The Form Book®

Flat Annual for 2009

Including all the 2008 returns

The BHA's Official Record

Complete record of Flat Racing
from 1 January to 31 December 2008

Associated Raceform products

The Form Book, is updated weekly. Subscribers receive a binder, together with all the early racing. Weekly sections and a new index are threaded into the binder to keep it up to date.

The data contained in The Form Book Flat Annual for 2009 is available in paper form or on computer disk. The disk service, Raceform Interactive, contains the same data as Raceform, The Form Book, and operates on any PC within a 'Windows' environment. The database is designed to allow access to the information in a number of different ways, and is extremely quick and easy to use.

Published in 2009 by Raceform Ltd
Compton, Newbury, Berkshire, RG20 6NL

A catalogue record for this book is available from the British Library,

ISBN 978-1-905153-95-4

Printed in the UK by CPI William Clowes Beccles NR34 7TL

Full details of all Raceform services and publications are available from:

Raceform Ltd, Compton, Newbury, Berkshire RG20 6NL
Tel: 01635 578080 • Fax: 01635 578101
Email: rfsubscription@racingpost.co.uk
www.racingpost.com

Cover photo: Yeats (Johnny Murtagh) winning his third successive Gold Cup at Royal Ascot © Edward Whitaker/Racing Post

CONTENTS

Editor: Graham Dench

Head of Analysis Team: Ashley Rumney

Race Analysts & Notebook Writers:
Gavin Beech, Dave Bellingham, Mark Brown, Steffan Edwards, Walter Glynn, Keith Hewitt, Richard Lowther, Lee McKenzie, Dave Moon, Sandra Noble, David Orton, Ashley Rumney, Desmond Stoneham, David Toft, Ron Wood, Richard Young.

Production: Ashley Rumney & Richard Lowther

The Official Scale of Weight, Age & Distance (Flat)

The following scale should only be used in conjunction with the Official ratings published in this book. Use of any other scale will introduce errors into calculations. The allowances are expressed as the number of pounds that is deemed the average horse in each group falls short of maturity at different dates and distances.

Dist		Jan		Feb		Mar		Apr		May		Jun		Jul		Aug		Sep		Oct		Nov		Dec	
(fur)	Age	1-15	16-31	1-14	15-28	1-15	16-31	1-15	16-30	1-15	16-31	1-15	16-30	1-15	16-31	1-15	16-31	1-15	16-30	1-15	16-31	1-15	16-30	1-15	16-31
5	2	-	-	-	-	-	47	44	41	38	36	34	32	30	28	26	24	22	20	19	18	17	17	16	16
	3	15	15	14	14	13	12	11	10	9	8	7	6	5	4	3	2	1	1	-	-	-	-	-	-
6	2	-	-	-	-	-	-	-	-	44	41	38	36	33	31	28	26	24	22	21	20	19	18	17	17
	3	16	16	15	15	14	13	12	11	10	9	8	7	6	5	4	3	2	2	1	1	-	-	-	-
7	2	-	-	-	-	-	-	-	-	-	-	-	-	38	35	32	30	27	25	23	22	21	20	19	19
	3	18	18	17	17	16	15	14	13	12	11	10	9	8	7	6	5	4	3	2	2	1	1	-	-
8	2	-	-	-	-	-	-	-	-	-	-	-	-	-	-	37	34	31	28	26	24	23	22	21	20
	3	20	20	19	19	18	17	15	14	13	12	11	10	9	8	7	6	5	4	3	3	2	2	1	1
9	3	22	22	21	21	20	19	17	15	14	13	12	11	10	9	8	7	6	5	4	4	3	3	2	2
	4	1	1	-	-	-	-	-	-	-	-	-	-	-	-	-	-	-	-	-	-	-	-	-	-
10	3	23	23	22	22	21	20	19	17	15	14	13	12	11	10	9	8	7	6	5	5	4	4	3	3
	4	2	2	1	1	-	-	-	-	-	-	-	-	-	-	-	-	-	-	-	-	-	-	-	-
11	3	24	24	23	23	22	21	20	19	17	15	14	13	12	11	10	9	8	7	6	6	5	5	4	4
	4	3	3	2	2	1	1	-	-	-	-	-	-	-	-	-	-	-	-	-	-	-	-	-	-
12	3	25	25	24	24	23	22	21	20	19	17	15	14	13	12	11	10	9	8	7	7	6	6	5	5
	4	4	4	3	3	2	2	1	1	-	-	-	-	-	-	-	-	-	-	-	-	-	-	-	-
13	3	26	26	25	25	24	23	22	21	20	19	17	15	14	13	12	11	10	9	8	8	7	7	6	6
	4	5	5	4	4	3	3	2	1	-	-	-	-	-	-	-	-	-	-	-	-	-	-	-	-
14	3	27	27	26	26	25	24	23	22	21	20	19	17	15	14	13	12	11	10	9	9	8	8	7	7
	4	6	6	5	5	4	4	3	2	1	-	-	-	-	-	-	-	-	-	-	-	-	-	-	-
15	3	28	28	27	27	26	25	24	23	22	21	20	19	17	15	14	13	12	11	10	9	8	8	7	7
	4	6	6	5	5	4	4	3	3	2	1	-	-	-	-	-	-	-	-	-	-	-	-	-	-
16	3	29	29	28	28	27	26	25	24	23	22	21	20	19	17	15	14	13	12	11	10	9	9	8	8
	4	7	7	6	6	5	5	4	4	3	2	1	-	-	-	-	-	-	-	-	-	-	-	-	-
18	3	31	31	30	30	29	28	27	26	25	24	23	22	21	20	18	16	14	13	12	11	10	10	9	9
	4	8	8	7	7	6	6	5	5	4	3	2	1	-	-	-	-	-	-	-	-	-	-	-	-
20	3	33	33	32	32	31	30	29	28	27	26	25	24	23	22	20	18	16	14	13	12	11	11	10	10
	4	9	9	8	8	7	7	6	6	5	4	3	2	1	-	-	-	-	-	-	-	-	-	-	-

The Form Book

Flat Racing Annual for 2009

Welcome to the 2009 edition of *The Form Book*, comprising the complete year's results from 2008.

Race details contain Racing Post Ratings assessing the merit of each individual performance, speed figures for every horse that clocks a worthwhile time, weight-for-age allowances, stall positions for every race and the starting price percentage, in addition to the traditional features.

Race Focus comments are printed below each race along with official explanations and notebook comments for all British races of Class 3 and above, all two-year-old races and foreign races. The comments provide an analysis of the winning performance and, where applicable, explain possible reasons for improvement or attempt to explain why any horse failed to run to its best. More importantly, our team will also indicate the conditions under which horses are likely to be seen to best advantage.

The official record

THE FORM BOOK records comprehensive race details of every domestic race, every major European Group race and every foreign event in which a British-trained runner participated. In the **NOTEBOOK** section, extended interpretation is provided for all runners worthy of a mention, including all placed horses and all favourites. Generally speaking, the higher the class of race, the greater the number of runners noted.

MEETING BACK REFERENCE NUMBER is the Raceform number of the last meeting run at the track and is shown to the left of the course name. Abandoned meetings are signified by a dagger.

THE GOING, The Official going, shown at the head of each meeting, is recorded as follows: Turf: Hard; Firm; Good to firm; Good; Good to soft; Soft; Heavy. All-Weather: Fast; Standard to fast; Standard; Standard to slow; Slow. There may be variations for non-British meetings

Where appropriate, a note is included indicating track bias and any differences to the official going indicated by race times.

THE WEATHER is shown below to th e date for selected meetings.

THE WIND is given as a strength and direction at the Winning Post, classified as follows:
Strength: gale; v.str; str; fresh; mod; slt; almost nil; nil.
Direction: (half) against; (half) bhd; (half) across from or towards stands.

VISIBILITY is good unless otherwise stated.

RACE NUMBERS for Foreign races carry the suffix 'a' in the race header and in the index.

RACE TITLE is the name of the race as shown in the Racing Calendar.

COMPETITIVE RACING CLASSIFICATIONS are shown on a scale from Class 1 to Class 7. All Pattern races are Class 1.

THE RACE DISTANCE is given for all races, and is accompanied by (s) for races run on straight courses and (r) for courses where there is a round track of comparable distance. On All-Weather courses (F) for Fibresand or (P) for Polytrack indicates the nature of the artificial surface on which the race is run.

OFFICIAL RACE TIME as published in the Racing Calendar is followed in parentheses by the time when the race actually started. This is followed by the race class, age restrictions, handicap restrictions and the official rating of the top weight.

PRIZE MONEY shows penalty values down to sixth place (where applicable).

THE POSITION OF THE STARTING STALLS is shown against each race, in the form of: High (H), Centre (C) or Low (L). If one stands at the start facing towards the finish, the stalls are numbered from left to right. If the stalls are placed adjacent to the left rail they are described as low, if against the right rail they are described as high. Otherwise they are central.

IN THE RACE RESULT, the figures to the far left of each horse (under FORM) show the most recent form figures. The figure in bold is the finishing position in this race as detailed below.

1...40 - finishing positions first to fortieth; **b** - brought down; **c** - carried out; **f** - fell; **p** - pulled up; **r** - refused; **ro** - ran out; **s** - slipped up; **u** - unseated rider; **v** - void race.

THE OFFICIAL DISTANCES between the horses are shown on the left-hand side immediately after their position at the finish.

NUMBER OF DAYS SINCE PREVIOUS RUN is the superscript figure immediately following the horse name and suffix.

PREVIOUS RACEFORM RACE NUMBER is the boxed figure to the right of the horse's name.

THE HORSE'S AGE is shown immediately before the weight carried.

WEIGHTS shown are actual weights carried.

OFFICIAL RATING is the figure in bold type directly after the horse's name in the race result. This figure indicates the Official BHB rating, at entry, after the following adjustments had been made:
(i) Overweight carried by the rider.
(ii) The number of pounds out of the handicap (if applicable).
(iii) Penalties incurred after the publication of the weights.
However, no adjustments have been made for:
(i) Weight-for-age.
(ii) Riders' claims.

HEADGEAR is shown immediately befoe the jockey's name and in parentheses and expressed as: **b** (blinkers); **v** (visor); **h** (hood); **e** (eyeshield); **c** (eyecover); **p** (sheepskin cheekpieces).

THE JOCKEY is shown for every runner followed, in superscript, by apprentice allowances in parentheses.

APPRENTICE ALLOWANCES The holders of apprentice jockeys' licences under the provisions of Rule 60(iii) are permitted to claim the following allowances in Flat races:
7lb until they have won 20 Flat races run under the Rules of any recognised Turf Authority; thereafter 5lb until they have won 50 such Flat races; thereafter 3lb until they have won 95 such Flat races. These allowances can be claimed in the Flat races set out below, with the exception of races confined to apprentice jockeys:
(a) All handicap handicaps other than those Rated stakes which are classified as listed races.
(b) All selling and claiming races.
(b) All weight-for-age races classified 3, 4, 5, 6 and 7.

THE DRAW for places at the start is shown after each jockey's name.

RACING POST RATINGS, which record the level of performance attained in this race for each horse, appear in the end column after each horse. These are the work of handicappers Simon Turner, Sam Walker and Paul Curtis, who head a dedicated team dealing with Flat races for Raceform and sister publication, the *Racing Post*.

THE TRAINER is shown for every runner.

COMMENT-IN-RUNNING is shown for each horse in an abbreviated form. Details of abbreviations appear later in this section.

STARTING PRICES appear below the jockey in the race result. The favourite indicator appears to the right of the Starting Price; 1 for the favourite, 2 for the second-favourite and 3 for third-favourite. Joint favourites share the same number.

RACE TIMES in Great Britain are official times which are electronically recorded and shown to 100th of a second. Figures in parentheses following the time show the number of seconds faster or slower than the Raceform Median Time for the course and distance.

RACEFORM MEDIAN TIMES are compiled from all races run over the course and distance in the preceding five years. Times equal to the median are shown as (0.00). Times under the median are preceded by minus, for instance, 1.8 seconds under the median would be shown (-1.8). Record times are displayed either referring to the juvenile record (1.2 under 2y best) or to the overall record (1.2 under best).

GOING CORRECTION appears against each race to allow for changing conditions of the ground. It is shown to a hundredth of a second and indicates the adjustment per furlong against the median time. The going based on the going correction is shown in parentheses and is recorded in the following stages:
Turf: HD (Hard); F (Firm); GF (Good to firm); G (Good); GS (Good to soft); S (Soft); HVY (Heavy). All-Weather: FST (Fast); SF (Standard to fast); STD (Standard); SS (Standard to slow); SLW (Slow)

WEIGHT-FOR-AGE allowances are given where applicable for mixed-age races.

STARTING PRICE PERCENTAGE follows the going correction and weight-for-age details, and gives the total SP percentage of all runners that competed. It precedes the number of runners taking part in the race.

SELLING DETAILS (where applicable) and details of any claim are given. Friendly claims are not detailed.

SPEED RATINGS appear below the race time and going correction. They are the work of time expert Dave Bellingham and differ from conventional ratings systems in that they are an expression of a horse's ability in terms of lengths-per-mile, as opposed to pounds in weight. They are not directly comparable with BHB and Racing Post ratings.

The ratings take no account of the effect of weight, either historically or on the day, and this component is left completely to the user's discretion. What is shown is a speed rating represented in its purest form, rather than one that has been altered for weight using a mathematical formula that treats all types of horses as if they were the same.

A comparison of the rating achieved with the 'par' figure for the grade of race - the rating that should be achievable by an everage winner in that class of race- will both provide an at-a-glance indication of whether or not a race was truly run and also highlight the value of the form from a time perspective.

In theory, if a horse has a best speed figure five points superior to another and both run to their best form in a race over a mile, the first horse should beat the second by five lengths. In a race run over two miles, the margin should be ten lengths and so on.

Before the speed figures can be calculated, it is necessary to establish a set of standard or median times for every distance at every track, and this is done by averaging the times of all winners over a particular trip going back several years. No speed ratings are produced when insufficient races have been run over a distance for a reliable median time to be calculated.

Once a meeting has taken place, a raw unadjusted speed rating is calculated for each winner by calculating how many lengths per mile the winning time was faster or slower than the median for the trip. A difference of 0.2 of a second equals one length. The raw speed ratings of all winners on the card are then compared to the 'par' figure for the class of race. The difference between the 'raw' speed rating and the 'par' figure for each race is then noted, and both the fastest and slowest races are discarded before the rest are averaged to produce the going allowance or track variant. This figure gives an idea as to how much the elements, of which the going is one, have affected the final times of each race.

The figure representing the going allowance is then used to adjust the raw speed figures and produce the final ratings, which represent how fast the winners would have run on a perfectly good surface with no external influences, including the weather. The ratings for beaten horses are worked out by taking the number of lengths they were behind the winner, adjusting that to take into account the distance of the race, and deducting that figure from the winner's rating. The reader is left with a rating which provides an instant impression of the value of a time performance.

The speed 'pars' below act as benchmark with which to compare the speed figures earned by each horse in each race. A horse that has already exceeded the 'par' for the class he is about to run in, is of special interest, especially if he has done it more than once, as are horses that have consistently earned higher figures than their rivals.

Class 1 Group One	117
Class 1 Group Two	115
Class 1 Group Three	113
Class 1 Listed	111
Class 2	109
Class 3	107
Class 4	105
Class 5	103
Class 6	101
Class 7	97

Allowances need to be made for younger horses and for fillies. These allowances are as follows.

MONTH	2yo	3yo
Jan / Feb	n/a	-6
Mar / Apr	-11	-5
May / Jun	-10	-4
Jul / Aug	-9	-3
Sep / Oct	-8	-2
Nov / Dec	-7	-1
Races contested by fillies only		-3

Allowances are cumulative. For example, using a combination of the above pars and allowances, the par figure for the Epsom Oaks would be 110. The Group One par is 117, then deduct 4 because the race is confined to three year olds and run in June, then subtract another 3 because the race is confined to fillies.

TOTE prices include £1 stake. Exacta dividends are shown in parentheses. The Computer Straight Forecast dividend is preceded by the letters CSF, Computer Tricast is preceded by CT and Tote Trio dividend is preceded by the word Trio. Jackpot, Placepot and Quadpot details appear at the end of the meeting to which they refer.

OWNER is followed by the breeder's name and the trainer's location.

STEWARDS' ENQUIRIES are included with the result, and any suspensions and/or fines incurred. Objections by jockeys and officials are included, where relevant.

HISTORICAL FOCUS details occasional points of historical significance.

FOCUS The Focus section has been enhanced to help readers distinguish good races from bad races and reliable form from unreliable form, by drawing together the opinions of handicapper, time expert and paddock watcher and interpreting their views in a punter-friendly manner.

NOTEBOOK horses marked with the diamond symbol are those deemed by our racereaders especially worthy of note in future races.

OFFICIAL EXPLANATIONS, where the horse is deemed to have run well above or below expectations

Abbreviations and their meanings

Paddock comments

gd sort - well made, above average on looks
h.d.w - has done well, improved in looks
wl grwn - well grown, has filled to its frame
lengthy - longer than average for its height
tall - tall
rangy - lengthy and tall but in proportion.
cl cpld - close coupled
scope - scope for physical development
str - strong, powerful looking
w'like - workmanlike, ordinary in looks
lt-f - light-framed, not much substance
cmpt - compact
neat - smallish, well put together
leggy - long legs compared with body
angular - unfurnished behind the saddle, not filled to frame
unf - unfurnished in the midriff, not filled to frame
narrow - not as wide as side appearance would suggest
small - lacks any physical scope
nt grwn - not grown
lw - looked fit and well
bkwd - backward in condition
t - tubed
swtg - sweating
b (off fore or nr fore) - bandaged in front
b.hind (off or nr) - bandaged behind

At the start

stdd s - jockey purposely reins back the horse
dwlt - missed the break and left for a short time
s.s - slow to start, left longer than a horse that dwelt
s.v.s - started very slowly
s.i.s - started on terms but took time to get going
ref to r - either does not jump off, or travels a few yards and then stops
rel to r - tries to pull itself up in mid-race
w.r.s - whipped round start

Position in the race

led - in lead on its own
disp ld - upsides the leader

w ldr - almost upsides the leader
w ldrs - in a line of three or more disputing the lead
prom - on the heels of the leaders, in the front third of the field
trckd ldr(s) - just in behind the leaders giving impression that it could lead if asked
chsd ldr - horse in second place
chsd clr ldrs - horse heads main body of field behind two clear leaders
chsd ldrs - horse is in the first four or five but making more of an effort to stay close to the pace than if it were tracking the leaders.
clsd - closed
in tch - close enough to have a chance
hdwy - making ground on the leader
gd hdwy - making ground quickly on the leader, could be a deliberate move
sme hdwy - making some ground but no real impact on the race
w.w - waited with
stdy hdwy - gradually making ground
ev ch - upsides the leaders when the race starts in earnest
rr - at the back of main group but not detached
bhd - detached from the main body of runners
hld up - restrained as a deliberate tactical move
nt rcvr - lost all chance after interference, mistake etc.
wknd - stride shortened as it began to tire
lost tch - had been in the main body but a gap appeared as it tired
lost pl - remains in main body of runners but lost several positions quickly

Riding

effrt - short-lived effort
pushed along - received urgings with hands only, jockey not using legs
rdn - received urgings from saddle, including use of whip
hrd rdn - received maximum assistance from the saddle including use of whip
drvn - received forceful urgings, jockey putting in a lot of effort and using whip
hrd drvn - jockey very animated, plenty of kicking, pushing and reminders

Finishing comments

jst failed - closing rapidly on the winner and probably would have led a stride after the line
r.o - jockey's efforts usually involved to produce an increase in pace without finding an appreciable turn of speed
r.o wl - jockey's efforts usually involved to produce an obvious increase in pace without finding an appreciable turn of speed
unable qckn - not visibly tiring but does not possess a sufficient change of pace
one pce - not tiring but does not find a turn of speed, from a position further out than unable qckn.
nt r.o. - did not consent to respond to pressure
styd on - going on well towards the end, utilising stamina
nvr able to chal - unable to produce sufficient to reach a challenging position
nvr nr to chal - in the opinion of the racereader, the horse was never in a suitable position to challenge.
nrst fin - nearer to the winner in distance beaten than at any time since the race had begun in earnest
nvr nrr - nearer to the winner position-wise than at any time since the race had begun in earnest
rallied - responded to pressure to come back with a chance having lost its place
no ex - unable to sustain its run
bttr for r - likely to improve for the run and experience
rn green - inclined to wander and falter through inexperience
too much to do - left with too much leeway to make up

Winning comments

v.easily - a great deal in hand
easily - plenty in hand
comf - something in hand, always holding the others
pushed out - kept up to its work with hands and heels without jockey resorting to whip or kicking along and wins fairly comfortably
rdn out - pushed and kicked out to the line, with the whip employed
drvn out - pushed and kicked out to the line, with considerable effort and the whip employed
all out - nothing to spare, could not have found any more
jst hld on - holding on to a rapidly diminishing lead, could not have found any more if passed
unchal - must either make all or a majority of the running and not be challenged from an early stage

Complete list of abbreviations

a - always
gng - going
qckn - quicken
a.p - always prominent
gp - group
r - race
abt - about
grad - gradually
racd - raced
appr - approaching
grnd - ground
rch - reach
awrdd - awarded
hd - head
rcvr - recover
b.b.v - broke blood-vessel
hdd - headed
rdn - ridden
b.d - brought down
hdwy - headway
rdr - rider
bdly - badly
hld - held
reard - reared
bef - before
hmpd - hampered
ref - refused
bhd - behind
imp - impression
rn - ran
bk - back
ins - inside
rnd - round
blkd - baulked
j.b - jumped badly
r.o - ran on
blnd - blundered
j.w - jumped well
rr - rear
bmpd - bumped

jnd - joined
rspnse - response
bnd - bend
jst - just
rt - right
btn- beaten
kpt - kept
s - start
bttr - better
l - length
sddle - saddle
c - came
ld - lead
shkn - shaken
ch - chance
ldr - leader
slt - slight
chal - challenged
lft - left
sme - some
chse - chase
m - mile
sn - soon
chsd - chased
m.n.s - made no show
spd- speed
chsng - chasing
mde - made

st - straight
circ - circuit
mod - moderate
stmbld - stumbled
cl - close
mid div - mid division
stdd - steadied
clr - clear
mstke - mistake
stdy - steady
clsd - closed
n.d - never dangerous
strly - strongly
comf - comfortably
n.g.t - not go through
styd - stayed
cpld - coupled
n.m.r - not much room
styng - staying
crse - course
nk - neck
s.u - slipped up
ct - caught
no ex - no extra
swtchd - switched
def - definite
nr - near
swvd - swerved

dismntd - dismounted
nrr - nearer
tk - took
disp - disputed
nrst fin - nearest finish
t.k.h - took keen hold
dist - distance
nt - not
t.o - tailed off
div - division
nvr - never
tch - touch
drvn - driven
one pce - one pace
thrght - throughout
dwlt - dwelt
out - from finish
trbld - troubled
edgd - edged
outpcd - outpaced
trckd - tracked
effrt - effort
p.u - pulled up
u.p - under pressure
ent - entering
pce - pace
u.str.p- under strong pressure

ev ch - every chance
pckd - pecked
w - with
ex - extra
pl - place
w.r.s - whipped round start
f - furlong
plcd - placed
wd - wide
fin - finished
plld - pulled
whn - when
fnd - found
press - pressure
wknd - weakened
fnl - final
prog - progress
wl - well
fr - from
prom - prominent
wnr - winner
gd - good
qckly - quickly
wnt - went
w.w - waited with
1/2-wy - halfway

Racing Post Ratings

Racing Post Ratings for each horse are shown in the right hand column, headed RPR, and indicate the actual level of performance attained in that race. The figure in the back index represents the BEST public form that Raceform's Handicappers still believe the horse capable of reproducing.

To use the ratings constructively in determining those horses best-in in future events, the following procedure should be followed:

(i) In races where all runners are the same age and are set to carry the same weight, no calculations are necessary. The horse with the highest rating is best-in.

(ii) In races where all runners are the same age but are set to carry different weights, add one point to the Raceform Rating for every pound less than 10 stone to be carried; deduct one point for every pound more than 10 stone.

For example,

Horse	Age & wt	Adjustment from 10st	Base rating	Adjusted rating
Treclare	3-10-1	-1	78	77
Buchan	3-9-13	+1	80	81
Paper Money	3-9-7	+7	71	78
Archaic	3-8-11	+17	60	77

Therefore Buchan is top-rated (best-in)

(iii) In races concerning horses of different ages the procedure in (ii) should again be followed, but reference must also be made to the Official Scale of Weight-For-Age.

For example,

12 furlongs, July 20th

Horse	Age & wt	Adjustment from 10st	Base rating	Adjusted rating	W-F-A deduct	Final rating
Orpheus	5-10-0	0	90	90	Nil	90
Lemonora	4-9-9	+5	88	88	Nil	88
Tamar	3-9-4	+10	85	95	-12	83
Craigangower	4-8-7	+21	73	94	Nil	94

Therefore Craigangower is top-rated (best-in)

(A 3-y-o is deemed 12lb less mature than a 4-y-o or older horse on 20th July over 12f. Therefore, the deduction of 12 points is necessary.)

The following symbols are used in conjunction with the ratings:

++: almost certain to prove better

+: likely to prove better

d: disappointing (has run well below best recently)

?: form hard to evaluate

t: tentative rating based on race-time rating may prove unreliable

Weight adjusted ratings for every race are published daily in Raceform Private Handicap and our new service Raceform Private handicap ONLINE (www.raceform.co.uk).

For subscription terms please contact the Subscription Department on (01635) 578080.

Effect of the draw

(R.H.) denotes right-hand and (L.H.) left-hand courses.

* Draw biases shown below apply to straight-course races unless otherwise stipulated.

** Most races (outside Festival meetings) are now restricted to 20 runners under a recently introduced BHB rule, which means it's now particularly worth looking at the stalls position, as many courses can accommodate more than that number.

ASCOT (R-H) - Following extensive redevelopment there were some pretty exaggerated draw biases in 2006. Jockeys reported the ground on the far side (high) to be more undulating and that was clearly not the place to be at the Royal Meeting, when low numbers enjoyed a distinct advantage.
However, watering then became the deciding factor and far too much was applied on more than one occasion. Further work is due to be carried out in a bid to level things out and it remains to be seen what effect the draw has at early meetings.
STALLS: Usually go up the stands' side (low).
BIASES: One side or other was often favoured last season but that could all change again.
SPLITS: Are common in big-field handicaps and occasionally will occur on soft ground in round-course races, when some head for the outside rail (covered by trees).

AYR (L-H) - Throughout the 90s high numbers were massively favoured in the
Gold and Silver Cups but things have become less clear-cut since. Traditionally the centre of the course has ridden slower, meaning low numbers were often favoured over 7f50y and 1m, but this didn't look the case on more than one occasion last year.
STALLS: Usually go up the stands' side (high) in sprints, but occasionally go on the other side. It wasn't uncommon last year for jockeys to switch from the far side to race down the centre or even come right across and this could well continue in the new season.
BIASES: There's ultimately not a lot between the two sides in big fields now.
SPLITS: Are becoming more common, having only usually occurred in the Silver and Gold Cups in the past.

BATH (L-H) - The draw is basically of far less importance than the pace at which races are run. In big fields, runners drawn low are often inclined to go off too fast to hold a rail position (the course turns left most of the way, including one major kink) and this can see hold-up horses drawn wide coming through late. Conversely, in smaller fields containing little pace, up front and on the inside is often the place to be.
STALLS: Always go on the inside (low).
SPLITS: Fields almost always stick together, but soft ground can see a split, with the outside rail (high) then favoured.

BEVERLEY (R-H) - A high draw is essential on good to soft or faster ground over 5f and also on the round course, particularly in races of 7f100y and 1m100y. In sprints, runners have to negotiate a right-handed jink not long after the start and it seems harder here than at any course for runners drawn low to get over to the favoured rail (there's also a camber). The course management experimented with moving stalls to the stands' side over 5f in 2002 (unsuccessfully, as it led to a huge low bias) and haven't done
so since.
STALLS: Go on the inside (high) at all distances.
BIASES: High numbers are massively favoured at 5f on good to soft or faster
ground and are also best on the round course.
SPLITS: Splits are rare and only likely over 5f on soft ground.

BRIGHTON (L-H) - There was a spell during the summer last year when it was a massive advantage to race against the outside rail (high) as this strip was brown and clearly hadn't been watered. Otherwise, much depends on the going and time of year; on good to soft or slower ground runners often head for the outside rail, while in late season it's usually just a case of whichever jockey finds the least cut-up strip of ground. Otherwise, low-drawn prominent-racers tend to hold sway in fast-ground sprints, with double figures always facing an uphill task over 5f59y.
STALLS: Always go on the inside (low) in sprints.
SPLITS: These occur frequently, as jockeys look for a fresh strip on ground that seems to churn up easily.

CARLISLE (R-H) - Runners racing with the pace and hardest against the inside rail (high) do well in big fields on decent ground. This is largely down to the fact that the Flat course and NH course are one and the same, and that those racing nearest the fence are running where the hurdle wings were positioned, while those wider out are on the raced-on surface. On soft ground, the bias swings completely, with runners racing widest (low) and grabbing the stands' rail in the straight favoured at all distances.
STALLS: Normally go on the inside (high) but can go down the middle in sprints (usually on slow ground).
BIASES: High numbers are best in fast-ground sprints. Look to back low numbers on soft/heavy ground.
SPLITS: Rarely will two groups form but, on easy ground, runners often spread out.

CATTERICK (L-H) - When the ground is testing, the stands' rail is definitely the place to be, which suits high numbers in 5f races and high-drawn prominent-racers at all other distances. However, when the ground is good to firm or faster, horses drawn on the inside (low) often hold the edge, and there have been several meetings over the last few seasons in which those racing prominently hardest against the inside rail have dominated (over all distances, presumably as a result of watering).
STALLS: Go on the inside (low) at all distances these days (they often used to go on the outer over 5f212y).
BIASES: Low numbers are best in sprints on fast ground (particularly watered firm going) but the stands' rail (high) rides faster under slower conditions.
SPLITS: Are common over 5f.

CHEPSTOW (L-H) - High numbers enjoyed a massive advantage in straight-course races in 2000 and the course management duly took steps to eradicate the faster strip, using the same 'earthquake' machine as had been employed at Goodwood in the late 90s. This has led to little in the way of a draw bias since.
STALLS: Always go on the stands' side (high) on the straight course.
BIASES: Have become hard to predict in recent times.
SPLITS: Splits are common and jockeys drawn low often head far side.

CHESTER (L-H) - It's well known that low numbers are favoured at all distances here, even in the 2m2f Chester Cup, and the bias is factored into the prices these days. That said sprints (and in particular handicaps) are still playable, as it often pays to stick to a runner drawn 1-3.
STALLS: Go on the inside (low) at all distances bar 1m2f75y and 2m2f117y (same starting point) when they go on the outside. Certain starters ask for the stalls to come off the inside rail slightly in sprints.
BIASES: Low numbers are favoured at all distances. Soft ground seems to accentuate the bias until a few races have been staged, when a higher draw becomes less of a disadvantage as the ground on the inside becomes chewed up.

DONCASTER (L-H) - The course has been closed for redevelopment and it remains to be seen whether the old biases remain. As a rule of thumb in the past, the stands' rail (high) always offered an advantage in sprints when the stalls were on the stands' side, with low numbers best the odd occasions they went on the far side.
STALLS: Can go either side but tend to go up the stands' side (high) whenever possible.
BIASES: Runners down the centre are usually worst off. The longer the trip on the straight course the better chance the far side (low) has against the stands' side in big fields.

EPSOM (L-H) - When the going is on the soft side, jockeys tack over to the stands' side for the better ground (this strip rides quicker in such conditions as the course cambers away from the stands' rail. In 5f races, the stalls are invariably placed on the stands' side, so when the going is soft the majority of the runners are on the best ground from the outset.
Prominent-racers drawn low in round-course races are able to take the shortest route around Tattenham Corner, and on faster ground have a decisive edge over 6f, 7f and 1m114y. Over 5f, high numbers used to hold quite an advantage, but the bias is not so great these days.
STALLS: Always go on the outside (high) over 5f and 6f (races over the latter trip start on a chute) and inside (low) at other distances, bar 1m4f10y (centre).
BIASES: Low-drawn prominent racers are favoured at between 6f and 1m114y.
SPLITS: Good to soft ground often leads to a few trying the stands'-side route.

FOLKESTONE (R-H) - Prior to 1998, Folkestone was never thought to have much in the way of a bias, but nowadays the draw is often crucial on the straight course (up to 7f). On easy ground, the far rail (high) rides faster than the stands' rail, which in turn rides quicker than the middle of the track. Runners now usually go across to the far side over 6f and 7f (jockeyship often playing a part, with several races going to whichever horse secures the front up the rail). However, over 5f, when the stalls are up the stands' rail, fields often split, with low numbers just about holding sway (it seems the ground lost by switching across over the minimum trip can't be regained from racing on the faster surface). On good to firm/firm ground runners tend to stay up the near side now (the ambulance used to go this side of the far rail but now goes the other side of the fence).
STALLS: Usually go up the stands' side (low) on the straight track, but occasionally down the centre.

BIASES: High numbers are favoured over 6f and 7f, and also over the minimum trip when 14 or more line up. However, very low numbers have a good record in smaller fields over 5f. Front-runners are well worth considering at all distances.
SPLITS: Often occur.

GOODWOOD (R-H) & (L-H) - The course management took steps to end the major high bias seen in the Stewards' Cup throughout the late 90s by breaking up the ground by machine in 1998. This led to the stands' side (low) dominating the race in 1999 before the far side gradually took over again.
STALLS: Invariably go on the stands' side (low).
BIASES: High numbers are best at between 7f-1m1f, and the faster the ground, the more pronounced the bias (keep an eye out for the rail on the home turn being moved during Glorious week, usually after the Thursday).
SPLITS: Although fields tend not to break into groups in most sprints, runners often spread out to about two-thirds of the way across in fields of around 20.

GREAT LEIGHS All-Weather, Polytrack surface (L-H) – The track only came online in April 2008 and the only aspect about the draw that has become noticeable as that a low stall is an advantage in sprints, especially so over 5f. Once into the straight there is an advantage in being brought out into the centre of the track for the run to the line.
STALLS: Go towards the inside rail (low).

HAMILTON (R-H) - Extensive drainage work was carried out in the winter of 2002 in a bid to level up the two sides of the track but, after encouraging early results, the natural bias in favour of high numbers (far side) kicked in again. This can be altered by watering on faster going, though, so be careful after a dry spell, as things can often swing in favour of low numbers. High numbers are best over 1m65y, thanks to runners encountering a tight right-handed loop soon after the start.
STALLS: It's not uncommon for the ground to become too soft for the use of stalls, but otherwise they go either side.
BIASES: High draws are best in soft/heavy-ground sprints, but the bias becomes middle to high otherwise (often switching to low on watered fast ground). Front-runners do particularly well at all distances.
SPLITS: Look for high numbers to peel off in fields of 8+ when the stalls are stands' side unless the ground is fast.

HAYDOCK (L-H) - High numbers used to enjoy a major advantage in soft-ground sprints, but that seems to have been turned full circle by drainage work carried out in the late 90s, with the far side (low) now best on very bad ground. Otherwise, runners usually head for the centre these days, the draw rarely making much of a difference (although very high numbers can be worst off in big fields on faster going).
STALLS: Usually go down the centre in the straight.

KEMPTON All-Weather, Polytrack surface (R-H) - A high draw is a big advantage over 5f (inner bend) and 6f (outer bend) with both starts about the same distance from the first right-hand turn. A high draw is still an advantage over 7f, but becomes less significant over further.
STALLS: Go towards the inside rail (high).

LEICESTER (R-H) - There was a four-year spell between 1998 and 2001 when the centre-to-far-side strip (middle to high) enjoyed a decisive advantage over the stands' rail, jockeys eventually choosing to avoid the near side. However, that's changed recently, with very low numbers more than holding their own.
STALLS: Invariably go up the stands' side (low).
SPLITS: Still occur occasionally.

LINGFIELD Turf (L-H) - The draw advantage is nothing like as defined as in years past, but the stands' rail (high) again went through a good spell in the second half of last season, as was the case the year before. The one factor that can have a massive effect on the draw is heavy rainfall on to firm ground. Presumably because of the undulating nature of the track and the fact that the far rail on the straight course is towards the bottom of a slope where it joins the round course, rainfall seems to make the middle and far side ride a deal slower. In these conditions, the top three or four stalls have a massive edge.
STALLS: Go up the stands' side (high) at between 5f and 7f and down the middle over 7f140y.
BIASES: High numbers are massively favoured on fast ground after recent rain, but otherwise the most recent meeting is often the best guide.
SPLITS: It's unusual to see two distinct groups, but runners often fan out centre to stands' side in big fields.

LINGFIELD All-Weather, Polytrack surface (L-H) - There is little bias over most trips, but it is an advantage to be drawn low over 6f and 1m 2f with both starts being situated very close to the first bend.
STALLS: Are against the outside rail (high) over 5f and 1m, but against the inside rail (low) for all other distances.
SPLITS: Due to the nature of the circuit, the fields never split though some horses can be forced very wide on the home bend.

MUSSELBURGH (R-H) - The bias in favour of low numbers over 5f isn't as pronounced as many believe, apart from on soft ground, while the bias in favour of high numbers at 7f and 1m also isn't that big.
STALLS: Usually go up the stands' side (low) over 5f nowadays, but they can be rotated.
SPLITS: Look out for runners drawn very high in big-field 5f races on fast ground, as they occasionally go right to the far rail.

NEWBURY (L-H) - There's basically little between the two sides these days, apart from on soft ground, in which case the stands' rail (high) is definitely the place to be. When the ground is testing it's not uncommon to see runners race wide down the back straight and down the side at between 1m3f56y and 2m (particularly over 1m5f61y). In such circumstances, a high draw becomes an advantage.
STALLS: Can go anywhere for straight-course races.
SPLITS: It's not often fields are big enough for a split to occur.

NEWCASTLE (L-H) - It's always been a case of high numbers best at up to and including 7f on good or firmer, and low numbers having the advantage when the ground is good to soft or softer. Over the straight 1m, the stands' rail (high) is the place to be apart from on very bad ground.
STALLS: Invariably go on the stands' side (high) only being switched to the inside under exceptional circumstances.
SPLITS: Two groups are usually formed when 14+ go to post, and often when 8-13 line up.

NEWMARKET July Course (R-H) - The major draw biases seen under the former Clerk of the Course have become a thing of the past since Michael Prosser took over and now only the occasional meeting will be affected. The course is permanently divided into two halves by a rail (the Racing Post now carry information regarding which side is to be used) and, as a rule of thumb, the two outside rails (stands' rail when they're on the stands'-side half, far rail when they're on the far-side half) ride faster than the dividing rail.
Stands'-side half - On fast ground (particularly watered) very high numbers are often favoured at up to 1m, when there's a narrow strip hard against the fence that rides quicker. However, on good to soft or slower ground, runners racing down the centre are favoured.
Far-side half - There's rarely much in the draw, apart from on slow ground, when the far side (low) rides faster.
STALLS: Can go either side on either half of the track.
SPLITS: Runners just about tend to form two groups in capacity fields, but are more likely to run to their draw here than at tracks such as Newcastle.

NEWMARKET Rowley Mile (R-H) - Similarly to the July Course, the draw seems to have been evened out since the Clerk of the Course change, although it's still generally a case of the further away from the stands' rail the better.
STALLS: Can go anywhere and are rotated.
BIASES: High numbers have dominated the 2m2f Cesarewitch in recent years, the logic here being that those on the inside can be switched off early, while low numbers have to work to get into position before the sole right-handed turn.
SPLIT: It's not unusual for jockeys to come stands' side on slow ground in round-course races.

NOTTINGHAM (L-H) - On the straight course, it used to be a case of low numbers being favoured when the stalls were on the far rail and high numbers when they were stands' side, with low being best when the stalls spanned the entire course. These days, though, it's less clear-cut and the going makes the biggest difference. On soft ground low numbers are usually best but high tend to be favoured on good to firm or faster.
STALLS: Tend to go on the stands' side (high) unless the ground is very soft.
SPLITS: Fields usually split in sprints when 14+ line up.

PONTEFRACT (L-H) - Low numbers have always been considered best here for the same reason as at Chester, in that the course has several distinct left-hand turns with a short home straight, but this is not always true. High numbers at least hold their own over 6f now, whatever the ground, but massively so on soft/heavy. Drainage work was carried out in the late 90s to try and eradicate the outside-rail bias on slow ground, and this worked immediately afterwards, but during the last few seasons there have been definite signs that it's now riding much faster.
STALLS: Go on the inside (low) unless the ground is very soft, when they're switched to the outside rail.
SPLITS: Although it's uncommon to see distinct groups, high numbers usually race wide these days on good to soft or slower ground.

REDCAR (L-H) - It's not unusual to see big fields throughout the season here and, while the draw has rarely played a part in the past, with runners inclined to converge towards the centre, high numbers were definitely best last year.
STALLS: Go towards the stands' side (high).
SPLITS: Splits are unusual.

RIPON (R-H) - The draw is often the sole deciding factor in big-field sprints and watering plays a major part. As a general rule, low numbers are best when the ground is good to firm or faster, while the far side is always best on softer going but, ultimately, the best guide here these days is the most recent meeting.
STALLS: Go on the stands' side (low) apart from under exceptional circumstances.
BIASES: Front-runners (particularly from high draws over 1m) have an excellent record and any horse trying to make ground from behind and out wide is always facing a tough task.

SPLITS: Fields tend to stay together in races of 12 or fewer, but a split is near guaranteed when 15 or more line up. Look for 'draw' jockeys who might chance going far side in fields of 13-14.

SALISBURY (R-H) - It's difficult to win from a single-figure draw in big-field fast-ground sprints, but proven stamina and race suitability become the most important factors over the testing straight 1m. This far-side bias is at its greatest early and late season, before and after the erection of a temporary rail (which usually goes up in July). The draw swings full circle on slower ground, as jockeys then invariably head towards the stands' rail (good to soft seems to be the cut-off point).
STALLS: Go on the far side (high) unless the ground is soft, when they're often moved to the near side.
BIASES: High numbers are best on the straight course on fast ground, there's not much in it on good to soft, while low take over on soft/heavy.
SPLITS: Fields only tend to divide on good to soft ground; otherwise they all converge towards either rail, dependant upon going.

SANDOWN (R-H) - On the 5f chute, when the going is on the soft side and the stalls are on the far side (high), high numbers enjoy a decisive advantage. On the rare occasions that the stalls are placed on the stands' side, low numbers enjoy a slight advantage when all the runners stay towards the stands' rail, but when a few break off and go to the far side high numbers comfortably hold the upper hand again. High numbers enjoy a decent advantage in double-figure fields over 7f and 1m on good going or faster, but jockeys invariably head for the stands' side on slow ground.
STALLS: Usually go far side (high) over 5f, as the course is more level that side.
SPLITS: It's unusual for runners to split over 5f, with capacity fields rare and jockeys all inclined to head for the far rail.

SOUTHWELL All-Weather, Fibresand surface (L-H) - Over most trips on the round track it is preferable to be drawn away from the extreme inside or outside. The exceptions are over 6f and 1m 3f, which both start close to the first bend and therefore it is better to be drawn low to middle. At most meetings the centre of the track rides faster than against either rail, though that can change in extreme weather when power-harrowing can even out the bias. A low to middle draw is preferable over the straight 5f and it is noticeable that even when a high draw wins, the horse concerned almost always giving the stands' rail a wide berth having been angled to its left to race more towards the centre.
STALLS: Are placed next to the inside rail (low), except over 5f where they are placed next to the stands' rail (high).
SPLITS: The fields do not tend to split into groups as such, but can fan right out and take varied routes once into the home straight. Even in big fields over the straight 5f, the runners basically stick to their draw and race as straight as they can from start to finish.

THIRSK (L-H) - This used to be the biggest draw course in the country, back in the days of the old watering system (which was badly affected by the wind) but, while biases still often show up, they're not as predictable as used to be the case. Field sizes, watering and going always have to be taken into account when 12 or more line up (11 or fewer runners and it's rare to see anything bar one group up the stands' rail, with high numbers best). Otherwise, either rail can enjoy the edge on watered fast ground (the one place not to be under any circumstances is down the middle). Low-drawn prominent-racers are well worth considering whatever the distance on the round course.
STALLS: Always go up the stands' side (high).
BIASES: High numbers are best in sprints when 11 or fewer line up, but it's hard to know which side is likely to do best in bigger fields on fast ground. The far (inside) rail is always best on slow going (the softer the ground, the greater the advantage).
SPLITS: Runners invariably stay towards the stands' side in sprints containing 12 or fewer runners (unless the ground is soft) and frequently when 13-14 line up. Any more and it becomes long odds-on two groups.

WARWICK (L-H) - Low numbers are favoured in fast-ground sprints, but not by as much as many believe, and the prices often over-compensate. However, when the ground is genuinely soft, high numbers can enjoy an advantage.
STALLS: Always go on the inside (low).

WINDSOR (Fig. 8) - It's typical to see large fields all season and the draw almost always plays a part. In sprints, things are set in stone, with high numbers best on good or faster going (particularly watered fast ground), not much between the two sides on good to soft, and the far side (low) taking over on soft or heavy ground. It can be difficult for runners who switch off the stands' rail to make up the leeway (because the course turns sharply left soon after the finish those pulled wide must think they're being asked to quicken up into a dead-end). On slower ground, jockeys head centre to far side, and right over to the far rail on genuine soft/heavy (again it's difficult to make ground from behind under such conditions).
STALLS: Can be positioned anywhere for sprints.
BIASES: High-drawn prominent-racers are favoured in fast-ground sprints, and also over 1m67y. On good to soft going, there's rarely much between the two sides, but it's a case of nearer to the far rail (low) the better on bad ground.
SPLITS: Splits only tend to occur on good to soft ground, and even then it's rare to see two defined groups.

WOLVERHAMPTON All-Weather, Polytrack surface since October 2004 (L-H) - The huge bias that used to exist towards those horses that raced away from the inside rail on the old Fibresand is a fading memory, but even though the Polytrack is relatively new, some biases are emerging. A low draw is a big advantage over 5f and 6f and low to middle is preferable over 7f. Beyond that it doesn't seem to matter, though it is never a good idea to race too wide on the home bends and those that do so rarely seem to make up the lost ground.
STALLS: Are placed against the outside rail (high) over 7f and against the inside rail (low) at all other distances.
SPLITS: Splits do not happen and most of the time the runners stay as close as they can next to the inside rail unless traffic problems force them wide.

YARMOUTH (L-H) - High numbers enjoyed a major advantage for much of the 90s, but this was put an end to by the course switching from pop-up sprinklers (which were affected by the off-shore breeze) to a Briggs Boom in '99. These days a bias will appear occasionally but it's hard to predict, and runners often head for the centre whatever the going.
STALLS: Go one side or the other.
SPLITS: It's common to see groups form, often including one down the centre, in big fields.

YORK (L-H) - The draw is nothing like as unpredictable in sprints as many believe, although things are never quite as clear-cut in September/October as earlier in the season. Essentially, on good or faster ground, the faster strip is to be found centre to far side, which means in capacity fields, the place to be is stall 6-12, while in fields of 12-14 runners drawn low are favoured (the course is only wide enough to house 20 runners). On soft/heavy ground, the stands' side (high) becomes the place to be, and high numbers often get the rail to themselves, as this is not a bias well known among jockeys. Low numbers are best on fast ground on the round course, although watering can reduce the bias.
STALLS: Can go anywhere.
BIASES: Prominent-racers drawn down the centre are favoured in fast-ground sprints, but high numbers take over on genuine soft/heavy ground. Low numbers are best in big fields on the round course, apart from on slower going, when runners leave the inside in the home straight.
SPLITS: Defined groups are rare.

Key to racereaders' initials

WG ....Walter Glynn
KH ....Keith Hewitt
RL ....Richard Lowther
LM...................Lee McKenzie
TM ....Tim Mitchell
JN............Jonathan Neesom
DO ....Darren Owen
SP ....Steve Payne
CR ....Colin Roberts
JR ....Joe Rowntree
JS.........................John Santer
ST ....Steve Taylor
RY ....Richard Young

SOUTHWELL (L-H)

Tuesday, January 1

OFFICIAL GOING: Standard

Wind: Light across Weather: Light rain

1 HAPPY NEW YEAR APPRENTICE MEDIAN AUCTION MAIDEN STKS — 1m 3f (F)

12:20 (12:22) (Class 6) 4-6-Y-O — **£1,911** (£564; £282) **Stalls** Low

Form				RPR
222-	1		**Wicked Daze (IRE)**[168] 3621 5-8-11 78 .... JackMitchell(5) 3	65+
			(Sir Mark Prescott) *trckd ldrs: led on bit over 4f out: clr fnl 2f: canter* **1/25**[1]	
0/	2	7	**Red Fama**[448] 5900 4-8-10 0 .... SladeO'Hara(3) 1	53
			(N Bycroft) *led early: chsd ldrs: rdn and lost tch 1/2-way: n.d after* **40/1**[3]	
60V-	3	4	**Lady's Law**[22] 7100 5-8-8 43 .... JamieJones(5) 5	41
			(Rae Guest) *chsd ldr: led 1/2-way: rdn and hdd over 4f out: wknd over 2f out* **20/1**[2]	
000-	4	27	**Long Gone**[12] 7199 5-8-6 27 .... (p) MarkCoumbe(5) 2	—
			(John A Harris) *s.i.s: sn rcvrd to ld: rdn and hdd 1/2-way: sn wknd* **66/1**	

2m 28.9s (0.90) **Going Correction** -0.20s/f (Stan)
WFA 4 from 5yo 3lb — **4** Ran SP% **104.8**
Speed ratings: **92,86,84,64**
CSF £3.35 TOTE £1.10; EX 3.60.
Owner Roger T Ferris **Bred** Bloomsbury Stud **Trained** Newmarket, Suffolk

FOCUS
The first race of the 2008 Flat season and things can only get better. This was an awful race and the form means very little in relation to future events.

2 MAKE YOUR RESOLUTION PONTIN'S (S) STKS — 1m (F)

12:55 (12:55) (Class 6) 4-Y-O+ — **£1,774** (£523; £262) **Stalls** Low

Form				RPR
206-	1		**Blue Empire (IRE)**[5] 7244 7-8-12 55 .... (p) AdamKirby 4	54
			(C R Dore) *led 7f out: rdn over 3f out: hdd over 1f out: rallied to ld and hung rt wl ins fnl f* **6/4**[1]	
000-	2	1/2	**Stepaside (IRE)**[11] 7209 4-8-5 42 .... (b) SBushby(7) 6	53
			(A D Brown) *prom: chsd wnr 5f out: rdn to ld and hung rt fr over 1f out: hdd wl ins fnl f* **12/1**	
423-	3	3 1/2	**Davidia (IRE)**[12] 7197 5-8-9 47 .... (p) AndrewElliott(3) 1	45
			(D W Thompson) *sn pushed along and prom: outpcd over 4f out: styd on fr over 1f out: nt trble ldrs* **7/4**[2]	
0L5-	4	9	**By Storm**[12] 7197 5-8-2 37 .... (p) KirstyMilczarek(5) 3	19
			(Miss J E Foster) *led 1f: rdn and wknd over 3f out* **15/2**[3]	
000-	5	8	**Susiedil (IRE)**[4] 7169 7-8-7 35 .... (b) PaulFessey 2	1
			(S T Mason) *sn pushed along and prom: rdn and wknd over 4f out* **20/1**	
600/	6	hd	**Chris Corsa**[230] 4605 5-8-12 63 .... (b[1]) PaulMulrennan 5	5
			(J R Weymes) *chsd ldrs: rdn 1/2-way: sn wknd* **8/1**	

1m 44.09s (0.39) **Going Correction** -0.20s/f (Stan) — **6** Ran SP% **111.7**
Speed ratings (Par 101): **94,93,90,81,73 72**
CSF £19.42 TOTE £2.00: £1.60, £4.00; EX 17.10.There was no bid for the winner.
Owner Mrs Jennifer Marsh **Bred** Yeomanstown Stud **Trained** West Pinchbeck, Lincs

FOCUS
Although this was a bit more competitive than the first race, it was still a bad seller and it was obvious from some way out that it only concerned the front pair. The winner did not need to be at his best.

3 HAPPY NEW YEAR AT PONTIN'S H'CAP — 1m 6f (F)

1:30 (1:30) (Class 5) (0-75,68) 4-Y-O+ — **£2,461** (£732; £365; £182) **Stalls** Low

Form				RPR
461-	1		**Clear Reef**[11] 7211 4-9-9 **68** .... TGMcLaughlin 4	77+
			(Jane Chapple-Hyam) *hld up: shkn up over 4f out: hdwy and nt clr run over 3f out: led over 1f out: rdn out* **11/8**[1]	
211-	2	1 1/2	**Victory Quest (IRE)**[14] 7178 8-10-0 **67** .... (v) DaneO'Neill 1	73
			(Mrs S Lamyman) *chsd ldrs: led over 6f out: rdn and hdd over 1f out: styd on same pce* **5/2**[2]	
454-	3	3 1/2	**Sand Repeal (IRE)**[18] 7135 6-9-6 **62** .... (v) JerryO'Dwyer(3) 5	63
			(Miss J Feilden) *chsd ldr: rdn over 4f out: hung lft and styd on same pce appr fnl f* **9/2**[3]	
	4	1/2	**Conclave (IRE)**[96] 5763 4-8-2 **54** .... MHarley(7) 3	54
			(Adrian Sexton, Ire) *chsd ldrs: rdn over 3f out: styd on same pce fnl 2f* **10/1**	
026-	5	8	**Exit To Luck (GER)**[33] 2839 7-9-10 **63** .... PaulMulrennan 2	52
			(S Gollings) *led tl over 6f out: rdn over 4f out: wknd over 2f out* **11/1**	

3m 9.89s (1.59) **Going Correction** -0.20s/f (Stan)
WFA 4 from 6yo+ 6lb — **5** Ran SP% **106.3**
Speed ratings (Par 103): **91,90,88,87,83**
CSF £4.60 TOTE £2.00: £1.40, £1.40; EX 3.80.
Owner Chapple-Hyam Serrell Tegel Ward **Bred** Hesmonds Stud Ltd **Trained** Lambourn, Berks

FOCUS
No great pace on for this staying handicap so not the test of stamina it might have been. Weak form behind the front pair.

4 BOOK NOW @ PONTINS.COM H'CAP — 6f (F)

2:05 (2:06) (Class 5) (0-75,73) 4-Y-O+ — **£2,593** (£765; £383) **Stalls** Low

Form				RPR
323-	1		**Tag Team (IRE)**[3] 7271 7-8-4 62 .... AndrewElliott(3) 5	73
			(John A Harris) *mde virtually all: edgd rt over 2f out: rdn out* **9/2**[3]	
213-	2	1/2	**Winthorpe (IRE)**[10] 7227 8-8-6 61 .... (p) LiamJones 4	71
			(J J Quinn) *chsd ldrs: rdn over 1f out: r.o* **7/2**[2]	
636-	3	hd	**Strathmore (IRE)**[3] 7271 4-8-8 63 .... PaulMulrennan 2	72
			(R A Fahey) *s.i.s: sn pushed along in rr: swtchd rt 2f out: hdwy u.p over 1f out: r.o* **7/2**[2]	
040-	4	3	**Cool Sands (IRE)**[4] 7253 6-8-12 67 .... (v) AdamKirby 9	66
			(D Shaw) *hld up: hdwy 2f out: sn rdn: no ex ins fnl f* **3/1**[1]	
515-	5	3/4	**Gone'N'Dunnett (IRE)**[3] 7265 9-8-4 59 oh7 .... (p) NeilPollard 7	56
			(Mrs C A Dunnett) *prom: rdn over 3f out: rdn and edgd lft 2f out: wknd fnl f* **14/1**	
106-	6	1 3/4	**Doubtful Sound (USA)**[11] 7212 4-9-4 73 .... PaulFessey 6	64
			(T D Barron) *w wnr tl hung rt 1/2-way: sn rdn: wknd fnl f* **14/1**	
500-	7	1 1/4	**Spoof Master (IRE)**[21] 7112 4-8-13 73 .... KirstyMilczarek(5) 1	60
			(N A Callaghan) *chsd ldrs 4f* **14/1**	
004-	8	7	**Eloquent Rose (IRE)**[40] 6907 4-8-9 67 .... AndrewMullen(3) 3	32
			(Mrs A Duffield) *sn pushed along and prom: rdn and wknd over 2f out* **10/1**	

1m 16.11s (-0.39) **Going Correction** -0.20s/f (Stan) — **8** Ran SP% **116.7**
Speed ratings (Par 103): **97,96,96,92,91 88,87,77**
CSF £21.13 CT £61.47 TOTE £5.00: £1.30, £1.40, £1.70; EX 15.80 Trifecta £32.90 Pool: £111.33 - 2.40 winning units..
Owner Cleartherm Glass Sealed Units Ltd **Bred** Miss Sally Hodgins **Trained** Eastwell, Leics

FOCUS
A modest sprint handicap and again those that raced up with the pace seemed to be at an advantage. Pretty sound form, with the winner rated back to his best.

5 RING IN THE NEW YEAR @ PONTIN'S H'CAP — 5f (F)

2:40 (2:40) (Class 2) (0-100,100) 4-Y-O+ — **£10,525** (£3,131; £1,564; £781) **Stalls** High

Form				RPR
323-	1		**Tartatartufata**[11] 7215 6-7-11 86 oh13 .... (v) PatrickDonaghy(7) 1	91
			(D Shaw) *led to 1/2-way: rdn over 1f out: edgd rt and led ins fnl f: r.o* **25/1**	
051-	2	1 1/4	**Northern Empire (IRE)**[21] 7112 5-8-4 86 oh2 .... PaulFessey 5	86
			(K A Ryan) *hld up in tch: rdn over 1f out: r.o* **11/2**	
023-	3	hd	**Pawan (IRE)**[14] 7179 8-8-1 88 oh8 ow2 .... (b) AnnStokell(5) 8	87
			(Miss A Stokell) *s.i.s: sn chsng ldrs: rdn and edgd lft over 1f out: rdr dropped reins ins fnl f: styd on* **16/1**	
201-	4	shd	**Aegean Dancer**[43] 6876 6-9-1 97 .... PhillipMakin 9	96
			(B Smart) *w ldrs tl led 1/2-way: rdn over 1f out: hdd and unable qck ins fnl f* **7/2**[2]	
312-	5	nk	**Turn On The Style**[4] 7255 6-9-3 99 .... (b) PaulMulrennan 6	97
			(J Balding) *w ldrs: racd keenly: rdn over 1f out: styd on same pce* **11/4**[1]	
003-	6	nk	**Yungaburra (IRE)**[21] 7112 4-8-0 87 oh1 ow1 .... (bt) KirstyMilczarek(5) 4	84
			(D J Murphy) *chsd ldrs: nt clr run over 1f out: styd on same pce fnl f* **11/2**	
050-	7	1 1/2	**Fyodor (IRE)**[45] 6851 7-9-4 100 .... LiamJones 3	91
			(W J Haggas) *dwlt: hld up: effrt over 1f out: no imp* **9/2**[3]	
000-	8	1	**Lethal**[21] 7112 5-8-4 86 oh1 .... DaleGibson 2	74
			(R A Fahey) *sn pushed along and prom: rdn 1/2-way: wknd fnl f* **33/1**	
130-	9	3	**Magic Glade**[21] 7112 9-8-6 88 oh2 ow2 .... LPKeniry 7	65
			(Peter Grayson) *hld up: rdn and wknd wl over 1f out* **16/1**	

59.35 secs (-0.35) **Going Correction** +0.05s/f (Slow) — **9** Ran SP% **116.4**
Speed ratings (Par 109): **109,107,106,106,106 105,103,101,96**
CSF £157.74 CT £2313.73 TOTE £17.00: £3.70, £2.00, £2.90; EX 210.10 Trifecta £168.80 Part won. Pool: £237.82 - 0.10 winning units..
Owner Danethorpe Racing Partnership **Bred** Dr A Ramkaran **Trained** Danethorpe, Notts

FOCUS
A valuable sprint handicap and a decent pace, but with the front three all out of the handicap, two of them very much so, there has to be a slight question mark over the form. One horse stuck to the stands' rail whilst the rest were inclined to race away from it and, as is usually the case over this straight 5f, the ability to lay up with the pace was key. The form has been rated at face value.

NOTEBOOK
Tartatartufata may have had a mountain to climb from 13lb out of the handicap, but crucially she possesses tremendous early pace and made full use of it from a stalls position that boasted impressive statistics before the floods came. The Handicapper is likely to make her pay for this, but this was a nice prize to net which in the meantime will help ease the burden. (op 33-1 tchd 22-1)
Northern Empire(IRE), raised 3lb for edging out Pawan over course and distance the previous month, was still 2lb wrong and although he finished in good style once again he could not get on terms with the winner. (tchd 7-1)
Pawan(IRE), 10lb wrong including his rider's overweight, was 5lb worse off with Northern Empire for a narrow defeat here last time. He had every chance and his rider getting into a muddle with her reins in the closing stages did not affect his chances of winning. In fact he probably put up an improved effort to go down by exactly the same margin to his old rival on these terms, but that is the story with him these days as he has only won once in almost three years, despite numerous efforts, and this performance will not give the Handicapper a reason to drop him. (op 20-1)
Aegean Dancer ◆, raised 5lb for his Wolverhampton victory, was drawn against the stands' rail and stayed there throughout. He ran fast for a very long way and it was only well inside the last furlong that he was beaten off. Before the flooding brought a halt to racing here the stands' rail was a no-go area, especially in these 5f sprints, and if that it still the case (the evidence is still limited since the resumption) then he has run a blinder and is very much one to keep on the right side of. (op 4-1)
Turn On The Style, who has not shown much in two previous tries over this straight 5f, raced up with the pace but was still under retraint and did not seem to like it. Once finally asked for maximum effort, the response was very limited. (tchd 3-1)
Yungaburra(IRE), 2lb wrong including the overweight, but still better off with both Northern Empire and Pawan having finished just behind them over course and distance last month, was unable to turn the form around with that pair. He did not have much room to play with when trying for a gap between Pawan and Turn On The Style over a furlong from home, but it made little difference to the result. (op 13-2 tchd 7-1)
Fyodor(IRE), 11lb higher than when taking this race last year but just 2lb higher than for his last win, was given his usual stalking ride but failed to pick up when asked. (op 7-2)

6 MAKE A DATE IN 2008 @ PONTIN'S H'CAP — 1m (F)

3:10 (3:13) (Class 2) (0-100,95) 4-Y-O+ — **£10,525** (£3,131; £1,564; £781) **Stalls** Low

Form				RPR
000-	1		**Partners In Jazz (USA)**[38] 6932 7-8-12 89 .... PhillipMakin 7	97
			(T D Barron) *hld up: hdwy over 2f out: sn rdn: styd on to ld wl ins fnl f* **4/1**[3]	
114-	2	1	**Kabeer**[5] 7241 10-8-5 85 .... (t) PatrickMathers(3) 2	91
			(A J McCabe) *s.i.s: hdwy over 5f out: chsd ldr over 3f out: led over 2f out: sn rdn: hdd and nt qckn wl ins fnl f* **7/1**	
410-	3	nk	**Vainglory (USA)**[38] 6931 4-8-9 91 .... KirstyMilczarek(5) 6	96
			(D M Simcock) *chsd ldrs: outpcd over 3f out: rallied over 1f out: r.o* **7/4**[1]	
225-	4	3/4	**Electric Warrior (IRE)**[115] 5221 5-8-9 86 .... PaulMulrennan 1	90
			(K R Burke) *chsd ldrs: rdn over 1f out: styd on same pce ins fnl f* **5/2**[2]	
042-	5	5	**Orpen Wide (IRE)**[10] 6539 6-8-5 87 .... (b) NicolPolli(5) 3	79
			(M C Chapman) *led: clr 5f out: sn hung rt: hdd over 2f out: rdn and wknd wl over 1f out* **6/1**	

1m 41.02s (-2.68) **Going Correction** -0.20s/f (Stan) — **5** Ran SP% **111.7**
Speed ratings (Par 109): **109,108,107,106,101**
CSF £29.24 TOTE £5.20: £2.20, £3.10; EX 36.80.
Owner Sporting Occasions Racing No 2 **Bred** Charles Nuckols Jr And Sons **Trained** Maunby, N Yorks

FOCUS
A decent handicap despite the two non-runners and a frantic early pace thanks to Orpen Wide, but the final time was ordinary. The form looks very solid indeed for the grade.

NOTEBOOK
Partners In Jazz(USA) ◆, winner of the 2006 Victoria Cup, was having only his third outing on sand in his 34th career start and only his second over this trip. Content to sit off the pace, he picked up really well when asked and the way the race was run gave him no place to hide with regards to his stamina. If an opportunity can be found, he can certainly win again under similar conditions now that he has proved he stays. (tchd 7-2 and 5-1)

Kabeer, disappointing in his hat-trick bid here the previous week, was up another 5lb here and emerges with plenty of credit especially after fluffing the start. The only negative was that he carried his head a shade high when in front halfway up the home straight before getting worn down and it may be that he needs a little break now. (op 5-1)
Vainglory(USA), 9lb higher than when winning at Wolverhampton two starts ago and outclassed in Listed company in the meantime, struggled to go with his rivals turning for home before staying on again late. The drop in trip looked as much of a problem as the inflated mark. (op 11-4)
Electric Warrior(IRE), still 7lb above his last winning mark, had every chance and may just have needed this after nearly four months off. (op 11-4)
Orpen Wide(IRE), back on the Flat after a spell over hurdles, is proven under these conditions but he went off far too fast and never had a prayer of lasting home. (op 9-2)

7 SOUTHWELL-RACECOURSE.CO.UK H'CAP 1m (F)
3:40 (3:40) (Class 6) (0-55,61) 4-Y-0+ **£1,911** (£564; £282) **Stalls** Low

Form RPR
104- 1 **Montemayorprincess (IRE)**[29] 7009 4-8-2 **48**......(p) AndrewElliott(3) 10 59
(D Haydn Jones) *chsd ldr tl rdn to ld over 3f out: hung lft towards fin: styd on* **11/1**
405- 2 ½ **Wodhill Gold**[35] 6956 7-8-1 **49**..............................(v) KirstyMilczarek(5) 9 59
(D Morris) *led over 4f: sn rdn: styd on* **11/2**[3]
001- 3 ¾ **Zabeel House**[3] 7275 5-9-4 **61** 6ex..................(p) DeanMcKeown 8 69
(John A Harris) *hld up: hdwy 1/2-way: rdn and hung lft fr over 1f out: nt qckn* **3/1**[2]
324- 4 6 **Ruffie (IRE)**[12] 7197 5-8-2 **50**..(e) NicolPolli(5) 6 44
(Miss Gay Kelleway) *hld up in tch: n.m.r and lost pl over 5f out: n.d after* **9/1**
312- 5 1 ¾ **Only A Grand**[5] 7244 4-8-7 **53**.................................(b) AndrewMullen(3) 4 43
(R Bastiman) *chsd ldrs: rdn over 3f out: edgd rt and wknd over 1f out* **11/4**[1]
002- 6 ½ **Shifty**[12] 7197 9-8-2 **52**.. JamieKyne(7) 5 41
(D Carroll) *prom: racd keenly: lost pl over 3f out: rdn over 2f out: no ch whn hmpd over 1f out* **15/2**
050- 7 1 **Ella Y Rossa**[23] 7083 4-8-4 **54**.. RichardEvans(7) 7 41
(P D Evans) *sn pushed along in rr: rdn over 2f out: n.d* **12/1**
004- 8 ¾ **Royal Orissa**[17] 7148 6-8-3 **46** oh1......................................(p) LiamJones 2 31
(D Haydn Jones) *s.i.s: sme hdwy over 4f out: wknd 3f out* **12/1**
054- 9 nk **Naledi**[5] 7244 4-8-12 **55**.. PaulMulrennan 1 39
(J R Norton) *prom over 5f* **20/1**
004- 10 2 ½ **Cove Mountain (IRE)**[11] 7219 6-8-3 **46** oh1..................... DaleGibson 3 25
(M G Rimell) *sn pushed along in rr: bhd fr 1/2-way* **28/1**

1m 41.95s (-1.75) **Going Correction** -0.20s/f (Stan) **10** Ran SP% **120.7**
Speed ratings (Par 101): **105,104,103,97,96 95,94,93,93,90**
CSF £72.97 CT £209.53 TOTE £14.40: £3.30, £2.00, £1.50; EX 98.90 TRIFECTA Not won. Place 6 £196.18, Place 5 £165.33.
Owner R Phillips **Bred** Thomas Morrin **Trained** Efail Isaf, Rhondda C Taff

FOCUS
A modest handicap, but this looks good form for the grade with the first three clear. They went a decent pace and the front pair were at the sharp end throughout.
T/Plt: £71.20 to a £1 stake. Pool: £32,563.25. 333.75 winning tickets. T/Qpdt: £31.90 to a £1 stake. Pool: £2,596.10. 60.10 winning tickets. CR

KEMPTON (A.W) (R-H)
Wednesday, January 2

OFFICIAL GOING: Standard
Wind: Moderate to strong, half behind Weather: Cold

8 TURFTV CLASSIFIED STKS 1m 2f (P)
6:20 (6:21) (Class 7) 4-Y-0+ **£1,365** (£403; £201) **Stalls** High

Form RPR
0/ 1 **Lough Beg (IRE)**[60] 6659 5-9-0 45...........................(t) DaneO'Neill 12 52
(Miss Tor Sturgis) *hld up in midfield: stdy prog 2f out to chse ldr 1f out: drvn and styd on to ld last 75yds* **5/1**[2]
050- 2 ½ **Fortune Point (IRE)**[20] 6529 10-9-0 45..................(p) RichardHughes 11 51
(A W Carroll) *led: drvn 2f out: worn down last 75yds* **8/1**
2/3- 3 ½ **Veneer (IRE)**[20] 7133 6-9-0 45............................ StephenDonohoe 14 50
(Mrs N S Evans) *lw: trckd ldrs: prog over 1f out: pressed ldrs fnl f: styng on but hld whn nt clr run last 75yds* **15/2**
042- 4 1 ½ **The Power Of Phil**[13] 7201 4-8-12 45..................... RichardKingscote 4 47
(Miss Joanne Priest) *wl in tch: prog over 2f out: clsd on ldrs 1f out: nt qckn fnl f* **15/2**
054- 5 nk **Big Ralph**[14] 7185 5-9-0 45..(p) JimCrowley 6 46
(D K Ivory) *trckd ldng trio: prog to chse ldr 2f out to 1f out: wknd* **9/2**[1]
2/0- 6 1 **Busy Man (IRE)**[23] 7098 9-9-0 45................................... PaulDoe 5 44+
(R C Guest) *stdd s: hld up in last pair: stl there but gng strly over 2f out: prog over 1f out to chse clr ldng quintet: styd on: hopeless task* **14/1**
005- 7 4 **Princess Zaha**[20] 7133 6-9-0 44................................ FergusSweeney 8 36
(A G Newcombe) *lw: hld up in midfield: rdn and no prog 2f out: fdd* **14/1**
404- 8 shd **Falcon Flyer**[17] 7166 4-8-12 45................................... SteveDrowne 3 36
(J R Best) *hld up in rr: sme prog 2f out: no imp over 1f out: wknd* **10/1**
056- 9 1 ¼ **Telling**[20] 7133 4-8-9 45..................................... AndrewMullen(3) 1 34
(Mrs A Duffield) *dwlt: rushed up to chse ldr: lost 2nd and wknd 2f out* **16/1**
050- 10 2 **War Feather**[22] 7069 6-9-0 44..(b[1]) AdamKirby 2 30
(T D McCarthy) *hld up towards rr on outer: sme prog over 2f out: wknd over 1f out* **20/1**
200- 11 7 **Montana Sky (IRE)**[35] 6969 5-9-0 45........................... TGMcLaughlin 9 16
(R A Harris) *lost pl and in rr fr 1/2-way: no prog 2f out: wknd* **7/1**[3]
000- 12 13 **Marker**[67] 5425 8-8-9 45.................................... HaddenFrost(5) 13 —
(J D Frost) *prom tl wknd over 2f out: t.o* **16/1**
/00- 13 dist **Ticking**[35] 6968 5-9-0 44.. MickyFenton 7 —
(T Keddy) *a last: bhd 4f out: virtually p.u fnl 2f* **16/1**

2m 9.57s (1.57) **Going Correction** -0.10s/f (Stan)
WFA 4 from 5yo+ 2lb **13** Ran SP% **126.8**
Speed ratings (Par 97): **93,92,92,91,90 89,86,86,85,84 78,68,—**
CSF £47.95 TOTE £6.00: £1.80, £3.50, £1.90; EX 64.40.
Owner M M McGrogan **Bred** Joe Fogarty **Trained** Lambourn, Berks

FOCUS
Ordinary form for the grade, rated through the runner-up who set only a modest pace. The first three were all drawn high.
War Feather Official explanation: jockey said gelding had no more to give
Ticking Official explanation: jockey said gelding was never travelling and hung right-handed

9 HAPPY NEW YEAR FROM KEMPTON PARK MAIDEN STKS 5f (P)
6:50 (6:52) (Class 5) 3-Y-0 **£2,590** (£770; £385; £192) **Stalls** High

Form RPR
1 **The Little Fizzer (IRE)** 3-8-12 0.............................. FergusSweeney 4 63
(K R Burke) *str: bit bkwd: trckd ldng pair: swtchd ins and effrt over 1f out: styd on fnl f to ld last strides* **11/1**[3]
2 hd **Hurricane Hen**[54] 6783 3-9-3 82................................ SteveDrowne 2 67
(D M Simcock) *trckd ldng pair: effrt wl over 1f out: shkn up to ld ent fnl f: fnd little in front: hdd last strides* **8/15**[1]
5- 3 ½ **Jane's Payoff (IRE)**[13] 7196 3-8-12 0........................ RichardThomas 1 60
(Mrs L C Jewell) *mde most tl ent fnl f: kpt on same pce* **66/1**
032- 4 shd **Orange Square (IRE)**[25] 7071 3-9-3 66........................ RichardHughes 7 65
(R Hannon) *settled in 5th: checked bnd 2f out: rdn and nt qckn over 1f out: styd on fnl f: nrst fin* **11/4**[2]
000- 5 7 **Far Song (IRE)**[12] 7216 3-8-12 57... LPKeniry 3 35
(A M Balding) *b.hind: pressed ldr tl wknd rapidly over 1f out* **16/1**
6 1 ¾ **Lady Amberlini** 3-8-12 0...................................... StephenDonohoe 5 29
(P D Evans) *bit bkwd: dwlt: outpcd and sn wl bhd: kpt on fnl f* **25/1**

61.30 secs (0.80) **Going Correction** -0.10s/f (Stan) **6** Ran SP% **111.5**
Speed ratings (Par 97): **88,87,86,86,75 72**
CSF £17.39 TOTE £8.40: £2.90, £1.20; EX 17.50.
Owner Fighttheban Partnership V **Bred** John McEnery **Trained** Middleham Moor, N Yorks

FOCUS
The first four finished in a heap in this ordinary event. The fourth may turn out to be the best guide to the form.

10 DIGIBET H'CAP 1m 2f (P)
7:20 (7:21) (Class 6) (0-52,57) 4-Y-0+ **£2,047** (£604; £302) **Stalls** High

Form RPR
304- 1 **Earl Kraul (IRE)**[28] 7028 5-8-12 **50**................................ AdamKirby 3 62
(G L Moore) *lw: hld up wl in rr: gd prog fr over 2f out: drvn and sustained effrt to ld last 100yds* **11/2**[2]
010- 2 ¾ **Under Fire (IRE)**[25] 7079 5-8-4 **49**............................ MarkCoumbe(7) 5 60
(A W Carroll) *chsd ldr: rdn to cl and led over 1f out: hdd last 100yds: kpt on* **33/1**
304- 3 1 ½ **Formidable Guest**[24] 7088 4-8-10 **50**........................... DaneO'Neill 11 58
(J Pearce) *dwlt: hld up in midfield: prog over 2f out: drifted lft over 1f out: hdwy w wnr after: nt qckn ins fnl f* **8/1**[3]
416- 4 ½ **Play Up Pompey**[5] 7257 6-9-0 **52**................................... AmirQuinn 6 59
(J J Bridger) *hld up in rr: n.m.r after 2f: effrt whn hmpd over 2f out: prog on inner over 1f out: styd on: unable to rch ldrs* **11/2**[2]
300- 5 1 ¾ **Bear Bottom**[17] 7167 4-8-12 **52**............................ TGMcLaughlin 14 55
(W J Musson) *lw: led: clr after 3f: hdd and no ex over 1f out* **8/1**[3]
020- 6 shd **Shaheer (IRE)**[21] 7115 6-9-0 **52**...............................(v) JimCrowley 10 55
(J Gallagher) *prom: rdn to chse ldng pair over 1f out: fdd ins fnl f* **10/1**
061- 7 2 ½ **Little Miss Tara (IRE)**[3] 7277 4-9-3 **57** 6ex...................(v) DavidKinsella 7 55
(A B Haynes) *hld up in midfield: effrt over 2f out: in tch but hanging whn hmpd over 1f out: no ch after* **9/1**
531- 8 shd **Noah Jameel**[14] 7186 6-8-13 **51**................................ FergusSweeney 8 49
(A G Newcombe) *trckd ldrs on outer: outpcd fr 2f out: n.d after* **4/1**[1]
360- 9 8 **Reveur**[33] 6979 5-8-11 **49**.. LiamJones 9 31
(M Mullineaux) *nvr beyond midfield: wknd 2f out: t.o* **20/1**
/00- 10 4 **Lady Firecracker (IRE)**[17] 7167 4-8-10 **50**...................... SteveDrowne 4 24
(J R Best) *a bhd: last and drvn 4f out: t.o* **33/1**
000- 11 5 **Charlie Bear**[67] 5094 7-8-11 **49**............................ AdrianMcCarthy 12 13
(Miss Z C Davison) *prom tl wknd rapidly 3f out: t.o* **50/1**
053- 12 3 **Josr's Magic (IRE)**[23] 7098 4-8-8 **53** ow3.................... HaddenFrost(5) 1 11
(H J Collingridge) *b: racd v wd in rr: prog on outer 4f out: wknd over 2f out: t.o* **8/1**[3]
000- 13 nk **Not Too Taxing**[147] 4272 4-8-10 **50**.................(vt[1]) RichardKingscote 13 7
(G A Ham) *prom tl wknd rapidly over 3f out: t.o* **66/1**
004- 14 4 **Only Hope**[17] 7168 4-8-10 **50**...................................(p) PaulEddery 2 —
(Miss Diana Weeden) *dwlt: a in rr: t.o* **25/1**

2m 6.70s (-1.30) **Going Correction** -0.10s/f (Stan)
WFA 4 from 5yo+ 2lb **14** Ran SP% **121.1**
Speed ratings (Par 101): **105,104,103,102,101 101,99,99,92,89 85,83,83,79**
CSF £189.61 CT £1463.82 TOTE £7.40: £2.40, £7.40, £2.40; EX 148.30.
Owner Miss Samantha Dare **Bred** Gerry Flannery **Trained** Woodingdean, E Sussex
■ Stewards' Enquiry : Adam Kirby caution: careless riding
Dane O'Neill two-day ban: careless riding (Jan 13-14)

FOCUS
A fairly competitive handicap and good form for the grade, rated through the second and fourth.
Play Up Pompey Official explanation: jockey said gelding was denied a clear run

11 DIGIBET CLASSIFIED STKS 1m (P)
7:50 (7:52) (Class 7) 4-Y-0+ **£1,365** (£403; £201) **Stalls** High

Form RPR
646- 1 **Future Deal**[28] 7034 7-9-0 44.. SimonWhitworth 7 52
(C A Horgan) *sn restrained in last trio: stdy prog fr over 2f out: drvn to chal ins fnl f: led last 50yds* **10/1**
030- 2 nk **Abbeygate**[20] 7133 7-9-0 44......................................(p) NickyMackay 13 51
(T Keddy) *drvn in rr early: sn rchd midfield: prog over 2f out: clsd on ldrs over 1f out but racd awkwardly: chal fnl f: jst hld* **10/3**[1]
400- 3 hd **Only If I Laugh**[3] 7278 7-9-0 43.............................. SteveDrowne 12 51
(M J Attwater) *chsd ldrs: rdn to take 2nd wl over 1f out: narrow ld ins fnl f: hdd and no ex last 50yds* **11/1**
220- 4 shd **Sion Hill (IRE)**[13] 7197 7-9-0 45..............................(p) DeanMcKeown 10 51
(John A Harris) *lw: led at str pce: 3 l clr 3f out: hrd pressed over 1f out: hdd ins fnl f: stl upsides 75yds out: no ex* **9/2**[2]
0/0- 5 3 ½ **Club Captain (USA)**[79] 6238 5-9-0 45............................ AdamKirby 14 43
(T D McCarthy) *b: v awkward s: mostly in last trio tl prog over 2f out: chsd ldrs over 1f out: one pce fnl f* **16/1**
006- 6 hd **Mucho Loco (IRE)**[23] 7098 5-9-0 45................................(b) DaneO'Neill 11 42
(R Curtis) *wl in rr: stdy prog over 2f out: shkn up and chsng ldrs over 1f out: no imp after* **8/1**[3]
000- 7 2 ½ **Golden Square**[36] 6311 6-8-9 43............................ KirstyMilczarek(5) 6 36
(A W Carroll) *prom: chsd ldr over 3f out to wl over 1f out: wknd rapidly ins fnl f* **8/1**[3]
0/5- 8 5 **Rhuby River (IRE)**[17] 7167 6-9-0 42.............................. MickyFenton 9 25
(R Dickin) *chsd ldrs: effrt 3f out: sn no imp: wknd wl over 1f out* **25/1**
020/ 9 3 **Tuscan Treaty**[610] 1395 8-9-0 43......................................(t) JimCrowley 3 18
(R W Price) *a towards rr: struggling wl over 2f out* **20/1**

00/- **10** 2 1/2 **Loaderfun (IRE)**[154] 6531 6-9-0 45..............................(e) DanielTudhope 2 12
(I W McInnes) *prom: effrt to chse ldng pair over 3f out: drvn wknd rapidly fnl 2f* **16/1**
000- **11** 3/4 **Tagula Sands (IRE)**[28] 7029 4-9-0 45.......................... RichardHughes 8 10
(J C Fox) *nvr beyond midfield: struggling wl over 2f out: wknd* **12/1**
000- **12** 5 **My Spring Rose**[17] 7167 4-9-0 42.................................... GregFairley 5 —
(J R Jenkins) *prom tl wknd wl over 2f out* **50/1**
000- **13** 16 **Pont Wood**[46] 6858 4-9-0 45...................................... StephenDonohoe 4 —
(Mrs N S Evans) *hld up in last trio: wknd 3f out: t.o* **16/1**
000- **14** dist **Christian Bendix**[22] 7107 6-9-0 42..............................(p) TGMcLaughlin 1 —
(P Howling) *chsd ldr to over 3f out: wknd rapidly: t.o* **33/1**

1m 39.8s **Going Correction** -0.10s/f (Stan) **14** Ran SP% **119.8**
Speed ratings (Par 97): **101,100,100,100,96 96,94,89,86,83 82,77,61,—**
CSF £41.31 TOTE £11.30: £4.00, £1.90, £4.70; EX 52.40.
Owner Mrs B Woodford **Bred** Mrs B Woodford **Trained** Uffcott, Wilts
■ Stewards' Enquiry : Steve Drowne two-day ban: used whip with excessive frequency (Jan 13-14)

FOCUS
They went a good pace in this very ordinary contest. Sound form for the grade.
Christian Bendix Official explanation: vet said gelding was distressed

12 DIGIBET SPORTS BETTING H'CAP 1m (P)
8:20 (8:21) (Class 5) (0-70,70) 3-Y-O **£2,590** (£770; £385; £192) **Stalls** High

Form RPR
005- **1** **Contessina (IRE)**[14] 7190 3-8-8 63.............................. TolleyDean(5) 4 67
(P F I Cole) *hld up in 6th: pushed along 1/2-way: prog to chse ldng pair over 1f out: styd on wl fnl f to ld last 50yds* **7/1**
302- **2** 3/4 **Leamington (USA)**[12] 7208 3-9-4 68.............................. GregFairley 2 70
(M Johnston) *lw: led: set stdy pce tl skipped at least 3 l clr 3f out: hung lft 2f out: hdd last 50yds* **9/2**[3]
543- **3** 1 **Tallulah Sunrise**[5] 7260 3-9-4 68.............................. DaneO'Neill 7 68
(M D I Usher) *hld up in 4th: prog to chse clr ldr over 2f out: clsd 1f out: nt qckn ins fnl f* **7/2**[2]
041- **4** 3 **Bridge Of Fermoy (IRE)**[109] 5423 3-9-2 66..................(t) MickyFenton 8 59
(Miss Gay Kelleway) *b.hind: mostly chsd ldr to over 2f out: nt qckn and sn btn: plugged on* **13/2**
050- **5** 1 **Hold That Call (USA)**[42] 6892 3-9-1 65...................... RichardHughes 1 56
(R Hannon) *heavily restrained s and hld up in last: effrt over 2f out and sme prog: shkn up and no hdwy over 1f out* **16/1**
361- **6** nk **Miss Phoebe (IRE)**[5] 7258 3-9-1 70 6ex.................... HaddenFrost(5) 3 60
(S Kirk) *trckd ldng pair: rdn over 3f out: lost pl and struggling over 2f out* **9/4**[1]
032- **7** nk **Alabama Spirit (USA)**[14] 7182 3-8-11 61.................... DeanMcKeown 5 50
(D Shaw) *rrd s: hld up in last: urged along and effrt over 2f out: no hdwy over 1f out* **12/1**
006- **8** 10 **Viola Rosa (IRE)**[14] 7182 3-8-1 54 oh9...................... DuranFentiman(3) 6 20
(D Shaw) *lw: hld up in 5th and racd on outer: rdn over 3f out: sn wknd and bhd* **12/1**

1m 40.52s (0.72) **Going Correction** -0.10s/f (Stan) **8** Ran SP% **118.3**
Speed ratings (Par 97): **97,96,95,92,91 90,90,80**
CSF £39.82 CT £131.70 TOTE £11.20: £3.00, £1.50, £2.00; EX 43.80.
Owner C Shiacolas **Bred** Christoph Amerian **Trained** Whatcombe, Oxon

FOCUS
They went a steady early gallop here and the race developed into something of a sprint. The form makes sense on figures but may not prove the most solid.
Contessina(IRE) Official explanation: trainer's rep said, regarding the improved forn shown, filly had benefited from the step up in trip to a mile
Miss Phoebe(IRE) Official explanation: jockey said filly never picked up
Viola Rosa(IRE) Official explanation: jockey said filly hung left-handed

13 KEMPTON.CO.UK H'CAP 6f (P)
8:50 (8:52) (Class 6) (0-55,55) 4-Y-O+ **£2,047** (£604; £302) **Stalls** High

Form RPR
020- **1** **Arfinnit (IRE)**[4] 7265 7-8-8 54..............................(p) KirstyMilczarek(5) 6 66
(Mrs A L M King) *lw: mde all: kicked clr wl over 1f out: unchal after* **12/1**
216- **2** 1 1/2 **Royal Envoy (IRE)**[29] 7023 5-9-0 55.............................. DeanMcKeown 4 62
(D Shaw) *lw: hld up in last trio: sme prog over 2f out: urged along and hdwy over 1f out: wnt 2nd last 100yds: nt rch wnr* **5/1**[2]
640- **3** 1 **Midmaar (IRE)**[3] 7278 7-8-9 50.............................. NickyMackay 12 54
(M Wigham) *lw: chsd wnr to over 3f out and again over 2f out: no imp over 1f out: lost 2nd ins fnl f* **9/2**[1]
462- **4** nk **Tilsworth Charlie**[21] 7118 5-8-13 54..........................(b) RichardHughes 11 57
(J R Jenkins) *cl up: rdn to dispute 2nd over 1f out: one pce and no imp wnr* **9/2**[1]
505- **5** 3 **Ishibee (IRE)**[29] 7013 4-9-0 55..............................(p) AmirQuinn 10 48
(J J Bridger) *t.k.h: hld up bhd ldrs: effrt on inner over 2f out: no imp over 1f out: wknd fnl f* **12/1**
041- **6** 1 1/4 **Is It Time (IRE)**[19] 7138 4-8-7 55.............................. NBazeley(7) 1 44
(Mrs P N Dutfield) *lw: plld hrd: hld up on outer tl prog to chse wnr over 3f out to over 2f out: sn btn* **16/1**
004- **7** nk **Lucius Verrus (USA)**[22] 7113 8-9-0 55..........................(v) DaneO'Neill 7 43
(D Shaw) *chsd ldrs: rdn and hanging over 2f out: fnd nil* **9/1**
000- **8** 3/4 **Fish Called Johnny**[14] 7192 4-8-12 53.............................. LPKeniry 8 39
(Peter Grayson) *prom: rdn and hanging over 2f out: sn wknd* **14/1**
005- **9** nk **Granakey (IRE)**[13] 7207 5-8-12 53.............................. JamieMackay 5 38
(M Wigham) *stdd s: hld up in last: shuffled along 2f out: nvr nr ldrs* **14/1**
561- **10** 3/4 **Lost All Alone**[39] 6925 4-8-3 51 ow1.............................. ChrisHough(7) 9 34
(D M Simcock) *lw: hld up in last trio: shkn up and hanging over 2f out: sn wknd* **7/1**[3]
413- **11** 2 **Mister Elegant**[12] 7209 6-8-11 52.............................. AdamKirby 3 28
(J L Spearing) *t.k.h: hld up: brief effrt on outer 1/2-way: wknd over 2f out* **8/1**

1m 13.27s (0.17) **Going Correction** -0.10s/f (Stan) **11** Ran SP% **121.2**
Speed ratings (Par 101): **98,96,94,94,90 88,88,87,86,85 83**
CSF £73.28 CT £325.35 TOTE £16.90: £5.50, £2.20, £2.70; EX 70.00.
Owner All The Kings Horses **Bred** Robert De Vere Hunt **Trained** Wilmcote, Warwicks
■ Stewards' Enquiry : Jamie Mackay 60-day ban: breach of Rule 157 in this race and in Granakey's previous race

FOCUS
An ordinary handicap run at a fair pace but dominated throughout by the leader. Sound form for the grade.
Granakey(IRE) Official explanation: 40-day ban (Mar 18-Apr 26); jockey said, regarding the running and riding, his orders were to jump out and get the best possible position, but that he missed the break and was outpaced; trainer added that mare probably wants further

14 FOLLOW YOUR MEETING WITH FLOODLIT RACING H'CAP 2m (P)
9:20 (9:20) (Class 6) (0-65,65) 4-Y-O+ **£2,047** (£604; £302) **Stalls** High

Form RPR
614- **1** **Snowberry Hill (USA)**[18] 7154 5-9-3 55.............................. NeilChalmers(3) 7 63
(Lucinda Featherstone) *hld up towards rr: prog 3f out: clsd on ldrs over 1f out: drvn ahd last 100yds* **33/1**
461- **2** nk **Prince Of Medina**[13] 7203 5-8-11 46.............................. SteveDrowne 8 53
(J R Best) *hld up in midfield: prog on inner over 2f out: rdn to chal and upsides fnl f: jst hld* **14/1**
224- **3** nk **Haatmey**[16] 7172 6-9-4 53..............................(v) LPKeniry 14 60
(P R Chamings) *mostly trckd ldr: led on inner wl over 2f out: sn drvn: hdd and no ex last 100yds* **8/1**
605- **4** 3 1/2 **Most Definitely (IRE)**[40] 4544 8-10-0 63.............................. RichardHughes 12 66
(R M Stronge) *dwlt: hld up in last pair: smooth prog fr 3f out: trckd ldrs over 1f out: rdn and fnd nil fnl f* **7/1**[3]
423- **5** nk **Sovereign Spirit (IRE)**[22] 6271 6-9-13 62..........................(t) JimCrowley 11 64
(C Gordon) *rn wout declared tongue-strap: wl plcd: effrt 3f out: pressing ldrs over 1f out: fdd ins fnl f* **8/1**
622- **6** 5 **Party Palace**[49] 6817 4-8-4 46.............................. AdrianMcCarthy 4 42
(H S Howe) *settled in midfield: prog over 3f out: u.p and lft bhd by ldrs fnl 2f* **20/1**
020- **7** 1 1/2 **Dubai Ace (USA)**[30] 7004 7-10-0 63..............................(p) DaneO'Neill 5 58
(Miss Sheena West) *reminders in rr after 2f: prog over 3f out to chse ldrs: wknd over 1f out* **25/1**
506- **8** 3 1/2 **Ghaill Force**[17] 7168 6-8-10 45.............................. RichardThomas 10 35
(P Butler) *s.v.s: mostly last tl kpt on fr over 2f out: no ch* **50/1**
021- **9** 5 **Bugsy's Boy**[25] 7081 4-9-7 63.............................. LiamJones 3 47
(P W D'Arcy) *led to wl over 2f out: sn wandering and wknd* **9/4**[1]
/55- **10** 2 1/2 **Grasp**[20] 2770 6-9-8 57..............................(b) GeorgeBaker 2 38
(G L Moore) *lw: hld up in midfield: prog to dispute 2nd over 4f out: wknd u.p over 2f out* **7/2**[2]
660- **11** 2 **Mr Excel (IRE)**[11] 7226 5-9-6 55.............................. RichardKingscote 13 34
(G A Ham) *mostly in midfield: rdn 3f out: sn wknd* **50/1**
103- **12** 6 **Stringsofmyheart**[12] 7211 4-9-9 65..............................(e) AdamKirby 1 37
(Miss Gay Kelleway) *lw: prom tl wknd 4f out* **16/1**
000- **13** 3/4 **Burnley (IRE)**[174] 3476 5-8-6 46.............................. RussellKennemore(5) 9 17
(Mrs A L M King) *a in rr: u.p and wkng wl over 3f out* **50/1**
650- **14** 41 **Sea Map**[320] 482 6-8-13 55.............................. HarryPoulton(7) 6 —
(Miss Sheena West) *b: a towards rr: wknd 5f out: t.o whn virtually p.u fnl 2f* **33/1**

3m 29.42s (-0.68) **Going Correction** -0.10s/f (Stan)
WFA 4 from 5yo+ 7lb **14** Ran SP% **120.6**
Speed ratings (Par 101): **100,99,99,97,97 95,94,92,90,89 88,85,84,64**
CSF £421.10 CT £4026.65 TOTE £34.80: £8.50, £4.30, £3.00; EX 256.50 Place 6 £129.34, Place 5 £47.25.
Owner J Roundtree **Bred** Russell S Fisher And Joe Sagginario **Trained** Atlow, Derbyshire

FOCUS
They went a good pace in this staying handicap and the main contenders at the finish were largely hold-up horses. Sound form despite the big-priced winner.
T/Plt: £117.90 to a £1 stake. Pool: £92,045.40. 569.70 winning tickets. T/Qpdt: £36.00 to a £1 stake. Pool: £5,865.90. 120.40 winning tickets. JN

WOLVERHAMPTON (A.W) (L-H)
Wednesday, January 2

OFFICIAL GOING: Standard
Wind: Fresh, half-against Weather: Overcast

15 HAPPY NEW YEAR @ PONTIN'S CLAIMING STKS 7f 32y(P)
1:20 (1:22) (Class 6) 4-Y-O+ **£2,047** (£604; £302) **Stalls** High

Form RPR
502- **1** **Obe Royal**[7] 7233 4-8-10 58..............................(b) RichardEvans(7) 6 77
(P D Evans) *hld up: hdwy over 2f out: led ins fnl f: rdn out* **6/1**[3]
056- **2** 2 **Sir Douglas**[25] 7073 5-9-5 70..............................(p) TGMcLaughlin 2 74
(R A Harris) *a.p: chsd ldr 5f out: rdn over 1f out: hung lft ins fnl f: nt run on* **8/1**
000- **3** 1 **Another Genepi (USA)**[7] 7233 5-8-8 66..................(b) PaulMulrennan 9 60
(K A Ryan) *sn rdn to ld: edgd rt over 1f out: hdd and no ex ins fnl f* **6/1**[3]
312- **4** nk **Alto Vertigo**[22] 7113 5-8-8 60.............................. PatrickDonaghy(7) 5 66
(P C Haslam) *prom: hung rt over 2f out: rdn and swtchd rt over 1f out: hung lft ins fnl f: nt trble ldrs* **2/1**[1]
540- **5** 3 1/2 **Satyricon**[23] 7094 4-8-13 72..............................(b) AshleyHamblett(5) 4 60
(M Botti) *hld up in tch: lost pl 5f out: n.d after* **6/1**[3]
005- **6** 1 1/4 **Gifted Flame**[7] 7233 9-8-7 42.............................. AnnStokell(5) 8 50
(Miss A Stokell) *s.i.s: hdwy over 5f out: wknd over 2f out* **40/1**
423- **7** 2 **Green Pirate**[7] 7233 6-8-11 62..............................(b[1]) LiamJones 7 44
(W M Brisbourne) *sn pushed along in rr: rdn over 2f out: no rspnse* **4/1**[2]
030- **8** 16 **Telepathic (IRE)**[140] 4494 8-8-12 38.............................. JamesDoyle 1 —
(A Berry) *led early: chsd ldr to 5f out: wknd over 2f out* **80/1**

1m 30.26s (0.66) **Going Correction** +0.075s/f (Slow) **8** Ran SP% **111.0**
Speed ratings (Par 101): **103,100,99,99,95 93,91,73**
CSF £49.36 TOTE £5.30: £1.50, £2.60, £1.80; EX 47.20 Trifecta £105.00 Pool: £276.56 - 1.87 winning units..
Owner Mrs I M Folkes **Bred** Helshaw Grange Stud Ltd **Trained** Pandy, Monmouths
■ Stewards' Enquiry : Paul Mulrennan one-day ban: failed to keep straight from stalls (Jan 13)

FOCUS
Probably only a modest claimer containing a few unconvincing characters. The winner is rated back to his best bit might have been flattered.
Green Pirate Official explanation: jockey said gelding would not face the first-time blinkers

16 WOLVERHAMPTON-RACECOURSE.CO.UK (S) STKS 5f 216y(P)
1:50 (1:51) (Class 6) 4-Y-O+ **£1,774** (£523; £262) **Stalls** Low

Form RPR
104- **1** **Mafaheem**[25] 7077 6-9-7 66.............................. GeorgeBaker 4 70
(A B Haynes) *mid-div: hdwy over 2f out: rdn to ld and hung lft ins fnl f: r.o* **15/8**[1]
220- **2** 1 1/2 **Macademy Royal (USA)**[32] 6993 5-8-13 62..............(t) TravisBlock(3) 2 60
(H Morrison) *chsd ldrs: rdn and nt clr run over 1f out: styd on same pce ins fnl f* **5/2**[2]

300- **3** ½ **Calloff The Search**[7] 7233 4-8-11 46.....(v) MickyFenton 5 53
(Stef Liddiard) *sn led: hdd 5f out: led again 4f out: rdn and edgd rt over 1f out: hdd and no ex ins fnl f* **14/1**

060- **4** 1¼ **Hart Of Gold**[29] 7020 4-9-7 63..... TGMcLaughlin 12 59
(R A Harris) *hld up: hmpd over 2f out: hdwy and hung lft over 1f out: nt trble ldrs* **17/2**

024- **5** nk **Phinerine**[19] 7138 5-8-11 51.....(p[1]) TolleyDean(5) 10 53
(Miss J E Foster) *outpcd: hdwy u.p over 1f out: styd on same pce fnl f* **16/1**

046- **6** ½ **Cyfrwys (IRE)**[25] 7077 7-9-2 44.....(p) RichardKingscote 8 52
(B Palling) *chsd ldrs: rdn and edgd lft over 1f out: no ex fnl f* **16/1**

045- **7** 1½ **Mind Alert**[3] 7276 7-9-7 48.....(v) DeanMcKeown 3 52
(D Shaw) *chsd ldrs: rdn over 1f out: wkng whn nt clr run ins fnl f* **8/1**[3]

005- **8** 1½ **Blushing Russian (IRE)**[14] 7188 6-8-9 42.....(p) PietroRomeo(7) 9 42
(J M Bradley) *sn outpcd: nvr nrr* **33/1**

400- **9** hd **Isobel Rose (IRE)**[22] 7113 4-8-6 48.....(b) LiamJones 11 32
(J L Spearing) *mid-div: hdwy and stmbld over 2f out: sn rdn: wkng whn hung lft fr over 1f out* **14/1**

000- **10** 2½ **Cayman Breeze**[14] 7192 8-9-10 42.....(b) BarrySavage(7) 1 49
(J M Bradley) *hld up: effrt over 1f out: wkng whn n.m.r ins fnl f* **66/1**

00P- **11** 5 **Diamond Josh**[11] 7226 6-8-4 42.....(be[1]) RossAtkinson(7) 7 13
(M Mullineaux) *led 5f out to 4f out: rdn and wknd over 1f out* **40/1**

400- **12** 3 **Obe One**[22] 7107 8-9-7 44.....(b) PaulMulrennan 6 13
(A Berry) *sn outpcd* **22/1**

1m 16.0s (1.00) **Going Correction** +0.075s/f (Slow) **12** Ran SP% **121.3**
Speed ratings (Par 101): **101,99,98,96,96 95,93,91,91,88 81,77**
CSF £6.35 TOTE £2.90: £1.40, £1.30, £5.70; EX 9.40 TRIFECTA Not won..The winner was bought in for 5,500gns.
Owner W Clifford **Bred** J H And J M Wall **Trained** Limpley Stoke, Bath

FOCUS
An ordinary-looking seller, best rated around the third and sixth.

17 ANDREW STEVENS 21ST BIRTHDAY CELEBRATION H'CAP 5f 216y(P)
2:25 (2:25) (Class 5) (0-70,69) 3-Y-O £2,730 (£806; £403) **Stalls** Low

Form RPR

446- **1** **Bertbrand**[5] 7260 3-8-11 **67**..... KirstyMilczarek(5) 3 75
(M Botti) *led 1f: chsd ldrs: led over 1f out: hung rt fnl f: rdn out* **16/1**

611- **2** 2½ **Caprio (IRE)**[35] 6966 3-9-2 **67**..... RichardKingscote 4 67+
(R Charlton) *outpcd: hdwy u.p over 1f out: chsd wnr ins fnl f: no imp* **11/8**[1]

320- **3** ¾ **Splash The Cash**[15] 7176 3-8-13 **64**..... PaulMulrennan 5 62+
(K A Ryan) *hld up: nt clr run over 1f out: r.o ins fnl f: nvr nrr* **15/2**[3]

415- **4** hd **Loose Caboose (IRE)**[56] 6722 3-9-0 **68**..... PatrickMathers(3) 9 65
(A J McCabe) *chsd ldr over 4f out: rdn and ev ch over 1f out: hung lft and no ex fnl f* **8/1**

422- **5** ¾ **Nice Wee Girl (IRE)**[7] 7232 3-8-13 **69**..... HaddenFrost(5) 6 64
(S Kirk) *prom: lost pl over 4f out: hdwy over 1f out: nt rch ldrs* **17/2**

300- **6** 1¾ **Fulford**[103] 5582 3-8-7 **58**..... DaleGibson 2 47
(M Brittain) *prom: racd keenly: rdn over 2f out: wknd ins fnl f* **25/1**

033- **7** 1½ **Andrasta**[6] 7243 3-8-7 **58**..... JamesDoyle 1 43
(A Berry) *hld up: sme hdwy over 1f out: wknd fnl f* **12/1**

212- **8** shd **Martingrange Boy (IRE)**[6] 7240 3-8-13 **69**.....(t) TolleyDean(5) 8 53
(D J Murphy) *led 5f out: rdn and hdd over 1f out: wknd ins fnl f* **4/1**[2]

005- **9** nk **Shabnaam**[27] 7043 3-8-9 **60**..... TonyHamilton 7 43
(K A Ryan) *prom: rdn over 2f out: wknd over 1f out* **33/1**

1m 16.37s (1.37) **Going Correction** +0.075s/f (Slow) **9** Ran SP% **115.9**
Speed ratings (Par 97): **99,95,94,94,93 91,89,88,88**
CSF £38.65 CT £190.75 TOTE £23.50: £6.20, £1.60, £2.20; EX 58.70 Trifecta £266.40 Part won. Pool: £375.27 - 0.37 winning units..
Owner Giuliano Manfredini **Bred** R F And S D Knipe **Trained** Newmarket, Suffolk

FOCUS
A modest event won nicely by Bertrand. The runner-up never figured until late on, while the third was hampered when making an effort.
Caprio(IRE) Official explanation: jockey said colt was slowly into stride
Fulford Official explanation: jockey said gelding hung right
Martingrange Boy(IRE) Official explanation: jockey said gelding hung right

18 CROC AROUND THE CLOCK @ PONTIN'S CLAIMING STKS 1m 4f 50y(P)
2:55 (2:55) (Class 6) 4-Y-O+ £2,047 (£604; £302) **Stalls** Low

Form RPR

662- **1** **Looks The Business (IRE)**[55] 4915 7-8-12 63..... JackDean(7) 1 66
(W G M Turner) *a.p: chsd ldr over 3f out: led over 1f out: edgd rt: rdn out* **7/2**[2]

033- **2** nk **Regency Red (IRE)**[4] 7273 10-8-7 55..... Julie-AnneCumine(7) 4 61
(W M Brisbourne) *chsd ldrs: shkn up and ev ch ins fnl f: edgd lft: styd on* **10/3**[1]

530- **3** 1¾ **Treetops Hotel (IRE)**[6] 7249 9-8-12 62..... RussellKennemore(5) 2 61
(R Hollinshead) *hld up: racd keenly: rdn over 3f out: hdwy over 2f out: styng on same pce whn nt clr run and switchd lft ins fnl f* **5/1**[3]

500- **4** 5 **Atlantic Gamble (IRE)**[11] 7226 8-8-13 58.....(p) AndrewElliott(3) 5 52
(K R Burke) *sn led: rdn and hdd over 1f out: sn wknd* **10/3**[1]

/61- **5** 7 **Shaydreambeliever**[18] 7150 5-9-2 62..... TonyHamilton 3 41
(R A Fahey) *chsd ldr over 8f: wknd 2f out* **7/2**[2]

000- **6** 1 **Smoothie (IRE)**[17] 7168 10-8-6 43..... TolleyDean(5) 6 34
(E G Bevan) *hld up: rdn over 4f out: wknd over 2f out* **25/1**

2m 45.99s (4.89) **Going Correction** +0.075s/f (Slow) **6** Ran SP% **111.1**
Speed ratings (Par 101): **91,90,89,86,81 80**
CSF £15.13 TOTE £4.00: £2.60, £2.30; EX 15.30.
Owner M J B Racing **Bred** Mrs M O'Callaghan **Trained** Sigwells, Somerset
■ Stewards' Enquiry : Jack Dean one-day ban: careless riding (Jan 13); caution: used whip with excessive frequency

FOCUS
A modest race run at a steady pace. The form has been rated through the runner-up but looks suspect.

19 BOOK EARLY @ PONTINS.COM MAIDEN STKS 5f 20y(P)
3:25 (3:25) (Class 5) 3-Y-O+ £2,457 (£725; £362) **Stalls** Low

Form RPR

530- **1** **Star Strider**[107] 5473 4-9-13 64..... GeorgeBaker 8 74
(Miss Gay Kelleway) *hmpd s: chsd ldrs: rdn to ld ins fnl f: edgd rt: r.o* **3/1**[2]

332- **2** 1 **Chivola (IRE)**[32] 7000 3-8-12 75..... PaulMulrennan 3 64
(B Smart) *sn led: rdn and hdd ins fnl f: nt qckn* **4/11**[1]

50- **3** 2½ **Lujiana**[115] 5252 3-8-2 0 ow2..... AdamCarter(7) 1 52
(M Brittain) *chsd ldrs: hung rt thrght: outpcd 1/2-way: r.o ins fnl f* **33/1**

44- **4** 4 **Plenty Of Action (USA)**[7] 7235 3-8-4 0 ow2..... TolleyDean(5) 2 38
(M J Wallace) *sn outpcd: nvr nrr* **14/1**[3]

062- **5** shd **Earl Compton (IRE)**[17] 7162 4-9-13 51.....(v[1]) MickyFenton 5 47
(Stef Liddiard) *wnt rt s: sn hung rt: chsd ldr over 3f out: rdn and hung lft over 1f out: nt run on* **14/1**[3]

00- **6** 7 **Bovered (IRE)**[102] 5625 4-9-5 29.....(b[1]) PatrickMathers(3) 7 16
(A Berry) *hmpd s: sn outpcd* **100/1**

000- **7** 9 **Ten For Tosca (IRE)**[12] 7209 4-9-13 40.....(p) TGMcLaughlin 4 —
(R A Harris) *wnt rt s: chsd ldrs: rdn 1/2-way: sn wknd* **80/1**

63.42 secs (1.12) **Going Correction** +0.075s/f (Slow)
WFA 3 from 4yo 15lb **7** Ran SP% **116.8**
Speed ratings (Par 103): **98,96,92,86,85 74,60**
CSF £4.59 TOTE £3.30: £2.50, £1.10; EX 10.20 Trifecta £75.10 Pool: £392.46 - 3.71 winning units..
Owner Holistic Racing Ltd **Bred** Snailwell Stud Co Ltd **Trained** Exning, Suffolk

FOCUS
A modest-looking maiden in which the winner returned to her best on her first run for a new yard.
Earl Compton(IRE) Official explanation: jockey said gelding hung badly left-handed in the straight

20 RING IN THE NEW YEAR @ PONTIN'S H'CAP 1m 1f 103y(P)
3:55 (3:55) (Class 6) (0-65,65) 3-Y-O £2,047 (£604; £302) **Stalls** Low

Form RPR

040- **1** **Duneen Dream (USA)**[21] 7117 3-8-9 53..... NeilPollard 6 57
(W J Musson) *hld up: hmpd over 4f out: hdwy over 3f out: rdn to ld and edgd lft 1f out: r.o* **13/2**

152- **2** 1¼ **Caltire (GER)**[13] 7204 3-9-2 65.....(b) JamieJones(5) 5 66
(M G Quinlan) *hld up: nt clr run over 2f out: hdwy over 1f out: sn rdn and edgd lft: r.o* **11/2**[3]

031- **3** hd **Ridgeway Jazz**[18] 7149 3-8-5 49..... NickyMackay 1 50
(M D I Usher) *hld up: hdwy over 1f out: n.m.r ins fnl f: r.o* **9/2**[2]

000- **4** ½ **Plaka (FR)**[6] 7245 3-8-12 56..... LiamJones 9 56
(W M Brisbourne) *a.p: chsd ldr over 2f out: rdn and hung lft over 1f out: styd on* **10/1**

000- **5** shd **Boomtown**[23] 7101 3-8-12 63..... MarieLussiana(7) 11 63
(M Johnston) *chsd ldr tl led over 2f out: rdn and edgd lft over 1f out: sn hdd: rdr dropped reins ins fnl f: styd on* **12/1**

003- **6** 1¾ **Silver Sprite**[18] 7149 3-8-10 54..... DeanMcKeown 3 50
(D Shaw) *mid-div: hdwy over 2f out: cl up whn hmpd over 1f out: styd on same pce* **7/1**

006- **7** ½ **Balais Folly (FR)**[30] 7010 3-8-4 53 ow1.....(p) TolleyDean(5) 8 48
(B Palling) *s.i.s: hld up: rdn over 3f out: hdwy over 2f out: hung lft over 1f out: styd on same pce* **12/1**

131- **8** 2 **Carry On Cleo**[5] 7259 3-9-2 60 6ex.....(b) SaleemGolam 7 51
(P D Evans) *mid-div: hdwy over 5f out: rdn over 2f out: wknd ins fnl f* **4/1**[1]

001- **9** 3½ **Ostinata (IRE)**[30] 7010 3-8-8 52..... WandersonD'Avila 2 35
(B W Duke) *hld up: rdn over 3f out: wknd over 2f out* **9/1**

000- **10** 20 **Mujinda**[105] 5526 3-8-2 46 oh1..... DaleGibson 4 —
(M Brittain) *chsd ldrs 6f* **50/1**

000- **P** **Super Starlet (IRE)**[25] 7070 3-8-0 49 oh1 ow3..... KirstyMilczarek(5) 10 —
(M Botti) *led 7f: eased wl over 1f out: p.u fnl f* **22/1**

2m 4.57s (2.87) **Going Correction** +0.075s/f (Slow) **11** Ran SP% **120.2**
Speed ratings (Par 95): **94,92,92,92,92 90,90,88,85,67** —
CSF £43.17 CT £181.30 TOTE £9.80: £3.40, £1.60, £1.70; EX 44.30 Trifecta £216.90 Pool: £369.75 - 1.21 winning units..
Owner EACH Partnership **Bred** Wayne G Lyster III Et Al **Trained** Newmarket, Suffolk

FOCUS
A modest handicap run at a reasonable tempo. Sound form, rated through the runner-up. Improved form from the winner.
Ostinata(IRE) Official explanation: trainer said filly ran flat
Super Starlet(IRE) Official explanation: jockey said filly lost her action, but returned sound

21 GO BOOK TODAY @ PONTIN'S APPRENTICE H'CAP 1m 141y(P)
4:25 (4:25) (Class 5) (0-75,73) 4-Y-O+ £2,457 (£725; £362) **Stalls** Low

Form RPR

231- **1** **Arthur's Edge**[33] 6979 4-8-5 60..... TolleyDean 7 69
(B Palling) *chsd ldr: rdn over 1f out: sn edgd lft and led: r.o* **3/1**[1]

412- **2** ¾ **Jord (IRE)**[12] 7213 4-9-0 69..... KirstyMilczarek 5 76
(A J McCabe) *wnt rt s: led: rdn and hdd 1f out: kpt on* **8/1**

053- **3** ½ **Happy As Larry (USA)**[6] 7241 6-9-2 73.....(t) JackMitchell(3) 3 82+
(D J Murphy) *hld up: hmpd 3f out: nt clr run over 2f out: swtchd rt and hdwy over 1f out: sn hung lft: r.o: nt rch ldrs* **3/1**[1]

231- **4** 3 **Putra Laju (IRE)**[27] 7047 4-8-13 68.....(p) PatrickHills 4 67
(J W Hills) *chsd ldrs: rdn over 2f out: no ex fnl f* **12/1**

260- **5** ¾ **Sol Rojo**[91] 5916 6-8-8 69.....(v) JosephineBruning(7) 9 66+
(J Pearce) *dwlt: hld up: edgd lft 3f out: styd on ins fnl f: nt trble ldrs* **22/1**

323- **6** nk **Casablanca Minx (IRE)**[4] 7274 5-8-2 61 ow2.....(b) RichardEvans(5) 10 57
(P D Evans) *hld up: hdwy over 5f out: rdn over 3f out: hung lft and styd on same pce appr fnl f* **5/1**[3]

7 2 **Passato (GER)**[86] 4-8-8 68..... DavidProbert(5) 2 60
(R A Harris) *hld up: rdn over 3f out: n.d* **28/1**

030- **8** 6 **Personify**[104] 5559 6-9-1 69..... RussellKennemore 6 47
(R A Harris) *hmpd s: hld up: rdn over 3f out: sn wknd* **14/1**

000- **9** 7 **Bahamian Duke**[14] 7188 5-8-0 59 oh9..... DeclanCannon(5) 1 21
(K R Burke) *prom 6f* **40/1**

1m 51.5s (1.00) **Going Correction** +0.075s/f (Slow)
WFA 4 from 5yo+ 1lb **9** Ran SP% **116.9**
Speed ratings (Par 103): **104,103,102,100,99 99,97,92,85**
CSF £27.51 CT £78.68 TOTE £4.10: £1.80, £2.40, £1.50; EX 26.60 Trifecta £155.20 Pool: £680.13 - 3.11 winning units. Place 6 £26.66, Place 5 £6.05.
Owner Mrs Annabelle Mason **Bred** Christopher J Mason **Trained** Tredodridge, Vale Of Glamorgan

FOCUS
A modest affair run at only a moderate pace. The front two were always prominent and look progressive, while the third was very unlucky not to get involved.
Happy As Larry(USA) Official explanation: jockey said gelding hung left in the straight
T/Plt: £43.00 to a £1 stake. Pool: £56,094.85. 951.40 winning tickets. T/Qpdt: £10.30 to a £1 stake. Pool: £4,512.20. 321.50 winning tickets. CR

LINGFIELD (L-H)
Thursday, January 3

OFFICIAL GOING: Standard

Wind: brisk, half-against Weather: Overcast, cold with snow flurries

22 SUPER FAMILY HOLIDAYS @ PONTINS.COM MAIDEN STKS 1m 2f (P)
12:35 (12:36) (Class 5) 4-Y-O+ £2,331 (£693; £346; £173) Stalls Low

Form RPR

645- 1 **Art Man**63 6603 5-9-5 72 GeorgeBaker 3 69
(G L Moore) *hld up in tch: trckd ldng pair over 2f out: asked for effrt but hanging over 1f out: rdn to ld ent fnl f: sn in command* **8/11**1

263- 2 1 1/2 **Sri Kuantan (IRE)**81 6211 4-9-3 66 ChrisCatlin 2 66
(P F I Cole) *t.k.h: trckd ldr: led 3f out: rdn over 1f out: hdd and outpcd ent fnl f* **4/1**2

033- 3 1 1/4 **Rollin 'n Tumblin**4 7282 4-8-12 47 KirstyMilczarek(5) 7 63
(W Jarvis) *trckd ldrs: wnt cl 2nd 3f out: rdn and nt qckn over 1f out: one pce after* **5/1**3

000- 4 1/2 **Movie Mogul**215 2261 4-8-12 65 AdamKirby 1 57
(M L W Bell) *cl up: sltly outpcd over 2f out: one pce and nvr rchd ldrs after* **16/1**

04- 5 hd **Flight Dream (FR)**17 7174 5-9-0 0 JamieJones(5) 4 62
(M G Quinlan) *in tch in last pair: effrt 3f out: nt qckn 2f out: kpt on fnl f* **8/1**

6 25 **Collateral**31 5-8-11 0 TravisBlock(3) 6 7
(J A Geake) *v s.i.s: t.k.h and sn in tch: rdn and wknd over 4f out: t.o* **66/1**

5- 7 nk **Jollys Joy**64 5637 4-8-9 0 JerryO'Dwyer(3) 5 6
(K F Clutterbuck) *led to 3f out: wkng rapidly whn hmpd over 2f out: eased: t.o* **100/1**

2m 5.94s (-0.66) **Going Correction** -0.075s/f (Stan)
WFA 4 from 5yo 2lb 7 Ran SP% **114.0**
Speed ratings (Par 103): **104,102,101,101,101 81,81**
CSF £3.97 TOTE £1.60: £1.10, £2.00; EX 3.90.
Owner Matthew Green **Bred** Lady Lonsdale **Trained** Woodingdean, E Sussex

FOCUS
Not a very competitive maiden and they finished very much as the market suggested they should, but at least the pace was a fair one and the winning time was 0.82 seconds faster than the later handicap over the same trip. The form looks sound enough rated around the placed horses.
Movie Mogul Official explanation: jockey said filly hung left

23 BOOK NOW @ PONTINS.COM H'CAP 7f (P)
1:05 (1:05) (Class 6) (0-60,57) 3-Y-O £1,876 (£554; £277) Stalls Low

Form RPR

003- 1 **Banjo Bandit (IRE)**52 6791 3-9-3 56 JohnEgan 8 63+
(J S Moore) *pushed along in rr 1st 2f: prog gng bttr 1/2-way: effrt on outer over 1f out: rdn to ld ent fnl f: sn clr* **11/2**3

055- 2 2 **Waterloo Dock**52 6800 3-9-3 56 ChrisCatlin 9 58
(M Quinn) *pressed ldr after 100yds: rdn to ld over 2f out: hdd and outpcd ent fnl f* **7/1**

050- 3 3/4 **Transcendent (IRE)**44 6884 3-8-6 48 AndrewElliott(3) 5 48
(J D Bethell) *wl in tch: trckd ldng pair 1/2-way: cl enough over 1f out: fnd little u.p* **13/2**

300- 4 1 **Ramblin Bob**15 7182 3-9-4 57 NeilPollard 6 54
(W J Musson) *led 100yds: settled to trck ldrs: effrt 2f out: one pce and no imp jst over 1f out* **9/2**2

040- 5 nk **Too Grand**15 7182 3-9-0 56 (v) NeilChalmers(3) 7 52
(J J Bridger) *mostly in last trio: effrt on outer 3f out but sn rdn: outpcd over 2f out: kpt on again fnl f* **6/1**

055- 6 1/2 **Seductive Witch**17 7170 3-8-10 54 PatrickHills(5) 4 49
(M D I Usher) *hld up in last trio: rdn over 2f out: kpt on fr over 1f out: nt pce to rch ldrs* **25/1**

044- 7 1/2 **Talamahana**5 7272 3-8-9 48 LPKeniry 3 42
(S Kirk) *nvr gng wl: chsd ldrs but pushed along over 4f out: u.p and struggling over 2f out* **4/1**1

050- 8 2 **Wynberg (IRE)**20 7136 3-8-8 52 KirstyMilczarek(5) 1 40
(N A Callaghan) *led after 100yds to over 2f out: wknd over 1f out* **15/2**

004- 9 2 **In Decorum**15 7182 3-8-6 45 (v) RichardThomas 2 28
(J A Geake) *a in rr: rdn and no prog over 2f out* **16/1**

1m 25.56s (0.76) **Going Correction** -0.075s/f (Stan) 9 Ran SP% **115.2**
Speed ratings (Par 95): **98,95,94,93,93 92,92,89,87**
CSF £43.48 CT £257.25 TOTE £4.80: £1.50, £2.70, £2.30; EX 37.30 Trifecta £135.70 Part won. Pool £191.26 - 0.37 winning units..
Owner K Bailey & J S Moore **Bred** Rathasker Stud **Trained** Upper Lambourn, Berks

FOCUS
A modest little handicap, but they went a very decent pace early which meant there was no hiding place. The form looks very solid for the grade rated around the third and fourth.
Wynberg(IRE) Official explanation: jockey said gelding hung left

24 RING PONTIN'S 0844 815 3647 (S) STKS 1m (P)
1:35 (1:37) (Class 6) 4-Y-O+ £1,774 (£523; £262) Stalls High

Form RPR

00- 1 **Dushstorm (IRE)**33 6996 7-8-9 63 KirstyMilczarek(5) 4 62
(M Botti) *trckd ldrs: prog to go 3rd wl over 2f out: effrt over 1f out: rdn to ld last 150yds: styd on wl* **10/3**3

042- 2 3/4 **Northern Desert (IRE)**6 7251 9-9-0 62 PaulDoe 6 60
(S Curran) *prom: trckd ldr 4f out: rdn to ld over 1f out: hdd and outpcd last 150yds* **3/1**2

066- 3 3/4 **Pab Special (IRE)**6 7253 5-9-0 70 (v) FergusSweeney 8 59
(K R Burke) *t.k.h: w ldr: led 5f out: hdd and nt qckn over 1f out* **2/1**1

134- 4 2 **Arctic Desert**21 7131 8-9-5 59 (t) AdamKirby 1 59
(Miss Gay Kelleway) *dwlt: t.k.h: hld up in last trio: prog to dispute cl 3rd 2f out: rdn and nt qckn over 1f out* **6/1**

056- 5 3 **Salvestro**38 6452 5-9-0 42 JamesDoyle 7 47
(A W Carroll) *hld up in rr: outpcd over 2f out: shkn up over 1f out: styd on: nvr on terms* **33/1**

140- 6 3 **Zaafira (SPA)**6 7251 4-9-0 51 StephenDonohoe 2 40
(E J Creighton) *chsd ldrs: rdn fr 4f out: outpcd over 2f out: no ch after: fdd* **14/1**

004- 7 nk **Bollywood (IRE)**4 7276 5-8-11 43 (p) NeilChalmers(3) 9 39
(J J Bridger) *hld up in rr and racd on outer: brief effrt 1/2-way: wl outpcd and btn over 2f out* **11/1**

060- 8 14 **Katie Coniston**71 6429 4-8-9 44 RichardThomas 5 —
(Dr J R J Naylor) *dwlt: detached in last after 2f: t.o* **80/1**

000- 9 3 **Pink Salmon**15 7189 4-8-9 40 (v1) LPKeniry 3 —
(Mrs L J Mongan) *led 3f: sn lost pl u.p: t.o* **50/1**

1m 37.36s (-0.84) **Going Correction** -0.075s/f (Stan) 9 Ran SP% **116.8**
Speed ratings (Par 101): **107,106,105,103,100 97,97,83,80**
CSF £13.89 TOTE £4.40: £1.50, £1.40, £1.20; EX 17.50 Trifecta £41.50 Pool £389.55 - 6.65 winning units..The winner was bought in for 3,200gns. Pab Special was claimed by B. R. Johnson for £6,000.
Owner Giuliano Manfredini **Bred** M Fahy **Trained** Newmarket, Suffolk

FOCUS
A modest seller on paper, but they went a good pace and the winning time was 2.91 seconds faster than the following three-year-old handicap over the same trip. However, the proximity of the fifth anchors the form.
Arctic Desert Official explanation: jockey said gelding did not pick up

25 BOOK PONTIN'S TODAY @ PONTINS.COM H'CAP 1m (P)
2:10 (2:15) (Class 4) (0-85,83) 3-Y-O £4,100 (£1,227; £613; £306; £152) Stalls High

Form RPR

301- 1 **Hucking Hero (IRE)**30 7016 3-8-12 73 JimCrowley 6 76+
(J R Best) *hld up in last pair: prog on outer 3f out: hanging briefly but led wl over 1f out: clr fnl f: pushed out* **2/1**1

542- 2 1 1/4 **Mcconnell (USA)**6 7252 3-8-13 74 SteveDrowne 4 74
(J R Best) *hld up in last pair: shkn up in 4th over 1f out: styd on to take 2nd nr fin: nvr nr wnr* **11/4**2

132- 3 nk **Dhhamaan (IRE)**20 7145 3-9-4 79 (v) GeorgeBaker 5 78
(C E Brittain) *trckd ldr after 3f: rdn to chal and upsides 2f out: outpcd by wnr 1f out: lost 2nd nr fin* **3/1**3

315- 4 6 **Hieroglyph**30 7016 3-8-11 72 GregFairley 3 58
(M Johnston) *led: set stdy pce to 1/2-way: hdd wl over 1f out: sn wknd* **11/2**

021- 5 4 **Yamanmickmccann**33 6990 3-9-3 78 DaneO'Neill 2 54
(R Hannon) *trckd ldr for 3f: rdn 3f out: wknd 2f out* **6/1**

1m 40.27s (2.07) **Going Correction** -0.075s/f (Stan) 5 Ran SP% **114.7**
Speed ratings (Par 99): **92,90,90,84,80**
CSF £8.19 TOTE £2.80: £1.40, £1.90; EX 8.50.
Owner Hucking Horses **Bred** Mrs A Hughes **Trained** Hucking, Kent
■ Geezers Colours was withdrawn (11/2, uns rdr & got loose before race). Deduct 15p in the £ under Rule 4. New market formed.

FOCUS
They went a dawdle early on in this handicap and the form is not that solid. It took the field 2.23 seconds longer to cover the first quarter-mile than in the seller and the final time was 2.91 seconds slower.

26 CAPTAIN CROC MAKES YOUR HOLIDAY ROCK H'CAP 7f (P)
2:45 (2:46) (Class 4) (0-80,80) 4-Y-O+ £4,100 (£1,227; £613; £306; £152) Stalls Low

Form RPR

121- 1 **Halsion Chancer**25 7087 4-9-3 79 JohnEgan 5 92
(J R Best) *t.k.h: hld up in midfield: prog 2f out: decisive move to ld ins fnl f: rdn out* **7/1**

562- 2 1 **Bazroy (IRE)**25 7087 4-9-2 78 (b) StephenDonohoe 3 88
(P D Evans) *hld up in midfield: effrt over 1f out: r.o wl to take 2nd last 75yds: nvr able to threaten wnr* **12/1**

/11- 3 1 **Den's Gift (IRE)**33 6996 4-9-4 80 AdamKirby 4 87
(C G Cox) *led 1f: styd prom: rdn and effrt on inner 2f out: cl up 1f out: styd on* **3/1**1

404- 4 1/2 **Super Frank (IRE)**6 7253 5-8-13 75 ChrisCatlin 13 81
(J Akehurst) *led after 1f: kicked on 2f out: hdd and fdd ins fnl f* **9/2**2

122- 5 1/2 **Smokin Joe**5 7269 7-9-0 76 (b) JimCrowley 7 81
(J R Best) *blindfold removed late and slowly away: hld up in last trio: effrt and tried to thread through over 1f out: styd on: no ch* **6/1**3

000- 6 shd **Precocious Star (IRE)**18 7165 4-9-4 80 (v1) FergusSweeney 6 84
(K R Burke) *hld up towards rr: rdn wl over 1f out: styd on fnl f: nt pce to trble ldrs* **20/1**

600- 7 shd **Moonlight Man**73 6391 7-9-3 79 LPKeniry 9 83
(C R Dore) *prom: trckd ldr 5f out: rdn to chal over 1f out: fnd nil: fdd* **33/1**

336- 8 1/2 **Best One**25 7087 4-8-8 70 PaulDoe 11 73
(C E Brittain) *prom: rdn in cl 3rd 2f out: fdd fnl f* **10/1**

320- 9 1/2 **Dudley Docker (IRE)**95 5840 6-8-10 75 TravisBlock(3) 1 76
(C R Dore) *dwlt: t.k.h: hld up in last trio: nt clr run wl over 1f out: no real prog: kpt on* **33/1**

551- 10 1/2 **Desert Dreamer (IRE)**24 7094 7-9-0 76 PaulMulrennan 8 76
(G A Butler) *hld up in last trio: shkn up on outer over 1f out: styd on last 150yds: no ch* **10/1**

054- 11 nk **Russian Symphony (USA)**25 7087 7-9-1 77 SteveDrowne 12 76
(C R Egerton) *hld up in midfield: nt clr run briefly wl over 1f out: hanging and btn after* **11/1**

540- 12 6 **China Cherub**25 7087 5-9-4 80 DaneO'Neill 2 63
(S Dow) *lost prom pl after 3f: drvn and in trble 3f out: wknd and eased fnl 2f* **33/1**

1m 23.69s (-1.11) **Going Correction** -0.075s/f (Stan) 12 Ran SP% **117.8**
Speed ratings (Par 105): **109,107,106,106,105 105,105,104,104,103 103,96**
CSF £83.37 CT £322.64 TOTE £7.70: £2.40, £4.40, £1.30; EX 48.80 Trifecta £181.70 Pool £547.70 - 2.14 winning units..
Owner Halsion Ltd **Bred** Mrs S Hansford **Trained** Hucking, Kent

FOCUS
A very competitive handicap and run at a solid pace too thanks to Super Frank. The form looks very decent and winners will come out of this race.

27 LINGFIELDPARK.CO.UK H'CAP 1m 5f (P)
3:15 (3:16) (Class 5) (0-70,70) 4-Y-O+ £2,331 (£693; £346; £173) Stalls Low

Form RPR

011- 1 **War Of The Roses (IRE)**6 7256 5-9-3 64 6ex PaulMulrennan 1 74+
(R Brotherton) *hld up in last trio: prog over 2f out: clsd to ld jst over 1f out: r.o wl* **6/4**1

630- 2 1 3/4 **Wait For The Will (USA)**43 6902 12-9-7 68 (b) GeorgeBaker 3 72
(G L Moore) *trckd ldrs: effrt and got through over 1f out: chsd wnr fnl f: readily outpcd* **14/1**

100- 3 2 **Pret A Porter (UAE)**195 2816 4-9-4 70 StephenDonohoe 5 71
(P D Evans) *rrd s: hld up in last trio: prog on outer over 2f out: nt qckn over 1f out: styd on fnl f to take 3rd last stride* **8/1**

061- 4 shd **Just Intersky (USA)**25 7083 5-9-1 62 (e) DeanMcKeown 2 63
(V Smith) *t.k.h: hld up in last trio on inner: swtchd wd and effrt over 2f out: chsd ldng gp over 1f out: shuffled along and kpt on* **8/1**

222- 5 nk **Calculating (IRE)**14 7198 4-8-13 70 PatrickHills(5) 7 70
(M D I Usher) *trckd ldrs: effrt over 2f out: hanging but led briefly over 1f out: sn outpcd by ldng pair: lost 2 pls nr fin* **5/1**2

016- **6** 3 **Dark Parade (ARG)**[45] 6875 7-9-0 **66**........................(b) JamieJones(5) 9 62
(G L Moore) *led at stop-s pce: hdd jst over 3f out: upsides again 2f out: wknd fnl f* **7/1**[3]
045- **7** 1 3/4 **Ocean Avenue (IRE)**[58] 6709 9-9-6 **67**........................ SimonWhitworth 4 60
(C A Horgan) *hld up in tch: effrt over 2f out: outpcd and n.d over 1f out* **16/1**
116- **8** 1 1/4 **Featherlight**[62] 6622 4-9-4 **70**........................(b) JohnEgan 8 61
(Jamie Poulton) *w ldrs: led on inner jst over 3f out: hdd & wknd over 1f out* **7/1**[3]
000- **9** 2 1/2 **Salut Saint Cloud**[15] 7194 7-8-7 **61**........................ JemmaMarshall(7) 6 49
(G L Moore) *prom early: lost pl over 5f out: struggling in last pair over 2f out* **33/1**
6/0- **10** 3 **Mustamad**[29] 1356 5-9-7 **68**........................ FergusSweeney 10 51
(Miss A M Newton-Smith) *ldng trio: rdn over 4f out: wknd over 2f out* **66/1**
2m 53.35s (7.35) **Going Correction** -0.075s/f (Stan)
WFA 4 from 5yo+ 5lb **10** Ran SP% **120.9**
Speed ratings (Par 103): **81,79,78,78,78 76,75,74,73,71**
CSF £27.30 CT £138.57 TOTE £2.20: £1.10, £3.20, £2.70; EX 20.40 Trifecta £108.20 Pool £757.47 - 4.97 winning units..
Owner P S J Croft **Bred** Mrs Jane Bailey **Trained** Elmley Castle, Worcs
FOCUS
This was not the test of stamina it might have been as the field virtually walked the first half-mile and it developed into a sprint. The winning time was understandably pedestrian and the way the race was run would not have suited several, so the form is a little dubious.
Featherlight Official explanation: trainer said filly was never travelling

28 JUMPING HERE TOMORROW H'CAP 1m 2f (P)
3:45 (3:45) (Class 5) (0-75,74) 4-Y-0+ **£1,680** (£1,680; £385; £192) **Stalls** Low

Form RPR
311- **1** **Mutamaasek (USA)**[15] 7194 6-8-8 **66**........................ KirstyMilczarek(5) 7 73
(Lady Herries) *trckd ldng pair: wl plcd whn pce qcknd over 2f out: rdn to chal fnl f: jnd ldr on line* **2/1**[1]
412- **1** dht **Kindlelight Blue (IRE)**[30] 7018 4-9-4 **73**........................ JamesDoyle 2 80
(N P Littmoden) *trckd ldrs: effrt on inner over 1f out: narrow ld ins fnl f: jnd on post* **11/4**[2]
043- **3** nk **Oakley Heffert (IRE)**[15] 7193 4-9-0 **74**..............(b) NataliaGemelova(5) 6 80
(R Hannon) *hld up in midfield: effrt on outer 2f out: styd on wl fnl f to take 3rd nr fin and clsng on ldng pair* **8/1**
106- **4** 1/2 **Prime Number (IRE)**[15] 7194 6-9-3 **70**........................ ChrisCatlin 3 75
(J Akehurst) *led after 2f and set v stdy pce: kicked on over 2f out: narrowly hdd ins fnl f: nt qckn* **8/1**
226- **5** shd **Meditation**[12] 7224 6-8-10 **68**........................ JamieJones(5) 8 73
(I A Wood) *led 2f: w ldr after: stl upsides ins fnl f: nt qckn* **20/1**
000- **6** shd **Prince Charlemagne (IRE)**[190] 2987 5-9-6 **73**.......... FergusSweeney 5 78
(K R Burke) *hld up in last trio: gng easily bhd ldrs 2f out: nt clr run briefly and hanging: shuffled along and fnd nil* **11/2**[3]
666- **7** 1 1/2 **Street Life (IRE)**[34] 6982 10-8-8 **61**........................ NeilPollard 1 63
(W J Musson) *dwlt: hld up in last: sltly outpcd over 2f out: shuffled along and kpt on steadily fnl f: nvr nr ldrs* **25/1**
300- **8** nk **Cavallini (USA)**[81] 6200 6-9-1 **68**........................ GeorgeBaker 4 69
(G L Moore) *t.k.h early: hld up in tch: outpcd and shkn up over 2f out: nvr on terms after* **12/1**
100- **9** 1 1/4 **Le Corvee (IRE)**[32] 4284 6-9-5 **72**........................ AdamKirby 9 71
(A W Carroll) *hld up in last trio: shkn up and outpcd over 2f out: nt on terms after* **22/1**
2m 6.76s (0.16) **Going Correction** -0.075s/f (Stan)
WFA 4 from 5yo+ 2lb **9** Ran SP% **118.3**
Speed ratings (Par 103): **101,101,100,100,100 100,99,98,97**W: KB £1.90, M £1.60; Pl:KB £1.60, M £1.60, OH £2.00; Ex: KB/M £3.80, M/KB £3.70; CSF: KB/M £4.32, M/KB £3.75. Tric: KB/M/OH £19.31, M/KB/OH £17.91 TRIFECTA KB/M/OH £12.70 - 19.87 winning units. M/KB/OH £8.30 - 30.41 winning units. Pool £71127 Owner.
Owner Lady Herries **Bred** Shadwell Farm LLC **Trained** Patching, W Sussex
FOCUS
A moderate early pace for this ordinary handicap and the winning time was 0.82 seconds slower than the earlier maiden. The first six finished in a heap and the form looks a little dubious, although the third and fifth were close to recent course form.
T/Plt: £24.20 to a £1 stake. Pool: £54,927.40. 1,650.25 winning tickets. T/Qpdt: £3.20 to a £1 stake. Pool: £4,610.40. 1,065.90 winning tickets. JN

[15]WOLVERHAMPTON (A.W) (L-H)
Thursday, January 3
OFFICIAL GOING: Standard
Wind: moderate, half-against Weather: Fine and cold

29 WOLVERHAMPTON-RACECOURSE.CO.UK H'CAP 5f 20y(P)
6:50 (6:50) (Class 6) (0-65,65) 4-Y-0+ **£1,774** (£523; £262) **Stalls** Low

Form RPR
064- **1** **Almaty Express**[13] 7215 6-8-8 **60**........................(b) AshleyHamblett(5) 3 77
(J R Weymes) *mde all: rdn 1f out: edgd lft wl ins fnl f: r.o wl* **9/2**[2]
015- **2** 2 1/2 **Sands Crooner (IRE)**[14] 7206 5-8-10 **62**....................(v) TolleyDean(5) 13 70
(D Shaw) *s.i.s: sn swtchd lft and outpcd: rdn and hdwy over 1f out: r.o ins fnl f: nt trble wnr* **12/1**
321- **3** 1 1/2 **Perlachy**[12] 7227 4-8-9 **59**........................(v) DuranFentiman(3) 8 62
(Mrs N Macauley) *a.p: rdn and edgd rt over 1f out: kpt on ins fnl f* **8/1**
250- **4** shd **Twosheetstothewind**[60] 6667 4-9-4 **65**........................ LiamJones 4 68
(C R Dore) *plld hrd: a.p: ev ch over 2f out: rdn over 1f out: one pce fnl f* **18/1**
230- **5** hd **Thoughtsofstardom**[25] 7082 5-8-5 **57**..............(be) KirstyMilczarek(5) 2 59
(G C Bravery) *chsd ldrs: rdn wl over 1f out: one pce fnl f* **9/1**
020- **6** 2 **Hythe Bay**[22] 7119 4-9-4 **65**........................ JimCrowley 12 60
(J R Best) *chsd ldrs tl rdn and wknd wl over 1f out* **20/1**
554- **7** 1 **Desert Light (IRE)**[15] 7183 7-8-10 **57**........................(v) DeanMcKeown 1 48
(D Shaw) *chsd ldrs tl wknd wl over 2f out* **13/2**[3]
006- **8** 1/2 **Egyptian Lord**[31] 7005 5-8-5 **57**........................ ColinHaddon(5) 10 46
(Peter Grayson) *racd wd: hld up: bhd fnl 3f* **33/1**
313- **9** 1 1/2 **Music Box Express**[14] 7206 4-8-13 **60**........................(e) JohnEgan 7 44
(D J Murphy) *s.i.s: pushed along over 3f out: hdwy on outside over 2f out: rdn and wknd wl over 1f out: eased ins fnl f* **13/8**[1]
166- **10** 9 **Stoneacre Boy (IRE)**[22] 7116 5-9-1 **62**........................ LPKeniry 5 14
(Peter Grayson) *chsd ldrs 2f: eased whn no ch ins fnl f* **25/1**
62.31 secs (0.01) **Going Correction** +0.025s/f (Slow) **10** Ran SP% **115.2**
Speed ratings (Par 101): **105,101,98,98,98 94,93,92,90,75**
CSF £54.62 CT £431.85 TOTE £6.70: £1.90, £4.50, £2.10; EX 90.40.
Owner Sporting Occasions Racing No 5 **Bred** P G Airey **Trained** Middleham Moor, N Yorks
FOCUS
A tightly-knit minor sprint handicap run at a sound pace.
Music Box Express Official explanation: jockey said gelding was fractious pre-race

30 BOOK ONLINE @ PONTINS.COM CLAIMING STKS 1m 141y(P)
7:20 (7:20) (Class 5) 3-Y-O **£2,457** (£725; £362) **Stalls** Low

Form RPR
411- **1** **Elusive Lady (IRE)**[8] 7234 3-8-12 67........................(p) ChrisCatlin 3 67
(J R Weymes) *hld up in tch: rdn to ld ins fnl f: r.o* **11/8**[1]
2- **2** 1 1/4 **Roundthetwist (IRE)**[8] 7235 3-9-2 0........................ AndrewElliott(3) 1 71
(K R Burke) *led: hdd 5f out: led over 3f out: rdn over 1f out: hdd and nt qckn ins fnl f* **9/2**[3]
431- **3** hd **Tiger Spice**[19] 7156 3-8-6 67........................(b) LiamJones 5 58
(W J Haggas) *half-rrd s: sn w ldr: led 5f out tl over 3f out: rdn wl over 1f out: kpt on same pce fnl f* **13/8**[2]
501- **4** 3/4 **Autumn Charm**[16] 7177 3-7-13 60........................ KirstyMilczarek(5) 4 54
(D W Chapman) *hld up: hung rt 3f out: rdn wl over 1f out: one pce* **9/1**
1m 53.61s (3.11) **Going Correction** +0.025s/f (Slow) **4** Ran SP% **108.4**
Speed ratings (Par 97): **92,90,90,90**
CSF £7.53 TOTE £2.30; EX 6.80.
Owner T A Scothern **Bred** Liam Queally **Trained** Middleham Moor, N Yorks
FOCUS
A competitive little claimer with three of the four runners successful on their previous outing and the other a promising second on debut.
Autumn Charm Official explanation: jockey said filly hung right

31 MAKE A DATE IN 2008 @ PONTIN'S H'CAP 1m 4f 50y(P)
7:50 (7:51) (Class 6) (0-60,60) 4-Y-0+ **£1,774** (£523; £262) **Stalls** Low

Form RPR
620- **1** **Fantasy Ride**[15] 7186 6-9-8 58........................ TGMcLaughlin 4 68
(J Pearce) *hld up in rr: hdwy over 3f out: rdn over 2f out: chalng whn hung lft ins fnl f: led cl home* **5/1**
363- **2** hd **Raquel White**[7] 7249 4-9-1 60........................ TolleyDean(5) 2 70
(J L Flint) *a.p: rdn over 2f out: led over 1f out: hdd cl home* **11/4**[2]
10/- **3** 6 **King's Fable (USA)**[46] 6317 5-9-1 54........................ JerryO'Dwyer(3) 1 54
(Karen George) *hld up in mid-div: hdwy over 4f out: swtchd rt over 2f out: sn rdn and hung lft: wknd fnl f* **14/1**
406- **4** hd **Cyril The Squirrel**[15] 7185 4-8-8 48 ow1........................ MickyFenton 9 48
(Karen George) *s.i.s: sn led: hung rt bnd 7f out: rdn over 3f out: hdd over 1f out: wknd ins fnl f* **20/1**
/32- **5** 1 1/4 **Twist Bookie (IRE)**[13] 7219 8-9-6 56........................ ChrisCatlin 5 54
(S Lycett) *hld up in mid-div: hdwy over 3f out: rdn and one pce whn nt clr run over 2f out* **9/4**[1]
313- **6** 6 **Oasis Sun (IRE)**[15] 7187 5-9-4 54........................(b) JohnEgan 3 42
(J R Best) *hld up towards rr: rdn and hdwy on ins over 2f out: wknd and eased ins fnl f* **7/2**[3]
060/ **7** 15 **Beauchamp Turbo**[899] 3589 6-8-12 48........................ DanielTudhope 6 12
(N Wilson) *t.k.h early in rr: lost tch fnl 3f* **25/1**
650- **8** 10 **Sea Frolic (IRE)**[48] 6835 7-8-9 45........................ PaulMulrennan 8 —
(Jennie Candlish) *hld up towards rr: hdwy over 5f out: rdn over 4f out: wknd over 3f out: sn lost tch* **20/1**
000- **9** 42 **One And Gone (IRE)**[19] 7153 4-8-2 45..................(b1) AndrewElliott(3) 7 —
(Miss M E Rowland) *sn chsng ldr: wknd over 4f out: sn t.o* **66/1**
2m 43.02s (1.92) **Going Correction** +0.025s/f (Slow)
WFA 4 from 5yo+ 4lb **9** Ran SP% **117.9**
Speed ratings (Par 101): **99,98,94,94,93 89,79,73,45**
CSF £18.73 CT £183.11 TOTE £8.40: £3.30, £1.40, £5.60; EX 30.20.
Owner M M Foulger **Bred** A J Holder **Trained** Newmarket, Suffolk
FOCUS
A poor contest in which the first two finished clear.
Oasis Sun(IRE) Official explanation: jockey said mare had no more to give
Sea Frolic(IRE) Official explanation: jockey said mare hung left

32 CROC AROUND THE CLOCK @ PONTIN'S H'CAP 7f 32y(P)
8:20 (8:21) (Class 6) (0-52,52) 4-Y-0+ **£1,774** (£523; £262) **Stalls** High

Form RPR
020- **1** **Aggbag**[26] 7077 4-8-4 47........................ AndrewElliott(3) 1 59
(B P J Baugh) *a.p: nt clr run and swtchd rt over 1f out: hrd rdn to ld nr fin* **10/1**
401- **2** hd **The Salwick Flyer (IRE)**[19] 7148 5-8-11 51........................ PhillipMakin 3 62
(Miss L A Perratt) *t.k.h: chsd ldr: led over 2f out: sn rdn: edgd rt wl ins fnl f: hdd nr fin* **4/1**[2]
405- **3** 1 1/2 **Snow Bunting**[31] 7006 10-8-9 52........................ TravisBlock(3) 12 59
(Jedd O'Keeffe) *hld up and bhd: rdn and hdwy over 1f out: r.o ins fnl f* **16/1**
600- **4** nk **Guadaloup**[134] 4705 6-8-8 51 ow2........................ MarkLawson(3) 8 57
(M Brittain) *hld up in tch: rdn and wnt 2nd over 1f out: no ex wl ins fnl f* **20/1**
000- **5** 2 1/2 **Balerno**[15] 7192 9-8-11 51........................ AmirQuinn 5 50
(Mrs L J Mongan) *hld up in mid-div: rdn over 2f out: hdwy over 1f out: one pce fnl f* **8/1**
006- **6** 1/2 **Wiltshire (IRE)**[30] 7024 6-8-12 52........................ MickyFenton 10 50
(P T Midgley) *hld up towards rr: pushed along over 3f out: hdwy over 1f out: rdn and one pce fnl f* **9/2**[3]
060- **7** 2 **Over Ice**[8] 5366 5-8-9 52 ow2........................ JerryO'Dwyer(3) 4 45
(Karen George) *s.i.s: in rr: pushed along over 4f out: nvr nr ldrs* **28/1**
062- **8** 3/4 **Claws**[7] 7250 5-8-8 48........................(p) JamesDoyle 6 39
(A J Lidderdale) *a.p: rdn to chse ldr 2f out tl over 1f out: wknd ins fnl f* **11/4**[1]
000- **9** 1/2 **Keon (IRE)**[17] 7169 6-8-9 49........................ JimCrowley 11 38
(R Hollinshead) *t.k.h in mid-div: c wd st: rdn and wknd over 1f out* **15/2**
420- **10** 1/2 **Prince Of Gold**[260] 1086 8-8-12 52........................(v) LPKeniry 9 40
(Ms N M Hugo) *s.s: rdn over 3f out: a in rr* **8/1**
00- **11** 1 **Pauvic (IRE)**[23] 7111 5-8-5 48........................(p) AndrewMullen(3) 2 33
(Mrs A Duffield) *led: rdn and hdd over 2f out: wknd wl over 1f out* **20/1**
1m 30.11s (0.51) **Going Correction** +0.025s/f (Slow) **11** Ran SP% **126.8**
Speed ratings (Par 101): **102,101,100,99,96 96,94,93,92,92 90**
CSF £52.54 CT £678.46 TOTE £13.80: £3.80, £2.60, £3.50; EX 81.70.
Owner Joe Singh **Bred** D R Tucker **Trained** Audley, Staffs
FOCUS
A closely-knit weak affair.

Prince Of Gold Official explanation: jockey said gelding missed the break

33 STAY AT THE WOLVERHAMPTON HOLIDAY INN CLASSIFIED STKS 7f 32y(P)

8:50 (8:50) (Class 7) 4-Y-0+ £1,365 (£403; £201) Stalls High

Form RPR

041- 1 **Epidaurian King (IRE)**[4] 7278 5-9-6 45..................(v) DeanMcKeown 11 58
(D Shaw) *hld up in rr: hdwy over 3f out: edgd lft 1f out: led ins fnl f: jst hld on* 5/2[2]

050- 2 *hd* **Mr Chocolate Drop (IRE)**[14] 7197 4-8-9 42.........(b) JamesO'Reilly(5) 1 51
(Miss M E Rowland) *prom whn nt clr run on ins and lost pl bnd after 1f: hld up: rdn over 2f out: swtchd rt and hdwy on outside over 1f out: fin wl* 33/1

004- 3 *1 1/4* **Temtation (IRE)**[23] 7108 4-8-9 44...................... RussellKennemore(5) 6 48
(J A Pickering) *led: rdn over 1f out: hdd and nt qckn ins fnl f* 22/1

354- 4 *1* **Desert Lover (IRE)**[7] 7250 6-8-9 45.........................(p) TolleyDean(5) 5 45
(R J Price) *hld up in mid-div: nt clr run over 5f out: rdn and hdwy on ins 3f out: one pce fnl f* 9/4[1]

032- 5 *1* **Kindkintyre (IRE)**[19] 7153 4-9-0 45.............................. TonyHamilton 10 43
(R A Fahey) *chsd ldr tl rdn wl over 1f out: no ex fnl f* 4/1[3]

000- 6 *nk* **Steel Grey**[98] 5756 7-8-11 44...................................... MarkLawson(3) 2 42
(M Brittain) *prom: reminder and lost pl 4f out: styd on ins fnl f* 33/1

066- 7 *1 1/2* **James Street (IRE)**[19] 7153 5-8-7 45.............................. RyanHill(7) 12 38
(Peter Grayson) *prom: rdn 2f out: wknd over 1f out* 14/1

360- 8 *3/4* **Pawn In Life (IRE)**[131] 4797 10-9-0 44...........................(v) PaulEddery 3 36
(D W Chapman) *s.i.s: bhd: pushed along 3f out: hdwy over 1f out: no further prog fnl f* 25/1

46-6 9 *4* **Cyfrwys (IRE)**[1] 16 7-9-0 44..(p) ChrisCatlin 9 25
(B Palling) *prom: rdn over 2f out: wknd over 1f out* 10/1

500- 10 *3/4* **Just Crystal**[7] 7248 4-9-0 43...................................... TGMcLaughlin 7 23
(B P J Baugh) *s.i.s: hdwy over 2f out: hung lft and wknd over 1f out* 20/1

56-0 11 *12* **Telling**[1] 8 4-8-11 45.. AndrewMullen(3) 8 —
(Mrs A Duffield) *s.i.s: hdwy over 5f out: rdn and edgd lft 4f out: sn wknd* 12/1

1m 31.29s (1.69) **Going Correction** +0.025s/f (Slow) 11 Ran SP% 121.6
Speed ratings (Par 97): **95,94,93,92,91 90,89,88,83,82 69**
CSF £95.06 TOTE £3.70: £1.30, £6.70, £3.80; EX 109.30.
Owner Derek Shaw **Bred** Shadwell Estate Company Limited **Trained** Danethorpe, Notts

FOCUS
A competitive race albeit at a very low level.
Kindkintyre(IRE) Official explanation: vet said gelding bled from the nose
Steel Grey Official explanation: jockey said gelding hung right

34 BOOK EARLY @ PONTINS.COM H'CAP 1m 141y(P)

9:20 (9:20) (Class 4) (0-85,85) 4-Y-0+ £4,210 (£1,252; £625; £312) Stalls Low

Form RPR

551- 1 **Scamperdale**[17] 7173 6-8-10 76.................................... PaulMulrennan 1 83
(B P J Baugh) *hld up: hdwy wl over 1f out: sn swtchd rt: rdn to ld wl ins fnl f: r.o* 4/1[3]

110- 2 *1 1/4* **Abbondanza (IRE)**[18] 7163 5-9-5 85...............................(p) PhillipMakin 6 89
(Miss L A Perratt) *led: rdn 2f out: hdd wl ins fnl f: nt qckn* 11/4[2]

666/ 3 *shd* **Claret And Amber**[504] 4521 6-8-10 76.............................. DaleGibson 2 80
(R A Fahey) *hld up: rdn wl over 1f out: kpt on ins fnl f* 11/1

152- 4 *shd* **Princess Cocoa (IRE)**[33] 7002 5-8-9 75.......................... TonyHamilton 4 79
(R A Fahey) *a.p: chsd ldr over 2f out tl rdn over 1f out: kpt on ins fnl f* 11/8[1]

216- 5 *2* **My Michelle**[28] 7047 7-8-5 71 oh5.................................... ChrisCatlin 5 70
(B Palling) *sn chsng ldr: rdn and lost 2nd over 2f out: one pce* 13/2

000- 6 *3* **Lopinot (IRE)**[4] 7281 5-8-11 77... LPKeniry 3 70
(M R Bosley) *hld up in rr: rdn wl over 1f out: no rspnse* 8/1

1m 50.22s (-0.28) **Going Correction** +0.025s/f (Slow) 6 Ran SP% 121.5
Speed ratings (Par 105): **107,105,105,105,103 101**
CSF £16.92 TOTE £3.10: £1.60, £3.10; EX 22.80 Place 6 £367.27, Place 5 £127.95..
Owner Saddle Up Racing **Bred** Mrs J A Prescott **Trained** Audley, Staffs

FOCUS
An interesting little handicap.
T/Plt: £559.30 to a £1 stake. Pool: £121,022.25. 157.95 winning tickets. T/Qpdt: £89.50 to a £1 stake. Pool: £8,018.80. 66.30 winning tickets. KH

[1]SOUTHWELL (L-H)

Friday, January 4

OFFICIAL GOING: Standard
Wind: Virtually nil Weather: Overcast

36 SOUTHWELL-RACECOURSE.CO.UK AMATEUR RIDERS' H'CAP (DIV I) 2m (F)

12:10 (12:10) (Class 6) (0-60,59) 4-Y-0+ £1,351 (£415; £207) Stalls Low

Form RPR

032- 1 **Cumbrian Knight (IRE)**[32] 7004 10-11-2 **59**........... MissNJefferson(5) 3 61
(J M Jefferson) *s.i.s and in rr: hdwy to trck ldr after 6f: pushed along 3f out: rdn to ld jst ins fnl f: styd on* 4/1[1]

506- 2 *1 3/4* **Countback (FR)**[6] 7273 9-10-9 **50** ow5..................(p) MrMJJSmith(3) 10 50
(A W Carroll) *trckd ldrs: hdwy 4f out and sn cl up: rdn to ld wl over 1f out: hdd jst ins fnl f and kpt on same pce* 9/1[3]

060- 3 *3/4* **Devilfishpoker Com**[9] 6561 4-9-11 **49** ow4.............(v) MrJohnWilley(7) 4 48
(R C Guest) *led: rdn along over 3f out: hdd wl over 1f out: kpt on same pce* 14/1

610- 4 *7* **Ice And Fire**[27] 7081 9-10-10 **48**.....................................(b) MrSDobson 1 42
(J T Stimpson) *hld up in rr: stdy hdwy on outer 5f out: hung rt and wd st to stands' rail: ev ch 2f: sn rdn and wknd over 1f out* 9/2[2]

000- 5 *4* **Gavanello**[7] 5698 5-10-0 **45**.....................................(t) MissSEilbeck(7) 6 31
(M C Chapman) *chsd ldrs: rdn along over 5f out and sn outpcd* 50/1

000- 6 *7* **Integration**[9] 6797 8-10-0 **45**.. MrKJames(7) 9 23
(Miss M E Rowland) *trckd ldrs: hdwy and cl up 1/2-way: rdn along over 3f out and sn wknd* 25/1

350- 7 *2 1/2* **Ronsard (IRE)**[4] 7285 6-11-3 **55**...................................... MissEFolkes 8 30
(P D Evans) *plld hrd: hld up in rr: sme hdwy 1/2-way: in tch and rdn along over 4f out: sn wknd* 4/1[1]

520- 8 *7* **On Every Street**[53] 6797 7-10-6 **49**...............................(vt) MissRBastiman(5) 7 15
(R Bastiman) *midfield: reminders 1/2-way: rdn along over 4f out and sn btn* 9/1[3]

464- 9 *12* **Mango Masher (IRE)**[31] 7012 4-10-5 **57**.......................(p) MrRPFlint(7) 2 9
(J L Flint) *hld up in tch on inner: pushed along 1/2-way: lost pl 6f out and sn bhd* 9/2[2]

400- 10 *dist* **Divine Love (IRE)**[97] 5819 4-10-6 **58**................................ MrLJohnson(7) 5 —
(T Wall) *prom tl rdn along and lost pl 1/2-way: t.o fnl 5f* 40/1

3m 52.0s (6.50) **Going Correction** +0.15s/f (Slow)
WFA 4 from 5yo+ 7lb 10 Ran SP% 111.3
Speed ratings (Par 101): **87,86,85,82,80 76,75,72,66,—**
CSF £37.71 CT £439.96 TOTE £4.50: £1.80, £2.80, £3.40; EX 40.20 TRIFECTA Not won..
Owner J M Jefferson **Bred** John P A Kenny **Trained** Norton, N Yorks

FOCUS
A poor race and also a real war of attrition for these amateurs. Although there was not much separating the front three at the line, the others finished spread out all over Nottinghamshire and the form is weak. The pace was a fair one and those that raced handily were at an advantage. The winning time was 1.62 seconds faster than the second division.
Ice And Fire Official explanation: jockey said gelding hung badly right throughout

37 SOUTHWELL-RACECOURSE.CO.UK AMATEUR RIDERS' H'CAP (DIV II) 2m (F)

12:40 (12:40) (Class 6) (0-60,59) 4-Y-0+ £1,351 (£415; £207) Stalls Low

Form RPR

250- 1 **Cragganmore Creek**[49] 6835 5-10-0 **45**...................... MrBMMorris(7) 6 55
(D Morris) *hld up in rr: gd hdwy on outer 1/2-way: led over 4f out: pushed clr 3f out: rdn wl over 1f out and styd on strly* 5/2[1]

000/ 2 *10* **Captain Smoothy**[396] 5925 8-10-2 **45**............................ MrRBirkett(5) 7 43
(Miss J Feilden) *trckd ldrs: hdwy 4f out: rdn along 3f out: drvn wl over 1f out: tk 2nd ins fnl f: no ch w wnr* 7/1

4/0- 3 *3* **Haoin An Bothar (IRE)**[96] 602 4-10-10 **55**...................... MrMFahey 1 49
(Adrian Sexton, Ire) *trckd ldrs: effrt on inner to chse wnr 3f out: sn rdn along and kpt on same pce fnl 2f* 9/2[2]

050- 4 *3/4* **Katie Kingfisher**[31] 7012 4-9-7 **45**..............................(p) MrJPearce(7) 8 39
(M Wigham) *s.i.s: t.k.h and hdwy to trck ldrs after 6f: pushed along wl over 2f out: sn rdn and one pce* 12/1

060- 5 *9* **The Mighty Ogmore**[16] 7187 4-9-7 **45**......................(p) MrCAHarris(7) 9 28
(R C Guest) *hld up in rr: sme hdwy 3f out: nvr a factor* 15/2

/00- 6 *2 1/2* **In Deep**[42] 4067 7-10-6 **49**... MrIPopham(5) 4 29
(Mrs P N Dutfield) *hld up in tch: effrt on inner over 5f out: sn rdn along and wknd* 7/1

000- 7 *8* **Mi Odds**[168] 3714 12-10-0 **45**.................................... MissKLMorgan(7) 3 15
(Mrs N Macauley) *led: rdn along 5f out: sn hdd & wknd* 66/1

0/0- 8 *58* **Zalzaar (IRE)**[7] 6797 6-10-5 **50**.. MrAWedge(7) 2 —
(R T Phillips) *prom: rdn along over 4f out: sn wknd* 40/1

152/ P **Countrywide Belle**[470] 642 5-10-7 **52**............................ MrRPFlint(7) 5 —
(J L Flint) *trckd ldrs: rdn along and wknd over 6f out: bhd whn p.u wl over 3f out* 5/1[3]

3m 53.62s (8.12) **Going Correction** +0.15s/f (Slow)
WFA 4 from 5yo+ 7lb 9 Ran SP% 111.8
Speed ratings (Par 101): **83,78,76,76,71 70,66,37,—**
CSF £19.56 CT £72.15 TOTE £3.50: £1.60, £1.80, £1.60; EX 24.80 Trifecta £144.10 Pool £355.41 - 1.75 winning units..
Owner Stag & Huntsman **Bred** Grovewood Stud **Trained** Newmarket, Suffolk
■ The first winner for 16-y-o rider Ben Morris, son of winning trainer Dave.

FOCUS
This looked even weaker than the first division and the early pace was much slower. It developed into something of a sprint over the last half-mile or so and in the end the winning time was just 1.62 seconds slower than division one. Even so, several of these found it too severe a test apart from the winner, who bolted up but only ran to his autumn form.
Cragganmore Creek Official explanation: trainer said, regarding the improved form, that gelding was better suited by the slow early pace and had possibly benefited from having had a seven-week break

38 CAPTAIN CROC MAKES PONTIN'S ROCK CLAIMING STKS 6f (F)

1:10 (1:11) (Class 6) 3-Y-0 £1,911 (£564; £282) Stalls Low

Form RPR

003- 1 **Ballycroy Boy (IRE)**[17] 7176 3-9-2 64.............................. MickyFenton 2 74
(A Bailey) *in tch: hdwy to trck ldrs 1/2-way: swtchd rt and effrt to ld wl over 1f out: rdn clr ent fnl f* 7/4[1]

141- 2 *6* **Valhillen**[18] 7171 3-8-10 65.. PatCosgrave 3 49
(M J Wallace) *disp ld: effrt over 2f out: sn rdn and ev ch tl drvn and one pce appr fnl f* 9/4[2]

005- 3 *1 3/4* **Bahamarama (IRE)**[18] 7171 3-8-5 52................................ ChrisCatlin 4 38
(R A Harris) *disp ld: rdn along over 2f out: drvn and hdd wl over 1f out: sn one pce* 22/1

4 *5* **Heavenly Encounter** 3-8-8 0.................................... AndrewElliott(3) 6 28
(K R Burke) *hld up: hdwy over 2f out: sn rdn and kpt on same pce* 14/1

016- 5 *2 1/2* **Night Robe**[14] 7210 3-8-6 50 ow1...............................(v[1]) MatthewHenry 8 15
(P D Evans) *chsd ldrs: rdn along wl over 2f out: sn outpcd* 14/1

33-0 6 *5* **Andrasta**[2] 17 3-8-3 58.. AndrewMullen(3) 7 —
(A Berry) *chsd ldrs: rdn along wl over 2f out: sn wknd* 10/1

625- 7 *5* **Her Name Is Rio (IRE)**[6] 7272 3-8-4 62 ow4..............(p) TolleyDean(5) 1 —
(J S Moore) *chsd ldrs: rdn along over 2f out and sn wknd* 7/1[3]

630- 8 *12* **Lady Bower**[16] 7182 3-8-12 58 ow1...............................(b[1]) AdamKirby 5 —
(J Ryan) *dwlt and a in rr* 12/1

1m 17.77s (1.27) **Going Correction** +0.15s/f (Slow) 8 Ran SP% 114.1
Speed ratings (Par 95): **100,92,89,83,79 73,66,50**
CSF £5.75 TOTE £2.40: £1.30, £1.10, £5.70; EX 7.00 Trifecta £84.30 Pool £373.11 - 3.14 winning units..Valhillen was claimed by M. D. I. Usher for £6,000.
Owner R T Collins **Bred** Paraic Fox **Trained** Newmarket, Suffolk

FOCUS
Not a great claimer, but they went a good pace and they finished very well spread out. Those that raced handily were at an advantage.
Her Name Is Rio(IRE) Official explanation: jockey said filly lost its action
Lady Bower Official explanation: jockey said filly stumbled leaving stalls

39 BOOK PONTIN'S NOW MAIDEN STKS 1m 4f (F)

1:40 (1:40) (Class 5) 4-Y-0+ £2,457 (£725; £362) Stalls Low

Form RPR

1 **She's The Lady**[229] 8-9-2 0.. ChrisCatlin 7 63+
(E J O'Neill) *s.i.s: sn pushed along and hdwy to ld after 2f: pushed clr 3f out: rdn wl over 1f out and styd on strly* 5/1

00- 2 *3* **Phone Call**[16] 6132 5-8-13 65.. TravisBlock(3) 2 61+
(Mouse Hamilton-Fairley) *hld up in tch on inner: nt clr run and lost pl over 3f out: hdwy to chse wnr over 1f out: sn drvn and no imp fnl f* 20/1

005- 3 *5* **Niqaab**[37] 6967 4-8-12 62.. NeilPollard 4 50
(W J Musson) *trckd ldrs: hdwy to chse wnr 3f out and sn rdn: drvn 2f out and sn one pce* 7/2[1]

4 4 *1* **Conclave (IRE)**[3] 3 4-8-9 0...................................... JerryO'Dwyer(3) 8 48
(Adrian Sexton, Ire) *hld up: hdwy 4f out: rdn along 3f out: sn drvn and kpt on same pce appr fnl f* 9/2[3]

030- **5** *2* **Weet For Ever (USA)**[36] 729 5-9-0 50 .... GabrielHannon(7) 6 50
(P A Blockley) *in rr: hdwy over 3f out: rdn over 2f out: sn drvn along and no imp* **17/2**

035- **6** *3* **Mariaverdi**[19] 7168 4-8-12 49 .... SteveDrowne 3 40
(P G Murphy) *chsd ldrs: pushed along 4f out: rdn 3f out and sn wknd* **4/1**[2]

002- **7** *1* **West End Lad**[23] 7125 5-9-7 54 ....(p) PhillipMakin 9 44
(S R Bowring) *in tch: hdwy on outer 1/2-way: rdn along over 3f out: sn wknd* **6/1**

000- **8** *nk* **Feeling Peckish (USA)**[29] 6055 4-8-12 38 ......(t) RussellKennemore(5) 1 43
(M C Chapman) *led 2f: prom tl rdn along over 4f out and sn wknd* **50/1**

9 *shd* **Eddystone (IRE)**[18] 4-9-3 0 ....(p) LPKeniry 10 43
(Mrs L C Jewell) *prom: rdn along over 4f out: wknd over 3f out* **50/1**

000- **10** *79* **Smiling Tiger**[249] 1353 4-9-3 20 .... StephenDonohoe 5 —
(M J Gingell) *sn outpcd in rr: wl bhd fr 1/2-way* **150/1**

2m 43.97s (2.97) **Going Correction** +0.15s/f (Slow)
WFA 4 from 5yo+ 4lb **10** Ran SP% **111.2**
Speed ratings (Par 103): **99,97,93,93,91 89,89,88,88,36**
CSF £95.75 TOTE £6.90: £2.70, £5.40, £1.20; EX 91.50 Trifecta £249.10 Part won. Pool £350.95 - 0.10 winning units..
Owner R S Brookhouse **Bred** Woodsway Stud & Chao Racing & Bloodstock Ltd **Trained** Averham Park, Notts

■ Stewards' Enquiry : Jerry O'Dwyer two-day ban: used whip with excessive frequency (Jan 15-16)

FOCUS
A very uncompetitive maiden, but at least the winner made it truer test than it might otherwise have been and the field finished very well spread out. There was very little encouragement from those outside the two mares and the form is not solid.
Feeling Peckish(USA) Official explanation: jockey said gelding hung right

40 GET A TASTE FOR PONTIN'S CLAIMING STKS 1m (F)
2:10 (2:10) (Class 6) 4-Y-0+ £1,774 (£523; £262) Stalls Low

Form RPR

253- **1** **Hucking Heat (IRE)**[7] 7251 4-9-7 64 ....(be1) PatCosgrave 5 70
(J R Boyle) *chsd ldrs: rdn along 3f out: drvn wl over 1f out: styd on to ld last 100yds* **2/1**[1]

030- **2** *1* **Rebellious Spirit**[8] 7241 5-8-13 68 .... PhillipMakin 6 60
(P W Hiatt) *led: rdn along 2f out: hung rt over 1f out: sn drvn: hdd and no ex last 100yds* **9/4**[2]

006- **3** *3/4* **Katie Lawson (IRE)**[32] 7006 5-8-6 50 ....(p) LiamJones 3 51
(D Haydn Jones) *s.i.s and sn rdn along in rr: hdwy over 2f out: sn drvn and styd on appr fnl f: nrst fin* **5/1**[3]

406- **4** *5* **Red Current**[9] 7237 4-9-4 62 .... ChrisCatlin 8 51
(R A Harris) *cl up: rdn 2f out and ev ch tl drvn and wknd appr fnl f* **7/1**

600- **5** *2* **Storm Mission (USA)**[48] 5511 4-8-9 40 ....(t) PaulMulrennan 7 38
(J Mackie) *cl up: rdn along 3f out: grad wknd* **12/1**

000- **6** *4* **Grey Vision**[109] 5487 5-8-3 45 .... AdamCarter(7) 2 30
(M Brittain) *in tch: rdn along over 3f out and sn wknd* **40/1**

046- **7** *9* **Wizby**[14] 7218 5-8-8 40 ow2 ....(v) StephenDonohoe 4 7
(P D Evans) *dwlt: a in rr* **12/1**

1m 44.81s (1.11) **Going Correction** +0.15s/f (Slow) **7** Ran SP% **111.1**
Speed ratings (Par 101): **104,103,102,97,95 91,82**
CSF £6.31 TOTE £2.70: £1.50, £1.60; EX 7.60 Trifecta £15.00 Pool £377.97 - 17.80 winning units..
Owner M Khan X2 **Bred** Thomas J Reid **Trained** Epsom, Surrey

■ Stewards' Enquiry : Pat Cosgrave two-day ban: used whip from above shoulder height (Jan 15-16)

FOCUS
Another uncompetitive claimer and they almost finished in perfect market order, but again they did go a fair pace up front which found out a few. The winner is rated to recent form with the third to last year's best. As in the first race, it did appear that any horse that came right over to the stands' rail in the home straight found the going tough.

41 HALF TERM HAPPY DEALS @ PONTIN'S H'CAP 6f (F)
2:40 (2:41) (Class 5) (0-70,67) 4-Y-0+ £2,593 (£765; £383) Stalls Low

Form RPR

131- **1** **Realt Na Mara (IRE)**[20] 7161 5-9-4 67 .... SteveDrowne 4 80
(H Morrison) *trckd ldrs: hdwy to chse ldr 2f out: rdn over 1f out: drvn and styd on ins fnl f to ld last 75yds* **2/1**[1]

466- **2** *1 1/4* **Xpres Maite**[20] 7155 5-8-13 62 ....(b) PhillipMakin 5 71
(S R Bowring) *led: rdn and edgd lft wl over 1f out: drvn ent fnl f: hdd and nt qckn last 75yds* **11/2**[3]

625- **3** *2 1/2* **Musical Script (USA)**[23] 7119 5-8-9 58 ....(p) JamieMackay 6 59
(Mouse Hamilton-Fairley) *chsd ldr: rdn along over 2f out: drvn and one pce appr fnl f* **7/1**

104- **4** *2* **Proud Killer**[17] 7179 5-9-1 67 .... JerryO'Dwyer(3) 1 62
(J R Jenkins) *chsd ldrs on inner: rdn along and lost pl 1/2-way: drvn and kpt on appr fnl f* **7/2**[2]

100- **5** *nk* **Trinculo (IRE)**[13] 7227 11-8-6 57 ....(b) ChrisCatlin 2 51
(R A Harris) *dwlt and sn rdn along in rr: hdwy over 2f out: sn drvn and no imp* **8/1**

223- **6** *2* **Quiet Times (IRE)**[24] 7108 9-9-2 65 ....(b) PaulMulrennan 8 52
(K A Ryan) *chsd ldrs on outer: rdn along over 2f out: sn edgd lft and btn wl over 1f out* **15/2**

030- **7** *1* **Campo Bueno (FR)**[31] 7025 6-8-3 55 .... AndrewMullen(3) 3 39
(A Berry) *chsd ldrs: n.m.r and lost pl over 3f out and sn in rr* **16/1**

1m 16.86s (0.36) **Going Correction** +0.15s/f (Slow) **7** Ran SP% **112.2**
Speed ratings (Par 103): **106,104,101,98,97 95,93**
CSF £12.82 CT £62.03 TOTE £2.60: £1.40, £3.50; EX 14.30 Trifecta £61.00 Pool £620.51 - 7.22 winning units..
Owner Mrs G C Maxwell & J D N Tillyard **Bred** J C Condon **Trained** East Ilsley, Berks

FOCUS
An ordinary sprint handicap, but they went a good pace and most of these were in trouble at halfway. The winning time was 0.91 seconds faster than the earlier claimer and the race can be rated higher, so the front pair can find further success on this surface.

42 GREAT VALUE GETAWAYS @ PONTIN'S H'CAP 7f (F)
3:10 (3:10) (Class 6) (0-60,60) 4-Y-0+ £1,911 (£564; £282) Stalls Low

Form RPR

651- **1** **Haroldini (IRE)**[20] 7153 6-9-2 58 ....(p) PaulMulrennan 2 71
(J Balding) *in tch: hdwy over 2f out: swtchd lft and rdn to ld ent fnl f: styd on* **7/2**[1]

026- **2** *2* **Solicitude**[34] 7003 5-8-8 53 ....(p) AndrewElliott(3) 10 61+
(D Haydn Jones) *s.i.s and bhd: hdwy wl over 2f out: rdn wl over 1f out: styd on ins fnl f: nt rch wnr* **11/2**

000- **3** *3/4* **Wodhill Schnaps**[70] 6479 7-8-7 49 ....(v) AdrianMcCarthy 4 55
(D Morris) *towards rr: hdwy on outer wl over 2f out: rdn to chse ldrs over 1f out: sn drvn and one pce ins fnl f* **22/1**

365- **4** *1/2* **Toms Laughter**[6] 7271 4-9-2 58 .... ChrisCatlin 6 63
(R A Harris) *cl up: led over 3f out: rdn wl over 1f out: drvn and hdd ent fnl f: kpt on same pce* **5/1**[3]

463- **5** *1* **Run Free**[17] 7180 4-9-3 59 .... DanielTudhope 8 61
(N Wilson) *in tch: hdwy over 2f out: sn rdn and kpt on same pce appr fnl f* **9/1**

001- **6** *hd* **Van Ruymbeke (IRE)**[8] 7239 4-8-9 51 6ex ....(t1) LiamJones 11 52
(D J Murphy) *in tch: effrt over 2f out: sn rdn and kpt on same pce* **14/1**

000- **7** *3/4* **Kingsmaite**[20] 7153 7-8-1 46 oh1 ....(b) DuranFentiman(3) 5 45
(S R Bowring) *chsd ldrs: rdn along 2f out: grad wknd* **28/1**

550- **8** *1* **Cleveland**[51] 6818 6-8-13 60 .... RussellKennemore(5) 12 57
(R Hollinshead) *trckd ldrs: hdwy 3f out: rdn to chal 2f out and ev ch: sn edgd rt: drvn and wknd* **4/1**[2]

000- **9** *2* **Government (IRE)**[8] 7244 7-8-1 46 oh1 .... DominicFox(3) 3 37
(M C Chapman) *led: rdn along and hdd over 3f out: sn drvn and wknd fnl 2f* **33/1**

000- **10** *2* **Silidan**[109] 5489 5-9-1 60 .... MarkLawson(3) 9 46
(M Brittain) *in tch: rdn along wl over 2f out and sn wknd* **50/1**

020- **11** *2 1/2* **Shadow Jumper (IRE)**[8] 7250 7-8-6 48 ....(v) DaleGibson 14 27
(J T Stimpson) *chsd ldrs: rdn wl over 2f out: grad wknd* **16/1**

100- **12** *1 3/4* **Shaftesbury Avenue (USA)**[145] 4427 5-8-10 57 .... JamesO'Reilly(5) 7 31
(J O'Reilly) *s.i.s: a in rr* **9/1**

006- **13** *nk* **Capital Lass**[23] 7124 5-7-13 46 oh1 .... NataliaGemelova(5) 13 20
(A J McCabe) *dwlt and towards rr: effrt and sme hdwy 3f out: sn wknd* **28/1**

600- **14** *15* **Prettilini**[148] 4324 5-8-5 47 .... JamieMackay 1 —
(A W Carroll) *cl up on inner: rdn along 1/2-way: sn wknd* **50/1**

1m 30.6s (0.30) **Going Correction** +0.15s/f (Slow) **14** Ran SP% **124.9**
Speed ratings (Par 101): **107,104,103,103,102 101,101,99,97,95 92,90,90,73**
CSF £22.05 CT £391.69 TOTE £4.00: £1.50, £2.20, £7.80; EX 27.90 Trifecta £355.90 Part won. Pool £501.32 - 0.57 winning units..
Owner Tykes And Terriers Racing Club **Bred** Michael O'Mahony **Trained** Scrooby, Notts

FOCUS
A moderate handicap on paper, but with a few confirmed front-runners in the field a rapid pace was always likely. The strong gallop resulted in a decent time for the grade, but it also helped those ridden patiently as the front three all came from off the pace.
Cleveland Official explanation: jockey said gelding failed to stay the 7f

43 SOUTHWELL GOLF CLUB H'CAP 7f (F)
3:40 (3:40) (Class 4) (0-85,84) 4-Y-0+ £4,210 (£1,252; £625; £312) Stalls Low

Form RPR

601- **1** **Red Romeo**[4] 7289 7-9-2 82 6ex .... DanielTudhope 2 91
(N Wilson) *trckd ldrs: hdwy on inner over 2f out: led wl over 1f out and sn rdn: drvn and edgd rt ins fnl f: hld on wl* **11/2**[3]

/01- **2** *1/2* **Crimson King (IRE)**[14] 7212 7-9-1 81 .... AdamKirby 4 89
(R W Price) *hld up in tch: hdwy on outer 2f out: rdn to chal ent fnl f: sn drvn: edgd lft and nt qckn towards fin* **4/5**[1]

113- **3** *2 1/2* **Tilapia (IRE)**[212] 2354 4-9-4 84 .... JamieMackay 5 85
(Sir Mark Prescott) *cl up: effrt 2f out and ev ch tl rdn and one pce ent fnl f* **10/3**[2]

001- **4** *nk* **Soviet Palace (IRE)**[25] 7104 4-8-9 75 ....(e) PaulMulrennan 1 75
(K A Ryan) *led: rdn along over 2f out: hdd wl over 1f out: sn drvn and wknd appr fnl f* **9/1**

126/ **5** *14* **Ela Aleka Mou**[517] 4146 4-9-3 83 .... MatthewHenry 3 45
(M A Jarvis) *cl up: rdn along over 2f out and grad wknd* **16/1**

1m 30.31s (0.01) **Going Correction** +0.15s/f (Slow) **5** Ran SP% **109.9**
Speed ratings (Par 105): **108,107,104,104,88**
CSF £10.49 TOTE £6.20: £2.60, £1.10; EX 11.30 Place 6 £16.91, Place 5 £5.44..
Owner Six Pound Note Club **Bred** J O'Mulloy **Trained** Flaxton, N Yorks

FOCUS
A decent little handicap despite the small field and run at a solid pace thanks to Soviet Palace. The form looks somewhat dubious though.
T/Jkpt: £7,100.00 to a £1 stake. Pool: £10,000.00. 1.00 winning ticket. T/Plt: £16.20 to a £1 stake. Pool: £52,489.10. 2,356.75 winning tickets. T/Qpdt: £5.00 to a £1 stake. Pool: £5,522.90. 807.50 winning tickets. JR

29 WOLVERHAMPTON (A.W) (L-H)
Friday, January 4

OFFICIAL GOING: Standard
Wind: Fresh behind Weather: Raining

44 HALF TERM HAPPY DEALS @ PONTIN'S APPRENTICE H'CAP 1m 1f 103y(P)
6:50 (6:50) (Class 6) (0-60,60) 4-Y-0+ £1,774 (£523; £262) Stalls Low

Form RPR

210- **1** **Hatch A Plan (IRE)**[16] 7186 7-9-5 59 .... TravisBlock 4 63
(Mouse Hamilton-Fairley) *prom: outpcd over 3f out: rallied 2f out: styd on u.p to ld post* **10/1**

201- **2** *shd* **Glenridding**[8] 7247 4-8-13 59 6ex .... JackMitchell(5) 6 63
(J G Given) *w ldr: racd keenly: led over 2f out: sn rdn: rdr dropped whip over 1f out: hdd post* **3/1**[1]

005- **3** *1/2* **Mujobliged (IRE)**[16] 7186 5-7-13 46 oh1 .... RossAtkinson(7) 2 49
(J R Best) *chsd ldrs: rdn over 1f out: hung lft: styd on* **18/1**

V50- **4** *1* **Western Roots**[6] 7274 7-9-3 60 ....(p) KirstyMilczarek(3) 7 63+
(M Appleby) *hld up: nt clr run wl over 1f out: hdwy whn hmpd 1f out: swtchd rt: r.o: nt rch ldrs* **13/2**[3]

23-6 **5** *1/2* **Casablanca Minx (IRE)**[2] 21 5-8-12 59 ....(b) RichardEvans(7) 3 59
(P D Evans) *hld up in tch: lost pl over 4f out: nt clr run 3f out: hdwy over 1f out: one pce fnl f* **9/2**[2]

650- **6** *1 1/4* **Lordswood (IRE)**[44] 6896 4-7-12 46 oh1 .... KierenFox(7) 10 43
(J R Best) *hld up: hdwy over 5f out: rdn and hung lft over 1f out: no ex* **14/1**

0/0- **7** *7* **Dark Society**[2] 6804 10-8-4 49 .... MarkCoumbe(5) 5 32
(A W Carroll) *s.i.s: a in rr* **50/1**

643- **8** *3* **Capania (IRE)**[28] 7057 4-9-5 60 .... MichaelJStainton 9 36
(P D Evans) *plld hrd: sddle slipped sn after s: trckd ldrs tl wknd over 2f out* **9/1**

120- **9** *2 1/2* **Mighty Mover (IRE)**[29] 7046 6-9-0 57 .... TolleyDean(3) 1 28
(B Palling) *led: rdn and hdd over 2f out: wknd over 1f out* **3/1**[1]

2m 4.16s (2.46) **Going Correction** +0.05s/f (Slow)
WFA 4 from 5yo+ 1lb **9** Ran SP% **114.5**
Speed ratings (Par 101): **95,94,94,93,93 92,85,83,80**
CSF £39.82 CT £539.38 TOTE £14.10: £3.70, £1.70, £3.60; EX 39.20.

The Form Book, Raceform Ltd, Compton, RG20 6NL

Owner Hamilton-Fairley Racing **Bred** Camogue Stud Ltd **Trained** Bramshill, Hants

FOCUS

A weak handicap, confined to apprentice riders, which was run at a moderate early pace. It resulted in a modest winning time and the form is limited by the proximity of the third and sixth racing from just out of the handicap.

Western Roots Official explanation: jockey said gelding was denied a clear run

Dark Society Official explanation: jockey said gelding had been hanging badly left

45 AND THEY'RE OFF TO PONTIN'S CLAIMING STKS 5f 20y(P)

7:20 (7:20) (Class 6) 4-Y-0+ £2,047 (£604; £302) Stalls Low

Form RPR

345- **1** **Compton Classic**[8] 7238 6-8-13 71 (v) HarryPoulton(7) 3 72
(J R Boyle) *chsd ldr: rdn to ld wl ins fnl f: r.o* **15/2**[3]

325- **2** 1 1/4 **Harry Up**[5] 7279 7-9-7 82 (p) FergalLynch 1 69
(K A Ryan) *led: rdn over 1f out: edgd rt and hdd wl ins fnl f* **30/100**[1]

62-5 **3** 1 **Earl Compton (IRE)**[2] 19 4-8-13 51 (v) MickyFenton 2 57
(Stef Liddiard) *dwlt: hdwy 1/2-way: rdn over 1f out: styd on same pce* **33/1**

224- **4** 2 **Chatshow (USA)**[42] 6910 7-8-10 62 MarkCoumbe(7) 4 54
(A W Carroll) *chsd ldrs: rdn 1/2-way: styd on same pce appr fnl f* **6/1**[2]

62.71 secs (0.41) **Going Correction** +0.05s/f (Slow) 4 Ran SP% **105.9**

Speed ratings (Par 101): **102,100,98,95**

CSF £10.38 TOTE £16.20; EX 12.40.

Owner M Khan X2 **Bred** James Thom And Sons And Peter Orr **Trained** Epsom, Surrey

FOCUS

A messy claimer and not particularly sound form for the grade.

46 HAVE A BREAK - HAVE A PONTIN'S BREAK H'CAP 5f 216y(P)

7:50 (7:51) (Class 6) (0-50,54) 4-Y-0+ £1,774 (£523; £262) Stalls Low

Form RPR

00-3 **1** **Calloff The Search**[2] 16 4-8-8 **46** (p) MickyFenton 8 58
(Stef Liddiard) *mde all: rdn clr and edgd rt fnl f* **3/1**[2]

660- **2** 5 **Avoncreek**[148] 4330 4-8-6 **47** AndrewElliott(3) 13 43+
(B P J Baugh) *hld up: plld hrd: hdwy over 1f out: r.o: no ch w wnr* **28/1**

616- **3** 1 **Silver Hotspur**[8] 7250 4-8-12 **50** NickyMackay 4 48+
(M Wigham) *hld up: nt clr run wl over 1f out: edgd lft and r.o fnl f: nvr nr to chal* **5/2**[1]

203- **4** 1/2 **Blackheath (IRE)**[27] 7077 12-8-12 **50** PaulFessey 5 41
(S T Mason) *trckd ldrs: rdn over 2f out: wknd ins fnl f* **5/1**[3]

400- **5** 1 1/2 **Mister Incredible**[175] 3498 5-8-7 **50** (v) TolleyDean(5) 1 36
(J M Bradley) *hld up: hmpd 5f out: hung rt over 2f out: hdwy sn after: wknd fnl f* **11/1**

400- **6** 1/2 **Tibinta**[16] 7188 4-8-8 **46** oh1 (b) StephenDonohoe 6 31
(P D Evans) *hmpd sn after s: hld up: hdwy over 1f out: n.d* **9/1**

00-0 **7** 1 3/4 **Cayman Breeze**[2] 16 8-8-8 **46** oh1 (b) PaulFitzsimons 11 25
(J M Bradley) *chsd ldrs: rdn over 2f out: edgd rt and wknd over 1f out* **25/1**

501- **8** shd **Ace Club**[4] 7283 7-8-9 **54** 6ex (b) MarkCoumbe(7) 10 33
(S Parr) *hld up: plld hrd: hdwy over 2f out: rdn and wknd over 1f out* **9/1**

000- **9** 6 **Spinning Game**[92] 5930 4-8-3 **46** oh1 (b) DanielleMcCreery(5) 3 6
(D W Chapman) *s.s: outpcd* **28/1**

/00- **10** 1/2 **White Ledger (IRE)**[159] 4008 9-8-9 **47** oh1 ow1 TGMcLaughlin 7 5
(R E Peacock) *hmpd sn after s: in rr: hdwy over 3f out: rdn over 2f out: wkng whn hmpd over 1f out* **40/1**

000- **11** 5 **Mujart**[21] 7138 4-8-8 **46** oh1 ChrisCatlin 2 —
(J A Pickering) *sn chsng ldrs: wknd over 2f out* **10/1**

1m 16.15s (1.15) **Going Correction** +0.05s/f (Slow) 11 Ran SP% **120.8**

Speed ratings (Par 101): **99,92,91,90,88 87,85,85,77,76 69**

CSF £93.15 CT £249.90 TOTE £4.10: £1.90, £5.50, £1.70; EX 195.50.

Owner Lobster & The Wizrat Busters **Bred** Mascalls Stud **Trained** Great Shefford, Berks

■ Stewards' Enquiry : Paul Fitzsimons seven-day ban: careless riding (Jan 15-21)

FOCUS

Solid enough form for the grade, with the improving winner rated back to his best. The placed horses both shaped better than the bare form.

White Ledger(IRE) Official explanation: jockey said gelding suffered interference in running

47 HBOS - PEOPLE DEVELOPMENT IS OUR PASSION H'CAP 1m 4f 50y(P)

8:20 (8:20) (Class 5) (0-75,76) 4-Y-0+ £2,590 (£770; £385; £192) Stalls Low

Form RPR

112- **1** **Fresh Mint (IRE)**[29] 7046 4-9-1 **69** DaneO'Neill 1 81+
(M J Wallace) *chsd ldr tl led 2f out: sn edgd lft: rdn clr fnl f* **9/4**[1]

231- **2** 3 1/2 **Fenners (USA)**[20] 7157 5-8-6 **63** NSLawes(7) 4 69
(M W Easterby) *a.p: rdn to chse wnr and hung lft over 1f out: styd on same pce fnl f* **11/2**[3]

002- **3** 2 1/2 **Touch Of Style (IRE)**[20] 7160 4-9-5 **73** (p) PatCosgrave 3 75
(J R Boyle) *hld up: edgd lft 4f out: rdn over 1f out: edgd lft: nt trble ldrs* **11/2**[3]

064- **4** 2 **Pocketwood**[32] 7004 6-9-0 **64** (p) FrankieMcDonald 6 63
(Jean-Rene Auvray) *hld up: rdn over 5f out: wknd over 2f out* **9/1**

002- **5** shd **Marsam (IRE)**[23] 7123 5-9-5 **72** JerryO'Dwyer(3) 2 71
(M G Quinlan) *led: rdn and hdd 2f out: wknd fnl f* **11/2**[3]

/11- **6** 3 **Friends Hope**[9] 7237 7-9-12 **76** 6ex FergalLynch 5 70
(P A Blockley) *dwlt: hld up: hmpd 4f out: rdn over 2f out: sn wknd* **7/2**[2]

2m 41.38s (0.28) **Going Correction** +0.05s/f (Slow)

WFA 4 from 5yo+ 4lb 6 Ran SP% **109.1**

Speed ratings (Par 103): **105,102,101,99,99 97**

CSF £13.95 TOTE £3.00: £1.90, £2.50; EX 8.70.

Owner Rick Barnes **Bred** Grange Con Holdings **Trained** Newmarket, Suffolk

■ Stewards' Enquiry : Pat Cosgrave two-day ban: careless riding (Jan 17-18)

FOCUS

A competitive little handicap run at a fair pace but very few got into it, and the winner remains an improving filly. The form is solid rated through the second and third.

48 BE BESIDE THE SEASIDE @ PONTIN'S MAIDEN STKS 7f 32y(P)

8:50 (8:52) (Class 5) 4-Y-0+ £2,457 (£725; £362) Stalls High

Form RPR

023- **1** **Tri Chara (IRE)**[60] 6695 4-8-12 62 RussellKennemore(5) 8 69
(R Hollinshead) *hld up in tch: nt clr run and swtchd rt over 2f out: rdn to ld and edgd lft over 1f out: r.o* **4/1**[3]

560- **2** 2 1/2 **Cow Girl (IRE)**[6] 7269 4-8-12 57 MickyFenton 11 57
(Miss Gay Kelleway) *s.i.s: hld up: hdwy over 2f out: rdn over 1f out: styd on same pce* **11/1**

000- **3** 4 **King Of Legend (IRE)**[168] 3710 4-9-3 63 ChrisCatlin 1 51
(A G Foster) *plld hrd and prom: rdn over 2f out: wknd fnl f* **7/1**

050- **4** 1 1/4 **Lily La Belle**[59] 6706 4-8-12 48 JamesDoyle 6 43
(A W Carroll) *plld hrd and prom: lost pl over 4f out: styd on appr fnl f* **33/1**

306- **5** 2 **Far Seeking**[18] 7174 4-9-3 55 TGMcLaughlin 3 43
(R A Harris) *led: racd keenly: rdn and hdd over 1f out: wknd fnl f* **18/1**

542- **6** shd **Fine Ruler (IRE)**[21] 7143 4-9-3 65 GeorgeBaker 10 42
(M R Bosley) *hld up in tch: plld hrd: rdn over 2f out: wknd over 1f out* **13/8**[1]

7 3 **Northstar Express (IRE)**[62] 6659 5-8-12 20 StephenDonohoe 5 29
(J L Spearing) *sn outpcd: nvr nrr* **80/1**

8 nk **Ella** 4-8-12 0 PaulMulrennan 7 28
(G A Swinbank) *chsd ldrs lots pl 1/2-way: wknd over 2f out* **3/1**[2]

/60- **9** nk **Miss Hoolie**[8] 7239 4-8-5 0 JackDean(7) 9 28
(W G M Turner) *plld hrd and prom: rdn and wknd over 2f out* **80/1**

10 shd **Newgate (UAE)** 4-9-3 0 PaulFessey 4 32
(D W Chapman) *chsd ldrs 5f* **16/1**

1m 30.51s (0.91) **Going Correction** +0.05s/f (Slow) 10 Ran SP% **120.5**

Speed ratings (Par 103): **101,98,93,92,89 89,86,85,85,85**

CSF £48.65 TOTE £5.80: £1.60, £2.50, £2.60; EX 41.00.

Owner The Tri Chara Partnership **Bred** High Bramley Grange Stud **Trained** Upper Longdon, Staffs

FOCUS

Most of this field had had a number of chances already and the form looks modest rated through the runner-up.

49 BOOK NOW @ PONTINS.COM H'CAP 7f 32y(P)

9:20 (9:20) (Class 5) (0-70,68) 4-Y-0+ £2,331 (£693; £346; £173) Stalls High

Form RPR

12-4 **1** **Alto Vertigo**[2] 15 5-8-3 60 PatrickDonaghy(7) 2 70
(P C Haslam) *s.i.s: sn rcvrd to ld: hrd rdn fr over 1f out: styd on* **3/1**[2]

225- **2** 3/4 **Tanforan**[21] 7143 6-8-12 62 DavidAllan 5 70
(B P J Baugh) *hld up: hdwy over 2f out: rdn and hung lft fr over 1f out: nt rch wnr* **12/1**

145- **3** 1 3/4 **Northern Boy (USA)**[29] 7047 5-8-13 63 PaulMulrennan 7 66
(M W Easterby) *prom: chsd wnr 1/2-way: rdn over 2f out: hung lft over 1f out: styd on same pce fnl f* **6/1**

02-1 **4** 1 **Obe Royal**[2] 15 4-8-7 64 6ex (b) RichardEvans(7) 6 65
(P D Evans) *hld up: hdwy over 1f out: edgd lft: nt trble ldrs* **2/1**[1]

236- **5** 1 **Wicked Uncle**[15] 7206 9-8-12 62 (v) ChrisCatlin 3 60
(S Gollings) *chsd ldrs: rdn over 2f out: wknd fnl f* **16/1**

010- **6** 1 1/2 **Carefree**[70] 6463 4-8-4 57 AndrewElliott(3) 1 51
(G A Swinbank) *led early: chsd wnr to 1/2-way: styd on same pce fnl 2f* **20/1**

662- **7** 1 3/4 **Theoretical**[13] 7227 4-8-3 56 (p) PatrickMathers(3) 4 45
(A J McCabe) *hld up in tch: plld hrd: lost pl 1/2-way: n.d after* **10/1**

123- **8** 2 **Millfield (IRE)**[20] 7160 5-9-4 68 GeorgeBaker 8 52
(P R Chamings) *hld up: rdn over 2f out: a in rr* **7/2**[3]

1m 29.5s (-0.10) **Going Correction** +0.05s/f (Slow) 8 Ran SP% **122.3**

Speed ratings (Par 103): **107,106,104,103,101 100,98,95**

CSF £41.16 CT £213.09 TOTE £4.50: £1.80, £2.80, £2.50; EX 46.60 Place 6 £640.21, Place 5£213.42.

Owner Middleham Park Racing XXXI **Bred** Ercan Dogan **Trained** Middleham Moor, N Yorks

■ Stewards' Enquiry : Patrick Donaghy two-day ban: used whip with excessive frequency (Jan 15-16)

FOCUS

A modest handicap dominated throughout by the forcefully-ridden winner. He recorded a fair winning time for the class, just over a second quicker than the maiden. The form is rated through the runner-up.

Theoretical Official explanation: jockey said gelding had hung right

Millfield(IRE) Official explanation: jockey said gelding had run flat

T/Plt: £338.10 to a £1 stake. Pool: £115,993.35. 250.40 winning tickets. T/Qpdt: £16.00 to a £1 stake. Pool: £9,960.30. 460.20 winning tickets. CR

[8]KEMPTON (A.W) (R-H)

Saturday, January 5

OFFICIAL GOING: Standard

Wind: Almost nil Weather: Cloudy

50 PANORAMIC BAR & RESTAURANT CLASSIFIED STKS 5f (P)

6:20 (6:22) (Class 7) 4-Y-0+ £1,295 (£385; £192; £96) Stalls High

Form RPR

0/0- **1** **Ask Jenny (IRE)**[364] 46 6-9-0 41 RichardHughes 9 52
(Patrick Morris, Ire) *trckd ldng pair: effrt and got through to ld last 150yds: rdn out* **16/1**

053- **2** 1/2 **Maraagel (USA)**[9] 7239 5-9-0 45 (t) J-PGuillambert 7 50+
(S C Williams) *dwlt: mostly in last pair: prog over 1f out: r.o fnl f to take 2nd nr fin* **9/4**[1]

504- **3** hd **Lady Hopeful (IRE)**[5] 7284 6-9-0 44 (b) LPKeniry 3 49
(Peter Grayson) *s.s: mostly last: prog and nt clr run over 1f out: swtchd lft: r.o ins fnl f: nrst fin* **9/1**

05-0 **4** nk **Blushing Russian (IRE)**[3] 16 6-9-0 42 (b[1]) PaulFitzsimons 10 48
(J M Bradley) *dwlt: pushed up and sn prom: effrt over 1f out: upsides ent fnl f: nt qckn* **8/1**

505- **5** 1/2 **Elvina**[107] 5564 7-9-0 45 DaneO'Neill 2 46
(A G Newcombe) *led 1f: pressed ldr: drvn to ld again 1f out: sn hdd: wknd nr fin* **11/2**[2]

506- **6** 3/4 **Time Share (IRE)**[17] 7192 4-9-0 44 (be) TGMcLaughlin 1 43
(G C Bravery) *dwlt: wl in rr: rousted along on wd outside and prog 2f out: chsd ldrs 1f out: no imp* **15/2**

000- **7** 1 **Dotty's Daughter**[75] 6390 4-9-0 43 (p) JimCrowley 12 40
(B Storey) *chsd ldrs but sn pushed along: nt qckn over 1f out: plugged on* **20/1**

266- **8** nk **Orchestration (IRE)**[5] 7284 7-8-11 45 (v) DominicFox(3) 5 39
(S Parr) *nvr bttr than midfield: lost pl and struggling over 1f out* **11/1**

046- **9** 3/4 **Kissi Kissi**[9] 7238 5-9-0 40 AdrianMcCarthy 6 36
(M J Attwater) *a in rr: outpcd in last over 1f out: modest late prog* **20/1**

003- **10** hd **Maromito (IRE)**[47] 6864 11-9-0 44 PatCosgrave 8 35
(R Bastiman) *led after 1f to 1f out: wknd rapidly* **7/1**[3]

040- **11** 1 1/2 **Yurchenko**[5] 7283 4-8-11 38 NeilChalmers(3) 4 30
(M Wellings) *racd towards outer: nvr bttr than midfield: rdn and fnd nil over 1f out: fdd* **33/1**

60.68 secs (0.18) **Going Correction** -0.10s/f (Stan) 11 Ran SP% **118.2**

Speed ratings (Par 97): **93,92,91,91,90 89,87,86,86,85 83**

CSF £51.15 TOTE £13.60: £4.20, £1.50, £3.10; EX 84.90.

Owner W J Crosbie **Bred** Mrs J Costelloe **Trained** Ruanbeg, Co. Kildare

FOCUS
A very moderate sprint but straightforward form rated around the third and fourth.

51 KEMPTON FOR CONFERENCES H'CAP — 1m 2f (P)
6:50 (6:56) (Class 5) (0-70,68) 4-Y-O+ — £2,590 (£770; £385; £192) Stalls High

Form — RPR

420- 1 **Blu Manruna**[8] 7257 5-9-0 62 ....(b) PaulDoe 6 67
(J Akehurst) *disp ld: def advantage over 2f out: hrd pressed fnl 2f: hld on: all out* 10/1

200- 2 *hd* **Sudden Impulse**[17] 7194 7-9-6 68 .... PaulMulrennan 8 73
(A D Brown) *hld up in midfield: smooth prog fr 3f out: clsd on ldrs over 1f out: drvn to chal last 100yds: jst hld* 20/1

010- 3 ½ **Fateful Attraction**[40] 6951 5-9-5 67 ....(bt) JamesDoyle 2 71
(I A Wood) *prom: pressed wnr over 2f out: nrly upsides fnl f: nt qckn nr fin* 14/1

011- 4 ½ **Mr Napoleon (IRE)**[8] 7257 6-9-4 66 .... GeorgeBaker 12 73+
(G L Moore) *sn hld up in rr: stdy prog 2f out: chsd ldrs and rdn 1f out: clsng whn nowhere to go 100yds out and snatched up* 1/1[1]

445- 5 ¾ **Boundless Prospect (USA)**[15] 7213 9-8-13 61 .... MickyFenton 10 62+
(Miss Gay Kelleway) *hld up and mostly last: shkn up on outer fr 2f out: styd on steadily over 1f out: nrst fin* 12/1

105- 6 1 ½ **Stark Contrast (USA)**[14] 7224 4-9-0 64 .... J-PGuillambert 11 62+
(J Akehurst) *t.k.h: hld up in midfield: lost pl on inner 3f out and wl in rr: rdn and kpt on fr over 1f out* 15/2[3]

006/ 7 *shd* **Startengo (IRE)**[30] 1081 5-9-2 64 .... SamHitchcott 14 62
(Miss Suzy Smith) *prom: drvn on inner over 2f out: one pce over 1f out: fdd* 50/1

633- 8 3 **Arena's Dream (USA)**[8] 7257 4-9-1 65 ....(e[1]) PatCosgrave 7 57
(J R Boyle) *settled in midfield: drvn over 2f out: no imp on ldrs over 1f out: fdd* 7/1[2]

556- 9 2 **Double Spectre (IRE)**[75] 4878 6-9-1 63 .... DaneO'Neill 3 51
(Jean-Rene Auvray) *dwlt: a in rr: rdn in last pair 2f out: no real prog* 33/1

600- 10 5 **Prince Of Charm (USA)**[26] 7099 4-9-1 65 ....(p) JimCrowley 9 43
(R A Teal) *dwlt: hld up in rr: struggling 2f out: wknd* 20/1

62U- 11 7 **Danehill Silver**[102] 5710 4-8-7 60 .... AndrewElliott[(3)] 13 24
(B Storey) *disp ld to over 2f out: wknd rapidly* 25/1

120- 12 *nk* **Dinner Date**[27] 7083 6-8-11 59 .... NickyMackay 5 22
(T Keddy) *nvr beyond midfield: wknd 2f out: heavily eased* 8/1

2m 7.61s (-0.39) **Going Correction** -0.10s/f (Stan)
WFA 4 from 5yo+ 2lb — **12** Ran SP% **127.1**
Speed ratings (Par 103): **101,100,100,100,99 98,98,95,94,90 84,84**
CSF £204.19 CT £2823.38 TOTE £12.70: £3.60, £7.80, £3.80; EX 258.60.
Owner Canisbay Bloodstock **Bred** Canisbay Bloodstock Ltd **Trained** Epsom, Surrey

FOCUS
A modest handicap run at a reasonable pace but somewhat messy form best rated through the third.
Double Spectre(IRE) Official explanation: jockey said gelding suffered interference in running

52 DIGIBET MAIDEN STKS — 1m (P)
7:20 (7:23) (Class 5) 3-Y-O — £2,590 (£770; £385; £192) Stalls High

Form — RPR

04- 1 **Grand Strategy (IRE)**[73] 6436 3-9-3 0 .... MatthewHenry 8 77+
(M A Jarvis) *t.k.h: trckd ldrs: wnt 2nd over 2f out: led wl over 1f out: briefly looked vulnerable fnl f: shuffled along and styd on wl* 5/4[1]

0- 2 1 **Finmore Queen (USA)**[63] 6648 3-8-12 0 .... AdamKirby 7 67+
(J R Fanshawe) *reluctant to enter stalls: in tch: rdn and prog over 2f out: chsd ldrs over 1f out: styd on fnl f to take 2nd last strides* 11/1[3]

03- 3 *nk* **Ocean Legend (IRE)**[131] 4883 3-9-0 0 .... JerryO'Dwyer[(3)] 5 71
(Miss J Feilden) *led after 2f to wl over 1f out: tried to rally u.p fnl f: hld last 100yds: lost 2nd fnl strides* 16/1

0- 4 ¾ **Bon Ton Roulet**[49] 6849 3-8-7 0 .... HaddenFrost[(5)] 10 64
(R Hannon) *stdd s: hld up: prog to trck ldng trio over 2f out: reminder sn after and over 1f out: kpt on steadily: do bttr* 33/1

5 3 ½ **Thankful** 3-8-12 0 .... ChrisCatlin 1 56+
(Rae Guest) *s.i.s: hld up towards rr and rn green: hung rt 2f out: kpt on fnl f: n.d* 50/1

333- 6 *hd* **Hit The Roof**[62] 6665 3-9-3 75 .... RichardHughes 4 61
(R Hannon) *t.k.h: led 2f: trckd ldr to over 2f out: sn btn* 13/8[2]

500- 7 4 **Forsyte Saga**[17] 7190 3-8-12 65 .... GregFairley 2 47
(M Johnston) *prom tl wknd jst over 2f out* 14/1

0- 8 ½ **Colleoni (IRE)**[57] 6740 3-9-3 0 .... TPQueally 9 50+
(G A Butler) *dwlt: hld up in last trio: shkn up whn carried bdly rt 2f out: no prog after* 33/1

- 9 7 **South Wales** 3-9-3 0 .... SaleemGolam 6 34
(S C Williams) *s.s: rn green and a bhd* 25/1

0- 10 5 **Caffe Coretto**[7] 7266 3-8-5 0 .... GabrielHannon[(7)] 3 18
(B G Powell) *chsd ldrs tl wknd 3f out* 100/1

1m 40.12s (0.32) **Going Correction** -0.10s/f (Stan) — **10** Ran SP% **116.1**
Speed ratings (Par 97): **99,98,97,96,93 93,89,88,81,76**
CSF £15.63 TOTE £2.20: £1.10, £3.00, £2.20; EX 25.30.
Owner Sheikh Ahmed Al Maktoum **Bred** Darley **Trained** Newmarket, Suffolk

FOCUS
Just an ordinary maiden best rated through the third.

53 DIGIBET CLAIMING STKS — 1m (P)
7:50 (7:50) (Class 6) 4-Y-O+ — £2,047 (£604; £302) Stalls High

Form — RPR

25-4 1 **Electric Warrior (IRE)**[4] 6 5-9-7 86 .... FergusSweeney 5 92
(K R Burke) *sn settled in 3rd: sneaked through on inner to ld 2f out: shkn up and sn clr* 8/15[1]

346- 2 3 ½ **Waterline Twenty (IRE)**[6] 7281 5-8-12 71 .... JohnEgan 2 75
(P D Evans) *sn pressed ldr: narrow ld briefly over 2f out: sn lft bhd by wnr* 4/1[2]

205- 3 ½ **Landucci**[63] 6646 7-9-2 78 ....(p) PatrickHills[(5)] 3 83
(J W Hills) *hld up in 4th: effrt 2f out: fnd little over 1f out and unable to pass runner-up fnl f* 5/1[3]

400- 4 2 ½ **Boogie Dancer**[8] 7253 4-8-6 63 ....(v[1]) AdrianMcCarthy 1 62
(H S Howe) *pushed up to ld: drvn and hdd over 2f out: sn btn* 25/1

000- 5 4 **Safe Investment (USA)**[33] 6232 4-9-2 69 ....(t) VinceSlattery 4 63
(B N Pollock) *a last: wknd 2f out* 50/1

1m 39.71s (-0.09) **Going Correction** -0.10s/f (Stan) — **5** Ran SP% **107.7**
Speed ratings (Par 101): **101,97,97,94,90**
CSF £2.82 TOTE £1.40: £1.10, £1.60; EX 3.00.The winner was subject to a friendly claim.
Owner Market Avenue Racing Club Ltd **Bred** Limestone Stud **Trained** Middleham Moor, N Yorks

FOCUS
A good claimer and a straightforward task for the well-in Landucci. Sound enough form.

54 DIGIBET H'CAP — 6f (P)
8:20 (8:21) (Class 6) (0-58,58) 4-Y-O+ — £2,047 (£604; £302) Stalls High

Form — RPR

031- 1 **Muktasb (USA)**[7] 7265 7-9-0 56 ....(v) AdamKirby 9 65
(D Shaw) *hld up in rr: prog on inner over 2f out: rdn to chal over 1f out: narrow ld ins fnl f: hld on* 5/1[2]

054- 2 ¾ **Radiator Rooney (IRE)**[16] 7206 5-9-2 58 ....(v[1]) RichardHughes 12 69+
(Patrick Morris, Ire) *trckd ldrs gng easily: swtchd rt over 1f out: tried for gap but no room sn after: stmbld and rdr nrly off: nt rcvr: fin 3rd: plcd 2nd* 11/2[3]

100- 3 *shd* **Reigning Monarch (USA)**[117] 5275 5-8-13 55 .... SamHitchcott 11 64
(Miss Z C Davison) *led: drvn 2f out: hdd ins fnl f: kpt on wl: jst hld: fin 2nd: disqualified & plcd 3rd* 8/1

500- 4 *shd* **Zazous**[7] 7269 7-8-12 57 .... NeilChalmers[(3)] 8 63
(J J Bridger) *hld up: n.m.r after 1f: prog over 2f out: chsd ldrs over 1f out but nt qckn: styd on ins fnl f* 14/1

422- 5 3 **Stormburst (IRE)**[32] 7013 4-8-12 57 .... TravisBlock[(3)] 5 53
(A G Newcombe) *a chsng ldrs: rdn and outpcd fr over 1f out* 5/1[2]

462- 6 *nk* **Rhapsilian**[17] 7183 4-9-1 57 .... SteveDrowne 7 52+
(J A Geake) *t.k.h and hld up in rr: nt clr run briefly over 2f out: sn outpcd: no ch after* 11/4[1]

30-5 7 3 **Thoughtsofstardom**[2] 29 5-8-10 57 .... KirstyMilczarek[(5)] 6 42
(G C Bravery) *stdd s: t.k.h and hld up in rr: rdn and outpcd fr 2f out* 8/1

/01- 8 *hd* **Sir Don (IRE)**[17] 7192 9-8-13 55 ....(p) StephenDonohoe 4 40
(E S McMahon) *chsd ldrs: outpcd fr 2f out: fdd fnl f* 25/1

301- 9 1 **Bens Georgie (IRE)**[16] 7207 6-8-11 58 .... JamesO'Reilly[(5)] 1 40
(D K Ivory) *stdd s: t.k.h on outer and sn wl there: wknd 2f out* 12/1

340- 10 2 ½ **Anfield Dream**[32] 7013 6-9-0 56 ....(t) MickyFenton 3 30
(J R Jenkins) *pressed ldr: upsides 2f out: btn over 1f out: wknd v rapidly fnl f* 25/1

1m 13.03s (-0.07) **Going Correction** -0.10s/f (Stan) — **10** Ran SP% **119.7**
Speed ratings (Par 101): **100,98,99,98,94 94,90,90,88,85**
CSF £33.65 CT £184.25 TOTE £6.10: £1.80, £2.40, £2.90; EX 35.50.
Owner Miss Claire Comery **Bred** Shadwell Farm LLC **Trained** Danethorpe, Notts
■ Stewards' Enquiry : Sam Hitchcott two-day ban: careless riding (Jan 16-17)

FOCUS
A moderate sprint handicap. The winning time was 0.76 seconds slower than the following 6f handicap. A somewhat messy race, but sound form overall.

55 KEMPTON.CO.UK H'CAP — 6f (P)
8:50 (8:51) (Class 5) (0-75,78) 4-Y-O+ — £2,590 (£770; £385; £192) Stalls High

Form — RPR

051- 1 **Mr Lambros**[8] 7261 7-9-7 78 ....(vt) MickyFenton 11 89+
(Miss Gay Kelleway) *hit side of stalls as they opened: rousted along to rcvr and sn t.k.h: led over 4f out: clr over 2f out: hld on all out nr fin* 11/4[1]

323- 2 *hd* **Maysarah (IRE)**[31] 7033 4-8-9 66 .... TPQueally 6 76
(G A Butler) *hld up in last trio gng wl: gd prog on outer fr 2f out to chse wnr over 1f out: hung rt but clsd and looked sure to win: jinked lft 50yds out: nt qckn* 13/2[3]

434- 3 *shd* **Mogok Ruby**[14] 7221 4-8-12 69 .... RichardHughes 9 79
(L Montague Hall) *hld up: rr s: hld up in last trio: nt clr run over 2f out: stdy prog fnl 2f: drvn to cl fr 1f out: jst hld* 13/2[3]

055- 4 2 **Louphole**[56] 6762 6-9-1 72 .... ChrisCatlin 5 76+
(P J Makin) *dwlt: mostly last and off the pce: rdn and r.o fr over 1f out: fin wl* 14/1

226- 5 ½ **Brandywell Boy (IRE)**[21] 7161 5-8-12 69 .... RichardThomas 12 71
(D J S Ffrench Davis) *cl up: rdn to dispute 2nd over 2f out: nt qckn over 1f out: fdd* 6/1[2]

000- 6 1 **Hucking Hill (IRE)**[36] 6970 4-8-11 68 ....(b) JimCrowley 10 67
(J R Best) *in tch: prog to chse wnr over 2f out to over 1f out: fdd* 9/1

053- 7 ¾ **Parkview Love (USA)**[8] 7261 7-8-13 70 ....(v) DeanMcKeown 7 66
(D Shaw) *towards rr: rdn over 2f out: no prog* 10/1

106- 8 1 **Norcroft**[8] 7261 6-8-4 66 ....(p) KirstyMilczarek[(5)] 3 59
(Mrs C A Dunnett) *wl away and pressed ldrs on outer: lost pl over 2f out: struggling after* 16/1

163- 9 ¾ **No Time (IRE)**[8] 7253 8-8-4 64 .... PatrickMathers[(3)] 2 55
(A J McCabe) *prom on outer: lost grnd fr 3f out: n.d fnl 2f* 12/1

016- 10 1 **Dvinsky (USA)**[20] 7164 7-8-13 70 ....(v) TGMcLaughlin 4 58
(P Howling) *led to over 4f out: chsd wnr to over 2f out: wknd over 1f out* 10/1

1m 12.27s (-0.83) **Going Correction** -0.10s/f (Stan) — **10** Ran SP% **116.0**
Speed ratings (Par 103): **105,104,104,101,101 99,98,97,96,95**
CSF £20.17 CT £106.43 TOTE £4.00: £1.60, £1.70, £2.60; EX 15.90.
Owner Winterbeck Manor Stud **Bred** Witney And Warren Enterprises Ltd **Trained** Exning, Suffolk

FOCUS
A fair sprint handicap run at a strong pace. The winning time was 0.76 seconds quicker than the previous 6f handicap. The winner was the only one of the first four to race prominently and is rated better than the bare form.

56 DAY TIME, NIGHT TIME, GREAT TIME H'CAP — 7f (P)
9:20 (9:20) (Class 6) (0-60,60) 4-Y-O+ — £2,047 (£604; £302) Stalls High

Form — RPR

212- 1 **Emma Jean Lad (IRE)**[68] 6533 4-9-3 59 .... JohnEgan 14 71
(J S Moore) *rousted along early to go prom: wnt 2nd on inner wl over 2f out: led 2f out and clr w runner-up: kpt on steadily fnl f* 5/2[1]

501- 2 ½ **Angel Voices (IRE)**[24] 7118 5-8-7 56 ....(p) DeclanCannon[(7)] 10 67
(K R Burke) *led: rdn and hdd 2f out but clr w wnr: kpt on wl fnl f but a hld* 12/1

320- 3 2 **Royal Embrace**[22] 7143 5-9-1 57 ....(v) DeanMcKeown 1 63+
(D Shaw) *stdd s: hld up in last pair: rdn and prog fr 2f out: fin wl fnl f to snatch 3rd on line* 12/1

165- 4 *shd* **Jools**[20] 7164 10-8-12 59 .... JamesO'Reilly[(5)] 5 64
(D K Ivory) *trckd ldrs: shkn up and nt qckn over 2f out: kpt on steadily fr over 1f out: n.d* 13/2[3]

630- 5 *shd* **Metropolitan Chief**[7] 7269 4-9-1 57 .... LPKeniry 12 62
(P Burgoyne) *trckd ldrs: prog to chse ldng pair 2f out: no imp: kpt on fnl f but lost pls nr fin* 20/1

421- 6 *shd* **Littledodayno (IRE)**[55] 6779 5-9-3 59 .... JamieMackay 13 64
(M Wigham) *hld up in rr: prog on inner 2f out: rdn and kpt on same pce fr over 1f out* 8/1

233- 7 ¾ **Majestical (IRE)**[45] 6895 6-8-10 55 ....(e) JerryO'Dwyer[(3)] 2 58
(V Smith) *wl in rr on outer: rdn and effrt over 2f out: styd on fnl f: nt rch ldrs* 12/1

The Form Book, Raceform Ltd, Compton, RG20 6NL

300- **8** *nk* **Dancing Duo**[7] 7268 4-8-7 **54**........................(v) TolleyDean(5) 8 56
(D Shaw) *rdn towards rr over 3f out: struggling after: kpt on fnl f* **12/1**

063- **9** *nk* **Mythical Charm**[6] 7278 9-8-10 **52**........................(t) TPQueally 6 53
(J J Bridger) *dwlt: hld up towards rr: shkn up on outer and no real prog fnl 2f* **16/1**

300- **10** *3* **Beneking**[16] 7207 8-8-10 **52**........................(p) ChrisCatlin 7 45
(D Burchell) *prom tl lost pl over 2f out: wl btn whn n.m.r ins fnl f* **16/1**

100- **11** *1* **Sagunt (GER)**[17] 7186 5-9-4 **60**........................ AdrianMcCarthy 11 50
(S Curran) *mostly in last pair: rdn and no prog over 2f out* **33/1**

134- **12** *hd* **Park Valley Prince**[16] 7207 4-8-11 **53**........................ PaulDoe 9 43
(W R Muir) *chsd ldr to wl over 2f out: wknd and wandered over 1f out* **5/1**[2]

000- **13** *11* **Prospect Place**[104] 5662 4-9-4 **60**........................ AmirQuinn 4 20
(M A Allen) *plld hrd early: hld up: prog on wd outside over 3f out: wknd wl over 2f out: t.o* **66/1**

1m 25.76s (-0.24) **Going Correction** -0.10s/f (Stan) 13 Ran SP% **121.4**
Speed ratings (Par 101): **101,100,98,98,97 97,96,96,96,92 91,91,78**
CSF £34.56 CT £326.95 TOTE £2.90: £1.60, £3.60, £3.90; EX 44.60 Place 6 £201.54, Place 5 £87.95.
Owner Roger Ambrose William Reilly Stan Moore **Bred** Mrs H D McCalmont **Trained** Upper Lambourn, Berks
■ Stewards' Enquiry : Dean McKeown caution: careless riding

FOCUS
A moderate handicap, run at an uneven pace. The first pair came clear and the runner-up to last year's best sets the level.
T/Plt: £377.50 to a £1 stake. Pool: £91,087.05. 176.10 winning tickets. T/Qpdt: £12.90 to a £1 stake. Pool: £6,734.10. 386.00 winning tickets. JN

22 LINGFIELD (L-H)
Saturday, January 5

OFFICIAL GOING: Standard
Wind: moderate, half behind

57 PLAY GOLF @ LINGFIELD PARK (S) STKS 1m 2f (P)
12:35 (12:35) (Class 6) 4-Y-O+ **£1,774** (£523; £262) **Stalls** Low

Form RPR

212- **1** **Bridgewater Boys**[55] 6774 7-9-7 60........................(b) GeorgeBaker 1 71
(G L Moore) *hld up in tch: rdn to go 2nd over 3f out: led wl over 1f out: r.o wl* **11/8**[1]

044- **2** *2* **Ryan's Future (IRE)**[6] 7277 8-9-2 69........................ JohnEgan 7 62
(J S Moore) *hld up in tch: hdwy over 2f out: swtchd lft bef st: r.o to chse wnr fnl f* **9/2**[2]

206- **3** *nk* **Katiypour (IRE)**[8] 7251 11-9-2 61........................ SebSanders 6 61
(B R Johnson) *in rr: hdwy on outside over 2f out: r.o fnl f* **5/1**[3]

334- **4** *3* **Musango**[14] 7226 5-9-7 65........................(t) PaulDoe 5 60
(Miss Gay Kelleway) *led tl hdd wl over 1f out: fdd ins fnl f* **13/2**

052- **5** *5* **Barry Island**[6] 7277 9-9-2 60........................ LPKeniry 2 45
(D R C Elsworth) *slowly away: a in rr* **6/1**

050- **6** *11* **Swayze (IRE)**[54] 6804 5-9-2 55........................ ChrisCatlin 4 23
(M Quinn) *trckd ldrs tl rdn and wknd 3f out* **25/1**

000- **7** *5* **Campbeltown (IRE)**[26] 7094 5-9-2 40........................(b) SamHitchcott 3 13
(A B Haynes) *trckd ldr tl rdn and wknd over 3f out* **100/1**

2m 4.56s (-2.04) **Going Correction** -0.20s/f (Stan) 7 Ran SP% **109.4**
Speed ratings (Par 101): **104,102,102,99,95 86,82**
CSF £7.04 TOTE £2.00: £1.30, £2.30; EX 7.20.The winner was bought in for 7,200gns.
Owner Matthew Green & Richard Green **Bred** Southill Stud **Trained** Woodingdean, E Sussex

FOCUS
Not many races are truly run over this trip here these days, but this was an exception thanks to Musango making it a true test and the form looks very solid for a seller. It was noticeable that the jockeys made sure they came down the centre of the track once into the straight and gave the inside rail a wide berth.
Musango Official explanation: jockey said, regarding the running and riding, his orders were to jump out and make the running, which he had done, until being passed in the home straight; trainer added that as gelding had won over 1m4f, this trip of 1m2f night otherwise have been too short

58 LINGFIELDPARK.CO.UK MAIDEN STKS 1m 2f (P)
1:05 (1:05) (Class 5) 3-Y-O **£2,331** (£693; £346; £173) **Stalls** Low

Form RPR

00- **1** **Pacifism (UAE)**[64] 6618 3-9-3 0........................ NCallan 5 94+
(M A Jarvis) *hld up in tch: hdwy and squeezed through gap to ld 2f out: styd on wl and in command after* **4/1**[1]

2 *½* **Electrolyser (IRE)** 3-9-3 0........................ AdamKirby 10 90+
(C G Cox) *s.i.s: rdn 1/2-way: gd hdwy to go 2nd 2f out: kpt on but a hld by wnr ins fnl f* **8/1**

3 *7* **Always Bold (IRE)** 3-9-3 0........................ GregFairley 1 76+
(M Johnston) *hld up: hdwy 2f out: swtchd lft ent fnl f: styd on to go 3rd ins fnl f* **7/1**

642- **4** *nk* **Flash Of Colour**[24] 7114 3-9-3 71........................ JimCrowley 6 75
(Mrs A J Perrett) *led for 2f: led again over 3f out tl hdd 2f out: wknd ins fnl f* **13/2**

0- **5** *2* **Mischief Making (USA)**[40] 6944 3-8-12 0........................ TGMcLaughlin 8 66
(E A L Dunlop) *slowly away: in rr: mde sme late hdwy but nvr on terms* **20/1**

045- **6** *2 ½* **Unlicensed**[40] 6948 3-9-3 72........................ RichardHughes 3 66
(R Hannon) *trckd ldrs: rdn over 2f out: sn btn* **5/1**[3]

00- **7** *2 ½* **Ski Sunday**[80] 6267 3-9-3 0........................ MatthewHenry 2 61
(M A Jarvis) *led after 2f: rdn and hdd over 3f out: wknd over 1f out* **16/1**

660- **8** *4* **I Certainly May**[24] 7117 3-9-3 62........................ JohnEgan 4 53
(S Dow) *hld up in rr: rdn 4f out: no hdwy after* **25/1**

6- **9** *2 ½* **Sacrilege**[17] 7191 3-9-3 0........................ LPKeniry 9 48
(D R C Elsworth) *trckd ldrs tl rdn and wknd over 2f out* **9/2**[2]

10 *8* **Ollie Fliptrik (USA)** 3-9-3 0........................ ChrisCatlin 7 32
(P F I Cole) *prom on outside tl rdn over 4f out: sn wknd* **16/1**

2m 5.40s (-1.20) **Going Correction** -0.20s/f (Stan) 10 Ran SP% **112.2**
Speed ratings (Par 97): **101,100,95,94,93 91,89,85,83,77**
CSF £34.63 TOTE £4.40: £2.20, £2.90, £1.90; EX 37.20 Trifecta £119.40 Pool: £232.22 - 1.38 winning tickets..
Owner Sheikh Ahmed Al Maktoum **Bred** Darley **Trained** Newmarket, Suffolk

FOCUS
The early pace was nothing like as strong as in the preceding seller over the same trip, the first half-mile was run 3.61 seconds slower, but the second half of the contest was much more strongly run and the final time was only 0.84 seconds slower. The front pair pulled a long way clear of the others and both look to have a bright future.
Always Bold(IRE) Official explanation: jockey said colt hung left
Unlicensed Official explanation: jockey said gelding hung right

59 ARENALEISUREPLC.COM H'CAP 5f (P)
1:40 (1:40) (Class 5) (0-70,70) 3-Y-O **£2,331** (£693; £346; £173) **Stalls** High

Form RPR

400- **1** **Cocabana**[28] 7072 3-8-9 **61**........................ JamesDoyle 1 67
(J G Portman) *chsd ldng pair: rdn and hdwy to go 2nd over 1f out: r.o u.p to ld ins fnl f* **9/2**[3]

005- **2** *2* **Baytown Blaze**[114] 5365 3-8-13 **70**........................ KirstyMilczarek(5) 2 69
(G C Bravery) *led: strly rdn whn rdr lost whip and hdd ins fnl f: no ex* **2/1**[1]

303- **3** *2* **Wild Bill Tracey**[9] 7240 3-8-13 **65**........................ PatCosgrave 4 61
(M J Wallace) *rdn and sn jnd ldr: hung rt fr 1/2-way: wknd ins fnl f* **9/4**[2]

004- **4** *1 ½* **Twilight Belle (IRE)**[18] 7176 3-8-1 **56** oh4........................(b) AndrewElliott(3) 5 42
(K R Burke) *s.i.s: outpcd: rdn and mde sme late hdwy* **5/1**

000- **5** *8* **Queen's Treasure (IRE)**[143] 4500 3-8-5 **57**........................ ChrisCatlin 3 14
(S Dow) *in tch tl rdn 1/2-way: eased whn wl btn ins fnl f* **8/1**

58.76 secs (-0.04) **Going Correction** -0.20s/f (Stan) 5 Ran SP% **110.1**
Speed ratings (Par 97): **100,96,93,91,78**
CSF £13.89 TOTE £5.30: £2.60, £1.30; EX 10.80.
Owner Hockham Racing **Bred** Catridge Farm Stud Ltd **Trained** Compton, Berks

FOCUS
A moderate sprint handicap, but the two market leaders went off like scalded cats and probably set it up for the winner.

60 LINGFIELD PARK FOR WEDDINGS MAIDEN STKS 6f (P)
2:15 (2:15) (Class 5) 3-Y-O **£2,331** (£693; £346; £173) **Stalls** Low

Form RPR

52- **1** **Requisite**[35] 6998 3-8-12 0........................ PatCosgrave 1 71
(Jane Chapple-Hyam) *a in tch on ins: led over 1f out: edgd rt ins fnl f but hld on wl* **3/1**[2]

3- **2** *hd* **Salt Of The Earth (IRE)**[45] 6897 3-9-3 0........................ JohnEgan 6 75
(T G Mills) *t.k.h: a.p: rdn to chse wnr ins fnl f but hld cl home* **5/6**[1]

56- **3** *2 ½* **Kingsgate Castle**[7] 7266 3-9-3 0........................ GeorgeBaker 9 67
(J R Best) *prom on outside: effrt over 1f out: one pce ins fnl f* **9/1**

62- **4** *¾* **Maggie Kate**[8] 7258 3-8-12 0........................ DavidKinsella 4 60
(R Ingram) *trckd ldr tl rdn over 2f out: one pce fnl f* **25/1**

32-4 **5** *1 ¼* **Orange Square (IRE)**[3] 9 3-9-3 66........................(t) RichardHughes 2 61
(R Hannon) *led tl rdn and hdd over 1f out: wknd ins fnl f* **7/1**[3]

- **6** *½* **Bye Baby Bunting** 3-8-12 0........................ DaneO'Neill 3 54
(B R Johnson) *s.i.s: a bhd* **66/1**

7 *1 ¼* **Martha (IRE)** 3-8-12 0........................ LPKeniry 7 50+
(D R C Elsworth) *slowly away: outpcd: a bhd* **14/1**

020- **8** *½* **Kaystar Ridge**[31] 7031 3-8-12 64........................(t) JamesO'Reilly(5) 8 54
(D K Ivory) *racd wd: trckd ldrs tl wknd over 1f out* **20/1**

400- **9** *4* **Bad Moon Rising**[17] 7191 3-9-3 63........................ ChrisCatlin 5 41
(J Akehurst) *hld up in mid-div: lost pl over 2f out* **33/1**

1m 12.54s (0.64) **Going Correction** -0.20s/f (Stan) 9 Ran SP% **121.8**
Speed ratings (Par 97): **93,92,89,88,86 86,84,83,78**
CSF £6.00 TOTE £3.50: £1.70, £1.10, £1.90; EX 8.30 Trifecta £102.30 Pool: £488.59 - 3.39 winning tickets..
Owner Franconson Partners **Bred** Darley **Trained** Lambourn, Berks

FOCUS
An ordinary sprint maiden in which the front pair pulled clear and, outside of that pair, the form probably does not add up to a great deal.

61 BOOK ONLINE @ LINGFIELDPARK.CO.UK H'CAP 1m 4f (P)
2:45 (2:45) (Class 2) (0-100,103) 4-Y-O+ **£9,971** (£2,985; £1,492; £747) **Stalls** Low

Form RPR

534- **1** **Millville**[14] 7225 8-9-11 103........................ NCallan 2 111
(M A Jarvis) *trckd ldr: led over 2f out: pushed out fnl f: readily* **9/4**[2]

322- **2** *¾* **Polish Power (GER)**[27] 7086 8-8-11 89........................ JohnEgan 5 96
(J S Moore) *hld up in last pl: rdn and hdwy to chse wnr over 1f out: kpt on but a hld* **15/8**[1]

231- **3** *½* **Mafeking (UAE)**[28] 7075 4-8-1 86 oh2........................ AndrewElliott(3) 1 92
(M R Hoad) *a in tch in 3rd pl: kpt on one pce fnl f* **7/2**

631- **4** *3* **Invasian (IRE)**[22] 7147 7-9-2 94........................ MickyFenton 4 95
(P W D'Arcy) *led tl hdd over 2f out: rdn and wknd ent fnl f* **10/3**[3]

2m 30.84s (-2.16) **Going Correction** -0.20s/f (Stan)
WFA 4 from 7yo+ 4lb 4 Ran SP% **110.9**
Speed ratings (Par 109): **103,102,102,100**
CSF £6.98 TOTE £2.80; EX 5.20.
Owner T G Warner **Bred** Red House Stud **Trained** Newmarket, Suffolk

FOCUS
A decent prize, but a race rendered less competitive by the two non-runners. The very early pace was stronger than it might have been due to confirmed front-runner Invasian, but even he had slowed things down considerably by halfway and the contest still developed into something of a sprint.

NOTEBOOK
Millville, back in a handicap after making the frame in a couple of 1m2f Listed events here, is probably even better suited by this trip on this surface and was only just beaten by the 2006 Winter Derby-winner Sri Diamond in this race last year off a 4lb higher mark. Always in a great position behind the pace-setter, he won the race when sent for home off the final bend and his rivals were never able to get to him. (op 6-4 tchd 11-4)
Polish Power(GER), who continues to edge up the weights despite not winning, was given his normal waiting ride before being delivered late, but despite putting in his usual power-packed finish the winner had got first run on him. These are his ideal conditions and he deserves to win more races than he actually does. (op 5-2)
Mafeking(UAE), raised 4lb for his recent victory here but also 2lb wrong, was trying this trip for the first time and was ridden to get it. The pace they went probably tested his stamina enough and the way he stayed on suggests he is with another go over it off his correct mark. (op 4-1)
Invasian(IRE), raised 4lb for his Wolverhampton win, attempted his usual forcing tactics on his first visit to this track. Front-runners have a torrid time over this trip here though, and despite getting his own way out in front and being able to slow things down and quicken up when he wanted to, still proved a sitting duck. He should not be judged too harshly on this and he remains capable of winning again with these tactics elsewhere. (op 9-2 tchd 3-1)

62 HOTEL COMING TO LINGFIELD PARK CONDITIONS STKS 1m (P)
3:20 (3:20) (Class 3) 4-Y-O+ **£6,624** (£1,982; £991; £495) **Stalls** High

Form RPR

010- **1** **Capricorn Run (USA)**[17] 7184 5-9-0 106........................(v) SebSanders 5 111
(A J McCabe) *s.i.s: hdwy to ld over 2f out: pushed out fnl f* **9/4**[2]

501- **2** *2* **Jack Sullivan (USA)**[14] 7223 7-9-4 109........................(t) TPQueally 2 110
(G A Butler) *t.k.h in 4th pl rdn over 1f out: r.o to go 2nd ins fnl f* **7/4**[1]

561- **3** *1* **Vortex**[8] 7254 9-9-0 103........................(t) GeorgeBaker 3 104
(Miss Gay Kelleway) *trckd ldr to 3f out: sn outpcd but kpt on ins fnl f* **10/3**[3]

125- **4** *nk* **Troubadour (IRE)**[14] 7225 7-9-0 97 .... NCallan 6 103
(W Jarvis) *led tl hdd over 2f out: wknd ins fnl f* **9/2**

1m 38.67s (0.47) **Going Correction** -0.20s/f (Stan) 4 Ran SP% **108.4**
Speed ratings (Par 107): **95,93,92,91**
CSF £6.54 TOTE £3.30; EX 6.80.
Owner Paul J Dixon And Placida Racing **Bred** Santa Rosa Partners **Trained** Babworth, Notts

FOCUS
Another valuable race which cut up, though the two non-runners would have had no chance anyway. They went no pace at all early and it developed into another sprint from the home bend resulting in a time 1.6 seconds slower than the following Class 5 handicap, but they finished in exactly the order that adjusted official ratings suggested they should, so it is hard to argue that the result was not the right one.

NOTEBOOK
Capricorn Run(USA), back on his favourite track after finishing unplaced in a Kempton Listed race, was settled off the modest pace early but his rider decided to take the race by the scruff of the neck by booting him into the lead starting the home turn. Once there he never looked like getting caught, but the way the race was run did not conclusively prove his stamina. He may go to Dubai now and he might return here for the Winter Derby in March, but his ability to see out 1m2f has to be a big question mark. (op 10-3 tchd 4-1)
Jack Sullivan(USA), conceding 4lb to his three rivals, was probably not done any favours by the moderate early tempo and he raced keenly enough out the back. He could not respond immediately when the winner was committed for home and, when he did eventually get into stride, it was far too late. He has enjoyed a fair amount of success in Dubai in recent years and will head back there again. (op 11-8)
Vortex, comfortable winner of a 7f handicap on his return to action here last month, had every chance but failed to quicken and he is another that was not really helped by the way the race was run. He was 3lb badly in with the winner and 2lb badly in with the runner-up, so he probably ran his race nonetheless. (op 9-4)
Troubadour(IRE), probably flattered by his effort in a slowly-run Listed race over 1m2f here last time, soon found himself on front and set just a modest pace, but he still proved a sitting duck. He was upwards of 6lb badly in with his three rivals compared to a handicap, so it is probably unfair to be too harsh. (op 6-1 tchd 4-1)

63 DINE IN THE TRACKSIDE CARVERY H'CAP 1m (P)
3:50 (3:50) (Class 5) (0-75,75) 4-Y-O+ **£2,590** (£770; £385; £192) **Stalls** High

Form RPR
563- **1** **Monkey Glas (IRE)**[5] 7289 4-9-1 **75** .... (v[1]) AndrewElliott(3) 2 85
(K R Burke) *mde all: sn clr: pushed out fnl f: unchal* **4/1**[2]
0/ **2** *1 3/4* **Marias Dream (IRE)**[157] 4087 6-9-3 **74** .... MCHussey 1 80
(John A Quinn, Ire) *trckd ldrs: wnt 2nd over 2f out: rdn but no ch w wnr fnl f* **9/1**
511- **3** *nk* **Ninth House (USA)**[8] 7251 6-9-4 **75** .... (bt) GeorgeBaker 7 80
(N P Littmoden) *in tch: hdwy whn short of room over 2f out: one pce fnl f* **5/1**[3]
012- **4** *3* **One Night In Paris (IRE)**[61] 6696 5-9-4 **75** .... DaneO'Neill 5 73
(M J Wallace) *hld up: outpcd over 2f out: effrt over 1f out: no hdwy after* **14/1**
53-3 **5** *2* **Happy As Larry (USA)**[3] 21 6-9-0 **71** .... (t) JohnEgan 6 65
(D J Murphy) *trckd ldrs: pushed along over 3f out: no hdwy fnl 2f* **15/8**[1]
531- **6** *shd* **Corlough Mountain**[7] 7269 4-8-12 **69** .... RichardHughes 8 62
(M J McGrath) *hld up on outside: rdn and wknd over 2f out* **6/1**
240- **7** *2 1/2* **Nicada (IRE)**[20] 7164 4-8-13 **70** .... MickyFenton 3 58
(Stef Liddiard) *chsd ldr tl wknd over 2f out* **10/1**

1m 37.07s (-1.13) **Going Correction** -0.20s/f (Stan) 7 Ran SP% **111.5**
Speed ratings (Par 103): **103,101,100,97,95 95,93**
CSF £36.49 CT £177.41 TOTE £5.00: £1.70, £3.60; EX 50.00 TRIFECTA Not won. Place 6 £70.92, Place 5 £51.20..
Owner Denis Fehan **Bred** D Bourke And Yuriy Meduedyev **Trained** Middleham Moor, N Yorks

FOCUS
The shape of this race was heavily influenced by the withdrawal of Meditation, whose presence would probably have meant a contested lead and quite possibly a different result. The early fractions were much faster than in the preceding conditions event over the same trip and the winning time was 1.6 seconds quicker.
T/Plt: £163.20 to a £1 stake. Pool: £50,256.90. 224.75 winning tickets. T/Qpdt: £50.50 to a £1 stake. Pool: £3,180.40. 46.60 winning tickets. JS

[36]SOUTHWELL (L-H)
Sunday, January 6

OFFICIAL GOING: Standard
Wind: almost nil Weather: Fine and sunny

64 CAPTAIN CROC MAKES PONTIN'S ROCK CLAIMING STKS 6f (F)
12:40 (12:40) (Class 6) 4-Y-O+ **£1,911** (£564; £282) **Stalls** Low

Form RPR
614- **1** **Dickie Le Davoir**[9] 7251 4-9-0 73 .... AndrewElliott(3) 11 78
(K R Burke) *s.i.s: outpcd and bhd: hdwy on wd outside over 2f out: led last 150yds: sn drvn clr* **11/4**[1]
004- **2** *2 1/2* **Goodbye Cash (IRE)**[7] 7279 4-8-9 75 .... RichardEvans(7) 5 69
(P D Evans) *chsd ldrs: led 2f out: hdd and no ex ins fnl f* **7/2**[2]
24-5 **3** *2 1/2* **Phinerine**[4] 16 5-8-6 51 .... (be) TolleyDean(5) 4 56
(Miss J E Foster) *hld up in rr: hdwy over 2f out: hung lft and kpt on fnl f* **25/1**
540- **4** *1 3/4* **Soba Jones**[236] 1753 11-8-11 50 .... DavidAllan 8 50
(J Balding) *w ldrs: t.k.h: wknd appr fnl f* **16/1**
13-0 **5** *1 3/4* **Mister Elegant**[4] 13 6-8-9 52 .... ChrisCatlin 6 43
(J L Spearing) *in tch: drvn over 2f out: one pce* **10/1**
/05- **6** *nk* **Aboustar**[346] 239 8-8-10 42 .... (b) MarkLawson(3) 3 46
(M Brittain) *t.k.h: led: hdd 2f out: hung rt and sn wknd* **80/1**
140- **7** *7* **Owed**[227] 1977 6-9-7 72 .... (tp) DanielTudhope 2 31
(R Bastiman) *w ldrs: lost pl over 1f out* **4/1**[3]
062- **8** *1/2* **Mozakhraf (USA)**[16] 7209 6-8-9 57 .... (b[1]) PaulMulrennan 9 18
(K A Ryan) *chsd ldrs on outer: lost pl 2f out: sn bhd: lame* **4/1**[3]
052- **9** *3* **George The Best (IRE)**[60] 6720 7-9-11 45 .... PaulFessey 1 24
(Micky Hammond) *in rr: drvn over 3f out: sme hdwy on inner over 2f out: lost pl and eased over 1f out* **33/1**

1m 16.24s (-0.26) **Going Correction** -0.075s/f (Stan) 9 Ran SP% **111.9**
Speed ratings (Par 101): **101,97,94,92,89 89,79,79,75**
CSF £11.81 TOTE £4.30: £1.30, £2.20, £5.60; EX 17.60 Trifecta £101.50 Part won. Pool £143.04 - 0.75 winning units..
Owner Bigwigs Bloodstock II **Bred** P And Mrs A G Venner **Trained** Middleham Moor, N Yorks

FOCUS
A fair claimer with the first two running somewhere near their best. The third and sixth set the level for the form.

Mozakhraf(USA) Official explanation: jockey said gelding finished lame in front

65 CHUCKLES THE MONKEY MAKES PONTIN'S FUNKY MAIDEN STKS 6f (F)
1:10 (1:11) (Class 5) 3-Y-O+ **£2,457** (£725; £362) **Stalls** Low

Form RPR
00-6 **1** **Fulford**[4] 17 3-8-9 58 ow1 .... MarkLawson(3) 10 65
(M Brittain) *hld up: hdwy on outer over 2f out: styd on to ld appr fnl f: hld on wl towards fin* **8/1**
052- **2** *1/2* **Cape Of Storms**[10] 7239 5-9-13 47 .... PaulMulrennan 8 66
(R Brotherton) *chsd ldrs: kpt on to chal ins fnl f: no ex* **7/1**[3]
004- **3** *4* **Pappas Image**[16] 7209 4-9-13 45 .... (p) DaleGibson 7 53
(A J McCabe) *mid-div: sn drvn along: hdwy over 2f out: kpt on fnl f* **14/1**
003- **4** *1 1/4* **Tenancy (IRE)**[23] 7137 4-9-10 45 .... (p) PatrickMathers(3) 13 49
(A J McCabe) *swtchd lft after s: led: edgd lft 2f out: hdd appr fnl f: sn wknd* **12/1**
5 *1 1/2* **Angharad** 3-8-3 0 .... AndrewElliott(3) 2 35
(K R Burke) *hmpd s: sn chsng ldrs: one pce fnl 2f* **9/2**[2]
6 *shd* **Be Free** 3-8-6 0 .... JamieMackay 12 35+
(Sir Mark Prescott) *s.v.s: bhd and green: hung lft over 2f out: wandered and styd on strly fnl f* **17/2**
5- **7** *nk* **Elusive Hawk (IRE)**[22] 7159 4-9-13 0 .... TPQueally 1 39+
(A P Stringer) *dwlt and hmpd s: hdwy on ins over 2f out: nvr nr ldrs* **12/1**
/00- **8** *3* **Shopfitter**[17] 7197 5-9-13 36 .... (b) FrankieMcDonald 4 34
(P T Midgley) *w ldr: lost pl and edgd rt over 2f out* **66/1**
3- **9** *5* **Dunmore Dodger (IRE)**[8] 7270 3-8-11 0 .... TonyHamilton 3 —
(R A Fahey) *swvd lft s: mid-div: sn drvn along: lost pl 3f out* **15/8**[1]
10 *4* **Maddison County** 3-7-13 0 .... DeclanCannon(7) 6 —
(K R Burke) *sn bhd and drvn along: nvr on terms* **25/1**
040- **11** *19* **Coleorton Dagger**[17] 7201 4-9-8 37 .... ChrisCatlin 11 —
(J R Holt) *chsd ldrs: lost pl over 2f out: bhd whn eased ins fnl f* **66/1**
3/ **12** *1 1/4* **Fiona Fox**[388] 6821 4-9-8 0 .... DavidAllan 5 —
(J Balding) *chsd ldrs: lost pl over 2f out: bhd whn eased ins fnl f* **18/1**

1m 17.65s (1.15) **Going Correction** -0.075s/f (Stan)
WFA 3 from 4yo+ 16lb 12 Ran SP% **121.2**
Speed ratings (Par 103): **92,91,86,84,82 82,81,77,71,65 40,38**
CSF £63.98 TOTE £8.60: £2.10, £1.80, £3.90; EX 60.10 TRIFECTA Not won..
Owner Mel Brittain **Bred** D Simpson **Trained** Warthill, N Yorks
■ Stewards' Enquiry : Patrick Mathers caution: used whip with excessive frequency

FOCUS
A poor sprint maiden and limited form with the runner-up rated just 47 and the third and fourth 45.
Be Free Official explanation: jockey said filly missed the break

66 TODD MARTIN 18TH BIRTHDAY CELEBRATIONS (S) STKS 7f (F)
1:40 (1:40) (Class 6) 3-Y-O+ **£1,774** (£523; £262) **Stalls** Low

Form RPR
510- **1** **Louisiade (IRE)**[17] 7197 7-9-9 63 .... (p) SebSanders 5 62+
(John A Harris) *chsd ldrs: rdn to ld 2f out: edgd lft and drew clr fnl f* **5/2**[1]
00-2 **2** *2 1/2* **Stepaside (IRE)**[5] 2 4-9-6 42 .... (b) AndrewElliott(3) 4 55
(A D Brown) *led: hdd 2f out: hung rt and one pce* **9/2**[3]
50-2 **3** *3/4* **Mr Chocolate Drop (IRE)**[3] 33 4-9-4 42 .... (b) JamesO'Reilly(5) 7 53
(Miss M E Rowland) *trckd ldrs: kpt on same pce fnl 2f* **5/1**
06-0 **4** *1 1/2* **Capital Lass**[2] 42 5-8-13 45 .... NataliaGemelova(5) 9 44
(A J McCabe) *prom: one pce fnl 2f* **25/1**
033- **5** *7* **Namroud (USA)**[11] 1066 9-9-9 65 .... DanielTudhope 1 30
(D Carroll) *stmbld s: hrd rdn and sme hdwy over 2f out: nvr on terms* **7/2**[2]
46-0 **6** *8* **Wizby**[2] 40 5-9-4 40 .... (v) StephenDonohoe 10 3
(P D Evans) *reminders after s: w ldrs on outer: lost pl over 2f out* **22/1**
7 *1 1/4* **Charlie Chan**[19] 7-9-9 0 .... (b[1]) LiamJones 8 5
(D W Chapman) *s.s: hdwy to chse ldrs over 4f out: lost pl 2f out* **100/1**
660- **8** *3* **Didactic**[43] 5688 4-9-6 43 .... PatrickMathers(3) 2 —
(A J McCabe) *chsd ldrs: lost pl over 4f out* **16/1**
405- **9** *3* **Dazzler Mac**[68] 6563 7-9-9 47 .... PaulMulrennan 6 —
(N Bycroft) *in rr: bhd and eased over 2f out: lame* **8/1**
000- **10** *shd* **Put It On The Card**[16] 7209 4-9-9 49 .... (v) TonyHamilton 3 —
(J S Wainwright) *chsd ldrs: lost pl over 3f out* **20/1**

1m 30.75s (0.45) **Going Correction** -0.075s/f (Stan) 10 Ran SP% **116.6**
Speed ratings (Par 101): **97,94,93,91,83 74,73,69,66,66**
CSF £13.24 TOTE £3.80: £1.30, £2.00, £2.10; EX 13.40 Trifecta £44.40 Pool £268.69 - 4.29 winning units..There was no bid for the winner.
Owner Mrs A E Harris **Bred** Mrs Noelle Walsh **Trained** Eastwell, Leics

FOCUS
It looked a two-horse race beforehand and the betting told the story with the winner well supported and Namroud friendless.
Namroud(USA) Official explanation: jockey said gelding stumbled on leaving the stalls
Dazzler Mac Official explanation: vet said gelding finished lame in front

67 SEE POSTMAN PAT @ PONTIN'S H'CAP 1m 6f (F)
2:10 (2:10) (Class 6) (0-60,60) 4-Y-O+ **£1,911** (£564; £282) **Stalls** Low

Form RPR
001- **1** **Legend Erry (IRE)**[25] 7120 4-9-6 57 .... JohnEgan 9 83+
(Jane Chapple-Hyam) *chsd ldrs: shkn up 6f out: led 3f out: drvn long way clr: kpt up to work* **11/8**[1]
436- **2** *16* **Park's Prodigy**[29] 7081 4-8-5 49 .... (tp) PatrickDonaghy(7) 3 53
(P C Haslam) *led after 1f: hdd 3f out: sn no ch w wnr: kpt on same pce* **7/2**[2]
636- **3** *1 1/2* **Tioga Gold (IRE)**[268] 1032 9-8-9 45 .... RussellKennemore(5) 6 47
(L R James) *hld up in rr: hdwy to join ldrs over 4f out: one pce fnl 3f* **11/1**
000- **4** *5* **Optimistic Alfie**[11] 6271 8-9-10 55 .... (b) VinceSlattery 10 50
(B G Powell) *in rr and sn drvn along: kpt on fnl 2f: nvr a factor* **25/1**
066- **5** *1 1/4* **Isa'Af (IRE)**[23] 7135 9-9-0 45 .... (p) ChrisCatlin 5 38
(P W Hiatt) *chsd ldrs: jnd ldrs 8f out: lost pl over 3f out* **28/1**
50-0 **6** *2* **Ronsard (IRE)**[2] 36 6-9-3 55 .... RichardEvans(7) 11 45
(P D Evans) *s.i.s: t.k.h and sn trcking ldrs: rdn and lost pl over 5f out* **8/1**[3]
050/ **7** *1/2* **Aqua Pura (GER)**[20] 750 9-9-0 45 .... TPQueally 2 35
(A P Stringer) *led 1f: w ldrs: rdn and hung rt over 5f out: lost pl over 3f out* **16/1**
030- **8** *3* **History Prize (IRE)**[18] 7187 5-9-1 46 .... StephenDonohoe 7 31
(A G Newcombe) *hld up in rr: hdwy on outer over 4f out: nvr nr ldrs* **28/1**
540- **9** *3* **Scaramouschca**[25] 7120 5-9-5 50 .... NeilPollard 8 31
(G C Bravery) *sn chsng ldrs: rdn over 5f out: lost pl over 3f out* **16/1**
505- **10** *26* **King Of Connacht**[25] 7125 5-8-11 45 .... (p) NeilChalmers(3) 4 —
(M Wellings) *chsd ldrs: drvn over 7f out: sn lost pl and bhd* **33/1**

The Form Book, Raceform Ltd, Compton, RG20 6NL

54- **11** *33* **Directa's Digger (IRE)**[11] 6259 4-9-4 60....................(v) TolleyDean(5) 1 —
(M Scudamore) *chsd ldrs: reminders after 4f: lost pl over 6f out: sn bhd: virtually p.u 2f out* **12/1**

3m 7.00s (-1.30) **Going Correction** -0.075s/f (Stan)
WFA 4 from 5yo+ 6lb **11** Ran SP% **117.3**
Speed ratings (Par 101): **104,94,94,91,90 89,89,87,85,70 51**
CSF £5.43 CT £37.13 TOTE £2.40: £1.10, £1.70, £2.40; EX 7.20 Trifecta £27.00 Pool £305.33 - 8.00 winning units..
Owner Elite Sports Organisation **Bred** Dermot Cantillon And Forenaghts Stud **Trained** Lambourn, Berks

FOCUS
A weak handicap and a one-horse race with the rider leaving nothing to chance.
Directa's Digger(IRE) Official explanation: jockey said colt was never travelling

68 MEET ZENA THE ZEBRA @ PONTIN'S H'CAP — 1m (F)
2:40 (2:40) (Class 5) (0-70,69) 4-Y-O+ **£2,593** (£765; £383) **Stalls** Low

Form RPR
111- **1** **Dado Mush**[10] 7244 5-8-13 69..............................(p) KirstyMilczarek(5) 6 79+
(T T Clement) *trckd ldrs: led over 1f out: rdn and edgd lft: styd on* **15/8**[1]
210- **2** *1 ¼* **My Mentor (IRE)**[173] 3622 4-9-1 66.............................. SebSanders 5 72+
(Sir Mark Prescott) *led: drvn 3f out: hdd over 1f out: styd on same pce: no real imp* **6/1**
326- **3** *nk* **Baan (USA)**[18] 7193 5-9-2 67..............................(v) GregFairley 7 72
(M Johnston) *in rr: hdwy over 3f out: sn chsng ldrs: kpt on same pce fnl f* **9/4**[2]
005- **4** *5* **Speed Dial Harry (IRE)**[10] 7241 6-8-9 60......................(v) LiamJones 4 54
(C R Dore) *chsd ldrs: drvn and outpcd over 3f out: edgd lft over 1f out: one pce* **11/1**
210- **5** *9* **Rigat**[20] 7173 5-8-11 62.............................. PaulFessey 2 35
(T D Barron) *dwlt: sn trcking ldrs: drvn over 2f out: lost pl over 1f out* **5/1**[3]
560- **6** *1 ¾* **Good Cause (IRE)**[10] 7239 7-8-9 60.............................. ChrisCatlin 8 29
(Mrs S Lamyman) *s.i.s: sn drvn along on outer: lost pl over 3f out* **66/1**
010- **7** *5* **Oakbridge (IRE)**[16] 7213 6-8-9 60.............................. VinceSlattery 3 18
(R Brotherton) *hld up in rr: lost pl over 4f out* **25/1**
516/ **8** *6* **Benayoun**[424] 6394 4-8-0 58.............................. DavidProbert(7) 1 —
(B J Llewellyn) *sn drvn along: sn chsng ldrs: lost pl over 2f out* **50/1**

1m 43.19s (-0.51) **Going Correction** -0.075s/f (Stan) **8** Ran SP% **112.1**
Speed ratings (Par 103): **104,102,102,97,88 86,81,75**
CSF £13.08 CT £25.37 TOTE £2.90: £1.40, £1.90, £1.10; EX 14.30 Trifecta £23.10 Pool £483.84 - 14.83 winning units..
Owner Dr M Edres **Bred** Bellow Hill Stud **Trained** Newmarket, Suffolk

FOCUS
The winner goes from strength to strength and the first three finished clear.

69 PONTIN'S BLUE COATS ARE THE BEST H'CAP — 1m 4f (F)
3:10 (3:10) (Class 6) (0-55,55) 4-Y-O+ **£1,911** (£564; £282) **Stalls** Low

Form RPR
230- **1** **Karmest**[27] 7098 4-8-4 **50**.............................. AndrewElliott(3) 10 54
(A D Brown) *hld up in rr: hdwy on outer 6f out: chal over 4f out: led over 2f out: kpt on gamely* **6/1**[2]
156- **2** *nk* **Nimello (USA)**[259] 1178 12-9-0 **53**.............................. SimonWhitworth 6 57
(A G Newcombe) *in rr: hdwy 3f out: chal over 1f out: hrd rdn and no ex towards fin* **9/1**
643- **3** *1 ¾* **Piano Key**[17] 7203 4-8-3 **46** oh1.............................. HayleyTurner 9 47
(M D I Usher) *chsd ldrs: outpcd 3f out: kpt on wl fnl f* **8/1**[3]
000/ **4** *1* **Bright Sparky (GER)**[11] 4734 5-8-4 **50**..............................(t) NSLawes(7) 2 49
(M W Easterby) *set modest pce: hdd over 4f out: edgd rt 2f out: kpt on same pce* **14/1**
040- **5** *7* **Anything Once (USA)**[16] 7219 5-8-7 **46**..............................(v) ChrisCatlin 1 34
(D Carroll) *trckd ldrs: drvn over 4f out: wknd over 1f out* **8/1**[3]
6/0- **6** *½* **Blue Opal**[85] 1362 6-8-7 **46** oh1..............................(p) PaulEddery 8 33
(Miss S E Hall) *trckd ldrs: t.k.h: narrow advantage over 4f out: hdd over 2f out: wknd over 1f out* **20/1**
000/ **7** *3* **Smoothly Does It**[368] 5831 7-8-13 **55**.............................. JamieMoriarty(3) 7 38
(R A Fahey) *hld up in rr: hdwy on outer over 5f out: effrt 3f out: sn outpcd and lost pl* **6/4**[1]
503- **8** *shd* **Island King (IRE)**[17] 7199 5-8-4 **46** oh1.............................. AndrewMullen(3) 4 28
(R Bastiman) *mid-div: drvn over 6f out: lost pl over 3f out* **25/1**
0/0- **9** *nk* **Interest (USA)**[334] 373 4-8-4 **47**..............................(b) PaulFessey 5 29
(T D Barron) *hld up in rr: hdwy on outer to chse ldrs over 5f out: lost pl over 2f out* **25/1**
040- **10** *27* **Tidy (IRE)**[22] 7155 8-9-0 **53**..............................(v) PaulMulrennan 11 —
(Micky Hammond) *hld up towards rr: effrt 4f out: sn lost pl and bhd* **20/1**
000- **11** *1 ¾* **Parchment (IRE)**[68] 6558 6-8-13 **52**.............................. TonyHamilton 3 —
(A J Lockwood) *hld up in rr: lost pl 4f out: sn bhd* **11/1**

2m 41.48s (0.48) **Going Correction** -0.075s/f (Stan)
WFA 4 from 5yo+ 4lb **11** Ran SP% **118.7**
Speed ratings (Par 101): **99,98,97,96,92 91,89,89,89,71 70**
CSF £55.82 CT £434.28 TOTE £6.40: £2.40, £2.00, £3.10; EX 44.60 Trifecta £209.10 Pool £329.86 - 1.12 winning units..
Owner David Logan **Bred** Charles B B Booth **Trained** Pickering, York
■ Stewards' Enquiry : Paul Fessey caution: used whip from above shoulder height

FOCUS
A very steady gallop for the first mile but in the end something of a war of attrition.
Parchment(IRE) Official explanation: trainer said gelding was found to be lame post race

70 SOUTHWELL GOLF CLUB H'CAP — 6f (F)
3:40 (3:40) (Class 6) (0-65,65) 3-Y-O **£1,911** (£564; £282) **Stalls** Low

Form RPR
221- **1** **Yankee Storm**[16] 7210 3-9-2 **63**.............................. PatCosgrave 9 73
(M J Wallace) *chsd ldrs on outer: led 3f out: hrd rdn and styd on gamely* **8/11**[1]
550- **2** *1 ¾* **Diademas (USA)**[39] 6966 3-8-11 **65**..............................(e) AshleyMorgan(7) 8 69
(V Smith) *hdwy on outside to chse ldrs over 4f out: wnt 2nd over 2f out: kpt on same pce fnl f* **7/1**[3]
044- **3** *5* **Dancing Maite**[23] 7139 3-8-13 **60**.............................. PaulEddery 2 48
(S R Bowring) *led tl 3f out: kpt on same pce* **16/1**
406- **4** *5* **Indecision**[135] 4783 3-8-13 **60**.............................. PaulMulrennan 4 32
(M W Easterby) *chsd ldrs: outpcd over 3f out: kpt on fnl 2f* **22/1**
060- **5** *5* **Caprima (IRE)**[111] 5484 3-8-4 **51**.............................. PaulFessey 6 7
(M Brittain) *chsd ldrs: outpcd and lost pl 4f out: sme hdwy 2f out: n.d* **40/1**
602- **6** *3 ½* **Galley Slave (IRE)**[10] 7243 3-8-8 **58**.............................. DominicFox(3) 5 —
(M C Chapman) *chsd ldrs: rdn: hung rt and lost pl 4f out: no threat after* **20/1**
04-4 **7** *hd* **Twilight Belle (IRE)**[1] 59 3-8-5 **52**..............................(p) DaleGibson 3 —
(K R Burke) *chsd ldrs: wknd 2f out* **12/1**
000- **8** *6* **Lunatico (GER)**[165] 3842 3-8-0 **52** oh6 ow1.............. KirstyMilczarek(5) 7 —
(S C Williams) *chsd ldrs on outer: drvn over 3f out: lost pl over 2f out* **12/1**
062- **9** *7* **Rich James (IRE)**[23] 7136 3-8-1 **51** oh1..................(p) AndrewElliott(3) 1 —
(J D Bethell) *prom: rdn and lost pl over 4f out: bhd fnl 3f* **6/1**[2]

1m 16.68s (0.18) **Going Correction** -0.075s/f (Stan) **9** Ran SP% **117.5**
Speed ratings (Par 95): **98,95,89,82,75 71,70,62,53**
CSF £6.29 CT £47.97 TOTE £1.50: £1.10, £2.30, £4.20; EX 7.10 Trifecta £87.80 Pool £526.95 - 4.26 winning units. Place 6 £50.36, Place 5 £25.79..
Owner Greenstead Hall Racing **Bred** Mark Johnston Racing Ltd **Trained** Newmarket, Suffolk

FOCUS
The winner had the outside draw to overcome and the runner-up deserves credit.
T/Jkpt: Not won. T/Plt: £69.00 to a £1 stake. Pool: £63,904.80. 675.60 winning tickets. T/Qpdt: £5.20 to a £1 stake. Pool: £5,253.60. 747.30 winning tickets. WG

64 SOUTHWELL (L-H)
Monday, January 7

OFFICIAL GOING: Standard
Wind: Fresh, half-behind Weather: Fine

71 SOUTHWELL GOLF CLUB H'CAP — 6f (F)
12:50 (12:50) (Class 6) (0-65,65) 4-Y-O+ **£2,047** (£604; £302) **Stalls** Low

Form RPR
36-3 **1** **Strathmore (IRE)**[6] 4 4-8-13 **63**.............................. JamieMoriarty(3) 2 71
(R A Fahey) *a.p: chsd ldr over 3f out: led ins fnl f: sn rdn: r.o* **10/3**[2]
032- **2** *hd* **Bentley**[7] 7283 4-8-6 **53**..............................(v) DeanMcKeown 4 60
(D Shaw) *chsd ldrs: rdn and edgd lft over 1f out: r.o* **6/1**[3]
23-6 **3** *nk* **Quiet Times (IRE)**[3] 41 9-9-4 **65**..............................(b) PaulMulrennan 5 71
(K A Ryan) *led: rdn and hdd ins fnl f: r.o* **10/1**
005- **4** *shd* **Guildenstern (IRE)**[16] 7227 6-8-8 **55**.............................. TGMcLaughlin 7 61
(P Howling) *hld up: hdwy u.p and hung lft over 1f out: r.o* **15/2**
230- **5** *1 ¾* **Zarzu**[66] 6625 9-9-3 **64**.............................. TPQueally 8 64
(C R Dore) *dwlt: hld up: rdn over 1f out: nt trble ldrs* **18/1**
13-2 **6** *nk* **Winthorpe (IRE)**[6] 4 8-9-0 **61**..............................(p) DanielTudhope 3 60
(J J Quinn) *chsd ldrs: pushed along over 3f out: rdn over 2f out: styd on same pce fnl f* **2/1**[1]
04-0 **7** *3* **Lucius Verrus (USA)**[5] 13 8-8-1 **55**..............................(v) PatrickDonaghy(7) 6 45
(D Shaw) *sn pushed along in rr: rdn: hung rt and outpcd over 2f out* **6/1**[3]

1m 16.78s (0.28) **Going Correction** 0.0s/f (Stan) **7** Ran SP% **111.1**
Speed ratings (Par 101): **100,99,99,99,96 96,92**
CSF £21.96 CT £171.17 TOTE £4.00: £1.80, £2.90; EX 24.00 Trifecta £117.90 Pool: £235.80 - 1.42 winning tickets..
Owner Jonathan Gill **Bred** M Sharkey **Trained** Musley Bank, N Yorks
■ Stewards' Enquiry : Dean McKeown caution: careless riding

FOCUS
A modest sprint handicap and a bunch finish. The form appears to make sense, through the fourth. The winning time was 0.81 seconds slower than the following 56-70.
Winthorpe(IRE) Official explanation: jockey said gelding suffered interference

72 HAPPY HALF TERM DEALS @ PONTINS.COM H'CAP — 6f (F)
1:20 (1:20) (Class 5) (0-70,70) 4-Y-O+ **£2,457** (£725; £362) **Stalls** Low

Form RPR
14- **1** **Sweet Pickle**[41] 6962 7-9-4 70..............................(e) PatCosgrave 5 85
(J R Boyle) *s.i.s: sn prom: chsd ldr over 4f out: rdn to ld 1f out: edgd lft: r.o* **6/1**
212- **2** *1 ½* **Grand Palace (IRE)**[9] 7271 5-8-10 62..............................(v) DeanMcKeown 4 72
(D Shaw) *led: rdn and hdd 1f out: edgd lft: styd on same pce* **11/4**[1]
112- **3** *2 ½* **Dasheena**[20] 7180 5-8-11 66..............................(be) PatrickMathers(3) 3 68
(A J McCabe) *s.i.s: hdwy over 3f out: rdn and edgd lft over 2f out: styd on same pce appr fnl f* **10/3**[3]
000- **4** *1 ¾* **Flores Sea (USA)**[61] 6727 4-9-1 67.............................. PaulFessey 2 63
(T D Barron) *chsd ldr over 1f: sn rdn: styd on same pce fnl 2f* **4/1**
001- **5** *2 ½* **Figaro Flyer (IRE)**[9] 7271 5-9-1 67.............................. SimonWhitworth 1 55
(P Howling) *hld up: plld hrd: rdn over 2f out: n.d* **3/1**[2]

1m 15.97s (-0.53) **Going Correction** 0.0s/f (Stan) **5** Ran SP% **109.0**
Speed ratings (Par 103): **106,104,100,98,95**
CSF £21.99 TOTE £7.20: £1.50, £1.80; EX 21.00.
Owner M Khan X2 **Bred** C T Van Hoorn **Trained** Epsom, Surrey

FOCUS
Just the five runners and an ordinary sprint handicap. The form is rated around the first two. The winning time was 0.81 seconds quicker than the opening 51-65.
Figaro Flyer(IRE) Official explanation: jockey said gelding suffered a breathing problem

73 SOUTHWELL-RACECOURSE.CO.UK (S) STKS — 1m (F)
1:50 (1:50) (Class 6) 3-Y-O **£1,774** (£523; £262) **Stalls** Low

Form RPR
322- **1** **Home**[10] 7259 3-8-11 72..............................(p) PatCosgrave 3 69+
(J R Boyle) *sn chsng ldr: led on bit over 3f out: shkn up 2f out: sn clr: eased ins fnl f* **4/11**[1]
234- **2** *7* **Just Mossie**[7] 7286 3-8-4 54.............................. JackDean(7) 1 48
(W G M Turner) *chsd ldrs: rdn over 4f out: chsd wnr 2f out: sn edgd lft and outpcd* **11/4**[2]
606- **3** *7* **Liz Long**[62] 6705 3-8-6 48.............................. SimonWhitworth 2 27
(P Howling) *led over 4f: wknd 2f out* **25/1**[3]

1m 45.72s (2.02) **Going Correction** 0.0s/f (Stan) **3** Ran SP% **103.8**
Speed ratings (Par 95): **94,87,80**
CSF £1.51 TOTE £1.10; EX 1.30.The winner was bought in for 10,000gns.
Owner M Khan X2 **Bred** A T Macdonald **Trained** Epsom, Surrey

FOCUS
Only three runners and an uncompetitive seller in which Home faced a straightforward task at the weights.

74 RACE TO PONTIN'S FOR GREAT BREAKS MAIDEN STKS — 7f (F)
2:20 (2:20) (Class 5) 3-Y-O **£2,730** (£806; £403) **Stalls** Low

Form RPR
204- **1** **Royal Applord**[59] 6740 3-9-3 71.............................. PaulMulrennan 6 65
(K A Ryan) *trckd ldr: led over 2f out: hrd rdn and edgd lft ins fnl f: all out* **3/1**[1]
63- **2** *½* **Inontime (IRE)**[31] 7058 3-8-9 0.............................. AndrewElliott(3) 5 59
(K R Burke) *led over 4f: sn rdn: r.o* **4/1**[2]
03- **3** *1* **Topflightrebellion**[17] 7216 3-8-12 0.............................. DaleGibson 9 56
(Mrs G S Rees) *chsd ldrs: outpcd 2f out: sn hung lft: r.o ins fnl f* **20/1**

2- **4** *hd* **Kool Katie**[17] 7216 3-8-5 0........ IanCraven(7) 7 58+
(Mrs G S Rees) *trckd ldrs: rdn over 1f out: n.m.r ins fnl f: styd on* **8/1**
5 *nk* **Helping Hand (IRE)** 3-8-12 0........ RussellKennemore(5) 8 60
(R Hollinshead) *sn trcking ldrs: racd keenly: rdn and ev ch fr over 2f out: edgd lft fr over 1f out: no ex towards fin* **10/1**
00U- **6** *3/4* **Traitor's Gate**[62] 6698 3-9-3 0........ GregFairley 4 58
(M Johnston) *chsd ldrs: rdn over 1f out: no ex ins fnl f* **11/1**
304- **7** *1 1/4* **Santa Clara**[24] 7136 3-8-12 61........ PatCosgrave 1 50
(Jane Chapple-Hyam) *hld up: hdwy 1/2-way: rdn over 2f out: styd on same pce* **5/1**[3]
03- **8** *3* **Amyann (IRE)**[18] 7196 3-8-12 0........ ChrisCatlin 3 41
(J R Holt) *s.i.s: sn pushed along in rr: rdn 1/2-way: sn outpcd* **25/1**
9 *2 1/2* **Ultimate Quest (IRE)** 3-9-3 0........ SebSanders 2 40
(Sir Mark Prescott) *s.i.s: outpcd* **5/1**[3]

1m 32.3s (2.00) **Going Correction** 0.0s/f (Stan) **9 Ran SP% 115.5**
Speed ratings (Par 97): **91,90,89,89,88 87,86,83,80**
CSF £14.90 TOTE £3.00: £1.30, £2.10, £6.20; EX 21.00 TRIFECTA Not won..
Owner Bull & Bell Partnership **Bred** Brick Kiln Stud And V A D'Haens **Trained** Hambleton, N Yorks

FOCUS
A modest maiden run in a slow time, and probably not form to take too literally. It is unlikely the winer had to match his best turf form.

75 GOLF AND RACING AT SOUTHWELL RACECOURSE APPRENTICE H'CAP 7f (F)
2:50 (2:50) (Class 6) (0-65,63) 4-Y-0+ **£2,047** (£604; £302) **Stalls Low**

Form RPR
3- **1** **Ginger Princess (IRE)**[24] 7143 6-8-3 52........(t) PatrickDonaghy(5) 7 70+
(Oliver McKiernan, Ire) *s.i.s: hld up: hdwy 1/2-way: led 2f out: hung lft: rdn clr* **11/4**[2]
00-0 **2** *6* **Government (IRE)**[3] 42 7-8-5 49 oh4........ AndrewElliott 4 51
(M C Chapman) *led: hdd over 5f out: rdn to ld over 2f out: sn hdd: styd on same pce* **6/1**
205- **3** *hd* **Elusive Warrior (USA)**[27] 7107 5-8-11 55........(p) JamieMoriarty 6 57
(R A Fahey) *prom: chsd wnr over 1f out: sn hrd rdn: wknd ins fnl f* **7/4**[1]
/42- **4** *7* **Pauline's Prince**[11] 7248 6-9-2 63........ RussellKennemore(3) 1 47
(R Hollinshead) *trckd ldrs: rdn over 2f out: wknd over 1f out* **4/1**[3]
006- **5** *3* **A Teen**[8] 7276 10-8-5 49 oh4........ DuranFentiman 3 25
(P Howling) *hld up in tch: rdn over 2f out: sn wknd* **40/1**
000- **6** *11* **Josh**[16] 7224 6-9-5 63........(b) AndrewMullen 5 10
(K A Ryan) *s.i.s: rcvrd to ld over 5f out: rdn and hdd over 2f out: sn wknd* **10/1**

1m 29.65s (-0.65) **Going Correction** 0.0s/f (Stan) **6 Ran SP% 108.8**
Speed ratings (Par 101): **106,99,98,90,87 74**
CSF £17.85 TOTE £3.90: £2.50, £2.70; EX 13.80.
Owner Mrs C McKiernan **Bred** John Boden & Willie Kane **Trained** Rathcoole, Co Dublin

FOCUS
A modest apprentice handicap, but the time was decent and the winner proved different class. The runner-up was 8lb out of the weights but there is no real reason to doubt the form.
Pauline's Prince Official explanation: jockey said horse ran flat

76 BOOK YOUR PONTIN'S HALF TERM BREAKS H'CAP 1m 4f (F)
3:20 (3:20) (Class 6) (0-50,51) 4-Y-0+ **£1,774** (£523; £262) **Stalls Low**

Form RPR
065- **1** **Zaffeu**[37] 6999 7-8-12 49 ow1........ VinceSlattery 9 66+
(A G Juckes) *sn pushed along and prom: led over 2f out: rdn and edgd lft over 1f out: styd on wl: eased wl ins fnl f* **25/1**
024- **2** *5* **Mid Valley**[19] 7187 5-8-10 47........ J-PGuillambert 5 54
(J R Jenkins) *s.i.s: hld up: plld hrd: hdwy over 3f out: chsd wnr 2f out: sn rdn and edgd lft: styd on same pce* **3/1**[2]
50-1 **3** *7* **Cragganmore Creek**[3] 37 5-9-0 51 6ex........ SaleemGolam 4 47
(D Morris) *hld up: hdwy over 3f out: rdn and wknd over 1f out* **11/8**[1]
000- **4** *2 1/2* **Tabulate**[67] 6613 5-8-9 46........ TGMcLaughlin 1 38
(P Howling) *hld up: rdn over 2f out: n.d* **12/1**
000- **5** *shd* **Valart**[135] 4802 5-8-10 47 ow2........ PaulMulrennan 7 39
(C Tinkler) *chsd ldrs: rdn and ev ch over 2f out: wknd over 1f out* **9/1**
0- **6** *4* **Jalandy (IRE)**[28] 7098 5-8-10 47........ PaulDoe 2 32
(S Curran) *chsd ldrs tl rdn and wknd over 2f out* **7/1**[3]
000- **7** *9* **Makfly**[39] 3035 5-8-6 48 ow1........ RussellKennemore(5) 8 19
(R Hollinshead) *trckd ldr: plld hrd: led 8f out: hdd 5f out: rdn and wknd over 3f out* **16/1**
000- **8** *5* **Bahhmirage (IRE)**[12] 7237 5-8-12 49........(p) ChrisCatlin 3 12
(C N Kellett) *led 4f: led again 5f out: rdn and hdd over 2f out: sn wknd* **40/1**
253- **9** *13* **Tip Toes (IRE)**[35] 1925 6-8-5 45........(be1) DuranFentiman(3) 10 —
(M J Gingell) *hld up: rdn 1/2-way: sn wknd* **16/1**

2m 40.9s (-0.10) **Going Correction** 0.0s/f (Stan)
WFA 4 from 5yo+ 4lb **9 Ran SP% 115.3**
Speed ratings (Par 101): **103,99,95,93,93 90,84,81,72**
CSF £99.11 CT £178.98 TOTE £29.00: £5.80, £1.30, £1.30; EX 110.60 TRIFECTA Not won..
Owner Whispering Winds **Bred** Patrick Eddery Ltd **Trained** Abberley, Worcs

FOCUS
A moderate handicap, but they went a reasonable pace with a wave of three battling for the lead for much of the way and they finished very well spread out. The form is a bit dubious but this rates as the winner's best run since he was a 3-y-o.
Zaffeu Official explanation: trainer said, regarding the improved form shown, gelding might have benefited from a return to the fibresand

77 CHUCKLES THE MONKEY MAKES PONTIN'S FUNKY H'CAP 1m 3f (F)
3:50 (3:50) (Class 6) (0-58,58) 4-Y-0+ **£1,774** (£523; £262) **Stalls Low**

Form RPR
665- **1** **Starcross Maid**[18] 7198 6-8-12 51........ PatrickMathers(3) 1 61+
(J F Coupland) *hld up: hdwy over 3f out: led over 1f out: rdn clr* **9/1**
640- **2** *5* **Don Pasquale**[66] 6627 6-8-13 49........(v) ChrisCatlin 8 48
(J T Stimpson) *s.i.s: hld up: hdwy over 4f out: led over 2f out: rdn and hdd over 1f out: styd on same pce fnl f* **10/3**[2]
003- **3** *shd* **Granary Girl**[8] 7277 6-8-13 49........ TGMcLaughlin 3 48
(J Pearce) *hld up in tch: lost pl 5f out: rdn and hung lft over 1f out: r.o ins fnl f* **8/1**
00-0 **4** *hd* **Mi Odds**[3] 37 12-8-6 45........ AndrewElliott(3) 4 44
(Mrs N Macauley) *chsd ldrs: outpcd over 3f out: r.o ins fnl f* **50/1**
503- **5** *1 1/2* **Sorbiesharry (IRE)**[11] 7244 9-8-6 45........(p) DuranFentiman(3) 6 42
(Mrs N Macauley) *chsd ldr tl rdn 3f out: wknd fnl f* **7/1**
050- **6** *1/2* **Boppys Pride**[31] 7060 5-8-12 51........(b1) JamieMoriarty(3) 7 47
(R A Fahey) *sn led: hdd over 2f out: sn rdn and hung lft: wknd over 1f out* **5/2**[1]
000- **7** *3 1/2* **Danelor (IRE)**[7] 7115 10-8-12 48........(p) DeanMcKeown 5 38
(D Shaw) *s.i.s: hld up: rdn over 3f out: a in rr* **11/2**[3]
200- **8** *nk* **Chiff Chaff**[61] 6719 4-9-5 58........ TPQueally 2 48
(C R Dore) *chsd ldrs: rdn over 3f out: wknd over 1f out* **8/1**

2m 29.76s (1.76) **Going Correction** 0.0s/f (Stan)
WFA 4 from 5yo+ 3lb **8 Ran SP% 113.7**
Speed ratings (Par 101): **96,92,92,92,91 90,88,87**
CSF £38.67 CT £252.02 TOTE £14.00: £3.20, £1.40, £2.00; EX 45.70 Trifecta £186.90 Part won. Pool: £263.37 - 0.60 winning tickets. Place 6 £56.74, Place 5 £15.61.
Owner J F Coupland **Bred** D M Beresford **Trained** East Ravendale, S Humberside

FOCUS
They went no pace early in this moderate handicap, but it still developed into a one-horse race. Not surprisingly, the winning time was modest even for a race like this. With the favourite running poorly the form is weak.
T/Plt: £96.80 to a £1 stake. Pool: £41,948.50. 316.05 winning tickets. T/Qpdt: £31.60 to a £1 stake. Pool: £2,585.50. 60.40 winning tickets. CR

71 SOUTHWELL (L-H)
Tuesday, January 8

OFFICIAL GOING: Standard
Wind: light across Weather: Dry and bright

78 RACE TO PONTIN'S FOR HALF TERM APPRENTICE H'CAP 1m 4f (F)
12:10 (12:10) (Class 5) (0-70,70) 4-Y-0+ **£2,457** (£725; £362) **Stalls Low**

Form RPR
122- **1** **Three Boars**[21] 7178 6-9-7 68........(b) JamieJones 2 74
(S Gollings) *hld up: hdwy on bit over 3f out: cl up 2f out: shkn up to ld ent fnl f: sn rdn and kpt on* **15/8**[1]
024- **2** *2* **Jackie Kiely**[28] 7110 7-9-9 70........(t) NeilBrown 5 73
(R Brotherton) *trckd ldng pair: hdwy to ld over 4f out: rdn along wl over 1f out: hdd ent fnl f: sn drvn and kpt on same pce* **15/8**[1]
053- **3** *3 1/2* **Global Traffic**[10] 7175 4-8-6 62........(v) RichardEvans(5) 3 59
(P D Evans) *t.k.h: trckd ldr: pushed along over 2f out: sn rdn and kpt on same pce* **9/2**[2]
531- **4** *9* **Summerofsixtynine**[11] 7262 5-8-11 58........(p) RussellKennemore 4 41
(J G M O'Shea) *t.k.h: set stdy pce: qcknd 1/2-way: rdn along whn hung rt over 4f out and sn hdd: drvn 3f out and sn wknd* **10/1**
336- **5** *2* **Punta Galera (IRE)**[12] 7249 5-8-11 63........ AndrewHeffernan(5) 1 43
(Paul Green) *t.k.h: hld up: effrt 1/2-way: rdn along over 3f out and sn btn* **8/1**[3]

2m 43.31s (2.31) **Going Correction** 0.0s/f (Stan)
WFA 4 from 5yo+ 4lb **5 Ran SP% 107.9**
Speed ratings (Par 103): **95,93,91,85,84**
CSF £5.24 TOTE £2.80: £1.50, £1.10; EX 5.60.
Owner P Whinham **Bred** J M Greetham **Trained** Scamblesby, Lincs

FOCUS
A modest middle-distance handicap. They went steady through the early stages, but this still proved a good test and they came home well-strung out. Weakish form.
Summerofsixtynine Official explanation: jockey said horse hung right

79 RING PONTIN'S NOW 0844 815 3648 H'CAP (DIV I) 6f (F)
12:40 (12:40) (Class 6) (0-52,51) 4-Y-0+ **£1,399** (£413; £206) **Stalls Low**

Form RPR
16-3 **1** **Silver Hotspur**[4] 46 4-8-11 50........ NickyMackay 10 67
(M Wigham) *hld up in tch on outer: smooth hdwy to trck ldrs over 2f out: effrt over 1f out: styd on ins fnl f to ld nr line* **3/1**[1]
52-2 **2** *hd* **Cape Of Storms**[2] 65 5-8-8 47........ PaulMulrennan 3 63
(R Brotherton) *trckd ldrs: hdwy to ld 3f out: rdn over 1f out: drvn ins fnl f: hdd and nt qckn nr line* **10/3**[2]
003- **3** *3* **Shava**[24] 7153 8-7-13 45........ DeclanCannon(7) 11 51
(H J Evans) *trckd ldrs on outer: hdwy 1/2-way: chal 2f out and ev ch tl rdn and one pce over 1f out* **9/2**[3]
04-3 **4** *3 1/2* **Pappas Image**[2] 65 4-8-3 45........(p) PatrickMathers(3) 6 40
(A J McCabe) *chsd ldrs: rdn along and edgd lft wl over 1f out: sn drvn and one pce* **10/1**
003- **5** *1 1/4* **Astorygoeswithit**[24] 7148 5-8-6 45........(be) LiamJones 7 36
(G C Bravery) *cl up: led briefly over 3f out: sn rdn and hdd: drvn over 2f out and grad wknd* **12/1**
006- **6** *3 1/2* **Jember Red**[12] 7239 5-8-6 45........(v) ChrisCatlin 1 25
(B Smart) *rdn along in rr 1/2-way: hdwy 2f out: sn drvn and nvr rchd ldrs* **40/1**
000- **7** *2 1/2* **Nabra**[108] 5627 4-8-9 51........ MarkLawson(3) 5 23
(M Brittain) *chsd ldrs to 1/2-way: sn wknd* **66/1**
442- **8** *hd* **Mickleberry (IRE)**[8] 7284 4-8-7 49........(p) AndrewElliott(3) 8 20
(J D Bethell) *dwlt: sn rdn along in rr: nvr a factor* **8/1**
20-0 **9** *shd* **Shadow Jumper (IRE)**[4] 42 7-8-9 48........(v) DaleGibson 2 19
(J T Stimpson) *in tch on inner: rdn along 1/2-way and sn wknd* **12/1**
04-3 **10** *nk* **Temtation (IRE)**[5] 33 4-8-3 45........ DuranFentiman(3) 9 15
(J A Pickering) *led: rdn along and hdd over 3f out: drvn and wknd 2f out* **20/1**
006- **11** *5* **Smash N'Grab (IRE)**[9] 7278 4-8-5 51........(v1) PatrickDonaghy(7) 4 5
(J R Jenkins) *reminders and sn pushed along in rr: hdwy and in tch 1/2-way: sn rdn and wknd* **20/1**

1m 16.59s (0.09) **Going Correction** 0.0s/f (Stan) **11 Ran SP% 115.3**
Speed ratings (Par 101): **102,101,97,93,91 86,83,83,83,82 75**
CSF £12.08 CT £44.16 TOTE £4.60: £1.60, £1.60, £1.90; EX 16.30 Trifecta £53.50 Pool £332.69 - 4.41 winning units..
Owner D Hassan **Bred** Theobalds Stud **Trained** Newmarket, Suffolk

FOCUS
A very moderate sprint handicap. The winner was close to his old form and the race should work out.

80 SOUTHWELL-RACECOURSE.CO.UK H'CAP 1m (F)
1:10 (1:10) (Class 6) (0-60,60) 4-Y-0+ **£1,911** (£564; £282) **Stalls Low**

Form RPR
05-2 **1** **Wodhill Gold**[7] 7 7-8-7 49........(v) HayleyTurner 8 68
(D Morris) *chsd ldrs: rdn along and outpcd 3f out: swtchd ins and gd hdwy 2f out: rdn to ld over 1f out and styd on strly* **2/1**[1]
054- **2** *5* **Krakatau (FR)**[10] 7268 4-8-12 54........ ChrisCatlin 1 62
(D J Wintle) *dwlt: hdwy 1/2-way: rdn to chse ldrs 2f out: ev ch over 1f out: sn drvn and one pce* **9/1**
403- **3** *3/4* **Justcallmehandsome**[42] 6956 6-8-9 56........(v) NataliaGemelova(5) 3 62
(D J S Ffrench Davis) *cl up: led 3f out: rdn wl over 1f out: drvn and hdd appr fnl f: kpt on same pce* **8/1**

024- **4** 3 **Soldier Field**[19] 7199 4-8-13 **55**....................(p) TonyHamilton 5 54
(J S Wainwright) *dwlt: sn trcking ldrs: smooth hdwy over 2f out: rdn wl over 1f out and sn one pce* **16/1**

323- **5** hd **Ours (IRE)**[18] 7218 5-9-1 **57**....................(p) StephenDonohoe 12 55
(John A Harris) *trckd ldrs: hdwy on outer 3f out: rdn and ev ch 2f out: sn hung lft and wknd* **7/2**[2]

05-4 **6** 2 1/2 **Speed Dial Harry (IRE)**[2] 68 6-9-4 **60**....................(v) LiamJones 4 53
(C R Dore) *led: rdn along and hdd 3f out: drvn and grad wknd fnl 2f* **12/1**

000- **7** 3 **Cape Dancer (IRE)**[18] 7209 4-8-4 **46** oh1....................(p) PaulFessey 6 32
(J S Wainwright) *chsd ldrs on inner: rdn over 2f out and sn wknd* **100/1**

001- **8** nk **Sir Bond (IRE)**[18] 7218 7-8-10 **57**.................... SladeO'Hara(5) 10 42
(G R Oldroyd) *chsd ldrs: rdn along wl over 2f out: sn wknd* **6/1**[3]

50-0 **9** 5 **Sea Frolic (IRE)**[5] 31 7-8-5 **47** oh1 ow1....................(v) SaleemGolam 7 21
(Jennie Candlish) *a towards rr* **40/1**

000- **10** 6 **Ali D**[83] 4427 10-7-11 **46** oh1.................... PatrickDonaghy(7) 2 6
(G Woodward) *a in rr* **50/1**

206- **11** 3 **Passionately Royal**[112] 5503 6-8-4 **46**.................... DaleGibson 9 —
(M Brittain) *s.i.s: a in rr* **20/1**

600- **12** 3/4 **Inflagrantedelicto (USA)**[181] 3411 4-8-2 **47** oh1 ow1(p) AndrewElliott(3) 11 —
(D W Chapman) *s.i.s: a in rr* **100/1**

1m 43.15s (-0.55) **Going Correction** 0.0s/f (Stan) 12 Ran SP% **115.7**
Speed ratings (Par 101): **107,102,101,98,98 95,92,92,87,81 78,77**
CSF £19.83 CT £120.85 TOTE £3.00: £1.70, £2.50, £2.50; EX 13.60 Trifecta £55.50 Pool £152.43 - 1.95 winning units..
Owner Miss S Graham **Bred** Wodhill Stud **Trained** Newmarket, Suffolk

FOCUS
A moderate handicap but a fair race for the grade with plenty arriving here in form. Wodhill Gold was back to the sort of form which saw him win this event a year ago.

81 PACKED FULL OF FUN THAT'S PONTIN'S CLAIMING STKS 7f (F)
1:40 (1:40) (Class 6) 3-Y-O **£1,911** (£564; £282) **Stalls** Low

Form RPR

01-4 **1** **Autumn Charm**[5] 30 3-8-6 **60**.................... LiamJones 4 60
(D W Chapman) *trckd ldrs: effrt 2f out: rdn to chse ldr wl over 1f out: styd on u.p ins fnl f to ld last 100yds* **9/2**[3]

252- **2** 1 1/2 **Copperbottomed (IRE)**[12] 7246 3-9-0 **67**....................(be) PatCosgrave 6 64
(J R Boyle) *trckd ldrs: hdwy to ld 2f out: rdn over 1f out: drvn ins fnl f: hdd and one pce fnl 100yds* **7/4**[1]

064- **3** 3 **Hawa Khana (IRE)**[36] 7010 3-8-3 **58**....................(p) AndrewElliott(3) 3 48
(N P Littmoden) *chsd ldr: rdn along over 2f out: sn drvn and kpt on same pce* **2/1**[2]

044- **4** 2 1/2 **Weetfromthechaff**[13] 7232 3-9-5 **56**.................... HayleyTurner 2 54
(R Hollinshead) *hld up in tch: hdwy to chse ldrs 3f out: rdn over 2f out and sn one pce* **11/1**

066- **5** 1 **Mujada**[204] 2710 3-8-1 **55**.................... AdamCarter(7) 1 40
(M Brittain) *led: rdn along and hdd over 2f out: sn wknd* **22/1**

16-5 **6** 7 **Night Robe**[4] 38 3-7-9 **50**....................(b1) NataliaGemelova(5) 5 13
(P D Evans) *sn rdn along in rr: a bhd* **10/1**

1m 31.85s (1.55) **Going Correction** 0.0s/f (Stan) 6 Ran SP% **109.7**
Speed ratings (Par 95): **94,92,88,86,84 76**
CSF £12.22 TOTE £4.40: £1.60, £1.50; EX 7.60.
Owner David W Chapman **Bred** Brick Kiln Farming **Trained** Stillington, N Yorks

FOCUS
A modest claimer in which only the winner could boast recent form. It is doubtful if she needed to improve.
Weetfromthechaff Official explanation: jockey said gelding hung left in straight
Night Robe Official explanation: vet said filly pulled up lame

82 RING PONTIN'S NOW 0844 815 3648 H'CAP (DIV II) 6f (F)
2:10 (2:10) (Class 6) (0-52,51) 4-Y-O+ **£1,399** (£413; £206) **Stalls** Low

Form RPR

45-0 **1** **Mind Alert**[6] 16 7-8-9 **48**....................(v) JamesDoyle 3 65
(D Shaw) *trckd ldrs: smooth hdwy over 2f out: shkn up to ld 1f out: sn rdn and styd on wl* **12/1**

4-53 **2** 4 **Phinerine**[2] 64 5-8-9 **51**....................(p) MichaelJStainton(3) 8 55
(Miss J E Foster) *towards rr: pushed along and hdwy 2f out: sn rdn: styd on u.p to chse wnr ins fnl f: no imp* **11/2**[3]

00-4 **3** 1 3/4 **Guadaloup**[5] 32 6-8-7 **49**.................... MarkLawson(3) 1 48
(M Brittain) *towards rr: hdwy on inner over 2f out: rdn and ch over 1f out: sn drvn and kpt on same pce* **7/1**

002- **4** shd **Blakeshall Quest**[28] 7111 8-8-6 **45**....................(b) PaulFessey 5 43
(R Brotherton) *cl up: led wl over 2f out: rdn over 1f out: drvn and hdd 1f out: wknd* **5/1**[2]

01-6 **5** hd **Van Ruymbeke (IRE)**[4] 42 4-8-9 **48**....................(t) LiamJones 10 46
(D J Murphy) *dwlt and in rr tl styd on fnl 2f: nvr nrr* **4/1**[1]

500- **6** 2 **Jojesse**[25] 7138 4-8-3 **45**.................... AndrewElliott(3) 9 36
(Jennie Candlish) *sn pushed along in rr: rdn along and hdwy on outer wl over 2f out: sn drvn and no imp* **12/1**

06-6 **7** hd **Time Share (IRE)**[3] 50 4-8-6 **45**.................... HayleyTurner 2 36
(G C Bravery) *towards rr: effrt and sme hdwy on inner over 2f out: sn rdn and btn* **14/1**

00-5 **8** 2 **Mister Incredible**[4] 46 5-8-11 **50**....................(v) PaulMulrennan 6 34
(J M Bradley) *trckd ldrs: effrt 2f out: sn rdn and grad wknd* **8/1**

000- **9** 3/4 **Edin Burgher (FR)**[53] 6831 7-7-13 **45**....................(v) AmyBaker(7) 11 27
(T T Clement) *chsd ldrs to 1/2-way: sn wknd* **33/1**

006- **10** 3 **Bold Nevison (IRE)**[18] 7209 4-8-6 **45**.................... ChrisCatlin 4 17
(B Smart) *chsd ldrs: rdn along 3f out and sn wknd* **25/1**

03-4 **11** 1 3/4 **Tenancy (IRE)**[2] 65 4-8-4 **46** ow1....................(p) PatrickMathers(3) 7 13
(A J McCabe) *led: rdn along and hdd over 2f out: sn wknd* **8/1**

1m 17.15s (0.65) **Going Correction** 0.0s/f (Stan) 33 Ran SP% **115.6**
Speed ratings (Par 101): **98,92,90,90,89 87,87,84,83,79 77**
CSF £75.40 CT £513.78 TOTE £11.70: £2.90, £2.60, £2.80; EX 78.30 Trifecta £157.30 Part won. Pool £221.55 - 0.20 winning units..
Owner R G Botham **Bred** P T Tellwright **Trained** Danethorpe, Notts

FOCUS
A weak handicap and despite what looked a decent early pace with Blakeshall Quest and Tenancy taking each other on from the start, the final time was 0.56 seconds slower than the first division. The winner is rated back to his best, with the second close to recent form.

Edin Burgher(FR) Official explanation: trainer said gelding lost a front shoe

83 BOOK YOUR TICKETS ON-LINE (S) STKS 1m 4f (F)
2:40 (2:40) (Class 6) 4-6-Y-O **£1,774** (£523; £262) **Stalls** Low

Form RPR

1 **Kanisorn (SWE)**[21] 6-9-8 **0**....................(bt) CColombi 6 72+
(A Barbagallo, Italy) *trckd ldrs: hdwy to ld over 4f out: rdn and hung rt to stands' rails 2f out: styd on strly* **4/6**[1]

60-3 **2** 10 **Devilfishpoker Com**[4] 36 4-8-13 **44**....................(v) ChrisCatlin 1 47
(R C Guest) *led: rdn along and hdd over 4f out: drvn over 2f out: plugged on same pce* **7/2**[2]

23-3 **3** 3 1/2 **Davidia (IRE)**[7] 2 5-9-0 **47**.................... AndrewElliott(3) 3 41
(D W Thompson) *trckd ldrs: hdwy to chse wnr over 2f out: sn rdn and outpcd over 1f out* **13/2**[3]

/0-0 **4** 1 1/2 **Interest (USA)**[2] 69 4-8-6 **47**....................(b) DeanHeslop(7) 5 39
(T D Barron) *hld up: hdwy to trck ldrs 1/2-way: rdn along over 3f out and sn wknd* **20/1**

526- **5** hd **Cool Isle**[17] 7226 5-8-12 **38**....................(b) TGMcLaughlin 4 34
(P Howling) *a in rr: rdn along and bhd fr 1/2-way* **12/1**

600- **6** 2 1/2 **Cumae (USA)**[18] 7219 4-8-8 **31**.................... LiamJones 2 30
(J Pearce) *cl up: rdn along 4f out: sn wknd* **80/1**

2m 42.18s (1.18) **Going Correction** 0.0s/f (Stan)
WFA 4 from 5yo+ 4lb 9 Ran SP% **109.2**
Speed ratings: **99,92,90,89,88 87**
CSF £3.01 TOTE £1.50: £1.20, £1.70; EX 3.50.The winner was sold to D W Chapman for 9,000gns.
Owner Scuderia San Giusto **Bred** Ostlund Gote **Trained** Italy

FOCUS
This would have been perhaps the world's worst-ever seller had it not been for the presence of the Italian-trained winner, as officially the highest rated of the five domestic runners was 47. The favourite duly bolted up and the form means nothing apart from him.

84 IF IT'S SHOWTIME IT'S PONTIN'S TIME H'CAP 5f (F)
3:10 (3:11) (Class 4) (0-85,85) 4-Y-O+ **£4,210** (£1,252; £625; £312) **Stalls** High

Form RPR

23-1 **1** **Tartatartufata**[7] 5 6-8-5 **79** 6ex....................(v) PatrickDonaghy(7) 5 89
(D Shaw) *trckd ldrs: hdwy wl over 1f out: rdn ent fnl f: styd on to ld last stride* **7/4**[1]

020- **2** shd **Diminuto**[27] 7126 4-8-4 **71** oh1.................... HayleyTurner 3 80
(M D I Usher) *prom: hdwy to chal over 1f out: rdn to ld ins fnl f: sn drvn: hdd and nt qckn last stride* **11/1**

024- **3** shd **Memphis Man**[11] 7261 5-8-5 **72**.................... SaleemGolam 2 81
(P D Evans) *hld up in tch: hdwy 2f out: rdn ent fnl f and sn ev ch: drvn and nt qckn nr fin* **8/1**[3]

045- **4** 1 1/2 **Godfrey Street**[21] 7179 5-8-11 **81**....................(b) AndrewMullen(3) 1 85
(K A Ryan) *led: rdn wl over 1f out: drvn and hdd ins fnl f: sn no ex* **12/1**

041- **5** 2 1/2 **Stolt (IRE)**[18] 7215 4-8-8 **75**.................... PaulMulrennan 10 70
(N Wilson) *chsd ldrs: rdn 2f out: sn drvn and wknd appr fnl f* **10/1**

004- **6** hd **Dancing Mystery**[27] 7116 14-8-5 **72**....................(b) ChrisCatlin 6 66
(E A Wheeler) *cl up: rdn along 2f out: grad wknd* **12/1**

03-6 **7** 3/4 **Yungaburra (IRE)**[7] 5 4-8-13 **85**.................... JamieJones(5) 4 76
(D J Murphy) *in midfield: rdn along and outpcd 1/2-way: sn hung lft: drvn and no imp fr wl over 1f out* **5/1**[2]

23-3 **8** nk **Pawan (IRE)**[7] 5 8-8-6 **78**....................(b) AnnStokell(5) 8 68
(Miss A Stokell) *sn pushed along: a towards rr* **9/1**

100/ **9** 2 **Supreme Speedster**[507] 4603 4-8-4 **71** oh1.................... DaleGibson 7 54
(M Brittain) *towards rr: rdn along 1/2-way and sn outpcd* **66/1**

655- **10** 9 **New York Oscar (IRE)**[18] 7212 4-8-9 **79**....................(p) PatrickMathers(3) 9 30
(A J McCabe) *stmbld s: a bhd* **11/1**

59.19 secs (-0.51) **Going Correction** -0.075s/f (Stan) 10 Ran SP% **116.8**
Speed ratings (Par 105): **105,104,104,102,98 97,96,96,93,78**
CSF £22.79 CT £126.19 TOTE £2.70: £1.50, £4.70, £2.90; EX 25.90 Trifecta £184.70 Part won. Pool £260.24 - 0.37 winning units..
Owner Danethorpe Racing Partnership **Bred** Dr A Ramkaran **Trained** Danethorpe, Notts

FOCUS
Unlike the previous contest this was a cracker with nothing separating the front three at the line. The race did once again expose a draw bias though, with the first four home starting from the five lowest stalls and all the action eventually unfolding centre to far side. The winner was well-in but did not match the form she showed when winning here a week earlier.
New York Oscar(IRE) Official explanation: jockey said gelding stumbled at start

85 ARENALEISUREPLC.COM H'CAP 6f (F)
3:40 (3:41) (Class 4) (0-85,85) 4-Y-O+ **£4,210** (£1,252; £625; £312) **Stalls** Low

Form RPR

002- **1** **Bonnie Prince Blue**[39] 6970 5-8-10 **77**....................(b) ChrisCatlin 2 90+
(B W Hills) *trckd ldrs: hdwy over 2f out: rdn to ld 1f out: sn clr: eased nr fin* **3/1**[1]

030- **2** 4 **Sand Cat**[30] 7087 5-8-9 **79**.................... MichaelJStainton(3) 1 79
(G L Moore) *chsd ldrs on inner: rdn along and outpcd wl over 1f out: styd on u.p to take 2nd ins fnl f: no ch w wnr* **7/1**

203- **3** 1 1/4 **Coleorton Dancer**[18] 7212 6-8-5 **75**.................... AndrewMullen(3) 7 71
(K A Ryan) *led: rdn along 2f out: drvn and hdd 1f out: kpt on same pce* **7/2**[2]

226- **4** 1/2 **Resplendent Alpha**[8] 7289 4-8-12 **79**.................... TGMcLaughlin 4 74
(P Howling) *dwlt and rr tl hdwy over 2f out: sn rdn and styd on ins fnl f: nrst fin* **4/1**[3]

420- **5** nk **Cornus**[39] 6981 6-8-12 **79**....................(be) JamesDoyle 8 73
(A J McCabe) *chsd ldrs: rdn along 2f out: drvn and wknd over 1f out* **7/1**

206- **6** 6 **River Thames**[27] 7126 5-8-8 **75**.................... PaulMulrennan 3 49
(K A Ryan) *cl up: effrt 2f out and ev ch tl rdn and wknd qckly over 1f out* **11/1**

403- **7** 5 **Tagula Sunrise (IRE)**[150] 4373 6-9-1 **85**.................... JamieMoriarty(3) 6 43
(R A Fahey) *s.i.s and sn rdn along: a in rr* **12/1**

436- **8** 3 1/2 **Prince Tum Tum (USA)**[329] 452 8-9-4 **85**.................... DanielTudhope 5 32
(D Shaw) *hld up: a in rr* **16/1**

1m 15.37s (-1.13) **Going Correction** 0.0s/f (Stan) 8 Ran SP% **114.1**
Speed ratings (Par 105): **110,104,103,102,101 93,87,82**
CSF £24.32 CT £76.01 TOTE £4.70: £2.10, £2.00, £1.50; EX 24.10 Trifecta £152.20 Pool £289.46 - 1.35 winning units. Place 6 £10.98, Place 5 £9.12..
Owner G J Hicks **Bred** George Joseph Hicks **Trained** Lambourn, Berks

FOCUS
A decent little handicap in which they went a serious pace and the time was decent. The field finished well spread out and the form looks pretty solid, with the winner back to his best.
T/Plt: £13.20 to a £1 stake. Pool: £36,593.75. 2,012.75 winning tickets. T/Qpdt: £7.10 to a £1 stake. Pool: £3,239.90. 335.30 winning tickets. JR

[50]KEMPTON (A.W) (R-H)

Wednesday, January 9

OFFICIAL GOING: Standard

Wind: Moderate, across Weather: Sunny

86 CITY & SUBURBAN PARKING CHRISTMAS PARTY H'CAP — 5f (P)

1:30 (1:30) (Class 6) (0-58,58) 4-Y-O+ — £2,047 (£604; £302) Stalls High

Form — RPR

044- **1** **Sir Loin**[11] 7265 7-7-12 **47**........(v) RossAtkinson(7) 3 — 56
(P Burgoyne) *mde all: rdn over 1f out: coaxed along fnl f: jst hld on* **8/1**

030- **2** *hd* **Minnow**[11] 7265 4-8-8 **50**........(p) SaleemGolam 2 — 58
(S C Williams) *towards rr: hdwy over 1f out: drvn to go 2nd ins fnl f: clsd on wnr: jst failed* **12/1**

403- **3** *¾* **Taboor (IRE)**[9] 7283 10-8-1 **48**........ KirstyMilczarek(5) 9 — 54
(R M H Cowell) *hld up in 6th: hdwy to chse ldrs over 1f out: kpt on fnl f* **8/1**

160- **4** *nk* **Commander Wish**[18] 7227 5-8-13 **58**........(tp) NeilChalmers(3) 7 — 67+
(Lucinda Featherstone) *hld up in rr: hdwy on rail whn hmpd over 1f out: swtchd lft: r.o wl fnl f* **4/1**[2]

050- **5** *nk* **Rosie Cross (IRE)**[43] 6962 4-9-2 **58**........ StephenCarson 4 — 61
(Eve Johnson Houghton) *in tch: sn pushed along: kpt on fnl 2f* **13/2**

006- **6** *½* **Ashes (IRE)**[10] 7279 6-8-11 **56**........(p) AndrewElliott(3) 8 — 58
(K R Burke) *prom: rdn over 1f out: one pce* **10/1**

41-6 **7** *1½* **Is It Time (IRE)**[7] 13 4-8-13 **55**........ RichardHughes 6 — 51
(Mrs P N Dutfield) *dwlt: hld up in rr: drvn along 2f out: nt rch ldrs* **5/1**[3]

602- **8** *15* **Fastrac Boy**[31] 7082 5-8-9 **51**........ JimCrowley 1 — —
(J R Best) *lw: prom tl v wd and wknd 2f out* **10/3**[1]

215- **9** *1¾* **Wibbadune (IRE)**[9] 7284 4-8-5 **52**........ ColinHaddon(5) 5 — —
(Peter Grayson) *prom tl wd and wknd 2f out* **25/1**

60.55 secs (0.05) **Going Correction** +0.025s/f (Slow) — **9** Ran SP% **115.9**
Speed ratings (Par 101): **99,98,97,97,96 95,93,69,66**
CSF £98.66 CT £799.00 TOTE £9.30: £2.80, £3.20, £3.20; EX 91.50.
Owner L Tomlin **Bred** Britton House Stud And C Gregson **Trained** Shepton Montague, Somerset
■ Stewards' Enquiry : Saleem Golam one-day ban: used whip with excessive force (Jan 20)

FOCUS
A very moderate sprint handicap rated around the third to his recent form.
Fastrac Boy Official explanation: trainer's rep had no explanation for the poor form shown

87 C. S. P. JOE FRIMPONG EMPLOYEE OF THE YEAR CLASSIFIED STKS — 6f (P)

2:00 (2:00) (Class 6) 4-Y-O+ — £2,047 (£604; £302) Stalls High

Form — RPR

00-2 **1** **Reigning Monarch (USA)**[4] 54 5-9-0 55........ SaleemGolam 6 — 60
(Miss Z C Davison) *mde all: hrd rdn over 1f out: hld on wl* **10/11**[1]

300- **2** *½* **Regal Royale**[10] 7276 5-8-9 50........ ColinHaddon(5) 7 — 59
(Peter Grayson) *prom: hrd rdn 2f out: r.o to chse wnr fnl 75yds: clsng at fin* **10/1**

/21- **3** *½* **Grand Assault**[27] 7134 5-9-0 54........(be) TGMcLaughlin 1 — 58
(G C Bravery) *stdd s: hdwy 4f out: hrd rdn and swtchd lft 2f out: styd on wl fnl f* **10/3**[2]

310- **4** *nk* **Crimson Fern (IRE)**[59] 6779 4-9-0 55........ MatthewHenry 4 — 56
(M S Saunders) *chsd wnr: rdn to chal ins fnl 2f: no ex fnl 100yds* **7/1**[3]

0- **5** *2½* **Kazakstan**[10] 7279 4-8-11 55........(p) JerryO'Dwyer(3) 5 — 48
(Mrs L C Jewell) *hld up: effrt over 2f out: no imp* **25/1**

46-0 **6** *3* **Kissi Kissi**[4] 50 5-9-0 40........ AmirQuinn 2 — 38
(M J Attwater) *in tch: pushed along and outpcd over 3f out: n.d after* **50/1**

600- **7** *nk* **Just Spike**[11] 7271 5-9-0 55........ StephenCarson 3 — 37
(B P J Baugh) *stdd s: hld up in rr: wd bnd 3f out: sn rdn and nt trble ldrs* **10/1**

1m 13.28s (0.18) **Going Correction** +0.025s/f (Slow) — 7 Ran SP% **112.0**
Speed ratings (Par 101): **103,102,101,101,97 93,93**
CSF £10.90 TOTE £1.90: £1.20, £3.90; EX 12.20.
Owner John Belsey **Bred** High Creek Farm **Trained** Hammerwood, E Sussex

FOCUS
A very moderate classified sprint but sound enough form for the grade rated through the second and third.

88 DIGIBET MEDIAN AUCTION MAIDEN STKS — 1m 3f (P)

2:30 (2:30) (Class 6) 4-6-Y-O — £2,047 (£604; £302) Stalls High

Form — RPR

33-3 **1** **Rollin 'n Tumblin**[6] 22 4-8-12 47........ KirstyMilczarek(5) 8 — 69+
(W Jarvis) *lw: chsd ldrs: rdn to ld 2f out: hld on wl fnl f* **9/4**[1]

35- **2** *nk* **Blue Eyed Eloise**[70] 3621 6-9-1 0........ StephenCarson 9 — 63
(B J McMath) *prom: rdn to chal fnl 2f: nt qckn fnl 50yds* **11/2**[3]

604- **3** *6* **Beech Games**[21] 7186 4-9-3 53........ TGMcLaughlin 2 — 57
(F Jordan) *s.i.s: sn in midfield on outside: hdwy to press ldrs whn wd st: one pce fnl 2f* **9/1**

452- **4** *hd* **Verbatim**[21] 7185 4-8-9 48........(v) NeilChalmers(3) 6 — 52
(A M Balding) *hld up in midfield: effrt over 2f out: hrd rdn over 1f out: nt pce to chal* **10/3**[2]

/04- **5** *4* **Todwick Owl**[26] 7144 4-9-3 54........ TPQueally 3 — 50
(J G Given) *prom: led 4f out tl 2f out: wknd over 1f out* **12/1**

0/ **6** *hd* **George Henson (IRE)**[438] 6214 4-9-3 0........ PaulMulrennan 10 — 49+
(M H Tompkins) *hld up in rr: sme hdwy whn nt clr run and swtchd rt 2f out: sn rdn and no imp* **15/2**

00-0 **7** *3* **Lady Firecracker (IRE)**[7] 10 4-8-12 50........ JimCrowley 7 — 39
(J R Best) *towards rr: rdn 4f out: n.d* **33/1**

204- **8** *7* **Red**[20] 7203 4-8-12 50........ RichardHughes 1 — 26
(R M Stronge) *s.s: rdn 3f out: a bhd* **17/2**

060- **9** *6* **Keagles (ITY)**[21] 7189 5-9-1 38........(p) NeilPollard 4 — 15
(J E Long) *chsd ldrs tl wknd over 3f out* **66/1**

600- **10** *7* **Haydock Express (IRE)**[21] 7185 4-8-12 41........ ColinHaddon(5) 5 — 8
(Peter Grayson) *led: t.k.h and restrained in front: hdd 4f out: wknd qckly over 2f out: eased* **66/1**

2m 21.66s (-0.24) **Going Correction** +0.025s/f (Slow)
WFA 4 from 5yo+ 3lb — **10** Ran SP% **115.1**
Speed ratings: **104,103,99,99,96 96,94,88,84,79**
CSF £14.58 TOTE £2.80: £1.30, £3.20, £2.10; EX 20.20.
Owner Canisbay Bloodstock **Bred** Canisbay Bloodstock Ltd **Trained** Newmarket, Suffolk

FOCUS
A quite terrible maiden rated around the third and fourth to a shade off recent levels.

89 DIGIBET FILLIES' H'CAP — 1m (P)

3:00 (3:00) (Class 6) (0-65,64) 4-Y-O+ — £2,047 (£604; £302) Stalls High

Form — RPR

026- **1** **Perfect Practice**[24] 7166 4-8-2 **53**........ KirstyMilczarek(5) 7 — 61
(C G Cox) *lw: mde all: hrd rdn over 1f out: in control fnl f: r.o wl* **5/2**[2]

04-0 **2** *2½* **Falcon Flyer**[7] 8 4-7-11 **50** oh5........ KierenFox(7) 5 — 52
(J R Best) *chsd ldr tl wl over 1f out: kpt on to regain 2nd nr fin* **12/1**

62-4 **3** *hd* **Tilsworth Charlie**[7] 13 5-8-8 **54**........(b) JimCrowley 2 — 56
(J R Jenkins) *bhd: rdn and hdwy over 2f out: chsd wnr wl over 1f out: one pce: lost 2nd nr fin* **9/4**[1]

63-0 **4** *1¾* **Mythical Charm**[4] 56 9-8-3 **52**........(t) NeilChalmers(3) 4 — 50
(J J Bridger) *lw: dwlt: hld up in 5th: hdwy on bit to dispute 2nd over 2f out: sn rdn and nt qckn* **9/2**[3]

50-4 **5** *4* **Lily La Belle**[5] 48 4-8-1 **50** oh2........ AndrewElliott(3) 1 — 38
(A W Carroll) *chsd ldrs: cornered bdly and lost pl 3f out: hrd rdn and no hdwy fnl 2f* **10/1**

100- **6** *1¾* **Fustaan (IRE)**[18] 7221 4-9-4 **64**........ TPQueally 3 — 48
(A G Newcombe) *t.k.h in rr: effrt over 2f out: wknd over 1f out* **14/1**

001- **7** *3* **Shantina's Dream (USA)**[27] 7133 4-7-11 **50** oh3... PatrickDonaghy(7) 6 — 27
(J R Boyle) *lw: dwlt: sn chsng ldrs: wknd qckly over 2f out* **7/1**

1m 41.03s (1.23) **Going Correction** +0.025s/f (Slow) — **7** Ran SP% **113.5**
Speed ratings (Par 98): **99,96,96,94,90 88,85**
CSF £30.84 TOTE £3.30: £2.50, £5.30; EX 40.40.
Owner The Perfect Partnership II **Bred** Dachel Stud **Trained** Lambourn, Berks

FOCUS
A very moderate fillies' handicap and dubious form given the steady early pace. It has been rated through the third.

90 DIGIBET SPORTS BETTING FILLIES' H'CAP — 7f (P)

3:30 (3:30) (Class 5) (0-75,73) 4-Y-O+ — £2,590 (£770; £385; £192) Stalls High

Form — RPR

01-2 **1** **Angel Voices (IRE)**[4] 56 5-7-11 **59** oh3........(p) DeclanCannon(7) 6 — 73
(K R Burke) *lw: mde all: drvn clr 2f out: readily* **5/2**[2]

000- **2** *4* **Neardown Beauty (IRE)**[40] 6981 5-9-3 **72**........(p) PaulMulrennan 3 — 75
(A J McCabe) *hld up in tch: effrt over 2f out: chsd wnr fnl f: no imp* **13/2**[3]

030- **3** *1¾* **Social Rhythm**[64] 6701 4-8-10 **70**........ KirstyMilczarek(5) 5 — 68
(H J Collingridge) *dwlt: hld up in rr: hdwy whn carried rt and swtchd lft 2f out: kpt on to take 3rd ins fnl f* **10/1**

361- **4** *nk* **Blackmalkin (USA)**[63] 6717 4-8-12 **67**........ TPQueally 4 — 64
(M Quinn) *chsd ldng pair: wnt 2nd over 2f out tl 1f out: no ex* **8/1**

201- **5** *2* **Reeling N' Rocking (IRE)**[12] 7253 5-9-4 **73**........ RichardHughes 2 — 65
(B W Hills) *in tch: hung lft bnd 1/2-way: hrd rdn and btn 2f out* **11/8**[1]

126- **6** *2½* **Onenightinlisbon (IRE)**[11] 7269 4-9-0 **69**........ PatCosgrave 1 — 54
(J R Boyle) *pressed wnr tl wknd over 2f out* **14/1**

1m 25.24s (-0.76) **Going Correction** +0.025s/f (Slow) — **6** Ran SP% **110.9**
Speed ratings (Par 100): **109,104,102,102,99 96**
CSF £18.08 TOTE £3.50: £1.70, £4.90; EX 19.60.
Owner Mrs Elaine M Burke **Bred** W Haggas And W Jarvis **Trained** Middleham Moor, N Yorks

FOCUS
A modest fillies' handicap, but they went a serious gallop and the winning time was very smart. The winner was in no danger from a long way out and has been rated back to the best of her two-year-old form.
Reeling N' Rocking(IRE) Official explanation: jockey said mare never travelled

91 C. S. P. ALF WOODS GETTING OUT H'CAP — 1m 4f (P)

4:00 (4:01) (Class 6) (0-65,64) 4-Y-O+ — £2,047 (£604; £302) Stalls Centre

Form — RPR

005- **1** **Resplendent Ace (IRE)**[12] 7257 4-9-2 **64**........ TGMcLaughlin 2 — 72
(P Howling) *chsd ldrs: rdn into narrow ld 1f out: jnd by runner-up ins fnl f: jst prevailed* **11/1**

513- **2** *hd* **Smokey The Bear**[12] 7256 6-8-6 **53**........ NeilChalmers(3) 11 — 66+
(Miss Sheena West) *lw: hld up in midfield: dropped towards rr over 3f out: gd hdwy over 1f out: jnd wnr ins fnl f: r.o* **9/4**[1]

05-4 **3** *½* **Most Definitely (IRE)**[7] 14 8-9-5 **63**........(p) RichardHughes 7 — 70
(R M Stronge) *lw: stdd s: t.k.h in midfield: hdwy on bit to trck ldrs over 1f out: shkn up and r.o fnl 100yds* **11/2**[2]

255- **4** *½* **Pocket Too**[28] 7123 5-8-11 **60**........(p) KirstyMilczarek(5) 8 — 66
(M Salaman) *led: rdn over 2f out: hdd 1f out: kpt on same pce* **9/1**

000- **5** *½* **Tancredi (SWE)**[26] 7143 6-9-1 **62**........ JerryO'Dwyer(3) 13 — 69+
(N B King) *hld up in tch: effrt over 2f out: nt clr run and swtchd rt over 1f out: disputing 4th and styng on whn nowhere to go fnl 75yds* **25/1**

042- **6** *1* **Whaxaar (IRE)**[21] 7187 4-8-10 **58** ow1........ StephenCarson 10 — 62
(R Ingram) *t.k.h: hdwy to trck ldrs 6f out: rdn 2f out: nt clr run ins fnl f: 6th and hld whn eased fnl 50yds* **15/2**[3]

240- **7** *nk* **Red Wine**[14] 5779 9-9-6 **64**........ PaulMulrennan 14 — 67
(A J McCabe) *stdd s: t.k.h towards rr: hdwy 2f out: sn rdn and nvr able to chal* **12/1**

555- **8** *½* **Bienheureux**[83] 6276 7-8-12 **59**........ AndrewElliott(3) 12 — 61
(Miss Gay Kelleway) *mid-div on rail: gd hdwy to chse ldrs 2f out: hrd rdn and no ex over 1f out* **10/1**

050- **9** *nk* **Amwell Brave**[91] 6102 7-9-0 **58**........ J-PGuillambert 5 — 60
(J R Jenkins) *stdd s: t.k.h towards rr: effrt over 2f out: hrd rdn over 1f out: nt rch ldrs* **16/1**

000/ **10** *1* **King Of Diamonds**[34] 5046 7-8-13 **57**........(t) FrankieMcDonald 1 — 57
(Jean-Rene Auvray) *stdd s: bhd: rdn 3f out: n.d* **50/1**

/30- **11** *¾* **Persona (IRE)**[70] 6577 6-8-13 **57**........ TPQueally 9 — 56
(B J McMath) *prom tl wknd over 1f out* **33/1**

150- **12** *1¼* **Key Partners (IRE)**[47] 6911 7-8-6 **57**........ GabrielHannon(7) 3 — 54
(P A Blockley) *stdd s: rdn 3f out: a bhd* **12/1**

200- **13** *2* **Desert Soul**[141] 4687 4-8-12 **60**........ NeilPollard 6 — 54
(R H York) *chsd ldr tl wknd 2f out* **25/1**

2m 37.69s (3.19) **Going Correction** +0.025s/f (Slow)
WFA 4 from 5yo+ 4lb — **13** Ran SP% **119.2**
Speed ratings (Par 101): **98,97,97,97,96 96,96,95,95,94 94,93,92**
CSF £34.59 CT £158.35 TOTE £15.30: £4.80, £1.70, £2.10; EX 47.20.
Owner Resplendent Racing Limited **Bred** Newlands House Stud **Trained** Newmarket, Suffolk

FOCUS
A competitive if moderate handicap, but they only went a steady pace and they finished in a bit of a heap. One or two did not enjoy the clearest of runs late on and it is unlikely that the form is solid, although by rating it around the third and fourth it looks alright.
Whaxaar(IRE) Official explanation: jockey said gelding ran too free

King Of Diamonds Official explanation: jockey said gelding hung right-handed

92 KEMPTON FOR WEDDINGS H'CAP 6f (P)
4:30 (4:32) (Class 6) (0-55,54) 3-Y-O £2,047 (£604; £302) Stalls High

Form RPR
000- 1 2 ½ **Regal Veil**[74] 6503 3-8-8 **48**.............................. SaleemGolam 4 49
(S C Williams) *lw: dwlt: hdwy to chse ldr after 2f: nt pce of wnr fnl f* **4/1**[2]
000- 2 ½ **Little Finch (IRE)**[13] 7243 3-8-5 **45**..............(b) PaulEddery 2 44
(R C Guest) *led 1f: chsd ldrs: rdn over 2f out: one pce appr fnl f* **13/2**[3]
505- 3 1 **Where's Killoran**[32] 7071 3-8-4 **49**.............. ColinHaddon(5) 7 45
(Peter Grayson) *t.k.h in rr: rdn over 2f out: styd on fnl f* **16/1**
44-0 4 ¾ **Talamahana**[6] 23 3-8-13 **53**..................(b) RichardHughes 1 47
(S Kirk) *led after 1f tl wl over 1f out: wknd fnl f* **2/1**[1]
55-6 5 ¾ **Seductive Witch**[6] 23 3-8-7 **54**.............. GabrielHannon(7) 5 45
(M D I Usher) *chsd ldrs: rdn over 2f out: sn btn* **4/1**[2]
456- 6 hd **La Varrosa**[13] 7240 3-8-8 **48**.............. TGMcLaughlin 3 39
(Mrs P N Dutfield) *s.i.s: in rr: rdn over 3f out: n.d fnl 2f* **11/1**
000- D **Bold Diva**[83] 6281 3-8-0 **45**..............(v[1]) KirstyMilczarek(5) 6 54
(A W Carroll) *t.k.h: trckd ldrs: led wl over 1f out: rdn clr fnl f* **17/2**

1m 14.72s (1.62) **Going Correction** +0.025s/f (Slow) 7 Ran SP% **111.4**
Speed ratings (Par 95): **90,90,88,87,86 86,94**
CSF £39.95 TOTE £10.20: £3.70, £2.30; EX 47.40 Place 6 £138.83, Place 5 £26.16.
Owner J W Parry **Bred** Old Mill Stud And Partners **Trained** Newmarket, Suffolk
■ Bold Diva completed a 107-1 treble for jockey Kirsty Milczarek.

FOCUS
A very moderate three-year-old handicap with the top weight rated just 54. The form makes some sense rated through the runner-up and third.
T/Plt: £184.60 to a £1 stake. Pool: £41,327.30. 163.40 winning tickets. T/Qpdt: £20.70 to a £1 stake. Pool: £3,343.20. 119.00 winning tickets. LM

[57]LINGFIELD (L-H)
Wednesday, January 9

OFFICIAL GOING: Standard
Wind: Strong, half behind Weather: Fine

93 CROCK AROUND THE CLOCK @ PONTIN'S APPRENTICE (S) STKS 6f (P)
12:50 (12:50) (Class 6) 3-Y-O £1,774 (£523; £262) Stalls Low

Form RPR
033- 1 **Lord Deevert**[11] 7272 3-8-13 62..............(v) JackDean(3) 3 65
(W G M Turner) *dwlt: chsd ldr over 4f out: rdn to chal 2f out: narrow ld ins fnl f: asserted nr fin* **7/1**[3]
023- 2 ¾ **Atephobia**[13] 7246 3-8-11 63.............. DeclanCannon(5) 4 63
(K R Burke) *led: drvn over 1f out: narrowly hdd ins fnl f: nt qckn* **5/4**[2]
212- 3 2 **Maybe I Wont**[26] 7142 3-8-13 64.............. JackMitchell(3) 1 56
(R M Stronge) *chsd ldr to over 4f out: rdn 2f out: cl up on inner 1f out: one pce* **1/1**[1]

1m 12.1s (0.20) **Going Correction** -0.125s/f (Stan) 3 Ran SP% **106.9**
Speed ratings (Par 95): **99,98,95**
CSF £15.05 TOTE £6.60; EX 13.00.There was no bid for the winner.
Owner Mrs M S Teversham **Bred** Mrs Monica Teversham **Trained** Sigwells, Somerset

FOCUS
Weak in numbers, but the three contestants had shown fair form, and were above-average for an All-Weather seller. The winner is rated back to his best.

94 RACE TO PONTIN'S 0844 815 3647 H'CAP 6f (P)
1:20 (1:21) (Class 5) (0-75,74) 4-Y-O+ £2,590 (£770; £385; £192) Stalls Low

Form RPR
041- 1 **Benllech**[10] 7279 4-8-12 **68** 6ex.............. SimonWhitworth 1 76
(M Wigham) *t.k.h: hld up bhd ldrs: easy passage on inner to ld 1f out: drvn out: jst hld on* **3/1**[2]
55-4 2 shd **Louphole**[4] 55 6-9-2 **72**.............. SebSanders 4 81+
(P J Makin) *t.k.h: hld up bhd ldrs: got through to chse wnr ins fnl f: clsng at fin: jst failed* **11/8**[1]
00-6 3 1 ½ **Hucking Hill (IRE)**[4] 55 4-8-12 **68**..............(b) HayleyTurner 3 71
(J R Best) *t.k.h: disp ld: stdy pce to 1/2-way: rdn and hdd 1f out: nt qckn* **15/2**[3]
010- 4 ½ **What Do You Know**[115] 5447 5-9-4 **74**.............. PatDobbs 5 75
(A M Hales) *t.k.h: disp ld: stdy pce to 1/2-way: hdd 1f out: edgd rt and fnd nil* **16/1**
63-0 5 1 **No Time (IRE)**[4] 55 8-8-5 **64**.............. PatrickMathers(3) 6 62
(A J McCabe) *trckd ldrs: rdn over 2f out: nt qckn over 1f out: btn after* **9/1**
600- 6 1 **Quality Street**[117] 5381 6-9-0 **70**..............(p) RichardThomas 7 65
(P Butler) *trckd ldrs on outer: rdn over 2f out: nt qckn over 1f out: fdd* **20/1**

1m 12.07s (0.17) **Going Correction** -0.125s/f (Stan) 6 Ran SP% **99.5**
Speed ratings (Par 103): **99,98,96,96,94 93**
CSF £5.82 TOTE £4.60: £2.20, £1.10; EX 7.40.
Owner R J Lorenz **Bred** Speedlith Group **Trained** Newmarket, Suffolk

FOCUS
A modest but competitive race considering the smallish field. The pace was steady and the form makes sense rated through the third.

95 GREAT GETAWAYS @ PONTINS.COM MAIDEN STKS 1m (P)
1:50 (1:50) (Class 5) 4-Y-O+ £2,331 (£693; £346; £173) Stalls High

Form RPR
442- 1 **Granary**[23] 7174 4-8-12 67.............. ChrisCatlin 9 65
(H Candy) *led: set stdy pce to 3f out: drvn and hdd over 1f out: kpt on wl to ld again ins fnl f: hld on* **7/1**
U03- 2 nk **North South Divide (IRE)**[35] 7029 4-9-3 0.............. SebSanders 4 69
(R A Teal) *restless in stalls: dwlt: t.k.h: hld up: sweeping run on wd outside over 2f out: led over 1f out: sn hrd drvn: hdd ins fnl f: no ex* **7/2**[2]
/44- 3 ½ **Denbera Dancer (USA)**[164] 3994 4-9-3 75.............. GregFairley 6 68+
(M Johnston) *t.k.h: trckd ldng pair: rdn 2f out: hanging and nt qckn over 1f out: plld out and r.o nr fin* **10/11**[1]
043- 4 1 ¾ **Saviour Sand (IRE)**[23] 7174 4-9-3 70.............. PatDobbs 1 64
(D R C Elsworth) *t.k.h: trckd ldr to 2f out: rdn and nt qckn after* **6/1**[3]
4U0- 5 3 **Ma Ridge**[24] 7167 4-9-3 50.............. RichardThomas 5 57?
(T D McCarthy) *hld up in tch: shkn up and outpcd over 2f out: no imp on ldrs after* **50/1**
0- 6 1 **Irish Cape**[72] 6546 5-8-12 0.............. JamesDoyle 2 50?
(Mrs N Smith) *t.k.h: hld up in last pair: outpcd over 2f out: no imp after* **80/1**
304- 7 nk **Mini Mosa**[49] 6901 4-8-12 66.............. DavidKinsella 8 49
(J H M Gosden) *hld up in tch: outpcd over 2f out: n.d after* **12/1**
240- 8 4 **Old Etonian (UAE)**[10] 7282 4-8-10 0.............. RyanHill(7) 7 45
(Peter Grayson) *t.k.h: hld up in tch: dropped away tamely 3f out* **25/1**

1m 38.19s (-0.01) **Going Correction** -0.125s/f (Stan) 8 Ran SP% **116.1**
Speed ratings (Par 103): **101,100,100,98,95 94,94,90**
CSF £31.90 TOTE £10.80: £2.20, £1.70, £1.02; EX 37.00 Trifecta £123.20 Pool: £263.91 - 1.52 winning tickets..
Owner Major M G Wyatt **Bred** W And R Barnett Ltd **Trained** Kingston Warren, Oxon

FOCUS
A routine maiden, run at a steady pace. Modest form, limited by the fifth.
Irish Cape Official explanation: jockey said mare ran too free

96 LINGFIELDPARK.CO.UK H'CAP 1m 4f (P)
2:20 (2:20) (Class 4) (0-85,85) 4-Y-O+ £4,100 (£1,227; £613; £306; £152) Stalls Low

Form RPR
22-1 1 **Wicked Daze (IRE)**[8] 1 5-9-1 **78**.............. SebSanders 3 89+
(Sir Mark Prescott) *mde all: set stdy pce to 4f out: pressed 2f out: rdn and styd on wl fr over 1f out* **2/1**[1]
301- 2 1 ¾ **Sgt Schultz (IRE)**[33] 7055 5-9-7 **84**.............. JohnEgan 10 92
(J S Moore) *t.k.h: hld up but sn prom: trckd wnr 3f out: clr of rest 2f out: drvn and readily hld fnl f* **9/2**[2]
064- 3 1 ¼ **Cold Turkey**[31] 7086 8-9-8 **85**.............. SimonWhitworth 2 93+
(G L Moore) *dwlt: hld up in last: nt clr run wl over 1f out tl ent fnl f: flashed home last 150yds to snatch 3rd fnl stride* **20/1**
500- 4 hd **Altilhar (USA)**[18] 6473 5-9-0 **77**..............(b) PatDobbs 8 83
(G L Moore) *chsd ldrs: rdn over 3f out and struggling: styd on fr 2f out to dispute 3rd fnl f: kpt on* **7/1**[3]
422- 5 ½ **Pass The Port**[14] 7236 7-9-5 **82**.............. HayleyTurner 7 87
(D Haydn Jones) *stdd s: hld up in last pair: prog on outer 3f out: chsd clr ldng pair over 1f out: no imp: one pce* **7/1**[3]
445- 6 shd **Resonate (IRE)**[36] 7018 10-8-10 **73**.............. StephenDonohoe 1 78
(A G Newcombe) *hld up in midfield: rdn over 3f out: nt clr run over 2f out: sme prog u.p over 1f out: no hdwy after* **12/1**
/44- 7 3 **Shogun Prince (IRE)**[77] 6422 5-8-13 **76**.............. MickyFenton 5 76
(W Jarvis) *hld up: effrt on outer over 2f out: hanging bdly and no prog over 1f out: n.d after* **8/1**
014- 8 4 **Vallemeldee (IRE)**[20] 7205 4-8-6 **73**.............. ChrisCatlin 6 67
(P W D'Arcy) *chsd wnr after 2f to 3f out: wknd 2f out* **16/1**
9 shd **Trachonitis (IRE)**[21] 4436 4-8-13 **80**.............. J-PGuillambert 9 73
(J R Jenkins) *t.k.h: hld up in rr: prog on outer over 3f out: chsd clr ldng pair over 2f out to over 1f out: n.m.r sn after: wknd* **33/1**
0/0- 10 10 **Sadler's Star (GER)**[39] 488 5-8-9 **72**..............(t) RichardKingscote 4 49
(B G Powell) *chsd wnr 2f: prom tl wknd 3f out* **8/1**

2m 29.63s (-3.37) **Going Correction** -0.125s/f (Stan)
WFA 4 from 5yo+ 4lb 10 Ran SP% **120.0**
Speed ratings (Par 105): **110,108,108,107,107 107,105,102,102,96**
CSF £11.04 CT £142.77 TOTE £3.10: £1.20, £1.90, £3.90; EX 11.80 Trifecta £82.90 Pool: £349.28 - 2.99 winning tickets..
Owner Roger T Ferris **Bred** Bloomsbury Stud **Trained** Newmarket, Suffolk

FOCUS
A fair All-Weather handicap, but run at a steady pace. The form looks sound and the first two are progressive types.
Vallemeldee(IRE) Official explanation: jockey said filly hung left

97 HOTEL ON IT'S WAY TO LINGFIELD PARK H'CAP 1m 2f (P)
2:50 (2:50) (Class 4) (0-85,85) 4-Y-O+ £4,100 (£1,227; £613; £306; £152) Stalls Low

Form RPR
531- 1 **Baylini**[55] 6822 4-8-13 **80**.............. JamesDoyle 6 99+
(Ms J S Doyle) *prom: trckd ldr 4f out: led over 2f out and sn clr: eased nr fin* **9/4**[1]
064- 2 6 **Mataram (USA)**[24] 7165 5-8-13 **78**.............. ChrisCatlin 9 83
(W Jarvis) *hld up bhd ldrs: already wl outpcd whn effrt 2f out: pushed into modest 2nd 1f out: no imp on wnr* **3/1**[2]
030- 3 3 **Fusili (IRE)**[24] 7163 5-8-13 **85**.............. HarryPoulton(7) 1 84
(N P Littmoden) *led to over 2f out: no ch w wnr after: jst hld on for 3rd* **14/1**
443- 4 hd **Generous Lad (IRE)**[26] 7147 5-8-10 **75**..............(p) DavidKinsella 2 74
(A B Haynes) *stdd s: hld up in last pair: outpcd wl over 2f out: prog on inner over 1f out: kpt on fnl f* **7/1**
000- 5 ½ **Risque Heights**[10] 7281 4-8-13 **80**.............. HayleyTurner 8 78
(G A Butler) *stdd s: plld hrd: hld up in last pair: outpcd over 2f out: n.d after* **9/2**[3]
400- 6 ½ **Transvestite (IRE)**[37] 6007 6-8-11 **76**..............(v) GregFairley 4 73
(J W Hills) *hld up towards rr: outpcd wl over 2f out: no ch after* **14/1**
250- 7 1 ¼ **Fregate Island (IRE)**[14] 7236 5-9-1 **80**.............. SebSanders 11 75
(J G Given) *chsd ldr to 4f out: sn lost pl u.p* **13/2**
030- 8 1 ¾ **Obrigado (USA)**[21] 7193 8-8-9 **74**.............. MickyFenton 7 65
(Karen George) *stdd s: t.k.h: hld up: prog to dispute 3rd over 2f out but outpcd: wknd over 1f out* **20/1**

2m 4.76s (-1.84) **Going Correction** -0.125s/f (Stan)
WFA 4 from 5yo+ 2lb 8 Ran SP% **117.9**
Speed ratings (Par 105): **107,102,99,99,99 98,97,96**
CSF £9.46 CT £75.91 TOTE £2.70: £1.02, £2.00, £5.90; EX 11.50 Trifecta £36.00 Pool: £357.60 - 7.05 winning tickets..
Owner Ms J S Doyle **Bred** Templeton Stud **Trained** Eastbury, Berks

FOCUS
A race of reasonable quaility, with a improving winner, but run at an ordinary gallop. The form is rated through the runner-up.
Obrigado(USA) Official explanation: jockey said gelding finished distressed

98 MEET POSTMAN PAT @ PONTIN'S H'CAP 1m (P)
3:20 (3:20) (Class 6) (0-60,60) 3-Y-O £1,876 (£554; £277) Stalls High

Form RPR
000- 1 **Ledgerwood**[28] 7117 3-9-4 60..............(p) JamesDoyle 6 62
(J W Hills) *t.k.h early: hld up in 5th: prog on outer over 3f out to press ldr over 2f out: sustained chal to ld nr fin* **14/1**
55-2 2 ½ **Waterloo Dock**[6] 23 3-9-0 56.............. ChrisCatlin 7 57
(M Quinn) *trckd ldr: led 3f out: pressed over 2f out: worn down nr fin* **2/1**[1]
600- 3 2 **Sistos Fascination**[56] 6812 3-9-3 59.............. JohnEgan 8 55
(M Botti) *a ldng trio: rdn to chse ldng pair over 2f out: kpt on but no real imp* **9/4**[2]
406- 4 1 **Lady Sandicliffe (IRE)**[28] 7117 3-9-0 56.............. SimonWhitworth 4 50
(Miss Jo Crowley) *hld up in last pair: outpcd 3f out: prog and rdn over 1f out: kpt on: nrst fin* **13/2**

256- **5** 2 **Miss Bouggy Wouggy**[36] 7022 3-9-4 60 PatDobbs 3 49
(M Blanshard) *hld up in midfield: outpcd 3f out: modest prog to chse ldng trio over 2f out: sn btn* **16/1**
006- **6** hd **Lancaster Lad (IRE)**[28] 7121 3-8-4 46 oh1 DavidKinsella 2 35
(A B Haynes) *hld up in last pair: outpcd 3f out: shkn up and no ch fnl 2f* **33/1**
442- **7** nk **Mairead's Boy (IRE)**[28] 7117 3-9-4 60 (v) RichardThomas 5 48
(P Butler) *hld up in rr: wl outpcd fr 3f out: plugged on fr over 1f out* **11/2**[3]
000- **8** shd **Victory Shout (USA)**[70] 6584 3-9-0 56 HayleyTurner 1 44
(J R Best) *sn rdn towards rr: nvr gng wl: nvr a factor* **20/1**
046- **9** 6 **Adam Eterno (IRE)**[30] 7101 3-8-13 55 (b) MickyFenton 9 29
(A B Haynes) *led at decent pce: hdd 3f out: sn wknd: t.o* **20/1**

1m 39.65s (1.45) **Going Correction** -0.125s/f (Stan) 9 Ran SP% **117.8**
Speed ratings (Par 95): **93,92,90,89,87 87,87,86,80**
CSF £42.32 CT £91.12 TOTE £20.60: £4.20, £1.30, £1.60; EX 65.00 Trifecta £357.70 Part won. Pool: £503.83 - 0.75 winning tickets..
Owner Gary & Linnet Woodward and Neil Ledger **Bred** Shutford Stud And O F Waller **Trained** Upper Lambourn, Berks
■ Stewards' Enquiry : Chris Catlin one-day ban: used whip with excessive force (Jan 20)

FOCUS
A low-grade handicap, run at a routine gallop. Not strong form overall, rated through the runner-up.
Lancaster Lad(IRE) Official explanation: jockey said colt hung left

99 PLAY GOLF @ LINGFIELD PARK H'CAP 1m (P)
3:50 (3:51) (Class 6) (0-50,50) 4-Y-0+ **£1,876** (£554; £277) **Stalls** High

Form RPR
50-6 **1** **Lordswood (IRE)**[5] 44 4-8-7 46 oh1 HayleyTurner 6 54+
(J R Best) *t.k.h: hld up in last trio: prog over 2f out: nt clr run briefly wl over 1f out: r.o fnl f to ld nr fin: won gng away* **4/1**[2]
150- **2** 1 1/4 **Jessica Wigmo**[35] 7028 5-8-9 48 JamesDoyle 5 53
(A W Carroll) *hld up in midfield: rapid prog 3f out to ld jst over 2f out and kicked on: worn down nr fin* **7/1**
404- **3** 2 **Riviera Red (IRE)**[10] 7278 8-8-7 46 oh1 ChrisCatlin 1 47
(L Montague Hall) *hld up towards rr: rdn and struggling over 3f out: styd on wl fnl f to snatch 3rd nr fin* **3/1**[1]
515- **4** nk **Maiden Investor**[11] 7275 5-8-11 50 MickyFenton 4 50
(Stef Liddiard) *hld up in midfield: prog over 2f out: rdn to chse ldr briefly 1f out: one pce after* **7/1**
010- **5** 3/4 **Kinsman (IRE)**[42] 6968 11-8-9 48 (p) JohnEgan 8 46
(T D McCarthy) *hld up in last trio: effrt on outer 3f out: sn outpcd: styd on fr over 1f out* **8/1**
602- **6** 1 **Ponte Vecchio (IRE)**[27] 7133 4-8-7 46 oh1 LiamJones 2 42
(J R Boyle) *chsd ldr to 3f out: sn lost pl u.p: one pce fr over 1f out* **5/1**[3]
00- **7** 3/4 **Newpark Spirit (IRE)**[81] 6348 5-8-7 46 oh1 (v[1]) NickyMackay 3 45+
(Emmanuel Hughes, Ire) *hld up in last trio: outpcd 3f out: effrt on inner and sme prog wl over 1f out: keeping on but n.d whn hmpd ins fnl f* **16/1**
000- **8** 1 3/4 **Frank's Quest (IRE)**[10] 7276 8-8-7 46 oh1 DavidKinsella 10 36
(A B Haynes) *led at str pce to jst over 2f out: wknd rapidly* **33/1**
300- **9** 4 **Blakeshall Hope**[11] 7274 6-8-7 46 oh1 GregFairley 7 27
(A J Chamberlain) *trckd ldng pair: chsd ldr 3f out to over 2f out: wknd rapidly over 1f out* **10/1**
500- **10** 7 **Stratn Jack**[12] 7251 4-8-11 50 VinceSlattery 9 15
(B G Powell) *chsd ldrs: rdn over 4f out: sn btn: wl bhd fnl 3f: t.o* **20/1**

1m 39.08s (0.88) **Going Correction** -0.125s/f (Stan) 10 Ran SP% **120.5**
Speed ratings (Par 101): **96,94,92,92,91 90,89,88,84,77**
CSF £33.47 CT £99.77 TOTE £5.40: £1.70, £3.10, £1.80; EX 45.40 Trifecta £203.90 Pool: £611.81 - 2.13 winning tickets. Place 6 £31.45, Place 5 £2.66.
Owner Rod Jordan **Bred** Blackdown Stud **Trained** Hucking, Kent

FOCUS
A selling-quality handicap and a rather messy affair run at a steady pace. The form does make sense.
Newpark Spirit(IRE) Official explanation: jockey said gelding was denied a clear run
T/Plt: £30.40 to a £1 stake. Pool: £52,827.45. 1,265.05 winning tickets. T/Qpdt: £2.70 to a £1 stake. Pool: £4,053.50. 1,078.20 winning tickets. JN

[44]WOLVERHAMPTON (A.W) (L-H)
Wednesday, January 9

OFFICIAL GOING: Standard to slow
Wind: Moderate, half behind Weather: Showers

100 STAY AT THE WOLVERHAMPTON HOLIDAY INN APPRENTICE CLASSIFIED STKS 5f 20y(P)
6:50 (6:52) (Class 7) 4-Y-0+ **£1,365** (£403; £201) **Stalls** Low

Form RPR
055- **1** **Dodaa (USA)**[9] 7283 5-9-0 43 AshleyHamblett 3 55
(N Wilson) *mde all: rdn over 1f out: r.o wl* **7/2**[1]
5-04 **2** 2 **Blushing Russian (IRE)**[4] 50 6-8-9 42 (b) BarrySavage[(5)] 6 48
(J M Bradley) *chsd ldrs: nt clr run on ins over 2f out: rdn and wnt 2nd wl over 1f out: no imp fnl f* **13/2**[3]
3 1 3/4 **Is Mise An Ri (IRE)**[35] 7036 6-8-9 37 JemmaMarshall[(5)] 7 42
(Emmanuel Hughes, Ire) *hld up towards rr: hdwy over 2f out: edgd lft fr jst over 1f out: one pce* **16/1**
66-0 **4** hd **Orchestration (IRE)**[4] 50 7-8-9 45 (v) MarkCoumbe[(5)] 13 41+
(S Parr) *in rr: swtchd lft and hdwy over 1f out: kpt on ins fnl f* **11/1**
540- **5** 1 **Ask No More**[13] 7250 5-8-11 45 (b) WilliamCarson[(3)] 11 44+
(J Ryan) *in rr: rdn and hdwy on ins 1f out: nt clr run ins fnl f: nt rcvr* **8/1**
000- **6** 1 1/4 **Borzoi Maestro**[71] 6565 7-9-0 42 HaddenFrost 9 33
(D G Bridgwater) *chsd ldrs: rdn over 2f out: no imp whn swtchd rt over 1f out* **22/1**
00-6 **7** 1 1/2 **Tibinta**[5] 46 4-8-9 43 RichardEvans[(5)] 4 27
(P D Evans) *rrd s and rdr lost iron briefly: nvr nr ldrs* **13/2**[3]
00-0 **8** hd **Dotty's Daughter**[4] 50 4-9-0 43 (p) NeilBrown 1 27
(B Storey) *towards rr: pushed along over 3f out: no hdwy whn carried lft over 1f out* **16/1**
066- **9** 1 1/2 **Prime Recreation**[26] 7137 11-9-0 41 JamesO'Reilly 10 21
(P S Felgate) *prom: wnt 2nd briefly 2f out: edgd rt 1f out: wknd ins fnl f* **25/1**
00V- **10** hd **Mind That Fox**[30] 7100 6-9-0 41 SladeO'Hara 5 21
(T Wall) *a in rr: hung lft over 1f out* **25/1**
00-0 **11** 1 **Mujart**[5] 46 4-9-0 44 (p) RussellKennemore 8 17
(J A Pickering) *s.i.s: sn mid-div: rdn and sme hdwy over 2f out: wknd over 1f out* **20/1**
050- **12** 1 1/2 **She's Our Beauty (IRE)**[26] 7138 5-8-11 43 (v) PatrickDonaghy[(3)] 2 12
(S T Mason) *chsd wnr tl rdn 2f out: wknd over 1f out* **5/1**[2]

64.01 secs (1.71) **Going Correction** +0.15s/f (Slow) 12 Ran SP% **113.6**
Speed ratings (Par 97): **96,92,90,89,88 86,83,83,80,80 79,76**
CSF £22.88 TOTE £5.60: £1.10, £2.40, £7.60; EX 23.50.
Owner Paul & Linda Dixon **Bred** Silverleaf Farm Inc **Trained** Flaxton, N Yorks

FOCUS
A very moderate contest won in good style by Dodaa. He may go close again but the rest cannot be trusted to reproduce their efforts next time.
Ask No More Official explanation: jockey said gelding was denied a clear run
Tibinta Official explanation: jockey said filly reared as stalls opened
Prime Recreation Official explanation: jockey said gelding hung right-handed

101 HAPPY HALF TERM BREAKS @ PONTINS.COM (S) STKS 1m 141y(P)
7:20 (7:20) (Class 6) 4-Y-0+ **£1,774** (£523; £262) **Stalls** Low

Form RPR
34-4 **1** **Arctic Desert**[6] 24 8-9-5 59 (t) HayleyTurner 8 64
(Miss Gay Kelleway) *t.k.h in rr: hdwy and swtchd rt over 2f out: wnt 2nd and edgd lft wl over 1f out: rdn to ld cl home* **5/2**[1]
542- **2** 1/2 **Climate (IRE)**[11] 7274 9-8-8 52 RussellKennemore[(5)] 10 57
(R Hollinshead) *hld up in mid-div: hdwy over 3f out: led and edgd lft 2f out: sn rdn and flashed tail: hdd cl home* **7/2**[2]
206- **3** 5 **Pianoforte (USA)**[26] 7143 6-8-13 63 (b) MickyFenton 4 45
(E J Alston) *hld up in mid-div: hdwy over 3f out: rdn over 2f out: wknd ins fnl f* **7/2**[2]
30-0 **4** 3 **Personify**[7] 21 6-8-13 69 (p) TGMcLaughlin 7 38
(R A Harris) *hld up in tch: rdn over 2f out: nt clr run briefly wl over 1f out: hung lft and wknd jst over 1f out* **7/1**[3]
000- **5** 3 1/2 **Stargazy**[10] 7279 4-8-12 49 LiamJones 6 30
(W G M Turner) *t.k.h: w ldr: led 4f out: rdn and hdd 2f out: sn sltly hmpd: wknd over 1f out* **33/1**
500- **6** 6 **Yenaled**[35] 6452 11-8-10 37 AndrewElliott[(3)] 2 17
(J M Bradley) *a towards rr* **50/1**
33-5 **7** 10 **Namroud (USA)**[3] 66 9-8-13 65 JimCrowley 1 —
(D Carroll) *rdn over 4f out: a towards rr* **8/1**
250- **8** 3 **Not Now Lewis (IRE)**[33] 7057 4-8-12 57 (b[1]) TPQueally 3 —
(J A Osborne) *led: hdd 4f out: sn rdn: wknd over 2f out* **8/1**
000- **9** 9 **Skiddaw Fox**[26] 7137 4-8-12 40 (p) DaleGibson 5 —
(Mrs L Williamson) *t.k.h: prom tl lost pl 4f out* **100/1**

1m 52.99s (2.49) **Going Correction** +0.15s/f (Slow)
WFA 4 from 6yo+ 1lb 9 Ran SP% **113.6**
Speed ratings (Par 101): **100,99,95,92,89 84,75,72,64**
CSF £11.02 TOTE £4.00: £1.50, £1.10, £1.50; EX 9.30.There was no bid for the winner. Climate was claimed by P. D. Evans for £5,500.
Owner Miss Gay Kelleway **Bred** Whatton Manor Stud **Trained** Exning, Suffolk

FOCUS
An ordinary seller in which the front two were nicely clear.
Not Now Lewis(IRE) Official explanation: jockey said gelding hung right-handed
Skiddaw Fox Official explanation: jockey said colt hung right-handed

102 CAPTAIN CROC MAKES PONTIN'S ROCK H'CAP 7f 32y(P)
7:50 (7:50) (Class 5) (0-70,70) 3-Y-0 **£2,331** (£693; £346; £173) **Stalls** High

Form RPR
651- **1** **Bookish**[35] 7031 3-9-2 68 GregFairley 5 75
(M Johnston) *chsd ldr: led wl over 2f out: clr whn rdn wl over 1f out: r.o* **9/4**[1]
612- **2** 1 1/2 **Rich Kid (IRE)**[50] 6880 3-9-4 70 TGMcLaughlin 6 73
(R A Harris) *hld up in tch: chsd wnr over 2f out: sn rdn: kpt on ins fnl f* **10/3**[2]
040- **3** 3 **Bury Treasure (IRE)**[136] 4854 3-8-11 63 HayleyTurner 4 58
(Miss Gay Kelleway) *s.i.s: in rr: hdwy and hung lft fr 2f out: one pce fnl f* **9/1**
414- **4** nk **Feeling Fresh (IRE)**[12] 7260 3-8-9 64 PatrickMathers[(3)] 3 61+
(Paul Green) *hld up: hdwy over 1f out: one pce fnl f* **7/2**[3]
5 11 **Moonlitesilhouette (IRE)**[33] 7062 3-8-12 64 MickyFenton 2 28
(Noel Lawlor, Ire) *hld up in tch: pushed along 4f out: sltly hmpd on ins 2f out: sn wknd* **9/2**
030- **6** 20 **Yattendon**[13] 7245 3-8-11 63 (v[1]) JamesDoyle 1 —
(S Kirk) *led: hdd wl over 2f out: sn wknd* **14/1**

1m 32.14s (2.54) **Going Correction** +0.15s/f (Slow) 6 Ran SP% **110.9**
Speed ratings (Par 97): **96,94,90,90,77 55**
CSF £9.70 TOTE £2.20: £1.02, £5.50; EX 10.30.
Owner Sheikh Hamdan Bin Mohammed Al Maktoum **Bred** Darley **Trained** Middleham Moor, N Yorks

FOCUS
Not a bad race for the grade, and the winner looks capable of collecting the hat-trick.
Bury Treasure(IRE) Official explanation: jockey said colt hung left-handed
Feeling Fresh(IRE) ♦ Official explanation: jockey said colt was denied a clear run

103 WOLVERHAMPTON-RACECOURSE.CO.UK CLAIMING STKS 7f 32y(P)
8:20 (8:20) (Class 5) 4-Y-0+ **£2,590** (£770; £385; £192) **Stalls** High

Form RPR
56-2 **1** **Sir Douglas**[7] 15 5-9-3 70 (b[1]) TGMcLaughlin 2 74
(R A Harris) *t.k.h: mde all: hung rt fr 2f out: rdn over 1f out: drvn out* **9/2**
2-14 **2** 1 1/4 **Obe Royal**[5] 49 4-8-10 62 (b) RichardEvans[(7)] 6 71+
(P D Evans) *hld up: swtchd rt over 2f out: hdwy whn nt clr run wl over 1f out: rdn and r.o ins fnl f: tk 2nd cl home* **3/1**[2]
122- **3** hd **One More Round (USA)**[10] 7279 10-9-4 83 (b) TPQueally 3 71
(Ollie Pears) *hld up: hdwy over 2f out: chsd wnr wl over 1f out: sn rdn: no ex towards fin* **5/4**[1]
016- **4** 2 **Circus Polka (USA)**[14] 7233 4-8-13 65 (bt) LiamJones 5 61
(W M Brisbourne) *sn pushed along: prom: chsd wnr 4f out tl rdn and hung lft wl over 1f out: hung lft ins fnl f: nt run on* **4/1**[3]
050- **5** 1 1/4 **Spy Gun (USA)**[29] 7111 8-8-0 45 (p) PatrickDonaghy[(7)] 1 51
(T Wall) *chsd wnr 3f: sn lost pl: n.d after* **40/1**
515- **6** 7 **Mountain Pass (USA)**[12] 7251 6-8-4 60 (p) DavidProbert[(7)] 4 36
(B J Llewellyn) *s.s: hld up: hdwy over 3f out: rdn over 2f out: wknd wl over 1f out* **16/1**

1m 32.05s (2.45) **Going Correction** +0.15s/f (Slow) 6 Ran SP% **115.9**
Speed ratings (Par 103): **96,94,94,92,90 82**
CSF £19.08 TOTE £5.70: £1.60, £2.20; EX 29.30.
Owner Leeway Group Limited **Bred** Overbury Partnership **Trained** Earlswood, Monmouths

The Form Book, Raceform Ltd, Compton, RG20 6NL

FOCUS
A very moderate claimer, where all of the horses wore some sort of headgear and gave the impression that they would rather not win if they could get away with it. The early fractions of the race were very quick in comparison with the other race at this distance on the night, but the latter stages were much slower.

104 TO PONTIN'S FOR HALF TERM H'CAP — 1m 1f 103y(P)
8:50 (8:50) (Class 5) (0-75,75) 4-Y-O+ — **£2,730** (£806; £403) **Stalls** Low

Form — RPR
203- **1** **Given A Choice (IRE)**[56] [6806] 6-9-5 **75**............................. TPQueally 2 89
(J G Given) *hld up: hdwy 3f out: wnt 2nd 2f out: led wl ins fnl f: pushed out* **7/1**
V44- **2** *1* **Alonso De Guzman (IRE)**[13] [7249] 4-7-12 **62**........ PatrickDonaghy(7) 5 74
(J R Boyle) *led: clr whn rdn wl over 1f out: edgd rt and hdd wl ins fnl f: no ex* **7/2**[3]
00-6 **3** *8* **Prince Charlemagne (IRE)**[6] [28] 5-9-0 **73**............ AndrewElliott(3) 1 68
(K R Burke) *a.p: chsd wnr wl over 3f out to 2f out: sn wknd* **11/4**[2]
2/0- **4** *13* **Kings Confession (IRE)**[251] [1440] 5-8-8 **64**.................. JimCrowley 4 32
(D Carroll) *hld up in tch: wknd 3f out* **40/1**
040- **5** *2 1/2* **Desert Leader (IRE)**[82] [6314] 7-8-11 **67**.......................... DaleGibson 3 30
(R W Price) *w ldr tl wknd qckly wl over 3f out* **14/1**
112- **6** *3* **Moment Of Clarity**[26] [7146] 6-8-2 **65**.....................(p) KrishGundowry(7) 6 21
(R C Guest) *a in rr: fin lame* **6/5**[1]

2m 2.27s (0.57) **Going Correction** +0.15s/f (Slow)
WFA 4 from 5yo+ 1lb — 6 Ran SP% **115.9**
Speed ratings (Par 103): **107,106,99,87,85 82**
CSF £32.55 TOTE £7.40: £2.50, £2.70; EX 29.20.
Owner Mike J Beadle **Bred** Rathasker Stud **Trained** Willoughton, Lincs

FOCUS
A fair event but both Moment Of Clarity (lame) and Prince Charlemagne (wrong course) ran below expectations.
Moment Of Clarity Official explanation: jockey said gelding ran flat; vet said gelding returned lame

105 PONTIN'S BRILLIANT BLUE COATS ARE BEST H'CAP — 1m 5f 194y(P)
9:20 (9:21) (Class 4) (0-85,85) 4-Y-O+ — **£4,533** (£1,348; £674; £336) **Stalls** Low

Form — RPR
121- **1** **Birkside**[14] [7236] 5-9-6 **85**.. JamieKyne(7) 7 96
(D Carroll) *stdd s: hld up in rr: hdwy over 3f out: swtchd rt ent st: led ins fnl f: edgd lft towards fin: styd on wl* **4/1**
213- **2** *2* **Jack Rolfe**[67] [6007] 6-8-11 **76**...................................... WilliamCarson(7) 5 84
(G L Moore) *hld up in tch: wnt 2nd 4f out: rdn to ld over 2f out: hdd and nt qckn ins fnl f* **3/1**[2]
4/1- **3** *1 1/4* **Tartan Tie**[225] [2118] 4-9-5 **83**.. GregFairley 1 89+
(M Johnston) *t.k.h: chsd ldr: led over 4f out: rdn and hdd over 2f out: no ex ins fnl f* **11/4**[1]
025- **4** *3* **Noble Minstrel**[14] [7236] 5-8-13 **71**....................................(t) JimCrowley 4 73
(S C Williams) *hld up towards rr: hdwy over 4f out: wknd over 1f out* **7/2**[3]
431- **5** *29* **Abounding**[20] [7205] 4-8-0 **67**.. AndrewElliott(3) 3 28
(M J Attwater) *s.i.s: pushed along over 4f out: a bhd: t.o* **11/1**
153- **6** *18* **Osolomio (IRE)**[109] [5623] 5-9-7 **79**..................................... DaleGibson 6 15
(Jennie Candlish) *t.k.h: led: hdd over 4f out: wknd wl over 3f out: t.o* **16/1**
502- **7** *35* **Bronze Dancer (IRE)**[81] [6325] 6-8-10 **68**......................... PaulMulrennan 2 —
(B Storey) *chsd ldrs: rdn over 6f out: wknd qckly over 5f out: sn t.o* **33/1**

3m 7.20s (1.20) **Going Correction** +0.15s/f (Slow)
WFA 4 from 5yo+ 6lb — 7 Ran SP% **111.0**
Speed ratings (Par 105): **106,104,104,102,85 75,55**
CSF £15.41 TOTE £4.80: £1.70, £2.30; EX 13.90 Place 6 £133.83, Place 5 £59.60.
Owner Document Express Ltd **Bred** Pendley Farm **Trained** Sledmere, E Yorks

FOCUS
A fair event on paper but one would suspect that the winner did not need to run anywhere near his current mark to win.
Bronze Dancer(IRE) Official explanation: jockey said gelding stopped very quickly
T/Plt: £68.00 to a £1 stake. Pool: £103,136.40. 1,106.75 winning tickets. T/Qpdt: £25.50 to a £1 stake. Pool: £5,860.60. 169.90 winning tickets. KH

[78]SOUTHWELL (L-H)
Thursday, January 10

OFFICIAL GOING: Standard
Wind: Strong, across Weather: Overcast and showers

106 HAVE A BREAK - HAVE A PONTIN'S BREAK APPRENTICE CLAIMING STKS — 5f (F)
12:40 (12:40) (Class 6) 4-Y-O+ — **£1,774** (£523; £262) **Stalls** High

Form — RPR
300- **1** **Grimes Faith**[13] [7261] 5-9-10 70...................................(b) AndrewMullen 4 79
(K A Ryan) *trckd ldrs: smooth hdwy 1/2-way and sn cl up: led 1f out: pushed clr ins fnl f* **10/3**[2]
000- **2** *1 3/4* **High Reach**[48] [6910] 8-8-12 52.. AndrewElliott 3 61
(J G M O'Shea) *cl up: led 1/2-way: rdn wl over 1f out: drvn and hdd 1f out: kpt on same pce* **9/2**[3]
24-4 **3** *5* **Chatshow (USA)**[6] [45] 7-9-1 62................................ MarkCoumbe(5) 6 51
(A W Carroll) *towards rr: pushed along 2f out: sn rdn and styd on ins fnl f* **2/1**[1]
6-60 **4** *nk* **Time Share (IRE)**[2] [82] 4-8-2 44.......................(be) KirstyMilczarek(3) 1 35
(G C Bravery) *sn cl up on outer: rdn along 2f out and grad wknd* **11/2**
003- **5** *1 1/2* **Creme Brulee**[27] [7138] 5-8-6 45 ow1.................... RussellKennemore(3) 7 33
(P T Dalton) *led to 1/2-way: sn rdn along and wknd over 1f out* **17/2**
05-6 **6** *1/2* **Aboustar**[4] [64] 8-9-9 42.......................................(b) AdamCarter(7) 2 38
(M Brittain) *cl up: rdn along 1/2-way: sn edgd lft and wknd* **12/1**
00-0 **7** *14* **Spinning Game**[6] [46] 4-8-2 44.............................(b) PatrickDonaghy(5) 5 —
(D W Chapman) *sn outpcd and a bhd* **40/1**

59.85 secs (0.15) **Going Correction** -0.25s/f (Stan) — 7 Ran SP% **110.6**
Speed ratings (Par 101): **93,90,82,81,79 78,56**
CSF £17.36 TOTE £3.90: £1.80, £2.50; EX 18.30.
Owner Mrs Angie Bailey **Bred** John Grimes **Trained** Hambleton, N Yorks

FOCUS
Moderate claiming form and, although the first two were having their first tries here, a race to be against overall.
Chatshow(USA) Official explanation: jockey said gelding didn't face the kickback

107 ARENALEISUREPLC.COM MAIDEN STKS — 1m 3f (F)
1:10 (1:11) (Class 5) 4-Y-O+ — **£2,457** (£725; £362) **Stalls** Low

Form — RPR
22-5 **1** **Calculating (IRE)**[7] [27] 4-9-3 70.................................... HayleyTurner 3 76+
(M D I Usher) *cl up: led 2f out: sn rdn clr: easily* **8/11**[1]
04-5 **2** *9* **Flight Dream (FR)**[7] [22] 5-9-6 0.. TPQueally 2 59
(M G Quinlan) *led: rdn along 3f out: hdd 2f out: sn drvn and kpt on same pce* **11/4**[2]
344- **3** *8* **Spares And Repairs**[14] [7242] 5-9-6 63.............................. ChrisCatlin 4 45
(Mrs S Lamyman) *hld up: hdwy to chse ldng pair over 4f out: rdn 3f out and sn outpcd* **13/2**[3]
0 **4** *6* **Newgate (UAE)**[6] [48] 4-9-3 0.. LiamJones 5 35
(D W Chapman) *hld up in rr: gd hdwy 4f out: chsd ldng pair 3f out: sn rdn and btn* **40/1**
5 *12* **Spellman**[50] 4-9-3 0... JamesDoyle 7 15
(N P Littmoden) *a in rr: bhd fnl 3f* **10/1**
6 *1/2* **Able Dara**[39] 5-9-6 0.. PaulMulrennan 6 14
(N Bycroft) *chsd ldng pair: rdn along 5f out and sn wknd* **40/1**
7 *nk* **Moorside Diamond** 4-8-9 0.. AndrewElliott(3) 1 8
(A D Brown) *chsd ldrs: rdn along over 4f out: sn wknd* **50/1**

2m 27.21s (-0.79) **Going Correction** -0.075s/f (Stan)
WFA 4 from 5yo 3lb — 7 Ran SP% **113.8**
Speed ratings (Par 103): **103,96,90,86,77 77,76**
CSF £2.88 TOTE £1.60: £1.10, £1.90; EX 3.50.
Owner Brian Rogan **Bred** Darley **Trained** Upper Lambourn, Berks

FOCUS
A weak maiden and they finished well strung out at the finish, with the form rated around the first two.
Able Dara Official explanation: jockey said gelding had no more to give

108 PACK YOUR SMILE FOR PONTIN'S (S) STKS — 7f (F)
1:40 (1:40) (Class 6) 3-Y-O — **£1,774** (£523; £262) **Stalls** Low

Form — RPR
25-0 **1** **Her Name Is Rio (IRE)**[6] [38] 3-8-7 62.............................. JohnEgan 3 57
(A Berry) *t.k.h: cl up: lft in ld after 2f: rdn along and hdd over 3f out: sn lost pl: swtchd rt and drvn 2f out: hdwy over 1f out: styd on to ld ins fnl f* **7/2**[2]
006- **2** *1 3/4* **Mama Leo**[27] [7136] 3-8-2 48................................(b[1]) KirstyMilczarek(5) 6 52
(J G M O'Shea) *cl up whn hmpd after 2f: hdwy to chal over 2f out: led wl over 1f out: rdn and hdd ins fnl f* **14/1**
52-2 **3** *2* **Copperbottomed (IRE)**[2] [81] 3-9-4 67...................(be) PatCosgrave 4 58
(J R Boyle) *dwlt: t.k.h and sn trcking ldrs: hmpd after 2f: hdwy to ld over 3f out: rdn along over 2f out: hdd wl over 1f out: sn drvn and kpt on one pce* **1/2**[1]
0- **4** *14* **Orphan Boy**[14] [7240] 3-8-12 0.. TPQueally 2 14
(M G Quinlan) *trckd ldrs: rdn along 3f out: outpcd fnl 2f* **33/1**
460- **U** **Sir Joey**[10] [7286] 3-8-12 52.. ChrisCatlin 5 —
(J T Stimpson) *led tl stmbld and uns rdr after 2f* **8/1**[3]

1m 32.93s (2.63) **Going Correction** -0.075s/f (Stan) — 5 Ran SP% **109.6**
Speed ratings (Par 95): **84,82,79,63,—**
CSF £40.29 TOTE £3.70: £1.10, £4.40; EX 36.00.The winner was sold to Nigel Underwood for 6,000gns.
Owner A B Parr **Bred** Tommy Newton **Trained** Cockerham, Lancs

FOCUS
Moderate form and not totally reliable given that the second and third were both hampered in the early part of the race by Sir Joey unseating his rider. The runner-up is the best guide to the form.

109 SOUTHWELL-RACECOURSE.CO.UK H'CAP — 6f (F)
2:10 (2:10) (Class 6) (0-60,60) 4-Y-O+ — **£1,911** (£564; £282) **Stalls** Low

Form — RPR
/41- **1** **Diriculous**[43] [6963] 4-9-3 59.. JohnEgan 3 73+
(T G Mills) *mde most: rdn wl over 1f out: kpt on wl fnl f* **6/4**[1]
002- **2** *1 3/4* **The Geester**[27] [7138] 4-8-8 50..................................(b) PaulEddery 11 55
(S R Bowring) *t.k.h: trckd ldrs on outer: effrt 2f out: effrt wl over 1f out and sn rdn: styd on ins fnl f* **20/1**
50-0 **3** *nk* **Cleveland**[6] [42] 6-8-13 60.................................. RussellKennemore(5) 7 64
(R Hollinshead) *t.k.h: cl up: rdn wl over 1f out: kpt on same pce* **5/2**[2]
006- **4** *1/2* **Imperial Sword**[23] [7180] 5-8-12 54.................................(b) PaulFessey 4 56
(T D Barron) *chsd ldrs: outpcd 1/2-way: rdn and hdwy to chse ldrs 2f out: drvn and one pce fnl f* **14/1**
000- **5** *1 1/2* **Plateau**[12] [7271] 9-9-3 59.. TPQueally 2 57
(C R Dore) *towards rr: hdwy on inner 2f out: sn rdn and no imp appr fnl f* **12/1**
40-4 **6** *hd* **Soba Jones**[4] [64] 11-8-9 51 ow1.................................. PaulMulrennan 5 48
(J Balding) *plld hrd: chsd ldrs: rdn 2f out and grad wknd* **7/1**[3]
020- **7** *1 3/4* **Boy Dancer (IRE)**[220] [2302] 5-8-12 54.............................. PatCosgrave 10 45
(J J Quinn) *sn pushed along: a towards rr* **7/1**[3]
000- **8** *9* **Minimum Fuss (IRE)**[14] [7238] 4-8-1 46 oh1.............(b) AndrewElliott(3) 9 9
(M C Chapman) *t.k.h: cl up: rdn along over 2f out and sn wknd* **80/1**
056- **9** *3 1/2* **Totally Free**[162] [4071] 4-9-2 58.....................................(v) HayleyTurner 8 9
(M D I Usher) *outpcd and in rr fr 1/2-way* **20/1**

1m 16.28s (-0.22) **Going Correction** -0.075s/f (Stan) — 9 Ran SP% **118.7**
Speed ratings (Par 101): **101,98,98,97,95 95,93,81,76**
CSF £38.55 CT £76.35 TOTE £2.80: £1.50, £2.50, £1.30; EX 26.20 Trifecta £43.90 Pool: £215.95 - 3.49 winning tickets..
Owner Sherwoods Transport Ltd **Bred** Sherwoods Transport Ltd **Trained** Headley, Surrey

FOCUS
A moderate handicap won by an unexposed performer but the form, rated through te runner-up, is pretty weak.
Soba Jones Official explanation: jockey said gelding was too free early stages

110 GREAT FAMILY HOLIDAY DEALS @ PONTINS.COM H'CAP — 1m (F)
2:40 (2:48) (Class 5) (0-70,75) 4-Y-O+ — **£2,593**

Form — RPR
30-2 **1** **Rebellious Spirit**[6] [40] 5-9-0 65.. ChrisCatlin 4 —
(P W Hiatt) *chsd ldrs tl p.u after 2f whn false s called: returned to starting post and later deemed to have walked over*

(-103.70) course record — 1 Ran

Owner Mrs Lucia Stockley & Ken Read **Bred** Car Colston Hall Stud **Trained** Hook Norton, Oxon
■ Stewards' Enquiry : Paul Mulrennan seven-day ban: ignored false start and recall flag (Jan 21-27)
Kirsty Milczarek seven-day ban: ignored false start and recall flag (Jan 21-27)
Andrew Elliott seven-day ban: ignored false start and recall flag (Jan 21-27)
Pat Cosgrave seven-day ban: ignored false start and recall flag (Jan 21-27)

FOCUS
A shambles of a contest in which a false start was signalled after Jord's stall opened early, but only Chris Catlin on Rebellious Spirit had the sense to pull up his mount. The other four ignored or did not see the recall flag and raced on, Jord making all from Rigat and Dado Mush with Hucking Heat tailed off. They were all deemed non-runners, having completed the course, but Rebellious Spirit was allowed to go back to the start and complete in his own time for a walkover. Bets were voided and the riders of the other four all received seven-day bans.

111 TREAT THE FAMILY @ PONTINS H'CAP — 7f (F)
3:10 (3:15) (Class 5) (0-75,76) 4-Y-0+ — **£2,593** (£765; £383) **Stalls** Low

Form — RPR
00-4 **1** **Flores Sea (USA)**[3] 72 4-8-10 67 PaulFessey 5 — 77
(T D Barron) *mde all: rdn over 2f out: drvn ent fnl f: hld on wl* **8/1**[3]
4-1 **2** *¾* **Sweet Pickle**[3] 72 7-9-5 76 6ex (e) PatCosgrave 4 — 84
(J R Boyle) *chsd ldng pair: hdwy to chal 2f out: sn rdn and ev ch tl drvn and no ex wl ins fnl f* **7/4**[1]
615- **3** *8* **Cha Cha Cha**[26] 7158 4-9-4 75 PaulMulrennan 3 — 61
(K A Ryan) *cl up: rdn along over 2f out: sn drvn and kpt on same pce fr wl over 1f out* **7/2**[2]
600- **4** *4* **Seneschal**[25] 7164 7-8-9 66 ow1 TPQueally 2 — 42
(A B Haynes) *hld up in tch: effrt 3f out: sn rdn and btn* **7/4**[1]

1m 28.45s (-1.85) **Going Correction** -0.075s/f (Stan) — **4** Ran SP% **106.1**
Speed ratings (Par 103): **110,109,100,95**
CSF £21.28 TOTE £8.90; EX 16.00.
Owner T D Barron **Bred** Beckie McLay-Irons **Trained** Maunby, N Yorks

FOCUS
A competitive contest on paper, but Flores Sea was able to dominate and caused a minor surprise in a race run at a good gallop.

112 SOUTHWELL RACECOURSE FOR CONFERENCES H'CAP — 5f (F)
3:40 (3:40) (Class 6) (0-60,60) 3-Y-0 — **£1,911** (£564; £282) **Stalls** High

Form — RPR
000- **1** **Orpen's Art (IRE)**[30] 7106 3-7-13 **46** oh1 KirstyMilczarek(5) 4 — 58
(N A Callaghan) *mde all: shkn up ent fnl f and kpt on* **2/1**[1]
043- **2** *2* **Holly Golightley**[21] 7195 3-8-13 **55** (b) PaulMulrennan 6 — 60
(K A Ryan) *trckd ldrs: smooth hdwy 1/2-way: chal over 1f out: sn rdn and kpt on same pce* **7/2**[2]
254- **3** *5* **Upstanding**[93] 6074 3-9-1 **60** MarkLawson(3) 2 — 47
(M Brittain) *chsd ldrs: rdn wl over 1f out: drvn and one pce ins fnl f* **4/1**[3]
300- **4** *1½* **East Coast Girl (IRE)**[57] 6812 3-9-4 **60** TGMcLaughlin 3 — 41
(S W Hall) *cl up: rdn along wl over 1f out: wknd appr fnl f* **12/1**
004- **5** *2½* **Westwood Dawn**[24] 7170 3-8-1 **46** oh1 DuranFentiman(3) 7 — 18
(Mrs N Macauley) *chsd ldrs: rdn along 2f out: sn wknd* **16/1**
010- **6** *1½* **Captain Crooner (IRE)**[13] 7260 3-8-5 **47** LiamJones 1 — 14
(D Shaw) *dwlt and wnt lft s: in tch and rdn along 1/2-way: sn no prog* **15/2**
02-6 **7** *1* **Galley Slave (IRE)**[4] 70 3-8-13 **58** AndrewElliott(3) 5 — 21
(M C Chapman) *s.i.s: a bhd* **13/2**

58.60 secs (-1.10) **Going Correction** -0.25s/f (Stan) — **7** Ran SP% **114.2**
Speed ratings (Par 95): **103,99,91,89,85 83,81**
CSF £9.11 TOTE £2.80: £1.60, £2.10; EX 8.40 Place 6 £136.82, Place 5 £55.51.
Owner Matthew Green **Bred** Fin A Co S R L **Trained** Newmarket, Suffolk

FOCUS
A poor handicap but a sound gallop and the form is rated around the principals.
T/Plt: £91.20 to a £1 stake. Pool: £50,910.90. 407.35 winning tickets. T/Qpdt: £42.20 to a £1 stake. Pool: £3,782.50. 66.30 winning tickets. JR

100 WOLVERHAMPTON (A.W) (L-H)
Thursday, January 10

OFFICIAL GOING: Standard
Wind: Moderate, behind

113 WOLVERHAMPTON-RACECOURSE.CO.UK H'CAP — 5f 20y(P)
6:50 (6:51) (Class 5) (0-75,71) 4-Y-0+ — **£2,457** (£725; £362) **Stalls** Low

Form — RPR
636- **1** **Baileys Outshine**[20] 7215 4-8-13 **66** TPQueally 4 — 76
(J G Given) *hld up in rr: rdn and hdwy appr fnl f: led fnl 75yds* **9/1**
15-2 **2** *1* **Sands Crooner (IRE)**[7] 29 5-8-2 **62** (v) PatrickDonaghy(7) 2 — 68
(D Shaw) *s.i.s: sn in tch: hrd rdn to ld appr fnl f: hdd fnl 75yds* **11/8**[1]
321- **3** *2* **Pegasus Dancer (FR)**[19] 7221 4-9-4 **71** (p) PaulMulrennan 1 — 70
(K A Ryan) *trckd ldr tl rdn over 1f out: one pce fnl f* **11/4**[2]
225- **4** *¾* **Fizzlephut (IRE)**[20] 7215 6-9-0 **67** JamesDoyle 3 — 63
(Miss J R Tooth) *led tl rdn and hdd appr fnl f: fdd ins fnl f* **3/1**[3]
040- **5** *6* **Hawaii Prince**[102] 5834 4-8-13 **66** PaulFessey 5 — 41
(S T Mason) *in tch on outside: rdn and wknd over 1f out* **18/1**

62.88 secs (0.58) **Going Correction** +0.15s/f (Slow) — **5** Ran SP% **109.0**
Speed ratings (Par 103): **105,103,100,99,89**
CSF £21.65 TOTE £16.30: £5.60, £1.10; EX 31.30.
Owner G R Bailey Ltd (Baileys Horse Feeds) **Bred** P And Mrs A G Venner **Trained** Willoughton, Lincs

FOCUS
A modest sprint and the form looks fair rated though the runner-up.

114 STAY AT THE WOLVERHAMPTON HOLIDAY INN MAIDEN STKS — 5f 20y(P)
7:20 (7:20) (Class 5) 3-Y-0+ — **£2,331** (£693; £346; £173) **Stalls** Low

Form — RPR
32-2 **1** **Chivola (IRE)**[8] 19 3-8-12 75 TomEaves 1 — 59
(B Smart) *mde all: rdn out ins fnl f* **4/5**[1]
2-53 **2** *1½* **Earl Compton (IRE)**[6] 45 4-9-13 51 (v) MickyFenton 3 — 60
(Stef Liddiard) *racd in 4th: rdn 2f out: styd on to go 2nd towards fin* **16/1**
42- **3** *½* **Moon Bound (IRE)**[12] 7264 3-8-12 0 TPQueally 4 — 52
(W R Muir) *t.k.h: in tch: chsd wnr 2f out tl one pce and lost 2nd nr fin* **2/1**[2]
40- **4** *5* **Miss Bronte**[147] 4522 3-8-7 0 HayleyTurner 2 — 29
(R Hollinshead) *trckd ldr to 2f out: rdn and wknd over 1f out* **10/1**[3]
/00- **5** *5* **Lady Fas (IRE)**[70] 6609 5-9-3 40 KirstyMilczarek(5) 5 — 17
(A W Carroll) *wnt rt s: racd wd: lost tch ins fnl 2f* **66/1**

63.50 secs (1.20) **Going Correction** +0.15s/f (Slow)
WFA 3 from 4yo+ 15lb — **5** Ran SP% **105.4**
Speed ratings (Par 103): **100,97,96,88,80**
CSF £12.89 TOTE £1.70: £1.10, £11.90; EX 9.00.
Owner Prime Equestrian **Bred** Mohammad Al-Qatami **Trained** Hambleton, N Yorks

FOCUS
A weak maiden. The form is put into perspective by the 51-rated runner-up with the first and third below their best.
Lady Fas(IRE) Official explanation: jockey said mare hung right

115 DINE IN THE HORIZONS RESTAURANT (S) STKS — 7f 32y(P)
7:50 (7:50) (Class 6) 4-Y-0+ — **£1,774** (£523; £262) **Stalls** High

Form — RPR
42-2 **1** **Northern Desert (IRE)**[7] 24 9-8-5 65 (p) KirstyMilczarek(5) 6 — 67
(S Curran) *a.p: smooth hdwy to ld over 1f out: edgd lft but sn clr: easily* **6/5**[1]
4-00 **2** *5* **Lucius Verrus (USA)**[3] 71 8-8-10 55 (v) DeanMcKeown 5 — 53
(D Shaw) *t.k.h: racd wd in rr: hdwy on outside ent fnl f: r.o to go 2nd nr fin* **11/1**
116- **3** *nk* **Dancing Deano (IRE)**[26] 7148 6-8-10 57 (v) RussellKennemore(5) 7 — 57
(R Hollinshead) *trckd ldr: led over 2f out: hdd over 1f out: kpt on but lost 2nd nr fin* **12/1**
50-5 **4** *½* **Spy Gun (USA)**[1] 103 8-8-3 45 (p) PatrickDonaghy(7) 1 — 51
(T Wall) *in rr: hdwy on outside over 1f out: r.o fnl f: nvr nrr* **33/1**
05-3 **5** *nk* **Snow Bunting**[7] 32 10-9-1 52 TPQueally 3 — 55
(Jedd O'Keeffe) *in rr: mde sme late hdwy* **10/1**
562- **6** *1* **Gifted Heir (IRE)**[21] 7001 4-8-10 56 MickyFenton 2 — 47
(A Bailey) *trckd ldrs tl rdn and lost pl 3f out: sn in rr* **7/2**[2]
502- **7** *3½* **The Jailer**[50] 6895 5-8-3 55 (p) MCGeran(7) 4 — 38
(J G M O'Shea) *set str pce tl hdd over 2f out: wknd rapidly* **5/1**[3]

1m 30.6s (1.00) **Going Correction** +0.15s/f (Slow) — **7** Ran SP% **112.4**
Speed ratings (Par 101): **104,98,97,97,97 95,91**
CSF £15.50 TOTE £2.30: £1.20, £4.80; EX 21.90.There was no bid for the winner.
Owner Miss N Henton **Bred** J P Hardiman **Trained** Hatford, Oxon

FOCUS
A typically poor seller. The winner scored as he was entitled to at the weights with the placed horses below their best and the next two limiting the form.
Gifted Heir(IRE) Official explanation: jockey said colt hung right

116 SPONSOR A RACE BY CALLING 0870 220 2442 H'CAP — 1m 141y(P)
8:20 (8:21) (Class 5) (0-75,73) 3-Y-0 — **£2,457** (£725; £362) **Stalls** Low

Form — RPR
00-5 **1** **Boomtown**[8] 20 3-8-8 **63** GregFairley 3 — 76+
(M Johnston) *trckd ldr: led wl over 2f out: clr over 1f out: easily* **7/4**[1]
1- **2** *6* **My Mate Max**[28] 7130 3-8-13 **73** RussellKennemore(5) 4 — 76+
(R Hollinshead) *in tch: short of room wl over 1f out: swtchd rt: r.o to go 2nd nr fin* **9/4**[2]
610- **3** *½* **Kryptonite (IRE)**[21] 7204 3-8-4 **66** GabrielHannon(7) 5 — 64
(J W Hills) *hld up: rdn to go 2nd wl over 1f out: one pce and lost 2nd nr fin* **6/1**
5 **4** *7* **Moonlitesilhouette (IRE)**[1] 102 3-8-9 **64** MickyFenton 6 — 46
(Noel Lawlor, Ire) *led tl hdd wl over 2f out: sn wknd* **16/1**
113- **5** *12* **Marino Prince (FR)**[21] 7204 3-8-9 **71** PatrickDonaghy(7) 1 — 25
(T Wall) *s.i.s: rdn to trck ldrs 6f out: lost tch over 2f out* **3/1**[3]

1m 52.59s (2.09) **Going Correction** +0.15s/f (Slow) — **5** Ran SP% **112.3**
Speed ratings (Par 97): **102,96,96,90,79**
CSF £6.16 TOTE £3.20: £1.60, £1.10; EX 4.60.
Owner Mark Johnston Racing Ltd **Bred** Gainsborough Stud Management Ltd **Trained** Middleham Moor, N Yorks

FOCUS
An ordinary handicap on paper but the form looks pretty sound.
Marino Prince(FR) Official explanation: jockey said colt never travelled

117 HOTEL & CONFERENCING AT WOLVERHAMPTON FILLIES' H'CAP — 1m 1f 103y(P)
8:50 (8:50) (Class 5) (0-75,74) 4-Y-0+ — **£2,457** (£725; £362) **Stalls** Low

Form — RPR
262- **1** **Chia (IRE)**[15] 7237 5-8-10 **65** (p) HayleyTurner 1 — 71
(D Haydn Jones) *mde all: set stdy pce: shkn up over 2f out: kpt on and in command fnl f* **7/4**[2]
0/2 **2** *1¼* **Marias Dream (IRE)**[5] 63 6-9-5 **74** PatCosgrave 2 — 77
(John A Quinn, Ire) *trckd wnr: rdn wl over 1f out: no imp fnl f* **5/6**[1]
310- **3** *1½* **Sforzando**[59] 6803 7-8-2 **64** KristinStubbs(7) 3 — 64
(Mrs L Stubbs) *t.k.h: a 3rd: rdn and one pce fr over 1f out* **14/1**
3-65 **4** *½* **Casablanca Minx (IRE)**[6] 44 5-8-1 **61** (v) KirstyMilczarek(5) 4 — 60
(P D Evans) *hld up in rr: effrt on outside 3f out: no hdwy ins fnl 2f* **7/1**[3]

2m 11.09s (9.39) **Going Correction** +0.15s/f (Slow) — **4** Ran SP% **110.1**
Speed ratings (Par 100): **68,66,65,65**
CSF £3.68 TOTE £3.00; EX 6.30.
Owner D Llewelyn **Bred** Shane Moroney **Trained** Efail Isaf, Rhondda C Taff

FOCUS
Just the four runners for this fillies' handicap and, with Chia allowed to dictate at a steady pace from the outset, this form is likely to prove unreliable.

118 BOOK TICKETS ONLINE H'CAP — 2m 119y(P)
9:20 (9:20) (Class 5) (0-75,73) 4-Y-0+ — **£2,457** (£725; £362) **Stalls** Low

Form — RPR
005- **1** **Mister Completely (IRE)**[23] 7178 7-9-6 **65** (v) JamesDoyle 4 — 73
(Ms J S Doyle) *in tch: wnt 2nd 5f out: led wl over 2f out: clr whn edgd lft ins fnl f* **3/1**[2]
323- **2** *2½* **Capitalise (IRE)**[10] 7285 5-8-8 **56** (v[1]) JerryO'Dwyer(3) 7 — 61
(V Smith) *hld up towards reaar: hdwy to go 2nd 3f out: rdn over 1f out: no imp ins fnl f* **2/1**[1]
266- **3** *8* **Is It Me (USA)**[74] 5725 5-8-12 **62** RussellKennemore(5) 1 — 57
(A W Carroll) *led tl hdd over 5f out: rdn over 2f out: one pce after* **8/1**[3]
330- **4** *1* **Flame Creek (IRE)**[26] 7154 12-10-0 **73** StephenDonohoe 5 — 67
(E J Creighton) *trckd ldrs: led over 5f out: hdd wl over 2f out: rdn and no hdwy fr over 1f out* **14/1**
0/0- **5** *12* **Impostor (IRE)**[14] 7242 5-9-6 **65** (p) TGMcLaughlin 6 — 45
(R A Harris) *trckd ldr to 7f out: wknd over 2f out* **40/1**
332- **6** *¾* **Altos Reales**[14] 7249 4-8-5 **57** DeanMcKeown 2 — 36
(D Shaw) *hld up in rr: rdn 3f out: no ch after* **2/1**[1]

3m 46.15s (4.35) **Going Correction** +0.15s/f (Slow)
WFA 4 from 5yo+ 7lb — **6** Ran SP% **111.9**
Speed ratings (Par 103): **98,96,93,92,86 86**
CSF £9.37 TOTE £3.60: £2.10, £1.10; EX 10.90 Place 6 £25.33, Place 5 £13.30.
Owner Ms J S Doyle **Bred** Eamonn Griffin **Trained** Eastbury, Berks

FOCUS
A modest staying handicap with the winner rated to the level of last year's course and distance win.
T/Plt: £35.70 to a £1 stake. Pool: £105,414.50. 2,149.70 winning tickets. T/Qpdt: £13.50 to a £1 stake. Pool: £6,343.50. 345.80 winning tickets. JS

86 **KEMPTON (A.W)** (R-H)

Friday, January 11

OFFICIAL GOING: Standard

Wind: virtually nil Weather: clear chilly

119 DIGIBET APPRENTICE CLASSIFIED STKS 6f (P)

6:20 (6:20) (Class 7) 4-Y-0+ £1,365 (£403; £201) Stalls High

Form RPR

064- 1 **Stoneacre Donny (IRE)**[11] 7283 4-8-7 37 RyanHill(7) 3 54
(Peter Grayson) *stdd s: hld up in last: gd hdwy on inner over 2f out: chsd ldr 2f out: pushed along to ld jst over 1f out: r.o strly* **20/1**

0-31 2 3 **Calloff The Search**[7] 46 4-9-6 45 (p) JackMitchell 5 50
(Stef Liddiard) *awkward leaving stalls: sn led: rdn over 2f out: hdd jst over 1f out: outpcd by wnr fnl f* **4/6**[1]

0-00 3 3 **Cayman Breeze**[7] 46 8-8-9 42 (v) BarrySavage(5) 1 34
(J M Bradley) *t.k.h: hld up in rr: drvn wl over 2f out: styd on to chse ldng pair 1f out: nvr able to chal* **20/1**

0-60 4 ¾ **Tibinta**[2] 100 4-8-9 43 RichardEvans(5) 6 32
(P D Evans) *in tch towards rr: rdn wl over 2f out: plugged on but no ch w ldrs* **11/1**

6-04 5 5 **Orchestration (IRE)**[2] 100 7-9-0 45 (v) JackDean 9 16
(S Parr) *chsd ldrs: rdn wl over 2f out: wl outpcd last 2f* **6/1**[3]

3 6 ½ **Is Mise An Ri (IRE)**[2] 100 6-8-11 37 JemmaMarshall(3) 8 14
(Emmanuel Hughes, Ire) *wnt rt s: chsd ldrs: rdn to chse ldr 3f out tl 2f out: sn wl outpcd* **12/1**

066- 7 ¾ **College Queen**[28] 7138 10-9-0 40 (b) JPHamblett 4 12
(S Gollings) *chsd ldr tl 3f out: sn rdn: wknd 2f out* **33/1**

606- 8 3 **King Of Charm (IRE)**[38] 7013 5-8-9 45 (b) RossAtkinson(5) 2 2
(G L Moore) *t.k.h: chsd ldrs on outer tl lost pl and rdn 3f out: sn wl bhd* **5/1**[2]

1m 13.37s (0.27) **Going Correction** -0.15s/f (Stan) 8 Ran SP% **119.4**
Speed ratings (Par 97): **96,92,88,87,80 79,78,74**
CSF £34.95 TOTE £14.20: £2.30, £1.10, £6.20; EX 26.40.
Owner Richard Teatum **Bred** John And Mrs Susan Flavin **Trained** Formby, Lancs

FOCUS
A very moderate classified contest restricted to apprentices who had not ridden more than ten winners. The winning time was 1.41 seconds slower than the later 46-52 handicap and the form has been rated slightly negatively.

120 DIGIBET.COM CLASSIFIED STKS 7f (P)

6:50 (6:50) (Class 7) 4-Y-0+ £1,365 (£403; £201) Stalls High

Form RPR

20-4 1 **Sion Hill (IRE)**[9] 11 7-9-0 45 (p) MickyFenton 8 53
(John A Harris) *mde all: kicked clr 2f out: sn in command: easily* **5/2**[1]

6-06 2 3 ½ **Wizby**[5] 66 5-9-0 40 JohnEgan 10 44
(P D Evans) *s.i.s: hld up wl in rr: edgd out lft fr wl over 2f out: hdwy 2f out: r.o to go 2nd ins fnl f: no ch w wnr* **10/1**

000- 3 ¾ **Noddledoddle (IRE)**[28] 7137 4-9-0 37 (bt) ChrisCatlin 12 42
(J Ryan) *chsd ldrs: wnt 2nd 3f out: rdn over 2f out: wl outpcd by wnr 2f out: lost 2nd ins fnl f* **25/1**

06-5 4 1 **A Teen**[4] 75 10-9-0 42 TGMcLaughlin 9 39
(P Howling) *hld up in tch on inner: rdn and hdwy to chse ldng pair over 2f out: kpt on same pce* **16/1**

00-3 5 nk **Only If I Laugh**[9] 11 7-9-0 43 DaleGibson 4 38
(M J Attwater) *hld up in towards rr on inner: n.m.r wl over 2f out: rdn and hdwy over 2f out: no imp wl over 1f out* **10/3**[2]

00-0 6 hd **Newpark Spirit (IRE)**[2] 99 5-8-11 37 (v) JerryO'Dwyer(3) 13 37
(Emmanuel Hughes, Ire) *hld up in rr: hdwy over 2f out: chsd ldrs and drvn jst over 2f out: kpt on same pce* **15/2**

56-5 7 5 **Salvestro**[8] 24 5-9-0 42 RichardHughes 3 24
(A W Carroll) *racd in midfield: rdn and effrt 3f out: wl btn over 2f out* **9/2**[3]

005- 8 nk **Tamworth (IRE)**[48] 6935 6-9-0 35 (v) StephenDonohoe 1 23
(E J Creighton) *s.i.s: hld up in rr: hdwy 3f out: nvr nr ldrs* **50/1**

00-0 9 hd **Tagula Sands (IRE)**[9] 11 4-9-0 45 PatDobbs 2 23
(J C Fox) *racd in midfield: effrt and rdn over 2f out: wknd 2f out* **25/1**

66-0 10 3 ½ **James Street (IRE)**[8] 33 5-8-7 45 (v) RyanHill(7) 6 13
(Peter Grayson) *chsd ldr tl 3f out: hanging rt and wknd over 2f out* **9/1**

560- 11 3 ½ **Maeve (IRE)**[27] 7148 4-8-11 40 AlanCreighton(3) 11 4
(E J Creighton) *chsd ldrs: rdn over 3f out: wknd wl over 2f out: t.o* **50/1**

000- 12 3 ½ **Merlins Quest**[44] 6963 4-9-0 42 (b) LiamJones 7 —
(J M Bradley) *t.k.h: chsd ldrs: rdn over 3f out: wknd qckly over 2f out: t.o* **33/1**

000/ 13 7 **Lady Lucinda**[431] 6376 7-8-9 36 JamieJones(5) 5 —
(C N Kellett) *s.i.s: a bhd: lost tch over 3f out: t.o* **100/1**

1m 25.58s (-0.42) **Going Correction** -0.15s/f (Stan) 13 Ran SP% **122.1**
Speed ratings (Par 97): **100,96,95,94,93 93,87,87,87,83 79,75,67**
CSF £28.10 TOTE £3.50: £1.10, £3.50, £6.90; EX 35.70.
Owner Peter Taylor **Bred** Joe Rogers **Trained** Eastwell, Leics

FOCUS
Like the opener, a very moderate classified contest and weak form.
James Street(IRE) Official explanation: jockey said gelding hung right-handed

121 REBECCA DRAPER BIRTHDAY CELEBRATION H'CAP 6f (P)

7:20 (7:20) (Class 6) (0-52,54) 4-Y-0+ £2,047 (£604; £302) Stalls High

Form RPR

5-01 1 **Mind Alert**[3] 82 7-9-1 54 6ex (v) JamesDoyle 8 68+
(D Shaw) *racd wl off the pce in midfield: hdwy jst over 2f out: chsd ldr ins fnl f: pushed along and led wl ins fnl f: sn in command* **2/1**[1]

00-2 2 1 ¼ **Regal Royale**[2] 87 5-8-11 50 (v) AdrianMcCarthy 6 60
(Peter Grayson) *led: rdn and clr over 1f out: edgd lft fnl f: hdd wl ins fnl f: nt pce of wnr* **4/1**[2]

00-5 3 1 ¼ **Balerno**[8] 32 9-8-12 51 AmirQuinn 2 57
(Mrs L J Mongan) *chsd ldng trio: rdn over 3f out: hdwy 2f out: chsd ldr over 1f out tl ins fnl f: kpt on same pce* **16/1**

244- 4 ½ **Davids Mark**[61] 6773 8-8-11 50 RichardHughes 1 54
(J R Jenkins) *wl bhd: hdwy over 2f out: chsd ldrs and rdn over 1f out: kpt on same pce ins fnl f* **9/2**[3]

346- 5 3 **Accolation**[13] 7265 4-8-9 48 (b[1]) PatDobbs 9 43
(Pat Eddery) *awkward leaving stalls: t.k.h: chsd ldng trio: rdn to chse ldr wl over 1f out tl over 1f out: wknd fnl f* **9/1**

660- 6 3 ½ **Piccostar**[33] 7082 5-8-9 48 (b) DavidKinsella 3 32
(A B Haynes) *chsd ldr: rdn over 3f out: wknd wl over 1f out* **25/1**

02-0 7 3 ½ **Fastrac Boy**[2] 86 5-8-12 51 JimCrowley 7 23
(J R Best) *t.k.h: hld up wl in rr: n.d* **11/2**

005- 8 ¾ **Mr Loire**[23] 7192 4-8-7 46 DeanMcKeown 4 16
(A J Chamberlain) *a bhd: no ch last 3f* **8/1**

1m 11.96s (-1.14) **Going Correction** -0.15s/f (Stan) 8 Ran SP% **117.7**
Speed ratings (Par 101): **105,103,101,101,97 92,87,86**
CSF £10.44 CT £100.69 TOTE £2.60: £1.10, £2.20, £3.20; EX 13.90.
Owner R G Botham **Bred** P T Tellwright **Trained** Danethorpe, Notts

FOCUS
A moderate handicap, but probably not bad form for the grade and they went a strong pace. The winning time was 1.41 seconds quicker than the opening 0-45 classified contest and the form is rated through the runner-up to his recent best.

122 DIGIBET.COM CLAIMING STKS 1m 3f (P)

7:50 (7:50) (Class 6) 4-Y-0+ £2,047 (£453; £453) Stalls High

Form RPR

000- 1 **Steely Dan**[14] 7251 9-9-6 70 (p) NeilPollard 10 66+
(Mrs L C Jewell) *s.i.s: t.k.h: hld up in last: gd hdwy over 2f out: upsides ldr gng best over 1f out: pushed into ld 1f out: pushed out* **20/1**

643- 2 ½ **Daring Affair**[16] 7237 7-8-11 65 JimCrowley 1 56
(K R Burke) *hld up in tch: hdwy 3f out: rdn to chse ldng pair over 1f out: kpt on u.p last 100yds* **2/1**[1]

315- 2 dht **Satindra (IRE)**[15] 7242 4-9-1 62 (tp) MickyFenton 9 63
(John A Harris) *t.k.h: hld up in midfield: hdwy to chse ldr wl over 2f out: rdn to ld wl over 1f out: hdd 1f out: kpt on same pce u.p* **5/1**

164- 4 5 **Sweet World**[24] 7175 4-9-3 63 AndrewElliott(3) 2 59
(A P Jarvis) *racd keenly: led: rdn over 2f out: hdd wl over 1f out: wknd fnl f* **3/1**[2]

000- 5 2 ½ **Hayley's Flower (IRE)**[21] 7218 4-8-10 47 PatDobbs 8 45
(J C Fox) *hld up in last trio: swtchd lft and hdwy wl over 2f out: chsd ldrs 2f out: sn outpcd* **50/1**

00-5 6 nk **Safe Investment (USA)**[6] 53 4-9-6 69 (t) VinceSlattery 5 54
(B N Pollock) *stdd s: t.k.h: hld up in rr: rdn and effrt wl over 2f out: nvr trbld ldrs* **33/1**

62-1 7 7 **Looks The Business (IRE)**[9] 18 7-8-13 63 JackDean(7) 3 40
(W G M Turner) *s.i.s: hdwy to chse ldrs 8f out: rdn over 3f out: wknd over 2f out: eased whn no ch fnl f* **4/1**[3]

000- 8 2 ½ **Revolve**[78] 6447 8-9-4 57 (b) AmirQuinn 4 33
(Mrs L J Mongan) *chsd ldrs: wnt 2nd over 4f out tl wl over 2f out: sn wknd* **16/1**

250/ 9 21 **Major Faux Pas (IRE)**[58] 6015 6-9-1 75 (b[1]) ChrisCatlin 7 —
(O Sherwood) *chsd ldr tl over 4f out: sn rdn: wknd 3f out: t.o fnl f* **12/1**

2m 20.6s (-1.30) **Going Correction** -0.15s/f (Stan)
WFA 4 from 6yo+ 3lb 9 Ran SP% **118.2**
Speed ratings (Par 101): **101,100,100,97,95 94,89,88,72**
TOTE £24.30: £4.20 TRIFECTA 2nd place DA £1.30, S 1.10; Ex SD-S 104.80, SD-DA 53.70; CSF SD-S 58.95, SD-DA 30.45.Daring Affair was claimed by R. A. Harris for £8,000
Owner E A Condon **Bred** Mrs S E Barclay And L B Snowden **Trained** Sutton Valence, Kent

FOCUS
A modest claimer run at a reasonable pace but the form looks dubious.

123 DIGIBET.COM H'CAP 1m (P)

8:20 (8:20) (Class 6) (0-55,55) 4-Y-0+ £2,047 (£604; £302) Stalls High

Form RPR

00-0 1 **Golden Square**[9] 11 6-8-0 46 oh1 KirstyMilczarek(5) 2 53
(A W Carroll) *sn led: rdn and hdd wl over 1f out: led ins ins fnl f: hld on wl* **25/1**

002- 2 nk **Napoletano (GER)**[13] 7268 7-9-0 55 (p) JohnEgan 5 61
(S Dow) *t.k.h: hld up in tch: hdwy over 2f out: ev ch 1f out: unable qckn wl ins fnl f* **13/2**

522- 3 ¾ **Simpsons Gamble (IRE)**[26] 7167 5-8-12 53 JimCrowley 8 57
(R A Teal) *trckd ldrs: hdwy to ld wl over 1f out: sn rdn: hdd ins fnl f: curled up towards fin* **7/2**[1]

540- 4 shd **Postmaster**[20] 7085 6-8-11 52 ChrisCatlin 4 56
(R Ingram) *hld up in midfield: swtchd lft over 2f out: drvn and hdwy over 1f out: styd on fnl f: nt quite rch ldrs* **9/2**[3]

0-61 5 ¾ **Lordswood (IRE)**[2] 99 4-8-3 51 6ex KierenFox(7) 7 53
(J R Best) *t.k.h: hld up in rr: shkn up and hdwy wl over 1f out: kpt on but nvr pce to rch ldrs* **4/1**[2]

/54- 6 nk **Micky Mac (IRE)**[15] 7248 4-8-9 53 DuranFentiman(3) 9 55
(T D Walford) *t.k.h: hld up in last: rdn and effrt 2f out: styd on fnl f: nvr trbld ldrs* **9/1**

60-2 7 4 **Cow Girl (IRE)**[7] 48 4-9-0 55 MickyFenton 11 47
(Miss Gay Kelleway) *plld hrd: hld up towards rr: rdn and effrt on inner over 2f out: wl btn wl over 1f out* **10/1**

4-02 8 2 ½ **Falcon Flyer**[2] 89 4-8-5 46 oh1 HayleyTurner 1 33
(J R Best) *chsd ldr: rdn over 2f out: wknd qckly jst over 2f out* **10/1**

/51- 9 7 **My Jeanie (IRE)**[26] 7167 4-8-13 54 PatDobbs 3 25
(J C Fox) *t.k.h: chsd ldrs on outer: rdn 3f out: sn lost pl: no ch last 2f* **12/1**

002- 10 1 ½ **Korty**[26] 7166 4-8-9 50 NeilPollard 6 17
(W J Musson) *t.k.h: chsd ldrs: rdn over 2f out: sn wknd* **14/1**

1m 40.21s (0.41) **Going Correction** -0.15s/f (Stan) 10 Ran SP% **120.1**
Speed ratings (Par 101): **96,95,94,94,94 93,89,87,80,78**
CSF £184.65 CT £740.46 TOTE £18.20: £4.30, £3.20, £1.30; EX 221.70.
Owner Mr & Mrs J B Bacciochi **Bred** J R And Mrs P Good **Trained** Cropthorne, Worcs

FOCUS
A very moderate handicap that makes sense rated around the placed horses. The time was 1.98 seconds slower than the following 71-85.
Golden Square Official explanation: trainer said, regarding apparent improvement in form, that the gelding is inconsistent and appeared to benefit from being able to dominate in front.

124 DIGIBET H'CAP 1m (P)

8:50 (8:50) (Class 4) (0-85,86) 4-Y-0+ £4,210 (£1,252; £625; £312) Stalls High

Form RPR

63-1 1 **Monkey Glas (IRE)**[6] 63 4-8-11 81 6ex (v) AndrewElliott(3) 6 94
(K R Burke) *dwlt: sn pushed up to ld: mde rest: hrd pressed fr 2f out: hld on gamely fnl f* **7/2**[2]

421- 2 shd **Alfresco**[12] 7281 4-9-5 86 6ex (b) RichardHughes 7 99
(I A Wood) *s.i.s: hld up in midfield: hdwy to trck ldrs over 1f out: shkn up to chal jst ins fnl f: hrd drvn and a jst hld after* **5/2**[1]

013- 3 3 **Will He Wish**[11] 7287 12-9-1 82 (b) ChrisCatlin 5 88
(S Gollings) *taken down early: chsd wnr: ev ch and rdn jst over 2f out: outpcd by ldng pair fnl f* **14/1**

001- 4 1 **Spring Goddess (IRE)**[41] 6997 7-8-8 75 JohnEgan 1 79
(A P Jarvis) *t.k.h: chsd ldrs: rdn over 2f out: wknd jst ins fnl f* **7/2**[2]

615- **5** ¾ **Secret Liaison**[62] 6765 5-9-3 **84**.. JamieMackay 4 86
(S Parr) *s.i.s: t.k.h: hld up in last trio: rdn and effrt wl over 1f out: kpt on but nvr pce to threaten ldrs* **14/1**

040- **6** *nk* **Buxton**[12] 7281 4-8-10 **77**.. PatDobbs 8 78
(R Ingram) *chsd wnr tl over 6f out: rdn jst over 2f out: wknd jst over 1f out* **14/1**

334- **7** *1* **Wavertree Warrior (IRE)**[13] 7267 6-8-11 **85**..........(b) HarryPoulton[(7)] 3 84
(N P Littmoden) *hld up in midfield: effrt on outer wl over 2f out: sn rdn: no imp 2f out* **13/2**[3]

623- **8** 2 ½ **Bobski (IRE)**[79] 6435 6-9-3 **84**..(p) AmirQuinn 10 77
(P J McBride) *s.i.s: plld hrd: hld up last: rdn and hung rt wl over 2f out: n.d* **12/1**

210- **9** ½ **Trivia (IRE)**[69] 6651 4-8-1 **75**.. SophieDoyle[(7)] 9 67
(Ms J S Doyle) *s.i.s: hld up in last trio: rdn and brief effrt over 2f out: n.d* **20/1**

1m 38.23s (-1.57) **Going Correction** -0.15s/f (Stan) **9** Ran SP% **118.8**
Speed ratings (Par 105): **106,105,102,101,101 100,99,97,96**
CSF £13.12 CT £109.91 TOTE £5.20: £1.60, £1.60, £3.00; EX 16.50.
Owner Denis Fehan **Bred** D Bourke And Yuriy Medeudeyev **Trained** Middleham Moor, N Yorks

FOCUS
A fair handicap but not the most solid despite the third and fourth being close to form. The winner's time was 1.98 seconds faster than the previous 46-55.
Bobski(IRE) Official explanation: jockey said gelding missed the break

125 DIGIBET SPORTS BETTING H'CAP 1m 4f (P)
9:20 (9:20) (Class 6) (0-55,55) 4-Y-0+ **£2,047** (£604; £302) **Stalls** High

Form RPR

515- **1** **Little Richard (IRE)**[11] 7285 9-9-2 **55**........................(p) RichardHughes 8 64
(M Wellings) *chsd ldrs: effrt on inner 2f out: drvn to ld narrowly 1f out: sn hdd: rallied gamely to ld again ins fnl f: hld on wl* **11/1**

10-2 **2** *nk* **Under Fire (IRE)**[9] 10 5-8-10 **49**.. HayleyTurner 9 58
(A W Carroll) *t.k.h: led: rdn over 2f out: narrowly hdd 1f out: ev ch tl no ex wl ins fnl f* **13/2**[3]

13-2 **3** *shd* **Smokey The Bear**[2] 91 6-8-11 **53**.. NeilChalmers[(3)] 5 61
(Miss Sheena West) *hld up in rr: hdwy over 2f out: rdn to chal 1f out: led narrowly jst ins fnl f: hdd ins fnl f: nt qckn towards fin* **6/5**[1]

/00- **4** *4* **Backlash**[70] 7-8-7 **46** oh1.. LiamJones 11 48
(A W Carroll) *t.k.h: hld up in midfield: rdn wl over 3f out: plugged on fnl f but nvr pce to rch ldrs* **33/1**

/55- **5** *shd* **Hiawatha (IRE)**[230] 416 9-8-4 **46**.. AndrewElliott[(3)] 2 48
(A M Hales) *t.k.h: hld up in rr: rdn and struggling over 3f out: styd on past btn horses fr over 1f out: nt rch ldrs* **25/1**

220- **6** *shd* **Mixing**[14] 7256 6-8-8 **52**.. KirstyMilczarek[(5)] 3 54
(J Akehurst) *t.k.h: chsd ldrs tl jnd ldrs 5f out: rdn over 2f out: wkng whn short of room ent fnl f* **7/1**

53-0 **7** *hd* **Josr's Magic (IRE)**[9] 10 4-8-7 **50**.. JohnEgan 7 51
(H J Collingridge) *t.k.h: hld up towards rr: rdn and effrt over 2f out: no imp whn edgd rt ins fnl f* **20/1**

060- **8** 2 ½ **Come What July (IRE)**[13] 7274 7-8-7 **46**........................(v) JamesDoyle 10 43
(D Shaw) *hld up in midfield: effrt and edgd lft wl over 2f out: no hdwy 2f out* **25/1**

555- **9** *1* **Autograph Hunter**[48] 6937 4-8-10 **53**........................ AdrianMcCarthy 1 49
(Peter Grayson) *taken down early: s.i.s: sn in tch in midfield: rdn to chse ldrs wl over 3f out: wknd over 2f out* **14/1**

021- **10** *2* **Winter Cruise (IRE)**[13] 7273 4-8-12 **55**.. ChrisCatlin 4 48
(Ian Williams) *chsd ldr: jnd ldr 5f out: rdn over 2f out: sn hung rt and wknd* **9/2**[2]

04-0 **11** *7* **Only Hope**[9] 10 4-8-7 **50**..(p) PaulEddery 6 31
(Miss Diana Weeden) *hld up in last trio: rdn and no hdwy over 2f out* **66/1**

2m 35.98s (1.48) **Going Correction** -0.15s/f (Stan)
WFA 4 from 5yo+ 4lb **11** Ran SP% **121.4**
Speed ratings (Par 101): **97,96,96,94,94 93,93,92,91,90 85**
CSF £78.18 CT £151.42 TOTE £11.10: £2.80, £2.90, £1.20; EX 76.30 Place 6 £ 29.91, Place 5 £ 19.06.
Owner Mark Wellings Racing **Bred** Rathbarry Stud **Trained** Six Ashes, Shropshire

FOCUS
A moderate handicap run at just a steady gallop and best rated through the runner-up who made the running.
Josr's Magic(IRE) Official explanation: jockey said gelding ran too free
Winter Cruise(IRE) Official explanation: trainer said gelding hung badly right-handed
Only Hope Official explanation: trainer said race had come too soon for the filly
T/Plt: £18.00 to a £1 stake. Pool: £97,406.30. 3,948.80 winning tickets. T/Qpdt: £9.70 to a £1 stake. Pool: £7,370.90. 557.70 winning tickets. SP

[113]WOLVERHAMPTON (A.W) (L-H)
Friday, January 11

OFFICIAL GOING: Standard
Wind: Fresh against Weather: Raining

126 STAY AT THE WOLVERHAMPTON HOLIDAY INN H'CAP 5f 20y(P)
1:00 (1:03) (Class 6) (0-65,70) 4-Y-0+ **£2,047** (£604; £302) **Stalls** Low

Form RPR

64-1 **1** **Almaty Express**[8] 29 6-9-0 **66** 6ex....................(b) AshleyHamblett[(5)] 2 80+
(J R Weymes) *mde all: rdn and edgd rt fnl f: r.o* **11/8**[1]

110- **2** 2 ½ **Bond Becks (IRE)**[20] 7227 8-8-10 **57**.. ChrisCatlin 6 62
(G R Oldroyd) *sn pushed along and prom: rdn to chse wnr 1/2-way: no imp fnl f* **14/1**

21-3 **3** ½ **Perlachy**[8] 29 4-8-9 **59**..(v) DuranFentiman[(3)] 7 62
(Mrs N Macauley) *chsd ldrs: rdn 1/2-way: edgd rt fnl f: styd on* **8/1**

30-1 **4** ½ **Star Strider**[9] 19 4-9-9 **70** 6ex.. MickyFenton 4 71
(Miss Gay Kelleway) *sn pushed along in rr: rdn and hung rt 2f out: r.o ins fnl f: nt rch ldrs* **9/1**

300- **5** *1* **Lord Of The Reins (IRE)**[13] 7271 4-9-3 **64**................ DeanMcKeown 5 62
(D Shaw) *edgd rt s: sn pushed along in rr: rdn and hung rt 1/2-way: n.d* **11/2**[3]

011- **6** *1* **Triskaidekaphobia**[11] 7284 5-9-0 **61** 6ex........................(t) JamesDoyle 1 55
(Miss J R Tooth) *chsd wnr to 1/2-way: wknd fnl f* **7/2**[2]

330/ **7** *5* **Tigim (IRE)**[79] 6441 9-9-4 **65**..(p) PatCosgrave 3 41
(Noel Henley, Ire) *sn outpcd* **25/1**

62.79 secs (0.49) **Going Correction** +0.20s/f (Slow) **7** Ran SP% **111.3**
Speed ratings (Par 101): **108,104,103,102,100 99,91**
CSF £21.45 TOTE £2.20: £1.60, £4.30; EX 21.40.
Owner Sporting Occasions Racing No 5 **Bred** P G Airey **Trained** Middleham Moor, N Yorks

FOCUS
A modest sprint but run at a good gallop and the positions did not change much throughout. The form looks solid enough rated around those in the frame behind the winner.

127 BOOK ONLINE AT WOLVERHAMPTON-RACECOURSE.CO.UK (S) STKS 1m 1f 103y(P)
1:30 (1:31) (Class 6) 4-Y-0+ **£1,774** (£523; £262) **Stalls** Low

Form RPR

1 **Mon Ami (IRE)**[71] 6-9-1 0..(t) CColombi 1 72+
(G Di Chio, Italy) *hld up: hdwy over 3f out: led over 1f out: rdn clr* **2/5**[1]

350- **2** *10* **Persian Fox (IRE)**[87] 6247 4-9-0 52.. VinceSlattery 5 51
(A G Juckes) *dwlt: hld up: hdwy over 2f out: hung lft fr over 1f out: styd on: no ch w wnr* **20/1**

063- **3** ¾ **Still Dreaming**[13] 6108 4-8-9 46..(b) TomEaves 8 44
(M Dods) *s.i.s: hdwy 7f out: outpcd over 3f out: rdn and hung lft over 1f out: n.d after* **14/1**

/56- **4** ¾ **Ocean Pride (IRE)**[16] 3083 5-8-10 68....................(bt) HaddenFrost[(5)] 2 48
(D E Pipe) *chsd ldrs: rdn over 2f out: wknd over 1f out* **17/2**[2]

030- **5** 2 ½ **Tobago Reef**[39] 7006 4-8-7 57..(p) KristinStubbs[(7)] 6 43
(Mrs L Stubbs) *led: rdn and hdd over 1f out: edgd lft and sn wknd* **9/1**[3]

0- **6** *shd* **Swimandyouwin (IRE)**[22] 7199 5-8-10 0................ KirstyMilczarek[(5)] 7 42
(Shaun Harley, Ire) *chsd ldr over 7f out: rdn and ev ch 2f out: wknd over 1f out* **33/1**

00-5 **7** *4* **Storm Mission (USA)**[7] 40 4-9-0 40........................(t) PaulMulrennan 4 34
(J Mackie) *plld hrd and prom: pushed along 5f out: wknd over 3f out* **40/1**

2m 3.60s (1.90) **Going Correction** +0.20s/f (Slow)
WFA 4 from 5yo+ 1lb **7** Ran SP% **108.8**
Speed ratings (Par 101): **103,94,93,92,90 90,86**
CSF £10.92 TOTE £1.20: £1.10, £6.30; EX 9.90 Trifecta £57.40 Pool: £213.45, 2.64 winning units.The winner was bought in for 14,500gns.
Owner P Cesello **Bred** Franco Castlefranci **Trained** Italy
■ Over Ice (20/1) was withdrawn. Rule 4 does not apply.

FOCUS
An uncompetitive seller turned into a procession by the Italian raider. The time was faster than the two handicaps over the trip athough it was hand timed.

128 SPONSOR A RACE BY CALLING 0870 220 2442 H'CAP 1m 1f 103y(P)
2:00 (2:01) (Class 6) (0-65,62) 4-Y-0+ **£2,047** (£604; £302) **Stalls** Low

Form RPR

430- **1** **Alexander Guru**[37] 7029 4-9-4 **62**.. JamesDoyle 4 69
(M Blanshard) *hld up: hdwy over 2f out: rdn to chal over 1f out: edgd lft: styd on to ld post* **16/1**

0/3- **2** *hd* **Breaker Morant (IRE)**[21] 7214 6-9-3 **60**........................(b) FMBerry 8 66
(J G Burns, Ire) *fly-leapt s: hld up: hdwy u.p over 2f out: hrd rdn fnl f: r.o reluctantly* **11/4**[1]

143- **3** *shd* **Waterloo Corner**[21] 7213 6-9-1 **58**.. PaulMulrennan 7 64
(R Craggs) *chsd ldr: led over 2f out: rdn and edgd rt over 1f out: hdd post* **11/4**[1]

50-4 **4** 1 ¾ **Western Roots**[7] 44 7-9-1 **58**.. JimmyQuinn 5 60
(M Appleby) *hld up: hdwy over 2f out: rdn over 1f out: styd on same pce ins fnl f* **13/2**[3]

5- **5** ½ **Amical Risks (FR)**[23] 7185 4-9-2 **60**.. NeilPollard 6 61
(W J Musson) *hld up: rdn over 2f out: hung lft and r.o ins fnl f: nvr nrr* **25/1**

056- **6** ½ **Kansas Gold**[25] 7173 5-9-5 **62**.. PatCosgrave 2 62
(J Mackie) *chsd ldrs: rdn over 2f out: nt clr run over 1f out: no ex ins fnl f* **11/2**[2]

055- **7** 3 ½ **Speagle (IRE)**[15] 7249 6-9-5 **62**.. DeanMcKeown 9 55
(A J Chamberlain) *hld up: plld hrd: hdwy 7f out: rdn and wknd over 2f out* **25/1**

004- **8** 3 ½ **Valley Observer (FR)**[27] 7155 4-9-4 **62**........................(v[1]) PatDobbs 3 48
(W R Swinburn) *led 7f: wknd over 1f out* **15/2**

200- **9** *4* **Corrib (IRE)**[29] 7131 5-9-4 **61**.. ChrisCatlin 1 38
(B Palling) *chsd ldrs 7f* **12/1**

2m 4.90s (3.20) **Going Correction** +0.20s/f (Slow)
WFA 4 from 5yo+ 1lb **9** Ran SP% **115.1**
Speed ratings (Par 101): **97,96,96,95,94 94,91,88,84**
CSF £59.80 CT £160.61 TOTE £22.70: £5.40, £1.20, £1.10; EX 94.30 TRIFECTA Not won..
Owner J M Beever **Bred** Redmyre Bloodstock And John Bourke **Trained** Upper Lambourn, Berks
■ Stewards' Enquiry : F M Berry two-day ban: used whip with excessive frequency (Jan 22-23)

FOCUS
A modest handicap that was run at a moderate gallop and produced a close finish. The form looks relatively weak rated around the placed horses.

129 HORIZONS (S) STKS 1m 5f 194y(P)
2:30 (2:30) (Class 6) 4-Y-0+ **£1,774** (£523; £262) **Stalls** Low

Form RPR

264- **1** **Champagne Shadow (IRE)**[53] 6875 7-9-3 75................(p) ChrisCatlin 2 59
(Miss Tor Sturgis) *hld up: pushed along 7f out: swtchd outside over 5f out: hdwy 4f out: led over 2f out: rdn clr fr over 1f out: eased nr fin* **4/6**[1]

663- **2** *6* **Perfect Storm**[11] 5835 9-8-10 50.. JackDean[(7)] 1 51
(W G M Turner) *prom: outpcd over 3f out: rallied and hung lft over 1f out: sn chsng wnr: no imp* **12/1**[3]

050- **3** 3 ½ **Snake Hips**[37] 7032 4-8-11 42..(v[1]) RichardKingscote 7 46
(B Palling) *chsd ldrs: rdn over 3f out: outpcd fnl 2f* **50/1**

4 ¾ **Starstruck Peter (IRE)**[37] 7040 4-8-8 57........................(t) JerryO'Dwyer[(3)] 6 45
(J G Coogan, Ire) *led after 1f: hdd 4f out: rdn over 2f out: sn wknd* **22/1**

6/4- **5** ½ **Flash Harry**[22] 6999 4-8-11 51..(b) TPQueally 10 44
(M G Quinlan) *prom: rdn over 2f out: wknd over 1f out* **25/1**

400- **6** *shd* **Reminiscent (IRE)**[11] 7285 9-9-3 50........................(p) DanielTudhope 4 44
(B P J Baugh) *s.i.s: hld up: hdwy over 2f out: wknd over 1f out* **20/1**

0/0- **7** *5* **Tanning**[14] 7157 6-8-12 40.. LiamJones 3 32
(M Appleby) *chsd ldrs: rdn 7f out: wknd over 3f out* **100/1**

34-4 **8** *nk* **Musango**[6] 57 5-9-4 65..(t) RussellKennemore[(5)] 8 43
(Miss Gay Kelleway) *led 1f: chsd ldr: led 4f out: rdn and hdd over 2f out: wknd over 1f out* **7/2**[2]

00-4 **9** *39* **Atlantic Gamble (IRE)**[9] 18 8-9-3 58....................(p) PaulMulrennan 9 —
(K R Burke) *hld up: hdwy over 5f out: wknd over 3f out: virtually p.u fnl 2f* **12/1**[3]

3m 8.51s (2.51) **Going Correction** +0.20s/f (Slow)
WFA 4 from 5yo+ 6lb **9** Ran SP% **113.5**
Speed ratings (Par 101): **104,100,98,98,97 97,94,94,72**
CSF £8.95 TOTE £1.80: £1.10, £2.40, £11.30; EX 12.00 Trifecta £110.80 Pool: £817.79, 5.24 winning units.The winner sold to Jeff Pearce for 10,000gns.
Owner James Roberts **Bred** Mrs Kate Watson **Trained** Lambourn, Berks

FOCUS
An uncompetitive seller but a sound pace and ultimately producing a runaway winner, although he was still well below his official mark.
Musango Official explanation: trainer said gelding was unsuited by the trip
Atlantic Gamble(IRE) Official explanation: jockey said gelding had no more to give

130 HOTEL & CONFERENCING AT WOLVERHAMPTON MAIDEN STKS 7f 32y(P)
3:00 (3:01) (Class 5) 3-Y-O+ **£2,457** (£725; £362) **Stalls** High

Form RPR
642- **1** **Taken (IRE)**[23] 7191 3-8-9 75 .... JamieSpencer 7 76+
(J R Fanshawe) *hld up: hdwy u.p over 2f out: rdn to ld over 1f out: edgd lft: r.o* **4/6**[1]
0- **2** *1* **Kibitzer**[23] 7191 3-8-9 0 .... JamesDoyle 4 69
(J W Hills) *a.p: led 2f out: rdn and hdd over 1f out: styd on same pce ins fnl f* **8/1**[3]
0- **3** *6* **Rio L'Oren (IRE)**[157] 4254 3-8-0 0 ow1 .... KirstyMilczarek(5) 6 52+
(N J Vaughan) *chsd ldrs: nt clr run and lost pl 3f out: edgd lft and styd on ins fnl f* **40/1**
4 *hd* **Infinity Bond** 3-8-8 0 ow4 .... SladeO'Hara(5) 2 56
(G R Oldroyd) *dwlt: hdwy over 4f out: sn outpcd: n.d after* **33/1**
06- **5** *2* **Neyraan**[32] 7097 3-8-4 0 .... GregFairley 3 42
(M Johnston) *led: hdd over 5f out: led 1/2-way: hdd 2f out: sn rdn and wknd* **12/1**
4- **6** *2 1/2* **Modern Practice (IRE)**[15] 7246 3-8-9 0 .... MickyFenton 5 40
(Miss V Haigh) *prom: n.m.r and lost pl over 5f out: bhd fr 1/2-way* **66/1**
432- **7** *1/2* **Bahamian Lad**[13] 7270 3-8-9 72 .... JimCrowley 1 39
(R Hollinshead) *s.i.s: hld up: hdwy 3f out: rdn and wknd over 1f out* **3/1**[2]
8 *21* **Takeanoteofthat (IRE)**[92] 6-9-13 0 .... VinceSlattery 8 —
(D Burchell) *s.i.s: plld hrd and hdwy to ld over 5f out: hdd 1/2-way: sn hung rt and wknd* **100/1**

1m 31.52s (1.92) **Going Correction** +0.20s/f (Slow)
WFA 3 from 6yo 18lb **8** Ran SP% **111.7**
Speed ratings (Par 103): **101,99,93,92,90 87,87,63**
CSF £6.49 TOTE £1.60: £1.02, £1.80, £8.30; EX 6.30 Trifecta £130.50 Pool: £406.41, 2.21 winning units.
Owner Mrs Denis Haynes **Bred** Wretham Stud **Trained** Newmarket, Suffolk
FOCUS
A fair maiden for the time of year and the first two came clear. The winner is the best guide to the form.

131 WOLVERHAMPTON-RACECOURSE.CO.UK H'CAP 1m 1f 103y(P)
3:30 (3:30) (Class 4) (0-85,80) 3-Y-O **£4,533** (£1,348; £674; £336) **Stalls** Low

Form RPR
02-2 **1** **Leamington (USA)**[9] 12 3-8-9 **68** .... GregFairley 2 81
(M Johnston) *disp ld tl def advantage 1/2-way: rdn and hung lft over 1f out: r.o* **3/1**[2]
021- **2** *3/4* **Martyr**[22] 7204 3-9-2 **80** .... HaddenFrost(5) 1 91
(R Hannon) *disp ld to 1/2-way: rdn over 2f out: hmpd over 1f out: r.o* **7/4**[1]
121- **3** *8* **Wiseman's Diamond (USA)**[39] 7007 3-8-10 **69** .... JamieSpencer 4 63
(K A Ryan) *hld up in tch: outpcd over 3f out: n.d after* **7/4**[1]
540- **4** *1* **Piermarini**[65] 6723 3-9-3 **76** .... DeanMcKeown 3 68
(M Johnston) *chsd ldrs: rdn 3f out: wknd over 1f out* **7/1**[3]

2m 4.22s (2.52) **Going Correction** +0.20s/f (Slow) **4** Ran SP% **110.2**
Speed ratings (Par 99): **100,99,92,91**
CSF £8.73 TOTE £3.90; EX 9.00.
Owner Sheikh Hamdan Bin Mohammed Al Maktoum **Bred** Gainsborough Farm Llc **Trained** Middleham Moor, N Yorks
FOCUS
A fair handicap despite the small field and rated fairly positively with the first two coming clear.

132 BOOK TICKETS AT WOLVERHAMPTON-RACECOURSE.CO.UK FILLIES' H'CAP 1m 4f 50y(P)
4:00 (4:00) (Class 5) (0-70,75) 4-Y-O+ **£2,457** (£725; £362) **Stalls** Low

Form RPR
12-1 **1** **Fresh Mint (IRE)**[7] 47 4-9-7 **75** 6ex .... JamieSpencer 4 79
(M J Wallace) *mde all: rdn over 1f out: hung lft fnl f: r.o* **4/6**[1]
300- **2** *2 1/2* **Berry Hill Lass (IRE)**[50] 5346 4-8-6 **60** ....(p) JimmyQuinn 2 60
(J G M O'Shea) *chsd wnr over 3f: remained handy: rdn over 2f out: styd on same pce fnl f* **25/1**
605- **3** *shd* **Medieval Maiden**[13] 7273 5-8-8 **58** ....(p) NeilPollard 3 58
(W J Musson) *chsd ldrs: rdn over 2f out: styd on same pce fnl f* **3/1**[2]
00-2 **4** *3/4* **Sudden Impulse**[6] 51 7-9-4 **68** .... PaulMulrennan 1 67
(A D Brown) *hld up: rdn over 2f out: hdwy over 1f out: no ex ins fnl f* **11/2**[3]
5- **5** *4* **Nora Chrissie (IRE)**[35] 7068 6-9-6 **70** ....(v) TPQueally 5 62
(Niall Moran, Ire) *s.i.s: hdwy to chse wnr over 8f out: rdn over 2f out: edgd lft and wknd fnl f* **12/1**

2m 46.32s (5.22) **Going Correction** +0.20s/f (Slow)
WFA 4 from 5yo+ 4lb **5** Ran SP% **111.9**
Speed ratings (Par 100): **95,93,93,92,90**
CSF £18.63 TOTE £1.40: £1.20, £7.20; EX 26.10 Place 6 £ 22.11, Place 5 £ 12.20.
Owner Rick Barnes **Bred** Grange Con Holdings **Trained** Newmarket, Suffolk
FOCUS
A fair fillies' handicap in which the early pace was steady and the race developed into something of a sprint. The winner did not need to improve to score.
T/Plt: £32.00 to a £1 stake. Pool: £49,172.55. 1,120.05 winning tickets. T/Qpdt: £18.70 to a £1 stake. Pool: £2,750.60. 108.60 winning tickets. CR

93 LINGFIELD (L-H)
Saturday, January 12

OFFICIAL GOING: Standard

133 HOTEL COMING TO LINGFIELD PARK CLAIMING STKS 1m 2f (P)
12:45 (12:50) (Class 6) 4-Y-O+ **£1,774** (£523; £262) **Stalls** Low

Form RPR
122- **1** **Sawwaah (IRE)**[24] 7189 11-9-5 74 ....(v) RichardKingscote 2 78+
(Tom Dascombe) *dwlt: hld up in 5th: prog to chse ldr 2f out: rdn to ld jst over 1f out: styd on wl* **1/1**[1]
564- **2** *3* **Inside Story (IRE)**[28] 7160 6-9-9 72 ....(b) ChrisCatlin 4 76
(M W Easterby) *hld up in 4th: prog to ld and gng wl over 2f out: hdd and outpcd jst over 1f out* **7/4**[2]
214- **3** *5* **Barton Sands (IRE)**[21] 7224 11-8-9 55 ....(t) JimCrowley 1 52+
(Andrew Reid) *hld up in 3rd: trapped bhd wkng rival 3f out: wnt 3rd again over 1f out: kpt on same pce* **11/2**[3]
20-6 **4** *6* **Shaheer (IRE)**[10] 10 6-9-1 50 ....(b) GregFairley 5 46
(J Gallagher) *pressed ldr: led 4f out tl over 2f out: wknd* **16/1**
030- **5** *2 1/2* **My Mirasol**[34] 7083 4-8-3 47 .... MatthewDavies(7) 3 38
(D E Cantillon) *led tl 4f out: wknd 3f out* **33/1**
340/ **6** *4* **Persian Khanoom (IRE)**[502] 6-8-12 45 .... PatDobbs 7 30
(D E Cantillon) *dwlt: a last: wknd 3f out* **66/1**

2m 3.94s (-2.66) **Going Correction** -0.20s/f (Stan)
WFA 4 from 6yo+ 2lb **6** Ran SP% **112.1**
Speed ratings (Par 101): **107,104,100,95,93 90**
CSF £2.95 TOTE £2.00: £1.20, £1.50; EX 3.00.
Owner Alan Solomon **Bred** Shadwell Estate Company Limited **Trained** Lambourn, Berks
FOCUS
An uncompetitive contest in which the 'big' two came clear. The pace was sound and the winner can rate higher, with the runner-up setting the standard.
Barton Sands(IRE) Official explanation: jockey said gelding hung left throughout

134 COME JUMPING HERE ON JANUARY 21ST MAIDEN STKS 1m 2f (P)
1:20 (1:22) (Class 5) 4-Y-O+ **£2,331** (£693; £346; £173) **Stalls** Low

Form RPR
63-2 **1** **Sri Kuantan (IRE)**[9] 22 4-9-3 66 ....(t) ChrisCatlin 5 75
(P F I Cole) *trckd ldr: led over 2f out: hrd rdn ins fnl f: jst hld on* **7/2**[3]
432- **2** *hd* **Emperor Court (IRE)**[13] 7282 4-9-3 65 .... SebSanders 2 74
(P J Makin) *cl up: hrd rdn over 2f out: chsd wnr over 1f out: str chal ins fnl f: jst hld* **7/4**[2]
L05- **3** *3/4* **Rose Row**[13] 7282 4-8-12 0 .... VinceSlattery 1 67
(Mrs Mary Hambro) *hld up in last: prog 3f out: wnt 3rd and hanging 1f out: r.o and clsng at fin* **20/1**
44-3 **4** *4* **Denbera Dancer (USA)**[3] 95 4-9-3 75 .... GregFairley 4 64
(M Johnston) *led tl over 2f out: folded tamely* **11/8**[1]
0 **5** *14* **Eddystone (IRE)**[8] 39 4-9-3 0 ....(p) PatDobbs 3 36
(Mrs L C Jewell) *cl up tl wknd 4f out: t.o* **66/1**
6 *11* **Eagle Nebula** 4-9-3 0 .... SimonWhitworth 6 14
(B R Johnson) *dwlt: t.k.h early: trckd ldrs tl wknd 4f out: t.o* **28/1**

2m 5.71s (-0.89) **Going Correction** -0.20s/f (Stan) **6** Ran SP% **110.4**
Speed ratings (Par 103): **100,99,99,96,84 76**
CSF £9.70 TOTE £4.80: £1.90, £1.50; EX 6.80.
Owner H R H Sultan Ahmad Shah **Bred** Pat Fullam **Trained** Whatcombe, Oxon
■ Stewards' Enquiry : Seb Sanders 16-day ban: (takes into account previous offences; four days deferred): improper riding - used whip with excessive frequency and without giving colt time to respond (Jan 25-Feb 5)
FOCUS
A tricky little contest and the form looks modest rated around the placed horses.

135 PLAY GOLF @ LINGFIELD PARK MEDIAN AUCTION MAIDEN STKS 1m (P)
1:55 (1:56) (Class 5) 3-Y-O **£2,457** (£725; £362) **Stalls** High

Form RPR
53- **1** **Rankayo Hitam (USA)**[15] 7252 3-9-3 0 ....(v1) JohnEgan 11 77
(J S Moore) *trckd ldr after 2f: led narrowly over 1f out: hrd rdn and kpt on* **7/2**[3]
322- **2** *1 1/4* **Miss Mujanna**[14] 7266 3-8-12 74 .... J-PGuillambert 10 69
(J Akehurst) *led: narrowly hdd over 1f out: pressed wnr tl no ex last 100yds* **10/3**[2]
42-2 **3** *shd* **Mcconnell (USA)**[9] 25 3-9-3 76 .... JimCrowley 8 74
(J R Best) *chsd ldrs: rdn over 2f out: clsd fnl f: nrst fin* **7/4**[1]
33-6 **4** *1 3/4* **Hit The Roof**[7] 52 3-8-12 74 .... HaddenFrost(5) 7 70
(R Hannon) *pushed along in rr: prog u.p 3f out: nrst fin* **8/1**
020- **5** *1 1/2* **Samurai Warrior**[81] 6404 3-9-3 77 .... SebSanders 12 66
(P J Makin) *t.k.h: trckd ldrs: rdn and reluctant fnl 2f* **13/2**
6 *6* **Dara Diva (IRE)** 3-8-12 0 .... LiamJones 5 47
(W J Haggas) *dwlt: wl in rr: modest prog fnl 3f* **33/1**
0- **7** *5* **Marie Claude**[22] 7216 3-8-12 0 .... TPQueally 2 36+
(J Noseda) *dwlt: nvr on terms: modest late prog* **33/1**
0- **8** *2 1/2* **Den's Boy**[166] 4014 3-9-3 0 .... PatCosgrave 1 35
(J R Boyle) *dwlt: sn rdn: a bhd* **66/1**
0- **9** *nk* **Always Attractive (IRE)**[102] 5882 3-8-12 0 .... GregFairley 3 30
(M Johnston) *in tch tl wknd 3f out* **20/1**
6- **10** *1 1/4* **Fortunes Maid (IRE)**[50] 6912 3-8-12 0 .... JimmyQuinn 6 27
(M H Tompkins) *dwlt: a bhd* **66/1**
5- **11** *5* **Walton House (USA)**[24] 7181 3-9-0 0 .... NeilChalmers(3) 9 20
(A M Balding) *chsd ldrs: wknd 3f out* **50/1**
0- **12** *3 1/2* **Piccolo Pride**[14] 7264 3-9-3 0 .... RichardKingscote 4 12
(B G Powell) *chsd ldr 2f: wknd rapidly 3f out* **66/1**

1m 37.81s (-0.39) **Going Correction** -0.20s/f (Stan) **12** Ran SP% **123.2**
Speed ratings (Par 97): **100,98,98,96,95 89,84,81,81,80 75,71**
CSF £15.59 TOTE £5.70: £1.80, £1.50, £1.20; EX 20.20 Trifecta £22.30 Pool: £220.62. 7.00 w/u.
Owner Uplands Acquisitions Limited **Bred** Phil Booker **Trained** Upper Lambourn, Berks
FOCUS
A modest maiden featuring mainly exposed sorts and rated around the placed horses, but it should produce the odd winner.

136 LINGFIELDPARK.CO.UK H'CAP 7f (P)
2:25 (2:27) (Class 4) (0-85,83) 3-Y-O **£4,416** (£1,321; £660; £330; £164) **Stalls** Low

Form RPR
121- **1** **Geezers Colours**[17] 7232 3-9-1 **83** .... AndrewElliott(3) 11 92+
(K R Burke) *trckd ldrs over 4f out: led wl over 1f out: hrd rdn and jst hld on* **10/3**[1]
122- **2** *hd* **Smokey Rye**[13] 7280 3-8-9 **74** ....(b) PatDobbs 1 83
(G L Moore) *hld up in midfield: prog over 2f out: chsd wnr jst over 1f out: hrd rdn and clsd: jst failed* **12/1**
3- **3** *4* **Chinese Temple (IRE)**[17] 7232 3-8-12 **80** .... JerryO'Dwyer(3) 2 78
(M G Quinlan) *dwlt: hld up: outpcd 3f out: prog 2f out: kpt on* **20/1**
010- **4** *nk* **Kalhan Sands (IRE)**[147] 4613 3-9-1 **83** .... PJMcDonald(3) 7 80+
(G A Swinbank) *dwlt: sn rdn in last: prog and wd 2f out: styd on* **12/1**
420- **5** *1* **Harry Gee**[77] 6486 3-9-1 **80** .... ChrisCatlin 9 74
(G Wragg) *sn rdn in rr: styd on over 1f out: nvr a danger* **9/2**[3]
310- **6** *nk* **Harbour Blues**[43] 6973 3-8-12 **77** ....(t) LiamJones 8 71
(A W Carroll) *led tl wl over 1f out: wknd* **12/1**
351- **7** *1 1/4* **Cross Fell (USA)**[37] 7044 3-8-13 **78** .... PatCosgrave 4 68
(J R Boyle) *chsd ldrs tl wknd 2f out* **4/1**[2]
13- **8** *7* **Burriscarra**[43] 6974 3-8-12 **77** ....(b1) BrettDoyle 6 48
(Eamon Tyrrell, Ire) *sn rdn in rr: nvr a factor* **15/2**
201- **9** *1 1/2* **Glittering Prize (UAE)**[12] 7288 3-8-8 **73** .... GregFairley 3 40
(M Johnston) *chsd ldrs tl over 4f out: wknd rapidly 2f out* **8/1**

21-5 **10** 5 **Yamanmickmccann**[9] 25 3-8-8 **78**.. HaddenFrost(5) 5 32
(R Hannon) *in tch to 1/2-way: wknd* **16/1**

1m 23.41s (-1.39) **Going Correction** -0.20s/f (Stan) **10** Ran SP% **117.9**
Speed ratings (Par 99): **106,105,101,100,99 99,97,89,88,82**
CSF £45.08 CT £715.10 TOTE £3.60: £1.90, £2.90, £4.80; EX 37.90 Trifecta £47.30 Pool: £280.04, 4.20 w/u.
Owner C Waters **Bred** Bloodhorse International Limited **Trained** Middleham Moor, N Yorks

FOCUS
A good, competitive handicap run at a decent gallop and sound form rated fairly positively.
Yamanmickmccann Official explanation: jockey said colt never travelled

137 ARENALEISUREPLC.COM CONDITIONS STKS 6f (P)
2:55 (2:55) (Class 3) 3-Y-O+
£6,543 (£1,959; £979; £490; £244; £122) **Stalls** Low

Form RPR
141- **1** **Bonus (IRE)**[24] 7184 8-9-12 104.. HayleyTurner 2 106+
(G A Butler) *hld up: smooth prog to trck clr ldrs wl over 1f out: rdn and r.o fnl f: led last 50yds* **1/1**[1]
511- **2** 1 **Silver Prelude**[36] 7059 7-9-0 79.. JamesO'Reilly(5) 8 96
(D K Ivory) *led and sn clr: 4 l up 1f out: collared last 50yds* **20/1**
335- **3** 1 ¾ **Qadar (IRE)**[15] 7255 6-9-5 95..(b) JimCrowley 5 90
(N P Littmoden) *hld up: effrt 2f out: styd on but nt pce to chal* **7/2**[2]
120- **4** 1 **Lucayos**[15] 7255 5-8-12 93.. KylieManser(7) 1 87
(Mrs H Sweeting) *chsd clr ldr tl wl over 1f out: hanging and nt qckn* **14/1**
551- **5** 1 **Gross Prophet**[23] 7202 3-8-6 89.. RichardKingscote 7 83
(Tom Dascombe) *chsd ldrs: lost pl 2f out: one pce after* **14/1**
204- **6** 1 **Dalkey Girl (IRE)**[70] 6652 3-7-12 89.. DavidKinsella 6 72
(V Smith) *hld up: racd wd: rdn and no imp over 1f out* **22/1**
014- **7** ½ **Red Cape (FR)**[273] 1034 5-9-5 98.. JohnEgan 3 79
(Jane Chapple-Hyam) *hld up: rdn and no rspnse over 2f out* **4/1**[3]

1m 11.04s (-0.86) **Going Correction** -0.20s/f (Stan)
WFA 3 from 5yo+ 16lb **7** Ran SP% **114.7**
Speed ratings (Par 107): **103,101,99,98,96 95,94**
CSF £25.03 TOTE £1.90: £1.90, £4.70; EX 18.40 Trifecta £42.50 Pool: £374.97, 6.25 winning units.
Owner The Bonus Partnership **Bred** A Stroud And J Hanly **Trained** Newmarket, Suffolk

FOCUS
They went a decent gallop and class act Bonus readily justified favouritism. The winner is rated slightly below his recent best.

NOTEBOOK
Bonus(IRE) has come right back to his best of late, narrowly scoring in a Listed contest at Kempton last time, and he was always likely to take the beating in this conditions event. Ridden confidently, he made his ground with ease and was produced late to score readily. The Polytrack has proved the making of him and he will now be aimed at next month's Wulfrun Stakes at Wolverhampton. (op 5-4)
Silver Prelude, on a hat-trick following handicap wins over 5f at this course and more recently Wolverhampton, was faced with a much stiffer task here and was always likely to be stretched by the extra furlong, but in-form sprinters often run above themselves and he ran a blinder under an enterprising ride. His rating may suffer as a result, but he remains capable of better back at 5f. (tchd 16-1)
Qadar(IRE) is often thereabouts in competitive races, but he does not find winning easy. He ran his race, keeping on in third, but is likely to remain hard to win with. (op 3-1)
Lucayos has been running well in handicaps, but he could not maintain his effort and failed to quicken under pressure. (op 10-1)
Red Cape(FR), off since finishing fourth in a decent conditions event at the course back in the spring, looked the favourite's biggest threat if fully wound up, but he found little under pressure and presumably needed the run. Official explanation: trainer said gelding had a breathing problem (op 9-2)

138 LINGFIELD PARK FOR PARTIES H'CAP 1m 2f (P)
3:25 (3:25) (Class 2) (0-100,95) 4-Y-O+ **£9,971** (£2,985; £1,492; £747; £372) **Stalls** Low

Form RPR
31-3 **1** **Mafeking (UAE)**[7] 61 4-8-6 86.. AndrewElliott(3) 2 93
(M R Hoad) *rrd s: sn led: qcknd after 2f: hld on gamely fnl f* **9/2**[3]
311- **2** 1 **Evident Pride (USA)**[27] 7163 5-9-6 95.. SebSanders 5 100
(B R Johnson) *dwlt: hld up: outpcd after 2f: rdn 4f out: styd on to take 2nd nr fin* **5/6**[1]
326- **3** hd **Lisathedaddy**[100] 5940 6-8-12 87.. RichardKingscote 3 92
(B G Powell) *hld up: outpcd after 2f: rdn 4f out: styd on fnl 2f: a hld* **10/1**
111- **4** ¾ **Atlantic Story (USA)**[14] 7267 6-9-4 93..(bt) ChrisCatlin 4 97
(M W Easterby) *chsd wnr: rdn over 2f out: kpt on but lost 2 pls fnl f* **7/2**[2]
30-3 **5** 6 **Fusili (IRE)**[3] 97 5-8-10 85.. JimCrowley 1 77
(N P Littmoden) *hld up: outpcd after 2f: rdn 4f out: no prog* **14/1**

2m 6.22s (-0.38) **Going Correction** -0.20s/f (Stan)
WFA 4 from 5yo+ 2lb **5** Ran SP% **110.7**
Speed ratings (Par 109): **98,97,97,96,91**
CSF £8.87 TOTE £5.40: £1.80, £1.30; EX 10.60.
Owner Mrs J E Taylor **Bred** Darley **Trained** Lewes, E Sussex

FOCUS
A good handicap but run at a steady gallop and Mafeking led throughout.

NOTEBOOK
Mafeking(UAE) hardly ever runs a bad race and he looked a leading player, having finished a close third off this mark at the course last time. Back in trip, he was able to lead at his own tempo and always looked to be in a good rhythm once his rider injected some pace. The favourite was never able to get to him and connections plan on giving this admirable gelding plenty of time, as they hope he will continue to get better with age. (op 11-2)
Evident Pride(USA), who narrowly beat the winner over course and distance in November, came into this on a hat-trick having scored at Kempton last time, but he was another 7lb higher and was caught out here by a canny ride from Mafeking's pilot. He can be rated a little better than the bare form and his stock continues to rise. (op Evens)
Lisathedaddy, having her first start of the year, comes from a stable that has had a great time of it recently and she ran above herself, keeping on nicely from the rear. She has not won since March, but this effort suggests another victory may not be far off. (op 9-1 tchd 8-1)
Atlantic Story(USA), on a four-timer following two wins here and one at Kempton, had been raised another 4lb but the bigger question mark hung over how he would cope with this distance. All his previous wins had come at shorter and, though he appeared to see it out, it was clear that he will do better returned to 1m. (op 10-3 tchd 4-1 in a place)
Fusili(IRE) has not won since this time last year and she did little here to suggest that losing run is about to end. (op 8-1)

139 LINGFIELD PARK FOR WEDDINGS H'CAP 1m 2f (P)
3:55 (3:58) (Class 5) (0-70,70) 4-Y-O+ **£2,331** (£693; £259; £259) **Stalls** Low

Form RPR
060- **1** **Sun Of The Sea**[43] 6982 4-9-1 70.. KirstyMilczarek(5) 5 83+
(N P Littmoden) *hld up: prog 2f out: led jst over 1f out: rdn clr* **5/2**[1]
61-4 **2** 2 ½ **Just Intersky (USA)**[9] 27 5-9-0 62..(e) DeanMcKeown 6 67
(V Smith) *stdd s: hld up in last: effrt on outer 2f out: nt qckn over 1f out: kpt on* **3/1**[2]
041- **3** nk **King After**[14] 7268 6-8-9 57..(v) JimCrowley 2 61
(J R Best) *t.k.h: hld up in tch: chal 2f out: nt qckn 1f out* **7/2**[3]
26-5 **3** dht **Meditation**[9] 28 6-9-6 68.. JamesDoyle 3 72
(I A Wood) *trckd clr ldr: prog to ld 2f out: hdd and nt qckn jst over 1f out* **9/2**
640- **5** 2 ½ **Burgundy**[56] 6848 11-9-4 66..(b) ChrisCatlin 4 65
(R A Teal) *dwlt and reminders: hld up: in tch 2f out: sn btn* **12/1**
64-4 **6** 2 **Sweet World**[1] 122 4-8-10 63.. AndrewElliott(3) 1 58
(A P Jarvis) *uns rdr and bolted bef s: led and clr: hdd 2f out: wknd* **7/1**

2m 6.03s (-0.57) **Going Correction** -0.20s/f (Stan)
WFA 4 from 6yo+ 1lb **6** Ran SP% **114.2**
Speed ratings (Par 103): **99,97,96,96,94 93**
CSF £10.56 TOTE £3.40: £1.90, £2.70; EX 16.10 Place 6 £11.65, Place 5 £10.47..
Owner Miss Vanessa Church **Bred** Red House Stud **Trained** Newmarket, Suffolk

FOCUS
A modest handicap and the form looks relatively modest.
T/Plt: £13.20 to a £1 stake. Pool: £64,450.20. 3,560.00 winning tickets. T/Qpdt: £4.00 to a £1 stake. Pool: £3,492.80. 633.70 winning tickets. JN

126 WOLVERHAMPTON (A.W) (L-H)
Saturday, January 12

OFFICIAL GOING: Standard
Wind: Fresh behind Weather: Raining

140 FUN FOR ALL THE FAMILY @ PONTIN'S APPRENTICE H'CAP 1m 141y(P)
6:50 (6:50) (Class 6) (0-58,58) 4-Y-O+ **£2,047** (£604; £302) **Stalls** Low

Form RPR
03-3 **1** **Justcallmehandsome**[4] 80 6-8-9 56..(v) BillyCray(7) 5 63
(D J S Ffrench Davis) *led: hdd 7f out: led over 1f out: rdn and hung lft ins fnl f: r.o* **6/4**[1]
001- **2** 2 **Grey Gurkha**[27] 7166 7-8-13 58.. DeclanCannon(5) 1 60
(I W McInnes) *racd keenly: led 7f out: rdn and hdd over 1f out: nt clr run ins fnl f: styd on same pce* **10/3**[3]
000- **3** shd **Cantique (IRE)**[14] 7274 4-8-0 46 oh1.. RossAtkinson(5) 4 48
(R J Price) *chsd ldrs: rdn over 1f out: styd on same pce ins fnl f* **28/1**
404- **4** 2 ½ **Norwegian**[14] 7274 7-8-9 54..(p) AshleyMorgan(5) 7 50
(Ian Williams) *chsd ldrs: rdn over 2f out: styd on same pce appr fnl f* **9/4**[2]
\- **5** 6 **Oh So (IRE)**[245] 1686 4-8-9 55.. RichardEvans(5) 6 38
(P A Blockley) *prom: rdn over 3f out: wknd 2f out* **28/1**
/00- **6** ¾ **Arthurs Dream (IRE)**[31] 1362 6-8-6 46 oh1.. MarkCoumbe 2 27
(A W Carroll) *s.s: hld up: rdn over 3f out: wknd 2f out* **10/1**

1m 52.16s (1.66) **Going Correction** +0.05s/f (Slow)
WFA 4 from 6yo+ 1lb **6** Ran SP% **109.8**
Speed ratings (Par 101): **100,98,98,95,90 89**
CSF £6.53 TOTE £3.00: £1.30, £2.00; EX 8.10.
Owner Mrs J E Taylor **Bred** Mrs J E Taylor **Trained** Lambourn, Berks
■ A first winner for 19-year-old Billy Cray.

FOCUS
A moderate contest and weak form, limited by the proximity of the third.
Arthurs Dream(IRE) Official explanation: jockey said gleding missed the break

141 CALL PONTIN'S NOW 0844 576 5938 H'CAP 7f 32y(P)
7:20 (7:21) (Class 6) (0-60,58) 3-Y-O **£2,388** (£705; £352) **Stalls** High

Form RPR
425- **1** **Weet By Far**[15] 7258 3-9-4 58.. HayleyTurner 8 63
(R Hollinshead) *hld up: hdwy over 1f out: led wl ins fnl f: r.o* **9/1**
000- **2** 1 **Whaston (IRE)**[83] 6358 3-9-1 55.. JimmyQuinn 10 57
(J D Bethell) *hld up: hdwy and nt clr run over 1f out: swtchd lft ins fnl f: r.o* **7/1**[2]
065- **3** 1 ¼ **Run From Nun**[65] 6736 3-8-10 50.. NeilPollard 5 49
(John Berry) *prom: rdn and ev ch fr over 1f out: sn hung lft: styd on same pce ins fnl f* **8/1**[3]
44-4 **4** 1 **Weetfromthechaff**[4] 81 3-9-2 56.. TGMcLaughlin 7 52
(R Hollinshead) *s.i.s: hld up: hdwy over 2f out: rdn and hung lft fr over 1f out: styd on same pce* **7/2**[1]
600- **5** hd **Don Picolo**[96] 6051 3-8-6 46..(b[1]) FrankieMcDonald 4 42
(P A Blockley) *led 6f out: rdn over 2f out: hdd and no ex wl ins fnl f* **17/2**
000- **6** 1 ½ **Magical Song**[52] 6899 3-8-10 50.. StephenDonohoe 11 42
(P A Blockley) *chsd ldrs: rdn over 4f out: edgd lft over 1f out: wknd ins fnl f* **11/1**
265- **7** shd **Miss Tilen**[223] 2271 3-8-10 53.. JerryO'Dwyer(3) 9 44
(V Smith) *chsd ldrs: rdn over 1f out: wknd ins fnl f* **28/1**
554- **8** ½ **John Potts**[16] 7245 3-9-3 57.. PaulMulrennan 6 47
(B P J Baugh) *hld up: rdn and hung lft fr over 1f out: nt trble ldrs* **7/2**[1]
000- **9** ¾ **Charlie Green (IRE)**[167] 3995 3-7-12 45.. AndrewHeffernan(7) 2 33
(Paul Green) *s.i.s: sn pushed along in rr: rdn 1/2-way: no ch whn hmpd 1f out* **40/1**
005- **10** 5 **Lella Beya**[24] 7182 3-9-2 56.. JamesDoyle 1 30
(S Kirk) *led 1f: chsd ldr tl rdn 2f out: wkng whn hmpd 1f out* **7/1**[2]
000- **11** 17 **Jazz Romance (IRE)**[121] 5363 3-7-12 45.. PatrickDonaghy(7) 3 —
(D Shaw) *s.s: outpcd* **50/1**

1m 32.28s (2.68) **Going Correction** +0.05s/f (Slow) **11** Ran SP% **117.3**
Speed ratings (Par 95): **91,89,88,87,87 85,85,84,83,78 58**
CSF £69.52 CT £543.15 TOTE £8.10: £1.60, £2.20, £2.70; EX 88.10.
Owner Ed Weetman **Bred** Jocelyn Targett **Trained** Upper Longdon, Staffs

FOCUS
Not one of these had previously won a race, but they had not had that many chances and the form looks fine for the grade, rated around the third and fourth.
John Potts Official explanation: jockey said gelding hung left

142 BOOK PONTIN'S & MAKE PONTIN'S GR8 H'CAP 5f 20y(P)
7:50 (7:50) (Class 6) (0-55,60) 4-Y-O+ **£2,047** (£604; £302) **Stalls** Low

Form RPR
366- **1** **Garlogs**[243] 1729 5-8-6 52.. RussellKennemore(5) 10 62
(R Hollinshead) *mde all: shkn up and edgd lft ins fnl f: r.o* **9/1**
32-2 **2** ½ **Bentley**[5] 71 4-8-13 54..(v) DeanMcKeown 1 62
(D Shaw) *chsd wnr: rdn and swtchd rt ins fnl f: r.o* **7/4**[1]
-532 **3** 3 ½ **Earl Compton (IRE)**[2] 114 4-8-13 54..(v) HayleyTurner 2 49
(Stef Liddiard) *hld up: hdwy over 1f out: rdn and hung lft ins fnl f: nt trble ldrs* **17/2**

040- **4** 1 1/4 **Paddywack (IRE)**[25] 7180 11-8-12 53..........(b) PaulMulrennan 6 44
(D W Chapman) *prom: rdn 1/2-way: sn outpcd* **20/1**
043- **5** 3/4 **Lawdy Miss Clawdy**[14] 7265 4-8-5 46 oh1.......... FrankieMcDonald 3 34
(D W P Arbuthnot) *chsd ldrs: rdn 1/2-way: outpcd fnl 2f* **8/1**[3]
-312 **6** 1 **Calloff The Search**[1] 119 4-9-0 55..........(p) MickyFenton 4 40+
(Stef Liddiard) *hit side of stalls whn gates opened: sn outpcd: nvr nrr* **9/4**[2]
000- **7** 1/2 **Ava's World (IRE)**[12] 7283 4-8-4 50.......... ColinHaddon(5) 11 33
(Peter Grayson) *s.s: outpcd* **33/1**
543- **8** 2 **Fern House (IRE)**[12] 7284 6-8-6 47..........(v[1]) PaulEddery 8 23
(Garry Moss) *s.i.s: hdwy over 3f out: rdn and wknd over 1f out* **9/1**

62.66 secs (0.36) **Going Correction** +0.05s/f (Slow) **8** Ran SP% **116.5**
Speed ratings (Par 101): **103,102,96,94,93 91,91,87**
CSF £25.73 CT £144.90 TOTE £12.70: £2.50, £1.20, £2.50; EX 47.80.
Owner Peter G Freeman **Bred** Peter Taplin **Trained** Upper Longdon, Staffs
■ Stewards' Enquiry : Russell Kennemore one-day ban: failing to ride to draw (Jan 23)

FOCUS
A moderate sprint handicap, run at a good pace, in which very few got competitive. The form looks sound, though.

143 IMPROVE YOUR BETTING WITH SMARTERSIG.COM H'CAP 1m 1f 103y(P)
8:20 (8:20) (Class 6) (0-52,52) 4-Y-0+ **£2,047** (£604; £302) **Stalls** Low

Form RPR
004- **1** **Buscador (USA)**[14] 7273 9-8-9 48.......... RichardKingscote 7 62+
(W M Brisbourne) *led over 8f out: rdn and hdd over 2f out: sn led again: drvn clr fnl f: eased nr fin* **4/1**[2]
342- **2** 3 **Winged Farasi**[14] 7275 4-8-12 52.......... LiamJones 9 58
(R A Harris) *edgd rt s: sn drvn along: chsd wnr 7f out: rdn to ld over 2f out: sn hdd: no ex whn hung lft ins fnl f* **4/1**[2]
04-3 **3** 2 1/2 **Formidable Guest**[10] 10 4-8-12 52.......... JimmyQuinn 8 53
(J Pearce) *hld up: hdwy over 3f out: sn rdn: no imp fnl 2f* **4/1**[2]
630- **4** 1 1/2 **Bobering**[51] 6906 8-8-6 48.......... AndrewElliott(3) 2 46
(B P J Baugh) *dwlt: hld up: hdwy over 1f out: nt rch ldrs* **6/1**[3]
660- **5** 1 1/2 **Bothar Brugha (IRE)**[45] 6967 4-8-7 52.......... RussellKennemore(5) 1 47
(J G M O'Shea) *sn pushed along in rr: styd on ins fnl f: nvr nrr* **50/1**
060- **6** 1 3/4 **Jarvo**[31] 7115 7-8-12 51..........(e[1]) DanielTudhope 3 42
(I W McInnes) *hld up: rdn over 3f out: n.d* **18/1**
50-6 **7** hd **Boppys Pride**[5] 77 5-8-12 51..........(v[1]) TonyHamilton 5 42
(R A Fahey) *chsd ldrs: rdn over 3f out: wknd 2f out* **8/1**
00-5 **8** 6 **Bear Bottom**[10] 10 4-8-12 52.......... TGMcLaughlin 6 30
(W J Musson) *hld up: hdwy u.p over 3f out: wknd wl over 1f out* **3/1**[1]
000- **9** 23 **Miss Sure Bond (IRE)**[51] 6906 5-8-3 45..........(p) DuranFentiman(3) 4 —
(G R Oldroyd) *led 1f: chsd ldrs tl rdn and wknd over 3f out* **28/1**

2m 2.27s (0.57) **Going Correction** +0.05s/f (Slow)
WFA 4 from 5yo+ 1lb **9** Ran SP% **121.1**
Speed ratings (Par 101): **103,100,98,96,95 93,93,88,67**
CSF £21.57 CT £69.86 TOTE £5.60: £1.90, £1.80, £2.10; EX 24.60.
Owner David Robson **Bred** William H Floyd **Trained** Great Ness, Shropshire

FOCUS
A competitive handicap but not strong form rated through the second and the first two dominated almost throughout.
Jarvo Official explanation: jockey said gelding was denied a clear run

144 PONTIN'S MAKE THE BEST FAMILY HOLIDAYS MAIDEN STKS 1m 4f 50y(P)
8:50 (8:50) (Class 5) 4-Y-0+ **£2,457** (£725; £362) **Stalls** Low

Form RPR
2- **1** **Steig (IRE)**[16] 7247 5-9-7 61.......... JamesDoyle 9 60
(Carl Llewellyn) *a.p: racd keenly: led over 1f out: sn rdn and hung lft: styd on: eased nr fin* **1/1**[1]
05-3 **2** 1 1/4 **Niqaab**[8] 39 4-8-5 60.......... DebraEngland(7) 8 54
(W J Musson) *hld up in tch: rdn over 1f out: nt clr run ins fnl f: styd on same pce* **9/2**[2]
30-5 **3** 1 1/4 **Weet For Ever (USA)**[8] 39 5-9-7 50.......... StephenDonohoe 7 56
(P A Blockley) *chsd ldrs: led over 3f out: rdn and hdd over 1f out: no ex ins fnl f* **12/1**
4 2 1/2 **Right You Are (IRE)**[76] 8-9-0 0.......... AndrewHeffernan(7) 6 52
(Paul Green) *s.s: hld up: racd keenly: hdwy over 3f out: rdn and edgd lft over 1f out: nt rch ldrs* **40/1**
0- **5** 2 1/2 **Hayley's Pearl**[26] 7174 9-9-2 0.......... HayleyTurner 2 43
(Mrs P Ford) *hld up: styd on ins fnl f: nvr nrr* **50/1**
303- **6** 3 **The Diamond Bond**[15] 7262 4-8-12 50.......... SladeO'Hara(5) 10 43
(G R Oldroyd) *led: rdn and hdd over 3f out: wknd 2f out* **9/1**
00- **7** 5 **Tewkesbury (IRE)**[16] 7239 4-9-3 0.......... VinceSlattery 5 35
(Mrs K Waldron) *chsd ldrs 8f* **100/1**
0/ **8** 2 **Tribiani (IRE)**[178] 3656 4-8-12 53.......... FrankieMcDonald 12 27
(P A Blockley) *swvd lft s: hld up: plld hrd: rdn and wknd 3f out* **20/1**
0/ **9** 24 **Son Of Samson (IRE)**[698] 403 7-9-7 0.......... LiamJones 3 —
(R J Price) *hld up: rdn 1/2-way: sme hdwy over 3f out: sn wknd* **100/1**
050/ **10** 2 1/2 **Art Historian (IRE)**[331] 6790 5-9-7 0.......... TGMcLaughlin 4 —
(E G Bevan) *hld up: a in rr* **11/1**
0-6 **11** 1 3/4 **Swimandyouwin (IRE)**[1] 127 5-9-0 0.......... PatrickDonaghy(7) 1 —
(Shaun Harley, Ire) *chsd ldrs over 8f* **11/2**[3]

2m 43.66s (2.56) **Going Correction** +0.05s/f (Slow)
WFA 4 from 5yo+ 4lb **11** Ran SP% **120.7**
Speed ratings (Par 103): **97,96,95,93,92 90,86,85,69,67 66**
CSF £5.61 TOTE £2.20: £1.10, £1.70, £2.10; EX 5.80.
Owner Something In The City 2 **Bred** Elisabeth And Neil Draper **Trained** Upper Lambourn, Berks
■ Stewards' Enquiry : James Doyle three-day ban: careless riding (Jan 23-25)

FOCUS
A very ordinary maiden run at a steady early pace. The third sets the standard but the proximity of the fifth raises doubts about the form.

145 STAY AT THE WOLVERHAMPTON HOLIDAY INN CLASSIFIED STKS 1m 4f 50y(P)
9:20 (9:20) (Class 7) 4-Y-0+ **£1,365** (£403; £201) **Stalls** Low

Form RPR
050- **1** **Qaasi (USA)**[96] 6069 6-8-11 45.......... MarkLawson(3) 8 55+
(M Brittain) *hld up in tch: nt clr run and lost pl over 3f out: hdwy 2f out: rdn to ld wl ins fnl f* **3/1**[2]
000- **2** 1 1/4 **Classic Blue (IRE)**[82] 6387 4-8-10 45.......... PaulEddery 12 53+
(Ian Williams) *hld up: hdwy over 2f out: rdn over 1f out: r.o* **16/1**
060- **3** 2 1/2 **Santera (IRE)**[15] 7133 4-8-7 41.......... AndrewMullen(3) 3 49
(Mrs A Duffield) *chsd ldrs: led over 2f out: rdn clr over 1f out: hdd wl ins fnl f* **20/1**
/60- **4** 5 **El Dee (IRE)**[35] 4124 5-9-0 40.......... DanielTudhope 10 41
(Jedd O'Keeffe) *hld up: hdwy over 3f out: wknd over 1f out* **8/1**
26-5 **5** 1 **Cool Isle**[4] 83 5-9-0 38..........(b) JimmyQuinn 7 39
(P Howling) *hld up in tch: rdn over 2f out: wknd over 1f out* **8/1**
00-6 **6** 14 **Yenaled**[3] 101 11-8-7 37.......... PietroRomeo(7) 9 17
(J M Bradley) *hld up: rdn over 3f out: wknd over 2f out* **33/1**
260- **7** 1 3/4 **Trackattack**[14] 7273 6-8-11 45..........(p) NeilChalmers(3) 6 14
(M Appleby) *sn rdn to ld: hdd 4f out: wkng whn hmpd over 3f out* **16/1**
/0- **8** 1/2 **Jajoleen (IRE)**[127] 5187 5-8-7 42.......... GabrielHannon(7) 4 13
(P A Blockley) *chsd ldrs tl rdn and wknd over 2f out* **20/1**
000- **9** 1/2 **Welsh Whisper**[26] 7169 9-9-0 38.......... LiamJones 2 13
(S A Brookshaw) *dwlt: hld up: rdn over 3f out: sn wknd* **50/1**
42-4 **10** 5 **The Power Of Phil**[10] 8 4-8-10 44.......... RichardKingscote 1 —
(Miss Joanne Priest) *chsd ldr tl led 4f out: rdn and hdd over 2f out: wknd and eased over 1f out* **9/4**[1]
/3-3 **11** 9 **Veneer (IRE)**[10] 8 6-9-1 46.......... StephenDonohoe 11 —
(Mrs N S Evans) *hld up: a in rr: wknd 3f out* **11/2**[3]

2m 43.65s (2.55) **Going Correction** +0.05s/f (Slow)
WFA 4 from 5yo+ 4lb **11** Ran SP% **119.6**
Speed ratings (Par 97): **97,96,94,91,90 81,80,79,79,76 70**
CSF £48.19 TOTE £4.10: £2.10, £4.70, £12.00; EX 211.40 Place 6 £78.34, Place 5 £46.96..
Owner Eyes Wide Open Partnership **Bred** George Strawbridge Jr **Trained** Warthill, N Yorks

FOCUS
A moderate contest and the form looks weak.
The Power Of Phil Official explanation: jockey said gelding became unbalanced on the final bend and was possibly unsuited by the left-handed track
Veneer(IRE) Official explanation: jockey said gelding was never travelling; vet said gelding finished lame
T/Plt: £44.60 to a £1 stake. Pool: £94,828.50. 1,549.00 winning tickets. T/Qpdt: £12.90 to a £1 stake. Pool: £6,187.80. 353.10 winning tickets. CR

119 KEMPTON (A.W) (R-H)
Sunday, January 13

OFFICIAL GOING: Standard
Wind: strong, behind Weather: overcast

146 RACING UK MAIDEN STKS 6f (P)
12:45 (12:47) (Class 5) 3-Y-O **£2,590** (£770; £385; £192) **Stalls** High

Form RPR
00- **1** **Sparton Duke (IRE)**[215] 2532 3-9-3 0.......... ChrisCatlin 8 74
(E J O'Neill) *racd in midfield: rdn and effrt 2f out: led ent fnl f: in command and pushed out after* **7/1**[2]
3-2 **2** 1 1/4 **Salt Of The Earth (IRE)**[8] 60 3-9-3 0.......... JohnEgan 11 70
(T G Mills) *chsd ldr: rdn wl over 2f out: ev ch jst over 1f out: chsd wnr fnl f: one pce* **30/100**[1]
5-3 **3** 1 1/2 **Jane's Payoff (IRE)**[11] 9 3-8-12 0.......... RichardThomas 6 60
(Mrs L C Jewell) *led: rdn and edgd lft wl over 1f out: hdd ent fnl f: hung lft and outpcd after* **20/1**
0- **4** 1/2 **Jalons Bridewell**[82] 6404 3-9-3 0.......... TPQueally 9 63
(M Quinn) *s.i.s: in tch in midfield: rdn to chse ldrs wl over 1f out: ev ch briefly 1f out: sn outpcd* **50/1**
0- **5** nk **Extreme North (USA)**[15] 7264 3-9-3 0.......... MickyFenton 7 62+
(Miss V Haigh) *racd off the pce in midfield: shkn up and rn green wl over 2f out: styd on fnl f: nt rch ldrs* **25/1**
6 1 1/2 **Wherry (USA)** 3-8-12 0.......... MatthewHenry 10 53+
(M A Jarvis) *s.i.s: bhd: rdn over 3f out: styd on fr over 1f out: nvr trbld ldrs* **7/1**[2]
7 hd **Marquis De Louvois (IRE)** 3-9-0 0.......... AndrewMullen(3) 1 57+
(Mrs A Duffield) *s.i.s and hmpd s: dropped in bhd: rdn and effrt on inner over 2f out: n.d* **33/1**
20-0 **8** nk **Kaystar Ridge**[8] 60 3-8-12 63..........(p) JamesO'Reilly(5) 3 56
(D K Ivory) *in tch in midfield: effrt and drvn jst over 2f out: wknd wl over 1f out* **14/1**[3]
00- **9** 5 **Hero Heart**[50] 6926 3-9-3 0.......... PatCosgrave 5 40
(Jane Chapple-Hyam) *chsd ldrs: rdn over 2f out: wknd qckly over 1f out* **25/1**
6- **10** 3/4 **Saunders Encore**[38] 7043 3-8-12 0.......... JimCrowley 4 33
(M S Saunders) *stdd s: a bhd* **50/1**
6- **11** 8 **Princess Zhukova (IRE)**[23] 7217 3-8-7 0.......... KirstyMilczarek(5) 2 7
(R J Price) *wnt lft s: a bhd: t.o* **50/1**

1m 13.63s (0.53) **Going Correction** -0.05s/f (Stan) **11** Ran SP% **129.9**
Speed ratings (Par 97): **98,96,94,93,93 91,91,90,83,82 72**
CSF £10.03 TOTE £10.20: £1.90, £1.02, £3.70; EX 21.80.
Owner Ballard Campbell,JC Fretwell & C Evans **Bred** Killarkin Stud **Trained** Averham Park, Notts

FOCUS
A modest maiden, run at a fair pace. The form is rated through the runner-up.

147 TURFTV CLASSIFIED STKS 1m (P)
1:15 (1:15) (Class 7) 4-Y-0+ **£1,365** (£403; £201) **Stalls** High

Form RPR
00-0 **1** **Frank's Quest (IRE)**[4] 99 8-9-0 39.......... DavidKinsella 5 51
(A B Haynes) *hld up towards rr: nt clr run and swtchd lft over 2f out: str run fr wl over 1f out: led ins fnl f: r.o wl* **20/1**
/0-5 **2** nk **Club Captain (USA)**[11] 11 5-9-0 45.......... TPQueally 8 50
(T D McCarthy) *chsd ldrs: rdn and edgd rt briefly jst over 2f out: led jst over 1f out: hdd ins fnl f: unable qckn towards fin* **15/2**
0-35 **3** 1 1/4 **Only If I Laugh**[2] 120 7-9-0 45.......... DaleGibson 10 47
(M J Attwater) *s.i.s: t.k.h and sn in midfield: swtchd lft and hdwy over 2f out: ev ch 1f out: outpcd last 100yds* **7/2**[2]
4 2 1/2 **Vintage Quest**[31] 6662 6-9-0 43.......... VinceSlattery 14 41
(D Burchell) *s.i.s: bhd: rdn over 3f out: styd on u.p fnl f: nvr trbld ldrs* **25/1**
000- **5** 1 1/4 **Mtoto Girl**[81] 6429 4-8-11 43.......... NeilChalmers(3) 11 38
(J J Bridger) *in tch in midfield: rdn and effrt over 2f out: kpt on same pce fnl f* **66/1**
/5-0 **6** nk **Rhuby River (IRE)**[11] 11 6-9-0 42.......... MickyFenton 4 38
(R Dickin) *chsd ldrs: rdn 3f out: wknd ent fnl f* **33/1**
0-22 **7** 1 3/4 **Stepaside (IRE)**[7] 66 4-9-1 49..........(b) AndrewElliott(3) 6 38
(A D Brown) *led narrowly tl rdn and hdd jst over 1f out: wknd qckly fnl f* **6/1**
000- **8** 1 1/2 **Straight Face (IRE)**[15] 5525 4-9-0 45.......... NickyMackay 7 30
(M Wigham) *in midfield tl dropped to rr 4f out: rdn 3f out: nvr trbld ldrs* **11/4**[1]
04-0 **9** 3 **Royal Orissa**[12] 7 6-9-0 41.......... HayleyTurner 13 23
(D Haydn Jones) *taken down early: sn pushed up to press ldr: rdn wl over 2f out: wknd qckly wl over 1f out* **5/1**[3]

50-2 **10** ½ **Fortune Point (IRE)**[11] 8 10-9-1 46....................(p) RichardHughes 3 23
(A W Carroll) *hld up towards rr: rdn and effrt on outer jst over 3f out: wknd 2f out: eased ins fnl f* **11/2**

1m 41.13s (1.33) **Going Correction** -0.05s/f (Stan) **10** Ran SP% **120.0**
Speed ratings (Par 97): **96,95,94,91,90 90,88,87,84,83**
CSF £161.49 TOTE £19.80: £4.20, £2.00, £1.30; EX 137.10.
Owner Ms C Berry **Bred** Rathasker Stud **Trained** Limpley Stoke, Bath

FOCUS
A dire classified event which saw the first pair come clear. The third helps to set the level.
Fortune Point(IRE) Official explanation: jockey said gelding missed the break and ran flat

148 DIGIBET H'CAP 1m (P)
1:45 (1:45) (Class 6) (0-65,67) 4-Y-0+ **£2,047** (£604; £302) **Stalls** High

Form RPR
00-4 **1** **Seneschal**[3] 111 7-9-4 **65**.................................. RichardHughes 5 72
(A B Haynes) *mde all: pushed clr over 1f out: drvn out ins fnl f* **6/1**[3]
501- **2** 1 **Wrighty Almighty (IRE)**[35] 7085 6-9-4 **65**...................... JimCrowley 10 74+
(P R Chamings) *dwlt: t.k.h: hld up in midfield: nt clr run on inner over 2f out tl over 1f out: swtchd rt jst over 1f out: r.o strly to chse wnr ins fnl f: clsng on wnr last 100yds* **6/1**[3]
201- **3** 1½ **Machinate (USA)**[17] 7248 6-9-3 **64**...................................... LiamJones 9 65
(W M Brisbourne) *t.k.h: trckd ldrs: rdn to chse wnr over 1f out: no imp: lost 2nd ins fnl f* **12/1**
000- **4** 1 **Copper King**[99] 6024 4-9-2 **63**... JamesDoyle 1 62
(J W Hills) *hld up towards rr: rdn and gd hdwy jst over 2f out: no imp fnl f* **25/1**
614- **5** *hd* **Magic Warrior**[16] 7257 8-9-1 **62**... PatDobbs 6 60
(J C Fox) *hld up in tch: rdn and effrt jst over 2f out: kpt on same pce fr over 1f out* **6/1**[3]
00-1 **6** *shd* **Dushstorm (IRE)**[10] 24 7-9-1 **67**.......................... KirstyMilczarek(5) 2 65
(M Botti) *in tch: rdn and effrt to chse ldrs over 2f out: no imp over 1f out* **7/2**[1]
01-3 **7** ¾ **Zabeel House**[12] 7 5-9-1 **62**......................................(p) TPQueally 3 59
(John A Harris) *s.i.s: bhd: rdn and hanging rt wl over 2f out: styd on fnl f: nvr trbld ldrs* **9/2**[2]
054- **8** 3 **Very Well Red**[23] 7213 5-8-13 **60**.. ChrisCatlin 8 50
(P W Hiatt) *chsd wnr tl over 1f out: wknd qckly jst over 1f out* **11/1**
050- **9** 2½ **Binnion Bay (IRE)**[34] 7099 7-9-1 **62**..........................(b) AmirQuinn 7 46
(J J Bridger) *v.s.a: gd hdwy on outer 4f out: chsd ldrs and rdn wl over 2f out: wknd 2f out* **12/1**
600- **10** 6 **Cavallo Di Ferro (IRE)**[14] 7277 4-8-11 **58**............. StephenDonohoe 11 28
(M J Gingell) *hmpd and dropped to rr sn after s: no ch last 2f* **40/1**
6V3- **11** 4 **Strike Force**[17] 7248 4-8-8 **60**............................ NataliaGemelova(5) 4 21
(K F Clutterbuck) *chsd ldrs tl lost pl over 3f out: wl bhd last 2f* **20/1**

1m 40.75s (0.95) **Going Correction** -0.05s/f (Stan) **11** Ran SP% **118.0**
Speed ratings (Par 101): **98,97,95,94,94 94,93,90,87,81 77**
CSF £41.09 CT £431.31 TOTE £6.80: £2.00, £2.60, £4.40; EX 48.90.
Owner P Cook **Bred** Michael E Broughton **Trained** Limpley Stoke, Bath

FOCUS
A fair event for the class, run at an uneven pace.
Wrighty Almighty(IRE) Official explanation: jockey said gelding was denied a clear run
Binnion Bay(IRE) Official explanation: jockey said gelding missed the break

149 DIGIBET SPORTS BETTING H'CAP 7f (P)
2:20 (2:21) (Class 6) (0-65,63) 4-Y-0+ **£2,047** (£604; £302) **Stalls** High

Form RPR
000- **1** **Unlimited**[16] 7251 6-8-8 **53**.. JimmyQuinn 8 64
(R Simpson) *chsd ldrs: effrt to chal 2f out: rdn to ld over 1f out: drvn and r.o strly fnl f* **33/1**
16-2 **2** 1¼ **Royal Envoy (IRE)**[11] 13 5-8-11 **56**............................ DeanMcKeown 9 64
(D Shaw) *hld up wl bhd: gd hdwy on inner over 2f out: ev ch ent fnl f: nt pce of wnr after* **3/1**[2]
413- **3** *hd* **Faithful Ruler (USA)**[15] 7269 4-9-3 **62**........................ RichardHughes 4 69+
(M A Magnusson) *chsd ldrs: rdn and effrt over 1f out: chsd ldng pair ins fnl f: kpt on u.p but nt pce to trble wnr* **5/4**[1]
03/- **4** 1 **Mister Trickster (IRE)**[261] 5748 7-8-8 **53** ow1............... MickyFenton 10 57
(R Dickin) *stdd s: detached last and rdn 3f out: no hdwy tl str run fnl f: fin strly: nt rch ldrs* **33/1**
503- **5** 1¼ **Imperium**[15] 7268 7-8-12 **57**...(b) PatDobbs 1 58
(Jean-Rene Auvray) *dropped in after s: hld up in rr: rdn and effrt over 2f out: kpt on u.p but nvr gng pce to rch ldrs* **20/1**
233- **6** 1½ **Ever Cheerful**[32] 7119 7-9-4 **63**...(p) TPQueally 5 60
(A B Haynes) *chsd ldr tl led 2f out: sn rdn and hdd: wknd jst over 1f out* **9/1**
030- **7** *nk* **Takitwo**[28] 7164 5-9-0 **59**.. SimonWhitworth 7 55
(P D Cundell) *squeezed s: towards rr: hdwy over 2f out: swtchd lft and rdn wl over 1f out: no imp* **11/2**[3]
430- **8** 2½ **Kempsey**[277] 1004 6-8-12 **60**.. NeilChalmers(3) 6 49
(J J Bridger) *racd off the pce in midfield: rdn and effrt wl over 2f out: wknd over 2f out* **33/1**
420- **9** 4 **Willhewiz**[25] 7183 8-9-1 **60**...(v) JimCrowley 2 39
(M S Saunders) *sn crossed over to ld: rdn and hdd 2f out: sn wknd* **16/1**
00-4 **10** ½ **Zazous**[8] 54 7-8-12 **57**... ChrisCatlin 3 34
(J J Bridger) *chsd ldrs rdn over 3f out: wknd 2f out* **16/1**

1m 25.78s (-0.22) **Going Correction** -0.05s/f (Stan) **10** Ran SP% **120.2**
Speed ratings (Par 101): **103,101,101,100,98 97,96,93,89,88**
CSF £130.58 CT £229.15 TOTE £60.90: £10.00, £1.50, £1.10; EX 341.40.
Owner Carnival Quest **Bred** J Wise **Trained** Lambourn, Berks

FOCUS
A moderate handicap, run at a solid pace. The runner-up sets the level.
Unlimited Official explanation: trainer said, regarding apparent improvement in form, that the gelding can be difficult, was apprentice ridden last time, and may have benefited from stronger handling and the removal of cheek pieces.
Mister Trickster(IRE) Official explanation: jockey said gelding was slowly away from the stalls

150 DIGIBET CASINO H'CAP 6f (P)
2:55 (2:57) (Class 5) (0-70,74) 4-Y-0+ **£2,590** (£770; £385; £192) **Stalls** High

Form RPR
34-3 **1** **Mogok Ruby**[8] 55 4-9-6 **72**.. RichardHughes 3 82+
(L Montague Hall) *stdd s: racd in midfield: hdwy on inner 2f out: rdn to ld ins fnl f: sn in command: rdn out* **5/2**[1]
40-4 **2** 1¼ **Cool Sands (IRE)**[12] 4 6-8-13 **65**........................(v) DeanMcKeown 5 71
(D Shaw) *in tch in midfield: hdwy over 2f out: rdn and ev ch over 1f out: kpt on but nt pce of wnr ins fnl f* **15/2**
20-6 **3** ¾ **Hythe Bay**[10] 29 4-8-11 **63**... JimCrowley 10 67
(J R Best) *pressed ldrs: rdn to ld 2f out: hdd ins fnl f: kpt on same pce* **14/1**
030- **4** 1½ **Waqaarr**[279] 973 4-8-12 **64**... JohnEgan 9 63+
(Lady Herries) *stdd sn after s: bhd: outpcd and rdn over 3f out: styd on fr over 1f out: nvr trbld ldrs* **15/2**
0-63 **5** ¾ **Hucking Hill (IRE)**[4] 94 4-8-7 **66**.......................(b) GihanArnolda(7) 2 62
(J R Best) *chsd ldrs: rdn over 2f out: wknd ent fnl f* **8/1**
6 5 **Artreju (GER)**[18] 5-9-2 **68**.. PatDobbs 4 48
(G L Moore) *chsd ldrs for 2f: in midfield and rdn over 2f out: sn wl outpcd* **25/1**
320- **7** *hd* **Tamino (IRE)**[16] 7253 5-9-4 **70**.. JimmyQuinn 7 50
(P Howling) *led narrowly tl over 4f out: led again 3f out tl rdn and hdd 2f out: wknd over 1f out* **13/2**[2]
664- **8** *hd* **Mine Behind**[36] 7073 8-9-1 **67**... HayleyTurner 6 46
(J R Best) *bhd: lost tch 4f out: wl bhd after* **13/2**[2]
006- **9** ¾ **Mambazo**[22] 7221 6-8-13 **65**..................................(e) RichardKingscote 8 42
(S C Williams) *rrd leaving stalls: bhd: rdn and no rspnse over 2f out* **7/1**[3]
6-21 **10** 3½ **Sir Douglas**[4] 103 5-9-8 **74** 6ex..................................(b) TGMcLaughlin 1 40
(R A Harris) *awkward leaving stalls: sn dashed up to press ldrs: led over 4f out tl 3f out: wknd qckly 2f out* **8/1**

1m 12.44s (-0.66) **Going Correction** -0.05s/f (Stan) **10** Ran SP% **124.0**
Speed ratings (Par 103): **106,104,103,101,100 93,93,93,92,87**
CSF £23.44 CT £236.28 TOTE £3.00: £1.30, £2.70, £4.00; EX 22.80 Trifecta £139.20 Pool £470.54 - 2.40 winning units..
Owner The Ruby Partnership **Bred** R Pain **Trained** Epsom, Surrey

FOCUS
A modest handicap, run at a decent early pace.
Mine Behind Official explanation: jockey said gelding would not face the kickback

151 DAY TIME, NIGHT TIME, GREAT TIME H'CAP 7f (P)
3:25 (3:26) (Class 6) (0-50,53) 4-Y-0+ **£2,047** (£604; £302) **Stalls** High

Form RPR
41-1 **1** **Epidaurian King (IRE)**[10] 33 5-8-12 **52**...................(v) DeanMcKeown 7 68+
(D Shaw) *dwlt: hld up in midfield: swtchd lft over 2f out: pushed along and str run to ld ins fnl f: sn clr: readily* **9/4**[1]
000- **2** 3½ **Patavium Prince (IRE)**[25] 7188 5-8-6 **46**................ SimonWhitworth 11 53
(Miss Jo Crowley) *t.k.h: chsd ldrs: rdn over 2f out: led jst over 1f out tl ins fnl f: no ch w wnr* **20/1**
400- **3** ½ **Double Valentine**[14] 7278 5-8-1 **46** oh1............... KirstyMilczarek(5) 3 52
(R Ingram) *s.i.s: racd in last trio: hdwy over 3f out: kpt on steadily u.p fnl f: nvr nr wnr* **8/1**
000- **4** 1¼ **Marmooq**[55] 6873 5-8-7 **47**... DaleGibson 5 49
(M J Attwater) *chsd ldr: rdn over 2f out: led wl over 1f out tl jst over 1f out: wknd ins fnl f* **12/1**
640- **5** *nk* **Sovereignty (JPN)**[14] 7278 6-8-8 **53** ow4.................. JamesO'Reilly(5) 2 54
(D K Ivory) *bhd on outer: pushed wd and dropped to rr bnd 4f out: rdn over 3f out: kpt on u.p: n.d* **13/2**
016- **6** 1¾ **Ai Hawa (IRE)**[27] 7169 5-8-8 **48** ow1..............................(b) BrettDoyle 9 45
(Eamon Tyrrell, Ire) *t.k.h: chsd ldrs: effrt u.p 2f out: wknd fnl f* **6/1**[3]
15-4 **7** 1¼ **Maiden Investor**[4] 99 5-8-10 **50**....................................... MickyFenton 4 43
(Stef Liddiard) *stdd s: t.k.h: hld up bhd: rdn and effrt on inner over 2f out: swtchd lft jst over 2f out: sn no hdwy* **16/1**
041- **8** 4 **Mister Always**[17] 7250 4-8-10 **50**.................................(e) JimCrowley 10 33
(I W McInnes) *towards rr: rdn wl over 2f out: nvr threatened ldrs* **4/1**[2]
00-0 **9** 3½ **Pauvic (IRE)**[10] 32 5-8-3 **46** oh1..........................(v) AndrewMullen(3) 8 19
(Mrs A Duffield) *led: rdn over 2f out: hdd wl over 1f out: wknd qckly* **25/1**
343- **10** 8 **The Carpet Man**[28] 7162 4-8-8 **48**.............................. RichardKingscote 6 —
(A W Carroll) *towards rr: rn wd and lost pl bnd 4f: n.d after: eased ins fnl f* **20/1**
666- **11** 2½ **Rafferty (IRE)**[25] 7188 9-8-7 **47**...(p) JohnEgan 1 —
(S Dow) *chsd ldrs: rdn wl over 2f out: sn struggling: eased whn no ch fnl f* **12/1**

1m 26.48s (0.48) **Going Correction** -0.05s/f (Stan) **11** Ran SP% **124.1**
Speed ratings (Par 101): **99,95,94,93,92 90,89,84,80,71 68**
CSF £58.39 CT £335.38 TOTE £2.80: £1.30, £6.60, £3.10; EX 80.00.
Owner Joe McCarthy **Bred** Shadwell Estate Company Limited **Trained** Danethorpe, Notts

FOCUS
A very weak handicap and the progressive winner rates value for a bit further than the winning margin.
Rafferty(IRE) Official explanation: jockey said gelding ran too free

152 PANORAMIC BAR & RESTAURANT H'CAP 2m (P)
3:55 (3:55) (Class 6) (0-50,50) 4-Y-0+ **£2,047** (£604; £151; £151) **Stalls** High

Form RPR
66-5 **1** **Isa'Af (IRE)**[7] 67 9-8-11 **46** oh1....................................(p) JimCrowley 7 50
(P W Hiatt) *chsd ldr: rdn and upsides jst over 2f out: led last 100yds: forged ahd towards fin* **25/1**
00/4 **2** 1¼ **Bright Sparky (GER)**[7] 69 5-8-8 **50**.............................(t) NSLawes(7) 11 52
(M W Easterby) *led: rdn and hrd pressed over 2f out: battled on gamely tl hdd last 100yds: no ex* **6/1**[2]
0/0- **3** *shd* **Optimum (IRE)**[18] 585 6-8-8 **48** ow2........................ JamesO'Reilly(5) 2 50
(J T Stimpson) *chsd ldrs: rdn over 3f out: no imp tl plugged on u.p fnl f: steadily clsng fnl f* **8/1**
234- **3** *dht* **Squirtle (IRE)**[13] 7285 5-8-11 **46**....................................... LiamJones 1 48
(W M Brisbourne) *s.i.s: hdwy into midfield 10f out: chsd ldng pair over 4f out: drvn over 3f out: plugged on but nvr quite gng pce to rch ldrs* **7/1**[3]
61-2 **5** 1¾ **Prince Of Medina**[11] 14 5-9-0 **49**................................... HayleyTurner 9 49
(J R Best) *t.k.h: hld up in midfield: hdwy 5f out: chsd ldrs 4f out: sn rdn: hrd drvn and v one pce last 3f* **11/10**[1]
06-2 **6** 2 **Countback (FR)**[9] 36 9-9-1 **50**.....................................(p) JamesDoyle 8 47
(A W Carroll) *hld up towards rr: hdwy 7f out: 6th and in tch over 3f out: rdn jst over 2f out: no hdwy and sn btn* **8/1**
000/ **7** 17 **Khadija**[139] 1006 7-8-11 **46** oh1.. MickyFenton 4 23
(R Dickin) *stdd s: bhd: rdn 5f out: sn lost tch: t.o wl over 2f out* **25/1**
054- **8** 3½ **The Slider**[36] 7069 4-8-1 **46** oh1................................. AndrewElliott(3) 5 19
(Mrs L C Jewell) *in tch in midfield: rdn over 4f out: sn struggling: t.o wl over 2f out* **20/1**
036- **9** 7 **Lord Nellsson**[49] 3927 12-8-4 **46**... PNolan(7) 12 10
(A B Haynes) *a wl bhd: rdn 7f out: lost tch 5f out: t.o* **18/1**

464- **10** *13* **Gouranga**[11] 7262 5-9-1 **50**.......... RichardHughes 6 —
(A W Carroll) *chsd ldrs: reminders after 3f: rdn over 5f out: wknd over 4f out: eased last 2f: t.o* **16/1**

3m 32.72s (2.62) **Going Correction** -0.05s/f (Stan)
WFA 4 from 5yo+ 7lb **10** Ran SP% **120.2**
Speed ratings (Par 101): **94,93,93,93,92 91,82,81,77,71**
Place: Optimum £1.40, Squirtle £1.00. Tricast: I/BS/O £664.68, I/BS/S £591.26. CSF £169.70 TOTE £20.60: £3.60, £2.20; EX 272.90 Place 6 £63.93, Place 5 £53.60..
Owner Phil Kelly **Bred** T Monaghan **Trained** Hook Norton, Oxon

FOCUS
A moderate handicap that turned into a proper test at the distance.
Gouranga Official explanation: jockey said mare had no more to give
T/Jkpt: Not won. T/Plt: £86.30 to a £1 stake. Pool: £102,294.85. 865.15 winning tickets. T/Qpdt: £15.10 to a £1 stake. Pool: £7,341.10. 358.10 winning tickets. SP

106 SOUTHWELL (L-H)
Monday, January 14

OFFICIAL GOING: Standard
Wind: Light across Weather: Cloudy

153 SPONSOR A RACE BY CALLING 0870 220 2332 AMATEUR RIDERS' H'CAP — 5f (F)
12:40 (12:40) (Class 6) (0-52,47) 4-Y-0+ **£1,714** (£527; £263) **Stalls** High

Form RPR
406- **1** **Savile's Delight (IRE)**[34] 7107 9-11-2 **45**.......... MissMSowerby[(3)] 9 53
(Tom Dascombe) *hld up: hdwy 2f out: hung lft and led 1f out: pushed out* **7/4**[1]
000- **2** *2½* **High Window (IRE)**[18] 7239 8-11-2 **45**.......... MissJCoward[(3)] 8 44
(G P Kelly) *prom: lost pl 4f out: hdwy over 1f out: r.o* **33/1**
-042 **3** *¾* **Blushing Russian (IRE)**[5] 100 6-10-12 **45**..........(b) MissHDavies[(7)] 3 41
(J M Bradley) *edgd rt s: led: hdd over 3f out: led again 1/2-way: rdn and hdd 1f out: styd on same pce* **7/2**[3]
400- **4** *1½* **Eastern Princess**[83] 6402 4-10-12 **45**..........(b[1]) MrSeanKerr[(7)] 6 36
(G H Yardley) *chsd ldrs: rdn 1/2-way: edgd rt over 1f out: wknd ins fnl f* **20/1**
400- **5** *¾* **Preskani**[19] 7233 6-10-12 **45**..........(p) MissKLMorgan[(7)] 1 33
(Mrs N Macauley) *chsd ldrs: rdn over 1f out: wknd ins fnl f* **12/1**
30-0 **6** *¾* **Telepathic (IRE)**[12] 15 8-11-0 **45**..........(b) MrAshleePrice[(5)] 4 31
(A Berry) *s.i.s and hmpd s: sn chsng ldrs: rdn over 1f out: wknd ins fnl f* **20/1**
000- **7** *5* **Percy Douglas**[14] 7283 8-11-0 **45**..........(b) MissLAllan[(5)] 2 13
(Miss A Stokell) *chsd ldrs: led over 3f out: hdd 1/2-way: rdn and wknd over 1f out* **25/1**
43-0 **8** *hd* **Fern House (IRE)**[2] 142 6-11-4 **47**..........(v) MrMJJSmith[(3)] 7 14
(Garry Moss) *s.s: outpcd* **11/4**[2]
000- **9** *shd* **Kitchen Sink (IRE)**[37] 7077 6-10-12 **45**..........(be) MissJMHindle[(7)] 5 11
(Jean-Rene Auvray) *hmpd s: a in rr* **14/1**

61.74 secs (2.04) **Going Correction** +0.325s/f (Slow) **9** Ran SP% **115.9**
Speed ratings (Par 101): **101,97,95,93,92 91,83,82,82**
CSF £73.91 CT £191.43 TOTE £2.30: £1.50, £8.10, £1.50; EX 73.10 TRIFECTA Not won..
Owner ONEWAY Partners **Bred** Romany Investments Ltd **Trained** Lambourn, Berks

FOCUS
This was basically a banded type contest with only one horse rated above 45 and running off its correct mark.
Fern House(IRE) Official explanation: jockey said gelding missed the break

154 GR8 DEALS @ PONTINS.COM H'CAP — 6f (F)
1:10 (1:10) (Class 6) (0-60,60) 3-Y-0 **£1,774** (£523; £262) **Stalls** Low

Form RPR
32-0 **1** *2½* **Alabama Spirit (USA)**[12] 12 3-8-13 **60**.......... TolleyDean[(5)] 5 64
(D Shaw) *hld up: hdwy over 2f out: rdn and ev ch over 1f out: styd on same pce ins fnl f* **11/2**[3]
000- **2** *1¼* **Note Perfect**[198] 3092 3-8-11 **53**.......... DaleGibson 3 53
(M W Easterby) *chsd ldrs: rdn to ld 2f out: hdd over 1f out: no ex ins fnl f* **9/1**
0-61 **3** *1¼* **Fulford**[8] 65 3-9-1 **60** 6ex.......... MarkLawson[(7)] 7 56
(M Brittain) *s.i.s: sn prom: rdn and ev ch 2f out: wknd ins fnl f* **7/4**[1]
066- **4** *2½* **Joshua**[19] 7235 3-8-5 **47**.......... LiamJones 6 35
(D E Cantillon) *edgd rt s: prom: racd keenly: lost pl over 4f out: n.d after* **12/1**
055- **5** *hd* **Countrywide Comet (IRE)**[24] 7210 3-9-3 **59**..........(b) TGMcLaughlin 4 46
(P Howling) *chsd ldrs: rdn over 2f out: hung lft and wknd over 1f out* **8/1**
05-3 **6** *hd* **Bahamarama (IRE)**[10] 38 3-8-8 **50**.......... ChrisCatlin 1 37
(R A Harris) *led: rdn and hdd 2f out: wknd fnl f* **13/2**
00-1 **D** **Bold Diva**[5] 92 3-8-4 **51** 6ex..........(v) KirstyMilczarek[(5)] 2 63
(A W Carroll) *trckd ldrs: racd keenly: led over 1f out: r.o wl* **5/1**[2]

1m 17.35s (0.85) **Going Correction** -0.175s/f (Stan) **7** Ran SP% **110.6**
Speed ratings (Par 95): **86,85,83,80,79 79,90**
CSF £29.95 TOTE £5.60: £3.30, £2.70; EX 24.60.
Owner The Circle Bloodstock I Limited **Bred** Mckee Stables Inc **Trained** Danethorpe, Notts

FOCUS
A fairly competitive low-grade handicap run in a modest winning time. It has been rated around the runner-up.

155 DINE IN THE QUEEN MOTHER RESTAURANT (S) STKS — 7f (F)
1:40 (1:40) (Class 6) 4-Y-0+ **£1,774** (£523; £262) **Stalls** Low

Form RPR
00-3 **1** **Another Genepi (USA)**[12] 15 5-8-12 **63**..........(b) NCallan 6 70
(K A Ryan) *mde all: rdn clr over 1f out: eased nr fin* **5/4**[1]
05-3 **2** *7* **Elusive Warrior (USA)**[7] 75 5-8-12 **55**..........(p) TonyHamilton 2 51
(R A Fahey) *chsd wnr: rdn over 2f out: wkng whn hung rt over 1f out* **13/8**[2]
05-6 **3** *2½* **Gifted Flame**[12] 15 9-8-7 **48**.......... AnnStokell[(5)] 7 44
(Miss A Stokell) *s.i.s: sn chsng ldrs: wknd over 1f out* **20/1**
665- **4** *2* **Local Poet**[55] 6882 7-8-12 **57**..........(bt) TomEaves 1 39
(Ollie Pears) *sn pushed along in rr: bhd fr 1/2-way* **9/2**[3]
00-0 **5** *8* **Obe One**[12] 16 8-8-12 **44**..........(b) StephenDonohoe 4 17
(A Berry) *s.i.s: sn prom: wknd 3f out* **33/1**

1m 29.27s (-1.03) **Going Correction** -0.175s/f (Stan) **5** Ran SP% **108.4**
Speed ratings (Par 101): **101,93,90,87,78**
CSF £3.42 TOTE £2.10: £1.30, £1.40; EX 3.60.There was no bid for the winner
Owner Hambleton Racing Ltd I **Bred** Joseph Lacombe Stables Inc **Trained** Hambleton, N Yorks

FOCUS
Not a great event even by selling standards. The runner-up and third have been rated close to their previous course and distance form.

156 BOOK TICKETS ONLINE CLAIMING STKS — 1m (F)
2:10 (2:10) (Class 6) 3-Y-0 **£2,047** (£604; £302) **Stalls** Low

Form RPR
22-1 **1** **Home**[7] 73 3-9-7 **72**..........(p) PatCosgrave 2 73
(J R Boyle) *chsd ldr: led over 1f out: edgd rt ins fnl f: pushed out* **9/4**[1]
1-41 **2** *½* **Autumn Charm**[6] 81 3-8-6 **60**.......... LiamJones 5 57
(D W Chapman) *chsd ldrs: led over 2f out: rdn and hdd over 1f out: styd on* **9/4**[1]
305- **3** *¾* **Tapas Lad (IRE)**[14] 7286 3-8-9 **57**..........(v) TGMcLaughlin 1 58
(V Smith) *s.s: bhd: hdwy u.p over 1f out: r.o* **8/1**[2]
001- **4** *7* **Berrynarbor**[55] 6880 3-8-12 **62**.......... FergusSweeney 6 45+
(A G Newcombe) *chsd ldrs: rdn over 4f out: hung lft fr over 2f out: wkng whn nt clr run over 1f out* **9/1**[3]
5-01 **5** *nk* **Her Name Is Rio (IRE)**[4] 108 3-8-4 **60**.......... ChrisCatlin 4 36
(Mrs S Lamyman) *plld hrd and prom: lost pl over 5f out: hdwy u.p 2f out: wknd fnl f* **8/1**[2]
003- **6** *2½* **Sharps Gold**[14] 7286 3-8-1 **55**..........(b[1]) DuranFentiman[(3)] 7 30
(P J McBride) *sn led: rdn and hdd over 2f out: wkng whn hung lft over 1f out* **14/1**
31-0 **7** *3½* **Carry On Cleo**[12] 20 3-8-9 **61** ow1..........(b) StephenDonohoe 3 27
(P D Evans) *sn pushed along in rr: bhd fnl 3f* **10/1**

1m 44.89s (1.19) **Going Correction** -0.175s/f (Stan) **7** Ran SP% **109.5**
Speed ratings (Par 95): **91,90,89,82,82 79,76**
CSF £6.34 TOTE £2.80: £1.10, £2.00; EX 7.10.The winner and Tapas Lad were the subject of friendly claims. Autumn Charm was claimed by Ms Lucinda Featherstone for £7,000.
Owner M Khan X2 **Bred** A T Macdonald **Trained** Epsom, Surrey

FOCUS
A modest winning time in a race where six of the seven runners could already boast victories here. The runner-up and third give the form a fairly solid look, but it is not sure to work out.
Berrynarbor Official explanation: jockey said filly hung left in straight
Carry On Cleo Official explanation: jockey said filly was unsuited by the kickback

157 BE BESIDE THE SEASIDE @ PONTIN'S H'CAP — 1m (F)
2:40 (2:40) (Class 5) (0-75,75) 3-Y-0 **£2,457** (£725; £362) **Stalls** Low

Form RPR
001- **1** **Especially (IRE)**[27] 7176 3-8-12 **69**.......... GregFairley 4 76
(M Johnston) *chsd ldrs: rdn to ld over 1f out: r.o* **15/8**[2]
231- **2** *1* **Safebreaker**[31] 7140 3-9-4 **75**.......... SebSanders 1 80+
(N Tinkler) *a.p: hmpd over 2f out: rdn to chse wnr over 1f out: sn hung lft: r.o* **5/4**[1]
006- **3** *5* **Terracos Do Pinhal**[128] 5227 3-8-10 **67**.......... DeanMcKeown 2 61
(M Johnston) *chsd ldr tl led 1/2-way: rdn and hdd over 1f out: wknd ins fnl f* **8/1**
03-6 **4** *11* **Silver Sprite**[12] 20 3-7-11 **61** oh7.......... PatrickDonaghy[(7)] 3 29
(D Shaw) *led to 1/2-way: sn rdn: hung lft over 2f out: wknd wl over 1f out* **9/2**[3]

1m 42.39s (-1.31) **Going Correction** -0.175s/f (Stan) **4** Ran SP% **108.5**
Speed ratings (Par 97): **104,103,98,87**
CSF £4.63 TOTE £2.70; EX 4.80.
Owner Sheikh Hamdan Bin Mohammed Al Maktoum **Bred** Darley **Trained** Middleham Moor, N Yorks

FOCUS
A decent winning time for a race like this and by far the fastest of the three races over the trip. The form looks reasonable but not bomb-proof.

158 BOOK PONTIN'S - BECAUSE YOU'RE WORTH IT MAIDEN STKS — 1m (F)
3:10 (3:12) (Class 5) 3-Y-0 **£2,457** (£725; £362) **Stalls** Low

Form RPR
536- **1** **Tevez**[25] 7204 3-9-3 **69**..........(b[1]) JimmyQuinn 4 69
(M H Tompkins) *trckd ldrs: shkn up to ld over 1f out: r.o wl: eased nr fin* **5/2**[2]
0- **2** *3* **Musical Feud (IRE)**[26] 7191 3-9-3 **0**.......... PatCosgrave 3 62
(Jane Chapple-Hyam) *s.i.s: sn chsng ldrs: rdn whn hmpd over 2f out: hung lft over 1f out: styd on same pce fnl f* **28/1**
325- **3** *hd* **Hellfire Bay**[31] 7140 3-9-3 **67**..........(p) NCallan 1 62
(K A Ryan) *chsd ldr tl led over 3f out: rdn and hdd over 1f out: hung rt and no ex fnl f* **13/8**[1]
4 *3½* **Kirkie (USA)** 3-9-3 **0**.......... JohnEgan 6 54
(D J Murphy) *prom: rdn and edgd lft over 1f out: wknd fnl f* **8/1**
0- **5** *3½* **Soxy Doxy (IRE)**[103] 5912 3-8-12 **0**.......... GregFairley 2 41
(M Johnston) *led over 4f: rdn and edgd rt over 2f out: wknd over 1f out* **10/3**[3]
6 *15* **Just Kenko** 3-9-3 **0**.......... SamHitchcott 5 11
(N J Vaughan) *s.s: outpcd: bhd fnl 3f* **20/1**

1m 43.88s (0.18) **Going Correction** -0.175s/f (Stan) **6** Ran SP% **109.1**
Speed ratings (Par 97): **96,93,92,89,85 70**
CSF £52.22 TOTE £3.20: £1.80, £8.60; EX 44.70.
Owner Sakal Family **Bred** P A And Mrs D G Sakal **Trained** Newmarket, Suffolk

FOCUS
A modest maiden that did not take much winning. It has been rated through the third.

159 TREAT THE FAMILY @ PONTIN'S H'CAP — 1m 4f (F)
3:40 (3:40) (Class 5) (0-75,75) 4-Y-0+ **£2,730** (£806; £403) **Stalls** Low

Form RPR
213- **1** **Noble Plum (IRE)**[25] 7205 4-9-4 **73**.......... SebSanders 1 88+
(Sir Mark Prescott) *hld up: racd keenly: hdwy to ld over 3f out: sn clr: hung lft 2f out: styd on wl: eased nr fin* **2/1**[2]
511- **2** *5* **Bentley Brook (IRE)**[18] 7242 6-8-8 **66**.......... GabrielHannon[(7)] 7 70
(P A Blockley) *prom: chsd ldr over 4f out: ev ch over 3f out: sn rdn: styng on same pce whn hung lft over 1f out* **11/2**[3]
11-2 **3** *hd* **Victory Quest (IRE)**[13] 3 8-9-5 **70**..........(v) ChrisCatlin 5 73
(Mrs S Lamyman) *led: rdn and hdd over 3f out: styd on same pce fnl 2f* **12/1**
24-2 **4** *2½* **Jackie Kiely**[6] 78 7-9-5 **70**..........(t) J-PGuillambert 2 70
(R Brotherton) *chsd ldr over 7f: sn rdn: styd on same pce fnl 2f* **17/2**
61-1 **5** *3* **Clear Reef**[13] 3 4-9-6 **75**.......... TGMcLaughlin 3 70
(Jane Chapple-Hyam) *hld up and bhd: nt clr run wl over 3f out: sn rdn: nvr trbld ldrs* **11/8**[1]

/6- **6** *35* **Jeu De Roseau (IRE)**[25] 7198 4-8-9 64 .... TPQueally 4 3
(A P Stringer) *chsd ldrs over 8f* **66/1**

2m 38.69s (-2.31) **Going Correction** -0.175s/f (Stan)
WFA 4 from 5yo+ 4lb **6 Ran SP% 110.5**
Speed ratings (Par 103): **104,100,100,98,96 73**
CSF £12.81 TOTE £3.70: £2.10, £2.50; EX 17.40 Place 6 £ 52.52, Place 5 £ 31.75.
Owner Sir Edmund Loder **Bred** Sir E J Loder **Trained** Newmarket, Suffolk

FOCUS
Most of these came into this interesting little handicap in decent form, but the unexposed winner came nicely clear and is value for even further than the five-length winning margin.
Clear Reef Official explanation: jockey said colt ran flat
T/Plt: £49.80 to a £1 stake. Pool: £55,813.95. 817.40 winning tickets. T/Qpdt: £16.60 to a £1 stake. Pool: £4,711.80. 208.90 winning tickets. CR

[146]KEMPTON (A.W) (R-H)

Tuesday, January 15

OFFICIAL GOING: Standard
Wind: fresh, half-behind Weather: Cloudy

160 SPONSOR AT KEMPTON CLASSIFIED STKS 1m 2f (P)

1:10 (1:15) (Class 7) 4-Y-O+ **£1,365** (£403; £201) **Stalls** High

Form RPR

020- **1** **Megalala (IRE)**[30] 7166 7-8-11 42 .... NeilChalmers(3) 9 53+
(J J Bridger) *prom: sltly outpcd 3f out: rallied and hmpd ent st: fnd gap on rail and r.o to ld fnl 100yds* **7/1**

03-5 **2** *1* **Sorbiesharry (IRE)**[8] 77 9-8-9 42 ....(p) KirstyMilczarek(5) 1 48
(Mrs N Macauley) *stdd s: hld up in rr: hdwy over 3f out: chsd ldrs over 1f out: kpt on* **7/1**

600- **3** *shd* **Ernmoor**[38] 7069 6-9-0 41 .... J-PGuillambert 7 48
(J R Jenkins) *mid-div: rdn and dropped towards rr 4f out: gd late hdwy* **14/1**

02-6 **4** *1 1/4* **Ponte Vecchio (IRE)**[6] 99 4-8-12 45 .... FergusSweeney 5 45
(J R Boyle) *w ldrs tl no ex fnl 100yds* **3/1**[1]

/0-6 **5** *hd* **Busy Man (IRE)**[13] 8 9-9-0 45 .... PaulDoe 10 45
(R C Guest) *stdd s: hdwy to chse ldrs 6f out: slt ld wl over 1f out: hdd and no ex fnl 100yds* **9/2**[3]

6-50 **6** *1 1/4* **Salvestro**[4] 120 5-9-0 45 .... NCallan 3 42
(A W Carroll) *cl up: jnd ldrs wl over 1f out: wknd ins fnl f* **7/2**[2]

006- **7** *3 1/2* **Elms Schoolboy**[16] 7277 6-9-0 40 ....(b) TGMcLaughlin 2 35
(P Howling) *stdd s and lost 6 l: bhd: rdn 3f out: nvr nr ldrs* **14/1**

00-0 **8** *7* **Straight Face (IRE)**[2] 147 4-8-12 45 .... SimonWhitworth 8 21
(M Wigham) *slt ld tl wl over 1f out: sn wknd* **9/2**[3]

000- **9** *8* **Marist Madame**[19] 7250 4-8-12 45 .... RobertHavlin 6 5
(T J Pitt) *in tch: rdn 6f out: wknd 3f out* **16/1**

0/0- **10** *17* **Boogie Magic**[25] 7213 8-9-0 40 .... SamHitchcott 4 —
(R W Price) *towards rr: drvn along 6f out: no ch and eased 2f out* **33/1**

2m 11.35s (3.35) **Going Correction** +0.25s/f (Slow)
WFA 4 from 5yo+ 2lb **10 Ran SP% 130.7**
Speed ratings (Par 97): **96,95,95,94,93 92,90,84,78,64**
CSF £62.37 TOTE £11.00: £3.20, £1.90, £6.60; EX 46.50.
Owner Tommy Ware **Bred** Joseph Gallagher **Trained** Liphook, Hants

FOCUS
A dire contest rated around the runner-up and fourth.
Ernmoor Official explanation: jockey said gelding hung right in behind winner close home and being concerned he would clip heels, he had to ease gelding in final strides
Boogie Magic Official explanation: jockey said mare never travelled

161 KEMPTON.CO.UK H'CAP 1m 2f (P)

1:40 (1:46) (Class 6) (0-50,50) 4-Y-O+ **£2,047** (£604; £302) **Stalls** High

Form RPR

/10- **1** **Sahf London**[10] 187 5-8-11 47 ....(b) FergusSweeney 1 58+
(G L Moore) *sn rdn up to chse ldrs: chal and carried rt over 1f out: led ins fnl f: drvn out* **5/2**[1]

00-5 **2** *3/4* **Hayley's Flower (IRE)**[4] 122 4-8-4 47 .... KirstyMilczarek(5) 3 54
(J C Fox) *hld up in midfield: hdwy over 2f out: led and edgd rt jst over 1f out: hdd ins fnl f: kpt on* **6/1**

60-0 **3** *2* **Come What July (IRE)**[4] 125 7-8-5 46 .... TolleyDean(5) 2 49
(D Shaw) *rdn early: towards rr: hdwy on rail 2f out: hrd rdn over 1f out: styd on* **8/1**

03-3 **4** *3 1/2* **Granary Girl**[8] 77 6-8-12 48 .... JimmyQuinn 6 44
(J Pearce) *in tch: effrt over 3f out: hrd rdn 2f out: one pce* **7/2**[2]

050- **5** *2 1/2* **Ruwain**[27] 7186 4-8-12 50 .... TPQueally 10 41
(W J Musson) *t.k.h in rr: rdn 3f out: nvr rchd ldrs* **4/1**[3]

0-20 **6** *3* **Fortune Point (IRE)**[2] 147 10-8-11 47 ow1 ....(p) NCallan 5 32
(A W Carroll) *sn rdn to ld: hrd rdn 2f out: hdd and squeezed on rail jst over 1f out: wknd* **7/1**

000/ **7** *1 1/2* **Glowing Dawn (IRE)**[775] 5975 6-8-12 48 .... JamesDoyle 7 30
(Miss J S Davis) *plld hrd: prom tl wknd qckly over 1f out* **33/1**

0-00 **8** *1 3/4* **Lady Firecracker (IRE)**[6] 88 4-8-0 45 ....(v[1]) KierenFox(7) 4 23
(J R Best) *mid-div: hmpd and dropped towards rr 3f out: rdn and n.d after* **33/1**

520- **9** *5* **Royal Guest**[16] 7276 4-8-12 50 ....(p) J-PGuillambert 8 18
(J R Jenkins) *restless stalls: s.s: rdn 4f out: a bhd* **8/1**

0/0- **10** *7* **Italstar (IRE)**[176] 3792 4-8-8 46 .... PaulEddery 9 —
(Miss D Mountain) *prom tl wknd qckly over 3f out* **50/1**

2m 10.67s (2.67) **Going Correction** +0.25s/f (Slow)
WFA 4 from 5yo+ 2lb **10 Ran SP% 127.6**
Speed ratings (Par 101): **99,98,96,94,92 89,88,87,83,77**
CSF £20.05 CT £113.63 TOTE £3.80: £1.40, £2.40, £3.10; EX 20.00.
Owner Longshot Racing **Bred** Vogue Development Company (kent) Ltd **Trained** Woodingdean, E Sussex

FOCUS
A poor contest, rated around the third, that is unlikely to produce anything other than the odd winner.
Glowing Dawn(IRE) Official explanation: jockey said mare ran too free

162 DAY TIME, NIGHT TIME, GREAT TIME H'CAP 5f (P)

2:10 (2:15) (Class 4) (0-85,85) 4-Y-O+ **£4,210** (£1,252; £625; £312) **Stalls** High

Form RPR

51-2 **1** **Northern Empire (IRE)**[14] 5 5-9-4 85 .... NCallan 7 93
(K A Ryan) *chsd ldrs: led 1f out: rdn out* **1/1**[1]

3-60 **2** *1/2* **Yungaburra (IRE)**[7] 84 4-9-4 85 ....(t) JamesDoyle 6 91
(D J Murphy) *hld up in rr: rdn 2f out: r.o to take 2nd fnl 50yds* **7/1**

00- **3** *1/2* **Dress To Impress (IRE)**[60] 6836 4-8-3 75 .... KirstyMilczarek(5) 5 79
(G A Butler) *t.k.h in 5th: effrt and hrd rdn over 1f out: styd on fnl f* **7/1**

216- **4** *1/2* **Financial Times (USA)**[38] 7078 6-8-13 80 ....(t) TPQueally 2 82
(Stef Liddiard) *pressed ldr: hrd rdn 2f out: one pce* **6/1**[3]

30-0 **5** *hd* **Magic Glade**[14] 5 9-9-1 82 .... LPKeniry 3 84
(Peter Grayson) *led: hrd rdn and hdd 1f out: no ex ins fnl f* **16/1**

450- **6** *3/4* **Diane's Choice**[18] 7255 5-9-4 85 .... DaneO'Neill 4 84
(J Akehurst) *chsd ldrs on outside: rdn 2f out: no ex over 1f out* **5/2**[2]

61.18 secs (0.68) **Going Correction** +0.25s/f (Slow) **6 Ran SP% 123.7**
Speed ratings (Par 105): **104,103,102,101,101 100**
CSF £10.48 TOTE £2.30: £1.30, £3.50; EX 12.20.
Owner Roger Peel **Bred** Denis McDonnell **Trained** Hambleton, N Yorks

FOCUS
A competitive sprint handicap but a bunched finish gives the form a muddling feel.
Dress To Impress(IRE) Official explanation: jockey said colt ran too free

163 MIX BUSINESS WITH PLEASURE MEDIAN AUCTION MAIDEN STKS 7f (P)

2:40 (2:46) (Class 5) 3-Y-O **£2,590** (£770; £385; £192) **Stalls** High

Form RPR

46- **1** **Steele Tango (USA)**[37] 7084 3-9-3 0 .... DaneO'Neill 4 78+
(R A Teal) *prom: lost pl over 2f out: rallied over 1f out: str run to ld fnl strides* **5/4**[1]

440- **2** *hd* **Autumn Blades (IRE)**[75] 6602 3-9-3 70 .... TPQueally 2 73
(J W Hills) *t.k.h in 5th: led on bit 2f out: rdn and edgd lft fnl f: ct fnl strides* **13/8**[2]

3 *5* **Micheals Boy (IRE)** 3-9-3 0 .... FergusSweeney 7 60
(J R Boyle) *hld up in 6th: hdwy to join ldr wl over 1f out: no ex ins fnl f* **12/1**

00- **4** *2 1/2* **Dear Will**[38] 7070 3-9-3 0 .... OscarUrbina 5 53
(J R Fanshawe) *hld up towards rr: effrt 2f out: wnt 4th 1f out: no imp* **10/1**[3]

5 *3 1/2* **Red Sonja (IRE)** 3-8-12 0 .... JamesDoyle 3 38
(M Blanshard) *chsd ldrs: disp 2nd over 2f out: sn rdn and wknd* **16/1**

4- **6** *1 1/4* **Hiss And Boo**[27] 7181 3-9-3 0 ....(b) TGMcLaughlin 6 40
(P Howling) *chsd ldr: hung rt and carried hd awkwardly over 2f out: sn wknd* **25/1**

\- **7** *hd* **Awesome Light (IRE)** 3-9-3 0 .... NCallan 8 39
(W R Muir) *dwlt: bhd: rdn over 3f out: nvr nr ldrs* **10/1**[3]

0-0 **8** *5* **Caffe Coretto**[10] 52 3-8-5 0 .... GabrielHannon(7) 1 21
(B G Powell) *led tl 2f out: sn hrd rdn and wknd: swished tail whn btn* **50/1**

1m 28.7s (2.70) **Going Correction** +0.25s/f (Slow) **8 Ran SP% 120.1**
Speed ratings (Par 97): **94,93,88,85,81 79,79,73**
CSF £3.71 TOTE £2.40: £1.20, £1.10, £2.90; EX 4.30.
Owner The Thirty Acre Racing Partnership **Bred** Tom Zwiesler **Trained** Ashtead, Surrey

FOCUS
A moderate maiden, with the runner-up the best guide to the level for now.

164 PANORAMIC BAR & RESTAURANT H'CAP 1m (P)

3:10 (3:15) (Class 6) (0-50,50) 4-Y-O+ **£2,047** (£604; £302) **Stalls** High

Form RPR

000- **1** **Certifiable**[18] 7257 7-8-6 47 .... RobynBrisland(5) 4 53
(Miss Z C Davison) *trckd ldr: led 2f out: drvn out* **13/2**

004- **2** *nk* **Jomus**[30] 7167 7-8-12 48 .... RobertHavlin 7 54
(L Montague Hall) *s.s: hld up in rr: gd hdwy over 1f out: r.o to press wnr fnl 50yds* **9/1**

10-5 **3** *3/4* **Kinsman (IRE)**[6] 99 11-8-12 48 ....(p) J-PGuillambert 5 52
(T D McCarthy) *t.k.h: trckd ldrs: effrt over 2f out: chsd wnr ins fnl f: nt qckn fnl 75yds* **12/1**

055- **4** *1 1/4* **Border Edge**[17] 7268 10-8-12 48 .... NCallan 8 49
(J J Bridger) *sn led and set sedate pce: qcknd ent st: hdd 2f out: no ex fnl f* **5/2**[1]

206- **5** *1 3/4* **Beckenham's Secret**[48] 6453 4-8-7 48 .... KirstyMilczarek(5) 2 45
(A W Carroll) *trckd ldrs: rdn over 2f out: one pce* **4/1**[2]

003- **6** *1 3/4* **Trickle (USA)**[30] 7166 4-8-12 48 ....(t) PaulEddery 6 41
(Miss D Mountain) *in tch: effrt and hrd rdn 2f out: wknd over 1f out* **6/1**[3]

46-1 **7** *2* **Future Deal**[13] 11 7-8-10 46 .... SimonWhitworth 3 34
(C A Horgan) *rdn 3f out: a bhd* **5/2**[1]

306- **8** *1 1/2* **Law Of The Land (IRE)**[51] 5542 4-8-7 50 .... GabrielHannon(7) 1 35
(B W Duke) *t.k.h in 6th: outpcd and hrd rdn 3f out: n.d after* **16/1**

1m 42.35s (2.55) **Going Correction** +0.25s/f (Slow) **8 Ran SP% 128.3**
Speed ratings (Par 101): **97,96,95,94,92 91,89,87**
CSF £70.26 CT £712.37 TOTE £9.30: £2.10, £2.90, £2.30; EX 70.40.
Owner Mrs S E Colville **Bred** A S Reid **Trained** Hammerwood, E Sussex

FOCUS
A very moderate handicap and the form is not worth dwelling on. The best guide to rating the race is probably the third, to his course and distance win in October.

165 KEMPTON FOR WEDDINGS H'CAP 6f (P)

3:40 (3:46) (Class 5) (0-70,70) 4-Y-O+ **£2,590** (£770; £385; £192) **Stalls** High

Form RPR

31-1 **1** **Muktasb (USA)**[10] 54 7-8-3 60 ow1 ....(v) TolleyDean(5) 8 71+
(D Shaw) *hld up towards rr: hdwy over 2f out: led wl over 1f out: drvn clr: readily* **7/2**[2]

160- **2** *2* **Monashee Prince (IRE)**[27] 7183 6-8-9 61 ....(v) JimmyQuinn 2 66
(J R Best) *hld up in rr: rdn and r.o fnl 2f: tk 2nd fnl strides* **12/1**

-635 **3** *nk* **Hucking Hill (IRE)**[2] 150 4-9-0 66 ....(b) NCallan 9 70
(J R Best) *dwlt: sn trcking ldrs on rail: drvn to go 2nd 1f out: nt qckn: lost 2nd fnl strides* **3/1**[1]

20-1 **4** *1/2* **Arfinnit (IRE)**[13] 13 7-8-2 59 ....(p) KirstyMilczarek(5) 7 61
(Mrs A L M King) *rrd s: hld up in 5th: effrt over 2f out: styd on fnl f* **4/1**[3]

1-33 **5** *nk* **Perlachy**[4] 126 4-8-4 59 ....(v) DuranFentiman(3) 6 60
(Mrs N Macauley) *led tl wl over 1f out: hrd rdn: one pce* **8/1**

16-0 **6** *nk* **Dvinsky (USA)**[10] 55 7-9-3 69 .... TGMcLaughlin 5 69
(P Howling) *chsd ldr: hrd rdn 2f out: one pce* **12/1**

45-1 **7** *5* **Compton Classic**[11] 45 6-8-11 70 ....(v) HarryPoulton(7) 4 54
(J R Boyle) *hld up in 6th: outpcd and drvn along wl over 2f out: n.d after* **15/2**

0-63 **8** *1 3/4* **Hythe Bay**[2] 150 4-8-11 63 .... RobertHavlin 1 42
(J R Best) *prom: hrd rdn over 2f out: sn wknd* **10/1**

626- **9** *6* **Inka Dancer (IRE)**[41] 7033 6-8-5 57 .... MatthewHenry 3 16
(B Palling) *sn pushed along: wd st: a bhd* **10/1**

1m 13.18s (0.08) **Going Correction** +0.25s/f (Slow) **9 Ran SP% 123.7**
Speed ratings (Par 103): **109,106,105,105,104 104,97,95,87**
CSF £48.33 CT £146.12 TOTE £4.00: £1.50, £4.40, £1.90; EX 48.00.
Owner Miss Claire Comery **Bred** Shadwell Farm LLC **Trained** Danethorpe, Notts

FOCUS
Just a modest handicap, but a fair winning time for the class. The form looks solid rated around the third.

166 KEMPTON FOR EVENTS CLASSIFIED STKS 2m (P)
4:10 (4:17) (Class 7) 4-Y-0+ £1,365 (£403; £201) Stalls High

Form RPR
000/ **1** **Fade To Grey (IRE)**[570] 2870 4-8-12 40..........(t) LPKeniry 4 55
(S Lycett) *dwlt: sn in tch: rdn to chse ldrs over 2f out: styd on to ld fnl 75yds* 8/1[3]
/00- **2** *nk* **Mujamead**[20] 1224 4-8-7 44..........(p) KirstyMilczarek[(5)] 2 55
(A W Carroll) *t.k.h: chsd ldr: led 5f out: rdn and hdd fnl 75yds: kpt on* 5/2[1]
260- **3** *1 1/2* **Slavonic Lake**[20] 7083 4-8-12 45..........(t) NCallan 12 53
(I A Wood) *chsd ldrs: wnt 2nd over 2f out: hrd rdn: styd on same pce* 5/2[1]
402- **4** *5* **Wavertree One Off**[3] 7203 6-9-5 43.......... NeilPollard 6 47
(J Ryan) *mid-div: hdwy on rail 4f out: no ex over 1f out* 16/1
0/4- **5** *1 3/4* **Sonoma (IRE)**[12] 4535 8-8-12 43..........(t) GabrielHannon[(7)] 13 45
(B G Powell) *towards rr: rdn over 4f out: styd on u.p fnl 2f: nvr rchd ldrs* 16/1
400- **6** *5* **Equilibria (USA)**[12] 3448 6-9-5 45.......... GeorgeBaker 5 39
(G L Moore) *prom tl wknd over 2f out* 10/3[2]
026- **7** *3 1/2* **Domenico (IRE)**[43] 4859 10-9-5 40.......... J-PGuillambert 9 35
(J R Jenkins) *hld up in rr: hdwy into midfield 4f out: hrd rdn over 2f out: no rspnse* 10/1
06-0 **8** *3* **Ghaill Force**[13] 14 6-9-0 40.......... NataliaGemelova[(5)] 7 31
(P Butler) *bhd: rdn along 6f out: passed btn horses fnl 3f* 33/1
060- **9** *22* **Welsh Guard (USA)**[24] 5384 5-9-5 45..........(v[1]) DaneO'Neill 1 —
(G P Enright) *mid-div: rdn 5f out: wknd over 3f out* 50/1
000- **10** *11* **Night Groove (IRE)**[18] 7256 5-8-12 41..........(tp) JackDean[(7)] 14 —
(P Butler) *t.k.h towards rr: rdn 5f out: sn bhd* 50/1
00-5 **11** *4* **Valart**[8] 76 5-9-5 40.......... FergusSweeney 10 —
(C Tinkler) *led tl 5f out: wknd over 3f out: eased whn btn fnl 2f* 25/1
0- **12** *2 1/2* **Mancebo (GER)**[27] 3901 5-9-5 41.......... JamesDoyle 11 —
(R Curtis) *in tch: wknd 5f out: bhd fnl 3f: eased whn no ch fnl 2f* 33/1
060- **13** *11* **Itsy Bitsy**[65] 6774 6-9-0 45.......... JamieJones[(5)] 3 —
(W J Musson) *in tch: hrd rdn over 3f out: sn wknd: eased whn no ch fnl 2f* 20/1

3m 33.53s (3.43) **Going Correction** +0.25s/f (Slow)
WFA 4 from 5yo+ 7lb 13 Ran SP% 130.6
Speed ratings (Par 97): **101,100,100,97,96 94,92,90,79,74 72,71,65**
CSF £29.33 TOTE £8.80: £3.30, £1.90, £1.30; EX 52.00 Place 6 £273.69, Place 5 £36.96..
Owner Bill Hinge & Gary Smallbone **Bred** Mount Coote Partnership **Trained** Naunton, Gloucs

FOCUS
Only a 0-45, but three of these had won over hurdles since they were last seen on the Flat, and the winner landed a huge gamble, so the form looks well above average for the grade. The early pace was steady but they still came home well strung out.
Fade To Grey(IRE) Official explanation: trainer said, regarding the improved form shown, gelding was having its first run for the yard and had benefited from the step up in trip (7f to 2m)
Night Groove(IRE) Official explanation: jockey said saddle slipped
Valart Official explanation: jockey said mare hung left
T/Plt: £289.30 to a £1 stake. Pool: £74,350.45. 187.55 winning tickets. T/Qpdt: £10.10 to a £1 stake. Pool: £6,155.00. 450.80 winning tickets. LM

[153]SOUTHWELL (L-H)
Tuesday, January 15

OFFICIAL GOING: Standard to slow
Wind: light, across Weather: Overcast and rain

167 HALF TERM HAPPY DEALS @ PONTINS.COM (S) STKS 5f (F)
1:00 (1:00) (Class 6) 4-Y-0+ £1,774 (£523; £262) Stalls High

Form RPR
00-2 **1** **High Reach**[5] 106 8-9-0 52.......... AndrewElliott 6 51
(J G M O'Shea) *chsd ldrs: rdn and hdwy over 1f out: led ent fnl f: sn drvn and hld on gamely* 5/6[1]
050- **2** *shd* **Charlotte Grey**[16] 7279 4-8-9 45.......... NickyMackay 7 45
(C N Allen) *cl up: effrt over 1f out: sn rdn and ev ch tl drvn and nt qckn nr fin* 4/1[2]
4-34 **3** *shd* **Pappas Image**[7] 79 4-9-0 45..........(p) VJanacek 3 50
(A J McCabe) *in tch: rdn along and hung lft over 2f out: hdwy and ev ch ent fnl f: sn drvn and nt qckn nr fin* 8/1[3]
000- **4** *1 3/4* **Maktavish**[32] 7137 9-9-0 42..........(b) PaulMulrennan 8 44
(R Brotherton) *led: rdn along wl over 1f out: hdd ent fnl f: wknd* 12/1
000- **5** *1 1/4* **Piccolo Prince**[208] 2791 7-8-11 43.......... TravisBlock[(3)] 5 39
(Mrs Marjorie Fife) *in tch: rdn along 1/2-way: sn one pce* 11/1
500- **6** *5* **Iron Pearl**[42] 7014 4-8-9 53..........(v[1]) ChrisCatlin 4 16
(J Ryan) *swtchd lft and rdn along after 1f: a in rr* 14/1
/00- **7** *2 1/2* **Geordie Dancer (IRE)**[134] 5083 6-8-11 37.......... PatrickMathers[(3)] 9 12
(A Berry) *chsd ldrs: rdn along and lost pl bef 1/2-way: sn bhd* 66/1

60.59 secs (0.89) **Going Correction** +0.225s/f (Slow) 7 Ran SP% 109.9
Speed ratings (Par 101): **101,100,100,97,95 87,83**
CSF £3.90 TOTE £1.80: £1.10, £2.80; EX 5.40 Trifecta £7.70 Pool £269.96 - 24.79 winning units..There was no bid for the winner.
Owner W R Baddiley **Bred** S R Hope **Trained** Elton, Gloucs

FOCUS
This was a very poor seller, but it did provide a very tight finish and they came home in almost perfect market order. As has been the case at most recent meetings here, the action all ultimately unfolded centre to far side of the track.

168 SOUTHWELL-RACECOURSE.CO.UK H'CAP 7f (F)
1:30 (1:31) (Class 6) (0-52,56) 4-Y-0+ £1,911 (£564; £282) Stalls Low

Form RPR
6-31 **1** **Silver Hotspur**[7] 79 4-9-4 56 6ex.......... NickyMackay 3 69+
(M Wigham) *hld up in tch on inner: hdwy over 2f out and sn cl up: shkn up to ld ins fnl f: kpt on* 15/8[1]
645- **2** *nk* **Palais Polaire**[16] 7278 6-8-9 50..........(p) TravisBlock[(3)] 1 62
(J A Geake) *trckd ldrs: hdwy to ld over 3f out: rdn over 2f out: drvn over 1f out: hdd ins fnl f: kpt on wl u.p* 12/1
055- **3** *4* **Mister Benji**[19] 7250 9-8-12 50 ow1..........(p) PhillipMakin 5 51
(B P J Baugh) *trckd ldrs: hdwy wl over 2f out: sn rdn and kpt on same pce appr fnl f* 8/1
224- **4** *2* **Having A Ball**[76] 6587 4-8-12 50.......... ChrisCatlin 11 46
(P D Cundell) *chsd ldrs: rdn along wl over 2f out: sn drvn and kpt on same pce* 15/2[3]
0-43 **5** *3* **Guadaloup**[7] 82 6-8-8 49.......... MarkLawson[(3)] 9 37
(M Brittain) *in rr: hdwy over 2f out: sn rdn: styd on appr fnl f: nvr nr ldrs* 8/1
00-0 **6** *3/4* **Keon (IRE)**[12] 32 6-8-9 47..........(p) HayleyTurner 7 33
(R Hollinshead) *dwlt: a towards rr* 12/1
-532 **7** *1* **Phinerine**[7] 82 5-8-9 50..........(e) MichaelJStainton[(3)] 8 33
(Miss J E Foster) *in rr: effrt and rdn along wl over 2f out: no hdwy* 11/2[2]
040- **8** *5* **Favouring (IRE)**[68] 5546 6-8-7 45..........(v) AndrewElliott 6 14
(M C Chapman) *led: hdd over 3f out: sn rdn and wknd over 2f out* 10/1
54-0 **9** *hd* **Naledi**[14] 7 4-8-12 50..........(v[1]) PaulMulrennan 4 19
(J R Norton) *a towards rr* 16/1
100- **10** *5* **Avontuur (FR)**[99] 6064 6-8-9 47..........(b) LiamJones 10 —
(D W Chapman) *dwlt: hdwy and cl up on outer after 2f: rdn along 3f out and sn wknd* 50/1

1m 30.36s (0.06) **Going Correction** 0.0s/f (Stan) 10 Ran SP% 116.5
Speed ratings (Par 101): **99,98,94,91,88 87,86,80,80,74**
CSF £26.56 CT £141.17 TOTE £2.20: £1.30, £2.90, £2.70; EX 25.30 Trifecta £113.90 Pool £205.52 - 1.20 winning units..
Owner D Hassan **Bred** Theobalds Stud **Trained** Newmarket, Suffolk
■ Stewards' Enquiry : Travis Block two-day ban: used whip with excessive frequency (Jan 26-27)

FOCUS
A modest handicap and the front pair, who came clear, were the only ones that mattered from a long way out. The winning time was 2.25 seconds slower than the later 56-76 handicap confined to fillies, but was still reasonable for a race like this.
Guadaloup Official explanation: jockey said mare was unsuited by the standard to slow ground

169 BOOK PONTIN'S NOW ON 0844 815 3648 H'CAP 2m (F)
2:00 (2:00) (Class 6) (0-60,63) 4-Y-0+ £1,911 (£564; £282) Stalls Low

Form RPR
01-1 **1** **Legend Erry (IRE)**[9] 67 4-9-12 63 6ex.......... JohnEgan 7 79+
(Jane Chapple-Hyam) *hld up: rapid hdwy on outer 4f out: led over 3f out and sn pushed wl clr: unchal* 1/6[1]
00-0 **2** *17* **Feeling Peckish (USA)**[11] 39 4-8-8 45..........(t) AndrewElliott 6 38
(M C Chapman) *cl up: pushed along and lost pl 1/2-way: rdn and hdwy over 2f out: drvn and styd on to take 2nd pl ins fnl f: no ch w wnr* 50/1
00/2 **3** *1 1/4* **Captain Smoothy**[11] 37 8-8-8 45.......... AmyBaker[(7)] 5 37
(Miss J Feilden) *trckd ldrs: pushed along and outpcd 4f out: styd on one pce u.p fnl 2f* 20/1
00-5 **4** *3* **Gavanello**[11] 36 5-8-10 45..........(bt) NicolPolli[(3)] 3 33
(M C Chapman) *cl up: rdn along 4f out: sn drvn and wknd fnl 2f* 50/1
43-3 **5** *5* **Piano Key**[9] 69 4-8-8 45.......... HayleyTurner 1 27
(M D I Usher) *led: rdn along 4f out: sn hdd and drvn: wknd fr over 2f out* 7/1[2]
00-4 **6** *11* **Optimistic Alfie**[9] 67 8-9-11 55..........(b) VinceSlattery 4 24
(B G Powell) *trckd ldrs: effrt over 5f out: rdn along 4f out and sn wknd* 16/1[3]

3m 46.51s (1.01) **Going Correction** 0.0s/f (Stan)
WFA 4 from 5yo+ 7lb 6 Ran SP% 112.8
Speed ratings (Par 101): **97,88,87,86,83 78**
CSF £19.39 TOTE £1.10: £1.02, £19.00; EX 15.70.
Owner Elite Sports Organisation **Bred** Dermot Cantillon And Forenaghts Stud **Trained** Lambourn, Berks

FOCUS
A very uncompetitive staying handicap, especially after the withdrawal of Hora, who would have been clear second-favourite. They crawled early, but even so the favourite scored very much as the Handicapper, and indeed the market, suggested he should. The form behind him adds up to very little though.

170 TAKE THE FAMILY TO PONTIN'S H'CAP 6f (F)
2:30 (2:31) (Class 5) (0-75,75) 3-Y-0 £2,593 (£765; £383) Stalls Low

Form RPR
022- **1** **Only A Game (IRE)**[18] 7260 3-9-1 72..........(p) AdamKirby 1 78
(Miss M E Rowland) *trckd ldrs on inner: hdwy to ld 2f out: rdn and hung rt over 1f out: drvn and wandered ins fnl f: kpt on* 10/1
50-2 **2** *3/4* **Diademas (USA)**[9] 70 3-8-1 65..........(be) AshleyMorgan[(7)] 3 69
(V Smith) *hld up in tch: hdwy on inner 2f out: rdn to chal ent fnl f and ev ch tl drvn and nt qckn nr fin* 5/1[3]
03-1 **3** *1/2* **Ballycroy Boy (IRE)**[11] 38 3-9-4 75.......... MickyFenton 2 77
(A Bailey) *trckd ldrs: pushed along 3f out: rdn and hdwy over 1f out: kpt on u.p ins fnl f* 9/4[2]
15-4 **4** *3* **Loose Caboose (IRE)**[13] 17 3-8-8 68..........(p) PatrickMathers[(3)] 4 60
(A J McCabe) *led: rdn along and hdd 2f out: sn drvn and wknd appr fnl f* 12/1
21-1 **5** *2* **Yankee Storm**[9] 70 3-8-12 69 6ex.......... PaulMulrennan 6 55
(M J Wallace) *cl up: rdn over 2f out: sn drvn and btn over 1f out* 11/8[1]
20-3 **6** *9* **Splash The Cash**[13] 17 3-8-7 64.......... ChrisCatlin 5 21
(K A Ryan) *chsd ldrs: rdn along over 2f out and sn wknd* 10/1
520- **U** **Spic 'n Span**[32] 7140 3-9-3 74..........(t) JohnEgan 7 —
(R A Harris) *rrd and uns rdr s* 33/1

1m 16.51s (0.01) **Going Correction** 0.0s/f (Stan) 7 Ran SP% 118.4
Speed ratings (Par 97): **99,98,97,93,90 78,—**
CSF £61.24 TOTE £12.80: £5.30, £3.90; EX 80.50.
Owner Hall Farm Racing **Bred** Maggie & Eric Hemming **Trained** Lower Blidworth, Notts

FOCUS
Quite a tight little handicap with a few of these well backed. The time was perfectly creditable, so the form should stand up.

171 BOOK EARLY AND MAKE 2008 PONTIN'S-TASTIC H'CAP 1m 4f (F)
3:00 (3:00) (Class 6) (0-60,58) 4-Y-0+ £1,911 (£564; £282) Stalls Low

Form RPR
000- **1** **Contra Mundum (USA)**[16] 1744 5-8-13 45.......... HayleyTurner 6 64+
(B G Powell) *trckd ldrs gng wl: smooth hdwy 3f out: led over 2f out: rdn clr over 1f out: easily* 5/1[3]
404- **2** *8* **Andorran (GER)**[26] 6265 5-9-1 47..........(v[1]) MickyFenton 5 53
(A Bailey) *hld up in rr: hdwy over 3f out: rdn to chse ldrs 2f out: drvn and kpt on same pce fr over 1f out* 6/1
65-1 **3** *1 1/4* **Starcross Maid**[8] 77 6-9-8 57 6ex.......... PatrickMathers[(3)] 3 61
(J F Coupland) *hld up in rr: smooth prog wl over 2f out: rdn to chse wnr over 1f out: sn drvn and no imp* 9/2[2]
65-1 **4** *2 1/2* **Zaffeu**[8] 76 7-9-8 54 6ex.......... VinceSlattery 9 54
(A G Juckes) *trckd ldrs: effrt 3f out and sn rdn: drvn over 2f out and sn one pce* 11/4[1]
030- **5** *2 1/2* **Kentucky Bullet (USA)**[238] 1934 12-8-10 45.......... TravisBlock[(3)] 1 41
(A G Newcombe) *hld up towards rr: hdwy 4f out: rdn along over 2f out and sn no imp* 9/1

00-0 **6** ½ **Chiff Chaff**[8] 77 4-9-8 **58** AdamKirby 2 53
(C R Dore) *led: rdn along 3f out: hdd over 2f out: sn drvn and wknd* **20/1**

50-0 **7** 8 **Ella Y Rossa**[14] 7 4-9-2 **52** StephenDonohoe 7 34
(P D Evans) *a towards rr* **8/1**

406/ **8** 7 **Sir Night (IRE)**[20] 4104 8-8-13 **45** PaulMulrennan 8 16
(Jedd O'Keeffe) *cl up: rdn along 4f out: sn wknd* **14/1**

/00- **9** 17 **Good Investment**[214] 2252 6-8-13 **45** (p) SaleemGolam 4 —
(Miss Tracy Waggott) *chsd ldng pair: rdn along 3f out and sn wknd* **50/1**

2m 39.22s (-1.78) **Going Correction** 0.0s/f (Stan)
WFA 4 from 5yo+ 4lb **9 Ran SP% 110.3**
Speed ratings (Par 101): **105,99,98,97,95 95,89,85,73**
CSF £32.48 CT £134.69 TOTE £6.20: £2.00, £2.60, £1.90; EX 42.80 Trifecta £176.10 Part won. Pool £248.07 - 0.86 winning units..
Owner D J Coles **Bred** Christopher Buckley **Trained** Upper Lambourn, Berks

FOCUS
A very moderate handicap. The easy winner is value for further and the overall form is somewhat suspect.
Sir Night(IRE) Official explanation: jockey said gelding hung left

172 ARENALEISUREPLC.COM MAIDEN STKS 1m (F)
3:30 (3:31) (Class 5) 3-Y-0+ **£2,457** (£725; £362) **Stalls** Low

Form RPR

04- **1** **Taikoo**[25] 7208 3-8-8 0 ChrisCatlin 8 77+
(H Morrison) *mde all: rdn wl over 2f out: styd on* **4/5**[1]

6 **2** 4 **Be Free**[9] 65 3-8-3 0 JamieMackay 7 62+
(Sir Mark Prescott) *trckd ldrs: hdwy to chse wnr and edgd lft over 2f out: sn rdn and wknd ent fnl f* **2/1**[2]

04- **3** shd **Gayanula (USA)**[15] 7288 3-8-3 0 HayleyTurner 1 62
(Miss J A Camacho) *chsd ldrs: hdwy over 2f out: rdn over 1f out: kpt on ins fnl f: nrst fin* **12/1**[3]

4 ¾ **Dovetail (IRE)** 3-8-3 0 NickyMackay 2 60
(V Smith) *cl up: rdn along over 2f out: sn one pce* **12/1**[3]

6 **5** 10 **Able Dara**[5] 107 5-9-9 0 SladeO'Hara(5) 3 46
(N Bycroft) *chsd ldrs: rdn along over 3f out and sn wknd* **66/1**

000- **6** 8 **Mays Louise**[66] 6766 4-9-2 35 SoniaEaton(7) 4 23
(B P J Baugh) *t.k.h: chsd ldrs: rdn along 3f out and sn wknd* **150/1**

0 **7** 17 **Charlie Chan**[9] 66 7-10-0 0 (b) LiamJones 6 —
(D W Chapman) *s.i.s: a in rr* **100/1**

P **T'Ai Chi**[20] 7-9-9 0 MickyFenton 5 —
(John A Harris) *s.i.s: a bhd: p.u over 2f out: dismntd* **40/1**

1m 44.48s (0.78) **Going Correction** 0.0s/f (Stan)
WFA 3 from 4yo+ 20lb **8 Ran SP% 109.9**
Speed ratings (Par 103): **96,92,91,91,81 73,56,—**
CSF £2.27 TOTE £1.40: £1.02, £1.10, £2.50; EX 2.60 Trifecta £4.20 Pool £1,248.18 - 206.88 winning units..
Owner Miss B Swire **Bred** Miss B Swire **Trained** East Ilsley, Berks

FOCUS
A moderate maiden but the form makes sense.
T'Ai Chi Official explanation: jockey said mare lost its action

173 SOUTHWELL RACECOURSE FOR CONFERENCES FILLIES' H'CAP 7f (F)
4:00 (4:00) (Class 5) (0-70,76) 4-Y-0+ **£2,593** (£765; £383) **Stalls** Low

Form RPR

050- **1** **Sophia Gardens**[17] 7268 4-8-4 **56** ChrisCatlin 3 68
(D W P Arbuthnot) *chsd ldrs on inner: swtchd rt and effrt wl over 1f out: rdn and edgd lft ent fnl f: sn drvn and styd on to ld towards fin* **8/1**

4-12 **2** ½ **Sweet Pickle**[5] 111 7-9-10 **76** 6ex (e) SebSanders 1 87
(J R Boyle) *trckd ldr: hdwy 2f out: rdn to ld ins fnl f: sn drvn: hdd and no ex towards fin* **15/8**[1]

551- **3** 1 ½ **Cerebus**[66] 6762 6-9-1 **67** (bt) StephenDonohoe 6 74
(A J McCabe) *led: rdn 2f out: drvn and hdd ins fnl f: one pce* **4/1**[3]

212- **4** 8 **The City Kid (IRE)**[42] 7025 5-8-9 **61** SaleemGolam 7 46
(S C Williams) *towards rr: hdwy 3f out: rdn and chsd ldrs over 2f out: sn drvn and no imp* **2/1**[2]

43-0 **5** 6 **Capania (IRE)**[11] 44 4-8-8 **60** VinceSlattery 5 29
(P D Evans) *a towards rr* **16/1**

00-6 **6** 8 **Fustaan (IRE)**[6] 89 4-8-9 **64** TravisBlock(3) 4 11
(A G Newcombe) *a in rr* **25/1**

300- **7** 11 **On The Map**[19] 6385 4-8-6 **58** (p) AndrewElliott 2 —
(Joss Saville) *chsd ldrs: rdn along 3f out and sn wknd* **40/1**

1m 28.11s (-2.19) **Going Correction** 0.0s/f (Stan) **7 Ran SP% 111.4**
Speed ratings (Par 100): **112,111,109,100,93 84,72**
CSF £22.25 TOTE £9.70: £3.50, £1.20; EX 18.90 Place 6 £34.85, Place 5 £30.55..
Owner Derrick C Broomfield **Bred** Stowell Hill Ltd **Trained** Compton, Berks

FOCUS
A moderate handicap, but it was a very decent winning time for the type of contest, 2.25 seconds faster than the earlier 45-56 handicap. Sound enough form for the class.
The City Kid(IRE) Official explanation: jockey said mare hung left
T/Plt: £23.60 to a £1 stake. Pool: £62,345.65. 1,920.95 winning tickets. T/Qpdt: £7.30 to a £1 stake. Pool: £3,967.20. 397.00 winning tickets. JR

160 KEMPTON (A.W) (R-H)
Wednesday, January 16

OFFICIAL GOING: Standard
Wind: Almost nil Weather: Dark

174 FOLLOW YOUR MEETING WITH EVENING RACING CLASSIFIED STKS 6f (P)
6:20 (6:21) (Class 7) 4-Y-0+ **£1,365** (£403; £201) **Stalls** High

Form RPR

00-3 **1** **Double Valentine**[3] 151 5-8-9 45 JackMitchell(5) 1 56
(R Ingram) *stdd s fr wd draw: hld up in last: gd prog 2f out: urged along to ld last 150yds: kpt on wl* **6/1**[3]

060- **2** 1 ½ **Avoca Dancer (IRE)**[68] 6752 5-9-0 45 JamieMackay 10 51
(M Wigham) *trckd ldr gng wl: nudged into ld wl over 1f out: hdd and nt qckn last 150yds* **15/8**[1]

06-0 **3** 1 **King Of Charm (IRE)**[5] 119 5-9-0 45 (bt) FergusSweeney 6 48
(G L Moore) *chsd ldrs: rdn 2f out: styd on same pce: nvr able to chal* **8/1**

300- **4** ¾ **Luloah**[33] 7137 5-9-0 45 (p) SebSanders 3 46
(J G M O'Shea) *led to wl over 1f out: one pce* **14/1**

0/-0 **5** nk **Loaderfun (IRE)**[14] 11 6-9-0 45 (e) GregFairley 9 45
(I W McInnes) *t.k.h bhd ldrs: nt qckn 2f out: one pce after* **14/1**

64-1 **6** 1 ¾ **Stoneacre Donny (IRE)**[5] 119 4-9-0 43 LPKeniry 5 39
(Peter Grayson) *dwlt: pushed along early then t.k.h in rr: brief effrt on inner over 2f out: sn btn* **2/1**[2]

000- **7** 1 ¼ **Diamond World**[98] 6097 5-9-0 44 SimonWhitworth 4 35
(C A Horgan) *nvr beyond midfield: rdn and struggling over 2f out: no imp after* **50/1**

00-3 **8** 9 **Noddledoddle (IRE)**[5] 120 4-9-0 37 (vt[1]) AdamKirby 2 6
(J Ryan) *t.k.h early: prom: rdn and no rspnse over 2f out: wknd rapidly* **25/1**

000/ **9** hd **Pinafore**[529] 4141 6-9-0 45 ChrisCatlin 8 6
(B R Millman) *rdn in rr 1/2-way: sn bhd* **33/1**

1m 13.3s (0.20) **Going Correction** -0.025s/f (Stan) **9 Ran SP% 115.6**
Speed ratings (Par 97): **97,95,93,92,92 89,88,76,76**
CSF £17.44 TOTE £7.00: £2.00, £1.10, £2.60; EX 20.40.
Owner Ellangowan Racing Partners **Bred** Ellangowan Racing Partners **Trained** Epsom, Surrey

FOCUS
Only two or three of these could be described as being in form, so this probably did not take a great deal of winning.

175 KEMPTON.CO.UK MAIDEN STKS 7f (P)
6:50 (6:51) (Class 5) 3-Y-0+ **£2,457** (£725; £362) **Stalls** High

Form RPR

2- **1** **King Of Dixie (USA)**[162] 4258 4-9-11 0 PaulDoe 6 97+
(W J Knight) *mde all: pushed along and wl in command fnl 2f: comf* **11/10**[1]

3- **2** 3 ½ **Bussell Up**[70] 6721 3-8-2 0 LiamJones 4 74
(S C Williams) *dwlt: t.k.h and sn prom: chsd wnr over 2f out: styd on steadily but no imp* **7/1**[3]

260- **3** 5 **Cavalry Guard (USA)**[19] 7253 4-9-11 70 FergusSweeney 8 70
(J R Boyle) *chsd ldrs: prog into 3rd over 1f out but already wl outpcd by ldng pair: kpt on* **12/1**

223- **4** 3 **Silent Master (USA)**[37] 7095 3-8-7 76 GregFairley 5 57
(M Johnston) *t.k.h: pressed wnr tl wknd u.p over 2f out* **2/1**[2]

6 **5** 1 **Lady Amberlini**[14] 9 3-8-2 0 HayleyTurner 1 49
(P D Evans) *s.s: hld up in last: pushed along 2f out: sme prog fnl f: running on at fin* **66/1**

46- **6** nk **Coloso**[42] 7029 4-9-11 0 SimonWhitworth 9 58
(P D Cundell) *dwlt: nvr beyond midfield: wl outpcd fr over 2f out* **33/1**

0- **7** hd **Usetheforce (IRE)**[18] 7266 3-8-7 0 ChrisCatlin 10 53
(M J Wallace) *dwlt: a in rr: struggling and outpcd over 2f out* **25/1**

62-4 **8** ½ **Maggie Kate**[11] 60 3-8-2 64 RichardThomas 3 47
(R Ingram) *chsd ldng trio to over 2f out: sn wknd* **25/1**

0-6 **9** 1 **Irish Cape**[7] 95 5-9-6 0 JamesDoyle 2 49
(Mrs N Smith) *chsd ldrs: rdn and fnd nil over 2f out: sn wknd* **66/1**

0 **10** 2 **Ultimate Quest (IRE)**[9] 74 3-8-7 0 JamieMackay 7 43
(Sir Mark Prescott) *dwlt: a in rr: t.o 3f out* **50/1**

1m 24.63s (-1.37) **Going Correction** -0.025s/f (Stan)
WFA 3 from 4yo+ 18lb **10 Ran SP% 116.7**
Speed ratings (Par 103): **106,102,96,92,91 91,91,90,89,87**
CSF £9.12 TOTE £1.90: £1.10, £1.50, £3.40; EX 7.10.
Owner Hesmonds Stud **Bred** Bee Zee LLC **Trained** Patching, W Sussex

FOCUS
This appeared to lie between two horses with enough form in the book to win, despite being fairly exposed, and a couple of dark ones that shaped with promise in one previous maiden start. In many ways, it was good to see the unexposed two fight out the finish. Both look very nice prospects.

176 DIGIBET H'CAP 1m (P)
7:20 (7:21) (Class 6) (0-52,52) 4-Y-0+ **£2,047** (£604; £302) **Stalls** High

Form RPR

650- **1** **High Class Problem (IRE)**[35] 7115 5-8-9 **52** TolleyDean(5) 7 61
(P Winkworth) *chsd ldng pair: wnt 2nd wl over 2f out to 2f out: styd on u.p to chal again 1f out: led last 100yds: drvn out* **7/1**

50-2 **2** 1 **Jessica Wigmo**[7] 99 5-8-10 **48** JamesDoyle 5 55
(A W Carroll) *hld up in 5th: smooth prog on inner to go 2nd 2f out: led jst over 1f out: hdd and nt qckn last 100yds* **8/1**

503- **3** nk **Batchworth Blaise**[31] 7167 5-8-9 **47** StephenCarson 8 53
(E A Wheeler) *t.k.h: hld up in last: effrt over 2f out: eased out over 1f out: rdn and r.o: nrly snatched 2nd but no ch of chalng wnr* **20/1**

-615 **4** 1 ½ **Lordswood (IRE)**[5] 123 4-8-13 **51** 6ex HayleyTurner 3 54
(J R Best) *hld up in 6th: pushed along over 2f out: no imp tl styd on fnl f: n.d* **3/1**[2]

260- **5** shd **Recalcitrant**[38] 7083 5-9-0 **52** DaneO'Neill 6 55
(S Dow) *led to jst over 1f out: fdd* **4/1**[3]

42-2 **6** ½ **Climate (IRE)**[7] 101 9-9-0 **52** (v) StephenDonohoe 4 53
(P D Evans) *hld up in 7th: effrt over 2f out: no imp on ldrs wl over 1f out: one pce after* **8/1**

42-2 **7** 6 **Winged Farasi**[4] 143 4-9-0 **52** LiamJones 2 40
(R A Harris) *pushed up to chse ldr: rdn over 3f out: lost 2nd and wknd over 2f out* **5/2**[1]

06-5 **8** 7 **Far Seeking**[12] 48 4-9-0 **52** (tp) TGMcLaughlin 1 24
(R A Harris) *s.s: rcvrd to chse ldng trio: wknd wl over 2f out* **20/1**

1m 39.76s (-0.04) **Going Correction** -0.025s/f (Stan) **8 Ran SP% 117.8**
Speed ratings (Par 101): **99,98,97,96,96 95,89,82**
CSF £62.82 CT £1059.19 TOTE £9.30: £2.50, £2.90, £4.60; EX 53.60.
Owner Ashplace Stud & Joshua Russell **Bred** Mrs Clare McGinn **Trained** Chiddingfold, Surrey

FOCUS
There was a certain amount of doubt before the off that there would be much early pace on here, considering the usual racing styles of these horses. However, the winning time was not that bad and Recalcitrant may have done a fair job in front.
Winged Farasi Official explanation: trainer said, regarding running, race may have come too soon

177 DIGIBET SPORTS BETTING H'CAP 1m (P)
7:50 (7:51) (Class 5) (0-70,70) 4-Y-0+ **£2,590** (£770; £385; £192) **Stalls** High

Form RPR

500- **1** **Blacktoft (USA)**[46] 6996 5-9-4 **70** (e) J-PGuillambert 6 81
(S C Williams) *stdd s: hld up in last: smooth prog 3f out: rousted along to cl on ldrs over 1f out: drvn to ld narrowly ins fnl f: kpt on* **20/1**

31-1 **2** hd **Arthur's Edge**[14] 21 4-8-9 **66** TolleyDean(5) 11 77
(B Palling) *prom: wnt 2nd over 3f out: drvn to cl and led 1f out: narrowly hdd ins fnl f: jst hld* **9/4**[1]

53-0 **3** 2 **Parkview Love (USA)**[11] 55 7-9-2 **68** (v) DeanMcKeown 8 74
(D Shaw) *hld up in midfield: smooth prog to trck ldrs over 2f out: urged along over 1f out: outpcd fnl f* **12/1**

26-6 **4** 1 1/4 **Onenightinlisbon (IRE)**[7] 90 4-8-10 **69**.................. HarryPoulton(7) 9 72
(J R Boyle) *s.i.s: settled wl in rr: rdn and sme prog 2f out but nt on terms: styd on fnl f: nrst fin* **25/1**

415- **5** 1/2 **Carlitos Spirit (IRE)**[36] 7113 4-8-13 **65**.................. ChrisCatlin 3 67
(B R Millman) *led: hanging but drvn 2 l clr over 2f out: hdd & wknd 1f out* **7/1**

50-0 **6** *hd* **Binnion Bay (IRE)**[3] 148 7-8-10 **62**..................(b) TPQueally 7 63
(J J Bridger) *towards rr: rdn over 2f out: styd on fr over 1f out: nrst fin* **12/1**

205- **7** 3/4 **Golden Prospect**[121] 5475 4-9-4 **70**.................. SebSanders 4 70
(J W Hills) *hld up wl in rr: prog on outer 2f out: chsng ldrs but nt on terms over 1f out: effrt petered out fnl f* **5/1**[2]

002- **8** 2 1/2 **Pietersen (IRE)**[31] 7164 4-9-0 **66**..................(b) PaulFessey 12 62
(T D Barron) *chsd ldrs: drvn wl over 2f out: grad lost pl: eased ins fnl f* **13/2**[3]

425- **9** 3 **Our Kes (IRE)**[21] 7237 6-9-0 **66**.................. SimonWhitworth 5 53
(P Howling) *racd on outer in midfield: lost pl wl over 2f out: no ch after* **16/1**

0 **9** *dht* **Passato (GER)**[14] 21 4-8-13 **65**..................(p) TGMcLaughlin 10 52
(R A Harris) *chsd ldrs: drvn on inner and cl up 2f out: wknd over 1f out* **50/1**

00-0 **11** 5 **Prince Of Charm (USA)**[11] 51 4-8-11 **63**..................(b) DaneO'Neill 1 39
(R A Teal) *a wl in rr: struggling fnl 3f* **20/1**

40-0 **12** 2 1/2 **Nicada (IRE)**[11] 63 4-9-1 **67**..................(p) MickyFenton 2 37
(Stef Liddiard) *chsd ldr to over 3f out: wknd u.p* **8/1**

1m 39.2s (-0.60) **Going Correction** -0.025s/f (Stan) 12 Ran SP% **121.0**
Speed ratings (Par 103): **102,101,99,98,98 97,97,94,91,91 86,84**
CSF £63.89 CT £607.15 TOTE £35.50: £9.10, £1.10, £5.00; EX 89.80.
Owner Chris Watkins And David N Reynolds **Bred** Paradigm Thoroughbreds Inc **Trained** Newmarket, Suffolk

FOCUS
Carlitos Spirit had a virtual freebie out in front and set, what seemed, only a fair gallop. The winning time was a shade quicker than the previous race, which was over the same distance.
Blacktoft(USA) Official explanation: trainer had no explanation for the apparent improvement in form
Carlitos Spirit(IRE) Official explanation: jockey said gelding hung right
Nicada(IRE) Official explanation: jockey said gelding ran flat

178 DIGIBET CASINO H'CAP 7f (P)
8:20 (8:20) (Class 5) (0-75,74) 3-Y-O **£2,590** (£770; £385; £192) **Stalls** High

Form RPR

013- **1** **American Art (IRE)**[138] 4991 3-9-4 **74**..................(t) SebSanders 4 90
(B W Hills) *chsd ldrs: prog on inner over 2f out: sn drvn: led over 1f out: styd on wl and sn clr* **9/4**[2]

22-2 **2** 6 **Smokey Rye**[4] 136 3-9-4 **74**..................(b) GeorgeBaker 3 74
(G L Moore) *t.k.h: hld up on outer: wnt 2nd 3f out: chal over 1f out: sn outpcd by wnr* **15/8**[1]

14- **3** 1 1/4 **Mafasina (USA)**[43] 7016 3-9-3 **73**.................. ChrisCatlin 1 70
(Christian Wroe) *t.k.h: led after 2f to over 1f out: sn outpcd by wnr* **11/1**

551- **4** 1 1/2 **Tiger's Rocket (IRE)**[20] 7245 3-8-7 **68**.................. HaddenFrost(5) 5 61
(R Hannon) *chsd ldrs: struggling wl over 2f out: plugged on* **14/1**

541- **5** 1 1/2 **Annes Rocket (IRE)**[21] 7235 3-8-13 **69**.................. PatDobbs 8 58
(J C Fox) *s.s: t.k.h: hld up in last pair: effrt over 2f out: one pce wl over 1f out* **20/1**

015- **6** *nk* **Kamal**[17] 7280 3-8-8 **64**.................. HayleyTurner 2 52
(W R Muir) *dwlt: t.k.h and hld up in last pair: effrt on outer over 2f out: sn one pce* **10/1**

062- **7** 3 1/2 **Stagecoach Topaz (USA)**[71] 6698 3-9-2 **72**.................. GregFairley 7 50
(M Johnston) *led 2f: chsd ldr to 3f out: wknd over 2f out* **5/1**[3]

1m 25.65s (-0.35) **Going Correction** -0.025s/f (Stan) 7 Ran SP% **111.1**
Speed ratings (Par 97): **101,94,92,91,89 88,84**
CSF £6.44 CT £32.40 TOTE £3.20: £2.50, £1.40; EX 6.90.
Owner Matthew Green & T Hyde **Bred** Albert Steigenberger **Trained** Lambourn, Berks

FOCUS
The race saw an impressive winner, who should go on to better things, but the winning time was about a second slower than the maiden earlier on the card. However, on balance, the first three look capable of maintaining this level of form and improve.

179 SPONSOR AT KEMPTON H'CAP 2m (P)
8:50 (8:50) (Class 6) (0-50,51) 4-Y-0+ **£2,047** (£604; £302) **Stalls** High

Form RPR

006- **1** **Otaki (IRE)**[28] 7186 4-8-3 **46** oh1.................. JamieMackay 7 56+
(Sir Mark Prescott) *hld up: smooth prog over 3f out: drvn and r.o to ld jst over 1f out: sn in command* **4/1**[3]

50/0 **2** 2 **Aqua Pura (GER)**[10] 67 9-8-10 **46** oh1..................(v[1]) TPQueally 4 53
(A P Stringer) *hld up bhd ldrs: gng wl 3f out: effrt on inner to dispute ld wl over 1f out to jst over 1f out: nt qckn* **14/1**

300- **3** 1/2 **Squiffy**[58] 6871 5-9-0 **50**.................. LPKeniry 3 57
(P D Cundell) *trckd ldrs: rdn over 5f out: responded to press and styd on to dispute ld wl over 1f out to jst over 1f out: one pce fnl f* **2/1**[1]

1-25 **4** 11 **Prince Of Medina**[3] 152 5-8-13 **49**.................. HayleyTurner 2 42
(J R Best) *hanging lft: led to wl over 1f out: wknd rapidly fnl f* **11/4**[2]

3/0- **5** 1 **Onefourseven**[65] 6798 15-8-7 **46** oh1..................(t) NeilChalmers(3) 5 38?
(Lucinda Featherstone) *hld up in last pair: sme prog and gng wl enough 4f out: outpcd over 2f out: hung lft after: fin lame* **50/1**

516- **6** 3 1/2 **Imminent Victory**[35] 7123 5-9-0 **50**..................(p) ChrisCatlin 10 38
(R M H Cowell) *rousted along early but sn in rr: prog on outer to chse ldr 5f out to 2f out: wknd rapidly* **12/1**

6-51 **7** *shd* **Isa'Af (IRE)**[3] 152 9-8-10 **51** 6ex..................(p) TolleyDean(5) 9 39
(P W Hiatt) *rousted along to go prom: in ldng trio tl lost pl wl over 4f out: sn struggling in rr* **5/1**

/00- **8** 15 **Nanosecond (USA)**[19] 7257 5-9-0 **50**.................. SimonWhitworth 8 20
(N A Callaghan) *stdd s: hld up in last: briefest of effrts 4f out: sn wknd rapidly: t.o* **16/1**

666- **9** 25 **Acosta**[13] 5311 4-7-10 **46** oh1..................(b) MatthewCosham(7) 1 —
(Dr J R J Naylor) *racd v wd: prom to 6f out: sn t.o* **40/1**

3m 30.45s (0.35) **Going Correction** -0.025s/f (Stan)
WFA 4 from 5yo+ 7lb 9 Ran SP% **121.3**
Speed ratings (Par 101): **98,97,96,91,90 89,88,81,68**
CSF £61.10 CT £146.53 TOTE £5.00: £2.50, £3.00, £2.00; EX 79.90.
Owner Lady O'Reilly **Bred** Castlemartin Stud And Skymarc Farm **Trained** Newmarket, Suffolk

FOCUS
Before the off this looked a battle between a couple of horses with good current form against a few that may have been capable of better than they had shown in recent runs. As it turned out, it was one of the least exposed that came home in front. The winning time was reasonably slow.
Otaki(IRE) ◆ Official explanation: trainer's rep said, regarding the improved form shown, filly had benefited from the step up in trip
Prince Of Medina Official explanation: jockey said gelding hung left
Onefourseven Official explanation: vet said gelding finished lame
Isa'Af(IRE) Official explanation: jockey said gelding ran flat

180 PANORAMIC BAR & RESTAURANT H'CAP 1m 3f (P)
9:20 (9:20) (Class 6) (0-60,59) 4-Y-0+ **£2,047** (£604; £302) **Stalls** High

Form RPR

632- **1** **Wind Flow**[35] 7115 4-9-1 **56**..................(b) AdrianMcCarthy 4 64
(C A Dwyer) *trckd ldr: led over 1f out and sn kicked 2 l clr: styd on wl* **4/1**[3]

04-3 **2** 1 1/4 **Beech Games**[7] 88 4-8-12 **53**.................. TGMcLaughlin 1 59
(F Jordan) *rel to r: in tch in last pair: prog fr 2f out: styd on wl fnl f to take 2nd nr fin* **25/1**

04-1 **3** 3/4 **Earl Kraul (IRE)**[14] 10 5-9-5 **57**.................. GeorgeBaker 7 62
(G L Moore) *hld up in tch: prog and swtchd lft wl over 2f out: chsd wnr fnl f: no imp: lost 2nd nr fin* **5/2**[1]

0-22 **4** 1 1/2 **Under Fire (IRE)**[5] 125 5-9-1 **53**.................. HayleyTurner 6 55
(A W Carroll) *led: drvn and hdd over 1f out: fdd fnl f* **6/1**

16-4 **5** *hd* **Play Up Pompey**[14] 10 6-9-1 **53**.................. SebSanders 8 55
(J J Bridger) *trckd ldng pair to over 4f out: styd cl up tl outpcd u.p over 1f out* **5/1**

66-0 **6** 1 3/4 **Street Life (IRE)**[13] 28 10-9-7 **59**.................. NeilPollard 5 58
(W J Musson) *wl in tch: pushed along over 3f out: hmpd wl over 2f out: n.d fnl 2f* **10/3**[2]

1/0- **7** *shd* **Artzola (IRE)**[331] 495 8-9-2 **54**.................. SimonWhitworth 2 53
(C A Horgan) *hld up in last pair: sme prog and gng wl fr 3f out: pushed along and no hdwy 2f out: nvr nr ldrs* **25/1**

100- **8** 13 **Raydan (IRE)**[50] 6871 6-9-3 **55**..................(b) MickyFenton 3 32
(D R Gandolfo) *prom on outer: wnt 3rd over 4f out: pushed along whn hmpd and stmbld wl over 2f out: nt rcvr: t.o* **25/1**

2m 23.19s (1.29) **Going Correction** -0.025s/f (Stan)
WFA 4 from 5yo+ 3lb 8 Ran SP% **114.1**
Speed ratings (Par 101): **94,93,92,91,91 90,89,80**
CSF £94.58 CT £293.92 TOTE £4.30: £1.50, £4.80, £1.10; EX 89.40 Place 6 £46.67, Place 5 £27.34.
Owner David L Bowkett **Bred** Lord Halifax **Trained** Burrough Green, Cambs
■ Stewards' Enquiry : George Baker four-day ban: careless riding (Jan 27-30)

FOCUS
There were not many in this that liked to force the pace, so the gallop looked a bit false out in front – the winning time suggests that was the case. The field was stacked up turning in, and a sprint took place up the home straight. There was some scrimmaging on that bend, but it did not affect the final result too much.
T/Plt: £134.30 to a £1 stake. Pool: £99,375.80. 539.80 winning tickets. T/Qpdt: £38.30 to a £1 stake. Pool: £6,794.20. 131.10 winning tickets. JN

[133] LINGFIELD (L-H)
Wednesday, January 16

OFFICIAL GOING: Standard
Wind: virtually nil Weather: partly cloudy

181 HAPPY HALF TERM DEALS @ PONTINS.COM APPRENTICE H'CAP 6f (P)
12:40 (12:45) (Class 6) (0-60,60) 4-Y-0+ **£1,876** (£554; £277) **Stalls** Low

Form RPR

060- **1** **Follow The Flag (IRE)**[18] 7269 4-9-5 60.................. JackMitchell 2 70
(C F Wall) *chsd ldng pair: rdn over 2f out: swtchd rt jst over 1f out: chsd ldr ins fnl f: r.o wl to ld last stride* **3/1**[1]

10-4 **2** *shd* **Crimson Fern (IRE)**[7] 87 4-9-0 55.................. JackDean 7 65
(M S Saunders) *t.k.h: chsd ldr tl rdn to ld wl over 1f out: edgd rt wl ins fnl f: hdd last stride* **10/1**

61-0 **3** 1 1/2 **Lost All Alone**[14] 13 4-8-4 50.................. ChrisHough(5) 5 55
(D M Simcock) *t.k.h: hld up in midfield: hdwy over 2f out: rdn to chse ldr jst over 1f out: carried rt and lost 2nd 1f out: keeping on same pce whn hit on nose by rivals whip ins fnl f* **7/1**

54-0 **4** 1/2 **Desert Light (IRE)**[13] 29 7-9-0 55..................(v) KellyHarrison 8 61+
(D Shaw) *hld up in rr: hdwy over 2f out: nt clr run wl over 1f out: kpt on fnl f: nt rch ldrs* **6/1**

25-3 **5** *shd* **Musical Script (USA)**[12] 41 5-9-2 57..................(p) JPHamblett 4 60
(Mouse Hamilton-Fairley) *hld up in rr: rdn and effrt on inner 2f out: kpt on same pce fnl f* **4/1**[2]

33-0 **6** 3/4 **Majestical (IRE)**[11] 56 6-8-8 54..................(e) AshleyMorgan(5) 6 55
(V Smith) *stdd s: hld up in last: hdwy on outer over 2f out: rdn jst over 2f out: nvr trbld ldrs* **5/1**[3]

651- **7** 1 3/4 **Monashee Brave (IRE)**[26] 7209 5-8-12 58.................. RossAtkinson(5) 1 53
(R A Harris) *sn led: clr 4f out: rdn and hdd wl over 1f out: fdd fnl f* **11/2**

1m 11.95s (0.05) **Going Correction** +0.075s/f (Slow) 7 Ran SP% **112.9**
Speed ratings (Par 101): **102,101,99,99,99 98,95**
CSF £32.25 CT £191.21 TOTE £3.80: £2.50, £3.00; EX 49.40 Trifecta £137.70 Pool £232.78 - 1.20 winning units..
Owner Follow The Flag Partnership **Bred** Martin Francis **Trained** Newmarket, Suffolk
■ Stewards' Enquiry : Jack Mitchell one-day ban: careless riding (Jan 27); two-day ban: careless riding (Jan 28-29)

FOCUS
A typically modest race of its type. After taking a furlong to sort themselvers out, Monashee Brave was soon taking them along at a decent gallop.

182 RACE TO PONTIN'S @ PONTINS.COM CLAIMING STKS 2m (P)
1:10 (1:15) (Class 6) 4-Y-0+ **£1,774** (£523; £262) **Stalls** Low

Form RPR

25-4 **1** **Noble Minstrel**[7] 105 5-9-12 71..................(t) NCallan 4 73
(S C Williams) *led for 5f: chsd ldr after tl led again over 3f out: rdn over 2f out: styd on wl* **7/4**[2]

111- **2** 1 3/4 **Nawamees (IRE)**[25] 7226 10-9-12 78..................(p) GeorgeBaker 1 71
(G L Moore) *hld up in tch: rdn and effrt wl over 2f out: chsd wnr over 2f out: hanging lft fr over 1f out: no imp fnl f* **4/7**[1]

2-10 **3** 1 3/4 **Looks The Business (IRE)**[5] 122 7-9-2 63.................. JackDean(7) 2 66
(W G M Turner) *hld up in tch: rdn 4f out: outpcd in last wl over 2f out: kpt on over 1f out: wnt 3rd ins fnl f: nt threaten ldng pair* **25/1**[3]

5/ **4** 1 3/4 **Indian Star (GER)**[16] 10-8-10 62..................(t) RichardEvans(7) 3 58
(P D Evans) *chsd ldr tl led after 5f: hdd over 3f out: shkn up and outpcd over 2f out: kpt on same pce* **33/1**

3m 28.45s (2.75) **Going Correction** +0.075s/f (Slow) 4 Ran SP% **106.8**
Speed ratings (Par 101): **96,95,94,93**
CSF £3.05 TOTE £2.50; EX 3.50.Noble Minstrel was claimed by J J Best for £15,000.
Owner Alasdair Simpson **Bred** Mrs M Lavell **Trained** Newmarket, Suffolk

FOCUS
A fair claimer, but lacking in numbers, and run at a weak pace until the last half-mile.
Nawamees(IRE) Official explanation: trainer said gelding bled from the nose

183 COME SEE US SOON @ PONTIN'S MEDIAN AUCTION MAIDEN STKS 6f (P)
1:45 (1:51) (Class 5) 3-5-Y-O £2,331 (£693; £346; £173) **Stalls** Low

Form RPR
42-3 **1** **Moon Bound (IRE)**[6] 114 3-8-10 0 NCallan 6 69+
(W R Muir) *mde all: qcknd clr over 2f out: in n.d after: easily* **10/11**[1]
65- **2** 3 ½ **Eleanor Eloise (USA)**[42] 7029 4-9-7 0 LiamJones 1 57
(J R Gask) *t.k.h: chsd wnr over 4f out tl wl over 2f out: readily outpcd by wnr over 2f out: regained 2nd ins fnl f: no ch w wnr* **11/1**
2-45 **3** ½ **Orange Square (IRE)**[11] 60 3-8-10 66 RichardHughes 7 56
(R Hannon) *t.k.h: prom: chsd wnr wl over 2f out: readily outpcd by wnr over 2f out: no ch w wnr after: lost 2nd insde fnl f* **15/8**[2]
4 1 ¾ **Prime Factor** 3-8-5 0 ow2 AshtonByles(7) 4 52+
(B W Hills) *stdd s: t.k.h: hld up in tch: rdn and wd bnd over 2f out: kpt on but n.d* **10/1**[3]
05- **5** 1 **Mad Man Will (IRE)**[34] 7129 3-8-10 0 SaleemGolam 5 47
(S C Williams) *hld up in tch: outpcd wl over 2f out: rdn over 2f out: n.d* **20/1**
50- **6** 3 ½ **Joe Rich**[17] 7282 4-9-12 0 (p) LPKeniry 3 40
(Mrs L C Jewell) *t.k.h: chsd wnr tl over 4f out: lost pl over 2f out: sn no ch* **66/1**
- **7** 3 ½ **Running Supreme** 4-9-7 0 JamesDoyle 2 24
(Mrs N Smith) *s.i.s: a bhd* **33/1**
1m 12.92s (1.02) **Going Correction** +0.075s/f (Slow)
WFA 3 from 4yo 16lb 7 Ran SP% **113.8**
Speed ratings (Par 103): **96,91,90,88,87 82,77**
CSF £12.23 TOTE £1.80: £1.20, £3.20; EX 13.70.
Owner A J De V Patrick & M J Caddy **Bred** Burns Farm Stud **Trained** Lambourn, Berks
FOCUS
A routine maiden, and a moderate winning time, almost a second slower than the earlier 50-60 handicap.

184 LET US ENTERTAIN YOU @ PONTIN'S H'CAP 1m 2f (P)
2:20 (2:26) (Class 6) (0-65,69) 3-Y-O £1,876 (£554; £277) **Stalls** Low

Form RPR
041- **1** **Sheer Fantastic**[58] 6865 3-9-4 64 (b) J-PGuillambert 2 70
(P C Haslam) *in tch: chsd ldr and rdn wl over 2f out: hld hd high but clsd to chal ins fnl f: pushed ahd nr fin* **6/1**[3]
0-51 **2** hd **Boomtown**[6] 116 3-9-9 69 6ex GregFairley 12 75+
(M Johnston) *sn led: hdd 8f out: pressed ldr tl led again 5f out: pushed clr over 2f out: 4 l clr 2f out: jnd ins fnl f: hdd nr fin* **6/4**[1]
03-1 **3** 3 **Banjo Bandit (IRE)**[13] 23 3-8-13 64 TolleyDean(5) 6 64
(J S Moore) *t.k.h early: stdd and hld up towards rr after 1f: rdn over 5f out: hdwy u.p 3f out: styd on to go 3rd last stride: nvr nr ldrs* **4/1**[2]
000- **4** shd **Anabaa's Secret (IRE)**[66] 6776 3-8-6 52 JamesDoyle 4 52
(J A Osborne) *hld up in midfield: hdwy over 3f out: chsd ldrs and rdn over 2f out: hanging lft over 1f out: kpt on: nvr able to chal* **25/1**
422- **5** ½ **Scientific**[16] 7286 3-8-11 57 (b) SaleemGolam 1 56
(G Prodromou) *t.k.h: hld up in midfield: rdn wl over 2f out: wnt 3rd 1f out: no imp: lost 2 pls nr fin* **16/1**
060- **6** 1 **Coral Shores**[35] 7121 3-8-4 50 oh2 AdrianMcCarthy 3 47
(P W Hiatt) *t.k.h: chsd ldr for 1f: chsd ldrs after: 3rd and rdn over 2f out: no imp on ldr: fdd ins fnl f* **40/1**
040- **7** 2 ½ **Threestoneburn (USA)**[38] 7084 3-8-11 64 HarryPoulton(7) 11 56
(J R Boyle) *hld up towards rr: sme hdwy over 4f out: rdn 3f out: nvr nr ldrs* **10/1**
06-4 **8** ¾ **Lady Sandicliffe (IRE)**[7] 98 3-8-10 56 SimonWhitworth 9 46
(Miss Jo Crowley) *hld up towards rr: rdn 5f out: nvr nr ldrs* **12/1**
606- **9** 1 **Black Heart**[26] 7208 3-8-11 62 (v[1]) KirstyMilczarek(5) 10 50
(M Botti) *t.k.h: chsd ldr after 1f: led 8f out tl 5f out: chsd ldr after tl wl over 2f out: wknd u.p over 2f out* **9/1**
060- **10** 3 **Tobouggornotobougg**[20] 7245 3-7-13 50 oh2 KellyHarrison(5) 8 32
(D Shaw) *hld up in rr: n.d: lost tch 3f out* **40/1**
00-0 **11** dist **Victory Shout (USA)**[7] 98 3-8-10 56 (v[1]) HayleyTurner 7 —
(J R Best) *in tch: rdn along briefly 9f out: lost pl qckly 5f out: t.o and virtually p.u last 2f* **66/1**
2m 5.92s (-0.68) **Going Correction** +0.075s/f (Slow) 11 Ran SP% **117.2**
Speed ratings (Par 95): **105,104,102,102,101 101,99,98,97,95** —
CSF £14.93 CT £41.23 TOTE £7.20: £1.90, £1.40, £1.90; EX 20.30 Trifecta £60.40 Pool £519.65 - 6.10 winning units..
Owner Middleham Park Racing Xviii **Bred** Newsells Park Stud Limited **Trained** Middleham Moor, N Yorks
FOCUS
In theory a modest race, but the first three home had all won their previous starts, so the form is probably better than the ratings suggest. This is backed up by a very decent winning time for a race like this, only just over half a second slower than the following Class 4 handicap for older horses.
Banjo Bandit(IRE) Official explanation: trainer said colt never travelled

185 PLAY GOLF @ LINGFIELD PARK H'CAP 1m 2f (P)
2:50 (2:56) (Class 4) (0-80,86) 4-Y-O+ £4,100 (£1,227; £613; £306; £152) **Stalls** Low

Form RPR
45-1 **1** **Art Man**[13] 22 5-9-0 72 GeorgeBaker 7 82+
(G L Moore) *stdd after s: hld up in last trio: rdn and gd hdwy on inner over 2f out: led jst over 2f out: edgd rt ins fnl f: in command and pushed out last 100yds* **7/1**[3]
43-3 **2** ¾ **Oakley Heffert (IRE)**[13] 28 4-9-1 75 (b) RichardHughes 8 81
(R Hannon) *hld up in last trio: rdn and hdwy over 2f out: drvn over 1f out: chsd wnr ins fnl f: kpt on but a hld* **8/1**
12-1 **3** 1 ¾ **Kindlelight Blue (IRE)**[13] 28 4-9-2 76 NCallan 2 79
(N P Littmoden) *in tch: rdn over 2f out: kpt on u.p over 1f out: wnt 3rd wl ins fnl f: nt pce to threaten wnr* **7/2**[2]
31-1 **4** nk **Baylini**[7] 97 4-9-12 86 6ex JamesDoyle 5 88
(Ms J S Doyle) *t.k.h: chsd ldrs on outer: hdwy to ld over 2f out: hdd jst over 2f out: drvn wl over 1f out: one pce after: lost 2 pls fnl f* **10/11**[1]
26-3 **5** 1 ½ **Baan (USA)**[10] 68 5-8-9 67 (v) GregFairley 4 66
(M Johnston) *w ldr tl led over 3f out: hdd over 2f out: sn drvn: outpcd over 1f out* **12/1**
135- **6** 6 **Lorikeet**[39] 7075 9-9-0 72 SimonWhitworth 3 59
(G L Moore) *led narrowly tl over 3f out: edging rt after: wknd qckly over 2f out* **20/1**
114- **7** 8 **Italian Romance**[19] 7263 5-9-1 73 AdamKirby 6 44
(J W Unett) *hld up in last trio: rdn over 3f out: sn lost tch* **25/1**
360- **8** 1 ½ **Three Thieves (UAE)**[41] 7046 5-8-9 67 FergusSweeney 1 35
(M S Saunders) *trckd ldrs on inner: rdn 3f out: sn struggling: no ch last 2f* **33/1**
2m 5.39s (-1.21) **Going Correction** +0.075s/f (Slow)
WFA 4 from 5yo+ 2lb 8 Ran SP% **117.5**
Speed ratings (Par 105): **107,106,105,104,103 98,92,91**
CSF £60.19 CT £231.13 TOTE £9.10: £2.80, £2.60, £1.60; EX 64.70 Trifecta £156.70 Pool £732.78 - 3.32 winning units..
Owner Matthew Green **Bred** Lady Lonsdale **Trained** Woodingdean, E Sussex
FOCUS
A well-contested race containing some in-form horses, but the pace was modest.
Baylini Official explanation: jockey said filly ran flat; trainer said filly was found to be coughing post race and had scoped dirty
Lorikeet Official explanation: jockey said gelding hung right

186 LINGFIELDPARK.CO.UK CLAIMING STKS 7f (P)
3:25 (3:30) (Class 6) 3-Y-O £1,774 (£523; £262) **Stalls** Low

Form RPR
612- **1** **Longoria (IRE)**[18] 7272 3-8-12 68 NCallan 2 68
(M G Quinlan) *mde all: rdn wl over 1f out: jst hld on* **8/11**[1]
12-3 **2** shd **Maybe I Wont**[7] 93 3-8-0 64 DeclanCannon(7) 1 63
(R M Stronge) *chsd wnr: rdn over 2f out: swtchd lft over 1f out: styd on wl: jst hld* **6/4**[2]
06-2 **3** 3 ½ **Mama Leo**[6] 108 3-8-1 48 (b) KirstyMilczarek(5) 4 52
(J G M O'Shea) *hld up in last: rdn and effrt 2f out: outpcd fnl f* **10/1**[3]
1m 26.74s (1.94) **Going Correction** +0.075s/f (Slow) 3 Ran SP% **107.0**
Speed ratings (Par 95): **91,90,86**
CSF £2.10 TOTE £1.60; EX 2.10.The winner was claimed by Ms Lucinda Featherstone for £10,000. Maybe I Wont was claimed by Ms P M Marks for £5,000.
Owner John Hanly **Bred** Cathal Ryan **Trained** Newmarket, Suffolk
FOCUS
A fair standard, but weak in numbers, and the pace was predictably steady.
Mama Leo Official explanation: jockey said filly ran flat

187 ARENALEISUREPLC.COM H'CAP 5f (P)
3:55 (4:00) (Class 5) (0-75,74) 4-Y-O+ £2,590 (£770; £385; £192) **Stalls** High

Form RPR
5-22 **1** **Sands Crooner (IRE)**[6] 113 5-8-3 64 ow2 (v) TolleyDean(5) 7 77
(D Shaw) *bhd: rdn and hdwy on inner 2f out: chsd ldr over 1f out: led ins fnl f: drvn out* **5/2**[1]
660- **2** nk **Fromsong (IRE)**[17] 7279 10-8-13 74 JamesO'Reilly(5) 3 86
(D K Ivory) *w ldr tl led 2f out: sn rdn: hdd ins fnl f: kpt on wl but a hld* **7/1**
403- **3** 2 ½ **After The Show**[25] 7221 7-8-10 66 ow1 NCallan 2 69
(Rae Guest) *trckd ldrs on inner: rdn and effrt 2f out: kpt on same pce u.p: wnt 3rd wl ins fnl f* **5/1**
011- **4** nk **Smokin Beau**[35] 7116 11-8-8 69 KirstyMilczarek(5) 1 71
(N P Littmoden) *sn led: rdn over 2f out: hdd 2f out: wknd ins fnl f* **4/1**[3]
10-4 **5** 3 **What Do You Know**[7] 94 5-9-4 74 (b) RichardHughes 4 65
(A M Hales) *towards rr: rdn and effrt 2f out: no hdwy: eased whn no ch ins fnl f* **3/1**[2]
106- **6** nk **Drifting Gold**[123] 5418 4-9-4 74 (b) AdamKirby 6 64
(C G Cox) *chsd ldrs: rdn and wd bnd jst over 2f out: sn struggling: eased ins fnl f* **12/1**
000- **7** 10 **Fairfield Princess**[112] 5722 4-8-12 68 FergusSweeney 8 22
(M S Saunders) *s.i.s: in tch on outer: rdn over 2f out: sn struggling* **33/1**
57.93 secs (-0.87) **Going Correction** +0.075s/f (Slow) 7 Ran SP% **113.4**
Speed ratings (Par 103): **109,108,104,104,99 98,82**
CSF £20.11 CT £80.12 TOTE £3.40: £2.10, £3.90; EX 24.50 TRIFECTA Pool £497.18 - 5.12 winning units. Place 6 £62.30, Place 5 £22.23..
Owner Danethorpe Racing Partnership **Bred** Peter Molony **Trained** Danethorpe, Notts
FOCUS
A fair sprint of its type, run at a decent 5f tempo.
What Do You Know Official explanation: vet said gelding returned lame right-fore
T/Plt: £176.50 to a £1 stake. Pool: £54,931.60. 227.15 winning tickets. T/Qpdt: £11.40 to a £1 stake. Pool: £4,473.50. 288.40 winning tickets. SP

167 SOUTHWELL (L-H)
Thursday, January 17

OFFICIAL GOING: Standard
Wind: Virtually nil Weather: Overcast and showers

188 SOUTHWELL-RACECOURSE.CO.UK APPRENTICE CLAIMING STKS 1m 4f (F)
1:30 (1:30) (Class 6) 4-Y-O+ £2,047 (£604; £302) **Stalls** Low

Form RPR
0/6 **1** **George Henson (IRE)**[8] 88 4-9-0 0 AshleyMorgan(5) 5 60
(M H Tompkins) *hld up: hdwy on outer 1/2-way: cl up 4f out: effrt over 2f out: led wl over 1f out: sn rdn and kpt on* **11/4**[2]
0/5- **2** ½ **Nabir (FR)**[9] 1178 8-9-4 56 PatrickDonaghy 6 54
(P D Niven) *hld up: hdwy 1/2-way: cl up 4f out: led 3f out: rdn and hdd wl over 1f out: sn drvn and kpt on u.p ins fnl f* **6/4**[1]
6/6- **3** 2 ½ **Aristi (IRE)**[18] 1229 7-8-5 41 RichardEvans(5) 4 42
(Evan Williams) *cl up: led over 4f out: rdn and hdd 3f out: drvn and one pce fnl 2f* **7/2**[3]
005- **4** 29 **Finnegans Rainbow**[60] 6569 6-8-12 44 SBushby(7) 3 5
(M C Chapman) *chsd ldng pair: pushed along 1/2-way: sn lost pl and bhd fnl 3f* **15/2**
300- **5** 3 ½ **Royal Axminster**[78] 6583 13-8-11 40 NBazeley(5) 2 —
(Mrs P N Dutfield) *led: rdn along and hdd wl over 4f out: sn wknd and bhd* **9/1**
2m 42.2s (1.20) **Going Correction** +0.075s/f (Slow)
WFA 4 from 5yo+ 4lb 5 Ran SP% **110.7**
Speed ratings (Par 101): **99,98,97,77,75**
CSF £7.37 TOTE £4.40: £2.50, £1.10; EX 8.00.The winner was calimed by S. Parr for £12,000.
Owner David Tompkins **Bred** Patrick Headon **Trained** Newmarket, Suffolk

FOCUS
A very poor affair which saw the two market leaders come clear. Weak form, rated through the second and third, with sizeable improvment from the winner.

189 BOOK HALF TERM NOW @ PONTINS.COM CLASSIFIED STKS 7f (F)
2:00 (2:00) (Class 7) 4-Y-0+ £1,706 (£503; £252) Stalls Low

Form RPR
0-02 1 **Government (IRE)**[10] 75 7-9-0 41 .... AndrewElliott 4 53
(M C Chapman) *cl up: rdn along and sltly outpcd 2f out: n.m.r and swtchd rt over 1f out: rdn and styd on wl fnl f to ld last 75yds* 7/2[2]
00-0 2 3/4 **Kingsmaite**[13] 42 7-9-0 43 .... (b) PhillipMakin 7 51
(S R Bowring) *trckd ldrs: hdwy 3f out: sn led: rdn wl over 1f out: drvn ins fnl f: hdd and no ex last 75yds* 4/1[3]
0-23 3 nk **Mr Chocolate Drop (IRE)**[11] 66 4-8-9 45 .... (b) JamesO'Reilly(5) 2 50
(Miss M E Rowland) *dwlt: sn in tch: hdwy on inner over 2f out: rdn to chal ent fnl f and ev ch tl drvn and no ex last 75yds* 3/1[1]
000- 4 1/2 **Jaassey**[16] 4082 5-9-0 42 .... (t) PaulMulrennan 10 49
(P Beaumont) *towards rr: hdwy 2f out: sn rdn and styd on wl fnl f: nrst fin* 40/1
000- 5 1 3/4 **Love You Always (USA)**[171] 4031 8-9-0 40 .... TGMcLaughlin 11 44
(Jane Chapple-Hyam) *s.i.s and bhd: hdwy on wd outside over 2f out: sn rdn and styd on appr fnl f: nrst fin* 8/1
050- 6 5 **Fistral**[21] 6908 4-9-0 44 .... (p) TomEaves 1 30
(P D Niven) *sn rdn along and outpcd in rr tl styd on u.p fnl 2f: nvr a factor* 10/1
03-5 7 nk **Astorygoeswithit**[9] 79 5-9-0 41 .... (p) AdamKirby 12 30
(G C Bravery) *chsd ldrs: rdn over 2f out: grad wknd* 13/2
000- 8 2 1/2 **Wodhill Be**[43] 7034 8-9-0 41 .... HayleyTurner 9 23
(D Morris) *midfield: hdwy over 2f out: rdn over 1f out: sn no imp* 11/1
66-0 9 10 **College Queen**[6] 119 10-9-0 40 .... ChrisCatlin 3 —
(S Gollings) *chsd ldrs on inner: rdn along wl over 2f out: sn wknd* 50/1
550- 10 1 **Cryptic Clue (USA)**[33] 7148 4-9-0 44 .... LiamJones 5 —
(D W Chapman) *led: rdn along 3f out: sn hdd & wknd* 33/1
/00- 11 7 **Bella Marie**[166] 4177 5-9-0 45 .... StephenDonohoe 6 —
(L R James) *s.i.s: a in rr* 66/1

1m 31.46s (1.16) **Going Correction** +0.075s/f (Slow) 11 Ran SP% 117.9
Speed ratings (Par 97): **96,95,94,94,92 86,86,83,71,70 62**
CSF £17.66 TOTE £4.90: £1.50, £1.70, £1.50; EX 18.00 Trifecta £25.90 Pool: £155.28 - 4.25 winning tickets..
Owner James Gordon-Hall **Bred** C H Wacker Iii **Trained** Market Rasen, Lincs
■ Stewards' Enquiry : James O'Reilly one-day ban: used whip with excessive frequency (Jan 28)

FOCUS
A dire affair which saw the first four come clear. The form looks orinary for the grade but sound enough among the first three.
Wodhill Be Official explanation: jockey said mare finished sore

190 LIFE IS ALWAYS A CABARET @ PONTIN'S H'CAP 7f (F)
2:30 (2:30) (Class 5) (0-75,79) 4-Y-0+ £3,276 (£967; £483) Stalls Low

Form RPR
00-2 1 **Neardown Beauty (IRE)**[8] 90 5-9-1 72 .... (p) JamesDoyle 1 91
(A J McCabe) *hld up in rr: swtchd lft and gd hdwy 2f out: led appr fnl f: sn rdn clr* 8/1
31-1 2 3 **Realt Na Mara (IRE)**[13] 41 5-9-0 71 .... SteveDrowne 2 82
(H Morrison) *chsd ldrs: pushed along 1/2-way: hdwy over 2f out: rdn to ld wl over 1f out: sn hung rt: hdd appr fnl f: drvn and one pce fnl f* 7/4[1]
51-1 3 1 1/2 **Haroldini (IRE)**[13] 42 6-8-7 64 .... (p) PaulMulrennan 7 71
(J Balding) *trckd ldrs: smooth hdwy whn nt clr run 2f out: effrt and n.m.r over 1f out: sn rdn and kpt on same pce ins fnl f* 5/2[2]
14-1 4 3 **Dickie Le Davoir**[11] 64 4-9-8 79 6ex .... AndrewElliott 3 78
(K R Burke) *dwlt and sn pushed along in rr: hdwy on outer 2f out: sn rdn and no imp fnl f* 11/2[3]
66-2 5 2 1/2 **Xpres Maite**[13] 41 5-8-5 62 .... (b) PaulEddery 4 54
(S R Bowring) *cl up: effrt over 2f out and ev ch tl rdn over 1f out and sn wknd* 10/1
01-4 6 7 **Soviet Palace (IRE)**[13] 43 4-9-4 75 .... (p) FergalLynch 6 48
(K A Ryan) *led: rdn along wl over 2f out: hdd wl over 1f out and wknd qckly* 10/1
202- 7 5 **Crow's Nest Lad**[33] 7155 4-8-3 63 oh1 ow2 .... PatrickMathers(3) 5 23
(J O'Reilly) *cl up: rdn along over 2f out: sn drvn and wknd* 20/1

1m 28.85s (-1.45) **Going Correction** +0.075s/f (Slow) 7 Ran SP% 114.4
Speed ratings (Par 103): **111,107,105,102,99 91,85**
CSF £22.51 TOTE £9.10: £3.80, £1.60; EX 25.30.
Owner Brian Morton **Bred** Mrs Joan M Langmead **Trained** Babworth, Notts

FOCUS
A decent little handicap for a Class 5 and they went a solid pace too. The field finished well spread out and the winning time was very smart for a race of its class, 2.61 seconds faster than the preceding classified event. Solid form.

191 PONTIN'S SMILES BETTER BY FAR H'CAP 5f (F)
3:00 (3:01) (Class 6) (0-60,65) 4-Y-0+ £2,457 (£725; £362) Stalls High

Form RPR
0-03 1 **Cleveland**[7] 109 6-9-2 58 .... HayleyTurner 3 71
(R Hollinshead) *chsd ldrs far side: hdwy 2f out: sn rdn and styd on to ld ins fnl f: drvn out* 7/1[3]
2-22 2 1 1/4 **Bentley**[5] 142 4-8-12 54 .... (v) DeanMcKeown 1 63
(D Shaw) *cl up far side: effrt over 1f out: rdn and ev ch ent fnl f tl drvn and nt qckn last 100yds* 9/2[2]
13-0 3 1 **Music Box Express**[14] 29 4-9-3 59 .... (e) SteveDrowne 5 64
(D J Murphy) *a.p far side: hdwy to ld wl over 1f out and sn rdn: drvn and hdd ins fnl f: kpt on same pce* 14/1
032- 4 1 1/4 **Kennington**[19] 7265 8-8-11 53 .... (b) NeilPollard 2 54
(Mrs C A Dunnett) *overall ldr far side: rdn along 2f out: hdd wl over 1f out and kpt on same pce* 14/1
41-1 5 1 **Diriculous**[7] 109 4-9-9 65 6ex .... ChrisCatlin 10 62+
(T G Mills) *dwlt and hmpd s: bhd tl hdwy and chsd ldrs 1/2-way: rdn wl over 1f out and sn one pce* 6/4[1]
02-2 6 nk **The Geester**[7] 109 4-8-8 50 .... (b) PaulEddery 7 46
(S R Bowring) *chsd ldrs in centre: rdn along 2f out: sn no imp* 12/1
01-0 7 2 1/2 **Ace Club**[13] 46 7-8-12 54 .... (b) TGMcLaughlin 4 41
(S Parr) *cl up far side: rdn along over 2f out: sn edgd lft and wknd* 33/1
06-0 8 1/2 **Egyptian Lord**[14] 29 5-8-12 54 .... LPKeniry 12 39
(Peter Grayson) *prom stands' rail: effrt 2f out: sn rdn and btn* 10/1
36-5 9 nk **Wicked Uncle**[13] 49 9-9-4 60 .... (v) PaulMulrennan 11 44
(S Gollings) *wnt badly lft s: a in rr* 22/1
3-40 10 1/2 **Tenancy (IRE)**[9] 82 4-8-3 48 oh1 ow2 .... (p) PatrickMathers(3) 8 30
(A J McCabe) *wnt rt and hmpd s: a towards rr* 40/1
1-60 11 1 1/4 **Is It Time (IRE)**[8] 86 4-8-13 55 .... RobertHavlin 14 33
(Mrs P N Dutfield) *dwlt: sn prom on stands' rail: rdn along 1/2-way and sn wknd* 33/1
050- 12 3/4 **Polar Force**[26] 7227 8-8-8 55 .... KirstyMilczarek(5) 9 30
(Mrs C A Dunnett) *midfield: rdn along 1/2-way: sn wknd* 25/1
200- 13 2 1/2 **Fly Time**[154] 4529 4-8-9 51 ow1 .... TomEaves 6 17
(Mrs L Williamson) *chsd ldrs: rdn along 1/2-way: sn wknd* 100/1

59.32 secs (-0.38) **Going Correction** -0.05s/f (Stan) 13 Ran SP% 118.3
Speed ratings (Par 101): **101,99,97,95,93 93,89,88,88,87 85,84,80**
CSF £35.66 CT £341.51 TOTE £10.10: £2.40, £1.50, £4.70; EX 38.00 Trifecta £317.30 Part won. Pool: £446.98 - 0.95 winning tickets..
Owner Mrs Susy Haslehurst **Bred** Darley **Trained** Upper Longdon, Staffs

FOCUS
A big field for this moderate handicap, but also a big draw bias with this straight 5f reverting to type. Those that race centre to far side held the advantage throughout and the first four horses home came from the five lowest stalls. Sound enough form amongst the principals.
Diriculous Official explanation: jockey said gelding suffered interference at start

192 TREAT THE KIDS AT HALF TERM @ PONTIN'S H'CAP 1m (F)
3:30 (3:31) (Class 5) (0-75,75) 4-Y-0+ £3,276 (£967; £483) Stalls Low

Form RPR
450- 1 **Intersky Charm (USA)**[18] 7282 4-8-8 65 .... DeanMcKeown 6 86
(R M Whitaker) *trckd ldrs: smooth hdwy 3f out: led wl over 2f out: rdn clr over 1f out: kpt on* 8/1
022- 2 7 **King's Ransom**[37] 7109 5-8-5 62 .... ChrisCatlin 3 67
(S Gollings) *cl up: effrt and ev ch over 2f out: drvn wl over 1f out: kpt on: no ch w wnr* 3/1[3]
15-3 3 6 **Cha Cha Cha**[7] 111 4-9-4 75 .... JimmyQuinn 2 66
(K A Ryan) *trckd ldrs: hdwy 3f out: rdn 2f out and sn one pce* 14/1
10-2 4 4 **My Mentor (IRE)**[11] 68 4-8-9 66 .... JamieMackay 1 48
(Sir Mark Prescott) *led: rdn along 3f out and sn hdd: drvn and wknd fnl 2f* 13/8[1]
/10- 5 8 **Subadar**[120] 5532 4-9-2 73 .... OscarUrbina 5 37
(M Botti) *a in rr* 33/1
12-2 6 1 1/4 **Jord (IRE)**[15] 21 4-9-2 73 .... AndrewElliott 4 34
(A J McCabe) *s.i.s: rapid hdwy to join ldrs after 1f: rdn along 1/2-way and wknd qckly: bhd fnl 2f* 11/4[2]

1m 43.2s (-0.50) **Going Correction** +0.075s/f (Slow) 6 Ran SP% 110.5
Speed ratings (Par 103): **105,98,92,88,80 78**
CSF £30.95 TOTE £8.60: £3.10, £2.00; EX 37.50.
Owner Intersky Bloodstock **Bred** Phil Booker **Trained** Scarcroft, W Yorks

FOCUS
With the first two in the betting disappointing badly, this probably took less winning than had looked likely. However, the winner was unexposed and is open to further improvement.
Intersky Charm(USA) Official explanation: trainer said, regarding apparent improvement in form, he was unable to explain the poor run last time but considered the colt to be better suited by the slower going.
Jord(IRE) Official explanation: jockey said filly went flat

193 ARENALEISUREPLC.COM H'CAP 1m (F)
4:00 (4:00) (Class 6) (0-50,50) 4-Y-0+ £2,252 (£664; £332) Stalls Low

Form RPR
265- 1 **Komreyev Star**[19] 7274 6-8-11 49 .... ChrisCatlin 2 58
(R E Peacock) *cl up: rdn to ld wl over 2f out: drvn and hdd ent fnl f: rallied u.p to ld last 75yds* 8/1
30-2 2 3/4 **Abbeygate**[15] 11 7-8-8 46 oh1 .... (p) NickyMackay 4 53
(T Keddy) *hld up in tch: gd hdwy wl over 2f out: rdn to ld ent fnl f: drvn: hdd and no ex last 75yds* 11/4[1]
00-3 3 1/2 **Wodhill Schnaps**[13] 42 7-8-11 49 .... (v) HayleyTurner 9 55
(D Morris) *midfield: smooth hdwy 3f out: rdn to chse ldrs over 1f out: kpt on u.p ins fnl f* 11/4[1]
00-6 4 1 1/4 **Steel Grey**[14] 33 7-8-8 49 oh1 ow3 .... MarkLawson(3) 10 52
(M Brittain) *in tch: rdn along and outpcd 1/2-way: hdwy over 2f out: sn drvn and kpt on fnl f* 11/1
02-6 5 3 **Shifty**[16] 7 9-8-12 50 .... DanielTudhope 6 46
(Jedd O'Keeffe) *led: hdd 3f out: sn rdn and grad wknd fnl 2f* 9/2[2]
00-0 6 2 1/2 **Cape Dancer (IRE)**[9] 80 4-8-8 46 oh1 .... (p) PaulFessey 5 36
(J S Wainwright) *chsd ldrs: rdn along 3f out: sn drvn and wknd* 50/1
60-0 7 3/4 **Pawn In Life (IRE)**[14] 33 10-8-8 46 oh1 .... (v) PaulEddery 7 35
(D W Chapman) *chsd ldrs: rdn along wl over 2f out: grad wknd* 33/1
500- 8 5 **Fuel Cell (IRE)**[147] 4739 7-8-9 47 .... PaulMulrennan 3 —
(J J Quinn) *a in rr* 13/2[3]
060- 9 1 1/4 **First Frost**[42] 6570 4-8-10 48 oh1 ow2 .... StephenDonohoe 11 —
(M J Gingell) *a in rr* 100/1
600- 10 9 **Raven Rascal**[20] 2116 4-8-5 46 .... PatrickMathers(3) 1 —
(J F Coupland) *in tch on inner: rdn along 3f out: sn wknd* 33/1
000- 11 1/2 **Knickyknackienoo**[51] 6956 7-8-3 46 oh1 .... KirstyMilczarek(5) 8 —
(T T Clement) *a in rr* 25/1
006- 12 1 3/4 **Reflective Glory (IRE)**[28] 7199 4-8-3 46 oh1 .... (v1) KellyHarrison(5) 12 —
(J S Wainwright) *chsd ldrs: rdn along over 3f out and sn wknd* 66/1

1m 44.45s (0.75) **Going Correction** +0.075s/f (Slow) 12 Ran SP% 118.5
Speed ratings (Par 101): **99,98,97,96,93 91,90,85,84,75 74,72**
CSF £29.11 CT £79.00 TOTE £8.60: £2.30, £1.30, £1.60; EX 37.00 Trifecta £42.00 Pool: £176.95 - 2.99 winning tickets. Place 6 £52.54, Place 5 £41.96.
Owner Garry Whittaker **Bred** G And Mrs Whittaker **Trained** Kyre Park, Worcs

FOCUS
Moderate handicap form.
Knickyknackienoo Official explanation: jockey said gelding missed the break
T/Jkpt: Not won. T/Plt: £51.30 to a £1 stake. Pool: £107,405.60. 1,528.00 winning tickets. T/Qpdt: £24.90 to a £1 stake. Pool: £5,247.30. 155.50 winning tickets. JR

140 WOLVERHAMPTON (A.W) (L-H)
Thursday, January 17

OFFICIAL GOING: Standard
Wind: Moderate, half behind Weather: Fine

194 SPONSOR A RACE BY CALLING 0870 220 2442 H'CAP 5f 216y(P)
6:50 (6:51) (Class 5) (0-75,75) 4-Y-0+ £2,331 (£693; £346; £173) Stalls Low

Form RPR
430- 1 **Distant Sun (USA)**[70] 6731 4-9-3 74 .... TomEaves 5 82
(Miss L A Perratt) *hld up: hdwy over 1f out: rdn to ld last strides* 14/1
24-3 2 shd **Memphis Man**[9] 84 5-8-8 72 .... RichardEvans(7) 4 79
(P D Evans) *s.i.s: hld up: hdwy on ins over 3f out: rdn over 1f out: led wl ins fnl f: hdd last strides* 3/1[2]

202- **3** 1 **Came Back (IRE)**[21] 7238 5-8-5 **65** .... MichaelJStainton(3) 6 69
(J Mackie) *t.k.h: hdwy over 2f out: led wl over 1f out: sn rdn: hdd wl ins fnl f: no ex* **9/2**

150- **4** 2 1/2 **Royal Challenge**[20] 7261 7-9-0 **71** .... DanielTudhope 3 75+
(I W McInnes) *prom: nt clr run wl over 1f out and ent fnl f: nt rcvr* **12/1**

01-5 **5** nk **Figaro Flyer (IRE)**[10] 72 5-8-10 **67** .... SimonWhitworth 2 62
(P Howling) *sn led: hdd over 2f out: led wl over 1f out: wknd ins fnl f* **4/1**[3]

03-3 **6** 6 **Coleorton Dancer**[9] 85 6-9-4 **75** ....(p) NCallan 1 51
(K A Ryan) *led early: w ldr: led over 2f out: rdn and hdd wl over 1f out: wknd fnl f: eased whn btn* **85/40**[1]

1m 15.46s (0.46) **Going Correction** +0.15s/f (Slow) **6** Ran SP% **109.5**
Speed ratings (Par 103): **102,101,100,97,96 88**
CSF £52.70 TOTE £16.30: £11.40, £2.30; EX 61.70.
Owner Gordon McDowall **Bred** Forging Oaks Llc **Trained** Carluke, S Lanarks
■ A first winner for Linda Perratt since taking over at the yard previously occupied by Ian Semple, who's now her assistant.

FOCUS
A closely-knit little handicap and the form looks pretty sound.
Royal Challenge ◆ Official explanation: jockey said gelding was denied a clear run
Coleorton Dancer Official explanation: jockey said gelding ran too freely

195 RINGSIDE CONFERENCE SUITE (S) STKS 1m 141y(P)
7:20 (7:21) (Class 6) 3-Y-O **£1,774** (£523; £262) **Stalls** Low

Form RPR

05-3 **1** **Tapas Lad (IRE)**[3] 156 3-9-0 57 ....(v) JimmyQuinn 5 58
(V Smith) *hld up: rdn and hdwy over 2f out: led 1f out: all out* **13/8**[2]

64-3 **2** 1/2 **Hawa Khana (IRE)**[9] 81 3-8-4 58 ....(p) KirstyMilczarek(5) 8 52
(N P Littmoden) *sn led: rdn and hdd 1f out: sn edgd rt: kpt on* **5/4**[1]

34-2 **3** 3/4 **Just Mossie**[10] 73 3-8-7 53 ....(p) JackDean(7) 4 55
(W G M Turner) *plld hrd: chsd ldr: rdn over 3f out: edgd rt ins fnl f: nt qckn* **8/1**[3]

400- **4** 3 1/2 **Novestar (IRE)**[34] 7140 3-9-0 50 .... SimonWhitworth 3 47
(G J Smith) *led early: chsd ldrs: rdn and one pce fnl 3f* **33/1**

000- **5** 3 1/2 **Never Sold Out (IRE)**[78] 6584 3-9-5 52 .... TPQueally 6 44
(J G M O'Shea) *hld up in tch: rdn over 2f out: wknd wl over 1f out* **20/1**

040- **6** 5 **Cherished Song**[105] 5944 3-8-6 63 ow2 .... JamieJones(5) 9 25
(M G Quinlan) *hld up: rdn 3f out: sn bhd* **8/1**[3]

000- **7** 5 **Hollow Dream (IRE)**[27] 7208 3-8-9 47 .... TGMcLaughlin 7 11
(R A Harris) *rdn over 4f out: a bhd* **66/1**

0 **8** 1 1/2 **Maddison County**[11] 65 3-8-9 0 .... AndrewElliott 1 8
(K R Burke) *hld up: rdn over 4f out: sn bhd* **25/1**

9 dist **Millers Saphire** 3-8-2 0 .... PatrickDonaghy(7) 2 —
(K G Wingrove) *s.v.s: rel to r: a wl t.o* **80/1**

1m 53.1s (2.60) **Going Correction** +0.15s/f (Slow) **9** Ran SP% **119.0**
Speed ratings (Par 95): **94,93,92,89,86 82,77,76,—**
CSF £3.95 TOTE £2.90: £1.10, £1.10, £1.60; EX 5.50.The winner was bought in for 5,500gns.
Owner Fran O'Brien **Bred** T F Moorhead **Trained** Exning, Suffolk

FOCUS
A very ordinary seller.

196 HOTEL & CONFERENCING AT WOLVERHAMPTON H'CAP 1m 1f 103y(P)
7:50 (7:50) (Class 5) (0-75,81) 4-Y-O+ **£2,331** (£693; £346; £173) **Stalls** Low

Form RPR

44-2 **1** **Alonso De Guzman (IRE)**[8] 104 4-7-12 **62** .... PatrickDonaghy(7) 3 70
(J R Boyle) *w ldr: led over 5f out: rdn wl over 1f out: drvn out* **2/1**[1]

051- **2** 3/4 **Pop Music (IRE)**[20] 7263 5-8-8 **64** ....(p) JamesDoyle 7 70
(Miss J Feilden) *hld up in tch: chsd wnr over 2f out: sn rdn: nt qckn ins fnl f* **8/1**

03-1 **3** nk **Given A Choice (IRE)**[8] 104 6-9-11 **81** 6ex .... TPQueally 6 87
(J G Given) *stdd s: hld up in rr: hdwy over 2f out: rdn and nt qckn ins fnl f* **11/4**[2]

140- **4** 3/4 **Without Excuse (USA)**[29] 7193 4-9-3 **74** ....(b) URispoli 1 78
(M Botti) *hld up in rr: c wd st: rdn over 1f out: kpt on ins fnl f: nt rch ldrs* **16/1**

62-1 **5** 4 **Chia (IRE)**[7] 117 5-9-1 **71** 6ex ....(p) HayleyTurner 5 67
(D Haydn Jones) *led: hdd over 5f out: rdn and wknd over 1f out* **8/1**

3-35 **6** 3/4 **Happy As Larry (USA)**[12] 63 6-9-5 **75** ....(t) NCallan 2 71
(D J Murphy) *hld up in tch: rdn over 2f out: wknd fnl f* **7/2**[3]

2m 2.20s (0.50) **Going Correction** +0.15s/f (Slow)
WFA 4 from 5yo+ 1lb **6** Ran SP% **110.3**
Speed ratings (Par 103): **103,102,102,101,97 97**
CSF £17.62 TOTE £3.50: £1.70, £3.50; EX 18.90.
Owner M Khan X2 **Bred** G And Mrs Middlebrook **Trained** Epsom, Surrey

FOCUS
A fair handicap for the grade with all six runners boasting previous course wins. Something of a bunch finish but pretty sound form all the same.
Happy As Larry(USA) Official explanation: jockey said gelding lost its action

197 STAY AT THE WOLVERHAMPTON HOLIDAY INN CLASSIFIED STKS 1m 4f 50y(P)
8:20 (8:21) (Class 7) 4-Y-O+ **£1,365** (£403; £201) **Stalls** Low

Form RPR

50-1 **1** **Qaasi (USA)**[5] 145 6-9-5 45 .... MarkLawson(3) 1 63
(M Brittain) *mde all: sn clr: given breather over 3f out: edgd rt over 1f out: rdn and r.o wl* **4/5**[1]

60-3 **2** 5 **Santera (IRE)**[5] 145 4-8-9 41 .... AndrewMullen(3) 7 49
(Mrs A Duffield) *hld up towards rr: stdy hdwy over 5f out: chsd wnr over 2f out: sn rdn: no imp fnl f* **10/3**[2]

60-0 **3** 12 **Trackattack**[5] 145 6-8-13 45 ....(p) NeilChalmers(3) 8 30
(M Appleby) *s.i.s: hdwy over 4f out: rdn over 3f out: wknd over 2f out* **22/1**

030- **4** 3 **Chart Oak**[220] 2520 5-9-2 45 .... TGMcLaughlin 5 25
(P Howling) *t.k.h: sn mid-div: short-lived effrt on outside over 2f out* **7/1**[3]

0-00 **5** 1/2 **Sea Frolic (IRE)**[9] 80 7-9-2 40 ....(v) HayleyTurner 6 24
(Jennie Candlish) *hld up: hdwy 6f out: rdn over 3f out: wknd over 2f out* **40/1**

/0-0 **6** 5 **Dark Society**[13] 44 10-8-9 44 .... MarkCoumbe(7) 9 16
(A W Carroll) *s.s: sn swtchd lft: rdn 3f out: a in rr: fin lame* **25/1**

-000 **7** 3 **Lady Firecracker (IRE)**[2] 161 4-8-12 45 ....(v) JimmyQuinn 2 11
(J R Best) *chsd wnr tl rdn and wknd over 2f out* **16/1**

00-6 **8** 51 **Smoothie (IRE)**[15] 18 10-8-11 41 .... TolleyDean(5) 4 —
(E G Bevan) *chsd ldrs: rdn over 4f out: wknd over 3f out: virtually p.u fnl f: fin w an over-rch* **14/1**

600- **9** 1 1/4 **Fashion Accessory**[49] 6090 4-8-12 35 .... SimonWhitworth 3 —
(M Appleby) *a in rr: t.o fnl 3f* **100/1**

2m 42.7s (1.60) **Going Correction** +0.15s/f (Slow)
WFA 4 from 5yo+ 4lb **9** Ran SP% **115.3**
Speed ratings (Par 97): **100,96,88,86,86 83,81,47,46**
CSF £3.36 TOTE £1.80: £1.10, £1.40, £7.90; EX 3.50.
Owner Eyes Wide Open Partnership **Bred** George Strawbridge Jr **Trained** Warthill, N Yorks

FOCUS
A dire event in which Qaasi was able to dictate against poor opposition. He still looks back to his winter best.
Dark Society Official explanation: vet said gelding finished lame
Lady Firecracker(IRE) Official explanation: jockey said filly had no more to give
Smoothie(IRE) Official explanation: vet said gelding finished with an over-reach

198 DINE IN THE HORIZONS RESTAURANT H'CAP 1m 5f 194y(P)
8:50 (8:51) (Class 6) (0-65,62) 4-Y-O+ **£1,774** (£523; £262) **Stalls** Low

Form RPR

55-4 **1** **Pocket Too**[8] 91 5-9-7 **60** ....(p) KirstyMilczarek(5) 3 71
(M Salaman) *led 1f: chsd ldr: led 8f out to 7f out: rdn over 2f out: led over 1f out: styd on* **9/2**[3]

103- **2** 2 1/2 **Blue Hills**[33] 7154 7-9-11 **59** ....(b) PhillipMakin 6 66
(P W Hiatt) *led after 1f to 8f out: led 7f out: rdn over 2f out: hdd over 1f out: one pce* **11/4**[1]

64-4 **3** 2 **Pocketwood**[13] 47 6-9-7 **62** ....(b[1]) GabrielHannon(7) 5 66
(Jean-Rene Auvray) *a.p: rdn over 2f out: one pce* **7/2**[2]

000- **4** 2 **Vanishing Dancer (SWI)**[17] 7285 11-9-6 **54** .... J-PGuillambert 1 55
(Mrs D Thomas) *hld up in tch: rdn and outpcd 4f out: styd on fnl 2f: nvr trbld ldrs* **28/1**

64-0 **5** 3 1/2 **Mango Masher (IRE)**[13] 36 4-8-10 **55** ....(p) TolleyDean(5) 4 52
(J L Flint) *hld up and bhd: rdn over 5f out: no rspnse* **8/1**

30-3 **6** 7 **Treetops Hotel (IRE)**[15] 18 9-9-12 **60** .... NCallan 7 47
(R Hollinshead) *hld up: hdwy 4f out: rdn and wknd over 2f out* **9/2**[3]

53-3 **7** nk **Global Traffic**[9] 78 4-9-1 **62** ....(v) RichardEvans(7) 2 48
(P D Evans) *hld up and bhd: hdwy on ins over 4f out: rdn and wknd 3f out* **13/2**

3m 8.24s (2.24) **Going Correction** +0.15s/f (Slow)
WFA 4 from 5yo+ 6lb **7** Ran SP% **113.1**
Speed ratings (Par 101): **99,97,96,95,93 89,89**
CSF £16.91 TOTE £5.30: £4.10, £2.00; EX 21.00.
Owner Oaktree Racing **Bred** M J Lewin **Trained** Baydon, Wilts
■ Stewards' Enquiry : Gabriel Hannon two-day ban: careless riding (Jan 28-29)

FOCUS
A low-key staying handicap, rated through the runner-up with the winner back to the level of last year's best.

199 WOLVERHAMPTON-RACECOURSE.CO.UK H'CAP 5f 20y(P)
9:20 (9:20) (Class 5) (0-75,72) 3-Y-O **£2,331** (£693; £346; £173) **Stalls** Low

Form RPR

41-2 **1** **Valhillen**[13] 38 3-8-9 **63** .... HayleyTurner 4 68+
(M D I Usher) *a.p: rdn to ld 1f out: r.o wl* **3/1**[1]

001- **2** 2 1/2 **Blakeshall Diamond**[63] 6820 3-8-10 **71** .... MarkCoumbe(7) 6 67
(A J Chamberlain) *led: rdn and hdd 1f out: one pce* **20/1**

421- **3** shd **A Wish For You**[19] 7270 3-8-13 **72** ....(p) JamesO'Reilly(5) 2 68+
(D K Ivory) *hmpd sn after s: bhd tl rdn and hdwy over 1f out: r.o ins fnl f* **3/1**[1]

300- **4** 1/2 **Montiboli (IRE)**[146] 4775 3-8-11 **65** .... NCallan 1 59
(K A Ryan) *hld up in tch: rdn over 1f out: one pce* **8/1**[3]

422- **5** 2 **Firewalker**[31] 7170 3-8-8 **62** .... TomEaves 3 49
(B Smart) *hld up in tch: rdn and btn whn edgd lft wl over 1f out* **7/2**[2]

031- **6** 3 1/2 **Mac Dalia**[21] 7240 3-8-13 **70** .... PatrickMathers(3) 5 44
(A J McCabe) *plld hrd: sn chsng ldr: rdn and wknd wl over 1f out* **3/1**[1]

63.26 secs (0.96) **Going Correction** +0.15s/f (Slow) **6** Ran SP% **113.1**
Speed ratings (Par 97): **98,94,93,93,89 84**
CSF £54.83 TOTE £4.20: £2.20, £5.30; EX 52.50 Place 6 £38.75, Place 5 £8.76.
Owner Saxon House Racing **Bred** Lady Hardy **Trained** Upper Lambourn, Berks

FOCUS
A tightly-knit modest event, and solid form. The winner had looked well handicapped on the form of his selling win here last month.
T/Plt: £37.40 to a £1 stake. Pool: £107,332.45. 2,090.00 winning tickets. T/Qpdt: £11.00 to a £1 stake. Pool: £7,289.80. 488.90 winning tickets. KH

NAD AL SHEBA (L-H)
Thursday, January 17

OFFICIAL GOING: Fast
Three of the six races were due to be run on the grass, but were switched to dirt after a record amount of rainfall rendered the turf track unraceable.
Weather: cloudy

200a BAHRI STKS (H'CAP) (F&M) (DIRT) 7f 110y(D)
3:55 (3:56) (90-105,102) 3-Y-O+
£33,165 (£11,055; £5,527; £2,763; £1,658; £1,105)

RPR

1 **Many Colours**[104] 5998 4-9-6 **102** .... LDettori 6 98+
(Saeed Bin Suroor) *sn led: trckd ldr after 2f: rdn 4 1/2f out: led 1 1/2f out: r.o wl* **9/4**[1]

2 1 3/4 **Olympic City (BRZ)**[103] 5-9-4 **100** .... JMoreira 4 90
(A Cintra Pereira, Brazil) *trckd ldr: t.k.h for 2f: led: hdd 1 1/2f out: r.o wl* **13/2**[3]

3 hd **Cat Belling (IRE)**[7] 8-8-5 **85** ....(t) TPO'Shea 1 77
(R Bouresly, Kuwait) *slowly away: settled in rr: rdn 3f out: r.o fnl 2f: nrst fin* **14/1**

4 9 1/4 **Tonic Star (FR)**[138] 5-8-13 **95** ....[1] RoystonFfrench 3 61
(Christian Wroe) *broke awkwardly: racd in mid-div: rdn 3f out: nvr able to chal* **7/1**

5 1/4 **Tulipa Di Job (BRZ)**[13] 6-8-5 **75** ....(t) RichardMullen 2 52
(A Selvaratnam, UAE) *in rr of mid-div: rdn to trck ldr 3f out: sn btn but kpt on* **40/1**

6 4 **Classy-Lady (BRZ)**[103] 4-8-2 **94** .... KLatham 7 39
(H J Brown, South Africa) *racd wd in mid-div: rdn along 5f out: nvr able to chal* **9/4**[1]

7 5 1/2 **Jet Past (SAF)**[13] 6-9-1 97 .... TedDurcan 5 37
(S Seemar, UAE) *mid-div: wd and rdn 3f out: nvr nr to chal* **9/2**[2]
1m 32.0s (0.70) **Going Correction** +0.30s/f (Slow) **7** Ran SP% **114.7**
Speed ratings: **108,106,106,96,96 92,87**

Owner Godolphin **Bred** Gainsborough Stud Management Ltd **Trained** Newmarket, Suffolk

FOCUS

This race was switched from the turf track to the dirt course after the declarations were made. Some nice fillies and mares lined up for this valuable handicap, but still a disappointing turnout numerically and, with some of these unproven on the surface, it would be unwise to get carried away with the bare form. The winning time was 0.78 seconds slower than the closing 95-110 handicap.

NOTEBOOK

Many Colours had never previously raced on dirt and there had to be a real question mark over whether she would handle the surface, but she coped with it just fine. She improved into quite a smart type on the turf for Jim Bolger last season, winning a Listed contest in September and, on this showing, she is continuing where she left off. Quickly away from the stalls, she showed plenty of early dash to dispute the lead with Olympic City through the opening stages, before eventually settling for a close second. She had to battle when getting back upsides the eventual runner-up at the top of the straight, but she eventually wore that one down and was a decisive winner. The form is nothing special, but her new connections will have plenty of options now she has proven herself on the surface. In the longer term, she should do well in the ever-expanding fillies' division back in Europe. (op 7/4)

Olympic City(BRZ), a dual Listed winner in Brazil last year, ran well on the dirt on this debut in Dubai. She showed plenty of natural speed to eventually lead outright and stuck on well for pressure in the straight, but Many Colours ultimately proved too strong. (op 6/1)

Cat Belling(IRE), a regular at the Carnival, was the only runner to make any impression from off the pace. This was her fourth start of the winter campaign, so she would have been spot-on and it would probably be wrong to expect much improvement next time.

Tonic Star(FR), just short of Listed class when trained in France, was fitted with a hood on her debut in Dubai/first start for new connections, but she was well held. Her best form has come on easy ground, so this surface was probably not ideal.

Classy-Lady(BRZ) could be considered disappointing considering she won on dirt in Brazil. (4/1)

Jet Past(SAF) managed to win on the dirt at Jebel Ali on her latest start, but she is better on turf. (op 4/1)

201a AL HAARTH STKS (CONDITIONS RACE) (FILLIES) (DIRT) 7f (D)

4:25 (4:26) 3-Y-O

£9,045 (£3,015; £1,507; £753; £452; £301)

RPR

1 **Fiesta Lady (ARG)**[103] 4-9-11 104 .... LDettori 2 102+
(Saeed Bin Suroor) *trckd ldng pair: led 1 1/2f out: easily* **11/8**[1]

2 3 1/4 **Cocoa Beach (CHI)**[229] 4-9-6 102 .... TedDurcan 8 87+
(Saeed Bin Suroor) *rdn along early strides: 12th 3f out: r.o fnl 2f: nvr able to chal: nrst fin* **4/1**[2]

3 1/4 **Olympic Glory (BRZ)**[67] 4-9-4 93 .... JMoreira 12 84
(A Cintra Pereira, Brazil) *settled in rr: 10th 3f out: r.o fnl 2f: nrst fin* **10/1**

4 1 3/4 **Queen Jock (USA)**[74] 6682 3-8-9 95 .... PShanahan 10 83
(Tracey Collins, Ire) *wl away: disp: hdd 1 1/2f out: lost 2nd fnl 1/2f* **20/1**

5 3 1/4 **Badaria (FR)**[44] 3-8-9 98 .... C-PLemaire 4 74
(E Charpy, UAE) *trckd ldng pair: rdn to chal 2 1/2f out: nt qckn fnl 1 1/2f* **12/1**

6 1 1/4 **Love Of Dubai (USA)**[89] 6336 3-8-9 97 .... MJKinane 3 71
(C E Brittain) *mid-div: gng wl 3 1/2f out: rdn to cl 2 1/2f out: ev ch fnl 1 1/2f: nt qckn* **10/1**

7 1/4 **Love Dancing (ARG)**[187] 4-9-6 99 .... WJSupple 13 68
(Saeed Bin Suroor) *mid-div: dropped to rr 4 1/2f out: prog to mid-div 3 1/2f out: r.o same pce* **7/1**[3]

8 8 3/4 **Swallow Star**[21] 3-8-9 70 .... (b) RoystonFfrench 5 45
(R Bouresly, Kuwait) *slowly away: nvr able to chal* **100/1**

9 1/2 **Miss Clonyn (IRE)**[21] 3-8-9 65 .... DO'Donohoe 9 44
(Doug Watson, UAE) *nvr bttr than mid-div* **100/1**

10 1/4 **Observatory Ridge**[85] 6433 3-8-9 50 .... DSmith 7 43
(R Bouresly, Kuwait) *outpcd for 1f: racd in rr: nvr able to chal* **250/1**

11 2 **Little Lady (GER)**[81] 3-8-9 90 .... (t) RyanMoore 1 38
(Frau Nina Bach, Germany) *slowly away but sn disp: hdd 2 1/2f out: wknd qckly* **20/1**

12 10 **Baby Princess (BRZ)**[236] 4-9-4 90 .... RHills 11 6
(J W Hills) *in rr of mid-div: rdn 4f out: nvr able to chal* **16/1**

13 3/4 **Lamistrelle (IRE)**[129] 5281 3-8-9 64 .... (b) GBirrer 6 8
(R Bouresly, Kuwait) *mid-div tl rdn 3f out: wknd* **200/1**

14 8 1/4 **Star Of Rosanna**[21] 3-8-9 76 .... MartinDwyer 14 —
(Doug Watson, UAE) *trckd ldrs: rdn 3f out: sn wknd* **25/1**

1m 25.11s (0.31) **Going Correction** +0.30s/f (Slow)
WFA 3 from 4yo 18lb **14** Ran SP% **122.6**
Speed ratings: **110,106,106,104,100 98,98,88,88,87 85,74,73,63**

Owner Godolphin **Bred** Haras La Esperanza **Trained** Newmarket, Suffolk

FOCUS

A fascinating conditions contest and the form looks strong. Admittedly a handful of these had no chance, but there were plenty of potentially smart fillies on show. Open to 3yos from either the northern or southern hemispheres, this was basically an early trial for the UAE 1,000 Guineas and, in the slightly longer term, the UAE Oaks.

NOTEBOOK

Fiesta Lady(ARG) ◆, picked up by Godolphin after winning the Argentine Oaks over 1m2f in October, was chosen by Frankie Dettori ahead of the two other Suroor horses. There had to be a danger she would get behind early on considering she was dropping in trip and drawn in stall two, but as it turned out the inside of the track was no disadvantage at all on this card (it usually pays to race out wide on this dirt course) and she was soon in a reasonable position just off the lead once finding her stride. She was slightly short of room at the top of the straight and was soon under the whip, but she stayed on strongly once getting a run against the inside rail and was ultimately an impressive winner. Indeed her jockey had a job pulling her up after the line and there is no doubt she can step forward again when back up in trip. Next stop will surely now be the UAE 1000 Guineas and she should be very hard to beat, with the step up to 1m in her favour. She will also be suited by the 1m1f of the UAE Oaks later in the Carnival, and could well do the double. (op 13/8)

Cocoa Beach(CHI), the winner's stablemate, looked to be going nowhere for much of the way and had just one behind her at the top of the straight, but she finished strongly to grab second once switched out to the centre of the track, away from the kickback. The champion three-year-old filly in Chile after winning all four starts - on turf and dirt - she is another interesting recruit to the Godolphin camp and can be expected to be a lot sharper next time, with her trainer reporting beforehand she would come on for the run. She will be suited by the step up to 1m in the UAE 1,000 Guineas and will no doubt reoppose the winner, but she will need to display more tactical speed if she is going to have any chance of reversing form. (op 100/30)

Olympic Glory(BRZ), ex-Brazilian, was slow to find her stride and was well off the pace for much of the way, but she ran on well in the straight when switched towards the inside. On this evidence she is going to be suited by further.

Queen Jock(USA), an Irish challenger who was Listed placed over 1m on the turf last year, took well to the dirt surface and ran a big race under a positive ride. She showed bags of early speed, but let the eventual winner up her inside early in the straight and could find only the one pace late on.

Badaria(FR), a winner on the sand at Deauville in December, travelled very nicely into the straight, but she did not find as much as one might have hoped. (op 11/1)

Love Of Dubai(USA), sixth in the Rockfel when last seen in October, was stuck towards the inside for most of the way and struggled to make an impression.

Love Dancing(ARG), a dual winner in Argentina, including in Group 3 company when last seen in July, seemed to lack the pace to get a handy position, but she was kept towards the outside and remained in touch. She could only find the one pace in the straight and was never a threat.

Baby Princess(BRZ) was hard to weigh up beforehand, with all of her previous runs coming in Brazil, and she was well beaten.

202a INTIKHAB STKS (H'CAP) (DIRT) 1m 1f (D)

5:05 (5:05) (90-105,104) 3-Y-O+

£33,165 (£11,055; £5,527; £2,763; £1,658; £1,105)

RPR

1 **Rampallion**[68] 6759 5-8-13 96 .... MJKinane 2 101+
(E Charpy, UAE) *racd in last: 12th 3f out: prog on rail 2 1/2f out: led 1f out: r.o wl* **16/1**

2 1 3/4 **Familiar Territory**[153] 4588 5-9-5 102 .... LDettori 4 106
(Saeed Bin Suroor) *trckd ldrs: gng wl 3f out: led 2f out: hdd 1f out: r.o wl* **4/1**[1]

3 7 **Impeller (IRE)**[103] 6011 9-8-13 96 .... JohnEgan 1 83
(J S Moore) *trckd ldng gp: rdn to chal 3f out: n.m.r 1 1/2f out: one pce* **16/1**

4 4 1/2 **Bennie Blue (SAF)**[21] 6-9-6 104 .... KShea 11 81
(M F De Kock, South Africa) *wl away: led then trckd ldr: led again 3 1/2f out: trckd 2f out: wknd* **4/1**[1]

5 1/4 **Acrobatic (USA)**[14] 5-8-11 95 .... GBirrer 3 71
(Doug Watson, UAE) *mid-div: rdn 4f out: nvr able to chal: r.o fnl 1 1/2f* **25/1**

6 1 **Consular**[14] 6-9-4 101 .... (t) TPO'Shea 6 76
(E Charpy, UAE) *settled in rr: rdn 4f out: sme prog fnl 3f: nvr nr to chal* **14/1**

7 1 1/4 **Mosaic**[35] 6-9-5 102 .... RoystonFfrench 9 74
(A Al Raihe, UAE) *racd in rr: no room 1/2f out: nvr able to chal* **12/1**

8 1 **Elmustanser**[56] 7-9-3 100 .... (t) RHills 8 70
(Doug Watson, UAE) *mid-div: rdn to cl 2 1/2f out: nvr nr to chal* **16/1**

9 3/4 **Limehouse (SAF)**[14] 5-9-5 102 .... WMLordan 5 71
(M F De Kock, South Africa) *trckd ldr: rdn 3f out: ev ch tl wknd fnl f* **20/1**

10 2 1/4 **Jonquil (IRE)**[14] 6-8-9 93 .... DO'Donohoe 14 56
(Doug Watson, UAE) *trckd ldrs wd: hrd rdn 3f out: wknd* **20/1**

11 5 1/2 **Purple Emperor (USA)**[166] 4147 4-8-6 90 .... TedDurcan 15 42
(Saeed Bin Suroor) *slowly away: led 7 1/2f out: rdn 4f out: sn wknd* **10/1**

12 nse **Dubai Honor**[41] 9-9-5 102 .... (e) MartinDwyer 7 54
(Doug Watson, UAE) *settled in rr: rdn 3 1/2f out: one pce: short of room fnl f* **8/1**[3]

13 6 1/2 **Remaadd (USA)**[27] 7-9-6 104 .... JMurtagh 10 42
(D Selvaratnam, UAE) *nvr able to chal* **7/1**[2]

14 6 1/4 **Mambo King (DEN)**[82] 6-9-3 100 .... (t) RichardMullen 12 25
(L Kelp, Denmark) *in rr of mid-div: nvr able to chal* **33/1**

15 shd **Naipe Marcado (URU)**[315] 643 5-9-5 102 .... (v) WJSupple 16 27
(Saeed Bin Suroor) *mid-div: dropped to rr 4 1/2f out: sn btn* **10/1**

16 dist **Impetious**[95] 6216 4-9-2 100 .... (b) BrettDoyle 13 —
(Eamon Tyrrell, Ire) *trckd ldr for 2f: sn rdn and wknd* **33/1**

1m 50.76s (0.96) **Going Correction** +0.30s/f (Slow)
WFA 4 from 5yo+ 1lb **16** Ran SP% **133.1**
Speed ratings: **107,105,99,95,95 94,93,92,91,89 84,84,78,73,73 —**

Owner Sheikh Ahmed Bin Mohammed Al Maktoum **Bred** Side Hill Stud **Trained** United Arab Emirates

FOCUS

A very good, competitive handicap and the pace was strong. The front two pulled well clear of the remainder, but the winning time was 0.53 seconds slower than the following handicap.

NOTEBOOK

Rampallion has always promised to develop into a nice horse, but he has been lightly raced – he ran just three times when with Godolphin last year – and has presumably had some problems. However, trying dirt for the first time on his debut for a new trainer, he produced a decent performance. He hardly looked to be in a promising position early on, stuck towards the inside well off the pace after being slowly away from stall two, and he was keen enough. However, he travelled smoothly through the middle part of the contest and, despite meeting some trouble, he managed to get into some sort of challenging position early in the straight, albeit he still had a few lengths to find. He eventually stayed on best of all and was nicely on top at the line. He will also have the option of switching back to turf and might be able to go some way to fulfilling his potential in the coming weeks.

Familiar Territory, like the winner, has been lightly raced over the years, but he has some smart form to his name. He has won on Polytrack, but this was his first start on dirt and he ran well. He enjoyed a much better trip than the winner and can have no excuses, but this first run of the year should sharpen him up.

Impeller(IRE) ◆, returning from over three months off the track, was no match for the front pair, but he ran well in defeat. It is interesting to note he ran twice on dirt at the beginning of last year's Carnival (including fifth in this race) and won at the first attempt when switched to turf.

Bennie Blue(SAF), a winner over 1m2f on dirt off a mark of 100 at last year's Carnival, was never too far away, but he lacked a change of pace in the straight.

Acrobatic(USA) ◆, ex-Roger Charlton, ran well on just his second start since returning from a long absence. He was not helped by stall three and can improve on this when stepped up in trip.

Purple Emperor(USA) rushed up to dispute the lead after starting slowly, but he soon weakened and probably used up too much energy getting into a handy position.

Naipe Marcado(URU), having his first run for Godolphin, was well beaten.

Impetious was in trouble a fair way out. She should be happier back on turf.

203a INVASOR STKS (H'CAP) (DIRT) 1m 1f (D)

5:35 (5:36) (100-112,108) 3-Y-O+

£52,763 (£17,587; £8,793; £4,396; £2,638; £1,758)

RPR

1 **Lucky Find (SAF)**[229] 5-8-11 102 .... (t) KShea 4 116+
(M F De Kock, South Africa) *trckd ldr: led gng wl 2 1/2f out: r.o wl: easily* **2/1**[1]

2 7 1/2 **Third Set (IRE)**[167] 4119 5-8-11 102 .... LDettori 9 100+
(Saeed Bin Suroor) *sn led: hdd 2 1/2f out: r.o but no ch w wnr* **5/2**[2]

3 3 **Rosberg (USA)**[27] 7-8-11 102 .... (t) TPO'Shea 8 92
(E Charpy, UAE) *mid-div: rdn 4f out: nvr able to chal* **12/1**

4 1 1/4 **Yasoodd**[27] 5-8-9 **100** .... RPCleary 3 87
(D Selvaratnam, UAE) *slowly away: mid-div on rail: rdn 4f out: nvr able to chal* **10/1**

5 shd **Arabian Prince (USA)**[131] 5-9-0 **105** .... DO'Donohoe 10 92
(Doug Watson, UAE) *trckd ldr: rdn 3f out: nt qckn* **14/1**

6 1/2 **Gharir (IRE)**[27] 6-8-11 **102** .... (bt) RHills 12 88
(E Charpy, UAE) *in rr of mid-div: rdn 3f out: nvr able to chal* **7/2**[3]

7 5 1/4 **Final Verse**[154] 4543 5-9-1 **106** .... JohnEgan 7 81
(J S Moore) *slowly away: racd in rr: nvr nr to chal* **14/1**

1m 50.23s (0.43) **Going Correction** +0.30s/f (Slow)
WFA 4 from 5yo+ 1lb **7** Ran SP% **114.2**
Speed ratings: **110,103,100,99,99 99,94**

Owner Sh Ahmed bin Mohd bin Khalifa Al Maktoum **Bred** Oldlands Stud **Trained** South Africa

FOCUS
Another race that had been scheduled to be run on turf and a depleted field as a result of the switch to the dirt course. Restricted to horses rated 100 or higher, this had promised to be a very good handicap, but the form obviously now needs treating with caution. They seemed to go just a steady pace through the early stages and not many got into this, but the winning time was still 0.53 seconds quicker than the earlier 90-105 handicap.

NOTEBOOK
Lucky Find(SAF) was obviously being lined up for a turf race for his first start in Dubai, but the decision to allow him to take his chance after the race was switched to dirt was fully justified with an impressive success. Returning from over seven months off the track, he travelled very sweetly just off early leader Third Set and cruised upsides that one at the top of the straight, before pulling well clear when asked for his effort. It would be silly to get carried away, with the form not what it might have been, but nevertheless he is clearly a very useful individual and he will have plenty of options now he has proven himself on this surface.
Third Set(IRE) improved to win three big handicaps on the turf for Roger Charlton last year, most notably the International at Ascot and the Totesport Mile at Goodwood when last seen in August. However, considering he was beaten off a mark of 85 on his last start on an artificial surface (Kempton's Polytrack) he was unlikely to be suited by this race being switched to dirt and he did not show his best form on his debut for Saeed Bin Suroor. He was allowed an easy time up front, but was quickly left behind when Lucky Find threw down a challenge early in the straight and carried his head a little high under pressure. He will be much happier back on turf when he will be suited by both a shorter trip and a stronger-run race.
Rosberg(USA) is a triple winner on dirt, so he would not have minded the switch, and this was a respectable effort.
Yasoodd is a better horse on turf and a steadily run race on dirt would not have suited.
Arabian Prince(USA) looked to have every chance if good enough, but he was entitled to need this first run in over four months.
Gharir(IRE) seemed a little keen early on and did not see his race out.
Final Verse has done well since joining Stan Moore, but he can be tricky and dirt racing clearly didn't suit. He was held up last off a steady pace and didn't want to know when asked to go through the kickback. He can leave this form behind back on turf.

204a SH MAKTOUM BIN RASHID AL MAKTOUM CHALLENGE R1 (GROUP 3) (DIRT) 1m (D)
6:05 (6:07) 3-Y-O+
£60,301 (£20,100; £10,050; £5,025; £3,015; £2,010)

RPR

1 **Happy Boy (BRZ)**[68] 5-9-0 102 .... JAparecido 1 117+
(P Nickel Filho, Brazil) *hmpd s: mid-div on rail: trckd ldrs 3f out: led gng wl 2 1/2f out: v easily* **20/1**

2 9 **Gloria De Campeao (BRZ)**[103] 6031 5-9-0 102 .... C-PLemaire 3 98
(P Bary, France) *mid-div: rdn to cl 3f out: r.o wl fnl 2f: nrst fin* **14/1**

3 hd **Frosty Secret (USA)**[14] 4-9-0 100 .... KShea 10 98
(M F De Kock, South Africa) *trckd ldrs: rdn to chse wnr 2f out: r.o but no ch w wnr: lost 2nd on line* **7/1**[3]

4 5 1/4 **Etihaad**[21] 6-9-0 98 .... (t) BrettDoyle 4 87
(R Bouresly, Kuwait) *trckd ldr: disp ld 6f out: hdd 2 1/2f out: r.o wl* **20/1**

5 shd **Salt Track (ARG)**[130] 8-9-0 99 .... (t) ESki 14 87
(Niels Petersen, Norway) *in rr: last of main gp 3f out but r.o wl fnl 2f: nrst fin* **33/1**

6 3/4 **Golden Arrow (IRE)**[315] 642 5-9-0 104 .... (bt) TPO'Shea 2 85
(E Charpy, UAE) *wnt lft s: mid-div: rdn 3f out: r.o one pce* **25/1**

7 1 3/4 **Imperialista (BRZ)**[322] 599 5-9-0 108 .... (v) LDettori 15 82
(Saeed Bin Suroor) *sn led: hdd 6f out: ev ch 3f out: nt qckn* **11/4**[1]

8 3 3/4 **Jet Express (SAF)**[14] 6-9-0 106 .... RoystonFfrench 5 74
(A Al Raihe, UAE) *trckng ldrs whn hmpd 4 1/2f out: nt rcvr* **8/1**

9 3/4 **Vortex**[12] 62 9-9-0 106 .... (t) JMurtagh 6 73
(Miss Gay Kelleway) *mid-div: rdn 3f out: nt qckn* **9/1**

10 3/4 **Calrissian (GER)**[74] 4-9-0 97 .... MartinDwyer 11 71
(L Kelp, Denmark) *mid-div: rdn 3f out: nt qckn* **25/1**

11 1 1/4 **All That And More (IRE)**[7] 6-9-0 90 .... (t) DO'Donohoe 8 69
(Doug Watson, UAE) *v.s.a: nvr nr to chal* **66/1**

12 1/2 **Forty Hablador (ARG)**[7] 7-9-0 85 .... (bt) AdrianTNicholls 7 68
(A Manuel, UAE) *nvr nr to chal* **100/1**

13 2 1/4 **Jack Sullivan (USA)**[12] 62 7-9-0 109 .... (t) MJKinane 16 63
(G A Butler) *mid-div: rdn 3 1/2f out: nvr able to chal* **4/1**[2]

14 4 3/4 **Esquire**[7] 6-9-0 88 .... AhmedAjtebi 9 54
(A Al Raihe, UAE) *trckd ldr: disp ld 6f out: hdd 2 1/2f out: wknd* **66/1**

15 shd **Boston Lodge**[292] 858 8-9-0 109 .... (vt) RyanMoore 12 54
(Doug Watson, UAE) *sn rdn in rr: nvr able to chal* **7/1**[3]

16 4 1/4 **State Shinto (USA)**[7] 12-9-0 85 .... (bt) GBirrer 13 45
(R Bouresly, Kuwait) *a in rr* **100/1**

1m 36.37s (-0.33) **Going Correction** +0.30s/f (Slow) **16** Ran SP% **124.6**
Speed ratings: **113,104,103,98,98 97,95,92,91,90 89,88,86,81,81 77**

Owner Roberto A L Reichert **Bred** Haras Torrao De Ouro **Trained** Brazil

FOCUS
The first round of the Maktoum Challenge, but this did not look like a strong race by Group 3 standards.

NOTEBOOK
Happy Boy(BRZ) was hard to weigh up beforehand, but he had beaten a couple of previous Grade 1 winners when landing a Grade 3 over 1m4f on ground described as heavy in Brazil on his most recent start, and he absolutely bolted up on his debut in Dubai, providing his country with a second straight success in this race. He was off the pace and against the inside rail for much of the way - often the worst place to be on this track but not on this card - and he was always travelling easily. He moved to the front with embarrassing ease and pulled well clear without his rider having to ask him any sort of question, indeed Aparecido was able to pat him down the neck near the line. This was a weak race, so it would silly to get too carried away, but it was hard not to be impressed. He will no doubt now contest the second round of the Maktoum Challenge and that should tell use whether he can develop into a World Cup horse, or whether the Godolphin Mile will be more his level. It would be no surprise if he was sold before his next run.
Gloria De Campeao(BRZ), ex-Brazilian, ran a creditable race, but was no match whatsoever for the easy winner.
Frosty Secret(USA), a winner on dirt in the US, had run to just a fair level of form when second over 6f on his debut in Dubai in a non-Carnival handicap at the beginning of the month, but this was a respectable effort.
Etihaad is bred to win a Dubai World Cup – he is a son of the great Dubai Millennium and a half-brother to Almutawakel – but he did not make the track until the end of last year, when he beat some useful types over this course and distance. Upped in class, he ran with credit and could step forward again as he gains further experience.
Salt Track(ARG), a dual Listed winner on an artificial surface in Sweden, is back at the Carnival for a second straight year and did not run badly.
Imperialista(BRZ) has not gone on since winning this race for Brazilian connections last year and he proved a major disappointment on his return from ten months off the track. He showed good speed out wide early on, but there was nothing there when Dettori asked him for an effort at the top of the straight. He looks like one to leave alone for the time being.
Vortex was well below his best, although in fairness he didn't seem to enjoy the best of trips.
Jack Sullivan(USA) was beaten in a conditions contest at Lingfield on his previous start and he was well beaten upped in class on his return to Dubai.

205a MARJU STKS (H'CAP) (DIRT) 7f 110y(D)
6:35 (6:38) (95-110,105) 3-Y-O+
£36,180 (£12,060; £6,030; £3,015; £1,809; £1,206)

RPR

1 **Happy Runner (BRZ)**[68] 5-8-8 **95** .... JAparecido 13 103
(P Nickel Filho, Brazil) *trckd ldrs: t.k.h: led 1 1/2f out: r.o wl: comf* **8/1**[3]

2 2 1/2 **Objeto De Arte (BRZ)**[101] 6071 5-9-0 **100** .... (t) C-PLemaire 5 103
(P Bary, France) *sn led: hdd 1 1/2f out: r.o wl* **8/1**[3]

3 3/4 **Azarole (IRE)**[131] 5213 7-9-0 **100** .... JohnEgan 1 101
(J S Moore) *mid-div on rail: rdn 3f out: r.o wl fnl 2f: nrst fin* **16/1**

4 1 3/4 **Ans Bach**[25] 5-9-3 **104** .... (e) JMurtagh 3 99
(D Selvaratnam, UAE) *mid-div: rdn 2 1/2f out: r.o same pce* **11/1**

5 2 **King Jock (USA)**[74] 6681 7-8-5 **91** .... WMLordan 2 82
(R J Osborne, Ire) *slowly away: mid-div: chsd ldrs 3f out: nt qckn fnl 1 1/2f* **11/1**

6 3/4 **Colorado Rapid (IRE)**[194] 3330 4-8-9 **96** .... TedDurcan 9 84
(Saeed Bin Suroor) *mid-div: rdn 3f out: n.d* **9/1**

7 1/4 **Fleeting Shadow (IRE)**[125] 5392 4-8-7 **99** .... AhmedAjtebi(6) 4 87
(A Al Raihe, UAE) *mid-div: hrd rdn 3f out: nvr able to chal* **12/1**

8 3 1/2 **Almuraad (IRE)**[21] 7-8-6 **93** .... RHills 7 71
(Doug Watson, UAE) *settled in rr: rdn 2 1/2f out: nvr able to chal* **11/2**[2]

9 1 1/4 **Topor (TUR)**[87] 4-8-11 **98** .... HKaratas 8 73
(H Demirkiran, Turkey) *settled in last: nvr nr to chal* **16/1**

10 4 3/4 **Fremen (USA)**[103] 6011 8-8-9 **96** .... AdrianTNicholls 11 59
(D Nicholls) *a in rr* **14/1**

11 4 1/4 **Brunel (IRE)**[679] 621 7-9-0 **100** .... (t) TPO'Shea 10 52
(E Charpy, UAE) *trckd ldrs tl rdn 3f out: sn wknd* **28/1**

12 1 3/4 **Sea Hunter**[21] 6-9-0 **100** .... (vt) RoystonFfrench 12 48
(A Al Raihe, UAE) *mid-div: rdn to cl 3 1/2f out: ev ch 3f out: wknd fnl 2f* **5/1**[1]

P **Heart Alone (BRZ)**[25] 7-9-0 **100** .... RichardMullen 6 —
(S Seemar, UAE) *rdn in rr 3f out: p.u 2 1/2f out* **11/2**[2]

1m 31.22s (-0.08) **Going Correction** +0.30s/f (Slow) **13** Ran SP% **125.9**
Speed ratings: **112,109,108,107,105 104,104,100,99,94 90,88,—**

Owner Roberto A L Reichert **Bred** Haras Torrao De Ouro **Trained** Brazil

FOCUS
Another race that was due to be run on the turf course at the time of declarations, so the switch to dirt would not have suited some of these, and the form looks ordinary for the grade. The winning time was 0.78 seconds quicker than the opening handicap won by Many Colours. The first and second were always on the pace.

NOTEBOOK
Happy Runner(BRZ) followed up his stablemate Happy Boy's success in the previous race. He had actually run at the same meeting as Happy Boy on his latest outing and he took to Dubai without any problems at all. He showed good speed to get a handy position from his wide draw and was possibly even a shade free through the early stages, but he had plenty left when it mattered and was a clear-cut winner. He should remain competitive and will also have the option of switching to turf.
Objeto De Arte(BRZ), formerly trained in Brazil, was always travelling nicely on the front end and this was a respectable effort on his debut in Dubai off the back of a 101-day break. This was Pascal Bary's second runner on the card and both horses acquitted themselves with real credit.
Azarole(IRE), a winner on the turf at the Carnival in 2006 but unsuccessful last year, raced off the pace towards the inside for much of the way, exactly where more than one of the winners on this card were positioned, and he kept on for a place in the straight. This should put him spot on for a return to turf.
Ans Bach, a Listed winner on the turf at Abu Dhabi on his most recent start, ran creditably in defeat switched to dirt.
King Jock(USA) is a much better horse on turf, so he would have been unsuited by the switch, but he ran okay and this should put him right.
Colorado Rapid(IRE), an improving handicapper for Mark Johnston last year, struggled to make an impression on his first start on dirt off the back of a 194-day break. He can be given another chance back on turf.
Fremen(USA) was never really seen with a chance and will probably be happier back on turf.

174 KEMPTON (A.W) (R-H)
Friday, January 18

OFFICIAL GOING: Standard
Wind: Strong, across Weather: Overcast, frequent showers

206 KEMPTON.CO.UK CLASSIFIED STKS 5f (P)
6:20 (6:20) (Class 7) 4-Y-O+ **£1,365** (£403; £201) **Stalls** High

Form RPR

55-1 1 **Dodaa (USA)**[9] 100 5-8-9 43 .... AshleyHamblett(5) 8 56
(N Wilson) *mde all: rdn clr over 1f out: 4 l ahd ent fnl f: unchal* **2/1**[2]

06-1 2 1 1/2 **Savile's Delight (IRE)**[4] 153 9-9-6 43 .... RichardKingscote 7 56+
(Tom Dascombe) *lw: settled in 5th: effrt over 1f out: chsd clr wnr 200yds out: clsng at fin: hopeless task* **5/4**[1]

04-3 3 2 1/2 **Lady Hopeful (IRE)**[13] 50 6-9-0 45 .... (b) LPKeniry 5 41
(Peter Grayson) *s.s: mostly last tl styd on fnl f to snatch 3rd last stride: no ch* **8/1**[3]

05-5 4 shd **Elvina**[13] 50 7-9-0 44 .... FergusSweeney 6 41
(A G Newcombe) *awkward s: sn rdn to chse ldng pair: disp 2nd briefly 1f out: one pce* **14/1**

065- 5 3/4 **Elizabeth Spirit (IRE)**[36] 7134 4-9-0 40 .... StephenDonohoe 2 38
(E S McMahon) *chsd wnr: no imp over 1f out: lost 2nd and wknd last 200yds* **10/1**

0423 **6** *2* **Blushing Russian (IRE)**[4] 153 6-8-9 44......................(b) TolleyDean(5) 1 31
(J M Bradley) *chsd ldng trio: rdn 1/2-way: wknd over 1f out* **16/1**
60.81 secs (0.31) **Going Correction** +0.025s/f (Slow) **6** Ran SP% **110.5**
Speed ratings (Par 97): **98,95,91,91,90 87**
CSF £4.69 TOTE £3.00: £3.30, £1.10; EX 10.20.
Owner Paul & Linda Dixon **Bred** Silverleaf Farm Inc **Trained** Flaxton, N Yorks

FOCUS
This was a bit stronger than is usual at this level, with the winner and second both in-form last-time-out winners. The winner got a good tactical ride from the front.
Blushing Russian(IRE) Official explanation: jockey said gelding ran flat

207 PANORAMIC BAR & RESTAURANT LOYALTY SCHEME H'CAP 1m 2f (P)
6:50 (6:50) (Class 6) (0-65,65) 4-Y-0+ **£2,047** (£604; £302) **Stalls** High

Form RPR
220- **1** **Watchmaker**[27] 7224 5-9-2 **61**.. ChrisCatlin 1 71
(Miss Tor Sturgis) *lw: t.k.h: pressed ldr: drvn to ld narrowly over 1f out: kpt on wl whn jnd 50yds out* **11/4**[1]
20-1 **2** *nk* **Blu Manruna**[13] 51 5-9-6 **65**.......................................(b) PaulDoe 9 74
(J Akehurst) *led: drvn and narrowly hdd over 1f out: battled on and upsides 50yds out: no ex last strides* **11/2**[3]
00-5 **3** *2 1/2* **Tancredi (SWE)**[9] 91 6-9-0 **62**.............................. JerryO'Dwyer(3) 10 66
(N B King) *trckd ldng pair after 2f: drvn 2f out: kpt on but no imp* **7/2**[2]
10-1 **4** *2* **Hatch A Plan (IRE)**[14] 44 7-8-13 **61**......................... NeilChalmers(3) 8 61
(Mouse Hamilton-Fairley) *chsd ldrs: same pce and no imp on ldng trio fr over 2f out* **8/1**
000- **5** *3 1/2* **Prime Contender**[30] 7194 6-9-2 **61**...............................(b) GeorgeBaker 2 54
(G L Moore) *hld up in last pair: reminder sn after s: rdn 3f out: modest prog fr 2f out: n.d* **11/2**[3]
6 *2* **Bandits Pistol (NZ)**[44] 8-9-1 **60**.............................. J-PGuillambert 5 49
(M Madgwick) *settled in rr: drvn 3f out: no real prog* **80/1**
00/0 **7** *1/2* **King Of Diamonds**[9] 91 7-8-12 **57**....................(b[1]) FrankieMcDonald 3 45
(Jean-Rene Auvray) *plld hrd and hld up last: stl pulling over 4f out: drvn and no rspnse 3f out: styd on fnl f* **33/1**
014- **8** *2 1/2* **Mister Fizzbomb (IRE)**[42] 7056 5-8-13 **61**...............(v) PJMcDonald(3) 7 44
(J S Wainwright) *prom 2f: chsd ldrs after: rdn 3f out: nt keen and losing pl over 1f out* **8/1**
56-0 **9** *3* **Double Spectre (IRE)**[13] 51 6-9-3 **62**.............................. DaneO'Neill 4 39
(Jean-Rene Auvray) *nvr bttr than midfield: u.p and struggling wl over 2f out: wknd over 1f out* **20/1**
06/0 **10** *1 3/4* **Startengo (IRE)**[13] 51 5-9-2 **61**.................................... SamHitchcott 6 35
(Miss Suzy Smith) *sn pushed along to chse ldrs: drvn and cl up over 3f out: wknd over 2f out* **10/1**
2m 7.19s (-0.81) **Going Correction** +0.025s/f (Slow) **10** Ran SP% **119.9**
Speed ratings (Par 101): **104,103,101,100,97 95,95,93,90,89**
CSF £18.52 CT £55.37 TOTE £4.70: £1.70, £1.60, £1.90; EX 25.30.
Owner Miss Ann Sturgis **Bred** Hesmonds Stud Ltd **Trained** Lambourn, Berks

FOCUS
A moderate handicap and the first two had ot between them virtually throughout, nothing ever getting into the race from off the pace.
King Of Diamonds Official explanation: jockey said gelding hung right
Mister Fizzbomb(IRE) Official explanation: jockey said gelding stopped quickly
Startengo(IRE) Official explanation: jockey said gelding bled from the nose

208 DIGIBET.COM CLAIMING STKS 1m (P)
7:20 (7:20) (Class 6) 4-Y-0+ **£2,047** (£604; £302) **Stalls** High

Form RPR
40-5 **1** **Satyricon**[16] 15 4-9-6 70.. URispoli 4 74
(M Botti) *lw: sn chsd ldr: hd high and no imp 2f out: cajoled along and styd on fnl f to ld last strides* **7/2**[3]
0-21 **2** *nk* **Rebellious Spirit**[8] 110 5-8-11 60.. ChrisCatlin 1 64
(P W Hiatt) *lw: led: drvn 2 l clr over 2f out: kpt on u.p: collared last strides* **9/4**[2]
020- **3** *1 1/4* **Shouldntbethere (IRE)**[22] 7241 4-9-0 61....................... RobertHavlin 2 64
(Mrs P N Dutfield) *stdd s: hld up in last: effrt over 2f out: nt qckn over 1f out: kpt on same pce after* **8/1**
46-2 **4** *1/2* **Waterline Twenty (IRE)**[13] 53 5-9-0 70................. RichardEvans(7) 3 70
(P D Evans) *racd wd thrght and mostly in 4th: bmpd along and kpt on same pce fnl 2f* **15/8**[1]
26/5 **5** *dist* **Ela Aleka Mou**[14] 43 4-8-13 80.............................. MatthewHenry 5 —
(M A Jarvis) *plld hrd and sn restrained in 3rd: carried hd to one side and reluctant over 2f out: wknd and eased: t.o* **10/1**
1m 40.81s (1.01) **Going Correction** +0.025s/f (Slow) **5** Ran SP% **108.0**
Speed ratings (Par 101): **95,94,93,92,—**
CSF £11.26 TOTE £3.90: £3.20, £1.80; EX 9.70.Rebellious Spirit was claimed by Adrian Swingler for £6,500.
Owner Effevi Snc Di Villa Felice & C **Bred** Sir Eric Parker **Trained** Newmarket, Suffolk
■ A first winner in Britain for Umberto Rispoli, 20, a lightweight said to have ridden well over 350 winners in his native Italy.
■ Stewards' Enquiry : U Rispoli two day ban: used whip with excessive frequency and without allowing colt time to respond (Jan 29-30)

FOCUS
Not a bad bunch by claiming standards, but the gallop was moderate and the form probably isn't that reliable. The runner-up is probably the best guide to the race.

209 DIGIBET SPORTS BETTING H'CAP 1m (P)
7:50 (7:50) (Class 6) (0-55,59) 4-Y-0+ **£2,047** (£604; £302) **Stalls** High

Form RPR
202- **1** **Takaamul**[19] 7278 5-8-9 **50**.. JamesDoyle 9 59
(K A Morgan) *hld up in midfield: prog 2f out: drvn to ld jst over 1f out: styd on wl* **10/1**
053- **2** *1* **Convallaria (FR)**[53] 6950 5-9-0 **55**.............................(t) SteveDrowne 10 62
(G Wragg) *lw: hld up in midfield on inner: prog over 2f out: chal over 1f out: chsd wnr fnl f: a hld* **4/1**[1]
26-1 **3** *1/2* **Perfect Practice**[9] 89 4-9-1 **59** 6ex........................ KirstyMilczarek(3) 7 67+
(C G Cox) *lw: trckd ldrs: effrt whn n.m.r 2f out: eased to outer over 1f out: edgd lft but styd on wl fnl f: nvr able to chal* **6/1**[2]
22-3 **4** *1 1/4* **Simpsons Gamble (IRE)**[7] 123 5-8-12 **53**....................(p) DaneO'Neill 2 56
(R A Teal) *t.k.h: hld up in tch on outer: poised to chal 2f out: rdn and fnd nil over 1f out: styd on fnl f* **8/1**
032- **5** *1 1/4* **Mon Petite Amour**[21] 7257 5-8-13 **54**......................... FergusSweeney 5 54
(D W P Arbuthnot) *t.k.h: pressed ldrs: effrt to ld narrowly on outer 2f out: hdd jst over 1f out: wknd ins fnl f* **8/1**
2-26 **6** *1 1/2* **Climate (IRE)**[2] 176 9-8-4 **52**..................................(v) RichardEvans(7) 12 49+
(P D Evans) *trckd ldrs: effrt over 2f out: cl up and trying to get through whn hmpd over 1f out: nt rcvr* **10/1**
02-2 **7** *hd* **Napoletano (GER)**[7] 123 7-8-7 **55**..........................(p) ThomasBubb(7) 4 51+
(S Dow) *lw: s.v.s: t.k.h and sn in tch in last trio: effrt over 2f out: bmpd along on inner and n.m.r over 1f out: no prog after* **10/1**
54-2 **8** *1/2* **Krakatau (FR)**[10] 80 4-8-13 **54**.. ChrisCatlin 11 49
(D J Wintle) *disp ld to 2f out: hanging and sn btn* **7/1**[3]
24-4 **9** *3/4* **Soldier Field**[10] 80 4-8-11 **55**...................................(v[1]) PJMcDonald(3) 3 48
(J S Wainwright) *pushed along in last trio: shkn up and no prog over 2f out* **16/1**
026- **10** *1 1/2* **Over To You Bert**[184] 3647 9-8-7 **53** ow1....................... HaddenFrost(5) 6 43
(R J Hodges) *t.k.h: disp ld to 2f out: wknd* **33/1**
00-0 **11** *3* **Dancing Duo**[13] 56 4-8-11 **52**....................................(v) DeanMcKeown 8 35
(D Shaw) *a in last trio: drvn and no prog over 2f out* **10/1**
006- **12** *8* **Baba Ghanoush**[44] 7028 6-8-12 **53**.. PaulDoe 1 18
(J Akehurst) *cl up on wd outside: hanging bdly bnd over 3f out: sn bhd: t.o* **20/1**
1m 39.98s (0.18) **Going Correction** +0.025s/f (Slow) **12** Ran SP% **119.0**
Speed ratings (Par 101): **100,99,98,97,96 94,94,93,93,91 88,80**
CSF £49.90 CT £268.35 TOTE £13.00: £4.20, £2.00, £2.50; EX 80.00.
Owner K A Morgan **Bred** Shadwell Estate Company Limited **Trained** Little Marcle, H'fords

FOCUS
This was a bit messy and the third was unlucky not to finish closer.
Perfect Practice Official explanation: jockey said filly was denied a clear run
Climate(IRE) Official explanation: jockey said gelding suffered interference in running

210 DIGIBET.COM H'CAP 6f (P)
8:20 (8:20) (Class 4) (0-80,79) 4-Y-0+ **£4,210** (£1,252; £625; £312) **Stalls** High

Form RPR
501- **1** **Distinctly Game**[49] 6970 6-9-4 **79**.. NCallan 7 90+
(K A Ryan) *lw: trckd ldr to 1/2-way: cl up whn hmpd 2f out and dropped to 5th: rallied over 1f out: drvn to ld last 100yds: sn clr* **9/4**[1]
234- **2** *1 1/2* **Westport**[37] 7126 5-9-3 **78**.. ChrisCatlin 6 79
(K A Ryan) *sn in last trio: rdn on outer bnd 3f out and struggling: styd on fr over 1f out to take 2nd nr fin* **11/2**[3]
51-0 **3** *nk* **Desert Dreamer (IRE)**[15] 26 7-9-0 **75**.............................. TPQueally 3 75
(G A Butler) *lw: hld up in last trio: rdn over 2f out: styd on wl fnl f to take 3rd last strides* **7/1**
/00- **4** *hd* **She's My Outsider**[19] 7281 6-8-9 **73**........................ KirstyMilczarek(3) 8 72
(A W Carroll) *trckd ldrs: clsd to ld wl over 1f out: hdd last 100yds: wkng nr fin* **16/1**
26-4 **5** *nk* **Resplendent Alpha**[10] 85 4-9-3 **78**................................... JimmyQuinn 1 76
(P Howling) *b: dwlt: hld up in last trio: rdn over 2f out: styd on fnl f: nvr able to chal* **8/1**
/21- **6** *hd* **Hello Man (IRE)**[45] 7026 5-9-0 **78**............................. JerryO'Dwyer(3) 4 76
(Eamon Tyrrell, Ire) *prom: trckd ldr 1/2-way: chal and upsides 2f out: nt qckn over 1f out: wknd last 100yds* **9/2**[2]
04-2 **7** *1* **Goodbye Cash (IRE)**[12] 64 4-8-4 **72**....................... RichardEvans(7) 9 73+
(P D Evans) *cl up on inner: pressing ldrs whn nowhere to go over 1f out and snatched up: sn last: swtchd to wd outside and kpt on nr fin* **10/1**
54-0 **8** *nk* **Russian Symphony (USA)**[15] 26 7-9-1 **76**..............(b) RobertHavlin 2 70
(C R Egerton) *led at str pce: hdd wl over 1f out: sn wknd* **9/1**
1m 12.85s (-0.25) **Going Correction** +0.025s/f (Slow) **8** Ran SP% **112.9**
Speed ratings (Par 105): **102,100,99,99,98 98,97,96**
CSF £14.32 CT £72.68 TOTE £3.50: £1.40, £1.90, £1.80; EX 14.00.
Owner Mr & Mrs Julian And Rosie Richer **Bred** J A Forsyth **Trained** Hambleton, N Yorks

FOCUS
This looked a fairly competitive handicap, and it was run at a good gallop, but the time was only 0.23sec quicker than the following handicap for horses rated 46-55. The winner has been rated to last year's best, and the second to the best of his AW form.
Goodbye Cash(IRE) Official explanation: jockey said filly was denied a clear run

211 DAY TIME, NIGHT TIME, GREAT TIME H'CAP 6f (P)
8:50 (8:50) (Class 6) (0-55,60) 4-Y-0+ **£2,047** (£604; £302) **Stalls** High

Form RPR
0-22 **1** **Regal Royale**[7] 121 5-8-9 **50**..................................(v) AdrianMcCarthy 8 61
(Peter Grayson) *mde virtually all: rdn 2f out: hrd pressed fnl f: styd on wl nr fin* **3/1**[1]
2-43 **2** *1* **Tilsworth Charlie**[9] 89 5-8-12 **53**.......................................(b) NCallan 2 61
(J R Jenkins) *stdd s: hld up in last pair: swtchd sharply to inner and prog 2f out: chsd wnr jst 1f out: str chal fnl f: no ex last 50yds* **13/2**[3]
-011 **3** *nk* **Mind Alert**[7] 121 7-9-5 **60** 12ex......................................(v) JamesDoyle 1 67+
(D Shaw) *lw: hld up and sn last: effrt and prog over 1f out: styd on all the way to the line: too much to do* **7/2**[2]
030- **4** *1/2* **Nautical**[90] 6344 10-8-11 **55**.................................. KirstyMilczarek(3) 7 60
(A W Carroll) *t.k.h: hld up in midfield: prog to dispute 2nd over 1f out: nt qckn fnl f* **7/2**[2]
05-0 **5** *2* **Mr Loire**[7] 121 4-8-5 **46**.......................................(b) DeanMcKeown 9 45
(A J Chamberlain) *lw: wl in tch: prog to dispute 2nd 2f out: nt qckn over 1f out: one pce after* **15/2**
000- **6** *hd* **Racing Stripes (IRE)**[33] 7164 4-8-10 **54**..................(b) NeilChalmers(3) 5 52
(K O Cunningham-Brown) *stdd s: hld up towards rr: effrt over 2f out: chsng ldrs and cl enough on inner over 1f out: fdd* **40/1**
000- **7** *1* **Devon Flame**[165] 4236 9-8-8 **54**.................................... HaddenFrost(5) 4 49
(R J Hodges) *settled in last trio: pushed along on outer wl over 2f out: one pce and no hdwy* **16/1**
620- **8** *5* **Mulberry Lad (IRE)**[19] 7276 6-8-12 **53**............................. ChrisCatlin 3 32
(P W Hiatt) *lw: cl up: disp 2nd 2f out to over 1f out: wknd rapidly* **10/1**
05U- **9** *5* **Vlasta Weiner**[308] 687 8-8-4 **52**.........................(b) PietroRomeo(7) 6 15
(J M Bradley) *t.k.h: racd wd: chsd wnr to 2f out: wknd rapidly u.p* **33/1**
1m 13.08s (-0.02) **Going Correction** +0.025s/f (Slow) **9** Ran SP% **114.9**
Speed ratings (Par 101): **101,99,99,98,95 95,94,87,81**
CSF £22.89 CT £70.53 TOTE £4.30: £2.00, £1.80, £1.10.
Owner S Kamis And Mrs S Grayson **Bred** Cheveley Park Stud Ltd **Trained** Formby, Lancs
■ Stewards' Enquiry : Adrian McCarthy one-day ban: used whip with excessive frequency (Jan 29)

FOCUS
A tight little handicap run at a good pace, and the time compared favourably with the better class handicap which preceded it. Solid form, with the winner a slight improver on recent efforts.

212 KEMPTON.CO.UK H'CAP 2m (P)
9:20 (9:20) (Class 6) (0-65,65) 4-Y-0+ **£2,047** (£604; £302) **Stalls** High

Form RPR
653- **1** **Alnwick**[146] 4809 4-9-0 **58**.. DaneO'Neill 12 71+
(P D Cundell) *wl plcd bhd ldrs: effrt 3f out: drvn to ld on inner over 1f out: styd on wl* **5/2**[1]
546- **2** *3* **Right Option (IRE)**[22] 7242 4-9-2 **65**............................. TolleyDean(5) 10 74
(J L Flint) *t.k.h: prom: wnt 2nd over 7f out: led over 5f out and stl taking t.k.h: drvn and hdd over 1f out: kpt on same pce* **5/1**

140/ **3** *5* **Gallantian (IRE)**[266] 6-9-6 **57**........ GeorgeBaker 1 60
(Alan Fleming) *wl plcd: trckd ldr over 5f out: drvn over 2f out: sn lost 2nd and fdd: jst hld on for 3rd* **12/1**

23-2 **4** *hd* **Capitalise (IRE)**[8] 118 5-9-2 **56**........ JerryO'Dwyer(3) 3 59
(V Smith) *hld up in last trio: prog to 6th 3f out and wl in tch: nt qckn 2f out and wl btn: kpt on again fnl f* **7/2**[2]

200- **5** *2* **Synonymy**[80] 6564 5-9-10 **61**........(b) JimmyQuinn 5 61
(M Blanshard) *hld up towards rr: prog and rchd 5th over 3f out: lft bhd fnl 2f* **8/1**

651- **6** *3* **Sir Haydn**[30] 7186 8-9-11 **62**........(v) J-PGuillambert 9 59
(J R Jenkins) *t.k.h: hld up in last pair: prog 5f out: 7th and in tch 3f out: nt clr run sn after: rdn and wknd tamely* **12/1**

24-3 **7** *½* **Haatmey**[16] 14 6-9-4 **55**........(v) LPKeniry 8 51
(P R Chamings) *hld up in midfield: prog to chse ldng pair over 4f out: wknd u.p 2f out* **9/2**[3]

00-0 **8** *6* **Desert Soul**[9] 91 4-9-2 **60**........ NeilPollard 7 49
(R H York) *hld up in last: sme prog to 8th 3f out and jst in tch: sn rdn and wknd* **50/1**

060- **9** *29* **Explosive Fox (IRE)**[23] 5426 7-8-9 **46**........(p) PaulDoe 11 —
(S Curran) *led to over 5f out: wknd: t.o* **20/1**

001- **10** *16* **Victory Mile (USA)**[16] 4757 4-9-0 **58**........ FergusSweeney 2 —
(M F Harris) *reminder in midfield after 7f: wknd over 4f out: t.o* **25/1**

/0-5 **11** *29* **Impostor (IRE)**[8] 118 5-10-0 **65**........(p) TGMcLaughlin 6 —
(R A Harris) *b: drvn to press ldr: lost pl u.p over 7f out: wknd over 5f out: wl t.o* **50/1**

3m 29.59s (-0.51) **Going Correction** +0.025s/f (Slow)
WFA 4 from 5yo+ 7lb **11** Ran SP% **124.7**
Speed ratings (Par 101): **102,100,98,97,96 95,95,92,77,69 55**
CSF £15.79 CT £132.16 TOTE £2.60: £1.10, £3.30, £6.40; EX 28.60 Place 6 £10.72, Place 5 £9.50..
Owner Entre Nous and P D Cundell **Bred** Roden House Stud **Trained** Compton, Berks

FOCUS
They finished well strung out here and the well backed and unexposed winner looks to be going the right way. The form could be rated higher, although those behind him don't look that solid.
Sir Haydn Official explanation: jockey said gelding hung right
T/Plt: £12.70 to a £1 stake. Pool: £108,312.05. 6,189.10 winning tickets. T/Qpdt: £8.50 to a £1 stake. Pool: £6,883.50. 593.00 winning tickets. JN

[194] WOLVERHAMPTON (A.W) (L-H)
Friday, January 18

OFFICIAL GOING: Standard
Wind: Fresh behind Weather: Overcast

213 SPONSOR A RACE BY CALLING 0870 220 2442 CLAIMING STKS 5f 216y(P)
1:20 (1:26) (Class 6) 4-Y-0+ **£2,047** (£604; £302) **Stalls** Low

Form RPR

04-1 **1** **Mafaheem**[16] 16 6-8-12 66........ TPQueally 9 66+
(A B Haynes) *hld up: hdwy to ld over 1f out: sn rdn: edgd rt nr fin: styd on* **11/8**[1]

4-43 **2** *hd* **Chatshow (USA)**[8] 106 7-8-7 60........ MarkCoumbe(7) 3 67
(A W Carroll) *chsd ldrs: rdn over 2f out: hung lft ins fnl f: r.o* **14/1**

22-5 **3** *2* **Stormburst (IRE)**[13] 54 4-8-7 57........ SimonWhitworth 6 54
(A G Newcombe) *a.p: rdn over 2f out: hung lft fnl f: styd on* **7/1**[3]

00-1 **4** *hd* **Grimes Faith**[8] 106 5-9-5 70........(b) NCallan 1 68+
(K A Ryan) *trckd ldrs: hmpd over 1f out: r.o: nvr able to chal* **11/4**[2]

06-6 **5** *¾* **Doubtful Sound (USA)**[17] 4 4-9-2 70........ PaulFessey 5 60
(T D Barron) *chsd ldr: rdn and ev ch whn hung lft over 1f out: no ex ins fnl f* **15/2**

50- **6** *1 ¾* **Now You See Me**[220] 2542 4-8-9 0........ ChrisCatlin 7 47
(K McAuliffe) *s.i.s: outpcd: nvr nrr* **66/1**

03-4 **7** *7* **Blackheath (IRE)**[14] 46 12-8-5 48........ KellyHarrison(5) 8 26
(S T Mason) *chsd ldrs: rdn and ev ch 2f out: wknd over 1f out* **33/1**

3126 **8** *1 ¼* **Calloff The Search**[6] 142 4-8-13 55........ MickyFenton 2 25
(Stef Liddiard) *led: rdn: hung rt and hdd over 1f out: sn wknd* **9/1**

1m 15.73s (0.73) **Going Correction** +0.20s/f (Slow) **8** Ran SP% **114.1**
Speed ratings (Par 101): **103,102,100,99,98 96,87,85**
CSF £23.19 TOTE £2.30: £1.20, £2.80, £2.00; EX 20.20 Trifecta £81.10 Pool £439.13 - 3.84 winning units..Stormburst was claimed by A J Chamberlain for £8,000.
Owner W Clifford **Bred** J H And J M Wall **Trained** Limpley Stoke, Bath

FOCUS
A typical claimer, run at a solid pace. The first pair came clear and the winner scored with a bit in hand.

214 DINE IN THE HORIZONS RESTAURANT H'CAP 1m 141y(P)
1:50 (1:55) (Class 6) (0-55,55) 4-Y-0+ **£1,774** (£523; £262) **Stalls** Low

Form RPR

01-2 **1** **The Salwick Flyer (IRE)**[15] 32 5-8-12 **53**........ PhillipMakin 10 64
(Miss L A Perratt) *hld up: hdwy over 2f out: rdn and edgd lft fr over 1f out: led ins fnl f: styd on* **4/1**[2]

000- **2** *hd* **Supercast (IRE)**[108] 5879 5-9-0 **55**........ SamHitchcott 7 66
(N J Vaughan) *hld up: hdwy 3f out: led over 1f out: hrd rdn and hdd ins fnl f: edgd lft: styd on u.p* **4/1**[2]

133- **3** *2 ½* **Private Soldier**[112] 5782 5-8-5 **51**........ JamieJones(5) 8 56
(N J Vaughan) *s.i.s: hld up: racd keenly: hdwy over 2f out: rdn and nt clr run ins fnl f: hung lft: styd on same pce* **2/1**[1]

350- **4** *3 ½* **Star Of The Desert (IRE)**[28] 7213 5-8-12 **53**........(b1) PaulMulrennan 3 50
(Mrs K Walton) *chsd ldr tl led 3f out: rdn and hdd over 1f out: wknd ins fnl f* **16/1**

10-6 **5** *1 ½* **Carefree**[14] 49 4-8-13 **55**........(t) NCallan 4 49
(G A Swinbank) *chsd ldrs: ev ch over 2f out: sn rdn: wknd fnl f* **13/2**[3]

20-1 **6** *3* **Aggbag**[15] 32 4-8-9 **51**........ AndrewElliott 1 38
(B P J Baugh) *chsd ldrs: nt clr run and lost pl wl over 2f out: n.d after* **9/1**

50-2 **7** *4* **Persian Fox (IRE)**[7] 127 4-8-10 **52**........ VinceSlattery 9 30
(A G Juckes) *hld up: nvr trbld ldrs* **16/1**

000- **8** *9* **Brynris**[228] 2304 4-8-4 **46** oh1........(b1) DaleGibson 6 —
(Mrs G S Rees) *plld hrd and prom: rdn and wknd over 2f out* **100/1**

050- **9** *10* **Beaumont Boy**[20] 6640 4-8-9 **51**........(p) ChrisCatlin 2 —
(A G Foster) *led over 5f: sn wknd* **33/1**

1m 50.61s (0.11) **Going Correction** +0.20s/f (Slow)
WFA 4 from 5yo+ 1lb **9** Ran SP% **112.4**
Speed ratings (Par 101): **107,106,104,101,100 97,93,85,77**
CSF £19.66 CT £39.70 TOTE £5.50: £1.90, £1.60, £1.30; EX 26.00 Trifecta £105.80 Pool £530.67 - 3.56 winning units..
Owner The Irish Mafia **Bred** Piercetown Stud **Trained** Carluke, S Lanarks
■ Stewards' Enquiry : Sam Hitchcott one-day ban: used whip with excessive frequency (Jan 29)

FOCUS
A moderate handicap, run at a sound pace. The form looks fair.

215 GET AWAY @ PONTIN'S 0844 576 5938 (S) H'CAP 1m 4f 50y(P)
2:20 (2:25) (Class 6) (0-55,53) 4-Y-0+ **£1,774** (£523; £262) **Stalls** Low

Form RPR

63-3 **1** **Still Dreaming**[7] 127 4-8-6 46........(b) DaleGibson 7 51
(M Dods) *chsd ldrs: led over 3f out: rdn over 1f out: hung rt ins fnl f: styd on wl* **8/1**[3]

00-6 **2** *4* **Arthurs Dream (IRE)**[6] 140 6-8-4 45........ KellyHarrison(5) 8 44
(A W Carroll) *hld up: hdwy over 4f out: chsd wnr over 2f out: no ex fnl f* **8/1**[3]

/00- **3** *3 ½* **Boulevin (IRE)**[28] 333 8-8-4 45........ TolleyDean(5) 5 38
(R J Price) *hld up: racd keenly: hdwy over 2f out: rdn and hung lft fr over 1f out: nt trble ldrs* **12/1**

440- **4** *1 ¾* **Carlton Scroop (FR)**[74] 6697 5-9-3 53........(b) PaulEddery 4 44
(J Jay) *prom: rdn and n.m.r 3f out: styd on same pce fnl 2f* **13/8**[1]

000- **5** *2 ½* **Floodlight Fantasy**[10] 6801 5-8-11 50........(b) TravisBlock(3) 3 37
(Jedd O'Keeffe) *chsd ldr over 8f: wknd fnl f* **8/1**[3]

00-0 **6** *½* **Inflagrantedelicto (USA)**[10] 80 4-8-5 45........(b) LiamJones 1 31
(D W Chapman) *s.i.s: hld up: rdn over 2f out: n.d* **66/1**

56-2 **7** *7* **Nimello (USA)**[12] 69 12-9-3 53........ SimonWhitworth 6 28
(A G Newcombe) *dwlt: hld up: nvr nr to chal* **5/2**[2]

0-04 **8** *14* **Interest (USA)**[10] 83 4-8-7 47........(b) PaulFessey 2 —
(T D Barron) *led: clr 7f out: hdd over 3f out: sn wknd* **14/1**

2m 44.88s (3.78) **Going Correction** +0.20s/f (Slow)
WFA 4 from 5yo+ 4lb **8** Ran SP% **115.9**
Speed ratings (Par 101): **95,92,90,88,87 86,82,72**
CSF £70.23 CT £766.86 TOTE £6.90: £1.90, £2.50, £2.30; EX 37.30 Trifecta £350.80 Part won. Pool £494.16 - 0.37 winning units..The winner was sold to Richard Price for 8,000gns.
Owner J A Wynn-Williams **Bred** Brook Stud Bloodstock Ltd **Trained** Denton, Co Durham

FOCUS
A typically poor selling handicap, run at an uneven pace. The winner rates full value for the winning margin, but this is weak form.
Floodlight Fantasy Official explanation: jockey said gelding ran too freely

216 RACE TO PONTIN'S FOR HALF TERM MAIDEN STKS 1m 141y(P)
2:55 (3:00) (Class 5) 4-Y-0+ **£2,457** (£725; £362) **Stalls** Low

Form RPR

206- **1** **Cape Velvet (IRE)**[96] 6199 4-8-12 64........ JamesDoyle 4 67+
(J W Hills) *stdd s: hld up and bhd: hdwy over 2f out: led 1f out: sn clr: eased towards fin* **11/10**[1]

3/0- **2** *3* **Lascelles**[122] 5494 4-9-3 70........ TPQueally 2 63+
(J A Osborne) *dwlt: hld up: nt clr run and outpcd over 2f out: sn hung lft: r.o ins fnl f: no ch w wnr* **9/4**[2]

04 **3** *2* **Newgate (UAE)**[8] 107 4-9-3 0........ LiamJones 5 55
(D W Chapman) *trckd ldr: led wl over 1f out: rdn and hdd 1f out: no ex* **14/1**

00-3 **4** *1 ¾* **King Of Legend (IRE)**[14] 48 4-9-3 60........ ChrisCatlin 3 51
(A G Foster) *led: rdn and hdd wl over 1f out: wknd ins fnl f* **7/2**[3]

0/0- **5** *17* **Fun Thai**[65] 6807 4-8-5 35........ MarkCoumbe(7) 1 7
(A J Chamberlain) *chsd ldrs 6f* **66/1**

1m 54.31s (3.81) **Going Correction** +0.20s/f (Slow) **5** Ran SP% **108.8**
Speed ratings (Par 103): **91,88,86,85,69**
CSF £3.72 TOTE £1.80: £1.10, £1.90; EX 4.30.
Owner Mrs Kingham Mrs Moore Mr Ellis **Bred** C Gavin **Trained** Upper Lambourn, Berks

FOCUS
A poor maiden, not strongly-run. The form is a bit dubious and the first two probably did not need to be at their best.
Lascelles Official explanation: jockey said colt hung left

217 MAKE A BREAK FOR PONTIN'S TODAY H'CAP 1m 141y(P)
3:30 (3:35) (Class 4) (0-85,83) 3-Y-O **£4,533** (£1,348; £674; £336) **Stalls** Low

Form RPR

1- **1** **Age Of Reason (UAE)**[21] 7252 3-9-4 **83**........ GregFairley 1 95+
(M Johnston) *mde all: rdn out* **1/1**[1]

00-1 **2** *2 ½* **Pacifism (UAE)**[13] 58 3-9-3 **82**........ SteveDrowne 3 88+
(M A Jarvis) *s.i.s: sn prom: chsd wnr 6f out: rdn and hung lft over 1f out: styd on same pce* **2/1**[2]

11-1 **3** *3 ½* **Elusive Lady (IRE)**[15] 30 3-8-9 **74**........(p) ChrisCatlin 4 72
(J R Weymes) *plld hrd and prom: rdn over 2f out: styd on same pce appr fnl f* **11/1**

341- **4** *2 ½* **Sweet Hope (USA)**[30] 7190 3-9-3 **82**........(b) NCallan 5 74
(K A Ryan) *plld hrd: trckd wnr over 2f: remained handy: rdn 2f out: nt clr run and swtchd rt over 1f out: wknd fnl f* **13/2**[3]

13-5 **5** *2* **Marino Prince (FR)**[8] 116 3-7-13 **71**........ PatrickDonaghy(7) 2 59
(T Wall) *hld up: rdn over 3f out: sn wknd* **20/1**

1m 51.36s (0.86) **Going Correction** +0.20s/f (Slow) **5** Ran SP% **109.8**
Speed ratings (Par 99): **104,101,98,96,94**
CSF £3.19 TOTE £1.90: £1.30, £1.30; EX 2.80.
Owner Sheikh Hamdan Bin Mohammed Al Maktoum **Bred** Darley **Trained** Middleham Moor, N Yorks

FOCUS
This could prove to be a decent little handicap for the track and grade. It featured four last-time-out winners and the impressive Age Of Reason rates a smart prospect.
Pacifism(UAE) Official explanation: jockey said gelding hung left

218 WOLVERHAMPTON-RACECOURSE.CO.UK H'CAP 1m 141y(P)
4:05 (4:10) (Class 4) (0-85,85) 4-Y-O+ **£4,533** (£1,348; £674; £336) **Stalls** Low

Form RPR

13-3 **1** **Will He Wish**[7] 124 12-8-10 **81**........(b) JamieJones(5) 3 89
(S Gollings) *chsd ldrs: hmpd and lost pl over 3f out: hdwy over 1f out: hung lft ins fnl f: r.o to ld post* **22/1**

203- **2** *shd* **Curzon Prince (IRE)**[33] 7165 4-9-0 **81**........ NCallan 6 89
(C F Wall) *hld up: hdwy over 3f out: rdn to ld over 1f out: edgd rt ins fnl f: hdd post* **5/2**[1]

52-4 **3** *1 ¼* **Princess Cocoa (IRE)**[15] 34 5-8-9 **75**........ TonyHamilton 2 80
(R A Fahey) *chsd ldr to over 6f out: wnt 2nd again over 3f out: rdn to ld wl over 1f out: sn hdd: edgd rt ins fnl f: styd on same pce* **7/1**[3]

415- **4** *shd* **Gaelic Princess**[18] 7287 8-8-10 **79**........ TravisBlock(3) 8 84
(A G Newcombe) *hld up: hdwy over 1f out: edgd lft ins fnl f: r.o* **20/1**

21-2 **5** *2* **Alfresco**[7] 124 4-9-2 **83**........(b) DaneO'Neill 7 83
(I A Wood) *hld up: hdwy over 5f out: ev ch over 1f out: rdn and hung lft ins fnl f: nt run on* **5/2**[1]

10-2 **6** 14 **Abbondanza (IRE)**[15] 34 5-9-5 85..............................(p) PhillipMakin 5 53
(Miss L A Perratt) *plld hrd and prom: trckd ldr over 6f out: led over 4f out: rdn and hdd wl over 1f out: wknd fnl f* **5/1**[2]

625- **7** 4 **Emerald Bay (IRE)**[20] 6746 6-8-11 77.................................. TomEaves 4 36
(Miss L A Perratt) *sn led: hdd over 4f out: wkng whn hmpd over 3f out* **7/1**[3]

2/6- **8** 21 **Victor Trumper**[41] 7075 4-8-12 79.............................. AdrianMcCarthy 1 —
(P W Chapple-Hyam) *hld up: rdn over 5f out: wknd wl over 3f out* **40/1**

1m 50.31s (-0.19) **Going Correction** +0.20s/f (Slow)
WFA 4 from 5yo+ 1lb **8 Ran SP% 110.4**
Speed ratings (Par 105): **108,107,106,106,104 92,88,70**
CSF £71.72 CT £418.36 TOTE £18.00: £3.90, £1.30, £1.90; EX 108.50 Trifecta £393.00 Part won. Pool £553.55 - 0.74 winning units..
Owner Mrs D Dukes **Bred** Mrs C Buckland **Trained** Scamblesby, Lincs

FOCUS
A competitive handicap and probably fair form for the grade, although it was not run at that strong a pace. The form makes some sense.

219 WISH I WAS @ PONTIN'S NOW AMATEUR RIDERS' H'CAP (DIV I) 1m 1f 103y(P)
4:35 (4:40) (Class 6) (0-55,55) 4-Y-0+ £1,249 (£387; £193; £96) Stalls Low

Form RPR
406/ **1** **Schinken Otto (IRE)**[41] 469 7-10-7 46 oh1.......... MissNJefferson(5) 11 57
(J M Jefferson) *hld up: hdwy 5f out: chsd ldr 2f out: styd on to ld nr fin* **9/2**[2]

04-1 **2** hd **Buscador (USA)**[6] 143 9-11-1 54 6ex................. MrBenBrisbourne(5) 8 65
(W M Brisbourne) *chsd ldrs: led over 2f out: rdn over 1f out: hdd nr fin* **10/11**[1]

0/0- **3** 3 1/2 **Take It There**[30] 6179 6-11-0 53.............................. MissZoeLilly(5) 9 57
(A J Lidderdale) *s.i.s: hld up: hdwy over 3f out: rdn over 1f out: no ex fnl f* **12/1**

000- **4** 7 **Christalini**[33] 7166 4-10-9 49....................... MissSarah-JaneDurman(5) 4 38
(J C Fox) *s.i.s: hld up: plld hrd: r.o ins fnl f: nvr nrr* **20/1**

006- **5** 3/4 **Anduril**[30] 7189 7-11-7 55.. MrSDobson 10 42
(I W McInnes) *hld up: hdwy and hung rt over 2f out: rdn and hung lft over 1f out: nvr trbld ldrs* **11/2**[3]

/03- **6** 1 1/2 **Tuning Fork**[19] 7276 8-10-5 46 oh1................................ MrWRich(7) 7 30
(M J Attwater) *chsd ldrs: led over 3f out: hdd over 2f out: hung lft and wknd over 1f out* **12/1**

206- **7** 1 **Alasil (USA)**[36] 6479 8-10-8 49.. MrMPrice(7) 2 31
(R J Price) *mid-div: rdn over 3f out: wknd over 2f out* **7/1**

000- **8** 14 **Tequila Sheila (IRE)**[12] 7148 6-10-8 47.................. MissAWallace(5) 6 —
(M A Allen) *sn led: hdd over 3f out: wknd over 2f out* **25/1**

00-0 **9** 5 **Bahhmirage (IRE)**[11] 76 5-10-10 49........ MissSusannahWileman(5) 3 —
(C N Kellett) *s.i.s: hld up: wknd over 3f out* **28/1**

0V-0 **10** 3 1/2 **Mind That Fox**[9] 100 6-10-5 46 oh1.................. MrAWEdwards(7) 5 —
(T Wall) *mid-div: wknd over 3f out* **80/1**

000- **11** 6 **Montiona**[344] 390 4-10-4 46 oh1.................................... MrRRamloll(7) 1 —
(R C Guest) *chsd ldrs 6f* **125/1**

2m 3.96s (2.26) **Going Correction** +0.20s/f (Slow)
WFA 4 from 5yo+ 1lb **11 Ran SP% 127.9**
Speed ratings (Par 101): **97,96,93,87,86 85,84,72,67,64 59**
CSF £9.46 CT £52.50 TOTE £4.30: £1.50, £1.30, £3.60; EX 10.50 Trifecta £292.00 Pool £814.43 - 1.98 winning units..
Owner John Donald **Bred** T Burns And Mrs P F N Fanning **Trained** Norton, N Yorks

FOCUS
A poor handicap and marginally the slower of the two divisions. Schinken Otto has improved over jumps since last running on the Flat and there could be a bit more to come.

220 WISH I WAS @ PONTIN'S NOW AMATEUR RIDERS' H'CAP (DIV II) 1m 1f 103y(P)
5:05 (5:10) (Class 6) (0-55,55) 4-Y-0+ £1,249 (£387; £193; £96) Stalls Low

Form RPR
053- **1** **Morbick**[20] 7275 4-10-12 52..................................... MrBenBrisbourne(5) 7 69+
(W M Brisbourne) *prom: chsd ldr 6f out: led over 3f out: rdn clr fnl 2f* **5/4**[1]

24-4 **2** 6 **Ruffie (IRE)**[17] 7 5-10-9 48.. MrRBirkett(5) 9 53
(Miss J Feilden) *hld up: hdwy over 2f out: rdn to go 2nd and hung lft 1f out: no ch w wnr* **6/1**

60-6 **3** 5 **Jarvo**[6] 143 7-11-3 51.. MrSDobson 5 45
(I W McInnes) *hld up in tch: chsd wnr over 2f out: sn rdn: wknd fnl f* **7/2**[2]

00-0 **4** 2 **Divine Love (IRE)**[14] 36 4-10-13 55.........................(p) MrLJohnson(7) 10 45
(T Wall) *s.i.s: hld up: rdn over 2f out: sn hung lft: n.d* **100/1**

040- **5** 1/2 **Theflyingscottie**[20] 7273 6-11-1 49..............................(v) MrsMMorris 6 38
(D Shaw) *hld up: hdwy over 2f out: rdn and wknd over 1f out* **6/1**

/V6- **6** nk **Candy Anchor (FR)**[20] 7274 9-10-5 45.................. MissSPeacock(7) 8 34
(R E Peacock) *s.i.s: hld up: nt clr run over 2f out: no ch whn hmpd 1f out* **25/1**

00-0 **7** 3 **Charlie Bear**[16] 10 7-10-5 45.................................(p) MrHGMiller(7) 1 28
(Miss Z C Davison) *chsd ldr: led over 7f out: hdd over 3f out: wknd wl over 1f out: sn hung lft* **16/1**

000/ **8** 1 3/4 **Shosolosa (IRE)**[467] 5831 6-11-0 55......................... MrCAHarris(7) 11 33
(R C Guest) *s.i.s: plld hrd and sn prom: wknd 2f out* **33/1**

600- **9** 5 **Heaven's Gates**[52] 5967 4-10-8 46..........................(p) MissARyan(3) 3 14
(K A Ryan) *s.i.s: hdwy over 6f out: rdn and wknd over 3f out* **5/1**[3]

500- **10** 10 **Minnie Mill**[91] 6311 4-10-4 45...................................... PeterHatton(7) 2 —
(B P J Baugh) *prom: hmpd and lost pl over 6f out: wknd over 3f out* **50/1**

01-0 **11** 7 **Shantina's Dream (USA)**[9] 89 4-10-5 47.................. MrBAdams(7) 4 —
(J R Boyle) *sn led: hdd over 7f out: rdn and wknd over 2f out* **11/1**

2m 3.53s (1.83) **Going Correction** +0.20s/f (Slow)
WFA 4 from 5yo+ 1lb **11 Ran SP% 135.9**
Speed ratings (Par 101): **99,93,89,87,87 86,84,82,78,69 62**
CSF £11.51 CT £27.07 TOTE £3.10: £1.40, £2.50, £1.90; EX 18.30 Trifecta £22.80 Pool £440.68 - 13.72 winning units. Place 6 £16.64, Place 5 £9.82..
Owner J R Salter **Bred** Mark C Collins And Keith West **Trained** Great Ness, Shropshire

FOCUS
A weak handicap, confined to amateur riders, which saw the field finish fairly strung out behind the decisive winner who showed improved form. The time was decent.
T/Plt: £63.10 to a £1 stake. Pool: £70,301.80. 813.30 winning tickets. T/Qpdt: £24.50 to a £1 stake. Pool: £4,271.70. 128.50 winning tickets. CR

181 LINGFIELD (L-H)
Saturday, January 19

OFFICIAL GOING: Standard
Wind: Strong, half behind Weather: Overcast

221 PARTYBETS.COM MAIDEN STKS (DIV I) 1m (P)
12:15 (12:25) (Class 5) 3-Y-O £1,845 (£549; £274; £137) Stalls High

Form RPR
5- **1** **Admiral Dundas (IRE)**[31] 7191 3-9-3 0........................ J-PGuillambert 7 74+
(W Jarvis) *trckd ldrs: prog to go 3rd over 2f out: sn rdn: styd on wl fnl f to ld last strides* **2/1**[1]

0-5 **2** shd **Mischief Making (USA)**[14] 58 3-8-12 0................... TGMcLaughlin 2 69+
(E A L Dunlop) *dwlt: hld up in last trio: pushed along and effrt 3f out: gd hdwy fnl f: w wnr last strides: jst pipped* **12/1**

3 1/2 **Shadowtime** 3-9-3 0... GregFairley 4 73+
(M Johnston) *w ldr: led after 2f: kicked 2 l clr over 2f out: wknd fnl f: hdd last strides* **3/1**[2]

03- **4** 2 1/2 **Benedict Spirit (IRE)**[29] 7217 3-9-3 0............................ JimmyQuinn 9 67
(M H Tompkins) *trckd ldrs: pushed along and outpcd wl over 2f out: kpt on one pce fr over 1f out* **7/2**[3]

00- **5** 1 **Love Empire (USA)**[35] 7152 3-9-3 0........................... DeanMcKeown 1 65
(M Johnston) *s.s: rcvrd to chse ldrs: wnt 2nd 3f out: rdn and no imp on wnr 2f out: hanging and wknd fnl f* **25/1**

0- **6** 7 **E'Cusson**[54] 6944 3-8-12 0.. MatthewHenry 5 43
(M A Jarvis) *led 2f: styd prom tl wknd over 2f out* **16/1**

0-4 **7** 1 1/4 **Bon Ton Roulet**[14] 52 3-8-7 0.................................. HaddenFrost(5) 6 41
(R Hannon) *plld hrd: w ldrs to 3f out: sn btn* **8/1**

0- **8** 4 **Hucking Harrier (IRE)**[108] 5895 3-9-3 0........................... JimCrowley 10 36
(J R Best) *hld up fr wd draw: pushed along and struggling bef 1/2-way: wl bhd fnl 3f* **66/1**

9 1 **Ten Hour Lunch** 3-9-3 0.. StephenDonohoe 8 34
(B J Meehan) *s.s: rn green and a last: wl bhd fnl 3f* **25/1**

1m 39.38s (1.18) **Going Correction** +0.05s/f (Slow) **9 Ran SP% 114.4**
Speed ratings (Par 97): **96,95,95,92,91 84,83,79,78**
CSF £27.08 TOTE £2.90: £1.30, £2.80, £1.60; EX 31.20 Trifecta £78.40 Part won. Pool: £110.50 - 0.70 winning tickets..
Owner Dr J Walker **Bred** John Hussey And Stephen Hillen **Trained** Newmarket, Suffolk

FOCUS
An ordinary maiden and the winning time was 0.31 seconds slower than the second division. The principals could rate higher.

222 SHAREN BLAQUIERE CELEBRATE A LIFE (S) STKS 6f (P)
12:45 (12:57) (Class 6) 3-Y-O £1,774 (£523; £262) Stalls Low

Form RPR
23-2 **1** **Atephobia**[10] 93 3-9-3 63.. FergusSweeney 9 69
(K R Burke) *mde all: clr w runner-up fr 2f out: rdn and kpt on wl fnl f* **11/8**[1]

33-1 **2** 1 1/4 **Lord Deevert**[10] 93 3-8-10 65.......................................(v) JackDean(7) 7 65
(W G M Turner) *chsd wnr: clr of rest 2f out: tried to cl 1f out: kpt on but no imp fnl f* **6/4**[2]

00-5 **3** 9 **Don Picolo**[7] 141 3-8-12 44......................................(b) FrankieMcDonald 5 31
(P A Blockley) *in tch: outpcd 1/2-way and drvn: plugged on to take remote 3rd nr fin* **14/1**

664- **4** 2 1/2 **Whitcombe Flyer (USA)**[28] 7220 3-8-12 55......................... JohnEgan 8 23
(Jamie Poulton) *reminders sn after s: chsd ldrs: outpcd wl over 2f out: modest 3rd and veering bdly fr over 1f out: wknd last 100yds* **8/1**[3]

6-0 **5** 5 **Saunders Encore**[6] 146 3-8-7 0.. LPKeniry 2 2
(M S Saunders) *chsd ldng pair: outpcd wl over 2f out: wknd wl over 1f out* **40/1**

0-0 **6** 1 **Piccolo Pride**[7] 135 3-8-5 0...................................... GabrielHannon(7) 1 4
(B G Powell) *sn pushed along to stay in tch: hanging and outpcd 1/2-way: bhd after* **40/1**

7 3 **Clear Call** 3-8-4 0.. KirstyMilczarek(3) 6 —
(R J Hodges) *sn outpcd and wl bhd* **12/1**

1m 11.6s (-0.30) **Going Correction** +0.05s/f (Slow) **7 Ran SP% 112.5**
Speed ratings (Par 95): **104,102,90,87,80 79,75**
CSF £3.55 TOTE £2.40: £1.60, £1.40; EX 3.20 Trifecta £10.40 Pool: £82.10 - 5.60 winning tickets..The winner was sold to R A Harris for 3,400gns.
Owner P Timmins & A Rhodes Haulage **Bred** Ms Z N Watkins **Trained** Middleham Moor, N Yorks

FOCUS
An uncompetitive seller in which the form pair finished clear. A career best from the winner.

223 PARTYBETS.COM MAIDEN STKS (DIV II) 1m (P)
1:20 (1:30) (Class 5) 3-Y-O £1,845 (£549; £274; £137) Stalls High

Form RPR
1 **Vettorenjoy** 3-9-3 0.. OscarUrbina 7 74+
(M Botti) *lost pl sn after s: wl in rr: pushed along and prog 3f out but stll plenty to do: rn green over 1f out: drvn and styd on wl to ld last 100yds: sn clr* **16/1**

03- **2** 3 **Ace Of Spies (IRE)**[36] 7145 3-9-3 0.................................. GregFairley 2 67
(M Johnston) *led: rdn 3 l clr 2f out: hanging over 1f out: wknd and hdd last 100yds* **8/15**[1]

3 nk **Too Risky** 3-8-12 0.. AdrianMcCarthy 3 61
(P W Chapple-Hyam) *dwlt: rcvrd to chse ldr after 3f: drvn and no imp 2f out: lost 2nd ent fnl f: plugged on* **9/2**[2]

06- **4** 2 1/2 **Treasure Islands (IRE)**[69] 6777 3-8-12 0........................... LiamJones 5 56
(S W Hall) *chsd ldr for 3f: drvn in 3rd fr over 3f out: no imp after* **16/1**

5 3 1/2 **Precision Break (USA)** 3-9-3 0...................................... JohnEgan 10 53+
(J S Moore) *dwlt: last of main gp and sn wl off the pce: no hdwy tl kpt on fnl f* **7/1**[3]

0-0 **6** 3/4 **Marie Claude**[7] 135 3-8-12 0..(v[1]) SebSanders 4 46
(J Noseda) *chsd ldrs: lost tch u.p 3f out* **14/1**

6-0 **7** 1 1/4 **Fortunes Maid (IRE)**[7] 135 3-8-12 0............................ JimmyQuinn 9 43
(M H Tompkins) *a wl off the pce: rdn and struggling by 1/2-way: no real prog* **50/1**

0-0 **8** 11 **Den's Boy**[7] 135 3-9-3 0... PatCosgrave 6 23
(J R Boyle) *chsd ldrs to 1/2-way: sn wknd u.p: t.o* **33/1**

9 12 **Too Much To Do** 3-9-3 0.. J-PGuillambert 1 —
(T D McCarthy) *s.s: rn green and a t.o* **50/1**

1m 39.07s (0.87) **Going Correction** +0.05s/f (Slow) **9 Ran SP% 121.2**
Speed ratings (Par 97): **97,94,93,91,87 86,85,74,62**
CSF £26.34 TOTE £20.90: £3.80, £1.02, £1.80; EX 54.00 Trifecta £156.40 Part won. Pool: £220.30 - 0.10 winning tickets..
Owner Giuliano Manfredini **Bred** James Robert Mitchell **Trained** Newmarket, Suffolk

FOCUS
Just a fair maiden. The form makes sense around the second and fourth and the winner should be capable of better. The winning time was 0.31 seconds faster than the first division.

224 PARTYBETS.COM LINGFIELD H'CAP 1m 4f (P)
1:55 (2:05) (Class 5) (0-70,70) 4-Y-0+ **£2,331** (£693; £346; £173) **Stalls** Low

Form				RPR
11-1	1		**Mutamaasek (USA)**[16] 28 6-9-4 **69**........................ KirstyMilczarek(3) 9	81+
			(Lady Herries) *prom: trckd ldr 1/2-way: led 2f out: rdn at least 2 l clr 1f out: all out nr fin* **11/4**[2]	
452-	2	½	**Motarjm (USA)**[80] 5342 4-9-0 **66**........................(t) SebSanders 3	74
			(H J Collingridge) *hld up in rr: prog over 3f out: hrd rdn to chse wnr 1f out: clsng at fin* **5/1**[3]	
40-0	3	¾	**Red Wine**[10] 91 9-8-12 **63**........................ PatrickMathers(3) 8	70
			(A J McCabe) *settled towards rr: pushed along and sme prog over 3f out: drvn 2f out: styd on fnl f: nvr able to chal* **8/1**	
411-	4	1 ¼	**Highest Esteem**[61] 6871 4-9-3 **69**........................(p) GeorgeBaker 7	74
			(G L Moore) *trckd ldrs: wnt 3rd over 3f out: effrt 2f out: disp 2nd jst over 1f out: nt qckn* **2/1**[1]	
55-0	5	1 ¾	**Bienheureux**[10] 91 7-8-10 **58**........................ HayleyTurner 1	60
			(Miss Gay Kelleway) *hld up in last pair: effrt over 3f out: nvr really on terms w ldrs: kpt on fnl f: n.d* **14/1**	
06-4	6	nk	**Prime Number (IRE)**[16] 28 6-9-8 **70**........................ J-PGuillambert 4	72
			(J Akehurst) *trckd ldr: led 1/2-way: rdn and hdd 2f out: wknd fnl f* **8/1**	
00-0	7	12	**Salut Saint Cloud**[16] 27 7-8-8 **56**........................ SimonWhitworth 2	38
			(G L Moore) *dwlt: hld up in last: no prog over 3f out: bhd after* **33/1**	
60-0	8	5	**Three Thieves (UAE)**[3] 185 5-9-5 **67**........................ FergusSweeney 5	41
			(M S Saunders) *chsd ldrs tl wknd over 3f out: t.o* **40/1**	
/0-0	9	20	**Mustamad**[16] 27 5-8-12 **60**........................ ChrisCatlin 10	—
			(Miss A M Newton-Smith) *led to 1/2-way: sn wknd: wl t.o* **66/1**	

2m 33.68s (0.68) **Going Correction** +0.05s/f (Slow)
WFA 4 from 5yo+ 4lb **9** Ran SP% **112.4**
Speed ratings (Par 103): **99,98,98,97,96 95,87,84,71**
CSF £16.23 CT £94.91 TOTE £3.40: £1.60, £1.60, £2.00; EX 17.90 Trifecta £73.60 Pool: £529.34 - 5.10 winning tickets..
Owner Lady Herries **Bred** Shadwell Farm LLC **Trained** Patching, W Sussex

FOCUS
They went just a steady pace early on, but that is usually the case round here and the form looks reasonable for the grade, rated through ther third.

225 PARTYPOKER.COM H'CAP 1m 2f (P)
2:25 (2:40) (Class 5) (0-75,73) 3-Y-0 **£2,590** (£770; £385; £192) **Stalls** Low

Form				RPR
-512	1		**Boomtown**[3] 184 3-9-4 **73**........................ GregFairley 2	80+
			(M Johnston) *mde all: set stdy pce to 1/2-way: stretched away fr 2f out: pushed out fnl f: unchal* **11/10**[1]	
634-	2	2 ½	**Wannabe Free**[31] 7190 3-9-2 **71**........................ SebSanders 1	73
			(J Noseda) *trckd ldng pair: rdn to chse wnr over 2f out: kpt on but no imp* **7/2**[2]	
000-	3	2	**Shaftesbury (IRE)**[54] 6948 3-8-11 **66**........................ DeanMcKeown 4	64
			(M Johnston) *hld up in midfield: prog on inner 2f out: urged along to take 3rd 1f out: no imp after* **16/1**	
020-	4	hd	**Alcimedes**[22] 7252 3-9-4 **73**........................ AdrianMcCarthy 8	71
			(P W Chapple-Hyam) *hld up in last trio in steadily run r: effrt over 2f out: styd on fnl f to press for 3rd: nvr pce to threaten* **16/1**	
2U5-	5	3	**Greek Theatre (USA)**[50] 6973 3-8-13 **68**........................(e) JamesDoyle 5	60
			(Mrs A J Perrett) *unruly bef s: t.k.h early: racd wd in tch: racd awkwardly fr 4f out: outpcd over 2f out* **8/1**	
40-0	6	nk	**Threestoneburn (USA)**[3] 184 3-8-9 **64**........................ PatCosgrave 3	55
			(J R Boyle) *t.k.h early: hld up bhd ldrs: rdn and outpcd over 2f out* **25/1**	
3-	7	1 ¾	**Henry James (IRE)**[31] 7181 3-9-1 **70**........................ JohnEgan 6	58
			(M Botti) *hld up in last in steadily run r: outpcd fr over 2f out: no ch after* **28/1**	
05-1	8	1	**Contessina (IRE)**[17] 12 3-8-9 **69**........................ TolleyDean(5) 7	55
			(P F I Cole) *t.k.h: trckd wnr tl wknd over 2f out* **11/2**[3]	

2m 8.98s (2.38) **Going Correction** +0.05s/f (Slow) **8** Ran SP% **115.4**
Speed ratings (Par 97): **92,90,88,88,85 85,84,83**
CSF £5.06 CT £37.25 TOTE £2.00: £1.10, £1.40, £4.10; EX 7.00 Trifecta £61.20 Pool: £414.23 - 4.80 winning tickets..
Owner Mark Johnston Racing Ltd **Bred** Gainsborough Stud Management Ltd **Trained** Middleham Moor, N Yorks

FOCUS
A modest handicap which did not look very competitive beforehand. The winner set a very steady early pace, but it looks sound form on paper nevertheless.

226 FREE £25 BET AT PARTYBETS.COM H'CAP 6f (P)
3:00 (3:17) (Class 2) (0-100,105) 4-Y-0+
£9,971 (£2,985; £1,492; £747; £372; £187) **Stalls** Low

Form				RPR
225-	1		**Come Out Fighting**[76] 6676 5-8-8 **90**........................ StephenDonohoe 5	100
			(P A Blockley) *mde all: hrd pressed fnl f: hld on wl* **10/1**	
261-	2	hd	**Ebraam (USA)**[22] 7255 5-8-8 **90**........................ DeanMcKeown 2	99
			(D Shaw) *prom: chsd wnr jst over 2f out: str chal fnl f: jst hld* **10/3**[2]	
41-1	3	hd	**Bonus (IRE)**[7] 137 8-9-8 **104**........................ HayleyTurner 4	113+
			(G A Butler) *hld up in rr: effrt and sme prog over 1f out: picked up last 100yds and fin fast: post c too sn* **6/4**[1]	
453-	4	1	**Orpsie Boy (IRE)**[22] 7255 5-8-10 **92**........................ JimCrowley 9	98
			(N P Littmoden) *stdd s: hld up in last trio: prog on inner over 1f out: looked dangerous ins fnl f: nt qckn last 100yds* **8/1**	
000-	5	¾	**Woodnook**[43] 7053 5-8-4 **89**........................ KirstyMilczarek(3) 1	92
			(J A R Toller) *hld up in midfield: prog on inner 2f out: wnt 3rd 1f out and cl enough: fdd last 100yds* **16/1**	
20-4	6	½	**Lucayos**[7] 137 5-8-3 **92**........................ GabrielHannon(7) 7	94
			(Mrs H Sweeting) *chsd wnr to jst over 2f out: bmpd along and fdd fnl f* **25/1**	
405-	7	¾	**Andronikos**[22] 7254 6-8-5 **87**........................(bt[1]) ChrisCatlin 3	86
			(P F I Cole) *t.k.h: hld up in last trio: rdn and effrt 2f out: one pce and no real imp on ldrs* **8/1**	
35-3	8	½	**Qadar (IRE)**[7] 137 6-8-12 **94**........................(b) SebSanders 8	92
			(N P Littmoden) *hld up towards rr: eased to outer and rdn 2f out: nt qckn and no imp on ldrs over 1f out* **7/1**[3]	
132-	9	nk	**Carcinetto (IRE)**[31] 7184 6-8-4 **86** oh1........................ SaleemGolam 11	83
			(P D Evans) *chsd ldrs: rdn 1/2-way: lost pl and btn wl over 1f out* **16/1**	
120-	10	1	**Saviours Spirit**[223] 2494 7-8-7 **89**........................ J-PGuillambert 6	82
			(T G Mills) *dwlt: hld up in last trio: effrt on wd outside over 2f out: lost grnd and btn wl over 1f out: fin lame* **20/1**	
010-	11	1 ¾	**Shustraya**[89] 6391 4-8-4 **86** oh2........................ JimmyQuinn 10	74
			(P J Makin) *chsd ldrs: rdn 1/2-way: wknd 2f out* **16/1**	

1m 10.68s (-1.22) **Going Correction** +0.05s/f (Slow) **11** Ran SP% **133.1**
Speed ratings (Par 109): **110,109,109,108,107 106,105,104,104,103 100**
CSF £49.29 CT £84.18 TOTE £13.10: £3.30, £1.50, £1.40; EX 65.20 Trifecta £698.70 Pool: £984.15 - 1.00 winning ticket..
Owner M J Wiley **Bred** G J Hamer **Trained** Lambourn, Berks

FOCUS
A very competitive handicap featuring a number of specialists around here, although few looked obviously well handicapped. It was not as strongly run as might have been expected and the fourth has been rated through the second and fourth.

NOTEBOOK
Come Out Fighting, who did not go unbacked, having been available at 16-1 in the morning, appreciated the return to 6f and made every yard. Things got a bit desperate late on but he just held on in a three-way photo. He ran well off 95 at Ascot last spring so there is a chance he can remain competitive off a higher mark. (op 12-1 tchd 9-1)
Ebraam(USA) was well placed turning in and threw down a determined challenge to the eventual winner, but he was always just held by Come Out Fighting, despite racing on the outside of him down the straight. He has made great progress this All-Weather campaign, but a mark in the 90s leaves him vulnerable. (op 9-2 tchd 5-1)
Bonus(IRE) looked to hold strong claims but he did not enjoy the best of runs. Behind a wall of horses turning in, he was still struggling for racing room inside the last, and although he flew home once switched he was never quite getting there. He looked an unlucky loser. (op 11-4, tchd 3-1 in a place)
Orpsie Boy(IRE) challenged up the far rail, which is not usually the best place to be, and made a good fist of it. He is another who remains vulnerable off a mark in the 90s. (op 6-1)
Woodnook, ridden by an in-form apprentice whose claim is now just 3lb, threatened towards the inside approaching the final furlong, but then dropped out.
Lucayos, who is on a 7lb higher mark than when last successful, showed pace to the turn in, but then began to weaken. Official explanation: jockey said gelding hung left (op 20-1)
Qadar(IRE) was in a position to mount a challenge down the outside in the straight, but it never really materialised. (op 8-1)
Saviours Spirit Official explanation: vet said gelding returned lame right-fore

227 PARTYBETS.COM H'CAP 1m (P)
3:35 (3:48) (Class 2) (0-100,106) 4-Y-0+
£9,971 (£2,985; £1,492; £747; £372; £187) **Stalls** High

Form				RPR
313-	1		**Fajr (IRE)**[21] 7267 6-9-10 **106**........................(b) GeorgeBaker 4	115+
			(Miss Gay Kelleway) *hld up in last pair: prog on outer 2f out: rdn to ld 1f out: styd on wl* **5/2**[1]	
252-	2	1 ½	**Orchard Supreme**[21] 7267 5-8-13 **100**........................ NataliaGemelova(5) 6	106
			(R Hannon) *mde most in narrow ld: hdd 1f out: kpt on to hold 2nd but no ch w wnr* **9/1**	
002-	3	nk	**Ektimaal**[22] 7254 5-8-5 **87**........................(t) JamieMackay 7	92
			(E A L Dunlop) *hld up in last: prog on inner over 1f out: chsd ldrs ent fnl f: nt qckn last 100yds* **3/1**[2]	
330-	4	hd	**Samarinda (USA)**[99] 6143 5-8-11 **93**........................ MickyFenton 3	98
			(Mrs P Sly) *rrd s: sn w ldrs: n.m.r over 5f out: drvn to chal and upsides jst over 1f out: nt qckn* **11/2**	
25-4	5	nk	**Troubadour (IRE)**[14] 62 7-9-1 **97**........................ SteveDrowne 1	102+
			(W Jarvis) *hld up in tch: effrt 2f out: rdn and nt qckn over 1f out: nt clr run briefly ent fnl f: kpt on* **5/1**[3]	
204-	6	1 ½	**Bahiano (IRE)**[31] 7184 7-8-5 **87**........................ LiamJones 8	88
			(C E Brittain) *trckd ldrs: rdn 2f out: nt qckn and lost pl over 1f out: no hdwy after* **8/1**	
P0-	7	shd	**Markab**[22] 7254 5-8-6 **88** oh2 ow2........................ JamesDoyle 2	88?
			(K A Morgan) *w ldr to wl over 1f out: wknd ins fnl f* **66/1**	
6/	8	2 ½	**Re Barolo (IRE)**[83] 5-9-5 **101**........................ JohnEgan 5	96?
			(M Botti) *in tch but nvr looked to be gng wl: brief effrt on outer 2f out: sn btn* **16/1**	

1m 37.27s (-0.93) **Going Correction** +0.05s/f (Slow) **8** Ran SP% **114.1**
Speed ratings (Par 109): **106,104,104,104,103 102,102,99**
CSF £25.69 CT £69.46 TOTE £3.20: £1.40, £2.00, £1.30; EX 21.40 Trifecta £52.50 Pool: £407.20 - 5.50 winning tickets..
Owner The New Dawn Partnership **Bred** Shadwell Estate Company Limited **Trained** Exning, Suffolk
■ Stewards' Enquiry : James Doyle two-day ban: failed to ride out for 6th place (Jan 30-31)

FOCUS
There will not be many better performances on the All-Weather this winter than this if the form can be trusted, but it was a steadily run race and the proximity of the seventh and eighth cast some doubt on the value of the form.

NOTEBOOK
Fajr(IRE) was unable to overcome a slow early pace here last month, but he did so this time. He travelled well out the back and, once brought wide with his challenge in the straight, found a smart turn of foot to run out an easy winner of what had looked a fairly tight handicap. In winning this off a mark of 106 he stamps himself as one of the best performers on the All-Weather this winter, and his trainer has dreams of winning the Royal Hunt Cup with him later this year. Although he will have to carry a big weight at Ascot, the big field and fast pace will definitely suit him, just as it did when he finished second in the Buckingham Palace Stakes last year. (op 3-1)
Orchard Supreme is ideally suited by being held up in a strongly-run race, but the slow early pace led to him taking up a prominent position. The way the race panned out it was not a bad place to be, and although he had no chance with the impressive winner, he kept on doggedly to retain second place. (op 8-1 tchd 10-1)
Ektimaal, held up at the tail of the field with the eventual winner, got a bit outpaced running down the hill, but nipped through on the inside turning into the straight and ran on well. It was a better effort than it looked and he remains capable of winning off this mark. (op 5-2 tchd 9-4)
Samarinda(USA), who reared up at the start and was chopped for room at the first turn, raced a touch keenly and was just edged out of the places at the finish. Things did not go his way this time but he is entitled to come on for this first outing in three months. (op 8-1)
Troubadour(IRE), who looked to have stronger prospects back in handicap company off a 4lb higher mark than when runner-up over this course and distance in November, did not see a lot of daylight in the straight. However, he could not be considered unlucky. (tchd 11-2)
Bahiano(IRE) did not convince over this extra furlong. (op 15-2)

228 PARTYPOKER.COM H'CAP 6f (P)
4:10 (4:15) (Class 4) (0-85,82) 3-Y-0 **£4,100** (£1,227; £613; £306; £152) **Stalls** Low

Form				RPR
4-	1		**Monadreen Flyer (IRE)**[43] 7062 3-9-0 **78**........................ SebSanders 3	79
			(Daniel Mark Loughnane, Ire) *led: reminders 1/2-way: drvn and hdd jst over 2f out: led again over 1f out: edgd rt after: hld on: all out* **9/4**[2]	
044-	2	shd	**Mister New York (USA)**[21] 7266 3-8-6 **70** oh2 ow2....... JosedeSouza 2	71
			(Noel T Chance) *hld up in last: prog on inner over 1f out: rdn and upsides ins fnl f: jst failed* **20/1**	
013-	3	hd	**The Game**[20] 7280 3-9-4 **82**........................ PatCosgrave 1	82
			(J R Boyle) *stdd s: hld up in 4th: effrt on outer wl over 1f out: chal ins fnl f: nt qckn nr fin* **5/2**[3]	

11-2 **4** ½ **Caprio (IRE)**[17] 17 3-8-6 **70**..........(b[1]) RichardKingscote 5 68
(R Charlton) *pressed wnr: narrow ld jst over 2f out to over 1f out: carried rt after and nt qckn* **2/1**[1]
2 **5** 5 **Hurricane Hen**[17] 9 3-8-13 **80**.......... KirstyMilczarek(3) 4 62
(D M Simcock) *plld hrd: pressed ldrs tl wknd over 1f out* **6/1**
1m 11.66s (-0.24) **Going Correction** +0.05s/f (Slow) **5** Ran SP% **111.7**
Speed ratings (Par 99): **103,102,102,101,95**
CSF £35.11 TOTE £3.50: £1.50, £2.10; EX 35.10 Place 6 £4.55, Place 5 £3.07..
Owner Quicksharp Syndicate **Bred** Thomas And Linda Heffernan **Trained** Trim, Co Meath
■ Stewards' Enquiry : Seb Sanders six-day ban (includes four deferred days): used whip with excessive frequency without giving gelding time to respond (Feb 6-11)
FOCUS
There was a bunch finish to this sprint handicap and the form does not amount to much. It has been rated around the winner to his best Irish form and the third to his recent efforts.
Hurricane Hen Official explanation: jockey said colt ran too free
T/Plt: £6.70 to a £1 stake. Pool: £97,162.25. 10,512.50 winning tickets. T/Qpdt: £4.00 to a £1 stake. Pool: £6,980.60. 1,277.20 winning tickets. JN

213 WOLVERHAMPTON (A.W) (L-H)

Saturday, January 19

OFFICIAL GOING: Standard
Wind: Light behind Weather: Raining first two races

229 WOLVERHAMPTON-RACECOURSE.CO.UK APPRENTICE (S) STKS 1f 103y(P)

6:50 (6:50) (Class 6) 4-Y-0+ **£1,774** (£523; £262) **Stalls** Low

Form RPR
62-6 **1** **Gifted Heir (IRE)**[9] 115 4-8-6 55.......... NatashaEaton(7) 5 55
(A Bailey) *a.p: wnt 2nd 6f out: led jst over 1f out: r.o* **3/1**[1]
40-0 **2** ½ **Tidy (IRE)**[13] 69 8-8-11 50..........(v) JackMitchell(3) 4 54
(Micky Hammond) *hld up and bhd: hdwy on ins over 2f out: sn rdn: ev ch ins fnl f: r.o* **10/1**
0V-3 **3** *nk* **Lady's Law**[18] 1 5-8-9 40.......... JamieJones 6 48
(Rae Guest) *hld up: rdn over 3f out: hdwy wl over 1f out: r.o ins fnl f* **8/1**
3-33 **4** 1 ¾ **Davidia (IRE)**[11] 83 5-9-0 45.......... JamesO'Reilly 7 49
(D W Thompson) *hld up in tch: rdn over 2f out: one pce fnl f* **5/1**[3]
56-4 **5** *nk* **Ocean Pride (IRE)**[8] 127 5-9-0 60..........(bt) HaddenFrost 1 49
(D E Pipe) *led: rdn over 2f out: hdd jst over 1f out: no ex ins fnl f* **5/1**[3]
030- **6** 2 **Welcome Cat (USA)**[19] 7285 4-8-10 57..........(b) PatrickDonaghy(3) 3 44
(A D Brown) *s.s: bhd tl stdy hdwy over 4f out: rdn and c wd st: wknd wl over 1f out* **9/2**[2]
40-6 **7** 8 **Zaafira (SPA)**[16] 24 4-8-11 48..........(t) SCreighton(3) 2 29
(E J Creighton) *t.k.h: w ldr to 6f out: rdn 3f out: wknd 2f out* **8/1**
2m 4.68s (2.98) **Going Correction** +0.25s/f (Slow)
WFA 4 from 5yo+ 1lb **7** Ran SP% **107.8**
Speed ratings (Par 101): **96,95,95,93,93 91,84**
CSF £29.30 TOTE £4.60: £2.10, £3.70; EX 51.50.
Owner Phil Buchanan **Bred** A Malone **Trained** Newmarket, Suffolk
■ Stewards' Enquiry : Jack Mitchell two-day ban: used whip with excessive frequency (Jan 30-31)
James O'Reilly two-day ban: used whip with excessive frequency (Jan 30-31)
FOCUS
A typically weak seller, confined to apprentice riders. The winner did not need to match his recent best.

230 GET AWAY @ PONTIN'S 0844 576 5938 H'CAP 5f 20y(P)

7:20 (7:20) (Class 6) (0-65,60) 4-Y-0+ **£2,388** (£705; £352) **Stalls** Low

Form RPR
11-6 **1** **Triskaidekaphobia**[8] 126 5-9-4 60..........(t) JamesDoyle 1 71
(Miss J R Tooth) *mde all: rdn and edgd rt ent fnl f: r.o wl* **11/2**[3]
431- **2** 1 ¼ **By The Edge (IRE)**[30] 7206 4-9-2 58.......... PhillipMakin 5 65
(T D Barron) *a.p: rdn 2f out: wnt 2nd jst ins fnl f: nt trble wnr* **11/4**[1]
6-50 **3** ¾ **Wicked Uncle**[2] 191 9-9-4 60..........(v) PaulMulrennan 7 64
(S Gollings) *bhd: rdn and hdwy over 1f out: r.o ins fnl f* **3/1**[2]
10-2 **4** 1 ¼ **Bond Becks (IRE)**[8] 126 8-9-1 57.......... ChrisCatlin 2 56
(G R Oldroyd) *chsd wnr: rdn wl over 1f out: no ex ins fnl f* **3/1**[2]
000- **5** 2 ½ **Sparkwell**[161] 4397 6-9-1 57.......... DeanMcKeown 3 47
(D Shaw) *s.i.s: hld up: shkn up over 1f out: nvr nr ldrs* **13/2**
1-00 **6** 5 **Ace Club**[2] 191 7-8-9 54..........(b) DominicFox(3) 4 26
(S Parr) *chsd ldrs tl rdn and wknd over 2f out* **20/1**
62.79 secs (0.49) **Going Correction** +0.25s/f (Slow) **6** Ran SP% **110.1**
Speed ratings (Par 101): **106,104,102,100,96 88**
CSF £20.10 TOTE £6.70: £2.70, £2.10; EX 17.50.
Owner Raymond Tooth And Steve Gilbey **Bred** K Bowen **Trained** Upper Lambourn, Berks
■ Stewards' Enquiry : Dominic Fox two-day ban: careless riding (Jan 30-31)
FOCUS
A moderate sprint, run at a decent pace. The winner put in his best display since his juvenile campaign, but was able to dominate and the form may not prove entirely reliable.

231 STAY AT THE WOLVERHAMPTON HOLIDAY INN H'CAP 1m 4f 50y(P)

7:50 (7:50) (Class 6) (0-50,54) 4-Y-0+ **£1,774** (£523; £262) **Stalls** Low

Form RPR
4-12 **1** **Buscador (USA)**[1] 219 9-9-0 **54**.......... RichardKingscote 2 64+
(W M Brisbourne) *mde all: rdn over 2f out: r.o wl* **15/8**[1]
35-6 **2** 1 ½ **Mariaverdi**[15] 39 4-8-3 **47**.......... FrancisNorton 1 53
(P G Murphy) *hld up: hdwy over 3f out: rdn over 2f out: wnt 2nd and edgd lft wl ins fnl f: nt trble wnr* **11/1**
0-53 **3** 2 ½ **Weet For Ever (USA)**[7] 144 5-8-12 **52**.......... StephenDonohoe 7 54
(P A Blockley) *hld up in tch: chsd wnr over 3f out: rdn and ev ch 2f out: no ex ins fnl f* **5/1**[3]
24-2 **4** 3 **Mid Valley**[12] 76 5-8-8 **48**.......... J-PGuillambert 3 45
(J R Jenkins) *hld up in rr: pushed along over 3f out: hdwy wl over 1f out: no further prog* **5/1**[3]
056- **5** ½ **Kirkhammerton (IRE)**[123] 5497 6-8-8 **48**..........(p) LPKeniry 6 44
(J T Stimpson) *chsd wnr tl over 3f out: sn rdn and wknd* **16/1**
0/3- **6** 1 ½ **Rebel Raider (IRE)**[35] 496 9-8-8 **48**.......... VinceSlattery 5 42
(B N Pollock) *prom tl rdn and wknd over 3f out* **11/4**[2]
2m 43.99s (2.89) **Going Correction** +0.25s/f (Slow)
WFA 4 from 5yo+ 4lb **6** Ran SP% **109.0**
Speed ratings (Par 101): **100,99,97,95,95 94**
CSF £21.18 TOTE £3.20: £1.80, £3.20; EX 37.50.
Owner David Robson **Bred** William H Floyd **Trained** Great Ness, Shropshire
FOCUS
A very weak affair, run at an uneven pace. The third helps to set the level.
Mid Valley Official explanation: jockey said gelding ran flat

232 TAKE A BREAK @ PONTIN'S H'CAP 7f 32y(P)

8:20 (8:21) (Class 6) (0-50,62) 4-Y-0+ **£1,774** (£523; £262) **Stalls** High

Form RPR
40-5 **1** **Sovereignty (JPN)**[6] 151 6-8-7 52 ow3.......... JamesO'Reilly(5) 3 63
(D K Ivory) *bhd: c wd st: hdwy over 1f out: hrd rdn and r.o wl to ld cl home* **7/2**[2]
0-41 **2** 1 ¼ **Sion Hill (IRE)**[8] 120 7-8-8 48..........(p) MickyFenton 7 56
(John A Harris) *sn led: rdn and flashed tail ins fnl f: hung rt and hdd cl home* **7/2**[2]
-311 **3** 2 **Silver Hotspur**[4] 168 4-9-8 62 6ex.......... NickyMackay 5 65
(M Wigham) *chsd ldrs: rdn over 1f out: one pce fnl f* **2/1**[1]
41-0 **4** 1 ¾ **Mister Always**[6] 151 4-8-10 50..........(v[1]) FergalLynch 8 48
(I W McInnes) *chsd ldrs: wnt 2nd 3f out: rdn wl over 1f out: no ex wl ins fnl f* **6/1**[3]
60-2 **5** 1 ¾ **Avoncreek**[15] 46 4-8-7 47.......... AndrewElliott 1 40
(B P J Baugh) *chsd ldrs: nt clr run over 2f out: sn rdn: wknd ins fnl f* **9/1**
5-40 **6** 2 **Maiden Investor**[6] 151 5-8-9 49..........(v[1]) HayleyTurner 4 37
(Stef Liddiard) *s.i.s: hld up and bhd: hdwy over 2f out: wknd wl over 1f out* **16/1**
-045 **7** 7 **Orchestration (IRE)**[8] 119 7-8-3 46 oh1..........(v) DominicFox(3) 2 15
(S Parr) *broke wl: led early: sn lost pl: rdn over 2f out: sn struggling* **33/1**
52-0 **8** 1 ¾ **George The Best (IRE)**[13] 64 7-8-6 46 oh1.......... DeanMcKeown 6 10
(Micky Hammond) *s.i.s: sn chsng ldr: swtchd lft over 4f out: nt clr run on ins and lost pl 3f out: sn bhd* **25/1**
1m 30.91s (1.31) **Going Correction** +0.25s/f (Slow) **8** Ran SP% **114.7**
Speed ratings (Par 101): **102,100,98,96,94 92,84,82**
CSF £16.27 CT £30.29 TOTE £3.60: £1.30, £2.00, £1.10; EX 24.80.
Owner Radlett Racing **Bred** Darley Stud Management, L L C **Trained** Radlett, Herts
FOCUS
A poor handicap, run at a decent early pace.
George The Best(IRE) Official explanation: jockey said gelding hung badly left-handed

233 PARTY PEOPLE LOVE PONTIN'S PARTIES H'CAP 7f 32y(P)

8:50 (8:50) (Class 4) (0-85,85) 4-Y-0+ **£4,533** (£1,348; £674; £336) **Stalls** High

Form RPR
51-1 **1** **Mr Lambros**[14] 55 7-9-1 **82**..........(t) MickyFenton 1 98+
(Miss Gay Kelleway) *mde all: pushed clr ins fnl f: r.o wl* **5/2**[1]
245- **2** 3 ½ **Divertimenti (IRE)**[19] 7289 4-8-7 **74**.......... LPKeniry 3 81
(C R Dore) *a.p: chsd wnr wl over 1f out: rdn and no imp fnl f* **15/2**
20-0 **3** 2 ½ **Dudley Docker (IRE)**[16] 26 6-8-8 **75**.......... LiamJones 2 75
(C R Dore) *hld up in mid-div: hdwy over 2f out: rdn over 1f out: one pce* **16/1**
202- **4** ½ **Danetime Lord (IRE)**[19] 7289 5-9-1 **82**..........(p) PaulMulrennan 8 81
(K A Ryan) *chsd wnr tl rdn wl over 1f out: wkg whn edgd lft ins fnl f* **7/2**[2]
210- **5** *hd* **Teasing**[19] 7289 4-8-13 **80**.......... RobertHavlin 7 78
(J Pearce) *hld up and bhd: rdn and hdwy over 1f out: swtchd lft and n.m.r ins fnl f: n.d* **7/1**
23-0 **6** 1 **Bobski (IRE)**[8] 124 6-9-1 **82**..........(p) AmirQuinn 5 78
(P J McBride) *s.i.s: t.k.h in rr: hung rt fr over 2f out: hdwy wl over 1f out: wknd ins fnl f* **12/1**
020- **7** 5 **Wessex (USA)**[145] 4886 8-9-4 **85**.......... GeorgeBaker 6 67
(P A Blockley) *hld up in mid-div: rdn 3f out: bhd fnl 2f* **14/1**
00-6 **8** 12 **Precocious Star (IRE)**[16] 26 4-8-11 **78**..........(v) FergusSweeney 4 28
(K R Burke) *hld up in tch: rdn and wknd over 2f out* **4/1**[3]
1m 28.85s (-0.75) **Going Correction** +0.25s/f (Slow) **8** Ran SP% **115.3**
Speed ratings (Par 105): **114,110,107,106,106 105,99,85**
CSF £22.20 CT £217.84 TOTE £2.80: £1.10, £2.90, £7.20; EX 15.50.
Owner Winterbeck Manor Stud **Bred** Witney And Warren Enterprises Ltd **Trained** Exning, Suffolk
FOCUS
A good handicap which saw the bang in-form winner decisively make all. The winning time was very smart indeed for the grade, 2.06 seconds faster than the preceding event. The third helps to set the level.
Bobski(IRE) Official explanation: jockey said, regarding the running and riding, his orders had been to get gelding out and settled, as it is inclined to race keenly, adding that gelding is well known to be an awkward ride, needs to be cajoled in its races, and is probably best suited to a fast-run race; he also said gelding was slow away but quickly made up ground to join the field and was able to get cover, then met traffic round the final bend but picked up at the head of the straight before flattening out approaching the furlong marker and starting to wander
Precocious Star(IRE) Official explanation: jockey said filly stumbled shortly after leaving stalls and never travelled thereafter

234 GR8 FAMILY MEMORIES @ PONTIN'S H'CAP 1m 141y(P)

9:20 (9:20) (Class 6) (0-60,60) 4-Y-0+ **£2,388** (£705; £352) **Stalls** Low

Form RPR
3-31 **1** **Justcallmehandsome**[7] 140 6-8-12 60..........(v) BillyCray(7) 8 71
(D J S Ffrench Davis) *a.p: chsd ldr over 6f out: led 3f out: clr whn rdn over 1f out: r.o wl* **4/1**[3]
300- **2** 2 **Forbidden (IRE)**[59] 6894 5-9-2 60..........(t) JerryO'Dwyer(3) 1 66
(Daniel Mark Loughnane, Ire) *chsd ldr tl over 6f out: prom: wnt 2nd wl over 1f out: rdn and kpt on ins fnl f: nt trble wnr* **10/1**
26-2 **3** 2 **Solicitude**[15] 42 5-9-0 55.......... HayleyTurner 2 56
(D Haydn Jones) *hld up: rdn and hdwy over 1f out: kpt on same pce fnl f* **7/2**[2]
01-2 **4** 1 ½ **Grey Gurkha**[7] 140 7-9-3 58.......... DanielTudhope 5 56
(I W McInnes) *stdd s: hld up in rr: hdwy on outside over 2f out: rdn and edgd lft over 1f out: one pce* **5/1**
520- **5** 1 ¼ **Kadouchski (FR)**[31] 7183 4-9-4 60.......... DeanMcKeown 4 55
(Miss E C Lavelle) *s.i.s: hld up and bhd: pushed along over 2f out: n.d* **10/1**
136- **6** *hd* **Charlottebutterfly**[23] 7248 8-9-1 56.......... RobertHavlin 3 51
(P J McBride) *hld up in tch: rdn to chse wnr over 2f out tl wl over 1f out: wknd ins fnl f* **14/1**
0-44 **7** 2 ½ **Western Roots**[8] 128 7-9-3 58..........(p) GeorgeBaker 6 47
(M Appleby) *hld up in mid-div: hdwy over 3f out: wknd wl over 1f out* **5/2**[1]
6- **8** ½ **Simple Jim (FR)**[17] 6911 4-9-3 59.......... AndrewElliott 7 47
(A D Brown) *led: hdd 3f out: sn rdn and wknd* **20/1**
1m 54.72s (4.22) **Going Correction** +0.25s/f (Slow)
WFA 4 from 5yo+ 1lb **8** Ran SP% **117.1**
Speed ratings (Par 101): **91,89,87,86,85 84,82,82**
CSF £44.01 CT £155.10 TOTE £4.80: £1.80, £1.90, £1.50; EX 95.00 Place 6 £58.28, Place 5 £20.47.
Owner Mrs J E Taylor **Bred** Mrs J E Taylor **Trained** Lambourn, Berks
FOCUS
A moderate handicap, run at just a modest pace. Not form to be taken at face value.
Western Roots Official explanation: jockey said gelding was unsuited by the slow early pace

T/Plt: £9.70 to a £1 stake. Pool: £6,869.60. 520.00 winning tickets. T/Qpdt: £74.70 to a £1 stake. Pool: £108,983.55. 1,063.65 winning tickets. KH

229 WOLVERHAMPTON (A.W) (L-H)

Sunday, January 20

OFFICIAL GOING: Standard

Wind: Light, behind Weather: Mainly wet

235 CATCH CAPTAIN CROC @ PONTIN'S H'CAP — 7f 32y(P)

1:50 (1:52) (Class 6) (0-65,65) 4-Y-0+ — **£2,047** (£604; £302) **Stalls** High

Form — RPR

6-25 **1** **Xpres Maite**^{3} [190] 5-9-1 62 (v^{1}) PhillipMakin 2 — 77
(S R Bowring) *led early: chsd ldr: led over 2f out: rdn clr 1f out: r.o wl* **15/2**

00-1 **2** *3* **Unlimited**^{7} [149] 6-8-12 59 6ex JimmyQuinn 9 — 66
(R Simpson) *sn prom: rdn to chse wnr jst over 1f out: no imp* **5/1**^{2}

451- **3** *hd* **Kensington (IRE)**^{33} [7180] 7-8-12 59 (p) StephenDonohoe 10 — 65
(P D Evans) *hld up in mid-div: rdn and hdwy over 1f out: kpt on ins fnl f* **10/1**

23-0 **4** *½* **Green Pirate**^{18} [15] 6-8-10 60 KirstyMilczarek$^{(3)}$ 7 — 65
(W M Brisbourne) *s.i.s: hld up and bhd: c wd st: rdn and hdwy over 1f out: edgd lft ins fnl f: nt qckn* **8/1**

301- **5** *1 ½* **Cornerstone**^{176} [3949] 4-8-3 57 (v) WilliamCarson$^{(7)}$ 8 — 58
(S C Williams) *hld up in tch: rdn over 1f out: wknd wl ins fnl f* **16/1**

330- **6** *¾* **Gilded Cove**^{22} [7271] 8-9-2 63 HayleyTurner 11 — 62
(R Hollinshead) *hld up in rr: rdn and kpt on fnl f: n.d* **20/1**

01-0 **7** *1 ¼* **Bens Georgie (IRE)**^{15} [54] 6-8-11 58 JimCrowley 12 — 54
(D K Ivory) *hld up in mid-div: rdn and sme hdwy 2f out: wknd ins fnl f* **22/1**

25-2 **8** *¾* **Tanforan**^{16} [49] 6-9-4 65 DavidAllan 3 — 59
(B P J Baugh) *mid-div: nt clr run on ins and lost pl bnd after 1f: rdn over 3f out: n.d* **6/1**^{3}

20-3 **9** *nk* **Royal Embrace**^{15} [56] 5-8-10 57 (v) DeanMcKeown 1 — 50
(D Shaw) *prom early: lost pl after 1f: sme hdwy over 2f out: wknd ins fnl f* **4/1**^{1}

04-0 **10** *3 ½* **Eloquent Rose (IRE)**^{19} [4] 4-9-0 64 AndrewMullen$^{(3)}$ 5 — 47
(Mrs A Duffield) *s.i.s: a in rr* **28/1**

2-41 **11** *1 ½* **Alto Vertigo**^{16} [49] 5-8-11 65 (p) PatrickDonaghy$^{(7)}$ 6 — 44
(P C Haslam) *sn led: hdd over 2f out: rdn over 1f out: wknd qckly fnl f* **5/1**^{2}

503- **12** *¾* **Prince Rossi (IRE)**^{47} [7025] 4-8-6 53 (p) PaulFessey 4 — 30
(A E Price) *prom tl wknd over 3f out* **20/1**

1m 29.47s (-0.13) **Going Correction** +0.175s/f (Slow) — **12** Ran SP% **122.8**
Speed ratings (Par 101): **107,103,103,102,101 100,98,97,97,93 91,91**
CSF £44.00 CT £394.00 TOTE £10.10: £3.20, £1.50, £3.80; EX 73.10 Trifecta £297.80 Part won. Pool: £419.52 - 0.10 winning tickets..
Owner Charterhouse Holdings Plc **Bred** S R Bowring **Trained** Edwinstowe, Notts

FOCUS
A moderate handicap, but a decent winning time for the class of contest. Those that raced handily appeared to be at an advantage.

236 LADBROKES SERIOUS ABOUT BUSINESS CLASSIFIED STKS — 7f 32y(P)

2:20 (2:20) (Class 7) 4-Y-0+ — **£1,365** (£403; £201) **Stalls** High

Form — RPR

600- **1** **Polish Prize**^{37} [7137] 4-8-9 45 JamieJones$^{(5)}$ 3 — 47
(W R Swinburn) *a.p: chsd ldr over 2f out: hung rt over 1f out: rdn to ld cl home* **12/1**

0-02 **2** *½* **Kingsmaite**^{3} [189] 7-9-0 43 (b) PhillipMakin 7 — 46
(S R Bowring) *led 1f: chsd ldr: led over 3f out: rdn wl over 1f out: hdd cl home* **9/4**^{1}

3 *1 ¼* **Hi Spec (IRE)**^{46} [7036] 5-9-0 40 AdamKirby 2 — 43
(Miss M E Rowland) *hld up towards rr: hdwy 3f out: c wd st: carried rt over 1f out: kpt on same pce fnl f* **22/1**

0/ **4** *1 ½* **Up Dee Creek**^{46} [7036] 6-8-11 40 (b^{1}) JerryO'Dwyer$^{(3)}$ 8 — 39
(Daniel Mark Loughnane, Ire) *prom: outpcd 3f out: rdn and rallied over 1f out: one pce fnl f* **8/1**

000- **5** *1* **Broad Town Girl**^{36} [7159] 5-8-7 38 KylieManser$^{(7)}$ 5 — 36
(Mrs H Sweeting) *dwlt: hld up in rr: rdn and r.o fnl f: nrst fin* **100/1**

0-06 **6** *¾* **Telepathic (IRE)**^{6} [153] 8-9-0 36 (b) StephenDonohoe 4 — 34
(A Berry) *s.i.s: hld up and bhd: rdn and hdwy 2f out: wknd ins fnl f* **50/1**

0-01 **7** *½* **Golden Square**^{9} [123] 6-9-0 48 KirstyMilczarek$^{(3)}$ 11 — 36
(A W Carroll) *s.i.s: hdwy over 5f out: rdn and wkng whn hung lft ent fnl f* **11/2**

54-4 **8** *2* **Desert Lover (IRE)**^{17} [33] 6-9-0 45 JimmyQuinn 10 — 27
(R J Price) *sn mid-div: wknd over 2f out* **5/1**^{3}

32-5 **9** *3* **Kindkintyre (IRE)**^{17} [33] 4-8-11 45 JamieMoriarty$^{(3)}$ 9 — 19+
(R A Fahey) *a towards rr* **7/2**^{2}

5-66 **10** *1 ¾* **Aboustar**^{10} [106] 8-8-11 45 (b) MarkLawson$^{(3)}$ 6 — 14
(M Brittain) *led after 1f: hdd over 3f out: rdn and wknd 2f out* **14/1**

1m 31.66s (2.06) **Going Correction** +0.175s/f (Slow) — **10** Ran SP% **117.8**
Speed ratings (Par 97): **95,94,93,91,90 89,88,86,83,81**
CSF £39.38 TOTE £12.20: £4.10, £1.10, £6.00; EX 48.70 Trifecta £384.10 Part won. Pool: £541.10 - 0.77 winning tickets..
Owner Polish Punters **Bred** Lady Legard & Sir Tatton Sykes **Trained** Aldbury, Herts

FOCUS
A poor contest and the form looks very weak.
Polish Prize Official explanation: trainer said, regarding the improved form shown, gelding had benefited from the drop in class

237 PONTINS.COM H'CAP — 5f 216y(P)

2:50 (2:50) (Class 6) (0-60,58) 3-Y-0 — **£2,266** (£674; £337; £168) **Stalls** Low

Form — RPR

-614 **1** **Fulford**^{6} [154] 3-8-12 55 MarkLawson$^{(3)}$ 6 — 62
(M Brittain) *hld up: hdwy over 2f out: rdn over 1f out: led ins fnl f: drvn out* **9/4**^{1}

0-11 **2** *1 ¾* **Bold Diva**^{6} [154] 3-9-1 58 6ex KirstyMilczarek$^{(3)}$ 1 — 60
(A W Carroll) *chsd ldr tl over 3f out: rdn over 1f out: kpt on to take 2nd post* **9/4**^{1}

50-0 **3** *hd* **Wynberg (IRE)**^{17} [23] 3-8-9 49 StephenDonohoe 8 — 50
(S A Callaghan) *t.k.h in tch: edgd lft wl over 3f out: led 3f out: rdn over 1f out: hdd and no ex ins fnl f* **5/1**^{2}

4-44 **4** *1* **Weetfromthechaff**^{8} [141] 3-9-4 58 (p) HayleyTurner 7 — 56
(R Hollinshead) *hld up in rr: rdn over 1f out: r.o fnl f: nt rch ldrs* **8/1**^{3}

00-3 **5** *3 ½* **Little Finch (IRE)**^{11} [92] 3-7-12 45 (b) KrishGundowry$^{(7)}$ 4 — 32
(R C Guest) *led 3f: rdn wl over 1f out: wknd fnl f* **22/1**

00-2 **6** *1 ¾* **Regal Veil**^{11} [92] 3-8-5 48 TolleyDean$^{(3)}$ 3 — 29
(S C Williams) *s.i.s: rdn and shortlived effrt over 2f out* **8/1**^{3}

3-06 **7** *½* **Andrasta**^{16} [38] 3-8-10 55 DanielleMcCreery$^{(5)}$ 2 — 34
(A Berry) *hld up in tch: rdn and wknd 2f out* **25/1**

624- **8** *13* **Liani (IRE)**^{24} [7243] 3-8-7 50 AndrewMullen$^{(3)}$ 5 — —
(J R Norton) *prom: hmpd and lost pl wl over 3f out: n.d after* **20/1**

1m 16.97s (1.97) **Going Correction** +0.175s/f (Slow) — **8** Ran SP% **113.4**
Speed ratings (Par 95): **93,90,90,89,84 82,81,64**
CSF £6.75 CT £21.19 TOTE £3.10: £1.80, £1.10, £1.50; EX 10.10 Trifecta £69.00 Pool: £654.00 - 6.72 winning tickets..
Owner Mel Brittain **Bred** D Simpson **Trained** Warthill, N Yorks

FOCUS
A moderate handicap.
Liani(IRE) Official explanation: jockey said filly lost her action

238 HALF TERM DEALS @ PONTINS.COM CLASSIFIED STKS — 1m 5f 194y(P)

3:20 (3:20) (Class 7) 4-Y-0+ — **£1,365** (£403; £201) **Stalls** Low

Form — RPR

00-2 **1** **Mujamead**^{5} [166] 4-8-9 44 JerryO'Dwyer$^{(3)}$ 2 — 55
(A W Carroll) *led early: hld up: stdy hdwy 6f out: rdn 3f out: wnt 2nd and hung lft over 1f out: led ins fnl f: r.o wl* **2/1**^{2}

0-11 **2** *2 ½* **Qaasi (USA)**^{3} [197] 6-9-10 48 MarkLawson$^{(3)}$ 3 — 61
(M Brittain) *t.k.h: sn chsng ldr: led 5f out: rdn over 2f out: hdd and no ex ins fnl f* **15/8**^{1}

035- **3** *5* **Jenny Soba**^{30} [7219] 5-9-4 41 (p) TGMcLaughlin 6 — 45
(Lucinda Featherstone) *s.i.s: hld up in rr: pushed along 4f out: rdn and sme hdwy over 2f out: styd on fnl f* **12/1**

60-3 **4** *2 ½* **Slavonic Lake**^{5} [166] 4-8-12 45 (t) FergalLynch 8 — 41
(I A Wood) *a.p: rdn and ev ch over 2f out: wknd over 1f out: fin lame* **11/4**^{3}

00-0 **5** *1 ½* **Tewkesbury (IRE)**^{8} [144] 4-8-12 32 (v^{1}) VinceSlattery 1 — 39
(Mrs K Waldron) *prom tl rdn and wknd over 2f out* **50/1**

603/ **6** *8* **Castle Frome (IRE)**^{20} [5965] 9-9-1 40 (p) NeilChalmers$^{(3)}$ 4 — 28
(A E Price) *led after 1f to 5f out: wknd over 3f out* **50/1**

00-6 **7** *3 ½* **Integration**^{16} [36] 8-9-4 42 SamHitchcott 5 — 23
(Miss M E Rowland) *hld up and bhd: hdwy 6f out: rdn and wknd over 3f out* **25/1**

60-5 **8** *7* **The Mighty Ogmore**^{16} [37] 4-8-12 38 (p) PaulEddery 7 — 13
(R C Guest) *hld up and bhd: rdn 4f out: sn struggling* **25/1**

3m 8.64s (2.64) **Going Correction** +0.175s/f (Slow)
WFA 4 from 5yo+ 6lb — **8** Ran SP% **114.1**
Speed ratings (Par 97): **99,97,94,93,92 87,85,81**
CSF £5.93 TOTE £2.90: £1.30, £1.30, £2.10; EX 8.00 Trifecta £33.00 Pool: £1,196.51 - 25.70 winning tickets..
Owner J T Billson **Bred** D R Tucker **Trained** Cropthorne, Worcs

FOCUS
A low-grade contest, but several in-form horses made for an interesting race.
Slavonic Lake Official explanation: vet said gelding finished lame

239 LADBROKES LOYALTY CARD MEDIAN AUCTION MAIDEN STKS — 1m 1f 103y(P)

3:50 (3:51) (Class 6) 4-6-Y-0 — **£2,047** (£604; £302) **Stalls** Low

Form — RPR

35-2 **1** **Blue Eyed Eloise**^{11} [88] 6-8-13 62 StephenCarson 6 — 57+
(B J McMath) *hld up and bhd: hdwy over 3f out: c wd st: shkn up to ld 1f out: r.o wl* **2/1**^{1}

305- **2** *3* **Orama's Ghost**^{162} [4392] 4-8-12 67 GregFairley 7 — 53
(M Botti) *hld up in tch: wnt 2nd 4f out: rdn over 2f out: led briefly over 1f out: one pce* **5/2**^{2}

02-0 **3** *3 ¾* **West End Lad**^{16} [39] 5-9-4 52 (p) PhillipMakin 8 — 52
(S R Bowring) *led: rdn 3f out: hdd over 1f out: no ex fnl f* **20/1**

4-32 **4** *nk* **Beech Games**^{4} [180] 4-9-3 53 TGMcLaughlin 2 — 51
(F Jordan) *hld up: rdn over 2f out: hdwy over 1f out: one pce fnl f* **11/2**^{3}

000- **5** *shd* **Harts In Mo Shun (IRE)**^{141} [5041] 4-8-12 41 (b) DanielleMcCreery$^{(5)}$ 4 — 51
(A Berry) *t.k.h: reminder over 1f out: kpt on towards fin* **100/1**

0 **6** *7* **Northstar Express (IRE)**^{16} [48] 5-8-13 37 StephenDonohoe 3 — 35
(J L Spearing) *chsd ldr to 4f out: rdn and wknd over 1f out* **66/1**

7 *27* **Last Chance Dance**^{46} [7041] 4-8-9 0 JerryO'Dwyer$^{(3)}$ 1 — —
(Andrew Oliver, Ire) *prom: rdn over 3f out: sn wknd: eased over 2f out* **5/2**^{2}

00/ **8** *½* **Boluisce (IRE)**^{697} [479] 5-8-6 0 TimothyMeadows$^{(7)}$ 5 — —
(W S Kittow) *plld hrd: swtchd rt after 1f: hdwy over 6f out: wknd over 3f out: eased whn no ch fnl 2f* **33/1**

2m 3.62s (1.92) **Going Correction** +0.175s/f (Slow)
WFA 4 from 5yo+ 1lb — **8** Ran SP% **116.0**
Speed ratings: **98,95,92,91,91 85,61,60**
CSF £7.27 TOTE £3.00: £1.10, £1.40, £3.50; EX 9.30 Trifecta £51.60 Pool: £1,136.10 - 15.61 winning tickets..
Owner Miss Marie Steele **Bred** Miss M E Steele **Trained** Newmarket, Suffolk

FOCUS
A weak maiden and the form looks far from solid.
Harts In Mo Shun(IRE) Official explanation: jockey said, regarding the running and riding, her orders were to sit handy and see how the race unfolded, adding that the gelding ran very keen in the early stages and she was unable to manoeuvre out wide in the back straight, then gelding hung right on the final bend
Last Chance Dance Official explanation: jockey said filly was never travelling

240 LADBROKES IN THE COMMUNITY CHARITABLE TRUST H'CAP — 1m 1f 103y(P)

4:20 (4:20) (Class 5) (0-70,68) 4-Y-0+ — **£2,590** (£770; £385; £192) **Stalls** Low

Form — RPR

01-2 **1** **Glenridding**^{16} [44] 4-8-11 61 JimCrowley 2 — 73
(J G Given) *set modest pce: qcknd clr 2f out: rdn over 1f out: r.o wl* **11/4**^{2}

214- **2** *3* **Alfie Tupper (IRE)**^{30} [7214] 5-9-5 68 PatCosgrave 5 — 74
(J R Boyle) *hld up: hdwy to chse wnr 2f out: rdn and no imp fnl f* **7/4**^{1}

6- **3** *1 ¼* **Rising Force (IRE)**^{43} [7080] 5-9-3 66 (b) AdamKirby 3 — 69
(J L Spearing) *hld up in rr: rdn and hdwy over 1f out: kpt on to take 3rd post* **8/1**

4 *shd* **Schelm (GER)**^{120} [5658] 6-9-0 63 JimmyQuinn 6 — 66
(Ronald O'Leary, Ire) *s.i.s: sn chsng ldr: lost 2nd over 4f out: rdn and wknd over 1f out* **12/1**

10-5 **5** *2 ½* **Rigat**^{14} [68] 5-8-12 61 PhillipMakin 1 — 59
(T D Barron) *plld hrd: rdn and bhd fnl 2f* **4/1**^{3}

302- **6** *3* **He's Mine Too**[23] 7263 4-9-3 **67**.. MickyFenton 4 58
(D G Bridgwater) *plld hrd early: prom: chsd wnr over 4f out tl over 2f out: wknd wl over 1f out* **8/1**

2m 3.80s (2.10) **Going Correction** +0.175s/f (Slow)
WFA 4 from 5yo+ 1lb **6** Ran SP% **112.9**
Speed ratings (Par 103): **97,94,93,93,90 88**
CSF £8.11 TOTE £3.10: £1.10, £1.60; EX 7.40.
Owner Tremousser Partnership **Bred** Bolton Grange **Trained** Willoughton, Lincs

FOCUS
A moderate handicap and the winner had the run of the race out in front.

241 DO THE CROCODILE ROCK @ PONTIN'S H'CAP 5f 216y(P)
4:50 (4:50) (Class 5) (0-70,69) 4-Y-0+ **£2,590** (£770; £288; £288) **Stalls** Low

Form RPR
-142 **1** **Obe Royal**[11] 103 4-8-11 69................................(b) RichardEvans(7) 6 77
(P D Evans) *hld up in rr: hdwy on ins wl over 1f out: rdn to ld wl ins fnl f: r.o* **12/1**
23-1 **2** *1/2* **Tag Team (IRE)**[19] 4 7-8-8 66........................... MarkCoumbe(7) 8 73
(John A Harris) *led: rdn and hdd 1f out: r.o* **9/1**
-432 **3** *hd* **Chatshow (USA)**[2] 213 7-8-4 58............................ KirstyMilczarek(3) 5 64
(A W Carroll) *hld up: c wd st: rdn and hdwy over 1f out: r.o towards fin* **10/3**[2]
-335 **3** *dht* **Perlachy**[5] 165 4-8-8 59..(v) JimmyQuinn 3 65
(Mrs N Macauley) *a.p: rdn over 1f out: r.o towards fin* **13/2**
332- **5** *nk* **Methaaly (IRE)**[36] 7161 5-9-3 68................................... GeorgeBaker 1 73
(M Mullineaux) *hld up: hdwy on ins over 2f out: rdn to ld 1f out: hdd wl ins fnl f* **9/4**[1]
30-5 **6** *2* **Zarzu**[13] 71 9-8-11 62.. LiamJones 7 61
(C R Dore) *hld up: rdn and no hdwy fnl f* **20/1**
12-2 **7** *1 3/4* **Grand Palace (IRE)**[13] 72 5-8-12 63.....................(v) DeanMcKeown 4 56
(D Shaw) *prom tl rdn and wknd over 1f out* **9/2**[3]
460- **8** *17* **Metal Guru**[31] 7206 4-8-11 62... HayleyTurner 2 1
(R Hollinshead) *sn prom: wknd over 3f out: lost tch fnl 2f* **9/1**

1m 15.28s (0.28) **Going Correction** +0.175s/f (Slow) **8** Ran SP% **117.8**
Speed ratings (Par 103): **105,104,104,104,103 101,98,76**WIN: Obe Royal £15.40. PL: OR £3.50, Tag Team £3.50, Perlachy £1.20, Chatshow £0.80. EX: £86.90. CSF: £116.09. TRIC: OR/TT/P £389.55, OR/TT/C £223.36. TRIF: Pool: £1,163.76. OR/TT/P £295.00 - 1.40 w/u, OR/TT/C £83.10 - 4.97 w/u. Plac27 Owner.
■ Stewards' Enquiry : Mark Coumbe one-day ban: failed to keep straight from stalls; four-day ban: careless riding (Jan 31-Feb 4)

FOCUS
A competitive handicap run at a decent pace despite the principals finishing in a heap.
T/Jkpt: £39,763.50 to a £1 stake. Pool: £196,017.59. 3.50 winning tickets. T/Plt: £25.60 to a £1 stake. Pool: £163,498.70. 4,654.55 winning tickets. T/Qpdt: £2.60 to a £1 stake. Pool: £9,847.40. 2,742.15 winning tickets. KH

206 KEMPTON (A.W) (R-H)
Monday, January 21

OFFICIAL GOING: Standard
Wind: brisk, across

242 DIGIBET.COM CLASSIFIED STKS 1m 2f (P)
1:50 (1:58) (Class 7) 4-Y-0+ **£1,365** (£403; £201) **Stalls** High

Form RPR
20-1 **1** **Megalala (IRE)**[6] 160 7-9-3 42.................................... NeilChalmers(3) 1 56
(J J Bridger) *t.k.h: trckd ldr: rdn to ld appr fnl f: hld on wl u.p* **9/2**[2]
00-3 **2** *nk* **Ernmoor**[6] 160 6-9-0 41.. J-PGuillambert 3 50
(J R Jenkins) *t.k.h in rr tl hdwy to trck ldrs 6f out: rdn: hung lft and styd on to chse wnr ins fnl f: one pce fnl 100yds* **6/1**[3]
2-64 **3** *2* **Ponte Vecchio (IRE)**[6] 160 4-8-12 45..................(p) FergusSweeney 11 46
(J R Boyle) *broke out of stalls bef s: led: rdn 2f out: hdd appr fnl f and sn outpcd by ldng duo* **7/2**[1]
04-0 **4** *shd* **Bollywood (IRE)**[18] 24 5-9-0 43... DaneO'Neill 8 46
(J J Bridger) *in tch: hdwy over 2f out: styd on fnl f but nvr gng pce to be competitive* **8/1**
050- **5** *1/2* **Height Of Spirits**[70] 6792 6-9-0 44..............................(p) RobertHavlin 6 45
(T D McCarthy) *t.k.h: chsd ldrs: rdn over 2f out: styd on same pce fnl f* **13/2**
0-65 **6** *1/2* **Busy Man (IRE)**[6] 160 9-9-0 45....................................... StephenDonohoe 2 44+
(R C Guest) *slowly away: t.k.h in rr: hdwy over 1f out: styd on ins fnl f but nvr in contention* **8/1**
06-0 **7** *nk* **Elms Schoolboy**[6] 160 6-9-0 40.......................................(b) JimCrowley 7 43
(P Howling) *t.k.h in rr: hdwy over 1f out: kpt on but nvr gng pce to be competitive* **16/1**
40/6 **8** *nk* **Persian Khanoom (IRE)**[9] 133 6-9-0 43.............................. PatDobbs 9 42
(D E Cantillon) *chsd ldrs: rdn over 2f out: wknd fnl f* **25/1**
-506 **9** *1 1/4* **Salvestro**[6] 160 5-9-0 45..(p) JohnEgan 12 40
(A W Carroll) *t.k.h in mid-div: sme hdwy 3f out: sn rdn and n.d* **7/1**
/00- **10** *3* **Yeldham Lady**[14] 179 6-9-0 30.. SteveDrowne 4 34
(A J Chamberlain) *chsd ldrs: rdn over 2f out: sn btn* **66/1**
/00- **11** *5* **Chart Express**[188] 3616 4-8-12 43.. TGMcLaughlin 13 24
(P Howling) *a towards rr* **50/1**
00-0 **12** *5* **Burnley (IRE)**[19] 14 5-9-0 42.. MickyFenton 10 14
(Mrs A L M King) *slowly away: a in rr* **16/1**
/0-5 **13** *16* **Fun Thai**[3] 216 4-8-12 35.. JamesDoyle 5 —
(A J Chamberlain) *in rr: brief effrt 3f out: sn dropped to rr again* **100/1**

2m 10.72s (2.72) **Going Correction** +0.20s/f (Slow)
WFA 4 from 5yo+ 2lb **13** Ran SP% **122.8**
Speed ratings (Par 97): **97,96,95,95,94 94,94,93,92,90 86,82,69**
CSF £32.22 TOTE £5.40: £2.00, £2.50, £1.50; EX 24.90.
Owner Tommy Ware **Bred** Joseph Gallagher **Trained** Liphook, Hants
■ This race was delayed firstly by some geese on the track, then by Ponte Vecchio bursting out of the stalls.

FOCUS
A typically weak affair for the class, run at just an average pace. The first pair came clear and the form makes sense.
Salvestro Official explanation: jockey said gelding ran too free
Yeldham Lady Official explanation: jockey said mare finished lame

243 DIGIBET SPORTS BETTING H'CAP 5f (P)
2:20 (2:23) (Class 5) (0-70,70) 3-Y-0 **£2,590** (£770; £385; £192) **Stalls** High

Form RPR
05-2 **1** **Baytown Blaze**[16] 59 3-9-4 **70**.. TGMcLaughlin 4 73
(M Wigham) *mde all: rdn and styd on u.p fnl f: all out* **4/1**[3]
00-1 **2** *nk* **Orpen's Art (IRE)**[11] 112 3-7-11 **56** oh2.................. DeclanCannon(7) 2 58
(S A Callaghan) *s.i.s: sn rcvrd: chsd wnr 2f out: hung rt sn after: styd on u.p and clsng fnl 50yds but a jst hld* **7/4**[1]
1 **3** *1 1/2* **The Little Fizzer (IRE)**[19] 9 3-8-12 **64**.................... FergusSweeney 1 61
(K R Burke) *chsd ldrs and sn hanging lft: wd bnd 2f out: swtchd sharply rt to ins wl over 1f out: no imp on ldng duo fnl f* **4/1**[3]
233- **4** *7* **Sempre Libera (IRE)**[23] 7264 3-9-0 **66**......................... J-PGuillambert 5 37
(P W Chapple-Hyam) *in rr: sn rdn: no imp on ldrs whn hmpd on rail wl over 1f out* **7/2**[2]
404- **5** *8* **Casla Beag (IRE)**[103] 6104 3-8-8 **63**.................................. TolleyDean(3) 3 6
(B Palling) *chsd wnr to 2f out: wkng whn hmpd on rail wl over 1f out* **9/1**

61.62 secs (1.12) **Going Correction** +0.20s/f (Slow) **5** Ran SP% **108.6**
Speed ratings (Par 97): **99,98,96,84,72**
CSF £11.13 TOTE £5.70: £2.20, £1.50; EX 10.50.
Owner Eventmaker Racehorses **Bred** Ms Clare Sharp **Trained** Newmarket, Suffolk
■ Stewards' Enquiry : T G McLaughlin one-day ban: used whip above shoulder height (Feb 1)

FOCUS
A modest little handicap, in which the winner set a sound pace and is rated back to something like her 2yo form.
The Little Fizzer(IRE) Official explanation: jockey said filly hung right

244 DIGIBET MEDIAN AUCTION MAIDEN STKS 7f (P)
2:50 (2:51) (Class 5) 3-Y-0 **£2,590** (£770; £385; £192) **Stalls** High

Form RPR
1 **Laddies Poker Two (IRE)** 3-8-12 0.................................... TPQueally 2 85+
(J Noseda) *s.i.s: sn in tch: smooth hdwy to chal 2f out: led sn after: c readily clr over 1f out: v easily* **11/4**[2]
03-3 **2** *6* **Ocean Legend (IRE)**[16] 52 3-9-0 74......................... JerryO'Dwyer(3) 5 71
(Miss J Feilden) *trckd ldrs: drvn to chal over 2f out: chsd wnr sn after but nvr any ch: kpt on to hold 2nd fnl f* **11/8**[1]
300- **3** *1 1/2* **Monsieur Reynard**[150] 4775 3-9-3 72......................... StephenDonohoe 7 67
(B J Meehan) *led: rdn and hdd jst ins fnl 2f: sn one pce* **11/4**[2]
-6 **4** *3* **Bye Baby Bunting**[16] 60 3-8-12 0.. DaneO'Neill 3 53
(B R Johnson) *chsd ldrs: rdn 3f out: wknd ins fnl 2f* **10/1**[3]
5 *3 1/2* **Circadian Rhythm** 3-8-12 0.. SaleemGolam 8 44
(S C Williams) *s.i.s: in rr but in tch tl wknd over 2f out* **16/1**
0- **6** *5* **Scots W'Hae**[61] 6897 3-9-3 0.. JimCrowley 6 36
(S C Williams) *a in rr* **33/1**
00- **7** *20* **Peter's Joy (USA)**[23] 7266 3-9-3 0........................... FrankieMcDonald 1 —
(Jean-Rene Auvray) *early spd: hung lft and bhd fnl 4f* **66/1**

1m 26.64s (0.64) **Going Correction** +0.20s/f (Slow) **7** Ran SP% **114.8**
Speed ratings (Par 97): **104,97,95,92,88 82,59**
CSF £6.99 TOTE £5.40: £2.40, £1.40; EX 7.80.
Owner Ladbrokes International Ltd **Bred** Jerry O'Sullivan **Trained** Newmarket, Suffolk

FOCUS
An ordinary maiden, run at a decent pace. The debutante winner was most impressive and rates value for a good deal further.
Peter's Joy(USA) Official explanation: jockey said gelding lost its action

245 DIGIBET.COM CLAIMING STKS 7f (P)
3:20 (3:20) (Class 6) 4-Y-0+ **£2,047** (£604; £302) **Stalls** High

Form RPR
460- **1** **Waterside (IRE)**[44] 7074 9-9-7 99.. GeorgeBaker 7 80+
(G L Moore) *trckd ldrs: qcknd to ld over 1f out: shkn up and styd on strly ins fnl f* **8/15**[1]
23-0 **2** *2* **Millfield (IRE)**[17] 49 5-9-0 67... JimCrowley 2 67+
(P R Chamings) *s.i.s: in rr tl gd hdwy over 3f out: n.m.r whn improving over 1f out: chsd wnr ins fnl f but a comf hld* **9/1**[3]
000- **3** *1* **Count Ceprano (IRE)**[22] 7279 4-9-1 77................................. DaneO'Neill 3 66
(M D I Usher) *in tch: rdn and hdwy fr 2f out: styd on to take 3rd ins fnl f but nvr gng pce of ldng duo* **16/1**
4 *1 1/2* **Mr Rev** 5-9-4 0.. SteveDrowne 1 65
(J M Bradley) *v.s.a and bhd: shkn up 3f out and hdwy over 1f out: styd on fnl f and gng on cl home but nvr in contention* **100/1**
1-21 **5** *nk* **Angel Voices (IRE)**[12] 90 5-8-6 65........................(p) DeclanCannon(7) 4 59
(K R Burke) *led 2f: styd chsng ldr and led over 2f out: soon rdn: hdd over 1f ouyt: wknd ins fnl f* **7/2**[2]
1-46 **6** *1 1/2* **Soviet Palace (IRE)**[4] 190 4-9-5 75..............................(e) FergalLynch 6 61
(K A Ryan) *t.k.h: chsd ldr tl led after 2f: rdn and hdd over 2f out: sn btn* **12/1**
0-5 **7** *2 1/2* **Kazakstan**[12] 87 4-8-10 48..(p) FergusSweeney 5 45
(Mrs L C Jewell) *a in rr* **100/1**

1m 26.88s (0.88) **Going Correction** +0.20s/f (Slow) **7** Ran SP% **113.0**
Speed ratings (Par 101): **102,99,98,96,96 94,91**
CSF £6.40 TOTE £1.60: £1.10, £3.00; EX 6.90.
Owner Nigel Shields **Bred** Yeomanstown Stud **Trained** Woodingdean, E Sussex

FOCUS
This claimer revolved totally around the 99-rated Waterside and he duly won, despite not having to be anywhere near his best.

246 DIGIBET H'CAP 1m (P)
3:50 (3:50) (Class 5) (0-75,75) 4-Y-0+ **£2,590** (£770; £385; £192) **Stalls** High

Form RPR
01-2 **1** **Wrighty Almighty (IRE)**[8] 148 6-8-8 **65**............................. JimCrowley 8 72+
(P R Chamings) *in rr: rdn and hdwy fr 2f out: drvn to ld fnl 100yds: kpt on wl* **4/1**[2]
256- **2** *1* **Last Sovereign**[165] 4313 4-9-3 **74**.................................... SteveDrowne 3 79
(R Charlton) *chsd ldrs: led 2f out: sn rdn hdd and one pce fnl 100yds* **4/1**[2]
432- **3** *nk* **Common Purpose (USA)**[227] 2425 4-9-1 **72**.............. TGMcLaughlin 4 76
(Jane Chapple-Hyam) *fly-leapt out of stalls: chsd ldrs: rdn and n.m.r 1f out: kpt on ins fnl f: gng on cl home* **7/1**
12-4 **4** *nk* **One Night In Paris (IRE)**[16] 63 5-9-4 **75**......................... DaneO'Neill 9 79
(M J Wallace) *in rr: hdwy over 1f out: kpt on wl u.p fnl f: gng on cl home* **9/1**
004- **5** *1 1/4* **Hanbrin Bhoy (IRE)**[43] 6997 4-8-10 **67**............................ MickyFenton 5 68
(R Dickin) *led 1f: styd chsng ldrs: rdn over 2f out: wknd ins fnl f* **5/1**[3]
00-6 **6** *2* **Lopinot (IRE)**[18] 34 5-9-2 **73**.. GeorgeBaker 1 69
(M R Bosley) *in rr: hdwy on outside to chse ldrs 3f out: sn rdn: wknd appr fnl f* **16/1**
12-1 **7** *3/4* **Emma Jean Lad (IRE)**[16] 56 4-8-7 **64**................................ JohnEgan 6 58
(J S Moore) *trckd ldrs: rdn along and sme ptogress over 1f out: sn n.m.r and lost position: mod late prog* **3/1**[1]

10-0 **8** 5 **Trivia (IRE)**[10] [124] 4-9-2 **73** JamesDoyle 2 56
(Ms J S Doyle) *led after 1f: hdd 2f out and wknd qckly* **25/1**
1m 40.77s (0.97) **Going Correction** +0.20s/f (Slow) 8 Ran SP% **113.9**
Speed ratings (Par 103): **103,102,101,101,100 98,97,92**
CSF £20.21 CT £107.75 TOTE £4.30: £1.20, £1.70, £2.50; EX 16.90.
Owner The Boccy Hall Evans Tyrrell Partnership **Bred** P Heffernan **Trained** Baughurst, Hants
FOCUS
A good handicap for the class, run at an ordinary pace. The winner is possibly better than the bare form, which makes sense.

247 DIGIBET.COM H'CAP 6f (P)
4:20 (4:20) (Class 6) (0-50,49) 4-Y-O+ £2,047 (£604; £302) Stalls High

Form RPR
44-4 **1** **Davids Mark**[10] [121] 8-8-12 **49** JimCrowley 3 55
(J R Jenkins) *mde all: drvn along 2f out: styd on strly thrght fnl f* **10/3**[2]
044- **2** 1 **Sherjawy (IRE)**[90] [6402] 4-8-12 **49** (b) SamHitchcott 6 52
(Miss Z C Davison) *disp 2nd: rdn over 2f out: chsd wnr ins fnl f but a hld* **14/1**
-406 **3** nk **Maiden Investor**[2] [232] 5-8-12 **49** (v) MickyFenton 8 51+
(Stef Liddiard) *in tch whn hmpd on rail after 2f and dropped to rr: rdn 2f out: hdwy appr fnl f and r.o ins fnl f but nvr quite gng pce to rch ldng duo* **5/1**[3]
0-30 **4** ¾ **Noddledoddle (IRE)**[5] [174] 4-8-8 **45** (v) SaleemGolam 9 45
(J Ryan) *disp 2nd: rdn 2f out: one pce ins fnl f* **25/1**
03-3 **5** nk **Taboor (IRE)**[12] [86] 10-8-11 **48** TPQueally 4 47
(R M H Cowell) *s.i.s: in rr and hmpd on rail after 2f: rdn over 2f out: styd on fr over 1f out but nvr gng pce to rch ldrs* **8/1**
0-53 **6** nk **Balerno**[10] [121] 9-8-12 **49** (p) AmirQuinn 7 50+
(Mrs L J Mongan) *in tch: rdn and styng on whn hmpd 1f out: nt rcvr but styd on again nr fin* **11/4**[1]
0-50 **7** ¾ **Mister Incredible**[13] [82] 5-8-8 **48** (v) TolleyDean(3) 2 43
(J M Bradley) *t.k.h in rr: hung lft whn rdn over 2f out: mod prog ins fnl f* **8/1**
43-0 **8** 1 **The Carpet Man**[8] [151] 4-8-11 **48** JohnEgan 5 40
(A W Carroll) *in tch: rdn and effrt over 2f out: nvr gng pce to rch ldrs but kpt on ins fnl f* **6/1**
00-5 **9** 2 ½ **Lady Fas (IRE)**[11] [114] 5-8-8 **45** JamesDoyle 1 29
(A W Carroll) *chsd ldrs: rdn over 2f out: wknd over 1f out* **100/1**
1m 15.04s (1.94) **Going Correction** +0.20s/f (Slow) 9 Ran SP% **114.4**
Speed ratings (Par 101): **95,93,93,92,91 91,90,89,85**
CSF £48.26 CT £231.40 TOTE £3.30: £1.40, £4.00, £2.10; EX 39.60.
Owner Mrs Wendy Jenkins **Bred** D Lowe **Trained** Royston, Herts
■ Stewards' Enquiry : Jim Crowley three-day ban: careless riding (Feb 1-3)
FOCUS
A weak handicap which saw the winner make all under a canny ride. Suspect form.
Balerno Official explanation: jockey said gelding suffered interference in running

248 DIGIBET CASINO APPRENTICE H'CAP 1m 3f (P)
4:50 (4:50) (Class 6) (0-65,62) 4-Y-O+ £2,047 (£604; £302) Stalls High

Form RPR
1-42 **1** **Just Intersky (USA)**[9] [139] 5-9-7 **62** (e) AshleyMorgan 6 69
(V Smith) *stdd s: in rr: rdn and gd hdwy 2f out: led jst ins fnl f: drvn out* **9/2**[3]
32-1 **2** 1 **Wind Flow**[5] [180] 4-9-4 **62** 6ex (b) BradleyRoper 3 67
(C A Dwyer) *t.k.h: c sharply rt and led after 2f: rdn over 2f out: hdd jst ins fnl f and one pce* **5/4**[1]
2-1 **3** ¾ **Steig (IRE)**[9] [144] 5-9-6 **61** RichardEvans 1 66
(Carl Llewellyn) *sn led: hmpd on ins and hdd after 2f: chsd ldrs: rdn and hung rt fr 2f out: kpt on ins fnl f but nvr gng pce to chal* **15/8**[2]
00-2 **4** 4 **Phone Call**[17] [39] 5-9-5 **60** DavidProbert 2 57
(Mouse Hamilton-Fairley) *chsd ldrs: chal over 3f out: rdn over 2f out: wknd appr fnl f* **16/1**
00-2 **5** 1 ½ **Berry Hill Lass (IRE)**[10] [132] 4-9-2 **60** (p) DeclanCannon 5 54
(J G M O'Shea) *chsd ldrs: chal over 3f out: sn rdn: wknd ins fnl 2f* **20/1**
2m 24.83s (2.93) **Going Correction** +0.20s/f (Slow)
WFA 4 from 5yo+ 3lb 5 Ran SP% **108.1**
Speed ratings (Par 101): **97,96,95,92,91**
CSF £10.25 TOTE £5.00: £2.00, £1.10; EX 8.10 Place 6 £19.31, Place 5 £12.05..
Owner Tapas Partnership & J Pepper **Bred** Dreamfields Inc And Don Brady **Trained** Exning, Suffolk
■ Stewards' Enquiry : Bradley Roper two-day ban: careless riding (Feb 1-2)
FOCUS
A weak handicap, confined to apprentice riders. It was run at an ordinary pace and the form can be rated through the third.
T/Plt: £15.90 to a £1 stake. Pool: £59,498.90. 2,723.55 winning tickets. T/Qpdt: £5.10 to a £1 stake. Pool: £2,801.10. 399.40 winning tickets. ST

235 WOLVERHAMPTON (A.W) (L-H)
Monday, January 21

OFFICIAL GOING: Standard
Wind: Moderate becoming strong behind Weather: An odd shower

249 BUY TICKETS ONLINE CLASSIFIED STKS 1m 141y(P)
2:00 (2:03) (Class 7) 4-Y-O+ £1,365 (£403; £201) Stalls Low

Form RPR
30-5 **1** **My Mirasol**[9] [133] 4-8-13 44 (p) LPKeniry 6 57+
(D E Cantillon) *sn led: pushed clr 2f out: unchal* **9/4**[1]
4 **2** 5 **Vintage Quest**[8] [147] 6-9-0 43 (p) VinceSlattery 4 43
(D Burchell) *hld up and bhd: hdwy over 2f out: r.o u.p to take 2nd wl ins fnl f: no ch w wnr* **16/1**
0-45 **3** ½ **Lily La Belle**[12] [89] 4-8-13 45 LiamJones 7 42
(A W Carroll) *chsd ldrs: wnt 2nd over 3f out: rdn over 2f out: one pce* **10/1**
/05- **4** nk **Me No Puppet**[35] [7174] 4-8-13 45 JimmyQuinn 2 41
(E J Alston) *hld up in mid-div: rdn and hdwy 3f out: one pce fnl 2f* **20/1**
0-00 **5** 2 **Bahhmirage (IRE)**[3] [219] 5-8-9 45 (b) JamieJones(5) 5 37
(C N Kellett) *s.i.s: bhd tl hdwy and hung lft wl over 1f out: no further prog* **20/1**
0-01 **6** 3 **Frank's Quest (IRE)**[8] [147] 8-8-13 39 HarryPoulton(7) 9 31
(A B Haynes) *nvr nr ldrs* **9/1**
06-6 **6** 2 **Mucho Loco (IRE)**[19] [11] 5-9-0 44 (b) ChrisCatlin 10 25
(R Curtis) *hld up and bhd: stdy hdwy over 4f out: wknd over 2f out* **7/2**[2]
00-3 **8** 1 ¼ **Cantique (IRE)**[9] [140] 4-8-13 45 SebSanders 11 22
(R J Price) *hld up in mid-div: hdwy over 4f out: rdn and wknd 2f out* **9/2**[3]
00-0 **9** shd **Makfly**[14] [76] 5-9-0 45 (p) HayleyTurner 1 22
(R Hollinshead) *chsd ldrs: pushed along 7f out: lost pl and reminder over 4f out: bhd fnl 3f* **13/2**
00-0 **10** 5 **Brynris**[3] [214] 4-8-13 36 (b) DaleGibson 3 10
(Mrs G S Rees) *led early: prom tl wknd over 3f out* **80/1**
00/0 **11** 7 **Lady Lucinda**[10] [120] 7-8-11 30 TravisBlock(3) 8 —
(C N Kellett) *sn chsng ldr: lost 2nd and rdn over 3f out: sn wknd: eased whn no ch ins fnl f* **100/1**
1m 52.19s (1.69) **Going Correction** +0.125s/f (Slow)
WFA 4 from 5yo+ 1lb 11 Ran SP% **121.2**
Speed ratings (Par 97): **97,92,92,91,90 85,88,84,84,79 73**
CSF £42.12 TOTE £3.50: £1.60, £4.40, £3.00; EX 59.10 TRIFECTA Not won..
Owner J A Bailie **Bred** J A Forsyth **Trained** Newmarket, Suffolk
FOCUS
A weak event in which the winner enjoyed an easy lead, but the form seems sound.
Cantique(IRE) Official explanation: jockey said filly had no more to give

250 HOTEL AND CONFERENCING AT WOLVERHAMPTON (S) STKS 1m 141y(P)
2:30 (2:30) (Class 6) 4-Y-O+ £2,047 (£604; £302) Stalls Low

Form RPR
4-41 **1** **Arctic Desert**[12] [101] 8-9-4 60 (t) HayleyTurner 5 71+
(Miss Gay Kelleway) *hld up in rr: smooth hdwy to chse ldr over 2f out: led on bit over 1f out: shkn up and sn clr: easily* **3/1**[2]
06-3 **2** 4 **Pianoforte (USA)**[12] [101] 6-8-13 59 (p) JimmyQuinn 6 54
(E J Alston) *hld up in rr: rdn over 3f out: hdwy whn nt clr run and swtchd rt over 1f out: tk 2nd last strides: no ch w wnr* **13/2**
10-1 **3** nk **Louisiade (IRE)**[15] [66] 7-8-11 63 (p) MarkCoumbe(7) 1 58
(John A Harris) *led early: hld up: rdn and hdwy whn hung lft over 1f out: kpt on same pce fnl f* **5/1**
16-4 **4** 1 ¾ **Circus Polka (USA)**[12] [103] 4-9-3 63 (bt) ChrisCatlin 7 54
(W M Brisbourne) *sn led: clr over 6f out: rdn over 2f out: hdd over 1f out: sn btn: edgd lft wl ins fnl f* **7/2**[3]
230- **5** 5 **Sarraaf (IRE)**[31] [7218] 12-8-13 52 TomEaves 4 38
(Miss L A Perratt) *a.p: chsd ldr 4f out tl over 2f out: wknd wl over 1f out* **20/1**
004/ **6** 3 **Spence's Choice (IRE)**[25] [6926] 4-8-5 0 NSLawes(7) 3 31
(G P Kelly) *sn chsng ldr: rdn and lost 2nd 4f out: sn wknd* **66/1**
2-21 **7** 1 **Northern Desert (IRE)**[11] [115] 9-9-4 65 (p) PaulDoe 2 34
(S Curran) *hld up: hdwy over 4f out: rdn and wknd 2f out* **2/1**[1]
1m 51.36s (0.86) **Going Correction** +0.125s/f (Slow)
WFA 4 from 6yo+ 1lb 7 Ran SP% **116.8**
Speed ratings (Par 101): **101,97,97,95,91 88,87**
CSF £23.44 TOTE £4.40: £2.20, £2.30; EX 24.30.There was no bid for the winner.
Owner Miss Gay Kelleway **Bred** Whatton Manor Stud **Trained** Exning, Suffolk
FOCUS
A disappointing run by the favourite in this fair seller, which casts doubts on the form. The winner was back to last winter's best on face value.
Northern Desert(IRE) Official explanation: jockey said gelding ran flat

251 PONTINS.COM H'CAP 1m 1f 103y(P)
3:00 (3:00) (Class 6) (0-50,50) 4-Y-O+ £1,774 (£523; £262) Stalls Low

Form RPR
0-63 **1** **Jarvo**[3] [220] 7-8-6 49 (v[1]) PatrickMathers(3) 9 56
(I W McInnes) *hld up: hdwy over 3f out: rdn over 2f out: nt clr run and swtchd rt over 1f out: hung lft and led nr fin* **6/1**
606- **2** ½ **Ermine Grey**[111] [5890] 7-8-10 50 HayleyTurner 2 56
(A W Carroll) *t.k.h: a.p: rdn to ld ins fnl f: hdd nr fin* **10/1**
0-60 **3** 1 ¼ **Boppys Pride**[9] [143] 5-8-9 49 ow2 (p) TonyHamilton 1 52
(R A Fahey) *hld up in tch: rdn over 3f out: kpt on ins fnl f* **9/2**[3]
006- **4** nk **Willie Ever**[25] [7247] 4-8-9 50 FrancisNorton 8 53
(W J Musson) *t.k.h: led: rdn and hdd over 1f out: no ex wl ins fnl f* **10/1**
30-4 **5** nk **Bobering**[9] [143] 8-8-1 48 SoniaEaton(7) 7 50+
(B P J Baugh) *hld up: rdn over 2f out: hdwy over 1f out: kpt on ins fnl f* **3/1**[1]
40-2 **6** 1 **Don Pasquale**[14] [77] 6-8-8 48 (v) ChrisCatlin 3 48
(J T Stimpson) *hld up and bhd: hdwy over 2f out: sn rdn: one pce fnl f* **4/1**[2]
00-0 **7** ¾ **Welsh Whisper**[9] [145] 9-8-6 46 oh1 JimmyQuinn 5 44?
(S A Brookshaw) *a.p: hrd rdn to ld over 1f out: hdd ins fnl f: wknd* **33/1**
55-0 **8** 13 **Autograph Hunter**[10] [125] 4-8-9 50 LPKeniry 6 21
(Peter Grayson) *s.i.s: a bhd: rdn over 3f out: hung lft fr over 2f out: eased fnl f* **6/1**
600- **9** 51 **Monmouthshire**[219] [2656] 5-8-6 46 (v) LiamJones 4 —
(R J Price) *plld hrd in tch: rdn over 3f out: sn wknd: t.o fnl 2f: fin lame* **14/1**
2m 3.62s (1.92) **Going Correction** +0.125s/f (Slow)
WFA 4 from 5yo+ 1lb 9 Ran SP% **119.5**
Speed ratings (Par 101): **96,95,94,94,93 93,92,80,35**
CSF £66.32 CT £299.62 TOTE £8.90: £3.30, £1.50, £2.20; EX 58.40 Trifecta £223.90 Part won. Pool £315.37 - 0.47 winning units..
Owner F S W Partnership **Bred** Lloyd Farm Stud **Trained** Catwick, E Yorks
FOCUS
A poor handicap in which the winner was back to his form of last spring.
Monmouthshire Official explanation: jockey said gelding finished lame

252 BETTER BOOK EARLY @ PONTIN'S CLAIMING STKS 1m 1f 103y(P)
3:30 (3:31) (Class 6) 4-Y-O+ £1,943 (£578; £288; £144) Stalls Low

Form RPR
22-1 **1** **Sawwaah (IRE)**[9] [133] 11-9-0 74 (v) RichardKingscote 3 77+
(Tom Dascombe) *a.p: wnt 2nd over 5f out: led on bit 2f out: cheekily* **11/4**[2]
3-13 **2** nk **Given A Choice (IRE)**[4] [196] 6-9-6 82 SebSanders 4 77
(J G Given) *led after 1f: rdn and hdd 2f out: kpt on towards fin: no ch w wnr* **8/11**[1]
11-3 **3** 2 ½ **Ninth House (USA)**[16] [63] 6-8-12 75 (bt) HarryPoulton(7) 2 71
(N P Littmoden) *hld up: stdy hdwy over 3f out: rdn over 2f out: kpt on same pce fnl f* **4/1**[3]
0-5 **4** 8 **Hayley's Pearl**[9] [144] 9-8-11 0 HayleyTurner 1 46?
(Mrs P Ford) *hld up: sme hdwy over 3f out: wknd over 2f out* **100/1**
61-5 **5** 1 ¼ **Shaydreambeliever**[19] [18] 5-8-9 60 ow1 TonyHamilton 5 41
(R A Fahey) *led 1f: chsd ldr tl over 5f out: wknd over 3f out* **25/1**
2m 2.43s (0.73) **Going Correction** +0.125s/f (Slow) 5 Ran SP% **109.4**
Speed ratings (Par 101): **101,100,98,91,90**
CSF £5.09 TOTE £4.50: £1.90, £1.10; EX 5.60.The winner was claimed by Declan Carroll for £10,000.
Owner Alan Solomon **Bred** Shadwell Estate Company Limited **Trained** Lambourn, Berks

The Form Book, Raceform Ltd, Compton, RG20 6NL

FOCUS
Only three really mattered here and the bookmakers went 25/1 bar that trio. The form does not look solid.

253 RACE TO PONTIN'S FOR HALF TERM H'CAP 7f 32y(P)
4:00 (4:02) (Class 4) (0-85,82) 3-Y-O **£4,533** (£1,348; £674; £336) **Stalls** High

Form RPR
611- **1** **Fathsta (IRE)**[22] 7280 3-9-1 **76** LPKeniry 1 79
(S Kirk) *a.p: rdn to ld ins fnl f: r.o wl* **7/4**[2]
132- **2** 1 1/4 **Grand Fleet**[121] 5624 3-9-7 **82** GregFairley 3 81+
(M Johnston) *led: hdd 5f out: w ldr: led 2f out: sn rdn: hdd and nt qckn ins fnl f* **1/1**[1]
04-1 **3** *shd* **Royal Applord**[14] 74 3-9-0 **75** FrancisNorton 2 74
(K A Ryan) *hld up: rdn and outpcd over 2f out: hdwy on ins over 1f out: n.m.r briefly ins fnl f: r.o* **16/1**
345- **4** *3* **Spice Trade**[31] 7217 3-8-11 **72** (v) ChrisCatlin 5 63
(J Noseda) *s.i.s: sn rcvrd: jnd ldr after 1f: slt ld 5f out to 2f out: sn rdn and hung lft: wknd wl ins fnl f* **8/1**[3]
1-13 **5** *6* **Elusive Lady (IRE)**[3] 217 3-8-8 **74** (p) AshleyHamblett(5) 4 49
(J R Weymes) *t.k.h: prom tl wknd 2f out* **10/1**

1m 30.65s (1.05) **Going Correction** +0.125s/f (Slow) **5** Ran SP% **112.4**
Speed ratings (Par 99): **99,97,97,94,87**
CSF £3.97 TOTE £2.60: £1.10, £1.30; EX 4.10.
Owner Speedlith Group **Bred** Brian Miller **Trained** Upper Lambourn, Berks

FOCUS
An interesting little handicap despite the fact they went 8/1 bar the first two. The winner continues to progress with the third the guide to the form.

254 WOLVERHAMPTON-RACECOURSE.CO.UK APPRENTICE CLASSIFIED STKS 5f 216y(P)
4:30 (4:31) (Class 7) 4-Y-O+ **£1,365** (£403; £201) **Stalls** Low

Form RPR
50-2 **1** **Charlotte Grey**[6] 167 4-9-0 45 JackMitchell 3 55
(C N Allen) *a.p: rdn over 1f out: led wl ins fnl f: r.o* **2/1**[1]
00-5 **2** 1 1/4 **Stargazy**[12] 101 4-8-11 39 MatthewDavies(3) 1 51
(W G M Turner) *bhd: rdn and hdwy over 1f out: r.o ins fnl f: tk 2nd post* **8/1**[3]
4-30 **3** *shd* **Temtation (IRE)**[13] 79 4-9-0 42 KellyHarrison 7 51
(J A Pickering) *broke wl: led: rdn over 1f out: hdd and nt qckn wl ins fnl f* **14/1**
6-00 **4** *3* **James Street (IRE)**[10] 120 5-8-9 44 (v) RyanHill(5) 11 41
(Peter Grayson) *bhd: c v wd st: sn rdn: r.o ins fnl f: nrst fin* **12/1**
00-2 **5** 1/2 **High Window (IRE)**[7] 153 8-8-9 40 NSLawes(5) 5 40
(G P Kelly) *bhd tl r.o ins fnl f: nvr nrr* **17/2**
40-5 **6** 1 1/4 **Ask No More**[12] 100 5-9-0 44 (b) WilliamCarson 10 36
(J Ryan) *a.p: wnt 2nd over 2f out: rdn over 1f out: wknd ins fnl f* **13/2**[2]
/-05 **7** 3/4 **Loaderfun (IRE)**[5] 174 6-9-0 45 (e) PatrickDonaghy 12 33
(I W McInnes) *mid-div: rdn and no hdwy fnl 2f* **17/2**
000- **8** *shd* **Cadogen Square**[81] 6609 6-9-0 40 (b) DanielleMcCreery 2 33+
(D W Chapman) *s.i.s: in rr: n.m.r on ins over 3f out: nt clr run over 2f out: nvr nrr* **50/1**
060- **9** *1* **Tang**[90] 6402 4-9-0 40 JackDean 9 30
(W G M Turner) *chsd ldrs: hung rt over 3f out: wknd over 2f out: c wd st* **16/1**
6-00 **10** *hd* **College Queen**[4] 189 10-9-0 37 MCGeran 8 29
(S Gollings) *mid-div: sme hdwy wl over 1f out: sn edgd lft: no further prog* **40/1**
000- **11** *6* **Grand View**[150] 4768 12-9-0 45 (p) JPHamblett 13 10
(J R Weymes) *bhd fnl 4f: eased fnl f* **14/1**
6-06 **12** 2 1/2 **Kissi Kissi**[12] 87 5-9-0 40 HarryPoulton 4 —+
(M J Attwater) *chsd ldrs: sddle slipped over 3f out: lost pl over 2f out: eased fnl f* **9/1**
00-6 **13** 3 1/2 **Borzoi Maestro**[12] 100 7-8-11 42 (p) KylieManser(3) 6 —
(D G Bridgwater) *w ldr over 2f: wknd over 2f out* **33/1**

1m 16.05s (1.05) **Going Correction** +0.125s/f (Slow) **13** Ran SP% **123.1**
Speed ratings (Par 97): **98,96,96,92,91 89,88,88,87,87 79,75,71**
CSF £18.38 TOTE £2.60: £1.10, £2.90, £5.10; EX 16.30 Trifecta £160.50 Pool £361.87 - 1.60 winning units..
Owner N Davies **Bred** Finbar Kent **Trained** Newmarket, Suffolk
■ Perhaps the last winner for Conrad Allen, who hands in his licence at the end of this month.

FOCUS
A definite case of quantity rather than quality. The winner ran just about to the pick of her form this winter.
Kissi Kissi Official explanation: jockey said saddle slipped

255 CATCH CAPTAIN CROC @ PONTIN'S H'CAP 5f 216y(P)
5:00 (5:00) (Class 6) (0-50,50) 4-Y-O+ **£1,774** (£523; £262) **Stalls** Low

Form RPR
00-0 **1** **Avontuur (FR)**[6] 168 6-8-9 47 (p) LiamJones 6 58
(D W Chapman) *sn prom: led after 1f: rdn wl over 1f out: drvn out* **12/1**
5-05 **2** 2 1/2 **Mr Loire**[3] 211 4-8-8 46 oh1 (b) DeanMcKeown 5 49
(A J Chamberlain) *hld up and bhd: c wd and bmpd ent st: hdwy over 1f out: rdn wl over 1f out: rdn wl over 1f out: edgd lft and wnt 2nd towards fin: nt trble wnr* **6/1**
/50- **3** 1 1/2 **Smirfys Systems**[32] 7207 9-8-10 48 TonyHamilton 7 46
(E S McMahon) *sn prom: chsd wnr 4f out: rdn 2f out: hung rt fnl f: one pce* **5/1**[3]
00-0 **4** 1/2 **Ava's World (IRE)**[9] 142 4-8-3 46 oh1 ColinHaddon(5) 4 43
(Peter Grayson) *s.i.s: hdwy on ins wl over 1f out: one pce fnl f* **25/1**
0-00 **5** 1/2 **Pauvic (IRE)**[8] 151 5-8-5 46 oh1 (v) AndrewMullen(3) 2 41
(Mrs A Duffield) *a.p: rdn and one pce fnl 2f* **6/1**
5-35 **6** *1* **Snow Bunting**[11] 115 10-8-9 50 TravisBlock(3) 1 42
(Jedd O'Keeffe) *chsd ldrs: rdn 4f out: wknd wl over 1f out* **7/2**[2]
1-03 **7** 1/2 **Lost All Alone**[5] 181 4-8-5 50 ChrisHough(7) 3 53+
(D M Simcock) *broke wl: hld up and sn bhd: nt clr run fr 3f out tl hmpd ent st: n.d* **3/1**[1]
00-0 **8** *2* **Fish Called Johnny**[19] 13 4-8-12 50 (b) LPKeniry 8 34
(Peter Grayson) *led 1f: prom: rdn over 2f out: wknd wl over 1f out* **9/1**

1m 15.6s (0.60) **Going Correction** +0.125s/f (Slow) **8** Ran SP% **114.0**
Speed ratings (Par 101): **101,97,95,95,94 93,92,89**
CSF £80.95 CT £410.36 TOTE £14.90: £3.10, £2.40, £1.60; EX 98.30 Trifecta £279.10 Part won. Pool £393.19 - 0.10 winning units. Place 6 £46.33, Place 5 £18.42..
Owner David W Chapman **Bred** Haras D'Etreham **Trained** Stillington, N Yorks

FOCUS
A weak handiap which did not take much winning. The favourite is rated better than the bare form.
Avontuur(FR) Official explanation: trainer said, regarding apparent improvement in form, that the gelding was better suited by the track and distance.

T/Plt: £66.00 to a £1 stake. Pool: £56,786.45. 627.55 winning tickets. T/Qpdt: £8.00 to a £1 stake. Pool: £4,093.50. 377.00 winning tickets. KH

188 SOUTHWELL (L-H)
Tuesday, January 22

OFFICIAL GOING: Standard
Wind: Virtually nil Weather: Fine and dry

256 ARENALEISUREPLC.COM H'CAP 6f (F)
1:00 (1:01) (Class 6) (0-55,58) 4-Y-O+ **£1,911** (£564; £282) **Stalls** Low

Form RPR
500- **1** **Hits Only Jude (IRE)**[52] 7003 5-8-11 **52** J-PGuillambert 2 82
(P A Blockley) *sn trcking ldrs: hdwy to chse ldr 4f out: led on bit 1 1/2f out: sn clr: easily* **4/1**[1]
00-5 **2** *10* **Trinculo (IRE)**[18] 41 11-9-0 **55** (b) TGMcLaughlin 3 53
(R A Harris) *led: rdn along over 2f out: hdd 1 1/2f out: kpt on same pce* **12/1**
0-46 **3** *3* **Soba Jones**[12] 109 11-8-8 **49** DavidAllan 6 37
(J Balding) *in tch: hdwy on outer over 2f out: sn rdn and styd on ins fnl f* **11/1**
40-0 **4** 1 1/4 **Favouring (IRE)**[7] 168 6-7-12 **46** oh1 (v) PatrickDonaghy(7) 7 30
(M C Chapman) *chsd ldrs: rdn along 3f out: drvn and one pce over 2f out* **28/1**
-022 **5** 3/4 **Kingsmaite**[2] 236 7-8-2 **46** oh1 (v) DuranFentiman(3) 1 28
(S R Bowring) *prom: rdn along over 2f out: sn drvn and grad wknd* **13/2**[3]
02-4 **6** 1/2 **Blakeshall Quest**[14] 82 8-8-2 **46** oh1 (b) AndrewMullen(3) 14 26
(R Brotherton) *prom: rdn along over 2f out and sn one pce* **22/1**
03-3 **7** 1 1/4 **Shava**[14] 79 8-7-12 **46** oh1 DeclanCannon(7) 5 22
(H J Evans) *chsd ldrs: rdn along over 2f out: grad wknd* **13/2**[3]
1-65 **8** 3/4 **Van Ruymbeke (IRE)**[14] 82 4-8-7 **48** (t) LiamJones 8 22
(D J Murphy) *nvr bttr than midfield* **17/2**
00-5 **9** 1 1/4 **Piccolo Prince**[7] 167 7-8-5 **46** oh1 FrancisNorton 13 16
(Mrs Marjorie Fife) *nvr bttr than midfield* **33/1**
5320 **10** 3/4 **Phinerine**[7] 168 5-8-8 **52** (p) TolleyDean(3) 9 20
(Miss J E Foster) *towards rr: effrt and sme hdwy 3f out: sn rdn and wknd* **16/1**
1-11 **11** *nk* **Epidaurian King (IRE)**[9] 151 5-9-3 **58** 6ex (v) DeanMcKeown 10 25
(D Shaw) *dwlt: a towards rr* **9/2**[2]
20-0 **12** *3* **Royal Guest**[7] 161 4-8-9 **50** ChrisCatlin 4 7
(J R Jenkins) *s.i.s: a in rr* **33/1**
06-4 **13** *9* **Imperial Sword**[12] 109 5-8-11 **52** (b) PaulFessey 12 —
(T D Barron) *dwlt: a towards rr* **8/1**

1m 14.96s (-1.54) **Going Correction** -0.10s/f (Stan) **13** Ran SP% **122.1**
Speed ratings (Par 101): **106,92,88,87,86 85,83,82,81,80 79,75,63**
CSF £51.79 CT £497.15 TOTE £5.70: £2.70, £4.20, £2.70; EX 95.50 TRIFECTA Not won..
Owner Lynne Whiting & Judith Kell Stone **Bred** Swordlestown Stud **Trained** Lambourn, Berks

FOCUS
A decent winning time for a race of its class and the easy winner rates value for even further than his wide-winning margin. It is very difficult to know exactly what he achieved but he is rated back to his old form.
Epidaurian King(IRE) Official explanation: jockey said gelding didn't handle the surface

257 SOUTHWELL-RACECOURSE.CO.UK (S) STKS 7f (F)
1:30 (1:30) (Class 6) 3-Y-O **£1,774** (£523; £262) **Stalls** Low

Form RPR
1 **So Sublime** 3-9-0 0 ChrisCatlin 3 69+
(E J O'Neill) *cl up: rdn over 2f out: led 1 1/2f out: sn drvn and kpt on ins fnl f* **2/1**[2]
232- **2** 1 1/4 **What's For Tea**[32] 7210 3-9-0 62 RichardKingscote 1 66
(Tom Dascombe) *trckd ldrs: hdwy over 2f out: sn rdn: drvn and kpt on ins fnl f: nt rch wnr* **11/8**[1]
0-53 **3** *5* **Don Picolo**[3] 222 3-9-0 44 (e[1]) FrankieMcDonald 7 52
(P A Blockley) *in rr: pushed along and hdwy over 2f out: sn rdn and styd on ins fnl f: nrst fin* **25/1**
055- **4** *shd* **Carnival Dream**[24] 7270 3-8-9 55 TGMcLaughlin 8 47
(R A Harris) *hld up in tch: hdwy over 2f out: sn rdn and kpt on ins fnl f: nrst fin* **12/1**
443- **5** *hd* **Wee Buns**[31] 7220 3-9-0 62 LPKeniry 9 51
(S Kirk) *led: rdn along wl over 2f out: hdd 1 1/2f out: sn drvn and wknd ins fnl f* **13/2**[3]
60-U **6** *4* **Sir Joey**[12] 108 3-9-0 48 (p) StephenDonohoe 4 40
(J T Stimpson) *in tch: rdn along 1/2-way: sn wknd* **50/1**
0- **7** *4* **Arkando (IRE)**[174] 4076 3-8-9 0 FergusSweeney 6 25
(K R Burke) *chsd ldrs: rdn along wl over 2f out: sn wknd* **9/1**
00-0 **8** *35* **Jazz Romance (IRE)**[10] 141 3-8-6 34 (v[1]) TolleyDean(3) 5 —
(D Shaw) *s.i.s: a outpcd and bhd* **150/1**

1m 30.97s (0.67) **Going Correction** -0.10s/f (Stan) **8** Ran SP% **112.9**
Speed ratings (Par 95): **92,90,84,84,84 79,75,35**
CSF £4.93 TOTE £3.40: £1.30, £1.10, £3.60; EX 6.50 Trifecta £105.60 Pool: £485.04, 3.26 winning units.The winner was sold to M C Chapman for 6,000gns. What's For Tea was the subject of a friendly claim.
Owner J C Fretwell **Bred** Red House Stud **Trained** Averham Park, Notts

FOCUS
A typically uncompetitive seller and ordinary form for the grade. The first pair came clear of the third, who holds down the form a little.
Don Picolo Official explanation: jockey said colt did not face the kickback

258 BOOK NOW @ PONTINS.COM H'CAP 1m (F)
2:00 (2:01) (Class 6) (0-65,64) 4-Y-O+ **£1,911** (£564; £282) **Stalls** Low

Form RPR
1-13 **1** **Haroldini (IRE)**[5] 190 6-9-1 64 (p) TolleyDean(3) 8 75
(J Balding) *hld up in tch: hdwy 3f out: rdn to chse ldr over 1f out: styd on ins fnl f to ld last 100yds* **7/2**[2]
13-3 **2** 1/2 **Faithful Ruler (USA)**[9] 149 4-9-2 62 FergusSweeney 5 72
(M A Magnusson) *trckd ldrs gng wl: smooth hdwy to chal over 2f out: shkn up to ld 1 1/2f out: sn rdn and hung lft: drvn ins fnl f: hdd and no ex last 100yds* **5/2**[1]
030- **3** *4* **Red Contact (USA)**[32] 7213 7-9-1 61 (b) PaulFessey 3 62
(A Dickman) *sn led: rdn along over 2f out: hdd 1 1/2f out: sn drvn and kpt on same pce* **8/1**[3]
04-1 **4** 1/2 **Montemayorprincess (IRE)**[21] 7 4-8-6 52 (p) HayleyTurner 6 52
(D Haydn Jones) *prom: effrt to chal over 2f out and ev ch tl rdn and one pce fr over 1f out* **7/2**[2]

255- **5** 1 ½ **Tour D'Amour (IRE)**[111] 5907 5-8-7 58 .... KellyHarrison(5) 7 54
(R Craggs) *chsd ldrs: pushed along 3f out: sn rdn and no imp fnl 2f* **16/1**

12-5 **6** ½ **Only A Grand**[21] 7 4-8-7 53 .... (b) SaleemGolam 10 48
(R Bastiman) *prom: rdn along wl over 2f out: sn one pce* **10/1**

460- **7** 11 **Mick Is Back**[48] 7028 4-8-10 56 .... (p) J-PGuillambert 2 26
(G G Margarson) *prom on inner: rdn along 1/2-way and sn wknd* **16/1**

064- **8** 5 **El Coto**[63] 6882 8-9-1 61 .... (p) ChrisCatlin 9 19
(J R Holt) *a towards rr* **14/1**

0/0- **9** 2 **Zendaro**[142] 4433 6-8-10 56 .... MickyFenton 4 10
(C C Bealby) *a outpcd in rr* **40/1**

1m 42.84s (-0.86) **Going Correction** -0.10s/f (Stan) **9** Ran SP% **114.1**
Speed ratings (Par 101): **100,99,95,95,93 93,82,77,75**
CSF £12.49 CT £63.85 TOTE £4.70: £1.50, £1.30, £1.80; EX 14.70 Trifecta £200.80 Pool: £687.39, 2.4.3 winning units.
Owner Tykes And Terriers Racing Club **Bred** Michael O'Mahony **Trained** Scrooby, Notts

FOCUS
A modest handicap, but two progressive sorts came clear and the form seems sound.
Mick Is Back Official explanation: jockey said gelding did not face the kickback

259 GET AWAY TO PONTIN'S H'CAP 7f (F)
2:30 (2:31) (Class 2) (0-100,97) 4-Y-0+ **£10,525** (£3,131; £1,564; £781) **Stalls** Low

Form RPR

14-2 **1** **Kabeer**[21] 6 10-8-1 85 .... (t) NataliaGemelova(5) 4 98
(A J McCabe) *cl up: rdn to ld wl over 1f out: drvn ent fnl f and kpt on wl* **5/1**[2]

003- **2** 1 ¾ **Evens And Odds (IRE)**[31] 7223 4-9-1 94 .... (b) JimmyQuinn 6 102
(K A Ryan) *tk keen f: sn led: rdn along 2f out: sn hdd: drvn and kpt on fnl f* **8/1**

5-41 **3** 2 ½ **Electric Warrior (IRE)**[17] 53 5-8-7 86 .... FergusSweeney 7 87
(K R Burke) *in tch: hdwy on outer over 2f out and sn rdn: drvn and no imp appr fnl f* **6/1**[3]

01-1 **4** nk **Red Romeo**[18] 43 7-8-7 86 .... MatthewHenry 3 86+
(N Wilson) *towards rr and pushed along 1/2-way: hdwy 2f out: kpt on u.p appr last: nrst fin* **7/1**

3-31 **5** 3 **Will He Wish**[4] 218 12-8-5 89 6ex ow2 .... (b) JamieJones(5) 5 81
(S Gollings) *chsd ldrs: rdn along over 2f out: grad wknd* **25/1**

02-1 **6** 5 **Bonnie Prince Blue**[14] 85 5-8-6 85 .... (b) ChrisCatlin 2 64
(B W Hills) *sn rdn along: a in rr* **11/10**[1]

000- **7** 6 **Lucky Kyllachy (USA)**[179] 3931 4-9-4 97 .... SebSanders 1 60
(Jane Chapple-Hyam) *chsd ldrs on inner: rdn along 3f out and sn wknd* **11/1**

400- **8** 2 ½ **Jamieson Gold (IRE)**[95] 6301 5-8-8 87 ow1 .... TomEaves 8 43
(Miss L A Perratt) *in tch: rdn along 1/2-way: sn wknd* **20/1**

1m 27.6s (-2.70) **Going Correction** -0.10s/f (Stan) **8** Ran SP% **119.1**
Speed ratings (Par 109): **111,109,106,105,102 96,89,86**
CSF £46.06 CT £249.06 TOTE £7.20: £1.50, £1.90, £1.70; EX 70.30 Trifecta £180.30 Pool: £736.61, 2.90 winning units.
Owner Placida Racing **Bred** Shadwell Estate Company **Trained** Babworth, Notts

FOCUS
Even with the hot favourite running a shocker, this was a decent contest and the pace was very strong with the front pair dominating from the start. The form is rock solid.

NOTEBOOK
Kabeer and Natalia Gemelova provide an extraordinary sight, the gelding a great brute of a horse whilst his rider is tiny, but the pair have proved a most effective combination this winter as this was their third success from five outings as a team since the middle of last month, and their fourth overall. Now 8lb higher than for his last win, he was unable to lead thanks to the positive ride given to Evens And Odds and he did show his strange head-carriage once in front, but apart from that it was all plain sailing and he always looked like getting the better of the runner-up. He may be ten years old now and can expect another rise for this which will make opportunities harder to find, but his liking for this surface will always make him a potent rival if races can be found. (op 6-1 tchd 13-2, tchd 7-1 in a place)
Evens And Odds(IRE) was trying Fibresand for the first time, a surface which always looked likely to suit his attacking style if he took to it, and he was duly allowed to stride on. Racing with his usual zest, he earned himself plenty of credit with the way he battled back against a proven course specialist after being headed, and it was only well inside the last furlong that he had to admit defeat. He can win on this surface if a race can be found, but he has remained stubbornly rooted to his current mark for a few runs now and this performance will hardly encourage the Handicapper to drop him. (op 9-1 tchd 10-1)
Electric Warrior(IRE), back in a handicap after making the most of a penalty kick in a Kempton claimer, had finished over a length behind Kabeer here in his previous outing, but was no better off at the weights. Always in about the same place, he had every chance and although he was beaten further by his old rival this time, he probably still ran his race. (op 7-1)
Red Romeo, up 4lb in his bid for a hat-trick, usually likes to race up with the pace but he struggled to lay up this time and although he tried to get into the race up the inside after turning in, was never able to get to the leaders. (op 8-1)
Will He Wish, carrying a 6lb penalty for his recent Wolverhampton win plus another 2lb overweight, was close enough early but was in trouble as soon as the field straightened up for home. In order to win off this mark he would need to be better than he has ever been at the age of 12. (op 22-1)
Bonnie Prince Blue was 8lb higher than when bolting up here a fortnight earlier, but although he was over an extra furlong here he has enough form over this trip for that not to have been the reason for this dismal effort. He seemed to be hating it from the start, refusing to face the kickback, and never remotely looked like getting involved. Official explanation: trainer said gelding never travelled (op 5-4)

260 PONTIN'S GREAT FUN, GREAT TIMES H'CAP 1m 4f (F)
3:00 (3:00) (Class 4) (0-85,81) 4-Y-0+ **£4,210** (£1,252; £625; £312) **Stalls** Low

Form RPR

013- **1** **Maslak (IRE)**[26] 7242 4-8-8 71 .... LPKeniry 11 94+
(P W Hiatt) *a cl up: led over 4f out: rdn 2f out: clr appr fnl f: styd on wl* **20/1**

2-51 **2** 5 **Calculating (IRE)**[12] 107 4-8-9 72 .... HayleyTurner 2 85
(M D I Usher) *trckd ldrs: hdwy 3f out: rdn 2f out: drvn and styd on ins fnl f: no ch w wnr* **10/1**[3]

11-2 **3** 1 ¼ **Bentley Brook (IRE)**[8] 159 6-8-2 68 oh1 ow1 .... GabrielHannon(7) 9 79
(P A Blockley) *in tch: hdwy 4f out: rdn to chse wnr wl over 1f out: drvn and one pce ent fnl f* **11/1**

13-1 **4** 4 **Noble Plum (IRE)**[8] 159 4-9-2 79 6ex .... SebSanders 6 84
(Sir Mark Prescott) *hld up towards rr: hdwy over 4f out: rdn to chse ldrs wl over 2f out: sn drvn and btn wl over 1f out* **4/7**[1]

22-5 **5** 1 ¾ **Pass The Port**[13] 96 7-9-8 81 .... RobertHavlin 8 83
(D Haydn Jones) *hld up in midfield: hdwy 4f out: rdn along wl over 2f out: sn no imp* **17/2**[2]

0 **6** 1 ¼ **Trachonitis (IRE)**[13] 96 4-8-13 76 .... J-PGuillambert 5 75
(J R Jenkins) *t.k.h: chsd ldrs: rdn along 3f out: wknd over 2f out* **66/1**

22-1 **7** ½ **Three Boars**[14] 78 6-8-12 76 .... (b) JamieJones(5) 10 74
(S Gollings) *a towards rr* **12/1**

312- **8** 5 **Kylkenny**[26] 7242 13-9-1 77 .... (t) TravisBlock(3) 1 67
(H Morrison) *sn led: rdn along and hdd over 4f out: sn wknd* **18/1**

1 **9** 3 ½ **Kanisorn (SWE)**[14] 83 6-9-4 77 .... (b) LiamJones 3 62
(D W Chapman) *s.i.s: a in rr* **33/1**

1-23 **10** 3 ½ **Victory Quest (IRE)**[8] 159 8-8-11 70 .... (v) ChrisCatlin 4 49
(Mrs S Lamyman) *chsd ldrs: rdn along over 5f out and sn wknd* **28/1**

100- **11** 14 **Turn Of Phrase (IRE)**[27] 6759 9-9-2 75 .... (b) MatthewHenry 7 32
(N Wilson) *hld up: a in rr: bhd fnl 3f* **50/1**

2m 36.67s (-4.33) **Going Correction** -0.10s/f (Stan)
WFA 4 from 6yo+ 4lb **11** Ran SP% **119.2**
Speed ratings (Par 105): **110,106,105,103,102 100,100,97,94,92 83**
CSF £199.86 CT £2325.29 TOTE £24.50: £5.80, £3.10, £3.20; EX 135.40 Trifecta £691.40 Part won. Pool: £973.85 - 0.10 winning units..
Owner Clive Roberts **Bred** Shadwell Estate Company Limited **Trained** Hook Norton, Oxon

FOCUS
A competitive handicap run at a solid pace resulting in a decent winning time for a race of its class. This was another contest where it paid to be handy. Improved form from the winner.
Noble Plum(IRE) Official explanation: trainer had no explanation for the poor form shown

261 RACE TO PONTIN'S FOR HALF TERM MAIDEN STKS 6f (F)
3:30 (3:33) (Class 5) 3-Y-0+ **£2,457** (£725; £362) **Stalls** Low

Form RPR

5 **1** **Helping Hand (IRE)**[15] 74 3-8-11 0 .... HayleyTurner 4 67
(R Hollinshead) *cl up: led after 2f: rdn 2f out: drvn ins fnl f: hld on gamely* **5/1**[3]

4 **2** nk **Kirkie (USA)**[8] 158 3-8-11 0 .... FrancisNorton 1 66
(D J Murphy) *dwlt and sn pushed along in rr: hdwy on inner wl over 2f out: rdn to chse ldng pair over 1f out: styd on wl u.p ins fnl f* **12/1**

243- **3** shd **Town And Gown**[59] 6926 3-8-6 71 .... RobertHavlin 2 61
(J H M Gosden) *trckd ldrs: hdwy to chal 2f out: sn rdn and ev ch tl drvn and no ex wl ins fnl f* **10/11**[1]

4 3 **Boss Hog** 3-8-11 0 .... FrankieMcDonald 7 57+
(P A Blockley) *dwlt: hld up in rr: hdwy over 2f out: swtchd lft and rdn over 1f out: styd on ins fnl f: nrst fin* **16/1**

222- **5** 1 ¾ **Molly Ann (IRE)**[22] 7288 3-8-6 67 .... PaulEddery 8 47
(T D Easterby) *chsd ldrs: effrt over 2f out and sn rdn: drvn and wknd over 1f out* **11/4**[2]

000- **6** 7 **Red Barnet**[81] 6627 4-9-13 43 .... LiamJones 10 31
(S W Hall) *a in rr* **66/1**

0 **7** ½ **Marquis De Louvois (IRE)**[9] 146 3-8-8 0 .... AndrewMullen(3) 9 29
(Mrs A Duffield) *chsd ldrs: rdn along 3f out: grad wknd* **25/1**

50/ **8** 8 **Miss Double Daisy**[420] 6649 5-9-8 0 .... TomEaves 5 —
(B Smart) *led 2f: cl up tl rdn and wknd wl over 2f out* **66/1**

1m 16.48s (-0.02) **Going Correction** -0.10s/f (Stan)
WFA 3 from 4yo+ 16lb **8** Ran SP% **116.1**
Speed ratings (Par 103): **96,95,95,91,89 79,79,68**
CSF £60.41 TOTE £7.40: £1.80, £2.50, £1.10; EX 39.50 Trifecta £267.00 Pool: £1,105.71, 2.94 winning units.
Owner N Chapman **Bred** P F Mulholland **Trained** Upper Longdon, Staffs

FOCUS
A modest sprint maiden. Not easy to assess, with doubts over the third and fifth.
Boss Hog Official explanation: jockey said noseband came undone

262 COME JUMP RACING HERE ON SUNDAY H'CAP 1m (F)
4:00 (4:01) (Class 6) (0-60,59) 3-Y-O **£1,911** (£564; £282) **Stalls** Low

Form RPR

00-6 **1** **Magical Song**[10] 141 3-8-7 48 .... GregFairley 8 49
(P A Blockley) *chsd ldrs on outer: hdwy 2f out and sn rdn: drvn to ld ent fnl f: kpt on gamely* **11/4**[1]

633- **2** ½ **Little Firecracker**[25] 7259 3-9-3 58 .... AdamKirby 6 58
(Miss M E Rowland) *mde most tl rdn: edgd lft ent fnl f and sn hdd: no ex nr fin* **4/1**[2]

004- **3** shd **Ten Spot (IRE)**[33] 7204 3-8-10 51 .... (v) MickyFenton 7 51
(Stef Liddiard) *cl up: rdn and ev ch 2f out: drvn and n.m.r appr fnl f: swtchd rt and kpt on ins fnl f* **15/2**

242- **4** 1 **Sunshine Lady (IRE)**[27] 7234 3-9-4 59 .... RobertHavlin 3 57
(D Haydn Jones) *a cl up on inner: rdn 2f out and ev ch tl drvn and one pce ent fnl f* **9/2**[3]

3-64 **5** shd **Silver Sprite**[8] 157 3-8-13 54 .... DeanMcKeown 4 53+
(D Shaw) *hld up in tch: hdwy whn n.m.r wl over 1f out: effrt and styng on whn nt clr run ent fnl f: nt rcvr* **5/1**

65-0 **6** 1 **Miss Tilen**[10] 141 3-8-7 51 .... JerryO'Dwyer(3) 5 46
(V Smith) *chsd ldrs: pushed along 3f out: sn rdn and n.m.r over 1f out: kpt on same pce* **16/1**

000- **7** 4 **Paul The Carpet (UAE)**[137] 5186 3-8-9 50 .... SimonWhitworth 2 36
(G L Moore) *a in rr* **10/1**

060- **8** 34 **Fu Wa (USA)**[117] 5751 3-9-3 58 .... DaleGibson 1 —
(M W Easterby) *t.k.h: chsd ldrs on inner tl rdn along 3f out and sn wknd* **28/1**

1m 44.32s (0.62) **Going Correction** -0.10s/f (Stan) **8** Ran SP% **111.7**
Speed ratings (Par 95): **92,91,91,90,90 89,85,51**
CSF £13.05 CT £69.12 TOTE £3.70: £1.50, £1.90, £3.00; EX 16.00 Trifecta £126.30 Pool: £964.58 - 5.42 winning units. Place 6 £ 110.28, Place 5 £ 37.97.
Owner The Classical Syndicate **Bred** Peter Balding **Trained** Lambourn, Berks

■ Stewards' Enquiry : Adam Kirby one-day ban: careless riding (Feb 2)

FOCUS
A very moderate handicap, but the form seems sound enough.
Magical Song ◆ Official explanation: trainer said, regarding the improved form shown, colt had benefited from the slower surface
Fu Wa(USA) Official explanation: jockey said filly lost its action

T/Jkpt: Not won. T/Plt: £310.30 to a £1 stake. Pool: £125,875.15. 296.10 winning tickets. T/Qpdt: £51.40 to a £1 stake. Pool: £10,915.30. 157.10 winning tickets. JR

[242]KEMPTON (A.W) (R-H)

Wednesday, January 23

OFFICIAL GOING: Standard

Wind: Moderate across

263 DIGIBET SPORTS BETTING H'CAP — 5f (P)

6:20 (6:20) (Class 6) (0-58,57) 4-Y-0+ — £2,047 (£604; £302) Stalls High

Form — RPR

5323 **1** **Earl Compton (IRE)**[11] 142 4-8-11 **52**........................(v) MickyFenton 7 60
(Stef Liddiard) *t.k.h: hld up in tch: str run u.p fnl f to ld fnl 50yds* **8/1**

5-35 **2** ½ **Musical Script (USA)**[7] 181 5-9-2 **57**............................(p) ChrisCatlin 5 64
(Mouse Hamilton-Fairley) *chsd ldrs: rdn and one pce over 1f out: styd on strly ins fnl f: gng on cl home but nt rch wnr* **3/1**[2]

30-2 **3** hd **Minnow**[14] 86 4-8-4 **52**..(p) WilliamCarson(7) 8 58
(S C Williams) *chsd ldr: rdn 2f out: no ex u.p ins fnl f* **5/2**[1]

44-1 **4** ½ **Sir Loin**[14] 86 7-8-2 **50**...(v) RossAtkinson(7) 4 54
(P Burgoyne) *sn led: rdn over 1f out: hdd and one pce fnl 50yds* **4/1**[3]

00-6 **5** nk **Racing Stripes (IRE)**[5] 211 4-8-10 **54**...................(b) NeilChalmers(3) 3 57
(K O Cunningham-Brown) *slowly away: bhd: rdn 2f out: hdwy fnl f: kpt on but nt rch ldrs* **14/1**

0-50 **6** ¾ **Thoughtsofstardom**[18] 54 5-9-0 **55**............................ TGMcLaughlin 1 55
(M Wigham) *chsd ldrs: rdn 2f out: one pce ins fnl f* **11/2**

05-5 **7** 6 **Ishibee (IRE)**[21] 13 4-8-10 **54**.......................................(p) TolleyDean(3) 6 33
(J J Bridger) *in rr: wd bnd 3f out: a bhd* **11/1**

60.48 secs (-0.02) **Going Correction** +0.075s/f (Slow) — **7** Ran SP% **115.1**

Speed ratings (Par 101): **103,102,101,101,100 99,89**

CSF £32.60 CT £78.09 TOTE £7.10: £3.00, £1.90; EX 32.70.

Owner Mrs Stef Liddiard **Bred** Deepwood Farm Stud **Trained** Great Shefford, Berks

FOCUS

A very low-grade affair run at a fair pace. The form seems solid enough but may not be worth following due to the questionable attitude of a few in the race.

Racing Stripes(IRE) Official explanation: jockey said gelding missed the break

264 FRANK EWINS MEMORIAL CLASSIFIED STKS — 6f (P)

6:50 (6:50) (Class 7) 4-Y-0+ — £1,365 (£403; £201) Stalls High

Form — RPR

60-2 **1** **Avoca Dancer (IRE)**[7] 174 5-9-0 45.............................. NickyMackay 9 56+
(M Wigham) *chsd ldrs: drvn to ld 1f out: styd on u.p thrght fnl f* **15/8**[1]

-052 **2** 1¼ **Mr Loire**[2] 255 4-9-0 45...(b) DeanMcKeown 1 52
(A J Chamberlain) *slowly away and swtchd to ins rail: hdwy on ins and n.m.r 2f out: str run to chse wnr ins fnl f but a hld* **9/1**

0-31 **3** ¾ **Double Valentine**[7] 174 5-9-1 45.......................... JackMitchell(5) 7 56+
(R Ingram) *in rr: rdn and hdwy over 1f out: str run fnl f and fin wl but nt rch ldrs* **3/1**[2]

43-5 **4** shd **Lawdy Miss Clawdy**[11] 142 4-9-0 42.......................... FergusSweeney 5 49
(D W P Arbuthnot) *chsd ldrs: rdn to ld 2f: hdd 1f out and sn one pce* **7/1**[3]

60-6 **5** nk **Piccostar**[12] 121 5-9-0 45.. SamHitchcott 2 48
(A B Haynes) *in rr: hdwy over 2f out: styd on u.p ins fnl f but nt rch ldrs* **20/1**

006- **6** 1¼ **Coastal Breeze**[38] 7167 5-9-0 43...............................(b) FrancisNorton 3 44
(A J Chamberlain) *in rr: rdn and sme hdwy fr 2f out: nt rch ldrs and one pce ins fnl f* **50/1**

00-0 **7** 2 **Edin Burgher (FR)**[15] 82 7-9-0 40........................(v) TGMcLaughlin 11 38
(T T Clement) *chsd ldr: rdn 2f out: wknd 1f out* **20/1**

4-00 **8** 1 **Royal Orissa**[10] 147 6-9-0 41...................................... HayleyTurner 4 35
(D Haydn Jones) *wd bnd 3f out: a towards rr* **14/1**

000- **9** 1 **Royal Senga**[142] 5090 5-9-0 45............................... SimonWhitworth 10 32
(C A Horgan) *a towards rr* **25/1**

00-0 **10** 1¼ **Prettilini**[19] 42 5-9-0 45... JimCrowley 8 28
(A W Carroll) *led tl hdd 2f out: sn wknd* **8/1**

1m 13.45s (0.35) **Going Correction** +0.075s/f (Slow) — **10** Ran SP% **115.4**

Speed ratings (Par 97): **100,98,97,97,96 95,92,91,89,88**

CSF £18.40 TOTE £2.70: £1.10, £2.30, £2.00; EX 20.00.

Owner Have A Go Syndicate & Michael Wigham **Bred** Frank Towey **Trained** Newmarket, Suffolk

■ Stewards' Enquiry : Nicky Mackay two-day ban: used whip with excessive frequency in an incorrect position (Feb 3-4)

FOCUS

This was probably a bit better than average for the lowly grade. The winner is up 5lb on her latest form.

Coastal Breeze Official explanation: jockey said gelding hung right

265 DIGIBET MAIDEN STKS — 7f (P)

7:20 (7:20) (Class 5) 3-Y-0+ — £2,730 (£806; £403) Stalls High

Form — RPR

44- **1** **Baron's Court**[33] 7217 3-8-9 0.................................... GregFairley 7 77
(M Johnston) *led: hdd 2f out: drvn to stay pressing ldr and forged ahd again fnl 75yds* **11/2**

234- **2** 1 **Tension Mounts (IRE)**[124] 5605 3-8-9 75........................ TPQueally 11 74
(J A Osborne) *chsd ldrs: rdn to ld 2f out: sn hung lft u.p: hrd drvn ins fnl f: hdd and one pce fnl 75yds* **7/2**[2]

2- **3** 1½ **Georgie The Fourth (IRE)**[203] 3213 3-8-4 0.................. ChrisCatlin 1 65
(E J O'Neill) *chsd ldrs: rdn over 2f out: styd on u.p fnl f but nvr gng pce to rch ldng duo* **7/4**[1]

6 **4** 3 **Eagle Nebula**[11] 134 4-9-13 0...................................... DaneO'Neill 14 67
(B R Johnson) *in tch: rdn and hdwy to chse ldrs over 2f out: kpt on same pce ins fnl f* **50/1**

00- **5** 1¾ **Mileaminutemurphy**[167] 4316 3-8-9 0......................... FrancisNorton 6 57
(R Hannon) *chsd ldrs: drvn over 2f out and styd on same pce* **33/1**

6 1¼ **Brave Hawk** 3-8-9 0.. MatthewHenry 8 54+
(M A Jarvis) *in rr: hdwy and nt clr run 2f out: shkn up and styd on fr over 1f out but nvr gng pce to be competitive* **10/1**

7 ¾ **Minerton Mountain** 3-8-9 0...................................... SimonWhitworth 2 52
(B R Millman) *in rr: hdwy fr 3f out: nvr gng pce to rch ldrs and one pce fr over 1f out* **33/1**

8 ½ **Film Queen (IRE)** 4-9-1 0....................................... KylieManser(7) 13 51+
(B G Powell) *in rr: stl plenty to do 2f out: styd on steadily fnl f nvr in contention* **33/1**

00 **9** ¾ **Ultimate Quest (IRE)**[7] 175 3-8-11 0 ow2........................ SebSanders 3 51+
(Sir Mark Prescott) *in rr: shkn up over 2f out and nvr in contention* **33/1**

60-3 **10** ½ **Cavalry Guard (USA)**[7] 175 4-9-13 70....................... FergusSweeney 5 52
(J R Boyle) *in tch: rdn and effrt 3f out: wknd 2f out* **9/2**[3]

000- **11** 1½ **Herrbee (IRE)**[146] 4963 3-8-9 56.................................... PaulDoe 10 43
(S Dow) *chsd ldrs tl wknd over 2f out* **33/1**

12 hd **Flying Seasons** 3-8-9 0.. RobertHavlin 4 43+
(B R Millman) *s.i.s: hdwy 3f out: rdn: hung rt and wknd 2f out* **33/1**

00- **13** 3½ **Hula Hula**[76] 6734 3-8-4 0... PaulEddery 12 28
(Miss D Mountain) *a in rr* **80/1**

14 13 **Camera Shy (IRE)** 4-9-13 0... JimmyQuinn 9 —
(K A Morgan) *slowly away: a wl bhd* **33/1**

1m 26.62s (0.62) **Going Correction** +0.075s/f (Slow)

WFA 3 from 4yo 18lb — **14** Ran SP% **125.0**

Speed ratings (Par 103): **99,97,96,92,90 89,88,87,87,86 84,84,80,65**

CSF £24.12 TOTE £6.30: £2.30, £1.40, £1.20; EX 25.10.

Owner Sheikh Hamdan Bin Mohammed Al Maktoum **Bred** Darley **Trained** Middleham Moor, N Yorks

FOCUS

A fair-looking maiden with quite a few eyecatching performances. Not an easy race to assess, with the runner-up perhaps the most solid guide.

Camera Shy(IRE) Official explanation: jockey said colt missed the break

266 DIGIBET.COM CLAIMING STKS — 1m (P)

7:50 (7:50) (Class 6) 3-Y-0 — £2,047 (£604; £302) Stalls High

Form — RPR

41-4 **1** **Bridge Of Fermoy (IRE)**[21] 12 3-9-5 65...............(vt[1]) MickyFenton 1 71
(Miss Gay Kelleway) *trckd ldr over 5f out: rdn over 2f out: led jst ins fnl f: pushed out* **11/4**[2]

403- **2** 1½ **Coole Dodger (IRE)**[49] 7030 3-8-9 66.......................... KylieManser(7) 4 65
(B G Powell) *led after 1f: shkn up 2f out: hdd jst ins fnl f: styd on same pce* **7/1**

2-11 **3** ¾ **Home**[9] 156 3-9-5 72..(p) GeorgeBaker 3 66
(J R Boyle) *trckd ldrs: rdn and hung bdly rt over 2f out: styd on fr over 1f out but nvr gng pce to be competitive* **13/8**[1]

40-5 **4** 2 **Too Grand**[20] 23 3-8-4 55...(v) NeilChalmers(3) 2 50
(J J Bridger) *in rr: rdn and hung rt over 2f out: mod prog cl home* **15/2**

1-50 **5** 2 **Yamanmickmccann**[11] 136 3-9-0 75...............................(b[1]) DaneO'Neill 5 52
(R Hannon) *led 1f: rdn over 3f out: sn btn* **7/2**[3]

1m 41.05s (1.25) **Going Correction** +0.075s/f (Slow) — **5** Ran SP% **111.2**

Speed ratings (Par 95): **96,94,93,91,89**

CSF £20.63 TOTE £3.60: £1.50, £4.40; EX 25.10.

Owner T & Z Racing Club **Bred** Tally-Ho Stud **Trained** Exning, Suffolk

FOCUS

A weak claimer, but at least the pace was reasonable thanks to the positive ride given to Coole Dodger. The front pair dominated throughout and the winner has in theory improved, although this form is none too solid.

267 DIGIBET CASINO H'CAP — 1m (P)

8:20 (8:21) (Class 6) (0-52,56) 4-Y-0+ — £2,047 (£604; £302) Stalls High

Form — RPR

300- **1** **Milton's Keen**[17] 5348 5-8-11 **51**.................................. TGMcLaughlin 5 59
(M Salaman) *s.i.s: in rr: rapid hdwy on ins over 2f out: led appr fnl f: drvn out* **14/1**

04-2 **2** 1 **Jomus**[8] 164 7-8-8 **48**...[1] RobertHavlin 8 54
(L Montague Hall) *in rr: stl last over 2f out: sn rdn: hdwy over 1f out: str run ins fnl f to chse wnr cl home but a hld* **11/2**[3]

050- **3** shd **Shunkawakhan (IRE)**[27] 7244 5-8-7 **47**...................(p) SaleemGolam 9 52
(G C H Chung) *t.k.h: chsd ldrs: rdn 2f out: styd on wl fnl f to press for 2nd but a hld by wnr* **8/1**

000- **4** 1 **Hey Presto**[35] 7186 8-8-6 **46** oh1.................................. HayleyTurner 7 49
(R Rowe) *slt ld tl hdd over 4f out: led again 2f out: hdd appr fnl f: one pce ins fnl f* **25/1**

40-4 **5** nk **Postmaster**[12] 123 6-8-7 **52**.. JackMitchell(5) 4 54
(R Ingram) *in rr: rdn over 2f out: hdwy over 1f out: kpt on same pce ins fnl f* **4/1**[2]

00-1 **6** ¾ **Certifiable**[8] 164 7-8-8 **53** 6ex.................................. RobynBrisland(5) 6 54
(Miss Z C Davison) *chsd ldrs: rdn over 2f out: outpcd ins fnl f* **7/1**

-062 **7** 2 **Wizby**[12] 120 5-8-6 **46** oh1... JimmyQuinn 2 42
(P D Evans) *chsd ldrs: rdn 3f out: wknd 2f out* **14/1**

02-1 **8** 2½ **Takaamul**[5] 209 5-8-9 **56** 6ex.................................. PatrickDonaghy(7) 1 46
(K A Morgan) *w ldr: led over 4f out: hdd 2f out: wknd qckly* **15/8**[1]

03-6 **9** 2 **Trickle (USA)**[8] 164 4-8-8 **48**.....................................(t) PaulEddery 3 34
(Miss D Mountain) *chsd ldrs early: bhd fnl 3f* **25/1**

1m 41.31s (1.51) **Going Correction** +0.075s/f (Slow) — **9** Ran SP% **114.8**

Speed ratings (Par 101): **95,94,93,92,92 91,89,87,85**

CSF £88.38 CT £665.03 TOTE £14.30: £3.60, £1.60, £3.10; EX 113.20.

Owner Oaktree Racing **Bred** Henry And Mrs Rosemary Moszkowicz **Trained** Baydon, Wilts

FOCUS

They went no pace early which resulted in a modest winning time, 0.26 seconds slower than the preceding three-year-old claimer. Despite that, those that were held up fared best with the front pair occupying the last two places turning for home. The form means nothing though, with an habitual loser and a 32-raced maiden occupying the places.

Takaamul Official explanation: vet said gelding lost a hind shoe

268 SERVASSURE H'CAP — 2m (P)

8:50 (8:50) (Class 4) (0-85,85) 4-Y-0+ — £4,210 (£1,252; £625; £312) Stalls High

Form — RPR

5-41 **1** **Pocket Too**[6] 198 5-8-6 **66** 6ex oh1...........................(p) NeilChalmers(3) 8 74
(M Salaman) *chsd ldrs: str run on ins to ld appr fnl f: hld on all out* **9/1**

13-2 **2** nk **Jack Rolfe**[14] 105 6-9-7 **78**....................................... GeorgeBaker 5 85
(G L Moore) *in tch: hdwy 1/2-way: trckd ldr over 4f out: slt ld 3 out: rdn over 2f out: hdd appr fnl f: kpt on but a jst hld by wnr* **11/4**[2]

2/3- **3** 1 **Masked (IRE)**[35] 7194 7-9-7 **78**...................................(b[1]) SebSanders 6 84
(R M Beckett) *plld hrd in rr: stdy hdwy over 2f out: styd on u.p to chse ldrs fnl f but a hld* **10/3**[3]

00-3 **4** 4 **Pret A Porter (UAE)**[20] 27 4-8-6 **70**............................. JimmyQuinn 7 71
(P D Evans) *in rr: hdwy 3f out: drvn to chse ldrs ins fnl 2f: wknd fnl f* **15/2**

1-11 **5** 2 **Legend Erry (IRE)**[8] 169 4-9-4 **82** 6ex......................... TGMcLaughlin 1 81
(Jane Chapple-Hyam) *in tch: hdwy 4f out: rdn to chse ldrs 2f out: wknd over 1f out* **9/4**[1]

100- **6** 3 **Linden Lime**[89] 6473 6-8-13 **70**...................................... PaulDoe 2 65
(Jamie Poulton) *in tch: rdn to chse ldrs over 3f out: wknd fr 2f out* **14/1**

66-3 **7** 4 **Is It Me (USA)**[13] 118 5-8-9 **66** oh6................................ ChrisCatlin 4 56
(A W Carroll) *led tl hdd 1/2-way: wknd 3f out* **20/1**

0/0- **8** 21 **Dont Call Me Derek**[17] 1822 7-10-0 **85**............................ AmirQuinn 3 50
(M A Allen) *chsd ldr: led 1/2-way: hdd 3f out: wknd qckly* **25/1**

3m 28.87s (-1.23) **Going Correction** +0.075s/f (Slow)

WFA 4 from 5yo+ 7lb — **8** Ran SP% **117.6**

Speed ratings (Par 105): **106,105,105,103,102 100,98,88**

CSF £35.06 CT £102.27 TOTE £10.00: £2.70, £1.10, £1.60; EX 39.00.

Owner Oaktree Racing **Bred** M J Lewin **Trained** Baydon, Wilts

FOCUS
They did not seem to go a great pace early in this staying handicap, but they were certainly travelling over the last couple of furlongs and the winning time was perfectly respectable. This was another race where the winner raced closest to the inside rail in the closing stages. Ordinary form, but sound enough.

269 DIGIBET.COM CLASSIFIED STKS 1m 4f (P)
9:20 (9:22) (Class 7) 4-Y-O+ £1,365 (£403; £201) **Stalls** Centre

Form RPR

244- **1** **Tiegs (IRE)**[41] 5187 6-9-2 44........ ChrisCatlin 2 52
(P W Hiatt) *led tl hdd over 2f out: rallied to ld again appr fnl f: hld on all out* **9/2**[3]

406- **2** *nk* **Kilmeena Magic**[28] 6896 6-9-2 44........ PatDobbs 11 52
(J C Fox) *hld up in mid-div: gd hdwy fr 2f out: styd on to press wnr ins fnl f but a jst hld* **17/2**

00-4 **3** *1 3/4* **Tabulate**[16] 76 5-9-2 44........ JimmyQuinn 1 49
(P Howling) *chsd ldr: led over 2f out: sn rdn: hdd appr fnl f: lost 2nd ins fnl f and wknd nr fin* **5/1**

053- **4** *shd* **Missie Baileys**[46] 7069 6-9-2 45........(v) TGMcLaughlin 13 49
(Mrs L J Mongan) *mid-div: rdn and hdwy fr 2f out: kpt on fr over 1f out but nvr gng pce to rch ldrs* **7/2**[1]

54-0 **5** *1/2* **The Slider**[10] 152 4-8-12 43........ LPKeniry 6 48
(Mrs L C Jewell) *chsd ldrs: rdn and effrt over 2f out: wknd ins fnl f* **12/1**

0/0- **6** *nk* **Fantasy Legend (IRE)**[20] 5542 5-8-11 45........ JamieJones(5) 8 47
(A M Hales) *in rr: rdn and stl plenty to do over 2f out: r.o ins fnl f but nvr in contention* **10/1**

00-4 **7** *1/2* **Backlash**[12] 125 7-9-2 44........ JimCrowley 4 46
(A W Carroll) *in rr: rdn over 3f out: sme prog fnl 2f* **4/1**[2]

400/ **8** *nk* **Tetragon (IRE)**[303] 5925 8-8-9 45........ PatrickDonaghy(7) 3 46
(A M Hales) *chsd ldrs: rdn 4f out: nt a danger fnl 3f* **14/1**

000- **9** *1 1/4* **Compton Express**[38] 7166 5-9-2 45........ SimonWhitworth 9 44
(Jamie Poulton) *in rr: hdwy 3f out: sn rdn: nvr in contention* **20/1**

5-06 **10** *3/4* **Rhuby River (IRE)**[10] 147 6-9-2 42........ MickyFenton 12 43
(R Dickin) *chsd ldrs: rdn 3f out: wknd 2f out* **33/1**

00-0 **11** *6* **Not Too Taxing**[21] 10 4-8-12 43........(t) VinceSlattery 7 33
(G A Ham) *a in rr* **50/1**

50-0 **12** *9* **War Feather**[21] 8 6-9-2 41........(b) RobertHavlin 10 19
(T D McCarthy) *nvr bttr than mid-div: bhd fnl 4f* **25/1**

/0-0 **13** *63* **Italstar (IRE)**[8] 161 4-8-12 45........(bt[1]) SaleemGolam 5 —
(Miss D Mountain) *a in rr: t.o* **50/1**

2m 36.7s (2.20) **Going Correction** +0.075s/f (Slow)
WFA 4 from 5yo+ 4lb 13 Ran SP% **126.5**
Speed ratings (Par 97): **95,94,93,93,93 93,92,92,91,91 87,81,39**
CSF £43.06 TOTE £6.00: £2.40, £2.90, £2.50; EX 65.00 Place 6 £ 73.32, Place 5 £ 28.08.
Owner The Fox Inn Partnership **Bred** Paradime Ltd **Trained** Hook Norton, Oxon

FOCUS
A typically modest Class 7 classified (banded) event run at an ordinary pace and yet another race where the winner raced closest to the inside rail on the run to the line. Weak form, but it makes sense amongst the principals.
T/Plt: £102.70 to a £1 stake. Pool: £93,318.65. 663.05 winning tickets. T/Qpdt: £25.90 to a £1 stake. Pool: £6,357.90. 181.30 winning tickets. ST

221 LINGFIELD (L-H)
Wednesday, January 23

OFFICIAL GOING: Standard
Wind: strong behind Weather: overcast

270 HOTEL COMING TO LINGFIELD PARK AMATEUR RIDERS' H'CAP 6f (P)
1:20 (1:20) (Class 6) (0-65,60) 4-Y-O+ £1,813 (£557; £278) **Stalls** Low

Form RPR

0-42 **1** **Crimson Fern (IRE)**[7] 181 4-11-1 **54**........ MrSWalker 1 66+
(M S Saunders) *t.k.h: hld up in tch: hdwy wl over 1f out: shkn up to chal 1f out: led ins fnl f: wl in command nr fin* **15/8**[1]

6-12 **2** *1/2* **Savile's Delight (IRE)**[5] 206 9-10-9 **51** 6ex........ MissMSowerby(3) 4 61
(Tom Dascombe) *tk keen hold: sn led: jnd ent fnl f: rdn and hdd ins fnl f: one pce* **5/2**[2]

20-0 **3** *1 1/4* **Mulberry Lad (IRE)**[5] 211 6-10-11 **53**........ MrsMarieKing(3) 7 59
(P W Hiatt) *hld up in tch: hdwy on outer wl over 2f out: ev ch 2f out: kpt on same pce fnl f* **8/1**

0-14 **4** *1/2* **Arfinnit (IRE)**[8] 165 7-10-13 **59**........(p) MrOJMurphy(7) 2 63
(Mrs A L M King) *t.k.h: trckd ldrs: rdn and effrt wl over 1f out: kpt on same pce after* **8/1**

3-06 **5** *1 1/4* **Majestical (IRE)**[7] 181 6-10-8 **54**........(e) MissTStone(7) 3 54
(V Smith) *stdd s: bhd: hdwy and in tch over 2f out: outpcd and wd on bnd 2f out: kpt on fnl f: nvr pce to trble ldrs* **14/1**

4-04 **6** *3/4* **Desert Light (IRE)**[7] 181 7-11-2 **55**........(v) MrsMMorris 5 53
(D Shaw) *stdd after s: hld up in last pair: rdn and effrt wl over 1f out: no imp* **9/2**[3]

V3-0 **7** *2 1/2* **Strike Force**[10] 148 4-11-2 **60**........(p) MissALHutchinson(5) 6 50
(K F Clutterbuck) *t.k.h: chsd ldr tl over 2f out wknd over 1f out* **16/1**

1m 14.27s (2.37) **Going Correction** +0.20s/f (Slow) 7 Ran SP% **116.3**
Speed ratings (Par 101): **92,91,89,89,87 86,83**
CSF £7.00 TOTE £2.40: £1.30, £1.90; EX 6.50.
Owner M S Saunders **Bred** David Brickley **Trained** Green Ore, Somerset

FOCUS
A moderate handicap, confined to amateur riders. The early pace was most sedate which dictates the form is messy, but the winner still rates value for a bit further. The third is the best guide to the form.

271 BOOK PONTIN'S HALF TERM HAPPY DEALS MAIDEN STKS 6f (P)
1:50 (1:50) (Class 5) 3-Y-O £2,331 (£693; £346; £173) **Stalls** Low

Form RPR

56-3 **1** **Kingsgate Castle**[18] 60 3-9-3 71........ GeorgeBaker 7 67
(J R Best) *trckd ldrs on outer: shkn up to chal 2f out: rdn over 1f out: led ins fnl f: styd on* **4/6**[1]

0-4 **2** *1/2* **Jalons Bridewell**[10] 146 3-9-3 0........ TPQueally 4 65
(M Quinn) *t.k.h: sn led: hrd pressed and rdn 2f out: kpt on wl tl hdd and no ex ins fnl f* **7/2**[2]

04- **3** *1 1/4* **Jazenio**[33] 7216 3-8-9 0........ AndrewMullen(3) 2 56
(K A Ryan) *t.k.h: hld up bhd ldrs on inner: rdn and effrt wl over 1f out: kpt on fnl f: nt pce to rch ldrs* **16/1**

300- **4** *1/2* **Evenstorm (USA)**[24] 7280 3-8-12 62........ GregFairley 5 54
(B Gubby) *t.k.h: hld up wl in tch: rdn and hanging lft fr over 1f out: kpt on same pce fnl f* **9/2**[3]

5 *1* **Princess Livius (IRE)** 3-8-12 0........ FergusSweeney 3 51
(G L Moore) *short of room and dropped to last sn after s: rdn and no imp over 2f out: kpt on but nvr pce to chal ldrs* **20/1**

6 *1/2* **Szaba** 3-8-12 0........ HayleyTurner 6 50
(J M P Eustace) *pressed ldr tl over 2f out: sn rdn and outpcd: kpt on same pce fnl f* **20/1**

1m 13.36s (1.46) **Going Correction** +0.20s/f (Slow) 6 Ran SP% **115.8**
Speed ratings (Par 97): **98,97,95,95,93 93**
CSF £3.55 TOTE £1.70: £1.50, £1.70; EX 3.00.
Owner John Mayne **Bred** Broughton Bloodstock **Trained** Hucking, Kent

FOCUS
A very moderate three-year-old maiden, run at an average pace. The winner has been rated as running to form.

272 AHEAD WITH PONTIN'S GET AWAYS H'CAP 2m (P)
2:20 (2:21) (Class 5) (0-75,71) 4-Y-O+ £2,331 (£693; £346; £173) **Stalls** Low

Form RPR

30-4 **1** **Flame Creek (IRE)**[13] 118 12-9-13 **70**........ HayleyTurner 4 81+
(E J Creighton) *stdd s: hld up bhd: shkn up and hdwy over 1f out: led ins fnl f: sn clr: readily* **14/1**

20-0 **2** *3 1/2* **Dubai Ace (USA)**[21] 14 7-9-0 **60**........(p) NeilChalmers(3) 2 66
(Miss Sheena West) *chsd ldr for 4f: chsd ldrs after tl rdn and outpcd over 2f out: rallied u.p over 1f out: styd on to go 2nd wl ins fnl f: no ch w wnr* **9/2**[3]

31-5 **3** *nk* **Abounding**[14] 105 4-9-2 **66**........ AdamKirby 3 72
(M J Attwater) *chsd ldr after 4f: led over 3f out: rdn over 2f out: hdd ins fnl f: sn outpcd by wnr: lost 2nd wl ins fnl f* **9/1**

064- **4** *3* **Mind How You Go (FR)**[28] 6131 10-10-0 **71**........ GeorgeBaker 7 73
(J R Best) *w.w in midfield: rdn wl over 3f out: hdwy to chse ldrs jst over 2f out: wknd 1f out* **2/1**[1]

31-4 **5** *1 1/2* **Summerofsixtynine**[15] 78 5-8-12 **55**........(p) TGMcLaughlin 6 56
(J G M O'Shea) *t.k.h: stdd s and hld up bhd: reminders 9f out: drvn and effrt on outer over 2f out: no hdwy last 2f* **12/1**

16-6 **6** *1 1/2* **Dark Parade (ARG)**[20] 27 7-9-3 **65**........(b) JamieJones(5) 1 64
(G L Moore) *travelled wl: hld up in tch: hdwy to chse ldr over 2f out: sn rdn: fdd tamely jst over 1f out* **7/2**[2]

1 **7** *14* **She's The Lady**[19] 39 8-9-9 **66**........ ChrisCatlin 5 48
(E J O'Neill) *led: rdn 4f out: hdd over 3f out: wknd 2f out* **5/1**

3m 24.36s (-1.34) **Going Correction** +0.20s/f (Slow)
WFA 4 from 5yo+ 7lb 7 Ran SP% **114.8**
Speed ratings (Par 103): **111,109,109,107,106 106,99**
CSF £75.41 TOTE £17.30: £5.60, £2.60; EX 65.30.
Owner E J Creighton **Bred** Kilcornan Stables **Trained** East Garston, Berks

FOCUS
A very decent winning time for a race of its class, but the form still looks just ordinary rated through the fifth.

273 PONTIN'S EARLY OFFERS @ PONTINS.COM MEDIAN AUCTION MAIDEN STKS 1m 4f (P)
2:50 (2:50) (Class 5) 4-6-Y-O £2,331 (£693; £346; £173) **Stalls** Low

Form RPR

42-6 **1** **Whaxaar (IRE)**[14] 91 4-9-3 57........ RobertHavlin 1 53+
(R Ingram) *hld up in last: rdn and hdwy jst over 2f out: chsd ldr over 1f out: led ins fnl f: sn in command: easily* **4/6**[1]

06-4 **2** *1 1/2* **Cyril The Squirrel**[20] 31 4-9-3 46........(p) MickyFenton 5 51
(Karen George) *rn green: led: rdn and clr jst over 2f out: hdd ins fnl f: sn btn* **4/1**[3]

035- **3** *3 1/2* **Dr Dream (IRE)**[34] 6480 4-9-3 50........(b) TGMcLaughlin 4 45
(J G M O'Shea) *chsd ldr: rdn 4f out: outpcd jst over 2f out: lost 2nd over 1f out: wl btn after* **10/3**[2]

0/ **4** *5* **Shanagolden Juan (IRE)**[23] 4931 5-9-7 0........ GeorgeBaker 2 37
(M R Bosley) *t.k.h: hld up in last pair: rdn over 3f out: wl outpcd over 2f out: no ch last 2f* **16/1**

5 *8* **Krismick (IRE)**[20] 4-8-12 0........ VinceSlattery 3 20
(G A Ham) *s.i.s: chsd ldrs: rdn 4f out: wknd wl over 2f out: sn bhd* **33/1**

6 *nk* **Sweet Demerara**[56] 4-8-12 0........ RichardThomas 6 19
(P Butler) *wnt rt s: chsd ldrs: rdn wl over 3f out: wknd wel over 2f out: no ch last 2f* **66/1**

2m 35.88s (2.88) **Going Correction** +0.20s/f (Slow)
WFA 4 from 5yo 4lb 6 Ran SP% **113.4**
Speed ratings: **98,97,94,91,86 85**
CSF £3.88 TOTE £1.20: £1.02, £3.20; EX 3.40.
Owner G F Chesneaux **Bred** Agricola Del Parco **Trained** Epsom, Surrey

FOCUS
A dire maiden, run at an average pace. The winner rates value for a good deal further but this is very weak form.

274 GREAT PONTIN'S BREAKS 0844 815 3647 H'CAP 1m (P)
3:20 (3:20) (Class 5) (0-75,75) 4-Y-O+ £2,590 (£770; £385; £192) **Stalls** High

Form RPR

054- **1** **Bee Stinger**[24] 7281 6-9-4 **75**........ DaneO'Neill 7 85+
(I A Wood) *hld up in tch: hdwy wl over 2f out: drvn to ld 1f out: in command last 50yds* **3/1**[1]

3-03 **2** *1 1/2* **Parkview Love (USA)**[7] 177 7-8-11 **68**........(v) DeanMcKeown 4 74
(D Shaw) *t.k.h: hld up wl in tch: trckd ldrs gng wl 2f out: rdn over 1f out: kpt on to go 2nd ins fnl f: nt pce of wnr* **9/2**[3]

6-64 **3** *nk* **Onenightinlisbon (IRE)**[7] 177 4-8-11 **68**........ FergusSweeney 2 74
(J R Boyle) *hld up in tch on inner: rdn and effrt 2f out: chsd ldrs jst over 1f out: kpt on u.p* **14/1**

203- **4** *3/4* **Lord Theo**[107] 6067 4-9-4 **75**........ GeorgeBaker 6 79
(N P Littmoden) *s.i.s: chsd ldr after 1f: rdn to ld 2f out: hdd 1f out: wknd last 100yds* **8/1**

060- **5** *nk* **Bertie Southstreet**[26] 7253 5-9-1 **72**........ JimmyQuinn 5 75+
(J R Best) *plld hrd for 1f: hld up in rr: rdn wl over 2f: sme hdwy over 1f out: nvr trbld ldrs* **11/2**

31-4 **6** *1 3/4* **Putra Laju (IRE)**[21] 21 4-8-3 **67**........(p) GabrielHannon(7) 8 66
(J W Hills) *rrd s: t.k.h: rdn and effrt on outer wl over 1f out: nvr trbld ldrs* **7/1**

606- **7** *nk* **Music Note (IRE)**[141] 5114 5-9-1 **72**........(t) MickyFenton 3 71
(Miss Gay Kelleway) *led: hung rt and hdd bnd 2f out: wknd over 1f out* **4/1**[2]

000- **8** *5* **Winged Flight (USA)**^{74} [6765] 4-8-13 **70**........................(b^{1}) GregFairley 1 57
(M Johnston) *chsd ldr for 1f: styd handy tl rdn and wknd jst over 2f out* **8/1**

1m 38.79s (0.59) **Going Correction** +0.20s/f (Slow) **8** Ran SP% **120.0**
Speed ratings (Par 103): **105,103,103,102,102 100,100,95**
CSF £17.64 CT £168.30 TOTE £4.40: £1.70, £2.60, £3.30; EX 17.20 Trifecta £123.90 Pool: £408.58, 2.34 winning units.
Owner Sporting Occasions No 11 **Bred** Templeton Stud **Trained** Upper Lambourn, Berks
■ Stewards' Enquiry : Greg Fairley one-day ban: failed to ride to draw (Feb 3)

FOCUS
A steadily run handicap in which the winner was a cut above his rivals on his best form. The form makes sense but is not solid given the lack of pace.
Bertie Southstreet Official explanation: jockey said gelding ran too free
Music Note(IRE) Official explanation: jockey said gelding hung right

275 LINGFIELDPARK.CO.UK H'CAP 7f (P)
3:50 (3:52) (Class 5) (0-70,71) 4-Y-0+ **£2,331** (£693; £346; £173) **Stalls** Low

Form RPR
450- **1** **Samuel Charles**^{25} [7269] 10-9-2 **67**..................................(b) LiamJones 3 75
(C R Dore) *chsd ldrs: hdwy to ld jst over 2f out: rdn over 1f out: kpt on* **6/1**^{3}
440- **2** *nk* **Gimme Some Lovin (IRE)**^{25} [7269] 4-8-9 **60**............. FergusSweeney 8 67
(D W P Arbuthnot) *racd towards rr on outer: hdwy 3f out: rdn over 2f out: chsd wnr 1f out: kpt on but nvr quite getting to wnr* **8/1**
41-3 **3** *3/4* **King After**^{11} [139] 6-8-6 **57**..................................(v) JimmyQuinn 6 62
(J R Best) *t.k.h: hld up in tch: rdn and effrt over 1f out: edgd lft but r.o fnl f: nt able to rch ldng pair* **9/2**^{2}
36-0 **4** *shd* **Best One**^{20} [26] 4-9-3 **68**.. HayleyTurner 9 73+
(C E Brittain) *s.i.s: hld up in rr: swtchd lft onto rail jst over 2f out: stl little room tl swtchd rt over 1f out: r.o wl fnl f: nt rch ldrs* **3/1**^{1}
0-42 **5** *1 1/2* **Cool Sands (IRE)**^{10} [150] 6-9-0 **65**.........................(v) DeanMcKeown 4 66
(D Shaw) *hld up in midfield on inner: rdn and effrt over 1f out: kpt on same pce* **6/1**^{3}
00-6 **6** *1/2* **Quality Street**^{14} [94] 6-9-4 **69**..............................(p) RichardThomas 10 68
(P Butler) *bhd: rdn wl over 3f out: kpt on u.p ins fnl f: nvr trbld ldrs* **16/1**
0-41 **7** *nk* **Seneschal**^{10} [148] 7-9-6 **71** 6ex................................ TPQueally 7 70
(A B Haynes) *chsd ldrs: wnt 2nd 4f out: rdn over 2f out: lost 2nd 1f out: fdd ins fnl f* **7/1**
250- **8** *2 1/2* **Hollow Jo**^{26} [7253] 8-9-0 **65**....................................... MickyFenton 1 57
(J R Jenkins) *sn led: hdd and rdn jst over 2f out: wknd over 1f out* **11/1**
64-0 **9** *1 3/4* **Mine Behind**^{10} [150] 8-9-2 **67**................................. GeorgeBaker 2 54
(J R Best) *s.i.s: rdn and hdwy on inner 3f out: n.m.r bnd jst over 2f out: nvr trbld ldrs* **10/1**
004- **10** *3/4* **Cheonmado (USA)**^{265} [1433] 4-9-0 **65**.........................(b^{1}) JimCrowley 5 50
(J R Gask) *chsd ldr tl 4f out: sn rdn and lost pl: bhd last 2f* **20/1**

1m 24.33s (-0.47) **Going Correction** +0.20s/f (Slow) **10** Ran SP% **123.4**
Speed ratings (Par 103): **110,109,108,108,106 106,106,103,101,100**
CSF £56.65 CT £248.00 TOTE £10.00: £3.10, £2.00, £2.00; EX 63.90 Trifecta £294.10 Pool: £546.83, 1.32 winning units.
Owner Chris Marsh **Bred** Sheikh Mohammed Obaid Al Maktoum **Trained** West Pinchbeck, Lincs

FOCUS
A strongly run race and a smart winning time for the grade, 2.48 seconds faster than the following apprentice handicap. Ordinary form, but pretty sound.
Hollow Jo Official explanation: vet said gelding had lost a shoe

276 PLAY GOLF @ LINGFIELD PARK APPRENTICE H'CAP 7f (P)
4:20 (4:20) (Class 6) (0-60,57) 4-Y-0+ **£1,876** (£554; £277) **Stalls** Low

Form RPR
0-22 **1** **Jessica Wigmo**^{7} [176] 5-8-10 48.................................. MarkCoumbe 7 56
(A W Carroll) *t.k.h: hld up in tch: hdwy on outer over 2f out: rdn to chal jst over 1f out: led ins fnl f: rdn out* **9/2**^{3}
03-5 **2** *hd* **Imperium**^{10} [149] 7-9-5 57..(b) KylieManser 9 64
(Jean-Rene Auvray) *t.k.h: hld up bhd ldrs: hdwy on inner 2f out: led briefly jst ins fnl f: unable qck towards fin* **9/2**^{3}
042- **3** *1/2* **Strut The Stage (IRE)**^{24} [7276] 4-8-10 53...............(tp) DavidProbert$^{(5)}$ 5 59
(B W Duke) *t.k.h: w ldrs: rdn and ev ch wl over 1f out: led jst over 1f out tl jst ins fnl f: one pce last 100yds* **11/2**
66-0 **4** *3/4* **Rafferty (IRE)**^{10} [151] 9-8-4 47..................................(p) ThomasBubb$^{(5)}$ 6 51
(S Dow) *t.k.h: prom: led over 2f out: rdn wl over 1f out: hdd jst over 1f out: one pce ins fnl f* **14/1**
005- **5** *1 1/2* **Nikki Bea (IRE)**^{25} [7269] 5-9-0 57.......................... AshleyMorgan$^{(5)}$ 1 57
(Jamie Poulton) *led narrowly tl over 2f out: rdn and ev ch wl over 1f out: wknd jst ins fnl f* **4/1**^{2}
00-0 **6** *4* **Sagunt (GER)**^{18} [56] 5-9-0 57.................................. RossAtkinson$^{(5)}$ 3 46
(S Curran) *in tch in rr: rdn and struggling wl over 3f out: no ch last 2f* **16/1**
45-2 **7** *3 1/2* **Palais Polaire**^{8} [168] 6-8-12 50...............................(p) MatthewDavies 8 29
(J A Geake) *s.i.s: a last: detached and rdn 4f out: sn lost tch* **9/4**^{1}

1m 26.81s (2.01) **Going Correction** +0.20s/f (Slow) **7** Ran SP% **115.1**
Speed ratings (Par 101): **96,95,95,94,92 88,84**
CSF £25.19 CT £113.20 TOTE £4.00: £1.70, £2.80; EX 19.60 Trifecta £53.80 Pool: £494.93 - 6.53 winning units. Place 6 £ 48.64, Place 5 £ 37.57.
Owner J Wigmore Racing Partnership **Bred** J Wigmore **Trained** Cropthorne, Worcs

FOCUS
A slowly run race and a modest winning time, 2.48 seconds slower than the preceding Class 5 handicap over the same trip. Weak, low-grade form.
Palais Polaire Official explanation: trainer's rep said mare had missed the break and was unable to dominate
T/Plt: £73.40 to a £1 stake. Pool: £49,595.30. 492.80 winning tickets. T/Qpdt: £22.90 to a £1 stake. Pool: £2,764.60. 89.20 winning tickets. SP

256 SOUTHWELL (L-H)
Thursday, January 24

OFFICIAL GOING: Standard
Wind: Fresh behind Weather: Fine

277 BOOK YOUR TICKETS ONLINE APPRENTICE H'CAP 1m 3f (F)
1:00 (1:00) (Class 6) (0-55,54) 4-Y-0+ **£1,774** (£523; £262) **Stalls** Low

Form RPR
30-1 **1** **Karmest**^{18} [69] 4-8-7 **54**... SBushby$^{(7)}$ 4 62+
(A D Brown) *hld up: racd keenly: hdwy over 2f out: led over 1f out: rdn clr fnl f* **9/2**^{2}
0/0- **2** *4* **Munching Mike (IRE)**^{24} [6380] 5-8-12 **54**.................. RichardEvans$^{(5)}$ 3 55
(K M Prendergast) *chsd ldrs: led wl over 1f out: sn rdn and hdd: styd on same pce fnl f* **7/2**^{1}
03-6 **3** *1 1/4* **The Diamond Bond**^{12} [144] 4-8-4 **47**................................ NSLawes$^{(3)}$ 5 46
(G R Oldroyd) *led: hdd over 9f out: led 6f out: rdn and hdd wl over 1f out: styd on same pce* **12/1**
00/0 **4** *5* **Smoothly Does It**^{18} [69] 7-8-13 **53**.......................... BMcHugh$^{(3)}$ 9 43
(R A Fahey) *hld up: hdwy over 3f out: rdn 2f out: wknd fnl f* **5/1**^{3}
001- **5** *6* **Meeting Of Minds**^{8} [7197] 4-8-5 **50**............................ JamieKyne$^{(5)}$ 2 30
(D Carroll) *hld up in tch: r keenly: stmbld after 1f: rdn over 2f out: sn wknd* **7/2**^{1}
3-35 **6** *1 1/4* **Piano Key**^{9} [169] 4-8-1 **46**.. RossAtkinson$^{(5)}$ 1 24
(M D I Usher) *hld up in tch: rdn and wknd 2f out* **5/1**^{3}
60-0 **7** *3 1/2* **First Frost**^{7} [193] 4-8-5 **45**.. DeanHeslop 7 17
(M J Gingell) *chsd ldrs: rdn over 3f out: wknd over 2f out* **100/1**
100- **8** *6* **Wickedish**^{57} [6570] 4-8-7 **52**......................................(t) AshleyMorgan$^{(5)}$ 6 14
(M J Gingell) *hld up: rdn over 3f out: sn wknd* **12/1**
600- **9** *9* **Scruffy (IRE)**^{40} [7148] 4-8-5 **45**..(p) MarkCoumbe 8 —
(John A Harris) *plld hrd and prom: led over 9f out: hdd 6f out: wknd over 3f out* **33/1**

2m 27.72s (-0.28) **Going Correction** -0.15s/f (Stan)
WFA 4 from 5yo+ 3lb **9** Ran SP% **115.3**
Speed ratings (Par 101): **95,92,91,87,83 82,79,75,68**
CSF £20.61 CT £175.91 TOTE £5.60: £1.70, £1.70, £3.20; EX 23.80 Trifecta £171.60 Part won. Pool £241.71 - 0.85 winning units..
Owner David Logan **Bred** Charles B B Booth **Trained** Pickering, York
■ A first winner on his 21st ride for jockey Sean Bushby.

FOCUS
A very moderate apprentice handicap and even though the pace was not strong they still finished very well spread out. The form looks weak, rated through the third.

278 SOUTHWELL-RACECOURSE.CO.UK CLAIMING STKS 5f (F)
1:30 (1:30) (Class 6) 4-Y-0+ **£1,774** (£523; £262) **Stalls** High

Form RPR
45-4 **1** **Godfrey Street**^{16} [84] 5-9-5 80..(b) FergalLynch 2 84
(K A Ryan) *mde all: pushed clr fnl f: eased nr fin* **5/4**^{1}
-400 **2** *6* **Tenancy (IRE)**^{7} [191] 4-8-7 43..............................(p) PatrickMathers$^{(3)}$ 1 54
(A J McCabe) *chsd ldrs: rdn 1/2-way: outpcd fr over 1f out* **33/1**
4-32 **3** *nk* **Memphis Man**^{7} [194] 5-8-11 74.............................. RichardEvans$^{(7)}$ 6 61
(P D Evans) *s.i.s: outpcd: styd on ins fnl f: nvr trbld ldrs* **2/1**^{2}
-343 **4** *1/2* **Pappas Image**^{9} [167] 4-8-9 44.......................................(p) VJanacek 5 50
(A J McCabe) *chsd wnr: rdn 1/2-way: edgd lft over 1f out: sn outpcd* **28/1**
-031 **5** *2* **Cleveland**^{7} [191] 6-9-3 59.. HayleyTurner 7 51
(R Hollinshead) *sn outpcd* **11/4**^{3}

57.14 secs (-2.56) **Going Correction** -0.425s/f (Stan) course record **5** Ran SP% **110.8**
Speed ratings (Par 95): **103,93,92,92,88**
CSF £32.63 TOTE £2.00: £1.60, £8.70; EX 37.00.The winner was claimed by M K Seymour for £15,000.
Owner Club ISM **Bred** Miss S N Ralphs **Trained** Hambleton, N Yorks
■ The first winner since July 2006 for jockey Fergal Lynch, who has recently resumed his riding career following a ban.

FOCUS
As uncompetitive a claimer as you can get, made all the more so by the two non-runners, which makes it all the more surprising that the course record fell. There was a fresh following wind which would have played its part. The time was decent and the form looks believable despite the runner-up's improvement.

279 ARENA LEISURE PLC (S) STKS 5f (F)
2:00 (2:00) (Class 6) 3-Y-O **£1,774** (£523; £262) **Stalls** High

Form RPR
31-6 **1** **Mac Dalia**^{7} [199] 3-8-9 70...(p) JerryO'Dwyer$^{(3)}$ 5 60
(A J McCabe) *trckd ldrs: rdn to ld ins fnl f: r.o* **8/11**^{1}
03-3 **2** *1/2* **Wild Bill Tracey**^{19} [59] 3-8-12 63.................................... ChrisCatlin 2 58
(M J Wallace) *led: rdn over 1f out: hdd ins fnl f: kpt on* **7/4**^{2}
-060 **3** *2 1/2* **Andrasta**^{4} [237] 3-8-7 55..................................(p) DanielleMcCreery$^{(5)}$ 4 49
(A Berry) *edgd lft s: chsd ldrs: rdn over 1f out: styd on same pce* **14/1**^{3}
005- **4** *1/2* **Silver Deal**^{28} [7240] 3-8-2 41..................................... KellyHarrison$^{(5)}$ 1 42
(J A Pickering) *chsd ldrs: rdn 1/2-way: no ex fnl f* **66/1**
000- **5** *8* **Distant Noble**^{45} [7101] 3-8-12 43.. PhillipMakin 3 18
(R Brotherton) *s.i.s and hmpd s: outpcd* **33/1**
005- **6** *7* **Flex**^{121} [5699] 3-8-12 54..(e^{1}) LiamJones 6 —
(D J Murphy) *prom: sn drvn along: wknd 3f out* **18/1**

59.13 secs (-0.57) **Going Correction** -0.425s/f (Stan) **6** Ran SP% **110.6**
Speed ratings (Par 95): **87,86,82,81,68 57**
CSF £2.10 TOTE £1.60: £1.10, £1.50; EX 2.00.The winner was bought in for 4,250gns
Owner Paul J Dixon & Brian Morton **Bred** Chippenham Lodge Stud **Trained** Babworth, Notts

FOCUS
A poor seller in which only the front pair had a chance according to the market and the winning time was moderate even for a race like this, a fraction under two seconds slower than the preceding older-horse claimer. The contest eventually panned out the way that adjusted official ratings suggested it should.
Distant Noble Official explanation: jockey said gelding suffered interference at start
Flex Official explanation: jockey said gelding was unsuited by the surface

280 SOUTHWELL RACING AND GOLF H'CAP 7f (F)
2:30 (2:30) (Class 4) (0-85,85) 4-Y-0+ **£4,210** (£1,252; £625; £312) **Stalls** Low

Form RPR
0-21 **1** **Neardown Beauty (IRE)**^{7} [190] 5-8-11 **78** 6ex....(p) StephenDonohoe 2 89+
(A J McCabe) *s.i.s: hld up: hdwy over 2f out: rdn to ld wl ins fnl f: r.o* **3/1**^{2}
20-0 **2** *1* **Wessex (USA)**^{5} [233] 8-9-4 **85**.. GeorgeBaker 4 93
(P A Blockley) *chsd ldr: led over 4f out: rdn over 1f out: edgd lft and hdd wl ins fnl f* **9/2**
30-2 **3** *nk* **Sand Cat**^{16} [85] 5-8-8 **78**.. MichaelJStainton$^{(3)}$ 6 85
(G L Moore) *chsd ldrs: rdn and ev ch ins fnl f: styd on same pce* **10/1**
50-1 **4** *1 1/2* **Intersky Charm (USA)**^{7} [192] 4-8-4 **71** 6ex.............. DeanMcKeown 5 74
(R M Whitaker) *led: hdd over 4f out: edgd rt over 3f out: sn rdn: styd on same pce fnl f* **9/4**^{1}
263- **5** *4* **Dichoh**^{25} [7281] 5-9-0 **81**..(p) MatthewHenry 1 77
(M A Jarvis) *chsd ldrs: lost pl over 4f out: rdn over 2f out: wknd and eased fnl f* **7/2**^{3}
15-5 **6** *5* **Secret Liaison**^{13} [124] 5-9-2 **83**...................................... HayleyTurner 3 62
(S Parr) *prom: rdn 1/2-way: wknd 2f out* **14/1**
03-0 **7** *8* **Tagula Sunrise (IRE)**^{16} [85] 6-8-10 **80**.................. JamieMoriarty$^{(3)}$ 7 37
(R A Fahey) *hld up in tch: racd keenly: rdn and wknd over 2f out* **33/1**

1m 28.25s (-2.05) **Going Correction** -0.15s/f (Stan) **7** Ran SP% **114.9**
Speed ratings (Par 105): **105,103,103,101,97 91,82**
CSF £17.05 TOTE £4.00: £1.70, £3.00; EX 17.90.
Owner Brian Morton **Bred** Mrs Joan M Langmead **Trained** Babworth, Notts

FOCUS
A decent handicap, though the pace was pretty average and the winner came from last. This is solid Fibresand form which should work out.
Dichoh Official explanation: jockey said gelding hung left and lost its action

281 ARENALEISUREPLC.COM H'CAP — 1m (F)
3:00 (3:00) (Class 5) (0-70,69) 3-Y-O — **£2,525** (£745; £372) **Stalls** Low

Form — RPR
602- **1** **Bookiebasher Babe (IRE)**[92] 6433 3-8-7 **58**............... FrancisNorton 3 — 67
(M Quinn) *mde all: rdn over 1f out: styd on* — **13/2**
15-4 **2** *1 ¾* **Hieroglyph**[21] 25 3-9-4 **69**.............................. GregFairley 2 — 74
(M Johnston) *a.p: rdn over 2f out: chsd wnr fr over 1f out: no imp* — **9/4**[2]
43-3 **3** *7* **Tallulah Sunrise**[22] 12 3-8-11 **69**........................ GabrielHannon(7) 4 — 58
(M D I Usher) *chsd wnr 7f out tl rdn over 1f out: wknd fnl f* — **2/1**[1]
624- **4** *11* **Natural Rhythm (IRE)**[29] 7234 3-9-1 **66**................(p) HayleyTurner 1 — 30
(D W Chapman) *chsd ldrs: rdn 1/2-way: wknd over 2f out* — **5/2**[3]
1m 43.39s (-0.31) **Going Correction** -0.15s/f (Stan) — **4** Ran SP% **106.0**
Speed ratings (Par 97): **95,93,86,75**
CSF £19.91 TOTE £10.70; EX 21.80.
Owner J Henry, J Blake & A Newby **Bred** Minch Bloodstock And Castletown Stud **Trained** Newmarket, Suffolk
FOCUS
A modest three-year-old handicap, but at least the winner made it a reasonable test. The form looks very ordinary, rated through the runner-up, with the winner up 6lb.

282 BOOK YOUR HOSPITALITY PACKAGES CLASSIFIED STKS — 1m 3f (F)
3:30 (3:30) (Class 7) 4-Y-O+ — **£1,365** (£403; £201) **Stalls** Low

Form — RPR
00-1 **1** **Contra Mundum (USA)**[9] 171 5-9-6 43..................... HayleyTurner 10 — 68+
(B G Powell) *hld up: hdwy over 4f out: led on bit over 1f out: sn clr: comf* — **4/6**[1]
004- **2** *7* **Matinee Idol**[29] 6700 5-9-0 43..(b¹) ChrisCatlin 7 — 45
(Mrs S Lamyman) *hld up: hdwy over 5f out: outpcd over 2f out: swtchd lft over 1f out: styd on ins fnl f* — **16/1**
/0-6 **3** *½* **Blue Opal**[18] 69 6-9-0 35...(p) PaulEddery 11 — 44
(Miss S E Hall) *prom: chsd wnr over 3f out: rdn and ev ch 2f out: styd on same pce* — **20/1**
20-0 **4** *1 ¼* **On Every Street**[20] 36 7-9-0 45.................................(p) LiamJones 12 — 42
(R Bastiman) *sn drvn along in rr: hdwy 8f out: rdn over 2f out: hung lft and wknd over 1f out* — **16/1**
0-04 **5** *1 ½* **Mi Odds**[17] 77 12-8-9 44... KellyHarrison(5) 14 — 39
(Mrs N Macauley) *hld up: hdwy over 3f out: sn rdn: nt trble ldrs* — **28/1**
50-3 **6** *¾* **Snake Hips**[13] 129 4-8-11 40..............................(v) RichardKingscote 5 — 38
(B Palling) *hld up: rdn over 2f out: n.d* — **10/1**
000/ **7** *1* **Secret Cavern (USA)**[51] 5988 6-8-11 42............... DuranFentiman(3) 13 — 37
(H J Evans) *plld hrd and prom: rdn over 3f out: wknd over 1f out* — **66/1**
54-5 **8** *2* **Big Ralph**[22] 8 5-8-9 45.. JamesO'Reilly(5) 6 — 33
(D K Ivory) *chsd ldr tl led over 4f out: rdn and hdd over 1f out: sn wknd* — **6/1**[2]
0-64 **9** *3* **Steel Grey**[7] 193 7-8-11 40.. MarkLawson(3) 9 — 28
(M Brittain) *chsd ldrs over 6f* — **15/2**[3]
60-0 **10** *1 ½* **Didactic**[18] 66 4-8-11 40..(p) VJanacek 2 — 25
(A J McCabe) *hld up: bhd fr 1/2-way* — **66/1**
520/ **11** *8* **Aggi Mac**[450] 6280 7-8-7 38.. KristinStubbs(7) 3 — 12
(L R James) *hld up: a in rr* — **100/1**
000/ **12** *29* **Haughton Hope**[444] 6373 5-9-0 37...................................(t) PhillipMakin 8 — —
(G Woodward) *sn led: rdn and hdd over 4f out: wknd over 3f out: eased* — **66/1**
/00- **13** *1 ¾* **Little Hotpotch**[16] 6792 4-8-11 43............... StephenDonohoe 1 — —
(M J Gingell) *prom: lost pl over 8f out: sn bhd* — **100/1**
206- **14** *1 ¼* **Littleton Aldor (IRE)**[20] 4460 8-8-11 42..................... TolleyDean(3) 4 — —
(Mark Gillard) *mid-div: lost pl over 8f out: sn bhd* — **33/1**
2m 26.72s (-1.28) **Going Correction** -0.15s/f (Stan)
WFA 4 from 5yo+ 3lb — **14** Ran SP% **124.5**
Speed ratings (Par 97): **98,92,92,91,90 90,89,87,85,84 78,57,56,55**
CSF £14.11 TOTE £1.70: £1.10, £3.10, £3.60; EX 18.40 Trifecta £165.90 Pool £165.90 - 1.52 winning units..
Owner D J Coles **Bred** Christopher Buckley **Trained** Upper Lambourn, Berks
FOCUS
The winning time was exactly a second faster than the earlier apprentice handicap, but this was still a poor race and certainly not as competitive as the numbers might suggest with an odds-on favourite and only two other horses starting at less than 10-1. The favourite duly dotted up and apart from him the form is unlikely to mean much outside of this grade.
Haughton Hope Official explanation: jockey said the gelding stopped very quickly

283 SOUTHWELL-RACECOURSE.CO.UK H'CAP — 2m (F)
4:00 (4:01) (Class 6) (0-65,61) 4-Y-O+ — **£1,774** (£523; £262) **Stalls** Low

Form — RPR
103- **1** **Hora**[37] 7178 4-9-4 **57**...(b¹) SebSanders 1 — 79+
(Sir Mark Prescott) *trckd ldrs: led over 4f out: clr fnl 3f: edgd lft over 1f out: eased ins fnl f* — **13/8**[1]
60-4 **2** *17* **El Dee (IRE)**[12] 145 5-8-8 **45**.............................. KellyHarrison(5) 10 — 43
(Jedd O'Keeffe) *hld up: hdwy over 3f out: sn rdn: no ch w wnr* — **16/1**
000- **3** *nk* **Just Waz (USA)**[73] 6308 6-9-6 **55**.......................... MichaelJStainton(5) 4 — 53
(R M Whitaker) *chsd ldrs: lost pl over 4f out: n.d after* — **25/1**
10-4 **4** *½* **Ice And Fire**[20] 36 9-9-0 **46**.......................................(b) MickyFenton 5 — 43
(J T Stimpson) *hld up: rdn 1/2-way: styd on fr over 1f out: n.d* — **10/1**
540- **5** *1 ¼* **Square Dealer**[26] 5626 7-9-4 **50**..................................(b) PhillipMakin 6 — 46
(J R Norton) *prom: rdn to chse wnr over 3f out: wknd over 2f out* — **40/1**
025- **6** *1 ¼* **Botham (USA)**[27] 7262 4-9-0 **53**..................................(e) FrancisNorton 3 — 47
(D J Murphy) *hld up: hdwy and nt clr run over 3f out: sn rdn and wknd* — **12/1**
44-3 **7** *½* **Spares And Repairs**[14] 107 5-10-0 **60**........................... ChrisCatlin 7 — 53
(Mrs S Lamyman) *sn pushed along and prom: rdn over 3f out: sn wknd* — **16/1**
21-0 **8** *5* **Bugsy's Boy**[22] 14 4-9-8 **61**... LiamJones 2 — 48
(P W D'Arcy) *chsd ldr tl rdn 4f out: wknd 3f out* — **5/2**[2]
050- **9** *18* **Al Moulatham**[96] 6341 9-9-3 **49**................................(bt) SamHitchcott 8 — 15
(R Ford) *sn led: rdn and hdd over 4f out: wknd 3f out: eased* — **11/1**
/4-5 **10** *½* **Sonoma (IRE)**[9] 166 8-8-13 **45**..............................(vt) HayleyTurner 9 — 10
(B G Powell) *sn pushed along in rr: bhd fnl 4f: eased fnl 3f* — **7/1**[3]
3m 38.92s (-6.58) **Going Correction** -0.15s/f (Stan)
WFA 4 from 5yo+ 7lb — **10** Ran SP% **122.3**
Speed ratings (Par 101): **110,101,101,101,100 99,99,97,88,87**
CSF £33.18 CT £510.76 TOTE £2.60: £1.30, £2.40, £7.90; EX 52.70 Trifecta £285.10 Part won. Pool £104.61 - 0.37 winning units. Place 6 £130.14, Place 5 £63.08..
Owner Dr Catherine Wills **Bred** St Clare Hall Stud **Trained** Newmarket, Suffolk
FOCUS
This was a moderate staying event, at least outside of the winner who hosed up hard held and is a filly on the up. The pace was a fair one thanks to habitual front-runner Al Moulatham.
Al Moulatham Official explanation: jockey said gelding hung left
T/Plt: £131.40 to a £1 stake. Pool: £41,990.55. 233.20 winning tickets. T/Qpdt: £28.60 to a £1 stake. Pool: £2,265.90. 58.50 winning tickets. CR

249 WOLVERHAMPTON (A.W) (L-H)
Thursday, January 24

OFFICIAL GOING: Standard
Wind: moderate, behind

284 BUY TICKETS ONLINE APPRENTICE H'CAP — 1m 141y(P)
6:50 (6:53) (Class 6) (0-60,66) 4-Y-O+ — **£1,774** (£523; £262) **Stalls** Low

Form — RPR
032- **1** **General Feeling (IRE)**[83] 6629 7-8-10 **53**................ DeclanCannon(3) 1 — 59
(S T Mason) *a in tch on ins: wnt 2nd over 2f out: rdn to ld ins fnl f* — **13/2**[3]
55-3 **2** *½* **Mister Benji**[9] 168 9-8-6 **49**................................(p) SoniaEaton(3) 9 — 54
(B P J Baugh) *plld hrd: led: rdn and edgd rt fr over 1f out: hdd ins fnl f* **8/1**
3 *3* **Kingoftheswingers (IRE)**[41] 6659 4-8-11 **57**.................. JamieKyne(5) 4 — 55
(Adrian McGuinness, Ire) *t.k.h: trckd ldrs: rdn over 2f out: kpt on one pce fnl f* — **8/1**
-311 **4** *½* **Justcallmehandsome**[5] 234 6-9-7 **66** 6ex...................(v) BillyCray(5) 5 — 63
(D J S Ffrench Davis) *rrd s: hld up: hdwy on outside into st: kpt on fnl f but nt rch ldrs* — **11/10**[1]
0-54 **5** *1 ¼* **Spy Gun (USA)**[14] 115 8-8-8 **48**......................................(p) KylieManser 7 — 42
(T Wall) *slowly away: in rr: rdn and hdwy over 1f out but nvr nr to chal* — **16/1**
-5 **6** *3* **Oh So (IRE)**[12] 140 4-8-4 **52**.. RyanRaftery(7) 8 — 39
(P A Blockley) *trckd ldr to over 2f out: wknd over 1f out* — **66/1**
7 *2 ½* **Much Reality (IRE)**[50] 7036 6-9-5 **59**.........................(t) DeanHeslop 2 — 40
(Gordon Elliott, Ire) *in tch tl wknd wl over 1f out* — **4/1**[2]
1m 51.35s (0.85) **Going Correction** +0.025s/f (Slow)
WFA 4 from 5yo+ 1lb — **7** Ran SP% **110.5**
Speed ratings (Par 101): **97,96,93,93,92 89,87**
CSF £51.94 CT £399.54 TOTE £6.10: £2.30, £3.00; EX 25.50.
Owner The Mason Racing Partnership I **Bred** John Graham And Leslie Laverty **Trained** Lanchester, Co. Durham
FOCUS
A very moderate and slowly run affair. Weak form, rated through the first two.
Justcallmehandsome Official explanation: jockey said, regarding the running and riding, his orders were to jump out and be prominent to keep out of the kickback, but gelding reared leaving stalls and because it has a quirky temperament it can't be bustled so he had to bide his time, keep wide and could only make his move in the straight when heading for home

285 RACE TO PONTIN'S FOR HALF TERM (S) STKS — 5f 216y(P)
7:20 (7:20) (Class 6) 3-Y-O+ — **£1,774** (£523; £262) **Stalls** Low

Form — RPR
4-11 **1** **Mafaheem**[6] 213 6-9-13 66.. TPQueally 6 — 70+
(A B Haynes) *s.i.s: hld up: swtchd rt and hdwy over 2f out: edgd lft bef led 1f out: sn clr* — **8/13**[1]
60-0 **2** *3* **Tang**[3] 254 4-8-10 40.. JackDean(7) 1 — 47
(W G M Turner) *a in tch on ins: ev ch appr fnl f: chsd wnr ins fnl f* — **40/1**
20-2 **3** *1* **Macademy Royal (USA)**[22] 16 5-9-5 60.................(t) TravisBlock(3) 3 — 49
(H Morrison) *racd keenly: trckd ldr: led over 2f out: rdn and hdd 1f out: no ex after* — **5/2**[2]
40-4 **4** *2* **Paddywack (IRE)**[12] 142 11-9-8 50...................................(b) LiamJones 2 — 43
(D W Chapman) *s.i.s: sn in tch: swtchd rt over 1f out: kpt on one pce* — **16/1**
00-0 **5** *1 ¾* **Geordie Dancer (IRE)**[9] 167 6-9-8 37.........................(b) FrancisNorton 4 — 37
(A Berry) *led tl hdd over 2f out: rdn and wknd wl over 1f out* — **100/1**
-002 **6** *1 ¼* **Lucius Verrus (USA)**[14] 115 8-9-5 53.....................(v) TolleyDean(3) 5 — 33
(D Shaw) *broke wl but sn rdn and outpcd: b.b.v* — **10/1**[3]
1m 15.53s (0.53) **Going Correction** +0.025s/f (Slow) — **6** Ran SP% **108.9**
Speed ratings (Par 101): **97,93,91,89,86 85**
CSF £27.37 TOTE £1.40: £1.10, £14.20; EX 60.90.
Owner W Clifford **Bred** J H And J M Wall **Trained** Limpley Stoke, Bath
■ Stewards' Enquiry : Liam Jones caution: careless riding
FOCUS
A weak seller in which the easy winner probably achieved little.
Lucius Verrus(USA) Official explanation: vet said gelding bled from the nose

286 GREAT VALUE HALF TERM PONTIN'S BREAKS H'CAP — 5f 20y(P)
7:50 (7:51) (Class 5) (0-70,70) 4-Y-O+ — **£2,590** (£770; £385; £192) **Stalls** Low

Form — RPR
00-5 **1** **Lord Of The Reins (IRE)**[13] 126 4-8-7 **62**................. TolleyDean(3) 7 — 72
(D Shaw) *in rr: hdwy on outside 2f out: rdn and r.o to ld wl ins fnl f* — **9/1**
6-31 **2** *½* **Strathmore (IRE)**[17] 71 4-8-10 **65**......................... JamieMoriarty(3) 3 — 73
(R A Fahey) *outpcd tl hdwy over 1f out: r.o wl fnl f to go 2nd post* — **5/1**[3]
552- **3** *shd* **Desert Opal**[33] 7221 8-9-4 **70**......................................(b) LiamJones 6 — 78
(C R Dore) *trckd ldrs: edgd lft and led over 1f out: hdd and lost 2nd nr fin* — **13/2**
030- **4** *½* **Multahab**[95] 6360 9-8-12 **64**...(t) JimmyQuinn 8 — 70
(M Wigham) *hld up: hdwy on outside over 2f out: kpt on one pce fnl f* — **14/1**
3-03 **5** *½* **Music Box Express**[7] 191 4-8-7 **59**..........................(be¹) FrancisNorton 1 — 63
(D J Murphy) *in rr: hdwy 2f out: kpt on: nvr nr to chal* — **7/4**[1]
25-4 **6** *2 ½* **Fizzlephut (IRE)**[14] 113 6-9-0 **66**.............................. PaulFitzsimons 4 — 61
(Miss J R Tooth) *wnt lft s: sn chsng ldrs: ev ch 0ver 1f out: wknd ins fnl f* — **8/1**
1-61 **7** *5* **Triskaidekaphobia**[5] 230 5-9-0 **66** 6ex.................................(t) LPKeniry 5 — 43
(Miss J R Tooth) *led tl rdn and hdd over 1f out: fdd ins fnl f: fin lame* — **9/2**[2]
40-5 **8** *11* **Hawaii Prince**[14] 113 4-8-11 **63**...................................... PhillipMakin 2 — —
(S T Mason) *w ldr tl wknd qckly over 1f out: eased ins fnl f* — **33/1**
61.93 secs (-0.37) **Going Correction** +0.025s/f (Slow) — **8** Ran SP% **115.3**
Speed ratings (Par 103): **103,102,102,101,100 96,88,70**
CSF £53.74 CT £317.82 TOTE £11.50: £3.90, £2.00, £2.30; EX 47.00.
Owner Danethorpe Racing Partnership **Bred** C Farrell **Trained** Danethorpe, Notts
■ Stewards' Enquiry : Liam Jones one-day ban: careless riding
FOCUS
This was run at a fast pace and the first two came from the rear. Sound form, with the winner back to his best.
Triskaidekaphobia Official explanation: vet said gelding finished lame behind

Hawaii Prince Official explanation: jockey said gelding lost its action

287 RACE AHEAD WITH ZENA @ PONTINS.COM H'CAP 1m 4f 50y(P)
8:20 (8:20) (Class 6) (0-55,55) 4-Y-0+ £1,774 (£523; £262) Stalls Low

Form RPR
004- 1 **Mandalay Prince**[48] 7060 4-8-11 54 TPQueally 1 69+
(W J Musson) *hld up: hdwy over 1f out: strly rdn to ld ins fnl f* 13/8[1]
00-2 2 1 1/4 **Classic Blue (IRE)**[12] 145 4-8-3 46 PaulEddery 10 58
(Ian Williams) *hld up: hdwy on outside over 2f out: led over 1f out: rdn and hdd ins fnl f* 11/2[3]
400- 3 8 **Sky Chart (IRE)**[26] 7275 4-8-3 51 DanielleMcCreery(5) 5 50
(N J Vaughan) *trckd ldr: led after 4f: rdn and hdd over 1f out: wknd ins fnl f* 10/1
00-4 4 3 **Vanishing Dancer (SWI)**[7] 198 11-9-1 54 J-PGuillambert 3 48
(Mrs D Thomas) *in rr: rdn and outpcd over 4f out: kpt on past btn horses fr over 1f out* 12/1
0-06 5 3/4 **Chiff Chaff**[9] 171 4-8-12 55 AdamKirby 2 48
(C R Dore) *led for 4f: wkng whn hmpd over 2f out* 7/1
0/42 6 shd **Bright Sparky (GER)**[11] 152 5-8-4 50 ow1 (t) NSLawes(7) 7 43
(M W Easterby) *mid-div: rdn over 3f out: no hdwy after* 5/1[2]
65-1 7 3 1/2 **Komreyev Star**[7] 193 6-9-2 55 6ex ChrisCatlin 4 42
(R E Peacock) *in rr: hdwy 7f out: rdn 3f out: wknd 2f out: reported to have the thumps post r* 15/2
U **Saint Eric (FR)**[775] 6-8-12 51 SamHitchcott 8 —
(Noel T Chance) *stmbld and uns rdr leaving stalls* 33/1

2m 40.06s (-1.04) **Going Correction** +0.025s/f (Slow)
WFA 4 from 5yo+ 4lb 8 Ran SP% **114.1**
Speed ratings (Par 101): **104,103,97,95,95 95,92,—**
CSF £10.73 CT £66.44 TOTE £2.20: £1.10, £1.70, £3.40; EX 11.90.
Owner McGregor Bloodstock and Gillings **Bred** Mrs D O Joly **Trained** Newmarket, Suffolk

FOCUS
This was run at an ordinary pace but the first two, who pulled a long way clear, both came from the rear. An improved effort from Mandalay Prince.
Komreyev Star Official explanation: vet said gelding had the thumps post-race

288 GO BOOK TODAY @ PONTIN'S H'CAP 1m 1f 103y(P)
8:50 (8:51) (Class 6) (0-60,63) 3-Y-0 £1,774 (£523; £262) Stalls Low

Form RPR
33-2 1 **Little Firecracker**[2] 262 3-9-2 58 AdamKirby 4 61
(Miss M E Rowland) *a in tch: rdn over 2f out: kpt on u.p to ld ins fnl f* 5/1[3]
00-0 2 1/2 **Ski Sunday**[19] 58 3-9-4 60 J-PGuillambert 5 62
(M A Jarvis) *hld up in rr: hdwy 3f out: led 2f out: one pce and hdd ins fnl f* 4/1[2]
40-1 3 nk **Duneen Dream (USA)**[22] 20 3-9-2 58 NeilPollard 6 60
(W J Musson) *hld up in rr: hdwy on outside over 2f out: rdn and one pce fnl f* 15/8[1]
054- 4 nk **Arabesque Dancer**[27] 7259 3-9-1 57 (b[1]) URispoli 9 58
(M Botti) *in rr: rdn 4f out: hdwy on outside over 2f out: kpt on one pce: nvr nrr* 22/1
5-31 5 3/4 **Tapas Lad (IRE)**[7] 195 3-9-7 63 6ex (v) JimmyQuinn 3 62
(V Smith) *in rr: effrt 2f out: kpt on one pce* 11/2
60-0 6 1/2 **Tobouggornotobougg**[8] 184 3-8-3 48 (v[1]) TolleyDean(3) 2 46
(D Shaw) *trckd ldr: led over 3f out: hdd 2f out: wknd appr fnl f* 40/1
0-61 7 5 **Magical Song**[2] 262 3-8-12 54 6ex (b) FrankieMcDonald 7 42
(P A Blockley) *trckd ldrs tl rdn and wknd over 2f out* 9/1
00-4 8 9 **Plaka (FR)**[22] 20 3-9-0 56 LiamJones 8 25
(W M Brisbourne) *led tl hdd over 3f out: sn wknd* 17/2
56-5 9 2 1/2 **Miss Bouggy Wouggy**[15] 98 3-9-1 57 TPQueally 1 21
(M Blanshard) *mid-div: rdn over 3f out: sn bhd* 14/1

2m 2.62s (0.92) **Going Correction** +0.025s/f (Slow) 9 Ran SP% **120.8**
Speed ratings (Par 95): **96,95,95,95,94 93,89,81,79**
CSF £26.64 CT £51.78 TOTE £7.60: £1.90, £1.70, £1.90; EX 33.80.
Owner Hall Farm Racing **Bred** Palm Tree Thoroughbreds **Trained** Lower Blidworth, Notts

FOCUS
A truly run race and sound form, limited by the fourth and fifth.
Miss Bouggy Wouggy Official explanation: jockey said filly had no more to give

289 SPONSOR A RACE BY CALLING 0870 220 2442 CLASSIFIED STKS 7f 32y(P)
9:20 (9:21) (Class 7) 4-Y-0+ £1,365 (£403; £201) Stalls High

Form RPR
0-52 1 **Stargazy**[3] 254 4-8-7 39 MatthewDavies(7) 5 53+
(W G M Turner) *hld up: rdn and hdwy over 2f out: edgd lft bef led ins fnl f: drvn out* 3/1[1]
4-40 2 2 **Desert Lover (IRE)**[4] 236 6-9-0 45 JimmyQuinn 2 48
(R J Price) *in tch: hrd rdn and led briefly ins fnl f: nt pce of wnr* 4/1[2]
-233 3 1 3/4 **Mr Chocolate Drop (IRE)**[7] 189 4-8-9 45 (b) JamesO'Reilly(5) 11 43
(Miss M E Rowland) *edgd lft fr outside draw after 1f: t.k.h: hdwy on outside 1/2-way: one pce fnl f* 5/1[3]
4 1/2 **Oberows Lady (IRE)**[148] 4955 6-8-11 35 JerryO'Dwyer(3) 3 42
(Adrian McGuinness, Ire) *trckd ldr: led 2f out: rdn and hdd ins fnl f: no ex* 16/1
-353 5 nk **Only If I Laugh**[11] 147 7-9-0 45 AdamKirby 8 41
(M J Attwater) *mid-div: rdn 3f out: one pce fnl f* 3/1[1]
000- 6 1 3/4 **Lizarazu (GER)**[24] 5121 9-9-0 43 ChrisCatlin 7 36
(D J Wintle) *hld up: rdn over 2f out: nvr nr to chal* 16/1
600- 7 2 **Buzzin'Boyzee (IRE)**[66] 6869 5-9-0 45 StephenDonohoe 4 31
(P D Evans) *slowly away: hdwy 1/2-way: rdn 2f out: wknd over 1f out* 13/2
-066 8 2 1/2 **Telepathic (IRE)**[4] 236 8-9-0 36 (b) FrancisNorton 10 24
(A Berry) *sn led: hdd 2f out: wknd over 1f out* 22/1
20/0 9 10 **Tuscan Treaty**[22] 11 8-8-11 43 (t) TolleyDean(3) 6 —
(R W Price) *a in rr* 40/1
00-6 10 7 **Mays Louise**[9] 172 4-8-7 35 SoniaEaton(7) 9 —
(B P J Baugh) *hmpd after 1f: a bhd* 80/1
00-6 11 8 **Bovered (IRE)**[22] 19 4-8-9 29 DanielleMcCreery(5) 1 —
(A Berry) *in tch tl sddle slipped and wknd 1/2-way* 100/1

1m 29.93s (0.33) **Going Correction** +0.025s/f (Slow) 11 Ran SP% **120.8**
Speed ratings (Par 97): **99,96,94,94,93 91,89,86,75,67 58**
CSF £15.25 TOTE £5.10: £2.40, £1.10, £1.70; EX 24.80 Place 6 £102.07, Place 5 £10.32..
Owner Kachina Racing **Bred** Bearstone Stud **Trained** Sigwells, Somerset

FOCUS
Not a bad race for the grade, with the runner-up the best guide. The winner is rated back to last winter's form.
Only If I Laugh Official explanation: trainer said gelding was found to have bled from the nose after race
Bovered(IRE) Official explanation: jockey said saddle slipped

T/Plt: £54.70 to a £1 stake. Pool: £106,556.40. 1,419.85 winning tickets. T/Qpdt: £9.20 to a £1 stake. Pool: £8,195.80. 658.80 winning tickets. JS

200 NAD AL SHEBA (L-H)
Thursday, January 24
OFFICIAL GOING: Turf course - good; dirt course - fast

290a MEYDAN HOTEL H'CAP (TURF) 6f 110y(T)
3:05 (3:07) (95-110,107) 3-Y-0+
£36,180 (£12,060; £6,030; £3,015; £1,809; £1,206)

RPR
1 **Drift Ice (SAF)**[21] 7-9-0 100 (b) KShea 3 98
(M F De Kock, South Africa) *mid-div: gng wl whn led over 2f out: qcknd clr 1 1/2f out: comf* 11/2[2]
2 1 1/2 **Algharb**[21] 6-8-11 98 RHills 1 91
(A Manuel, UAE) *broke awkwardly: no room on rail 2 1/2f out: r.o once clr 2f out: no ch w wnr* 10/3[1]
3 1 1/4 **Santiago Atitlan**[60] 6-9-4 105 MJKinane 7 95
(P Schiergen, Germany) *in rr of main gp: rdn 2f out: r.o: nrst fin* 6/1[3]
4 1/4 **Stetchworth Prince**[32] 6-8-10 97 TPO'Shea 8 86
(E Charpy, UAE) *trckd ldr: wd 3f out: led briefly 2 1/2f out: ev ch fnl 2f: r.o same pce* 11/1
5 shd **Grand Vista**[137] 5259 4-9-2 102 RyanMoore 6 92
(H J Brown, South Africa) *slowly away: settled in rr: gng wl 3f out: sn short of room: nrst fin* 7/1
6 2 **Indian Trail**[124] 5616 8-9-6 107 AdrianTNicholls 10 90
(D Nicholls) *restrained in mid-div: bmpd 2 1/2f out: nt qckn fnl 1 1/2f* 8/1
7 hd **Ripples Maid**[97] 6300 5-8-10 97 RoystonFfrench 2 79
(J A Geake) *mid-div on rail: trckd ldr 2f out: sn no room and btn* 7/1
8 4 1/4 **Machynleth**[21] 8-8-8 95 (t) WayneSmith 9 65
(M Al Muhairi, UAE) *sn led: rdn and hdd 2 1/2f out: wknd* 12/1
9 3 3/4 **T-Bird (SAF)**[144] 7-9-1 101 (t) DO'Donohoe 5 62
(Doug Watson, UAE) *racd in last: rdn 3 1/2f out: nvr able to chal* 8/1
10 dist **Cartography (IRE)**[686] 619 7-8-12 99 BrettDoyle 4 —
(R Bouresly, Kuwait) *trckd ldr tl short of room 2f out: wknd: t.o* 25/1

1m 18.74s (1.24) **Going Correction** +0.375s/f (Good) 10 Ran SP% **119.8**
Speed ratings: **107,105,103,103,103 101,100,96,91,—**
Win: 6.10; PL 1.80, 1.60, 1.90; CSF 24.92; TRI 116.65.
Owner Sh Rashid bin Humaid Al Nuaimi **Bred** Lammerskraal Stud **Trained** South Africa

FOCUS
A safety limit of ten meant there were not as many runners as this sort of handicap would attract in Britain, and it was less competitive as a result, so it would be unwise to get carried away with the form. They went a strong pace, setting this up for those who raced off the lead, and the winning time was 0.65 secs quicker than the following handicap run over the same trip.

NOTEBOOK
Drift Ice(SAF) had only ever raced on dirt in Dubai, including when down the field in a non-Carnival handicap at the beginning of the year, but he has won on turf in his native South Africa and proved well suited by the switch of surface. The good early gallop seemed to suit and, having travelled well in mid-division, he got a good run in the straight, before pulling away for a decisive victory. This was a weak race for this level, so one would not want to take too short a price about him following up, but his trainer's runners will always be worthy of respect round here. (op 6/1)
Algharb has been in good form in non-Carnival handicaps over slightly further on the dirt recently, but he is just as effective over this shorter trip on turf, as he showed when trained in Britain by William Haggas, and he ran well. (op 4/1)
Santiago Atitlan, a Listed winner in Germany back in 2006, was representing the same connections as last year's multiple Carnival winner Quijano. Returning from a two-month break, he struggled to go the early pace, but he found his stride in the second half of the contest and looked a real danger when switched out wide in the straight. His effort eventually flattened out, but this was still a promising enough showing. He gives the impression some sort of headgear might just sharpen him, which is not unusual for a son of Stravinsky. (op 11/2)
Stetchworth Prince chased the strong pace for much of the way and was vulnerable to those ridden with more patience. (op 10/1)
Grand Vista, winless since his two-year-old days when trained in France by Andre Fabre, ran with credit on his debut for new connections off the back of over four months off the track.
Indian Trail was conceding weight all round, but he could still have been expected to find this slightly less competitive than some of the handicaps he contested in Britain last year. He ran okay, but will need to improve on this first run in four months to pick up a similar event. This extended 6f probably just stretched him as well. (op 7/1)
Ripples Maid, returning from over three months off the track, looked a little short of room inside the final furlong, but she was well held at the time.

291a MEYDAN BUSINESS PARK H'CAP (TURF) 6f 110y(T)
3:35 (3:37) (95-110,109) 3-Y-0+
£36,180 (£12,060; £6,030; £3,015; £1,809; £1,206)

RPR
1 1/2 **Prince Tamino**[150] 4886 5-8-9 98 RoystonFfrench 3 100+
(A Al Raihe, UAE) *slowly away: hmpd by wnr 1f out: fin 2nd, 1/2l: awrdd r* 8/1
2 **Mariol (FR)**[59] 6954 5-9-2 105 TPO'Shea 6 105
(E Charpy, UAE) *settled in last: gng wl 3f out: r.o fnl 1 1/2f: led 1f out: fin 1st: disq: plcd 2nd* 6/1
3 2 1/4 **Loyalist (SAF)**[336] 528 7-8-11 100 RichardMullen 5 94
(S Seemar, UAE) *mid-div: rdn 2 1/2f out: n.m.r 1f out: r.o* 25/1
4 1/2 **Beckermet (IRE)**[96] 6338 6-9-6 109 TedDurcan 4 102
(R F Fisher) *wl away: sn led: hdd 1 1/2f out but r.o wl* 11/2[3]
5 1 1/4 **Machinist (IRE)**[154] 4747 8-8-10 99 DO'Donohoe 8 88
(D Nicholls) *trckd ldr: led 1 1/2f out: hdd 1f out: wknd* 15/2
6 2 3/4 **Conceal**[28] 10-8-11 100 BrettDoyle 2 81
(R Bouresly, Kuwait) *mid-div: rdn 2 1/2f out: nt qckn and short of room 1f out* 8/1
7 2 1/2 **Something (IRE)**[128] 5512 6-9-1 104 AdrianTNicholls 7 78
(D Nicholls) *mid-div: rdn to chse ldr 2f out: bdly hmpd 1f out: nt rcvr* 4/1[1]
8 3 1/4 **Taqseem (IRE)**[28] 5-9-0 102 (t) RHills 9 68
(M Al Muhairi, UAE) *mid-div: rdn to chal 2f out: u.p whn bdly hmpd 1f out* 16/1
9 1/2 **San Domenico**[103] 4-8-8 97 MartinDwyer 1 61
(Doug Watson, UAE) *settled in rr: hmpd 4f out: n.d* 5/1[2]

1m 19.39s (1.89) **Going Correction** +0.375s/f (Good) 9 Ran SP% **110.1**
Speed ratings: **103,104,100,100,98 95,92,89,88**
Win: 12.40; PL 3.30, 1.70, 8.50; CSF 50.17; TRI 981.79.
Owner H R H Princess Haya Of Jordan **Bred** The National Stud **Trained** UAE

FOCUS
This was basically another division of the 3.05 and, just like the opener, the form is not what one would expect for such a valuable sprint handicap in Europe. Again the pace was strong, with the leaders appearing to go off a little too fast. The winning time was 0.65 secs slower than the opening handicap run over the same trip.

NOTEBOOK
Prince Tamino was second past the post, but he had his ground taken by Mariol around a furlong out when just beginning to stay on and, after the Stewards took a look, he was awarded the race. He traded at odds on in the inquiry betting and it looked the correct decision, for although there was not actually a great deal of contact between the two horses, there can be little doubt he would have won with a clear run. He had proved disappointing at last year's Carnival, and was held in a couple of starts in Britain for Godolphin, but he was much more like his old self this time on his debut for new connections off the back of a 150-day break. This was not much of a race, but he has always promised to develop into a smart type. (tchd 15/2)
Mariol(FR), twice successful in French handicaps when trained by Robert Collet last year, posted a very useful effort on his first start in Dubai, even if he did eventually lose the race. There could be a little more to come in time and he might be able to gain compensation.
Loyalist(SAF) had not been seen for the best part of a year, but this was a respectable effort and he can obviously be expected to come on for the run.
Beckermet(IRE) was allowed a clear lead, but he was kept honest and probably ended up going off a little too fast. This was a reasonable effort after three months off the track. (op 6/1)
Machinist(IRE) was never that far away from the strong gallop and he could find only the one pace late on. (op 8/1)
Conceal was a winner at last year's Carnival and this was a creditable showing.
Something(IRE) was not at his best on his debut for David Nicholls off the back of a 128-day break, but he can be expected to come on for this. (op 100/30 tchd 3/1)

292a MEYDAN MARINA STKS (CONDITIONS RACE) (DIRT) 7f (D)
4:05 (4:08) 3-Y-O
£9,045 (£3,015; £1,507; £753; £452; £301)

RPR
1 **Honour Devil (ARG)**^{314} 4-9-4 104 .... JMurtagh 11 110
(M F De Kock, South Africa) *disp ld: rdn 2 1/2f out: led 1 1/2f out: r.o wl: comf* **7/2**^{2}
2 *5 1/4* **My Indy (ARG)**^{115} 4-9-8 100 .... LDettori 15 101+
(Saeed Bin Suroor) *mid-div: rdn 3f out: r.o fnl 2f: nrst fin* **10/3**^{1}
3 *1/2* **Aquino (URU)**^{284} 4-9-4 100 ....(t) MJKinane 10 96
(Doug Watson, UAE) *disp ld: rdn 2 1/2f out: hdd 1 1/2f out: wknd fnl 1/2f* **7/2**^{2}
4 *4 1/4* **Lizard Island (USA)**^{116} [5845] 3-9-0 113 .... JohnEgan 13 94
(J S Moore) *mid-div: rdn 3f out: wnt 3rd 1 1/2f out: one pce* **7/1**^{3}
5 *3 1/4* **Paveroc**^{21} 3-8-9 93 .... AdrianTNicholls 12 81
(A Manuel, UAE) *slowly away: mid-div: rdn 3f out: nvr able to chal but r.o fnl 1 1/2f* **40/1**
6 *2 1/2* **Basko De Zarautz (ARG)**^{213} 4-9-4 102 ....(t) TedDurcan 2 70
(Saeed Bin Suroor) *settled in rr: 14th 3f out: r.o fnl 1 1/2f: nrst fin* **14/1**
7 *2 1/4* **Jasmines Hero (USA)**^{21} 3-8-9 76 ....(t) MartinDwyer 6 69
(A Manuel, UAE) *mid-div on rail: rdn 3f out: nvr able to chal: r.o fnl 1 1/2f* **100/1**
8 *1 1/4* **Free Tussy (ARG)**^{154} 4-9-6 100 ....(t) RyanMoore 14 62
(H J Brown, South Africa) *disp tl 3 1/2f out: rdn 3f out: wknd* **9/1**
9 *1* **Change Alley (USA)**^{21} 3-8-9 87 .... RoystonFfrench 7 63
(A Al Raihe, UAE) *trckd ldng gp: rdn 3f out: r.o same pce* **50/1**
10 *1/4* **Call For Liberty (USA)**^{20} 3-8-9 82 .... TPO'Shea 8 62
(E Charpy, UAE) *in rr of mid-div: rdn 4f out: nvr able to chal* **66/1**
11 *1 3/4* **Toolittleyourlate (USA)**^{155} [4724] 3-8-9 91 .... RichardMullen 16 58
(S Seemar, UAE) *mid-div: wd: rdn 3f out: n.d* **50/1**
12 *1 1/2* **Yem Kinn**^{127} [5536] 3-8-9 91 ....(t) WayneSmith 4 54
(S Seemar, UAE) *trckd ldrs on rail: rdn 3 1/2f out: wknd 2 1/2f out* **40/1**
13 *1 1/2* **Choisky (IRE)**^{85} [6588] 3-8-10 66 ow1 .... BrettDoyle 3 51
(R Bouresly, Kuwait) *a in rr* **100/1**
14 *3/4* **Bain Douche (BRZ)**^{75} 4-9-8 95 .... RSchistl 9 47
(R Colombo, Brazil) *stmbld sn after s: nvr able to chal* **33/1**
15 *3/4* **Ukrainian (BRZ)**^{87} 4-9-4 98 .... RHills 5 41
(A Cintra Pereira, Brazil) *nvr nr to chal* **11/1**
16 *1/2* **Yahrab (IRE)**^{103} [6170] 3-8-9 106 .... PJSmullen 1 45
(C E Brittain) *slowly away: nvr nr to chal* **12/1**

1m 24.45s (-0.35) **Going Correction** +0.175s/f (Slow)
WFA 3 from 4yo 18lb **16** Ran SP% **127.9**
Speed ratings: **109,103,102,97,93 91,88,87,85,85 83,81,80,79,78 77**
Win: 5.30; PL 2.10, 1.70, 1.20; CSF 15.90.
Owner Sheikh Mohammed Bin Khalifa Al Maktoum **Bred** Firmamento **Trained** South Africa

FOCUS
A trial for the UAE 2000 Guineas – won last year by Triple Crown winner Asiatic Boy and in 2005 by subsequent Guineas winner Stagelight – and this looked a seriously good renewal.

NOTEBOOK
Honour Devil(ARG), representing the same connections as Asiatic Boy, could not have been more impressive and his trainer looks to have unearthed another star. He had just a maiden win in Argentina back in March 2007 to his name coming into this, but the five-length runner-up that day went on to win in Listed and Group 3 company, and he recorded a time over two seconds quicker than an older-horse conditions contest, and exactly the same time as a dual Group 1 winner. Having helped force the early pace after being quickly into his stride, he looked set for a prolonged battle with Aquino, another potential top notcher, when those two were upsides at the top of the straight, but he left that rival behind in fine style late on. His rider said afterwards he was still a little green, so there should be plenty more to come as the Carnival progresses and, barring injury, he could well emulate his stablemate Asiatic Boy and land the UAE Triple Crown. (op 100/30)
My Indy(ARG) was bought by Godolphin after winning both his starts in Argentina, including a 1m1f Grade 2 on ground described as heavy when last seen in October. Having raced a little way off the early leaders, he appeared to lack the pace to move into a challenging position at the top of the straight and the winner was long gone by the time he switched into the clear. He will be suited by the 1m of the UAE 2000 Guineas, as well as the 1m1f of the other two legs of the Triple Crown, so he will be worthy of respect if taking his chance in those races, but his trainer indicated in a stable tour that Etched may well be their main hope for those types of races.
Aquino(URU) was a Listed winner in Uruguay by a wide margin when last seen in April and was the subject of very bullish comments from his trainer in the build-up to this race. He looked set to battle it out with Honour Devil all the way up the straight, but he eventually gave best and may have needed this. He remains an exciting prospect, but he will have his stamina to prove if taking his chance in the UAE Guineas, particularly with the likelihood of some strong stayers in opposition.
Lizard Island(USA) won last year's Group 2 Railway Stakes, but was held thereafter, including when only sixth when favourite for the Beresford Stakes, and has since been bought privately out of Aidan O'Brien's yard. He ran with real credit on his first start on dirt and should continue to give a good account in races like the UAE Guineas and Derby.
Paveroc, who used to be trained by Stan Moore, had the benefit of previous experience on dirt and came through the kickback to post a reasonable effort in defeat.
Basko De Zarautz(ARG) joined Godolphin after winning his only start by ten lengths in Argentina back in June, but he has not been seen since and his trainer felt he might need the run. He lacked the speed of some of these and met some trouble when trying to stay on, but he did do some reasonable late work and is going to be suited by further. (op 12/1)
Free Tussy(ARG) joined Herman Brown after landing his last two starts on the dirt in Argentina, including a Group 3 by seven lengths when last seen in August, but he dropped out tamely after disputing the early lead with the eventual winner and third. (op 17/2)
Yahrab(IRE), third in the Group 3 Autumn Stakes at Ascot on his final start at two, fell out of the stalls and was never seen with a chance.

293a MEYDAN CITY H'CAP (TURF) 1m 4f (T)
4:45 (4:46) (100-110,110) 3-Y-O+
£52,763 (£17,587; £8,793; £4,396; £2,638; £1,758)

RPR
1 **Book Of Music (IRE)**^{111} [5976] 5-9-3 **107** ....(v) WJSupple 2 111
(Saeed Bin Suroor) *settled in rr: rdn to cl 3f out: r.o wl fnl f: led nr line* **14/1**
2 *1/4* **Gravitas**^{102} [6198] 5-8-12 **102** .... TedDurcan 1 106
(Saeed Bin Suroor) *mid-div on rail: swtchd off rail 1 1/2f out: led briefly 110yds out: hdd cl home* **11/2**^{3}
3 *1 1/4* **Longville (GER)**^{94} [6400] 4-8-6 **100** .... MartinDwyer 7 102
(Mario Hofer, Germany) *led: qcknd clr 4 1/2f out: rdn 2f out: hdd 110yds out: r.o wl* **4/1**^{2}
4 *1 1/2* **New Guinea**^{75} [6759] 5-9-1 **105** .... LDettori 10 105
(Saeed Bin Suroor) *trckd ldr after 2f: gng wl 3f out: ev ch but nt qckn fnl f* **3/1**^{1}
5 *1/4* **Snoqualmie Boy**^{110} [6011] 5-8-12 **102** .... JohnEgan 3 101
(J S Moore) *settled in rr: rdn 2 1/2f out: nvr able to chal* **16/1**
6 *1 1/4* **Great Plains**^{21} 6-9-0 **104** .... RHills 8 101
(E Charpy, UAE) *settled in rr: gng wl but no room 2 1/2f out: swtchd wd: one pce fnl f* **11/1**
7 *3/4* **Lake Poet (IRE)**^{116} [5830] 5-8-10 **100** .... MJKinane 9 96
(C E Brittain) *trckd ldrs: rdn 3f out: no room 2f out: nt rcvr* **10/1**
8 *1 3/4* **Hard Top (IRE)**^{152} [4803] 6-9-1 **105** .... RyanMoore 11 98
(H J Brown, South Africa) *hld up last: trckd ldr 2f out: no room 1f out: n.d* **8/1**
9 *4 1/4* **Mulaqat**^{34} 5-9-6 **110** .... JMurtagh 4 96
(D Selvaratnam, UAE) *trckd ldrs on rail: rdn 2 1/2f out: sn btn* **15/2**
10 *1/4* **Mosaic**^{7} [202] 6-8-12 **102** .... RoystonFfrench 6 88
(A Al Raihe, UAE) *mid-div: wd: rdn 3f out: n.d* **20/1**
11 *8 1/2* **Dono Da Raia (BRZ)**^{329} [598] 6-9-1 **105** ....(t) DO'Donohoe 5 77
(Saeed Bin Suroor) *trckd ldr: rdn 3f out: wknd fnl 2 1/2f* **25/1**

2m 35.52s (4.52) **Going Correction** +0.375s/f (Good)
WFA 4 from 5yo+ 4lb **11** Ran SP% **121.8**
Speed ratings: **99,98,98,97,96 96,95,94,91,91 85**
Win:18.90; PL 2.50, 2.60, 1.50; CSF 92.46; TRI 376.86.
Owner H R H Princess Haya Of Jordan **Bred** Wentworth Racing Pty Ltd **Trained** Newmarket, Suffolk

FOCUS
A high-class middle-distance handicap on paper, but all bar one of these were five or six years of age and most of them came into this pretty well exposed. The pace seemed steady through the early stages, with Longville able to dictate on his own terms, but it increased significantly when that one was sent into a clear lead leaving the back straight.

NOTEBOOK
Book Of Music(IRE) was not at his best in two runs in Britain last year, but he had dropped to the same mark as when winning at last year's Carnival as a result and he just proved good enough. The steady early pace would not have been ideal as he was held up through the early stages, but he made good ground when the tempo increased and eventually responded to strong pressure to get up close home. He might follow up, but does not really appeal as one to be backing to do so.
Gravitas was last seen beating just one rival home in a 1m conditions contest at Bath in October, but this sort of trip is much more suitable and he ran well behind his stablemate. However, it is worth noting he ran second off a mark of 110 on his first start at the Carnival last year and failed to progress.
Longville(GER), German trained, improved nicely last season and finished the year with a second in a French Listed race (the winner of that race went on to win again in Listed company). The youngest horse in the line-up, he took the field along at a steady pace through the early stages and looked like he might take a bit of catching when kicking clear rounding the final bend. However, it is hard to make all over these sorts of distances round here, with the long straight surely a big factor, and he was just pegged back. (op 9/2)
New Guinea seemed inclined to edge to his left under pressure and, ridden with just hands and heels late on, he did not totally convince that he was striding out as well as he can after being a little short of room over a furlong out.
Snoqualmie Boy, who ran in the 2006 Derby, had failed to win in 11 runs since taking that year's Listed Hampton Court Stakes, but he was bought out of David Elsworth's yard for 75,000gns at the Newmarket Horses in Training sale. He could only plug on at the one pace after being asked to come from well back and he would have appreciated a stronger gallop.
Great Plains compromised his chance by hanging left under pressure. (op 9/1)
Lake Poet(IRE) is better than he was able to show as he was short of room when looking to stay on around two furlongs out.
Hard Top(IRE), who has failed to win since landing the 2005 Great Voltigeur for Sir Michael Stoute, was staying on from a long way back when short of room in the straight. He can do better off a stronger pace.
Dono Da Raia(BRZ) dropped out tamely and has plenty to prove.

294a MEYDAN RACECOURSE H'CAP (TURF) 7f 110y(D)
5:20 (5:20) (100-118,118) 3-Y-O+
£52,763 (£17,587; £8,793; £4,396; £2,638; £1,758)

RPR
1 **Linngari (IRE)**^{95} [6372] 6-9-6 **118** .... RyanMoore 2 119+
(H J Brown, South Africa) *settled in rr: rdn to cl 2 1/2f out: no room 1 1/2f out: r.o and led 55yds out* **3/1**^{2}
2 *1 1/4* **Divine Jury (SAF)**^{327} 5-9-0 **111** .... KShea 11 109
(M F De Kock, South Africa) *settled in rr: gng wl 3f out: rdn to chal 1 1/2f out: led briefly 110yds out: sn hdd* **5/4**^{1}
3 *3/4* **Visionist (IRE)**^{28} 6-8-5 **100** .... WayneSmith 4 98
(M Al Muhairi, UAE) *led main gp: led overall 2f out: r.o wl: hdd 110yds out* **33/1**
4 *3/4* **With Interest**^{449} [6299] 5-8-5 **102** .... TedDurcan 5 96+
(Saeed Bin Suroor) *slowly away: settled in rr: gng wl on rail 3f out: no room 2f out: r.o wl fnl f* **13/2**^{3}
5 *3 1/4* **Traffic Guard (USA)**^{137} [5265] 4-8-7 **105** ....(p) JohnEgan 3 90
(J S Moore) *sn led: rdn and hdd 2 1/2f out: kpt on same pce* **8/1**
6 *3/4* **Mandobi (IRE)**^{32} 7-8-5 **100** ....(vt) RPCleary 6 87
(D Selvaratnam, UAE) *mid-div: rdn to chal 2 1/2f out: sn btn* **20/1**

7 1 1/4 **Emirates Gold (IRE)**46 5-8-7 **105**.....(t) TPO'Shea 8 86
(E Charpy, UAE) *racd in last: nvr able to chal* **20/1**
8 1/2 **Dickensian (IRE)**328 5-8-5 **100**.....(t) DBadel 9 82
(E Charpy, UAE) *settled in rr: rdn 3f out: nvr able to chal* **50/1**
9 1/4 **Appalachian Trail (IRE)**57 6965 7-9-0 **111**.....(b) TomEaves 1 91
(I Semple) *mid-div: chsd ldrs 2 1/2f out: nt qckn* **14/1**
10 3 1/4 **Alpacco (IRE)**179 4012 6-8-6 **104**.....KLatham 10 75
(Frau Nina Bach, Germany) *trckd ldr: rdn 3 1/2f out: sn btn* **66/1**
11 1/2 **Desert Realm (IRE)**11 5-8-5 **100**.....RoystonFfrench 7 73
(A Al Raihe, UAE) *mid-div: rdn 3f out: sn wknd* **25/1**

1m 31.85s (0.25) **Going Correction** +0.375s/f (Good) 11 Ran SP% **120.3**
Speed ratings: **113,111,111,110,107 106,105,104,104,101 100**
Win: 3.20; PL 1.20, 1.20, 12.50; CSF 6.71; TRI 102.48.
Owner The Bayern Syndicate & Peter Walichnowski **Bred** His Highness The Aga Khan's Studs S C **Trained** South Africa

FOCUS
A really high-class handicap and a quite tremendous performance from Linngari, who managed to defy a handicap mark of 118. The early pace was fair.

NOTEBOOK
Linngari(IRE) seemed happy enough towards the rear through the early stages, but he needed plenty of luck to get a run in the straight once making his move, with Ryan Moore having little choice but to challenge towards the inside. Things got a little tight and he lost a length or so when squeezed up around a furlong from the finish. That looked to have well and truly handed the initiative to the favourite, but he produced a fine late burst once switched to get up and win going away. He has done fantastically well at the last two Carnivals for this trainer, landing consecutive runnings of the Group 2 Al Fahidi Fort before running second in the Dubai Duty Free last March, and he gained a deserved first Group 1 success in Italy for Alain de Royer-Dupre when last seen in October. Now back with Herman Brown, he showed himself as good as ever, if not better, and will surely now be geared towards a third straight success in the Al Fahidi Fort, although he will have a 6lb penalty this year. After that, he will no doubt bid to go one place better than last year in the Dubai Duty Free. (op 100/30)
Divine Jury(SAF), a multiple winner in his native South Africa, including in Group 1 company, came into this with a big reputation and was being talked up as a Dubai Duty Free horse by his trainer. Forced to race wider than the eventual winner throughout, he looked set to justify favouritism when quickening into the lead down the outside halfway up the straight, especially with Linngari being a little short of room, but he began to tire late on and was picked off near the post. This was his first run since last March, so he can be expected to improve, and he might even benefit from being held on to a little longer next time. He remains an exciting prospect. (op 11/8)
Visionist(IRE), a winner on the dirt at last year's Carnival, ran a stormer in defeat behind a couple of high-class rivals. (op 20/1)
With Interest has always promised to be a smart sort, but he was off for over a year before winning a conditions race at Nottingham on his debut for Godolphin and then missed the whole of last season. This was a pleasing return to action and he could progress if he can be kept sound. He looks as though he will appreciate a little further.
Traffic Guard(USA), returning from a 137-day break, took them along at a good pace but gave way in the straight. (op 17/2)
Appalachian Trail(IRE) was a little too keen early on. (op 12/1)

295a AL SHINDAGHA SPRINT (SPONSORED BY MEYDAN) (GROUP 3) (DIRT) 6f (D)
5:55 (5:55) 3-Y-0+

£60,301 (£20,100; £10,050; £5,025; £3,015; £2,010)

RPR
1 **Asiatic Boy (ARG)**156 4693 5-9-5 120.....JMurtagh 9 113+
(M F De Kock, South Africa) *trckd ldrs: no room 3f out and again 2f out: r.o once clr: led 110yds out* **10/11**1
2 1 1/4 **Salaam Dubai (AUS)**28 7-9-1 107.....(v) RichardMullen 8 104
(A Selvaratnam, UAE) *trckd ldrs: led 1f out: r.o: hdd 100yds out: no ch w wnr* **12/1**3
3 3 1/2 **Malayeen (AUS)**21 6-9-1 87.....(v) AhmedAjtebi 5 93
(A Selvaratnam, UAE) *trckd ldrs: led 1 1/2f out: hdd 1f out* **66/1**
4 shd **Diabolical (USA)**180 5-9-5 113.....LDettori 3 97
(Saeed Bin Suroor) *stmbld start: prom in centre: ev ch 3f out: rdn 2f out: r.o same pce* **13/8**2
5 2 1/2 **Sea Hunter**7 205 6-9-1 100.....(vt) RoystonFfrench 2 85
(A Al Raihe, UAE) *racd in centre: rdn 2 1/2f out: wknd fnl f* **33/1**
6 1/2 **Botanical (USA)**307 7-9-1 95.....(vt) TPO'Shea 7 84
(E Charpy, UAE) *slowly away: nvr able to chal but r.o fnl 1 1/2f* **66/1**
7 3 1/2 **Valiance (USA)**258 1623 4-9-1 95.....KShea 1 73
(M F De Kock, South Africa) *racd in centre: rdn 3f out: nvr able to chal* **40/1**
8 1/2 **Terrific Challenge (USA)**28 6-9-1 109.....(bt) TedDurcan 4 72
(Doug Watson, UAE) *mid-div: gng wl 4f out: rdn 2 1/2f out: nt qckn* **12/1**3
9 3 1/2 **Mercury Chief (SAF)**34 7-9-1 95.....(t) AdrianTNicholls 10 61
(A Manuel, UAE) *trckd ldrs: rdn 3f out: one pce* **66/1**
10 hd **Power Politics (USA)**21 5-9-1 95.....(t) WayneSmith 6 61
(M Al Muhairi, UAE) *sn led: hdd 1 1/2f out: wknd* **40/1**

1m 11.27s (1.07) **Going Correction** +0.525s/f (Slow) 10 Ran SP% **118.2**
Speed ratings: **113,111,106,106,103 102,97,97,92,92**
Win: 2.40; PL 1.70, 4.30, 1.80; CSF 13.52.
Owner Sheikh Mohammed Bin Khalifa Al Maktoum **Bred** Haras Arroyo De Luna **Trained** South Africa

FOCUS
There can often be a draw bias on the straight track, but they all raced middle to stands' side this time and there was no advantage to be had. It is more than fair to say that Asiatic Boy didn't have a great deal to beat, with this Group 3 seriously lacking strength in depth – the third home, Malayeen, was successful off just 72 on his previous start – and his only serious rival on paper, Diabolical, losing his race at the start. However, one could not fail to be impressed by the manner of his victory.

NOTEBOOK
Asiatic Boy(ARG) endured an horrendous trip, having to overcome all sorts of traffic problems over a distance short of his optimum. He showed enough early speed to sit just off the leaders and he travelled nicely enough, but the trouble began when he looked to make his move in the second half of the contest, as he was forced to switch left twice in order to get into the clear. He bounded away when finally seeing daylight inside the final furlong and was value for significantly more than the winning margin suggests. Last year's UAE Triple Crown winner acquitted himself with credit in a couple of turf Group 1s in the summer, but dirt racing is clearly his game and he is being targeted at the Dubai World Cup. He might contest one leg of the Maktoum Challenge before World Cup night. (tchd 5/6)
Salaam Dubai(AUS) is a very smart sprinter on his day, as he showed when third in last year's Group 1 Golden Shaheen Stakes, and this was a good effort in second. He is, though, flattered to get so close to the winner. (op 10/1)
Malayeen(AUS)'s two recent wins in handicap company have come off marks of just 65 and 72, so his proximity has to hold the form down somewhat, but he is clearly improving fast. (op 50/1)
Diabolical(USA) has some smart sprinting form in the US to his name – he won a Grade 2 when last seen in July – and he looked the only serious danger to the favourite beforehand, but he lost his race when stumbling badly leaving the stalls. He did well to stay on his feet, let alone go on to compete, and he will be worth another chance. (op 7/4)

296a MEYDAN RACES TO THE FUTURE H'CAP (TURF) 1m 2f (T)
6:30 (6:30) (95-110,106) 3-Y-0+

£36,180 (£12,060; £6,030; £3,015; £1,809; £1,206)

RPR
1 **Al Shemali**207 3142 4-9-3 **104**.....(t) LDettori 11 113+
(Saeed Bin Suroor) *trckd ldrs: rdn to chse ldrs 3f out: led 2f out: r.o wl: easily* **6/4**1
2 2 1/2 **Teslin (IRE)**110 6011 4-9-1 **102**.....(t) TedDurcan 2 102+
(Saeed Bin Suroor) *in rr of mid-div: rdn 2 1/2f out: r.o fnl 1 1/2f: nrst fin* **9/2**2
3 1 1/2 **Hazeymm (IRE)**21 5-9-3 **102**.....JMurtagh 7 99
(D Selvaratnam, UAE) *sn led: hdd 2f out but r.o wl at same pce* **25/1**
4 hd **Engrupido (ARG)**349 410 5-9-2 **101**.....KShea 5 98
(M F De Kock, South Africa) *mid-div: rdn 3f out: r.o fnl 1 1/2f: nrst fin* **7/1**3
5 1 3/4 **Mister Fasliyev (IRE)**63 6909 6-9-5 **105**.....PJSmullen 4 97
(E Charpy, UAE) *t.k.h in mid-div: gng wl 2 1/2f out: no room 1 1/2f out: one pce* **50/1**
6 1/4 **Where With All (IRE)**14 6-8-12 **98**.....TPO'Shea 6 90
(E Charpy, UAE) *trckd ldng trio: rdn 2 1/2f out: nt qckn* **15/2**
7 1 1/4 **Etihaad**7 204 6-8-12 **98**.....(t) BrettDoyle 9 87
(R Bouresly, Kuwait) *mid-div: wd 3f out: nvr nr to chal* **20/1**
8 1/2 **Coeur De Lionne (IRE)**122 5686 4-8-11 **99**.....SteveDrowne 12 87
(E A L Dunlop) *settled in rr: nvr nr to chal* **8/1**
9 1 1/4 **European Dream (IRE)**19 6655 5-9-3 **102**.....(p) MJKinane 1 89
(R C Guest) *settled in rr: last 3f out: n.d* **10/1**
10 4 1/4 **Silverlord (FR)**120 5744 4-8-10 **98**.....(t) KLatham 10 75
(Frau Nina Bach, Germany) *settled in last: nvr able to chal* **25/1**
11 1 3/4 **Dynamic Saint (USA)**21 5-9-4 **104**.....RyanMoore 8 78
(Doug Watson, UAE) *trckd ldrs: rdn 3f out: sn btn* **20/1**
12 4 **Anani (USA)**34 8-9-6 **106**.....(t) RichardMullen 3 72
(S Seemar, UAE) *mid-div on rail: rdn 2 1/2f out: one pce: wknd fnl f* **16/1**

2m 6.00s (1.50) **Going Correction** +0.375s/f (Good)
WFA 4 from 5yo+ 2lb 12 Ran SP% **127.7**
Speed ratings: **109,107,105,105,104 104,103,102,101,98 96,93**
Win: 2.00; PL 1.20, 2.10, 12.80; CSF 8.06; TRI 133.61; Placepot: £37.40 to a £1 stake. Pool: £11,542.50. 224.95 winning tickets..
Owner Godolphin **Bred** Minster Stud **Trained** Newmarket, Suffolk

FOCUS
A decent handicap, but they went steady early on.

NOTEBOOK
Al Shemali was below form in the Irish Derby on his final start for Sir Michael Stoute last July, but he had previously achieved an RPR of 111 when third to Authorized in the Dante, and an RPR of 112 when runner-up in the Hampton Court at Royal Ascot, so he looked well treated off an official mark of 104. That proved to be the case, as his rider never had to get that serious with him, before eventually easing him down near the line, and he can be rated value for over double the winning margin. He deserves another chance in Pattern company and, while that will obviously be tougher, he should be very competitive. (op 7/4)
Teslin(IRE) was having his first start since being picked up out of Brian Ellison's yard after his third in the Cambridgeshire. He stayed on nicely from off the modest pace to take second, but he was never a danger and should do better in a stronger-run race.
Hazeymm(IRE), given a pipe-opener on the dirt at the beginning of the year, was allowed to dictate just a steady pace and he battled on well in the straight.
Engrupido(ARG) was having his first start since last February and he can be expected to come on a little for this.
Mister Fasliyev(IRE) made a respectable debut for new connections on his first start in Dubai. (op 40/1)
Etihaad ran nicely in a Group 3 on dirt the previous week and he is probably a little better than he was able to show on his first-ever start on turf, as he made his move out wide. His challenge flattened out late on, but he is not one to give up on.
Coeur De Lionne(IRE), three times a winner on the Polytrack over 1m3f-1m4f for Roger Charlton last year, lacked the pace to get involved off a career-high mark on his debut for Ed Dunlop. A stronger gallop over 1m4f should suit better. (op 15/2)
European Dream(IRE), an improved hurdler of late, was never involved on his return to the Flat and he looks at his best when the ground is testing. (tchd 11/1)

263 KEMPTON (A.W) (R-H)
Friday, January 25

OFFICIAL GOING: Standard
Wind: Moderate, across Weather: Fine

297 DIGIBET CLASSIFIED STKS 5f (P)
6:20 (6:20) (Class 7) 4-Y-0+ £1,365 (£403; £201) **Stalls High**

Form RPR
6-03 1 **King Of Charm (IRE)**9 174 5-9-0 45.....(b) FergusSweeney 6 53
(G L Moore) *cl up on inner: chsd ldr over 1f out: led jst ins fnl f: urged along and sn clr* **15/8**1
4-33 2 2 1/2 **Lady Hopeful (IRE)**7 206 6-9-0 45.....(b) LPKeniry 5 44
(Peter Grayson) *s.s: in tch in last pair after 2f: effrt over 1f out: styd on to take 2nd last 50yds: no ch w wnr* **5/2**2
0-60 3 nk **Borzoi Maestro**4 254 7-9-0 42.....(vt) MickyFenton 2 43
(D G Bridgwater) *led: drvn and hdd jst ins fnl f: sn btn: lost 2nd last 50yds* **14/1**
-604 4 1 1/4 **Time Share (IRE)**15 106 4-9-0 42.....(be) TGMcLaughlin 4 38
(M Wigham) *s.i.s and drvn early: chsd ldng trio: rdn and no rspnse over 1f out: btn after* **3/1**3
0-50 5 nk **Lady Fas (IRE)**4 247 5-8-9 40.....KellyHarrison(5) 3 37
(A W Carroll) *t.k.h early: chsd ldr to over 1f out: wknd tamely* **33/1**
0-04 6 4 **Ava's World (IRE)**4 255 4-9-0 45.....(b1) AdrianMcCarthy 1 23
(Peter Grayson) *s.s: a last: wknd wl over 1f out* **8/1**

60.93 secs (0.43) **Going Correction** +0.025s/f (Slow) 6 Ran SP% **109.1**
Speed ratings (Par 97): **97,93,92,90,90 83**
CSF £6.38 TOTE £2.70: £1.10, £1.50; EX 7.00.
Owner Greystar Partnership **Bred** David Commins **Trained** Woodingdean, E Sussex

FOCUS
Weak form and not a race to dwell on.

Ava's World(IRE) Official explanation: jockey said filly missed the break

298 DIGIBET SPORTS BETTING H'CAP — 5f (P)
6:50 (6:51) (Class 6) (0-55,55) 3-Y-0 — £2,047 (£604; £302) Stalls High

Form — RPR

0-03 **1** **Wynberg (IRE)**[5] 237 3-8-8 **49** JimCrowley 1 56+
(S A Callaghan) *hld up off the pce on outer: gd prog over 1f out: led jst ins fnl f: nudged clr* **4/6**[1]

0-35 **2** 1 1/4 **Little Finch (IRE)**[5] 237 3-8-5 **46** oh1 (b) PaulEddery 3 44
(R C Guest) *pressed ldr: rdn to ld jst over 1f out: hdd and outpcd jst ins fnl f* **9/1**[3]

64-4 **3** 1 1/4 **Whitcombe Flyer (USA)**[6] 222 3-9-0 **55** (b) PaulDoe 8 49
(Jamie Poulton) *drvn in last and nt keen: styd on reuctantly fr over 1f out to take 3rd nr fin* **5/1**[2]

000- **4** nk **Miss Deeds (IRE)**[138] 5252 3-8-5 **46** RichardThomas 4 38
(N P Littmoden) *dwlt: t.k.h and hld up bhd ldrs: rdn and nt qckn over 1f out* **11/1**

000- **5** 1/2 **Ballyhealy Lady**[154] 4756 3-8-6 **52** JamesO'Reilly(5) 6 43
(D K Ivory) *bmpd s: plld hrd and hld up in last pair: rdn over 1f out: no rspnse* **16/1**

006- **6** 1/2 **Ocean Glory (IRE)**[36] 7195 3-8-10 **51** LPKeniry 7 40
(Peter Grayson) *wnt lft s: mde most to jst over 1f out: wknd* **12/1**

006- **7** 4 **Stoneacre Baby (USA)**[81] 6692 3-8-5 **46** oh1 AdrianMcCarthy 5 20
(Peter Grayson) *dwlt: sn trckd ldrs on inner: hanging and wknd over 1f out* **40/1**

00-5 **8** 3/4 **Far Song (IRE)**[23] 9 3-8-12 **53** (b1) FergusSweeney 2 25
(A M Balding) *pressed ldng pair on outer tl wknd wl over 1f out* **16/1**

62.65 secs (2.15) **Going Correction** +0.025s/f (Slow) — **8** Ran SP% **116.9**
Speed ratings (Par 95): **83,81,79,78,77 76,70,69**
CSF £8.04 CT £19.65 TOTE £1.70: £1.10, £2.50, £1.40; EX 5.90.
Owner Cast Hinge Searchfield & Smallbone 1 **Bred** Ged O'Leary **Trained** Newmarket, Suffolk
■ A first winner for Simon Callaghan, who recently took over from his father Neville.

FOCUS
Not strong form and the winning time was very slow, even for a race like this, but the winner looks to be going the right way.
Miss Deeds(IRE) Official explanation: jockey said filly ran too free
Stoneacre Baby(USA) Official explanation: jockey said filly hung right in straight

299 DIGIBET.COM H'CAP — 1m 2f (P)
7:20 (7:21) (Class 6) (0-52,53) 4-Y-0+ — £2,047 (£604; £302) Stalls High

Form — RPR

0/1 **1** **Lough Beg (IRE)**[23] 8 5-8-10 **48** (t) DaneO'Neill 12 59
(Miss Tor Sturgis) *wl plcd: prog to ld over 1f out: rdn out and wl in command fnl f* **4/1**[1]

10-1 **2** 2 **Sahf London**[10] 161 5-9-1 **53** 6ex (b) GeorgeBaker 2 60
(G L Moore) *led: drvn and hdd over 1f out: nt qckn and readily hld by wnr after* **5/1**[2]

0-64 **3** 1 1/2 **Shaheer (IRE)**[13] 133 6-8-12 **50** JimCrowley 1 54
(J Gallagher) *mistimed s: sn rcvrd: chsd wnr to over 1f out: one pce u.p* **8/1**

600- **4** 1/2 **Rawaabet (IRE)**[13] 3035 6-8-7 **45** AdrianMcCarthy 7 48
(P W Hiatt) *dwlt: t.k.h in midfield: rdn 3f out: no prog tl styd on ins fnl f* **33/1**

0-22 **5** 1/2 **Abbeygate**[8] 193 7-8-7 **45** (p) NickyMackay 6 47
(T Keddy) *hld up towards rr: rdn and fnd nil wl over 1f out: kpt on fnl f* **5/1**[2]

0-26 **6** 1 **Don Pasquale**[4] 251 6-8-10 **48** (v) MickyFenton 8 48+
(J T Stimpson) *hld up in last trio: effrt and c wdst of all bnd 2f out: plugged on fnl f: n.d* **10/1**

006- **7** nk **Theatre Royal**[27] 7275 5-8-7 **48** (b) NeilChalmers(3) 11 47
(Mouse Hamilton-Fairley) *chsd ldng pair to wl over 1f out: wknd* **14/1**

04-3 **8** hd **Riviera Red (IRE)**[16] 99 8-8-9 **47** ow2 TGMcLaughlin 9 46
(L Montague Hall) *hld up on inner in midfield: struggling to hold pl over 2f out: sn btn* **9/1**

440- **9** 1/2 **Dot's Delight**[53] 7009 4-8-12 **52** (b) RichardThomas 4 50
(Jim Best) *in tch in midfield: rdn 3f out: struggling fr 2f out* **12/1**

05-3 **10** nk **Mujobliged (IRE)**[21] 44 5-8-9 **47** JimmyQuinn 3 44
(J R Best) *rrd s: hld up wl in rr: last over 1f out: shkn up and no ch* **7/1**[3]

0-52 **11** 3 **Hayley's Flower (IRE)**[10] 161 4-8-2 **47** KevinGhunowa(5) 5 38
(J C Fox) *chsd ldng trio tl wknd wl over 1f out* **12/1**

360- **12** 1/2 **Royal Auditon**[225] 2595 7-8-11 **49** (p) SaleemGolam 10 39
(T T Clement) *wl in rr: drvn and brief effrt 3f out: sn wknd* **33/1**

2m 7.84s (-0.16) **Going Correction** +0.025s/f (Slow)
WFA 4 from 5yo+ 2lb — **12** Ran SP% **124.0**
Speed ratings (Par 101): **101,99,98,97,97 96,96,96,95,95 93,92**
CSF £24.56 CT £157.01 TOTE £4.90: £1.50, £2.00, £4.00; EX 29.40.
Owner M M McGrogan **Bred** Joe Fogarty **Trained** Lambourn, Berks

FOCUS
An ordinary handicap dominated largey by those who raced to the fore. Solid form for the grade.

300 DIGIBET CASINO H'CAP — 1m 2f (P)
7:50 (7:52) (Class 6) (0-65,65) 4-Y-0+ — £2,047 (£604; £302) Stalls High

Form — RPR

12-1 **1** **Bridgewater Boys**[20] 57 7-9-6 **63** (b) GeorgeBaker 2 71
(G L Moore) *trckd ldr: led wl over 1f out: sn pressed and rdn: kpt on wl fnl f* **10/11**[1]

32-5 **2** 1/2 **Mon Petite Amour**[7] 209 5-8-11 **54** FergusSweeney 4 61
(D W P Arbuthnot) *hld up and sn last: prog on wd outside over 2f out to chse wnr over 1f out: chal fnl f: a 1/2 l down and nt qckn* **13/2**

530- **3** 2 **Bramcote Lorne**[45] 7109 5-8-10 **53** StephenDonohoe 5 56
(R C Guest) *led: set slow pce for 4f: rdn and hdd wl over 1f out: steadily outpcd fnl f* **14/1**

14-5 **4** 1/2 **Magic Warrior**[12] 148 8-9-5 **62** PatDobbs 3 64+
(J C Fox) *t.k.h: hld up in tch: rdn and nt qckn wl over 1f out: n.d after* **6/1**[3]

30-1 **5** nk **Alexander Guru**[14] 128 4-9-6 **65** JimmyQuinn 6 66
(M Blanshard) *trckd ldng pair: rdn and nt qckn wl over 1f out: fdd* **8/1**

6-45 **6** 2 1/2 **Play Up Pompey**[9] 180 6-8-7 **53** NeilChalmers(3) 9 49
(J J Bridger) *s.s: t.k.h and hld up in last pair: checked jst over 3f out and detached in last: n.d after* **8/1**

15-2 **7** nk **Satindra (IRE)**[14] 122 4-9-5 **64** (tp) MickyFenton 1 60
(John A Harris) *t.k.h: sn trckd ldrs: rdn and wknd wl over 1f out* **5/1**[2]

2m 10.31s (2.31) **Going Correction** +0.025s/f (Slow)
WFA 4 from 5yo+ 2lb — **7** Ran SP% **125.6**
Speed ratings (Par 101): **91,90,89,88,88 86,86**
CSF £8.99 CT £59.65 TOTE £1.70: £1.10, £4.00; EX 11.00.
Owner Matthew Green & Richard Green **Bred** Southill Stud **Trained** Woodingdean, E Sussex

FOCUS
A modest handicap run at a very steady early pace. The winning time was unsurprisingly very moderate. The winner did not need to improve.
Play Up Pompey Official explanation: jockey said gelding suffered interference in running

301 DIGIBET H'CAP — 5f (P)
8:20 (8:21) (Class 4) (0-85,80) 4-Y-0+ — £4,210 (£1,252; £625; £312) Stalls High

Form — RPR

60-2 **1** **Fromsong (IRE)**[9] 187 10-8-7 **74** JamesO'Reilly(5) 5 87
(D K Ivory) *mde all: pressed wl over 1f out: drvn and drew clr sn after: styd on wl* **7/2**[2]

25-2 **2** 3 1/2 **Harry Up**[21] 45 7-9-3 **79** (p) DaneO'Neill 1 79
(K A Ryan) *pressed wnr: tried to chal wl over 1f out: sn btn: wknd ins fnl f: jst hld on for 2nd* **7/2**[2]

-221 **3** nk **Sands Crooner (IRE)**[9] 187 5-8-5 **70** 6ex (v) TolleyDean(3) 6 69
(D Shaw) *s.i.s: outpcd in last and rdn: styd on fr jst over 1f out: nrly snatched 2nd* **4/1**[3]

00-3 **4** 1 1/2 **Dress To Impress (IRE)**[10] 162 4-8-13 **75** AdamKirby 8 69
(G A Butler) *in tch: chsd ldng pair 1/2-way: rdn and no imp over 1f out: fdd* **5/2**[1]

04-6 **5** 1 **Dancing Mystery**[17] 84 14-8-8 **70** (b) StephenCarson 7 60
(E A Wheeler) *t.k.h: snatched up after 1f: nvr gng pce to trble ldrs after* **14/1**

/00- **6** nk **Nigella**[188] 3749 5-9-1 **77** StephenDonohoe 2 66
(E S McMahon) *chsd ldng pair to 1/2-way: sn rdn: outpcd fnl 2f* **20/1**

41-5 **7** 2 **Stolt (IRE)**[17] 84 4-8-13 **75** JimmyQuinn 3 57
(N Wilson) *plld hrd: rn v wd bnd over 3f out: nvr on terms after* **5/1**

59.34 secs (-1.16) **Going Correction** +0.025s/f (Slow) — **7** Ran SP% **121.1**
Speed ratings (Par 105): **110,104,103,101,99 99,96**
CSF £17.51 CT £52.33 TOTE £5.40: £2.50, £1.90; EX 13.50.
Owner Dean Ivory **Bred** Mrs Teresa Bergin **Trained** Radlett, Herts
■ Stewards' Enquiry : Adam Kirby one-day ban: careless riding (Feb 5)

FOCUS
A fair little sprint handicap run at a good gallop. The winner recorded a decent winning time for the grade and is rated to his best form of the last year or so.
Dress To Impress(IRE) Official explanation: jockey said colt hung left

302 DIGIBET.COM CLAIMING STKS — 1m (P)
8:50 (8:52) (Class 6) 4-Y-0+ — £2,047 (£604; £302) Stalls High

Form — RPR

6-24 **1** **Waterline Twenty (IRE)**[7] 208 5-9-2 70 StephenDonohoe 6 70
(P D Evans) *mostly chsd ldr: rdn over 2f out: clsd over 1f out: narrow ld ins fnl f: hld on wl* **5/1**

00-4 **2** hd **Copper King**[12] 148 4-8-13 63 TQuinn 1 67
(J W Hills) *settled in last: rdn and effrt over 2f out: clsd to chal fnl f: pressed wnr hrd: jst hld* **13/2**

00-3 **3** 1/2 **Count Ceprano (IRE)**[4] 245 4-8-8 77 GabrielHannon(7) 5 68
(M D I Usher) *cl up: rdn on inner over 2f out: clsd to chal 1f out: upsides ins fnl f: nt qckn* **9/4**[2]

-410 **4** 1 1/4 **Seneschal**[2] 275 7-9-7 65 TPQueally 4 71
(A B Haynes) *led at decent pce: gng best 2f out: rdn over 1f out: collared and wknd ins fnl f* **3/1**[3]

53-1 **5** 13 **Hucking Heat (IRE)**[21] 40 4-9-0 68 (p) GeorgeBaker 3 34
(J R Boyle) *nvr gng wl: rdn on outer 1/2-way: wknd over 2f out* **2/1**[1]

1m 38.95s (-0.85) **Going Correction** +0.025s/f (Slow) — **5** Ran SP% **119.1**
Speed ratings (Par 101): **105,104,104,103,90**
CSF £36.29 TOTE £7.30: £3.00, £5.60; EX 21.20.
Owner Waterline Racing Club **Bred** Mountarmstrong Stud **Trained** Pandy, Monmouths

FOCUS
There was a good pace on here but the overall form is slightly dubious.
Hucking Heat(IRE) Official explanation: jockey said gelding ran flat

303 DIGIBET.COM CLASSIFIED STKS — 1m 3f (P)
9:20 (9:22) (Class 7) 4-Y-0+ — £1,365 (£403; £201) Stalls High

Form — RPR

0-11 **1** **Contra Mundum (USA)**[1] 282 5-9-13 43 TQuinn 12 67+
(B G Powell) *trckd ldr to over 5f out: effrt to ld over 2f out: clr over 1f out: pushed out: comf* **8/13**[1]

0-11 **2** 3 1/2 **Megalala (IRE)**[4] 242 7-9-10 42 NeilChalmers(3) 9 59
(J J Bridger) *led to over 2f out: sn outpcd by wnr: kpt on and hld on for 2nd* **9/2**[2]

0-32 **3** nk **Ernmoor**[4] 242 6-9-1 41 J-PGuillambert 1 46
(J R Jenkins) *heavily restrained s: hld up in detached last: urged along and prog on wd outside over 2f out: r.o fnl f: nrly snatched 2nd* **8/1**[3]

0-62 **4** 1 1/2 **Arthurs Dream (IRE)**[7] 215 6-8-10 39 KellyHarrison(5) 2 44
(A W Carroll) *hld up in midfield: prog 3f out: disp 2nd 2f out: fdd fnl f* **14/1**

430- **5** 3 **Rubilini**[85] 6607 4-8-7 44 NataliaGemelova(5) 8 38
(Miss Sheena West) *racd wd: trckd ldrs: rdn 3f out: outpcd fr over 2f out* **20/1**

00-5 **6** 4 **Mtoto Girl**[12] 147 4-8-12 43 DaneO'Neill 6 31
(J J Bridger) *hld up towards rr: gng wl enough 3f out: rdn and no rspnse over 2f out* **33/1**

0-03 **7** 3 1/2 **Come What July (IRE)**[10] 161 7-8-12 44 TolleyDean(3) 5 25
(D Shaw) *hld up in last pair: rdn over 3f out: struggling and btn over 2f out* **8/1**[3]

000- **8** hd **Ashmolian (IRE)**[67] 6866 5-9-1 45 (b1) SamHitchcott 4 25
(Miss Z C Davison) *t.k.h: prog to chse ldr over 5f out to 3f out: wknd u.str.p* **20/1**

0-00 **9** 4 **War Feather**[2] 269 6-9-1 41 (b) TPQueally 7 17
(T D McCarthy) *dwlt: in tch: rdn 3f out: wknd over 2f out* **50/1**

000- **10** 1 1/2 **For Eileen**[36] 5710 4-8-12 42 VinceSlattery 11 15
(D Burchell) *t.k.h: cl up: 3rd 3f out: sn wknd u.p* **50/1**

2m 21.03s (-0.87) **Going Correction** +0.025s/f (Slow)
WFA 4 from 5yo+ 3lb — **10** Ran SP% **125.4**
Speed ratings (Par 97): **104,101,101,100,97 95,92,92,89,88**
CSF £3.83 TOTE £1.60: £1.02, £1.90, £2.40; EX 5.70 Place 6 £61.92, Place 5 £48.49 .
Owner D J Coles **Bred** Christopher Buckley **Trained** Upper Lambourn, Berks

FOCUS
The pace was not overly strong but the form looks solid rated through the runner-up.
Ashmolian(IRE) Official explanation: jockey said gelding ran too free
T/Plt: £57.90 to a £1 stake. Pool: £94,771.35. 1,193.05 winning tickets. T/Qpdt: £38.10 to a £1 stake. Pool: £6,736.90. 130.70 winning tickets. JN

284 WOLVERHAMPTON (A.W) (L-H)

Friday, January 25

OFFICIAL GOING: Standard

Wind: Fresh, half-behind

304 PONTIN'S HALF TERM DEALS 0844 576 5938 H'CAP 5f 20y(P)
1:40 (1:40) (Class 6) (0-62,66) 4-Y-0+ £2,047 (£604; £302) Stalls Low

Form RPR

31-2 1 **By The Edge (IRE)**[6] 230 4-8-12 58 PhillipMakin 7 69
(T D Barron) *trckd ldr: led ins fnl f: drvn out* 3/1[3]

60-4 2 ¾ **Commander Wish**[16] 86 5-8-9 58 (tp) NeilChalmers(3) 2 66
(Lucinda Featherstone) *in tch whn n.m.r on ins 1/2-way: sn rdn: swtchd rt coming into st: r.o to go 2nd wl ins fnl f* 9/4[2]

00-5 3 2 **Sparkwell**[6] 230 6-8-8 57 TolleyDean(3) 5 58
(D Shaw) *t.k.h: trckd ldrs: rdn over 1f out: one pce fnl f: b.b.v* 8/1

66-1 4 1½ **Garlogs**[13] 142 5-8-5 56 RussellKennemore(5) 4 52
(R Hollinshead) *led tl rdn and hdd ins fnl f: no ex* 15/8[1]

000- 5 1 **Overstayed (IRE)**[36] 7206 5-8-11 60 (be) JohnMcAuley(3) 6 52
(M Mullineaux) *in tch tl rdn and wknd over 1f out* 11/1

56-0 6 8 **Totally Free**[15] 109 4-8-12 58 (v) HayleyTurner 1 21
(M D I Usher) *s.i.s: rdn and outpcd* 33/1

61.69 secs (-0.61) **Going Correction** +0.05s/f (Slow) 6 Ran SP% **112.9**

Speed ratings (Par 101): **106,104,101,99,97 84**

CSF £10.33 TOTE £4.00: £1.50, £1.90; EX 10.80.

Owner J Starbuck **Bred** A M Burke **Trained** Maunby, N Yorks

FOCUS

A moderate sprint handicap. The front pair give the form a solid look.

Commander Wish Official explanation: jockey said gelding suffered interference on bend

Sparkwell Official explanation: vet said gelding bled from the nose

305 WOLVERHAMPTON RACECOURSE FOR HOTEL & CONFERENCING (S) STKS 7f 32y(P)
2:15 (2:16) (Class 6) 4-Y-0+ £1,774 (£523; £262) Stalls High

Form RPR

3-04 1 **Green Pirate**[5] 235 6-8-12 60 (p) RichardKingscote 9 62
(W M Brisbourne) *settled in rr fr wd draw: hdwy on outside 3f out: rdn and edgd lft bef led 1f out: sn in command* 6/5[1]

3 2 3 **Kingoftheswingers (IRE)**[1] 284 4-8-12 57 AdamKirby 3 54
(Adrian McGuinness, Ire) *a in tch: rdn 2f out: styd on to go 2nd ins fnl f* 5/2[2]

50-6 3 ¾ **Now You See Me**[7] 213 4-8-7 0 ChrisCatlin 1 47
(K McAuliffe) *led tl rdn and hdd 1f out: one pce and lost 2nd ins fnl f* 8/1

16/0 4 1½ **Benayoun**[19] 68 4-8-5 53 DavidProbert(7) 7 48
(B J Llewellyn) *in rr: hdwy whn rdn and hung lft over 1f out: kpt on fnl f: nvr nrr* 40/1

00-4 5 nk **Marmooq**[12] 151 5-8-12 47 (p) DaleGibson 5 47
(M J Attwater) *trckd ldrs: wnt 2nd 1/2-way: rdn and wknd over 1f out* 7/1[3]

4 6 1 **Oberows Lady (IRE)**[1] 289 6-8-7 35 LPKeniry 6 39
(Adrian McGuinness, Ire) *hld up in rr: rdn over 2f out: edgd lft and wknd over 1f out* 20/1

0660 7 nk **Telepathic (IRE)**[1] 289 8-8-7 36 (b) DanielleMcCreery(5) 2 44
(A Berry) *t.k.h: a in rr* 50/1

6-04 8 11 **Capital Lass**[19] 66 5-8-7 42 HayleyTurner 8 9
(A J McCabe) *chsd ldrs: rdn over 2f out: sn wknd* 16/1

0/0- 9 33 **Sharp Tune (USA)**[293] 721 6-8-8 35 ow1 (b[1]) HaddenFrost(5) 4 —
(J D Frost) *trckd ldr to 1/2-way: rdn and wknd qckly: virtually p.u fnl f: t.o* 100/1

1m 30.25s (0.65) **Going Correction** +0.05s/f (Slow) 9 Ran SP% **113.7**

Speed ratings (Par 101): **98,94,93,92,91 90,90,77,39**

CSF £3.99 TOTE £2.10: £1.30, £1.60, £2.00; EX 5.40 Trifecta £33.20 Pool £538.75 - 11.51 winning units..There was no bid for the winner.

Owner J Babb **Bred** Hrh Princess Michael Of Kent **Trained** Great Ness, Shropshire

FOCUS

An uncompetitive seller, and weak form. The winning time was 1.57 seconds quicker than the following 46-55, but they went no pace in that race, so comparisons are misleading.

Marmooq Official explanation: jockey said gelding lost its action in closing stages

306 ROGER THOMPSON 70TH CELEBRATION H'CAP 7f 32y(P)
2:50 (2:51) (Class 6) (0-55,55) 3-Y-0 £2,047 (£604; £302) Stalls High

Form RPR

4-05 1 **Talamahana**[16] 92 3-8-9 50 (b) LPKeniry 9 55
(S Kirk) *a.p: edgd lft bef led over 1f out: rdn out* 15/2

000- 2 1 **Rhode Island Red (USA)**[154] 4756 3-9-0 55 (v[1]) RichardKingscote 1 57
(H J L Dunlop) *slowly away in rr tl hdwy on outside 2f out: hung lft but r.o to go 2nd ins fnl f* 12/1

50-3 3 1½ **Transcendent (IRE)**[22] 23 3-8-7 48 JimmyQuinn 8 46
(J D Bethell) *mid-div: hdwy on ins over 2f out: short of room and swtchd rt over 1f out: r.o ins fnl f* 9/4[1]

65-3 4 1¼ **Run From Nun**[13] 141 3-8-9 50 NeilPollard 3 45
(John Berry) *a.p: rdn over 1f out: one pce after* 10/3[2]

5-66 5 nk **Seductive Witch**[16] 92 3-8-9 50 HayleyTurner 7 44
(M D I Usher) *towards rr: effrt over 1f out: nvr nrr* 12/1

06-5 6 1¼ **Neyraan**[14] 130 3-9-0 55 GregFairley 2 46
(M Johnston) *t.k.h: led tl rdn and hdd over 1f out: wknd after* 4/1[3]

000- 7 2½ **Amazing Spirit**[135] 5322 3-8-5 46 oh1 LiamJones 5 30
(Miss V Haigh) *trckd ldr: hld whn hmpd over 1f out: no ch after* 12/1

05-4 8 5 **Where's Killoran**[16] 92 3-8-1 47 ColinHaddon(5) 4 17
(Peter Grayson) *sn bhd: lost tch 2f out* 16/1

1m 31.82s (2.22) **Going Correction** +0.05s/f (Slow) 8 Ran SP% **114.6**

Speed ratings (Par 95): **89,87,86,84,84 82,80,74**

CSF £90.96 CT £268.38 TOTE £8.60: £1.90, £2.50, £1.20; EX 60.70 Trifecta £215.50 Pool £564.58 - 1.86 winning units..

Owner M Nicolson, G Doran, A Wilson **Bred** Mrs D Du Feu **Trained** Upper Lambourn, Berks

FOCUS

A very moderate handicap and weak form. They went pretty steady through the opening stages and the winning time was 1.57 seconds slower than the earlier seller.

307 HAPPY HALF TERM @ PONTIN'S CLAIMING STKS 5f 20y(P)
3:25 (3:25) (Class 5) 3-Y-0+ £2,457 (£725; £362) Stalls Low

Form RPR

6-65 1 **Doubtful Sound (USA)**[7] 213 4-9-8 70 NeilBrown(5) 1 79
(T D Barron) *racd in 3rd pl: rdn over 2f out: swtchd rt ent fnl f: hung lft and led ins fnl f: won gng away* 4/1[3]

21-3 2 2½ **Pegasus Dancer (FR)**[15] 113 4-9-13 71 (p) FergalLynch 3 70
(K A Ryan) *chsd ldr: ev ch whn bmpd ent fnl f: nt qckn ins fnl f* 4/5[1]

0-22 3 ½ **Diademas (USA)**[10] 170 3-8-2 68 (be) AshleyMorgan(7) 2 59
(V Smith) *s.i.s: racd in last pl: hung lft over 1f out: r.o ins fnl f: nvr nrr* 9/4[2]

15-0 4 1½ **Wibbadune (IRE)**[16] 86 4-9-2 49 (b[1]) LPKeniry 4 52
(Peter Grayson) *led: sn clr: rdn and edgd rt ent fnl f: hung lft and hdd ins fnl f: no ex* 25/1

61.52 secs (-0.78) **Going Correction** +0.05s/f (Slow)

WFA 3 from 4yo 15lb 4 Ran SP% **110.2**

Speed ratings (Par 103): **108,104,103,100**

CSF £7.94 TOTE £4.20; EX 9.00.

Owner Miss N J Barron **Bred** Millsec, Ltd **Trained** Maunby, N Yorks

FOCUS

Only four runners, but the front three in the betting were separated by just 1lb and this is reasonable claiming form. The outsider, Wibbadune, went off too quickly.

308 CAPTAIN CROC MAKES PONTIN'S ROCK CONDITIONS STKS 1m 141y(P)
4:00 (4:00) (Class 2) 4-Y-0+ £9,971 (£2,985; £1,492; £747; £372) Stalls Low

Form RPR

321- 1 **Baharah (USA)**[55] 6992 4-8-11 102 HayleyTurner 1 108+
(G A Butler) *in tch tl hmpd and lost pl over 4f out: hdwy over 2f out: wnt 2nd over 1f out: rdn to ld ins fnl f* 15/8[2]

10-1 2 1¾ **Capricorn Run (USA)**[20] 62 5-9-5 109 (v) AdamKirby 3 111
(A J McCabe) *in tch: led 5f out: rdn over 1f out: hdd ins fnl f: nt pce of wnr* 10/3[3]

064- 3 3½ **Murfreesboro**[55] 6992 5-9-0 90 (be) DeanMcKeown 5 98
(K J Burke) *trckd ldrs: rdn over 1f out: edgd lft and one pce after* 25/1

13-1 4 1¼ **Fajr (IRE)**[6] 227 6-9-0 106 (b) GeorgeBaker 2 95
(Miss Gay Kelleway) *led tl hdd 5f out: rdn wl over 1f out: wknd fnl f* 6/5[1]

50/ 5 71 **Neveronamonday (IRE)**[512] 4956 4-8-8 0 DanielleMcCreery 4 —
(A Berry) *disp ld early: edgd lft and wknd over 4f out: t.o* 500/1

1m 50.42s (-0.08) **Going Correction** +0.05s/f (Slow)

WFA 4 from 5yo+ 1lb 5 Ran SP% **107.4**

Speed ratings (Par 109): **102,100,97,96,33**

CSF £7.97 TOTE £2.80: £1.80, £1.50; EX 9.40 TRIFECTA Pool £515.10 - 1.35 winning units..

Owner Erik Penser **Bred** Darley **Trained** Newmarket, Suffolk

FOCUS

Only four of the five runners counted, but still a very good conditions contest, with three of these rated over 100. The early pace was steady, which did not suit the favourite. Not really form to take too literally.

NOTEBOOK

Baharah(USA) ◆ looked a nice prospect when getting off the mark at the third attempt in a similar event over 7f at Kempton on her previous start and she confirmed herself a very smart filly in the making with another ready success. She looked in real trouble when losing her place badly around half a mile from the finish, dropping a good six or so lengths off the lead, but she quickly came back on the bridle and her rider appeared confident enough. There was a lot to like about the way she made up the lost ground and she readily accounted for Capricorn Run in the straight, without her rider having to resort to the whip, although she did wander slightly when asked to go by. That was probably down to greenness, so she can be given the benefit of the doubt for now, but it is something to keep an eye on in future. It would be unwise to get too carried away, as there were doubts about the runner-up's stamina for this trip, and Fajr did not have the race run to suit, but this was still a taking performance. She could well be a Group-class filly in the making if she continues to go the right way and she could face an early test at that level with the Godolphin Mile at Nad Al Sheba in March being mentioned as a possible target. (op 13-8)

Capricorn Run(USA) improved throughout 2007 and showed himself still on the up at the beginning of this year when winning a similar event over 1m at Lingfield on his latest start. However, they went no pace that day and, with all his previous best form coming over 6f-7f, there had to be a doubt about his stamina for this trip in a strongly run race. As it turned out, the pace was not that strong and, having ended up towards the front much sooner than his rider would probably have liked, he failed to see out his race anywhere near as well as the winner. On this evidence, he will be suited by a return to shorter trips. (op 11-4 tchd 5-2 and 7-2)

Murfreesboro finished a little closer to today's winner than he had managed at Kempton on his previous start, and he reversed form with Fajr, but he was still well held. He will be better off in handicap company off his current sort of mark. (op 22-1)

Fajr(IRE) produced a decent turn of foot when coming from off the pace in a slowly run handicap off a mark of 106 at Lingfield on his previous start, but this track rides totally different and his rider clearly didn't want him out the back this time with no pace on again. As it turned out the change in tactics failed to have the desired effect and he was some way below form. Official explanation: trainer said race came too soon for gelding (op 7-4)

309 HOTEL & CONFERENCING AT WOLVERHAMPTON H'CAP 1m 1f 103y(P)
4:30 (4:30) (Class 4) (0-85,82) 4-Y-0+ £4,533 (£1,348; £674; £336) Stalls Low

Form RPR

51-1 1 **Scamperdale**[22] 34 6-9-3 79 TPQueally 4 86+
(B P J Baugh) *hld up in rr: hdwy on ins over 2f out: r.o to ld ins fnl f: drvn out* 4/1[3]

64-2 2 hd **Mataram (USA)**[16] 97 5-9-2 78 ChrisCatlin 3 85
(W Jarvis) *t.k.h: in tch: led and edgd lft u.p over 1f out: hdd ins fnl f: kpt on* 10/3[2]

204- 3 hd **Tufton**[104] 6175 5-9-1 77 StephenDonohoe 7 84
(Ian Williams) *hld up: rdn and hdwy 2f out: ev ch ins fnl f: kpt on* 10/1

111- 4 1¾ **Confidentiality (IRE)**[43] 7131 4-9-5 82 NickyMackay 2 88+
(M Wigham) *hld up towards rr: hdwy whn n.m.r ent fnl f: swtchd rt: kpt on but nt nr to chal* 2/1[1]

/00- 5 1 **Freeloader (IRE)**[176] 1767 8-8-12 81 BMcHugh(7) 1 82
(R A Fahey) *led for 1f: rdn and ever ch ent fnl f: wknd ins fnl f* 16/1

460- 6 3 **Rock Anthem (IRE)**[113] 5941 4-8-8 74 TravisBlock(3) 5 69
(Mike Murphy) *sn trckd ldr: ev ch appr fnl f: wknd ins fnl f* 33/1

341- 7 5 **Pearl (IRE)**[51] 7032 4-8-8 71 LiamJones 8 55
(I A Wood) *sn in tch on outside: wknd over 2f out* 11/1

351- 8 hd **Gloucester**[28] 5296 5-8-9 71 JimmyQuinn 6 55
(J J Quinn) *led after 1f: rdn and hmpd whn hdd over 1f out: wknd qckly* 5/1

2m 1.58s (-0.12) **Going Correction** +0.05s/f (Slow)

WFA 4 from 5yo+ 1lb 8 Ran SP% **119.3**

Speed ratings (Par 105): **102,101,101,100,99 96,92,91**

CSF £18.67 CT £126.71 TOTE £4.40: £1.30, £1.50, £2.50; EX 18.00 Trifecta £270.90 w/u.

Owner Saddle Up Racing **Bred** Mrs J A Prescott **Trained** Audley, Staffs

■ Stewards' Enquiry : Nicky Mackay 16-day ban (takes into account previous offences; four days deferred): careless riding (Feb 9-20)

FOCUS
A fair, competitive handicap on paper, but it turned into a sprint following a steady early pace and the form needs treating with caution. The winner could still have more improvement in him.

310 HALF PRICE BREAKS @ PONTINS.COM MAIDEN STKS 1m 1f 103y(P)
5:00 (5:02) (Class 5) 3-Y-O £2,590 (£770; £385; £192) Stalls Low

Form RPR
43- **1** **Caribana**[35] 7208 3-8-12 0 .... J-PGuillambert 4 75
(M A Jarvis) *in tch: wnt 2nd 2f out: rdn to ld ent fnl f: pushed out* 5/2[2]
\- **2** 1 **Montfjord (IRE)** 3-9-3 0 .... ChrisCatlin 2 78
(E J O'Neill) *led tl edgd rt and hdd ent fnl f: kpt on* 5/1[3]
3 5 **Boy Racer (IRE)** 3-9-3 0 .... GregFairley 3 67
(M Johnston) *trckd ldrs: disp 2nd briefly 2f out: fdd ins fnl f* 6/5[1]
20-5 **4** 7 **Samurai Warrior**[13] 135 3-9-3 76 .... TPQueally 5 53
(P J Makin) *trckd ldrs: wnt 2nd over 3f out to 2f out: rdn and wknd over 1f out* 7/1
0- **5** hd **Pie O My (IRE)**[76] 6763 3-9-3 0 .... AdamKirby 6 52
(J Jay) *slowly away: effrt over 2f out: nvr on terms* 100/1
6- **6** 9 **Grail Knight**[41] 7152 3-9-3 0 .... HayleyTurner 7 33
(Miss Gay Kelleway) *dwlt and wnt rt leaving stalls: a bhd* 40/1
7 4 **Lucky Character** 3-9-3 0 .... SamHitchcott 1 25
(N J Vaughan) *w ldrs tl wknd over 3f out* 18/1

2m 1.12s (-0.58) **Going Correction** +0.05s/f (Slow) 7 Ran SP% 111.9
Speed ratings (Par 97): **104,103,98,92,92 84,80**
CSF £14.69 TOTE £3.20: £1.80, £2.60; EX 16.60 Place 6 £97.51, Place 5 £50.63..
Owner Miss K Rausing **Bred** Miss K Rausing **Trained** Newmarket, Suffolk
FOCUS
Probably ordinary form, and not easy to rate, but an interesting enough maiden.
T/Plt: £67.80 to a £1 stake. Pool: £49,664.95. 534.40 winning tickets. T/Qpdt: £33.50 to a £1 stake. Pool: £2,945.40. 64.90 winning tickets. JS

270 LINGFIELD (L-H)
Saturday, January 26

OFFICIAL GOING: Standard
Wind: Fresh, half behind

311 ARENALEISUREPLC.COM MAIDEN STKS 1m (P)
12:40 (12:42) (Class 5) 3-Y-O+ £2,331 (£693; £346; £173) Stalls High

Form RPR
546- **1** **Garden Party**[119] 5819 4-9-13 65 .... TGMcLaughlin 7 76
(Jane Chapple-Hyam) *trckd ldr: nosed ahd 2f out: edgd lft fnl f: all out* 13/2[3]
256- **2** nk **Oberlin (USA)**[93] 6451 3-8-7 72 .... GregFairley 3 71
(M Johnston) *trckd ldrs: rdn and styd on to go 2nd appr fnl f: kpt on u.p* 10/11[1]
6 **3** 3/4 **Wherry (USA)**[13] 146 3-8-2 0 .... MatthewHenry 4 64
(M A Jarvis) *a in tch: rdn 2f out: styd on fnl f* 8/1
04- **4** 1 1/4 **Jal Music**[178] 4070 3-8-2 0 .... KevinGhunowa(5) 2 66
(R A Harris) *mid-div: hung lft fr 3f out: rdn 2f out: kpt on one pce fnl f* 50/1
223- **5** 1/2 **Hamalka (IRE)**[122] 5734 3-8-2 72 .... ChrisCatlin 8 60
(B W Hills) *led tl hdd 2f out: wknd 1f out* 3/1[2]
5 **6** 5 **Precision Break (USA)**[7] 223 3-8-7 0 .... JohnEgan 6 53
(J S Moore) *slowly away: a in rr* 12/1
0 **7** 1 **Ten Hour Lunch**[7] 221 3-8-7 0 .... StephenDonohoe 5 51
(B J Meehan) *sn bhd on outside: rdn along: nvr on terms* 66/1
-0 **8** 1 3/4 **South Wales**[21] 52 3-8-7 0 .... SaleemGolam 1 47
(S C Williams) *slowly away: a bhd* 66/1

1m 38.75s (0.55) **Going Correction** +0.075s/f (Slow)
WFA 3 from 4yo 20lb 8 Ran SP% 114.5
Speed ratings (Par 103): **100,99,98,97,97 92,91,89**
CSF £12.90 TOTE £9.00: £1.50, £1.10, £1.60; EX 14.40 Trifecta £123.10 Part won. Pool: £173.52, 0.50 winning units..
Owner Mrs Ruth M Serrell **Bred** The Queen **Trained** Lambourn, Berks
FOCUS
A modest maiden run at an ordinary early pace. The winning time was 1.74 seconds slower than the later 71-85 handicap.

312 HOTEL COMING TO LINGFIELD PARK H'CAP 6f (P)
1:10 (1:10) (Class 5) (0-75,72) 4-Y-O+ £2,590 (£770; £385; £192) Stalls Low

Form RPR
41-1 **1** **Benllech**[17] 94 4-9-4 72 .... SimonWhitworth 5 82+
(M Wigham) *hld up in tch: rdn to go 2nd 2f out: led over 1f out: pushed out: comf* 15/8[1]
1-11 **2** 1 1/4 **Muktasb (USA)**[11] 165 7-8-13 67 .... (v) AdamKirby 1 73
(D Shaw) *hld up in rr: hdwy on outside over 1f out: r.o to go 2nd nr fin* 11/4[2]
30-0 **3** nk **Kempsey**[13] 149 6-8-4 58 .... (b) ChrisCatlin 4 63
(J J Bridger) *led tl rdn and hdd over 1f out: kpt on: lost 2nd nr fin* 6/1
0-66 **4** 3/4 **Quality Street**[3] 275 6-9-1 69 .... (p) RichardThomas 3 72
(P Butler) *trckd ldr to 2f out: rallied and kpt on fnl f* 8/1
4-00 **5** 1 1/4 **Mine Behind**[3] 275 8-8-11 65 .... JimmyQuinn 2 64
(J R Best) *racd in 4th: effrt on ins over 1f out: no ex ins fnl f* 4/1[3]

1m 11.2s (-0.70) **Going Correction** +0.075s/f (Slow) 5 Ran SP% 106.8
Speed ratings (Par 103): **107,105,104,103,102**
CSF £6.76 TOTE £3.20: £1.60, £1.30; EX 6.20.
Owner R J Lorenz **Bred** Speedlith Group **Trained** Newmarket, Suffolk
FOCUS
Just the five runners and, although the first two home came into this in real good order, this was not a very competitive handicap. That said, the form looks solid. The early pace was strong, thanks to Kempsey, but seemed to slow just before the home turn.

313 PLAY GOLF @ LINGFIELD PARK H'CAP 7f (P)
1:45 (1:45) (Class 4) (0-80,80) 4-Y-O+ £4,100 (£1,227; £613; £306; £152) Stalls Low

Form RPR
530- **1** **Sailor King (IRE)**[96] 6391 6-8-10 77 .... JamesO'Reilly(5) 8 88
(D K Ivory) *hld up in rr: rdn over 1f out: qcknd to ld wl ins fnl f: won gng away* 15/2
04-4 **2** 1 1/2 **Super Frank (IRE)**[23] 26 5-8-11 73 .... ChrisCatlin 2 80
(J Akehurst) *stmbld leaving stalls and bhd: rdn in rr 2f out: r.o wl fnl f to go 2nd towards fin* 13/8[1]
20-5 **3** 1/2 **Cornus**[18] 85 6-9-1 77 .... (be) JamesDoyle 7 83
(A J McCabe) *in tch on outside: rdn 2f out: kpt on fnl f* 10/1
62-2 **4** nk **Bazroy (IRE)**[23] 26 4-9-4 80 .... (b) StephenDonohoe 4 85
(P D Evans) *trckd ldr: led 3f out: rdn and hdd wl ins fnl f: no ex cl home* 11/4[2]
6-45 **5** 1 3/4 **Resplendent Alpha**[8] 210 4-9-1 77 .... JimmyQuinn 6 77
(P Howling) *in tch tl rdn and wknd ins fnl f* 11/2[3]
640- **6** 1 **Buy On The Red**[26] 7289 7-9-4 80 .... (p) HayleyTurner 1 77
(W R Muir) *led tl hdd 3f out: wl there tl wknd ins fnl f* 16/1
05-3 **7** nk **Landucci**[21] 53 7-8-11 78 .... (p) PatrickHills(5) 3 75
(J W Hills) *trckd ldrs on ins tl rdn and wknd over 1f out* 12/1

1m 23.38s (-1.42) **Going Correction** +0.075s/f (Slow) 7 Ran SP% 114.6
Speed ratings (Par 105): **111,109,108,108,106 105,104**
CSF £20.28 CT £124.35 TOTE £10.30: £2.30, £1.70; EX 27.60 TRIFECTA Not won..
Owner John Stocker **Bred** Janus Bloodstock **Trained** Radlett, Herts
FOCUS
A fair handicap and solid form for the grade. The early gallop was not that strong, yet the finish was dominated by those who raced off the pace.
Super Frank(IRE) Official explanation: jockey said gelding stumbled on leaving stalls

314 LINGFIELDPARK.CO.UK H'CAP 1m (P)
2:20 (2:20) (Class 4) (0-85,84) 4-Y-O+ £4,100 (£1,227; £613; £306; £152) Stalls High

Form RPR
006- **1** **Highland Harvest**[101] 6269 4-8-6 72 .... HayleyTurner 1 81
(D R C Elsworth) *trckd ldr: rdn to ld 1f out: edgd lft: kpt on wl* 14/1
1-33 **2** 3/4 **Ninth House (USA)**[5] 252 6-8-9 75 .... (bt) JimCrowley 4 83
(N P Littmoden) *towards rr: hdwy on outside over 1f out: fin strly to go 2nd towards fin* 7/1[3]
11-4 **3** 3/4 **Confidentiality (IRE)**[1] 309 4-9-2 82 .... NickyMackay 5 88
(M Wigham) *s.i.s: sn in mid-div: hdwy 2f out: swtchd towards ins over 1f out: r.o fnl f: nt qckn towards fin* 5/2[2]
60-5 **4** nk **Bertie Southstreet**[3] 274 5-8-6 72 .... JimmyQuinn 7 77
(J R Best) *led tl rdn and hdd 1f out: kpt on but nt qckn ins fnl f* 7/1[3]
00-0 **5** 1 1/2 **Moonlight Man**[23] 26 7-8-11 77 .... LPKeniry 8 79
(C R Dore) *trckd ldrs: rdn over 1f out: no ex ins fnl f* 20/1
0-03 **6** 1 **Dudley Docker (IRE)**[7] 233 6-8-8 74 .... LiamJones 3 74
(C R Dore) *s.i.s: t.k.h: a towards rr* 12/1
602- **7** 2 1/2 **Apache Dawn**[41] 7165 4-9-4 84 .... GeorgeBaker 2 78
(G L Moore) *s.i.s: sn in tch: rdn over 2f out: wknd fnl f* 9/4[1]
34-0 **8** nk **Wavertree Warrior (IRE)**[15] 124 6-9-3 83 .... TGMcLaughlin 6 76
(N P Littmoden) *a in rr: rdn over 2f out and nvr on terms* 8/1

1m 37.01s (-1.19) **Going Correction** +0.075s/f (Slow) 8 Ran SP% 114.6
Speed ratings (Par 105): **108,107,106,106,104 103,101,100**
CSF £107.23 CT £332.32 TOTE £14.90: £3.10, £1.90, £1.30; EX 81.70 TRIFECTA Not won..
Owner J Wotherspoon **Bred** John Wotherspoon **Trained** Newmarket, Suffolk
FOCUS
An ordinary handicap for the level, and sound form. The start was very ragged, with all bar three of these missing the kick to some extent and, with few wanting to press on, the pace was modest. The winning time, though, was still 1.74 seconds quicker than the opening maiden.
Confidentiality(IRE) Official explanation: jockey said filly missed the break
Apache Dawn Official explanation: jockey said gelding stumbled on leaving stalls

315 LINGFIELD PARK FOR CONFERENCES H'CAP 1m 2f (P)
2:50 (2:51) (Class 2) (0-100,98) 4-Y-O+
£9,971 (£2,985; £1,492; £747; £372; £187) Stalls Low

Form RPR
121- **1** **Silver Pivotal (IRE)**[253] 1824 4-9-6 98 .... HayleyTurner 10 109+
(G A Butler) *in tch: hdwy 2f out: swtchd to ins over 1f out: r.o wl to ld ins fnl f* 7/2[2]
211- **2** 1 **Alpes Maritimes**[53] 7018 4-8-5 83 .... FergusSweeney 4 92+
(G L Moore) *hld up: hdwy over 2f out: r.o to go 2nd wl ins fnl f* 9/4[1]
01-2 **3** nk **Sgt Schultz (IRE)**[17] 96 5-8-10 86 .... JohnEgan 11 95+
(J S Moore) *trckd ldrs: short of room over 1f out: swtchd rt: fin wl* 12/1
206- **4** 3/4 **Speedy Sam**[28] 6995 5-8-13 89 .... JimCrowley 9 96
(K R Burke) *a.p: led over 2f out: hdd ins fnl f: no ex nr fin* 9/1
26-3 **5** shd **Lisathedaddy**[14] 138 6-8-11 87 .... TQuinn 8 94
(B G Powell) *mid-div: rdn and hdwy to hold ev ch ent fnl f: nt qckn towards fin* 16/1
0-35 **6** hd **Fusili (IRE)**[14] 138 5-8-6 82 oh1 .... (b[1]) JamesDoyle 7 89
(N P Littmoden) *in tch: rdn and outpcd over 2f out: fin wl fnl f* 33/1
021- **7** 1 3/4 **Greek Easter (IRE)**[35] 7224 5-7-13 82 oh8 .... PatrickDonaghy(7) 5 85
(David P Myerscough, Ire) *fly-jmpd s: in rr tl hdwy over 1f out: nvr nr to chal* 14/1
64-3 **8** 1/2 **Cold Turkey**[17] 96 8-8-10 86 .... SimonWhitworth 6 88
(G L Moore) *hld up: sme late hdwy but nvr on terms* 16/1
/1-3 **9** 1 1/4 **Tartan Tie**[17] 105 4-8-5 83 .... GregFairley 1 83
(M Johnston) *trckd ldr to over 2f out: rdn and wknd appr fnl f* 9/2[3]
135- **10** 1 1/2 **Master Pegasus**[27] 7281 5-8-1 82 .... JackMitchell(5) 3 79
(C F Wall) *plld hrd: racd wd: rdn and fdd appr fnl f* 14/1
4/4- **11** 9 **King's Head (IRE)**[248] 944 5-9-6 96 .... GeorgeBaker 12 75
(G L Moore) *led tl hdd over 2f out: wknd over 1f out* 33/1
1-31 **12** 33 **Mafeking (UAE)**[14] 138 4-8-11 89 .... ChrisCatlin 2 2
(M R Hoad) *hld up: a bhd: t.o whn eased fnl f* 10/1

2m 4.16s (-2.44) **Going Correction** +0.075s/f (Slow)
WFA 4 from 5yo+ 2lb 12 Ran SP% 128.9
Speed ratings (Par 109): **112,111,110,110,110 110,108,108,107,106 98,72**
CSF £12.95 CT £90.71 TOTE £4.60: £1.90, £1.90, £3.20; EX 14.70 Trifecta £189.70 Part won. Pool: £267.26, 0.20 winning units..
Owner The Distaff Partnership **Bred** Stratford Place Stud **Trained** Newmarket, Suffolk
FOCUS
A very good handicap and, although the pace was just ordinary, that's typical Lingfield and this form should work out well. The first three can all rate higher. The winning time was 4.38 seconds quicker than the following 56-70.
NOTEBOOK
Silver Pivotal(IRE) ◆ had been off the track since winning a 1m fillies' Listed contest at York last May, but she had won her maiden at Wolverhampton, so this surface was never going to pose her any problems, and she returned to action with a terrific effort on this step up in trip. A fine-looking filly with plenty of scope, she was always cruising under the impressive Hayley Turner, but needed a bit of luck in running in the straight after things got a little tight rounding the final bend. She eventually got a run against the far rail, which is by no means ideal round here, but she responded well to pressure and was a decisive winner. She can be expected to come on for this and will now be aimed at the Winter Derby Trial, before going for the big race itself back here in March. On this evidence, Gentleman's Deal and co. might have a job stopping her. (tchd 4-1, tchd 9-2 in a place)
Alpes Maritimes came into this looking for the hat-trick having won both his starts over this course and distance since joining Gary Moore's yard, but he was 7lb higher than for his latest success and found Silver Pivotal too good. This still rates as a useful effort in defeat. He seemed slightly unbalanced rounding the final bend and took longer than expected to engage top gear, but it made no difference to the result. (op 11-4 tchd 10-3)

Sgt Schultz(IRE) ◆ looked unlucky not to finish second as he was short of room at the top of the straight and had to be switched out with his effort. He can win over 1m2f, but might be an even better horse over 1m4f and seems to still be improving. He looks worth keeping on side. (op 11-1 tchd 9-1)
Speedy Sam, back on the Flat after an unsuccessful spin over hurdles, seemed to have his chance and ran well. (op 12-1)
Lisathedaddy is a useful mare and this was a good effort in defeat. (tchd 14-1)
Fusili(IRE) was stuck towards the inside for much of the way and got going too late when switched out. She can be rated a little better than the bare form.
Greek Easter(IRE), from 8lb out of the handicap, was effectively 14lb higher than when winning a much weaker race over course and distance on her previous start. She was never that well placed after appearing to fly jump as the stalls opened and she struggled to land a telling blow, but this was still a creditable effort. She will be one to look out for if turned out off her correct mark before she is reassessed. (tchd 16-1)
Cold Turkey ◆ was the slowest away from the stalls and that set the theme for the race. He was given far too much to do over an inadequate trip, but caught the eye running on when the race was all over. He is beginning to look nicely handicapped and will be one to look out for when stepped back up in trip.
Tartan Tie ran disappointingly on this drop back in trip. (op 7-1)
Mafeking(UAE) Official explanation: jockey said gelding finished distressed

316 LINGFIELD PARK FOR WEDDINGS H'CAP 1m 2f (P)
3:25 (3:25) (Class 5) (0-70,68) 4-Y-O+ **£2,331** (£693; £346; £173) **Stalls** Low

Form RPR
3-21 **1** **Sri Kuantan (IRE)**[14] 134 4-9-2 **66**.................................(t) ChrisCatlin 5 79+
(P F I Cole) *trckd ldrs: swtchd rt wl over 1f out: led 1f out: qcknd clr* **7/2**[2]
11-4 **2** *4* **Mr Napoleon (IRE)**[21] 51 6-9-6 **68**................................ GeorgeBaker 3 73+
(G L Moore) *hld up in tch on outside: hdwy 3f out: rdn and r.o fnl f to go 2nd post* **11/10**[1]
6-53 **3** *shd* **Meditation**[14] 139 6-9-5 **67**.................................... JamesDoyle 6 72
(I A Wood) *led tl hdd 2f out: kpt on and r.o wl fnl f* **16/1**
05-6 **4** *shd* **Stark Contrast (USA)**[21] 51 4-8-13 **63**...................... J-PGuillambert 8 68
(J Akehurst) *trckd ldr: led 2f out: edgd lft and hdd 1f out: nt qckn nr fin* **8/1**
1-33 **5** *hd* **King After**[3] 275 6-8-9 **57**...(v) JimCrowley 4 61
(J R Best) *mid-div: rdn over 1f out: kpt on fnl f* **9/2**[3]
135- **6** *1 ½* **Lord Of Dreams (IRE)**[71] 6837 6-8-10 **63**.................. JamieJones(5) 1 64
(G L Moore) *hld up: effrt on ins over 1f out: wknd ins fnl f* **14/1**
351- **7** *hd* **Moonlight Fantasy (IRE)**[28] 7274 5-9-0 **62**................. TGMcLaughlin 2 63
(Lucinda Featherstone) *slowly away: a in rr* **16/1**
10-3 **8** *1 ¼* **Fateful Attraction**[21] 51 5-9-6 **68**...............................(b) DaneO'Neill 7 66
(I A Wood) *t.k.h: in tch: rdn and wkng whn sltly hmpd wl over 1f out* **12/1**

2m 8.54s (1.94) **Going Correction** +0.075s/f (Slow)
WFA 4 from 5yo+ 2lb **8 Ran SP% 125.3**
Speed ratings (Par 103): **95,91,91,91,91 90,90,89**
CSF £8.59 CT £58.46 TOTE £5.50: £1.60, £1.10, £3.70; EX 10.30 Trifecta £73.70 Pool: £187.98, 1.81 winning units.
Owner H R H Sultan Ahmad Shah **Bred** Pat Fullam **Trained** Whatcombe, Oxon
■ Stewards' Enquiry : Chris Catlin caution: careless riding

FOCUS
A modest handicap and, with the pace steady, the form needs treating with caution, although the progressive winner impressed. The winning time was 4.38 seconds slower than the earlier 86-100.

317 LINGFIELD PARK FOR EXHIBITIONS MAIDEN STKS 1m 4f (P)
4:00 (4:00) (Class 5) 4-Y-O+ **£2,331** (£693; £346; £173) **Stalls** Low

Form RPR
1 **Outlandish**[38] 5-9-7 0... ChrisCatlin 9 67+
(Andrew Turnell) *sn led: mde rest: clr over 1f out: pushed out: eased nr fin* **11/8**[1]
022- **2** *2* **Aphrodisia**[129] 5531 4-8-12 60...................................... J-PGuillambert 6 56
(S C Williams) *hld up in tch: hdwy over 3f out: wnt 2nd over 1f out: kpt on but no imp on wnr* **7/4**[2]
4-52 **3** *1* **Flight Dream (FR)**[16] 107 5-9-2 65.........................(b1) JamieJones(5) 7 59
(M G Quinlan) *in tch: chsd wnr 4f out to over 1f out: one pce after* **17/2**
4 *¾* **Mondial Jack (FR)**[19] 9-9-0 0.....................................(v) RichardEvans(7) 2 58
(P D Evans) *in rr: hdwy over 4f out: kpt on fnl f* **33/1**
400- **5** *1 ¾* **My Monna**[53] 7012 4-8-12 46... JimCrowley 1 50
(Miss Sheena West) *in tch to 3f out: n.d after* **20/1**
5-32 **6** *hd* **Niqaab**[14] 144 4-8-12 58.. JohnEgan 4 50
(W J Musson) *prom: trckd ldr 7f out to over 3f out: wknd 2f out* **11/2**[3]
7 *1 ¼* **Allez Melina**[249] 7-8-13 0.. NeilChalmers(3) 5 48
(Mouse Hamilton-Fairley) *slowly away: a in rr* **66/1**
64-0 **8** *4* **Gouranga**[13] 152 5-9-2 47..(v1) HayleyTurner 3 42
(A W Carroll) *chsd wnr to 7f out: rdn and wknd over 3f out* **50/1**
9 *7* **Renege The Joker**[364] 5-9-0 0..............................(t) WilliamCarson(7) 8 35
(S Regan) *a bhd* **33/1**

2m 34.96s (1.96) **Going Correction** +0.075s/f (Slow)
WFA 4 from 5yo+ 4lb **9 Ran SP% 118.5**
Speed ratings (Par 103): **96,94,94,93,92 92,91,88,84**
CSF £3.92 TOTE £2.40: £1.30, £1.10, £2.50; EX 5.30 Trifecta £96.20 Pool: £407.99 - 3.01 winning units. Place 6 £11.60, Place 5 £8.37.
Owner L G Kimber **Bred** Darley **Trained** Broad Hinton, Wilts

FOCUS
A weak older-horse maiden and the form is very limited, although Outlandish did it well.
Renege The Joker Official explanation: jockey said gelding gurgled
T/Plt: £21.40 to a £1 stake. Pool: £61,836.75. 2,106.45 winning tickets. T/Qpdt: £15.20 to a £1 stake. Pool: £3,391.40. 164.10 winning tickets. JS

304 WOLVERHAMPTON (A.W) (L-H)
Saturday, January 26
OFFICIAL GOING: Standard
Wind: Fresh, behind Weather: Cloudy

318 JO WILCOXSON BIRTHDAY CELEBRATION H'CAP 5f 20y(P)
6:50 (6:51) (Class 6) (0-50,52) 4-Y-O+ **£1,774** (£523; £262) **Stalls** Low

Form RPR
1 **Miss Curly (IRE)**[57] 6983 8-8-8 **46** oh1.............................(t) ChrisCatlin 6 56+
(Gerard Keane, Ire) *mid-div: rdn 1/2-way: hdwy over 1f out: r.o to ld post* **8/1**[3]
320- **2** *hd* **Twinned (IRE)**[98] 6340 5-8-12 **50**.. AdamKirby 7 59
(M J Wilkinson) *a.p: chsd ldr 2f out: rdn to ld ins fnl f: edgd rt towards fin: hdd post* **9/2**[2]
5-11 **3** *2* **Dodaa (USA)**[8] 206 5-8-9 **52**................................ AshleyHamblett(5) 5 54+
(N Wilson) *s.i.s: sn rcvrd to ld: rdn over 1f out: hdd and no ex ins fnl f* **11/10**[1]
000- **4** *½* **Town House**[124] 5672 6-8-1 **46** oh1.................................. SoniaEaton(7) 1 46
(B P J Baugh) *led early: chsd ldrs: rdn over 1f out: styd on same pce* **16/1**
000- **5** *1 ¾* **Stoneacre Gareth (IRE)**[26] 7283 4-8-12 **50**........................ LPKeniry 8 44
(Peter Grayson) *s.s: in rr: nt claer run wl over 1f out: r.o ins fnl f: nvr nrr* **8/1**[3]
3-00 **6** *shd* **The Carpet Man**[5] 247 4-8-9 **47**......................................(v1) LiamJones 2 40
(A W Carroll) *sn pushed along in rr: styd on fr over 1f out: n.d* **9/1**
000- **7** *4* **Signor Panettiere**[115] 5908 7-8-5 **50**.............................(t) SBushby(7) 9 29
(A D Brown) *chsd ldr 3f: wknd over 1f out* **14/1**
00-0 **8** *½* **Percy Douglas**[12] 153 8-8-9 **52** oh1 ow6.....................(b) AnnStokell(5) 3 29
(Miss A Stokell) *chsd ldrs: lost pl 3f out: wknd over 1f out* **66/1**
00-0 **9** *1* **Fly Time**[9] 191 4-8-10 **48** ow1... TomEaves 10 22
(Mrs L Williamson) *chsd ldrs over 3f* **33/1**

62.70 secs (0.40) **Going Correction** +0.125s/f (Slow) **9 Ran SP% 115.0**
Speed ratings (Par 101): **101,100,97,96,93 93,87,86,84**
CSF £43.68 CT £69.98 TOTE £6.80: £2.70, £1.30, £1.10; EX 42.30.
Owner P J Lohan **Bred** P J Lohan **Trained** Trim, Co Meath

FOCUS
A very moderate sprint handicap ut the form is solid enough despite the winner being out of the weights. The winning time was 1.06 seconds quicker than the following maiden.
Signor Panettiere Official explanation: trainer said gelding had a breathing problem

319 BOOK A PONTIN'S BREAK TO REMEMBER MEDIAN AUCTION MAIDEN STKS 5f 20y(P)
7:20 (7:20) (Class 6) 4-6-Y-O **£2,047** (£604; £302) **Stalls** Low

Form RPR
1 **Alexander Huricane (IRE)** 4-9-3 0.................................. ChrisCatlin 4 50+
(K A Ryan) *s.i.s: sn chsng ldr: outpcd 1/2-way: rallied over 1f out: r.o.u.p to ld post* **2/7**[1]
000- **2** *nk* **Kilvickeon (IRE)**[26] 7284 4-9-3 43...................................(b) LPKeniry 3 49
(Peter Grayson) *led: rdn over 1f out: edgd rt ins fnl f: hdd post* **8/1**[3]
3 *1 ¼* **Emacolali (IRE)** 4-9-0 0.. JerryO'Dwyer(3) 2 45
(Gerard Keane, Ire) *dwlt: hung lft thrght: plld hrd and sn prom: rdn and ev ch 1f out: no ex towards fin* **11/2**[2]
0- **4** *12* **Mystic Spin (IRE)**[81] 6704 4-9-3 0.........................(b1) CatherineGannon 1 1
(K J Burke) *sn outpcd* **33/1**

63.76 secs (1.46) **Going Correction** +0.125s/f (Slow) **4 Ran SP% 107.2**
Speed ratings: **93,92,90,71**
CSF £3.09 TOTE £1.20; EX 2.80.
Owner N O'Callaghan, R Fagan & R O'Callaghan **Bred** Mrs M Fox **Trained** Hambleton, N Yorks

FOCUS
Surely one of the worst maidens ever run. The winning time was 1.06 seconds slower than the previous 46-50 handicap.
Emacolali(IRE) Official explanation: jockey said gelding hung left throughout

320 GARY HANKINSON 40TH BIRTHDAY H'CAP 1m 5f 194y(P)
7:50 (7:51) (Class 5) (0-75,74) 4-Y-O+ **£2,590** (£770; £385; £192) **Stalls** Low

Form RPR
362- **1** **Opera Writer (IRE)**[26] 7285 5-8-13 **56**................................ JimCrowley 1 65
(R Hollinshead) *a.p: chsd ldr over 1f out: rdn to ld ins fnl f: edgd lft: styd on* **3/1**[2]
20-1 **2** *1 ¾* **Fantasy Ride**[23] 31 6-9-7 **64**.. TGMcLaughlin 8 71
(J Pearce) *hld up: hdwy over 2f out: rdn over 1f out: styd on* **15/2**[3]
251- **3** *hd* **Young Scotton**[26] 7285 8-9-5 **62**..................................... JimmyQuinn 4 69
(J D Bethell) *hld up in tch: chsd ldr over 3f out: rdn and edgd rt over 1f out: hdd and no ex ins fnl f* **11/4**[1]
150- **4** *5* **Morning Farewell**[40] 6669 4-9-11 **74**................................ TPQueally 2 74
(P W Chapple-Hyam) *led: rdn and hdd over 2f out: wknd fnl f* **3/1**[2]
5 *12* **Positive Move (IRE)**[20] 3935 4-8-7 **56**..........................(p) ChrisCatlin 5 39
(Gerard Keane, Ire) *sn pushed along in rr: effrt over 3f out: wknd over 2f out* **12/1**
053- **6** *hd* **Rosie's Glory (USA)**[15] 5472 4-8-11 **60**.....................(b) FrancisNorton 3 43
(M F Harris) *chsd ldr tl rdn over 3f out: wknd over 2f out* **25/1**
00-0 **7** *2* **Le Corvee (IRE)**[23] 28 6-9-13 **70**..................................... JamesDoyle 6 50
(A W Carroll) *hld up: effrt over 3f out: n.m.r and wknd over 2f out* **20/1**
165/ **8** *103* **Nounou**[476] 2739 7-9-10 **70**...................................... TolleyDean(3) 7 —
(Miss J E Foster) *chsd ldrs: pushed along 7f out: wknd over 5f out* **16/1**

3m 5.92s (-0.08) **Going Correction** +0.125s/f (Slow)
WFA 4 from 5yo+ 6lb **8 Ran SP% 110.6**
Speed ratings (Par 103): **105,104,103,101,94 94,92,—**
CSF £23.86 CT £63.46 TOTE £4.00: £1.60, £1.90, £2.00; EX 32.60.
Owner John L Marriott **Bred** J Davison **Trained** Upper Longdon, Staffs

FOCUS
A modest staying handicap in which Opera Writer reversed recent C/D form with Young Scotton at the revised weights.
Fantasy Ride Official explanation: vet said gelding returned lame

321 PONTIN'S THE FAMILY FAVOURITE HOLIDAY H'CAP 1m 141y(P)
8:20 (8:21) (Class 6) (0-65,65) 3-Y-O **£2,047** (£604; £302) **Stalls** Low

Form RPR
40-3 **1** **Bury Treasure (IRE)**[17] 102 3-9-0 **61**.............................. MickyFenton 1 62
(Miss Gay Kelleway) *trckd ldrs: racd keenly: rdn to ld wl ins fnl f: r.o* **9/2**[3]
00-2 **2** *¾* **Whaston (IRE)**[14] 141 3-8-11 **58**................................... JimmyQuinn 4 57
(J D Bethell) *hld up in tch: rdn over 1f out: r.o* **15/8**[1]
003- **3** *½* **Hollow Point (IRE)**[26] 7288 3-9-2 **63**.............................. GregFairley 2 61
(M Johnston) *led: rdn over 1f out: hdd wl ins fnl f* **7/1**
54-0 **4** *nk* **John Potts**[14] 141 3-8-10 **57**.. TPQueally 5 54
(B P J Baugh) *hld up: hdwy over 2f out: sn rdn: styd on* **8/1**
043- **5** *shd* **Afton View (IRE)**[30] 7245 3-9-3 **64**...........................(e) FrancisNorton 3 63+
(D J Murphy) *s.i.s: hld up: nt clr run wl over 1f out: sn rdn: r.o nr fin: nt rch ldrs* **7/2**[2]
00-1 **6** *3 ½* **Ledgerwood**[17] 98 3-9-4 **65**...(b1) JamesDoyle 6 54
(J W Hills) *chsd ldr tl rdn over 2f out: wknd fnl f* **7/1**

1m 54.61s (4.11) **Going Correction** +0.125s/f (Slow) **6 Ran SP% 111.3**
Speed ratings (Par 95): **86,85,84,84,84 81**
CSF £13.16 TOTE £5.80: £2.50, £1.30; EX 14.00.
Owner M M Foulger P Andrews Deauville Daze Pship **Bred** John Bernard O'Connor **Trained** Exning, Suffolk

FOCUS
A modest handicap and, with the pace ordinary, they finished in a bunch. The winning time was very ordinary and it is hard to rate the form any more positively.
Afton View(IRE) Official explanation: jockey said gelding was denied a clear run

Ledgerwood Official explanation: jockey said gelding ran too freely and didn't face the first-time blinkers

322 GO PONTIN'S FOR GREAT VALUE CLASSIFIED STKS 2m 119y(P)
8:50 (8:51) (Class 7) 4-Y-0+ £1,365 (£403; £201) Stalls Low

Form RPR

0-21 **1** **Mujamead**[6] 238 4-9-8 52 (p) JerryO'Dwyer(3) 4 68
(A W Carroll) *a.p: led 3f out: rdn and edgd rt over 1f out: styd on* **5/2**[2]

000/ **2** *2* **Saipan (FR)**[9] 2563 7-9-5 45 ChrisCatlin 12 53
(Gerard Keane, Ire) *hld up in tch: chsd wnr over 2f out: sn rdn: styd on same pce fnl f* **6/1**[3]

0/02 **3** *1 1/4* **Aqua Pura (GER)**[10] 179 9-9-10 50 (v) TPQueally 1 56
(A P Stringer) *a.p: rdn over 1f out: no ex ins fnl f* **11/1**

06-1 **4** *3* **Otaki (IRE)**[10] 179 4-9-9 56 J-PGuillambert 8 59
(Sir Mark Prescott) *hld up: hdwy over 4f out: rdn over 2f out: wknd ins fnl f* **5/4**[1]

/6-3 **5** *2* **Aristi (IRE)**[9] 188 7-8-12 40 RichardEvans(7) 10 45
(Evan Williams) *chsd ldrs: rdn over 2f out: wknd over 1f out* **28/1**

02-4 **6** *4* **Wavertree One Off**[11] 166 6-9-5 45 AdamKirby 2 40
(J Ryan) *hld up: hdwy 6f out: rdn and wknd 2f out* **16/1**

03/6 **7** *1* **Castle Frome (IRE)**[6] 238 9-9-5 40 (p) PaulFitzsimons 3 39
(A E Price) *hld up: rdn over 2f out: n.d* **100/1**

/0-0 **8** *5* **Tanning**[15] 129 6-9-2 37 (p) NeilChalmers(3) 11 33
(M Appleby) *chsd ldr tl led over 5f out: hdd 3f out: wknd 2f out* **100/1**

/4-5 **9** *27* **Flash Harry**[15] 129 4-8-12 45 (b) FrancisNorton 7 —
(M G Quinlan) *sn rdn to ld: hdd over 5f out: wknd over 3f out* **16/1**

0-36 **10** *9* **Snake Hips**[2] 282 4-8-12 40 (v) RichardKingscote 9 —
(B Palling) *hld up: rdn over 3f out: sn wknd* **20/1**

/06- **11** *6* **Francescas Boy (IRE)**[70] 5389 5-9-5 44 (p) TomEaves 5 —
(P D Niven) *sn pushed along and prom: lost pl 7f out: wknd over 5f out* **66/1**

00-4 **12** *76* **Long Gone**[25] 1 5-9-5 32 (p) MickyFenton 6 —
(John A Harris) *s.i.s: hld up: bhd fnl 6f* **150/1**

3m 43.2s (1.40) **Going Correction** +0.125s/f (Slow)
WFA 4 from 5yo+ 7lb 12 Ran SP% **119.7**
Speed ratings (Par 97): **101,100,99,98,97 95,94,92,79,75 72,36**
CSF £17.56 TOTE £3.70: £1.50, £2.70, £3.50; EX 20.60.
Owner J T Billson **Bred** D R Tucker **Trained** Cropthorne, Worcs

FOCUS
A good staying contest for the lowly grade, and solid form.
Long Gone Official explanation: jockey said mare hung right

323 CALL PONTIN'S FAMILY BREAKS 0844 576 5938 H'CAP 1m 1f 103y(P)
9:20 (9:20) (Class 6) (0-58,61) 4-Y-0+ £2,047 (£604; £302) Stalls Low

Form RPR

53-1 **1** **Morbick**[8] 220 4-9-5 61 TGMcLaughlin 3 77
(W M Brisbourne) *chsd ldrs: led over 2f out: rdn out* **5/4**[1]

00-2 **2** *1 3/4* **Supercast (IRE)**[8] 214 5-9-2 57 SamHitchcott 7 69
(N J Vaughan) *a.p: rdn to chse wnr fnl f: styd on same pce* **9/2**[2]

-121 **3** *3 1/2* **Buscador (USA)**[7] 231 9-9-4 59 RichardKingscote 1 64
(W M Brisbourne) *chsd ldr over 2f: remained handy: rdn over 2f out: no ex fnl f* **15/2**

04-4 **4** *3* **Norwegian**[14] 140 7-8-11 52 (p) PaulEddery 8 50
(Ian Williams) *hld up: hdwy over 3f out: rdn and wknd over 1f out* **11/2**[3]

55-0 **5** *3/4* **Speagle (IRE)**[15] 128 6-9-3 58 DeanMcKeown 2 55
(A J Chamberlain) *prom: chsd ldr 6f out tl rdn over 2f out: wknd over 1f out:* **12/1**

5-46 **6** *1/2* **Speed Dial Harry (IRE)**[18] 80 6-9-2 57 (v) LiamJones 10 53
(C R Dore) *hld up: rdn over 3f out: nvr trbld ldrs* **33/1**

20-0 **7** *hd* **Mighty Mover (IRE)**[22] 44 6-9-1 56 ChrisCatlin 5 51
(B Palling) *led: rdn and hdd over 2f out: wknd fnl f* **20/1**

005- **8** *nk* **Tina's Ridge (IRE)**[29] 7263 4-9-1 57 JimCrowley 4 52
(R Hollinshead) *mid-div: rdn over 3f out: wknd 2f out* **16/1**

0-04 **9** *1/2* **Divine Love (IRE)**[8] 220 4-8-1 50 (p) PatrickDonaghy(7) 9 44
(T Wall) *s.i.s: rdn 1/2-way: n.d* **100/1**

06-5 **10** *2* **Anduril**[8] 219 7-8-11 52 (b) FergalLynch 6 41
(I W McInnes) *hld up: rdn over 2f out: a in rr* **14/1**

50/0 **11** *17* **Art Historian (IRE)**[14] 144 5-8-7 48 PaulFitzsimons 11 2
(E G Bevan) *hld up: a in rr: wknd 3f out* **100/1**

2m 1.24s (-0.46) **Going Correction** +0.125s/f (Slow)
WFA 4 from 5yo+ 1lb 11 Ran SP% **119.7**
Speed ratings (Par 101): **107,105,102,99,99 98,98,98,97,95 80**
CSF £6.77 CT £31.09 TOTE £2.30: £1.50, £1.40, £1.30; EX 9.10 Place 6 £7.19, Place 5 £5.66.
Owner J R Salter **Bred** Mark C Collins And Keith West **Trained** Great Ness, Shropshire

FOCUS
A decent handicap for the grade and the winning time was decent. Solid form.
T/Plt: £12.00 to a £1 stake. Pool: £107,443.00. 6,497.50 winning tickets. T/Qpdt: £7.20 to a £1 stake. Pool: £6,087.00. 623.00 winning tickets. CR

[297] KEMPTON (A.W) (R-H)
Sunday, January 27

OFFICIAL GOING: Standard
Wind: Light, across Weather: Fine

324 DIGIBET CLAIMING STKS 5f (P)
1:25 (1:25) (Class 6) 3-Y-O £2,047 (£604; £302) Stalls High

Form RPR

611- **1** **Ten Down**[50] 7072 3-9-5 78 TPQueally 5 79
(J A Osborne) *mde all and mostly 2 l clr: drvn over 1f out: jst hld on* **4/5**[1]

25 **2** *shd* **Hurricane Hen**[8] 228 3-9-2 77 SteveDrowne 2 76
(D M Simcock) *stdd s: hld up in 3rd: chsd wnr wl over 1f out: clsd grad fnl f: jst failed* **6/1**[3]

-453 **3** *7* **Orange Square (IRE)**[11] 183 3-8-12 66 RichardHughes 3 51
(R Hannon) *chsd wnr to wl over 1f out: sn btn: eased last 100yds* **8/1**

21-3 **4** *2* **A Wish For You**[10] 199 3-8-8 72 (p) JamesO'Reilly(5) 1 40
(D K Ivory) *stdd s: sn drvn in last: nvr able to go the pce: wknd over 1f out* **9/4**[2]

59.94 secs (-0.56) **Going Correction** 0.0s/f (Stan) 4 Ran SP% **111.7**
Speed ratings (Par 95): **104,103,92,89**
CSF £6.23 TOTE £2.00; EX 5.30.Hurricane Hen was claimed by M Khan for £12,000
Owner Piers Pottinger And Ten **Bred** Baydon House Stud **Trained** Upper Lambourn, Berks

FOCUS
Not a bad little claimer, run at a solid pace. The form looks fair enough with the first pair coming clear.

325 DIGIBET.COM H'CAP 1m 2f (P)
1:55 (1:56) (Class 6) (0-65,65) 3-Y-O £2,047 (£604; £302) Stalls High

Form RPR

0-02 **1** **Ski Sunday**[3] 288 3-9-2 60 SteveDrowne 10 66+
(M A Jarvis) *t.k.h: trckd ldng pair: led over 1f out: shkn up and sn wl in command* **11/10**[1]

54-4 **2** *1 3/4* **Arabesque Dancer**[3] 288 3-8-13 57 (b) URispoli 7 60
(M Botti) *hld up in last pair: checked on inner 6f out: rdn and prog 3f out: styd on to take 2nd last 50yds: no ch w wnr* **7/1**[3]

00-4 **3** *nk* **Anabaa's Secret (IRE)**[11] 184 3-8-8 52 TPQueally 2 54
(J A Osborne) *trckd ldr: led 2f out to over 1f out: sn no ch w wnr: kpt on nr fin* **5/1**[2]

60-0 **4** *nk* **I Certainly May**[22] 58 3-9-2 60 JohnEgan 8 61
(S Dow) *settled in midfield: rdn over 4f out: clsd over 2f out: nt clr run sn after: chsd wnr briefly ins fnl f: wknd nr fin* **25/1**

10-3 **5** *1 1/2* **Kryptonite (IRE)**[17] 116 3-9-7 65 JamesDoyle 5 63
(J W Hills) *hld up in last pair: wl adrift fr 1/2-way: hrd rdn 3f out: swtchd wd 1f out: plugged on* **9/1**

60-6 **6** *1 1/2* **Coral Shores**[11] 184 3-8-3 47 AdrianMcCarthy 3 42
(P W Hiatt) *t.k.h: trckd ldrs: cl enough 2f out: sn wknd* **16/1**

31-3 **7** *1 1/4* **Tiger Spice**[24] 30 3-9-7 65 (b) LiamJones 6 58
(W J Haggas) *led at gd pce to 2f out: wknd over 1f out* **8/1**

006- **8** *hd* **Tobago Bay**[118] 5863 3-8-3 50 NeilChalmers(3) 4 43
(Miss Sheena West) *dwlt: rousted along early: a in rr: struggling fnl 4f* **25/1**

000- **9** *5* **Ba Dreamflight**[90] 6543 3-8-8 52 ChrisCatlin 1 35
(H Morrison) *lost prom pl after 3f and sn struggling: wl bhd fnl 3f* **14/1**

2m 8.31s (0.31) **Going Correction** 0.0s/f (Stan) 9 Ran SP% **118.1**
Speed ratings (Par 95): **98,96,96,96,94 93,92,92,88**
CSF £9.69 CT £27.87 TOTE £1.90: £1.40, £1.90, £1.60; EX 11.80.
Owner Sheikh Ahmed Al Maktoum **Bred** New England, Stanley House & Mount Coote Studs **Trained** Newmarket, Suffolk

FOCUS
A moderate three-year-old handicap, run at a sound pace. The form looks straightforward and the winner was vaue for further.
Tobago Bay Official explanation: jockey said gelding missed the break

326 DIGIBET MEDIAN AUCTION MAIDEN STKS 6f (P)
2:30 (2:32) (Class 6) 4-6-Y-O £2,047 (£604; £302) Stalls High

Form RPR

2-34 **1** **Simpsons Gamble (IRE)**[9] 209 5-9-3 53 (p) DaneO'Neill 6 63
(R A Teal) *hld up in last pair: prog and cruising bhd ldrs 2f out: produced to ld last 150yds: cajoled along and kpt on* **7/2**[2]

30-4 **2** *3/4* **Waqaarr**[14] 150 4-9-3 64 JohnEgan 1 61
(Lady Herries) *trckd ldrs: rdn to go 2nd 1/2-way: led u.p over 1f out: hdd and nt qckn last 150yds* **4/9**[1]

4 **3** *1/2* **Mr Rev**[6] 245 5-9-3 0 SteveDrowne 4 59
(J M Bradley) *hld up: outpcd 1/2-way: prog u.p 2f out: clsd on ldrs 1f out: one pce last 150yds* **5/1**[3]

-304 **4** *6* **Noddledoddle (IRE)**[6] 247 4-8-12 38 (vt) ChrisCatlin 3 35
(J Ryan) *led to over 1f out: wknd* **20/1**

600/ **5** *5* **Daniel O'Donnell**[977] 2001 6-9-3 58 SaleemGolam 5 24
(S C Williams) *chsd ldrs: wknd rapidly wl over 1f out* **16/1**

0 **6** *1 1/2* **Takeanoteofthat (IRE)**[16] 130 6-9-3 0 VinceSlattery 2 19
(D Burchell) *hld up: plld hrd and sn pressed ldr: wd and hanging: wknd 1/2-way* **100/1**

1m 13.17s (0.07) **Going Correction** 0.0s/f (Stan) 6 Ran SP% **119.8**
Speed ratings: **99,98,97,89,82 80**
CSF £5.89 TOTE £4.30: £1.70, £1.20; EX 6.10.
Owner Chris Simpson **Bred** D And Mrs D Veitch **Trained** Ashtead, Surrey

FOCUS
A weak maiden which saw the first three come clear. The 38-rated fourth put the form into perspective.

327 DIGIBET H'CAP 7f (P)
3:05 (3:06) (Class 6) (0-55,62) 4-Y-O+ £2,047 (£604; £302) Stalls High

Form RPR

0-51 **1** **Sovereignty (JPN)**[8] 232 6-8-10 56 JamesO'Reilly(5) 3 66+
(D K Ivory) *hld up in rr: effrt over 2f out on outer: hanging but r.o fr over 1f out: led last 50yds: won gng away* **5/2**[1]

250- **2** *3/4* **Contented (IRE)**[53] 7028 6-8-11 52 (p) LPKeniry 2 60
(Mrs L C Jewell) *hld up in midfield: prog on outer 2f out: rdn to ld 1f out: hdd and outpcd last 50yds* **16/1**

00-2 **3** *1 1/4* **Patavium Prince (IRE)**[14] 151 5-8-7 48 SimonWhitworth 4 53
(Miss Jo Crowley) *prom: disp 2nd over 2f out: chal and upsides 1f out: nt qckn* **9/1**

21-3 **4** *hd* **Grand Assault**[18] 87 5-8-13 54 (p) AdamKirby 7 58
(G C Bravery) *trckd ldrs: chsng ldr whn nt clr run over 1f out: styd on same pce fnl f* **9/2**[2]

400- **5** *1 1/2* **Task Complete**[67] 6895 5-8-11 52 HayleyTurner 12 52
(Jean-Rene Auvray) *sn prom: disp 2nd 3f out to over 1f out: nt qckn* **25/1**

05-4 **6** *3/4* **Guildenstern (IRE)**[20] 71 6-9-0 55 TGMcLaughlin 1 53
(P Howling) *dropped in fr wd draw: t.k.h and hld up in last trio: outpcd over 2f out: kpt on but no ch fr over 1f out* **8/1**[3]

-110 **7** *1/2* **Epidaurian King (IRE)**[5] 256 5-9-7 62 (v) DeanMcKeown 6 59+
(D Shaw) *stdd s: hld up on inner: cl up over 2f out: nt qckn over 1f out: keeping on but nt pce to chal whn bdly hmpd jst ins fnl f* **5/2**[1]

0-03 **8** *1 1/4* **Mulberry Lad (IRE)**[4] 270 6-8-11 52 ChrisCatlin 11 45
(P W Hiatt) *mde most at stdy pce: kicked on over 2f out: hdd & wknd 1f out* **9/1**

5-50 **9** *1/2* **Ishibee (IRE)**[4] 263 4-8-10 54 (p) TolleyDean(3) 9 46
(J J Bridger) *hld up wl in rr: sme prog on inner over 2f out: wknd jst over 1f out* **25/1**

005- **10** *shd* **Montzando**[215] 2972 5-8-7 48 ow1 (p) RobertHavlin 8 40
(B R Millman) *stdd s: t.k.h and hld up wl in rr: outpcd over 2f out: no ch after* **20/1**

00-6 **11** *2* **Iron Pearl**[12] 167 4-8-5 46 oh1 (e[1]) LiamJones 10 32
(J Ryan) *t.k.h: hld up in last trio: outpcd over 2f out: no ch after* **50/1**

5U-0 **12** *15* **Vlasta Weiner**[9] 211 8-8-9 50 (b) SteveDrowne 5 —
(J M Bradley) *dwlt: t.k.h and sn w ldr: wknd 3f out: t.o* **50/1**

1m 26.84s (0.84) **Going Correction** 0.0s/f (Stan) 12 Ran SP% **128.7**
Speed ratings (Par 101): **95,94,92,92,90 89,89,87,87,87 84,67**
CSF £50.43 CT £286.14 TOTE £4.10: £1.40, £5.00, £2.40; EX 63.90.

The Form Book, Raceform Ltd, Compton, RG20 6NL

Owner Radlett Racing **Bred** Darley Stud Management, L L C **Trained** Radlett, Herts

FOCUS
A moderate handicap, run at an ordinary pace. The form seems to make sense.
Epidaurian King(IRE) Official explanation: jockey said gelding suffered interference in running
Vlasta Weiner Official explanation: jockey said gelding ran too free

328 HAPPY 91ST BIRTHDAY JOAN AYRES H'CAP 1m (P)
3:35 (3:37) (Class 6) (0-50,50) 4-Y-0+ £2,047 (£604; £302) Stalls High

Form RPR
50-0 **1** **Not Now Lewis (IRE)**[18] 101 4-8-12 **50**.............................. TPQueally 4 58
(J A Osborne) *hld up in midfield: prog into 5th over 3f out: chsd ldr 2f out: styd on to ld ins fnl f: hld on* **12/1**
24-4 **2** *nk* **Having A Ball**[12] 168 4-8-11 **49**.............................. DaneO'Neill 3 56
(P D Cundell) *hld up wl in rr: taken to outer and rdn over 2f out: prog over 1f out: styd on to take 2nd and press wnr nr fin* **9/2**[2]
55-4 **3** *nk* **Border Edge**[12] 164 10-8-5 **46**.............................. NeilChalmers(3) 6 52
(J J Bridger) *chsd ldng pair: pushed along bef 1/2-way: nt qckn 2f out: styd on wl again fnl f: nrst fin* **10/1**
06-2 **4** *1* **Ermine Grey**[6] 251 7-8-12 **50**.............................. HayleyTurner 2 54
(A W Carroll) *sn in midfield: rdn and effrt over 2f out: styd on fr over 1f out to take 4th nr fin: no real danger* **4/1**[1]
245- **5** *½* **Johnston's Glory (IRE)**[44] 7144 4-8-12 **50**.............................. MickyFenton 10 53
(E J Alston) *chsd clr ldr: clsd to ld over 2f out: hdd & wknd ins fnl f* **7/1**[3]
4-22 **6** *½* **Jomus**[4] 267 7-8-11 **49**.............................. RobertHavlin 11 51
(L Montague Hall) *stdd s: hld up in last: no real prog tl consented to run on jst over 1f out: no ch of rching ldrs* **4/1**[1]
0620 **7** *nk* **Wizby**[4] 267 5-8-8 **46** oh1.............................. JamesDoyle 8 49+
(P D Evans) *stdd s: hld up wl in rr: prog fr 2f out: nvr pce to rch ldrs: 6th whn short of room nr fin* **16/1**
0-00 **8** *½* **Royal Guest**[5] 256 4-8-10 **48**..............................(v) GregFairley 13 48
(J R Jenkins) *dwlt and rousted early: then t.k.h: prog fr 3f out: chsd ldng pair over 1f out: wknd last 100yds* **16/1**
4-04 **9** *shd* **Bollywood (IRE)**[6] 242 5-8-8 **46** oh1.............................. JohnEgan 9 46
(J J Bridger) *hld up in midfield: prog on inner over 2f out: chsng ldrs over 1f out: wknd ins fnl f* **9/1**
0-00 **10** *1 ¼* **Charlie Bear**[9] 220 7-8-8 **46** oh1..............................(b[1]) AdrianMcCarthy 14 43
(Miss Z C Davison) *hld up wl in rr: effrt on inner 2f out: no imp on ldrs over 1f out: wknd ins fnl f* **25/1**
0-53 **11** *1 ½* **Kinsman (IRE)**[12] 164 11-8-9 **47**..............................(p[1]) J-PGuillambert 1 40
(T D McCarthy) *racd on outer in rr: effrt and sme prog over 2f out: wknd over 1f out* **16/1**
00-0 **12** *1 ½* **Blakeshall Hope**[18] 99 6-8-8 **46** oh1.............................. DeanMcKeown 12 36
(A J Chamberlain) *chsd ldng pair: losing pl whn hmpd and snatched up wl over 1f out* **50/1**
0-00 **13** *½* **Shadow Jumper (IRE)**[19] 79 7-8-2 **47**..............................(v) PatrickDonaghy(7) 5 36
(J T Stimpson) *led at str pce and sn 3 l clr: hdd & wknd over 2f out* **25/1**
5-63 **14** *nk* **Gifted Flame**[13] 155 9-8-6 **49** ow1.............................. AnnStokell(5) 7 37
(Miss A Stokell) *racd wd: mostly in rr: struggling on wd outside over 2f out* **20/1**

1m 39.32s (-0.48) **Going Correction** 0.0s/f (Stan) 14 Ran SP% **129.5**
Speed ratings (Par 101): **102,101,101,100,99 99,99,98,98,97 95,94,93,93**
CSF £67.70 CT £590.36 TOTE £18.00: £4.40, £2.00, £3.80; EX 89.40.
Owner Morsethehorse Syndicate **Bred** Michael And John Fahy **Trained** Upper Lambourn, Berks

FOCUS
A very weak handicap which resulted in a driving finish between the first three. The runner-up helps to set the level but there are doubts over the strength of the form.

329 DIGIBET SPORTS BETTING H'CAP 6f (P)
4:05 (4:07) (Class 4) (0-85,87) 4-Y-0+ £4,210 (£1,252; £625; £312) Stalls High

Form RPR
2-24 **1** **Bazroy (IRE)**[1] 313 4-8-13 **80**..............................(b) StephenDonohoe 5 93
(P D Evans) *hld up in rr: prog over 2f out: squeezed through fnl f to ld last 75yds: drvn out* **11/2**[2]
340- **2** *½* **Bo McGinty (IRE)**[92] 6487 7-8-6 **73**..............................(b) DaleGibson 3 84
(R A Fahey) *blasted off and led to over 3f out: pressed ldr after: upsides fnl f: kpt on but jst hld last 50yds* **20/1**
4-31 **3** *hd* **Mogok Ruby**[14] 150 4-8-11 **78**.............................. RichardHughes 1 89
(L Montague Hall) *dropped in fr wd draw and hld up in last: effrt 2f out: prog over 1f out: styd on wl fnl f: nrst fin* **7/2**[1]
00-0 **4** *1* **Lethal**[26] 5 5-8-12 **82**.............................. JamieMoriarty(3) 7 90
(R A Fahey) *pressed ldr: narrow ld over 3f out: drvn over 1f out: hdd and fdd last 75yds* **10/1**
00-4 **5** *¾* **She's My Outsider**[9] 210 6-8-6 **73**.............................. HayleyTurner 11 78
(A W Carroll) *t.k.h: trckd ldrs: wl plcd to chal 2f out: nt qckn over 1f out* **16/1**
1-03 **6** *1* **Desert Dreamer (IRE)**[9] 210 7-8-8 **75**.............................. TPQueally 2 77
(G A Butler) *racd wd and hld up: struggling over 2f out: styd on fnl f: n.d* **10/1**
5-42 **7** *nk* **Louphole**[18] 94 6-8-8 **75**..............................(p) ChrisCatlin 9 76
(P J Makin) *dwlt: hld up in rr: prog on inner over 2f out: looked dangerous over 1f out: effrt petered out tamely fnl f* **7/2**[1]
050- **8** *1 ¼* **Secret Night**[39] 7184 5-9-1 **82**.............................. RobertHavlin 8 79
(J A R Toller) *hld up in midfield: effrt towards inner over 2f out: no imp on ldrs over 1f out: wknd ins fnl f* **12/1**
-602 **9** *3* **Yungaburra (IRE)**[12] 162 4-9-6 **87**..............................(bt) JohnEgan 4 74
(D J Murphy) *chsd ldrs on outer but hanging and difficult to steer: steadily wknd fnl 2f* **7/1**[3]
206- **10** *3* **Trees Of Green (USA)**[100] 6309 4-8-5 **72**.............................. NickyMackay 6 50
(M Wigham) *nvr on terms w ldrs: rdn and struggling fr 1/2-way* **10/1**
300- **11** *nk* **Grand Show**[47] 7112 6-9-1 **82**..............................(p) AdamKirby 10 59
(W R Swinburn) *chsd ldrs: rdn over 2f out: wknd rapidly over 1f out* **8/1**

1m 12.2s (-0.90) **Going Correction** 0.0s/f (Stan) 11 Ran SP% **129.0**
Speed ratings (Par 105): **106,105,105,103,102 101,101,99,95,91 90**
CSF £120.07 CT £455.66 TOTE £8.10: £2.10, £4.40, £1.80; EX 191.90.
Owner Barry McCabe **Bred** P D Savill **Trained** Pandy, Monmouths

FOCUS
A good sprint handicap, run at a strong early pace. Sound form which should work out.
Desert Dreamer(IRE) Official explanation: jockey said gelding hung left
Trees Of Green(USA) Official explanation: jockey said colt ran flat

330 DIGIBET AMATEUR JOCKEYS ASSOCIATION H'CAP (FOR AMATEUR RIDERS) 1m 3f (P)
4:40 (4:42) (Class 6) (0-60,59) 4-Y-0+ £1,977 (£608; £304) Stalls High

Form RPR
06/1 **1** **Schinken Otto (IRE)**[9] 219 7-10-11 **52**.............................. MissNJefferson(5) 7 61
(J M Jefferson) *s.s: rcvrd and led after 2f: mde rest: pushed along and kpt on steadily fnl 2f* **4/1**[2]
/16- **2** *1 ¼* **Ndola**[55] 6583 9-11-0 **50**..............................(v) MrSDobson 5 57
(P Butler) *trckd ldrs on inner: effrt to chse wnr wl over 1f out: kpt on but no imp fnl f* **20/1**
2-61 **3** *1 ½* **Gifted Heir (IRE)**[8] 229 4-10-9 **55**.............................. MissRLLockie(7) 10 59
(A Bailey) *racd towards outer in midfield: effrt 3f out: kpt on fnl 2f to take 3rd nr fin: nvr able to chal* **14/1**
/46- **4** *nk* **Inn For The Dancer**[32] 1592 6-10-8 **49**..... MissSarah-JaneDurman(5) 13 52+
(J C Fox) *hld up in last trio: sme prog over 2f out: no imp over 1f out: r.o fnl f: nrst fin* **20/1**
0-12 **5** *½* **Sahf London**[2] 299 5-10-10 **53**..............................(b) MrJoshuaMoore(7) 8 56
(G L Moore) *t.k.h: trckd ldrs: pushed along and nt qckn 2f out: fdd ins fnl f* **9/4**[1]
5-05 **6** *hd* **Bienheureux**[8] 224 7-10-13 **56**..............................(bt) MissOMaylam(7) 1 58
(Miss Gay Kelleway) *stdd s: hld up in last trio: sme prog fr over 2f out: nvr rchd ldrs* **14/1**
00-0 **7** *1* **Ashmolian (IRE)**[2] 303 5-10-6 **45**..........(b) MissGDGracey-Davison(7) 9 46
(Miss Z C Davison) *t.k.h: hld up in midfield: chsng ldrs 2f out: one pce after* **66/1**
4-42 **8** *nk* **Ruffie (IRE)**[9] 220 5-10-5 **46**.............................. MrRBirkett(5) 4 46
(Miss J Feilden) *led 2f: chsd wnr to wl over 1f out: wknd fnl f* **10/1**[3]
-440 **9** *7* **Western Roots**[8] 234 7-11-0 **57**..............................(v[1]) MrJGoss(7) 2 45
(M Appleby) *racd wd towards rr: lost tch over 2f out* **33/1**
4/0- **10** *4* **Take A Mile (IRE)**[17] 4544 6-10-9 **52**.............................. MrRElliott(5) 6 33
(B G Powell) *s.v.s and then restrained in last pair: racd wd fr 7f out: nvr a factor* **12/1**
000/ **11** *1* **Canni Thinkaar (IRE)**[390] 2636 7-10-4 **45**..............(p) MrBMMorris(5) 12 25
(P Butler) *nvr on terms: lost tch wl over 2f out* **80/1**
4- **12** *½* **Ramvaswani (IRE)**[13] 5898 5-11-0 **55**..............................(p) MissZoeLilly(5) 11 34
(N B King) *v s.i.s: rcvrd and prom after 3f: drvn and wknd over 3f out* **16/1**
656- **13** *nk* **Cavendish**[23] 6902 4-10-13 **59**..............................(b) MrDJEustace(7) 3 37
(J M P Eustace) *v awkward s and slowly away: rapid prog on wd outside to chse ldrs after 3f: wknd over 3f out* **20/1**
106- **14** *dist* **Blue Hedges**[30] 7256 6-11-7 **57**.............................. MrSWalker 14 —
(H J Collingridge) *reluctant to enter stalls: hld up towards rr on inner: wknd rapidly over 3f out: virtually p.u* **4/1**[2]

2m 23.78s (1.88) **Going Correction** 0.0s/f (Stan)
WFA 4 from 5yo+ 3lb 14 Ran SP% **126.7**
Speed ratings (Par 101): **93,92,91,90,90 90,89,89,84,81 80,80,80,—**
CSF £92.69 CT £1061.84 TOTE £4.80: £1.90, £6.60, £4.90; EX 93.20 Place 6 £30.32, Place 5 £16.82..
Owner John Donald **Bred** T Burns And Mrs P F N Fanning **Trained** Norton, N Yorks
■ Stewards' Enquiry : Mr B M Morris one-day ban: used whip when out of contention (Feb 18)

FOCUS
A moderate handicap, confined to amateur riders. The first two were always prominent and this is modest form.
T/Plt: £34.50 to a £1 stake. Pool: £57,622.65. 1,218.30 winning tickets. T/Qpdt: £24.70 to a £1 stake. Pool: £3,898.30. 116.70 winning tickets. JN

324 KEMPTON (A.W) (R-H)
Monday, January 28

OFFICIAL GOING: Standard
Wind: Nil Weather: Dull, misty

331 KEMPTON.CO.UK CLAIMING STKS 1m 2f (P)
1:50 (1:51) (Class 6) 4-Y-0+ £1,774 (£523; £262) Stalls High

Form RPR
60-1 **1** **Waterside (IRE)**[7] 245 9-9-7 99.............................. JimCrowley 2 77
(G L Moore) *t.k.h: hld up in midfield: rdn and effrt 2f out: chsd ldr ins fnl f: r.o to ld on post* **8/11**[1]
50-0 **2** *shd* **Fregate Island (IRE)**[19] 97 5-9-7 75.............................. TPQueally 1 77
(J G Given) *sn led: rdn 2f out: kpt on u.p tl hdd on line* **7/1**[3]
3-23 **3** *½* **Smokey The Bear**[17] 125 6-9-1 57.............................. NeilChalmers(3) 5 73
(Miss Sheena West) *trckd ldrs: hdwy on inner wl over 1f out: rdn to chse ldr over 1f out tl one pce last 100yds* **16/1**
3-15 **4** *1* **Hucking Heat (IRE)**[3] 302 4-8-12 68.............................. PatCosgrave 4 67
(J R Boyle) *t.k.h: chsd ldr after 1f: rdn jst over 2f out: outpcd ins fnl f* **12/1**
40-4 **5** *nk* **Without Excuse (USA)**[11] 196 4-9-2 73..............................(b) URispoli 6 70
(M Botti) *s.i.s: hld up in last pair: rdn and effrt 2f out: hung rt after: kpt on but nt pce to trble ldrs* **3/1**[2]
45-5 **6** *½* **Boundless Prospect (USA)**[23] 51 9-8-13 61............ MickyFenton 7 64
(Miss Gay Kelleway) *hld up in last pair: rdn and effrt wl over 1f out: kpt on same pce* **16/1**

2m 8.85s (0.85) **Going Correction** +0.05s/f (Slow)
WFA 4 from 5yo+ 2lb 6 Ran SP% **114.9**
Speed ratings (Par 101): **98,97,97,96,96 96**
CSF £7.00 TOTE £1.60: £1.10, £3.30; EX 7.80.The winner was claimed by M. J. Gingell for £18,000.
Owner Nigel Shields **Bred** Yeomanstown Stud **Trained** Woodingdean, E Sussex

FOCUS
An uncompetitive claimer, run at a steady early pace. The favourite just got there and the form should be treated with some caution, with the proximity of the third a worry.
Without Excuse(USA) Official explanation: jockey said gelding hung right

332 KEMPTON FOR WEDDINGS H'CAP 1m 4f (P)
2:20 (2:20) (Class 6) (0-60,60) 4-Y-0+ £1,774 (£523; £262) Stalls Centre

Form RPR
20-6 **1** **Mixing**[17] 125 6-8-9 **50**.............................. KirstyMilczarek(3) 9 58
(J Akehurst) *t.k.h: trckd ldrs: wnt 2nd over 3f out: rdn to ld jst over 1f out: clr ins fnl f: rdn out* **10/3**[2]
553- **2** *1 ¼* **Wee Charlie Castle (IRE)**[31] 7186 5-9-3 **55**.................. OscarUrbina 3 61+
(G C H Chung) *hld up in midfield tl lost pl 4f out: hdwy wl over 2f out: rdn jst over 2f out: kpt on to chse wnr ins fnl f: r.o* **7/2**[3]
50-0 **3** *¾* **Amwell Brave**[19] 91 7-9-5 **57**.............................. JimCrowley 2 62
(J R Jenkins) *hld up towards rr: hdwy wl over 2f out: styd on u.p over 1f out: wnt 3rd wl ins fnl f: nt rch wnr* **8/1**

15-1 **4** *shd* **Little Richard (IRE)**[17] [125] 9-9-8 **60**..............................(p) AdamKirby 8 65
(M Wellings) *chsd ldrs: rdn and edgd lft on inner over 2f out: kpt on same pce fnl f* **7/1**

05-3 **5** *1 ½* **Medieval Maiden**[17] [132] 5-9-6 **58**..............................(p) TPQueally 5 60
(W J Musson) *sn led: rdn jst over 2f out: hdd jst over 1f out: wknd fnl f* **11/4**[1]

0/00 **6** *3 ½* **King Of Diamonds**[10] [207] 7-9-0 **52**..............................(b) FrankieMcDonald 4 49
(Jean-Rene Auvray) *t.k.h: hld up wl in tch: hdwy to chse ldrs over 3f out: rdn and hanging rt wl over 1f out: wknd jst over 1f out* **33/1**

0/61 **7** *¾* **George Henson (IRE)**[11] [188] 4-8-1 **50**.............................. MCGeran(7) 1 46
(S Parr) *stdd s: hld up in last: shkn up over 4f out: rdn 3f out: nvr pce to threaten ldrs* **9/2**

6 **8** *5* **Bandits Pistol (NZ)**[10] [207] 8-9-3 **55**.............................. J-PGuillambert 7 43
(M Madgwick) *t.k.h: chsd ldr tl over 3f out: sn rdn: wknd wl over 2f out* **33/1**

00-0 **9** *2* **Raydan (IRE)**[12] [180] 6-9-2 **54**..............................(b) MickyFenton 6 38
(D R Gandolfo) *stdd s: hld up in rr: effrt on outer 3f out: sn no imp and wl btn* **33/1**

2m 33.77s (-0.73) **Going Correction** +0.05s/f (Slow)
WFA 4 from 5yo+ 4lb **9** Ran SP% **122.6**
Speed ratings (Par 101): **104,103,102,102,101 99,98,95,94**
CSF £16.35 CT £86.12 TOTE £4.70: £1.10, £1.50, £2.40; EX 18.30.
Owner Canisbay Bloodstock **Bred** Juddmonte Farms **Trained** Epsom, Surrey
■ Stewards' Enquiry : Jim Crowley £130 fine: late arrival in parade ring

FOCUS
An ordinary handicap, run at a sound enough pace. Theform is sound and the fourth helps to set the standard.
George Henson(IRE) Official explanation: jockey said gelding hung right

333 KEMPTON FOR CONFERENCES H'CAP 6f (P)
2:50 (2:50) (Class 6) (0-60,60) 3-Y-0 **£1,774** (£523; £262) **Stalls** High

Form RPR

-031 **1** **Wynberg (IRE)**[3] [298] 3-8-13 **55** 6ex.............................. JimCrowley 1 62+
(S A Callaghan) *plld hrd: hld up in tch: pushed along and hdwy over 1f out: qcknd to ld 1f out: rdn out* **5/4**[1]

2-02 **2** *½* **Alabama Spirit (USA)**[14] [154] 3-9-1 **60**.............................. TolleyDean(3) 6 63
(D Shaw) *t.k.h: trckd ldrs: rdn 2f out: ev ch and edgd lft u.p 1f out: chsd wnr fnl f: unable qck* **6/1**

0-26 **3** *1 ¼* **Regal Veil**[8] [237] 3-8-6 **48**.............................. SaleemGolam 3 47
(S C Williams) *led at v stdy gallop: rdn over 2f out: hdd 1f out: no ex last 100yds* **16/1**

-112 **4** *hd* **Bold Diva**[8] [237] 3-8-13 **58**..............................(v) KirstyMilczarek(3) 4 62+
(A W Carroll) *stdd s: plld hrd: hld up in tch: swtchd rt and hdwy wl over 1f out: running on whn nt clr run 1f out: unable to rcvr* **2/1**[2]

443- **5** *2* **Llab Nala**[65] [6928] 3-8-13 **55**..............................(v) ChrisCatlin 5 47
(M R Channon) *t.k.h: chsd ldr: rdn to chal and hung lft 2f out: kpt on same pce u.p* **11/2**[3]

065- **6** *5* **Dickie Valentine**[33] [7235] 3-8-6 **48**..............................(v) HayleyTurner 2 24
(M R Bosley) *stdd and dropped in after s: a last: rdn and lost tch over 2f out* **16/1**

1m 16.67s (3.57) **Going Correction** +0.05s/f (Slow) **6** Ran SP% **119.2**
Speed ratings (Par 95): **78,77,75,75,72 66**
CSF £10.43 TOTE £3.30: £1.40, £3.30; EX 10.90.
Owner Cast Hinge Searchfield & Smallbone 1 **Bred** Ged O'Leary **Trained** Newmarket, Suffolk
■ Stewards' Enquiry : Saleem Golam four-day ban: used whip with excessive force (Feb 8-11)

FOCUS
A weak handicap, run at a crawling early pace. The first two still make sense and the fourth must be rated better than the bare form.
Bold Diva Official explanation: jockey said filly was denied a clear run and lost a shoe

334 TFM NETWORKS H'CAP 6f (P)
3:20 (3:21) (Class 5) (0-70,70) 4-Y-0+ **£2,331** (£693; £346; £173) **Stalls** High

Form RPR

6-22 **1** **Royal Envoy (IRE)**[15] [149] 5-8-3 **58** ow2.............................. TolleyDean(3) 3 65
(D Shaw) *racd in midfield off the pce: hdwy 2f out: rdn to ld 1f out: r.o wl* **3/1**[1]

3-02 **2** *¾* **Millfield (IRE)**[7] [245] 5-9-1 **67**.............................. JimCrowley 5 72
(P R Chamings) *hld up wl in rr: rdn and hdwy wl over 1f out: r.o strly fnl f: wnt 2nd towards fin: nt rch wnr* **10/3**[2]

0-14 **3** *½* **Star Strider**[17] [126] 4-9-2 **68**.............................. MickyFenton 6 71
(Miss Gay Kelleway) *wnt lft s: chsd ldng pair: effrt over 2f out: ev ch u.p over 1f out: unable qck ins fnl f* **11/1**

6-06 **4** *½* **Dvinsky (USA)**[13] [165] 7-9-2 **68**..............................(b) TGMcLaughlin 7 70
(P Howling) *pressed ldr clr of remainder: rdn over 2f out: ev ch tl no ex jst ins fnl f* **10/1**

6353 **5** *nk* **Hucking Hill (IRE)**[13] [165] 4-9-0 **66**..............................(b) DaneO'Neill 4 67
(J R Best) *s.i.s: hld up wl bhd: c wd over 3f out: rdn and hdwy 2f out: r.o: nt rch ldrs* **13/2**

500- **6** *nk* **Linda Green**[62] [6962] 7-8-12 **64**.............................. ChrisCatlin 8 64
(M R Channon) *s.i.s: sn in midfield: rdn and effrt over 2f out: kpt on same pce fnl f* **16/1**

60-2 **7** *½* **Monashee Prince (IRE)**[13] [165] 6-8-10 **62**..............................(v) HayleyTurner 1 60
(J R Best) *t.k.h: hld up bhd on outer: swtchd to rail over 3f out: rdn over 2f out: kpt on u.p but nt pce to rch ldrs* **7/1**

030- **8** *2 ½* **Hill Of Lujain**[31] [7261] 4-8-6 **58**.............................. PaulEddery 9 48
(Ian Williams) *led at fast gallop: clr w one rival: rdn wl over 1f out: hdd 1f out: sn wknd* **25/1**

444- **9** *21* **Interactive (IRE)**[30] [7269] 5-9-1 **70**.............................. KirstyMilczarek(3) 2 —
(Andrew Turnell) *racd off the pce in midfield: rdn over 2f out: sn wknd: virtually p.u ins fnl f* **11/2**[3]

1m 12.12s (-0.98) **Going Correction** +0.05s/f (Slow) **9** Ran SP% **116.4**
Speed ratings (Par 103): **108,107,106,105,105 104,104,100,72**
CSF £13.22 CT £95.88 TOTE £3.70: £1.60, £1.50, £3.00; EX 14.70.
Owner The Circle Bloodstock I Limited **Bred** Northern Lights Bloodstock **Trained** Danethorpe, Notts

FOCUS
A modest handicap, run at a decent pace. The form looks solid enough for the class rated through the second and fourth.
Interactive(IRE) Official explanation: jockey said gelding lost its action; vet said gelding had an irregular heartbeat

335 PANORAMIC BAR & RESTAURANT H'CAP 1m (P)
3:50 (3:50) (Class 6) (0-60,59) 3-Y-0 **£1,774** (£523; £262) **Stalls** High

Form RPR

00-3 **1** **Sistos Fascination**[19] [98] 3-9-4 **59**.............................. OscarUrbina 7 63+
(M Botti) *hld up in bhd ldrs: wnt 2nd over 3f out: plld out over 2f out: sn chalng: carried bdly rt fr over 1f out: led last 100yds: rdn out* **5/2**[1]

4-32 **2** *¾* **Hawa Khana (IRE)**[11] [195] 3-8-11 **55**..............................(p) KirstyMilczarek(3) 6 57
(N P Littmoden) *t.k.h: led: hrd pressed and rdn 2f out: sn hung bdly lft: hdd last 100yds: no ex* **3/1**[2]

000- **3** *¾* **Ray Diamond**[90] [6574] 3-8-11 **52**.............................. J-PGuillambert 1 52
(M Madgwick) *s.i.s: sn pushed up to chse ldrs: rdn over 2f out: carried lft over 1f out: sn swtchd rt: kpt on same pce fnl f* **33/1**

00-0 **4** *1 ¾* **Herrbee (IRE)**[5] [265] 3-9-1 **56**.............................. PaulDoe 2 52
(S Dow) *hld up wl bhd in last: rdn and gd hdwy wl over 2f out: chsd ldrs over 1f out: kpt on same pce fnl f* **20/1**

-645 **5** *½* **Silver Sprite**[6] [262] 3-8-13 **54**.............................. DeanMcKeown 5 49
(D Shaw) *racd in midfield: rdn 3f out: nvr pce to trble ldrs* **9/2**

22-5 **6** *5* **Scientific**[12] [184] 3-9-2 **57**..............................(b) SaleemGolam 4 40+
(G Prodromou) *hld up: stmbld bdly after 1f and bhd after rdn and effrt on inner over 3f out: nvr nr ldrs* **6/1**

500- **7** *6* **Ricci De Mare**[68] [6897] 3-9-0 **55**.............................. StephenDonohoe 3 25
(Sir Mark Prescott) *s.i.s: sn pushed up to chse ldr: rdn over 4f out: lost pl over 3f out: hung rt 2f out: sn wl bhd* **4/1**[3]

1m 41.61s (1.81) **Going Correction** +0.05s/f (Slow) **7** Ran SP% **113.7**
Speed ratings (Par 95): **92,91,90,88,88 83,77**
CSF £10.14 TOTE £3.50: £2.10, £2.30; EX 8.50.
Owner Giuliano Manfredini **Bred** Newsells Park Stud **Trained** Newmarket, Suffolk
■ Stewards' Enquiry : Kirsty Milczarek four-day ban: careless riding (Feb 8-11)

FOCUS
A modest handicap run at an ordinary pace. Weakish form and this probably took little winning. The winning time was 3.15 seconds slower than the following 81-95.
Scientific Official explanation: jockey said gelding clipped heels

336 SPONSOR AT KEMPTON H'CAP 1m (P)
4:20 (4:20) (Class 3) (0-95,93) 4-Y-0+
£6,543 (£1,959; £979; £490; £244; £122) **Stalls** High

Form RPR

335- **1** **Capable Guest (IRE)**[72] [6852] 6-8-13 **88**.............................. ChrisCatlin 4 97
(M R Channon) *racd in midfield: niggled along at times: sltly outpcd 2f out: drvn and hdwy over 1f out: ev ch 1f out: led nr fin* **9/2**[3]

016- **2** *hd* **Gallantry**[85] [6674] 6-8-11 **86**.............................. DeanMcKeown 3 95
(D Shaw) *t.k.h: hld up wl in tch in last trio: hdwy between horses 2f out: rdn to ld ins fnl f: hdd nr fin* **8/1**

1-25 **3** *1* **Alfresco**[10] [218] 4-9-2 **91**..............................(b) DaneO'Neill 7 99+
(I A Wood) *s.i.s: t.k.h: hld up wl in tch in rr: nt clr run on inner fr over 2f out: swtchd lft ins fnl f: r.o and snatched 3rd on line* **8/1**

11-4 **4** *shd* **Atlantic Story (USA)**[16] [138] 6-9-4 **93**..............................(bt) AdamKirby 1 99
(M W Easterby) *t.k.h: hld up on outer: hdwy u.p over 1f out: wnt 3rd last 100yds: no imp after: lost 3rd on line* **11/4**[2]

640- **5** *¾* **Tender The Great (IRE)**[43] [7165] 5-8-8 **83**.............................. TQuinn 6 88
(B G Powell) *t.k.h: hld up in bhd ldrs: rdn to chal on inner over 1f out: unable qck ins fnl f* **7/1**

P0-0 **6** *nk* **Markab**[9] [227] 5-8-9 **84**.............................. JimCrowley 5 88
(K A Morgan) *w ldr tl led 4f out: rdn over 1f out: hdd ins fnl f: fdd last 100yds* **16/1**

212- **7** *½* **Dream Lodge (IRE)**[99] [6359] 4-9-3 **92**.............................. TPQueally 2 95
(J G Given) *sn led: hdd 4f out: styd w ldr: drvn and ev ch over 2f out: fdd jst ins fnl f* **5/2**[1]

1m 38.46s (-1.34) **Going Correction** +0.05s/f (Slow) **7** Ran SP% **114.0**
Speed ratings (Par 107): **108,107,106,106,105 105,105**
CSF £38.89 TOTE £5.70: £3.70, £5.70; EX 45.50.
Owner John Guest **Bred** Mountarmstrong Stud **Trained** West Ilsley, Berks

FOCUS
A good handicap, but they went an ordinary early gallop and finished in a bit of a bunch. Despite the lack of pace in the opening stages, the winning time was still 3.15 seconds quicker than the previous 46-60. The form makes sense.

NOTEBOOK
Capable Guest(IRE) had the visor left off on his return from over two months off the track and he just proved good enough. He obviously responded well enough to pressure to get the verdict, but his rider was having to keep at him from an early stage and it would be no surprise to see headgear given another go next time. He is now two from four on Polytrack and appeals as one to keep on side. (tchd 4-1)
Gallantry ran very well considering he was keen off the modest early tempo and would have preferred a stronger gallop. There could be more to come. (tchd 9-1)
Alfresco had nowhere to go when trying to make his move around a furlong out and could be considered an unlucky loser. He was a little keen early on and would have preferred a stronger pace, so this rates as a decent effort off a career-high mark. (op 15-2)
Atlantic Story(USA) would have appreciated the return to this trip, but the steady early pace was against him. (op 9-4 tchd 3-1 in a places)
Tender The Great(IRE) is probably a better horse over 7f. (op 15-2)
Dream Lodge(IRE), racing off a career-high mark, seemed well placed considering how the race was run, but he dropped out tamely. (op 3-1)

337 MIX BUSINESS WITH PLEASURE H'CAP 6f (P)
4:50 (4:50) (Class 2) (0-100,107) 4-Y-0+ **£10,363** (£3,083; £1,540; £769) **Stalls** High

Form RPR

53-4 **1** **Orpsie Boy (IRE)**[9] [226] 5-8-7 **92**.............................. KirstyMilczarek(3) 8 99
(N P Littmoden) *hld up wl in tch: hdwy to ld over 1f out: in command fnl f: pushed out* **5/2**[2]

1-13 **2** *¾* **Bonus (IRE)**[9] [226] 8-9-11 **107**.............................. HayleyTurner 2 115+
(G A Butler) *wnt lft s: dropped in bhd: clsd over 3f out: hdwy inner and nt clr run over 1f out: sn swtchd lft: r.o to chse wnr ins fnl f but unable to chal* **11/8**[1]

50-0 **3** *1* **Fyodor (IRE)**[27] [5] 7-9-1 **97**.............................. TPQueally 1 98
(W J Haggas) *stdd s and dropped in bhd: hdwy over 1f out: rdn to chse ldng pair ins fnl f: no imp last 100yds* **20/1**

5-30 **4** *½* **Qadar (IRE)**[9] [226] 6-8-10 **92**..............................(b) JimCrowley 3 92
(N P Littmoden) *racd in midfield: plld out and drvn over 2f out: kpt on u.p but nt pce to threaten wnr* **14/1**

1-11 **5** *3* **Mr Lambros**[9] [233] 7-8-8 **90**..............................(vt) MickyFenton 5 80
(Miss Gay Kelleway) *sn pressing ldr tl led over 3f out: rdn wl over 1f out: hdd over 1f out: wknd fnl f* **9/2**[3]

0-46 **6** *1 ½* **Lucayos**[9] [226] 5-8-8 **90**.............................. RichardKingscote 7 79
(Mrs H Sweeting) *led tl over 3f out: w ldr after: rdn over 2f out: wknd 1f out: eased ins fnl f* **25/1**

25-1 **7** *nk* **Come Out Fighting**[9] [226] 5-8-12 **94**.............................. StephenDonohoe 4 82
(P A Blockley) *awkward leaving stalls: sn chsng ldrs: rdn over 2f out: wknd over 1f out* **13/2**

1m 11.72s (-1.38) **Going Correction** +0.05s/f (Slow) **7** Ran SP% **117.5**
Speed ratings (Par 109): **111,110,108,108,104 103,102**
CSF £6.64 CT £52.61 TOTE £2.90: £1.50, £1.60; EX 6.30 Place 6 £60.08, Place 5 £41.19.
Owner Miss Vanessa Church **Bred** Minch Bloodstock **Trained** Newmarket, Suffolk

FOCUS
A very good sprint handicap. The form seems sound enough and Bonus has been rated a narrow winner.

NOTEBOOK
Orpsie Boy(IRE) ◆ was able to reverse recent Lingfield form with both Come Out Fighting and Bonus and this rates as a career best. Admittedly the runner-up was a little unlucky, but he did well to hold that one at bay throughout the final furlong and may well have won regardless. He is still very much on the up and is a sprinter to keep on side. (op 4-1)
Bonus(IRE) was possibly an unlucky loser as he was short of room when just beginning to make his move around a furlong out and the winner very much got first run. Official explanation: jockey said gelding was denied a clear run (op 6-4 tchd 7-4 tchd 15-8 in places)
Fyodor(IRE) ◆ was another who looked unlucky not to finish closer as he was given plenty to do and had to wait before he could make his move. He is a smart sprinter at his best and appeals as one to keep on side in the coming weeks.
Qadar(IRE) ran a creditable race in defeat, but he is hard to win with these days. (op 12-1)
Mr Lambros was 8lb higher than when successful at Wolverhampton on his previous start and 17lb higher than when starting his winning run, and the Handicapper looks in charge now. (op 3-1)
Come Out Fighting was only 4lb higher than when winning at Lingfield on his previous start (Orpsie Boy fourth, Bonus third), but he was unable to dominate after starting awkwardly and was nowhere near that level this time. (op 6-1 tchd 7-1)
T/Plt: £77.00 to a £1 stake. Pool: £50,658.30. 480.15 winning tickets. T/Qpdt: £55.80 to a £1 stake. Pool: £3,307.00. 43.80 winning tickets. SP

318 WOLVERHAMPTON (A.W) (L-H)
Monday, January 28

OFFICIAL GOING: Standard
Wind: Almost nil Weather: Fine

338 RACE AHEAD WITH ZENA @ PONTIN'S FILLIES' H'CAP 5f 216y(P)
2:10 (2:10) (Class 6) (0-60,64) 4-Y-0+ **£2,047** (£604; £302) **Stalls** Low

Form				RPR
-421	1		**Crimson Fern (IRE)**[5] 270 4-9-10 64 6ex ... FergusSweeney 7 (M S Saunders) *hld up: hdwy 3f out: led wl over 1f out: sn hung lft: edgd rt cl home: drvn out* **11/10**[1]	69+
00-0	2	1 3/4	**Cadogen Square**[7] 254 6-8-5 45 ... (b) LiamJones 6 (D W Chapman) *led after 1f: hdd wl over 1f out: sn swtchd rt: r.o one pce fnl f* **25/1**	44
3-05	3	1	**Capania (IRE)**[13] 173 4-9-4 58 ... VinceSlattery 4 (P D Evans) *bhd: rdn and hdwy 1f out: r.o to take 3rd cl home* **10/1**	54
0-00	4	nk	**Prettilini**[5] 264 5-8-0 45 ... KellyHarrison(5) 1 (A W Carroll) *a.p: rdn over 2f out: kpt on same pce fnl f* **14/1**	40
0/0-	5	3/4	**Shafrons Canyon (IRE)**[45] 7143 5-8-12 55 ... (t) JerryO'Dwyer(3) 5 (P M Rogers, Ire) *hld up: hmpd 3f out: rdn over 2f out: hdwy over 1f out: one pce fnl f* **12/1**	47
6044	6	3/4	**Time Share (IRE)**[3] 297 4-8-5 45 ... JimmyQuinn 8 (M Wigham) *led early: prom: n.m.r and swtchd rt over 3f out: no hdwy fnl 2f* **9/1**	35
0-20	7	1/2	**Cow Girl (IRE)**[17] 123 4-8-8 53 ... NataliaGemelova(5) 3 (Miss Gay Kelleway) *s.i.s: hld up: hdwy on outside over 2f out: c wd st: rdn over 1f out: no further prog* **4/1**[2]	41
00-0	8	4	**On The Map**[13] 173 4-9-0 54 ... (v) LPKeniry 2 (Joss Saville) *sn led: hdd after 1f: rdn over 2f out: sn wknd* **25/1**	30
640-	9	6	**Briery Blaze**[55] 7025 5-8-9 49 ... (b) SteveDrowne 9 (J W Unett) *prom tl rdn and wknd over 2f out* **5/1**[3]	5

1m 16.33s (1.33) **Going Correction** +0.175s/f (Slow) 9 Ran SP% **125.4**
Speed ratings (Par 98): **98,95,94,93,92 91,91,85,77**
CSF £40.65 CT £210.57 TOTE £1.60: £1.10, £7.20, £4.20; EX 33.90 Trifecta £170.10 Pool: £297.08 - 1.24 winning units..
Owner M S Saunders **Bred** David Brickley **Trained** Green Ore, Somerset

FOCUS
Only the winner really came into this weak handicap in good form. She is on the up and the form is rated through the second.

339 HORIZONS RESTAURANT CLAIMING STKS 5f 216y(P)
2:40 (2:40) (Class 6) 3-Y-0 **£2,047** (£604; £302) **Stalls** Low

Form				RPR
10-6	1		**Harbour Blues**[16] 136 3-9-7 74 ... (t) LiamJones 2 (A W Carroll) *mde all: rdn over 1f out: r.o wl* **11/8**[1]	79
2-32	2	3 1/2	**Maybe I Wont**[12] 186 3-8-11 63 ... SteveDrowne 3 (P G Murphy) *chsd wnr: rdn over 1f out: no imp* **9/2**	58
3-13	3	1 1/4	**Ballycroy Boy (IRE)**[13] 170 3-9-0 77 ... (v1) AshleyMorgan(7) 1 (A Bailey) *hld up in tch: rdn jst over 1f out: one pce* **4/1**[3]	64
3-12	4	1/2	**Lord Deevert**[9] 222 3-8-4 65 ... (b1) JackDean(7) 5 (W G M Turner) *prom: rdn and edgd rt wl over 1f out: sn btn* **3/1**[2]	52
-444	5	1 1/4	**Weetfromthechaff**[8] 237 3-9-1 58 ... (p) LPKeniry 4 (R Hollinshead) *hld up: rdn over 1f out: no rspnse* **28/1**	52

1m 15.7s (0.70) **Going Correction** +0.175s/f (Slow) 5 Ran SP% **108.7**
Speed ratings (Par 95): **102,97,95,95,93**
CSF £7.70 TOTE £1.90: £1.70, £2.40; EX 7.30.Maybe I Won't was the subject of a friendly claim
Owner B Ward **Bred** Ewar Stud Farms **Trained** Cropthorne, Worcs

FOCUS
A moderate little claimer in which the winner set a good pace and is rated back to form.

340 THE FAMILY ARE OFF TO PONTIN'S FILLIES' H'CAP 1m 1f 103y(P)
3:10 (3:10) (Class 5) (0-70,68) 4-Y-0+ **£2,730** (£806; £403) **Stalls** Low

Form				RPR
000-	1		**Wasalat (USA)**[100] 6343 6-9-0 63 ... FergalLynch 4 (D W Barker) *s.i.s: hld up in rr: hdwy wl over 1f out: sn rdn: led wl ins fnl f: drvn out* **5/1**[2]	68
120-	2	nk	**Satin Braid**[43] 7164 4-8-11 68 ... AmyBaker(7) 7 (D R C Elsworth) *t.k.h: sn in tch: rdn to ld over 1f out: hdd wl ins fnl f* **7/2**[1]	73
2-15	3	nk	**Chia (IRE)**[11] 196 5-9-5 68 ... (p) RobertHavlin 2 (D Haydn Jones) *a.p: led over 2f out: rdn and hdd over 1f out: kpt on* **7/2**[1]	72
10-3	4	1	**Sforzando**[18] 117 7-8-6 62 ... KristinStubbs(7) 3 (Mrs L Stubbs) *hld up: hdwy on ins over 4f out: pushed along over 3f out: n.m.r 2f out: ev ch 1f out: nt qckn* **14/1**[3]	64
6-13	5	4	**Perfect Practice**[10] 209 4-8-5 60 ... JamieJones(5) 5 (C G Cox) *led: hdd and edgd rt over 2f out: wknd over 1f out* **7/2**[1]	54
-533	6	nk	**Meditation**[2] 316 6-9-4 67 ... JamesDoyle 6 (I A Wood) *sn chsng ldr: hmpd briefly and lost 2nd over 2f out: wknd wl over 1f out* **7/2**[1]	60

2m 5.25s (3.55) **Going Correction** +0.175s/f (Slow)
WFA 4 from 5yo+ 1lb 6 Ran SP% **112.2**
Speed ratings (Par 100): **91,90,90,89,86 85**
CSF £22.56 TOTE £6.80: £2.90, £2.80; EX 32.90.
Owner Miss Daphne Downes **Bred** Darley **Trained** Scorton, N Yorks

FOCUS
A slowly-run tight little handicap. Modest, but sound form.
Perfect Practice Official explanation: jockey said filly had no more to give

341 HALF TERM HAPPY DEALS @ PONTINS.COM CLAIMING STKS 1m 141y(P)
3:40 (3:40) (Class 6) 4-Y-0+ **£2,047** (£604; £302) **Stalls** Low

Form				RPR
01-3	1		**Machinate (USA)**[15] 148 6-9-5 64 ... LiamJones 7 (W M Brisbourne) *hld up in tch: n.m.r 2f out: led wl over 1f out: sn rdn: edgd rt ins fnl f: drvn out* **5/4**[1]	64
-613	2	1 1/2	**Gifted Heir (IRE)**[1] 330 4-8-10 55 ... NatashaEaton(7) 1 (A Bailey) *a.p: nt clr run on ins 2f out: r.o ins fnl f: tk 2nd last strides* **7/2**[2]	59
006-	3	hd	**Holyfield Warrior (IRE)**[91] 6532 4-8-13 43 ... JamesDoyle 6 (I A Wood) *w ldr: led over 2f out: sn rdn and edgd lft: hdd wl over 1f out: kpt on same pce fnl f* **66/1**	55
005-	4	1/2	**Chasing Memories (IRE)**[21] 7226 4-8-4 50 ... JimmyQuinn 2 (W K Goldsworthy) *hld up: hdwy 2f out: rdn over 1f out: one pce fnl f* **5/1**	45
-266	5	1 1/4	**Climate (IRE)**[10] 209 9-9-0 50 ... SteveDrowne 5 (P D Evans) *hld up in rr: carried wd bnd after 1f: hdwy over 2f out: rdn and hung lft over 1f out: no ex wl ins fnl f* **9/2**[3]	51
0-04	6	4	**Personify**[19] 101 6-8-9 62 ... (b1) KevinGhunowa(5) 3 (R A Harris) *hld up: bmpd bnd after 1f: rdn over 3f out: sn struggling* **12/1**	42
500-	7	5	**Tracer**[19] 6640 4-9-3 58 ... DaleGibson 4 (M W Easterby) *t.k.h: led: rdn and hdd over 2f out: wknd over 1f out* **14/1**	34

1m 52.12s (1.62) **Going Correction** +0.175s/f (Slow)
WFA 4 from 6yo+ 1lb 7 Ran SP% **117.4**
Speed ratings (Par 101): **99,97,97,97,95 92,87**
CSF £6.17 TOTE £1.90: £1.10, £3.10; EX 7.70.Chasing Memories was claimed by A M Hales for £4,000
Owner D Slingsby **Bred** Gaines-Gentry Thoroughbreds & William Condren **Trained** Great Ness, Shropshire
■ Stewards' Enquiry : Dale Gibson two-day ban: careless riding (Feb 8-9)

FOCUS
This moderate claimer was run at a modest pace. The form is rated through the third.
Personify Official explanation: jockey said gelding was hampered
Tracer Official explanation: jockey said gelding hung left throughout

342 WOLVERHAMPTON-RACECOURSE.CO.UK H'CAP 7f 32y(P)
4:10 (4:10) (Class 5) (0-75,74) 4-Y-0+ **£2,457** (£725; £362) **Stalls** High

Form				RPR
-251	1		**Xpres Maite**[8] 235 5-8-12 68 6ex ... (v) PhillipMakin 10 (S R Bowring) *hld up in tch: rdn wl over 1f out: r.o to ld towards fin* **7/2**[2]	78
163-	2	3/4	**Bel Cantor**[47] 7126 5-8-6 67 ... (p) KellyHarrison(5) 8 (W J H Ratcliffe) *led early: chsd ldr: led wl over 1f out: sn rdn: hdd towards fin* **15/2**	75
000-	3	1 1/4	**Celtic Step**[33] 7236 4-9-1 71 ... (b) GregFairley 7 (M Johnston) *wnt lft s: hld up in mid-div: hdwy wl over 1f out: rdn and edgd lft wl ins fnl f: nt qckn* **14/1**	76
-210	4	1	**Sir Douglas**[15] 150 5-8-9 70 ... (p) KevinGhunowa(5) 1 (R A Harris) *hung rt thrght: sn led: hdd wl over 1f out: kpt on towards fin* **16/1**	72
45-2	5	nk	**Divertimenti (IRE)**[9] 233 4-9-4 74 ... LPKeniry 9 (C R Dore) *hld up in tch: rdn and one pce fnl f* **5/2**[1]	75
30-3	6	1	**Social Rhythm**[19] 90 4-8-12 68 ... JamesDoyle 4 (H J Collingridge) *hld up towards rr: rdn and hdwy on ins wl over 1f out: wknd wl ins fnl f* **8/1**	66
32-5	7	1/2	**Methaaly (IRE)**[8] 241 5-8-5 68 ... EJMcNamara(7) 2 (M Mullineaux) *s.i.s: hld up: hdwy on outside over 2f out: c wd st: rdn and wknd ins fnl f* **6/1**	65
45-3	8	nk	**Northern Boy (USA)**[24] 49 5-8-7 63 ... DaleGibson 5 (M W Easterby) *s.i.s: hld up: hdwy over 4f out: rdn and wknd over 2f out* **4/1**[3]	59
0/0-	9	3	**Grenane (IRE)**[44] 7158 5-9-0 70 ... SteveDrowne 6 (P D Evans) *bmpd s: a bhd* **66/1**	58

1m 29.71s (0.11) **Going Correction** +0.175s/f (Slow) 9 Ran SP% **122.0**
Speed ratings (Par 103): **106,105,103,102,102 101,100,100,96**
CSF £31.93 CT £338.05 TOTE £4.50: £1.70, £1.80, £4.60; EX 39.20 TRIFECTA Not won..
Owner Charterhouse Holdings Plc **Bred** S R Bowring **Trained** Edwinstowe, Notts
■ Stewards' Enquiry : James Doyle two-day ban: careless riding (Feb 8-9)

FOCUS
A decent clip led to the best time of the meeting compared with standard. Fairly sound form, with a career best from Xpres Maite.
Sir Douglas Official explanation: jockey said horse hung right-handed

343 SPONSOR A RACE BY CALLING 0870 220 2442 MAIDEN STKS 7f 32y(P)
4:40 (4:41) (Class 5) 3-Y-0 **£2,457** (£725; £362) **Stalls** High

Form				RPR
-	1		**Mr Macattack** 3-9-3 0 ... PatDobbs 10 (N J Vaughan) *hld up: hdwy over 5f out: rdn to ld and edgd rt over 1f out: r.o wl* **13/8**[1]	65
	2	1 1/4	**West Lorne (USA)** 3-8-12 0 ... GregFairley 5 (M Johnston) *sn led: hdd over 1f out: rdn and nt qckn ins fnl f* **7/4**[2]	56
	3	hd	**Tripod Molly (IRE)** 3-8-12 0 ... (t) FrancisNorton 9 (P J McBride) *a.p: rdn over 1f out: nt qckn ins fnl f* **28/1**	56
-0	4	nk	**Awesome Light (IRE)**[13] 163 3-9-3 0 ... JamesDoyle 4 (W R Muir) *broke wl: hld up and sn mid-div: hdwy on ins over 1f out: rdn and nt qckn ins fnl f* **22/1**	60
00-	5	1	**Moscow Oznick**[90] 6574 3-9-3 0 ... SamHitchcott 3 (N J Vaughan) *t.k.h towards rr: hdwy on outside over 2f out: edgd lft over 1f out: one pce fnl f* **13/2**[3]	57
03-	6	3	**Little Lovely (IRE)**[74] 6820 3-8-12 0 ... FergusSweeney 1 (A G Newcombe) *hmpd on ins sn after s: sn bhd: n.d after* **13/2**[3]	44
645-	7	3 1/2	**Doric Dream**[38] 7216 3-8-12 60 ... TomEaves 7 (B Smart) *led early: chsd ldr: ev ch over 2f out: wkng whn hung lft over 1f out* **12/1**	35
	8	5	**Rightcar Hull (IRE)** 3-8-12 0 ... LPKeniry 2 (Peter Grayson) *pushed along 4f out: a bhd* **50/1**	21

1m 32.29s (2.69) **Going Correction** +0.175s/f (Slow) 8 Ran SP% **118.6**
Speed ratings (Par 97): **91,89,89,89,87 84,80,74**
CSF £4.88 TOTE £2.50: £1.20, £1.10, £7.30; EX 6.40 Trifecta £223.90 Pool: £552.04 - 1.75 winning units..
Owner Owen Promotions Limited **Bred** Hascombe And Valiant Studs **Trained** Hampton Heat, Cheshire

FOCUS
A steadily-run maiden with the first three all newcomers so the value of the form remains to be seen.

344 BOOK PONTIN'S FOR HALF TERM 0844 576 5938 H'CAP 1m 4f 50y(P)
5:10 (5:10) (Class 5) (0-75,74) 4-Y-0+ £2,730 (£806; £403) Stalls Low

Form RPR
520- 1 **Casual Affair**[94] 6473 5-8-9 63 JimmyQuinn 4 77
(J D Bethell) *hld up towards rr: hdwy on ins over 4f out: led jst over 1f out: rdn and r.o wl ins fnl f* 4/1[3]
2-13 2 4 **Steig (IRE)**[7] 248 5-8-7 61 JamesDoyle 8 69
(Carl Llewellyn) *t.k.h: led 1f: w ldr: led 7f out tl jst over 1f out: wknd ins fnl f* 5/1
0/3- 3 1/2 **Mexican Pete**[29] 3407 8-9-4 72 SteveDrowne 1 79
(A King) *a.p: chsd ldr over 4f out tl rdn over 3f out: one pce fnl 2f* 7/2[2]
44-0 4 3 **Shogun Prince (IRE)**[19] 96 5-9-6 74 FergusSweeney 2 76
(W Jarvis) *hld up in mid-div: hdwy 4f out: rdn over 2f out: sn wknd* 9/2
31-2 5 5 **Fenners (USA)**[24] 47 5-8-11 65 DaleGibson 3 59
(M W Easterby) *t.k.h in tch: pushed along and lost pl over 4f out: n.d after* 5/2[1]
000- 6 1 1/4 **Top Spec (IRE)**[70] 6878 7-8-9 70 JosephineBruning(7) 5 62
(J Pearce) *s.i.s: hld up in rr: pushed along over 4f out: nvr nr ldrs* 50/1
0-00 7 1 **Three Thieves (UAE)**[9] 224 5-8-6 60 SimonWhitworth 7 51
(M S Saunders) *hld up in rr: rdn and short-lived effrt over 2f out* 25/1
350/ 8 10 **Taxman (IRE)**[24] 6602 6-9-0 68 (p) LPKeniry 6 43
(A G Newcombe) *prom tl rdn and wknd over 3f out* 22/1
104- 9 shd **Jazrawy**[20] 811 6-8-13 74 JamieKyne(7) 9 49
(D Carroll) *plld hrd: led after 1f to 7th out: w ldr tl rdn and wknd over 3f out* 14/1

2m 40.17s (-0.93) **Going Correction** +0.175s/f (Slow) 9 Ran SP% 122.5
Speed ratings (Par 103): **110,107,107,105,101 100,100,93,93**
CSF £25.48 CT £79.11 TOTE £6.70: £1.90, £1.30, £1.70; EX 34.90 Trifecta £176.20 Pool: £625.73 - 2.52 winning units. Place 6 £37.89, Place 5 £20.02.
Owner Peter J Mitchell **Bred** Ian Neville Marks **Trained** Middleham Moor, N Yorks
FOCUS
They went no great gallop in this low-key handicap. The form looks sound enough despite the favourite's disappointing effort.
T/Plt: £133.50 to a £1 stake. Pool: £53,055.15. 290.05 winning tickets. T/Qpdt: £34.10 to a £1 stake. Pool: £3,889.60. 84.20 winning tickets. KH

277 SOUTHWELL (L-H)
Tuesday, January 29

OFFICIAL GOING: Standard
Wind: Light, across Weather: Overcast

345 HAPPY HALF TERM @ PONTIN'S AMATEUR RIDERS' H'CAP 1m 6f (F)
1:30 (1:30) (Class 6) (0-65,63) 4-Y-0+ £1,846 (£567; £283) Stalls Low

Form RPR
36-3 1 **Tioga Gold (IRE)**[23] 67 9-9-11 45 MrKJames(7) 10 57
(L R James) *hld up in rr: stdy hdwy on outer over 3f out: rdn over 1f out: styd on wl fnl f to ld last 50yds* 25/1
54-3 2 3/4 **Sand Repeal (IRE)**[28] 3 6-11-0 60 (v) MrRBirkett(5) 13 71
(Miss J Feilden) *hld up in tch: hdwy over 4f out: chsd ldr over 3f out: rdn to ld wl over 1f out: drvn ins fnl f: hdd and no ex last 50yds* 12/1
03-1 3 6 **Hora**[5] 283 4-10-11 63 6ex (b) MrBMMorris(5) 12 65
(Sir Mark Prescott) *trckd ldrs: hdwy 1/2-way: led 5f out: rdn along wl over 2f out: hdd wl over 1f out and kpt on same pce* 8/15[1]
0-06 4 5 **Ronsard (IRE)**[23] 67 6-10-9 50 MissEFolkes 14 45
(P D Evans) *s.i.s and in rr: hdwy on outer 5f out: rdn along wl over 2f out: sn no imp* 16/1
0-02 5 6 **Feeling Peckish (USA)**[4] 169 4-9-5 45 (t) MissSEilbeck(7) 2 32
(M C Chapman) *chsd ldrs: rdn along over 5f out: plugged on same pce fnl 3f* 66/1
00-6 6 4 **Reminiscent (IRE)**[18] 129 9-9-13 45 (v) MissAWallace(5) 11 26
(B P J Baugh) *in midfield: sme hdwy over 3f out: sn rdn along and nvr a factor* 66/1
03-2 7 shd **Blue Hills**[12] 198 7-11-2 60 (b) MrsMarieKing(3) 4 41
(P W Hiatt) *led: rdn along and hdd 5f out: grad wknd* 11/2[2]
100- 8 3 **Orchard House (FR)**[190] 3795 5-10-6 54 (b) MrSHoughton(7) 5 31
(J Jay) *chsd ldrs: rdn along 4f out: sn wknd* 25/1
004- 9 11 **I'll Do It Today**[52] 6797 7-10-8 54 MissNJefferson(5) 9 16
(J M Jefferson) *prom: rdn along over 4f out and sn wknd* 17/2[3]
04-2 10 3/4 **Andorran (GER)**[14] 171 5-10-2 50 (v) MissRLLockie(7) 1 11
(A Bailey) *a towards rr* 20/1
U00/ 11 16 **Subsidise (IRE)**[64] 3999 5-10-1 47 MrCJCallow(5) 8 —
(F P Murtagh) *chsd ldrs 3f: sn lost pl and bhd: t.o fnl 4f* 100/1

3m 8.74s (0.44) **Going Correction** -0.075s/f (Stan)
WFA 4 from 5yo+ 6lb 11 Ran SP% 121.1
Speed ratings (Par 101): **95,94,91,88,84 82,82,80,74,74 64**
CSF £284.01 CT £453.55 TOTE £31.20: £5.40, £3.30, £1.10; EX 274.70 Trifecta £256.90 Part won. Pool £361.85 - 0.20 winning units..
Owner L R James Limited **Bred** Rathasker Stud **Trained** Norton, N Yorks
■ The first winner for rider Kyle James.
FOCUS
A moderate handicap which looked pretty uncompetitive beforehand, but there was a good gallop on and the winner came from well of the pace. He recorded his best figure since he was a 2yo, with the runner-up rated to last year's form. The favourite was a big disappointment.

346 SOUTHWELL-RACECOURSE.CO.UK CLAIMING STKS 6f (F)
2:00 (2:00) (Class 6) 4-Y-0+ £1,774 (£523; £262) Stalls Low

Form RPR
0-14 1 **Grimes Faith**[11] 213 5-9-11 70 (b) ChrisCatlin 3 79
(K A Ryan) *plld hrd: chsd ldng pair tl led over 3f out and sn clr: rdn ent fnl f: sn drvn and edgd lft: hld on wl towards fin* 10/3[2]
4-14 2 3/4 **Dickie Le Davoir**[12] 190 4-9-7 72 AndrewElliott 2 73
(K R Burke) *sn outpcd and chsd along after 2f: rdn and hdwy over 2f out: drvn over 1f out: styd on u.p ins fnl f: nt rch wnr* 4/6[1]
40-0 3 3 1/2 **Owed**[23] 64 6-9-11 70 PatCosgrave 5 66
(R Bastiman) *led: hdd over 3f out: rdn over 2f out: drvn and one pce appr fnl f* 16/1
4-20 4 2 1/2 **Goodbye Cash (IRE)**[11] 210 4-8-11 69 RichardEvans(7) 4 51
(P D Evans) *chsd ldrs: rdn along wl over 2f out: sn one pce* 9/2[3]
405- 5 7 **Swallow Senora (IRE)**[84] 6702 6-8-4 39 (t) PatrickDonaghy(7) 1 21
(M C Chapman) *chsd ldng pair: rdn along 1/2-way: sn wknd* 100/1

1m 16.88s (0.38) **Going Correction** -0.075s/f (Stan) 5 Ran SP% 108.1
Speed ratings (Par 101): **94,93,88,85,75**
CSF £5.78 TOTE £3.90: £1.90, £1.10; EX 6.20.Dickie Le Davoir was claimed by I. W. McInnes for £10,000.
Owner Mrs Angie Bailey **Bred** John Grimes **Trained** Hambleton, N Yorks
FOCUS
Something of a tactical affair, with the winner getting first run on the more patiently ridden favourite. The form has been rated at face value.

347 MAKE A DATE WITH PONTIN'S IN 2008 H'CAP 6f (F)
2:30 (2:30) (Class 6) (0-65,63) 4-Y-0+ £1,911 (£564; £282) Stalls Low

Form RPR
00-1 1 **Hits Only Jude (IRE)**[7] 256 5-8-13 58 6ex DeanMcKeown 5 78+
(P A Blockley) *trckd ldrs: effrt 2f out: nt clr run over 1f out: rdn and qcknd to ld ins fnl f: comf* 8/13[1]
3-1 2 2 **Ginger Princess (IRE)**[22] 75 6-8-10 62 (t) PatrickDonaghy(7) 6 74
(Oliver McKiernan, Ire) *hld up: hdwy on outer 1/2-way: rdn to ld wl over 1f out: drvn and hdd ins fnl f: nt pce of wnr* 11/2[2]
0-01 3 3 **Avontuur (FR)**[8] 255 6-8-8 53 6ex (p) LiamJones 4 55
(D W Chapman) *dwlt: led after 1f: rdn along over 2f out: drvn and hdd over 1f out: kpt on same pce* 40/1
30-4 4 1/2 **Nautical**[11] 211 10-8-7 55 KirstyMilczarek(3) 3 55
(A W Carroll) *led 1f: cl up on inner: rdn and ev ch 2f out: drvn and wknd ent fnl f* 25/1
3113 5 1 1/2 **Silver Hotspur**[10] 232 4-9-1 60 NickyMackay 2 56
(M Wigham) *hld up: hdwy over 2f out: sn rdn and no imp* 13/2[3]
3-26 6 1 1/4 **Winthorpe (IRE)**[22] 71 8-9-4 63 (p) GrahamGibbons 7 55
(J J Quinn) *cl up: ev ch 2f out: sn rdn and wknd over 1f out* 14/1
0113 7 4 **Mind Alert**[11] 211 7-9-3 62 (v) JamesDoyle 1 41
(D Shaw) *hld up: a in rr* 11/1

1m 15.49s (-1.01) **Going Correction** -0.075s/f (Stan) 7 Ran SP% 111.9
Speed ratings (Par 101): **103,100,96,95,93 92,86**
CSF £4.18 TOTE £1.40: £1.30, £2.70; EX 5.10.
Owner Lynne Whiting & Judith Kell Stone **Bred** Swordlestown Stud **Trained** Lambourn, Berks
FOCUS
Strong form for the grade, worth taking positively. The winner was 7lb well in and there should be more to come from him.
Mind Alert Official explanation: jockey said gelding hung right

348 ARENA LEISURE PLC (S) STKS 1m 4f (F)
3:00 (3:01) (Class 6) 4-Y-0+ £1,774 (£523; £262) Stalls Low

Form RPR
650- 1 **Maria Antonia (IRE)**[46] 7135 5-8-9 48 StephenDonohoe 5 62
(P A Blockley) *hld up in tch: hdwy to trck ldr over 4f out: led over 2f out and sn clr: rdn and kpt on ins fnl f* 11/4[2]
10 2 2 1/2 **Kanisorn (SWE)**[7] 260 6-9-5 77 (b) LiamJones 2 68
(D W Chapman) *trckd ldng pair: hdwy to ld 5f out: rdn along and hdd over 2f out: sn outpcd: styd on u.p ins fnl f* 4/6[1]
5/4 3 18 **Indian Star (GER)**[13] 182 10-8-7 60 RichardEvans(7) 1 34
(P D Evans) *led to 1/2-way: sn rdn along and plugged on one pce fnl 3f* 7/1[3]
000- 4 17 **Mejhar (IRE)**[71] 6878 8-9-0 50 HayleyTurner 4 7
(E J Creighton) *a in rr* 12/1
0-54 5 3/4 **Gavanello**[14] 169 5-8-7 39 (vt[1]) KMay(7) 3 6
(M C Chapman) *cl up: led 1/2-way: rdn and hdd 5f out: wknd 4f out* 33/1

2m 39.52s (-1.48) **Going Correction** -0.075s/f (Stan) 5 Ran SP% 109.8
Speed ratings (Par 101): **101,99,87,76,75**
CSF £4.96 TOTE £4.20: £1.50, £1.40; EX 6.70.There was no bid for the winner.
Owner Pedro Rosas **Bred** J McElroy **Trained** Lambourn, Berks
FOCUS
Weak form and it was a two-horse race from the turn out of the back straight. There is some doubt over what the winner actually achieved.

349 PONTINS.COM FOR BEST PRICE BREAKS FILLIES' H'CAP 6f (F)
3:30 (3:31) (Class 5) (0-70,67) 4-Y-0+ £2,593 (£765; £383) Stalls Low

Form RPR
51-3 1 **Cerebus**[14] 173 6-9-4 67 (bt) StephenDonohoe 5 79
(A J McCabe) *mde all: rdn over 1f out: styd on strly ins fnl f* 6/5[1]
61-4 2 3 1/2 **Blackmalkin (USA)**[20] 90 4-9-4 67 TPQueally 4 68
(M Quinn) *chsd wnr: rdn and ch over 1f out: sn drvn and one pce ins fnl f* 7/2[2]
0-00 3 2 **Dancing Duo**[11] 209 4-7-11 53 oh4 (v) PatrickDonaghy(7) 2 47
(D Shaw) *sn outpcd and bhd: rdn along and hdwy on inner wl over 1f out: styd on ins fnl f: nrst fin* 22/1
-432 4 2 **Tilsworth Charlie**[11] 211 5-8-6 55 (b) ChrisCatlin 1 43
(J R Jenkins) *stmbld s: chsd ldrs on inner: rdn along over 2f out and sn one pce* 7/2[2]
410- 5 2 1/2 **Dematraf (IRE)**[141] 5272 6-8-8 64 RichardEvans(7) 3 44
(P D Evans) *sn outpcd and a in rr* 9/1[3]
400- 6 4 **Controvento (IRE)**[97] 6441 6-9-4 67 (b) TGMcLaughlin 6 34
(Eamon Tyrrell, Ire) *chsd ldng pair: rdn along over 2f out and sn wknd* 14/1

1m 15.78s (-0.72) **Going Correction** -0.075s/f (Stan) 6 Ran SP% 110.9
Speed ratings (Par 100): **101,96,93,91,87 82**
CSF £5.47 TOTE £2.00: £1.50, £2.60; EX 5.70.
Owner Paul J Dixon **Bred** Rookley Holdings **Trained** Babworth, Notts
FOCUS
A modest handicap for fillies and probably not strong form. The winner is rated back to her best.

350 KIDS ARE ALWAYS HAPPY @ PONTIN'S MAIDEN STKS 1m (F)
4:00 (4:01) (Class 5) 3-Y-0 £2,457 (£725; £362) Stalls Low

Form RPR
03-4 1 **Benedict Spirit (IRE)**[10] 221 3-8-12 71 NicolPolli(5) 5 74
(M H Tompkins) *trckd ldrs: hdwy on inner 3f out: chal wl over 1f out: rdn to ld appr fnl f: kpt on wl u.p* 5/2[2]
2 1 1/2 **Key News (IRE)** 3-8-12 0 MatthewHenry 1 66
(M A Jarvis) *sn led: jnd and rdn along over 2f out: drvn over 1f out: hdd appr fnl f: kpt on same pce* 8/1
62 3 7 **Be Free**[14] 172 3-8-12 0 J-PGuillambert 4 50
(Sir Mark Prescott) *s.i.s: hdwy 1/2-way: rdn to chse ldrs wl over 1f out: styd on u.p ins fnl f: nrst fin* 7/1[3]

5- **4** 1 3/4 **Yes Mr President (IRE)**[39] 7208 3-9-3 0 .... GregFairley 7 51
(M Johnston) *cl up on outer: rdn along over 2f out: sn drvn and wknd over 1f out* **5/4**[1]

00-4 **5** 5 **Novestar (IRE)**[12] 195 3-9-3 49 .... ChrisCatlin 3 39
(G J Smith) *cl up: rdn along 3f out: drvn over 2f out and sn wknd* **66/1**

6 17 **Opening Hand** 3-8-10 0 .... KMay(7) 6 —
(B J Meehan) *towards rr: hdwy over 3f out: sn rdn along and wknd over 2f out* **18/1**

6 **7** 2 1/2 **Dara Diva (IRE)**[17] 135 3-8-12 0 .... LiamJones 2 —
(W J Haggas) *in tch and sn rdn along: lost pl 1/2-way: sn bhd* **12/1**

1m 42.66s (-1.04) **Going Correction** -0.075s/f (Stan) 7 Ran SP% **111.1**
Speed ratings (Par 97): **102,100,93,91,86 69,67**
CSF £21.10 TOTE £2.40: £1.90, £4.10; EX 21.10.
Owner Miss Fiona Corrigan **Bred** Allevamento Pian Di Neve Srl **Trained** Newmarket, Suffolk

FOCUS
A modest maiden and not easy to rate, although it should throw up a winner or two. Probably improved form from Benedict Spirit.
Dara Diva(IRE) Official explanation: jockey said filly would not face the kickback

351 SOUTHWELL RACECOURSE FOR CONFERENCES H'CAP 1m (F)
4:30 (4:30) (Class 5) (0-75,74) 4-Y-0+ **£2,593** (£765; £383) **Stalls** Low

Form RPR

50-1 **1** **Sophia Gardens**[14] 173 4-8-4 **60** .... ChrisCatlin 3 68+
(D W P Arbuthnot) *trckd ldrs: hdwy and cl up 3f out: rdn to ld wl over 1f out: drvn and hdd ins fnl f: rallied strly under hrd driving to ld again nr line* **15/8**[1]

-036 **2** 1/2 **Dudley Docker (IRE)**[3] 314 6-9-4 **74** .... LiamJones 4 81
(C R Dore) *t.k.h: trckd ldrs: hdwy on bit 2f out and sn cl up: slt ld briefly ins fnl f: shkn up and nt qckn nr line* **5/1**

11-1 **3** 8 **Dado Mush**[23] 68 5-9-1 **74** .... (p) KirstyMilczarek(3) 1 62
(T T Clement) *cl up: effrt 2f out and ev ch tl rdn and wknd appr fnl f* **11/4**[2]

5-21 **4** 3/4 **Wodhill Gold**[21] 80 7-8-4 **60** oh1 .... (v) HayleyTurner 2 47
(D Morris) *broke wl: sn rdn along and lost pl after 2f: bhd after* **10/3**[3]

260- **5** 2 **Robinzal**[54] 7045 6-7-11 **60** .... AmyBaker(7) 5 42
(A W Carroll) *led: rdn along over 2f out: hdd wl over 1f out: sn drvn and grad wknd* **16/1**

1m 41.87s (-1.83) **Going Correction** -0.075s/f (Stan) 5 Ran SP% **107.1**
Speed ratings (Par 103): **106,105,97,96,94**
CSF £10.72 TOTE £3.40: £1.90, £1.90; EX 11.40 Place 6 £4.39, Place 5 £3.12..
Owner Derrick C Broomfield **Bred** Stowell Hill Ltd **Trained** Compton, Berks

FOCUS
Fairly modest handicap form, but the winner is progressing nicely on this surface. The runner-up found less than looked likely.
T/Plt: £10.50 to a £1 stake. Pool: £47,369.30. 3,281.10 winning tickets. T/Qpdt: £7.80 to a £1 stake. Pool: £2,462.40. 231.95 winning tickets. JR

311 LINGFIELD (L-H)
Wednesday, January 30

OFFICIAL GOING: Standard
Wind: Moderate, half against Weather: Fine

352 HOT TO TROTT DEALS @ PONTINS.COM H'CAP 1m 2f (P)
1:25 (1:26) (Class 6) (0-58,57) 4-Y-0+ **£1,876** (£554; £277) **Stalls** Low

Form RPR

6154 **1** **Lordswood (IRE)**[14] 176 4-8-9 50 .... HayleyTurner 14 61
(J R Best) *stdd s: hld up wl in rr: stdy prog fr 3f out: eased out over 1f out to chse ldr fnl f: wl-timed chal to ld last 75yds* **8/1**[3]

14-3 **2** 1 **Barton Sands (IRE)**[18] 133 11-9-2 55 .... (t) JimCrowley 3 64
(Andrew Reid) *settled in midfield: pushed along over 4f out: prog over 2f out: rdn to ld over 1f out: hdd and outpcd last 75yds* **9/2**[1]

3-00 **3** 2 1/2 **Josr's Magic (IRE)**[19] 125 4-8-8 49 .... ChrisCatlin 1 53
(H J Collingridge) *trckd ldrs: effrt but nt qckn 2f out: kpt on fnl f: nt pce to trble ldng pair* **16/1**

-603 **4** nk **Boppys Pride**[9] 251 5-8-10 49 ow2 .... (p) TonyHamilton 2 52
(R A Fahey) *hld up wl in rr: gng wl whn nt clr run over 2f out: effrt wl over 1f out: kpt on but only at one pce* **7/1**[2]

500- **5** 1 1/2 **Siena Star (IRE)**[33] 7257 10-9-3 56 .... MickyFenton 6 56
(Stef Liddiard) *led for 3f: pressed ldrs after: rdn over 2f out: outpcd on inner fnl f* **8/1**[3]

00-0 **6** 1 1/2 **Revolve**[19] 122 8-9-2 55 .... (b) TGMcLaughlin 10 52
(Mrs L J Mongan) *plld hrd early: prom: effrt to ld over 2f out: hdd & wknd over 1f out* **25/1**

40-4 **7** 2 **Carlton Scroop (FR)**[12] 215 5-8-13 52 .... StephenDonohoe 4 45
(J Jay) *nvr beyond midfield: u.p and no prog 3f out* **10/1**

-533 **8** 1 1/4 **Weet For Ever (USA)**[11] 231 5-8-12 51 .... GregFairley 8 42
(P A Blockley) *plld v hrd early: hld up in last trio: gng wl enough over 2f out: nt clr run wl over 1f out: nvr a factor* **8/1**[3]

000- **9** 1/2 **Competitor**[239] 2332 7-9-2 55 .... (v) DaneO'Neill 5 45
(J Akehurst) *hld up in rr: stl there 2f out: bmpd wl over 1f out: n.d* **16/1**

4-20 **10** 1 **Krakatau (FR)**[12] 209 4-9-0 55 .... VinceSlattery 7 43
(D J Wintle) *hld up towards rr on outer: rdn wl over 2f out: no real prog fnl 2f* **12/1**

000- **11** nk **Lay The Cash (USA)**[142] 5269 4-9-2 57 .... TQuinn 11 44
(B G Powell) *hld up in last: reminders 7f out: stl last over 2f out: no ch* **16/1**

4-13 **12** 1 1/4 **Earl Kraul (IRE)**[14] 180 5-9-4 57 .... (v[1]) AdamKirby 12 42
(G L Moore) *t.k.h: hld up in midfield on outer: rdn wl over 2f out: wknd over 1f out* **8/1**[3]

61-0 **13** 2 1/2 **Little Miss Tara (IRE)**[28] 10 4-9-1 56 .... DavidKinsella 13 36
(A B Haynes) *pressed ldr: u.p over 3f out: wknd over 2f out* **14/1**

5-30 **14** 13 **Mujobliged (IRE)**[5] 299 5-8-8 47 .... JimmyQuinn 9 —
(J R Best) *dwlt: rousted along then plld hrd: prog to ld after 3f: hdd & wknd rapidly over 2f out: t.o* **14/1**

2m 5.63s (-0.97) **Going Correction** +0.20s/f (Slow)
WFA 4 from 5yo+ 2lb 14 Ran SP% **126.7**
Speed ratings (Par 101): **111,110,108,107,106 105,103,102,102,101 101,100,98,88**
CSF £46.19 CT £588.69 TOTE £9.70: £2.50, £2.60, £5.40; EX 64.20 Trifecta £71.70 Part won. Pool: £101.11 - 0.30 winning tickets.
Owner Rod Jordan **Bred** Blackdown Stud **Trained** Hucking, Kent

FOCUS
Sound form for the grade rated around the third and fourth.
Weet For Ever(USA) Official explanation: jockey said gelding was denied a clear run
Earl Kraul(IRE) Official explanation: jockey said gelding ran too free

353 CROC MAKES PONTIN'S HALF TERM ROCK (S) STKS 6f (P)
1:55 (2:01) (Class 6) 4-Y-0+ **£1,774** (£523; £262) **Stalls** Low

Form RPR

-030 **1** **Mulberry Lad (IRE)**[3] 327 6-9-2 52 .... (p) ChrisCatlin 3 54
(P W Hiatt) *chsd ldng pair: rdn over 2f out: chal over 1f out: upsides after w all the others: won on the nod* **5/2**[2]

0-02 **2** shd **Tang**[6] 285 4-8-4 40 .... MatthewDavies(7) 4 49
(W G M Turner) *led at stdy pce: jnd on all sides fnl f: btn on the nod* **12/1**

00-5 **3** shd **Plateau**[20] 109 9-9-2 57 .... LPKeniry 6 54
(C R Dore) *t.k.h: pressed ldr: upsides 1f out: nt qckn nr fin* **11/4**[3]

0-65 **4** nk **Piccostar**[7] 264 5-8-11 45 .... SamHitchcott 5 48
(A B Haynes) *hld up bhd ldrs: effrt on outer 2f out: upsides ins fnl f: nt qckn nr fin* **16/1**

-005 **5** shd **Mine Behind**[4] 312 8-9-2 65 .... DaneO'Neill 1 52
(J R Best) *hld up in last: effrt on inner over 1f out: upsides 100yds out: no ex nr fin* **1/1**[1]

1m 14.06s (2.16) **Going Correction** +0.20s/f (Slow) 5 Ran SP% **118.8**
Speed ratings (Par 101): **93,92,92,92,92**
CSF £29.32 TOTE £3.70: £1.20, £4.90; EX 21.80.There was no bid for the winner.
Owner P W Hiatt **Bred** Mountarmstrong Stud **Trained** Hook Norton, Oxon

FOCUS
They went no pace here and all five were in a line a furlong out. They finished in similar fashion and the form is hardly solid.

354 PONTIN'S MAKES THE WORLD GO ROUND MAIDEN STKS 6f (P)
2:25 (2:28) (Class 5) 3-Y-0+ **£2,331** (£693; £346; £173) **Stalls** Low

Form RPR

3-2 **1** **Bussell Up**[14] 175 3-8-5 0 .... SaleemGolam 4 84+
(S C Williams) *trckd ldng pair: tried for gap and nowhere to go wl over 1f out: got through to ld last 150yds: drvn clr* **6/4**[2]

3-22 **2** 3 1/2 **Salt Of The Earth (IRE)**[17] 146 3-8-10 76 .... JimCrowley 1 75
(T G Mills) *led 1f: w ldr tl led again 2f out: drvn and hdd last 150yds: outpcd* **1/1**[1]

00/ **3** 3 1/2 **Judge 'n Jury**[461] 6188 4-9-7 0 .... KevinGhunowa(5) 2 68
(R A Harris) *narrow ld after 1f to 2f out: btn 1f out: wknd last 100yds* **25/1**

0-5 **4** 1/2 **Extreme North (USA)**[17] 146 3-8-10 0 .... MickyFenton 6 62
(Miss V Haigh) *chsd ldng trio: rdn and outpcd 2f out: kpt on nr fin* **12/1**

0- **5** 2 1/2 **Rossini Byline (IRE)**[133] 5540 3-8-2 0 .... KirstyMilczarek(3) 7 49
(J L Spearing) *hld up: wl outpcd and bhd bef 1/2-way: plugged on fr over 1f out* **10/1**[3]

0- **6** 2 **Flemish Art (IRE)**[159] 4782 3-8-10 0 .... PatCosgrave 5 48
(M J Wallace) *hld up in rr: outpcd by 1/2-way: no ch after: wknd fnl f* **25/1**

0-0 **7** 3 **Hucking Harrier (IRE)**[11] 221 3-8-10 0 .... HayleyTurner 8 38
(J R Best) *immediately outpcd: t.o after 2f: styd on fnl f* **50/1**

5/ **8** 2 1/2 **Tiara Boom De Ay (IRE)**[639] 1347 4-9-7 0 .... VinceSlattery 3 29
(D J Wintle) *dwlt: hld up: outpcd and bhd bef 1/2-way: no ch after* **40/1**

1m 11.6s (-0.30) **Going Correction** +0.20s/f (Slow)
WFA 3 from 4yo 16lb 8 Ran SP% **118.9**
Speed ratings (Par 103): **110,105,100,100,96 94,90,86**
CSF £3.37 TOTE £3.00: £1.40, £1.02, £5.10; EX 3.70 Trifecta £166.50 Pool: £417.63 - 1.78 winning tickets..
Owner Wardour St Properties **Bred** Baroness Bloodstock **Trained** Newmarket, Suffolk

FOCUS
The runner-up and third set a fair pace out in front and, to a point, set it up for the winner. The form looks solid enough, with improvement from the winner.

355 COME STAY WITH US @ PONTIN'S H'CAP 7f (P)
2:55 (2:58) (Class 5) (0-75,75) 3-Y-O **£2,590** (£770; £385; £192) **Stalls** Low

Form RPR

544- **1** **Southwest Star (IRE)**[31] 7280 3-8-8 65 .... LPKeniry 3 64
(J S Moore) *w ldr in v slowly run r: led jst over 2f out and qcknd: rdn out and a jst holding on* **7/2**[3]

40-2 **2** nk **Autumn Blades (IRE)**[15] 163 3-9-1 72 .... SteveDrowne 1 70
(J W Hills) *hld up bhd ldng pair: rdn to chse wnr over 1f out: clsd but a jst hld* **11/4**[2]

400- **3** 1/2 **Affirmatively**[61] 6973 3-9-1 72 .... TQuinn 4 69
(D R C Elsworth) *t.k.h: hld up bhd ldng pair: lost 2 l whn wnr qcknd 2f out: hanging lft over 1f out: styd on fnl f: nvr quite able to chal* **10/1**

51-1 **4** 3 **Bookish**[21] 102 3-9-4 75 .... JamieSpencer 2 64
(M Johnston) *led at slow pce: hdd jst over 2f out: fnd nil and btn over 1f out* **5/6**[1]

1m 31.12s (6.32) **Going Correction** +0.20s/f (Slow) 4 Ran SP% **112.5**
Speed ratings (Par 97): **71,70,70,66**
CSF £13.28 TOTE £4.90; EX 12.60.
Owner Wall To Wall Partnership **Bred** T J Hurley And Simon And Mrs S Marriot **Trained** Upper Lambourn, Berks

FOCUS
A steadily-run handicap that developed into a bit of a sprint.
Bookish Official explanation: trainer's rep had no explanation for the poor form shown

356 PLAY GOLF @ LINGFIELD PARK H'CAP 1m (P)
3:25 (3:28) (Class 6) (0-60,60) 4-Y-0+ **£1,876** (£554; £277) **Stalls** High

Form RPR

000- **1** **Safari Sundowner (IRE)**[66] 6407 4-9-1 57 .... JimCrowley 2 66
(P Winkworth) *chsd ldr to over 3f out: 2nd again over 2f out: drvn wl over 1f out: styd on wl fnl f to ld last strides* **16/1**

041- **2** nk **Dawson Creek (IRE)**[31] 7276 4-9-0 56 .... GregFairley 10 64
(B Gubby) *led: kicked on 2f out: drvn fnl f: collared last strides* **3/1**[1]

42-3 **3** 1 3/4 **Strut The Stage (IRE)**[7] 276 4-8-8 53 .... (tp) DJMoran(3) 4 57
(B W Duke) *trckd ldrs: effrt to go 3rd over 2f out: tried to chal on inner 1f out: one pce last 150yds* **8/1**

2-20 **4** shd **Napoletano (GER)**[12] 209 7-9-0 56 .... (p) JamieSpencer 7 60+
(S Dow) *s.s: t.k.h: hld up in last trio: plenty to do 2f out: coaxed along and prog over 1f out: keeping on whn jockey dropped whip last 75yds* **6/1**[3]

-335 **5** nk **King After**[4] 316 6-9-1 57 .... (v) DaneO'Neill 5 60
(J R Best) *t.k.h: hld up bhd ldrs: effrt 2f out: nt qckn over 1f out: one pce after* **10/3**[2]

000- **6** 2 **White Bear (FR)**[65] 6947 6-9-4 60 .... (b) AdamKirby 3 59
(C R Dore) *settled in midfield: rdn and nt qckn 2f out: one pce and no imp after* **16/1**

540- **7** 1/2 **Silver Blue (IRE)**[140] 5341 5-8-13 55 .... (b) LPKeniry 1 53
(C R Dore) *dwlt: settled in midfield on inner: rdn and limited prog wl over 1f out: sn btn* **20/1**

53-2 **8** 3/4 **Convallaria (FR)**[12] [209] 5-9-1 57................................(t) SteveDrowne 9 53
(G Wragg) *nvr bttr than midfield on outer: rdn over 2f out: no prog* **15/2**
/0-3 **9** 1 1/4 **Take It There**[12] [219] 6-8-11 53...........................(t) StephenDonohoe 11 46
(A J Lidderdale) *a in rr: rdn and no prog 2f out* **16/1**
-020 **10** 1 3/4 **Falcon Flyer**[19] [123] 4-8-6 48.. HayleyTurner 6 37
(J R Best) *s.i.s: sn prom: chsd ldr over 3f out to over 2f out: wknd* **25/1**
51-0 **11** 3 **Monashee Brave (IRE)**[14] [181] 5-9-2 58.................................. PaulDoe 8 40
(M A Allen) *plld hrd: hld up in last trio: last and wl bhd over 2f out* **25/1**
1m 38.01s (-0.19) **Going Correction** +0.20s/f (Slow) **11** Ran SP% **115.3**
Speed ratings (Par 101): **108,107,105,105,105 103,103,102,101,99 96**
CSF £60.98 CT £427.71 TOTE £13.40: £3.80, £1.40, £2.80; EX 91.00 TRIFECTA Not won..
Owner P Winkworth **Bred** Michael Phelan **Trained** Chiddingfold, Surrey

FOCUS
A low-grade handicap but the form looks sound, with the winner back to his 2yo level.
Safari Sundowner(IRE) Official explanation: trainer's rep said, regarding the improved form shown, gelding had benefited from the drop in trip
White Bear(FR) Official explanation: jockey said gelding hung right
Convallaria(FR) Official explanation: jockey said mare hung right

357 LINGFIELDPARK.CO.UK H'CAP 1m (P)
3:55 (3:57) (Class 4) (0-80,81) 4-Y-0+ **£4,100** (£1,227; £613; £306; £152) **Stalls** High

Form RPR
04-5 **1** **Hanbrin Bhoy (IRE)**[9] [246] 4-8-2 67........................ KirstyMilczarek(3) 5 73
(R Dickin) *trckd ldrs on outer: effrt 2f out: rdn to ld 1f out: styd on wl and a holding on* **8/1**
66/3 **2** nk **Claret And Amber**[27] [34] 6-9-0 76............................. TonyHamilton 1 81
(R A Fahey) *trckd ldrs: effrt on inner wl over 1f out: got through to press wnr last 100yds: a hld* **4/1[2]**
4-34 **3** nk **Denbera Dancer (USA)**[18] [134] 4-8-10 72.................. JamieSpencer 4 77
(M Johnston) *led to over 6f out: trckd ldrs after: chal and upsides 1f out: nt qckn u.p* **13/2**
000- **4** shd **Zafonical Storm (USA)**[33] [7254] 4-9-1 80....................(t) DJMoran(3) 7 84
(B W Duke) *t.k.h: trckd ldr over 6f out: drvn to ld briefly jst over 1f out: kpt on same pce u.p fnl f and a hld* **33/1**
54-1 **5** hd **Bee Stinger**[7] [274] 6-9-5 81 6ex.. DaneO'Neill 3 88+
(I A Wood) *hld up bhd ldrs: effrt and clsng whn nt clr run over 1f out and ins fnl f: styd on but nt rcvr* **5/2[1]**
10-5 **6** 1/2 **Teasing**[11] [233] 4-9-3 79.. RobertHavlin 8 82
(J Pearce) *hld up in last pair: prog on outer 2f out: cl enough 1f out: nt qckn fnl f* **10/1**
0- **7** 3/4 **Australia Day (IRE)**[31] [5460] 5-8-8 70............................. ChrisCatlin 6 71
(P R Webber) *plld hrd: led over 6f out: tried to kick on 2f out: hdd jst over 1f out: sn btn* **5/1[3]**
22-5 **8** 2 **Smokin Joe**[27] [26] 7-9-0 76..(b) JimCrowley 2 72
(J R Best) *dwlt: t.k.h: hld up in last: rdn and no rspnse over 2f out* **7/1**
1m 39.79s (1.59) **Going Correction** +0.20s/f (Slow) **8** Ran SP% **114.2**
Speed ratings (Par 105): **100,99,99,99,99 98,97,95**
CSF £39.86 CT £223.00 TOTE £10.70: £2.60, £1.40, £1.70; EX 64.20 Trifecta £229.60 Part won. Pool: £323.46 - 0.37 winning tickets..
Owner John Hanley John Brindley **Bred** A Lyons Bloodstock **Trained** Atherstone on Stour, Warwicks

FOCUS
A race to treat with caution as a steady pace led to a bunch finish. The form is unlikely to work out.

358 GO PONTIN'S H'CAP 1m 5f (P)
4:25 (4:27) (Class 5) (0-75,77) 4-Y-0+ **£2,590** (£770; £385; £192) **Stalls** Low

Form RPR
1-11 **1** **Mutamaasek (USA)**[11] [224] 6-9-6 73...................... KirstyMilczarek(3) 5 83
(Lady Herries) *trckd ldng trio: effrt on outer 2f out: led jst over 1f out: shkn up and styd on wl* **5/2[1]**
11-1 **2** nk **War Of The Roses (IRE)**[27] [27] 5-9-6 70.................. J-PGuillambert 8 80
(R Brotherton) *hld up in last: effrt on outer over 2f out: nt qckn over 1f out: styd on wl fnl f to take 2nd nr fin* **11/4[2]**
13-1 **3** 1/2 **Maslak (IRE)**[8] [260] 4-9-8 77 6ex... LPKeniry 1 86
(P W Hiatt) *trckd ldng pair: effrt to ld wl over 1f out to jst over 1f out: kpt on same pce* **9/2**
000- **4** 1 1/4 **Zamboozle (IRE)**[31] [2833] 6-9-5 69.................................. DaneO'Neill 4 76
(A King) *hld up in last pair: effrt 2f out: nt qckn over 1f out: kpt on same pce after* **20/1**
52-2 **5** 2 **Motarjm (USA)**[11] [224] 4-8-13 68..............................(t) JamieSpencer 2 72
(H J Collingridge) *a in same pl: rdn and nt qckn over 1f out: no imp after* **3/1[3]**
35-6 **6** 2 1/2 **Lorikeet**[14] [185] 9-9-6 70.. SimonWhitworth 7 71
(G L Moore) *led to over 2f out: fdd over 1f out* **16/1**
612- **7** hd **Rickety Bridge (IRE)**[64] [6961] 5-9-6 70............................ JimCrowley 3 70
(P R Chamings) *trckd ldr: led over 2f out to wl over 1f out: wknd fnl f* **11/1**
2m 47.85s (1.85) **Going Correction** +0.20s/f (Slow)
WFA 4 from 5yo+ 5lb **7** Ran SP% **117.4**
Speed ratings (Par 103): **102,101,101,100,99 97,97**
CSF £10.16 CT £28.92 TOTE £3.40: £1.20, £2.80; EX 7.00 Trifecta £22.80 Pool: £506.67 - 15.76 winning tickets. Place 6 £307.30, Place 5 £113.67.
Owner Lady Herries **Bred** Shadwell Farm LLC **Trained** Patching, W Sussex

FOCUS
Another steadily-run contest, but this is decent form with the first three all winners last time.
T/Plt: £379.20 to a £1 stake. Pool: £37,143.35. 71.50 winning tickets. T/Qpdt: £68.00 to a £1 stake. Pool: £2,861.80. 31.10 winning tickets. JN

338 WOLVERHAMPTON (A.W) (L-H)
Wednesday, January 30

OFFICIAL GOING: Standard
Wind: Fresh, behind Weather: Fine

359 WOLVERHAMPTON-RACECOURSE.CO.UK H'CAP 5f 20y(P)
6:50 (6:52) (Class 5) (0-75,75) 4-Y-0+ **£2,590** (£770; £385; £192) **Stalls** Low

Form RPR
06-6 **1** **Drifting Gold**[14] [187] 4-9-1 72....................................(b) AdamKirby 6 81+
(C G Cox) *s.i.s: hld up: hdwy 2f out: nt clr run ins fnl f: edgd rt: r.o to ld towards fin* **14/1**
1-50 **2** 1/2 **Stolt (IRE)**[5] [301] 4-9-4 75... JimmyQuinn 1 83
(N Wilson) *chsd ldrs: rdn to ld ins fnl f: hdd towards fin* **9/2[3]**
4-11 **3** nk **Almaty Express**[19] [126] 6-8-12 74.....................(b) AshleyHamblett(5) 3 81
(J R Weymes) *led: rdn over 1f out: hdd ins fnl f: sn hung rt: styd on same pce* **7/4[1]**
-425 **4** 1 1/4 **Cool Sands (IRE)**[7] [275] 6-8-9 66..............................(v) DeanMcKeown 5 68
(D Shaw) *s.i.s: outpcd: hdwy over 1f out: nt trble ldrs* **8/1**
223- **5** nk **Chjimes (IRE)**[95] [6492] 4-9-4 75... LiamJones 2 76
(C R Dore) *trckd ldrs: racd keenly: hung lft fr over 1f out: styd on same pce* **3/1[2]**
20-2 **6** 5 **Diminuto**[22] [84] 4-9-2 73... HayleyTurner 7 56
(M D I Usher) *chsd ldrs: rdn and wknd over 1f out* **8/1**
5-46 **7** 2 1/2 **Fizzlephut (IRE)**[6] [286] 6-8-9 66................................ PaulFitzsimons 4 40
(Miss J R Tooth) *s.i.s: sn chsng ldrs: wknd 2f out* **12/1**
62.78 secs (0.48) **Going Correction** +0.25s/f (Slow) **7** Ran SP% **116.1**
Speed ratings (Par 103): **106,105,104,102,102 94,90**
CSF £77.02 TOTE £18.50: £12.30, £4.10; EX 61.30.
Owner Martin C Oliver **Bred** Witney And Warren Enterprises Ltd **Trained** Lambourn, Berks
■ Stewards' Enquiry : Adam Kirby caution: careless riding

FOCUS
A fair sprint, run at a solid pace. The form looks sound.
Chjimes(IRE) Official explanation: jockey said gelding hung left
Fizzlephut(IRE) Official explanation: jockey said gelding ran flat

360 TREAT THE FAMILY @ PONTIN'S CLAIMING STKS 1m 1f 103y(P)
7:20 (7:20) (Class 5) 3-Y-0 **£2,590** (£770; £385; £192) **Stalls** Low

Form RPR
51-4 **1** **Tiger's Rocket (IRE)**[14] [178] 3-8-9 67........................ HaddenFrost(5) 4 71
(R Hannon) *trckd ldrs: racd keenly: rdn over 1f out: hung lft and led ins fnl f: styd on* **16/1**
5121 **2** 1/2 **Boomtown**[11] [225] 3-9-6 81.. GregFairley 5 76
(M Johnston) *trckd ldrs: racd keenly: led 3f out: rdn and stmbld over 1f out: hdd ins fnl f: styd on same pce* **2/7[1]**
324- **3** 1 1/2 **Mujahope**[49] [7121] 3-9-0 67..(p) OscarUrbina 2 67
(M Botti) *trckd ldrs: plld hrd: rdn over 2f out: edgd rt over 1f out: styd on same pce* **6/1[2]**
-315 **4** 1 1/2 **Tapas Lad (IRE)**[6] [288] 3-8-11 59.................................(v) DavidKinsella 1 61
(V Smith) *hld up: hdwy 3f out: nt clr run over 2f out: rdn and hung lft over 1f out: no ex fnl f* **9/1[3]**
6 **5** 16 **Just Kenko**[16] [158] 3-9-2 0.. SamHitchcott 3 32
(N J Vaughan) *s.i.s: sn led: rdn and hdd 3f out: wkng whn n.m.r sn after* **66/1**
2m 4.65s (2.95) **Going Correction** +0.25s/f (Slow) **5** Ran SP% **109.4**
Speed ratings (Par 97): **96,95,94,92,78**
CSF £21.72 TOTE £10.00: £5.70, £1.02; EX 27.50.Boomtown was claimed by Heather Dalton for £16,000.
Owner Michael Mulholland **Bred** Bryan Ryan **Trained** East Everleigh, Wilts

FOCUS
A moderate claimer, run at an average early pace. The form can be rated through the third.

361 PONTIN'S HALF TERM HAPPY DEALS H'CAP 1m 1f 103y(P)
7:50 (7:50) (Class 5) (0-75,80) 4-Y-0+ **£2,590** (£770; £385) **Stalls** Low

Form RPR
1-21 **1** **Glenridding**[10] [240] 4-8-11 67 6ex.. JimCrowley 3 69+
(J G Given) *mde all: rdn and edgd rt over 1f out: styd on: eased towards fin* **2/11[1]**
3/0- **2** 2 **Inspirina (IRE)**[83] [6731] 4-8-11 70........................ KirstyMilczarek(3) 4 67
(R Ford) *hld up in tch: rdn over 3f out: edgd rt ins fnl f: nt trble wnr* **7/1[2]**
10-5 **3** nk **Subadar**[13] [192] 4-8-12 68.. OscarUrbina 2 64
(M Botti) *trckd wnr: rdn 3f out: styd on same pce fnl 2f* **12/1[3]**
2m 5.68s (3.98) **Going Correction** +0.25s/f (Slow)
WFA 4 from 6yo+ 1lb **3** Ran SP% **104.8**
Speed ratings (Par 103): **92,90,89**
CSF £1.75 TOTE £1.20; EX 1.90.
Owner Tremousser Partnership **Bred** Bolton Grange **Trained** Willoughton, Lincs

FOCUS
This modest handicap was weakened by the three non-runners and the in-form winner should be rated value for at least double his winning margin. He did not need to match the form of his last win though.

362 CROC MAKES PONTIN'S HALF TERM ROCK H'CAP 7f 32y(P)
8:20 (8:20) (Class 6) (0-60,64) 4-Y-0+ **£2,047** (£604; £302) **Stalls** High

Form RPR
002- **1** **Mineral Rights (USA)**[117] [5982] 4-9-3 54.............................. PhillipMakin 1 61
(Miss L A Perratt) *mde all: rdn over 1f out: edgd rt ins fnl f: r.o* **8/1[3]**
0-11 **2** 1 **Hits Only Jude (IRE)**[1] [347] 5-9-13 64 12ex............... DeanMcKeown 2 68
(P A Blockley) *a.p: rdn to chse wnr 2f out: styd on* **1/3[1]**
05-4 **3** 1 1/4 **Chasing Memories (IRE)**[2] [341] 4-8-13 50......................... LPKeniry 3 51
(A M Hales) *hld up in tch: rdn over 1f out: styd on: nt trble ldrs* **25/1**
043 **4** 1 3/4 **Newgate (UAE)**[12] [216] 4-9-4 55.. LiamJones 5 51
(D W Chapman) *prom: rdn over 2f out: no ex fnl f* **33/1**
-402 **5** 3/4 **Desert Lover (IRE)**[6] [289] 6-8-8 45.................................. JimmyQuinn 4 39
(R J Price) *chsd wnr tl rdn 2f out: no ex fnl f* **13/2[2]**
1m 31.84s (2.24) **Going Correction** +0.25s/f (Slow) **5** Ran SP% **106.3**
Speed ratings (Par 101): **97,95,94,92,91**
CSF £10.64 TOTE £13.50: £3.00, £1.10; EX 14.30.
Owner Belstane Park Racing **Bred** Budget Stable **Trained** Carluke, S Lanarks

FOCUS
A slight surprise here with hat-trick seeking Hits Only Jude only managing second behind all-the-way winner Mineral Rights. The pace was ordinary and the form has a weakish look to it.

363 SPONSOR A RACE BY CALLING 0870 220 2442 CLASSIFIED STKS 5f 20y(P)
8:50 (8:50) (Class 7) 4-Y-0+ **£1,365** (£403; £201) **Stalls** Low

Form RPR
0522 **1** **Mr Loire**[7] [264] 4-9-0 45..(b) DeanMcKeown 6 55
(A J Chamberlain) *s.i.s: hld up: hdwy 2f out: led over 1f out: sn rdn: jst hld on* **2/1[1]**
00-0 **2** shd **White Ledger (IRE)**[26] [46] 9-9-0 41.............................. JimmyQuinn 11 55
(R E Peacock) *s.i.s: hld up: hdwy over 1f out: r.o wl* **33/1**
-303 **3** 5 **Temtation (IRE)**[9] [254] 4-8-9 42............................ KellyHarrison(5) 1 37
(J A Pickering) *chsd ldrs: rdn over 1f out: styd on same pce* **7/2[2]**
5-54 **4** 1/2 **Elvina**[12] [206] 7-9-0 43.. TPQueally 4 35
(A G Newcombe) *chsd ldr: led over 3f out: rdn and hdd over 1f out: edgd rt and wknd ins fnl f* **11/2[3]**
65-5 **5** 1/2 **Elizabeth Spirit (IRE)**[12] [206] 4-9-0 40.................... StephenDonohoe 3 33
(E S McMahon) *chsd ldrs: rdn 1/2-way: wknd over 1f out* **15/2**
0-00 **6** 1/2 **Percy Douglas**[4] [318] 8-8-9 37..............................(b) AnnStokell(5) 2 31
(Miss A Stokell) *mid-div: sn pushed along: hdwy 1/2-way: wknd over 1f out* **40/1**

03-0 **7** 3/4 **Maromito (IRE)**25 50 11-9-0 43 .....(b) PatCosgrave 5 29
(R Bastiman) *led: hdd over 3f out: rdn and ev ch over 1f out: wknd fnl f* **12/1**

4236 **8** 1/2 **Blushing Russian (IRE)**12 206 6-9-0 44 .....(b) PaulFitzsimons 7 27
(J M Bradley) *sn pushed along in rr: sme hdwy over 1f out: wknd fnl f* **11/2**3

40-0 **9** *nk* **Yurchenko**25 50 4-8-11 38 .....(p) NeilChalmers(3) 9 26
(M Wellings) *chsd ldrs over 3f* **66/1**

0-00 **10** *1* **Dotty's Daughter**21 100 4-8-11 41 .....(v) PJMcDonald(3) 8 22
(B Storey) *sn outpcd: bhd whn hung lft ins fnl f* **10/1**

66-0 **11** *4* **Prime Recreation**21 100 11-9-0 40 ..... RichardThomas 10 8
(P S Felgate) *chsd ldrs: hung rt and wknd 1/2-way* **80/1**

63.73 secs (1.43) **Going Correction** +0.25s/f (Slow) **11** Ran SP% **123.0**
Speed ratings (Par 97): **98,97,89,89,88 87,86,85,84,83 76**
CSF £84.24 TOTE £3.50: £1.40, £13.90, £1.10; EX 68.00.
Owner Miss J M Foran **Bred** Harts Farm And Stud **Trained** Ashton Keynes, Wilts

FOCUS
A bad contest in which the front pair came clear. Both were suited by being held up off the strong pace.
Prime Recreation Official explanation: jockey said gelding hung right throughout

364 HOT TO TROTT DEALS @ PONTIN'S H'CAP 5f 216y(P)
9:20 (9:21) (Class 5) (0-75,74) 3-Y-O £1,768 (£1,768; £403) Stalls Low

Form RPR

52-1 **1** **Requisite**25 60 3-9-2 72 ..... PatCosgrave 6 76
(Jane Chapple-Hyam) *a.p: rdn and hung rt over 1f out: ev ch ins fnl f: r.o to join wnr post* **2/1**1

1 *dht* **Sovine (IRE)**56 7035 3-9-4 74 ..... TPQueally 2 78
(M G Holden, Ire) *hld up in tch: rdn over 1f out: r.o to ld wl ins fnl f: jnd post* **11/2**3

5-44 **3** *1* **Loose Caboose (IRE)**15 170 3-8-11 67 .....(p) StephenDonohoe 7 68
(A J McCabe) *led: rdn over 1f out: hdd wl ins fnl f* **8/1**

140- **4** 3/4 **Asian Power (IRE)**95 6502 3-9-1 71 ..... OscarUrbina 5 70
(P J O'Gorman) *a.p: chsd ldr over 2f out: rdn over 1f out: no ex ins fnl f* **15/2**

1-21 **5** *1* **Valhillen**13 199 3-9-0 70 ..... HayleyTurner 1 65
(M D I Usher) *chsd ldr tl rdn over 2f out: wknd ins fnl f* **6/1**

41-5 **6** 1 3/4 **Annes Rocket (IRE)**14 178 3-8-13 69 ..... PatDobbs 3 59
(J C Fox) *s.i.s: hld up: plld hrd: rdn over 2f out: n.d* **16/1**

46-1 **7** *9* **Bertbrand**28 17 3-9-1 74 ..... KirstyMilczarek(3) 4 35
(M Botti) *hld up: plld hrd: hung rt fr 1/2-way: sn bhd* **3/1**2

1m 16.19s (1.19) **Going Correction** +0.25s/f (Slow) **7** Ran SP% **116.8**
Speed ratings (Par 97): **102,102,100,99,98 96,84**
WIN: Sovine £2.80, Requisite £1.80; PL: Sovine £3.50, Requisite £2.40; EX: Sovine £6.70, Requisite £8.50; CSF: Sovine £8.80; Requisite £7.03 Place 6 £27.00, Place 5 £2.60.
Owner C Gallagher **Bred** Barouche Stud Ireland Ltd **Trained** Mullinavat, Co Kilkenny
Owner Franconson Partners **Bred** Darley **Trained** Lambourn, Berks

FOCUS
A modest handicap dominated by a couple of in-form sprinters who produced a dead-heat. Sound form.
Bertbrand Official explanation: jockey said colt hung right
T/Plt: £37.10 to a £1 stake. Pool: £77,319.30. 1,519.10 winning tickets. T/Qpdt: £2.80 to a £1 stake. Pool: £5,101.70. 1,330.10 winning tickets. CR

345 SOUTHWELL (L-H)
Thursday, January 31

OFFICIAL GOING: Standard
Wind: Strong across Weather: Fine and dry, but windy

365 RACE ALL THE FAMILY TO PONTIN'S APPRENTICE CLASSIFIED STKS 1m (F)
1:20 (1:20) (Class 7) 4-Y-O+ £1,365 (£403; £201) Stalls Low

Form RPR

30-5 **1** **Rubilini**6 303 4-9-0 44 .....(p) KylieManser 5 51
(Miss Sheena West) *s.i.s and towards rr: hdwy over 4f out: trckd ldrs over 2f out: swtchd rt and rdn to ld wl over 1f out: styd on wl u.p ins fnl f* **9/2**3

0-00 **2** *1* **Pawn In Life (IRE)**14 193 10-9-0 42 .....(v) DeanHeslop 9 49
(D W Chapman) *in tch: hdwy on wd outside over 2f out: rdn to chse wnr over 1f out and ev ch tl one pce ins fnl f* **8/1**

05-0 **3** *3* **Princess Zaha**29 8 6-8-9 43 .....(p) RossAtkinson(5) 12 42
(A G Newcombe) *in tch: hdwy on inner over 2f out: rdn to chse ldrs wl over 1f out: sn drvn and kpt on same pce fnl f* **10/1**

0225 **4** 1/2 **Kingsmaite**9 256 7-8-9 45 .....(b) AshleyMorgan(5) 6 41
(S R Bowring) *cl up: led wl over 2f out: rdn and hdd wl over 1f out: wknd appr fnl f* **11/4**1

00-4 **5** *3* **Jaassey**14 189 5-8-11 43 .....(t) DeclanCannon(3) 7 34
(P Beaumont) *trckd ldrs: hdwy 3f out: rdn along over 2f out and sn one pce* **4/1**2

0-04 **6** *5* **Favouring (IRE)**9 256 6-8-9 42 .....(v) SBushby(5) 1 23
(M C Chapman) *led: rdn along 3f out: sn hdd and grad wknd fnl 2f* **8/1**

000- **7** 3 1/2 **Piquet**46 7166 10-8-9 40 .....(p) BradleyRoper(5) 10 15
(G F Bridgwater) *in tch on outer: rdn along over 3f out: sn wknd* **33/1**

00-0 **8** 1 1/4 **Raven Rascal**14 193 4-8-9 40 ..... KrishGundowry(5) 8 12
(J F Coupland) *chsd ldrs: rdn along over 3f out and sn wknd* **33/1**

3 **9** *1* **Hi Spec (IRE)**11 236 5-8-9 40 ..... JamieKyne(5) 4 9
(Miss M E Rowland) *chsd ldrs: rdn along wl over 2f out: sn wknd* **7/1**

000- **10** *7* **Classic Hall (IRE)**17 5683 5-8-7 35 ..... MJMurphy(7) 3 —
(T Keddy) *s.i.s: a bhd* **100/1**

00/0 **11** *5* **Pinafore**15 174 6-9-0 43 ..... JemmaMarshall 11 —
(B R Millman) *sn outpcd and a bhd* **33/1**

000- **12** *29* **Wilford Maverick (IRE)**328 653 6-9-0 40 .....(v) DTDaSilva 2 —
(S Parr) *dwlt: chsd along and in tch after 2f: rdn along bef 1/2-way: sn wknd and bhd* **50/1**

1m 46.64s (2.94) **Going Correction** +0.075s/f (Slow) **12** Ran SP% **120.4**
Speed ratings (Par 97): **88,87,84,83,80 75,72,70,69,62 57,28**
CSF £39.62 TOTE £8.10: £2.30, £2.30, £2.50; EX 61.60 TRIFECTA Not won..
Owner Heart Of The South Racing **Bred** John And Mrs Caroline Penny **Trained** Falmer, E Sussex

FOCUS
A typically very weak event for the class. The form is rated around the placed horses.

366 ARENA LEISURE PLC H'CAP 1m (F)
1:50 (1:50) (Class 5) (0-70,69) 3-Y-O £2,730 (£806; £403) Stalls Low

Form RPR

5-42 **1** **Hieroglyph**7 281 3-9-4 69 ..... GregFairley 5 76
(M Johnston) *trckd ldr: effrt 2f out: rdn to chal over 1f out: drvn ins fnl f and styd on to ld nr fin* **2/1**2

400- **2** 1/2 **Park Royal (UAE)**88 6665 3-9-3 68 ..... AndrewElliott 1 73
(M Johnston) *led: rdn along 2f out: drvn ent fnl f: hdd and no ex nr fin* **16/1**

5-10 **3** *6* **Contessina (IRE)**12 225 3-9-0 68 ..... TolleyDean(3) 6 60
(P F I Cole) *stdd s and hld up in rr: hdwy on inner wl over 2f out: sn rdn and ch tl drvn and one pce appr fnl f* **4/1**3

064- **4** *1* **Duke Of Touraine (IRE)**83 6750 3-8-11 69 ..... PatrickDonaghy(7) 3 58
(P C Haslam) *trckd ldrs: hdwy 3f out: rdn along 2f out: sn drvn and wknd appr fnl f* **7/4**1

24-4 **5** *2* **Natural Rhythm (IRE)**7 281 3-9-2 67 ..... LiamJones 2 52
(D W Chapman) *trckd ldrs: effrt over 2f out: sn rdn and btn* **14/1**

3-0 **6** *nk* **Henry James (IRE)**12 225 3-9-1 66 ..... URispoli 4 50
(M Botti) *chsd ldrs: rdn along over 2f out: sn wknd* **14/1**

1m 44.74s (1.04) **Going Correction** +0.075s/f (Slow) **6** Ran SP% **108.9**
Speed ratings (Par 97): **97,96,90,89,87 87**
CSF £28.62 TOTE £2.80: £2.50, £8.00; EX 19.70.
Owner Sheikh Hamdan Bin Mohammed Al Maktoum **Bred** Gainsborough Stud Management Ltd **Trained** Middleham Moor, N Yorks

FOCUS
A modest handicap, run at a sound pace. The Mark Johnston stable companions came clear and are rated to their turf form.

367 CALL PONTIN'S NOW 0844 815 3648 CLAIMING STKS 7f (F)
2:20 (2:20) (Class 6) 4-Y-O+ £2,047 (£604; £302) Stalls Low

Form RPR

0-13 **1** **Louisiade (IRE)**10 250 7-8-10 63 .....(p) StephenDonohoe 3 69
(John A Harris) *chsd ldr after 3f: rdn over 2f out: drvn over 1f out: styd on u.str.p ins fnl f to ld nr line* **5/2**2

0-31 **2** *nk* **Another Genepi (USA)**17 155 5-8-5 65 .....(b) ChrisCatlin 5 63
(K A Ryan) *led and sn clr: rdn wl over 1f out: drvn ins fnl f: hdd and no ex nr fin* **4/9**1

-040 **3** *9* **Capital Lass**6 305 5-8-3 42 ..... HayleyTurner 2 37
(A J McCabe) *s.i.s: in tch after 2f: hdwy to chse ldng pair over 2f out: sn rdn and no imp* **33/1**

-021 **4** *4* **Government (IRE)**14 189 7-8-10 47 ..... PatrickDonaghy(7) 1 40
(M C Chapman) *chsd ldr 3f: rdn along 3f out and sn wknd* **14/1**3

1m 30.02s (-0.28) **Going Correction** +0.075s/f (Slow) **4** Ran SP% **107.4**
Speed ratings (Par 101): **104,103,93,88**
CSF £4.02 TOTE £3.70; EX 4.70.Another Genepi (USA) was claimed by I. W. McInnes for £7,000
Owner Shaun Taylor **Bred** Mrs Noelle Walsh **Trained** Eastwell, Leics

FOCUS
This claimer revolved around the two market leaders and the pair duly dominated.

368 HOSPITALITY PACKAGES AVAILABLE H'CAP 1m 3f (F)
2:50 (2:50) (Class 5) (0-70,72) 4-Y-O+ £2,730 (£806; £403) Stalls Low

Form RPR

4-24 **1** **Jackie Kiely**17 159 7-9-7 69 .....(t) J-PGuillambert 4 79
(R Brotherton) *dwlt: hld up in rr: hdwy over 3f out: effrt and n.m.r 2f out and sn rdn to chal: led appr last: drvn and styd on wl* **6/1**

-111 **2** 2 1/2 **Contra Mundum (USA)**6 303 5-9-10 72 12ex ..... HayleyTurner 2 78
(B G Powell) *led 3f: trckd ldr: hdwy 3f out: rdn to chal 2f out and ev ch tl drvn and one pce ent fnl f* **3/1**2

0-11 **3** *2* **Karmest**7 277 4-7-11 55 oh1 ..... PatrickDonaghy(7) 5 57+
(A D Brown) *cl up: led after 3f: rdn along over 2f out and sn jnd: drvn and hdd over 1f out: one pce ins fnl f* **6/4**1

5-13 **4** *5* **Starcross Maid**16 171 6-8-10 58 ..... PatrickMathers 1 51
(J F Coupland) *hld up in tch: hdwy on inner 4f out: cl up over 2f out and ev ch tl rdn and wknd over 1f out* **9/1**

60-6 **5** *nk* **Good Cause (IRE)**25 68 7-8-7 55 ..... ChrisCatlin 3 48
(Mrs S Lamyman) *chsd ldrs: rdn along over 4f out: sn wknd* **50/1**

43-3 **6** 2 1/2 **Waterloo Corner**20 128 6-8-9 60 ..... MarkLawson(3) 6 48
(R Craggs) *trckd ldrs: effrt on outer 4f out: rdn wl over 2f out and sn wknd* **4/1**3

2m 26.85s (-1.15) **Going Correction** +0.075s/f (Slow)
WFA 4 from 5yo+ 3lb **6** Ran SP% **111.2**
Speed ratings (Par 103): **107,105,103,100,99 98**
CSF £23.71 TOTE £8.80: £2.90, £2.00; EX 21.90.
Owner P S J Croft **Bred** Mrs M Chaworth Musters **Trained** Elmley Castle, Worcs

FOCUS
A moderate handicap, run at a fair pace. The field came home fairly strung out and with the placed horses having been in good form recently, a race that could work out.

369 BOOK HALF PRICE BREAKS @ PONTIN'S MEDIAN AUCTION MAIDEN STKS 1m (F)
3:20 (3:20) (Class 6) 4-6-Y-O £2,047 (£604; £302) Stalls Low

Form RPR

04-5 **1** **Todwick Owl**22 88 4-9-3 52 ..... TPQueally 7 53
(J G Given) *trckd ldrs on outer: smooth hdwy over 2f out: led on bit over 1f out: shkn up ins fnl f: sn rdn and edgd lft: kpt on* **5/2**2

2-03 **2** *2* **West End Lad**11 239 5-9-3 52 .....(p) PhillipMakin 1 48
(S R Bowring) *led to 1/2-way: rdn along and outpcd 2f out: styd on u.p on inner ent fnl f: tk 2nd last 75yds* **7/4**1

0- **3** 1/2 **Fifth Zak**164 4659 4-9-3 0 ..... PaulEddery 6 47
(S R Bowring) *chsd ldrs: pushed along 3f out: rdn and hdwy on outer 2f out: styd on to chse wnr ent fnl f: sn drvn and one pce* **40/1**

026/ **4** *2* **Welcome Releaf**549 3999 5-9-3 0 ..... AdamKirby 4 42
(G C Bravery) *cl up: led 1/2-way: rdn along 2f out: drvn and hdd over 1f out: wknd ent fnl f* **4/1**3

000- **5** *2* **Measured Response**33 6598 6-9-3 50 ..... AndrewElliott 2 38
(J G M O'Shea) *cl up: effrt over 2f out and ev ch tl rdn over 1f out and grad wknd* **6/1**

60-5 **6** *5* **Bothar Brugha (IRE)**19 143 4-8-12 50 ..... RussellKennemore(5) 3 26
(J G M O'Shea) *in tch: rdn along 3f out and sn outpcd* **12/1**

65 **7** *2* **Able Dara**16 172 5-8-12 0 .....(b1) SladeO'Hara(5) 5 22
(N Bycroft) *s.i.s and a wl bhd* **40/1**

1m 45.04s (1.34) **Going Correction** +0.075s/f (Slow) **7** Ran SP% **111.8**
Speed ratings: **96,94,93,91,89 84,82**
CSF £6.92 TOTE £4.50: £2.00, £1.60; EX 7.30.

Owner Tremousser Partnership **Bred** Chippenham Lodge Stud Ltd **Trained** Willoughton, Lincs
FOCUS
A very moderate maiden, run at an average pace. The form looks straightforward enough but is weak.

370 GOLDEN MEMORIES ARE MADE AT PONTIN'S H'CAP 5f (F)
3:50 (3:50) (Class 6) (0-65,65) 4-Y-O+ **£2,047** (£453; £453) **Stalls** High

Form RPR
2-20 **1** **Grand Palace (IRE)**[11] 241 5-9-2 **63**........................(v) DeanMcKeown 9 73
(D Shaw) *cl up: rdn 2f out: led wl over 1f out: drvn out* **7/1**
-312 **2** ½ **Strathmore (IRE)**[7] 286 4-9-4 **65**.................................. TonyHamilton 6 73
(R A Fahey) *in tch: hdwy over 2f out: drvn to chse ldrs over 1f out: kpt on u.p ins fnl f* **3/1**[1]
3-50 **2** *dht* **Astorygoeswithit**[14] 189 5-8-4 **51** oh6..........................(be) LiamJones 5 59
(G C Bravery) *cl up: led 1/2-way: rdn and hdd wl over 1f out: drvn and kpt on same pce ins fnl f* **18/1**
00/0 **4** 2½ **Supreme Speedster**[23] 84 4-9-1 **65**........................ MarkLawson(3) 8 64
(M Brittain) *dwlt: hdwy and in tch after 1f: rdn along 2f out: kpt on u.p ins fnl f: nrst fin* **25/1**
-222 **5** ¾ **Bentley**[14] 191 4-8-6 **56**..(v) TolleyDean(3) 7 52
(D Shaw) *chsd ldrs: rdn along and outpcd 1/2-way: styd on u.p appr fnl f: nt rch ldrs* **3/1**[1]
15-5 **6** *shd* **Gone'N'Dunnett (IRE)**[30] 4 9-8-2 **52**..............(p) KirstyMilczarek(3) 2 48
(Mrs C A Dunnett) *rdn along and outpcd after 2f: sme hdwy u.p over 1f out: nvr a factor* **4/1**[2]
205- **7** 1½ **Guto**[58] 7020 5-8-11 **65**..(b) PatrickDonaghy(7) 3 56
(W J H Ratcliffe) *sn outpcd and a towards rr* **6/1**[3]
0-50 **8** 1¼ **Hawaii Prince**[7] 286 4-9-2 **63**..(p) PaulFessey 4 49
(S T Mason) *s.i.s: sn chsng ldrs: rdn over 2f out: drvn and wknd wl over 1f out* **40/1**
106- **9** 3 **Umpa Loompa (IRE)**[93] 6559 4-8-13 **60**...................(v) PaulMulrennan 1 35
(D Nicholls) *led: rdn along and hdd 1/2-way: sn wknd* **12/1**

59.65 secs (-0.05) **Going Correction** +0.025s/f (Slow) **9 Ran SP% 116.0**
Speed ratings (Par 101): **101,100,100,96,95 94,92,90,85**
2nd Pl S 1.60, A 4.80; Ex GP-S 22.00, GP-A 82.50; CSF GP-S 14.23, GP-A 61.04; T/C GP-S-A 184.24, GP-A-S 230.47 TOTE £6.30: £2.00 Trifecta £154.90 Part won. Pool £436.52. GP-S-A - 0.95 winning units; GP-A-S - 0.10 winning units..
Owner ownaracehorse.co.uk (Shakespeare) **Bred** D McDonnell And Tower Bloodstock **Trained** Danethorpe, Notts
FOCUS
A moderate sprint. The form is rated through the consistent third and looks reasonable.
Guto Official explanation: jockey said gelding suffered interference at start
Hawaii Prince Official explanation: jockey said gelding had no more to give
Umpa Loompa(IRE) Official explanation: jockey said gelding hung right

371 SOUTHWELL-RACECOURSE.CO.UK H'CAP 6f (F)
4:20 (4:21) (Class 6) (0-50,50) 4-Y-O+ **£2,047** (£604; £302) **Stalls** Low

Form RPR
4002 **1** **Tenancy (IRE)**[7] 278 4-8-7 **45**....................................(p) PatrickMathers 5 53
(A J McCabe) *t.k.h: chsd ldrs: hdwy to chal over 2f out: rdn to ld over 1f out: drvn ins fnl f and hld on wl towards fin* **5/1**[3]
2-46 **2** *hd* **Blakeshall Quest**[9] 256 8-8-7 **45**...................................(b) PaulFessey 1 52
(R Brotherton) *led: rdn along 2f out: edgd lft and hdd over 1f out: sn drvn and kpt on wl fnl f: jst hld* **15/2**
3434 **3** ¾ **Pappas Image**[7] 278 4-8-7 **45**...(p) VJanacek 2 50
(A J McCabe) *chsd ldrs on inner: hdwy to chal 2f out and ev ch tl drvn and nt qckn wl ins fnl f* **4/1**[2]
-435 **4** *hd* **Guadaloup**[16] 168 6-8-9 **50** ow2.. MarkLawson(3) 7 54
(M Brittain) *dwlt and squeezed s: towards rr tl gd hdwy wl over 2f out: rdn to chse ldrs and n.m.r over 1f out: sn drvn and one pce ins fnl f* **5/1**[3]
-463 **5** *shd* **Soba Jones**[9] 256 11-8-8 **49**.. TolleyDean(3) 8 53
(J Balding) *chsd ldrs: rdn along and outpcd wl over 2f out: styd on u.p ent fnl f: nrst fin* **5/2**[1]
0-25 **6** 1½ **High Window (IRE)**[10] 254 8-8-10 **48** ow3................ PaulMulrennan 3 47
(G P Kelly) *cl up: ev ch over 2f out: sn rdn: edgd rt and grad wknd* **12/1**
50-0 **7** 8 **Cryptic Clue (USA)**[14] 189 4-8-7 **45**..................................(p) LiamJones 6 18
(D W Chapman) *wnt rt s: sn cl up on outer: rdn along wl over 2f out: drvn and wknd wl over 1f out* **33/1**
250/ **8** 4 **Sergeant Slipper**[618] 1914 11-8-7 **45**..........................(v) DeanMcKeown 4 5
(C Smith) *s.i.s and a in rr* **33/1**
00-5 **9** ½ **Preskani**[17] 153 6-8-4 **45**..(p) DuranFentiman(3) 9 4
(Mrs N Macauley) *sn outpcd and a in rr* **12/1**

1m 16.4s (-0.10) **Going Correction** +0.075s/f (Slow) **9 Ran SP% 114.9**
Speed ratings (Par 101): **103,102,101,101,101 99,88,83,82**
CSF £41.92 CT £162.48 TOTE £6.20: £1.30, £2.90, £2.10; EX 32.70 Trifecta £87.50 Pool: £276.11. 2.24 winning units. Place 6 £ 255.14, Place 5 £ 82.37.
Owner Paul J Dixon **Bred** G A E And J Smith Bloodstock **Trained** Babworth, Notts
■ Cryptic Clue was the final runner of a long career for David Chapman. His granddaughter Ruth Clark takes over the licence.
■ Stewards' Enquiry : Patrick Mathers three-day ban: used whip with excessive frequency (Feb 11-13)
FOCUS
A weak handicap that saw the first five closely covered at the finish. The time was reasonable and the form appears reliable for the grade.
High Window(IRE) Official explanation: trainer later said gelding had been struck into during the race
T/Plt: £384.60 to a £1 stake. Pool: £45,182.10. 85.75 winning tickets. T/Qpdt: £30.50 to a £1 stake. Pool: £3,395.90. 82.30 winning tickets. JR

359 WOLVERHAMPTON (A.W) (L-H)
Thursday, January 31

OFFICIAL GOING: Standard
Wind: Fresh behind Weather: Fine

372 BOOK A PONTIN'S BREAK TO REMEMBER H'CAP 5f 20y(P)
6:50 (6:50) (Class 6) (0-55,55) 4-Y-O+ **£1,684** (£501; £250; £125) **Stalls** Low

Form RPR
01-0 **1** **Sir Don (IRE)**[26] 54 9-9-0 **55**................................(p) StephenDonohoe 9 63
(E S McMahon) *led after 1f: rdn over 1f out: edgd rt ins fnl f: drvn out* **7/1**
6-00 **2** *shd* **Egyptian Lord**[14] 191 5-8-9 **50**..(b) LPKeniry 1 58
(Peter Grayson) *plld hrd: sn prom: rdn and ev ch ins fnl f: r.o* **7/2**[2]
-506 **3** 1½ **Thoughtsofstardom**[8] 263 5-9-0 **55**...................(be) TGMcLaughlin 3 57
(M Wigham) *t.k.h: hmpd and lost pl after 1f: c wd st: rdn and r.o ins fnl f* **4/1**[3]
5221 **4** *shd* **Mr Loire**[1] 363 4-8-11 **52** 6ex...(b) DeanMcKeown 8 54
(A J Chamberlain) *s.i.s: sn swtchd lft: hdwy on ins 2f out: rdn and nt qckn ins fnl f* **5/2**[1]
300- **5** 3 **Highland Song (IRE)**[58] 7026 5-8-8 **49**................................ ChrisCatlin 7 40
(R F Fisher) *prom tl rdn and wknd over 1f out* **6/1**
-006 **6** 1¼ **Percy Douglas**[1] 363 8-8-6 **52** oh1 ow6..........................(b) AnnStokell(5) 2 39
(Miss A Stokell) *led 1f: chsd ldr: rdn and wknd ins fnl f* **33/1**
-006 **7** ¾ **The Carpet Man**[5] 318 4-8-6 **47**..(p) LiamJones 4 31
(A W Carroll) *prom: n.m.r and lost pl after 1f: bhd whn rdn and hung lft fr over 1f out* **10/1**
4-16 **8** *nk* **Stoneacre Donny (IRE)**[15] 174 4-8-9 **50**........................ TPQueally 6 33
(Peter Grayson) *s.i.s: rdn and c v wd st: a bhd* **9/1**

63.36 secs (1.06) **Going Correction** +0.30s/f (Slow) **8 Ran SP% 119.6**
Speed ratings (Par 101): **103,102,100,100,95 93,92,91**
CSF £33.29 CT £114.83 TOTE £8.40: £2.70, £1.80, £1.30; EX 40.50.
Owner Mrs Dian Plant **Bred** C And R O'Brien **Trained** Lichfield, Staffs
FOCUS
A weak handicap rated through the fourth to course form.
Stoneacre Donny(IRE) Official explanation: jockey said colt hung right

373 AHEAD WITH ZENA @ PONTIN'S (S) STKS 1m 1f 103y(P)
7:20 (7:20) (Class 6) 4-Y-O+ **£1,684** (£501; £250; £125) **Stalls** Low

Form RPR
6-32 **1** **Pianoforte (USA)**[10] 250 6-9-6 59..................................(b) JimmyQuinn 5 65
(E J Alston) *hld up in tch: led jst over 1f out: edgd lft ins fnl f: rdn out* **9/2**[3]
100- **2** 1¼ **Bethanys Boy (IRE)**[109] 6199 7-9-6 60.............................. NickyMackay 2 62
(M Wigham) *hld up: hdwy over 3f out: kpt on u.p to take 2nd towards fin* **10/3**[2]
-411 **3** ¾ **Arctic Desert**[10] 250 8-9-11 60..(t) HayleyTurner 6 65
(Miss Gay Kelleway) *chsd ldr: led over 4f out: rdn and hdd jst over 1f out: no ex ins fnl f* **5/6**[1]
3-34 **4** 6 **Granary Girl**[16] 161 6-9-1 48... TPQueally 1 43
(J Pearce) *prom: lost pl over 4f out: n.d after* **18/1**
-56 **5** 2½ **Oh So (IRE)**[7] 284 4-8-7 52.. ManavNem(7) 7 38
(P A Blockley) *stdd s: t.k.h in rr: rdn over 2f out: nvr nr ldrs* **50/1**
0-36 **6** 1¼ **Treetops Hotel (IRE)**[14] 198 9-9-1 59................ RussellKennemore(5) 4 40
(R Hollinshead) *hld up: hdwy over 4f out: hrd rdn over 3f out: wknd over 2f out* **12/1**
405/ **7** 2½ **Archirondel**[452] 1666 10-9-6 0.. DanielTudhope 3 35
(B P J Baugh) *led: hdd over 4f out: wknd 3f out* **40/1**

2m 5.14s (3.44) **Going Correction** +0.30s/f (Slow)
WFA 4 from 6yo+ 1lb **7 Ran SP% 113.2**
Speed ratings (Par 101): **96,94,94,88,86 85,83**
CSF £19.41 TOTE £6.00: £1.40, £2.10; EX 22.50.There was no bid for the winner. Arctic Desert was the subject of a friendly claim
Owner Edges Farm Racing Stables Ltd **Bred** Cashmark Farm **Trained** Longton, Lancs
FOCUS
The three major players fought out the finish of this falsely-run seller. The form appears dubious although the front pair seemed to run to their marks.

374 HALF TERM HAPPY DEALS @ PONTINS.COM H'CAP 2m 119y(P)
7:50 (7:50) (Class 6) (0-55,55) 4-Y-O+ **£1,684** (£501; £250; £125) **Stalls** Low

Form RPR
4 **1** **Starstruck Peter (IRE)**[20] 129 4-8-10 **52**............................(t) PaulDoe 9 59
(S Curran) *sn prom: wnt 2nd over 8f out: led 5f out: rdn and styd on fnl f* **16/1**
-065 **2** 1 **Chiff Chaff**[7] 287 4-8-8 **50**.. LPKeniry 8 56
(C R Dore) *hld up in mid-div: hdwy over 7f out: chsd wnr 3f out: rdn wl over 1f out: styd on same pce fnl f* **12/1**
3-24 **3** ¾ **Capitalise (IRE)**[13] 212 5-9-5 **54**.................................... GeorgeBaker 11 59
(V Smith) *hld up and bhd: stdy hdwy over 5f out: rdn and hung lft 1f out: nt qckn* **3/1**[2]
4-05 **4** ¾ **Mango Masher (IRE)**[14] 198 4-8-7 **52**........................ TolleyDean(3) 5 56
(J L Flint) *hld up: sn towards rr: hdwy on ins over 2f out: rdn wl over 1f out: styd on one pce fnl f* **16/1**
152- **5** 2 **Easibet Dot Net**[40] 7226 8-9-6 **55**................................(p) PhillipMakin 6 57
(Miss L A Perratt) *s.i.s: hld up in rr: rdn and hdwy over 2f out: no real prog fnl f* **2/1**[1]
-254 **6** 5 **Prince Of Medina**[15] 179 5-8-13 **48**................................ HayleyTurner 7 44
(J R Best) *t.k.h in rr: hdwy after 4f: rdn and wknd 2f out* **7/1**[3]
4/6- **7** 5 **Cayman Calypso (IRE)**[58] 7012 7-8-11 **46** oh1.............. MickyFenton 2 36
(Mrs P Sly) *hld up in mid-div: rdn over 3f out: hdwy 2f out: wknd fnl f* **7/1**[3]
/0-3 **8** 5 **Optimum (IRE)**[16] 152 6-8-13 **48**.................................... PatCosgrave 3 32
(J T Stimpson) *hld up in tch: rdn and wknd wl over 2f out* **14/1**
100- **9** 1¼ **Mystified (IRE)**[33] 6703 5-9-6 **55**..(b) ChrisCatlin 1 37
(R F Fisher) *led early: chsd ldr tl over 8f out: wknd over 4f out* **20/1**
0-44 **10** 14 **Vanishing Dancer (SWI)**[7] 287 11-9-2 **51**.................... J-PGuillambert 12 17
(Mrs D Thomas) *hld up and bhd: rdn over 5f out: eased whn no ch over 2f out* **12/1**
600- **11** 45 **Don Jose (USA)**[31] 7285 5-8-6 **46**........................ DanielleMcCreery(5) 10 —
(N J Vaughan) *sn led: hdd 5f out: wknd over 3f out: t.o fnl 2f* **7/1**[3]

3m 46.02s (4.22) **Going Correction** +0.30s/f (Slow)
WFA 4 from 5yo+ 7lb **11 Ran SP% 134.4**
Speed ratings (Par 101): **102,101,101,100,99 97,95,92,92,85 64**
CSF £220.38 CT £757.18 TOTE £16.10: £9.30, £5.70, £1.10; EX 225.80.
Owner Mrs K Devlin **Bred** Barouche Stud Ireland Ltd **Trained** Hatford, Oxon
FOCUS
A poor staying handicap in which the pace picked up in the final half a mile. The overall time was reasonable and the form looks sound.
Vanishing Dancer(SWI) Official explanation: jockey said gelding never travelled

375 BOOK PONTIN'S FOR HALF TERM 0844 576 5938 FILLIES' H'CAP 7f 32y(P)
8:20 (8:21) (Class 6) (0-60,58) 4-Y-O+ **£1,684** (£501; £250; £125) **Stalls** High

Form RPR
6-23 **1** **Solicitude**[12] 234 5-9-1 **55**..(p) RobertHavlin 4 65+
(D Haydn Jones) *hld up in mid-div: hdwy over 2f out: led 1f out: drvn out* **5/2**[1]
1-00 **2** 1 **Bens Georgie (IRE)**[11] 235 6-9-4 **58**................................ JimCrowley 8 62
(D K Ivory) *anticipated s: led: hdd over 5f out: chsd ldr: led over 2f out: rdn and hdd 1f out: kpt on same pce* **10/3**[2]
0-30 **3** *nk* **Cantique (IRE)**[10] 249 4-8-5 **45**...................................... JimmyQuinn 10 48
(R J Price) *s.i.s: sn swtchd lft: hld up: hdwy 2f out: rdn over 1f out: r.o towards fin* **25/1**
45-5 **4** *nk* **Johnston's Glory (IRE)**[4] 328 4-8-10 **50**........................ MickyFenton 1 52
(E J Alston) *t.k.h: a.p: rdn 1f out: nt qckn cl home* **4/1**[3]

015- **5** *2 ½* **Fairdonna**[215] 3110 5-9-2 **56**.................................... AdamKirby 3 52
(Seamus Fahey, Ire) *hld up in mid-div: hdwy on ins 2f out: rdn over 1f out: one pce fnl f* **13/2**

00/0 **6** *1 ¾* **Shosolosa (IRE)**[13] 220 6-8-5 **52**.................... KrishGundowry(7) 2 43
(R C Guest) *s.i.s: bhd tl rdn and hdwy over 1f out: n.d* **33/1**

060- **7** *¾* **Gee Ceffyl Bach**[57] 7028 4-8-12 **52**.................... StephenDonohoe 6 41
(R C Guest) *hld up in mid-div: rdn and wknd 2f out* **20/1**

000- **8** *8* **Pulsate**[203] 3447 4-9-1 **55**.. LPKeniry 7 22
(E F Vaughan) *prom tl wknd 2f out* **20/1**

-200 **9** *1 ¾* **Cow Girl (IRE)**[3] 338 4-8-13 **53**............................(p) HayleyTurner 5 16
(Miss Gay Kelleway) *w ldr: led over 5f out tl over 2f out: wknd wl over 1f out* **8/1**

0/0 **10** *shd* **Tribiani (IRE)**[19] 144 4-8-3 **50**.................................. ManavNem(7) 11 12
(P A Blockley) *s.v.s: a in rr* **33/1**

050- **11** *1* **Castle Durrow (IRE)**[55] 7066 4-8-7 **47**.....................(b) ChrisCatlin 9 7
(Seamus Fahey, Ire) *s.i.s: sn carried lft: rdn over 2f out: a bhd* **14/1**

1m 31.71s (2.11) **Going Correction** +0.30s/f (Slow) **11** Ran SP% **122.0**
Speed ratings (Par 98): **99,97,97,97,94 92,91,82,80,80 79**
CSF £10.37 CT £171.95 TOTE £4.30: £1.20, £1.50, £7.30; EX 12.70.

Owner David Llewelyn Partnership **Bred** Mrs M L Parry **Trained** Efail Isaf, Rhondda C Taff

FOCUS
A moderate contest but weak form and the placed horses look high enough in the weights now.

Johnston's Glory(IRE) Official explanation: jockey said filly ran too freely

Fairdonna Official explanation: jockey said mare ran too freely

376 PONTINS.COM H'CAP 1m 141y(P)
8:50 (8:50) (Class 4) (0-85,83) 3-Y-0 **£4,210** (£1,252; £625; £312) **Stalls** Low

Form RPR

04-1 **1** **Grand Strategy (IRE)**[26] 52 3-9-4 **78**.................... MatthewHenry 6 87+
(M A Jarvis) *chsd ldr 7f out: led over 2f out: drvn out* **11/8**[1]

36-1 **2** *hd* **Tevez**[17] 158 3-8-12 **72**...(b) JimmyQuinn 3 78
(M H Tompkins) *s.i.s: sn hld up in tch: hrd rdn and ev ch whn edgd rt ins fnl f: r.o* **10/1**

01-1 **3** *1 ¾* **Especially (IRE)**[17] 157 3-8-12 **72**.............................. GregFairley 1 74
(M Johnston) *led: hdd over 2f out: rdn over 1f out: no ex towards fin* **7/2**[2]

32-3 **4** *3* **Dhhamaan (IRE)**[28] 25 3-9-6 **80**............................(v) HayleyTurner 4 75
(C E Brittain) *prom tl rdn and wknd wl over 1f out* **8/1**

3-3 **5** *2* **Chinese Temple (IRE)**[19] 136 3-9-0 **77**.................... JerryO'Dwyer(3) 2 68
(M G Quinlan) *hld up in rr: pushed along 2f out: no rspnse* **9/2**[3]

10-4 **6** *shd* **Kalhan Sands (IRE)**[19] 136 3-9-6 **83**........................ PJMcDonald(3) 5 73
(G A Swinbank) *prom: stdd and lost pl 7f out: rdn wl over 1f out: no rspnse* **5/1**

1m 53.61s (3.11) **Going Correction** +0.30s/f (Slow) **6** Ran SP% **119.4**
Speed ratings (Par 99): **98,97,96,93,91 91**
CSF £17.83 TOTE £2.50: £2.50, £2.00; EX 36.30.

Owner Sheikh Ahmed Al Maktoum **Bred** Darley **Trained** Newmarket, Suffolk

■ Stewards' Enquiry : Jimmy Quinn one-day ban: used whip with excessive frequency (Feb 11)

FOCUS
An interesting handicap featuring some unexposed types in a race that developed into a sprint from the 3f pole. The fourth is the best guide to the level.

377 COME STAY WITH US @ PONTIN'S CLASSIFIED STKS 1m 4f 50y(P)
9:20 (9:20) (Class 7) 4-Y-0+ **£1,295** (£385; £192; £96) **Stalls** Low

Form RPR

003/ **1** **Wizard Of Us**[31] 6300 8-9-2 **45**................................ JimCrowley 10 52
(M Mullineaux) *chsd ldr: led over 2f out: rdn wl over 1f out: r.o wl* **4/1**[2]

V6-6 **2** *2 ½* **Candy Anchor (FR)**[13] 220 9-9-2 **44**........................ HayleyTurner 11 48
(R E Peacock) *s.i.s: hld up in rr: hdwy over 3f out: rdn wl over 1f out: styd on fnl f: edgd rt and tk 2nd nr fin* **11/1**

3/60 **3** *½* **Castle Frome (IRE)**[5] 322 9-9-2 **40**.....................(p) PaulFitzsimons 6 47
(A E Price) *t.k.h: hld up in tch: wnt 2nd over 3f out: rdn and ev ch 2f out: one pce* **40/1**

0-32 **4** *2 ½* **Santera (IRE)**[14] 197 4-8-12 **41**................................(p) TPQueally 4 43
(Mrs A Duffield) *hld up in mid-div: hdwy over 3f out: rdn over 1f out: one pce* **6/4**[1]

6-55 **5** *10* **Cool Isle**[19] 145 5-9-2 **35**......................................(b) JimmyQuinn 1 27
(P Howling) *hld up towards rr: styd on fnl 2f: nvr nr ldrs* **12/1**

03-0 **6** *10* **Island King (IRE)**[25] 69 5-9-2 **42**.............................. PatCosgrave 5 11
(R Bastiman) *s.i.s: hld up towards rr: rdn and sme hdwy 3f out: wknd over 1f out* **25/1**

0-40 **7** *1* **Backlash**[8] 269 7-9-2 **44**.. LiamJones 9 9
(A W Carroll) *sn prom: rdn and wknd wl over 2f out* **12/1**

30-0 **8** *shd* **History Prize (IRE)**[25] 67 5-9-2 **42**...........................(p) LPKeniry 8 9
(A G Newcombe) *hld up in mid-div: rdn over 3f out: sn struggling* **18/1**

064- **9** *17* **Procrastinate (IRE)**[57] 5782 6-9-2 **45**........................ ChrisCatlin 2 —
(R F Fisher) *prom: rdn over 4f out: sn wknd* **7/1**[3]

30-4 **10** *¾* **Chart Oak**[14] 197 5-9-2 **42**.. TGMcLaughlin 3 —
(P Howling) *led: rdn and hdd over 4f out: wkng whn n.m.r on ins over 3f out* **7/1**[3]

60/0 **11** *22* **Beauchamp Turbo**[28] 31 6-9-2 **45**............................ DanielTudhope 12 —
(N Wilson) *hld up in mid-div: rdn over 3f out: sn struggling: t.o* **33/1**

2m 44.84s (3.74) **Going Correction** +0.30s/f (Slow)
WFA 4 from 5yo+ 4lb **11** Ran SP% **123.2**
Speed ratings (Par 97): **99,97,97,95,88 82,81,81,69,69 54**
CSF £49.22 TOTE £5.20: £1.40, £3.50, £8.60; EX 57.40 Place 6 £ 207.11, Place 5 £ 121.67.

Owner P Currey **Bred** S Mellor **Trained** Alpraham, Cheshire

■ Stewards' Enquiry : Jim Crowley one-day ban: careless riding (Feb 11)

FOCUS
A dire affair and weak form.

T/Plt: £305.90 to a £1 stake. Pool: £103,705.10. 247.45 winning tickets. T/Qpdt: £37.70 to a £1 stake. Pool: £7,462.50. 146.30 winning tickets. KH

[290]NAD AL SHEBA (L-H)
Thursday, January 31
OFFICIAL GOING: Dirt course - fast; turf course - good

378a DUBAI INGOT H'CAP (DIRT) 5f (D)
3:15 (3:17) (90-105,104) 3-Y-0+
£33,165 (£11,055; £5,527; £2,763; £1,658; £1,105)

RPR

1 **New Freedom (BRZ)**[28] 7-8-9 **93**................................ TPO'Shea 15 99
(A Selvaratnam, UAE) *prom nr rail: rdn 2f out: r.o wl and led 110yds out: comf* **12/1**[3]

2 *6 ¼* **Sarissa (BRZ)**[86] 5-9-1 **98**.. JMurtagh 2 83
(P Bary, France) *led far side: clr 2f out: hdd 110yds out: r.o* **9/2**[2]

3 *½* **Drayton (IRE)**[141] 5325 4-9-6 **104**.............................. WMLordan 13 86
(M F De Kock, South Africa) *bmpd at s: trckd ldrs nr side: ev ch 3f out: nt qckn fnl 1 1/2f* **4/1**[1]

4 *½* **Conroy (USA)**[314] 10-8-11 **95**.................................. RyanMoore 16 75
(A Selvaratnam, UAE) *slowly away: prom nr side: ev ch 2f out: r.o* **14/1**

5 *¾* **Select Reason (BRZ)**[61] 4-8-7 **95**............................(t) MJKinane 10 69
(A Cintra Pereira, Brazil) *trckd ldrs: rdn 2 1/2f out: nt qckn* **4/1**[1]

6 *shd* **Almaram (USA)**[41] 8-8-12 **96**...................................(e) RPCleary 6 73
(D Selvaratnam, UAE) *sn rdn in mid-div: r.o fnl 1 1/2f* **12/1**[3]

7 *1 ¼* **Canadian Danehill (IRE)**[116] 6036 6-8-12 **96**..............(p) LDettori 12 69
(R M H Cowell) *slowly away: racd prom: rdn 3f out: sn btn* **14/1**

8 *½* **Rockets 'n Rollers (IRE)**[350] 471 8-8-11 **95**.......(p) RoystonFfrench 14 66
(A Manuel, UAE) *hmpd s: chsd ldrs 2 1/2f out: one pce* **33/1**

9 *1 ¼* **Big Spartan (BRZ)**[28] 5-8-8 **91**................................ DO'Donohoe 11 58
(Doug Watson, UAE) *prom in centre: rdn 3f out: one pce* **16/1**

10 *1 ¾* **Attilius (BRZ)**[13] 6-8-7 **90**..(t) DBadel 8 51
(E Charpy, UAE) *sn rdn in mid-div: n.d* **18/1**

11 *4 ½* **Doctor Hilary**[35] 6-8-9 **93**....................................(vt) TedDurcan 1 37
(S Seemar, UAE) *trckd ldrs for 2f: wknd* **14/1**

12 *hd* **Chaplinesque (USA)**[1049] 9-8-10 **94**........................ CharlotteKerton 3 37
(A Selvaratnam, UAE) *nvr nr to chal* **100/1**

13 *1 ¾* **Buachaill Dona (IRE)**[131] 5616 5-9-3 **100**................ AdrianTNicholls 7 38
(D Nicholls) *a struggling in rr* **14/1**

14 *9 ¼* **Cartography (IRE)**[7] 290 7-9-0 **97**.........................(t) RichardMullen 4 2
(R Bouresly, Kuwait) *a in rr* **66/1**

15 *1* **Junction Line**[28] 10-9-0 **97**.....................................(t) WayneSmith 9 —
(M Al Muhairi, UAE) *sn struggling in rr* **12/1**[3]

P **League Champion (USA)**[357] 394 5-9-5 **102**................... WJSupple 5 —
(R Bouresly, Kuwait) *p.u after 2f* **33/1**

57.45 secs (-0.95) **Going Correction** +0.05s/f (Slow) **16** Ran SP% **127.4**
Speed ratings: **109,99,98,97,96 96,94,93,91,88 81,80,78,63,61** —
Win: 27.50; PL 6.20, 2.20, 1.40; CSF 67.10; TRI 267.42.
Owner Freedom Fighters **Bred** Haras Belmont Ltda **Trained** United Arab Emirates

FOCUS
It was hard to make a serious case about many of these beforehand and this looked like an ordinary sprint handicap for the grade. They raced middle to stands' side, but there seemed to track bias.

NOTEBOOK
New Freedom(BRZ), posted in stall 15, stuck to the stands' rail throughout and ran out a most decisive winner. He could manage only eighth in a non-Carnival handicap over 6f at the beginning of the year, but that race was has worked out exceptionally well and, suited by the drop in trip, he was able to gain his first success since switching to Dubai from Brazil.
Sarissa(BRZ), the nine-length winner of an extended 6f conditions contest in Brazil on her most recent start, showed bags of speed up the centre of the track, but she was no match whatsoever for the winner, who raced well away from her on the stands' rail. (tchd 4/1)
Drayton(IRE) was a dual Listed winner at two and, although failing to win last season, he ran some creditable races in defeat, including round here on the turf and when a fine fifth in the Golden Jubilee Stakes at Royal Ascot. Trying dirt for the first time, he showed plenty of early speed, but just found a couple too strong in the later stages. This was a respectable effort under top weight. (op 5/1)
Conroy(USA) ran with real credit on his return from a 314-day absence.
Select Reason(BRZ), a Brazilian challenger who was successful over 6f on a track described as sloppy on his previous start, seemed to lose about a length with an awkward start, but he recovered to chase the pace and was not unlucky.
Canadian Danehill(IRE) had a career-high mark to contend with on his debut in Dubai and was well held. This was his first run in just short of four months and he is entitled to be sharper next time.
Buachaill Dona(IRE) failed to show anywhere near enough to speed to get a handy position and was never seen with a chance.

379a DUBAI TROPHY (H'CAP) (TURF) 1m (T)
3:55 (3:55) (95-110,108) 3-Y-0+
£36,180 (£12,060; £6,030; £3,015; £1,809; £1,206)

RPR

1 **River Tiber**[117] 6011 5-8-12 **100**.................................. WJSupple 2 105
(Saeed Bin Suroor) *trckd ldr: smooth prog to ld 1f out: r.o wl* **12/1**

2 *½* **Dijeerr (USA)**[96] 6491 4-9-0 **101**..............................(v) TedDurcan 11 106
(Saeed Bin Suroor) *sn led: rdn 3f out: hdd 1f out but r.o wl* **13/2**[2]

3 *nk* **Big Timer (USA)**[43] 7184 4-8-12 **100**............................ TomEaves 9 103
(I Semple) *mid-div on rail: smooth prog 2 1/2f out: no room 2f out: r.o once clr: nrst fin* **25/1**

4 *½* **Jet Express (SAF)**[14] 204 6-9-3 **105**..................... RoystonFfrench 3 107
(A Al Raihe, UAE) *trckd ldrs: rdn to chse wnr 2f out: r.o same pce* **14/1**

5 *2 ¾* **Metropolitan Man**[117] 6009 5-9-6 **108**.................... MartinDwyer 12 104
(D M Simcock) *mid-div: no room 2f out: r.o fnl f* **14/1**

6 *nk* **Instant Recall (IRE)**[21] 7-8-9 **97**..........................(vt) WayneSmith 6 92
(M Al Muhairi, UAE) *trckd ldr: t.k.h: ev ch 1 1/2f out: wknd fnl 110yds* **14/1**

7 *shd* **Lucky Dance (BRZ)**[39] 6-8-12 **100**.............................. RyanMoore 4 95
(H J Brown, South Africa) *settled in rr: rdn 3f out: r.o fnl 2f: nrst fin* **8/1**[3]

8 *2 ¼* **Ea (USA)**[187] 3940 4-8-12 **100**....................................(v) LDettori 5 90
(Saeed Bin Suroor) *settled in rr: n.m.r 3f out: nvr able to chal fr 2 1/2f out* **6/4**[1]

9 *3 ¾* **Limehouse (SAF)**[14] 202 5-8-12 **100**............................ JMurtagh 10 81
(M F De Kock, South Africa) *mid-div: rdn 3f out: one pce fnl 2f* **11/1**

10 *½* **Yorokobi (BRZ)**[41] 5-8-7 **95**.. KLatham 8 75
(H J Brown, South Africa) *slowly away: nvr able to chal* **40/1**

11 *2 ¼* **Aqmaar**[21] 4-8-7 **95**.. RHills 7 70
(E Charpy, UAE) *trckd ldrs ev ch whn rdn 2 1/2f out: wknd fnl f* **12/1**

12 1 3/4 **Alpacco (IRE)**[7] 294 6-9-1 **102**................(b) AStarke 15 74
(Frau Nina Bach, Germany) *settled in rr: nvr able to chal* **50/1**
13 4 1/2 **Valiance (USA)**[7] 295 4-8-7 **95**................ MJKinane 1 55
(M F De Kock, South Africa) *settled in last: nvr able to chal* **14/1**
14 8 **Hurricane James (IRE)**[18] 6-8-8 **96**................(t) TPO'Shea 14 38
(E Charpy, UAE) *racd in rr: nvr nr to chal* **16/1**
15 9 **Momtic (IRE)**[480] 5845 7-8-11 **99**................ RichardMullen 13 20
(S Seemar, UAE) *mid-div: rdn 4f out: n.d* **33/1**

1m 38.31s (0.01) **Going Correction** +0.20s/f (Good) **15** Ran SP% **131.9**
Speed ratings: **107,106,106,105,102 102,102,100,96,96 93,92,87,79,70**
Win: 27.80; PL 4.00, 3.10, 8.90; CSF 90.09; TRI 1,978.45.
Owner Sheikh Majid Bin Mohammed al Maktoum **Bred** D G Hardisty Bloodstock **Trained** Newmarket, Suffolk

FOCUS
A decent handicap on paper with some interesting types on show, but they went a steady pace through the early stages, putting those who raced handy at an advantage, and the form needs treating with caution.

NOTEBOOK
River Tiber looked Saeed Bin Suroor's third string strictly on jockey bookings, but he progressed into a smart handicapper for Luca Cumani last season, and he continued his progression with a hard-fought success on his debut for new connections. Having been well placed considering the modest pace, he got first run on the possibly unlucky Big Timer when getting a gap in the straight and battled on well to get the better of long-time leader and stablemate Dijeerr. There could be even more to come in a stronger-run race.
Dijeerr(USA), fitted with a visor for the first time, slowed the pace significantly when getting to the front soon after the start and very much had the run of the race, although he was continually pestered by the free-running Instant Recall. He battled on well when strongly challenged in the straight, but eventually had to give best. He is a class act on his day, as he showed when winning the 2006 Horris Hill for Michael Jarvis. (op 6/1)
Big Timer(USA) failed to progress after enjoying a fantastic juvenile campaign, but he showed real signs of a revival with a solid effort in defeat, and he could even be considered a little unlucky. Having raced keenly off the steady pace, he was short of room when looking to make his move early in the straight, with the eventual winner getting the gap he seemed to be going for, and his run just flattened out a touch when finally in the clear late on. A stronger-run race should suit better.
Jet Express(SAF) has been in tremendous form on the dirt this winter, winning three non-Carnival events, and this was a decent effort switched to turf.
Metropolitan Man had no easy task under top weight and he would have benefited from a stronger pace, so this was a creditable effort.
Instant Recall(IRE) was too free for his own good.
Lucky Dance(BRZ) got going too late and is yet another who would have appreciated a stronger-run race.
Ea(USA), a progressive three-year-old handicapper for Sir Michael Stoute last year, had a visor on for the first time, but was held up in a slowly-run race and could never land a blow. It is probably best to put a line through this and he can do better when getting the race run to suit. (op 13/8)

380a DUBAL POTLINE H'CAP (DIRT) 1m 2f (D)
4:25 (4:25) (90-105,102) 3-Y-O+
£33,165 (£11,055; £5,527; £2,763; £1,658; £1,105)

RPR
1 **Igor Protti**[130] 5670 6-9-6 **102**................(b) LDettori 3 104+
(Saeed Bin Suroor) *mid-div: wd: smooth prog 3f out: led 1 1/2f out: easily* **6/1**[2]
2 3 1/2 **Bennie Blue (SAF)**[14] 202 6-9-6 **102**................ KShea 11 95+
(M F De Kock, South Africa) *trckd ldrs: dropped to mid-div 3f out: r.o wl fnl 2f: no ch w wnr* **13/2**[3]
3 2 1/4 **Acrobatic (USA)**[14] 202 5-8-10 **93**................ RyanMoore 7 80
(Doug Watson, UAE) *trckd ldr: rdn 2 1/2f out: r.o same pce* **14/1**
4 1/2 **Vainglory (USA)**[30] 6 4-8-1 **91**................ AhmedAjtebi(6) 4 78
(D M Simcock) *trckd ldr on rail: rdn to chse 2 1/2f out: kpt on same pce* **14/1**
5 1/2 **Leaving Alone (BRZ)**[21] 5-8-10 **93**................ WJSupple 6 78
(Doug Watson, UAE) *sn led: clr 4f out: hdd 1 1/2f out: kpt on* **14/1**
6 1 **Safety Investments (AUS)**[46] 9-9-4 **100**................(t) MJKinane 5 84
(J Lau, Macau) *mid-div on rail: nvr nr to chal* **14/1**
7 shd **Morghim (IRE)**[28] 5-8-11 **94**................(bt) MartinDwyer 2 76
(E Charpy, UAE) *a in mid-div* **14/1**
8 1/2 **Consular**[14] 202 6-9-4 **100**................(t) TPO'Shea 9 82
(E Charpy, UAE) *mid-div: rdn 3f out: r.o same pce fnl 2f* **16/1**
9 3 3/4 **Chinkara**[21] 8-8-12 **95**................(t) DO'Donohoe 8 69
(Doug Watson, UAE) *settled in rr: nvr nr to chal: r.o fnl f* **12/1**
10 nse **Mosaic**[7] 293 6-9-4 **100**................ RoystonFfrench 13 75
(A Al Raihe, UAE) *nvr nr to chal but r.o fr rr fnl 2f* **33/1**
11 1/2 **Elmustanser**[14] 202 7-9-2 **98**................(t) RHills 14 72
(Doug Watson, UAE) *settled in rr: nvr able to chal* **20/1**
12 1 1/4 **Kayak (SAF)**[28] 6-9-4 **100**................ JMurtagh 16 71
(M F De Kock, South Africa) *mid-div: wd: rdn 4f out: nvr able to chal* **11/4**[1]
13 1 **Impeller (IRE)**[14] 202 9-9-0 **96**................ JohnEgan 1 65
(J S Moore) *mid-div: rdn 3f out: wknd* **10/1**
14 9 1/4 **Hando**[28] 4-8-10 **95**................ BrettDoyle 15 45
(Christian Wroe) *nvr nr to chal* **33/1**
15 1 **Hunters' Glen (USA)**[21] 5-8-10 **93**................(t) RichardMullen 10 41
(Doug Watson, UAE) *slowly away: hrd rdn in mid-div 3f out: wknd* **33/1**
16 dist **Parasol (IRE)**[343] 529 9-9-4 **100**................(bt) TedDurcan 12 —
(Doug Watson, UAE) *v.s.a: sn rdn in last: nvr able to chal* **33/1**

2m 2.50s (0.20) **Going Correction** +0.225s/f (Slow)
WFA 4 from 5yo+ 2lb **16** Ran SP% **126.8**
Speed ratings: **108,105,103,103,102 101,101,101,98,98 97,96,96,88,87** —
Win: 7.70; PL 2.20, 2.00, 3.80; CSF 44.01; TRI 528.96.
Owner Godolphin **Bred** Giorgio Barsotti And V De Siero **Trained** Newmarket, Suffolk

FOCUS
Well over half the field were upwards of six years of age and most of these were well exposed, so the form of this handicap is nothing special. The pace was pretty ordinary and it proved hard to make up significant amounts of ground.

NOTEBOOK
Igor Protti, last seen finishing last of six in a German Group 2, took to dirt extremely well at the first attempt and made a winning debut for Godolphin. Never too far away from the modest pace, he made his way to the front very easily and only had to be pushed out by Dettori late on, although he was possibly beginning to tire a little close home. This is ordinary form for the level and a rise in the weights will obviously make things a lot tougher, but he is at least unexposed on dirt.
Bennie Blue(SAF) appreciated front-running tactics when winning over course and distance off a 2lb lower mark at last year's Carnival, so it was disappointing he didn't put pressure on the early leader considering the lack of pace. He unsurprisingly did his best work late on and can do better when ridden more positively.
Acrobatic(USA) shaped nicely when fifth over 1m1f here on his previous start, and he confirmed that promise with a good effort in defeat. This was only his third start since returning from a long absence and there could yet be even more to come.
Vainglory(USA) tracked the early leader throughout and seemed well enough placed if good enough.
Leaving Alone(BRZ), back on dirt, was allowed a very soft lead and can have no excuses.
Safety Investments(AUS) was asked to come from well back off the steady gallop after racing keenly and met some trouble when trying to make his move off the home bend, so he can be rated a little better than the bare form. (op 16/1)
Kayak(SAF) was beaten some way out and was very disappointing.
Impeller(IRE) will be happier back on turf and, interestingly enough, he won on the grass at last year's Carnival off the back of two runs on dirt.

381a DUBAL CASTHOUSE H'CAP (TURF) 1m 4f (T)
4:55 (4:57) (95-110,105) 3-Y-O+
£36,180 (£12,060; £6,030; £3,015; £1,809; £1,206)

RPR
1 **Mourilyan (IRE)**[89] 6660 4-8-7 **95**................ MJKinane 7 107+
(John M Oxx, Ire) *settled in rr: smooth prog wd 3f out: r.o wl to ld 100yds out: despite running green* **13/2**[2]
2 3 1/4 **Doubnov (FR)**[151] 5078 5-8-12 **97**................ LDettori 12 102
(Saeed Bin Suroor) *trckd ldrs: t.k.h: smooth prog 3f out: led ins fnl 2f: hdd 100yrds out: r.o same pace but no ch with winner* **13/2**[2]
3 2 1/4 **Remaadd (USA)**[14] 202 7-9-3 **101**................ JMurtagh 10 103
(D Selvaratnam, UAE) *mid-div: rdn to chse ldrs 3f out: r.o same pce* **28/1**
4 1 1/2 **Lundy's Lane (IRE)**[82] 6759 8-8-11 **96**................ MartinDwyer 4 95
(A M Balding) *settled in rr: n.m.r 3f out: r.o once clr: nrst fin* **28/1**
5 1 1/4 **Hard Top (IRE)**[7] 293 6-9-6 **105**................ RyanMoore 6 102
(H J Brown, South Africa) *settled in rr: trckd wnr 2 1/2f out: one pce* **20/1**
6 3 1/4 **Gower Song**[82] 6757 5-9-3 **101**................ TedDurcan 5 93
(D R C Elsworth) *mid-div: rdn to chse ldrs 3f out: one pce* **20/1**
7 1 1/2 **Kerashan (IRE)**[28] 6-8-10 **95**................(t) RoystonFfrench 2 84
(A Al Raihe, UAE) *racd in rr: n.m.r in mid-div 2 1/2f out: nt qckn* **40/1**
8 1 3/4 **Before You Go (IRE)**[123] 5830 5-8-12 **97**................(v) DO'Donohoe 9 83
(Saeed Bin Suroor) *trckd ldr: rdn 2 1/2f out: wknd* **25/1**
9 1 1/4 **Snoqualmie Boy**[7] 293 5-9-4 **102**................ JohnEgan 15 87
(J S Moore) *settled in last: nvr nr to chal* **20/1**
10 hd **Coeur De Lionne (IRE)**[7] 296 4-8-10 **99**................ SteveDrowne 8 83+
(E A L Dunlop) *mid-div rail: trckd ldrs whn no room 1 1/2f out: nt rcvr* **25/1**
11 1 1/4 **Silverlord (FR)**[7] 296 4-8-8 **97**................(t) RichardMullen 1 79
(Frau Nina Bach, Germany) *in rr of mid-div: nvr nr to chal* **50/1**
12 nk **L'Amico Steve (BRZ)**[165] 5-9-5 **104**................ TPO'Shea 3 85
(A Cintra Pereira, Brazil) *mid-div on rail: rdn 3 1/2f out: nvr able to chal* **1/1**[1]
13 nk **Filios (IRE)**[224] 2790 4-8-8 **97**................ WJSupple 14 78
(Saeed Bin Suroor) *in rr of mid-div: rdn to cl 3f out: nvr able to chal* **15/2**[3]
14 2 1/4 **Lake Poet (IRE)**[7] 293 5-9-2 **100**................ PJSmullen 11 78
(C E Brittain) *mid-div: ev ch whn trckd ldr 2 1/2f out: nt qckn* **20/1**
15 2 3/4 **Mutasallil (USA)**[28] 8-9-0 **98**................(t) RHills 16 72
(Doug Watson, UAE) *sn led: hdd 1 1/2f out: wknd* **50/1**
16 dist **Nepotista (BRZ)**[329] 648 6-9-2 **100**................(b) AdrianTNicholls 13 —
(J S Moore) *slowly away: trckd ldr: wknd 3 1/2f out* **25/1**

2m 31.02s (0.02) **Going Correction** +0.20s/f (Good)
WFA 4 from 5yo+ 4lb **16** Ran SP% **132.3**
Speed ratings: **107,104,103,102,101 99,98,97,96,96 95,95,94,93,91** —
Win: 6.80; PL 2.20, 1.80, 4.60; CSF 43.53; TRI 1,157.93.
Owner H H Aga Khan **Bred** His Highness The Aga Khan's Studs S C **Trained** Currabeg, Co Kildare

FOCUS
A big field for this 95-110, and a very interesting handicap. Admittedly there were the usual handful who could be easily dismissed, but there were plenty of very useful types on show and this looks like decent form. The pace increased significantly down the back straight and this race should work out.

NOTEBOOK
Mourilyan(IRE) ◆ was a seriously impressive winner and took this in the style of a Group horse. He has been lightly raced to date, but showed plenty of ability when third on his only start at two behind Soldier Of Fortune and then when third behind Mores Wells on his three-year-old reappearance. His two subsequent wins were gained in just ordinary company, so it was difficult to get a real handle on him beforehand, but he crept into this at the bottom of the weights and made a mockery of his handicap mark. Held up out the back on this step up in trip, the decent tempo was to his liking and he was absolutely tanking along on the turn into the home straight. He was forced to make his move out widest, but that was no bother to him and Mick Kinane's only worry seemed to be not to get there too soon. The result was inevitable when he was finally given his head. He will be extremely hard to beat if turned out in another handicap and, in the slightly longer term, something like the Group 3 Dubai City Of Gold Stakes back over this course and distance later in the Carnival could be a good target. (op 6/1)
Doubnov(FR), a multiple winner in France, got to the front travelling quite easily, but he was no match whatsoever for the well above-average winner. This was a creditable effort on his first start for Saeed Bin Suroor. (op 6/1)
Remaadd(USA), a winner on the dirt at last year's Carnival, battled on well to claim a place on what was a rare turf start. He is an honest performer and should continue to go well on both surfaces. (tchd 33/1)
Lundy's Lane(IRE) is on a long losing run, but he ran a solid-enough race on his return to Dubai off the back of a near three-month break. He was a little short of room at the top of the straight, but was not unlucky. (op 25/1)
Hard Top(IRE) had no easy task under top weight, but he stayed on from a long way back to post a respectable effort in defeat.
Gower Song travelled quite nicely into the straight, but found a few too strong late on. She gives the impression she might be better back over 1m2f. (tchd 18/1)
Before You Go(IRE), having his first start since leaving Terry Mills, was well enough placed but failed to pick up.
Snoqualmie Boy briefly looked a threat, but his effort soon flattened out.
Coeur De Lionne(IRE) ◆, back up in trip, can be rated much better than the bare form as he was badly hampered when trying to make his move against the far rail in the straight.
L'Amico Steve(BRZ), a Grade 1 winner in Brazil, had twice finished in front of recent impressive Carnival winner Happy Boy in his homeland, and was duly heavily supported on his debut in Dubai, but he was never seen with a chance. (op 5/4)
Filios(IRE), ex-Luca Cumani, travelled reasonably well into the straight, but did not see his race out and may have needed this first run in 224 days.
Lake Poet(IRE) shaped with some promise on his previous start, but he dropped out disappointingly this time.

Nepotista(BRZ) ran as though something was amiss and caused some trouble in behind when weakening. (op 22/1)

382a DUBAI BILLET H'CAP (DIRT) 1m (D)

5:30 (5:30) (90-105,105) 3-Y-0+

£33,165 (£11,055; £5,527; £2,763; £1,658; £1,105)

RPR

1 **Blackat Blackitten (IRE)**[119] 5950 4-8-10 **95**......................... LDettori 4 107+
(Saeed Bin Suroor) *mid-div: smooth prog 2 1/2f out: led 1 1/2f out: comf* **5/4**[1]

2 *2 1/2* **Akona Matata (USA)**[28] 6-8-10 **95**......................... DO'Donohoe 13 100
(Doug Watson, UAE) *mid-div: wd: smooth prog to ld briefly 2f out: r.o but no ch w wnr* **25/1**

3 *3* **Gongidas**[111] 6155 4-8-8 **93**.........................(v) TedDurcan 1 91
(Saeed Bin Suroor) *v.s.a: rdn in rr 4f out: n.d but r.o fnl 2f: nrst fin* **16/1**

4 *2 1/2* **Skywards**[28] 6-8-8 **93**.........................(t) TPO'Shea 12 85
(E Charpy, UAE) *trckd ldrs: wd 3f out: led briefly 2 1/2f out: r.o* **9/1**[3]

5 *1/2* **Opportunist (IRE)**[28] 9-8-8 **93**.........................(vt) MartinDwyer 3 84
(Doug Watson, UAE) *mid-div on rail: ev ch fnl 2f: one pce* **12/1**

6 *1 1/2* **Vortex**[14] 204 9-9-6 **105**.........................(t) RyanMoore 7 93
(Miss Gay Kelleway) *racd in rr: rdn to cl 2 1/2f out: ev ch nt qckn but r.o fnl 1 1/2f* **10/1**

7 *1/2* **Montalba (USA)**[62] 8-8-7 **91**.........................(be) MJKinane 9 79
(J Lau, Macau) *trckd ldrs: rdn 3f out: ev ch 2f out: nt qckn* **16/1**

8 *3/4* **Salt Track (ARG)**[14] 204 8-9-1 **99**.........................(t) ESki 8 85
(Niels Petersen, Norway) *s.i.s: racd in last: rdn 3f out: r.o but n.d* **18/1**

9 *1 1/4* **Quorum (GER)**[18] 5-8-6 **90**.........................(v) WayneSmith 2 73
(M Al Muhairi, UAE) *prom on rail tl btn 2 1/2f out* **9/1**[3]

10 *1/2* **Fleeting Shadow (IRE)**[14] 205 4-8-12 **97**......... RoystonFfrench 11 78
(A Al Raihe, UAE) *trckd ldrs: rdn 2 1/2f out: r.o same pce* **33/1**

11 *8 1/4* **Naipe Marcado (URU)**[14] 202 5-9-0 **98**.........................(v) WJSupple 5 61
(Saeed Bin Suroor) *disp ld in centre tl 3f out: wknd* **33/1**

12 *7 3/4* **Azarole (IRE)**[14] 205 7-9-2 **100**......................... JohnEgan 6 45
(J S Moore) *rdn in rr of mid-div 3f out: sn btn* **8/1**[2]

13 *2 1/2* **Bo Bid (USA)**[406] 8-9-0 **98**.........................(t) RichardMullen 10 37
(S Seemar, UAE) *in rr of mid-div: rdn 3f out: n.d* **14/1**

1m 36.52s (-0.18) **Going Correction** +0.225s/f (Slow) **13 Ran SP% 125.8**
Speed ratings: **109,106,103,101,100 99,98,97,96,96 87,80,77**
Win: 2.00; PL 1.10, 5.30, 4.40; CSF 46.25; TRI 384.60.
Owner Godolphin **Bred** Conor Murphy **Trained** Newmarket, Suffolk

FOCUS
Perhaps not quite as strong a race as one might hope for the level, but there were still some interesting types on show.

NOTEBOOK
Blackat Blackitten(IRE) ◆ was a nice, improving handicapper both on turf and Polytrack for Gerard Butler last season and he showed he is still very much on the up with a convincing success on his debut for Godolphin. This was his first start on dirt proper, but he handled it well and travelled nicely in behind the leaders for much of the way. He had to wait for a gap at the top of the straight, very much allowing Akona Matata first run, but there was a lot to like about the way he regained his momentum to get up and win going away. Seemingly fully effective on most surfaces, he will have plenty of options and should continue to progress. (op 6/4)

Akona Matata(USA) travelled well just off the lead out wide and looked the one to beat when moving to the front around horses at the top of the straight, but he ultimately had to give best. This was a blinding effort on just his second start since returning from a long absence.

Gongidas, trying dirt for the first time, blew his chance with a really slow start, losing five or so lengths, but he went the shortest way round in a bid to make up the lost ground and eventually ran on for third.

Skywards travelled nicely on the pace for much of the way, but he was forced out extremely wide rounding the final bend and found a few too strong in the straight.

Opportunist(IRE), a winner over course and distance two starts back, had every chance and ran reasonably. (op 14/1)

Vortex was never really a danger after taking time to find his stride. (op 9/1)

Naipe Marcado(URU) dropped out tamely after showing good early speed.

Azarole(IRE) was never really involved and will be suited by a return to turf.

383a AL RASHIDIYA STKS (GROUP 3) (TURF) 1m 194y(T)

6:00 (6:01) 3-Y-0+

£60,301 (£20,100; £10,050; £5,025; £3,015; £2,010)

RPR

1 **Lord Admiral (USA)**[88] 6681 7-9-0 111.........................(b) MJKinane 1 112+
(Charles O'Brien, Ire) *mid-div on rail: gng wl 3f out: rdn to chal 2f out: led 1 1/2f out: easily* **6/1**[3]

2 *3 3/4* **Gharir (IRE)**[14] 203 6-9-0 105.........................(bt) RHills 5 102+
(E Charpy, UAE) *slowly away: racd in last: stl last 3f out: r.o but no ch w wnr* **25/1**

3 *2 1/2* **Yasoodd**[14] 203 5-9-0 111......................... JMurtagh 9 97
(D Selvaratnam, UAE) *trckd ldr: ev ch 2f out: nt qckn fnl f* **13/2**

4 *2 1/2* **Senor Dali (IRE)**[329] 642 5-9-0 109......................... TPO'Shea 2 92
(E Charpy, UAE) *settled in rr: rdn on rail 2 1/2f out: no room 1 1/2f out: r.o wl fnl f* **14/1**

5 *nk* **King Jock (USA)**[14] 205 7-9-0 107......................... PShanahan 7 91
(R J Osborne, Ire) *settled in rr: nvr nr to chal but r.o fnl 1 1/2f: nrst fin* **14/1**

6 *nk* **Jay Peg (SAF)**[208] 5-9-6 112......................... RyanMoore 6 96
(H J Brown, South Africa) *sn led: rdn 3f out: hdd 1 1/2f out: wknd* **13/8**[1]

7 *3 3/4* **Montpellier (IRE)**[145] 5221 5-9-0 88......................... RoystonFfrench 4 82
(A Al Raihe, UAE) *mid-div: rdn to chse ldrs 3fm out: wknd fnl f* **66/1**

7 *dht* **The Pirate (DEN)**[109] 5-9-0 99.........................(t) ESki 3 82
(Niels Petersen, Norway) *in rr of mid-div: nvr nr to chal* **50/1**

9 *2 1/4* **Teslin (IRE)**[7] 296 4-9-0 104.........................(t) LDettori 8 79
(Saeed Bin Suroor) *in rr of mid-div: chsng ldrs whn no room 1f out: nt rcvr* **3/1**[2]

10 *4 1/4* **Davidoff (GER)**[120] 5929 4-9-0 108......................... AStarke 10 70
(P Schiergen, Germany) *trckd ldr tl rdn 2 1/2f out: wknd* **12/1**

1m 49.34s (-0.66) **Going Correction** +0.20s/f (Good)
WFA 4 from 5yo+ 1lb **10 Ran SP% 119.0**
Speed ratings: **110,106,104,102,101 101,98,98,96,92**
Win: £6.40; PL £2.00, £4.30, £2.50; CSF £142.97.
Owner Dr M V O'Brien **Bred** London Thrghbrd Services/Derry **Trained** Straffan, Co Kildare

FOCUS
The fourth year this race has held Group 3 status, but the finish was dominated by mainly exposed types and this looked an ordinary renewal.

NOTEBOOK
Lord Admiral(USA) gained his first success in Dubai on his third visit to the Carnival, and he did so in style too. Always going well just off the pace, he showed a smart change of gear when asked to go and win his race and proved far too good. It would be no surprise to see him now take a familiar path and go for the Al Fahidi Fort Stakes, in which he was second in 2006 and sixth last year, before possibly going for the Jebel Hatta Stakes, a race in which he took second place in 2006 and sixth last season

Gharir(IRE), back on turf, compromised his chance with a slow start, but he went the shortest way round against the inside rail and stayed on well for second. He cannot be considered unlucky, but possibly wants rating better than the bare form.

Yasoodd, switched from dirt to turf, was a little keen early on, but he was given absolutely every chance and ran well to claim a place.

Senor Dali(IRE) often leads, but he was ridden with restraint this time and ran a very respectable race in fourth, especially considering he was short of room inside the final two furlongs. (op 12/1)

King Jock(USA), back on turf having been unsuited by the dirt last time, travelled enthusiastically, as he usually does, but he was never able to get in a blow.

Jay Peg(SAF), a multiple winner in South Africa, including the Cape Guineas and Derby, looked like the one they all had to beat beforehand, but he ran disappointingly. He was asked to make the running, which might not be his ideal style of racing, and he was in trouble at the top of the straight. He can be given another chance under more patient tactics. (tchd 7/4)

The Pirate(DEN)

Teslin(IRE) could not build on the form he showed when second in a 1m2f handicap here the previous week. He met some trouble in the straight, but cannot be considered unlucky. (op 11/4)

Davidoff(GER) also met with some trouble and is better than this run suggests.

384a DUBAI ALUMINIUM H'CAP (TURF) 1m (T)

6:30 (6:30) (95-110,110) 3-Y-0+

£36,180 (£12,060; £6,030; £3,015; £1,809; £1,206)

RPR

1 **Sentinelese (IRE)**[172] 4443 5-8-6 **96**......................... TedDurcan 6 102+
(Saeed Bin Suroor) *led main gp: smooth prog to trck runner-up 2 1/2f out: led 1 1/2f out: easily* **7/1**[2]

2 *2 1/4* **Glen Nevis (USA)**[224] 2789 4-8-8 **98**.........................(v) WJSupple 2 98
(Saeed Bin Suroor) *disp ld on rail: trckd ldr: led briefly 2f out: hdd 1 1/2f out: no ch w wnr* **25/1**

3 *1 1/4* **Almuraad (IRE)**[14] 205 7-8-9 **99**......................... RHills 1 96
(Doug Watson, UAE) *mid-div: rdn 3f out: r.o same pce* **12/1**[3]

4 *1/2* **Fremen (USA)**[14] 205 8-8-6 **96**......................... AdrianTNicholls 10 92
(D Nicholls) *settled in rr: rdn 2 1/2f out: r.o wl fnl f: nrst fin* **12/1**[3]

5 *hd* **Dark Islander (IRE)**[166] 4600 5-9-6 **110**......................... MJKinane 4 106
(J W Hills) *settled in rr: swtchd wd 3f out: r.o wl fnl f: nrst fin* **14/1**

6 *shd* **Latino Magic (IRE)**[69] 6920 8-8-10 **100**......................... PJSmullen 7 95
(D K Weld, Ire) *mid-div: rdn on rail 2 1/2f out: r.o wl fnl f* **12/1**[3]

7 *2 1/4* **The Illies (IRE)**[117] 6011 4-8-10 **100**......................... LDettori 11 90
(Saeed Bin Suroor) *broke awkwardly: settled in rr: nvr nr to chal* **2/1**[1]

8 *3/4* **King Charles**[125] 5764 4-8-5 **95**......................... MartinDwyer 13 83
(E A L Dunlop) *mid-div: rdn 2 1/2f out: r.o same pce* **12/1**[3]

9 *2 3/4* **Ans Bach**[14] 205 5-9-0 **104**.........................(e) JMurtagh 9 86
(D Selvaratnam, UAE) *mid-div: nvr nr to chal* **7/1**[2]

10 *nk* **Earl's Court**[35] 6-8-10 **100**.........................(t) TPO'Shea 5 81
(E Charpy, UAE) *disp: t.k.h: led 5f out: hdd 2f out: wknd* **40/1**

11 *nk* **Mezel (USA)**[343] 532 5-8-10 **100**......................... RichardMullen 3 81
(S Seemar, UAE) *mid-div on rail: rdn 2f out: wknd* **40/1**

12 *nk* **Tonic Star (FR)**[14] 200 5-8-5 **95**......................... RoystonFfrench 15 75
(Christian Wroe) *in rr: nvr nr to chal* **40/1**

13 *2* **Final Verse**[14] 203 5-9-2 **106**......................... JohnEgan 8 81
(J S Moore) *mid-div: nvr able to chal* **25/1**

14 *1/2* **Money Bags (SAF)**[336] 601 6-8-12 **102**.........................(bt) KShea 12 76
(M F De Kock, South Africa) *settled in rr: nvr involved* **7/1**[2]

15 *nk* **Starpix (FR)**[53] 6-8-10 **100**.........................(t) RyanMoore 14 74
(H J Brown, South Africa) *settled last: nvr able to chal* **20/1**

1m 37.7s (-0.60) **Going Correction** +0.20s/f (Good) **15 Ran SP% 128.0**
Speed ratings: **111,108,107,107,106 106,104,103,100,100 100,100,98,97,97**
Win £8.70; Pl £2.30, £9.70, £4.00; CSF 186.44; TRI £2,085.34; Placepot: £475.40 to a £1 stake. Pool 11,853.30 - 18.20 winning units..
Owner Godolphin **Bred** Peter Thome **Trained** Newmarket, Suffolk

FOCUS
A high-class handicap on paper, but the first three home were always close up and not many got involved.

NOTEBOOK
Sentinelese(IRE) landed a Listed handicap in France on his final start for John Hammond last August and continued his progression with a comfortable victory on his debut for Godolphin. Always well positioned just in behind the leaders, he travelled very strongly into the straight and found plenty when asked to record a straightforward success. The Handicapper clearly underestimated him, so he is likely to be hit quite hard for this, and that will make things tougher, but he is clearly an improver.

Glen Nevis(USA), fitted with a visor on his return from a 224-day absence, was always in a good position and, despite proving no match for his stablemate, he battled on well to the line. He is entitled to come on for this.

Almuraad(IRE), back on turf, was never too far away and kept on to the line to take third.

Fremen(USA) was well beaten on the dirt two weeks previously, but the return to turf suited and he fared best of those held up. He could improve on this.

Dark Islander(IRE) ◆ briefly looked a danger when switched out with his run, but it proved hard to make up ground and his effort flattened out. This was his first run in over five months and, with normal improvement, he could well find a similar race.

Latino Magic(IRE), a winner on the Polytrack at Dundalk when last seen in November, ran a respectable race in defeat.

The Illies(IRE), having his first start since leaving Barry Hills, was dropped in from his wide draw and was far too keen early on. He was left with an impossible task at the top of the straight, with the leaders not stopping, and he could make no impression.

King Charles did not convince when asked for his effort and failed to pick up. He could be best left for the time being.

Final Verse, back on turf, was another who didn't really go anywhere for pressure.

CAGNES-SUR-MER

Thursday, January 31

OFFICIAL GOING: Very soft

385a PRIX DES BOULEAUX MAIDEN (C&G) 7f 110y

1:05 (1:05) 3-Y-O **£6,985** (£2,794; £2,096; £1,397; £699)

RPR

1 **Pelvoux (FR)** 3-9-2 DBoeuf 5 84
(Robert Collet, France)

2 *nk* **My Shadow**[34] 7252 3-9-2 J-BEyquem 2 83
(S Dow) *racd in 2nd: disp ld 2f out tl led 1 1/2f out: hdd 150yds out: r.o* **83/10**[1]

3 *1 1/2* **Maroni (IRE)** 3-9-2 F-XBertras 1 80
(F Rohaut, France)

4 *3* **Izanagi (USA)**[70] 3-8-13 JAuge 8 70
(J E Hammond, France)

5 *5* **Colombey (FR)** 3-8-13 (b) SRichardot 4 58
(K Borgel, France)

6 *11* **Catch A Fire (FR)** 3-8-13 JVictoire 7 33
(C Scandella, France)

7 *2 1/2* **Canari Blue (FR)** 3-8-6 (b) TPiccone(3) 6 23
(P Tual, France)

8 *4* **Takemor (FR)** 3-8-13 (b) WMongil 9 18
(J-J Boutin, France)

9 *9* **Tchic Cove (FR)** 3-8-9 FBlondel 3 —
(A Junk, France)

1m 35.69s (95.69) **9 Ran SP% 10.8**
PARI-MUTUEL (including 1 Euro stake): WIN 2.30; PL 1.10, 1.90, 1.30; DF 10.80.
Owner K Valvis **Bred** Kastro Stud Farm **Trained** Chantilly, France

NOTEBOOK
My Shadow ran really well on his first encounter with soft ground, and only just got run out of it, keeping on after being headed inside the final furlong.

331 KEMPTON (A.W) (R-H)

Friday, February 1

OFFICIAL GOING: Standard
Wind: Fresh, across Weather: Cold

386 TURFTV CLAIMING STKS 5f (P)

6:20 (6:20) (Class 6) 4-Y-O+ **£2,047** (£453; £453) **Stalls** High

Form RPR

/0-1 1 **Ask Jenny (IRE)**[27] 50 6-8-8 47 LPKeniry 2 59
(Patrick Morris, Ire) *chsd ldng pair: wnt 2nd over 1f out: styd on to ld ins fnl f: drvn out* **13/2**[3]

5-10 2 *1* **Compton Classic**[17] 165 6-8-13 68 (v) HarryPoulton(7) 3 67
(J R Boyle) *stdd s: hld up in last and off the pce: clsd over 1f out: sn rdn and nt qckn: kpt on same pce* **9/4**[2]

-141 2 *dht* **Grimes Faith**[3] 346 5-9-6 70 (b) ChrisCatlin 4 67
(K A Ryan) *blasted of in front: rdn over 1f out: wknd and hdd ins fnl f* **4/7**[1]

00 4 *3 1/2* **Yurchenko**[2] 363 4-8-4 39 ow1 (p) NeilChalmers(3) 1 42
(M Wellings) *pestered ldr tl wknd over 1f out* **50/1**

61.15 secs (0.65) **Going Correction** +0.15s/f (Slow) **4 Ran SP% 109.7**
Speed ratings (Par 101): **100,98,98,92**
WIN: £5.50. EX: Ask Jenny/Compton Classic £9.20, Ask Jenny/Grimes Faith £7.30. CSF: AJ/CC £10.38, AJ/GF £5.61..
Owner W J Crosbie **Bred** Mrs J Costelloe **Trained** Ruanbeg, Co. Kildare

FOCUS
Just the four runners, but no hanging around. The runner-up and third were below their best and the fourth is the best guide.

387 RACING UK H'CAP 1m 2f (P)

6:50 (6:53) (Class 6) (0-55,55) 4-Y-O+ **£2,047** (£604; £302) **Stalls** High

Form RPR

0-22 1 **Classic Blue (IRE)**[8] 287 4-8-5 46 PaulEddery 7 56
(Ian Williams) *sn towards rr: rdn over 3f out: prog u.p over 2f out: wnt 2nd jst ins fnl f: clsd on ldr: won on the nod* **9/2**[3]

-224 2 *shd* **Under Fire (IRE)**[16] 180 5-8-9 52 KirstyMilczarek(3) 8 62
(A W Carroll) *led: fought off chalr over 1f out: kpt on fnl f: pipped on the nod* **3/1**[2]

0/-3 3 *1 3/4* **King's Fable (USA)**[29] 31 5-8-9 52 JerryO'Dwyer(3) 1 58
(Karen George) *pressed ldr after 2f: rdn to chal wl over 1f out: edgd lft and fnd little: one pce after* **7/1**

0/11 4 *1 1/2* **Lough Beg (IRE)**[7] 299 5-9-0 54 6ex (t) DaneO'Neill 4 57
(Miss Tor Sturgis) *wl in tch: chsd ldng pair 3f out: rdn and nt qckn wl over 1f out: btn after* **6/4**[1]

400- 5 *3* **Istead Rise (IRE)**[163] 3365 4-9-0 55 StephenDonohoe 3 52
(P A Blockley) *reluctant to enter stalls: stdd s: hld up in detached last: shkn up over 2f out: passed two rivals fnl f: nvr nr ldrs* **20/1**

0- 6 *3 1/2* **Lord Orpen (IRE)**[150] 5125 4-8-6 47 (v[1]) JimmyQuinn 6 37
(Patrick Morris, Ire) *chsd ldr 2f: rdn and lost pl over 3f out: struggling after* **12/1**

200- 7 *3 1/2* **Scar Tissue**[162] 4742 4-8-6 47 JamesDoyle 5 30
(E J Creighton) *a in rr: u.p over 3f out: sn btn* **33/1**

2m 8.86s (0.86) **Going Correction** +0.15s/f (Slow)
WFA 4 from 5yo 1lb **7 Ran SP% 111.1**
Speed ratings (Par 101): **102,101,100,99,96 94,91**
CSF £16.53 CT £69.47 TOTE £4.60: £1.70, £2.10; EX 15.60.
Owner Boston R S Ian Bennett **Bred** Michael Conlon **Trained** Portway, Worcs
■ Willie Ever was withdrawn (8/1, refused to enter stalls). R4 applies, deduct 10p in the £.

FOCUS
Moderate fare, but at least it featured some in-form horses, two of which were ahead of the Handicapper. The form looks sound enough rated around the placed horses.

388 KEMPTON.CO.UK CLAIMING STKS 1m 4f (P)

7:20 (7:20) (Class 6) 4-Y-O+ **£2,047** (£604; £302) **Stalls** Centre

Form RPR

-233 1 **Smokey The Bear**[4] 331 6-9-7 57 NeilChalmers(3) 5 72
(Miss Sheena West) *led 1f: stdd into 3rd: trckd ldr over 2f out: rdn to chal over 1f out: edgd ahd ins fnl f* **2/1**[2]

300- 2 *nk* **Critical Stage (IRE)**[50] 6811 9-8-9 63 HaddenFrost(5) 1 62
(J D Frost) *led after 1f: rdn over 2f out: worn down ins fnl f* **5/1**[3]

64-1 3 *4* **Champagne Shadow (IRE)**[21] 129 7-9-6 75 ChrisCatlin 4 63
(J Pearce) *nvr gng that wl: rdn over 4f out and sn last: laboured effrt to chse ldng pair 2f out: btn over 1f out* **1/1**[1]

/610 4 *6* **George Henson (IRE)**[4] 332 4-9-4 50 DominicFox(3) 2 56
(S Parr) *trckd ldr after 3f tl over 2f out: wknd* **10/1**

0-56 5 *3* **Safe Investment (USA)**[21] 122 4-9-7 57 (t) VinceSlattery 3 51
(B N Pollock) *t.k.h: hld up in last: effrt 4f out: rdn and no rspnse over 2f out: wknd* **20/1**

2m 37.82s (3.32) **Going Correction** +0.15s/f (Slow)
WFA 4 from 6yo+ 3lb **5 Ran SP% 113.9**
Speed ratings (Par 101): **94,93,91,87,85**
CSF £12.47 TOTE £2.80: £1.30, £4.20; EX 10.70.
Owner Graham Flight **Bred** A P Jones **Trained** Falmer, E Sussex

FOCUS
An uncompetitive claimer run in a modest time and not easy to pin down the form.

389 KEMPTON FOR OUTDOOR PURSUITS ON 01932 782292 H'CAP 1m (P)

7:50 (7:50) (Class 6) (0-55,55) 4-Y-O+ **£2,047** (£604; £302) **Stalls** High

Form RPR

06-3 1 **Katiypour (IRE)**[27] 57 11-9-0 55 DaneO'Neill 9 64
(B R Johnson) *trckd ldrs: effrt to ld narrowly 2f out: drvn and asserted fnl f* **7/2**[2]

54-6 2 *2* **Micky Mac (IRE)**[21] 123 4-8-11 52 GrahamGibbons 4 57
(T D Walford) *plld hrd early: hld up in last pair: effrt on outer over 2f out: sn nt qckn: styd on fnl f w reins in a tangle to take 2nd last stride* **5/1**[3]

0-45 3 *shd* **Postmaster**[9] 267 6-8-11 52 RobertHavlin 5 56
(R Ingram) *hld up in last pair: prog on inner to ld briefly over 2f out: nt qckn and hld by wnr 1f out: lost 2nd last stride* **7/2**[2]

455- 4 *1* **Royal Amnesty**[67] 6951 5-9-0 55 PhillipMakin 3 57
(Miss L A Perratt) *sn trckd ldrs on outer: cl up over 2f out: sn rdn and nt qckn* **9/4**[1]

066- 5 *3/4* **Espejo (IRE)**[169] 4550 4-9-0 55 NeilPollard 6 55
(W J Musson) *in tch: lost pl and last wl over 2f out: shuffled along and modest late prog: nvr nr ldrs* **25/1**

-010 6 *1 1/2* **Golden Square**[12] 236 6-8-4 48 KirstyMilczarek(3) 2 45
(A W Carroll) *led to jst over 2f out: wknd over 1f out* **6/1**

06-0 7 *3/4* **Baba Ghanoush**[14] 209 6-8-7 48 PaulDoe 1 43
(J Akehurst) *trckd ldr to over 2f out: sn btn* **16/1**

1m 40.89s (1.09) **Going Correction** +0.15s/f (Slow) **7 Ran SP% 115.9**
Speed ratings (Par 101): **100,98,97,96,96 94,93**
CSF £21.83 CT £65.24 TOTE £5.60: £2.60, £2.10; EX 23.20.
Owner Peter Crate **Bred** His Highness The Aga Khan's Studs S C **Trained** Ashtead, Surrey

FOCUS
A weak handicap in which very few could be fancied, and it provided a great opportunity for the winner on his 101st and final racecourse appearance and he is the best guide to the level.

390 FOLLOW YOUR MEETING WITH FLOODLIT RACING FILLIES' H'CAP 1m (P)

8:20 (8:20) (Class 4) (0-85,84) 4-Y-O+ **£4,210** (£1,252; £625; £312) **Stalls** High

Form RPR

-211 1 **Neardown Beauty (IRE)**[8] 280 5-9-6 84 6ex (p) JamesDoyle 4 91+
(A J McCabe) *hld up in last: prog on inner over 2f out: led over 1f out: coaxed along and styd on wl* **2/1**[2]

1-43 2 *3/4* **Confidentiality (IRE)**[6] 314 4-9-4 82 NickyMackay 3 88
(M Wigham) *hld up in 3rd: effrt on outer to chal wl over 1f out: nt qckn and readily hld fnl f* **7/4**[1]

2-44 3 *3/4* **One Night In Paris (IRE)**[11] 246 5-8-11 75 DaneO'Neill 1 79
(M J Wallace) *trckd ldr: led after 3f: rdn and hdd over 1f out: kpt on same pce* **5/2**[3]

4 *3 1/2* **Bassinet (USA)**[80] 4-8-5 72 KirstyMilczarek(3) 2 68
(J A R Toller) *led 3f: restrained: trckd ldr to over 2f out: wknd over 1f out* **7/1**

1m 40.34s (0.54) **Going Correction** +0.15s/f (Slow) **4 Ran SP% 110.8**
Speed ratings (Par 102): **103,102,101,98**
CSF £6.02 TOTE £2.50; EX 4.50.
Owner Brian Morton **Bred** Mrs Joan M Langmead **Trained** Babworth, Notts

FOCUS
Only four runners, but three of them were in good order and the form makes sense with the first three to their marks.

391 RACINGUK.TV H'CAP 6f (P)

8:50 (8:50) (Class 6) (0-60,60) 4-Y-O+ **£2,047** (£604; £302) **Stalls** High

Form RPR

21-6 1 **Littledodayno (IRE)**[27] 56 5-9-3 59 NickyMackay 2 70
(M Wigham) *hld up in last and wl off the pce: stdy prog over 2f out: sustained effrt on inner to ld last 75yds* **10/3**[1]

06-0 2 *1/2* **Mambazo**[19] 150 6-8-11 60 (e) WilliamCarson(7) 8 69
(S C Williams) *led and sn clr: 5l ahd 1/2-way: reeled in fr over 1f out: hdd last 75yds* **10/1**

-352 3 *1* **Musical Script (USA)**[9] 263 5-9-0 56 (p) ChrisCatlin 3 62
(Mouse Hamilton-Fairley) *chsd ldng trio: rdn 1/2-way: effrt u.p to go 2nd over 1f out tl jst ins fnl f: nt qckn* **9/2**[3]

-046 4 *1 1/2* **Desert Light (IRE)**[9] 270 7-8-9 54 (v) TolleyDean(3) 5 55
(D Shaw) *off the pce towards rr: rdn wl over 2f out: kpt on fr over 1f out: nvr pce to rch ldrs* **13/2**

5 *3* **Nell's Girl (IRE)**[180] 4209 4-8-13 55 LPKeniry 6 46
(Patrick Morris, Ire) *stdd s: sn taking t.k.h in last pair: effrt on outer over 2f out: effrt fizzled out over 1f out* **4/1**[2]

0-21 6 *1/2* **Reigning Monarch (USA)**[23] 87 5-9-1 57 SamHitchcott 1 47
(Miss Z C Davison) *disp 2nd pl bhd clr ldr to over 1f out: wknd fnl f* **9/2**[3]

3353 7 *1/2* **Perlachy**[12] 241 4-9-3 59 (v) JimmyQuinn 4 47
(Mrs N Macauley) *disp 2nd pl bhd clr ldr tl over 1f out: wknd* **5/1**

/00- 8 *8* **Eau Sauvage**[33] 7282 4-8-5 47 oh1 ow1 PaulDoe 7 10
(J Akehurst) *a in rr: last and wkng over 2f out* **50/1**

1m 13.66s (0.56) **Going Correction** +0.15s/f (Slow) **8 Ran SP% 120.5**
Speed ratings (Par 101): **102,101,100,98,94 93,92,82**
CSF £39.62 CT £156.27 TOTE £5.00: £2.10, £2.80, £1.40; EX 63.20.
Owner W L Bamforth & John Williams P'ship **Bred** Lodge Park Stud **Trained** Newmarket, Suffolk

The Form Book, Raceform Ltd, Compton, RG20 6NL

FOCUS
Not a bad little race, for besides several runners with decent recent form, it featured a couple more who were particularly well treated if they recaptured the best of last year's form. The form looks solid rated around the third and fourth.

392 **PANORAMIC BAR & RESTAURANT LOYALTY SCHEME CLASSIFIED STKS** **7f (P)**
9:20 (9:21) (Class 7) 4-Y-0+ **£1,365** (£403; £201) **Stalls High**

Form RPR
3-30 **1** **Shava**[10] 256 8-8-7 44 DeclanCannon(7) 12 56
(H J Evans) *hld up in midfield: prog on inner 3f out: led over 1f out: styd on u.str.p* **7/2**[2]
03-6 **2** *1 1/4* **Tuning Fork**[14] 219 8-8-11 45 KirstyMilczarek(3) 11 53
(M J Attwater) *trckd ldrs: wnt 2nd 3f out: led 2f out: hdd over 1f out: kpt on same pce* **11/2**[3]
00-1 **3** *5* **Polish Prize**[12] 236 4-9-1 45 JamieJones(5) 5 45
(W R Swinburn) *hld up in midfield: prog and gng wl enough 3f out: outpcd 2f out: kpt on to take 3rd 1f out: no imp on ldng pair* **8/1**
3-54 **4** *3 1/2* **Lawdy Miss Clawdy**[9] 264 4-9-0 42 FergusSweeney 10 30
(D W P Arbuthnot) *dwlt: rcvrd and sn led: hdd 2f out: fdd* **11/2**[3]
-521 **5** *nk* **Stargazy**[8] 289 4-8-13 39 MatthewDavies(7) 7 35
(W G M Turner) *dwlt: wl in rr: effrt on outer over 2f out: plugged on but no ch* **13/8**[1]
00-4 **6** *1/2* **Hey Presto**[9] 267 8-9-0 35 JimmyQuinn 6 27
(R Rowe) *mostly in midfield: effrt to chse ldrs over 2f out: sn outpcd and btn* **12/1**
50-5 **7** *1/2* **Height Of Spirits**[11] 242 6-9-0 44 (p) RobertHavlin 4 26
(T D McCarthy) *nvr beyond midfield: effrt on outer over 2f out: no real prog* **16/1**
-453 **8** *hd* **Lily La Belle**[11] 249 4-9-0 45 JamesDoyle 9 26
(A W Carroll) *nvr beyond midfield: outpcd and wl btn over 2f out* **10/1**
655/ **9** *10* **Grezie**[438] 6542 6-9-0 44 PaulDoe 2 —
(L A Dace) *prom on outer: disp 2nd 3f out: wknd rapidly over 2f out* **33/1**
00-5 **10** *3/4* **Broad Town Girl**[12] 236 5-8-7 38 KylieManser(7) 3 —
(Mrs H Sweeting) *s.v.s: a wl bhd* **33/1**
0-60 **11** *11* **Iron Pearl**[5] 327 4-9-0 45 ChrisCatlin 8 —
(J Ryan) *chsd ldr to 1/2-way: wknd: t.o* **40/1**
00-0 **12** *10* **Tequila Sheila (IRE)**[14] 219 6-9-0 43 AmirQuinn 1 —
(M A Allen) *dwlt: a bhd: t.o* **40/1**

1m 27.26s (1.26) **Going Correction** +0.15s/f (Slow) **12** Ran SP% **135.6**
Speed ratings (Par 97): **98,96,90,86,86 85,85,85,73,72 60,48**
CSF £26.52 TOTE £7.20: £2.30, £3.60, £3.00; EX 38.40 Place 6 £759.11, Place 5 £89.79 .
Owner Mrs J Evans & D W Stockton **Bred** Slatch Farm Stud **Trained** Honeybourne, Worcs

FOCUS
This was a very low-grade classified stakes confined to horses rated no higher than 45, though it did include two last-time-out winners and the form looks pretty good for the level.
T/Plt: £660.30 to a £1 stake. Pool: £82,584.90. 91.30 winning tickets. T/Qpdt: £42.70 to a £1 stake. Pool: £7,477.80. 129.30 winning tickets. JN

[372]WOLVERHAMPTON (A.W) (L-H)
Friday, February 1

OFFICIAL GOING: Standard
The final two races were abandoned for safety reasons due to a snowstorm.
Wind: Strong, half-behind Weather: Fine

393 **RACE ALL THE FAMILY TO PONTIN'S CLAIMING STKS** **7f 32y(P)**
2:05 (2:06) (Class 6) 3-Y-O **£2,388** (£705; £352) **Stalls High**

Form RPR
-322 **1** **Maybe I Wont**[4] 339 3-8-6 63 JackMitchell(5) 4 68
(P G Murphy) *broke wl: plld hrd: stdd and dropped to rr 6f out: hdwy over 2f out: led over 1f out: sn hung lft: rdn out* **5/1**[3]
2-2 **2** *1 3/4* **Rich Kid (IRE)**[23] 102 3-8-13 72 JamieSpencer 1 66
(S A Callaghan) *s.i.s: sn prom: chsd ldr 5f out: led over 2f out: rdn: hdd and hung lft over 1f out: styd on same pce* **4/6**[1]
511- **3** *9* **Shepherds Warning (IRE)**[34] 7272 3-9-2 69 RichardKingscote 3 44
(N J Vaughan) *led: hdd over 2f out: sn rdn: wknd and eased fnl f* **11/4**[2]
00-0 **4** *6* **Mujinda**[30] 20 3-8-8 40 ow2 (b[1]) MarkLawson(3) 5 23
(M Brittain) *chsd ldr 2f: rdn and wknd over 2f out* **150/1**
00-0 **5** *4* **Amazing Spirit**[7] 306 3-8-8 45 MickyFenton 6 9
(Miss V Haigh) *hld up: hdwy 1/2-way: rdn and wknd over 2f out* **40/1**
4 **6** *5* **Heavenly Encounter**[28] 38 3-8-12 0 AndrewElliott 2 —
(K R Burke) *chsd ldrs: rdn 1/2-way: wknd over 2f out* **33/1**

1m 32.24s (2.64) **Going Correction** +0.275s/f (Slow) **6** Ran SP% **109.4**
Speed ratings (Par 95): **95,93,82,75,71 65**
CSF £8.45 TOTE £6.70: £1.90, £1.10; EX 11.80.The winner was claimed by Ms Lucinda Featherstone for £7,000. Rich Kid was claimed by R A Harris for £8,000.
Owner Ms P M Marks **Bred** Wheelersland Stud **Trained** East Garston, Berks

FOCUS
They went a fair pace here and, in a pattern repeated throughout the afternoon, those that set the pace struggled as they battled the wind, and the race was set up for a closer. The winner is rated to his autumn form and the race is worth viewing positively.

394 **BOOK HALF TERM @ PONTIN'S (S) H'CAP** **2m 119y(P)**
2:40 (2:40) (Class 6) (0-60,60) 4-Y-0+ **£1,774** (£523; £262) **Stalls Low**

Form RPR
5-14 **1** **Zaffeu**[17] 171 7-9-6 58 VinceSlattery 5 59
(A G Juckes) *s.i.s: sn chsng ldrs: chal over 2f out: styd on u.p to ld wl ins fnl f* **9/2**[3]
63-2 **2** *2* **Perfect Storm**[21] 129 9-8-5 50 JackDean(7) 8 48
(W G M Turner) *hld up: hdwy over 5f out: chsd ldr over 4f out: led over 2f out: rdn and hung lft fr over 1f out: hdd wl ins fnl f* **6/4**[1]
5/43 **3** *nk* **Indian Star (GER)**[3] 348 10-9-1 60 (t) RichardEvans(7) 6 58
(P D Evans) *chsd ldr tl led 10f out: rdn and hdd over 2f out: styd on u.p* **9/1**
0-03 **4** *shd* **Trackattack**[15] 197 6-8-5 46 oh1 NeilChalmers(3) 3 44
(M Appleby) *prom: outpcd over 3f out: styd on ins fnl f* **9/1**
-510 **5** *27* **Isa'Af (IRE)**[16] 179 9-8-11 49 ow1 PhillipMakin 2 14
(P W Hiatt) *led to over 6f out: rdn over 5f out: wknd 4f out* **5/2**[2]
000/ **6** *25* **Tiffin Deano (IRE)**[20] 2536 6-8-5 46 oh1 TolleyDean(3) 4 —
(H J Manners) *hld up: rdn 1/2-way: bhd fnl 5f* **66/1**

3m 48.07s (6.27) **Going Correction** +0.275s/f (Slow) **6** Ran SP% **108.2**
Speed ratings (Par 101): **96,95,94,94,82 70**
CSF £10.86 CT £47.76 TOTE £6.30: £1.80, £1.20; EX 14.90 Trifecta £53.70 Pool £397.47 - 5.25 winning units..There was no bid for the winner.
Owner Whispering Winds **Bred** Patrick Eddery Ltd **Trained** Abberley, Worcs

FOCUS
A moderate staying handicap in which those who enjoyed a bit of cover early dominated at the finish. The form is rated through the third to recent marks.

395 **RACE ALL THE FAMILIES TO PONTIN'S H'CAP** **1m 141y(P)**
3:10 (3:11) (Class 6) (0-65,70) 4-Y-0+ **£2,047** (£604; £302) **Stalls Low**

Form RPR
06-1 **1** **Cape Velvet (IRE)**[14] 216 4-9-3 64 JamesDoyle 2 69+
(J W Hills) *hld up: hdwy over 2f out: led over 1f out: sn rdn and hung lft: r.o* **15/8**[1]
25-0 **2** *1* **Our Kes (IRE)**[16] 177 6-9-4 65 SimonWhitworth 8 68
(P Howling) *hld up: hdwy 2f out: sn rdn: r.o* **6/1**
135- **3** *shd* **Pelham Crescent (IRE)**[79] 6816 5-9-4 65 CatherineGannon 6 68
(B Palling) *hld up: hdwy u.p over 1f out: r.o* **11/2**[3]
1-31 **4** *nk* **Machinate (USA)**[4] 341 6-9-9 70 6ex LiamJones 4 72
(W M Brisbourne) *chsd ldrs: rdn over 2f out: hung lft over 1f out: styd on* **5/1**[2]
5-20 **5** *1/2* **Tanforan**[12] 235 6-9-4 65 DavidAllan 7 66
(B P J Baugh) *trckd ldr: led over 3f out: rdn and hdd over 1f out: no ex towards fin* **13/2**
15-5 **6** *10* **Fairdonna**[1] 375 5-8-10 57 ow1 PatDobbs 1 35
(Seamus Fahey, Ire) *trckd ldrs: racd keenly: hmpd over 3f out: sn rdn and wknd* **15/2**
050- **7** *5* **Golden Spectrum (IRE)**[143] 5307 9-8-11 63 (b) KevinGhunowa(5) 9 29
(R A Harris) *trckd ldrs: racd keenly: ev ch over 2f out: sn rdn and wknd* **16/1**
310/ **8** *6* **Princelywallywogan**[813] 6302 6-9-1 62 AndrewElliott 5 15
(John A Harris) *led 5f: rdn and wknd over 2f out* **12/1**

1m 53.59s (3.09) **Going Correction** +0.275s/f (Slow) **8** Ran SP% **119.8**
Speed ratings (Par 101): **97,96,96,95,95 86,81,76**
CSF £14.41 CT £55.11 TOTE £2.40: £1.20, £1.50, £1.80; EX 18.20 Trifecta £75.60 Pool £447.39 - 4.48 winning units..
Owner Mrs Kingham Mrs Moore Mr Ellis **Bred** C Gavin **Trained** Upper Lambourn, Berks

FOCUS
A modest handicap in which the hold-up performers once again came out on top. The time was moderate and the form does not feel solid.

396 **HAVE A BLAST @ PONTIN'S MAIDEN STKS** **1m 1f 103y(P)**
3:45 (3:46) (Class 5) 3-Y-0+ **£2,457** (£725; £362) **Stalls Low**

Form RPR
0- **1** **Man Of Gwent (UAE)**[252] 2005 4-9-12 0 JamesDoyle 3 74
(P D Evans) *hld up: hdwy over 3f out: rdn to ld wl ins fnl f: eased last strides* **6/1**[3]
43-4 **2** *1 1/4* **Saviour Sand (IRE)**[23] 95 4-9-12 70 PatDobbs 4 71
(D R C Elsworth) *led: rdn and hung lft fr over 1f out: hdd wl ins fnl f* **11/2**[2]
333- **3** *1* **Tenjack King**[132] 5646 3-8-5 73 FrancisNorton 2 64
(J A Osborne) *a.p: rdn to chse ldr over 2f out: styd on same pce ins fnl f* **5/6**[1]
0-0 **4** *12* **Colleoni (IRE)**[27] 52 3-8-5 0 HayleyTurner 1 39
(G A Butler) *hld up: pushed along over 3f out: nvr nr ldrs* **8/1**
60 **5** *2* **Dara Diva (IRE)**[3] 350 3-8-0 0 LiamJones 10 30
(W J Haggas) *chsd ldrs: rdn over 3f out: wknd 2f out* **25/1**
3- **6** *1 1/2* **Ginger Minx (IRE)**[35] 7258 3-7-9 0 DanielleMcCreery(5) 7 26
(N J Vaughan) *trckd ldrs: racd keenly: rdn and wknd over 2f out* **7/1**
7 *12* **Meadow Cottage (IRE)**[32] 5-9-12 0 CatherineGannon 6 11
(Mrs P Ford) *s.i.s: a bhd* **125/1**
0- **8** *7* **Mystik Megan**[64] 4334 7-9-7 0 GeorgeBaker 5 —
(M Mullineaux) *mid-div: hdwy 4f out: wknd 3f out* **50/1**
0/0 **P** **Son Of Samson (IRE)**[20] 144 7-9-9 0 TolleyDean(3) 8 —
(R J Price) *prom to 1/2-way: bhd whn p.u over 2f out* **20/1**

2m 3.05s (1.35) **Going Correction** +0.275s/f (Slow)
WFA 3 from 4yo+ 21lb **9** Ran SP% **119.2**
Speed ratings (Par 103): **105,103,103,92,90 89,78,72,—**
CSF £38.67 TOTE £9.50: £2.10, £1.80, £1.10; EX 38.80 Trifecta £132.80 Pool £712.67 - 3.81 winning units..
Owner K J Mercer **Bred** And Mrs K J Mercer **Trained** Pandy, Monmouths

FOCUS
A modest maiden featuring a gambled-on winner. The pace was sound and the runner-up is probably the best guide to the level.
Son Of Samson(IRE) Official explanation: jockey said gelding lost its action

397 **CALL PONTIN'S NOW 0844 576 5938 H'CAP** **5f 216y(P)**
4:15 (4:16) (Class 6) (0-65,65) 3-Y-O **£2,047** (£604; £302) **Stalls Low**

Form RPR
054- **1** **Vigano (IRE)**[51] 7117 3-9-4 65 (v[1]) GeorgeBaker 7 71
(S Kirk) *sn pushed along in rr: hdwy 1/2-way: led over 1f out: sn rdn and edgd lft: eased towards fin* **15/8**[1]
4445 **2** *2 1/2* **Weetfromthechaff**[4] 339 3-8-11 58 (v[1]) HayleyTurner 1 56
(R Hollinshead) *hld up: hdwy over 1f out: rdn to chse wnr fnl f: no imp* **7/2**[3]
54-3 **3** *1/2* **Upstanding**[22] 112 3-8-9 59 MarkLawson(3) 4 52
(M Brittain) *chsd ldrs: rdn and ev ch over 1f out: no ex ins fnl f* **17/2**
13 **4** *1 3/4* **The Little Fizzer (IRE)**[11] 243 3-9-3 64 FergusSweeney 3 52
(K R Burke) *chsd ldrs: led over 2f out: rdn and hdd over 1f out: wknd ins fnl f* **5/2**[2]
22-5 **5** *2 1/2* **Firewalker**[15] 199 3-9-0 61 PaulMulrennan 2 41
(B Smart) *chsd ldrs: rdn whn n.m.r over 2f out: wknd fnl f* **7/1**
05-5 **6** *1 1/2* **Mad Man Will (IRE)**[16] 183 3-8-10 57 SaleemGolam 8 32
(S C Williams) *sn pushed along: a in rr* **11/1**
360- **7** *3* **Jastaanhi**[35] 7258 3-7-13 51 oh2 KellyHarrison(5) 5 16
(J A Pickering) *prom: lost pl 4f out: wknd 2f out* **33/1**
04-5 **8** *19* **Casla Beag (IRE)**[11] 243 3-9-2 63 CatherineGannon 6 —
(B Palling) *led over 3f: wknd over 1f out* **40/1**

1m 17.04s (2.04) **Going Correction** +0.275s/f (Slow) **8** Ran SP% **122.3**
Speed ratings (Par 95): **97,93,91,89,86 84,80,54**
CSF £9.62 CT £47.10 TOTE £2.30: £1.20, £1.90, £2.30; EX 9.90 Trifecta £198.90 Pool £369.90 - 1.32 winning units. Place 6 £5.69, Place 5 £4.27..
Owner Norman Ormiston **Bred** John Bernard O'Connor **Trained** Upper Lambourn, Berks

FOCUS
This was run in a snowstorm and they went a good pace with the winner back to his best. Once again being covered up out of the elements paid dividends.

398 CROC MAKES PONTIN'S HALF TERM ROCK H'CAP 5f 216y(P)
() (Class 6) (0-52,) 4-Y-0+ £

399 WOLVERHAMPTON-RACECOURSE.CO.UK AMATEUR RIDERS' H'CAP 1m 4f 50y(P)
() (Class 5) (0-70,) 4-Y-0+ £

T/Plt: £5.70 to a £1 stake. Pool: £57,949.60. 7,328.95 winning tickets. T/Qpdt: £3.10 to a £1 stake. Pool: £3,692.20. 864.10 winning tickets. CR

386 KEMPTON (A.W) (R-H)
Saturday, February 2

OFFICIAL GOING: Standard
Wind: Light, across Weather: Dark

400 KEMPTON.CO.UK CLASSIFIED STKS 1m 2f (P)
6:20 (6:23) (Class 7) 4-Y-0+ £1,365 (£403; £201) Stalls High

Form RPR
0-43 1 **Tabulate**[10] 269 5-8-13 45 JimmyQuinn 8 53
(P Howling) *chsd ldrs: prog on inner 2f out: led over 1f out: drvn out* 7/2[1]
0-51 2 1 **My Mirasol**[12] 249 4-9-3 57 (p) MatthewDavies(7) 9 63+
(D E Cantillon) *pressed ldr and racd freely: led bnd 2f out and rn wd: hdd over 1f out: plugged on* 4/1[2]
6200 3 nk **Wizby**[6] 328 5-8-13 40 JamesDoyle 13 51
(P D Evans) *stdd s: hld up in last and wl off the pce: prog on outer fr 1/2-way: drvn 2f out: kpt on: nvr quite able to chal* 10/1
00-5 4 1 1/4 **Love You Always (USA)**[16] 189 8-8-13 40 (t) TGMcLaughlin 1 48
(Jane Chapple-Hyam) *settled in midfield: racd v awkwardly fr 3f out and lost pl u.p: hld hd v high and hanging but styd on again fr over 1f out* 9/2[3]
-030 5 1/2 **Come What July (IRE)**[8] 303 7-8-10 43 (v) TolleyDean(3) 4 47
(D Shaw) *settled in midfield: lost pl over 4f out: last wl over 1f out: styd on again fnl f* 9/1
42 6 nk **Vintage Quest**[12] 249 6-9-0 46 (p) VinceSlattery 6 47
(D Burchell) *chsd clr ldrs: rdn 3f out: effrt to chse ldng pair over 1f out and checked sltly: wknd ins fnl f* 16/1
3-52 7 nk **Sorbiesharry (IRE)**[18] 160 9-8-8 45 (p) ColinHaddon(5) 11 51+
(Mrs N Macauley) *hld up in midfield: nt clr run fr over 2f out to over 1f out: kpt on fnl f: no ch to rcvr* 7/1
020- 8 hd **Hester Brook (IRE)**[100] 6452 4-8-12 43 TPQueally 12 47+
(J G M O'Shea) *stdd s: hld up in last trio: gng wl 2f out: nt clr run over 1f out and swtchd lft: styd on fnl f: no ch* 20/1
000- 9 1 **Pearl Of Esteem**[111] 6211 5-8-13 38 ChrisCatlin 10 43
(J Pearce) *dwlt: hld up in last trio: rdn 2f out: no real prog* 50/1
0000 10 hd **Lady Firecracker (IRE)**[16] 197 4-8-12 40 (v) HayleyTurner 2 43
(J R Best) *settled towards rr: prog into midfield 3f out: no hdwy over 1f out: wknd ins fnl f* 40/1
5060 11 1 3/4 **Salvestro**[12] 242 5-8-10 41 (p) KirstyMilczarek(3) 5 40
(A W Carroll) *chsd ldng pair to wl over 1f out: wknd* 8/1
660- 12 6 **Sadler's Hill (IRE)**[45] 7187 4-8-12 44 LPKeniry 7 28
(M J McGrath) *chsd clr ldrs tl wknd over 2f out* 22/1
-060 13 1 3/4 **Rhuby River (IRE)**[10] 269 6-8-13 41 MickyFenton 3 24
(R Dickin) *led at gd clip: hdd 2f out: wkng rapidly whn n.m.r 1f out* 16/1

2m 8.19s (0.19) **Going Correction** +0.15s/f (Slow)
WFA 4 from 5yo+ 1lb 13 Ran SP% 128.4
Speed ratings (Par 97): **105,104,103,102,102 102,102,101,101,100 99,94,93**
CSF £17.97 TOTE £4.30: £1.90, £2.20, £4.10; EX 22.10.
Owner Richard Berenson **Bred** Millsec Limited **Trained** Newmarket, Suffolk

FOCUS
A very moderate classified contest, but they did go a good pace and the form looks sound enough.

401 RASHER FRITH MEMORIAL CLASSIFIED STKS 1m (P)
6:50 (6:52) (Class 7) 4-Y-0+ £1,365 (£403; £201) Stalls High

Form RPR
-656 1 **Busy Man (IRE)**[12] 242 9-9-0 43 StephenDonohoe 12 50
(R C Guest) *dwlt: sn in tch towards rr: prog over 2f out: chsd ldr fnl f: drvn and styd on to ld last 50yds* 13/2[3]
-000 2 nk **Charlie Bear**[6] 328 7-9-0 41 (b) AdrianMcCarthy 10 50
(Miss Z C Davison) *s.i.s and rousted along early: wl in rr: prog over 2f out: r.o fnl f: tk 2nd last strides* 12/1
4-50 3 nk **Big Ralph**[9] 282 5-8-9 42 JamesO'Reilly(5) 9 49
(D K Ivory) *trckd ldng pair: effrt to ld over 1f out: worn down last 50yds* 5/1[2]
-005 4 1 1/4 **Bahhmirage (IRE)**[12] 249 5-9-0 42 (p) JimmyQuinn 11 46
(C N Kellett) *wl in tch in midfield: drvn to try to cl on outer over 2f out: nt qckn over 1f out: kpt on fnl f* 40/1
000- 5 hd **Mr Belvedere**[98] 6175 7-9-0 45 (tp) JamesDoyle 13 46
(A J Lidderdale) *disp ld after 3f tl led 3f out: hd high over 2f out: hdd over 1f out: wknd ins fnl f* 10/1
0-45 6 3/4 **Marmooq**[8] 305 5-9-0 45 (e[1]) ChrisCatlin 6 44
(M J Attwater) *t.k.h: hld up in rr: last 3f out: prog over 2f out: chsd ldrs but nt qckn over 1f out: kpt on* 5/1[2]
0/4 7 2 **Up Dee Creek**[13] 236 6-9-0 40 LiamJones 3 39
(W M Brisbourne) *trckd ldng pair: rdn over 2f out: stl chsng wl over 1f out: edgd rt and wknd* 12/1
/60- 8 1 3/4 **Whos Counting**[96] 6532 4-8-9 42 HaddenFrost(5) 4 35
(R J Hodges) *nvr on terms w ldrs: rdn and no real prog over 2f out* 33/1
06-5 9 1 1/2 **Beckenham's Secret**[18] 164 4-8-11 45 KirstyMilczarek(3) 7 32
(A W Carroll) *led or disp ld to 3f out: edgd lft 2f out: wknd* 4/1[1]
0/60 10 1 3/4 **Persian Khanoom (IRE)**[12] 242 6-9-0 41 PatDobbs 8 28
(D E Cantillon) *hld up in rr: rdn 3f out: brief effrt over 2f out: sn btn* 16/1
06 11 1 1/2 **Northstar Express (IRE)**[13] 239 5-9-0 37 SamHitchcott 14 24
(J L Spearing) *nvr bttr than midfield on inner: struggling over 2f out* 66/1
00-0 12 2 1/2 **For Eileen**[8] 303 4-9-0 37 VinceSlattery 1 19
(D Burchell) *t.k.h on outer in midfield: rdn over 3f out: sn btn* 100/1
0-52 13 3/4 **Club Captain (USA)**[20] 147 5-9-0 45 TPQueally 2 17
(T D McCarthy) *wl in tch on outer: rdn 3f out: wknd over 2f out* 4/1[1]
000- 14 5 **Rangali Belle**[66] 6963 4-9-0 42 (e[1]) SimonWhitworth 5 5
(C A Horgan) *plld hrd on outer and hld up: wknd over 2f out* 33/1

1m 40.9s (1.10) **Going Correction** +0.15s/f (Slow) 14 Ran SP% 127.8
Speed ratings (Par 97): **100,99,99,98,97 97,95,93,91,90 88,86,85,80**
CSF £85.22 TOTE £7.10: £2.20, £4.10, £2.50; EX 88.70.
Owner James Roche **Bred** Nicholas Roche **Trained** Carburton, Notts

■ Stewards' Enquiry : James O'Reilly three-day ban: used whip with excessive force above shoulder height (Feb 13-15)

FOCUS
A very moderate classified event, but they went a decent pace. Weak form.
Up Dee Creek Official explanation: jockey said mare hung right

402 DIGIBET H'CAP 7f (P)
7:20 (7:21) (Class 6) (0-52,52) 4-Y-0+ £2,047 (£604; £302) Stalls High

Form RPR
26-0 1 **Over To You Bert**[15] 209 9-8-7 52 ow1 HaddenFrost(5) 3 63
(R J Hodges) *w ldr: led over 2f out: hrd pressed over 1f out: kpt on wl: asserted last 75yds* 14/1
-313 2 1 **Double Valentine**[10] 264 5-8-7 50 KirstyMilczarek(3) 10 58
(R Ingram) *dwlt: hld up in last pair: gd prog over 2f out to press wnr over 1f out: nt qckn and hld wl ins fnl f* 4/1[2]
460- 3 1 **Mix N Match**[80] 4532 4-8-9 49 ChrisCatlin 6 54
(R M Stronge) *wl in rr: rdn 3f out: no real prog tl styd on fnl f to take 3rd nr fin* 16/1
0-16 4 1/2 **Certifiable**[10] 267 7-8-4 49 (v[1]) RobynBrisland(5) 9 53
(Miss Z C Davison) *plld hrd: trckd ldrs: rdn and nt qckn 2f out: one pce after* 8/1
06-6 5 3 **Wiltshire (IRE)**[30] 32 6-8-10 50 MickyFenton 1 46
(P T Midgley) *dwlt: towards rr on outer: wd bnd 3f out: tried to cl on ldrs 2f out: no imp 1f out: gng v slowly nr fin* 7/1[3]
-221 6 1 3/4 **Jessica Wigmo**[10] 276 5-8-10 50 JamesDoyle 5 41+
(A W Carroll) *awkward s: hld up in rr: forced v wd bnd 3f out: nvr on terms after* 7/2[1]
5-20 7 2 1/2 **Palais Polaire**[10] 276 6-8-9 52 (p) TravisBlock(3) 7 36
(J A Geake) *trckd ldng gp: prog on inner over 2f out: hanging v bdly fnl 2f: wknd* 8/1
U0-5 8 1/2 **Ma Ridge**[24] 95 4-8-10 50 TPQueally 2 33
(T D McCarthy) *chsd ldrs: lost pl u.p wl over 2f out: sn btn* 12/1
-412 9 1 **Sion Hill (IRE)**[14] 232 7-8-8 48 (p) JimmyQuinn 4 28
(John A Harris) *t.k.h on outer: prom tl wknd over 2f out* 4/1[2]
300- 10 5 **Suhayl Star (IRE)**[94] 6587 4-8-10 50 LPKeniry 8 17
(P Burgoyne) *led: hdd and hanging bdly over 2f out: sn wknd* 20/1

1m 27.07s (1.07) **Going Correction** +0.15s/f (Slow) 10 Ran SP% 121.9
Speed ratings (Par 101): **99,97,96,96,92 90,87,87,86,80**
CSF £72.59 CT £958.72 TOTE £18.20: £3.80, £2.80, £8.80; EX 108.00.
Owner R J Hodges **Bred** J K S Cresswell **Trained** Charlton Mackrell, Somerset

FOCUS
A slow-motion finish to this very moderate handicap, which had been run at an even gallop.
Double Valentine Official explanation: jockey said mare was denied a clear run
Certifiable Official explanation: vet said gelding bled from the nose

403 DIGIBET.COM CLAIMING STKS 6f (P)
7:50 (7:50) (Class 6) 3-Y-0 £2,047 (£604; £302) Stalls High

Form RPR
43-5 1 **Wee Buns**[11] 257 3-8-3 62 ChrisCatlin 6 61
(S Kirk) *trckd ldng pair: clsd on inner to dispute ld over 1f out: rdn and in command fnl f* 15/8[1]
4533 2 1 1/2 **Orange Square (IRE)**[6] 324 3-8-6 66 PatrickHills(5) 1 64
(R Hannon) *trckd ldr: clsd to dispute ld over 1f out: fnd nil and btn fnl f* 15/2
2-23 3 2 1/2 **Copperbottomed (IRE)**[23] 108 3-8-9 67 (be) PatCosgrave 5 54
(J R Boyle) *hld up in last pair: rdn and no rspnse over 2f out: plugged on to take 3rd ent fnl f* 5/2[2]
03-2 4 3 **Coole Dodger (IRE)**[10] 266 3-8-10 68 KylieManser(7) 4 52
(B G Powell) *led: hdd & wknd over 1f out* 5/1
50-5 5 4 **Hold That Call (USA)**[31] 12 3-8-12 63 HaddenFrost(5) 2 40
(R Hannon) *restless stalls: dwlt: plld hrd early: hld up: wknd tamely over 2f out* 4/1[3]

1m 14.55s (1.45) **Going Correction** +0.15s/f (Slow) 5 Ran SP% 111.8
Speed ratings (Par 95): **96,94,90,86,81**
CSF £15.86 TOTE £2.80: £1.60, £2.30; EX 15.70.The winner was claimed by Ms P M Marks for £5,000.
Owner Club ISM & S Kirk **Bred** M J Hills **Trained** Upper Lambourn, Berks

FOCUS
A weak claimer, but run at a decent pace. The winner was seemingly back to his best and the second to form.
Hold That Call(USA) Official explanation: jockey said gelding had no more to give

404 DIGIBET SPORTS BETTING H'CAP 6f (P)
8:20 (8:22) (Class 5) (0-70,71) 4-Y-0+ £2,590 (£770; £385; £192) Stalls High

Form RPR
54-3 1 **Radiator Rooney (IRE)**[28] 54 5-8-6 58 (v) ChrisCatlin 6 67+
(Patrick Morris, Ire) *t.k.h: trckd ldr: urged along to ld over 1f out w hd to one side: kpt on wl fnl f* 2/1[1]
1130 2 1 **Mind Alert**[4] 347 7-8-10 62 (v) JamesDoyle 3 68
(D Shaw) *hld up in last pair: drvn and prog on inner fr 2f out: wnt 2nd last 100yds: no real imp on wnr* 16/1
120- 3 nk **Red Rudy**[135] 5568 6-8-11 66 KirstyMilczarek(3) 2 71+
(A W Carroll) *hld up in fnl pair: sltly checked over 2f out: stl last over 1f out: gd prog ent fnl f: kpt on same pce last 75yds to snatch 3rd on line* 16/1
1421 4 shd **Obe Royal**[13] 241 4-8-12 71 (b) RichardEvans(7) 8 76
(P D Evans) *t.k.h and sn trckd ldng pair: shkn up and nt qckn 2f out: kpt on same pce after* 6/1
3535 5 shd **Hucking Hill (IRE)**[5] 334 4-9-0 66 (b) HayleyTurner 5 70
(J R Best) *hld up bhd ldrs: shkn up 2f out: nt qckn over 1f out: kpt on same pce after* 7/1
20-0 6 1 1/2 **Tamino (IRE)**[20] 150 5-8-13 65 (t) JimmyQuinn 7 65
(P Howling) *led: rdn and hdd over 1f out: chsd wnr tl wknd last 100yds* 11/2[3]
-112 7 1/2 **Muktasb (USA)**[7] 312 7-8-13 68 (v) TolleyDean(3) 4 66
(D Shaw) *settled in last trio: rdn and no prog over 2f out: no imp after* 11/2[3]
2-50 8 3 **Methaaly (IRE)**[5] 342 5-9-2 68 GeorgeBaker 1 56
(M Mullineaux) *trckd ldrs: rdn 3f out: qckn 2f out: wknd fnl f* 9/2[2]

1m 12.74s (-0.36) **Going Correction** +0.15s/f (Slow) 8 Ran SP% 120.8
Speed ratings (Par 103): **108,106,106,106,106 104,103,99**
CSF £40.28 CT £426.13 TOTE £3.00: £1.30, £3.30, £3.40; EX 61.20.
Owner Hogs Syndicate **Bred** Barry Lyons **Trained** Ruanbeg, Co. Kildare

FOCUS
A decent race for the grade on paper, but the early pace was surprisingly steady, which didn't suit some of these, and the form needs treating with caution. The winner was always well placed but looks back to his best

405 RASHER FRITH MEMORIAL H'CAP 2m (P)
8:50 (8:51) (Class 4) (0-85,81) 4-Y-0+ £4,210 (£1,252; £625; £312) Stalls High

Form RPR
3-22 1 **Jack Rolfe**[10] 268 6-10-0 81 GeorgeBaker 8 86
(G L Moore) *trckd ldng trio: lost pl 5f out: effrt on inner over 2f out: led over 1f out: drvn out: jst hld on* 7/4[1]
6/0- 2 ½ **Moon Mix (FR)**[27] 5578 5-9-13 80 J-PGuillambert 3 88+
(J R Jenkins) *dropped in and hld up in last: repeatedly rn into trble fr over 2f out to over 1f out: plld wd jst over 1f out: flew home fnl f: jst failed: unlucky* 25/1
1-53 3 1 ½ **Abounding**[10] 272 4-8-7 66 ChrisCatlin 6 69
(M J Attwater) *t.k.h: trckd ldr to over 4f out: cl up and stl keen 3f out: nt qckn 2f out: kpt on to chse wnr ins fnl f: no imp: lost 2nd nr fin* 9/2[3]
006- 4 1 ½ **Stoop To Conquer**[37] 3273 8-9-6 76 KirstyMilczarek(3) 2 77
(A W Carroll) *t.k.h: hld up in midfield: prog 3f out: jnd wnr over 1f out: sn outpcd* 8/1
2/5- 5 1 ¼ **At The Money**[12] 1793 5-9-1 68 HayleyTurner 5 68
(J M P Eustace) *led: set slow pce to 4f out: drvn and hdd over 1f out: wknd fnl f* 4/1[2]
00-6 6 ½ **Linden Lime**[10] 268 6-9-0 67 PaulDoe 9 66
(Jamie Poulton) *hld up towards rr: started pulling hrd 7f out: rdn and nt qckn over 2f out: one pce after* 6/1
0-41 7 6 **Flame Creek (IRE)**[10] 272 12-9-8 75 EdwardCreighton 7 67
(E J Creighton) *hld up in last pair but wl in tch: nt qckn over 2f out: wknd rapidly fnl f* 9/1
440- 8 1 ¾ **Montosari**[207] 3397 9-8-9 62 IanMongan 4 52
(R A Teal) *trckd ldng pair tl jnd ldr 4f out: wknd jst over 2f out* 16/1

3m 41.94s (11.84) **Going Correction** +0.15s/f (Slow)
WFA 4 from 5yo+ 6lb 8 Ran SP% **119.7**
Speed ratings (Par 105): **76,75,75,74,73 73,70,69**
CSF £54.13 CT £181.67 TOTE £3.10: £1.10, £3.90, £1.60; EX 63.90.
Owner Mrs Sarah Diamandis & Mrs Celia Woollett **Bred** W H F Carson **Trained** Woodingdean, E Sussex

FOCUS
This looked like an ordinary staying handicap for the grade beforehand and the race itself turned into a bit of a farce, with the pace very steady for the first ten furlongs or so. A few of these raced keenly as a result and the form needs to be treated with caution.

406 BRIAN CULLOM 60TH BIRTHDAY H'CAP 1m 3f (P)
9:20 (9:24) (Class 5) (0-70,75) 4-Y-0+ £2,590 (£770; £385; £192) Stalls High

Form RPR
6-3 1 **Rising Force (IRE)**[13] 240 5-9-0 64 (b) LiamJones 6 70
(J L Spearing) *hld up in midfield: stdy prog gng wl fr over 2f out: rdn to ld 1f out: hung lft but asserted nr fin* 20/1
-211 2 ½ **Sri Kuantan (IRE)**[7] 316 4-9-9 75 (t) ChrisCatlin 5 80+
(P F I Cole) *t.k.h: led at stdy pce: qcknd over 2f out: hdd 1f out: kpt on but hld nr fin* 7/4[1]
5-43 3 1 **Most Definitely (IRE)**[24] 91 8-9-0 64 JamesDoyle 3 67
(R M Stronge) *hld up in last trio: stdy prog fr 2f out: rdn ent fnl f and sn wnt 3rd: no ch to chal* 9/1
6 4 ¾ **Artreju (GER)**[20] 150 5-9-4 68 FergusSweeney 8 70+
(G L Moore) *t.k.h: hld up in last pair: effrt over 2f out: styd on fnl f to take 4th nr fin: nvr any ch* 25/1
11-4 5 ½ **Highest Esteem**[14] 224 4-9-2 68 (p) GeorgeBaker 9 69
(G L Moore) *cl up: chsd ldr over 2f out to over 1f out: fdd ins fnl f* 9/4[2]
600- 6 shd **Sir Liam (USA)**[155] 5014 4-9-3 69 IanMongan 4 70
(R A Teal) *t.k.h: hld up in midfield: effrt to chse ldrs and cl enough 2f out: nt qckn over 1f out: one pce after5* 6/1[3]
3-31 7 nk **Rollin 'n Tumblin**[24] 88 4-8-9 64 KirstyMilczarek(3) 1 64
(W Jarvis) *hld up in midfield: clsd on ldrs 4f out: rdn 2f out: nt qckn and sn btn* 6/1[3]
8 1 **Foreign King (USA)**[58] 4821 4-8-11 63 JimmyQuinn 2 62
(J W Mullins) *chsd ldr to over 2f out: sn btn* 40/1
20-5 9 1 ¼ **Kadouchski (FR)**[14] 234 4-8-7 59 DeanMcKeown 7 56
(Miss E C Lavelle) *s.s: t.k.h: hld up in last pair: shuffled along and no prog over 2f out* 14/1

2m 25.52s (3.62) **Going Correction** +0.15s/f (Slow)
WFA 4 from 5yo+ 2lb 9 Ran SP% **123.4**
Speed ratings (Par 103): **92,91,90,90,90 89,89,88,88**
CSF £58.22 CT £369.71 TOTE £17.80: £5.60, £1.20, £3.10; EX 88.80 TRIFECTA Price £199.53, Price 5 £100.99..
Owner Masonaires **Bred** Moyglare Stud Farm Ltd **Trained** Kinnersley, Worcs

FOCUS
This looked like an ordinary handicap for the grade and they went a steady pace for much of the way.
T/Plt: £204.20 to a £1 stake. Pool: £111,818.90. 399.55 winning tickets. T/Qpdt: £33.40 to a £1 stake. Pool: £7,470.60. 165.40 winning tickets. JN

352 LINGFIELD (L-H)
Saturday, February 2

OFFICIAL GOING: Standard
Wind: Moderate, half-behind

407 LINGFIELD PARK FOR EXHIBITIONS APPRENTICE H'CAP 7f (P)
1:10 (1:10) (Class 6) (0-65,65) 4-Y-0+ £1,876 (£554; £277) Stalls Low

Form RPR
33-6 1 **Ever Cheerful**[20] 149 7-8-11 62 (p) PNolan(5) 1 71
(A B Haynes) *t.k.h: mde all: rdn ent fnl f: kpt on* 11/1
2-10 2 nk **Emma Jean Lad (IRE)**[12] 246 4-9-1 64 JackDean(3) 3 72
(J S Moore) *sn in tch: wnt 2nd over 2f out: rdn and kpt on fnl f* 5/1[3]
60-1 3 2 **Follow The Flag (IRE)**[17] 181 4-9-1 64 JackMitchell(3) 4 67
(C F Wall) *in tch: rdn over 2f out: kpt on one pce fnl f* 9/4[1]
353- 4 nk **Convivial Spirit**[56] 7073 4-9-5 65 (t) NicolPolli 5 67
(E F Vaughan) *in rr: c wd into st: r.o fnl f: nvr nrr* 3/1[2]
0-42 5 nk **Copper King**[8] 302 4-9-5 65 PatrickHills 2 66
(Miss Tor Sturgis) *trckd ldr to over 2f out: sn rdn: wknd ins fnl f* 5/1[3]
020- 6 shd **Juzilla (IRE)**[122] 5917 4-9-3 63 JamieJones 6 64
(W R Swinburn) *s.i.s: hld up: rdn over 1f out: a in rr* 16/1
3-52 7 1 **Imperium**[10] 276 7-8-7 58 KylieManser(5) 7 56
(Jean-Rene Auvray) *hld up: effrt wl over 1f out: sn btn* 11/1

1m 24.48s (-0.32) **Going Correction** -0.025s/f (Stan) 7 Ran SP% **111.7**
Speed ratings (Par 101): **100,99,97,97,96 96,95**
CSF £61.13 TOTE £13.10: £5.90, £2.70; EX 65.40.
Owner Abacus Employment Services Ltd **Bred** Southill Stud **Trained** Limpley Stoke, Bath

FOCUS
A modest handicap restricted to apprentices who had not ridden more than 50 winners. The winning time was 2.96 seconds quicker than the later maiden and the form looks fairly sound.
Imperium Official explanation: jockey said, regarding running and riding, her orders were to drop in and make ground throughout, and adding that as the gelding was drawn wide not to come wide and stay up near the pace, further adding that she was denied a clear run until 180yds out.

408 PLAY GOLF @ LINGFIELD PARK (S) STKS 1m (P)
1:40 (1:40) (Class 6) 4-Y-0+ £1,774 (£523; £262) Stalls High

Form RPR
0-16 1 **Dushstorm (IRE)**[20] 148 7-9-2 67 (p) KirstyMilczarek(3) 2 72+
(M Botti) *in tch: wnt 2nd over 2f out: led appr fnl f: pushed out* 4/5[1]
02-0 2 1 ¾ **The Jailer**[23] 115 5-9-0 55 TPQueally 1 63
(J G M O'Shea) *set stdy pce: rdn 2f out: hdd appr fnl f: one pce after* 10/3[3]
124- 3 9 **Defi (IRE)**[58] 7047 6-9-5 60 (b) PhillipMakin 3 54
(Miss L A Perratt) *trckd ldr tl rdn over 2f out: wknd ent fnl f: eased* 5/2[2]

1m 37.5s (-0.70) **Going Correction** -0.025s/f (Stan) 3 Ran SP% **107.2**
Speed ratings (Par 101): **102,100,91**
CSF £3.56 TOTE £1.70; EX 3.40.The winner was bought in for 6,800gns.
Owner Giuliano Manfredini **Bred** M Fahy **Trained** Newmarket, Suffolk

FOCUS
Just the three runners and quite obviously an uncompetitive seller. The pace was reasonable considering the small field.

409 LINGFIELDPARK.CO.UK H'CAP 1m 2f (P)
2:15 (2:15) (Class 4) (0-85,84) 4-Y-0+ £4,100 (£1,227; £613; £306; £152) Stalls Low

Form RPR
4-22 1 **Mataram (USA)**[8] 309 5-9-1 79 ChrisCatlin 3 89+
(W Jarvis) *in tch tl short of room and swtchd rt over 1f out: str run fnl f to ld nr fin* 4/1[3]
5-11 2 nk **Art Man**[17] 185 5-9-1 79 GeorgeBaker 1 87
(G L Moore) *hld up on ins: hdwy on ins 2f out: led over 1f out: rdn and hdd nr fin* 9/4[1]
022- 3 nk **Basra (IRE)**[34] 7281 5-9-4 82 DaneO'Neill 7 89
(Miss Jo Crowley) *trckd ldrs: rdn and ev ch ent fnl f: kpt on u.p* 9/2
-356 4 shd **Fusili (IRE)**[7] 315 5-9-0 81 (b) KirstyMilczarek(3) 5 88
(N P Littmoden) *in tch tl lost pl on outside ent st: hdwy appr fnl f: r.o wl* 7/1
050- 5 nk **Crossbow Creek**[104] 6169 10-9-5 83 LPKeniry 2 89
(M G Rimell) *hld up: hdwy on ins over 1f out: r.o: nvr nrr* 20/1
102- 6 ½ **Northern Spy (USA)**[48] 7163 4-9-5 84 PatDobbs 4 89
(S Dow) *trckd ldr tl rdn and one pce appr fnl f* 11/4[2]
426- 7 7 **Dragon Slayer (IRE)**[48] 7163 6-8-13 77 FrankieMcDonald 6 68
(P A Blockley) *t.k.h: led tl hdd & wknd over 1f out* 25/1

2m 3.69s (-2.91) **Going Correction** -0.025s/f (Stan)
WFA 4 from 5yo+ 1lb 7 Ran SP% **116.7**
Speed ratings (Par 105): **110,109,109,109,109 108,103**
CSF £13.96 TOTE £4.70: £2.30, £1.70; EX 15.60.
Owner Sales Race 2001 Syndicate **Bred** Ben P Walden Jr And James Anthony **Trained** Newmarket, Suffolk

FOCUS
A good, competitive handicap. The first six finished in a bunch, but this still looks reliable form and the winner was perhaps value for a bit further, having had to wait for a run.

410 BOOK ONLINE @ LINGFIELDPARK.CO.UK H'CAP 1m 4f (P)
2:45 (2:46) (Class 2) (0-100,106) 4-Y-0+
£9,971 (£2,985; £1,492; £747; £372; £187) Stalls Low

Form RPR
050- 1 **John Terry (IRE)**[43] 6759 5-8-10 89 TPQueally 2 97
(Mrs A J Perrett) *led for 2f: styd prom on ins: rdn to ld ins fnl f: hld on wl* 8/1
2-11 2 nk **Wicked Daze (IRE)**[24] 96 5-8-7 86 J-PGuillambert 4 93
(Sir Mark Prescott) *sn trckd ldr: led 3f out: hdd 1f out: rallied wl and kpt on to line* 3/1[1]
1-23 3 nk **Sgt Schultz (IRE)**[7] 315 5-8-8 87 LPKeniry 5 95+
(J S Moore) *hld up: rdn and hdwy over 2f out: short of room and swtchd rt over 1f out: r.o wl ins fnl f* 10/3[2]
34-1 4 ¾ **Millville**[28] 61 8-9-13 106 SteveDrowne 3 112
(M A Jarvis) *in tch: wnt 2nd over 2f out: led briefly 1f out: no ex fnl 50yds* 10/3[2]
000- 5 1 ¾ **Kames Park (IRE)**[132] 5664 6-8-11 90 PhillipMakin 8 93
(Miss L A Perratt) *hld up: hdwy to chal on outside 2f out: one pce fnl f* 16/1
22-2 6 3 ½ **Polish Power (GER)**[28] 61 8-8-8 90 TolleyDean(3) 1 87
(J S Moore) *in rr: rdn 7f out: effrt over 2f out: wknd appr fnl f* 11/2[3]
42- 7 8 **Eumene (IRE)**[50] 7147 5-8-8 87 ChrisCatlin 6 72
(C C Bealby) *prom on outside: rdn 3f out: wknd 2f out* 18/1
31-4 8 6 **Invasian (IRE)**[28] 61 7-9-0 93 MickyFenton 7 68
(P W D'Arcy) *plld hrd: led after 2f: hdd 3f out: wknd qckly* 16/1

2m 28.19s (-4.81) **Going Correction** -0.025s/f (Stan) course record 8 Ran SP% **114.7**
Speed ratings (Par 109): **115,114,114,114,112 110,105,101**
CSF £32.39 CT £96.50 TOTE £10.50: £2.20, £1.80, £1.50; EX 40.90 Trifecta £142.60 Pool £387.75 - 1.93 winning units..
Owner A D Spence **Bred** Dr T A Ryan **Trained** Pulborough, W Sussex

FOCUS
There was no pace early before Invasian rushed up to increase the tempo heading out on the final circuit, but the gallop slowed once again when the leader dropped away before the turn for home. Nevertheless, these were a decent bunch and the form looks sound enough, with the winner to last year's turf form and the progressive second up another 4lb.

NOTEBOOK
John Terry(IRE), last of six on his hurdling debut in a Grade 2 at Ascot in December, returned to the Flat at the top of his game. He was probably a fortunate winner, with the third looking an unlucky loser, but this still cannot have been far off a career-best effort. Often a spin over hurdles can freshen up a horse's mind so, whilst the form needs treating with a little caution, it would be no surprise to see him remain competitive off higher marks. (op 12-1)
Wicked Daze(IRE) was just denied the hat-trick off a mark 8lb higher than when making all in slightly lesser company over course and distance on his previous start. He would probably have preferred a strong end-to-end gallop and looks the type to keep improving. (op 5-2 tchd 10-3)

Sgt Schultz(IRE) ◆, who looked a little unlucky when third over 1m2f round here the previous week, again found trouble and would have won with anything like a clear run. Having been waited with, he was short of room when the pace slowed before the turn for home and, quite a big horse, he was unable to organise himself in time to take a gap early in the straight, with Wicked Daze shutting it in his face. He eventually switched out wide, but again took time to find top gear and just got going too late. Considering he was totally unsuited by the way the race was run, yet still would have won with a better trip suggests he is a little way ahead of the Handicapper. Official explanation: jockey said gelding was denied a clear run (op 11-4)

Millville was 3lb higher than when winning a less competitive handicap over course and distance on his previous start and had no easy task conceding upwards of 13lb all round. This was a decent effort in defeat. (op 4-1)

Kames Park(IRE) had won his last two starts on Polytrack, with both victories gained off a slow pace round here, so he would not have minded the way the race was run. This was his first start for a new trainer and he might have needed this first run in over four months. (op 14-1)

Polish Power(GER) looked in trouble a fair way out and was well below form. (op 6-1)

Invasian(IRE) Official explanation: jockey said gelding hung left in final 4f

411 ARENALEISUREPLC.COM H'CAP 5f (P)

3:20 (3:21) (Class 2) (0-100,105) 4-Y-0+

£9,971 (£2,985; £1,492; £747; £372; £187) **Stalls** High

Form — RPR

61-2 **1** **Ebraam (USA)**[14] 226 5-8-8 **93** TolleyDean(3) 9 104+
(D Shaw) *hld up in rr and swtchd to ins fr wd draw early on: hdwy over 1f out: strong run fnl f to ld cl home* **7/2**[2]

000- **2** *nk* **Johnstown Lad (IRE)**[57] 7063 4-7-11 **86** oh2 (t) MHarley(7) 5 96
(Niall Moran, Ire) *chsd ldrs: wnt 2nd over 1f out: ev ch wl ins fnl f: ct by wnr cl home* **12/1**

11-2 **3** *½* **Silver Prelude**[21] 137 7-8-1 **86** oh1 KirstyMilczarek(3) 2 94
(D K Ivory) *led tl hdd wl ins fnl f: lost 2nd nr fin* **5/1**

231- **4** *½* **First Order**[56] 7078 7-8-4 **86** oh3 (v) PaulHanagan 6 92
(Miss L A Perratt) *a.p: rdn and nt qckn ins fnl f* **8/1**

1-21 **5** *¾* **Northern Empire (IRE)**[18] 162 5-8-7 **89** JamieSpencer 3 93
(K A Ryan) *hld up: hdwy over 1f out: r.o fnl f: nvr nrr* **10/3**[1]

0-03 **6** *hd* **Fyodor (IRE)**[5] 337 7-9-1 **97** TPQueally 4 103+
(W J Haggas) *hld up: r.o ins fnl f: nvr nrr* **9/2**[3]

0-05 **7** *1 ¼* **Magic Glade**[18] 162 9-8-4 **86** oh6 AdrianMcCarthy 1 84
(Peter Grayson) *in tch: rdn and wknd fnl f* **33/1**

414- **8** *nk* **Maltese Falcon**[36] 7255 8-9-9 **105** (t) ChrisCatlin 7 102
(P F I Cole) *chsd ldrs: wknd fnl f* **8/1**

50-6 **9** *1 ½* **Diane's Choice**[18] 162 5-8-4 **86** oh2 JimmyQuinn 8 78
(J Akehurst) *in rr: lost tch over 1f out* **25/1**

3-11 **10** *hd* **Tartatartufata**[25] 84 6-8-0 **89** (v) PatrickDonaghy(7) 10 80
(D Shaw) *prom on outside tl wknd wl over 1f out* **20/1**

57.64 secs (-1.16) **Going Correction** -0.025s/f (Stan) **10** Ran SP% **121.6**
Speed ratings (Par 109): **108,107,106,105,104 104,102,101,99,99**
CSF £45.80 CT £220.29 TOTE £4.80: £1.70, £3.60, £1.60; EX 83.40 Trifecta £487.30 Pool £487.30 - 1.18 winning units..
Owner The Circle Bloodstock I Limited **Bred** Shadwell Farm LLC **Trained** Danethorpe, Notts

FOCUS
A very good sprint handicap, despite half the field racing from out of the weights, and seriously competitive. Predictably enough they went a very strong pace, and the winning time was 1.86 seconds quicker than the three-year-old maiden. Another improved effort from the winner, and there's a chance his new RPR may still underestimate him.

NOTEBOOK
Ebraam(USA) had a career-high mark to contend with - 3lb higher than when second over 6f here last time and 7lb higher than when winning over 6f round here two starts back - but he showed he remains very much on the up with a narrow victory. Dropping back in trip, he was ridden with loads of confidence by Tolley Dean and still had plenty to find at the top of the straight, but he flew home and got up near the line. He is clearly a sprint handicapper to keep on side. (op 4-1 tchd 11-2)

Johnstown Lad(IRE), in good form in defeat on the Polytrack at Dundalk towards the end of last year, ran a blinder in defeat from 2lb out of the handicap. He was always well placed and looked to have his chance, but his 7lb claimer was not the strongest late on and he was reeled in. (tchd 14-1)

Silver Prelude, just pegged back after going off very quickly in a 6f conditions contest round here on his previous start, tried to repeat the tactics and ran another stormer in defeat. From 1lb out of the handicap he was effectively 15lb higher than when winning at Wolverhampton two starts back and, bizarrely enough, he looks to have found significant improvement at the age of seven. (op 4-1 tchd 7-2)

First Order was 8lb higher (including 3lb out of the handicap) than when winning at Wolverhampton on his previous start and ran well. (tchd 9-1)

Northern Empire(IRE) struggled to get competitive and was unable to defy a mark 4lb higher than when winning at Kempton on his previous start. (op 13-2)

Fyodor(IRE) looked to be full of running at the top of the straight, but he made only limited progress once in the clear and, if anything, his run flattened out late on. (op 4-1 tchd 10-3)

412 HOTEL COMING TO LINGFIELD PARK MAIDEN STKS 5f (P)

3:50 (3:50) (Class 5) 3-Y-0

£2,331 (£693; £346; £173) **Stalls** High

Form — RPR

05- **1** **Stoneacre Pat (IRE)**[42] 7220 3-9-3 0 GeorgeBaker 4 63
(Peter Grayson) *mde all: drvn out fnl f* **40/1**

2 *¾* **Stoneacre Chris (USA)** 3-8-12 0 LPKeniry 2 55
(Peter Grayson) *a in tch on ins: chsd wnr over 1f out: kpt on* **20/1**

3 *¾* **Allium (IRE)** 3-8-12 0 JamieSpencer 5 52+
(B W Hills) *t.k.h: hld up: hdwy 1/2-way: r.o fnl f* **11/8**[2]

0- **4** *½* **Premier Yank (USA)**[124] 5856 3-9-3 0 TPQueally 9 67+
(J A Osborne) *s.i.s: hmpd 2f out: c wd into st: r.o wl ins fnl f* **5/4**[1]

0- **5** *hd* **Capriccioso**[45] 7190 3-8-12 0 FergusSweeney 6 50
(G L Moore) *trckd wnr tl rdn and wknd ent fnl f* **9/2**[3]

0 **6** *½* **Rightcar Hull (IRE)**[5] 343 3-8-12 0 AdrianMcCarthy 1 48
(Peter Grayson) *mid-div: outpcd over 2f out: kpt on ins fnl f* **66/1**

0- **7** *5* **Stoneacre Ma**[99] 6477 3-8-5 0 RyanHill(7) 8 30
(Peter Grayson) *prom on outside tl wknd appr fnl f* **33/1**

0- **8** *3* **Tilly Ann (IRE)**[43] 7216 3-8-7 0 ColinHaddon(5) 3 19
(Peter Grayson) *prom: rdn over 2f out: wknd over 1f out* **40/1**

9 *3 ½* **Gelert (IRE)** 3-9-3 0 DaneO'Neill 7 12
(Peter Grayson) *outpcd: a in rr* **12/1**

59.50 secs (0.70) **Going Correction** -0.025s/f (Stan) **9** Ran SP% **126.5**
Speed ratings (Par 97): **93,91,90,89,89 88,80,75,70**
CSF £637.70 TOTE £20.40: £6.10, £4.00, £1.02; EX 83.10 Trifecta £219.40 Part won. Pool £309.14 - 0.85 winning units..
Owner R Teatum And Mrs S Grayson **Bred** J Kinsella **Trained** Formby, Lancs

FOCUS
A bizarre race to analyse, with Peter Grayson saddling six of the nine runners including the first two, but the winning time was respectable, only 1.86 seconds slower than the 86-100 handicap. While the gut feeling is that it was a modest race, it could have been rated significantly higher.

413 LINGFIELD PARK FOR WEDDINGS MAIDEN STKS 7f (P)

4:25 (4:25) (Class 5) 3-Y-0+

£2,331 (£693; £346; £86; £86) **Stalls** Low

Form — RPR

53- **1** **Liberty Valance (IRE)**[38] 7235 3-8-10 0 LPKeniry 5 74+
(S Kirk) *in tch: t.k.h: hdwy on outside to ld appr fnl f: rdn out* **7/2**[2]

66- **2** *1 ½* **Always Certain (USA)**[113] 6156 3-8-10 0 JamieSpencer 4 68
(M Johnston) *led tl rdn and hdd appr fnl f: kpt on one pce* **4/5**[1]

3 **3** *3* **Micheals Boy (IRE)**[18] 163 3-8-10 0 FergusSweeney 6 60
(J R Boyle) *racd on outside: trckd ldr to over 1f out: one pce after* **8/1**

4 *hd* **Snow Bounty** 3-8-10 0 TPQueally 7 59+
(J A Osborne) *s.i.s: hld up: effrt over 1f out but nvr on terms* **4/1**[3]

0 **4** *dht* **Film Queen (IRE)**[10] 265 4-9-1 0 KylieManser(7) 3 54
(B G Powell) *hld up: mde hdwy fnl f but nvr on terms* **33/1**

0-6 **6** *1 ¼* **Scots W'Hae**[12] 244 3-8-10 0 J-PGuillambert 2 56
(S C Williams) *t.k.h: trckd ldrs: wknd over 1f out* **40/1**

1m 27.44s (2.64) **Going Correction** -0.025s/f (Stan)
WFA 3 from 4yo 17lb **6** Ran SP% **114.3**
Speed ratings (Par 103): **83,81,77,77,77 76**
CSF £6.90 TOTE £5.10: £2.30, £1.10; EX 10.40 Place 6 £185.69, Place 5 £32.56.
Owner J C Smith **Bred** T Stack and Stan Cosgrove **Trained** Upper Lambourn, Berks

FOCUS
An ordinary maiden. It was slowly run and the winning time was 2.96 seconds slower than the earlier 51-65 handicap. Questionable form, but the winner showed a nice turn of foot.

Scots W'Hae Official explanation: jockey said colt hung right

T/Plt: £61.20 to a £1 stake. Pool: £63,758.30. 759.35 winning tickets. T/Qpdt: £6.30 to a £1 stake. Pool: £4,474.00. 522.10 winning tickets. JS

400 KEMPTON (A.W) (R-H)

Sunday, February 3

OFFICIAL GOING: Standard
Wind: Strong, half-behind Weather: Fine but cloudy

414 PANORAMIC BAR & RESTAURANT H'CAP 5f (P)

1:50 (1:51) (Class 6) (0-60,60) 4-Y-0+

£2,047 (£604; £302) **Stalls** High

Form — RPR

4-14 **1** **Sir Loin**[11] 263 7-8-1 **50** (v) RossAtkinson(7) 12 61
(P Burgoyne) *mde all and sn at least 2l clr: tired fnl f: a jst holding on* **10/1**

0-03 **2** *nk* **Kempsey**[8] 312 6-9-2 **58** (b) ChrisCatlin 6 67
(J J Bridger) *chsd wnr: drvn and no imp over 1f out: grad clsd fnl f: nt quite get up* **8/1**[3]

00-5 **3** *¾* **Overstayed (IRE)**[9] 304 5-8-12 **57** (be) JohnMcAuley(3) 11 64
(M Mullineaux) *chsd ldng pair: rdn 1/2-way: clsd grad fnl f: a hld* **14/1**

4-31 **4** *¾* **Radiator Rooney (IRE)**[1] 404 5-9-8 **58** 6ex (v) JamieSpencer 8 68
(Patrick Morris, Ire) *t.k.h early: trckd ldng trio: rdn and hanging over 1f out: nt qckn: kpt on nr fin* **5/4**[1]

-031 **5** *1 ¼* **King Of Charm (IRE)**[9] 297 5-8-7 **49** (b) FergusSweeney 2 49
(G L Moore) *hld up in last: rdn over 1f out: kpt on fnl f: n.d* **14/1**

66-0 **6** *½* **Stoneacre Boy (IRE)**[31] 29 5-9-4 **60** LPKeniry 10 58
(Peter Grayson) *dwlt: rcvrd to midfield after 2f but nvr on terms w ldrs: no imp over 1f out* **20/1**

-221 **7** *hd* **Regal Royale**[16] 211 5-8-13 **55** (v) AdrianMcCarthy 4 52
(Peter Grayson) *nvr on terms w ldrs: struggling in rr 2f out* **8/1**[3]

065- **8** *½* **Camissa**[208] 3394 4-8-13 **60** JamesO'Reilly(5) 1 55
(D K Ivory) *dwlt: racd wd towards rr and sn struggling: nvr a factor* **33/1**

6-02 **9** *nk* **Mambazo**[2] 391 6-8-11 **60** (e) WilliamCarson(7) 9 54+
(S C Williams) *hld up: 6th and gng strly wl over 1f out: nt clr run briefly jst over 1f out: allowed to coast home after* **7/2**[2]

0-65 **10** *4* **Racing Stripes (IRE)**[11] 263 4-8-7 **52** (b) NeilChalmers(3) 7 32
(K O Cunningham-Brown) *wnt lft s: a towards rr: wknd over 1f out* **14/1**

59.92 secs (-0.58) **Going Correction** +0.075s/f (Slow) **10** Ran SP% **125.7**
Speed ratings (Par 101): **107,106,105,104,102 101,101,100,99,93**
CSF £94.26 CT £1182.73 TOTE £16.00: £3.20, £2.10, £5.40; EX 98.10.
Owner L Tomlin **Bred** Britton House Stud And C Gregson **Trained** Shepton Montague, Somerset
■ Stewards' Enquiry : William Carson 14-day ban: failed to take all reasonable and permissable measures throughout (Feb 14-27)

FOCUS
A moderate sprint handicap but the form appears solid enough for the grade.

Radiator Rooney(IRE) Official explanation: vet said gelding bled from the nose

Mambazo Official explanation: jockey said, regarding running and riding, his orders were to make the running if possible, but if he missed the break make sure he got to the rail and make his effort in home straight; he added gelding had been slowly away and been denied a clear run from turn for home; trainer confirmed, but added that he was dissatisfied with the effort made in the home straight.

415 FREDERICK MOTSON 21ST BIRTHDAY CLASSIFIED STKS 1m 3f (P)

2:20 (2:22) (Class 7) 4-Y-0+

£1,365 (£403; £201) **Stalls** High

Form — RPR

100- **1** **Trysting Grove (IRE)**[271] 1570 7-9-0 45 SaleemGolam 13 55
(E G Bevan) *t.k.h: trckd ldrs: effrt to ld over 2f out: drvn and styd on stoutly fnl f* **9/1**

-323 **2** *3* **Ernmoor**[9] 303 6-9-0 45 J-PGuillambert 3 51
(J R Jenkins) *stdd s: hld up in detached last: prog fr 3f out: drvn and styd on to go 2nd over 1f out: no threat to wnr* **11/4**[1]

-624 **3** *1 ¾* **Arthurs Dream (IRE)**[9] 303 6-8-9 43 KellyHarrison(5) 5 47
(A W Carroll) *hld up in last pair: sme prog over 2f out: styd on to take 3rd ins fnl f: no ch w ldng pair* **7/1**[3]

2-46 **4** *½* **Wavertree One Off**[8] 322 6-9-0 43 (b) AdamKirby 7 46
(J Ryan) *prom: pressed ldr 4f out to over 2f out: nt qckn u.p after* **7/1**[3]

6-00 **5** *3* **Elms Schoolboy**[13] 242 6-9-0 42 (b) JimmyQuinn 9 41
(P Howling) *stdd s: t.k.h: hld up: effrt and sme prog over 2f out: no hdwy over 1f out* **20/1**

06-2 **6** *4* **Kilmeena Magic**[11] 269 6-9-3 48 PatDobbs 11 37
(J C Fox) *hld up in rr: rdn and prog on outer over 2f out: floundering over 1f out: wknd* **3/1**[2]

0-6 **7** *4* **Lord Orpen (IRE)**[2] 387 4-8-12 42 (p) JamesDoyle 4 27
(Patrick Morris, Ire) *led to over 2f out: wknd rapidly over 1f out* **9/1**

-000 **8** *1 ½* **War Feather**[9] 303 6-9-0 37 TPQueally 12 25
(T D McCarthy) *chsd ldrs: wknd over 2f out* **33/1**

The Form Book, Raceform Ltd, Compton, RG20 6NL

-040 **9** 1 **Bollywood (IRE)**[7] 328 5-9-0 43 .... DaneO'Neill 1 23
(J J Bridger) *chsd ldrs: rdn and struggling 4f out: sn lost pl and btn* **8/1**

4-05 **10** 1 ½ **The Slider**[11] 269 4-8-12 44 .... (p) LPKeniry 6 21
(Mrs L C Jewell) *chsd ldr to 4f out: wknd rapidly* **11/1**

0-56 **P** **Mtoto Girl**[9] 303 4-8-9 38 .... NeilChalmers(3) 8 —
(J J Bridger) *sddle slipped sn after s: unsteerable fr 7f out: t.o whn p.u over 1f out* **40/1**

2m 22.78s (0.88) **Going Correction** +0.075s/f (Slow)
WFA 4 from 5yo+ 2lb **11** Ran SP% **126.3**
Speed ratings (Par 97): **99,96,95,95,93 90,87,86,85,84** —
CSF £35.99 TOTE £11.20: £3.20, £1.30, £2.60; EX 32.50.

Owner E G Bevan **Bred** Knocktoran Stud **Trained** Ullingswick, H'fords

FOCUS
A lowly contest and weak form rated around the first three.

Mtoto Girl Official explanation: jockey said saddle slipped

416 DIGIBET MEDIAN AUCTION MAIDEN STKS 1m (P)
2:50 (2:53) (Class 6) 3-Y-O **£2,047** (£604; £302) **Stalls** High

Form RPR

60- **1** **Gallic Charm (IRE)**[55] 7097 3-8-12 0 .... TQuinn 13 71+
(D R C Elsworth) *v keen early: hld up in 5th: effrt 2f out: drvn to ld last 150yds: sn clr* **20/1**

2 1 ½ **Maadraa (IRE)** 3-9-3 0 .... MatthewHenry 11 72
(M A Jarvis) *dwlt: rushed up and sn led: pressed 2f out: hdd and outpcd last 150yds* **10/1**

22-2 **3** *shd* **Miss Mujanna**[22] 135 3-8-12 73 .... J-PGuillambert 12 67
(J Akehurst) *trckd ldng pair: effrt on inner to chse ldr 2f out: drvn and upsides ent fnl f: nt qckn* **9/4**[1]

65 **4** ½ **Lady Amberlini**[18] 175 3-8-12 0 .... StephenDonohoe 6 66+
(P D Evans) *hld up wl in rr: shkn up over 2f out: stdy prog fr wl over 1f out: styd on* **33/1**

0- **5** *hd* **Driven Snow**[190] 3962 3-8-12 0 .... PatCosgrave 1 65
(Jane Chapple-Hyam) *dwlt: sn in midfield: prog over 3f out: rdn and nt qckn over 2f out: kpt on fr over 1f out* **9/4**[1]

6 ½ **Snowdrop Princess** 3-8-12 0 .... LiamJones 2 64
(W J Haggas) *s.i.s: wl in rr: sme prog on outer over 3f out: hanging and green over 2f out: kpt on fnl f* **25/1**

3- **7** 1 **Parson's Punch**[76] 6868 3-9-3 0 .... DaneO'Neill 5 67+
(P D Cundell) *dwlt: hld up in rr on outer: rn green over 2f out: shkn up briefly wl over 1f out: kpt on steadily* **4/1**[2]

3- **8** *hd* **Silver Waters**[89] 6705 3-9-3 0 .... NeilPollard 10 66
(D R C Elsworth) *dwlt: towards rr on inner: pushed along over 3f out: sme prog over 1f out: nvr rchd ldrs* **20/1**

9 *nk* **Boy On A Swing (USA)** 3-9-3 0 .... TPQueally 3 66+
(J A Osborne) *rn green and sn last: shkn up 3f out: no prog tl styd on fnl f: nrst fin* **14/1**

6- **10** 1 ¼ **Asmodea**[37] 7258 3-8-12 0 .... JimmyQuinn 4 58
(D J Coakley) *nvr bttr than midfield: shkn up and no prog 2f out: fdd fnl f* **50/1**

62-0 **11** 1 ½ **Stagecoach Topaz (USA)**[18] 178 3-9-3 70 .... JamieSpencer 7 59
(M Johnston) *chsd ldr to 2f out: wknd rapidly over 1f out* **8/1**[3]

0 **12** 2 **Minerton Mountain**[11] 265 3-9-3 0 .... SimonWhitworth 9 55
(B R Millman) *t.k.h early: hld up in rr: struggling over 2f out* **50/1**

5 **13** 1 **Red Sonja (IRE)**[19] 163 3-8-12 0 .... JamesDoyle 8 48
(M Blanshard) *chsd ldng trio tl wknd over 2f out* **50/1**

1m 43.0s (3.20) **Going Correction** +0.075s/f (Slow) **13** Ran SP% **130.6**
Speed ratings (Par 95): **87,85,85,84,84 84,83,83,82,81 79,77,76**
CSF £212.61 TOTE £27.50: £4.00, £4.20, £1.50; EX 233.50.

Owner The Bramfield Racing Syndicate **Bred** Limestone And Tara Studs **Trained** Newmarket, Suffolk

FOCUS
They went a noticeably steady pace early on, so the form needs treating with some caution, but this looked like an interesting maiden beforehand and the race should produce some winners.

417 LONDON MILE H'CAP (QUALIFIER) 1m (P)
3:20 (3:22) (Class 4) (0-85,86) 4-Y-0+ **£4,210** (£1,252; £625; £312) **Stalls** High

Form RPR

-241 **1** **Bazroy (IRE)**[7] 329 4-9-5 86 6ex .... (b) StephenDonohoe 1 97+
(P D Evans) *hld up in 5th/6th: effrt gng strly over 2f out: led over 1f out: sn rdn clr: eased nr fin* **8/1**

-315 **2** 1 ¾ **Will He Wish**[12] 259 12-8-11 83 .... (b) JamieJones(5) 8 89
(S Gollings) *hld up in 5th/6th: rdn and nt qckn over 2f out: styd on wl fnl f to take 2nd nr fin* **12/1**

11-3 **3** ½ **Den's Gift (IRE)**[31] 26 4-8-13 80 .... AdamKirby 4 85
(C G Cox) *trckd ldng pair: effrt over 2f out: led briefly wl over 1f out: sn outpcd by wnr: lost 2nd nr fin* **6/5**[1]

0-56 **4** ¾ **Teasing**[4] 357 4-8-12 79 .... JamieSpencer 2 82
(J Pearce) *s.s: hld up in last pair: pushed along and no prog 2f out: shkn up and styd on fnl f: no ch* **12/1**

00-1 **5** 1 ¼ **Blacktoft (USA)**[18] 177 5-8-8 75 .... (e) J-PGuillambert 7 75
(S C Williams) *stdd s: hld up in last pair: rdn and nt qckn over 2f out: plugged on same pce after* **9/1**

242- **6** *nk* **Lawyers Choice**[71] 6929 4-8-12 79 .... DaneO'Neill 3 79
(Pat Eddery) *sn led: hdd after 2f: pressed ldr after: upsides wl over 1f out: fdd* **11/1**

00-5 **7** *shd* **Risque Heights**[25] 97 4-8-11 78 .... (p) HayleyTurner 6 77
(G A Butler) *t.k.h: led after 2f: hdd wl over 1f out: hanging rt and nt keen after* **6/1**[2]

500- **8** 2 **Granston (IRE)**[128] 5776 7-9-4 85 .... TQuinn 5 80+
(J D Bethell) *trckd ldng pair: effrt on inner over 2f out: shkn up whn trapped bhd rivals fr over 1f out: no ch to rcvr* **7/1**[3]

1m 39.6s (-0.20) **Going Correction** +0.075s/f (Slow) **8** Ran SP% **117.1**
Speed ratings (Par 105): **104,102,101,101,99 99,99,97**
CSF £98.79 CT £198.01 TOTE £9.00: £3.00, £3.00, £1.10; EX 87.80.

Owner Barry McCabe **Bred** P D Savill **Trained** Pandy, Monmouths

■ Stewards' Enquiry : Stephen Donohoe two-day ban: careless riding (Feb 14-15)
Dane O'Neill two-day ban: careless riding (Feb 14-15)

FOCUS
A fair handicap and the form looks reasonable rated around the second and fourth.

Risque Heights Official explanation: jockey said gelding hung right throughout

418 DIGIBET.COM LADYBIRD STKS (LISTED RACE) 1m (P)
3:50 (3:51) (Class 1) 4-Y-0+
£14,762 (£5,595; £2,800; £1,396; £699; £351) **Stalls** High

Form RPR

061- **1** **Medicine Path**[88] 6726 4-9-0 103 .... JamieSpencer 6 111+
(E J O'Neill) *hld up in last: prog 2f out: swooping run to ld 1f out: pushed clr* **6/4**[2]

21-1 **2** 2 **Baharah (USA)**[9] 308 4-8-9 102 .... HayleyTurner 3 101+
(G A Butler) *hld up in 4th: shkn up 2f out: clsng on ldrs over 1f out but wnr sn stormed past: drvn to take 2nd nr fin* **11/10**[1]

0-12 **3** 1 **Capricorn Run (USA)**[9] 308 5-9-0 109 .... (v) SteveDrowne 1 104
(A J McCabe) *led 100yds: trckd ldr: led again 2f out: hdd and easily outpcd 1f out: lost 2nd nr fin* **9/2**[3]

5-45 **4** 1 **Troubadour (IRE)**[15] 227 7-9-0 97 .... TQuinn 7 102
(W Jarvis) *trckd ldng pair: effrt on inner over 2f out: nt qckn wl over 1f out: sn outpcd* **16/1**

261- **5** 4 **St Savarin (FR)**[47] 7175 7-9-0 94 .... DaneO'Neill 4 93
(B R Johnson) *pushed up to ld after 100yds: hdd & wknd 2f out* **25/1**

32-0 **6** 2 **Carcinetto (IRE)**[15] 226 6-8-9 85 .... TGMcLaughlin 2 83
(P D Evans) *in tch: rdn over 3f out: wknd over 2f out* **25/1**

1m 38.24s (-1.56) **Going Correction** +0.075s/f (Slow) **6** Ran SP% **119.4**
Speed ratings (Par 111): **110,108,107,106,102 100**
CSF £3.83 TOTE £3.50: £1.40, £1.10; EX 5.20.

Owner J C Fretwell **Bred** Jenny Hall Bloodstock Ltd **Trained** Averham Park, Notts

FOCUS
An ordinary Listed contest. The pace was fair, without being frantic and the fourth is the best guide to the level.

NOTEBOOK
Medicine Path did not progress as expected after running third to Authorized in the 2006 Racing Post Trophy, but he finished last season with a confidence-boosting success in a conditions event at Doncaster and confirmed he is back on track with a ready success on this step back up in grade. This was his first run in almost three months and he was said to be having a little blow afterwards, so he is entitled to come on for this. He could yet fulfil the potential he showed at two. (op 2-1 tchd 9-4 in places)

Baharah(USA) created a really good impression when landing back-to-back conditions contests, the first over 7f round here and the latest coming over an extended 1m at Wolverhampton, but she was not in quite the same form this time. She looked rather laboured when asked for her effort and had no answer to the winner's strong challenge. This was just her fifth start and she can be given another chance to prove herself up to this level. (op 10-11 tchd 5-4 in places)

Capricorn Run(USA) could not reverse recent Wolverhampton form with Baharah, even allowing for that filly running below form, and he looks better over shorter. (tchd 6-1)

Troubadour(IRE) ran reasonably, but he is not up to this level and should be better off back in handicaps. (op 14-1)

St Savarin(FR), claimed out of Richard Fahey's yard for £15,000 after winning over 1m3f at Southwell on his previous start, was dropping back to 1m for the first time in two years. This was asking a bit much. (op 20-1)

419 RASHER FRITH MEMORIAL H'CAP 7f (P)
4:20 (4:20) (Class 6) (0-65,71) 3-Y-O **£2,047** (£604; £302) **Stalls** High

Form RPR

666- **1** **Rapidity**[170] 4578 3-9-2 63 .... ChrisCatlin 1 80+
(E J O'Neill) *wl away fr wd draw: mde all: rdn clr fr over 2f out: in n.d over 1f out: styd on wl* **6/1**[3]

2-40 **2** 6 **Maggie Kate**[18] 175 3-9-1 62 .... (p) SteveDrowne 3 63
(R Ingram) *prom: rdn to chse wnr 2f out: no ch sn after: hld on for 2nd* **16/1**

1124 **3** ¾ **Bold Diva**[6] 333 3-8-11 61 .... (v) KirstyMilczarek(3) 10 60+
(A W Carroll) *hld up in last pair: gng wl enough over 2f out but wl off the pce: rdn and styd on after: tk 3rd nr fin* **6/1**[3]

44-1 **4** ¾ **Southwest Star (IRE)**[4] 355 3-9-3 71 6ex .... JackDean(7) 11 68
(J S Moore) *s.i.s: mostly midfield: rdn and struggling wl over 2f out: plugged on fr over 1f out* **7/2**[1]

450- **5** *nk* **A Dream Come True**[152] 5117 3-8-10 62 .... JamesO'Reilly(5) 7 58
(D K Ivory) *trckd ldng trio: u.p fr 1/2-way: no imp 2f out* **12/1**

0-54 **6** 1 ¾ **Too Grand**[11] 266 3-8-4 54 ow1 .... NeilChalmers(3) 4 45
(J J Bridger) *s.s: settled in last pair: sme prog on inner fr over 2f out: no hdwy fnl f* **12/1**

655- **7** ¾ **Oceana Blue**[38] 7245 3-8-9 63 .... (v) DavidProbert(7) 5 52
(A M Balding) *mostly chsd wnr to 2f out: wknd* **25/1**

15-6 **8** 3 **Kamal**[18] 178 3-9-2 63 .... HayleyTurner 2 44
(W R Muir) *stdd s: t.k.h on outer: rdn 3f out: sn btn* **13/2**

560- **9** ½ **Challow Hills (USA)**[92] 6650 3-9-1 62 .... TQuinn 8 42
(B W Hills) *t.k.h early: hld up: last and struggling over 2f out* **9/2**[2]

562- **10** 8 **Funseeker (UAE)**[52] 7130 3-9-3 64 .... JamieSpencer 6 22
(M Johnston) *chsd ldng trio: rdn 1/2-way: sn btn: t.o* **9/2**[2]

1m 26.48s (0.48) **Going Correction** +0.075s/f (Slow) **10** Ran SP% **125.6**
Speed ratings (Par 95): **100,93,92,91,91 89,88,84,84,75**
CSF £102.74 CT £627.22 TOTE £9.60: £2.20, £5.20, £2.00; EX 172.30.

Owner Premspace Ltd **Bred** Angmering Park Stud **Trained** Averham Park, Notts

■ Stewards' Enquiry : James O'Reilly one-day ban: careless riding (Feb 16)

FOCUS
A modest three-year-old handicap. The early pace seemed just ordinary and the winner got the field well-strung out when increasing the tempo rounding the final bend. The runner-up is probably the best guide to the form.

Rapidity ◆ Official explanation: trainer's rep said, regarding the improved form shown, colt was weak as a 2yo and has now strengthened up

Bold Diva Official explanation: jockey said filly was denied a clear run

Too Grand Official explanation: jockey said filly suffered interference in running

Challow Hills(USA) Official explanation: jockey said filly suffered interference after start

420 TFM NETWORKS H'CAP 1m 4f (P)
4:50 (4:51) (Class 6) (0-52,52) 4-Y-0+ **£2,047** (£604; £151; £151) **Stalls** Centre

Form RPR

/0-0 **1** **Take A Mile (IRE)**[7] 330 6-8-13 52 .... TQuinn 8 59
(B G Powell) *sn settled towards rr: shkn up and prog over 2f out: drvn to ld 1f out: styd on wl nr fin* **7/1**

403- **2** ¾ **Magic Amigo**[53] 7120 7-8-7 46 .... SimonWhitworth 7 52
(J R Jenkins) *cl up: effrt to ld wl over 1f out: narrowly hdd 1f out: edgd lft and nt qckn nr fin* **6/1**[3]

16-2 **3** 2 ½ **Ndola**[7] 330 9-8-11 50 .... (v) HayleyTurner 1 52
(P Butler) *hld up: last 3f out: effrt over 2f out but no prog tl drvn and styd on fr over 1f out: nrst fin* **10/3**[1]

610- **3** *dht* **Lord Laing (USA)**[67] 6969 5-8-10 **49** .... PatDobbs 2 51
(H J Collingridge) *trckd ldr over 7f out: rdn to chal and upsides 2f out: outpcd over 1f out* **7/2**[2]

0-40 **5** *2 ½* **Carlton Scroop (FR)**[4] 352 5-8-13 **52** ....(b) StephenDonohoe 3 50
(J Jay) *stdd s: hld up towards rr: rdn over 2f out: no imp on ldrs: plugged on* **7/2**[2]

00-5 **6** *nk* **My Monna**[8] 317 4-8-5 **50** .... NeilChalmers(3) 6 48
(Miss Sheena West) *dwlt: rcvrd and led for 3f: rdn over 3f out: struggling fnl 2f* **16/1**

5-62 **7** *3* **Mariaverdi**[15] 231 4-8-8 **50** ow1 ....(p) SteveDrowne 5 43
(P G Murphy) *led after 3f to wl over 1f out: sn wknd* **13/2**

5-00 **8** *8* **Autograph Hunter**[13] 251 4-8-7 **49** ow1 ....(v¹) LPKeniry 4 29
(Peter Grayson) *in tch in rr tl wknd over 2f out* **14/1**

2m 38.12s (3.62) **Going Correction** +0.075s/f (Slow)
WFA 4 from 5yo+ 3lb **8** Ran SP% **120.2**
Speed ratings (Par 101): **90,89,87,87,86 85,83,78**
CSF £50.81 TOTE £8.40: £2.40, £2.30; EX 61.30 TRIFECTA 3rd place Tote Ndola 1.50, Lord Laing 0.90. T/C TAM-MA-N 84.44; TAM-MA-LL 87.68. Place 6 £213.87, Place 5 £28.07..
Owner R E Williams **Bred** Gerry Flannery **Trained** Upper Lambourn, Berks

FOCUS
A very moderate middle-distance handicap with the runner-up rated to recent course form backed up by the third.
Take A Mile(IRE) Official explanation: trainer's rep said, regarding apparent improvement in form, that the gelding missed the break last time, and had been better suited by a stronger ride
T/Jkpt: Not won. T/Plt: £101.10 to a £1 stake. Pool: £63,352.80. 457.25 winning tickets. T/Qpdt: £12.30 to a £1 stake. Pool: £4,105.90. 245.70 winning tickets. JN

ST MORITZ (R-H)
Sunday, February 3

OFFICIAL GOING: Frozen

421a GRAND PRIX HANDELS & GEWERBEVEREIN ST MOTITZ (ICE) 5f 110y
11:45 (11:50) 4-Y-0+ **£4,267** (£1,707; £1,280; £853; £427)

RPR

1 **Coseadrom (IRE)**[22] 6-9-0 .... RPiechulek 9 —
(C Von Der Recke, Germany)

2 *1 ¼* **Atlantic Dancer (GER)**[463] 5-9-5 .... OPlacais 8 —
(A Schennach, Switzerland)

3 *nk* **Zoom (GER)**[70] 5-9-1 .... TMundry 10 —
(C Von Der Recke, Germany)

4 *¾* **Tobanjaro (HUN)** 5-9-0 ....(b) SGeorgiev 3 —
(Z Nagy, Hungary)

5 *hd* **Fulminant (IRE)**[107] 7-9-5 ....(b) TCastanheira 4 —
(Karin Suter, Switzerland)

6 *2* **Hart Of Gold**[32] 16 4-9-0 .... FrancisNorton 6 —
(R A Harris) *mid-div: hdwy appr st: sltly blkd fnl turn: styd on again cl home* **62/10**[1]

7 *2* **Assam (GER)**[107] 6-9-9 .... GBocskai 7 —
(Carmen Bocskai, Switzerland)

8 *1* **Humbolt (IRE)**[1291] 8-9-7 .... RobertHavlin 1 —
(M Weiss, Switzerland)

9 *hd* **Mystic Ways (IRE)** 4-8-5 .... SilviaCasanova(7) 2 —
(Traugott Stauffer, Switzerland)

10 *1* **Investor (IRE)**[364] 356 9-8-12 .... TLukasek 5 —
(G Martin, Austria)

69.69 secs (69.69) **10** Ran SP% **13.9**
(Including SFr 1 stake): WIN 24.80; PL 4.40, 1.70, 2.40; DF 72.80.
Owner F T M Meyer **Bred** David Hanley And James Egan **Trained** Weilerswist, Germany

422a GRAND PRIX AMERICAN AIRLINES (ICE) 1m
1:15 (1:27) 4-Y-0+ **£3,200** (£1,280; £960; £640; £320)

RPR

1 **Rushing Dasher (GER)**[67] 6-9-0 .... JBojko 10 —
(A Wohler, Germany)

2 *22* **Vegano (FR)**[255] 7-9-0 .... TMundry 3 —
(C Von Der Recke, Germany)

3 *nk* **Song Of Victory (GER)**[238] 2503 4-9-6 ....(b) MiguelLopez(7) 1 —
(M Weiss, Switzerland)

4 *1 ½* **Daring Affair**[23] 122 7-9-10 .... FrancisNorton 8 —
(R A Harris) *racd in 3rd or 4th to appr st: sltly outpcd ent st but styd on again fnl stages to take 4th* **51/10**[1]

5 *5* **Shiraz (GER)**[364] 355 8-9-4 .... RobertHavlin 5 —
(M Weiss, Switzerland)

6 *9* **Dixigold (FR)**[350] 493 7-9-0 .... ChantalZollet 4 —
(Carmen Bocskai, Switzerland)

7 *3 ½* **Milord Du Bourg (FR)**[504] 5-9-11 .... OPlacais 9 —
(K Schafflutzel, Switzerland)

8 *nk* **Royal Honor (GER)**[875] 5165 5-9-2 ....(b) PScharer(4) 6 —
(T Vana)

9 *12* **Royal Fire (GER)**[350] 494 9-8-7 .... HelenIsler-Kopalek(7) 2 —
(Miss A Casotti, Switzerland)

10 *24* **Vallorcine (FR)** 5-9-1 .... TLukasek 7 —
(G Martin, Austria)

1m 47.6s (107.60) **10** Ran SP% **16.4**
WIN 3.90; PL 1.50, 1.30, 1.30; DF 2.80.
Owner Stall Weissenstein **Bred** H K Gutschow **Trained** Germany

423a GRAND PRIX SPORT MIND (ICE) 1m 1f
1:45 (2:05) 4-Y-0+ **£4,907** (£1,963; £1,472; £981; £491)

RPR

1 **Balor (FR)**[155] 5-9-8 .... RobertHavlin 12 —
(M Weiss, Switzerland)

2 *3 ½* **Ailton (GER)**[98] 4-9-3 .... GBocskai 4 —
(Carmen Bocskai, Switzerland)

3 *2* **Quiron (IRE)**[350] 493 7-9-6 .... TMundry 6 —
(Carmen Bocskai, Switzerland)

4 *2* **Britannic**[85] 5-8-13 .... RPiechulek 3 —
(C Von Der Recke, Germany)

5 *5* **Wassiljew (IRE)**[90] 4-9-7 .... OPlacais 11 —
(K Schafflutzel, Switzerland)

6 *5* **Cupid's Glory**[34] 7287 6-8-13 .... RichardThomas 7 —
(Mrs L C Jewell) *mid-div: n.d* **22/1**[2]

7 *3* **First Time (GER)**[350] 493 5-9-5 .... TCastanheira 5 —
(Karin Suter, Switzerland)

8 *6* **Collow (GER)**[350] 493 8-9-4 .... CStefan 2 —
(M Weiss, Switzerland)

9 *½* **Simonas (IRE)**[123] 5929 9-8-13 .... JBojko 10 —
(A Wohler, Germany)

10 *15* **Lucky Girl (GER)** 7-8-12 .... HelenIsler-Kopalek 8 —
(Miss A Casotti, Switzerland)

11 *12* **Arturius (IRE)**[269] 783 6-8-13 .... FrancisNorton 1 —
(R A Harris) *n.d* **77/10**[1]

12 *10* **Simplex (FR)**[364] 355 7-9-8 .... MSautjeau 9 —
(K Schafflutzel, Switzerland)

2m 34.94s (154.94) **12** Ran SP% **15.8**
WIN 10.30; PL 3.80, 2.70, 2.20; DF 92.00.
Owner F & B Bartschi **Bred** Famille Niarchos **Trained** Switzerland

407 LINGFIELD (L-H)
Monday, February 4

OFFICIAL GOING: Standard
Wind: Fresh, half behind Weather: Fine

424 BACK HERE ON WEDNESDAY FILLIES' (S) STKS 1m (P)
1:40 (1:43) (Class 6) 3-Y-0 **£1,774** (£523; £262) Stalls High

Form RPR

32-2 **1** **What's For Tea**[13] 257 3-9-4 62 .... RichardKingscote 5 61+
(Tom Dascombe) *mde virtually all: rdn 2l clr and in command over 1f out: kpt on* **1/1**[1]

2 *2* **Solaria (IRE)** 3-8-12 0 .... LPKeniry 4 50
(E J O'Neill) *dwlt: t.k.h and trckd ldng pair after 2f: nt qckn 2f out: kpt on to take 2nd ins fnl f* **9/2**[3]

3 *¾* **Queen Macha (IRE)** 3-8-12 0 .... JamieSpencer 8 49
(M J Wallace) *stdd bhd ldrs: effrt to chse wnr 3f out: sn rdn: hd high and fnd nil u.str.p: lost 2nd ins fnl f* **4/1**[2]

1-00 **4** *½* **Carry On Cleo**[21] 156 3-9-4 60 ....(b) JamesDoyle 2 54
(P D Evans) *stmbld and uns rdr on way to post then bolted: hld up in last: outpcd over 2f out: plugged on fnl f* **8/1**

066- **5** *½* **Nothing Likea Dame**[35] 7286 3-8-12 52 ....(v¹) JimmyQuinn 6 46
(D J Coakley) *in tch in rr: outpcd over 2f out: no imp on ldrs after: plugged on* **10/1**

060- **6** *8* **Diamond Seeker**[63] 7007 3-8-9 46 .... JerryO'Dwyer(3) 7 28
(V Smith) *pressed wnr: rdn 1/2-way: lost pl and wknd 3f out: sn bhd: eased last 100yds* **25/1**

0 **7** *4* **Clear Call**[16] 222 3-8-9 0 .... KirstyMilczarek(3) 3 19
(R J Hodges) *nvr gng wl: dropped to last and rdn bef 1/2-way: t.o* **33/1**

1m 39.24s (1.04) **Going Correction** -0.025s/f (Stan) **7** Ran SP% **115.2**
Speed ratings (Par 92): **93,91,90,89,89 81,77**
CSF £5.99 TOTE £2.00: £1.30, £2.40; EX 7.80 Trifecta £14.00 Pool £579.05 - 29.23 winning units..The winner was sold to P Butler for 6,200gns. Queen Macha was claimed by A. M. Hales for £6,000. Solaria was the subject of a friendly claim.
Owner Alan Solomon **Bred** Helshaw Grange Farms Ltd **Trained** Lambourn, Berks

FOCUS
A modest seller, but at least the favourite made sure it was run at a reasonable pace. The form makes plenty of sense.
Queen Macha(IRE) Official explanation: vet said filly finished distressed
Nothing Likea Dame Official explanation: jockey said filly missed the break
Clear Call Official explanation: jockey said filly suffered interference in running

425 LINGFIELDPARK.CO.UK H'CAP 6f (P)
2:10 (2:10) (Class 6) (0-58,64) 3-Y-0 **£1,215** (£1,215; £277) Stalls Low

Form RPR

-665 **1** **Seductive Witch**[10] 306 3-8-6 **48** .... JamesDoyle 2 53
(M D I Usher) *led: drvn over 1f out: hdd ins fnl f: kpt on wl to join ldr on line* **13/2**[3]

0311 **1** *dht* **Wynberg (IRE)**[7] 333 3-9-5 **64** 6ex .... KirstyMilczarek(3) 5 73+
(S A Callaghan) *stdd s: hld up in last pair: prog on inner over 1f out: cajoled along to ld ins fnl f: wknd and jnd post* **8/11**[1]

-051 **3** *2* **Talamahana**[10] 306 3-8-13 **55** ....(b) LPKeniry 1 54
(S Kirk) *cl up: chsd ldr 2f out to over 1f out: nt qckn and hld after* **3/1**[2]

05-0 **4** *5* **Shabnaam**[33] 17 3-8-12 **54** .... TGMcLaughlin 4 37
(P Howling) *rrd s: last tl effrt on outer over 2f out: wknd over 1f out* **14/1**

400- **5** *2 ½* **Whistful Miss**[77] 6872 3-8-6 **48** .... JimmyQuinn 3 23
(P Howling) *pressed ldr: rdn 1/2-way: lost 2nd and wknd 2f out* **25/1**

1m 12.72s (0.82) **Going Correction** -0.025s/f (Stan) **5** Ran SP% **106.8**
Speed ratings (Par 95): **93,93,90,83,80**
WIN: Wynberg £0.80, Seductive Witch £3.80; PL: W £1.10, SW £2.10; EX: W/SW £2.20, SW/W £6.40; CSF W/SW £2.77, SW/W £5.59..
Owner Bryan Fry And The Toerags **Bred** B Minty **Trained** Upper Lambourn, Berks
Owner Cast Hinge Searchfield & Smallbone 1 **Bred** Ged O'Leary **Trained** Newmarket, Suffolk

FOCUS
A modest sprint handicap in which the pace was ordinary, but the outcome was quite dramatic for such a low-key event. Seductive Witch has been rated to form but fellow dead-heater Wynberg idled in front.

426 RACE ALL THE FAMILY TO PONTIN'S FILLIES' H'CAP 1m (P)
2:40 (2:40) (Class 5) (0-70,68) 4-Y-0+ **£2,331** (£693; £346; £173) Stalls High

Form RPR

236- **1** **Paradise Dancer (IRE)**[36] 7282 4-9-4 **68** .... GeorgeBaker 3 77
(J A R Toller) *mde all: set mod gallop: qcknd over 2f out: in n.d fr over 1f out* **3/1**[2]

-643 **2** *3* **Onenightinlisbon (IRE)**[12] 274 4-8-11 **68** .... HarryPoulton(7) 1 70
(J R Boyle) *trckd wnr 2f: rdn to go 2nd again over 2f out: nt qckn and no imp fr over 1f out* **7/2**[3]

40-2 **3** *¾* **Gimme Some Lovin (IRE)**[12] 275 4-8-12 **62** .... FergusSweeney 4 62
(D W P Arbuthnot) *hld up in last: effrt on outer to go 3rd over 2f out: sn rdn and nt qckn: one pce after* **15/8**[1]

-654 **4** *6* **Casablanca Minx (IRE)**[25] 117 5-8-9 **59** ....(v) JamieSpencer 2 54
(P D Evans) *chsd wnr after 2f tl over 2f out: sn btn: eased whn no ch* **3/1**[2]

1m 38.5s (0.30) **Going Correction** -0.025s/f (Stan) **4** Ran SP% **107.0**
Speed ratings (Par 100): **97,94,93,87**
CSF £12.62 TOTE £4.10; EX 12.70.
Owner John Drew and Dr Bridget Drew **Bred** N Cheng & A Smith **Trained** Newmarket, Suffolk

FOCUS
A modest fillies' handicap and they went very steadily in the early stages, which rather played into the hands of the winner. Not form that can be taken at face value.
Casablanca Minx(IRE) Official explanation: jockey said mare ran flat

427 SUNSHINE ALL THE WAY @ PONTIN'S H'CAP 6f (P)
3:10 (3:10) (Class 5) (0-75,75) 4-Y-O+ £2,590 (£770; £385; £192) Stalls Low

Form RPR
40-6 1 **Buxton**[24] 124 4-9-4 75 (t) RobertHavlin 2 85
(R Ingram) *chsd ldng pair: wnt 2nd on inner over 1f out: drvn to ld ins fnl f: styd on wl* 9/2[3]
000- 2 1 **Don't Tell Sue**[219] 3086 5-8-8 65 FergusSweeney 1 71
(D W P Arbuthnot) *led: drvn over 1f out: hdd and one pce ins fnl f* 14/1
23-5 3 3/4 **Chjimes (IRE)**[5] 359 4-9-4 75 LPKeniry 6 79
(C R Dore) *hld up in 6th: prog to chse ldng trio over 2f out: rdn and hanging lft over 1f out: wnt 3rd fnl f but stl hanging and no imp* 3/1[1]
0055 4 1 3/4 **Mine Behind**[5] 353 8-8-2 62 KirstyMilczarek(3) 8 60
(J R Best) *settled in last: rdn over 2f out: stl last over 1f out: styd on fnl f: n.d* 8/1
0-20 5 3/4 **Monashee Prince (IRE)**[7] 334 6-8-5 62 (v) JimmyQuinn 4 58
(J R Best) *a abt same pl: rdn over 2f out: no imp on ldrs over 1f out* 4/1[2]
-664 6 1/2 **Quality Street**[9] 312 6-8-10 67 (p) RichardThomas 3 61
(P Butler) *chsd ldng trio to 1/2-way: sn lost pl and struggling* 10/1
06- 7 nk **George The Second**[59] 7054 5-8-13 70 RichardKingscote 7 63
(Mrs H Sweeting) *chsd ldr to over 1f out: wknd rapidly fnl f* 6/1
36-1 8 1 **Baileys Outshine**[25] 113 4-9-1 72 JimCrowley 5 62
(J G Given) *n.m.r sn after s: a in last trio: rdn and no prog over 2f out* 9/1

1m 10.68s (-1.22) **Going Correction** -0.025s/f (Stan) 8 Ran SP% **114.3**
Speed ratings (Par 103): **107,105,104,102,101 100,100,98**
CSF £63.40 CT £218.72 TOTE £6.50: £1.90, £4.30, £1.50; EX 110.20 Trifecta £385.20 Part won. Pool £542.60 - 0.40 winning units..
Owner Peter J Burton **Bred** Sharon Ingram **Trained** Epsom, Surrey
■ Stewards' Enquiry : Richard Kingscote one-day ban: careless riding (Feb 15)
FOCUS
An ordinary handicap, but they went a decent pace and the winning time was over two seconds faster than the earlier three-year-old handicap over the same trip. The winner is rated back to his best and the second to his old sand mark.
Chjimes(IRE) Official explanation: jockey said gelding hung left throughout

428 BOOK HALF PRICE BREAKS @ PONTINS.COM H'CAP 1m 4f (P)
3:40 (3:40) (Class 4) (0-85,85) 4-Y-O+ £4,100 (£1,227; £613) Stalls Low

Form RPR
4-30 1 **Cold Turkey**[9] 315 8-9-7 85 SimonWhitworth 3 93
(G L Moore) *hld up in 3rd: chsd ldr over 2f out: urged along to ld jst ins fnl f: styd on wl* 13/8[2]
60-1 2 2 **Sun Of The Sea**[23] 139 4-8-6 76 KirstyMilczarek(3) 5 81
(N P Littmoden) *trckd ldr: led wl over 2f out: drvn and hdd jst ins fnl f: no ex* 5/2[3]
2-11 3 5 **Fresh Mint (IRE)**[24] 132 4-8-13 80 JamieSpencer 1 77
(M J Wallace) *led: rdn 3f out: sn hdd and btn* 6/4[1]

2m 29.14s (-3.86) **Going Correction** -0.025s/f (Stan) course record
WFA 4 from 5yo+ 3lb 3 Ran SP% **106.7**
Speed ratings (Par 105): **111,109,106**
CSF £5.38 TOTE £2.70; EX 5.80.
Owner A Grinter **Bred** Worksop Manor Stud **Trained** Woodingdean, E Sussex
FOCUS
A tiny field after two non-runners, but any worries of a slow pace were dismissed by the positive ride given to the favourite and the winning time was less than a second off the course record. Sound form, Cold Turkey rated to his winter best.
Fresh Mint(IRE) Official explanation: trainer said regarding the poor form shown filly may be feeling effects of running several times in recent weeks

429 PLAY GOLF @ LINGFIELD PARK CLAIMING STKS 7f (P)
4:10 (4:10) (Class 6) 4-Y-O+ £1,774 (£523; £262) Stalls Low

Form RPR
-332 1 **Ninth House (USA)**[9] 314 6-9-9 76 (bt) JimCrowley 3 81+
(N P Littmoden) *hld up in 4th: prog whn carried v wd bnd 2f out and lost grnd: rallied to chal 1f out: drvn to ld last 100yds* 11/8[1]
-036 2 hd **Desert Dreamer (IRE)**[8] 329 7-9-6 75 (p) KirstyMilczarek(3) 4 78
(G A Butler) *taken down early: hld up in 5th: lft chalng bnd wl over 1f out: led sn after: r.o but worn down last 100yds* 7/4[2]
-064 3 3 **Dvinsky (USA)**[7] 334 7-9-5 68 (b) TGMcLaughlin 6 66
(P Howling) *trckd ldng pair: hmpd by hanging ldr 2f out and lost grnd: kpt on to take 3rd fnl f* 6/1[3]
6-04 4 1 **Rafferty (IRE)**[12] 276 9-8-4 45 (p) JackMitchell(5) 5 53
(S Dow) *s.s: hld up in last: effrt on inner over 1f out: sn outpcd* 33/1
0-33 5 nk **Count Ceprano (IRE)**[10] 302 4-8-12 68 GabrielHannon(7) 1 62
(M D I Usher) *trckd ldr: lft in ld bnd wl over 1f out: sn hdd & wknd* 12/1
104 6 3 1/2 **Sir Douglas**[7] 342 5-9-4 70 (b) KevinGhunowa(5) 2 57
(R A Harris) *taken down early: led: hanging rt thrght: hung v wd bnd 2f out: sn hdd & wknd* 12/1

1m 23.46s (-1.34) **Going Correction** -0.025s/f (Stan) 6 Ran SP% **116.7**
Speed ratings (Par 101): **106,105,102,101,100 96**
CSF £4.31 TOTE £2.80: £1.50, £1.80; EX 5.00.Desert Dreamer was claimed by T. Dascombe for £13,000. Ninth House was the subject of a friendly claim.
Owner Nigel Shields **Bred** Juddmonte Farms Inc **Trained** Newmarket, Suffolk
FOCUS
They went a good pace in this and despite a few taking a wayward course rounding the home bend, the finish was still dominated by the pair best in at the weights who also dominated the market. The form is pretty solid for the grade.
Count Ceprano(IRE) Official explanation: jockey said gelding hung right
Sir Douglas Official explanation: jockey said gelding hung badly right throughout

430 HAVE A BLAST @ PONTIN'S H'CAP 1m 2f (P)
4:40 (4:40) (Class 6) (0-65,65) 4-Y-O+ £2,331 (£693; £346; £173) Stalls Low

Form RPR
-003 1 **Josr's Magic (IRE)**[5] 352 4-8-4 51 oh2 JimmyQuinn 4 56
(H J Collingridge) *t.k.h: mde all: set v stdy pce tl kicked on over 2f out: hrd rdn fnl f: jst hld on* 7/1
2-52 2 shd **Mon Petite Amour**[10] 300 5-8-9 55 FergusSweeney 2 60
(D W P Arbuthnot) *trckd ldng pair on inner: gd run through wl over 1f out and sn chsd wnr: str chal fnl f: jst failed* 11/4[1]
5-02 3 1/2 **Our Kes (IRE)**[3] 395 6-9-5 65 SimonWhitworth 6 72+
(P Howling) *hld up in 5th: trapped bhd rivals whn pce qcknd 2f out: got out jst over 1f out: r.o but nt quite rch ldng pair* 7/1
0-03 4 1 **Red Wine**[16] 224 9-9-4 64 PatrickMathers 1 66+
(A J McCabe) *hld up in last pair: bdly plcd whn pce lifted over 2f out: rdn and styd on fr over 1f out: nvr able to rch ldrs* 13/2[3]
35-6 5 nk **Lord Of Dreams (IRE)**[9] 316 6-8-10 61 JamieJones(5) 8 62+
(G L Moore) *hld up in 6th: short of room whn pce qcknd 2f out: pushed along and styd on steadily fnl f: nvr nr ldrs* 9/1
520- 6 1/2 **Pactolos Way**[107] 6344 5-9-4 64 JimCrowley 5 64
(P R Chamings) *trckd ldng trio: prog to chse wnr jst over 2f out to over 1f out: wknd tamely* 15/2
3355 7 3/4 **King After**[5] 356 6-8-7 56 (v) KirstyMilczarek(3) 7 55
(J R Best) *tk fierce hold: trckd wnr to jst over 2f out: sn lost pl and btn* 7/2[2]
0-15 8 nk **Alexander Guru**[10] 300 4-9-4 65 JamesDoyle 3 63
(M Blanshard) *hld up in last pair: prog on outer over 2f out: hanging wl over 1f out: wknd fnl f* 15/2

2m 10.32s (3.72) **Going Correction** -0.025s/f (Stan)
WFA 4 from 5yo+ 1lb 8 Ran SP% **120.8**
Speed ratings (Par 101): **84,83,83,82,82 82,81,81**
CSF £28.23 CT £145.30 TOTE £11.00: £2.70, £1.90, £1.90; EX 43.60 Trifecta £293.40 Part won. Pool £413.33 - 0.95 winning units. Place 6 £49.59, Place 5 £34.64..
Owner Ken Tyre & Lee Tyre **Bred** Bryan Ryan **Trained** Exning, Suffolk
FOCUS
A moderate handicap run at an early dawdle and that enabled the winner to steal it from the front. Unsurprisingly the winning time was pedestrian. The form is rated around the first two, and the next three all shaped better than the bare form.
King After Official explanation: jockey said gelding ran too free
T/Plt: £86.90 to a £1 stake. Pool: £83,324.05. 699.90 winning tickets. T/Qpdt: £49.10 to a £1 stake. Pool: £3,948.30. 59.50 winning tickets. JN

365 SOUTHWELL (L-H)
Monday, February 4

OFFICIAL GOING: Standard
Wind: Light across Weather: Showers

431 RACE TO PONTIN'S FOR GR8 GETAWAYS H'CAP 7f (F)
1:20 (1:25) (Class 5) (0-70,73) 4-Y-O+ £2,457 (£725; £362) Stalls Low

Form RPR
1135 1 **Silver Hotspur**[6] 347 4-8-11 **60** FrancisNorton 4 79+
(M Wigham) *a gng wl: led jst ins fnl f: easily* 10/3[3]
0-11 2 2 1/2 **Sophia Gardens**[6] 351 4-9-3 **66** 6ex ChrisCatlin 3 78
(D W P Arbuthnot) *s.i.s: hdwy and wnt 2nd over 3f out: led over 2f out: rdn over 1f out: hdd jst ins fnl f: no ex* 15/8[2]
1-31 3 9 **Cerebus**[6] 349 6-9-10 **73** 6ex (bt) StephenDonohoe 1 61
(A J McCabe) *led: rdn and hdd over 2f out: wknd 1f out* 7/4[1]
060- 4 4 **Intersky Sports (USA)**[56] 7104 4-8-9 **58** (p) DeanMcKeown 2 35
(K J Burke) *chsd ldr tl over 4f out: wkng whn hung lft over 2f out* 8/1

1m 29.11s (-1.19) **Going Correction** -0.075s/f (Stan) 4 Ran SP% **105.3**
Speed ratings (Par 103): **103,100,89,85**
CSF £9.37 TOTE £3.60; EX 9.30.
Owner D Hassan **Bred** Theobalds Stud **Trained** Newmarket, Suffolk
FOCUS
Two of the four runners were penalised for wins over a different distance here last week. The pace was decent despite the small field and the form looks sound enough with the first pair progressive.

432 SOUTHWELL-RACECOURSE.CO.UK (S) STKS 7f (F)
1:50 (1:55) (Class 6) 3-Y-O+ £1,774 (£523; £262) Stalls Low

Form RPR
00-0 1 **Buzzin'Boyzee (IRE)**[11] 289 5-8-12 45 RichardEvans(7) 6 58
(P D Evans) *hld up: nt clr run on ins over 3f out: hdwy over 2f out: rdn over 1f out: led ins fnl f: r.o* 25/1
-131 2 hd **Louisiade (IRE)**[4] 367 7-10-0 60 (p) StephenDonohoe 4 66
(John A Harris) *a.p: rdn to ld wl over 1f out: sn hung lft: hdd ins fnl f: r.o* 10/11[1]
0-53 3 3 1/2 **Plateau**[5] 353 9-9-10 57 TPQueally 7 53
(C R Dore) *hld up: hdwy 3f out: rdn and hung lft over 1f out: one pce fnl f* 7/2[2]
0-16 4 2 **Aggbag**[17] 214 4-9-7 51 DeclanCannon(7) 2 52
(B P J Baugh) *hld up in tch: bmpd after 1f: rdn over 2f out: no imp fnl f* 9/1
0403 5 3 **Capital Lass**[4] 367 5-9-5 40 HayleyTurner 3 35
(A J McCabe) *chsd ldr: rdn and ev ch 2f out: wknd over 1f out* 16/1
040- 6 5 **Ginger Pop**[54] 7118 4-9-10 60 NeilPollard 8 26
(G G Margarson) *t.k.h: led: rdn and hung lft whn hdd wl over 1f out: sn wknd* 14/1
4-23 7 8 **Just Mossie**[18] 195 3-8-3 56 ow3 (p) JackDean(7) 1 7
(W G M Turner) *prom: n.m.r on ins and bmpd after 1f: rdn over 3f out: wknd over 2f out* 8/1[3]
00 8 24 **Charlie Chan**[20] 172 7-9-10 0 (b) DaleGibson 5 —
(Mrs R A Carr) *s.i.s: a in rr: lost tch 4f out* 100/1

1m 30.46s (0.16) **Going Correction** -0.075s/f (Stan)
WFA 3 from 4yo+ 17lb 8 Ran SP% **113.1**
Speed ratings (Par 101): **96,95,91,89,86 80,71,43**
CSF £47.69 TOTE £19.90: £5.20, £1.10, £1.40; EX 74.30.There was no bid for the winner.
Owner Mrs I M Folkes **Bred** Golden Vale Stud **Trained** Pandy, Monmouths
FOCUS
A modest time even for a seller. Ordinary form but sound enough for the grade.
Ginger Pop Official explanation: jockey said gelding hung left up the straight

433 SPONSOR A RACE BY CALLING 01636 814481 CLAIMING STKS 1m (F)
2:20 (2:25) (Class 6) 4-Y-O+ £2,047 (£604; £302) Stalls Low

Form RPR
50-1 1 **Samuel Charles**[12] 275 10-9-3 70 (b) TPQueally 3 74
(C R Dore) *s.i.s: sn prom: rdn over 1f out: led towards fin: r.o* 13/8[1]
-212 2 nk **Rebellious Spirit**[17] 208 5-8-13 60 ChrisCatlin 1 69
(John A Harris) *led: rdn over 1f out: hdd towards fin* 10/3[3]
-154 3 2 1/2 **Hucking Heat (IRE)**[7] 331 4-9-0 68 (e[1]) PatCosgrave 4 65
(J R Boyle) *a.p: hrd rdn over 1f out: one pce fnl f* 2/1[2]
65-4 4 3/4 **Local Poet**[21] 155 7-8-9 55 ow2 (b) PaulMulrennan 2 58
(Ollie Pears) *w ldr: rdn over 1f out: no ex fnl f* 12/1
00- 5 3 1/2 **Besi**[10] 2254 6-8-9 60 FrancisNorton 6 50
(A Berry) *hld up: struggling over 3f out: btn whn hung lft wl over 1f out* 18/1

0-4 **6** *61* **Mystic Spin (IRE)**[9] 319 4-8-9 0 (b) CatherineGannon 5 —
(K J Burke) *a in rr: pushed along over 4f out: lost tch and eased over 2f out* **100/1**

1m 42.36s (-1.34) **Going Correction** -0.075s/f (Stan) **6** Ran SP% **108.5**
Speed ratings (Par 101): **103,102,100,99,95 34**
CSF £6.87 TOTE £2.70: £1.50, £1.80; EX 7.30.Rebellious Spirit was claimed by J. M. (Sean) Curran for £8,000.
Owner Chris Marsh **Bred** Sheikh Mohammed Obaid Al Maktoum **Trained** West Pinchbeck, Lincs

FOCUS
The three in-form contenders finished in the prize money in this ordinary claimer. The form has been rated through the runner-up.

434 RACE AHEAD WITH ZENA @ PONTIN'S H'CAP 1m 3f (F)
2:50 (2:55) (Class 5) (0-75,72) 3-Y-O **£2,457** (£725; £362) **Stalls** Low

Form RPR
2-21 **1** **Leamington (USA)**[24] 131 3-9-6 71 GregFairley 1 84
(M Johnston) *mde all: clr over 1f out: r.o wl* **15/8**[2]
-021 **2** *9* **Ski Sunday**[8] 325 3-9-3 68 6ex SteveDrowne 4 65
(M A Jarvis) *hld up: hdwy 3f out: wnt 2nd 2f out: sn rdn and edgd lft: no ch w wnr* **5/4**[1]
00-3 **3** *nk* **Shaftesbury (IRE)**[16] 225 3-9-0 65 DeanMcKeown 2 61
(M Johnston) *chsd wnr 3f: pushed along over 3f out: rdn and hung lft fnl 2f: one pce* **6/1**[3]
20-4 **4** *3* **Alcimedes**[16] 225 3-9-7 72 AdrianMcCarthy 3 63
(P W Chapple-Hyam) *prom: chsd wnr after 3f tl rdn 2f out: wknd over 1f out* **7/1**

2m 26.4s (-1.60) **Going Correction** -0.075s/f (Stan) **4** Ran SP% **106.0**
Speed ratings (Par 97): **102,95,95,93**
CSF £4.44 TOTE £2.70; EX 4.60.
Owner Sheikh Hamdan Bin Mohammed Al Maktoum **Bred** Gainsborough Farm Llc **Trained** Middleham Moor, N Yorks
■ With this winner Mark Johnston became the fastest Flat trainer to reach the 2,000th career winner milestone.

FOCUS
A fair winning time for the type of contest with the winner the only one to have previous experience of this surface. This looked a fair race and Leamington is progressive, up 3lb on her previous best.
Shaftesbury(IRE) Official explanation: jockey said gelding hung left up the straight

435 BOOK TICKETS ONLINE AT SOUTHWELL-RACECOURSE.CO.UK MAIDEN STKS 1m 4f (F)
3:20 (3:25) (Class 5) 4-Y-O+ **£2,457** (£725; £362) **Stalls** Low

Form RPR
0/ **1** **Basalt (IRE)**[316] 785 4-9-3 68 GregFairley 2 72+
(T J Pitt) *chsd ldr: led over 2f out: rdn and edgd rt over 1f out: drew clr fnl f: styd on wl* **7/4**[1]
63- **2** *9* **My Friend Fritz**[370] 305 8-9-6 0 PhillipMakin 1 58
(P W Hiatt) *led: rdn and hdd over 2f out: one pce* **9/1**
0 **3** *1* **Ella**[31] 48 4-8-9 0 PJMcDonald[(3)] 4 51+
(G A Swinbank) *dwlt: bhd: hung rt over 4f out: hdwy over 3f out: styd on one pce fnl 2f* **17/2**
0/2 **4** *hd* **Red Fama**[34] 1 4-8-12 0 SladeO'Hara[(5)] 9 56
(N Bycroft) *hld up in mid-div: hdwy 8f out: rdn over 3f out: one pce fnl 2f* **33/1**
4 **5** *3* **Mondial Jack (FR)**[9] 317 9-8-13 0 (v) RichardEvans[(7)] 6 51
(P D Evans) *hld up in mid-div: hdwy 3f out: sn hrd rdn: no further prog: b.b.v* **8/1**[3]
04-2 **6** *¾* **Matinee Idol**[11] 282 5-9-1 42 (b) ChrisCatlin 8 45
(Mrs S Lamyman) *prom tl rdn and wknd 2f out* **8/1**[3]
/0-2 **7** *6* **Lascelles**[17] 216 4-9-3 65 TPQueally 10 40
(J A Osborne) *plld hrd towards rr: rdn and swtchd rt over 2f out: no rspnse* **11/4**[2]
055/ **8** *11* **Rambo Honours (IRE)**[429] 6670 4-9-3 52 FrankieMcDonald 5 23
(P A Blockley) *t.k.h in tch: rdn over 4f out: wknd over 3f out* **28/1**
0 **9** *5* **Allez Melina**[9] 317 7-8-12 0 NeilChalmers[(3)] 7 10
(Mouse Hamilton-Fairley) *bhd: rdn 5f out: sn toiling* **50/1**
0/0- **10** *64* **La Nuage**[182] 4229 4-8-12 0 SaleemGolam 3 —
(T J Etherington) *prom: rdn over 5f out: wknd over 4f out: eased whn no ch over 2f out* **66/1**

2m 39.67s (-1.33) **Going Correction** -0.075s/f (Stan)
WFA 4 from 5yo+ 3lb **10** Ran SP% **115.6**
Speed ratings (Par 103): **101,95,94,94,92 91,87,80,77,34**
CSF £18.05 TOTE £2.70: £1.50, £3.00, £2.20; EX 21.60.
Owner Tim Kelly **Bred** John M Weld **Trained** Norton, N Yorks
■ This was the first winner to Tim Pitt in his second spell as a trainer.

FOCUS
A weak maiden with the second favourite most disappointing, but the well-bred winner won easily and should not be hit too hard by the handicapper for this.
Mondial Jack(FR) Official explanation: jockey said gelding had bled from the nose

436 MEET CHUCKLES THE MONKEY @ PONTIN'S H'CAP 1m 6f (F)
3:50 (3:55) (Class 6) (0-60,60) 4-Y-O+ **£2,047** (£604; £302) **Stalls** Low

Form RPR
3-20 **1** **Blue Hills**[6] 345 7-9-7 60 (b) PhillipMakin 7 71
(P W Hiatt) *a.p: led over 5f out: rdn over 2f out: hld on wl ins fnl f* **10/3**[1]
6104 **2** *nk* **George Henson (IRE)**[3] 388 4-8-3 50 DominicFox[(3)] 3 60
(S Parr) *hld up in tch: rdn and str chal fnl f: nt qckn nr fin* **8/1**[3]
0-24 **3** *4* **Phone Call**[14] 248 5-9-2 58 NeilChalmers[(3)] 9 62
(Mouse Hamilton-Fairley) *hld up towards rr: stdy hdwy over 5f out: rdn and ev ch wl over 1f out: one pce whn rdr dropped whip jst ins fnl f* **8/1**[3]
004- **4** *11* **Bulberry Hill**[54] 7123 7-8-10 49 EdwardCreighton 4 38
(R W Price) *t.k.h in tch: chsd ldr over 5f out tl rdn over 3f out: wknd over 2f out* **13/2**[2]
053- **5** *5* **Grizebeck (IRE)**[38] 7125 6-9-7 60 ChrisCatlin 8 42
(R F Fisher) *led: hdd over 5f out: wknd over 4f out* **10/3**[1]
5-35 **6** *2* **Medieval Maiden**[7] 332 5-9-4 57 (p) HayleyTurner 2 36
(W J Musson) *chsd ldr 3f: rdn over 5f out: wknd over 4f out* **8/1**[3]
00-0 **7** *23* **Orchard House (FR)**[6] 345 5-9-1 54 (b) StephenDonohoe 5 1
(J Jay) *a in rr: lost tch 7f out* **13/2**[2]
/6-6 **8** *1 ¼* **Jeu De Roseau (IRE)**[21] 159 4-8-12 56 TPQueally 6 1
(A P Stringer) *a bhd* **20/1**
0-06 **9** *17* **Inflagrantedelicto (USA)**[17] 215 4-8-2 46 oh1 (b) DaleGibson 1 —
(Mrs R A Carr) *s.i.s: sn mid-div: bhd fnl 6f: t.o* **100/1**

3m 6.72s (-1.58) **Going Correction** -0.075s/f (Stan)
WFA 4 from 5yo+ 5lb **9** Ran SP% **111.9**
Speed ratings (Par 101): **101,100,98,92,89 88,75,74,64**
CSF £29.64 CT £192.89 TOTE £4.70: £1.50, £2.70, £2.60; EX 29.60.
Owner Tom Pratt **Bred** Darley **Trained** Hook Norton, Oxon

FOCUS
A distinctly modest handicap but one run at a good pace. The winner was close to his best but the form outside the first two is shaky.

437 BOOK YOUR BEST BREAK @ PONTIN'S H'CAP 5f (F)
4:20 (4:25) (Class 6) (0-65,56) 4-Y-O+ **£2,047** (£604; £151; £151) **Stalls** High

Form RPR
-122 **1** **Savile's Delight (IRE)**[12] 270 9-9-0 52 HayleyTurner 4 68+
(Tom Dascombe) *hld up: hdwy 2f out: led over 1f out: comf* **3/1**[2]
32-4 **2** *2 ½* **Kennington**[18] 191 8-9-1 53 (b) NeilPollard 2 57
(Mrs C A Dunnett) *led: hrd rdn and hdd over 1f out: kpt on one pce* **6/1**[3]
5063 **3** *¾* **Thoughtsofstardom**[4] 372 5-8-9 54 (be) MJMurphy[(7)] 7 55
(M Wigham) *plld hrd: hdwy 3f out: ev ch wl over 1f out: one pce fnl f* **12/1**
00-5 **3** *dht* **Highland Song (IRE)**[4] 372 5-8-11 49 ChrisCatlin 1 50
(R F Fisher) *w ldrs: rdn and ev ch wl over 1f out: one pce fnl f* **16/1**
-002 **5** *1* **Egyptian Lord**[4] 372 5-8-12 50 (b) AdrianMcCarthy 5 47
(Peter Grayson) *half-rrd s: jnd ldrs and plld hrd 3f out: ev ch wl over 1f out: sn rdn: no ex fnl f* **11/10**[1]
5-56 **6** *7* **Gone'N'Dunnett (IRE)**[4] 370 9-8-7 52 (p) KMay[(7)] 8 24
(Mrs C A Dunnett) *bhd fnl 3f* **14/1**
-006 **7** *hd* **Ace Club**[16] 230 7-8-12 53 (b) DominicFox[(3)] 3 24
(S Parr) *w ldrs tl wknd over 2f out* **28/1**
520- **8** *32* **Union Jack Jackson (IRE)**[209] 3408 6-9-4 56 (p) StephenDonohoe 6 —
(John A Harris) *prom: lost pl over 3f out: sn bhd: t.o* **11/1**

60.38 secs (0.68) **Going Correction** +0.175s/f (Slow) **8** Ran SP% **118.9**
Speed ratings (Par 101): **101,97,95,95,94 83,82,31**
PL: Thoughtsofstardom £1.50, Highland Song £1.70; TRI: £97.72 (Thoughtsofstardom), £125.76 (Highland Song) CSF £22.41 TOTE £3.60: £1.10, £1.80; EX 20.70 Place 6 £134.39, Place 5 £20.18..
Owner ONEWAY Partners **Bred** Romany Investments Ltd **Trained** Lambourn, Berks

FOCUS
A tightly-knit, low-grade sprint handicap. Reasonable form for the grade despite the disappointing effort of the favourite, and the winner continues to improve for this yard.
T/Jkpt: £12,894.30 to a £1 stake. Pool: £18,161.00. 0.50 winning tickets. T/Plt: £137.90 to a £1 stake. Pool: £62,361.65. 330.10 winning tickets. T/Qpdt: £18.50 to a £1 stake. Pool: £4,544.80. 181.00 winning tickets. KH

431 SOUTHWELL (L-H)
Tuesday, February 5

OFFICIAL GOING: Standard
Wind: Fresh across Weather: Cloudy, giving way to showers

438 ARENA LEISURE PLC AMATEUR RIDERS' H'CAP 1m 3f (F)
1:40 (1:41) (Class 6) (0-52,58) 4-Y-O+ **£1,714** (£527; £263) **Stalls** Low

Form RPR
0-13 **1** **Cragganmore Creek**[29] 76 5-11-0 **50** (v) MrBMMorris[(5)] 2 61
(D Morris) *a.p: chsd ldr 8f out: led 5f out: rdn and hung lft over 1f out: styd on* **9/2**[2]
50-1 **2** *1 ¼* **Maria Antonia (IRE)**[7] 348 5-11-4 **54** 6ex MrAshleePrice[(5)] 9 63
(P A Blockley) *hld up: hdwy 6f out: chsd wnr over 3f out: rdn over 1f out: styd on* **9/2**[2]
6/11 **3** *12* **Schinken Otto (IRE)**[9] 330 7-11-10 **58** 6ex MissNJefferson[(3)] 7 46
(J M Jefferson) *led 6f: rdn over 3f out: wknd over 2f out* **10/3**[1]
0-00 **4** *1 ½* **Ashmolian (IRE)**[9] 330 5-10-12 **46** oh1 (p) MissGDGracey-Davison[(3)] 6 32
(Miss Z C Davison) *mid-div: lost pl 1/2-way: n.d after* **16/1**
-466 **5** *1 ¾* **Speed Dial Harry (IRE)**[10] 323 6-11-7 **52** (v) MrSDobson 14 35
(C R Dore) *hld up: sme hdwy over 3f out: sn rdn: n.d* **5/1**[3]
-064 **6** *½* **Ronsard (IRE)**[7] 345 6-11-5 **50** MissEFolkes 12 32
(P D Evans) *s.i.s: hld up: n.d* **17/2**
6-62 **7** *1* **Candy Anchor (FR)**[5] 377 9-10-8 **46** oh1 MissSPeacock[(7)] 3 26
(R E Peacock) *prom over 6f* **22/1**
00/- **8** *hd* **Pure Brief (IRE)**[76] 2726 11-10-8 **46** oh1 MissStefaniaGandola[(7)] 13 26
(R Hollinshead) *sn pushed along in rr: hdwy over 6f out: wknd over 4f out* **50/1**
015- **9** *1 ¾* **Simply St Lucia**[164] 4003 6-10-11 **49** MrBlakeStorrie[(7)] 1 26
(J R Weymes) *chsd ldr 3f: wknd 6f out* **25/1**
-045 **10** *8* **Mi Odds**[12] 282 12-10-8 **46** oh1 MissKLMorgan[(7)] 5 9
(Mrs N Macauley) *a in rr: bhd fnl 7f* **40/1**
406- **11** *2 ½* **Sovietta (IRE)**[60] 6643 7-10-11 **49** (t) MrJRavenall[(7)] 8 8
(Ian Williams) *hld up: wknd 5f out* **14/1**
L5-4 **12** *4* **By Storm**[35] 2 5-10-10 **46** oh1 MissJFoster[(5)] 11 —
(Miss J E Foster) *prom 7f* **100/1**
6-00 **13** *5* **Telling**[33] 33 4-10-6 **46** oh1 MrCFeely[(7)] 10 —
(Mrs A Duffield) *hld up: hdwy 6f out: wknd 4f out* **66/1**
50-4 **14** *½* **Katie Kingfisher**[32] 37 4-10-6 **46** oh1 (p) MrJPearce[(7)] 4 —
(M Wigham) *hld up: a in rr: bhd fnl 6f* **25/1**

2m 30.57s (2.57) **Going Correction** -0.20s/f (Stan)
WFA 4 from 5yo+ 2lb **14** Ran SP% **118.1**
Speed ratings (Par 101): **82,81,72,71,70 69,68,68,67,61 59,56,53,52**
CSF £23.00 CT £76.74 TOTE £6.50: £1.50, £2.20, £2.10; EX 30.10 Trifecta £61.80 Pool: £316.25, 3.63 winning units.
Owner Stag & Huntsman **Bred** Grovewood Stud **Trained** Newmarket, Suffolk
■ Stewards' Enquiry : Miss J Foster two-day ban: used whip when out of contention (Feb 18, Mar 3)
Miss G D Gracey-Davison three-day ban; careless riding (Feb 18, Mar 3,17)

FOCUS
Very few got into this, with the first three pulling clear leaving the back straight. It was run in a slow time, even for an amateur event, almost six seconds slower than the later Class 5 handicap, but the form looks straightforward rated around the first two.

439 BOOK HALF PRICE BREAKS @ PONTINS.COM MAIDEN H'CAP 1m (F)
2:10 (2:11) (Class 6) (0-55,55) 3-Y-O **£1,774** (£523; £262) **Stalls** Low

Form RPR
-322 **1** **Hawa Khana (IRE)**[8] 335 3-8-11 55 (p) KirstyMilczarek[(3)] 6 63
(N P Littmoden) *trckd ldrs: rdn to ld 2f out: styd on wl: swvd rt towards fin* **11/2**[2]
0-66 **2** *3* **Coral Shores**[9] 325 3-8-6 47 (v[1]) ChrisCatlin 9 48
(P W Hiatt) *s.i.s: hdwy 5f out: rdn over 2f out: hung lft over 1f out: styd on same pce* **14/1**
0-43 **3** *¾* **Anabaa's Secret (IRE)**[9] 325 3-8-11 52 JamesDoyle 12 51
(J A Osborne) *hld up: hdwy over 3f out: rdn over 2f out: sn hung lft: styd on: nt rch ldrs* **3/1**[1]
0-06 **4** *1 ½* **Tobouggornotobougg**[12] 288 3-8-4 48 oh1 ow2 (v) TolleyDean[(3)] 3 44
(D Shaw) *chsd ldr: led 5f out: rdn and hdd 2f out: no ex fnl f* **10/1**

020- **5** *6* **Grapes Of Wrath (UAE)**[40] 7245 3-8-11 52...................... GregFairley 8 34
(M Johnston) *prom: lost pl 7f out: outpcd over 4f out: styd on appr fnl f: nt trble ldrs* **6/1**[3]

00-0 **6** *2* **Hero Heart**[23] 146 3-9-0 55...................................... PatCosgrave 10 32
(Jane Chapple-Hyam) *hld up in tch: rdn over 2f out: hung lft and wknd over 1f out* **12/1**

6-56 **7** *2 1/2* **Neyraan**[11] 306 3-8-12 53...................................... DeanMcKeown 7 25
(M Johnston) *s.s: outpcd: nvr nrr* **16/1**

006- **8** *2 1/2* **Lechero (IRE)**[67] 6980 3-8-12 53........................... StephenDonohoe 13 19
(P A Blockley) *trckd ldrs: rdn over 3f out: wknd over 2f out* **15/2**

0-45 **9** *hd* **Novestar (IRE)**[7] 350 3-8-8 49.......................... FrankieMcDonald 1 14
(G J Smith) *prom: lost pl over 5f out: bhd fr 1/2-way* **25/1**

0-06 **10** *1* **Marie Claude**[17] 223 3-8-11 52.................................(vt) TPQueally 5 15
(J Noseda) *s.i.s: outpcd* **16/1**

5-06 **11** *2* **Miss Tilen**[14] 262 3-8-8 49...................................... MickyFenton 11 8
(V Smith) *prom over 5f* **16/1**

600- **12** *1* **Sweet Andromeda**[55] 7117 3-8-5 46 oh1...................... PaulHanagan 2 2
(T J Fitzgerald) *led 3f: rdn and wknd over 2f out* **50/1**

600- **13** *1* **Colmar Magic (IRE)**[104] 6427 3-8-8 49........................ PaulEddery 4 3
(Miss D Mountain) *hld up: bhd fr 1/2-way* **50/1**

1m 45.27s (1.57) **Going Correction** -0.20s/f (Stan) **13** Ran SP% **115.3**
Speed ratings (Par 95): **84,81,80,78,72 70,68,65,65,64 62,61,60**
CSF £76.12 CT £280.82 TOTE £4.80: £1.70, £4.20, £1.90; EX 86.10 Trifecta £85.20 Pool: £165.66, 1.38 winning units.
Owner Miss Vanessa Church **Bred** P Larkin **Trained** Newmarket, Suffolk
■ Stewards' Enquiry : Paul Eddery one-day ban; used whip when out of contention (Feb 16)

FOCUS
A weak handicap run in a very moderate time, even for a race like this, and the form is sound but limited.

440 BOOK YOUR TICKETS ON LINE (S) STKS 5f (F)
2:40 (2:41) (Class 6) 4-Y-0+ **£1,774** (£523; £262) **Stalls High**

Form RPR

44-2 **1** **Sherjawy (IRE)**[15] 247 4-8-12 49..............................(b) SamHitchcott 11 56
(Miss Z C Davison) *s.i.s: hdwy over 3f out: rdn to ld 1f out: r.o* **10/1**

00-4 **2** *1 3/4* **Maktavish**[21] 167 9-8-12 42.......................................(b) PhillipMakin 7 49
(R Brotherton) *led: rdn and hdd 1f out: styd on same pce* **6/1**[2]

4343 **3** *1* **Pappas Image**[5] 371 4-8-12 45......................................(p) VJanacek 10 46
(A J McCabe) *a.p: chsd wnr 1/2-way: rdn over 1f out: no ex ins fnl f* **7/2**[1]

3-40 **4** *2 1/2* **Blackheath (IRE)**[18] 213 12-8-7 45........................... KellyHarrison[(5)] 1 37
(S T Mason) *s.i.s: hdwy 1/2-way: no imp fnl f* **15/2**[3]

133- **5** *3/4* **Magic Amour**[290] 1163 10-8-5 58...............................(b) ManavNem[(7)] 4 34+
(P A Blockley) *dwlt: outpcd: r.o wl ins fnl f: nrst fin* **7/2**[1]

3-00 **6** *3/4* **Maromito (IRE)**[6] 363 11-8-7 43.......................... DanielleMcCreery[(5)] 8 31
(R Bastiman) *s.i.s sn chsng ldrs: rdn 1/2-way: wknd fnl f: eased nr fin* **25/1**

065- **7** *2* **Dunn Deal (IRE)**[53] 7138 8-8-12 44............................(b[1]) PaulMulrennan 6 24
(J Balding) *prom to 1/2-way* **12/1**

00-4 **8** *3* **Luloah**[20] 174 5-8-4 43.......................................(p) KirstyMilczarek[(3)] 12 8
(J G M O'Shea) *sn hung lft and outpcd* **8/1**

506- **9** *2 1/2* **Baytown Paikea**[379] 219 4-8-2 50 ow2........................... JackDean[(7)] 9 1
(W G M Turner) *chsd ldrs: hung lft and wknd over 1f out* **25/1**

-603 **10** *6* **Borzoi Maestro**[11] 297 7-8-12 42.................................(vt) MickyFenton 5 —
(D G Bridgwater) *sn pushed along and prom: wknd 1/2-way: sn hung lft* **20/1**

60.51 secs (0.81) **Going Correction** +0.05s/f (Slow) **10** Ran SP% **110.8**
Speed ratings (Par 101): **95,92,90,86,85 84,81,76,72,62**
CSF £63.43 TOTE £10.90: £2.70, £2.50, £1.40; EX 77.70 Trifecta £186.80 Pool: £323.63, 1.23 winning units.There was no bid for the winner
Owner John Belsey **Bred** Darley **Trained** Hammerwood, E Sussex
■ Stewards' Enquiry : Danielle McCreery caution: allowed gelding to coast home with no assistance from the saddle

FOCUS
A modest time, even for a seller, 0.73 seconds slower than the later Class 6 handicap for three-year-olds. the runner-up sets the level with the third a length off.
Magic Amour Official explanation: jockey said, regarding running and riding, that his orders were to jump the gelding out and ride the race as he found it, however it started sluggishly, moved poorly and hung; trainer confirmed, adding that gelding needs a longer trip
Maromito(IRE) Official explanation: caution: allowed gelding to coast home with no assistance
Dunn Deal(IRE) Official explanation: jockey said gelding bled from the nose
Borzoi Maestro Official explanation: jockey said gelding had a breathing problem

441 CALL PONTIN'S 0870 604 5620 MAIDEN STKS 6f (F)
3:10 (3:11) (Class 5) 3-Y-0+ **£2,457** (£725; £362) **Stalls Low**

Form RPR

5-0 **1** **Elusive Hawk (IRE)**[30] 65 4-9-13 0...................................... TPQueally 4 71+
(A P Stringer) *dwlt: plld hrd and sn prom: chsd ldr over 2f out: led over 1f out: rdn out* **7/1**

0-42 **2** *shd* **Jalons Bridewell**[13] 271 3-8-12 68.............................. FrancisNorton 3 67
(M Quinn) *led: rdn: hung lft and hdd over 1f out: r.o u.p* **10/3**[3]

00 **3** *4* **Marquis De Louvois (IRE)**[14] 261 3-8-12 0................... SaleemGolam 6 54
(Mrs A Duffield) *chsd ldr over 3f: sn rdn: styd on same pce appr fnl f* **25/1**

4 *1 1/4* **Article** 3-8-9 0.. DuranFentiman[(3)] 2 50+
(T D Easterby) *s.s: hdwy over 3f out: sn rdn: edgd rt wl over 1f out: styd on same pce* **16/1**

0- **5** *2* **Stand Guard**[290] 1143 4-9-10 0.. TolleyDean[(3)] 9 48
(D Shaw) *trckd ldrs: rdn 1/2-way: edgd lft and wknd over 1f out* **2/1**[1]

6 *5* **Sazerac (USA)** 3-8-12 0.. DeanMcKeown 5 28+
(D Shaw) *s.s: outpcd: hdwy 2f out: wknd over 1f out: eased* **9/1**

7 *22* **Easily Naimd** 4-9-6 0.. LeeTopliss[(7)] 1 —
(D Shaw) *prom: lost pl over 4f out: sn bhd* **50/1**

8 *5* **Trusted Friend (USA)** 3-8-12 0.. GregFairley 8 —+
(M Johnston) *dwlt: hdwy over 3f out: wkng whn n.m.r wl over 1f out: eased* **3/1**[2]

1m 17.6s (1.10) **Going Correction** -0.22s/f (Stan)
WFA 3 from 4yo 15lb **8** Ran SP% **115.6**
Speed ratings (Par 103): **83,82,77,75,73 66,37,30**
CSF £30.96 TOTE £12.20: £3.50, £1.10, £3.90; EX 29.00 Trifecta £311.10 Pool: £495.16, 1.13 winning units.
Owner Curley Leisure **Bred** J Fike **Trained** Newmarket, Suffolk
■ A first winner in his second spell as a trainer for Andrew Stringer, who has taken over the licence from Barney Curley.

FOCUS
A very poor maiden in which the front pair pulled right away. The winning time was pedestrian, a massive 3.37 seconds slower than the following Class 3 handicap, and the form, rated around the placed horses, is unlikely to amount to much amongst the principals, though a couple of inexperienced horses further back could improve.

Trusted Friend(USA) Official explanation: jockey said colt lost its action

442 DO THE CROCODILE ROCK @ PONTIN'S H'CAP 6f (F)
3:40 (3:41) (Class 3) (0-90,89) 4-Y-0+ **£7,124** (£2,119; £1,059; £529) **Stalls Low**

Form RPR

051- **1** **Ingleby Arch (USA)**[55] 7126 5-8-13 84.............................. PaulFessey 6 95
(T D Barron) *mde all: rdn over 1f out: r.o* **2/1**[1]

4-21 **2** *3/4* **Kabeer**[14] 259 10-8-13 89................................(t) NataliaGemelova[(5)] 4 98
(A J McCabe) *mid-div: hdwy over 3f out: rdn to chse wnr over 1f out: edgd lft: r.o* **9/1**

0-23 **3** *3* **Sand Cat**[12] 280 5-8-4 78...................................(b[1]) MichaelJStainton[(3)] 5 77
(G L Moore) *prom: chsd wnr over 3f out tl rdn over 1f out: no ex ins fnl f* **8/1**

4254 **4** *1* **Cool Sands (IRE)**[6] 359 6-7-11 75 oh9...............(v) PatrickDonaghy[(7)] 3 71
(D Shaw) *chsd ldrs: rdn over 2f out: styd on same pce appr fnl f* **33/1**

05-0 **5** *shd* **Andronikos**[17] 226 6-9-0 85..(t) TQuinn 8 80
(P F I Cole) *hld up: hdwy over 2f out: rdn over 1f out: hung lft and no ex fnl f* **10/1**

-323 **6** *3/4* **Memphis Man**[12] 278 5-8-4 75 oh1......................... CatherineGannon 7 68
(P D Evans) *s.i.s: hld up: rdn over 2f out: nt trble ldrs* **20/1**

2-16 **7** *1 1/4* **Bonnie Prince Blue**[14] 259 5-9-0 85.............................(b) ChrisCatlin 10 74
(B W Hills) *chsd ldrs: rdn over 2f out and lost pl over 3f out: n.d after* **15/2**[3]

060- **8** *3* **Imperial Echo (USA)**[87] 6753 7-8-4 78........................... TolleyDean[(3)] 1 57
(D Shaw) *hld up in tch: rdn over 2f out: wknd over 1f out* **6/1**[2]

0-02 **9** *2* **Wessex (USA)**[12] 280 8-9-1 86................................. StephenDonohoe 9 59
(P A Blockley) *rrd s: outpcd* **6/1**[2]

1m 14.23s (-2.27) **Going Correction** -0.20s/f (Stan) **9** Ran SP% **111.6**
Speed ratings (Par 107): **107,106,102,100,100 99,97,93,91**
CSF £19.78 CT £114.45 TOTE £2.30: £1.10, £2.90, £3.10; EX 29.40 Trifecta £148.60 Pool: £531.72, 2.54 winning units.
Owner Dave Scott **Bred** Alexander-Groves Thoroughbreds **Trained** Maunby, N Yorks

FOCUS
A decent sprint handicap run at a true pace and the form looks rock solid. Those that raced handily were at an advantage and it proved very hard for those that tried to come from off the pace.

NOTEBOOK
Ingleby Arch(USA), raised 7lb for his course-and-distance victory in December, adopted the same powerful front-running tactics here and the result was the same. This was a much better field he disposed of though, and he has won off a 3lb higher mark on turf. (op 11-4)
Kabeer does love it here, but he was racing over the shortest trip he has ever tried in his 41st Flat outing off a career-high mark. Not asked to race as prominently as usual over this shorter distance, he put in a strong late effort and, although never quite able to get to the favourite, pulled right away from the others. This was a cracking effort under the circumstances and he remains in great heart. (op 7-1)
Sand Cat, tried in first-time blinkers, was always in about the same place but could never get on terms with the winner. He continues to perform well, but his losing run continues to grow and this effort will not give the Handicapper much reason to drop him.
Cool Sands(IRE) likes it here and was far from disgraced from 9lb wrong, but he could be in trouble if the Handicapper takes this form at face value.
Andronikos, without the blinkers this time, could never get to the principals in a race where it proved hard to come from off the pace. He remains without a win in almost three years. (op 9-1 tchd 11-1)
Memphis Man, 1lb wrong, usually misses the break and that was always going to prove too big a handicap in this contest.
Bonnie Prince Blue, back at the trip he was successful over two starts back and 9lb worse off with his nearest victim Sand Cat on that running, did not detach himself like he did over an extra furlong last time but he was making hard work of it from some way out. (op 7-1 tchd 8-1)
Imperial Echo(USA), making his debut both for the yard and on sand in his 54th outing, was a major gamble earlier in the day but was a big drifter on the track. He broke well enough and was close enough turning in, but the writing was on the wall before reaching the 2f pole. (op 7-2)
Wessex(USA) has done most of his recent racing over further though his last win came over this course and distance two years ago. However, on this occasion he lost all chance at the start. Official explanation: jockey said gelding reared when leaving stalls (op 10-1)

443 BEST HOLIDAY DEALS @ PONTINS.COM H'CAP 1m 3f (F)
4:10 (4:10) (Class 5) (0-75,74) 4-Y-0+ **£2,593** (£765; £383) **Stalls Low**

Form RPR

1-23 **1** **Bentley Brook (IRE)**[14] 260 6-9-2 68.......................... StephenDonohoe 1 82
(P A Blockley) *chsd ldrs: led over 4f out: rdn over 2f out: edgd lft fr over 1f out: all out* **3/1**[1]

06 **2** *shd* **Trachonitis (IRE)**[14] 260 4-9-2 70................................. J-PGuillambert 2 84
(J R Jenkins) *hld up: hdwy over 5f out: chsd wnr over 2f out: sn rdn: edgd rt and hmpd ins fnl f: r.o* **10/1**

-512 **3** *2* **Calculating (IRE)**[14] 260 4-9-6 74.................................. HayleyTurner 6 84
(M D I Usher) *hld up: hdwy over 6f out: rdn over 2f out: styd on same pce fnl f* **4/1**[2]

205- **4** *7* **Black Falcon (IRE)**[229] 2511 8-9-4 70.............................. MickyFenton 7 71
(M A Peill) *hld up and bhd: hdwy 2f out: sn rdn: edgd lft: wknd and eased* **11/1**

5 *nk* **Leyte Gulf (USA)**[11] 5-8-13 65... ChrisCatlin 4 63
(C C Bealby) *sn led: hdd over 8f out: rdn and wknd over 3f out* **33/1**

2-10 **6** *5* **Three Boars**[14] 260 6-9-0 71..(b) JamieJones[(5)] 3 61
(S Gollings) *pushed along in rr: rdn over 3f out: sn wknd* **5/1**[3]

503- **7** *1* **Don Pietro**[48] 6774 5-9-2 68...................................... FrankieMcDonald 5 56
(P A Blockley) *chsd ldrs: chal over 4f out: rdn over 2f out: sn wknd* **13/2**

105- **8** *2* **Petrosian**[270] 1624 4-8-11 65....................................... DeanMcKeown 8 49
(M Johnston) *chsd ldr tl led over 8f out: hdd over 4f out: rdn and wknd 2f out* **11/2**

2m 24.63s (-3.37) **Going Correction** -0.20s/f (Stan)
WFA 4 from 5yo+ 2lb **8** Ran SP% **110.8**
Speed ratings (Par 103): **104,103,102,97,97 93,92,91**
CSF £31.48 CT £113.96 TOTE £3.90: £1.30, £2.70, £1.70; EX 35.50 Trifecta £82.40 Pool: £467.05, 4.02 winning units.
Owner John Wardle **Bred** Christopher Maye **Trained** Lambourn, Berks

FOCUS
A fair handicap and another race in which they went a good pace and finished well spread out. The form looks solid with hte winner and third close to previous course form.

444 SOUTHWELL-RACECOURSE.CO.UK H'CAP 5f (F)
4:40 (4:40) (Class 6) (0-65,65) 3-Y-0 **£1,911** (£564; £282) **Stalls High**

Form RPR

50-3 **1** **Lujiana**[34] 19 3-8-8 55.. MarkLawson[(3)] 5 64+
(M Brittain) *s.i.s: sn chsng ldrs: rdn to ld over 1f out: r.o wl: hung rt towards fin* **25/1**

3-32 **2** *3* **Wild Bill Tracey**[12] 279 3-9-2 60...................................... ChrisCatlin 3 58
(M J Wallace) *chsd ldr: rdn and hung lft over 1f out: edgd rt ins fnl f: styd on same pce* **5/2**[2]

0-12 **3** *nk* **Orpen's Art (IRE)**[15] 243 3-8-11 **58** KirstyMilczarek[(3)] 6 55
(S A Callaghan) *led: racd keenly: rdn and hdd over 1f out: no ex ins fnl f* **4/5**[1]

214- **4** *3 1/2* **Golden Dane (IRE)**[67] 6977 3-9-7 **65** LiamJones 2 38
(C R Dore) *chsd ldrs: sn rdn along: wknd 1/2-way: fin 5th, 3l, nk, 3l and 3 1/2l: plcd 4th* **6/1**[3]

2-60 **5** *1 1/2* **Galley Slave (IRE)**[26] 112 3-8-4 **55** PatrickDonaghy[(7)] 1 22
(M C Chapman) *s.i.s: outpcd: fin 6th, 3l, nk, 3l, 3 1/2l and 1 1/2l: plcd 5th* **50/1**

0603 **D** *3* **Andrasta**[12] 279 3-8-4 **53** DanielleMcCreery[(5)] 4 39
(A Berry) *s.i.s: hdwy 1/2-way: wknd over 1f out: fin 4th, 3l, nk and 3l: disq: weighed in light* **28/1**

59.88 secs (0.18) **Going Correction** +0.05s/f (Slow) **6** Ran SP% **107.7**
Speed ratings (Par 95): **100,95,94,81,89 89**
CSF £79.85 TOTE £18.20: £4.30, £1.40; EX 32.50 Place 6 £ 29.02, Place 5 £ 21.61.
Owner Mel Brittain **Bred** Bearstone Stud **Trained** Warthill, N Yorks
■ Stewards' Enquiry : Danielle McCreery three-day ban: Rule 161 (iii), failed to draw correct weight (Feb 16-18)

FOCUS
Not a very competitive race on paper, but a shock result as things turned out and a fair time for a race like this, 0.73 seconds quicker than the earlier older-horse seller. The form is moderate with the exposed runner-up to previous course and distance form.
T/Jkpt: Not won. T/Plt: £24.80. Pool £74,086.95, 2,179.45 winning units T/Qpdt: £15.00. Pool £3,720, 183.50 winning units CR

414 KEMPTON (A.W) (R-H)
Wednesday, February 6

OFFICIAL GOING: Standard
Wind: Almost nil Weather: Clear

445 TURFTV CLASSIFIED STKS — 6f (P)
6:20 (6:22) (Class 7) 4-Y-0+ **£1,365** (£403; £201) **Stalls** High

Form RPR

00-0 **1** **Isobel Rose (IRE)**[35] 16 4-9-0 **45** (b) AdamKirby 5 54
(J L Spearing) *chsd ldrs: prog on outer over 2f out: rdn to ld ins fnl f: styd on wl* **9/1**

-654 **2** *1 1/4* **Piccostar**[7] 353 5-9-0 **43** (b) SamHitchcott 8 50
(A B Haynes) *t.k.h: hld up in last pair: hanging but prog fr over 2f out: kpt on rather reluctantly fnl f to take 2nd nr fin* **8/1**[3]

004 **3** *1/2* **Prettilini**[9] 338 5-8-11 **40** KirstyMilczarek[(3)] 11 48
(A W Carroll) *led: pressed 2f out: hdd and no ex ins fnl f* **11/2**[2]

2214 **4** *3/4* **Mr Loire**[6] 372 4-9-6 **45** (b) DeanMcKeown 12 52
(P A Blockley) *trckd ldrs: n.m.r on inner 1/2-way: prog and darted to far rail over 2f out: sn pressed ldr: nt qckn fnl f* **6/4**[1]

-022 **5** *1/2* **Tang**[7] 353 4-8-7 **44** JackDean[(7)] 3 44
(W G M Turner) *chsd ldrs on outer: outpcd u.p over 2f out: kpt on again fnl f* **9/1**

-004 **6** *1/2* **James Street (IRE)**[16] 254 5-8-7 **44** (v) RyanHill[(7)] 6 43+
(Peter Grayson) *awkward s: hld up in last pair: hanging fr over 2f out: pushed along and plugged on fr over 1f out* **9/1**

0060 **7** *1* **The Carpet Man**[6] 372 4-9-0 **45** LiamJones 9 40
(A W Carroll) *chsd ldng pair to over 2f out: steadily fdd* **14/1**

50-6 **8** *1 1/4* **Joe Rich**[21] 183 4-9-0 **45** (p) DaneO'Neill 10 36
(Mrs L C Jewell) *lost midfield pl over 3f out: rdn in rr over 2f out: plugged on: n.d* **25/1**

3044 **9** *5* **Noddledoddle (IRE)**[10] 326 4-9-0 **42** (vt) ChrisCatlin 4 20
(J Ryan) *chsd ldr to over 2f out: hanging and wknd* **16/1**

-600 **10** *1* **Iron Pearl**[5] 392 4-8-11 **45** (bt[1]) JerryO'Dwyer[(3)] 7 16
(J Ryan) *nvr beyond midfield: wknd 2f out* **33/1**

000/ **11** *nk* **Old Time Dancing**[763] 30 5-9-0 **45** JimCrowley 2 15
(J F Panvert) *a in rr: no ch fnl 2f* **33/1**

000- **12** *nk* **Doctor Ned**[122] 5886 4-9-0 **40** NeilChalmers 1 14
(Miss Sheena West) *dwlt: racd wd: nvr beyond midfield: wknd 2f out* **40/1**

1m 13.6s (0.50) **Going Correction** +0.10s/f (Slow) **12** Ran SP% **121.2**
Speed ratings (Par 97): **100,98,97,96,96 95,94,92,85,84 83,83**
CSF £78.24 TOTE £12.70: £3.30, £2.20, £2.50; EX 100.80.
Owner Mrs R F Knipe **Bred** John Brown & Megan Dennis **Trained** Kinnersley, Worcs

FOCUS
A moderate field as would be expected for a race like this, but the pace was solid and those that raced handily seemed to be at an advantage. Not that many got into it but the form is sound for the grade.

446 KEMPTON.CO.UK H'CAP — 7f (P)
6:50 (6:52) (Class 6) (0-65,65) 4-Y-0+ **£2,047** (£604; £302) **Stalls** High

Form RPR

42-6 **1** **Fine Ruler (IRE)**[33] 48 4-9-4 **65** GeorgeBaker 5 75
(M R Bosley) *hld up in last trio: prog over 2f out: rdn and sustained effrt to ld ins fnl f: sn clr* **14/1**

1100 **2** *1 1/2* **Epidaurian King (IRE)**[10] 327 5-9-1 **62** (v) DeanMcKeown 9 68
(D Shaw) *lw: hld up in midfield: prog over 2f out to chse ldng pair over 1f out: sn chalng: edgd lft and fnd nil: kpt on to take 2nd nr fin* **8/1**

0-12 **3** *1/2* **Unlimited**[17] 235 6-8-12 **59** JimmyQuinn 10 64
(R Simpson) *plld hrd early: trckd ldr: narrow ld 2f out: fnd little in front: hdd and nt qckn ins fnl f* **11/4**[2]

1-55 **4** *nk* **Figaro Flyer (IRE)**[20] 194 5-9-4 **65** SimonWhitworth 1 69
(P Howling) *dropped in to last pair fr wd draw and plld hrd: prog over 2f out: clsd on ldrs over 1f out: one pce fnl f* **6/1**

15-5 **5** *1/2* **Carlitos Spirit (IRE)**[21] 177 4-9-3 **64** ChrisCatlin 2 66
(B R Millman) *keen: led at mod pce: narrowly hdd 2f out: styd w ldr tl wknd ins fnl f* **9/2**[3]

01-5 **6** *4* **Cornerstone**[17] 235 4-8-10 **57** (v) JimCrowley 7 49
(S C Williams) *lw: pressed ldng pair: rdn wl over 2f out: bmpd sn after: fdd* **9/1**

-511 **7** *hd* **Sovereignty (JPN)**[10] 327 6-8-10 **62** 6ex JamesO'Reilly[(5)] 6 53
(D K Ivory) *t.k.h: hld up in tch: rdn over 2f out: sn struggling* **9/4**[1]

04-4 **8** *2 1/2* **Proud Killer**[33] 41 5-9-1 **65** JerryO'Dwyer[(3)] 8 49
(J R Jenkins) *lw: stdd s: plld hrd and hld up in last pair: rdn 3f out: no prog and sn btn* **16/1**

0-40 **9** *1 3/4* **Zazous**[24] 149 7-8-10 **57** NeilChalmers 3 37
(J J Bridger) *chsd ldrs and racd on outer: rdn over 2f out: sn wknd* **25/1**

1m 25.93s (-0.07) **Going Correction** +0.10s/f (Slow) **9** Ran SP% **127.4**
Speed ratings (Par 101): **104,102,101,101,100 96,96,93,91**
CSF £132.33 CT £414.35 TOTE £15.10: £3.40, £2.70, £1.60; EX 190.70.
Owner Mrs Jean M O'Connor **Bred** Gainsborough Stud Management Ltd **Trained** Lockeridge, Wilts

FOCUS
Not a bad little sprint handicap, but a few of these pulled their chances away. The form is sound enough rated around thefour immediately behind the winner.
Proud Killer Official explanation: jockey said gelding was never travelling

447 DIGIBET MAIDEN STKS — 1m (P)
7:20 (7:20) (Class 5) 3-Y-0+ **£2,457** (£725; £362) **Stalls** High

Form RPR

6 **1** **Snowdrop Princess**[3] 416 3-8-4 0 LiamJones 4 71+
(W J Haggas) *s.i.s: hld up in last: prog to trck ldng pair over 1f out: led ins fnl f: hung lft but styd on wl* **6/1**

2 *1 3/4* **Trimaran (IRE)** 3-8-4 0 GregFairley 2 67+
(M Johnston) *w'like: bit bkwd: trckd ldr: led over 2f out and rn green: rdn and hung bdly lft fnl f: sn hdd and btn* **3/1**[2]

32-3 **3** *nk* **Common Purpose (USA)**[16] 246 4-10-0 **72** PatCosgrave 3 76
(Jane Chapple-Hyam) *lw: trckd ldrs gng easily: wnt 2nd 2f out and sn chalng: edgd lft and nt qckn fnl f* **11/10**[1]

5-0 **4** *13* **Walton House (USA)**[25] 135 3-8-9 0 (v[1]) NeilChalmers 5 41
(A M Balding) *led to over 2f out: wknd rapidly wl over 1f out* **25/1**

2- **5** *3 1/2* **Dancing Wizard**[53] 7159 4-10-0 0 AdamKirby 1 38
(C G Cox) *lw: in tch: rdn over 3f out: sn wknd and bhd* **5/1**[3]

5-0 **6** *9* **Jollys Joy**[34] 22 4-9-9 0 JamesDoyle 6 12
(K F Clutterbuck) *cl up tl wknd rapidly over 2f out: t.o* **66/1**

1m 40.08s (0.28) **Going Correction** +0.10s/f (Slow)
WFA 3 from 4yo 19lb **6** Ran SP% **108.9**
Speed ratings (Par 103): **102,100,99,86,83 74**
CSF £22.70 TOTE £7.70: £2.90, £1.60; EX 13.60.
Owner Snowdrop Stud Co Limited **Bred** Snowdrop Stud Co Limited **Trained** Newmarket, Suffolk

FOCUS
A fairly uncompetitive maiden in which the front three pulled right away from the other trio despite all hanging badly out to their left. The time was fair though and there may be a bit more to come from the front pair.

448 DIGIBET.COM H'CAP — 1m (P)
7:50 (7:50) (Class 6) (0-65,65) 4-Y-0+ **£2,047** (£604; £302) **Stalls** High

Form RPR

00-1 **1** **Safari Sundowner (IRE)**[7] 356 4-9-2 **63** 6ex JimCrowley 5 74+
(P Winkworth) *lw: mde all: set stdy pce tl increased tempo over 3f out: pressed over 2f out: rdn over 1f out: drew clr fnl f* **7/2**[2]

53-4 **2** *1 3/4* **Convivial Spirit**[4] 407 4-9-4 **65** (t) LPKeniry 6 72
(E F Vaughan) *t.k.h: trckd ldng pair: effrt on inner to press wnr over 1f out: drvn and one pce* **10/3**[1]

00-2 **3** *3/4* **Forbidden (IRE)**[18] 234 5-8-10 **60** (t) JerryO'Dwyer[(3)] 4 65
(Daniel Mark Loughnane, Ire) *lw: trckd wnr: rdn to chal over 2f out: hld and lost 2nd over 1f out: one pce fnl f* **6/1**

46-6 **4** *nk* **Coloso**[21] 175 4-8-13 **60** SimonWhitworth 3 64
(P D Cundell) *t.k.h: hld up in 5th in steadily run r: effrt over 2f out: kpt on fr over 1f out: nvr able to chal* **20/1**

0-30 **5** *2 1/2* **Royal Embrace**[17] 235 5-8-10 **57** (v) DeanMcKeown 7 56
(D Shaw) *stdd s: hld up in last in moderately run r: struggling once pce lifted fr over 3f out* **4/1**[3]

0-06 **6** *1 1/4* **Binnion Bay (IRE)**[21] 177 7-8-13 **60** (b) ChrisCatlin 1 56
(J J Bridger) *dwlt: sn in 4th: rdn over 2f out: sn lost pl and wl btn* **7/2**[2]

20-3 **7** *shd* **Shouldntbethere (IRE)**[19] 208 4-9-0 **61** RobertHavlin 2 56
(Mrs P N Dutfield) *hld up in 6th in steadily run r: outpcd over 2f out: no imp after* **9/1**

1m 41.27s (1.47) **Going Correction** +0.10s/f (Slow) **7** Ran SP% **116.6**
Speed ratings (Par 101): **96,94,93,93,90 89,89**
CSF £16.16 TOTE £4.90: £2.70, £2.60; EX 21.40.
Owner P Winkworth **Bred** Michael Phelan **Trained** Chiddingfold, Surrey

FOCUS
They went a very steady early pace in this, which suited those that raced handily, and it took them over two seconds longer to cover the first 2f than in the preceding maiden over the same trip. Although things quickened up later, the winning time was still 1.19 seconds slower and that would have helped the all-the-way winner no end. The form is rated around theplaced horses to their recent marks.

449 DIGIBET SPORTS BETTING CLAIMING STKS — 1m 3f (P)
8:20 (8:20) (Class 6) 4-Y-0+ **£2,047** (£604; £302) **Stalls** High

Form RPR

-132 **1** **Given A Choice (IRE)**[16] 252 6-9-0 **82** TPQueally 2 82+
(J G Given) *lw: hld up in 3rd: wnt 2nd over 2f out: clsd to ld ins fnl f: nt extended* **4/7**[1]

1543 **2** *1* **Hucking Heat (IRE)**[2] 433 4-8-8 **68** JimCrowley 4 67
(J R Boyle) *mde most: drvn and tried to assert 2f out: hdd and brushed aside ins fnl f* **4/1**[2]

50-0 **3** *5* **Key Partners (IRE)**[28] 91 7-8-10 **54** StephenDonohoe 3 58
(P A Blockley) *stdd s: hld up in last: rdn over 2f out: plugged on into modest 3rd over 1f out* **16/1**

220- **4** *7* **Best Selection**[46] 7224 4-9-1 **68** IanMongan 1 52
(Mrs L J Mongan) *chsd ldr tl wknd u.p over 2f out* **9/2**[3]

2m 23.72s (1.82) **Going Correction** +0.10s/f (Slow)
WFA 4 from 6yo+ 2lb **4** Ran SP% **107.7**
Speed ratings (Par 101): **97,96,92,87**
CSF £3.14 TOTE £1.80; EX 3.00.The winner was claimed by Jeff Pearce for £12,000.
Owner Mike J Beadle **Bred** Rathasker Stud **Trained** Willoughton, Lincs

FOCUS
An uncompetitive claimer and the result was very much as adjusted official ratings suggested it should be. They went a dawdle in the early part of this contest and the tempo did not pick up until after half a mile.

450 TURFTV SHOWING BEST RACECOURSES' H'CAP — 1m 3f (P)
8:50 (8:50) (Class 4) (0-80,79) 4-Y-0+ **£4,210** (£1,252; £625; £312) **Stalls** High

Form RPR

640- **1** **Rationale (IRE)**[117] 6158 5-9-4 **79** J-PGuillambert 4 89+
(S C Williams) *s.s: hld up in last pair: prog on inner over 2f out: got through over 1f out: led ins fnl f: drvn and r.o wl* **13/2**

0-02 **2** *1 1/2* **Fregate Island (IRE)**[9] 331 5-9-0 **75** TPQueally 6 83
(J G Given) *lw: chsd clr ldr: clsd 4f out: drvn to ld over 1f out: hdd and outpcd ins fnl f* **11/2**

-231 **3** *2* **Bentley Brook (IRE)**[1] 443 6-8-13 **74** 6ex StephenDonohoe 7 78
(P A Blockley) *lw: settled in 5th: rdn and effrt over 2f out: kpt on to take 3rd ins fnl f: nt pce to chal* **3/1**[1]

45-6 **4** *3/4* **Resonate (IRE)**[28] 96 10-8-11 **72** DaneO'Neill 3 75
(A G Newcombe) *hld up in 4th: effrt and cl up over 2f out: drvn and nt qckn over 1f out: fdd* **9/2**[3]

1/0- **5** *hd* **Inch Lodge**[334] [652] 6-9-3 **78**........................ MickyFenton 1 81
(Miss D Mountain) *b: b.hind: sn led and set str pce: clr after 3f: rdn over 2f out: hdd over 1f out: wknd ins fnl f* **20/1**

010- **6** *6* **Garrulous (UAE)**[41] [1609] 5-8-5 **66**........................ FergusSweeney 2 58
(G L Moore) *stdd s: hld up in last pair: rdn and btn wl over 2f out* **7/2**[2]

6-46 **7** *3* **Prime Number (IRE)**[18] [224] 6-8-7 **68**........................ ChrisCatlin 5 55
(J Akehurst) *chsd ldng pair: hanging bnd over 3f out: wknd over 2f out* **6/1**

2m 19.29s (-2.61) **Going Correction** +0.10s/f (Slow) 7 Ran SP% **113.2**
Speed ratings (Par 105): **113,111,110,109,109 105,103**
CSF £40.52 TOTE £6.00: £3.20, £2.00; EX 56.10.
Owner Alasdair Simpson **Bred** Middle Park Stud Ltd **Trained** Newmarket, Suffolk

FOCUS
A much stronger pace in this handicap than the two races either side of it over the same trip. The winning time was 4.43 seconds faster than the earlier claimer and 6.68 seconds faster than the later Class 6 handicap, so the form looks solid and should work out.
Garrulous(UAE) Official explanation: jockey said gelding hung left handed

451 DAY TIME, NIGHT TIME, GREAT TIME H'CAP — 1m 3f (P)
9:20 (9:21) (Class 6) (0-60,60) 4-Y-O+ **£2,047** (£604; £302) **Stalls** High

Form RPR

32-6 **1** **Altos Reales**[27] [118] 4-9-0 **56**........................ DeanMcKeown 7 62
(D Shaw) *hld up in 4th: prog to chse ldr over 2f out: shoved along and styd on fnl f to ld last strides* **7/2**[2]

5-5 **2** *nk* **Amical Risks (FR)**[26] [128] 4-9-3 **59**........................ TPQueally 6 65
(W J Musson) *hld up in 3rd: prog to ld 4f out: kicked on over 2f out: worn down last strides* **9/2**[3]

4-54 **3** *2* **Magic Warrior**[12] [300] 8-9-6 **60**........................ PatDobbs 2 62
(J C Fox) *hld up in 5th in slowly run r: effrt over 2f out: wnt 3rd over 1f out: nt pce to trble ldng pair* **11/2**

614/ **4** *nk* **Ocean Rock**[410] [6936] 7-8-12 **52**........................ SimonWhitworth 3 54
(C A Horgan) *stdd s: t.k.h: hld up in last in slowly run r: pushed along and plugged on fnl 2f: nvr nr ldrs* **13/2**

040- **5** *2* **Starr Flyer**[111] [4391] 4-7-11 **46**........................ NatashaEaton(7) 5 44
(A Bailey) *reluctant ldr at slow pce: hdd narrowly 4f out: fdd fnl 2f* **10/1**

00-5 **6** *6* **Prime Contender**[9] [207] 6-9-3 **57**........................(b) GeorgeBaker 1 44
(G L Moore) *trckd ldr to 1/2-way: nt gng wl after: rdn and wl btn over 2f out* **7/4**[1]

2m 25.97s (4.07) **Going Correction** +0.10s/f (Slow)
WFA 4 from 6yo+ 2lb 6 Ran SP% **114.6**
Speed ratings (Par 101): **89,88,87,87,85 81**
CSF £19.86 TOTE £4.00: £2.90, £3.00; EX 17.50 Place 6 £340.16, Place 5 £134.29..
Owner Danethorpe Racing Partnership **Bred** Goldford Stud And P E Clinton **Trained** Danethorpe, Notts

FOCUS
Unlike the previous race, but exactly like the contest before that, they went no pace at all early here as those that found themselves in front did not want to be there. As a result it developed into a messy sprint and the time was very slow and the third is the best guide to the form.
T/Plt: £184.30 to a £1 stake. Pool: £75,615.55. 299.50 winning tickets. T/Qpdt: £29.50 to a £1 stake. Pool: £5,789.70. 144.90 winning tickets. JN

[424] LINGFIELD (L-H)
Wednesday, February 6

OFFICIAL GOING: Standard
Wind: fresh against Weather: cloudy with some bright spells

452 LET US ENTERTAIN YOU @ PONTIN'S H'CAP — 1m (P)
1:30 (1:30) (Class 5) (0-75,75) 4-Y-O+ **£2,331** (£693; £346; £173) **Stalls** High

Form RPR

205- **1** **Reballo (IRE)**[112] [6269] 5-8-9 **66**........................ JamieSpencer 5 73+
(J R Fanshawe) *t.k.h: hld up wl in tch in rr: plld out and rdn wl over 1f out: str run fnl f to ld on line* **7/2**[1]

1-21 **2** *shd* **Wrighty Almighty (IRE)**[16] [246] 6-8-12 **69**........................ JimCrowley 4 76
(P R Chamings) *lw: s.i.s: t.k.h: sn in tch in midfield: rdn 3f out: r.o wl u.p fnl f: snatched 2nd on line* **7/2**[1]

46-1 **3** *shd* **Garden Party**[11] [311] 4-9-2 **73**........................ TGMcLaughlin 2 80
(Jane Chapple-Hyam) *s.i.s: sn prom: rdn and lost pl on inner jst over 2f out: rallied ins fnl f: led towards fin: hdd and lost 2 pls last strides* **11/1**

3-32 **4** *shd* **Faithful Ruler (USA)**[15] [258] 4-8-9 **66**........................(b) FergusSweeney 10 72
(M A Magnusson) *lw: stdd and dropped in after s: t.k.h: hld up wl in tch in rr: hdwy 2f out: swtchd rt 1f out: r.o: nt quite rch ldrs* **4/1**[2]

0-05 **5** *shd* **Moonlight Man**[11] [314] 7-9-4 **75**........................ LPKeniry 6 81
(C R Dore) *in tch: hdwy to press ldrs wl over 2f out: rdn over 2f out: led ins fnl f: hdd and no ex towards fin* **15/2**[3]

0-51 **6** *nk* **Satyricon**[19] [208] 4-8-13 **70**........................ URispoli 9 75
(M Botti) *lw: hld up in tch on outer: rdn 2f out: kpt on fnl f: nt quite rch ldrs* **11/1**

31-6 **7** *hd* **Corlough Mountain**[32] [63] 4-8-12 **69**........................ JimmyQuinn 8 74
(M J McGrath) *led: rdn 2f out: hdd ins fnl f: btn whn n.m.r nr fin* **16/1**

-032 **8** *1* **Parkview Love (USA)**[14] [274] 7-8-8 **68**........................(v) TolleyDean(3) 3 71
(D Shaw) *t.k.h: chsd ldr: ev ch and rdn over 2f out: one pce ins fnl f* **8/1**

335- **9** *½* **Chief Exec**[40] [7253] 6-8-4 **68**........................ DavidProbert(7) 7 70
(J R Gask) *hld up in tch: effrt to chse ldrs jst over 2f out: rdn 2f out: fdd last 100yds* **16/1**

1m 38.42s (0.22) **Going Correction** +0.05s/f (Slow) 9 Ran SP% **115.8**
Speed ratings (Par 103): **100,99,99,99,99 99,99,98,97**
CSF £15.75 CT £120.91 TOTE £3.90: £1.90, £1.30, £3.50; EX 18.80 Trifecta £97.60 Pool £222.71 - 1.62 winning units.
Owner Clipper Logistics **Bred** Barouche Stud Ireland Ltd **Trained** Newmarket, Suffolk

FOCUS
A modest handicap, run at a steady early pace, which resulted in the first seven being very closely covered at the finish. With them finishing in a heap the bare form is very ordinary, with the seventh maybe the best guide.

453 ARENALEISUREPLC.COM H'CAP — 7f (P)
2:00 (2:00) (Class 6) (0-58,58) 4-Y-O+ **£1,876** (£554; £277) **Stalls** Low

Form RPR

101- **1** **Joy And Pain**[72] [6950] 7-8-13 **55**........................(p) IanMongan 3 65+
(M J Attwater) *hld up wl in tch: rdn 2f out: drvn to chse ldr ins fnl f: r.o to ld towards fin* **10/1**

41-2 **2** *hd* **Dawson Creek (IRE)**[7] [356] 4-9-0 **56**........................ GregFairley 7 65
(B Gubby) *led: rdn 2f out: kpt on wl tl hdd and no ex towards fin* **11/8**[1]

05-5 **3** *1¼* **Nikki Bea (IRE)**[14] [276] 5-8-7 **56**........................ HarryPoulton(7) 6 62
(Jamie Poulton) *chsd ldr: rdn and tried to chal over 1f out: kpt on same pce fnl f* **14/1**

-520 **4** *1¼* **Imperium**[4] [407] 7-9-2 **58**........................ DaneO'Neill 4 61
(Jean-Rene Auvray) *t.k.h: trckd ldrs: rdn and effrt 2f out: chsd ldrs 1f out: sn edgd lft: outpcd last 100yds* **9/1**

-204 **5** *1* **Napoletano (GER)**[7] [356] 7-9-0 **56**........................(p) JamieSpencer 1 56
(S Dow) *t.k.h: hld up in last tl hdwy on outer to chse ldrs over 4f out: rdn 2f out: sn outpcd and btn* **11/2**[3]

3550 **6** *shd* **King After**[2] [430] 6-9-0 **56**........................(v) JimCrowley 2 58+
(J R Best) *broke wl but sn stdd bk and hld up in rr: effrt on inner 2f out: styng on whn nt clr run and snatched up jst ins fnl f: no ch after* **9/2**[2]

1-34 **7** *nk* **Grand Assault**[10] [327] 5-8-12 **54**........................(be) AdamKirby 5 53
(G C Bravery) *in tch tl dropped to rr and rdn over 3f out: nvr trbld ldrs after* **7/1**

1m 25.38s (0.58) **Going Correction** +0.05s/f (Slow) 7 Ran SP% **113.9**
Speed ratings (Par 101): **98,97,96,94,93 93,93**
CSF £24.15 TOTE £10.30: £5.20, £1.60; EX 21.60.
Owner Phones Direct Partnership **Bred** Jonathan Shack **Trained** Epsom, Surrey
■ Stewards' Enquiry : Dane O'Neill one-day ban: careless riding (Feb 17)

FOCUS
A moderate handicap, run at a fair pace. The runner-up helps to set the level and the winner could build on this.
Imperium Official explanation: trainer said gelding lost a shoe

454 LINGFIELDPARK.CO.UK MAIDEN STKS — 1m 2f (P)
2:30 (2:30) (Class 5) 3-Y-O **£2,331** (£693; £346; £173) **Stalls** Low

Form RPR

2 **1** **Electrolyser (IRE)**[32] [58] 3-9-3 0........................ AdamKirby 1 82+
(C G Cox) *trckd ldrs: rdn and effrt jst over 2f out: led jst over 1f out: in command and pushed out fnl f* **1/2**[1]

2 *1½* **Red Linnet** 3-8-12 0........................ HayleyTurner 2 72
(M L W Bell) *leggy: in tch: rdn over 2f out: chsd wnr 1f out: edgd rt and nt pce of wnr fnl f* **16/1**

22- **3** *4* **The Riddler (IRE)**[136] [5663] 3-9-3 79........................ TPQueally 3 69
(J A Osborne) *led: jnd 3f out: sn rdn: hdd jst over 1f out: sn btn* **4/1**[2]

625- **4** *4* **Clovis**[48] [7204] 3-9-3 73........................ JamieSpencer 6 61
(M Johnston) *lw: restless in stalls: chsd ldr: upsides 3f out: rdn jst over 2f out: wknd qckly wl over 1f out* **11/2**[3]

0-5 **5** *4* **Pie O My (IRE)**[12] [310] 3-9-3 0........................ StephenDonohoe 5 53
(J Jay) *a bhd: rdn and lost tch over 3f out: no ch whn rn wd bnd 2f out* **66/1**

6 *2* **Royal Soverin** 3-9-3 0........................ PatCosgrave 4 49
(M J Wallace) *w'like: bit bkwd: s.i.s: sn bustled along: a bhd: drvn and lost tch wl over 3f out: no ch after* **33/1**

0-00 **7** *dist* **Den's Boy**[18] [223] 3-8-10 42........................ HarryPoulton(7) 7 —
(J R Boyle) *chsd ldrs tl lost pl over 4f out: t.o and eased last 2f* **100/1**

2m 6.23s (-0.37) **Going Correction** +0.05s/f (Slow) 7 Ran SP% **113.4**
Speed ratings (Par 97): **103,101,98,95,92 90,—**
CSF £10.68 TOTE £1.60: £1.10, £4.20; EX 9.80.
Owner Mr And Mrs P Hargreaves **Bred** Darley **Trained** Lambourn, Berks

FOCUS
The first pair came clear in this fair maiden and the winner looks a useful prospect. It was a decent winning time for a race of its type.
The Riddler(IRE) Official explanation: jockey said colt hung right
Clovis Official explanation: jockey said gelding hung right

455 NEXT MEETING ON SATURDAY CLAIMING STKS — 1m 5f (P)
3:05 (3:06) (Class 6) 4-Y-O+ **£1,774** (£523; £262) **Stalls** Low

Form RPR

4-13 **1** **Champagne Shadow (IRE)**[5] [388] 7-9-7 75........................ ChrisCatlin 2 65+
(J Pearce) *trckd ldrs: rdn to ld over 1f out: sn clr: comf* **1/1**[1]

050- **2** *3½* **Amnesty**[63] [4534] 9-8-13 40........................(v[1]) JimmyQuinn 8 49
(L A Dace) *stdd s: hld up in rr: stdy hdwy fr 5f out: chsd ldrs 2f out: rdn to chse wnr 1f out: no imp* **14/1**

40-0 **3** *3½* **Montosari**[4] [405] 9-9-3 62........................ IanMongan 6 48
(R A Teal) *in tch: chsd ldr 7f out: rdn to ld over 2f out: hdd over 1f out: sn btn* **11/4**[2]

503/ **4** *¾* **Barnbrook Empire (IRE)**[514] [3896] 6-8-9 0........................ KylieManser(7) 1 46
(L A Dace) *in tch: rdn over 1f out: sn outpcd* **33/1**

01-0 **5** *1* **Victory Mile (USA)**[19] [212] 4-8-9 56........................(b[1]) SteveDrowne 7 41
(M F Harris) *chsd ldr tl 7f out: lost pl over 2f out: bhd and swtchd rt over 1f out: plugged on past btn horses ins fnl f* **8/1**[3]

53-6 **6** *2* **Rosie's Glory (USA)**[11] [320] 4-8-4 56........................(v) HayleyTurner 5 33
(M F Harris) *led: rdn and hdd 2f out: wknd qckly over 1f out* **8/1**[3]

00-0 **7** *2* **Pink Salmon**[34] [24] 4-8-10 35........................ TGMcLaughlin 3 36
(Mrs L J Mongan) *t.k.h: trckd ldrs tl dropped to rr 4f out: tried to rally u.p over 1f out: nvr nr ldrs* **66/1**

2m 47.77s (1.77) **Going Correction** +0.05s/f (Slow)
WFA 4 from 6yo+ 4lb 7 Ran SP% **110.0**
Speed ratings (Par 101): **96,93,91,91,90 89,88**
CSF £15.85 TOTE £1.70: £1.20, £4.20; EX 18.00 Trifecta £69.50 Pool £522.74 - 5.34 winning units..
Owner Miss Audrey Lanham **Bred** Mrs Kate Watson **Trained** Newmarket, Suffolk

FOCUS
A very weak claimer and dubious form, with the winner not needing to be anywhere near his best.

456 KIDS ARE ALWAYS HAPPY @ PONTIN'S H'CAP — 7f (P)
3:35 (3:35) (Class 4) (0-85,92) 4-Y-O+ **£4,100** (£1,227; £613; £306; £152) **Stalls** Low

Form RPR

2411 **1** **Bazroy (IRE)**[3] [417] 4-9-12 92 12ex........................(b) StephenDonohoe 4 106+
(P D Evans) *hld up in last: stl last jst over 2f out: plld out and hdwy wl over 1f out: edgd lft but r.o strly fnl f to ld towards fin* **6/1**[3]

4-42 **2** *¾* **Super Frank (IRE)**[11] [313] 5-8-8 74........................ ChrisCatlin 9 86
(J Akehurst) *lw: chsd ldr tl led over 2f out: rdn 2f out: hdd and nt pce of wnr towards fin* **7/2**[2]

0-53 **3** *1* **Cornus**[11] [313] 6-8-11 77........................(be) JamesDoyle 3 86
(A J McCabe) *trckd ldrs: rdn 2f out: edgd sltly rt 1f out: kpt on u.p fnl f* **14/1**

02-4 **4** *1* **Danetime Lord (IRE)**[18] [233] 5-9-2 82........................(p) FergalLynch 2 89
(K A Ryan) *stdd s: hld up in rr: rdn and effrt on inner wl over 1f out: chsd ldrs 1f out: no imp last 100yds* **11/1**

40-5 **5** *shd* **Tender The Great (IRE)**[9] [336] 5-9-3 83........................ TQuinn 6 90+
(B G Powell) *t.k.h: hld up towards rr: hdwy 2f out: swtchd rt over 1f out: running on whn short of room and snatched up ins fnl f: unable to rcvr* **10/1**

21-1 **6** 1 1/4 **Halsion Chancer**[34] 26 4-9-4 84 GeorgeBaker 5 89+
(J R Best) *t.k.h: chsd ldrs: rdn and effrt 2f out: chsd ldr briefly 1f out: wkng whn squeezed out and snatched up ins fnl f* **7/4**[1]
0-04 **7** 3/4 **Lethal**[10] 329 5-9-2 82 PaulHanagan 1 83
(R A Fahey) *lw: led tl over 2f out: rdn 2f out: wknd ins fnl f* **11/1**
00-3 **8** 2 **Celtic Step**[9] 342 4-8-5 71 (b) GregFairley 7 67
(M Johnston) *chsd ldrs: rdn and struggling jst over 2f out: btn whn sltly hmpd over 1f out* **16/1**
2-50 **9** 3 **Smokin Joe**[7] 357 7-8-10 76 (b) JimCrowley 8 63
(J R Best) *lw: hld up towards rr: rdn and effrt over 2f out: wknd over 1f out* **20/1**

1m 22.93s (-1.87) **Going Correction** +0.05s/f (Slow) course record **9** Ran SP% **115.9**
Speed ratings (Par 105): **112,111,110,108,108 107,106,104,100**
CSF £27.42 CT £285.99 TOTE £6.10: £2.10, £2.00, £3.30; EX 32.50 Trifecta £131.30 Pool £636.32 - 3.44 winning units..
Owner Barry McCabe **Bred** P D Savill **Trained** Pandy, Monmouths
FOCUS
A decent handicap for the grade, run at a solid pace. The winner continues on the up and produced a very smart winning time indeed, 2.45 seconds quicker than the earlier handicap over the same trip. A positive view has been taken of the form.

457 FUN-BELIEVABLE - THAT'S PONTIN'S FAMILY HOLIDAYS H'CAP 6f (P)
4:10 (4:16) (Class 4) (0-85,83) 3-Y-O **£4,100** (£1,227; £613; £306; £152) **Stalls** Low

Form RPR
44-2 **1** **Mister New York (USA)**[18] 228 3-8-3 71 KirstyMilczarek(3) 3 76
(Noel T Chance) *lw: trckd ldrs: rdn to ld on inner wl over 1f out: styd on wl* **3/1**[1]
4-1 **2** 1 **Monadreen Flyer (IRE)**[18] 228 3-9-1 80 ChrisCatlin 1 82
(Daniel Mark Loughnane, Ire) *led: hung rt 3f out and again bnd 2f out: sn hdd: kpt on u.p* **5/1**[3]
216- **3** 1 1/2 **Rockfield Lodge (IRE)**[141] 5509 3-8-12 77 TPQueally 8 74+
(J A Osborne) *hmpd s: t.k.h: hld up in rr: hdwy over 2f out: carried wd bnd 2f out: kpt on to go 3rd ins fnl f: nt trble ldng pair* **8/1**
01-1 **4** nk **Hucking Hero (IRE)**[34] 25 3-8-13 78 JimCrowley 2 74
(J R Best) *awkward leaving stalls: hld up in tch: rdn and hdwy inner over 1f out: chsd ldng pair 1f out: no imp after* **10/3**[2]
6-31 **5** 1 3/4 **Kingsgate Castle**[14] 271 3-8-5 70 JimmyQuinn 5 61
(J R Best) *lw: hmpd s: sn chsng ldr: rdn and ev ch whn carried wd bnd 2f out: wknd fnl f* **3/1**[1]
100- **6** 2 **Geoffdaw**[124] 5974 3-8-12 77 DaneO'Neill 4 61
(M J Wallace) *wnt rt s: in tch: rdn over 2f out: outpcd over 1f out* **8/1**

1m 12.36s (0.46) **Going Correction** +0.05s/f (Slow) **6** Ran SP% **112.0**
Speed ratings (Par 99): **98,96,94,94,91 89**
CSF £17.99 CT £105.21 TOTE £3.30: £2.00, £2.20; EX 14.60 Trifecta £70.90 Pool £708.04 - 7.09 winning units..
Owner Mrs M Chance **Bred** J S McDonald **Trained** Upper Lambourn, Berks
FOCUS
A fair sprit handicap, featuring four last-time-out winners, which was run at a decent pace. Slight improvement from the winner.

458 MEET CAPTAIN CROC @ PONTIN'S H'CAP 1m (P)
4:40 (4:45) (Class 5) (0-75,75) 3-Y-O **£2,590** (£770; £385; £192) **Stalls** High

Form RPR
506- **1** **Rockfield Tiger (IRE)**[161] 4947 3-9-1 72 SteveDrowne 2 80+
(J A Osborne) *hld up in rr: swtchd rt over 1f out: pushed along and r.o wl to ld last strides* **17/2**
032- **2** shd **Segal (IRE)**[81] 6850 3-9-2 73 TPQueally 3 79+
(J Noseda) *lw: in tch: plld out 3f out: rdn to ld 1f out: hdd last strides* **5/4**[1]
4-13 **3** 2 1/2 **Royal Applord**[16] 253 3-9-4 75 FergalLynch 6 75
(K A Ryan) *chsd ldr: upsides ldr and rdn 2f out: led narrowly over 1f out: hdd 1f out: outpcd by ldng pair: kpt on* **8/1**
301- **4** nk **Easy Wonder (GER)**[90] 6734 3-8-13 70 RichardThomas 7 69
(I A Wood) *led: jnd 2f out: rdn and hdd over 1f out: outpcd by ldng pair fnl f: kpt on* **33/1**
42-1 **5** nk **Taken (IRE)**[26] 130 3-9-4 75 JamieSpencer 5 74+
(J R Fanshawe) *stdd s: hld up in last: c wd and effrt bnd 2f out: sn rdn and hanging lft: kpt on but nvr trbld ldrs* **11/4**[2]
03-3 **6** 1 1/2 **Hollow Point (IRE)**[11] 321 3-8-6 63 GregFairley 1 58
(M Johnston) *s.i.s: sn chsng ldrs: rdn and outpcd jst over 2f out: no ch after* **25/1**
31-2 **7** 1/2 **Safebreaker**[23] 157 3-9-4 75 JimCrowley 4 69
(N Tinkler) *lw: hld up towards rr: pushed along 4f out: rdn and effrt jst over 2f out: sn outpcd and btn* **5/1**[3]

1m 38.86s (0.66) **Going Correction** +0.05s/f (Slow) **7** Ran SP% **116.2**
Speed ratings (Par 97): **98,97,95,95,94 93,92**
CSF £20.29 TOTE £10.20: £3.20, £1.70; EX 33.30 Place 6 £27.25, Place 5 £15.40..
Owner Michael O'Flynn & Mrs John Nesbitt **Bred** Castlefarm Stud **Trained** Upper Lambourn, Berks
FOCUS
A fair three-year-old handicap, run at a fair pace. The form looks sound based around the third and fourth, with the first pair coming clear.
T/Plt: £22.30 to a £1 stake. Pool: £58,185.60. 1,897.60 winning tickets. T/Qpdt: £6.20 to a £1 stake. Pool: £3,202.10. 377.45 winning tickets. SP

438 SOUTHWELL (L-H)
Thursday, February 7

OFFICIAL GOING: Standard
Wind: Moderate, across Weather: Fine and dry

459 BOOK BEST BREAKS @ PONTINS.COM H'CAP 5f (F)
1:30 (1:30) (Class 5) (0-75,73) 4-Y-0+ **£2,593** (£765; £383) **Stalls** High

Form RPR
40-2 **1** **Bo McGinty (IRE)**[11] 329 7-9-4 73 (b) PaulHanagan 2 84
(R A Fahey) *cl up: rdn 2f out: led 1f out: drvn: edgd rt and hdd wl ins fnl f: rallied ld nr line* **15/8**[1]
00-0 **2** shd **Spoof Master (IRE)**[37] 4 4-9-1 70 JimCrowley 1 81
(S A Callaghan) *cl up: effrt 2f out: rdn to chal over 1f out: drvn and slt ld wl ins fnl f: hdd and no ex nr line* **3/1**[2]
0-51 **3** 1 1/2 **Lord Of The Reins (IRE)**[14] 286 4-8-7 65 TolleyDean(3) 4 70
(D Shaw) *in tch: swtchd lft and hdwy 2f out: rdn to chse ldng pair ins fnl f: drvn and nt qckn last 100yds* **8/1**
-651 **4** 1 1/2 **Doubtful Sound (USA)**[13] 307 4-8-13 73 NeilBrown(5) 3 73
(T D Barron) *trckd ldrs: effrt 2f out: sn rdn and one pce* **13/2**
03-3 **5** 2 **After The Show**[22] 187 7-8-9 64 (p) JamesDoyle 6 57
(Rae Guest) *led: rdn along 2f out: drvn and hdd over 1f out: sn wknd* **5/1**[3]
52-3 **6** 2 1/2 **Desert Opal**[14] 286 8-9-1 70 (b) TPQueally 5 54
(C R Dore) *chsd ldrs: rdn along 2f out: sn btn* **8/1**

59.59 secs (-0.11) **Going Correction** +0.075s/f (Slow) **6** Ran SP% **112.0**
Speed ratings (Par 103): **103,102,100,98,94 90**
CSF £7.64 TOTE £2.70: £1.60, £2.00; EX 7.40.
Owner Paddy McGinty & Bo Turnbull **Bred** Stephen Breen **Trained** Musley Bank, N Yorks
FOCUS
A fair sprint that looks straightforward and solid form for the grade.

460 SOUTHWELL-RACECOURSE.CO.UK CLAIMING STKS 6f (F)
2:00 (2:00) (Class 6) 4-Y-0+ **£1,774** (£523; £262) **Stalls** Low

Form RPR
02-3 **1** **Came Back (IRE)**[21] 194 5-9-3 65 GeorgeBaker 6 78+
(J Mackie) *trckd ldrs gng wl: hdwy on bit to join ldr 1 1/2f out: rdn to ld ent fnl f: styd on* **3/1**[2]
-142 **2** 2 **Dickie Le Davoir**[9] 346 4-9-9 72 FergalLynch 3 77
(I W McInnes) *hld up in rr: hdwy on 2f out: rdn to chse ldrs over 1f out: kpt on u.p ins fnl f: tk 2nd on line* **3/1**[2]
0315 **3** hd **Cleveland**[14] 278 6-8-10 64 RussellKennemore(5) 4 69
(R Hollinshead) *cl up: rdn to ld wl over 1f out: sn drvn and hdd ent fnl f: kpt on same pce* **11/4**[1]
0-44 **4** hd **Nautical**[9] 347 10-8-10 55 KirstyMilczarek(3) 8 66
(A W Carroll) *in tch: hdwy over 2f out: sn rdn and styd on u.p fnl f: nrst fin* **11/1**
1-32 **5** 5 **Pegasus Dancer (FR)**[13] 307 4-9-7 70 (p) DarryllHolland 2 58
(K A Ryan) *led: rdn along over 2f out: drvn and hdd wl over 1f out: grad wknd* **7/1**[3]
6-45 **6** 3/4 **Ocean Pride (IRE)**[19] 229 5-8-7 50 (bt) HayleyTurner 7 42
(D E Pipe) *towards rr: rdn along 1/2-way: kpt on fr over 1f out: n.d* **25/1**
1-00 **7** 3 **Monashee Brave (IRE)**[8] 356 5-8-11 58 JimmyQuinn 10 36
(M A Allen) *chsd ldrs: rdn along over 2f out: sn drvn and wknd* **22/1**
0-03 **8** 1/2 **Owed**[9] 346 6-9-11 70 PatCosgrave 1 48
(R Bastiman) *n.m.r on inner sn after s: chsd ldng pair: hdwy over 2f out: rdn and ch wl over 1f out: sn drvn and wknd* **12/1**
6-06 **9** 3 1/2 **Totally Free**[13] 304 4-8-4 55 (v) PatrickHills(5) 5 21
(M D I Usher) *s.i.s: a in rr* **40/1**

1m 16.16s (-0.34) **Going Correction** -0.10s/f (Stan) **9** Ran SP% **115.8**
Speed ratings (Par 101): **98,95,95,94,88 87,83,82,77**
CSF £12.21 TOTE £3.60: £1.50, £1.50, £1.50; EX 13.90 Trifecta £63.40 Pool: £209.17 - 2.34 winning units..The winner was claimed by P. A. Blockley for £10,000.
Owner W I Bloomfield **Bred** Yeomanstown Stud **Trained** Church Broughton , Derbys
■ Stewards' Enquiry : Darryll Holland one-day ban: careless riding (Feb 18)
FOCUS
Not a bad claimer and competitive enough on the figures. They went a good pace and the form looks sound rated around the placed horses.
Cleveland Official explanation: jockey said gelding ran too freely

461 MAD FOR IT AT PONTIN'S H'CAP 2m (F)
2:30 (2:30) (Class 6) (0-65,62) 4-Y-0+ **£1,911** (£564; £282) **Stalls** Low

Form RPR
-211 **1** **Mujamead**[12] 322 4-9-4 62 (p) JerryO'Dwyer(3) 7 71+
(A W Carroll) *trckd ldrs: pushed along over 4f out: hdwy to ld 2f out: rdn over 1f out: drvn and edgd lft ins fnl f: hld on gamely* **10/3**[2]
00-3 **2** shd **Squiffy**[22] 179 5-9-4 53 DaneO'Neill 3 62+
(P D Cundell) *a cl up: led 3f out: rdn and hdd 2f out: rallied u.p ins fnl f and ev ch tl drvn and nt qckn nr line* **2/1**[1]
06-0 **3** 4 **Sovietta (IRE)**[2] 438 7-9-0 49 (t) StephenDonohoe 10 53
(Ian Williams) *hld up in tch: smooth hdwy 3f out: rdn and ev ch 2f out tl drvn and one pce appr fnl f* **18/1**
0-00 **4** 1 3/4 **Salut Saint Cloud**[19] 224 7-9-1 50 (p) SimonWhitworth 6 52
(G L Moore) *hld up and bhd: hdwy 4f out: sn pushed along: styd on u.p fnl 2f: nt rch ldrs* **9/2**[3]
0-42 **5** 1 **El Dee (IRE)**[14] 283 5-8-5 45 KellyHarrison(5) 8 46
(Jedd O'Keeffe) *hld up towards rr: hdwy over 4f out: rdn along wl over 2f out: sn no imp* **10/1**
/60- **6** 1 3/4 **Pochard**[2156] 5-9-13 62 HayleyTurner 2 61
(J M P Eustace) *mde most tl rdn along and hdd 3f out: sn drvn and grad wknd* **22/1**
0652 **7** 8 **Chiff Chaff**[7] 374 4-8-7 48 LPKeniry 4 37
(C R Dore) *trckd ldrs: effrt over 3f out: sn rdn and btn over 2f out* **11/2**
8 3 1/2 **Aston (USA)**[8] 4354 8-8-10 45 (v) GrahamGibbons 5 30
(R C Guest) *reminders sn after s: in tch tl hdwy on outer and cl up after 4f: rdn along over 5f out and sn wknd* **40/1**
/60- **9** 1/2 **Salawat**[80] 6875 5-8-7 45 KirstyMilczarek(3) 9 29
(T T Clement) *hld up: a in rr* **100/1**
0-65 **10** 6 **Good Cause (IRE)**[7] 368 7-9-6 55 PaulHanagan 1 32
(Mrs S Lamyman) *trckd ldrs on inner: rdn along 4f out: wknd wl over 2f out* **25/1**

3m 43.59s (-1.91) **Going Correction** -0.10s/f (Stan)
WFA 4 from 5yo+ 6lb **10** Ran SP% **116.0**
Speed ratings (Par 101): **100,99,97,97,96 95,91,89,89,86**
CSF £9.99 CT £101.57 TOTE £3.80: £1.90, £1.30, £3.40; EX 12.20 Trifecta £77.00 Pool: £260.42 - 2.40 winning units..
Owner J T Billson **Bred** D R Tucker **Trained** Cropthorne, Worcs
■ Stewards' Enquiry : Dane O'Neill three-day ban: used whip with excessive frequency (Feb 18-20)
FOCUS
An ordinary handicap in which the pace was not too strong, and the field was well bunched entering the straight. The form does not look that solid.

462 CAPTAIN CROC MAKES PONTIN'S HOLIDAYS ROCK (S) STKS 7f (F)
3:00 (3:00) (Class 6) 3-Y-O **£1,774** (£523; £262) **Stalls** Low

Form RPR
-233 **1** **Copperbottomed (IRE)**[5] 403 3-9-3 67 (e) JimCrowley 2 64
(J R Boyle) *cl up: led over 2f out: pushed along fnl f: kpt on* **5/6**[1]
-450 **2** 3/4 **Novestar (IRE)**[2] 439 3-8-11 49 SimonWhitworth 4 56
(G J Smith) *cl up on outer: effrt 2f out: sn rdn and chsd wnr ent fnl f: drvn and kpt on* **17/2**
40-6 **3** 1 1/2 **Cherished Song**[21] 195 3-8-6 57 GregFairley 5 47
(M G Quinlan) *chsd ldrs: rdn along 2f out: drvn and one pce appr fnl f* **5/1**[3]
06-0 **4** 1 3/4 **Lechero (IRE)**[2] 439 3-8-11 53 StephenDonohoe 1 47
(P A Blockley) *led: rdn along and hdd over 2f out: sn drvn and wknd over 1f out* **10/3**[2]

The Form Book, Raceform Ltd, Compton, RG20 6NL

00-5 **5** *14* **Whistful Miss**[3] 425 3-8-6 48 JimmyQuinn 3 —
(P Howling) *sn outpcd and a bhd* **16/1**
1m 30.83s (0.53) **Going Correction** -0.10s/f (Stan) **5** Ran SP% **110.7**
Speed ratings (Par 95): **92,91,89,87,71**
CSF £8.74 TOTE £1.40: £1.10, £4.00; EX 8.00.The winner was bought in for 6,000gns.
Owner M Khan X2 **Bred** Paul McEnery **Trained** Epsom, Surrey
FOCUS
A weak seller and the form looks dubious with the runner-up rated to his best recent form.

463 GO ACTIVE @ PONTIN'S HOLIDAY CENTRES H'CAP 7f (F)
3:30 (3:31) (Class 4) (0-80,80) 4-Y-0+ **£4,210** (£1,252; £625; £312) **Stalls** Low

Form RPR
002- **1** **Yakimov (USA)**[51] 7175 9-9-4 80 VinceSlattery 1 91
(D J Wintle) *trckd ldrs on inner: rdn along and hdwy 2f out: led wl over 1f out: drvn 2l clr ent fnl f: styd on wl* **12/1**
0362 **2** *1 1/2* **Dudley Docker (IRE)**[9] 351 6-8-11 73 (p) LiamJones 2 81
(C R Dore) *plld hrd: hld up on heels of ldrs: hdwy 2f out and sn ev ch: rdn to chse wnr whn edgd lft ins fnl f: kpt on u.p towards fin* **4/5**[1]
4214 **3** *2* **Obe Royal**[5] 404 4-8-2 71 (b) RichardEvans(7) 3 74
(P D Evans) *cl up: ev ch 2f out: sn rdn and sltly outpcd over 1f out: kpt on u.p ins fnl f* **7/2**[2]
460- **4** *hd* **Kelamon**[100] 6568 4-8-3 70 PatrickHills(5) 5 72
(M D I Usher) *chsd ldng pair: hdwy on outer 3f out: chal and ev ch 2f out: sn rdn and one pce appr fnl f* **13/2**[3]
504- **5** *2* **High 'n Dry (IRE)**[59] 7094 4-8-4 66 JimmyQuinn 4 64
(M A Allen) *led: rdn along 2f out: drvn and hdd wl over 1f out: wknd appr fnl f* **9/1**
1m 28.53s (-1.77) **Going Correction** -0.10s/f (Stan) **5** Ran SP% **108.8**
Speed ratings (Par 105): **106,104,102,101,99**
CSF £22.16 TOTE £9.80: £3.50, £1.50; EX 28.00.
Owner B E T Partnership **Bred** Jane & Jeff Wooder **Trained** Naunton, Gloucs
FOCUS
An ordinary handicap rated around the runner-up to his latest mark.

464 SOUTHWELL FOR RACING AND GOLF H'CAP 1m 3f (F)
4:00 (4:00) (Class 5) (0-70,67) 3-Y-0 **£2,593** (£765; £383) **Stalls** Low

Form RPR
0-52 **1** **Mischief Making (USA)**[19] 221 3-9-4 67 TGMcLaughlin 8 80+
(E A L Dunlop) *hld up and bhd: hdwy on outer over 4f out: rdn along 3f out: hung bdly lft wl over 1f out: drvn and styd on to ld ins fnl f: sn clr* **9/4**[1]
04-3 **2** *2 1/2* **Gayanula (USA)**[23] 172 3-8-10 59 HayleyTurner 9 67
(Miss J A Camacho) *hld up in midfield: hdwy over 4f out: rdn to chal on outer 2f out: led 1 1/2f out: drvn and hdd ins fnl f: kpt on same pce* **14/1**
004- **3** *6* **Whitcombe Spirit**[57] 7114 3-9-3 66 RobertHavlin 1 64+
(Jamie Poulton) *hld up in rr: hdwy whn hmpd wl over 1f out and sn rdn: swtchd lft ent fnl f and styd on* **9/2**[3]
230- **4** *1 1/4* **Space Pirate**[66] 7010 3-8-8 57 (v[1]) JimmyQuinn 6 53
(J Pearce) *hld up: hdwy 1/2-way: chsd ldrs 4f out: rdn along over 2f out: hmpd wl over 1f out: drvn and kpt on one pce after* **16/1**
02-1 **5** *1* **Bookiebasher Babe (IRE)**[14] 281 3-9-0 63 TPQueally 3 57
(M Quinn) *led: rdn along and hdd 3f out: led again 2f out: drvn and hdd 1 1/2f out: sn wknd* **3/1**[2]
3154 **6** *1 1/4* **Tapas Lad (IRE)**[8] 360 3-8-13 62 (v) PatCosgrave 4 54
(V Smith) *cl up: rdn to ld 3f out: drvn and hdd 2f out: sn wknd* **13/2**
00-0 **7** *3/4* **Paul The Carpet (UAE)**[16] 262 3-8-4 53 oh7 GregFairley 5 44
(G L Moore) *chsd ldrs 4f: rdn along and wknd over 4f out* **16/1**
06-4 **8** *5* **Treasure Islands (IRE)**[19] 223 3-8-13 62 LiamJones 7 45
(S W Hall) *chsd ldng pair: pushed along 4f out: rdn over 3f out and sn wknd* **33/1**
6455 **9** *1 1/4* **Silver Sprite**[10] 335 3-8-4 56 ow3 TolleyDean(3) 2 36
(D Shaw) *chsd ldrs: rdn along on inner 4f out: wknd wl over 2f out* **12/1**
2m 26.92s (-1.08) **Going Correction** -0.10s/f (Stan) **9** Ran SP% **116.3**
Speed ratings (Par 97): **99,97,92,91,91 90,89,86,85**
CSF £36.18 CT £133.71 TOTE £3.10: £1.40, £2.20, £1.90; EX 20.70 Trifecta £76.60 Pool: £263.50 - 2.44 winning units..
Owner Cliveden Stud **Bred** Clivedon Stud Ltd **Trained** Newmarket, Suffolk
■ Stewards' Enquiry : T G McLaughlin caution: careless riding
FOCUS
A modest handicap but it featured a few unexposed sorts and was run at a decent pace, resulting in the hold-up horses dominating at the finish. The form looks good for the grade.

465 ARENALEISUREPLC.COM H'CAP 1m (F)
4:30 (4:36) (Class 6) (0-50,50) 4-Y-0+ **£1,911** (£564; £282) **Stalls** Low

Form RPR
6-50 **1** **Anduril**[12] 323 7-8-10 48 (p) FergalLynch 4 57
(I W McInnes) *cl up: effrt and ev ch 2f out: sn rdn: drvn ent fnl f: styd on u.p to ld nr line* **12/1**
4-42 **2** *hd* **Having A Ball**[11] 328 4-8-11 49 DaneO'Neill 1 58
(P D Cundell) *cl up: led 2f out: rdn wl over 1f out: drvn ins fnl f: hdd and no ex nr line* **4/1**[3]
-003 **3** *1 3/4* **Dancing Duo**[9] 349 4-8-8 49 (v) TolleyDean(3) 6 54
(D Shaw) *hld up in rr: hdwy on inner wl over 2f out: rdn to chse ldng pair over 1f out: kpt on same pce fnl f* **16/1**
0-33 **4** *3/4* **Wodhill Schnaps**[21] 193 7-8-11 49 (v) HayleyTurner 5 52
(D Morris) *cl up: effrt on outer and ev ch 2f out and sn rdn: drvn over 1f out and kpt on same pce* **10/3**[2]
-002 **5** *2* **Pawn In Life (IRE)**[7] 365 10-8-1 46 oh1 (v) DeanHeslop(7) 7 45
(Mrs R A Carr) *in tch: rdn along and outpcd wl over 2f out: kpt on u.p appr fnl f* **25/1**
5-32 **6** *nk* **Mister Benji**[14] 284 9-8-12 50 (p) PhillipMakin 8 48
(B P J Baugh) *chsd ldrs on outer: rdn along 1/2-way: drvn wl over 2f out and sn btn* **5/2**[1]
2-65 **7** *3 1/2* **Shifty**[21] 193 9-8-10 48 PaulHanagan 3 38
(Jedd O'Keeffe) *led: rdn along 3f out: drvn and hdd 2f out: sn wknd* **10/1**
0-51 **8** *6* **Rubilini**[7] 365 4-8-3 46 oh1 (p) NataliaGemelova(5) 9 22
(Miss Sheena West) *hld up: hdwy and in tch 3f out: rdn over 2f out and sn wknd* **6/1**
1m 42.74s (-0.96) **Going Correction** -0.10s/f (Stan) **8** Ran SP% **112.4**
Speed ratings (Par 101): **100,99,98,97,95 95,91,85**
CSF £57.46 CT £779.60 TOTE £12.50: £2.90, £1.50, £3.90; EX 54.20 Trifecta £327.40 Part won. Pool: £461.24 - 0.10 winning units. Place 6 £4.87, Place 5 £3.55..
Owner Ivy House Racing **Bred** Miss K Rausing **Trained** Catwick, E Yorks
FOCUS
A poor handicap but sound enough form for the grade withthe three immediately behind the principals close to recent course form.
T/Plt: £9.20 to a £1 stake. Pool: £49,077.00. 3,855.35 winning tickets. T/Qpdt: £3.80 to a £1 stake. Pool: £2,964.80. 564.90 winning tickets. JR

393 WOLVERHAMPTON (A.W) (L-H)
Thursday, February 7

OFFICIAL GOING: Standard
Wind: Light, behind Weather: Fine

466 HORIZONS RESTAURANT APPRENTICE H'CAP 5f 216y(P)
6:50 (6:50) (Class 5) (0-70,68) 4-Y-0+ **£2,331** (£693; £346; £173) **Stalls** Low

Form RPR
63-2 **1** **Bel Cantor**[10] 342 5-9-1 67 (p) KellyHarrison(3) 5 80
(W J H Ratcliffe) *mde all: rdn ins fnl f: r.o* **15/8**[1]
4323 **2** *1* **Chatshow (USA)**[18] 241 7-8-9 58 RussellKennemore 4 68
(A W Carroll) *a.p: chsd wnr 3f out: rdn 2f out: kpt on towards fin* **4/1**[3]
-500 **3** *3 1/2* **Methaaly (IRE)**[5] 404 5-9-0 68 RossAtkinson(5) 3 67
(M Mullineaux) *hld up: hdwy over 2f out: rdn and one pce fnl f* **13/2**
-013 **4** *2* **Avontuur (FR)**[9] 347 6-8-2 54 oh1 (p) DanielleMcCreery(3) 1 46
(Mrs R A Carr) *s.i.s: sn prom: rdn wl over 1f out: wknd ins fnl f* **14/1**
-111 **5** *2 1/2* **Mafaheem**[14] 285 6-8-12 66 PNolan(5) 6 50
(A B Haynes) *prom: rdn over 2f out: wkng whn edgd lft fr over 1f out* **7/1**
3122 **6** *1 3/4* **Strathmore (IRE)**[7] 370 4-8-12 66 BMcHugh(5) 8 45
(R A Fahey) *sn prom: t.k.h: rdn over 2f out: wknd wl over 1f out* **11/4**[2]
10-5 **7** *4* **Dematraf (IRE)**[9] 349 6-8-10 64 RichardEvans(5) 2 30
(P D Evans) *s.i.s: rdn and rdr lost whip 3f out: a in rr* **20/1**
1m 15.48s (0.48) **Going Correction** +0.20s/f (Slow) **7** Ran SP% **118.7**
Speed ratings (Par 103): **104,102,98,95,92 89,84**
CSF £10.40 CT £41.04 TOTE £1.80: £1.20, £2.00; EX 8.50.
Owner W J H Ratcliffe **Bred** Henry And Mrs Rosemary Moszkowicz **Trained** Wensley, N Yorks
FOCUS
A modest handicap but solid enough with the runner-up to recent form and the winner capable of goin higher.
Dematraf(IRE) Official explanation: jockey said mare never travelled

467 STAY AT THE WOLVERHAMPTON HOLIDAY INN (S) STKS 5f 20y(P)
7:20 (7:20) (Class 6) 3-Y-0 **£1,774** (£523; £262) **Stalls** Low

Form RPR
5332 **1** **Orange Square (IRE)**[5] 403 3-8-7 66 PatrickHills(5) 2 50
(R Hannon) *mde all: rdn fnl f: drvn out* **4/6**[1]
5-30 **2** *1/2* **Bahamarama (IRE)**[24] 154 3-8-12 48 PaulHanagan 1 48
(R A Harris) *chsd ldrs: wnt 2nd wl over 1f out: rdn and kpt on ins fnl f* **9/4**[2]
10-6 **3** *4* **Captain Crooner (IRE)**[28] 112 3-9-0 46 TolleyDean(3) 4 39
(D Shaw) *s.i.s: sn outpcd: wnt 3rd ins fnl f: n.d* **6/1**[3]
05-4 **4** *4* **Silver Deal**[14] 279 3-8-2 45 KellyHarrison(5) 3 14
(J A Pickering) *w wnr tl wl over 1f out: sn rdn: wknd fnl f* **12/1**
64.11 secs (1.81) **Going Correction** +0.20s/f (Slow) **4** Ran SP% **112.7**
Speed ratings (Par 95): **93,92,85,79**
CSF £2.61 TOTE £2.10; EX 1.40.The winner was sold to David Barker for 6,500gns.
Owner N A Woodcock,D Pody, M McGee & J Ball **Bred** Mrs P Grubb **Trained** East Everleigh, Wilts
FOCUS
A poor seller and the form is weak rated through the runner-up.

468 SPONSOR A RACE BY CALLING 0870 220 2442 H'CAP 1m 1f 103y(P)
7:50 (7:50) (Class 6) (0-50,50) 4-Y-0+ **£1,774** (£523; £262) **Stalls** Low

Form RPR
003- **1** **Joe Jo Star**[250] 1210 6-8-8 46 oh1 AndrewElliott 6 53
(B P J Baugh) *hld up in tch: rdn and edgd lft wl over 1f out: r.o to ld last strides* **18/1**
6-24 **2** *nk* **Ermine Grey**[11] 328 7-8-9 50 KirstyMilczarek(3) 1 56
(A W Carroll) *a.p: nt clr run over 2f out: rdn to ld jst ins fnl f: hdd last strides* **7/2**[1]
-640 **3** *shd* **Steel Grey**[14] 282 7-8-8 49 oh1 ow3 MarkLawson(3) 10 55
(M Brittain) *w ldr: rdn to ld over 2f out: hdd jst ins fnl f: r.o* **40/1**
4-44 **4** *1 1/4* **Norwegian**[12] 323 7-8-12 50 (p) StephenDonohoe 3 53
(Ian Williams) *hld up in mid-div: hdwy over 2f out: n.m.r wl over 1f out: kpt on ins fnl f* **7/2**[1]
0/2- **5** *1 1/2* **Nassar (IRE)**[339] 616 5-8-11 49 AdrianMcCarthy 5 49
(G Prodromou) *a.p: rdn and ev ch 1f out: fdd towards fin* **7/1**[2]
-643 **6** *1 1/2* **Shaheer (IRE)**[13] 299 6-8-12 50 JimCrowley 11 47
(J Gallagher) *hld up in mid-div: hdwy over 2f out: rdn wl over 1f out: wknd ins fnl f* **7/1**[2]
00-5 **7** *5* **Floodlight Fantasy**[20] 215 5-8-10 48 (p) HayleyTurner 8 34
(Dr R D P Newland) *bhd: rdn 3f out: nvr nr ldrs* **10/1**
400- **8** *2* **Rotuma (IRE)**[20] 4972 9-8-10 48 (b) PhillipMakin 9 30
(M Dods) *bhd: rdn 3f out: n.d* **7/1**[2]
-643 **9** *2* **Ponte Vecchio (IRE)**[17] 242 4-8-8 46 oh1 (v[1]) FergusSweeney 2 24
(J R Boyle) *led: rdn and hdd over 2f out: wknd wl over 1f out* **8/1**[3]
0-45 **10** *1 1/2* **Bobering**[17] 251 8-8-1 46 SoniaEaton(7) 7 21
(B P J Baugh) *a towards rr* **7/1**[2]
02-0 **11** *5* **Korty**[27] 123 4-8-12 50 (t) SteveDrowne 4 14
(W J Musson) *s.s whn rdr late removing blind fold: a in rr* **12/1**
2m 3.40s (1.70) **Going Correction** +0.20s/f (Slow) **11** Ran SP% **123.4**
Speed ratings (Par 101): **100,99,99,98,97 95,91,89,87,86 82**
CSF £84.22 CT £2577.23 TOTE £16.70: £3.90, £1.90, £16.20; EX 170.00.
Owner Joe Singh **Bred** B J And Mrs Crangle **Trained** Audley, Staffs
■ Stewards' Enquiry : Adrian McCarthy one-day ban: careless riding (Feb 18)
FOCUS
A plating-class affair and the form is sound but limited.
Ermine Grey Official explanation: jockey said gelding was denied a clear run

469 HOTEL & CONFERENCING AT WOLVERHAMPTON H'CAP 5f 216y(P)
8:20 (8:21) (Class 6) (0-50,51) 4-Y-0+ **£1,774** (£523; £262) **Stalls** Low

Form RPR
50-3 **1** **Smirfys Systems**[17] 255 9-8-9 47 (p) StephenDonohoe 7 59
(E S McMahon) *a.p: led over 4f out: clr 2f out: sn rdn: r.o* **15/2**
0-21 **2** *2* **Avoca Dancer (IRE)**[15] 264 5-8-11 49 NickyMackay 3 58+
(M Wigham) *hld up and bhd: hdwy 2f out: rdn to chse wnr 1f out: edgd lft: no imp* **2/1**[2]
00-0 **3** *1 3/4* **Nabra**[30] 79 4-8-9 50 MarkLawson(3) 4 50
(M Brittain) *bhd: hdwy on outside over 2f out: rdn over 1f out: one pce* **16/1**
0-25 **4** *2* **Avoncreek**[19] 232 4-8-8 46 oh1 AndrewElliott 2 40
(B P J Baugh) *sn led: hdd over 4f out: chsd wnr tl rdn 1f out: wknd* **7/1**
043 **5** *nk* **Prettilini**[1] 445 5-8-5 46 oh1 KirstyMilczarek(3) 5 39
(A W Carroll) *w ldrs tl rdn and wknd 2f out* **13/2**[3]

-060 6 shd **Kissi Kissi**[17] 254 5-8-8 46 oh1 .... AdrianMcCarthy 1 38
(M J Attwater) *s.i.s: rdn over 2f out: sn bhd* **25/1**
0-21 7 5 **Charlotte Grey**[17] 254 4-8-7 50 .... JackMitchell(5) 6 26
(P J McBride) *led early: prom tl rdn and wknd over 2f out* **15/8**[1]
1m 16.22s (1.22) **Going Correction** +0.20s/f (Slow) 7 Ran SP% **115.4**
Speed ratings (Par 101): **99,96,94,91,90 90,84**
CSF £23.42 CT £237.05 TOTE £7.80: £2.30, £1.70; EX 25.80.
Owner Mrs Dian Plant **Bred** Gerard Bingham **Trained** Lichfield, Staffs
FOCUS
A low-grade handicap with the runner-up offering solid recent form but slightly disappointing.
Charlotte Grey Official explanation: jockey said filly ran flat

470 WOLVERHAMPTON-RACECOURSE.CO.UK H'CAP 5f 20y(P)
8:50 (8:50) (Class 4) (0-85,83) 3-Y-O £4,210 (£1,252; £625; £312) Stalls Low

Form RPR
050- 1 **Soopacal (IRE)**[89] 6756 3-9-2 78 .... PaulHanagan 5 89+
(B Smart) *bmpd s: hld up and bhd: rdn and hdwy over 1f out: led ins fnl f: r.o wl* **7/2**[2]
13-3 2 3 **The Game**[19] 228 3-9-7 83 .... PatCosgrave 2 83
(J R Boyle) *t.k.h: rdn and edgd rt over 1f out: kpt on to take 2nd towards fin* **3/1**[1]
146- 3 1 **Fast Feet**[39] 7280 3-9-1 77 ....(p) FergalLynch 1 73
(K A Ryan) *chsd wnr tl rdn and hung rt 1f out: one pce* **3/1**[1]
5-21 4 hd **Baytown Blaze**[17] 243 3-8-12 74 .... TGMcLaughlin 4 70
(M Wigham) *wnt rt s: led: clr over 2f out: edgd rt and c wd st: rdn over 1f out: hdd ins fnl f: one pce* **13/2**
111- 5 nk **Weet A Surprise**[42] 7243 3-9-0 76 .... HayleyTurner 6 71
(R Hollinshead) *bhd: swtchd lft wl over 1f out: rdn 1f out: nvr able to chal* **5/1**[3]
-443 6 nk **Loose Caboose (IRE)**[8] 364 3-8-5 67 ....(p) PatrickMathers 3 61
(A J McCabe) *chsd ldrs: rdn over 2f out: btn whn hung lft wl over 1f out* **13/2**
62.38 secs (0.08) **Going Correction** +0.20s/f (Slow) 6 Ran SP% **115.6**
Speed ratings (Par 99): **107,102,100,100,99 99**
CSF £14.95 TOTE £4.60: £3.30, £1.70; EX 10.50.
Owner Brian Grieve & Jeff Evans **Bred** Paul Trainor **Trained** Hambleton, N Yorks
FOCUS
This fair handicap was run at a fast clip which suited the winner who came from off the pace. The form looks solid with the placed horses consistent of late and the winner quite impressive although being suited by the way the race was run.

471 BOOK TICKETS ONLINE CLASSIFIED STKS 2m 119y(P)
9:20 (9:20) (Class 7) 4-Y-O+ £1,365 (£403; £201) Stalls Low

Form RPR
/3-6 1 **Rebel Raider (IRE)**[19] 231 9-8-13 45 ....(v1) RussellKennemore(5) 1 50
(B N Pollock) *mde all: rdn clr over 1f out: styd on wl* **7/2**[2]
066- 2 7 **Watch Out**[8] 4036 4-8-9 41 ow2 .... HaddenFrost(5) 4 44+
(G A Ham) *hld up and bhd: rdn and hdwy over 2f out: styd on to take 2nd towards fin: no ch w wnr* **9/2**[3]
0-05 3 1 ½ **Tewkesbury (IRE)**[18] 238 4-8-12 35 ....(t) VinceSlattery 2 40
(Mrs K Waldron) *hld up in tch: rdn over 2f out: one pce* **8/1**
0-40 4 nk **Chart Oak**[7] 377 5-9-4 42 .... HayleyTurner 6 39
(P Howling) *t.k.h: chsd wnr 3f: prom: wnt 2nd 5f out: rdn over 2f out: one pce* **8/1**
050- 5 11 **Phoenix Hill (IRE)**[38] 7285 6-9-4 45 .... SteveDrowne 9 26
(D R Gandolfo) *chsd ldrs: rdn over 2f out: wknd wl over 1f out* **2/1**[1]
050/ 6 6 **Kimoe Warrior**[40] 3282 10-9-4 30 ....(be) JimCrowley 7 19
(M Mullineaux) *hld up towards rr: hdwy over 3f out: wkng whn hung rt over 2f out* **16/1**
530- 7 5 **Gertie (IRE)**[163] 4914 4-8-12 45 .... EdwardCreighton 8 13
(E J Creighton) *hld up towards rr: hdwy over 3f out: sn rdn: wknd over 2f out* **8/1**
600/ 8 29 **Impero**[91] 857 10-9-1 32 .... DominicFox(3) 5 —
(G F Bridgwater) *mid-div: pushed along after 6f: bhd fnl 6f* **66/1**
00-0 9 1 ¾ **Chart Express**[17] 242 4-8-12 41 .... TGMcLaughlin 10 —
(P Howling) *a bhd* **33/1**
00-0 10 8 **Piquet**[7] 365 10-9-13 40 ow14 .... AdrianScholes(5) 11 —
(G F Bridgwater) *hld up in tch: chsd wnr after 3f to 5f out: wknd 4f out* **33/1**
300/ 11 28 **Lara's Girl**[39] 6700 6-9-4 39 ....(p) FergalLynch 3 —
(S Wynne) *sn bhd: t.o fnl 6f* **28/1**
3m 46.32s (4.52) **Going Correction** +0.20s/f (Slow)
WFA 4 from 5yo+ 6lb 11 Ran SP% **123.8**
Speed ratings (Par 97): **97,93,93,92,87 84,82,68,68,64 51**
CSF £20.36 TOTE £5.00: £2.10, £2.10, £3.60; EX 22.00 Place 6 £90.10, Place 5 £50.71.
Owner Mrs Zoe Pruhs **Bred** Ivan And Mrs Eileen Heanen **Trained** Medbourne, Leics
FOCUS
A very poor affair run at an ordinary gallop and rated around the placed horses to form.
T/Plt: £95.00 to a £1 stake. Pool: £86,602.30. 665.25 winning tickets. T/Qpdt: £30.30 to a £1 stake. Pool: £6,781.60. 165.60 winning tickets. KH

378 NAD AL SHEBA (L-H)
Thursday, February 7
OFFICIAL GOING: Turf course - good; dirt course - fast

472a INVASOR STKS (H'CAP) (TURF) 6f 110y(T)
3:45 (3:46) (100-113,113) 3-Y-O+
£52,763 (£17,587; £8,793; £4,396; £2,638; £1,758)

RPR
1 **So Will I**[350] 528 7-8-9 102 ....(t) RHills 3 109
(Doug Watson, UAE) *trckd ldng pair: led 1 1/2f out: r.o wl* **16/1**
2 ½ **Law Lord**[151] 5259 4-8-10 104 ....(v) LDettori 4 109
(Saeed Bin Suroor) *slowly away: t.k.h in mid-div: trckd ldrs 2 1/2f out: no room 1 1/2f out: r.o once clr* **5/1**[2]
3 ¾ **Beaver Patrol (IRE)**[124] 6003 6-8-9 102 ....(v) MJKinane 11 105
(Eve Johnson Houghton) *mid-div: rdn to chse ldrs 2 1/2f out: r.o: nrst fin* **7/1**
4 ½ **Prince Tamino**[14] 291 5-8-9 102 .... RoystonFfrench 2 103
(A Al Raihe, UAE) *trckd ldr: led 2 1/2f out: hdd 1 1/2f out: r.o same pce* **7/1**
5 ½ **Mariol (FR)**[14] 291 5-9-0 107 .... TPO'Shea 10 107
(E Charpy, UAE) *settled in rr: smooth prog wd 2f out: r.o: nrst fin* **13/2**[3]
6 ¾ **Grand Vista**[14] 290 4-8-9 102 ....(t) RyanMoore 6 100
(H J Brown, South Africa) *settled in rr: nvr able to chal but r.o fnl 1 1/2f* **8/1**
7 ¾ **Drift Ice (SAF)**[14] 290 7-8-12 106 ....(b) KShea 8 101
(M F De Kock, South Africa) *mid-div: rdn to chse ldrs 2 1/2f out: ev ch 1 1/2f out: nt qckn* **7/2**[1]
8 1 ¼ **Terrific Challenge (USA)**[14] 295 6-8-12 106 ....(bt) TedDurcan 5 97
(Doug Watson, UAE) *mid-div on rail: rdn 2 1/2f out: no room 1 1/2f out: nt rcvr* **20/1**
9 ¾ **Hurricane Spirit (IRE)**[278] 1473 4-8-9 102 .... JohnEgan 12 92
(J R Best) *settled in rr: nvr nr to chal* **16/1**
10 1 **Archipenko (USA)**[151] 5261 4-9-6 113 .... JMurtagh 9 100
(M F De Kock, South Africa) *racd in last: nvr nr to chal* **9/1**
11 2 ½ **T-Bird (SAF)**[14] 290 7-8-7 100 ....(t) WJSupple 7 80
(Doug Watson, UAE) *in rr of mid-div: rdn 3 1/2f out: n.d* **33/1**
12 2 ¼ **Conceal**[14] 291 10-8-7 100 .... PaulEddery 1 73
(R Bouresly, Kuwait) *sn led: hdd 2 1/2f out: wknd* **33/1**
1m 18.87s (1.37) **Going Correction** +0.35s/f (Good) 12 Ran SP% **120.7**
Speed ratings: **106,105,104,104,103 102,101,100,99,98 95,92**
CSF 94.14; TRI 625.24.
Owner Hamdan Al Maktoum **Bred** Mrs M Campbell Andenaes **Trained** United Arab Emirates
FOCUS
An ordinary sprint handicap for the grade.
NOTEBOOK
So Will I ended a losing run stretching back to a Listed success for Marcus Tregoning in 2004. He does, though, have to be considered a fortunate winner, as he very much had the run of the race, whereas the runner-up was continually denied a clear run in the straight. He had struggled in similar races in the past, so this was hard to predict, and it will be a surprise if he follows up.
Law Lord, a Listed winner at two when trained in France by Andre Fabre, looked an unlucky loser on his debut for Godolphin. He travelled strongly into the straight, but was continually denied a clear run and could not recover his momentum by the time he was finally in the clear. This was not much of a race for the level, but he looks up to winning a similar event. (tchd 11/2)
Beaver Patrol(IRE), having his first start in Dubai off the back of a four-month break, was under pressure at the top of the straight but kept on to the line. He should be sharper next time.
Prince Tamino was ridden much more forcefully than on his previous start over this course and distance (finished second to Mariol, awarded the race in the Stewards' room) and he could find only the one pace late on. A return to more patient tactics should suit. (op 13/2)
Mariol(FR) had to be switched around two furlongs out and could not quite get there. (tchd 7/1)
Grand Vista was well below the form he showed when winning over course and distance on his previous start. (op 9/1)
Hurricane Spirit(IRE) could make no impression on his first start since failing to beat a rival in last year's 2000 Guineas at Newmarket.
Archipenko(USA), last year's Derrinstown Stud Derby Trial winner when trained by Aidan O'Brien, was totally unsuited by this significant drop in trip on his debut for new connections and offered little. Having proved reluctant to load, it was disconcerting to see that he carried his head high under pressure.

473a SWAIN STKS (H'CAP) (DIRT) 7f (D)
4:15 (4:15) (90-105,102) 3-Y-O+
£33,165 (£11,055; £5,527; £2,763; £1,658; £1,105)

RPR
1 **Almaram (USA)**[7] 378 8-8-12 95 ....(e) JMurtagh 14 99+
(D Selvaratnam, UAE) *trckd ldng pair: rdn to chal 2f out: led 110yds out: jst hld on* **16/1**
2 nk **Frosty Secret (USA)**[21] 204 4-9-4 100 .... KShea 7 105
(M F De Kock, South Africa) *disp on rail: led 3f out: hdd 110yds out: rallied: jst failed* **9/2**[2]
3 2 ¼ **Skywards**[7] 382 6-8-9 91 ....(t) TPO'Shea 15 89
(E Charpy, UAE) *mid-div: wd 3f out: r.o fnl 2 1/2f: nrst fin* **20/1**
4 1 ½ **Green Coast (IRE)**[364] 395 5-8-12 95 .... DO'Donohoe 2 88
(Doug Watson, UAE) *mid-div on rail: trckd runner-up 2 1/2f out: r.o wl* **14/1**
5 1 ¼ **Minefield (USA)**[223] 4-8-12 95 .... LDettori 9 85
(Saeed Bin Suroor) *in rr of mid-div: rdn 3f out: r.o fnl 1 1/2f: nrst fin* **13/8**[1]
6 1 ½ **Lavarone (ARG)**[28] 5-8-10 93 ....(t) RyanMoore 6 78
(H J Brown, South Africa) *trckd ldng pair: rdn 3f out: nt qckn* **20/1**
7 shd **Select Reason (BRZ)**[7] 378 4-8-5 95 .... WJSupple 8 73
(A Cintra Pereira, Brazil) *slowly away: sn trckd ldrs: ev ch 3f out: kpt on same pce* **16/1**
8 1 **Love Dancing (ARG)**[21] 201 4-8-7 97 .... KerrinMcEvoy 11 72
(Saeed Bin Suroor) *nvr nr to chal but r.o fnl 2f* **14/1**
9 1 ¼ **Aqmaar**[7] 379 4-8-12 95 .... MartinDwyer 3 74
(E Charpy, UAE) *slowly away: racd in rr: nvr nr to chal* **33/1**
10 3 ¼ **Calrissian (GER)**[21] 204 4-9-1 97 .... TedDurcan 13 68
(L Kelp, Denmark) *mid-div: rdn 2 1/2f out: wknd fnl 1 1/2f* **40/1**
11 ½ **Algharb**[14] 290 6-9-3 99 .... RHills 1 68
(A Manuel, UAE) *slowly away: settled in rr: nvr nr to chal* **16/1**
12 ¼ **Fleeting Shadow (IRE)**[7] 382 4-8-10 93 .... RoystonFfrench 4 60
(A Al Raihe, UAE) *rdn in rr 3f out: n.d* **40/1**
13 nse **Montalba (USA)**[7] 382 8-8-9 91 ....(be) MJKinane 5 59
(J Lau, Macau) *racd in last: t.k.h: nvr able to chal* **20/1**
14 ¼ **Happy Runner (BRZ)**[21] 205 5-9-6 102 .... JAparecido 10 69
(P Nickel Filho, Brazil) *disp tl 3 1/2 out: wknd* **6/1**[3]
15 4 ¼ **Comandante Xara (BRZ)**[35] 5-8-8 90 ....(v) LisaJones 16 46
(A Selvaratnam, UAE) *mever nr to chal* **40/1**
16 2 ¾ **Valiance (USA)**[7] 379 4-8-12 95 .... PDevlin 12 42
(M F De Kock, South Africa) *mid-div: wd: rdn 3f out: sn btn* **50/1**
1m 23.94s (-0.86) **Going Correction** +0.125s/f (Slow) 16 Ran SP% **128.0**
Speed ratings: **109,108,106,104,102 101,101,99,98,94 94,93,93,93,88 85**
CSF 83.25; TRI 1,509.85.
Owner Sheikh Ahmed Al Maktoum **Bred** Darley Stud Management Llc **Trained** United Arab Emirates
FOCUS
An ordinary handicap for the level, but it was at least competitive, and it provided an exciting finish.
NOTEBOOK
Almaram(USA) had been well held over 5f round here on his previous start, but the step back up in trip suited and he ran out a game winner. Having travelled well on the speed throughout, he had a protracted dual with Frosty Secret for much of the way up the straight, before eventually just edging ahead near the line. This was a very useful effort off a mark 5lb higher than when winning over 6f at last year's Carnival, but he does not appeal as one to back to follow up. (op 14/1)
Frosty Secret(USA), third in the first round of the Maktoum Challenge over 1m round here on his previous start, proved suited by the drop in trip and was just held.
Skywards ◆ has been in good form lately and this was another decent effort. He ran on nicely to claim third after taking the home bend extremely wide and it would be no surprise to see him pick up a similar event in due course if things fall a little more kindly.
Green Coast(IRE) had been off the track for a year and left Godolphin since he was last seen. He was never too far away from his inside draw, but got tired late on. (op 12/1)

Minefield(USA) ◆ struggled to get a good early position and had plenty to do at the top of the straight as a result. He looked set to finish well back when hitting a flat spot inside the final three furlongs, but he eventually responded to pressure late on and came home in quite good style. He was passing tired horses, so it would be unwise to get carried away, but he is entitled to come on for this first run since last June and may also be suited by a step up in trip. He is lightly raced and should improve on this if he can be kept sound. (op 15/8)
Love Dancing(ARG) was in trouble from an early stage. (op 12/1)
Happy Runner(BRZ), 7lb higher than when winning over an extended 7f round here last time, went out like a light in the straight.

474a JAZIL STKS (H'CAP) (TURF) 7f 110y(D)
4:45 (4:48) (95-110,109) 3-Y-0+

£36,180 (£12,060; £6,030; £3,015; £1,809; £1,206)

RPR
1 **Instant Recall (IRE)**^{7} [379] 7-8-7 **96**.....................(vt) WayneSmith 1 103
(M Al Muhairi, UAE) *trckd ldr: t.k.h: rdn 1 1/2f out: r.o wl fnl f: led 55yds out* **22/1**
2 1/4 **Almuraad (IRE)**^{7} [384] 7-8-9 **98**..................... RHills 2 104
(Doug Watson, UAE) *mid-div: gng wl 2 1/2f out: rdn 2f out: r.o: nrst fin* **11/1**
3 3/4 **Wise Dennis**^{71} [6965] 6-9-1 **104**..................... JohnEgan 11 108
(A P Jarvis) *settled in rr: gng wl: swtchd wd 2 1/2f out: r.o wl: nrst fin* **12/1**
4 shd **Racer Forever (USA)**^{124} [6018] 5-9-2 **105**.....................(b) RyanMoore 8 109
(J H M Gosden) *sn led: clr 2 1/2f out: hdd cl home* **10/1**
5 1/4 **African Appeal (SAF)**^{194} 7-9-6 **109**..................... JMurtagh 5 112
(M F De Kock, South Africa) *settled in rr: prog on rail 2 1/2f out: no room 2f out or 1f out: unlucky* **2/1**^{1}
6 1/2 **Escape Route (USA)**^{124} [6011] 4-8-6 **95**..................... RichardMullen 13 97
(J H M Gosden) *settled in rr: rdn 2 1/2f out: one pce* **9/1**^{3}
7 3/4 **Big Timer (USA)**^{7} [379] 4-8-12 **101**..................... TomEaves 7 101+
(I Semple) *mid-div: rdn whn no room 1 1/2f out: nt rcvr* **4/1**^{2}
8 6 3/4 **Emirates Gold (IRE)**^{14} [294] 5-9-1 **104**.....................(t) TPO'Shea 10 87
(E Charpy, UAE) *racd in rr of mid-div: n.d* **40/1**
9 hd **Vortex**^{7} [382] 9-9-1 **104**.....................(t) MartinDwyer 6 87
(Miss Gay Kelleway) *settled in rr: no room 2 1/2f out or 1 1/2f out* **10/1**
10 3/4 **Checkit (IRE)**^{357} [470] 8-8-8 **97** ow2..................... BrettDoyle 9 78
(R Bouresly, Kuwait) *trckd ldr tl wknd 1f out* **40/1**
11 3/4 **Bain Douche (BRZ)**^{14} [292] 4-8-2 **97** ow2..................... JMoreira 3 70
(R Colombo, Brazil) *settled in rr: no room 2 1/2f out: nvr nr to chal* **22/1**
12 1 1/4 **Topor (TUR)**^{21} [205] 4-8-9 **98**..................... BKurdu 4 74
(H Demirkiran, Turkey) *mid-div: rdn 2 1/2f out: sn wknd* **25/1**
13 2 1/4 **Desert Realm (IRE)**^{14} [294] 5-8-11 **100**..................... RoystonFfrench 14 70
(A Al Raihe, UAE) *mid-div: chsd ldrs 2 1/2f out: wknd fnl 1 1/2f* **40/1**
14 1 3/4 **Mandobi (IRE)**^{14} [294] 7-8-11 **100**.....................(tp) RPCleary 12 66
(D Selvaratnam, UAE) *slowly away: mid-div 3f out: nt qckn fnl 1 1/2f* **20/1**

1m 32.19s (0.59) **Going Correction** +0.35s/f (Good) **14** Ran SP% **122.2**
Speed ratings: **111,110,109,109,109 109,108,101,101,100 99,98,96,94**
CSF 234.38; TRI 3,036.09.
Owner Salman Mussallam Al Shalahi **Bred** Frank Dunne **Trained** UAE

FOCUS
A decent handicap on paper and the pace seemed fair enough, but they finished in a bit of a bunch.

NOTEBOOK
Instant Recall(IRE) ◆ had been much too keen when ridden handy over 1m round here on his previous start, and he again pulled hard, but crucially he managed to get a lead this time. He found just enough to come out on top in a close finish and should continue to go well in similar company. (op 20/1)
Almuraad(IRE), taking a slight drop in trip, had to wait for a gap early in the straight, but he was in the clear for long enough if good enough. (op 10/1)
Wise Dennis ◆, having his first start in Dubai, looked a slightly unlucky loser. He was travelling noticeably strongly at the top of the straight, but had been set plenty to do having been dropped in from a wide draw and had to wait an age for a gap. He finished strongly once finally in the clear, but the line was always going to come too soon. He can win a similar event.
Racer Forever(USA), making his debut in Dubai off the back of a four-month break, ran a good race from the front and is entitled to come on a little for this. (op 9/1)
African Appeal(SAF) ◆, a South African Grade 1 winner returning from over six months off the track, was another who looked pretty unlucky loser, although it would probably be unwise to get too carried away. A little keen towards the inside early on, he was continually denied a clear run in the straight and got going too late once in the clear. He will probably be a short price next time and it is worth remembering this was a bunch finish, and he was not the only horse short of room at some stage. (op 15/8)
Escape Route(USA), mid-division in the Cambridgeshire when last seen in October, was under pressure a fair way out but kept on. He should be sharper next time and is likely to be suited by a step up in trip.
Big Timer(USA) did not enjoy the best of runs in the straight and is a little better than he was able to show. (op 9/2)
Vortex never threatened on this return to turf.

475a CAPE VERDI STKS (LISTED RACE) (F&M) (TURF) 1m (T)
5:20 (5:20) 3-Y-0+

£45,226 (£15,075; £7,537; £3,768; £2,261; £1,507)

RPR
1 **Sun Classique (AUS)**^{215} 5-9-9 107..................... KShea 1 116
(M F De Kock, South Africa) *mid-div on rail: smooth prog to chal 2f out: led over 1f out: comf* **10/3**^{2}
2 2 1/4 **Many Colours**^{21} [200] 4-9-3 105..................... LDettori 4 105
(Saeed Bin Suroor) *broke awkwardly: mid-div: rdn to chse ldrs 2f out: r.o: no ch w wnr* **5/4**^{1}
3 1/4 **Classy-Lady (BRZ)**^{21} [200] 4-8-8 94..................... RyanMoore 2 95
(H J Brown, South Africa) *settled in rr: rdn 2 1/2f out: r.o fnl 1 1/2f: nrst fin* **16/1**
4 1/2 **Sweet Lilly**^{111} [6299] 4-9-3 110..................... TedDurcan 5 103
(M R Channon) *slowly away: settled last: rdn 2 1/2f out: r.o fnl 2f: nrst fin* **4/1**^{3}
5 2 **Whazzis**^{102} [6524] 4-9-5 104..................... JMurtagh 10 101
(D Selvaratnam, UAE) *settled in rr: nvr able to chal but r.o fnl 2f* **12/1**
6 4 3/4 **Olympic City (BRZ)**^{21} [200] 5-9-3 100..................... RoystonFfrench 7 88
(A Cintra Pereira, Brazil) *sn led: rdn 2 1/2f out: hdd 1 1/2f out: wknd* **12/1**
7 3 1/4 **Jet Past (SAF)**^{21} [200] 6-9-3 97..................... RichardMullen 6 80
(S Seemar, UAE) *mid-div: rdn 2 1/2f out: wknd* **40/1**
8 5 **Cat Belling (IRE)**^{21} [200] 8-9-3 90.....................(t) PaulEddery 9 69
(R Bouresly, Kuwait) *trckd ldrs tl 2 1/2f out: wknd* **80/1**
9 hd **Impetious**^{21} [202] 4-9-3 100.....................(b) BrettDoyle 11 68
(Eamon Tyrrell, Ire) *nvr bttr than mid-div* **40/1**
10 2 **Tulipa Di Job (BRZ)**^{21} [200] 6-9-3 90.....................(t) TPO'Shea 3 64
(A Selvaratnam, UAE) *trckd ldrs tl 4 1/2f out: wknd* **150/1**

1m 40.05s (1.75) **Going Correction** +0.35s/f (Good) **10** Ran SP% **115.6**
Speed ratings: **105,102,102,101,99 95,91,86,86,84**
CSF 7.71.
Owner L Cohen & W V Rippon **Bred** L Cohen **Trained** South Africa

FOCUS
The third straight year the Cape Verdi Stakes has held Listed status and this looked like a good renewal. They looked to go a good pace.

NOTEBOOK
Sun Classique(AUS) ◆ was conceding weight all round on account of her Grade 1 victory over 1m3f in South Africa, but she proved much too good for this lot. This shorter trip had to be a slight concern beforehand, but she was always travelling easily and picked up in good style when sent on in the straight. There is another Listed race over 1m1f later in the month, the Balanchine Stakes for fillies and mares, but it would be no surprise to see her step up to Group company for something like the Al Fahidi Fort, or a race on Super Thursday in March. (op 5/2)
Many Colours, successful on the dirt in a race transferred from turf off a mark of 102 on her debut for Godolphin, travelled well enough in the straight, but she could not match the winner's acceleration. This looks as good as she is. (op 11/8 tchd 6/5)
Classy-Lady(BRZ), returned to turf, was getting weight all round and ran a good race in third.
Sweet Lilly, soon out the back after missing the kick, stayed on in the straight, but was far from convincing, both edging left and appearing to carry her head at a slight angle. This was a decent effort strictly on the figures, but she might be best left for the time being. (op 9/2)
Whazzis, a Listed and Group 3 winner for William Haggas, was plenty keen enough early on and did not show her best on her debut for new connections. (op 10/1)
Impetious was again well held. (op 33/1)

476a SH MAKTOUM BIN RASHID AL MAKTOUM CHALLENGE R2 (GROUP 3) (DIRT) 1m 1f (D)
5:55 (5:55) 3-Y-0+

£60,301 (£20,100; £10,050; £5,025; £3,015; £2,010)

RPR
1 **Lucky Find (SAF)**^{21} [203] 5-9-0 111..................... KShea 7 116
(M F De Kock, South Africa) *trckd ldr: eased ahd 1 1/2f out: comf* **7/4**^{1}
2 2 1/4 **Kandidate**^{75} [6942] 6-9-0 110.....................(t) RyanMoore 12 111
(C E Brittain) *sn led: wd: hdd 1 1/2f out: r.o wl but no ch w wnr* **5/1**^{3}
3 7 **Imperial Star (IRE)**^{152} [5220] 5-9-0 109..................... KerrinMcEvoy 6 96
(Saeed Bin Suroor) *settled in rr: wd 3f out: r.o fnl 2f but nvr nr to chal* **10/1**
4 hd **Jack Sullivan (USA)**^{21} [204] 7-9-0 109.....................(tp) MJKinane 10 96
(G A Butler) *in rr of mid-div: rdn 3f out: r.o same pce* **10/1**
5 2 1/2 **Quorum (GER)**^{7} [382] 5-9-0 88..................... WayneSmith 5 91
(M Al Muhairi, UAE) *trckd ldng gp on rail: rdn 3f out: r.o wl fnl 1 1/2f* **66/1**
6 1/2 **Delude (IRE)**^{6} 10-9-0 90..................... BrettDoyle 4 90
(R Bouresly, Kuwait) *settled in rr: nvr able to chal* **100/1**
7 1 1/4 **Boscobel**^{170} [4692] 4-9-0 115..................... LDettori 11 87
(Saeed Bin Suroor) *trckd ldr: ev ch 3f out: nt qckn: wknd fnl 1 1/2f* **3/1**^{2}
8 shd **Etihaad**^{14} [296] 6-9-0 96.....................(t) PaulEddery 1 87
(R Bouresly, Kuwait) *slowly away: sme prog 2 1/2f out but nvr nr to chal* **33/1**
9 1/2 **Sahara Sphinx (USA)**^{6} 5-9-0 90.....................(p) DSmith 2 86
(M Al Muhairi, UAE) *mid-div: t.k.h: wknd 4f out* **100/1**
10 4 **Rampallion**^{21} [202] 5-9-0 102..................... TPO'Shea 3 77
(E Charpy, UAE) *settled in rr: nvr nr to chal* **14/1**
11 8 1/4 **Eu Tambem (BRZ)**^{313} [859] 5-9-0 113..................... WJSupple 9 60
(Saeed Bin Suroor) *trckd ldrs tl rdn over 4f out: wknd qckly* **12/1**
12 3 1/2 **West Virginia (USA)**^{474} 7-9-0 104.....................(t) TedDurcan 8 53
(S Seemar, UAE) *mid-div: rdn in rr 3f out: sn btn* **14/1**

1m 49.06s (-0.74) **Going Correction** +0.125s/f (Slow) **12** Ran SP% **123.7**
Speed ratings: **108,106,99,99,97 96,95,95,95,91 84,81**
CSF 11.26.
Owner Sh Ahmed bin Mohd bin Khalifa Al Maktoum **Bred** Oldlands Stud **Trained** South Africa

FOCUS
The second round of the Maktoum Challenge but, although the winners of the last three renewals lined up, this race lacked strength in depth and looked like just an ordinary Group 3.

NOTEBOOK
Lucky Find(SAF), whose trainer won this race in 2004 with Victory Moon, followed up his recent handicap success in battling style. He had to work hard to see off early leader Kandidate, but he eventually wore that one down and was well on top at the line. He is well named, because it is unlikely he would have even run in this race had things worked out differently. He had actually been due to race on turf at the beginning of this year's Carnival and only took his chance on dirt after the race was switched, but he proved well suited by the surface, easily defying a mark of 102. This was tougher, but he confirmed himself a high-class dirt performer. The third round of the Maktoum Challenge is the next logical step, but he will need to improve significantly to be seriously considered for the Dubai World Cup. (op 2/1)
Kandidate, allowed an easy lead when winning this race last year, tried to repeat the tactics, but he was made to work a little harder to dominate this time and found one too strong in the straight. He goes very well fresh, so he is no sure thing to build on this. (op 11/2)
Imperial Star(IRE), without the visor on his first start since leaving John Gosden, was not an obvious type to be suited by this surface having suffered with back problems in the past. He ran on from the back to take third, but he was a mile off the front two. (op 9/1)
Jack Sullivan(USA), the winner of this race in both 2005 and 2006, stepped up significantly on the form he showed in round one of the Maktoum Challenge on his previous start. (op 9/1)
Quorum(GER) is not really up to this level, but he ran well in defeat without his usual visor. (tchd 100/1)
Boscobel was well below form switched to dirt on his first start since leaving Mark Johnston. He is much better suited by middle distances on turf and it would be silly to hold this against him. (op 11/4)
Rampallion was nowhere near the form he showed when winning over course and distance off a mark of 96 on his previous start.
Eu Tambem(BRZ), winner of the third round of the Maktoum Challenge last year, offered absolutely nothing on his first start since running seventh in last season's UAE Derby.

477a ALJABR STKS (H'CAP) (TURF) 1m 2f (T)
6:30 (6:30) (95-110,107) 3-Y-0+

£36,180 (£12,060; £6,030; £3,015; £1,809; £1,206)

RPR
1 **Before You Go (IRE)**^{7} [381] 5-8-10 **97**.....................(v) KerrinMcEvoy 10 97
(Saeed Bin Suroor) *mid-div: rdn to trck ldrs 2 1/2f out: led cl home* **22/1**
2 1/2 **Hallhoo (IRE)**^{28} 6-8-11 **98**..................... JMurtagh 14 97
(D Selvaratnam, UAE) *sn led: kicked clr 3f out: r.o wl but hdd cl home* **8/1**^{3}
3 1 1/2 **Engrupido (ARG)**^{14} [296] 5-9-1 **101**..................... KShea 1 98
(M F De Kock, South Africa) *trckd ldr: ev ch 3f out: r.o wl fnl 1 1/2f* **4/1**^{1}

4 ½ **The Illies (IRE)**[7] 384 4-8-12 **100** LDettori 3 95
(Saeed Bin Suroor) *in rr of mid-div: gng wl whn no room 3f out: r.o once clr: nrst fin* **4/1**[1]

5 1 ¼ **Lake Poet (IRE)**[7] 381 5-8-11 **98** (b) TedDurcan 13 91
(C E Brittain) *mid-div: rdn to chse ldrs 2 1/2f out: nt qckn* **20/1**

6 4 ¼ **Greek Well (IRE)**[124] 6011 5-8-8 **95** TPO'Shea 2 79
(E Charpy, UAE) *settled in rr: gng wl but n.m.r 2 1/2f out: nt qckn* **8/1**[3]

7 1 ¼ **Arabian Prince (USA)**[21] 203 5-9-3 **104** MJKinane 6 86
(Doug Watson, UAE) *mid-div: hrd rdn 2 1/2f out: r.o same pce* **10/1**

8 2 ½ **Hando**[7] 380 4-8-7 **95** TomEaves 11 72
(Christian Wroe) *trckd ldng gp: rdn 3f out: nt qckn* **66/1**

9 shd **Impeller (IRE)**[7] 380 9-8-9 **96** JohnEgan 8 73
(J S Moore) *mid-div: rdn 2 1/2f out: n.d* **12/1**

10 1 ¾ **Courageous Duke (USA)**[326] 9-8-8 **95** DO'Donohoe 4 68
(Doug Watson, UAE) *settled in rr: nvr able to chal* **33/1**

11 3 ¾ **Fenice (IRE)**[336] 643 5-8-12 **99** (t) RichardMullen 7 65
(S Seemar, UAE) *in rr of mid-div: rdn 3f out: n.d* **16/1**

12 8 ½ **Championship Point (IRE)**[110] 6334 5-9-6 **107** RyanMoore 5 56
(M R Channon) *settled in rr: nvr nr to chal* **15/2**[2]

13 14 **Mambo King (DEN)**[21] 202 6-9-0 **100** (t) MartinDwyer 12 22
(L Kelp, Denmark) *trckd ldr tl over 5f out: wknd* **50/1**

14 8 ¼ **Malahem (IRE)**[28] 6-8-8 **95** (t) RHills 9 —
(E Charpy, UAE) *mid-div: dropped to rr 2 1/2f out: eased fnl 1 1/2f* **10/1**

2m 5.53s (1.03) **Going Correction** +0.35s/f (Good)
WFA 4 from 5yo+ 1lb **14** Ran SP% **121.2**
Speed ratings: **109,108,107,107,106 102,101,99,99,98 95,88,77,70**
CSF 183.30; TRI 867.42. Placepot: £281.40 to a £1 stake. Pool £14,707.60 - 38.15 winning units. Quadpot: £23.90 to a £1 stake. Pool £398.10 - 12.30 winning units..
Owner Sheikh Ahmed Bin Mohammed Al Maktoum **Bred** The Niarchos Family **Trained** Newmarket, Suffolk

FOCUS
Just an ordinary handicap for the level, but they seemed to go a reasonable pace.

NOTEBOOK
Before You Go(IRE) could make no impression in a stronger race over 1m4f the previous week on his first start since leaving Terry Mills, but that run clearly brought him on and this drop in trip did him no harm. Having travelled well throughout, it was just a question of whether he would go through with his effort, and he picked up the long-timer leader Hallhoo without too much hesitation. It might just be that this was his day and he does not appeal as one to back to follow up. (tchd 25/1)
Hallhoo(IRE), back up in trip, set a reasonable pace in front, but crucially he was left alone, and he very nearly lasted home. This is as good as he is. (op 15/2)
Engrupido(ARG) ran well in defeat without really improving on the form he showed when fourth over course and distance on his return from a long break last time.
The Illies(IRE), stepping up in trip having failed to land a blow over 1m on his first start since leaving Barry Hills last time, raced keenly early, not helping his rider at all, and then failed to pick up as one might have hoped in the straight, failing to convince with his attitude.
Lake Poet(IRE) could make no impression over 1m4f last time, but he had previously shaped with some promise and this was better, although his effort rather flattened out late on.
Greek Well(IRE) ran a respectable on his first start since leaving Sir Michael Stoute and is entitled to come on for this considering he had been off for four months. (op 9/1)
Impeller(IRE) won the corresponding race last year following two runs on dirt and he came into this off the same preparation, but he failed to run up to his best.
Championship Point(IRE) was another who was below form - he was eased in the straight - and has yet to show his best round Nad Al Sheba. (op 7/1)

[459]SOUTHWELL (L-H)
Friday, February 8

OFFICIAL GOING: Standard
Wind: Virtually nil Weather: Fine and dry

478 MEET CAPTAIN CROC @ PONTIN'S FILLIES' H'CAP 1m (F)
1:20 (1:20) (Class 6) (0-60,55) 4-Y-0+ **£1,911** (£564; £282) **Stalls** Low

Form RPR

-420 **1** **Ruffie (IRE)**[12] 330 5-8-2 46 AmyBaker(7) 5 54
(Miss J Feilden) *towards rr: gd hdwy wl over 2f out: swtchd lft and rdn to ld over 1f out: styd on wl u.p fnl f* **7/2**[2]

2-56 **2** 2 **Only A Grand**[17] 258 4-9-0 51 (b) PhillipMakin 6 55
(R Bastiman) *trckd ldng pair: hdwy to ld 3f out: rdn 2f out: hdd over 1f out: sn drvn and kpt on same pce* **7/2**[2]

003- **3** 1 ¼ **Sparky Vixen**[102] 6537 4-8-7 47 DuranFentiman(3) 7 48
(C J Teague) *chsd ldrs: hdwy wl over 2f out: rdn wl over 1f out and kpt on same pce appr last* **14/1**

0-06 **4** 1 ¼ **Cape Dancer (IRE)**[22] 193 4-8-8 45 (p) PaulFessey 2 43
(J S Wainwright) *chsd ldrs: rdn along wl over 2f out and sn one pce* **33/1**

55-5 **5** 3 ½ **Tour D'Amour (IRE)**[17] 258 5-9-4 55 FergalLynch 4 45
(R Craggs) *in tch: pushed along on outer 1/2-way: rdn wl over 2f out and sn no imp* **11/4**[1]

-510 **6** 11 **Rubilini**[1] 465 4-8-3 45 (p) NataliaGemelova(5) 3 10
(Miss Sheena West) *sn chsng ldr: rdn along 3f out and sn wknd* **9/2**[3]

0-02 **7** 7 **Cadogen Square**[11] 338 6-8-8 45 (b) LiamJones 8 —
(Mrs R A Carr) *sn led: pushed along and hdd 3f out: sn rdn and wknd* **20/1**

000- **8** 29 **Maid Of Ale (IRE)**[162] 4960 4-9-2 53 StephenDonohoe 1 —
(D J Wintle) *a in rr: wl bhd fnl 3f* **12/1**

1m 42.45s (-1.25) **Going Correction** -0.15s/f (Stan) **8** Ran SP% **111.4**
Speed ratings (Par 98): **100,98,96,95,92 81,74,45**
CSF £15.28 CT £143.52 TOTE £4.20: £1.90, £1.70, £3.20; EX 17.80 Trifecta £178.80 Part won. Pool: £251.85 - 0.95 winning tickets..
Owner Hoofbeats Racing Club **Bred** Fergus Jones **Trained** Exning, Suffolk

FOCUS
A moderate fillies' handicap in which the pace was fair and, unusually for races over this trip here, the winner came from a long way back. The form probably does not amount to a great deal and does not look solid.
Rubilini Official explanation: trainer said filly had come into season

479 RACE TO PONTIN'S FOR GREAT SHORT BREAKS CLAIMING STKS 5f (F)
1:55 (1:55) (Class 6) 4-Y-0+ **£1,684** (£501; £250; £125) **Stalls** High

Form RPR

05-0 **1** **Guto**[8] 370 5-8-10 65 KellyHarrison(5) 2 66
(W J H Ratcliffe) *mde all: rdn wl over 1f out: edgd rt ins fnl f: drvn out* **85/40**[2]

-444 **2** ¾ **Nautical**[1] 460 10-8-10 55 JerryO'Dwyer(3) 6 61
(A W Carroll) *trckd ldrs: hdwy to chal wl over 1f out: drvn ent fnl f and ev ch tl nt qckn last 100yds* **3/1**[3]

-325 **3** 2 ½ **Pegasus Dancer (FR)**[1] 460 4-9-1 70 (p) FergalLynch 5 54
(K A Ryan) *cl up: rdn along 2f out: sn edgd lft and one pce ent fnl f* **7/4**[1]

0450 **4** 1 ¾ **Orchestration (IRE)**[20] 232 7-8-8 40 (v) MarkCoumbe(7) 4 48
(S Parr) *cl up: rdn along 2f out: drvn and wknd appr fnl f* **14/1**

5-04 **5** 2 ½ **Wibbadune (IRE)**[14] 307 4-8-3 49 (b) LiamJones 1 27
(Peter Grayson) *swtchd to r alone far side: prom tl rdn along 2f out and sn wknd* **9/1**

05-5 **6** 3 **Swallow Senora (IRE)**[10] 346 6-7-9 39 KMay(7) 3 15
(M C Chapman) *chsd ldrs: rdn along 1/2-way: sn outpcd* **50/1**

60.07 secs (0.37) **Going Correction** +0.075s/f (Slow) **6** Ran SP% **112.0**
Speed ratings (Par 101): **100,98,94,92,88 83**
CSF £8.89 TOTE £3.80: £1.80, £2.00; EX 9.30.
Owner W J H Ratcliffe **Bred** H B Hughes **Trained** Wensley, N Yorks

FOCUS
A moderate claimer and as usual over this straight 5f, the ability to race handily was a big asset. This did not take a great deal of winning and is best rated around the first two.

480 BE BESIDE THE SEASIDE @ PONTINS.COM H'CAP 6f (F)
2:25 (2:26) (Class 6) (0-65,63) 3-Y-O **£1,911** (£564; £282) **Stalls** Low

Form RPR

00-3 **1** **Note Perfect**[25] 154 3-8-7 52 (b[1]) ChrisCatlin 6 54
(M W Easterby) *cl up: led wl over 2f out: rdn over 1f out: drvn ins fnl f: hld on gamely towards fin* **4/1**[2]

00-4 **2** shd **Montiboli (IRE)**[22] 199 3-9-4 63 FergalLynch 1 65
(K A Ryan) *stdd s: hld up in rr: hdwy on inner 2f out: rdn over 1f out: styd on wl fnl f: jst failed* **9/1**

1243 **3** hd **Bold Diva**[5] 419 3-8-11 61 (v) KellyHarrison(5) 7 62
(A W Carroll) *s.i.s and hld up in rr: hdwy on outer 1/2-way: rdn to chse ldrs over 1f out: drvn and ev ch whn edgd lft ins fnl f: kpt on wl towards fin* **7/2**[1]

66-5 **4** shd **Mujada**[31] 81 3-8-6 51 JimmyQuinn 3 52
(M Brittain) *trckd ldrs: hdwy over 2f out: rdn to chal over 1f out and ev ch tl drvn ins fnl f and nt qckn towards fin* **13/2**

-022 **5** 2 **Alabama Spirit (USA)**[11] 333 3-9-0 62 TolleyDean(3) 8 57
(D Shaw) *hld up: hdwy and nt clr run wl over 1f out: effrt and n.m.r ins fnl f: kpt on towards fin* **11/2**

5-60 **6** ¾ **Kamal**[5] 419 3-9-4 63 HayleyTurner 4 55
(W R Muir) *t.k.h: chsd ldrs: hdwy 2f out and sn rdn: drvn and wknd ent fnl f* **9/2**[3]

04-0 **7** 1 **Santa Clara**[32] 74 3-9-2 61 PatCosgrave 2 50
(Jane Chapple-Hyam) *led: pushed along and hdd wl over 2f out: sn rdn and wknd over 1f out* **11/1**

4-40 **8** 5 **Twilight Belle (IRE)**[33] 70 3-8-4 49 oh1 (b) AndrewElliott 5 22
(K R Burke) *chsd ldrs on outer: rdn along over 2f out: sn drvn and wknd wl over 1f out* **20/1**

1m 16.94s (0.44) **Going Correction** -0.15s/f (Stan) **8** Ran SP% **112.2**
Speed ratings (Par 95): **91,90,90,90,87 86,85,78**
CSF £37.72 CT £136.31 TOTE £5.50: £2.10, £2.70, £1.20; EX 42.20 Trifecta £126.10 Pool: £646.75 - 3.64 winning tickets..
Owner Mrs Jean Turpin **Bred** Mrs Jean Turpin **Trained** Sheriff Hutton, N Yorks
■ Stewards' Enquiry : Chris Catlin two-day ban: used whip in incorrect place (Feb 19-20)

FOCUS
An ordinary sprint handicap and with the first four all finishing in a heap, the form is probably only modest and hard to rate positively.
Bold Diva Official explanation: jockey said filly missed the break

481 COME SEE US SOON @ PONTIN'S CLAIMING STKS 1m 4f (F)
3:00 (3:00) (Class 6) 4-Y-0+ **£1,774** (£523; £262) **Stalls** Low

Form RPR

3-30 **1** **Global Traffic**[22] 198 4-9-1 58 (b) StephenDonohoe 6 64
(P D Evans) *midfield: hdwy over 4f out: rdn along 3f out: rdn and hdwy on inner wl over 1f out: led ins fnl f: drvn out* **3/1**[2]

00-2 **2** 2 **Bethanys Boy (IRE)**[8] 373 7-8-10 60 NickyMackay 7 58+
(M Wigham) *hld up in tch: smooth hdwy 4f out: effrt on bit to chal 2f out: led over 1f out: hdd and shkn up ins fnl f: one pce* **1/1**[1]

/5-2 **3** 1 ¾ **Nabir (FR)**[22] 188 8-9-2 52 (p) PaulHanagan 5 56
(P D Niven) *cl up: led over 4f out: rdn over 2f out: drvn and hdd over 1f out: kpt on same pce* **7/1**[3]

5330 **4** 6 **Weet For Ever (USA)**[9] 352 5-9-2 51 HayleyTurner 2 46
(P A Blockley) *trckd ldrs: hdwy over 3f out: rdn to chal over 2f out and ev ch tl drvn and wknd appr fnl f* **8/1**

15-0 **5** 8 **Simply St Lucia**[3] 438 6-8-11 49 ChrisCatlin 1 29
(J R Weymes) *led: rdn along and hdd over 4f out: sn drvn and wknd* **14/1**

0- **6** 17 **Topwell**[9] 6700 7-8-9 0 (p) NataliaGemelova(5) 3 4
(R C Guest) *sn outpcd and a in rr* **33/1**

7 2 **Art Of Being (IRE)**[14] 4-9-0 0 (p) PatrickDonaghy(7) 9 11
(M C Chapman) *chsd ldrs: rdn along 5f out: sn wknd* **100/1**

0450 **8** 13 **Mi Odds**[3] 438 12-8-12 42 AndrewElliott 4 —
(Mrs N Macauley) *a in rr* **40/1**

9 15 **Cantley Spirit**[72] 5-8-0 0 DanielleMcCreery(5) 8 —
(T J Pitt) *s.i.s: a bhd* **50/1**

2m 38.25s (-2.75) **Going Correction** -0.15s/f (Stan)
WFA 4 from 5yo+ 3lb **9** Ran SP% **113.6**
Speed ratings (Par 101): **103,101,100,96,91 79,78,69,59**
CSF £6.12 TOTE £3.80: £1.40, £1.10, £1.80; EX 8.10 Trifecta £29.60 Pool: £712.68 - 17.07 winning tickets..The winner was claimed by Derek Shaw for £9,000. Bethanys Boy was claimed by A. M. Hales for £5,000.
Owner Mrs Folkes & Mrs Madden **Bred** P F I Cole **Trained** Pandy, Monmouths

FOCUS
What looked an ordinary claimer became the most talked about race of the day after what looked an horrendous piece of showboating from the rider of the hot favourite. In terms of form, this was a routine Fibresand claimer in which half the field had little or no chance. The winner, backed up by the third, sets the standard.
Bethanys Boy(IRE) Official explanation: jockey said, regarding running and riding, that his orders were to hold onto the gelding as long as possible in order to get the trip, adding that he was aware of two runners on his right and noticed the winner coming to his left at the 1f mark, adding further that having started to ride it was outpaced.

482 ARENA LEISURE PLC H'CAP 5f (F)
3:30 (3:31) (Class 4) (0-85,85) 4-Y-0+ **£4,210** (£1,252; £625; £312) **Stalls** High

Form RPR

5-41 **1** **Godfrey Street**[15] 278 5-8-13 **80** (b) FergalLynch 3 88
(A G Newcombe) *mde all: rdn over 1f out: drvn and edgd rt ins fnl f: hld on gamely* **2/1**[1]

0-21 **2** shd **Bo McGinty (IRE)**[1] 459 7-8-12 **79** 6ex (b) PaulHanagan 2 87
(R A Fahey) *prom: rdn to chal ins fnl f: sn drvn and kpt on: jst hld* **9/4**[2]

0-26 **3** 1 1/4 **Diminuto**[9] 359 4-8-6 **73** HayleyTurner 1 76
(M D I Usher) *rdn along and outpcd after 2f: hdwy wl over 1f out: styd on u.p ins fnl f* **7/1**

01-1 **4** 1/2 **Distinctly Game**[21] 210 6-8-13 **85** KellyHarrison(5) 6 86
(K A Ryan) *chsd ldrs: rdn along 2f out: sn wknd* **7/2**[3]

500- **5** 2 **Misaro (GER)**[119] 6141 7-8-8 **80** (b) KevinGhunowa(5) 7 74
(R A Harris) *cl up: rdn along over 2f out: sn drvn and wknd over 1f out* **20/1**

6514 **6** 1 3/4 **Doubtful Sound (USA)**[1] 459 4-8-6 **73** PaulFessey 5 61
(T D Barron) *chsd ldr: rdn 2f out: drvn and wknd over 1f out* **7/1**

59.29 secs (-0.41) **Going Correction** +0.075s/f (Slow) **6** Ran SP% **116.1**
Speed ratings (Par 105): **106,105,103,103,99 97**
CSF £7.18 TOTE £2.90: £1.40, £1.90; EX 7.50.
Owner M K F Seymour **Bred** Miss S N Ralphs **Trained** Yarnscombe, Devon
■ Stewards' Enquiry : Paul Hanagan caution: used whip with excessive frequency

FOCUS
A fair little handicap and the favourite making all meant that both races over the straight 5f at the meeting had been won from the front. Low draws again dominated, but the form still looks very solid for the grade with the time decent.

483 SOUTHWELL-RACECOURSE.CO.UK MAIDEN STKS 7f (F)
4:05 (4:06) (Class 5) 3-Y-0+ **£2,457** (£725; £362) **Stalls** Low

Form RPR

006- **1** **Little Wing (IRE)**[197] 3878 3-8-10 70 TPQueally 3 74+
(J A Osborne) *t.k.h: trckd ldrs: hdwy to chal 2f out: rdn to ld over 1f out: hung bdly rt ins fnl f: kpt on* **2/1**[2]

04-4 **2** 3 1/2 **Jal Music**[13] 311 3-8-5 67 KevinGhunowa(5) 9 65
(R A Harris) *cl up: effrt and ev ch over 2f out: sn rdn: drvn and kpt on ins fnl f* **11/2**[3]

2 **3** nk **West Lorne (USA)**[11] 343 3-8-5 0 GregFairley 6 59
(M Johnston) *led: rdn along over 2f out: drvn and hdd over 1f out: kpt on same pce* **6/4**[1]

4 3/4 **Nags To Riches (IRE)** 3-8-10 0 ChrisCatlin 2 62+
(J A Osborne) *towards rr: pushed along 1/2-way: hdwy 2f out: rdn and styd on appr fnl f* **9/1**

5 1/2 **Days Of Pleasure (IRE)** 3-8-10 0 MickyFenton 8 61
(J A Osborne) *chsd ldrs: rdn along over 2f out: one pce fr over 1f out* **22/1**

0- **6** 1 **To Bubbles**[113] 6281 3-8-5 0 PaulFessey 7 53
(T D Barron) *towards rr: hdwy on outer 2f out: sn rdn and no imp appr fnl f* **33/1**

50- **7** 12 **Uno Dos Tres**[81] 6868 3-8-10 0 (t) PatCosgrave 5 26
(Jane Chapple-Hyam) *chsd ldrs on outer: rdn along over 2f out: sn wknd* **7/1**

8 1/2 **Sharp Indian** 4-9-8 0 PaulHanagan 4 19
(W J H Ratcliffe) *s.i.s: rn green and a bhd* **40/1**

000- **9** 6 **Josama**[78] 6904 4-9-8 37 PhillipMakin 1 3
(R Bastiman) *chsd ldng pair: rdn along 3f out: sn drvn and wknd* **150/1**

1m 29.22s (-1.08) **Going Correction** -0.15s/f (Stan)
WFA 3 from 4yo 17lb **9** Ran SP% **121.6**
Speed ratings (Par 103): **100,96,95,94,94 93,79,78,71**
CSF £14.07 TOTE £2.70: £1.20, £2.00, £1.10; EX 17.40 Trifecta £80.80 Pool: £992.47 - 8.72 winning tickets..
Owner Mountgrange Stud **Bred** Andrew Coonan And Thomas J K Clarke **Trained** Upper Lambourn, Berks

FOCUS
An ordinary maiden, but a couple of these are open to improvement. The form is rated around the placed horses and could have rated higher.

484 SPONSOR A RACE AT SOUTHWELL H'CAP 7f (F)
4:35 (4:35) (Class 5) (0-70,69) 3-Y-0 **£2,593** (£765; £383) **Stalls** Low

Form RPR

66-1 **1** **Rapidity**[5] 419 3-9-4 69 6ex ChrisCatlin 3 87
(E J O'Neill) *mde all: rdn clr wl over 1f out: unchal* **2/7**[1]

63-2 **2** 14 **Inontime (IRE)**[32] 74 3-9-3 **68** AndrewElliott 1 49
(K R Burke) *hld up: hdwy 3f out: rdn 2f out: kpt on u.p: no ch w wnr* **9/1**[2]

0U-6 **3** shd **Traitor's Gate**[32] 74 3-9-2 **67** GregFairley 2 47
(M Johnston) *prom: rdn along and sltly outpcd over 2f out: kpt on u.p appr fnl f* **16/1**

423- **4** 1 1/4 **Tamasou (IRE)**[90] 6763 3-9-0 **68** DominicFox(3) 5 45
(S Parr) *chsd ldrs: rdn along over 2f out: sn one pce* **9/1**[2]

1-61 **5** 2 1/2 **Mac Dalia**[15] 279 3-9-1 **69** (p) JerryO'Dwyer(3) 4 39
(A J McCabe) *t.k.h: cl up: rdn over 2f out: hung rt and wknd qckly over 1f out* **10/1**[3]

1m 28.52s (-1.78) **Going Correction** -0.15s/f (Stan) **5** Ran SP% **112.7**
Speed ratings (Par 97): **104,88,87,86,83**
CSF £3.95 TOTE £1.20: £1.10, £2.40; EX 4.00 Place 6 £10.39, Place 5 £3.70.
Owner Premspace Ltd **Bred** Angmering Park Stud **Trained** Averham Park, Notts

FOCUS
A very uncompetitive handicap and ultimately a one-horse race. The winning time was smart for the type of contest, 0.7 seconds faster than the preceding maiden.
T/Plt: £19.20 to a £1 stake. Pool: £49,410.50. 1,871.15 winning tickets. T/Qpdt: £2.10 to a £1 stake. Pool: £3,820.60. 1,294.70 winning tickets. JR

466 WOLVERHAMPTON (A.W) (L-H)
Friday, February 8

OFFICIAL GOING: Standard
Wind: Almost nil Weather: Fine

485 GOLD PONTIN'S FOR THE OVER 50'S APPRENTICE H'CAP 1m 4f 50y(P)
6:50 (6:50) (Class 6) (0-60,60) 4-Y-0+ **£2,047** (£604; £302) **Stalls** Low

Form RPR

220- **1** **Ardmaddy (IRE)**[53] 6534 4-8-9 **53** (b) JemmaMarshall(3) 9 63+
(G L Moore) *a.p: chsd ldr over 5f out: led 3f out: clr 2f out: pushed out* **3/1**[1]

3-31 **2** 1 3/4 **Still Dreaming**[21] 215 4-8-6 **52** (b) RossAtkinson(5) 6 58
(R J Price) *hld up towards rr: hdwy over 3f out: sn nt clr run: rdn over 2f out: styd on to take 2nd ins fnl f: nt rch wnr* **9/1**

6132 **3** 1 1/2 **Gifted Heir (IRE)**[11] 341 4-8-9 **55** NatashaEaton(5) 1 59
(A Bailey) *chsd ldr tl over 5f out: wnt 2nd again over 2f out tl ins fnl f: nt qckn* **7/2**[2]

00-3 **4** 3 **Sky Chart (IRE)**[15] 287 4-8-9 **50** (t) DanielleMcCreery 3 49+
(N J Vaughan) *s.s: t.k.h in rr: hdwy on outside wl over 1f out: styd on and edgd lft fnl f: nvr nrr* **10/1**

U **5** 2 1/2 **Saint Eric (FR)**[15] 287 6-8-10 **51** KylieManser(3) 5 46
(Noel T Chance) *hld up in mid-div: hdwy 7f out: rdn 2f out: wkng whn edgd lft jst over 1f out* **40/1**

20- **6** 2 1/2 **Ilviz (FR)**[41] 7273 6-8-12 **55** BMcHugh(5) 4 46
(Ollie Pears) *hld up in mid-div: n.m.r 3f out: n.d after* **3/1**[1]

-000 **7** 4 **Three Thieves (UAE)**[11] 344 5-9-8 **60** JackDean 7 45
(M S Saunders) *hld up and bhd: rdn and shortlived effrt on outside over 2f out* **14/1**

/20- **8** 3 **Dream Forest (IRE)**[388] 148 5-9-3 **55** PatrickDonaghy 8 35
(P R Webber) *s.i.s: hld up towards rr: rdn over 2f out: no rspnse: swtchd rt over 1f out* **8/1**[3]

134/ **9** 2 1/2 **Liberty Seeker (FR)**[582] 2452 9-9-5 **60** MarkCoumbe(3) 2 36
(John A Harris) *set slow pce: hdd 3f out: sn wknd* **8/1**[3]

2m 45.89s (4.79) **Going Correction** +0.275s/f (Slow)
WFA 4 from 5yo+ 3lb **9** Ran SP% **122.6**
Speed ratings (Par 101): **95,93,92,90,89 87,84,82,81**
CSF £33.22 CT £102.38 TOTE £6.20: £1.10, £3.50, £1.60; EX 35.60.
Owner Blue Crocodile **Bred** Frank Dunne **Trained** Woodingdean, E Sussex
■ Stewards' Enquiry : Jack Dean one-day ban: used whip with excessive force (Feb 19)

FOCUS
A poor handicap that was slowly run and the form looks weak rated through the exposed third.

486 WOLVERHAMPTON-RACECOURSE.CO.UK (S) STKS 5f 216y(P)
7:20 (7:20) (Class 6) 3-Y-0 **£2,047** (£604; £302) **Stalls** Low

Form RPR

0-0 **1** **Arkando (IRE)**[17] 257 3-8-12 0 (b[1]) DarrenWilliams 4 51+
(K R Burke) *a gng wl: wnt 2nd over 2f out: led over 1f out: sn rdn and edgd lft: r.o wl* **4/1**[2]

0-0 **2** 3 **Tilly Ann (IRE)**[6] 412 3-8-12 0 LPKeniry 8 41
(Peter Grayson) *t.k.h in rr: hdwy over 2f out: rdn over 1f out: wnt 2nd wl ins fnl f: no ch w wnr* **50/1**

666- **3** 3/4 **O'Casey (IRE)**[214] 3364 3-9-3 49 TGMcLaughlin 9 48+
(J G M O'Shea) *bhd: nt clr run on ins over 2f out: hdwy on ins whn bdly hmpd wl over 1f out: sn swtchd rt: kpt on ins fnl f* **4/1**[2]

000- **4** hd **Avian Flew**[129] 5888 3-8-7 49 RussellKennemore(5) 3 38
(J A Pickering) *led: rdn over 2f out: hdd over 1f out: no ex ins fnl f* **11/1**

5 2 1/2 **Foxy Jane** 3-8-9 0 MarkLawson(3) 1 30
(M Brittain) *s.s: hdwy on ins over 3f out: rdn over 2f out: hung lft wl over 1f out: sn btn* **7/1**[3]

6-23 **6** 8 **Mama Leo**[23] 186 3-8-9 54 (v) TolleyDean(3) 7 4
(J G M O'Shea) *bhd fnl 4f* **11/4**[1]

1U0- **7** 2 1/2 **Amazing Day**[193] 4027 3-8-10 65 (p) MarkCoumbe(7) 2 1
(John A Harris) *chsd ldrs tl rdn and wknd over 3f out* **4/1**[2]

0-4 **8** 1 1/4 **Orphan Boy**[29] 108 3-9-0 0 JerryO'Dwyer(3) 5 —
(M G Quinlan) *chsd ldr tl rdn over 2f out: wknd wl over 1f out* **14/1**

1m 18.17s (3.17) **Going Correction** +0.275s/f (Slow) **8** Ran SP% **116.1**
Speed ratings (Par 95): **89,85,84,83,80 69,66,64**
CSF £155.43 TOTE £6.30: £2.60, £6.50, £2.50; EX 246.10.There was no bid for the winner.
Owner Market Avenue Racing Club Ltd **Bred** Michael Mullins **Trained** Middleham Moor, N Yorks
■ Darren Williams' first winner since his recent return to the saddle.

FOCUS
A weak seller weakened further by the favourite failing to run her race. The third is rated to his turf form and sets the level.
Amazing Day Official explanation: jockey said gelding hung both ways

487 GET A GREAT DEAL @ PONTINS.COM MEDIAN AUCTION MAIDEN STKS 5f 20y(P)
7:50 (7:50) (Class 5) 3-Y-0 **£2,590** (£770; £385; £192) **Stalls** Low

Form RPR

5 **1** **Princess Livius (IRE)**[16] 271 3-8-12 0 FergusSweeney 1 66
(G L Moore) *hld up and bhd: hdwy and swtchd rt over 1f out: sn rdn and hung rt: r.o wl to ld cl home* **10/3**[3]

04-3 **2** 1 1/4 **Jazenio**[16] 271 3-8-12 60 ChrisCatlin 2 61
(K A Ryan) *chsd ldrs: rdn to ld ins fnl f: hdd cl home* **9/2**

020- **3** 3 1/2 **Lady Vibeeka**[107] 6425 3-8-5 64 KylieManser(3) 6 48
(Mrs H Sweeting) *led after 1f: hrd rdn wl over 1f out: hdd & wknd ins fnl f* **8/1**

2-4 **4** nk **Kool Katie**[32] 74 3-8-5 0 IanCraven(7) 5 47
(Mrs G S Rees) *chsd ldrs: rdn and outpcd over 2f out: kpt on towards fin* **3/1**[2]

00- **5** nk **Cool Fashion (IRE)**[56] 7139 3-8-9 0 (v[1]) JamieMoriarty(3) 4 46
(Ollie Pears) *led 1f: chsd ldr tl rdn over 1f out: wknd ins fnl f* **40/1**

60- **6** hd **Swallow Forest**[179] 4447 3-8-12 0 PhillipMakin 3 46+
(T D Barron) *hld up and bhd: rdn and outpcd over 2f out: hung lft over 1f out: sme late prog* **15/8**[1]

63.88 secs (1.58) **Going Correction** +0.275s/f (Slow) **6** Ran SP% **114.6**
Speed ratings (Par 97): **98,96,90,89,89 89**
CSF £18.96 TOTE £4.40: £1.80, £2.30; EX 12.50.
Owner James S McMahon **Bred** Ivan And Mrs Eileen Heanen **Trained** Woodingdean, E Sussex
■ Stewards' Enquiry : Kylie Manser two-day ban: used whip with excessive frequency (Feb 19-20)

FOCUS
This modest median auction did not take much winning. The form has been rated cautiously.

488 STRATSTONE LAND ROVER WOLVERHAMPTON H'CAP 5f 20y(P)
8:20 (8:20) (Class 6) (0-65,65) 4-Y-0+ **£2,218** (£654; £327) **Stalls** Low

Form RPR

30-4 **1** **Multahab**[15] 286 9-9-4 **64** (t) JimmyQuinn 4 74
(M Wigham) *chsd ldrs: led over 1f out: drvn out* **7/2**[3]

-020 **2** 1 1/4 **Mambazo**[5] 414 6-9-0 **60** (e) AdamKirby 5 66
(S C Williams) *sn outpcd: hdwy over 2f out: nt clr run and swtchd lft jst over 1f out: chsd wnr ins fnl f: rdn and kpt on towards fin* **5/2**[2]

2210 **3** 2 1/2 **Regal Royale**[5] 414 5-8-9 **55** (v) AdrianMcCarthy 3 52
(Peter Grayson) *s.i.s: outpcd in rr: hrd rdn and hdwy on ins 1f out: no ex towards fin* **8/1**

4211 **4** 1 3/4 **Crimson Fern (IRE)**[11] 338 4-9-5 **65** 6ex FergusSweeney 6 55
(M S Saunders) *chsd ldrs gng wl: rdn and flashed tail ins fnl f: fnd nil* **9/4**[1]

610 **5** 3 1/2 **Triskaidekaphobia**[15] 286 5-9-4 **64** (t) PaulFitzsimons 2 42
(Miss J R Tooth) *w ldr: ev ch 2f out: sn rdn: wknd fnl f* **8/1**

-113 **6** 1 3/4 **Dodaa (USA)**[13] 318 5-8-1 **52** AshleyHamblett(5) 1 23
(N Wilson) *led: rdn and hdd over 1f out: wknd fnl f* **15/2**

62.43 secs (0.13) **Going Correction** +0.275s/f (Slow) **6** Ran SP% **115.5**
Speed ratings (Par 101): **109,107,103,100,94 91**
CSF £13.20 TOTE £5.30: £1.60, £1.40; EX 10.90.
Owner P J Burke and Dave Anderson **Bred** Shadwell Estate Company Limited **Trained** Newmarket, Suffolk

FOCUS
A modest sprint but a very decent time for the grade with the leading pair cutting their own throats.

489 BE BESIDE THE SEASIDE @ PONTIN'S H'CAP 7f 32y(P)
8:50 (8:51) (Class 4) (0-85,80) 3-Y-O £4,533 (£1,348; £674; £336) Stalls High

Form RPR
51-0 **1** **Cross Fell (USA)**[27] [136] 3-9-4 78............................(p) FergusSweeney 1 83
(J R Boyle) *mde all: rdn jst over 1f out: r.o wl* **8/1**
22-1 **2** *1 3/4* **Only A Game (IRE)**[24] [170] 3-9-3 77..............................(p) AdamKirby 3 77
(Miss M E Rowland) *chsd wnr: rdn and hung rt and lft fr wl over 1f out: hld whn rdr dropped rein towards fin* **7/1**
00-1 **3** *nk* **Sparton Duke (IRE)**[26] [146] 3-9-5 79................................ ChrisCatlin 5 78
(E J O'Neill) *hld up in tch: rdn over 2f out: sltly hmpd wl over 1f out: one pce fnl f* **2/1**[2]
1- **4** *3/4* **Upper Class (IRE)**[232] [2804] 3-9-3 77............................ GregFairley 7 74+
(M Johnston) *hld up: rdn over 1f out: nvr able to chal* **11/2**[3]
11-1 **5** *hd* **Fathsta (IRE)**[18] [253] 3-9-6 80.. LPKeniry 2 77
(S Kirk) *plld hrd in tch: rdn over 1f out: no hdwy* **13/8**[1]
51 **6** *7* **Helping Hand (IRE)**[17] [261] 3-8-11 76.............. RussellKennemore(5) 4 54
(R Hollinshead) *hld up and bhd: nt clr run and swtchd rt 3f out: short-lived effrt on outside over 2f out* **20/1**

1m 29.99s (0.39) **Going Correction** +0.275s/f (Slow) **6** Ran SP% **115.2**
Speed ratings (Par 99): **108,106,105,104,104 96**
CSF £61.08 TOTE £8.60: £2.40, £2.70; EX 65.90.
Owner M Khan X2 **Bred** Darley **Trained** Epsom, Surrey
FOCUS
Quite an interesting little tightly-knit handicap and another smart winning time for a race of its type. Despite this there are some doubts over the reliability of the form.
Fathsta(IRE) Official explanation: jockey said colt ran too freely

490 GO ACTIVE @ PONTIN'S IN 2008 FILLIES' H'CAP 1m 1f 103y(P)
9:20 (9:22) (Class 6) (0-60,60) 4-Y-O+ £2,047 (£604; £302) Stalls Low

Form RPR
-522 **1** **Mon Petite Amour**[4] [430] 5-8-13 55.............................. FergusSweeney 1 57+
(D W P Arbuthnot) *hld up in tch: wnt 2nd over 3f out: led over 2f out: rdn over 1f out: r.o* **10/11**[1]
6544 **2** *2* **Casablanca Minx (IRE)**[4] [426] 5-8-10 59..............(v) RichardEvans(7) 4 56
(P D Evans) *hld up: hdwy over 1f out: rdn and r.o to take 2nd nr fin* **7/2**[2]
60-0 **3** *shd* **Over Ice**[36] [32] 5-8-4 46 oh1.. JimmyQuinn 5 43
(Karen George) *played up in stalls: s.i.s: swtchd rt and hdwy to ld after 1f: hdd over 4f out: rdn over 2f out: chsd wnr fnl f: no imp* **4/1**[3]
000- **4** *1* **Naughty Thoughts (IRE)**[42] [7257] 4-9-4 60.......................... AlanDaly 8 55
(Andrew Turnell) *a.p: swtchd rt wl over 1f out: rdn and one pce fnl f* **13/2**
0-54 **5** *1 1/2* **Hayley's Pearl**[18] [252] 9-7-11 46 oh1......................... RossAtkinson(7) 6 38
(Mrs P Ford) *hld up: hdwy over 3f out: rdn over 2f out: wknd ins fnl f* **14/1**
-040 **6** *1* **Divine Love (IRE)**[13] [323] 4-7-12 47 oh1 ow1.....(b) PatrickDonaghy(7) 7 37
(T Wall) *s.i.s: hdwy over 5f out: led over 4f out: rdn and hdd over 2f out: wknd ins fnl f* **28/1**
000- **7** *4* **Miss Wolf**[65] [5982] 8-8-1 46 oh1.. DominicFox(3) 2 27
(G H Jones) *led 1f: lost pl over 5f out: bhd whn rdn over 3f out* **66/1**
3-66 **8** *20* **Rosie's Glory (USA)**[2] [455] 4-9-0 56..............................(b) ChrisCatlin 3 —
(M F Harris) *hdwy over 6f out: rdn and wknd over 3f out* **11/1**

2m 4.80s (3.10) **Going Correction** +0.275s/f (Slow) **8** Ran SP% **127.9**
Speed ratings (Par 98): **97,95,95,94,92 92,88,70**
CSF £5.24 CT £10.56 TOTE £1.50: £1.10, £1.30, £2.20; EX 4.10 Place 6 £364.62, Place 5 £198.07.
Owner Noel Cronin **Bred** Branston Stud Ltd **Trained** Compton, Berks
FOCUS
They went no pace early on in this dreadful fillies' handicap. It is doubtful the winner had to run up to recent form to score.
T/Plt: £563.70 to a £1 stake. Pool: £95,019.55. 123.05 winning tickets. T/Qpdt: £69.60 to a £1 stake. Pool: £6,800.60. 72.30 winning tickets. KH

472 NAD AL SHEBA (L-H)
Friday, February 8

OFFICIAL GOING: Turf course - good; dirt course - fast

491a MEYDAN CITY STKS (H'CAP) (TURF) 1m 4f (T)
3:05 (3:05) (100-111,111) 3-Y-O+
£52,763 (£17,587; £8,793; £4,396; £2,638; £1,758)

RPR
1 **Gravitas**[15] [293] 5-9-0 105.. LDettori 2 110+
(Saeed Bin Suroor) *led main gp: t.k.h: smooth prog to ld 1 1/2f out: easily* **11/4**[2]
2 *3 1/4* **Illustrious Blue**[97] [6645] 5-9-3 108..................................... PaulDoe 1 108+
(W J Knight) *slowly away: settled in rr: rdn 2 1/2f out: r.o: no ch w wnr* **9/2**
3 *1 1/2* **New Guinea**[15] [293] 5-9-0 105.. TedDurcan 4 102
(Saeed Bin Suroor) *trckd ldr: rdn 4f out: chsd ldr 2 1/2f out: nt qckn but r.o* **6/1**
4 *3/4* **Mulaqat**[15] [293] 5-9-3 108..(b) JMurtagh 5 104
(D Selvaratnam, UAE) *restrained in last: rdn 2 1/2f out: stl in rr whn no room 1f out: swtchd: r.o* **14/1**
5 *3 1/4* **Longville (GER)**[15] [293] 4-8-7 101 ow1............................ RyanMoore 3 92
(H J Brown, South Africa) *set stdy pce: qcknd 4f out: hdd 1 1/2f out: wknd* **5/2**[1]
6 *4 1/4* **Book Of Music (IRE)**[15] [293] 5-9-6 111....................(v) KerrinMcEvoy 6 96
(Saeed Bin Suroor) *racd in 4th: wnt 3rd 7f out: rdn 2 1/2f out: one pce* **4/1**[3]

2m 35.37s (4.37) **Going Correction** +0.30s/f (Good)
WFA 4 from 5yo 3lb **6** Ran SP% **114.4**
Speed ratings: **97,94,93,93,91 88**
CSF: £15.79..
Owner Godolphin **Bred** Exors Of The Late Gerald W Leigh **Trained** Newmarket, Suffolk
FOCUS
A disappointing turnout numerically, but some sort of case could be made for all six runners and this was a good middle-distance handicap. The pace was steady to the first bend, but Longville soon upped the tempo and set a decent enough gallop considering the lack of runners.
NOTEBOOK
Gravitas, suited by the strong pace, improved on the form he showed when second to Book Of Music over course and distance on his previous start with a clear-cut success. Having moved into contention travelling well early in the straight, he found plenty when asked for his effort to come nicely clear of his five rivals. He has not always been the most consistent - his last success was gained when trained in France in 2006 - but he seems to have got his act together now.
Illustrious Blue, successful over an extended 1m at last year's carnival off a 6lb lower mark, showed he gets this longer trip when third in a Listed event on the Polytrack at Kempton when last seen in November. He ran a respectable race, but was no match whatsoever for the convincing winner. (op 5/1)
New Guinea, racing off the same mark as when fourth behind Book Of Music over course and distance on his previous start, was under pressure before the straight but to his credit he kept responding. (op 11/2)
Mulaqat ran a little better than when down the field over course and distance on his previous start, but he was still well held. He had to be switched inside the final furlong, but was not unlucky. (tchd 16/1)
Longville(GER) has left Mario Hofer's yard since running third behind both Book Of Music and Gravitas over course and distance on his previous start. Ridden from the front once again, it looked as if he might take a bit of passing when still moving well at the top of the straight, but he offered disappointingly little once challenged. (op 3/1)
Book Of Music(IRE) had four of today's rivals behind, including Gravitas, when winning off a 4lb lower mark over course and distance on his previous start, so this was disappointing. All of his wins have been gained in fields of ten or more. (op 7/2)

492a MEYDAN STKS (H'CAP) (TURF) 6f (T)
3:35 (3:37) (95-110,110) 3-Y-O+
£36,180 (£12,060; £6,030; £3,015; £1,809; £1,206)

RPR
1 **Turn On The Style**[38] [5] 6-8-10 100............................(b) PaulMulrennan 4 107
(J Balding) *trckd ldr: rdn to ld 1 1/2f out: r.o wl* **7/1**[3]
2 *1 1/2* **Admiralofthefleet (USA)**[181] [4412] 4-9-6 110.................... JMurtagh 12 113
(M F De Kock, South Africa) *settled in rr: smooth prog to chse wnr 1 1/2f out: nt qckn fnl 110yds* **8/1**
3 *1/2* **Buachaill Dona (IRE)**[8] [378] 5-8-10 100........................ FrancisNorton 2 101
(D Nicholls) *slowly away: settled in rr: r.o wl fnl 1 1/2f: nrst fin* **20/1**
4 *1/2* **Indian Trail**[15] [290] 8-9-3 107..................................(v) AdrianTNicholls 8 107
(D Nicholls) *settled in rr: trckd runner-up 1 1/2f out: r.o: nrst fin* **8/1**
5 *1 1/2* **Attilius (BRZ)**[8] [378] 6-8-5 95....................................(t) TPO'Shea 1 90
(E Charpy, UAE) *mid-div on rail: rdn 2 1/2f out: r.o fnl f: nrst fin* **33/1**
6 *3/4* **Rochdale**[29] 5-7-13 95... AhmedAjtebi(6) 10 88
(A Al Raihe, UAE) *trckd ldr 3f out: ev ch 1 1/2f out: one pce* **12/1**
7 *1 1/4* **Checkit (IRE)**[1] [474] 8-8-5 95.. PaulEddery 3 84
(R Bouresly, Kuwait) *mid-div: rdn to cl 2f out: r.o same pce* **40/1**
8 *1/4* **Rockets 'n Rollers (IRE)**[8] [378] 8-8-10 100..........(p) RoystonFfrench 11 88
(A Manuel, UAE) *mid-div: wd: chsd ldrs 2f out: wknd fnl f* **33/1**
9 *2 1/4* **Grantley Adams**[104] [6491] 5-8-5 95.................................. TedDurcan 7 76
(Saeed Bin Suroor) *racd in last: gng wl 3f out: swtchd wd: nvr nr to chal* **6/4**[1]
10 *3* **Canadian Danehill (IRE)**[8] [378] 6-8-6 96..................(p) RichardMullen 9 68
(R M H Cowell) *trckd ldr: ev ch 2f out: wknd fnl f* **16/1**
11 *6 3/4* **Shmookh (USA)**[146] [5416] 4-8-9 99.................................. RHills 6 51
(Doug Watson, UAE) *mid-div: rdn whn no room 1 1/2f out: nt rcvr* **4/1**[2]
12 *13* **Heart Alone (BRZ)**[22] [205] 7-8-10 100.................................. PDevlin 5 13
(S Seemar, UAE) *rdn to ld: rdn 3f out: hdd 2 1/2f out: wknd* **50/1**

1m 12.06s (0.06) **Going Correction** +0.30s/f (Good) **12** Ran SP% **123.3**
Speed ratings: **111,109,108,107,105 104,103,102,99,95 86,69**
CSF: £61.25. TRI: £1,092.96..
Owner The Haydock Badgeholders **Bred** J And Mrs Bowtell **Trained** Scrooby, Notts
FOCUS
This looked like an ordinary sprint handicap for the level, basically another division of the seventh race.
NOTEBOOK
Turn On The Style provided Britain with a belated first winner at this year's carnival. He was reluctant to load, but displayed a most willing attitude in the race itself. Having got a good lead for much of the way, he found a dream run against the far rail in the straight and stayed on strongly for pressure to readily hold off Admiralofthefleet. He started last season rated just 76, but has progressed into a smart sprinter and this was arguably a career-best performance.
Admiralofthefleet(USA) ◆ struggled after winning last season's Dee Stakes at Chester for Aidan O'Brien and he had plenty to prove dropped back to a sprint trip for the first time, but he ran a stormer off top weight. Although his run rather flattened out close home, he produced an impressive burst of speed to move from near last to second halfway up the straight and this must rate as a very pleasing return to action. He looks capable of fulfilling his potential for his new connections and appeals as one to keep onside.
Buachaill Dona(IRE), down the field on the dirt over 5f on his previous start, was suited by the return to turf and looked unlucky not to finish a little closer. Held up for much of the way, he was denied a clear run when initially trying to make a move and got in the clear too late to threaten the front two.
Indian Trail struggled to land a blow over an extended 6f round here on his previous start, but this was better. He did not enjoy the best of trips and had to be switched with his effort, so this was encouraging.
Attilius(BRZ), back on turf, is a little bit better than he was able to show as he was short of room in the straight and had to be switched. (op 25-1)
Grantley Adams was 1lb lower than when winning an extended 6f handicap at last year's carnival for Mick Channon, but he was held up in last and never looked like picking up.
Canadian Danehill(IRE) looks too high in the weights. (tchd 18-1)
Shmookh(USA), an improved sprinter for John Dunlop last season, was badly hampered halfway up the straight on his debut for new connections and can be forgiven this.

493a MEYDAN MARINA STKS (H'CAP) (DIRT) 1m 110y
4:10 (4:10) (90-105,104) 3-Y-O+
£33,165 (£11,055; £5,527; £2,763; £1,658; £1,105)

RPR
1 **Jalil (USA)**[119] [6143] 4-8-8 91................................ KerrinMcEvoy 13 102+
(Saeed Bin Suroor) *mid-div: wd: trckd runner-up 3f out: rdn 1 1/2f out: led 110yds out: easily* **5/2**[1]
2 *3* **Aleutian**[344] [601] 8-9-5 102...(e) MartinDwyer 6 105
(F Nass, Bahrain) *trckd ldrs: led 1 1/2f out: r.o wl: no ch w wnr* **16/1**
3 *3 3/4* **Imperialista (BRZ)**[22] [204] 5-9-6 104................................(v) LDettori 14 99
(Saeed Bin Suroor) *sn led: rdn 2 1/2f out: hdd 1 1/2f out: r.o wl* **6/1**[2]
4 *6* **Delude (IRE)**[1] [476] 10-8-8 91 ow1.................................. BrettDoyle 4 75
(R Bouresly, Kuwait) *in rr of mid-div: rdn 3f out: r.o wl fnl 1 1/2f: nrst fin* **25/1**
5 *1 1/4* **Quebec Citizen (BRZ)**[7] 5-8-11 95..............................(p) WayneSmith 5 75
(M Al Muhairi, UAE) *trckd ldrs: rdn 3f out: r.o same pce* **12/1**
6 *2 3/4* **Kayak (SAF)**[8] [380] 6-9-1 98..(b) KShea 2 74
(M F De Kock, South Africa) *wl away: trckd ldr on rail: rdn 4f out: r.o same pce* **13/2**[3]
7 *1 3/4* **Opportunist (IRE)**[8] [382] 9-8-8 91..............................(vt) RichardMullen 7 63
(Doug Watson, UAE) *mid-div: rdn 2 1/2f out: r.o same pce but n.d* **8/1**
8 *nse* **Etihaad**[1] [476] 6-8-12 96..(t) PaulEddery 9 67
(R Bouresly, Kuwait) *mid-div: rdn 3f out: nvr able to chal* **20/1**

9 1 3/4 **Purple Emperor (USA)**[22] 202 4-8-7 **90** .... DO'Donohoe 12 58
(Saeed Bin Suroor) *racd in rr: n.d* **14/1**
10 1 1/4 **Estihdaaf (USA)**[7] 7-8-1 **90** .... (tp) AhmedAjtebi(6) 8 56
(A Al Raihe, UAE) *in rr of main gp: nvr nr to chal* **33/1**
11 1 1/4 **Yorokobi (BRZ)**[8] 379 5-8-7 **90** .... RyanMoore 11 53
(H J Brown, South Africa) *sn rdn in rr: nvr able to chal* **25/1**
12 1/2 **Kerashan (IRE)**[8] 381 6-8-11 **95** .... (t) RoystonFfrench 1 56
(A Al Raihe, UAE) *slowly away: a in rr* **33/1**
13 3 1/2 **Tonic Star (FR)**[8] 384 5-8-11 **95** .... TomEaves 3 49
(Christian Wroe) *slowly away: mid-div on rail: rdn 4f out: wknd fnl 1 1/2f* **40/1**
14 1 1/2 **Night Hour (IRE)**[104] 6490 6-8-8 **91** .... TedDurcan 10 43
(Saeed Bin Suroor) *a in rr* **11/1**
15 3 1/4 **Extreme Measures**[118] 6185 5-8-7 **90** .... (t) WJSupple 15 36
(Saeed Bin Suroor) *racd in last: nvr nr to chal* **25/1**

1m 42.15s (102.15) **Going Correction** +0.075s/f (Slow) **15** Ran SP% **120.5**
Speed ratings: **110,107,104,98,97 95,93,93,91,90 89,89,86,84,81**
CSF: £42.02. TRI: £226.71..
Owner Godolphin **Bred** Mr & Mrs Martin J Wygod **Trained** Newmarket, Suffolk

FOCUS
A weak handicap for the level and Saeed Bin Suroor very much held the key, saddling five of the 15 runners, including the favourite. They went a strong pace and the field were soon well-strung out.

NOTEBOOK
Jalil(USA) justified favouritism in workmanlike style. He is a horse with a big reputation, thanks to his $9,700,000 price tag rather that what he has actually achieved on a racecourse, but his previous form still entitled him to go close, and the switch to dirt was also expected to suit. Having been well off the fast early pace through the opening stages, he moved into a challenging position travelling strongly at the top of the straight, but took longer than expected to pick up. He seemed to hit a flat spot when first coming under pressure, but he was well on top at the line and this ought to have boosted his confidence. He should be suited by a step back up in trip. (op 2-1)
Aleutian, returning from almost a year off the track, was never too far away and kept on to the line, but the winner was too strong.
Imperialista(BRZ) has not gone on since winning the first round of the Maktoum Challenge last year, but he was given every chance from the front and this was a respectable effort under top weight.
Delude(IRE) ran well turned out a day after running sixth in the second round of the Maktoum Challenge.
Purple Emperor(USA) was never really seen with a chance and will probably be happier back on turf.
Night Hour(IRE) was never really seen with a chance and is another that may be happier back on grass.
Extreme Measures, like a couple of his stable companions, may have more to offer back on turf.

494a MEYDAN RACECOURSE STKS (H'CAP) (TURF) 1m 194y(T)
4:40 (4:40) (100-118,118) 3-Y-0+

£52,763 (£17,587; £8,793; £4,396; £2,638; £1,758)

RPR
1 **Oracle West (SAF)**[110] 6374 7-9-6 **118** .... JMurtagh 6 116
(M F De Kock, South Africa) *mid-div: smooth prog to chal 2f out: led 1 1/2f out: r.o wl* **5/2**[2]
2 1 1/4 **Sushisan (AUS)**[285] 6-9-4 **116** .... RyanMoore 2 111
(H J Brown, South Africa) *in rr of main gp: rdn to cl on wnr 1 1/2f out: r.o but no ch w wnr* **9/4**[1]
3 shd **Eddie Jock (IRE)**[146] 5412 4-8-12 **110** .... (v) LDettori 5 105
(Saeed Bin Suroor) *sn led: hdd 1 1/2f out: kpt on wl* **9/2**
4 1 1/4 **Traffic Guard (USA)**[15] 294 4-8-7 **105** .... (p) JohnEgan 3 97
(J S Moore) *trckd ldr: rdn 2 1/2f out: wknd fnl 1 1/2f* **9/1**
5 2 1/2 **Gun Salute (USA)**[77] 6-8-10 **108** .... (bt) MJKinane 1 95
(Doug Watson, UAE) *mid-div on rail: rdn 2 1/2f out: r.o same pce* **4/1**[3]
6 7 **Money Bags (SAF)**[8] 384 6-8-5 **102** .... (b) WMLordan 4 76
(M F De Kock, South Africa) *slowly away: settled in last: rdn 3f out: nvr nr to chal* **25/1**

1m 51.05s (1.05) **Going Correction** +0.30s/f (Good) **6** Ran SP% **111.4**
Speed ratings: **107,105,105,104,102 96**
CSF: £8.41..
Owner A Geemooi **Bred** Langeberg Stud **Trained** South Africa

FOCUS
Just the six runners, which was disappointing, but those that turned up still made for a high-class handicap. The pace seemed fair enough considering the small field.

NOTEBOOK
Oracle West(SAF) is probably best suited by 1m4f, as last year's second in the Sheema Classic indicates, but he is versatile with regards trip and was able to defy a mark of 118 over this extended 1m on his first start since running fifth in the Canadian International last October. Always well enough placed, he showed a nice change of pace when asked to challenge and was a decisive winner. The Group 3 Dubai City Of Gold Stakes, which he won in 2006 and finished second in last year, could be a suitable target, before having another go at the Sheema Classic.
Sushisan(AUS), a winner over 1m2f off a mark of 107 round here before running fifth in the Sheema Classic last year, had been off the track since finishing fifth in a Group 1 at Sha Tin. The winner was too good, but this still rates as a very smart effort off the back of such a long break and he can be expected to improve significantly. (op 2-1)
Eddie Jock(IRE), the winner of the Britannia Stakes off 104 for Michael Bell last season, was allowed the run of the race out in front on his debut for new connections and can have few excuses. This was his first run in almost five months and he can be expected to come on a little. (op 4-1)
Traffic Guard(USA), fifth to Linngari over an extended 7f round here on his previous start, seemed to have his chance but failed to pick up.
Gun Salute(USA), winner of the Grade 1 Secretariat Stakes in 2005 when trained in the US, dropped out rather tamely on his first start for new connections. (op 9-2)
Money Bags(SAF), with the tongue-tie left off this time, did not offer a great deal, but then this was a hot race. (op 16-1)

495a MEYDAN BUSINESS PARK STKS (H'CAP) (TURF) 1m (T)
5:20 (5:20) (95-110,110) 3-Y-0+

£36,180 (£12,060; £6,030; £3,015; £1,809; £1,206)

RPR
1 **Third Set (IRE)**[22] 203 5-8-12 **102** .... LDettori 3 113+
(Saeed Bin Suroor) *mid-div: swtchd wd 2f out: r.o wl: led 110yds out: easily* **15/8**[1]
2 2 1/4 **King Jock (USA)**[8] 383 7-9-3 **107** .... PShanahan 8 112
(R J Osborne, Ire) *mid-div: trckd ldr 2f out: r.o fnl f: no ch w wnr* **16/1**
3 1/2 **Colorado Rapid (IRE)**[22] 205 4-8-6 **96** .... (v) KerrinMcEvoy 2 100
(Saeed Bin Suroor) *settled in rr: nvr able to chal but r.o wl fnl f: nrst fin* **11/2**[2]
4 1/2 **Hazeymm (IRE)**[15] 296 5-8-11 **101** .... (v) JMurtagh 6 104
(D Selvaratnam, UAE) *trckd ldng duo: t.k.h: led 1 1/2f out: hdd 110yds out: wknd* **14/1**
5 1/4 **Pride Of Nation (IRE)**[111] 6332 6-9-4 **108** .... MJKinane 4 110
(J W Hills) *settled in rr: mid-div on rail whn n.m.r 1 1/2f out: r.o* **16/1**
6 shd **Glen Nevis (USA)**[8] 384 4-8-8 **98** .... (v) TedDurcan 1 100
(Saeed Bin Suroor) *settled in rr: mid-div whn n.m.r ent fnl f: r.o* **10/1**
7 1 3/4 **Ragheed (USA)**[146] 5431 4-8-9 **99** .... RHills 9 97
(E Charpy, UAE) *sn led: hdd 1f out: wknd* **8/1**[3]
8 1/4 **River Tiber**[8] 379 5-9-0 **104** .... WJSupple 10 101
(Saeed Bin Suroor) *trckd ldrs tl rdn 2f out: wknd* **10/1**
9 2 3/4 **Fremen (USA)**[8] 384 8-8-6 **96** .... AdrianTNicholls 7 87
(D Nicholls) *mid-div: t.k.h: nvr nr to chal* **9/1**
10 2 3/4 **Diamond Quest (SAF)**[230] 2856 7-9-6 **110** .... KLatham 12 95
(H J Brown, South Africa) *settled in rr: nvr nr to chal* **20/1**
11 3 1/4 **Lucky Dance (BRZ)**[8] 379 6-8-10 **100** .... RyanMoore 13 77
(H J Brown, South Africa) *mid-div: t.k.h: rdn 3f out: nvr able to chal* **16/1**
12 2 1/4 **Dickensian (IRE)**[15] 294 5-8-10 **100** .... (t) DBadel 5 72
(E Charpy, UAE) *slowly away: racd in rr: n.d* **50/1**
13 1/4 **Mister Fasliyev (IRE)**[15] 296 6-9-1 **105** .... TPO'Shea 11 76
(E Charpy, UAE) *mid-div: rdn 2 1/2f out: nt qckn: wknd fnl 1 1/2f* **25/1**
14 9 1/4 **Obe Brave**[111] 6338 5-8-10 **100** .... TomEaves 14 50
(I Semple) *trckd ldr: wknd 2 1/2f out* **50/1**

1m 39.44s (1.14) **Going Correction** +0.30s/f (Good) **14** Ran SP% **126.3**
Speed ratings: **106,103,103,102,102 102,100,100,97,94 91,89,89,79**
CSF: £37.13. TRI: £153.91..
Owner Sultan Ali **Bred** A Stroud And J Hanly **Trained** Newmarket, Suffolk

FOCUS
Many of these types of carnival handicaps lack strength in depth, but this was a very good race, arguably one of the most competitive of its type this year. The pace was fair.

NOTEBOOK
Third Set(IRE) was some way below the pick of the form he showed for Roger Charlton last season when second on the dirt on his debut for Saeed Bin Suroor, but he was well suited by the return to turf and ran out a most decisive winner. He had to be switched with his challenge in the straight, but he picked up well once in the clear without his rider having to get overly serious. It has to be noted he again carried his head high, and also edged left once in front, but while that was hardly ideal, it did not seem to slow him down at all. On this evidence he will be worth his place in a Pattern race. (op 9-4)
King Jock(USA), dropped in class, was ridden closer to the pace this time and ran on to the line, but he ultimately proved no match for the classy winner.
Colorado Rapid(IRE) ◆ was suited by the return to turf having run well below form on dirt on his first start since leaving Mark Johnston's yard last time but, ridden with a lot of patience as usual, he was given plenty to do and arrived on the scene too late having had to wait for an opening early in the straight. He can be rated a little better than the bare form. (op 6-1)
Hazeymm(IRE), unable to dictate this time, raced very keenly just off the lead and did well to finish so close.
Pride Of Nation(IRE), a Group 3 winner for Luca Cumani last season, ran on in the straight without matching the speed of some of these and gave the impression he will be much sharper next time.
River Tiber was well below the form he showed when winning a similar race on his previous start. (op 8-1)
Fremen(USA) looked a little unlucky when fourth over course and distance on his previous start, but he can have no real excuses this time. (op 10-1)
Obe Brave offered little on his first start since leaving Mick Channon.

496a UAE 1000 GUINEAS - MEYDAN (LISTED RACE) (FILLIES) (DIRT) 1m (D)
5:55 (5:55) 3-Y-0

£75,376 (£25,125; £12,562; £6,281; £3,768; £2,512)

RPR
1 **Cocoa Beach (CHI)**[22] 201 4-9-4 **102** .... (v) TedDurcan 8 105+
(Saeed Bin Suroor) *s.i.s: sn trcking ldrs: rdn to chse ldr 2 1/2f out: led 110yds out: comf* **11/4**[2]
2 5 1/4 **Fiesta Lady (ARG)**[22] 201 4-9-4 108 .... LDettori 10 96+
(Saeed Bin Suroor) *trckd ldr: led gng wl 3f out: hdd 110yds out* **2/5**[1]
3 11 **Love Of Dubai (USA)**[22] 201 3-8-9 97 .... MJKinane 2 76
(C E Brittain) *settled in rr: nvr nr to chal but r.o fnl 2f* **25/1**
4 3/4 **Patio**[142] 5524 3-8-9 79 .... WJSupple 13 75
(Doug Watson, UAE) *trckd ldrs: rdn to chse wnr 2 1/2f out: kpt on same pce* **66/1**
5 3 1/4 **Star Of Rosanna**[22] 201 3-8-9 76 .... MartinDwyer 11 68
(Doug Watson, UAE) *in rr of mid-div: r.o fnl 2 1/2f: nrst fin* **100/1**
6 1 3/4 **Dalkey Girl (IRE)**[27] 137 3-8-9 91 .... RyanMoore 6 65
(V Smith) *racd in rr: r.o fnl 2f but n.d* **50/1**
7 1 1/2 **Olympic Glory (BRZ)**[22] 201 4-9-4 96 .... RoystonFfrench 12 57
(A Cintra Pereira, Brazil) *mid-div: wd: rdn 3f out: r.o same pce* **12/1**[3]
8 shd **Miss Clonyn (IRE)**[22] 201 3-8-9 65 .... DO'Donohoe 7 61
(Doug Watson, UAE) *trckd ldr: rdn 3f out: wknd* **150/1**
9 4 1/2 **Queen Jock (USA)**[22] 201 3-8-9 95 .... PShanahan 1 52
(Tracey Collins, Ire) *settled in rr: nvr nr to chal* **16/1**
10 7 **Badaria (FR)**[22] 201 3-8-9 98 .... TPO'Shea 3 38
(E Charpy, UAE) *settled in rr: nvr able to chal* **33/1**
11 2 1/2 **Baby Princess (BRZ)**[22] 201 4-9-4 90 .... RHills 9 28
(J W Hills) *sn led on rail: hdd 3f out: wknd* **66/1**
12 1 1/4 **Swallow Star**[22] 201 3-8-9 70 .... PaulEddery 5 31
(R Bouresly, Kuwait) *chsd ldrs for 3f: wknd* **150/1**

1m 37.66s (0.96) **Going Correction** +0.075s/f (Slow)
WFA 3 from 4yo 19lb **12** Ran SP% **125.7**
Speed ratings: **108,102,91,91,87 86,84,84,79,72 70,69**
CSF: £4.34..
Owner H R H Princess Haya Of Jordan **Bred** Haras La Obra **Trained** Newmarket, Suffolk

FOCUS
The eighth running of the UAE 1,000 Guineas, although the race still only carries Listed status. This year's renewal was lacking in strength or depth and Saeed Bin Suroor, who had won this race six times in the past, looked to hold the key with his pair, Fiesta Lady and Cocoa Beach, very much looking the form picks having run first and second respectively in a trial for this race over 7f on their previous starts.

NOTEBOOK
Cocoa Beach(CHI) provided a slight turn up, reversing form with her better-fancied stablemate despite being 5lb worse off for a three-and-a-quarter-length beating. She had been found out by her lack of early speed in the trial, getting going far too late having struggled to lay up early on, but that race clearly brought her on and the step up was very much in her favour. She was again a little slow into her stride, but she soon recovered to chase the early leaders and, although running in snatches somewhat, she was much better placed this time. She was under pressure much sooner than Fiesta Lady, but stamina is clearly her strong suit and she readily picked up that rival in the straight. There has to be a suspicion the runner-up was not quite at her best, and with very few other serious contenders in the line-up it would be unwise to get carried away, but she gives the impression there is more to come. She will be suited by the 1m1f of the UAE Oaks and could well do the double. (op 3-1)

Fiesta Lady(ARG) looked the most likely winner when travelling very strongly into the straight and her rider seemed confident, allowing her to coast into a clear lead, but she did not find quite as much as had looked likely when coming under pressure. She responded to her rider's urgings after changing her legs at the 400m pole, but her stride shortened inside the final furlong and she seemed to finish quite tired. It would be silly to be too harsh, as she easily confirmed form with all the other fillies who ran in the trial, but this effort will still leave her with something to prove if she takes her chance in the UAE Oaks.
Love Of Dubai(USA) kept on from the back to claim third, but she was never any danger at all to the front pair.
Patio, having her first start since winning a Beverley maiden for Amanda Perrett last September, ran about as well as could have been expected.
Dalkey Girl(IRE) was well held on her first start on dirt.
Queen Jock(USA), who ran well to be fourth in the trial, was never going.
Baby Princess(BRZ) again offered little.

497a MEYDAN RACES TO THE FUTURE STKS (H'CAP) (TURF) 6f (T)
6:30 (6:32) (95-110,109) 3-Y-0+
£36,180 (£12,060; £6,030; £3,015; £1,809; £1,206)

RPR
1 **Mutamarres**[64] 5-8-5 **95** ... MartinDwyer 1 99
(Doug Watson, UAE) *sn led: clr 2 1/2f out: r.o and hld on wl* **12/1**
2 ¾ **Machinist (IRE)**[15] 291 8-8-9 **99** ... FrancisNorton 5 100
(D Nicholls) *mid-div on rail: rdn to chse wnr 2f out: r.o: nrst fin* **9/2**[2]
3 ¼ **Botanical (USA)**[15] 295 7-8-5 **95** ...(vt) TPO'Shea 2 96
(E Charpy, UAE) *slowly away: racd in last: no room 3f out: r.o wl whn clr: nrst fin* **20/1**
4 ¼ **Ripples Maid**[15] 290 5-8-7 **97** ... RyanMoore 11 97
(J A Geake) *racd in rr: rdn 3f out: ev ch 1 1/2f out: nt qckn fnl f* **14/1**
5 nse **Drayton (IRE)**[8] 378 4-9-0 **104** ... WMLordan 4 104
(M F De Kock, South Africa) *slowly away: sn trckd ldr: ev ch 2 1/2f out: nt qckn but r.o same pce* **10/3**[1]
6 2½ **Loyalist (SAF)**[15] 291 7-8-10 **100** ... RichardMullen 3 92
(S Seemar, UAE) *mid-div: rdn 2 1/2f out: r.o fnl f* **6/1**[3]
7 ½ **Sunrise Safari (IRE)**[90] 6758 5-8-10 **100** ...(v) TomEaves 9 91
(I Semple) *racd in rr: swtchd wd and rdn 2 1/2f out: r.o but n.d* **9/2**[2]
8 1 **Beckermet (IRE)**[15] 291 6-9-5 **109** ... TedDurcan 10 97
(R F Fisher) *mid-div: wd: trckd ldr 3f out: ev ch fnl 2f: nt qckn* **6/1**[3]
9 nk **Conceal**[1] 472 10-8-10 **100** ... PaulEddery 12 87
(R Bouresly, Kuwait) *settled in rr: rdn 3f out: nvr nr to chal* **50/1**
10 14 **Borehan**[601] 2658 5-8-5 **95** ... RPCleary 6 40
(D Selvaratnam, UAE) *racd v keenly bhd ldrs for 2f: wknd fnl 2 1/2f* **16/1**
11 1¼ **Mercury Chief (SAF)**[15] 295 7-8-5 **95** ...(t) AdrianTNicholls 7 36
(A Manuel, UAE) *trckd ldrs: rdn 3f out: wknd fnl 2f* **33/1**

1m 12.39s (0.39) **Going Correction** +0.30s/f (Good) **11 Ran SP% 117.9**
Speed ratings: **109,108,107,107,107 103,103,101,101,82 81**
CSF: £64.41. TRI: £1,090.36. Placepot: £41.60 to a £1 stake. Pool £12,550.00 - 220 winning units. Quadpot: £4.30 to a £1 stake. Pool £423.90 - 72.30 winning units..
Owner Hamdan Al Maktoum **Bred** Shadwell Estate Co Ltd **Trained** United Arab Emirates

FOCUS
This looked like a weak sprint handicap for both the level and prize money, basically another division of the second race.

NOTEBOOK
Mutamarres finished last in a non-carnival handicap on the dirt on his previous start, but he was given a positive ride on this return to turf and found plenty under pressure in the straight to make just about every yard. He was formerly a useful handicapper for Sir Michael Stoute, but one suspects a rise in the weights might be enough to stop him following up.
Machinist(IRE) stayed on from off the pace to take second, but he never quite looked likely to reach the winner. He was short of room rounding the final bend, but it did not cost him the race. This was an improvement on the form he showed over an extended 6f round here on his previous start. (op 5-1)
Botanical(USA), having a rare outing on turf, ran on from off the pace to take third, but he does not win very often. (op 16-1)
Ripples Maid was still last at the top of the straight and was forced to make her move out wide. She stayed on, but was never going to get there.
Drayton(IRE) is probably better when able to dominate.
Sunrise Safari(IRE) was under strong pressure at the top of the straight and never looked likely to get involved, but he did stay on late.
Beckermet(IRE) was forced to come much wider than ideal round the final bend and did not see his race out.

[452]LINGFIELD (L-H)
Saturday, February 9

OFFICIAL GOING: Standard
Wind: Very modest, behind Weather: Bright and sunny

498 LINGFIELD PARK FOR WEDDINGS MAIDEN STKS 5f (P)
1:00 (1:01) (Class 5) 3-Y-0+ £2,457 (£725; £362) Stalls High

Form RPR
00/3 1 **Judge 'n Jury**[10] 354 4-9-8 65 ...(t) KevinGhunowa(5) 2 80+
(R A Harris) *mde all: rdn clr over 1f out: in control fnl f: readily* **9/2**[2]
252 2 2½ **Hurricane Hen**[13] 324 3-8-13 75 ... PatCosgrave 3 65+
(J R Boyle) *t.k.h: hld up in tch: hdwy on outer bnd 2f out: hung lft over 1f out: chsd wnr ins fnl f: no imp* **8/11**[1]
0 3 2 **Martha (IRE)**[35] 60 3-8-8 0 ... LPKeniry 4 53
(D R C Elsworth) *s.i.s: racd in last pl: rdn and effrt over 1f out: kpt on to go 3rd nr fin: nvr trbld ldrs* **11/1**
00-4 4 hd **Evenstorm (USA)**[17] 271 3-8-8 60 ... GregFairley 6 52
(B Gubby) *prom: rdn to chse wnr over 2f out: outpcd over 1f out: lost 2 pls ins fnl f* **6/1**[3]
6 5 nk **Szaba**[17] 271 3-8-8 0 ... HayleyTurner 5 51
(J M P Eustace) *chsd wnr tl over 2f out: sn rdn: outpcd over 1f out: no ch fnl f* **25/1**
300- 6 2 **Heron (IRE)**[87] 6813 3-8-13 66 ...(b[1]) JimCrowley 1 49
(N P Littmoden) *t.k.h: trckd ldrs: drvn to dispute 2nd over 1f out: wknd jst ins fnl f* **8/1**

58.38 secs (-0.42) **Going Correction** 0.0s/f (Stan)
WFA 3 from 4yo 14lb **6 Ran SP% 113.7**
Speed ratings (Par 103): **103,99,95,95,95 91**
CSF £8.40 TOTE £7.00: £1.90, £1.50; EX 10.20.
Owner Mrs Ruth M Serrell **Bred** C A Cyzer **Trained** Earlswood, Monmouths

FOCUS
A modest event in which the winner made all. The form makes sense.

499 LINGFIELD PARK FOR CONFERENCES H'CAP 1m 4f (P)
1:30 (1:30) (Class 6) (0-50,51) 4-Y-0+ £1,876 (£554; £277) Stalls Low

Form RPR
2546 1 **Prince Of Medina**[9] 374 5-8-8 46 ... JimCrowley 4 49
(J R Best) *chsd ldrs: nt clr run bnd jst over 2f out: drvn and hdwy over 1f out: led 1f out: drvn out* **3/1**[2]
6-23 2 1 **Ndola**[6] 420 9-8-13 51 ...(v) HayleyTurner 6 52
(P Butler) *chsd ldr: clsd up 7f out: rdn wl over 2f out: hrd rdn to ld narrowly jst over 1f out: sn hdd and one pce* **11/4**[1]
6-42 3 nk **Cyril The Squirrel**[17] 273 4-8-9 50 ...(b[1]) MickyFenton 5 51
(Karen George) *led: clr tl 7f out: rdn over 2f out: hdd jst over 1f out: one pce after* **4/1**
6-26 4 nk **Countback (FR)**[27] 152 9-8-11 49 ...(p) CatherineGannon 1 50
(A W Carroll) *racd in midfield: hdwy 6f out: chsd ldrs and rdn 2f out: fnd little tl styd on ins fnl f* **7/1**
0305 5 nk **Come What July (IRE)**[7] 400 7-8-5 46 oh1 ...(v) TolleyDean(3) 2 46
(D Shaw) *racd in midfield: rdn 4f out: hdwy on outer to chse ldrs over 2f out: outpcd u.p over 1f out: kpt on ins fnl f* **7/2**[3]
4-00 6 nk **Only Hope**[29] 125 4-8-7 48 ...(v) PaulEddery 3 48
(Miss Diana Weeden) *stdd s: hld up in last: hdwy 6f out: rdn and effrt over 1f out: sn hung lft and no imp* **25/1**

2m 32.51s (-0.49) **Going Correction** 0.0s/f (Stan)
WFA 4 from 5yo+ 3lb **6 Ran SP% 110.2**
Speed ratings (Par 101): **101,100,100,99,99 99**
CSF £11.20 TOTE £2.80: £1.70, £2.10; EX 13.10.
Owner G G Racing **Bred** Slatch Farm Stud **Trained** Hucking, Kent

FOCUS
A low-grade handicap run at a steady pace, and they finished in a bit of a heap. Weak form with the third and fourth running to recent marks.

500 HOTEL COMING HERE TO LINGFIELD PARK MAIDEN STKS 1m (P)
2:05 (2:05) (Class 5) 3-Y-0 £2,457 (£725; £362) Stalls High

Form RPR
1 **Throne Of Power (USA)** 3-9-3 0 ... FergusSweeney 1 84+
(M A Magnusson) *dwlt: sn trcking ldrs: wnt 2nd 4f out: upsides gng wl 2f out: rdn to ld over 1f out: sn clr: easily* **3/1**[2]
0 2 2½ **Boy On A Swing (USA)**[6] 416 3-9-3 0 ... TPQueally 2 75+
(J A Osborne) *towards rr: rdn and hdwy wl over 3f out: chsd ldng trio wl over 2f out: wnt 2nd 1f out: r.o but nt trble wnr* **6/1**
3 4 **Gang Show (IRE)** 3-9-3 0 ... ChrisCatlin 3 66
(W J Musson) *t.k.h: hld up in rr: hdwy to chse ldng pair wl over 3f out: rdn 2f out: wl outpcd by ldng pair fnl f* **33/1**
03-2 4 2 **Ace Of Spies (IRE)**[21] 223 3-9-3 78 ... GregFairley 9 61
(M Johnston) *led: jnd 2f out: sn rdn: hdd 1f out: sn wknd* **2/1**[1]
5 1 **Fairfield Flame (GER)** 3-8-12 0 ... TQuinn 5 54+
(D R C Elsworth) *towards rr on outer: last and rdn over 4f out: sn lost tch: styd on past btn horses fnl f: n.d* **14/1**
245- 6 nk **Copperwood**[121] 6126 3-9-3 77 ... PaulDoe 4 58
(M Blanshard) *t.k.h: hld up in rr: pushed along and lost tch wl over 3f out: no ch after* **9/2**[3]
6 7 ¾ **Brave Hawk**[17] 265 3-9-3 0 ... MatthewHenry 8 56
(M A Jarvis) *chsd ldrs tl lost pl 4f out: wl bhd last 2f* **6/1**
0- 8 22 **Station Place**[61] 7097 3-8-12 0 ... SteveDrowne 6 1
(A B Haynes) *t.k.h: chsd ldr tl 4f out: sn wknd: t.o last 2f* **66/1**

1m 37.65s (-0.55) **Going Correction** 0.0s/f (Stan) **8 Ran SP% 116.2**
Speed ratings (Par 97): **102,99,95,93,92 92,91,69**
CSF £21.79 TOTE £3.00: £1.10, £2.30, £7.50; EX 22.90 Trifecta £192.30 Part won. Pool: £270.95 - 0.30 winning units..
Owner Eastwind Racing Ltd and Martha Trussell **Bred** Mineola Farm II Partnership Et Al **Trained** Upper Lambourn, Berks

FOCUS
A fair winning time for the type of race, and a potentially decent maiden although the favourite was clearly not at his best. The first two are rated better than the bare form.

501 LINGFIELD PARK FOR EXHIBITIONS CLAIMING STKS 1m (P)
2:35 (2:35) (Class 6) 3-Y-0 £1,774 (£523; £262) Stalls High

Form RPR
4 1 **Snow Bounty**[7] 413 3-9-7 0 ... TPQueally 1 58
(J A Osborne) *s.i.s: chsd ldrs: rdn and c wd wl over 1f out: edgd lft over 1f out: styd on wl fnl f to ld towards fin* **11/10**[1]
43-5 2 nk **Llab Nala**[12] 333 3-8-12 55 ... MatthewDavies(7) 3 55
(M R Channon) *t.k.h: set stdy pce: pushed along over 1f out: hdd and no ex towards fin* **10/3**[3]
46-0 3 1¼ **Adam Eterno (IRE)**[31] 98 3-9-0 53 ... DavidKinsella 5 47
(A B Haynes) *chsd ldr: rdn and ev ch jst over 2f out: wknd last 100yds* **13/2**
2-56 4 hd **Scientific**[12] 335 3-9-4 57 ...(b) DMylonas 4 51
(G Prodromou) *hld up in tch: rdn and outpcd over 2f out: kpt on fnl f* **11/4**[2]

1m 41.22s (3.02) **Going Correction** 0.0s/f (Stan) **4 Ran SP% 110.7**
Speed ratings (Par 95): **84,83,82,82**
CSF £5.18 TOTE £1.90; EX 3.30.The winner was claimed by J. S. Moore for £12,000.
Owner Mountgrange Stud **Bred** Redmyre Bloodstock & Gareth Jones Bloodstock **Trained** Upper Lambourn, Berks

FOCUS
A very slowly-run race which produced a moderate winning time, even for a race like this. Weak form, best rated through the runner-up.

502 LINGFIELDPARK.CO.UK H'CAP 1m 2f (P)
3:10 (3:10) (Class 2) (0-100,97) 4-Y-0+
£9,971 (£2,985; £1,492; £747; £372; £187) Stalls Low

Form RPR
30-4 1 **Samarinda (USA)**[21] 227 5-9-1 93 ... MickyFenton 5 99
(Mrs P Sly) *t.k.h: chsd ldrs: wnt 2nd over 2f out: rdn to ld over 1f out: all out nr fin* **4/1**[2]
12-0 2 shd **Dream Lodge (IRE)**[12] 336 4-8-13 92 ... TPQueally 7 98
(J G Given) *led at stdy pce: jnd and rdn jst over 2f out: hdd over 1f out: rallied u.p ins fnl f: jst hld* **6/1**[3]
3152 3 hd **Will He Wish**[6] 417 12-8-5 83 ...(b) ChrisCatlin 2 88
(S Gollings) *t.k.h: chsd ldrs: rdn 2f out: kpt on u.p ins fnl f* **9/1**

 The Form Book, Raceform Ltd, Compton, RG20 6NL

000- **4** ½ **Regional Counsel**[135] [5761] 4-8-4 **83** .... GregFairley 6 87
(K J Burke) *t.k.h: hld up in midfield: rdn and hdwy over 2f out: chsd ldrs wl over 1f out: kpt on same pce u.p fnl f* **25/1**

-454 **5** *shd* **Troubadour (IRE)**[6] [418] 7-9-5 **97** .... SteveDrowne 3 101
(W Jarvis) *hld up in last pair: rdn and effrt 2f out: swtchd ins and hdwy jst over 1f out: no imp towards fin* **4/1**[2]

6-35 **6** *nk* **Lisathedaddy**[14] [315] 6-8-9 **87** .... TQuinn 1 91
(B G Powell) *bustled along early: bhd: hdwy on outer jst over 2f out: styd on u.p fnl f: nt rch ldrs* **7/2**[1]

7 3½ **Dakiyah (IRE)**[73] 4-8-4 **83** oh1 .... HayleyTurner 4 80
(Mrs L J Mongan) *racd in midfield: nt clr run and lost pl jst over 2f out: bhd and hmpd bnd 2f out: sn hung lft and no imp* **33/1**

06-4 **8** *9* **Speedy Sam**[14] [315] 5-8-11 **89** ....(v) AndrewElliott 8 68
(K R Burke) *t.k.h: chsd ldr tl over 2f out: wknd qckly jst over 2f out: sn bhd: eased ins fnl f* **7/2**[1]

2m 5.51s (-1.09) **Going Correction** 0.0s/f (Stan)
WFA 4 from 5yo+ 1lb **8** Ran SP% **115.5**
Speed ratings (Par 109): **104,103,103,103,103 103,100,93**
CSF £28.45 CT £203.36 TOTE £5.90: £1.60, £2.20, £2.60; EX 38.70 Trifecta £173.40 Pool: £422.55 - 1.73 winning units..
Owner D Bayliss, T Davies, G Libson & P Sly **Bred** Gainsborough Farm Llc **Trained** Thorney, Cambs

FOCUS
A steadily-run handicap in which the first two are rated to form, although there are doubts over its reliability.

NOTEBOOK
Samarinda(USA), who had been confined to trips of a mile for the last year, was sharper for his recent return to the track. He got to the front approaching the final furlong and stuck his head out gamely to hold on. A crack at the Lincoln is possible next month, and he penalty he picked up here will help his chances of getting into the race. (op 10-3 tchd 9-2)
Dream Lodge(IRE), responsible for the very moderate gallop, was headed by the winner approaching the final furlong but was coming back again towards the line. He appeared to stay this longer trip, albeit in what was not a truly-run race. (op 13-2 tchd 11-2)
Will He Wish, an admirable veteran, is running well at present and he was clawing back the two in front of him at the line to suggest he is well worth another try at this longer trip. (op 8-1 tchd 10-1)
Regional Counsel won the Group 2 Anglesey Stakes at the Curragh for Kevin Prendergast as a two-year-old, but lost his way last season and was making his debut for this yard after more than four months off the track. Tackling 1m2f for the first time, he was keeping on at the end and this was a step in the right direction. (op 16-1)
Troubadour(IRE), held up off a slow pace on this step up in trip, was a bit short of room before the home turn and, despite running on up the rail, was never able to get to the leaders. Things did not really go for him here. (op 6-1)
Lisathedaddy was very slow to find her stride and looked reluctant to race for a few seconds. In a moderately run race, she was staying on just that bit too late. (op 4-1 tchd 3-1 tchd 9-2 in a place)
Speedy Sam failed to settle in the re-applied visor and was the first beaten. (op 10-3 tchd 3-1)

503 ARENALEISUREPLC.COM H'CAP 6f (P)
3:45 (3:45) (Class 4) (0-85,82) 4-Y-0+ **£4,100** (£1,227; £613; £306; £152) **Stalls** Low

Form RPR

0-21 **1** **Fromsong (IRE)**[15] [301] 10-8-12 **81** .... JamesO'Reilly(5) 7 94
(D K Ivory) *taken down early: mde all: rdn over 1f out: edgd rt fnl f: styd on wl* **7/2**[3]

1-11 **2** *1* **Benllech**[14] [312] 4-9-0 **78** .... SimonWhitworth 2 88+
(M Wigham) *chsd wnr: clsd wl over 1f out: rdn and half a l down whn struck on nose by rivals whip ins fnl f: btn after* **11/4**[2]

-313 **3** 3½ **Mogok Ruby**[13] [329] 4-9-2 **80** .... IanMongan 5 79
(L Montague Hall) *racd off the pce in midfield: rdn and effrt 2f out: no imp on ldng pair* **5/2**[1]

5-25 **4** *nk* **Divertimenti (IRE)**[12] [342] 4-8-10 **74** .... LPKeniry 1 72
(C R Dore) *chsd ldng pair: rdn jst over 2f out: no imp* **6/1**

3-06 **5** *2* **Bobski (IRE)**[21] [233] 6-9-4 **82** .... AmirQuinn 4 73
(P J McBride) *awkward leaving stalls and wnt rt s: a bhd: n.d* **8/1**

2213 **6** ½ **Sands Crooner (IRE)**[15] [301] 5-8-3 **70** ow1 ....(v) TolleyDean(3) 3 60
(D Shaw) *hld up in last pair: rdn and effrt on inner 2f out: no hdwy* **8/1**

1m 10.29s (-1.61) **Going Correction** 0.0s/f (Stan) course record **6** Ran SP% **114.0**
Speed ratings (Par 105): **110,108,104,103,100 100**
CSF £13.86 TOTE £4.70: £3.30, £1.30; EX 13.30.
Owner Dean Ivory **Bred** Mrs Teresa Bergin **Trained** Radlett, Herts

FOCUS
A fair winning time for the grade. Only the first two got into this and the order barely changed. The form makes sense.
Bobski(IRE) Official explanation: jockey said gelding missed the break

504 PLAY GOLF @ LINGFIELD PARK H'CAP 1m 2f (P)
4:20 (4:20) (Class 5) (0-75,77) 4-Y-0+ **£2,590** (£770; £385; £192) **Stalls** Low

Form RPR

32-2 **1** **Emperor Court (IRE)**[28] [134] 4-8-8 **65** .... SteveDrowne 2 76
(P J Makin) *t.k.h: chsd ldr for 2f: styd handy: rdn and hdwy inner wl over 1f out: led over 1f out: r.o wl* **9/4**[1]

0-12 **2** 1¼ **Blu Manruna**[22] [207] 5-8-13 **69** ....(b) PaulDoe 1 77
(J Akehurst) *led at stdy pce: pushed along and qcknd 3f out: drvn jst over 2f out: hdd over 1f out: kpt on same pce fnl f* **7/1**

5-64 **3** 1½ **Stark Contrast (USA)**[14] [316] 4-8-5 **62** .... SimonWhitworth 3 67
(J Akehurst) *t.k.h: hld up in midfield: shuffled bk and lost position over 2f out: rdn and hdwy on inner over 1f out: kpt on but nt pce to rch ldrs* **12/1**

0-63 **4** *hd* **Prince Charlemagne (IRE)**[31] [104] 5-9-2 **72** ....(p) FergusSweeney 6 77
(K R Burke) *t.k.h: hld up in rr: rdn and effrt 2f out: styd on fnl f: nvr trbld ldrs* **11/2**[3]

60-6 **5** *1* **Rock Anthem (IRE)**[15] [309] 4-8-10 **70** .... TravisBlock(3) 4 73
(Mike Murphy) *t.k.h: hld up in last: hdwy on outer wl over 2f out: wd and rdn bnd 2f out: wknd jst ins fnl f* **12/1**

2112 **6** *nk* **Sri Kuantan (IRE)**[7] [406] 4-9-6 **77** ....(t) ChrisCatlin 5 79
(P F I Cole) *t.k.h: chsd ldrs: rdn to press ldr jst over 2f out: wknd jst ins fnl f* **11/4**[2]

14-2 **7** 2½ **Alfie Tupper (IRE)**[20] [240] 5-8-12 **68** .... PatCosgrave 7 65
(J R Boyle) *hld up in rr: hdwy wl over 2f out: chsd ldrs and rdn 2f out: wknd over 1f out* **15/2**

/00- **8** *6* **Esteem**[153] [3215] 5-9-2 **72** .... MickyFenton 8 57
(D G Bridgwater) *t.k.h: chsd ldr 8f out tl jst over 2f out: sn wknd* **33/1**

2m 6.59s (-0.01) **Going Correction** 0.0s/f (Stan)
WFA 4 from 5yo 1lb **8** Ran SP% **115.4**
Speed ratings (Par 103): **100,99,97,97,96 96,94,89**
CSF £18.90 CT £154.87 TOTE £3.00: £1.40, £2.20, £2.80; EX 22.20 Trifecta £334.20 Pool: £532.01 - 1.13 winning units. Place 6 £60.22, Place 5 £45.63.
Owner Four Seasons Racing Ltd **Bred** John O'Connor **Trained** Ogbourne Maisey, Wilts

FOCUS
Another steadily run race and the form will probably not prove that reliable. The winner produced a career best and the second ran to form.
Esteem Official explanation: jockey said gelding ran too free and lost its action on the bend
T/Plt: £121.40 to a £1 stake. Pool: £57,446.75. 345.30 winning tickets. T/Qpdt: £58.10 to a £1 stake. Pool: £2,916.10. 37.10 winning tickets. SP

485 WOLVERHAMPTON (A.W) (L-H)
Saturday, February 9

OFFICIAL GOING: Standard
Wind: Slight, behind

505 CALL PONTIN'S NOW ON 0844 576 5938 MAIDEN STKS 5f 216y(P)
6:50 (6:50) (Class 5) 3-Y-0 **£2,457** (£725; £362) **Stalls** Low

Form RPR

32-0 **1** **Bahamian Lad**[29] [130] 3-8-12 **72** .... RussellKennemore(5) 5 75
(R Hollinshead) *mde all: clr fnl f: pushed out* **7/4**[2]

2 *3* **Thebes** 3-9-3 **0** .... GregFairley 4 65+
(M Johnston) *s.i.s: sn trckd wnr: hung rt ent fnl f: one pce* **10/11**[1]

3 *nk* **Young Gladiator (IRE)** 3-9-3 **0** .... PhillipMakin 3 64+
(Miss J A Camacho) *hld up: rdn 2f out: kpt on fnl f: nvr nrr* **10/1**[3]

0- **4** 2½ **Arrabiata**[45] [7235] 3-8-12 **0** .... JimmyQuinn 7 51
(C N Kellett) *in rr: rdn over 1f out: one pce after* **50/1**

6 **5** *shd* **Sazerac (USA)**[4] [441] 3-9-3 **0** .... DeanMcKeown 1 56
(D Shaw) *in tch tl rdn and wknd fnl f* **16/1**

06 **6** *9* **Rightcar Hull (IRE)**[7] [412] 3-8-12 **0** .... LPKeniry 6 22
(Peter Grayson) *t.k.h: trckd ldrs tl wknd 2f out* **25/1**

1m 16.04s (1.04) **Going Correction** +0.15s/f (Slow) **6** Ran SP% **109.5**
Speed ratings (Par 97): **99,95,94,91,91 79**
CSF £3.44 TOTE £2.30: £1.10, £1.30; EX 3.10.
Owner J D Graham **Bred** J D Graham **Trained** Upper Longdon, Staffs

FOCUS
The market principals dominated what could turn out to be a fair race with the winner's greater experience proving his trump card. The form just about makes sense.

506 MIKE AND SAM SCRIMSHAW WEDDING H'CAP 7f 32y(P)
7:20 (7:20) (Class 5) (0-75,74) 4-Y-0+ **£2,457** (£725; £362) **Stalls** High

Form RPR

05-0 **1** **Golden Prospect**[24] [177] 4-8-8 **69** .... PatrickHills(5) 5 79
(J W Hills) *stdd s: hdwy 2f out: edgd lft bef strly rdn to ld nr fin* **8/1**

51-3 **2** ¾ **Kensington (IRE)**[20] [235] 7-8-7 **63** oh1 ow3........(p) StephenDonohoe 6 71
(P D Evans) *sn trckd ldr: led 3f out: kpt on u.str.p: hdd nr fin* **10/3**[1]

0320 **3** 1¼ **Parkview Love (USA)**[3] [452] 7-8-12 **68** ....(v) DeanMcKeown 7 73
(D Shaw) *hld up: rdn and hdwy on outside 2f out: kpt on one pce ins fnl f* **10/3**[1]

034- **4** *hd* **Hypocrisy**[56] [7158] 5-9-1 **71** .... MickyFenton 2 75
(Garvan Donnelly, Ire) *prom: rdn to chse ldr over 1f out: no ex ins fnl f* **11/2**[2]

160- **5** ½ **Hits Only Cash**[114] [6293] 6-8-10 **66** .... JimmyQuinn 3 69
(J Pearce) *hld up: rdn and hdwy over 1f out: nt qckn ins fnl f* **8/1**

000- **6** *3* **Raza Cab (IRE)**[166] [4259] 6-8-13 **72** .... JerryO'Dwyer(3) 1 67
(Karen George) *led for 1f: rdn over 2f out: wknd fnl f* **10/1**

02-0 **7** ¾ **Pietersen (IRE)**[24] [177] 4-8-9 **65** ....(b) PaulFessey 4 58
(T D Barron) *led after 1f: hdd 3f out: wknd over 1f out* **13/2**[3]

364- **8** ¾ **Inca Soldier (FR)**[42] [7271] 5-8-4 **60** oh1 .... PaulEddery 8 51
(R C Guest) *t.k.h: trckd ldrs: wknd over 2f out* **8/1**

9 *4* **Tyrana (GER)**[2] 5-9-4 **74** .... VinceSlattery 9 54
(G F Bridgwater) *a bhd: lost tch 3f out* **66/1**

1m 30.11s (0.51) **Going Correction** +0.15s/f (Slow) **9** Ran SP% **118.8**
Speed ratings (Par 103): **103,102,100,100,99 96,95,94,90**
CSF £35.93 CT £109.07 TOTE £13.70: £3.80, £1.20, £1.50; EX 60.20.
Owner Michael Wauchope And Partners **Bred** D E And Mrs J Cash **Trained** Upper Lambourn, Berks

FOCUS
An ordinary handicap of its type, but quite competitive. Sound form.

507 SANDMAN @ ALLWEATHERTIPS.COM (S) STKS 1m 1f 103y(P)
7:50 (7:50) (Class 6) 4-6-Y-0 **£1,774** (£523; £262) **Stalls** Low

Form RPR

0054 **1** **Bahhmirage (IRE)**[7] [401] 5-8-8 **42** ....(p) JimmyQuinn 6 49
(C N Kellett) *led tl hdd 6f out: led again 2f out: rdn out fnl f* **14/1**

6243 **2** 1¼ **Arthurs Dream (IRE)**[6] [415] 6-8-8 **43** .... KellyHarrison(5) 4 51
(A W Carroll) *hld up: hdwy 3f out: rdn to chse wnr fnl f* **4/1**[3]

0-20 **3** *5* **Persian Fox (IRE)**[22] [214] 4-8-13 **52** .... VinceSlattery 3 41
(A G Juckes) *t.k.h in rr: mde late hdwy: nvr nrr* **5/2**[2]

660- **4** ½ **Imperial Amber**[58] [6904] 6-8-8 **52** ....(p) HayleyTurner 1 35
(Karen George) *trckd ldrs tl rdn and lost pl 2f out: n.d after* **10/1**

40-0 **5** ¾ **Silver Blue (IRE)**[10] [356] 5-8-13 **53** ....(b) LPKeniry 5 38
(C R Dore) *trckd ldr: ev ch 2f out: wknd ent fnl f* **9/4**[1]

-334 **6** *10* **Davidia (IRE)**[21] [229] 5-8-13 **47** ....(v[1]) AndrewElliott 2 17
(D W Thompson) *in rr tl rapid hdwy to ld 6f out: hdd 2f out: wknd qckly* **11/2**

2m 4.99s (3.29) **Going Correction** +0.15s/f (Slow) **6** Ran SP% **110.5**
Speed ratings: **91,89,85,85,84 75**
CSF £65.56 TOTE £14.90: £5.40, £1.70; EX 41.30.There was no bid for the winner
Owner Miss S Walley **Bred** Centaur Bloodstock Agency **Trained** Woodlane, Staffs

FOCUS
This was a poor contest and the winning time was very moderate, even for a seller. The form has been rated negatively.

508 BOOK YOUR PONTIN'S SHORT BREAK NOW H'CAP 1m 141y(P)
8:20 (8:20) (Class 6) (0-60,60) 4-Y-0+ **£2,047** (£604; £302) **Stalls** Low

Form RPR

0-34 **1** **King Of Legend (IRE)**[22] [216] 4-8-12 **54** .... RobertHavlin 2 63
(A G Foster) *mde all: rdn out fnl f* **8/1**

00-6 **2** ¾ **White Bear (FR)**[10] [356] 6-9-0 **56** ....(b) LPKeniry 3 63
(C R Dore) *hld up in tch: hdwy on ins 2f out: swtchd rt 1f out to chse wnr: kpt on* **8/1**

0/06 **3** *2* **Shosolosa (IRE)**[9] [375] 6-8-6 **48** .... PaulFessey 1 51
(R C Guest) *hld up: hdwy on ins over 1f out: kpt on: nvr nr to chal* **16/1**

-303 **4** ¾ **Cantique (IRE)**[9] [375] 4-8-4 **46** oh1 .... JimmyQuinn 7 47
(R J Price) *trckd wnr tl rdn 2f out: kpt on one pce after* **12/1**

-444 **5** ¾ **Norwegian**[2] [468] 7-8-8 **50** ....(p) StephenDonohoe 6 49
(Ian Williams) *in tch: rdn over 3f out: swtchd rt 1f out: one pce after* **6/4**[1]

-041 **6** 2 **Green Pirate**[15] [305] 6-9-4 **60**....(p) RichardKingscote 5 55
(W M Brisbourne) *trckd ldrs tl rdn and wknd over 1f out* **10/3[2]**

-053 **7** 2 ½ **Capania (IRE)**[12] [338] 4-9-0 **56**.... VinceSlattery 8 45
(P D Evans) *racd wd: hd up: rdn 3f out: nvr on terms* **5/1[3]**

8 2 **Suburban Cool**[43] [5961] 4-8-4 **46**....(bt) HayleyTurner 4 30
(Thomas O'Neill, Ire) *s.i.s: effrt 3f out: nvr on terms* **28/1**

1m 52.67s (2.17) **Going Correction** +0.15s/f (Slow) 8 Ran SP% **119.0**
Speed ratings (Par 101): **96,95,93,92,92 90,88,86**
CSF £72.14 CT £733.39 TOTE £8.00: £3.20, £3.10, £5.40; EX 92.40.
Owner Joshua Snellings **Bred** Golden Vale Stud **Trained** Cousland, Midlothian

FOCUS
The winner was allowed to dominate at his own tempo in this moderate handicap and the time was modest as a result.

509 RACE AHEAD TO PONTIN'S H'CAP 1m 141y(P)
8:50 (8:50) (Class 5) (0-75,75) 4-Y-0+ **£2,457** (£725; £362) **Stalls** Low

Form RPR

-055 **1** **Moonlight Man**[3] [452] 7-9-4 **75**.... LPKeniry 3 83
(C R Dore) *w.w: rdn to go 3rd 2f out: r.o u.p to ld nr fin* **6/1**

-211 **2** ¾ **Glenridding**[10] [361] 4-8-13 **70**.... JimCrowley 7 76
(J G Given) *led: rdn over 1f out: hdd nr fin and jst hld on for 2nd* **7/2[3]**

06-1 **3** shd **Highland Harvest**[14] [314] 4-9-4 **75**.... HayleyTurner 1 81
(D R C Elsworth) *a in tch on ins: wnt 2nd 3f out and ev ch ins fnl f: no ex nr fin* **11/4[1]**

16-5 **4** 3 **My Michelle**[37] [34] 7-8-9 **66**.... CatherineGannon 2 65
(B Palling) *hld up: rdn over 3f out: styd on but no ch w first 3 fr over 1f out* **10/1**

/0-0 **5** 16 **Grenane (IRE)**[12] [342] 5-8-5 **62**.... JimmyQuinn 6 24
(P D Evans) *v.s.a: outpcd in rr: nvr on terms* **22/1**

-314 **6** 14 **Machinate (USA)**[8] [395] 6-8-9 **66**.... LiamJones 8 —
(W M Brisbourne) *hld up: rdn over 3f out: sn wknd* **13/2**

03-4 **7** 9 **Lord Theo**[17] [274] 4-9-3 **74**.... GeorgeBaker 5 —
(N P Littmoden) *racd keenly: chsd wnr 7f out to 3f out: wknd qckly* **10/3[2]**

1m 50.05s (-0.45) **Going Correction** +0.15s/f (Slow) 7 Ran SP% **113.0**
Speed ratings (Par 103): **108,107,107,104,90 77,69**
CSF £26.53 CT £69.85 TOTE £8.40: £3.20, £2.40; EX 41.40.
Owner Liam Breslin **Bred** P T Tellwright **Trained** West Pinchbeck, Lincs
■ Stewards' Enquiry : L P Keniry two-day ban: used whip with excessive frequency (Feb 20-21)
Hayley Turner two-day ban: used whip with excessive frequency (Feb 20-21)

FOCUS
They went a decent clip in this which resulted in a decent winning time for the class. The form looks sound.
Lord Theo Official explanation: jockey said gelding lost its action

510 DISCOUNT DEALS ONLINE @ PONTINS.COM H'CAP 1m 4f 50y(P)
9:20 (9:20) (Class 5) (0-75,74) 4-Y-0+ **£2,457** (£725; £362) **Stalls** Low

Form RPR

0/1 **1** **Basalt (IRE)**[5] [435] 4-9-8 74 6ex.... GregFairley 5 91+
(T J Pitt) *sn led: rdn 2f out: in command fr over 1f out* **4/6[1]**

05-3 **2** 1 ¾ **Rose Row**[28] [134] 4-8-7 59.... HayleyTurner 2 67
(Mrs Mary Hambro) *t.k.h: trckd ldrs: wnt 2nd over 2f out: kpt on but no ch w wnr fr over 1f out* **8/1[3]**

0-34 **3** 5 **Pret A Porter (UAE)**[17] [268] 4-9-3 69....(b) StephenDonohoe 1 69
(P D Evans) *hld up: rdn 3f out: kpt on to go 3rd ins fnl f but nvr nr to chal* **12/1**

123- **4** 3 ½ **The King And I (IRE)**[45] [7236] 4-9-7 73....(b) GeorgeBaker 3 67
(Miss E C Lavelle) *hld up: effrt over 2f out: one pce after* **3/1[2]**

5 4 **Nil Bleu (USA)**[28] 4-9-0 66.... SamHitchcott 6 54
(Noel T Chance) *hld up: rdn 4f out: no hdwy fnl 2f* **33/1**

14-0 **6** 2 ½ **Vallemeldee (IRE)**[31] [96] 4-9-5 71.... MickyFenton 4 55
(P W D'Arcy) *chsd wnr after 3f: rdn 3f out: hung lft and sn wknd* **16/1**

2m 41.77s (0.67) **Going Correction** +0.15s/f (Slow) 6 Ran SP% **112.6**
Speed ratings (Par 103): **103,101,98,96,93 91**
CSF £7.07 TOTE £1.60: £1.60, £2.90; EX 7.10 Place 6 £ 230.73, Place 5 £ 214.14.
Owner Tim Kelly **Bred** John M Weld **Trained** Norton, N Yorks

FOCUS
A fair little handicap run at a solid pace and the winner looks progressive. The form is rated through the runner-up.
Vallemeldee(IRE) Official explanation: jockey said filly hung left
T/Plt: £277.40 to a £1 stake. Pool: £92,648.50. 243.80 winning tickets. T/Qpdt: £160.30 to a £1 stake. Pool: £5,721.50. 26.40 winning tickets. JS

511 - (Foreign Racing) - See Raceform Interactive

445 KEMPTON (A.W) (R-H)
Sunday, February 10

OFFICIAL GOING: Standard
Wind: Almost nil

512 TURFTV CLAIMING STKS 1m 2f (P)
2:10 (2:10) (Class 6) 4-Y-0+ **£2,047** (£604; £302) **Stalls** High

Form RPR

2331 **1** **Smokey The Bear**[9] [388] 6-9-10 69.... NeilChalmers 8 79
(Miss Sheena West) *trckd ldr: led appr fnl f: r.o wl* **10/3[2]**

0-45 **2** 1 ¾ **Without Excuse (USA)**[13] [331] 4-9-7 70....(v[1]) URispoli 5 73
(M Botti) *trckd ldrs: rdn to ld wl over 1f out: hdd appr fnl f: kpt on* **11/2[3]**

5-56 **3** ½ **Boundless Prospect (USA)**[13] [331] 9-9-0 61.... HayleyTurner 3 64
(Miss Gay Kelleway) *hld up: hdwy over 1f out: r.o wl to go 3rd ins fnl f* **6/1**

64-2 **4** nk **Inside Story (IRE)**[29] [133] 6-9-10 72....(b) DaneO'Neill 1 73
(M W Easterby) *in tch: hdwy to chse ldrs 2f out: one pce and lost 3rd ins fnl f* **13/8[1]**

005- **5** 3 **Swift Cut (IRE)**[54] [7180] 4-9-3 55.... ChrisCatlin 6 61
(A P Jarvis) *in rr: mde sme hdwy 2f out: nvr nr to chal* **33/1**

4-46 **6** nk **Sweet World**[29] [139] 4-9-3 61.... AndrewElliott 7 61
(A P Jarvis) *plld hrd: sn trckd ldr: rdn 2f out: wknd appr fnl f* **12/1**

-206 **7** 8 **Fortune Point (IRE)**[26] [161] 10-8-8 45 ow1....(p) JerryO'Dwyer(3) 2 38
(A W Carroll) *led tl rdn and hdd wl over 1f out: wknd qckly* **66/1**

01/ **8** 6 **Portland**[664] [1048] 5-8-10 70....(bt[1]) DeanMcKeown 4 25
(K J Burke) *rrd up leaving stalls: a struggling in rr* **8/1**

2m 5.90s (-2.10) **Going Correction** +0.05s/f (Slow)
WFA 4 from 5yo+ 1lb 8 Ran SP% **114.1**
Speed ratings (Par 101): **110,108,108,107,105 105,98,94**
CSF £21.89 TOTE £2.90: £1.40, £1.90, £1.60; EX 22.60.The winner was the subject of a friendly claim
Owner Graham Flight **Bred** A P Jones **Trained** Falmer, E Sussex

FOCUS
A fair race for the class and run in a decent winning time for the type of contest. Sound form among the principals.

513 KEMPTON.CO.UK MEDIAN AUCTION MAIDEN STKS 1m 3f (P)
2:40 (2:42) (Class 6) 4-6-Y-0 **£2,047** (£604; £302) **Stalls** High

Form RPR

/0-2 **1** **Inspirina (IRE)**[11] [361] 4-9-3 68.... HayleyTurner 2 69
(R Ford) *trckd ldr: led 3f out: drvn out fnl f* **7/4[1]**

05-2 **2** 1 ¾ **Orama's Ghost**[21] [239] 4-8-12 62....(v[1]) GregFairley 1 61
(M Botti) *slowly away: sn in tch: hdwy 3f out: rdn to go 2nd 2f out: no imp fnl f* **9/4[2]**

40-0 **3** 4 **Dot's Delight**[16] [299] 4-8-12 50.... DeanMcKeown 5 54
(K J Burke) *trckd ldrs: hung lft over 2f out and no ch w first 2 after* **5/1[3]**

20-0 **4** 6 **Hester Brook (IRE)**[8] [400] 4-8-12 43.... AndrewElliott 4 44
(J G M O'Shea) *s.i.s: t.k.h in rr: effrt over 2f out: one pce fnl 2f* **8/1**

0-56 **5** shd **Bothar Brugha (IRE)**[10] [369] 4-8-12 45....(p) RussellKennemore(5) 3 49
(J G M O'Shea) *reminders after 2f: prom on outside: c wd into st and no ch after* **40/1**

0/4 **6** 4 **Shanagolden Juan (IRE)**[18] [273] 5-9-0 0....(t) HaddenFrost(5) 7 42
(M R Bosley) *led tl hdd 3f out: wknd qckly* **40/1**

7 9 **Simply The Quest** 4-8-12 0.... JimmyQuinn 6 22
(R Simpson) *v.s.a: a bhd: lost tch 3f out* **8/1**

8 13 **Bessie Smith (IRE)**[12] [3512] 5-9-0 0.... SteveDrowne 8 —
(D R Gandolfo) *t.k.h: in tch tl wknd over 3f out* **14/1**

2m 23.96s (2.06) **Going Correction** +0.05s/f (Slow)
WFA 4 from 5yo 2lb 8 Ran SP% **117.6**
Speed ratings: **94,92,89,85,85 82,75,66**
CSF £6.07 TOTE £2.30: £1.20, £1.30, £1.90; EX 6.00.
Owner Miss Gill Quincey **Bred** Mohammad Al-Qatami **Trained** Cotebrook, Cheshire

FOCUS
A steadily run maiden and the winning time was unsurprisingly modest. This was a weak race and the winner did not need to improve.
Orama's Ghost Official explanation: jockey said filly missed the break
Dot's Delight Official explanation: jockey said filly hung left
Bothar Brugha(IRE) Official explanation: jockey said gelding hung badly
Shanagolden Juan(IRE) Official explanation: jockey said gelding lost its action

514 PANORAMIC BAR & RESTAURANT MEDIAN AUCTION MAIDEN STKS 6f (P)
3:10 (3:10) (Class 5) 3-5-Y-0 **£2,590** (£770; £385; £192) **Stalls** High

Form RPR

4 **1** **Prime Factor**[25] [183] 3-8-11 0.... MichaelHills 1 71+
(B W Hills) *trckd ldrs: led over 2f out: fnd ex whn chal appr fnl f: rdn out* **3/1[2]**

0-22 **2** ¾ **Autumn Blades (IRE)**[11] [355] 3-8-11 72.... TQuinn 5 69
(J W Hills) *in tch: hdwy over 2f out: chal appr fnl f: no imp ins fnl f* **4/5[1]**

43 **3** 3 **Mr Rev**[14] [326] 5-9-12 0.... SteveDrowne 2 63
(J M Bradley) *t.k.h: hld up: hdwy on outside over 1f out: r.o wl: nvr nrr* **4/1[3]**

00- **4** 2 **Tiepie**[134] [5815] 3-8-11 0.... DaneO'Neill 3 53
(J Akehurst) *bmpd leaving stalls: hld up: hdwy on ins over 2f out: one pce fr over 1f out* **18/1**

060- **5** 2 ½ **Honest Value (IRE)**[109] [6426] 3-8-8 52.... JerryO'Dwyer(3) 6 45
(Mrs L C Jewell) *trckd ldr tl wknd over 1f out* **12/1**

4-6 **6** 5 **Hiss And Boo**[26] [163] 3-8-11 0....(b) FergalLynch 4 29
(P Howling) *led tl hdd over 2f out: hung lft and wknd qckly* **40/1**

0 **7** 1 ¼ **Easily Naimd**[5] [441] 4-9-12 0.... DeanMcKeown 7 29
(D Shaw) *stdd s: a bhd: lost tch 1/2-way* **40/1**

1m 13.19s (0.09) **Going Correction** +0.05s/f (Slow)
WFA 3 from 4yo+ 15lb 7 Ran SP% **118.4**
Speed ratings (Par 103): **101,100,96,93,90 83,81**
CSF £6.07 TOTE £3.80: £1.80, £1.40; EX 6.90.
Owner Mrs W Falle & M Franklin **Bred** Slatch Farm Stud **Trained** Lambourn, Berks

FOCUS
An ordinary maiden rated around the third, but not the most solid of form.

515 KEMPTON FOR WEDDINGS H'CAP 6f (P)
3:40 (3:41) (Class 6) (0-65,64) 4-Y-0+ **£2,590** (£770; £385; £192) **Stalls** High

Form RPR

3232 **1** **Chatshow (USA)**[3] [466] 7-8-5 **58**.... MarkCoumbe(7) 7 68
(A W Carroll) *mid-div: rdn and hdwy over 1f out: r.o to ld fnl strides* **11/2[2]**

-205 **2** ½ **Monashee Prince (IRE)**[6] [427] 6-9-1 **61**....(v) JimmyQuinn 9 69
(J R Best) *trckd ldr: led appr fnl f: r.o: hdd fnl strides* **10/1**

-032 **3** ½ **Kempsey**[7] [414] 6-8-12 **58**....(b) ChrisCatlin 11 64
(J J Bridger) *led tl rdn and hdd appr fnl f: kpt on* **11/2[2]**

-123 **4** nk **Unlimited**[4] [446] 6-8-6 **59**.... SophieDoyle(7) 5 64
(R Simpson) *a.p: nt qckn ins fnl f* **5/1[1]**

50-2 **5** hd **Contented (IRE)**[14] [327] 6-8-9 **55**....(p) LPKeniry 1 60
(Mrs L C Jewell) *mid-div: hdwy over 1f out to chse ldrs fnl f* **10/1**

50-0 **6** 1 **Hollow Jo**[18] [275] 8-9-4 **64**.... MickyFenton 3 66
(J R Jenkins) *a.p: no ex ins fnl f* **11/2[2]**

0464 **7** hd **Desert Light (IRE)**[9] [391] 7-8-6 **52**....(v) DeanMcKeown 12 53
(D Shaw) *t.k.h: in rr: r.o fnl f: nvr nr to chal* **10/1**

1-61 **8** nk **Littledodayno (IRE)**[9] [391] 5-8-11 **64**.... MJMurphy(7) 2 64+
(M Wigham) *swtchd over to ins fr wd draw after s: hdwy on ins 2f out: nvr nr to chal* **9/1**

-144 **9** 1 ½ **Arfinnit (IRE)**[18] [270] 7-8-12 **58**....(p) HayleyTurner 10 53
(Mrs A L M King) *hld up: rdn 1/2-way: nvr on terms* **10/1**

2225 **10** hd **Bentley**[10] [370] 4-8-7 **56**....(v) TolleyDean(3) 8 51
(D Shaw) *trckd ldr tl rdn and wknd 2f out* **14/1**

00-0 **11** 2 **Devon Flame**[23] [211] 9-8-8 **54** ow2.... SteveDrowne 6 42
(R J Hodges) *a in rr* **33/1**

1302 **12** 5 **Mind Alert**[8] [404] 7-9-2 **62**....(v) JamesDoyle 4 34
(D Shaw) *a bhd* **8/1[3]**

1m 12.49s (-0.61) **Going Correction** +0.05s/f (Slow) 12 Ran SP% **129.9**
Speed ratings (Par 101): **106,105,104,104,104 102,102,102,100,99 97,90**
CSF £65.88 CT £332.02 TOTE £7.10: £2.50, £3.50, £2.30; EX 92.70.
Owner One Under Par Racing **Bred** Juddmonte Farms Inc **Trained** Cropthorne, Worcs
■ Stewards' Enquiry : Mark Coumbe two-day ban: careless riding (Feb 21-22)

FOCUS
An ordinary handicap in which it proved an advantage to race fairly prominently. This is fairly sound form and the time was fair for the class.

Desert Light(IRE) Official explanation: jockey said gelding suffered interference in running

516 MIX BUSINESS WITH PLEASURE H'CAP 7f (P)
4:15 (4:16) (Class 6) (0-55,55) 4-Y-0+ £2,047 (£604; £302) Stalls High

Form RPR
5-46 **1** **Guildenstern (IRE)**[14] 327 6-8-13 **54** JimmyQuinn 14 63+
(P Howling) *trckd ldr: led jst ins fnl f: rdn out* **4/1**[1]
6-01 **2** *nk* **Over To You Bert**[8] 402 9-8-9 **55** HaddenFrost[(5)] 1 63
(R J Hodges) *led tl rdn and hdd jst ins fnl f: kpt on* **10/1**
060- **3** *1 1/2* **Lindbergh**[104] 6531 6-8-11 **55** JerryO'Dwyer[(3)] 12 59
(J Ryan) *trckd ldrs: rdn and ev ch over 1f out: kpt on* **50/1**
000- **4** *2* **Just Dust**[129] 5936 4-9-0 **55** DaneO'Neill 3 54
(M W Easterby) *in tch: r.o fnl f* **5/1**[2]
0-00 **5** *hd* **Edin Burgher (FR)**[18] 264 7-8-5 **46** oh1 (e[1]) HayleyTurner 8 44
(T T Clement) *trckd ldr to over 2f out: kpt on one pce after* **33/1**
000- **6** *hd* **Buzbury Rings**[285] 1373 4-9-0 **55** NeilChalmers 9 52
(A M Balding) *stdd s: nvr bttr than mid-div* **22/1**
0-01 **7** *1/2* **Buzzin'Boyzee (IRE)**[6] 432 5-8-3 **51** 6ex RichardEvans[(7)] 13 47
(P D Evans) *in rr: t.k.h: effrt on ins over 2f out: nvr nr to chal* **14/1**
020- **8** *hd* **Drum Dance (IRE)**[75] 6957 6-8-11 **52** JamesDoyle 6 48+
(M Hill) *t.k.h: in rr: sme hdwy over 1f out: n.d* **11/2**[3]
-000 **9** *1 1/2* **Royal Guest**[14] 328 4-8-6 **47** (b[1]) GregFairley 5 39
(J R Jenkins) *racd wd: a towards rr* **20/1**
0106 **10** *1 1/4* **Golden Square**[9] 389 6-8-2 **48** KellyHarrison[(5)] 11 36
(A W Carroll) *slowly away: clipped heels after 1f: a bhd* **20/1**
020- **11** *nk* **Julian Joachim (USA)**[190] 4157 4-9-0 **55** (v[1]) DeanMcKeown 7 42
(D Shaw) *chsd ldrs tl rdn and wknd over 1f out* **11/2**[3]
03-3 **12** *hd* **Batchworth Blaise**[25] 176 5-8-6 **47** ChrisCatlin 2 34
(E A Wheeler) *in rr: rdn over 2f out: nvr on terms* **13/2**
0-50 **13** *3* **Kazakstan**[20] 245 4-8-7 **48** LPKeniry 4 27
(Mrs L C Jewell) *mid-div tl wknd over 2f out* **28/1**
5-43 **P** **Chasing Memories (IRE)**[11] 362 4-8-9 **50** (p) AndrewElliott 10 —
(A M Hales) *in rr whn struck into after 1f: sn p.u* **16/1**

1m 27.29s (1.29) **Going Correction** +0.05s/f (Slow) **14** Ran SP% **124.6**
Speed ratings (Par 101): **94,93,91,89,89 89,88,88,86,85 84,84,81,—**
CSF £42.17 CT £1835.31 TOTE £5.50: £2.10, £3.60, £14.50; EX 54.00.
Owner David Andrew Brown **Bred** Peter E Daly **Trained** Newmarket, Suffolk
■ Stewards' Enquiry : Hadden Frost one-day ban: failed to keep straight from stalls (Feb 21)

FOCUS
They went no pace early on in this moderate handicap, and the winning time was modest. Those who raced prominently dominated.
Just Dust Official explanation: jockey said gelding hung left
Buzbury Rings Official explanation: jockey said gelding ran too free
Julian Joachim(USA) Official explanation: jockey said gelding had a breathing problem
Chasing Memories(IRE) Official explanation: jockey said filly lost its action

517 SPONSOR AT KEMPTON H'CAP 1m (P)
4:45 (4:45) (Class 6) (0-55,55) 4-Y-0+ £2,047 (£604; £302) Stalls High

Form RPR
2242 **1** **Under Fire (IRE)**[9] 387 5-8-12 **54** HayleyTurner 5 62
(A W Carroll) *trckd ldrs: wnt 2nd 3f out: led over 1f out: drvn out* **9/4**[1]
60-3 **2** *1/2* **Mix N Match**[8] 402 4-8-7 **49** ChrisCatlin 4 56
(R M Stronge) *hld up in rr: swtchd lft over 2f out: sustained run on outside to go 2nd ins fnl f: clsng on wnr at line* **13/2**
-226 **3** *1 1/4* **Jomus**[14] 328 7-8-8 **50** ow2 FergalLynch 2 54
(L Montague Hall) *hld up in rr: hdwy on ins over 2f out: r.o to go 3rd ins fnl f* **9/1**
30-3 **4** *1* **Bramcote Lorne**[16] 300 5-8-4 **53** ow3 (p) MarkCoumbe[(7)] 9 55
(R C Guest) *trckd ldr to 3f out: styd prom: kpt on fnl f* **15/2**
300- **5** *1/2* **Camolin (IRE)**[58] 7146 5-8-9 **51** (b) MickyFenton 7 52
(Michael McElhone, Ire) *led tl rdn and hdd over 1f out: no ex ins fnl f* **14/1**
-453 **6** *3/4* **Postmaster**[9] 389 6-8-9 **51** RobertHavlin 6 50
(R Ingram) *hld up in mid-div: rdn and sme hdwy 2f out: wknd fnl f* **4/1**[3]
0-06 **7** *1/2* **Revolve**[11] 352 8-8-11 **53** (b) IanMongan 1 51
(Mrs L J Mongan) *prom: rdn 1/2-way: wknd over 1f out* **12/1**
/00- **8** *2* **Sorrel Point**[110] 6413 5-8-13 **55** JimmyQuinn 10 48
(H J Collingridge) *in tch tl wknd appr fnl f* **7/2**[2]
00-0 **9** *3 1/2* **Cavallo Di Ferro (IRE)**[28] 148 4-8-8 **55** RussellKennemore[(5)] 8 40
(M J Gingell) *in tch tl rdn 3f out: sn wknd* **28/1**
050- **10** *14* **Benellino**[11] 5341 5-8-6 **48** ow1 SimonWhitworth 3 —
(R M Stronge) *in rr: wl bhd whn eased over 1f out* **50/1**

1m 39.15s (-0.65) **Going Correction** +0.05s/f (Slow) **10** Ran SP% **127.9**
Speed ratings (Par 101): **105,104,103,102,101 101,100,98,95,81**
CSF £19.78 CT £121.19 TOTE £4.60: £1.40, £3.30, £3.10; EX 18.70.
Owner Marita Bayley and Trevor Turner **Bred** Mrs Marita Bayley **Trained** Cropthorne, Worcs
■ Stewards' Enquiry : Chris Catlin one-day ban:careless riding (Feb 21)

FOCUS
A weak handicap run at an ordinary gallop. The form is not solid.

518 PANORAMIC BAR & RESTAURANT LOYALTY SCHEME CLASSIFIED STKS 1m (P)
5:15 (5:15) (Class 7) 4-Y-0+ £1,365 (£403; £201) Stalls High

Form RPR
-456 **1** **Marmooq**[8] 401 5-9-0 45 (e) AdrianMcCarthy 9 47
(M J Attwater) *trckd ldrs: led appr fnl f: all out* **8/1**[2]
-503 **2** *hd* **Big Ralph**[8] 401 5-9-0 44 OscarUrbina 10 47
(D K Ivory) *mid-div: hdwy over 1f out: hung lft but pressed wnr ins fnl f* **2/1**[1]
2003 **3** *nk* **Wizby**[8] 400 5-9-0 45 CatherineGannon 4 46+
(P D Evans) *hld up: wnt rt and hdwy on ins over 1f out: pressed first 2 ins fnl f* **8/1**[2]
0000 **4** *1* **Lady Firecracker (IRE)**[8] 400 4-9-0 39 (v) StephenCarson 3 44
(J R Best) *prom tl outpcd 2f out: styd on ins fnl f* **33/1**
-56P **5** *1* **Mtoto Girl**[7] 415 4-9-0 38 NeilChalmers 8 42
(J J Bridger) *mid-div: outpcd over 2f out: styd on ins fnl f* **50/1**
6561 **6** *3/4* **Busy Man (IRE)**[8] 401 9-9-1 46 PaulEddery 2 41
(R C Guest) *stdd s: hdwy 2f out: one pce fnl f* **8/1**[2]
-431 **7** *shd* **Tabulate**[8] 400 5-9-3 48 FergalLynch 6 43
(P Howling) *hld up: hdwy over 1f out: nvr nr to chal* **2/1**[1]
505- **8** *3/4* **Hornpipe**[51] 7218 6-8-7 42 (e[1]) GabrielHannon[(7)] 5 38
(M Hill) *led tl rdn and hdd over 1f out: wknd ins fnl f* **16/1**[3]
0600 **9** *nk* **Salvestro**[8] 400 5-8-11 39 JerryO'Dwyer[(3)] 11 37
(A W Carroll) *in rr: hdwy over 2f out: wkng whn hmpd over 1f out* **20/1**
600- **10** *2 1/2* **Pajada**[63] 7088 4-9-0 39 (v) RichardThomas 7 32
(M D I Usher) *t.k.h: trckd ldr after 1f: wknd over 1f out* **16/1**[3]

1m 40.91s (1.11) **Going Correction** +0.05s/f (Slow) **10** Ran SP% **121.4**
Speed ratings (Par 97): **96,95,95,94,93 92,92,91,91,89**
CSF £25.23 TOTE £10.80: £2.30, £1.50, £2.60; EX 30.90 Place 6 £ 53.11, Place 5 £ 17.96.
Owner The Attwater Partnership **Bred** Matthews Breeding And Racing Ltd **Trained** Epsom, Surrey
■ Stewards' Enquiry : Oscar Urbina two-day ban: careless riding (Feb 21-22)

FOCUS
A slowly run classified race and the form looks pretty unreliable.
Tabulate Official explanation: jockey said mare ran flat
T/Plt: £17.00 to a £1 stake. Pool: £52,826.90. 2,267.85 winning tickets. T/Qpdt: £5.80 to a £1 stake. Pool: £2,887.80. 364.60 winning tickets. JS

505 WOLVERHAMPTON (A.W) (L-H)
Monday, February 11

OFFICIAL GOING: Standard
Wind: Almost nil Weather: Sunny

521 STAY AT THE WOLVERHAMPTON HOLIDAY INN H'CAP 7f 32y(P)
1:50 (1:50) (Class 6) (0-52,58) 4-Y-0+ £1,774 (£523; £262) Stalls High

Form RPR
-164 **1** **Aggbag**[7] 432 4-8-4 **51** DeclanCannon[(7)] 4 61
(B P J Baugh) *wnt lft s: chsd ldrs: rdn over 2f out: led wl over 1f out: rdn out* **12/1**
2-20 **2** *1 1/2* **Winged Farasi**[26] 176 4-8-7 **52** KevinGhunowa[(5)] 3 58
(R A Harris) *mid-div: rdn 5f out: hdwy 2f out: r.o ins fnl f: tk 2nd last strides* **9/1**[3]
4354 **3** *nk* **Guadaloup**[11] 371 6-8-8 **51** ow2 MarkLawson[(3)] 11 56
(M Brittain) *hld up and bhd: hdwy whn swtchd lft wl over 1f out: chsd wnr fnl f: rdn and nt qckn* **14/1**
2-26 **4** *1/2* **The Geester**[25] 191 4-8-10 **50** (b) PaulEddery 7 54
(S R Bowring) *chsd ldrs: nt qckn ins fnl f* **12/1**
1221 **5** *3/4* **Savile's Delight (IRE)**[7] 437 9-9-4 **58** 6ex RichardKingscote 12 64+
(Tom Dascombe) *hld up and bhd: c v wd st: rdn and hdwy 1f out: hung lft ins fnl f: nt rch ldrs* **11/1**
4120 **6** *3* **Sion Hill (IRE)**[9] 402 7-8-8 **48** (p) AndrewElliott 1 42
(John A Harris) *led: rdn and hdd wl over 1f out: wknd fnl f* **5/1**[2]
2000 **7** *nk* **Cow Girl (IRE)**[11] 375 4-8-9 **49** MickyFenton 2 42
(Miss Gay Kelleway) *n.m.r s: mid-div: hdwy on ins wl over 1f out: rdn and wknd ins fnl f* **33/1**
1-04 **8** *3/4* **Mister Always**[23] 232 4-8-8 **48** (v) FergalLynch 8 39
(I W McInnes) *hld up and bhd: c wd st: rdn and shortlived effrt over 1f out* **10/1**
6/04 **9** *3 1/2* **Benayoun**[17] 305 4-8-3 **50** DavidProbert[(7)] 10 31
(B J Llewellyn) *hld up towards rr: rdn wl over 1f out: no rspnse* **50/1**
33-3 **10** *3* **Private Soldier**[24] 214 5-8-11 **51** SamHitchcott 6 24
(N J Vaughan) *w ldr: rdn and ev ch over 2f out: wknd wl over 1f out* **13/8**[1]
50-4 **11** *1* **Star Of The Desert (IRE)**[24] 214 5-8-10 **50** (b) ChrisCatlin 9 21
(Mrs K Walton) *rdn over 2f out: a bhd* **12/1**

1m 29.87s (0.27) **Going Correction** +0.025s/f (Slow) **11** Ran SP% **116.8**
Speed ratings (Par 101): **99,97,96,96,95 92,91,90,86,83 82**
CSF £114.80 CT £1569.69 TOTE £19.10: £4.40, £3.30, £2.60; EX 135.10 Trifecta £204.10 Part won. Pool: £287.57 - 0.10 winning units..
Owner Joe Singh **Bred** D R Tucker **Trained** Audley, Staffs

FOCUS
A moderate handicap run at a good pace. The winner was always well placed and is rated back to his best. The form is pretty solid.
Savile's Delight(IRE) Official explanation: jockey said, regarding running and riding, his orders were to get to the rail and go the shortest way round, however, having been drawn 12, and considering there might be too much pace, he decided to take a pull trying to drop gelding in on the rail, he was unable to execute his orders due to the slow early pace, then met tiring horses down back straight and was forced wide entering home straight; trainer's rep confirmed orders and expressed dissatisfaction with the ride; vet said gelding lost right front shoe
Cow Girl(IRE) Official explanation: jockey said filly reared as stalls opened
Private Soldier Official explanation: trainer had no explanation for the poor form shown

522 RACE AHEAD TO PONTIN'S H'CAP 5f 20y(P)
2:20 (2:20) (Class 6) (0-50,50) 4-Y-0+ £1,774 (£523; £262) Stalls Low

Form RPR
1 **1** **Alexander Huricane (IRE)**[16] 319 4-8-9 **47** ChrisCatlin 9 62+
(K A Ryan) *led after 1f: rdn over 1f out: rdn out* **15/8**[1]
-404 **2** *3/4* **Blackheath (IRE)**[6] 440 12-8-3 **46** oh1 KellyHarrison[(5)] 8 58
(S T Mason) *led 1f: w wnr: rdn and ev ch ins fnl f: nt qckn* **12/1**
00-4 **3** *2 1/2* **Town House**[16] 318 6-8-1 **46** oh1 SoniaEaton[(7)] 1 49
(B P J Baugh) *chsd ldrs: rdn and one pce fnl f* **12/1**
000- **4** *1 3/4* **Melandre**[188] 4252 6-8-9 **50** MarkLawson[(3)] 3 47
(M Brittain) *mid-div: hdwy whn hung rt wl over 1f out: one pce fnl f* **18/1**
0315 **5** *4* **King Of Charm (IRE)**[8] 414 5-8-11 **49** (b) FergusSweeney 10 32
(G L Moore) *nvr nr ldrs* **5/1**[3]
00-5 **6** *1/2* **Stoneacre Gareth (IRE)**[16] 318 4-8-10 **48** (b) LPKeniry 4 29
(Peter Grayson) *chsd ldrs: rdn over 2f out: wkng whn bmpd wl over 1f out* **8/1**
-160 **7** *1 1/2* **Stoneacre Donny (IRE)**[11] 372 4-8-5 **48** (b[1]) ColinHaddon[(5)] 2 23
(Peter Grayson) *s.i.s: outpcd* **11/1**
00-4 **8** *1* **Eastern Princess**[28] 153 4-8-5 **50** oh1 ow4 (b) MarkCoumbe[(7)] 7 22
(G H Yardley) *bhd fnl 3f* **25/1**
4063 **9** *7* **Maiden Investor**[21] 247 5-8-10 **48** (vt) MickyFenton 5 —
(Stef Liddiard) *s.v.s: a wl in rr* **9/2**[2]

61.78 secs (-0.52) **Going Correction** +0.025s/f (Slow) **9** Ran SP% **113.6**
Speed ratings (Par 101): **105,103,99,97,90 89,87,85,74**
CSF £26.09 CT £211.99 TOTE £2.60: £1.10, £3.80, £4.00; EX 21.60 Trifecta £169.50 Part won. Pool: £238.81 - 0.75 winning units..
Owner N O'Callaghan, R Fagan & R O'Callaghan **Bred** Mrs M Fox **Trained** Hambleton, N Yorks

FOCUS
A very moderate sprint handicap in which the first two dominated. Solid enough form.

523 WOLVERHAMPTON-RACECOURSE.CO.UK (S) STKS 5f 216y(P)
2:55 (2:55) (Class 6) 3-Y-0+ £1,774 (£523; £262) Stalls Low

Form RPR
4442 **1** **Nautical**[3] 479 10-9-5 54 JerryO'Dwyer[(3)] 6 64
(A W Carroll) *hld up in tch: led ins fnl f: pushed out* **11/4**[1]
565- **2** *2 1/2* **Punching**[64] 7082 4-9-13 58 StephenCarson 4 61
(Eve Johnson Houghton) *led: rdn and hung lft 1f out: hdd ins fnl f: no ex* **11/4**[1]

-533 **3** 1 1/2 **Plateau**[7] 432 9-9-8 55 LPKeniry 10 51
(C R Dore) *hld up: sn bhd: hdwy wl over 1f out: rdn and r.o one pce fnl f* **6/1**[2]
0-63 **4** 2 1/2 **Now You See Me**[17] 305 4-9-3 48 (e[1]) DaneO'Neill 8 38
(K McAuliffe) *t.k.h: chsd ldr: rdn 2f out: wknd fnl f* **8/1**[3]
0-55 **5** 3 **Hold That Call (USA)**[9] 403 3-8-2 60 (t) PatrickHills(5) 5 34
(R Hannon) *s.i.s: t.k.h towards rr: hdwy on outside over 2f out: rdn and wknd over 1f out* **17/2**
050- **6** 1 1/2 **La Belle Joannie**[79] 6928 3-8-2 52 AndrewElliott 7 24
(S Curran) *t.k.h in rr: rdn wl over 1f out: nvr nr ldrs* **40/1**
0-00 **7** 2 1/2 **Mujart**[33] 100 4-8-12 40 RussellKennemore(5) 9 16
(J A Pickering) *t.k.h: prom tl rdn and wknd wl over 1f out* **66/1**
0301 **8** 1 **Mulberry Lad (IRE)**[12] 353 6-9-13 51 (p) DarrenWilliams 11 23
(P W Hiatt) *hld up in mid-div: wknd wl over 1f out* **9/1**
000- **9** 1/2 **Freudian Slip**[79] 6928 3-8-2 59 (p) AdrianMcCarthy 1 11
(S Curran) *s.i.s: rdn over 3f out: a bhd* **16/1**
0-00 **10** 3/4 **Brynris**[21] 249 4-9-8 33 (bt) GrahamGibbons 3 14
(Mrs G S Rees) *chsd ldrs tl rdn and wknd over 2f out* **100/1**
0600 **11** nk **The Carpet Man**[5] 445 4-9-8 43 LiamJones 2 13
(A W Carroll) *swtchd lft wl over 1f out: a bhd* **20/1**

1m 15.14s (0.14) **Going Correction** +0.025s/f (Slow)
WFA 3 from 4yo+ 15lb 11 Ran SP% **114.8**
Speed ratings (Par 101): **100,96,94,91,87 85,82,80,80,79 78**
CSF £8.92 TOTE £3.30: £1.40, £1.10, £2.40; EX 12.70 Trifecta £64.10 Pool: £717.40 - 7.94 winning units..There was no bid for the winner. Punching was claimed by Miss Gay Kelleway for £5,500
Owner J T Billson **Bred** Sheikh Mohammed Bin Rashid Al Maktoum **Trained** Cropthorne, Worcs
FOCUS
A reasonable seller, and the form looks sound with Nautical rated close to his winter best.

524 TIME FOR A PONTIN'S GET AWAY MAIDEN STKS 1m 4f 50y(P)
3:30 (3:30) (Class 5) 4-Y-0+ **£2,457** (£725; £362) **Stalls** Low

Form RPR
2-25 **1** **Motarjm (USA)**[12] 358 4-9-3 68 (t) ChrisCatlin 2 72+
(H J Collingridge) *chsd ldr: led over 2f out: clr over 1f out: r.o wl* **11/8**[1]
40- **2** 10 **Power Shared (IRE)**[18] 6235 4-9-3 65 SteveDrowne 5 56
(P G Murphy) *led: hdd over 2f out: rdn and btn over 1f out* **11/4**[2]
45 **3** 3 **Mondial Jack (FR)**[7] 435 9-8-13 0 (v) RichardEvans(7) 6 51
(P D Evans) *hld up: hdwy 5f out: one pce fnl 2f* **14/1**
4 **4** 3/4 **Right You Are (IRE)**[30] 144 8-8-13 0 AndrewHeffernan(7) 4 50
(Paul Green) *hld up: hdwy on ins over 2f out: one pce* **22/1**
00 **5** 3 1/2 **Allez Melina**[7] 435 7-9-1 0 NeilChalmers 1 39
(Mouse Hamilton-Fairley) *nvr nr ldrs* **100/1**
20- **6** nk **Ready To Crown (USA)**[43] 7282 4-8-12 0 AlanDaly 9 39
(Andrew Turnell) *hld up in mid-div: hdwy 5f out: wknd wl over 1f out* **3/1**[3]
0- **7** 1/2 **Fortuitous (IRE)**[258] 2118 4-9-3 0 DanielTudhope 8 43
(I W McInnes) *a bhd* **28/1**
0-3 **8** 11 **Fifth Zak**[11] 369 4-9-3 0 PaulEddery 3 25
(S R Bowring) *hld up in tch: rdn and wknd over 3f out* **16/1**
0- **9** 105 **Ela Mario (CYP)**[73] 6975 4-8-10 0 (t) KylieManser(7) 7 —
(Mrs H Sweeting) *prom 6f: t.o* **100/1**

2m 40.54s (-0.56) **Going Correction** +0.025s/f (Slow)
WFA 4 from 7yo+ 3lb 9 Ran SP% **116.1**
Speed ratings (Par 103): **102,95,93,92,90 90,89,82,—**
CSF £5.20 TOTE £2.00: £1.10, £1.10, £2.70; EX 6.20 Trifecta £29.70 Pool: £767.66 - 18.35 winning units..
Owner P D Band **Bred** Darley **Trained** Exning, Suffolk
FOCUS
A very weak maiden and it is doubtful whether Motarjm had to improve on his recent handiacp form.
Ela Mario(CYP) Official explanation: jockey said gelding lost its action

525 CAPTAIN CROC MAKES YOUR PONTIN'S ROCK APPRENTICE H'CAP 1m 1f 103y(P)
4:05 (4:05) (Class 4) (0-80,79) 4-Y-0+ **£4,533** (£1,348; £674; £336) **Stalls** Low

Form RPR
2-43 **1** **Princess Cocoa (IRE)**[24] 218 5-8-11 **74** BMcHugh(3) 7 82
(R A Fahey) *hld up: hdwy over 3f out: rdn whn sltly hmpd wl over 1f out: led ins fnl f: drvn out* **3/1**[2]
3-11 **2** 1 1/4 **Morbick**[16] 323 4-8-8 **68** DeanHeslop 4 73
(W M Brisbourne) *a.p: ev ch 2f out: rdn and edgd lft over 1f out: kpt on towards fin* **5/4**[1]
3114 **3** nk **Justcallmehandsome**[18] 284 6-8-2 **67** (v) BillyCray(5) 2 71
(D J S Ffrench Davis) *led: edgd rt wl over 1f out: hung lft and hdd ins fnl f: nt qckn* **10/1**
660- **4** 4 **Latif (USA)**[199] 3926 7-8-1 **66** AndrewHeffernan(5) 3 62
(Paul Green) *dwlt: hld up in rr: rdn and hdwy over 1f out: no imp fnl f* **20/1**
3-32 **5** 1 1/4 **Oakley Heffert (IRE)**[26] 185 4-8-13 **78** (b) CharlesEddery(5) 8 71
(R Hannon) *hld up in tch: rdn 3f out: hung lft and wknd wl over 1f out* **9/2**[3]
60-5 **6** 1 1/4 **Sol Rojo**[40] 21 6-8-0 **67** JosephineBruning(7) 5 58
(J Pearce) *hld up: rdn over 2f out: no rspnse* **33/1**
605- **7** 3/4 **Red Lancer**[121] 6185 7-9-2 **79** AdeleRothery(3) 6 68
(D Nicholls) *chsd ldr to 3f out: sn wknd* **10/1**

2m 1.44s (-0.26) **Going Correction** +0.025s/f (Slow) 7 Ran SP% **113.5**
Speed ratings (Par 105): **102,100,100,97,95 94,94**
CSF £7.02 CT £29.97 TOTE £3.50: £1.60, £1.30; EX 7.00 Trifecta £33.30 Pool: £839.67 - 17.89 winning units..
Owner P Ashton **Bred** Corduff Stud **Trained** Musley Bank, N Yorks
FOCUS
A fair handicap restricted to apprentices who had not ridden more than ten winners. They went a fair pace and the winning time was 0.24 seconds quicker than the following 51-65. The form is best rated through the third.

526 HOTEL & CONFERENCING @ WOLVERHAMPTON H'CAP 1m 1f 103y(P)
4:35 (4:35) (Class 6) (0-65,65) 4-Y-0+ **£2,047** (£604; £302) **Stalls** Low

Form RPR
4 **1** **Schelm (GER)**[22] 240 6-8-11 61 JerryO'Dwyer(3) 9 69+
(Ronald O'Leary, Ire) *half-rrd s: hld up towards rr: nt clr run on ins briefly 3f out: hdwy 2f out: rdn and edgd rt over 1f out: r.o to ld cl home* **7/1**[2]
-130 **2** hd **Earl Kraul (IRE)**[12] 352 5-8-10 57 FergusSweeney 1 64
(G L Moore) *mid-div: hdwy on ins over 2f out: rdn and hung rt jst over 1f out: hung lft ins fnl f: r.o* **12/1**
-132 **3** nk **Steig (IRE)**[14] 344 5-9-0 61 JamesDoyle 3 68
(Carl Llewellyn) *led: clr over 6f out: rdn over 2f out: ct cl home* **2/1**[1]
36-5 **4** 1/2 **Punta Galera (IRE)**[34] 78 5-8-13 60 NeilChalmers 12 66+
(Paul Green) *hld up towards rr: c v wd st: rdn and hdwy over 1f out: hung lft ins fnl f: r.o* **15/2**[3]
00-1 **5** 3 **Wasalat (USA)**[14] 340 6-9-4 65 FergalLynch 13 64+
(D W Barker) *swtchd lft sn after s: hld up in rr: hdwy and swtchd lft over 1f out: nvr trbld ldrs* **9/1**
35-3 **6** 1/2 **Pelham Crescent (IRE)**[10] 395 5-9-4 65 CatherineGannon 2 63
(B Palling) *hld up in tch: rdn over 2f out: wnt 2nd briefly wl over 1f out: wknd ins fnl f* **8/1**
00 **7** 2 1/2 **Passato (GER)**[26] 177 4-8-10 62 KevinGhunowa(5) 10 55
(R A Harris) *hld up in mid-div: hdwy 4f out: rdn over 2f out: wknd wl over 1f out* **28/1**
633- **8** 1/2 **Airman (IRE)**[15] 6612 5-9-2 63 (p) TPQueally 7 55
(B P J Baugh) *hld up in tch: rdn over 2f out: c wd st: wkng whn nt clr run over 1f out* **17/2**
0-14 **9** shd **Hatch A Plan (IRE)**[24] 207 7-9-0 61 ChrisCatlin 8 53
(Mouse Hamilton-Fairley) *n.d* **9/1**
64-0 **10** 1 1/4 **El Coto**[20] 258 8-8-11 58 (b) SteveDrowne 5 47
(J R Holt) *prom: chsd clr ldr over 3f out tl wl over 1f out: sn wknd* **18/1**
11 5 **Amarillo Slim (IRE)**[143] 5611 4-8-11 58 PaulDoe 11 37
(S Curran) *hld up and bhd: shortlived effrt over 3f out* **50/1**
5-20 **12** 1 1/4 **Satindra (IRE)**[17] 300 4-9-3 64 (tp) MickyFenton 4 40
(John A Harris) *chsd ldr tl over 3f out: wknd over 2f out* **16/1**
054/ **13** shd **Mozayada (USA)**[516] 5287 4-9-0 64 MarkLawson(3) 6 40
(M Brittain) *bhd fnl 3f* **33/1**

2m 1.68s (-0.02) **Going Correction** +0.025s/f (Slow) 13 Ran SP% **126.4**
Speed ratings (Par 101): **101,100,100,100,97 97,94,94,94,93 88,87,87**
CSF £92.39 CT £236.04 TOTE £7.80: £2.40, £3.90, £1.30; EX 149.60 TRIFECTA Not won..
Owner Paul Hillis **Bred** E Jahns **Trained** Killaloe, Co. Clare
■ Stewards' Enquiry : Fergus Sweeney caution: careless riding in two incidents
FOCUS
A modest handicap run at a fair pace. The winning time was 0.24 seconds slower than the previous 66-80. Something ofa bunch finish but the form should work out.

527 CALL 0844 576 5938 FOR BEST PONTIN'S DEALS H'CAP 1m 141y(P)
5:05 (5:05) (Class 6) (0-70,75) 3-Y-O **£2,457** (£725; £362) **Stalls** Low

Form RPR
6-11 **1** **Rapidity**[3] 484 3-9-11 **75** 12ex ChrisCatlin 2 83
(E J O'Neill) *mde all: rdn fnl f: r.o wl* **1/2**[1]
0-31 **2** 1 1/4 **Bury Treasure (IRE)**[16] 321 3-9-0 **64** MickyFenton 4 69
(Miss Gay Kelleway) *a.p: chsd wnr jst over 2f out: rdn over 1f out: kpt on towards fin* **9/1**[3]
540- **3** 3 **Calistos Quest**[168] 4876 3-9-3 **67** GregFairley 8 65+
(M Botti) *hld up in tch: rdn wl over 1f out: one pce* **6/1**[2]
-004 **4** 1 **Carry On Cleo**[7] 424 3-8-10 **60** (v) CatherineGannon 3 56
(P D Evans) *hld up and bhd: hdwy wl over 1f out: one pce fnl f* **33/1**
4-04 **5** 2 **John Potts**[16] 321 3-8-6 **56** AndrewElliott 7 47+
(B P J Baugh) *hld up towards rr: swtchd lft wl over 1f out: edgd lft ins fnl f: nvr trbld ldrs* **20/1**
530- **6** 1/2 **Kiwi Princess**[94] 6750 3-8-6 **56** DeanMcKeown 5 46
(M Brittain) *chsd wnr tl jst over 2f out: wknd wl over 1f out* **40/1**
3-55 **7** 2 **Marino Prince (FR)**[24] 217 3-8-11 **68** PatrickDonaghy(7) 1 54
(T Wall) *mid-div: edgd rt wl over 1f out: sn wknd* **20/1**
25-3 **8** shd **Hellfire Bay**[28] 158 3-9-1 **65** FergalLynch 6 50
(K A Ryan) *s.i.s: a towards rr* **9/1**[3]

1m 51.4s (0.90) **Going Correction** +0.025s/f (Slow) 8 Ran SP% **115.9**
Speed ratings (Par 97): **97,95,93,92,90 90,88,88**
CSF £5.50 CT £15.18 TOTE £1.40: £1.02, £1.90, £2.30; EX 6.00 Trifecta £37.40 Pool: £369.68 - 7.00 winning units. Place 6 £30.22, Place 5 £3.82.
Owner Premspace Ltd **Bred** Angmering Park Stud **Trained** Averham Park, Notts
FOCUS
A modest handicap, but a decent winner in the form of the progressive Rapidity who set an ordinary pace.
Hellfire Bay Official explanation: jockey said colt reared as the stalls opened
T/Jkpt: Not won. T/Plt: £65.50 to a £1 stake. Pool: £59,768.10. 665.70 winning tickets. T/Qpdt: £3.60 to a £1 stake. Pool: £5,470.00. 1,098.30 winning tickets. KH

478 SOUTHWELL (L-H)
Tuesday, February 12

OFFICIAL GOING: Standard
Wind: Almost nil Weather: Fine

528 SOUTHWELL-RACECOURSE.CO.UK H'CAP 6f (F)
1:50 (1:51) (Class 6) (0-55,53) 4-Y-0+ **£1,911** (£564; £282) **Stalls** Low

Form RPR
4635 **1** **Soba Jones**[12] 371 11-8-6 **48** TolleyDean(3) 6 64
(J Balding) *trckd ldr: rdn to ld and edgd lft wl ins fnl f: r.o* **13/2**
11 **2** 1 **Alexander Huricane (IRE)**[1] 522 4-9-0 **53** 6ex NCallan 8 66+
(K A Ryan) *chsd ldrs: rdn to ld over 1f out: edgd lft: hdd wl ins fnl f* **15/8**[1]
3433 **3** 3 1/2 **Pappas Image**[7] 440 4-8-7 **46** ow1 (p) StephenDonohoe 3 48
(A J McCabe) *hld up in tch: rdn over 2f out: no ex fnl f* **4/1**[2]
-462 **4** 2 **Blakeshall Quest**[12] 371 8-8-8 **47** (b) PaulFessey 4 42
(R Brotherton) *led: rdn and hdd over 1f out: wknd ins fnl f* **11/2**[3]
-046 **5** 2 1/2 **Favouring (IRE)**[12] 365 6-7-13 **45** (v) PatrickDonaghy(7) 5 32
(M C Chapman) *sn outpcd: nvr nrr* **11/1**
-065 **6** 6 **Majestical (IRE)**[20] 270 6-8-13 **52** (e) ChrisCatlin 1 20
(V Smith) *s.i.s: swtchd rt sn after s: outpcd* **17/2**
-020 **7** 1/2 **Cadogen Square**[4] 478 6-8-6 **45** (b) LiamJones 2 11
(Mrs R A Carr) *chsd ldrs: rdn whn hmpd 1/2-way: sn wknd* **50/1**
600- **8** 3 **Bodden Bay**[146] 5546 6-9-0 **53** DanielTudhope 9 10
(I W McInnes) *sn outpcd* **11/1**

1m 16.92s (0.42) **Going Correction** +0.10s/f (Slow) 8 Ran SP% **112.7**
Speed ratings (Par 101): **101,99,95,92,89 81,80,76**
CSF £18.53 CT £54.81 TOTE £7.00: £1.90, £1.10, £1.50; EX 20.70 Trifecta £75.60 Pool: £322.95 - 3.03 winning tickets..
Owner R L Crowe **Bred** Mrs M J Hills **Trained** Scrooby, Notts

FOCUS
A moderate sprint run 2.25sec slower than the later Class 3 handicap. The form seems solid with the winner back to his winter best. There is more to come from the second who matched his form of the previous day.

529 MAKE A DATE WITH PONTIN'S MAIDEN STKS 1m (F)
2:20 (2:22) (Class 5) 3-Y-0+ **£2,457** (£725; £362) **Stalls** Low

Form RPR
1 **William Blake** 3-8-8 0 GregFairley 11 79+
(M Johnston) *chsd ldrs: rdn and hung rt over 2f out: led over 1f out: hung lft fnl f: r.o* **9/1**
4 2 3 **Nags To Riches (IRE)**[4] 483 3-8-8 0 TPQueally 10 68
(J A Osborne) *led 7f out: hdd over 5f out: led 1/2-way: rdn and hdd over 1f out: styd on same pce* **4/1**[2]
4 3 ¾ **Boss Hog**[21] 261 3-8-8 0 StephenDonohoe 7 66+
(P A Blockley) *chsd ldrs: rdn over 2f out: styd on u.p* **7/1**[3]
035- 4 hd **Moral Code (IRE)**[77] 6959 4-9-13 63 ChrisCatlin 9 71
(E J O'Neill) *sn chsng ldrs: led over 5f out: hdd 1/2-way: rdn over 2f out: no ex ins fnl f* **7/1**[3]
5 5 ½ **Days Of Pleasure (IRE)**[4] 483 3-8-8 0 MickyFenton 1 65+
(J A Osborne) *hld up: rdn 1/2-way: hdwy 3f out: styd on: nt rch ldrs* **20/1**
3-42 6 2 **Saviour Sand (IRE)**[11] 396 4-9-13 70 SebSanders 6 65+
(D R C Elsworth) *prom: sn drvn along: lost pl 7f out: hdwy u.p and hung lft over 2f out: n.d* **7/4**[1]
7 10 **Great Destination** 3-8-8 0 PaulHanagan 13 37
(B Smart) *led: racd keenly: hdd 7f out: rdn 1/2-way: wknd over 2f out: sn hung lft* **11/1**
5 8 3 ½ **Thankful**[38] 52 3-8-3 0 JimmyQuinn 8 24
(Rae Guest) *hld up: in tch: rdn over 3f out: sn wknd* **14/1**
9 1 ¼ **Shenandoah Girl** 5-9-1 0 GabrielHannon[(7)] 5 26
(M D I Usher) *s.i.s: a in rr* **100/1**
0 10 10 **Moorside Diamond**[33] 107 4-9-8 0 AndrewElliott 3 —
(A D Brown) *s.i.s: hdwy over 6f out: rdn and wknd over 2f out* **100/1**
11 5 **Kenland (IRE)** 3-8-8 0 LiamJones 2 —
(S W Hall) *dwlt: a in rr* **33/1**
12 2 ½ **Majestic Issue (IRE)**[32] 4-9-13 0 PhillipMakin 12 —
(M Dods) *chsd ldrs: lost pl over 5f out: bhd fnl 3f* **50/1**

1m 44.5s (0.80) **Going Correction** +0.10s/f (Slow)
WFA 3 from 4yo+ 19lb **12 Ran SP% 118.0**
Speed ratings (Par 103): **100,97,96,96,95 93,83,80,78,68 63,61**
CSF £43.43 TOTE £10.50: £2.80, £2.00, £1.70; EX 43.10 TRIFECTA Not won..
Owner Sheikh Hamdan Bin Mohammed Al Maktoum **Bred** Gainsborough Stud Management Ltd **Trained** Middleham Moor, N Yorks

FOCUS
A modest maiden which lost some of its interest with the defection of the 78-rated McConnell. The time was 1.4sec slower than the later older-horse handicap and the form is probably nothing special although the form among the first six might prove a bit better than the bare figures.

530 SOUTHWELL GOLF CLUB (S) STKS 7f (F)
2:50 (2:51) (Class 6) 4-Y-0+ **£1,774** (£523; £262) **Stalls** Low

Form RPR
33-5 1 **Magic Amour**[7] 440 10-8-12 58 (b) StephenDonohoe 9 61
(P A Blockley) *chsd ldr tl led over 4f out: rdn over 2f out: styd on* **6/4**[1]
-220 2 3 **Stepaside (IRE)**[30] 147 4-8-5 47 (b) SBushby[(7)] 4 53
(A D Brown) *led: hdd over 4f out: rdn over 2f out: no imp fnl f* **11/1**
0026 3 1 ½ **Lucius Verrus (USA)**[19] 285 8-8-12 52 (v) NCallan 8 49
(D Shaw) *chsd ldrs: rdn over 4f out: styd on u.p* **5/1**[2]
6-50 4 1 ½ **Far Seeking**[27] 176 4-8-7 47 KevinGhunowa[(5)] 2 45
(R A Harris) *s.i.s: sn prom: rdn 1/2-way: styd on same pce fnl 2f* **14/1**
-010 5 nk **Buzzin'Boyzee (IRE)**[2] 516 5-8-6 45 RichardEvans[(7)] 3 45+
(P D Evans) *s.i.s and rdr lost iron sn after s: bhd: hdwy u.p over 1f out: nt trble ldrs* **8/1**
5333 6 1 ¼ **Plateau**[1] 523 9-8-12 55 LPKeniry 5 41
(C R Dore) *prom: rdn 4f out: wknd fnl f* **11/2**[3]
4025 7 1 ¾ **Desert Lover (IRE)**[13] 362 6-8-12 45 (v) JimmyQuinn 6 36
(R J Price) *chsd ldrs: rdn 1/2-way: wknd over 2f out* **9/1**
4035 8 ½ **Capital Lass**[8] 432 5-8-7 40 VJanacek 7 30
(A J McCabe) *s.s: n.d* **40/1**
-060 9 1 ¾ **Totally Free**[5] 460 4-8-12 55 (v) DaneO'Neill 1 30
(M D I Usher) *chsd ldrs 4f* **25/1**
0-50 10 27 **Fun Thai**[22] 242 4-8-7 28 GregFairley 10 —
(A J Chamberlain) *s.i.s: outpcd* **100/1**

1m 31.31s (1.01) **Going Correction** +0.10s/f (Slow) **10 Ran SP% 115.4**
Speed ratings (Par 101): **98,94,92,91,90 89,87,86,84,53**
CSF £19.41 TOTE £2.30: £1.40, £2.60, £1.70; EX 24.30 Trifecta £87.40 Pool: £161.32 - 1.31 winning tickets..There was no bid for the winner.
Owner Joe McCarthy **Bred** Juddmonte Farms **Trained** Lambourn, Berks

FOCUS
An uncompetitive seller and a race in which it paid to race close to the pace. The time was 0.42 secs faster than the closing three-year-old handicap. The form seems sound enough although the winner did not need to run to his best.

531 I LOVE, YOU LOVE, WE LOVE PONTIN'S H'CAP 1m (F)
3:20 (3:20) (Class 4) (0-85,85) 4-Y-0+ **£4,210** (£1,252; £625; £312) **Stalls** Low

Form RPR
-343 1 **Denbera Dancer (USA)**[13] 357 4-8-5 72 GregFairley 4 89+
(M Johnston) *led: hdd 7f out: remained handy: chsd ldr 3f out: rdn to ld over 1f out: r.o wl* **9/1**
0-14 2 3 ½ **Intersky Charm (USA)**[19] 280 4-8-12 79 DeanMcKeown 1 88
(R M Whitaker) *chsd ldrs: outpcd over 2f out: rallied and hung rt fr over 1f out: no ch w wnr* **9/2**[2]
13-3 3 1 ¼ **Tilapia (IRE)**[39] 43 4-9-3 84 (b[1]) SebSanders 3 90
(Sir Mark Prescott) *led 7f out: rdn and hung rt 2f out: sn hdd: styd on same pce fnl f* **13/8**[1]
35-0 4 ½ **Master Pegasus**[17] 315 5-8-13 80 NCallan 6 85
(C F Wall) *hld up: racd keenly: hdwy over 3f out: rdn over 1f out: styd on same pce* **5/1**[3]
000- 5 ½ **Kildare Sun (IRE)**[117] 6293 6-8-4 71 oh1 PaulFessey 2 75
(J Mackie) *hld up: pushed along over 4f out: sme hdwy over 1f out: nvr trbld ldrs* **18/1**
00-0 6 3 **Granston (IRE)**[9] 417 7-9-4 85 JimmyQuinn 5 82
(J D Bethell) *chsd ldr tl rdn 3f out: wknd over 1f out* **8/1**
6/32 7 ½ **Claret And Amber**[13] 357 6-8-10 77 PaulHanagan 7 73
(R A Fahey) *chsd ldrs over 5f* **15/2**

1m 43.1s (-0.60) **Going Correction** +0.10s/f (Slow) **7 Ran SP% 111.1**
Speed ratings (Par 105): **107,103,102,101,101 98,97**
CSF £45.90 TOTE £10.90: £3.50, £2.40; EX 49.50.
Owner Syndicate 2005 **Bred** Quay Bloodstock And The Niarchos Family **Trained** Middleham Moor, N Yorks

FOCUS
A decent handicap for the money and run 1.40secs faster than the earlier maiden. The form, best rated through the third, is not all that solid.

532 LOVE EVERY DAY @ PONTIN'S H'CAP 6f (F)
3:50 (3:56) (Class 3) (0-95,94) 4-Y-0+ **£7,124** (£2,119; £1,059; £529) **Stalls** Low

Form RPR
03-2 1 **Evens And Odds (IRE)**[21] 259 4-9-4 94 (b) NCallan 1 111+
(K A Ryan) *mde all: rdn clr over 1f out: eased towards fin* **4/1**[3]
-212 2 5 **Bo McGinty (IRE)**[4] 482 7-8-5 81 6ex (b) PaulHanagan 7 80
(R A Fahey) *prom: rdn to chse wnr 2f out: sn outpcd* **8/1**
-212 3 2 **Kabeer**[7] 442 10-8-8 89 (t) NataliaGemelova[(5)] 3 82
(A J McCabe) *dwlt: hdwy over 3f out: rdn and edgd lft over 2f out: styd on same pce* **5/2**[2]
000- 4 1 ¾ **Sandrey (IRE)**[111] 6437 4-8-9 85 AdrianMcCarthy 6 72
(P W Chapple-Hyam) *chsd wnr tl rdn 2f out: wknd fnl f* **16/1**
01-2 5 5 **Crimson King (IRE)**[39] 43 7-8-8 84 ChrisCatlin 2 55
(R W Price) *s.i.s: sn pushed along in rr: rdn over 2f out: n.d* **2/1**[1]
-466 6 nk **Lucayos**[15] 337 5-8-5 88 KylieManser[(7)] 5 58
(Mrs H Sweeting) *prom: lost pl 4f out: bhd fr 1/2-way* **25/1**
-533 7 1 **Cornus**[6] 456 6-8-4 80 oh3 (be) JimmyQuinn 4 47
(A J McCabe) *chsd ldrs tl rdn and wknd over 2f out* **14/1**

1m 14.67s (-1.83) **Going Correction** +0.10s/f (Slow) **7 Ran SP% 109.4**
Speed ratings (Par 107): **116,109,106,104,97 97,95**
CSF £31.89 TOTE £4.30: £2.50, £3.60; EX 28.70.
Owner Mrs Catherine O'Flynn **Bred** Old Carhue Stud **Trained** Hambleton, N Yorks

FOCUS
The feature race on the card looked a decent race for the track and again it paid to race prominently. The time was 2.25secs faster than the opening Class 6 handicap. Evens And Odds did it well but the form may not stand up away from Southwell.

NOTEBOOK
Evens And Odds(IRE) ◆ made all from the inside stall and came right away in the last furlong. The son of Johannesburg was 4lb better off for just under two lengths with Kabeer compared with their meeting over 7f here in January, but he turned that around in taking fashion and looks capable of following up. (tchd 10-3)
Bo McGinty(IRE) has been running consistently of late but was no match for the winner on this step up grade. This was his third outing in six days but he is likely to be kept on the go having only returned from a break at the end of last month, and he could well go in again against lesser company. (op 15-2 tchd 13-2)
Kabeer lost his chance with a tardy start and, although unable to run anywhere near previous form with the winner, in the circumstances did well to reach the placings in a race where nothing else came from behind. (tchd 2-1 and 11-4 in places)
Sandrey(IRE) seems to have had his problems of late and his runs have been well spread out, but he looked a decent sort last spring and this was a fair effort against battle-hardened sprinters after a four-month absence. He could well build on this if his troubles are behind him. (op 9-1)
Crimson King(IRE) has a good record here but missed the kick and was always struggling from that point. He is better than this effort suggests. Official explanation: trainer said, regarding running, that the gelding appeared outpaced over 6f and may appreciate a longer trip and more patient riding tactics (op 11-4 tchd 3-1 in places)

533 START A LOVE AFFAIR WITH PONTIN'S H'CAP 1m 4f (F)
4:20 (4:25) (Class 6) (0-65,65) 4-Y-0+ **£1,911** (£564; £282) **Stalls** Low

Form RPR
26-5 1 **Exit To Luck (GER)**[42] 3 7-9-3 61 (b) ChrisCatlin 5 71
(S Gollings) *chsd ldr: rdn to ld over 1f out: styd on* **22/1**
102 2 1 **Kanisorn (SWE)**[14] 348 6-9-7 65 (bt) LiamJones 2 73
(Mrs R A Carr) *led: rdn and hdd over 1f out: kpt on* **12/1**
0-03 3 1 ¼ **Amwell Brave**[15] 332 7-8-12 56 NCallan 7 62
(J R Jenkins) *hld up: hdwy over 3f out: rdn over 2f out: styd on* **10/3**[2]
-034 4 ½ **Red Wine**[8] 430 9-9-6 64 JamesDoyle 3 69
(A J McCabe) *hld up: hdwy over 2f out: swtchd rt over 1f out: sn rdn: nt rch ldrs* **5/2**[1]
/66- 5 5 **Zed Candy (FR)**[93] 6780 5-9-4 62 MickyFenton 8 59
(J T Stimpson) *s.i.s: sn chsng ldrs: rdn over 2f out: wknd over 1f out* **12/1**
6-0 6 ¾ **Simple Jim (FR)**[24] 234 4-8-9 56 AndrewElliott 4 52
(A D Brown) *hld up: rdn over 4f out: styd on ins fnl f: nvr nrr* **33/1**
00-5 7 13 **Istead Rise (IRE)**[11] 387 4-8-6 53 ow1 StephenDonohoe 6 28
(P A Blockley) *mid-div: rdn over 4f out: nt clr run over 3f out: sn wknd* **8/1**
21-0 8 12 **Winter Cruise (IRE)**[32] 125 4-8-7 54 PaulHanagan 9 10
(Ian Williams) *hld up: hdwy over 6f out: rdn and wknd over 4f out* **15/2**
51-3 9 1 **Young Scotton**[17] 320 8-9-5 63 JimmyQuinn 10 17
(J D Bethell) *chsd ldrs: rdn over 4f out: wknd 3f out: eased* **9/2**[3]

2m 41.82s (0.82) **Going Correction** +0.10s/f (Slow)
WFA 4 from 5yo+ 3lb **9 Ran SP% 115.4**
Speed ratings (Par 101): **101,100,99,99,95 95,86,78,78**
CSF £257.92 CT £1111.75 TOTE £19.50: £4.00, £3.70, £1.40; EX 212.60 Trifecta £251.90 Part won. Pool: £354.87 - 0.10 winning tickets..
Owner P J MArtin **Bred** H K Gutschow **Trained** Scamblesby, Lincs

FOCUS
A moderate handicap in which the first two held those positions throughout. Ordinary, but sound form.
Young Scotton Official explanation: trainer said gelding appears unsuited by the fibresand surface

534 ARENA LEISURE PLC H'CAP 7f (F)
4:50 (4:55) (Class 6) (0-60,63) 3-Y-O **£1,911** (£564; £282) **Stalls** Low

Form RPR
-533 1 **Don Picolo**[21] 257 3-8-10 50 (b) FrankieMcDonald 5 59
(P A Blockley) *dwlt: sn prom: lost pl over 5f out: hdwy over 2f out: rdn to ld ins fnl f: r.o wl* **8/1**
3221 2 3 ½ **Hawa Khana (IRE)**[7] 439 3-9-6 63 6ex (p) KirstyMilczarek[(3)] 2 62
(N P Littmoden) *a.p: trckd ldr 1/2-way: led 2f out: rdn and hung rt fr over 1f out: hdd and no ex ins fnl f* **7/4**[1]
06-4 3 2 ½ **Indecision**[37] 70 3-9-4 58 DaneO'Neill 3 50
(M W Easterby) *chsd ldr to 1/2-way: rdn and ev ch 2f out: hmpd sn after: wknd ins fnl f* **4/1**[3]
0-33 4 ½ **Transcendent (IRE)**[18] 306 3-8-8 48 JimmyQuinn 7 39
(J D Bethell) *hld up in tch: rdn over 1f out: wknd ins fnl f* **5/2**[2]
-015 5 5 **Her Name Is Rio (IRE)**[29] 156 3-9-4 58 ChrisCatlin 6 36
(Mrs S Lamyman) *chsd ldrs: rdn over 4f out: wknd 2f out* **9/1**
566- 6 shd **Invincible Rose (IRE)**[157] 5226 3-8-7 47 DeanMcKeown 4 24
(M Brittain) *s.s: hld up: a bhd* **22/1**

60-5 **7** 3 **Caprima (IRE)**[37] 70 3-8-9 **49** ow1 MickyFenton 1 18
(M Brittain) *led: rdn and hdd 2f out: sn wknd* **33/1**

1m 31.73s (1.43) **Going Correction** +0.10s/f (Slow) **7** Ran SP% **113.3**
Speed ratings (Par 95): **95,91,88,87,81 81,78**
CSF £22.09 TOTE £8.80: £3.30, £1.40; EX 30.30 Place 6 £283.32, Place 5 £195.77.
Owner Pedro Rosas **Bred** C D S Bryce And Mrs M Bryce **Trained** Lambourn, Berks

FOCUS
A moderate handicap little better than a seller and the time was 0.42secs slower than the earlier contest of that grade. The form seems solid enough.
T/Plt: £326.30 to a £1 stake. Pool: £55,751.85. 124.70 winning tickets. T/Qpdt: £95.50 to a £1 stake. Pool: £3,653.90. 28.30 winning tickets. CR

[512]KEMPTON (A.W) (R-H)

Wednesday, February 13

OFFICIAL GOING: Standard
Wind: Almost nil Weather: Clear

535 BOOK NOW FOR RACING POST CHASE DAY CLASSIFIED STKS 7f (P)
6:20 (6:21) (Class 7) 4-Y-0+ **£1,365** (£403; £201) **Stalls** High

Form RPR

2333 **1** **Mr Chocolate Drop (IRE)**[20] 289 4-9-0 45 (b) AdamKirby 7 53
(Miss M E Rowland) *trckd ldng pair: effrt on inner to ld over 1f out: drvn out* **5/1**[3]

0033 **2** 1 1/2 **Wizby**[3] 518 5-9-0 45 JamesDoyle 9 49
(P D Evans) *stdd s: hld up towards rr: prog 2f out to chse wnr jst over 1f out: kpt on but no real imp* **3/1**[2]

00-0 **3** 4 **Doctor Ned**[7] 445 4-9-0 40 NeilChalmers 1 38
(Miss Sheena West) *t.k.h: hld up in last pair: gng easily over 2f out: prog over 1f out: wnt 3rd ins fnl f but ldng pair gone beyond recall* **50/1**

0225 **4** 1/2 **Tang**[7] 445 4-8-7 44 JackDean(7) 2 37
(W G M Turner) *plld hrd early on outer: chsd ldrs: u.p over 2f out: kpt on: n.d* **16/1**

53-2 **5** nk **Maraagel (USA)**[39] 50 5-9-0 45 (t) J-PGuillambert 6 50+
(S C Williams) *t.k.h: trckd ldrs: nt clr run 2f out and sn wl outpcd: plugged on again fnl f* **5/2**[1]

-544 **6** hd **Lawdy Miss Clawdy**[12] 392 4-9-0 43 JimCrowley 4 35
(D W P Arbuthnot) *stdd s: t.k.h and hld up in last: drvn over 1f out: plugged on fnl f* **7/1**

6-00 **7** 1/2 **Baba Ghanoush**[12] 389 6-9-0 45 PaulDoe 8 34
(J Akehurst) *mde most to over 1f out: wknd* **9/1**

05-0 **8** 1/2 **Montzando**[17] 327 5-9-0 45 (p) ChrisCatlin 5 33
(B R Millman) *t.k.h: pressed ldr: upsides 2f out: sn wknd* **8/1**

06-6 **9** 2 1/2 **Coastal Breeze**[21] 264 5-9-0 42 (b) FrancisNorton 3 26
(A J Chamberlain) *t.k.h: trckd ldrs: wknd 2f out* **16/1**

1m 28.01s (2.01) **Going Correction** +0.15s/f (Slow) **9** Ran SP% **117.6**
Speed ratings (Par 97): **94,92,87,87,86 86,86,85,82**
CSF £20.81 TOTE £6.20: £1.90, £1.10, £3.10; EX 16.60.
Owner Dean R Mitchell **Bred** P J Munnelly **Trained** Lower Blidworth, Notts

FOCUS
A poor contest run at just a steady gallop. The winner is rated to recent form.

536 JOIN THE KEMPTON PARK PUNTERS CLUB CLAIMING STKS 7f (P)
6:50 (6:50) (Class 6) 4-Y-0+ **£2,047** (£604; £302) **Stalls** High

Form RPR

1422 **1** **Dickie Le Davoir**[6] 460 4-9-3 72 FergalLynch 1 79
(I W McInnes) *hld up in last: prog on inner fr 2f out to ld over 1f out: rdn out and a holding on* **4/1**[2]

2-44 **2** 3/4 **Danetime Lord (IRE)**[7] 456 5-9-6 82 (p) NCallan 5 80
(K A Ryan) *trckd ldng pair: sltly short of room as wnr mde his move wl over 1f out: wnt 2nd 1f out: cl enough after but nt qckn* **11/10**[1]

000- **3** 1 1/2 **Love On Sight**[145] 5585 4-9-1 75 AndrewElliott 4 71
(A P Jarvis) *t.k.h: trckd ldrs: effrt to chal 2f out: nt qckn fnl f* **12/1**

2321 **4** 1 1/4 **Chatshow (USA)**[3] 515 7-8-7 58 MarkCoumbe(7) 6 67
(A W Carroll) *t.k.h: hld up in tch: effrt 2f out: sn nt qckn and hld* **15/2**[3]

4104 **5** 1 3/4 **Seneschal**[19] 302 7-8-13 70 RichardHughes 3 61
(A B Haynes) *led to 1/2-way: trckd ldr: led again 2f out to over 1f out: wknd and eased fnl f* **4/1**[2]

00-0 **6** 6 **Suhayl Star (IRE)**[11] 402 4-8-10 47 LPKeniry 2 42
(P Burgoyne) *t.k.h: w ldr: led 1/2-way to 2f out: hanging and wknd rapidly* **66/1**

005- **7** 1 **Galaxy Stars**[211] 3622 4-8-12 68 DaneO'Neill 7 41
(R A Teal) *dwlt: t.k.h: hld up: struggling over 2f out: sn bhd* **20/1**

1m 26.41s (0.41) **Going Correction** +0.15s/f (Slow) **7** Ran SP% **113.3**
Speed ratings (Par 101): **103,102,100,99,97 90,89**
CSF £8.64 TOTE £5.60: £3.10, £1.10; EX 10.00.Danetime Lord (IRE) was claimed by Mustafa Khan for £16,000
Owner Ivy House Racing **Bred** P And Mrs A G Venner **Trained** Catwick, E Yorks

FOCUS
A fair contest for the grade. The form seems fairly sound with the winner and fourth close to recent marks.

537 DIGIBET CASINO H'CAP 1m (P)
7:20 (7:21) (Class 6) (0-60,60) 4-Y-0+ **£2,047** (£604; £302) **Stalls** High

Form RPR

2421 **1** **Under Fire (IRE)**[3] 517 5-8-12 60 6ex MarkCoumbe(7) 11 69
(A W Carroll) *mde all: rdn and pressed 2f out: pushed out and asserted fnl f: gamely* **4/1**[2]

200- **2** 1 **Wisdom's Kiss**[133] 5900 4-8-9 50 (p) JimmyQuinn 8 57
(J D Bethell) *prom: chsd wnr jst over 2f out: sn trying to chal: nt qckn u.p over 1f out and hld fnl f* **33/1**

0-42 **3** 1/2 **Waqaarr**[17] 326 4-9-3 58 SebSanders 9 64
(Lady Herries) *t.k.h: hld up in midfield: prog to go 3rd 2f out: drvn and kpt on same pce* **3/1**[1]

2045 **4** nk **Napoletano (GER)**[7] 453 7-9-1 56 (p) NCallan 7 61
(S Dow) *awkward s: t.k.h and hld up in 7th: rdn and kpt on rather reluctantly fnl 2f: nvr chal* **9/1**

1-24 **5** 1/2 **Grey Gurkha**[25] 234 7-9-2 57 FergalLynch 2 61+
(I W McInnes) *hld up and sn last: plenty to do whn effrt 3f out: styd on fnl 2f: nt rch ldrs* **7/1**

54-0 **6** 1/2 **Very Well Red**[31] 148 5-9-3 58 ChrisCatlin 3 61
(P W Hiatt) *trckd ldng trio: rdn and effrt on outer over 2f out: no imp over 1f out: fdd ins fnl f* **14/1**

-305 **7** 2 1/2 **Royal Embrace**[7] 448 5-9-2 57 (v) DaneO'Neill 4 54
(D Shaw) *stdd s: hld up in last pair: rdn 3f out and sn struggling: no real prog after* **6/1**[3]

0-62 **8** shd **White Bear (FR)**[4] 508 6-9-1 56 (b) LPKeniry 1 53
(C R Dore) *hld up in 8th: shkn up and no prog over 2f out* **6/1**[3]

5-43 **9** 1 3/4 **Border Edge**[17] 328 10-8-7 48 NeilChalmers 6 41
(J J Bridger) *rn in snatches in midfield: struggling over 2f out: no ch after* **12/1**

-135 **10** 1/2 **Perfect Practice**[16] 340 4-9-4 59 AdamKirby 5 50
(C G Cox) *chsd wnr to jst over 2f out: steadily wknd* **9/1**

1m 40.99s (1.19) **Going Correction** +0.15s/f (Slow) **10** Ran SP% **123.4**
Speed ratings (Par 101): **100,99,98,98,97 97,94,94,92,92**
CSF £129.94 CT £412.76 TOTE £5.80: £1.30, £6.90, £1.60; EX 187.00.
Owner Marita Bayley and Trevor Turner **Bred** Mrs Marita Bayley **Trained** Cropthorne, Worcs

FOCUS
A moderate handicap dominated by recent course-and-distance winner Under Fire. The form seems sound enough at face value.

538 DIGIBET H'CAP 6f (P)
7:50 (7:50) (Class 5) (0-75,74) 3-Y-0 **£2,457** (£725; £362) **Stalls** High

Form RPR

40-4 **1** **Asian Power (IRE)**[14] 364 3-9-0 70 OscarUrbina 6 75+
(P J O'Gorman) *hld up in last pair: clsd fr 2f out: rdn and styd on wl fnl f to ld last strides* **15/8**[2]

53-1 **2** hd **Liberty Valance (IRE)**[11] 413 3-9-4 74 LPKeniry 1 79
(S Kirk) *trckd clr ldr: clsd over 2f out: led over 1f out: edgd lft fnl f: hdd last strides* **13/8**[1]

0-54 **3** 2 1/2 **Extreme North (USA)**[14] 354 3-8-4 65 (v[1]) SCreighton(5) 2 62
(Miss V Haigh) *blasted off in front and sn 4 l clr: c bk to field over 2f out: hdd over 1f out: grad fdd* **10/1**

6-10 **4** 1/2 **Bertbrand**[14] 364 3-9-4 74 URispoli 3 69
(M Botti) *chsd clr ldr: clsd 2f out: rdn and one pce after* **7/1**

00-3 **5** 4 **Affirmatively**[14] 355 3-9-2 72 TQuinn 4 54
(D R C Elsworth) *t.k.h: hld up in last pair: rdn and hung lft over 2f out: btn after* **11/2**[3]

1m 14.61s (1.51) **Going Correction** +0.15s/f (Slow) **5** Ran SP% **109.9**
Speed ratings (Par 97): **95,94,91,90,85**
CSF £5.29 TOTE £2.80: £1.80, £1.30; EX 5.30.
Owner N S Yong **Bred** Luke O'Reilly **Trained** Newmarket, Suffolk
■ Stewards' Enquiry : L P Keniry two-day ban: careless riding (Feb 24-25)

FOCUS
A decent contest, despite the small field, and two progressive types fought it out. The winner may prove a little better than the bare form.

539 DIGIBET.COM H'CAP 6f (P)
8:20 (8:20) (Class 5) (0-70,69) 4-Y-0+ **£2,590** (£770; £385; £192) **Stalls** High

Form RPR

0643 **1** **Dvinsky (USA)**[9] 429 7-9-2 67 (b) JimmyQuinn 2 78
(P Howling) *chsd ldr: clsd to chal 2f out: narrow ld 1f out but looked vulnerable: battled on wl* **11/1**

204- **2** hd **Mr Cellophane**[70] 7033 5-9-1 66 JimCrowley 10 76
(J R Jenkins) *trckd ldng pair: clsd 2f out: chal ent fnl f and looked likely wnr: did nt find enough and jst hld* **12/1**

-221 **3** 1 **Royal Envoy (IRE)**[16] 334 5-8-8 62 TolleyDean(3) 3 69
(D Shaw) *n.m.r s: hld up in last trio: rdn over 2f out: gd prog jst over 1f out: styd on: nrst fin* **9/2**[1]

20-3 **4** nk **Red Rudy**[11] 404 6-8-12 66 KirstyMilczarek(3) 8 72+
(A W Carroll) *dwlt: plld hrd and hld up in last: prog on inner 2f out: kpt on same pce u.p fnl f* **9/2**[1]

0-36 **5** nk **Social Rhythm**[16] 342 4-9-1 66 ChrisCatlin 5 71
(H J Collingridge) *dwlt: hld up in midfield: prog to cl on ldrs and look dangerous over 1f out: effrt petered out ins fnl f* **10/1**

232- **6** nk **Monte Major (IRE)**[55] 7206 7-9-2 67 DeanMcKeown 11 71
(D Shaw) *led at str pce: jnd 2f out: hdd 1f out: wkng whn eased last strides* **11/1**

-204 **7** 1 1/4 **Goodbye Cash (IRE)**[15] 346 4-9-3 68 StephenDonohoe 6 68
(P D Evans) *chsd clr ldng trio: rdn bef 1/2-way: struggling over 2f out: plugged on fnl f* **14/1**

-143 **8** hd **Star Strider**[16] 334 4-9-3 68 GeorgeBaker 12 70+
(Miss Gay Kelleway) *trckd clr ldrs: clsd fr over 2f out: cl up over 1f out: hld whn nowhere to go and snatched up last 150yds* **5/1**[2]

-610 **9** 3/4 **Littledodayno (IRE)**[3] 515 5-8-13 64 SimonWhitworth 7 61
(M Wigham) *hld up in last trio: shkn up over 1f out: nvr nr ldrs* **15/2**[3]

2544 **10** nk **Cool Sands (IRE)**[8] 442 6-9-0 65 (v) DaneO'Neill 1 61
(D Shaw) *dwlt: hld up in rr: struggling and btn over 2f out* **10/1**

2-53 **11** 7 **Stormburst (IRE)**[26] 213 4-8-5 56 FrancisNorton 4 30
(A J Chamberlain) *a in rr: wknd over 2f out: t.o* **20/1**

1m 12.97s (-0.13) **Going Correction** +0.15s/f (Slow) **11** Ran SP% **118.8**
Speed ratings (Par 103): **106,105,104,104,103 103,101,101,100,99 90**
CSF £137.05 CT £699.11 TOTE £10.20: £4.10, £3.80, £1.60; EX 96.90.
Owner Richard Berenson **Bred** Eclipse Bloodstock & Tipperary Bloodstock **Trained** Newmarket, Suffolk

FOCUS
A fair handicap which was run at a good pace, and the form looks pretty solid.

540 PANORAMIC BAR & RESTAURANT LOYALTY SCHEME H'CAP 1m 4f (P)
8:50 (8:51) (Class 5) (0-75,75) 4-Y-0+ **£2,590** (£770; £288; £288) **Stalls** Centre

Form RPR

3311 **1** **Smokey The Bear**[3] 512 6-9-8 75 6ex NeilChalmers 3 85+
(Miss Sheena West) *hld up in midfield: plld out and gd prog over 2f out: swept into ld over 1f out and then idled: plld out more whn chal fnl f* **9/2**[2]

-433 **2** 3/4 **Most Definitely (IRE)**[11] 406 8-8-11 64 RichardHughes 4 71
(R M Stronge) *stdd s: hld up: last 3f out: gd prog fr 2f out to chse wnr fnl f: hrd rdn and nt qckn* **15/2**[3]

5-66 **3** shd **Lorikeet**[14] 358 9-9-0 67 JimCrowley 10 74
(G L Moore) *led: rdn and hdd over 1f out: kpt on wl u.p* **16/1**

523- **3** dht **They All Laughed**[55] 7198 5-8-13 66 ChrisCatlin 12 73
(P W Hiatt) *hld up and sn last: rdn and stl wl in rr 3f out: gd prog over 1f out: nrst fin* **9/1**

-023 **5** hd **Our Kes (IRE)**[9] 430 6-8-12 65 SimonWhitworth 11 72
(P Howling) *trckd ldrs: wnt 2nd over 2f out to wl over 1f out: nt clrest of runs after: shoved along and kpt on* **14/1**

20-1 **6** 1 1/4 **Casual Affair**[16] 344 5-9-3 70 JimmyQuinn 8 79+
(J D Bethell) *hld up towards rr on inner: prog over 2f out: clsng whn gap clsd over 1f out: nowhere to go after and fin w plenty lft* **15/8**[1]

The Form Book, Raceform Ltd, Compton, RG20 6NL

000- **7** 1 ¾ **One To Follow**[112] 6421 4-8-11 **67** AdamKirby 9 69
(C G Cox) *mostly in midfield: effrt to chse ldrs and wl in tch 2f out: wknd jst over 1f out* **14/1**

423- **8** 3 **Turner's Touch**[119] 6261 6-8-7 **67** (b) RossAtkinson(7) 6 64
(G L Moore) *stdd s: hld up: prog to trck ldrs 4f out: disp 2nd briefly over 2f out: sn btn* **14/1**

9 ¾ **Ambitious Genes (IRE)**[139] 4-9-4 **74** JamesDoyle 2 70
(J W Hills) *rn in snatches: in tch tl wknd 2f out* **33/1**

50/0 **10** 2 ½ **Taxman (IRE)**[16] 344 6-8-12 **65** (p) DaneO'Neill 5 57
(A G Newcombe) *hld up wl in rr: rdn and no prog wl over 2f out* **50/1**

06-4 **11** ½ **Stoop To Conquer**[11] 405 8-9-4 **74** KirstyMilczarek(3) 7 65
(A W Carroll) *sn trckd ldrs: disp 2nd 3f out: wknd rapidly 2f out* **12/1**

1112 **12** 2 ½ **Contra Mundum (USA)**[13] 368 5-9-6 **73** HayleyTurner 1 60
(B G Powell) *mostly chsd ldr to over 2f out: wknd rapidly* **8/1**

2m 35.02s (0.52) **Going Correction** +0.15s/f (Slow)
WFA 4 from 5yo+ 3lb **12** Ran SP% **124.3**
Speed ratings (Par 103): **104,103,103,103,103 102,101,99,98,97 96,95**
3rd place tote - Lorikeet £2.30, They All Laughed £1.60. T/C Lorikeet £256.95; They All Laughed £151.30 CSF £40.47 TOTE £4.20: £2.10, £2.20; EX 48.30.
Owner Graham Flight **Bred** A P Jones **Trained** Falmer, E Sussex

FOCUS
This was run at an ordinary pace. Sound form, rated through the runner-up and the fifth.
Casual Affair Official explanation: jockey said gelding was denied a clear run

541 THE DAY TIME, NIGHT TIME, GREAT TIME H'CAP 1m 3f (P)
9:20 (9:20) (Class 6) (0-55,56) 4-Y-O+ **£2,047** (£604; £302) **Stalls** High

Form RPR

31-0 **1** **Noah Jameel**[42] 10 6-8-11 **51** DaneO'Neill 11 60
(A G Newcombe) *hld up bhd ldrs: effrt on inner over 2f out: prog to ld over 1f out: drvn out* **4/1**[2]

53-2 **2** 1 **Wee Charlie Castle (IRE)**[16] 332 5-9-1 **55** OscarUrbina 9 62
(G C H Chung) *hld up in midfield: effrt and prog 2f out: chsd wnr ent fnl f: styd on but nvr really able to chal* **2/1**[1]

00-5 **3** 1 ¼ **Siena Star (IRE)**[14] 352 10-9-0 **54** MickyFenton 7 59
(Stef Liddiard) *trckd ldr to 1/2-way: styd cl up: led 2f out: drvn and hdd over 1f out: one pce* **17/2**

/0-0 **4** nk **Artzola (IRE)**[28] 180 8-9-0 **54** SimonWhitworth 12 58
(C A Horgan) *stdd s: hld up in last: plenty to do whn effrt over 2f out: prog wl over 1f out: styd on: nrst fin* **14/1**

-631 **5** 1 ¼ **Jarvo**[23] 251 7-8-11 **51** (v) FergalLynch 1 53
(I W McInnes) *hld up wl in rr: effrt over 2f out: kpt on same pce fr over 1f out: n.d* **12/1**

-112 **6** ¾ **Megalala (IRE)**[19] 303 7-8-13 **53** NeilChalmers 2 53
(J J Bridger) *fly leapt s: sn led: edgd lft and hdd 2f out: fdd* **15/2**

10-3 **7** 2 **Lord Laing (USA)**[10] 420 5-8-9 **49** PatDobbs 6 46
(H J Collingridge) *prom: wnt 2nd 1/2-way: edgd lft over 2f out: sn lost pl: fdd* **8/1**

/10- **8** 2 **Cheveley Flyer**[188] 4340 5-8-12 **52** JimmyQuinn 10 45
(J Pearce) *settled midfield: rdn 3f out: sn lost pl and struggling* **14/1**

0-01 **9** 2 ½ **Take A Mile (IRE)**[10] 420 6-9-2 **56** 6ex TQuinn 3 45
(B G Powell) *chsd ldrs: rdn over 3f out: sn struggling and btn* **7/1**[3]

6436 **10** 6 **Shaheer (IRE)**[6] 468 6-8-2 **49** (v) SineadLogush(7) 5 27
(J Gallagher) *racd wd thrght: t.k.h: in tch tl wknd over 2f out* **22/1**

603/ **11** 20 **Hat Trick Man**[574] 6564 7-8-10 **50** VinceSlattery 4 —
(D Burchell) *hld up: wknd 4f out: t.o* **50/1**

2m 24.92s (3.02) **Going Correction** +0.15s/f (Slow)
WFA 4 from 5yo+ 2lb **11** Ran SP% **126.6**
Speed ratings (Par 101): **95,94,93,93,92 91,90,88,86,82 68**
CSF £13.44 CT £69.41 TOTE £5.60: £2.20, £1.10, £3.20; EX 17.40 Place 6 £ 57.30, Place 5 £ 17.73.
Owner S Langridge **Bred** Michael Ng **Trained** Yarnscombe, Devon

FOCUS
A steadily run handicap and very modest form. The winner is rated up 5lb on his previous best.
Take A Mile(IRE) Official explanation: jockey said gelding ran flat
T/Plt: £47.40 to a £1 stake. Pool: £79,203.05. 1,219.10 winning tickets. T/Qpdt: £14.10 to a £1 stake. Pool: £6,329.20. 330.20 winning tickets. JN

498 LINGFIELD (L-H)
Wednesday, February 13

OFFICIAL GOING: Standard
Wind: Nil Weather: bright and suny

542 LOVE IS IN THE AIR @ PONTIN'S CLAIMING STKS 1m (P)
1:40 (1:41) (Class 6) 4-Y-O+ **£1,774** (£523; £262) **Stalls** High

Form RPR

06-3 **1** **Holyfield Warrior (IRE)**[16] 341 4-8-11 50 JamesDoyle 5 53
(I A Wood) *hld up in tch: rdn wl over 1f out: r.o strly to ld towards fin: jst hld on* **20/1**

66-3 **2** shd **Pab Special (IRE)**[41] 24 5-9-3 65 DaneO'Neill 2 59
(B R Johnson) *stdd after s: hld up in last: stl last over 1f out: rdn and str run fnl f: jst hld* **11/4**[2]

0416 **3** nk **Green Pirate**[4] 508 6-8-9 60 (p) RichardKingscote 6 50
(W M Brisbourne) *hld up in last pair: rdn and hdwy over 2f out: drvn 2f out: r.o to ld ins fnl f: sn hdd and unable qck* **15/2**

33-0 **4** ¾ **Arena's Dream (USA)**[39] 51 4-9-1 65 JamieSpencer 1 54
(J R Boyle) *led: rdn jst over 2f out: hdd and no ex wl ins fnl f* **10/3**[3]

0-11 **5** shd **Samuel Charles**[9] 433 10-9-4 70 (b) LiamJones 4 57
(C R Dore) *t.k.h: chsd ldr: upsides jst over 2f out: rdn and hung lft over 1f out: nt run on* **6/4**[1]

00-5 **6** shd **Mr Belvedere**[11] 401 7-8-2 42 (tp) SophieDoyle(7) 3 48
(A J Lidderdale) *s.i.s: sn chsng ldrs: rdn jst over 2f out: ev ch jst ins fnl f: fdd last 50yds* **66/1**

60-5 **7** 2 ½ **Robinzal**[15] 351 6-9-11 57 VinceSlattery 7 58
(A W Carroll) *t.k.h: in tch: rdn 2f out: chsd ldrs 1f out: wknd ins fnl f* **33/1**

1m 38.85s (0.65) **Going Correction** +0.075s/f (Slow) **7** Ran SP% **110.7**
Speed ratings (Par 101): **99,98,98,97,97 97,95**
CSF £69.90 TOTE £24.40: £8.20, £2.20; EX 104.20.The winner was claimed by Miss Sheena West for £7,000.
Owner Neardown Stables **Bred** A Malone **Trained** Upper Lambourn, Berks

FOCUS
A typically moderate claimer, run at just a steady pace. The winner did not have to improve much and the form is worth treating with some caution.

543 I LOVE PONTIN'S FAMILY HOLIDAY CENTRES MAIDEN STKS 7f (P)
2:10 (2:11) (Class 5) 3-Y-O **£2,457** (£725; £362) **Stalls** Low

Form RPR

44- **1** **Top Draw (USA)**[112] 6434 3-8-12 0 JamieSpencer 4 68+
(M L W Bell) *t.k.h: chsd ldr tl led over 2f out: edgd rt wl over 1f out: r.o wl* **6/5**[1]

2 1 **Crafty Dealer (IRE)** 3-9-3 0 JamesDoyle 2 68
(J W Hills) *in tch in midfield: hdwy over 2f out: chsd wnr over 1f out: kpt on but nt pce to chal wnr* **20/1**

3 ½ **Seasonal Cross** 3-8-12 0 SebSanders 10 62+
(S Dow) *s.i.s: in tch in midfield: rdn wl over 2f out: hdwy wl over 1f out: chsd ldng pair 1f out: kpt on* **20/1**

4 ¾ **Eastern Hills** 3-9-3 0 GregFairley 7 72+
(M Johnston) *chsd ldrs: nt clr run and shuffled bk bnd 2f out: swtchd lft jst over 1f out: styd on: nt trble ldrs* **9/4**[2]

0-6 **5** ¾ **Flemish Art (IRE)**[14] 354 3-9-3 0 PatCosgrave 11 63+
(M J Wallace) *t.k.h: hld up in tch in midfield: lost pl and rdn over 2f out: styd on fnl f: nvr trbld ldrs* **33/1**

3 **6** hd **Tripod Molly (IRE)**[16] 343 3-8-12 0 (t) EdwardCreighton 9 57
(P J McBride) *t.k.h: hld up in midfield: rdn and effrt 2f out: kpt on same pce after* **12/1**

6- **7** 1 ¼ **Polychrome**[74] 6998 3-8-12 0 NeilPollard 8 54
(John Berry) *chsd ldrs: rdn wl over 2f out: wknd 1f out* **66/1**

8 1 ¼ **Thankuforthemusic (IRE)** 3-9-3 0 TPQueally 3 55+
(J A Osborne) *s.i.s: sn in tch in midfield: pushed along over 3f out: outpcd over 2f out: kpt on same pce after* **10/1**[3]

660- **9** 3 **Elegant Step**[114] 6379 3-8-12 65 LiamJones 6 42
(A W Carroll) *led tl over 2f out: wknd qckly over 1f out* **12/1**

10 ¾ **Stoneacre Sarah** 3-8-12 0 AdamKirby 12 40
(Peter Grayson) *stdd after s: bhd: c wd bnd 2f out: nvr nr ldrs* **33/1**

11 4 **Musharahb** 3-9-3 0 NeilChalmers 1 34
(M Appleby) *s.i.s: a bhd* **100/1**

12 16 **Kay Tee Jo (IRE)** 3-8-12 0 LPKeniry 5 —
(Peter Grayson) *bhd: rdn over 4f out: lost tch 3f out: t.o* **66/1**

1m 28.61s (3.81) **Going Correction** +0.075s/f (Slow) **12** Ran SP% **120.1**
Speed ratings (Par 97): **81,79,79,78,77 77,75,74,71,70 65,47**
CSF £34.07 TOTE £2.30: £1.10, £3.30, £3.90; EX 28.90 TRIFECTA Not won..
Owner Sheikh Marwan Al Maktoum **Bred** Darley **Trained** Newmarket, Suffolk

FOCUS
This was probably an average maiden, run at an ordinary early pace in a very slow time. With little previous form to go on the race is rated around the winner.
Eastern Hills ◆ Official explanation: jockey said colt was denied a clear run
Stoneacre Sarah Official explanation: jockey said filly hung right from 3f out

544 MY HEART BELONGS TO PONTIN'S H'CAP 2m (P)
2:40 (2:40) (Class 6) (0-60,60) 4-Y-O+ **£1,876** (£554; £277) **Stalls** Low

Form RPR

0-02 **1** **Dubai Ace (USA)**[21] 272 7-9-10 **60** (p) NeilChalmers 3 71
(Miss Sheena West) *hld up towards rr: rdn 3f out: hdwy over 2f out: led over 1f out: swished tail u.p fnl f: styd on wl* **5/1**

-004 **2** 1 ½ **Salut Saint Cloud**[6] 461 7-8-7 **50** (p) JemmaMarshall(7) 8 58
(G L Moore) *hld up in midfield: hdwy 7f out: chsd ldrs and rdn 3f out: styd on over 2f out: pressed wnr and ev ch over 1f out: no ex last 100yds* **7/2**[2]

6520 **3** 5 **Chiff Chaff**[6] 461 4-8-8 **50** LPKeniry 5 52
(C R Dore) *hld up and bhd: rdn over 4f out: kpt on u.p to chse ldng pair ins fnl f: nvr able to chal* **14/1**

000- **4** 1 ½ **Lysander's Quest (IRE)**[41] 6811 10-8-10 **46** oh1 RobertHavlin 1 46
(R Ingram) *in tch tl lost pl and dropped to rr over 3f out: styd on past btn horses u.p fnl f: nvr threatened ldrs* **33/1**

-400 **5** hd **Backlash**[13] 377 7-8-10 **46** oh1 LiamJones 7 47+
(A W Carroll) *t.k.h: hld up in rr: hdwy 5f out: rdn 4f out: plugging on whn nt clr run over 1f out: nvr trbld ldrs* **50/1**

250- **6** 1 **Arabian Sun**[93] 6802 4-9-3 **59** (v) IanMongan 2 58
(M J Attwater) *chsd ldr for 3f: styd chsng ldrs: rdn 3f out: wknd 2f out* **15/2**

41 **7** shd **Starstruck Peter (IRE)**[13] 374 4-8-12 **54** (t) PaulDoe 6 53
(S Curran) *chsd ldrs: wnt 2nd 6f out: drvn to ld 2f out: hdd over 1f out: sn btn* **9/2**[3]

-054 **8** 1 ¼ **Mango Masher (IRE)**[13] 374 4-8-5 **50** TolleyDean(3) 4 47
(J L Flint) *hld up and bhd: nvr nr ldrs* **11/1**

6-14 **9** 3 ½ **Otaki (IRE)**[18] 322 4-8-12 **54** SebSanders 11 47
(Sir Mark Prescott) *led: rdn 3f out: hdd 2f out: sn btn and nt pushed* **10/3**[1]

454- **10** 10 **Rose Bien**[235] 2887 6-9-9 **59** (p) EdwardCreighton 10 40
(P J McBride) *hld up in tch in midfield: lost pl and rdn 5f out: wl bhd last 3f: t.o and eased ins fnl f* **14/1**

1-05 **11** 70 **Victory Mile (USA)**[7] 455 4-9-0 **56** (b) SteveDrowne 9 —
(M F Harris) *slowly into strde: bustled along and hdwy to chse ldr after 3f tl 6f out: sn dropped out: t.o last 2f* **66/1**

3m 21.42s (-4.28) **Going Correction** +0.075s/f (Slow)
WFA 4 from 6yo+ 6lb **11** Ran SP% **120.0**
Speed ratings (Par 101): **113,112,109,109,108 108,108,107,105,100 65**
CSF £23.18 CT £235.49 TOTE £6.60: £1.80, £1.90, £3.30; EX 24.30 Trifecta £63.90 Pool: £180.10 - 2.00 winning tickets..
Owner Mucky Duck II Partnership **Bred** Gainsborough Farm Llc **Trained** Falmer, E Sussex

FOCUS
A moderate staying handicap, run at a solid pace in a very decent time for the grade. The form looks fair with the first pair coming clear, the winner rated to form.

545 EVERYBODY LOVES PONTIN'S BRILLIANT BLUE COATS MAIDEN STKS 1m 5f (P)
3:10 (3:10) (Class 5) 4-Y-O+ **£2,331** (£693; £346; £173) **Stalls** Low

Form RPR

364- **1** **Crispian (IRE)**[230] 3041 4-9-3 67 LiamJones 7 55
(W J Haggas) *stdd s: hld up in tch: hdwy to trck ldrs 5f out: chal over 2f out: rdn to ld wl over 1f out: hld on u.p: all out* **2/1**[2]

0- **2** hd **National Day (IRE)**[45] 7282 4-8-12 0 TQuinn 3 50+
(D R C Elsworth) *plld hrd: hld up towards rr: hdwy over 4f out: chsd ldng pair over 1f out: chsd wnr ins fnl f: kpt on* **5/1**[3]

22-2 **3** ½ **Aphrodisia**[18] 317 4-8-12 60 J-PGuillambert 10 49
(S C Williams) *t.k.h: led after 1f: jnd and rdn jst over 2f out: hdd over 1f out: ev ch tl unable qck towards fin* **15/8**[1]

4 hd **Brave Bugsy (IRE)**54 5-9-7 0 NeilChalmers 2 54
(M Appleby) *hld up towards rr: hdwy over 5f out: chsd ldrs and rdn over 2f out: kpt on same pce u.p fnl f* **33/1**

-523 5 nk **Flight Dream (FR)**18 [317] 5-9-2 63 (b) JamieJones(5) 9 53
(M G Quinlan) *t.k.h: hld up in rr: hdwy 6f out: chsd ldrs and rdn 2f out: kpt on same pce fnl f* **7/1**

6 4 **Site Sentry (IRE)**17 5-9-7 0 SteveDrowne 4 47
(M F Harris) *hld up in tch in midfield: lost pl and dropped to rr over 4f out: rdn and outpcd 3f out: kpt on but n.d after* **33/1**

05 7 shd **Eddystone (IRE)**32 [134] 4-9-3 0 (p) LPKeniry 8 47
(Mrs L C Jewell) *chsd ldrs: wnt 2nd 6f out tl over 2f out: sn rdn: wknd 2f out* **66/1**

/0-6 8 nk **Fantasy Legend (IRE)**21 [269] 5-9-7 45 AndrewElliott 6 47
(A M Hales) *chsd ldr after 1f tl 6f out: rdn over 4f out: lost pl over 3f out: kpt on u.p but n.d after* **14/1**

000/ P **Lord Of Adventure (IRE)**310 [545] 6-9-7 53 (p) PatDobbs 1 —
(Mrs L C Jewell) *led for 1f out: rdn 8f out: dropped to last 5f out: sn t.o: p.u and dismntd 2f out* **100/1**

2m 50.17s (4.17) **Going Correction** +0.075s/f (Slow)
WFA 4 from 5yo+ 4lb **9** Ran SP% **112.3**
Speed ratings (Par 103): **90,89,89,89,89 86,86,86,—**
CSF £11.81 TOTE £2.90: £1.10, £2.10, £1.10; EX 12.60 Trifecta £31.60 Pool: £153.55 - 3.44 winning tickets..
Owner Wentworth Racing (pty) Ltd **Bred** Forenaghts Stud **Trained** Newmarket, Suffolk

FOCUS
A moderate staying maiden, run at just a steady early pace. The form looks worth treating with a fair degree of caution with the winner not having to match his previous best and some poor hurdlers too close for comfort.
Lord Of Adventure(IRE) Official explanation: vet said gelding pulled up lame

546 LINGFIELDPARK.CO.UK H'CAP 1m 2f (P)
3:40 (3:40) (Class 5) (0-70,69) 4-Y-0+ **£2,331** (£693; £346; £173) **Stalls** Low

Form RPR
0-11 1 **Safari Sundowner (IRE)**7 [448] 4-9-3 **67** 6ex JimCrowley 2 82+
(P Winkworth) *trckd ldrs: wnt 2nd wl over 3f out: rdn 2f out: led 1f out: sn in command: rdn out* **4/1**2

5-65 2 2 1/2 **Lord Of Dreams (IRE)**9 [430] 6-8-7 **61** JamieJones(5) 9 68
(G L Moore) *hld up in rr: hdwy over 3f out: swtchd lft bnd 2f out: rdn to chse wnr ins fnl f: no imp* **8/1**

1541 3 2 1/2 **Lordswood (IRE)**14 [352] 4-8-6 **56** HayleyTurner 4 58
(J R Best) *hld up in tch in midfield: hdwy to chse ldng pair over 2f out: rdn over 1f out: outpcd fnl f* **9/4**1

0-24 4 3/4 **My Mentor (IRE)**27 [192] 4-9-2 **66** SebSanders 1 67
(Sir Mark Prescott) *sn pushed into ld: rdn 4f out: hrd pressed 2f out: hdd 1f out: sn btn* **9/2**3

0 5 1 3/4 **Foreign King (USA)**11 [406] 4-8-12 **62** MickyFenton 8 59
(J W Mullins) *in tch in midfield: rdn over 4f out: wknd jst over 2f out* **50/1**

52-5 6 shd **Barry Island**39 [57] 9-8-8 **57** NeilPollard 6 54
(D R C Elsworth) *stdd after s: hld up in rr: rdn and effrt 2f out: sn hung lft: n.d* **14/1**

00-6 7 1/2 **Sir Liam (USA)**11 [406] 4-9-5 **69** IanMongan 3 65
(R A Teal) *chsd ldrs: rdn over 3f out: wknd 2f out* **15/2**

0-30 8 3 1/2 **Fateful Attraction**18 [316] 5-9-5 **68** (b) DaneO'Neill 5 57
(I A Wood) *w.w in tch in midfield: rdn and lost pl over 3f out: n.d after* **16/1**

336 9 6 **Meditation**16 [340] 6-9-1 **64** JamesDoyle 7 41
(I A Wood) *chsd ldr tl over 3f out: sn rdn and wknd* **12/1**

2m 3.76s (-2.84) **Going Correction** +0.075s/f (Slow)
WFA 4 from 5yo+ 1lb **9** Ran SP% **114.0**
Speed ratings (Par 103): **114,112,110,109,108 107,107,104,99**
CSF £35.40 CT £87.67 TOTE £5.20: £1.80, £2.70, £1.20; EX 40.40 Trifecta £166.80 Pool: £368.92 - 1.57 winning tickets..
Owner P Winkworth **Bred** Michael Phelan **Trained** Chiddingfold, Surrey

FOCUS
A modest handicap, but the pace was sound and the winning time was very smart. The form looks solid for the class, with the winner continuing on the upgrade and the second back to something like his best.
Foreign King(USA) Official explanation: jockey said gelding hung left

547 ARENALEISUREPLC.COM H'CAP 1m 2f (P)
4:10 (4:10) (Class 6) (0-65,64) 3-Y-0 **£1,781** (£529; £264; £132) **Stalls** Low

Form RPR
50-5 1 **A Dream Come True**10 [419] 3-9-5 **62** DaneO'Neill 1 68+
(D K Ivory) *trckd ldrs: nt clr run and shuffled bk bnd 2f out: rdn and hdwy on inner wl over 1f out: hung rt but led ins fnl f: r.o strly* **7/2**2

00-5 2 1 3/4 **Love Empire (USA)**25 [221] 3-9-6 **63** (b1) DeanMcKeown 3 64
(M Johnston) *chsd ldr: rdn to ld over 2f out: hdd ins fnl f: nt pce of wnr last 100yds* **9/4**1

000- 3 1 **Jemiliah**112 [6432] 3-8-13 **56** RobertHavlin 6 55
(B J Meehan) *towards rr: rdn and hdwy on outer 4f out: chsd ldrs over 2f out: outpcd 2f out: kpt on u.p fnl f* **9/1**

0-04 4 nk **I Certainly May**17 [325] 3-9-3 **60** SebSanders 2 59
(S Dow) *sn pushed up to ld: rdn and jnd over 3f out: hdd over 2f out: outpcd jst ins fnl f* **9/4**1

0-40 5 3/4 **Bon Ton Roulet**25 [221] 3-9-2 **64** HaddenFrost(5) 4 61
(R Hannon) *hld up in last pair: hdwy on inner 2f out: rdn over 1f out: no imp* **13/2**3

0-05 6 2 **Amazing Spirit**12 [393] 3-8-2 **45** AdrianMcCarthy 5 38?
(Miss V Haigh) *led briefly after s: sn stdd bk: chsd ldrs: rdn to chse ldng pair jst over 2f out: wknd over 1f out* **50/1**

000- 7 13 **Honest Yankee (USA)**88 [6857] 3-8-2 **45** (p) RichardThomas 8 12
(Mrs L C Jewell) *a last: rdn over 4f out: lost tch 3f out: t.o* **33/1**

2m 7.68s (1.08) **Going Correction** +0.075s/f (Slow) **7** Ran SP% **112.0**
Speed ratings (Par 95): **98,96,95,95,94 93,82**
CSF £11.30 CT £61.75 TOTE £4.20: £2.30, £1.40; EX 16.10 Trifecta £150.90 Pool: £337.98 - 1.59 winning tickets..
Owner Dean Ivory **Bred** D K Ivory **Trained** Radlett, Herts

FOCUS
Another steadily-run handicap and messy form which may not prove reliable. The winner is better than the bare form and the fourth looks the best guide.

548 PLAY GOLF @ LINGFIELD PARK H'CAP 1m (P)
4:40 (4:40) (Class 5) (0-75,75) 4-Y-0+ **£2,457** (£725; £362) **Stalls** High

Form RPR
6-13 1 **Highland Harvest**4 [509] 4-9-4 75 HayleyTurner 2 82
(D R C Elsworth) *plld hrd: chsd ldr: rdn to chal over 1f out: r.o wl to ld towards fin* **7/4**1

36-1 2 nk **Paradise Dancer (IRE)**9 [426] 4-9-3 74 6ex GeorgeBaker 3 80
(J A R Toller) *led: hrd pressed and rdn wl over 1f out: hdd and no ex towards finsh* **7/2**3

-212 3 2 **Wrighty Almighty (IRE)**7 [452] 6-8-12 69 JimCrowley 4 71
(P R Chamings) *t.k.h: hld up in last pair: hdwy over 2f out: rdn 2f out: chsd ldng pair ins fnl f: outpcd last 100yds* **9/4**2

1002 4 3/4 **Epidaurian King (IRE)**7 [446] 5-8-5 62 (v) DeanMcKeown 1 62
(D Shaw) *t.k.h: hld up in tch: hdwy on inner over 2f out: rdn over 1f out: outpcd fnl f* **15/2**

6432 5 1/2 **Onenightinlisbon (IRE)**9 [426] 4-8-11 68 PatCosgrave 5 67
(J R Boyle) *chsd ldng pair: rdn and outpcd 2f out: kpt on same pce after* **10/1**

1m 38.39s (0.19) **Going Correction** +0.075s/f (Slow) **5** Ran SP% **110.2**
Speed ratings (Par 103): **102,101,99,98,98**
CSF £8.19 TOTE £3.20: £1.80, £1.70; EX 9.30 Place 6 £46.72, Place 5 £9.78.
Owner J Wotherspoon **Bred** John Wotherspoon **Trained** Newmarket, Suffolk

FOCUS
A modest little handicap, run at an uneven pace. The form is not that solid, rated around the second and the fifth.
T/Plt: £57.30 to a £1 stake. Pool: £46,220.95. 588.65 winning tickets. T/Qpdt: £6.10 to a £1 stake. Pool: £3,635.60. 436.50 winning tickets. SP

385 CAGNES-SUR-MER
Wednesday, February 13

OFFICIAL GOING: Very soft

549a PRIX D'ISOLA 2000 (MAIDEN) (C&G) 7f 110y
2:20 (2:21) 3-Y-0 **£6,985** (£2,794; £2,096; £1,397; £699)

RPR
1 **Maroni (IRE)**13 [385] 3-9-2 SPasquier 7 82
(F Rohaut, France)
2 1 1/2 **My Shadow**13 [385] 3-9-2 J-BEyquem 1 79
(S Dow) *led: hrd rdn appr fnl f: hdd last 100yds: no ex* **13/10**1
3 2 **Chock Dee (FR)** 3-8-13 LProietti 2 71
(X Betron, France)
4 4 **For Pro (GER)**77 3-9-2 THuet 8 65
(G Martin, Austria)
5 1 **Tchic Cove (FR)**13 [385] 3-8-13 ACrastus 3 60
(A Junk, France)
6 2 **Volo Prince (FR)**77 3-8-13 JParize 5 55
(J Parize, France)
7 2 1/2 **Speed Skater (FR)**112 3-8-10 YLetondeur(3) 6 49
(N Clement, France)
8 11 **Vahhare (FR)** 3-8-4 BCantieri(5) 4 20
(J-P Perruchot, France)

1m 36.16s (96.16) **8** Ran SP% **43.5**
PARI-MUTUEL (including 1 Euro stake): WIN 3.00; PL 1.10, 1.10, 1.20; DF 1.60.
Owner M Perret **Bred** Janus Bloodstock Inc & Chevin Bloodstock Ltd **Trained** Sauvagnon, France

NOTEBOOK
My Shadow, runner-up here at the end of last month, filled the same place again but was unable to confirm previous form with the winner despite meeting him on the same terms. Perhaps making the running left him vulnerable to a late challenge.

528 SOUTHWELL (L-H)
Thursday, February 14

OFFICIAL GOING: Standard
Wind: Almost nil Weather: Overcast, dull, damp and on the cold side

550 SOUTHWELL-RACECOURSE.CO.UK APPRENTICE H'CAP 1m (F)
1:40 (1:40) (Class 6) (0-58,58) 4-Y-0+ **£1,774** (£523; £262) **Stalls** Low

Form RPR
03-3 1 **Sparky Vixen**6 [478] 4-8-1 **47** JamieKyne(5) 1 56
(C J Teague) *hld up: hdwy on ins to ld 2f out: sn rdn and edgd rt: kpt on wl fnl f* **8/1**

-225 2 1 1/4 **Abbeygate**20 [299] 7-8-1 **47** (b) AshleyMorgan(5) 4 53
(T Keddy) *t.k.h: effrt 3f out: sn chsng ldrs: kpt on to take 2nd ins fnl f: no real imp* **4/1**1

01-0 3 1 3/4 **Sir Bond (IRE)**37 [80] 7-8-12 **56** NSLawes(3) 5 58
(G R Oldroyd) *trckd ldrs: kpt on same pce fnl f* **9/2**2

05-0 4 hd **Tina's Ridge (IRE)**19 [323] 4-8-7 **53** (p) DavidProbert(5) 2 55
(R Hollinshead) *sn chsng ldrs: led over 2f out: sn hdd: kpt on same pce appr fnl f* **10/1**

4-51 5 6 **Todwick Owl**14 [369] 4-9-3 **58** MatthewDavies 3 46
(J G Given) *set modest pce: qcknd over 3f out: hdd and rdr lost whip over 2f out: lost pl over 1f out* **9/2**2

32-1 6 hd **General Feeling (IRE)**21 [284] 7-9-2 **57** DeclanCannon 7 44
(S T Mason) *s.v.s: hdwy to chse ldrs over 5f out: wknd over 1f out* **11/2**3

26/4 7 3 1/2 **Welcome Releaf**14 [369] 5-8-11 **52** MarkCoumbe 8 31
(P Leech) *trckd ldrs: t.k.h: wknd over 1f out* **12/1**

0025 8 14 **Pawn In Life (IRE)**7 [465] 10-8-5 **46** oh1 (v) DeanHeslop 9 —
(Mrs R A Carr) *sn chsng ldrs on outside: effrt over 3f out: lost pl over 2f out: sn bhd* **22/1**

0214 9 13 **Government (IRE)**14 [367] 7-8-6 **54** ow7 MJMurphy(7) 6 —
(M C Chapman) *hld up: effrt over 3f out: lost pl over 2f out: sn bhd* **9/1**

1m 45.24s (1.54) **Going Correction** +0.25s/f (Slow) **9** Ran SP% **114.0**
Speed ratings (Par 101): **102,100,99,98,92 92,89,75,62**
CSF £39.49 CT £163.52 TOTE £9.90: £3.50, £1.10, £2.40; EX 37.20 TRIFECTA Not won..
Owner G T Carlton **Bred** Mrs G Slater **Trained** Station Town, Co Durham

FOCUS
No gallop and several pulled hard. Modest but sound form.

Sir Bond(IRE) Official explanation: jockey said gelding lost a hind shoe
Government(IRE) Official explanation: jockey said gelding bled from the nose

551 DINE IN THE QUEEN MOTHER RESTAURANT CLAIMING STKS 1m 4f (F)
2:10 (2:10) (Class 6) 4-Y-0+ **£1,774** (£523; £262) **Stalls** Low

Form RPR
63-2 **1** **My Friend Fritz**[10] 435 8-9-2 0 .... PhillipMakin 4 62
(P W Hiatt) *led: rdn 3f out: hld on towards fin* **4/1**[3]
6-06 **2** *nk* **Simple Jim (FR)**[2] 533 4-9-3 56 .... AndrewElliott 1 66
(A D Brown) *trckd ldrs: effrt over 2f out: kpt on wl ins fnl f* **8/1**
0-12 **3** *¾* **Maria Antonia (IRE)**[9] 438 5-8-2 55 .... ManavNem(7) 2 54
(P A Blockley) *s.s: tk fierce hold in last: plld outside over 5f out: chal over 2f out: sn rdn: no ex ins fnl f* **2/1**[2]
00-2 **4** *3* **Critical Stage (IRE)**[13] 388 9-8-9 58 .... HaddenFrost(5) 3 54
(J D Frost) *chsd ldrs: outpcd over 3f out: kpt on fnl 2f* **13/8**[1]
4-26 **5** *7* **Matinee Idol**[10] 435 5-8-9 42 ....(b) ChrisCatlin 5 38
(Mrs S Lamyman) *sn w wnr: lost pl over 2f out* **12/1**

2m 44.66s (3.66) **Going Correction** +0.25s/f (Slow)
WFA 4 from 5yo+ 3lb 5 Ran SP% **110.2**
Speed ratings (Par 101): **97,96,96,94,89**
CSF £31.66 TOTE £3.60: £1.70, £3.50; EX 25.20.Maria Antonia was claimed by Mustafa Khan for £7,000.
Owner P W Hiatt **Bred** Butts Enterprises Limited **Trained** Hook Norton, Oxon
FOCUS
The winner was given his own way out in front and benefited from a well judged ride, setting just a steady pace. The third and fourth were below par and the runner-up is the best guide.

552 YOU'LL LOVE DEALS ON PONTINS.COM MEDIAN AUCTION MAIDEN STKS 1m 4f (F)
2:40 (2:40) (Class 6) 4-6-Y-0 **£1,911** (£564; £282) **Stalls** Low

Form RPR
0-03 **1** **Dot's Delight**[4] 513 4-8-12 50 .... DeanMcKeown 1 47
(K J Burke) *trckd ldrs: led over 2f out: drvn rt out* **5/2**[2]
000/ **2** *2 ½* **Huggle**[471] 6272 5-9-6 0 .... LiamJones 4 48
(P Leech) *led tl 8f out: w ldrs: led 4f out tl over 2f out: edgd rt and kpt on same pce* **33/1**
00/- **3** *1* **Kofi**[21] 1429 6-9-3 45 .... JerryO'Dwyer(3) 2 47
(Karen George) *w ldrs: lost pl over 7f out: reminders over 5f out: kpt on fnl 2f* **15/2**
3-63 **4** *½* **The Diamond Bond**[21] 277 4-8-12 45 .... SladeO'Hara(5) 5 46
(G R Oldroyd) *w ldrs: led 8f out tl 4f out: one pce fnl 2f* **3/1**[3]
0/24 **5** *4* **Red Fama**[10] 435 4-9-3 0 .... ChrisCatlin 3 40
(N Bycroft) *sn chsng ldrs: outpcd over 2f out: no threat after* **6/4**[1]

2m 44.77s (3.77) **Going Correction** +0.25s/f (Slow)
WFA 4 from 5yo+ 3lb 5 Ran SP% **108.3**
Speed ratings: **97,95,94,94,91**
CSF £48.50 TOTE £4.00: £1.30, £8.30; EX 39.30.
Owner Michael Kelly **Bred** M W And Mrs B A Littlewort **Trained** Northleach, Gloucs
FOCUS
A selling-class maiden race in which Dot's Delight did not even need to match her poor recent form.
Red Fama Official explanation: trainer had no explanation for the poor form shown

553 LOVE IS IN THE AIR @ PONTIN'S (S) STKS 1m (F)
3:15 (3:15) (Class 6) 4-Y-0+ **£1,774** (£523; £262) **Stalls** Low

Form RPR
1312 **1** **Louisiade (IRE)**[10] 432 7-8-10 65 ....(p) MarkCoumbe(7) 2 65
(John A Harris) *sn w ldrs: led over 1f out: edgd lft: drew clr* **8/11**[1]
5-44 **2** *4* **Local Poet**[10] 433 7-8-9 55 ow1 ....(b) JamieMoriarty(3) 5 51
(Ollie Pears) *led: edgd rt over 2f out: hdd over 1f out: kpt on same pce* **9/2**[2]
-650 **3** *1 ½* **Shifty**[7] 465 9-8-11 48 .... PaulHanagan 6 46
(Jedd O'Keeffe) *w ldrs on outer: t.k.h: lost pl over 3f out: kpt on fnl 2f* **9/1**
4530 **4** *2 ½* **Lily La Belle**[13] 392 4-8-6 44 .... LiamJones 8 36
(A W Carroll) *w ldrs: drvn over 3f out: wknd over 1f out* **20/1**
0 **5** *5* **Art Of Being (IRE)**[6] 481 4-8-4 0 ....(p) PatrickDonaghy(7) 1 29
(M C Chapman) *s.s: sn chsng ldrs: outpcd and drvn 4f out: sn btn* **100/1**
000- **6** *½* **Pre Eminance (IRE)**[68] 7081 7-8-6 37 .... RussellKennemore(5) 4 28
(L R James) *w ldrs on outer: effrt over 3f out: sn btn* **50/1**
000- **7** *5* **Music Celebre (IRE)**[85] 6412 8-8-11 47 ....(b) PaulDoe 7 16
(S Curran) *w ldrs on wd outside: lost pl over 4f out: sn bhd* **5/1**[3]

1m 45.83s (2.13) **Going Correction** +0.25s/f (Slow) 7 Ran SP% **110.5**
Speed ratings (Par 101): **99,95,93,91,86 85,80**
CSF £3.92 TOTE £1.70: £1.10, £2.80; EX 4.50 Trifecta £8.30 Pool: £388.91 - 33.07 winning units..There was no bid for the winner.
Owner James Gordon-Hall **Bred** Mrs Noelle Walsh **Trained** Eastwell, Leics
■ Stewards' Enquiry : Jamie Moriarty one-day ban: failed to ride to draw (Feb 25)
Liam Jones one-day ban: failed to ride to draw (Feb 25)
FOCUS
The winner had 3lb in hand of the runner-up on official figures and made no mistake. Neither of the first two was at their best, the third limiting the form.

554 MY HEART BELONGS TO PONTIN'S H'CAP 5f (F)
3:50 (3:51) (Class 5) (0-70,70) 4-Y-0+ **£2,593** (£765; £383) **Stalls** High

Form RPR
2215 **1** **Savile's Delight (IRE)**[3] 521 9-8-6 58 6ex .... RichardKingscote 1 76+
(Tom Dascombe) *chsd ldrs: outpcd 3f out: hdwy to ld appr fnl f: v readily* **11/4**[2]
0-02 **2** *2 ½* **Spoof Master (IRE)**[7] 459 4-9-4 70 ....(p) JimCrowley 2 77
(S A Callaghan) *led tl appr fnl f: no ch w wnr* **2/1**[1]
-201 **3** *½* **Grand Palace (IRE)**[14] 370 5-9-0 66 ....(v) DeanMcKeown 4 71
(D Shaw) *bmpd s: sn chsng ldrs: kpt on same pce fnl f* **6/1**[3]
4-40 **4** *½* **Proud Killer**[8] 446 5-8-13 65 ....(v) ChrisCatlin 3 68
(J R Jenkins) *stl had blindfold on whn stalls opened: hdwy and edgd lft over 1f out: kpt on fnl f* **14/1**
60-4 **5** *nk* **Kelamon**[7] 463 4-8-13 70 .... PatrickHills(5) 7 72
(M D I Usher) *chsd ldrs: kpt on same pce appr fnl f* **12/1**
3-12 **6** *3* **Tag Team (IRE)**[25] 241 7-8-7 66 .... MarkCoumbe(7) 5 57
(John A Harris) *chsd ldrs: wknd over 1f out: lame* **6/1**[3]
0-53 **7** *¾* **Overstayed (IRE)**[11] 414 5-8-2 57 ....(be) JohnMcAuley(3) 6 46
(M Mullineaux) *sn outpcd and in rr* **11/1**
-502 **8** *3* **Astorygoeswithit**[14] 370 5-8-4 56 oh4 ....(be) LiamJones 8 34
(G C Bravery) *chsd ldrs: wknd over 1f out* **25/1**

60.48 secs (0.78) **Going Correction** +0.25s/f (Slow) 8 Ran SP% **115.1**
Speed ratings (Par 101): **103,99,98,97,96 92,90,86**
CSF £8.74 CT £28.97 TOTE £3.80: £1.40, £1.10, £2.30; EX 10.30 Trifecta £61.80 Pool: £450.41 - 5.17 winning units..
Owner ONEWAY Partners **Bred** Romany Investments Ltd **Trained** Lambourn, Berks
FOCUS
The winner has been a revelation over this trip here this winter and he took this in smashing style. He is rated back to his late 2005 form and there could be more to come from him here. Sound enough form overall.
Tag Team(IRE) Official explanation: jockey said gelding finished lame

555 EVERYBODY LOVES PONTIN'S BRILLIANT BLUE COATS H'CAP 7f (F)
4:25 (4:25) (Class 5) (0-70,70) 4-Y-0+ **£2,593** (£574; £574) **Stalls** Low

Form RPR
1-32 **1** **Kensington (IRE)**[5] 506 7-8-7 59 ....(p) JamesDoyle 3 62+
(P D Evans) *set modest pce and plld v hrd: hdd over 5f out: slt ld ins fnl f: hld on nr fin* **6/4**[1]
06-0 **2** *hd* **Music Note (IRE)**[22] 274 5-9-3 69 .... HayleyTurner 5 71
(Miss Gay Kelleway) *w ldr: led over 5f out: qcknd 3 out: hdd ins fnl f: no ex nr fin* **13/2**[2]
1351 **2** *dht* **Silver Hotspur**[10] 431 4-9-0 66 6ex .... FrancisNorton 6 68+
(M Wigham) *hld up on heels of ldrs: swtchd lft over 1f out: chal ins fnl f: nt qckn nr fin* **6/4**[1]
0033 **4** *¾* **Dancing Duo**[7] 465 4-7-11 56 oh7 ....(v) PatrickDonaghy(7) 1 56
(D Shaw) *s.i.s: sn chsng ldrs: effrt over 2f out: kpt on same pce fnl f* **20/1**
100- **5** *15* **Elusive Dreams (USA)**[139] 5768 4-9-0 66 .... DeanMcKeown 4 26
(D Shaw) *s.s: hld up in last: effrt over 2f out: sn lost pl and bhd: eased* **11/1**[3]

1m 31.31s (1.01) **Going Correction** +0.25s/f (Slow) 5 Ran SP% **106.4**
Speed ratings (Par 103): **104,103,103,102,85**
PL: Music Note £1.10, Silver Hotspur £0.60; EX: Music Note £5.00, Silver Hotspur £1.90; CSF: Music Note £5.49, Silver Hotspur £1.78 TOTE £2.40: £1.40.
Owner Derek Buckley **Bred** Mountarmstrong Stud **Trained** Pandy, Monmouths
■ Stewards' Enquiry : Hayley Turner two-day ban: used whip with excessive frequency without giving gelding time to respond (Feb 25-26)
FOCUS
A modest early pace and in reality just a three-furlong sprint with three in line inside the last.

556 ARENA LEISURE PLC H'CAP 1m (F)
4:55 (4:55) (Class 6) (0-60,63) 3-Y-0 **£1,911** (£564; £282) **Stalls** Low

Form RPR
04-3 **1** **Ten Spot (IRE)**[23] 262 3-8-11 52 ....(v) MickyFenton 6 64
(Stef Liddiard) *trckd ldrs: led 2f out: sn wnt clr: eased ins fnl f* **8/1**
-662 **2** *5* **Coral Shores**[9] 439 3-8-4 45 ....(v) ChrisCatlin 5 46
(P W Hiatt) *sn led: hdd over 5f out: led 3f out tl 2f out: kpt on: no ch w wnr* **4/1**[2]
00-2 **3** *4* **Rhode Island Red (USA)**[20] 306 3-9-3 58 ....(v) RichardKingscote 2 49
(H J L Dunlop) *in rr: sn drvn along: plld wd over 5f out: edgd lft over 2f out: kpt on* **14/1**
000- **4** *hd* **Hits Only Time**[108] 6530 3-9-4 59 .... DeanMcKeown 3 50
(J Pearce) *trckd ldrs: t.k.h: effrt over 2f out: one pce* **9/4**[1]
0-40 **5** *5* **Plaka (FR)**[21] 288 3-9-1 56 .... LiamJones 7 35
(W M Brisbourne) *w ldrs: drvn over 4f out: lost pl 2f out* **20/1**
2212 **6** *3 ½* **Hawa Khana (IRE)**[2] 534 3-9-5 63 6ex ....(p) KirstyMilczarek(3) 1 34
(N P Littmoden) *led after 1f tl 3f out: sn edgd rt and wknd* **9/4**[1]
-064 **7** *16* **Tobouggornotobougg**[9] 439 3-8-3 47 ow2 ....(v) TolleyDean(3) 4 —
(D Shaw) *broke first: sn hdd: drvn and dropped to rr over 5f out: sn bhd: eased ins fnl f* **15/2**[3]

1m 44.95s (1.25) **Going Correction** +0.25s/f (Slow) 7 Ran SP% **115.8**
Speed ratings (Par 95): **103,98,94,93,88 85,69**
CSF £40.76 TOTE £10.90: £3.30, £2.10; EX 33.40 Place 6 £47.84, Place 5 £26.33.
Owner Mrs Felicity Ashfield **Bred** Kilshannig Stud **Trained** Great Shefford, Berks
FOCUS
A low-grade handicap run at a steady pace until the final turn. Improved form from Ten Spot, rated through the runner-up.
Tobouggornotobougg Official explanation: trainer said having been restrained at start gelding sulked
T/Plt: £53.80 to a £1 stake. Pool: £42,300.75. 573.50 winning tickets. T/Qpdt: £3.10 to a £1 stake. Pool: £3,128.00. 737.50 winning tickets. WG

521 WOLVERHAMPTON (A.W) (L-H)
Thursday, February 14

OFFICIAL GOING: Standard
Racing was delayed half an hour by a power cut.
Wind: Light, half-against Weather: Overcast

557 LADBROKES REWARDS LOYALTY H'CAP 5f 216y(P)
6:50 (7:20) (Class 6) (0-60,61) 3-Y-0 **£1,774** (£523; £262) **Stalls** Low

Form RPR
6651 **1** **Seductive Witch**[10] 425 3-8-11 54 6ex .... JamesDoyle 4 57
(M D I Usher) *mde all: rdn over 1f out: edgd lft: r.o* **15/2**
62-0 **2** *1 ½* **Rich James (IRE)**[39] 70 3-8-7 50 .... JimmyQuinn 5 48
(J D Bethell) *chsd wnr: rdn over 1f out: styd on* **17/2**
0-31 **3** *hd* **Lujiana**[9] 444 3-9-1 61 6ex .... MarkLawson(3) 7 59+
(M Brittain) *stmbld s: hld up: hung rt 1/2-way: hdwy over 2f out: rdn and hung lft fnl f: r.o* **7/4**[1]
4452 **4** *hd* **Weetfromthechaff**[13] 397 3-9-0 57 ....(v) HayleyTurner 2 54
(R Hollinshead) *trckd ldrs: rdn over 1f out: no ex ins fnl f* **3/1**[2]
4-43 **5** *1* **Whitcombe Flyer (USA)**[20] 298 3-8-9 52 ....(b) LPKeniry 3 46
(Miss M E Rowland) *prom: rdn and nt clr run wl over 1f out: styd on same pce* **13/2**[3]
034- **6** *1 ½* **Planet Paradise (IRE)**[206] 3788 3-7-11 47 oh1 ow1 PatrickDonaghy(7) 6 36
(D Shaw) *hld up: plld hrd: rdn 1/2-way: hung lft over 1f out: nt trble ldrs* **25/1**
00-4 **7** *1 ¼* **Miss Deeds (IRE)**[20] 298 3-8-3 46 oh1 .... RichardThomas 8 31
(N P Littmoden) *chsd ldrs: rdn over 2f out: wknd ins fnl f* **12/1**
30-6 **8** *nk* **Yattendon**[36] 102 3-8-10 60 .... MatthewBirch(7) 1 44
(S Kirk) *stdd s: hld up: sme hdwy over 1f out: wknd ins fnl f* **14/1**

1m 17.39s (2.39) **Going Correction** +0.20s/f (Slow) 8 Ran SP% **115.2**
Speed ratings (Par 95): **92,90,89,89,88 86,84,84**
CSF £68.94 CT £160.73 TOTE £5.20: £1.20, £3.10, £1.10; EX 60.80.
Owner Bryan Fry And The Toerags **Bred** B Minty **Trained** Upper Lambourn, Berks
FOCUS
A modest three-year-old sprint in which a couple compromised their own chances, whilst the winner had the run of the race and made all off a steady pace. Weak form

Lujiana ◆ Official explanation: jockey said filly stumbled at the start and hung right throughout

558 DOUBLE POINTS BONUSES LOYALTY CARD (S) STKS 5f 20y(P)
7:20 (7:45) (Class 6) 3-Y-O+ £1,774 (£523; £262) Stalls Low

Form RPR
0-05 1 **Geordie Dancer (IRE)**[21] 285 6-9-2 37..........(b) DanielleMcCreery(5) 5 46
(A Berry) *s.i.s: hld up: hdwy 1/2-way: chsd ldr over 1f out: rdn to ld wl ins fnl f* 16/1
0-53 2 ¾ **Highland Song (IRE)**[10] 437 5-9-7 47.......................... ChrisCatlin 4 43
(R F Fisher) *chsd ldrs: led 1/2-way: sn edgd lft: rdn over 1f out: hung rt and hdd wl ins fnl f* 8/13[1]
6000 3 1 ¾ **The Carpet Man**[3] 523 4-9-4 43.................. KirstyMilczarek(3) 1 37
(A W Carroll) *sn outpcd: nt clr run 1/2-way: hdwy over 1f out: sn rdn and hung lft: nt rch ldrs* 3/1[2]
6/55 4 7 **Ela Aleka Mou**[27] 208 4-9-2 70.......................... PaulEddery 2 7
(Miss D Mountain) *s.i.s: sn drvn along: hdwy to ld over 3f out: hdd 1/2-way: n.m.r sn after: wknd over 1f out* 6/1[3]
06-0 5 2 **Baytown Paikea**[9] 440 4-8-9 50.......................... JackDean(7) 3 —
(W G M Turner) *led: hdd over 3f out: hmpd 1/2-way: wknd wl over 1f out* 12/1

64.84 secs (2.54) **Going Correction** +0.20s/f (Slow) 5 Ran SP% 114.8
Speed ratings (Par 101): **87,85,83,71,68**
CSF £28.41 TOTE £12.90: £5.00, £1.10; EX 30.20.There was no bid for the winner.
Owner Alan Berry **Bred** Ronnie Boland **Trained** Cockerham, Lancs

FOCUS
Sellers do not come much worse than this and it produced a shock result with a six-year-old gelding rated just 37 beating the odds-on favourite. Dubious form. A three-horse war for the lead probably played into the hands of the winner.

559 LADBROKES, LOYALTY CARD H'CAP 1m 1f 103y(P)
7:50 (8:10) (Class 6) (0-60,60) 4-Y-O+ £1,774 (£523; £262) Stalls Low

Form RPR
4-62 1 **Micky Mac (IRE)**[13] 389 4-8-10 **52**.......................... GrahamGibbons 9 64
(T D Walford) *hld up in tch: racd keenly: rdn to ld over 1f out: styd on* 5/1
0-00 2 ½ **Mighty Mover (IRE)**[19] 323 6-8-13 **55**.......................... CatherineGannon 3 66
(B Palling) *led: rdn: edgd rt and hdd over 1f out: styd on* 11/1
140- 3 3 **Terminate (GER)**[49] 6458 6-8-12 **54**.......................... ChrisCatlin 5 59
(Ian Williams) *mid-div: pushed along 6f out: hdwy u.p over 1f out: nrst fin* 15/2
1213 4 ½ **Buscador (USA)**[19] 323 9-9-1 **57**.......................... RichardKingscote 7 61
(W M Brisbourne) *prom: chsd ldr over 4f out: rdn over 2f out: styd on same pce appr fnl f* 5/2[1]
-321 5 hd **Pianoforte (USA)**[14] 373 6-9-2 **58**..........................(b) JimmyQuinn 2 61
(E J Alston) *hld up in tch: rdn to chse ldr 2f out: no ex fnl f* 4/1[3]
5-52 6 4 **Amical Risks (FR)**[8] 451 4-9-3 **59**.......................... TPQueally 8 54
(W J Musson) *s.i.s: hld up: rdn over 3f out: hung lft over 1f out: nvr trbld ldrs* 7/2[2]
0-02 7 1 ½ **Tidy (IRE)**[26] 229 8-8-5 **52** ow2..........................(v) JackMitchell(5) 4 44
(Micky Hammond) *hld up: n.d* 25/1
00-5 8 nk **Besi**[10] 433 6-9-1 **60**.......................... MarkLawson(3) 6 51
(A Berry) *chsd ldrs: rdn over 3f out: wknd 2f out* 50/1
060- 9 3 ½ **Alekhine (IRE)**[106] 6598 7-9-3 **59**.......................... VinceSlattery 1 43
(J W Unett) *s.i.s: a in rr* 40/1
660- 10 36 **Grey Light (IRE)**[22] 1624 4-9-4 **60**..........................(p) PaulHanagan 10 —
(L Lungo) *chsd ldr 5f: sn rdn and wknd* 18/1

2m 2.73s (1.03) **Going Correction** +0.20s/f (Slow) 10 Ran SP% 121.1
Speed ratings (Par 101): **103,102,99,99,99 95,94,94,91,59**
CSF £59.89 CT £418.03 TOTE £7.30: £2.80, £3.90, £3.90; EX 79.00.
Owner A M McArdle **Bred** Stephen O'Rourke **Trained** Sheriff Hutton, N Yorks
■ A first winner back following a three-month ban for failing a breathalyser test for jockey Graham Gibbons.

FOCUS
Quite a competitive handicap of its type and with a couple of established front-runners in the field the pace was a solid one. Fairly sound form, the winner up 4lb.

560 POINTS MEAN PRIZES LOYALTY CARD H'CAP 1m 141y(P)
8:20 (8:36) (Class 6) (0-60,60) 4-Y-O+ £1,774 (£523; £262) Stalls Low

Form RPR
0-22 1 **Supercast (IRE)**[19] 323 5-9-4 **60**.......................... SamHitchcott 1 68+
(N J Vaughan) *trckd ldrs: swtchd rt wl over 1f out: rdn to ld 1f out: r.o* 15/8[1]
-242 2 nk **Ermine Grey**[7] 468 7-8-5 **50**.......................... KirstyMilczarek(3) 9 57+
(A W Carroll) *s.i.s: hld up: hdwy over 1f out: hung lft and r.o ins fnl f* 9/2[3]
-200 3 1 ¾ **Krakatau (FR)**[15] 352 4-8-12 **54**.......................... VinceSlattery 5 57
(D J Wintle) *chsd ldrs: rdn over 2f out: styd on u.p* 14/1
1-21 4 nk **The Salwick Flyer (IRE)**[27] 214 5-9-0 **56**.......................... PhillipMakin 7 58
(Miss L A Perratt) *hld up: plld hrd: hdwy over 2f out: sn rdn: styng on same pce whn nt clr run ins fnl f* 11/4[2]
330- 5 shd **Muncaster Castle (IRE)**[72] 7023 4-8-13 **55**.......................... ChrisCatlin 4 57
(R F Fisher) *chsd ldr tl led over 2f out: rdn and hdd 1f out: no ex towards fin* 12/1
66-5 6 ½ **Espejo (IRE)**[13] 389 4-8-12 **54**.......................... NeilPollard 3 55
(W J Musson) *s.i.s: hld up: rdn over 2f out: hung lft fr over 1f out: nt rch ldrs* 16/1
50-0 7 1 **Golden Spectrum (IRE)**[13] 395 9-8-12 **59**..........(b) KevinGhunowa(5) 2 58
(R A Harris) *hld up: plld hrd: rdn over 2f out: styd on same pce fnl f* 16/1
5-54 8 1 **Johnston's Glory (IRE)**[14] 375 4-8-8 **50**.......................... JimmyQuinn 8 46
(E J Alston) *hld up: nt clr run 2f out: hdwy over 1f out: no ex fnl f* 7/1
40-0 9 3 ½ **Briery Blaze**[17] 338 5-8-10 **52** ow4.......................... GrahamGibbons 6 40
(J W Unett) *led: rdn and hdd over 2f out: wknd over 1f out* 25/1

1m 52.66s (2.16) **Going Correction** +0.20s/f (Slow) 9 Ran SP% 122.1
Speed ratings (Par 101): **98,97,96,95,95 95,94,93,90**
CSF £11.46 CT £96.22 TOTE £3.20: £1.20, £2.60, £9.80; EX 17.70.
Owner Stephen Walker **Bred** J Egan, J Corcoran And J Judd **Trained** Hampton Heat, Cheshire

FOCUS
A modest handicap and the early pace was not strong. As a result the whole field were within a couple of lengths of each other approaching the furlong pole. It is doubtful if the winner had to improve on his latest effort but both he and the second shaped better than the bare form here.

561 JOIN THE ODDS ON CLUB AT LADBROKES H'CAP 1m 5f 194y(P)
8:50 (9:00) (Class 4) (0-85,83) 4-Y-O+ £4,210 (£1,252; £625; £312) Stalls Low

Form RPR
2/3- 1 **Buster Hyvonen (IRE)**[49] 1272 6-9-7 **76**.......................... OscarUrbina 4 88
(J R Fanshawe) *hld up: racd keenly: hdwy over 3f out: led and hung lft fr over 1f out: drvn out* 4/1[2]
5123 2 ¾ **Calculating (IRE)**[9] 443 4-9-0 **74**.......................... HayleyTurner 7 85
(M D I Usher) *chsd ldrs: rdn over 3f out: ev ch whn carried lft over 1f out: n.m.r ins fnl f: styd on* 11/2
-343 3 7 **Pret A Porter (UAE)**[5] 510 4-8-9 **69**.......................... JimmyQuinn 3 70
(P D Evans) *chsd ldrs: rdn over 3f out: wknd 2f out* 5/1[3]
645/ 4 2 **Rehearsal**[282] 5361 7-10-0 **83**.......................... PaulHanagan 8 81
(L Lungo) *led: rdn and hdd over 2f out: wknd over 1f out* 14/1
3-14 5 1 ½ **Noble Plum (IRE)**[23] 260 4-9-8 **82**.......................... SebSanders 1 78
(Sir Mark Prescott) *chsd ldr tl led over 2f out: rdn and hdd over 1f out: sn wknd* 9/4[1]
2-55 6 7 **Pass The Port**[23] 260 7-9-11 **80**.......................... RobertHavlin 6 67
(D Haydn Jones) *hld up: rdn over 3f out: n.d* 4/1[2]
040- 7 1 ¾ **Petrovich (USA)**[69] 7055 5-9-4 **78**..........................(t) KevinGhunowa(5) 5 62
(R A Harris) *chsd ldrs: sn pushed along: wknd over 4f out* 50/1
62-1 8 hd **Opera Writer (IRE)**[19] 320 5-8-2 **64** oh3.......................... PatrickDonaghy(7) 2 48
(R Hollinshead) *hld up: hdwy over 5f out: rdn and wknd wl over 3f out* 9/1

3m 5.40s (-0.60) **Going Correction** +0.20s/f (Slow)
WFA 4 from 5yo+ 5lb 8 Ran SP% 121.4
Speed ratings (Par 105): **109,108,104,103,102 98,97,97**
CSF £28.07 CT £115.38 TOTE £4.70: £2.00, £1.40, £1.80; EX 24.50.
Owner Simon Gibson **Bred** Hollington Stud **Trained** Newmarket, Suffolk
■ Stewards' Enquiry : Oscar Urbina one-day ban: careless riding (Feb 25)

FOCUS
A fair handicap and the decent pace set by Rehearsal, constantly hassled by Noble Plum, led to a fair winning time for the grade. This rather set the race up for the finishers and the front pair pulled right away. Sound form.
Petrovich(USA) Official explanation: jockey said horse became unbalanced

562 WILL YOU MARRY ME RICHARD? CLASSIFIED STKS 5f 20y(P)
9:20 (9:25) (Class 7) 4-Y-O+ £1,365 (£403; £201) Stalls Low

Form RPR
4042 1 **Blackheath (IRE)**[3] 522 12-8-9 45.......................... KellyHarrison(5) 3 61
(S T Mason) *chsd ldr: hmpd over 3f out: led over 1f out: rdr dropped whip ins fnl f: r.o wl* 13/8[1]
0-42 2 4 **Maktavish**[9] 440 9-9-0 42..........................(b) PhillipMakin 5 46
(R Brotherton) *led: edgd lft over 3f out: rdn: edgd rt and hdd over 1f out: no ex fnl f* 4/1[3]
004- 3 3 ½ **Desert Hunter (IRE)**[156] 5295 5-9-0 45.......................... JimmyQuinn 7 34+
(Micky Hammond) *s.i.s: outpcd: styd on ins fnl f: nrst fin* 11/4[2]
-332 4 ½ **Lady Hopeful (IRE)**[20] 297 6-9-0 45..........................(b) LPKeniry 4 32
(Peter Grayson) *chsd ldrs: rdn 2f out: wkng whn hung rt fnl f* 6/1
-000 5 ¾ **Dotty's Daughter**[15] 363 4-8-11 38..........................(p) PJMcDonald(3) 6 29
(B Storey) *chsd ldrs 3f* 28/1
000- 6 3 **Alexia Rose (IRE)**[65] 7108 6-8-9 39.......................... DanielleMcCreery(5) 1 19
(A Berry) *s.s: outpcd* 33/1
2-00 7 1 ½ **George The Best (IRE)**[26] 232 7-9-0 43.......................... DeanMcKeown 2 13
(Micky Hammond) *prom: lost pl wl over 3f out: sn bhd* 11/1
-505 8 5 **Lady Fas (IRE)**[20] 297 5-8-11 39.......................... KirstyMilczarek(3) 8 —
(A W Carroll) *mid-div: rdn over 3f out: wknd 1/2-way* 18/1

62.74 secs (0.44) **Going Correction** +0.20s/f (Slow) 8 Ran SP% 119.0
Speed ratings (Par 97): **104,97,92,91,90 85,82,74**
CSF £8.96 TOTE £2.40: £1.90, £1.10, £1.50; EX 11.90 Place 6 £53.84, Place 5 £28.94.
Owner Middleham Park Racing XX **Bred** John McKay **Trained** Lanchester, Co. Durham

FOCUS
About as modest a "banded" event as you could ask for and fairly routine for the favourite. The pace was a decent one though, and the winning time was over two seconds faster than the earlier seller. The form is rated through the first two.
Alexia Rose(IRE) Official explanation: jockey said mare missed the break
George The Best(IRE) Official explanation: jockey said gelding hung badly left
Lady Fas(IRE) Official explanation: jockey said saddle slipped
T/Plt: £52.00 to a £1 stake. Pool: £81,443.05. 1,141.25 winning tickets. T/Qpdt: £21.80 to a £1 stake. Pool: £4,991.50. 169.40 winning tickets. CR

[491] NAD AL SHEBA (L-H)
Thursday, February 14
OFFICIAL GOING: Turf course - good; dirt course - fast

563a WHEELS H'CAP (DIRT) 7f 110y(D)
3:30 (3:30) (95-110,100) 3-Y-O+
£36,180 (£12,060; £6,030; £3,015; £1,809; £1,206)

RPR
1 **Drift Ice (SAF)**[7] 472 7-9-2 **98**..........................(b) KShea 4 100
(M F De Kock, South Africa) *trckd ldr on rail: no room 2 1/2f out: swtchd 1 1/2f out: led 100yds out: r.o wl* 11/2[3]
2 ¼ **Almaram (USA)**[7] 473 8-9-3 **99**..........................(e) JMurtagh 8 100
(D Selvaratnam, UAE) *sn led on rail: rdn clr 2f out: hdd fnl f: battled bk* 7/2[2]
3 1 ¼ **Ukrainian (BRZ)**[21] 292 4-8-4 **95**.......................... RichardMullen 6 84+
(A Cintra Pereira, Brazil) *settled in rr: wd 3f out: r.o wl fnl f: nrst fin* 12/1
4 3 ½ **Stepping Up (IRE)**[13] 5-9-4 **100**..........................(t) TPO'Shea 10 90
(E Charpy, UAE) *mid-div: rdn and hung 2 1/2f out: r.o same pce* 14/1
5 2 ¼ **San Domenico**[21] 291 4-9-1 **97**.......................... RyanMoore 9 81
(Doug Watson, UAE) *trckd ldr: rdn and ev ch 2f out: wknd fnl f* 20/1
6 1 ½ **Rockets 'n Rollers (IRE)**[6] 492 8-8-12 **95**..........(p) RoystonFfrench 5 75
(A Manuel, UAE) *mid-div: rdn 3f out: nvr able to chal* 20/1
7 ¼ **Akona Matata (USA)**[14] 382 6-9-1 **97**.......................... DO'Donohoe 2 77
(Doug Watson, UAE) *slowly away: rdn in rr 2 1/2f out: nvr nr to chal* 11/4[1]
8 3 ½ **Safety Investments (AUS)**[14] 380 9-9-4 **100**..........(t) MJKinane 3 72
(J Lau, Macau) *settled in rr: nvr able to chal* 11/2[3]
9 3 ¼ **Latino Magic (IRE)**[14] 384 8-9-4 **100**.......................... PJSmullen 1 64
(D K Weld, Ire) *slowly away: in rr on rail 3f out: nvr able to chal* 7/1
10 1 ¾ **Mezel (USA)**[14] 384 5-9-4 **100**..........................(v) TedDurcan 7 60
(S Seemar, UAE) *slowly away: trckd ldrs: rdn 3f out: sn wknd* 33/1

1m 30.09s (-1.21) **Going Correction** +0.075s/f (Slow) 10 Ran SP% 119.0
Speed ratings: **109,108,107,103,101 100,99,96,93,91**
CSF 24.97; TRI 226.25.
Owner Sh Rashid bin Humaid Al Nuaimi **Bred** Lammerskraal Stud **Trained** South Africa

FOCUS
Just an ordinary handicap for the level, but run at a sound pace.

NOTEBOOK

Drift Ice(SAF) gained his second win of this year's carnival due to a good bit of placing by his trainer. Having won on the turf off a mark of 100 two starts back, he could make no impression off his new rating of 106 last time but, returned to dirt, he was able to race off just 98, and he took full advantage. This trip was a slight concern beforehand, with his best previous efforts coming over shorter, but he saw his race out well. Having tracked Almaram through for much of the way, he had to switch off the rail and come round that rival in the straight, but he kept responding to pressure and just got the call. A rise in the weights will bring his dirt mark more in line with his turf rating and that should be enough to stop him following up. (op 5/1)

Almaram(USA) was only 4lb higher than when a narrow winner over the bare 7f here the previous week and he was just held. He had the run of the race and a further rise in the weights for this could make him hard to win with. (op 4/1)

Ukrainian(BRZ) made up for a no-show in a 2000 Guineas trial on his debut in Dubai, but he is a dual winner on the dirt in Brazil and this was better. He looked dangerous when produced wide at the top of the straight, but his effort flattened out late on.

Stepping Up(IRE) was having just his second start since returning from a long absence and this was a creditable effort.

San Domenico, switched to dirt having shown little on the turf on his debut in Dubai, had every chance if good enough.

Akona Matata(USA) was nowhere near the form he showed when second over 1m round here on his previous start and, considering this was his third outing after being given two runs in the space of a month since returning from over a year off, he might have bounced. (tchd 5/2)

Latino Magic(IRE) was never a factor on this switch to dirt.

564a GNADS4U H'CAP (DIRT) — 1m (D)

4:10 (4:10) (90-105,104) 3-Y-O+

£33,165 (£11,055; £5,527; £2,763; £1,658; £1,105)

RPR

1 **Blackat Blackitten (IRE)**[14] 382 4-9-6 **104** .... LDettori 8 113+
(Saeed Bin Suroor) *mid-div: rdn 2 1/2f out: swtchd wd: r.o: led cl home* **1/1**[1]

2 *3/4* **Golden Arrow (IRE)**[13] 5-9-3 **100** .... (bt) PJSmullen 11 106
(E Charpy, UAE) *trckd ldrs: led 1f out: hdd last strides* **20/1**

3 *1 1/4* **Halkin (USA)**[657] 6-8-11 **95** .... MO'Callaghan 9 97
(F Nass, Bahrain) *mid-div: smooth prog to chal 2 1/2f out: led 1 1/2f out: sn hdd: r.o* **50/1**

4 *1 1/4* **Escape Route (USA)**[7] 474 4-8-11 **95** .... RichardMullen 15 94
(J H M Gosden) *mid-div: wd: rdn 3f out: r.o fnl 2f* **14/1**

5 *1 1/4* **Mulaqat**[6] 491 5-9-3 **100** .... (e) JMurtagh 10 97
(D Selvaratnam, UAE) *racd in rr: r.o fnl 1 1/2f: nvr able to chal* **25/1**

6 *1 1/2* **Montpellier (IRE)**[14] 383 5-8-7 **90** .... RoystonFfrench 13 84
(A Al Raihe, UAE) *trckd ldrs: t.k.h 3f out: ev ch 2 1/2f out: wknd fnl f* **28/1**

7 *3/4* **Accountforthegold (USA)**[207] 6-9-5 **102** .... KerrinMcEvoy 14 94
(Saeed Bin Suroor) *trckd ldrs: wd 3f out: n.d afterwards* **7/1**[3]

8 *hd* **Salt Track (ARG)**[14] 382 8-8-11 **95** .... (t) ESki 2 86
(Niels Petersen, Norway) *sn last: r.o fnl 1 1/2f: nvr able to chal* **28/1**

9 *shd* **Roman's Run (USA)**[13] 4-8-11 **95** .... (t) MartinDwyer 1 85
(Doug Watson, UAE) *disp on rail: rdn 3f out: wknd 2f out* **14/1**

10 *2 1/4* **Ketter (BRZ)**[707] 7-8-9 **93** .... DSmith 6 78
(R Bouresly, Kuwait) *a in rr* **66/1**

11 *1/2* **Gongidas**[14] 382 4-8-9 **93** .... (v) TedDurcan 3 77
(Saeed Bin Suroor) *slowly away: sn trckd ldrs: rdn 3f out: nvr a threat* **6/1**[2]

12 *4 3/4* **Skywards**[7] 473 6-8-8 **91** .... (t) TPO'Shea 12 65
(E Charpy, UAE) *mid-div: rdn 2 1/2f out: nvr able to chal* **11/1**

13 *1 1/4* **Montalba (USA)**[7] 473 8-8-7 **90** .... (be) DO'Donohoe 4 61
(J Lau, Macau) *trckd ldr: t.k.h for 3f: sn btn* **40/1**

14 *4 3/4* **Naipe Marcado (URU)**[14] 382 5-8-11 **95** .... (v) WJSupple 5 54
(Saeed Bin Suroor) *disp to 3f out: wknd* **50/1**

1m 36.34s (-0.36) **Going Correction** +0.075s/f (Slow) **14** Ran SP% **121.8**
Speed ratings: **104,103,102,100,99 98,97,97,96,94 94,89,88,83**
CSF 30.06; TRI 693.50.

Owner Sheikh Hamdan Bin Mohammed Al Maktoum **Bred** Conor Murphy **Trained** Newmarket, Suffolk

FOCUS

A decent race, certainly a stronger race than many of the dirt handicaps at this year's carnival.

NOTEBOOK

Blackat Blackitten(IRE) looked to have plenty on his plate having been raised 9lb for his recent course-and-distance success, particularly with the runner-up that day finishing well behind in the first race on this card, but he is highly progressive and defied his new mark a shade cosily. He was under pressure a fair way out and seemed to hit a bit of a flat spot when in the clear early in the straight, but he picked up well late on and was nicely on top at the line. This was a smart effort, but he gives the impression he might do even better once returned to turf. (op 5/4)

Golden Arrow(IRE), runner-up in a 1m Listed event at Jebel Ali on his previous start, was always well placed and stayed on to the line, but the winner was ultimately too strong. (op 18/1)

Halkin(USA), a multiple Group winner on the turf in Bahrain in 2006, ran a massive race switched to dirt on his debut in Dubai off the back of a 657-day absence. Having travelled well in behind the leaders, he looked the most likely winner when produced with a strong challenge halfway up the straight, but he understandably got tired late on. (op 33/1)

Escape Route(USA), trying dirt for the first time, stayed on from off the pace without ever looking like getting there. (op 12/1)

Mulaqat, dropped in trip with an eyeshield replacing blinkers, met trouble after getting outpaced turning for home, but he ran on in the straight. A return to further should help and he seems in good order.

Montpellier(IRE), tried on dirt for the first time, was tanking along turning for home, but he did not see his race out.

Accountforthegold(USA), a multiple winner in the USA, including in Grade 3 company, was disappointing off the back of a 207-day break on his debut for Godolphin. He seemed a little keen towards the outside early on and failed to land a blow. (op 6/1)

Gongidas was rushed up after again starting slowly, but offered little under pressure.

565a SPORT EXTRA H'CAP (TURF) — 1m 2f (T)

4:50 (4:50) (100-115,115) 3-Y-O+

£52,763 (£17,587; £8,793; £4,396; £2,638; £1,758)

RPR

1 **With Interest**[21] 294 5-8-9 **102** .... LDettori 7 99
(Saeed Bin Suroor) *mid-div: smooth prog to ld 1 1/2f out: sn hdd: led nr line* **5/4**[1]

2 *hd* **Gower Song**[14] 381 5-8-8 **101** .... TedDurcan 6 98
(D R C Elsworth) *settled in rr: trckd wnr 3f out: led 1f out: r.o wl but hdd last strides* **15/2**

3 *5 1/4* **Yasoodd**[14] 383 5-9-4 **111** .... (e) JMurtagh 5 98
(D Selvaratnam, UAE) *mid-div: trckd wnr 2f out: r.o same pce* **6/1**[2]

4 *1 1/2* **Halicarnassus (IRE)**[81] 6943 4-9-6 **115** .... DarryllHolland 4 98
(M R Channon) *settled in rr: no room 2 1/2f out: swtchd and r.o last 1 1/2f* **13/2**[3]

5 *3 1/4* **Arqaam**[13] 4-8-12 **107** .... MartinDwyer 3 83
(Doug Watson, UAE) *slowly away: settled in last: nvr nr to chal* **14/1**

6 *12* **Arabian Prince (USA)**[7] 477 5-8-8 **101** .... (v) MJKinane 2 54
(Doug Watson, UAE) *trckd ldr: rdn 3f out: sn wknd* **9/1**

7 *shd* **Great Plains**[21] 293 6-8-10 **104** .... RHills 1 56
(E Charpy, UAE) *sn led: t.k.h: rdn 2 1/2f out: hdd 1 1/2f out: wknd* **7/1**

2m 7.65s (3.15) **Going Correction** +0.625s/f (Yiel)
WFA 4 from 5yo+ 1lb **7** Ran SP% **113.0**
Speed ratings: **112,111,107,106,103 94,94**
CSF 11.02.

Owner Godolphin **Bred** George Strawbridge **Trained** Newmarket, Suffolk

FOCUS

A slightly disappointing turnout numerically, with just the seven lining up, but still a very good handicap and the time was good.

NOTEBOOK

With Interest had shaped well on his return from a long absence over an extended 7f round here on his previous start and was able to confirm that promise, with the longer trip no problem to him, but he was made to work very hard. Having had to be niggled before the turn for home, he came back on the bridle and seemed to be travelling well early in the straight, but he could only find the one pace once let down. To his credit he kept finding, which enabled him to peg back the weak-finishing Gower Song and get up the near the line. He will need to step forward again to make the jump up to Pattern company, but he has always promised to develop into a very smart sort and there could be more to come when there is a bit of give underfoot. (op 11/8)

Gower Song gave the impression she would be suited by the drop back to this trip when failing to see out her race over 1m4f on her debut in Dubai and she looked set to win quite well when going on after travelling well around two furlongs from the finish, but she again finished her race weakly and was reeled in near the line. She does not look ungenuine, but she just looks to have a burst of speed that lasts about 100 yards or so and she will want holding on to for longer next time. (tchd 8/1)

Yasoodd, third in an ordinary Group 3 over an extended 1m round here on his previous start, could find only the one pace under pressure and was no match for the front two.

Halicarnassus(IRE) had no easy task off top weight and was well held. He took a while to get going and might have fared better ridden closer to the pace, but he is entitled to come on for this first run in nearly three months. (tchd 7/1)

Arqaam, a lightly-raced colt, never threatened on his return to turf.

Arabian Prince(USA), with a visor on this time, was well beaten. (op 8/1)

Great Plains was allowed his own way in front, but never really settled and set a reasonable pace considering the small field. (op 6/1)

566a XPRESS SPRINT (CONDITIONS RACE) (DIRT) — 5f (D)

5:25 (5:25) 3-Y-O+

£33,165 (£11,055; £5,527; £2,763; £1,658; £1,105)

RPR

1 **Star Crowned (USA)**[27] 5-9-4 87 .... (t) BrettDoyle 4 100
(R Bouresly, Kuwait) *trckd ldr: led 2f out: r.o wl* **14/1**

2 *3/4* **Sir Edwin Landseer (USA)**[42] 8-8-12 91 .... (p) PaulMulrennan 12 91
(Christian Wroe) *mid-div: trckd wnr 2 1/2f out: r.o wl fnl 1 1/2f: nrst fin* **25/1**

3 *1/2* **Salaam Dubai (AUS)**[21] 295 7-9-4 107 .... (v) RichardMullen 11 95
(A Selvaratnam, UAE) *mid-div on rail: rdn 3f out: r.o fnl 1 1/2f: nrst fin* **4/6**[1]

4 *3/4* **Malayeen (AUS)**[21] 295 6-8-12 100 .... (v) AhmedAjtebi(6) 2 93
(A Selvaratnam, UAE) *led: hdd 2f out: one pce* **5/1**[2]

5 *1 1/4* **Belpasso (IRE)**[13] 5-8-12 68 .... (t) DarryllHolland 14 82
(A Selvaratnam, UAE) *racd in rr: n.d but r.o fnl 2f* **33/1**

6 *1/2* **Conceal**[6] 497 10-8-12 90 .... DSmith 9 80
(R Bouresly, Kuwait) *racd in rr: rdn 2 1/2f out: r.o fnl 1 1/2f* **20/1**

7 *1 1/2* **Guertino (IRE)**[42] 3-8-2 85 ow1 .... TPO'Shea 6 79
(E Charpy, UAE) *slowly away: mid-div: no room 2 1/2f out: r.o fnl 1 1/2f* **33/1**

8 *1/2* **Raging Creek (USA)**[13] 9-8-12 63 .... (t) DO'Donohoe 13 73
(R Bouresly, Kuwait) *nvr nr to chal: mod prog* **100/1**

9 *2 1/2* **Canadian Danehill (IRE)**[6] 492 6-9-4 95 .... (p) LDettori 3 70
(R M H Cowell) *broke awkwardly: racd alone in centre: rdn bhd ldrs 2f out: wknd* **11/1**[3]

10 *3/4* **Rochdale**[6] 492 5-8-12 85 .... RoystonFfrench 1 61
(A Al Raihe, UAE) *mid-div: nvr nr to chal* **20/1**

11 *1/2* **Chaplinesque (USA)**[14] 378 9-8-12 94 .... CharlotteKerton 10 60
(A Selvaratnam, UAE) *a in rr* **66/1**

12 *6 1/4* **New Art (USA)**[912] 4456 5-8-12 80 .... MartinDwyer 8 37
(R Bouresly, Kuwait) *in rr of mid-div: nvr able to chal* **20/1**

13 *1/2* **Melhor Impossivel (BRZ)**[35] 7-9-4 82 .... TedDurcan 7 41
(A Selvaratnam, UAE) *a struggling* **18/1**

56.30 secs (-2.10) **Going Correction** -0.15s/f (Stan)
WFA 3 from 5yo+ 14lb **13** Ran SP% **123.4**
Speed ratings: **110,108,108,106,104 104,101,100,96,95 94,84,84**
CSF 318.53.

Owner Bouresly Racing Syndicate **Bred** Carl Rosen Associates **Trained** Kuwait

FOCUS

As has tended to be the theme on the straight course this year, they raced middle to stands' side and those towards the near rail looked to be at an advantage. Four of the first six home were drawn in the top six stalls. This was just an ordinary sprint contest and Aditiyan Selvaratnam and Rashed Bouresly accounted for nine of the 13 runners.

NOTEBOOK

Star Crowned(USA) had been off the track for well over a year after winning a 1m maiden at Windsor for Brian Meehan in 2006, but he showed he retains plenty of ability when defying a mark of 78 in a 6f handicap at Jebel Ali last month and was able to follow up over this shorter trip. As it turned out, he was not ideally drawn in stall four, and he was ridden along as soon as the gates opened, but he responded well to display plenty of speed and gradually edged towards the seemingly favoured stands' side. He kept on to the line and is clearly progressive.

Sir Edwin Landseer(USA) refused to enter the stalls when due to run on the turf the previous week, but he was in a better frame of mind this time and ran well from his favourable draw.

Salaam Dubai(AUS) was another well drawn and had the benefit of the rail, but he was below the form he showed when runner-up to Asiatic Boy in a Group 3 over 6f here on his previous start. He was, though, able to confirm form with stablemate Malayeen.

Malayeen(AUS) showed good speed but was not helped by a low draw.

Belpasso(IRE) was drawn against the rail, but he lacked the early speed of some of these and was never a factor after having to be switched.

Canadian Danehill(IRE) was soon stuck out towards the middle of the track after appearing to stumble as the stalls opened and this run is best forgotten.

567a UAE 2000 GUINEAS - GULF NEWS (GROUP 3) (DIRT) 1m (D)
6:00 (6:01) 3-Y-O

£75,376 (£25,125; £12,562; £6,281; £3,768; £2,512)

RPR

1 **Honour Devil (ARG)**[21] 292 4-9-4 110 .... JMurtagh 6 111
(M F De Kock, South Africa) *disp for 2f: trckd ldr: rdn to ld again 2 1/2f out: r.o wl* **7/4**[1]

2 *1/2* **Royal Vintage (SAF)**[257] 4-9-4 98 .... KShea 13 110
(M F De Kock, South Africa) *trckd ldrs: rdn to chse wnr 2f out: r.o wl* **6/1**[2]

3 *3 3/4* **My Indy (ARG)**[21] 292 4-9-4 102 .... KerrinMcEvoy 15 101
(Saeed Bin Suroor) *trckd ldng gp: mid-div 3f out: rdn 2 1/2f out: r.o but no ch w first two* **12/1**

4 *1 3/4* **Etched (USA)**[109] 3-8-9 108 ....(b) LDettori 4 107
(Saeed Bin Suroor) *trckd ldrs: rdn 3f out: r.o but nvr able to chal* **7/4**[1]

5 *2 3/4* **Numaany (USA)**[104] 3-8-9 90 .... TedDurcan 9 101
(Saeed Bin Suroor) *mid-div: rdn and wd 2 1/2f out: nt qckn but kpt on* **9/1**[3]

6 *2 1/2* **Paveroc**[21] 292 3-8-9 93 .... JohnEgan 1 95
(A Manuel, UAE) *disp: led briefly 3f out: sn btn* **50/1**

7 *1 3/4* **Mutabayen (USA)**[42] 3-8-9 90 ....(b) WayneSmith 14 91
(A Al Raihe, UAE) *rdn to ld after 2 1/2f: hdd 3f out: wknd* **100/1**

8 *1/4* **New Jersey (IRE)**[131] 6017 3-8-9 93 .... MartinDwyer 8 90
(Doug Watson, UAE) *mid-div on rail: rdn 3f out: one pce* **100/1**

9 *1* **Aquino (URU)**[21] 292 4-9-4 100 ....(t) MJKinane 10 78
(Doug Watson, UAE) *racd in rr: rdn 3f out: nvr able to chal* **14/1**

10 *3/4* **Change Alley (USA)**[21] 292 3-8-9 87 ....(e) RoystonFfrench 3 86
(A Al Raihe, UAE) *rdn in mid-div on rail 4f out: n.d* **100/1**

11 *1/4* **Free Tussy (ARG)**[21] 292 4-9-4 97 ....(t) RyanMoore 7 75
(H J Brown, South Africa) *rdn bhd ldrs after 3f: sn btn* **50/1**

12 *5 1/2* **Siberian Tiger (IRE)**[95] 6782 3-8-9 105 .... DarryllHolland 2 73
(M R Channon) *nvr nr to chal* **25/1**

13 *5* **Choisky (IRE)**[21] 292 3-8-9 70 .... BrettDoyle 11 61
(R Bouresly, Kuwait) *slowly away: nvr able to chal* **250/1**

14 *3/4* **Ablaan (USA)**[42] 3-8-9 95 .... PDevlin 5 60
(M F De Kock, South Africa) *racd in last: t.k.h: nvr able to chal* **33/1**

15 *1/4* **Toolittleyourlate (USA)**[21] 292 3-8-9 91 .... RichardMullen 16 59
(S Seemar, UAE) *nvr able to chal* **100/1**

1m 34.8s (-1.90) **Going Correction** +0.075s/f (Slow)
WFA 3 from 4yo 19lb **15** Ran SP% **126.4**
Speed ratings: **112,111,107,106,103 100,99,98,97,96 96,91,86,85,85**
CSF 13.86.
Owner Sheikh Mohammed Bin Khalifa Al Maktoum **Bred** Firmamento **Trained** South Africa
■ Mike De Kock produced a magnificent training performance to saddle the first two home.

FOCUS
This race has varied in quality since the inaugural running in 2000, but it has been won by some top-class performers, most notably subsequent Dubai World Cup winner Street Cry in 2001, and three of the eight winners went on to land the UAE Derby. A field of 15 was just one off the biggest in the race's history and this looked an outstanding renewal. There were plenty of smart horses in the line up from the Northern Hemisphere, but for the third straight year the race went to a horse from the Southern Hemisphere, indeed the first three home were bred in that part of the world.

NOTEBOOK
Honour Devil(ARG) ◆ confirmed the impression he made when an impressive winner of the trial for this race over 7f on his debut in Dubai. Always travelling really well within himself, he was nicely placed throughout, but he was pushed all the way by his stablemate, Royal Vintage, and was forced to work hard late on to keep that one at bay. (op 13/8)
Royal Vintage(SAF), although a longer price than his winning stablemate, was the subject of some very positive reports and a big run was expected. The winner of both his starts in South Africa last year, including in Grade 2 company when last seen, he produced a fine effort to finish a clear second. It looked at one stage as though he might go by, but he was ultimately just held and probably got a little tired late on. (op 13/2)
My Indy(ARG), runner-up to Honour Devil in the trial, was produced with every chance at the top of the straight, but the De Kock pair proved too strong. (op 10/1)
Etched(USA) won both his starts when trained in the US by Kiaran McLaughlin last year, including a six-and-a-half-length thrashing of a subsequent Grade 2 winner in a Grade 3 on his final start, but he could manage only fourth. Both his wins were gained in much smaller fields and he was very much entitled to need this experience, so a better run can be expected next time. (op 15/8 tchd 2/1)
Numaany(USA) ◆, who did incredibly well to win his maiden on his final start in the US last November having spooked badly and lost his momentum when in front, ran with credit upped in grade. He was never seen with a chance having lacked the speed of some of these, but kept on for pressure late on and should improve for a step back up in trip. He could do better in the next two legs of the Triple Crown. (op 11/1)
Siberian Tiger(IRE) is smart on turf, as he showed when winning a Listed race at Pontefract last season, but he was never involved on his dirt debut.

568a GNB H'CAP (DIRT) 1m 2f (D)
6:35 (6:35) (95-110,105) 3-Y-O+

£36,180 (£12,060; £6,030; £3,015; £1,809; £1,206)

RPR

1 **Familiar Territory**[28] 202 5-9-5 **105** .... LDettori 9 110+
(Saeed Bin Suroor) *mid-div: gng wl 3f out: smooth prog 2 1/2f out: rdn to ld 100yds out* **6/5**[1]

2 *3 1/4* **Dynamic Saint (USA)**[21] 296 5-9-4 **104** ....(e) RyanMoore 1 102
(Doug Watson, UAE) *trckd ldrs: led 2 1/2f out: r.o wl but no ch w wnr* **16/1**

3 *6 1/4* **Mutasallil (USA)**[14] 381 8-8-12 **98** ....(t) RHills 5 82
(Doug Watson, UAE) *trckd ldr: led 4 1/2f out: rdn 2 1/2f out: hdd 100yds: kpt on same pce* **33/1**

4 *6 1/4* **Bennie Blue (SAF)**[14] 380 6-9-3 **102** .... KShea 11 74
(M F De Kock, South Africa) *racd in rr: rdn 3f out: nvr able to chal* **7/2**[2]

5 *1* **Consular**[14] 380 6-9-0 **99** ....(t) TPO'Shea 8 69
(E Charpy, UAE) *trckd ldr: wd: rdn 3f out: wknd* **14/1**

6 *1/4* **The Pirate (DEN)**[14] 383 5-9-0 **99** ....(t) ESki 4 68
(Niels Petersen, Norway) *broke awkwardly: settled in rr: nvr involved* **33/1**

7 *2 1/2* **Elmustanser**[14] 380 7-8-9 **95** ....(vt) MartinDwyer 7 58
(Doug Watson, UAE) *mid-div: rdn 4f out: nvr able to chal* **33/1**

8 *14* **Reve Lunaire (USA)**[13] 5-9-1 **100** .... TedDurcan 10 36
(S Seemar, UAE) *sn rdn in rr of mid-div: nvr able to chal* **16/1**

9 *2 1/4* **Remaadd (USA)**[14] 381 7-9-1 **100** .... JMurtagh 3 32
(D Selvaratnam, UAE) *sn led: hdd 4 1/2f out: sn btn* **11/2**[3]

10 *1/4* **Chinkara**[14] 380 8-8-9 **95** ....(t) WJSupple 2 25
(Doug Watson, UAE) *sn rdn along: n.d* **16/1**

11 *dist* **Dubai Honor**[13] 9-8-12 **98** ....(e) DO'Donohoe 6 —
(Doug Watson, UAE) *racd in last: n.d* **20/1**

2m 0.40s (-1.90) **Going Correction** +0.075s/f (Slow) **11** Ran SP% **121.0**
Speed ratings: **110,107,102,97,96 96,94,83,81,81** —
CSF 24.33; TRI 425.58. Placepot: £14.50 to a £1 stake. Pool £10,725.05 - 538.70 winning units. Quadpot: £8.70 to a £1 stake. Pool £297.80 - 25.30 winning units..
Owner Sheikh Saeed Bin Mohammed Al Maktoum **Bred** P & Mrs Venner **Trained** Newmarket, Suffolk

FOCUS
An ordinary handicap, but the pace was good and that suited the favourite.

NOTEBOOK
Familiar Territory confirmed the promise he showed when second over 1m1f round here on his debut in Dubai. Ridden with patience, he had a few lengths to find on the leaders at the top of the straight, but his rider never looked worried and he found plenty when finally asked for his effort to get up and win going away. He is progressing and, every bit as effective on turf, he should have plenty of options.
Dynamic Saint(USA), back on dirt with eye-shields fitted, raced enthusiastically in behind the leaders for much of the way and kept on for pressure in the straight, but he was ultimately no match for the winner.
Mutasallil(USA), another switching from turf to dirt, ran with credit but has not won since November 2006.
Bennie Blue(SAF) ran a strange race as he has often shown his best form when ridden really positively, but he never seemed to be going that well this time and found himself well back. He eventually ran on in the straight, but the race was all over by that point.
Consular was again well held and is not progressing. He has won on dirt, but might be worth switching back to turf.

542 LINGFIELD (L-H)
Friday, February 15

OFFICIAL GOING: Standard
Wind: moderate, half-against

569 CROCS SNAPPY HAPPY HOLIDAYS @ PONTIN'S APPRENTICE (S) STKS 1m 4f (P)
1:45 (1:45) (Class 6) 4-Y-O+ **£1,774** (£523; £262) **Stalls** Low

Form RPR

00-0 **1** **Competitor**[16] 352 7-9-5 54 ....(b) KirstyMilczarek 6 59
(J Akehurst) *mde all: stdd pce over 2f out: shkn up to go clr over 1f out: v easily* **9/2**[3]

3-22 **2** *4* **Perfect Storm**[14] 394 9-9-0 50 .... JackDean(5) 3 54+
(W G M Turner) *trckd wnr to 3f out: short of room and swtchd rt 1f out: rallied and styd on to go 2nd again ins fnl f* **11/4**[2]

4-40 **3** *1 1/2* **Musango**[35] 129 5-9-7 60 ....(t) RussellKennemore(3) 5 56
(Miss Gay Kelleway) *stdd s: chsd wnr 3f out: hung lft ent fnl f: one pce and lost 2nd ins fnl f* **5/4**[1]

006- **4** *3* **Honduras (SWI)**[16] 6819 7-9-0 70 ....(be) JemmaMarshall(5) 1 46
(G L Moore) *hld up: rdn over 2f out: one pce after* **13/2**

60-4 **5** *7* **Intersky Sports (USA)**[11] 431 4-8-11 58 ....(be) PatrickDonaghy(5) 4 35
(K J Burke) *chsd ldrs tl rdn and lost tch wl over 2f out* **14/1**

2m 35.52s (2.52) **Going Correction** +0.075s/f (Slow)
WFA 4 from 5yo+ 3lb **5** Ran SP% **109.3**
Speed ratings (Par 101): **94,91,90,88,83**
CSF £16.73 TOTE £5.10: £3.10, £2.00; EX 17.70.There was no bid for the winner.
Owner John Akehurst **Bred** Cheveley Park Stud Ltd **Trained** Epsom, Surrey

FOCUS
A standard apprentice seller on paper, but the winner was allowed his own way and set a stop-start gallop, so the form needs treating with caution.
Musango Official explanation: jockey said gelding hung badly left

570 PLAY GOLF @ LINGFIELD PARK MEDIAN AUCTION MAIDEN STKS 1m 2f (P)
2:15 (2:15) (Class 6) 3-Y-O **£1,943** (£578; £288; £144) **Stalls** Low

Form RPR

1 **Rowan Rio** 3-9-3 0 .... LiamJones 2 74+
(W J Haggas) *hld up in rr: hdwy over 1f out: r.o wl to ld fnl 1/2f* **11/1**

0- **2** *1 1/4* **Might Be Magic**[133] 5977 3-9-3 0 .... AdrianMcCarthy 5 71
(P W Chapple-Hyam) *trckd ldr: rdn and ev ch ins fnl f: nt pce of wnr* **8/1**[3]

0- **3** *1* **Nowzdetime (IRE)**[48] 7266 3-8-12 0 .... JamieJones(5) 3 69
(M G Quinlan) *led: rdn 3f out: hdd 1/2f out: no ex* **14/1**

02 **4** *hd* **Boy On A Swing (USA)**[6] 500 3-9-3 0 .... TPQueally 1 69
(J A Osborne) *trckd ldrs: chal on ins appr fnl f but nt clr run* **4/9**[1]

3-0 **5** *3* **Silver Waters**[12] 416 3-9-3 0 .... NeilPollard 4 63
(D R C Elsworth) *in tch tl rdn and outpcd over 2f out: no hdwy after* **6/1**[2]

6 *4* **Code Violation** 3-8-12 0 .... FrankieMcDonald 7 50
(Jean-Rene Auvray) *hld up in rr: rdn and wknd over 2f out* **66/1**

0- **U** **Malt Empress (IRE)**[68] 7084 3-8-5 0 .... GabrielHannon(7) 8 —
(B W Duke) *jinked lft and uns rdr sn after s* **66/1**

2m 8.01s (1.41) **Going Correction** +0.075s/f (Slow) **7** Ran SP% **112.6**
Speed ratings (Par 95): **97,96,95,95,92 89,**—
CSF £89.54 TOTE £9.40: £2.80, £2.40; EX 59.30 Trifecta £163.30 Part won. Pool £230.02 - 0.37 winning units..
Owner Rowan Stud Partnership 1 **Bred** Rowan Farm Stud **Trained** Newmarket, Suffolk

FOCUS
The bare form of this maiden is probably just fair, but some powerful stables were represented and the race should produce winners in time. The pace was just ordinary for much of the way, but still reasonable enough by Lingfield's usual standards.

571 BE BESIDE THE SEASIDE @ PONTIN'S FILLIES' H'CAP 7f (P)
2:45 (2:46) (Class 6) (0-60,60) 4-Y-O+ **£1,876** (£554; £277) **Stalls** Low

Form RPR

3132 **1** **Double Valentine**[13] 402 5-8-6 51 .... KirstyMilczarek(3) 8 61
(R Ingram) *hld up in rr: gd hdwy on outside to go 2nd 1f out: r.o wl to ld nr fin* **6/1**

2-02 **2** *3/4* **The Jailer**[13] 408 5-8-13 55 ....(p) TPQueally 4 63
(J G M O'Shea) *led: clr over 1f out: kpt on: hdd nr fin* **9/2**[3]

-002 **3** *3* **Bens Georgie (IRE)**[15] 375 6-9-2 58 .... JimCrowley 6 58
(D K Ivory) *in tch on outside: rdn 3f out: hung lft appr fnl f: kpt on on ins but no ch w first 2* **9/2**[3]

-231 **4** *nk* **Solicitude**[15] 375 5-9-2 58 ....(p) RobertHavlin 7 57+
(D Haydn Jones) *towards rr: hdwy whn short of room over 1f out: swtchd rt: kpt on one pce fnl f* **3/1**[1]

310- **5** *2* **Alucica**[235] 2937 5-8-5 50 ....(v) TolleyDean(3) 3 44
(D Shaw) *hld up in rr: outpcd 2f out: passed btn horses ins fnl f* **20/1**

5-53 **6** *hd* **Nikki Bea (IRE)**[9] [453] 5-9-0 56..(b[1]) PaulDoe 2 49
(Jamie Poulton) *t.k.h in rr: effrt on ins over 1f out: one pce after* **4/1**[2]

50-5 **7** *1 1/4* **Rosie Cross (IRE)**[37] [86] 4-8-10 57.............................. PatrickHills(5) 5 47
(Eve Johnson Houghton) *trckd ldr to 3f out: regained 2nd over 1f out: wknd fnl f* **11/1**

65-2 **8** *2* **Eleanor Eloise (USA)**[30] [183] 4-9-4 60.............................. LiamJones 1 44
(J R Gask) *trckd ldrs: wnt 2nd 3f out to over 1f out: wknd qckly* **16/1**

1m 24.88s (0.08) **Going Correction** +0.075s/f (Slow) **8** Ran SP% **114.6**
Speed ratings (Par 98): **102,101,97,97,95 94,93,91**
CSF £33.16 CT £133.71 TOTE £5.10: £1.30, £1.90, £2.00; EX 23.20 Trifecta £77.10 Pool £318.18 - 2.93 winning units..
Owner Ellangowan Racing Partners **Bred** Ellangowan Racing Partners **Trained** Epsom, Surrey

FOCUS
A moderate fillies' handicap run at an even tempo but the winner's form is pretty sound with the runner-up back to her best.

572 RACE TO PONTIN'S NOW CLAIMING STKS 7f (P)
3:20 (3:20) (Class 6) 3-Y-O **£1,774** (£523; £262) **Stalls** Low

Form RPR

3-64 **1** **Hit The Roof**[34] [135] 3-9-4 75.. RichardHughes 4 65
(R Hannon) *hld up: rdn over 2f out: hdwy to ld 1f out: rdn out* **6/4**[1]

3-52 **2** *1 1/2* **Llab Nala**[6] [501] 3-8-7 55.............................. MatthewDavies(7) 2 57
(M R Channon) *hld up in rr: hdwy to press wnr fnl f: no imp fnl 50yds* **12/1**

331 **3** *nk* **Copperbottomed (IRE)**[8] [462] 3-8-11 65....................(e) JimCrowley 1 53
(J R Boyle) *trckd ldrs: disp 2nd 1/2-way: short of room wl over 1f out: kpt on one pce fnl f* **4/1**[3]

5-30 **4** *3/4* **Hellfire Bay**[4] [527] 3-9-2 65..(b[1]) NCallan 3 56
(K A Ryan) *slowly away: rapid hdwy to ld after 1f: hung lft wl over 1f out: hdd 1f out: no ex* **9/2**

2-2 **5** *3/4* **Roundthetwist (IRE)**[43] [30] 3-9-5 0.............................. AndrewElliott 5 57
(K R Burke) *led for 1f: prom tl rdn and wknd appr fnl f* **7/2**[2]

1m 25.85s (1.05) **Going Correction** +0.075s/f (Slow) **5** Ran SP% **108.1**
Speed ratings (Par 95): **97,95,94,94,93**
CSF £18.19 TOTE £2.40: £1.30, £2.50; EX 18.40.The winner was claimed by Derek Shaw for £14,000.
Owner A F M (Holdings) Ltd **Bred** Cothi Bloodstock **Trained** East Everleigh, Wilts

FOCUS
A modest claimer run at a good pace but the proximity of the 55-rated runner-up raises doubts about the form.
Copperbottomed(IRE) Official explanation: jockey said gelding was denied a clear run

573 MAYO WYNNE BAXTER H'CAP 1m (P)
3:55 (3:55) (Class 4) (0-85,82) 3-Y-O **£4,100** (£1,227; £613; £306; £152) **Stalls** High

Form RPR

-111 **1** **Rapidity**[4] [527] 3-9-6 81 18ex.............................. ChrisCatlin 3 94+
(E J O'Neill) *mde all: rdn clr over 1f out: kpt up to work: impressive* **11/4**[1]

003- **2** *3* **Hansinger (IRE)**[154] [5374] 3-9-3 78.............................. NCallan 7 81
(B I Case) *s.i.s: in rr: styd on fr over 1f out to go 2nd nr fin* **10/1**

56-2 **3** *nk* **Oberlin (USA)**[20] [311] 3-8-11 72.............................. GregFairley 4 74
(M Johnston) *trckd wnr to over 2f out: wnt 2nd again ins fnl f tl no ex nr fin* **5/1**[3]

1-14 **4** *1 1/2* **Hucking Hero (IRE)**[9] [457] 3-9-3 78.............................. GeorgeBaker 1 77
(J R Best) *hld up: hdwy on ins 2f out: fdd ins fnl f* **5/1**[3]

06-1 **5** *shd* **Rockfield Tiger (IRE)**[9] [458] 3-9-3 78 6ex.............................. SteveDrowne 6 77
(J A Osborne) *t.k.h: hld up on outside: rdn and outpcd fnl f* **10/3**[2]

1 **6** *hd* **Vettorenjoy**[27] [223] 3-9-7 82.............................. OscarUrbina 5 82+
(M Botti) *in tch: rdn over 2f out: outpcd fr over 1f out* **7/1**

2-23 **7** *nk* **Miss Mujanna**[12] [416] 3-8-12 73.............................. J-PGuillambert 2 71
(J Akehurst) *trckd ldrs: chsd wnr over 2f out tl wknd fnl f* **14/1**

1m 36.75s (-1.45) **Going Correction** +0.075s/f (Slow) **7** Ran SP% **111.3**
Speed ratings (Par 99): **110,107,106,105,105 104,104**
CSF £28.64 TOTE £3.70: £2.10, £4.50; EX 38.00.
Owner Premspace Ltd **Bred** Angmering Park Stud **Trained** Averham Park, Notts

FOCUS
This looked like a decent handicap beforehand, but nothing could live the progressive Rapidity. The form looks solid rated around the placed horses.

574 BOOK YOUR SHORT BREAK @ PONTINS.COM H'CAP 6f (P)
4:30 (4:30) (Class 4) (0-80,80) 4-Y-O+ **£4,100** (£1,227; £613; £306; £152) **Stalls** Low

Form RPR

-112 **1** **Benllech**[6] [503] 4-9-2 78.............................. SimonWhitworth 2 86+
(M Wigham) *trckd ldrs: led 1f out: rdn out* **15/8**[1]

215 **2** *3/4* **Angel Voices (IRE)**[25] [245] 5-8-4 66 oh1....................(p) AndrewElliott 1 72
(K R Burke) *led tl rdn and hdd 1f out: kpt on but no imp on wnr* **8/1**

3-53 **3** *3/4* **Chjimes (IRE)**[11] [427] 4-8-13 75.............................. LPKeniry 3 79+
(C R Dore) *s.i.s: t.k.h: hdwy and rdn whn short of room ent fnl f: kpt on* **8/1**

34-2 **4** *1 1/2* **Westport**[28] [210] 5-9-2 78.............................. NCallan 4 77
(K A Ryan) *trckd ldr tl edgd lft over 1f out: fdd ins fnl f* **5/2**[2]

3133 **5** *1/2* **Mogok Ruby**[6] [503] 4-9-4 80.............................. RichardHughes 6 77+
(L Montague Hall) *stdd s: hdwy whn n.m.r over 1f out: no imp after* **4/1**[3]

-513 **6** *1 1/2* **Lord Of The Reins (IRE)**[8] [459] 4-8-3 68 oh1 ow2.......... TolleyDean(3) 5 60
(D Shaw) *in tch: rdn and effrt on outside wl over 1f out: sn btn* **11/1**

1m 12.24s (0.34) **Going Correction** +0.075s/f (Slow) **6** Ran SP% **113.9**
Speed ratings (Par 105): **100,99,98,96,95 93**
CSF £17.70 TOTE £2.60: £1.10, £2.70; EX 15.90.
Owner R J Lorenz **Bred** Speedlith Group **Trained** Newmarket, Suffolk

FOCUS
A fair sprint handicap, but just the six runners and they went a steady pace early on. The form looks reasonable rated around the placed horses.
Chjimes(IRE) Official explanation: jockey said gelding was denied a clear run
Lord Of The Reins(IRE) Official explanation: jockey said gelding ran too free

575 LINGFIELDPARK.CO.UK H'CAP 1m 5f (P)
5:00 (5:00) (Class 6) (0-60,59) 4-Y-O+ **£1,876** (£554; £277) **Stalls** Low

Form RPR

-243 **1** **Capitalise (IRE)**[15] [374] 5-9-2 53.............................. GeorgeBaker 7 55
(V Smith) *bhd: hdwy over 3f out: styd on u.p to ld nr fin* **11/4**[1]

5461 **2** *nk* **Prince Of Medina**[6] [499] 5-9-1 52 6ex.............................. SteveDrowne 1 53
(J R Best) *trckd ldrs: wnt 2nd over 2f out: rdn to ld briefly wl ins fnl f: hdd cl home* **10/3**[3]

0-25 **3** *nk* **Berry Hill Lass (IRE)**[25] [248] 4-9-3 58..........................(p) AndrewElliott 4 59
(J G M O'Shea) *led after 2f: rdn and hdd wl ins fnl f and lost 2nd sn after* **16/1**

-056 **4** *1* **Bienheureux**[19] [330] 7-9-4 55..(bt) NCallan 3 55
(Miss Gay Kelleway) *mid-div: rdn 2f out: styd on fnl f: nvr nrr* **11/4**[1]

5-14 **5** *shd* **Little Richard (IRE)**[18] [332] 9-9-8 59..........................(p) RichardHughes 6 60+
(M Wellings) *led for 2f: swtchd rt over 1f out: hld whn squeezed out ins fnl f* **3/1**[2]

-006 **6** *1 1/4* **Only Hope**[6] [499] 4-8-7 48..(p) PaulEddery 5 45
(Miss Diana Weeden) *stdd s: in rr: mde sme late hdwy* **33/1**

03/4 **7** *12* **Barnbrook Empire (IRE)**[9] [455] 6-8-8 45.............................. PaulDoe 2 24
(L A Dace) *prom tl rdn and wknd over 2f out: eased whn btn ins fnl f* **20/1**

2m 46.73s (0.73) **Going Correction** +0.075s/f (Slow)
WFA 4 from 5yo+ 4lb **7** Ran SP% **115.0**
Speed ratings (Par 101): **100,99,99,99,98 98,90**
CSF £12.47 TOTE £2.90: £2.10, £2.90; EX 10.80 Place 6 £466.33, Place 5 £176.26..
Owner Tilen Electrics Ltd **Bred** Dan Daly **Trained** Exning, Suffolk
■ Stewards' Enquiry : Steve Drowne caution: careless riding

FOCUS
A moderate staying handicap run at a good pace after a couple of furlongs or so but the form looks weak.
T/Plt: £694.00 to a £1 stake. Pool: £50,055.50. 52.65 winning tickets. T/Qpdt: £27.70 to a £1 stake. Pool: £4,114.60. 109.90 winning tickets. JS

557 WOLVERHAMPTON (A.W) (L-H)
Friday, February 15

OFFICIAL GOING: Standard
Wind: Light, half-against Weather: Cloudy

576 HOTEL & CONFERENCING AT WOLVERHAMPTON H'CAP 7f 32y(P)
6:50 (6:50) (Class 6) (0-65,65) 4-Y-O+ **£2,047** (£604; £302) **Stalls** High

Form RPR

0-13 **1** **Follow The Flag (IRE)**[13] [407] 4-8-12 64.............................. JackMitchell(5) 2 74
(C F Wall) *chsd ldrs: rdn over 1f out: r.o to ld wl ins fnl f* **8/1**

0-23 **2** *1* **Gimme Some Lovin (IRE)**[11] [426] 4-9-1 62...........(p) FrancisNorton 11 69+
(D W P Arbuthnot) *hld up: rdn 1/2-way: hdwy u.p over 1f out: edgd lft: r.o* **7/1**

4163 **3** *nk* **Green Pirate**[2] [542] 6-8-13 60..(p) JamesDoyle 3 66
(W M Brisbourne) *hld up in tch: rdn over 2f out: nt clr run over 1f out: r.o* **13/2**[3]

-312 **4** *nk* **Another Genepi (USA)**[15] [367] 5-9-2 63..........................(b) FergalLynch 4 68
(I W McInnes) *led: rdn over 1f out: hdd wl ins fnl f* **5/1**[1]

-554 **5** *nk* **Figaro Flyer (IRE)**[9] [446] 5-9-4 65.............................. JimmyQuinn 9 70+
(P Howling) *s.i.s: hld up: hdwy and nt clr run over 1f out: swtchd lft: r.o: nt rch ldrs* **7/1**

5110 **6** *hd* **Sovereignty (JPN)**[9] [446] 6-9-0 61.............................. DanielTudhope 7 69+
(D K Ivory) *hld up: hdwy and nt clr run over 1f out: running on whn hmpd ins fnl f: nvr able to chal* **9/1**

416- **7** *2* **Cabourg (IRE)**[48] [7268] 5-8-13 60.............................. PatCosgrave 10 59
(R Bastiman) *hld up: hdwy 1/2-way: rdn and edgd lft over 1f out: styng on same pce whn nt clr run ins fnl f* **14/1**

02-1 **8** *nk* **Mineral Rights (USA)**[16] [362] 4-8-12 59.............................. PhillipMakin 12 57
(Miss L A Perratt) *hld up: rdn over 1f out: sn hung lft: r.o ins fnl f: nrst fin* **12/1**

0134 **9** *2* **Avontuur (FR)**[8] [466] 6-8-6 53..(p) LiamJones 5 45
(Mrs R A Carr) *chsd ldr: rdn over 2f out: edgd rt over 1f out: wknd fnl f* **25/1**

30-0 **10** *nk* **Takitwo**[33] [149] 5-8-11 58.............................. HayleyTurner 8 50
(P D Cundell) *prom: rdn and lost pl 5f out: n.d after* **6/1**[2]

30-6 **11** *shd* **Gilded Cove**[26] [235] 8-8-10 62.............................. RussellKennemore(5) 6 53
(R Hollinshead) *hld up: rdn over 2f out: n.d* **14/1**

-425 **12** *5* **Copper King**[13] [407] 4-9-2 63.............................. AdamKirby 1 41
(Miss Tor Sturgis) *chsd ldrs: rdn 1/2-way: wknd 2f out* **13/2**[3]

1m 29.9s (0.30) **Going Correction** +0.175s/f (Slow) **12** Ran SP% **128.6**
Speed ratings (Par 101): **105,103,103,103,102 102,100,99,97,97 97,91**
CSF £68.69 CT £406.49 TOTE £11.50: £2.20, £3.40, £1.80; EX 61.80.
Owner Follow The Flag Partnership **Bred** Martin Francis **Trained** Newmarket, Suffolk

FOCUS
Just an ordinary handicap, but it was competitive enough and it was certainly truly run, with Another Genepi and Avontuur going hard up front. A few found trouble in the straight, notably Sovereignty, but the form is solid, with the third the best guide.
Figaro Flyer(IRE) Official explanation: jockey said gelding missed the break
Sovereignty(JPN) Official explanation: jockey said gelding was denied a clear run
Copper King Official explanation: jockey said gelding never travelled

577 YOU'LL LOVE THE DEALS ON PONTINS.COM CLAIMING STKS 1m 141y(P)
7:20 (7:20) (Class 5) 4-Y-O+ **£2,914** (£867; £433; £216) **Stalls** Low

Form RPR

3321 **1** **Ninth House (USA)**[11] [429] 6-9-3 76..........................(bt) JimCrowley 7 82
(N P Littmoden) *trckd ldrs: led: over 2f out: drvn out* **3/1**[3]

-443 **2** *1 1/2* **One Night In Paris (IRE)**[14] [390] 5-8-12 75.............................. PatCosgrave 4 73
(M J Wallace) *chsd ldr tl led 3f out: sn rdn and hdd: styd on same pce ins fnl f* **15/8**[1]

5442 **3** *1* **Casablanca Minx (IRE)**[7] [490] 5-8-4 59..............(v) CatherineGannon 2 63
(P D Evans) *chsd ldrs: rdn over 2f out: styd on same pce fnl f* **11/1**

4113 **4** *1 3/4* **Arctic Desert**[15] [373] 8-8-8 63.............................. HayleyTurner 3 63
(Miss Gay Kelleway) *s.i.s: hld up: plld hrd: hdwy over 2f out: rdn over 1f out: no ex fnl f* **3/1**[3]

2-11 **5** *3/4* **Sawwaah (IRE)**[25] [252] 11-8-10 79..........................(v) JamieKyne(7) 6 70
(D Carroll) *hld up: racd keenly: nt clr run over 2f out: rdn and hung lft over 1f out: nt trble ldrs* **5/2**[2]

050/ **6** *15* **Eyes To The Right (IRE)**[73] [394] 9-8-5 34.............................. JimmyQuinn 1 24
(D Burchell) *led over 5f: wknd over 2f out* **28/1**

1m 53.25s (2.75) **Going Correction** +0.175s/f (Slow) **6** Ran SP% **125.1**
Speed ratings (Par 103): **94,92,91,90,89 76**
CSF £10.41 TOTE £4.60: £2.70, £1.20; EX 9.90.
Owner Nigel Shields **Bred** Juddmonte Farms Inc **Trained** Newmarket, Suffolk

FOCUS
This was a decent claimer, but there was no real pace on and it became something of a tactical affair. The form cannot be taken at face value.

578 DINE IN THE HORIZONS RESTAURANT CLASSIFIED STKS 1m 1f 103y(P)
7:50 (7:50) (Class 7) 4-Y-O+ **£1,365** (£403; £201) **Stalls** Low

Form RPR

03-1 **1** **Joe Jo Star**[8] [468] 6-8-13 43.............................. DeclanCannon(7) 5 57
(B P J Baugh) *a.p: led and edgd lft wl over 1f out: rdn and hung lft ins fnl f: styd on* **5/1**[3]

305- **2** 1 ½ **Faraday (IRE)**[77] 6979 5-9-0 45........(b[1]) TPQueally 3 48
(A P Stringer) *trckd ldrs: plld hrd: rdn and n.m.r ins fnl f: styd on same pce* **15/8**[1]

2-40 **3** ½ **The Power Of Phil**[34] 145 4-9-0 41........ HayleyTurner 6 47
(Miss Joanne Priest) *a.p: chsd ldr over 6f out: led over 2f out: rdn and hdd wl over 1f out: styd on same pce fnl f* **10/1**

2432 **4** 3 **Arthurs Dream (IRE)**[6] 507 6-8-9 43........ KellyHarrison(5) 4 49+
(A W Carroll) *broke wl: plld hrd: stdd and lost pl after 1f: hmpd 3f out: nt clr run wl over 1f out: swtchd rt: r.o ins fnl f: nt trble ldrs* **15/2**

-324 **5** 2 ½ **Santera (IRE)**[15] 377 4-8-11 41........ AndrewMullen(3) 7 35
(Mrs A Duffield) *hld up: hdwy 5f out: rdn over 2f out: sn ev ch: wknd fnl f* **6/1**

0406 **6** nk **Divine Love (IRE)**[7] 490 4-8-7 43........(p) PatrickDonaghy(7) 12 35
(T Wall) *sn pushed along in rr: rdn over 2f out: n.d* **66/1**

0/00 **7** hd **Tribiani (IRE)**[15] 375 4-9-0 45........ FrankieMcDonald 8 34
(P A Blockley) *s.s: bhd: hdwy over 2f out: rdn and wkng whn hung lft over 1f out* **4/1**[2]

0/40 **8** 1 ½ **Up Dee Creek**[13] 401 6-9-0 39........(b) LiamJones 2 31
(W M Brisbourne) *hld up: hmpd 3f out: n.d* **40/1**

6403 **9** ¾ **Steel Grey**[8] 468 7-8-11 45........ MarkLawson(3) 1 29
(M Brittain) *led 1f: pushed along 6f out: wknd over 2f out* **7/1**

05/0 **10** 3 **Archirondel**[15] 373 10-8-7 45........ SoniaEaton(7) 13 23
(B P J Baugh) *chsd ldrs: rdn over 2f out: sn wknd* **100/1**

-005 **11** shd **Elms Schoolboy**[12] 415 6-9-0 42........(b) JimmyQuinn 9 23
(P Howling) *hld up: a in rr* **16/1**

-565 **12** 1 ¾ **Oh So (IRE)**[15] 373 4-8-7 45........ GabrielHannon(7) 11 19
(P A Blockley) *led over 8f out: hdd over 2f out: hmpd and wknd wl over 1f out* **66/1**

00-0 **13** 28 **Miss Sure Bond (IRE)**[34] 143 5-8-9 40........ SladeO'Hara(5) 10 —
(G R Oldroyd) *hld up in tch: racd keenly: sddle slipped sn after s: wknd over 2f out* **33/1**

2m 4.26s (2.56) **Going Correction** +0.175s/f (Slow) **13** Ran SP% **134.3**
Speed ratings (Par 97): **95,93,93,90,88 88,87,86,85,83 83,81,56**
CSF £16.57 TOTE £7.60: £1.50, £1.60, £4.10; EX 31.00.
Owner Joe Singh **Bred** B J And Mrs Crangle **Trained** Audley, Staffs

FOCUS
Not a bad race of its type and the form looks sound, rated around the winner and third.
Tribiani(IRE) Official explanation: jockey said filly missed the break
Up Dee Creek Official explanation: jockey said mare was denied a clear run
Miss Sure Bond(IRE) Official explanation: jockey said saddle slipped

579 RACE THE FAMILY TO PONTIN'S NOW FILLIES' H'CAP 1m 1f 103y(P)
8:20 (8:20) (Class 6) (0-60,61) 4-Y-O+ £2,218 (£654; £327) Stalls Low

Form RPR
-512 **1** **My Mirasol**[13] 400 4-9-4 **58**........(p) ChrisCatlin 1 64
(D E Cantillon) *led: hdd over 1f out: rallied to ld wl ins fnl f* **3/1**[2]

00-1 **2** hd **Trysting Grove (IRE)**[12] 415 7-8-11 **51** 6ex........ SaleemGolam 3 56
(E G Bevan) *hld up: hdwy over 2f out: rdn and ev ch ins fnl f: r.o* **13/2**

5221 **3** ¾ **Mon Petite Amour**[7] 490 5-9-4 **61** 6ex........ KirstyMilczarek(3) 6 65
(D W P Arbuthnot) *chsd ldrs: led over 1f out: rdn: edgd lft and hdd wl ins fnl f* **11/4**[1]

0530 **4** 2 ½ **Capania (IRE)**[6] 508 4-9-2 **56**........(v[1]) JimCrowley 8 54
(P D Evans) *chsd wnr tl rdn over 1f out: no ex fnl f* **6/1**[3]

4201 **5** 3 ½ **Ruffie (IRE)**[7] 478 5-8-4 **51** 6ex........ AmyBaker(7) 4 42
(Miss J Feilden) *hld up: racd keenly: hdwy over 2f out: rdn and hung lft over 1f out: wknd fnl f* **3/1**[2]

426 **6** nk **Vintage Quest**[13] 400 6-8-5 **45**........ CatherineGannon 2 35
(D Burchell) *s.i.s: hld up: rdn over 2f out: n.d* **18/1**

36-6 **7** 7 **Charlottebutterfly**[27] 234 8-9-0 **54**........ RobertHavlin 5 30
(P J McBride) *hld up: rdn over 2f out: n.d* **8/1**

0-00 **8** 21 **Welsh Whisper**[25] 251 9-8-5 **45**........ JimmyQuinn 7 —
(S A Brookshaw) *chsd ldrs: rdn over 3f out: wknd over 2f out* **25/1**

2m 2.75s (1.05) **Going Correction** +0.175s/f (Slow) **8** Ran SP% **124.5**
Speed ratings (Par 98): **102,101,101,98,95 95,89,70**
CSF £25.26 CT £62.22 TOTE £4.50: £2.00, £2.30, £1.20; EX 47.50.
Owner J A Bailie **Bred** J A Forsyth **Trained** Newmarket, Suffolk

FOCUS
Just a moderate fillies' handicap, but several of the runners arrived here in good form. The pace was reasonable but the form is modest.
Welsh Whisper Official explanation: jockey said mare had no more to give

580 A BREAK TO REMEMBER @ PONTIN'S H'CAP 5f 20y(P)
8:50 (8:50) (Class 4) (0-80,79) 4-Y-O+ £4,533 (£1,348; £674; £336) Stalls Low

Form RPR
30-1 **1** **Distant Sun (USA)**[29] 194 4-9-2 77........ PhillipMakin 1 89
(Miss L A Perratt) *hld up: hdwy 1/2-way: rdn over 1f out: r.o to ld wl ins fnl f* **6/1**

6-4 **2** 1 ¼ **Financial Times (USA)**[31] 162 6-9-4 79........(t) MickyFenton 5 86
(Stef Liddiard) *chsd ldrs: rdn over 1f out: ev ch ins fnl f: unable qckn towards fin* **9/1**

00-6 **3** nk **Nigella**[21] 301 5-8-12 73........ GrahamGibbons 7 79
(E S McMahon) *chsd ldr: rdn over 1f out: led ins fnl f: sn hdd: styd on same pce* **3/1**[1]

2-36 **4** ½ **Desert Opal**[8] 459 8-8-9 70........(b) LiamJones 9 74
(C R Dore) *hld up: rdn 3f out: r.o ins fnl f: nt rch ldrs* **12/1**

2136 **5** hd **Sands Crooner (IRE)**[6] 503 5-8-5 69........(v) TolleyDean(3) 4 76+
(D Shaw) *dwlt: outpcd: rdn over 1f out: running on whn nt clr run ins fnl f: nvr able to chal* **10/1**

-502 **6** ¾ **Stolt (IRE)**[16] 359 4-9-0 75........ DanielTudhope 6 76
(N Wilson) *chsd ldrs: rdn 1/2-way: edgd lft over 1f out: no ex fnl f* **5/1**[3]

5-22 **7** ½ **Harry Up**[21] 301 7-8-10 78........(p) BMcHugh(7) 2 77
(K A Ryan) *led: rdn over 1f out: hdd and no ex ins fnl f* **3/1**[1]

-113 **8** 2 ½ **Almaty Express**[16] 359 6-8-8 74........(b) AshleyHamblett(5) 3 64+
(J R Weymes) *n.m.r sn after s: in rr: rdn over 1f out: n.d* **4/1**[2]

6-10 **9** shd **Baileys Outshine**[11] 427 4-8-11 72........ TPQueally 8 62
(J G Given) *s.i.s: outpcd* **20/1**

62.15 secs (-0.15) **Going Correction** +0.175s/f (Slow) **9** Ran SP% **132.5**
Speed ratings (Par 105): **108,106,105,104,104 103,102,98,98**
CSF £67.56 CT £204.49 TOTE £9.80: £2.60, £1.80, £2.20; EX 79.30.
Owner Gordon McDowall **Bred** Forging Oaks Llc **Trained** Carluke, S Lanarks

FOCUS
A fair handicap run at a sound pace. The progressive winner is up another 7lb, with the second rated to form.
Almaty Express Official explanation: jockey said gelding missed the break

581 BOOK BEST DEALS EVER @ PONTIN'S H'CAP 5f 216y(P)
9:20 (9:21) (Class 6) (0-60,60) 4-Y-O+ £2,218 (£654; £327) Stalls Low

Form RPR
640- **1** **Howards Tipple**[104] 6639 4-9-3 58........ PhillipMakin 7 66
(Miss L A Perratt) *a.p: rdn over 1f out: r.o to ld towards fin* **9/1**

64-0 **2** nk **Inca Soldier (FR)**[6] 506 5-8-11 59........ MarkCoumbe(7) 3 66
(R C Guest) *dwlt: hld up: hdwy and hung lft fr over 1f out: r.o* **5/1**[3]

0-24 **3** nk **Bond Becks (IRE)**[27] 230 8-9-2 57........ ChrisCatlin 1 63
(G R Oldroyd) *led: rdn over 1f out: hdd towards fin* **11/2**

20-2 **4** 1 ¾ **Twinned (IRE)**[20] 318 5-8-11 52........ AdamKirby 2 52+
(M J Wilkinson) *a.p: chsd ldr 2f out: sn rdn: no ex ins fnl f* **11/1**

3231 **5** 1 ¼ **Earl Compton (IRE)**[23] 263 4-9-0 55........(v) MickyFenton 5 51
(Stef Liddiard) *s.i.s and n.m.r s: hdwy over 3f out: rdn over 2f out: no ex fnl f* **7/1**

4421 **6** nk **Nautical**[4] 523 10-9-2 60 6ex........ JerryO'Dwyer(3) 10 55
(A W Carroll) *hld up: hdwy over 2f out: rdn and edgd lft over 1f out: styd on same pce* **9/4**[1]

3530 **7** nk **Perlachy**[14] 391 4-9-3 58........(v) JimmyQuinn 4 52
(Mrs N Macauley) *chsd ldrs: rdn over 2f out: no ex fnl f* **9/2**[2]

2250 **8** hd **Bentley**[5] 515 4-8-12 56........(v) TolleyDean(3) 8 50
(D Shaw) *hld up: plld hrd: rdn over 2f out: styd on same pce appr fnl f* **11/1**

4640 **9** 1 ¾ **Desert Light (IRE)**[5] 515 7-8-11 52........(v) DeanMcKeown 9 40
(D Shaw) *sn outpcd* **13/2**

1m 16.2s (1.20) **Going Correction** +0.175s/f (Slow) **9** Ran SP% **133.5**
Speed ratings (Par 101): **99,98,98,95,94 93,93,93,90**
CSF £62.09 CT £289.40 TOTE £11.50: £3.40, £2.00, £3.10; EX 125.70 Place 6 £123.17, Place 5 £27.44.
Owner Gordon McDowall **Bred** New Hall Stud **Trained** Carluke, S Lanarks
■ Stewards' Enquiry : Mark Coumbe three-day ban: used whip with excessive frequency without giving gelding time to respond (Feb 26-28)

FOCUS
A very moderate handicap. The winner was well in on his improved form of last autumn and the next two ran to form.
Twinned(IRE) Official explanation: jockey said gelding hung right all the way
T/Plt: £305.60 to a £1 stake. Pool: £114,013.90. 272.30 winning tickets. T/Qpdt: £81.40 to a £1 stake. Pool: £7,960.10. 72.30 winning tickets. CR

535 KEMPTON (A.W) (R-H)
Saturday, February 16

OFFICIAL GOING: Standard
Wind: Light, half behind Weather: Clear, cold

582 JOIN THE KEMPTON PARK PUNTERS CLUB CLAIMING STKS 6f (P)
6:20 (6:20) (Class 6) 3-Y-O £2,047 (£604; £302) Stalls High

Form RPR
121- **1** **Ike Quebec (FR)**[51] 7246 3-9-2 78........ HaddenFrost(5) 2 76
(J R Boyle) *mde all: set stdy pce to 1/2-way: hrd rdn over 1f out: hld on wl* **9/4**[1]

-223 **2** ½ **Diademas (USA)**[22] 307 3-8-12 68........(p) NCallan 5 66
(V Smith) *t.k.h: disp 2nd to 2f out: drvn and kpt on to chse wnr ins fnl f: clsng grad at fin* **5/2**[2]

3-51 **3** hd **Wee Buns**[14] 403 3-8-7 63 ow2........ JackMitchell(5) 4 65
(P G Murphy) *t.k.h: disp 2nd tl chsd wnr 2f out: urged along and hld 1f out: sn lost 2nd: kpt on nr fin* **11/4**[3]

005- **4** 3 **Little Knickers**[122] 6270 3-9-2 60........ JimCrowley 3 59
(Andrew Reid) *hld up in last pair: rdn 2f out: nt qckn and no imp after* **10/3**

0-60 **5** 1 **Yattendon**[2] 557 3-8-9 60........(t) LPKeniry 1 49
(S Kirk) *plld hrd: hld up in last pair: rdn and nt qckn over 2f out* **20/1**

1m 15.2s (2.10) **Going Correction** +0.15s/f (Slow) **5** Ran SP% **113.8**
Speed ratings (Par 95): **92,91,91,87,85**
CSF £8.56 TOTE £2.10: £1.10, £1.30; EX 8.50.
Owner J-P Lim & Keith Marsden **Bred** Elevage De Bois Carrouges **Trained** Epsom, Surrey

FOCUS
A competitive little claimer, but it was slowly run. The winning time was 0.54 seconds slower than the following three-year-old 46-55, and 2.28 seconds slower than the older-horse 46-55. Fairly sound form.

583 PANORAMIC BAR AND RESTAURANT LOYALTY SCHEME H'CAP 6f (P)
6:50 (6:54) (Class 6) (0-55,58) 3-Y-O £2,047 (£604; £302) Stalls High

Form RPR
0513 **1** **Talamahana**[12] 425 3-8-9 **55**........(b) HaddenFrost(5) 5 60
(S Kirk) *trckd ldng pair: clsd 2f out: rdn to ld 1f out: styd on wl* **4/1**[3]

-263 **2** 2 **Regal Veil**[19] 333 3-8-5 **46**........ SaleemGolam 2 45
(S C Williams) *disp ld at str pce tl led over 1f out: hdd 1f out: no ex* **9/2**

-435 **3** nk **Whitcombe Flyer (USA)**[2] 557 3-8-11 **52**........(b) AdamKirby 3 50
(Miss M E Rowland) *dwlt: pushed along in last: rdn and hanging fr over 2f out: styd on reluctantly to take 3rd ins fnl f* **7/2**[2]

0-31 **4** 1 **Note Perfect**[8] 480 3-8-13 **54**........(b) ChrisCatlin 6 48
(M W Easterby) *disp ld at str pce to over 1f out: fdd* **15/8**[1]

5-34 **5** 3 **Run From Nun**[22] 306 3-8-9 **50**........ NeilPollard 7 35
(John Berry) *chsd ldng trio: rdn and no imp over 2f out: wknd fnl f* **15/2**

00-5 **6** 1 ¼ **Ballyhealy Lady**[22] 298 3-8-11 **52** ow2........ PatDobbs 4 33
(D K Ivory) *mostly in 4th or 5th: wknd over 1f out* **14/1**

1m 14.66s (1.56) **Going Correction** +0.15s/f (Slow) **6** Ran SP% **113.6**
Speed ratings (Par 95): **95,92,91,90,86 84**
CSF £22.33 CT £67.69 TOTE £4.80: £1.40, £3.20; EX 15.80.
Owner M Nicolson, G Doran, A Wilson **Bred** Mrs D Du Feu **Trained** Upper Lambourn, Berks

FOCUS
A moderate sprint handicap. Modest form, but improvement from the winner. The winning time was 0.54 seconds quicker than the three-year-old claimer, but 1.74 seconds slower than the following older-horse 46-55.

584 TERESA ARMSTRONG'S 21 AGAIN BIRTHDAY BASH H'CAP 6f (P)
7:20 (7:22) (Class 6) (0-55,55) 4-Y-O+ £2,047 (£604; £302) Stalls High

Form RPR
60-3 **1** **Lindbergh**[6] 516 6-8-11 **55**........(v[1]) JerryO'Dwyer(3) 8 65
(J Ryan) *mde all at str pce: 3 l clr over 2f out: c bk to rivals fnl f but nvr in serious danger* **7/1**

4324 **2** ¾ **Tilsworth Charlie**[18] 349 5-8-13 **54**....(b) NCallan 1 61
(J R Jenkins) *s.s: prog fr rr after 2f: effrt to chse wnr over 1f out: clsd fnl f but nvr able to chal* **11/2**[3]

030- **3** 1 **Compulsion**[80] 6963 5-9-0 **55**.... PatDobbs 2 59
(Pat Eddery) *stdd s: hld up in last trio: effrt over 2f out: styd on to take 3rd nr fin: no ch* **25/1**

3-05 **4** ½ **Mister Elegant**[41] 64 6-8-9 **50**.... LiamJones 9 52
(J L Spearing) *t.k.h: chsd wnr after 2f to over 1f out: one pce* **10/1**

20-0 **5** nk **Drum Dance (IRE)**[6] 516 6-8-8 **52**.... TravisBlock(3) 4 53
(M Hill) *chsd wnr for 2f: rdn 1/2-way: no imp after: plugged on* **11/2**[3]

-341 **6** nk **Simpsons Gamble (IRE)**[20] 326 5-8-12 **53**....(p) DaneO'Neill 7 53
(R A Teal) *hld up in midfield: shuffled along and no rspnse over 2f out: no ch after* **11/4**[1]

0656 **7** nk **Majestical (IRE)**[4] 528 6-8-11 **52**....(p) JamieSpencer 3 52
(V Smith) *hld up in last and wl off the pce: rdn and nt keen over 2f out: no ch after* **13/2**

-301 **8** 3½ **Shava**[15] 392 8-8-4 **52**.... DeclanCannon(7) 6 40
(H J Evans) *plld hrd: hld up bhd ldrs: wknd 2f out* **9/2**[2]

1m 12.92s (-0.18) **Going Correction** +0.15s/f (Slow) **8** Ran SP% **114.4**
Speed ratings (Par 101): **107,106,104,104,103 103,102,98**
CSF £45.01 CT £914.92 TOTE £6.00: £1.90, £1.60, £4.40; EX 28.00.
Owner J Ryan **Bred** Lady Whent, Mrs B Burchett & R Hannon **Trained** Newmarket, Suffolk

FOCUS
A moderate sprint handicap, and fairly sound form rated around the second and third. The winning time was 2.28 seconds quicker than the opening claimer, and 1.74 seconds faster than the previous 46-55, although both of those races were for three-year-olds only.

585 KEMPTON FOR WEDDINGS CLASSIFIED STKS 1m 4f (P)
7:50 (7:51) (Class 7) 4-Y-0+ £1,365 (£403; £201) Stalls Centre

Form RPR

004- **1** **Chimes At Midnight (USA)**[247] 2595 11-8-12 42..(b) JerryO'Dwyer(3) 6 51
(Luke Comer, Ire) *stdd s: hld up wl bhd: prog fr 3f out: drvn and r.o fr over 1f out to ld last 100yds: won gng away* **12/1**

0-04 **2** 1½ **On Every Street**[23] 282 7-9-1 42....(p) PatCosgrave 4 49
(R Bastiman) *trckd ldrs: clsd over 2f out: rdn to chal wl over 1f out: upsides ins fnl f: outpcd by wnr* **12/1**

3055 **3** ¾ **Come What July (IRE)**[7] 499 7-9-2 46....(v) NCallan 9 49
(D Shaw) *trckd ldrs: prog over 2f out: rdn to ld narrowly over 1f out: hdd and outpcd last 100yds* **8/1**

3232 **4** ¾ **Ernmoor**[13] 415 6-9-1 45.... J-PGuillambert 14 51+
(J R Jenkins) *heavily restrained s: hld up in last and wl bhd: prog over 3f out: hanging 2f out: trckd ldrs over 1f out but nowhere to go after: nt rcvr* **9/4**[1]

50-2 **5** shd **Amnesty**[10] 455 9-9-6 50....(v) JimmyQuinn 11 51
(L A Dace) *hld up towards rr: prog on inner over 2f out: rdn to chal over 1f out and upsides: fdd last 150yds* **14/1**

3-61 **6** 1¼ **Rebel Raider (IRE)**[9] 471 9-8-13 48....(v) RussellKennemore(5) 13 47
(B N Pollock) *t.k.h: trckd ldng pair: wnt 2nd wl over 3f out: led over 2f out to over 1f out: fdd fnl f* **6/1**[3]

000/ **7** ¾ **Ben Bacchus (IRE)**[467] 6375 6-9-1 43.... ChrisCatlin 7 43
(P W Hiatt) *trckd ldrs: cl enough 2f out: grad fdd fr over 1f out* **16/1**

50-5 **8** nk **Phoenix Hill (IRE)**[9] 471 6-9-1 43....(t) JamieSpencer 2 43
(D R Gandolfo) *stdd s: hld up and bhd: limited prog on inner over 2f out: eased to outer and drvn over 1f out: hanging but kpt on fnl f* **4/1**[2]

60-0 **9** 1 **Royal Auditon**[22] 299 7-9-1 45....(p) AdamKirby 10 41
(T T Clement) *dwlt: wl in rr: rdn 3f out: plugged on fnl 2f: n.d* **28/1**

00-0 **10** 7 **Compton Express**[24] 269 5-9-1 43.... SimonWhitworth 12 30
(Jamie Poulton) *trckd ldrs: n.m.r then hmpd jst over 2f out: fdd: eased fnl f* **66/1**

60-0 **11** 10 **Explosive Fox (IRE)**[16] 212 7-9-1 42....(p) PaulDoe 8 14
(S Curran) *hld up in midfield: wkng whn forced wd bnd 3f out: sn t.o* **20/1**

05-0 **12** 2 **Hornpipe**[6] 518 6-8-8 42....(e) GabrielHannon(7) 1 11
(M Hill) *sn led: hdd & wknd rapidly over 2f out: t.o* **25/1**

5-03 **13** 9 **Princess Zaha**[16] 365 6-9-1 43.... DaneO'Neill 3 —
(A G Newcombe) *stdd s: hld up towards rr: forced wd bnd 3f out: wknd: t.o* **16/1**

000- **14** 6 **Peas 'n Beans (IRE)**[253] 2430 5-9-1 43.... LiamJones 5 —
(T Keddy) *trckd ldr tl wknd rapidly over 3f out: t.o* **20/1**

2m 35.52s (1.02) **Going Correction** +0.15s/f (Slow) **14** Ran SP% **128.3**
Speed ratings (Par 97): **102,101,100,100,99 99,98,98,97,93 86,85,79,75**
CSF £148.20 TOTE £18.50: £3.30, £5.00, £2.90; EX 308.40.
Owner Luke Comer **Bred** Calumet Farm **Trained** Dunboyne, Co Meath

FOCUS
A very moderate classified event, but the pace was sound and this is solid form for the grade which should prove reliable. The fourth has been rated as dead-heating with veteran winner Chimes At Midnight.
Ernmoor Official explanation: jockey said gelding was denied a clear run
Rebel Raider(IRE) Official explanation: trainer said gelding was unsuited by the track
Royal Auditon Official explanation: jockey said mare never travelled

586 BOOK NOW FOR RACING POST CHASE DAY H'CAP 1m 3f (P)
8:20 (8:21) (Class 5) (0-75,74) 4-Y-0+ £2,590 (£770; £385; £192) Stalls High

Form RPR

601- **1** **Ryedale Ovation (IRE)**[15] 6719 5-8-8 **65**.... TravisBlock(3) 4 72+
(M Hill) *stdd s: hld up in 6th: prog on outer 2f out: drvn to ld last 150yds: jst hld on* **8/1**

235- **2** hd **Royal Fantasy (IRE)**[100] 6738 5-9-6 **74**.... JamieSpencer 8 83+
(J R Fanshawe) *hld up in last: effrt: nt clr run over 1f out and swtchd lft sn after: r.o and gaining on wnr fin: too much to do* **3/1**[2]

4332 **3** 1½ **Most Definitely (IRE)**[3] 540 8-8-10 **64**.... JamesDoyle 7 68
(R M Stronge) *hld up in 5th: prog on inner 2f out: led over 1f out: carried hd in most unattractive fashion: hdd and hung lft last 150yds* **7/2**[3]

6-31 **4** nk **Rising Force (IRE)**[14] 406 5-9-0 **68**....(b) LiamJones 2 72
(J L Spearing) *trckd ldng trio: effrt to chal 2f out: upsides 1f out: nt qckn after* **7/1**

0-24 **5** hd **Sudden Impulse**[36] 132 7-9-2 **70**.... DaneO'Neill 5 76+
(A D Brown) *trckd ldng pair: nt clr run and snatched up 2f out: nt clr run again over 1f out and dropped to last: r.o fnl 150yds* **14/1**

20-1 **6** 2 **Watchmaker**[29] 207 5-8-13 **67**.... ChrisCatlin 1 67
(Miss Tor Sturgis) *t.k.h: trckd ldr: upsides 2f out: sn rdn and nt qckn: fdd fnl f* **9/4**[1]

63-2 **7** shd **Raquel White**[44] 31 4-8-6 **65**.... TolleyDean(3) 3 65
(J L Flint) *led: set stdy pce to 4f out: drvn over 2f out: hdd and outpcd over 1f out* **8/1**

2m 24.45s (2.55) **Going Correction** +0.15s/f (Slow)
WFA 4 from 5yo+ 2lb **7** Ran SP% **119.4**
Speed ratings (Par 103): **96,95,94,94,94 92,92**
CSF £34.11 CT £102.45 TOTE £11.60: £6.00, £1.90; EX 31.50.
Owner Martin Hill **Bred** Hascombe And Valiant Studs **Trained** Littlehempston, Devon

FOCUS
A modest handicap run at a steady pace, and messy form. The winner has more to offer on his old form, the runner-up was probably unlucky and the fifth is rated as finishing third.

587 MIX BUSINESS WITH PLEASURE H'CAP 1m (P)
8:50 (8:50) (Class 6) (0-55,55) 4-Y-0+ £2,047 (£604; £302) Stalls High

Form RPR

0-01 **1** **Not Now Lewis (IRE)**[20] 328 4-8-10 **54**.... JerryO'Dwyer(3) 10 63+
(J A Osborne) *hld up towards rr: effrt and eased to outer over 1f out: drvn and r.o wl to ld nr fin* **13/2**

50-3 **2** ½ **Shunkawakhan (IRE)**[24] 267 5-8-7 **48**....(p) SaleemGolam 7 56
(G C H Chung) *led 1f: restrained bhd ldrs: effrt 2f out: rdn to ld last 100yds: hdd nr fin* **16/1**

0-05 **3** ¾ **Silver Blue (IRE)**[7] 507 5-8-8 **49**....(b) LPKeniry 12 55
(C R Dore) *hld up towards rr: prog on inner 2f out: drvn to chal over 1f out: upsides fnl f: outpcd last 75yds* **25/1**

-012 **4** shd **Over To You Bert**[6] 516 9-8-9 **55**.... HaddenFrost(5) 2 61
(R J Hodges) *led after 1f: jnd over 2f out: battled on wl tl hdd and no ex last 100yds* **5/1**[3]

-422 **5** 1 **Having A Ball**[9] 465 4-8-11 **52**.... DaneO'Neill 8 56
(P D Cundell) *cl up: stl chsng ldrs over 1f out: nt qckn fnl f* **7/2**[2]

00-4 **6** 1¼ **Just Dust**[6] 516 4-9-0 **55**.... JamieSpencer 5 56
(M W Easterby) *t.k.h: pressed ldr after 1f: upsides fr over 2f out tl wknd last 100yds* **3/1**[1]

20-0 **7** 3 **Julian Joachim (USA)**[6] 516 4-9-0 **55**....(t) DeanMcKeown 4 49
(D Shaw) *stdd s: hld up in last: shuffled along and sme prog 2f out: nvr nr ldrs* **20/1**

-164 **8** nk **Certifiable**[14] 402 7-8-3 **49**....(p) RobynBrisland(5) 3 42
(Miss Z C Davison) *t.k.h: hld up cl bhd ldrs: rdn over 2f out: wknd over 1f out* **25/1**

60-0 **9** 1¾ **Mick Is Back**[25] 258 4-8-13 **54**....(p) NCallan 6 43
(G G Margarson) *nvr beyond midfield: rdn and no prog over 2f out: struggling after* **11/1**

0-32 **10** 6 **Mix N Match**[6] 517 4-8-8 **49**.... ChrisCatlin 1 24
(R M Stronge) *hld up in midfield: lost pl u.p over 2f out: sn bhd* **13/2**

0000 **11** 1 **Royal Guest**[6] 516 4-8-7 **48** ow1....(be) SimonWhitworth 11 21
(J R Jenkins) *s.v.s: plld hrd and hld up in rr: hanging and no prog 2f out: wknd* **50/1**

-565 **12** 9 **Safe Investment (USA)**[15] 388 4-9-0 **55**....(vt[1]) VinceSlattery 9 7
(B N Pollock) *s.i.s: sn rcvrd into ldng trio: wknd rapidly 3f out: t.o* **25/1**

1m 40.51s (0.71) **Going Correction** +0.15s/f (Slow) **12** Ran SP% **123.0**
Speed ratings (Par 101): **102,101,100,100,99 98,95,95,93,87 86,77**
CSF £100.20 CT £2504.08 TOTE £8.10: £2.80, £5.10, £8.70; EX 92.10.
Owner Morsethehorse Syndicate **Bred** Michael And John Fahy **Trained** Upper Lambourn, Berks

FOCUS
Modest fare, but the winner came from well off the pace off a steady gallop and is probably value for more than the official margin of victory. Sound form rated through the fourth and fifth.

588 GOFFS BREEZE UP SALE MARCH 7TH H'CAP 2m (P)
9:20 (9:21) (Class 5) (0-70,85) 4-Y-0+ £2,590 (£770; £385; £192) Stalls High

Form RPR

062 **1** **Trachonitis (IRE)**[11] 443 4-9-12 **74**.... NCallan 5 82
(J R Jenkins) *t.k.h early: hld up in 6th: prog over 2f out: drvn to ld 1f out: styd on wl* **6/1**[3]

46-2 **2** ½ **Right Option (IRE)**[29] 212 4-9-3 **68**.... TolleyDean(3) 9 75
(J L Flint) *t.k.h: trckd ldng trio: wnt 2nd wl over 2f out: drvn to ld briefly over 1f out: edgd lft fnl f: kpt on but a hld* **10/1**

53-1 **3** 2 **Alnwick**[29] 212 4-9-3 **65**.... DaneO'Neill 3 70
(P D Cundell) *hld up in 5th: clsd on ldrs 2f out: chal over 1f out: sn nt qckn: kpt on* **11/4**[2]

6/5- **4** 1¼ **Savannah**[280] 1688 5-9-11 **70**.... JerryO'Dwyer(3) 7 73
(Luke Comer, Ire) *hld up in last pair: effrt over 2f out: sme prog to chse ldrs over 1f out: kpt on: nt pce to chal* **20/1**

-533 **5** 2½ **Abounding**[14] 405 4-9-4 **66**.... JamesDoyle 8 66
(M J Attwater) *led at mod pce: hdd & wknd over 1f out* **9/1**

0/11 **6** 7 **Basalt (IRE)**[7] 510 4-10-2 **85**.... PatrickDonaghy(7) 2 77
(T J Pitt) *trckd ldng pair: effrt 3f out: wknd over 2f out* **1/1**[1]

154/ **7** 19 **Riff Raff**[532] 5022 5-9-3 **59**.... ChrisCatlin 4 28
(C J Gray) *t.k.h: hld up in last: wknd over 3f out: t.o* **33/1**

500- **8** 14 **First Friend (IRE)**[9] 6598 7-8-8 **55**.... HaddenFrost(5) 6 7
(M Hill) *trckd ldr to wl over 2f out: wknd rapidly: t.o* **33/1**

3m 34.69s (4.59) **Going Correction** +0.15s/f (Slow)
WFA 4 from 5yo+ 6lb **8** Ran SP% **120.7**
Speed ratings (Par 103): **94,93,92,92,90 87,77,70**
CSF £63.90 CT £203.21 TOTE £8.20: £2.20, £2.60, £1.10; EX 74.10 Place 6 £2,536.78, Place 5 £1,637.12 .
Owner Jim McCarthy **Bred** D H W Dobson **Trained** Royston, Herts
■ Stewards' Enquiry : Patrick Donaghy one-day ban: failed to ride to draw (Feb 27)

FOCUS
A slowly run handicap which turned into something of a sprint. The form is rated around the fifth but is a bit messy with both the third and sixth disappointing.
First Friend(IRE) Official explanation: jockey said gelding had no more to give
T/Plt: £1,077.20 to a £1 stake. Pool: £72,678.05. 49.25 winning tickets. T/Qpdt: £302.40 to a £1 stake. Pool: £7,070.10. 17.30 winning tickets. JN

569 LINGFIELD (L-H)
Saturday, February 16

OFFICIAL GOING: Standard
Wind: Moderate, half against

589 BETDAQ THE BETTING EXCHANGE CLAIMING STKS 1m (P)
1:40 (1:40) (Class 6) 3-Y-O £1,774 (£523; £262) Stalls High

Form RPR

2-21 **1** **What's For Tea**[12] 424 3-8-7 63.... RichardKingscote 6 59
(P Butler) *led for 1f: led again over 2f out: in command fnl f* **5/2**[2]

1-41 **2** 1 3/4 **Tiger's Rocket (IRE)**[17] 360 3-8-13 70 HaddenFrost(5) 2 66
(R Hannon) *t.k.h in tch: rdn over 2f out: kpt on to go 2nd ent fnl f* **2/1**[1]

1-41 **3** 2 1/2 **Bridge Of Fermoy (IRE)**[24] 266 3-9-8 74 (vt) MickyFenton 4 64
(Miss Gay Kelleway) *led after 1f: hdd over 2f out: rdn and lost 2nd ent fnl f: one pce after* **11/4**[3]

0- **4** nk **Littonfountain (IRE)**[127] 6156 3-9-0 0 DarrenWilliams 1 55
(K R Burke) *s.i.s: in rr: styd on fnl f: nvr nrr* **20/1**

0044 **5** 2 **Carry On Cleo**[5] 527 3-8-5 56 (b) CatherineGannon 3 42
(P D Evans) *trckd ldrs: rdn over 2f out: wknd over 1f out* **7/1**

000- **6** nk **Dhaka Dazzle**[149] 5572 3-8-5 48 MCGeran(7) 5 48
(M R Channon) *hld up: a struggling in rr* **20/1**

1m 38.64s (0.44) **Going Correction** +0.05s/f (Slow) **6** Ran SP% **110.6**
Speed ratings (Par 95): **99,97,94,94,92 92**
CSF £7.67 TOTE £2.60: £1.80, £1.30; EX 7.10.The winner was subject to a friendly claim.
Owner Mrs E Lucey-Butler **Bred** Helshaw Grange Farms Ltd **Trained** East Chiltington, E Sussex

FOCUS
Half the field had won last-time out and this was a reasonable claimer. The pace was good and the winning time was 0.93 seconds quicker than the closing three-year-old maiden, but 3.44 seconds quicker than older-horse 81-95 handicap. The proximity of the fourth and sixth suggest the principals were not at their best.

590 BETDAQ.CO.UK MAIDEN STKS 6f (P)
2:15 (2:17) (Class 5) 3-Y-O+ **£2,331** (£693; £346; £173) **Stalls** Low

Form RPR

244- **1** **Silver Guest**[218] 3486 3-8-11 98 EdwardCreighton 7 76+
(M R Channon) *trckd ldrs: led appr fnl f: sn clr: pushed out* **5/4**[1]

04 **2** 6 **Film Queen (IRE)**[14] 413 4-9-0 0 KylieManser(7) 10 56
(B G Powell) *mid-div: hdwy on ins over 1f out: r.o fnl f to go 2nd nr fin* **66/1**

052- **3** shd **Complete Frontline (GER)**[217] 3560 3-8-11 68 AndrewElliott 4 57
(K R Burke) *sn led: hdd over 2f: rn wd into st: r.o fnl f* **7/2**[2]

00-5 **4** hd **Mileaminutemurphy**[24] 265 3-8-6 62 PatrickHills(5) 1 56
(R Hannon) *trckd ldr after 2f: led over 2f out: hdd appr fnl f: kpt on towards fin* **10/1**

0- **5** 3/4 **Sunley Smiles**[80] 6964 3-8-6 0 ChrisCatlin 8 49+
(D R C Elsworth) *towards rr: rdn 2f out: styd on fr over 1f out: nvr nrr* **14/1**

65 **6** 1 **Sazerac (USA)**[7] 505 3-8-11 0 DeanMcKeown 11 50
(D Shaw) *mid-div: hdwy 2f out: kpt on one pce fnl f* **33/1**

64 **7** shd **Eagle Nebula**[24] 265 4-9-12 0 DaneO'Neill 5 54
(B R Johnson) *sn trckd ldr: lost pl 2f out and c wd: n.d after* **11/1**

0-0 **8** 1 **Usetheforce (IRE)**[31] 175 3-8-11 0 PatCosgrave 6 50+
(M J Wallace) *slowly away: in rr whn hmpd over 1f out: nvr on terms* **14/1**

5/0 **9** 1/2 **Tiara Boom De Ay (IRE)**[17] 354 4-9-7 0 VinceSlattery 3 44
(D J Wintle) *mid-div: wknd wl over 1f out* **50/1**

0- **10** 1 1/2 **Art Exhibition (IRE)**[93] 6820 3-8-11 0 SebSanders 2 40
(J Noseda) *sn rdn in rr: nvr on terms* **6/1**[3]

1m 12.69s (0.79) **Going Correction** +0.05s/f (Slow)
WFA 3 from 4yo 15lb **10** Ran SP% **118.1**
Speed ratings (Par 103): **96,88,87,87,86 85,85,83,83,81**
CSF £126.12 TOTE £1.70: £1.02, £20.80, £1.90; EX 67.40 Trifecta £321.70 Pool: £462.18 - 1.02 winning tickets..
Owner John Guest **Bred** Timber Hill Racing Partnership **Trained** West Ilsley, Berks

FOCUS
An uncompetitive sprint maiden and Silver Guest was in a different league to this lot. The form is rated around the third and fourth for now.
Sazerac(USA) ◆ Official explanation: jockey said, regarding running and riding, having been drawn wide, his orders were to drop in, get some cover and then come home as best he could, as the gelding had failed to get home previously, adding that he was able to carry them out and stayed on under a hands-and-heels ride

591 BET FA CUP - BETDAQ H'CAP 1m 4f (P)
2:55 (2:55) (Class 4) (0-95,83) 4-Y-O+ **£4,100** (£1,227; £613; £306; £152) **Stalls** Low

Form RPR

3-13 **1** **Maslak (IRE)**[17] 358 4-9-1 80 ChrisCatlin 4 92
(P W Hiatt) *w.w: gd hdwy on outside to ld 3f out: rdn out fnl f* **5/1**[3]

3564 **2** 1 **Fusili (IRE)**[14] 409 5-9-5 81 (b) NCallan 3 92+
(N P Littmoden) *trckd ldrs: rdn 2f out: kpt in and n.m.r bend: styd on to go 2nd ins fnl f* **13/2**

-111 **3** 2 1/4 **Mutamaasek (USA)**[17] 358 6-8-13 78 KirstyMilczarek(3) 5 85
(Lady Herries) *hld up in rr: hdwy on outside to chse wnr over 2f out: one pce and lost 2nd ins fnl f* **6/4**[1]

2-13 **4** 6 **Kindlelight Blue (IRE)**[31] 185 4-8-11 76 JamesDoyle 1 73
(N P Littmoden) *hld up in rr: hdwy on ins whn n.m.r over 2f out: kpt on but n.d after* **3/1**[2]

3433 **5** 3 1/2 **Pret A Porter (UAE)**[2] 561 4-8-4 69 oh2 CatherineGannon 2 61
(P D Evans) *rrd s: sn led: hdd 3f out: wkng and n.m.r sn after* **12/1**

000- **6** nk **Bazart**[14] 6759 6-9-0 83 DeclanCannon(7) 6 74
(K R Burke) *trckd ldr to 3f out: sn wknd* **17/2**

2m 30.21s (-2.79) **Going Correction** +0.05s/f (Slow)
WFA 4 from 5yo+ 3lb **6** Ran SP% **113.2**
Speed ratings (Par 105): **111,110,108,104,102 102**
CSF £36.26 TOTE £6.60: £2.40, £2.60; EX 25.50.
Owner Clive Roberts **Bred** Shadwell Estate Company Limited **Trained** Hook Norton, Oxon

FOCUS
Poor prize money meant this 81-95 carried just Class 4 status and, with the following race a 1m2f handicap open to horses of exactly the same ratings, yet worth an extra £4,000, it was hardly surprising only six turned up. The contest itself looks ordinary form for the level, rated around the winner and third, but the pace was reasonable.

592 TRY BETDAQ FOR AN EXCHANGE H'CAP 1m 2f (P)
3:30 (3:30) (Class 3) (0-95,93) 4-Y-O+ **£6,800** (£2,023; £1,011; £505) **Stalls** Low

Form RPR

065- **1** **Philatelist (USA)**[175] 4799 4-9-1 89 NCallan 3 101+
(M A Jarvis) *trckd ldrs: c wd and led ent fnl f: hung rt but in command ins fnl f* **11/4**[1]

1-14 **2** 2 1/4 **Baylini**[31] 185 4-9-5 93 JamesDoyle 7 102+
(Ms J S Doyle) *in rr: hdwy on outside 2f out: wnt 2nd whn carried rt by wnr ent fnl f: swtchd lft ins fnl f: styd on whn hld to hang on for 2nd* **15/2**

40-1 **3** hd **Rationale (IRE)**[10] 450 5-8-11 84 J-PGuillambert 6 91
(S C Williams) *hld up in rr: hdwy on ins 2f out: r.o fnl f* **7/1**

-233 **4** 1/2 **Sgt Schultz (IRE)**[14] 410 5-9-2 89 LPKeniry 8 95
(J S Moore) *trckd ldr: led over 4f out: rdn and hdd ent fnl f: no ex fnl 50yds* **13/2**[3]

4-15 **5** 1 1/2 **Bee Stinger**[17] 357 6-8-9 82 ow1 JamieSpencer 5 85
(I A Wood) *led tl hdd over 4f out: fdd ins fnl f* **10/1**

6-40 **6** hd **Speedy Sam**[7] 502 5-9-1 88 JimCrowley 2 91
(K R Burke) *hld up: rdn and hdwy over 2f out: wknd over 1f out* **12/1**

00-5 **7** 1 **Freeloader (IRE)**[22] 309 8-8-6 79 JimmyQuinn 1 80
(R A Fahey) *in tch: rdn over 2f out: outpcd over 1f out* **8/1**

-221 **8** shd **Mataram (USA)**[14] 409 5-8-9 82 ChrisCatlin 4 82
(W Jarvis) *t.k.h: trckd ldrs: rdn over 2f out: wknd over 1f out* **10/3**[2]

2m 6.35s (-0.25) **Going Correction** +0.05s/f (Slow)
WFA 4 from 5yo+ 1lb **8** Ran SP% **115.2**
Speed ratings (Par 107): **103,101,101,100,99 99,98,98**
CSF £24.10 CT £130.57 TOTE £3.50: £1.50, £1.90, £3.70; EX 38.40 Trifecta £104.90 Pool: £418.32 - 2.83 winning tickets..
Owner Gary A Tanaka **Bred** Darley **Trained** Newmarket, Suffolk

FOCUS
A decent handicap on paper, but they went no pace at all for about the first six furlongs or so and the form, although rated at face value, needs treating with a little caution.

NOTEBOOK
Philatelist(USA), without the blinkers on his return from a six-month break, was well backed throughout the day and justified the support with a hard-fought victory, although he did have to survive a Stewards' enquiry after hanging right close home and hampering the staying-on Baylini. Well covered up in the middle of the pack, the steady pace did not bother him and this was a very useful effort, although it was a little worrying to see him hang under pressure. He is now two from two round here, but is just as effective on turf and looks capable of going on from this, even if he has some quirks. He is entered in the Winter Derby. (op 7-2 tchd 4-1)
Baylini ◆ was 7lb higher than when disappointing (10/11) over course and distance on her previous start, but she left that form behind and was possibly even a little unlucky. Held up last, the steady pace was totally against her and she was forced to make her move very wide round the final bend. She kept responding, but was hampered by the eventual winner inside the final furlong and lost all momentum. Another in the Winter Derby, she can rate higher. (op 7-1 tchd 10-1)
Rationale(IRE), 5lb higher than when winning over 1m3f at Kempton on his previous start, was keen early on and got going too late when it mattered, so it is fair to say he did not have the race run to suit. (op 6-1)
Sgt Schultz(IRE) had looked a little bit better than the bare form of his recent efforts, but this steadily run 1m2f did not suit him. He basically wants 1m4f and, although he was ridden nice and handy, he could not pick up in the straight. (op 4-1)
Bee Stinger, an unlucky loser over 1m round here on his previous start, was trying 1m2f for the first time, but he found himself in front with nothing else wanting to lead and set a very steady pace. He failed to quicken and looks a better horse when waited with. (op 8-1)
Mataram(USA), 3lb higher than when winning a slightly lesser race over course and distance on his previous start, raced keenly off the steady pace and was well below form. Official explanation: jockey said gelding was unsuited by the slow pace (op 9-2 tchd 3-1)

593 BETDAQPOKER.CO.UK H'CAP 5f (P)
4:05 (4:05) (Class 2) (0-100,98) 4-Y-O+
£9,971 (£2,985; £1,492; £747; £372; £187) **Stalls** High

Form RPR

040- **1** **Ajigolo**[71] 7053 5-8-12 92 EdwardCreighton 6 100
(M R Channon) *in rr: hdwy 1/2-way: r.o down outside fnl f to ld cl home* **14/1**

-215 **2** hd **Northern Empire (IRE)**[14] 411 5-8-9 89 ow1 NCallan 3 96
(K A Ryan) *trckd ldrs: rdn to ld ent fnl f: ct cl home* **7/2**[2]

1-21 **3** nk **Ebraam (USA)**[14] 411 5-9-1 98 TolleyDean(3) 5 104
(D Shaw) *in rr: str hdwy fnl f: nvr nrr* **2/1**[1]

-036 **4** 3/4 **Fyodor (IRE)**[14] 411 7-9-1 95 TPQueally 2 99
(W J Haggas) *s.i.s: hdwy on ins to hold ev ch 1f out: nt qckn nr fin* **4/1**[3]

-110 **5** 1/2 **Tartatartufata**[14] 411 6-8-2 89 (v) PatrickDonaghy(7) 7 91
(D Shaw) *chsd ldrs: ev ch appr fnl f: no ex ins fnl f* **25/1**

1-23 **6** 2 1/2 **Silver Prelude**[14] 411 7-8-9 89 ow2 JamieSpencer 4 82
(D K Ivory) *chsd ldr: led 2f out: hdd ent fnl f: no ex* **9/2**

-411 **7** 3 **Godfrey Street**[8] 482 5-8-4 84 (b) ChrisCatlin 1 66
(A G Newcombe) *led tl hdd 2f out: wknd fnl f* **7/1**

58.52 secs (-0.28) **Going Correction** +0.05s/f (Slow) **7** Ran SP% **116.8**
Speed ratings (Par 109): **104,103,103,102,101 97,92**
CSF £64.34 TOTE £15.40: £5.70, £2.30; EX 41.40.
Owner Timberhill Racing Partnership **Bred** Timber Hill Racing Partnership **Trained** West Ilsley, Berks

FOCUS
An ordinary sprint handicap for the grade and the pace, although still decent, was not as strong as one might have expected. Both Silver Prelude and Godfrey Street are confirmed front runners, but neither blasted off, possibly wary of getting in a speed duel, and the form is a little messy as a result.

NOTEBOOK
Ajigolo's last five wins had all come over 6f, but he made good headway when the pace eased up a touch just before the home bend and stayed on strongest of all in the straight to get up literally on the line. He would usually be run off his feet over 5f and, although that was not the case this time, he still gave the impression he will be suited by a return to 6f. This is the highest mark he has ever won off, but he was rated 111 back in the 2006 and can remain competitive. (tchd 16-1)
Northern Empire(IRE), well placed early on, was produced with absolutely every chance in the straight and can have no excuses. (op 9-2)
Ebraam(USA) had four of today's rivals behind when winning over course and distance on his previous start, including Northern Empire, but he got going too late this time off a 5lb higher mark. He would have preferred an even stronger end-to-end gallop. (op 5-2 tchd 11-4)
Fyodor(IRE) flattened out late on having looked dangerous over course and distance on his previous start and this was a similar story, although he did make his move against the often unfavoured far rail. (tchd 3-1)
Tartatartufata failed to beat a rival over course and distance on her previous start, but this was a lot better.
Silver Prelude had shown improved form when able to dominate in recent starts, including when third behind Ebraam over course and distance on his latest outing, but he was not ridden from the front this time, with his rider possibly keen to avoid a dual with Godfrey Street, and he failed to show his best. He also carried 2lb overweight. Official explanation: jockey said gelding lost its action (tchd 11-2)
Godfrey Street, chasing the hat-trick after a couple of wins in lesser company at Southwell, found this company a bit much. (op 11-2)

594 BET MULTIPLES - BETDAQ H'CAP 1m (P)
4:35 (4:36) (Class 3) (0-95,98) 4-Y-O+ **£6,800** (£2,023; £1,011; £505) **Stalls** High

Form RPR

-253 **1** **Alfresco**[19] 336 4-9-0 91 (b) NCallan 12 101
(I A Wood) *hld up in rr: hdwy on ins over 1f out: r.o to ld wl ins fnl f* **10/1**

16-2 **2** nk **Gallantry**[19] 336 6-8-10 87 DeanMcKeown 8 96
(D Shaw) *s.i.s: sn mid-div: hdwy over 2f out: r.o to go 2nd ins fnl f* **16/1**

3-11 **3** 1/2 **Monkey Glas (IRE)**[36] 124 4-8-10 87 (v) AndrewElliott 6 95
(K R Burke) *led: clr 1/2-way: hung rt over 1f out: hdd ins fnl f: kpt on but lost 2nd nr fin* **12/1**

1-44 **4** *1 1/4* **Atlantic Story (USA)**[19] 336 6-9-2 93......................(bt) JamieSpencer 4 100+
(M W Easterby) *hld up in tch: n.m.r bef swtchd rt appr fnl f: r.o ins fnl f* **9/2**[2]

000- **5** *hd* **Plum Pudding (IRE)**[112] 6499 5-8-12 89...................... RichardHughes 7 94
(R Hannon) *trckd ldrs: wnt 2nd 3f out: ev ch whn hung lft ent fnl f: no ex ins fnl f* **7/2**[1]

2111 **6** *3/4* **Neardown Beauty (IRE)**[15] 390 5-8-13 90...............(p) JamesDoyle 11 93
(A J McCabe) *hld up in rr: styd on fnl f: nvr nrr* **14/1**

365- **7** *1* **Councellor (FR)**[49] 7267 6-8-11 88..................................(t) MickyFenton 2 89
(Stef Liddiard) *trckd ldr to 3f out: styd in tch: one pce fnl f* **25/1**

30-1 **8** *1 1/4* **Sailor King (IRE)**[21] 313 6-8-6 83 ow1............................ JimCrowley 5 81
(D K Ivory) *hld up: sme hdwy on outside over 2f out: nvr nr to chal* **7/1**[3]

600- **9** *3/4* **Bomber Command (USA)**[107] 6606 5-8-13 90....................(p) TQuinn 3 86
(J W Hills) *chsd ldrs: rdn over 2f out: wknd over 1f out* **14/1**

35-1 **10** *1/2* **Capable Guest (IRE)**[19] 336 6-8-13 90.......................... ChrisCatlin 10 85
(M R Channon) *racd wd: rdn 1/2-way: no ch ins fnl 2f* **8/1**

60-0 **11** *nk* **Imperial Echo (USA)**[11] 442 7-8-3 83 oh5 ow2........... TolleyDean(3) 9 77
(D Shaw) *a bhd* **33/1**

4111 **12** *1* **Bazroy (IRE)**[10] 456 4-9-7 98.................................(b) StephenDonohoe 1 90
(P D Evans) *t.k.h in rr: rdn over 2f out and effrt over 1f out: sn btn* **9/2**[2]

1m 35.2s (-3.00) **Going Correction** +0.05s/f (Slow) course record **12** Ran SP% **125.0**
Speed ratings (Par 107): **117,116,116,114,114 114,113,111,111,110 110,109**
CSF £167.97 CT £1991.65 TOTE £9.90: £2.30, £3.90, £4.60; EX 119.00 TRIFECTA Not won..
Owner Mrs A M Riney **Bred** Usk Valley Stud **Trained** Upper Lambourn, Berks

FOCUS

A very good, competitive handicap in which five of the 12 runners had won on their previous start. They went a strong pace from the off and the winning time, a new course record, was 3.44 seconds quicker than the claimer, and 4.37 seconds faster than the following maiden, although both of those races were for three-year-olds only. The form looks solid and should prove reliable.

NOTEBOOK

Alfresco looked a little unlucky when third behind both Capable Guest and Gallantry at Kempton on his previous start, but he enjoyed a better trip this time and took full advantage. The strong pace suited and he made rapid headway to move into a challenging position before staying on best of all, breaking the track record by 0.20 seconds in the process. His effort is all the more creditable considering he made his move against the often unfavoured far rail and also looked to idle once in front. He is clearly very useful when things go his way and his form figures over this course and distance now read 11411. The Winter Derby is apparently now the target, although he is likely to be out again in the meantime. (tchd 11-1)

Gallantry, 1lb higher than when second to Capable Guest over 1m at Kempton on his previous start, ran his race but was just unable to confirm form with Alfresco. He is at the top of his game. (op 14-1)

Monkey Glas(IRE) came into this chasing the hat-trick, but he was 1lb worse off with Alfresco for a short-head defeat of that rival at Kempton on his latest start. Racing off a mark 12lb higher than when starting his winning run over this course and distance, and 6lb higher than at Kempton, he adopted his usual front-running tactics and was soon setting a very strong pace in a clear lead. It looked at one stage as though he may have gone off a little too quickly but, just as on his previous start, he stuck on really for pressure and went down fighting.

Atlantic Story(USA), a close fourth behind Capable Guest, Gallantry and Alfresco at Kempton on his previous start, only had two in front on him turning for home, so it was a poor show from his rider that he found trouble. He was probably a little unlucky not to finish closer, but he basically just lacked the speed of some of these when the race got serious. Official explanation: jockey said gelding was denied a clear run (op 6-1)

Plum Pudding(IRE) ◆, 6lb lower than when last seen on the All-Weather, failed to justify market support but this was still a creditable effort. He was forced to do a lot of the donkey work to try and peg back the clear leader, Monkey Glas, but this was his first run in over three months and he understandably got tired. He can improve on this. (op 9-2 tchd 5-1 in places)

Neardown Beauty(IRE) has been in tremendous form in slightly smaller fields of late at both Southwell and Kempton and came into this bidding for a four-timer, but she was up 6lb for her latest success and 18lb higher than when starting her winning run. Held up well off the pace, not for the first time she carried her head high under pressure and struggled to get involved, but she was running on at the finish. (op 10-1)

Sailor King(IRE) was 6lb higher than when winning over 7f round here on his previous start and he found this much tougher. (tchd 6-1)

Capable Guest(IRE) had today's winner and runner-up behind when successful at Kempton on his previous start, and he was only 2lb higher, so this was very disappointing.

Bazroy(IRE) has made rapid improvement in recent starts, rattling up a hat-trick with wins between 6f-1m round here and at Kempton, but he was 6lb higher than when scoring over 7f here on his latest start, and 18lb higher than when beginning his winning run. He was well below form and his recent exertions have taken their toll. Official explanation: trainer said gelding was unsuited by the fast pace and consequently failed to stay the trip (op 7-2 tchd 5-1 and 6-1 in a place)

595 ALL NEW @ BETDAQ.CO.UK MAIDEN STKS 1m (P)

5:05 (5:06) (Class 5) 3-Y-O £2,331 (£693; £346; £173) Stalls High

Form RPR

32-2 **1** **Segal (IRE)**[10] 458 3-9-3 79.. TPQueally 2 76+
(J Noseda) *mde virtually all: shkn up to go clr over 1f out: comf* **1/2**[1]

30- **2** *4* **Cathedral Walk (USA)**[136] 5903 3-9-3 0......................... AndrewElliott 3 65
(K R Burke) *disp ld w wnr early: outpcd over 1f out: hld on wl for 2nd* **12/1**

654 **3** *shd* **Lady Amberlini**[13] 416 3-8-12 70.............................. StephenDonohoe 1 60
(P D Evans) *mid-div: rdn over 2f out: hdwy over 1f out: r.o fnl f* **14/1**

-04 **4** *nk* **Awesome Light (IRE)**[19] 343 3-9-3 0.............................. JamesDoyle 6 64+
(W R Muir) *hld up: hdwy over 1f out: kpt on fnl f* **16/1**

4- **5** *1* **Si Belle (IRE)**[63] 7152 3-8-12 0.. SebSanders 5 57
(Rae Guest) *t.k.h on outside: clsd on ldrs 1/2-way: wknd over 1f out* **4/1**[2]

6 *1/2* **Ambrix (IRE)** 3-8-12 0... ChrisCatlin 8 56
(M R Channon) *hld up on outside: outpcd over 2f out* **20/1**

7 *hd* **El Masir** 3-9-3 0.. GregFairley 7 60+
(M Johnston) *v.s.a: rdn 3f out: no hdwy after* **7/1**[3]

00- **8** *2 1/2* **Admirals Way**[116] 6409 3-9-3 0.. JimmyQuinn 4 54
(C N Kellett) *t.k.h: prom early: wknd over 2f out* **50/1**

1m 39.57s (1.37) **Going Correction** +0.05s/f (Slow) **8** Ran SP% **126.1**
Speed ratings (Par 97): **95,91,90,90,89 89,88,86**
CSF £10.37 TOTE £1.60: £1.10, £3.00, £3.50; EX 14.70 Trifecta £138.80 Pool: £410.59 - 2.10 winning tickets. Place 6 £403.29, Place 5 £308.23.
Owner Wood Hall Stud Limited **Bred** Wood Hall Stud Limited **Trained** Newmarket, Suffolk

FOCUS

An uncompetitive maiden run at a steady pace. The winning time was 0.93 seconds slower than the opening three-year-old claimer, and 4.37 seconds slower than the older-horse 81-95 handicap and the form is rated slightly negatively.

El Masir ◆ Official explanation: jockey said colt missed the break and was denied a clear run

T/Plt: £337.60 to a £1 stake. Pool: £44,357.05. 95.90 winning tickets. T/Qpdt: £154.10 to a £1 stake. Pool: £2,333.00. 11.20 winning tickets. JS

550 SOUTHWELL (L-H)

Sunday, February 17

OFFICIAL GOING: Standard to slow

-5c overnight and after the track has been worked all night and then rolled the surface was 'very slow, very hard work, the quicker part up the centre'.

Wind: Almost nil Weather: fine and sunny

596 BRILLIANT BLUE COATS @ PONTIN'S H'CAP 5f (F)

2:00 (2:01) (Class 6) (0-60,66) 4-Y-0+ £1,911 (£564; £282) Stalls High

Form RPR

6-14 **1** **Garlogs**[23] 304 5-8-9 56.. RussellKennemore(5) 8 73
(R Hollinshead) *mde all in centre: clr over 1f out: unchal* **9/2**[2]

000- **2** *2 1/2* **Limonia (GER)**[102] 6720 6-7-12 47.................................. JamieKyne(7) 11 55
(Mike Murphy) *hld up in rr: hdwy 2f out: styd on to take 2nd ins fnl f* **50/1**

2151 **3** *1 1/2* **Savile's Delight (IRE)**[3] 554 9-9-10 66 6ex.......... RichardKingscote 10 69
(Tom Dascombe) *sn bhd on stands' side: hdwy 2f out: styd on wl ins fnl f* **7/2**[1]

400- **4** *1 3/4* **Jilly Why (IRE)**[50] 7271 7-9-2 58..............................(b) PatrickMathers 9 54
(Paul Green) *chsd wnr: wknd fnl f* **16/1**

2-42 **5** *3/4* **Kennington**[13] 437 8-8-11 53.....................................(b) HayleyTurner 14 47
(Mrs C A Dunnett) *sn outpcd and bhd stands' side: hdwy and edgd lft 2f out: nvr nr ldrs* **10/1**

06-0 **6** *1/2* **Umpa Loompa (IRE)**[17] 370 4-8-13 55.......................(v) JimmyQuinn 6 47
(D Nicholls) *chsd wnr: wknd appr fnl f* **25/1**

000- **7** *1 1/2* **Stir Crazy (IRE)**[116] 6424 4-8-12 54.................................. FergalLynch 7 40
(D W Barker) *prom: outpcd after 2f: hdwy and edgd lft over 1f out: sn wknd* **11/1**

000- **8** *nk* **Bungie**[59] 7206 4-7-13 48.. AndrewHeffernan(7) 3 33
(Paul Green) *outpcd and in rr after 2f* **40/1**

5020 **9** *hd* **Astorygoeswithit**[3] 554 5-8-10 52..............................(p) LiamJones 12 37
(G C Bravery) *prom: lost pl over 1f out* **22/1**

101- **10** *3* **Brut**[103] 6702 6-9-1 57...(p) TonyHamilton 1 31
(D W Barker) *chsd ldrs on outer: wknd over 1f out* **5/1**[3]

20-0 **11** *10* **Union Jack Jackson (IRE)**[13] 437 6-8-6 55.......(p) MarkCoumbe(7) 13 —
(John A Harris) *sn outpcd: wl bhd fnl 2f* **33/1**

000- **12** *7* **Tombalina**[207] 3837 5-8-0 47 oh1 ow1........................... KellyHarrison(5) 2 —
(C J Teague) *prom 2f: sn lost pl and bhd* **100/1**

61.73 secs (2.03) **Going Correction** +0.45s/f (Slow) **12** Ran SP% **96.9**
Speed ratings (Par 101): **101,97,94,91,90 89,87,86,86,81 65,54**
CSF £152.42 CT £462.43 TOTE £3.80: £1.60, £12.20, £1.10; EX 226.00 Trifecta £89.60 Part won. Pool: £126.26 - 0.50 winning tickets..
Owner Peter G Freeman **Bred** Peter Taplin **Trained** Upper Longdon, Staffs
■ Egyptian Lord was withdrawn (4/1, unruly in the stalls). R4 applies, deduct 20p in the £.

FOCUS

A fair sprint handicap, the gamble landed in clear-cut fashion and the winner is rated back to his best. The stands'-side rail was not the place to be.

597 BACK OR LAY AT BETDAQ (S) STKS 1m (F)

2:30 (2:30) (Class 6) 3-Y-O £1,774 (£523; £262) Stalls Low

Form RPR

4502 **1** **Novestar (IRE)**[10] 462 3-8-7 49 ow1.............................. JamieJones(5) 2 53
(G J Smith) *mde all: sddle slipped 2f out: hld on towards fin* **9/2**[2]

04- **2** *1/2* **Spitfire Jane (IRE)**[72] 7058 3-8-6 0............................... AndrewElliott 8 46
(K R Burke) *trckd ldrs: effrt over 2f out: no ex ins fnl f* **6/5**[1]

65-6 **3** *1/2* **Dickie Valentine**[20] 333 3-8-13 45 ow2......................(b[1]) AdamKirby 1 52
(M R Bosley) *s.s: hdwy over 3f out: chsd ldrs fnl f: no ex* **22/1**

5-04 **4** *5* **Shabnaam**[13] 425 3-8-6 52.. JimmyQuinn 4 34
(P Howling) *trckd ldrs: drvn over 4f out: edgd rt and wknd over 1f out* **10/1**

004- **5** *1 1/2* **Landed Gent (IRE)**[59] 7196 3-8-6 44................................ SCreighton(5) 6 35
(Miss V Haigh) *chsd ldrs: drvn 4f out: edgd lft over 2f out: sn wknd* **40/1**

0-63 **6** *5* **Cherished Song**[10] 462 3-8-6 49..................................(b[1]) GregFairley 5 19
(M G Quinlan) *w wnr: wknd 2f out* **11/2**[3]

00-6 **7** *11* **Dhaka Dazzle**[1] 589 3-8-11 48... ChrisCatlin 7 —
(M R Channon) *chsd ldrs on outside: drvn over 5f out: lost pl over 2f out: sn bhd* **7/1**

U0-0 **8** *21* **Amazing Day**[9] 486 3-8-9 62.....................................(p) MarkCoumbe(7) 3 —
(John A Harris) *in rr: drvn and reminders after 2f: sn lost pl and bhd: t.o over 3f out* **22/1**

1m 49.77s (6.07) **Going Correction** +0.425s/f (Slow) **8** Ran SP% **111.7**
Speed ratings (Par 95): **86,85,85,80,78 73,62,41**
CSF £9.77 TOTE £5.60: £1.60, £1.30, £4.50; EX 13.30 Trifecta £209.90 Pool: £360.81 - 1.22 winning tickets..The winner was bought in for 4,250gns. Landed Gent was claimed by R. C. Guest for £5,000.
Owner Graham Smith **Bred** Mrs Eithne Thompson **Trained** Six Hills, Leics

FOCUS

A run-of-the-mill seller but a slow time and the form is not solid. The in-form winner overcame a slipping saddle, the well-backed runner-up looked a shade reluctant and the third, in first-time blinkers, did well after a slow start.

598 CROC MAKES HOLIDAYS ROCK @ PONTIN'S MAIDEN STKS 6f (F)

3:00 (3:02) (Class 5) 4-Y-O+ £2,457 (£725; £362) Stalls Low

Form RPR

2-22 **1** **Cape Of Storms**[40] 79 5-9-3 52.. PhillipMakin 8 67
(R Brotherton) *chsd ldr: led over 2f out: hld on wl* **1/1**[1]

5- **2** *1 1/4* **Frisbee**[320] 908 4-8-5 0.. RobbieEgan(7) 9 58
(C J Teague) *chsd ldrs: chal over 1f out: kpt on same pce ins fnl f* **16/1**

060- **3** *8* **Ducal Regancy Red**[162] 5231 4-8-7 37............................ KellyHarrison(5) 5 32
(C J Teague) *led: hdd over 2f out: wknd fnl f* **40/1**

3/0- **4** *1 1/2* **Not Another Cat (USA)**[212] 3710 4-9-3 76................... DarrenWilliams 3 33
(K R Burke) *sn drvn along: sn chsng ldrs: outpcd over 2f out* **5/4**[2]

5 *2 1/2* **Walragnek**[47] 4-9-3 0... AndrewElliott 4 25
(J G M O'Shea) *dwlt: t.k.h: sn trcking ldrs: lost pl over 2f out* **16/1**

00- **6** *8* **Raihanah**[90] 6877 4-8-5 0.. LeeTopliss(7) 7 —
(D Shaw) *sn drvn along: lost pl over 4f out: sn bhd* **33/1**

00/5 **7** *3 1/2* **Daniel O'Donnell**[21] 326 6-9-3 52................................... SaleemGolam 2 —
(S C Williams) *lost pl over 4f out: sn bhd* **14/1**[3]

00 **8** *1 1/2* **Easily Naimd**[7] 514 4-9-3 0.. DeanMcKeown 6 —
(D Shaw) *chsd ldrs: sn drvn along: lost pl over 3f out* **40/1**

1m 19.35s (2.85) **Going Correction** +0.425s/f (Slow) **8** Ran SP% **120.7**
Speed ratings (Par 103): **98,96,85,83,80 69,65,63**
CSF £20.36 TOTE £2.00: £1.10, £2.10, £5.60; EX 23.60 Trifecta £93.10 Pool: £647.98 - 4.94 winning tickets..

Owner P S J Croft **Bred** R J Turner **Trained** Elmley Castle, Worcs

FOCUS

A weak maiden saw the consistent 52-rated Cape of Storms open his account at the 24th attempt. The form is rated around the first two.

599 RACE AHEAD WITH ZENA @ PONTIN'S CLAIMING STKS 6f (F)

3:30 (3:30) (Class 6) 4-Y-0+ £1,774 (£523; £262) **Stalls** Low

Form RPR

2-31 **1** **Came Back (IRE)**[10] 460 5-8-13 69.................... FergalLynch 7 87
(P A Blockley) *trckd ldrs: led on bit over 2f out: clr 1f out: drvn out* **1/1**[1]

3153 **2** *6* **Cleveland**[10] 460 6-8-9 63.................... HayleyTurner 5 64
(R Hollinshead) *stmbld s: led: t.k.h: hdd over 2f out: edgd rt: kpt on: no ch w wnr* **7/2**[2]

1412 **3** *2* **Grimes Faith**[16] 386 5-9-3 73....................(b) NCallan 4 66
(K A Ryan) *sn trcking ldrs: effrt over 2f out: kpt on same pce* **7/2**[2]

-030 **4** *2 1/2* **Owed**[10] 460 6-9-2 65....................(p) PatCosgrave 6 57
(R Bastiman) *trckd ldrs: effrt over 2f out: sn outpcd* **16/1**

4333 **5** *2 1/2* **Pappas Image**[5] 528 4-8-8 45....................(p) PatrickMathers 3 41
(A J McCabe) *in tch: drvn 4f out: sn outpcd* **25/1**

00-6 **6** *4* **Linda Green**[20] 334 7-9-1 63.................... ChrisCatlin 2 35
(M R Channon) *last and sn drvn along: lost pl over 3f out* **10/1**[3]

1m 17.75s (1.25) **Going Correction** +0.425s/f (Slow) **6** Ran SP% **113.3**

Speed ratings (Par 101): **108,100,97,94,90 85**

CSF £4.89 TOTE £1.90: £1.10, £2.60; EX 5.20.The winner was claimed by K. A. Ryan for £11,000.

Owner Mrs Joanna Hughes **Bred** Yeomanstown Stud **Trained** Lambourn, Berks

FOCUS

A fair claimer and the winner made this look simple on his first outing for this trainer. When he next appears it will be for his third trainer in three starts.

600 ANDREW WOODWARD'S 50TH BIRTHDAY CELEBRATIONS H'CAP 1m 6f (F)

4:00 (4:00) (Class 6) (0-65,66) 4-Y-0+ £1,911 (£564; £282) **Stalls** Low

Form RPR

404- **1** **Dreams Jewel**[53] 7198 8-8-11 50.................... NeilChalmers 9 62
(C Roberts) *hld up in rr: stdy hdwy 6f out: led 2f out: rdn and styd on* **22/1**

1022 **2** *3* **Kanisorn (SWE)**[5] 533 6-9-12 65....................(bt) LiamJones 3 73
(Mrs R A Carr) *mid-div: drvn and outpcd over 4f out: hdwy on ins 3f out: styd on to take 2nd ins fnl f* **7/1**

4-32 **3** *1 1/2* **Sand Repeal (IRE)**[19] 345 6-9-7 63....................(v) JerryO'Dwyer(3) 13 69
(Miss J Feilden) *hld up: hdwy to trck ldrs after 4f: kpt on same pce fnl 2f* **9/2**[2]

-201 **4** *8* **Blue Hills**[13] 436 7-9-13 66....................(b) PhillipMakin 8 61
(P W Hiatt) *trckd ldrs: chal over 4f out: wknd over 1f out* **9/1**

5/4- **5** *shd* **Tayman (IRE)**[92] 4322 6-9-11 64.................... JamesDoyle 7 59
(Carl Llewellyn) *w ldr: led over 5f out tl 2f out: wknd fnl f* **11/2**[3]

00-3 **6** *4* **Just Waz (USA)**[24] 283 6-8-13 55.................... MichaelJStainton(3) 10 44
(R M Whitaker) *prom: effrt over 3f out: wknd over 1f out* **22/1**

-265 **7** *2 1/2* **Matinee Idol**[3] 551 5-8-7 46 oh1.................... PaulHanagan 11 31
(Mrs S Lamyman) *sn detached and pushed along: sme hdwy over 3f out: nvr on terms* **40/1**

40-5 **8** *1/2* **Square Dealer**[24] 283 7-8-9 48....................(b) JimmyQuinn 1 33
(J R Norton) *chsd ldrs: wknd over 2f out* **33/1**

244- **9** *1 1/2* **Muntami (IRE)**[106] 4490 7-9-12 65.................... StephenDonohoe 4 48
(John A Harris) *s.i.s: sme hdwy over 4f out: nvr on terms* **12/1**

6/0- **10** *shd* **Little Lily Morgan**[23] 62 5-8-11 50.................... PatCosgrave 6 33
(R Bastiman) *chsd ldrs: rdn 8f out: wknd over 2f out* **100/1**

6-31 **11** *30* **Tioga Gold (IRE)**[19] 345 9-8-6 50.................... RussellKennemore(5) 2 —
(L R James) *s.s: sme hdwy on wd outside 7f out: lost pl 4f out: sn bhd and virtually p.u* **11/1**

0-32 **12** *3* **Squiffy**[10] 461 5-9-3 56.................... NCallan 12 —
(P D Cundell) *chsd ldrs: lost pl over 3f out: sn bhd and virtually p.u* **3/1**[1]

10 **13** *6* **She's The Lady**[25] 272 8-9-11 64.................... ChrisCatlin 5 —
(E J O'Neill) *led tl over 5f out: lost pl over 4f out: sn bhd and virtually p.u* **12/1**

3m 13.59s (5.29) **Going Correction** +0.425s/f (Slow) **13** Ran SP% **119.9**

Speed ratings (Par 101): **101,99,98,93,93 91,90,89,88,88 71,70,66**

CSF £163.61 CT £835.22 TOTE £25.80: £5.60, £2.30, £1.90; EX 272.30 Trifecta £85.70 Pool: £362.19 - 3.00 winning tickets..

Owner Allan Ashcroft **Bred** Allan Ashcroft **Trained** Coedkernew, Newport

FOCUS

A low-grade stayers' handicap run at a sound pace and they came home well strung out. An improved effort from the winner and the form looks sound at this level.

Tioga Gold(IRE) Official explanation: jockey said gelding dwelt and never travelled

Squiffy Official explanation: trainer had no explanation for the poor form shown

601 KIDS ARE ALWAYS HAPPY @ PONTIN'S H'CAP 1m (F)

4:30 (4:30) (Class 5) (0-70,70) 4-Y-0+ £2,593 (£765; £383) **Stalls** Low

Form RPR

5-10 **1** **Komreyev Star**[24] 287 6-8-4 56 oh4.................... JimmyQuinn 4 60
(R E Peacock) *led 1f: w ldrs: led over 1f out: hrd rdn and hld on towards fin* **15/2**

3121 **2** *nk* **Louisiade (IRE)**[3] 553 7-8-11 70 6ex....................(p) MarkCoumbe(7) 2 73
(M C Chapman) *trckd ldrs: chal 2f out: no ex towards fin* **9/1**

22-2 **3** *1/2* **King's Ransom**[31] 192 5-8-10 62.................... ChrisCatlin 1 64
(S Gollings) *hdwy on ins to ld after 1f: hdd over 1f out: hrd rdn and styd on same pce ins fnl f* **5/2**[1]

1-30 **4** *3* **Zabeel House**[35] 148 5-8-10 62....................(p) DeanMcKeown 9 57
(John A Harris) *chsd ldrs on outer: one pce fnl 3f* **5/1**[3]

-131 **5** *1* **Haroldini (IRE)**[26] 258 6-9-1 70....................(p) TolleyDean(3) 7 63
(J Balding) *t.k.h in rr: hdwy on outside over 2f out: kpt on: nvr a threat* **3/1**[2]

60-4 **6** *1* **Latif (USA)**[6] 525 7-9-0 66.................... SamHitchcott 5 56
(Paul Green) *s.s: hmpd on ins bnd over 4f out: hdwy 3f out: kpt on: nvr trbld ldrs* **11/1**

10/0 **7** *11* **Princelywallywogan**[16] 395 6-8-8 60.................... AndrewElliott 3 25
(John A Harris) *trckd ldrs: lost pl 3f out: sn bhd* **40/1**

5-04 **8** *hd* **Tina's Ridge (IRE)**[3] 550 4-7-11 56 oh3....................(p) DavidProbert(7) 8 21
(R Hollinshead) *hld up in rr: n.m.r and swtchd outside over 2f out: lost pl over 1f out* **9/1**

1m 46.64s (2.94) **Going Correction** +0.425s/f (Slow) **8** Ran SP% **112.8**

Speed ratings (Par 103): **102,101,101,98,97 96,85,85**

CSF £69.71 CT £214.89 TOTE £8.40: £2.70, £1.70, £1.50; EX 81.90 Trifecta £350.60 Part won. Pool: £493.91 - 0.85 winning tickets..

Owner Garry Whittaker **Bred** G And Mrs Whittaker **Trained** Kyre Park, Worcs

■ Stewards' Enquiry : Mark Coumbe two-day ban: careless riding (Feb 29-Mar 1); three-day ban: used whip with excessive frequency (Mar 3-5)

FOCUS

A modest handicap and not easy to rate with the third, who enjoyed the run of the race, perhaps the best guide.

602 BET FA CUP - BETDAQ H'CAP 1m 4f (F)

5:00 (5:00) (Class 6) (0-60,60) 4-Y-0+ £1,911 (£564; £282) **Stalls** Low

Form RPR

4-24 **1** **Mid Valley**[29] 231 5-8-10 46.................... J-PGuillambert 6 59+
(J R Jenkins) *s.i.s: hld up: stdy hdwy over 4f out: wnt 2nd 3f out: led over 1f out: eased ins fnl f* **4/1**[2]

5-05 **2** *3* **Speagle (IRE)**[22] 323 6-9-5 55.................... DeanMcKeown 4 63
(P A Blockley) *led: hdd over 1f out: kpt on same pce* **9/4**[1]

-301 **3** *8* **Global Traffic**[9] 481 4-9-2 60....................(v) PatrickHills(5) 8 54
(D Shaw) *s.i.s: detached in rr: hdwy 4f out: wnt modest 3rd over 1f out* **4/1**[2]

5-23 **4** *3/4* **Nabir (FR)**[9] 481 8-9-2 52....................(p) PaulHanagan 2 45
(P D Niven) *chsd ldrs: drvn over 4f out: hung lft and one pce* **7/1**[3]

042- **5** *6* **Shandelight (IRE)**[198] 4139 4-8-9 51.................... AndrewMullen(3) 5 34
(Mrs A Duffield) *rrd s: sn chsng ldrs: drvn over 4f out: wknd over 2f out* **15/2**

4665 **6** *1 1/2* **Speed Dial Harry (IRE)**[12] 438 6-9-0 50....................(v) AdamKirby 7 30
(C R Dore) *mid-div: reminders after 3f: lost pl over 4f out* **12/1**

030- **7** *7* **Bolckow**[59] 7198 5-9-4 54.................... MickyFenton 1 22
(J T Stimpson) *chsd ldrs: drvn over 4f out: lost pl over 2f out* **10/1**

34/0 **8** *36* **Liberty Seeker (FR)**[9] 485 9-9-7 57.................... StephenDonohoe 3 —
(John A Harris) *in rr: detached 7f out: t.o 3f out* **28/1**

2m 44.46s (3.46) **Going Correction** +0.425s/f (Slow)

WFA 4 from 5yo+ 3lb **8** Ran SP% **115.3**

Speed ratings (Par 101): **105,103,97,97,93 92,87,63**

CSF £13.57 CT £37.57 TOTE £5.80: £2.00, £1.50, £1.50; EX 16.90 Trifecta £56.40 Pool: £679.56 - 8.54 winning tickets. Place 6 £26.97, Place 5 £15.94.

Owner M Ng **Bred** Michael Ng **Trained** Royston, Herts

FOCUS

A moderate contest run at a strong gallop which seemed to suit the winner, and the form appears solid for the grade. The runner-up has changed stables and is a stone lower than his last success.

T/Plt: £25.20 to a £1 stake. Pool: £118,865.10. 3,429.80 winning tickets. T/Qpdt: £10.50 to a £1 stake. Pool: £6,491.50. 456.40 winning tickets. WG

421 ST MORITZ (R-H)

Sunday, February 17

OFFICIAL GOING: Frozen

603a GRAND PRIX CORPORATE EVENTS/NEWMARKET RACES (ICE) 5f 110y

11:45 (11:49) 4-Y-0+ £6,400 (£2,560; £1,920; £1,280; £640)

RPR

1 **Atlantic Dancer (GER)**[14] 421 5-8-11 .... OPlacais 6 —
(A Schennach, Switzerland) **7/2**[2]

2 *nk* **Rushing Dasher (GER)**[7] 6-9-4 .... JBojko 10 —
(A Wohler, Germany) **21/10**[1]

3 *1 1/4* **Assam (GER)**[14] 421 6-9-4 .... GBocskai 4 —
(Carmen Bocskai, Switzerland) **86/10**

4 *3/4* **Hart Of Gold**[14] 421 4-8-11 .... KevinGhunowa 5 —
(R A Harris) *cl up: hdwy to press ldrs whn hung lft off fnl bnd 1 1/2f out: lost pl: r.o wl clsng stages* **146/10**

5 *nk* **Fulminant (IRE)**[14] 421 7-9-2 ....(b) TCastanheira 1 —
(Karin Suter, Switzerland) **48/10**

6 *5* **Tobanjaro (HUN)**[14] 421 5-8-9 ....(b) SGeorgiev 8 —
(Z Nagy, Hungary) **175/10**

7 *nk* **Smarten Die (IRE)** 5-8-11 .... DPorcu 3 —
(Frau E Mader, Germany) **173/10**

8 *2* **Coseadrom (IRE)**[14] 421 6-9-2 .... RPiechulek 9 —
(C Von Der Recke, Germany) **46/10**[3]

9 *1/2* **Zoom (GER)**[14] 421 5-8-12 .... TMundry 2 —
(C Von Der Recke, Germany) **7/2**[2]

10 *1 1/4* **Radames (GER)**[1018] 9-8-9 .... RobertHavlin 7 —
(U Bosshard, Switzerland) **177/10**

65.24 secs (65.24) **10** Ran SP% **144.8**

(including 1 Swiss Franc stake): WIN 4.50; PL 1.40, 1.30, 1.60;DF 10.40.

Owner Stall Leonardo **Bred** Frau S Kubatta **Trained** Switzerland

NOTEBOOK

Hart Of Gold, who was slightly baulked when running here earlier in the month, looked unlucky as he ran wide off the final bend before finishing well. He looks capable of scoring on this surface.

604a GRAND PRIX AXA WINTERTHUR VERSICHERUNGEN (ICE) 1m 1f

1:25 (1:27) 4-Y-0+ £3,200 (£1,280; £960; £640; £320)

RPR

1 **Vlavianus (CZE)**[371] 439 7-9-2 ....(b) MiguelLopez(7) 2 —
(M Weiss, Switzerland) **6/5**[1]

2 *2 1/2* **Daring Affair**[14] 422 7-9-6 .... KevinGhunowa 4 —
(R A Harris) *led to ins fnl f: one pce after* **9/1**

3 *2 1/2* **Puro (CZE)**[364] 494 6-9-9 .... RobertHavlin 5 —
(M Weiss, Switzerland) **21/10**[2]

4 *1* **Congrio Dorado (USA)**[364] 494 6-8-12 .... TMundry 3 —
(C Von Der Recke, Germany) **191/10**

5 *5* **Dixigold (FR)**[14] 422 7-8-10 .... ChantalZollet 1 —
(Carmen Bocskai, Switzerland) **72/10**[3]

6 *15* **Demonious**[185] 9-9-8 .... SilviaCasanova(7) 7 —
(R Pritchard-Gordon, France) **122/10**

7 *4* **Royal Fire (GER)**[14] 422 9-8-6 ow3.................... HelenIsler-Kopalek(7) 6 —
(Miss A Casotti, Switzerland) **106/10**

8 *1 1/4* **Simonas (IRE)**[14] 423 9-9-0 .... JBojko 8 —
(A Wohler, Germany) **76/10**

9 *5* **Festero (GER)** 5-8-10 .... RPiechulek 9 —
(C Von Der Recke, Germany) **76/10**

1m 58.7s (118.70) **9** Ran SP% **144.3**

WIN 2.20; PL 1.20, 1.90, 1.20; DF 10.30.

Owner Stall Schachen **Bred** Stall Schachen **Trained** Switzerland

The Form Book, Raceform Ltd, Compton, RG20 6NL

NOTEBOOK
Daring Affair, well beaten here early in the month, seemed happier making the running and held on until inside the last furlong.

605a GUBELIN GROSSER PREIS VON SAINT MORITZ (ICE) 1m 2f
1:55 (1:59) 4-Y-0+ £23,704 (£9,481; £7,111; £4,785; £2,372)

RPR
1 **First Time (GER)**[14] 423 5-8-11 .... TCastanheira 7 —
(Karin Suter, Switzerland) **11/1**
2 *nk* **Cupid's Glory**[14] 423 6-8-12 .... SteveDrowne 6 —
(Mrs L C Jewell) *cl up tl led 1/2-way: hdd and no ex cl home* **35/1**
3 *3* **Collow (GER)**[14] 423 8-9-4 .... OPlacais 13 —
(M Weiss, Switzerland) **17/1**
4 *10* **Salattus (GER)**[124] 7-9-7 .... PScharer 12 —
(G Raveneau, Switzerland) **12/1**
5 *1 3/4* **Vegano (FR)**[14] 422 7-8-12 .... MKolb 9 —
(C Von Der Recke, Germany) **31/1**
6 *7* **Balor (FR)**[14] 423 5-9-9 .... RobertHavlin 2 —
(M Weiss, Switzerland) **17/10**[1]
7 *1 3/4* **Rockbranglen (USA)**[481] 5-9-0 .... JJohansen 1 —
(F Reuterskiold, Sweden) **14/1**
8 *8* **Quiron (IRE)**[14] 423 7-9-9 .... TMundry 3 —
(Carmen Bocskai, Switzerland) **59/10**[3]
9 *1 1/2* **Personal Power (GER)**[28] 5-8-12 .... DPorcu 4 —
(C Von Der Recke, Germany) **20/1**
10 *nk* **Ailton (GER)**[14] 423 4-8-13 .... GBocskai 8 —
(Carmen Bocskai, Switzerland) **51/10**[2]
11 *dist* **Home Call (USA)**[273] 6-9-0 .... JBojko 5 —
(C Von Der Recke, Germany) **49/1**
12 *2* **Britannic**[14] 423 5-8-12 .... RPiechulek 11 —
(C Von Der Recke, Germany) **10/1**
0 **Arturius (IRE)**[14] 423 6-8-12 .... KevinGhunowa 10 —
(R A Harris) *4th over 4f out: wknd qckly* **100/1**

2m 7.32s (127.32)
WFA 4 from 5yo+ 1lb 13 Ran SP% **118.9**
WIN 12.00; PL 4.70, 8.20, 4.70; DF 123.40.
Owner Stall S V H **Bred** Gestut Elite **Trained** Switzerland

NOTEBOOK
Cupid's Glory ran much better than on his debut here under a positive ride and was only just caught.

589 LINGFIELD (L-H)
Monday, February 18

OFFICIAL GOING: Standard
Wind: Almost nil Weather: Sunny

606 FAMILY TO PONTIN'S AMATEUR RIDERS' H'CAP 1m 4f (P)
1:20 (1:21) (Class 6) (0-52,51) 4-Y-0+ £1,813 (£557; £278) Stalls Low

Form RPR
000/ 1 **Wizard Looking**[612] 2612 7-11-6 **50** .... MrSWalker 3 59+
(D E Cantillon) *hld up bhd ldrs: prog on inner to go 2nd 4f out: trckd ldr tl rdn to ld ins fnl f: jst hld on* **7/2**[1]
00/0 2 *hd* **Ben Bacchus (IRE)**[2] 585 6-10-12 **45** .... MrsMarieKing(3) 1 53
(P W Hiatt) *prom: led 6f out: clr w two rivals fr over 3f out: pushed along and hdd ins fnl f: kpt on wl* **10/1**
-344 3 *5* **Granary Girl**[18] 373 6-10-13 **46** .... SimonPearce(3) 10 46
(J Pearce) *hld up in midfield: n.m.r and snatched up over 4f out: prog over 3f out but already lost tch w ldng trio: r.o to take 3rd nr fin* **7/1**[3]
-405 4 *1/2* **Carlton Scroop (FR)**[15] 420 5-10-13 **50** .... (b) MrSHoughton(7) 5 49
(J Jay) *trckd ldrs: reminder 5f out: prog to chse ldng pair over 3f out and sn clr of rest: bmpd along and no imp 2f out: lost 3rd nr fin* **8/1**
-232 5 *2 1/2* **Ndola**[9] 499 9-11-2 **51** .... (v) MissZoeLilly(5) 15 46
(P Butler) *hld up in rr: prog to chse clr ldng trio over 2f out: urged along and no imp: fdd fnl f* **9/1**
0050 6 *1* **Elms Schoolboy**[3] 578 6-10-10 **45** .... (b) MissAWallace(5) 8 39
(P Howling) *s.s: hld up wl in rr: prog 4f out but ldrs already clr: bmpd along and no imp fnl 2f* **25/1**
0/-0 7 *3* **Pure Brief (IRE)**[13] 438 11-10-8 **45** .... MissStefaniaGandola(7) 2 34
(R Hollinshead) *mde most at stdy pce to 6f out: steadily fdd fr over 3f out* **40/1**
00-4 8 *nk* **Christalini**[31] 219 4-10-9 **47** .... MissSarah-JaneDurman(5) 13 35
(J C Fox) *hld up and sn detached in last pair: stl in last pair 3f out and wl bhd: styd on wl fnl 2f* **10/1**
0646 9 *1/2* **Ronsard (IRE)**[13] 438 6-11-1 **45** .... MissEFolkes 16 33
(P D Evans) *hld up towards rr: wl bhd 3f out: styd on u.p fr over 1f out* **12/1**
005- 10 *hd* **Krasivi's Boy (USA)**[7] 7256 6-10-10 **47** .... (b) MrJoshuaMoore(7) 9 34
(G L Moore) *in tch: outpcd over 3f out: no ch after: plugged on* **5/1**[2]
0-00 11 *2 1/2* **Piquet**[11] 471 10-10-8 **45** .... MrSeanKerr(7) 14 28
(G F Bridgwater) *nvr beyond midfield: lft bhd fr 4f out* **66/1**
6-00 12 *3 1/2* **Ghaill Force**[15] 166 6-11-1 **45** .... MissEJJones 11 23
(P Butler) *s.v.s: sn in tch in rr: outpcd over 3f out: no ch after* **14/1**
-034 13 *3* **Trackattack**[17] 394 6-10-8 **45** .... (p) MrRJKirk(7) 12 18
(M Appleby) *racd v wd thrght: w ldrs to over 4f out: sn btn* **16/1**
5106 14 *1/2* **Rubilini**[10] 478 4-10-6 **46** .... (p) MissTHall(7) 4 18
(Miss Sheena West) *t.k.h: hld up wl in rr: effrt and extremely wd over 3f out: sn wknd* **16/1**
0-40 15 *1 1/2* **Katie Kingfisher**[13] 438 4-10-5 **45** .... (p) MrJPearce(7) 7 15
(M Wigham) *w ldrs tl wknd rapidly 4f out* **25/1**
000- 16 *23* **Fulvio (USA)**[160] 5310 8-10-8 **45** .... (v) MissAlexWells(7) 6 —
(P Howling) *w ldrs tl wknd rapidly over 4f out: t.o* **33/1**

2m 34.48s (1.48) **Going Correction** +0.025s/f (Slow)
WFA 4 from 5yo+ 3lb 16 Ran SP% **131.4**
Speed ratings (Par 101): **96,95,92,92,90 89,87,87,87,87 85,83,81,80,79 64**
CSF £40.45 CT £250.32 TOTE £4.70: £1.60, £3.70, £1.10, £2.50; EX 75.10 TRIFECTA Not won..
Owner T H Heckingbottom **Bred** J G Phillips **Trained** Newmarket, Suffolk

FOCUS
Some of these amateurs were less than convincing and the form needs treating with caution. They hacked through the first couple of furlongs, but the pace was increased down the back straight and they finished strung out. The winner was well in on his old form and could defy a rise in the weights.

Ghaill Force Official explanation: jockey said gelding missed the break

607 GREAT FAMILY MEMORIES @ PONTIN'S HOLIDAYS (S) STKS 1m (P)
1:55 (1:55) (Class 6) 3-Y-0+ £1,774 (£523; £262) Stalls High

Form RPR
00-4 1 **Naughty Thoughts (IRE)**[10] 490 4-9-3 56 .... AlanDaly 5 50
(Andrew Turnell) *t.k.h early: trckd ldrs: 6th whn rdn 2f out: r.o u.p fr over 1f out: led last stride* **8/1**
-210 2 *shd* **Northern Desert (IRE)**[28] 250 9-10-0 65 .... (p) PaulDoe 10 61
(S Curran) *t.k.h: trckd ldrs: gng wl 2f out: led jst over 1f out: drvn and plugged on fnl f: hdd last stride* **6/1**[3]
1134 3 *shd* **Arctic Desert**[3] 577 8-10-0 63 .... (t) HayleyTurner 11 60
(Miss Gay Kelleway) *racd wd: hld up: prog over 3f out: drvn over 1f out: r.o to chal last 100yds: jst hld* **11/4**[2]
1546 4 *1 1/4* **Tapas Lad (IRE)**[11] 464 3-8-9 61 .... (v) DavidKinsella 4 51
(V Smith) *pressed ldr: rdn over 2f out: stl cl enough over 1f out: one pce ins fnl f* **12/1**
5 *1/2* **Sendreni (FR)**[98] 4-9-8 69 .... PatCosgrave 3 50
(D E Cantillon) *t.k.h: mde most: hrd rdn and hdd jst over 1f out: fdd* **15/8**[1]
0-03 6 *1* **Doctor Ned**[5] 535 4-9-8 35 .... NeilChalmers 6 48
(Miss Sheena West) *trckd ldrs: rdn and cl enough 2f out: swtchd off rail 1f out: no imp after* **33/1**
00-0 7 *2 1/2* **Stratn Jack**[7] 99 4-9-1 40 .... GabrielHannon(7) 8 42
(B G Powell) *a in last trio: urged along and outpcd over 3f out* **66/1**
-500 8 *nk* **Kazakstan**[8] 516 4-9-5 48 .... (p) JerryO'Dwyer(3) 1 42
(Mrs L C Jewell) *towards rr: reminders wl over 3f out: sn outpcd: no imp on ldrs after* **33/1**
135- 9 *12* **Blue Quiver (IRE)**[122] 6316 8-9-8 58 .... SimonWhitworth 9 14
(C A Horgan) *hld up in last: lost tch over 3f out: shkn up over 2f out and no prog: eased fnl f* **8/1**

1m 38.35s (0.15) **Going Correction** +0.025s/f (Slow)
WFA 3 from 4yo+ 19lb 9 Ran SP% **113.0**
Speed ratings (Par 101): **100,99,99,98,98 97,94,94,82**
CSF £53.16 TOTE £10.60: £2.30, £1.30, £1.60; EX 40.00 Trifecta £96.20 Pool £239.96 - 1.77 winning units..The winner was sold to Tom Dascombe for 8,800gns. Sendreni was the subject of a friendly claim.
Owner Mrs Claire Hollowood **Bred** Dr John Hollowood And Aiden Murphy **Trained** Broad Hinton, Wilts

FOCUS
A competitive enough seller, but it was slowly run and the form looks dubious, with the sixth and seventh not beaten far.

Blue Quiver(IRE) Official explanation: jockey said gelding ran flat

608 BE BESIDE SEASIDE @ PONTIN'S MAIDEN STKS 7f (P)
2:25 (2:26) (Class 5) 3-Y-0+ £2,331 (£693; £346; £173) Stalls Low

Form RPR
2- 1 **Orientalist Art**[268] 2041 3-8-9 0 .... SebSanders 2 77+
(P W Chapple-Hyam) *trckd ldng pair: effrt and got through to ld jst over 1f out: pressed fnl f: rdn and r.o wl* **30/100**[1]
23-4 2 *nk* **Silent Master (USA)**[33] 175 3-8-9 77 .... GregFairley 5 76
(M Johnston) *trckd ldrs on outer: effrt over 1f out: pressed wnr fnl f: r.o but a hld* **8/1**[3]
544- 3 *3* **Atheer Dubai (IRE)**[121] 6328 3-8-9 79 .... LiamJones 6 68
(C E Brittain) *led: narrowly hdd 2f out: stl upsides jst over 1f out: sn outpcd* **13/2**[2]
44-0 4 *1/2* **Interactive (IRE)**[21] 334 5-9-12 70 .... ChrisCatlin 7 73
(Andrew Turnell) *pressed ldr: narrow ld 2f out to jst over 1f out: outpcd u.p* **16/1**
5 *3/4* **Bahamian Bliss** 3-8-3 0 ow2 .... KirstyMilczarek(3) 3 62
(J A R Toller) *hld up in last trio: pushed along over 2f out: rn green over 1f out: no imp* **66/1**
54- 6 *1/2* **Thermidor (USA)**[146] 5714 5-9-12 0 .... RichardKingscote 1 69+
(Lady Herries) *hld up in last trio: pushed along 2f out: no imp on ldrs after: do bttr* **33/1**
7 *8* **Ramprakash** 3-8-9 0 .... HayleyTurner 4 42
(M L W Bell) *dwlt: rn green and sn pushed along: a last: lost tch 2f out* **33/1**

1m 23.5s (-1.30) **Going Correction** +0.025s/f (Slow)
WFA 3 from 5yo 17lb 7 Ran SP% **114.6**
Speed ratings (Par 103): **108,107,104,103,102 102,93**
CSF £3.53 TOTE £1.30: £1.10, £2.70; EX 3.50.
Owner Matthew Green **Bred** Lady Bamford **Trained** Newmarket, Suffolk

FOCUS
An ordinary maiden and a decent winning time for the type of race. Sound form, rated through the second and fourth. Orientalist Art did not need to match the form of his debut last year and can obviously rate a good deal higher.

609 PEGGY'S 90TH BIRTHDAY CELEBRATION H'CAP 7f (P)
3:00 (3:01) (Class 5) (0-75,70) 4-Y-0+ £2,590 (£770; £385; £192) Stalls Low

Form RPR
-335 1 **Count Ceprano (IRE)**[14] 429 4-8-7 **66** .... GabrielHannon(7) 8 75
(M D I Usher) *hld up towards rr: gng wl 2f out: swtchd ins 1f out: pushed into ld last 100yds: kpt on wl* **10/1**
04-2 2 *1/2* **Mr Cellophane**[5] 539 5-9-0 **66** .... JimCrowley 5 73
(J R Jenkins) *sn led: tried to kick on over 1f out: kpt on u.p fnl f: hdd last 100yds* **10/3**[2]
01-1 3 *1/2* **Joy And Pain**[12] 453 7-8-7 **59** .... (p) IanMongan 2 65
(M J Attwater) *trckd ldrs: rdn and effrt over 1f out: clsd and looked dangerous ent fnl f: nt qckn* **13/2**
6-04 4 *2 1/2* **Best One**[26] 275 4-9-2 **68** .... HayleyTurner 6 67
(C E Brittain) *w ldr: rdn wl over 1f out: nt qckn ent fnl f: wknd* **2/1**[1]
2143 5 *hd* **Obe Royal**[11] 463 4-8-11 **70** .... (b) RichardEvans(7) 7 69
(P D Evans) *hld up in last trio: n.m.r over 5f out: wl off the pce 2f out: styd on fnl f* **8/1**
165- 6 *1 1/2* **Wadnagin (IRE)**[103] 6717 4-8-10 **62** .... JamesDoyle 3 57
(I A Wood) *a in last trio: rdn and struggling in last 2f out* **12/1**
1-60 7 *hd* **Corlough Mountain**[12] 452 4-9-3 **69** .... JimmyQuinn 4 63
(M J McGrath) *trckd ldng pair: rdn and nt qckn 2f out: fdd on inner fnl f* **5/1**[3]
0-30 8 *nk* **Cavalry Guard (USA)**[26] 265 4-9-4 **70** .... PatCosgrave 1 63
(J R Boyle) *trckd ldrs: rdn over 2f out: wknd over 1f out* **25/1**

1m 23.46s (-1.34) **Going Correction** +0.025s/f (Slow) 8 Ran SP% **118.2**
Speed ratings (Par 103): **108,107,106,104,103 102,101,101**
CSF £44.88 CT £242.08 TOTE £12.80: £3.30, £1.20, £1.90; EX 56.20 Trifecta £101.10 Pool £712.09 - 5.00 winning units..
Owner I Sheward **Bred** Pendley Farm **Trained** Upper Lambourn, Berks

FOCUS
An ordinary handicap, but they went a decent-enough pace and the winning time was a creditable one for the class. Just modest form, the winner taking advantage of having dropped to a good mark.
Obe Royal Official explanation: jockey said gelding suffered interference in running

610 BET CHAMPIONS LEAGUE - BETDAQ MAIDEN STKS 1m 2f (P)
3:35 (3:36) (Class 5) 3-Y-O+ **£2,331** (£693; £346; £173) **Stalls** Low

Form RPR
3- **1** **General Blucher (IRE)**[61] 7191 3-8-5 0.............................. AlanMunro 4 64+
(P W Chapple-Hyam) *trckd ldr: led narrowly 2f out: hd high over 1f out: drvn and kpt on fnl f* **8/11**[1]
2 ¾ **Smooth Sovereign (IRE)** 3-8-5 0.............................. GregFairley 3 63+
(M Johnston) *trckd ldng pair: gng wl 2f out: nt clr run on inner over 1f out and swtchd rt: styd on fnl f to take 2nd nr fin* **7/2**[2]
066- **3** *nk* **Hawk House**[132] 6080 3-8-5 64.............................. ChrisCatlin 7 59
(B W Hills) *led at stdy pce: rdn and hdd 2f out: pressed wnr after: hld ins fnl f: edgd rt and lost 2nd nr fin* **7/2**[2]
4 *1* **Our Jane** 3-8-0 0.............................. DavidKinsella 1 52
(P G Murphy) *hld up in last pair: rdn and effrt 2f out: chsng ldrs over 1f out: kpt on same pce* **80/1**
6 **5** *1 ¼* **Royal Soverin**[12] 454 3-8-5 0.............................. LiamJones 5 55
(M J Wallace) *trckd ldng pair: effrt 2f out: wandered and green over 1f out: fdd* **33/1**[3]
5 **6** *5* **Spellman**[39] 107 4-9-12 0.............................. JamesDoyle 2 50?
(N P Littmoden) *a in last pair: rdn and lost tch over 2f out* **33/1**[3]

2m 7.45s (0.85) **Going Correction** +0.025s/f (Slow)
WFA 3 from 4yo 22lb **6 Ran SP% 109.5**
Speed ratings (Par 103): **97,96,96,95,94 90**
CSF £3.35 TOTE £1.70: £1.20, £1.40; EX 3.80.
Owner P W Chapple-Hyam **Bred** Philip Brady **Trained** Newmarket, Suffolk
■ A winner for Alan Munro on his first ride in Britain following an 18-month lay-off.

FOCUS
This was basically a three-horse race and the trio duly filled the frame, but it was also a bit of a messy contest and there was not much pace on early. The form looks ordinary with the close-up third rated just 64 but the first two should prove better than the bare form.

611 BOOK PONTIN'S - BECAUSE YOU'RE WORTH IT H'CAP 1m 2f (P)
4:10 (4:11) (Class 6) (0-55,55) 4-Y-O+ **£1,876** (£554; £277) **Stalls** Low

Form RPR
2665 **1** **Climate (IRE)**[21] 341 9-8-8 49 ow1.............................. StephenDonohoe 11 60
(P D Evans) *hld up towards rr: prog 3f out: rdn and hanging over 1f out: styd on to ld ins fnl f* **10/1**
0-53 **2** *1* **Siena Star (IRE)**[5] 541 10-8-13 54.............................. MickyFenton 5 63
(Stef Liddiard) *trckd ldng pair: narrow ld over 2f out: drvn over 1f out: hdd ins fnl f: nt qckn* **7/2**[1]
0-22 **3** *1* **Bethanys Boy (IRE)**[10] 481 7-9-0 55.............................. NCallan 12 62
(A M Hales) *s.s: sn in midfield: rdn to chse ldrs 2f out: kpt on u.p but nvr pce to chal* **7/2**[1]
2263 **4** *shd* **Jomus**[8] 517 7-8-8 49 ow1.............................. RobertHavlin 1 57+
(L Montague Hall) *stdd s: hld up in last: plenty to do over 2f out: prog whn nt clr run jst over 1f out and swtchd rt: styd on: nrst fin* **10/1**
4400 **5** *1 ¼* **Western Roots**[22] 330 7-8-13 54.............................. ChrisCatlin 3 58
(M Appleby) *s.i.s: hld up in last trio: prog fr 3f out: chsng ldrs 2f out: fdd fnl f* **10/1**
-456 **6** *½* **Play Up Pompey**[24] 300 6-8-11 52.............................. NeilChalmers 2 58+
(J J Bridger) *dwlt: hld up in rr: nt qckn over 2f out and plenty to do: styng on but no ch whn squeezed out ins fnl f* **8/1**
0031 **7** *2* **Josr's Magic (IRE)**[14] 430 4-8-12 54.............................. JimmyQuinn 7 53
(H J Collingridge) *t.k.h: trckd ldrs fast pce: led over 3f out to over 2f out: sn btn* **6/1**[3]
030- **8** *1 ¼* **Gyration (IRE)**[142] 5817 4-8-5 47.............................. AndrewElliott 8 44
(G A Swinbank) *trckd ldng pair: rdn to chal over 2f out: wknd over 1f out* **4/1**[2]
60 **9** *2* **Bandits Pistol (NZ)**[21] 332 8-8-9 50..............................(b[1]) J-PGuillambert 9 43
(M Madgwick) *nvr beyond midfield: pushed along over 4f out: struggling in rr 2f out* **25/1**
40-0 **10** *7* **Old Etonian (UAE)**[40] 95 4-8-3 50..............................(p) ColinHaddon[(5)] 10 29
(Peter Grayson) *racd v freely in ld: hdd over 3f out and immediately dropped out* **20/1**

2m 4.96s (-1.64) **Going Correction** +0.025s/f (Slow)
WFA 4 from 5yo+ 1lb **10 Ran SP% 125.7**
Speed ratings (Par 101): **107,106,105,105,104 103,102,101,99,94**
CSF £48.67 CT £155.09 TOTE £11.50: £3.80, £1.50, £1.60; EX 50.80 Trifecta £110.40 Pool £516.32 - 3.32 winning units..
Owner J E Abbey **Bred** Mrs A Naughton **Trained** Pandy, Monmouths
■ Stewards' Enquiry : Robert Havlin two-day ban: careless riding (Feb 29-Mar 1)

FOCUS
A poor handicap, but they went a fair pace after a couple of furlongs and the winning time was a decent one for the class. Modest form, but sound enough.
Bethanys Boy(IRE) Official explanation: jockey said gelding hung right

612 BEST VALUE FOR ASIAN H'CAPS - BETDAQ HANDICAP 5f (P)
4:40 (4:40) (Class 5) (0-55,70) 3-Y-O **£2,331** (£693; £346; £173) **Stalls** High

Form RPR
-123 **1** **Orpen's Art (IRE)**[13] 444 3-8-3 58.............................. KirstyMilczarek[(3)] 6 66+
(S A Callaghan) *hld up in last pair: nt clr run wl over 1f out: prog sn after: pushed along and r.o wl to ld last 50yds* **9/4**[1]
6511 **2** *¾* **Seductive Witch**[4] 557 3-8-6 58 6ex.............................. JamesDoyle 7 60
(M D I Usher) *disp ld: def advantage 1f out: kpt on: hdd and outpcd last 50yds* **13/2**
-215 **3** *1* **Valhillen**[19] 364 3-8-13 70.............................. PatrickHills[(5)] 2 68
(M D I Usher) *hld up in tch: effrt on inner over 1f out: styd on fnl f but nt pce to chal* **7/2**[2]
330- **4** *nk* **Ben**[135] 6017 3-9-1 67.............................. RobertHavlin 1 64
(P G Murphy) *disp ld to 1f out: fdd last 100yds* **5/1**
05-1 **5** *nk* **Stoneacre Pat (IRE)**[16] 412 3-8-5 62.............................. ColinHaddon[(5)] 3 58
(Peter Grayson) *t.k.h: hld up in last: effrt 2f out: nt qckn over 1f out: one pce after* **16/1**
14-5 **6** *1 ¾* **Golden Dane (IRE)**[13] 444 3-8-11 63.............................. LiamJones 5 53
(C R Dore) *racd wd: chsd ldrs: rdn 2f out: struggling over 1f out* **9/2**[3]
20-3 **7** *1 ½* **Lady Vibeeka**[10] 487 3-8-10 62.............................. HayleyTurner 4 46
(Mrs H Sweeting) *chsd ldrs: lost pl 2f out: sn wknd* **25/1**

59.99 secs (1.19) **Going Correction** +0.025s/f (Slow) **7 Ran SP% 110.9**
Speed ratings (Par 97): **91,89,88,87,87 84,82**
CSF £16.29 TOTE £3.20: £1.50, £2.50; EX 16.40 Place 6 £27.72, Place 5 £13.20..
Owner Matthew Green **Bred** Fin A Co S R L **Trained** Newmarket, Suffolk

FOCUS
A competitive enough contest, but the winning time was moderate. A career best from the winner, who is rated better than the bare form which is only modest.
Lady Vibeeka Official explanation: jockey said filly lost its action
T/Jkpt: £16,295.70 to a £1 stake. Pool: £275,421.41. 12.00 winning tickets. T/Plt: £20.60 to a £1 stake. Pool: £128,159.35. 4,523.20 winning tickets. T/Qpdt: £4.90 to a £1 stake. Pool: £9,449.30. 1,425.40 winning tickets. JN

596 SOUTHWELL (L-H)
Tuesday, February 19

OFFICIAL GOING: Standard to slow
Wind: Nil Weather: Misty and cold

613 LADBROKES.COM LEADS THE WAY APPRENTICE H'CAP 1m 3f (F)
2:10 (2:10) (Class 6) (0-60,59) 4-Y-O+ **£1,911** (£564; £282) **Stalls** Low

Form RPR
-113 **1** **Karmest**[19] 368 4-9-2 59.............................. SBushby[(5)] 5 69+
(A D Brown) *hld up in rr: hdwy on outer 4f out: qcknd to ld 3f out and sn clr: rdn wl over 1f out: kpt on ins fnl f* **5/4**[1]
30-5 **2** *2 ½* **Kentucky Bullet (USA)**[35] 171 12-8-4 45.............................. RossAtkinson[(5)] 4 48
(A G Newcombe) *hld up in tch: pushed along 3f out: hdwy 2f out: chsd wnr over 1f out: kpt on same pce* **5/1**[2]
-356 **3** *3 ½* **Piano Key**[26] 277 4-8-2 45.............................. BillyCray[(5)] 1 42
(M D I Usher) *prom: rdn along 3f out: kpt on same pce fnl 2f* **8/1**
60-0 **4** *½* **Itsy Bitsy**[35] 166 6-8-4 45.............................. DebraEngland[(5)] 6 41
(W J Musson) *prom: chsd ldr 1/2-way: rdn along wl over 2f out: grad wknd fr 1 1/2f out* **12/1**
20-0 **5** *6* **Dream Forest (IRE)**[11] 485 5-9-0 53..............................(v[1]) BMcHugh[(3)] 3 38
(P R Webber) *chsd ldrs: pushed along and hdwy on inner over 2f out: sn rdn and wknd over 1f out* **6/1**[3]
0-50 **6** *3* **Besi**[5] 559 6-9-1 51.............................. DeclanCannon 2 31
(A Berry) *led: pushed along and hdd 3f out: sn rdn and wknd wl over 1f out* **10/1**
600- **7** *11* **Book Of Facts (FR)**[14] 3824 4-9-0 59..............................(b) GemmaElford[(7)] 7 19
(S W Hall) *s.i.s: a bhd* **12/1**

2m 35.62s (7.62) **Going Correction** +0.45s/f (Slow)
WFA 4 from 5yo+ 2lb **7 Ran SP% 111.0**
Speed ratings (Par 101): **90,88,85,85,80 78,70**
CSF £7.16 TOTE £1.90: £1.30, £2.50; EX 6.20.
Owner David Logan **Bred** Charles B B Booth **Trained** Pickering, York

FOCUS
They went an ordinary gallop in this moderate handicap and the time was slow. Really weak form, with the second, third and fourth all wrong at the weights, although the winner is worth better than the bare figure.

614 RACE TO PONTINS.COM (S) STKS 5f (F)
2:40 (2:40) (Class 6) 3-Y-O **£1,774** (£523; £262) **Stalls** High

Form RPR
-615 **1** **Mac Dalia**[11] 484 3-8-10 67..............................(p) JerryO'Dwyer[(3)] 3 55
(A J McCabe) *cl up: led 1/2-way: rdn over 1f out: drvn ins fnl f: kpt on* **8/11**[1]
00-4 **2** *hd* **East Coast Girl (IRE)**[40] 112 3-8-7 55..............................(b[1]) LiamJones 4 49
(S W Hall) *cl up: effrt to chal wl over 1f out and sn rdn: drvn and edgd lft and rt ins fnl f: ev ch tl n.g.t w effrt towards fin* **9/2**[3]
60-0 **3** *3 ½* **Jastaanhi**[18] 397 3-8-0 45.............................. StacyRenwick[(7)] 5 36
(J A Pickering) *led to 1/2-way: cl up tl rdn wl over 1f out: wknd ent fnl f* **16/1**
3321 **4** *1 ½* **Orange Square (IRE)**[12] 467 3-9-4 64.............................. TonyHamilton 6 42
(D W Barker) *cl up: rdn along 2f out: sn drvn and wknd appr fnl f* **4/1**[2]
5 *13* **Feeling Pretty** 3-8-9 0 ow2.............................. MickyFenton 1 —
(C Smith) *wnt bdly lft s: a rdn along and bhd* **28/1**
0-63 **6** *½* **Captain Crooner (IRE)**[12] 467 3-8-11 46..............................(v) PatrickDonaghy[(7)] 2 —
(D Shaw) *stmbld s: sn rdn along a outpcd towards rr* **20/1**

64.01 secs (4.31) **Going Correction** +0.75s/f (Slow) **6 Ran SP% 110.2**
Speed ratings (Par 95): **95,94,89,86,65 65**
CSF £4.17 TOTE £1.70: £1.10, £2.20; EX 4.50.There was no bid for the winner.
Owner Paul J Dixon & Brian Morton **Bred** Chippenham Lodge Stud **Trained** Babworth, Notts
■ Stewards' Enquiry : Jerry O'Dwyer one-day ban: used whip in incorrect place (Mar 1)
Liam Jones one-day ban: used whip without allowing filly time to respond (Mar 1)

FOCUS
A weak seller in which neither of the front pair looked too keen, and the second and third hold down the winner's form.

615 CROC'S SNAPPY HAPPY HOLIDAYS @ PONTIN'S CLASSIFIED CLAIMING STKS 6f (F)
3:10 (3:10) (Class 6) 4-Y-O+ **£1,774** (£523; £262) **Stalls** Low

Form RPR
6351 **1** **Soba Jones**[7] 528 11-8-5 48.............................. TolleyDean[(3)] 4 63+
(J Balding) *mde all: pushed clr 2f out: rdn and kpt on wl fnl f* **3/1**[3]
3214 **2** *2* **Chatshow (USA)**[6] 536 7-8-13 60.............................. MarkCoumbe[(7)] 7 67
(A W Carroll) *trckd ldrs: hdwy 2f out: rdn to chse wnr over 1f out: kpt on u.p ins fnl f* **11/4**[2]
0263 **3** *1 ½* **Lucius Verrus (USA)**[7] 530 8-7-11 52 ow2..........(v) PatrickDonaghy[(7)] 8 46
(D Shaw) *chsd ldrs on outer: rdn along 1/2-way: drvn wl over 1f out: kpt on same pce u.p appr fnl f* **13/2**
3-51 **4** *5* **Magic Amour**[7] 530 10-8-9 58 ow1..............................(b) StephenDonohoe 1 35
(P A Blockley) *cl up and sn pushed along to hold position on inner: rdn over 2f out: sn drvn and wknd wl over 1f out* **13/8**[1]
000- **5** *hd* **Jabraan (USA)**[18] 6738 6-8-2 39..............................(b) LiamJones 2 27
(Mrs R A Carr) *chsd ldrs: rdn along over 2f out: drvn and wknd wl over 1f out* **33/1**
0105 **6** *15* **Buzzin'Boyzee (IRE)**[7] 530 5-8-6 55.............................. CatherineGannon 5 —
(P D Evans) *rrd s: sn rdn along and a in rr* **10/1**

1m 18.88s (2.38) **Going Correction** +0.45s/f (Slow) **6 Ran SP% 115.1**
Speed ratings (Par 101): **102,99,97,90,90 70**
CSF £12.11 TOTE £4.70: £1.90, £1.60; EX 14.10 Trifecta £39.30 Pool: £624.69 - 11.26 winning units..
Owner R L Crowe **Bred** Mrs M J Hills **Trained** Scrooby, Notts

FOCUS
A pretty competitive claimer run at an ordinary gallop. The favourite ran poorly and Soba Jones probably did not need to improve on his latest form.
Magic Amour Official explanation: jockey said gelding was unsuited by slow surface

Buzzin'Boyzee(IRE) Official explanation: jockey said mare reared leaving stalls

616 TREAT YOUR FAMILY TO PONTIN'S MAIDEN STKS 6f (F)
3:40 (3:41) (Class 5) 3-Y-O **£2,457** (£725; £362) **Stalls** Low

Form RPR
2 **1** **Thebes**[10] 505 3-9-3 0 .... GregFairley 2 86+
(M Johnston) *mde all: rdn clr over 1f out: edgd lft ins fnl f* **4/6**[1]
5- **2** *6* **Flying Sommelier (USA)**[251] 2562 3-9-3 0 .... PhillipMakin 1 61
(T D Barron) *cl up: rdn wl over 2f out: drvn wl over 1f out and sn one pce* **9/2**[2]
3 *nk* **Orpenella** 3-8-12 0 .... NCallan 5 55+
(K A Ryan) *dwlt: t.k.h and trcking ldrs whn hung rt home turn: rdn and styd on to take 2nd ins fnl f: no ex and lost 2nd nr fin* **11/2**[3]
4 *12* **Wildcat Island (IRE)** 3-8-12 0 .... DavidAllan 6 17
(T D Easterby) *chsd ldng pair: rdn along over 2f out: sn wknd* **18/1**
4 **5** *19* **Article**[14] 441 3-9-0 0 .... DuranFentiman(3) 3 —
(T D Easterby) *in tch: rdn along 1/2-way: sn wknd* **12/1**
1m 20.15s (3.65) **Going Correction** +0.45s/f (Slow) 5 Ran SP% **106.5**
Speed ratings (Par 97): **93,85,84,68,43**
CSF £3.62 TOTE £1.50: £1.10, £2.00; EX 3.60.
Owner Sheikh Hamdan Bin Mohammed Al Maktoum **Bred** Whitsbury Manor Stud And Mrs M E Slade **Trained** Middleham Moor, N Yorks

FOCUS
Modest maiden form, rated through the runner-up. The winner can rate higher than the bare form.

617 GREAT VALUE GOLD BREAKS @ PONTIN'S H'CAP 1m 4f (F)
4:10 (4:10) (Class 5) (0-70,70) 4-Y-O+ **£2,593** (£765; £383) **Stalls** Low

Form RPR
23-3 **1** **They All Laughed**[6] 540 5-9-3 66 .... PhillipMakin 5 79+
(P W Hiatt) *hld up in rr: hdwy over 4f out: rdn along over 3f out: styd on to ld wl over 1f out: edgd lft and clr ins fnl f* **6/4**[1]
6-20 **2** *6* **Nimello (USA)**[32] 215 12-8-7 56 .... SimonWhitworth 3 59
(A G Newcombe) *hld up in tch: hdwy over 2f out: rdn to chse wnr over 1f out: sn drvn and kpt on same pce* **11/1**
-243 **3** *5* **Phone Call**[15] 436 5-8-9 58 .... NeilChalmers 2 51
(Mouse Hamilton-Fairley) *cl up: led over 7f out: rdn along over 3f out: hdd wl over 1f out: sn drvn and wknd* **5/1**
0-03 **4** *14* **Key Partners (IRE)**[13] 449 7-8-9 58 oh2 ow2 .... StephenDonohoe 4 29
(P A Blockley) *t.k.h: hld up: hdwy and cl up over 4f out: ev ch tl rdn over 2f out and sn wknd* **9/2**[3]
/10- **5** *114* **Foursquare Flyer (IRE)**[17] 153 6-9-7 70 .... (t) NCallan 1 —
(J Mackie) *led over 4f: rdn along and lost pl over 4f out: sn wl bhd* **10/3**[2]
2m 45.42s (4.42) **Going Correction** +0.45s/f (Slow) 5 Ran SP% **106.3**
Speed ratings (Par 103): **103,99,95,86,—**
CSF £16.25 TOTE £2.20: £1.30, £3.40; EX 14.50.
Owner Clive Roberts **Bred** T G And B B Mills **Trained** Hook Norton, Oxon

FOCUS
They went a fair pace here and the winner came from last to first, rated up 6lb. However this probably took little winning with only the first two running their race.
Foursquare Flyer(IRE) Official explanation: jockey said gelding had a breathing problem

618 LADBROKES 24/7 FREEPHONE BETTING 0800 777 888 H'CAP 7f (F)
4:40 (4:40) (Class 4) (0-85,78) 4-Y-O+ **£4,210** (£1,252; £625; £312) **Stalls** Low

Form RPR
3512 **1** **Silver Hotspur**[5] 555 4-8-7 67 .... FrancisNorton 3 81+
(M Wigham) *trckd ldrs: hdwy to chse ldr over 2f out: rdn to ld and edgd lft appr fnl f: rdn clr* **11/8**[1]
3236 **2** *4* **Memphis Man**[14] 442 5-8-13 73 .... StephenDonohoe 2 75
(P D Evans) *hld up: hdwy on outer over 2f out: rdn to chse ldng pair wl over 1f out: sn drvn and styd on ins fnl f to take 2nd nr line* **9/2**[3]
3622 **3** *nk* **Dudley Docker (IRE)**[12] 463 6-9-3 77 .... (b) NCallan 4 78
(C R Dore) *plld hrd: chsd ldrs tl led 1/2-way: jnd and rdn 2f out: drvn and hdd appr fnl f: kpt on same pce* **9/4**[2]
5330 **4** *10* **Cornus**[7] 532 6-9-4 78 .... (be) JamesDoyle 1 52
(A J McCabe) *chsd ldr: rdn along wl over 2f out and sn outpcd* **13/2**
2040 **5** *2* **Goodbye Cash (IRE)**[6] 539 4-8-8 68 .... CatherineGannon 5 37
(P D Evans) *led: hdd 1/2-way: sn rdn along and wknd wl over 2f out* **14/1**
1m 32.03s (1.73) **Going Correction** +0.45s/f (Slow) 5 Ran SP% **111.1**
Speed ratings (Par 105): **108,103,103,91,89**
CSF £8.04 TOTE £1.80: £1.60, £1.70; EX 6.40.
Owner D Hassan **Bred** Theobalds Stud **Trained** Newmarket, Suffolk

FOCUS
A steadily run handicap, and pretty weak form. A fairly straightforward task for Silver Hotspur.

619 BET IN PLAY AT LADBROKES.COM H'CAP 7f (F)
5:10 (5:10) (Class 5) (0-75,75) 3-Y-O **£2,593** (£765; £383) **Stalls** Low

Form RPR
06-1 **1** **Little Wing (IRE)**[11] 483 3-9-4 75 .... TPQueally 6 93+
(J A Osborne) *t.k.h: trckd ldrs: smooth hdwy 3f out: led 2f out: sn clr: easily* **5/6**[1]
4436 **2** *8* **Loose Caboose (IRE)**[12] 470 3-8-10 67 .... PatrickMathers 7 61
(A J McCabe) *dwlt: hld up towards rr: god hdwy on outer wl over 2f out: rdn to chse wnr over 1f out: sn drvn and no imp* **14/1**
-133 **3** *1* **Ballycroy Boy (IRE)**[22] 339 3-9-4 75 .... MickyFenton 2 66
(A Bailey) *prom tl rdn along and outpcd 3f out: hdwy on inner 2f out: drvn and kpt on appr fnl f* **4/1**[2]
530- **4** *nk* **One Called Alice**[113] 6536 3-7-11 61 .... PatrickDonaghy(7) 4 52
(A W Carroll) *dwlt: hdwy 3f out and sn rdn: drvn to chse ldrs 2f out: sn one pce* **20/1**
2433 **5** *shd* **Bold Diva**[11] 480 3-8-2 62 .... (v) KirstyMilczarek(3) 1 52
(A W Carroll) *in rr: hdwy 3f out: rdn over 2f out: sn drvn and kpt on same pce* **8/1**
01-4 **6** *1 1/4* **Easy Wonder (GER)**[13] 458 3-8-13 70 .... JamesDoyle 3 57
(I A Wood) *led: rdn along 3f out: hdd 2f out: sn drvn and grad wknd* **15/2**[3]
U-63 **7** *4* **Traitor's Gate**[11] 484 3-8-10 67 .... GregFairley 5 43
(M Johnston) *prom: rdn along 3f out: wknd over 2f out* **14/1**
1m 31.78s (1.48) **Going Correction** +0.45s/f (Slow) 7 Ran SP% **115.5**
Speed ratings (Par 97): **109,99,98,98,98 96,92**
CSF £15.16 TOTE £2.00: £1.20, £6.50; EX 23.10 Place 6 £7.42, Place 5 £6.04.
Owner Mountgrange Stud **Bred** Andrew Coonan And Thomas J K Clarke **Trained** Upper Lambourn, Berks
■ Stewards' Enquiry : Kirsty Milczarek three-day ban: failed to ride out filly that could have finished 4th (Mar 1,3-4)

FOCUS
A soundly run handicap run in a good time and an impressive performance from the unexposed winner. There is some doubt over what he beat, though.

T/Plt: £16.70 to a £1 stake. Pool: £69,677.65. 3,045.60 winning tickets. T/Qpdt: £10.30 to a £1 stake. Pool: £3,477.30. 248.10 winning tickets. JR

582 KEMPTON (A.W) (R-H)
Wednesday, February 20

OFFICIAL GOING: Standard
Wind: Nil

620 GOFFS BREEZE UP AT KEMPTON MARCH 7TH H'CAP 5f (P)
6:20 (6:21) (Class 6) (0-65,64) 4-Y-O+ **£2,047** (£604; £302) **Stalls** High

Form RPR
0-06 **1** **Hollow Jo**[10] 515 8-9-4 64 .... MickyFenton 8 75
(J R Jenkins) *chsd ldrs: rdn 2f out: str run u.p fnl f to ld cl home* **10/3**[2]
5-01 **2** *nk* **Guto**[12] 479 5-8-11 62 .... KellyHarrison(5) 1 72
(W J H Ratcliffe) *led: rdn fnl f: ct cl home* **5/1**
-530 **3** *1* **Overstayed (IRE)**[6] 554 5-8-11 57 .... TPQueally 7 63
(M Mullineaux) *chsd ldr: rdn 2f out: no imp fnl f and outpcd into 3rd cl home* **9/4**[1]
0323 **4** *1 1/2* **Kempsey**[10] 515 6-9-0 60 .... (v) NeilChalmers 4 61
(J J Bridger) *chsd ldrs: rdn 2f out: one pce fr over 1f out* **4/1**[3]
6-06 **5** *hd* **Stoneacre Boy (IRE)**[17] 414 5-8-13 59 .... (b) AdamKirby 5 59
(Peter Grayson) *s.i.s: in rr: hdwy 2f out: kpt on same pce ins fnl f* **16/1**
-530 **6** *hd* **Stormburst (IRE)**[7] 539 4-8-3 56 .... MarkCoumbe(7) 6 55
(A J Chamberlain) *s.i.s: in rr tl drvn and styd on fr over 1f out* **20/1**
00-0 **7** *1 1/2* **Fairfield Princess**[35] 187 4-9-2 62 .... SimonWhitworth 3 56
(M S Saunders) *in rr: rdn and sme hdwy over 1f out: nvr in contention* **33/1**
-460 **8** *nk* **Fizzlephut (IRE)**[21] 359 6-9-2 62 .... PaulFitzsimons 2 55
(Miss J R Tooth) *chsd ldrs: rdn 2f out: wknd fnl f* **12/1**
60.53 secs (0.03) **Going Correction** +0.075s/f (Slow) 8 Ran SP% **111.8**
Speed ratings (Par 101): **102,101,99,97,97 96,94,94**
CSF £19.40 CT £43.29 TOTE £5.50: £1.80, £2.30, £1.60; EX 21.30.
Owner Jim McCarthy **Bred** K J Reddington **Trained** Royston, Herts

FOCUS
A competitive little contest run at a good pace. Solid forn, Hollow Jo rated to his winter best.
Stoneacre Boy(IRE) Official explanation: jockey said gelding hung right-handed.

621 PANORAMIC BAR & RESTAURANT CLASSIFIED STKS 7f (P)
6:50 (6:50) (Class 7) 4-Y-O+ **£1,365** (£302; £302) **Stalls** High

Form RPR
3331 **1** **Mr Chocolate Drop (IRE)**[7] 535 4-9-6 45 .... (b) AdamKirby 10 55
(Miss M E Rowland) *chsd ldrs: led ins fnl 2f: rdn and hld on all out ins fnl f* **3/1**[1]
55/0 **2** *3/4* **Grezie**[19] 392 6-9-0 42 .... PaulDoe 7 47
(L A Dace) *awkward s: towards rr: hdwy 2f out: styd on to chse wnr fnl f but a hld* **33/1**
405- **2** *dht* **Fun In The Sun**[116] 6505 4-9-0 43 .... TPQueally 11 47+
(A B Haynes) *in tch: n.m.r and outpcd 2f out: rallied 1f out: kpt on u.p ins fnl f to dead heat for 2nd cl home but nt rch wnr* **9/2**[2]
0332 **4** *nk* **Wizby**[7] 535 5-9-0 45 .... CatherineGannon 9 46
(P D Evans) *chsd ldrs: carried lft 2f out and lost pl: rallied ins fnl f and kpt on cl home* **7/1**
-044 **5** *1* **Rafferty (IRE)**[16] 429 9-9-0 45 .... (p) SebSanders 1 46+
(S Dow) *hld up in rr: hmpd 2f out and again fnl f tl fnlly got run cl home but nt rcvr* **11/2**[3]
3535 **6** *3/4* **Only If I Laugh**[27] 289 7-9-0 44 .... IanMongan 3 41
(M J Attwater) *chsd ldrs: chalng whn hung lft 2f out: rcvrd and kpt on ins fnl f: nt rch ldrs* **13/2**
6-54 **7** *shd* **A Teen**[40] 120 10-9-0 38 .... JimmyQuinn 5 41
(P Howling) *in tch: effrt whn hmpd 2f out: kpt on again cl home* **25/1**
00-0 **8** *1/2* **Pajada**[10] 518 4-8-7 39 .... (p) GabrielHannon(7) 4 40
(M D I Usher) *in rr: sme prog whn hmpd 2f out: sme prog fnl f* **33/1**
-005 **9** *nk* **Edin Burgher (FR)**[10] 516 7-9-0 40 .... (e) SamHitchcott 6 39
(T T Clement) *led tl hdd over 2f out: wknd fnl f* **12/1**
0-56 **10** *1/2* **Mr Belvedere**[7] 542 7-9-0 42 .... (tp) JamesDoyle 2 38
(A J Lidderdale) *chsd ldrs: slt ld over 2f out: sn hdd: wknd ins fnl f* **13/2**
1m 26.78s (0.78) **Going Correction** +0.075s/f (Slow) 10 Ran SP% **115.2**
Speed ratings (Par 97): **98,97,97,96,95 94,94,94,93,93**
WIN: Mr Chocolate Drop £3.70. PL: £1.20, Fun In The Sun £1.90, Grezie £7.60. EX: MCD/FITS £9.60, MCD/G £71.60. CSF: MCD/FITS £7.84, MCD/G £56.41..
Owner Dean R Mitchell **Bred** P J Munnelly **Trained** Lower Blidworth, Notts

FOCUS
An ultra-competitive heat and virtually all the runners held a chance with a furlong to run. Sound form for the lowly grade, the winner rated back to his best.

622 DIGIBET CLAIMING STKS 1m 4f (P)
7:20 (7:21) (Class 6) 4-Y-O+ **£2,047** (£604; £302) **Stalls** Centre

Form RPR
-022 **1** **Fregate Island (IRE)**[14] 450 5-9-7 75 .... TPQueally 5 79
(J G Given) *mde all: pushed along and styd on fr 2f out: unchal* **6/4**[2]
1321 **2** *1 3/4* **Given A Choice (IRE)**[14] 449 6-9-7 82 .... SebSanders 4 76
(J Pearce) *trckd ldrs: chsd wnr fr 5f out: rdn and no imp fnl 2f* **10/11**[1]
05-5 **3** *5* **Swift Cut (IRE)**[10] 512 4-8-12 55 .... AndrewElliott 3 62
(A P Jarvis) *in rr: hdwy into 3rd 3f out: styd on same pce fr over 2f out* **20/1**
0- **4** *15* **Dilmoun (IRE)**[201] 4138 6-9-1 0 .... VinceSlattery 2 38
(Mrs A M Thorpe) *s.i.s: plld hrd: stdd in tch: rdn 3f out and sn wknd* **40/1**
030- **5** *114* **Bed Fellow (IRE)**[117] 6475 4-9-2 72 .... NeilPollard 1 —
(A P Jarvis) *chsd wnr to 5f out: wknd over 3f out: t.o* **8/1**[3]
2m 34.38s (-0.12) **Going Correction** +0.075s/f (Slow)
WFA 4 from 5yo+ 3lb 5 Ran SP% **110.7**
Speed ratings (Par 101): **103,101,98,88,—**
CSF £3.21 TOTE £3.40: £1.40, £1.10; EX 3.10.The winner was claimed by A. G. Newcombe for £16,000.
Owner Mr & Mrs G Middlebrook **Bred** G And Mrs Middlebrook **Trained** Willoughton, Lincs

FOCUS
A fair claimer but a tactical race and as a result the form is not entirely reliable.

Bed Fellow(IRE) Official explanation: vet said gelding bled from the nose.

623 DIGIBET H'CAP — 1m (P)
7:50 (7:50) (Class 6) (0-55,56) 3-Y-O — £2,047 (£604; £302) Stalls High

Form — RPR

420- 1 **Silca Destination**[70] 7117 3-9-0 55 .... EdwardCreighton 6 56
(M R Channon) *chsd ldr: chal 4f out: led 3f out: hdd and outpcd jst ins fnl 2f: rallied and styd on fnl f to ld last stride* 10/3[2]

03-6 2 shd **Sharps Gold**[37] 156 3-9-0 55 .... (bt) AmirQuinn 1 56
(P J McBride) *hld up in tch: qcknd to ld jst ins fnl 2f: rdn ins fnl f: hdd last stride* 12/1

00-3 3 ½ **Ray Diamond**[23] 335 3-8-11 52 .... J-PGuillambert 4 52
(M Madgwick) *chsd ldrs: rdn and hung rt over 2f out: r.o ins fnl f but nver quite gng pce to get to ldng duo* 7/2[3]

6-03 4 5 **Adam Eterno (IRE)**[11] 501 3-8-9 50 ow1 .... (b) TPQueally 7 38
(A B Haynes) *led: rdn and hdd 3f out: wknd fnl f* 14/1

66-3 5 1 **O'Casey (IRE)**[12] 486 3-8-8 49 .... TGMcLaughlin 8 35
(J G M O'Shea) *s.i.s: t.k.h: in tch: hdwy 2f out: sn one pce* 12/1

0-02 6 2 **Tilly Ann (IRE)**[12] 486 3-8-5 46 .... LiamJones 5 27
(Peter Grayson) *slowly away: in rr: rdn 4f out: nvr in contention* 20/1

5331 7 1½ **Don Picolo**[8] 534 3-9-1 56 6ex .... FrankieMcDonald 3 34
(P A Blockley) *chsd ldrs: rdn 3f out: wknd fr 2f out* 5/2[1]

0-04 8 1½ **Herrbee (IRE)**[23] 335 3-8-13 54 .... PaulDoe 2 29
(S Dow) *rdn and hung rt 3f out: a towards rr* 13/2

1m 42.18s (2.38) **Going Correction** +0.075s/f (Slow) 8 Ran SP% **114.0**
Speed ratings (Par 95): **91,90,90,85,84 82,80,79**
CSF £41.78 CT £148.61 TOTE £4.50: £1.50, £4.70, £1.70; EX 66.00.
Owner Aldridge Racing Partnership **Bred** E Aldridge **Trained** West Ilsley, Berks

FOCUS
A weak handicap run at a steady pace and the form looks dubious.
Don Picolo Official explanation: trainer's rep said colt appears better suited by wearing headgear

624 DIGIBET SPORTS BETTING H'CAP — 7f (P)
8:20 (8:22) (Class 6) (0-50,50) 4-Y-O+ — £2,047 (£604; £302) Stalls High

Form — RPR

2216 1 **Jessica Wigmo**[18] 402 5-8-5 50 .... MarkCoumbe(7) 1 60
(A W Carroll) *in rr: hdwy fr 2f out: chsd wnr u.p ins fnl f: led fnl 50yds: drvn out* 9/1

1206 2 ½ **Sion Hill (IRE)**[9] 521 7-8-10 48 .... (p) MickyFenton 9 56
(John A Harris) *led: rdn over 1f out: hdd and no ex fnl 50yds* 4/1[3]

3-62 3 1½ **Tuning Fork**[19] 392 8-8-8 49 .... KirstyMilczarek(3) 5 53
(M J Attwater) *chsd ldrs: rdn 2f out: styd on u.p fnl f but nt pce to rch ldng duo* 3/1[1]

10-5 4 shd **Alucica**[5] 571 5-8-12 50 .... (v) DeanMcKeown 2 54
(D Shaw) *in rr: rdn 3f out: styd on fr over 1f out: kpt on ins fnl f but nt rch ldrs* 11/1

3-30 5 ½ **Batchworth Blaise**[10] 516 5-8-10 48 ow1 .... StephenCarson 4 52+
(E A Wheeler) *in rr: rdn and hung rt over 2f out: kpt on ins fnl f but n.d* 8/1

0-23 6 1¼ **Patavium Prince (IRE)**[24] 327 5-8-10 48 .... SimonWhitworth 8 47
(Miss Jo Crowley) *chsd ldrs: rdn over 2f out: wknd fnl 100yds* 7/2[2]

0-06 7 1 **Suhayl Star (IRE)**[7] 536 4-8-2 47 .... RossAtkinson(7) 6 44
(P Burgoyne) *chsd ldr: chal fr 3f out tl over 1f out: wknd ins fnl f* 20/1

060- 8 2½ **Wattys The Craic**[120] 6415 4-8-10 48 .... SaleemGolam 10 38
(G Prodromou) *chsd ldrs tl rdn and outpcd over 2f out* 33/1

00-5 9 shd **Task Complete**[24] 327 5-8-12 50 .... NeilChalmers 7 40
(Jean-Rene Auvray) *a towards rr* 9/1

600- 10 5 **County Kerry (UAE)**[140] 5894 4-8-12 50 .... FrankieMcDonald 3 26
(Jean-Rene Auvray) *s.i.s: a towards rr* 25/1

1m 26.22s (0.22) **Going Correction** +0.075s/f (Slow) 10 Ran SP% **118.2**
Speed ratings (Par 101): **101,100,98,98,98 96,95,92,92,86**
CSF £44.57 CT £139.86 TOTE £10.30: £3.20, £1.60, £1.90; EX 22.20.
Owner J Wigmore Racing Partnership **Bred** J Wigmore **Trained** Cropthorne, Worcs

FOCUS
A weak handicap, run at a fair pace. The form seems sound with the runner-up setting the level.

625 DAY TIME, NIGHT TIME, GREAT TIME H'CAP — 6f (P)
8:50 (8:52) (Class 6) (0-52,52) 4-Y-O+ — £2,047 (£604; £302) Stalls High

Form — RPR

6-65 1 **Wiltshire (IRE)**[18] 402 6-8-9 51 ow1 .... (v) MickyFenton 8 65+
(P T Midgley) *plld hrd early and stdd in tch: qcknd ins fnl 2f to ld appr fnl f: sn in command: readily* 9/4[1]

600- 2 1½ **Decider (USA)**[177] 4881 5-8-5 52 .... KevinGhunowa(5) 4 61
(R A Harris) *led: rdn 2f out: hdd appr fnl f: sn outpcd by wnr but kpt on wl for 2nd* 13/2

-212 3 1¼ **Avoca Dancer (IRE)**[13] 469 5-8-8 50 .... SimonWhitworth 1 55
(M Wigham) *s.i.s and swtchd rt to ins rail: rdn and hdwy over 1f out: kpt on ins fnl f but nt pce to rch ldng duo* 11/4[2]

4-41 4 nk **Davids Mark**[30] 247 8-8-10 52 .... JimCrowley 7 56
(J R Jenkins) *in rr: rdn 2f out: styd on ins fnl f but n.d* 3/1[3]

-566 5 1¾ **Gone'N'Dunnett (IRE)**[16] 437 9-8-8 50 .... (v) TGMcLaughlin 5 48
(Mrs C A Dunnett) *chsd ldrs: rdn to chal over 2f out and sn hung rt: wknd ins fnl f* 25/1

50-0 6 2½ **Polar Force**[34] 191 8-8-10 52 .... IanMongan 2 42
(Mrs C A Dunnett) *chsd ldrs: rdn over 2f out: wknd fnl f* 20/1

6542 7 3½ **Piccostar**[14] 445 5-8-4 46 oh1 .... (b) DavidKinsella 3 25
(A B Haynes) *towards rr but in tch: rdn 3f out and sme prog: sn wknd* 12/1

1m 12.83s (-0.27) **Going Correction** +0.075s/f (Slow) 7 Ran SP% **112.1**
Speed ratings (Par 101): **104,102,100,99,97 94,89**
CSF £16.71 CT £40.21 TOTE £2.90: £1.80, £3.20; EX 22.60.
Owner David Mann **Bred** John Perotta **Trained** Westow, N Yorks

FOCUS
A moderate handicap, run at a decent pace. The form looks solid for the class.

626 CITY & SUBURBAN PARKING H'CAP — 1m 3f (P)
9:20 (9:20) (Class 4) (0-85,85) 4-Y-O+ — £4,210 (£1,252; £625; £312) Stalls High

Form — RPR

3-33 1 **Tilapia (IRE)**[8] 531 4-9-3 84 .... SebSanders 7 93
(Sir Mark Prescott) *trckd ldrs: edgd rt over 1f out: sn drvn to ld: styd on strly* 11/4[1]

0-1 2 ½ **Man Of Gwent (UAE)**[19] 396 4-8-10 77 .... JamesDoyle 3 88+
(P D Evans) *faltered bnd after 2f: in rr but in tch: hdwy on ins whn bdly hmpd over 1f out: rallied and r.o strly to take 2nd cl home but nt rcvr* 10/1

0/5- 3 1¼ **Jagger**[73] 7086 8-9-6 85 .... TPQueally 1 91
(G A Butler) *stdd s: in rr: rdn over 2f out: kpt on wl fnl f but nt pce to rch ldng duo* 20/1

-431 4 hd **Princess Cocoa (IRE)**[9] 525 5-8-9 74 .... PaulHanagan 5 79
(R A Fahey) *chsd ldrs: rdn and kpt on fnl f but nvr gng pce to chal* 9/2

053- 5 hd **Awatuki (IRE)**[5] 7163 5-9-2 81 .... NeilPollard 6 86
(A P Jarvis) *chsd ldr: rdn over 2f out: one pce ins fnl f* 10/3[2]

3111 6 1¼ **Smokey The Bear**[7] 540 6-9-3 82 12ex .... NeilChalmers 4 85
(Miss Sheena West) *in rr: hdwy and n.m.r fr 2f out: nvr gng pce to rch ldrs and fdd ins fnl f* 7/2[3]

/0-5 7 nk **Inch Lodge**[14] 450 6-8-11 76 .... PaulEddery 2 78
(Miss D Mountain) *led: edgd rt u.p over 1f out: sn hdd: wknd ins fnl f* 11/1

2m 22.74s (0.84) **Going Correction** +0.075s/f (Slow)
WFA 4 from 5yo+ 2lb 7 Ran SP% **112.3**
Speed ratings (Par 105): **99,98,97,97,97 96,96**
CSF £29.32 TOTE £2.80: £2.20, £3.20; EX 42.50 Place 6 £12.56, Place 5 £8.97.
Owner G D Waters **Bred** G D Waters **Trained** Newmarket, Suffolk

FOCUS
A good handicap for the class. The early pace was only ordinary, however, and the runner-up has to rate unlucky. The fifth is perhaps the best guide to the form.
Man Of Gwent(UAE) ◆ Official explanation: jockey said gelding suffered interference in running.
T/Jkpt: Not won. T/Plt: £51.40 to a £1 stake. Pool: £86,032.15. 1,220.10 winning tickets. T/Qpdt: £12.50 to a £1 stake. Pool: £5,785.10. 342.10 winning tickets. ST

606 LINGFIELD (L-H)
Wednesday, February 20

OFFICIAL GOING: Standard
Wind: Modest, across Weather: hazy sun

627 HOP TO PONTIN'S 0844 815 3647 CLAIMING STKS — 5f (P)
1:50 (1:50) (Class 6) 4-Y-O+ — £1,774 (£523; £262) Stalls High

Form — RPR

0-34 1 **Dress To Impress (IRE)**[26] 301 4-9-7 74 .... (p) PatCosgrave 2 66
(G A Butler) *chsd ldr: upsides 2f out: rdn to ld over 1f out: drvn out* 1/2[1]

-634 2 ½ **Now You See Me**[9] 523 4-8-8 48 .... AlanMunro 4 51
(K McAuliffe) *chsd ldrs: outpcd bnd 2f out: rdn and rallied over 1f out: styd on wl to chse wnr ins fnl f: nvr quite rching wnr* 9/1[3]

0-56 3 1½ **Stoneacre Gareth (IRE)**[9] 522 4-8-6 48 .... (b) ColinHaddon(5) 1 49
(Peter Grayson) *led: rdn and hdd over 1f out: kpt on same pce fnl f* 20/1

040- 4 1¼ **Night Prospector**[178] 4853 8-8-12 70 .... (p) KevinGhunowa(5) 3 50
(R A Harris) *rdn thrght: in tch: kpt on same pce last 2f* 3/1[2]

58.90 secs (0.10) **Going Correction** 0.0s/f (Stan) 4 Ran SP% **106.4**
Speed ratings (Par 101): **99,98,95,93**
CSF £5.33 TOTE £1.40; EX 3.60.Stoneacre Gareth was claimed by Jonathan Jay for £7,000.
Owner M Khan X2 **Bred** K Molloy **Trained** Newmarket, Suffolk

FOCUS
A weakish claimer and only half the field came into this in any sort of form. The winner did not need to be anywhere near his best to beat a couple of rivals officially rated 48.
Night Prospector Official explanation: jockey said gelding was never travelling.

628 BET CHAMPIONS LEAGUE - BETDAQ H'CAP — 6f (P)
2:25 (2:25) (Class 6) (0-65,65) 4-Y-O+ — £1,876 (£554; £277) Stalls Low

Form — RPR

3523 1 **Musical Script (USA)**[19] 391 5-8-10 57 .... (b) NCallan 1 65
(Mouse Hamilton-Fairley) *t.k.h: trckd ldrs: hdwy to chal jst over 2f out: hung rt fr over 1f out: led wl ins fnl f: styd on* 5/1[3]

0633 2 ½ **Thoughtsofstardom**[16] 437 5-8-2 52 .... KirstyMilczarek(3) 2 58
(M Wigham) *stdd s: plld hrd: hld up wl in tch in last trio: gd hdwy on inner 2f out: ev ch ins fnl f: uanble to qckn towards fin* 9/2[2]

152 3 shd **Angel Voices (IRE)**[5] 574 5-8-11 65 .... (p) DeclanCannon(7) 3 71
(K R Burke) *led: hrd pressed and rdn wl over 1f out: hdd wl ins fnl f: no ex* 5/2[1]

2052 4 shd **Monashee Prince (IRE)**[10] 515 6-9-0 61 .... (v) JimmyQuinn 5 67
(J R Best) *hld up in tch: rdn and hdwy jst over 2f out: ev ch ins fnl f: nt qckn nr fin* 5/1[3]

-400 5 shd **Zazous**[14] 446 7-8-8 55 .... NeilChalmers 4 60
(J J Bridger) *s.i.s: sn chsng ldr: rdn and outpcd jst over 2f out: rallied u.p 1f out: kpt on* 17/2

3020 6 1¼ **Mind Alert**[10] 515 7-9-1 62 .... (v) JamesDoyle 7 63
(D Shaw) *stdd s: hld up in rr: outpcd and rdn 2f out: styd on steadily fnl f: nt rch ldrs* 16/1

0202 7 1¼ **Mambazo**[12] 488 6-8-11 63 .... (e) PatrickHills(5) 6 60
(S C Williams) *taken down early: stdd s: t.k.h: hld up in midfield: rdn 2f out: no imp over 1f out: keeping on same pce whn eased towards fin* 6/1

2103 8 5 **Regal Royale**[12] 488 5-8-2 54 .... (v) ColinHaddon(5) 8 35
(Peter Grayson) *wnt rt s: hdwy on outer 3f out: wd and lost pl bnd jst over 2f out: sn bhd* 14/1

1m 11.97s (0.07) **Going Correction** 0.0s/f (Stan) 8 Ran SP% **117.4**
Speed ratings (Par 101): **99,98,98,98,97 96,94,87**
CSF £28.55 CT £69.69 TOTE £5.40: £1.80, £1.40, £1.60; EX 31.00 Trifecta £180.00 Pool: £552.90 - 2.18 winning tickets..
Owner The Composers **Bred** Juddmonte Farms Inc **Trained** Bramshill, Hants
■ Stewards' Enquiry : N Callan two-day ban: careless riding (Mar 3-4)

FOCUS
A modest sprint handicap, but certainly a more competitive race than the first and there were four in a line across the track passing the furlong pole. The pace had been steady though and this is muddling form.
Musical Script(USA) Official explanation: jockey said gelding hung right throughout

629 GREAT FAMILY DEALS @ PONTINS.COM H'CAP — 6f (P)
3:00 (3:01) (Class 5) (0-70,70) 3-Y-O — £2,331 (£693; £346; £173) Stalls Low

Form — RPR

4-14 1 **Southwest Star (IRE)**[17] 419 3-9-2 68 .... SebSanders 2 72
(J S Moore) *trckd ldrs: rdn and effrt on inner 2f out: led last 100yds: r.o wl* 3/1[1]

-402 2 nk **Maggie Kate**[17] 419 3-8-10 62 .... (p) RobertHavlin 6 65
(R Ingram) *chsd ldr: rdn jst over 2f out: ev ch fr over 1f out: kpt on* 11/2[3]

-422 3 hd **Jalons Bridewell**[15] 441 3-9-2 68 .... FrancisNorton 5 70
(M Quinn) *led: hrd pressed and rdn wl over 1f out: hdd last 100yds: no ex* 6/1

0-36 4 1 **Splash The Cash**[36] 170 3-8-10 62 .... NCallan 4 61
(K A Ryan) *hld up in bhd ldrs: rdn and outpcd 2f out: styd on steadily fnl f: nt pce to rch ldrs* 7/2[2]

0-66 5 3½ **Scots W'Hae**[18] 413 3-8-5 57 .... GregFairley 1 45
(P J McBride) *stdd s: t.k.h: hld up in tch: rdn jst over 2f out: outpcd wl over 1f out* 16/1

The Form Book, Raceform Ltd, Compton, RG20 6NL

004- **6** *2* **Karmei**[90] 6903 3-8-13 65........ JamesDoyle 9 46
(J W Hills) *in tch in midfield on outer: rdn over 2f out: wknd jst over 2f out* **8/1**

0-01 **7** *6* **Arkando (IRE)**[12] 486 3-8-4 56 oh2........(b) AndrewElliott 7 18
(K R Burke) *stdd s: hmpd over 5f out: bhd and struggling after: lost tch over 2f out* **16/1**

0-54 **8** *54* **Mileaminutemurphy**[4] 590 3-8-5 62........ PatrickHills(5) 3 —
(R Hannon) *clipped heels and stmbld over 5f out: a bhd after: eased fr wl over 2f out: t.o* **13/2**

1m 11.37s (-0.53) **Going Correction** 0.0s/f (Stan) **8** Ran SP% **113.1**
Speed ratings (Par 97): **103,102,102,101,96 93,85,13**
CSF £19.31 CT £91.98 TOTE £4.30: £1.70, £1.80, £1.70; EX 16.30 Trifecta £84.90 Pool: £601.66 - 5.03 winning tickets..
Owner Wall To Wall Partnership **Bred** T J Hurley And Simon And Mrs S Marriot **Trained** Upper Lambourn, Berks

FOCUS
Another reasonably competitive sprint handicap, this time restricted to three-year-olds. The winning time was 0.6 seconds faster than the preceding handicap for older horses and not many ever got into it. The form seems sound enough with the first two close to their Kempton form behind Rapidity.
Karmei Official explanation: jockey said colt ran too free
Arkando(IRE) Official explanation: jockey said filly suffered interference and was never travelling thereafter
Mileaminutemurphy Official explanation: jockey said gelding stumbled and lost its action on the first bend.

630 TREAT YOUR FAMILY TO PONTIN'S H'CAP 2m (P)
3:35 (3:35) (Class 4) (0-85,87) 4-Y-0+ **£4,100** (£1,227; £613; £306; £152) **Stalls** Low

Form RPR

-112 **1** **Wicked Daze (IRE)**[18] 410 5-10-1 **87**........ SebSanders 6 95+
(Sir Mark Prescott) *hld up in last: gd hdwy on outer 3f out: chsd ldr jst over 2f out: rdn to ld ins fnl f: styd on strly* **11/4**[1]

1-12 **2** *1* **War Of The Roses (IRE)**[21] 358 5-9-1 **73**........ J-PGuillambert 4 80+
(R Brotherton) *trckd ldng pair: hdwy to ld travelling wl 3f out: rdn jst over 2f out: hdd and no ex ins fnl f* **9/2**[2]

/3-3 **3** *nk* **Masked (IRE)**[28] 268 7-9-8 **80**........ AdamKirby 5 87
(R M Beckett) *stdd s: hld up in rr: hdwy jst over 2f out: edgd rt u.p briefly jst ins fnl f: r.o: nt rch ldrs* **8/1**

-221 **4** *1 1/2* **Jack Rolfe**[18] 405 6-9-12 **84**........ GeorgeBaker 3 89
(G L Moore) *hld up in tch: rdn wl over 2f out: chsd ldng pair 2f out: kpt on same pce: lost 3rd ins fnl f* **13/2**

023- **5** *5* **High Point (IRE)**[153] 5573 10-9-0 **72**........ SimonWhitworth 1 71
(G P Enright) *led at stdy pce: rdn wl over 3f out: hdd 3f out: wknd wl over 1f out* **40/1**

05-1 **6** *5* **Mister Completely (IRE)**[41] 118 7-8-11 **69**........(v) JamesDoyle 8 62
(Ms J S Doyle) *in tch in midfield: rdn 3f out: wknd qckly 2f out* **20/1**

/0-2 **7** *1* **Moon Mix (FR)**[18] 405 5-9-13 **85**........ NCallan 2 77
(J R Jenkins) *stdd s: t.k.h: hdwy on inner 4f out: rdn jst over 2f out: sn wl btn* **5/1**[3]

-021 **8** *1 3/4* **Dubai Ace (USA)**[7] 544 7-8-8 **66** 6ex........(p) NeilChalmers 7 56
(Miss Sheena West) *chsd ldr: rdn 4f out: wkng whn short of room jst over 2f out: wl bhd after* **9/2**[2]

3m 24.21s (-1.49) **Going Correction** 0.0s/f (Stan) **8** Ran SP% **111.3**
Speed ratings (Par 105): **103,102,102,101,99 96,96,95**
CSF £14.29 CT £82.81 TOTE £3.40: £1.20, £1.70, £2.70; EX 18.30 Trifecta £162.50 Pool: £718.78 - 3.14 winning tickets..
Owner Roger T Ferris **Bred** Bloomsbury Stud **Trained** Newmarket, Suffolk

FOCUS
A decent staying handicap on paper with the majority of these coming into it in decent form, but unfortunately it was nowhere near a proper test of stamina as the field dawdled until well past halfway and that may have helped both the front pair. The form may not prove the most solid but the winner should have more to offer at this trip.

631 PONTIN'S BREAKS ARE THE BEST @ EASTER (S) STKS 1m 2f (P)
4:10 (4:10) (Class 6) 4-Y-0+ **£1,774** (£523; £262) **Stalls** Low

Form RPR

-652 **1** **Lord Of Dreams (IRE)**[7] 546 6-8-10 61........ JamieJones(5) 5 61+
(G L Moore) *hld up wl in tch in last: pild out 3f out: gd hdwy over 2f out: led jst over 1f out: edgd lft ins fnl f: pushed out* **10/11**[1]

0-01 **2** *1 1/2* **Competitor**[5] 569 7-8-12 54........(v) KirstyMilczarek(3) 7 58
(J Akehurst) *chsd ldrs tl led 7f out: rdn 2f out: hdd jst over 1f out: nt pce of wnr fnl f* **3/1**[2]

3-04 **3** *1 1/4* **Arena's Dream (USA)**[7] 542 4-9-0 65........(p) PatCosgrave 3 56
(J R Boyle) *t.k.h: hld up in tch: rdn and effrt wl over 1f out: chsd ldng pair ins fnl f: one pce* **7/2**[3]

-222 **4** *3/4* **Perfect Storm**[5] 569 9-8-8 50........ JackDean(7) 8 54
(W G M Turner) *in tch: hdwy to dispute ld 7f out: ev ch and drvn 2f out: wknd fnl f* **14/1**

/040 **5** *3* **Benayoun**[9] 521 4-9-0 50........ StephenDonohoe 1 48
(B J Llewellyn) *led after 1f tl 7f out: chsd ldrs after: rdn 5f out: wknd wl over 1f out* **33/1**

-060 **6** *1/2* **Revolve**[10] 517 8-9-1 53........ IanMongan 2 47
(Mrs L J Mongan) *led for 1f: in tch after: rdn wl over 2f out: wkng whn short of room bnd 2f out* **20/1**

2m 5.66s (-0.94) **Going Correction** 0.0s/f (Stan)
WFA 4 from 6yo+ 1lb **6** Ran SP% **114.0**
Speed ratings (Par 101): **103,101,100,100,97 97**
CSF £4.03 TOTE £2.00: £1.30, £1.90; EX 4.00 Trifecta £8.20 Pool: £737.80 - 63.67 winning tickets..The winner was brought in for 7,600gns.
Owner N J Jones **Bred** B Ryan **Trained** Woodingdean, E Sussex
■ Stewards' Enquiry : Jamie Jones one-day ban: careless riding (Mar 3)

FOCUS
A pretty weak seller, and straightforward for the winner. They went no pace at all early and the race turned into something of a sprint over the last half-mile.
Revolve Official explanation: vet said gelding bled from the nose.

632 ALL NEW @ BETDAQ.CO.UK H'CAP 1m 2f (P)
4:40 (4:40) (Class 4) (0-85,82) 3-Y-0 **£4,100** (£1,227; £613; £306; £152) **Stalls** Low

Form RPR

21-2 **1** **Martyr**[40] 131 3-9-6 81........ PatDobbs 7 86+
(R Hannon) *chsd ldr: rdn to challlenge 2f out: led 1f out: drvn ins fnl f: hld on cl home* **2/1**[1]

0-52 **2** *hd* **Love Empire (USA)**[7] 547 3-8-2 63........(b) JimmyQuinn 5 65
(M Johnston) *s.i.s: hld up in last pair: hdwy over 2f out: chsd ldng pair over 1f out: styd on wl to go 2nd towards fin: hld cl home* **11/1**

20-5 **3** *hd* **Harry Gee**[39] 136 3-9-5 80........ SteveDrowne 1 82
(G Wragg) *chsd ldng pair: rdn and outpcd jst over 2f out: rallied u.p and swtchd rt jst over 1f out: styd on wl fnl f* **7/1**

34-2 **4** *1/2* **Wannabe Free**[32] 225 3-8-12 73........ SebSanders 2 74
(J Noseda) *led at stdy pce: hrd pressed and rdn 2f out: hdd 1f out: one pce and lost 2 pls towards fin* **6/1**[3]

43-1 **5** *3/4* **Caribana**[26] 310 3-9-0 75........ NCallan 3 75
(M A Jarvis) *t.k.h: hld up wl in tch: rdn to chse ldng pair jst over 2f out: one pce u.p after* **9/4**[2]

14- **6** *5* **Jim Martin**[190] 4482 3-9-7 82........ JimCrowley 4 72
(J R Weymes) *taken down early: plld hrd: hld up wl in tch in rr: rdn over 2f out: sn outpcd and bhd* **12/1**

415- **7** *nk* **Redsensor**[91] 6899 3-8-10 71........ FrancisNorton 6 60
(M Quinn) *plld hrd: hld up wl in tch: rdn over 2f out: sn outpcd and bhd* **20/1**

2m 6.71s (0.11) **Going Correction** 0.0s/f (Stan) **7** Ran SP% **111.7**
Speed ratings (Par 99): **99,98,98,98,97 93,93**
CSF £23.17 TOTE £3.00: £1.20, £3.90; EX 20.00.
Owner Highclere Thoroughbred Racing (Delilah) **Bred** D Maroun **Trained** East Everleigh, Wilts

FOCUS
Not a bad little three-year-old handicap and a few of these still have the potential for improvement. This was another race where they went a very steady pace though, and the winning time was just over a second slower than the preceding older-horse seller. The fourth is the best guide to the form.

633 BETDAQPOKER.CO.UK MAIDEN STKS 1m (P)
5:10 (5:12) (Class 5) 3-Y-0+ **£2,331** (£693; £346; £173) **Stalls** High

Form RPR

5- **1** **Haydens Mark**[161] 5337 3-8-9 0........ LiamJones 3 83+
(W J Haggas) *t.k.h: stdd and dropped in bhd ldrs after s: hdwy over 2f out: chsd ldr over 1f out: led ins fnl f: styd on strly* **2/1**[2]

2 *1 3/4* **Maslaha** 3-8-4 0........ MatthewHenry 4 74+
(M A Jarvis) *chsd ldrs: hdwy to join ldrs over 2f out: led 2f out: hdd ins fnl f: nt pce of wnr last 100yds* **7/1**[3]

3 *5* **Twelfth Night (IRE)** 4-9-9 0........ JimCrowley 5 68+
(J R Best) *hld up in last: rdn and outpcd over 2f out: plugged on to go modest 3rd ins fnl f* **33/1**

3 **4** *1 1/4* **Shadowtime**[32] 221 3-8-9 0........ GregFairley 2 65
(M Johnston) *sn pressing ldr: led over 2f out: rdn and hdd 2f out: wknd qckly over 1f out* **4/6**[1]

5 *2 1/2* **Canary Islands** 3-8-9 0........ TGMcLaughlin 1 59
(E A L Dunlop) *t.k.h: led narrowly tl hdd over 2f out: wknd qckly 2f out* **12/1**

6 *36* **Emerging Light**[17] 6-10-0 0........ SebSanders 6 —
(S Dow) *in tch in rr: rdn wknd qckly over 2f out: eased last 2f: t.o* **25/1**

1m 37.44s (-0.76) **Going Correction** 0.0s/f (Stan)
WFA 3 from 4yo+ 19lb **6** Ran SP% **120.3**
Speed ratings (Par 103): **103,101,96,95,92 56**
CSF £17.60 TOTE £3.30: £1.60, £2.70; EX 18.30 Place 6 £8.34, Place 5 £5.58.
Owner Mrs J Dye **Bred** A J And Mrs Dye **Trained** Newmarket, Suffolk
■ Stewards' Enquiry : T G McLaughlin one-day ban; not riding to draw (Mar 3)

FOCUS
This looked a modest maiden beforehand with very little form to go on and half the field seeing the racecourse for the first time, but some big stables were represented and as things turned out the contest may have produced a couple of decent types. However the favourite was below par.
Shadowtime Official explanation: jockey said the saddle slipped
Emerging Light Official explanation: jockey said gelding lost its action
T/Plt: £12.20 to a £1 stake. Pool: £97,536.85. 5,802.85 winning tickets. T/Qpdt: £6.00 to a £1 stake. Pool: £7,063.70. 870.20 winning tickets. SP

613 SOUTHWELL (L-H)
Thursday, February 21

OFFICIAL GOING: Standard to slow
Wind: Virtually nil Weather: Overcast and dry

634 BET UEFA CUP - BETDAQ MAIDEN STKS 5f (F)
2:00 (2:01) (Class 5) 3-Y-0+ **£2,457** (£725; £362) **Stalls** High

Form RPR

0-4 **1** **Premier Yank (USA)**[19] 412 3-8-13 0........ TPQueally 12 71+
(J A Osborne) *in tch: smooth hdwy 2f out: rdn to ld ent fnl f: edgd lft and sn clr* **9/4**[1]

60-3 **2** *4* **Ducal Regancy Red**[4] 598 4-9-3 37........ KellyHarrison(5) 1 57
(C J Teague) *cl up: rdn 2f out and ev ch tl drvn and one pce ent fnl f* **16/1**

3 **3** *2* **Allium (IRE)**[19] 412 3-8-8 0........ MichaelHills 4 44
(B W Hills) *sn led: rdn over 1f out: hdd ent fnl f: sn wknd* **9/2**[3]

06- **4** *4* **Rossini's Dancer**[122] 6386 3-8-13 0........ PaulHanagan 5 35
(R A Fahey) *sn outpcd and bhd: hdwy wl over 1f out: styd on strly ins fnl f: nrst fin* **8/1**

005- **5** *1* **Princess Charlmane (IRE)**[180] 4795 5-9-8 37........ JimmyQuinn 8 32
(C J Teague) *towards rr: hdwy 2f out: sn rdn and kpt on appr fnl f: nrst fin* **33/1**

6 *3/4* **Champagne Lawn (USA)** 3-8-8 0........ PaulFessey 11 23
(T D Barron) *chsd ldrs: rdn along and sltly outpcd 2f out: kpt on ins fnl f* **20/1**

- **7** *nk* **Meinardus (IRE)** 3-8-13 0........ PhillipMakin 7 27
(T D Barron) *midfield: hdwy 2f out: sn rdn and one pce* **13/2**

00- **8** *shd* **Petite Music (IRE)**[125] 6306 3-8-5 0........ DuranFentiman(3) 13 22
(T D Easterby) *in tch: rdn along 2f out: grad wknd* **50/1**

4524 **9** *1 3/4* **Weetfromthechaff**[7] 557 3-8-13 57........(v) NCallan 9 21
(R Hollinshead) *chsd ldrs: rdn along 1/2-way and sn wknd* **4/1**[2]

5050 **10** *1/2* **Lady Fas (IRE)**[7] 562 5-9-5 39........ JerryO'Dwyer(3) 6 20
(A W Carroll) *midfield: rdn along and hdwy 2f out: wknd over 1f out* **50/1**

3/0 **11** *7* **Fiona Fox**[46] 65 4-9-5 0........ TolleyDean(3) 2 —
(J Balding) *chsd ldrs: rdn along 1/2-way: sn wknd* **33/1**

12 *2 1/2* **Amber May**[36] 5-9-5 0........ PJMcDonald(3) 3 —
(J P L Ewart) *s.i.s: a bhd* **50/1**

000/ **13** *8* **Dancing Moonlight (IRE)**[463] 6490 6-9-3 27........ ColinHaddon(5) 10 —
(Mrs N Macauley) *sn outpcd and bhd* **200/1**

60.50 secs (0.80) **Going Correction** +0.25s/f (Slow)
WFA 3 from 4yo+ 14lb **13** Ran SP% **116.3**
Speed ratings (Par 103): **103,96,93,87,85 84,83,83,80,79 68,64,51**
CSF £39.45 TOTE £3.20: £1.50, £3.80, £1.60; EX 30.50 Trifecta £126.30 Part won. Pool: £178.02 - 0.38 winning units..
Owner J Browne **Bred** Doyle Williams **Trained** Upper Lambourn, Berks

FOCUS
Very few got into this weak maiden. While the favourite did it well, he beat little with a 37-rated rival finishing second and there is very little to go on.

635 PONTIN'S EASTER BREAKS ARE BEST CLAIMING STKS 6f (F)
2:30 (2:30) (Class 6) 3-Y-O **£1,774** (£523; £262) **Stalls** Low

Form RPR

1333 **1** **Ballycroy Boy (IRE)**[2] 619 3-9-7 75 MickyFenton 3 77
(A Bailey) *led: rdn along and hdd 2f out: led again over 1f out: drvn ins fnl f and kpt on* **13/8**[1]

313 **2** *1* **Copperbottomed (IRE)**[6] 572 3-8-11 65 (e) JimCrowley 5 64
(J R Boyle) *chsd ldng pair: hdwy to chal 2f out: sn rdn and ev ch tl drvn and kpt on same pce ins fnl f* **3/1**[3]

2232 **3** *2* **Diademas (USA)**[5] 582 3-9-2 68 (p) NCallan 4 63
(V Smith) *trckd ldrs: smooth hdwy to ld 2f out: sn rdn: hdd over 1f out: sn drvn and one pce* **9/4**[2]

6151 **4** *11* **Mac Dalia**[2] 614 3-8-8 67 ow1 (p) JerryO'Dwyer(3) 1 22
(A J McCabe) *t.k.h: hld up in rr: effrt over 2f out: sn rdn and nvr a factor* **15/2**

46 **5** *16* **Heavenly Encounter**[20] 393 3-8-7 0 KellyHarrison(5) 2 —
(K R Burke) *cl up on inner: rdn along 1/2-way: sn wknd* **50/1**

1m 18.88s (2.38) **Going Correction** +0.225s/f (Slow) **5** Ran SP% **107.6**
Speed ratings (Par 95): **93,91,89,74,53**
CSF £6.47 TOTE £2.50: £2.40, £1.30; EX 6.90.
Owner R T Collins **Bred** Paraic Fox **Trained** Newmarket, Suffolk

FOCUS
A fair claimer rated through the winner to form.

636 BET GOLF - BETDAQ H'CAP 6f (F)
3:00 (3:00) (Class 5) (0-75,74) 4-Y-O+ **£2,593** (£765; £383) **Stalls** Low

Form RPR

-112 **1** **Hits Only Jude (IRE)**[22] 362 5-8-12 68 DeanMcKeown 7 89
(P A Blockley) *qckly away: mde all: rdn clr over 1f out: comf* **9/4**[2]

1-12 **2** *6* **Realt Na Mara (IRE)**[35] 190 5-9-4 74 SteveDrowne 5 76
(H Morrison) *in tch: rdn along 1/2-way: hdwy to chal 2f out: sn drvn and one pce appr fnl f* **2/1**[1]

0-45 **3** *½* **Kelamon**[7] 554 4-8-8 69 PatrickHills(5) 6 69
(M D I Usher) *trckd ldrs on outer: hdwy and ev ch 2f out: sn rdn and one pce appr fnl f* **12/1**

3-36 **4** *2* **Coleorton Dancer**[35] 194 6-9-3 73 NCallan 2 67
(K A Ryan) *prom: effrt and ev ch 2f out: sn rdn and wknd over 1f out* **7/1**

0/04 **5** *¾* **Supreme Speedster**[21] 370 4-8-6 62 JimmyQuinn 8 53
(M Brittain) *chsd wnr: rdn along wl over 2f out: sn wknd* **25/1**

0-54 **6** *6* **Bertie Southstreet**[26] 314 5-9-1 71 GeorgeBaker 4 43
(J R Best) *hld up: a in rr* **10/1**

2511 **7** *2* **Xpres Maite**[24] 342 5-9-2 72 (v) PhillipMakin 1 38
(S R Bowring) *chsd ldrs on inner: rdn along 1/2-way: sn lost pl and bhd* **11/2**[3]

1m 17.17s (0.67) **Going Correction** +0.225s/f (Slow) **7** Ran SP% **112.6**
Speed ratings (Par 103): **104,96,95,92,91 83,81**
CSF £6.93 CT £39.68 TOTE £3.20: £1.90, £1.50; EX 4.70 Trifecta £62.00 Pool: £223.00 - 2.55 winning units..
Owner Lynne Whiting & Judith Kell Stone **Bred** Swordlestown Stud **Trained** Lambourn, Berks

FOCUS
A fair handicap won in good style and the winner could be value for a little more.

637 TO PONTIN'S THIS EASTER (S) STKS 1m 4f (F)
3:35 (3:35) (Class 6) 4-Y-O+ **£1,774** (£523; £262) **Stalls** Low

Form RPR

5432 **1** **Hucking Heat (IRE)**[15] 449 4-9-2 63 PatCosgrave 3 66+
(J R Boyle) *mde all: pushed clr 2f out: unchal* **4/9**[1]

2650 **2** *6* **Matinee Idol**[4] 600 5-8-9 41 (b) PaulHanagan 2 38
(Mrs S Lamyman) *hld up: hdwy 1/2-way: chsd wnr 3f out: sn rdn and kpt on: no ch w wnr* **3/1**[2]

0-50 **3** *17* **The Mighty Ogmore**[32] 238 4-8-6 35 (e[1]) PaulFessey 5 11
(R C Guest) *chsd wnr: rdn along over 4f out: drvn 3f out and plugged on same pce* **14/1**[3]

00-0 **4** *18* **Pearl Of Esteem**[19] 400 5-8-9 39 JimmyQuinn 1 —
(J Pearce) *trckd ldng pair: rdn along 4f out: sn drvn and wknd over 2f out* **25/1**

2m 49.77s (8.77) **Going Correction** +0.225s/f (Slow)
WFA 4 from 5yo 3lb **4** Ran SP% **104.8**
Speed ratings (Par 101): **79,75,63,51**
CSF £1.83 TOTE £1.50; EX 1.90.The winner was sold to Mr E. Weetman for 12,000gns.
Owner M Khan X2 **Bred** Thomas J Reid **Trained** Epsom, Surrey

FOCUS
An uncompetitive seller and a pedestrian time, even for a race like this, resulting in a breeze for the odds-on Hucking Heat.

638 THERE'S NO PLACE QUITE LIKE PONTIN'S H'CAP 1m 6f (F)
4:05 (4:05) (Class 5) (0-75,75) 4-Y-O+ **£2,593** (£765; £383) **Stalls** Low

Form RPR

2313 **1** **Bentley Brook (IRE)**[15] 450 6-9-9 72 StephenDonohoe 6 89
(P A Blockley) *hld up in tch: gd hdwy 1/2-way: led over 4f out: jnd 3f out: rdn 2f out: drvn over 1f out: hld on gamely u.p ins fnl f* **5/2**[2]

1-15 **2** *hd* **Clear Reef**[38] 159 4-9-6 74 TGMcLaughlin 2 91
(Jane Chapple-Hyam) *hld up in rr: stdy hdwy 5f out: jnd wnr 3f out: rdn and edgd lft over 1f out: sn drvn and ev ch tl no ex towards fin* **2/1**[1]

-410 **3** *28* **Flame Creek (IRE)**[19] 405 12-9-11 74 EdwardCreighton 1 52
(E J Creighton) *hld up: stdy hdwy over 4f out: chsd ldng pair 3f out: sn rdn and outpcd* **12/1**

12-0 **4** *½* **Kylkenny**[30] 260 13-9-9 75 (t) TravisBlock(3) 7 52
(H Morrison) *trckd ldrs: pushed along 4f out: rdn 3f out and sn btn* **17/2**

-230 **5** *18* **Victory Quest (IRE)**[30] 260 8-9-5 68 (v) PaulHanagan 4 20
(Mrs S Lamyman) *led to over 5f out: sn wknd* **7/2**[3]

520/ **6** *¾* **Nessen Dorma (IRE)**[19] 2975 7-9-4 70 (v) PJMcDonald(3) 3 21
(J S Wainwright) *chsd ldng pair: rdn along 1/2-way: sn lost pl and bhd* **9/1**

000- **7** *2½* **Alisar (IRE)**[28] 6292 8-8-0 56 oh11 (t) KMay(7) 5 3
(E J Creighton) *cl up: led over 5f out tl over 4f out: sn wknd* **100/1**

3m 9.47s (1.17) **Going Correction** +0.225s/f (Slow)
WFA 4 from 6yo+ 5lb **7** Ran SP% **113.3**
Speed ratings (Par 103): **105,104,88,88,78 77,76**
CSF £7.78 TOTE £4.10: £1.80, £1.60; EX 6.30.
Owner John Wardle **Bred** Christopher Maye **Trained** Lambourn, Berks
■ Stewards' Enquiry : P J McDonald three-day ban: used whip when out of contention (Mar 3-5)

FOCUS
Just a fair staying handicap, but with Victory Quest and Alisar duelling for the lead from the start this was run at a proper pace, and the front pair pulled a mile clear of the others. The form is rated fairly positively.

639 BACK OR LAY AT BETDAQ H'CAP 7f (F)
4:40 (4:40) (Class 6) (0-65,70) 4-Y-O+ **£1,911** (£564; £282) **Stalls** Low

Form RPR

-214 **1** **Wodhill Gold**[23] 351 7-8-13 59 (v) NCallan 6 71
(D Morris) *cl up: led over 2f out: rdn over 1f out and kpt on wl* **4/1**[2]

3124 **2** *1¾* **Another Genepi (USA)**[6] 576 5-9-3 63 (b) FergalLynch 8 70
(I W McInnes) *sn led: rdn along 3f out: hdd over 2f out: drvn over 1f out and kpt on same pce* **11/4**[1]

1212 **3** *5* **Louisiade (IRE)**[4] 601 7-9-7 70 6ex (p) RussellKennemore(3) 5 64
(M C Chapman) *chsd ldrs: rdn 2f out: sn drvn and one pce appr fnl f* **4/1**[2]

04-5 **4** *1¾* **High 'n Dry (IRE)**[14] 463 4-9-3 63 (p) PaulDoe 7 52
(M A Allen) *hld up in tch: hdwy to chse ldrs over 2f out: sn rdn and no imp fr wl over 1f out* **14/1**

6-40 **5** *¾* **Imperial Sword**[30] 256 5-8-4 50 (b) PaulFessey 3 37
(T D Barron) *chsd ldrs: rdn along over 2f out: sn drvn and wknd wl over 1f out* **20/1**

2-00 **6** *5* **Pietersen (IRE)**[12] 506 4-8-11 64 (b) DeanHeslop(7) 1 37
(T D Barron) *dwlt: sn rdn along and outpcd in rr tl styd on fnl 2f* **9/1**

0-06 **7** *nk* **Tamino (IRE)**[19] 404 5-9-2 62 (t) JimmyQuinn 4 34
(P Howling) *chsd ldrs on inner: rdn along wl over 2f out and sn wknd* **5/1**[3]

013- **8** *4* **Penel (IRE)**[149] 5704 7-8-9 55 ow3 (p) MickyFenton 2 17
(P T Midgley) *sn outpcd and a bhd* **10/1**

1m 31.66s (1.36) **Going Correction** +0.225s/f (Slow) **8** Ran SP% **113.9**
Speed ratings (Par 101): **101,99,93,91,90 84,84,79**
CSF £15.29 CT £45.60 TOTE £4.70: £1.60, £1.60, £1.60; EX 19.30 Trifecta £36.90 Pool: £336.89 - 6.48 winning units..
Owner Miss S Graham **Bred** Wodhill Stud **Trained** Newmarket, Suffolk

FOCUS
A modest handicap and very few ever got into it. The form is ordinary with the runner-up to her plating mark.

640 PONTIN'S GREAT FUN, GREAT TIMES H'CAP 1m (F)
5:10 (5:10) (Class 6) (0-52,52) 4-Y-O+ **£1,911** (£564; £282) **Stalls** Low

Form RPR

06-1 **1** **Blue Empire (IRE)**[51] 2 7-8-13 51 (p) StephenDonohoe 8 65
(John A Harris) *in tch: gd hdwy on outer 3f out: led over 2f out: rdn and hung lft ent fnl f: sn drvn and styd on* **7/1**

-334 **2** *1¼* **Wodhill Schnaps**[14] 465 7-8-11 49 (b) NCallan 14 60
(D Morris) *a.p: effrt 2f out: rdn and ch whn sltly hmpd ent fnl f: sn drvn and one pce* **5/1**[2]

-562 **3** *2½* **Only A Grand**[13] 478 4-8-13 51 (b) PatCosgrave 12 56
(R Bastiman) *trckd ldrs: hdwy 3f out: rdn to chse ldng pair whn n.m.r and swtchd rt over 1f out: sn drvn and one pce* **8/1**

003- **4** *1¾* **Ming Vase**[138] 6019 6-8-8 46 oh1 FrankieMcDonald 11 47
(P T Midgley) *trckd ldrs: hdwy 2f out: sn rdn and hung lft over 1f out: kpt on same pce u.p ins fnl f* **25/1**

2422 **5** *2½* **Ermine Grey**[7] 560 7-8-9 50 KirstyMilczarek(3) 5 46
(A W Carroll) *chsd ldrs: rdn along over 3f out: kpt on same pce u.p fnl 2f* **4/1**[1]

-501 **6** *3* **Anduril**[14] 465 7-9-0 52 (p) FergalLynch 6 41
(I W McInnes) *trckd ldrs: effrt over 2f out: sn rdn and kpt on same pce* **8/1**

6503 **7** *¾* **Shifty**[7] 553 9-8-8 46 oh1 PaulHanagan 10 33
(Jedd O'Keeffe) *hld up in midfield: effrt and nt clr run over 1f out: sn swtchd rt and rdn: n.d* **16/1**

4030 **8** *2½* **Steel Grey**[6] 578 7-8-11 49 (b[1]) DavidAllan 9 30
(M Brittain) *led to 1/2-way: cl up tl led again 3f out: rdn and hdd over 2f out: sn drvn and wknd* **16/1**

/063 **9** *2½* **Shosolosa (IRE)**[12] 508 6-8-8 46 PaulFessey 7 21
(R C Guest) *midfield: wd st: rdn over 2f out and no imp* **20/1**

3-31 **10** *2½* **Sparky Vixen**[7] 550 4-8-1 46 JamieKyne(7) 1 16+
(C J Teague) *midfield: wd st: rdn over 2f out and no hdwy* **6/1**[3]

03-0 **11** *9* **Prince Rossi (IRE)**[32] 235 4-9-0 52 JimCrowley 4 —
(A E Price) *cl up on inner: led 1/2-way: rdn and hdd 3f out: sn wknd* **16/1**

12 *5* **Wall To Wall (IRE)**[76] 7066 5-8-5 46 oh1 (p) AndrewMullen(3) 3 —
(Patrick Carey, Ire) *s.i.s: a in rr* **16/1**

50-6 **13** *31* **Swayze (IRE)**[47] 57 5-9-0 52 TPQueally 2 —
(M Quinn) *a outpcd: wl bhd fnl 3f* **25/1**

1m 45.65s (1.95) **Going Correction** +0.225s/f (Slow) **13** Ran SP% **121.7**
Speed ratings (Par 101): **99,97,95,93,91 88,87,84,82,79 70,65,34**
CSF £41.58 CT £290.23 TOTE £9.80: £2.70, £2.70, £2.90; EX 105.70 Trifecta £138.40 Part won. Pool: £194.98 - 0.10 winning units. Place 6 £3.96, Place 5 £2.49.
Owner Shaun Taylor **Bred** Yeomanstown Stud **Trained** Eastwell, Leics

FOCUS
A big field, but a poor race with the top-weights rated just 52. They went a fair early pace though and again it paid to race handily. The form looks straightforward rated around the first two.
Wall To Wall(IRE) Official explanation: jockey said mare was slowly away
T/Plt: £3.20 to a £1 stake. Pool: £51,352.15. 11,571.80 winning tickets. T/Qpdt: £1.80 to a £1 stake. Pool: £2,497.20. 990.70 winning tickets. JR

576 WOLVERHAMPTON (A.W) (L-H)
Thursday, February 21

OFFICIAL GOING: Standard
Wind: Moderate becoming strong, behind Weather: Fine

641 BETDAQ BETTING EXCHANGE H'CAP 5f 20y(P)
6:50 (6:50) (Class 6) (0-50,51) 4-Y-O+ **£1,684** (£501; £250; £125) **Stalls** Low

Form RPR

1136 **1** **Dodaa (USA)**[13] 488 5-8-7 50 AshleyHamblett(5) 5 58
(N Wilson) *mde all: rdn wl over 1f out: r.o* **7/2**[1]

0-43 **2** *nk* **Town House**[10] 522 6-8-1 46 oh1 SoniaEaton(7) 6 53
(B P J Baugh) *chsd wnr: rdn and edgd lft 1f out: kpt on* **6/1**

0630 **3** *nk* **Maiden Investor**[10] 522 5-8-10 48 (vt) MickyFenton 3 54+
(Stef Liddiard) *s.i.s: hdwy over 1f out: rdn and edgd lft ins fnl f: r.o to take 3rd post* **8/1**

3-35 **4** *shd* **Taboor (IRE)**[31] 247 10-8-10 48 AlanMunro 2 54
(R M H Cowell) *a.p: swtchd lft ins fnl f: rdn and kpt on towards fin* **11/2**

The Form Book, Raceform Ltd, Compton, RG20 6NL

1 **5** *1 1/4* **Miss Curly (IRE)**[26] 318 8-8-11 **49**..........(t) TGMcLaughlin 8 50
(Gerard Keane, Ire) *s.i.s: hld up: hdwy on outside over 2f out: rdn and kpt on one pce fnl f* **4/1**[2]

00-4 **6** *1 1/2* **Melandre**[10] 522 6-8-9 **50**.......... MarkLawson(3) 1 46
(M Brittain) *n.m.r on ins after s: bhd: swtchd rt wl over 1f out: nvr trbld ldrs* **12/1**

-051 **7** *nk* **Geordie Dancer (IRE)**[7] 558 6-8-8 **51** 6ex......(b) DanielleMcCreery(5) 4 46
(A Berry) *mid-div: hdwy on ins 2f out: wknd 1f out* **14/1**

U-00 **8** *7* **Vlasta Weiner**[25] 327 8-8-8 **46** oh1..........(p) PaulFitzsimons 9 15
(J M Bradley) *chsd ldrs: reminders after 1f: rdn over 2f out: wknd wl over 1f out* **40/1**

0-02 **9** *3* **White Ledger (IRE)**[22] 363 9-8-11 **49**.......... JimmyQuinn 7 8
(R E Peacock) *chsd ldrs tl wknd over 2f out* **9/2**[3]

62.52 secs (0.22) **Going Correction** +0.125s/f (Slow) 9 Ran SP% **118.0**
Speed ratings (Par 101): **103,102,102,101,99 97,97,85,81**
CSF £25.44 CT £158.81 TOTE £4.30: £1.50, £3.50, £4.60; EX 45.50.
Owner Paul & Linda Dixon **Bred** Silverleaf Farm Inc **Trained** Flaxton, N Yorks

FOCUS
A weak sprint handicap, run at a strong early pace. The first four were closely bunched at the finish but the form looks straighforward rated around the runner-up, fourth and sixth.
White Ledger(IRE) Official explanation: trainer said gelding ran flat

642 BET FOOTBALL - BETDAQ CLASSIFIED STKS 5f 216y(P)
7:20 (7:21) (Class 7) 4-Y-0+ **£1,365** (£403; £201) **Stalls** Low

Form RPR
0421 **1** **Blackheath (IRE)**[7] 562 12-9-1 45.......... KellyHarrison(5) 7 61
(S T Mason) *a.p: led jst over 1f out: pushed out* **11/10**[1]

005- **2** *3/4* **Bahamian Bay**[114] 6565 6-8-11 43.......... MarkLawson(3) 3 53
(M Brittain) *bhd: rdn and hdwy over 1f out: r.o ins fnl f: nt rch wnr* **33/1**

0435 **3** *1 1/4* **Prettilini**[14] 469 5-8-11 42.......... KirstyMilczarek(3) 5 49
(A W Carroll) *chsd ldrs: rdn wl over 1f out: kpt on one pce fnl f* **7/1**[2]

3033 **4** *2 1/2* **Temtation (IRE)**[22] 363 4-8-11 45.......... RussellKennemore(3) 9 41
(J A Pickering) *led: rdn and hdd whn edgd rt jst over 1f out: wknd ins fnl f* **12/1**

-500 **5** *3/4* **Mister Incredible**[31] 247 5-9-0 45..........(v) PaulFitzsimons 6 39
(J M Bradley) *hld up in tch: rdn wl over 1f out: one pce* **14/1**

46 **6** *nk* **Oberows Lady (IRE)**[27] 305 6-8-11 40.......... JerryO'Dwyer(3) 4 38
(Adrian McGuinness, Ire) *hld up and bhd: hdwy on ins over 1f out: no further prog fnl f* **17/2**

-254 **7** *1* **Avoncreek**[14] 469 4-9-0 43..........(p) AndrewElliott 10 34
(B P J Baugh) *hld up towards rr: c wd st: rdn over 1f out: n.d* **8/1**[3]

8 *4* **Fraizer (IRE)**[76] 7065 4-9-0 42.......... FergalLynch 13 22
(Adrian McGuinness, Ire) *hld up and bhd: sme hdwy on wd outside over 2f out: wkng whn hung bdly lft over 1f out* **25/1**

/ **9** *1* **Da Luego (IRE)**[97] 6842 4-9-0 42.......... JimmyQuinn 2 18
(Patrick Allen, Ire) *hld up in mid-div: rdn over 2f out: wknd wl over 1f out* **12/1**

2254 **10** *2 1/2* **Tang**[8] 535 4-8-7 44..........(p) JackDean(7) 1 10
(W G M Turner) *s.i.s: outpcd* **10/1**

6/0- **11** *7* **Wotavadun (IRE)**[180] 4795 5-9-0 40.......... PatrickMathers 12 —
(I W McInnes) *chsd ldrs: rdn over 3f out: wknd over 2f out* **50/1**

1m 16.22s (1.22) **Going Correction** +0.125s/f (Slow) 11 Ran SP% **121.6**
Speed ratings (Par 97): **96,95,93,90,89 88,87,81,80,77 67**
CSF £55.39 TOTE £2.10: £1.40, £9.40, £2.20; EX 59.30.
Owner Middleham Park Racing XX **Bred** John McKay **Trained** Lanchester, Co. Durham

FOCUS
A very weak affair but straightforward for the grade rated around the winner and third.

643 BETDAQPOKER.CO.UK CLAIMING STKS 7f 32y(P)
7:50 (7:50) (Class 5) 4-Y-0+ **£2,331** (£693; £346; £173) **Stalls** High

Form RPR
5-30 **1** **Landucci**[26] 313 7-8-12 75..........(p) PatrickHills(5) 5 83
(J W Hills) *stdd s: hld up in rr: hdwy over 1f out: rdn and edgd lft ins fnl f: sn led: r.o wl* **15/8**[2]

4221 **2** *1 1/2* **Dickie Le Davoir**[8] 536 4-9-0 70.......... FergalLynch 4 76
(I W McInnes) *hld up in tch: wnt 2nd 2f out: rdn over 1f out: ev ch ins fnl f: nt qckn* **1/1**[1]

00-6 **3** *1 1/4* **Raza Cab (IRE)**[12] 506 6-9-1 71.......... JimmyQuinn 2 74
(Karen George) *led: rdn over 1f out: hdd and no ex wl ins fnl f* **4/1**[3]

2-5 **4** *6* **Dancing Wizard**[15] 447 4-8-11 0.......... AdamKirby 1 53
(C G Cox) *hld up in tch: rdn and wknd over 1f out* **14/1**

00 **5** *6* **Moorside Diamond**[9] 529 4-8-2 0.......... AndrewElliott 3 28
(A D Brown) *chsd ldr 5f: sn wknd* **80/1**

1m 31.37s (1.77) **Going Correction** +0.125s/f (Slow) 5 Ran SP% **112.7**
Speed ratings (Par 103): **94,92,90,84,77**
CSF £4.25 TOTE £2.60: £1.10, £1.50; EX 4.70.Dickie Le Davoir was claimed by John Harris for £13,000.
Owner R J Tufft **Bred** D J And Mrs Deer **Trained** Upper Lambourn, Berks

FOCUS
The top three in the weights stood out in this claimer and they duly played out the finish. The winning time was moderate but the form looks sound enough rated around the first two.

644 TRY BETDAQ FOR AN EXCHANGE H'CAP 1m 4f 50y(P)
8:20 (8:20) (Class 6) (0-60,59) 3-Y-0 **£1,774** (£523; £262) **Stalls** Low

Form RPR
0-00 **1** **Paul The Carpet (UAE)**[14] 464 3-8-4 45..........(b1) JimmyQuinn 1 51
(G L Moore) *t.k.h: sn led: clr over 9f out: hung rt bnd 7f out: rdn over 2f out: drvn out* **10/1**

605 **2** *2 1/2* **Dara Diva (IRE)**[20] 396 3-8-8 **54**..........(bt1) PatrickHills(5) 5 56
(W J Haggas) *hld up in rr: rdn and hdwy on ins over 2f out: chsd wnr wl over 1f out: no imp* **16/1**

5021 **3** *nk* **Novestar (IRE)**[4] 597 3-8-9 **55** 6ex.......... JamieJones(5) 4 56
(G J Smith) *led early: chsd wnr tl over 9f out: wnt 2nd again over 4f out: rdn over 2f out: one pce fnl 2f* **12/1**

4-42 **4** *3/4* **Arabesque Dancer**[25] 325 3-9-3 **58**..........(b) URispoli 2 58
(M Botti) *t.k.h early: hld up in tch in chsng gp: hrd rdn over 1f out: one pce fnl f* **7/2**[2]

000- **5** *5* **Jemima's Art**[193] 4422 3-8-6 **47**.......... DaleGibson 3 39
(M W Easterby) *bhd: rdn over 3f out: sme hdwy over 2f out: wkng whn hung lft wl over 1f out* **8/1**

-433 **6** *6* **Anabaa's Secret (IRE)**[16] 439 3-8-11 **52**.......... TPQueally 7 34
(J A Osborne) *hld up in tch in chsng gp: rdn over 3f out: wknd over 2f out* **3/1**[1]

003- **7** *2* **Dawn Wind**[169] 5127 3-9-4 **59**.......... NCallan 8 38
(I A Wood) *hld up: lost pl and n.m.r over 4f out: rdn and bhd whn hmpd over 3f out* **13/2**[3]

4-31 **P** **Ten Spot (IRE)**[7] 556 3-9-3 58 6ex..........(v) MickyFenton 6 —
(Stef Liddiard) *prom: chsd wnr 8f out tl edgd lft over 4f out: sn wknd: p.u over 2f out* **3/1**[1]

2m 42.91s (1.81) **Going Correction** +0.125s/f (Slow) 8 Ran SP% **119.3**
Speed ratings (Par 95): **98,96,96,95,92 88,86,—**
CSF £156.56 CT £1945.54 TOTE £12.40: £2.30, £4.30, £3.90; EX 87.90.
Owner A Grinter **Bred** Darley **Trained** Woodingdean, E Sussex

FOCUS
A poor handicap in which the winner looked to outstay his rivals. The form appears sound rated around the third and fourth.
Paul The Carpet(UAE) Official explanation: trainer's rep said, regarding the apparent improvement in form, that the gelding had benefited from the application of blinkers
Ten Spot(IRE) Official explanation: trainer said filly choked

645 BETDAQ.CO.UK MEDIAN AUCTION MAIDEN STKS 1m 141y(P)
8:50 (8:51) (Class 5) 3-Y-O **£2,331** (£693; £346; £173) **Stalls** Low

Form RPR
1 **Dream Desert (IRE)** 3-9-3 0.......... EdwardCreighton 5 77+
(M R Channon) *s.i.s: t.k.h: sn hld up in tch: rdn to ld jst ins fnl f: r.o wl* **8/1**[3]

2 **2** *1 1/2* **Maadraa (IRE)**[18] 416 3-9-3 0.......... NCallan 8 74
(M A Jarvis) *sn led: rdn over 1f out: hdd jst ins fnl f: nt qckn* **4/6**[1]

3 *1 3/4* **Apt Son (USA)**[170] 5123 3-9-3 0.......... J-PGuillambert 3 70
(Francis Ennis, Ire) *a.p: wnt 2nd over 6f out: rdn over 2f out: one pce fnl f* **7/4**[2]

6 **4** *2 1/2* **Ambrix (IRE)**[5] 595 3-8-5 0.......... MatthewDavies(7) 6 59
(M R Channon) *s.s: bhd: hdwy over 2f out: rdn and edgd lft over 1f out: wknd fnl f* **20/1**

65 **5** *7* **Just Kenko**[22] 360 3-9-3 0.......... StephenDonohoe 2 48
(N J Vaughan) *led early: chsd ldr tl over 6f out: rdn and wknd over 3f out* **66/1**

0 **6** *1/2* **Lucky Character**[27] 310 3-9-3 0..........(t) SamHitchcott 7 47
(N J Vaughan) *hld up in tch: rdn over 3f out: wknd over 2f out* **50/1**

- **7** *8* **Admiral Troy** 3-8-10 0.......... GabrielHannon(7) 1 29
(M D I Usher) *s.i.s: a bhd* **50/1**

0- **8** *1 3/4* **Whenineedyou**[121] 6401 3-8-12 0..........(t) JamesDoyle 4 20
(I A Wood) *prom early: hld up: rdn over 3f out: sn bhd* **80/1**

1m 52.77s (2.27) **Going Correction** +0.125s/f (Slow) 8 Ran SP% **118.9**
Speed ratings (Par 97): **94,92,91,88,82 82,75,73**
CSF £14.51 TOTE £9.00: £2.00, £1.10, £1.10; EX 14.70.
Owner Jaber Abdullah **Bred** Gainsborough Stud Management Ltd **Trained** West Ilsley, Berks

FOCUS
A modest maiden but the form, although ordinary, should work out.

646 MAKE IT PAY AT BETDAQ H'CAP 1m 1f 103y(P)
9:20 (9:23) (Class 6) (0-65,65) 4-Y-0+ **£1,774** (£523; £262) **Stalls** Low

Form RPR
2-23 **1** **King's Ransom**[4] 601 5-8-10 **62**.......... JamieJones(5) 7 70
(S Gollings) *a.p: led 2f out: rdn and edgd lft towards fin: r.o* **2/1**[1]

1323 **2** *3/4* **Gifted Heir (IRE)**[13] 485 4-8-8 **55**.......... LiamJones 1 61
(A Bailey) *a.p: led over 2f out: sn hdd: rdn over 1f out: kpt on ins fnl f* **6/1**

2134 **3** *nk* **Buscador (USA)**[7] 559 9-8-10 **57**.......... RichardKingscote 2 63
(W M Brisbourne) *chsd ldr: led over 7f out: rdn and hdd over 2f out: edgd rt ins fnl f: kpt on* **7/2**[3]

5-21 **4** *hd* **Blue Eyed Eloise**[32] 239 6-9-1 **62**.......... StephenCarson 5 67
(B J McMath) *hld up: rdn and hdwy on ins over 2f out: swtchd rt wl over 1f out: r.o wl towards fin* **3/1**[2]

5-36 **5** *2 1/2* **Pelham Crescent (IRE)**[10] 526 5-9-4 **65**..........(p) CatherineGannon 4 65
(B Palling) *hld up: rdn over 2f out: no real prog* **13/2**

00- **6** *2 1/2* **Top Seed (IRE)**[53] 3407 7-8-9 **56** ow1.......... StephenDonohoe 3 51
(Ian Williams) *a in rr* **14/1**

3360 **7** *9* **Meditation**[8] 546 6-9-3 **64**.......... JamesDoyle 6 40
(I A Wood) *led: hdd over 7f out: rdn over 3f out: hmpd wl over 2f out: sn wknd* **16/1**

2m 2.53s (0.83) **Going Correction** +0.125s/f (Slow) 7 Ran SP% **120.7**
Speed ratings (Par 101): **101,100,100,99,97 95,87**
CSF £15.97 TOTE £3.40: £1.10, £5.20; EX 21.80 Place 6 £62.13, Place 5 £28.82.
Owner Mrs D Dukes **Bred** Darley **Trained** Scamblesby, Lincs
■ Stewards' Enquiry : Jamie Jones caution: careless riding

FOCUS
Not a bad race for the class, run at a sound pace. The form is ordinary rated around the placed horses.
T/Plt: £163.80 to a £1 stake. Pool: £83,337.40. 371.25 winning tickets. T/Qpdt: £39.20 to a £1 stake. Pool: £6,347.40. 119.80 winning tickets. KH

563 NAD AL SHEBA (L-H)
Thursday, February 21

OFFICIAL GOING: Dirt course - fast; turf course - good

647a TADAWUL STKS (H'CAP) (DIRT) 7f 110y(D)
3:40 (3:41) (95-110,108) 3-Y-0+
£36,180 (£12,060; £6,030; £3,015; £1,809; £1,206)

RPR
1 **Green Coast (IRE)**[14] 473 5-8-7 **95**.......... WJSupple 7 102+
(Doug Watson, UAE) *trckd ldr: wd: led 3f out: clr 2f out: comf* **4/1**[2]

2 *4 1/4* **Marbush (IRE)**[6] 7-9-6 **108**..........(e) JMurtagh 4 104
(D Selvaratnam, UAE) *trckd ldr: rdn 4 1/2f out: 5th 3f out: r.o fnl 2f: no ch w wnr* **2/1**[1]

3 *1 1/4* **Stepping Up (IRE)**[7] 563 5-8-9 **97**..........(t) TPO'Shea 2 90
(E Charpy, UAE) *trckd ldr on rail: no room 4 1/2f out: dropped bk: r.o wl fnl 2 1/2f* **8/1**

4 *4 1/4* **Accountforthegold (USA)**[7] 564 6-9-1 **102**.......... KerrinMcEvoy 6 87
(Saeed Bin Suroor) *trckd ldr: rdn 3f out: nt qckn* **9/2**[3]

5 *1 3/4* **Grand Hombre (USA)**[1083] 571 8-8-12 **100**.......... BrettDoyle 5 80
(R Bouresly, Kuwait) *broke awkwardly: sn struggling: rdn 4f out: mod prog last 2 1/2f* **22/1**

6 *5 1/2* **Ekhtiaar**[140] 5950 4-8-7 **95**.......... RoystonFfrench 3 63
(A Al Raihe, UAE) *slowly away: trckd ldr: rdn 3 1/2f out: one pce* **5/1**

7 *1 3/4* **Olympic City (BRZ)**[14] 475 5-8-6 **100**.......... AhmedAjtebi(6) 1 64
(A Cintra Pereira, Brazil) *led on rail tl 3f out: wknd* **8/1**

1m 30.8s (-0.50) **Going Correction** +0.225s/f (Slow) 7 Ran SP% **114.8**
Speed ratings: **111,106,105,101,99 94,92**
CSF 12.55.

Owner Mohsin Al Tajir **Bred** Hadi Al Tajir **Trained** United Arab Emirates

FOCUS

Just the seven runners and this looked like a pretty ordinary handicap for the level. Despite the small field, the pace was strong and they finished strung out.

NOTEBOOK

Green Coast(IRE), fourth over the bare 7f round here on his return from a year off and first start since leaving Godolphin last time, improved on that form and did this easily. Well away from the widest stall, he was always travelling strongly close to the pace and had this won when taking over on the bridle at the top of the straight. This was an ordinary contest, but he is lightly raced and is clearly capable of producing a smart level of form.

Marbush(IRE)'s recent second over 5f at Jebel Ali on his return from over a year off the track didn't really amount to a great deal, but he was expected to be suited by this step up in trip and was extremely well backed. He was no match whatsoever for the easy winner, but this was still a smart performance off a mark of 108. (op 5/2)

Stepping Up(IRE) can be rated better than the bare form as he lost his place when hampered against the rail by Marbush a couple of furlongs or so after the start. (op 7/1)

Accountforthegold(USA), formerly trained in the US, offered little on his first start in Dubai the previous week and this was another tame effort. (op 4/1)

Grand Hombre(USA) was fourth in the 2004 Dubai World Cup when with Godolphin, but he had run just once since then, taking third in the third round of the Maktoum Challenge in 2005, and his absence totalled 1083 days. Now with new connections, he was quickly detached from his six rivals after being slow to find his stride, but he closed up slightly rounding the final bend and ran on in the straight to pass a couple of tiring rivals. He is obviously not the force of old, but he seems to retain some ability at least and will be suited by a step back up in trip. (op 20/1)

Ekhtiaar is two from two on Polytrack, but he failed to prove himself on dirt on his first start since leaving John Gosden.

648a VISA INFINITE STKS (H'CAP) (DIRT) 1m 110y(D)

4:10 (4:11) (95-110,102) 3-Y-O+

£36,180 (£12,060; £6,030; £3,015; £1,809; £1,206)

			RPR
1		**Rosberg (USA)**[35] [203] 7-9-4 **100**......(bt) TPO'Shea 6 (E Charpy, UAE) *trckd ldr: gng wl 3f out: led 2 1/2f out: r.o wl: comf* **6/1**	106
2	2 3/4	**Miswaatt (KSA)**[76] 5-9-2 **98**......(t) JBeitia 9 (J Gardel, Saudi Arabia) *mid-div: rdn to chse wnr 2 1/2f out: r.o: no ch w wnr* **25/1**	100
3	2 3/4	**Imperialista (BRZ)**[13] [493] 5-9-6 **102**......(v) LDettori 1 (Saeed Bin Suroor) *sn led: hdd 2 1/2f out: r.o same pce* **7/2**[2]	99
4	4 3/4	**Minefield (USA)**[14] [473] 4-8-12 **95**......(vt) KerrinMcEvoy 4 (Saeed Bin Suroor) *racd in rr: rdn 3f out: r.o fnl f* **5/2**[1]	80
5	2 1/4	**Mambo King (DEN)**[14] [477] 6-8-9 **97**......(t) AhmedAjtebi(6) 5 (L Kelp, Denmark) *trckd ldng pair: rdn 3f out: r.o one pce* **40/1**	78
6	1 1/4	**Ukrainian (BRZ)**[7] [563] 4-8-4 **96**...... RichardMullen 8 (A Cintra Pereira, Brazil) *racd in rr: rdn 3f out: nvr nr to chal* **13/2**	65
7	2 1/2	**Mister Fasliyev (IRE)**[13] [495] 6-9-6 **102**...... MJKinane 2 (E Charpy, UAE) *nvr nr to chal* **20/1**	76
8	6	**Jonquil (IRE)**[20] 6-9-6 **102**......(v) WJSupple 3 (Doug Watson, UAE) *s.i.s: mid-div on rail: rdn 3f out: wknd* **9/1**	64
9	3 3/4	**Almaram (USA)**[7] [563] 8-9-5 **101**......(e) JMurtagh 7 (D Selvaratnam, UAE) *racd in rr: nvr able to chal* **4/1**[3]	55

1m 42.86s (-1.14) **Going Correction** +0.225s/f (Slow) **9** Ran SP% **119.5**

Speed ratings: **114,111,109,104,102 101,99,94,90**

CSF 144.97; TRI 610.14.

Owner Sheikh Majid Bin Mohammed al Maktoum **Bred** Addison Racing Ltd **Trained** United Arab Emirates

FOCUS

An average handicap for the level.

NOTEBOOK

Rosberg(USA) was beaten a long way into third over 1m1f round here on his previous start, but the winner that day, Lucky Find, followed up in a better race, and the runner-up, Third Set, won well switched to turf next time. This was easier and, having travelled kindly on the speed with the blinkers re-fitted, he found plenty for pressure in the straight. A rise in the weights will make things tougher and he will do well to follow up. (op 11/2)

Miswaatt(KSA), a 1m dirt winner in Saudi Arabia, moved quite well into the straight, but the winner got first run and he was always being held.

Imperialista(BRZ) showed signs of a revival when third in what looked a better race than this over course and distance on his previous start, but he was unable to build on that promise. Having been rushed up to lead from the inside stall, he was kept busy by the eventual winner and offered disappointingly little when asked for his effort.

Minefield(USA) looked better than the bare form of his fifth over 7f round here on his first start since switching from the US and he was well backed on this step up in trip, with a visor and tongue-tie fitted, but things didn't go his way. Having taken an age to find his stride, he soon found himself well back towards the inside and did not appear to face the kickback. He must have been around 12 lengths off the lead and had only one behind when switched out wide at the top of the straight, but he eventually ran on to take fourth. He doesn't look the most straightforward, and he is obviously not one to take a short price about in future, but it would be no surprise to see him leave this form behind when things fall more kindly. (op 11/4)

Mambo King(DEN), back on dirt, stepped up on his two previous efforts at this year's Carnival, but was still well held.

649a CBD MORTGAGE STKS (H'CAP) (TURF) 6f (T)

4:45 (4:46) (95-110,107) 3-Y-O+

£36,180 (£12,060; £6,030; £3,015; £1,809; £1,206)

			RPR
1		**Prince Tamino**[14] [472] 5-8-10 **101**...... RoystonFfrench 5 (A Al Raihe, UAE) *mid-div: smooth prog 2f out: led 1f out: easily* **8/1**	110+
2	2 1/2	**Ripples Maid**[13] [497] 5-8-6 **97**...... RichardMullen 6 (J A Geake) *mid-div: no room 2 1/2f out: r.o wl once clr: nrst fin* **15/2**	99
3	1/2	**Beaver Patrol (IRE)**[14] [472] 6-8-11 **102**......(v) MJKinane 1 (Eve Johnson Houghton) *mid-div on rail: no room 1 1/2f out: r.o fnl 100yds: nrst fin* **10/3**[1]	102
4	1 1/4	**Turn On The Style**[13] [492] 6-9-0 **105**......(b) PaulMulrennan 2 (J Balding) *trckd ldr: t.k.h: rdn to ld 1 1/2f out: sn hdd* **7/2**[2]	101
5	shd	**Mariol (FR)**[14] [472] 5-9-0 **105**...... TPO'Shea 10 (E Charpy, UAE) *taken to rail: settled last: no room 2f out or 1f out: r.o once clr* **7/1**[3]	101
6	1 1/2	**Massive (IRE)**[20] 4-8-11 **102**...... WJSupple 4 (D Selvaratnam, UAE) *racd in rr: n.d but r.o fnl f* **33/1**	93
7	1 1/4	**Happy Runner (BRZ)**[14] [473] 5-8-9 **100**...... JAparecido 9 (P Nickel Filho, Brazil) *sn led: hdd 1 1/2f out: wknd fnl f* **16/1**	88
8	1 1/2	**Beckermet (IRE)**[13] [497] 6-9-2 **107**...... TedDurcan 3 (R F Fisher) *trckd ldr: rdn 3f out: sn wknd* **7/1**[3]	90
9	1 3/4	**Brave Tin Soldier (USA)**[137] [6038] 4-8-11 **102**...... KShea 7 (M F De Kock, South Africa) *nvr nr to chal* **14/1**	80
10	6 3/4	**Instant Recall (IRE)**[14] [474] 7-8-10 **101**......(vt) WayneSmith 8 (M Al Muhairi, UAE) *mid-div: trckd ldrs and ev ch 2 1/2f out: sn btn* **15/2**	59

1m 13.23s (1.23) **Going Correction** +0.45s/f (Yiel) **10** Ran SP% **120.4**

Speed ratings: **109,105,105,103,103 101,99,97,95,86**

CSF 68.95; TRI 243.53.

Owner H R H Princess Haya Of Jordan **Bred** The National Stud **Trained** UAE

FOCUS

A decent sprint handicap run at a fair pace.

NOTEBOOK

Prince Tamino had too much use made of him when only fourth (Beaver Patrol third) over an extended 6f round here on his previous start, but the return to more patient tactics suited and he ran out a clear-cut winner. Both Beaver Patrol and Mariol were denied clear runs, so the winning margin probably flatters him, but he looked the winner on merit such was the manner of his success. He found himself a little wider than ideal early on and had to make his move around horses turning for home, but he arrived on the scene travelling easily and found plenty when asked. He was runner-up in a Listed race at Newmarket back in 2006 and there is no doubt he is pattern class when in this sort of form.

Ripples Maid stayed on well after having to be switched out more towards the centre of the track when short of room inside the final couple of furlongs, but she basically just ran into a better one on the day.

Beaver Patrol(IRE) was stopped in his run when just beginning to pick up around two furlongs from the finish and looked very unlucky not to finish considerably closer.

Turn On The Style, 5lb higher than when winning over course and distance on his debut in Dubai two weeks previously, was always close to the pace and had every chance when getting a run against the far rail early in the straight.

Mariol(FR), like Beaver Patrol, had nowhere to go against the far rail for much of the final two furlongs and he was another unlucky not to finish considerably closer.

Massive(IRE) lacked the pace to pose a threat and needs further.

Happy Runner(BRZ) found a few too strong after leading early on.

Beckermet(IRE) was one of the first beaten and was held when short of room in the closing stages.

650a ZAWAJ STKS (H'CAP) (DIRT) 1m 2f (D)

5:15 (5:16) (90-105,102) 3-Y-O+

£33,165 (£11,055; £5,527; £2,763; £1,658; £1,105)

			RPR
1		**Jalil (USA)**[13] [493] 4-9-4 **100**...... LDettori 16 (Saeed Bin Suroor) *settled in rr: smooth prog 2 1/2f out: sn led: r.o wl* **5/6**[1]	119
2	2 1/2	**Gloria De Campeao (BRZ)**[35] [204] 5-9-6 **102**...... C-PLemaire 10 (P Bary, France) *trckd ldr: rdn to chal 2 1/2f out: r.o but no ch w wnr* **12/1**	115
3	5 3/4	**Dynamic Saint (USA)**[7] [568] 5-9-6 **102**......(e) RyanMoore 12 (Doug Watson, UAE) *mid-div: wd 3f out: rdn to chse wnr 2 1/2f out: r.o* **11/1**[3]	104
4	1 1/2	**Halkin (USA)**[7] [564] 6-9-1 **97**...... MO'Callaghan 6 (F Nass, Bahrain) *mid-div: rdn to chse ldrs 2 1/2f out: r.o same pce* **12/1**	96
5	4 1/4	**Acrobatic (USA)**[21] [380] 5-8-10 **93**...... WJSupple 2 (Doug Watson, UAE) *sn led: rdn 3f out: hdd 1 1/2f out: kpt on same pce* **20/1**	82
6	1 1/4	**Mulaqat**[7] [564] 5-9-2 **98**......(be) JMurtagh 9 (D Selvaratnam, UAE) *a in mid-div* **16/1**	86
7	shd	**Escape Route (USA)**[7] [564] 4-8-12 **95**...... RichardMullen 13 (J H M Gosden) *racd in rr: rdn 3f out: r.o fnl 1 1/2f* **12/1**	82
8	1 1/2	**Vainglory (USA)**[21] [380] 4-8-3 **91**...... AhmedAjtebi(6) 14 (D M Simcock) *trckd ldr: rdn 3f out: sn btn* **25/1**	76
9	2 3/4	**Great Plains**[7] [565] 6-9-6 **102**...... MartinDwyer 11 (E Charpy, UAE) *slowly away: nvr nr to chal* **33/1**	81
10	4 1/2	**Bain Douche (BRZ)**[14] [474] 4-8-1 **95**...... VLeal 8 (R Colombo, Brazil) *trckd ldr tl 3 1/2f out: wknd* **50/1**	54
11	hd	**Rampallion**[14] [476] 5-9-5 **101**...... TPO'Shea 7 (E Charpy, UAE) *racd in last: nvr nr to chal but r.o fnl 2 1/2f* **20/1**	70
12	1 1/4	**Seabow (USA)**[117] [6499] 5-8-11 **94**......(t) WayneSmith 4 (M Al Muhairi, UAE) *mid-div on rail: rdn 3f out: wknd* **33/1**	60
13	13	**Public Forum**[42] 6-8-12 **95**......(tp) TedDurcan 3 (M Al Muhairi, UAE) *nvr bttr than mid-div* **20/1**	35
14	3	**Chinkara**[7] [568] 8-8-10 **93**......(t) DO'Donohoe 15 (Doug Watson, UAE) *racd in rr: nvr nr to chal* **40/1**	27
15	17	**Basko De Zarautz (ARG)**[28] [292] 4-8-5 **98**......(t) KerrinMcEvoy 5 (Saeed Bin Suroor) *nvr nr to chal* **10/1**[2]	—
16	1 3/4	**Tabadul (IRE)**[205] [4043] 7-9-2 **98**...... RHills 1 (M Al Muhairi, UAE) *mid-div: rdn 3 1/2f out: n.d* **33/1**	—

2m 1.81s (-0.49) **Going Correction** +0.225s/f (Slow)

WFA 4 from 5yo+ 1lb **16** Ran SP% **132.3**

Speed ratings: **110,108,103,102,98 97,97,96,94,90 90,89,79,76,63 61**

CSF 11.12; TRI 88.97.

Owner Godolphin **Bred** Mr & Mrs Martin J Wygod **Trained** Newmarket, Suffolk

FOCUS

The market could only have one horse - rightly so as it turned out - but this looked like a good race on paper, certainly one of the stronger handicaps to be run on dirt at this year's Carnival. The first three home were drawn in double-figure stalls.

NOTEBOOK

Jalil(USA) showed himself well suited to this surface when winning over the extended 1m on his debut in Dubai last time and, stepped up in trip, he improved on the bare form of that effort with a most convincing display off a 9lb higher mark. Having travelled strongly quite a way off the pace and wide of the kickback, he made noticeable headway before the turn for home and picked up in good style when asked for his effort in the straight to readily seal the race. This was just his sixth start and he is progressing into a very smart dirt performer. He deserves his chance in better company now. (op 11/10)

Gloria De Campeao(BRZ), a nine-length second to Happy Boy over 1m in the first round of the Maktoum Challenge on his first start in Dubai, did the form of that race no harm at all with a good effort in second. He kept on well when headed by the winner and was nicely clear of the remainder. (op 11/1)

Dynamic Saint(USA) was ridden from a little further back than when runner-up over course and distance the previous week and he could only plod on at the one pace. (op 10/1)

Halkin(USA), just as when third on his return from a long absence over 1m round here the previous week, travelled with great enthusiasm, but he again got tired in the straight, which is understandable.

Acrobatic(USA), in good form in defeat since returning from a long absence, held a clear lead at the top of the straight, but he folded rather tamely.

Escape Route(USA) was never seen with a chance but he did keep on in the straight.

Vainglory(USA) could not confirm the promise he showed when fourth over course and distance on his first start in Dubai. (op 22/1)

The Form Book, Raceform Ltd, Compton, RG20 6NL

Basko De Zarautz(ARG) shaped as though this sort of trip would suit when sixth in a UAE 2000 Guineas trial behind Honour Devil, but he was a bitter disappointment. He was soon well off the pace, struggling to face the kickback, and looked rather slow. (op 9/1)

651a AL FAHIDI FORT - SPONSORED BY COMMERCIAL BANK OF DUBAI (GROUP 2) (TURF) 1m (T)

5:55 (5:56) 3-Y-0+

£75,376 (£25,125; £12,562; £6,281; £3,768; £2,512)

RPR

1 **Archipenko (USA)**[14] 472 4-9-0 113 (bt) KShea 8 121
(M F De Kock, South Africa) *mid-div: swtchd wd and rdn 2 1/2f out: r.o wl fnl 1 1/2f: led cl home* **14/1**

2 2 **Royal Oath (USA)**[169] 5142 5-9-0 112 (b) RichardMullen 6 117
(J H M Gosden) *mid-div: trckd ldr gng wl 2 1/2f out: led 1f out: hdd last 50yds* **8/1**

3 4 1/4 **Lord Admiral (USA)**[21] 383 7-9-0 113 (b) MJKinane 4 107
(Charles O'Brien, Ire) *trckd ldr: led 2 1/2f out: hdd 1f out: kpt on* **5/1**[3]

4 3 1/4 **Linngari (IRE)**[28] 294 6-9-6 121 RyanMoore 1 106
(H J Brown, South Africa) *mid-div w wnr 2 1/2f out: rdn 1 1/2f out: nt qckn* **11/8**[1]

5 3 3/4 **Dark Islander (IRE)**[21] 384 5-9-0 110 LDettori 10 91
(J W Hills) *settled last: stl towards rr 2f out: r.o fnl 1 1/2f: nrst fin* **10/1**

6 1/2 **Danak (IRE)**[194] 4414 5-9-0 113 RHills 3 90
(Doug Watson, UAE) *mid-div on rail: rdn 3 1/2f out: hrd rdn 2f out: wknd* **3/1**[2]

7 3 1/4 **Warriors Key (IRE)**[90] 6920 4-9-0 96 TedDurcan 5 82
(S Seemar, UAE) *slowly away: racd in rr: nvr nr to chal* **66/1**

8 2 1/2 **Big Timer (USA)**[14] 474 4-9-0 101 TomEaves 2 77
(I Semple) *sn led: keen: hdd 2 1/2f out: wknd* **25/1**

9 8 3/4 **Quebec Citizen (BRZ)**[13] 493 5-9-0 93 WayneSmith 7 56
(M Al Muhairi, UAE) *settled in rr: nvr able to chal: eased* **100/1**

10 11 **Etihaad**[13] 493 6-9-0 95 (t) BrettDoyle 9 31
(R Bouresly, Kuwait) *mid-div: rdn 4f out: sn btn: eased* **100/1**

1m 39.31s (1.01) **Going Correction** +0.45s/f (Yiel) **10 Ran SP% 118.0**
Speed ratings: **112,110,105,102,98 98,95,92,83,72**
CSF 119.75.
Owner Sh Mohd Khalifa Al Maktoum & DR AH Parker **Bred** Eagle Holdings **Trained** South Africa

FOCUS
Probably just an ordinary renewal of this Group 2 contest and the pace was by no means frantic.

NOTEBOOK
Archipenko(USA) had offered absolutely nothing on his debut for Mike De Kock in an extended 6f handicap round here two weeks previously, even allowing for that trip being well short of his optimum, having both proved reluctant to load and carried his head high under pressure. However, his master trainer clearly knew what he was doing and, fitted with both blinkers and a tongue-tie for the first time, the colt returned to the sort of form that saw him win last year's Derrinstown Stud Derby Trial at Leopardstown. Having been positioned in the mid-field through the early stages, he took a few strides to pick up when first coming under pressure early in the straight, but he soon responded and stayed on strongest of all to win going away. It would be no surprise to see him take his chance in the Jebel Hatta Stakes, a Group 2 over 1m1f round here on Super Thursday, and the Group 1 Dubai Duty Free Stakes on World Cup night will surely be on his agenda as well.
Royal Oath(USA), a four-length winner of last year's Royal Hunt Cup, was always close up and had his chance, but he just found one too good. This was a decent effort off the back of a 169-day break on his first start in Dubai. (op 7/1)
Lord Admiral(USA), second in this race in 2006 and sixth last year, came into this off the back of a Group 3 success over 1m1f round here and ran well. He is another who could go for the Jebel Hatta Stakes, having taken second in that race in 2006, and finished sixth last year.
Linngari(IRE) won this race both last year and in 2006, but he had a 6lb penalty to contend with this time having won a Group 1 in Italy last year. He showed himself as good as ever when defying a handicap mark of 118 over an extended 7f on his return to Dubai last time, but he failed to produce his very best on this occasion. He did not pick up as one might have hoped in the straight and probably would have preferred a stronger pace to run at. (op 6/4)
Dark Islander(IRE), fifth in a course-and-distance handicap off a mark of 110 on his debut in Dubai, fared best of those held up and this was a very respectable effort. The Listed Zabeel Mile back over this course and distance could be suitable target. (op 9/1)
Danak(IRE), sold by the Aga Khan to Hamdan Al Maktoum and switched from John Oxx to Doug Watson since he was last seen over six months previously, ran disappointingly. (tchd 100/30)
Big Timer(USA) had a bit to find in this company and was well held after helping to force the pace. (tchd 28/1)

652a MUSTAQBALI STKS (H'CAP) (TURF) 1m 4f (T)

6:30 (6:30) (95-110,105) 3-Y-0+

£36,180 (£12,060; £6,030; £3,015; £1,809; £1,206)

RPR

1 **Mourilyan (IRE)**[21] 381 4-9-1 **105** MJKinane 8 111
(John M Oxx, Ire) *slowly away: settled last: stl last 3f out: rdn 1 1/2f out: led last strides* **8/15**[1]

2 1 **Hard Top (IRE)**[21] 381 6-9-2 **104** RyanMoore 4 107
(H J Brown, South Africa) *in rr of mid-div: smooth prog to trck ldr 3f out: led 1f out: hdd cl home* **25/1**

3 1 1/4 **Doubnov (FR)**[21] 381 5-8-12 **100** LDettori 10 101+
(Saeed Bin Suroor) *in rr of mid-div: gng wl 3f out: wd: r.o but nvr able to chal* **4/1**[2]

4 hd **New Guinea**[13] 491 5-9-2 **104** KerrinMcEvoy 3 105
(Saeed Bin Suroor) *trckd ldng trio: led briefly 2f out: r.o same pce* **16/1**

5 1 1/4 **Lake Poet (IRE)**[14] 477 5-8-9 **97** (b) DarryllHolland 2 96
(C E Brittain) *settled in rr: n.m.r 2 1/2f out: sn rdn: nt qckn* **25/1**

6 1 1/4 **Rohaani (USA)**[363] 541 6-8-10 **98** RHills 9 95
(Doug Watson, UAE) *led main gp: led 2 1/2f out: sn rdn and hdd: kpt on* **25/1**

7 12 **Coeur De Lionne (IRE)**[21] 381 4-8-9 **99** TedDurcan 1 77
(E A L Dunlop) *mid-div: rdn to chse ldr 2 1/2f out: sn btn* **16/1**

8 2 3/4 **L'Amico Steve (BRZ)**[21] 381 5-9-2 **104** VLeal 6 77
(A Cintra Pereira, Brazil) *sn led: trckd ldrs: rdn 3f out: sn wknd* **10/1**[3]

9 17 **Nepotista (BRZ)**[21] 381 6-8-7 **95** JohnEgan 5 41
(A Manuel, UAE) *trckd ldr: led after 2f: rdn and hdd 2 1/2f out: wknd* **66/1**

10 4 3/4 **Dono Da Raia (BRZ)**[28] 293 6-8-12 **100** (t) DO'Donohoe 7 38
(Saeed Bin Suroor) *mid-div: nvr able to chal: eased fnl 1 1/2f* **66/1**

2m 33.22s (2.22) **Going Correction** +0.45s/f (Yiel)
WFA 4 from 5yo+ 3lb **10 Ran SP% 120.6**
Speed ratings: **110,109,108,108,107 106,98,96,85,82**
CSF 26.23; TRI £37.89. Placepot: £29.00 to a £1 stake. Pool £13,004.40 - 327.20 winning units. Quadpot: £5.30 to a £1 stake. Pool £332.80 - 46.40 winning units..
Owner H H Aga Khan **Bred** His Highness The Aga Khan's Studs S C **Trained** Currabeg, Co Kildare

FOCUS
A very good middle-distance handicap and, with the pace decent from the start, the form looks solid.

NOTEBOOK
Mourilyan(IRE) was able to defy a 10lb rise in the weights for an impressive success over this course and distance on his debut in Dubai, and make it four wins on the bounce in total. He was made to work much harder this time, but that was to be expected. He was still last at the top of the straight, and had a good three lengths to make up on Hard Top passing the 400m pole, but he responded well to strong pressure to reel that rival in close home. This was a smart effort off a mark of 105 (less 2lb weight for age allowance) and he deserves to take his chance in the Group 3 Dubai City Of Gold Stakes back over this course and distance on Super Thursday. That will be tougher and will require improvement, but he is clearly most progressive. (op 8/13)
Hard Top(IRE) was only fifth behind today's winner in a similar event over course and distance on his previous start, but the strong pace suited and he made Mourilyan work after getting first run on that rival. He is not quite as good as he used to be, but is obviously still very smart when things go his way. (op 20/1)
Doubnov(FR) was 8lb better off with Mourilyan for a three and a quarter-length defeat over this course and distance last time, but he could not reverse form. He seemed to race a little keener than ideal and, having been taken wide with his challenge, he took a while to pick up when first coming under pressure. (tchd 7/2)
New Guinea posted another decent effort in defeat, but he is probably a little vulnerable off his current sort of mark. (op 14/1)
Lake Poet(IRE) would have appreciated the good pace and this was a respectable showing. (op 20/1)
Rohaani(USA) ran with credit on his return from a year off the track, showing up well before getting tired. He is a big horse, so plenty of improvement can be expected.
Coeur De Lionne(IRE) looked unlucky not to finish closer behind today's winner on his previous start, but he finished rather tamely this time. (op 14/1)
Dono Da Raia(BRZ) offered nothing. (op 50/1)

634 SOUTHWELL (L-H)

Friday, February 22

OFFICIAL GOING: Standard to slow
Wind: Moderate half-behind Weather: Fine and dry

653 BET SIX NATIONS RUGBY - BETDAQ CLAIMING STKS 1m (F)

1:40 (1:40) (Class 6) 4-Y-0+ **£1,774** (£523; £262) Stalls Low

Form RPR

02-1 1 **Yakimov (USA)**[15] 463 9-9-7 85 VinceSlattery 2 93+
(D J Wintle) *trckd ldrs: smooth hdwy to ld over 2f out: sn clr: heavily eased towards fin* **2/5**[1]

-466 2 12 **Sweet World**[12] 512 4-9-3 61 (v[1]) AndrewElliott 4 51
(A P Jarvis) *trckd ldng pair: effrt over 2f out and sn rdn along: swtchd rt and drvn ent fnl f: styd on u.p to take 2nd towards fin: no ch w wnr* **17/2**[3]

35-4 3 3/4 **Moral Code (IRE)**[10] 529 4-9-7 63 ChrisCatlin 5 54
(E J O'Neill) *led: rdn along and hdd over 2f out: sn drvn and plugged on one pce: lost 2nd wl ins fnl f* **9/2**[2]

3-50 4 6 **Namroud (USA)**[44] 101 9-8-0 57 (v[1]) JamieKyne[(7)] 3 26
(D Carroll) *t.k.h: rapid hdwy and cl up after 2f: pushed along 3f out: sn wknd* **14/1**

0-00 5 22 **Raven Rascal**[22] 365 4-8-4 36 (b[1]) PatrickMathers 1 —
(J F Coupland) *a in rr: bhd fr 1/2-way* **100/1**

1m 45.7s (2.00) **Going Correction** +0.30s/f (Slow) **5 Ran SP% 107.8**
Speed ratings (Par 101): **102,90,89,83,61**
CSF £4.29 TOTE £1.50: £1.02, £3.30; EX 3.50.
Owner B E T Partnership **Bred** Jane & Jeff Wooder **Trained** Naunton, Gloucs

FOCUS
An uncompetitive claimer won by the favourite in the expected manner. The winner is rated back to his best and is value for more than the official margin.

654 MEET CAPTAIN CROC @ PONTIN'S H'CAP 1m 4f (F)

2:10 (2:10) (Class 6) (0-55,59) 4-Y-0+ **£1,774** (£523; £262) Stalls Low

Form RPR

600- 1 **Coda Agency**[49] 4531 5-8-9 48 JimCrowley 9 61
(D W P Arbuthnot) *in tch: pushed along to chse ldrs 4f out: rdn to chse ldr over 2f out: swtchd rt and drvn ent fnl f: styd on gamely to ld on line* **5/2**[1]

3-21 2 shd **My Friend Fritz**[8] 551 8-9-6 59 6ex PhillipMakin 8 72+
(P W Hiatt) *in tch: smooth hdwy to ld over 4f out: pushed clr over 2f out: rdn over 1f out: hung lft ent fnl f: sn drvn: hdd on line* **3/1**[2]

300- 3 13 **Blushing Hilary (IRE)**[28] 5364 5-9-2 55 (p) PaulHanagan 4 47
(Miss J A Camacho) *chsd ldrs: rdn along and outpcd over 4f out: styd on u.p fnl 2f: tk remote 3rd wl ins fnl f* **9/2**[3]

0-63 4 8 **Blue Opal**[29] 282 6-8-7 46 oh1 (p) PaulEddery 10 25
(Miss S E Hall) *hld up towards rr: hdwy on outer 1/2-way: chsd ldr 3f out: sn rdn and wknd fnl 2f* **11/1**

00/2 5 5 **Huggle**[8] 552 5-8-13 52 LiamJones 1 23
(P Leech) *led 4f: prom tl rdn along 4f out and grad wknd* **16/1**

/603 6 13 **Castle Frome (IRE)**[22] 377 9-8-7 46 oh1 (p) PaulFitzsimons 5 —
(A E Price) *cl up: rdn along over 4f out and sn wknd* **16/1**

-234 7 2 1/2 **Nabir (FR)**[5] 602 8-8-10 52 (p) PJMcDonald[(3)] 3 —
(P D Niven) *cl up: led after 4f: rdn along and hdd over 4f out: sn wknd* **8/1**

000- 8 9 **Boppys Dancer**[73] 7109 5-8-8 47 oh1 ow1 (t) MickyFenton 6 —
(P T Midgley) *chsd ldrs: rdn along 1/2-way: wknd 4f out* **25/1**

10-0 9 23 **Oakbridge (IRE)**[47] 68 6-9-2 55 VinceSlattery 2 —
(R Brotherton) *a in rr: bhd fnl 4f* **20/1**

2m 42.82s (1.82) **Going Correction** +0.30s/f (Slow) **9 Ran SP% 111.6**
Speed ratings (Par 101): **105,104,96,90,87 78,77,71,55**
CSF £9.45 CT £29.43 TOTE £3.60: £1.30, £1.40, £2.10; EX 13.20 Trifecta £42.90 Pool £250.92 - 4.15 winning units.
Owner Banfield, Thompson **Bred** Baydon House Stud **Trained** Compton, Berks

FOCUS
There was a good gallop on here and the winner came from off the pace. The form is sound enough in a weak race.
Oakbridge(IRE) Official explanation: trainer said he had no explanation for the poor form shown

655 RACE TO PONTIN'S FOR EASTER DEALS (S) STKS 6f (F)

2:45 (2:46) (Class 6) 3-Y-0+ **£1,774** (£523; £262) Stalls Low

Form RPR

3511 1 **Soba Jones**[3] 615 11-9-10 48 TolleyDean[(3)] 1 64
(J Balding) *trckd ldr: cl up 1/2-way: chal 2f out: rdn to ld over 1f out: drvn ins fnl f and hld on gamely towards fin* **8/13**[1]

4216 2 nk **Nautical**[7] 581 10-9-10 57 JerryO'Dwyer[(3)] 2 63
(A W Carroll) *trckd ldng pair: pushed along and sltly outpcd over 2f out: rdn and hdwy to chal ent fnl f: sn drvn and ev ch tl no ex towards fin* **5/2**[2]

0-21 **3** *3* **High Reach**[38] [167] 8-9-13 52 .... AndrewElliott 4 53
(J G M O'Shea) *led: jnd and rdn 2f out: drvn and hdd over 1f out: edgd rt and wknd ins fnl f* **6/1**[3]

0- **4** *66* **Monasheemini (IRE)**[181] [4795] 5-8-12 0 .... ColinHaddon(5) 5 —
(Mrs N Macauley) *sn outpcd and wl bhd fr 1/2-way* **100/1**

1m 18.23s (1.73) **Going Correction** +0.30s/f (Slow) **4** Ran SP% **105.8**
Speed ratings (Par 101): **100,99,95,7**
CSF £2.27 TOTE £1.60; EX 2.90.There was no bid for the winner.
Owner R L Crowe **Bred** Mrs M J Hills **Trained** Scrooby, Notts

FOCUS
This turned out to be quite a competitive little seller in the end but not a race to be too positive about.

656 BET CARLING CUP FINAL - BETDAQ H'CAP 7f (F)
3:20 (3:21) (Class 6) (0-65,64) 3-Y-O **£1,911** (£564; £282) **Stalls** Low

Form RPR

-610 **1** **Magical Song**[29] [288] 3-8-4 **50** .... FrankieMcDonald 4 56+
(P A Blockley) *trckd ldrs: hdwy on outer 3f out: chal 2f out: rdn to ld and edgd lft ent fnl f: sn drvn and kpt on* **5/2**[1]

000- **2** *nk* **Hennessy Island (USA)**[75] [7084] 3-8-10 **56** .... JimCrowley 6 61+
(T G Mills) *cl up: led 2f out: sn rdn: drvn and hdd ent fnl f: rallied wl towards fin* **11/4**[2]

500- **3** *5* **Scruffy Skip (IRE)**[125] [6329] 3-9-4 **64** .... LiamJones 5 56
(C R Dore) *sn rdn along and outpcd in rr: bhd 1/2-way: hdwy wl over 1f out: styd on u.p ins fnl f: nrst fin* **14/1**

350- **4** *shd* **Low Flyer (USA)**[188] [4612] 3-9-2 **62** .... PaulFessey 1 54
(T D Barron) *cl up on inner: led 1/2-way: rdn and hdd 2f out: grad wknd* **7/2**[3]

25-1 **5** *5* **Weet By Far**[41] [141] 3-9-3 **63** .... HayleyTurner 3 41
(R Hollinshead) *trckd ldrs: chsd along after: 2f: effrt and cl up over 2f out: sn drvn and wknd* **4/1**

0640 **6** *6* **Tobouggornotobougg**[8] [556] 3-7-11 **50** oh4......(v) PatrickDonaghy(7) 2 12
(D Shaw) *led to 1/2-way: cl up tl rdn wl over 2f out and sn wknd* **14/1**

1m 33.05s (2.75) **Going Correction** +0.30s/f (Slow) **6** Ran SP% **110.8**
Speed ratings (Par 95): **96,95,89,89,84 77**
CSF £9.41 TOTE £3.10: £1.50, £2.80; EX 10.00 TRIFECTA Pool £356.25 - 4.71 winning units..
Owner The Classical Syndicate **Bred** Peter Balding **Trained** Lambourn, Berks

FOCUS
A decent race for the grade and sound form. The race could be better than average and should throw up winners.

657 ENJOY EASTER @ PONTIN'S MAIDEN STKS 1m 3f (F)
3:55 (3:56) (Class 5) 3-Y-0+ **£2,457** (£725; £362) **Stalls** Low

Form RPR

6-23 **1** **Oberlin (USA)**[7] [573] 3-8-5 72 .... AndrewElliott 1 58+
(M Johnston) *mde most: rdn over 2f out: drvn over 1f out: kpt on u.p ins fnl f* **1/2**[1]

6622 **2** *1 3/4* **Coral Shores**[8] [556] 3-8-2 48 ow2 ....(v) ChrisCatlin 6 51
(P W Hiatt) *a.p: effrt 3f out and sn cl up: rdn 2f out and ev ch tl drvn and nt qckn wl ins fnl f* **6/1**[2]

3 *1 1/2* **Azabu Juban (IRE)** 3-8-1 0 ow1 .... LiamJones 8 47
(J Jay) *hld up towards rr: gd hdwy over 4f out: chsd ldng pair over 3f out: drvn and styd on appr fnl f: nrst fin* **33/1**

0-6 **4** *7* **Topwell**[14] [481] 7-9-9 0 .... NataliaGemelova(5) 4 42
(R C Guest) *bhd: sme hdwy 4f out: styd on fnl 2f: nvr a factor* **100/1**

045/ **5** *10* **Tirol Livit (IRE)**[21] [3258] 5-9-7 0 .... SamuelDrury(7) 5 24
(N Wilson) *prom: rdn along over 5f out and sn wknd* **25/1**

3304 **6** *4* **Weet For Ever (USA)**[14] [481] 5-10-0 47 .... HayleyTurner 3 17
(P A Blockley) *chsd ldrs: rdn along over 3f out and sn outpcd* **9/1**[3]

300- **7** *6* **Hunting Haze**[74] [6259] 5-10-0 52 .... PaulEddery 7 6
(Miss S E Hall) *midfield: rdn along 4f out: sn outpcd* **14/1**

20/0 **8** *23* **Aggi Mac**[29] [282] 7-9-2 35 .... KristinStubbs(7) 9 —
(L R James) *prom: cl up after 4f tl rdn along and wknd over 4f out* **100/1**

9 *158* **Flamingo Land (GER)** 4-9-12 0 .... TPQueally 2 —
(A P Stringer) *s.i.s: a in rr: detached fr 1/2-way and virtually p.u over 2f out* **6/1**[2]

2m 30.53s (2.53) **Going Correction** +0.30s/f (Slow)
WFA 3 from 4yo 23lb 4 from 5yo+ 2lb **9** Ran SP% **120.7**
Speed ratings (Par 103): **102,100,99,94,87 84,80,63,—**
CSF £4.34 TOTE £1.50: £1.02, £1.60, £7.40; EX 3.50 Trifecta £53.70 w/u.
Owner Sheikh Hamdan Bin Mohammed Al Maktoum **Bred** Gainsborough Farm Llc **Trained** Middleham Moor, N Yorks

FOCUS
An uncompetitive maiden on paper and the form is no better than plating class based on the performance of the exposed second.

658 GO BOOK PONTIN'S TODAY H'CAP 1m 3f (F)
4:30 (4:31) (Class 5) (0-70,69) 4-Y-0+ **£2,593** (£765; £383) **Stalls** Low

Form RPR

6-51 **1** **Exit To Luck (GER)**[10] [533] 7-9-12 **67** 6ex ....(b) ChrisCatlin 4 79
(S Gollings) *trckd ldng pair: pushed along to chse ldr 3f out: rdn to ld wl over 1f out: pushed out* **6/4**[1]

-034 **2** *6* **Key Partners (IRE)**[3] [617] 7-8-13 **54** .... StephenDonohoe 2 54
(P A Blockley) *led: rdn along 3f out: hdd 2f out: sn drvn and one pce* **4/1**[3]

-134 **3** *3* **Starcross Maid**[22] [368] 6-9-2 **57** .... PatrickMathers 1 51
(J F Coupland) *hld up: hdwy over 4f out: rdn and ch over 2f out: sn drvn and one pce* **4/1**[3]

4321 **4** *27* **Hucking Heat (IRE)**[1] [637] 4-9-5 **69** 6ex .... PatrickDonaghy(7) 3 9
(J R Boyle) *chsd ldr: rdn along over 4f out and sn wknd* **9/4**[2]

2m 31.93s (3.93) **Going Correction** +0.30s/f (Slow)
WFA 4 from 6yo+ 2lb **4** Ran SP% **110.8**
Speed ratings (Par 103): **97,92,90,70**
CSF £7.73 TOTE £2.20; EX 4.60 TRIFECTA Pool £229.06 - 4.50 winning units..
Owner P J MArtin **Bred** H K Gutschow **Trained** Scamblesby, Lincs

FOCUS
A modest handicap which did not take much winning in the end. The form is weak with the third the best guide.

659 BET MULTIPLES - BETDAQ H'CAP 1m (F)
5:00 (5:02) (Class 5) (0-70,73) 4-Y-0+ **£2,593** (£765; £383) **Stalls** Low

Form RPR

060- **1** **Exit Smiling**[139] [6016] 6-8-8 **60** .... MickyFenton 6 76
(P T Midgley) *hdwy to trck ldr after 2f: effrt to chal over 2f out: rdn over 1f out: styd on to ld jst ins fnl f: sn drvn and kpt on wl* **9/2**[3]

-244 **2** *3/4* **My Mentor (IRE)**[9] [546] 4-9-0 **66** ....(b[1]) SebSanders 8 80
(Sir Mark Prescott) *led: rdn along 2f out and sn hung lft: drvn and hung rt ent fnl f: sn hdd and no ex towards fin* **3/1**[2]

5121 **3** *3* **Silver Hotspur**[3] [618] 4-9-7 **73** 6ex .... SimonWhitworth 7 80
(M Wigham) *stdd s: hld up in rr: hdwy on inner 3f out: chal and ev ch wl over 1f out: sn rdn and one pce ins fnl f* **7/4**[1]

00-5 **4** *7* **Kildare Sun (IRE)**[10] [531] 6-9-4 **70** .... DaleGibson 1 61
(J Mackie) *chsd ldrs: rdn along over 2f out: sn drvn and wknd over 1f out* **12/1**

244- **5** *1/2* **Superior Star**[30] [5620] 5-8-13 **65** ....(b) GrahamGibbons 3 55
(N Wilson) *chsd ldrs on outer: rdn along wl over 2f out and sn wknd* **11/2**

21/ **6** *2* **Babieca (USA)**[573] [3940] 4-9-4 **70** .... PhillipMakin 5 55
(T D Barron) *prom: rdn along after 3f: sn lost pl and bhd* **8/1**

1m 45.31s (1.61) **Going Correction** +0.30s/f (Slow) **6** Ran SP% **113.7**
Speed ratings (Par 103): **103,102,99,92,91 89**
CSF £18.68 CT £31.53 TOTE £5.70: £3.50, £1.70; EX 21.70 Trifecta £36.10 Place 6 £5.40, Place 5 £4.33..
Owner Peter Mee **Bred** Mrs D O Joly **Trained** Westow, N Yorks

FOCUS
A fair handicap run at a good gallop which eventually found out the favourite, whose stamina was in doubt beforehand. The form is only modest for the grade.
T/Plt: £13.10 to a £1 stake. Pool: £45,288.10. 2,514.05 winning tickets. T/Qpdt: £9.10 to a £1 stake. Pool: £1,568.90. 126.20 winning tickets. JR

641 WOLVERHAMPTON (A.W) (L-H)
Friday, February 22

OFFICIAL GOING: Standard
Wind: Fresh behind Weather: Cloudy

660 ENJOY EASTER @ PONTIN'S APPRENTICE H'CAP 1m 141y(P)
6:50 (6:50) (Class 5) (0-75,73) 4-Y-0+ **£2,590** (£770; £385; £192) **Stalls** Low

Form RPR

1143 **1** **Justcallmehandsome**[11] [525] 6-8-5 66 ....(v) BillyCray(7) 1 74
(D J S Ffrench Davis) *a.p: chsd ldr 4f out: led 2f out: rdn and hung lft 1f out: jst hld on* **15/2**

650- **2** *hd* **Urban Warrior**[139] [4909] 4-8-10 67 .... HaddenFrost(3) 7 74
(Ian Williams) *chsd ldrs: rdn to chse wnr fnl f: edgd lft: r.o* **10/1**

1-46 **3** *1* **Putra Laju (IRE)**[30] [274] 4-8-9 66 ....(p) PatrickHills(3) 6 71
(J W Hills) *s.i.s: hld up: nt clr run over 2f out: hdwy u.p over 1f out: edgd lft ins fnl f: r.o* **4/1**[2]

1323 **4** *nk* **Steig (IRE)**[11] [526] 5-8-7 61 .... KirstyMilczarek 3 65
(Carl Llewellyn) *sn led: clr 6f out: rdn and hdd 2f out: nt clr run 1f out: styd on* **5/4**[1]

213- **5** *5* **Encores**[105] [6749] 4-8-10 67 .... JamieJones(3) 2 60
(M G Quinlan) *hld up: rdn over 1f out: nvr trbld ldrs* **5/1**[3]

506- **6** *nk* **King Of The Moors (USA)**[105] [6744] 5-9-0 73 .... DeanHeslop(5) 4 65
(T D Barron) *chsd ldr over 4f: sn rdn: wknd over 1f out* **16/1**

30-5 **7** *6* **Muncaster Castle (IRE)**[8] [560] 4-8-2 59 oh4 .... NicolPolli(3) 5 37
(R F Fisher) *hld up: rdn over 2f out: sn wknd* **25/1**

1m 51.58s (1.08) **Going Correction** +0.225s/f (Slow) **7** Ran SP% **111.7**
Speed ratings (Par 103): **104,103,102,102,98 97,92**
CSF £72.65 TOTE £7.90: £3.10, £3.10; EX 117.20.
Owner Mrs J E Taylor **Bred** Mrs J E Taylor **Trained** Lambourn, Berks
■ Stewards' Enquiry : Kirsty Milczarek one-day ban: used whip with excessive frequency (Mar 5)
Hadden Frost caution: used whip with excessive frequency

FOCUS
A moderate affair though the pace was sound. Pretty ordinary form, rated around the second and third.
Muncaster Castle(IRE) Official explanation: jockey said gelding hung left-handed throughout

661 COME EVENING RACING TOMORROW CLASSIFIED STKS 2m 119y(P)
7:20 (7:22) (Class 7) 4-Y-0+ **£1,365** (£403; £201) **Stalls** Low

Form RPR

3563 **1** **Piano Key**[3] [613] 4-8-5 42 .... PatrickHills(5) 8 47
(M D I Usher) *hld up: hdwy over 5f out: led over 2f out: rdn out* **6/1**[3]

6460 **2** *1 1/2* **Ronsard (IRE)**[4] [606] 6-9-2 45 .... StephenDonohoe 5 45
(P D Evans) *s.s: hld up: hdwy and hmpd wl over 3f out: edgd lft and styd on fnl f: nt rch wnr* **4/1**[1]

66-2 **3** *nk* **Watch Out**[15] [471] 4-8-7 42 ow2 .... HaddenFrost(5) 2 47
(G A Ham) *hld up in tch: lost pl over 11f out: hdwy 3f out: rdn over 1f out: styd on* **9/2**[2]

0-66 **4** *2 1/2* **Reminiscent (IRE)**[24] [345] 9-9-2 42 ....(v) TPQueally 3 42
(B P J Baugh) *dwlt: hld up: nt clr run and swtchd rt 4f out: hdwy 3f out: rdn over 1f out: styd on* **10/1**

0/-3 **5** *hd* **Kofi**[8] [552] 6-8-13 45 .... JerryO'Dwyer(3) 7 42
(Karen George) *w ldr tl led 6f out: rdn and hdd over 2f out: styd on same pce* **7/1**

0340 **6** *5* **Trackattack**[4] [606] 6-9-2 45 .... NeilChalmers 12 36
(M Appleby) *hld up: hdwy 6f out: rdn over 3f out: wknd 2f out* **18/1**

5-05 **7** *9* **Simply St Lucia**[14] [481] 6-9-2 45 ....(v[1]) PhillipMakin 11 25
(J R Weymes) *chsd ldrs: rdn over 3f out: wknd 2f out* **20/1**

000/ **8** *5* **Desert Tommy**[6] [651] 7-8-11 40 .... JackMitchell(5) 6 19
(A Sadik) *hld up: bhd fnl 10f* **14/1**

4066 **9** *6* **Divine Love (IRE)**[7] [578] 4-8-10 41 ....(p) DeanMcKeown 10 12
(T Wall) *hld up: rdn 1/2-way: wknd over 4f out* **40/1**

0 **10** *6* **Aston (USA)**[15] [461] 8-8-11 42 ....(be) JamieJones(5) 9 4
(R C Guest) *s.i.s: hld up: rdn 1/2-way: wknd over 5f out* **33/1**

-053 **11** *5* **Tewkesbury (IRE)**[15] [471] 4-8-10 38 ....(t) VinceSlattery 13 —
(Mrs K Waldron) *prom: rdn over 5f out: edgd lft and wknd wl over 3f out* **14/1**

6-35 **12** *nk* **Aristi (IRE)**[27] [322] 7-8-9 41 .... RichardEvans(7) 1 —
(Evan Williams) *led: rdn and hdd 6f out: wknd over 3f out* **14/1**

600/ **13** *48* **Mythical Air (IRE)**[1582] [5725] 7-9-2 44 .... LPKeniry 4 —
(S Lycett) *rn wout declared tongue strap: chsd ldrs: rdn over 4f out: sn edgd lft: wkng whn hmpd sn after* **6/1**[3]

3m 44.25s (2.45) **Going Correction** +0.225s/f (Slow)
WFA 4 from 6yo+ 6lb **13** Ran SP% **123.7**
Speed ratings (Par 97): **103,102,102,100,100 98,94,91,89,86 83,83,61**
CSF £30.74 TOTE £7.50: £2.60, £1.90, £2.20; EX 34.50.
Owner Donaghey Usher **Bred** Juddmonte Farms Ltd **Trained** Upper Lambourn, Berks
■ Stewards' Enquiry : Patrick Hills seven-day ban: used whip with excessive frequency and in incorrect place (Mar 4-6,7-8,11-12)

FOCUS
A desperate contest, though the time was not bad for a race like this.

Mythical Air(IRE) Official explanation: trainer said mare ran without a tongue strap, because it became upset in the preliminaries and may have suffered from the loss of the strap at the start which adversely affected its performance

662 VISIT PONTINS.COM FOR GREAT DEALS MAIDEN STKS 7f 32y(P)
7:50 (7:51) (Class 5) 3-Y-O £2,590 (£770; £385; £192) **Stalls** High

Form RPR

0-3 **1** **Rio L'Oren (IRE)**[42] [130] 3-8-12 0 JimmyQuinn 7 62
(N J Vaughan) *mde all: rdn over 1f out: all out* **12/1**

55 **2** *shd* **Days Of Pleasure (IRE)**[10] [529] 3-9-3 0 MickyFenton 4 67
(J A Osborne) *chsd ldrs: rdn over 2f out: r.o wl nr fin* **13/2**[3]

3 *1 1/2* **Always A Rock (IRE)** 3-9-3 0 AndrewElliott 1 71+
(M Johnston) *s.i.s: sn pushed along in rr: nt clr run over 2f out: rdn over 1f out: r.o wl ins fnl f: nt rch ldrs* **3/1**[2]

0-2 **4** *3/4* **Kibitzer**[42] [130] 3-9-3 0 SteveDrowne 6 61
(J W Hills) *sn trcking wnr: racd keenly: rdn and hung lft over 1f out: styd on same pce* **4/6**[1]

00- **5** *8* **Mistress Rio (IRE)**[188] [4611] 3-8-12 0 TPQueally 3 34
(J G Given) *hung lft sn after s: prom: rdn over 3f out: wknd over 2f out* **50/1**

0-6 **6** *6* **To Bubbles**[14] [483] 3-8-12 0 PaulFessey 5 18
(T D Barron) *hld up in tch: wknd over 2f out* **28/1**

1m 32.79s (3.19) **Going Correction** +0.225s/f (Slow) 6 Ran SP% **111.4**
Speed ratings (Par 97): **90,89,88,87,78 71**
CSF £81.72 TOTE £10.80: £5.00, £2.20; EX 94.20.
Owner Super Saturday Syndicate **Bred** Camogue Stud Ltd **Trained** Hampton Heat, Cheshire

FOCUS
An average maiden which was slowly run, and the time was moderate. The form is rated around the runner-up and the favourite was almost certainly below form.

663 JIM MCNICHOLAS 40TH BIRTHDAY CELEBRATION H'CAP 7f 32y(P)
8:20 (8:21) (Class 6) (0-55,60) 4-Y-O+ £1,774 (£523; £262) **Stalls** High

Form RPR

3543 **1** **Guadaloup**[11] [521] 6-8-8 **52** ow3 MarkLawson(3) 2 58
(M Brittain) *led: hdd over 6f out: chsd ldr tl led over 2f out: rdn over 1f out: all out* **9/2**[1]

2-33 **2** *nk* **Strut The Stage (IRE)**[23] [356] 4-8-5 **53** (tp) GabrielHannon(7) 4 58
(B W Duke) *chsd ldrs: nt clr run over 2f out: rdn over 1f out: r.o* **6/1**[3]

1056 **3** *hd* **Buzzin'Boyzee (IRE)**[3] [615] 5-8-7 **55** RichardEvans(7) 12 59
(P D Evans) *hld up: racd keenly: hdwy 2f out: rdn over 1f out: r.o* **20/1**

5215 **4** *1 1/4* **Stargazy**[21] [392] 4-8-0 **48** MatthewDavies(7) 10 49
(W G M Turner) *hld up: hdwy over 2f out: sn edgd lft: rdn over 1f out: no ex ins fnl f* **6/1**[3]

-461 **5** *shd* **Guildenstern (IRE)**[12] [516] 6-9-5 **60** 6ex JimmyQuinn 6 61+
(P Howling) *hld up: nt clr run over 3f out: hdwy and nt clr run over 1f out: rdn and swtchd rt ins fnl f: hung lft: r.o* **11/2**[2]

1-56 **6** *1 1/4* **Cornerstone**[16] [446] 4-8-13 **54** (v) SteveDrowne 1 51
(S C Williams) *chsd ldr tl led over 5f out: rdn and hdd over 2f out: n.m.r and no ex ins fnl f* **9/2**[1]

-326 **7** *1 1/4* **Mister Benji**[15] [465] 9-8-9 **50** (p) AndrewElliott 7 44
(B P J Baugh) *hld up: hdwy 4f out: hmpd over 2f out: sn rdn and edgd lft: no imp fnl f* **6/1**[3]

60-0 **8** *nk* **Gee Ceffyl Bach**[22] [375] 4-8-3 **47** KirstyMilczarek(3) 8 40
(R C Guest) *chsd ldrs: rdn over 2f out: styng on same pce whn hung lft over 1f out* **16/1**

0334 **9** *2* **Dancing Duo**[8] [555] 4-8-5 **49** (v) TolleyDean(3) 9 42+
(D Shaw) *s.i.s: hld up: rdn over 2f out: n.d* **7/1**

050- **10** *5* **Meathop (IRE)**[219] [3636] 4-8-7 **48** ChrisCatlin 3 22
(R F Fisher) *hld up in tch: wknd over 2f out* **33/1**

0600 **11** *1 3/4* **Totally Free**[10] [530] 4-8-8 **52** (p) TravisBlock(3) 5 22
(M D I Usher) *chsd ldrs: rdn 4f out: wknd 3f out* **33/1**

1m 31.11s (1.51) **Going Correction** +0.225s/f (Slow) 11 Ran SP% **123.6**
Speed ratings (Par 101): **100,99,99,98,97 96,95,94,92,86 84**
CSF £32.57 CT £508.93 TOTE £6.10: £2.30, £2.50, £5.60; EX 37.80.
Owner Northgate Red **Bred** Cheveley Park Stud Ltd **Trained** Warthill, N Yorks

FOCUS
A competitive little race and the winning time was 1.68 seconds faster than the preceding maiden, but still only ordinary for the grade. The winner was pretty much back to her best form in making all.
Gee Ceffyl Bach Official explanation: jockey said filly was unruly in stalls
Dancing Duo Official explanation: jockey said filly was denied a clear run

664 RACE THE FAMILY TO PONTIN'S @ EASTER H'CAP 1m 4f 50y(P)
8:50 (8:50) (Class 6) (0-65,65) 4-Y-O+ £2,047 (£604; £302) **Stalls** Low

Form RPR

/-33 **1** **King's Fable (USA)**[21] [387] 5-8-8 52 ow1 (p) TGMcLaughlin 6 60
(Karen George) *s.i.s: hld up: nt clr run over 2f out: hdwy over 1f out: led ins fnl f: rdn out: swvd rt towards fin* **17/2**

-312 **2** *1 1/2* **Still Dreaming**[14] [485] 4-8-1 55 (b) RossAtkinson(7) 3 61
(R J Price) *s.i.s: sn trcking ldrs: rdn over 1f out: edgd rt: styd on* **7/1**

2-61 **3** *3* **Altos Reales**[16] [451] 4-8-13 60 DeanMcKeown 2 61
(D Shaw) *hld up: hdwy over 3f out: rdn over 1f out: styd on same pce fnl f* **7/1**

53-5 **4** *1/2* **Grizebeck (IRE)**[18] [436] 6-8-13 57 ChrisCatlin 1 57
(R F Fisher) *led: rdn and hdd over 2f out: rallied to ld over 1f out: hdd and no ex ins fnl f* **11/2**[3]

-112 **5** *5* **Qaasi (USA)**[33] [238] 6-8-13 60 MarkLawson(3) 4 52
(M Brittain) *trckd ldr tl led over 2f out: rdn: edgd rt and hdd over 1f out: wknd ins fnl f* **9/4**[1]

050/ **6** *2 1/2* **Piran (IRE)**[482] [6181] 6-9-0 65 RichardEvans(7) 8 53
(Evan Williams) *hld up: a in rr: wknd over 3f out* **20/1**

4-30 **7** *3 1/2* **Haatmey**[35] [212] 6-8-9 53 GrahamGibbons 5 35
(N Wilson) *chsd ldrs: rdn over 2f out: wknd wl over 1f out* **4/1**[2]

500- **8** *5* **Fossgate**[147] [5777] 7-9-7 65 JimmyQuinn 7 39
(J D Bethell) *sn pushed along and prom: wknd over 2f out* **8/1**

2m 42.34s (1.24) **Going Correction** +0.225s/f (Slow)
WFA 4 from 5yo+ 3lb 8 Ran SP% **117.6**
Speed ratings (Par 101): **104,103,101,100,97 95,93,90**
CSF £67.81 CT £444.31 TOTE £12.10: £2.90, £3.30, £3.10; EX 56.20.
Owner Mrs Frank George **Bred** Karen Suzanne Farrar **Trained** Higher Easingdon, Devon
■ Stewards' Enquiry : T G McLaughlin one-day ban: used whip with excessive frequency without giving gelding time to respond (Mar 4)

FOCUS
An ordinary handicap, but the time was perfectly creditable. The winenr is rated back to his best.

Qaasi(USA) Official explanation: jockey said gelding ran flat; trainer said gelding was struck into

665 WISH YOU WERE HERE @ PONTIN'S H'CAP 1m 1f 103y(P)
9:20 (9:20) (Class 6) (0-60,65) 3-Y-O £2,047 (£604; £302) **Stalls** Low

Form RPR

0-51 **1** **A Dream Come True**[9] [547] 3-9-4 65 6ex PatrickHills(5) 6 68
(D K Ivory) *hld up in tch: chsd ldr 2f out: rdn to ld 1f out: r.o* **2/1**[2]

-045 **2** *1/2* **John Potts**[11] [527] 3-9-0 56 AndrewElliott 1 58
(B P J Baugh) *hld up in tch: hmpd and lost pl 7f out: hdwy and nt clr run over 1f out: swtchd lft: r.o* **10/1**

006- **3** *1/2* **Star Grazer**[107] [6714] 3-8-13 60 JackMitchell(5) 2 61+
(C F Wall) *chsd ldrs: rdn and edgd rt over 1f out: r.o* **7/1**[3]

01-0 **4** *hd* **Ostinata (IRE)**[51] [20] 3-8-2 51 GabrielHannon(7) 5 52
(B W Duke) *chsd ldrs: rdn over 3f out: hmpd ins fnl f: kpt on* **16/1**

-060 **5** *1 3/4* **Miss Tilen**[17] [439] 3-7-13 48 (p) AshleyMorgan(7) 10 45
(V Smith) *chsd ldr tl led over 7f out: rdn and hdd 1f out: edgd rt and no ex* **33/1**

0-13 **6** *1* **Duneen Dream (USA)**[29] [288] 3-9-3 59 NeilPollard 9 54+
(W J Musson) *hld up: nt clr run over 2f out: swtchd lft and hdwy over 1f out: rdn: hung rt no ex ins fnl f* **11/8**[1]

-405 **7** *1 1/4* **Plaka (FR)**[8] [556] 3-9-0 56 LiamJones 7 48
(W M Brisbourne) *hld up: plld hrd: rdn over 2f out: n.d* **20/1**

0445 **8** *1/2* **Carry On Cleo**[6] [589] 3-9-0 56 (b) StephenDonohoe 8 47
(P D Evans) *hld up: rdn 3f out: n.d* **16/1**

-056 **9** *shd* **Amazing Spirit**[9] [547] 3-8-4 46 oh1 AdrianMcCarthy 3 37
(Miss V Haigh) *led: plld hrd: hdd over 7f out: chsd ldrs tl rdn and wknd over 1f out: nt clr run ins fnl f* **66/1**

2m 5.48s (3.78) **Going Correction** +0.225s/f (Slow) 9 Ran SP% **118.0**
Speed ratings (Par 95): **92,91,91,90,89 88,87,86,86**
CSF £22.60 CT £121.26 TOTE £3.10: £1.10, £2.60, £1.80; EX 34.20 Place 6 £3937.13, Place 5 £ 370.37.
Owner Dean Ivory **Bred** D K Ivory **Trained** Radlett, Herts
■ Stewards' Enquiry : Ashley Morgan one-day ban: careless riding (Mar 4)
Neil Pollard caution: careless riding

FOCUS
This did not take a lot of winning, especially with Duneen Dream a bit below par. The form reads sound enough despite the ordinary pace.
Duneen Dream(USA) Official explanation: jockey said gelding hung right throughout
T/Plt: £457.10 to a £1 stake. Pool £98,074.90. 156.60 winning tickets T/Qpdt: £65.30 to a £1 stake. Pool £7,033.00. 79.60 winning tickets CR

647 NAD AL SHEBA (L-H)
Friday, February 22
OFFICIAL GOING: Dirt course - fast; turf course - good

666a ETISALAT WASEL STKS (H'CAP) (TURF) 6f 110y(T)
3:05 (3:05) (95-110,110) 3-Y-O+
£36,180 (£12,060; £6,030; £3,015; £1,809; £1,206)

RPR

1 **Mutamarres**[14] [497] 5-8-9 **99** RHills 1 104
(Doug Watson, UAE) *sn led: set stdy pce: rdn clr 1 1/2f out: r.o wl: comf* **7/2**[1]

2 *1 1/4* **Grand Vista**[15] [472] 4-8-10 **100** (t) RyanMoore 2 101
(H J Brown, South Africa) *slowly away: settled in rr: gng wl on rail 3f out: r.o wl fnl 1 1/2f: nrst fin* **15/2**

3 *1 1/4* **Loyalist (SAF)**[14] [497] 7-8-8 **98** RichardMullen 6 96
(S Seemar, UAE) *trckd ldr: rdn 2 1/2f out: r.o same pce* **10/1**

4 *1 1/4* **Drayton (IRE)**[14] [497] 4-9-0 **104** KShea 4 98
(M F De Kock, South Africa) *slowly away: settled in rr: t.k.h: gng wl 3f out: rdn 2f out: r.o: nvr able to chal* **4/1**[2]

5 *1/2* **Appalachian Trail (IRE)**[29] [294] 7-9-6 **110** (b) TomEaves 9 103
(I Semple) *racd in rr: rdn 2 1/2f out: r.o: n.d* **7/1**

6 *hd* **Hurricane Spirit (IRE)**[15] [472] 4-8-12 **102** TedDurcan 3 94
(J R Best) *trckd ldng pair: ev ch on rail 2f out: one pce fnl f* **16/1**

7 *3/4* **Indian Trail**[14] [492] 8-9-2 **106** (v) AdrianTNicholls 5 96
(D Nicholls) *mid-div: rdn to chse ldrs 2 1/2f out: r.o same pce* **6/1**[3]

8 *2 1/2* **Subpoena**[351] [644] 6-8-12 **102** (v) RoystonFfrench 8 85
(A Al Raihe, UAE) *slowly away: mid-div: rdn 2 1/2f out: nvr able to chal* **14/1**

9 *4 1/2* **T-Bird (SAF)**[15] [472] 7-8-6 **96** (t) WJSupple 10 66
(Doug Watson, UAE) *racd in rr: nvr nr to chal* **33/1**

10 *13* **Botanical (USA)**[14] [497] 7-8-7 **97** (bt) TPO'Shea 7 31
(E Charpy, UAE) *mid-div: rdn 3f out: wknd qckly* **6/1**[3]

1m 20.3s (2.80) **Going Correction** +0.30s/f (Good) 10 Ran SP% **119.6**
Speed ratings: **96,94,93,91,91 90,90,87,82,67**
CSF 31.08; T/C 250.31.
Owner Hamdan Al Maktoum **Bred** Shadwell Estate Co Ltd **Trained** United Arab Emirates

FOCUS
This looked like an ordinary sprint handicap and the winner made all at a steady pace, so the form needs treating with caution. Basically another division of the 4.15 contest., but the winning time was 0.76 seconds slower.

NOTEBOOK
Mutamarres was 4lb higher than when winning over the bare 6f round here on his previous start but, again drawn in stall one, he was once more allowed an easy lead and followed up in good style. He is obviously quite smart when able to dominate, but he will not always get things his own way and a further rise in the weights should make things tougher.
Grand Vista raced a little keenly under restraint off the steady pace and, although staying on well once switched in the straight, he was never going to peg the winner back. (op 8-1)
Loyalist(SAF), sixth behind today's winner on his previous start, was always well placed and can have no excuses whatsoever. (op 9-1)
Drayton(IRE), fifth behind Mutamarres on his previous outing, was noted doing some good late work and might be one to back when it looks as though he will be able to dominate.
Appalachian Trail(IRE), dropped back in trip, ran a big race under top weight considering the steady pace was totally against him. Held up out the back, he was always going to struggle to pick up off the steady gallop, but he stayed on as well as could have been expected.
Hurricane Spirit(IRE) tracked the eventual winner into the straight, but he could find only the one pace under pressure. (op 14-1)

Indian Trail did not pick up and needs a strong pace to run at. (13/2)

667a ETISALAT WEYAK STKS (H'CAP) (DIRT) 1m 1f (D)
3:40 (3:41) (95-110,110) 3-Y-0+

£36,180 (£12,060; £6,030; £3,015; £1,809; £1,206)

RPR

1 **Mutasallil (USA)**[8] 568 8-8-5 **95**.....................(t) RHills 6 99
(Doug Watson, UAE) *sn led: kicked clr 3f out: r.o wl: comf* **7/1**[3]

2 3 ¾ **Aleutian**[14] 493 8-9-0 **104**.....................(e) WayneSmith 5 100
(F Nass, Bahrain) *settled in rr: rdn 2 1/2f out: r.o: no ch w wnr* **9/2**[2]

3 ¾ **Igor Protti**[22] 380 6-9-6 **110**.....................(b) LDettori 4 104
(Saeed Bin Suroor) *restrained early: settled in rr: wd 3f out: rdn 2 1/2f out: r.o: nvr able to chal* **8/13**[1]

4 3 ¼ **Kayak (SAF)**[14] 493 6-8-7 **98** ow1..................... KShea 2 85
(M F De Kock, South Africa) *trckd ldr: rdn 4f out: r.o same pce* **9/1**

5 8 ½ **West Virginia (USA)**[15] 476 7-8-10 **100**.....................(t) TedDurcan 1 70
(S Seemar, UAE) *trckd ldr on rail: rdn 3f out: sn btn* **20/1**

6 4 ¾ **Pearly King (USA)**[351] 648 5-8-11 **101**..................... MJKinane 3 61
(M Al Muhairi, UAE) *settled in rr: rdn 3f out: nvr able to chal* **16/1**

1m 50.05s (0.25) **Going Correction** +0.175s/f (Slow) **6** Ran SP% **113.2**
Speed ratings: **105,101,101,98,90 86**
CSF 38.09.

Owner Hamdan Al Maktoum **Bred** Shadwell Farm LLC **Trained** United Arab Emirates

FOCUS

An ordinary handicap for the grade and, with Mutasallil able to dictate at a steady pace, the form does not look very reliable.

NOTEBOOK

Mutasallil(USA) was on a losing run stretching back to November 2006, but he ran okay when third in a better race than this over 1m2f the previous week and took full advantage of being gifted the lead. A rise in the weights will make things tougher and he is unlikely to have things fall so kindly in future. (op 13-2)

Aleutian shaped well when a three-length third to the improving Jalil over an extended 1m round here on his return from almost a year off the track last time, but he did not have the race run to suit on this occasion. He stayed on from off the pace to take second, but the winner, having led at a steady pace, was not stopping. (op 7-2)

Igor Protti, 8lb higher than when winning over 1m2f round here on his debut for Godolphin, was another who did not have the race run to suit and he was unable to follow up. He was ridden with restraint having been the slowest to find his stride but, such was the lack of pace, he would have been better served racing closer to the lead and, as it turned out, he was forced six wide round the final bend. While things obviously didn't go his way, it's worth noting his recent success was gained against mainly exposed types and the Handicapper looks to have been very harsh. (op 10-11)

Kayak(SAF) was well placed considering the lack of pace, but he failed to pick up for pressure and has so far not taken to racing in Dubai. (op 6-1)

668a ETISALAT AHLAN STKS (H'CAP) (TURF) 6f 110y(T)
4:15 (4:15) (95-110,107) 3-Y-0+

£36,180 (£12,060; £6,030; £3,015; £1,809; £1,206)

RPR

1 **Racer Forever (USA)**[15] 474 5-9-2 **106**.....................(b) RyanMoore 5 116
(J H M Gosden) *mid-div on rail: smooth prog to ld 1f out: r.o wl* **4/1**[2]

2 ¾ **Ragheed (USA)**[14] 495 4-8-9 **99**..................... RHills 1 107+
(E Charpy, UAE) *racd in rr: last on rail 3f out: swtchd wd and r.o wl: nrst fin* **8/1**[3]

3 2 ¼ **Law Lord**[15] 472 4-9-3 **107**.....................(v) LDettori 6 109
(Saeed Bin Suroor) *mid-div: rdn to cl 3f out: r.o but nt qckn fnl 1 1/2f* **6/5**[1]

4 2 ½ **Calrissian (GER)**[15] 473 4-7-13 **95**..................... AhmedAjtebi(6) 2 90
(L Kelp, Denmark) *trckd ldr: led 2f out: hdd 1f out: wknd fnl 100yds* **66/1**

5 3 ¾ **Buachaill Dona (IRE)**[14] 492 5-8-10 **100**..................... AdrianTNicholls 8 84
(D Nicholls) *settled in rr: rdn to chse ldrs 2 1/2f out: ev ch 1 1/2f out: nt qckn* **8/1**[3]

6 2 ½ **Ans Bach**[22] 384 5-8-12 **102**.....................(e) JMurtagh 4 79
(D Selvaratnam, UAE) *mid-div on rail: rdn to chal 2 1/2f out: nt qckn* **12/1**

7 11 **Shmookh (USA)**[14] 492 4-8-9 **99**..................... MartinDwyer 9 45
(Doug Watson, UAE) *mid-div: wd and rdn 3f out: nvr able to chal* **10/1**

8 hd **League Champion (USA)**[22] 378 5-8-12 **102**.....................(b) BrettDoyle 10 48
(R Bouresly, Kuwait) *sn led: t.k.h: hdd 2f out: wknd* **50/1**

9 2 ½ **Obe Brave**[14] 495 5-8-10 **100**..................... TomEaves 7 39
(I Semple) *mid-div: rdn 3f out: nt qckn* **14/1**

10 1 **San Domenico**[8] 563 4-8-7 **97**..................... WJSupple 3 33
(Doug Watson, UAE) *trckd ldr tl rdn 3f out: wknd* **16/1**

1m 19.54s (2.04) **Going Correction** +0.30s/f (Good) **10** Ran SP% **120.5**
Speed ratings: **100,99,96,93,89 86,74,73,70,69**
CSF 37.48; T/C 61.23.

Owner Mohamed Obaida **Bred** Gainsborough Farm Llc **Trained** Newmarket, Suffolk

FOCUS

Basically another division of the 3.05, but this looked a stronger race – reasonable form for the level – and, with the pace much better than in the opener, the winning time was 0.76 seconds quicker.

NOTEBOOK

Racer Forever(USA) ◆ is probably not the most straightforward and he was winless since landing a Listed race at Epsom in June 2006, but the drop back to a sprint trip suited and he benefited from a lovely ride from Ryan Moore. He was ridden from the front when fourth over an extended 7f round here on his first start in Dubai two weeks previously, but his jockey was more patient on this drop in trip and the new tactics worked a treat. If anything he was a touch keen, but he saved ground by making his move against the far rail and, although idling once in front, the line came in time. He has always had plenty of ability and the drop back to sprint distances might just be the making of him. He very much gives the impression he will be just as effective over the bare 6f, and he might even be suited by a strongly run 5f. (tchd 9-2)

Ragheed(USA) ◆, mid-division in a very hot 1m handicap on his first start since leaving William Haggas, ran a fine race dropped back to his shortest trip since making his debut over 6f, and he could even be considered unlucky, although the winner was probably idling in front. Having been given time to find his stride, he was last at halfway and was denied a clear run when trying to stay on in the straight, eventually having to switch out wide with his challenge, by which time Racer Forever had already made his move. He had a progressive profile in Britain last year and remains on an upward curve.

Law Lord, raised 3lb for an unlucky defeat over course and distance on his debut for Godolphin/first start in Dubai, did not look to have any excuses this time. He raced alongside the eventual winner through the early stages, but made his move a little wider and lacked that one's turn of foot. (op 5-4, tchd 11-10)

Calrissian(GER), switched from dirt to turf, fared best of those to race handy.

Buachaill Dona(IRE), ridden with patience, could not sustain his effort in the straight.

Obe Brave showed little over 1m on his previous start and this was another modest effort. He did not convince that he was putting it all in under pressure, although he did race wider than ideal.

669a ETISALAT BLACKBERRY STKS (H'CAP) (TURF) 1m 2f (T)
4:45 (4:45) (95-110,110) 3-Y-0+

£36,180 (£12,060; £6,030; £3,015; £1,809; £1,206)

RPR

1 **Engrupido (ARG)**[15] 477 5-8-12 **102**..................... KShea 8 102
(M F De Kock, South Africa) *trckd ldr: rdn 3f out: led 1 1/2f out: r.o wl: jst hld on* **3/1**[1]

2 shd **Alpacco (IRE)**[22] 379 6-8-8 **98**..................... KLatham 1 98
(H J Brown, South Africa) *sn led on rail: hdd 1 1/2f out: r.o bravely: jst failed* **50/1**

3 ¼ **Diamond Quest (SAF)**[14] 495 7-9-6 **110**..................... RyanMoore 7 109
(H J Brown, South Africa) *settled in rr: gng wl 3f out: r.o wl fnl 1 1/2f: nrst fin* **12/1**

4 ½ **The Illies (IRE)**[15] 477 4-8-10 **100**..................... LDettori 9 99
(Saeed Bin Suroor) *mid-div: wd 2 1/2f out: r.o wl fnl 1 1/2f: nrst fin* **3/1**[1]

5 1 ¼ **Championship Point (IRE)**[15] 477 5-9-1 **105**..................... DarryllHolland 2 101
(M R Channon) *settled in rr: wd and rdn 3f out: nvr able to chal* **12/1**

6 ¾ **Safety Investments (AUS)**[8] 563 9-8-7 **97**.....................(e) MJKinane 4 91
(J Lau, Macau) *trckd ldrs: t.k.h: mid-div after 2f: rdn to chse ldrs 2f out: wknd* **18/1**

7 1 ¼ **Davidoff (GER)**[22] 383 4-9-4 **108**.....................(v) AStarke 3 101
(P Schiergen, Germany) *settled in rr: prog on rail 2 1/2f out: n.d* **14/1**

8 12 **Courageous Duke (USA)**[15] 477 9-8-5 **95**..................... WJSupple 6 63
(Doug Watson, UAE) *slowly away: no room 2 1/2f out: nvr nr to chal* **33/1**

9 11 **Hazeymm (IRE)**[14] 495 5-8-10 **100**.....................(v) JMurtagh 10 46
(D Selvaratnam, UAE) *mid-div: wd: rdn 2 1/2f out: sn btn* **11/2**[3]

10 ¾ **Ea (USA)**[22] 379 4-8-10 **100**.....................(v) KerrinMcEvoy 5 45
(Saeed Bin Suroor) *trckd ldrs: rdn 2 1/2f out: sn wknd* **4/1**[2]

2m 6.44s (1.94) **Going Correction** +0.30s/f (Good)
WFA 4 from 5yo+ 1lb **10** Ran SP% **117.6**
Speed ratings: **104,103,103,103,102 101,100,91,82,81**
CSF 157.35, T/C 1598.82.

Owner Sheikh Mohammed Bin Khalifa Al Maktoum **Bred** Haras Rio Claro **Trained** South Africa

FOCUS

A good, competitive handicap on paper, pretty much another division of the 6.45. However, the pace was just steady early on and, although the tempo increased down the back straight, the first two home were in the first two pretty much throughout, and the principals finished in a bit of a bunch. The winning time was 1.75 seconds slower than the last race.

NOTEBOOK

Engrupido(ARG) had run well on two previous starts at this year's Carnival and built on those efforts to run out a narrow winner. He was always nicely positioned close to the pace and stayed on strongly for pressure to get the verdict, displaying a willing attitude in the process.

Alpacco(IRE) had shown very little on his first two starts this year but, stepped back up in trip and with the blinkers left off, he was allowed the run of the race in front and was just denied. He was a winner at last year's Carnival off a mark of 100 and is clearly very capable when things fall right.

Diamond Quest(SAF) improved on the form he showed over 1m on his return to Dubai last time and was possibly a little unlucky. He had to wait for a run at the top of the straight, but picked up well once in the clear and fared best of those held up.

The Illies(IRE) had not convinced with his attitude in recent starts and this was another suspect effort. He didn't really drop his head for much of the way and failed to totally convince once placed under maximum pressure in the straight.

Championship Point(IRE) finished strongly and was not beaten that far; a good effort considering he would have been much better suited by a stronger end-to-end gallop.

Safety Investments(AUS), switching from dirt to turf, was much too keen early on.

Hazeymm(IRE) was another far too keen.

Ea(USA) looked better than the bare form of his recent effort over 1m on his debut for Godolphin, but this was very disappointing.

670a ETISALAT HOTSPOT STKS (H'CAP) (DIRT) 6f (D)
5:15 (5:16) (95-105,105) 3-Y-0+

£36,180 (£12,060; £6,030; £3,015; £1,809; £1,206)

RPR

1 **Frosty Secret (USA)**[15] 473 4-9-3 **102**..................... KShea 1 105
(M F De Kock, South Africa) *wl away: a.p gng wl 3f out: rdn 1 1/2f out: r.o wl: led last 50yds* **5/1**[3]

2 hd **Sarissa (BRZ)**[22] 378 5-8-12 **98**..................... JMurtagh 10 100
(P Bary, France) *led nr rail: r.o wl: hdd last 50m* **7/2**[2]

3 1 ¾ **Elusive Warning (USA)**[329] 4-9-1 **100**..................... LDettori 2 97
(Saeed Bin Suroor) *nvr far away: ev ch whn rdn 2f out: one pce* **3/1**[1]

4 shd **Star Crowned (USA)**[8] 566 5-9-3 **102**.....................(t) BrettDoyle 6 99
(R Bouresly, Kuwait) *led in centre: ev ch but nt qckn fnl f* **10/1**

5 5 ¾ **Sir Edwin Landseer (USA)**[8] 566 8-8-10 **96**.........(p) PaulMulrennan 11 75
(Christian Wroe) *settled in mid-div: rdn 2 1/2f out: r.o same pce* **11/1**

6 3 **Select Reason (BRZ)**[15] 473 4-8-5 **95**.....................(b) RichardMullen 8 61
(A Cintra Pereira, Brazil) *mid-div: rdn 3f out: chsd ldrs briefly: wknd* **20/1**

7 ½ **Terrific Challenge (USA)**[15] 472 6-9-4 **104**.....................(bt) TedDurcan 9 72
(Doug Watson, UAE) *mid-div: rdn 2 1/2f out: r.o same pce* **20/1**

8 1 ¼ **Sunrise Safari (IRE)**[14] 497 5-9-1 **100**.....................(v) TomEaves 12 66
(I Semple) *trckd ldr nr side: rdn 3f out: nvr able to chal* **16/1**

9 2 ¼ **Desert Diplomat (IRE)**[119] 7-9-5 **105**.....................(bt) JBeitia 5 63
(A B Aziz, UAE) *slowly away: sn rdn in rr: r.o once swtchd to far side fnl 3f* **20/1**

10 2 ½ **Borehan**[14] 497 5-8-9 **95**..................... WJSupple 7 45
(D Selvaratnam, UAE) *mid-div: rdn 3f out: n.d* **50/1**

11 ¾ **Algharb**[15] 473 6-8-10 **96**..................... RHills 3 44
(A Manuel, UAE) *slowly away: mid-div in centre: rdn 3f out: nt qckn* **20/1**

12 ½ **Machinist (IRE)**[14] 497 8-9-2 **101**..................... FrancisNorton 4 49
(D Nicholls) *a in mid-div* **10/1**

69.75 secs (-0.45) **Going Correction** +0.175s/f (Slow) **12** Ran SP% **117.3**
Speed ratings: **110,109,107,107,99 95,94,93,90,86 85,85**
CSF 21.72, T/C 63.67.

Owner Elsadig Elhag **Bred** Carl Bowling **Trained** South Africa

FOCUS

Sprint races on the dirt course at the Carnival are often pretty weak, but this looked like a decent handicap, certainly quite competitive on paper. There has been a bias towards high drawn horses on the straight track so far this year, with most of the action taking place middle to stands' side, and that's where the majority of these raced.

NOTEBOOK

Frosty Secret(USA) had the worst draw of all in stall one, so this effort was particularly creditable. He was stuck out towards the centre of the track for much of the way, but edged closer to the near rail inside the final furlong and narrowly got the call over a horse drawn against the rail. He wants rating better than the bare form.

Sarissa(BRZ), who ran well from an unfavourable draw when second over 5f on her first start since switching from Brazil, had the best stall of all this time and had every chance against the favoured rail. She showed good speed throughout, but was just denied. (op 4-1)
Elusive Warning(USA), two from two in the US last year, was not ideally drawn, but he showed plenty of speed and had his chance. This was his first run since last March and he is entitled to come on a fair bit. (op 11-4)
Star Crowned(USA), a surprise winner of a 5f conditions event here the previous week, was 25lb higher than when winning a non-Carnival handicap at Jebel Ali two starts back, and he ran well, managing to confirm recent course form with Sir Edwin Landseer. (op 9-1)
Sunrise Safari(IRE) raced against the rail and reversed recent course-and-distance form with Machinist.
Machinist(IRE) was stuck out in the middle of the track and was well beaten. (op 7-1)

671a ETISALAT GREENTUNE STKS (H'CAP) (TURF) 1m 194y(T)
5:45 (5:45) (100-112,112) 3-Y-0+

£52,763 (£17,587; £8,793; £4,396; £2,638; £1,758)

RPR
1 **Wise Dennis**[15] 474 6-8-9 **105** TedDurcan 7 113
(A P Jarvis) *settled in rr: t.k.h: rdn 2 1/2f out whn last: r.o wl fnl 1 1/2f: led cl home* **13/2**[3]
2 *1* **Dijeerr (USA)**[22] 379 4-8-7 **102** (v) KerrinMcEvoy 5 109
(Saeed Bin Suroor) *led main gp: rdn to chal 2f out: led 1f out: hdd fnl 50yds* **6/1**[2]
3 *nk* **Jay Peg (SAF)**[22] 383 5-9-3 **112** RyanMoore 2 118+
(H J Brown, South Africa) *mid-div: rdn to chse ldrs 2f out: r.o: nrst fin* **7/1**
4 *5 1/4* **Mashaahed**[111] 6653 5-9-3 **112** (t) RHills 4 107
(E Charpy, UAE) *racd in clr 2nd: led 2 1/2f out: hdd 1f out: kpt on* **9/1**
5 *3 1/4* **Jet Express (SAF)**[22] 379 6-8-8 **104** RoystonFfrench 10 91
(A Al Raihe, UAE) *mid-div: rdn to chse ldrs 2 1/2f out: sn btn* **20/1**
6 *3 1/4* **Senor Dali (IRE)**[22] 383 5-8-12 **108** TPO'Shea 3 87
(E Charpy, UAE) *in rr of mid-div: nvr able to chal* **20/1**
7 *3 1/4* **African Appeal (SAF)**[15] 474 7-9-2 **111** JMurtagh 1 84
(M F De Kock, South Africa) *settled in rr: no room on rail 2 1/2f out: n.d* **6/4**[1]
8 *4 1/2* **Traffic Guard (USA)**[14] 494 4-8-8 **104** (p) JohnEgan 8 66
(A Manuel, UAE) *sn led: hdd 2 1/2f out: wknd qckly* **20/1**
R **Gharir (IRE)**[22] 383 6-8-11 **107** (bt) MartinDwyer 6 —
(E Charpy, UAE) *ref to r* **16/1**

1m 49.73s (-0.27) **Going Correction** +0.30s/f (Good) **9** Ran SP% **110.3**
Speed ratings: **113,112,111,107,104 101,98,94,—**
CSF 37.37, T/C 203.07.
Owner Allen B Pope, Andrew J King **Bred** J And Mrs Bowtell **Trained** Twyford, Bucks
■ Eddie Jock was withdrawn (6/1, deduct 10p in the £ under Rule 4.)

FOCUS
A very good, competitive handicap and, with the pace strong throughout, the form looks reliable. The winning time was 2.50 seconds faster than the following fillies & mares Listed contest, but they didn't go as quick in that race.

NOTEBOOK
Wise Dennis looked very unlucky when third over the extended 7f round here on his previous start and gained compensation in determined style, coping just fine with the longer trip. He was dropped in last of all soon after the start, so the good gallop was very much to his liking and he stayed on powerfully once switched wide with his challenge in the straight. While this was a decent race, it's probably fair to say things will get a lot tougher when he returns to the UK, but he was Listed placed towards the end of last year and seems as good as ever.
Dijeerr(USA), a close second over the bare 1m on his debut in Dubai three weeks previously, again had to settle for second. He raced much closer to the strong pace than Wise Dennis and could not resist that one's strong challenge late on. (op 5-1)
Jay Peg(SAF), a dual Grade 1 winner in South Africa, was probably unsuited by making the running when only sixth in a course-and-distance Group 3 on his first start in Dubai and, ridden with more patience this time, he ran a lot better. This was a very smart effort off a mark of 112. (op 13-2)
Mashaahed could not sustain his effort after chasing the decent gallop. This was his first start since landing a Listed race at Newmarket for Barry Hills last November and he is entitled to come on for the run. (tchd 10-1)
Jet Express(SAF), drawn in stall ten, raced wider round the final bend than ideal and ran well in the circumstances. (op 16-1)
African Appeal(SAF), another South African Grade 1 winner, had looked unlucky when fifth (Wise Dennis also unlucky third) over the extended 7f round here on his debut in Dubai, and he was expected to be suited by this longer trip, but he ran below expectations. He was a little short of room early in the straight, but was basically not good enough on the day to take the gaps. (op 7-4)

672a BALANCHINE STKS (SPONSORED BY ETISALAT) (LISTED RACE) (F&M) (TURF) 1m 194y(T)
6:15 (6:16) 3-Y-0+

£45,226 (£15,075; £7,537; £3,768; £2,261; £1,507)

RPR
1 **Sun Classique (AUS)**[15] 475 5-9-11 113 KShea 7 118+
(M F De Kock, South Africa) *mid-div on rail: gng wl 2 1/2f out: no room 2f out: swtchd: r.o to ld line* **4/6**[1]
2 *1/4* **Many Colours**[15] 475 4-9-4 105 LDettori 5 108
(Saeed Bin Suroor) *sn led: kicked clr 3f out: r.o wl but hdd cl home* **7/1**[3]
3 *1* **Light Green (BRZ)**[139] 4-9-2 99 MJKinane 10 104
(P Nickel Filho, Brazil) *mid-div: rdn to chse ldr 2f out: led briefly fnl f out: nt qckn last 50yds* **11/2**[2]
4 *1 1/4* **Gower Song**[8] 565 5-9-4 104 TedDurcan 4 104
(D R C Elsworth) *in rr of mid-div: trckd wnr 2 1/2f out: ev ch fnl f: one pce last 50yds* **8/1**
5 *3 1/4* **Classy-Lady (BRZ)**[15] 475 4-8-9 100 RyanMoore 1 88
(H J Brown, South Africa) *settled in rr: nvr nr to chal* **16/1**
6 *nse* **Crossing**[98] 6843 7-9-4 102 PaulMulrennan 2 97
(William J Fitzpatrick, Ire) *trckd ldr: rdn 2 1/2f out: wknd* **50/1**
7 *1/2* **Whazzis**[15] 475 4-9-6 104 (v) JMurtagh 6 98
(D Selvaratnam, UAE) *slowly away: settled in rr: r.o fnl 1 1/2f: nvr nr to chal* **16/1**
8 *2 3/4* **Impetious**[15] 475 4-9-4 97 BrettDoyle 9 90
(Eamon Tyrrell, Ire) *settled in rr: r.o fnl 2f: nvr nr to chal* **100/1**
9 *1 1/2* **Sweet Lilly**[15] 475 4-9-4 110 DarryllHolland 3 87
(M R Channon) *mid-div: rdn 2 1/2f out: one pce* **8/1**
10 *3 3/4* **Jet Past (SAF)**[15] 475 6-9-4 95 (v) RichardMullen 8 79
(S Seemar, UAE) *trckd ldr: rdn 3f out: wknd* **100/1**

1m 52.23s (2.23) **Going Correction** +0.30s/f (Good) **10** Ran SP% **125.8**
Speed ratings: **102,101,100,99,96 96,96,93,92,89**
CSF 7.06.
Owner L Cohen & W V Rippon **Bred** L Cohen **Trained** South Africa
■ A third winner of this race for trainer Mike De Kock.

FOCUS
The third straight year the Balanchine Stakes has held Listed status and this looked like a very good renewal. The pace was just ordinary, with Many Colours leading on her own terms, and the winning time was 2.5 seconds slower than the 100-112 handicap run over the trip.

NOTEBOOK
Sun Classique(AUS) was a short-price favourite to follow up her recent success in the Cape Verdi Stakes, but she had to overcome serious trouble in running to do so. Well placed just off the modest gallop early on, everything went smoothly until she tried to angle off the rail inside the final two furlongs. She was kept in by Light Green and had to be switched out wide with her challenge, only getting in the clear a furlong out. The way she regained her momentum to get up and win was most impressive, not least because she was conceding upwards of 5lb all round, and she is clearly a high-class individual. She has already won in the highest grade in South Africa and looks ready for a step back up in class. The Group 2 Jebel Hatta Stakes on Super Thursday could be a suitable target, and she will also have options on World Cup night, with either the Dubai Duty Free Stakes or the Sheema Classic on the agenda. (op 8-11)
Many Colours, representing Saeed Bin Suroor, who won the inaugural running of this race with Gonfilia in 2004, enjoyed the run of things out in front, but she was just unable to reverse recent form with Sun Classique.
Light Green(BRZ), a Grade 1 winner in Brazil, ran very well on her debut in Dubai, although she is no sure thing to build on this. (op 5-1)
Gower Song was worth a try at this trip having finished her races quite weakly over 1m2f-1m4f lately, and she ran well. Things got a little tight against the far rail in the straight, but she was basically just not quick enough to take the gap. She will probably be suited by a hold-up ride back over 1m2f
Classy-Lady(BRZ) ran a respectable race, but was still well held.
Impetious made no impression.
Sweet Lilly offered disappointingly little.

673a ETISALAT STKS (H'CAP) (TURF) 1m 2f (T)
6:45 (6:45) (95-110,109) 3-Y-0+

£36,180 (£12,060; £6,030; £3,015; £1,809; £1,206)

RPR
1 **Glen Nevis (USA)**[14] 495 4-8-9 **98** (v) TedDurcan 2 104
(Saeed Bin Suroor) *in rr of mid-div: trckd runner-up 2 1/2f out: hrd rdn and r.o to ld cl home* **8/1**
2 *1 1/4* **Imperial Star (IRE)**[15] 476 5-9-6 **109** LDettori 7 112
(Saeed Bin Suroor) *mid-div: rdn to chal 2f out: ev ch fnl f: r.o wl* **15/8**[1]
3 *shd* **King Charles**[22] 384 4-8-6 **95** AdrianTNicholls 3 99
(E A L Dunlop) *mid-div: gng wl 3f out: rdn to ld 1 1/2f out: hdd cl home* **8/1**
4 *4 3/4* **Hallhoo (IRE)**[15] 477 6-8-12 **101** JMurtagh 10 94
(D Selvaratnam, UAE) *sn led: hdd 2f out: one pce fnl 1 1/2f* **5/1**[3]
5 *1/4* **Lucky Dance (BRZ)**[14] 495 6-8-8 **97** RyanMoore 9 90
(H J Brown, South Africa) *settled in last: wd and rdn 2 1/2f out: r.o fnl 1 1/2f: nrst fin* **16/1**
6 *1 1/4* **Consular**[8] 568 6-8-8 **97** (t) TPO'Shea 4 87
(E Charpy, UAE) *trckd ldr: rdn 2 1/2f out: no room 1 1/2f out: one pce fnl f* **12/1**
7 *6 1/4* **Before You Go (IRE)**[15] 477 5-9-0 **102** (v) KerrinMcEvoy 1 81
(Saeed Bin Suroor) *mid-div: rdn 2 1/2f out: nt qckn* **9/2**[2]
8 *1* **Gun Salute (USA)**[14] 494 6-9-5 **108** (b) WJSupple 5 84
(Doug Watson, UAE) *trckd ldr: rdn 2 1/2f out: sn wknd* **10/1**
9 *3 1/4* **Fleeting Shadow (IRE)**[15] 473 4-8-10 **99** RoystonFfrench 8 69
(A Al Raihe, UAE) *racd in rr: nvr nr to chal* **25/1**
10 *1 1/4* **Money Bags (SAF)**[14] 494 6-8-11 **100** WMLordan 6 67
(M F De Kock, South Africa) *s.i.s: racd in rr: pushed along 4 1/2f out: nvr able to chal* **25/1**

2m 4.69s (0.19) **Going Correction** +0.30s/f (Good)
WFA 4 from 5yo+ 1lb **10** Ran SP% **122.2**
Speed ratings: **111,110,109,106,105 104,99,99,96,95**
CSF 24.53, T/C 129.15 PLACEPOT: £122.40. Pool £12,274.50, 73.15 winning tickets; QUADPOT £9.80. Pool £335.50, 25.30 winning units.
Owner Sh Zayed Bin Marwan Al Maktoum **Bred** Nutbush Farm **Trained** Newmarket, Suffolk

FOCUS
A good handicap, although essentially another division of the 4.45. The pace seemed just modest, yet the winning time was 1.75 seconds quicker than the 4.45.

NOTEBOOK
Glen Nevis(USA) had beaten just one rival on his only previous attempt at this trip and he was no sure thing to stay on pedigree – his dam was a dual 6f winner – but he saw his race out well, very much confirming the promise he showed when runner-up over 1m round here on his return from a break.
Imperial Star(IRE) was not at his best in a Group 3 on dirt on his previous start, but the return to turf suited and he ran a respectable race, although he didn't pick up quite as well as one might have hoped. He travelled nicely, but lacked a change of pace when coming off the bridle and never looked like getting there. (op 2-1)
King Charles battled on well when headed and this was a big improvement on the form he showed when eighth (Glen Nevis second) over 1m on his debut in Dubai.
Hallhoo(IRE) had the run of the race but was still below form. He was, though, able to reverse recent course-and-distance placings with Before You Go.
Lucky Dance(BRZ), upped in trip, would have preferred a stronger pace to run at, but this was still an improvement on his two previous efforts at this year's Carnival. (op 20-1)
Before You Go(IRE), 5lb higher than when winning over course and distance on his previous start, failed to give his running.

[627] LINGFIELD (L-H)
Saturday, February 23

OFFICIAL GOING: Standard
Wind: Moderate, half-behind.

674 OWN A RACEHORSE WITH DIAMOND RACING MAIDEN STKS 1m 4f (P)
2:00 (2:02) (Class 5) 3-Y-0 **£2,331** (£693; £346; £173) **Stalls Low**

Form RPR
2 1 **Red Linnet**[17] 454 3-8-12 0 HayleyTurner 7 58+
(M L W Bell) *trckd ldr: rdn 4f out: styd on to ld wl over 1f out: pushed out fnl f* **6/4**[2]
3 2 *2* **Always Bold (IRE)**[49] 58 3-9-3 0 NCallan 1 59+
(M Johnston) *lw: led: qcknd pce 3f out: rdn and hdd wl over 1f out: kpt on but no imp fnl f* **5/4**[1]
0- 3 *5* **Dubai's Wonder (IRE)**[113] 6616 3-9-3 0 MichaelHills 4 51+
(B W Hills) *in rr: hdwy over 2f out: styd on to go 3rd ins fnl f* **11/2**[3]
06-0 4 *1 1/2* **Tobago Bay**[27] 325 3-9-3 47 (b[1]) NeilChalmers 5 49
(Miss Sheena West) *chsd ldrs: rdn 4f out: one pce and lost 3rd ins fnl f* **50/1**

5 4 **Maria Di Scozia** 3-8-12 0 .... AlanMunro 8 38
(P W Chapple-Hyam) *leggy: scope: s.i.s: nvr on terms* **14/1**

6 ½ **Visconte (GER)** 3-9-3 0 .... GeorgeBaker 3 42
(J Pearce) *leggy: bit bkwd: slowly away: a bhd* **25/1**

0- 7 2½ **Mr Plod**[98] [6850] 3-9-3 0 .... JimCrowley 6 38
(Andrew Reid) *in tch tl wknd over 2f out* **50/1**

00-0 8 9 **Honest Yankee (USA)**[10] [547] 3-9-3 36 .... (v[1]) RichardThomas 2 23
(Mrs L C Jewell) *slowly away: sn mid-div: wknd wl over 2f out* **66/1**

2m 34.61s (1.61) **Going Correction** -0.025s/f (Stan) **8** Ran SP% **115.8**
Speed ratings (Par 97): **93,91,88,87,84 84,82,76**
CSF £3.69 TOTE £2.80: £1.10, £1.20, £2.00; EX 3.60 Trifecta £14.10 Pool £331.62 - 16.71 winning units..
Owner Sheikh Marwan Al Maktoum **Bred** Darley **Trained** Newmarket, Suffolk

FOCUS
A steadily run maiden in which the form horses pulled clear in the straight. The relatively good effort from the fourth suggests the bare form should not be rated too highly.

675 NORMAN FREETHY IS 75 TODAY H'CAP 1m 5f (P)
2:35 (2:35) (Class 5) (0-70,69) 4-Y-0+ **£2,590** (£770; £385; £192) **Stalls** Low

Form RPR

-310 1 **Rollin 'n Tumblin**[21] [406] 4-8-9 **63** .... KirstyMilczarek(3) 5 68
(W Jarvis) *trckd ldrs: rdn over 1f out: rdn and edgd rt bef led wl ins fnl f: all out* **8/1**

022- 2 nk **Jago (SWI)**[55] [6848] 5-9-3 **64** .... LPKeniry 6 69
(A M Hales) *t.k.h: trckd ldrs: rdn and led briefly ins fnl f: kpt on* **16/1**

0344 3 ¾ **Red Wine**[11] [533] 9-9-2 **63** .... JamesDoyle 1 67
(A J McCabe) *hld up in rr: hdwy over 1f out: r.o strly to go 2nd cl home* **7/2**[1]

-145 4 nk **Little Richard (IRE)**[8] [575] 9-8-11 **58** .... (p) NeilChalmers 8 61
(M Wellings) *trckd ldr: led over 2f out: rdn and hdd ins fnl f: squeezed out and lost 3rd cl home* **12/1**

30-2 5 1¼ **Wait For The Will (USA)**[51] [27] 12-9-8 **69** .... (b) GeorgeBaker 9 71+
(G L Moore) *hld up in rr: rdn and hdwy over 1f out: r.o fnl f: nvr nrr* **11/2**[2]

5413 6 nk **Lordswood (IRE)**[10] [546] 4-8-5 **56** .... HayleyTurner 4 57
(J R Best) *hld up in rr: sme hdwy fnl f* **13/2**

1-25 7 nk **Fenners (USA)**[26] [344] 5-8-10 **64** .... NSLawes(7) 2 65
(M W Easterby) *set stdy pce: qcknd 3f out: hdd over 2f out: wknd ins fnl f* **11/2**[2]

05-1 8 hd **Resplendent Ace (IRE)**[45] [91] 4-9-2 **67** .... TGMcLaughlin 7 67
(P Howling) *mid-div: rdn 2f out: wknd ins fnl f* **6/1**[3]

0564 9 nk **Bienheureux**[8] [575] 7-8-8 **55** oh2 .... (bt) AlanMunro 3 55
(Miss Gay Kelleway) *b: b.hind: mid-div: rdn wl over 1f out: wknd ins fnl f* **15/2**

2m 50.7s (4.70) **Going Correction** -0.025s/f (Stan)
WFA 4 from 5yo+ 4lb **9** Ran SP% **117.1**
Speed ratings (Par 103): **84,83,83,83,82 82,82,81,81**
CSF £126.69 CT £531.59 TOTE £11.70: £3.80, £4.50, £1.70; EX 146.90 Trifecta £265.30 Part won. Pool £373.77 - 0.10 winning units..
Owner Canisbay Bloodstock **Bred** Canisbay Bloodstock Ltd **Trained** Newmarket, Suffolk
■ Stewards' Enquiry : Kirsty Milczarek two-day ban: carless riding (Mar 6-7)

FOCUS
They went no pace and the race turned into a sprint from the turn into the straight. The form is slightly messy with the runner-up the best guide to the level.
Little Richard(IRE) Official explanation: jockey said gelding suffered interference in running

676 DOUG GROUT 60TH BIRTHDAY H'CAP 5f (P)
3:10 (3:11) (Class 4) (0-85,85) 4-Y-0+ **£4,100** (£1,227; £613; £306; £152) **Stalls** High

Form RPR

1-16 1 **Halsion Chancer**[17] [456] 4-9-3 **84** .... GeorgeBaker 8 92+
(J R Best) *a in tch: rdn and hdwy on ins over 2f out: r.o to ld nr fin* **10/3**[1]

-211 2 nk **Fromsong (IRE)**[14] [503] 10-9-4 **85** .... JimCrowley 9 92
(D K Ivory) *lw: in rr on outside: hdwy 1/2-way: r.o wl to go 2nd nr fin* **9/2**[3]

300- 3 nk **Merlin's Dancer**[131] [6231] 8-9-1 **82** .... SebSanders 2 88
(S Dow) *led tl rdn and hdd wl ins fnl f: lost 2nd cl home* **7/1**

-42 4 ½ **Financial Times (USA)**[8] [580] 6-8-13 **80** .... (t) MickyFenton 6 84
(Stef Liddiard) *lw: s.i.s: hdwy over 1f out: n.m.r and swtchd rt ins fnl f: r.o cl home* **4/1**[2]

1365 5 nk **Sands Crooner (IRE)**[8] [580] 5-7-11 **71** oh2 .... (v) PatrickDonaghy(7) 1 74
(D Shaw) *lw: slowly away: in rr tl r.o ins fnl f: nvr nrr* **12/1**

0/31 6 ½ **Judge 'n Jury**[14] [498] 4-8-3 **75** .... (t) KevinGhunowa(5) 4 76
(R A Harris) *lw: trckd ldr tl rdn: wknd and lost 2nd ins fnl f* **4/1**[2]

-263 7 shd **Diminuto**[15] [482] 4-8-6 **73** .... HayleyTurner 3 74
(M D I Usher) *chsd ldrs tl wknd wl ins fnl f* **16/1**

0-45 8 nk **What Do You Know**[38] [187] 5-8-5 **72** .... (b) AndrewElliott 7 72
(A M Hales) *in tch on outside: wknd ins fnl f* **16/1**

6020 9 1 **Yungaburra (IRE)**[27] [329] 4-9-1 **85** .... (p) DNolan(3) 5 81
(S Parr) *broke wl: sn outpcd: a bhd* **16/1**

57.72 secs (-1.08) **Going Correction** -0.025s/f (Stan) **9** Ran SP% **119.1**
Speed ratings (Par 105): **107,106,106,105,104 103,103,103,101**
CSF £19.13 CT £101.07 TOTE £4.40: £1.60, £1.30, £2.80; EX 18.80 Trifecta £82.40 Pool £386.74 - 3.33 winning units..
Owner Halsion Ltd **Bred** Mrs S Hansford **Trained** Hucking, Kent
■ Stewards' Enquiry : Patrick Donaghy one-day ban: used whip without giving gelding time to respond (Mar 5)

FOCUS
A competitive handicap run at a good gallop, and the form looks reliable rated through the fourth and fifth.

677 DIAMONDRACING.CO.UK CLEVES STKS (LISTED RACE) 6f (P)
3:45 (3:46) (Class 1) 4-Y-0+
£14,762 (£5,595; £2,800; £1,396; £699; £351) **Stalls** Low

Form RPR

000- 1 **Excusez Moi (USA)**[119] [6491] 6-9-0 96 .... LiamJones 4 114
(C E Brittain) *lw: hld up: hdwy on outside over 1f out: edgd lft and led ins fnl f* **16/1**

331- 2 1½ **Ceremonial Jade (UAE)**[98] [6851] 5-9-0 98 .... (tp) OscarUrbina 3 109
(M Botti) *lw: mid-div: hdwy and hung lft fr over 1f out: kpt on to go 2nd ins fnl f* **6/1**[3]

-132 3 ¾ **Bonus (IRE)**[26] [337] 8-9-3 108 .... HayleyTurner 1 110
(G A Butler) *lw: mid-div: rdn and hdwy on ins over 1f out: kpt on* **7/4**[1]

14-0 4 1½ **Maltese Falcon**[21] [411] 8-9-3 103 .... (t) NelsonDeSouza 6 105
(P F I Cole) *lw: led tl hdd ins fnl f: no ex* **12/1**

00-5 5 ¾ **Woodnook**[35] [226] 5-8-9 88 .... TPQueally 5 95+
(J A R Toller) *slowly away: in rr tl r.o wl fnl f: nvr nrr* **33/1**

-213 6 nk **Ebraam (USA)**[7] [593] 5-9-0 98 .... TolleyDean 11 99+
(D Shaw) *hld up towards rr: hdwy on outside over 1f out: rdn and r.o ins fnl f: nvr nrr* **10/1**

001- 7 ¾ **Kostar**[189] [4614] 7-9-0 102 .... AdamKirby 9 96
(C G Cox) *chsd ldrs tl wknd ins fnl f* **25/1**

3-21 8 ¾ **Evens And Odds (IRE)**[11] [532] 4-9-0 94 .... (b) JamieSpencer 8 99+
(K A Ryan) *trckd ldr tl hmpd and snatched up ins fnl f: nt rcvr* **4/1**[2]

412/ 9 2 **Baby Strange**[483] [6229] 4-9-0 106 .... PhillipMakin 10 87
(D Shaw) *s.i.s: in rr on outside: nvr nr to chal* **14/1**

5-10 10 ½ **Come Out Fighting**[26] [337] 5-9-0 94 .... StephenDonohoe 2 86
(P A Blockley) *trckd ldrs: rdn over 2f out: wknd ent fnl f* **20/1**

510- 11 2½ **King Orchisios (IRE)**[119] [6487] 5-9-0 106 .... (p) NCallan 12 78
(K A Ryan) *trckd ldrs on outside: wknd appr fnl f* **9/1**

3242 12 1½ **Tilsworth Charlie**[7] [584] 5-8-9 54 .... (b) PaulDoe 7 68?
(J R Jenkins) *s.i.s: a outpcd in rr* **100/1**

69.61 secs (-2.29) **Going Correction** -0.025s/f (Stan) course record **12** Ran SP% **122.5**
Speed ratings (Par 111): **114,112,111,109,108 107,106,105,102,102 98,96**
CSF £109.26 TOTE £13.70: £4.00, £2.50, £1.10; EX 89.80 Trifecta £323.80 Part won. Pool £456.15 - 0.50 winning units..
Owner Sheikh Hamdan Bin Mohammed Al Maktoum **Bred** Lyons Demesne **Trained** Newmarket, Suffolk
■ Stewards' Enquiry : Liam Jones caution: careless riding
Oscar Urbina caution: careless riding

FOCUS
A decent race and sound form for the grade, with the fifth the best guide. The track record was beaten by 0.19 seconds.

NOTEBOOK
Excusez Moi(USA) had not won a race since the Great St Wilfrid back in 2006, but he had finished second in a couple of Listed races last spring so perhaps he should not have been as big a price as he was. Only Ceremonial Jade travelled as well as him rounding the turn into the straight and, although he edged left under pressure, he ran on really well and was comfortably on top at the finish. A son of Fusaichi Pegasus, he is unexposed on this surface, and further success at this level would not be a surprise. (op 25-1)
Ceremonial Jade(UAE), who won a competitive handicap nicely off 95 when dropped back to sprinting here in November, looked to have a lot more on his plate up in grade against rivals rated in the 100s, but he was solid in the market and ran as many expected, travelling smoothly into the straight before finding one too good in the closing stages. He has a good race in him on this surface. (op 7-1 tchd 15-2)
Bonus(IRE) is not an easy ride as he has to be delivered late and requires luck in running, but he has been in top form this winter and was sent off a relatively short price to make up for a couple of recent near-misses. He challenged near the rail in the straight, which is not normally the best place to be, and ran on well, but the first two always had his measure. (op 13-8)
Maltese Falcon, at his best when getting his own way out in front, set a track-record making pace and it is to his credit that he held on to fourth place. (op 16-1)
Woodnook was never a danger to the principals but she did get a run up the inside in the straight and kept on well enough for fifth. A fairly reliable mare, she helps set the level of the race. (tchd 40-1)
Ebraam(USA), who has progressed through the handicapping ranks this winter, ran well on his first start in Listed grade. Held up in the early stages, he finished well down the outside and was never nearer than at the line. (tchd 9-1 and 11-1)
Kostar has gone well fresh in the past but he looked as though he would come on for the run beforehand. He was weakening when the winner hung left, carrying Ceremonial Jade into him and forcing his rider to snatch up. He would have finished a bit closer with a clear run. (op 20-1)
Evens And Odds(IRE), whose improvement this winter has coincided with him switching to Fibresand, was also hampered in the same incident, but he too was weakening at the time. Official explanation: jockey said colt suffered interference and lost its action (tchd 5-1 in a place)

678 DIAMOND RACING ALONGSIDE HENRY CECIL WINTER DERBY TRIAL STKS (LISTED RACE) 1m 2f (P)
4:15 (4:16) (Class 1) 4-Y-0+
£14,762 (£5,595; £2,800; £1,396; £699; £351) **Stalls** Low

Form RPR

511- 1 **Dansant**[84] [6994] 4-9-2 114 .... JamieSpencer 4 103+
(G A Butler) *lw: mid-div: hdwy over 1f out: r.o to ld nr fin* **11/10**[1]

024- 2 hd **Dubai's Touch**[125] [6372] 4-9-2 109 .... J-PGuillambert 12 103
(M Johnston) *lw: trckd ldrs: rdn and hung lft bef led briefly ins fnl f: hdd nr fin* **7/1**[2]

-142 3 1 **Baylini**[7] [592] 4-8-8 93 .... JamesDoyle 10 93
(Ms J S Doyle) *hld up on outside: hdwy 2f out: r.o wl ins fnl f* **12/1**

2-02 4 1 **Dream Lodge (IRE)**[14] [502] 4-8-13 93 .... TPQueally 8 96
(J G Given) *trckd ldr: rdn 2f out: ev ch 1f out: no ex wl ins fnl f* **20/1**

264- 5 nk **Yarqus**[140] [6011] 5-9-0 90 .... (t) HayleyTurner 1 95
(C E Brittain) *led tl rdn and hdd ins fnl f: no ex* **20/1**

22-3 6 ½ **Basra (IRE)**[21] [409] 5-9-0 82 .... AdamKirby 6 94+
(Miss Jo Crowley) *hld up in rr: hdwy fnl f: nvr nrr* **33/1**

453- 7 ½ **Voliere**[63] [7225] 5-8-9 95 .... JimCrowley 9 88
(S C Williams) *in rr: kpt on fnl f: nvr nr to chal* **16/1**

3-14 8 ½ **Fajr (IRE)**[29] [308] 6-9-0 110 .... (b) GeorgeBaker 5 92
(Miss Gay Kelleway) *in tch: rdn over 1f out: one pce fnl f* **9/1**

4545 9 ½ **Troubadour (IRE)**[14] [502] 7-9-0 97 .... AlanMunro 11 91
(W Jarvis) *hld up in tch: ev ch 2f out: wknd 1f out* **16/1**

012- 10 shd **Grand Passion (IRE)**[63] [7225] 8-9-3 105 .... SteveDrowne 13 94
(G Wragg) *lw: stdd s: hld up in rr: nvr got into r* **15/2**[3]

-123 11 ½ **Capricorn Run (USA)**[20] [418] 5-9-0 106 .... (v) SebSanders 2 90
(A J McCabe) *in rr: rdn 2f out: one pce fnl f* **9/1**

1116 12 1 **Smokey The Bear**[3] [626] 6-9-0 70 .... NeilChalmers 3 88?
(Miss Sheena West) *lw: trckd ldrs: rdn 2f out: wknd qckly fnl f* **50/1**

2m 4.43s (-2.17) **Going Correction** -0.025s/f (Stan)
WFA 4 from 5yo+ 1lb **12** Ran SP% **125.8**
Speed ratings (Par 111): **107,106,106,105,105 104,104,103,103,103 102,102**
CSF £9.28 TOTE £2.00: £1.20, £2.80, £3.40; EX 12.30 Trifecta £249.00 Part won. Pool £350.78 - 0.50 winning units..
Owner Mrs Barbara M Keller **Bred** Mrs Cino Del Duca **Trained** Newmarket, Suffolk

FOCUS
A good race but unreliable form as they went an ordinary pace at best in the early stages and the winner is better than the bare form suggests.

NOTEBOOK
Dansant, the highest-rated horse in the field, did not really have the race run to suit but he got the necessary luck in running and picked up well between horses in the straight to get his nose in front near the finish. He is better than the bare form of this performance suggests, and in a stronger-run race he will be even more effective. His connections are hoping for an invitation to the Dubai Sheema Classic as that is a far more valuable event than the Winter Derby. (op 6-4 after 7-4 in a place and 13-8 in a place)

Dubai's Touch, a winner of each of his previous three starts in Listed company, including on Polytrack, was having his first outing since October. He hung when first asked for his effort in the straight, not looking the most straightforward of rides, but then ran on well to be only narrowly denied. He should once again pay his way at this sort of level on turf this season. (op 13-2 tchd 15-2)

Baylini, who has improved through handicaps around here this winter, captured some valubale black type with a good run down the outside in the straight. Given the way the race was run she is could well be flattered by the bare form, but one would imagine that that will not bother her connections. (tchd 14-1)

Dream Lodge(IRE) raced in second for most of the race and that meant he was well placed for when the sprint to the line began. He certainly looks flattered by his proximity to the first two. (op 25-1)

Yarqus, running for the first time since finishing fourth in the Cambridgeshire, made the running at a sedate pace and as such he very much had the run of things. He is another who looks flattered by the bare form. (op 25-1)

Basra(IRE) was the second lowest rated runner in the race, but he travelled out the back like a better horse than that and, while he took a while to pick up, he was staying on at the finish. His poor strike-rate is offputting but he has the ability to win a handicap off his current mark.

Voliere, a confirmed hold-up performer, needs a stronger pace than she got here.

Fajr(IRE), who has done all his winning over shorter, did not have his stamina fully tested in this steadily run affair. (op 8-1 tchd 10-1)

Grand Passion(IRE) had to give weight all round but he won this race in 2004 and 2006 and was again fancied to go well. He failed to show his true form in this tactical affair, though. (op 7-1 tchd 8-1)

Capricorn Run(USA) came into the race with big stamina doubts. (op 12-1)

679 TRUE RACEHORSE OWNERSHIP WITH DIAMOND RACING H'CAP — 7f (P)

4:45 (4:51) (Class 2) (0-100,99) 4-Y-O+

£9,971 (£2,985; £1,492; £747; £372; £187) **Stalls** Low

Form — RPR

-444 **1** **Atlantic Story (USA)**[7] 594 6-8-12 **93**........(bt) JamieSpencer 4 — 104
(M W Easterby) *lw: led for 1f: trckd ldr: rdn to ld ins fnl f: hld on wl* **7/2[1]**

-115 **2** ½ **Mr Lambros**[26] 337 7-8-8 **89**........(t) MickyFenton 12 — 99
(Miss Gay Kelleway) *b: b.hind: led after 1f: rdn over 1f out: hdd ins fnl f: kpt on* **16/1**

3-41 **3** 2 **Orpsie Boy (IRE)**[26] 337 5-8-12 **96**........ KirstyMilczarek(3) 1 — 101
(N P Littmoden) *a in tch: styd on to go 3rd ins fnl f* **4/1[2]**

6/0 **4** ¾ **Re Barolo (IRE)**[35] 227 5-9-4 **99**........(t) NCallan 2 — 104+
(M Botti) *trckd ldrs: making hdwy whn hmpd and swtchd rt ins fnl f: styd on* **33/1**

02-3 **5** ½ **Ektimaal**[35] 227 5-8-6 **87**........(t) AlanMunro 11 — 88+
(E A L Dunlop) *hld up on outside: r.o wl fnl f: nvr nrr* **4/1[2]**

1116 **6** *hd* **Neardown Beauty (IRE)**[7] 594 5-8-8 **89**........(p) JamesDoyle 9 — 90+
(A J McCabe) *swtchd lft fr outside draw after s in rr tl styd on fnl f* **12/1**

-304 **7** 1 **Qadar (IRE)**[26] 337 6-8-9 **90**........(b) JimCrowley 6 — 88
(N P Littmoden) *s.i.s: sn chsd ldrs: edgd lft and fdd ins fnl f* **10/1[3]**

010- **8** 1¼ **Resplendent Nova**[157] 5545 6-8-6 **87**........ HayleyTurner 10 — 82
(P Howling) *chsd ldrs tl rdn and wknd appr fnl f* **25/1**

0364 **9** *nk* **Fyodor (IRE)**[7] 593 7-8-13 **94**........ TPQueally 5 — 88
(W J Haggas) *stmbld leaving stalls: a in rr* **20/1**

0-11 **10** ¾ **Waterside (IRE)**[26] 331 9-9-4 **99**........ GeorgeBaker 8 — 91
(S Curran) *a in rr* **20/1**

2123 **11** *nk* **Kabeer**[11] 532 10-8-11 **92**........(t) SebSanders 7 — 83
(A J McCabe) *trckd ldrs: wknd 1f out* **12/1**

0/0- **12** 3 **Fictional**[294] 1474 7-8-7 **88** ow1........ GrahamGibbons 3 — 71
(E J O'Neill) *in rr: rdn 1/2-way: sn outpcd* **40/1**

1m 22.48s (-2.32) **Going Correction** -0.025s/f (Stan) course record **12** Ran SP% **111.3**
Speed ratings (Par 109): **112,111,109,108,107 107,106,104,104,103 103,99**
CSF £44.65 CT £155.22 TOTE £4.00: £1.40, £6.30, £1.80; EX 80.10 TRIFECTA Not won..
Owner Matthew Green **Bred** Arthur I Appleton **Trained** Sheriff Hutton, N Yorks
■ King Of Dixie was withdrawn (9/2, broke out of stalls). R4 applies, deduct 15p in the £.

FOCUS
A good handicap and they seemed to go a fair pace, but very few got into it, with the leaders quickening off the front. Those who were held up proved to be at a big disadvantage. The third is the best guide to the form with the first two improving on recent efforts.

NOTEBOOK
Atlantic Story(USA), unlucky in running in a strong handicap over a mile here a week earlier, was backed into favouritism to make amends. Always well placed in a race in which the prominent racers dominated, he quickened up well in the closing stages to get the better of Mr Lambros, and he looks to be still improving. (op 5-1 tchd 6-1)

Mr Lambros was allowed to do his own thing and when he quickened off the front only the eventual winner could go with him. He has regained his form this winter and put up one of his best efforts so far in defeat. (op 14-1)

Orpsie Boy(IRE) is probably most effective over sprint distances but he still ran well, having tracked the leader on the rail for most of the race. (op 5-1 tchd 7-2)

Re Barolo(IRE), a multiple winner in Italy at around a mile, ran a lot better than on his debut in this country last month. He might have finished a bit closer but for being hampered, and looks the type to improve again. Official explanation: jockey said horse suffered interference 1f out

Ektimaal let his supporters down again, although once again he can be excused as the race was dominated by prominent racers and he did quite well in relation to the other hold-up types. (op 5-1)

Neardown Beauty(IRE), another hold-up performer, did not really have the race run to suit, but she might well be high enough in the weights now anyway. (tchd 11-1 and 14-1)

Qadar(IRE) threatened to challenge down the outside in the straight but his run flattened out. (op 12-1 tchd 9-1)

Kabeer had every chance the way the race panned out, but he weakened tamely in the straight. While he has won here three times before, it is at Southwell that he has improved tremendously this winter, and that galloping track does seem to suit him better. (tchd 14-1)

680 CALL DIAMOND RACING ON 01525 853667 CONDITIONS STKS — 1m (P)

5:10 (5:15) (Class 3) 4-Y-O+ **£6,624** (£1,982; £991; £495; £246) **Stalls** High

Form — RPR

-204 **1** **Jack Sullivan (USA)**[16] 476 7-9-6 0........(b) JamieSpencer 5 — 106
(G A Butler) *t.k.h early: trckd ldr after 2f: tk narrow ld on outside 2f out: rdn out fnl f* **1/1[1]**

2531 **2** 1 **Alfresco**[7] 594 4-9-0 91........(b) NCallan 6 — 98
(I A Wood) *lw: hld up in rr: hdwy over 2f out: rdn to go 2nd wl ins fnl f* **5/2[2]**

-113 **3** *nk* **Monkey Glas (IRE)**[7] 594 4-9-0 87........(v) AndrewElliott 3 — 97
(K R Burke) *led tl hdd 2f out: kpt on u.p: lost 2nd wl ins fnl f* **6/1[3]**

3060 **4** 3 **Vortex**[16] 474 9-9-0 0........(t) GeorgeBaker 2 — 90
(Miss Gay Kelleway) *b: b.hind: hld up in rr: rdn and kpt on fnl f: nvr nr to chal* **8/1**

04-6 **5** *nk* **Bahiano (IRE)**[35] 227 7-9-0 85........ HayleyTurner 1 — 89
(C E Brittain) *trckd ldr for 2f: outpcd 2f out: n.d after* **20/1**

/06- **6** 1¾ **Stevie Gee (IRE)**[294] 1476 4-8-11 92........ PJMcDonald(3) 4 — 85
(G A Swinbank) *slowly away: hld up in tch: rdn 2f out: wknd over 1f out* **20/1**

1m 36.63s (-1.57) **Going Correction** -0.025s/f (Stan) **6** Ran SP% **113.5**
Speed ratings (Par 107): **106,105,104,101,101 99**
CSF £3.77 TOTE £1.70: £1.40, £1.50; EX 4.20 Place 6 £14.12, Place 5 £13.47..
Owner The International Carnival Partnership **Bred** Hermitage Farm Llc **Trained** Newmarket, Suffolk

FOCUS
The winner made hard work of beating lesser rivals off an ordinary pace. The form has been rated around the second and third.

NOTEBOOK
Jack Sullivan(USA), fourth but well held in a Group 3 race in Dubai 16 days earlier, was only workmanlike in beating inferior rivals back on his own patch. He swung quite wide into the straight and took a while to assert his authority, but he was well on top at the finish. (op 11-8)

Alfresco, who has improved a good 10lb this winter, was held up in last in a race that was run at a fairly ordinary pace. He stayed on to take second place late on, but a stronger gallop would have suited this confirmed hold-up performer better. (op 3-1 tchd 9-4)

Monkey Glas(IRE) looked likely to get his own way in front in this small field and so it proved. He could not quite make that advantage tell over a classy rival like Jack Sullivan, but he gave it a good go and certainly made things hard for the favourite. (tchd 13-2)

Vortex, another who has been out in Dubai recently, was also held up out the back in what turned out to be a fairly tactical affair. He was never a threat and is far from at the top of his game at the moment. (op 6-1)

Bahiano(IRE), worst in at the weights in this conditions event, has a poor strike-rate.

T/Plt: £18.40 to a £1 stake. Pool: £66,013.45. 2,604.90 winning tickets. T/Qpdt: £5.90 to a £1 stake. Pool: £2,658.35. 329.10 winning tickets. JS

660 WOLVERHAMPTON (A.W) (L-H)

Saturday, February 23

OFFICIAL GOING: Standard
Wind: Fresh behind Weather: Overcast

681 VORSPRUNG DURCH TECHNIK H'CAP — 5f 216y(P)

6:50 (6:50) (Class 6) (0-60,62) 4-Y-O+ **£2,047** (£604; £302) **Stalls** Low

Form — RPR

65-4 **1** **Toms Laughter**[50] 42 4-8-10 **57**........ KevinGhunowa(5) 7 — 68+
(R A Harris) *chsd ldrs: led over 2f out: rdn over 1f out: styd on* **7/2[1]**

04-3 **2** 1¼ **Desert Hunter (IRE)**[9] 562 5-8-4 **46** oh1........ JimmyQuinn 3 — 53
(Micky Hammond) *a.p: rdn to chse wnr fnl f: no imp* **14/1**

1340 **3** 1 **Avontuur (FR)**[8] 576 6-8-10 **52**........(p) RichardKingscote 4 — 56
(Mrs R A Carr) *dwlt: hdwy over 2f out: rdn and edgd lft over 1f out: r.o* **8/1**

2-10 **4** 1¼ **Mineral Rights (USA)**[8] 576 4-9-3 **59**........ PhillipMakin 10 — 59
(Miss L A Perratt) *chsd ldr tl led over 4f out: rdn and hdd over 2f out: no ex fnl f* **5/1[2]**

15 **5** 1¼ **Miss Curly (IRE)**[2] 641 8-8-7 **49**........(t) ChrisCatlin 8 — 45
(Gerard Keane, Ire) *prom: rdn over 2f out: styd on same pce appr fnl f* **10/1**

5300 **6** 1½ **Perlachy**[8] 581 4-8-12 **57**........(v) DuranFentiman(3) 2 — 48
(Mrs N Macauley) *hld up: nt clr run over 2f out: styd on u.p fr over 1f out: nvr nrr* **17/2**

2142 **7** 1 **Chatshow (USA)**[4] 615 7-8-13 **62**........ MarkCoumbe(7) 5 — 50
(A W Carroll) *chsd ldrs: lost pl 1/2-way: n.d after* **7/2[1]**

5303 **8** 1½ **Overstayed (IRE)**[3] 620 5-9-1 **57**........(be) LPKeniry 9 — 40
(M Mullineaux) *led: hdd over 4f out: rdn over 2f out: wkng whn hung lft over 1f out* **13/2[3]**

0-00 **9** 1¾ **Devon Flame**[13] 515 9-8-6 **48**........ DavidKinsella 1 — 26
(R J Hodges) *hld up: bhd fr 1/2-way* **33/1**

0/0- **10** 11 **Longy The Lash**[36] 6732 5-7-11 **46** oh1........ DavidProbert(7) 6 — —
(Paul Murphy) *sn pushed along in rr: bhd fr 1/2-way* **100/1**

1m 15.4s (0.40) **Going Correction** +0.075s/f (Slow) **10** Ran SP% **115.8**
Speed ratings (Par 101): **100,98,97,95,93 91,90,88,86,71**
CSF £55.03 CT £367.88 TOTE £4.80: £2.10, £3.80, £3.40; EX 42.80.
Owner Five To Follow **Bred** Mrs D J Hughes **Trained** Earlswood, Monmouths

FOCUS
A moderate but competitive-enough handicap and the form looks pretty solid rated around the placed horses.

682 BEECHWOOD AUDI CLAIMING STKS — 1m 4f 50y(P)

7:20 (7:20) (Class 5) 4-Y-O+ **£2,590** (£770; £385; £192) **Stalls** Low

Form — RPR

1343 **1** **Buscador (USA)**[2] 646 9-8-11 56........ RichardKingscote 6 — 69
(W M Brisbourne) *mde all: rdn clr over 3f out: eased nr fin* **6/1[3]**

4-20 **2** 7 **Alfie Tupper (IRE)**[14] 504 5-9-5 67........ PatCosgrave 2 — 66
(J R Boyle) *s.i.s: hld up: hdwy to chse wnr over 2f out: sn rdn and hung lft: wknd fnl f* **11/4[2]**

-131 **3** 2½ **Champagne Shadow (IRE)**[17] 455 7-9-0 70........(p) ChrisCatlin 5 — 57
(J Pearce) *chsd ldrs: pushed along 7f out: rdn over 3f out: wkng whn n.m.r over 2f out* **4/6[1]**

430- **4** 1¼ **Dante's Diamond (IRE)**[7] 3922 6-8-8 59........(bt[1]) JimmyQuinn 1 — 49
(R Lee) *hld up: effrt over 3f out: wknd over 2f out* **16/1**

0-40 **5** 2 **Atlantic Gamble (IRE)**[43] 129 8-8-11 53 ow1........(p) PhillipMakin 3 — 49
(K R Burke) *trckd ldrs: wnt 2nd over 4f out: rdn and wknd over 2f out* **33/1**

/433 **6** 5 **Indian Star (GER)**[22] 394 10-8-10 60........(t) StephenDonohoe 4 — 40
(P D Evans) *chsd wnr over 7f: rdn and wknd over 2f out* **25/1**

2m 40.71s (-0.39) **Going Correction** +0.075s/f (Slow) **6** Ran SP% **113.6**
Speed ratings (Par 103): **104,99,97,96,95 92**
CSF £23.21 TOTE £6.70: £3.10, £1.70; EX 15.10.
Owner David Robson **Bred** William H Floyd **Trained** Great Ness, Shropshire

FOCUS
A moderate claimer and, with the winner allowed a soft lead, the form needs treating with caution.

683 SHREWSBURY AUDI H'CAP — 7f 32y(P)

7:50 (7:50) (Class 5) (0-70,72) 4-Y-O+ **£2,730** (£806; £403) **Stalls** High

Form — RPR

-321 **1** **Kensington (IRE)**[9] 555 7-8-13 **65**........(p) StephenDonohoe 2 — 80
(P D Evans) *trckd ldr: plld hrd: led over 5f out: drvn out* **7/2[2]**

34-4 **2** 1½ **Hypocrisy**[14] 506 5-8-11 **70**........ PaulPickard(7) 1 — 81
(D Carroll) *led: hdd over 5f out: chsd wnr: nt clr run over 2f out: rdn over 1f out: styd on same pce fnl f* **7/1**

3203 **3** *nk* **Parkview Love (USA)**[14] 506 7-9-1 **67**........(v) DeanMcKeown 3 — 77
(D Shaw) *prom: outpcd over 2f out: rallied over 1f out: r.o* **11/1**

-115 **4** 1 **Samuel Charles**[10] 542 10-9-4 **70**........(b) LPKeniry 4 — 77
(C R Dore) *chsd ldrs: rdn and hung lft over 1f out: styd on same pce* **17/2**

021- **5** 1 3/4 **Four Tel**[71] 7143 4-9-2 **68** .... SamHitchcott 7 71
(N J Vaughan) *s.i.s: sn chsng ldrs: rdn over 2f out: styd on same pce appr fnl f* **11/8**[1]
2-61 **6** nk **Fine Ruler (IRE)**[17] 446 4-8-12 **69** .... HaddenFrost(5) 5 71
(M R Bosley) *hld up: plld hrd: rdn over 2f out: no imp* **5/1**[3]
1m 30.89s (1.29) **Going Correction** +0.075s/f (Slow) **6** Ran SP% **112.4**
Speed ratings (Par 103): **95,93,92,91,89 89**
CSF £26.99 TOTE £4.50: £1.90, £3.10; EX 24.10.
Owner Derek Buckley **Bred** Mountarmstrong Stud **Trained** Pandy, Monmouths

FOCUS
A modest handicap and the winning time was ordinary, only 0.15 seconds quicker than the following 0-45 classified contest. The form makes sense with the front three finishing in the same order as over course and distance earlier in the month.
Four Tel Official explanation: jockey said gelding never travelled
Fine Ruler(IRE) Official explanation: jockey said gelding ran too freely

684 SUTTON COLDFIELD AUDI CLASSIFIED STKS 7f 32y(P)
8:20 (8:21) (Class 7) 4-Y-0+ **£1,365** (£403; £201) **Stalls** High

Form RPR
30 **1** **Hi Spec (IRE)**[23] 365 5-9-0 42 ....(p) AdamKirby 5 51
(Miss M E Rowland) *a.p: chsd ldr 2f out: rdn to ld ins fnl f: r.o* **7/1**
0250 **2** 1 **Desert Lover (IRE)**[11] 530 6-9-0 44 ....(v) JimmyQuinn 10 48
(R J Price) *hld up: nt clr run wl over 2f out: hdwy over 1f out: edgd lft: r.o* **9/2**[2]
000- **3** 3/4 **Bonnet O'Bonnie**[80] 7034 4-9-0 43 .... PatCosgrave 12 46
(J Mackie) *hld up: hdwy over 2f out: rdn and hung lft fr over 1f out: r.o* **4/1**[1]
0 **4** 2 **Fraizer (IRE)**[2] 642 4-9-0 42 .... FergalLynch 3 41
(Adrian McGuinness, Ire) *led: rdn over 1f out: hdd and no ex ins fnl f* **16/1**
/ **5** 1/2 **Say Anything (IRE)**[112] 6662 7-9-0 41 .... LPKeniry 11 40
(Patrick Allen, Ire) *s.i.s: hld up: rdn over 2f out: nt clr run and swtchd rt over 1f out: r.o ins fnl f: nvr nrr* **22/1**
5304 **6** 3 **Lily La Belle**[9] 553 4-8-11 44 .... KirstyMilczarek(3) 8 31
(A W Carroll) *chsd ldrs: rdn over 2f out: wkng whn hung lft over 1f out: hmpd sn after* **5/1**[3]
-000 **7** shd **Shadow Jumper (IRE)**[27] 328 7-8-11 45 ....(v) RussellKennemore(3) 7 31
(J T Stimpson) *prom: rdn 1/2-way: wknd fnl f* **6/1**
-000 **8** 1 **George The Best (IRE)**[9] 562 7-9-0 42 .... DeanMcKeown 9 28
(Micky Hammond) *s.i.s: hld up: n.d* **22/1**
0200 **9** 1 3/4 **Cadogen Square**[11] 528 6-9-0 43 ....(b) LiamJones 1 24
(Mrs R A Carr) *chsd ldr: rdn over 2f out: wkng whn hung lft wl over 1f out: hung rt 1f out* **25/1**
466 **10** 2 **Oberows Lady (IRE)**[2] 642 6-8-11 40 .... JerryO'Dwyer(3) 4 18
(Adrian McGuinness, Ire) *chsd ldrs: rdn over 2f out: wknd wl over 1f out* **4/1**[1]
000- **11** shd **Cost Analysis (IRE)**[88] 6959 6-9-0 40 .... PaulFitzsimons 6 18
(Mrs P Ford) *hld up: rdn over 2f out: wknd wl over 1f out* **66/1**
1m 31.04s (1.44) **Going Correction** +0.075s/f (Slow) **11** Ran SP% **121.6**
Speed ratings (Par 97): **94,92,92,89,89 85,85,84,82,80 80**
CSF £38.33 TOTE £6.90: £2.40, £2.00, £2.40; EX 30.70.
Owner Hall Farm Racing **Bred** Mrs Marita Rogers **Trained** Lower Blidworth, Notts

FOCUS
A typically moderate classified event. The winning time was 0.15 seconds slower than the 56-70 handicap and the form is weak rated around the runner-up.
Desert Lover(IRE) Official explanation: jockey said gelding was denied a clear run
George The Best(IRE) Official explanation: jockey said gelding hung left-handed

685 WOLVERHAMPTON AUDI H'CAP 1m 141y(P)
8:50 (8:50) (Class 6) (0-65,65) 4-Y-0+ **£2,047** (£604; £302) **Stalls** Low

Form RPR
2122 **1** **Rebellious Spirit**[19] 433 5-9-0 **61** .... PaulDoe 2 73
(S Curran) *mde all: rdn and hung rt fr over 1f out: styd on gamely* **10/3**[1]
20-6 **2** hd **Juzilla (IRE)**[21] 407 4-8-13 **60** .... AdamKirby 7 72
(W R Swinburn) *trckd ldrs: racd keenly: rdn over 2f out: ev ch and carried rt ins fnl f: r.o* **7/2**[2]
3146 **3** 3 **Machinate (USA)**[14] 509 6-9-4 **65** .... LiamJones 5 70
(W M Brisbourne) *a.p: chsd wnr 1f out: rdn and edgd rt jst ins fnl f: nt clr run sn after: no ex* **11/2**
4423 **4** 1 1/4 **Casablanca Minx (IRE)**[8] 577 5-8-12 **59** ....(v) StephenDonohoe 1 61
(P D Evans) *hld up: hdwy u.p over 1f out: wknd ins fnl f* **9/2**[3]
60-5 **5** 1 **Hits Only Cash**[14] 506 6-9-4 **65** .... JimmyQuinn 6 65
(J Pearce) *hld up: rdn 1/2-way: wknd over 1f out* **10/3**[1]
6-54 **6** 3 1/2 **My Michelle**[14] 509 7-9-4 **65** .... CatherineGannon 4 57
(B Palling) *chsd wnr tl rdn over 2f out: n.m.r and wknd wl over 1f out* **7/1**
1m 50.92s (0.42) **Going Correction** +0.075s/f (Slow) **6** Ran SP% **114.4**
Speed ratings (Par 101): **101,100,98,97,96 93**
CSF £15.68 TOTE £4.10: £2.30, £2.30; EX 17.80.
Owner Colin Hill **Bred** Car Colston Hall Stud **Trained** Hatford, Oxon
■ Stewards' Enquiry : Paul Doe one-day ban: careless riding (Mar 5)

FOCUS
A modest handicap and weak form for the grade with the third the best guide.

686 QUATTRO CUP H'CAP 1m 1f 103y(P)
9:20 (9:20) (Class 6) (0-60,60) 4-Y-0+ **£2,047** (£604; £302) **Stalls** Low

Form RPR
55-4 **1** **Royal Amnesty**[22] 389 5-8-12 **54** ....(b) PhillipMakin 8 66+
(Miss L A Perratt) *hld up: nt clr run over 2f out: hdwy over 1f out: rdn to ld and hung lft ins fnl f: r.o* **6/1**[3]
-002 **2** 2 **Mighty Mover (IRE)**[9] 559 6-9-2 **58** .... CatherineGannon 1 66
(B Palling) *sn led: rdn over 1f out: hdd and unable qckn ins fnl f* **13/2**
-621 **3** 1 **Micky Mac (IRE)**[9] 559 4-9-1 **57** .... GrahamGibbons 3 63
(T D Walford) *trckd ldrs: swtchd lft after 1f: rdn to chse ldr 2f out: rdn and nt clr run ins fnl f: rdr dropped reins sn after: styd on same pce* **10/3**[2]
3013 **4** 2 1/2 **Global Traffic**[6] 602 4-8-13 **60** ....(v) PatrickHills(5) 7 61
(D Shaw) *s.i.s: hld up: hmpd after 1f: hdwy over 2f out: sn rdn: no ex fnl f* **14/1**
3232 **5** 5 **Gifted Heir (IRE)**[2] 646 4-8-13 **55** .... LiamJones 2 45
(A Bailey) *chsd ldr tl rdn over 2f out: wknd over 1f out* **2/1**[1]
3-11 **6** 2 **Joe Jo Star**[8] 578 6-8-5 **54** .... DeclanCannon(7) 4 40
(B P J Baugh) *chsd ldrs: rdn over 2f out: hung rt and wknd wl over 1f out* **6/1**[3]
4310 **7** 8 **Tabulate**[13] 518 5-8-6 **48** .... JimmyQuinn 5 17
(P Howling) *hld up: hmpd over 2f out: sn wknd* **10/1**
-620 **8** 31 **White Bear (FR)**[10] 537 6-9-0 **56** ....(b) LPKeniry 6 —
(C R Dore) *hld up: hung rt fr over 5f out: sn wknd* **16/1**
2m 1.88s (0.18) **Going Correction** +0.075s/f (Slow) **8** Ran SP% **120.0**
Speed ratings (Par 101): **102,100,99,97,92 90,83,56**
CSF £46.63 CT £154.18 TOTE £6.60: £1.90, £2.50, £1.40; EX 74.00 Place 6 £158.66, Place 5 £57.95..
Owner Mrs Francesca Mitchell **Bred** Brick Kiln Stud, Mrs L Hicks & Partners **Trained** Carluke, S Lanarks
■ Stewards' Enquiry : Graham Gibbons three-day ban: careless riding (Mar 5-7)

FOCUS
A moderate handicap and the form looks sound rated around the placed horses.
Tabulate Official explanation: jockey said mare suffered interference on bend
White Bear(FR) Official explanation: jockey said saddle slipped
T/Plt: £190.50 to a £1 stake. Pool: £88,792.20. 340.25 winning tickets. T/Qpdt: £25.00 to a £1 stake. Pool: £6,110.50. 180.20 winning tickets. CR

[549]CAGNES-SUR-MER
Saturday, February 23
OFFICIAL GOING: Turf course - soft; all-weather - standard

687a PRIX DE LA PRINCIPAUTE DE MONACO (ALL-WEATHER) 6f 110y
12:40 (12:42) 3-Y-0 **£11,765** (£4,706; £3,529; £2,353; £1,176)

RPR
1 **Cee Bargara**[155] 5583 3-9-0 .... SPasquier 6 94
(J A Osborne) *sn pressing ldr: rdn to ld ins fnl f: r.o wl* **41/10**[3]
2 1 **Trevelez (IRE)**[67] 3-9-0 .... TThulliez 3 91
(F-X de Chevigny, France) **5/4**[1]
3 4 **Roscoff (IRE)**[7] 3-9-1 ....(b) DBoeuf 1 81
(Robert Collet, France) **9/4**[2]
4 1 1/2 **Voitudon**[140] 3-8-5 .... ACardine(5) 5 72
(D Prod'Homme, France) **52/10**
5 3 **Pentacle (FR)** 3-9-0 .... ACrastus 4 67
(J-Y Beaurain, France) **14/1**
6 3 **Sandy Road (FR)** 3-7-13 .... GMasure(8) 2 52
(C Boutin, France) **50/1**
1m 18.1s (78.10) **6** Ran SP% **119.6**
PARI-MUTUEL (including one euro stakes): WIN 5.10; PL 2.40, 1.60; SF 14.60.
Owner A Taylor **Bred** Mrs R Pease **Trained** Upper Lambourn, Berks

NOTEBOOK
Cee Bargara, a decent juvenile last year with winning form on Polytrack, got off the mark on this seasonal debut and first outing since September. He was gelded after his last run and, as there are few opportunities for him in Britain in the near future, he will be sent to race in California now.

688 - 689a (Foreign Racing) - See Raceform Interactive

[620]KEMPTON (A.W) (R-H)
Sunday, February 24
OFFICIAL GOING: Standard
Wind: Slight, behind

690 KEMPTON.CO.UK H'CAP 5f (P)
2:05 (2:05) (Class 6) (0-55,59) 4-Y-0+ **£1,943** (£578; £288; £144) **Stalls** High

Form RPR
6332 **1** **Thoughtsofstardom**[4] 628 5-8-6 **52** .... KellyHarrison(5) 6 67+
(M Wigham) *in tch: led gng wl jst ins fnl f: r.o wl* **7/2**[1]
0-24 **2** 2 1/2 **Twinned (IRE)**[9] 581 5-8-12 **53** ow1 .... AdamKirby 2 59
(M J Wilkinson) *trckd ldrs: led briefly ent fnl f: nt pce of wnr* **9/1**
0-31 **3** 1/2 **Lindbergh**[8] 584 6-9-1 **59** ....(v) JerryO'Dwyer(3) 4 63
(J Ryan) *mid-div: rdn and hdwy over 1f out: nvr nrr* **9/2**[2]
2500 **4** shd **Bentley**[9] 581 4-8-13 **54** ....(v) DeanMcKeown 12 61+
(D Shaw) *trckd ldrs: effrt whn short of room ins fnl f and nt trble ldrs after* **9/2**[2]
6-00 **5** 2 1/2 **Prime Recreation**[25] 363 11-8-5 **46** oh1 .... RichardThomas 8 41
(P S Felgate) *mid-div: rdn and styd on fnl f* **66/1**
04 **6** shd **Yurchenko**[23] 386 4-8-5 **46** oh1 ....(b[1]) LiamJones 10 40
(M Wellings) *s.i.s: hdwy on outside wl over 1f out: nvr nr to chal* **50/1**
315 **7** nk **Earl Compton (IRE)**[9] 581 4-9-0 **55** ....(v) TPQueally 3 48
(Stef Liddiard) *v.s.a: mde sme late hdwy: n.d* **13/2**
030- **8** nk **One Way Ticket**[95] 6890 8-8-6 **47** ....(b) HayleyTurner 11 39
(J M Bradley) *led tl rdn and hdd ent fnl f: wknd qckly* **10/1**
0003 **9** 1/2 **The Carpet Man**[10] 558 4-8-3 **47** oh1 ow1 .... KirstyMilczarek(3) 5 38
(A W Carroll) *a in rr* **25/1**
2-00 **10** 2 1/2 **Fastrac Boy**[44] 121 5-8-2 **50** .... KierenFox(7) 9 41+
(J R Best) *a struggling in rr* **12/1**
-141 **11** 3/4 **Sir Loin**[21] 414 7-8-6 **54** ....(v) RossAtkinson(7) 7 33
(P Burgoyne) *t.k.h: w ldr on outside tl wknd rapidly over 1f out: b.b.v* **6/1**[3]
000- **12** 3 **Millenium Sun (IRE)**[189] 4635 4-8-13 **54** .... EdwardCreighton 1 22
(E J Creighton) *a bhd* **66/1**
60.61 secs (0.11) **Going Correction** +0.175s/f (Slow) **12** Ran SP% **121.8**
Speed ratings (Par 101): **106,102,101,101,97 96,96,95,95,91 89,85**
CSF £36.48 CT £147.65 TOTE £5.30: £1.90, £3.30, £1.70; EX 52.80.
Owner Eventmaker Racehorses **Bred** B Bargh **Trained** Newmarket, Suffolk

FOCUS
A strongly-run handicap and solid form rated through the runner-up, third and fourth.
Bentley Official explanation: jockey said gelding was denied a clear run
Prime Recreation Official explanation: jockey said gelding hung right throughout
Earl Compton(IRE) Official explanation: jockey said gelding missed the break
Sir Loin Official explanation: jockey said gelding bled from the nose

691 PANORAMIC BAR AND RESTAURANT CLASSIFIED STKS 1m 2f (P)
2:35 (2:38) (Class 7) 4-Y-0+ **£1,295** (£385; £192; £96) **Stalls** High

Form RPR
0541 **1** **Bahhmirage (IRE)**[15] 507 5-9-0 43 .... JimmyQuinn 8 50
(C N Kellett) *trckd ldrs: rdn to ld over 1f out: edgd rt ins fnl f: hld on* **15/2**
3324 **2** 1/2 **Wizby**[4] 621 5-9-0 45 .... StephenDonohoe 7 49
(P D Evans) *hld up in rr: swtchd rt 2f out: rdn and rapid hdwy on ins to go 2nd ins fnl f: hld nr fin* **9/2**[3]
000- **3** 1/2 **Itsawindup**[56] 7276 4-8-13 42 ....(t) JamesDoyle 3 48
(Miss Sheena West) *a.p: wnt 2nd 1/2-way tl ins fnl f: hld whn squeezed out cl home* **7/1**
-450 **4** 1 1/4 **Bobering**[17] 468 8-8-7 45 .... SoniaEaton(7) 2 46
(B P J Baugh) *mid-div: styd on ins fnl f* **11/2**[3]

2060 **5** *5* **Fortune Point (IRE)**[14] 512 10-8-11 45 JerryO'Dwyer(3) 1 36
(A W Carroll) *sn trckd ldr: led after 3f: rdn and hdd over 1f out: sn wknd* **10/1**

56P5 **6** *¾* **Mtoto Girl**[14] 518 4-8-13 40 NeilChalmers 6 34
(J J Bridger) *in rr: nvr nrr* **25/1**

0-54 **7** *1* **Love You Always (USA)**[22] 400 8-9-0 43 (t) TGMcLaughlin 4 32
(Jane Chapple-Hyam) *hld up in rr: sme hdwy over 2f out: rdn and hung rt over 1f out: readily btn: b.b.v* **11/4**[1]

0-66 **8** *1¼* **Yenaled**[43] 145 11-8-7 34 JakePayne(7) 10 30
(J M Bradley) *a bhd* **40/1**

-050 **9** *shd* **The Slider**[21] 415 4-8-13 42 (p) SteveDrowne 9 29
(Mrs L C Jewell) *hld up in mid-div: rdn over 2f out: wknd appr fnl f* **16/1**

60-0 **10** *½* **Whos Counting**[22] 401 4-8-8 39 HaddenFrost(5) 5 28
(R J Hodges) *t.k.h: led for 3f: wknd 3f out* **11/1**

2m 10.87s (2.87) **Going Correction** +0.175s/f (Slow)
WFA 4 from 5yo+ 1lb **10** Ran SP% **120.9**
Speed ratings (Par 97): **95,94,94,93,89 88,87,86,86,86**
CSF £31.46 TOTE £7.20: £2.10, £1.30, £3.00; EX 27.00.
Owner Miss S Walley **Bred** Centaur Bloodstock Agency **Trained** Woodlane, Staffs
■ Stewards' Enquiry : Jimmy Quinn two-day ban: careless riding (Mar 6-7)

FOCUS
They went a steady pace in this weak event and the first two look the best guide to the level of the form.
Love You Always(USA) Official explanation: trainer said gelding bled from the nose

692 GREAT LEIGHS H'CAP 1m 2f (P)
3:05 (3:07) (Class 4) (0-85,83) 4-Y-O+ **£4,210** (£1,252; £625; £312) **Stalls High**

Form RPR

1-11 **1** **Scamperdale**[30] 309 6-9-4 **82** TPQueally 11 92+
(B P J Baugh) *a.p: rdn to ld ins fnl f: r.o wl* **4/1**[2]

-155 **2** *1¾* **Bee Stinger**[8] 592 6-9-3 **81** JamesDoyle 7 87
(I A Wood) *trckd ldrs: led over 2f out: rdn and hdd ins fnl f* **8/1**

0-15 **3** *hd* **Blacktoft (USA)**[21] 417 5-8-11 **75** (e) J-PGuillambert 6 81
(S C Williams) *slowly away: sn trckd ldrs: swtchd rt and hdwy over 1f out: no ex wl ins fnl f* **14/1**

-432 **4** *nk* **Confidentiality (IRE)**[23] 390 4-9-4 **83** FrancisNorton 2 88
(M Wigham) *hld up in rr: hdwy over 1f out: r.o: nvr nrr* **15/2**[3]

-112 **5** *hd* **Art Man**[22] 409 5-9-2 **80** GeorgeBaker 9 85+
(G L Moore) *a in mid-div: carried lft on outside over 1f out: kpt on fnl f* **5/4**[1]

0551 **6** *1* **Moonlight Man**[15] 509 7-9-1 **79** SteveDrowne 3 82
(C R Dore) *hld up: effrt over 1f out: nvr nr to chal* **12/1**

0 **7** *nk* **Dakiyah (IRE)**[15] 502 4-9-1 **80** IanMongan 4 82
(Mrs L J Mongan) *in tch tl hung rt over 1f out: sn btn* **50/1**

-115 **8** *shd* **Sawwaah (IRE)**[9] 577 11-8-6 **77** (v) JamieKyne(7) 10 79
(D Carroll) *plld hrd: a in rr* **16/1**

211- **9** *2½* **Wild Fell Hall (IRE)**[22] 2994 5-9-5 **83** AdamKirby 8 80
(A D Brown) *led tl rdn and hdd over 2f out: sn wknd* **16/1**

01-5 **10** *1½* **Reeling N' Rocking (IRE)**[46] 90 5-8-8 **72** MichaelHills 5 66
(B W Hills) *stdd s: plld hrd: hdwy over 3f out: wknd 2f out* **8/1**

2m 9.54s (1.54) **Going Correction** +0.175s/f (Slow)
WFA 4 from 5yo+ 1lb **10** Ran SP% **126.5**
Speed ratings (Par 105): **100,98,98,98,98 97,97,96,94,93**
CSF £39.62 CT £427.73 TOTE £5.00: £1.80, £2.20, £4.60; EX 43.10.
Owner Saddle Up Racing **Bred** Mrs J A Prescott **Trained** Audley, Staffs

FOCUS
A decent handicap but perhaps not the most solid of form as the pace down the back straight was not that strong, but the winner is a progressive sort.

693 DAY TIME, NIGHT TIME, GREAT TIME CLASSIFIED STKS 1m (P)
3:40 (3:41) (Class 7) 4-Y-O+ **£1,295** (£385; £192; £96) **Stalls High**

Form RPR

4561 **1** **Marmooq**[14] 518 5-9-1 46 (e) IanMongan 8 56
(M J Attwater) *a in tch: wnt 2nd over 4f out: nosed ahd wl ins fnl f: jst hld on* **10/3**[2]

0-00 **2** *hd* **Straight Face (IRE)**[40] 160 4-9-0 42 (b[1]) FrancisNorton 7 55
(M Wigham) *led: rdn and hdd wl ins fnl f: battled bk gamely: jst failed* **14/1**

05-2 **3** *1¼* **Faraday (IRE)**[9] 578 5-9-0 45 (b) TPQueally 4 52
(A P Stringer) *t.k.h in mid-div: hdwy to go 3rd 2f out: rdn and no imp on first 2 fnl f* **6/5**[1]

0004 **4** *nk* **Lady Firecracker (IRE)**[14] 518 4-9-0 42 (v) StephenCarson 11 51
(J R Best) *mid-div: styd on ins fnl 2f* **25/1**

-560 **5** *¾* **Mr Belvedere**[4] 621 7-9-0 45 (tp) JamesDoyle 10 49
(A J Lidderdale) *a in tch: rdn 3f out: one pce fnl 2f* **16/1**

-520 **6** *2½* **Club Captain (USA)**[22] 401 5-9-0 45 J-PGuillambert 6 44
(T D McCarthy) *rdn to chal over 2f out: sn btn* **12/1**

0-56 **7** *hd* **Ask No More**[34] 254 5-9-0 43 AdamKirby 3 43
(J Ryan) *plld hrd: in tch tl lost pl 3f out: n.d after* **16/1**

0002 **8** *1½* **Charlie Bear**[22] 401 7-9-0 45 (b) AdrianMcCarthy 5 40
(Miss Z C Davison) *in rr: outpcd 1/2-way: nvr on terms after* **11/2**[3]

6000 **9** *hd* **Salvestro**[14] 518 5-8-11 39 JerryO'Dwyer(3) 1 39
(A W Carroll) *hld up: a in rr* **25/1**

00-0 **10** *15* **Scar Tissue**[23] 387 4-9-0 45 (b[1]) EdwardCreighton 12 —
(E J Creighton) *s.i.s: a bhd: lost tch 2f out* **33/1**

1m 41.39s (1.59) **Going Correction** +0.175s/f (Slow) **10** Ran SP% **120.7**
Speed ratings (Par 97): **99,98,97,97,96 94,93,92,92,77**
CSF £49.65 TOTE £3.90: £1.50, £4.00, £1.10; EX 71.80.
Owner The Attwater Partnership **Bred** Matthews Breeding And Racing Ltd **Trained** Epsom, Surrey

FOCUS
Not many got into this and the form looks pretty weak rated around the winner to this year's best.
Charlie Bear Official explanation: jockey said horse missed the break

694 KEMPTON.CO.UK MEDIAN AUCTION MAIDEN FILLIES' STKS 1m (P)
4:10 (4:12) (Class 5) 3-5-Y-O **£2,590** (£770; £385; £192) **Stalls High**

Form RPR

1 **Mrs Jefferson (IRE)** 3-8-9 0 JamesDoyle 6 66+
(J G Portman) *a in tch: hdwy over 2f out: led appr fnl f: rdn clr* **20/1**

00- **2** *1¼* **Milanollo**[158] 5527 3-8-9 0 HayleyTurner 5 61+
(M L W Bell) *in tch: outpcd over 2f out: rdn and hdwy over 1f out: styd on to go 2nd ins fnl f* **6/1**

3 *nk* **Turtle Dove** 3-8-9 0 OscarUrbina 1 60+
(M Botti) *in rr: hdwy over 1f out: shkn up and r.o nr fin* **7/1**

4 *1¾* **Princess Raya** 3-8-6 0 KirstyMilczarek(3) 8 56
(M Botti) *mid-div: hdwy over 1f out: kpt on one pce* **3/1**[1]

5 *1½* **Kitto Katsu** 4-10-0 0 JimmyQuinn 7 58
(D J Coakley) *t.k.h: chsd ldrs: chal over 1f out: one pce ins fnl f* **12/1**

00-3 **6** *nk* **Love On Sight**[11] 536 4-10-0 72 AndrewElliott 3 57
(A P Jarvis) *w ldr on outside: led wl over 1f out: rdn and hdd appr fnl f: nt qckn* **10/3**[2]

6543 **7** *5* **Lady Amberlini**[8] 595 3-8-9 66 StephenDonohoe 11 43
(P D Evans) *led tl hdd wl over 1f out: wknd fnl f* **9/2**[3]

0 **8** *1¼* **Shenandoah Girl**[12] 529 5-9-7 0 GabrielHannon(7) 9 42
(M D I Usher) *a bhd* **50/1**

9 *½* **Baileys Benchmark** 3-8-9 0 TPQueally 10 35
(J G Given) *a bhd* **8/1**

10 *1½* **Estella Mai** 3-8-9 0 NeilChalmers 4 31
(J J Bridger) *chsd ldrs tl lost pl over 3f out* **66/1**

1m 41.47s (1.67) **Going Correction** +0.175s/f (Slow)
WFA 3 from 4yo+ 19lb **10** Ran SP% **120.1**
Speed ratings (Par 100): **98,96,96,94,93 92,87,86,86,84**
CSF £137.99 TOTE £19.80: £3.90, £2.10, £3.10; EX 301.40.
Owner J G B Portman **Bred** M Hosokawa **Trained** Compton, Berks

FOCUS
There was a decent gallop on here and the leaders fell in a hole in the straight. Not an easy race to rate so treated cautiously with the sixth and seventh well below their official marks.

695 KEMPTON FOR WEDDINGS H'CAP 1m 4f (P)
4:40 (4:41) (Class 6) (0-55,55) 4-Y-O+ **£1,943** (£578; £288; £144) **Stalls Centre**

Form RPR

-356 **1** **Medieval Maiden**[20] 436 5-9-0 **53** IanMongan 3 62
(Mrs L J Mongan) *in tch on outside: hdwy over 3f out: rdn to ld ins fnl f: drvn out* **15/2**[3]

55-5 **2** *½* **Hiawatha (IRE)**[44] 125 9-8-7 **46** AndrewElliott 6 54
(A M Hales) *in tch: hdwy over 2f out: ev ch appr fnl f and ins fnl f: no ex towards fin* **12/1**

0-12 **3** *¾* **Trysting Grove (IRE)**[9] 579 7-8-13 **52** SaleemGolam 4 59
(E G Bevan) *trckd ldrs: led over 2f out: kpt on but hdd and lost 2nd ins fnl f* **6/1**[2]

-125 **4** *2½* **Sahf London**[28] 330 5-9-2 **55** GeorgeBaker 1 58
(G L Moore) *trckd ldrs thrght: styd on one pce ins fnl 2f* **11/4**[1]

32 **5** *2½* **Kingoftheswingers (IRE)**[30] 305 4-8-11 **53** DeanMcKeown 13 52
(K J Burke) *towards rr: hdwy on ins to chse ldrs over 2f out: wknd fnl f* **10/1**

13-6 **6** *2* **Oasis Sun (IRE)**[52] 31 5-9-0 **53** (b) HayleyTurner 2 49
(J R Best) *towards rr: sme hdwy over 1f out: nvr nr to chal* **8/1**

04-4 **7** *shd* **Bulberry Hill**[20] 436 7-8-9 **48** ow1 EdwardCreighton 8 43
(R W Price) *in rr: rdn over 2f out: one pce after* **20/1**

000- **8** *1* **Northern Dune (IRE)**[130] 469 4-8-8 **50** TPQueally 9 44
(A P Stringer) *hld up: rdn and hdwy over 3f out: wknd over 1f out* **20/1**

0-25 **9** *½* **Amnesty**[8] 585 9-8-9 **48** (v) JimmyQuinn 5 41
(L A Dace) *hld up: a in rr* **16/1**

-440 **10** *nk* **Vanishing Dancer (SWI)**[24] 374 11-8-2 **48** PatrickDonaghy(7) 12 41
(Mrs D Thomas) *trckd ldr: rdn 3f out: sn wknd* **33/1**

0000 **11** *1* **Three Thieves (UAE)**[16] 485 5-8-13 **52** (v[1]) FrancisNorton 11 43
(M S Saunders) *t.k.h in mid-div: wknd over 2f out* **10/1**

-423 **12** *5* **Cyril The Squirrel**[15] 499 4-8-9 **51** ow1 (p) TGMcLaughlin 7 34
(Karen George) *led tl hdd over 2f out: sn wknd* **12/1**

14/4 **13** *3½* **Ocean Rock**[18] 451 7-8-13 **52** SimonWhitworth 10 29
(C A Horgan) *a bhd* **10/1**

2m 35.94s (1.44) **Going Correction** +0.175s/f (Slow)
WFA 4 from 5yo+ 3lb **13** Ran SP% **124.8**
Speed ratings (Par 101): **102,101,101,99,97 96,96,95,95,95 94,91,88**
CSF £96.20 CT £589.81 TOTE £8.60: £2.30, £4.90, £2.70; EX 91.40.
Owner Condover Racing **Bred** Eclipse Bloodstock Ltd **Trained** Epsom, Surrey

FOCUS
It proved difficult to make up ground from off the pace here but the form looks sound enough rated around the first three.
Ocean Rock Official explanation: jockey said gelding ran flat

696 SUNBURY APPRENTICE H'CAP 6f (P)
5:10 (5:10) (Class 6) (0-50,49) 4-Y-O+ **£1,943** (£578; £288; £144) **Stalls High**

Form RPR

4-21 **1** **Sherjawy (IRE)**[19] 440 4-8-6 **49** (b) RossAtkinson(5) 2 63
(Miss Z C Davison) *w.w: hdwy on ins over 2f out: led over 1f out: r.o wl and sn clr* **6/4**[1]

5005 **2** *3* **Mister Incredible**[3] 642 5-8-7 **45** (v) MCGeran 8 49
(J M Bradley) *in tch: rdn to ld 2f out: hdd over 1f out: nt pce of wnr* **13/2**

0446 **3** *nk* **Time Share (IRE)**[27] 338 4-8-7 **45** KellyHarrison 4 48
(M Wigham) *hld up in tch: chal over 1f out: one pce fnl f* **5/1**[3]

0046 **4** *2* **James Street (IRE)**[18] 445 5-8-6 **49** ow4 (v) RyanHill(5) 3 46
(Peter Grayson) *wl bhd: hdwy over 2f out: kpt on to go 4th ins fnl f: nvr nrr* **6/1**

4353 **5** *3* **Prettilini**[3] 642 5-8-7 **45** MarkCoumbe 7 32
(A W Carroll) *led tl rdn and hdd 2f out: wknd fnl f* **4/1**[2]

-000 **6** *1* **Vlasta Weiner**[3] 641 8-8-2 **45** (b) PietroRomeo(5) 5 29
(J M Bradley) *a in rr: effrt over 2f out but nvr on terms* **40/1**

0440 **7** *hd* **Noddledoddle (IRE)**[18] 445 4-8-3 **46** ow1 (vt) RichardEvans(5) 6 30
(J Ryan) *chsd ldrs tl wknd appr fnl f* **16/1**

050- **8** *1½* **Boisdale (IRE)**[57] 7265 10-8-4 **45** LanceBetts(3) 1 24
(P S Felgate) *chsd ldrs tl rdn and wknd 2f out* **16/1**

1m 13.57s (0.47) **Going Correction** +0.175s/f (Slow) **8** Ran SP% **118.5**
Speed ratings (Par 101): **103,99,98,95,91 90,90,88**
CSF £12.62 CT £41.16 TOTE £2.20: £1.20, £2.40, £1.50; EX 12.20 Place 6 £232.90, Place 5 £129.96.
Owner John Belsey **Bred** Darley **Trained** Hammerwood, E Sussex

FOCUS
They went a decent pace in this sprint handicap. The race is best rated through the winner as both the second and third have been largely out of form for some time.

T/Plt: £377.60 to a £1 stake. Pool: £65,859.20. 127.30 winning tickets. T/Qpdt: £138.30 to a £1 stake. Pool: £2,356.40. 12.60 winning tickets. JS

681 WOLVERHAMPTON (A.W) (L-H)

Monday, February 25

OFFICIAL GOING: Standard

A number of new distances were introduced to British racing today, with Almaty Express winning by an official three and a quarter lengths.

Wind: Fresh behind Weather: Overcast

697 BETDAQ BETTING EXCHANGE APPRENTICE H'CAP 1m 1f 103y(P)

2:40 (2:40) (Class 5) (0-75,75) 4-Y-0+ **£2,730** (£806; £403) **Stalls** Low

Form RPR

-112 **1** **Morbick**[14] [525] 4-8-12 **68** .... AshleyHamblett 5 78
(W M Brisbourne) *chsd ldrs: rdn to ld over 1f out: r.o* **13/8**[1]

3234 **2** *2 1/2* **Steig (IRE)**[3] [660] 5-8-7 **63** .... PatrickHills 7 68
(Carl Llewellyn) *led: rdn and hdd over 1f out: styd on same pce ins fnl f* **7/2**[3]

4-04 **3** *1* **Shogun Prince (IRE)**[28] [344] 5-9-2 **72** .... JackMitchell 4 75
(W Jarvis) *hld up: hdwy over 3f out: swtchd rt wl over 1f out: sn rdn and hung lft: no ex ins fnl f* **9/1**

6-54 **4** *3* **Punta Galera (IRE)**[14] [526] 5-8-0 **61** .... AndrewHeffernan(5) 6 59
(Paul Green) *hld up: hdwy over 3f out: sn rdn: styd on same pce* **20/1**

660- **5** *3/4* **Dancing Lyra**[30] [6490] 7-9-0 **75** .... BMcHugh(5) 3 71
(R A Fahey) *s.i.s: hld up: rdn over 2f out: n.d* **9/4**[2]

V23- **6** *6* **Kingsholm**[59] [7263] 6-8-13 **69** .... KellyHarrison 2 54
(I W McInnes) *trckd ldr: racd keenly: rdn over 2f out: wknd fnl f* **14/1**

-140 **7** *7* **Hatch A Plan (IRE)**[14] [526] 7-8-2 **61** oh1 .... PatrickDonaghy(3) 1 33
(Mouse Hamilton-Fairley) *s.i.s: sn prom: wknd over 3f out* **33/1**

2m 1.57s (-0.13) **Going Correction** +0.15s/f (Slow) **7** Ran SP% **115.5**
Speed ratings (Par 103): **106,103,102,100,99 94,88**
CSF £7.90 TOTE £2.00: £1.30, £2.50; EX 8.40.
Owner J R Salter **Bred** Mark C Collins And Keith West **Trained** Great Ness, Shropshire

FOCUS
A modest handicap. The winner is progressive and the form is rated through the second and third.

698 WOLVERHAMPTON RACECOURSE MEDIAN AUCTION MAIDEN STKS 1m 141y(P)

3:10 (3:12) (Class 5) 3-4-Y-0 **£2,331** (£693; £346; £173) **Stalls** Low

Form RPR

0-2 **1** **Might Be Magic**[10] [570] 3-8-7 0 .... AdrianMcCarthy 8 71
(P W Chapple-Hyam) *trckd ldr: racd keenly: rdn to ld over 1f out: r.o* **2/1**[2]

2 *1 1/4* **Crystal Spirit (IRE)**[150] [5786] 3-8-2 0 .... CDHayes 2 63
(Enda Kelly, Ire) *chsd ldrs: rdn over 1f out: r.o* **14/1**

42 **3** *nk* **Nags To Riches (IRE)**[13] [529] 3-8-7 0 .... TPQueally 3 67
(J A Osborne) *chsd ldrs: rdn 2f out: r.o* **1/1**[1]

0- **4** *2 3/4* **Lawton**[156] [5633] 3-8-7 0 .... RobertHavlin 7 61
(Miss J R Tooth) *led: rdn and hdd over 1f out: no ex ins fnl f* **66/1**

-044 **5** *4 1/2* **Awesome Light (IRE)**[9] [595] 3-8-7 68 .... JamesDoyle 6 51
(W R Muir) *hld up: rdn over 3f out: hung lft over 1f out: nt trble ldrs* **6/1**[3]

0- **6** *1 1/2* **Woodland Mist**[165] [5363] 3-8-2 0 .... DaleGibson 5 42
(M Dods) *hld up: rdn over 3f out: wknd wl over 1f out* **22/1**

05-4 **7** *shd* **Me No Puppet**[35] [249] 4-9-9 45 .... JimmyQuinn 4 48
(E J Alston) *hld up in tch: rdn over 2f out: wknd over 1f out* **20/1**

0 **8** *13* **Majestic Issue (IRE)**[13] [529] 4-9-7 0 .... JohnCavanagh(7) 1 23
(M Dods) *sn outpcd* **150/1**

1m 51.77s (1.27) **Going Correction** +0.15s/f (Slow)
WFA 3 from 4yo 21lb **8** Ran SP% **115.6**
Speed ratings (Par 103): **100,98,98,96,92 90,90,79**
CSF £27.16 TOTE £3.10: £1.20, £4.60, £1.10; EX 39.10 Trifecta £95.50 Pool £724.04 - 5.38 winning units..
Owner Jaber Abdullah **Bred** Gainsborough Stud Management Ltd **Trained** Newmarket, Suffolk

FOCUS
An ordinary maiden, run at a fair pace. The form is rated through the winner and third.

699 CALL 0844 576 5938 FOR GREAT PONTIN'S DEALS H'CAP 5f 20y(P)

3:40 (3:40) (Class 5) (0-75,75) 4-Y-0+ **£2,730** (£806; £403) **Stalls** Low

Form RPR

1130 **1** **Almaty Express**[10] [580] 6-9-3 **74** .... (b) ChrisCatlin 2 85
(J R Weymes) *mde all: rdn over 1f out: r.o wl* **7/2**[2]

32-6 **2** *3 1/4* **Monte Major (IRE)**[12] [539] 7-8-10 **67** .... DeanMcKeown 5 66
(D Shaw) *chsd ldrs: rdn over 1f out: styd on same pce* **7/2**[2]

00-4 **3** *1 1/4* **Jilly Why (IRE)**[8] [596] 7-7-11 **61** oh3 .... AndrewHeffernan(7) 4 56
(Paul Green) *hld up: hdwy over 1f out: styd on same pce ins fnl f* **20/1**

/316 **4** *nk* **Judge 'n Jury**[2] [676] 4-8-13 **75** .... (t) KevinGhunowa(5) 6 69
(R A Harris) *sn chsng wnr: rdn and edgd rt over 1f out: no ex fnl f* **11/4**[1]

-364 **5** *2 1/4* **Desert Opal**[10] [580] 8-8-13 **70** .... (b) TPQueally 3 56
(C R Dore) *dwlt: outpcd: bhd whn rdn and hung lft fr over 1f out* **15/2**[3]

6-61 **6** *nk* **Drifting Gold**[26] [359] 4-9-4 **75** .... (b) AdamKirby 1 60
(C G Cox) *chsd ldrs: hung lft 1/2-way: wknd over 1f out* **11/4**[1]

62.38 secs (0.08) **Going Correction** +0.15s/f (Slow) **6** Ran SP% **114.3**
Speed ratings (Par 103): **105,99,97,97,93 93**
CSF £16.47 TOTE £5.60: £2.60, £1.80; EX 18.90.
Owner Sporting Occasions Racing No 5 **Bred** P G Airey **Trained** Middleham Moor, N Yorks

FOCUS
A modest sprint, run at a solid pace. The winner was recording his ninth win over course and distance and looks better than ever, although he could be found out from his revised mark.

700 ALL NEW @ BETDAQ.CO.UK MAIDEN STKS 5f 216y(P)

4:10 (4:11) (Class 5) 3-Y-0+ **£2,457** (£725; £362) **Stalls** Low

Form RPR

200- **1** **Invincible Lad (IRE)**[198] [4384] 4-9-13 50 .... JimmyQuinn 6 71
(E J Alston) *chsd ldrs: rdn to ld wl ins fnl f: r.o* **12/1**

4-42 **2** *3/4* **Jal Music**[17] [483] 3-8-7 67 .... KevinGhunowa(5) 4 65
(R A Harris) *led: rdn over 1f out: hdd wl ins fnl f* **6/4**[1]

3 **3** *1 1/2* **Young Gladiator (IRE)**[16] [505] 3-8-12 0 .... PhillipMakin 3 61
(Miss J A Camacho) *chsd ldr tl rdn over 1f out: hung lft ins fnl f: styd on* **13/8**[2]

00- **4** *6* **Felicia**[58] [7264] 3-8-7 0 .... SaleemGolam 8 38
(S C Williams) *prom: rdn over 2f out: wknd over 1f out* **14/1**

0-5 **5** *1/2* **Stand Guard**[20] [441] 4-9-13 0 .... DeanMcKeown 2 45+
(D Shaw) *hld up: shkn up over 2f out: n.d* **15/2**[3]

0-4 **6** *2* **Arrabiata**[16] [505] 3-8-8 0 ow1 .... TGMcLaughlin 7 31
(C N Kellett) *hld up: effrt over 2f out: sn wknd* **40/1**

7 *13* **Notforloveormoney** 3-8-7 0 .... RobertHavlin 1 —
(A G Foster) *s.s: a in rr: wknd over 2f out* **25/1**

8 *1 1/4* **Super Al** 3-8-7 0 ow2 .... MJMurphy(7) 5 —
(M Wigham) *s.i.s: hld up: shkn up 1/2-way: sn wknd* **16/1**

1m 16.71s (1.71) **Going Correction** +0.15s/f (Slow)
WFA 3 from 4yo 15lb **8** Ran SP% **116.4**
Speed ratings (Par 103): **94,93,91,83,82 79,62,60**
CSF £31.12 TOTE £10.10: £2.50, £1.30, £1.10; EX 31.20 Trifecta £194.00 Pool £390.93 - 1.43 winning units.
Owner Con Harrington **Bred** Mrs Chris Harrington **Trained** Longton, Lancs

FOCUS
A modest maiden, run at a fair pace. The form is worth treating with a little caution and the winner is sure to pay for his defeat of a 67-rated rival.

701 BOOK YOUR EASTER BREAK @ PONTIN'S H'CAP 1m 4f 50y(P)

4:40 (4:40) (Class 5) (0-75,73) 4-Y-0+ **£2,730** (£806; £403) **Stalls** Low

Form RPR

-251 **1** **Motarjm (USA)**[14] [524] 4-9-5 **73** .... (t) ChrisCatlin 4 87+
(H J Collingridge) *chsd ldrs: led 3f out: rdn out* **6/4**[1]

0-21 **2** *3 3/4* **Inspirina (IRE)**[15] [513] 4-8-11 **68** .... KirstyMilczarek(3) 3 75
(R Ford) *s.i.s: hld up in tch: racd keenly: rdn to chse wnr over 1f out: no imp* **11/2**[3]

41 **3** *3 1/2* **Schelm (GER)**[14] [526] 6-8-10 **64** .... JerryO'Dwyer(3) 2 66
(Ronald O'Leary, Ire) *hld up: racd keenly: nt clr run wl over 2f out: hdwy u.p and hung rt over 1f out: hung lft fnl f: nt trble ldrs* **9/4**[2]

00-0 **4** *4 1/2* **Fossgate**[3] [664] 7-9-0 **65** .... (p) JimmyQuinn 6 60
(J D Bethell) *led: hdd over 3f out: sn outpcd* **16/1**

23-4 **5** *hd* **The King And I (IRE)**[16] [510] 4-8-11 **72** .... (b) KrishGundowry(7) 5 67
(Miss E C Lavelle) *trckd ldrs: hung rt over 2f out: sn rdn: wknd over 1f out* **6/1**

3/0- **6** *6* **Archimboldo (USA)**[15] [4352] 5-8-4 **62** .... (b) PatrickDonaghy(7) 7 48
(T Wall) *s.i.s: sn rdn to chse ldr: led over 3f out: sn hdd & wknd* **16/1**

0-46 **7** *3/4* **Latif (USA)**[8] [601] 7-8-13 **64** .... PatrickMathers 1 49
(Paul Green) *hld up: effrt over 2f out: sn wknd* **16/1**

2m 42.63s (1.53) **Going Correction** +0.15s/f (Slow)
WFA 4 from 5yo+ 3lb **7** Ran SP% **118.1**
Speed ratings (Par 103): **100,97,95,92,92 88,87**
CSF £11.07 TOTE £2.70: £1.40, £3.50; EX 12.60.
Owner P D Band **Bred** Darley **Trained** Exning, Suffolk

■ Stewards' Enquiry : Krish Gundowry four-day ban: failed to ride out gelding which would have been placed 4th (Mar 7-8, 11-12)

FOCUS
A modest handicap which saw the three last-time-out winners play out the finish. The winner is progressive and the second was back to his best, but the race was run at just a steady pace.

702 BE BESIDE THE SEASIDE @ PONTIN'S MAIDEN STKS 1m 1f 103y(P)

5:10 (5:10) (Class 5) 3-Y-0 **£2,457** (£725; £362) **Stalls** Low

Form RPR

5-4 **1** **Yes Mr President (IRE)**[27] [350] 3-9-3 0 .... JoeFanning 3 82+
(M Johnston) *chsd ldrs: nt clr run over 2f out: led over 1f out: shkn up and sn clr* **11/4**[2]

-2 **2** *7* **Montfjord (IRE)**[31] [310] 3-9-3 0 .... ChrisCatlin 4 68+
(E J O'Neill) *led: hung rt over 7f out: rdn: edgd rt and hdd over 1f out: sn outpcd* **4/11**[1]

3-6 **3** *11* **Ginger Minx (IRE)**[24] [396] 3-8-12 0 .... FrancisNorton 5 40
(N J Vaughan) *trckd ldr: hmpd over 7f out: rdn over 2f out: wkng whn swvd rt wl over 1f out* **16/1**[3]

0 **4** *3* **Musharahb**[12] [543] 3-9-3 0 .... NeilChalmers 2 39
(M Appleby) *sn pushed along in rr: lost tch fnl 3f* **125/1**

2m 3.75s (2.05) **Going Correction** +0.15s/f (Slow) **4** Ran SP% **106.7**
Speed ratings (Par 97): **96,89,80,77**
CSF £4.13 TOTE £2.80; EX 4.70.
Owner T J Monaghan **Bred** T J Monaghan **Trained** Middleham Moor, N Yorks

■ A winner for Joe Fanning on his first ride since sustaining back injuries at Glorious Goodwood last year.

FOCUS
This maiden revolved around the two market leaders and the winner won decisively. The runner-up looked very quirky, however, and this is difficult form to pin down.

703 GO ACTIVE @ PONTINS.COM H'CAP 1m 141y(P)

5:40 (5:40) (Class 6) (0-60,60) 4-Y-0+ **£2,047** (£604; £302) **Stalls** Low

Form RPR

00-2 **1** **Wisdom's Kiss**[12] [537] 4-8-10 52 .... (p) JimmyQuinn 7 59
(J D Bethell) *trckd ldrs: plld hrd: wnt 2nd over 4f out: rdn over 1f out: led ins fnl f: r.o* **11/2**

3-20 **2** *nk* **Convallaria (FR)**[26] [356] 5-9-0 56 .... (t) SteveDrowne 2 62
(G Wragg) *hld up in tch: rdn over 1f out: r.o* **3/1**[2]

-341 **3** *2 1/2* **King Of Legend (IRE)**[16] [508] 4-9-1 57 .... RobertHavlin 3 58
(A G Foster) *trckd ldr: racd keenly: led over 6f out: rdn and hung lft over 1f out: hdd and nt qckn ins fnl f* **9/4**[1]

0-50 **4** *5* **Robinzal**[12] [542] 6-8-13 55 .... (t) VinceSlattery 4 45
(A W Carroll) *hld up: rdn over 3f out: nvr trbld ldrs* **20/1**

000- **5** *2 1/4* **Soul Blazer (USA)**[183] [4860] 5-9-4 60 .... ChrisCatlin 5 46
(Miss Gay Kelleway) *s.i.s: outpcd* **25/1**

0-00 **6** *4 1/2* **Golden Spectrum (IRE)**[11] [560] 9-8-8 55 .... (b) KevinGhunowa(5) 6 31
(R A Harris) *hld up in tch: plld hrd: rdn: hung rt and wknd over 2f out* **15/2**

446- **7** *13* **Empire Dancer (IRE)**[77] [7104] 5-9-2 58 .... FergalLynch 1 7
(I W McInnes) *led: hdd over 6f out: chsd ldr to over 4f out: rdn and wknd wl over 1f out* **10/3**[3]

1m 51.38s (0.88) **Going Correction** +0.15s/f (Slow) **7** Ran SP% **114.6**
Speed ratings (Par 101): **102,101,99,95,93 89,77**
CSF £22.44 TOTE £6.20: £2.70, £2.10; EX 19.10 Place 6 £43.62, Place 5 £25.18.
Owner Ms Linda J Hipkiss **Bred** Snowdrop Stud Co Ltd **Trained** Middleham Moor, N Yorks

FOCUS
A moderate handicap, run at a sound pace. The first pair came clear and the form looks reliable, if modest.

Empire Dancer(IRE) Official explanation: jockey said gelding stopped quickly

T/Plt: £28.80 to a £1 stake. Pool: £57,234.50. 1,450.35 winning tickets. T/Qpdt: £13.60 to a £1 stake. Pool: £2,641.70. 143.70 winning tickets. CR

674 LINGFIELD (L-H)
Tuesday, February 26

OFFICIAL GOING: Standard
Wind: Strong, across Weather: Fine

704 GO PONTIN'S THIS EASTER CLAIMING STKS 1m 2f (P)
2:00 (2:00) (Class 6) 3-Y-O £1,774 (£523; £262) Stalls Low

Form RPR
6222 1 **Coral Shores**[4] 657 3-8-6 48....................(v) AdrianMcCarthy 5 51
(P W Hiatt) *trckd ldrs: rdn to ld over 2f out: hld on wl fnl f: all out* 10/3[1]
0- 2 *nse* **Poppy Red**[131] 6289 3-8-8 0.................... PaulFitzsimons 2 53
(Miss J R Tooth) *hld up in midfield: hdwy 3f out: str chal fnl f: kpt on wl nr fin: jst hld* 100/1
0 3 *1 1/4* **Thankuforthemusic (IRE)**[13] 543 3-8-11 0.................... TPQueally 3 54
(J A Osborne) *towards rr: drvn along over 4f out: hdwy over 2f out: styd on u.p fnl f* 10/1
5464 4 *shd* **Tapas Lad (IRE)**[8] 607 3-8-7 61....................(v) DavidKinsella 1 49
(V Smith) *towards rr: rdn and hdwy 2f out: chsd ldrs over 1f out: kpt on same pce fnl 100yds* 7/2[2]
06-6 5 *1/2* **Lancaster Lad (IRE)**[48] 98 3-8-13 42.................... DaneO'Neill 7 54
(A B Haynes) *bhd: rdn over 5f out: styd on wl fnl 2f: hung lft: nrst fin* 66/1
050- 6 *4* **Has To Be Abacus (IRE)**[76] 7114 3-8-13 53.................... SteveDrowne 8 47
(A B Haynes) *bhd: drvn along over 3f out: mod effrt over 1f out: nt pce to chal* 22/1
2 7 *4 1/2* **Solaria (IRE)**[22] 424 3-8-8 0.................... ChrisCatlin 4 33
(E J O'Neill) *trckd ldrs tl rdn and wknd over 2f out* 5/1
24-3 8 *3 3/4* **Mujahope**[27] 360 3-9-3 67....................(p) OscarUrbina 6 35
(M Botti) *trckd ldr: led 4f out: hrd rdn and hdd over 2f out: wknd over 1f out* 9/2[3]
102- 9 *15* **Rosy Dawn**[99] 6865 3-9-2 52....................(b) JamesDoyle 9 6+
(Ms J S Doyle) *dwlt: sn rdn up to ld: hdd 4f out: hrd rdn and wknd 3f out* 16/1
2126 10 *24* **Hawa Khana (IRE)**[12] 556 3-8-7 61....................(p) KirstyMilczarek(3) 10 —
(N P Littmoden) *sn prom: lost pl 4f out: bhd whn virtually p.u 2f out* 13/2

2m 7.95s (1.35) **Going Correction** +0.025s/f (Slow) 10 Ran SP% 115.3
Speed ratings (Par 95): **95,94,93,93,93 90,86,83,71,52**
CSF £322.60 TOTE £4.70: £1.30, £14.10, £3.70; EX 247.50 TRIFECTA Not won..Poppy Red was subject to a friendly claim. Tapas Lad was claimed by Graham Smith for £5,000.
Owner P W Hiatt **Bred** Cheveley Park Stud Ltd **Trained** Hook Norton, Oxon
■ Coral Shores is the first winner in Britain to win by the new official minimum margin of a nose.
■ Stewards' Enquiry : Adrian McCarthy four-day ban: used whip with excessive frequency (Mar 8, 11-13)

FOCUS
A really weak race run in strong crosswinds. Only the winner featured at the finish among those who had raced prominently. Not form to be with in any way.
Lancaster Lad(IRE) Official explanation: jockey said colt hung left throughout
Rosy Dawn Official explanation: trainer said filly was in season
Hawa Khana(IRE) Official explanation: jockey said filly lost its action

705 CAPTAIN CROC MAKES PONTIN'S ROCK MAIDEN STKS 7f (P)
2:30 (2:32) (Class 5) 3-Y-O+ £2,331 (£693; £346; £173) Stalls Low

Form RPR
1 **Underworld** 3-8-9 0.................... JoeFanning 9 86+
(M Johnston) *trckd ldr: led wl over 1f out: drvn clr fnl f* 9/2[2]
60 2 *3* **Brave Hawk**[17] 500 3-8-9 0....................(b[1]) NCallan 2 78
(M A Jarvis) *prom: rdn over 2f out: kpt on to take 2nd ins fnl f: nt pce of wnr* 10/1
0- 3 *1 1/4* **Baunagain (IRE)**[184] 4854 3-8-10 0 ow1.................... JamieSpencer 10 76+
(M J Wallace) *led at gd pce tl wl over 1f out: one pce appr fnl f* 6/1[3]
34-2 4 *2 1/4* **Tension Mounts (IRE)**[34] 265 3-8-9 75.................... TPQueally 3 69
(J A Osborne) *chsd ldrs: hrd rdn over 1f out: no ex* 11/10[1]
036- 5 *6* **Agglestone Rock**[126] 6401 3-8-2 64.................... JackDean(7) 12 53
(W G M Turner) *mid-div: drvn along over 4f out: no imp fnl 3f* 40/1
0- 6 *3/4* **Cape Colony**[164] 5417 3-8-9 0.................... PatDobbs 6 53+
(R Hannon) *dwlt: outpcd towards rr: n.m.r and snatched up bnd over 2f out: styd on fnl f: bit slipped* 25/1
0-5 7 *1/2* **Sunley Smiles**[10] 590 3-8-4 0.................... ChrisCatlin 1 45
(D R C Elsworth) *in tch: rdn 3f out: sn outpcd* 12/1
460- 8 *nk* **Ruby Delta**[168] 5314 3-8-9 70.................... SimonWhitworth 7 49
(P D Cundell) *outpcd and bhd: mod effrt over 2f out: n.d* 12/1
-0 9 *6* **Running Supreme**[41] 183 4-9-7 0.................... JamesDoyle 11 35
(Mrs N Smith) *outpcd: a bhd* 100/1
-00 10 *10* **South Wales**[31] 311 3-8-9 0.................... SaleemGolam 5 —
(S C Williams) *s.i.s: outpcd: a bhd* 33/1

1m 23.88s (-0.92) **Going Correction** +0.025s/f (Slow)
WFA 3 from 4yo 17lb 10 Ran SP% 114.8
Speed ratings (Par 103): **106,102,101,98,91 90,90,89,83,71**
CSF £46.00 TOTE £4.10: £1.80, £3.00, £2.00; EX 41.20 Trifecta £170.00 Part won. Pool: £239.51 - 0.48 winning tickets..
Owner Sheikh Hamdan Bin Mohammed Al Maktoum **Bred** St Clare Hall Stud **Trained** Middleham Moor, N Yorks

FOCUS
A mixed bunch, but the winner looks useful. They went a good gallop, and the fact the the first four dominated throughout confirms their superiority over the other runners. The winning time was very smart, over a second quicker than the later handicap for older horses and over four seconds quicker than the three-year-old handicap.
Cape Colony Official explanation: jockey said bit went through colt's mouth
Running Supreme Official explanation: jockey said filly hung right

706 RACE AHEAD WITH ZENA @ PONTIN'S MAIDEN STKS 6f (P)
3:00 (3:00) (Class 5) 3-Y-O £2,331 (£693; £346; £173) Stalls Low

Form RPR
032- 1 **Young Ivanhoe**[110] 6734 3-9-3 74.................... AdrianMcCarthy 7 68
(C A Dwyer) *pressed ldr: drvn to ld over 1f out: hld on wl fnl f: all out* 9/2[2]
2 *nse* **Opus Maximus (IRE)** 3-9-3 0.................... JoeFanning 5 68+
(M Johnston) *dwlt: sn in 4th: effrt whn hung rt and wd st: str chal fnl f: jst hld* 5/1[3]
0- 3 *2 1/4* **Firespin (USA)**[60] 7258 3-8-12 0....................(t) OscarUrbina 3 56
(M Botti) *dwlt: sn in tch: rdn 3f out: kpt on fnl f* 14/1
20-U 4 *1 1/2* **Spic 'n Span**[42] 170 3-8-12 72.................... KevinGhunowa(5) 1 56
(R A Harris) *led: hrd rdn and hdd over 1f out: wknd ins fnl f* 10/1
440- 5 *1/2* **Fly In Johnny (IRE)**[125] 6419 3-9-3 71.................... PatDobbs 8 54+
(R Hannon) *trckd ldrs: rdn 3f out: no ex fnl f* 11/4[1]
03 6 *3 1/4* **Martha (IRE)**[17] 498 3-8-12 0....................(b[1]) SebSanders 2 39+
(D R C Elsworth) *dwlt: early reminders and sn in tch: rdn 3f out: sn outpcd* 11/4[1]
7 *4* **Breathe**[144] 5987 3-8-12 0.................... SteveDrowne 4 26
(R T Phillips) *sn outpcd and bhd* 33/1
8 *1 1/2* **Big Boom** 3-9-3 0.................... PatCosgrave 6 26
(M J Wallace) *s.v.s: a wl bhd* 12/1

1m 12.63s (0.73) **Going Correction** +0.025s/f (Slow) 8 Ran SP% 114.6
Speed ratings (Par 97): **96,95,92,90,90 85,80,78**
CSF £27.26 TOTE £4.00: £1.10, £2.30, £5.00; EX 24.90 Trifecta £195.80 Pool: £518.58 - 1.88 winning tickets..
Owner S B Components (international) Ltd **Bred** Plantation Stud **Trained** Burrough Green, Cambs

FOCUS
A routine Polytrack maiden. The form seems sound with the winner rated to his previous level.
Big Boom Official explanation: jockey said gelding was slowly away

707 KIDS ARE ALWAYS HAPPY @ PONTIN'S H'CAP 6f (P)
3:30 (3:32) (Class 4) (0-85,85) 4-Y-O+ £4,100 (£1,227; £613; £306; £152) Stalls Low

Form RPR
0-61 1 **Buxton**[22] 427 4-8-13 80....................(t) RobertHavlin 3 89
(R Ingram) *sn 4th and pushed along: wnt 2nd 1f out: hrd drvn to ld fnl 100yds: hld on nr fin* 4/1[1]
-233 2 *nk* **Sand Cat**[21] 442 5-8-7 77....................(b) MichaelJStainton(3) 4 85
(G L Moore) *mod 5th tl drvn along and gd hdwy over 1f out: r.o to chal fnl 100yds: jst hld* 6/1[3]
00-5 3 *1* **Misaro (GER)**[18] 482 7-8-6 78....................(b) KevinGhunowa(5) 7 83
(R A Harris) *led: sn 5 l clr: hdd and no ex fnl 100yds* 25/1
4666 4 *2 1/4* **Lucayos**[14] 532 5-8-11 85.................... KylieManser(7) 5 83
(Mrs H Sweeting) *chsd clr ldr tl 1f out: one pce* 8/1
-040 5 *2* **Lethal**[20] 456 5-8-13 80.................... JamieSpencer 8 72+
(R A Fahey) *stdd s: hld up off the pce in 6th: rdn 3f out: edgd rt 1f out: nt rch ldrs* 9/2[2]
1120 6 *3/4* **Muktasb (USA)**[24] 404 7-7-12 72 oh3 ow1....................(v) PatrickDonaghy(7) 1 62+
(D Shaw) *s.s and lost 7 l: remote last tl rdn and sme hdwy over 1f out: n.d* 16/1
21-6 7 *17* **Hello Man (IRE)**[39] 210 5-8-11 78.................... NCallan 6 17
(Eamon Tyrrell, Ire) *prom in chsng gp tl wknd qckly 2f out* 7/1

1m 11.1s (-0.80) **Going Correction** +0.025s/f (Slow) 7 Ran SP% 85.8
Speed ratings (Par 105): **106,105,104,101,98 97,74**
CSF £15.18 CT £170.65 TOTE £3.60: £2.00, £2.00; EX 16.30 Trifecta £141.80 Pool: £285.71 - 1.43 winning tickets..
Owner Peter J Burton **Bred** Sharon Ingram **Trained** Epsom, Surrey
■ Benllech was withdrawn (9/4F, lost shoe on way to post). R4 applies, deduct 30p in the £.

FOCUS
A fair handicap run at a solid sprint pace. Weakish form for the grade, rated through the front two.
Lethal ◆ Official explanation: jockey said gelding hung right

708 TRY BETDAQ FOR AN EXCHANGE H'CAP 7f (P)
4:00 (4:00) (Class 6) (0-60,60) 4-Y-O+ £1,876 (£554; £277) Stalls Low

Form RPR
1-13 1 **Joy And Pain**[8] 609 7-9-3 59....................(p) IanMongan 1 67
(M J Attwater) *trckd ldng pair: effrt over 2f out: drvn to ld fnl 50yds* 10/3[2]
1-22 2 *1/2* **Dawson Creek (IRE)**[20] 453 4-9-3 59.................... NCallan 6 66
(B Gubby) *chsd ldr: drvn to ld 1f out: hdd fnl 50yds: kpt on* 13/8[1]
5204 3 *nk* **Imperium**[20] 453 7-9-1 57....................(p) DaneO'Neill 5 63
(Jean-Rene Auvray) *towards rr: hrd rdn and hdwy over 1f out: fin strly: clsng at fin* 14/1
544- 4 *2 1/4* **Murrisk**[107] 6778 4-8-10 52.................... DavidKinsella 10 52
(Eamon Tyrrell, Ire) *led: hrd rdn and hdd 1f out: no ex fnl f* 12/1
-066 5 *1 1/4* **Binnion Bay (IRE)**[20] 448 7-9-2 58....................(b) ChrisCatlin 7 55
(J J Bridger) *bhd: drvn along over 3f out: styd on wl appr fnl f: nvr nrr* 8/1[3]
0454 6 *1 1/2* **Napoletano (GER)**[13] 537 7-8-13 55....................(p) SebSanders 9 48
(S Dow) *stdd s and missed break: plld hrd and bhd: effrt and sme hdwy on rail ent st: no imp* 10/1
-245 7 *3/4* **Grey Gurkha**[13] 537 7-9-0 56.................... FergalLynch 2 47
(I W McInnes) *mid-div: rdn to go fair 4th over 2f out: wknd over 1f out* 8/1[3]
3034 8 *nk* **Cantique (IRE)**[17] 508 4-8-3 48 oh1 ow2.................... KirstyMilczarek(3) 3 38
(R J Price) *t.k.h: in tch: rdn over 2f out: sn btn* 25/1
042 9 *1 1/2* **Film Queen (IRE)**[10] 590 4-8-11 60.................... KylieManser(7) 8 46
(B G Powell) *a towards rr: rdn and n.d fnl 2f* 33/1
0-50 10 *1 3/4* **Kadouchski (FR)**[24] 406 4-9-0 56.................... DeanMcKeown 4 38
(Miss E C Lavelle) *in tch: outpcd 1/2-way: losing pl whn rn wd bnd 2f out* 25/1

1m 24.95s (0.15) **Going Correction** +0.025s/f (Slow) 10 Ran SP% 117.5
Speed ratings (Par 101): **100,99,99,96,95 93,92,92,90,88**
CSF £8.98 CT £67.64 TOTE £4.10: £1.70, £1.10, £3.40; EX 9.40 Trifecta £47.80 Pool: £673.96 - 10.00 winning tickets..
Owner Phones Direct Partnership **Bred** Jonathan Shack **Trained** Epsom, Surrey

FOCUS
A modest race, run at a decent pace. Solid form with the front two both coming here in good heart.
Napoletano(GER) Official explanation: jockey said gelding missed the break
Cantique(IRE) Official explanation: jockey said filly ran too free
Kadouchski(FR) Official explanation: jockey said gelding hung right throughout

709 BET SMART - BETDAQ FILLIES' H'CAP 7f (P)
4:30 (4:30) (Class 6) (0-60,61) 3-Y-O £1,876 (£554; £277) Stalls Low

Form RPR
20-1 1 **Silca Destination**[6] 623 3-9-5 61 6ex.................... EdwardCreighton 5 69+
(M R Channon) *sn led and dictated modest tempo: qcknd over 2f out: 4 l clr over 1f out: pushed out* 9/4[2]
-546 2 *2 1/2* **Too Grand**[23] 419 3-8-9 51.................... NeilChalmers 1 51
(J J Bridger) *hld up in 4th: effrt on outside 2f out: kpt on to take 2nd fnl 75yds: no ch w wnr* 9/2[3]
5131 3 *1* **Talamahana**[10] 583 3-9-4 60....................(b) JamieSpencer 3 57
(A B Haynes) *hld up in 3rd: wnt 2nd over 2f out: nt pce of wnr: lost 2nd fnl 75yds* 1/1[1]
000- 4 *3 1/2* **Last Angel (IRE)**[147] 5888 3-8-4 46 oh1.................... FrancisNorton 2 34
(M Wigham) *chsd wnr tl over 2f out: sn rdn and outpcd: wknd over 1f out* 8/1
34-6 5 *1/2* **Planet Paradise (IRE)**[12] 557 3-7-11 46 oh1.................... PatrickDonaghy(7) 4 33
(D Shaw) *t.k.h in rr: rdn 3f out: sn outpcd* 25/1

1m 28.15s (3.35) **Going Correction** +0.025s/f (Slow) 5 Ran SP% 113.9
Speed ratings (Par 92): **81,78,77,73,72**
CSF £12.88 TOTE £2.40: £1.10, £1.90; EX 10.80.
Owner Aldridge Racing Partnership **Bred** E Aldridge **Trained** West Ilsley, Berks

FOCUS
A weak turnout in quality and numbers, but the winner is on the upgrade. She was able to dictate a very modest pace and the winning time was very slow, well over three seconds slower than the handicap for older horses and more than four seconds slower than the three-year-old maiden.

710 BETDAQ.CO.UK APPRENTICE H'CAP — 2m (P)
5:00 (5:00) (Class 5) (0-70,67) 4-Y-0+ £2,331 (£693; £346; £173) Stalls Low

Form RPR
320- 1 **Josh You Are**[182] 4925 5-9-12 65 KirstyMilczarek 4 75
(D E Cantillon) *stdd s: hld up in rr: hdwy 4f out: led over 1f out: drvn clr fnl f* 11/8[2]
-663 2 2 1/2 **Lorikeet**[13] 540 9-9-9 67 JemmaMarshall(5) 5 74
(G L Moore) *t.k.h in 3rd: wnt 2nd 5f out: led and qcknd 2f out: hdd over 1f out: nt pce of wnr* 10/11[1]
-031 3 8 **Dot's Delight**[12] 552 4-8-0 50 DanielleMcCreery(5) 1 47
(K J Burke) *hld up in tch: outpcd 2f out: sn btn* 16/1
044- 4 3 1/4 **Fondness**[18] 4531 5-8-13 52 (v[1]) AndrewElliott 7 46
(B G Powell) *w ldr: led 1/2-way: hrd rdn over 3f out: hdd 2f out: sn wknd* 11/1[3]
5 7 **Guilt**[331] 4092 8-8-13 57 (t) PatrickDonaghy(5) 2 42
(K J Burke) *led and set modest pce: hdd 1/2-way: drvn along 3f out: sn outpcd* 50/1

3m 24.81s (-0.89) **Going Correction** +0.025s/f (Slow)
WFA 4 from 5yo+ 6lb 5 Ran SP% **110.7**
Speed ratings (Par 103): **103,101,97,96,92**
CSF £2.96 TOTE £2.30: £1.10, £1.40; EX 3.00 Place 6 £134.99, Place 5 £45.96.
Owner Don Cantillon **Bred** Phil Jen Racing **Trained** Newmarket, Suffolk
FOCUS
A moderate race, run at a modest tempo. Not a race to place too much faith in, with no strength in depth behind the first two.
T/Plt: £124.20 to a £1 stake. Pool: £64,355.00. 378.00 winning tickets. T/Qpdt: £6.90 to a £1 stake. Pool: £5,173.50. 553.20 winning tickets. LM

690 KEMPTON (A.W) (R-H)
Wednesday, February 27

OFFICIAL GOING: Standard
Wind: Virtually nil

711 PANORAMIC BAR & RESTAURANT APPRENTICE H'CAP — 1m (P)
6:20 (6:20) (Class 6) (0-50,50) 4-Y-0+ £2,047 (£604; £302) Stalls High

Form RPR
2062 1 **Sion Hill (IRE)**[7] 624 7-8-9 47 (p) KellyHarrison 7 59+
(John A Harris) *mde all: c clr ins fnl 2f: pushed out: unchal* 10/3[1]
-053 2 5 **Silver Blue (IRE)**[11] 587 5-8-11 49 (b) AshleyHamblett 1 50
(C R Dore) *hld up in rr: hdwy over 2f out: n.m.r whn styd on to chse wnr jst ins fnl f but nvr any ch* 4/1[3]
-530 3 2 **Kinsman (IRE)**[31] 328 11-8-9 47 (p) HaddenFrost 9 45+
(T D McCarthy) *chsd ldrs: rdn and no ch w wnr fr over 2f out: one pce whn n.m.r ins fnl f and eased* 14/1
3242 4 1 1/2 **Wizby**[3] 691 5-8-3 46 oh1 RossAtkinson(5) 8 39
(P D Evans) *s.i.s: hld up in rr: hdwy on ins fr 3f out: n.m.r ins fnl 2f: wknd fnl f* 7/2[2]
-305 5 1 1/4 **Batchworth Blaise**[7] 624 5-8-9 47 JackMitchell 3 38
(E A Wheeler) *v.s.a: latched on to main gp after 2f: styd on same pce fnl 2f* 13/2
0-54 6 nse **Alucica**[7] 624 5-8-12 50 (v) PatrickHills 2 40
(D Shaw) *in rr: sme prog on outside 3f out: nvr nr ldrs and sn hung lft: rdn and hung rt ins fnl f* 13/2
0-00 7 5 **Pajada**[7] 621 4-8-3 46 oh1 (p) BillyCray(5) 4 25
(M D I Usher) *in rr: rdn 3f out: nvr in contention* 33/1
1060 8 nse **Golden Square**[17] 516 6-8-10 48 RussellKennemore 6 27
(A W Carroll) *early spd: bhd fnl 3f* 16/1
-010 9 21 **Frank's Quest (IRE)**[37] 249 8-8-3 46 PNolan(5) 5 —
(A B Haynes) *prom early: bhd fnl 3f* 25/1

1m 39.67s (-0.13) **Going Correction** +0.05s/f (Slow) 9 Ran SP% **111.3**
Speed ratings (Par 101): **102,97,95,93,92 92,87,87,66**
CSF £15.92 CT £155.35 TOTE £4.00: £1.10, £1.40, £3.40; EX 15.20.
Owner Peter Taylor **Bred** Joe Rogers **Trained** Eastwell, Leics
■ Stewards' Enquiry : Russell Kennemore caution: used whip with whip arm above shoulder height.
Ashley Hamblett four-day ban: careless riding (Mar 11-14)
FOCUS
A very moderate apprentices' contest in which Sion Hill dominated throughout at a steady pace. The form is very limited.
Batchworth Blaise Official explanation: jockey said gelding missed the break

712 JUMP RACING HERE ON SATURDAY CLAIMING STKS — 1m (P)
6:50 (6:50) (Class 6) 3-Y-0 £2,047 (£604; £302) Stalls High

Form RPR
-413 1 **Bridge Of Fermoy (IRE)**[11] 589 3-9-5 73 (bt[1]) GeorgeBaker 1 71
(Miss Gay Kelleway) *hld up in tch: hdwy 3f out: chsd ldr 2f out: drvn to ld over 1f out: drvn and styd on on wl* 11/4[1]
40- 2 1 3/4 **Montefiore (IRE)**[119] 6578 3-9-1 0 (t) KirstyMilczarek(3) 4 66+
(M Botti) *t.k.h: hld up in rr: hdwy 2f out: rdn and styd on to chse wnr ins fnl f but nvr gng pce to be competitive: edgd rt cl home* 20/1
412 3 nk **Tiger's Rocket (IRE)**[11] 589 3-9-5 70 PatDobbs 8 66
(R Hannon) *chsd ldrs tl rdn and lost pl 3f out: styd on u.p fr 2f out: chsd ldrs and one pce wl ins fnl f: pushed rt cl home* 11/4[1]
-113 4 4 1/2 **Home**[35] 266 3-9-5 74 (p) PatCosgrave 7 56
(J R Boyle) *chsd ldr 5f out: rdn over 2f out: wknd fnl f* 9/2[2]
0- 5 1 1/4 **Beneath The Trees (USA)**[177] 5091 3-8-12 0 DaneO'Neill 6 46
(J A Osborne) *s.i.s: in rr: drvn along after 2f: reminders 5f out: hrd drvn fr 3f out: styd on fnl f but nvr a danger* 16/1
0-4 6 1 3/4 **Littonfountain (IRE)**[11] 589 3-9-4 0 DarrenWilliams 3 49
(K R Burke) *in rr: sme hdwy over 2f out: nvr gng pce to be competitive and nvr any ch w ldrs* 10/1
3-24 7 1/2 **Coole Dodger (IRE)**[25] 403 3-8-6 67 ow1 KylieManser(7) 9 42
(B G Powell) *led: 3 l clr ins fnl 3f: rdn 2f out: hdd over 1f out: wknd qckly* 9/1
05-4 8 5 **Little Knickers**[11] 582 3-9-0 73 JimCrowley 2 32
(Andrew Reid) *a towards rr* 16/1
000- 9 5 **Fareeha**[112] 6715 3-8-9 65 SamHitchcott 10 16
(B R Johnson) *chsd ldrs: rdn 3f out: wknd qckly 2f out* 8/1[3]

1m 40.43s (0.63) **Going Correction** +0.05s/f (Slow) 9 Ran SP% **118.2**
Speed ratings (Par 95): **98,96,95,91,90 88,87,82,77**
CSF £64.28 TOTE £3.80: £1.80, £7.00, £1.50; EX 67.70.
Owner T & Z Racing Club **Bred** Tally-Ho Stud **Trained** Exning, Suffolk
FOCUS
A competitive enough claimer that is rated on the positive side despite the moderate time.

713 DIGIBET.COM CLASSIFIED STKS — 6f (P)
7:20 (7:20) (Class 7) 4-Y-0+ £1,365 (£403; £201) Stalls High

Form RPR
5420 1 **Piccostar**[7] 625 5-8-7 43 PNolan(7) 6 52
(A B Haynes) *chsd ldrs: rdn 2f out: pressed ldr ins fnl f: drvn to ld fnl 30yds: all out* 9/2[3]
-060 2 1/2 **Suhayl Star (IRE)**[7] 624 4-9-0 45 DaneO'Neill 1 51
(P Burgoyne) *plld hrd: towards rr but in tch: stl str hold 3f out: qcknd fr 2f out to ld over 1f out: kpt on u.p tl hdd and no ex fnl 30yds* 4/1[2]
5/02 3 5 **Grezie**[7] 621 6-9-0 42 JimCrowley 5 36
(L A Dace) *t.k.h: chsd ldrs tl n.m.r on rails: hmpd and lost pl appr fnl 2f: styd on again ins fnl f but nvr gng pce to trble ldng duo* 7/2[1]
0030 4 1 1/2 **The Carpet Man**[3] 690 4-8-11 41 KirstyMilczarek(3) 2 31
(A W Carroll) *in rr: c wd into st sn rdn: mod last prog to take 4th ins fnl f* 7/1
-036 5 3/4 **Doctor Ned**[9] 607 4-8-11 36 AndrewMullen(3) 7 29
(Miss Sheena West) *slt ld tl hdd over 1f out: wknd qckly ins fnl f* 13/2
-003 6 1 **Cayman Breeze**[47] 119 8-9-0 42 SteveDrowne 4 26
(J M Bradley) *chsd ldrs: rdn over 2f out: wknd fnl f* 10/1
0-60 7 nk **Joe Rich**[21] 445 4-8-11 45 (p) JerryO'Dwyer(3) 3 25
(Mrs L C Jewell) *a towards rr* 25/1
056/ 8 16 **Chiracahua (IRE)**[174] 5183 6-9-0 42 NCallan 8 —
(P Butler) *w ldr over 3f: wknd qckly appr fnl 2f* 5/1

1m 13.63s (0.53) **Going Correction** +0.05s/f (Slow) 8 Ran SP% **115.8**
Speed ratings (Par 97): **98,97,90,88,87 86,85,64**
CSF £23.19 TOTE £5.80: £2.00, £2.50, £1.50; EX 17.50.
Owner Ms C Berry **Bred** Catridge Farm Stud Ltd **Trained** Limpley Stoke, Bath
■ Stewards' Enquiry : P Nolan two-day ban: used whip down shoulder in forehand position (Mar 11-12)
Dane O'Neill 28-day ban (takes into account previous offences; 9 days deferred): used whip with excessive frequency, down the shoulder in the forehand position and without giving gelding time to respond (Mar 14-Apr 4)
FOCUS
A weak contest and not a race to place any great faith in.
Grezie Official explanation: jockey said mare was denied a clear run

714 DIGIBET SPORTS BETTING H'CAP — 6f (P)
7:50 (7:50) (Class 6) (0-65,65) 3-Y-0 £2,047 (£604; £302) Stalls High

Form RPR
-513 1 **Wee Buns**[11] 582 3-9-4 65 SteveDrowne 12 68
(P G Murphy) *sn chsng clr ldr: styd on u.p fnl 2f to ld fnl 100yds: hld on wl* 8/1
-543 2 1/2 **Extreme North (USA)**[14] 538 3-8-11 63 (b[1]) SCreighton(5) 2 65
(Miss V Haigh) *led: sn clr and 5l ahd 3f out: rdn 2f out: hdd and no ex fnl 100yds but hld on wl for 2nd* 20/1
1231 3 3/4 **Orpen's Art (IRE)**[9] 612 3-9-0 64 6ex KirstyMilczarek(3) 10 63
(S A Callaghan) *s.i.s: sn rcvrd into mid-div and hdwy 2f out: styd on to go 3rd fnl f and nvr gng pce to rch ldng duo* 5/2[1]
0225 4 1 1/4 **Alabama Spirit (USA)**[19] 480 3-8-12 62 TolleyDean(3) 11 58
(D Shaw) *in tch: hdwy and drvn over 2f out: styd on fnl f but nvr gng pce to be competitive* 14/1
0-42 5 3/4 **Montiboli (IRE)**[19] 480 3-9-3 64 NCallan 6 57+
(K A Ryan) *in rr: rdn over 2f out: r.o fnl f and fin wl but nvr in contention* 3/1[2]
00-4 6 nse **Tiepie**[17] 514 3-8-11 58 DaneO'Neill 5 51+
(J Akehurst) *towards rr: hdwy over 2f out: kpt on fnl f but nvr in contention* 14/1
4-56 7 1 1/4 **Golden Dane (IRE)**[9] 612 3-9-2 63 AdamKirby 9 52
(C R Dore) *chsd ldrs: rdn 3f out: wknd fnl f* 11/2
002- 8 4 **Desiderio**[98] 6892 3-8-5 57 PatrickHills(5) 8 34
(R Hannon) *outpcd most of way* 4/1[3]
003 9 2 1/2 **Marquis De Louvois (IRE)**[22] 441 3-8-12 62 AndrewMullen(3) 3 32
(Mrs A Duffield) *sn outpcd* 25/1
0-56 10 4 **Ballyhealy Lady**[11] 583 3-8-4 51 oh4 (tp) ChrisCatlin 7 9
(D K Ivory) *plld hrd early: bhd most of way* 50/1
60-0 11 hd **Elegant Step**[14] 543 3-9-2 63 LiamJones 4 20
(A W Carroll) *a in rr* 33/1

1m 13.51s (0.41) **Going Correction** +0.05s/f (Slow) 11 Ran SP% **126.9**
Speed ratings (Par 95): **99,98,97,95,94 94,92,87,84,78 78**
CSF £165.14 CT £536.73 TOTE £9.60: £2.60, £5.30, £1.10; EX 233.70.
Owner Ms P M Marks **Bred** M J Hills **Trained** East Garston, Berks
FOCUS
A competitive handicap but the standard looks modest.
Elegant Step Official explanation: jockey said filly never travelled

715 DIGIBET MEDIAN AUCTION MAIDEN STKS — 1m 3f (P)
8:20 (8:20) (Class 6) 4-6-Y-0 £2,047 (£604; £302) Stalls High

Form RPR
00-3 1 **Itsawindup**[3] 691 4-9-3 42 (t) JamesDoyle 6 50
(Miss Sheena West) *in tch: hdwy over 3f out: drvn to ld 2f out: styd on wl thrght fnl f* 9/4[2]
-404 2 2 1/4 **Chart Oak**[20] 471 5-9-5 38 HayleyTurner 4 47
(P Howling) *in tch: hdwy 4f out: drvn to chse wnr over 1f out: kpt on ins fnl f but a hld* 11/2
6430 3 3 1/2 **Ponte Vecchio (IRE)**[20] 468 4-9-3 43 (p) FergusSweeney 1 42
(J R Boyle) *led 2f: chsd ldr: led again 3f out: rdn and hdd 2f out: wknd fnl f* 15/8[1]
06 4 13 **Takeanoteofthat (IRE)**[31] 326 6-9-5 0 VinceSlattery 5 24
(D Burchell) *plld hrd and led after 2f: hdd 3f out and sn wknd* 33/1
0- 5 5 **Highlands Skye**[105] 6807 4-8-12 0 LPKeniry 2 12
(L Montague Hall) *a in rr* 33/1
6 29 **Youmeanddupree (IRE)**[19] 6-9-5 0 NCallan 3 —
(K J Burke) *slowly away: bhd: rdn and lost tch 1/2-way: eased fnl 2f* 7/2[3]

2m 21.96s (0.06) **Going Correction** +0.05s/f (Slow)
WFA 4 from 5yo+ 2lb 6 Ran SP% **109.0**
Speed ratings: **101,99,96,87,83 62**
CSF £13.87 TOTE £2.00: £1.60; EX 9.80.
Owner W R B Racing 46 (wrbracing.com) **Bred** J A And Mrs Duffy **Trained** Falmer, E Sussex

FOCUS
A strong contender for worst maiden of all time and not a race to dwell on.
Highlands Skye Official explanation: jockey said filly had a breathing problem

716 EVERGREEN H'CAP 1m 3f (P)
8:50 (8:51) (Class 6) (0-60,60) 4-Y-0+ £2,047 (£604; £302) Stalls High

Form RPR
3-66 1 **Oasis Sun (IRE)**[3] 695 5-8-13 53 (b) JimCrowley 1 61
(J R Best) *in tch: hdwy fr 2f out: str run u.p fnl f to ld fnl 75yds* 14/1
0-61 2 1 **Mixing**[30] 332 6-8-9 52 KirstyMilczarek(3) 8 58
(J Akehurst) *t.k.h: chsd ldrs: drvn to ld 1f out: hdd and no ex fnl 75yds* 3/1[1]
3 nk **Annapurna Sunrise (IRE)**[147] 5925 4-8-10 52 (b[1]) DavidKinsella 6 58
(Eamon Tyrrell, Ire) *chsd ldr: rdn 3f out: chal appr fnl f: styd on same pce ins fnl f* 25/1
0-20 4 nk **Lascelles**[23] 435 4-9-4 60 TPQueally 11 66+
(J A Osborne) *in rr: gd hdwy over 2f out: styng on whn nt clr run and swtchd lft ins fnl f: kpt on cl home but nvr quite gng pce to rch ldrs* 12/1
-532 5 ¾ **Siena Star (IRE)**[9] 611 10-8-13 53 MickyFenton 13 57
(Stef Liddiard) *led: rdn over 2f out: hdd 1f out: wknd fnl 100yds* 8/1
-331 6 1 ¼ **King's Fable (USA)**[5] 664 5-9-3 57 6ex (p) TGMcLaughlin 3 59
(Karen George) *s.i.s: in rr: hdwy fr 2f out: styd on wl fnl f but nt rch ldrs* 9/2[2]
-123 7 ¾ **Maria Antonia (IRE)**[13] 551 5-9-1 55 StephenDonohoe 10 56
(M J Gingell) *chsd ldrs: rdn 3f out: wknd ins fnl f* 16/1
04-1 8 hd **Chimes At Midnight (USA)**[11] 585 11-8-9 52 ow2(b) JerryO'Dwyer(3) 2 52
(Luke Comer, Ire) *in rr: rdn along over 3f out: r.o ins fnl f but nt a danger* 16/1
645- 9 1 ¾ **The Dagger**[338] 790 4-9-4 60 GeorgeBaker 12 58
(G L Moore) *in tch: chsd ldrs 3f out: rdn 2f out: wknd ins fnl f* 11/2[3]
-543 10 nk **Magic Warrior**[21] 451 8-9-6 60 PatDobbs 7 57
(J C Fox) *chsd ldrs tl wknd over 1f out* 16/1
0-04 11 ¾ **Artzola (IRE)**[14] 541 8-9-0 54 SimonWhitworth 5 50
(C A Horgan) *s.i.s: in rr tl sme late prog* 9/1
-200 12 hd **Satindra (IRE)**[16] 526 4-9-4 60 (tp) LiamJones 9 56
(John A Harris) *t.k.h: towards rr most of way* 33/1
-563 13 hd **Boundless Prospect (USA)**[17] 512 9-9-6 60 (p) HayleyTurner 4 55
(Miss Gay Kelleway) *nvr bttr than mid-div* 14/1

2m 24.18s (2.28) **Going Correction** +0.05s/f (Slow)
WFA 4 from 5yo+ 2lb 13 Ran SP% **125.1**
Speed ratings (Par 101): **93,92,92,91,91 90,89,89,88,88 87,87,87**
CSF £58.34 CT £1097.73 TOTE £16.80: £5.20, £2.00, £6.50; EX 138.60.
Owner Mrs J Schabacker **Bred** Peter Jones And G G Jones **Trained** Hucking, Kent

FOCUS
They went just a steady gallop in what was an open event and it turned into something of a sprint in the straight. The winning time was moderate as a result, 2.28 seconds slower than the preceding maiden, but the form appears sound enough on paper.

717 FREE EVENINGS FOR GIRLS IN APRIL H'CAP 7f (P)
9:20 (9:20) (Class 4) (0-85,85) 4-Y-0+ £4,210 (£1,252; £625; £312) Stalls High

Form RPR
-422 1 **Super Frank (IRE)**[21] 456 5-8-10 77 TPQueally 5 86
(J Akehurst) *led: rdn and narrowly hdd ins fnl 2f: chal and hung lft fnl f: led fnl 100yds: all out* 9/4[1]
-413 2 hd **Electric Warrior (IRE)**[36] 259 5-9-4 85 FergusSweeney 2 94
(K R Burke) *chsd wnr 4f out: rdn to take slt ld ins fnl 2f: carried lft fr 1f out: hdd fnl 100yds: no ex cl home* 11/4[2]
3351 3 1 ¾ **Count Ceprano (IRE)**[9] 609 4-8-5 72 6ex HayleyTurner 7 76
(M D I Usher) *in rr: hdwy fr 2f out: rdn and styd on wl fnl f but nvr gng pce of ldng duo* 9/1
0-63 4 hd **Raza Cab (IRE)**[6] 643 6-8-4 71 JimmyQuinn 1 75
(Karen George) *s.i.s: in rr: hdwy over 3f out: chsd ldrs and rdn 2f out: kpt on fnl f but nvr gng pce to chal* 25/1
2362 5 1 **Memphis Man**[8] 618 5-8-6 73 JamesDoyle 3 74
(P D Evans) *t.k.h in rr: hdwy fr 2f out: kpt on ins fnl f but nvr gng pce to be competitive* 10/1
0-10 6 1 ¾ **Sailor King (IRE)**[11] 594 6-9-1 82 JimCrowley 6 79
(D K Ivory) *chsd ldrs: rdn over 2f out: wknd ins fnl f* 11/2
02-0 7 hd **Apache Dawn**[32] 314 4-9-2 83 GeorgeBaker 4 79
(G L Moore) *chsd ldrs: rdn 2f out: wknd fnl f* 5/1[3]

1m 26.52s (0.52) **Going Correction** +0.05s/f (Slow) 7 Ran SP% **112.4**
Speed ratings (Par 105): **99,98,96,96,95 93,93**
CSF £8.31 TOTE £2.50: £2.20, £3.10; EX 7.00 Place 6 £48.27, Place 5 £25.60.
Owner A D Spence **Bred** A Butler **Trained** Epsom, Surrey

FOCUS
A fair contest in which Super Frank won his first race in a year. The form is rated around the placed horses and looks solid enough.
T/Plt: £38.30 to a £1 stake. Pool: £8,661.30. 1,650.40 winning tickets. T/Qpdt: £17.20 to a £1 stake. Pool: £6,878.10. 295.40 winning tickets. ST

[697]WOLVERHAMPTON (A.W) (L-H)
Wednesday, February 27

OFFICIAL GOING: Standard
Wind: Light, behind Weather: Fine

718 COME STAY WITH US @ PONTIN'S H'CAP 5f 216y(P)
2:30 (2:30) (Class 6) (0-55,58) 4-Y-0+ £1,774 (£523; £262) Stalls Low

Form RPR
00-2 1 **Decider (USA)**[7] 625 5-8-4 52 KevinGhunowa(5) 5 64
(R A Harris) *mde all: rdn over 1f out: drvn out* 11/4[2]
221 2 1 **Cape Of Storms**[10] 598 5-9-1 58 6ex PhillipMakin 9 67
(R Brotherton) *a.p: rdn over 3f out: outpcd over 2f out: c wd st: rallied ins fnl f: tk 2nd last strides* 6/1
-651 3 nk **Wiltshire (IRE)**[7] 625 6-8-13 56 6ex (v) MickyFenton 4 64
(P T Midgley) *plld hrd: sn in tch: rdn over 1f out: ev ch ins fnl f: no ex cl home* 9/4[1]
0-31 4 1 **Smirfys Systems**[20] 469 9-8-11 54 (p) StephenDonohoe 2 59
(E S McMahon) *sn prom: chsd wnr 3f out: rdn over 1f out: nt qckn ins fnl f* 11/2[3]
00-0 5 2 **Just Spike**[49] 87 5-8-9 52 AndrewElliott 1 51
(B P J Baugh) *s.i.s: hld up: hdwy on ins over 2f out: rdn over 1f out: one pce* 20/1
6400 6 3 ½ **Desert Light (IRE)**[12] 581 7-8-8 51 (v) DeanMcKeown 3 40
(D Shaw) *hld up: n.m.r after 1f: sn bhd: rdn over 1f out: n.d* 12/1
0-50 7 ¾ **Rosie Cross (IRE)**[12] 571 4-8-5 55 DanielBlackett(7) 7 41
(Eve Johnson Houghton) *bhd fnl 3f* 16/1
05-2 8 nk **Bahamian Bay**[6] 642 6-8-3 46 oh1 JimmyQuinn 8 31
(M Brittain) *w wnr 3f: wknd 2f out* 12/1
00/ 9 5 **Moverra (IRE)**[116] 6656 4-8-10 53 FrancisNorton 6 23+
(M Wigham) *bhd fnl 4f* 6/1

1m 15.94s (0.94) **Going Correction** +0.225s/f (Slow) 9 Ran SP% **127.4**
Speed ratings (Par 101): **102,100,100,98,96 91,90,90,83**
CSF £22.32 CT £46.17 TOTE £4.10: £1.40, £2.10, £2.00; EX 31.30 Trifecta £18.00 Pool: £337.76 - 13.31 winning tickets..
Owner Robert Bailey **Bred** Green Willow Farms **Trained** Earlswood, Monmouths

FOCUS
A modest handicap but pretty strong for the grade.

719 BACK OR LAY AT BETDAQ (S) STKS 5f 20y(P)
3:00 (3:00) (Class 6) 4-Y-0+ £1,774 (£523; £262) Stalls Low

Form RPR
030- 1 **Rann Na Cille (IRE)**[105] 6810 4-8-9 60 MickyFenton 2 54
(P T Midgley) *led early: chsd ldr: rdn to ld ins fnl f: r.o* 15/8[1]
-000 2 hd **Monashee Brave (IRE)**[20] 460 5-9-5 55 (p) AmirQuinn 1 63
(M A Allen) *sn led: hrd rdn fr wl over 1f out: hdd ins fnl f: r.o* 10/1
2162 3 1 ¾ **Nautical**[5] 655 10-9-2 58 JerryO'Dwyer(3) 6 57
(A W Carroll) *hld up: hdwy wl over 1f out: kpt on one pce fnl f* 9/4[2]
0-23 4 ¾ **Macademy Royal (USA)**[34] 285 5-8-9 57 (t) KellyHarrison(5) 3 49
(M Wigham) *hld up in tch: no ex wl ins fnl f* 11/4[3]
-532 5 1 ¼ **Highland Song (IRE)**[13] 558 5-9-0 47 ChrisCatlin 4 45
(R F Fisher) *chsd ldrs: no hdwy fnl 2f* 13/2
00-5 6 ¾ **Jabraan (USA)**[8] 615 6-9-0 39 (b) LiamJones 5 42
(Mrs R A Carr) *s.i.s: a bhd* 22/1

63.78 secs (1.48) **Going Correction** +0.225s/f (Slow) 6 Ran SP% **119.0**
Speed ratings (Par 101): **97,96,93,92,90 89**
CSF £22.43 TOTE £2.90: £1.50, £5.80; EX 15.80.The winner was bought in for 4,800gns.
Owner P T Midgley **Bred** Donal Mac A Bhaird **Trained** Westow, N Yorks
■ Stewards' Enquiry : Amir Quinn four-day ban: used whip with excessive frequency, in incorrect place down shoulder, in forehand position (Mar 11-14)

FOCUS
An ordinary seller and not a race to be with.

720 HOP TO IT AT PONTIN'S H'CAP 1m 4f 50y(P)
3:30 (3:30) (Class 6) (0-60,60) 4-Y-0+ £2,047 (£604; £302) Stalls Low

Form RPR
-052 1 **Speagle (IRE)**[10] 602 6-9-2 55 DeanMcKeown 4 65
(D Shaw) *mde all: rdn over 1f out: r.o* 5/2[1]
1454 2 1 ½ **Little Richard (IRE)**[4] 675 9-9-5 58 (p) NeilChalmers 3 66
(M Wellings) *hld up: rdn over 3f out: hdwy over 2f out: brought wd st: styd on ins fnl f: tk 2nd nr fin* 3/1[2]
3-54 3 ¾ **Grizebeck (IRE)**[5] 664 6-9-4 57 J-PGuillambert 8 64
(R F Fisher) *sn prom: chsd wnr over 3f out: rdn over 2f out: no ex wl ins fnl f* 8/1
U5 4 3 ¾ **Saint Eric (FR)**[19] 485 6-8-7 46 ChrisCatlin 2 47
(Noel T Chance) *hld up and bhd: rdn 4f out: styd on fnl f: nvr nrr* 16/1
1125 5 hd **Qaasi (USA)**[5] 664 6-9-4 60 MarkLawson(3) 1 61
(M Brittain) *hld up and bhd: sme hdwy over 2f out: rdn over 1f out: no imp whn edgd lft jst ins fnl f* 5/1[3]
-033 6 3 ¼ **Amwell Brave**[15] 533 7-9-1 54 StephenDonohoe 5 50
(J R Jenkins) *hld up: hdwy over 3f out: rdn wl over 1f out: wkng whn edgd lft jst ins fnl f* 5/1[3]
03/1 7 1 **Wizard Of Us**[11] 377 8-9-2 55 JimCrowley 7 50
(M Mullineaux) *chsd wnr tl over 3f out: wknd over 2f out* 5/1[3]
-062 8 8 **Simple Jim (FR)**[13] 551 4-9-4 60 (p) AndrewElliott 6 43
(A D Brown) *prom: rdn over 3f out: sn wknd* 16/1

2m 43.01s (1.91) **Going Correction** +0.225s/f (Slow)
WFA 4 from 6yo+ 3lb 8 Ran SP% **126.4**
Speed ratings (Par 101): **102,101,100,98,97 95,95,89**
CSF £11.57 CT £56.20 TOTE £3.40: £2.20, £1.10, £2.90; EX 15.90 Trifecta £48.90 Pool: £480.99 - 6.98 winning tickets..
Owner Christopher Chell **Bred** Mrs Sheila Morrissey **Trained** Danethorpe, Notts
■ Stewards' Enquiry : Dean McKeown one-day ban: used whip with excessive frequency (Mar 11)

FOCUS
A moderate contest run at a modest pace and best assessed through the runner-up.

721 BETDAQ.CO.UK MAIDEN STKS 5f 20y(P)
4:00 (4:01) (Class 5) 3-Y-O £2,457 (£725; £362) Stalls Low

Form RPR
4-33 1 **Upstanding**[26] 397 3-8-9 58 MarkLawson(3) 7 63
(M Brittain) *w ldr: led wl over 1f out: sn rdn: drvn out* 5/1[2]
4223 2 ¾ **Jalons Bridewell**[7] 629 3-9-3 68 FrancisNorton 3 65
(M Quinn) *a.p: hung lft jst over 1f out: rdn and ev ch ins fnl f: nt qckn* 13/8[1]
0- 3 nse **Gracious Girl (IRE)**[115] 6680 3-8-12 71 CDHayes 1 60
(Enda Kelly, Ire) *s.s: sn chsng ldrs: rdn wl over 1f out: ev ch ins fnl f: nt qckn* 13/8[1]
4-32 4 1 ¼ **Jazenio**[19] 487 3-8-12 62 FergalLynch 5 56
(K A Ryan) *hld up: hdwy on outside over 2f out: rdn and flashed tail whn edgd lft over 1f out: one pce fnl f* 15/2[3]
5 3 ¼ **Many Welcomes** 3-8-12 0 AndrewElliott 2 44
(B P J Baugh) *s.i.s: carried lft over 1f out: nvr nr ldrs* 40/1
- 6 2 ½ **Hardcase** 3-9-3 0 TPQueally 6 40
(M Quinn) *sn outpcd* 12/1
656 7 2 ¾ **Sazerac (USA)**[11] 590 3-9-3 0 DeanMcKeown 4 30
(D Shaw) *led: hdd wl over 1f out: sn hung lft: wkng whn hung rt ins fnl f* 8/1

64.10 secs (1.80) **Going Correction** +0.225s/f (Slow) 7 Ran SP% **125.9**
Speed ratings (Par 97): **94,92,92,90,85 81,77**
CSF £15.33 TOTE £9.50: £4.60, £1.10; EX 22.60.
Owner Mel Brittain **Bred** The Hon Mrs R Pease **Trained** Warthill, N Yorks

FOCUS
A minor maiden in which the winner showed slight improvement.

722 MEET CAPTAIN CROC @ PONTIN'S H'CAP 1m 5f 194y(P)
4:30 (4:30) (Class 6) (0-65,63) 4-Y-0+ £2,047 (£604; £302) Stalls Low

Form RPR
023- 1 **Rare Coincidence**[60] 7008 7-9-12 63 (p) ChrisCatlin 7 73
(R F Fisher) *sn led: rdn and hld on wl ins fnl f* 3/1[1]

1-30 **2** 3/4 **Young Scotton**[15] 533 8-9-11 62 JimmyQuinn 1 71
(J D Bethell) *a.p: chsd wnr over 1f out: rdn and nt qckn ins fnl f* **15/2**

2-10 **3** 6 **Opera Writer (IRE)**[13] 561 5-9-8 59 TPQueally 2 60
(R Hollinshead) *a.p: rdn wl over 1f out: wknd fnl f* **3/1**[1]

04-1 **4** 2 **Dreams Jewel**[10] 600 8-9-5 56 6ex NeilChalmers 3 54
(C Roberts) *s.i.s: hld up in tch: rdn 3f out: n.m.r on ins whn hung rt and wknd bnd over 2f out* **7/2**[2]

-620 **5** 8 **Mariaverdi**[24] 420 4-8-5 47 (p) FrancisNorton 5 34
(P G Murphy) *t.k.h in tch: pushed along and shortlived effrt 3f out* **12/1**

1-00 **6** 10 **Winter Cruise (IRE)**[15] 533 4-8-8 50 StephenDonohoe 6 23
(Ian Williams) *hld up: hdwy over 4f out: wknd wl over 2f out* **4/1**[3]

5 **7** 18 **Nil Bleu (USA)**[18] 510 4-9-5 61 LPKeniry 4 8
(Noel T Chance) *led early: hld up in tch: wknd over 3f out* **16/1**

3m 8.01s (2.01) **Going Correction** +0.225s/f (Slow)
WFA 4 from 5yo+ 5lb **7 Ran SP% 117.6**
Speed ratings (Par 101): **103,102,99,98,93 87,77**
CSF £27.03 TOTE £3.60: £1.10, £2.90; EX 19.30.

Owner A Kerr **Bred** D R Tucker **Trained** Ulverston, Cumbria

FOCUS
A slowly-run, modest handicap but the first two came clear and the form looks solid.

723 BOOK EASTER @ PONTIN'S NOW H'CAP 7f 32y(P)
5:00 (5:01) (Class 4) (0-85,82) 3-Y-O **£4,533** (£1,348; £674; £336) **Stalls** High

Form RPR

1-4 **1** **Upper Class (IRE)**[19] 489 3-9-2 77 JoeFanning 6 88+
(M Johnston) *led over 1f: w ldr: rdn over 2f out: led wl over 1f out: hung lft 1f out: r.o wl* **7/2**[2]

1-15 **2** 2 1/2 **Fathsta (IRE)**[19] 489 3-9-5 80 LPKeniry 1 84
(S Kirk) *wnt rt s: t.k.h: sn w ldr: led over 5f out: edgd rt and hdd wl over 1f out: sn rdn: swtchd rt ins fnl f: one pce* **13/2**[3]

3-21 **3** 1/2 **Bussell Up**[28] 354 3-9-4 79 SaleemGolam 5 81
(S C Williams) *t.k.h: a.p: rdn over 2f out: one pce fnl f* **7/2**[2]

216- **4** 2 **Naughty Frida (IRE)**[122] 6525 3-9-5 80 OscarUrbina 2 77
(M Botti) *s.i.s: t.k.h towards rr: hdwy 2f out: rdn and wandered fr over 1f out: one pce* **16/1**

6-11 **5** 1/2 **Little Wing (IRE)**[8] 619 3-9-6 81 6ex TPQueally 3 77+
(J A Osborne) *sltly hmpd s: hdwy over 5f out: rdn and edgd lft over 1f out: btn whn carried rt ins fnl f* **5/6**[1]

624- **6** 1 1/4 **Ocean Transit (IRE)**[134] 6251 3-9-0 82 JackDean(7) 7 74
(W G M Turner) *prom: rdn and wknd over 2f out: hung lft over 1f out* **25/1**

114- **7** 3 1/4 **Ten Pole Tudor**[79] 7095 3-9-0 80 KevinGhunowa(5) 4 64
(R A Harris) *s.i.s: swtchd rt over 1f out: a in rr* **20/1**

-641 **8** 1/2 **Hit The Roof**[12] 572 3-8-12 73 DeanMcKeown 8 55
(D Shaw) *bhd fnl 3f* **33/1**

1m 30.89s (1.29) **Going Correction** +0.225s/f (Slow) **8 Ran SP% 129.8**
Speed ratings (Par 99): **101,98,97,95,94 93,89,89**
CSF £29.50 CT £91.95 TOTE £5.30: £1.80, £2.20, £1.40; EX 19.30 Trifecta £121.60 Pool: £440.44 - 2.57 winning tickets..

Owner Sheikh Hamdan Bin Mohammed Al Maktoum **Bred** Darley **Trained** Middleham Moor, N Yorks

FOCUS
There were some unexposed and improving types in this interesting handicap. Although the third and fifth did not run up to their pre-race form the race should work out.

724 HOTEL & CONFERENCING AT WOLVERHAMPTON APPRENTICE H'CAP 1m 141y(P)
5:30 (5:30) (Class 6) (0-58,57) 4-Y-O+ **£1,774** (£523; £262) **Stalls** Low

Form RPR

6651 **1** **Climate (IRE)**[9] 611 9-8-10 **54** 6ex RichardEvans(4) 10 64
(P D Evans) *hld up in mid-div: swtchd rt and hdwy over 1f out: squeezed through to ld ins fnl f: r.o wl* **10/3**[2]

0630 **2** 1 1/2 **Shosolosa (IRE)**[6] 640 6-8-2 **46** KrishGundowry(4) 1 53
(R C Guest) *hld up and bhd: hdwy wl over 1f out: rdn and hung lft ins fnl f: r.o* **14/1**

1641 **3** 3/4 **Aggbag**[16] 521 4-9-1 **55** DeclanCannon 8 60
(B P J Baugh) *hld up in tch: rdn to ld 1f out: hdd ins fnl f: nt qckn* **6/1**[3]

1-03 **4** 1 1/4 **Sir Bond (IRE)**[13] 550 7-8-11 **55** NSLawes(4) 3 57
(G R Oldroyd) *hld up: lost pl on ins over 6f out: hdwy over 2f out: rdn over 1f out: one pce whn carried lft towards fin* **3/1**[1]

3260 **5** 1 1/2 **Mister Benji**[5] 663 9-8-6 **50** SoniaEaton(4) 4 49
(B P J Baugh) *led: rdn and hdd 1f out: fdd wl ins fnl f* **8/1**

2-16 **6** 2 **General Feeling (IRE)**[13] 550 7-9-3 **57** LanceBetts 2 52
(S T Mason) *s.s: hld up: hdwy over 6f out: c wd st: rdn over 1f out: wknd ins fnl f* **13/2**

0-50 **7** 1/2 **Muncaster Castle (IRE)**[5] 660 4-9-0 **54** MatthewDavies 5 48
(R F Fisher) *chsd ldr: ev ch wl over 1f out: n.m.r ent fnl f: wknd* **16/1**

006- **8** nse **The Gaikwar (IRE)**[147] 5917 9-8-7 **51** (b) DavidProbert(4) 7 45
(R A Harris) *hld up: hdwy and plld hrd over 6f out: rdn over 2f out: wknd ins fnl f* **14/1**

000- **9** 3 **The Bonus King**[162] 5503 8-8-11 **57** NatalieJankiewicz(6) 9 45
(J Jay) *hld up in tch: wknd over 2f out* **20/1**

0-05 **10** 2 3/4 **Grenane (IRE)**[18] 509 5-8-10 **54** AshleyMorgan(4) 11 36
(P D Evans) *s.v.s: a in rr: b.b.v* **25/1**

-006 **11** 2 1/2 **Golden Spectrum (IRE)**[2] 703 9-8-11 **55** (b) CharlesEddery(4) 6 32
(R A Harris) *s.v.s: plld hrd: pushed along over 3f out: a in rr* **12/1**

1m 54.13s (3.63) **Going Correction** +0.225s/f (Slow) **11 Ran SP% 122.3**
Speed ratings (Par 101): **92,90,90,88,87 85,85,85,82,80 77**
CSF £52.02 CT £282.84 TOTE £4.70: £1.50, £5.20, £2.40; EX 87.50 Trifecta £195.20 Part won. Pool: £275.01 - 0.20 winning tickets. Place 6 £48.78, Place 5 £32.77.

Owner J E Abbey **Bred** Mrs A Naughton **Trained** Pandy, Monmouths

FOCUS
A stop-start gallop resulted in a very moderate winning time for this poor handicap. Despite that the form appears solid enough.

Grenane(IRE) Official explanation: trainer said gelding was slowly away and bled from the nose

Golden Spectrum(IRE) Official explanation: jockey said gelding was slowly away

T/Plt: £42.50 to a £1 stake. Pool: £51,564.75. 884.50 winning tickets. T/Qpdt: £9.00 to a £1 stake. Pool: £3,337.50. 272.95 winning tickets. KH

711 KEMPTON (A.W) (R-H)
Thursday, February 28

OFFICIAL GOING: Standard
Wind: Virtually nil

725 KEMPTON.CO.UK CLASSIFIED STKS 5f (P)
6:50 (6:51) (Class 7) 4-Y-O+ **£1,295** (£385; £192; £96) **Stalls** High

Form RPR

0-32 **1** **Ducal Regancy Red**[7] 634 4-8-9 37 KellyHarrison(5) 6 51+
(C J Teague) *trckd ldr: rdn and styd on thrght fnl f to ld cl home: hld on all out* **2/1**[2]

4463 **2** shd **Time Share (IRE)**[4] 696 4-9-0 41 TGMcLaughlin 2 51
(M Wigham) *hld up in rr but in tch: hdwy over 1f out: str run ins fnl f: fin wl: jst failed* **4/1**[3]

-422 **3** nk **Maktavish**[14] 562 9-9-0 44 (b) PhillipMakin 7 50
(R Brotherton) *led: rdn over 1f out: kpt on ins fnl f tl ct cl home* **7/4**[1]

3324 **4** 1 1/4 **Lady Hopeful (IRE)**[14] 562 6-9-0 43 (b) LPKeniry 4 45+
(Peter Grayson) *s.i.s: sn rcvrd and in tch: hdwy on ins over 1f out: styng on whn n.m.r and eased wl ins fnl f* **14/1**

5-00 **5** 1 **Montzando**[15] 535 5-9-0 43 (v) AlanMunro 5 41
(B R Millman) *chsd ldrs: wd into st: sn rdn: kpt on ins fnl f but nver gng pce to be competitive* **7/1**

60.83 secs (0.33) **Going Correction** -0.05s/f (Stan) **5 Ran SP% 118.0**
Speed ratings (Par 97): **95,94,94,92,90**
CSF £9.70 TOTE £2.60: £1.30, £2.60; EX 15.50.

Owner Regancy Bloodstock **Bred** Paul Wyatt Ranby Hall **Trained** Station Town, Co Durham
■ Stewards' Enquiry : T G McLaughlin one-day ban: used whip with excessive frequency (Mar 11)

FOCUS
A dire event and not a race to be with. The first three came home in a blanket finish.

Lady Hopeful(IRE) Official explanation: jockey said mare was denied a clear run

726 JUMP RACING HERE ON SATURDAY CLAIMING STKS 5f (P)
7:20 (7:21) (Class 5) 4-Y-O+ **£2,331** (£693; £346; £173) **Stalls** High

Form RPR

-220 **1** **Harry Up**[13] 580 7-9-5 77 (p) NCallan 5 83+
(K A Ryan) *mde all: pushed clr appr fnl f: unchal* **6/4**[1]

-022 **2** 2 1/4 **Spoof Master (IRE)**[14] 554 4-8-12 73 (p) JimCrowley 1 68
(S A Callaghan) *chsd wnr thrght: rdn 2f out and sn no imp* **6/4**[1]

-100 **3** 1 3/4 **Baileys Outshine**[13] 580 4-8-6 70 JoeFanning 6 56
(J G Given) *chsd ldrs in 3rd thrght: rdn and one pce fnl 2f* **11/2**[2]

6342 **4** 1/2 **Now You See Me**[8] 627 4-8-6 47 AlanMunro 3 54
(K McAuliffe) *in rr: rdn over 2f out: sme prog fnl f but nvr in contention* **16/1**[3]

150 **5** 2 **Earl Compton (IRE)**[4] 690 4-9-1 55 (v) MickyFenton 4 56
(Stef Liddiard) *s.i.s: sn in tch in 5th: sme hdwy over 2f out: nvr in contention and sn wknd* **25/1**

-234 **6** 2 **Macademy Royal (USA)**[1] 719 5-8-3 57 (t) KellyHarrison(5) 2 41
(M Wigham) *racd in 4th: rdn and no prog over 2f out: wknd over 1f out* **20/1**

59.72 secs (-0.78) **Going Correction** -0.05s/f (Stan) **6 Ran SP% 109.9**
Speed ratings (Par 103): **104,100,97,96,93 90**
CSF £3.59 TOTE £1.90: £1.10, £2.00; EX 4.60.Spoof Master was claimed by C R Dore for £9,000.

Owner The Fishermen **Bred** J E Rose **Trained** Hambleton, N Yorks

FOCUS
A modest little claiming sprint, run at a solid pace. The form is assessed through the fourth.

727 KEMPTON FOR WEDDINGS MAIDEN STKS 1m 2f (P)
7:50 (7:52) (Class 5) 3-Y-O+ **£2,590** (£770; £385; £192) **Stalls** High

Form RPR

526- **1** **Greylami (IRE)**[139] 6138 3-8-6 81 JimCrowley 6 74+
(T G Mills) *in tch: hdwy 3f out: str run to ld appr fnl f: sn clr: easily* **7/4**[2]

3-05 **2** 5 **Silver Waters**[13] 570 3-8-6 67 AlanMunro 11 65
(D R C Elsworth) *chsd ldrs: rdn over 2f out: styd on to chse wnr ins fnl f but no ch* **33/1**

3 nk **Deer Daylami (IRE)** 3-8-6 0 EdwardCreighton 1 64+
(M R Channon) *s.i.s: in rr: pushed along 5f out: rdn over 2f out: styd on wl fnl f to take 3rd nr fin* **4/1**[3]

0/ **4** 3/4 **Songmaster (USA)**[621] 2655 5-10-0 0 DaneO'Neill 3 68+
(A King) *in rr: rdn along 1/2-way: styd on fr over 1f out and styd on ins fnl f: gng on cl home* **50/1**

06- **5** nse **Scripted (USA)**[224] 3685 4-9-13 0 (t) GeorgeBaker 2 68
(C F Wall) *led tl hdd appr fnl f: sn no ch w wnr: wknd cl home* **20/1**

23-5 **6** 2 3/4 **Hamalka (IRE)**[33] 311 3-8-1 66 ChrisCatlin 5 53
(B W Hills) *in rr: pushed along 1/2-way: rdn and hdwy over 1f out: fin wl but nvr in contention* **20/1**

4 **7** 3 **Eastern Hills**[15] 543 3-8-6 0 JoeFanning 4 53
(M Johnston) *racd in 2nd: rdn over 2f out and nt pce to rch ldr: wknd qckly fnl f* **11/8**[1]

00- **8** 3 1/2 **Sir Jake**[206] 4235 4-9-13 0 TGMcLaughlin 9 51
(T T Clement) *in tch: dropped towards rr 1/2-way: sme prog fnl f* **100/1**

50- **9** 1 **Whatalotofbuts**[244] 3043 3-8-6 0 HayleyTurner 10 45
(B De Haan) *t.k.h: in tch: rdn 3f out: nvr in contention after* **66/1**

10 5 **Hold Fire** 4-9-5 0 JerryO'Dwyer(3) 8 36
(A W Carroll) *s.i.s: a wl bhd* **100/1**

0-2 **11** 5 **National Day (IRE)**[15] 545 4-9-8 0 SebSanders 7 27
(D R C Elsworth) *chsd ldrs: t.k.h: rdn 3f out: sddle slipped and wknd ins fnl 2f: virtually p.u cl home* **10/1**

2m 7.31s (-0.69) **Going Correction** -0.05s/f (Stan)
WFA 3 from 4yo 22lb 4 from 5yo 1lb **11 Ran SP% 125.5**
Speed ratings (Par 103): **100,96,95,95,95 92,90,87,86,82 78**
CSF £68.37 TOTE £3.30: £1.10, £6.40, £1.60; EX 142.00.

Owner J Daniels **Bred** Barouche Stud Ireland Ltd **Trained** Headley, Surrey

FOCUS
A modest maiden. The winner is value for further, but the overall form looks a little suspect.

National Day(IRE) Official explanation: jockey said filly lost its action and hung badly right

728 BURGUNDY LONG AND HAPPY RETIREMENT H'CAP 1m 2f (P)
8:20 (8:21) (Class 6) (0-65,67) 4-Y-O+ **£2,047** (£604; £302) **Stalls** High

Form RPR

1221 **1** **Rebellious Spirit**[5] 685 5-9-5 **67** 6ex KirstyMilczarek(3) 4 77
(S Curran) *chsd ldrs: c wd into st and str run fr over 1f out: fin wl to ld fnl 30yds: all out* **6/1**[3]

1126 **2** ½ **Megalala (IRE)**[15] 541 7-8-10 **55** .... NeilChalmers 2 64
(J J Bridger) *chsd ldr: challenged fr 3f out tl slt advantage jst ins fnl 2f: hdd ins fnl f: rallied to chal fnl 50yds: no ex cl home* **33/1**

40-5 **3** ¾ **Burgundy**[47] 139 11-9-4 **63** .... (b) IanMongan 10 71
(R A Teal) *chsd ldrs: rdn to ld ins fnl f: hdd and no ex fnl 30yds* **20/1**

2-12 **4** 1 ¾ **Wind Flow**[38] 248 4-9-3 **63** .... (b) AdrianMcCarthy 11 67
(C A Dwyer) *led: rdn and hdd jst ins fnl 2f: styd pressing ldrs tl wknd ins fnl f* **7/2**[1]

2442 **5** ½ **My Mentor (IRE)**[6] 659 4-9-5 **65** .... (b) SebSanders 8 68
(Sir Mark Prescott) *chsd ldrs: rdn over 2f out: one pce fnl f* **7/2**[1]

6-32 **6** 1 **Pab Special (IRE)**[15] 542 5-9-5 **64** .... DaneO'Neill 13 65
(B R Johnson) *s.i.s: in rr: wd into st and hdwy over 1f out: kpt on wl cl home but nvr a danger* **7/1**

1302 **7** ¾ **Earl Kraul (IRE)**[17] 526 5-9-0 **59** .... FergusSweeney 14 59
(G L Moore) *mid-div: rdn and hdwy over 2f out: no imp on ldrs fnl f* **5/1**[2]

2634 **8** nk **Jomus**[10] 611 7-8-7 **52** ow2 .... RobertHavlin 12 51
(L Montague Hall) *in rr: sme prog fr over 1f out: nvr in contention* **12/1**

0-53 **9** nk **Subadar**[29] 361 4-9-5 **65** .... OscarUrbina 6 63
(M Botti) *in tch: hdwy 4f out: nvr gng pce to rch ldrs: wknd ins fnl 2f* **25/1**

0-00 **10** 3 ½ **Julian Joachim (USA)**[12] 587 4-8-5 **54** ow1 .... (t) TolleyDean(3) 5 45
(D Shaw) *a towards rr* **33/1**

42-5 **11** 2 ½ **Shandelight (IRE)**[11] 602 4-8-2 **51** .... AndrewMullen(3) 1 37
(Mrs A Duffield) *s.i.s: a towards rr* **33/1**

2-10 **12** ¾ **Takaamul**[36] 267 5-8-9 **54** .... JamesDoyle 7 39
(K A Morgan) *towards rr most of way* **10/1**

2m 7.21s (-0.79) **Going Correction** -0.05s/f (Stan)
WFA 4 from 5yo+ 1lb **12** Ran SP% **122.1**
Speed ratings (Par 101): **101,100,100,98,98 97,96,96,96,93 91,90**
CSF £187.49 CT £3186.59 TOTE £5.70: £2.50, £5.00, £5.40; EX 173.60.
Owner Colin Hill **Bred** Car Colston Hall Stud **Trained** Hatford, Oxon

FOCUS
A moderate handicap, run at a fair pace. The form makes sense with the third and fourth suggesting it is sound.
Megalala(IRE) Official explanation: jockey said gelding hung left

729 TFM SOLUTIONS H'CAP 6f (P)
8:50 (8:51) (Class 5) (0-75,75) 4-Y-0+ **£2,590** (£770; £385; £192) **Stalls** High

Form RPR

1-15 **1** **Diriculous**[42] 191 4-8-8 **65** .... JimCrowley 9 78+
(T G Mills) *chsd ldrs: led ins fnl 2f: drvn and hld on wl fnl f* **15/8**[1]

0-34 **2** ¾ **Red Rudy**[15] 539 6-8-6 **66** .... KirstyMilczarek(3) 1 74
(A W Carroll) *in rr: rapid hdwy on outside over 1f out: fin strly ins fnl f but nt rch wnr* **14/1**

1435 **3** 1 ¼ **Obe Royal**[10] 609 4-8-6 **70** .... (b) RichardEvans(7) 2 74+
(P D Evans) *in rr: hdwy whn hmpd 1f out: styd on ins fnl f but nt rch ldrs* **20/1**

5355 **4** nk **Hucking Hill (IRE)**[26] 404 4-8-8 **65** .... (b) HayleyTurner 11 68+
(J R Best) *in rr: rdn and hdwy whn hmpd 1f out: kpt on again ins fnl f* **12/1**

150- **5** 2 **Bobby Rose**[121] 6575 5-9-0 **71** .... RobertHavlin 10 68
(D K Ivory) *chsd ldrs: rdn 2f out: outpcd fnl f* **20/1**

4123 **6** ¾ **Grimes Faith**[11] 599 5-9-2 **73** .... (b) NCallan 6 68
(K A Ryan) *chsd ldrs: rdn over 2f out: r.o ins fnl f but nvr gng pce to be competitive* **16/1**

-546 **7** shd **Bertie Southstreet**[7] 636 5-9-0 **71** .... SebSanders 12 66
(J R Best) *slt ld: jnd after 2f: rdn and hdd ins fnl 2f: wknd ins fnl f* **10/1**

-455 **8** shd **Resplendent Alpha**[33] 313 4-9-4 **75** .... (b[1]) JimmyQuinn 5 78+
(P Howling) *s.i.s: swtchd to ins rail: effrt and nt clr run fr over 1f out: fin on bit* **8/1**

0524 **9** 1 ¼ **Monashee Prince (IRE)**[8] 628 6-8-6 **63** .... (v) AlanMunro 4 54
(J R Best) *in rr: hdwy and hung rt 1f out: nvr in contention* **25/1**

4-22 **10** ¾ **Mr Cellophane**[10] 609 5-8-11 **68** .... FergalLynch 7 57
(J R Jenkins) *w ldr after 2f and upsides tl rdn 2f out: wknd over 1f out* **9/2**[2]

-254 **11** 3 ¾ **Divertimenti (IRE)**[19] 503 4-9-1 **72** .... RobertWinston 8 49
(C R Dore) *chsd ldrs: rdn and wknd 2f out* **13/2**[3]

00-2 **12** 12 **Don't Tell Sue**[24] 427 5-8-10 **67** .... FergusSweeney 3 8
(D W P Arbuthnot) *chsd ldrs over 3f* **10/1**

1m 12.03s (-1.07) **Going Correction** -0.05s/f (Stan) **12** Ran SP% **129.2**
Speed ratings (Par 103): **105,104,102,101,99 98,98,98,96,95 90,74**
CSF £34.46 CT £454.64 TOTE £3.00: £1.80, £5.60, £4.90; EX 48.40.
Owner Sherwoods Transport Ltd **Bred** Sherwoods Transport Ltd **Trained** Headley, Surrey
■ Stewards' Enquiry : Alan Munro three-day ban: careless riding (Mar 11-13)

FOCUS
A modest sprint, run at a strong early pace and those in the frame behind the winner set a sound standard.
Resplendent Alpha Official explanation: jockey said gelding was denied a clear run

730 GOFFS BREEZE UP SALE HERE MARCH 7TH H'CAP 1m (P)
9:20 (9:20) (Class 5) (0-70,70) 4-Y-0+ **£2,590** (£770; £385; £192) **Stalls** High

Form RPR

231 **1** **King's Ransom**[7] 646 5-8-11 **68** 6ex .... JamieJones(5) 3 78
(S Gollings) *mde all: hrd drvn and hld on gamely thrght fnl f* **8/1**

5-55 **2** ¾ **Carlitos Spirit (IRE)**[22] 446 4-8-11 **63** .... AlanMunro 7 71
(B R Millman) *chsd ldrs: wnt 2nd 2f out: rdn and a hld by wnr thrght fnl f* **11/2**

4211 **3** 1 **Under Fire (IRE)**[15] 537 5-8-9 **64** .... JerryO'Dwyer(3) 6 70
(A W Carroll) *chsd ldrs: rdn and kpt on fr over 1f out but nvr gng pce of ldng duo* **7/1**

-102 **4** 1 ¼ **Emma Jean Lad (IRE)**[26] 407 4-9-1 **67** .... LPKeniry 10 70
(J S Moore) *hld up towards rr: hdwy on ins 2f out: sn rdn outpcd fnl f* **5/1**[3]

1431 **5** nk **Justcallmehandsome**[6] 660 5-6-7 **66** .... (v) BillyCray(7) 8 69
(D J S Ffrench Davis) *in rr: hdwy to chse ldrs 4f out: wd into st and outpcd: rallied and r.o again ins fnl f but no ch w ldrs* **7/2**[1]

-241 **6** ¾ **Waterline Twenty (IRE)**[34] 302 5-9-3 **69** .... StephenDonohoe 4 70
(P D Evans) *chsd ldrs: wnt 2nd over 3f out: sn rdn: no imp 2f out: wknd fnl f* **10/1**

-516 **7** ½ **Satyricon**[22] 452 4-9-4 **70** .... URispoli 5 70
(M Botti) *mid-div: sme hdwy over 2f out: sn btn* **13/2**

2123 **8** 4 ½ **Wrighty Almighty (IRE)**[15] 548 6-9-3 **69** .... JimCrowley 2 58
(P R Chamings) *plld hrd in rr: nvr bttr than mid-div* **9/2**[2]

0 **9** 1 **Tyrana (GER)**[19] 506 5-9-4 **70** .... VinceSlattery 9 57
(G F Bridgwater) *a in rr* **66/1**

00-5 **10** 3 **Elusive Dreams (USA)**[14] 555 4-8-11 **66** .... TolleyDean(3) 1 46
(D Shaw) *s.i.s: a bhd* **33/1**

1m 38.8s (-1.00) **Going Correction** -0.05s/f (Stan) **10** Ran SP% **122.9**
Speed ratings (Par 103): **103,102,101,100,99 98,98,93,92,89**
CSF £54.54 CT £333.47 TOTE £7.30: £2.40, £1.90, £2.10; EX 96.80 Place 6 £318.19, Place 5 £161.91.
Owner Mrs D Dukes **Bred** Darley **Trained** Scamblesby, Lincs

FOCUS
A modest handicap, run at a sound pace. The form looks fair and solid enough.
T/Plt: £308.90 to a £1 stake. Pool: £96,388.60. 227.75 winning tickets. T/Qpdt: £248.10 to a £1 stake. Pool: £7,746.60. 23.10 winning tickets. ST

704 LINGFIELD (L-H)
Thursday, February 28

OFFICIAL GOING: Standard
Wind: Virtually nil Weather: cloudy

731 MEMORABLE FAMILY TIMES @ PONTIN'S APPRENTICE H'CAP 1m (P)
2:10 (2:10) (Class 5) (0-75,73) 4-Y-0+ **£2,590** (£770; £385; £192) **Stalls** High

Form RPR

616- **1** **Mia's Boy**[194] 4608 4-9-5 73 .... JPHamblett 2 80+
(C A Dwyer) *stdd s: hld up in last pair: rdn and hdwy on outer bnd 2f out: r.o wl to ld last 100yds: sn in command: readily* **2/1**[1]

1045 **2** 2 ½ **Seneschal**[15] 536 7-8-9 68 .... PNolan(5) 5 69
(A B Haynes) *chsd ldr: hdwy to chal 2f out: rdn over 1f out: kpt on same pce: wnt 2nd nr fin* **3/1**[2]

-044 **3** hd **Best One**[10] 609 4-8-9 68 .... DebraEngland(5) 6 69
(C E Brittain) *led: pressed and pushed along wl over 1f out: hdd last 100yds: sn outpcd by wnr: lost 2nd nr fin* **2/1**[1]

0-00 **4** 5 **Trivia (IRE)**[38] 246 4-9-2 70 .... SophieDoyle 7 59
(Ms J S Doyle) *t.k.h: hld up bhd ldng pair: rdn and outpcd jst over 2f out: n.d after* **16/1**

000- **5** nk **Paraguay (USA)**[164] 5476 5-8-5 59 oh1 .... SCreighton 4 47
(Miss V Haigh) *stdd after s: hld up in last pair: rdn and effrt 2f out: sn outpcd and wl btn* **8/1**[3]

1m 37.5s (-0.70) **Going Correction** +0.025s/f (Slow) **5** Ran SP% **108.7**
Speed ratings (Par 103): **104,101,101,96,96**
CSF £8.05 TOTE £2.60: £1.10, £2.20; EX 8.90.
Owner Iraj Parvizi **Bred** Sir Eric Parker **Trained** Burrough Green, Cambs

FOCUS
A moderate race weakened further by the two non-runners, but despite what appeared to be a modest early pace the final time was not at all bad. Just fair form overall, but no crabbing the winner, who might be able to step up on this.

732 BETDAQ.CO.UK CLAIMING STKS 7f (P)
2:40 (2:41) (Class 6) 3-Y-0 **£1,774** (£523; £262) **Stalls** Low

Form RPR

2-34 **1** **Dhhamaan (IRE)**[28] 376 3-9-8 80 .... (v) HayleyTurner 5 78
(C E Brittain) *prom: chsd ldr 5f out: led 4f out: mde rest: rdn wl over 1f out: hld on wl towards fin* **11/10**[1]

5131 **2** nk **Wee Buns**[1] 714 3-8-10 65 .... SteveDrowne 4 65
(P G Murphy) *t.k.h: hld up trcking ldrs: hdwy to chse wnr wl over 2f out: rdn 2f out: str chal fnl f: unable qck and hld towards fin* **15/8**[2]

-522 **3** 3 ¼ **Llab Nala**[13] 572 3-8-5 57 .... MatthewDavies(7) 3 59
(M R Channon) *hld up in last: rdn and effrt jst over 2f out: chsd ldng pair over 1f out: no imp fnl f* **7/1**[3]

-540 **4** 8 **Mileaminutemurphy**[8] 629 3-8-12 64 .... PatrickHills(5) 2 43
(R Hannon) *w ldr tl bmpd 5f out: rdn over 2f out: wknd over 1f out* **20/1**

00- **5** 14 **Racie Gracie**[132] 6295 3-8-2 0 .... AdrianMcCarthy 1 —
(C A Dwyer) *led tl 4f out: chsd wnr tl rdn and wknd wl over 2f out: sn wl bhd: t.o* **12/1**

1m 25.67s (0.87) **Going Correction** +0.025s/f (Slow) **5** Ran SP% **107.4**
Speed ratings (Par 95): **96,95,91,82,66**
CSF £3.17 TOTE £2.10: £1.30, £1.50; EX 3.80.
Owner C E Brittain **Bred** D Veitch And Musagd Abo Salim **Trained** Newmarket, Suffolk

FOCUS
An uncompetitive claimer with only two seriously fancied in the market, and the pace was ordinary to boot. The race only concerned the two market leaders from some way out, and the winner has been rated to form, with the second and third to their recent level.

733 RACE THE FAMILY TO PONTIN'S FILLIES' H'CAP 7f (P)
3:10 (3:10) (Class 4) (0-85,85) 4-Y-0+ **£4,100** (£1,227; £613; £306; £152) **Stalls** Low

Form RPR

50-0 **1** **Secret Night**[32] 329 5-8-12 **79** .... AlanMunro 4 85
(J A R Toller) *hld up in tch: hdwy to trck ldrs 2f out: pushed along to ld ins fnl f: rdn out* **7/2**[2]

42-6 **2** ¾ **Lawyers Choice**[25] 417 4-8-11 **78** .... NCallan 5 82
(Pat Eddery) *chsd ldr: rdn to chal 2f out: ev ch tl nt pce of wnr ins fnl f: wnt 2nd nr fin* **3/1**[1]

410- **3** ½ **Crystal Gazer (FR)**[145] 6006 4-8-13 **85** .... HaddenFrost(5) 2 88
(R Hannon) *led: hrd pressed 2f out: rdn wl over 1f out: hdd ins fnl f: one pce and lost 2nd nr fin* **8/1**[3]

2-06 **4** 1 **Carcinetto (IRE)**[25] 418 6-9-4 **85** .... StephenDonohoe 1 85
(P D Evans) *trckd ldrs: rdn 2f out: outpcd wl over 1f out: kpt on ins fnl f: nt pce to trble ldrs* **7/2**[2]

10-0 **5** 1 ¼ **Shustraya**[40] 226 4-9-2 **83** .... SebSanders 6 80
(P J Makin) *stdd s: t.k.h: hld up in tch: hdwy 3f out: chsd ldrs and rdn 2f out: outpcd wl over 1f out: kpt on same pce after* **3/1**[1]

3-00 **6** 1 **Tagula Sunrise (IRE)**[35] 280 6-8-8 **75** .... PaulHanagan 3 69
(R A Fahey) *s.i.s: hld up in last: rdn and no hdwy wl over 2f out: kpt on ins fnl f: nvr trbld ldrs* **14/1**

1m 24.77s (-0.03) **Going Correction** +0.025s/f (Slow) **6** Ran SP% **112.2**
Speed ratings (Par 102): **101,100,99,98,97 95**
CSF £14.35 TOTE £5.20: £2.80, £1.40; EX 15.30.
Owner Hants and Herts **Bred** Worksop Manor Stud **Trained** Newmarket, Suffolk

FOCUS
An ordinary fillies' handicap, and the early pace was even slower than the preceding claimer, though with the tempo increasing in the second half of the contest the final time was almost a second quicker. Not form to get too enthusiastic about.

734 BETDAQPOKER.CO.UK MAIDEN STKS — 5f (P)
3:40 (3:40) (Class 5) 3-Y-0+ £2,331 (£693; £346; £173) Stalls High

Form — RPR

0 **1** **Stoneacre Sarah**[15] 543 3-8-8 0 ... LiamJones 1 64+
(Peter Grayson) *s.i.s: sn trcking ldrs: edgd out 2f out: edgd rt over 1f out: rdn to ld ins fnl f: r.o strly: readily* **7/2**[2]

2 **2** 3 ½ **Stoneacre Chris (USA)**[26] 412 3-8-8 0 ... LPKeniry 7 51
(Peter Grayson) *led: rdn 2f out: hdd ins fnl f: nt pce of wnr but kpt on* **8/1**

3 ½ **Rightcar Dominic** 3-8-13 0 ... AdamKirby 3 55+
(Peter Grayson) *bhd: pushed along and outpcd over 2f out: r.o wl fnl f: wnt 3rd wl ins fnl f: nvr nr wnr* **11/4**[1]

33 **4** 1 ¼ **Allium (IRE)**[7] 634 3-8-8 0 ... MichaelHills 9 45
(B W Hills) *towards rr: hdwy on outer over 3f out: rdn 2f out: kpt on one pce fnl f* **4/1**[3]

0 **5** ¾ **Gelert (IRE)**[26] 412 3-8-13 0 ... DaneO'Neill 2 47+
(Peter Grayson) *t.k.h: hld up in tch tl outpcd and rdn over 2f out: swtchd rt 1f out: styd on but nvr able to chal* **50/1**

0-5 **6** hd **Capriccioso**[26] 412 3-8-8 0 ... FergusSweeney 5 42
(G L Moore) *pressed ldr: ev ch and rdn 2f out tl ins fnl f: wknd last 100yds* **4/1**[3]

0-0 **7** nk **Stoneacre Ma**[26] 412 3-8-8 0 ... HayleyTurner 8 41
(Peter Grayson) *chsd ldrs: rdn 2f out: kpt on same pce fr over 1f out* **33/1**

8 ¾ **Stoneacre Paddy (IRE)** 3-8-6 0 ... RyanHill(7) 6 43+
(Peter Grayson) *in tch: pushed along and hung lft over 1f out: no hdwy fr over 1f out* **14/1**

9 22 **Sevenovus (IRE)** 3-8-13 0 ... AdrianMcCarthy 10 —
(Peter Grayson) *sn outpcd in detached last: t.o last 2f* **25/1**

60.40 secs (1.60) **Going Correction** +0.025s/f (Slow) 9 Ran SP% **115.4**
Speed ratings (Par 103): **88,82,81,79,78 78,77,76,41**
CSF £30.83 TOTE £6.00: £1.60, £2.10, £1.10; EX 47.40 Trifecta £410.70 Part won. Pool £578.56 - 0.68 winning units..
Owner R Teatum And Mrs S Grayson **Bred** Gainsborough Stud Management Ltd **Trained** Formby, Lancs

FOCUS
Almost a private race with Peter Grayson, responsible for seven of the nine runners, filling the first three places. The winning time was moderate, and though the winner did it nicely the future does not look that bright for the beaten horses.
Rightcar Dominic Official explanation: jockey said due to a neck injury he was unable to ride out fully to the line
Gelert(IRE) Official explanation: jockey said colt hung left

735 ENJOY A CRACKING EASTER @ PONTIN'S H'CAP — 1m 4f (P)
4:10 (4:10) (Class 4) (0-85,88) 4-Y-0+ £4,100 (£1,227; £613; £306; £152) Stalls Low

Form — RPR

-131 **1** **Maslak (IRE)**[12] 591 4-9-5 84 ... ChrisCatlin 2 94+
(P W Hiatt) *t.k.h: chsd ldng pair: hdwy to ld 3f out: rdn clr 2f out: styd on wl and in command after* **2/1**[1]

-634 **2** 1 ¾ **Prince Charlemagne (IRE)**[19] 504 5-8-9 71 ... (p) JamesDoyle 4 75
(K R Burke) *hld up in last pair: hdwy 3f out: chsd wnr u.p over 2f out: kpt on but nvr pce to trble wnr* **10/1**[3]

104- **3** 1 ½ **La Estrella (USA)**[45] 7236 5-9-6 82 ... PatDobbs 5 84
(D E Cantillon) *led tl hdd and rdn 3f out: outpcd by ldng pair over 1f out: kpt on same pce* **3/1**[2]

43-4 **4** 3 **Generous Lad (IRE)**[50] 97 5-8-11 73 ... (p) DaneO'Neill 1 70
(A B Haynes) *in tch: rdn and outpcd over 2f out: kpt on same pce fr over 1f out* **12/1**

-331 **5** ½ **Tilapia (IRE)**[8] 626 4-9-9 88 6ex ... SebSanders 7 85
(Sir Mark Prescott) *stdd s: hld up in rr: rdn and effrt on outer over 2f out: drvn 2f out: sn hanging lft and no hdwy: nvr nr ldrs* **3/1**[2]

00-6 **6** 3 **Bazart**[12] 591 6-9-4 80 ... FergusSweeney 6 72
(K R Burke) *w ldr tl 3f out: wknd u.p 2f out* **33/1**

043- **7** 14 **Art Modern (IRE)**[138] 6175 6-9-2 78 ... GeorgeBaker 8 49
(G L Moore) *hld up in tch on outer: rdn and outpcd wl over 2f out: eased ins fnl f: t.o* **12/1**

2m 30.69s (-2.31) **Going Correction** +0.025s/f (Slow)
WFA 4 from 5yo+ 3lb 7 Ran SP% **110.8**
Speed ratings (Par 105): **108,106,105,103,103 101,92**
CSF £21.48 CT £55.03 TOTE £3.00: £1.80, £4.80; EX 20.60 Trifecta £241.60 Pool £422.04 - 1.24 winning units..
Owner Clive Roberts **Bred** Shadwell Estate Company Limited **Trained** Hook Norton, Oxon

FOCUS
A nice handicap, and the pace set by La Estrella was a decent one, which made this a proper test over the trip. The winner goes from strength to strength and always in charge. He could still be competitive when reassessed.
Bazart Official explanation: jockey said gelding hung right
Art Modern(IRE) Official explanation: jockey said gelding had no more to give

736 BACK OR LAY AT BETDAQ FILLIES' H'CAP — 1m 2f (P)
4:40 (4:40) (Class 5) (0-70,69) 4-Y-0+ £2,331 (£693; £346; £173) Stalls Low

Form — RPR

600 **1** **Meditation**[7] 646 6-8-13 62 ... NCallan 6 69
(I A Wood) *mde all: rdn and qcknd wl over 2f out: styd on wl* **14/1**

24/- **2** ½ **Tinnarinka**[506] 5891 4-9-4 68 ... PatDobbs 3 74+
(R Hannon) *hld up in tch: rdn and effrt on inner wl over 1f out: styd on to chse wnr wl ins fnl f: nvr quite getting to wnr* **9/4**[1]

505- **3** ¾ **Keidas (FR)**[131] 6343 4-9-4 68 ... AlanMunro 1 73
(C F Wall) *chsd ldr tl 5f out and again wl over 2f out: sn rdn: kpt on same pce fnl f: edgd rt towards fin* **3/1**[2]

2213 **4** ¾ **Mon Petite Amour**[13] 579 5-8-11 60 ... FergusSweeney 8 63
(D W P Arbuthnot) *in tch: hdwy 3f out: rdn and chsd ldrs 2f out: unable qck u.p ins fnl f* **4/1**[3]

4 **5** 1 ½ **Bassinet (USA)**[27] 390 4-9-5 69 ... GeorgeBaker 2 69
(J A R Toller) *stdd s: t.k.h: hld up in tch in rr: rdn and effrt over 2f out: no real hdwy tl styd on ins fnl f: nvr nr to chal* **12/1**

2-23 **6** 1 ½ **Aphrodisia**[15] 545 4-8-10 60 ... JimCrowley 5 57
(S C Williams) *stdd s: t.k.h: hld up in tch in rr: nt clr run and swtchd rt jst over 2f out: c wd bnd 2f out: sn rdn and no imp* **9/2**

1-00 **7** ½ **Little Miss Tara (IRE)**[29] 352 4-8-5 55 ... DavidKinsella 4 52
(A B Haynes) *chsd ldrs tl wnt 2nd 5f tl wl over 2f out: wknd u.p jst over 2f out* **25/1**

4234 **8** ½ **Casablanca Minx (IRE)**[5] 685 5-8-10 59 ... (v) StephenDonohoe 7 55
(P D Evans) *s.i.s: hld up in last: rdn and no hdwy over 2f out: kpt on same pce* **16/1**

2m 6.87s (0.27) **Going Correction** +0.025s/f (Slow)
WFA 4 from 5yo+ 1lb 8 Ran SP% **118.0**
Speed ratings (Par 100): **99,98,98,97,96 95,94,94**
CSF £47.38 CT £125.59 TOTE £13.90: £3.20, £1.60, £1.50; EX 70.10 Trifecta £222.10 Pool £2,331.90 - 44.20 winning units..
Owner Paddy Barrett **Bred** P E Barrett **Trained** Upper Lambourn, Berks

FOCUS
A modest fillies' handicap in which they crawled for most of the contest, very much playing into the hands of the well-ridden winner. Not many ever got into it and the standard is pretty ordinary.
Meditation Official explanation: trainer said, regarding apparent improvement in form, that the mare likes to dominate unchallenged as she was able to do today

737 CALL 0844 815 3647 FOR PONTIN'S DEALS H'CAP — 1m (P)
5:10 (5:10) (Class 5) (0-75,75) 3-Y-O £2,590 (£770; £385; £192) Stalls High

Form — RPR

60-1 **1** **Gallic Charm (IRE)**[25] 416 3-9-2 73 ... SebSanders 6 81+
(D R C Elsworth) *t.k.h: stdd after s and hld up in last: hdwy on outer over 2f out: rdn wl over 1f out: str run fnl f to ld towards fin* **13/2**

33-3 **2** ½ **Tenjack King**[27] 396 3-8-13 70 ... TPQueally 2 77
(J A Osborne) *w ldrs: wnt 2nd over 4f out: upsides ldr over 2f out: drvn to ld narrowly over 1f out: hdd and no ex nr fin* **15/8**[1]

3-35 **3** ½ **Chinese Temple (IRE)**[28] 376 3-9-1 75 ... JerryO'Dwyer(3) 3 81
(M G Quinlan) *chsd ldrs tl led after 1f: hrd pressed over 2f out: rdn wl over 1f out: hdd over 1f out: ev ch tl no ex towards fin* **9/2**[3]

-222 **4** 1 ¾ **Salt Of The Earth (IRE)**[29] 354 3-9-3 74 ... JimCrowley 4 76
(T G Mills) *t.k.h: hld up in tch: rdn over 2f out: kpt on same pce u.p fnl f* **2/1**[2]

-211 **5** ½ **What's For Tea**[12] 589 3-8-8 65 ... RichardKingscote 1 66
(P Butler) *led for 1f: chsd ldr tl over 4f out: styd handy: rdn over 2f out: wknd 1f out* **8/1**

41 **6** 5 **Snow Bounty**[19] 501 3-8-5 62 ... SimonWhitworth 5 51
(J S Moore) *stdd after s: t.k.h: hld up in rr: rdn jst over 2f out: wknd wl over 1f out* **20/1**

1m 37.21s (-0.99) **Going Correction** +0.025s/f (Slow) 6 Ran SP% **115.5**
Speed ratings (Par 97): **105,104,104,102,101 96**
CSF £19.91 TOTE £7.00: £2.20, £1.70; EX 18.00 Place 6 £11.49, Place 5 £6.63..
Owner The Bramfield Racing Syndicate **Bred** Limestone And Tara Studs **Trained** Newmarket, Suffolk

FOCUS
Not a bad little handicap and the winning time was 0.29 seconds faster than the earlier older-horse handicap over the same trip. It was noticeable that the principals all came out towards the centre of the track on reaching the home straight.
T/Plt: £54.60 to a £1 stake. Pool: £52,749.15. 705.10 winning tickets. T/Qpdt: £39.00 to a £1 stake. Pool: £2,331.90. 44.20 winning tickets. SP

666 NAD AL SHEBA (L-H)
Thursday, February 28

OFFICIAL GOING: Turf course - good: dirt course - fast

738a AL QUOZ SPRINT (DIV I) (SPONSORED BY LAND ROVER) (LISTED RACE) (TURF) — 6f (T)
3:15 (3:17) 3-Y-0+

£60,301 (£20,100; £10,050; £5,025; £3,015; £2,010)

RPR

1 **Mutamarres**[6] 666 5-9-0 105 ... RHills 2 113
(Doug Watson, UAE) *sn led: clr 2 1/2f out: r.o wl: comf* **4/1**[3]

2 2 ¾ **Big Timer (USA)**[7] 651 4-9-0 101 ... TomEaves 1 104
(I Semple) *trckd ldr: rdn 2 1/2f out: r.o wl but no ch w wnr* **16/1**

3 ¼ **Grand Vista**[6] 666 4-9-0 102 ... (t) RyanMoore 7 103
(H J Brown, South Africa) *slowly away: settled in rr: rdn 2 1/2f out: r.o wl fnl f: nrst fin* **9/1**

4 ¼ **Prince Tamino**[7] 649 5-9-0 107 ... RoystonFfrench 4 102
(A Al Raihe, UAE) *mid-div: gng wl 2 1/2f out: rdn 2f out: one pce* **7/2**[2]

5 3 **Loyalist (SAF)**[6] 666 7-9-0 97 ... MJKinane 8 93
(S Seemar, UAE) *mid-div: rdn 2 1/2f out: nvr able to chal* **25/1**

6 2 ¾ **Racer Forever (USA)**[6] 668 5-9-0 111 ... (b) RichardMullen 3 84
(J H M Gosden) *mid-div on rail: trckd wnr 3f out: rdn 2f out: wknd fnl f* **5/2**[1]

7 1 ½ **Ragheed (USA)**[6] 668 4-9-0 104 ... MartinDwyer 6 79
(E Charpy, UAE) *sn pushed along: racd in rr: wd 3f out: r.o same pce* **7/1**

8 5 **Grantley Adams**[20] 492 5-9-0 95 ... (b) LDettori 5 63
(Saeed Bin Suroor) *slowly away: settled in rr: gng wl 3f out: rdn 2f out: nt qckn* **12/1**

9 2 ¼ **Valiance (USA)**[13] 4-9-0 95 ... KShea 10 56
(M F De Kock, South Africa) *mid-div: rdn 2 1/2f out: nvr able to chal* **33/1**

10 ½ **Comandante Xara (BRZ)**[13] 5-9-0 100 ... KLatham 9 54
(A Selvaratnam, UAE) *trckd ldr tl wknd 3f out* **25/1**

1m 12.81s (0.81) **Going Correction** +0.45s/f (Yiel) 10 Ran SP% **117.5**
Speed ratings: **112,108,108,107,103 100,98,91,88,87**
CSF: 64.08.
Owner Hamdan Al Maktoum **Bred** Shadwell Estate Co Ltd **Trained** United Arab Emirates

FOCUS
A competitive sprint handicap.

NOTEBOOK
Mutamarres maintained his unbeaten record at this year's carnival. The Doug Watson-trained five-year-old was bidding for a hat-trick following two all-the-way wins in course handicaps (one of which was last Friday) and he again looked ideally berthed for a front-runner. This represented a stiffer task and he had to do a bit more to lead on this occasion, but Hills began to quicken the tempo off the home bend and he had them all in trouble racing into the final quarter-mile. He is clearly at the peak of his powers at the moment and it is a shame there is no suitable race on World Cup night for the son of Green Desert. (op 9/2)
Big Timer(USA), who has been racing at further, looked a shade unfortunate on his debut here in January and again got little luck next time. Far too keen when upped to Group 2 level latest, this return to sprinting looked a step in the right direction and he was soon tracking Mutamarres towards the inside. However, he got caught flat-footed when the winner kicked and, despite keeping on willingly under pressure, was never able to get back at him. This was a return to his best.
Grand Vista, who looked a little unfortunate not to get closer to the winner last week, was again well in rear early and, despite staying on under pressure, found his old rival home and hosed by the time he reached top gear.

Prince Tamino has returned to the carnival an improved performer this year, winning two of his three starts in handicaps, and the way in which he bolted up over course and distance last time entitled him to go close despite the rise in grade. However, he took a fierce grip in the early stages and was unable to quicken under strong pressure, just keeping on at the one pace. He is probably a bit better than this.

Loyalist(SAF) kept plugging away under pressure having been outpaced off the home bend, but has now finished behind Mutamarres in each of his three wins.

Racer Forever(USA) has sometimes had his finishing effort questioned, but he ran well over 1m on his carnival debut and appreciated the strong gallop set when scoring over and extended 6f next time. He had more to do on this rise in class though, and having tried to go in pursuit of the winner over two out, it soon became apparent he was running on empty. This was not his best form, but it is not easy to predict when he is going to show it. (op 9/4)

Ragheed(USA), second to Racer Forever last week, was soon being niggled to keep up and he never really threatened to get involved.

Grantley Adams had blinkers on this time, having flopped on his recent debut for the yard, but they failed to make any difference and he dropped right out inside the final quarter-mile.

739a FERRARI TROPHY (H'CAP) (TURF) — 1m 2f (T)

3:45 (3:45) (100-116,116) 3-Y-0+

£52,763 (£17,587; £8,793; £4,396; £2,638; £1,758)

RPR

1 — **With Interest**[14] 565 5-8-11 **107** .... LDettori 7 — 111
(Saeed Bin Suroor) *mid-div: rdn 2 1/2f out: r.o wl fnl 1 1/2f: led cl home* — **11/4**[2]

2 ¾ **Alpacco (IRE)**[6] 669 6-8-7 **102** ow1 .... KLatham 3 — 105
(H J Brown, South Africa) *sn led: rdn 2 1/2f out: hdd 1 1/2f out: r.o bravely fnl f* — **9/1**

3 2¼ **Sushisan (AUS)**[20] 494 6-9-6 **116** .... (p) RyanMoore 2 — 115
(H J Brown, South Africa) *mid-div: smooth prog to ld 1 1/2f out: hdd ins fnl f: wknd* — **5/2**[1]

4 2¼ **Teslin (IRE)**[28] 383 4-8-8 **104** .... (t) KerrinMcEvoy 9 — 98
(Saeed Bin Suroor) *mid-div: dropped to rr 5f out: rdn 3 1/2f out: r.o fnl 1 1/2f: nrst fin* — **5/1**[3]

5 1¼ **Advice**[56] 7-8-9 **105** .... RichardMullen 5 — 96
(S Seemar, UAE) *slowly away: racd in rr of mid-div: rdn 2 1/2f out: r.o same pce* — **33/1**

6 2 **Snoqualmie Boy**[28] 381 5-8-5 **100** .... JohnEgan 1 — 88
(A Manuel, UAE) *trckd ldr: t.k.h: rdn 2 1/2f out: sn btn* — **28/1**

7 1¼ **The Illies (IRE)**[6] 669 4-8-5 **100** .... TedDurcan 4 — 86
(Saeed Bin Suroor) *trckd ldr: rdn 3f out: ev ch 2f out: wknd* — **9/1**

8 1 **Championship Point (IRE)**[6] 669 5-8-8 **104** .... DarryllHolland 10 — 86
(M R Channon) *settled last: rdn 3f out: nvr nr to chal* — **9/1**

9 ¼ **Wild Savannah**[357] 645 6-8-12 **108** .... TPO'Shea 6 — 90
(E Charpy, UAE) *mid-div: rdn to chse ldrs 3f out: sn btn* — **16/1**

10 6¼ **European Dream (IRE)**[35] 296 5-8-5 **100** .... (p) MartinDwyer 8 — 70
(R C Guest) *settled in rr: rdn 3f out: nvr able to chal* — **20/1**

2m 7.10s (2.60) **Going Correction** +0.45s/f (Yiel)
WFA 4 from 5yo+ 1lb — 10 Ran SP% **118.9**
Speed ratings: **107,106,104,102,101 100,99,98,98,93**
CSF: 27.80; TRI: 70.42.

Owner Godolphin **Bred** George Strawbridge **Trained** Newmarket, Suffolk

FOCUS
This handicap looked competitive enough beforehand, but they did not go a great gallop early and few got into it.

NOTEBOOK
With Interest has not been the easiest to train over the years, but he is gradually climbing the ladder and this fourth win from five starts probably marks the end of his career in handicaps. He really began to pick up from two furlongs out, won a shade cosily in the end and will deserve his place in Listed company when he resumes his career in Britain.

Alpacco(IRE), not for the first time, showed how dangerous he can be when allowed the run of the race out in front. He set a steady early pace before winding it up rounding the turn into the straight. That was soon enough given the advantage he had been given, and had his rider left it a bit longer before picking up the pace he may have proved very difficult to pass. As it was he rallied after being headed by his stable companion Sushisan, but could not hold off the winner's late challenge. (op 8/1)

Sushisan(AUS), who wore cheekpieces this time, had shaped with promise behind Oracle West on his reappearance and made what looked a race-winning move when he nipped through on the inside two furlongs out. He appeared to throw in the towel once he hit the front, though. (op 11/4)

Teslin(IRE) was disappointing last time out, but he was making a quick return to the track after his seasonal reappearance that day and the competition was weaker this time. A stronger all-round pace would have seen him in a better light as he was staying on all too late. (op 9/2)

Advice, well beaten on dirt on his reappearance, ran a better race back on turf, especially considering that he was keen enough in the early stages.

Snoqualmie Boy was always well placed towards the front end and can have few excuses.

The Illies(IRE) was similarly prominent throughout and had every chance given the way the race was run.

Championship Point(IRE) did not have the race run to suit and should not be judged too harshly.

European Dream(IRE) was another unsuited by the steady early gallop.

740a MASERATI TROPHY (H'CAP) (TURF) — 1m 4f (T)

4:15 (4:15) (100-115,115) 3-Y-0+

£52,763 (£17,587; £8,793; £4,396; £2,638; £1,758)

RPR

1 — **Hard Top (IRE)**[7] 652 6-8-9 **105** .... RyanMoore 6 — 107
(H J Brown, South Africa) *mid-div: trckd ldrs 2f out: rdn to ld fnl f out: r.o wl* — **7/2**[1]

2 ½ **Doubnov (FR)**[7] 652 5-8-5 **100** .... TedDurcan 5 — 102
(Saeed Bin Suroor) *mid-div: trckd ldrs 3f out: ev ch fnl 2f: hung bhd wnr fnl f out: r.o* — **7/2**[1]

3 1¾ **New Guinea**[7] 652 5-8-7 **102** .... KerrinMcEvoy 3 — 101
(Saeed Bin Suroor) *sn led: pushed clr 5f out: hdd fnl f out: kpt on* — **8/1**

4 3½ **Book Of Music (IRE)**[20] 491 5-9-1 **110** .... (vt) WJSupple 2 — 104
(Saeed Bin Suroor) *slowly away: racd in last: n.d: r.o fnl 1 1/2f: nrst fin* — **10/1**

5 shd **Halicarnassus (IRE)**[14] 565 4-9-4 **115** .... DarryllHolland 7 — 109
(M R Channon) *settled in rr: rdn 3 1/2f out: wd 3f out: r.o fnl 1 1/2f: nvr able to chal* — **10/1**

6 ½ **Illustrious Blue**[20] 491 5-8-12 **108** .... PaulDoe 8 — 100
(W J Knight) *mid-div: rdn 3f out: nvr nr to chal* — **5/1**[3]

7 1 **Boscobel**[21] 476 4-9-4 **115** .... LDettori 4 — 107
(Saeed Bin Suroor) *trckd ldr: rdn 3f out whn ev ch: r.o same pce fnl f* — **4/1**[2]

8 2 **Pearly King (USA)**[6] 667 5-8-6 **101** .... (bt) WayneSmith 1 — 89
(M Al Muhairi, UAE) *trckd ldr: t.k.h: rdn and wknd 3f out* — **20/1**

2m 36.08s (5.08) **Going Correction** +0.45s/f (Yiel)
WFA 4 from 5yo+ 3lb — 8 Ran SP% **115.2**
Speed ratings: **101,100,99,97,97 96,96,94**
CSF: 15.98; TRI: 90.30.

Owner The Bayern Syndicate & Des Scott **Bred** Ballymacoll Stud Farm Ltd **Trained** South Africa

FOCUS
A quality handicap run at a steady gallop.

NOTEBOOK
Hard Top(IRE) has improved a little with each run at the carnival, getting mowed down late on by the smart Mourilyan last week, and he was able to confirm the placings with Doubnov and record his first victory since August 2005. There is no doubting he has been a disappointment over the years, but seems to have got his act together out here and there may be even more to come from the six-year-old.

Doubnov(FR) is the younger of the pair, but he does not seem quite as progressive. Ridden more positively on this occasion, he had every chance but could not quicken and, though he did his best to get back at the winner, Hard Top was always doing enough. This ex-French performer may need a slower surface to be seen at his best.

New Guinea is a tough and consistent sort, but he really needs further than this and continues to get done for a change of speed at the end of his races.

Book Of Music(IRE), a course-and-distance winner last month, failed to run to form behind a couple of these last time and he again looked vulnerable to more progressive types. He ran on late having still been last over a furlong out, but was a bit adrift of the front three.

Halicarnassus(IRE) looked vulnerable to less-exposed types off joint top-weight and, despite keeping on, never posed a serious threat to the principals. (op 12/1)

Illustrious Blue has a decent record at the carnival and he returned with a fine effort to finish second earlier in the month (ahead of both New Guinea and Book Of Music) but was unable to build on that performance and ran rather flat.

Boscobel, a high-class middle-distance three-year-old for Mark Johnston last season, he failed to adapt to the dirt when only seventh in a Group 3 here earlier in the month, but looked to have every chance on this return to turf and the step back up in trip. However, having tracked New Guinea early on he became outpaced as the tempo quickened three out and eventually dropped away. He has yet to recapture his best form, but may do better returned to Britain.

741a AL QUOZ SPRINT (DIV II) (SPONSORED BY AL TAYER MOTORS) (LISTED RACE) (TURF) — 6f (T)

4:45 (4:45) 3-Y-0+

£60,301 (£20,100; £10,050; £5,025; £3,015; £2,010)

RPR

1 — **Instant Recall (IRE)**[7] 649 7-9-0 101 .... (vt) WayneSmith 4 — 103
(M Al Muhairi, UAE) *trckd ldr: led 2f out: hdd ins fnl f out: led again fnl strides* — **20/1**

2 shd **Calrissian (GER)**[6] 668 4-9-0 93 .... RyanMoore 10 — 103
(L Kelp, Denmark) *settled in rr: trckd 3rd 2f out: rdn to ld ins fnl f out: hdd cl home* — **33/1**

3 ½ **Munaddam (USA)**[211] 4058 6-9-0 110 .... RHills 6 — 102
(E Charpy, UAE) *mid-div on rail: smooth prog to chal 2f out: r.o same pce fnl f* — **11/4**[1]

4 ½ **Beaver Patrol (IRE)**[7] 649 6-9-0 102 .... (v) MJKinane 2 — 100
(Eve Johnson Houghton) *mid-div: trckd wnr 2 1/2f out: nt qckn fnl 1 1/2f* — **7/2**[2]

5 ¼ **Mariol (FR)**[7] 649 5-9-0 105 .... JMurtagh 9 — 99
(E Charpy, UAE) *settled in rr: swtchd wd 2 1/2f out: prog to chal 2f out: nt qckn fnl f* — **5/1**

6 ¼ **Ripples Maid**[7] 649 5-8-9 97 .... RichardMullen 3 — 94
(J A Geake) *mid-div: rdn 2 1/2f out: r.o fnl 1 1/2f: nrst fin* — **6/1**

7 2½ **Subpoena**[6] 666 6-9-0 102 .... (v) AhmedAjtebi 8 — 91
(A Al Raihe, UAE) *mid-div: nvr able to chal* — **20/1**

8 2½ **Turn On The Style**[7] 649 6-9-0 105 .... (b) PaulMulrennan 5 — 84
(J Balding) *mid-div: nvr able to chal* — **9/2**[3]

9 3¾ **Hurricane Spirit (IRE)**[6] 666 4-9-0 100 .... WJSupple 7 — 72
(J R Best) *slowly away: a in rr* — **16/1**

10 3¾ **League Champion (USA)**[6] 668 5-9-0 95 .... (b) TPO'Shea 1 — 61
(R Bouresly, Kuwait) *sn led: hdd 2f out: wknd* — **66/1**

1m 13.09s (1.09) **Going Correction** +0.45s/f (Yiel) — 10 Ran SP% **117.9**
Speed ratings: **110,109,109,108,108 107,104,101,96,91**
CSF: 524.08.

Owner Salman Mussallam Al Shalahi **Bred** Frank Dunne **Trained** UAE

FOCUS
There was not a lot to choose between a few of these on their previous efforts at the carnival and that was borne out by the result, a bunched finish and a winning time 0.28sec slower than the first division.

NOTEBOOK
Instant Recall(IRE) ran way below his best on the drop back to sprinting last time out, but his previous win over 7f gave him every chance if bouncing back to his best. The winner hit the front at the top of the straight and, although headed, would not give in and kept on in determined fashion to edge ahead again near the line. His will to win cannot be faulted and, like the winner of the first division, he was recording his third success of the carnival.

Calrissian(GER), a Danish challenger, improved for a switch to turf last time out and once again showed his preference for this surface. He was going well turning in and got a dream run up the inside rail, and was only denied on the line.

Munaddam(USA), narrowly beaten in this race last year, has a fair record when fresh, but his trainer did express concerns beforehand that he was a big, stuffy horse who would probably come on for the run. He was 5lb clear of his nearest challenger on official ratings and ran well, but was a little one paced in the closing stages having been brought with a well-timed challenge, and his trainer's fear was probably realised.

Beaver Patrol(IRE) did not enjoy much luck in running last time out behind Prince Tamino, but despite benefiting from a favourable low draw and having a clearer run this time, he ran to a similar level. (op 4/1)

Mariol(FR) was another who had looked unlucky here last week, but he had absolutely no excuse this time, as he quickened up well a furlong and a half out, but once he got a sniff of the lead he downed tools. He looks one for the in-running layers.

Ripples Maid also had her excuses behind Prince Tamino, but despite things going kinder for her this time she still finished up running close to her old rival Beaver Patrol.

Turn On The Style ran a bit below his recent form and perhaps he is in need of a break now. (op 4/1)

Hurricane Spirit(IRE) has yet to return to his best after getting injured in last year's 2000 Guineas.

742a JAGUAR TROPHY (H'CAP) (DIRT) 1m 2f (D)

5:15 (5:15) (100-129,129) 3-Y-0+

£52,763 (£17,587; £8,793; £4,396; £2,638; £1,758)

RPR

1 **Curlin (USA)**[124] 6514 4-9-6 **129**........(t) RAlbarado 2 130+
(S Asmussen, U.S.A) *trckd ldr: t.k.h: swtchd wd 7f out: smooth prog to ld 2f out: easily* **30/100**[1]

2 *2 1/4* **Familiar Territory**[14] 568 5-8-5 **109**........ KerrinMcEvoy 3 107
(Saeed Bin Suroor) *broke awkwardly: mid-div: trckd wnr 2f out: no ch w wnr* **7/2**[2]

3 *4 1/4* **Jet Express (SAF)**[6] 671 6-8-5 **104**........ RoystonFfrench 6 98
(A Al Raihe, UAE) *settled in rr: rdn 4f out: nvr able to chal: r.o fnl 2f* **50/1**

4 *3 1/4* **Arqaam**[14] 565 4-8-6 **101** ow1........ RHills 1 94
(Doug Watson, UAE) *settled last: nvr nr to chal* **66/1**

5 *1 1/4* **Imperialista (BRZ)**[7] 648 5-8-5 **100**........(v) TedDurcan 5 89
(Saeed Bin Suroor) *sn led: rdn 3f out: hdd 2f out: wknd* **20/1**

6 *1 1/4* **Engrupido (ARG)**[6] 669 5-8-5 **106**........ WMLordan 4 87
(M F De Kock, South Africa) *trckd ldng duo tl 4 1/2f out: wknd* **16/1**[3]

2m 0.60s (-1.70) **Going Correction** +0.15s/f (Slow)
WFA 4 from 5yo+ 1lb **6** Ran SP% **113.2**
Speed ratings: **112,110,106,104,103 102**
CSF: 1.69.
Owner Stonestreet Stables LLC & Midnight Cry Stables **Bred** Fares Farm Inc **Trained** USA

FOCUS
An impressive reappearance from Breeders' Cup Classic winner Curlin.

NOTEBOOK
Curlin(USA), the 2007 US Horse Of The Year, was making his eagerly anticipated UAE debut and bidding to enhance his already obvious World Cup claims. Hero of last season's Breeders' Cup Classic, his official rating of 129 means he is the best horse to run at the Dubai Carnival since Cigar (the inaugural World Cup winner) and he showed here just why he is the top dirt horse in the world with a stylish weight-carrying performance. A bull of a horse, the winner was happy to track pace-setter Imperialista through and, having been woken up with a few nudges over two out, he proceeded to canter home under a sympathetic ride from Alborado. He had reportedly been shaping nicely in his work and this would have felt like nothing more than an exercise canter to the son of Smart Strike, having contested some of the roughest and toughest races around in his homeland last season. Although clearly straight enough, he can be expected to be a lot sharper come World Cup night and, assuming he runs to his capabilities, it would be a mighty surprise were he to be beaten. (op 1/3)
Familiar Territory did it easily in a course-and-distance handicap two weeks ago, but this was a completely different ball game and second was best he could have hoped for. As expected he proved no match for the classy winner and was flattered to finish so close, but seems to be progressing and it is just hoped this effort does not affect his handicap mark too much.
Jet Express(SAF) ran on late past beaten horses.
Engrupido(ARG) dropped out tamely late on.

743a ZABEEL MILE (DIV I) (SPONSORED BY FORD) (LISTED RACE) (TURF) 1m (T)

5:45 (3:45) 3-Y-0+

£60,301 (£20,100; £10,050; £5,025; £3,015; £2,010)

RPR

1 **Wise Dennis**[6] 671 6-9-4 110........ TedDurcan 4 112
(A P Jarvis) *in rr of mid-div: rdn to chse runner-up 2 1/2f out: led fnl f out: r.o wl: jst hld on* **4/1**[2]

2 *shd* **Dijeerr (USA)**[6] 671 4-9-4 105........(v) LDettori 3 112
(Saeed Bin Suroor) *sn led: rdn clr 2 1/2f out: r.o but hdd fnl f: kpt on wl* **9/2**[3]

3 *4 1/2* **Divine Jury (SAF)**[35] 294 5-9-11 112........ KShea 8 110
(M F De Kock, South Africa) *settled in rr: smooth prog to chse ldrs 2 1/2f out: nt qckn fnl f* **5/4**[1]

4 *4* **Emirates Gold (IRE)**[21] 474 5-9-4 101........(t) TPO'Shea 6 92
(E Charpy, UAE) *slowly away: settled last: r.o fnl 1 1/2f: nvr able to chal* **33/1**

5 *1/4* **Yahrab (IRE)**[35] 292 3-8-6 106........ MJKinane 10 93
(C E Brittain) *settled in rr: last 3f out: nvr nr to chal* **25/1**

6 *1/2* **Final Verse**[28] 384 5-9-4 102........ JohnEgan 1 90
(A Manuel, UAE) *trckd ldr: t.k.h: rdn 2 1/2f out: sn btn* **40/1**

7 *1/2* **King Jock (USA)**[20] 495 7-9-4 108........ PShanahan 7 89
(R J Osborne, Ire) *mid-div: rdn to chse ldrs 2 1/2f out: nt qckn fnl 1 1/2f* **13/2**

8 *4 1/2* **Latino Magic (IRE)**[14] 563 8-9-4 100........ PJSmullen 5 79
(D K Weld, Ire) *trckd ldrs tl 3f out: sn btn* **22/1**

9 *8 1/4* **River Tiber**[20] 495 5-9-4 104........ KerrinMcEvoy 9 60
(Saeed Bin Suroor) *trckd ldrs tl 3 1/2f out: wknd* **16/1**

R **Gharir (IRE)**[6] 671 6-9-4 107........(bt) RHills 2 —
(E Charpy, UAE) *ref to r: styd in stall* **20/1**

1m 39.27s (0.97) **Going Correction** +0.45s/f (Yiel)
WFA 3 from 4yo+ 19lb **10** Ran SP% **120.2**
Speed ratings: **113,112,108,104,104 103,103,98,90,—**
CSF: 21.45.
Owner Allen B Pope, Andrew J King **Bred** J And Mrs Bowtell **Trained** Twyford, Bucks

FOCUS
There was a chance that this would be tactical and so it proved.

NOTEBOOK
Wise Dennis beat Dijeer by a length last time while conceding 2lb, so had every chance of confirming the form off levels, but in contrast to the last time they met this was a more tactical affair. Given his preference for a strongly-run race, he deserves extra credit for this narrow victory, although the runner-up's string of defeats does suggest he is vulnerable to a tougher rival. (op 9/2)
Dijeerr(USA) very much got the run of the race in front under a fine ride from Dettori, who slowed things down rounding the turn into the straight, began to wind it up gradually and kept enough in reserve to respond when strongly challenged in the latter stages. However, his mount had a question mark next to his name after finishing runner-up in six of his previous nine starts, and he added another second placing to his name despite everything going his way. (op 11/2)
Divine Jury(SAF), whose trainer Mike de Kock won this race last year with Kapil, had to shoulder a Grade 1 penalty but still looked to hold strong claims having chased home Linngari on his reappearance. The first two stole a march on him though, and while he briefly looked a threat a furlong and a half out, he was soon one paced. A stronger gallop would undoubtedly have suited him, but his Dubai Duty Free claims were not enhanced.
Emirates Gold(IRE) had not shown much in his previous two starts at the carnival but he was a Listed winner in Abu Dhabi in December.
Yahrab(IRE), who was placed in Group company last autumn, showed nothing on dirt last time out, but he shaped better back on turf against his elders. He is bred to make up into a middle-distance horse this year.
Final Verse paid for racing keenly and would have preferred a stronger pace. (op 33/1)
King Jock(USA) threatened to get into it at the top of the straight, but soon flattened out. He was another who would have probably done better in a more strongly run race. (op 11/2)

744a UAE OAKS (SPONSORED BY AL TAYER MOTORS) (LISTED RACE) (DIRT) (FILLIES) 1m 1f (D)

6:15 (6:15) 3-Y-0

£75,376 (£25,125; £12,562; £6,281; £3,768; £2,512)

RPR

1 **Cocoa Beach (CHI)**[20] 496 4-9-4 109........(v) TedDurcan 9 96+
(Saeed Bin Suroor) *mid-div: wd: gng wl 3f out: smooth prog to ld 2f out: r.o easily* **8/13**[1]

2 *6* **Love Of Dubai (USA)**[20] 496 3-8-9 93........ MJKinane 6 85
(C E Brittain) *settled in rr: trckd wnr 3f out: r.o wl fnl 1 1/2f: no ch w wnr* **25/1**

3 *1 1/4* **Love Dancing (ARG)**[21] 473 4-9-4 95........ KerrinMcEvoy 11 77
(Saeed Bin Suroor) *trckd ldrs: rdn 3 1/2f out: r.o but no ch w wnr* **25/1**

4 *1* **Patio**[20] 496 3-8-9 85........ WJSupple 3 80
(Doug Watson, UAE) *mid-div: rdn 3f out: r.o same pce* **40/1**

5 *1 1/2* **Miss Clonyn (IRE)**[20] 496 3-8-9 75........ DO'Donohoe 10 77
(Doug Watson, UAE) *disp in centre: led 3f out: hdd 2f out: r.o same pce* **150/1**

6 *1 1/4* **Classy-Lady (BRZ)**[6] 672 4-9-4 100........ RyanMoore 2 69
(H J Brown, South Africa) *s.i.s: mid-div: trckd ldrs 4f out: sn btn* **16/1**[3]

7 *1/4* **Star Of Rosanna**[20] 496 3-8-9 80........ MartinDwyer 7 74
(Doug Watson, UAE) *settled in rr: nvr nr to chal* **50/1**

8 *3 1/4* **Dalkey Girl (IRE)**[20] 496 3-8-9 91........ DarryllHolland 1 67
(V Smith) *disp on rail: rdn 3f out: sn wknd* **66/1**

9 *1 1/4* **Fiesta Lady (ARG)**[20] 496 4-9-4 105........ LDettori 4 59
(Saeed Bin Suroor) *settled in rr: wd 2 1/2f out: mid-div: nvr able to chal* **15/8**[2]

10 *14* **Olympic Glory (BRZ)**[20] 496 4-9-4 90........ JMurtagh 8 30
(A Al Raihe, UAE) *settled in rr: last and rdn 3f out: n.d* **33/1**

1m 49.09s (-0.71) **Going Correction** +0.15s/f (Slow)
WFA 3 from 4yo 21lb **10** Ran SP% **119.8**
Speed ratings: **109,103,102,101,100 99,99,96,95,82**
CSF: 26.61.
Owner H R H Princess Haya Of Jordan **Bred** Haras La Obra **Trained** Newmarket, Suffolk

FOCUS
This was basically a re-run of the UAE 1000 Guineas with the first eight home all taking their chance again over the extra furlong. Saeed Bin Suroor has developed something of a stranglehold on the race in its seven-year history, winning no less than four renewals prior to this, and with it looking a straight match on paper between two of his representatives Cocoa Beach and Fiesta Lady, there was a strong chance his fine record was going to be enhanced further. The expected dual did not develop, though, with the latter being eased right off late on as though something was amiss.

NOTEBOOK
Cocoa Beach(CHI) had been held by stablemate Fiesta Lady over 7f on their respective UAE debuts last month, getting well behind early, but the application of a visor and step up to 1m enabled her to reverse the form with ease in the 1000 Guineas and this additional furlong was not expected to represent a problem. Durcan maintained the partnership and, having travelled supremely well towards the outside, he found himself looking around for dangers as he prepared to send the filly on over two out. The response was instant and she quickly sprinted into an unassailable lead, having the luxury of being eased in the final 75 yards. With her only serious market rival failing to run her race it would be unwise to get carried away, but it was visually very impressive and she would be perfectly entitled to take her chance against the boys in the UAE Derby on World Cup night, just as Folk did (albeit unsuccessfully) having won this last year. A trip to the US will no doubt be on the agenda at some stage in the season. (op 4/6)
Love Of Dubai(USA) confirmed the promise of her sixth placing behind Fiesta Lady by taking third in the 1000 Guineas and she stepped up again with a game effort in second. She was finishing behind the winner for the third consecutive occasion. (op 22/1)
Love Dancing(ARG) was expected to be suited by this step up in trip and she kept on well under pressure to hold third. This represented a marked improvement in form and a further rise in distance would probably help further.
Patio appeared to run above herself when fourth in the 1000 Guineas, but this effort seemed to confirm it was no fluke.
Classy-Lady(BRZ) looked the biggest threat to the Bin Suroor challengers, having twice run well behind the smart Sun Classique, but she found little for pressure in the straight and perhaps found this run coming too soon after last week's efforts. (op 14/1)
Fiesta Lady(ARG), who is not that big, was a top-class filly in Argentina, romping away with their Oaks in October, and she looked good when beating Cocoa Beach over 7f last month. However, she failed to confirm the form when readily held in the 1000 Guineas and this effort was too bad to be true. It would not surprise to learn that all was not well, but there is also a chance she has not trained on. (op 7/4)

745a ZABEEL MILE (DIV II) (SPONSORED BY AL TAYER MOTORS) (LISTED RACE) (TURF) 1m (T)

6:45 (6:46) 3-Y-0+

£60,301 (£20,100; £10,050; £5,025; £3,015; £2,010)

RPR

1 **Third Set (IRE)**[20] 495 5-9-4 110........ LDettori 2 114+
(Saeed Bin Suroor) *slowly away: settled in rr: gng wl 2 1/2f out: rdn to cl 2f out: led fnl f: r.o: easily* **8/15**[1]

2 *1 1/2* **Metropolitan Man**[28] 379 5-9-4 108........ RichardMullen 8 111+
(D M Simcock) *settled last: trckd wnr 3f out: smooth prog 1 1/2f out: r.o wl: no ch w wnr* **12/1**[3]

3 *1 1/2* **Beckermet (IRE)**[7] 649 6-9-4 105........ JMurtagh 4 107
(R F Fisher) *sn led: clr 4 1/2f out: chal 2 1/2f out: r.o gamely* **33/1**

4 *1/2* **Almuraad (IRE)**[21] 474 7-9-4 101........ RHills 7 106
(Doug Watson, UAE) *settled in rr: r.o fnl 2f: nrst fin* **14/1**

5 *3/4* **Golden Arrow (IRE)**[14] 564 5-9-4 104........(bt) TPO'Shea 6 104
(E Charpy, UAE) *trckd ldr: rdn 4f out: r.o same pce* **12/1**[3]

6 *hd* **Law Lord**[6] 668 4-9-4 107........(v) KerrinMcEvoy 5 104
(Saeed Bin Suroor) *led main gp: chsd ldr 2 1/2f out whn ev ch: nt qckn* **9/1**[2]

7 *2* **Crossing**[6] 672 7-9-0 102........ PaulMulrennan 3 95
(William J Fitzpatrick, Ire) *mid-div: rdn 3f out: btn w no room 1 1/2f out* **33/1**

8 *2 1/4* **The Pirate (DEN)**[14] 568 5-9-4 99........(t) ESki 1 94
(Niels Petersen, Norway) *slowly away: nvr able to chal* **66/1**

9 *3 1/4* **Albabilia (IRE)**[167] 5395 3-8-4 105........ RoystonFfrench 9 92
(C E Brittain) *mid-div: wd: rdn 3f out: n.d* **20/1**

10 *dist* **Pride Of Nation (IRE)**[20] 495 6-9-6 108........................ MJKinane 10 —
(J W Hills) *mid-div: rdn 3f out: n.d* **9/1**[2]

1m 39.63s (1.33) **Going Correction** +0.45s/f (Yiel)
WFA 3 from 4yo+ 19lb 10 Ran SP% **119.4**
Speed ratings: **111,109,108,107,106 106,104,102,99,—**
CSF: 8.21.
Owner Sultan Ali **Bred** A Stroud And J Hanly **Trained** Newmarket, Suffolk

FOCUS
They went a decent pace here thanks to Beckermet, who is better known as a sprinter.

NOTEBOOK
Third Set(IRE), held up towards the back of the field in the early stages, came there travelling strongly two furlongs out and quickened clear inside the last. He enjoyed the strong pace and very much had things fall his way, but he has looked much improved this winter and is an exciting prospect for Group-race honours back in Europe this year. (op 8/13)
Metropolitan Man also benefited from the good gallop and, like the winner, came from way off the pace. He is a very useful horse, but is hard to place, and things are hardly likely to get any easier for him on that front back in Britain.
Beckermet(IRE) ran very well to hold on for third place having set a proper gallop over a trip that stretches his stamina to the limit.
Almuraad(IRE), another to stay on from well off the pace, has not won for years but had the race run to suit.
Golden Arrow(IRE), who ran well on dirt last time, paid for chasing the strong pace. (op 10/1)
Law Lord, whose last-time-out third behind Racer Forever and Ragheed had not been given much of a boost when those two blew out in the first race on this card, also paid the price for trying to keep tabs on the trailblazing leader. (op 7/1)
Albabilia(IRE) faced a stiff task on her reappearance against older horses. (op 16/1)
Pride Of Nation(IRE) weakened quickly a furlong and a half out as though something may have been amiss.

725 KEMPTON (A.W) (R-H)

Friday, February 29

OFFICIAL GOING: Standard
Wind: Fresh, across Weather: Damp

746 JUMP RACING HERE TOMORROW H'CAP 5f (P)

6:50 (6:51) (Class 6) (0-65,68) 4-Y-O+ **£2,047** (£604; £151; £151) **Stalls** High

Form RPR
110- **1** **Fast Freddie**[80] 7107 4-9-1 **63**........................(e) DNolan(3) 1 73
(S Parr) *mde all: rdn clr ins fnl 2f: in n.d after: pushed out* **7/1**
000- **2** *2* **Rocker**[109] 6794 4-9-4 **63**........................(v) DaneO'Neill 5 66
(B R Johnson) *hld up in rr: rdn and hdwy over 1f out: hmpd jst ins fnl f: swtchd lft: r.o to take 2nd nr fin* **7/2**[3]
-061 **3** *nk* **Hollow Jo**[9] 620 8-9-9 **68** 6ex........................ FergusSweeney 6 70
(J R Jenkins) *hld up in 4th: drvn along and nt qckn 2f out: kpt on fnl f* **2/1**[1]
3234 **3** *dht* **Kempsey**[9] 620 6-8-8 **60**........................(b) PatrickDonaghy(7) 7 62
(J J Bridger) *hld up in 5th: drvn along and outpcd 2f out: kpt on fnl f* **10/3**[2]
3-35 **5** *3/4* **After The Show**[22] 459 7-9-3 **62**........................(p) AlanMunro 4 61
(Rae Guest) *hld up in 6th: effrt and hung rt wl over 1f out: plld outside: styd on fnl f: nvr nrr* **11/2**
020- **6** *nse* **Nightstrike (IRE)**[216] 3950 5-8-12 **57**........................(b) EdwardCreighton 3 56
(Luke Comer, Ire) *chsd wnr: rdn 1/2-way: lost 2nd and no ex ins fnl f* **28/1**
4600 **7** *nk* **Fizzlephut (IRE)**[9] 620 6-9-3 **62**........................(b[1]) PaulFitzsimons 2 60
(Miss J R Tooth) *prom: effrt and hung rt into rail wl over 1f out: no ex fnl 100yds* **33/1**

61.20 secs (0.70) **Going Correction** +0.10s/f (Slow) 7 Ran SP% **112.9**
Speed ratings (Par 101): **98,94,94,94,93 93,92**
CSF £30.76 TOTE £9.50: £2.90, £2.40; EX 27.90.
Owner Gordon Crawford **Bred** New Hall Stud **Trained** Bawtry, S Yorks
■ Stewart Parr's first winner since moving to Bawtry to take over from Danny Murphy, & David Nolan's first after a year's ban.

FOCUS
A moderate sprint handicap, but a clear-cut winner in Fast Freddie, who got an uncontested lead and then kicked off the turn. A personal best from the winner and the form could rate higher, but the race is best rated arouns those in the frame behind him.

747 PANORAMIC BAR & RESTAURANT LOYALTY SCHEME H'CAP 1m 2f (P)

7:20 (7:22) (Class 4) (0-80,80) 4-Y-O+ **£4,210** (£1,252; £625; £312) **Stalls** High

Form RPR
-460 **1** **Prime Number (IRE)**[23] 450 6-8-7 **66**........................ JoeFanning 7 75
(J Akehurst) *mde all: chal by runner-up fnl 2f: rdn and hld on wl* **7/1**
3-40 **2** *1/2* **Lord Theo**[20] 509 4-8-12 **72**........................ JamesDoyle 3 80
(N P Littmoden) *chsd wnr: drvn to chal fnl 2f: unable to get past* **20/1**
0-16 **3** *3/4* **Watchmaker**[13] 586 5-8-7 **66**........................ ChrisCatlin 6 73
(Miss Tor Sturgis) *chsd ldrs: rdn over 2f out: kpt on fnl f* **7/2**[2]
5516 **4** *1 1/2* **Moonlight Man**[5] 692 7-9-6 **79**........................ RobertWinston 11 83
(C R Dore) *mid-div: drvn along and sme hdwy over 1f out: kpt on fnl f* **3/1**[1]
/5-4 **5** *nk* **Savannah**[13] 588 5-8-11 **70**........................(b) MickyFenton 1 73
(Luke Comer, Ire) *prom 2f: sn towards rr: rdn and r.o again fnl 2f* **25/1**
-500 **6** *nk* **Smokin Joe**[23] 456 7-9-1 **74**........................(b) JimCrowley 4 77
(J R Best) *s.s: hld up in last pl: shkn up and styd on fnl 2f: nt rch ldrs* **12/1**
06F- **7** *nk* **Krugerrand (USA)**[160] 5620 9-9-2 **75**........................ AlanMunro 10 77
(W J Musson) *hld up towards rr: weaved though and hdwy over 1f out: no imp fnl f* **25/1**
006- **8** *3* **Shabahar (IRE)**[114] 6727 4-8-8 **75**........................ DeclanCannon(7) 8 71
(M J McGrath) *t.k.h in midfield: effrt over 2f out: wknd over 1f out* **8/1**
30-0 **9** *2* **Obrigado (USA)**[51] 97 8-8-10 **72**........................(t) JerryO'Dwyer(3) 2 65
(Karen George) *s.s: hld up in rr: wd bnd into st: rdn and nt pce to rch ldrs* **20/1**
1160 **10** *4 1/2* **Smokey The Bear**[6] 678 6-9-7 **80**........................ NeilChalmers 9 64
(Miss Sheena West) *prom tl wknd wl over 1f out* **9/2**[3]
/21- **11** *nk* **Sarwin (USA)**[371] 539 5-8-9 **68**........................ FergusSweeney 5 51
(W J Musson) *hdwy to chse ldrs 6f out: wknd 2f out* **12/1**

2m 6.59s (-1.41) **Going Correction** +0.10s/f (Slow)
WFA 4 from 5yo+ 1lb 11 Ran SP% **121.6**
Speed ratings (Par 105): **109,108,108,106,106 106,106,103,102,98 98**
CSF £144.16 CT £575.41 TOTE £7.90: £2.60, £7.20, £1.60; EX 27.90.
Owner A D Spence **Bred** Ballylinch Stud **Trained** Epsom, Surrey

FOCUS
A fair handicap featuring several dropping in the weights. The winning time was decent for the grade and the placed horses set a solid standard.
Savannah Official explanation: jockey said horse lost its action
Smokey The Bear Official explanation: jockey said gelding lost its action

748 DIGIBET.COM MAIDEN STKS 1m (P)

7:50 (7:51) (Class 5) 3-Y-O **£2,590** (£770; £385; £192) **Stalls** High

Form RPR
2 **1** **Trimaran (IRE)**[23] 447 3-8-12 0........................ JoeFanning 6 69+
(M Johnston) *trckd ldr: led over 2f out: rdn clr over 1f out: readily* **3/1**[2]
2 *1 1/4* **Mekong Melody (IRE)** 3-8-12 0........................ RichardThomas 5 66+
(C G Cox) *dwlt: hdwy and prom after 2f: rdn over 2f out: kpt on to take 2nd fnl 75yds* **1/1**[1]
3 **3** *2 1/4* **Gang Show (IRE)**[20] 500 3-9-3 0........................ NeilPollard 12 66
(W J Musson) *cl up: rdn to chse wnr wl over 1f out: edgd lft: one pce appr fnl f: lost 2nd fnl 75yds* **16/1**
4 *nse* **Arts Guild (USA)** 3-9-3 0........................ FergusSweeney 9 66
(W J Musson) *s.s: hld up in rr of midfield: rdn and hdwy on outside 2f out: styd on fnl f* **66/1**
5 *nk* **Director's Chair** 3-9-0 0........................ JerryO'Dwyer(3) 1 65
(Miss J Feilden) *s.s: hdwy and in tch on outside after 2f: effrt and hung bdly rt in st: kpt on u.p* **100/1**
6 *shd* **Moon Crystal** 3-8-12 0........................(t) StephenDonohoe 4 60
(E A L Dunlop) *s.s: hld up in rr: shkn up and r.o fnl 2f: nrst fin* **33/1**
5 **7** *nk* **Fairfield Flame (GER)**[20] 500 3-8-12 0........................ AlanMunro 7 59
(D R C Elsworth) *hld up in midfield: rdn over 2f out: styd on same pce* **8/1**
6-0 **8** *3/4* **Asmodea**[26] 416 3-8-12 0........................ EdwardCreighton 10 58
(D J Coakley) *in tch: rdn and sltly outpcd over 2f out: tried to rally over 1f out: disputing 6th and btn whn hmpd nr fin* **80/1**
4-5 **9** *3/4* **Si Belle (IRE)**[13] 595 3-8-12 0........................ ChrisCatlin 11 56+
(Rae Guest) *hld up towards rr: shkn up over 2f out: r.o fnl f* **25/1**
0-0 **10** *2 1/4* **Art Exhibition (IRE)**[13] 590 3-9-3 0........................ SebSanders 14 56
(J Noseda) *hld up in midfield: effrt and n.m.r on rail over 2f out: sn rdn and btn* **40/1**
00-2 **11** *1 1/2* **Park Royal (UAE)**[29] 366 3-8-12 70........................ PatCosgrave 8 48
(D E Cantillon) *led tl over 2f out: wknd wl over 1f out* **7/1**[3]
12 *2* **Emshabb** 3-8-12 0........................ LiamJones 3 43
(W J Haggas) *a towards rr: n.d fnl 3f* **28/1**
13 *19* **Hatter's Way** 3-8-12 0........................ DaneO'Neill 13 2
(R A Farrant) *s.s: rn green: a bhd: no ch and eased fnl 2f* **100/1**

1m 41.48s (1.68) **Going Correction** +0.10s/f (Slow) 13 Ran SP% **121.9**
Speed ratings (Par 97): **95,93,91,91,91 91,90,90,89,87 85,83,64**
CSF £6.15 TOTE £3.70: £1.20, £1.50, £3.60; EX 9.00.
Owner Sheikh Hamdan Bin Mohammed Al Maktoum **Bred** Gainsborough Stud Management Ltd **Trained** Middleham Moor, N Yorks

FOCUS
An interesting maiden with several big stables represented, featuring mainly inexperienced sorts, the majority of whom were fillies. However, only four were supported in the market and it was 16-1 and more the rest, and they effectively dominated the contest. The time was moderate and the form is rated around the winner and third.
Director's Chair Official explanation: jockey said colt hung right in home straight

749 DIGIBET SPORTS BETTING H'CAP 7f (P)

8:20 (8:21) (Class 6) (0-60,60) 4-Y-O+ **£2,047** (£604; £302) **Stalls** High

Form RPR
0-25 **1** **Contented (IRE)**[19] 515 6-8-13 **55**........................(p) LPKeniry 6 66
(Mrs L C Jewell) *hld up in tch: effrt over 2f out: rdn to ld ins fnl f* **12/1**
-313 **2** *1 1/4* **Lindbergh**[5] 690 6-9-0 **59**........................(v) JerryO'Dwyer(3) 14 66
(J Ryan) *prom: led after 2f tl ins fnl f: nt qckn* **13/2**[2]
0124 **3** *1/2* **Over To You Bert**[13] 587 9-8-10 **57**........................ HaddenFrost(5) 7 63
(R J Hodges) *chsd ldrs: hrd rdn 2f out: kpt on same pce* **13/2**[2]
0-32 **4** *shd* **Shunkawakhan (IRE)**[13] 587 5-8-8 **50**........................(p) SaleemGolam 9 56
(G C H Chung) *chsd ldrs: effrt on rail ins fnl 2f: one pce fnl f: lost 3rd on line* **12/1**
30-3 **5** *1/2* **Compulsion**[13] 584 5-8-12 **54**........................ ChrisCatlin 11 58
(Pat Eddery) *in tch: n.m.r on rail and lost pl after 2f: rdn and r.o again fnl 2f* **8/1**[3]
20-0 **6** *1/2* **Boy Dancer (IRE)**[50] 109 5-8-12 **54**........................ SebSanders 8 58+
(J J Quinn) *dwlt: hld up towards rr: rdn and hdwy 2f out: styd on same pce* **8/1**[3]
2450 **7** *1 1/4* **Grey Gurkha**[3] 708 7-9-0 **56**........................ FergalLynch 1 56
(I W McInnes) *s.s: hld up and bhd: shkn up and styd on steadily fnl 2f: nrst fin* **16/1**
1234 **8** *hd* **Unlimited**[19] 515 6-9-3 **59**........................ JimmyQuinn 13 58
(R Simpson) *prom: hrd rdn over 1f out: sn wknd* **7/2**[1]
16-0 **9** *3 1/4* **Cabourg (IRE)**[14] 576 5-9-3 **59**........................(p) PatCosgrave 2 49
(R Bastiman) *mid-div: rdn and no hdwy fnl 2f* **16/1**
0023 **10** *3 3/4* **Bens Georgie (IRE)**[14] 571 6-9-2 **58**........................ DaneO'Neill 3 38
(D K Ivory) *hld up towards rr: rdn 3f out: wl btn whn hmpd wl over 1f out* **16/1**
30-5 **11** *1* **Metropolitan Chief**[55] 56 4-9-1 **57**........................ FergusSweeney 4 35
(P Burgoyne) *a towards rr: rdn and n.d fnl 2f* **12/1**
000/ **12** *5* **Zorn**[668] 1388 9-8-11 **53**........................ JoeFanning 10 17
(P Howling) *prom: led after 2f: prom tl wknd qckly 2f out* **50/1**
3340 **13** *3/4* **Dancing Duo**[7] 663 4-8-6 **55**........................(v) PatrickDonaghy(7) 12 17
(D Shaw) *missed break and lost 15l: a wl bhd: drvn along and no ch fnl 3f* **33/1**
656- **14** *3/4* **Baylaw Star**[186] 4891 7-9-4 **60**........................ RobertWinston 5 20
(I W McInnes) *mid-div: wd st: sn bhd* **25/1**

1m 26.16s (0.16) **Going Correction** +0.10s/f (Slow) 14 Ran SP% **120.6**
Speed ratings (Par 101): **103,101,101,100,100 99,98,98,94,90 88,83,82,81**
CSF £86.88 CT £578.83 TOTE £13.20: £3.90, £2.30, £3.60; EX 143.20.
Owner O J C Shannon Mrs Linda Beasley **Bred** Barry Noonan And Denis Noonan **Trained** Sutton Valence, Kent

FOCUS
A moderate handicap but competitive enough on paper. The form looks solid enough rated through the four immediately behind the winner.
Dancing Duo Official explanation: jockey said filly missed the break
Baylaw Star Official explanation: jockey said gelding moved badly and hung right

750 DIGIBET APPRENTICE CLAIMING STKS 1m (P)

8:50 (8:50) (Class 5) 4-Y-O+ **£2,457** (£725; £362) **Stalls** High

Form RPR
-452 **1** **Without Excuse (USA)**[19] 512 4-9-3 69........................(v) AshleyHamblett 3 55+
(M Botti) *chsd ldng pair: led 1f out: drvn 2l up: jst hld on* **11/8**[1]
3212 **2** *hd* **Given A Choice (IRE)**[9] 622 6-9-2 82........................(p) JosephineBruning(7) 4 61+
(J Pearce) *hld up in 5th: plld outside and pushed along 2f out: r.o wl fnl f: jst failed* **6/4**[2]

0-05 3 1 3/4 **Dream Forest (IRE)**[10] 613 5-9-7 53 PatrickDonaghy(3) 6 58
(P R Webber) *dwlt: sn drvn up to ld and set modest pce: qcknd 3f out: hdd 1f out: no ex* 33/1

60-4 4 nse **Imperial Amber**[20] 507 6-8-10 45 ow5 (p) HaddenFrost 1 44
(Karen George) *chsd ldr: drvn along over 2f out: no ex fnl f* 50/1

0-30 5 3/4 **Shouldntbethere (IRE)**[23] 448 4-9-1 59 JackMitchell 2 47
(Mrs P N Dutfield) *hld up in 4th: effrt 2f out: one pce fnl f* 14/1

100- 6 4 1/2 **Hansomelle (IRE)**[8] 5114 6-8-9 73 (p) JPHamblett(3) 5 34
(Miss Sheena West) *a last: outpcd and lost tch 3f out* 5/1[3]

1m 42.19s (2.39) **Going Correction** +0.10s/f (Slow) 6 Ran SP% 110.3
Speed ratings (Par 103): **92,91,90,90,89 84**
CSF £3.56 TOTE £2.20: £1.30, £1.80; EX 4.00.
Owner A Nencini **Bred** Cashmark Farms Inc **Trained** Newmarket, Suffolk
■ Stewards' Enquiry : Ashley Hamblett caution: used whip down shoulder in forehand position.

FOCUS
A small field for this apprentice claimer and the time was 0.71sec slower than the earlier three-year-old maiden. The principals were below their form as a result, the proximity of the next two testimony to that.

751 KEMPTON PARK FOR OUTDOOR EVENTS CLASSIFIED STKS 1m 4f (P)
9:20 (9:20) (Class 7) 4-Y-O+ £1,365 (£403; £201) Stalls Centre

Form RPR

0/02 1 **Ben Bacchus (IRE)**[11] 606 6-9-1 42 ChrisCatlin 6 55+
(P W Hiatt) *led 3f: pressed ldr tl led again 5f out: rdn and in control fnl 2f* 11/10[1]

-042 2 4 **On Every Street**[13] 585 7-9-1 45 (p) PatCosgrave 7 49
(R Bastiman) *chsd ldng pair: wnt 2nd over 4f out: nt pce of wnr fnl 2f* 11/4[2]

000- 3 5 **Sparkbridge (IRE)**[22] 5187 5-8-8 35 (tp) SoniaEaton(7) 4 42
(S C Burrough) *hld up and bhd: hdwy into fair 3rd over 2f out: pushed along: no imp* 66/1

60-0 4 3 1/2 **Sadler's Hill (IRE)**[27] 400 4-8-12 38 JimmyQuinn 3 36
(M J McGrath) *hld up in 6th: hrd rdn over 2f out: nvr nr to chal* 20/1

0553 5 nk **Come What July (IRE)**[13] 585 7-8-12 45 (v) TolleyDean(3) 2 36
(D Shaw) *hld up in 5th: hrd rdn over 2f out: sn btn* 11/2[3]

0066 6 12 **Only Hope**[14] 575 4-8-12 45 (p) DaneO'Neill 1 18
(Miss Diana Weeden) *t.k.h: hld up in 4th: effrt over 3f out: wknd over 2f out* 8/1

/00- 7 dist **Caliban (IRE)**[19] 514 10-8-12 32 JerryO'Dwyer(3) 5 —
(A W Carroll) *led after 3f: hrd rdn and hdd 5f out: sn wknd: wl bhd and virtually p.u fnl 3f* 16/1

2m 35.5s (1.00) **Going Correction** +0.10s/f (Slow)
WFA 4 from 5yo+ 3lb 7 Ran SP% 112.9
Speed ratings (Par 97): **100,97,94,91,91 83,—**
CSF £4.13 TOTE £1.70: £1.70, £1.80; EX 5.10 Place 6 £50.16, Place 5 £11.06.
Owner J W Hedges **Bred** Elisabeth And Neil Draper **Trained** Hook Norton, Oxon

FOCUS
A poor race but an authoritative first success for Ben Bacchus. The winner apart, it seems quite unlikely that any of these will be putting their nose in front in the near future, with the runner-up setting the level.
Caliban(IRE) Official explanation: jockey said gelding lost interest
T/Plt: £74.00 to a £1 stake. Pool: £83,188.15. 819.85 winning tickets. T/Qpdt: £5.40 to a £1 stake. Pool: £6,657.10. 910.80 winning tickets. LM

718 WOLVERHAMPTON (A.W) (L-H)
Friday, February 29

OFFICIAL GOING: Standard
Wind: fresh behind

752 BETDAQ THE BETTING EXCHANGE H'CAP 1m 141y(P)
2:20 (2:20) (Class 5) (0-75,74) 4-Y-O+ £2,590 (£770; £385; £192) Stalls Low

Form RPR

066- 1 **Yes One (IRE)**[133] 6314 4-8-11 67 NCallan 2 78+
(K A Ryan) *a.p: wnt 2nd 2f out: led 1f out: rdn and r.o wl* 7/2[2]

-111 2 3/4 **Safari Sundowner (IRE)**[16] 546 4-9-4 74 JimCrowley 4 82
(P Winkworth) *chsd ldr: led 4f out: rdn and hung lft wl over 1f out: hdd 1f out: nt qckn* 11/10[1]

1463 3 1 **Machinate (USA)**[6] 685 6-8-9 65 LiamJones 3 71
(W M Brisbourne) *hld up: hdwy on ins wl over 1f out: rdn fnl f: kpt on towards fin* 10/1

6-13 4 3 3/4 **Garden Party**[23] 452 4-9-3 73 TGMcLaughlin 5 71
(Jane Chapple-Hyam) *hld up: rdn and effrt over 2f out: wknd wl over 1f out* 5/1[3]

-544 5 shd **Punta Galera (IRE)**[4] 697 5-8-5 61 (v) FrancisNorton 7 59
(Paul Green) *hld up in tch: chsd ldr over 3f out to 2f out: wknd over 1f out* 15/2

2-26 6 4 1/2 **Jord (IRE)**[43] 192 4-9-3 73 PatrickMathers 1 62
(A J McCabe) *hd down whn stalls opened and s.s: in rr: rdn and short-lived effrt on outside over 2f out* 12/1

1/0- 7 25 **Outlook**[76] 7158 5-8-11 70 (b) JamieMoriarty(3) 6 6
(P T Midgley) *led: hdd 4f out: sn wknd: eased whn no ch fnl f* 50/1

1m 51.46s (0.96) **Going Correction** +0.275s/f (Slow) 7 Ran SP% 117.0
Speed ratings (Par 103): **106,105,104,101,101 97,74**
CSF £8.07 TOTE £4.30: £2.00, £1.70; EX 9.60.
Owner Mrs J Ryan **Bred** Carl Holt **Trained** Hambleton, N Yorks

FOCUS
A steadily-run modest little handicap with the runner-up rated to his recent level.

753 HOTEL & CONFERENCING AT WOLVERHAMPTON RACECOURSE (S) STKS 1m 141y(P)
2:50 (2:50) (Class 6) 4-Y-O+ £1,774 (£523; £262) Stalls Low

Form RPR

2102 1 **Northern Desert (IRE)**[11] 607 9-9-1 65 (p) KirstyMilczarek(3) 4 68
(S Curran) *a.p: wnt 2nd over 4f out: led jst over 1f out: edgd lft ins fnl f: r.o* 6/1[2]

3215 2 3/4 **Pianoforte (USA)**[15] 559 6-9-4 56 (b) JimmyQuinn 8 66
(E J Alston) *hld up in tch: rdn to chal whn edgd lft ins fnl f: nt run on* 12/1[3]

1343 3 1 **Arctic Desert**[11] 607 8-9-4 61 (t) HayleyTurner 1 64
(Miss Gay Kelleway) *t.k.h in tch: swtchd rt ins fnl f: rdn and r.o* 6/1[2]

5304 4 1/2 **Capania (IRE)**[14] 579 4-8-7 52 StephenDonohoe 5 52
(P D Evans) *led: hdd jst over 1f out: rdn whn bmpd ins fnl f: no ex* 20/1

4432 5 1 1/2 **One Night In Paris (IRE)**[14] 577 5-8-13 75 JamieSpencer 3 55
(M J Wallace) *chsd ldr tl over 4f out: rdn over 2f out: no imp fnl f* 8/15[1]

4005 6 11 **Western Roots**[11] 611 7-8-12 54 (p) ChrisCatlin 7 31
(M Appleby) *hld up: bhd fnl 2f* 14/1

00/0 7 33 **Dancing Moonlight (IRE)**[8] 634 6-8-7 27 LiamJones 2 —
(Mrs N Macauley) *stdd s: plld hrd in rr: struggling 3f out: t.o* 100/1

1m 54.95s (4.45) **Going Correction** +0.275s/f (Slow) 7 Ran SP% 113.9
Speed ratings (Par 101): **91,90,89,89,87 77,48**
CSF £70.47 TOTE £7.40: £2.30, £3.70; EX 61.90 Trifecta £138.80 Pool £537.81 - 2.75 winning units..There was no bid fro the winner. One Night In Paris was claimed by Diamond Racing Ltd for £5,500.
Owner Miss N Henton **Bred** J P Hardiman **Trained** Hatford, Oxon

FOCUS
This was 3.5 seconds slower than the previous handicap with a slow pace leading to a very moderate time, even for a seller. the form is rated around the first two and the fourth.
One Night In Paris(IRE) Official explanation: jockey said mare moved poorly

754 CALL 0844 576 5938 FOR PONTIN'S BEST DEALS H'CAP 2m 119y(P)
3:25 (3:25) (Class 6) (0-65,65) 4-Y-O+ £2,047 (£604; £302) Stalls Low

Form RPR

1-00 1 **Bugsy's Boy**[36] 283 4-9-0 59 (p) RobertWinston 9 73
(P W D'Arcy) *sn led: clr over 3f out: rdn and edgd lft over 1f out: styd on* 7/1[3]

505/ 2 2 1/2 **Rainbow Dash (IRE)**[90] 3145 9-9-3 56 (p) PatCosgrave 1 67
(T G McCourt, Ire) *a.p: rdn and sltly outpcd over 4f out: rallied over 2f out: styd on to take 2nd last strides* 20/1

20-1 3 shd **Josh You Are**[3] 710 5-9-9 65 KirstyMilczarek(3) 3 76+
(D E Cantillon) *s.s: hld up in rr: smooth hdwy 4f out: rdn over 2f out: chsd wnr wl over 1f out: sn edgd lft: no imp fnl f* 10/11[1]

6-03 4 9 **Sovietta (IRE)**[22] 461 7-8-9 48 (t) StephenDonohoe 4 48
(Ian Williams) *hld up: sn mid-div: hdwy 6f out: chsd wnr over 3f out tl wl over 1f out: sn wknd* 25/1

4336 5 1 **Indian Star (GER)**[6] 682 10-9-0 60 (t) RichardEvans(7) 5 61+
(P D Evans) *hld up towards rr: rdn over 4f out: nvr nr ldrs* 50/1

52-5 6 3 1/4 **Easibet Dot Net**[29] 374 8-9-0 53 (p) PhillipMakin 10 48
(Miss L A Perratt) *hld up and bhd: sme hdwy 6f out: rdn over 4f out: nt clr run briefly wl over 3f out: sn wknd* 6/1[2]

50-6 7 4 1/2 **Arabian Sun**[16] 544 4-8-12 57 (v) IanMongan 12 47
(M J Attwater) *led early: chsd wnr tl rdn 6f out: wknd over 3f out* 8/1

0222 8 4 1/2 **Kanisorn (SWE)**[12] 600 6-9-12 65 (bt) LiamJones 7 49
(Mrs R A Carr) *hld up in tch: rdn 6f out: wknd wl over 2f out* 8/1

300- 9 32 **Market Watcher (USA)**[101] 6883 7-8-13 55 (t) JamieMoriarty(3) 13 —
(Seamus Fahey, Ire) *hld up in tch: chsd wnr 6f out tl over 3f out: sn wknd* 20/1

005 10 nk **Allez Melina**[18] 524 7-8-11 50 NeilChalmers 11 —
(Mouse Hamilton-Fairley) *a bhd: rdn and lost tch 4f out* 100/1

54/0 11 1 1/4 **Riff Raff**[13] 588 5-9-3 56 ChrisCatlin 8 —
(C J Gray) *plld hrd towards rr: rdn 6f out: lost tch 4f out* 50/1

3m 46.56s (4.76) **Going Correction** +0.275s/f (Slow)
WFA 4 from 5yo+ 6lb 11 Ran SP% 119.7
Speed ratings (Par 101): **99,97,97,93,93 91,89,87,72,72 71**
CSF £138.79 CT £245.64 TOTE £10.40: £2.30, £4.80, £1.40; EX 147.30 TRIFECTA Not won..
Owner Seaton Stud Limited **Bred** Mrs R S Evans **Trained** Newmarket, Suffolk
■ This was the first winner for Robert Winston since he returned from his year-long suspension.

FOCUS
An uncompetitive low-grade staying handicap. The first two give the form a straightforward appearance with the third not helped by a slow start.

755 FAMILY FUN ALL DAY @ PONTIN'S H'CAP 7f 32y(P)
4:00 (4:01) (Class 5) (0-70,71) 4-Y-O+ £2,331 (£693; £346; £173) Stalls High

Form RPR

35-0 1 **Chief Exec**[23] 452 6-9-0 66 (b[1]) LiamJones 4 81+
(J R Gask) *hld up and bhd: hdwy 2f out: rdn to ld jst over 1f out: qcknd clr and hung lft ins fnl f: r.o wl* 8/1

-131 2 2 1/2 **Follow The Flag (IRE)**[14] 576 4-8-11 68 JackMitchell(5) 12 76
(C F Wall) *hld up in rr: hdwy and c v wd wl over 1f out: sn rdn: edgd lft and wnt 2nd ins fnl f: no ch w wnr* 6/1

1106 3 3/4 **Sovereignty (JPN)**[14] 576 6-8-9 61 JimCrowley 9 67+
(D K Ivory) *hld up in rr: nt clr run and swtchd rt wl over 1f out: gd hdwy fnl f: nrst fin* 9/2[1]

-453 4 nk **Kelamon**[8] 636 4-8-11 68 PatrickHills(5) 5 73+
(M D I Usher) *hld up in tch: n.m.r and lost pl over 5f out: hdwy 2f out: rdn over 1f out: kpt on one pce fnl f* 10/1

0024 5 1 **Epidaurian King (IRE)**[16] 548 5-8-11 63 (v) DeanMcKeown 6 65
(D Shaw) *t.k.h: sn chsng ldrs: rdn to ld wl over 1f out: sn edgd lft and hdd: no ex fnl f* 16/1

3-61 6 4 1/2 **Ever Cheerful**[27] 407 7-9-0 66 (p) JamieSpencer 7 56
(A B Haynes) *led after 1f: rdn and hdd wl over 1f out: sn carried lft and wknd* 11/2[3]

013- 7 3 **Sedge (USA)**[120] 6610 8-9-1 70 JamieMoriarty(3) 10 52
(P T Midgley) *hld up in mid-div: hdwy 2f out: wknd fnl f* 16/1

2033 8 1 1/4 **Parkview Love (USA)**[6] 683 7-9-1 67 (v) NCallan 3 46
(D Shaw) *led early: a.p: swtchd lft wl over 1f out: sn wknd* 5/1[2]

430- 9 3 **Marko Jadeo (IRE)**[180] 5064 10-8-10 67 KevinGhunowa(5) 2 38
(R A Harris) *hld up in tch: rdn and wknd over 3f out* 33/1

3211 10 1/2 **Kensington (IRE)**[6] 683 7-9-5 71 6ex (p) StephenDonohoe 8 40
(P D Evans) *prom: ev ch over 2f out: wknd over 1f out* 5/1[2]

433 11 7 **Mr Rev**[19] 514 5-8-13 65 SteveDrowne 1 15
(J M Bradley) *sn led: hdd after 1f: prom: rdn over 3f out: wknd over 2f out* 20/1

1m 30.69s (1.09) **Going Correction** +0.275s/f (Slow) 11 Ran SP% 120.9
Speed ratings (Par 103): **104,101,100,99,98 93,90,88,85,84 76**
CSF £57.06 CT £252.29 TOTE £10.50: £3.90, £2.10, £2.40; EX 85.80 TRIFECTA Not won..
Owner Horses First Racing Limited **Bred** C A Cyzer **Trained** Sutton Veny, Wilts
■ A first win for trainer Jeremy Gask.

FOCUS
A modest but competitive handicap with plenty in with a chance turning for home.The form looks solid rated around the placed horses.
Ever Cheerful Official explanation: jockey said gelding hung right entering straight

756 TIME TO BOOK YOUR PONTIN'S BREAK H'CAP 5f 216y(P)
4:35 (4:35) (Class 4) (0-85,83) 3-Y-O £4,533 (£1,348; £674; £336) Stalls Low

Form RPR

4-21 1 **Mister New York (USA)**[23] 457 3-8-12 77 KirstyMilczarek(3) 10 81
(Noel T Chance) *hld up and bhd: rdn and str run whn edgd lft ins fnl f: r.o wl to ld nr fin* 3/1[1]

The Form Book, Raceform Ltd, Compton, RG20 6NL

2153 **2** ¾ **Valhillen**[11] 612 3-8-3 **70**.......... PatrickHills(5) 3 72
(M D I Usher) *a.p: ev ch whn rdr dropped whip 1f out: edgd lft ins fnl f: r.o* **14/1**
1-01 **3** shd **Cross Fell (USA)**[21] 489 3-9-7 **83**..........(p) PatCosgrave 1 85
(J R Boyle) *led: rdn over 1f out: hdd nr fin* **9/2**[3]
41 **4** ½ **Prime Factor**[19] 514 3-8-12 **74**.......... MichaelHills 7 74
(B W Hills) *hld up: sn in tch: rdn over 1f out: kpt on towards fin* **7/2**[2]
6141 **5** nk **Fulford**[40] 237 3-8-2 **64**.......... DaleGibson 5 63
(M Brittain) *s.i.s: bhd: rdn and hdwy on ins over 1f out: styng on whn nt clr run cl home* **16/1**
16-3 **6** 1¼ **Rockfield Lodge (IRE)**[23] 457 3-9-1 **77**.......... TPQueally 6 72
(J A Osborne) *t.k.h towards rr: sme hdwy wl over 1f out: sn hung lft: no further prog* **11/2**
2-01 **7** nk **Bahamian Lad**[20] 505 3-8-7 **72**.......... RussellKennemore(3) 9 66
(R Hollinshead) *a.p: ev ch over 2f out: rdn over 1f out: fdd wl ins fnl f* **9/1**
401- **8** ½ **Storey Hill (USA)**[115] 6705 3-8-13 **75**.......... DeanMcKeown 2 67
(D Shaw) *prom: rdn over 1f out: fdd ins fnl f* **12/1**
060- **9** 9 **Feeling Proud (USA)**[147] 5974 3-9-2 **78**.......... JimmyQuinn 12 42
(Jane Chapple-Hyam) *hld up in tch: wknd over 2f out* **33/1**
0-41 **10** 3¾ **Asian Power (IRE)**[16] 538 3-8-12 **74**.......... OscarUrbina 8 26
(P J O'Gorman) *hld up towards rr: n.m.r and bmpd over 2f out: sn struggling* **7/1**

1m 17.05s (2.05) **Going Correction** +0.275s/f (Slow) **10 Ran SP% 126.5**
Speed ratings (Par 99): **97,96,95,95,94 93,92,92,80,75**
CSF £51.43 CT £203.08 TOTE £4.10: £1.90, £2.70, £2.10; EX 48.30 Trifecta £271.40 Part won. Pool £382.38 - 0.50 winning units..
Owner Mrs M Chance **Bred** J S McDonald **Trained** Upper Lambourn, Berks
FOCUS
A typically open-looking sprint handicap and the form has been rated positively.
Fulford Official explanation: jockey said gelding was denied a clear run

757 RACE TO PONTIN'S FOR EASTER H'CAP 1m 4f 50y(P)
5:05 (5:06) (Class 2) (0-100,106) 4-Y-0+ **£10,363** (£3,083; £1,540; £769) **Stalls** Low

Form RPR
4-14 **1** **Millville**[27] 410 8-9-12 **106**.......... NCallan 2 113
(M A Jarvis) *a.p: wnt 2nd 3f out: rdn wl over 1f out: r.o to ld towards fin* **5/2**[1]
2-26 **2** ½ **Polish Power (GER)**[27] 410 8-8-9 **89**.......... LPKeniry 1 95
(J S Moore) *led: rdn wl over 1f out: edgd lft ins fnl f: hdd towards fin* **8/1**
111- **3** 6 **Grande Caiman (IRE)**[82] 7086 4-8-3 **93**.......... CharlesEddery(7) 4 90+
(R Hannon) *hld up towards rr: hdwy wl over 1f out: hung lft and tk 3rd wl ins fnl f: nvr nr ldrs* **8/1**
101/ **4** 1¼ **Permanent Way (IRE)**[254] 5-8-10 **90**.......... JamieSpencer 11 85
(B J Meehan) *hld up in tch: rdn and edgd rt over 1f out: one pce* **9/1**
006- **5** 5 **Kings Quay**[20] 6302 6-8-7 **87** ow1..........(t) GrahamGibbons 8 75
(J J Quinn) *hld up towards rr: hdwy over 3f out: rdn wl over 1f out: no further prog* **12/1**
350/ **6** 1½ **Profit's Reality (IRE)**[518] 5657 6-9-1 **95**.......... IanMongan 6 81
(P A Blockley) *hld up in rr: styd on fr over 1f out: n.d* **7/1**[3]
-301 **7** 1¼ **Cold Turkey**[25] 428 8-8-9 **89**.......... SimonWhitworth 10 73
(G L Moore) *chsd ldr to 3f out: wknd 2f out* **5/1**[2]
452- **8** 6 **New Beginning (IRE)**[217] 3912 4-8-4 **87**.......... PaulHanagan 3 62
(Mrs S Lamyman) *hld up in mid-div: rdn and wknd over 2f out* **15/2**
00-5 **9** 5 **Kames Park (IRE)**[27] 410 6-8-10 **90**.......... PhillipMakin 9 57
(Miss L A Perratt) *s.i.s: rdn 3f out: a bhd* **7/1**[3]
1230 **10** 16 **Kabeer**[6] 679 10-8-12 **92**..........(t) PatrickMathers 7 35
(A J McCabe) *t.k.h in rr: pushed along 4f out: rdn and struggling 3f out* **25/1**

2m 42.11s (1.01) **Going Correction** +0.275s/f (Slow)
WFA 4 from 5yo+ 3lb **10 Ran SP% 125.8**
Speed ratings (Par 109): **107,106,102,101,98 97,96,92,89,78**
CSF £25.57 CT £149.88 TOTE £3.40: £1.60, £2.60, £2.30; EX 31.40 Trifecta £69.20 Pool £671.27 - 6.88 winning units..
Owner T G Warner **Bred** Red House Stud **Trained** Newmarket, Suffolk
FOCUS
A good handicap and a decent turnout for some good prizemoney. The form looks rock-solid with the first two clear.
NOTEBOOK
Millville continues in good form and always gave the impression that he was going to wear down the front-running Polish Power despite his big weight. (op 3-1)
Polish Power(GER) put a disappointing run last time behind him after being beaten three quarters of a length by the winner on 3lb worse terms at Lingfield on his previous start. He adopted totally different tactics and they very nearly paid off. (tchd 15-2)
Grande Caiman(IRE) had been raised a total of 21lb for completing a hat-trick and was meeting the second on 8lb worse terms than when beaten a length at Lingfield in December. Given an awful lot to do, it has to be said that he was not helping his young rider in the latter stages. Official explanation: jockey said, regarding running and riding, that his orders were to drop the colt in and to settle in mid-division, adding that it suffered interference, was shuffled back turning out of the back straight and was unable to hold its position; trainer's rep confirmed instructions adding that the colt has a sensitive mouth and is a difficult ride at home. (op 7-1)
Permanent Way(IRE) finished tailed off on soft ground at Dieppe in June on his only run last year and would be entitled to come on for this outing. (tchd 10-1)
Kings Quay had finished last in the totesport Trophy hurdle at Newbury earlier in the month, never got involved having been held up. (op 8-1)
Profit's Reality(IRE) ◆ was a real springer in the market on what was only his second outing on Polytrack. Having his first run since September he had presumably been showing something at home and it may be prudent to keep an eye on him. (op 20-1)

758 TRY BETDAQ FOR AN EXCHANGE MAIDEN STKS 1m 4f 50y(P)
5:35 (5:36) (Class 5) 3-Y-0+ **£2,457** (£725; £362) **Stalls** Low

Form RPR
32 **1** **Always Bold (IRE)**[6] 674 3-8-4 0.......... GregFairley 7 81+
(M Johnston) *mde all clr over 2f out: eased ins fnl f* **4/5**[1]
240- **2** 5 **Guardian Of Truth (IRE)**[18] 4113 4-9-11 71.......... GeorgeBaker 8 74
(G L Moore) *a.p: rdn and wnt 2nd 3f out: no ch w wnr* **7/4**[2]
0-5 **3** 10 **Soxy Doxy (IRE)**[46] 158 3-7-13 0.......... JimmyQuinn 9 51
(M Johnston) *hld up in tch: pushed along 6f out: rdn over 3f out: wknd over 2f out* **25/1**
4 **4** 16 **Brave Bugsy (IRE)**[16] 545 5-10-0 0.......... SimonWhitworth 3 35
(M Appleby) *hld up towards rr: rdn 4f out: styd on to take poor 4th wl ins fnl f* **20/1**
5/ **5** 2 **No Supper (IRE)**[429] 6950 4-9-6 0.......... JamieJones(5) 10 32
(M G Quinlan) *chsd wnr tl rdn 3f out: sn wknd* **10/1**[3]
6 **6** 2 **Site Sentry (IRE)**[16] 545 5-10-0 0.......... SteveDrowne 4 29
(M F Harris) *hld up in tch: wknd 4f out* **33/1**
7 1¾ **Brave Boogie** 3-8-1 0 ow2.......... FrancisNorton 5 20
(H J L Dunlop) *a in rr: no ch fnl 5f* **33/1**
56 **8** hd **Spellman**[11] 610 4-9-11 0.......... IanMongan 1 26
(N P Littmoden) *hld up towards rr: rdn 5f out: sn no ch* **25/1**
006- **9** hd **Zach's Harmoney (USA)**[195] 4591 4-9-11 69..........(t) JamieSpencer 6 25
(M Appleby) *hld up in mid-div: hdwy 5f out: wknd over 3f out* **16/1**
0 **10** nk **Meadow Cottage (IRE)**[28] 396 5-10-0 0.......... HayleyTurner 12 25
(Mrs P Ford) *s.s: a in rr: no ch fnl 5f* **100/1**
44 **11** 2½ **Right You Are (IRE)**[18] 524 8-10-0 0.......... PatrickMathers 11 21
(Paul Green) *s.s: hld up towards rr: rdn 4f out: sn struggling* **40/1**
0-0 **12** 9 **Mystik Megan**[28] 396 7-9-9 0.......... TPQueally 2 —
(M Mullineaux) *a in rr: no ch fnl 5f* **100/1**

2m 42.42s (1.32) **Going Correction** +0.275s/f (Slow)
WFA 3 from 4yo 24lb 4 from 5yo+ 3lb **12 Ran SP% 129.6**
Speed ratings (Par 103): **106,102,96,85,84 82,81,81,81,81 79,73**
CSF £2.40 TOTE £2.00: £1.10, £1.10, £3.90; EX 3.10 Trifecta £14.00 Pool £274.55 - 13.90 winning units. Place 6 £68.21, Place 5 £51.60.
Owner Always Trying Partnership V **Bred** R N Auld **Trained** Middleham Moor, N Yorks
FOCUS
This did not take much winning but it was a fair time for a race of its type. The form is not easy to assess.
T/Plt: £113.60 to a £1 stake. Pool: £53,919.65. 346.20 winning tickets. T/Qpdt: £9.10 to a £1 stake. Pool: £5,063.80. 408.60 winning tickets. KH

759 - 765a (Foreign Racing) - See Raceform Interactive

752
WOLVERHAMPTON (A.W) (L-H)
Saturday, March 1

OFFICIAL GOING: Standard
Wind: Fresh behind Weather: Overcast

766 MAUREEN COWBOURNE CELEBRATION SPECIAL APPRENTICE H'CAP 5f 216y(P)
6:50 (6:50) (Class 6) (0-65,65) 4-Y-0+ **£2,047** (£604; £302) **Stalls** Low

Form RPR
3403 **1** **Avontuur (FR)**[7] 681 6-8-6 **52**..........(p) MCGeran 5 61
(Mrs R A Carr) *s.i.s: hdwy over 2f out: styd on u.p to ld wl ins fnl f* **14/1**
-035 **2** hd **Music Box Express**[37] 286 4-8-9 **58**..........(t) MatthewDavies(3) 1 66
(George Baker) *sn led: rdn and hdd wl ins fnl f* **11/4**[1]
2020 **3** 1¼ **Mambazo**[10] 628 6-8-11 **62**..........(e) BMcHugh(5) 9 67
(S C Williams) *chsd ldrs: rdn over 1f out: styd on* **12/1**[3]
-211 **4** ½ **Sherjawy (IRE)**[6] 696 4-8-4 **55** 6ex..........(b) RossAtkinson(5) 3 58
(Miss Z C Davison) *a.p: chsd ldr 1/2-way: rdn over 1f out: styd on same pce* **11/4**[1]
4-02 **5** 3½ **Inca Soldier (FR)**[15] 581 5-8-9 **60**.......... KrishGundowry(5) 4 53
(R C Guest) *dwlt: bhd: nvr nrr* **9/2**[2]
5545 **6** 1½ **Figaro Flyer (IRE)**[15] 576 5-9-5 **65**.......... SCreighton 8 53
(P Howling) *plld hrd: led early: trckd ldr to 1/2-way: wknd fnl f* **9/2**[2]
6100 **7** 1½ **Littledodayno (IRE)**[17] 539 5-8-10 **63**.......... MJMurphy(7) 7 47
(M Wigham) *hld up: rdn over 2f out: a in rr* **18/1**
/045 **8** 9 **Supreme Speedster**[9] 636 4-8-8 **59**.......... AdamCarter(5) 6 16
(M Brittain) *chsd ldrs over 3f* **16/1**

1m 14.89s (-0.11) **Going Correction** +0.15s/f (Slow) **8 Ran SP% 115.2**
Speed ratings (Par 101): **106,105,104,103,98 96,94,82**
CSF £53.03 CT £491.74 TOTE £16.20: £4.00, £1.50, £2.90; EX 59.90.
Owner David W Chapman **Bred** Haras D'Etreham **Trained** Stillington, N Yorks
■ A first winner for trainer Ruth Carr since she took over the licence from her grandfather David Chapman.
FOCUS
A fair winning time for a race like this and reliable form rated around the runner-up.

767 MUM KNOWS THAT PONTIN'S IS BEST H'CAP 5f 20y(P)
7:20 (7:20) (Class 6) (0-60,64) 3-Y-0 **£2,388** (£705; £352) **Stalls** Low

Form RPR
-331 **1** **Upstanding**[3] 721 3-9-5 **64** 6ex.......... MarkLawson(3) 9 66
(M Brittain) *a.p: chsd ldr over 1f out: sn rdn: r.o to ld post* **15/8**[1]
60-5 **2** hd **Honest Value (IRE)**[20] 514 3-8-10 **52**..........(p) NeilPollard 3 53
(Mrs L C Jewell) *led: rdn over 1f out: edgd rt: hdd post* **16/1**
4-65 **3** 1 **Planet Paradise (IRE)**[4] 709 3-7-13 **46** oh1.......... KellyHarrison(5) 10 44+
(D Shaw) *s.i.s: hld up: rdn over 1f out: r.o ins fnl f: nt rch ldrs* **50/1**
450- **4** shd **Thomas Malory (IRE)**[128] 6454 3-8-10 **57**.......... SCreighton(5) 5 54
(Miss V Haigh) *edgd rt s: mid-div: rdn 1/2-way: hdwy over 1f out: styd on* **11/1**
066 **5** 1 **Rightcar Hull (IRE)**[21] 505 3-8-8 **50**.......... LPKeniry 1 44
(Peter Grayson) *mid-div: sn pushed along: hdwy u.p over 1f out: styd on* **25/1**
0-03 **6** nk **Jastaanhi**[11] 614 3-7-11 **46** oh1.......... StacyRenwick(7) 7 39
(J A Pickering) *chsd ldrs: rdn over 1f out: no ex ins fnl f* **33/1**
-606 **7** 1 **Kamal**[22] 480 3-9-4 **60**.......... HayleyTurner 4 49
(W R Muir) *hld up: nt clr run over 2f out: hdwy and nt clr run over 1f out: styd on same pce ins fnl f* **5/2**[2]
4353 **8** 1¾ **Whitcombe Flyer (USA)**[14] 583 3-8-9 **51**..........(b) JimmyQuinn 8 34
(Miss M E Rowland) *hld up: rdn 1/2-way: n.d* **13/2**[3]
40-4 **9** 3½ **Miss Bronte**[51] 114 3-8-10 **55**.......... RussellKennemore(3) 2 25
(R Hollinshead) *chsd ldrs: rdn over 1f out: sn wknd* **8/1**
400- **10** 6 **Bellas Chicas (IRE)**[150] 5903 3-8-12 **54**.......... MickyFenton 6 3
(P T Midgley) *bmpd s: chsd ldrs: rdn and hung lft over 1f out: sn wknd* **20/1**
-352 **11** 1¾ **Little Finch (IRE)**[36] 298 3-8-5 **47**..........(b) ChrisCatlin 13 —
(R C Guest) *rrd s: outpcd* **16/1**

63.81 secs (1.51) **Going Correction** +0.15s/f (Slow) **11 Ran SP% 121.4**
Speed ratings (Par 96): **93,92,91,90,89 88,87,84,78,69 66**
CSF £34.49 CT £1192.22 TOTE £3.20: £1.40, £3.90, £14.20; EX 61.00.
Owner Mel Brittain **Bred** The Hon Mrs R Pease **Trained** Warthill, N Yorks
■ Stewards' Enquiry : Mark Lawson one-day ban: used whip with excessive frequency (Mar 12)
FOCUS
A weak handicap based on the performances of the modest trio who followed the winner home.
Kamal Official explanation: jockey said gelding was denied a clear run
Bellas Chicas(IRE) Official explanation: jockey said filly lost its action
Little Finch(IRE) Official explanation: jockey said filly missed the break

768 PONTIN'S - THE MOTHER OF ALL HOLIDAYS CLAIMING STKS 1m 141y(P)
7:50 (7:50) (Class 5) 4-Y-0+ **£2,590** (£770; £385; £192) **Stalls** Low

Form RPR
3211 **1** **Ninth House (USA)**[15] 577 6-9-3 77..........(bt) JimCrowley 2 84+
(N P Littmoden) *trckd ldr tl led over 3f out: clr 2f out: comf* **4/7**[1]

4-24 **2** 4 ½ **Inside Story (IRE)**[20] 512 6-9-3 72........................(b) ChrisCatlin 3 73
(M W Easterby) *prom: rdn to chse wnr over 2f out: hung lft and no imp fr over 1f out* **9/4**[2]
3050 **3** 3 ¾ **Royal Embrace**[17] 537 5-8-1 55........................(v) KellyHarrison(5) 4 54
(D Shaw) *hld up: rdn and hung lft fr over 1f out: n.d* **25/1**
6-44 **4** 4 **Circus Polka (USA)**[40] 250 4-8-10 59........................(bt) TGMcLaughlin 5 50
(W M Brisbourne) *sn led: racd keenly: rdn and hdd over 3f out: wknd over 1f out* **9/1**[3]
00-6 **5** 2 ¼ **Grey Vision**[57] 40 5-8-2 40........................(b) JimmyQuinn 1 37
(M Brittain) *prom: racd keenly: rdn and wknd over 2f out* **50/1**
1m 51.71s (1.21) **Going Correction** +0.15s/f (Slow) **5** Ran SP% **110.2**
Speed ratings (Par 103): **100,96,92,89,87**
CSF £2.09 TOTE £1.70: £1.20, £1.30; EX 1.60.The winner was the subject of a friendly claim
Owner Nigel Shields **Bred** Juddmonte Farms Inc **Trained** Newmarket, Suffolk
FOCUS
Not a competitive claimer, and the standard is governed by the fifth.

769 MUM'S THE WORD @ PONTINS.COM H'CAP 1m 1f 103y(P)
8:20 (8:21) (Class 6) (0-52,52) 4-Y-O+ £1,774 (£523; £262) Stalls Low

Form RPR
6315 **1** **Jarvo**[17] 541 7-8-11 51........................(v) PatrickMathers 9 58
(I W McInnes) *hld up in tch: shkn up over 3f out: hrd rdn fr over 1f out: hung lft and styd on to ld wl ins fnl f* **5/1**[3]
-020 **2** ½ **Tidy (IRE)**[16] 559 8-8-10 50........................(v) DeanMcKeown 5 56
(Micky Hammond) *hld up: nt clr run over 3f out: sn rdn: r.o ins fnl f: nt rch wnr* **11/1**
0-34 **3** ½ **Bramcote Lorne**[20] 517 5-8-10 50........................(p) StephenDonohoe 3 55
(R C Guest) *led: rdn clr over 1f out: hdd wl ins fnl f* **7/2**[1]
2252 **4** ½ **Abbeygate**[16] 550 7-8-0 47........................(p) AshleyMorgan(7) 11 51
(T Keddy) *hld up: hdwy and edgd lft fr over 2f out: sn rdn: styd on* **5/1**[3]
-266 **5** 2 **Don Pasquale**[36] 299 6-8-6 46........................(v) ChrisCatlin 1 46
(J T Stimpson) *hld up: hdwy u.p over 1f out: kpt on* **9/2**[2]
3100 **6** 1 ¾ **Tabulate**[7] 686 5-8-6 46........................ JimmyQuinn 4 43
(P Howling) *chsd ldrs: rdn over 1f out: no ex fnl f* **13/2**
066- **7** ¾ **Kielty's Folly**[82] 7103 4-8-9 49........................ AndrewElliott 8 45
(B P J Baugh) *prom: rdn over 2f out: hmpd sn after: hung lft and wknd over 1f out* **16/1**
-203 **8** 1 ¼ **Persian Fox (IRE)**[21] 507 4-8-7 47........................ VinceSlattery 10 40
(A G Juckes) *hld up: nt clr run over 2f out: effrt and nt clr run over 1f out: swtchd lft: nvr trbld ldrs* **10/1**
240/ **9** 2 ¼ **House Martin**[468] 6279 6-8-6 46 oh1........................(p) HayleyTurner 2 35
(C R Dore) *chsd ldr tl rdn over 2f out: wknd over 1f out* **33/1**
/400 **10** 15 **Up Dee Creek**[15] 578 6-8-3 46 oh1........................(b) DuranFentiman(3) 6 6
(W M Brisbourne) *chsd ldrs: rdn over 2f out: wknd over 2f out* **25/1**
2m 3.26s (1.56) **Going Correction** +0.15s/f (Slow) **10** Ran SP% **117.2**
Speed ratings (Par 101): **99,98,98,97,95 94,93,92,90,77**
CSF £59.07 CT £218.44 TOTE £5.30: £2.10, £3.20, £1.60; EX 79.20.
Owner F S W Partnership **Bred** Lloyd Farm Stud **Trained** Catwick, E Yorks
FOCUS
Modest form rated around the first four home and not a race to be with.

770 PAUL HEATH ELECTRICAL JOHN LAVERTY MEMORIAL CLASSIFIED STKS 1m 1f 103y(P)
8:50 (8:51) (Class 7) 4-Y-O+ £1,365 (£403; £201) Stalls Low

Form RPR
5411 **1** **Bahhmirage (IRE)**[6] 691 5-9-6 43........................ JimmyQuinn 13 58
(C N Kellett) *mid-div: rdn over 3f out: hdwy and swtchd lft over 1f out: styd on u.p to ld towards fin* **11/1**
040- **2** nk **High Five Society**[121] 6609 4-9-0 43........................(bt) PhillipMakin 12 51
(S R Bowring) *led over 7f out: rdn clr 2f out: hdd towards fin* **14/1**
4324 **3** ¾ **Arthurs Dream (IRE)**[15] 578 6-8-9 45........................ KellyHarrison(5) 1 50
(A W Carroll) *hld up in tch: rdn over 1f out: edgd lft: r.o* **6/1**[3]
6036 **4** nk **Castle Frome (IRE)**[8] 654 9-9-0 42........................(p) PaulFitzsimons 2 49
(A E Price) *trckd ldrs: racd keenly: rdn over 1f out: kpt on* **25/1**
-620 **5** 3 ½ **Candy Anchor (FR)**[25] 438 9-9-0 43........................ ChrisCatlin 5 42
(R E Peacock) *hld up in tch: racd keenly: stdd and lost pl 7f out: rdn over 2f out: r.o ins fnl f* **16/1**
/60- **6** ½ **High Country (IRE)**[273] 215 8-9-0 45........................ DeanMcKeown 3 41
(Micky Hammond) *hld up: styd on ins fnl f: nvr nrr* **20/1**
-563 **7** nk **Stoneacre Gareth (IRE)**[10] 627 4-9-0 45........................ JimCrowley 11 41
(J Jay) *prom: chsd ldr over 5f out: rdn over 2f out: wknd ins fnl f* **3/1**[1]
06-0 **8** nk **Passionately Royal**[53] 80 6-8-11 45........................ MarkLawson(3) 9 40
(M Brittain) *chsd ldrs: rdn over 2f out: hung lft over 1f out: styd on same pce* **20/1**
-403 **9** ½ **The Power Of Phil**[15] 578 4-9-0 44........................ RichardKingscote 4 39
(Miss Joanne Priest) *led 1f: chsd ldrs: rdn over 2f out: wknd ins fnl f* **11/2**[2]
000- **10** ½ **The London Gang**[228] 3629 5-9-0 43........................ TGMcLaughlin 8 38
(W M Brisbourne) *hld up: sme hdwy over 2f out: wknd fnl f* **14/1**
-540 **11** ½ **Love You Always (USA)**[6] 691 8-9-0 43........................(t) HayleyTurner 7 37
(Jane Chapple-Hyam) *in rr: did not look to face kickback: styng on whn nt clr run ins fnl f: n.d* **17/2**
4266 **12** 3 ½ **Vintage Quest**[15] 579 6-9-0 45........................(v[1]) VinceSlattery 10 31
(D Burchell) *s.i.s: sme hdwy over 2f out: wknd fnl f* **25/1**
5616 **13** 2 ½ **Busy Man (IRE)**[20] 518 9-9-0 45........................ StephenDonohoe 6 26
(R C Guest) *s.i.s: hld up: a in rr* **6/1**[3]
2m 2.93s (1.23) **Going Correction** +0.15s/f (Slow) **13** Ran SP% **124.2**
Speed ratings (Par 97): **100,99,99,98,95 95,94,94,94,93 93,90,88**
CSF £152.95 TOTE £7.00: £3.10, £5.60, £2.40; EX 85.40.
Owner Miss S Walley **Bred** Centaur Bloodstock Agency **Trained** Woodlane, Staffs
■ Stewards' Enquiry : Jimmy Quinn caution: used whip without giving mare time to respond
FOCUS
Moderate form but solid enough, rated around the four who chased the winner home.
Passionately Royal Official explanation: jockey said gelding hung left-handed
The Power Of Phil Official explanation: jockey said gelding had no more to give

771 MUM'S GONE TO PONTIN'S H'CAP 1m 4f 50y(P)
9:20 (9:20) (Class 6) (0-60,64) 4-Y-O+ £2,047 (£604; £302) Stalls Low

Form RPR
40-3 **1** **Terminate (GER)**[16] 559 6-8-11 53........................ StephenDonohoe 9 64+
(Ian Williams) *hld up: hdwy over 2f out: led wl over 1f out: styd on wl* **5/1**[3]
3431 **2** 3 **Buscador (USA)**[7] 682 9-9-1 57........................ RichardKingscote 3 64
(W M Brisbourne) *led: rdn over 3f out: hdd wl over 1f out: edgd lft and no ex fnl f* **13/8**[1]
1131 **3** 2 ½ **Karmest**[11] 613 4-9-1 64........................ KellyHarrison(5) 2 67
(A D Brown) *hld up: hdwy over 3f out: rdn and edgd lft fr over 1f out: no ex fnl f* **8/1**
3122 **4** ½ **Still Dreaming**[8] 664 4-8-6 57........................(b) RossAtkinson(7) 5 59
(R J Price) *hld up in tch: rdn over 2f out: no ex fnl f* **13/2**
1255 **5** 5 **Qaasi (USA)**[3] 720 6-9-0 59........................ MarkLawson(3) 1 54
(M Brittain) *prom: racd keenly: chsd ldr 4f out: rdn over 1f out: wknd fnl f* **9/2**[2]
063- **6** 1 ½ **Berbatov**[198] 4526 4-8-2 46........................ PatrickMathers 4 38
(Paul Green) *s.i.s: hld up: rdn over 2f out: nvr nrr* **12/1**
/06- **7** 2 **River City (IRE)**[65] 6709 11-8-13 55........................ VinceSlattery 7 44
(Noel T Chance) *hld up: hdwy over 5f out: wknd 3f out* **33/1**
56-0 **8** 1 **Cavendish**[34] 330 4-8-13 57........................ DaleGibson 8 45
(J M P Eustace) *chsd ldrs 7f* **20/1**
5/00 **9** 20 **Archirondel**[15] 578 10-7-11 46 oh1........................ SoniaEaton(7) 6 4
(B P J Baugh) *trckd ldrs: plld hrd: wknd over 2f out* **66/1**
50/6 **10** 48 **Eyes To The Right (IRE)**[15] 577 9-8-4 46 oh1........................ JimmyQuinn 10 —
(D Burchell) *chsd ldrs over 7f* **66/1**
2m 42.0s (0.90) **Going Correction** +0.15s/f (Slow)
WFA 4 from 6yo+ 2lb **10** Ran SP% **115.8**
Speed ratings (Par 101): **103,101,99,99,95 94,93,92,79,47**
CSF £13.07 CT £63.05 TOTE £4.60: £2.10, £1.40, £1.80; EX 15.00 Place 6 £ 60.19, Place 5 £ 20.31.
Owner Dr Marwan Koukash & P J Legros **Bred** Gestut Hofgut Mappen **Trained** Portway, Worcs
FOCUS
A modest handicap made up mostly of badly handicapped horses, but the form looks solid enough for the grade rated around the second, third and fourth.
Eyes To The Right(IRE) Official explanation: jockey said gelding had no more to give
T/Plt: £56.10 to a £1 stake. Pool: £104,858.00. 1,363.50 winning tickets. T/Qpdt: £6.10 to a £1 stake. Pool: £8,688.90. 1,047.20 winning tickets. CR

[731] LINGFIELD (L-H)
Monday, March 3

OFFICIAL GOING: Standard
Wind: Brisk, half-behind Weather: Fine

772 BET MULTIPLES - BETDAQ MAIDEN STKS 7f (P)
2:10 (2:10) (Class 5) 3-Y-O+ £2,331 (£693; £346; £173) Stalls Low

Form RPR
3-42 **1** **Silent Master (USA)**[14] 608 3-8-11 77........................ JoeFanning 10 80+
(M Johnston) *mde virtually all: clr over 2f out: pushed along and in total command after* **5/6**[1]
636- **2** 4 ½ **Clifton Four (USA)**[161] 5682 3-8-6 73........................ DavidKinsella 6 63
(R Hannon) *mostly chsd wnr: lft bhd fr over 2f out: plugged on and jst hld on for 2nd* **11/1**
3 shd **Bartercard (USA)**[62] 7-9-13 0........................ MickyFenton 3 74
(Stef Liddiard) *dwlt: wl in rr: pushed along and wl off the pce 3f out: prog on outer over 1f out: r.o wl fnl f* **28/1**
64 **4** hd **Ambrix (IRE)**[11] 645 3-7-13 0........................ MatthewDavies(7) 5 62
(M R Channon) *in tch in midfield: outpcd over 2f out: drvn and styd on fr over 1f out* **25/1**
0- **5** 1 **Precipice**[157] 5785 3-8-6 0........................ AlanMunro 11 60
(D Carroll) *pressed ldrs: nt qckn over 2f out: one pce and no real imp over 1f out* **11/2**[2]
6 hd **Dream Rainbow**[276] 2226 3-8-11 0........................ TPQueally 7 64
(N Nevin, Ire) *hld up bhd ldrs: nt qckn 2f out: in chsng bunch after and no ch w wnr: n.m.r nr fin* **7/1**[3]
532- **7** 1 **Monashee Rock (IRE)**[120] 6664 3-8-6 75........................ LiamJones 1 57
(R Simpson) *chsd ldng pair: outpcd over 2f out: wknd ins fnl f* **11/2**[2]
8 2 ¼ **Bonne** 3-8-6 0........................ NeilPollard 2 51
(M L W Bell) *nvr beyond midfield: struggling over 2f out: n.d after* **20/1**
9 17 **Sweet Refrain** 3-8-6 0........................ PaulDoe 4 —
(J Akehurst) *s.s: a wl in rr: t.o* **50/1**
00-0 **10** 8 **Eau Sauvage**[31] 391 4-9-5 37........................ TolleyDean(3) 8 —
(J Akehurst) *last and rdn over 4f out: t.o* **66/1**
00- **11** 3 ½ **Ubiquitous Bounty**[160] 5706 3-8-6 0........................ RobynBrisland(5) 9 —
(Miss Z C Davison) *awkward s: racd wd: bhd fr 1/2-way: t.o* **66/1**
1m 24.13s (-0.67) **Going Correction** 0.0s/f (Stan)
WFA 3 from 4yo+ 16lb **11** Ran SP% **123.2**
Speed ratings (Par 103): **103,97,97,97,96 96,95,92,73,63 59**
CSF £11.61 TOTE £1.80: £1.10, £2.70, £5.60; EX 12.80.
Owner Sheikh Hamdan Bin Mohammed Al Maktoum **Bred** Darley **Trained** Middleham Moor, N Yorks
■ Stewards' Enquiry : Matthew Davies caution: careless riding
FOCUS
This was certainly not as competitive a maiden as the numbers would suggest and there was limited promise amongst those behind the odds-on favourite, several of whom were returning from layoffs. The winner's effort could have been rated higher than the bare form.

773 BETDAQPOKER.CO.UK MEDIAN AUCTION MAIDEN STKS 1m 2f (P)
2:40 (2:40) (Class 6) 3-5-Y-O £2,266 (£674; £337; £168) Stalls Low

Form RPR
306- **1** **Kyrie Eleison (IRE)**[185] 5002 3-8-3 73 ow3........................ PatrickHills(5) 5 64
(R Hannon) *dwlt: hld up in last pair: prog on inner over 2f out: urged along and sustained effrt to ld last 100yds* **11/8**[2]
66 **2** ½ **Site Sentry (IRE)**[3] 758 5-9-12 0........................ SteveDrowne 4 65
(M F Harris) *led: pressed 3f out: urged along over 2f out: hdd and nt qckn last 100yds* **14/1**
552 **3** 1 ¼ **Days Of Pleasure (IRE)**[10] 662 3-8-5 65........................ DavidKinsella 1 58
(J A Osborne) *trckd ldr: chal fr 3f out: rdn and nt qckn 2f out: btn and lost 2nd fnl f* **5/4**[1]
0 **4** 1 ¾ **Ramprakash**[14] 608 3-8-5 0........................ AndrewElliott 3 54+
(M L W Bell) *dwlt: trckd ldng pair: rn green and wd bnd 2f out: btn after: kpt on* **7/1**[3]
50 **5** 5 **Red Sonja (IRE)**[29] 416 3-8-0 0........................ LiamJones 2 40
(M Blanshard) *cl up: rdn over 2f out: hanging and wknd over 1f out* **33/1**
6 1 ¾ **Hoar Frost** 3-8-0 0........................ CatherineGannon 6 37
(M R Channon) *a in last pair: rdn 4f out: struggling over 2f out* **16/1**
2m 10.04s (3.44) **Going Correction** 0.0s/f (Stan)
WFA 3 from 5yo 21lb **6** Ran SP% **114.5**
Speed ratings (Par 101): **86,85,84,83,79 77**
CSF £20.59 TOTE £2.00: £1.30, £4.10; EX 19.40.
Owner Mrs J Wood **Bred** And Mrs B Firestone **Trained** East Everleigh, Wilts

FOCUS
A moderate maiden with only two seriously backed and a moderate pace resulted in a very slow winning time. The form looks sound through the winner and third but the runner-up was stepping up considerably on his previous efforts.

774 TRY BETDAQ FOR AN EXCHANGE H'CAP 5f (P)
3:10 (3:10) (Class 6) (0-55,59) 4-Y-O+ £2,252 (£664; £332) Stalls High

Form RPR
1361 **1** **Dodaa (USA)**[11] 641 5-8-6 **52** AshleyHamblett(5) 3 60
(N Wilson) *mde all: drvn over a l clr 1f out: hld on* **5/1**[3]
3321 **2** *nk* **Thoughtsofstardom**[8] 690 5-8-11 **59** 6ex MJMurphy(7) 2 66
(M Wigham) *hld up bhd ldng trio gng wl: effrt on inner to go 2nd jst ins fnl f: sn rdn: clsd but post c too sn* **2/1**[1]
1505 **3** *2* **Earl Compton (IRE)**[4] 726 4-9-0 **55** (v) MickyFenton 6 55
(Stef Liddiard) *trckd wnr after 2f: rdn and fnd nil over 1f out* **8/1**
-000 **4** *1* **Fastrac Boy**[8] 690 5-8-2 **50** KierenFox(7) 4 46
(J R Best) *hld up in midfield: urged along over 1f out: kpt on same pce* **16/1**
30-0 **5** *1 1/4* **One Way Ticket**[8] 690 8-8-6 **47** (b) LiamJones 7 39
(J M Bradley) *trckd wnr for 2f: lost pl over 1f out: n.d after* **16/1**
5004 **6** *hd* **Bentley**[8] 690 4-8-13 **54** (v) DaneO'Neill 5 45
(D Shaw) *chsd ldrs on outer: rdn 3f out: hanging and btn over 1f out* **9/4**[2]
-500 **7** *1/2* **Rosie Cross (IRE)**[5] 718 4-8-9 **55** (b[1]) PatrickHills(5) 8 44
(Eve Johnson Houghton) *a in same pl: unable to go early pce and a struggling* **8/1**
000 **8** *23* **Easily Naimd**[15] 598 4-8-4 **48** oh1 ow2 (v[1]) TolleyDean(3) 1 —
(D Shaw) *sn wl bhd: t.o* **66/1**
58.20 secs (-0.60) **Going Correction** 0.0s/f (Stan) **8** Ran SP% **116.2**
Speed ratings (Par 101): **104,103,100,98,96 96,95,58**
CSF £15.73 CT £79.76 TOTE £5.60: £1.90, £1.10, £2.40; EX 12.60.
Owner Paul & Linda Dixon **Bred** Silverleaf Farm Inc **Trained** Flaxton, N Yorks

FOCUS
A strongly run sprint and very few ever got into it. Sound form rated around the first two.

775 BET CHAMPIONS LEAGUE - BETDAQ H'CAP 7f (P)
3:40 (3:40) (Class 5) (0-75,75) 4-Y-O+ £2,914 (£867; £433; £216) Stalls Low

Form RPR
0362 **1** **Desert Dreamer (IRE)**[28] 429 7-9-3 **74** (t) RichardKingscote 1 83
(Tom Dascombe) *dwlt: sn trckd ldrs on inner: effrt 2f out: rdn to ld ins fnl f: hld on* **9/2**[1]
3513 **2** *nk* **Count Ceprano (IRE)**[5] 717 4-8-6 **70** GabrielHannon(7) 7 79+
(M D I Usher) *hld up in rr: stl in last pair 2f out: bmpd along and threaded through fr over 1f out: fin wl: nt rch wnr* **9/2**[1]
-022 **3** *3/4* **Millfield (IRE)**[35] 334 5-8-11 **68** JimCrowley 5 74
(P R Chamings) *hld up in last trio: prog on inner 2f out: clsd to chal ins fnl f: nt qckn last 100yds* **13/2**
6431 **4** *hd* **Dvinsky (USA)**[19] 539 7-8-13 **70** (b) TPQueally 2 76
(P Howling) *led after 1f: narrowly hdd jst over 1f out: stl ch ins fnl f: one pce* **16/1**
6-12 **5** *nk* **Paradise Dancer (IRE)**[19] 548 4-9-4 **75** GeorgeBaker 6 80
(J A R Toller) *led 1f: pressed ldr: rdn to ld jst over 1f out: hdd and folded tamely ins fnl f* **5/1**[2]
2213 **6** *1/2* **Royal Envoy (IRE)**[19] 539 5-8-4 **64** ow2 TolleyDean(3) 3 68
(D Shaw) *chsd ldrs: rdn over 2f out: kpt on u.p but nvr able to chal* **6/1**[3]
5006 **7** *nk* **Smokin Joe**[3] 747 7-9-3 **74** (b) SteveDrowne 4 77
(J R Best) *t.k.h: hld up towards rr: stl gng strly 2f out: rdn and fnd nil over 1f out: kpt on nr fin* **14/1**
603- **8** *1 3/4* **Scarlet Flyer (USA)**[138] 6269 5-9-0 **71** FergusSweeney 8 70
(G L Moore) *hld up in last pair: rdn 2f out: no prog* **15/2**
-232 **9** *1 1/2* **Gimme Some Lovin (IRE)**[17] 576 4-8-7 **64** (p) AlanMunro 9 59
(D W P Arbuthnot) *prom on outer tl lost pl fnl 2f* **8/1**
1m 24.1s (-0.70) **Going Correction** 0.0s/f (Stan) **9** Ran SP% **116.1**
Speed ratings (Par 103): **104,103,102,102,102 101,101,99,97**
CSF £24.78 CT £132.06 TOTE £7.10: £1.80, £2.30, £2.60; EX 26.00.
Owner ONEWAY Partners **Bred** Gainsborough Stud Management Ltd **Trained** Lambourn, Berks

FOCUS
A competitive handicap but the pace was only fair despite Paradise Dancer and Dvinsky duelling for the lead from the start. There was very little separating the front seven at the line but the form does make plenty of sense.

776 ALL NEW @ BETDAQ.CO.UK CLASSIFIED STKS 1m 5f (P)
4:10 (4:10) (Class 7) 4-Y-O+ £1,943 (£578; £288; £144) Stalls Low

Form RPR
4042 **1** **Chart Oak**[5] 715 5-9-2 38 TPQueally 1 50
(P Howling) *hld up towards rr: stdy prog on inner fr 5f out: trckd ldng pair over 2f out: rdn to ld jst ins fnl f: sn clr* **9/2**[2]
0422 **2** *2* **On Every Street**[3] 751 7-9-2 45 (p) PatCosgrave 5 47
(R Bastiman) *prom: led 3f out: rdn and hdd 2f out: kpt on fnl f but outpcd by wnr* **7/4**[1]
3/40 **3** *3/4* **Barnbrook Empire (IRE)**[17] 575 6-9-2 45 PaulDoe 6 46
(L A Dace) *dwlt: hld up in rr: rapid prog on outer over 4f out: pressed ldr 3f out: led 2f out: hdd and fdd jst ins fnl f* **16/1**
0666 **4** *1* **Only Hope**[3] 751 4-8-13 45 (p) PaulEddery 4 45
(Miss Diana Weeden) *dwlt: hld up: last over 4f out: prog to chse clr ldng trio jst over 2f out: kpt on but nvr able to chal* **12/1**
/00- **5** *3 1/2* **Escobar (POL)**[24] 7012 7-9-2 45 (t) AlanMunro 9 40
(Mrs P Townsley) *hld up in midfield: gng wl enough but lost pl over 4f out: wl in rr 3f out: shkn up and styd on fnl 2f: no ch* **8/1**
-555 **6** *2 3/4* **Cool Isle**[32] 377 5-9-2 33 (b) JimCrowley 7 36
(P Howling) *settled wl in rr: outpcd fr 3f out: plugged on fnl 2f: no ch* **14/1**
0-00 **7** *3 1/2* **Chart Express**[25] 471 4-8-13 38 AlanDaly 10 31
(P Howling) *nvr bttr than midfield: u.p on outer over 3f out: n.d after* **50/1**
00-0 **8** *1 1/2* **Peas 'n Beans (IRE)**[16] 585 5-9-2 36 (p) LiamJones 3 29
(T Keddy) *hld up in rr: outpcd over 3f out: no real imp after* **50/1**
0-50 **9** *4 1/2* **Valart**[48] 166 5-9-2 36 MickyFenton 2 23
(C Tinkler) *led: stdd pce 8f out: hdd 3f out: wknd rapidly fnl 2f* **16/1**
0-00 **10** *12* **Royal Auditon**[16] 585 7-9-2 42 (p) JoeFanning 11 6
(T T Clement) *s.i.s: prog to go prom 10f out: rdn and wknd 4f out: t.o* **8/1**
0-00 **11** *5* **Stratn Jack**[14] 607 4-8-6 45 (p) GabrielHannon(7) 8 —
(B G Powell) *plld hrd: prom tl wknd over 4f out: t.o* **33/1**
050/ **12** *8* **Achilles Wings (USA)**[978] 3315 12-9-2 42 (p) SamHitchcott 13 —
(Karen George) *stdd s: plld hrd: hld up in last tl rapid prog to go 2nd over 6f out: wknd 4f out: t.o* **20/1**
/-35 **P** **Kofi**[10] 661 6-8-9 45 (p) MGrossett(7) 12 —
(Karen George) *cl up tl dropped out and p.u 5f out: dismntd: b.b.v* **7/1**[3]
2m 46.05s (0.05) **Going Correction** 0.0s/f (Stan)
WFA 4 from 5yo+ 3lb **13** Ran SP% **127.0**
Speed ratings (Par 97): **99,97,97,96,94 92,90,89,87,79 76,71,—**
CSF £13.19 TOTE £4.70: £1.60, £1.40, £6.30; EX 10.10.
Owner Mrs A K Petersen & Chart Oak Partners **Bred** Kentavr (uk) Ltd **Trained** Newmarket, Suffolk

FOCUS
A bad race and most of these would struggle to get out of their own way. This also proved too much of a test of stamina for many and they finished very well spread out. The runner-up helps set the level.
Kofi Official explanation: vet said gelding bled from the nose

777 BETDAQ BETTING EXCHANGE MAIDEN STKS 6f (P)
4:40 (4:40) (Class 5) 3-Y-O+ £2,331 (£693; £346; £173) Stalls Low

Form RPR
2 **1** **Opus Maximus (IRE)**[6] 706 3-8-12 0 JoeFanning 1 74+
(M Johnston) *t.k.h: pressed ldr: chal fr 2f out: urged into ld over 1f out: kpt on* **10/11**[1]
4-04 **2** *1 1/4* **Interactive (IRE)**[14] 608 5-9-12 69 AlanDaly 10 74
(Andrew Turnell) *trckd ldng pair: clr of rest over 2f out: swtchd ins and effrt over 1f out: kpt on wl but unable to chal* **8/1**[3]
3 *1/2* **Maid Of Ailsa (USA)** 3-8-7 0 LiamJones 9 67+
(W J Haggas) *s.s: hld up in last trio: sme prog 2f out but stl wl off the pce: shuffled along and r.o wl fnl f: improve* **5/2**[2]
4 *1* **Mask Of Conspiracy (IRE)**[172] 5369 3-8-12 0 TPQueally 5 66+
(N Nevin, Ire) *sn rdn in rr: wl off the pce 1/2-way: styd on fr over 1f out: nrst fin* **33/1**
300- **5** *3/4* **Miss Firefly**[160] 5705 3-8-7 69 EdwardCreighton 2 58
(M R Channon) *led: drvn and hdd over 1f out: wknd ins fnl f* **14/1**
45-6 **6** *2 1/2* **Copperwood**[23] 500 3-8-12 70 PaulDoe 4 56
(M Blanshard) *dwlt: mostly in last pair: drvn on outer and bhd 1/2-way: kpt on fr over 1f out* **20/1**
30-4 **7** *2* **Ben**[14] 612 3-8-12 67 RobertHavlin 3 50
(P G Murphy) *hld up in midfield: outpcd 1/2-way: sn rdn and no rspnse* **33/1**
06-0 **8** *2 1/2* **Trees Of Green (USA)**[36] 329 4-9-12 69 OscarUrbina 7 46
(M Wigham) *chsd ldrs: outpcd fr 1/2-way: no ch fnl 2f* **20/1**
5/3- **9** *1* **Zeeuw (IRE)**[302] 1501 4-9-12 69 DaneO'Neill 11 43
(D J Coakley) *a in last trio: outpcd and no ch fr 1/2-way* **25/1**
52-3 **10** *shd* **Complete Frontline (GER)**[16] 590 3-8-12 65 AndrewElliott 8 39
(K R Burke) *chsd ldrs: rdn after 2f: wknd wl over 2f out* **16/1**
1m 11.79s (-0.11) **Going Correction** 0.0s/f (Stan)
WFA 3 from 4yo+ 14lb **10** Ran SP% **123.9**
Speed ratings (Par 103): **100,98,97,96,95 92,89,86,84,84**
CSF £9.35 TOTE £2.10: £1.30, £1.20, £1.30; EX 8.80 Place 6 £12.23, Place 5 £7.30.
Owner Jim McGrath And Reg Griffin **Bred** Mrs Anne Marie Burns **Trained** Middleham Moor, N Yorks
■ Stewards' Enquiry : Alan Daly two-day ban: used whip without giving gelding time to respond (Mar 14-15)

FOCUS
Only a few could be fancied in this maiden and not many ever got into the race. A couple did offer some promise for the future though, particularly the winner and third. The runner-up sets the standard.
T/Plt: £13.80 to a £1 stake. Pool: £54,425.80. 2,868.40 winning tickets. T/Qpdt: £2.90 to a £1 stake. Pool: £3,637.30. 919.10 winning tickets. JN

766 WOLVERHAMPTON (A.W) (L-H)
Monday, March 3

OFFICIAL GOING: Standard
Wind: Fresh half-behind Weather: Overcast

778 AHEAD WITH ZENA @ PONTIN'S AMATEUR RIDERS' H'CAP (DIV I) 1m 5f 194y(P)
1:50 (1:50) (Class 5) (0-70,70) 4-Y-O+ £1,879 (£577; £288) Stalls Low

Form RPR
4-14 **1** **Dreams Jewel**[5] 722 8-10-0 **56** MissIsabelTompsett(7) 12 67
(C Roberts) *a.p: chsd ldr 9f out: led over 2f out: rdn over 1f out: all out* **14/1**
-543 **2** *nse* **Grizebeck (IRE)**[5] 720 6-10-3 **55** HarryHaynes(3) 8 66
(R F Fisher) *chsd ldr: led 12f out: hdd over 2f out: sn rdn: ev ch fr over 1f out: styd on* **11/4**[2]
-004 **3** *4 1/2* **Ashmolian (IRE)**[27] 438 5-9-9 **51** oh6 MrHGMiller(7) 6 56
(Miss Z C Davison) *chsd ldrs: rdn over 2f out: styd on same pce appr fnl f* **25/1**
00-6 **4** *1 3/4* **Top Spec (IRE)**[35] 344 7-11-2 **68** SimonPearce(3) 1 70
(J Pearce) *s.i.s: hld up: hdwy over 4f out: rdn over 2f out: hung rt and wknd fnl f* **16/1**
/30- **5** *3/4* **According To Pete**[37] 6473 7-11-4 **70** MissNJefferson(3) 4 71+
(J M Jefferson) *hld up: hdwy over 6f out: lost pl over 4f out: r.o ins fnl f* **6/4**[1]
-250 **6** *1 1/4* **Fenners (USA)**[9] 675 5-10-8 **62** MissJoannaMason(5) 10 61
(M W Easterby) *chsd ldrs: rdn over 2f out: hung lft and wknd over 1f out* **11/2**[3]
/0-6 **7** *2 1/2* **Archimboldo (USA)**[7] 701 5-10-6 **62** MrAWEdwards(7) 3 58
(T Wall) *hld up: hdwy over 4f out: wknd over 2f out* **33/1**
400- **8** *15* **Star Berry**[35] 6501 5-9-9 **51** oh6 (p) MrLJohnson(7) 2 26
(T Wall) *chsd ldrs over 10f* **150/1**
453 **9** *1/2* **Mondial Jack (FR)**[7] 524 9-10-11 **60** (v) MissEFolkes 7 34
(P D Evans) *hld up: rdn and wknd over 3f out* **14/1**
0050 **10** *9* **Allez Melina**[3] 754 7-9-11 **51** oh1 MrKJames(5) 5 13
(Mouse Hamilton-Fairley) *mid-div: dropped to rr over 8f out: wknd over 3f out* **150/1**
000- **11** *14* **Niza D'Alm (FR)**[89] 6561 7-9-9 **51** oh6 (p) MrJRichards(7) 9 —
(A Crook) *mid-div: wknd over 4f out* **200/1**
400- **12** *10* **King Of The Beers (USA)**[220] 3901 4-10-9 **67** (p) MissJodieHughes(5) 11 —
(W K Goldsworthy) *racd wd: led 2f: chsd ldrs tl wknd over 4f out* **14/1**
3m 7.79s (1.79) **Going Correction** +0.15s/f (Slow)
WFA 4 from 5yo+ 4lb **12** Ran SP% **116.5**
Speed ratings (Par 103): **100,99,97,96,95 95,93,85,84,79 71,66**
CSF £51.16 CT £980.64 TOTE £11.40: £3.30, £1.10, £5.80; EX 50.00 Trifecta £211.50 Part won. Pool £297.91 - 0.78 winning units..
Owner Allan Ashcroft **Bred** Allan Ashcroft **Trained** Coedkernew, Newport
■ The first winner under rules for successful point-to-point rider Isabel Tompsett.

FOCUS
This first division of the amateur riders' handicap was a typically moderate affair for a race of its type. The first pair came clear and dictate the level of the form. The time was 1.53sec faster than that for the second division.

779 AHEAD WITH ZENA @ PONTIN'S AMATEUR RIDERS' H'CAP (DIV II) 1m 5f 194y(P)
2:20 (2:20) (Class 5) (0-70,69) 4-Y-0+ **£1,879** (£577; £288) **Stalls** Low

Form RPR
2014 **1** **Blue Hills**[15] 600 7-11-4 **64**....(b) MrsMarieKing(3) 5 74
(P W Hiatt) *chsd ldrs: led 4f out: rdn over 1f out: styd on* **8/1**
2433 **2** 2 ½ **Phone Call**[13] 617 5-10-13 **56**.... MissFayeBramley 4 63
(Mouse Hamilton-Fairley) *hld up: hdwy over 5f out: chsd wnr over 1f out: sn rdn and hung lft: styd on same pce ins fnl f* **12/1**
32-1 **3** 3 ¼ **Cumbrian Knight (IRE)**[59] 36 10-11-2 **62**.... MissNJefferson(3) 2 64
(J M Jefferson) *s.s: hld up: hdwy 5f out: chsd wnr over 2f out tl rdn over 1f out: wknd ins fnl f* **4/1**[1]
14-1 **4** 1 **Snowberry Hill (USA)**[61] 14 5-10-11 **59**.... JPFeatherstone(5) 10 60
(Lucinda Featherstone) *hld up: hdwy 4f out: rdn over 2f out: hung rt and wknd fnl f* **6/1**[3]
3/10 **5** 1 ¾ **Wizard Of Us**[5] 720 8-10-7 **55**.... MissMMullineaux(5) 8 53
(M Mullineaux) *led: hdd 11f out: chsd ldrs tl wknd over 2f out* **22/1**
0660 **6** ½ **Divine Love (IRE)**[10] 661 4-9-5 **45**....(tp) MrLJohnson(7) 12 42
(T Wall) *s.i.s: outpcd: hdwy over 2f out: nvr trbld ldrs* **150/1**
23-1 **7** ½ **Rare Coincidence**[5] 722 7-11-9 **69** 6ex....(p) HarryHaynes(3) 7 66
(R F Fisher) *chsd ldr: led 11f out: hdd 4f out: rdn and wknd over 1f out* **5/1**[2]
/-00 **8** 9 **Pure Brief (IRE)**[14] 606 11-9-9 **45**.... MissStefaniaGandola(7) 3 29
(R Hollinshead) *prom: lost pl after 2f: n.d after* **100/1**
433- **9** 9 **Tension Point**[130] 209 4-11-4 **65**....(t) MissLHorner 11 37
(D L Williams) *mid-div: hdwy over 6f out: wkng whn n.m.r over 3f out* **16/1**
-323 **10** 9 **Sand Repeal (IRE)**[15] 600 6-11-1 **63**....(v) MrRBirkett(5) 1 22
(Miss J Feilden) *hld up in tch: lost pl 7f out: rdn and wknd over 3f out* **4/1**[1]
4602 **11** 5 **Ronsard (IRE)**[10] 661 6-10-2 **45**.... MissEFolkes 9 —
(P D Evans) *prom: racd keenly: lost pl 7f out: wknd 4f out* **15/2**
2325 **12** 3 ¾ **Ndola**[14] 606 9-10-1 **51** ow1....(v) MissMBryant(7) 6 —
(P Butler) *prom 10f* **20/1**

3m 9.32s (3.32) **Going Correction** +0.15s/f (Slow)
WFA 4 from 5yo+ 4lb **12 Ran SP% 118.2**
Speed ratings (Par 103): **96,94,92,92,91 90,90,85,80,75 72,70**
CSF £96.49 CT £444.87 TOTE £10.50: £2.60, £4.30, £1.70; EX 91.80 TRIFECTA Not won..
Owner Tom Pratt **Bred** Darley **Trained** Hook Norton, Oxon
■ Stewards' Enquiry : Mrs Marie King three-day ban: careless riding (Mar 17,31, Apr 4)

FOCUS
This was the more competitive of the two divisions but the time was 1.53sec slower. The winner was back to his best and the third was right up to form.

780 MEET CAPTAIN CROC @ PONTINS.COM (S) STKS 5f 216y(P)
2:50 (2:51) (Class 6) 3-Y-0 **£1,774** (£523; £262) **Stalls** Low

Form RPR
0-04 **1** **Mujinda**[31] 393 3-8-8 38....(b) JimmyQuinn 6 50
(M Brittain) *in rr and bmpd nt long after s: hdwy over 1f out: styd on u.p to ld wl ins fnl f* **40/1**
2-02 **2** 2 **Rich James (IRE)**[18] 557 3-8-13 50.... RobertWinston 4 49
(J D Bethell) *a.p: chsd ldr over 2f out: rdn to ld ins fnl f: sn hdd and unable qck* **5/1**[2]
00-6 **3** 4 **Heron (IRE)**[23] 498 3-8-13 60....(b) JamesDoyle 7 37
(N P Littmoden) *led: rdn over 1f out: wknd and hdd ins fnl f* **13/2**
0-65 **4** 1 ¼ **Flemish Art (IRE)**[19] 543 3-8-13 67.... SebSanders 1 33
(M J Wallace) *sn pushed along in mid-div: hdwy u.p over 2f out: no imp fnl f* **6/5**[1]
00-0 **5** 1 **Petite Music (IRE)**[11] 634 3-8-5 45....(b[1]) DuranFentiman(3) 8 25
(T D Easterby) *prom: rdn over 2f out: sn outpcd* **50/1**
-302 **6** 6 **Bahamarama (IRE)**[25] 467 3-8-9 48.... KevinGhunowa(5) 3 13
(R A Harris) *mid-div: n.m.r over 3f out: sn rdn: n.d* **14/1**
5240 **7** 2 ½ **Weetfromthechaff**[11] 634 3-8-13 57....(v) FergalLynch 5 5
(R Hollinshead) *chsd ldr over 3f: rdn and wknd over 1f out* **6/1**[3]
-026 **8** 4 **Tilly Ann (IRE)**[12] 623 3-8-8 43.... LPKeniry 9 —
(Peter Grayson) *sn outpcd* **50/1**
-010 **9** 3 ½ **Arkando (IRE)**[12] 629 3-9-0 52....(b) DarrenWilliams 11 —
(K R Burke) *s.i.s: sn chsng ldrs: rdn and wknd over 2f out* **16/1**
00-4 **10** 17 **Avian Flew**[24] 486 3-8-5 45.... RussellKennemore(3) 10 —
(J A Pickering) *sn outpcd* **50/1**
5 **11** 4 **Feeling Pretty**[13] 614 3-8-8 0.... ChrisCatlin 2 —
(C Smith) *s.s: outpcd* **100/1**

1m 16.81s (1.81) **Going Correction** +0.15s/f (Slow) **11 Ran SP% 111.6**
Speed ratings (Par 96): **93,90,85,83,82 74,70,65,60,38 32**
CSF £217.84 TOTE £59.60: £13.50, £1.40, £2.10; EX 272.50 TRIFECTA Not won..There was no bid for the winner. Flemish Art was claimed by R A Harris for £6,000. Heron was claimed by A M Hales for £6,000.
Owner Mel Brittain **Bred** Worksop Manor Stud **Trained** Warthill, N Yorks

FOCUS
This was weak, even by selling standards. The winner, officially rated just 38, stepped up greatly on her previous form to score.
Mujinda Official explanation: trainer said, regarding apparent improvement in form, that the filly benefited from being dropped in rather than ridden in a handier position.
Avian Flew Official explanation: jockey filly did not face the kick-back

781 BACK OR LAY AT BETDAQ CLAIMING STKS 1m 1f 103y(P)
3:20 (3:20) (Class 5) 4-Y-0+ **£2,331** (£693; £346) **Stalls** Low

Form RPR
1150 **1** **Sawwaah (IRE)**[8] 692 11-9-13 77....(v) DanielTudhope 5 73+
(D Carroll) *hld up: chsd clr ldr over 4f out: led on bit wl over 1f out: easily* **1/4**[1]
00-0 **2** 2 ¾ **Silidan**[59] 42 5-8-6 56.... AdamCarter(7) 3 46
(M Brittain) *plld hrd: led and sn clr: rdn 3f out: sn hung rt: hdd wl over 1f out: flattered by proximety to wnr* **7/2**[2]
00-0 **3** 14 **Miss Wolf**[24] 490 8-8-3 30.... DominicFox(3) 2 12
(G H Jones) *chsd clr ldr to over 4f out: sn rdn: n.d* **33/1**[3]

2m 3.60s (1.90) **Going Correction** +0.15s/f (Slow) **3 Ran SP% 105.2**
Speed ratings (Par 103): **97,94,82**
CSF £1.35 TOTE £1.40; EX 1.20.
Owner Document Express Ltd **Bred** Shadwell Estate Company Limited **Trained** Sledmere, E Yorks

FOCUS
This claimer was weakened by two non-runners. Sawwaah did not have to run near to his best to score.

782 BET CRICKET - BETDAQ H'CAP 5f 216y(P)
3:50 (3:50) (Class 5) (0-70,68) 4-Y-0+ **£2,457** (£725; £362) **Stalls** Low

Form RPR
112 **1** **Alexander Huricane (IRE)**[20] 528 4-8-8 **58**.... JamieSpencer 8 78+
(K A Ryan) *mde all: rdn and hung rt ins fnl f: r.o* **11/8**[1]
5456 **2** 3 ½ **Figaro Flyer (IRE)**[2] 766 5-9-1 **65**.... SimonWhitworth 6 74
(P Howling) *hld up: hdwy over 1f out: sn rdn and edgd lft: no ch w wnr* **6/1**[3]
0203 **3** 1 ¾ **Mambazo**[2] 766 6-8-5 **62**....(e) BMcHugh(7) 3 65
(S C Williams) *s.i.s: hdwy over 4f out: chsd wnr over 3f out: rdn over 2f out: wknd ins fnl f* **13/2**
-464 **4** 3 ½ **Hart Of Gold**[15] 603 4-8-3 **58**.... KevinGhunowa(5) 4 50
(R A Harris) *plld hrd: trckd wnr to over 3f out: wknd over 1f out* **9/1**
5003 **5** nk **Methaaly (IRE)**[25] 466 5-8-8 **65**.... RossAtkinson(7) 2 56
(M Mullineaux) *chsd ldrs: rdn over 2f out: wknd over 1f out* **7/1**
1206 **6** ¾ **Muktasb (USA)**[6] 707 7-9-4 **68**....(v) AdamKirby 1 57
(D Shaw) *hld up: rdn over 2f out: n.d* **16/1**
-365 **7** ¾ **Social Rhythm**[19] 539 4-9-1 **65**.... ChrisCatlin 5 51
(H J Collingridge) *prom: rdn over 2f out: wknd wl over 1f out* **5/1**[2]

1m 14.92s (-0.08) **Going Correction** +0.15s/f (Slow) **7 Ran SP% 114.8**
Speed ratings (Par 103): **106,101,99,94,93 92,91**
CSF £10.21 CT £40.15 TOTE £2.20: £1.20, £2.70; EX 10.30 Trifecta £39.50 Pool £589.85 - 10.60 winning units..
Owner N O'Callaghan, R Fagan & R O'Callaghan **Bred** Mrs M Fox **Trained** Hambleton, N Yorks

FOCUS
A moderate sprint. The progressive Alexander Hurricane is well ahead of the handicapper and can rate higher still. The second and third help pin down the form.
Hart Of Gold Official explanation: jockey said gelding ran too freely

783 CALL 0844 576 5938 FOR PONTIN'S EASTER BREAKS CLAIMING STKS 5f 216y(P)
4:20 (4:20) (Class 6) 4-Y-0+ **£2,047** (£604; £302) **Stalls** Low

Form RPR
1633 **1** **Green Pirate**[17] 576 6-8-9 61....(p) JamesDoyle 4 67
(W M Brisbourne) *hld up: hdwy over 2f out: rdn to ld ins fnl f: styd on* **4/1**[3]
1242 **2** ¾ **Another Genepi (USA)**[11] 639 5-8-10 63....(b) FergalLynch 2 66
(I W McInnes) *chsd ldrs: led over 2f out: rdn over 1f out: hdd and unable qck ins fnl f* **11/4**[2]
0405 **3** 1 ¾ **Goodbye Cash (IRE)**[13] 618 4-8-1 66.... RossAtkinson(7) 7 58
(P D Evans) *bhd: hdwy over 1f out: sn rdn: styd on same pce ins fnl f* **17/2**
1115 **4** ¾ **Mafaheem**[25] 466 6-8-13 65.... SebSanders 5 61
(A B Haynes) *hld up in tch: rdn over 1f out: styd on* **5/2**[1]
-466 **5** shd **Soviet Palace (IRE)**[42] 245 4-9-0 74....(p) BMcHugh(7) 8 68
(K A Ryan) *hld up: hdwy 1/2-way: rdn over 1f out: no ex fnl f* **15/2**
0-03 **6** 11 **Nabra**[25] 469 4-8-4 47.... AdamCarter(7) 1 23
(M Brittain) *chsd ldr: led 4f out: edgd rt and hdd over 2f out: wknd over 1f out* **33/1**
64-0 **7** 1 ¼ **Procrastinate (IRE)**[32] 377 6-8-7 42.... ChrisCatlin 3 15
(R F Fisher) *led 2f: wknd over 2f out* **66/1**
1046 **8** 3 **Sir Douglas**[28] 429 5-9-7 68....(b) PaulHanagan 6 19
(R A Harris) *chsd ldrs: hung rt fr 1/2-way: sn wknd* **13/2**

1m 15.21s (0.21) **Going Correction** +0.15s/f (Slow) **8 Ran SP% 115.3**
Speed ratings (Par 101): **104,103,100,99,99 84,83,79**
CSF £15.60 TOTE £5.00: £1.50, £1.60, £2.40; EX 19.50 Trifecta £116.20 Pool £411.01 - 2.51 - winning units..Green Pirate was claimed by C R Dore for £6,000.
Owner J Babb **Bred** Hrh Princess Michael Of Kent **Trained** Great Ness, Shropshire

FOCUS
A typically moderate claimer, run at a sound pace. The runner-up sets the level.
Sir Douglas Official explanation: jockey said gelding hung badly right on bend

784 WOLVERHAMPTON-RACECOURSE.CO.UK H'CAP 1m 4f 50y(P)
4:50 (4:51) (Class 5) (0-70,66) 3-Y-0 **£2,730** (£806; £403) **Stalls** Low

Form RPR
0-35 **1** **Kryptonite (IRE)**[36] 325 3-9-2 **64**.... JamesDoyle 5 67
(J W Hills) *hld up: hdwy over 3f out: chsd ldr over 2f out: sn rdn: hung rt and styd on u.p to ld wl ins fnl f* **4/1**
000- **2** nk **Pepper's Ghost**[164] 5599 3-8-12 **60**.... DMylonas 1 63
(Miss J Feilden) *hld up: bhd 8f out: hdwy over 3f out: rdn over 1f out: edgd rt: styd on* **14/1**
40-3 **3** 2 ½ **Calistos Quest**[21] 527 3-9-4 **66**.... GregFairley 4 65
(M Botti) *trckd ldr: racd keenly: led over 3f out: rdn and edgd lft over 1f out: hdd wl ins fnl f* **2/1**[1]
-001 **4** 9 **Paul The Carpet (UAE)**[11] 644 3-8-4 **52** oh2....(b) JimmyQuinn 2 38
(G L Moore) *led: rdn and hdd over 3f out: wknd over 2f out* **10/3**[3]
4-32 **5** 25 **Gayanula (USA)**[25] 464 3-8-13 **61**.... TomEaves 3 9
(Miss J A Camacho) *chsd ldrs 9f* **5/2**[2]

2m 41.82s (0.72) **Going Correction** +0.15s/f (Slow) **5 Ran SP% 111.7**
Speed ratings (Par 98): **103,102,101,95,78**
CSF £46.31 TOTE £3.90: £1.50, £3.60; EX 39.50.
Owner R J Tufft **Bred** Pat Jones **Trained** Upper Lambourn, Berks

FOCUS
A modest little handicap, run at a solid pace. It was a fair winning time for the type of race, but the form still looks a little suspect. Not a race to be with.

785 MAKE EASTER EGG-STRA SPECIAL @ PONTIN'S H'CAP 1m 141y(P)
5:20 (5:21) (Class 6) (0-65,65) 3-Y-0 **£2,047** (£604; £302) **Stalls** Low

Form RPR
2-15 **1** **Bookiebasher Babe (IRE)**[25] 464 3-9-2 **63**.... FrancisNorton 2 68
(M Quinn) *w ldr tl led 6f out: rdn over 1f out: jst hld on* **3/1**[1]
00-0 **2** shd **Forsyte Saga**[58] 52 3-9-1 **62**.... GregFairley 7 67
(M Johnston) *chsd ldrs: rdn over 1f out: r.o* **10/1**
040- **3** 2 **Little Toto**[117] 6715 3-9-1 **62**.... AdamKirby 1 63
(C G Cox) *sn led: hdd 6f out: rdn over 2f out: styd on* **3/1**[1]
30-4 **4** 1 ½ **One Called Alice**[13] 619 3-8-10 **60**.... JerryO'Dwyer(3) 5 57
(A W Carroll) *hld up: hdwy 2f out: rdn over 1f out: edgd lft fnl f: styd on same pce* **12/1**
43-5 **5** 1 **Afton View (IRE)**[37] 321 3-9-3 **64**....(e) DarrenWilliams 9 59
(S Parr) *hld up: hdwy over 2f out: rdn and hung lft fr over 1f out: no ex fnl f* **13/2**[3]
0-22 **6** 6 **Whaston (IRE)**[37] 321 3-8-12 **59**.... RobertWinston 3 42+
(J D Bethell) *hld up in tch: hmpd 4f out: wknd wl over 1f out* **3/1**[1]

The Form Book, Raceform Ltd, Compton, RG20 6NL

000- **7** *2* **Northgate Lodge (USA)**[176] 5251 3-8-6 **53**.................... JimmyQuinn 4 32
(M Brittain) *chsd ldrs: swicthed lft 4f out: sn rdn: wknd over 1f out: eased* **25/1**

-550 **8** *1 1/4* **Marino Prince (FR)**[21] 527 3-9-4 **65**.................................. ChrisCatlin 6 41
(T Wall) *hld up: a in rr: wknd over 2f out* **16/1**

00-3 **9** *7* **Scruffy Skip (IRE)**[10] 656 3-9-3 **64**.................................. DaleGibson 8 25
(C R Dore) *sn bhd and pushed along: wknd 3f out* **7/2[2]**

1m 51.47s (0.97) **Going Correction** +0.15s/f (Slow) **9** Ran SP% **137.1**
Speed ratings (Par 96): **101,100,99,97,96 91,89,88,82**
CSF £41.92 CT £108.29 TOTE £5.10: £1.80, £4.10, £1.70; EX 67.50 TRIFECTA Not won. Place 6 £100.69, Place 5 £33.60.
Owner J Henry, J Blake & A Newby **Bred** Minch Bloodstock And Castletown Stud **Trained** Newmarket, Suffolk

FOCUS
A moderate three-year-old handicap. It was a creditable winning time for a contest of its type and the form can be rated through the second and third.
T/Plt: £93.70 to a £1 stake. Pool: £49,932.10. 388.95 winning tickets. T/Qpdt: £13.80 to a £1 stake. Pool: £4,083.40. 217.50 winning tickets. CR

653 SOUTHWELL (L-H)
Tuesday, March 4

OFFICIAL GOING: Standard
Wind: Strong, half behind Weather: Dry and sunny

786 BET CHAMPIONS LEAGUE - BETDAQ H'CAP 5f (F)
2:10 (2:10) (Class 5) (0-70,67) 4-Y-0+ **£2,593** (£765; £383) **Stalls** High

Form RPR

-141 **1** **Garlogs**[16] 596 5-8-12 **64**.................................. RussellKennemore(3) 3 75
(R Hollinshead) *mde all: rdn ent fnl f: drvn and hld on wl towards fin* **85/40[2]**

1513 **2** *nse* **Savile's Delight (IRE)**[16] 596 9-9-4 **67**.................. RichardKingscote 1 78
(Tom Dascombe) *chsd ldrs: rdn along wl over 1f out: drvn to chal wl ins fnl f: jst hld* **15/8[1]**

0304 **3** *1 3/4* **Owed**[16] 599 6-8-11 **60**..(tp) PatCosgrave 2 65
(R Bastiman) *prom: rdn along wl over 1f out: one pce ins fnl f* **18/1**

6000 **4** *1 1/2* **Fizzlephut (IRE)**[4] 746 6-8-10 **59**.................................. PaulFitzsimons 4 58
(Miss J R Tooth) *prom: rdn along 2f out: sn edgd lft and one pce* **25/1**

2013 **5** *2 1/4* **Grand Palace (IRE)**[19] 554 5-9-3 **66**...........................(v) DeanMcKeown 8 57+
(D Shaw) *chsd ldrs: rdn along 2f out: sn no imp* **11/2[3]**

-012 **6** *4* **Guto**[13] 620 5-8-12 **64**.. AndrewMullen(3) 6 41+
(W J H Ratcliffe) *stmbld s: a in rr* **6/1**

0-56 **7** *3 3/4* **Jabraan (USA)**[6] 719 6-7-11 **53** oh8.............................(v[1]) MCGeran(7) 7 16+
(Mrs R A Carr) *s.i.s: a bhd* **66/1**

-630 **8** *4 1/2* **Hythe Bay**[49] 165 4-8-12 **61**.......................................(v[1]) JimCrowley 5 8+
(J R Jenkins) *s.i.s: sn rdn along: a bhd* **10/1**

59.02 secs (-0.68) **Going Correction** -0.05s/f (Stan) **8** Ran SP% **116.1**
Speed ratings (Par 103): **103,102,100,97,94 87,81,74**
CSF £6.65 CT £52.56 TOTE £2.70: £1.20, £1.10, £4.90; EX 7.20 Trifecta £144.30 Pool: £609.96 - 3.00 winning units..
Owner Peter G Freeman **Bred** Peter Taplin **Trained** Upper Longdon, Staffs

FOCUS
A modest sprint but straightforward form rated around the first three home. The pace was towards the far side, and consequently those drawn low dominated throughout.
Guto Official explanation: jockey said gelding stumbled on leaving stalls

787 BET ALL WEATHER RACING - BETDAQ CLAIMING STKS 1m 6f (F)
2:40 (2:40) (Class 6) 4-Y-0+ **£1,774** (£523; £262) **Stalls** Low

Form RPR

-141 **1** **Zaffeu**[32] 394 7-9-1 60.. VinceSlattery 7 62
(A G Juckes) *hld up in tch: hdwy to trck ldrs 1/2-way: chsd ldr 4f out: rdn over 2f out: styd on to ld over 1f out: sn drvn and styd on* **9/4[2]**

2220 **2** *2 1/4* **Kanisorn (SWE)**[4] 754 6-9-9 67....................................(bt) LiamJones 3 67
(Mrs R A Carr) *led: rdn along over 3f out: drvn and hdd over 1f out: kpt on same pce* **6/5[1]**

6502 **3** *9* **Matinee Idol**[12] 637 5-8-11 37 ow1...........................(b) RobertWinston 2 43
(Mrs S Lamyman) *hld up in rr: stdy hdwy 1/2-way: chsd ldrs 4f out: rdn along 3f out: sn drvn and kpt on same pce fnl 2f* **16/1**

0313 **4** *1/2* **Dot's Delight**[7] 710 4-8-5 50 ow1.................................. DeanMcKeown 6 41
(K J Burke) *trckd ldrs: effrt 4f out: sn rdn along and kpt on same pce fnl 2f* **13/2[3]**

-616 **5** *29* **Rebel Raider (IRE)**[17] 585 9-9-6 48..............(v) RussellKennemore(3) 1 17
(B N Pollock) *chsd ldr: rdn along 5f out: drvn and wknd 3f out* **12/1**

60-0 **6** *27* **Salawat**[26] 461 5-8-10 26.. SamHitchcott 5 —
(T T Clement) *a in rr: t.o fnl 4f* **100/1**

506- **7** *3* **Francesco**[169] 5472 4-8-7 52......................................(t) ChrisCatlin 4 —
(J R Weymes) *trckd ldrs: rdn along 1/2-way: sn wknd: t.o fnl 4f* **12/1**

6 **8** *38* **Youmeanddupree (IRE)**[6] 715 6-9-3 0.............................. GregFairley 8 —
(K J Burke) *chsd ldng pair: rdn along and lost pl 1/2-way: t.o fnl 4f* **40/1**

3m 13.07s (4.77) **Going Correction** +0.30s/f (Slow)
WFA 4 from 5yo+ 4lb **8** Ran SP% **114.3**
Speed ratings (Par 101): **98,96,91,91,74 59,57,35**
CSF £5.27 TOTE £3.80: £1.30, £1.10, £2.50; EX 6.40 Trifecta £49.90 Pool: £397.78 - 5.65 winning units..
Owner Whispering Winds **Bred** Patrick Eddery Ltd **Trained** Abberley, Worcs

FOCUS
A modest claimer rated around the first two.

788 BETDAQ.CO.UK (S) STKS 1m 3f (F)
3:10 (3:11) (Class 6) 4-6-Y-0 **£1,774** (£523; £262) **Stalls** Low

Form RPR

03-4 **1** **Ming Vase**[12] 640 6-8-11 42.................................. MickyFenton 4 55
(P T Midgley) *hld up in tch: hdwy 5f out: led over 3f out: rdn 2f out: edgd rt and kpt on u.p ins fnl f* **6/1[3]**

230/ **2** *1 1/4* **Ruling Reef**[40] 5166 6-8-6 45.................................. JimmyQuinn 5 48
(M D I Usher) *hld up towards rr: stdy hdwy over 4f out: rdn over 2f out: chsd wnr over 1f out: swtchd lft and drvn ent fnl f: kpt on* **16/1**

0405 **3** *10* **Benayoun**[13] 631 4-8-10 48...(b[1]) ChrisCatlin 8 37
(B J Llewellyn) *prom: led over 4f out: hdd over 3f out and sn rdn: drvn and one pce fr wl over 1f out* **11/1**

0134 **4** *1 1/4* **Global Traffic**[10] 686 4-9-0 57..............................(v) DeanMcKeown 7 39
(D Shaw) *in tch: hdwy to trck ldrs 1/2-way: rdn along 4f out: drvn 3f out and sn one pce* **5/4[1]**

56-5 **5** *11* **Kirkhammerton (IRE)**[17] 231 6-8-11 46..............................(p) LPKeniry 3 17
(J T Stimpson) *chsd ldr: led briefly wl over 4f out: sn rdn and hdd: wknd wl over 3f out* **12/1**

-403 **6** *35* **Musango**[18] 569 5-9-1 57..(t) DarrylIHolland 1 —
(Miss Gay Kelleway) *hld up in rr: hdwy 1/2-way: in tch and pushed along over 3f out: sn rdn: btn: eased over 2f out* **9/4[2]**

05 **7** *3 3/4* **Art Of Being (IRE)**[19] 553 4-8-3 0.......................................(p) KMay(7) 2 —
(M C Chapman) *chsd ldrs: rdn along after 4f: sn lost pl and bhd* **100/1**

5650 **8** *1/2* **Oh So (IRE)**[18] 578 4-8-2 38 ow2........................... KevinGhunowa(5) 6 —
(P A Blockley) *led: pushed along 1/2-way: hdd wl over 4f out and sn wknd* **50/1**

2m 31.44s (3.44) **Going Correction** +0.30s/f (Slow)
WFA 4 from 5yo+ 1lb **8** Ran SP% **114.4**
Speed ratings: **99,98,90,89,81 56,53,53**
CSF £92.87 TOTE £7.00: £1.40, £3.10, £2.10; EX 75.60 Trifecta £200.50 Pool: £353.04 - 1.25 winning units..There was no bid for the winner.
Owner Michael Ng **Bred** Cheveley Park Stud Ltd **Trained** Westow, N Yorks

FOCUS
A poor seller in which the front two in the betting did not give their running and the form looks weak.
Global Traffic Official explanation: trainer had no explanation for the poor form shown
Musango Official explanation: jockey said gelding hung left throughout

789 SPRING TO IT AT PONTIN'S H'CAP 1m 4f (F)
3:40 (3:40) (Class 6) (0-65,71) 4-Y-0+ **£1,911** (£564; £282) **Stalls** Low

Form RPR

-212 **1** **My Friend Fritz**[11] 654 8-9-6 **65**.................................. PhillipMakin 6 76+
(P W Hiatt) *trckd ldr: led 4f out: rdn over 2f out: drvn ent fnl f: styd on wl* **3/1[1]**

-241 **2** *1* **Mid Valley**[16] 602 5-8-9 **54**.. J-PGuillambert 7 64
(J R Jenkins) *hld up in rr: hdwy over 4f out: effrt to chse wnr 3f out: rdn to chal over 1f out and ev ch tl drvn and no ex wl ins fnl f* **4/1[3]**

00-1 **3** *1 3/4* **Coda Agency**[11] 654 5-8-9 **54**.. JimCrowley 3 61
(D W P Arbuthnot) *trckd ldrs: effrt over 3f out: rdn to chse ldng pair over 2f out: drvn over 1f out and kpt on same pce* **10/3[2]**

1230 **4** *10* **Maria Antonia (IRE)**[6] 716 5-8-7 **55**.................. RussellKennemore(3) 5 47
(M J Gingell) *hld up in rr: hdwy over 4f out: rdn along to chse ldrs 3f out: drvn 2f out and sn one pce* **16/1**

66-5 **5** *4* **Zed Candy (FR)**[21] 533 5-9-1 **60**.................................. DaleGibson 1 46
(J T Stimpson) *chsd ldrs on inner: rdn along 5f out: sn wknd* **16/1**

44-0 **6** *28* **Muntami (IRE)**[16] 600 7-9-1 **60**.................................. RobertWinston 4 4
(John A Harris) *hld up: effrt and sme hdwy over 5f out: sn rdn and wknd* **8/1**

311 **7** *12* **King's Ransom**[5] 730 5-9-12 **71** 6ex.............................. ChrisCatlin 2 —
(S Gollings) *led: rdn along and hdd 4f out: sn wknd* **4/1[3]**

2m 44.07s (3.07) **Going Correction** +0.30s/f (Slow) **7** Ran SP% **111.0**
Speed ratings (Par 101): **101,100,99,92,89 71,63**
CSF £14.30 TOTE £4.10: £1.60, £2.50; EX 17.40.
Owner P W Hiatt **Bred** Butts Enterprises Limited **Trained** Hook Norton, Oxon

FOCUS
A moderate handicap but the first three came clear and the form looks reliable for the grade of race.
Muntami(IRE) Official explanation: jockey said gelding ran flat

790 MAKE A DATE AT PONTIN'S H'CAP 6f (F)
4:10 (4:12) (Class 6) (0-50,50) 4-Y-0+ **£1,911** (£564; £282) **Stalls** Low

Form RPR

-264 **1** **The Geester**[22] 521 4-8-11 **49**....................................(b) PhillipMakin 1 63
(S R Bowring) *mde all: rdn wl over 1f out: kpt on strly fnl f* **7/2[1]**

00-2 **2** *2* **Limonia (GER)**[16] 596 6-8-3 **48**.................................. JamieKyne(7) 6 56
(Mike Murphy) *dwlt: in tch on inner: hdwy wl over 2f out: sn rdn and kpt on same pce ins fnl f* **13/2[3]**

4624 **3** *1* **Blakeshall Quest**[21] 528 8-8-9 **47**..........................(b) PaulMulrennan 11 52
(R Brotherton) *chsd wnr: rdn 2f out: drvn over 1f out: one pce ins fnl f* **7/1**

-405 **4** *1 1/2* **Imperial Sword**[12] 639 5-8-3 **48**..........................(b) DeanHeslop(7) 12 48+
(T D Barron) *towards rr: pushed along and hdwy on outer 1/2-way: rdn over 2f out: edgd lft over 1f out: kpt on ins fnl f: nrst fin* **10/1**

6/40 **5** *1 3/4* **Welcome Releaf**[19] 550 5-8-12 **50**.................................. LiamJones 3 44
(P Leech) *rrd s and bhd tl styd on fnl 2f: nrst fin* **8/1**

0052 **6** *3/4* **Mister Incredible**[9] 696 5-8-1 **46** oh1...........................(v) MCGeran(7) 5 38
(J M Bradley) *chsd ldng pair: rdn along 2f out: drvn over 1f out: wknd ent fnl f* **8/1**

3335 **7** *nk* **Pappas Image**[16] 599 4-8-8 **46** oh1.................................(p) VJanacek 7 37
(A J McCabe) *chsd ldrs: rdn along over 2f out and sn no imp* **12/1**

-054 **8** *1 1/4* **Mister Elegant**[17] 584 6-8-11 **49**.................................. AdamKirby 4 36
(J L Spearing) *a towards rr* **9/2[2]**

035- **9** *1 1/2* **Duke Of Milan (IRE)**[114] 6773 5-8-11 **49**.................. RobertWinston 9 31
(G C Bravery) *a in rr* **8/1**

05-5 **10** *10* **Princess Charlmane (IRE)**[12] 634 5-8-8 **46** oh1.......... JimmyQuinn 8 —
(C J Teague) *plld hrd: chsd ldrs: rdn along 3f out: wknd 2f out* **40/1**

50/0 **11** *5* **Sergeant Slipper**[33] 371 11-8-8 **46** oh1.........................(v) ChrisCatlin 10 —
(C Smith) *a in rr* **66/1**

1m 17.7s (1.20) **Going Correction** +0.30s/f (Slow) **11** Ran SP% **120.3**
Speed ratings (Par 101): **104,101,100,98,95 94,94,92,90,77 70**
CSF £26.99 CT £157.24 TOTE £4.50: £1.40, £2.30, £2.90; EX 35.40 Trifecta £200.80 Part won. Pool: £282.93 - 0.50 winning units..
Owner Mrs Anne & Fred Cowley **Bred** P O'Boyle **Trained** Edwinstowe, Notts
■ Stewards' Enquiry : V Janacek two-day ban: careless riding (Mar 15,17)

FOCUS
A very moderate contest rated through the runner-up to her recent course form.
Welcome Releaf Official explanation: jockey said gelding hung right

791 BOOK NOW FOR EASTER @ PONTIN'S H'CAP 1m (F)
4:40 (4:40) (Class 4) (0-85,85) 4-Y-0+ **£4,210** (£1,252; £625; £312) **Stalls** Low

Form RPR

1213 **1** **Silver Hotspur**[11] 659 4-8-8 **75**.................................. FrancisNorton 5 90+
(M Wigham) *trckd ldrs on outer gng wl: smooth hdwy 2f out: rdn to chal over 1f out: led ins fnl f and styd on wl* **6/1**

3431 **2** *2 1/2* **Denbera Dancer (USA)**[21] 531 4-8-11 **78**.......................... GregFairley 6 87+
(M Johnston) *cl up: led over 2f out and sn rdn: jnd and drvn over 1f out: hdd ins fnl f and one pce* **5/4[1]**

-020 **3** *4* **Wessex (USA)**[28] 442 8-9-4 **85**.. JimCrowley 2 85
(P A Blockley) *trckd ldrs: effrt over 2f out: sn rdn: drvn and wknd appr fnl f* **5/1[3]**

2123 **4** *nk* **Louisiade (IRE)**[12] 639 7-7-13 71....(p) NicolPolli(5) 3 71
(M C Chapman) *chsd ldrs: rdn along over 2f out: drvn and kpt on same pce fr over 1f out* **16/1**

06-6 **5** *½* **Stevie Gee (IRE)**[10] 680 4-9-4 85.... RobertWinston 1 83
(G A Swinbank) *hld up in rr: hdwy on outer over 2f out: rdn and ev ch wl over 1f out: sn edgd lft and wknd appr fnl f* **9/1**

6-02 **6** *4½* **Music Note (IRE)**[19] 555 5-8-4 71 oh1.... ChrisCatlin 4 60
(Miss Gay Kelleway) *led: rdn along and hdd over 2f out: sn wknd* **4/1**[2]

1m 43.99s (0.29) **Going Correction** +0.30s/f (Slow) 6 Ran SP% **111.3**
Speed ratings (Par 105): **110,107,103,103,102 98**
CSF £13.80 TOTE £8.30: £2.70, £1.30; EX 16.60.
Owner D Hassan **Bred** Theobalds Stud **Trained** Newmarket, Suffolk

FOCUS
A fairly decent handicap run in a good time and the form looks believable rated around the third and fourth.

792 JOIN THE EASTER PARADE @ PONTIN'S 0844 815 3648 H'CAP 7f (F)
5:10 (5:11) (Class 6) (0-52,52) 4-Y-O+ **£1,911** (£564; £282) **Stalls** Low

Form RPR

660- **1** **Ugenius**[90] 7034 4-8-2 47 oh1 ow1.... KevinGhunowa(5) 8 53
(P A Blockley) *chsd ldrs: effrt 2f out and sn rdn: drvn over 1f out: styd on wl u.p ins fnl f to ld nr fin* **20/1**

5623 **2** *nk* **Only A Grand**[12] 640 4-8-11 51....(b) PatCosgrave 7 56
(R Bastiman) *prom: chsd ldr 3f out: led wl over 1f out and sn rdn clr: drvn ins fnl f: wknd and hdd towards fin* **11/4**[1]

000- **3** *6* **Attacca**[127] 6533 7-8-12 52.... DarryllHolland 5 41
(J R Weymes) *midfield: hdwy over 2f out: rdn to chse ldrs and edgd rt wl over 1f out: drvn and kpt on same pce fnl f* **8/1**

006- **4** *hd* **Karma Llama (IRE)**[137] 6310 4-8-12 52....(v[1]) RobertWinston 6 40
(George Baker) *s.i.s and bhd: hdwy 2f out: swtchd lft and rdn wl over 1f out: kpt on u.p ins fnl f: nrst fin* **7/1**[3]

6000 **5** *1¾* **Totally Free**[11] 663 4-8-2 49....(b[1]) GabrielHannon(7) 1 33
(M D I Usher) *cl up on inner: pushed along and outpcd 3f out: swtchd rt over 2f out: sn rdn and hung rt over 1f out: kpt on ins fnl f* **40/1**

2633 **6** *2½* **Lucius Verrus (USA)**[14] 615 8-8-8 48....(v) DeanMcKeown 12 25
(D Shaw) *in tch: hdwy on outer to chse ldrs over 2f out: sn rdn and no imp* **12/1**

0/0- **7** *2* **Oh Gracious Me (IRE)**[290] 1838 4-8-10 50.... GregFairley 13 21
(P A Blockley) *led: rdn along over 2f out: hdd wl over 1f out and sn wknd* **7/1**[3]

3311 **8** *nse* **Mr Chocolate Drop (IRE)**[13] 621 4-8-12 52....(b) AdamKirby 10 23
(Miss M E Rowland) *towards rr: effrt 1/2-way: sn rdn along and nvr a factor* **7/2**[2]

0000 **9** *3¼* **Shadow Jumper (IRE)**[10] 684 7-8-6 46 oh1....(v) ChrisCatlin 9 8
(J T Stimpson) *chsd ldrs: rdn along 1/2-way: sn wknd* **7/1**[3]

2140 **10** *4½* **Government (IRE)**[19] 550 7-8-2 47.... NicolPolli(5) 3 —
(M C Chapman) *chsd ldrs: rdn along 3f out and sn wknd* **16/1**

0-50 **11** *5* **Preskani**[33] 371 6-8-3 46 oh1....(p) DuranFentiman(3) 2 —
(Mrs N Macauley) *chsd ldrs 2f: sn rdn and wknd 1/2-way* **33/1**

0250 **12** *1½* **Pawn In Life (IRE)**[19] 550 10-7-13 46 oh1....(v) DeanHeslop(7) 4 —
(Mrs R A Carr) *s.i.s: a bhd* **40/1**

0-00 **13** *6* **Union Jack Jackson (IRE)**[16] 596 6-8-12 52....(p) MickyFenton 11 —
(John A Harris) *a outpcd and bhd* **22/1**

1m 32.5s (2.20) **Going Correction** +0.30s/f (Slow) 13 Ran SP% **128.0**
Speed ratings (Par 101): **99,98,91,91,89 86,84,84,80,75 69,68,61**
CSF £76.49 CT £510.12 TOTE £25.70: £6.00, £1.70, £3.90; EX 224.30 TRIFECTA Not won. Place 6 £33.44, Place 5 £23.41.
Owner Three Acres Racing **Bred** Three Acres Stud **Trained** Lambourn, Berks

FOCUS
A moderate contest and ordinary form rated around the runner-up to her recent efforts at this track.
Mr Chocolate Drop(IRE) Official explanation: jockey said gelding never travelled
T/Plt: £129.50 to a £1 stake. Pool: £57,256.10. 322.70 winning tickets. T/Qpdt: £56.40 to a £1 stake. Pool: £2,663.50. 34.90 winning tickets. JR

772 LINGFIELD (L-H)
Wednesday, March 5

OFFICIAL GOING: Standard
Wind: Moderate, across Weather: Fine

793 BET CHAMPIONS LEAGUE - BETDAQ APPRENTICE H'CAP 2m (P)
2:10 (2:10) (Class 5) (0-75,72) 4-Y-O+ **£2,590** (£770; £385; £192) **Stalls** Low

Form RPR

3101 **1** **Rollin 'n Tumblin**[11] 675 4-9-2 65.... TolleyDean 2 77+
(W Jarvis) *hld up and mostly in 3rd: effrt 2f out: led over 1f out: sn clr: abt 4 l up fnl f: heavily eased nr fin* **11/4**[2]

3-13 **2** *1* **Alnwick**[18] 588 4-9-2 65.... WilliamBuick 1 72
(P D Cundell) *trckd ldr to over 3f out: sn rdn: lost pl 2f out: rallied to go 2nd again last 100yds: flattered by proximity to wnr* **6/5**[1]

042- **3** *¾* **Dash Of Grey (IRE)**[68] 7256 9-9-1 65....(b) RPWalsh(6) 4 71
(Ruaidhri Joseph Tierney, Ire) *led and sn clr: stdd 1/2-way: narrowly hdd over 3f out: led again over 2f out: hdd over 1f out: outpcd* **6/1**[3]

5640 **4** *2½* **Bienheureux**[11] 675 7-8-7 53 oh1....(t) NicolPolli(2) 6 56
(Miss Gay Kelleway) *stdd s: hld up in last: rdn over 3f out: no real prog* **9/1**

4103 **5** *1¾* **Flame Creek (IRE)**[13] 638 12-9-10 72.... SCreighton(4) 3 73
(E J Creighton) *hld up in 4th: prog to ld narrowly over 3f out to over 2f out: wknd over 1f out* **7/1**

3m 24.05s (-1.65) **Going Correction** +0.05s/f (Slow)
WFA 4 from 7yo+ 5lb 5 Ran SP% **108.9**
Speed ratings (Par 103): **106,105,105,103,103**
CSF £6.34 TOTE £2.70: £1.60, £1.20; EX 5.40.
Owner Canisbay Bloodstock **Bred** Canisbay Bloodstock Ltd **Trained** Newmarket, Suffolk

FOCUS
A modest staying handicap, run at an uneven pace. The winner rates value for plenty further and the form seems solid enough.

794 SPRING IS IN THE AIR @ PONTIN'S CLAIMING STKS 1m 4f (P)
2:40 (2:40) (Class 6) 4-Y-O+ **£1,774** (£523; £262) **Stalls** Low

Form RPR

23-0 **1** **Turner's Touch**[21] 540 6-9-11 65....(b) GeorgeBaker 6 70
(G L Moore) *hld up in last pair: cajoled along and prog over 2f out to ld jst over 1f out: sn in command: tried to pull himself up nr fin* **6/1**[3]

3561 **2** *½* **Medieval Maiden**[10] 695 5-9-4 53.... IanMongan 9 62
(Mrs L J Mongan) *trckd ldr after 2f: led 7f out: drvn and hdd jst over 1f out: kpt on as ldr slowed nr fin* **15/2**

-103 **3** *1¼* **Looks The Business (IRE)**[24] 182 7-8-10 63.... JackDean(7) 4 59
(W G M Turner) *led after 1f out to 7f out: pressed ldrs after: rdn and nt qckn over 1f out* **16/1**

-223 **4** *1* **Bethanys Boy (IRE)**[16] 611 7-9-5 55.... RichardHughes 5 60
(A M Hales) *hld up towards rr: pushed along 2f out: nt clr run shortly after: one pce and nvr nr ldrs* **8/1**

6342 **5** *nse* **Prince Charlemagne (IRE)**[6] 735 5-9-11 71....(p) JamesDoyle 8 66
(K R Burke) *cl up: chsd ldr 6f out: hrd rdn 2f out: nt qckn and btn 1f out* **2/1**[1]

4-32 **6** *2* **Barton Sands (IRE)**[35] 352 11-8-9 57....(t) JimCrowley 1 47
(Andrew Reid) *trckd ldrs: rdn over 2f out: nt qckn and btn over 1f out: fdd* **5/2**[2]

5-53 **7** *15* **Swift Cut (IRE)**[14] 622 4-9-3 55.... AndrewElliott 3 34
(A P Jarvis) *plld hrd: hld up: wknd over 2f out: t.o* **16/1**

0-00 **8** *2½* **Compton Express**[18] 585 5-8-1 41.... WilliamBuick(3) 2 16
(Jamie Poulton) *led 1f: stdd: sn dropped to last pair and nvr gng wl after: t.o over 2f out* **50/1**

2m 34.0s (1.00) **Going Correction** +0.05s/f (Slow)
WFA 4 from 5yo+ 2lb 8 Ran SP% **112.8**
Speed ratings (Par 101): **98,97,96,96,96 94,84,83**
CSF £48.40 TOTE £6.00: £1.40, £2.80, £4.20; EX 54.30 Trifecta £137.60 Pool: £292.75 - 1.51 winning tickets..
Owner G L Moore **Bred** Hedgeholme Stud **Trained** Woodingdean, E Sussex
■ Stewards' Enquiry : James Doyle ten-day ban (takes into account previous offences): failed to ride out for 4th place (Mar 17-20, 22-27)

FOCUS
A claimer full of enigmatic sorts, run at a steady early pace. The first two and the fourth, plus the modest time, set the level.

795 MAKE EASTER EGG-STRA SPECIAL @ PONTIN'S H'CAP 1m (P)
3:10 (3:11) (Class 6) (0-52,52) 4-Y-O+ **£1,876** (£554; £277) **Stalls** High

Form RPR

6-60 **1** **Charlottebutterfly**[19] 579 8-8-12 52.... AdamKirby 10 61
(P J McBride) *trckd ldrs: effrt 2f out: led jst over 1f out: rdn and styd on wl* **20/1**

0621 **2** *¾* **Sion Hill (IRE)**[7] 711 7-8-10 50....(p) MickyFenton 5 57
(John A Harris) *hanging rt but sn led: wd bnd 2f out: hdd jst over 1f out: styd on but hld nr fin* **11/4**[1]

4566 **3** *½* **Play Up Pompey**[16] 611 6-8-11 51.... RichardHughes 4 57
(J J Bridger) *dwlt: sn trckd ldrs: cl enough over 1f out: rdn and kpt on same pce* **9/2**[2]

040- **4** *¾* **Da Bookie (IRE)**[179] 5237 8-8-9 49....(tp) LPKeniry 11 54
(Jean-Rene Auvray) *t.k.h: hld up in last pair: shkn up over 1f out: styd on fnl f: nvr nr ldrs* **33/1**

-236 **5** *½* **Patavium Prince (IRE)**[14] 624 5-8-8 48.... SimonWhitworth 7 52
(Miss Jo Crowley) *racd wd in midfield: rdn and effrt over 2f out: nt qckn over 1f out: kpt on* **12/1**

2-00 **6** *½* **Korty**[27] 468 4-8-8 48....(t) ChrisCatlin 1 50
(W J Musson) *t.k.h: hld up in last quartet: pushed along over 1f out: kpt on steadily: nvr nr ldrs* **25/1**

4536 **7** *½* **Postmaster**[7] 517 6-8-10 50.... RobertHavlin 3 51
(R Ingram) *hld up in last quartet: pushed along and no prog over 1f out: styd on ins fnl f: no ch* **6/1**

0532 **8** *hd* **Silver Blue (IRE)**[7] 711 5-8-4 49....(b) AshleyHamblett(5) 12 50
(C R Dore) *hld up in last pair: effrt on wd outside wl over 1f out: kpt on but nt pce to threaten* **7/1**

-623 **9** *shd* **Tuning Fork**[14] 624 8-8-6 49.... TolleyDean(3) 8 50
(M J Attwater) *mostly chsd ldr: carried wd bnd wl over 1f out: sn lost pl and btn* **12/1**

002- **10** *hd* **Bold Phoenix (IRE)**[307] 1435 7-8-7 47....(p) TPQueally 2 47
(A P Stringer) *cl up on inner: shkn up 3f out: stl cl up on inner over 1f out: wknd fnl f* **11/2**[3]

356- **11** *4* **Slo Mo Shun**[23] 5688 4-8-8 48.... JimCrowley 9 39
(C Gordon) *pressed ldrs tl wknd 2f out* **16/1**

000- **12** *¾* **Hallings Overture (USA)**[200] 4592 9-8-12 52.... PaulEddery 6 42
(C A Horgan) *stdd s: hld up towards rr and t.k.h: pushed along and no rspnse 2f out* **50/1**

1m 38.07s (-0.13) **Going Correction** +0.05s/f (Slow) 12 Ran SP% **121.8**
Speed ratings (Par 101): **102,101,100,100,99 99,98,98,98,98 94,93**
CSF £74.44 CT £312.71 TOTE £29.90: £6.60, £1.80, £1.70; EX 89.00 Trifecta £212.70 Part won. Pool: £299.67 - 0.38 winning tickets..
Owner Future Electrical Services Ltd **Bred** J T O'Neill **Trained** Newmarket, Suffolk

FOCUS
A weak handicap, run at a solid pace. Solid but very limited form, with the winner back to her best.
Charlottebutterfly Official explanation: trainer said, regarding apparent improvement in form, that the mare may have been suited by the shorter trip, a return to Lingfield and a fast run race.

796 SPRING TO IT @ PONTIN'S MAIDEN STKS 7f (P)
3:40 (3:43) (Class 5) 3-Y-O **£2,457** (£725; £362) **Stalls** Low

Form RPR

50- **1** **Commander Cave (USA)**[133] 6436 3-9-3 0.... JamieSpencer 4 84+
(R Hannon) *trckd ldr: rdn wl over 1f out: r.o wl fnl f to ld last strides* **7/2**[2]

2 *nk* **August Gale (USA)** 3-9-3 0.... JoeFanning 3 83+
(M Johnston) *led at mod pce: kicked on 2f out: r.o fnl f but hdd last strides* **3/1**[1]

6- **3** *6* **Irish Music (IRE)**[67] 7264 3-9-3 0.... NeilPollard 5 65
(A P Jarvis) *hld up bhd ldrs: effrt over 2f out: easily outpcd fr over 1f out: kpt on to take 3rd last stride* **7/1**[3]

-64 **4** *hd* **Bye Baby Bunting**[44] 244 3-8-12 0.... DaneO'Neill 1 59
(B R Johnson) *cl up on inner: chsd ldng pair 2f out: sn outpcd: lost 3rd last stride* **8/1**

36 **5** *1¾* **Tripod Molly (IRE)**[21] 543 3-8-12 0....(t) EdwardCreighton 2 55
(P J McBride) *hld up towards rr: sme prog 2f out: outpcd and wl btn over 1f out* **14/1**

40-5 **6** *½* **Fly In Johnny (IRE)**[8] 706 3-9-3 71.... RichardHughes 11 58
(R Hannon) *chsd ldrs: rdn and effrt over 2f out: easily outpcd fr over 1f out* **7/2**[2]

7 *½* **Lucullus** 3-9-3 0.... SteveDrowne 7 57+
(M Blanshard) *s.i.s: hld up in rr: outpcd fr 2f out: shkn up over 1f out: kpt on fnl f* **33/1**

00- **8** *3* **Hla Tun (USA)**[125] 6602 3-9-3 0.... AdamKirby 12 49
(W R Swinburn) *hld up in rr: nvr on terms: outpcd fnl 2f* **9/1**

00- **9** *2* **Buddy Holly**[141] 6252 3-9-3 0 PatDobbs 10 44
(Pat Eddery) *hld up and sn last: pushed along and no prog over 2f out: no ch after* **8/1**
10 *nk* **Sidestreet** 3-9-3 0 ChrisCatlin 8 43
(K McAuliffe) *a in rr: rdn 3f out: struggling after* **16/1**
00- **11** *1* **Patsymartin**[274] 2333 3-9-0 0 JerryO'Dwyer(3) 6 40
(M G Quinlan) *mostly chsd ldng pair tl wknd 2f out* **33/1**

1m 25.92s (1.12) **Going Correction** +0.05s/f (Slow) 11 Ran SP% **132.6**
Speed ratings (Par 98): **95,94,87,87,85 85,84,81,78,78 77**
CSF £16.62 TOTE £5.20: £2.00, £2.00, £2.90; EX 17.40 Trifecta £105.30 Pool: £397.80 - 2.68 winning tickets..
Owner Sir David Seale **Bred** R D Hubbard **Trained** East Everleigh, Wilts

FOCUS
A decent maiden, run at a sound pace. The form looks straightforward with the first pair coming well clear.

797 BOOK EASTER @ PONTINS.COM H'CAP 7f (P)
4:10 (4:11) (Class 6) (0-60,65) 3-Y-O **£1,876** (£554; £277) **Stalls** Low

Form RPR
640- **1** **Johnny Friendly**[145] 6150 3-9-1 **57** AndrewElliott 10 65
(K R Burke) *sn pressed ldr: rdn to ld narrowly 2f out: kpt on u.p fr over 1f out* **12/1**
0-46 **2** *½* **Tiepie**[7] 714 3-9-2 **58** DaneO'Neill 6 65
(J Akehurst) *rdn in midfield fr over 4f out: prog u.p 2f out: wnt 2nd ent fnl f: clsng steadily at fin* **9/2**[3]
0-11 **3** *1 ¼* **Silca Destination**[8] 709 3-9-9 **65** 6ex EdwardCreighton 4 69
(M R Channon) *prom on inner: rdn and tried to chal over 1f out: nt qckn and hld after* **9/4**[1]
02-0 **4** *hd* **Desiderio**[7] 714 3-9-1 **57** RichardHughes 3 60
(R Hannon) *settled in midfield: reminders 3f out: sme prog u.p over 1f out: nt pce to chal* **5/2**[2]
1313 **5** *nse* **Talamahana**[8] 709 3-9-4 **60** (b) LPKeniry 9 63
(A B Haynes) *hld up bhd ldrs: cl enough 2f out: rdn and fnd nil over 1f out* **8/1**
55-6 **6** *3 ¼* **Countrywide Comet (IRE)**[51] 154 3-9-1 **57** (b) RobertWinston 8 51
(P Howling) *mde most to 2f out: wknd fnl f* **12/1**
00-0 **7** *hd* **Admirals Way**[18] 595 3-8-10 **52** JimCrowley 12 45
(C N Kellett) *t.k.h: hld up but sn plld way through to press ldng pair: wknd over 1f out* **20/1**
-040 **8** *1* **Herrbee (IRE)**[14] 623 3-8-11 **53** IanMongan 1 44
(S Dow) *hld up in last pair early: rdn over 2f out: no real prog* **10/1**
240- **9** *1 ¼* **Secret Meaning**[194] 4762 3-8-11 **60** (p) JackDean(7) 11 48
(W G M Turner) *drvn towards rr over 4f out: struggling and no ch after* **16/1**
-605 **10** *2 ¼* **Yattendon**[18] 582 3-8-13 **55** (t) PatDobbs 5 36
(S Kirk) *hld up in last trio: shkn up and no prog over 2f out* **25/1**
6406 **11** *18* **Tobouggornotobougg**[12] 656 3-8-4 **49** oh1 ow3 (v) TolleyDean(3) 7 —
(D Shaw) *sn wl in rr: t.o over 2f out* **50/1**

1m 25.5s (0.70) **Going Correction** +0.05s/f (Slow) 11 Ran SP% **129.6**
Speed ratings (Par 96): **98,97,96,95,95 91,91,90,88,85 64**
CSF £70.88 CT £177.33 TOTE £18.30: £3.30, £1.90, £1.40; EX 110.20 Trifecta £195.10 Part won. Pool: £274.81 - 0.50 winning tickets..
Owner U N Syndicate & Mrs E Burke **Bred** Southill Stud **Trained** Middleham Moor, N Yorks

FOCUS
A moderate handicap, run at a sound early pace. The penalised third sets the level but this does not look like a race to place too much faith in.

798 TRY BETDAQ FOR AN EXCHANGE H'CAP 5f (P)
4:40 (4:40) (Class 4) (0-85,81) 3-Y-O **£4,100** (£1,227; £613; £306; £152) **Stalls** High

Form RPR
431- **1** **Style Award**[117] 6741 3-8-13 **76** RichardHughes 5 87
(W J H Ratcliffe) *trckd ldrs on inner: effrt and led jst over 1f out: sn clr* **11/2**
11-1 **2** *3* **Ten Down**[38] 324 3-9-1 **78** TPQueally 2 78
(J A Osborne) *w ldr: wd bnd 2f out: nt qckn over 1f out: no ch w wnr after* **2/1**[1]
045- **3** *½* **Barraland**[143] 6195 3-8-9 **72** EdwardCreighton 3 70
(M R Channon) *trckd ldng pair: rdn fr 1/2-way: one pce fr over 1f out* **10/3**[2]
1532 **4** *½* **Valhillen**[5] 756 3-8-4 **70** WilliamBuick(3) 6 67
(M D I Usher) *bdly outpcd after 1f and bhd: no prog tl r.o fnl f: gaining on plcd horses at fin* **4/1**[3]
-214 **5** *1 ¼* **Baytown Blaze**[27] 470 3-8-11 **74** TGMcLaughlin 1 66
(M Wigham) *t.k.h: mde most: hanging rt and wd bnd 2f out: nt rcvr and hdd jst over 1f out* **10/1**
000- **6** *4 ½* **Nawaaff**[120] 6699 3-9-4 **81** ChrisCatlin 4 57
(M R Channon) *sn bdly outpcd: a last and nvr a factor* **15/2**

58.40 secs (-0.40) **Going Correction** +0.05s/f (Slow) 6 Ran SP% **112.7**
Speed ratings (Par 100): **105,100,99,98,96 89**
CSF £17.09 TOTE £7.00: £3.70, £1.10; EX 17.50.
Owner Bolton Hall Partnership 1 **Bred** Mrs S F Dibben **Trained** Wensley, N Yorks

FOCUS
A fair sprint, run at a strong pace. The improved winner did the job comfortably and the form looks believable.

799 MAKE IT PAY AT BETDAQ H'CAP 1m 2f (P)
5:10 (5:10) (Class 4) (0-85,85) 3-Y-O **£4,100** (£1,227; £613; £306; £152) **Stalls** Low

Form RPR
1 **1** **William Blake**[22] 529 3-8-13 **77** JoeFanning 1 79+
(M Johnston) *led at stdy pce: hrd pressed fr over 2f out: hdd ins fnl f: styd on wl to ld again last strides* **11/8**[1]
2-15 **2** *nse* **Taken (IRE)**[28] 458 3-8-11 **75** JamieSpencer 4 77
(J R Fanshawe) *cl up: n.m.r briefly over 2f out: wnt 2nd over 1f out and drvn: led ins fnl f: hung rt and fnd little: hdd last strides* **7/2**[2]
-144 **3** *½* **Hucking Hero (IRE)**[19] 573 3-8-13 **77** JimCrowley 3 78
(J R Best) *s.i.s: hld up in last: asked for effrt and hanging over 2f out: prog over 1f out: styd on wl fnl f: gaining at fin* **8/1**
301- **4** *¾* **Straight And Level (CAN)**[74] 7222 3-9-0 **78** AdamKirby 2 77
(Miss Jo Crowley) *wl in tch: rdn and effrt 2f out: styd on fr over 1f out but nt pce to chal* **18/1**
015- **5** *½* **Mganga**[154] 5914 3-8-2 **66** CatherineGannon 5 64
(M R Channon) *mostly in last pair: rdn wl over 2f out: effrt on inner over 1f out: kpt on but nvr able to rch ldrs* **20/1**
0-53 **6** *hd* **Harry Gee**[14] 632 3-9-3 **81** SteveDrowne 6 79
(G Wragg) *trckd wnr: chal over 2f out and upsides: hanging and nt qckn over 1f out: sn btn* **7/2**[2]
111- **7** *nk* **Hilbre Court (USA)**[82] 7145 3-9-7 **85** IanMongan 7 82
(B J Meehan) *pressed ldng pair on outer: rdn 2f out: lost pl and one pce over 1f out* **15/2**[3]

2m 9.08s (2.48) **Going Correction** +0.05s/f (Slow) 7 Ran SP% **119.5**
Speed ratings (Par 100): **92,91,91,90,90 90,90**
CSF £6.92 TOTE £2.30: £1.70, £2.00; EX 8.30 Place 6 £33.33, Place 5 £28.24.
Owner Sheikh Hamdan Bin Mohammed Al Maktoum **Bred** Gainsborough Stud Management Ltd **Trained** Middleham Moor, N Yorks

FOCUS
A fair three-year-old handicap, but the pace was only moderate and it resulted in a blanket finish. The winner is rated better than the bare form and there should be more to come from him.
Taken(IRE) Official explanation: vet said gelding had been struck into
T/Plt: £72.30 to a £1 stake. Pool: £61,685.45. 622.70 winning tickets. T/Qpdt: £4.20 to a £1 stake. Pool: £3,998.80. 688.70 winning tickets. JN

778 WOLVERHAMPTON (A.W) (L-H)
Wednesday, March 5

OFFICIAL GOING: Standard
Wind: Moderate, behind Weather: Fine

800 RACE THE FAMILY TO PONTIN'S @ EASTER CLAIMING STKS 5f 20y(P)
6:50 (6:50) (Class 5) 3-Y-O+ **£2,730** (£806; £403) **Stalls** Low

Form RPR
5146 **1** **Doubtful Sound (USA)**[26] 482 4-9-8 69 PhillipMakin 3 78
(T D Barron) *w ldr: rdn over 1f out: led ins fnl f: r.o* **6/4**[1]
1236 **2** *1 ¼* **Grimes Faith**[6] 729 5-9-10 70 (b) NCallan 1 76
(K A Ryan) *a.p: rdn and swtchd rt over 1f out: nt qckn wl ins fnl f* **9/4**[2]
2522 **3** *2 ¾* **Hurricane Hen**[25] 498 3-8-12 73 FergusSweeney 2 67
(J R Boyle) *led: rdn over 1f out: hdd and no ex ins fnl f* **5/2**[3]
5053 **4** *3* **Earl Compton (IRE)**[2] 774 4-9-10 55 (v) MickyFenton 4 55
(Stef Liddiard) *wnt rt s: hld up: pushed along over 3f out: rdn over 1f out: no rspnse* **16/1**

62.74 secs (0.44) **Going Correction** +0.20s/f (Slow)
WFA 3 from 4yo+ 13lb 4 Ran SP% **105.2**
Speed ratings (Par 103): **104,102,97,92**
CSF £4.85 TOTE £2.30; EX 4.40.Doubtful Sound was claimed by John A. Harris for £10,000.
Owner Miss N J Barron **Bred** Millsec, Ltd **Trained** Maunby, N Yorks

FOCUS
Only 2lb separated the first three on adjusted official ratings. The fourth, plus the time, dictate the level.

801 BET GOLF - BETDAQ H'CAP 5f 216y(P)
7:20 (7:21) (Class 5) (0-75,75) 4-Y-O+ **£2,730** (£806; £403) **Stalls** Low

Form RPR
0035 **1** **Methaaly (IRE)**[2] 782 5-8-1 **65** RossAtkinson(7) 5 73
(M Mullineaux) *chsd ldr: led wl over 1f out: rdn and edgd lft ins fnl f: jst hld on* **11/1**
212 **2** *hd* **Dickie Le Davoir**[13] 643 4-9-1 **72** NCallan 4 79
(John A Harris) *hld up and bhd: hdwy on ins over 2f out: rdn fnl f: r.o wl towards fin: jst failed* **4/1**[2]
3-21 **3** *2* **Bel Cantor**[27] 466 5-8-12 **72** (p) AndrewMullen(3) 6 73
(W J H Ratcliffe) *led: rdn and hdd wl over 1f out: no ex wl ins fnl f* **13/8**[1]
50-4 **4** *2 ¼* **Royal Challenge**[48] 194 7-9-0 **71** FergalLynch 2 66
(I W McInnes) *hld up in tch: rdn wl over 1f out: wknd fnl f* **6/1**
-025 **5** *4 ½* **Inca Soldier (FR)**[4] 766 5-8-4 **61** oh1 JimmyQuinn 7 42
(R C Guest) *hld up in rr: rdn over 2f out: sn struggling* **9/1**
-533 **6** *5* **Chjimes (IRE)**[19] 574 4-9-4 **75** RobertWinston 1 41
(C R Dore) *prom: hung lft over 3f out: rdn and wknd over 2f out* **9/2**[3]

1m 15.34s (0.34) **Going Correction** +0.20s/f (Slow) 6 Ran SP% **108.9**
Speed ratings (Par 103): **105,104,102,99,93 86**
CSF £50.33 TOTE £14.60: £4.80, £1.70; EX 72.90.
Owner The Bellflower Methaaly Partnership **Bred** Scuderia Golden Horse S R L **Trained** Alpraham, Cheshire
■ Stewards' Enquiry : Ross Atkinson caution: used whip down shoulder in forehand position

FOCUS
An ordinary little handicap. Modest, but solid form.
Methaaly(IRE) Official explanation: trainer's rep said, regarding apparent improvement in form, that the gelding got the run of the race and was allowed to dominate.

802 MAKE EASTER EGG-STRA SPECIAL @ PONTIN'S H'CAP 1m 4f 50y(P)
7:50 (7:50) (Class 6) (0-65,65) 4-Y-O+ **£2,047** (£604; £302) **Stalls** Low

Form RPR
22-2 **1** **Jago (SWI)**[11] 675 5-9-6 **65** LPKeniry 6 72
(A M Hales) *hld up in tch: led wl over 1f out: sn hung lft: hrd rdn: all out* **7/2**[2]
-123 **2** *nk* **Trysting Grove (IRE)**[10] 695 7-8-7 **52** SaleemGolam 4 59
(E G Bevan) *hld up: hdwy over 2f out: hrd rdn ins fnl f: kpt on* **15/2**
0235 **3** *1 ¼* **Our Kes (IRE)**[21] 540 6-9-6 **65** SimonWhitworth 5 70
(P Howling) *hld up in rr: hdwy on outside over 3f out: rdn wl over 1f out: nt qckn towards fin* **5/1**[3]
04-1 **4** *¾* **Mandalay Prince**[41] 287 4-8-8 **62** DebraEngland(7) 2 66
(W J Musson) *prom: nt clr run on ins and lost pl 3f out: swtchd rt over 2f out: edgd lft jst over 1f out: styd on towards fin* **7/2**[2]
015- **5** *2 ¼* **Princely Ted (IRE)**[99] 6961 7-8-13 **58** DaneO'Neill 8 58
(D Burchell) *chsd ldr: led 3f out: rdn and hdd wl over 1f out: wknd ins fnl f* **16/1**
0521 **6** *6* **Speagle (IRE)**[7] 720 6-9-4 **63** 6ex DeanMcKeown 3 54
(D Shaw) *set stdy pce: hdd 3f out: sn nt clr run on ins: wknd over 2f out* **2/1**[1]

2m 43.47s (2.37) **Going Correction** +0.20s/f (Slow)
WFA 4 from 5yo+ 2lb 6 Ran SP% **112.1**
Speed ratings (Par 101): **100,99,98,98,96 92**
CSF £28.32 CT £128.16 TOTE £3.20: £2.40, £6.50; EX 20.20.
Owner Four Counties Partnership **Bred** Gestut Sohrenhof **Trained** Preston Capes, Northants

FOCUS
A low-grade handicap run at a modest pace with the tempo quickening inside the last half-mile. Modest form, especially with the favourite below par, but the winner's best run yet in Britain.
Speagle(IRE) Official explanation: trainer had no explanation for the poor form shown

803 JOIN THE EASTER PARADE @ PONTIN'S H'CAP 1m 1f 103y(P)
8:20 (8:21) (Class 6) (0-65,65) 3-Y-O **£2,047** (£604; £302) **Stalls** Low

Form RPR
01- **1** **Mission Control (IRE)**[65] 7286 3-9-4 **62** PatCosgrave 8 65
(J R Boyle) *s.i.s: hdwy after 2f: hrd rdn 3f out: r.o to ld wl ins fnl f* **11/10**[1]

0452 **2** 1 1/4 **John Potts**[12] [665] 3-9-0 **58** AndrewElliott 4 59
(B P J Baugh) *chsd ldr: rdn to ld jst over 1f out: hdd wl ins fnl f: nt qckn* **9/1**

606- **3** 1 1/4 **Persistent (IRE)**[82] [7140] 3-8-13 **57** MickyFenton 7 55
(P T Midgley) *hld up towards rr: hdwy 2f out: rdn over 1f out: edgd lft wl ins fnl f: kpt on* **20/1**

3-21 **4** 1 1/4 **Little Firecracker**[41] [288] 3-9-4 **62** AdamKirby 2 58
(Miss M E Rowland) *a.p: rdn 3f out: nt clr run briefly wl over 1f out: no ex wl ins fnl f* **10/3**[2]

6-50 **5** 2 1/4 **Miss Bouggy Wouggy**[41] [288] 3-8-9 **53** (b[1]) LPKeniry 10 45
(M Blanshard) *hld up in tch: n.m.r over 2f out: rdn and wkng whn edgd rt jst over 1f out* **40/1**

-405 **6** shd **Bon Ton Roulet**[21] [547] 3-9-3 **61** PatDobbs 11 52
(R Hannon) *swtchd lft sn after s: t.k.h in rr: rdn over 2f out: nvr trbld ldrs* **25/1**

-334 **7** shd **Transcendent (IRE)**[22] [534] 3-8-3 **47** JimmyQuinn 5 38
(J D Bethell) *t.k.h in mid-div: sme hdwy on ins 2f out: hrd rdn and hung lft over 1f out: no further prog* **8/1**

3-55 **8** 1/2 **Afton View (IRE)**[2] [785] 3-9-3 **64** (e) DNolan(3) 1 54
(S Parr) *led: rdn over 2f out: hdd jst over 1f out: wknd ins fnl f* **7/1**[3]

5500 **9** 10 **Marino Prince (FR)**[2] [785] 3-9-7 **65** DaneO'Neill 6 36
(T Wall) *a bhd* **25/1**

00-0 **10** 6 **Charlie Green (IRE)**[53] [141] 3-8-2 **46** oh1 LiamJones 9 6
(Paul Green) *hld up in mid-div: rdn over 4f out: bhd fnl 3f* **66/1**

2m 4.51s (2.81) **Going Correction** +0.20s/f (Slow) **10** Ran SP% **120.7**
Speed ratings (Par 96): **95,93,92,91,89 89,89,89,80,74**
CSF £12.09 CT £139.48 TOTE £2.30: £1.50, £2.40, £6.30; EX 17.00.

Owner M Khan X2 **Bred** Darley **Trained** Epsom, Surrey

■ Stewards' Enquiry : L P Keniry three-day ban: careless riding (Mar 17-19)

FOCUS
This turned out to be rather more competitive than the betting suggested. Solid but modest form, the favourite making rather hard work of this.

Little Firecracker Official explanation: jockey said filly hung both ways

Charlie Green(IRE) Official explanation: jockey said gelding never travelled

804 TREAT THE FAMILY TO EASTER @ PONTIN'S CLASSIFIED STKS 1m 141y(P)
8:50 (8:51) (Class 7) 4-Y-0+ **£1,365** (£403; £201) **Stalls** Low

Form RPR

40-2 **1** **High Five Society**[4] [770] 4-9-0 43 (bt) PhillipMakin 11 64+
(S R Bowring) *chsd ldr: led 3f out: rdn 2f out: edgd rt over 1f out: drew clr fnl f: eased towards fin* **6/5**[1]

0-06 **2** 7 **Keon (IRE)**[50] [168] 6-8-11 45 (p) RussellKennemore(3) 5 45
(R Hollinshead) *t.k.h in mid-div: hdwy 4f out: chsd wnr wl over 2f out: sn rdn: btn whn edgd rt ins fnl f* **5/1**[2]

45/5 **3** 1/2 **Tirol Livit (IRE)**[12] [657] 5-8-9 45 (b[1]) AshleyHamblett(5) 10 44
(N Wilson) *a.p: rdn over 2f out: one pce* **9/1**

064 **4** 3 **Cape Dancer (IRE)**[26] [478] 4-9-0 41 (p) FergalLynch 1 38
(J S Wainwright) *hld up in tch: n.m.r on ins after 1f: rdn 3f out: sn wknd* **15/2**[3]

0044 **5** 3/4 **Lady Firecracker (IRE)**[10] [693] 4-9-0 42 (v) StephenCarson 3 36
(J R Best) *prom: rdn over 3f out: sn wknd* **10/1**

5-40 **6** 2 **Me No Puppet**[9] [698] 4-9-0 45 JimmyQuinn 8 32
(E J Alston) *hld up in tch: rdn over 3f out: sn wknd* **8/1**

00-0 **7** 5 **Ticking**[63] [8] 5-8-7 35 AshleyMorgan(7) 7 22
(T Keddy) *t.k.h towards rr: hung rt fr over 2f out: nvr nr ldrs* **80/1**

065- **8** 2 1/4 **Franky'N'Jonny**[13] [7247] 5-9-0 38 AlanDaly 6 17
(G J Smith) *stdd s: hld up: a towards rr* **25/1**

00-6 **9** nk **Lizarazu (GER)**[41] [289] 9-9-0 41 VinceSlattery 4 16
(D J Wintle) *led: rdn and hdd 3f out: sn wknd* **20/1**

0-50 **10** 19 **Broad Town Girl**[33] [392] 5-8-7 36 (v[1]) KylieManser(7) 13 —
(Mrs H Sweeting) *s.s: plld hrd in rr: n.m.r on ins over 4f out: sn struggling: t.o* **50/1**

00-0 **11** 12 **Josama**[26] [483] 4-9-0 35 PatCosgrave 12 —
(R Bastiman) *wnt rt s: rdn over 4f out: a bhd: t.o* **66/1**

1m 52.76s (2.26) **Going Correction** +0.20s/f (Slow) **11** Ran SP% **117.4**
Speed ratings (Par 97): **97,90,90,87,87 85,80,78,78,61 50**
CSF £6.74 TOTE £1.90: £1.40, £1.90, £2.30; EX 12.10.

Owner The High Five Partnership **Bred** A C M Spalding **Trained** Edwinstowe, Notts

FOCUS
The ultimately easy winner apart, this was a weak event even by Class 7 standards.

Broad Town Girl Official explanation: jockey said mare ran too freely

805 BACK OR LAY AT BETDAQ H'CAP 1m 141y(P)
9:20 (9:20) (Class 5) (0-75,73) 4-Y-0+ **£2,730** (£806; £403) **Stalls** Low

Form RPR

16-1 **1** **Mia's Boy**[6] [731] 4-8-11 **73** JPHamblett(7) 4 85+
(C A Dwyer) *hld up in tch: shkn up to ld wl over 1f out: easily* **8/11**[1]

60-1 **2** 2 3/4 **Exit Smiling**[12] [659] 6-8-10 **65** MickyFenton 1 69
(P T Midgley) *led early: chsd ldr: ev ch wl over 1f out: sn rdn: one pce* **3/1**[2]

/0-4 **3** 1 **Not Another Cat (USA)**[17] [598] 4-9-0 **69** (t) DarrenWilliams 2 71
(K R Burke) *sn led: rdn and hdd wl over 1f out: one pce* **16/1**

-463 **4** nk **Putra Laju (IRE)**[12] [660] 4-8-4 **66** (p) GabrielHannon(7) 3 67
(J W Hills) *hld up in tch: ev ch wl over 1f out: one pce* **4/1**[3]

1m 56.4s (5.90) **Going Correction** +0.20s/f (Slow) **4** Ran SP% **108.8**
Speed ratings (Par 103): **81,78,77,77**
CSF £3.21 TOTE £2.00; EX 2.70 Place 6 £105.92, Place 5 £49.48.

Owner Iraj Parvizi **Bred** Sir Eric Parker **Trained** Burrough Green, Cambs

FOCUS
This developed into a sprint from the three-furlong pole and the time was 3.64 seconds slower than the Class 7 classified event. The winner is on the up but this was not a strong race.

T/Plt: £227.00 to a £1 stake. Pool: £82,221.40. 264.35 winning tickets. T/Qpdt: £8.00 to a £1 stake. Pool: £6,816.80. 629.10 winning tickets. KH

800 WOLVERHAMPTON (A.W) (L-H)
Thursday, March 6

OFFICIAL GOING: Standard
Wind: Light, behind Weather: Fine

806 BET UEFA CUP - BETDAQ H'CAP 5f 216y(P)
6:50 (6:51) (Class 6) (0-60,60) 4-Y-0+ **£1,774** (£523; £262) **Stalls** Low

Form RPR

342- **1** **Strabinios King**[69] [7261] 4-9-4 **60** FrancisNorton 2 74+
(M Wigham) *hld up in mid-div: hdwy and n.m.r over 1f out: hrd rdn to ld last strides* **11/4**[2]

0-60 **2** nse **Gilded Cove**[20] [576] 8-9-1 **60** RussellKennemore(3) 10 70
(R Hollinshead) *hld up towards rr: c v wd st: rdn and hdwy over 1f out: led ins fnl f: hdd last strides* **16/1**

212 **3** 3/4 **Cape Of Storms**[8] [718] 5-8-13 **55** PaulMulrennan 5 63
(R Brotherton) *a.p: rdn to ld over 1f out: hdd and edgd rt ins fnl f: nt qckn* **4/1**[3]

4-54 **4** hd **High 'n Dry (IRE)**[14] [639] 4-9-4 **60** (p) PaulDoe 12 67
(M A Allen) *hld up in mid-div: hdwy on outside over 2f out: rdn wl over 1f out: ev ch whn edgd rt ins fnl f: nt qckn* **25/1**

5-20 **5** 2 1/4 **Eleanor Eloise (USA)**[20] [571] 4-9-1 **57** (p) LiamJones 13 57
(J R Gask) *hld up and bhd: hdwy on ins wl over 1f out: rdn fnl f: nvr able to chal* **66/1**

0352 **6** shd **Music Box Express**[5] [766] 4-9-2 **58** (t) RobertWinston 1 58
(George Baker) *s.i.s: hld up and bhd: hdwy on ins wl over 1f out: rdn and edgd rt ins fnl f: no ex* **9/4**[1]

014- **7** 1 3/4 **Scarlett Heart (IRE)**[82] [7161] 4-9-0 **56** ChrisCatlin 4 51
(J G Burns, Ire) *hld up and bhd: hdwy whn nt clr run wl over 1f out: nt clr run briefly ins fnl f: nvr trbld ldrs* **10/1**

1260 **8** 1 1/2 **Calloff The Search**[48] [213] 4-8-10 **52** (v) MickyFenton 11 42
(Stef Liddiard) *led over 2f: led over 2f out tl over 1f out: sn rdn: wknd ins fnl f* **33/1**

40-1 **9** 1/2 **Howards Tipple**[20] [581] 4-9-4 **60** PhillipMakin 7 49
(Miss L A Perratt) *in tch: lost pl after 1f: n.d after* **6/1**

0-43 **10** 2 **Jilly Why (IRE)**[10] [699] 7-9-0 **56** (b) NeilChalmers 9 39
(Paul Green) *hld up in tch: wknd wl over 1f out* **20/1**

00-0 **11** 7 **Stir Crazy (IRE)**[18] [596] 4-8-10 **52** FergalLynch 3 14
(D W Barker) *prom tl wknd wl over 1f out* **25/1**

0002 **12** 2 3/4 **Monashee Brave (IRE)**[8] [719] 5-8-13 **55** (p) AmirQuinn 8 8
(M A Allen) *w ldr: led over 3f out: rdn and hdd over 2f out: wknd over 1f out* **33/1**

3006 **13** 26 **Perlachy**[12] [681] 4-8-10 **55** (p) DuranFentiman(3) 6 —
(Mrs N Macauley) *s.v.s: a t.o* **25/1**

1m 15.28s (0.28) **Going Correction** +0.20s/f (Slow) **13** Ran SP% **130.4**
Speed ratings (Par 101): **106,105,104,104,101 101,99,97,96,93 84,80,46**
CSF £46.68 CT £195.41 TOTE £4.80: £2.60, £6.00, £1.80; EX 87.60.

Owner Val Kelly **Bred** Newsells Park Stud Limited **Trained** Newmarket, Suffolk

FOCUS
A moderate sprint handicap, but a strongly run one and the winning time was creditable. Despite that, the bulk of the field were still within a couple of lengths of each other with every chance starting up the home straight. The race is rated through the front pair's recent form.

Music Box Express Official explanation: jockey said gelding missed the break

Perlachy Official explanation: jockey said gelding missed the break

807 BET FA CUP - BETDAQ CLAIMING STKS 7f 32y(P)
7:20 (7:20) (Class 6) 4-Y-0+ **£1,774** (£523; £262) **Stalls** High

Form RPR

-442 **1** **Danetime Lord (IRE)**[22] [536] 5-9-4 80 (p) PatCosgrave 3 89
(J R Boyle) *chsd ldrs: nt clr run over 1f out: led ins fnl f: r.o wl* **7/4**[1]

-564 **2** 2 1/2 **Teasing**[32] [417] 4-9-2 78 RobertHavlin 1 81
(J Pearce) *hld up in rr: rdn over 2f out: hdwy over 1f out: edgd lft and wnt 2nd towards fin: nt trble wnr* **11/4**[2]

000- **3** 1 1/2 **Moayed**[177] [5312] 9-8-13 74 (b) JimCrowley 2 74
(N P Littmoden) *hld up: hdwy on ins over 2f out: led jst over 1f out: rdn and hdd ins fnl f: one pce* **10/1**

0-36 **4** 2 **Love On Sight**[11] [694] 4-8-13 72 (v[1]) AndrewElliott 4 69
(A P Jarvis) *t.k.h: sn led: edgd rt over 1f out: sn hdd: wknd ins fnl f* **25/1**

-301 **5** 1 **Landucci**[14] [643] 7-9-5 75 (p) JamesDoyle 6 73
(J W Hills) *broke wl: led early: sn stdd and bhd: rdn wl over 1f out: nvr trbld ldrs* **13/2**

4665 **6** 3 1/2 **Soviet Palace (IRE)**[3] [783] 4-9-3 74 (p) NCallan 5 62
(K A Ryan) *sn chsng ldr: ev ch whn edgd lft over 1f out: edgd rt ent fnl f: wknd* **7/2**[3]

626- **7** 1 1/2 **Zennerman (IRE)**[69] [7141] 5-8-13 70 (p) PaulMulrennan 7 54
(Miss J E Foster) *rdn over 3f out: a bhd* **25/1**

1m 30.66s (1.06) **Going Correction** +0.20s/f (Slow) **7** Ran SP% **115.4**
Speed ratings (Par 101): **101,98,96,94,93 89,87**
CSF £6.91 TOTE £2.80: £1.20, £1.80; EX 9.20.The winner was claimed by J. R. Gask for £15,000.

Owner M Khan X2 **Bred** P J Murphy **Trained** Epsom, Surrey

FOCUS
A fair little claimer with the winner rated 80 and the seven runners were within 10lb of each other on adjusted official ratings. The early pace was not strong despite the leader racing keenly and the early fractions were slower than the following classified event, though the final time was 0.79 seconds faster. The winner is the best guide to the form.

808 BET SIX NATIONS RUGBY - BETDAQ CLASSIFIED STKS 7f 32y(P)
7:50 (7:51) (Class 7) 4-Y-0+ **£1,365** (£403; £201) **Stalls** High

Form RPR

5-20 **1** **Bahamian Bay**[8] [718] 6-8-11 45 MarkLawson(3) 7 53
(M Brittain) *broke wl: sn stdd and bhd: hdwy on outside over 2f out: rdn over 1f out: led ins fnl f: r.o* **8/1**

0602 **2** 1 **Suhayl Star (IRE)**[8] [713] 4-9-0 45 DaneO'Neill 9 51
(P Burgoyne) *t.k.h in tch: rdn over 1f out: nt qckn ins fnl f* **9/2**

30-0 **3** 1 1/2 **Gyration (IRE)**[17] [611] 4-9-0 45 (p) RobertWinston 3 47
(G A Swinbank) *sn led: hdd over 5f out: led over 3f out: edgd lft wl over 1f out: rdn and hdd ins fnl f: no ex* **5/2**[1]

/023 **4** 2 3/4 **Grezie**[8] [713] 6-9-0 45 PaulDoe 10 40
(L A Dace) *hld up and bhd: nt clr run on ins over 2f out: swtchd rt ent st: hdwy over 1f out: rdn and hung lft ins fnl f: one pce* **12/1**

2502 **5** 1 3/4 **Desert Lover (IRE)**[12] [684] 6-9-0 45 (v) NCallan 1 36
(R J Price) *chsd ldrs: rdn over 2f out: edgd lft 1f out: wknd ins fnl f* **4/1**[3]

5630 **6** 1 1/4 **Stoneacre Gareth (IRE)**[5] 770 4-9-0 45 JimCrowley 5 33
(J Jay) *led early: prom: n.m.r over 2f out: rdn and wknd wl over 1f out* **10/3**[2]

0334 **7** 7 **Temtation (IRE)**[14] 642 4-8-11 44 RussellKennemore(3) 8 16
(J A Pickering) *prom: led over 5f out tl over 3f out: wknd wl over 1f out* **12/1**

60-0 **8** 6 **Wattys The Craic**[15] 624 4-9-0 45 (v[1]) SaleemGolam 4 1
(G Prodromou) *s.i.s: a bhd* **40/1**

000- **9** 10 **Cadi May**[207] 4416 4-9-0 45 LiamJones 6 —
(W M Brisbourne) *t.k.h: prom tl wknd 3f out* **25/1**

1m 31.45s (1.85) **Going Correction** +0.20s/f (Slow) **9** Ran SP% **122.6**
Speed ratings (Par 97): **97,95,94,91,89 87,79,72,61**
CSF £46.72 TOTE £13.60: £3.80, £1.90, £1.50; EX 71.00.
Owner Northgate Lodge Racing Club **Bred** The National Stud **Trained** Warthill, N Yorks

FOCUS
A typically bad race of its type and although the early fractions were faster than the preceding claimer, the winning time was 0.79 seconds slower. Not many ever got into it and the market got it right as the front three were all backed. Weak form, but it makes sense.
Temtation(IRE) Official explanation: jockey said filly hung left

809 BETDAQ.CO.UK H'CAP 1m 141y(P)
8:20 (8:20) (Class 5) (0-70,67) 4-Y-0+ £2,331 (£693; £346; £173) Stalls Low

Form RPR
0-54 **1** **Kildare Sun (IRE)**[13] 659 6-9-4 **67** PatCosgrave 1 75
(J Mackie) *mde all: pushed along over 2f out: rdn wl over 1f out: drvn out* **6/1**

/3-2 **2** nk **Breaker Morant (IRE)**[55] 128 6-8-12 **61** (b) ChrisCatlin 3 68
(J G Burns, Ire) *chsd wnr: rdn and ev ch ins fnl f: nt qckn* **5/2**[1]

6-11 **3** nse **Cape Velvet (IRE)**[34] 395 4-9-4 **67** JamesDoyle 4 74
(J W Hills) *hld up in last: hdwy 2f out: edgd lft over 1f out: sn rdn: r.o wl towards fin* **10/3**[2]

320- **4** 1 1/2 **Bivouac (UAE)**[234] 3587 4-8-4 **53** PaulHanagan 2 57
(G A Swinbank) *a.p: rdn 2f out: swtchd rt over 1f out: nt qckn fnl f* **11/2**

-304 **5** 3 **Zabeel House**[18] 601 5-8-12 **61** (p) DeanMcKeown 5 58
(John A Harris) *hld up in tch: btn over 2f out* **9/2**[3]

6511 **6** 7 **Climate (IRE)**[8] 724 9-8-5 **54** CatherineGannon 6 37
(P D Evans) *hld up in tch: wknd over 2f out* **11/2**

1m 53.99s (3.49) **Going Correction** +0.20s/f (Slow) **6** Ran SP% **114.9**
Speed ratings (Par 103): **92,91,91,90,87 81**
CSF £22.02 TOTE £6.60: £3.30, £1.60; EX 26.00.
Owner Mrs Barbara Woodworth **Bred** Gordan Woodworth **Trained** Church Broughton , Derbys

FOCUS
They went very slowly early in this handicap and it developed into something of a 3f sprint, resulting in a moderate winning time for the grade. Weakish form.

810 BET CHELTENHAM FESTIVAL - BETDAQ H'CAP 2m 119y(P)
8:50 (8:50) (Class 4) (0-85,78) 4-Y-0+ £4,210 (£1,252; £625; £312) Stalls Low

Form RPR
1232 **1** **Calculating (IRE)**[21] 561 4-9-10 **77** DaneO'Neill 1 88
(M D I Usher) *hld up in tch: led over 2f out: rdn and hung lft over 1f out: clr whn edgd rt ins fnl f: styd on* **2/1**[2]

0621 **2** 8 **Trachonitis (IRE)**[19] 588 4-9-11 **78** NCallan 2 83+
(J R Jenkins) *t.k.h in last: hdwy to chse wnr over 2f out: rdn wl over 1f out: sn no imp: eased whn btn wl ins fnl f* **6/4**[1]

6-40 **3** 4 **Stoop To Conquer**[22] 540 8-9-7 **72** JerryO'Dwyer(3) 4 69+
(A W Carroll) *chsd wnr: led 4f out: rdn and hdd over 2f out: wknd wl over 1f out* **10/1**

2/5- **4** 46 **The Nawab (IRE)**[29] 3145 6-10-0 **76** PaulMulrennan 3 17+
(Barry Potts, Ire) *led: rdn and hdd 4f out: wknd 3f out: sn eased: fin lame* **11/4**[3]

3m 45.29s (3.49) **Going Correction** +0.20s/f (Slow)
WFA 4 from 6yo+ 5lb **4** Ran SP% **109.1**
Speed ratings (Par 105): **99,95,93,71**
CSF £5.43 TOTE £3.10; EX 6.40.
Owner Brian Rogan **Bred** Darley **Trained** Upper Lambourn, Berks

FOCUS
This was not a true test of stamina over the trip and the race only began in earnest over the last 5f. The time was therefore ordinary, but they still finished very well spread out. The winner remains on the up but effectively only had two to beat.
The Nawab(IRE) Official explanation: vet said gelding finished lame

811 BET MULTIPLES - BETDAQ H'CAP 1m 1f 103y(P)
9:20 (9:20) (Class 6) (0-65,71) 4-Y-0+ £1,774 (£523; £262) Stalls Low

Form RPR
2211 **1** **Rebellious Spirit**[7] 728 5-9-10 **71** 6ex PaulDoe 6 85
(S Curran) *chsd ldr: rdn to ld wl over 1f out: edgd lft ent fnl f: drvn out* **8/1**

5-41 **2** 1/2 **Royal Amnesty**[12] 686 5-8-13 **60** (b) PhillipMakin 3 73+
(Miss L A Perratt) *hld up and bhd: hdwy on ins 2f out: rdn 1f out: kpt on to take 2nd post* **15/8**[1]

-221 **3** shd **Supercast (IRE)**[21] 560 5-9-3 **64** SamHitchcott 4 77
(N J Vaughan) *chsd clr ldng pair: rdn over 2f out: wnt 2nd wl over 1f out: ev ch ins fnl f: nt qckn cl home* **9/2**[3]

202 **4** 6 **Alfie Tupper (IRE)**[12] 682 5-9-3 **64** PatCosgrave 7 65
(J R Boyle) *hld up: hdwy over 2f out: edgd lft over 1f out: sn rdn: wknd wl ins fnl f* **5/2**[2]

-150 **5** 3/4 **Alexander Guru**[31] 430 4-9-2 **63** JamesDoyle 2 63
(M Blanshard) *hld up and bhd: hdwy over 2f out: rdn wl over 1f out: sn edgd lft: no imp fnl f* **10/1**

5235 **6** 3 1/2 **Flight Dream (FR)**[22] 545 5-9-1 **65** (b) JerryO'Dwyer(3) 9 58
(M G Quinlan) *led: rdn 3f out: hdd wl over 1f out: wknd fnl f* **28/1**

6-06 **7** hd **Street Life (IRE)**[14] 180 10-8-10 **57** NeilPollard 8 50
(W J Musson) *s.i.s: a bhd* **16/1**

0-15 **8** 3 **Wasalat (USA)**[24] 526 6-9-4 **65** FergalLynch 5 52
(D W Barker) *a bhd* **12/1**

-460 **9** 7 **Latif (USA)**[10] 701 7-9-1 **62** NeilChalmers 10 36
(Paul Green) *dwlt: hld up: hdwy over 3f out: rdn and wknd over 2f out* **40/1**

0/00 **10** 9 **Princelywallywogan**[18] 601 6-8-9 **56** ow1 MickyFenton 1 13
(John A Harris) *a in rr* **66/1**

2m 2.18s (0.48) **Going Correction** +0.20s/f (Slow) **10** Ran SP% **122.7**
Speed ratings (Par 101): **105,104,104,99,98 95,95,92,86,78**
CSF £24.48 CT £80.99 TOTE £8.70: £2.10, £1.40, £2.00; EX 17.80 Place 6 £59.53, Place 5 £22.66 .
Owner Colin Hill **Bred** Car Colston Hall Stud **Trained** Hatford, Oxon

FOCUS
They went a very decent pace in this and the field were soon well spread out. The front three eventually pulled right away and the form looks solid and fair for the grade.

T/Plt: £98.90 to a £1 stake. Pool: £97,131.25. 716.45 winning tickets. T/Qpdt: £32.00 to a £1 stake. Pool: £5,984.70. 138.30 winning tickets. KH

738 NAD AL SHEBA (L-H)
Thursday, March 6
OFFICIAL GOING: Turf course - good; dirt course - fast

812a SHADWELL ESTATE (RATED CONDITIONS RACE) (DIRT) 7f (D)
3:40 (3:40) 3-Y-O
£9,045 (£3,015; £1,507; £753; £452; £301)

RPR
1 **Ukrainian (BRZ)**[14] 648 4-9-4 95 RichardMullen 2 93
(A Cintra Pereira, Brazil) *sn rdn in rr: 8th 2 1/2f out: r.o wl 1 1/2f out: led last 100yds* **5/1**[3]

2 1 1/4 **Select Reason (BRZ)**[13] 670 4-9-4 90 (bt) MJKinane 9 90
(A Cintra Pereira, Brazil) *mid-div: wd: smooth prog to ld 1f out: r.o: hdd last 100yds* **14/1**

3 1/4 **Lizard Island (USA)**[42] 292 3-9-0 107 (e) JohnEgan 8 94
(A Manuel, UAE) *mid-div: rdn to chse ldrs 2 1/2f out: r.o fnl 1 1/2f: nrst fin* **13/8**[1]

4 2 3/4 **Change Alley (USA)**[21] 567 3-8-5 89 (b) RoystonFfrench 1 77
(A Al Raihe, UAE) *disp on rail: led 3f out: hdd 1f out: wknd* **11/1**

5 2 3/4 **Choisky (IRE)**[21] 567 3-8-5 78 PDevlin 6 70
(R Bouresly, Kuwait) *slowly away: racd in rr: nvr nr to chal* **50/1**

6 5 1/4 **New Jersey (IRE)**[21] 567 3-8-9 93 MartinDwyer 4 59
(Doug Watson, UAE) *disp: rdn 2 1/2f out: sn btn* **10/1**

7 1 **Ablaan (USA)**[21] 567 3-8-9 95 (b) KShea 5 56
(M F De Kock, South Africa) *trckd ldrs: rdn 2 1/2f out: sn btn* **11/4**[2]

8 1/4 **Swallow Star**[27] 496 3-8-5 70 DO'Donohoe 10 51
(R Bouresly, Kuwait) *settled in rr: nvr able to chal* **50/1**

9 dist **Beetuna (IRE)**[20] 3-8-5 70 (b) TPO'Shea 3 —
(E Charpy, UAE) *disp: rdn 3f out: wknd qckly* **33/1**

10 dist **Palm Court**[63] 3-8-3 87 AhmedAjtebi(6) 7 —
(A Al Raihe, UAE) *settled in last: virtually p.u after 2f* **14/1**

1m 24.92s (0.12) **Going Correction** +0.20s/f (Slow)
WFA 3 from 4yo 16lb **10** Ran SP% **119.0**
Speed ratings: **107,105,105,102,99 93,91,91,—,—**
CSF: 72.49.
Owner Alfredo Leonardo Arnaldo Crabbia **Bred** Haras Santa Luzia Da Agua Branca **Trained** Brazil

FOCUS
An ordinary conditions contest, but certainly competitive enough and they went a good pace.

NOTEBOOK
Ukrainian(BRZ)'s form had been patchy since arriving from Brazil, where he was a dual winner on dirt, but he had a squeak judged on his third in an extended 7f handicap off a mark of 95 two starts back, and he proved the answer. He still had plenty to do at the top of the straight, but produced a sustained effort inside the final two furlongs to get on top near the line.
Select Reason(BRZ), stepped back up in trip with a tongue-tie added, picked up well from off the pace to lead around a furlong out and traded at 1.03 on Betfair, but he was reeled in late on. This would appear to be the limit of his stamina.
Lizard Island(USA) was below the pick of the form he showed on the turf for Aidan O'Brien last season when fourth in a UAE 2000 Guineas trial over the bare 7f round here for Stan Moore and, now with another trainer, he was again below par. Fitted with eye-shields this time, he kept responding to pressure all the way up the straight, but never looked like doing enough and will probably be happier back on turf. (op 7-4)
Change Alley(USA), with blinkers replacing eye-shields, found this easier than the UAE 2000 Guineas and ran well. He was only passed at the furlong pole and could do even better when there is less pressure on the lead. (op 10-1)
Choisky(IRE) came into this fully exposed as just a modest maiden after 13 starts and his proximity suggests the form is limited.
Ablaan(USA), who had blinkers on this time, showed good early speed, but weakened out of contention very tamely.

813a AL BASTAKIYA - MUJAHID (LISTED RACE) (DIRT) 1m 1f (D)
4:15 (4:15) 3-Y-O
£45,226 (£15,075; £7,537; £3,768; £2,261; £1,507)

RPR
1 **Royal Vintage (SAF)**[21] 567 4-9-8 113 KShea 7 115
(M F De Kock, South Africa) *trckd ldr: rdn to ld 2f out: r.o wl: hust hld on* **11/8**[2]

2 hd **Honour Devil (ARG)**[21] 567 4-9-6 115 JMurtagh 3 112+
(M F De Kock, South Africa) *mid-div: hrd rdn to chse wnr 2f out: hung: r.o wl fnl f: jst failed* **5/6**[1]

3 1 1/2 **Numaany (USA)**[21] 567 3-8-9 98 LDettori 2 107
(Saeed Bin Suroor) *sn led: hdd 2f out: r.o wl* **15/2**[3]

4 16 **Paveroc**[21] 567 3-8-9 93 (e) JohnEgan 4 73
(A Manuel, UAE) *racd in rr: nvr able to chal* **50/1**

5 11 **Mutabayen (USA)**[21] 567 3-8-9 91 (b) RoystonFfrench 1 50
(A Al Raihe, UAE) *mid-div tl 3 1/2f out: wknd* **66/1**

6 18 **Aquino (URU)**[21] 567 4-9-4 100 (t) RyanMoore 6 —
(Doug Watson, UAE) *mid-div: rdn 4 1/2f out: nvr nr to chal* **33/1**

7 12 **Toolittleyourlate (USA)**[21] 567 3-8-9 85 RichardMullen 5 —
(S Seemar, UAE) *racd in last: nvr nr to chal* **150/1**

1m 48.68s (-1.12) **Going Correction** +0.20s/f (Slow)
WFA 3 from 4yo 20lb **7** Ran SP% **115.5**
Speed ratings: **112,111,110,96,86 70,59**
CSF: 2.91.
Owner Sh Mohd bin Khalifa Al Maktoum/RMG Syndicate **Bred** E Foster **Trained** South Africa
■ Just as in the Guineas, Mike de Kock saddled the first two home.

FOCUS
The second leg of the UAE Triple Crown – the other two being the 2,000 Guineas and the Derby – and the race carried Listed status for the first time. This looked like a good renewal, with the first two home from the Guineas re-opposing, but the race itself was unsatisfactory, as the first two home both had very hard races.

NOTEBOOK
Royal Vintage(SAF) narrowly reversed Guineas form with Honour Devil, despite being 2lb worse off for half a length. He was entitled to improve for his recent second placing considering that was his first run for eight months, but there is no doubt he enjoyed a much better trip than his stablemate, and anyone who backed the runner-up is entitled to feel hard done by. He also had a very hard race and does not appeal as one to back at a short price for the UAE Derby, even if he is one of the main 'form' horses.

Honour Devil(ARG) was restrained soon after the start to race just in behind both the eventual winner and the third home, Numaany, with his rider perhaps reluctant to engage in a speed duel, but the tactic backfired as, after racing keenly through the early stages, he was caught flat-footed off the home bend, allowing Royal Vintage a couple or so lengths' head start. He then proceeded to carry his head awkwardly under pressure, perhaps showing his inexperience of chasing horses, before finally knuckling down inside the final furlong to very nearly reel in the tiring winner. He probably would have won under a more positive ride, and it would be no surprise to see him reverse form with Royal Vintage on World Cup night, but both horses had very hard races. (tchd 10-11)

Numaany(USA) ◆ looked better than the bare form of fifth behind today's first and second in the UAE 2000 Guineas and he duly got a lot closer this time although, like the winner, he enjoyed the run of things under a positive ride. He gives the impression he is still learning and could do better again in the UAE Derby, although stamina is very much his strong suit and he will again need plenty of use made of him. His stable also have both My Indy and Etched, third and fourth respectively in the Guineas, for the Derby, and it would be no surprise to see Godolphin land that particular prize. (op 13-2)

Paveroc had been running with credit in similar company lately, but he probably didn't have the stamina for this trip. (op 40-1)

814a MAHAB AL SHIMAAL - GREEN DESERT (GROUP 3) (DIRT) 6f (D)

4:45 (4:49) 3-Y-0+

£60,301 (£20,100; £10,050; £5,025; £3,015; £2,010)

				RPR
1		**Diabolical (USA)**[42] 295 5-9-4 113 ... KerrinMcEvoy 1 (Saeed Bin Suroor) *trckd ldrs: led 1f out: easily* **6/1**[3]		119
2	4½	**Star Crowned (USA)**[13] 670 5-9-0 102 ... (t) MJKinane 8 (R Bouresly, Kuwait) *trckd ldrs: outpcd 3f out: r.o wl fnl 1 1/2f: nrst fin* **12/1**		101
3	nse	**New Freedom (BRZ)**[35] 378 7-9-0 105 ... TPO'Shea 5 (A Selvaratnam, UAE) *sn led: rdn 3f out: r.o same pce* **11/1**		101
4	1	**Sarissa (BRZ)**[13] 670 5-8-9 102 ... C-PLemaire 3 (P Bary, France) *led in centre: rdn 2 1/2f out: hdd 1f out: kpt on same pce* **8/1**		93
5	3¼	**Salaam Dubai (AUS)**[21] 566 7-9-0 107 ... (v) RichardMullen 2 (A Selvaratnam, UAE) *trckd ldrs: rdn 3f out: nt qckn* **8/1**		88
6	2¾	**Drayton (IRE)**[13] 666 4-9-0 102 ... (bt) JMurtagh 14 (M F De Kock, South Africa) *slowly away: n.d: r.o fnl 1 1/2f* **10/1**		80
7	¾	**Prince Tamino**[7] 738 5-9-0 107 ... RoystonFfrench 13 (A Al Raihe, UAE) *nvr nr to chal* **18/1**		78
8	shd	**Malayeen (AUS)**[21] 566 6-9-0 100 ... (v) AhmedAjtebi 10 (A Selvaratnam, UAE) *trckd ldrs tl rdn 3f out: wknd* **28/1**		77
9	shd	**Frosty Secret (USA)**[13] 670 4-9-0 108 ... KShea 15 (M F De Kock, South Africa) *trckd ldrs: rdn 3f out: sn btn* **7/2**[1]		77
10	1¼	**Sea Hunter**[42] 295 6-9-0 98 ... (vt) TedDurcan 11 (A Al Raihe, UAE) *nvr able to chal* **25/1**		73
11	3¾	**Botanical (USA)**[13] 666 7-9-0 95 ... (bt) DBadel 4 (E Charpy, UAE) *prom in centre for 2f* **66/1**		62
12	nk	**Subpoena**[7] 741 6-9-0 100 ... (v) LisaJones 9 (A Al Raihe, UAE) *nvr nr to chal* **50/1**		61
13	¾	**Olympic City (BRZ)**[14] 647 5-8-9 98 ... DSmith 7 (A Al Raihe, UAE) *nvr able to chal* **66/1**		54
14	1¼	**Conroy (USA)**[35] 378 10-9-0 95 ... DWhyte 4 (A Selvaratnam, UAE) *nvr able to chal* **25/1**		55
15	nk	**Afrashad (USA)**[166] 6-9-0 107 ... (t) LDettori 6 (Saeed Bin Suroor) *slowly away: nvr nr to chal* **5/1**[2]		54
16	¾	**Grand Vista**[7] 738 4-9-0 102 ... (t) RyanMoore 16 (H J Brown, South Africa) *nvr nr to chal* **16/1**		52

69.59 secs (-0.61) **Going Correction** +0.20s/f (Slow) **16** Ran SP% **127.7**
Speed ratings: **112,106,105,104,100 96,95,95,95,93 88,88,87,85,85 84**
CSF: 75.71.
Owner Godolphin **Bred** Longleaf Pine Farm **Trained** Newmarket, Suffolk

FOCUS
The draw has tended to play a strong part in results over sprint distances on this dirt course and most of the field were keen to cross over to the stands'-side rail.

NOTEBOOK
Diabolical(USA) was drawn in stall one and ended up racing up the centre of the track. Twice a Graded winner over this trip in the US, he could be forgiven being beaten into fourth by Asiatic Boy on his debut in Dubai after stumbling exiting the stalls, and he showed his true form this time, tracking the pace until edging ahead a furlong and a half out and quickening clear inside the last to score impressively. He gave weight and a beating to a fair field here, but the competition will be much hotter in the Golden Shaheen on World Cup night, with some crack American sprinters expected to be in opposition. (op 13-2)

Star Crowned(USA) was campaigned over distances in excess of a mile when racing on turf in Britain but has improved out of all recognition since dropped back to sprinting on dirt. This was another career-best performance. (op 10-1)

New Freedom(BRZ), who bolted up in a handicap over 5f here last time, had more on his plate in this company, but he showed good early speed to cross over from stall seven and lead on the stands'-side rail, and was only denied second place close home. His performance helps set the level of the form. (op 9-1)

Sarissa(BRZ) once again showed plenty of early toe to drag the field along. She weakened quite badly inside the last, but this was still a fair effort up in grade.

Salaam Dubai(AUS), who was third at a big price in last year's Golden Shaheen, was unexpectedly beaten by Star Crowned over 5f last time and was unable to reverse the form over this extra distance.

Drayton(IRE), who wore a tongue-tie and blinkers, does not look as good on dirt as he is on turf.

Prince Tamino is another who looks a better horse on turf.

Frosty Secret(USA), who had beaten Sarissa and Star Crowned last time, was just never going and clearly failed to run to form. (op 4-1)

Afrashad(USA), the supposed Godolphin first-string, appeared to lose his action and can be forgiven this. His rider reported that the horse had been too fresh on his first outing since September.

815a BURJ NAHAAR - MUHTATHIR (GROUP 3) (DIRT) 1m (D)

5:15 (5:18) 3-Y-0+

£60,301 (£20,100; £10,050; £5,025; £3,015; £2,010)

			RPR
1		**Elusive Warning (USA)**[13] 670 4-9-0 100 ... KerrinMcEvoy 11 (Saeed Bin Suroor) *trckd ldrs: led over 2f out: r.o wl* **16/1**	112
2	½	**Blackat Blackitten (IRE)**[21] 564 4-9-0 110 ... LDettori 5 (Saeed Bin Suroor) *trckd ldrs: rdn 4 1/2f out: ev ch fnl 2f: nt qckn fnl f* **9/2**[2]	111
3	2¾	**Asiatic Boy (ARG)**[42] 295 5-9-4 120 ... JMurtagh 12 (M F De Kock, South Africa) *trckd ldrs: rdn 3f out: ev ch 2f out: nt qckn fnl f* **2/5**[1]	109
4	3¾	**Halkin (USA)**[14] 650 6-9-0 97 ... MO'Callaghan 8 (F Nass, Bahrain) *mid-div: chsd ldrs 2 1/2f out: r.o wl* **66/1**	96
5	1½	**Jet Express (SAF)**[7] 742 6-9-0 104 ... RoystonFfrench 14 (A Al Raihe, UAE) *mid-div: wd: ev ch 2 1/2f out: r.o same pce* **50/1**	93
6	1¼	**Brave Tin Soldier (USA)**[14] 649 4-9-0 102 ... (b) KLatham 13 (M F De Kock, South Africa) *racd in rr: r.o fnl 2f: nvr nr to chal* **50/1**	90
7	shd	**Green Coast (IRE)**[14] 647 5-9-0 102 ... WJSupple 2 (Doug Watson, UAE) *mid-div on rail: hmpd 5f out: sn rdn: nvr nr to chal* **20/1**	90
8	¾	**Beckermet (IRE)**[7] 745 6-9-0 105 ... TedDurcan 4 (R F Fisher) *sn led: hdd 2 1/2f out: wknd* **50/1**	88
9	1¼	**Roman's Run (USA)**[6] 4-9-0 100 ... (vt) DO'Donohoe 3 (Doug Watson, UAE) *slowly away: racd in rr: no room 5f out: nt rcvr* **50/1**	86
10	2	**Watch What Happens (FR)**[54] 5-9-0 104 ... DWhyte 10 (S P C Woods, Hong Kong) *mid-div: wd: nvr able to chal* **11/1**[3]	81
11	nk	**Etihaad**[14] 651 6-9-0 93 ... (t) AdrianTNicholls 1 (R Bouresly, Kuwait) *settled last: nvr nr to chal* **100/1**	81
12	3¼	**Marbush (IRE)**[14] 647 7-9-0 105 ... (e) MJKinane 7 (D Selvaratnam, UAE) *trckd ldrs: rdn 3f out: wknd* **20/1**	73
13	2¾	**Drift Ice (SAF)**[21] 563 7-9-0 102 ... (b) KShea 9 (M F De Kock, South Africa) *in rr of mid-div: nvr able to chal* **25/1**	67
14	¾	**Boston Lodge**[49] 204 8-9-0 107 ... (vt) MartinDwyer 6 (Doug Watson, UAE) *racd in rr of mid-div: n.d* **50/1**	66

1m 35.43s (-1.27) **Going Correction** +0.20s/f (Slow) **14** Ran SP% **129.5**
Speed ratings: **114,113,110,107,105 104,104,103,102,100 99,96,93,93**
CSF: 87.55.
Owner Godolphin **Bred** Robert Raphaelson **Trained** Newmarket, Suffolk

FOCUS
The third straight year the Burj Nahaar has held Group 3 status and this looked a decent renewal beforehand, but it failed to go the way most people expected with Asiatic Boy, second favourite for the Dubai World Cup at the start of the day, turned over.

NOTEBOOK
Elusive Warning(USA) improved markedly on the form he showed when third in a 6f handicap round here off a mark of 100 on his debut for Godolphin. He was hard to pick beforehand, with his two wins in the US coming in ordinary company over 6f, and Dettori favoured Blackat Blackitten, but the step up to 1m clearly suited. Having been well placed from the offset, he took over early in the straight without his rider having to ask for everything and, having got first run on his stablemate, he battled on well to keep that one at bay. On this evidence 1m is probably the limit of his stamina and he looks well worth a crack at the Godolphin Mile on World Cup night. (tchd 18-1)

Blackat Blackitten(IRE), successful twice in handicap company over this course and distance at this year's Carnival, firstly off 95 and then off 104, continued his improvement with a good second on this step up in class. He could even be considered a little unlucky, as he was forced to wait for a gap against the rail at the top of the straight, allowing his stablemate first run. The Godolphin Mile could be a suitable target and, in the longer term, he should prove just as effective back on turf. (op 4-1)

Asiatic Boy(ARG), having been settled three or so lengths off the lead out wide early on, briefly looked dangerous when brought with his challenge about four horses off the rail round the final bend, but he soon came under strong pressure and failed to pick up as one would have expected. He plugged on for third, but was no match at all for the Suroor pair and was well below his best. He was previously unbeaten at Nad Al Sheba, this being his first defeat at the track in six starts. His trainer thinks he might have left something to work on, but it is hard to see how he can win the World Cup off the back of this showing and he was pushed out to 10-1 with some bookmakers. (op 4-7)

Halkin(USA) has run some big races since returning from a long absence and this was another good effort. He was a little way off the pace turning for home, but he responded well to pressure to close up, before tiring late on.

Jet Express(SAF) came wide round the final bend and could not sustain his effort.

Beckermet(IRE), having just his second start on dirt, showed his customary early speed before fading in the straight.

816a DUBAI CITY OF GOLD - HAAFHD (GROUP 3) (TURF) 1m 4f (T)

5:50 (5:50) 4-Y-0+

£60,301 (£20,100; £10,050; £5,025; £3,015; £2,010)

			RPR
1		**Gower Song**[13] 672 5-8-7 104 ... RHills 4 (D R C Elsworth) *settled in rr: 10th 3f out: r.o fnl 1 1/2f: led cl home* **20/1**	111
2	½	**Mourilyan (IRE)**[14] 652 4-8-10 110 ... MJKinane 9 (John M Oxx, Ire) *settled in rr: rdn 4f out: r.o wl fnl 2 1/2f: nrst fin* **9/4**[1]	115
3	hd	**Oracle West (SAF)**[27] 494 7-8-11 119 ... JMurtagh 6 (M F De Kock, South Africa) *mid-div: smooth prog to chse ldr 2 1/2f out: ev ch fnl 1 1/2f* **5/2**[2]	114
4	shd	**Gravitas**[27] 491 5-8-11 109 ... LDettori 1 (Saeed Bin Suroor) *mid-div: trckd ldr 1 1/2f out: led 1f out: r.o: hdd cl home* **10/1**	114
5	2	**Quijano (GER)**[88] 7090 6-9-4 119 ... AStarke 3 (P Schiergen, Germany) *trckd ldr: led 2f out: wknd fnl f* **10/3**[3]	118
6	¾	**Crime Scene (IRE)**[131] 6496 5-8-11 112 ... TedDurcan 11 (Saeed Bin Suroor) *trckd ldr: rdn 3f out: nt qckn* **16/1**	109
7	¾	**Imperial Star (IRE)**[13] 673 5-8-11 110 ... (p) KerrinMcEvoy 10 (Saeed Bin Suroor) *set stdy gallop: hdd 2f out: wknd* **16/1**	108
8	¾	**Illustrious Blue**[7] 740 5-8-11 108 ... MartinDwyer 12 (W J Knight) *hld up in rr: nvr nr to chal* **33/1**	107
9	hd	**Diamond Quest (SAF)**[13] 669 7-8-11 111 ... RyanMoore 2 (H J Brown, South Africa) *mid-div: nvr able to chal* **16/1**	107
10	5½	**Fleeting Shadow (IRE)**[13] 673 4-8-10 95 ... (bt) RoystonFfrench 7 (A Al Raihe, UAE) *mid-div: nvr able to chal* **150/1**	99
11	¼	**Halicarnassus (IRE)**[7] 740 4-8-10 113 ... TPO'Shea 8 (M R Channon) *in rr of mid-div: rdn 3f out: nvr able to chal* **28/1**	98

2m 30.1s (-0.90) **Going Correction** +0.275s/f (Good)
WFA 4 from 5yo+ 2lb **11** Ran SP% **121.0**
Speed ratings: **114,113,113,113,112 111,111,110,110,106 106**
CSF: 65.43.
Owner Usk Valley Stud **Bred** R E Crutchley **Trained** Newmarket, Suffolk

FOCUS
Just a fair Group 3 race on paper and as no-one wanted to go on it was run at a fairly steady early pace. The result was something of a sprint finish.

NOTEBOOK
Gower Song is a smart mare but a very tricky ride as she has one short burst of speed and needs delivering right on the line. Ted Durcan got there too soon on her a couple of starts back when she was beaten by With Interest, but Richard Hills judged the challenge to perfection this time, no doubt aided by the fact that she was denied a clear run until well inside the last. The bunched finish suggests the form is not at all that solid, but she certainly deserves to take her chance in the Sheema Classic now. (op 25-1)

Mourilyan(IRE), whose handicap win last month was franked when the runner-up Hard Top won next time out, has looked a most progressive colt this winter, and his turn of foot is a valuable asset. He finished just as fast as the winner from off the pace and would undoubtedly have been better suited by a stronger pace. He will have good claims of reversing the form with the winner if they meet in the Sheema Classic.

Oracle West(SAF), who won this race in 2006 and was runner-up in it last year, looked to hold strong claims, having shown his wellbeing when successful on his reappearance last month. He had every chance, but no doubt his trainer will have left something to work on for the Sheema Classic, in which he was runner-up last year, and a stronger pace there will suit him as well. (op 9-4)

Gravitas had more to do than when winning a handicap last time in receipt of weight from the likes of Illustrious Blue, but he got a dream run through on the inside in the straight and led entering the final furlong, only to be swamped close home. It is possible that he is flattered by the bare result. (op 12-1)

Quijano(GER) won this race last year but, as a result of winning the Group 1 Grosser Preis von Baden last September, he had to give 7lb plus to all his rivals. Well placed throughout in a race that was fairly steadily run in the early stages, he ran a perfectly satisfactory trial for the Sheema Classic, and he should strip fitter for this first outing in three months.

Crime Scene(IRE) is another who should come on for the run as he had not been seen since winning the St Simon Stakes at Newbury in October.

Imperial Star(IRE) was handed an uncontested lead and perhaps should have done better, but he has done all his winning over 1m2f and that is probably his ideal trip.

Illustrious Blue was not good enough to land a blow from off the pace.

Halicarnassus(IRE) was another unable to get close enough to throw down a challenge, having been held up towards the back as usual.

817a AL MAKTOUM CHALLENGE R3 - SAKHEE (GROUP 2) (DIRT) 1m 2f (D)

6:20 (6:22) 3-Y-O+

£90,452 (£30,150; £15,075; £7,537; £4,522; £3,015)

RPR

1 **Jalil (USA)**[14] [650] 4-9-0 108 ... LDettori 10 120+
(Saeed Bin Suroor) *mid-div: trckd ldr 3f out: led 1f out: r.o wl: comf* **9/4**[2]

2 1 1/2 **Gloria De Campeao (BRZ)**[14] [650] 5-9-0 104 ... C-PLemaire 1 117
(P Bary, France) *mid-div: trckd ldr whn no room 2f out: swtchd 1f out: r.o: nrst fin* **20/1**

3 1 **Lucky Find (SAF)**[28] [476] 5-9-0 116 ... KShea 3 115
(M F De Kock, South Africa) *trckd ldr: led 2 1/2f out: rdn 1 1/2f out: hdd 1f out: wknd nr fin* **13/8**[1]

4 8 **Mutasallil (USA)**[13] [667] 8-9-0 102 ... (t) RHills 6 99
(Doug Watson, UAE) *sn led: hdd 2 1/2f out: r.o same pce* **33/1**

5 2 **Dynamic Saint (USA)**[14] [650] 5-9-0 100 ... (e) WJSupple 4 95
(Doug Watson, UAE) *settled in rr: r.o fnl 2 1/2f: nvr nr to chal* **33/1**

6 hd **Igor Protti**[13] [667] 6-9-0 108 ... (b) KerrinMcEvoy 12 95
(Saeed Bin Suroor) *mid-div: wd 3f out: sn rdn: nvr able to chal* **16/1**

7 2 3/4 **Singing Poet (IRE)**[341] [858] 7-9-0 104 ... (bt) TPO'Shea 2 89
(E Charpy, UAE) *mid-div on rail: rdn 3f out: wknd 2f out* **50/1**

8 nse **Latency (ARG)**[82] 7-9-0 113 ... JCMendez 13 89
(J B Udaondo, Argentina) *settled in rr: rdn 3f out: hung and sn btn* **4/1**[3]

9 9 1/2 **Aleutian**[13] [667] 8-9-0 102 ... (e) WayneSmith 7 70
(F Nass, Bahrain) *mid-div: no room after 3f: n.d* **25/1**

10 5 1/2 **Rohaani (USA)**[14] [652] 6-9-0 98 ... MartinDwyer 9 59
(Doug Watson, UAE) *in rr of mid-div: nvr nr to chal* **33/1**

11 1 3/4 **Delude (IRE)**[6] 10-9-0 87 ... DO'Donohoe 11 56
(R Bouresly, Kuwait) *sn rdn in last: nvr involved* **150/1**

U **Kandidate**[28] [476] 6-9-0 110 ... (t) RyanMoore 8 —
(C E Brittain) *uns rdr at s* **9/1**

2m 0.35s (-1.95) **Going Correction** +0.20s/f (Slow) **12** Ran SP% **124.8**
Speed ratings: **115,113,113,106,105 104,102,102,95,90 89,—**
CSF: 53.63.
Owner Godolphin **Bred** Mr & Mrs Martin J Wygod **Trained** Newmarket, Suffolk

FOCUS

Since the turn of the millennium three of the eight winners of the third round of the Maktoum Challenge – Dubai Millennium, Street Cry and Electrocutionist – went on to to win the Dubai World Cup, and two others have placed. However, this looked like just an ordinary renewal. The first three finished clear.

NOTEBOOK

Jalil(USA), since switching to dirt, has started to go some way to justifying his $9,700,000 price tag, winning a couple of handicaps to earn this step up in grade, and he is now three from three on this surface, but it is hard to assess the true merit of this performance. It is most noteworthy that he recorded a faster time than Curlin managed the previous week in his World Cup prep, but strictly from a form perspective one cannot get carried away, as everything went his way in what looked like a sub-standard race for the grade. For example the runner-up was racing off only 102 when filling the same position behind Jalil in a handicap on his previous start, and the third home ran like a non-stayer. Whatever the case, ridden closer to the pace this time, Jalil ranged upsides Lucky Find going well early in the straight and found enough when asked to record a convincing success. He was trimmed to 6-1 for the Dubai World Cup by some firms but, whilst he is clearly improving, it will be hard to see him playing anything other than a supporting role if Curlin turns up at the top of his game. In the longer term, considering his improvement has coincided with a switch to dirt, it would make sense to see him continue his career in the US.

Gloria De Campeao(BRZ) would have been unlucky had he not got up for second, as he was short of room early in the straight and had to be switched off the rail, but he was never going to reverse recent handicap form with the winner. (op 16-1)

Lucky Find(SAF), winner of a handicap off a mark of 102 over 1m1f before following up over that course and distance in the second round of the Maktoum Challenge, looked to be going every bit as well as the eventual winner at the top of the straight, but was running on empty in the final furlong and did not appear to see out this extra furlong. (op 15-8)

Mutasallil(USA), allowed an easy lead when winning a 1m1f handicap off a mark of 95 round here on his previous start, again went from the front, but the opposition was tougher this time and he finished up well held.

Igor Protti, the winner's stablemate, looked to be found out on this step up in class. (op 14-1)

Kandidate's race was over before it had even started, as he got rid of his rider when stumbling on leaving the stalls. (op 8-1)

818a JEBEL HATTA - NAYEF (GROUP 2) (TURF) 1m 194y(T)

6:55 (6:55) 3-Y-O+

£75,376 (£25,125; £12,562; £6,281; £3,768; £2,512)

RPR

1 **Lord Admiral (USA)**[14] [651] 7-9-0 112 ... (b) MJKinane 4 116
(Charles O'Brien, Ire) *settled in rr: stl in rr 2 1/2f out: r.o wl fnl 1 1/2f: led nr line* **9/1**

2 1 **Jay Peg (SAF)**[13] [671] 5-9-6 113 ... (b) RyanMoore 11 120
(H J Brown, South Africa) *led: t.k.h: r.o wl fnl 2f: hdd cl home* **12/1**

3 shd **Traffic Guard (USA)**[13] [671] 4-9-0 102 ... JohnEgan 3 114
(A Manuel, UAE) *mid-div: rdn 2 1/2f out: swtchd to rail 1 1/2f out: r.o wl: nrst fin* **50/1**

4 1/2 **Viva Macau (FR)**[33] 5-9-0 108 ... (tp) DBeadman 5 113
(J Moore, Hong Kong) *mid-div: rdn 2 1/2f out: r.o wl fnl 1 1/2f: nrst fin* **10/1**

5 1/2 **Royal Oath (USA)**[14] [651] 5-9-0 112 ... (b) LDettori 9 112
(J H M Gosden) *mid-div: smooth prog to chse ldrs 2f out: nt qckn fnl f* **3/1**[2]

6 shd **Seachange (NZ)**[26] [511] 6-9-2 112 ... TedDurcan 16 113
(R Manning, New Zealand) *wl away: trckd ldr: rdn 1 1/2f out: ev ch 1f out: wknd fnl f* **6/1**[3]

7 3 **Yasoodd**[21] [565] 5-9-0 110 ... C-PLemaire 7 105
(D Selvaratnam, UAE) *trckd ldr tl 2f out: wknd* **16/1**

8 1 1/4 **Alpacco (IRE)**[7] [739] 6-9-0 105 ... KLatham 2 103
(H J Brown, South Africa) *mid-div: rdn 3f out: n.d* **33/1**

9 shd **Admiralofthefleet (USA)**[27] [492] 4-9-0 111 ... JMurtagh 15 102
(M F De Kock, South Africa) *mid-div: rdn 3f out: nt qckn* **11/4**[1]

10 2 1/4 **Almuraad (IRE)**[7] [745] 7-9-0 104 ... MartinDwyer 12 98
(Doug Watson, UAE) *settled in rr: nvr able to chal* **33/1**

11 3/4 **Advice**[7] [739] 7-9-0 102 ... RichardMullen 6 96
(S Seemar, UAE) *mid-div: nvr able to chal* **50/1**

12 nse **Warriors Key (IRE)**[14] [651] 4-9-0 96 ... WayneSmith 8 96
(S Seemar, UAE) *slowly away: nvr nr to chal* **66/1**

13 1 3/4 **Grand Hombre (USA)**[14] [647] 8-9-0 100 ... AdrianTNicholls 1 92
(R Bouresly, Kuwait) *racd in last: nvr nr to chal* **66/1**

14 1/4 **Racinger (FR)**[152] [6031] 5-9-0 116 ... RHills 10 92
(Doug Watson, UAE) *trckd ldrs: rdn 2 1/2f out: wknd 1 1/2f out* **8/1**

15 9 3/4 **Senor Dali (IRE)**[13] [671] 5-9-0 106 ... TPO'Shea 14 71
(E Charpy, UAE) *mid-div: nvr able to chal* **33/1**

16 3/4 **African Appeal (SAF)**[13] [671] 7-9-6 111 ... KShea 13 76
(M F De Kock, South Africa) *mid-div: wd 3f out: sn rdn: nt qckn* **33/1**

1m 49.32s (-0.68) **Going Correction** +0.275s/f (Good) **16** Ran SP% **128.4**
Speed ratings: **114,113,113,112,112 112,109,108,108,106 105,105,103,103,95 94**
CSF: 112.50. PLACEPOT: £13.50 to a £1 stake. Pool: £12,197.55. 656.30 winning tickets.
QUADPOT: £4.50 to a £1 stake. Pool: £385.90. 62.50 winning tickets..
Owner Dr M V O'Brien **Bred** London Thrghbrd Services/Derry **Trained** Straffan, Co Kildare

FOCUS

A big field for this Group 2 race over the same course and distance that will be used for the $5m Dubai Duty Free, and the draw played an important role.

NOTEBOOK

Lord Admiral(USA) won in fine style but, having been drawn in stall four, he benefited from being able to race on the inside for much of the race before being switched to the outside in the straight. He found a smart turn of foot to pass a number of rivals inside the final furlong and record his first win at this level and, although a seven-year-old, he actually seems to be improving. He will presumably have booked his ticket for a shot at the Dubai Duty Free on World Cup night with this success.

Jay Peg(SAF), who had to carry a penalty, wore blinkers this time and was quickly away. Given a good front-running ride, he responded to pressure and battled on gamely in the straight, only being collared by the fast-finishing winner close home. He comes out of the race as the best horse on the figures.

Traffic Guard(USA) had too much use made of him last time, but he was ridden more patiently on this occasion. Favourably drawn in three, he nipped through on the inside in the closing stages to nick third place.

Viva Macau(FR) will have given his connections plenty of confidence for the chances of Viva Pataca in the Sheema Classic with this performance as he is very much inferior to his stable-companion. Another who had the benefit of a low draw, he looked to run up to his best on his debut in Dubai.

Royal Oath(USA) did not enjoy the benefit of racing on the rail at any stage and, while he looked a danger two furlongs out, his run flattened out inside the last. He probably ran better than the bare form suggests. (op 100-30)

Seachange(NZ) did well to get to the rail from her wide draw and she looked to be going like the winner entering the straight, but she did not look happy once she came under pressure and perhaps the ground was quicker than she would have liked. Her form in New Zealand, where she is a winner of four Grade 1s since September, came on good ground or softer.

Yasoodd is a consistent sort and, always well placed towards the front end, ran his race once again.

Admiralofthefleet(USA) had shaped with plenty of promise over an inadequate trip on his reappearance, but he had a poor draw to overcome here and ended up racing quite wide. It would probably be wise not to judge him too harshly on this fairly disappointing effort. (op 5-2)

Racinger(FR), who was having his first run since October, has shown all his best form with plenty of give in the ground.

806 WOLVERHAMPTON (A.W) (L-H)

Friday, March 7

OFFICIAL GOING: Standard

Wind: moderate, behind

819 BET SIX NATIONS RUGBY - BETDAQ H'CAP 7f 32y(P)

6:50 (6:50) (Class 5) (0-70,72) 4-Y-O+ **£2,590** (£770; £385; £192) **Stalls** High

Form RPR

4534 1 **Kelamon**[7] [755] 4-9-0 **68** ... WilliamBuick[(3)] 8 77
(M D I Usher) *a.p on outside: led 2f out: rdn over 1f out: r.o wl* **13/2**

-634 2 3/4 **Raza Cab (IRE)**[9] [717] 6-9-3 **68** ... DarryllHolland 4 75
(Karen George) *a in tch: rdn to chse wnr ent fnl f* **10/1**

1063 3 1/2 **Sovereignty (JPN)**[7] [755] 6-8-10 **61** ... JimCrowley 5 67
(D K Ivory) *a in tch: kpt on fnl f* **9/1**

5-01 4 nk **Chief Exec**[7] [755] 6-9-7 **72** 6ex ... (b) LiamJones 7 77
(J R Gask) *s.i.s: swtchd lft and r.o ins fnl f: nvr nrr* **2/1**[1]

3-42 5 1 3/4 **Convivial Spirit**[30] [448] 4-8-13 **64** ... (t) LPKeniry 3 65
(E F Vaughan) *in tch tl rdn and wknd over 1f out* **6/1**[3]

-616 6 nse **Fine Ruler (IRE)**[13] [683] 4-9-4 **69** ... GeorgeBaker 1 70
(M R Bosley) *t.k.h: a in rr* **10/1**

1154 7 3 1/2 **Samuel Charles**[13] [683] 10-9-4 **69** ... (b) RobertWinston 6 61
(C R Dore) *in tch: rdn over 2f out: wknd wl over 1f out* **16/1**

006- 8 3/4 **Briannsta (IRE)**[130] [6531] 6-8-13 **69** ... NataliaGemelova[(5)] 2 59
(J E Long) *led tl rdn and hdd 2f out: wknd qckly* **12/1**

1m 30.65s (1.05) **Going Correction** +0.20s/f (Slow) **8** Ran SP% **117.7**
Speed ratings (Par 103): **102,101,100,100,98 98,94,93**
CSF £70.18 CT £238.53 TOTE £10.30: £3.00, £2.30, £1.90; EX 79.70.
Owner Mr & Mrs Richard Hames And Friends **Bred** R And Mrs Hames **Trained** Upper Lambourn, Berks

FOCUS

A modest handicap, run at an average pace. The principals set the level.

820 JOIN THE EASTER PARADE @ PONTIN'S CLAIMING STKS 1m 141y(P)

7:20 (7:20) (Class 5) 3-Y-O **£2,590** (£770; £385; £192) **Stalls** Low

Form RPR

4131 1 **Bridge Of Fermoy (IRE)**[9] [712] 3-9-6 73 ... (bt) GeorgeBaker 8 74+
(Miss Gay Kelleway) *sn trckd ldr: led 2f out: rdn clr ent fnl f: comf* **11/10**[1]

0-16 **2** *2 1/4* **Ledgerwood**[41] 321 3-9-3 65..........(p) JamesDoyle 5 64
(J W Hills) *trckd ldrs: rdn 2f out: kpt on to go 2nd ins fnl f: no imp on wnr* **8/1**

0 **3** *1 1/4* **Emshabb**[7] 748 3-8-10 0.......... LiamJones 2 55
(W J Haggas) *hld up in rr: hdwy over 2f out: faltered ent fnl f: r.o ins fnl f to go 3rd nr fin* **16/1**

36-5 **4** *1/2* **Agglestone Rock**[10] 705 3-8-7 64.......... JackDean(7) 4 58
(W G M Turner) *led tl hdd 2f out: chsd wnr tl fdd ins fnl f* **22/1**

04-2 **5** *1 1/2* **Spitfire Jane (IRE)**[19] 597 3-8-6 62..........(p) AndrewElliott 7 46
(K R Burke) *racd on outside: nvr bttr than finishing position* **13/2[3]**

4644 **6** *3/4* **Tapas Lad (IRE)**[10] 704 3-8-7 61.......... JamieJones(5) 10 51
(G J Smith) *in rr: rdn 3f out: nvr nr to chal* **17/2**

-0 **7** *11* **Admiral Troy**[15] 645 3-8-5 0 ow1.......... GabrielHannon(7) 1 28
(M D I Usher) *prom tl wknd over 2f out* **66/1**

0-5 **8** *5* **Beneath The Trees (USA)**[9] 712 3-8-7 0.......... ChrisCatlin 9 12
(J A Osborne) *in rr: rdn 3f out: nvr on terms* **12/1**

6410 **9** *5* **Hit The Roof**[9] 723 3-9-0 73.......... TolleyDean(3) 3 12
(D Shaw) *a in rr: no rspnse whn rdn 3f out* **9/2[2]**

1m 52.66s (2.16) **Going Correction** +0.20s/f (Slow) **9** Ran SP% **120.2**
Speed ratings (Par 98): **98,96,94,94,93 92,82,78,73**
CSF £11.57 TOTE £1.80: £1.30, £2.20, £4.40; EX 12.30.

Owner T & Z Racing Club **Bred** Tally-Ho Stud **Trained** Exning, Suffolk

FOCUS
A moderate claimer that did not take much winning. The winner remains progressive and along with the third sets the standard.

Hit The Roof Official explanation: jockey said colt never travelled

821 BOOK EASTER NOW @ PONTINS.COM CLASSIFIED STKS 1m 1f 103y(P)
7:50 (7:54) (Class 7) 4-Y-O+ £1,365 (£403; £201) Stalls Low

Form RPR

0-44 **1** **Imperial Amber**[7] 750 6-9-0 45..........(p) DarryllHolland 11 48+
(Karen George) *sn prom: hdwy to ld over 5f out: clr whn hung lft over 1f out: r.o ins fnl f: easily* **15/2**

3243 **2** *7* **Arthurs Dream (IRE)**[6] 770 6-8-9 45..........(p) KellyHarrison(5) 3 35
(A W Carroll) *a in tch: short of room and swtchd rt over 3f out: styd on to chse wnr fnl f* **7/4[1]**

005 **3** *1 1/4* **Moorside Diamond**[15] 643 4-9-0 30.......... AndrewElliott 8 32
(A D Brown) *in tch: hdwy over 1f out: kpt on to go 3rd cl home* **40/1**

5/53 **4** *3/4* **Tirol Livit (IRE)**[2] 804 5-8-9 45..........(b[1]) AshleyHamblett(5) 6 31
(N Wilson) *v.s.a: rapid hdwy over 6f out: chsd wnr over 4f out tl no ex wknd fnl f* **3/1[2]**

4303 **5** *1 1/4* **Ponte Vecchio (IRE)**[9] 715 4-9-0 43..........(p) JimCrowley 12 29
(J R Boyle) *racd on outside and c wd into st: kpt on one pce after* **5/1[3]**

000/ **6** *5* **Love Academy**[280] 2229 13-8-11 32.......... JerryO'Dwyer(3) 1 19+
(Luke Comer, Ire) *a towards rr* **40/1**

000- **7** *3* **Xpres Boy (IRE)**[386] 463 5-9-0 37..........(bt) PhillipMakin 5 13
(S R Bowring) *in tch tl lost pl 6f out: in rr after* **16/1**

000/ **8** *15* **Time Dancer (IRE)**[432] 6996 4-9-0 30.......... PatrickMathers 2 —
(H A McWilliams) *mid-div: rdn 4f out: sn btn* **80/1**

40/0 **9** *2 1/2* **House Martin**[6] 769 6-9-0 41..........(p) LiamJones 10 —
(C R Dore) *trckd ldr early: rdn and wknd over 3f out* **40/1**

65-0 **10** *hd* **Franky'N'Jonny**[2] 804 5-9-0 38.......... AlanDaly 9 —
(G J Smith) *led tl hdd over 5f out: sn rdn and wknd* **33/1**

0/00 **11** *24* **Lady Lucinda**[46] 249 7-9-0 25.......... SamHitchcott 13 —
(C N Kellett) *a bhd: lost tch over 4f out* **100/1**

2m 4.25s (2.55) **Going Correction** +0.20s/f (Slow) **11** Ran SP% **125.9**
Speed ratings (Par 97): **96,89,88,88,86 82,79,66,64,64 42**
CSF £16.45 TOTE £7.00: £1.60, £1.10, £9.00; EX 19.30.

Owner Miss Karen George **Bred** C And Mrs Wilson **Trained** Higher Easington, Devon

■ Ektishaaf (8/1, ref to ent stalls) & Tribiani (14,1, bolted & uns rdr on way to s) were withdrawn. R4 applies, deduct 15p in the £.

FOCUS
A dire affair that saw an easy winner, who is value for further than the winning margin with the time helping to dictate the level.

Tirol Livit(IRE) Official explanation: jockey said gelding missed the break

House Martin Official explanation: vet said mare finished lame on left-fore

Lady Lucinda Official explanation: vet said mare finished lame in front

822 BET FA CUP - BETDAQ H'CAP 1m 1f 103y(P)
8:20 (8:20) (Class 6) (0-50,52) 4-Y-O+ £1,774 (£523; £262) Stalls Low

Form RPR

-405 **1** **Atlantic Gamble (IRE)**[13] 682 8-8-7 **49**..........(p) AndrewElliott 2 59
(K R Burke) *chsd ldrs: rdn to ld over 1f out: wnt clr fnl f* **6/1**

0202 **2** *3 1/4* **Tidy (IRE)**[6] 769 8-8-8 **50**..........(v) JimCrowley 5 56+
(Micky Hammond) *in rr: hdwy whn bmpd over 2f out: styd on u.p to go 2nd ins fnl f* **9/2[3]**

3443 **3** *1* **Granary Girl**[18] 606 6-8-4 **46**.......... ChrisCatlin 8 48
(J Pearce) *in rr and rdn along fr 1/2-way: hdwy on ins over 1f out: kpt on to go 3rd ins fnl f* **9/2[3]**

0-03 **4** *3/4* **Over Ice**[28] 490 5-8-1 **46** oh1.......... WilliamBuick(3) 9 47
(Karen George) *trckd ldr: led over 2f out: rdn and hdd over 1f out: no ex fnl f* **10/1**

4504 **5** *hd* **Bobering**[12] 691 8-8-4 **46** oh1.......... PatrickMathers 7 46
(B P J Baugh) *hld up in rr: hdwy over 2f out: kpt on one pce fnl f* **8/1**

-343 **6** *nk* **Bramcote Lorne**[6] 769 5-8-3 **52** ow2..........(b[1]) MarkCoumbe(7) 6 52
(R C Guest) *led tl hdd over 2f out: one pce fnl f* **4/1[2]**

053- **7** *1 1/2* **Pegasus Prince (USA)**[153] 6026 4-8-6 **48**.......... PaulHanagan 10 45+
(Miss J A Camacho) *hmpd s: a in rr* **7/2[1]**

0- **8** *1 1/2* **Spa Wells (IRE)**[179] 5286 7-8-2 **47**.......... AndrewMullen(3) 3 41
(Barry Potts, Ire) *in tch tl rdn over 3f out: sn btn* **12/1**

4000 **9** *14* **Up Dee Creek**[6] 769 6-8-4 **46** oh1..........(b) LiamJones 1 13
(W M Brisbourne) *mid-div tl wknd over 2f out* **50/1**

600- **10** *2 1/4* **Hill Of Clare (IRE)**[118] 6766 6-8-1 **46** oh1.......... DominicFox(3) 4 9
(G H Jones) *mid-div tl rdn over 3f out: sn bhd* **80/1**

2m 2.56s (0.86) **Going Correction** +0.20s/f (Slow) **10** Ran SP% **124.4**
Speed ratings (Par 101): **104,101,100,99,99 99,97,96,84,82**
CSF £35.62 CT £138.46 TOTE £7.80: £2.80, £2.50, £1.20; EX 52.40.

Owner R G Greaney **Bred** Larry Ryan **Trained** Middleham Moor, N Yorks

FOCUS
A poor handicap, run at a strong early pace and the winner bounced back after looking to be on the downgrade.

823 RACE TO PONTIN'S FOR EASTER MAIDEN STKS 1m 4f 50y(P)
8:50 (8:51) (Class 5) 3-Y-O+ £2,457 (£725; £362) Stalls Low

Form RPR

4-24 **1** **Wannabe Free**[16] 632 3-7-11 72.......... WilliamBuick(3) 2 73+
(J Noseda) *mde all: qcknd 3f out: rdn over 1f out: in command fnl f: unchal* **1/1[1]**

25- **2** *2 1/4* **Cybersnow (USA)**[251] 3084 4-9-12 0.......... PaulMulrennan 7 77
(Barry Potts, Ire) *in tch: wnt 2nd over 4f out: awkward on bnd turning into st: no imp on wnr fnl f* **2/1[2]**

44 **3** *12* **Brave Bugsy (IRE)**[7] 758 5-10-0 0.......... NeilChalmers 3 60+
(M Appleby) *hld up in rr: hdwy to go modeate 3rd over 2f out: no ch w first 2* **8/1**

6 **4** *14* **Visconte (GER)**[13] 674 3-8-5 0.......... ChrisCatlin 4 35
(J Pearce) *trckd ldrs: rdn over 4f out: sn btn* **6/1[3]**

5 *3 3/4* **Honkey Tonk Tony (IRE)**[7] 760 3-8-0 0.......... NicolPolli(5) 8 30+
(Luke Comer, Ire) *a towards rr* **12/1**

0-0 **6** *7* **Fortuitous (IRE)**[25] 524 4-9-12 0.......... PatrickMathers 6 22
(I W McInnes) *mid-div: rdn 5f out: sn btn* **20/1**

7 *7* **Mollie Blackburn**[21] 4-9-7 0.......... AndrewElliott 9 3
(A D Brown) *a bhd* **33/1**

0 **8** *3 3/4* **Hatter's Way**[7] 748 3-8-1 0 ow1.......... FrankieMcDonald 5 —
(R A Farrant) *trckd ldr tl wknd qckly over 4f out* **33/1**

2m 44.0s (2.90) **Going Correction** +0.20s/f (Slow)
WFA 3 from 4yo 23lb 4 from 5yo 2lb **8** Ran SP% **127.1**
Speed ratings (Par 103): **98,96,88,79,76 72,67,64**
CSF £3.64 TOTE £1.80: £1.02, £1.40, £2.40; EX 3.80.

Owner B McAllister **Bred** Chippenham Lodge Stud Ltd **Trained** Newmarket, Suffolk

FOCUS
No strength in depth here and the first pair came well clear. The winner did not need to be at her best to score and the placed horses set the level.

824 TREAT THE FAMILY TO EASTER @ PONTIN'S H'CAP 5f 216y(P)
9:20 (9:20) (Class 4) (0-85,83) 4-Y-O+ £4,533 (£1,348; £674; £336) Stalls Low

Form RPR

424 **1** **Financial Times (USA)**[13] 676 6-9-1 **80**..........(t) MickyFenton 8 90
(Stef Liddiard) *hld up: gd hdwy on ins over 1f out: led jst ins fnl f: rdn out* **6/1**

1121 **2** *3/4* **Benllech**[21] 574 4-9-3 **82**.......... SimonWhitworth 1 90
(M Wigham) *hld up: swtchd rt ent st: str run to hold ev ch jst ins fnl f: nt pce of wnr nr fin* **4/1[2]**

0-11 **3** *1* **Distant Sun (USA)**[21] 580 4-9-4 **83**.......... PhillipMakin 7 89+
(Miss L A Perratt) *hld up: hdwy over 1f out: n.m.r and swtchd rt ins fnl f: r.o wl* **5/1[3]**

0-53 **4** *3/4* **Misaro (GER)**[10] 707 7-8-8 **78**..........(b) KevinGhunowa(5) 5 80
(R A Harris) *sn led: rdn and hdd jst ins fnl f: no ex* **12/1**

0200 **5** *nk* **Yungaburra (IRE)**[13] 676 4-9-1 **83**..........(p) DNolan(3) 2 84
(S Parr) *broke wl: sn hdd: wnt 3rd 2f out: one pce fnl f* **16/1**

-213 **6** *nk* **Bel Cantor**[2] 801 5-8-4 **72**..........(p) AndrewMullen(3) 3 72
(W J H Ratcliffe) *chsd ldr to over 1f out: fdd ins fnl f* **3/1[1]**

3304 **7** *3/4* **Cornus**[17] 618 6-8-13 **78**..........(be) JamesDoyle 4 76
(A J McCabe) *chsd ldrs tl rdn and wknd over 1f out* **6/1**

3625 **8** *1 1/2* **Memphis Man**[9] 717 5-8-4 **72**.......... WilliamBuick(3) 6 65
(P D Evans) *in rr and a outpcd* **5/1[3]**

040- **9** *12* **The Lord**[287] 1986 8-8-8 **80**.......... JackDean(7) 9 34
(W G M Turner) *chsd ldrs tl wknd wl over 1f out: eased ins fnl f* **33/1**

1m 15.06s (0.06) **Going Correction** +0.20s/f (Slow) **9** Ran SP% **123.4**
Speed ratings (Par 105): **107,106,104,103,103 102,101,99,83**
CSF £32.51 CT £134.68 TOTE £4.50: £2.60, £2.70, £2.20; EX 43.30 Place 6 £44.61, Place 5 £17.39.

Owner Mrs Stef Liddiard **Bred** Patricia Elia And Christopher Elia **Trained** Great Shefford, Berks

FOCUS
A good sprint for the grade, run at a strong pace. The form is solid with the first two close to recent form.

Memphis Man Official explanation: jockey said gelding missed the break

T/Plt: £14.90 to a £1 stake. Pool: £104,061.30. 5,080.55 winning tickets. T/Qpdt: £2.80 to a £1 stake. Pool: £7,314.60. 1,892.90 winning tickets. JS

825 - (Foreign Racing) - See Raceform Interactive

759

DUNDALK (A.W) (L-H)
Friday, March 7

OFFICIAL GOING: Standard

826a GUINNESS (C & G) MAIDEN 7f
7:10 (7:12) 3-Y-O £6,351 (£1,479; £652; £376)

RPR

1 **High Court Drama (IRE)**[200] 4680 3-9-0 .... WJSupple 4 86+
(P D Deegan, Ire) *prom: 3rd ent st: prog to ld under 2f out: strly pressed ins fnl f: styd on wl cl home* **4/1[2]**

2 *1/2* **Fay Street (USA)**[91] 7064 3-9-0 75.......... RMBurke 6 85
(K J Condon, Ire) *trckd ldrs: rn freely: 5th ent st: prog into 2nd over 1f out: sn chal: no ex cl home* **20/1**

3 *3* **Cathedral Walk (USA)**[20] 595 3-9-0 .... FergusSweeney 13 77
(K R Burke) *trckd ldrs: 5th 1/2-way: 4th ent st: wnt 3rd over 1f out: kpt on one pce* **10/1**

4 *1 1/4* **Leo's Pride (IRE)**[223] 3979 3-9-0 .... PJSmullen 11 73
(D K Weld, Ire) *mid-div: 8th ent st: 4th over 1f out: no ex* **9/2[3]**

5 *1 1/4* **Blue Law (IRE)**[7] 760 3-9-0 .... JAHeffernan 1 70
(Andrew Oliver, Ire) *led: hdd under 2f out: no ex* **8/1**

6 *1/2* **Ros Cuire (IRE)**[85] 7130 3-9-2 ow2.......... WJLee 8 70?
(W A Murphy, Ire) *in rr: sme hdwy on inner 2f out: hmpd over 1f out: kpt on wl ins fnl f* **50/1**

7 *3/4* **Porto Santana (IRE)**[124] 6680 3-9-0 80.......... CDHayes 5 66
(Edward Lynam, Ire) *chsd ldrs: 6th 1/2-way: edgd lft under 2f out: kpt on* **25/1**

8 *hd* **Arizona John (IRE)**[137] 6394 3-9-0 .... FMBerry 9 66
(John M Oxx, Ire) *mid-div: 7th on outer ent st: sn rdn: no imp fr 1 1/2f out: eased whn btn ins fnl f* **7/4[1]**

9 *3* **Mosman Park (FR)**[223] 3979 3-9-0 .... NGMcCullagh 7 57
(Charles O'Brien, Ire) *nvr bttr than mid-div* **20/1**

10 nk **Invincible Joe (IRE)**[131] 6520 3-9-0 80 .... KJManning 12 56
(G M Lyons, Ire) *mid-div: 6th ent st: no ex fr 2f out* **8/1**
11 nk **Tyrur Ted**[266] 2642 3-9-0 72 .... CO'Donoghue 14 55
(John A Quinn, Ire) *nvr a factor* **25/1**
12 1 1/4 **Maxabillion (IRE)**[7] 760 3-9-0 .... RPCleary 3 52
(Edward Lynam, Ire) *nvr a factor* **33/1**
13 3 **Dealmaker Frank (USA)**[178] 5317 3-8-4 73 ....(t) CPHarrison(10) 10 44
(Niall Moran, Ire) *a towards rr* **25/1**
14 5 **Reward Of Faith (IRE)**[138] 6365 3-8-11 ....(b[1]) DJMoran(3) 2 30
(Liam Roche, Ire) *prom: wknd over 2f out: eased* **50/1**
1m 25.3s (85.30) **14** Ran SP% **133.8**
CSF £92.03 TOTE £4.60: £1.80, £7.10, £2.90; DF 159.80.
Owner Chris McHale **Bred** Budget Stables **Trained** The Curragh, Co Kildare

NOTEBOOK
Cathedral Walk(USA) failed to quicken when it really mattered on this drop back a furlong, but still managed to turn in just about his best effort to date in defeat. He is probably better off moving into handicaps now. (op 8/1)
Ros Cuire(IRE) Official explanation: jockey said colt did not have a clear run in the closing stages

829a CARLSBERG H'CAP 1m
8:40 (8:41) 4-Y-O+ **£12,445** (£3,651; £1,739; £592)

RPR
1 **Electric Warrior (IRE)**[9] 717 5-8-13 87 .... FergusSweeney 9 94
(K R Burke) *trcd ldrs: 3rd 3f out: led 2f out: kpt on wl u.p ins fnl f* **5/2**[1]
2 1/2 **Baynes Cross (IRE)**[7] 763 5-8-5 79 ....(b) CDHayes 6 85
(Ms Joanna Morgan, Ire) *mid-div: 6th 3f out: prog to go 2nd 1 1/2f out: kpt on wl ins fnl f* **5/1**[2]
3 2 1/2 **Essexford (IRE)**[105] 6922 4-8-8 82 .... NGMcCullagh 8 82
(John M Oxx, Ire) *chsd ldrs: 4th 3f out: wnt 3rd under 2f out: no ex fr 1f out* **12/1**
4 3/4 **Royal Island (IRE)**[98] 6987 6-8-11 85 .... PJSmullen 5 83
(Michael Cunningham, Ire) *in rr of mid-div: hdwy 2f out: 4th over 1f out: kpt on wout threatening ldrs* **7/1**
5 3 1/2 **Quinmaster (USA)**[96] 4237 6-10-5 107 .... PCarberry 3 98
(M Halford, Ire) *led and disp ld: hdd 2f out: sn no ex: wknd* **8/1**
6 1 1/2 **Little White Lie (IRE)**[215] 4211 4-9-4 99 .... EJMcNamara(7) 10 86
(G M Lyons, Ire) *towards rr: 8th ent st: kpt on fr over 1f out wout threatening ldrs* **7/1**
7 shd **Crooked Throw (IRE)**[137] 6398 9-10-0 102 .... WJLee 2 89
(C F Swan, Ire) *s.i.s: in rr of mid-div: kpt on one pce fr 2f out* **16/1**
8 3 **Infinite Charm (IRE)**[7] 765 5-8-12 86 ....(b) WMLordan 12 67
(M J P O'Brien, Ire) *in rr: 9th on outer over 2f out: no ex* **6/1**[3]
9 nk **An Tadh (IRE)**[152] 6038 5-10-4 106 .... KJManning 13 86
(G M Lyons, Ire) *disp ld: hdd 2f out: sn wknd* **14/1**
10 3 **Incline (IRE)**[7] 765 9-9-11 102 .... DJMoran(3) 11 75
(R McGlinchey, Ire) *nvr a factor: no imp on outer in st* **12/1**
11 1 1/4 **Giant Slalom**[98] 6987 4-8-7 81 .... WJSupple 1 52
(T G McCourt, Ire) *mid-div: 5th ent st: wknd fr 2f out* **14/1**
1m 36.4s (96.40) **13** Ran SP% **130.2**
CSF £16.46 CT £139.01 TOTE £3.10: £1.70, £2.60, £3.80; DF 34.70.
Owner Market Avenue Racing Club Ltd **Bred** Limestone Stud **Trained** Middleham Moor, N Yorks

NOTEBOOK
Electric Warrior(IRE), very well backed, turned in a career-best effort to score on this return to 1m. He was given a no-nonsense ride and does possess a decent attitude, but the Handicapper will bump him up accordingly for this now. (op 3/1 tchd 7/2)

830 - 831a (Foreign Racing) - See Raceform Interactive

[819] WOLVERHAMPTON (A.W) (L-H)
Saturday, March 8

OFFICIAL GOING: Standard
A marathon card, with extra races helping to replace the cancelled meeting which had been scheduled for Great Leighs.
Wind: Strong behind Weather: Overcast, turning to light rain after race 3

832 WILLIAMHILL.CO.UK LADY WULFRUNA STKS (LISTED RACE) 7f 32y(P)
2:25 (2:26) (Class 1) 4-Y-O+
£14,762 (£5,595; £2,800; £1,396; £699; £351) **Stalls** High

Form RPR
2041 1 **Jack Sullivan (USA)**[14] 680 7-9-3 107 ....(b) JamieSpencer 7 116
(G A Butler) *chsd ldrs: rdn to ld and edgd lft over 1f out: r.o wl* **10/3**[2]
2 2 3/4 **War Artist (AUS)**[237] 5-9-10 0 .... RyanMoore 2 116
(J M P Eustace) *hld up: hdwy over 2f out: rdn and ev ch over 1f out: styd on same pce ins fnl f* **5/1**[3]
100- 3 3/4 **Lovelace**[140] 6332 4-9-8 109 .... JoeFanning 1 112
(M Johnston) *trckd ldrs: wnt 2nd 1/2-way: rdn and ev ch whn edgd lft 1f out: no ex ins fnl f* **11/4**[1]
1323 4 2 1/4 **Bonus (IRE)**[14] 677 8-9-6 108 .... HayleyTurner 8 104
(G A Butler) *hld up: rdn 1/2-way: hdwy u.p over 1f out: styd on same pce fnl f* **5/1**[3]
-210 5 3/4 **Evens And Odds (IRE)**[14] 677 4-9-3 104 ....(b) NCallan 3 101+
(K A Ryan) *led: rdn and hdd over 1f out: hmpd and wknd sn after* **7/1**
1166 6 3 3/4 **Neardown Beauty (IRE)**[14] 679 5-8-12 89 ....(p) JamesDoyle 4 84+
(A J McCabe) *in rr whn hmpd over 6f out: n.d* **33/1**
65-0 7 1 1/2 **Councellor (FR)**[21] 594 6-9-3 86 ....(t) MickyFenton 5 85
(Stef Liddiard) *chsd ldr to 1/2-way: rdn and wknd 2f out* **50/1**
1230 8 7 **Capricorn Run (USA)**[14] 678 5-9-3 105 ....(v) SebSanders 9 66
(A J McCabe) *s.s: hdwy 1/2-way: wknd 2f out* **7/1**
12/0 9 7 **Baby Strange**[14] 677 4-9-3 104 .... PaulHanagan 6 47
(D Shaw) *mid-div: rdn 1/2-way: wknd over 2f out* **18/1**
1m 28.18s (-1.42) **Going Correction** +0.125s/f (Slow) **9** Ran SP% **118.2**
Speed ratings (Par 111): **113,109,109,106,105 101,99,91,83**
CSF £21.04 TOTE £3.30: £1.40, £1.70, £1.50; EX 21.10 Trifecta £47.80 Pool: £705.85 - 10.47 winning units..
Owner The International Carnival Partnership **Bred** Hermitage Farm Llc **Trained** Newmarket, Suffolk

FOCUS
A reasonable Listed race run at a strong pace throughout. The winning time was 1.42 seconds quicker than the following 71-85 handicap. Jack Sullivan ran up to his best form of recent years and the runner-up made a very encouraging Britsih debut.

NOTEBOOK
Jack Sullivan(USA) stepped up on the bare form of his recent success in a 1m conditions race at Lingfield, taking this tougher contest in convincing style. He edged left under strong pressure close home, slightly hampering Lovelace, but he had the race in the bag by that point. He is now likely to be aimed the Winter Derby, a race in which his trainer has a very strong hand and, although he has never won beyond 1m1f, he should stay the easy 1m2f at Lingfield. (op 7-2 tchd 3-1)
War Artist(AUS) ◆, an Australian-bred Grade 1 winner over 6f in South Africa last year, ran a terrific race on his debut for new connections off the back of an eight-month break. Conceding weight to some very smart rivals, and both stepping up in trip and trying Polytrack for the first time, he shaped with real promise. Having travelled sweetly a little way off the strong gallop, he was produced with his chance against the far rail in the straight, but just found to the race-fit Jack Sullivan, who was getting 7lb, too strong. This longer trip did not pose him any problems and he should prove versatile in that department. He can make his mark in Group company this year. (op 7-2)
Lovelace, who improved from handicap company to win the Group 3 Supreme Stakes at Goodwood last September, made a respectable return from a near five-month break on his first start on Polytrack. Carrying a penalty, although still getting weight from War Artist, he got tired in the straight after chasing the strong pace from the offset. He was slightly hampered by the winner around a furlong out, but was held at the time and can be expected to come on a little for the run. (op 3-1 tchd 7-2)
Bonus(IRE) only stayed on when the race was all over and never posed a threat. He might have found this company a bit too hot. (op 11-2)
Evens And Odds(IRE) took them along at a good pace, but he could not sustain his effort and it was always going to prove difficult to make all in such a hot race. Official explanation: jockey said colt suffered interference (op 10-1)
Neardown Beauty(IRE) had plenty to find in this company and she was never seen with a chance. (tchd 40-1)
Capricorn Run(USA) lost his race with a very slow start. (op 12-1)

833 WILLIAMHILLPOKER.COM H'CAP 7f 32y(P)
3:00 (3:00) (Class 4) (0-85,85) 4-Y-O+ **£4,533** (£1,348; £674; £336) **Stalls** High

Form RPR
2111 1 **Ninth House (USA)**[7] 768 6-8-10 77 ....(bt) JimCrowley 8 89
(N P Littmoden) *hld up in tch: led over 1f out: sn rdn and edgd lft: r.o wl* **3/1**[1]
-065 2 5 **Bobski (IRE)**[28] 503 6-8-13 80 ....(tp) AmirQuinn 2 80
(P J McBride) *s.s: hld up: hdwy over 2f out: rdn and hung lft fr over 1f out: nt trble wnr* **9/1**
1121 3 1 1/4 **Hits Only Jude (IRE)**[16] 636 5-8-13 80 .... FergalLynch 10 77
(P A Blockley) *sn led: hdd over 5f out: led over 2f out: rdn and hdd over 1f out: styd on same pce* **8/1**
4-65 4 nk **Bahiano (IRE)**[14] 680 7-9-4 85 .... RyanMoore 4 81
(C E Brittain) *hld up: rdn over 1f out: styd on ins fnl f: nvr nrr* **4/1**[2]
6223 5 hd **Dudley Docker (IRE)**[18] 618 6-8-9 76 ....(b) LiamJones 5 71
(C R Dore) *hld up: r.o ins fnl f: nvr nr to chal* **16/1**
-064 6 nk **Carcinetto (IRE)**[9] 733 6-8-10 84 .... RichardEvans(7) 6 79
(P D Evans) *chsd ldrs: rdn over 2f out: styd on same pce appr fnl f* **16/1**
0203 7 3/4 **Wessex (USA)**[4] 791 8-9-4 85 .... NCallan 7 78
(P A Blockley) *s.i.s: hld up: rdn over 1f out: n.d* **8/1**
0-00 8 shd **Imperial Echo (USA)**[21] 594 7-8-4 74 .... TolleyDean(3) 3 67+
(D Shaw) *hld up: hdwy over 2f out: hmpd wl over 1f out: wknd fnl f* **20/1**
10-0 9 3 **Resplendent Nova**[14] 679 6-9-4 85 .... JimmyQuinn 1 70
(P Howling) *chsd ldrs: rdn over 2f out: wknd over 1f out* **11/2**[3]
550- 10 3/4 **Harare**[208] 4455 7-8-8 75 ....(v) JamesDoyle 12 58
(R J Price) *hdwy to ld over 5f out: hdd over 2f out: sn rdn: wknd over 1f out* **50/1**
00-0 11 4 **Jamieson Gold (IRE)**[46] 259 5-9-4 85 .... TomEaves 11 59
(Miss L A Perratt) *s.i.s: sn mid-div: rdn 1/2-way: wknd over 2f out* **33/1**
000- 12 nk **Moody Tunes**[148] 6155 5-9-4 85 .... AndrewElliott 9 58
(K R Burke) *prom over 4f* **22/1**
1m 29.6s **Going Correction** +0.125s/f (Slow) **12** Ran SP% **118.4**
Speed ratings (Par 105): **105,99,97,97,97 96,96,95,92,91 87,86**
CSF £29.24 CT £202.88 TOTE £4.20: £1.50, £3.60, £2.10; EX 38.10 Trifecta £236.60 Part won. Pool: £333.27 - 0.10 winning units..
Owner Nigel Shields **Bred** Juddmonte Farms Inc **Trained** Newmarket, Suffolk
■ Stewards' Enquiry : Amir Quinn caution: careless riding

FOCUS
A fair handicap on paper, and the pace was good, but Ninth House routed the field. He is rated back to his best but is likely to face a big hike. Solid form in behind. The winning time was 1.42 seconds slower than the Listed contest won by Jack Sullivan.
Bobski(IRE) Official explanation: jockey said gelding missed the break
Dudley Docker(IRE) Official explanation: jockey said saddle slipped

834 WILLIAMHILL.CO.UK LINCOLN TRIAL STKS (HERITAGE H'CAP) 1m 141y(P)
3:35 (3:35) (Class 2) (0-105,105) 4-Y-O+
£31,160 (£9,330; £4,665; £2,335; £1,165; £585) **Stalls** Low

Form RPR
6/04 1 **Re Barolo (IRE)**[14] 679 5-9-4 99 ....(t) SebSanders 12 109
(M Botti) *a.p: rdn and hung lft fr over 1f out: r.o to ld post* **8/1**
00-5 2 nk **Plum Pudding (IRE)**[21] 594 5-8-7 88 .... RichardHughes 8 97
(R Hannon) *led: qckнd 2f out: sn rdn: hdd post* **4/1**[1]
5450 3 1 1/2 **Troubadour (IRE)**[14] 678 7-9-2 97 ....(b[1]) SteveDrowne 4 103+
(W Jarvis) *hld up: nt clr run and swtchd rt wl over 1f out: edgd lft and r.o ins fnl f: nt rch ldrs* **7/1**
4 2 1/4 **Classic Port (FR)**[332] 4-9-7 102 .... JimmyQuinn 5 103
(M Wigham) *trckd ldrs: rdn over 2f out: styd on same pce fnl f* **16/1**
64-5 5 nk **Yarqus**[14] 678 5-8-9 90 ....(t) HayleyTurner 13 90
(C E Brittain) *chsd ldr: ev ch over 2f out: sn rdn: no ex fnl f* **9/1**
400- 6 hd **Danehillsundance (IRE)**[126] 6654 4-8-10 91 .... RyanMoore 3 91+
(R Hannon) *hld up: nt clr run over 1f out: r.o ins fnl f: nvr nrr* **11/2**[3]
00-0 7 2 **Bomber Command (USA)**[21] 594 5-8-7 88 ....(v) JamesDoyle 10 84
(J W Hills) *hld up in tch: rdn 2f out: hung lft and wknd fnl f* **12/1**
5312 8 1 **Alfresco**[14] 680 4-9-0 95 ....(b) NCallan 11 89
(I A Wood) *hld up: rdn and hung lft over 1f out: n.d* **13/2**
64-3 9 3 1/4 **Murfreesboro**[43] 308 5-8-9 90 ....(be) GregFairley 7 77
(K J Burke) *hld up: effrt over 2f out: sn wknd* **40/1**
605- 10 1 1/4 **Charlie Tokyo (IRE)**[45] 6153 5-9-10 105 ....(v) PaulHanagan 2 89
(R A Fahey) *chsd ldrs: rdn over 2f out: wknd over 1f out* **20/1**
0-41 11 10 **Samarinda (USA)**[28] 502 5-9-0 95 .... MickyFenton 9 58
(Mrs P Sly) *dwlt: hld up: a in rr: bhd whn hung lft over 1f out* **5/1**[2]
1m 50.1s (-0.40) **Going Correction** +0.125s/f (Slow) **11** Ran SP% **119.8**
Speed ratings (Par 109): **106,105,104,102,102 101,100,99,96,95 86**
CSF £40.79 CT £245.99 TOTE £9.10: £2.80, £2.10, £3.00; EX 65.30 Trifecta £152.60 Pool: £595.42 - 2.77 winning units..
Owner Effevi Snc Di Villa Felice & C **Bred** Luciano Bosio **Trained** Newmarket, Suffolk

FOCUS
Just a reasonable renewal of the Lincoln Trial, but the race was spoilt somewhat by a lack of pace with Plum Pudding, allowed an easy lead, setting an ordinary gallop. However, the winning time was still 1.94 seconds quicker than the later maiden. Re Barolo looks a talented recruit and the next two ran up to their best.
NOTEBOOK
Re Barolo(IRE), a multiple winner in Italy, shaped well when fourth in a competitive 7f handicap at Lingfield on just his second start in this country and he stepped forward again the land this valuable contest. He was never too far away from the modest pace, but he was forced to race at least three wide for much of the way and did well to pick up in the straight and reel in the long-time leader. He is not in the Lincoln itself, but should prove just as effective on turf, although he probably won't want the ground too fast. (tchd 15-2)
Plum Pudding(IRE) probably needed the run when only fifth at Lingfield on his return from a break last time and he duly stepped up on that effort this time. He was, though, gifted a surprisingly easy lead and set very ordinary fractions before quickening off the bend. He is reasonably handicapped on the pick of his form, but things are unlikely to fall as kindly too often in the future. He is in the Lincoln. (op 6-1)
Troubadour(IRE), fitted with blinkers for the first time, was unable to get to the front two, but he still fared best of those held up and this was a decent effort in defeat. He is entered in both the Winter Derby and the Lincoln. (op 12-1 tchd 14-1)
Classic Port(FR) ◆ won two of his first three starts when trained in France by Andre Fabre for Sheikh Mohammed, but he has been off the track since last April and was picked up by his new connections for 20,000gns. This must rate as a very pleasing return to action considering he was racing off a mark of 102 and conceding weight to all bar one of his rivals. He is in the Lincoln and if the ground comes up on the soft side the 33/1 on offer ante-post could look massive. (op 14-1)
Yarqus, possibly flattered by his fifth in the Winter Derby Trial, had every chance and can have no excuses. (op 8-1 tchd 12-1)
Danehillsundance(IRE), returning from a four-month break, was held up in a steadily run race and can do better. (op 5-1 tchd 9-2)
Bomber Command(USA) was 5lb lower than when running second in this race last year, so this could be considered a little disappointing.
Alfresco was below form and has yet to show his best in three runs at this track. The lack of pace probably didn't suit either. (op 7-1 tchd 6-1)
Samarinda(USA) got upset in the stalls and missed the break. He can be forgiven this. Official explanation: jockey said gelding hit its head on leaving stalls (op 13-2)

835 FREEPHONE WILLIAM HILL ON 0800 44 40 40 CLAIMING STKS 5f 20y(P)
4:10 (4:10) (Class 5) 3-Y-O **£2,730** (£806; £403) **Stalls** Low

Form				RPR
1-12	**1**		**Ten Down**[3] 798 3-9-3 78 .... TPQueally 1	80
			(J A Osborne) *mde all: edgd rt over 1f out: hrd rdn ins fnl f: r.o* **4/7**[1]
6060	**2**	2 ½	**Kamal**[7] 767 3-8-10 60 .... (b[1]) HayleyTurner 3	64
			(W R Muir) *chsd ldrs: rdn over 1f out: styd on same pce ins fnl f* **11/2**[3]
1312	**3**	nse	**Wee Buns**[9] 732 3-8-10 68 .... SteveDrowne 5	64+
			(P G Murphy) *chsd wnr: rdn and nt clr run over 1f out: styd on same pce fnl f* **3/1**[2]
0100	**4**	7	**Arkando (IRE)**[5] 780 3-8-4 52 .... (p) AndrewElliott 2	33
			(K R Burke) *dwlt: outpcd* **33/1**
6050	**5**	5	**Yattendon**[3] 797 3-8-9 55 .... (t) LPKeniry 4	20
			(S Kirk) *chsd ldrs: rdn over 3f out: wknd 2f out* **50/1**

62.73 secs (0.43) **Going Correction** +0.125s/f (Slow) **5** Ran SP% **108.9**
Speed ratings (Par 98): **101,97,96,85,77**
CSF £4.18 TOTE £1.60: £1.10, £2.70; EX 3.90.The winner was claimed by Gay Kelleway for £15,000.
Owner Piers Pottinger And Ten **Bred** Baydon House Stud **Trained** Upper Lambourn, Berks
FOCUS
An uncompetitive claimer in which the clear form pick faced a straightforward task. Solid enough form.

836 WILLIAMHILLCASINO.COM H'CAP 5f 216y(P)
4:45 (4:45) (Class 2) (0-100,98) 4-Y-O+ **£10,363** (£3,083; £1,540; £769) **Stalls** Low

Form				RPR
-413	**1**		**Orpsie Boy (IRE)**[14] 679 5-8-13 96 .... KirstyMilczarek[(3)] 1	107
			(N P Littmoden) *hld up: hdwy over 1f out: r.o to ld wl ins fnl f* **3/1**[1]
3640	**2**	¾	**Fyodor (IRE)**[14] 679 7-9-0 94 .... LiamJones 5	103
			(W J Haggas) *hld up: hdwy over 1f out: rdn and ev ch wl ins fnl f: styd on* **14/1**
1-14	**3**	1 ¼	**Distinctly Game**[29] 482 6-8-4 84 .... JimmyQuinn 4	89
			(K A Ryan) *chsd ldrs: rdn to ld ins fnl f: sn hdd and unable qck* **11/1**
001-	**4**	nk	**Curtail (IRE)**[113] 6836 5-8-8 88 .... TomEaves 11	92
			(Miss L A Perratt) *mid-div: hdwy over 2f out: rdn over 1f out: styd on* **14/1**
2122	**5**	¾	**Bo McGinty (IRE)**[25] 532 7-8-4 84 oh2 .... (b) PaulHanagan 2	86
			(R A Fahey) *trckd ldrs: plld hrd: rdn over 1f out: no ex towards fin* **14/1**
1110	**6**	shd	**Bazroy (IRE)**[21] 594 4-9-4 98 .... (b) TGMcLaughlin 9	100
			(P D Evans) *hld up: hdwy over 2f out: rdn and edgd rt over 1f out: styd on same pce fnl f* **10/1**
-236	**7**	¾	**Silver Prelude**[21] 593 7-8-7 87 .... ChrisCatlin 7	87
			(D K Ivory) *led: rdn over 1f out: hdd and no ex ins fnl f* **16/1**
3040	**8**	1 ¼	**Qadar (IRE)**[14] 679 6-8-8 88 .... (b) JimCrowley 8	84
			(N P Littmoden) *hld up: hdwy over 2f out: rdn over 1f out: wknd ins fnl f* **11/2**[3]
40-1	**9**	1 ½	**Ajigolo**[21] 593 5-9-1 95 .... EdwardCreighton 10	86
			(M R Channon) *prom: chsd ldr over 3f out: rdn over 1f out: wknd ins fnl f* **11/2**[3]
-100	**10**	16	**Come Out Fighting**[14] 677 5-8-13 93 .... (b[1]) RyanMoore 3	36
			(P A Blockley) *s.i.s: sn trcking ldrs: wknd 2f out* **4/1**[2]

1m 14.38s (-0.62) **Going Correction** +0.125s/f (Slow) **10** Ran SP% **119.1**
Speed ratings (Par 109): **109,108,106,105,104 104,103,102,100,78**
CSF £48.30 CT £416.87 TOTE £3.60: £1.60, £3.10, £2.90; EX 41.10 Trifecta £248.20 Part won. Pool: £349.65 - 0.38 winning units..
Owner Miss Vanessa Church **Bred** Minch Bloodstock **Trained** Newmarket, Suffolk
FOCUS
A very good sprint handicap run at a decent pace. Solid form which should work out, the winner recording a career best. The winning time was 2.12 seconds faster than the claimer won by the 63-rated Another Genepi.
NOTEBOOK
Orpsie Boy(IRE) looked to have it all to do at the top of the straight, but the leaders came back to the field and he stayed on strongest of all when getting a dream run inside the final furlong. His long-term aim is the Wokingham at Royal Ascot. (tchd 11-4 and 10-3)
Fyodor(IRE) has not been convincing with his attitude in recent starts, but he was well produced by Liam Jones and was just denied. (op 10-1)
Distinctly Game had every chance if good enough, but he was run out of it by a couple of strong finishers. (op 10-1 tchd 9-1)
Curtail(IRE) ◆, 4lb higher than when winning over course and distance when last seen in November, wants rating better than the bare form as he raced much wider than ideal pretty much throughout. (op 10-1)
Bo McGinty(IRE), back on Polytrack, ran well from 2lb out of the handicap, but he did not help his chances of lasting home by racing very enthusiastically just off the lead. On this evidence he will be happier back over 5f. (op 16-1)
Bazroy(IRE) was forced to make his move out wide and this was a respectable effort in the circumstances. (tchd 14-1)
Silver Prelude was always going to have difficulty containing such a hot field. (tchd 20-1)
Ajigolo was only 3lb higher than when winning over 5f at Lingfield on his previous start, but he was not in the same form this time. (op 13-2 tchd 7-1 and 5-1)
Come Out Fighting ran a stinker and might not have faced the first-time blinkers. Official explanation: jockey said horse ran too freely in first-time blinkers (op 6-1)

837 WILLIAMHILLPOKER.COM MAIDEN STKS 1m 141y(P)
5:20 (5:22) (Class 5) 3-Y-O+ **£2,590** (£770; £385; £192) **Stalls** Low

Form				RPR
1		**Al Samha (USA)** 3-8-8 0 .... JoeFanning 5	75+
			(M Johnston) *s.i.s: sn rcvrd to ld: rdn and hung rt fr over 1f out: r.o* **11/4**[1]
2-	**2**	1 ¾	**Two Left Feet**[115] 6805 3-8-8 0 .... SaleemGolam 3	71
			(W R Swinburn) *chsd ldrs: rdn over 2f out: edgd rt fnl f: styd on same pce* **3/1**[2]
22	**3**	2	**Maadraa (IRE)**[16] 645 3-8-8 0 .... NCallan 11	67
			(M A Jarvis) *chsd ldrs: rdn 2f out: edgd lft fr over 1f out: styd on same pce* **3/1**[2]
024	**4**	nk	**Boy On A Swing (USA)**[22] 570 3-8-8 75 .... (t) TPQueally 13	66
			(J A Osborne) *chsd wnr: rdn and hung lft over 1f out: styd on same pce* **11/2**[3]
-540	**5**	½	**Johnston's Glory (IRE)**[23] 560 4-9-9 48 .... JimmyQuinn 4	66?
			(E J Alston) *hld up: plld hrd: hdwy over 2f out: rdn over 1f out: styd on same pce* **50/1**
5	**6**	shd	**Canary Islands**[17] 633 3-8-8 0 .... TGMcLaughlin 6	65+
			(E A L Dunlop) *s.i.s: hld up: hdwy and swtchd lft fnl f: nvr nr to chal* **14/1**
3-	**7**	shd	**Baaher (USA)**[385] 492 4-10-0 0 .... GregFairley 12	71
			(T J Pitt) *dwlt: hdwy 7f out: rdn over 3f out: no ex fnl f* **8/1**
0-6	**8**	6	**Cape Colony**[11] 705 3-8-8 0 .... RichardHughes 8	51
			(R Hannon) *hld up: rdn over 1f out: n.d* **20/1**
9	1 ¾	**Amber Moon** 3-8-3 0 .... HayleyTurner 10	42
			(M L W Bell) *plld hrd and prom: rdn and wknd over 2f out* **33/1**
-5	**10**	2 ¾	**Rossini Byline (IRE)**[38] 354 3-8-3 0 .... LiamJones 1	35
			(J L Spearing) *plld hrd and prom: stdd and lost pl over 7f out: rdn over 3f out: n.d after* **50/1**
600-	**11**	7	**Sultan Of The Sand**[220] 4077 3-8-8 50 .... PatrickMathers 7	24
			(C C Bealby) *hld up: racd keenly: hdwy over 5f out: rdn over 3f out: sn wknd* **100/1**
12	42	**Come On Molly** 4-9-9 0 .... J-PGuillambert 2	—
			(R Brotherton) *s.i.s: sn outpcd* **100/1**

1m 52.04s (1.54) **Going Correction** +0.125s/f (Slow)
WFA 3 from 4yo 20lb **12** Ran SP% **123.4**
Speed ratings (Par 103): **98,96,94,94,93 93,93,88,86,84 78,40**
CSF £11.31 TOTE £4.40: £1.70, £1.80, £1.40; EX 15.80 Trifecta £101.50 Pool: £515.14 - 3.60 winning units..
Owner Sheikh Hamdan Bin Mohammed Al Maktoum **Bred** Gainsborough Farm Llc **Trained** Middleham Moor, N Yorks
FOCUS
The winning time was 1.94 seconds slower than the Lincoln Trial and the form is nothing special, with the 48-rated Johnston's Glory finishing close up, but the winner is very likely to prove better than the bare result suggests.

838 WILLIAMHILLBINGO.COM H'CAP 1m 5f 194y(P)
5:50 (5:50) (Class 4) (0-85,85) 4-Y-O+ **£4,533** (£1,348; £674; £336) **Stalls** Low

Form				RPR
2511	**1**		**Motarjm (USA)**[12] 701 4-9-2 80 .... (t) ChrisCatlin 4	88+
			(H J Collingridge) *trckd ldr: racd keenly: led over 2f out: rdn clr over 1f out: edgd rt ins fnl f: styd on* **10/3**[1]
0-16	**2**	1 ¼	**Casual Affair**[24] 540 5-8-10 70 .... JimmyQuinn 7	76
			(J D Bethell) *a.p: chsd wnr over 2f out: rdn over 1f out: styd on* **7/2**[2]
3-33	**3**	hd	**Masked (IRE)**[17] 630 7-9-8 82 .... SebSanders 9	88
			(R M Beckett) *hld up: hdwy over 3f out: rdn over 1f out: styd on* **4/1**[3]
-556	**4**	¾	**Pass The Port**[23] 561 7-9-4 78 .... JamieSpencer 6	83
			(D Haydn Jones) *s.i.s: hld up: hdwy over 2f out: rdn over 1f out: kpt on* **15/2**
/5-3	**5**	1 ¾	**Jagger**[17] 626 8-9-11 85 .... TPQueally 1	87
			(G A Butler) *s.i.s: hld up: hdwy u.p and hung lft ins fnl f: n.d* **15/2**
-325	**6**	2 ½	**Oakley Heffert (IRE)**[15] 525 4-8-12 76 .... (b) RichardHughes 5	75
			(R Hannon) *chsd ldrs: nt clr run over 2f out: sn rdn and outpcd* **10/1**
0-66	**7**	2 ¼	**Bazart**[9] 735 6-9-3 77 .... FergusSweeney 3	73
			(K R Burke) *sn led: rdn and hdd over 2f out: wknd over 1f out* **33/1**
3131	**8**	1 ½	**Bentley Brook (IRE)**[16] 638 6-9-6 80 .... FergalLynch 2	73
			(P A Blockley) *hld up: rdn over 3f out: wknd 2f out* **15/2**

3m 7.43s (1.43) **Going Correction** +0.125s/f (Slow)
WFA 4 from 5yo+ 4lb **8** Ran SP% **112.6**
Speed ratings (Par 105): **100,99,99,98,97 96,95,94**
CSF £14.74 CT £46.34 TOTE £4.40: £1.70, £1.80, £1.50; EX 17.60 Trifecta £84.40 Pool: £264.13 - 2.22 winning units..
Owner P D Band **Bred** Darley **Trained** Exning, Suffolk
FOCUS
A fairly steadily run race but another good performance from Motarjm, who is clearly progressive. The form looks sound enough rated through the placed horses.
Bazart Official explanation: jockey said gelding hung right

839 WILLIAMHILLARCADE.COM CLAIMING STKS 5f 216y(P)
6:20 (6:20) (Class 5) 3-Y-O+ **£2,331** (£693; £346; £173) **Stalls** Low

Form				RPR
2422	**1**		**Another Genepi (USA)**[5] 783 5-9-2 63 .... (b) FergalLynch 7	66
			(I W McInnes) *a.p: rdn to chse ldr over 1f out: sn hung lft: r.o to ld wl ins fnl f* **7/2**[3]
2362	**2**	1 ¼	**Grimes Faith**[3] 800 5-9-10 70 .... (p) NCallan 6	70
			(K A Ryan) *w ldr tl led over 4f out: rdn clr over 1f out: hdd wl ins fnl f* **15/8**[1]
1154	**3**	2	**Mafaheem**[5] 783 6-9-6 65 .... GeorgeBaker 4	60+
			(A B Haynes) *s.i.s: hdwy over 4f out: rdn whn nt clr run and swtchd lft over 1f out: styd on* **7/2**[3]
0405	**4**	1 ¾	**Lethal**[11] 707 5-9-13 78 .... (e) PaulHanagan 1	62
			(R A Fahey) *led: hdd over 4f out: rdn over 1f out: wknd ins fnl f* **5/2**[2]
4053	**5**	1 ¾	**Goodbye Cash (IRE)**[5] 783 4-8-8 66 .... (p) RichardEvans[(7)] 5	45
			(P D Evans) *s.i.s: hld up: effrt over 2f out: wknd over 1f out* **10/1**

/0-0 **6** *32* **Longy The Lash**[14] 681 5-8-10 35............(p) DavidProbert(7) 8 —
(Paul Murphy) *sn pushed along in rr: bhd fr 1/2-way* **100/1**

1m 16.5s (1.50) **Going Correction** +0.125s/f (Slow)
WFA 3 from 4yo+ 14lb **6** Ran SP% **117.9**
Speed ratings (Par 103): **95,93,90,88,86 43**
CSF £11.22 TOTE £4.90: £1.50, £1.60; EX 13.60 Trifecta £39.70 Pool: £469.38 - 8.39 winning units.The winner was claimed by A S Reid for £9,000.
Owner Ivy House Racing **Bred** Joseph Lacombe Stables Inc **Trained** Catwick, E Yorks

FOCUS
There was not a lot to choose between five of the six at the weights, and the market reflected that competitiveness. The winning time was 2.12 seconds slower than the earlier 86-100 handicap and the form is modest, rated around the third.
Lethal Official explanation: jockey said gelding hung right

840 EVERY MINUTE, EVERY MATCH - BETLIVE@WILLIAMHILL.CO.UK H'CAP 5f 20y(P)
6:50 (6:50) (Class 5) (0-75,82) 4-Y-0+ £2,457 (£725; £362) Stalls Low

Form RPR
3655 **1** **Sands Crooner (IRE)**[14] 676 5-8-12 **69**............(v) DaneO'Neill 3 80
(D Shaw) *hld up: hung lft and r.o to ld wl ins fnl f* **8/1**
324- **2** *1 1/2* **Cosmic Destiny (IRE)**[135] 6450 6-8-13 **70**............ LPKeniry 5 76
(E F Vaughan) *hld up: racd keenly: hdwy over 1f out: rdn and ev ch wl ins fnl f: unable qck* **22/1**
1301 **3** *1/2* **Almaty Express**[12] 699 6-9-11 **82**............(b) ChrisCatlin 1 86
(J R Weymes) *led: rdn over 1f out: hdd wl ins fnl f* **5/1**[3]
4353 **4** *shd* **Obe Royal**[9] 729 4-8-6 **70**............(b) RichardEvans(7) 8 73
(P D Evans) *s.i.s: outpcd: r.o ins fnl f: nrst fin* **9/1**
0-41 **5** *3/4* **Multahab**[29] 488 9-8-13 **70**............(t) JimmyQuinn 2 71
(M Wigham) *chsd ldrs: rdn over 1f out: edgd rt and styd on same pce fnl f* **9/2**[2]
3645 **6** *hd* **Desert Opal**[12] 699 8-8-11 **68**............(b) LiamJones 9 68+
(C R Dore) *chsd ldrs: rdn 1/2-way: styng on same pce whn hmpd ins fnl f* **20/1**
2-62 **7** *3/4* **Monte Major (IRE)**[12] 699 7-8-6 **66**............ TolleyDean(3) 7 63
(D Shaw) *mid-div: sn pushed along: n.d* **7/1**
10-1 **8** *1/2* **Fast Freddie**[8] 746 4-8-10 **70**............(e) DNolan(3) 6 66+
(S Parr) *chsd ldrs: rdn over 1f out: no ex whn n.m.r ins fnl f* **10/1**
0-63 **9** *1* **Nigella**[22] 580 5-9-2 **73**............ GrahamGibbons 4 65
(E S McMahon) *chsd ldrs: rdn over 1f out: wknd fnl f* **11/4**[1]
020- **10** *3 1/4* **Kings College Boy**[112] 6860 8-8-6 **63**............(b) PaulHanagan 10 43
(R A Fahey) *prom 3f* **40/1**

62.30 secs **Going Correction** +0.125s/f (Slow) **10** Ran SP% **115.8**
Speed ratings (Par 103): **105,102,101,101,100 100,98,98,96,91**
CSF £168.19 CT £968.92 TOTE £9.70: £2.70, £4.10, £2.60; EX 95.50 Trifecta £251.80 Part won: Pool: £354.70 - 0.70 winning units..
Owner Danethorpe Racing Partnership **Bred** Peter Molony **Trained** Danethorpe, Notts

FOCUS
They went a strong gallop here and the winner came from way off the pace. The form looks sound rated through the third.
Multahab Official explanation: jockey said gelding hung right

841 BE IN THE GAME! BETLIVE@WILLIAMHILL.CO.UK APPRENTICE H'CAP 1m 1f 103y(P)
7:20 (7:20) (Class 6) (0-60,60) 4-Y-0+ £1,774 (£523; £262) Stalls Low

Form RPR
0-41 **1** **Naughty Thoughts (IRE)**[19] 607 4-9-0 **56**............ RossAtkinson 4 64
(Tom Dascombe) *stdd s: hld up: hdwy 3f out: chsd ldr 2f out: styd on u.p to ld post* **3/1**[1]
4225 **2** *hd* **Ermine Grey**[16] 640 7-8-10 **52**............ BMcHugh 5 60
(A W Carroll) *chsd ldrs: led over 2f out: rdn and edgd rt over 1f out: hdd post* **7/1**[3]
5121 **3** *7* **My Mirasol**[22] 579 4-9-4 **60**............(p) AshleyMorgan 8 55
(D E Cantillon) *chsd ldrs: nt clr run over 2f out: sn rdn: styd on same pce* **3/1**[1]
2340 **4** *1* **Casablanca Minx (IRE)**[9] 736 5-8-13 **55**............(v) BillyCray 3 48
(P D Evans) *hld up: hdwy over 1f out: swtchd lft and r.o ins fnl f: n.d* **8/1**
2325 **5** *nse* **Gifted Heir (IRE)**[14] 686 4-8-13 **55**............ NatashaEaton 1 48
(A Bailey) *hld up: hdwy 2f out: sn rdn: styd on same pce* **8/1**
-116 **6** *5* **Joe Jo Star**[14] 686 6-8-12 **54**............ SoniaEaton 2 37
(B P J Baugh) *plld hrd and prom: wknd over 2f out* **14/1**
2152 **7** *1 3/4* **Pianoforte (USA)**[8] 753 6-8-11 **58**............(p) PaulPickard(5) 6 38
(E J Alston) *prom: chsd ldr 6f out: rdn and wknd over 1f out* **5/1**[2]
-613 **8** *2 1/4* **Altos Reales**[15] 664 4-9-2 **58**............ JamieKyne 9 34
(D Shaw) *sn pushed along in rr: hdwy over 5f out: wknd over 2f out* **16/1**
3044 **9** *2 3/4* **Capania (IRE)**[8] 753 4-8-8 **50**............(p) DavidProbert 10 20
(P D Evans) *led: hdd over 2f out: wknd over 1f out* **20/1**

2m 2.03s (0.33) **Going Correction** +0.125s/f (Slow) **9** Ran SP% **118.7**
Speed ratings (Par 101): **103,102,96,95,95 91,89,87,85**
CSF £25.51 CT £69.11 TOTE £3.60: £1.50, £2.70, £1.40; EX 33.00 Trifecta £42.40 Pool £322.78 - 5.40 winning units. Place 6 £17.79, Place 5 £11.92.
Owner 123 Racing Partnership **Bred** Dr John Hollowood And Aiden Murphy **Trained** Lambourn, Berks
■ Stewards' Enquiry : David Probert four-day ban: careless riding (Mar 19-20, 22-23)

FOCUS
The front two finished well clear and the form looks sound for the grade.
T/Plt: £17.00 to a £1 stake. Pool: £84,285.45. 3,609.55 winning tickets. T/Qpdt: £7.60 to a £1 stake. Pool: £3,670.50. 357.10 winning tickets. CR

786 SOUTHWELL (L-H)
Tuesday, March 11

OFFICIAL GOING: Standard
Wind: Fresh, half-behind Weather: Overcast

843 BETDAQ THE BETTING EXCHANGE APPRENTICE H'CAP 1m 4f (F)
1:50 (1:50) (Class 6) (0-55,54) 4-Y-0+ £1,774 (£523; £262) Stalls Low

Form RPR
-202 **1** **Nimello (USA)**[21] 617 12-9-2 **54**............ KellyHarrison 9 65+
(A G Newcombe) *hld up: hdwy over 6f out: led over 1f out: shkn up and r.o* **7/1**
30/2 **2** *1 1/4* **Ruling Reef**[7] 788 6-8-2 **45**............ BillyCray(5) 12 54
(M D I Usher) *hld up in tch: led over 2f out: rdn and hdd over 1f out: styd on* **11/2**[3]
/021 **3** *7* **Ben Bacchus (IRE)**[11] 751 6-9-1 **53**............ JamieJones 4 52
(P W Hiatt) *chsd ldrs: rdn over 2f out: sn outpcd* **13/8**[1]
000- **4** *7* **Miss Havisham (IRE)**[169] 5676 4-8-8 **48**............ HaddenFrost 8 36
(J R Weymes) *trckd ldr: led over 7f out: hdd over 4f out: hung lft and wknd over 1f out* **25/1**
0-30 **5** *1* **Fifth Zak**[29] 524 4-8-9 **52**............(p) JackDean(3) 10 39
(S R Bowring) *hld up: hdwy over 3f out: rdn and wknd over 2f out* **16/1**
6404 **6** *1 1/2* **Bienheureux**[6] 793 7-9-0 **52**............(t) NicolPolli 3 36
(Miss Gay Kelleway) *chsd ldrs: rdn over 4f out: wknd over 2f out* **7/2**[2]
604- **7** *1* **Acapulco Bay**[97] 6464 4-8-3 **46**............(p) MCGeran(3) 7 29
(Miss J A Camacho) *led: racd keenly: hdd over 7f out: led over 4f out: rdn and hdd over 2f out: sn wknd* **13/2**
0-64 **8** *13* **Topwell**[18] 657 7-8-2 **45**............(p) StacyRenwick(5) 1 8
(R C Guest) *s.i.s: hld up: rdn 1/2-way: wknd over 4f out* **20/1**
000- **9** *13* **Watermill (IRE)**[293] 1942 5-8-2 **45**............(b) DeanHeslop(5) 11 —
(Mrs R A Carr) *s.i.s: hld up: a in rr: wknd over 4f out* **66/1**
0 **10** *26* **Amarillo Slim (IRE)**[29] 526 4-8-9 **54**............ KylieManser(5) 2 —
(S Curran) *chsd ldrs over 8f* **40/1**

2m 44.3s (3.30) **Going Correction** +0.30s/f (Slow)
WFA 4 from 5yo+ 2lb **10** Ran SP% **120.0**
Speed ratings (Par 101): **101,100,95,90,90 89,88,79,71,53**
CSF £44.91 CT £93.83 TOTE £5.70: £1.40, £1.80, £1.20; EX 33.00 Trifecta £65.30 Pool: £161.92 - 1.76 winning units..
Owner Mrs Jayne Bramhill **Bred** Glencrest Farm **Trained** Yarnscombe, Devon
■ Kentucky Bullet was withdrawn (7/1, no suitable jockey available). R4, deduct 10p in the £. New market formed.

FOCUS
A very poor race in which the pace was honest. That proved too much for the vast majority of these with the field finishing very well spread out. The first two finished well clear and could be vulnerable when reassessed.

844 BET "CHAMPION HURDLE" - BETDAQ CLASSIFIED CLAIMING STKS 1m (F)
2:25 (2:25) (Class 6) 4-Y-0+ £1,774 (£523; £262) Stalls Low

Form RPR
-032 **1** **West End Lad**[40] 369 5-8-11 54 ow1............(b[1]) PhillipMakin 7 61
(S R Bowring) *hld up: hdwy over 2f out: rdn over 1f out: styd on u.p to ld towards fin* **14/1**
4225 **2** *nk* **Having A Ball**[24] 587 4-8-6 52............ JamieJones(5) 8 60
(P D Cundell) *a.p: led over 2f out: rdn and edgd lft fr over 1f out: hdd towards fin* **5/1**[2]
0-45 **3** *3* **Jaassey**[40] 365 5-8-6 43............(t) PaulFessey 10 49
(P Beaumont) *hld up: hdwy over 2f out: rdn over 1f out: edgd lft: styd on* **33/1**
5016 **4** *2* **Anduril**[19] 640 7-8-12 52............(p) FergalLynch 11 50
(I W McInnes) *hld up: hdwy over 3f out: rdn and hung lft 2f out: no ex fnl f* **7/1**[3]
-202 **5** *1 3/4* **Winged Farasi**[29] 521 4-8-5 52............ KevinGhunowa(5) 14 44
(R A Harris) *dwlt and reluctant in rr: hdwy over 2f out: sn rdn no ex fnl f* **9/1**
-040 **6** *2* **Tina's Ridge (IRE)**[23] 601 4-9-0 50............(p) RobertWinston 5 44
(R Hollinshead) *s.i.s: outpcd: hdwy over 1f out: wknd ins fnl f* **16/1**
5320 **7** *1* **Silver Blue (IRE)**[6] 795 5-8-4 49............(b) LiamJones 9 32
(C R Dore) *s.i.s: outpcd: nt clr run over 3f out: hdwy 2f out: wknd fnl f* **9/1**
60-1 **8** *3/4* **Ugenius**[7] 792 4-8-7 41............ GrahamGibbons 2 33
(P A Blockley) *chsd ldrs: rdn over 2f out: wknd over 1f out* **7/2**[1]
-442 **9** *3/4* **Local Poet**[26] 553 7-8-5 52............(b) PaulHanagan 12 30
(Ollie Pears) *chsd ldrs: led over 3f out: rdn and hdd over 2f out: wknd over 1f out* **5/1**[2]
6336 **10** *10* **Lucius Verrus (USA)**[7] 792 8-7-13 48............(v) KellyHarrison(5) 3 7
(D Shaw) *hld up in tch: lost pl over 5f out: nt clr run over 3f out: wknd over 2f out* **28/1**
600- **11** *2 1/4* **Feelin Irie (IRE)**[6] 6587 5-8-10 49 ow2............ StephenDonohoe 13 8
(M J Gingell) *chsd ldrs: rdn over 3f out: sn wknd* **40/1**
-504 **12** *4* **Robinzal**[15] 703 6-8-8 52............(t) VinceSlattery 4 —
(A W Carroll) *s.i.s: outpcd* **22/1**
000- **13** *1/2* **El Capitan (FR)**[225] 4031 5-8-10 52............(b) HayleyTurner 6 —
(Miss Gay Kelleway) *chsd ldrs over 5f* **14/1**
0005 **14** *1 3/4* **Totally Free**[7] 792 4-8-4 49............(v) JimmyQuinn 1 —
(M D I Usher) *s.i.s: sn rcvrd to ld: hdd over 3f out: wknd 2f out* **50/1**

1m 46.49s (2.79) **Going Correction** +0.30s/f (Slow) **14** Ran SP% **122.4**
Speed ratings (Par 101): **98,97,94,92,90 88,87,87,86,76 74,70,69,67**
CSF £80.26 TOTE £15.60: £3.80, £2.20, £12.90; EX 103.20 TRIFECTA Not won..
Owner K Nicholls **Bred** Keith Nicholls **Trained** Edwinstowe, Notts

FOCUS
A bad race featuring several whose best days are behind them - if they ever had any - and the front pair pulled clear. The principals set the level.
Lucius Verrus(USA) Official explanation: jockey said gelding lost its action
Totally Free Official explanation: jockey said gelding had no more to give

845 BET CHELTENHAM FESTIVAL - BETDAQ (S) STKS 7f (F)
3:00 (3:00) (Class 6) 3-Y-0 £1,774 (£523; £262) Stalls Low

Form RPR
132 **1** **Copperbottomed (IRE)**[19] 635 3-9-4 62............(e) JimCrowley 8 67+
(J R Boyle) *trckd ldrs: led on bit over 2f out: rdn clr over 1f out: eased ins fnl f* **6/5**[1]
3530 **2** *6* **Whitcombe Flyer (USA)**[10] 767 3-8-12 50............(b) JimmyQuinn 4 46+
(Miss M E Rowland) *s.i.s: hld up: hmpd 1/2-way: sn rdn: styd on fr over 1f out: no ch w wnr* **12/1**[3]
0-6 **3** *3 1/2* **Woodland Mist**[15] 698 3-8-7 0............ TomEaves 3 32
(M Dods) *trckd ldrs: rdn 2f out: wkng whn nt clr run over 1f out* **16/1**
3310 **4** *1 1/2* **Don Picolo**[20] 623 3-9-4 56............(b) FrankieMcDonald 1 40
(P A Blockley) *s.i.s: hld up: rdn over 1f out: n.d* **7/2**[2]
6-43 **5** *1 3/4* **Indecision**[28] 534 3-8-12 56............ PaulMulrennan 7 29
(M W Easterby) *disp ld over 4f: sn rdn and wknd* **7/2**[2]
0-05 **6** *3 3/4* **Petite Music (IRE)**[8] 780 3-8-4 45............(b) DuranFentiman(3) 5 15
(T D Easterby) *disp ld over 4f out: sn rdn and wknd* **28/1**
00- **7** *2 1/2* **Barbossa**[225] 4020 3-8-12 0............ PatrickMathers 6 14
(A J McCabe) *s.i.s: hld up: plld hrd: hdwy 1/2-way: rdn over 2f out: sn wknd* **25/1**
02- **8** *13* **Just Puddie**[236] 3681 3-8-3 0 ow3............ JackDean(7) 2 —
(W G M Turner) *chsd ldrs: rdn 1/2-way: wknd wl over 2f out* **33/1**

1m 32.39s (2.09) **Going Correction** +0.30s/f (Slow) **8** Ran SP% **113.7**
Speed ratings (Par 96): **100,93,89,87,85 81,78,63**
CSF £17.31 TOTE £1.70: £1.30, £2.20, £2.60; EX 14.70 Trifecta £76.10 Pool: £640.65 - 5.97 winning units..The winner was bought in for 7,000gns.
Owner M Khan X2 **Bred** Paul McEnery **Trained** Epsom, Surrey

FOCUS
An awful seller and ultimately a one-horse race. Copperbottomed has been rated to his previous best.

846 BETDAQ.CO.UK H'CAP 5f (F)
3:40 (3:40) (Class 6) (0-60,64) 4-Y-0+ £1,911 (£564; £282) Stalls High

Form RPR
0-21 1 **Decider (USA)**13 718 5-8-10 57 KevinGhunowa(5) 1 77
(R A Harris) *led: hdd over 3f out: rdn to ld wl over 1f out: r.o wl: eased nr fin* 5/2[2]
1121 2 3 1/4 **Alexander Huricane (IRE)**8 782 4-9-8 64 6ex NCallan 2 72
(K A Ryan) *sn chsng wnr: led over 3f out: rdn and hdd wl over 1f out: styd on same pce* 11/10[1]
3043 3 1 1/4 **Owed**7 786 6-9-4 60 (tp) PatCosgrave 4 64
(R Bastiman) *s.i.s: outpcd: hdwy u.p over 1f out: nt rch ldrs* 9/1[3]
3350 4 nk **Pappas Image**7 790 4-8-4 46 oh1 (v) NeilPollard 7 49
(A J McCabe) *chsd ldrs: rdn 1/2-way: no ex fnl f* 33/1
4211 5 1 1/2 **Blackheath (IRE)**19 642 12-8-7 54 KellyHarrison(5) 6 51
(S T Mason) *chsd ldrs over 3f out: hmpd 1/2-way: n.d after* 20/1
400- 6 1 1/4 **Piccleyes**280 2343 7-7-11 46 oh1 (b) StacyRenwick(7) 8 39
(A J McCabe) *sn outpcd: nvr nrr* 100/1
5-32 7 3 **Elusive Warrior (USA)**57 155 5-8-11 53 (be1) StephenDonohoe 5 35
(A J McCabe) *s.i.s and hmpd s: outpcd* 10/1
-560 8 1/2 **Jabraan (USA)**7 786 6-7-12 47 oh1 ow1 (p) MCGeran(7) 10 27
(Mrs R A Carr) *sn outpcd* 100/1
0021 9 nk **Tenancy (IRE)**40 371 4-8-6 48 (p) PatrickMathers 9 27
(A J McCabe) *chsd ldrs: rdn 1/2-way: wknd over 1f out* 12/1
0534 F **Earl Compton (IRE)**6 800 4-8-13 55 (b) MickyFenton 3 —
(Stef Liddiard) *chsd ldrs tl broke leg & fell 1/2-way: dead* 16/1

59.09 secs (-0.61) **Going Correction** -0.075s/f (Stan) 10 Ran SP% 118.5
Speed ratings (Par 101): **101,95,93,93,90 88,84,83,82,—**
CSF £5.55 CT £19.57 TOTE £3.60: £1.70, £1.30, £1.80; EX 7.30 Trifecta £40.80 Pool: £802.09 - 13.95 winning units..
Owner Robert Bailey **Bred** Green Willow Farms **Trained** Earlswood, Monmouths

FOCUS
A moderate sprint, though a strong pace and the winner proved different class to the others. The front pair disputed the lead throughout the contest and little else ever got involved. Solid form, with the first two on an upward curve.

847 BET UEFA CUP - BETDAQ H'CAP 1m 4f (F)
4:25 (4:25) (Class 5) (0-75,73) 4-Y-0+ £2,593 (£765; £383) Stalls Low

Form RPR
4425 1 **My Mentor (IRE)**12 728 4-8-12 67 SebSanders 6 75
(Sir Mark Prescott) *sn pushed along in rr: reminders 9f out: hdwy over 7f out: led over 4f out: rdn 3f out: all out* 4/1[2]
2-04 2 1 1/4 **Kylkenny**19 638 13-9-2 72 (t) TravisBlock(3) 3 78
(H Morrison) *prom: rdn over 4f out: sn outpcd: hdwy to chse wnr over 2f out: styd on* 20/1
-511 3 13 **Exit To Luck (GER)**18 658 7-9-6 73 (b) ChrisCatlin 5 60
(S Gollings) *chsd ldrs: led over 6f out: rdn and hdd over 4f out: wknd over 2f out* 4/1[2]
2121 4 15 **My Friend Fritz**7 789 8-9-4 71 6ex PhillipMakin 2 35
(P W Hiatt) *chsd ldrs: rdn 1/2-way: sn swtchd rt and wknd* 6/5[1]
04-0 5 3 **Jazrawy**10 344 6-9-4 71 DanielTudhope 7 31
(D Carroll) *s.i.s: sn rcvrd to ld: hdd over 6f out: rdn and wknd over 4f out* 9/1
045- 6 67 **Active Asset (IRE)**142 6357 6-9-3 70 StephenDonohoe 1 —
(A J McCabe) *s.i.s: sn chsng ldrs: lost pl over 7f out: sn bhd: t.o fnl 5f* 17/2[3]

2m 44.13s (3.13) **Going Correction** +0.30s/f (Slow)
WFA 4 from 6yo+ 2lb 6 Ran SP% 110.7
Speed ratings (Par 103): **101,100,91,81,79 34**
CSF £64.73 TOTE £5.60: £2.20, £2.90; EX 34.30.
Owner Mr And Mrs Arthur Finn **Bred** B D Burnett **Trained** Newmarket, Suffolk
■ Stewards' Enquiry : Seb Sanders five-day ban: used whip with excessive frequency (Mar 22-26)

FOCUS
A very strange race in which they went a furious pace early, but they were virtually walking at the end. The early tempo certainly sorted out the men from the boys. The form is rated through the runner-up.
My Friend Fritz Official explanation: jockey said gelding hung right and lost its action back straight
Jazrawy Official explanation: jockey said gelding finished lame

848 BET MULTIPLES - BETDAQ MAIDEN STKS 6f (F)
5:05 (5:07) (Class 5) 3-Y-0+ £2,457 (£725; £362) Stalls Low

Form RPR
02- 1 **Minus Fifteen (IRE)**122 6755 3-8-13 0 NCallan 6 85+
(K A Ryan) *s.i.s: sn chsng ldrs: led over 3f out: rdn clr over 1f out: eased ins fnl f* 8/11[1]
33 2 5 **Young Gladiator (IRE)**15 700 3-8-13 0 TomEaves 5 66
(Miss J A Camacho) *trckd ldrs: plld hrd: rdn 1/2-way: chsd wnr 2f out: sn hung lft: styd on same pce* 9/1[3]
00- 3 2 1/2 **Fujin Dancer (FR)**145 6281 3-8-13 0 PaulHanagan 8 59
(R A Fahey) *s.i.s: hld up in tch: rdn over 2f out: sn outpcd* 14/1
03- 4 1 **Fools Gold**88 7139 3-8-13 0 PaulEddery 3 56
(G D Blake) *chsd ldrs over 3f* 16/1
-422 5 5 **Jal Music**15 700 3-8-8 67 (p) KevinGhunowa(5) 4 41
(R A Harris) *led: hdd over 3f out: rdn and wknd over 1f out* 3/1[2]
6 8 **Moonage Daydream (IRE)** 3-8-13 0 DavidAllan 2 17
(T D Easterby) *s.i.s: outpcd* 50/1
036- 7 1 **Swindon Town Flyer (IRE)**139 6419 3-8-13 68 SamHitchcott 7 14
(A B Haynes) *chsd ldrs over 3f* 12/1
8 58 **One Way Love** 3-8-2 0 ow1 JackDean(7) 1 —
(W G M Turner) *sn outpcd* 66/1

1m 18.26s (1.76) **Going Correction** +0.30s/f (Slow) 8 Ran SP% 116.6
Speed ratings (Par 103): **100,93,90,88,82 71,70,—**
CSF £8.97 TOTE £1.50: £1.40, £1.90, £2.70; EX 8.00 Trifecta £45.60 Pool: £322.80 - 5.02 winning units..
Owner Clipper Logistics **Bred** Denis McDonnell **Trained** Hambleton, N Yorks

FOCUS
A very modest maiden, won easily by the odds-on favourite with little to get excited about amongst the rest. The winner looks the type to progress.
Jal Music Official explanation: jockey said gelding hung left

849 TRY BETDAQ FOR AN EXCHANGE H'CAP 6f (F)
5:40 (5:41) (Class 5) (0-70,69) 3-Y-0 £2,593 (£765; £383) Stalls Low

Form RPR
025- 1 **Lieutenant Pigeon**102 6977 3-9-0 65 PaulEddery 8 80+
(G D Blake) *trckd ldr: led over 1f out: rdn clr* 6/1[3]
4362 2 6 **Loose Caboose (IRE)**21 619 3-9-2 67 (p) SebSanders 6 64
(A J McCabe) *chsd ldrs: rdn over 2f out: sn hung lft: styd on same pce fnl f* 5/2[1]
-314 3 1 1/4 **Note Perfect**24 583 3-8-4 55 oh1 (b) DaleGibson 2 48
(M W Easterby) *led: rdn and hdd over 1f out: no ex* 10/1
21-3 4 1 3/4 **Wiseman's Diamond (USA)**60 131 3-9-4 69 NCallan 3 57
(K A Ryan) *chsd ldrs: rdn over 2f out: wknd over 1f out* 9/1
4335 5 1 **Bold Diva**21 619 3-8-8 62 (v) KirstyMilczarek(3) 4 47
(A W Carroll) *hld up in tch: rdn over 2f out: hung lft and wknd over 1f out* 7/1
6101 6 1 1/2 **Magical Song**18 656 3-8-4 55 oh2 FrankieMcDonald 1 36
(P A Blockley) *sn outpcd* 3/1[2]
603- 7 6 **Minwir (IRE)**159 5939 3-9-1 66 FrancisNorton 5 29
(M Quinn) *sn pushed along in rr: bhd fr 1/2-way* 6/1[3]
435- 8 2 **Turn And River (IRE)**224 4041 3-8-6 57 TWilliams 7 14
(M Brittain) *prom: sn drvn along: wknd over 2f out* 33/1

1m 16.96s (0.46) **Going Correction** +0.30s/f (Slow) 8 Ran SP% 116.7
Speed ratings (Par 98): **108,100,98,96,94 92,84,82**
CSF £21.90 CT £150.53 TOTE £9.40: £1.70, £1.30, £2.90; EX 28.50 Trifecta £271.20 Part won. Pool: £382.10 - 0.50 winning units. Place 6 £68.92, Place 5 £44.28.
Owner P A Mason **Bred** P A Mason **Trained** Aylesbury, Bucks
■ A winner with only his second GB runner - his first was in the previous race - for Gavin Blake, previously based in S. Africa.

FOCUS
A moderate handicap, but a very impressive winner and the time was smart, 1.3 seconds faster than the preceding maiden. Those that raced up with the pace were very much at an advantage. Big improvement from the winner but the form looks worth taking at face value.
Magical Song Official explanation: jockey said colt never travelled
T/Plt: £64.70 to a £1 stake. Pool: £47,558.55. 536.00 winning tickets. T/Qpdt: £12.80 to a £1 stake. Pool: £2,860.30. 164.60 winning tickets. CR

843 SOUTHWELL (L-H)
Wednesday, March 12

OFFICIAL GOING: Standard
Wind: Strong half behind, becoming moderate Weather: Dry and sunny

850 BET CHELTENHAM FESTIVAL - BETDAQ H'CAP 7f (F)
1:50 (1:52) (Class 5) (0-75,81) 4-Y-0+ £2,593 (£765; £383) Stalls Low

Form RPR
2131 1 **Silver Hotspur**8 791 4-9-10 81 6ex FrancisNorton 9 94+
(M Wigham) *trckd ldr: led wl over 1f out: pushed out* 4/6[1]
2540 2 1 1/4 **Divertimenti (IRE)**13 729 4-8-13 70 RobertWinston 4 80
(C R Dore) *bmpd s: t.k.h and hld up: hdwy 1/2-way: rdn to chal over 1f out: sn drvn and one pce ins fnl f* 6/1[2]
12-3 3 4 1/2 **Dasheena**65 72 5-8-9 66 (be) PatrickMathers 1 65
(A J McCabe) *in tch: hdwy wl over 2f out: rdn to chse ldng pair wl over 1f out: sn drvn and no imp* 15/2[3]
-313 4 2 1/2 **Cerebus**37 431 6-9-1 72 (bt) StephenDonohoe 6 65
(A J McCabe) *led: rdn along over 2f out: hdd wl over 1f out and sn wknd* 9/1
000- 5 7 **Oi Vay Joe (IRE)**170 5684 4-9-4 75 GregFairley 3 50
(W Jarvis) *a in rr* 16/1
030- 6 1/2 **Indian's Feather (IRE)**149 6232 7-8-13 70 TomEaves 5 44
(N Tinkler) *chsd ldng pair: rdn along 1/2-way: hung lft over 2f out and sn wknd* 8/1

1m 30.92s (0.62) **Going Correction** +0.375s/f (Slow) 6 Ran SP% 113.0
Speed ratings (Par 103): **111,109,104,101,93 93**
CSF £5.30 CT £15.95 TOTE £1.50: £1.30, £2.60; EX 6.70 Trifecta £22.80 Pool: £436.20, 13.53 winning units.
Owner D Hassan **Bred** Theobalds Stud **Trained** Newmarket, Suffolk

FOCUS
Not a particularly competitive handicap especially with the three non-runners, but they went a good pace thanks to Cerebus and the winning time was smart. The first two pulled right away from the others and the winner ran right up to his latest form.

851 BET MULTIPLES - BETDAQ CLAIMING STKS 1m 3f (F)
2:25 (2:25) (Class 6) 4-Y-0+ £1,774 (£523; £262) Stalls Low

Form RPR
2-11 1 **Yakimov (USA)**19 653 9-9-8 85 VinceSlattery 2 84+
(D J Wintle) *hld up: smooth hdwy 4f out: led 2f out: sn pushed clr: easily* 4/9[1]
1343 2 4 1/2 **Starcross Maid**19 658 6-8-9 55 ChrisCatlin 6 59
(J F Coupland) *trckd ldng pair: hdwy 4f out: led briefly over 2f out: sn rdn and hdd 2f out: drvn over 1f out: kpt on: no ch w wnr* 4/1[2]
134 3 6 **Dot's Delight**8 787 4-8-4 45 (p) GregFairley 5 45
(K J Burke) *chsd ldr: led over 3f out: rdn and hdd over 2f out: plugged on same pce* 14/1
1344 4 3 1/4 **Global Traffic**8 788 4-8-9 57 (v) StephenDonohoe 1 45
(D Shaw) *hld up and bhd: hdwy 3f out: rdn over 2f out and sn no imp* 15/2[3]
00-0 5 4 1/2 **Wickedish**7 277 4-7-13 50 (t) WilliamBuick(3) 4 31
(M J Gingell) *chsd ldrs: rdn along 4f out: sn wknd* 33/1
0-00 6 41 **Cavallo Di Ferro (IRE)**7 517 4-8-4 52 DuranFentiman(3) 3 —
(M J Gingell) *led: rdn along 4f out: sn hdd & wknd* 33/1

2m 32.83s (4.83) **Going Correction** +0.375s/f (Slow)
WFA 4 from 6yo+ 1lb 6 Ran SP% 113.6
Speed ratings (Par 101): **97,93,89,87,83 53**
CSF £2.67 TOTE £1.50: £1.10, £1.60; EX 2.90.The winner was claimed by Ollie Pears for £12,000
Owner B E T Partnership **Bred** Jane & Jeff Wooder **Trained** Naunton, Gloucs

FOCUS
A routine claimer run at an ordinary pace and the favourite turned it into a procession. The second and third help pin down the level.

852 BET "CHAMPION BUMPER" - BETDAQ H'CAP 1m (F)
3:00 (3:00) (Class 5) (0-75,72) 4-Y-0+ £2,593 (£765; £383) Stalls Low

Form RPR
0-65 **1** **Rock Anthem (IRE)**[32] 504 4-9-0 68 ChrisCatlin 6 77
(Mike Murphy) *hld up: hdwy on outer 1/2-way: cl up 3f out: rdn to ld wl over 1f out: styd on* **6/1**
101- **2** 1 1/4 **Ansells Pride (IRE)**[124] 6746 5-9-4 72 TomEaves 4 78
(B Smart) *t.k.h: hld up: hdwy 3f out: sn rdn to chse ldng pair and outpcd over 2f out: styd on wl appr fnl f: tk 2nd last 75yds* **3/1**[3]
66-1 **3** 2 **Yes One (IRE)**[12] 752 4-9-3 71 NCallan 2 73+
(K A Ryan) *trckd ldr: hdwy to ld 3f out: rdn over 2f out: drvn: edgd rt and hdd wl over 1f out: wknd ins fnl f* **15/8**[1]
-266 **4** 10 **Jord (IRE)**[12] 752 4-9-2 70 AndrewElliott 5 50
(A J McCabe) *led: rdn along over 3f out: sn hdd & wknd* **16/1**
2342 **5** 1 1/2 **Steig (IRE)**[16] 697 5-8-8 62 JamesDoyle 1 39
(Carl Llewellyn) *chsd ldng pair on inner: rdn along over 3f out: sn wknd* **11/4**[2]
06-6 **6** 3 **King Of The Moors (USA)**[19] 660 5-9-3 71 PhillipMakin 3 41
(T D Barron) *chsd ldrs: rdn along over 3f out and sn wknd* **16/1**
1m 46.11s (2.41) **Going Correction** +0.375s/f (Slow) 6 Ran SP% **112.5**
Speed ratings (Par 103): **102,100,98,88,87 84**
CSF £24.26 TOTE £7.00: £2.50, £2.10; EX 38.80.
Owner Ronald Bright **Bred** Mervyn Stewkesbury **Trained** Westoning, Beds

FOCUS
A modest handicap run at a sound pace and the front trio pulled miles clear of the others. Solid enough form which should stand up.
Steig(IRE) Official explanation: trainer's rep had no explanation for the poor form shown

853 BETDAQ THE BETTING EXCHANGE (S) STKS 1m (F)
3:40 (3:40) (Class 6) 3-Y-0 £1,774 (£523; £262) Stalls Low

Form RPR
40-0 **1** **Secret Meaning**[7] 797 3-8-6 60 (p) JackDean(7) 6 47
(W G M Turner) *trckd ldrs: hdwy to chse ldr 3f out and sn rdn: drvn over 1f out: styd on ins fnl f to ld last 100yds* **5/2**[1]
5-63 **2** nk **Dickie Valentine**[24] 597 3-8-12 48 (b) AdamKirby 4 45
(M R Bosley) *hld up: effrt 3f out: sn rdn and outpcd: styd on wl u.p appr fnl f: tk 2nd nr fin* **11/4**[2]
00-5 **3** nk **Distant Noble**[48] 279 3-8-12 40 PaulMulrennan 5 44
(R Brotherton) *chsd ldrs: rdn along wl over 2f out: kpt on u.p appr fnl f* **16/1**
3104 **4** nk **Don Picolo**[1] 845 3-9-4 56 (b) FrankieMcDonald 3 50
(P A Blockley) *t.k.h: cl up: led wl over 3f out: pushed clr 2f out: rdn: hung lft and wknd ins fnl f: hdd last 100yds* **5/2**[1]
0-46 **5** 23 **Littonfountain (IRE)**[14] 712 3-8-12 59 (v[1]) DarrenWilliams 2 —
(K R Burke) *led: pushed along and hdd wl over 3f out: sn rdn and wknd* **7/2**[3]
1m 50.45s (6.75) **Going Correction** +0.375s/f (Slow) 5 Ran SP% **111.9**
Speed ratings (Par 96): **81,80,80,80,57**
CSF £9.86 TOTE £3.60: £1.80, £1.70; EX 11.20.There was no bid for the winner.
Owner Sparsholt Stud **Bred** P C Hunt **Trained** Sigwells, Somerset

FOCUS
A bad seller run at a moderate early pace and a race of changing fortunes with Don Picolo looking sure to score, but then stopping dramatically late on. The first four were separated by necks and this is not form to be with. The winning time was very slow, 4.34 seconds slower than the preceding handicap.
Littonfountain(IRE) Official explanation: jockey said gelding moved poorly in straight

854 ALL NEW @ BETDAQ.CO.UK H'CAP 1m 6f (F)
4:25 (4:26) (Class 5) (0-75,73) 4-Y-0+ £2,457 (£725; £362) Stalls Low

Form RPR
3-31 **1** **They All Laughed**[22] 617 5-9-9 71 ChrisCatlin 2 82+
(P W Hiatt) *trckd ldng pair: hdwy to ld over 3f out: rdn clr over 1f out: kpt on* **5/6**[1]
5113 **2** 3 1/2 **Exit To Luck (GER)**[1] 847 7-9-6 73 (b) JamieJones(5) 4 78
(S Gollings) *trckd ldr: hdwy to ld over 4f out: rdn and hdd over 3f out: sn drvn and kpt on same pce u.p appr fnl f* **7/2**[3]
3443 **3** 5 **Red Wine**[10] 675 9-9-1 63 StephenDonohoe 5 62
(A J McCabe) *hld up: hdwy 3f out: ch wl over 1f out: sn rdn and btn* **11/4**[2]
2305 **4** 45 **Victory Quest (IRE)**[20] 638 8-9-5 67 (v) RobertWinston 1 7+
(Mrs S Lamyman) *led: rdn along and hdd over 4f out: sn drvn and wknd: eased over 2f out* **9/1**
3m 15.93s (7.63) **Going Correction** +0.375s/f (Slow) 4 Ran SP% **113.4**
Speed ratings (Par 103): **93,91,88,62**
CSF £4.40 TOTE £1.80; EX 4.20.
Owner Clive Roberts **Bred** T G And B B Mills **Trained** Hook Norton, Oxon

FOCUS
A small field and modest handicap form. The winner is progressing but did not need to find much to follow up his recent victory.

855 BETDAQPOKER.CO.UK MAIDEN STKS 6f (F)
5:05 (5:08) (Class 5) 3-Y-0 £2,457 (£725; £362) Stalls Low

Form RPR
0-3 **1** **Baunagain (IRE)**[15] 705 3-9-3 0 PatCosgrave 2 76+
(M J Wallace) *trckd ldrs on inner: hdwy 1/2-way: rdn to ld 2f out: sn clr* **7/2**[3]
600- **2** 6 **Black Dahlia**[129] 6665 3-8-12 66 NCallan 3 49
(A J McCabe) *cl up: led wl over 2f out: sn rdn and hdd 2f out: drvn and sn one pce* **15/8**[2]
3 1 1/2 **Hot Bertie** 3-9-0 0 TravisBlock(3) 6 50
(Jedd O'Keeffe) *chsd ldrs: rdn along wl over 2f out: kpt on same pce* **16/1**
2232 **4** 3 3/4 **Jalons Bridewell**[14] 721 3-9-3 70 FrancisNorton 1 38
(M Quinn) *led: rdn along 1/2-way: sn hdd and drvn: btn wl over 1f out* **6/4**[1]
50- **5** 11 **Notepad**[277] 2457 3-8-12 0 LPKeniry 5 —
(W Jarvis) *sn rdn along and outpcd in rr: bhd fr 1/2-way* **10/1**
6 31 **Marysedge** 3-8-12 0 PaulMulrennan 4 —
(R Brotherton) *s.i.s: a in rr: wl bhd fr 1/2-way* **33/1**
1m 18.38s (1.88) **Going Correction** +0.375s/f (Slow) 6 Ran SP% **114.9**
Speed ratings (Par 98): **102,94,92,87,72 31**
CSF £10.89 TOTE £4.00: £1.90, £1.40; EX 15.00.
Owner P Ransley **Bred** Patrick Doyle **Trained** Newmarket, Suffolk

FOCUS
A modest maiden and not easy form to rate, with the favourite not running his race, but the winner looks a fairly promising type.

856 BACK OR LAY AT BETDAQ FILLIES' H'CAP 6f (F)
5:40 (5:40) (Class 6) (0-65,69) 4-Y-0+ £1,774 (£523; £262) Stalls Low

Form RPR
4221 **1** **Another Genepi (USA)**[4] 839 5-9-10 69 6ex (b) FergalLynch 5 83+
(Andrew Reid) *chsd ldrs: hdwy 1/2-way: led 2f out: sn rdn clr* **13/8**[1]
0-22 **2** 7 **Limonia (GER)**[8] 790 6-7-11 49 oh1 JamieKyne(7) 7 42
(Mike Murphy) *in rr: hdwy wl over 2f out: sn rdn and styd on appr fnl f: no ch w wnr* **15/8**[2]
455- **3** 5 **Silly Gilly (IRE)**[159] 5970 4-8-12 57 AndrewElliott 1 35
(R E Barr) *led for 1f: sn rdn along and outpcd 1/2-way: kpt on u.p fnl 2f* **20/1**
2000 **4** 1 3/4 **Cadogen Square**[18] 684 6-8-4 49 oh4 (b) LiamJones 6 22
(Mrs R A Carr) *chsd ldng pair: hdwy to ld 1/2-way: sn rdn and hdd 2f out: wknd over 1f out* **33/1**
3400 **5** 1 1/2 **Dancing Duo**[12] 749 4-8-7 55 (v) TolleyDean(3) 2 23
(D Shaw) *in rr tl sme late hdwy* **10/1**
0-00 **6** 7 **Fly Time**[46] 318 4-8-1 49 oh4 (p) WilliamBuick(3) 3 —
(Mrs L Williamson) *cl up: led after 1f: hdd 1/2-way and sn wknd* **33/1**
060- **7** 5 **Dressed To Dance (IRE)**[148] 6256 4-9-4 63 (v) NCallan 4 —
(N Tinkler) *chsd ldrs to 1/2-way: sn wknd* **7/2**[3]
1m 16.65s (0.15) **Going Correction** +0.375s/f (Slow) 7 Ran SP% **114.8**
Speed ratings (Par 98): **114,104,98,95,93 84,77**
CSF £4.94 TOTE £2.60: £1.70, £1.40; EX 5.20 Place 6 £ 25.98, Place 5 £ 22.44.
Owner A S Reid **Bred** Joseph Lacombe Stables Inc **Trained** Mill Hill, London NW7

FOCUS
Not a strong handicap on paper, but it was run in a very smart time indeed, 1.73 seconds quicker than the preceding maiden. Another Genepi came here in good form and this win could have been rated higher.
T/Plt: £62.90 to a £1 stake. Pool: £82,541.00. 956.95 winning tickets. T/Qpdt: £35.60 to a £1 stake. Pool: £4,435.40. 92.00 winning tickets. JR

832 WOLVERHAMPTON (A.W) (L-H)
Wednesday, March 12

OFFICIAL GOING: Standard
Wind: Fresh, across

857 BET UEFA CUP - BETDAQ H'CAP 5f 20y(P)
6:50 (6:52) (Class 6) (0-50,50) 4-Y-0+ £1,774 (£523; £262) Stalls Low

Form RPR
3424 **1** **Now You See Me**[13] 726 4-8-5 47 ChrisCatlin 7 58
(K McAuliffe) *chsd ldrs: strly rdn 2f out: led ins fnl f: drvn out* **7/2**[2]
-020 **2** 1 1/4 **White Ledger (IRE)**[20] 641 9-8-7 49 JimmyQuinn 1 55
(R E Peacock) *hld up: rdn and hdwy on ins over 1f out: chsd wnr ins fnl f* **14/1**
-321 **3** 1 1/2 **Ducal Regancy Red**[13] 725 4-8-3 50 KellyHarrison(5) 6 51
(C J Teague) *wnt rt s: sn trckd ldrs: ev ch over 1f out: edgd rt ins fnl f* **9/2**[3]
-354 **4** 1 **Taboor (IRE)**[20] 641 10-8-6 48 PaulHanagan 8 45
(R M H Cowell) *s.i.s: sn in tch on outside: rdn over 2f out: one pce fnl f* **13/2**
-432 **5** 1/2 **Town House**[20] 641 6-7-13 48 ow1 DeclanCannon(7) 5 43
(B P J Baugh) *led: rdn over 1f out: hdd and fdd ins fnl f* **5/2**[1]
000- **6** 1 1/4 **Beamsley Beacon**[131] 6629 7-8-3 48 ow1 KirstyMilczarek(3) 4 39
(Miss Tracy Waggott) *trckd ldrs rdn 3f out: sn wknd* **8/1**
0-46 **7** 2 1/2 **Melandre**[20] 641 6-8-5 47 TWilliams 2 29
(M Brittain) *s.i.s: t.k.h: bhd after 2f* **8/1**
300- **8** 1 3/4 **Beechside (IRE)**[89] 7137 4-8-6 48 PaulDoe 3 23
(W A Murphy, Ire) *rrd s: a bhd* **22/1**
5/00 **9** 1 **Tiara Boom De Ay (IRE)**[25] 590 4-8-8 50 VinceSlattery 9 22
(D J Wintle) *carried sltly rt s: effrt over 1f out: a bhd* **20/1**
62.78 secs (0.48) **Going Correction** +0.075s/f (Slow) 9 Ran SP% **120.3**
Speed ratings (Par 101): **99,97,94,93,92 90,86,83,81**
CSF £53.47 CT £231.59 TOTE £4.00: £1.70, £2.50, £1.90; EX 61.30.
Owner K W J McAuliffe **Bred** Gainsborough Stud Management Ltd **Trained** Fernham, Oxon

FOCUS
A weak handicap in which the winner built on her recent form in claiming company.
Melandre Official explanation: jockey said mare ran too freely

858 BETDAQ.CO.UK H'CAP 5f 216y(P)
7:20 (7:22) (Class 6) (0-52,55) 4-Y-0+ £1,774 (£523; £262) Stalls Low

Form RPR
2123 **1** **Avoca Dancer (IRE)**[21] 625 5-8-10 50 FrancisNorton 6 58+
(M Wigham) *mid-div: hdwy bef edgd rt over 1f out: rdn to ld ins fnl f* **9/2**
2600 **2** 2 **Calloff The Search**[6] 806 4-8-12 52 (p) MickyFenton 12 54
(Stef Liddiard) *led for 1f: styd prom: led again over 1f out: hdd ins fnl f: nt pce of wnr* **16/1**
2641 **3** 1/2 **The Geester**[8] 790 4-9-1 55 6ex (b) PhillipMakin 7 57+
(S R Bowring) *s.i.s: hdwy on ins over 2f out: edgd lft but r.o ins fnl f* **7/2**[2]
0340 **4** hd **Cantique (IRE)**[15] 708 4-8-0 47 oh1 ow1 RossAtkinson(7) 4 47
(R J Price) *in rr: rdn bef hdwy on ins over 2f out: r.o: nvr nrr* **25/1**
3535 **5** nk **Prettilini**[17] 696 5-8-3 46 oh1 KirstyMilczarek(3) 10 45
(A W Carroll) *a in tch: ev ch on ins ent fnl f: nt qckn* **20/1**
/0-0 **6** hd **Oh Gracious Me (IRE)**[8] 792 4-8-11 51 ow1 (b[1]) StephenDonohoe 1 49
(P A Blockley) *trckd ldrs: rdn 2f out: edgd lft and bmpd 1f out: fdd ins fnl f* **18/1**
4-32 **7** 1 **Desert Hunter (IRE)**[18] 681 5-8-7 47 JimmyQuinn 5 42
(Micky Hammond) *hld up: rdn 2f out: r.o fnl f: nvr nr to chal* **10/3**[1]
3336 **8** hd **Plateau**[29] 530 9-8-12 52 RobertWinston 9 47
(C R Dore) *mid-div: rdn over 2f out: one pce fr over 1f out* **12/1**
00/0 **9** nk **Zorn**[12] 749 9-8-10 50 PatCosgrave 2 44
(P Howling) *a towards rr* **50/1**
44-4 **10** 1 3/4 **Murrisk**[15] 708 4-8-10 50 DavidKinsella 3 39
(Eamon Tyrrell, Ire) *racd on ins: effrt over 1f out: nvr on terms* **4/1**[3]
0-00 **11** 1 **Briery Blaze**[27] 560 5-8-4 49 ow1 (b) JackMitchell(5) 13 34
(J W Unett) *racd on ins: rdn over 2f out: wknd over 1f out* **50/1**
030- **12** 1/2 **White's Ruby**[161] 5897 4-8-8 48 (b) PaulEddery 8 32
(G D Blake) *s.i.s but led after 1f: hdd over 1f out: wkng whn hmpd and bmpd ins fnl f* **15/2**

-036 **13** *3 ¾* **Nabra**[9] 783 4-8-7 **47** TWilliams 11 20
(M Brittain) *in tch on outside tl wknd 2f out* **50/1**
1m 15.79s (0.79) **Going Correction** +0.075s/f (Slow) **13** Ran SP% **128.6**
Speed ratings (Par 101): **97,94,93,93,93 92,91,91,90,88 87,86,81**
CSF £76.24 CT £300.19 TOTE £5.30: £1.50, £4.90, £2.50; EX 66.80.
Owner Have A Go Syndicate & Michael Wigham **Bred** Frank Towey **Trained** Newmarket, Suffolk
FOCUS
A moderate sprint that was relatively competitive. The winner has been in good heart and the form is best rated through the runner-up.
Oh Gracious Me(IRE) Official explanation: jockey said colt lost its action

859 BET CHELTENHAM FESTIVAL - BETDAQ CLAIMING STKS 1m 4f 50y(P)
7:50 (7:50) (Class 5) 4-Y-0+ **£2,590** (£770; £385; £192) **Stalls** Low

Form RPR
0-50 **1** **Kames Park (IRE)**[12] 757 6-9-1 **87** TomEaves 4 79+
(Miss L A Perratt) *stdd s and hld up in rr: hdwy on outside to go 2nd over 2f out: carried rt but led ins fnl f: rdn and jst hld on* **6/5**[1]
241- **2** *shd* **Salute (IRE)**[102] 6999 9-9-5 **77** RobertHavlin 6 83
(P G Murphy) *trckd ldr: led 4f out: rdn 2f out: edgd rt and hdd ins fnl f: no ex cl home* **11/4**[2]
1033 **3** *12* **Looks The Business (IRE)**[7] 794 7-8-8 **63** JackDean[(7)] 3 61
(W G M Turner) *trckd ldrs: rdn 4f out: wknd over 2f out* **20/1**
4312 **4** *4* **Buscador (USA)**[11] 771 9-8-13 **58** RichardKingscote 5 53
(W M Brisbourne) *led tl hdd 4f out: wknd 3f out* **5/1**[3]
4051 **5** *5* **Atlantic Gamble (IRE)**[5] 822 8-8-11 **49** (p) AndrewElliott 1 44
(K R Burke) *hld up: hdwy over 4f out: rdn and ev ch over 3f out: wknd over 2f* **13/2**
2m 39.53s (-1.57) **Going Correction** +0.075s/f (Slow) **5** Ran SP% **106.9**
Speed ratings (Par 103): **108,107,99,97,93**
CSF £4.37 TOTE £1.80: £1.30, £1.70; EX 4.70.Kames Park was claimed by Adrian Swingler for £10,000.
Owner Mrs June Delaney **Bred** Pat Beirne **Trained** Carluke, S Lanarks
■ Stewards' Enquiry : Tom Eaves two-day ban: used whip with excessive force (Mar 23,24)
FOCUS
An uncompetitive claimer in which the runners finished in the order official ratings suggested. The time was decent though and the first two came right away, with the runner-up's recent form perhaps the best guide.

860 BET "RYANAIR CHASE" - BETDAQ H'CAP 1m 1f 103y(P)
8:20 (8:20) (Class 5) (0-75,75) 4-Y-0+ **£2,590** (£770; £385; £192) **Stalls** Low

Form RPR
-426 **1** **Saviour Sand (IRE)**[29] 529 4-8-13 **70** HayleyTurner 4 77
(D R C Elsworth) *t.k.h: mde all: fnd ex whn chal ins fnl f* **6/1**
-541 **2** *¾* **Kildare Sun (IRE)**[6] 809 6-9-2 **73** 6ex PatCosgrave 5 79
(J Mackie) *in tch: hdwy over 3f out: wnt 2nd over 1f out bef chal ins fnl f: hld nr fin* **11/4**[2]
-163 **3** *1* **Watchmaker**[12] 747 5-8-11 **68** PaulDoe 8 72
(Miss Tor Sturgis) *trckd wnr: rdn 3f out: lost 2nd over 1f out: kpt on one pce fnl f* **8/1**
2122 **4** *½* **Given A Choice (IRE)**[12] 750 6-9-4 **75** (p) ChrisCatlin 2 78
(J Pearce) *s.i.s: in rr: rdn over 3f out: hdwy over 1f out: r.o fnl f: nvr nrr* **3/1**[2]
1121 **5** *nk* **Morbick**[16] 697 4-9-2 **73** TGMcLaughlin 6 76
(W M Brisbourne) *mid-div: sltly hmpd 3f out: nvr on terms* **2/1**[1]
150- **6** *1* **Final Tune (IRE)**[221] 4153 5-9-3 **74** AdamKirby 3 75
(Miss M E Rowland) *trckd ldrs: rdn over 2f out: wknd over 1f out* **9/1**
0- **7** *2 ½* **Mac Don (IRE)**[135] 6553 4-8-11 **68** RobertHavlin 1 64
(Eamon Tyrrell, Ire) *mid-div: reminders 4f out: nvr nr to chal* **66/1**
235- **8** *12* **Timber Treasure (USA)**[161] 5915 4-9-2 **73** (e[1]) FrancisNorton 7 46
(Paul Green) *t.k.h: in rr whn rdn 3f out: eased whn btn ent fnl f* **12/1**
2m 1.29s (-0.41) **Going Correction** +0.075s/f (Slow) **8** Ran SP% **118.3**
Speed ratings (Par 103): **104,103,102,102,101 100,98,87**
CSF £40.18 CT £269.46 TOTE £7.90: £1.60, £2.40, £1.90; EX 58.90.
Owner The Save Your Sand Partnership **Bred** Michael Munnelly **Trained** Newmarket, Suffolk
■ Stewards' Enquiry : Adam Kirby caution: used whip without giving gelding time to respond
FOCUS
A fair handicap in which the winner sset an ordinary pace and returned to his best form.
Final Tune(IRE) Official explanation: jockey said gelding hung left

861 BET "PERTEMPS FINAL HURDLE" - BETDAQ H'CAP 7f 32y(P)
8:50 (8:50) (Class 6) (0-60,60) 4-Y-0+ **£2,047** (£604; £302) **Stalls** High

Form RPR
200- **1** **Playtotheaudience**[145] 6304 5-8-7 **49** (v[1]) PaulHanagan 4 59
(R A Fahey) *in tch: rdn 3f out: drvn to ld ins fnl f* **12/1**
233- **2** *½* **Cap St Jean (IRE)**[109] 6567 4-9-0 **59** RussellKennemore[(3)] 3 68
(R Hollinshead) *hld up in rr: hdwy over 2f out: rdn to go 2nd nr fin* **4/1**[1]
-104 **3** *½* **Mineral Rights (USA)**[18] 681 4-9-2 **58** TomEaves 9 66+
(Miss L A Perratt) *trckd ldr: led over 2f out: rdn and hdd ins fnl f: lost 2nd nr fin* **6/1**[3]
6-00 **4** *1* **Cabourg (IRE)**[12] 749 5-9-1 **57** PatCosgrave 12 62
(R Bastiman) *trckd ldrs: rdn and swtchd lft over 1f out: ev ch tl fdd ins fnl f* **15/2**
-444 **5** *nk* **Circus Polka (USA)**[11] 768 4-8-13 **55** (bt) TGMcLaughlin 6 59
(W M Brisbourne) *trckd ldrs: rdn over 2f out: wknd fnl f* **8/1**
6413 **6** *1 ½* **Aggbag**[14] 724 4-9-0 **56** AndrewElliott 11 56
(B P J Baugh) *in rr: r.o fnl f: nvr nrr* **15/2**
00- **7** *1 ½* **Ashleigh Anderson (FR)**[195] 4978 4-8-12 **54** RobertHavlin 5 50
(Eamon Tyrrell, Ire) *mid-div: outpcd over 2f out: kpt on but nvr on terms after* **20/1**
5431 **8** *nk* **Guadaloup**[19] 663 6-8-11 **53** TWilliams 1 48
(M Brittain) *led tl hdd over 2f out: fdd ins fnl f* **9/2**[2]
0563 **9** *3 ¼* **Buzzin'Boyzee (IRE)**[19] 663 5-8-6 **55** RichardEvans[(7)] 10 42
(P D Evans) *hld up on outside: rdn over 2f out: nvr on terms after* **20/1**
0-50 **10** *1* **Elusive Dreams (USA)**[13] 730 4-9-1 **60** TolleyDean[(3)] 2 44
(D Shaw) *a in rr and hung lft fr over 1f out* **33/1**
00-3 **11** *¾* **Attacca**[8] 792 7-8-10 **52** ChrisCatlin 7 34
(J R Weymes) *mid-div: rdn 1/2-way: sn btn* **8/1**
2003 **12** *¾* **Krakatau (FR)**[27] 560 4-8-11 **53** VinceSlattery 8 33
(D J Wintle) *prom on outside tl rdn 1/2-way: wknd 2f out* **10/1**
1m 29.53s (-0.07) **Going Correction** +0.075s/f (Slow) **12** Ran SP% **127.5**
Speed ratings (Par 101): **103,102,101,100,100 98,96,96,92,91 90,90**
CSF £62.67 CT £338.03 TOTE £16.50: £4.10, £2.20, £1.80; EX 120.70.
Owner David M Knaggs & Mel Roberts **Bred** Dunchurch Lodge Stud Co **Trained** Musley Bank, N Yorks
■ Stewards' Enquiry : Paul Hanagan two-day ban: used whip with excessive frequency (Mar 23,24)

FOCUS
A moderate handicap run at a decent gallop. The first help set the level of the form.
Aggbag Official explanation: jockey said, regarding running and riding, that his orders were to drop in, keep the gelding covered up and try to get a run through horses, adding that he was badly drawn and there was no point in rushing up on the outside, adding further that it got a good run up the inside, ran well, but was beaten by the draw; trainer confirmed adding that the gelding is a bridle horse and needs cover.

862 BET GOLF - BETDAQ CLASSIFIED STKS 1m 141y(P)
9:20 (9:20) (Class 7) 4-Y-0+ **£1,365** (£403; £201) **Stalls** Low

Form RPR
0-21 **1** **High Five Society**[7] 804 4-9-6 **44** (bt) PhillipMakin 13 64+
(S R Bowring) *sn led: hdd over 5f out: led again over 2f out: sn clr: easily* **4/6**[1]
-062 **2** *3* **Keon (IRE)**[7] 804 6-8-11 **45** (p) RussellKennemore[(3)] 9 48
(R Hollinshead) *hld up: hdwy and swtchd lft over 1f out: kpt on u.p to go 2nd nr fin* **6/1**[2]
4030 **3** *hd* **The Power Of Phil**[11] 770 4-9-0 **44** HayleyTurner 10 47
(Miss Joanne Priest) *hld up: rdn over 3f out: styd on wl fnl f: nvr nrr* **10/1**
0364 **4** *hd* **Castle Frome (IRE)**[11] 770 9-9-0 **43** (p) PaulFitzsimons 2 47
(A E Price) *t.k.h: chsd ldrs: wnt 2nd over 1f out tl no ex fnl stages* **8/1**
000- **5** *3 ¾* **Ingleby Hill (IRE)**[30] 4943 4-9-0 **42** JimmyQuinn 5 39
(Micky Hammond) *mid-div: rdn over 2f out: n.d after* **33/1**
205- **6** *4 ½* **Almowj**[381] 557 5-9-0 **44** PaulEddery 6 30
(G H Jones) *mid-div: hdwy to trck ldrs over 3f out: wknd over 1f out* **40/1**
00-3 **7** *¾* **Bonnet O'Bonnie**[18] 684 4-9-0 **43** PatCosgrave 11 28
(J Mackie) *in tch: rdn 4f out: wknd over 2f out* **7/1**[3]
0-60 **8** *2 ¼* **Lizarazu (GER)**[7] 804 9-9-0 **41** VinceSlattery 3 23
(D J Wintle) *mid-div: rdn over 2f out: sn bhd* **66/1**
3046 **9** *1 ½* **Lily La Belle**[18] 684 4-8-11 **42** JerryO'Dwyer[(3)] 7 20
(A W Carroll) *broke wl: sn hdd: prom tl wknd wl over 1f out* **40/1**
/06- **10** *nk* **Crimson Flame (IRE)**[167] 180 5-9-0 **41** StephenDonohoe 4 19
(G F Bridgwater) *in rr: effrt whn swtchd rt over 2f out: nvr on terms* **100/1**
002/ **11** *11* **Royal Lustre**[677] 1460 7-9-0 **45** RobertWinston 12 —
(Miss Tracy Waggott) *sn trckd ldr: led over 5f out: hdd over 2f out: wknd qckly* **33/1**
1m 51.92s (1.42) **Going Correction** +0.075s/f (Slow) **11** Ran SP% **120.2**
Speed ratings (Par 97): **96,93,93,92,89 85,84,82,81,81 71**
CSF £4.98 TOTE £1.80: £1.02, £2.20, £3.30; EX 5.80 Place 6 £58.00, Place 5 £23.34.
Owner The High Five Partnership **Bred** A C M Spalding **Trained** Edwinstowe, Notts
FOCUS
A typical classified stakes but the winner looks above that grade. The placed horses dictate the level of the form.
Keon(IRE) Official explanation: jockey said gelding was denied a clear run
Royal Lustre Official explanation: jockey said gelding had no more to give
T/Plt: £123.50 to a £1 stake. Pool: £115,425.60. 682.05 winning tickets. T/Qpdt: £20.90 to a £1 stake. Pool: £6,500.70. 229.60 winning tickets. JS

850 SOUTHWELL (L-H)
Thursday, March 13

OFFICIAL GOING: Standard
Wind: Moderate behind Weather: Overcast and dry

863 BET SIX NATIONS RUGBY - BETDAQ H'CAP 1m 3f (F)
2:40 (2:41) (Class 6) (0-60,57) 4-Y-0+ **£1,911** (£564; £282) **Stalls** Low

Form RPR
053- **1** **Me Fein**[89] 7157 4-9-2 **55** TPQueally 14 67+
(A P Stringer) *trckd ldrs: hdwy 4f out: led wl over 2f out: rdn clr ent fnl f: styd on* **13/8**[1]
2000 **2** *2 ½* **Satindra (IRE)**[15] 716 4-9-4 **57** (tp) MickyFenton 5 65
(John A Harris) *cl up: led wl over 3f out: rdn and hdd wl over 2f out: sn drvn and kpt on same pce appr fnl f* **20/1**
2234 **3** *2* **Bethanys Boy (IRE)**[8] 794 7-9-3 **55** LPKeniry 6 60
(A M Hales) *hld up in midfield: hdwy 3f out: rdn over 2f out: drvn and styd on appr fnl f: nrst fin* **7/2**[2]
-500 **4** *nk* **Kadouchski (FR)**[16] 708 4-9-0 **53** (e[1]) OscarUrbina 13 57
(Miss E C Lavelle) *chsd ldrs on outer: hdwy 3f out: rdn over 2f out: drvn and one pce fr over 1f out* **4/1**[3]
5030 **5** *3 ¾* **Shifty**[21] 640 9-8-7 **45** PaulHanagan 9 43
(Jedd O'Keeffe) *hld up in midfield: hdwy over 3f out: rdn to chse ldrs over 2f out: sn drvn and one pce* **28/1**
1060 **6** *2 ¾* **Rubilini**[24] 606 4-8-7 **46** ow1 (p) NeilChalmers 7 40
(Miss Sheena West) *s.i.s and bhd: hdwy 5f out: rdn wl over 2f out: drvn and no imp fr over 1f out* **40/1**
000- **7** *1 ¼* **Noble Edge**[195] 5000 5-8-10 **48** (p) JoeFanning 12 40
(Karen McLintock) *hld up towards rr: hdwy over 3f out: rdn over 2f out: no imp* **16/1**
00-0 **8** *shd* **Hunting Haze**[20] 657 5-8-11 **49** (p) PaulEddery 2 41
(Miss S E Hall) *chsd ldrs: rdn along 3f out: drvn and wknd fnl 2f* **66/1**
-030 **9** *5* **Princess Zaha**[26] 585 6-8-7 **45** FergusSweeney 4 29
(A G Newcombe) *chsd ldrs: pushed along 5f out and sn wknd* **80/1**
636/ **10** *7* **Shami**[660] 1911 9-8-0 **45** (tp) DeanHeslop[(7)] 10 18
(Mrs R A Carr) *a in rr* **40/1**
053- **11** *hd* **Falimar**[160] 5967 4-8-5 **49** KellyHarrison[(5)] 3 21
(C W Fairhurst) *cl up on inner: rdn along over 4f out: sn wknd* **66/1**
5216 **12** *21* **Speagle (IRE)**[8] 802 6-8-12 **57** MarkCoumbe[(7)] 11 —
(D Shaw) *led: rdn along over 4f out: hdd wl over 3f out and sn wknd* **7/2**[2]
00-0 **13** *88* **Watermill (IRE)**[2] 843 5-8-0 **45** (b) MCGeran[(7)] 1 —
(Mrs R A Carr) *sn in rr: rdn along and bhd 1/2-way: t.o fnl 3f* **100/1**
2m 28.15s (0.15) **Going Correction** +0.125s/f (Slow)
WFA 4 from 5yo+ 1lb **13** Ran SP% **126.7**
Speed ratings (Par 101): **104,102,100,100,97 95,94,94,91,86 85,70,6**
CSF £43.76 CT £114.77 TOTE £2.70: £1.30, £6.80, £1.60; EX 59.60 Trifecta £234.90 Pool £453.45 - 1.37 winning units..
Owner Curley Leisure **Bred** Irish National Stud **Trained** Newmarket, Suffolk
■ Stewards' Enquiry : Mark Coumbe three-day ban: careless riding (Mar 24-26)
T P Queally two-day ban: careless riding (Mar 24-25)
FOCUS
A moderate contest with few serious contenders but the pace was sound. The winner bounced back to the level of his easy win last August.

The Form Book, Raceform Ltd, Compton, RG20 6NL

Rubilini Official explanation: jockey said filly missed the break

864 BETDAQ.CO.UK (S) STKS 1m (F)
3:15 (3:16) (Class 6) 3-Y-O+ **£1,774** (£523; £262) **Stalls** Low

Form RPR

5630 **1** **Boundless Prospect (USA)**[15] 716 9-9-12 58......... RosieJessop[(7)] 2 67+
(Miss Gay Kelleway) *s.i.s and bhd: gd hdwy to trck ldrs after 3f: cl up 3f out: rdn to ld wl over 1f out: edgd lft and clr ins fnl f* **5/1**[3]

050- **2** *2 3/4* **Rambling Socks**[83] 2535 5-9-8 41.................................(p) PhillipMakin 8 50
(S R Bowring) *cl up: led 3f out: rdn over 2f out: hdd over 1f out and kpt on same pce* **66/1**

3 *1/2* **Zeffirelli** 3-8-9 0.. LiamJones 3 48
(J L Spearing) *in tch: hdwy over 3f out and sn rdn along: kpt on u.p appr fnl f: nrst fin* **25/1**

6-11 **4** *1* **Blue Empire (IRE)**[21] 640 7-9-12 57.....................(p) MarkCoumbe[(7)] 1 57
(John A Harris) *stdd s and hld up in rr: hdwy on outer 3f out: rdn to chse ldrs and hung lft wl over 1f out: sn no imp* **6/4**[1]

2030 **5** *2 3/4* **Persian Fox (IRE)**[12] 769 4-9-13 47.........................(p) VinceSlattery 5 45
(A G Juckes) *chsd ldrs: rdn along over 2f out: sn drvn and no imp* **16/1**

0560 **6** *6* **Amazing Spirit**[20] 665 3-8-4 39 ow5.............................. SCreighton[(5)] 4 25
(Miss V Haigh) *a in rr: wl bhd fnl 3f* **40/1**

0-10 **7** *1/2* **Ugenius**[2] 844 4-10-0 41................................... KevinGhunowa[(5)] 7 36
(P A Blockley) *led: rdn along and hdd 3f out: sn drvn and wknd fnl 2f* **15/8**[2]

/0-0 **8** *10* **Outlook**[13] 752 5-9-13 63.. MickyFenton 6 7
(P T Midgley) *cl up: rdn along 1/2-way and sn wknd* **17/2**

1m 45.7s (2.00) **Going Correction** +0.125s/f (Slow)
WFA 3 from 4yo+ 18lb **8** Ran SP% **115.6**
Speed ratings (Par 101): **95,92,91,90,88 82,81,71**
CSF £267.17 TOTE £7.10: £2.00, £8.90, £5.00; EX 261.20 TRIFECTA Not won..There was no bid for the winner.
Owner M M Foulger A Maclennan **Bred** Mrs Edgar Scott Jr & Mrs Lawrence Macelree **Trained** Exning, Suffolk
■ A first winner on her first ride for 18-year-old Rosie Jessop.

FOCUS
An uncompetitive seller and not a race to be with, although the winner is better than this level.
Ugenius Official explanation: jockey said gelding ran flat
Outlook Official explanation: jockey said gelding moved badly

865 BET CHELTENHAM FESTIVAL - BETDAQ CLAIMING STKS 1m 3f (F)
3:50 (3:50) (Class 6) 3-Y-O **£1,774** (£523; £262) **Stalls** Low

Form RPR

1134 **1** **Home**[15] 712 3-9-3 72...(p) PatCosgrave 1 70+
(J R Boyle) *hld up: smooth hdwy 4f out: led over 2f out: sn rdn clr* **5/4**[1]

2221 **2** *6* **Coral Shores**[16] 704 3-8-10 59..(v) ChrisCatlin 3 49
(P W Hiatt) *trckd ldrs: hdwy to ld wl over 3f out: rdn and hdd over 2f out: sn drvn and one pce* **7/4**[2]

6-04 **3** *3/4* **Tobago Bay**[19] 674 3-8-11 52.......................................(b) NeilChalmers 5 49
(Miss Sheena West) *cl up: led after 3f: rdn along and hdd over 3f out: sn drvn and kpt on same pce* **16/1**

0213 **4** *17* **Novestar (IRE)**[21] 644 3-8-8 55 ow1.............................. JamieJones[(5)] 4 24
(G J Smith) *led 1f: sn rdn along: lost pl and bhd: hdwy on outer and cl up over 4f out: rdn 3f out and sn wknd* **4/1**[3]

04 **5** *100* **Musharahb**[17] 702 3-8-10 0.. SimonWhitworth 2 —
(M Appleby) *led after 1f tl 8f out: rdn along 1/2-way: lost pl 5f out and sn bhd* **80/1**

2m 30.17s (2.17) **Going Correction** +0.125s/f (Slow) **5** Ran SP% **107.9**
Speed ratings (Par 96): **97,92,92,79,—**
CSF £3.53 TOTE £1.80: £1.20, £1.50; EX 3.30.The winner was the subject of a friendly claim.
Owner M Khan X2 **Bred** A T Macdonald **Trained** Epsom, Surrey

FOCUS
An uncompetitive claimer that was turned into a procession by Home, who was the clear pick of the weights.

866 BET UEFA CUP - BETDAQ H'CAP 5f (F)
4:25 (4:25) (Class 2) (0-100,94) 4-Y-O+ **£10,687** (£3,179; £1,191; £1,191) **Stalls** High

Form RPR

-000 **1** **Canadian Danehill (IRE)**[28] 566 6-9-1 **91**.......................(p) ChrisCatlin 6 99
(R M H Cowell) *cl up: rdn ent fnl f: drvn and qcknd to ld last 100yds* **11/1**

2152 **2** *nk* **Northern Empire (IRE)**[26] 593 5-9-1 **91**................................ NCallan 3 98
(K A Ryan) *trckd ldrs: hdwy 2f out: rdn to chal ent fnl f: ev ch tl drvn: edgd rt and nt qckn nr fin* **9/4**[2]

1225 **3** *1 1/4* **Bo McGinty (IRE)**[5] 836 7-8-6 **82**................................(b) PaulHanagan 1 84
(R A Fahey) *cl up: rdn along and sltly outpcd wl over 1f out: kpt on wl u.p ins fnl f* **7/2**[3]

500- **3** *dht* **Classic Encounter (IRE)**[224] 4090 5-9-3 **93**.............. FergusSweeney 7 95
(D M Simcock) *led: rdn over 1f out: drvn ins fnl f: hdd and no ex last 100yds* **33/1**

6402 **5** *nse* **Fyodor (IRE)**[5] 836 7-9-4 **94**...(p) LiamJones 5 96
(W J Haggas) *dwlt and bmpd s: hdwy to trck ldrs 2f out: swtchd rt and rdn over 1f out: kpt on u.p ins fnl f* **2/1**[1]

060- **6** *3/4* **Luscivious**[138] 6487 4-8-1 **80**...................................(b) WilliamBuick[(3)] 4 80
(A J McCabe) *dwlt and wnt rt s: in rr tl styd on ins fnl f* **11/1**

1105 **7** *1* **Tartatartufata**[26] 593 6-8-5 **88**.........................(v) PatrickDonaghy[(7)] 2 84
(D Shaw) *chsd ldrs: rdn along over 2f out: sn one pce* **16/1**

200- **8** *3* **Cape Royal**[138] 6487 8-9-1 **91**.....................................(bt) PaulFitzsimons 8 76
(J M Bradley) *dwlt: sn cl up: rdn along 2f out: sn wknd* **50/1**

4110 **9** *5* **Godfrey Street**[26] 593 5-8-8 **84**.................................(b) FergalLynch 9 51
(A G Newcombe) *chsd ldrs on outer: rdn along 1/2-way: sn wknd* **12/1**

58.82 secs (-0.88) **Going Correction** +0.05s/f (Slow) **9** Ran SP% **121.5**
Speed ratings (Par 109): **109,108,106,106,106 105,103,98,90**
Place: Classic Encounter £3.90, Bo McGinty £1.00. Tricast: CD/NE/CE £420.08, CD/NE/BM £55.77 CSF £38.02 CT £420.08 TOTE £18.80: £4.10, £1.10; EX 47.40 TRIFECTA CD/NE/BM £98.10 Part won - 0.10 winning units; CD/NE/CE Not won. Pool: £276.42..
Owner T W Morley **Bred** Skymarc Farm Inc And Dr A J O'Reilly **Trained** Six Mile Bottom, Cambs

FOCUS
A good, competitive sprint handicap run at a good pace and resulting in a close finish. Canadian Danehill is rated back to his best and this form should work out.

NOTEBOOK
Canadian Danehill(IRE), who has recently returned from the Dubai Carnival, was clearly none the worse for the travelling and put up a game effort to score. He has yet to be out of the frame in seven runs at this course now, including three wins. (op 8-1)
Northern Empire(IRE), a winner and runner-up on his two previous runs on this track, maintained his good record here and lost nothing in defeat. (op 11-4 tchd 2-1)
Bo McGinty(IRE), another recent course-and-distance winner, ran well again and rallied after looking beaten, his stamina coming into play. (op 4-1 tchd 5-1)
Classic Encounter(IRE) ◆, who had been absent since weakening quickly tried in blinkers in a Group 3 at Glorious Goodwood, showed his usual blinding speed on this first race on Fibresand and only got run out of it in the closing stages. With fitness on his side he could make all in a similar contest. (op 4-1 tchd 5-1)
Fyodor(IRE), in the first-time cheekpieces, missed the break and got a bump early, so did well to finish as close as he did. He has not won for over two years but is knocking at the door. (op 5-2 tchd 11-4)
Godfrey Street Official explanation: jockey said gelding moved badly

867 BET MULTIPLES - BETDAQ MAIDEN STKS 1m (F)
5:05 (5:05) (Class 5) 3-Y-O **£2,457** (£725; £362) **Stalls** Low

Form RPR

3-32 **1** **Ocean Legend (IRE)**[52] 244 3-9-0 72.......................... JerryO'Dwyer[(3)] 5 74
(Miss J Feilden) *a.p: cl up 3f out: rdn to ld wl over 1f out: drvn ins fnl f and kpt on wl* **12/1**

0- **2** *1/2* **Pentathlon (IRE)**[85] 7191 3-9-3 0.. JoeFanning 7 73
(M Johnston) *in tch: pushed along over 3f out: hdwy wl over 1f out: rdn and edgd lft ins fnl f: kpt on* **11/4**[2]

0- **3** *1 1/4* **Allied Powers (IRE)**[149] 6248 3-9-0 0.......................... LukeMorris[(3)] 10 70+
(M L W Bell) *in midfield: hdwy over 2f out: sn rdn and styd on ins fnl f: nrst fin* **50/1**

2 **4** *nk* **Key News (IRE)**[44] 350 3-8-12 0.. NCallan 2 64
(M A Jarvis) *led: rdn along over 2f out: hdd wl over 1f out: sn drvn and wknd ent fnl f* **11/8**[1]

42 **5** *1/2* **Kirkie (USA)**[51] 261 3-9-0 0... DNolan[(3)] 12 68
(S Parr) *chsd ldrs: cl up on outer 3f out: rdn 2f out: drvn: edgd lft and one pce ins fnl f* **5/1**[3]

6 *3 1/4* **Murcar** 3-9-3 0.. AdamKirby 3 61
(C G Cox) *dwlt: sn in midfield: rdn along and outpcd on inner over 3f out: kpt on fnl 2f* **8/1**

7 *11* **Chevaliers Dream (IRE)** 3-9-3 0.. DavidAllan 8 37
(T D Easterby) *s.i.s: a towards rr* **100/1**

43 **8** *3/4* **Boss Hog**[30] 529 3-9-3 0.. StephenDonohoe 1 35
(P A Blockley) *chsd ldrs: rdn along wl over 2f out and grad wknd* **18/1**

9 *12* **Profumo Affair** 3-9-3 0.. HayleyTurner 11 9
(M L W Bell) *sn outpcd and bhd* **40/1**

10 *3/4* **Saintsylvadene** 3-9-3 0.. GrahamGibbons 4 7
(T D Walford) *cl up: rdn along 1/2-way: sn wknd* **80/1**

00 **11** *3/4* **Ten Hour Lunch**[47] 311 3-9-3 0... ChrisCatlin 6 6
(B J Meehan) *a bhd* **100/1**

0- **12** *4* **Trawlerman (IRE)**[174] 5598 3-8-10 0.......................... AshleyMorgan[(7)] 9 —
(M H Tompkins) *s.i.s: a in rr* **18/1**

1m 44.1s (0.40) **Going Correction** +0.125s/f (Slow) **12** Ran SP% **122.4**
Speed ratings (Par 98): **103,102,101,100,100 97,86,85,73,72 71,67**
CSF £46.51 TOTE £15.20: £2.30, £1.40, £11.40; EX 88.20 TRIFECTA Not won..
Owner Ocean Trailers Ltd **Bred** Mark Commins **Trained** Exning, Suffolk

FOCUS
A fair maiden with several who had already hinted at ability plus a couple of interesting newcomers. However, there was little between the first five at the finish. The form should work out.

868 BETDAQ THE BETTING EXCHANGE H'CAP 7f (F)
5:40 (5:41) (Class 6) (0-65,65) 4-Y-O+ **£2,047** (£604; £302) **Stalls** Low

Form RPR

3433 **1** **Arctic Desert**[13] 753 8-9-2 **63**...(t) HayleyTurner 6 67
(Miss Gay Kelleway) *t.k.h: trckd ldrs: rdn over 2f out: drvn appr fnl f: styd on wl to ld last 100yds* **10/1**

5-43 **2** *nk* **Moral Code (IRE)**[20] 653 4-9-4 **65**..................................(p) ChrisCatlin 4 68
(E J O'Neill) *led: rdn along and hdd 3f out: drvn over 1f out: rallied to have ev ch ins fnl f: no ex towards fin* **3/1**[2]

1532 **3** *shd* **Cleveland**[25] 599 6-8-12 **62**................................ RussellKennemore[(3)] 2 65
(R Hollinshead) *plld hrd: cl up: led 3f out: rdn wl over 1f out: drvn ent fnl f: hdd and no ex last 100yds* **7/4**[1]

2500 **4** *2* **Pawn In Life (IRE)**[9] 792 10-8-4 **51** oh6.........................(v) PaulEddery 5 49
(Mrs R A Carr) *hld up in tch: hdwy 2f out: sn rdn and kpt on ins fnl f: nrst fin* **40/1**

-515 **5** *4 1/2* **Todwick Owl**[28] 550 4-8-11 **58**... TPQueally 3 45
(J G Given) *chsd ldrs: effrt over 2f out: sn swtchd lft and rdn wl over 1f out: no imp* **3/1**[2]

-320 **6** *5* **Elusive Warrior (USA)**[2] 846 5-8-6 **53**........................(be[1]) NeilPollard 1 27
(A J McCabe) *cl up: rdn along 1/2-way: wknd over 2f out* **7/1**[3]

1m 31.75s (1.45) **Going Correction** +0.125s/f (Slow) **6** Ran SP% **110.4**
Speed ratings (Par 101): **96,95,95,93,88 82**
CSF £38.45 TOTE £6.90: £2.60, £1.90; EX 41.50 Place 6 £182.26, Place 5 £112.02..
Owner Miss Gay Kelleway **Bred** Whatton Manor Stud **Trained** Exning, Suffolk

FOCUS
A modest handicap and a small field but a close finish. Weakish form, held down by the fourth.
Cleveland Official explanation: jockey said gelding ran too free
T/Plt: £201.00 to a £1 stake. Pool: £47,654.60. 173.00 winning tickets. T/Qpdt: £20.30 to a £1 stake. Pool: £2,939.60. 107.00 winning tickets. JR

857 WOLVERHAMPTON (A.W) (L-H)
Thursday, March 13

OFFICIAL GOING: Standard
Wind: Fresh behind Weather: Overcast

869 BET CHELTENHAM FESTIVAL - BETDAQ APPRENTICE H'CAP 1m 5f 194y(P)
6:50 (6:52) (Class 6) (0-65,64) 4-Y-O+ **£2,047** (£604; £302) **Stalls** Low

Form RPR

5432 **1** **Grizebeck (IRE)**[10] 778 6-9-6 **56**.. MatthewDavies 3 63+
(R F Fisher) *mde all: rdn over 2f out: edgd lft over 1f out: styd on* **9/4**[1]

-300 **2** *hd* **Haatmey**[20] 664 6-8-9 **50**..(bt[1]) SamuelDrury[(5)] 4 57
(N Wilson) *chsd wnr: rdn and ev ch over 2f out: edgd lft fnl f: styd on: fin 3rd, 1/2l & hd: plcd 2nd* **9/2**[2]

6020 **3** *1/2* **Ronsard (IRE)**[10] 779 6-8-9 **45**... RichardEvans 1 52+
(P D Evans) *s.i.s: hld up: hdwy 2f out: nt clr run fr over 1f out tl r.o wl nr fin: nt rch wnr: fin 2nd, 1/2l: disq: plcd 3rd* **12/1**

-664 **4** *1 1/2* **Reminiscent (IRE)**[20] 661 9-8-9 **45**..............................(v) DeclanCannon 8 50+
(B P J Baugh) *hld up: hdwy over 5f out: rdn and nt clr run fr over 1f out: no ex wl towards fin* **10/1**

5631 **5** *nk* **Piano Key**[20] 661 4-8-2 **47**.. BillyCray[(5)] 6 51
(M D I Usher) *chsd ldrs: rdn over 2f out: styd on* **11/2**[3]

U54 **6** *1/2* **Saint Eric (FR)**[15] 720 6-8-9 **45**....................................... KylieManser 5 48
(Noel T Chance) *s.i.s: hld up and hid: hdwy and hung lft fr over 1f out: nt clr run ins fnl f: swtchd rt: nt rch ldrs* **9/1**

1313 **7** *hd* **Champagne Shadow (IRE)**[19] [682] 7-9-7 64.(p) JosephineBruning(7) 7 67
(J Pearce) *hld up: pushed along 5f out: r.o ins fnl f: n.d* **9/2**[2]
6606 **8** *3* **Divine Love (IRE)**[10] [779] 4-8-5 45..........(p) RossAtkinson 2 43
(T Wall) *s.i.s: sn chsng ldrs: outpcd fr over 2f out* **40/1**
3 **9** *3 3/4* **Annapurna Sunrise (IRE)**[15] [716] 4-8-6 53..........(b) IPLynch(7) 9 46
(Eamon Tyrrell, Ire) *prom: rdn over 3f out: wknd over 1f out* **9/1**
3m 6.57s (0.57) **Going Correction** +0.05s/f (Slow)
WFA 4 from 6yo+ 4lb 9 Ran SP% **121.7**
Speed ratings (Par 101): **100,99,99,98,98 98,98,96,94**
CSF £13.19 CT £103.79 TOTE £3.90: £1.02, £2.10, £6.00; EX 18.60.
Owner Sporting Occasions **Bred** John Killeen **Trained** Ulverston, Cumbria
■ Stewards' Enquiry : Richard Evans two-day ban: careless riding (Mar 24,25)
FOCUS
A very moderate apprentice handicap run at an ordinary pace and things got pretty tight late on. The winner came here in good form, and the second and fourth are both better than the bare facts to some extent.
Saint Eric(FR) Official explanation: jockey said, regarding running and riding, her orders were to drop the gelding in and gradually creep into the race, adding it was slowly away, hung left and was denied a clear run

870 BET "GOLD CUP" - BETDAQ CLAIMING STKS 7f 32y(P)
7:20 (7:20) (Class 5) 4-Y-0+ £2,590 (£770; £385; £192) **Stalls High**

Form RPR
5642 **1** **Teasing**[7] [807] 4-9-2 78..........(p) RobertHavlin 4 77+
(J Pearce) *hld up in tch: rdn over 1f out: r.o to ld post* **9/2**[3]
3621 **2** *shd* **Desert Dreamer (IRE)**[10] [775] 7-9-6 74..........(t) RichardKingscote 3 81+
(Tom Dascombe) *trckd ldrs: racd keenly: rdn over 1f out: sn edgd rt: led ins fnl f: hdd post* **11/8**[2]
-110 **3** *1 1/4* **Waterside (IRE)**[19] [679] 9-9-7 93.......... PaulDoe 1 79+
(S Curran) *chsd ldr tl led 2f out: sn rdn: edgd lft 1f out: sn hdd and unable qck* **10/11**[1]
6-60 **4** *4* **Cyfrwys (IRE)**[70] [33] 7-8-2 45..........(p) CatherineGannon 2 50
(B Palling) *led: rdn and hdd over 2f out: nt clr run 1f out: sn btn* **25/1**
1m 30.42s (0.82) **Going Correction** +0.05s/f (Slow) 4 Ran SP% **116.5**
Speed ratings (Par 103): **97,96,95,90**
CSF £11.97 TOTE £4.20; EX 12.00.
Owner D Leech **Bred** Chippenham Lodge Stud Ltd **Trained** Newmarket, Suffolk
FOCUS
Even though there were just the four runners, there was a wide spread of abilities judged on official ratings. Despite the small field, the pace was reasonable enough. The fourth sets the level, with the first three all capable of better.
Waterside(IRE) Official explanation: jockey said, regarding running and riding, his orders were to jump out, be handy and do his best; vet said gelding finished lame.

871 BET "COUNTY HURDLE" - BETDAQ CLASSIFIED STKS 5f 20y(P)
7:50 (7:50) (Class 7) 4-Y-0+ £1,365 (£403; £201) **Stalls Low**

Form RPR
-005 **1** **Montzando**[14] [725] 5-9-0 41..........(v) GrahamGibbons 1 50
(B R Millman) *led: rdn: hdd and hmpd over 1f out: rallied to ld ins fnl f: r.o* **13/2**
3244 **2** *nk* **Lady Hopeful (IRE)**[14] [725] 6-9-0 43..........(b) LPKeniry 7 49
(Peter Grayson) *s.i.s: hld up: swtchd lft sn after s: hdwy over 1f out: sn rdn: r.o* **11/2**[3]
-005 **3** *hd* **Pauvic (IRE)**[52] [255] 5-8-11 42..........(v) AndrewMullen(3) 9 48
(Mrs A Duffield) *chsd ldrs: rdn to ld and hung lft over 1f out: hdd ins fnl f: r.o* **5/1**[2]
4632 **4** *1/2* **Time Share (IRE)**[14] [725] 4-8-9 45.......... KellyHarrison(5) 11 46
(M Wigham) *hld up: plld hrd: hdwy 1/2-way: rdn over 1f out: r.o* **3/1**[1]
5600 **5** *1 1/4* **Jabraan (USA)**[2] [846] 6-8-7 39..........(p) MCGeran(7) 10 42
(Mrs R A Carr) *s.i.s: in rr: rdn over 1f out: r.o ins fnl f: nt trble ldrs* **20/1**
5325 **6** *1/2* **Highland Song (IRE)**[15] [719] 5-8-9 45.......... KevinGhunowa(5) 6 40
(R F Fisher) *chsd ldrs: hmpd wl over 3f out: sn rdn: hung lft over 1f out: no imp* **3/1**[1]
0006 **7** *nk* **Vlasta Weiner**[18] [696] 8-9-0 40..........(b) PaulFitzsimons 2 39
(J M Bradley) *s.i.s: hdwy over 3f out: rdn over 1f out: edgd rt and no ex ins fnl f* **22/1**
5-50 **8** *1 3/4* **Princess Charlmane (IRE)**[9] [790] 5-9-0 37..........(t) JimmyQuinn 3 33
(C J Teague) *s.i.s: hld up: plld hrd: nvr trbld ldrs* **14/1**
2360 **9** *nk* **Blushing Russian (IRE)**[43] [363] 6-8-7 43..........(p) PietroRomeo(7) 5 31
(J M Bradley) *mid-div: drvn along 1/2-way: styd on same pce appr fnl f* **11/1**
-006 **10** *7* **Maromito (IRE)**[37] [440] 11-9-0 40.......... PatCosgrave 8 6
(R Bastiman) *chsd ldr: edgd lft wl over 3f out: rdn 1/2-way: wknd over 1f out* **12/1**
62.99 secs (0.69) **Going Correction** +0.05s/f (Slow) 10 Ran SP% **127.2**
Speed ratings (Par 97): **96,95,95,94,92 91,91,88,87,76**
CSF £46.28 TOTE £6.80: £2.90, £1.10, £2.80; EX 31.70.
Owner The Links Partnership **Bred** Peter Baldwin **Trained** Kentisbeare, Devon
■ Stewards' Enquiry : Graham Gibbons two-day ban: used whip with excessive force (Mar 24-25)
Andrew Mullen caution: careless riding
FOCUS
A poor race but competitive enough. The fact that there was little covering the principals at the line suggests the form will mean little outside this level. The form is rated through the first two.

872 EDDIE COLLIER 50TH BIRTHDAY JOLLY H'CAP 1m 141y(P)
8:20 (8:21) (Class 6) (0-60,60) 4-Y-0+ £2,047 (£604; £302) **Stalls Low**

Form RPR
-166 **1** **General Feeling (IRE)**[15] [724] 7-8-6 55..........(p) DeclanCannon(7) 2 59
(S T Mason) *rousted along leaving stalls: sn hld up: hdwy over 2f out: rdn to ld over 1f out: edgd rt: r.o* **20/1**
0-21 **2** *nk* **Wisdom's Kiss**[17] [703] 4-9-0 56..........(p) JimmyQuinn 8 59
(J D Bethell) *chsd ldr: rdn over 2f out: nt clr run and swtchd lft over 1f out: r.o u.p* **4/1**[3]
06-4 **3** *nse* **Karma Llama (IRE)**[9] [792] 4-8-3 52..........(v) MatthewDavies(7) 9 55
(George Baker) *chsd ldrs: rdn over 1f out: r.o* **14/1**
-310 **4** *1* **Sparky Vixen**[21] [640] 4-8-4 51.......... KellyHarrison(5) 4 52
(C J Teague) *chsd ldrs: rdn over 1f out: r.o* **14/1**
3404 **5** *nse* **Casablanca Minx (IRE)**[5] [841] 5-8-6 55..........(v) RichardEvans(7) 3 56
(P D Evans) *hld up: nt clr run over 1f out: r.o wl ins fnl f: nt rch ldrs* **7/1**
000- **6** *hd* **It's A Dream (FR)**[175] [5559] 5-9-4 60.......... DaleGibson 1 60
(M W Easterby) *hld up in tch: lost pl 4f out: hdwy over 1f out: sn rdn: r.o* **7/2**[2]
0022 **7** *1/2* **Mighty Mover (IRE)**[19] [686] 6-9-2 58.......... CatherineGannon 5 57
(B Palling) *led: rdn and hdd over 1f out: edgd rt fnl f: styd on same pce* **5/2**[1]
-034 **8** *2 3/4* **Sir Bond (IRE)**[15] [724] 7-8-8 55 ow1.......... SladeO'Hara(5) 10 48
(G R Oldroyd) *s.i.s: hdwy over 5f out: rdn over 2f out: wknd fnl f* **13/2**
2605 **9** *3* **Mister Benji**[15] [724] 9-8-6 48..........(v) AndrewElliott 11 34
(B P J Baugh) *mid-div: rdn over 2f out: wknd over 1f out* **14/1**
620- **10** *14* **Giovanni D'Oro (IRE)**[245] [3469] 4-8-12 54.......... AdamKirby 7 8
(Miss M E Rowland) *mid-div: lost pl 1/2-way: sn rdn: wknd wl over 2f out* **20/1**
-000 **11** *2* **Union Jack Jackson (IRE)**[9] [792] 6-8-4 53 ow1.(v[1]) MarkCoumbe(7) 6 2
(John A Harris) *sn outpcd* **28/1**
1m 50.39s (-0.11) **Going Correction** +0.05s/f (Slow) 11 Ran SP% **129.6**
Speed ratings (Par 101): **102,101,101,100,100 100,100,97,95,82 80**
CSF £106.00 CT £1238.92 TOTE £25.20: £9.80, £2.20, £5.60; EX 170.40.
Owner The Mason Racing Partnership I **Bred** John Graham And Leslie Laverty **Trained** Lanchester, Co. Durham
■ Stewards' Enquiry : Catherine Gannon one-day ban: careless riding (Mar 24)
Matthew Davies three-day ban: used whip with excessive frequency (Mar 24-26)
FOCUS
An ordinary handicap in which they finished in a heap despite what looked a solid pace. Probably not form to be with.
Union Jack Jackson(IRE) Official explanation: jockey said gelding never travelled

873 BETDAQPOKER.CO.UK H'CAP 1m 141y(P)
8:50 (8:51) (Class 6) (0-60,60) 3-Y-0 £1,774 (£523; £262) **Stalls Low**

Form RPR
000- **1** **Wogan's Sister**[127] [6714] 3-8-10 52.......... ChrisCatlin 1 57+
(I A Wood) *a.p: racd keenly: rdn to ld ins fnl f: r.o* **16/1**
4-50 **2** *1* **Si Belle (IRE)**[13] [748] 3-9-4 60.......... SebSanders 6 63+
(Rae Guest) *hld up: hdwy over 1f out: r.o* **13/8**[1]
00-4 **3** *1 1/2* **Last Angel (IRE)**[16] [709] 3-8-4 46 oh1.......... FrancisNorton 12 45
(M Wigham) *edgd rt s: sn led: rdn over 1f out: hdd and unable qck ins fnl f* **14/1**
0-44 **4** *shd* **One Called Alice**[10] [785] 3-9-1 60.......... JerryO'Dwyer(3) 4 59
(A W Carroll) *trckd ldr: ev ch fr over 2f out: rdn over 1f out: no ex ins fnl f* **8/1**
-564 **5** *shd* **Scientific**[33] [501] 3-8-11 53..........(v[1]) J-PGuillambert 2 52
(G Prodromou) *prom: nt clr run over 2f out: rdn and ev ch ins fnl f: styd on same pce* **13/2**[3]
-665 **6** *1 1/2* **Scots W'Hae**[22] [629] 3-8-13 55..........(t) AdamKirby 10 50
(P J McBride) *hld up: hdwy over 2f out: sn rdn: no ex fnl f* **8/1**
1016 **7** *2 1/4* **Magical Song**[2] [849] 3-8-11 53.......... FrankieMcDonald 8 43
(P A Blockley) *mid-div: hdwy over 3f out: rdn and edgd lft over 1f out: wknd ins fnl f* **3/1**[2]
0-23 **8** *13* **Rhode Island Red (USA)**[28] [556] 3-9-0 56..........(v) DaneO'Neill 11 16
(H J L Dunlop) *s.i.s: hdwy over 5f out: rdn over 3f out: wknd over 2f out: eased* **11/1**
5-56 **9** *7* **Mad Man Will (IRE)**[41] [397] 3-8-13 55.......... SaleemGolam 7 —
(S C Williams) *prom: rdn over 3f out: wknd wl over 1f out* **14/1**
0-46 **10** *1 1/4* **Arrabiata**[17] [700] 3-8-8 50.......... JimmyQuinn 5 —
(C N Kellett) *hld up: rdn over 3f out: sn wknd* **33/1**
0 **11** *1 1/4* **Breathe**[16] [706] 3-9-0 56.......... TPQueally 9 —
(R T Phillips) *hdwy over 6f out: rdn and wknd over 2f out* **22/1**
1m 52.28s (1.78) **Going Correction** +0.05s/f (Slow) 11 Ran SP% **133.5**
Speed ratings (Par 96): **94,93,91,91,91 90,88,76,70,69 68**
CSF £48.06 CT £437.87 TOTE £21.30: £6.20, £1.40, £5.30; EX 112.90.
Owner Neardown Stables **Bred** Mrs J A Gawthorpe **Trained** Upper Lambourn, Berks
FOCUS
A very moderate contest and just a fair pace, but a few of these were unexposed including the front pair. Better can be expected from those two, but overall this is not a race to be positive about.
Wogan's Sister ◆ Official explanation: trainer said, regarding apparent improvement in form, that the filly had strengthened up from 2yo to 3yo
Arrabiata Official explanation: jockey said filly failed to handle the bend
Breathe Official explanation: jockey said filly lost its action

874 BETDAQ.CO.UK H'CAP 1m 1f 103y(P)
9:20 (9:21) (Class 6) (0-65,65) 4-Y-0+ £2,047 (£604; £302) **Stalls Low**

Form RPR
2353 **1** **Our Kes (IRE)**[8] [802] 6-9-4 65.......... TPQueally 3 73
(P Howling) *hld up: hdwy over 1f out: r.o u.p to ld post* **9/4**[2]
0-53 **2** *nk* **Tancredi (SWE)**[17] [207] 6-8-12 62..........(t) JerryO'Dwyer(3) 2 69
(N B King) *trckd ldr: led over 2f out: rdn over 1f out: hdd post* **4/1**[3]
1213 **3** *nk* **My Mirasol**[5] [841] 4-8-13 60..........(p) ChrisCatlin 6 67
(D E Cantillon) *led: hdd over 2f out: sn rdn: r.o* **13/8**[1]
/114 **4** *1 1/4* **Lough Beg (IRE)**[41] [387] 5-8-9 56..........(t) DaneO'Neill 4 60
(Miss Tor Sturgis) *chsd ldrs: rdn over 2f out: edgd lft and styd on same pce fnl f* **9/2**
06-0 **5** *3 1/4* **Zach's Harmoney (USA)**[13] [758] 4-9-4 65..........(t) JimmyQuinn 1 63
(M Appleby) *trckd ldrs: plld hrd: rdn over 2f out: wknd fnl f* **25/1**
-365 **6** *2 1/2* **Pelham Crescent (IRE)**[21] [646] 5-9-2 63.......... CatherineGannon 7 57
(B Palling) *s.i.s: hld up: rdn over 2f out: sn wknd* **15/2**
2m 1.66s (-0.04) **Going Correction** +0.05s/f (Slow) 6 Ran SP% **122.7**
Speed ratings (Par 101): **102,101,101,100,97 95**
CSF £13.09 TOTE £4.20: £1.70, £1.50; EX 17.80 Place 6 £542.07, Place 5 £295.02..
Owner S J Hammond **Bred** Yeomanstown Stud **Trained** Newmarket, Suffolk
FOCUS
An ordinary handicap, but with My Mirasol on the field the pace was always likely to be solid enough and that would have helped the winner. Modest but solid form.
T/Plt: £561.00 to a £1 stake. Pool: £85,540.60. 111.30 winning tickets. T/Qpdt: £65.80 to a £1 stake. Pool: £6,547.10. 73.60 winning tickets. CR

746 KEMPTON (A.W) (R-H)
Friday, March 14

OFFICIAL GOING: Standard
Wind: Virtually nil

875 JOIN THE MILLIONAIRES AT 32RED.COM H'CAP 5f (P)
6:20 (6:20) (Class 6) (0-65,65) 4-Y-0+ £2,047 (£604; £302) **Stalls High**

Form RPR
5-41 **1** **Toms Laughter**[20] [681] 4-8-10 62..........(p) KevinGhunowa(5) 9 74+
(R A Harris) *a in tch: rdn over 1f out: drvn to ld ins fnl f: edgd lft nr fin* **11/2**[2]
3030 **2** *1 1/2* **Overstayed (IRE)**[20] [681] 5-8-9 56..........(be) LiamJones 10 63
(M Mullineaux) *led rdn over 1f out: hdd and edgd lft ins fnl f* **9/1**
5136 **3** *3/4* **Lord Of The Reins (IRE)**[28] [574] 4-9-4 65.......... AdamKirby 11 69
(D Shaw) *hld up: rdn and hdwy over 1f out: r.o to go 3rd ins fnl f* **7/1**

3212 **4** 2 1/4 **Thoughtsofstardom**[11] 774 5-8-8 **60**........................ KellyHarrison(5) 1 56
(M Wigham) *t.k.h: trckd ldrs on outside: hung rt but kpt on fnl f: nvr nrr* **6/1**[3]

20-6 **5** 1/2 **Nightstrike (IRE)**[14] 746 5-8-9 **59** ow3..................(b) JerryO'Dwyer(3) 6 53
(Luke Comer, Ire) *towards rr: nt clr run and swtchd lft over 1f out: r.o wl ins funal f* **33/1**

5231 **6** 1 **Musical Script (USA)**[23] 628 5-8-13 **60**........................(b) ChrisCatlin 7 50
(Mouse Hamilton-Fairley) *in rr: swtchd lft over 1f out: r.o fnl f* **9/2**[1]

-355 **7** 1/2 **After The Show**[14] 746 7-8-13 **60**........................ AlanMunro 3 49
(Rae Guest) *a towards rr and nvr on terms* **12/1**

0004 **8** 1/2 **Fizzlephut (IRE)**[10] 786 6-8-12 **59**........................ PaulFitzsimons 2 46
(Miss J R Tooth) *trckd ldrs: rdn 1/2-way: wknd ins fnl f* **16/1**

00-2 **9** nk **Rocker**[14] 746 4-9-2 **63**........................ SimonWhitworth 4 49
(B R Johnson) *trckd ldr tl rdn and wknd over 1f out* **7/1**

2343 **10** 1 1/2 **Kempsey**[14] 746 6-8-9 **59**........................(b) TolleyDean(3) 8 39
(J J Bridger) *in tch: rdn 2f out: wknd appr 1f out: eased ins fnl f* **12/1**

2033 **11** shd **Mambazo**[11] 782 6-8-12 **62**........................(e) WilliamBuick(3) 5 42
(S C Williams) *towards rr on outside: c wd into st: a bhd* **13/2**

600- **12** 1 3/4 **Black Moma (IRE)**[83] 7221 4-8-8 **62**........................ PNolan(7) 12 36
(A B Haynes) *mid-div on ins: rdn 2f out: sn wknd* **20/1**

59.84 secs (-0.66) **Going Correction** +0.025s/f (Slow) **12** Ran SP% **125.2**
Speed ratings (Par 101): **106,103,102,98,98 96,95,94,94,91 91,88**
CSF £57.75 CT £287.54 TOTE £8.50: £1.90, £5.00, £3.10; EX 143.00.
Owner Five To Follow **Bred** Mrs D J Hughes **Trained** Earlswood, Monmouths

FOCUS
A moderate sprint with the winner improving and the form looks solid.

876 £100 BONUS AT 32RED.COM H'CAP 6f (P)
6:50 (6:51) (Class 6) (0-60,60) 3-Y-O **£2,047** (£604; £302) **Stalls** High

Form RPR

50-4 **1** **Thomas Malory (IRE)**[13] 767 3-8-10 **57**........................ SCreighton(5) 6 65+
(Miss V Haigh) *mid-div: hdwy over 2f out: rdn and r.o fnl f to ld nr fin* **10/1**

0-00 **2** 3/4 **Admirals Way**[9] 797 3-8-10 **52**........................ IanMongan 9 57
(C N Kellett) *trckd ldr: rdn 2f out: led jst ins fnl f: hdd nr fin* **11/2**[3]

0602 **3** 2 1/4 **Kamal**[6] 835 3-9-4 **60**........................(b) HayleyTurner 5 58
(W R Muir) *trckd ldrs: short of room on ins and swtchd lft over 1f out: r.o to snatch 3rd cl home* **11/4**[1]

2632 **4** nk **Regal Veil**[27] 583 3-8-4 **46**........................ SaleemGolam 10 43
(S C Williams) *led tl edgd rt and hdd jst ins fnl f: no ex and lost 3rd cl home* **5/1**[2]

5462 **5** 3/4 **Too Grand**[17] 709 3-8-9 **51**........................ NeilChalmers 8 46
(J J Bridger) *hld up: hdwy over 1f out: r.o wl: nvr nrr* **11/2**[3]

-653 **6** 1 1/2 **Planet Paradise (IRE)**[13] 767 3-7-13 **46**........................ KellyHarrison(5) 7 36
(D Shaw) *hld up in mid-div: making no imp whn bmpd 1f out* **16/1**

6-54 **7** 3 **Mujada**[35] 480 3-8-8 **53** ow1........................ MarkLawson(3) 3 34
(M Brittain) *in rr: rdn and hung rt 1/2-way: nvr on terms* **7/1**

3135 **8** 1/2 **Talamahana**[9] 797 3-9-4 **60**........................(b) LPKeniry 4 40
(A B Haynes) *prom: rdn over 2f out: wknd over 1f out* **15/2**

340- **9** 3 1/4 **Nestor Protector (IRE)**[214] 4461 3-8-9 **58**........................ PNolan(7) 2 28
(A B Haynes) *a in rr* **16/1**

0-00 **10** 2 1/2 **Elegant Step**[16] 714 3-8-13 **58**........................ LukeMorris(3) 1 21
(A W Carroll) *swtchd rt fr wd draw s: a struggling in rr* **25/1**

1m 13.13s (0.03) **Going Correction** +0.025s/f (Slow) **10** Ran SP% **123.1**
Speed ratings (Par 96): **100,99,96,95,94 92,88,87,83,80**
CSF £67.81 CT £198.79 TOTE £11.40: £2.50, £3.30, £1.30; EX 76.70.
Owner R J Budge **Bred** Ralph And Helen O'Brien **Trained** Wiseton, Notts

FOCUS
A moderate but competitive handicap and the form looks reasonable.
Elegant Step Official explanation: jockey said filly never travelled

877 $500 BONUS AT 32REDPOKER.COM CLASSIFIED STKS 7f (P)
7:20 (7:20) (Class 7) 4-Y-O+ **£1,365** (£403; £201) **Stalls** High

Form RPR

05-2 **1** **Fun In The Sun**[23] 621 4-9-0 45........................ TPQueally 4 51
(A B Haynes) *in tch: rdn over 1f out: edgd rt u.p but led ins fnl f* **5/2**[1]

-540 **2** 3/4 **A Teen**[23] 621 10-9-0 40........................ JimmyQuinn 6 49
(P Howling) *in tch: short of room over 2f out: rdn and squeezed through to hold ev ch ins fnl f: no ex cl home* **16/1**

5356 **3** 3/4 **Only If I Laugh**[23] 621 7-9-0 42........................ IanMongan 1 47
(M J Attwater) *mid-div: rdn over 1f out: r.o wl fnl f to go 3rd nr fin* **8/1**

0365 **4** nk **Doctor Ned**[16] 713 4-9-0 45........................ NeilChalmers 14 46
(Miss Sheena West) *trckd ldrs: ev ch 2f out: kpt on but lost 3rd nr fin* **12/1**

6022 **5** nk **Suhayl Star (IRE)**[8] 808 4-9-0 45........................ LPKeniry 5 45
(P Burgoyne) *t.k.h: prom on outside: rdn to ld over 2f out: hdd ins fnl f and short of room nr fin* **4/1**[2]

6P56 **6** nk **Mtoto Girl**[19] 691 4-8-11 40........................ TolleyDean(3) 10 45
(J J Bridger) *hld up: rdn over 2f out hdwy over 1f out: r.o fnl f: nvr nrr* **20/1**

-201 **7** hd **Bahamian Bay**[8] 808 6-9-3 45........................ MarkLawson(3) 3 50
(M Brittain) *in rr: rdn 3f out: r.o fnl f: nvr nr to chal* **5/1**[3]

0036 **8** 3/4 **Cayman Breeze**[16] 713 8-9-0 40........................ JimCrowley 12 42
(J M Bradley) *in rr: hdwy over 2f out: rdn and wknd ins fnl f* **20/1**

6/ **9** 1 1/4 **Divinshki (IRE)**[196] 5022 8-9-0 43........................ ChrisCatlin 8 39
(Irene J Monaghan, Ire) *hmpd s: sn in mid-div: rdn 3f out: wknd over 1f out* **12/1**

0304 **10** 5 **The Carpet Man**[16] 713 4-8-11 40........................ LukeMorris(3) 2 27
(A W Carroll) *a in rr* **12/1**

0445 **11** hd **Lady Firecracker (IRE)**[9] 804 4-9-0 42........................(v) StephenCarson 7 26
(J R Best) *prom: rdn and wknd over 1f out* **6/1**

-600 **12** 1 **Joe Rich**[16] 713 4-8-11 40........................(p) JerryO'Dwyer(3) 9 24
(Mrs L C Jewell) *led: rdn and hdd over 2f out: sn wknd* **7/1**

1m 26.7s (0.70) **Going Correction** +0.025s/f (Slow) **12** Ran SP% **141.6**
Speed ratings (Par 97): **97,96,95,94,94 94,94,93,91,86 85,84**
CSF £58.78 TOTE £4.30: £1.30, £5.40, £3.80; EX 44.50.
Owner W Clifford **Bred** Miss L Johnstone **Trained** Limpley Stoke, Bath

FOCUS
A poor race but still a most competitive handicap and they finished up well bunched. The placed horses set the level.

878 32RED.COM MEDIAN AUCTION MAIDEN STKS 1m (P)
7:50 (7:51) (Class 6) 4-6-Y-O **£2,047** (£604; £302) **Stalls** High

Form RPR

1 1/2 **Miss Marauder** 4-8-12 0........................ OscarUrbina 6 59+
(M Botti) *trckd ldrs: wnt 2nd wl over 1f out: chalng whn short of room and snatched up ins fnl f: swtchd lft and r.o cl home: fin 2nd, 1/2l: awrdd r* **6/4**[2]

5 **2** **Kitto Katsu**[19] 694 4-8-12 0........................ JimmyQuinn 3 57+
(D J Coakley) *hld up in tch: hdwy to ld 2f out: rdn and hung rt fnl f: r.o: fin 1st, 1/2l: disq: plcd 2nd* **11/8**[1]

060 **3** 5 **Northstar Express (IRE)**[41] 401 5-8-12 37........................ AdamKirby 4 46
(J L Spearing) *in rr: nvr on terms but kpt on to snatch 3rd on line* **8/1**

00/0 **4** nse **Boluisce (IRE)**[54] 239 5-8-12 50........................ ChrisCatlin 7 46
(P W Hiatt) *led tl rdn and hdd 2f out: sn wknd* **11/1**

5 **2** **Coco L'Escargot**[28] 4-8-12 0........................ JimCrowley 2 41
(J R Jenkins) *trckd ldr: rdn over 3f out: wknd over 2f out* **7/1**[3]

1m 41.43s (1.63) **Going Correction** +0.025s/f (Slow) **5** Ran SP% **114.0**
Speed ratings: **91,92,86,86,84**
CSF £4.14 TOTE £2.90: £1.40, £1.10; EX 3.80.
Owner Mrs Sally Doyle **Bred** Mrs Sally Doyle **Trained** Newmarket, Suffolk
■ Stewards' Enquiry : Jimmy Quinn four-day ban: careless riding (Mar 25-28)

FOCUS
A contest low on quality but there was plenty of drama with Miss Marauder being awarded the race in the Stewards' room. The fact that the 37-rated third was relatively close raises doubts about the form.

879 MOBILE ROULETTE TEXT "32" TO 89932 H'CAP 1m (P)
8:20 (8:21) (Class 6) (0-65,65) 4-Y-O+ **£2,047** (£604; £302) **Stalls** High

Form RPR

20-0 **1** **Dinner Date**[69] 51 6-8-12 **59**........................ J-PGuillambert 9 68+
(T Keddy) *hld up: hmpd 2f out: swtchd rt 1f out: r.o wl to ld cl home* **14/1**

230- **2** nk **Billy One Punch**[161] 5983 6-8-13 **65**........................ KellyHarrison(5) 13 72
(D Shaw) *a.p: led ins fnl f: r.o: hdd cl home* **7/1**[3]

-011 **3** 3/4 **Not Now Lewis (IRE)**[27] 587 4-8-11 **58**........................ TPQueally 6 63
(J A Osborne) *mid-div: hdwy over 1f out: r.o to go 3rd post* **4/1**[2]

2043 **4** hd **Imperium**[17] 708 7-8-10 **57**........................(p) FrankieMcDonald 8 62
(Jean-Rene Auvray) *a.p: wnt 2nd over 1f out: ev ch tl wknd wl ins fnl f* **14/1**

-532 **5** 1 1/4 **Tancredi (SWE)**[1] 874 6-8-12 **62**........................(t) JerryO'Dwyer(3) 10 64
(N B King) *slowly away: gd hdwy on outside over 1f out: r.o: no ex nr fin* **7/2**[1]

2113 **6** hd **Under Fire (IRE)**[15] 730 5-8-10 **64**........................ MarkCoumbe(7) 5 65
(A W Carroll) *trckd ldr: rdn over 2f out: one pce fnl f* **7/1**[3]

-530 **7** 2 1/4 **Subadar**[15] 728 4-8-10 **60**........................(p) KirstyMilczarek(3) 3 56+
(M Botti) *led: rdn and hdd ins fnl f: wkng whn hmpd cl home* **10/1**

04-0 **8** 2 1/2 **Cheonmado (USA)**[51] 275 4-9-1 **62**........................(t) LiamJones 2 53
(J R Gask) *in rr: nvr on terms* **25/1**

4250 **9** 1 1/2 **Copper King**[28] 576 4-9-0 **61**........................(t) ChrisCatlin 11 48
(Miss Tor Sturgis) *a in rr* **7/1**[3]

-131 **10** 1/2 **Joy And Pain**[17] 708 7-9-1 **62**........................(p) IanMongan 4 48
(M J Attwater) *trckd ldrs tl wknd 2f out* **10/1**

-251 **11** 1 1/4 **Contented (IRE)**[14] 749 6-8-12 **59**........................(p) LPKeniry 7 42
(Mrs L C Jewell) *t.k.h: rdn over 2f out: wknd over 1f out* **7/1**[3]

00 **12** 1 1/4 **Tyrana (GER)**[8] 730 5-9-4 **65**........................ VinceSlattery 14 45
(G F Bridgwater) *a bhd* **50/1**

0-55 **13** 7 **Stand Guard**[18] 700 4-8-10 **60**........................ TolleyDean(3) 12 38
(D Shaw) *a bhd* **20/1**

1m 39.66s (-0.14) **Going Correction** +0.025s/f (Slow) **13** Ran SP% **134.3**
Speed ratings (Par 101): **101,100,99,99,98 98,96,93,92,91 90,89,88**
CSF £120.26 CT £500.83 TOTE £22.60: £5.60, £4.00, £2.30; EX 271.10.
Owner Mrs H Keddy **Bred** J M Greetham **Trained** Newmarket, Suffolk
■ Stewards' Enquiry : J-P Guillambert caution: careless riding

FOCUS
A fair contest for the grade with the winner rated back to form.
Subadar Official explanation: jockey said gelding ran too free
Joy And Pain Official explanation: jockey said gelding ran flat

880 32REDPOKER.COM $20K ELEVATOR H'CAP 2m (P)
8:50 (8:50) (Class 5) (0-75,70) 4-Y-O+ **£2,590** (£770; £385; £192) **Stalls** High

Form RPR

1011 **1** **Rollin 'n Tumblin**[9] 793 4-8-13 **65**........................ KirstyMilczarek(3) 7 77+
(W Jarvis) *hld up: gd hdwy on ins to ld over 2f out: in command fnl f* **11/8**[1]

6632 **2** 3 **Lorikeet**[17] 710 9-9-10 **68**........................ GeorgeBaker 4 74
(G L Moore) *trckd ldrs: rdn over 3f out: ev ch 2f out: kpt on one pce* **9/2**[3]

5-16 **3** 1 1/4 **Mister Completely (IRE)**[23] 630 7-9-9 **67**........................(v) JamesDoyle 2 72
(Ms J S Doyle) *hld up: rdn and hdwy 2f out: styd on: nvr nr to chal* **25/1**

16-0 **4** 1 1/2 **Featherlight**[71] 27 4-9-5 **68**........................(b) RobertHavlin 1 71
(Jamie Poulton) *hld up: hdwy on outside over 2f out: kpt on one pce fnl f* **16/1**

5-45 **5** 2 **Savannah**[14] 747 5-9-9 **70**........................(b) JerryO'Dwyer(3) 8 70
(Luke Comer, Ire) *trckd ldr: led after 6f to 6f out: led again 5f out tl rdn and hdd over 2f out: sn wknd* **16/1**

-132 **6** 3 **Alnwick**[9] 793 4-8-11 **65**........................ JamieJones(5) 3 62
(P D Cundell) *led for 6f: prom tl rdn and wknd over 2f out* **4/1**[2]

00-0 **7** 1 3/4 **One To Follow**[30] 540 4-9-2 **65**........................ AdamKirby 5 60
(C G Cox) *mid-div: rdn over 2f out: wknd over 1f out* **4/1**[2]

23-5 **8** 5 **High Point (IRE)**[23] 630 10-9-12 **70**........................ SimonWhitworth 6 59
(G P Enright) *in tch: led briefly 6f out: rdn 4f out: wknd qckly* **12/1**

3m 30.61s (0.51) **Going Correction** +0.025s/f (Slow)
WFA 4 from 5yo+ 5lb **8** Ran SP% **123.6**
Speed ratings (Par 103): **99,97,96,96,95 93,92,90**
CSF £8.84 CT £114.65 TOTE £2.40: £1.10, £1.90, £5.70; EX 9.60.
Owner Canisbay Bloodstock **Bred** Canisbay Bloodstock Ltd **Trained** Newmarket, Suffolk

FOCUS
An uncompetitive staying handicap in which Rollin 'n Tumblin readily completed the hat-trick.
One To Follow Official explanation: jockey said gelding ran too free

881 FREE £10 AT 32REDBINGO.COM H'CAP 1m 4f (P)
9:20 (9:20) (Class 6) (0-65,65) 4-Y-O+ **£2,047** (£604; £302) **Stalls** Centre

Form RPR

356/ **1** **Saraba (FR)**[22] 4191 7-9-5 **62**........................ GeorgeBaker 14 70
(Mrs L J Mongan) *trckd ldrs: led 2f out: edgd rt but hld on wl fnl f* **22/1**

5-10 **2** 3/4 **Resplendent Ace (IRE)**[20] 675 4-9-6 **65**........................ JimmyQuinn 8 71
(P Howling) *a.p: rdn over 2f out: r.o to go 2nd ins fnl f* **7/1**[3]

-612 **3** nk **Mixing**[16] 716 6-8-7 **53**........................ KirstyMilczarek(3) 10 59
(J Akehurst) *hld up: hdwy 2f out: rdn and str run fnl f to go 3rd fin* **7/4**[1]

3316 **4** shd **King's Fable (USA)**[16] 716 5-9-0 **57**........................(p) TGMcLaughlin 12 63
(Karen George) *a in tch: rdn and short of room whn swtchd lft ins fnl f: kpt on cl home* **8/1**

1262 **5** 2 **Megalala (IRE)**[15] 728 7-9-2 **59**........................ NeilChalmers 9 62
(J J Bridger) *led tl hdd 2f out: edgd lft and one pce ins fnl f* **14/1**

20-4 **6** 1 ¾ **Best Selection**[37] 449 4-9-6 **65** .... IanMongan 5 65
(Mrs L J Mongan) *towards rr: rdn over 1f out: r.o one pce* **14/1**

-204 **7** 1 **Lascelles**[16] 716 4-9-2 **61** .... TPQueally 13 63+
(J A Osborne) *hld up: hdwy over 2f out: running on whn bdly hmpd ins fnl f: nt rcvr* **11/2**[2]

6/00 **8** 2 **Startengo (IRE)**[56] 207 5-9-3 **60** .... SimonWhitworth 11 56+
(Miss Suzy Smith) *in tch: wkng whn hmpd ins fnl f* **25/1**

001- **9** 3 **Royal Premier (IRE)**[86] 7187 5-8-13 **59** ....(v) JerryO'Dwyer(3) 4 50
(H J Collingridge) *prom: rdn 3f out: wknd 2f out* **7/1**[3]

2-61 **10** ½ **Whaxaar (IRE)**[51] 273 4-8-12 **57** .... RobertHavlin 6 47
(R Ingram) *s.i.s: in rr: brief effrt 2f out: sn btn* **7/1**[3]

-661 **11** 1 ¾ **Oasis Sun (IRE)**[16] 716 5-9-0 **57** ....(b) JimCrowley 2 45
(J R Best) *mid-div: wknd over 2f out* **7/1**[3]

00-0 **12** 5 **County Kerry (UAE)**[23] 624 4-8-4 **49** oh2........(t) FrankieMcDonald 1 29
(Jean-Rene Auvray) *v.s.a: hdwy on outside over 3f out: wknd over 2f out* **50/1**

00-0 **13** *nk* **Lay The Cash (USA)**[4] 352 4-8-9 **54** ....(p) HayleyTurner 3 34
(B G Powell) *racd wd: mid-div: wknd over 3f out* **25/1**

2m 34.6s (0.10) **Going Correction** +0.025s/f (Slow)
WFA 4 from 5yo+ 2lb **13** Ran SP% **140.2**
Speed ratings (Par 101): **100,99,99,99,97 96,96,94,92,92 91,87,87**
CSF £190.97 CT £430.58 TOTE £32.10: £7.10, £3.30, £1.10; EX 442.40 Place 6 £ 89.55, Place 5 £ 21.93.
Owner Mrs P J Sheen **Bred** S A Aga Khan **Trained** Epsom, Surrey

FOCUS
A moderate handicap. The form looks solid for the grade with the first four coming clear.
Mixing Official explanation: jockey said gelding was denied a clear run
T/Plt: £135.50 to a £1 stake. Pool: £78,131.00. 420.70 winning tickets. T/Qpdt: £6.90 to a £1 stake. Pool: £7,112.90. 761.60 winning tickets. JS

793 LINGFIELD (L-H)
Friday, March 14

OFFICIAL GOING: Standard
Wind: modest half behind Weather: overcast

882 LINGFIELDPARK.CO.UK H'CAP 5f (P)
2:00 (2:00) (Class 6) (0-65,65) 3-Y-O **£2,590** (£770; £385; £192) **Stalls** High

Form RPR

2313 **1** **Orpen's Art (IRE)**[16] 714 3-9-0 **64** .... KirstyMilczarek(3) 8 74
(S A Callaghan) *stdd s: hld up in rr: hdwy over 2f out: qcknd to ld on inner jst over 1f out: rdn clr: readily* **2/1**[2]

5112 **2** 3 ¾ **Seductive Witch**[25] 612 3-9-0 **61** .... JamesDoyle 6 58
(J Balding) *w ldrs: rdn jst over 2f out: kpt on u.p to go 2nd wl ins fnl f: no ch w wnr* **15/2**

01 **3** ½ **Stoneacre Sarah**[15] 734 3-9-4 **65** .... LPKeniry 5 60
(Peter Grayson) *cl up: wnt 2nd wl over 2f out: rdn and ev ch 2f out: outpcd by wnr fnl f: kpt on same pce* **15/8**[1]

5432 **4** 1 ¼ **Extreme North (USA)**[16] 714 3-8-12 **64** ....(b) SCreighton(5) 7 54
(Miss V Haigh) *w ldr on outer tl led 3f out: rdn 2f out: hdd jst over 1f out: wknd ins fnl f* **5/1**[3]

6560 **5** ¾ **Sazerac (USA)**[16] 721 3-8-7 **57** .... TolleyDean(3) 3 45
(D Shaw) *t.k.h: prom tl stdd and dropped to last pair 4f out: rdn over 2f out: kpt on ins fnl f but nvr a threat* **14/1**

0665 **6** 1 ¼ **Rightcar Hull (IRE)**[13] 767 3-8-4 **51** oh3........ ChrisCatlin 2 34
(Peter Grayson) *dwlt: sn pushed up to ld narrowly: hdd 3f out: rdn and wknd jst over 2f out* **20/1**

0-00 **7** *nse* **Stoneacre Ma**[15] 734 3-8-4 **51** oh4........ HayleyTurner 1 34
(Peter Grayson) *sn bustled along and outpcd in rr: nvr a factor* **33/1**

59.66 secs (0.86) **Going Correction** +0.15s/f (Slow) **7** Ran SP% **110.9**
Speed ratings (Par 96): **99,93,92,90,89 87,86**
CSF £16.19 CT £29.55 TOTE £2.90: £1.90, £3.10; EX 14.40 Trifecta £33.90 Pool: £826.98, 17.27 winning units.
Owner Matthew Green **Bred** Fin A Co S R L **Trained** Newmarket, Suffolk

FOCUS
A modest sprint. The winner remains progressive and the placed horses indicate the form should stand up.

883 BETDAQ THE BETTING EXCHANGE H'CAP 5f (P)
2:35 (2:35) (Class 6) (0-52,52) 4-Y-0+ **£1,876** (£554; £277) **Stalls** High

Form RPR

-045 **1** **Wibbadune (IRE)**[35] 479 4-8-10 **48** .... NCallan 3 58
(D Shaw) *mde all: hung rt fr jst over 2f out: hld on wl* **16/1**

6324 **2** *nk* **Time Share (IRE)**[1] 871 4-8-3 **46** oh1........ KellyHarrison(5) 1 55
(M Wigham) *taken down early: stdd s: t.k.h: hld up in rr: gd hdwy on inner over 1f out: pressed ldrs ins fnl f: wnt 2nd towards fin: nt quite rch wnr* **10/1**

4201 **3** *nk* **Piccostar**[16] 713 5-8-11 **49** ow2........ SebSanders 5 57
(A B Haynes) *chsd ldng pair: rdn wl over 1f out: ev ins fnl f: unable qckn last 50yds* **5/1**[3]

35-0 **4** ½ **Duke Of Milan (IRE)**[10] 790 5-8-11 **49** .... RobertWinston 9 55
(G C Bravery) *s.i.s: bhd: hdwy over 1f out: r.o wl fnl f: nt rch ldrs* **8/1**

0-05 **5** 1 **One Way Ticket**[11] 774 8-8-8 **46** oh1........(p) ChrisCatlin 7 49
(J M Bradley) *pressed wnr: ev ch and rdn over 1f out: fdd last 50yds* **14/1**

000- **6** 1 ¼ **Charming Ballet (IRE)**[143] 6415 5-8-10 **48** .... FergusSweeney 2 46
(G L Moore) *racd in midfield: rdn over 2f out: hdwy to chse ldrs jst over 1f out: wknd last 100yds* **3/1**[1]

0025 **7** ¾ **Egyptian Lord**[39] 437 5-9-0 **52** ....(b) LPKeniry 4 47+
(Peter Grayson) *s.i.s: sn chsng ldrs: rdn over 2f out: wknd over 1f out: eased towards fin* **4/1**[2]

6002 **8** *nk* **Calloff The Search**[2] 858 4-9-0 **52** ....(p) MickyFenton 6 46
(Stef Liddiard) *sn rdn along in midfield: outpcd wl over 2f out: no ch after* **5/1**[3]

0004 **9** ¾ **Fastrac Boy**[11] 774 5-8-3 **48** .... KierenFox(7) 8 40
(J R Best) *racd wd: in tch in midfield tl lost pl bnd jst over 2f out: hung lft and no ch after* **12/1**

58.96 secs (0.16) **Going Correction** +0.15s/f (Slow) **9** Ran SP% **118.8**
Speed ratings (Par 101): **104,103,103,102,100 98,97,96,95**
CSF £168.77 CT £935.08 TOTE £29.70: £4.30, £2.80, £1.40; EX 191.00 Trifecta £530.40 Part won. Pool: £747.15, 0.38 winning units..
Owner Simon Mapletoft Racing I **Bred** Ballyhane Stud **Trained** Danethorpe, Notts

FOCUS
A very weak sprint. The form looks fair enough for the class with the placed horses setting a modest but solid standard.

884 BOOK PONTIN'S FOR A CRACKING EASTER (S) STKS 6f (P)
3:15 (3:15) (Class 6) 4-Y-0+ **£1,774** (£523; £262) **Stalls** Low

Form RPR

30-0 **1** **Marko Jadeo (IRE)**[14] 755 10-8-7 65 .... KevinGhunowa(5) 2 64
(R A Harris) *taken down early: dwlt: in tch in midfield: hdwy on inner wl over 1f out: led 1f out: kpt on wl u.p* **7/1**[3]

40-4 **2** ½ **Night Prospector**[23] 627 8-8-12 65 ....(p) AlanMunro 4 62
(R A Harris) *chsd ldng pair: hdwy to chal over 1f out: ev ch tl no ex towards fin* **5/1**[2]

65-0 **3** ¾ **Camissa**[40] 414 4-8-7 57 .... HayleyTurner 6 55
(D K Ivory) *chsd ldr: rdn and ev ch over 1f out: unable qckn wl ins fnl f* **10/1**

4006 **4** 1 ½ **Desert Light (IRE)**[16] 718 7-8-12 49 ....(v) NCallan 8 56
(D Shaw) *towards rr: hdwy over 2f out: n.m.r 2f out: swtchd rt over 1f out: edgd lft but r.o fnl f: nt rch ldrs* **10/1**

0020 **5** ¾ **Monashee Brave (IRE)**[8] 806 5-9-3 58 ....(p) PaulDoe 3 58
(M A Allen) *led: rdn jst over 2f out: hdd 1f out: wknd fnl f* **12/1**

65-2 **6** ½ **Punching**[32] 523 4-9-3 57 ....(b) GeorgeBaker 9 57
(Miss Gay Kelleway) *t.k.h: hld up in tch: hdwy to press ldrs over 1f out: drvn 1f out: fnd little: wknd last 100yds* **5/4**[1]

5446 **7** 3 ¾ **Lawdy Miss Clawdy**[30] 535 4-8-7 43 .... FergusSweeney 5 36
(D W P Arbuthnot) *stdd s: t.k.h: hld up in rr: rdn and effrt on outer bnd 2f out: nvr on terms* **11/1**

3010 **8** 1 **Mulberry Lad (IRE)**[32] 523 6-9-3 50 .... ChrisCatlin 10 43
(P W Hiatt) *in tch: rdn and struggling over 2f out: n.d after* **12/1**

2346 **9** 11 **Macademy Royal (USA)**[15] 726 5-8-6 52 ow1........(t) MJMurphy(7) 7 6
(M Wigham) *restless stalls: awkward and slowly away: racd wd: a bhd: lost tch over 2f out* **10/1**

1m 12.12s (0.22) **Going Correction** +0.15s/f (Slow) **9** Ran SP% **124.6**
Speed ratings (Par 101): **104,103,102,100,99 98,93,92,77**
CSF £45.39 TOTE £9.00: £2.70, £1.40, £3.80; EX 29.80 Trifecta £170.00 Pool: £538.94, 2.25 winning units.There was no bid for the winner
Owner Ron Harris & David Thornton **Bred** P Casey **Trained** Earlswood, Monmouths
■ Stewards' Enquiry : M J Murphy three-day ban: used whip when out of contention (Mar 25-27)

FOCUS
A typically poor seller and a race to be against, with the fourth limiting the form.
Punching Official explanation: jockey said gelding ran too free
Macademy Royal(USA) Official explanation: trainer said gelding lost a left front shoe

885 GET EASTER CRACKING @ PONTIN'S MAIDEN FILLIES' STKS 7f (P)
3:55 (4:00) (Class 5) 3-Y-0+ **£2,331** (£693; £346; £173) **Stalls** Low

Form RPR

2 **1** **Maslaha**[23] 633 3-8-9 0 .... PhilipRobinson 8 82+
(M A Jarvis) *chsd ldr: chal gng wl over 1f out: shkn up to ld jst over 1f out: sn clr: readily* **10/11**[1]

5 **2** 3 ½ **Bahamian Bliss**[25] 608 3-8-6 0 .... KirstyMilczarek(3) 4 70
(J A R Toller) *wnt lft s: sn led: rdn over 1f out: hdd jst over 1f out: no ch w wnr but kpt on* **15/2**

344- **3** 4 **Candle Sahara (IRE)**[192] 5110 3-8-9 79 .... EdwardCreighton 1 59
(M R Channon) *chsd ldrs: rdn wl over 2f out: outpcd over 2f out: plugged on fnl f: no ch w ldng pair* **3/1**[2]

0 **4** 1 ½ **Bonne**[11] 772 3-8-9 0 .... HayleyTurner 3 55+
(M L W Bell) *bmpd s: hld up in midfield: rdn and effrt over 2f out: sn outpcd by ldrs: kpt on steadily fnl f* **33/1**

0-50 **5** ¾ **Sunley Smiles**[17] 705 3-8-9 55 .... AlanMunro 5 53
(D R C Elsworth) *in tch in midfield: rdn over 2f out: sn outpcd* **25/1**

3 **6** ½ **Seasonal Cross**[30] 543 3-8-11 0 ow2........ SebSanders 7 54
(S Dow) *stdd s: hld up in rr: hdwy over 3f out: rdn over 2f out: no hdwy and n.d* **12/1**

7 *shd* **Angels Quest** 3-8-2 0 .... SophieDoyle(7) 9 51
(R Simpson) *t.k.h: in midfield on outer: rdn and effrt over 2f out: sn outpcd* **66/1**

0- **8** 1 ¼ **The Dragon (IRE)**[183] 5357 3-8-9 0 .... FergusSweeney 11 48
(M Quinn) *a bhd: sme modest late hdwy: n.d* **66/1**

9 *nse* **Kijivu** 3-8-2 0 .... MatthewDavies(7) 10 48
(M R Channon) *a bhd* **50/1**

0420 **10** 1 ½ **Film Queen (IRE)**[17] 708 4-9-4 58 .... KylieManser(7) 6 50
(B G Powell) *bhd: rdn over 2f out: sn outpcd and wl btn* **50/1**

23 **11** *nk* **West Lorne (USA)**[35] 483 3-8-9 0 .... JoeFanning 13 43
(M Johnston) *chsd ldrs: rdn over 2f out: sn outpcd: wknd wl over 1f out* **7/1**[3]

1m 25.17s (0.37) **Going Correction** +0.15s/f (Slow)
WFA 3 from 4yo 16lb **11** Ran SP% **123.0**
Speed ratings (Par 100): **103,99,94,92,91 91,91,89,89,87 87**
CSF £9.06 TOTE £1.90: £1.20, £2.10, £1.70; EX 9.30 Trifecta £39.10 Pool: £833.31, 15.12 winning units.
Owner Sheikh Ahmed Al Maktoum **Bred** Darley **Trained** Newmarket, Suffolk

FOCUS
An ordinary fillies' maiden but the time was reasonable and the form should work out with the fifth the best guide.

886 TRY BETDAQ FOR AN EXCHANGE H'CAP 1m 5f (P)
4:25 (4:25) (Class 5) (0-75,72) 4-Y-0+ **£2,590** (£770; £385; £192) **Stalls** Low

Form RPR

2431 **1** **Capitalise (IRE)**[16] 575 5-8-5 **54** .... WilliamBuick(3) 5 62+
(V Smith) *hld up in last pair: clsd and in tch fr 6f out: stl last 2f out: smooth hdwy to go 2nd ins fnl f: pushed into ld towards fin: cleverly* **3/1**[3]

0-13 **2** ¾ **Josh You Are**[14] 754 5-9-10 **70** .... OscarUrbina 4 75
(M Wigham) *hld up in 3rd pl: hdwy to join ldr 5f out: led 3f out: drvn 2f out: styd on wl tl hdd and no ex towards fin* **9/4**[1]

0-25 **3** 1 ½ **Wait For The Will (USA)**[20] 675 12-9-9 **69** ....(b) GeorgeBaker 1 72
(G L Moore) *chsd ldr: clsd 7f out: dropped to 3rd 5f out: shkn up to chse ldr 2f out: one pce u.p fnl f* **7/1**

3-44 **4** 7 **Generous Lad (IRE)**[15] 735 5-9-12 **72** ....(p) SebSanders 3 65
(A B Haynes) *t.k.h: led: clr tl stdd and reduced ld 7f out: jnd 5f out and sn rdn: hdd 3f out: wknd over 1f out* **5/2**[2]

4136 **5** 4 **Lordswood (IRE)**[20] 675 4-8-6 **55** .... HayleyTurner 2 43
(J R Best) *stdd s: hld up in last: clsd and in tch 6f out: rdn and effrt jst over 2f out: sn wknd* **11/2**

2m 49.37s (3.37) **Going Correction** +0.15s/f (Slow)
WFA 4 from 5yo+ 3lb **5** Ran SP% **112.2**
Speed ratings (Par 103): **95,94,93,89,86**
CSF £10.36 TOTE £3.70: £2.20, £1.20; EX 12.20.

The Form Book, Raceform Ltd, Compton, RG20 6NL

Owner Tilen Electrics Ltd **Bred** Dan Daly **Trained** Exning, Suffolk
FOCUS
A modest little handicap in which the form looks straightforward enough rated around the placed horses.

887 RACE TO PONTIN'S CALL 0870 604 5620 H'CAP 6f (P)
5:10 (5:11) (Class 4) (0-80,86) 4-Y-O+ £4,100 (£1,227; £613; £306; £152) **Stalls** Low

Form RPR
-311 1 **Came Back (IRE)**[26] 599 5-9-0 **76** NCallan 3 88+
(K A Ryan) *t.k.h: trckd ldrs: hdwy to ld 1f out: rdn clr and sn in command: comf* **9/4**[1]
241 2 1¼ **Financial Times (USA)**[7] 824 6-9-10 **86** 6ex (t) MickyFenton 2 90
(Stef Liddiard) *t.k.h: hld up in rr: hdwy over 1f out: r.o wl to chse wnr ins fnl f: unable to chal* **7/2**[2]
2332 3 ½ **Sand Cat**[17] 707 5-9-1 **80** (b) MichaelJStainton(3) 5 83
(G L Moore) *v.s.a: wl bhd in last: c wd over 1f out: r.o strly fnl f: nt rch ldrs* **4/1**[3]
4550 4 ½ **Resplendent Alpha**[15] 729 4-8-13 **75** (b) JimmyQuinn 1 76
(P Howling) *s.i.s: pushed up into midfield and t.k.h after 1f: rdn 2f out: hdwy u.p over 1f out: one pce last 100yds* **5/1**
014- 5 ½ **Cativo Cavallino**[131] 6667 5-8-11 **78** NataliaGemelova(5) 10 78
(J E Long) *in tch: hdwy to chse ldrs over 2f out: drvn wl over 1f out: kpt on same pce* **10/1**
150- 6 ½ **Impromptu**[163] 5923 4-8-13 **75** SteveDrowne 11 73
(P G Murphy) *stdd and dropped in after s: hdwy jst over 2f out: sn rdn and unable qck: kpt on ins fnl f: nvr pce to trble ldrs* **20/1**
06-0 7 ½ **George The Second**[39] 427 5-8-6 **68** RichardKingscote 7 65
(Mrs H Sweeting) *chsd ldr: rdn to ld wl over 1f out: hdd 1f out: fdd fnl f* **20/1**
523 8 ¾ **Angel Voices (IRE)**[23] 628 5-7-12 **67** (p) DeclanCannon(7) 4 61
(K R Burke) *led: rdn and hdd wl over 1f out: wknd fnl f* **10/1**
060- 9 2¼ **Teen Ager (FR)**[139] 6492 4-8-13 **75** LPKeniry 6 63
(P Burgoyne) *t.k.h early: hld up in midfield: rdn jst over 2f out: wknd wl over 1f out* **25/1**

1m 12.01s (0.11) **Going Correction** +0.15s/f (Slow) **9** Ran SP% **121.2**
Speed ratings (Par 105): **105,103,102,102,101 100,100,99,96**
CSF £10.45 CT £30.71 TOTE £2.60: £1.20, £1.80, £1.70; EX 8.30 Trifecta £21.50 Pool: £433.24, 14.29 winning units.
Owner Mrs Ger O'Driscoll **Bred** Yeomanstown Stud **Trained** Hambleton, N Yorks
FOCUS
A fair sprint run at a decent pace. The form looks sound rated through the penalised runner-up and backed up by the third.

888 TIME TO GET EGG-CITED @ PONTIN'S H'CAP 1m 2f (P)
5:40 (5:40) (Class 4) (0-80,78) 4-Y-O+ £4,100 (£1,227; £613; £306; £152) **Stalls** Low

Form RPR
1112 1 **Safari Sundowner (IRE)**[14] 752 4-9-1 **75** JimCrowley 3 85+
(P Winkworth) *trckd ldr: rdn to ld jst over 2f out: clr 1f out: readily* **9/4**[1]
0-12 2 1¾ **Sun Of The Sea**[39] 428 4-8-12 **75** KirstyMilczarek(3) 6 82
(N P Littmoden) *t.k.h: hld up in tch: effrt and wanting to hang lft over 1f out: wnt 2nd ins fnl f: no ch w wnr* **9/4**[1]
-153 3 nk **Blacktoft (USA)**[19] 692 5-9-1 **75** (e) J-PGuillambert 4 81
(S C Williams) *plld hrd: hld up wl in tch in last pl: rdn and effrt 2f out: hung lft fr over 1f out: kpt on to go 3rd wl ins fnl f but nvr pce to threaten wnr* **7/1**[3]
4312 4 ¾ **Denbera Dancer (USA)**[10] 791 4-9-4 **78** JoeFanning 2 83
(M Johnston) *led at slow gallop: hdd and rdn jst over 2f out: one pce and lost 2 pls ins fnl f* **3/1**[2]
1-42 5 1¾ **Mr Napoleon (IRE)**[48] 316 6-8-8 **68** FergusSweeney 5 70
(G L Moore) *t.k.h: hld up in tch: rdn 2f out: kpt on same pce u.p* **7/1**[3]
-300 6 9 **Cavalry Guard (USA)**[25] 609 4-8-8 **68** PatCosgrave 1 53
(J R Boyle) *t.k.h: hld up in 3rd: rdn jst over 2f out: sn wl outpcd* **20/1**

2m 12.33s (5.73) **Going Correction** +0.15s/f (Slow) **6** Ran SP% **116.3**
Speed ratings (Par 105): **83,81,81,80,79 72**
CSF £7.96 TOTE £3.70: £2.20, £1.80; EX 7.50 Place 6 £ 61.05, Place 5 £ 27.64.
Owner P Winkworth **Bred** Michael Phelan **Trained** Chiddingfold, Surrey
FOCUS
A fair handicap, but the form should be treated with some caution due to the steady early pace that resulted in a moderate time.
T/Plt: £43.30 to a £1 stake. Pool: £58,553.85. 986.15 winning tickets. T/Qpdt: £11.10 to a £1 stake. Pool: £2,805.30. 187.00 winning tickets. SP

889 - 895a (Foreign Racing) - See Raceform Interactive

875 KEMPTON (A.W) (R-H)
Saturday, March 15

OFFICIAL GOING: Standard
Wind: Brisk, behind

896 32RED.COM CLAIMING STKS 6f (P)
6:20 (6:20) (Class 6) 4-Y-O+ £2,047 (£604; £302) **Stalls** High

Form RPR
-364 1 **Love On Sight**[9] 807 4-8-12 65 (v) NeilPollard 4 75
(A P Jarvis) *trckd ldrs: wnt 2nd 2f out: led over 1f out: styd on wl* **16/1**
-342 2 2½ **Red Rudy**[16] 729 6-9-0 70 LukeMorris(3) 2 72
(A W Carroll) *in rr: rdn and hdwy over 1f out: styd on u.p fnl f to take 2nd fnl 30yds but no ch w wnr* **10/11**[1]
3132 3 1 **Lindbergh**[15] 749 6-8-10 60 (v) JerryO'Dwyer(3) 5 65
(J Ryan) *led: hdd over 1f out: outpcd ins fnl f and lost 2nd fnl 30yds* **10/3**[2]
00-3 4 1¾ **Moayed**[9] 807 9-9-3 72 (b) IanMongan 1 63
(N P Littmoden) *s.i.s: in rr: rdn over 2f out: styd on fnl f but nvr in contention* **9/2**[3]
1420 5 2¼ **Chatshow (USA)**[21] 681 7-9-0 61 MarkCoumbe(7) 3 60
(A W Carroll) *chsd ldr 4f: sn wknd* **14/1**

1m 11.58s (-1.52) **Going Correction** -0.075s/f (Stan) **5** Ran SP% **106.2**
Speed ratings (Par 101): **107,103,102,100,97**
CSF £29.65 TOTE £13.00: £2.20, £1.30; EX 30.10. The winner was subject to a friendly claim.
Owner Mrs Ann Jarvis **Bred** Millsec Limited **Trained** Twyford, Bucks
■ Stewards' Enquiry : Luke Morris caution: used whip with arm above shoulder height

FOCUS
A reasonable claimer, and solid enough form. The winning time was almost identical to the later 56-70 handicap.

897 32REDMOBILE.COM MEDIAN AUCTION MAIDEN STKS 7f (P)
6:50 (6:50) (Class 5) 3-Y-O £2,457 (£725; £362) **Stalls** High

Form RPR
222- 1 **Elizabeth Swann**[163] 5949 3-8-12 82 RichardHughes 6 72+
(R Hannon) *hld up in rr: stdy hdwy fr 3f out: qcknd to chse ldr over 1f out: str run to ld fnl 100yds: readily* **4/6**[1]
- 2 1 **Erlydors (IRE)** 3-8-12 0 AdamKirby 4 68+
(W R Swinburn) *chsd ldrs: led over 2f out: drvn over 1f out: hdd and outpcd fnl 100yds* **7/2**[2]
-044 3 5 **Shabnaam**[27] 597 3-8-12 47 JimmyQuinn 9 49
(P Howling) *sn trcking ldrs: rdn over 2f out: styd on fnl f but no ch w ldng duo* **20/1**
60- 4 ¾ **Night Premiere (IRE)**[184] 5357 3-8-7 0 HaddenFrost(5) 5 47
(R Hannon) *prom early: lost pl and pushed along 1/2-way: styd on fr over 1f out and edgd rt: gng on cl home but nvr in contention* **10/1**
-240 5 shd **Coole Dodger (IRE)**[17] 712 3-8-10 64 KylieManser(7) 8 52
(B G Powell) *s.i.s: plld hrd in rr: hdwy over 2f out: kpt on ins fnl f but nvr gng pce to be competitive* **14/1**
0- 6 nk **Arniecoco**[234] 3849 3-9-3 0 TPQueally 3 51
(Miss J R Gibney) *chsd ldrs: outpcd over 3f out: drvn and styd on fr over 1f out: kpt on cl home but nvr a threat* **28/1**
0 7 ¾ **Estella Mai**[20] 694 3-8-9 0 TolleyDean(3) 11 44
(J J Bridger) *led tl hdd over 2f out: wknd over 1f out* **100/1**
8 1 **Veni Bidi Vici** 3-8-12 0 NeilChalmers 2 41
(A M Balding) *s.i.s: a in rr* **8/1**[3]
0 9 ½ **Sidestreet**[10] 796 3-9-3 0 ChrisCatlin 7 45
(K McAuliffe) *rdn over 3f out: a towards rr* **50/1**

1m 26.87s (0.87) **Going Correction** -0.075s/f (Stan) **9** Ran SP% **120.2**
Speed ratings (Par 98): **92,90,85,84,84 83,82,81,81**
CSF £3.27 TOTE £1.50: £1.10, £1.30, £3.50; EX 4.30.
Owner Richard Morecombe **Bred** Stourbank Stud **Trained** East Everleigh, Wilts
FOCUS
A modest maiden. The bare form is not worth a great deal with the third rated only 47, but the front pair are better than the bare facts. The winning time was 1.06 seconds slower than the following 46-52 handicap, and 0.86 seconds slower than the later 56-70 fillies' contest.

898 FREE £10 AT 32REDBINGO.COM H'CAP 7f (P)
7:20 (7:20) (Class 6) (0-52,56) 4-Y-O+ £2,047 (£604; £302) **Stalls** High

Form RPR
-546 1 **Alucica**[17] 711 5-8-9 **49** (v) JimCrowley 10 56
(D Shaw) *t.k.h: edgd rt after 1f: mid-div: hdwy 2f out: str run fnl f and upsides fnl 100yds: led last strides: all out* **10/1**
5611 2 nk **Marmooq**[20] 693 5-8-7 **47** (e) IanMongan 1 53
(M J Attwater) *chsd ldrs: rdn 2f out: led over 1f out: styd on u.p whn chal fnl f: hdd last strides* **11/2**[3]
1231 3 1¾ **Avoca Dancer (IRE)**[3] 858 5-9-2 **56** 6ex TGMcLaughlin 12 60+
(M Wigham) *bdly hmpd and dropped to rr after 1f: stl plenty to do fr 2f out: r.o wl fnl f: gng on cl home* **3/1**[1]
0/00 4 1 **Zorn**[3] 858 9-8-10 **50** JimmyQuinn 7 49
(P Howling) *led: rdn over 2f out: hdd over 1f out: wknd ins fnl f* **33/1**
3055 5 ½ **Batchworth Blaise**[17] 711 5-8-7 **47** LPKeniry 9 45
(E A Wheeler) *in rr: hdwy and n.m.r over 1f out: kpt on ins fnl f but nt rch ldrs* **14/1**
6230 6 1 **Tuning Fork**[10] 795 8-8-5 **48** TolleyDean(3) 8 44
(M J Attwater) *t.k.h: in rr: rdn and hdwy fr 2f out: nt pce to rch ldrs* **7/1**
5040 7 2½ **Robinzal**[4] 844 6-8-9 **52** (t) LukeMorris(3) 6 41
(A W Carroll) *towards rr: sme prog u.p fr over 1f out: n.d* **12/1**
00-6 8 hd **Buzbury Rings**[34] 516 4-8-12 **52** FrancisNorton 11 41
(A M Balding) *t.k.h: chsd ldrs: rdn 2f out and sn btn* **7/2**[2]
-000 9 4½ **Julian Joachim (USA)**[16] 728 4-8-7 **47** (t) PaulHanagan 4 25
(D Shaw) *sn bhd* **16/1**
6/0 10 5 **Divinshki (IRE)**[1] 877 8-8-6 **46** oh1 (t) ChrisCatlin 5 11
(Irene J Monaghan, Ire) *pressed ldr to 3f out: sn btn* **16/1**
0600 11 5 **Golden Square**[17] 711 6-8-3 **46** KirstyMilczarek(3) 2 —
(A W Carroll) *nvr bttr than mid-div* **16/1**

1m 25.81s (-0.19) **Going Correction** -0.075s/f (Stan) **11** Ran SP% **119.1**
Speed ratings (Par 101): **98,97,95,94,93 92,89,89,84,78 73**
CSF £65.06 CT £212.87 TOTE £13.40: £3.80, £2.00, £1.20; EX 86.90.
Owner Shakespeare Racing **Bred** D R Tucker **Trained** Danethorpe, Notts
FOCUS
A very moderate handicap but the form is solid enough. The winning time was 1.06 seconds quicker than the previous three-year-old maiden, and 0.20 seconds faster than the following 56-70 fillies' handicap.
Avoca Dancer(IRE) ◆ Official explanation: jockey said mare suffered interference in running
Buzbury Rings Official explanation: jockey said gelding ran too free
Julian Joachim(USA) Official explanation: jockey said gelding had a breathing problem

899 $500 BONUS AT 32REDPOKER.COM FILLIES' H'CAP 7f (P)
7:50 (7:51) (Class 5) (0-70,70) 3-Y-O+ £2,590 (£770; £385; £192) **Stalls** High

Form RPR
-230 1 **Miss Mujanna**[29] 573 3-9-0 **69** J-PGuillambert 11 74
(J Akehurst) *chsd ldrs: edgd lft and rt over 1f out: qcknd smartly ins fnl f and sn led: readily* **17/2**
020- 2 1¾ **Anthill**[142] 6455 4-9-9 **62** GeorgeBaker 9 68
(I A Wood) *w ldr tl slt advantage over 1f out: hdd ins fnl f: sn outpcd by wnr but kpt on wl for 2nd* **22/1**
5-40 3 ½ **Little Knickers**[17] 712 3-8-13 **68** HayleyTurner 14 67
(Andrew Reid) *towards rr: stl plenty to do 2f out: rapid hdwy over 1f out: gng on cl home* **50/1**
2320 4 ½ **Gimme Some Lovin (IRE)**[12] 775 4-9-10 **63** (p) FrancisNorton 7 66
(D W P Arbuthnot) *in rr: hdwy over 1f out: kpt on ins fnl f but nvr quite gng pce to chal* **13/2**[3]
0-35 5 ½ **Affirmatively**[31] 538 3-9-1 **70** AlanMunro 12 66
(D R C Elsworth) *chsd ldrs: str chal fr over 1f out tl ins fnl f: wknd nr fin* **16/1**
51 6 nse **Princess Livius (IRE)**[36] 487 3-8-12 **67** FergusSweeney 3 63
(G L Moore) *in rr: hdwy over 1f out: r.o ins fnl f: nt rch ldrs* **12/1**
1 7 ½ **Mrs Jefferson (IRE)**[20] 694 3-9-1 **70** JamesDoyle 10 64
(J G Portman) *in tch: rdn over 2f out: kpt on same pce ins fnl f* **14/1**
-004 8 shd **Trivia (IRE)**[16] 731 4-10-0 **67** TGMcLaughlin 4 67
(Ms J S Doyle) *s.i.s: bhd: hdwy on ins fnl 2f: kpt on ins fnl f but nvr in contention* **33/1**

2211 **9** *1* **Another Genepi (USA)**3 856 5-10-2 **69** 6ex................(b) FergalLynch 1 66
(Andrew Reid) *slowly away: in rr: kpt on fr over 1f out but nvr in contention* **3/1**1

1-42 **10** *2 1/4* **Blackmalkin (USA)**46 349 4-9-13 **66**.................................. TPQueally 8 57
(M Quinn) *nvr in contention* **5/1**2

4022 **11** *nk* **Maggie Kate**24 629 3-8-9 **64**.............................(p) RobertHavlin 13 49
(R Ingram) *led and kpt slt advantage tl hdd over 1f out: sn wknd* **8/1**

660- **12** *1* **Rakeekah**119 6849 3-8-12 **67**.. RHills 5 49
(J H M Gosden) *in tch: hdwy on outside 3f out: wknd over 1f out* **8/1**

1-46 **13** *5* **Easy Wonder (GER)**25 619 3-9-0 **69**...................................... JoeFanning 2 37
(I A Wood) *chsd ldrs: chal ins fnl 2f: sn wknd* **20/1**

206- **14** *3 1/4* **River Gleam (IRE)**154 6177 3-8-12 **67**........................ RichardHughes 6 27
(A P Jarvis) *chsd ldrs over 4f* **25/1**

1m 26.01s (0.01) **Going Correction** -0.075s/f (Stan)
WFA 3 from 4yo+ 16lb **14** Ran SP% **125.8**
Speed ratings (Par 100): **96,94,93,92,92 92,91,91,90,87 87,86,80,76**
CSF £194.58 CT £8583.24 TOTE £12.00: £3.50, £9.90, £5.50; EX 267.60.
Owner Green Pastures Partnership **Bred** Green Pastures Farm **Trained** Epsom, Surrey

FOCUS
A modest fillies' handicap in which the winner produced an improved effort. The winning time was 0.86 seconds faster than the earlier three-year-old maiden, but 0.20 seconds slower than the 46-52 handicap.
Trivia(IRE) Official explanation: jockey said filly missed the break
Another Genepi(USA) Official explanation: jockey said mare missed the break

900 MOBILE ROULETTE TEXT "32" TO 89932 H'CAP — 1m (P)
8:20 (8:20) (Class 5) (0-75,75) 3-Y-O **£2,590** (£770; £385; £192) **Stalls High**

Form RPR

3-32 **1** **Tenjack King**16 737 3-9-1 **72**.. TPQueally 7 80
(J A Osborne) *trckd ldrs: swtchd rt ins fnl 2f: wnt rt to rails over 1f out: sn qcknd to ld ins fnl f: drvn out* **2/1**1

66- **2** *1 1/4* **Irish Artist (FR)**144 6410 3-8-11 **68**...................... RichardHughes 1 73
(R Hannon) *in rr: hdwy over 2f out: str run to chse wnr ins fnl f but a hld* **10/1**

2-04 **3** *1 1/2* **Desiderio**10 797 3-7-11 **61** oh4...............................(p) CharlesEddery(7) 5 63
(R Hannon) *led: rdn over 2f out: kpt slt advantage tl hdd under 1f out: sn outpcd* **25/1**

1311 **4** *1 1/4* **Bridge Of Fermoy (IRE)**8 820 3-9-4 **75**..................(bt) GeorgeBaker 4 74
(Miss Gay Kelleway) *sn trcking ldrs: rdn over 2f out: nvr quite gng pce to chal: wknd ins fnl f* **5/1**2

21 **5** *2 1/4* **Trimaran (IRE)**15 748 3-9-0 **71**.................................... JoeFanning 2 66+
(M Johnston) *trckd ldrs: rdn to chal fr 2f out: wkng whn n.m.r 1f out* **2/1**1

400- **6** *2* **Mr Fantozzi (IRE)**225 4130 3-8-7 **64**..................................... DMylonas 6 54
(Miss J Feilden) *outpcd most of way* **33/1**

023- **7** *3/4* **It's Josr**94 7121 3-8-11 **68**... AdamKirby 9 56
(I A Wood) *in tch: rdn 3f out: sn btn* **16/1**

40-2 **8** *5* **Montefiore (IRE)**17 712 3-8-10 **70**.......................(t) KirstyMilczarek(3) 8 47
(M Botti) *s.i.s: in rr whn hmpd ins fnl 4f: nvr in contention after* **7/1**3

4100 **9** *14* **Hit The Roof**8 820 3-8-8 **68**.. TolleyDean(3) 3 14
(D Shaw) *bhd fr 1/2-way* **33/1**

1m 39.11s (-0.69) **Going Correction** -0.075s/f (Stan) **9** Ran SP% **120.5**
Speed ratings (Par 98): **100,98,97,96,93 91,91,86,72**
CSF £25.83 CT £393.66 TOTE £3.30: £1.50, £3.40, £4.20; EX 38.20.
Owner Robert Goldsack & Ten **Bred** Cheveley Park Stud Ltd **Trained** Upper Lambourn, Berks
■ Stewards' Enquiry : Richard Hughes three-day ban: careless riding (Mar 26-28)
T P Queally one-day ban: used whip with excessive force (Mar 28)

FOCUS
A fair handicap that should produce a few winners. An easy race to assess with the first two running to form.

901 £100 BONUS AT 32RED.COM H'CAP — 6f (P)
8:50 (8:50) (Class 5) (0-70,70) 4-Y-O+ **£2,590** (£770; £385; £192) **Stalls High**

Form RPR

2136 **1** **Royal Envoy (IRE)**12 775 5-8-7 **62**.................................... TolleyDean(3) 7 73
(D Shaw) *in tch: rdn 2f out: hdwy over 1f out: led fnl 110yds: drvn out* **4/1**2

4314 **2** *1* **Dvinsky (USA)**12 775 7-9-4 **70**....................................(b) JimmyQuinn 4 78
(P Howling) *chsd ldrs: rdn and str chal 1f out: stl upsides ins fnl f: outpcd by wnr fnl 110yds* **13/2**3

0613 **3** *shd* **Hollow Jo**15 746 8-9-1 **67**.. MickyFenton 12 75
(J R Jenkins) *chsd ldrs: rdn 2f out: narrow ld 1f out: hdd and no ex fnl 110yds* **13/2**3

1000 **4** *2 1/4* **Littledodayno (IRE)**14 766 5-8-10 **62**............................... FrancisNorton 6 66+
(M Wigham) *in rr: hdwy: nt clr run and swtchd lft over 1f out: kpt on cl home but nvr gng pce to be competitive* **15/2**

300- **5** *1 1/2* **Game Lady**126 6762 4-8-13 **65**.. JoeFanning 8 61
(I A Wood) *led: kpt slt advantage tl hdd 1f out: sn wknd* **20/1**

505- **6** *hd* **Sun Catcher (IRE)**144 6406 5-9-2 **68**........................... RobertHavlin 10 64
(P G Murphy) *in rr: hdwy over 1f out: fin wl but nvr in contention* **7/1**

0206 **7** *nk* **Mind Alert**24 628 7-8-10 **62**...(v) JamesDoyle 9 57
(D Shaw) *in rr: sme prog fr over 1f out: nvr in contention* **16/1**

611- **8** *1 3/4* **Rabbit Fighter (IRE)**87 7183 4-9-4 **70**.......................(v) PaulHanagan 11 60
(D Shaw) *s.i.s: nvr in contention* **7/2**1

500- **9** *2 3/4* **Gleaming Spirit (IRE)**137 6575 4-9-1 **67**......................... AndrewElliott 5 48
(A P Jarvis) *w ldr: rdn over 2f out: wknd over 1f out* **14/1**

600- **10** *15* **Namir (IRE)**170 5747 6-9-0 **69**.................................(vt) DuranFentiman(3) 2 5
(D Shaw) *t.k.h: bhd most of way* **25/1**

461- **11** *5* **Hollywood George**323 1281 4-9-2 **68**................................... AdamKirby 3 —
(Miss M E Rowland) *in tch: to 1/2-way* **16/1**

1m 11.57s (-1.53) **Going Correction** -0.075s/f (Stan) **11** Ran SP% **120.2**
Speed ratings (Par 103): **107,105,105,102,100 100,99,97,93,73 67**
CSF £31.10 CT £172.32 TOTE £5.60: £1.50, £2.00, £2.50; EX 36.40.
Owner The Circle Bloodstock I Limited **Bred** Northern Lights Bloodstock **Trained** Danethorpe, Notts

FOCUS
A modest sprint handicap, but solid form which ought to prove reliable. The winning time was almost identical to the earlier claimer.
Hollywood George Official explanation: jockey said colt stopped quickly

902 32RED.COM BEST CASINO SINCE 2003 CONDITIONS STKS — 1m 1f (P)
9:20 (9:20) (Class 2) 3-Y-O **£16,192** (£4,817; £2,407; £1,202) **Stalls High**

Form RPR

410- **1** **Campanologist (USA)**168 5795 3-9-3 **92**........................... JoeFanning 2 102+
(M Johnston) *sn trcking ldr: led ins fnl 2f: c clr ins fnl f: readily* **10/3**2

41- **2** *1 3/4* **Whitcombe Minister (USA)**77 7266 3-9-3 **83**............................ JohnEgan 6 96
(Jamie Poulton) *chsd ldrs: rdn and styd on fr 2f out: tk 2nd ins fnl f but no ch w wnr* **7/1**

016- **3** *1* **Cordell (IRE)**148 6297 3-9-3 **82**.. RichardHughes 5 93
(R Hannon) *led: rdn 3f out: hdd ins fnl 2f: no ch w wnr 1f out: lost 2nd ins fnl f* **14/1**

15-0 **4** *3 1/4* **Siberian Tiger (IRE)**30 567 3-9-3 **0**................................ EdwardCreighton 4 87+
(M R Channon) *towards rr: hdwy on outside over 2f out: styd on fnl f but nvr in contention* **7/1**

215- **5** *2 1/2* **Pegasus Again (USA)**196 5048 3-9-3 **95**............................ JimCrowley 1 80
(T G Mills) *in rr: rdn 3f out: mod prog fr over 1f out* **7/4**1

350- **6** *1 1/4* **Ellmau**185 5324 3-9-3 **100**... ChrisCatlin 7 77
(E J O'Neill) *chsd ldrs: rdn 3f out: wknd 2f out* **7/2**3

025- **7** *1 1/4* **Randama Bay (IRE)**129 6714 3-9-3 **75**.............................. AdamKirby 3 73
(I A Wood) *a towards rr* **50/1**

0-0 **8** *12* **Mr Plod**21 674 3-9-3 **0**... HayleyTurner 8 48
(Andrew Reid) *bhd fr 1/2-way* **66/1**

1m 54.19s (114.19) **8** Ran SP% **116.8**
CSF £27.48 TOTE £5.00: £1.50, £1.90, £3.60; EX 37.80 Place 6 £176.33, Place 5 £106.70 .
Owner Sheikh Hamdan Bin Mohammed Al Maktoum **Bred** Darley **Trained** Middleham Moor, N Yorks

FOCUS
A decent three-year-old contest. The form can be rated around the third and the winner is progressive.

NOTEBOOK
Campanologist(USA) ◆, a dual winner at two, showed he has wintered well and did the job in good style on this All-Weather debut. He had disappointed on his final outing last year, but that was in the Group 2 Royal Lodge Stakes on soft ground, and there is little doubt that he needs a sound surface to shine. He is also entitled to come on a deal for the run and, in very good hands, he looks worthy of another try in Pattern company this year. (op 11-4)
Whitcombe Minister(USA) ◆, last seen making all in a 7f Lingfield maiden 77 days previously, turned in his best effort to date on this step up in trip and class. He got the distance well enough and, considering he is rated officially 9lb inferior to the winner, his connections will no doubt be delighted with this effort. (op 15-2 tchd 8-1)
Cordell(IRE), making his three-year-old debut, had won on his only previous outing at the track. He was another to perform with real credit, only tiring at the business end, and should come on nicely for the run. (op 16-1)
Siberian Tiger(IRE) improved on the lacklustre level of his debut on dirt in Dubai a month ago and was not disgraced. However, he still has to truly prove he retains the ability that saw him run well in Group 1 company on his final outing last term. (op 9-2)
Pegasus Again(USA), whose third and final outing last season was in the Group 3 Solario Stakes over 7f, produced a laboured effort on this return to action and never looked like justifying favouritism. He has something to prove now. (op 2-1)
Ellmau has the highest official rating of these lot and met support in the betting ring on this first run for six months, but he was eventually done with shortly after entering the home straight. (op 6-1)
Mr Plod Official explanation: jockey said gelding hung left
T/Plt: £461.70 to a £1 stake. Pool: £76,923.15. 121.60 winning tickets. T/Qpdt: £148.10 to a £1 stake. Pool: £6,106.40. 30.50 winning tickets. ST

882 LINGFIELD (L-H)
Saturday, March 15

OFFICIAL GOING: Standard
Wind: Moderate, across Weather: Overcast, light rain race 5

903 LIFESTYLESERVICES.UK.COM MAIDEN STKS — 1m 2f (P)
1:40 (1:42) (Class 4) 3-Y-O **£4,731** (£1,416; £708; £354; £176) **Stalls Low**

Form RPR

0- **1** **Summer Winds**204 4761 3-9-3 .... JamieSpencer 5 73
(T G Mills) *chsd ldrs: led 1f out: hrd rdn fnl f: jst hld on* **7/2**1

03 **2** *hd* **Emshabb**8 820 3-8-12 .... LiamJones 3 68+
(W J Haggas) *hld up in midfield: hdwy on rail 2f out: r.o wl fnl f: jockey momentarily stopped riding 25 yds out: jst failed* **25/1**

3- **3** *1/2* **Princess Lomi (IRE)**224 4162 3-8-12 .... ChrisCatlin 1 67
(E J O'Neill) *in tch on rail: pushed along 5f out: drvn to chse ldrs over 1f out: r.o fnl f* **7/1**3

- **4** *hd* **Vice Consul** 3-9-3 .... JoeFanning 11 72
(M Johnston) *dwlt: hdwy to press ldr after 3f: led over 3f out tl over 2f out: one pce fnl f* **4/1**2

0-3 **5** *3/4* **Nowzdetime (IRE)**29 570 3-8-12 .... JamieJones(5) 14 70
(M G Quinlan) *led tl over 3f out: led over 2f out tl 1f out: no ex ins fnl f* **15/2**

6 *nk* **Barring Decree (IRE)** 3-8-12 .... DPMcDonogh 4 65+
(E J O'Neill) *mid-div: hrd rdn over 2f out: styd on fnl f: nvr nrr* **8/1**

7 *3* **Every Whisper (IRE)** 3-8-12 .... JimCrowley 2 59
(Mrs A J Perrett) *dwlt: rn green in rr: pushed along and styd on steadily fnl 3f: should improve* **11/1**

50 **8** *hd* **Fairfield Flame (GER)**15 748 3-8-12 .... AlanMunro 7 58
(D R C Elsworth) *chsd ldrs: rdn over 4f out: sn outpcd* **7/1**3

522- **9** *1 1/2* **No To Trident**154 6184 3-9-3 **75**.............................. StephenDonohoe 10 60
(P D Evans) *t.k.h: chsd ldrs tl wknd ent st* **7/1**3

3 **10** *3/4* **Azabu Juban (IRE)**22 657 3-8-5 .... NatalieJankiewicz(7) 8 54
(J Jay) *dwlt: restrained towards rr: r.o fnl 2f: can do bttr* **25/1**

0-U **11** *nk* **Malt Empress (IRE)**29 570 3-8-9 .... DJMoran(3) 9 53
(B W Duke) *t.k.h: prom tl wknd over 1f out* **100/1**

0-0 **12** *5* **Wheninneedyou**23 645 3-8-12 ....(t) NCallan 13 43
(I A Wood) *mid-div: effrt and hrd rdn over 2f out: wknd over 1f out* **100/1**

0- **13** *8* **Amphibalus (IRE)**173 5679 3-9-3 .... HayleyTurner 6 32
(D K Ivory) *dwlt: rdn 4f out: a bhd* **40/1**

00- **14** *4 1/2* **Mums The Best**302 1814 3-8-9 .... LukeMorris(3) 12 18
(A B Coogan) *dwlt: t.k.h towards rr: rdn 4f out: sn bhd* **100/1**

2m 10.07s (3.47) **Going Correction** +0.125s/f (Slow) **14** Ran SP% **124.0**
Speed ratings (Par 100): **91,90,90,90,89 89,87,86,85,85 84,80,74,70**
CSF £102.28 TOTE £4.10: £1.40, £8.30, £2.20; EX 131.80 TRIFECTA Not won..
Owner John Humphreys **Bred** Beechgrove Stud **Trained** Headley, Surrey
■ Stewards' Enquiry : Natalie Jankiewicz 14-day ban: breach of Rule 158 (Mar 26-29, 31, Apr 1-5, 7-10)
Liam Jones ten-day ban: failed to ride out for first place (Mar 26-29, 31, Apr 1-5)

FOCUS
A fair maiden run, but it was run at a moderate gallop - the time was 6.46secs slower than the Winter Derby - and produced a close finish. Difficult to be that positive about the form, although there were several eye-catching performances.

Azabu Juban(IRE) Official explanation: jockey said, regarding running and riding, her orders were to make the running, but she was unable to do so as the filly was slowly away, adding that she was unable to take closer order and did not get the best of runs; trainer confirmed orders but was dissatisfied the jockey did not achieve an early prominent position, this being her third ride in public, that she could have made more of an effort in running.

904 DIAMONDRACING.CO.UK H'CAP — 7f (P)

2:10 (2:12) (Class 2) (0-100,103) 4-Y-0+

£12,464 (£3,732; £1,866; £934; £466; £234) **Stalls** Low

Form	Pos	Btn	Horse	RPR
4441	1		**Atlantic Story (USA)**^{21} [679] 6-9-2 **98**.....................(bt) JamieSpencer 5 (M W Easterby) *chsd ldr: led 1f out: rdn out* **7/2**^{2}	107
6-22	2	1 1/4	**Gallantry**^{28} [594] 6-8-5 **90**........................ TolleyDean(3) 3 (D Shaw) *disp 4th: effrt and hrd rdn over 1f out: r.o to take 2nd fnl 100yds* **13/2**	96
1133	3	nk	**Monkey Glas (IRE)**^{21} [680] 4-8-8 **90**.....................(v) AndrewElliott 2 (K R Burke) *led: rdn over 2f out: hdd 1f out: one pce* **9/2**^{3}	95
31-2	4	1	**Ceremonial Jade (UAE)**^{21} [677] 5-9-6 **102**...............(tp) OscarUrbina 7 (M Botti) *dwlt: towards rr: rdn and styd on fnl 2f: nt rch ldrs* **10/3**^{1}	104+
551-	5	1	**Purus (IRE)**^{133} [6651] 6-8-5 **87**........................ ChrisCatlin 1 (R A Teal) *chsd ldng pair: rdn over 2f out: wknd fnl f* **14/1**	87
0400	6	2 1/4	**Qadar (IRE)**^{7} [836] 6-8-1 **86** oh1.....................(p) WilliamBuick(3) 4 (N P Littmoden) *hld up in rr: mod effrt on rail ent st: no imp* **6/1**	80
0604	7	1/2	**Vortex**^{21} [680] 9-9-7 **103**........................(t) GeorgeBaker 8 (Miss Gay Kelleway) *dwlt: hld up in tch disputing 4th: rdn 2f out: wknd over 1f out* **14/1**	96
1106	8	9	**Bazroy (IRE)**^{7} [836] 4-9-1 **97**.....................(b) StephenDonohoe 6 (P D Evans) *t.k.h in 6th: rdn 2f out: sn bhd* **10/1**	66

1m 23.69s (-1.11) **Going Correction** +0.125s/f (Slow) **8 Ran SP% 113.5**
Speed ratings (Par 109): **111,109,109,108,106 104,103,93**
CSF £26.00 CT £102.50 TOTE £3.30: £1.50, £2.00, £2.00; EX 21.90 Trifecta £64.50 Pool: £948.04 - 10.42 winning tickets..

Owner Matthew Green **Bred** Arthur I Appleton **Trained** Sheriff Hutton, N Yorks

FOCUS
A high-class handicap run in a time 1.31 secs faster than the following Listed race. The form looks solid.

NOTEBOOK
Atlantic Story(USA) is a very effective performer on the All-Weather and took his record to ten wins in 15 starts with a straightforward success in this good handicap. He got a good lead from Monkey Glas until going on at the furlong mark and was never in danger from that point. A winner on all four All-Weather tracks, he is not far short of Listed class on this evidence. (op 3-1 tchd 11-4)

Gallantry, narrowly beaten in his two races since the turn of the year, put up another fine effort but again arrived on the scene a little too late. He ran pretty close with the winner to their Kempton form from February last year and deserves to pick up a decent race, so possibly Kempton's new 1m1f track may provide him with a suitable opportunity. (op 6-1 tchd 7-1)

Monkey Glas(IRE), closely matched with the runner-up on last month's course and distance form, ran very close to that mark under a positive ride. He is holding his form well despite a rising handicap mark; the visor having made the difference. (op 11-2)

Ceremonial Jade(UAE), who ran well in a Listed race over 6f here last time, looked to have a sound chance in this handicap with the trip likely to be in his favour. However, he could never land a serious blow in the straight after having missed the break and had to race wide from his high draw. (op 5-2)

Purus(IRE), a progressive sort on turf last season, was racing off his highest mark to date on this first outing since November. He did not run badly and this should sharpen him up for a return to the grass. (op 16-1 tchd 12-1)

Qadar(IRE), with cheekpieces replacing the usual blinkers, was the subject of market support despite being a pound out of the handicap. He never really figured, having been held up out the back in a race in which it was difficult to come from behind. (op 14-1)

905 BETDIRECT.COM SPRING CUP (LISTED RACE) — 7f (P)

2:40 (2:41) (Class 1) 3-Y-0

£34,068 (£12,912; £6,462; £3,222; £1,614; £810) **Stalls** Low

Form	Pos	Btn	Horse	RPR
311-	1		**Paco Boy (IRE)**^{134} [6621] 3-9-1 93........................ RichardHughes 3 (R Hannon) *stdd s: patiently rdn fr last pl: fnd gap and rapid hdwy over 1f out: qcknd wl to ld fnl 50yds: impressive* **3/1**^{1}	101+
410-	2	1 3/4	**Tasdeer (USA)**^{162} [5972] 3-9-1 90........................ RHills 10 (M A Jarvis) *t.k.h: in tch on outside: pressed ldrs 3f out: led over 1f out: hdd and nt pce of wnr fnl 50yds* **7/2**^{2}	93
21-1	3	shd	**Geezers Colours**^{63} [136] 3-9-1 88........................ FergusSweeney 2 (K R Burke) *trckd ldrs: effrt over 1f out: kpt on fnl f* **13/2**	93
44-1	4	1 3/4	**Silver Guest**^{28} [590] 3-9-1 98........................ EdwardCreighton 4 (M R Channon) *hld up in midfield: swtchd to rail and hdwy to chse ldrs whn nt clr run over 1f out: rallied and r.o fnl f* **6/1**	93+
12-	5	nk	**King Hafhafah**^{121} [6823] 3-9-1 79........................ NCallan 9 (I A Wood) *dwlt: towards rr: effrt on outside over 2f out: rdn and styd on same pce* **22/1**	87
42-	6	1 1/2	**Tathkaar**^{161} [6015] 3-8-10 0........................ SebSanders 8 (C E Brittain) *pressed ldr: led 2f out tl over 1f out: wknd fnl f* **16/1**	79+
104-	7	3/4	**Ruff Diamond (USA)**^{245} [3522] 3-9-1 93........................ GeorgeBaker 6 (J R Best) *chsd ldrs: rdn over 3f out: btn over 1f out* **16/1**	82
00-1	8	1/2	**Cee Bargara**^{21} [687] 3-9-1 93........................ TPQueally 5 (J A Osborne) *led tl 2f out: wknd 1f out* **11/2**^{3}	80
-211	9	shd	**Mister New York (USA)**^{15} [756] 3-9-1 81........................ KirstyMilczarek 1 (Noel T Chance) *hld up towards rr: effrt whn nt clr run and hmpd over 1f out: swtchd rt: nvr able to chal* **8/1**	83+
16-4	10	hd	**Naughty Frida (IRE)**^{17} [723] 3-8-10 78........................ OscarUrbina 7 (M Botti) *in tch: rdn and outpcd over 2f out: wknd over 1f out* **33/1**	74

1m 25.0s (0.20) **Going Correction** +0.125s/f (Slow) **10 Ran SP% 120.4**
Speed ratings (Par 106): **103,101,100,98,98 96,95,95,95,95**
CSF £13.99 TOTE £3.50: £1.70, £2.00, £2.40; EX 15.00 Trifecta £135.80 Pool: £700.07 - 3.66 winning tickets..

Owner The Calvera Partnership No 2 **Bred** Mrs Joan Browne **Trained** East Everleigh, Wilts

■ Stewards' Enquiry : T P Queally two-day ban: careless riding (Mar 26-27)

FOCUS
A decent Listed race, featuring several interestting runners, but run 1.31secs slower than the preceding handicap for older horses. The winner was highly impressive and is one to be positive about.

NOTEBOOK
Paco Boy(IRE) ◆, who won twice on turf last year after a Polytrack debut, was stepping up in trip on this seasonal debut. He was held up at the back and Hughes looked to have overdone the waiting tactics when the gap did not immediately appear off the home turf, but once in the clear he picked up in highly impressive fashion to score going away. He is built like a sprinter but, now he has proved he stays this trip, will be aimed at either the Greenham or the Free Handicap. He looks as if he needs a sound surface, but providing he gets it he will take some beating on this evidence. (op 11-4 tchd 10-3 and 7-2 in a place)

Tasdeer(USA), who disappointed when tried in a Group 3 on his last outing of last season, was well supported on this return to action. He did not settle that well but travelled smoothly into contention and looked the most likely winner when going to the front. However, he could not respond when the winner arrived on the scene and barely held on for second. (op 11-4 tchd 5-2)

Geezers Colours has been most progressive this winter, rising by 21lb in the handicap, but he still had something to find judged on official ratings on this first try at Listed level. He ran his race though and probably represents the best guide to the form. (op 8-1)

Silver Guest ◆ had the highest official rating in the contest and had shown he handles this surface when scoring here on his return to action. He lost lengths when stopped in his run against the rail and although he rallied really well, he could never get in a blow. He might well have finished second had things gone his way and the longer trip did not seem to be a problem. (op 9-1 tchd 12-1)

King Hafhafah, who had not been seen since narrowly failing to give 10lb to today's runner-up in a course and distance nursery back in November, ran a decent race on this return to action, especially considering he missed the break. He should be sharper for this and could be up to winning a good handicap if the assessor does not raise him too much for this. (op 25-1 tchd 20-1)

Tathkaar, a maiden making her All-Weather debut, faced a big task against the colts on this step up in grade but showed up until headed by the runner-up in the straight. She can win a maiden against her own sex and, being related to stayers, may appreciate further in time. (op 22-1)

Ruff Diamond(USA), who had not raced since July, appears to have done well during his absence. He shaped as if this was needed and was not disgraced. Sprinting could be his game. Official explanation: jockey said colt hung left in straight (tchd 14-1)

Cee Bargara, an All-Weather winner at Cagnes-Sur-Mer recently, was reportedly due to go to California afterwards but instead took his chance here. He made the running, as he did in France, but was brushed aside in the straight. Held in six attempts at Listed and Group level now, the American option may offer his best chance of further success. (op 13-2)

906 BETDIRECT.COM WINTER DERBY (3RD LEG OF THE EUROPEAN ALL WEATHER SERIES) (GROUP 3) — 1m 2f (P)

3:15 (3:18) (Class 1) 4-Y-0+

£56,780 (£21,520; £10,770; £5,370; £2,690; £1,350) **Stalls** Low

Form	Pos	Btn	Horse	RPR
140-	1		**Hattan (IRE)**^{132} [6689] 6-9-0 105........................ SebSanders 7 (C E Brittain) *chsd ldrs: effrt over 2f out: led 1f out: drvn clr* **14/1**	115
21-1	2	2	**Silver Pivotal (IRE)**^{49} [315] 4-8-11 105........................ JamieSpencer 14 (G A Butler) *hld up in rr: rdn 2f out: gd late hdwy: tk 2nd nr fin: nt rch wnr* **7/2**^{1}	111+
004-	3	nk	**Great Hawk (USA)**^{175} [5634] 5-9-0 98.....................(v) JimmyFortune 5 (Sir Michael Stoute) *trckd ldrs: effrt over 1f out: drvn to chse wnr ins fnl f: kpt on: lost 2nd nr fin* **22/1**	111
24-2	4	3/4	**Dubai's Touch**^{21} [678] 4-9-0 109........................ JoeFanning 1 (M Johnston) *t.k.h: chsd ldr: led briefly over 1f out: one pce fnl f* **9/2**^{3}	109
12-0	5	hd	**Grand Passion (IRE)**^{21} [678] 8-9-0 105........................ SteveDrowne 11 (G Wragg) *in rr of mid-div: pushed along 5f out: styd on u.p fnl 2f: nvr nrr* **20/1**	109
52-2	6	1	**Orchard Supreme**^{56} [227] 5-9-0 100........................ RichardHughes 9 (R Hannon) *hld up in rr: sme hdwy 2f out: hrd rdn over 1f out: nt pce to chal* **33/1**	107
1423	7	1	**Baylini**^{21} [678] 4-8-11 94........................ JamesDoyle 6 (Ms J S Doyle) *prom: led over 2f out tl over 1f out: wknd fnl f* **20/1**	102
-024	8	1 1/4	**Dream Lodge (IRE)**^{21} [678] 4-9-0 93........................ TPQueally 2 (J G Given) *led tl over 2f out: wknd fnl f* **66/1**	103
11-2	9	6	**Evident Pride (USA)**^{63} [138] 5-9-0 96........................ ChrisCatlin 10 (B R Johnson) *hld up in midfield: tk clsr order and in tch 4f out: rdn 2f out: sn btn* **10/1**	91
65-1	10	1/2	**Philatelist (USA)**^{28} [592] 4-9-0 94........................ NCallan 3 (M A Jarvis) *t.k.h: in tch on rail: rdn over 3f out: chsd ldrs over 1f out: sn hrd rdn: n.m.r and wknd: eased whn btn fnl 100yds* **11/2**	92+
3120	11	1 3/4	**Alfresco**^{7} [834] 4-9-0 95.....................(b) GeorgeBaker 12 (I A Wood) *s.s: towards rr: mod effrt over 2f out: n.d* **33/1**	87
05-0	12	4 1/2	**Charlie Tokyo (IRE)**^{7} [834] 5-9-0 105.....................(v) PaulHanagan 4 (R A Fahey) *s.i.s: towards rr: hrd rdn 3f out: sn bhd* **66/1**	78
1-	13	2	**Red Moloney (USA)**^{127} [6786] 4-9-0........................ DPMcDonogh 8 (Kevin Prendergast, Ire) *prom: rdn 3f out: sn wknd* **8/1**	75+
322-	14	6	**Zaham (USA)**^{167} [5831] 4-9-0 113........................ RHills 13 (M Johnston) *stmbld s: racd wd: hdwy and in tch after 3f: wnt prom 4f out: wknd 3f out: eased whn no ch over 1f out* **4/1**^{2}	63+

2m 3.61s (-2.99) **Going Correction** +0.125s/f (Slow) **14 Ran SP% 125.4**
Speed ratings (Par 113): **116,114,114,113,113 112,111,110,106,105 104,100,99,94**
CSF £61.01 TOTE £20.20: £4.90, £1.60, £7.20; EX 93.80 Trifecta £761.70 Pool: £1,394.74 - 1.30 winning tickets..

Owner Saeed Manana **Bred** Darley **Trained** Newmarket, Suffolk

FOCUS
A competitive renewal of the highlight of the All-Weather season. It was run at a good gallop and the time was 6.46secs faster than the opening maiden. The winner and thoroughly exposed fifth set the standard.

NOTEBOOK
Hattan(IRE), tenth in this race last year following a campaign in Dubai, had been given the winter off this time and the break had the desired effect, as he took this valuable race with authority. This was his first Group success since winning the Chester Vase as a three-year-old but, as he is well suited by the Roodeye, having also won a Listed race there last season, the Huxley Stakes or even the Ormonde Stakes at the May meeting look logical targets. (tchd 16-1)

Silver Pivotal(IRE) ◆, a Listed winner at York last season, had shown she handles the trip and track when scoring here on her return to action last month. However, she was drawn on the wide outside of her field and as a result had to be held up at the back. Having had a lot to do straightening up she finished really well for second, but the winner had already gone beyond recall. She looks more than capable of winning a race at this level, and quite possibly something even better. (op 11-4 tchd 5-2)

Great Hawk(USA), who had shown in the past he handles Polytrack, was back at 1m2f for this seasonal debut. He ran well until his effort flattened out in the closing stages and this should set him up for a return to turf, with his rider believing that a step back up to 1m4f would not go amiss. (op 20-1)

Dubai's Touch has a good record on Polytrack, having won a Kempton Listed race and been narrowly beaten by Dansant in the trial for this contest. He ran his race again but was quite keen early and, although he appears to stay, has yet to prove conclusively he is as effective at this trip as he is at a mile. (op 11-2)

Grand Passion(IRE), running in this race for the fifth successive year, having been runner-up in both of the last two renewals, put up another fine effort, staying on well in the closing stages. At his age his chance of winning this has probably gone now, but he is still very effective at Listed level and the Magnolia Stakes at Kempton, in which he finished runner-up last season, looks an obvious target. (tchd 25-1)
Orchard Supreme, eighth in this last year, ran his race again but is probably most effective in good handicaps at around a mile. (tchd 40-1)
Baylini, third behind Dansant and Dubai's Touch in the trial for this race, was 5lb worse off but ran well and showed ahead turning for home before being run out of it. She is another who is capable of picking up decent handicaps on this surface. (op 33-1 tchd 18-1)
Evident Pride(USA) was gambled on and moved particularly well to post, but he was no danger in the straight. (op 20-1 tchd 17-2)
Philatelist(USA) was well backed after beating Baylini over course and distance last time and being unbeaten in two runs on Polytrack. However, he was up in grade here and appeared to be found out in this company, although he did not really settle early and was eased when short of room in the straight, which may explain why he was beaten as far as he was. (op 7-1)
Zaham(USA) was the disappointment of the race. However, he stumbled leaving the stalls and was forced to race five wide for most of the way, and could not respond when the race began in earnest. He was eased when his chance had gone and was found to have suffered an overreach, so this usually consistent individual can be given another chance. Official explanation: vet said gelding suffered an overreach on right-fore (op 9-2 tchd 5-1)

907 BETDIRECT.COM HEVER SPRINT STKS (LISTED RACE) 5f (P)
3:50 (3:52) (Class 1) 4-Y-0+

£17,034 (£6,456; £3,231; £1,611; £807; £405) **Stalls** High

Form					RPR
300-	**1**		**Conquest (IRE)**[154] 6183 4-9-0 97 (v[1]) JimmyFortune 1 (W J Haggas) *chsd ldrs: effrt over 1f out: drvn to ld ins fnl f* **4/1[2]**		112
164-	**2**	2	**Matsunosuke**[140] 6487 6-9-0 96 SebSanders 6 (A B Coogan) *towards rr: rdn and hdwy over 1f out: r.o to take 2nd nr fin* **8/1**		105
010-	**3**	nk	**Stoneacre Lad (IRE)**[163] 5953 5-9-0 95 (b) LPKeniry 5 (Peter Grayson) *prom: led over 1f out: hung lft: hdd and one pce ins fnl f* **33/1**		104
00-1	**4**	hd	**Excusez Moi (USA)**[21] 677 6-9-3 106 LiamJones 8 (C E Brittain) *missed break and lost 5l: bhd tl rdn and r.o fnl 2f: nrst fin* **2/1[1]**		106+
4-04	**5**	2	**Maltese Falcon**[21] 677 8-9-3 102 (t) NelsonDeSouza 7 (P F I Cole) *in tch: rdn over 2f out: one pce appr fnl f* **7/1**		99
2360	**6**	½	**Silver Prelude**[7] 836 7-9-0 87 ChrisCatlin 3 (D K Ivory) *led: hdd and hmpd over 1f out: wknd fnl f* **16/1**		94
00-3	**7**	¾	**Merlin's Dancer**[21] 676 8-9-0 83 IanMongan 10 (S Dow) *chsd ldr tl over 1f out: wknd fnl f* **40/1**		91
1050	**8**	¾	**Tartatartufata**[2] 866 6-8-9 88 (v) FrancisNorton 2 (D Shaw) *in tch: rdn 2f out: wkng whn hmpd ins fnl f* **33/1**		89+
10-0	**9**	1 ½	**King Orchisios (IRE)**[21] 677 5-9-0 106 (p) NCallan 4 (K A Ryan) *in tch: hmpd and dropped to rr after 150yds: rallied over 1f out: no imp whn hmpd ins fnl f* **9/2[3]**		93+
230-	**10**	3	**Esteem Machine (USA)**[153] 6205 4-9-0 87 JoeFanning 9 (R A Teal) *hld up in midfield on outside: rdn and rn wd bnd into st: sn bhd* **11/1**		72

58.38 secs (-0.42) **Going Correction** +0.125s/f (Slow) **10** Ran SP% **117.7**
Speed ratings (Par 111): **108,104,104,104,100 100,98,97,95,90**
CSF £35.77 TOTE £5.60: £2.00, £2.60, £5.30; EX 43.90 Trifecta £343.20 Pool: £754.25 - 1.56 winning tickets..
Owner Highclere Thoroughbred Racing XXXVIII **Bred** Gerrardstown House Stud **Trained** Newmarket, Suffolk

FOCUS
A decent enough Listed sprint, although more like a high-class handicap in its make-up. The winner was well suited by the way the race developed and might not find it easy with his Listed penalty. The second is a good yardstick.

NOTEBOOK
Conquest(IRE) has never looked straightforward and has often worn blinkers or a tongue strap. This time he was fitted with a visor, and it enabled him to gain his first win since the 2006 Gimcrack. He hit the front inside the final furlong and was soon in charge, although he again carried his head high. He reportedly took a while to get over being gelded last year but looks to have come back to himself, and connections have races like the Abernant and the Palace House in mind for him. (op 7-1)
Matsunosuke, who was rated just 69 when scoring at Sandown last August, improved considerably afterwards and came into this unbeaten in two previous runs on Polytrack. This was arguably a personal best and he should give connections plenty of fun again this term on the evidence of this seasonal debut. (op 5-1)
Stoneacre Lad(IRE), another making his reappearance, was a surprise winner of a valuable Ascot sprint last backend and, effective on soft ground, could well be one to follow in early-season sprints. (op 25-1)
Excusez Moi(USA) ◆, who was impressive over 6f here on his reappearance, was dropping to 5f and lost all chance when he missed the break badly and was left with too much ground to make up in the short straight. He did well to get so close and is well worth another chance. (op 7-4 tchd 9-4)
Maltese Falcon, whose wins on this surface have all been over another furlong, was unable to lead this time and could only keep on at the one speed. (op 8-1)
Silver Prelude set a good pace as usual but had a good deal to find judged on official ratings and will be better off racing from his proper mark in handicaps. Official explanation: jockey said gelding hung left (tchd 20-1)
Tartatartufata Official explanation: jockey said mare hung left
King Orchisios(IRE), another who likes to make it, was short of room and lost his chance in the early stages. He also suffered again when making headway in the straight and this can safely be ignored. Official explanation: jockey said gelding suffered interference in runing (op 5-1)

908 CORTAFLEX H'CAP 1m 4f (P)
4:20 (4:20) (Class 3) (0-95,92) 4-Y-0+

£9,348 (£2,799; £1,399; £700; £349; £175) **Stalls** Low

Form				RPR
2334	**1**		**Sgt Schultz (IRE)**[28] 592 5-9-1 89 TolleyDean(3) 7 (J S Moore) *hld up towards rr: wd bnd into st: gd hdwy to ld 1f out: drvn out* **7/2[2]**	97
11-3	**2**	nk	**Grande Caiman (IRE)**[15] 757 4-9-5 92 RichardHughes 8 (R Hannon) *hld up towards rr: rdn and hdwy over 1f out: r.o to take 2nd fnl 30yds: nt catch wnr* **7/4[1]**	100
4-30	**3**	hd	**Murfreesboro**[7] 834 5-8-12 86 WilliamBuick(3) 5 (K J Burke) *dwlt: hld up and bhd: rdn and r.o wl fr over 1f out: nrst fin* **33/1**	93
50-1	**4**	1	**John Terry (IRE)**[42] 410 5-9-6 91 TPQueally 9 (Mrs A J Perrett) *dwlt: hdwy to join ldr after 2f: slt ld jst over 1f out: sn hdd and hrd rdn: little rspnse* **4/1[3]**	97
00-4	**5**	¾	**Regional Counsel**[21] 502 4-8-10 83 GregFairley 4 (K J Burke) *plld hrd: prom: rdn 2f out: one pce appr fnl f* **22/1**	88
3315	**6**	shd	**Tilapia (IRE)**[16] 735 4-9-1 88 (v[1]) SebSanders 3 (Sir Mark Prescott) *chsd ldrs on rail: rdn over 1f out: no ex fnl f* **8/1**	92
-262	**7**	2	**Polish Power (GER)**[15] 757 8-9-6 91 LPKeniry 1 (J S Moore) *led: hrd rdn and hdd jst over 1f out: wknd fnl f* **6/1**	92
5642	**8**	3 ¾	**Fusili (IRE)**[28] 591 5-8-12 83 (b) NCallan 6 (N P Littmoden) *chsd ldrs tl wknd ent st* **12/1**	79

2m 30.84s (-2.16) **Going Correction** +0.125s/f (Slow)
WFA 4 from 5yo+ 2lb **8** Ran SP% **119.0**
Speed ratings (Par 107): **112,111,111,111,110 110,109,106**
CSF £10.52 CT £173.57 TOTE £5.20: £1.40, £1.40, £5.10; EX 11.50 Trifecta £283.90 Part won. Pool: £399.90 - 0.69 winning tickets..
Owner Jim Barnes **Bred** Frank Dunne **Trained** Upper Lambourn, Berks

FOCUS
Another good, competitive handicap and a close finish once again. The pace was sound and the first three came from the rear. Slight personal bests from the winner, who is a course specialist, and the second.

NOTEBOOK
Sgt Schultz(IRE) has done all of his winning here and gained his fifth course and distance success. Held up at the back, he came with a strong run to lead a furlong out and then held off the late challengers. He is a consistent sort but his opportunities will be more limited as the spring goes on. (op 5-1 tchd 11-2)
Grande Caiman(IRE), another who has gained all his wins around here, has come back from a break in good heart and finished strongly, but like the winner his options are limited and he may have to try turf once again. (op 13-8 tchd 2-1)
Murfreesboro ◆, who has been running over a mile or shorter for all of his career, was taking a big step up in trip and saw it out with no problem. The headgear was done away with on this occasion and, as he has been given a chance by the Handicapper, he could be one to follow in the short-term. (op 25-1)
John Terry(IRE), a course and distance winner on his All-Weather debut last time, was 2lb higher and was always in the right place. He looked the likeliest winner as they turned for home but could not respond when the late finishers arrived on the scene. (op 7-2 tchd 9-2 in places)
Regional Counsel was again quite keen on this step up in trip and paid the penalty in the straight. (op 25-1 tchd 20-1)
Tilapia(IRE) travelled well in the re-fitted headgear and looked a possible danger on the inner starting up the straight, but he did not find as much as he might have done.

909 CEMPLAS MAIDEN STKS 1m (P)
4:55 (4:57) (Class 5) 3-Y-0+ **£4,731** (£1,416; £708; £354; £176) **Stalls** High

Form				RPR
3-	**1**		**Sundowner (IRE)**[134] 6618 3-8-10 0 JamieSpencer 5 (G A Butler) *trckd ldrs: qcknd to ld jst ins fnl f: rdn out: shade comf* **5/4[1]**	82+
3	**2**	¾	**Always A Rock (IRE)**[22] 662 3-8-10 0 JoeFanning 12 (M Johnston) *led tl over 3f out: led over 1f out tl jst ins fnl f: kpt on: a hld* **13/2[3]**	78
56	**3**	nse	**Canary Islands**[7] 837 3-8-10 0 TGMcLaughlin 3 (E A L Dunlop) *hld up in midfield: hdwy and rdn ent st: r.o wl fnl f: clsng at fin* **20/1**	80+
233-	**4**	hd	**Green Wadi**[153] 6194 3-8-10 83 EdwardCreighton 10 (M R Channon) *prom: led over 3f out tl over 1f out: nt qckn fnl f* **7/2[2]**	78
44-3	**5**	2 ½	**Atheer Dubai (IRE)**[26] 608 3-8-10 76 (b) SebSanders 9 (C E Brittain) *sn prom: hrd rdn over 1f out: one pce* **7/2[2]**	72
3	**6**	1 ¼	**Bartercard (USA)**[12] 772 7-10-0 MickyFenton 8 (Stef Liddiard) *wd: hld up in midfield: outpcd over 2f out: styd on again fnl f* **12/1**	74
4-22	**7**	2	**My Shadow**[31] 549 3-8-10 70 IanMongan 4 (S Dow) *t.k.h in rr: rdn and struggling 3f out: styd on fnl f* **25/1**	64+
0-	**8**	½	**Yes Eighteen (IRE)**[211] 4571 3-8-10 0 RHills 7 (J W Hills) *s.i.s: swtchd wd early: sn in midfield: outpcd 3f out: sme late hdwy* **33/1**	63
0	**9**	8	**Camera Shy (IRE)**[52] 265 4-10-0 0 JamesDoyle 11 (K A Morgan) *prom: rdn and outpcd over 3f out: wknd 2f out* **66/1**	50
05-	**10**	4	**Laurentian Lad**[254] 3244 4-10-0 0 ChrisCatlin 1 (Rae Guest) *a bhd: no ch fnl 3f* **66/1**	41
	11	1	**La Zarza** 3-8-5 0 SaleemGolam 6 (S C Williams) *plld hrd in midfield: rdn 3f out: wknd 2f out* **50/1**	28
6	**12**	dist	**Sweet Demerara**[52] 273 4-9-4 0 JamieJones(5) 2 (P Butler) *s.s: plld hrd: sn in midfield: wknd 4f out: sn wl bhd: eased fnl 2f* **100/1**	—

1m 38.7s (0.50) **Going Correction** +0.125s/f (Slow)
WFA 3 from 4yo+ 18lb **12** Ran SP% **127.4**
Speed ratings (Par 103): **102,101,101,101,98 97,95,94,86,82 81,—**
CSF £10.99 TOTE £2.30: £1.10, £2.30, £6.50; EX 13.80 Trifecta £94.60 Pool: £630.33 - 4.73 winning tickets..
Owner A D Spence **Bred** Des Swan **Trained** Newmarket, Suffolk

FOCUS
A fair maiden run, but run at a modest early gallopand in a time 0.88secs slower than the closing handicap. The overall level looks pretty solid.

910 LINGFIELD PARK FOR WEDDINGS H'CAP 1m (P)
5:30 (5:32) (Class 4) (0-85,88) 4-Y-0+

£6,232 (£1,866; £933; £467; £233; £117) **Stalls** High

Form				RPR
2235	**1**		**Dudley Docker (IRE)**[7] 833 6-8-9 76 (b) LiamJones 9 (C R Dore) *s.i.s: plld hrd in rr: hdwy ent st: r.o to ld fnl 50yds* **20/1**	84
63-5	**2**	½	**Dichoh**[51] 280 5-8-13 80 (b) JamieSpencer 1 (M A Jarvis) *dwlt: sn trckng ldrs on rail: rdn to ld ins fnl f: hdd and nt qckn fnl 50yds* **11/2**	87
2-62	**3**	1 ½	**Lawyers Choice**[16] 733 4-8-12 79 PatDobbs 12 (Pat Eddery) *hld up in last pl: rdn and hdwy over 1f out: r.o fnl f* **20/1**	83
-131	**4**	nk	**Highland Harvest**[31] 548 4-8-10 77 HayleyTurner 10 (D R C Elsworth) *prom: led ent st: hdd and one pce ins fnl f* **10/3[1]**	80
41-	**5**	hd	**Twilight Star (IRE)**[230] 4007 4-8-13 80 ChrisCatlin 4 (R A Teal) *s.s: hld up towards rr: hdwy on rail ent st: shkn up and styd on fnl f: should improve* **16/1**	82+
610-	**6**	2	**Hessian (IRE)**[132] 6677 4-8-5 72 JimmyQuinn 2 (M D Squance) *in tch: hmpd and bmpd over 2f out: no imp over 1f out* **16/1**	70+
1552	**7**	1	**Bee Stinger**[20] 692 6-9-0 81 SebSanders 11 (I A Wood) *towards rr: effrt and v wd st: drvn along and nvr able to chal* **6/1**	77
200-	**8**	2	**Trimlestown (IRE)**[153] 6209 5-8-10 77 NCallan 6 (K A Ryan) *in tch: bmpd over 2f out: wknd ent st* **9/2[3]**	68+
1111	**9**	½	**Ninth House (USA)**[7] 833 6-9-7 88 (bt) JimCrowley 8 (N P Littmoden) *wd: in tch: pressed ldrs 3f out: rdn and wknd 2f out* **4/1[2]**	78

The Form Book, Raceform Ltd, Compton, RG20 6NL

2-00 **10** *nk* **Apache Dawn**^{17} [717] 4-9-1 **82**.. GeorgeBaker 5 71
(G L Moore) *led tl ent st: sn wknd* **20/1**

00-4 **11** *1 3/4* **Zafonical Storm (USA)**^{45} [357] 4-8-10 **80**......................(t) DJMoran$^{(3)}$ 7 65
(B W Duke) *prom: rdn over 2f out: wknd over 1f out* **25/1**

1m 37.82s (-0.38) **Going Correction** +0.125s/f (Slow) **11** Ran SP% **120.8**
Speed ratings (Par 105): **106,105,104,103,103 101,100,98,98,97 95**
CSF £123.78 CT £2312.17 TOTE £27.30: £6.50, £2.30, £5.10; EX 195.30 TRIFECTA Not won. Place 6 £110.56, Place 5 £46.42..
Owner Sean J Murphy **Bred** Nuri Fuat Basak **Trained** West Pinchbeck, Lincs
■ Stewards' Enquiry : Jamie Spencer five-day ban: careless riding (Mar 26-29, 31)

FOCUS
A competitive handicap. It was run 0.88secs faster than the preceding maiden and once again the principals all came from off the pace. Solid, though unspectacular, form and a personal best from the hard-to-predict winner.
T/Plt: £90.60 to a £1 stake. Pool: £109,650.15. 883.30 winning tickets. T/Qpdt: £53.60 to a £1 stake. Pool: £4,838.40. 66.70 winning tickets. LM

911 - (Foreign Racing) - See Raceform Interactive

842 SAINT-CLOUD (L-H)
Saturday, March 15

OFFICIAL GOING: Heavy

912a PRIX EXBURY (GROUP 3) 1m 2f
2:45 (2:46) 4-Y-0+ **£29,412** (£11,765; £8,824; £5,882; £2,941)

RPR

1 **Spirit One (FR)**^{181} [5466] 4-8-12 .... CSoumillon 3 116
(P Demercastel, France) *racd in cl 2nd: racd in centre to 5f out: chalng st: led over 2f out: wnt clr fr over 1 1/2f out: easily* **1/1**^{1}

2 *3* **Balius (IRE)**^{119} [6862] 5-8-12 ....(b) MBlancpain 1 111
(C Laffon-Parias, France) *trckd Claire et Bleu on rail: 3rd st: wnt 2nd 2f out: drvn to chse wnr: no imp* **39/10**^{3}

3 *6* **Aspectus (IRE)**^{146} [6372] 5-9-0 .... SPasquier 4 103
(A Fabre, France) *racd in 4th in centre: pushed along st: rdn and styd on to take 3rd appr fnl f: nvr in contention* **26/10**^{2}

4 *2* **Claire Et Bleu (FR)**^{131} 4-8-6 .... AlexisBadel 2 92
(Mme M Bollack-Badel, France) *led on rail to over 2f out: one pce fr over 1 1/2f out* **12/1**

5 *8* **Davidoff (GER)**^{22} [669] 4-9-0 .... JVictoire 6 86
(P Schiergen, Germany) *hld up disputing last in centre: 5th st: effrt 2f out: no imp* **79/10**

6 *2* **Elasos (FR)**^{136} [6600] 6-8-12 .... DBonilla 5 81
(D Sepulchre, France) *hld up disputing last in centre: last st: n.d* **39/10**^{3}

2m 12.8s (-3.20) **6** Ran SP% **137.5**
PARI-MUTUEL: WIN 2.00; PL 1.40, 2.70; SF 9.10.
Owner B Chehboub **Bred** K & B Chehboub **Trained** France

NOTEBOOK
Spirit One(FR) never looked in danger of tasting defeat. He looked well in the paddock and was winning his first Group race since his juvenile days. Always prominent, none of the other runners could go with him from two out and he was in a class of his own. His trainer already has his eye on the Prince of Wales's Stakes at Royal Ascot and a run before in the Ganay is also on the cards. He looks back to his very best form.
Balius(IRE), who did not look as forward as the winner in the paddock, he was given every possible chance but could only manage to stay on one paced in the closing stages. He will certainly benefit from the outing and looks capable of winning a Group 3 contest during the season.
Aspectus(IRE), well supported on the Pari Mutuel, was given every chance but was being niggled at coming into the straight and could not quicken in the latter stages. He is another who is sure to benefit from the outing and better ground in the future could be an advantage.
Claire Et Bleu(FR) tried to make all the running. She stuck to her task until the straight but is not really up to this level.

913 - (Foreign Racing) - See Raceform Interactive

869 WOLVERHAMPTON (A.W) (L-H)
Monday, March 17

OFFICIAL GOING: Standard
Wind: Light, against Weather: Cloudy with sunny spells

914 HAVE A HAPPY EASTER @ PONTIN'S AMATEUR RIDERS' CLAIMING STKS (DIV I) 1m 141y(P)
2:00 (2:00) (Class 6) 4-Y-0+ **£1,483** (£456; £228) **Stalls** Low

Form RPR

15-6 **1** **Mountain Pass (USA)**^{68} [103] 6-10-10 58...(p) MissIsabelTompsett$^{(5)}$ 8 66
(B J Llewellyn) *s.i.s: hld up: plld hrd: hdwy over 2f out: rdn and hung lft ins fnl f: r.o to ld towards fin* **16/1**

0/00 **2** *1/2* **Arturius (IRE)**^{29} [605] 6-11-7 88.................................(p) MrSWalker 9 71
(R A Harris) *s.i.s: plld hrd and sn trcking ldr: rdn to ld ins fnl f: hdd towards fin* **5/1**^{3}

4633 **3** *1 1/2* **Machinate (USA)**^{17} [752] 6-10-8 64........................ MrBenBrisbourne$^{(5)}$ 7 61+
(W M Brisbourne) *chsd ldrs: rdn over 2f out: ev ch ins fnl f: styng on same pce whn n.m.r towards fin* **9/4**^{1}

26-0 **4** *1 1/2* **Zennerman (IRE)**^{11} [807] 5-10-10 65..........................(p) MissJFoster$^{(5)}$ 3 59
(Miss J E Foster) *led: rdn over 1f out: hdd and no ex ins fnl f* **10/1**

-530 **5** *3 1/4* **Swift Cut (IRE)**^{12} [794] 4-10-8 53.......................... MissKellyBurke$^{(5)}$ 11 50
(A P Jarvis) *dwlt: hld up: hdwy over 5f out: rdn over 1f out: hung lft ins fnl f: nt trble ldrs* **10/1**

6-66 **6** *3 1/4* **Mucho Loco (IRE)**^{56} [249] 5-10-2 42...................(v^{1}) MrSPHanson$^{(5)}$ 10 37
(R Curtis) *chsd ldrs 6f* **20/1**

1021 **7** *1 1/4* **Northern Desert (IRE)**^{17} [753] 9-10-4 65............(p) MissLCGriffiths$^{(7)}$ 6 39
(S Curran) *chsd ldrs: rdn over 2f out: sn wknd* **13/2**

620/ **8** *3/4* **Naughty Girl (IRE)**^{732} [648] 8-9-11 41........................... MrKJames$^{(5)}$ 2 28
(John A Harris) *chsd ldrs: lost pl 7f out: rdn over 3f out: wknd over 2f out* **50/1**

4331 **9** *nk* **Arctic Desert**^{4} [868] 8-10-2 63...................................(t) MissOMaylam$^{(7)}$ 5 34
(Miss Gay Kelleway) *s.s: hld up: plld hrd: swtchd rt 4f out: rdn over 1f out: n.d* **11/4**^{2}

3250 **10** *15* **Ndola**^{14} [779] 9-11-0 48..(v) MissMBryant$^{(7)}$ 1 15
(P Butler) *chsd ldrs: rdn over 3f out: sn wknd* **25/1**

0000 **11** *10* **Easily Naimd**^{14} [774] 4-10-9 35.......................................(v) MrsMMorris 4 —
(D Shaw) *unruly in stalls: hld up: rdn over 3f out: sn wknd* **66/1**

1m 52.84s (2.34) **Going Correction** +0.075s/f (Slow) **11** Ran SP% **123.6**
Speed ratings (Par 101): **92,91,90,88,86 83,82,81,81,67 58**
CSF £96.12 TOTE £19.30: £4.90, £1.80, £1.10; EX 54.20 Trifecta £265.50 Part won. Pool: £373.96 - 0.10 winning units..
Owner B J Llewellyn **Bred** Marablue Farm **Trained** Fochriw, Caerphilly
■ Stewards' Enquiry : Miss Isabel Tompsett caution: careless riding

FOCUS
A very moderate race and with the early pace so slow several were inclined to take a hold. The front four pulled clear, but the form looks moderate.
Swift Cut(IRE) Official explanation: jockey said gelding banged its head on the stalls, lost a tooth and was slow away

915 HAVE A HAPPY EASTER @ PONTIN'S AMATEUR RIDERS' CLAIMING STKS (DIV II) 1m 141y(P)
2:30 (2:30) (Class 6) 4-Y-0+ **£1,483** (£456; £228) **Stalls** Low

Form RPR

116- **1** **Blue Sky Thinking (IRE)**^{287} [2298] 9-10-6 74............ MissLEBurke$^{(7)}$ 8 72
(K R Burke) *chsd clr ldr tl led on bit over 2f out: sn clr: pushed out* **7/2**^{3}

4045 **2** *5* **Casablanca Minx (IRE)**^{4} [872] 5-10-8 53...............(v) MissEFolkes 9 57
(P D Evans) *hld up: hdwy over 2f out: rdn to chse wnr over 1f out: hung lft: styd on* **6/1**

3422 **3** *5* **Red Rudy**^{2} [896] 6-11-4 70................................... MrMJJSmith$^{(3)}$ 11 59
(A W Carroll) *s.s and rdr lost iron leaving stalls: bhd: hdwy over 1f out: hung lft: nvr nrr* **10/3**^{2}

0503 **4** *1* **Royal Embrace**^{16} [768] 5-10-7 53.................................(v) MrsMMorris 6 43
(D Shaw) *hld up: hdwy over 2f out: rdn and nt clr run over 1f out: wknd fnl f* **8/1**

2015 **5** *3/4* **Ruffie (IRE)**^{31} [579] 5-10-1 50.. MrRBirkett$^{(5)}$ 2 40
(Miss J Feilden) *hld up: hdwy over 3f out: rdn over 1f out: wknd fnl f* **6/1**

0-03 **6** *9* **Miss Wolf**^{14} [781] 8-9-11 30.......................... MissSarah-JayneDavies$^{(7)}$ 3 20
(G H Jones) *chsd clr ldrs tl wknd 3f out* **66/1**

4445 **7** *3/4* **Circus Polka (USA)**^{5} [861] 4-10-6 55.............(bt) MrBenBrisbourne$^{(5)}$ 5 25
(W M Brisbourne) *rdn to ld and sn clr: hdd over 2f out: edgd rt and wknd over 1f out* **11/4**^{1}

0-40 **8** *7* **Christalini**^{28} [606] 4-11-2 44.......................... MissSarah-JaneDurman$^{(5)}$ 7 20
(J C Fox) *s.i.s: a in rr* **20/1**

00-0 **9** *6* **El Capitan (FR)**^{6} [844] 5-10-6 52...........................(b) MissOMaylam$^{(7)}$ 1 —
(Miss Gay Kelleway) *chsd clr ldrs 5f* **16/1**

00-0 **10** *8* **Night Groove (IRE)**^{34} [166] 5-10-12 40.......................... MissZoeLilly$^{(5)}$ 4 —
(P Butler) *mid-div: wknd 1/2-way* **25/1**

0-06 **11** *53* **Longy The Lash**^{9} [839] 5-10-0 30..................................(p) MrCFeely$^{(7)}$ 10 —
(Paul Murphy) *mid-div: lost pl over 5f out: sn bhd* **100/1**

1m 51.42s (0.92) **Going Correction** +0.075s/f (Slow) **30** Ran SP% **128.6**
Speed ratings (Par 101): **98,93,89,88,87 79,78,72,67,60 13**
CSF £26.89 TOTE £4.50: £1.70, £3.10, £1.40; EX 28.40 Trifecta £93.50 Pool: £283.16 - 2.15 winning units..The winner was subject to a friendly claim.
Owner Mrs Elaine M Burke **Bred** Thomas J Murphy **Trained** Middleham Moor, N Yorks
■ A first winner for Lucy Burke, daughter of the successful trainer Karl and granddaughter of trainer Alan Jarvis.

FOCUS
The winning time was 1.42 seconds faster than the first division, but the early pace was so frantic that they covered the first couple of furlongs around two and a half seconds quicker than in division one. As a result very few ever got into it. The form is rated around the runner-up and the sixth.
Red Rudy Official explanation: jockey said he lost a stirrup

916 BOOK ONLINE AT WOLVERHAMPTON-RACECOURSE.CO.UK H'CAP 1m 141y(P)
3:00 (3:00) (Class 6) (0-60,59) 4-Y-0+ **£2,047** (£604; £302) **Stalls** Low

Form RPR

4-14 **1** **Montemayorprincess (IRE)**^{55} [258] 4-8-11 **52**........(p) AndrewElliott 3 60
(D Haydn Jones) *a.p: chsd ldr 2f out: rdn and hung lft over 1f out: r.o to ld wl ins fnl f* **5/2**^{1}

5116 **2** *nk* **Climate (IRE)**^{11} [809] 9-8-11 **59**.................................. RichardEvans$^{(7)}$ 5 66
(P D Evans) *hld up: hdwy over 2f out: rdn and edgd lft ins fnl f: r.o* **9/2**^{2}

006- **3** *3/4* **Time To Regret**^{96} [7127] 8-9-2 **57**.................................(p) DanielTudhope 7 62
(I W McInnes) *sn led: hdd 5f out: led again over 3f out: rdn clr 2f out: hdd wl ins fnl f* **13/2**^{3}

600- **4** *8* **Franksalot (IRE)**^{174} [5701] 8-9-3 **58**.................................. FergalLynch 4 47+
(I W McInnes) *chsd ldrs: rdn over 2f out: wknd over 1f out* **8/1**

0060 **5** *3 1/2* **Golden Spectrum (IRE)**^{19} [724] 9-8-8 **52**............(b) KevinGhunowa$^{(3)}$ 1 33
(R A Harris) *chsd ldr tl led 5f out: hdd over 3f out: sn rdn: wknd over 1f out* **10/1**

2524 **6** *nk* **Abbeygate**^{16} [769] 7-8-6 **47**..(p) LiamJones 6 28
(T Keddy) *sn pushed along in rr: n.d* **5/2**^{1}

36/0 **7** *1 1/2* **Shami**^{4} [863] 9-8-4 **45**..(bt) ChrisCatlin 8 22
(Mrs R A Carr) *prom: rdn over 3f out: sn wknd* **16/1**

000/ **8** *2 1/4* **Ath Tiomain (IRE)**^{14} [5429] 5-8-6 **47**.............................. RichardThomas 2 20
(D J S Ffrench Davis) *hld up: a in rr: wknd 3f out* **20/1**

1m 51.12s (0.62) **Going Correction** +0.075s/f (Slow) **8** Ran SP% **119.5**
Speed ratings (Par 101): **100,99,99,91,88 88,87,85**
CSF £14.81 CT £67.29 TOTE £2.80: £1.40, £1.60, £2.10; EX 16.50 Trifecta £92.70 Pool: £331.80 - 2.54 winning units..
Owner R Phillips **Bred** Thomas Morrin **Trained** Efail Isaf, Rhondda C Taff

FOCUS
A moderate handicap in which the front three finished clear. The form is rated around them.
Abbeygate Official explanation: jockey said gelding was never travelling

917 JOIN THE EASTER PARADE @ PONTIN'S (S) STKS 5f 20y(P)
3:30 (3:31) (Class 6) 3-Y-O **£1,774** (£523; £262) **Stalls** Low

Form RPR

5223 **1** **Hurricane Hen**^{12} [800] 3-8-12 68.. PatCosgrave 10 58
(J R Boyle) *edgd lft s: sn trcking ldrs: rdn to ld and edgd lft wl ins fnl f* **11/8**^{1}

-560 **2** *3/4* **Golden Dane (IRE)**^{19} [714] 3-9-4 60...........................(p) RobertWinston 4 61
(C R Dore) *prom: hmpd wl over 3f out: sn rdn: hung lft and r.o ins fnl f: nt rch wnr* **9/4**^{2}

3026 **3** *shd* **Bahamarama (IRE)**^{14} [780] 3-8-10 48..................(p) KevinGhunowa$^{(3)}$ 7 56
(R A Harris) *chsd ldrs: edgd lft wl over 3f out: rdn over 1f out: r.o* **20/1**

0-63 **4** *1 1/4* **Heron (IRE)**^{14} [780] 3-8-7 55..................................(b) JamieJones$^{(5)}$ 3 51
(A M Hales) *sn led: rdn over 1f out: hdd and unable qck wl ins fnl f* **8/1**

60-6 **5** *2* **Swallow Forest**^{38} [487] 3-8-7 60.......................................(b^{1}) PaulFessey 5 38
(T D Barron) *sn outpcd: rdn and hung lft ins fnl f: r.o: nt rch ldrs* **8/1**

643- **6** *nk* **Queens Mantle**^{100} [7071] 3-8-7 53.. ChrisCatlin 6 37
(P J Makin) *prom: rdn 1/2-way: no ex fnl f* **13/2**^{3}

-036 **7** *6* **Jastaanhi**^{16} [767] 3-8-0 44.. StacyRenwick$^{(7)}$ 2 16
(J A Pickering) *chsd ldrs: hmpd wl over 3f out: wknd 2f out* **20/1**

0-40 **8** *6* **Miss Bronte**^{16} [767] 3-8-7 52.. HayleyTurner 8 —
(R Hollinshead) *s.i.s and hmpd s: outpcd* **18/1**

-6 **9** 4 **Hardcase**[19] 721 3-8-12 0 FrancisNorton 1 —
(M Quinn) *s.i.s: sn outpcd* **10/1**

62.92 secs (0.62) **Going Correction** +0.075s/f (Slow) **9** Ran SP% **132.3**
Speed ratings (Par 96): **98,96,96,94,91 90,81,71,65**
CSF £5.51 TOTE £2.60: £1.10, £1.40, £3.70; EX 7.20 Trifecta £106.00 Pool: £391.22 - 2.62 winning units..The winner was sold to David Evans for 7,000gns.
Owner M Khan X2 **Bred** Aston Mullins Stud **Trained** Epsom, Surrey
■ Stewards' Enquiry : Kevin Ghunowa three-day ban: careless riding (Mar 28-29,31)

FOCUS
A weak race bar the winner, who made hard work of it. The second and third are rated just above their recent levels. The early pace was strong.

918 GET EGG-CITED FOR EASTER @ PONTIN'S H'CAP 7f 32y(P)
4:00 (4:00) (Class 5) (0-70,70) 3-Y-O **£2,457** (£725; £362) **Stalls** High

Form RPR
21 **1** **Thebes**[27] 616 3-9-4 70 GregFairley 9 93+
(M Johnston) *chsd ldrs: led and edgd lft 6f out: rdn clr fnl 2f* **7/4**[1]
020- **2** 7 **Greystoke Prince**[155] 6201 3-8-11 63 AdamKirby 10 67
(W R Swinburn) *chsd ldrs: rdn over 2f out: sn outpcd* **5/2**[2]
40-1 **3** ¾ **Johnny Friendly**[12] 797 3-8-9 61 AndrewElliott 3 63
(K R Burke) *chsd ldrs: hmpd wl over 5f out: sn pushed along: rdn over 2f out: sn outpcd* **5/1**[3]
200- **4** 3 ¾ **Mahadee (IRE)**[146] 6410 3-9-2 68 HayleyTurner 8 60
(C E Brittain) *chsd ldrs: n.m.r wl over 5f out: hung lft over 3f out: sn rdn: wkng whn hung lft fr over 1f out* **14/1**
225- **5** ½ **Liberty Ship**[204] 4844 3-9-4 70 RobertWinston 4 61
(J D Bethell) *hld up: hdwy and hung lft over 1f out: n.d* **8/1**
15-0 **6** ½ **Redsensor**[26] 632 3-9-4 70 FrancisNorton 12 59
(M Quinn) *mid-div: rdn 1/2-way: wknd over 2f out* **16/1**
04-6 **7** ½ **Karmei**[26] 629 3-8-10 62 AlanMunro 11 50
(J W Hills) *s.i.s: nvr nrr* **20/1**
050- **8** nse **Arcetri (IRE)**[165] 5949 3-8-8 60 FergalLynch 7 48+
(K A Ryan) *s.i.s: hld up: nt clr run over 2f out: n.d* **16/1**
644 **9** 7 **Ambrix (IRE)**[14] 772 3-8-4 63 MCGeran(7) 2 32
(M R Channon) *s.i.s: sn prom: rdn and wknd over 2f out* **14/1**
650- **10** 5 **Casino Night**[169] 5837 3-8-11 63 ChrisCatlin 5 18
(J R Weymes) *prom: lost pl over 5f out: wknd over 3f out* **16/1**
015- **11** 3 ½ **Spinning Ridge (IRE)**[152] 6263 3-9-1 70 KevinGhunowa(3) 1 16
(R A Harris) *led 1f: chsd wnr tl rdn and wknd 2f out: eased* **8/1**

1m 28.61s (-0.99) **Going Correction** +0.075s/f (Slow) **11** Ran SP% **139.6**
Speed ratings (Par 98): **108,100,99,94,94 93,93,93,85,79 75**
CSF £7.60 CT £23.08 TOTE £2.60: £1.70, £1.70, £1.60; EX 9.50 Trifecta £22.50 Pool: £432.00 - 13.29 winning units..
Owner Sheikh Hamdan Bin Mohammed Al Maktoum **Bred** Whitsbury Manor Stud And Mrs M E Slade **Trained** Middleham Moor, N Yorks

FOCUS
An ordinary handicap, but a seriously impressive performance from Thebes, who recorded a very decent winning time. He will be raised by at least a stone but warrants it. Solid form.
Arcetri(IRE) Official explanation: jockey said filly was denied a clear run

919 SPONSOR A RACE BY CALLING 01902 390009 MAIDEN STKS 1m 4f 50y(P)
4:30 (4:30) (Class 5) 3-Y-O+ **£2,457** (£725; £362) **Stalls** Low

Form RPR
0244 **1** **Boy On A Swing (USA)**[9] 837 3-8-4 72 (t) ChrisCatlin 6 74
(J A Osborne) *chsd ldrs: led over 1f out: shkn up and styd on wl* **7/2**[3]
325- **2** 5 **Spanish Diva**[169] 5839 4-9-5 75 JamieSpencer 10 64
(S C Williams) *led over 10f out: clr 6f out: rdn and hdd over 1f out: styd on same pce* **13/8**[1]
40-4 **3** 1 ¼ **Piermarini**[66] 131 3-8-4 72 GregFairley 1 65
(M Johnston) *led: hdd over 10f out: chsd ldr to over 4f out: rdn over 2f out: styd on same pce appr fnl f* **9/4**[2]
4 5 **Spanish Cruise (IRE)**[11] 4-9-10 0 AlanDaly 9 59
(Andrew Turnell) *prom: chsd ldr over 4f out: rdn over 2f out: wknd fnl f* **13/2**
5 4 **Night Orbit**[283] 4-9-3 0 AmyBaker(7) 8 53+
(Miss J Feilden) *hld up: rdn over 2f out: nvr nrr* **50/1**
6 3 ½ **Just Dennis**[22] 4-9-7 0 DNolan(3) 5 48
(D G Bridgwater) *hld up: plld hrd: rdn over 2f out: n.d* **66/1**
00- **7** ½ **Royal Rainbow**[159] 6109 4-9-10 0 DarrenWilliams 11 47
(P W Hiatt) *hld up: hdwy 1/2-way: rdn and wknd over 2f out* **50/1**
0 **8** 5 **Brave Boogie**[17] 758 3-8-1 0 ow2 FrancisNorton 7 35
(H J L Dunlop) *chsd ldrs: rdn 1/2-way: wknd over 3f out* **80/1**
5/ **9** 2 ¼ **The Music Queen**[577] 4549 7-9-4 0 (b[1]) WilliamBuick(3) 2 31
(C W J Farrell, Ire) *hld up in tch: racd keenly: rdn over 4f out: wknd over 3f out* **20/1**
6 **10** 3 **Hoar Frost**[14] 773 3-7-13 0 CatherineGannon 3 25
(M R Channon) *hld up: bhd fnl 5f* **50/1**
00 **11** shd **Meadow Cottage (IRE)**[17] 758 5-9-12 0 (p) HayleyTurner 4 32
(Mrs P Ford) *hld up: bhd fnl 5f* **100/1**
4 **12** 24 **Our Jane**[28] 610 3-7-13 0 DavidKinsella 12 —
(P G Murphy) *s.i.s: hld up: hdwy 7f out: rdn and wknd 4f out* **14/1**

2m 40.66s (-0.44) **Going Correction** +0.075s/f (Slow)
WFA 3 from 4yo 22lb 4 from 5yo+ 2lb **12** Ran SP% **125.4**
Speed ratings (Par 103): **104,100,99,96,93 91,91,87,86,84 84,68**
CSF £9.96 TOTE £4.20: £1.30, £1.10, £1.50; EX 10.10 Trifecta £28.00 Pool: £386.23 - 9.77 winning units..
Owner Mountgrange Stud **Bred** Green Gates Farm **Trained** Upper Lambourn, Berks

FOCUS
A weak middle-distance maiden. The winner stepped up on recent efforts but the second was disappointing.

920 GET CRACKING AND BOOK NOW @ PONTIN'S H'CAP 1m 1f 103y(P)
5:00 (5:00) (Class 5) (0-75,75) 3-Y-O **£2,752** (£818; £409; £204) **Stalls** Low

Form RPR
-521 **1** **Mischief Making (USA)**[39] 464 3-9-4 75 TGMcLaughlin 7 84
(E A L Dunlop) *sn pushed along in rr: rdn 3f out: hdwy to chse ldr 2f out: edgd lft fnl f: styd on u.p to ld nr fin* **11/4**[2]
602 **2** shd **Brave Hawk**[20] 705 3-8-12 69 (b) PhilipRobinson 1 78
(M A Jarvis) *led: hdd 6f out: led again over 3f out: rdn and hung lft ins fnl f: hdd nr fin* **7/4**[1]
1-20 **3** 4 ½ **Safebreaker**[40] 458 3-9-4 75 JimCrowley 2 74
(N Tinkler) *hld up in tch: rdn over 2f out: styd on same pce appr fnl f* **7/1**
0-02 **4** 3 ¾ **Forsyte Saga**[14] 785 3-8-9 66 JoeFanning 3 57
(M Johnston) *chsd ldr: rdn over 2f out: wknd over 1f out* **7/2**[3]
2-25 **5** 1 ¼ **Roundthetwist (IRE)**[31] 572 3-9-1 72 AndrewElliott 4 61
(K R Burke) *trckd ldrs: racd keenly: outpcd over 3f out: n.d after* **8/1**
031- **6** 1 ¾ **Alfredtheordinary**[127] 6776 3-8-9 66 SamHitchcott 6 51
(M R Channon) *hld up in tch: led 6f out: hdd over 3f out: rdn and wknd over 1f out* **6/1**

2m 3.04s (1.34) **Going Correction** +0.075s/f (Slow) **6** Ran SP% **123.1**
Speed ratings (Par 98): **97,96,92,89,88 86**
CSF £9.03 CT £31.55 TOTE £4.20: £2.20, £1.50; EX 8.90 Trifecta £31.30 Pool: £356.82 - 8.07 winning units. Place 6 £7.60, Place 5 £4.00.
Owner Cliveden Stud **Bred** Clivedon Stud Ltd **Trained** Newmarket, Suffolk

FOCUS
A fair handicap in which the first two finished clear. Reliable form which should work out.
T/Jkpt: £4,733.30 to a £1 stake. Pool: £10,000.00. 1.50 winning tickets. T/Plt: £5.30 to a £1 stake. Pool: £82,805.95. 11,356.15 winning tickets. T/Qpdt: £2.00 to a £1 stake. Pool: £4,839.10. 1,742.80 winning tickets. CR

896 KEMPTON (A.W) (R-H)
Tuesday, March 18

OFFICIAL GOING: Standard
Wind: Almost Nil Weather: Overcast

921 KEMPTON.CO.UK APPRENTICE H'CAP 1m 4f (P)
2:00 (2:00) (Class 5) (0-75,73) 4-Y-O+ **£2,457** (£725; £362) **Stalls** Centre

Form RPR
0-56 **1** **Sol Rojo**[36] 525 6-8-6 65 JosephineBruning(7) 3 71
(J Pearce) *mde all: t.k.h after 2f and sn wl clr: 30 l ahd 4f out: unchal* **14/1**
1 **2** 16 **Outlandish**[52] 317 5-9-2 73 BillyCray(5) 1 55
(Andrew Turnell) *a 2nd but wnr sn wl clr: no effrt tl 3f out: nvr any ch* **11/10**[1]
3-01 **3** 1 ¾ **Turner's Touch**[13] 794 6-9-0 66 (b) RossAtkinson 4 45
(G L Moore) *hld up: no effrt tl 3f out: nvr any ch* **15/8**[2]
-444 **4** 13 **Generous Lad (IRE)**[4] 886 5-9-1 72 (p) PNolan(5) 2 32
(A B Haynes) *hld up: nvr any ch: wknd fnl 2f* **4/1**[3]

2m 36.85s (2.35) **Going Correction** +0.075s/f (Slow) **4** Ran SP% **109.1**
Speed ratings (Par 103): **95,84,83,74**
CSF £30.43 TOTE £22.60; EX 38.40.
Owner Mrs Jennifer Marsh **Bred** Mrs A Yearley **Trained** Newmarket, Suffolk
■ Josephine Bruning was riding her first winner, and in extraordinary circumstances.
■ Stewards' Enquiry : Ross Atkinson 12-day ban: in breach of Rule 156 (iv) (Mar 29,31, Apr 1-5, 7-11)
Billy Cray 12-day ban: in breach of Rule 156 (iv) (Mar 29,31, Apr 1-5, 7-11)
P Nolan 10-day ban: in breach of Rule 156 (iv) (Mar 29,31, Apr 1-5, 7-9)

FOCUS
A farce of a race with Sol Rojo, totally ignored by his three rivals, winning unchallenged. The form is not worth the paper it is written on.
Outlandish Official explanation: jockey said, regarding the running and riding, his orders were to sit in and get an easy lead
Turner's Touch Official explanation: jockey said, regarding the running and riding, his orders were to drop in and come late; trainer said he felt the instructions had been overdone
Generous Lad(IRE) Official explanation: jockey said, regarding the running and riding, his orders were to drop in as gelding had run too free in its previous race; trainer said gelding was not a straightforward ride

922 THE PANORAMIC BAR & RESTAURANT CLASSIFIED STKS 7f (P)
2:30 (2:30) (Class 7) 4-Y-O+ **£1,365** (£403; £201) **Stalls** High

Form RPR
002 **1** **Straight Face (IRE)**[23] 693 4-9-0 45 (b) FrancisNorton 8 57
(V Smith) *mde all: rdn and pressed over 1f out: styd on wl and gng away nr fin* **6/1**
316- **2** 1 ¾ **Prince Valentine**[138] 6607 7-9-0 45 FergusSweeney 6 53
(G L Moore) *t.k.h: hld up in midfield: prog 2f out: chsd wnr 1f out: nt qckn and hld after* **4/1**[2]
5-21 **3** 1 ½ **Fun In The Sun**[4] 877 4-9-6 45 TPQueally 11 55
(A B Haynes) *trckd ldng pair: rdn on inner over 1f out: hld whn n.m.r jst ins fnl f: kpt on* **2/1**[1]
3563 **4** hd **Only If I Laugh**[4] 877 7-9-0 42 (p) IanMongan 10 48
(M J Attwater) *trckd wnr: rdn to chal over 1f out: sn nt qckn and hld: wknd ins fnl f* **9/2**[3]
0360 **5** 1 ½ **Cayman Breeze**[4] 877 8-9-0 40 (b) JimCrowley 5 45
(J M Bradley) *t.k.h: hld up in midfield: rdn 2f out: one pce and no imp* **25/1**
0234 **6** 1 **Grezie**[12] 808 6-9-0 44 (p) PaulDoe 7 42
(L A Dace) *s.i.s: hld up in midfield: rdn and fnd nil 2f out: btn after* **11/1**
405- **7** 1 ¼ **Raise Again (IRE)**[82] 7244 5-8-8 45 ow1 NBazeley(7) 3 40
(Mrs P N Dutfield) *stdd s: hld up in last pair: shkn up over 2f out: modest late prog* **10/1**
5402 **8** ¾ **A Teen**[4] 877 10-9-0 40 JimmyQuinn 4 37
(P Howling) *hld up in midfield: rdn over 2f out: wknd over 1f out* **12/1**
3654 **9** 4 **Doctor Ned**[4] 877 4-9-0 45 NeilChalmers 9 27
(Miss Sheena West) *chsd ldrs tl wknd 2f out* **14/1**
00-6 **10** 4 **Raihanah**[30] 598 4-9-0 25 DeanMcKeown 1 17
(D Shaw) *s.s: a in last pair: bhd fnl 2f* **40/1**

1m 25.81s (-0.19) **Going Correction** +0.075s/f (Slow) **10** Ran SP% **123.9**
Speed ratings (Par 97): **104,102,100,100,98 97,95,94,90,85**
CSF £32.31 TOTE £8.20: £2.20, £2.00, £1.60; EX 41.70.
Owner Michael Wigham **Bred** P J Towell **Trained** Exning, Suffolk
■ First leg of a double for Vince Smith with horses switched from temporarily banned Michael Wigham, who owns this one too.
■ Stewards' Enquiry : Fergus Sweeney one-day ban: careles riding (Mar 29)

FOCUS
Pretty strong form for the lowly grade and the winning time was 0.08 seconds quicker than the later three-year-old 81-95 handicap.
Grezie Official explanation: jockey said mare hung both ways

923 KEMPTON.CO.UK MEDIAN AUCTION MAIDEN STKS 6f (P)
3:00 (3:02) (Class 6) 3-5-Y-O **£2,047** (£604; £302) **Stalls** High

Form RPR
002- **1** **Emperors Jade**[136] 6641 3-8-7 76 JamieSpencer 5 64+
(A P Jarvis) *led: awkward bnd 3f out: jinked rt jst over 2f out: sn hdd: hanging over 1f out: edgd lft fnl f: drvn to ld again nr fin* **13/8**[2]
4330 **2** nk **Mr Rev**[18] 755 5-9-6 62 PaulFitzsimons 3 65
(J M Bradley) *trckd ldrs: effrt over 1f out: rdn and upsides last 100yds: edgd lft: jst outpcd* **20/1**
0-3 **3** nk **Firespin (USA)**[21] 706 3-8-2 0 (t) JimmyQuinn 2 55
(M Botti) *trckd ldr: led 2f out: hrd pressed fnl f: hdd & wknd nr fin* **6/1**[3]

4-24 **4** ¾ **Tension Mounts (IRE)**[21] 705 3-8-7 73 .... TPQueally 6 58
(J A Osborne) *cl up: sltly hmpd jst over 2f out: rdn and nt qckn over 1f out: one pce after* **6/5**[1]

5 ½ **Al Gillani (IRE)** 3-8-8 0 ow1 .... PatCosgrave 1 57
(J R Boyle) *s.s: sn in tch: shkn up 2f out: kpt on but nvr able to chal* **20/1**

6 5 **Pure Inspiration** 3-8-2 0 .... ChrisCatlin 4 36
(P Howling) *sn last and a struggling: wknd 2f out* **25/1**

1m 14.46s (1.36) **Going Correction** +0.075s/f (Slow)
WFA 3 from 5yo 13lb **6** Ran SP% **111.2**
Speed ratings (Par 101): **93,92,92,91,90 83**
CSF £30.76 TOTE £2.20: £1.10, £7.70; EX 23.50.
Owner Eurostrait Ltd **Bred** Simon Dutfield & William Harrison-Allan **Trained** Twyford, Bucks

FOCUS
A modest maiden in which the first five finished in a heap, and this looks form to be against. That said, the winner can probably do better. The winning time was 1.15 seconds slower than the following 61-75 three-year-old handicap, and 2.68 seconds off the time recorded in the older-horse 81-95 handicap.

924 THE PANORAMIC BAR & RESTAURANT H'CAP 6f (P)
3:30 (3:31) (Class 5) (0-75,75) 3-Y-O £2,457 (£725; £362) **Stalls** High

Form RPR

25-1 **1** **Lieutenant Pigeon**[7] 849 3-9-0 **71** 6ex .... PaulEddery 1 77+
(G D Blake) *fast away fr wd draw: mde all: rdn over 1f out: styd on steadily* **7/2**[2]

5324 **2** 1 **Valhillen**[13] 798 3-8-9 **71** .... PatrickHills(5) 11 74
(M D I Usher) *prom: drvn over 2f out: no imp over 1f out: styd on fnl f to snatch 2nd last strides* **13/2**[3]

-410 **3** shd **Asian Power (IRE)**[18] 756 3-9-3 **74** .... OscarUrbina 12 77
(P J O'Gorman) *prom: rdn to dispute 2nd fr 2f out: tried to cl 1f out: kpt on same pce* **8/1**

-141 **4** shd **Southwest Star (IRE)**[27] 629 3-9-0 **71** .... SebSanders 7 74
(J S Moore) *dwlt: hld up in last: taken to wd outside over 2f out: str run over 1f out: nt rch ldrs* **3/1**[1]

0-56 **5** 1 ¼ **Fly In Johnny (IRE)**[13] 796 3-8-8 **65** .... RichardHughes 10 64
(R Hannon) *hld up in last trio: gd prog on inner to press ldrs over 1f out: shkn up and one pce fnl f* **14/1**

216- **6** 1 ¼ **Tobar Suil Lady (IRE)**[136] 6635 3-9-2 **73** .... FergalLynch 4 68
(K A Ryan) *hld up in midfield: rdn over 2f out: no imp over 1f out: kpt on* **10/1**

3123 **7** nk **Wee Buns**[10] 835 3-8-4 **68** .... RossAtkinson(7) 5 62
(P Burgoyne) *a in midfield: rdn over 2f out: one pce* **14/1**

6-36 **8** nk **Rockfield Lodge (IRE)**[18] 756 3-9-4 **75** .... TPQueally 8 68+
(J A Osborne) *hld up in last trio: repeatedly denied clr run fr over 2f out: no ch to rcvr: fin w plenty lft* **7/1**

000- **9** hd **Wave Hill (IRE)**[146] 6419 3-8-8 **65** .... RobertHavlin 9 58
(B J Meehan) *n.m.r s: hld up towards rr: rdn over 2f out: one pce and no real prog* **20/1**

01-0 **10** nk **Storey Hill (USA)**[18] 756 3-9-2 **73** .... DeanMcKeown 2 65
(D Shaw) *chsd ldng pair to 2f out: steadily fdd* **14/1**

32-1 **11** 2 ¾ **Young Ivanhoe**[21] 706 3-9-3 **74** .... AdrianMcCarthy 3 58
(C A Dwyer) *mostly chsd wnr to 2f out: wknd fnl f* **14/1**

1m 13.31s (0.21) **Going Correction** +0.075s/f (Slow) **11** Ran SP% **124.7**
Speed ratings (Par 98): **101,99,99,99,97 96,95,95,95,94 90**
CSF £28.60 CT £181.60 TOTE £3.90: £2.00, £1.60, £3.10; EX 32.60.
Owner P A Mason **Bred** P A Mason **Trained** Aylesbury, Bucks

FOCUS
A fair sprint handicap and solid form, with more to come likely from the winner. The winning time was 1.15 seconds quicker than the previous maiden, but 1.53 seconds slower than the following older-horse 81-95.
Rockfield Lodge(IRE) Official explanation: jockey said gelding had been denied a clear run

925 BOOK NOW FOR EASTER SATURDAY H'CAP 6f (P)
4:00 (4:02) (Class 3) (0-95,95) 4-Y-O+
£6,543 (£1,959; £979; £490; £244; £122) **Stalls** High

Form RPR

1212 **1** **Benllech**[11] 824 4-8-7 **84** .... SimonWhitworth 4 92
(V Smith) *cl up: rdn to ld jst over 2f out: styd on wl* **6/1**

0-10 **2** ½ **Ajigolo**[10] 836 5-9-4 **95** .... EdwardCreighton 6 101+
(M R Channon) *t.k.h: hld up in last pair: cruising at bk of main gp over 1f out: swtchd lft and effrt: styd on to take 2nd last strides: too much to do* **7/2**[2]

-143 **3** nk **Distinctly Game**[10] 836 6-8-7 **84** .... FergalLynch 1 89
(K A Ryan) *racd wd bhd ldrs: rdn to chal wl over 1f out: nt qckn ent fnl f: kpt on* **5/1**[3]

2112 **4** nk **Fromsong (IRE)**[24] 676 10-8-10 **87** .... JimCrowley 3 91
(D K Ivory) *led at str pce: drvn over 2f out: hdd jst over 1f out: kpt on same pce* **5/1**[3]

10-3 **5** ½ **Crystal Gazer (FR)**[19] 733 4-8-8 **85** .... RichardHughes 8 88
(R Hannon) *hld up in midfield: effrt to chse ldrs over 1f out: one pce fnl f* **5/1**[3]

2412 **6** 1 ¾ **Financial Times (USA)**[4] 887 6-8-8 **85** ....(t) MickyFenton 9 82
(Stef Liddiard) *hld up in midfield: effrt on inner 2f out: nt qckn and hld 1f out: fdd* **10/3**[1]

2/00 **7** ½ **Baby Strange**[10] 832 4-9-4 **95** .... FergusSweeney 2 91
(D Shaw) *chsd ldr to 2f out: sn lost pl and btn* **14/1**

050- **8** 14 **Tony James (IRE)**[115] 6932 6-8-11 **88** .... SebSanders 5 42+
(K O Cunningham-Brown) *hld up in last pair: wknd 2f out: eased: t.o* **11/1**

1m 11.78s (-1.32) **Going Correction** +0.075s/f (Slow) **8** Ran SP% **124.6**
Speed ratings (Par 107): **111,110,109,109,108 106,105,87**
CSF £29.96 CT £118.75 TOTE £9.50: £2.30, £1.70, £2.30; EX 50.50.
Owner R J Lorenz **Bred** Speedlith Group **Trained** Exning, Suffolk

FOCUS
A competitive handicap run in a time 2.68 seconds quicker than the earlier maiden, and 1.53 seconds faster than the three-year-old 61-75 handicap. The form looks very solid with another fine effort from the winner.

NOTEBOOK
Benllech, another 2lb higher, was running for Vince Smith as Michael Wigham is currently banned from training. Well placed tracking the pace on the rail, he won a bit more comfortably than the winning margin suggests and remains at the top of his game. (tchd 13-2)
Ajigolo raced keenly but was still going well approaching the final furlong. He ran on well down the outside to take second, but he was never quite getting there this time. A strongly run race sees him at his best and there will be other days. (op 6-1)
Distinctly Game, drawn worst of all, has looked held since being raised onto a mid-80s mark. He ran well but remains vulnerable. (op 9-2)
Fromsong(IRE), who is now on a mark 6lb higher than when last successful, set a good gallop which resulted in a decent time. He probably finds getting home over 6f at Lingfield easier than here, where the surface is slightly slower. (op 9-2)
Crystal Gazer(FR) kept on well enough, but this was a rise in class as she had done all her previous winning in Class 5 and Class 4 races, and she just found it a bit too tough. (tchd 11-2)
Financial Times(USA) had the best draw, but he proved disappointing, weakening out of things inside the last. His form at this track is not as good as at Lingfield and Wolverhampton. (op 4-1 tchd 9-2)

926 JOIN THE KEMPTON PARK PUNTERS CLUB H'CAP 7f (P)
4:30 (4:31) (Class 3) (0-95,92) 3-Y-O
£6,543 (£1,959; £979; £490; £244; £122) **Stalls** High

Form RPR

220- **1** **Always Ready**[159] 6120 3-8-7 **81** .... HayleyTurner 6 85
(C E Brittain) *cl up on inner: effrt to ld wl over 1f out: drvn and hung bdly lft after: styd on wl* **7/1**[3]

2110 **2** 1 ¼ **Mister New York (USA)**[3] 905 3-8-4 **81** .... KirstyMilczarek(3) 7 83+
(Noel T Chance) *hld up in last pair: prog to chse ldrs whn hmpd over 1f out: kpt on to take 2nd nr fin* **10/11**[1]

004- **3** hd **Tia Mia**[213] 4613 3-9-4 **92** .... OscarUrbina 2 93
(M Botti) *hld up in last pair: smooth prog on outer to chal and upsides wnr 1f out: carried lft and nt qckn: wknd nr fin* **14/1**

32-2 **4** 3 **Grand Fleet**[57] 253 3-8-8 **82** .... JoeFanning 3 75
(M Johnston) *racd wd bhd ldrs: rdn over 2f out: cl up and n.m.r briefly over 1f out: wknd* **5/2**[2]

045- **5** 1 **Tadalavil**[129] 6756 3-8-4 **85** .... MatthewDavies(7) 4 76
(M R Channon) *t.k.h: trckd ldr: led over 2f out to wl over 1f out: wknd* **15/2**

51-5 **6** 1 ¼ **Gross Prophet**[66] 137 3-9-1 **89** .... RichardKingscote 5 76
(Tom Dascombe) *led to over 2f out: wknd wl over 1f out* **8/1**

1m 25.89s (-0.11) **Going Correction** +0.075s/f (Slow) **6** Ran SP% **123.0**
Speed ratings (Par 102): **103,101,101,97,96 95**
CSF £15.51 TOTE £8.10: £3.10, £1.30; EX 19.80.
Owner Saeed Manana **Bred** Miss S N Ralphs **Trained** Newmarket, Suffolk
■ Stewards' Enquiry : Hayley Turner three-day ban: careless riding (Mar 29,31, Apr 1)

FOCUS
Not a bad handicap on paper but they went fairly steady early on and the winning time was 0.08 seconds slower than the earlier older-horse 0-45. The runner-up seems the best guide to the form.

NOTEBOOK
Always Ready ran poorly on his final start at two at this track, but his turf form gave him a solid chance off 81, and his stable has been in good heart recently. Well placed on the rail behind the leader, he nipped through at the intersection and, although hanging left in the closing stages, held off the others in good style. He had to survive a stewards' enquiry but was the deserved winner. (op 8-1 tchd 17-2)
Mister New York(USA), outclassed in Listed company last time, was back at a more realistic level here and ran right up to his best in defeat. His momentum was checked slightly when the eventual winner hung across him approaching the final furlong and he ran on well afterwards to take second. (op 6-4)
Tia Mia, off the track since August, was competing in a handicap and racing on sand for the first time. She was also stepping up in distance on her debut for her new stable and looked to have work to do off a mark of 92. However, she ran a promising race, especially as she was carried slightly left by the hanging winner in the closing stages. (tchd 12-1)
Grand Fleet, beaten at a short price off this mark last time, was again found out and appears to have his limitations. (op 7-4 tchd 11-4)
Tadalavil, who became exposed off marks in the mid 80s at two, may be difficult to place this season and he still has to prove he gets beyond 6f. (op 12-1)
Gross Prophet, back against his own age-group, had the run of the race out in front but could not make the most of it against some less-exposed types. He is another probably at his best over 6f, though. (op 13-2)

927 FREE EVENINGS FOR GIRLS IN APRIL H'CAP 1m 3f (P)
5:00 (5:00) (Class 4) (0-85,85) 4-Y-O+
£4,050 (£1,212; £606; £303; £151; £76) **Stalls** High

Form RPR

1125 **1** **Art Man**[23] 692 5-9-0 **80** .... FergusSweeney 1 87
(G L Moore) *stdd s: hld up in last: shkn up and no prog 2f out: cajoled and r.o fnl f to ld last strides* **9/2**[3]

53-5 **2** hd **Awatuki (IRE)**[27] 626 5-9-1 **81** .... RichardHughes 2 88
(A P Jarvis) *trckd ldr to 6f out: styd cl up: effrt on inner over 1f out: led last 75yds: hdd fnl strides* **9/2**[3]

35-2 **3** shd **Royal Fantasy (IRE)**[31] 586 5-8-11 **77** .... JamieSpencer 6 84
(J R Fanshawe) *sn chsd ldng trio: rdn to cl 2f out: upsides ins fnl f: nt qckn last 50yds* **6/4**[1]

4601 **4** hd **Prime Number (IRE)**[18] 747 6-8-5 **71** .... JoeFanning 3 77
(J Akehurst) *led at stdy pce: kicked on over 2f out: hrd pressed 1f out: hdd and lost 3 pls last 75yds* **4/1**[2]

-356 **5** hd **Lisathedaddy**[38] 502 6-9-5 **85** .... TQuinn 4 91
(B G Powell) *trckd ldng pair tl wnt 2nd 6f out: rdn over 2f out: chal and upsides 1f out: no ex last 75yds* **5/1**

50-5 **6** ¾ **Crossbow Creek**[45] 409 10-9-0 **83** .... LukeMorris(3) 5 88
(M G Rimell) *hld up in 5th: rdn 2f out: trying to cl whn nt clr run ent fnl f: kpt on* **7/1**

2m 22.23s (0.33) **Going Correction** +0.075s/f (Slow) **6** Ran SP% **125.5**
Speed ratings (Par 105): **101,100,100,100,100 99**
CSF £27.76 TOTE £4.80: £2.50, £3.10; EX 29.70 Place 6 £384.63, Place 5 £24.04.
Owner Matthew Green **Bred** Lady Lonsdale **Trained** Woodingdean, E Sussex

FOCUS
They went a fairly steady early pace which resulted in something of a sprint finish, with the six separated by little more than a length at the line. The form clearly has limitations.
T/Plt: £804.30 to a £1 stake. Pool: £51,676.55. 46.90 winning tickets. T/Qpdt: £18.90 to a £1 stake. Pool: £4,581.90. 178.60 winning tickets. JN

921 KEMPTON (A.W) (R-H)
Wednesday, March 19

OFFICIAL GOING: Standard
Wind: Moderate, against

928 JOIN THE KEMPTON PARK PUNTERS CLUB MEDIAN AUCTION MAIDEN STKS 5f (P)
6:20 (6:20) (Class 6) 3-5-Y-O £2,047 (£604; £302) **Stalls** High

Form RPR

443- **1** **The Magic Blanket (IRE)**[194] 5199 3-8-12 68 .... MickyFenton 4 60
(Stef Liddiard) *trckd ldrs: wnt 2nd over 1f out: rdn and led ins fnl f: r.o* **15/8**[1]

0-52 **2** ¾ **Honest Value (IRE)**[18] 767 3-8-12 55 ....(p) NeilPollard 6 57
(Mrs L C Jewell) *led: rdn over 1f out: hdd ins fnl f: kpt on* **10/1**

0-40 **3** ½ **Ben**[16] 777 3-8-12 66 .... SteveDrowne 2 56
(P G Murphy) *in tch: rdn over 1f out: r.o to go 3rd ins fnl f* **2/1**[2]
304- **4** ¾ **Shatter Resistant (IRE)**[202] 4970 3-8-12 65 .... LiamJones 1 53
(J R Gask) *s.i.s: t.k.h in rr: r.o fnl f: nvr nrr* **5/1**[3]
5 **5** 1 ¼ **Walragnek**[31] 598 4-9-10 0 .... AndrewElliott 3 53
(J G M O'Shea) *s.i.s: outpcd in rr: rdn over 1f out: r.o fnl f:* **33/1**
22 **6** shd **Stoneacre Chris (USA)**[20] 734 3-8-7 0 .... HayleyTurner 5 43
(Peter Grayson) *chsd ldr to over 1f out: wknd ins fnl f* **11/2**

60.74 secs (0.24) **Going Correction** +0.025s/f (Slow)
WFA 3 from 4yo 12lb **6** Ran SP% **112.2**
Speed ratings (Par 101): **99,97,97,95,93 93**
CSF £20.39 TOTE £2.60: £1.20, £6.70; EX 23.00.
Owner David Gilbert **Bred** Mrs M Shenkin **Trained** Great Shefford, Berks

FOCUS
A weak sprint maiden, run at an average pace. The race is rated around the winner but this is not form to be confident about. .

929 KEMPTON FOR OUTDOOR EVENTS H'CAP 1m 2f (P)
6:50 (6:51) (Class 3) (0-95,89) 4-Y-0+ **£6,800** (£2,023; £1,011; £505) **Stalls** High

Form RPR
030- **1** **Mr Aviator (USA)**[144] 6499 4-9-4 **89** .... RichardHughes 4 101
(R Hannon) *mde all qckng over 2f out: rdn out fnl f: readily* **2/1**[1]
505- **2** 1 ¾ **Ballinteni**[144] 6499 6-9-1 **86** .... MickyFenton 6 95
(Miss Gay Kelleway) *trckd ldrs: wnt 2nd over 1f out: kpt on but no imp on wnr* **13/2**
-111 **3** 1 ¼ **Scamperdale**[24] 692 6-9-2 **87** .... TPQueally 7 93
(B P J Baugh) *stdd s: sn racd in 4th pl: rdn and r.o fnl f: nvr nrr* **9/2**[3]
2210 **4** ½ **Mataram (USA)**[32] 592 5-8-11 **82** .... AlanMunro 8 87
(W Jarvis) *t.k.h: in tch: rdn over 1f out: kpt on fnl f* **11/4**[2]
240- **5** shd **Rapid City**[333] 1145 5-8-11 **85** .... JerryO'Dwyer(3) 2 90
(Miss J Feilden) *hld up: rdn and r.o fnl f but nvr nr to chal* **5/1**
0-45 **6** nk **Regional Counsel**[4] 908 4-8-12 **83** .... GregFairley 3 87
(K J Burke) *trckd wnr to over 1f out: fdd ins fnl f* **10/1**
1666 **7** 1 **Neardown Beauty (IRE)**[11] 832 5-9-4 **89** ....(p) SteveDrowne 1 91
(A J McCabe) *a in rr* **20/1**

2m 8.89s (0.89) **Going Correction** +0.025s/f (Slow) **7** Ran SP% **122.0**
Speed ratings (Par 107): **97,95,94,94,94 93,93**
CSF £17.33 CT £55.54 TOTE £2.80: £1.60, £4.60; EX 18.90.
Owner Mrs Sue Brendish **Bred** Dr Tom Keenan & Dr H G White Jr **Trained** East Everleigh, Wilts

FOCUS
A good handicap, run at an uneven pace which the winner was able to dictate. The form can be rated through the second and third.

NOTEBOOK
Mr Aviator(USA), a progressive three-year-old last year, showed he has wintered well and got his new campaign off to a winning start with a ready effort from the front. He was allowed an easy lead, but it was clear entering the final furlong he was going to score and this looks likely to prove his ideal trip now. It will be interesting to see how the Handicapper assesses him for this. (op 9-4 tchd 5-2)
Ballinteni, well in front of the winner when last seen at Newbury back in October last year, tried his best to gain on that rival inside the final furlong and probably ran right up to par. He should come on for the run and is probably a better horse on turf. (op 12-1)
Scamperdale, very easy to back in this quest for a five-timer, would have ideally enjoyed a more truly-run race. He has to now prove the Handicapper has now not finally got the better of him, however. (op 3-1)
Mataram(USA) again refused to settle through the early parts, but this was certainly one of his better efforts in defeat. He goes some way to helping set the standard of this form. (op 9-2)
Rapid City, having his first run since disappointing on turf back in April last year, was far from disgraced on this return to the track and should really come on a bundle for the run. (op 11-2 tchd 6-1)

930 DIGIBET CLASSIFIED STKS 1m 4f (P)
7:20 (7:22) (Class 7) 4-Y-0+ **£1,365** (£403; £201) **Stalls** Centre

Form RPR
-034 **1** **Sovietta (IRE)**[19] 754 7-9-0 45 ....(t) StephenDonohoe 6 54
(Ian Williams) *a in tch: wnt 2nd 2f out: led appr fnl f: rdn out* **8/1**[3]
5-23 **2** 1 **Faraday (IRE)**[24] 693 5-9-0 45 .... TPQueally 1 52
(A P Stringer) *led: rdn and edgd lft bef hdd appr fnl f: jst hld on for 2nd* **4/1**[2]
00-0 **3** shd **Nanosecond (USA)**[63] 179 5-9-0 45 .... JimCrowley 11 52
(S A Callaghan) *hld up in rr: hdwy whn swtchd lft over 2f out: r.o wl fnl f: nvr nrr* **11/4**[1]
343 **4** 3 ¼ **Dot's Delight**[7] 851 4-8-12 43 ....(p) GregFairley 8 47
(K J Burke) *towards rr tl hdwy on ins over 2f out: styd on one pce fnl f* **14/1**
00/0 **5** 2 ½ **Tetragon (IRE)**[15] 269 8-8-9 45 .... JamieJones(5) 14 43
(A M Hales) *a.p: trckd ldr over 4f out to 2f out: fdd fnl f* **33/1**
0-31 **6** nk **Itsawindup**[21] 715 4-8-12 45 ....(t) NeilChalmers 3 43
(Miss Sheena West) *mid-div: lost pl 4f out: hdwy over 2f out: kpt on one pce* **4/1**[2]
0303 **7** 2 ¼ **The Power Of Phil**[7] 862 4-8-12 44 .... HayleyTurner 12 39
(Miss Joanne Priest) *in tch: rdn 2f out: one pce after* **8/1**[3]
0/25 **8** 2 **Huggle**[26] 654 5-8-7 45 .... MarkCoumbe(7) 9 36
(P Leech) *a towards rr: mod late prog* **16/1**
6205 **9** 2 ¼ **Mariaverdi**[21] 722 4-8-12 45 .... SteveDrowne 4 32
(P G Murphy) *a towards rr* **20/1**
-250 **10** nk **Amnesty**[24] 695 9-9-0 45 ....(v) JimmyQuinn 10 32
(L A Dace) *mi-div: no hdwy ins fnl 3f* **14/1**
0606 **11** 1 ¼ **Rubilini**[6] 863 4-8-5 43 ....(p) KylieManser(7) 13 30
(Miss Sheena West) *in rr: effrt over 2f out: sn btn* **50/1**
60-6 **12** 5 **High Country (IRE)**[18] 770 8-9-0 43 .... JoeFanning 5 22
(Micky Hammond) *trckd ldr tl rdn over 4f out: wknd over 2f out* **20/1**
0/0- **13** 5 **Musical Affair**[275] 1432 4-8-12 45 .... TGMcLaughlin 2 14
(F Jordan) *a bhd* **50/1**
0500 **14** 5 **Allez Melina**[16] 778 7-9-0 45 ....(p) ChrisCatlin 7 6
(Mouse Hamilton-Fairley) *slowly away: sn prom: wknd over 3f out* **100/1**

2m 34.25s (-0.25) **Going Correction** +0.025s/f (Slow)
WFA 4 from 5yo+ 2lb **14** Ran SP% **125.5**
Speed ratings (Par 97): **101,100,100,98,96 96,94,93,91,91 90,87,84,80**
CSF £39.41 TOTE £11.70: £2.50, £1.40, £1.70; EX 35.80.
Owner Ian Williams **Bred** Lawn Stud **Trained** Portway, Worcs

FOCUS
A typically very weak classified event, run at a sound pace. The placed horses set the level.
Dot's Delight Official explanation: vet said filly lost a shoe
High Country(IRE) Official explanation: trainer said gelding scoped dirty

931 DIGIBET.COM MAIDEN FILLIES' STKS 1m (P)
7:50 (7:52) (Class 5) 3-Y-0+ **£2,590** (£578; £578; £192) **Stalls** High

Form RPR
6 **1** **Moon Crystal**[19] 748 3-8-7 0 ....(t) StephenDonohoe 11 63
(E A L Dunlop) *s.i.s: sn in mid-div: str hdwy over 1f out: led wl ins fnl f: r.o* **15/2**
3 **2** 1 ½ **Turtle Dove**[24] 694 3-8-7 0 .... OscarUrbina 5 59
(M Botti) *t.k.h: in tch: rdn and r.o fnl f to share 2nd on line* **9/2**[1]
343- **2** dht **Dream Sea**[182] 5524 3-8-7 75 .... EdwardCreighton 1 59
(M R Channon) *led after 1f: rdn over 2f out: hdd wl ins fnl f* **5/1**[2]
330- **4** 1 ½ **Ile Royale**[83] 7245 3-8-7 49 .... NeilPollard 4 60+
(B R Johnson) *bucked leaving stalls and wl bhd tl hdwy on ins 2f out: chsd ldr appr fnl f tl one pce towards fin* **66/1**
5 ½ **Music Party (USA)** 3-8-7 0 .... JoeFanning 3 55
(M Johnston) *sn trckd ldr: rdn over 2f out: one pce fnl f* **16/1**
50 **6** 1 **Thankful**[36] 529 3-8-7 0 .... ChrisCatlin 2 53
(Rae Guest) *in rr: hdwy on ins fnl f: nvr nrr* **33/1**
3 **7** nk **Queen Macha (IRE)**[44] 424 3-8-7 0 .... AndrewElliott 10 52
(A M Hales) *disp ld for 1f: prom tl no hdwy ins fnl f* **33/1**
0 **8** ½ **Hold Fire**[20] 727 4-9-3 0 .... MarkCoumbe(7) 8 56
(A W Carroll) *s.i.s: a in rr* **100/1**
00- **9** nk **Tell Me What (FR)**[237] 3878 3-8-7 0 .... RichardSmith 6 50
(R Hannon) *disp ld early: styd prom: rdn 2f out: wknd ent fnl f* **66/1**
10 1 ½ **Star Acclaim** 3-8-7 0 .... AlanMunro 7 47
(T Keddy) *t.k.h: prom: wknd appr fnl f* **7/1**[3]

1m 40.53s (0.73) **Going Correction** +0.025s/f (Slow)
WFA 3 from 4yo 17lb **10** Ran SP% **74.9**
Speed ratings (Par 100): **97,95,95,94,93 92,92,91,91,89**
PL: Dream Sea £1.30, Turtle Dove £1.10; EX: Dream Sea £8.50, Turtle Dove £8.30; CSF: Dream Sea £8.53, Turtle Dove £7.92 TOTE £7.60: £2.10.
Owner Eurostrait Ltd **Bred** Eurostrait Ltd **Trained** Newmarket, Suffolk
■ Stewards' Enquiry : Edward Creighton five-day ban: failed to ride out for (Mar 31-Apr 4)

FOCUS
A modest maiden weakened further by the late withdrawal of the favourite Tinnarinka who became stuck in the stalls (11/8F, deduct 40p in the £ under Rule 4). The form is held down by the proximity of the 49-rated fourth who also gave away a huge amount of ground at the start, but a couple of these do have a bit of scope for improvement. The race has been rated negatively.

932 DIGIBET SPORTS BETTING CLAIMING STKS 7f (P)
8:20 (8:20) (Class 6) 3-Y-0 **£2,047** (£604; £302) **Stalls** High

Form RPR
-341 **1** **Dhhamaan (IRE)**[20] 732 3-9-1 80 ....(b[1]) DebraEngland(7) 3 77
(C E Brittain) *hmpd sn after s and swtchd lft: led after 2f: rdn out ins fnl 2f* **11/8**[2]
1-24 **2** 2 ¼ **Caprio (IRE)**[60] 228 3-9-3 70 .... PatCosgrave 2 66
(J R Boyle) *edgd rt sn after s: led for 2f: rdn over 2f out: no imp on wnr fnl f* **1/1**[1]
5404 **3** 5 **Mileaminutemurphy**[20] 732 3-8-7 62 .... PatrickHills(5) 4 49
(R Hannon) *hmpd sn after s: racd in 3rd thrght: outpcd over 2f out* **8/1**[3]
-000 **4** nk **Stoneacre Ma**[5] 882 3-8-8 47 .... HayleyTurner 1 44
(Peter Grayson) *stdd s: a last: outpcd 1/2-way: rdn over 2f out though sme late hdwy* **33/1**

1m 26.48s (0.48) **Going Correction** +0.025s/f (Slow) **4** Ran SP% **106.2**
Speed ratings (Par 96): **98,95,89,89**
CSF £2.98 TOTE £3.00; EX 2.90.
Owner C E Brittain **Bred** D Veitch And Musagd Abo Salim **Trained** Newmarket, Suffolk
■ Stewards' Enquiry : Pat Cosgrave four-day ban: careless riding (Mar 31-Apr 3)

FOCUS
A straight match on paper and Dhhamaan proved too classy for Caprio. Not a race in which we learned a great deal, with the winner basically to form.

933 BOOK NOW FOR EASTER SATURDAY H'CAP 6f (P)
8:50 (8:50) (Class 6) (0-55,55) 4-Y-0+ **£2,047** (£604; £302) **Stalls** High

Form RPR
0064 **1** **Desert Light (IRE)**[5] 884 7-8-5 **49** ....(v) TolleyDean(3) 12 60
(D Shaw) *a in tch: rdn to ld ins fnl f: r.o wl* **6/1**[2]
2420 **2** 1 **Tilsworth Charlie**[25] 677 5-9-0 **55** ....(b) JimCrowley 5 63
(J R Jenkins) *stdd s: hld up in rr: hdwy 2f out: r.o wl fnl f to go 2nd cl home* **6/1**[2]
3416 **3** nse **Simpsons Gamble (IRE)**[32] 584 5-8-12 **53** ....(p) ChrisCatlin 11 61
(R A Teal) *in rr: rdn over 2f out: str run fnl f: nrst fin* **8/1**[3]
050- **4** nk **Greenwood**[140] 6579 10-8-12 **53** .... RobertHavlin 2 60
(P G Murphy) *trckd ldrs: ev ch ent fnl f: nt qckn towards fin* **16/1**
0020 **5** 1 ½ **Calloff The Search**[5] 883 4-8-9 **50** ....(p) MickyFenton 10 52
(Stef Liddiard) *led tl rdn and edgd rt bef hdd ins fnl f: fdd nr fin* **8/1**[3]
1030 **6** ¾ **Regal Royale**[28] 628 5-8-12 **53** ....(v) AdamKirby 4 52
(Peter Grayson) *trckd ldrs: ev ch over 1f out: fdd ins fnl f* **10/1**
2013 **7** hd **Piccostar**[5] 883 5-8-1 **49** ow2 .... PNolan(7) 9 48+
(A B Haynes) *mid-div: running on whn short of room and swtchd lft appr fnl f: r.o* **9/1**
2114 **8** 1 ¼ **Sherjawy (IRE)**[18] 766 4-9-0 **55** ....(b) SamHitchcott 8 56+
(Miss Z C Davison) *trckd ldrs: wl there whn hmpd on ins appr fnl f: nt rcvr* **11/2**[1]
-320 **9** 1 **Desert Hunter (IRE)**[7] 858 5-8-6 **47** .... JoeFanning 3 39+
(Micky Hammond) *stdd s: t.k.h: a bhd* **11/2**[1]
5306 **10** 3 **Stormburst (IRE)**[28] 620 4-8-5 **53** .... MarkCoumbe(7) 7 35
(A J Chamberlain) *a in rr* **20/1**
/004 **11** nse **Zorn**[4] 898 9-8-9 **50** .... JimmyQuinn 1 32
(P Howling) *trckd ldr tl rdn 3f out: wknd wl over 1f out* **16/1**

1m 12.19s (-0.91) **Going Correction** +0.025s/f (Slow) **17** Ran SP% **117.2**
Speed ratings (Par 101): **107,105,105,105,103 102,101,100,98,94 94**
CSF £41.76 CT £297.73 TOTE £8.70: £2.40, £2.50, £2.80; EX 49.60.
Owner ownaracehorse.co.uk (Shaw) **Bred** Anthony M Cahill **Trained** Danethorpe, Notts
■ Stewards' Enquiry : Micky Fenton two-day ban: careless riding (Mar 31-Apr 1)

FOCUS
A decent winning time for a race like this. Low-grade form rated around the first three.
Desert Hunter(IRE) Official explanation: trainer said gelding scoped dirty

934 KEMPTON FOR WEDDINGS H'CAP 1m 4f (P)
9:20 (9:22) (Class 6) (0-60,59) 4-Y-0+ **£2,047** (£604; £302) **Stalls** Centre

Form RPR
4433 **1** **Granary Girl**[12] 822 6-8-8 **46** .... JimmyQuinn 4 56
(J Pearce) *rdn over 2f out: hdwy to ld 1f out: all out* **16/1**

The Form Book, Raceform Ltd, Compton, RG20 6NL

4542 **2** nk **Little Richard (IRE)**[21] 720 9-9-6 **58**....................(p) AdamKirby 6 68
(M Wellings) *a.p: led over 1f out: heaaded 1f out: r.o gamely u.p* **8/1**

5612 **3** 3 **Medieval Maiden**[14] 794 5-9-5 **57**.................... IanMongan 11 62
(Mrs L J Mongan) *chsd ldrs: rdn over 2f out: r.o to go 3rd ins fnl f* **4/1**[1]

000/ **4** ½ **Meohmy**[611] 3592 5-8-0 **45**.................... MCGeran(7) 14 49
(M R Channon) *mid-div: rdn over 1f out: r.o fnl f: nvr nrr* **33/1**

3444 **5** hd **Global Traffic**[7] 851 4-9-1 **55**....................(v) StephenDonohoe 5 59
(D Shaw) *mid-div: hdwy over 1f out: no imp fnl f* **25/1**

2324 **6** hd **Ernmoor**[32] 585 6-8-8 **46**.................... J-PGuillambert 8 51+
(J R Jenkins) *t.k.h: hld up in rr: hdwy 3f out: styd on fnl f* **15/2**[3]

00-0 **7** ½ **Sir Jake**[20] 727 4-8-7 **50**.................... KirstyMilczarek(3) 9 53
(T T Clement) *led after 1f: rdn and hdd over 1f out: fdd ins fnl f* **16/1**

000- **8** ½ **Love Angel (USA)**[13] 1888 6-8-11 **49**.................... NeilChalmers 12 51
(J J Bridger) *towards rr: hdwy over 2f out: wknd 1f out* **33/1**

2412 **9** hd **Mid Valley**[15] 789 5-9-3 **55**.................... JimCrowley 3 57+
(J R Jenkins) *hld up: rdn over 1f out: kpt on but n.d* **6/1**[2]

4/40 **10** nk **Ocean Rock**[24] 695 7-8-12 **50**.................... SteveDrowne 7 56+
(C A Horgan) *hld up in rr: sme hdwy whn n.m.r over 1f out* **25/1**

146- **11** nk **Summer Bounty**[91] 7187 12-9-2 **54**.................... TGMcLaughlin 2 58+
(F Jordan) *stdd s: a in rr* **33/1**

00/1 **12** 3½ **Wizard Looking**[30] 606 7-9-4 **56**.................... ChrisCatlin 13 52
(D E Cantillon) *t.k.h: trckd ldrs tl wknd over 1f out* **4/1**[1]

062- **13** ½ **Star Of Pompey**[147] 6430 4-9-5 **59**.................... SamHitchcott 1 54
(A B Haynes) *stdd s: hdwy to chse ldrs over 7f out: wknd over 2f out* **20/1**

5-52 **14** nse **Hiawatha (IRE)**[24] 695 9-8-10 **48**.................... AndrewElliott 10 43
(A M Hales) *led for 1f: treacked ldr to wl over 1f out: wknd rapidly fnl f* **17/2**

2m 34.93s (0.43) **Going Correction** +0.025s/f (Slow)
WFA 4 from 5yo+ 2lb **14** Ran SP% **120.7**
Speed ratings (Par 101): **99,98,96,96,96 96,95,95,95,95 95,92,92,92**
CSF £127.63 CT £616.94 TOTE £8.40: £3.90, £2.80, £1.90; EX 88.10 Place 6 £64.79, Place 5 £30.00.
Owner Mrs P O'Shea **Bred** Barry Minty **Trained** Newmarket, Suffolk

FOCUS
There was not much pace on early for what was a competitive handicap and the field was compressed at the line as a result. Solid form, rated around the second and third.
Ocean Rock Official explanation: jockey said gelding was denied a clear run
T/Plt: £53.20 to a £1 stake. Pool: £72,362.60. 991.60 winning tickets. T/Qpdt: £11.00 to a £1 stake. Pool: £5,852.00. 392.20 winning tickets. JS

903 LINGFIELD (L-H)
Wednesday, March 19

OFFICIAL GOING: Standard
Wind: Medium, against Weather: Overcast

935 PUT ON YOUR EASTER BONNET @ PONTIN'S (S) STKS 1m 2f (P)
2:30 (2:30) (Class 6) 4-Y-0+ **£1,774** (£523; £262) **Stalls** Low

Form RPR

-012 **1** **Competitor**[28] 631 7-8-9 61....................(v) KirstyMilczarek(3) 5 67+
(J Akehurst) *led for 1f: chsd ldng pair after tl jnd ldr gng wl 3f out: led over 2f out: sn rdn clr: comf* **5/1**[3]

3425 **2** 3½ **Prince Charlemagne (IRE)**[14] 794 5-8-12 72....................(p) AndrewElliott 7 60
(K R Burke) *hld up in tch: hdwy wl over 2f out: chsd wnr jst over 2f out: rdn and no imp fr over 1f out* **9/4**[2]

-326 **3** 2¼ **Pab Special (IRE)**[20] 728 5-8-12 63.................... NeilPollard 4 56+
(B R Johnson) *hld up towards rr: hdwy on inner jst over 2f out: kpt on u.p but nvr pce to trble ldng pair* **5/1**[3]

060- **4** ½ **Ground Patrol**[149] 5120 7-8-9 52.................... TolleyDean(3) 6 55
(N R Mitchell) *stdd s: hld up in last: hdwy over 2f out: kpt on u.p fr over 1f out: nvr pce to trble ldng pair* **33/1**

6521 **5** ¾ **Lord Of Dreams (IRE)**[28] 631 6-8-12 64.................... JamieJones(5) 2 62+
(G L Moore) *hld up in tch in midfield: hdwy whn short of room and jostled over 2f out: rdn and no imp over 1f out* **15/8**[1]

00-6 **6** ½ **Hansomelle (IRE)**[19] 750 6-8-7 65....................(b[1]) NeilChalmers 1 48
(Miss Sheena West) *bustled along early: racd in last pair: c wd and effrt bnd over 2f out: kpt on but nvr a threat* **16/1**

-441 **7** 12 **Imperial Amber**[12] 821 6-8-12 51....................(p) JimmyQuinn 9 30
(Karen George) *t.k.h: led after 1f: sn hdd: chsd ldr after: rdn wl over 3f: wkng whn edgd lft u.p over 2f out: eased towards fin* **20/1**

-000 **8** 1¾ **Stratn Jack**[16] 776 4-8-5 42.................... GabrielHannon(7) 8 27
(B G Powell) *led over 8f out: rdn and jnd 3f out: hdd over 2f out: sn wknd: eased towards fin* **66/1**

410- **9** 2 **Sekula Pata (NZ)**[133] 6713 9-9-3 55....................(v) EdwardCreighton 3 28
(E J Creighton) *in tch: rdn wl over 2f out: wkng whn edgd rt over 2f out: sn wl btn: eased towards fin* **22/1**

2m 5.33s (-1.27) **Going Correction** +0.075s/f (Slow) **9** Ran SP% **118.3**
Speed ratings (Par 101): **108,105,103,103,102 102,92,91,89**
CSF £16.51 TOTE £5.40: £1.60, £1.50, £1.50; EX 18.00 Trifecta £81.30 Pool: £747.81 - 6.53 winning units..There was no bid for the winner. Prince Charlemagne was claimed by Robert Stronge for £6,000.
Owner John Akehurst **Bred** Cheveley Park Stud Ltd **Trained** Epsom, Surrey

FOCUS
A fair seller run in a decent winning time for a race of this type, 2.73 seconds faster than the later Class 5 handicap. The form looks solid for the grade.

936 JOIN THE EASTER PARADE @ PONTIN'S MAIDEN STKS 7f (P)
3:00 (3:01) (Class 5) 3-4-Y-0 **£2,331** (£693; £346; £173) **Stalls** Low

Form RPR

0 **1** **Lucullus**[14] 796 3-8-12 0.................... SteveDrowne 1 70+
(M Blanshard) *chsd ldr: shkn up to chal wl over 1f out: rdn 1f out: led ins fnl f: r.o wl* **12/1**[3]

\- **2** ½ **Christophers Quest** 3-8-12 0.................... JimmyQuinn 3 69
(R Simpson) *dwlt: racd in 4th pl: hdwy and rdn over 1f out: r.o to chse wnr ins fnl f: kpt on* **25/1**

0-24 **3** 1¼ **Kibitzer**[26] 662 3-8-12 70....................(t) TQuinn 4 66
(J W Hills) *t.k.h: hld up in 3rd pl: swtchd ins and rdn over 1f out: one pce u.p fnl f* **10/3**[2]

66-2 **4** nk **Always Certain (USA)**[46] 413 3-8-12 72.................... JoeFanning 2 65
(M Johnston) *led: rdn wl over 1f out: drvn 1f out: hdd ins fnl f: fdd last 50yds* **2/5**[1]

5 3½ **Sunny Spells** 3-8-12 0.................... SaleemGolam 5 57
(S C Williams) *s.i.s: a last: rdn jst over 2f out: kpt on same pce* **25/1**

1m 26.26s (1.46) **Going Correction** +0.075s/f (Slow) **5** Ran SP% **109.9**
Speed ratings (Par 103): **94,93,92,91,87**
CSF £171.09 TOTE £14.00: £6.30, £13.20; EX 147.70.
Owner Messrs Oliver, Gale, Ward & Roberts **Bred** Pillar To Post Racing **Trained** Upper Lambourn, Berks

FOCUS
A slightly muddling affair run in a time 1.18 seconds slower than the following 46-55 handicap. The form is rated around the third and fourth, with the winner building on his debut effort.

937 EASTER EGG-STRAVAGANZA @ PONTIN'S H'CAP 7f (P)
3:35 (3:36) (Class 6) (0-55,55) 4-Y-0+ **£2,047** (£604; £302) **Stalls** Low

Form RPR

4546 **1** **Napoletano (GER)**[22] 708 7-8-13 54....................(p) NCallan 7 61
(S Dow) *s.i.s: t.k.h: hld up in rr: hdwy gng wl over 2f out: nt clr run over 1f out: swtchd rt jst over 1f out: str run to ld nr fin* **8/1**

0-50 **2** ½ **Metropolitan Chief**[19] 749 4-9-0 55.................... TQuinn 3 61
(P Burgoyne) *in tch: hdwy jst over 2f out: wnt 2nd over 1f out: sn ev ch: led wl ins fnl f: hdd towards fin* **9/1**

4005 **3** hd **Zazous**[28] 628 7-9-0 55.................... NeilChalmers 6 60
(J J Bridger) *s.i.s: hld up in tch: rdn and hdwy over 2f out: led jst ins fnl f: hdd and no ex wl ins fnl f* **10/1**

0-50 **4** hd **Ma Ridge**[46] 402 4-8-6 47.................... RichardThomas 1 52
(T D McCarthy) *chsd ldrs: rdn jst over 2f out: hung lft and kpt on same pce ins fnl f* **33/1**

1321 **5** 1¼ **Double Valentine**[33] 571 5-8-11 55.................... KirstyMilczarek(3) 4 58+
(R Ingram) *towards rr: last but wl in tch jst over 2f out: nt clr run over 1f out: swtchd lft and hdwy jst ins fnl f: nt clr run again last 50yds: nvr able to chalenge* **4/1**[1]

2306 **6** ¾ **Tuning Fork**[4] 898 8-8-4 48.................... TolleyDean(3) 9 47
(M J Attwater) *prom: rdn and ev ch over 2f out tl wknd ins fnl f* **12/1**

-332 **7** nk **Strut The Stage (IRE)**[26] 663 4-8-5 53....................(tp) GabrielHannon(7) 8 52
(B W Duke) *t.k.h: chsd ldr tl led wl over 2f out: sn rdn: hdd jst ins fnl f: wknd last 100yds* **11/2**[3]

-536 **8** 1 **Balerno**[58] 247 9-8-8 49.................... IanMongan 10 45
(Mrs L J Mongan) *hld up in midfield: shuffled bk and lost pl over 2f out: rdn over 1f out: carried sltly rt jst over 1f out: kpt on but nvr able to chal* **15/2**

2161 **9** 4½ **Jessica Wigmo**[28] 624 5-8-6 54.................... MarkCoumbe(7) 2 38
(A W Carroll) *stmbld leaving stalls and s.i.s: hld up in last pair: hdwy on outer jst over 2f out: no hdwy and wl btn over 1f out* **7/1**

0-35 **10** 3½ **Compulsion**[19] 749 5-8-13 54.................... PatDobbs 5 29
(Pat Eddery) *led tl rdn and hdd wl over 2f out: wknd jst over 2f out: sn bhd* **5/1**[2]

1m 25.08s (0.28) **Going Correction** +0.075s/f (Slow) **10** Ran SP% **117.2**
Speed ratings (Par 101): **101,100,100,99,98 97,97,96,91,87**
CSF £78.14 CT £732.28 TOTE £8.80: £2.60, £3.90, £3.30; EX 100.70 Trifecta £346.60 Pool: £488.17 - 1.00 winning units..
Owner Miss Helen Chamberlain **Bred** Gestut Hof Ittlingen **Trained** Epsom, Surrey

FOCUS
A very moderate handicap, but it was competitive enough and the form is solid. The is winning time was 1.18 seconds quicker than the previous maiden.
Zazous Official explanation: jockey said gelding missed the break
Double Valentine Official explanation: jockey said mare was denied a clear run
Jessica Wigmo Official explanation: jockey said mare stumbled leaving stalls and missed the break, and also stumbled a furlong later

938 JOHN FERGUSON 40TH BIRTHDAY H'CAP 1m (P)
4:10 (4:12) (Class 6) (0-60,60) 4-Y-0+ **£2,047** (£604; £302) **Stalls** High

Form RPR

-544 **1** **High 'n Dry (IRE)**[13] 806 4-9-4 **60**....................(p) PaulDoe 3 73+
(M A Allen) *hld up towards rr on outer: hdwy over 3f out: jnd ldrs jst over 2f out: led wl over 1f out: rdn forged clr fnl f* **11/2**[3]

-222 **2** 2½ **Dawson Creek (IRE)**[22] 708 4-9-4 **60**....................(p) NCallan 11 67
(B Gubby) *chsd ldrs: wnt 2nd wl over 2f out: rdn to ld jst over 2f out: hdd wl over 1f out: nt pce of wnr ins fnl f* **3/1**[1]

0665 **3** 1 **Binnion Bay (IRE)**[22] 708 7-9-0 **56**....................(b) ChrisCatlin 2 61
(J J Bridger) *s.i.s: hld up bhd: rdn along wl over 3f out: gd hdwy 1f out: r.o strly to go 3rd nr fin: nvr nr ldrs* **8/1**

0310 **4** ½ **Josr's Magic (IRE)**[30] 611 4-8-12 **54**.................... JimmyQuinn 12 58
(H J Collingridge) *in tch in midfield: hdwy and rdn jst over 2f out: chsd ldng pair wl over 1f out: kpt on same pce u.p fnl f* **12/1**

2340 **5** nse **Unlimited**[19] 749 6-9-2 **58**.................... GeorgeBaker 4 62
(R Simpson) *t.k.h: chsd ldrs: lost pl jst over 2f out: kpt on u.p fnl f but nvr nr enough to chal* **10/1**

-423 **6** ½ **Waqaarr**[35] 537 4-9-2 **58**.................... JamieSpencer 6 61
(Lady Herries) *s.i.s: hld up wl bhd: hdwy and rdn jst over 2f out: c v wd st: r.o fnl f: nvr on terms* **9/2**[2]

1162 **7** ¾ **Climate (IRE)**[2] 916 9-8-10 **59**.................... RichardEvans(7) 1 60
(P D Evans) *hld up in rr: shkn up and effrt on inner over 1f out: nvr trbld ldrs* **7/1**

-601 **8** 1¼ **Charlottebutterfly**[14] 795 8-8-13 **55**.................... AdamKirby 9 53
(P J McBride) *sn bustled along: reminders over 4f out: rdn and no hdwy over 2f out* **14/1**

4005 **9** 1 **Dancing Duo**[7] 856 4-8-10 **55**....................(v) TolleyDean(3) 7 51
(D Shaw) *s.i.s: hld up in last pair: rdn over 3f out: nvr on terms* **40/1**

5300 **10** ½ **Subadar**[5] 879 4-9-1 **60**....................(p) KirstyMilczarek(3) 5 55
(M Botti) *hld up in midfield: lost pl over 2f out: n.d after* **8/1**

-053 **11** 1½ **Dream Forest (IRE)**[19] 750 5-8-13 **55**.................... JoeFanning 8 46
(P W Hiatt) *led for 1f: chsd ldr after tl over 2f out: sn rdn and wknd* **25/1**

3/2- **12** hd **Ali Bruce**[410] 341 8-9-2 **58**.................... AndrewElliott 10 49
(M R Hoad) *t.k.h: led after 1f: hdd jst over 2f out: sn dropped out and bhd* **50/1**

1m 37.42s (-0.78) **Going Correction** +0.075s/f (Slow) **12** Ran SP% **125.0**
Speed ratings (Par 101): **106,103,102,102,101 101,100,99,98,97 96,96**
CSF £23.34 CT £140.47 TOTE £6.50: £1.80, £2.00, £2.70; EX 25.60 Trifecta £219.10 Part won. Pool: £308.70 - 0.88 winning units..
Owner Miss Sarah Anne Phillips **Bred** Darley **Trained** Findon, W Sussex
■ A first winner for Mark Allen, who has been training for several years.

FOCUS
Just a moderate handicap, but solid form for the grade. The pace was reasonable.
Charlottebutterfly Official explanation: jockey said mare was never travelling
Ali Bruce Official explanation: jockey said gelding ran too free

939 TIME TO GET EGG-CITED @ PONTIN'S H'CAP 5f (P)
4:45 (4:45) (Class 5) (0-75,74) 4-Y-0+ **£2,590** (£770; £385; £192) **Stalls** High

Form RPR

6551 **1** **Sands Crooner (IRE)**[11] 840 5-9-4 74....................(v) NCallan 3 81
(D Shaw) *s.i.s: sn pushed up into midfield: rdn and hdwy over 2f out: chsd ldr 1f out: led ins fnl f: drvn out* **13/8**[1]

3430 **2** ½ **Kempsey**[5] 875 6-8-4 60 oh1 ....(v) ChrisCatlin 2 65
(J J Bridger) *dwlt: sn rdn along: chsd ldrs: sltly outpcd wl over 1f out: r.o u.p fr 1f out: wnt 2nd nr fin* **7/1**

105 **3** ¾ **Triskaidekaphobia**[40] 488 5-8-8 64 ....(t) PaulFitzsimons 4 67
(Miss J R Tooth) *led: sn clr: rdn wl over 1f out: hdd ins fnl f: no ex and lost 2nd nr fin* **7/1**

-102 **4** nse **Compton Classic**[47] 386 6-8-2 65 ....(v) PatrickDonaghy(7) 6 67+
(J R Boyle) *hld up in 5th pl: shkn up over 1f out: rdn and r.o ins fnl f: nvr quite getting to ldrs* **9/2[2]**

00-5 **5** hd **Game Lady**[4] 901 4-8-6 65 .... KirstyMilczarek(3) 1 67
(I A Wood) *chsd ldr: rdn and clsd over 1f out: kpt on same pce ins fnl f* **13/2**

0-20 **6** 9 **Don't Tell Sue**[20] 729 5-8-11 67 .... FergusSweeney 5 36+
(D W P Arbuthnot) *rrd in stalls and v.s.a: a bhd* **5/1[3]**

58.75 secs (-0.05) **Going Correction** +0.075s/f (Slow) **6** Ran SP% **111.3**
Speed ratings (Par 103): **103,102,101,100,100 86**
CSF £13.28 TOTE £2.20: £1.10, £4.90; EX 11.20.
Owner Danethorpe Racing Partnership **Bred** Peter Molony **Trained** Danethorpe, Notts

FOCUS
A modest sprint handicap and the form does not look strong. They went a strong pace.
Don't Tell Sue Official explanation: jockey said gelding reared in the stalls and missed the break

940 DLA PIPER H'CAP — 1m 4f (P)
5:20 (5:20) (Class 6) (0-65,65) 3-Y-O — **£2,047** (£604; £302) **Stalls** Low

Form — RPR

633- **1** **Warming Up (IRE)**[159] 6150 3-9-1 62 .... JamieSpencer 4 67
(C E Brittain) *hld up in midfield: nt clr run and swtchd rt over 2f out: hdwy to ld 2f out: hrd pressed over 1f out: hld on wl u.p: all out* **15/8[1]**

020- **2** nse **Lord's Bidding**[123] 6857 3-8-7 54 .... RobertHavlin 1 59
(R Ingram) *s.i.s: hld up towards rr: reminders over 5f out: rdn over 4f out: hdwy 3f out: chal wnr wl over 1f out: kpt on wl but a jst hld* **33/1**

-522 **3** 3 **Love Empire (USA)**[28] 632 3-9-4 65 ....(v[1]) JimmyQuinn 2 65
(M Johnston) *s.i.s: hld up in last: hdwy 3f out: rdn over 2f out: chsd ldng pair over 1f out: kpt on same pce u.p fnl f* **2/1[2]**

04-3 **4** 4 **Whitcombe Spirit**[41] 464 3-9-4 65 .... PaulDoe 5 59+
(Jamie Poulton) *hld up in midfield rdn 4f out: sltly hmpd and lost pl over 2f out: kpt on steadily over 1f out: wnt modest 4th ins fnl f* **9/1**

-044 **5** 2 **I Certainly May**[35] 547 3-8-12 59 .... IanMongan 9 50
(S Dow) *s.i.s: sn chsng ldrs: hdwy to ld over 5f out: rdn and hdd over 3f out: chsd ldrs after tl wknd over 1f out* **7/1[3]**

2212 **6** 1 ¾ **Coral Shores**[6] 865 3-8-12 59 ....(v) ChrisCatlin 6 47
(P W Hiatt) *plld hrd: hld up in bhd ldrs: rdn and wknd jst over 2f out* **8/1**

03-0 **7** hd **Dawn Wind**[27] 644 3-8-10 57 ....(p) NCallan 3 50+
(I A Wood) *t.k.h: hld up towards rr: short of room whn snatched up and eased jst over 2f out: pushed along and kpt on again fnl f: no ch* **16/1**

-043 **8** nse **Tobago Bay**[6] 865 3-8-5 52 ....(b) NeilChalmers 8 43+
(Miss Sheena West) *chsd ldr: rdn 4f out: wkng whn bmpd jst over 2f out: no ch after* **16/1**

02-0 **9** 11 **Rosy Dawn**[22] 704 3-8-5 52 ow1 ....(b) SaleemGolam 7 24
(Ms J S Doyle) *t.k.h early: led tl over 5f out: led again over 3f out: rdn and hdd 2f out: sn wknd* **25/1**

2m 34.82s (1.82) **Going Correction** +0.075s/f (Slow) **9** Ran SP% **120.3**
Speed ratings (Par 96): **96,95,93,91,89 88,88,88,81**
CSF £66.79 CT £143.02 TOTE £3.00: £1.30, £6.40, £1.20; EX 87.80 Trifecta £197.30 Part won. Pool: £277.90 - 0.39 winning units..
Owner Saeed Manana **Bred** Millsec Limited **Trained** Newmarket, Suffolk
■ Stewards' Enquiry : Jamie Spencer one-day ban: careless riding ban (Apr 2)

FOCUS
A moderate middle-distance handicap run at a steady pace. The first two showed improved form.
Love Empire(USA) Official explanation: jockey said colt was slowly away
Rosy Dawn Official explanation: trainer said filly was unsuited by the trip

941 PLAY GOLF @ LINGFIELD PARK H'CAP — 1m 2f (P)
5:50 (5:51) (Class 5) (0-70,70) 4-Y-0+ — **£2,457** (£725; £362) **Stalls** Low

Form — RPR

-043 **1** **Shogun Prince (IRE)**[23] 697 5-9-3 69 .... TQuinn 1 77+
(W Jarvis) *t.k.h: chsed ldr tl 8f out: rdn to chse ldr again over 2f out: led ins fnl f: styd on wl* **5/2[1]**

06-5 **2** ½ **Scripted (USA)**[20] 727 4-9-0 66 ....(t) NCallan 9 73
(C F Wall) *led: rdn and pushed clr wl over 1f out: hdd ins fnl f: no ex* **9/2[3]**

45 **3** ¾ **Bassinet (USA)**[20] 736 4-8-12 67 .... KirstyMilczarek(3) 10 73
(J A R Toller) *hld up in rr: rdn and effrt bnd jst over 2f out: styd on u.p fnl f: wnt 3rd nr fin: nt rch ldng pair* **16/1**

-425 **4** ½ **Mr Napoleon (IRE)**[5] 888 6-9-2 68 .... GeorgeBaker 8 73
(G L Moore) *chsd ldrs: rdn 2f out: unable qck wl over 1f out: kpt on ins fnl f: nt pce to threaten ldrs* **3/1[2]**

3323 **5** nk **Most Definitely (IRE)**[32] 586 8-8-12 64 ....(p) AdamKirby 5 68
(R M Stronge) *s.i.s: t.k.h: hld up in midfield: hdwy over 3f out: drvn to chse ldng pair over 1f out: one pce fnl f* **12/1**

0-00 **6** 1 **Obrigado (USA)**[19] 747 8-9-3 69 ....(t) JamieSpencer 3 73+
(Karen George) *s.i.s: hld up in last: hdwy jst over 2f out: swtchd lft jst over 1f out: styng on whn nt clr run and swtchd rt wl ins fnl f: nvr able to chal* **12/1**

2416 **7** ½ **Waterline Twenty (IRE)**[20] 730 5-9-2 68 .... StephenDonohoe 6 69
(P D Evans) *hld up in rr: effrt on outer jst over 2f out: kpt on but nvr pce to chal* **16/1**

/02- **8** 2 **Calming Waters**[282] 2520 5-9-4 70 .... ChrisCatlin 2 67
(D W P Arbuthnot) *t.k.h: chsd ldrs: wnt 2nd 8f out tl over 2f out: sn rdn: wknd jst over 1f out* **11/1**

-643 **9** nk **Stark Contrast (USA)**[23] 504 4-8-9 61 ....(p) JoeFanning 7 58
(J Akehurst) *hld up in midfield: rdn and effrt on inner wl over 1f out: no hdwy* **7/1**

660- **10** 2 **Nothingtodeclaire**[172] 5816 4-8-12 64 .... RobertHavlin 4 57
(V Smith) *t.k.h: hld up in rr: rdn and outpcd over 2f out: no ch last 2f* **40/1**

2m 8.06s (1.46) **Going Correction** +0.075s/f (Slow) **10** Ran SP% **122.2**
Speed ratings (Par 103): **97,96,96,95,95 94,94,92,92,90**
CSF £14.81 CT £154.69 TOTE £3.60: £1.60, £1.60, £4.30; EX 17.10 Trifecta £315.00 Part won. Pool: £443.76 - 0.59 winning units. Place 6 £1,353.70, Place 5 £758.90.
Owner M C Banks **Bred** Forenaghts Stud Co Ltd **Trained** Newmarket, Suffolk

FOCUS
A modest handicap and, with the pace steady for much of the way, the form needs treating with some caution. The winning time was 2.73 seconds slower than the earlier seller.
Obrigado(USA) Official explanation: jockey said gelding was unsuited by the slow pace
T/Plt: £1,039.40 to a £1 stake. Pool: £62,578.95. 43.95 winning tickets. T/Qpdt: £26.10 to a £1 stake. Pool: £4,925.90. 139.50 winning tickets. SP

863 SOUTHWELL (L-H)
Thursday, March 20

OFFICIAL GOING: Standard
Wind: Nil Weather: Overcast and raining

949 SOUTHWELL-RACECOURSE.CO.UK FILLIES' H'CAP — 1m (F)
2:10 (2:10) (Class 5) (0-70,70) 4-Y-0+ — **£2,457** (£725; £362) **Stalls** Low

Form — RPR

30-6 **1** **Indian's Feather (IRE)**[8] 850 7-8-13 70 .... HaddenFrost(5) 3 76
(N Tinkler) *trckd ldrs: hdwy on inner 3f out: chal 2f out and sn rdn: drvn to ld wl ins fnl f: kpt on* **5/1[3]**

2664 **2** nk **Jord (IRE)**[8] 852 4-9-4 70 .... AndrewElliott 6 75
(A J McCabe) *chsd ldr: rdn to take slt ld 2f out: drvn over 1f out: hdd wl ins fnl f: kpt on* **11/1**

2-33 **3** 1 ¾ **Dasheena**[8] 850 5-9-0 66 ....(be) PatrickMathers 1 67
(A J McCabe) *hld up in rr: hdwy 3f out: rdn to chse ldrs over 1f out: swtchd lft and styd on ins fnl f: nrst fin* **15/2**

2110 **4** nk **Another Genepi (USA)**[5] 899 5-9-3 69 6ex ....(b) FergalLynch 2 70
(Andrew Reid) *t.k.h: chsd ldng pair: hdwy to chal over 2f out: sn rdn and ev ch tl drvn ent fnl f and sn wknd* **11/4[2]**

050- **5** 5 **Lauro**[138] 6640 8-8-7 59 .... TomEaves 7 49
(Miss J A Camacho) *dwlt: hld up: effrt halfway: sn rdn along and outpcd wl over 2f out* **5/1[3]**

6232 **6** 9 **Only A Grand**[16] 792 4-8-4 56 oh1 ....(b) PaulHanagan 4 26
(R Bastiman) *led: rdn along 3f out: hdd 2f out and sn wknd* **9/4[1]**

1m 43.13s (-0.57) **Going Correction** -0.05s/f (Stan) **6** Ran SP% **110.9**
Speed ratings (Par 100): **100,99,97,97,92 83**
CSF £51.79 TOTE £6.50: £2.60, £4.00; EX 57.90.
Owner James Marshall & Mrs Susan Marshall **Bred** The Duke Of Roxburghe's Stud, Beckhampton House St **Trained** Langton, N Yorks
■ Stewards' Enquiry : Patrick Mathers two-day ban: used whip with excessive force (Mar 31, Apr 1)

FOCUS
A modest fillies' handicap and a weak race form-wise. The winning time was 0.39 seconds faster than the following 46-60 three-year-old handicap.
Only A Grand Official explanation: trainer said, regarding the disappointing run, that having been scoped the filly was found to have mucus on its lungs

950 SPONSOR A RACE AT SOUTHWELL (S) H'CAP — 1m (F)
2:40 (2:40) (Class 6) (0-60,55) 3-Y-O — **£1,774** (£523; £262) **Stalls** Low

Form — RPR

00-0 **1** **Ricci De Mare**[52] 335 3-9-4 55 .... SebSanders 2 58
(A B Haynes) *dwlt: sn trcking ldrs: hdwy on inner 3f out: rdn wl over 1f out: drvn ins fnl f and styd on wl to ld nr fin* **16/1**

2134 **2** hd **Novestar (IRE)**[7] 865 3-9-1 55 .... KevinGhunowa(3) 6 58
(G J Smith) *led 1f: cl up tl led again wl over 2f out: rdn wl over 1f out: drvn and hung bdly lft ent fnl f: hdd and no ex nr fin* **11/4[2]**

0-43 **3** 2 ¼ **Last Angel (IRE)**[7] 873 3-8-8 45 .... FrancisNorton 1 43
(V Smith) *cl up: led after 1f: rdn along and hdd wl over 2f out: ev ch tl drvn ent fnl f and kpt on same pce* **5/2[1]**

000- **4** 4 **Moss Way**[207] 4854 3-8-8 45 .... NeilPollard 4 34
(W J Musson) *towards rr: rdn along 1/2-way: hdwy on outer to chse ldrs over 2f out: sn drvn and one pce* **10/1**

5302 **5** nse **Whitcombe Flyer (USA)**[9] 845 3-8-13 50 ....(b) JimmyQuinn 5 39
(Miss M E Rowland) *chsd ldrs: rdn along 2f out: drvn over 1f out and sn one pce* **3/1[3]**

0-53 **6** 11 **Distant Noble**[8] 853 3-8-9 46 ow1 .... PaulMulrennan 8 11
(R Brotherton) *chsd ldrs: rdn along 1/2-way: wknd 3f out* **9/1**

000- **7** 1 ½ **Whodouthinkur (IRE)**[181] 5605 3-8-11 48 ....(p) TGMcLaughlin 7 10
(Mrs C A Dunnett) *sn rdn along: a bhd* **16/1**

00-5 **8** 7 **Mistress Rio (IRE)**[27] 662 3-8-8 45 .... TPQueally 3 —
(J G Given) *chsd ldrs: rdn along and wknd 1/2-way: sn bhd* **18/1**

1m 43.52s (-0.18) **Going Correction** -0.05s/f (Stan) **8** Ran SP% **116.4**
Speed ratings (Par 96): **98,97,95,91,91 80,79,72**
CSF £61.10 CT £153.76 TOTE £13.50: £2.80, £1.50, £1.30; EX 46.90 Trifecta £251.50 Part won. Pool: £354.30, 0.99 winning units..The winner was bought-in for 4,750gns
Owner Ms C Berry **Bred** Belgrave Bloodstock Ltd **Trained** Limpley Stoke, Bath

FOCUS
A moderate contest, as one would expect for a selling handicap, and form to have reservations about. The winning time was 0.39 seconds slower than the previous older-horse 56-70 handicap.
Ricci De Mare Official explanation: trainer said, regarding apparent improvement in form, that the filly was having its first run for the yard
Mistress Rio(IRE) Official explanation: jockey said filly hung left throughout

951 HAVE A HAPPY EASTER @ PONTIN'S CLAIMING STKS — 5f (F)
3:10 (3:10) (Class 6) 4-Y-0+ — **£1,774** (£523; £262) **Stalls** High

Form — RPR

520- **1** **Russian Rocket (IRE)**[89] 7227 6-8-13 60 .... ChrisCatlin 2 59
(Mrs C A Dunnett) *prom: rdn along and sltly outpcd wl over 1f out: drvn and styd on ent fnl f to ld nr fin* **14/1[3]**

5132 **2** hd **Savile's Delight (IRE)**[16] 786 9-9-3 70 .... RichardKingscote 3 62
(Tom Dascombe) *pushed along in rr 1/2-way: swtchd lft and hdwy 2f out: rdn to ld and hung lft over 1f out: drvn ins fnl f: hdd and nt qckn nr fin* **4/6[1]**

3504 **3** ¾ **Pappas Image**[9] 846 4-8-9 44 ....(v) NeilPollard 1 52
(A J McCabe) *chsd ldrs: hdwy wl over 1f out: drvn and ev ch ins fnl f: no ex towards fin* **33/1**

0210 **4** ½ **Tenancy (IRE)**[9] 846 4-8-11 48 ....(p) PatrickMathers 5 52
(A J McCabe) *in rr and pushed along 1/2-way: sn rdn: styd on u.p ins fnl f: nrst fin* **25/1**

4223 **5** hd **Maktavish**[21] 725 9-8-11 44 ....(b) PaulMulrennan 4 51
(R Brotherton) *led: rdn along wl over 1f out: drvn and hdd appr 1f out: kpt on u.p ins fnl f* **25/1**

3622 **6** 1 **Grimes Faith**[12] 839 5-9-7 69 ....(p) NCallan 6 57
(K A Ryan) *cl up: rdn wl over 1f out: wknd ent fnl f* **15/8[2]**

58.06 secs (-1.64) **Going Correction** -0.30s/f (Stan) **6** Ran SP% **112.1**
Speed ratings (Par 101): **101,100,99,98,98 96**
CSF £24.31 TOTE £11.60: £3.80, £1.10; EX 36.50.
Owner Mrs Christine Dunnett **Bred** Tally-Ho Stud **Trained** Hingham, Norfolk

The Form Book, Raceform Ltd, Compton, RG20 6NL

FOCUS
A modest claimer, but weak form they finished in a bit of a bunch. The winning time was 0.29 seconds quicker than the following 56-70 three-year-old handicap and the third is the best guide to the level.

952 EASTER IS EGG-STRA SPECIAL @ PONTIN'S H'CAP 5f (F)
3:40 (3:40) (Class 5) (0-70,67) 3-Y-O £2,457 (£725; £362) Stalls High

Form RPR
3622 **1** **Loose Caboose (IRE)**[9] 849 3-9-4 67........................(p) SebSanders 2 74
(A J McCabe) *prom: hdwy to chse ldr over 2f out: rdn over 1f out: styd on u.p to ld ins fnl f* **5/2**[2]
2323 **2** 2 **Diademas (USA)**[28] 635 3-9-2 65........................(v[1]) SimonWhitworth 6 65
(V Smith) *sn led and clr: rdn along 1 1/2f out: drvn and hdd ins fnl ft: no ex* **9/4**[1]
6536 **3** 2 **Planet Paradise (IRE)**[6] 876 3-7-13 53 oh7.............. KellyHarrison(5) 1 46
(D Shaw) *rdn along and outpcd in rr after 2f: hdwy wl over 1f out: sn rdn and kpt on ins fnl f: nrst fin* **20/1**
-425 **4** 1 1/4 **Montiboli (IRE)**[22] 714 3-9-1 64..(b[1]) NCallan 4 52+
(K A Ryan) *sn rdn along and outpcd after 2f: styd on u.p appr fnl f: nvr a factor* **7/2**[3]
1514 **5** 2 1/4 **Mac Dalia**[28] 635 3-8-11 63..................................(p) JerryO'Dwyer(3) 3 43
(A J McCabe) *t.k.h: hld up in tch: hdwy to chse ldrs after 2f: rdn along 2f out and sn wknd* **6/1**
5-15 **6** 3 1/2 **Stoneacre Pat (IRE)**[31] 612 3-8-11 60................................ LPKeniry 5 28
(Peter Grayson) *in rr and sn rdn along: bhd whn hung lft 1/2-way* **8/1**

58.35 secs (-1.35) **Going Correction** -0.30s/f (Stan) 6 Ran SP% **111.7**
Speed ratings (Par 98): **98,94,91,89,86 80**
CSF £8.47 TOTE £2.80: £1.20, £1.80; EX 7.60.
Owner Paul J Dixon & Greg McCabe **Bred** Paradime Ltd **Trained** Babworth, Notts

FOCUS
An ordinary handicap and the winning time was 0.29 seconds slower than the preceding older-horse claimer and so not a race to be with. Only the front pair ever really got into the race.

953 JOIN THE EASTER PARADE @ PONTIN'S MEDIAN AUCTION MAIDEN STKS 7f (F)
4:10 (4:10) (Class 6) 3-5-Y-O £1,774 (£523; £262) Stalls Low

Form RPR
5523 **1** **Days Of Pleasure (IRE)**[17] 773 3-8-12 65........................ TPQueally 7 64
(J A Osborne) *mde all: rdn clr 2f out: drvn ins fnl f and kpt on* **11/8**[1]
6 **2** 1 1/4 **Moonage Daydream (IRE)**[9] 848 3-8-12 0........................ DavidAllan 9 61+
(T D Easterby) *in tch: hdwy to chse ldrs 3f out: rdn wl over 1f out: kpt pn wl u.p ins fnl f* **28/1**
0-5 **3** 3/4 **Precipice**[17] 772 3-8-0 70.. PaulPickard(7) 8 54
(D Carroll) *a.p: rdn along 2f out: drvn over 1f out: kpt on* **3/1**[3]
0 **4** 2 1/4 **Chevaliers Dream (IRE)**[7] 867 3-8-12 0........................ FergalLynch 1 53
(T D Easterby) *s.i.s and bhd: hdwy on outer over 2f out: rdn to chse ldrs over 1f out: no imp ins fnl f* **16/1**
3 **5** 1 **Hot Bertie**[8] 855 3-8-9 0.. TravisBlock(3) 4 51
(Jedd O'Keeffe) *t.k.h: chsd wnr: rdn along wl over 2f out and grad wknd* **11/4**[2]
00- **6** 1/2 **Lady Florence**[138] 6648 3-8-4 0.. LukeMorris(3) 2 45
(A B Coogan) *chsd ldrs on inner: rdn along and outpcd 1/2-way: kpt on u.p fnl 2f* **11/1**
00 **7** 1 **Shenandoah Girl**[25] 694 5-9-8 0.. RichardSmith 3 42
(M D I Usher) *a towards rr* **28/1**
-00 **8** 1 3/4 **Admiral Troy**[13] 820 3-8-5 0.. GabrielHannon(7) 5 43
(M D I Usher) *chsd ldrs: rdn along 1/2-way: wknd over 2f out* **50/1**
0- **9** 28 **Lady Aviator**[311] 1713 3-8-4 0.. DuranFentiman(3) 6 —
(T D Easterby) *s.i.s: plld hrd in rr: bhd and rn wd st* **33/1**

1m 30.99s (0.69) **Going Correction** -0.05s/f (Stan)
WFA 3 from 5yo 15lb 9 Ran SP% **119.8**
Speed ratings (Par 101): **94,92,91,89,88 87,86,84,52**
CSF £52.40 TOTE £2.00: £1.10, £3.50, £1.40; EX 31.30 Trifecta £51.90 Pool: £1,147.22, 15.69 winning units.
Owner Cavendish Star Racing **Bred** Shay White **Trained** Upper Lambourn, Berks

FOCUS
A very modest maiden in which only three seriously counted as far as the market was concerned. This was another race dominated by those that raced handily.
Lady Aviator Official explanation: jockey said filly ran too free

954 CROC MAKES EASTER EGG-CITING @ PONTIN'S H'CAP 2m (F)
4:40 (4:40) (Class 5) (0-75,70) 4-Y-O+ £2,593 (£765; £383) Stalls Low

Form RPR
-106 **1** **Three Boars**[44] 443 6-9-5 68..(b) JamieJones(5) 5 76
(S Gollings) *hld up in rr: smooth hdwy over 4f out: chsd ldr over 2f out: rdn to chal ent fnl f: sn drvn and styd on to ld last 75yds* **3/1**[2]
-141 **2** 3/4 **Dreams Jewel**[15] 778 8-9-2 60.. NeilChalmers 2 67
(C Roberts) *hld up in rr: smooth hdwy over 4f out: effrt to ld 3f out and sn rdn clr: drvn over 1f out: jnd ent fnl f: hdd and no ex last 75yds* **9/4**[1]
0141 **3** 9 **Blue Hills**[11] 779 7-9-12 70..(b) PhillipMakin 6 66
(P W Hiatt) *a.p: rdn along wl over 2f out: drvn wl over 1f out kpt on same pce* **7/2**[3]
5 **4** 9 **Leyte Gulf (USA)**[44] 443 5-9-2 60.. ChrisCatlin 4 45
(C C Bealby) *cl up: led over 5f out: rdn along and hdd 3f out: sn outpcd* **10/1**
000- **5** 6 **Pheidias (IRE)**[44] 6109 4-8-9 58.. MickyFenton 1 36
(Mrs P Sly) *led rdn along and hdd over 5f out: sn wknd* **7/1**
040/ **6** 23 **Habitual Dancer**[44] 1184 7-8-12 59.. TravisBlock(3) 3 10
(Jedd O'Keeffe) *chsd ldng pair: rdn along 1/2-way: sn lost pl and bhd fnl 4f* **7/1**

3m 40.03s (-5.47) **Going Correction** -0.05s/f (Stan)
WFA 4 from 5yo+ 5lb 6 Ran SP% **112.1**
Speed ratings (Par 103): **111,110,106,101,98 87**
CSF £10.15 TOTE £4.20: £2.20, £1.30; EX 12.40 Place 6 £ 25.15, Place 5 £ 3.45.
Owner P Whinham **Bred** J M Greetham **Trained** Scamblesby, Lincs
■ Stewards' Enquiry : Jamie Jones one-day ban: used whip from above shoulder height (Mar 31)

FOCUS
Despite the small field and the fact that the majority of the runners stayed within close touch for most of the contest, the pace was a good one. They eventually finished very well spread out and the final time was decent but as most of these are exposed it is unlikely the first two have improved.
T/Plt: £75.40 to a £1 stake. Pool: £63,884.15. 617.75 winning tickets. T/Qpdt: £4.20 to a £1 stake. Pool: £4,060.50. 704.80 winning tickets. JR

DONCASTER (L-H)
Saturday, March 22

OFFICIAL GOING: Straight course - good to soft; round course - good (good to soft in places)
The start of the turf season was back at Doncaster after two years away, and the meeting has been reduced to a single day.
Wind: Strong, across Weather: Sunny and dry

957 WILLIAMHILLPOKER.COM BROCKLESBY CONDITIONS STKS 5f
2:15 (2:16) (Class 4) 2-Y-O £9,715 (£2,890; £1,444; £721) Stalls High

Form RPR
1 **Sally's Dilemma** 2-8-3 0.. TolleyDean(3) 19 81
(W G M Turner) *led on stands' rail: hdd 2f out: rdn to ld ins fnl f: pushed out* **7/1**[2]
2 1/2 **Doncaster Rover (USA)** 2-8-11 0........................ DarrenWilliams 14 84+
(S Parr) *cl up stands' side: effrt to ld 2f out: rdn and hdd ins fnl f: kpt on* **10/1**
3 3 **Knavesmire (IRE)** 2-8-6 0.. TWilliams 13 67
(M Brittain) *in tch stands' side: hdwy 2f out: sn rdn to chse ldng pair: styd on ins fnl f* **25/1**
4 3 3/4 **Lagan Handout** 2-8-11 0.. FergusSweeney 16 57
(Dr J R J Naylor) *in tch stands' side: hdwy over 2f out: sn rdn and kpt on same pce ent fnl f* **66/1**
5 hd **Riflessione** 2-8-11 0.. AdamKirby 20 56+
(J S Moore) *midfield: hdwy over 2f out: rdn and kpt on appr fnl f: nrst fin* **16/1**
6 1 3/4 **Northern Tour** 2-8-11 0.. TQuinn 7 53+
(P F I Cole) *s.i.s and bhd: hdwy 2f out: rdn and kpt on wl fnl f: nrst fin* **8/1**
7 1/2 **Calypso Girl (IRE)** 2-8-7 0 ow1........................ StephenDonohoe 5 43
(P D Evans) *in tch stands' side: rdn along 2f out: kpt on u.p appr fnl f* **12/1**
8 1 3/4 **Igoyougo** 2-8-11 0.. MickyFenton 10 40
(P T Midgley) *prom stands' side: rdn along 2f out: grad wknd* **14/1**
9 2 1/2 **Saxford** 2-8-11 0.. TomEaves 3 30+
(Mrs L Stubbs) *racd towards far side: in rr tl styd on fnl 2f: nvr nr ldrs* **33/1**
10 1/2 **Nchike** 2-8-11 0.. AdrianTNicholls 15 28+
(D Nicholls) *s.i.s and bhd tl sme late hdwy* **20/1**
11 shd **Richo** 2-8-11 0.. RobertWinston 11 28+
(D H Brown) *nvr bttr than midfield* **16/1**
12 1/2 **Another Luke (IRE)** 2-8-8 0.. PJMcDonald(3) 18 26
(T J Etherington) *sn outpcd and a towards rr* **20/1**
13 1 3/4 **Bad Beat** 2-8-10 0 ow2.. JerryO'Dwyer(3) 8 21
(V Smith) *in tch on outer: rdn along 1/2-way: sn wknd* **25/1**
14 1 3/4 **Mr Melodious** 2-8-11 0.. MichaelHills 4 12
(B W Hills) *s.i.s: a in rr* **11/2**[1]
15 1 1/4 **Olympic Dream** 2-8-11 0.. PaulHanagan 12 7
(R A Fahey) *sn rdn along and a towards rr* **7/1**[2]
16 hd **Shadow Bay (IRE)** 2-8-11 0.. ChrisCatlin 21 6
(M R Channon) *chsd ldrs stands' side: pushed along after 2f: sn rdn and wknd* **15/2**[3]
17 nk **Amosite** 2-8-6 0.. LiamJones 9 —
(J R Jenkins) *chsd ldrs stands' side: rdn along over 2f out and sn wknd* **66/1**
18 10 **Ballarina** 2-8-6 0.. JimmyQuinn 2 —
(E J Alston) *racd alone far rail: a in rr* **16/1**
19 3 **Diamond Blade** 2-8-11 0.. DavidAllan 6 —
(T D Easterby) *s.i.s: a in rr* **25/1**

62.66 secs (2.16) **Going Correction** +0.50s/f (Yiel) **19** Ran SP% **131.3**
Speed ratings (Par 94): **102,101,96,90,90 87,86,83,79,78 78,77,75,72,70 70,69,53,48**
CSF £72.17 TOTE £8.90: £2.90, £3.00, £8.20; EX 121.90 TRIFECTA Not won..
Owner E A Brook **Bred** K Benson **Trained** Sigwells, Somerset

FOCUS
The first two-year-old contest of the season and it was a clean sweep for those in a double-figure stall. The winning time was decent for the type of contest and interestingly fillies claimed two of the first three places home. The race should produce its usual plethora of winners.

NOTEBOOK
Sally's Dilemma, representing a yard with an excellent record with their early-season juveniles, including in this contest, cost just 3,800gns but her dam was a triple 5f winner and it was soon clear she is all about speed, racing out of the gates and grabbing the stands'-side rail. She was headed by the eventual runner-up racing into the final quarter mile, but showed a willing attitude and battled back to gain a hard-fought victory. The front pair came three lengths clear of the third and she should be capable of winning again, probably in a novice stakes. (tchd 15-2)
Doncaster Rover(USA) ◆, who should get further than 5f in time, was rather more costly than the winner at the sales - 35,000gns - and he would have been an appropriately named winner, but found the filly too strong in the closing stages. He travelled strongly and looked the winner when edging ahead, so should have little trouble winning a maiden. (op 8-1)
Knavesmire(IRE) ◆, a first runner for sire One Cool Cat, is another who will require further than this in time and she made a highly promising debut, keeping on for pressure and pulling clear of the fourth. She too can come on for this experience and win a maiden. (op 40-1)
Lagan Handout, whose dam won over a mile, comes from a yard who are hardly renowned for their success with juveniles, but he made a highly satisfactory debut back in fourth and ran way above market expectation. He showed enough speed to suggest he can win at this distance, but 6f will be required in time.
Riflessione ◆, a 13,000gns son of mudlark Captain Rio, is quite a late foal and as a result this has to go down as a promising start. He was doing his best work late and the fact he looked in need of the experience suggests a markedly improved effort is to be expected next time. He should win a maiden. (op 20-1)
Northern Tour ◆, whose yard have traditionally done well with their juveniles, is related to numerous middle-distance performers and he did not look an obvious early-season 5f type. Those fears proved founded, but there were only positives to take from this first run as he got behind following a slow start and it was pleasing to see him going on nicely under a sympathetic ride late on. He should learn a lot from this and, although likely to be seen at his best over further, he can probably win a 5f maiden.
Calypso Girl(IRE), a 28,000euros purchase, comes from a yard who can get a fast early-season juvenile, as we saw with Vhujon last term, and she made a satisfactory debut, keeping on at the one pace under pressure. The experience should not be lost on her.
Igoyougo, a January foal, is likely to want a bit further than this in time, but he still managed to show plenty of early speed. He should learn from the experience. (op 20-1)
Saxford, already a gelding, was taken off his feet early before making some late headway. He will want a bit further in time.
Nchike, related to a host of fast winners, is another to have been gelded and he blew his chance here with a slow start. He was trying to run on towards the end of his race though and is another likely type for a maiden.

Mr Melodious, who is bred to stay trips in excess of 1m in time, comes from a yard who have a decent enough record in this contest without actually winning it and he was strongly supported just before the race, coming right in to favourite. However, those who followed him did not get much of a run for their money as he was very slowly away and could never get involved. He is obviously thought to be capable of much better and deserves another chance, albeit there still have to be reservations about him having the speed for this trip. (op 9-1)

Olympic Dream, a 52,000gns son of Kyllachy, has more stamina on the dam's side and he failed to make any impact on this debut, soon getting outpaced and never really picking up. He was clearly in need of the experience. (op 5-1)

Shadow Bay(IRE), who cost 18,500gns, was representing a top two-year-old yard and he showed plenty of early toe, but stopped quickly under strong pressure and proved most disappointing. (tchd 7-1)

958 WILLIAM HILL SPRING MILE (H'CAP) 1m (S)

2:50 (2:52) (Class 2) 4-Y-0+

£24,928 (£7,464; £3,732; £1,868; £932; £468) **Stalls** High

Form	Pos	Dist	Horse / Details	RPR
151-	1		**Don't Panic (IRE)**160 6203 4-9-8 **92** AlanMunro 17 (P W Chapple-Hyam) *racd stands' side: hld up in tch: racd keenly: led that gp and overall ldr over 2f out: rdn clr of that side over 1f out: r.o wl* **13/2**2	114+
500-	2	4	**Benandonner (USA)**168 6011 5-9-5 **89** PaulHanagan 1 (R A Fahey) *racd far side: trckd ldrs: led that gp over 1f out: sn rdn: r.o: no ch w wnr* **16/1**	101+
100-	3	7	**Trafalgar Square**170 5950 6-9-3 **87** PaulDoe 2 (J Akehurst) *racd far side: chsd ldrs: led that gp over 2f out to over 1f out: no ex: 2nd of 8 in gp* **16/1**	84
013-	4	½	**Zaahid (IRE)**162 6155 4-9-8 **92** RHills 21 (B W Hills) *racd stands' side: hld up: hdwy over 2f out: chsd wnr over 1f out: sn rdn and no imp: 2nd of 13 in gp* **9/4**1	88
640-	5	½	**Regal Parade**175 5805 4-9-2 **86** AdrianTNicholls 4 (D Nicholls) *racd far side: hld up: hld up: hdwy over 1f out: nvr trbld ldrs: 3rd of 8 in gp* **33/1**	80
006-	6	2½	**Skhilling Spirit**162 6155 5-9-9 **93** PaulFessey 19 (T D Barron) *racd stands' side: dwlt: hld up: hdwy over 2f out: sn swtchd lft: nt rch ldrs: 3rd of 13 in gp* **25/1**	82
0-52	7	4	**Plum Pudding (IRE)**14 834 5-9-0 **89** HaddenFrost(5) 18 (R Hannon) *racd stands' side: chsd ldrs: led that side and overall ldr over 3f out: hdd over 2f out: wknd fnl f: 4th of 13 in gp* **8/1**3	69
00-1	8	1¼	**Partners In Jazz (USA)**81 6 7-9-8 **92** PhillipMakin 5 (T D Barron) *racd far side: hld up: hdwy over 2f out: rdn over 1f out: wknd fnl f: 4th of 8 in gp* **16/1**	69
00-0	9	3	**Moody Tunes**14 833 5-9-1 **85** AndrewElliott 7 (K R Burke) *racd far side: prom: rdn over 3f out: wknd over 1f out: 5th of 8 in gp* **28/1**	56
/01-	10	3	**Pelican Waters (IRE)**96 7174 4-9-3 **87** NCallan 15 (E F Vaughan) *racd stands' side: hld up: hdwy u.p over 2f out: wknd over 1f out: 5th of 13 in gp* **20/1**	51
500-	11	8	**White Deer (USA)**182 5615 4-9-9 **93** SilvestreDeSousa 22 (D Nicholls) *racd stands' side: prom: rdn 1/2-way: wknd over 2f out: 6th of 13 in gp* **50/1**	40
000-	12	3	**Fortunate Isle (USA)**20 4814 6-9-5 **89** (p) TonyHamilton 20 (R A Fahey) *racd stands' side: led that gp and overall ldr: hdd over 5f out: rdn over 2f out: sn wknd: 7th of 13 in gp* **33/1**	29
640-	13	nk	**Heywood**176 5765 4-8-9 **86** OliveGaule(7) 9 (D Nicholls) *racd far side: w ldr tl led 6f out: hdd 3f out: wknd wl over 1f out: 6th of 8 in gp* **100/1**	25
4503	14	7	**Troubadour (IRE)**14 834 7-9-8 **92** (b) TQuinn 16 (W Jarvis) *racd stands' side: s.i.s: hld up: hdwy u.p over 2f out: sn wknd: 8th of 13 in gp* **16/1**	16
-410	15	6	**Samarinda (USA)**14 834 5-9-9 **93** 5ex MickyFenton 11 (Mrs P Sly) *racd stands' side: mid-div: rdn 1/2-way: wknd 2f out: eased fnl f: 9th of 13 in gp* **33/1**	4
122-	16	11	**Ella Woodcock (IRE)**148 6474 4-9-4 **88** JimmyQuinn 6 (E J Alston) *s.i.s: swtchd to r stands' side: hld up: hdwy u.p over 2f out: sn wknd: 10th of 13 in gp* **12/1**	—
2-26	17	1¼	**Orchard Supreme**7 906 5-9-3 **87** RichardHughes 3 (R Hannon) *racd far side: led 2f: chsd ldrs: rdn and wknd 2f out: 7th of 8 in gp* **11/1**	—
114-	18	15	**Lap Of Honour (IRE)**189 5431 4-8-11 **84** WilliamBuick(3) 12 (Jennie Candlish) *racd stands' side: chsd ldrs: led over all over 5f out: hdd over 3f out: wknd over 2f out: 11th of 13 in gp* **18/1**	—
030-	19	3¾	**Minority Report**147 6491 8-9-3 **94** AdeleRothery(7) 13 (D Nicholls) *racd stands' side: chsd ldrs over 5f: 12th of 13 in gp* **50/1**	—
111-	20	1½	**Hoh Wotanite**82 7287 5-8-13 **86** (v) RussellKennemore(3) 8 (R Hollinshead) *racd far side: hld up: rdn 1/2-way: wknd 3f out: last of 8 in gp* **33/1**	—
0240	21	31	**Dream Lodge (IRE)**7 906 4-9-8 **92** JimmyFortune 14 (J G Given) *racd stands' side: mid-div: rdn 1/2-way: sn wknd: last of 13 in gp* **20/1**	—

1m 41.42s (2.12) **Going Correction** +0.50s/f (Yiel) **21** Ran SP% **133.5**

Speed ratings (Par 109): **109,105,98,97,97 94,90,89,86,83 75,72,71,64,58 47,46,31,27,26**

CSF £100.29 CT £1677.84 TOTE £7.40: £1.90, £4.30, £4.10, £1.60; EX 178.20 Trifecta £1209.60 Part won. Pool: £1,703.68 - 0.10 winning units..

Owner A B S Webb **Bred** Bernard Colclough **Trained** Newmarket, Suffolk

FOCUS

With its prize fund boosted by £10,000 this looked a very competitive renewal of the Lincoln consolation, especially with some of the more progressive types having failed to get into the main race, but Don't Panic ran out a most authoritative winner and it is hard to believe he would not have gone very close to winning the 'big' one later on the card had he made the cut, a theory backed up by the winning time which was almost a second quicker. Runner-up Benandonner in turn was seven lengths clear of the remainder. The form looks strong and Don't Panic looks ready to make an impact in Group races. Thirteen, including the winner, raced on the stands' side and eight took the far-side route, and there appeared to be little advantage either way.

NOTEBOOK

Don't Panic(IRE) ◆, a most progressive type once gelded last season who capped things off with an impressive performance in soft ground at Goodwood, was reappearing off a 9lb higher mark and would have been most interesting in the Lincoln itself had he made the cut. Quite keen early on, he still looked full of running as he came through to lead just over quarter of a mile out and fairly burst clear of the field once asked to go and win his race, pulling over 11 lengths clear of his nearest persuer Zaahid on the stands' side. An indication of just how easily he won can be taken from the fact that Munro had trouble pulling him up as the horse tanked on as though he was ready for another circuit. On this evidence he would have gone close to winning the Lincoln had he got in and the fact the time was almost a second quicker than the later race suggests Don't Panic is a horse going places. His trainer has no targets in mind and expects the handicapper to clobber him for this, but it seems likely he will be capable of winning at Listed/Group 3 level when he gets his ground. (op 7-1 tchd 15-2)

Benandonner(USA), who ran creditably for a long way in last season's Cambridgeshire, excelled himself in second and destroyed everything else on his side, but did not count on bumping into the winner. His hand has now been shown without reward and things will be a lot more difficult next time. (op 18-1)

Trafalgar Square only ran three times last year, winning on his reappearance at Newmarket, so it was no surprise to see him run well on this seasonal reappearance. He did best of the rest in the far-side group and may yet be open to further improvement.

Zaahid(IRE), favourite for the Lincoln until missing the cut, had been most progressive at three and looked the one to beat in this consolation race despite being 7lb higher than when last winning. Odds of 9/4 looked plenty short enough though and having made good headway to move into third on the stands' side he was simply left for dust by the winner. It is possible he will come on for this, but being by top-class middle-distance runner Sakhee there is every chance he requires 1m2f now. (op 11-4)

Regal Parade, who rattled up a quick hat-trick for Mark Johnston early last year, struggled off marks in the 90s during the peak season and was subsequently sold. He has joined a yard adept at doing well with other people's horses and he made a highly promising start, running on under pressure to claim third in the far-side group.

Skhilling Spirit is best known as a sprinter, but he rounded off last season with a creditable effort over this distance and judging by this performance the mile is definitely no problem. He is on something of a losing run, but remains capable of better at his new distance. (op 33-1)

Plum Pudding(IRE), claimed late on in the recent Lincoln Trial at Wolverhampton, was made plenty of use of and ran well. He could not match the principals at the business end but is on a decent mark and can find a race before too long. Official explanation: jockey said gelding lost its action

Samarinda(USA) Official explanation: jockey said gelding had no more to give

Ella Woodcock(IRE) Official explanation: jockey said gelding hit its head in stalls and was never travelling

Orchard Supreme Official explanation: jockey said gelding lost its action

Hoh Wotanite Official explanation: jockey said horse was unsuited by the ground - too holding

Dream Lodge(IRE) Official explanation: jockey said colt never travelled

959 WILLIAMHILL.CO.UK CAMMIDGE TROPHY (LISTED RACE) 6f

3:25 (3:25) (Class 1) 3-Y-0+

£17,034 (£6,456; £3,231; £1,611; £807; £405) **Stalls** High

Form	Pos	Dist	Horse / Details	RPR
140-	1		**Aahayson**166 6071 4-9-2 104 FergusSweeney 16 (K R Burke) *mde all on stands' rail: rdn and edgd lft over 1f out: drvn and edgd rt ins fnl f: kpt on gamely* **14/1**	113
400-	2	nk	**Sonny Red (IRE)**167 6039 4-9-2 105 RichardHughes 9 (R Hannon) *a.p: effrt 2f out and sn ev ch: rdn ins fnl f and nt qckn towards fin* **9/2**1	112
450-	3	1½	**Wi Dud**196 5214 4-9-2 109 NCallan 17 (K A Ryan) *trckd ldrs on stands' rail: effrt and nt clr run over 1f out and ins fnl f: swtchd lft and rdn: kpt on towards fin* **5/1**2	111+
530-	4	1¼	**Prime Defender**174 5832 4-9-2 108 MichaelHills 3 (B W Hills) *trckd ldrs: hdwy 2f out: rdn over 1f out: kpt on same pce ins fnl f* **7/1**3	104+
313-	5	3¼	**Tax Free (IRE)**170 5953 6-9-7 110 AdrianTNicholls 18 (D Nicholls) *midfield: hdwy 2f out: rdn and kpt on ins fnl f: nrst fin* **15/2**	99+
0426	6	1	**Ripples Maid**23 741 5-9-0 0 ChrisCatlin 15 (J A Geake) *towards rr: hdwy nr stands' rail 2f out: sn rdn and kpt on ins fnl f: nrst fin* **25/1**	89+
301-	7	¾	**Lady Grace (IRE)**155 6300 4-9-0 101 LiamJones 8 (W J Haggas) *towards rr: hdwy 2f out: sn rdn and kpt on ins fnl f: nrst fin* **12/1**	87+
00-3	8	¾	**Lovelace**14 832 4-9-7 109 JoeFanning 12 (M Johnston) *hld up in rr: effrt whn nt clr run wl over 1f out: swtchd rt ent fnl f: kpt on: nrst fin* **7/1**3	95+
635-	9	1¼	**Knot In Wood (IRE)**119 6930 6-9-2 103 PaulHanagan 1 (R A Fahey) *in tch on outer: rdn along over 2f out and grad wknd* **20/1**	83
5-05	10	4½	**Appalachian Trail (IRE)**29 666 7-9-5 0 (b) TomEaves 7 (Miss L A Perratt) *chsd ldrs: rdn along 2f out: sn edgd lft and wknd* **16/1**	72
006-	10	dht	**Rising Shadow (IRE)**133 6758 7-9-2 100 JimmyQuinn 2 (N Wilson) *midfield on outer: rdn along 2f out and no hdwy* **20/1**	69
050-	12	4	**Strike Up The Band**147 6487 5-9-2 98 SilvestreDeSousa 4 (D Nicholls) *prom on outer: rdn along over 2f out: sn wknd* **50/1**	57
520-	13	½	**Advanced**133 6758 5-9-2 111 PaulMulrennan 14 (K A Ryan) *chsd ldrs: rdn along 2f out and sn btn* **10/1**	56
420-	14	5	**Hinton Admiral**307 1876 4-9-2 105 JamieMoriarty 10 (R A Fahey) *a in midfield* **40/1**	41
620-	15	½	**Hoh Hoh Hoh**154 6338 6-9-2 104 DarryllHolland 6 (R J Price) *cl up: rdn along wl over 2f out and sn wknd* **22/1**	39

1m 14.5s (0.90) **Going Correction** +0.50s/f (Yiel) **15** Ran SP% **123.1**

Speed ratings (Par 111): **114,113,111,109,105 104,103,102,100,94 94,89,88,81,81**

CSF £70.61 TOTE £17.00: £4.90, £2.10, £2.50; EX 110.10 Trifecta £780.20 Part won. Pool: £1,098.88 - 0.20 winning units..

Owner Mrs Maura Gittins **Bred** Whitsbury Manor Stud And Mrs M E Slade **Trained** Middleham Moor, N Yorks

FOCUS

A good quality event and the winning time was very solid for a Listed race. The winner made all, posting a career best, and nothing got into it from off the speed. A few were below form, but the race should produce winners.

NOTEBOOK

Aahayson, a progressive handicapper last season who was not disgraced in a couple of back-end pattern contests, needed to have made significant strides over the winter to take a race of this nature, but the fact he was backed right in to 14/1, having been available at up to 50/1 in the morning, suggested he was fancied to run a big race. He did just that, leading right from the off on the stands' rail and willingly sticking out his neck to thwart the persistent Sonny Red. The winner is an imposing individual so it would not surprise to see him progress again and the Abernant Stakes was mentioned as his next intended target. (op 33-1)

Sonny Red(IRE), runner-up in last season's Craven, has proved adaptable in terms of trip and, although he could make no impact in the Abbaye on his final start last year, this looked a much more winnable contest. Never too far from the speed, he came to have every chance and ran on right the way to the line, but Aahayson was always just doing enough. The Abernant would appear an obvious target for him aswell. (tchd 4-1)

Wi Dud did not race outside of Group company last season, thrice at Group 1 level, and although he had yet to win at this distance, he looked a major player. He would have claims for being a little unlucky as having travelled strongly just in behind the winner he found no room on the rail when trying to come with his run and then could not regather himself in time. He should have been closer, but would probably have still finished third. (op 11-2)

Prime Defender has proved a solid performer at this level and he ran well from his low draw, keeping on at the same pace. This was his first start of the season and he can be expected to improve, especially back on fast ground. (op 11-2)

Tax Free(IRE) enjoyed a fine time of it last season, winning twice at Group 3 level, but he looked vulnerable under the penalty and ran about as well as could have been expected. He was going on nicely close home and should come on for the run. (op 8-1)

Ripples Maid has been running some good races in defeat in Dubai and she shaped promisingly here, running on well late having been in rear early. She is not the easiest to place. (op 33-1)

Lady Grace(IRE), off since winning a 6f Listed contest at Newmarket in October, was a little tapped for toe early but came home to good effect and should come on for this outing. She stay further and there is more success in her at this level. (tchd 14-1)

Lovelace, a tough and progressive sort at 7f last season, shaped as though in need of the run on his recent reappearance at Wolverhampton and he looked a shade unlucky not to finish closer on this drop in trip. He was just beginning to pick up when denied a clear run and deserves some credit as he was shouldering a Group 3 penalty. Official explanation: jockey said colt was denied a clear run (op 10-1)

Advanced, who defied top weight to land the 2007 Ayr Gold Cup, has no great record fresh and should leave this running behind in time. (op 8-1)

Hinton Admiral, a dual Listed winner for Mark Johnston, has joined a good yard but he was always going to struggle to make an impact here and really needs some assistance from the Handicapper. He is not going to be easy to place. (op 50-1)

960 WILLIAM HILL LINCOLN (HERITAGE H'CAP) 1m (S)

4:00 (4:03) (Class 2) 4-Y-0+

£77,900 (£23,325; £11,662; £5,837; £2,912; £1,462) Stalls High

Form				RPR
451-	1		**Smokey Oakey (IRE)**[140] 6637 4-8-9 **95** .... JimmyQuinn 12 (M H Tompkins) *racd stands' side: hld up: hdwy and swtchd lft over 1f out: rdn to ld overall ins fnl f: rdr dropped reins: r.o* **10/1**	105
430-	2	1 1/4	**Blythe Knight (IRE)**[11] 6298 8-9-3 **110** .... BMcHugh(7) 3 (J J Quinn) *racd far side: trckd ldrs: led far side over 2f out: sn rdn: styd on: 1st of 10 in gp* **22/1**	117
260-	3	1	**Babodana**[115] 6965 8-8-12 **98** .... NCallan 16 (M H Tompkins) *racd stands' side: chsd ldrs: led that gp well over 1f out: edgd rt: hdd and unable qck ins fnl f: 2nd of 11 in gp* **28/1**	103
300-	4	hd	**Rio Riva**[168] 6011 6-9-0 **100** .... TomEaves 5 (Miss J A Camacho) *racd far side: hld up in tch: lost pl over 4f out: hdwy u.p over 1f out: r.o: 2nd of 10 in gp* **17/2**[3]	104
-640	5	1 3/4	**Escape Route (USA)**[30] 650 4-8-9 **95** .... (p) RobertHavlin 4 (J H M Gosden) *racd far side: hld up in tch: rdn to chse ldr that side over 1f out: styd on same pce: 3rd of 10 in gp* **16/1**	96
460-	6	1 1/4	**Mine (IRE)**[175] 5797 10-9-4 **104** .... (v) DarryllHolland 13 (J D Bethell) *racd stands' side: hld up: hdwy over 2f out: rdn over 1f out: styd on same pce fnl f: 3rd of 11 in gp* **50/1**	102
150-	7	1 3/4	**Yeaman's Hall**[259] 3330 4-8-11 **100** .... WilliamBuick(3) 21 (A M Balding) *trckd ldrs stands' side: rdn over 1f out: no ex ins fnl f: 4th of 11 in gp* **6/1**[1]	94
-040	8	3/4	**Fremen (USA)**[43] 495 8-8-10 **96** .... AdrianTNicholls 1 (D Nicholls) *racd far side: hld up: hdwy and n.m.r over 1f out: r.o: nt trble ldrs: 4th of 10 in gp* **20/1**	88
040-	9	2	**Annemasse**[168] 6011 4-8-11 **97** .... PaulHanagan 2 (R A Fahey) *racd far side: chsd ldrs: rdn over 1f out: edgd rt and wknd ins fnl f: 5th of 10 in gp* **25/1**	85
442-	10	2 1/2	**Vitznau (IRE)**[155] 6301 4-8-11 **97** .... RichardHughes 9 (R Hannon) *racd far side: hld up: hdwy over 2f out: sn rdn: wknd ins fnl f: 6th of 10 in gp* **7/1**[2]	79
23-6	11	1/2	**Little White Lie (IRE)**[15] 829 4-8-13 **99** .... TQuinn 6 (G M Lyons, Ire) *racd far side: hld up: rdn over 2f out: n.d: 7th of 10 in gp* **12/1**	80
332-	11	dht	**Raptor (GER)**[91] 7223 5-9-2 **102** .... FergusSweeney 19 (K R Burke) *racd stands' side: broke wl: stdd and lost pl 7f out: hdwy over 2f out: wknd fnl f: 5th of 11 in gp* **12/1**	83+
0-00	13	3/4	**European Dream (IRE)**[23] 739 5-9-3 **103** .... (p) PhillipMakin 20 (R C Guest) *racd stands' side: hld up: sme hdwy u.p over 2f out: wknd over 1f out: 6th of 11 in gp* **12/1**	83
100-	14	4 1/2	**Very Wise**[115] 6965 6-9-0 **100** .... JimmyFortune 17 (W J Haggas) *overall ldr stands' side: rdn and hdd well over 1f out: not much room sn after: wknd fnl f: 7th of 11 in gp* **11/1**	70
500-	15	6	**Dhaular Dhar (IRE)**[133] 6758 6-8-9 **95** .... DanielTudhope 15 (J S Goldie) *racd stands' side: chsd ldrs: rdn over 2f out: wknd over 1f out: 8th of 11 in gp* **40/1**	52
210/	16	1 1/4	**Clipperdown (IRE)**[426] 7-9-5 **105** .... (t) EdwardCreighton 11 (E J Creighton) *racd stands' side: hld up in tch: rdn over 2f out: wknd over 1f out: 9th of 11 in gp* **100/1**	59
0-30	17	2 3/4	**Azarole (IRE)**[51] 382 7-9-0 **100** .... JohnEgan 18 (Jane Chapple-Hyam) *racd stands' side: plld hrd and prom: rdn and wknd over 2f out: 10th of 11 in gp* **40/1**	48
-140	18	1 3/4	**Fajr (IRE)**[28] 678 6-9-7 **107** .... (b) GeorgeBaker 7 (Miss Gay Kelleway) *trckd ldr far side: led that gp 1/2-way: rdn and hdd over 2f out: wknd over 1f out: 8th of 10 in gp* **25/1**	51
0/3-	19	9	**Prince Forever (IRE)**[301] 2043 4-9-6 **106** .... PhilipRobinson 10 (M A Jarvis) *led far side to 1/2-way: wknd over 2f out: 9th of 10 in gp* **9/1**	30
4	20	10	**Classic Port (FR)**[14] 834 4-9-2 **102** .... MickyFenton 14 (J Ryan) *racd stands' side: chsd ldrs 5f: last of 11 in gp* **16/1**	4
/10-	21	13	**Temple Place (IRE)**[311] 1767 7-8-8 **94** .... (t) RobertWinston 8 (D McCain Jnr) *racd far side: s.s: hdwy 1/2-way: wknd over 2f out: last of 10 in gp* **50/1**	—

1m 42.38s (3.08) **Going Correction** +0.50s/f (Yiel) **21 Ran SP% 129.6**

Speed ratings (Par 109): **104,102,101,101,99 98,96,96,94,91 91,91,90,85,79 78,75,74,65,55 42**

CSF £224.84 CT £6003.17 TOTE £9.70: £2.70, £4.80, £5.80, £3.20; EX 539.30 Trifecta £8654.40 Part won. Pool: £12,189.43 - 0.70 winning units..

Owner Judi Dench and Bryan Agar **Bred** Hyde Park Stud **Trained** Newmarket, Suffolk

■ Stewards' Enquiry : N Callan two-day ban: careless riding (Apr 5,7)

FOCUS

Leading ante-post fancies Zaahid (ran in the Spring Mile), Lang Shining and Heaven Knows failed to make the cut and, while the minimum rating required to get in was 94 this was perhaps not a vintage renewal of the race, the fact that the winning time was nearly a second slower than the Spring Mile bolstering that argument. However, the form does look very solid with progressive four-year-old Smokey Oakey beating two previous winners of the race and last year's runner-up claiming fourth. There seemed to be little in the draw and, as had been the case in the earlier Spring Mile, the best horse won.

NOTEBOOK

Smokey Oakey(IRE), a proven soft-ground performer, had done nearly all his racing at three over 1m2f, but the drop back to 1m in testing conditions brought about an impressive performance at Ayr on his final outing in November and, despite contesting this much more competitive contest off a 9lb higher mark, he looked one of the likelier winners for a yard who have enjoyed success in this contest before. A middle draw meant his rider had the option of which side to go and, having travelled strongly in the rear of the stands' side group, he came through with a strong winning challenge once switched, showing a good turn of pace in the process. His rider dropped his reins having been struck on the hand by the third-placed jockey's whip, but thankfully for connections it made no difference to the result. Further progress will be required if he is to defy another rise however and the John Smith's Cup at York is a mid-term target, assuming he gets his favoured slow surface. (op 12-1)

Blythe Knight(IRE), 15lb higher than when winning this at Redcar back in 2006, has been enduring mixed fortunes in the face of stiff opposition over hurdles, most recenty finishing down the field in the Champion Hurdle, but he showed himself to be most progressive on turf last season by winning the Group 3 Diomed Stakes at Epsom on Derby Day and his relatively inexperienced jockey taking off 7lb was an obvious help. Always going nicely, he went on over two out and quickly put the race on his side to bed, but it became clear from inside the final furlong that the winner was motoring and he could do nothing as he sailed by on the opposite side of the track. This run suggests he is as good as ever, if not better, and he may be capable of winning another small pattern race at some stage this season, albeit he will carry a Group 3 penalty in Listed company. (op 25-1)

Babodana, winner of the Lincoln as a four-year-old back in 2004, had only contested the race once more since when performing creditably behind Blythe Knight in 2006. Off a mark 9lb lower than when gaining his famous victory, he looked a most unlikely winner at the age of eight, but ran a storming race and kept battling away once hitting the front, just found wanting for a change of speed by his stable companion. The fire evidently still burns bright, but he will remain hard to place. (op 33-1)

Rio Riva, 3lb higher than when finishing second in this at Newcastle last year, often attracts support in these big-field handicaps, especially when there is some juice in the ground, and he performed creditably. Held up in the far group, he found himself shuffled back at halfway but kept plugging on and found only Blythe Knight too strong on his side. He is sure to win in his turn again at some stage this season. (op 8-1 tchd 9-1 in a place)

Escape Route(USA), one of a few to have been trying their luck in Dubai, has been running creditably behind some capable sorts out there and the first-time cheekpieces looked worth a shot for this underachiever. He looked a possible threat at one stage, but could not quicken sufficiently to challenge and perhaps a return to further is the answer. (op 14-1)

Mine(IRE) has plundered many a decent handicap in his time and he was another of the veterans to cover themselves in glory. He remains 2lb higher than when winning his last handicap, but was running on late and the ten-year-old evidently still has an appetite for the game.

Yeaman's Hall, although interesting as one of the least exposed in the field, looked a big, raw horse last season and there had to be a doubt as to whether he was battle-hardened enough to win a race of this nature on what was just the fifth start of his career. The answer was 'no' as having been up there on the stands' side he came under strong pressure and could not respond. His pedigree is a blend of speed and stamina (by Derby winner Galileo, out of a Dayjur mare) and it remains to be seen what his trip is. (op 13-2 tchd 7-1 in a place)

Fremen(USA), a late developer who had not really had things go his way in Dubai recently, likes to get his toe in and he looked one of the more interesting outsiders, but needs a really decent gallop to be seen at his best and he did not get it. He ran on to claim a creditable eighth and perhaps a little assistance from the handicapper would not go amiss.

Annemasse, a tough individual who more than paid his way for the Mark Johnston yard last season, ran a cracker to be beaten just over six lengths in last year's Cambridgeshire and was 1lb lower here, but he was not obviously fancied in the market and the way he ran suggests this run was needed. He probably needs to drop a few pounds in the weights before he is back winning.

Vitznau(IRE) was quite a popular selection on this seasonal debut, but came into this 13lb higher than when last winning and never threatened to get into it. He is going to remain vulnerable off this sort of mark. (op 8-1 tchd 9-1)

Little White Lie(IRE), the sole Irish representative, enjoyed a nice pipe-opener at Dundalk the other day and had the cut in the ground he required, but was never sighted in the race. (tchd 14-1)

Raptor(GER), fourth in last year's race, ran a little better than his finishing position suggests although a mark of 102 is going to continue to make life difficult in handicaps. (tchd 14-1)

European Dream(IRE) was no less than 26lb higher than when landing the Spring Mile at Newcastle a year ago and could never get into the race.

Very Wise, 9lb higher than when taking the race at Newcastle a year ago, had had no prep this time around and, despite again finding himself in front early, he was readily brushed aside at the business end. Official explanation: jockey said gelding had no more to give (op 14-1)

Fajr(IRE) has been on the go through the winter, winning a couple of times at Lingfield, and he was made plenty of use of on the far side, but it came as no surprise to see him swept aside when things started to really heat up.

Prince Forever(IRE), as was the case with Yeaman's Hall, could have looked interesting simply because he was well bred and unexposed, but a mark of 106 left him with a lot to prove and it all seemed too competitive for him in the end, dropping out tamely having set the early pace on the far side. This was only the fourth start of his career and he has clearly not been easy to train. Official explanation: jockey said colt hung right (op 8-1)

Classic Port(FR), an ex-French performer who shaped well in the recent Lincoln Trial at Wolverhampton, was another who looked vulnerable off a high mark and he failed to make an impact.

Temple Place(IRE) Official explanation: jockey said gelding had no more to give

961 WILLIAM HILL 0800 444040 MAIDEN STKS 1m 2f 60y

4:35 (4:35) (Class 4) 3-Y-0 £4,533 (£1,348; £674; £336) Stalls Low

Form				RPR
22-0	1		**No To Trident**[7] 903 3-8-10 80 .... RichardEvans(7) 7 (P D Evans) *trckd ldrs on inner: pushed along and outpcd wl ovcer 2f out: rdn to chse ldrs and hung lft over 1f out: n.m.r and swtchd rt jst ins fnl f: styd on to ld last 75yds* **33/1**	79
2-	2	1 1/4	**Fiulin**[136] 6723 3-9-3 0 .... NCallan 11 (M Botti) *hld up in tch: stdy hdwy on outer 4f out: rdn 2f out: styd on to chse ldr ins fnl f: drvn and hld whn n.m.r nr fin* **11/4**[1]	77
200-	3	3/4	**Internationaldebut (IRE)**[147] 6489 3-9-0 95 .... DNolan(3) 5 (S Parr) *cl up: led after 2f: qcknd clr over 2f out: rdn over 1f out: wknd qckly wl ins fnl f: wandered and hdd last 75yds* **9/2**	75+
30	4	1 1/4	**Azabu Juban (IRE)**[7] 903 3-8-9 0 .... LukeMorris(3) 3 (J Jay) *hld up towards rr: hdwy wl over 2f out: rdn wl over 1f out: styd on ins fnl f: nrst fin* **40/1**	68+
003-	5	hd	**Tharawaat (IRE)**[141] 6616 3-9-3 78 .... RHills 8 (B W Hills) *trckd ldrs: smooth hdwy over 3f out: rdn to chse ldr 2f out: drvn ent fnl f and one pce* **7/2**[2]	73

2 **6** 2 1/4 **Mekong Melody (IRE)**[22] 748 3-8-12 0 PhilipRobinson 12 63
(C G Cox) *trckd ldrs: smooth hdwy 3f out: rdn to chse ldr wl over 1f out: sn drvn and wknd ent fnl f* **4/1**[3]

500- **7** 6 **Sabre Light**[149] 6449 3-9-3 62 LeeEnstone 2 56
(P T Midgley) *midfield whn hmpd after 1f: hld up: hdwy and in tch 3f out: rdn over 2f out and kpt on same pce* **100/1**

0 **8** 3/4 **El Masir**[35] 595 3-9-3 0 JoeFanning 4 55
(M Johnston) *led 2f: cl up tl rdn along over 2f out and grad wknd* **25/1**

9 3 3/4 **Little Sark (IRE)** 3-9-3 0 StephenDonohoe 13 47
(P D Evans) *a towards rr* **100/1**

63- **10** 1/2 **Amanjena**[136] 6724 3-8-9 0 WilliamBuick(3) 14 41
(A M Balding) *nvr bttr than midfield* **16/1**

11 5 **Capal Dubh Alainn (IRE)** 3-9-3 0 RobertWinston 10 36
(T J Pitt) *s.i.s: a in rr* **66/1**

0- **12** shd **Kuriyama (IRE)**[155] 6296 3-9-3 0 JimmyQuinn 6 36
(M H Tompkins) *chsd ldrs on inner: rdn along 3f out and sn wknd* **50/1**

13 3/4 **Always Cruising (USA)** 3-9-3 0 DarryllHolland 1 34
(M Johnston) *dwlt: hdwy on inner whn hmpd after 1f: bhd after* **9/1**

405- **14** 3 3/4 **Eton Fable (IRE)**[143] 6593 3-9-0 68 AndrewMullen(3) 15 27
(W J H Ratcliffe) *a in rr* **100/1**

15 24 **Martingrange Lass (IRE)** 3-8-12 0 DarrenWilliams 9 —
(S Parr) *a bhd* **80/1**

2m 19.36s (8.16) **Going Correction** +0.80s/f (Soft) **15** Ran SP% **119.8**
Speed ratings (Par 100): **99,98,97,96,96 94,89,89,86,85 81,81,80,77,58**
CSF £119.80 TOTE £42.60: £6.40, £1.60, £1.90; EX 168.00 Trifecta £304.80 Part won. Pool: £429.42 - 0.20 winning units..
Owner G E Amey **Bred** G E Amey **Trained** Pandy, Monmouths

FOCUS
This was just a fair maiden, perhaps below the standard usually associated with this fixture, and No To Trident caused a shock in winning although he was not far off this level last season. A modest time, 2.6 seconds slower than the following handicap.

962 WILLIAMHILLCASINO.COM MARCH H'CAP 1m 2f 60y
5:10 (5:10) (Class 4) (0-85,85) 4-Y-0+ £6,477 (£1,927; £963; £481) Stalls Low

Form RPR

0-06 **1** **Granston (IRE)**[39] 531 7-9-1 82 RobertWinston 5 89
(J D Bethell) *chsd ldr: rdn to ld over 1f out: edgd lft: styd on* **25/1**

430- **2** 1/2 **First Buddy**[20] 5978 4-8-12 79 NCallan 20 85+
(G A Swinbank) *hld up: plld hrd: swtchd rt and hdwy over 2f out: rdn over 1f out: edgd lft: r.o: nt rch wnr* **8/1**[3]

400- **3** nse **Quince (IRE)**[147] 6490 5-8-11 78 (v) JimmyQuinn 4 84
(J Pearce) *s.i.s: sn pushed along and prom: rdn over 2f out: styd on* **18/1**

511- **4** 1 1/4 **Suits Me**[140] 6636 5-9-3 84 MickyFenton 2 88
(T P Tate) *led: rdn and hdd over 1f out: styd on same pce ins fnl f* **6/1**[2]

220- **5** 3 3/4 **Cleaver**[245] 3753 7-8-11 78 RichardHughes 6 75
(Lady Herries) *hld up: hdwy over 2f out: rdn over 1f out: nt rch ldrs* **11/2**[1]

2-36 **6** 4 **Basra (IRE)**[28] 678 5-9-1 82 AdamKirby 8 72
(Miss Jo Crowley) *hld up in tch: rdn over 2f out: sn edgd lft: wknd fnl f* **10/1**

02-6 **7** 1 1/4 **Northern Spy (USA)**[49] 409 4-9-2 83 PatDobbs 19 71
(S Dow) *hld up in tch: rdn over 2f out: wknd over 1f out* **14/1**

6F-0 **8** 1 **Krugerrand (USA)**[22] 747 9-8-7 74 FergusSweeney 9 60
(W J Musson) *hld up: hdwy over 2f out: nt trble ldrs* **14/1**

01- **9** 1 1/4 **Painted Sky**[10] 7045 5-8-9 76 PaulHanagan 1 60
(R A Fahey) *hld up in tch: rdn over 2f out: wknd over 1f out* **8/1**[3]

500- **10** hd **Lucayan Dancer**[161] 6180 8-8-12 79 SilvestreDeSousa 13 62
(D Nicholls) *hld up: rdn over 2f out: no ch whn swtchd rt over 1f out* **40/1**

405- **11** 3/4 **Cruise Director**[311] 1771 8-9-1 82 PaulEddery 7 64
(Ian Williams) *hld up: nt clr run over 2f out: n.d* **22/1**

5/1- **12** 3 1/4 **Lunar Promise (IRE)**[434] 117 6-8-8 75 StephenDonohoe 12 51
(Ian Williams) *hld up: plld hrd: hdwy 1/2-way: rdn and wkng whn hmpd 2f out* **20/1**

055- **13** 7 **Davenport (IRE)**[136] 6727 6-8-8 75 (p) AlanMunro 17 38
(B R Millman) *hld up: hdwy over 3f out: rdn and wknd over 1f out* **16/1**

06-5 **14** 1 1/2 **Kings Quay**[22] 757 6-9-4 85 (tp) GrahamGibbons 14 46
(J J Quinn) *prom: rdn over 2f out: sn wknd* **12/1**

-142 **15** 3 3/4 **Intersky Charm (USA)**[39] 531 4-8-12 79 DeanMcKeown 11 33
(R M Whitaker) *hld up in tch: plld hrd: rdn and wknd 2f out* **18/1**

202- **16** 7 **Prince Samos (IRE)**[148] 6475 6-8-8 75 AdrianTNicholls 10 16
(D Nicholls) *hld up: rdn over 3f out: sn wknd* **8/1**[3]

000- **17** 14 **Old Romney**[136] 6727 4-8-4 71 DaleGibson 15 —
(M W Easterby) *hld up: rdn 1/2-way: sn lost tch* **50/1**

2m 16.76s (5.56) **Going Correction** +0.80s/f (Soft) **17** Ran SP% **126.9**
Speed ratings (Par 103): **109,108,108,107,104 101,100,99,98,98 97,95,89,88,85 79,68**
CSF £211.24 CT £3727.42 TOTE £26.40: £4.30, £3.20, £4.20, £2.10; EX 311.80 TRIFECTA Not won..
Owner The Four Players Partnership **Bred** Yeomanstown Stud **Trained** Middleham Moor, N Yorks

FOCUS
A most competitive handicap where a low draw proved an advantage. An average race for the grade, but solid form.
Painted Sky Official explanation: jockey said gelding hung right
Prince Samos(IRE) Official explanation: jockey said gelding had no more to give

963 WILLIAMHILL.CO.UK APPRENTICE H'CAP 1m 4f
5:40 (5:40) (Class 5) (0-70,74) 4-Y-0+ £3,412 (£1,007; £504) Stalls Low

Form RPR

4433 **1** **Red Wine**[10] 854 9-8-8 62 EJMcNamara(5) 10 75
(A J McCabe) *hld up in rr: smooth hdwy on outer over 3f out: led over 2f out: shkn up ins fnl f and kpt on* **17/2**

60- **2** 1 1/4 **Puy D'Arnac (FR)**[59] 5738 5-8-8 60 GaryBartley(3) 18 71
(G A Swinbank) *t.k.h: trckd ldrs: hdwy over 2f out: rdn to chse wnr ent fnl f: kpt on* **11/1**

351- **3** 4 **Calzaghe (IRE)**[38] 5388 4-9-0 70 (v) DeclanCannon(5) 4 75
(K R Burke) *in tch: hdwy 3f out: rdn over 1f out: kpt on ins fnl f* **11/1**

-526 **4** 1 1/4 **Amical Risks (FR)**[37] 559 4-8-3 59 DebraEngland(5) 17 63+
(W J Musson) *stdd s and bhd: stdy hdwy on wd outside over 3f out: chal 2f out and ev ch tl rdn and wknd ent fnl f* **20/1**

1035 **5** shd **Flame Creek (IRE)**[17] 793 12-8-13 65 SCreighton(3) 13 68
(E J Creighton) *hld up in rr: hdwy over 3f out: rdn 2f out: kpt on ins fnl f: nrst fin* **33/1**

1313 **6** 1 **Karmest**[21] 771 4-8-12 63 NeilBrown 5 64
(A D Brown) *hld up and bhd: hdwy on inner over 2f out: sn rdn and styd on ins fnl f: nrst fin* **12/1**

0-64 **7** nk **Top Spec (IRE)**[19] 778 7-8-2 56 SimonPearce(5) 9 57
(J Pearce) *s.i.s and bhd: hdwy 3f out: rdn 2f out: kpt on ins fnl f: nt rch ldrs* **5/1**[1]

041- **8** nk **Dream Of Fortune (IRE)**[157] 6272 4-9-5 70 (t) JamieJones 1 71
(M G Quinlan) *hld up towards rr: hdwy 3f out: rdn 2f out: kpt on ins fnl f: nt rch ldrs* **7/1**[3]

650- **9** 1 3/4 **Parnassian**[171] 5917 8-8-13 62 (v) HaddenFrost 16 60
(J A Geake) *t.k.h: chsd ldr: effrt and ev ch 3f out: sn rdn and wknd* **12/1**

030- **10** 10 **Sir Arthur (IRE)**[225] 4072 5-9-2 70 LanceBetts(5) 14 53
(B Ellison) *t.k.h: led: rdn along over 3f out: hdd over 2f out and grad wknd* **22/1**

0 **11** 4 1/2 **Ambitious Genes (IRE)**[38] 540 4-9-5 70 PatrickHills 2 46
(J W Hills) *chsd ldrs on inner: rdn along 4f out and sn wknd* **20/1**

020- **12** 3/4 **Penang Cinta**[189] 5415 5-9-2 70 RichardEvans(5) 7 45
(P D Evans) *chsd ldrs: rdn along over 2f out: grad wknd* **17/2**

123- **13** 2 **John Dillon (IRE)**[11] 4332 4-9-0 68 (v) PatrickDonaghy(3) 3 40
(P C Haslam) *s.i.s: a in rr* **6/1**[2]

6123 **14** nse **Mixing**[8] 881 6-8-4 56 AmyBaker(3) 6 28
(J Akehurst) *midfield: pushed along 4f out: rdn 3f out and sn wknd* **9/1**

0-04 **15** 3 3/4 **Fossgate**[26] 701 7-8-6 60 (p) BMcHugh(5) 12 26
(J D Bethell) *midfield: hdwy to chse ldrs 4f out: rdn along wl over 2f out and sn wknd* **16/1**

00-0 **16** 13 **Turn Of Phrase (IRE)**[60] 260 9-9-2 70 (b) SamuelDrury(5) 8 17
(N Wilson) *prom: rdn along over 3f out and sn wknd* **50/1**

2m 43.56s (8.46) **Going Correction** +0.80s/f (Soft)
WFA 4 from 5yo+ 2lb **16** Ran SP% **131.2**
Speed ratings (Par 103): **103,102,99,98,98 97,97,97,96,89 86,86,84,84,82 73**
CSF £99.74 CT £1071.40 TOTE £10.40: £1.80, £2.80, £2.60, £8.30; EX 140.40 Trifecta £269.00 Part won. Pool: £378.95 - 0.50 winning units. Place 6 £676.77, Place 5 £131.42..
Owner Paul J Dixon **Bred** Genesis Green Stud Ltd **Trained** Babworth, Notts

FOCUS
A low-grade event and Red Wine rolled back the years to score. The first two finished clear and this is solid if unspectacular form.
Parnassian Official explanation: jockey said gelding had no more to give
Penang Cinta Official explanation: jockey said gelding was unsuited by the ground
John Dillon(IRE) Official explanation: jockey said gelding had no more to give
T/Jkpt: Not won. T/Plt: £452.20 to a £1 stake. Pool: £177,938.75. 287.25 winning tickets. T/Qpdt: £60.00 to a £1 stake. Pool: £10,150.30. 125.10 winning tickets. JR

928 KEMPTON (A.W) (R-H)
Saturday, March 22

OFFICIAL GOING: Standard
There was a major bias towards those that raced handily at this meeting. Four of the winners made all whilst two others raced prominently.
Wind: Strong, ahead

964 INTERCASINO.CO.UK H'CAP 6f (P)
2:10 (2:10) (Class 6) (0-65,68) 4-Y-0+ £2,047 (£604; £302) Stalls High

Form RPR

-411 **1** **Toms Laughter**[8] 875 4-9-4 68 (p) KevinGhunowa(3) 1 78+
(R A Harris) *trckd ldrs: shkn up over 1f out: qcknd to ld ins fnl f: readily* **4/1**[1]

000- **2** 1/2 **Bertie Swift**[273] 2878 4-8-13 60 JimCrowley 3 68
(J Gallagher) *lw: mid-div: rdn 3f out: hdwy over 1f out: styd on wl fnl f: tk 2nd cl home but a hld by wnr* **25/1**

2060 **3** nk **Mind Alert**[7] 901 7-8-13 60 (v) FrancisNorton 4 67
(D Shaw) *in rr: pushed along over 2f out: hdwy appr fnl f: kpt on thrght fnl f but nvr gng pce to trble wnr* **25/1**

4562 **4** nk **Figaro Flyer (IRE)**[19] 782 5-9-4 65 TPQueally 6 71
(P Howling) *hld up in rr: pushed along 2f out: hdwy over 1f out: squeezed through ins fnl f and fin wl* **9/2**[2]

5440 **5** hd **Cool Sands (IRE)**[38] 539 6-9-2 63 (v) SteveDrowne 11 68
(D Shaw) *in ouch: rdn and hdwy fr 2f out: styd on ins fnl f but nvr quite gng pce to chal* **6/1**[3]

-216 **6** shd **Reigning Monarch (USA)**[50] 391 5-8-10 57 SamHitchcott 12 62
(Miss Z C Davison) *led tl hdd ins fnl f: sn wknd* **7/1**

0-66 **7** 1 1/4 **Linda Green**[34] 599 7-8-8 62 MatthewDavies(7) 2 63
(M R Channon) *in tch: rdn to chse ldrs over 2f out: wknd fnl f* **16/1**

06-0 **8** 2 3/4 **Briannsta (IRE)**[15] 819 6-8-13 65 NataliaGemelova(5) 10 58
(J E Long) *lw: rdn over 2f out: wknd appr fnl f* **10/1**

1323 **9** nk **Lindbergh**[7] 896 6-8-6 60 (v) MCGeran(7) 7 52
(J Ryan) *lw: w ldr over 3f: wknd over 1f out* **7/1**

1440 **10** hd **Arfinnit (IRE)**[41] 515 7-8-7 57 (p) KirstyMilczarek(3) 8 48
(Mrs A L M King) *lw: rrd stalls: a in rr* **8/1**

0245 **11** 4 **Epidaurian King (IRE)**[22] 755 5-9-1 62 (v) TGMcLaughlin 5 41
(D Shaw) *lw: stdd stalls and swtchd rt to rails: a towards rr* **8/1**

1m 12.74s (-0.36) **Going Correction** -0.025s/f (Stan) **11** Ran SP% **122.4**
Speed ratings (Par 101): **101,100,99,99,99 99,97,93,93,93 87**
CSF £109.76 CT £1582.76 TOTE £4.60: £1.90, £6.10, £5.30; EX 124.70.
Owner Five To Follow **Bred** Mrs D J Hughes **Trained** Earlswood, Monmouths

FOCUS
A competitive little sprint handicap in which the early pace was solid and the form looks sound rated around the placed horses. However, the final time was only fractionally faster than the following three-year-old maiden which suggests the form is ordinary.
Arfinnit(IRE) Official explanation: jockey said gelding was never travelling

965 INTERCASINO.CO.UK MAIDEN STKS 6f (P)
2:45 (2:47) (Class 4) 3-Y-O £4,210 (£1,252; £625; £312) Stalls High

Form RPR

0- **1** **Mullein**[239] 3895 3-8-12 0 JimCrowley 4 82+
(R M Beckett) *lw: mde virtually all: pushed along and qcknd over 1f out: c clr ins fnl f: comf* **7/4**[1]

6-3 **2** 4 **Irish Music (IRE)**[17] 796 3-9-3 0 NeilPollard 3 73
(A P Jarvis) *chsd ldrs: rdn to go 2nd 1f out: kpt on but no ch w wnr ins fnl f* **12/1**

3 2 1/4 **Sir Billy Nick** 3-9-3 0 TPQueally 9 66+
(J Noseda) *w'like: outpcd and pushed along in rr 1/2-way: styd on fr over 1f out: r.o to take 3rd cl home but no ch w ldng duo* **11/4**[3]

60-4 **4** 3/4 **Night Premiere (IRE)**[7] 897 3-8-12 60 RyanMoore 8 59
(R Hannon) *chsd wnr to 1/2-way and again over 2f out but no ch: wknd ins fnl f and lost 3rd cl home* **16/1**

5 1 3/4 **Espy** 3-9-3 0 MartinDwyer 6 59
(S Kirk) *w'like: bit bkwd: in rr: hdwy over 2f out: nvr in contention and styd on same pce fr over 1f out* **25/1**

0-U4 **6** *5* **Spic 'n Span**[25] 706 3-9-0 70........ KevinGhunowa(3) 1 44
(R A Harris) *chsd ldrs: t.k.h and wnt 2nd 3f out: rn wd sn after and wknd fr 2f out* **20/1**

42- **7** *2 1/2* **Fastella (IRE)**[119] 6926 3-8-12 0........ JamieSpencer 2 31
(G A Butler) *slowly away: a outpcd in rr* **2/1**[2]

8 *26* **Hibou De Nuit (IRE)** 3-9-3 0........ PatCosgrave 5 —
(J R Boyle) *w'like: bit bkwd: slowly away and rdr lost iron: sn hanging rt and wl bhd w no ch* **50/1**

1m 12.79s (-0.31) **Going Correction** -0.025s/f (Stan) **8** Ran SP% **120.5**
Speed ratings (Par 100): **101,95,92,91,89 82,79,44**
CSF £24.79 TOTE £2.80: £1.10, £2.50, £1.50; EX 29.30.
Owner Landmark Racing Limited **Bred** C D S Bryce And Mrs M Bryce **Trained** Whitsbury, Hants

FOCUS
A modest maiden and ony three mattered in the market, but with two of them not running their races for various reasons there appears little strength in depth to the form behind the winner. The runner-up and fourth are the best guides to the level.
Spic 'n Span Official explanation: jockey said gelding ran too free and hung left

966 IAN MCCLELLAND MEMORIAL H'CAP (LONDON MILE QUALIFIER) 1m (P)
3:15 (3:17) (Class 4) (0-85,85) 3-Y-O **£4,210** (£1,252; £625; £312) **Stalls** High

Form RPR

16-3 **1** **Cordell (IRE)**[7] 902 3-9-4 **85**........ RyanMoore 7 98+
(R Hannon) *lw: mde virtually all: pushed along whn chal 2f out: forged clr and edgd lft ins fnl f: readily* **7/2**[1]

321- **2** *2 3/4* **Formation (USA)**[139] 6675 3-8-13 **80**........ JamieSpencer 4 87+
(E A L Dunlop) *sn trcking wnr: chal over 2f out: drvn and swished tail continuously sn after: no ch fnl f but kpt on for clr 2nd* **5/1**[3]

221- **3** *3 1/4* **Atabaas Pride**[194] 5281 3-8-13 **80**........ GregFairley 10 80
(M Johnston) *chsd ldrs in 3rd most of way: rdn over 2f out: kpt on same pce* **4/1**[2]

430- **4** *1/2* **Jollyhockeysticks**[140] 6652 3-8-5 **72**........ CatherineGannon 2 71+
(M R Channon) *in rr: pushed along over 2f out: hdwy over 1f out: styd on thrght fnl f to take 4th ins fnl f: nt trble ldrs* **33/1**

03-2 **5** *3/4* **Hansinger (IRE)**[36] 573 3-8-12 **79**........ RichardKingscote 8 76
(B I Case) *lw: in tch: hdwy fr 3f out: nvr gng pce to rch ldrs: one pce ins fnl 2f* **13/2**

5-1 **6** *1* **Admiral Dundas (IRE)**[63] 221 3-8-6 **73**........ J-PGuillambert 5 68
(W Jarvis) *chsd ldrs: rdn over 2f out: wknd over 1f out* **7/2**[1]

16 **7** *1 1/2* **Vettorenjoy**[36] 573 3-8-10 **80**........ KirstyMilczarek(3) 3 72+
(M Botti) *lw: in rr: racd on outside: sme prog over 3f out: nvr in contention* **8/1**

031- **8** *2* **Moment's Notice**[134] 6750 3-8-12 **79**........ LPKeniry 12 66
(S Kirk) *lw: chsd ldrs: rdn 3f out: wknd 2f out* **25/1**

502- **9** *1 1/2* **Averoo**[154] 6329 3-8-11 **78**........ TGMcLaughlin 9 62
(M D Squance) *fly j. stalls: t.k.h: a in rr* **50/1**

214- **10** *3/4* **Lady Sorcerer**[155] 6297 3-8-11 **78**........ NeilPollard 6 60
(A P Jarvis) *chsd ldrs: rdn 3f out: wknd 2f out* **33/1**

1m 39.21s (-0.59) **Going Correction** -0.025s/f (Stan) **10** Ran SP% **117.2**
Speed ratings (Par 100): **101,98,95,94,93 92,91,89,87,87**
CSF £20.69 CT £74.78 TOTE £4.90: £1.80, £1.40, £1.80; EX 22.20.
Owner Mrs J Wood **Bred** Scea Haras De La Poterie **Trained** East Everleigh, Wilts

FOCUS
A fair handicap of its type, but one dominated by those that raced handily as the first three home occupied those positions throughout. The form looks solid with the first two clear.

967 PLAY ROULETTE AT INTERCASINO.CO.UK H'CAP 6f (P)
3:50 (3:50) (Class 4) (0-85,82) 3-Y-O **£4,210** (£1,252; £625; £312) **Stalls** High

Form RPR

211 **1** **Thebes**[5] 918 3-8-12 **76** 6ex........ GregFairley 8 91+
(M Johnston) *mde all: shkn up over 1f out: pushed clr fnl f: easily* **1/2**[1]

130- **2** *2 1/4* **Wigram's Turn (USA)**[238] 3938 3-9-2 **80**........ FrancisNorton 1 82+
(A M Balding) *in rr: rdn and hdwy on outside fr 2f out: r.o u.p to chse wnr jst ins fnl f but no ch* **9/2**[3]

100- **3** *1/2* **Artistic License (IRE)**[162] 6154 3-8-0 **71**........ MatthewDavies(7) 2 71
(M R Channon) *lw: chsd ldrs: rdn over 2f out: styd on same pce fnl f* **28/1**

21-1 **4** *1/2* **Ike Quebec (FR)**[35] 582 3-9-0 **78**........ RyanMoore 4 77
(J R Boyle) *lw: chsd wnr: rdn over 2f out: sn no imp: wknd fnl 110yds* **10/1**

4103 **5** *1/2* **Asian Power (IRE)**[4] 924 3-8-10 **74**........ OscarUrbina 7 71
(P J O'Gorman) *chsd ldrs: rdn to disp 2nd over 2f out but nvr any ch w wnr: wknd ins fnl f* **16/1**

004- **6** *1 1/4* **Sofia's Star**[163] 6128 3-9-4 **82**........ JimCrowley 6 75
(P Winkworth) *t.k.h: in tch: rdn over 2f and outpcd: styd on again ins fnl f* **20/1**

1414 **7** *1/2* **Southwest Star (IRE)**[4] 924 3-8-7 **71**........ LPKeniry 3 62
(J S Moore) *in rr: sme prog 2f out: kpt on fnl f but nvr remotely in contention* **9/1**[3]

301- **8** *hd* **Van Bossed (CAN)**[206] 4937 3-9-0 **78**........ JamieSpencer 5 69
(D Nicholls) *stdd s: t.k.h in rr: sme hdwy over 2f out: nvr rchd ldrs and wknd fnl f* **12/1**

1m 12.87s (-0.23) **Going Correction** -0.025s/f (Stan) **8** Ran SP% **125.7**
Speed ratings (Par 100): **100,97,96,95,95 93,92,92**
CSF £3.81 CT £36.76 TOTE £1.70: £1.02, £1.60, £7.60; EX 5.10.
Owner Sheikh Hamdan Bin Mohammed Al Maktoum **Bred** Whitsbury Manor Stud And Mrs M E Slade **Trained** Middleham Moor, N Yorks

FOCUS
An uncompetitive handicap and the hot-favourite proved different class. The form is rated around those in the frame behind the winner.

968 INTERCASINO.CO.UK DRAGONFLY STKS (LISTED RACE) 1m 4f (P)
4:25 (4:25) (Class 1) 4-Y-O+
£14,762 (£5,595; £2,800; £1,396; £699; £351) **Stalls** Centre

Form RPR

011- **1** **Malt Or Mash (USA)**[133] 6759 4-9-0 105........ RyanMoore 2 109+
(R Hannon) *h.d.w: hld up in rr: hdwy fr 4f out: drvn and styd on wl to chse ldr ins fnl 3f: led wl over 1f out: r.o strly* **8/11**[1]

4- **2** *2 1/4* **Miramare (GER)**[140] 6645 4-8-9 0........ TPQueally 3 99
(A P Stringer) *lw: led: pushed along over 2f out: hdd wl over 1f out: kpt on wl for clr 2nd but a hld by wnr* **6/1**[3]

-141 **3** *15* **Millville**[22] 757 8-9-2 110........ SteveDrowne 1 81
(M A Jarvis) *lw: chsd ldrs: wnt 2nd 1m out to 6f out: rdn and outpcd 3f out: styd on again for mod 3rd appr fnl f* **9/4**[2]

61-5 **4** *nk* **St Savarin (FR)**[19] 418 7-9-2 94........ NeilPollard 6 81
(B R Johnson) *chsd ldrs: rdn over 3f out: wknd over 2f out* **25/1**

-303 **5** *5* **Murfreesboro**[7] 908 5-9-2 86........ GregFairley 5 74
(K J Burke) *chsd ldr 4f and again 6f out: lost 2nd ins fnl 3f: lost mod 3rd over 1f out* **16/1**

-501 **6** *3/4* **Kames Park (IRE)**[10] 859 6-9-2 87........ MarkCoumbe 4 72
(R C Guest) *s.i.s: a in rr* **33/1**

2m 31.32s (-3.18) **Going Correction** -0.025s/f (Stan)
WFA 4 from 5yo+ 2lb **6** Ran SP% **115.6**
Speed ratings (Par 111): **109,107,97,97,93 93**
CSF £6.31 TOTE £1.60: £1.10, £2.50; EX 5.00.
Owner A P Patey **Bred** Delahanty Stock Farm **Trained** East Everleigh, Wilts

FOCUS
The majority of this race was run in a blizzard, though it ended in sunshine. Not a particularly strong Listed race, containing a wide range of abilities, and the front pair dominated it completely with the runner-up rated to his British debut form. The early pace was a decent one though and it proved too much for a few.

NOTEBOOK
Malt Or Mash(USA), having his first run since winning last season's November Handicap, had run well at a more modest level here in his only previous try on sand, but he has improved a great deal since then. Held up as usual, he had a bit to do rounding the home bend, but he got stronger as the race progressed and was the only one to emerge from the pack and get to the clear leader. In the end he won with a bit in hand and looks ready for a step up to Group company now, but on the evidence of last season he will probably need fast ground. He looked beforehand as though he would improve for the run. (op Evens)
Miramare(GER) ran an almost identical race to her British debut over this course and distance in November, blasting off in front and setting a decent gallop, and then battling back very gamely even after being headed. She obviously has plenty of ability and there should be a race like this in her. (tchd 5-1)
Millville, in good form on Polytrack already this year, could never get on terms with the eventual runner-up and only just got up for third from a horse whom he was meeting on 16lb better terms compared with handicaps. He has fallen just short of this level before, but a bigger problem is that he is just not the same horse going right-handed. (op 15-8)
St Savarin(FR), back on the Flat after finishing third in a Stratford maiden hurdle, ran about as well as he was entitled to but he is on an awkward mark these days.
Murfreesboro, who ran well when stepped up to this trip in a Lingfield handicap last time, found this level a totally different kettle of fish. (op 20-1)
Kames Park(IRE), narrow winner of a Wolverhampton claimer last time, is better than that level but is nowhere near good enough for this and never figured. Official explanation: jockey said gelding finished distressed (op 25-1)

969 BIG JACKPOTS AT INTERCASINO.CO.UK H'CAP 7f (P)
5:00 (5:00) (Class 4) (0-85,85) 4-Y-O+ **£4,210** (£1,252; £625; £312) **Stalls** High

Form RPR

0-06 **1** **Markab**[54] 336 5-9-1 **82**........ PatCosgrave 7 92
(K A Morgan) *mde all: drvn along over 2f out: styd on grimly u.p thrght fnl f: all out* **16/1**

5132 **2** *1/2* **Count Ceprano (IRE)**[19] 775 4-8-4 **71**........ HayleyTurner 11 80+
(M D I Usher) *in rr: hdwy 2f out: str run fr over 1f out: tk 2nd wl ins fnl f and clsng on wnr but a jst hld* **15/2**

0-00 **3** *1* **Resplendent Nova**[14] 833 6-9-3 **84**........ FrancisNorton 6 90
(P Howling) *chsd ldrs: rdn to dispute 2nd fr 2f out: nvr quite gng pce to rch wnr and kpt on same pce ins fnl f* **10/1**

606- **4** *shd* **Kyle (IRE)**[160] 6205 4-8-13 **80**........ RyanMoore 12 86
(R Hannon) *lw: chsd ldrs: rdn and hdwy to chse wnr appr fnl f: nvr quite gng pce to chal and wknd nr fin* **6/1**

01-4 **5** *1 1/2* **Spring Goddess (IRE)**[71] 124 7-8-8 **75**........ RichardThomas 1 77
(A P Jarvis) *in rr: rdn and hdwy fr 2f out: kpt on ins fnl f but nvr in contention* **25/1**

0-00 **6** *1* **Bomber Command (USA)**[14] 834 5-9-4 **85**........ SteveDrowne 9 84
(J W Hills) *chsd ldrs: rdn over 2f out: nvr quite gng pce to chal: wknd ins fnl f* **11/2**[3]

030- **7** *1* **Our Blessing (IRE)**[191] 5356 4-8-11 **78**........ NeilPollard 10 75
(A P Jarvis) *chsd ldrs: rdn 3f out: wknd over 1f out* **33/1**

435- **8** *1/2* **Mcnairobi**[280] 2670 5-8-13 **80**........ JamieSpencer 4 79+
(P D Cundell) *s.i.s: in rr: hdwy whn nt clr run ins fnl 2f: styng on again whn hmpd and swtchd rt over 1f out: nt rcvr* **4/1**[2]

4221 **9** *1/2* **Super Frank (IRE)**[24] 717 5-8-13 **80**........ TPQueally 5 74
(J Akehurst) *lw: chsd wnr: rdn 3f out: wknd appr fnl f* **7/2**[1]

4006 **10** *2 1/4* **Qadar (IRE)**[7] 904 6-9-2 **83**........(p) JimCrowley 8 71
(N P Littmoden) *chsd ldrs: rdn 3f out: wknd 2f out* **11/1**

-611 **11** *1 3/4* **Buxton**[25] 707 4-9-3 **84**........(t) DavidKinsella 3 67
(R Ingram) *in rr: sme hdwy 4f out: sn btn* **12/1**

10-6 **12** *1/2* **Hessian (IRE)**[7] 910 4-8-4 **71**........ MartinDwyer 2 53
(M D Squance) *s.i.s: bhd most of way* **20/1**

1m 24.37s (-1.63) **Going Correction** -0.025s/f (Stan) **12** Ran SP% **126.2**
Speed ratings (Par 105): **108,107,106,106,104 103,102,101,101,98 96,95**
CSF £136.64 CT £1312.37 TOTE £26.00: £6.20, £2.00, £3.80; EX 273.70.
Owner Tight Lines Partnership **Bred** Shadwell Estate Company Limited **Trained** Little Marcle, H'fords

FOCUS
A very competitive handicap run at a strong pace though not many got into it and the runner-up sets the level backed up by the time. This was another race on the card where it paid to be handy.
Mcnairobi Official explanation: jockey said mare was denied a clear run

970 PLAY BLACKJACK AT INTERCASINO.CO.UK H'CAP 1m 4f (P)
5:35 (5:35) (Class 5) (0-75,75) 4-Y-O+ **£2,590** (£770; £385; £192) **Stalls** Centre

Form RPR

6/1- **1** **The Carlton Cannes**[83] 7282 4-9-6 **75**........ SteveDrowne 4 87+
(G Wragg) *lw: trckd ldrs: wnt 2nd over 2f out: hrd drvn and styd on over 1f out: led fnl 110yds: won gng away* **1/1**[1]

12 **2** *1 1/2* **Outlandish**[4] 921 5-9-6 **73**........ AlanDaly 6 81
(Andrew Turnell) *led: rdn over 2f out: kpt on tl hdd and outpcd fnl 110yds* **8/1**

3531 **3** *2 3/4* **Our Kes (IRE)**[9] 874 6-9-0 **67**........ TPQueally 7 72+
(P Howling) *hld up towards rr but in tch: hdwy to go 3rd over 1f out but no imp on ldng duo* **8/1**

301- **4** *1* **Hatton Flight**[145] 6534 4-8-10 **65**........(b) FrancisNorton 1 67
(A M Balding) *chsd ldrs: rdn and outpcd 3f out: styd on again u.p fr over 1f out: tk 4th ins fnl f but nvr in contention* **7/2**[2]

053- **5** *nk* **Wheelavit (IRE)**[21] 4910 5-8-8 **61**........ JimCrowley 3 63
(B G Powell) *t.k.h: chsd ldr 1m out: rdn over 2f out: wknd over 1f out* **9/2**[3]

040/ **6** *1* **Miss Pebbles (IRE)**[482] 6008 8-8-5 **61** ow1........ KirstyMilczarek(3) 2 61
(R Dickin) *in rr thrght but in tch: hung lft u.p and one pce 2f out* **33/1**

1V4- 7 21 **Crazy Bear (IRE)**77 [7132] 5-8-13 66 .... GregFairley 5 35
(K J Burke) *in rr but in tch: rdn 4f out: wknd qckly 3f out* **16/1**

2m 36.58s (2.08) **Going Correction** -0.025s/f (Stan)
WFA 4 from 5yo+ 2lb 7 Ran SP% **121.4**
Speed ratings (Par 103): **92,91,89,88,88 87,73**
CSF £11.44 TOTE £2.30: £1.40, £4.20; EX 14.30 Place 6 £58.89, Place 5 £17.77.
Owner J L C Pearce **Bred** J L C Pearce **Trained** Newmarket, Suffolk

FOCUS
An ordinary handicap and the early pace was modest which caused a few to pull but the front two are potentially progressive. The winning time was 5.26 seconds slower than the earlier Listed race.
T/Plt: £107.70 to a £1 stake. Pool: £50,215.10. 340.10 winning tickets. T/Qpdt: £11.80 to a £1 stake. Pool: £3,010.20. 188.20 winning tickets. ST

914 WOLVERHAMPTON (A.W) (L-H)
Saturday, March 22

OFFICIAL GOING: Standard
Wind: Moderate, half against

971 EASTER IS EGG-STRA SPECIAL @ PONTIN'S H'CAP 5f 20y(P)
6:50 (6:50) (Class 6) (0-58,67) 4-Y-0+ **£2,047** (£604; £302) **Stalls** Low

Form RPR
2115 1 **Blackheath (IRE)**11 [846] 12-8-7 54 .... KellyHarrison(5) 1 69
(S T Mason) *hld up in tch: hdwy to go 2nd 2f out: r.o to go 2nd ins fnl f: sn clr* **15/2**
3611 2 4 **Dodaa (USA)**19 [774] 5-8-9 56 .... AshleyHamblett(5) 3 57
(N Wilson) *led: strly rdn over 1f out: hdd ins fnl f: outpcd by wnr* **3/1**2
0046 3 ½ **Bentley**19 [774] 4-8-8 53 ....(v) TolleyDean(3) 2 52
(D Shaw) *s.i.s: in rr tl styd on to go 3rd ins fnl f* **5/1**3
0060 4 1 **Perlachy**16 [806] 4-8-10 55 ....(v) DuranFentiman(3) 6 51
(Mrs N Macauley) *in rr: rdn and outpcd: kpt on fnl f: nvr nr to chal* **16/1**
-211 5 ½ **Decider (USA)**11 [846] 5-9-8 67 .... KevinGhunowa(3) 7 61
(R A Harris) *prom on outside tl wknd over 1f out* **11/8**1
4325 6 5 **Town House**10 [857] 6-8-5 47 .... AndrewElliott 4 23
(B P J Baugh) *chsd ldr to 2f out: sn wknd* **14/1**
000- 7 3¼ **Lithaam (IRE)**164 [6101] 4-8-12 54 .... PaulFitzsimons 5 18
(J M Bradley) *chsd ldrs tl wknd over 1f out* **40/1**

61.72 secs (-0.58) **Going Correction** -0.10s/f (Stan) 7 Ran SP% **110.5**
Speed ratings (Par 101): **100,93,92,91,90 82,77**
CSF £28.17 TOTE £5.40: £3.40, £2.40; EX 35.50.
Owner Middleham Park Racing XX **Bred** John McKay **Trained** Lanchester, Co. Durham

FOCUS
A moderate sprint handicap run at a good early pace, although the overall time was moderate. The winner is rated back to his old form.
Decider(USA) Official explanation: jockey said gelding ran flat and hung

972 WOLVERHAMPTON-RACECOURSE.CO.UK CLASSIFIED STKS 5f 216y(P)
7:20 (7:20) (Class 7) 4-Y-0+ **£1,365** (£403; £201) **Stalls** Low

Form RPR
50-2 1 **Rambling Socks**9 [864] 5-9-4 49 ....(p) PhillipMakin 1 56
(S R Bowring) *t.k.h: trckd ldrs: rdn 2f out: led ins fnl f: hld on* **9/1**
0225 2 shd **Suhayl Star (IRE)**8 [877] 4-9-0 45 .... TQuinn 11 52
(P Burgoyne) *mid-div: hung lft thrght: hdwy on outside 3f out: hung lft but ev ch ins fnl f: jst hld* **7/2**1
0622 3 2 **Keon (IRE)**10 [862] 6-8-11 43 ....(p) RussellKennemore(3) 2 46
(R Hollinshead) *a in tch on ins: hdwy over 1f out to hold ev ch ins fnl f: nt qckn nr fin* **7/2**1
4504 4 nk **Orchestration (IRE)**43 [479] 7-8-7 45 ....(v) MarkCoumbe(7) 3 45
(Garry Moss) *a.p: nt clr run and swtchd rt appr 1f out: kpt on in ins fnl f* **20/1**
3340 5 1¼ **Temtation (IRE)**16 [808] 4-8-7 42 .... StacyRenwick(7) 6 41
(J A Pickering) *led tl rdn and hdd ins fnl f: no ex* **25/1**
5355 6 1½ **Prettilini**10 [858] 5-8-11 44 .... LukeMorris(3) 10 37
(A W Carroll) *wnt rt s: sn trckd ldrs: wknd over 1f out* **12/1**
-006 7 shd **Fly Time**10 [856] 4-8-11 41 ....(p) TolleyDean(3) 7 37
(Mrs L Williamson) *t.k.h: trckd ldrs: rdn over 2f out: no hdwy after* **33/1**
0053 8 ¾ **Pauvic (IRE)**9 [871] 5-8-11 44 ....(v) AndrewMullen(3) 5 34
(Mrs A Duffield) *mid-div: rdn over 2f out: nvr on terms* **8/1**3
2540 9 1¼ **Avoncreek**30 [642] 4-9-0 41 .... AndrewElliott 4 31
(B P J Baugh) *t.k.h: in rr: effrt over 1f out: nvr nr to chal* **14/1**
0051 10 ¾ **Montzando**9 [871] 5-9-1 46 ....(v) TGMcLaughlin 9 34+
(B R Millman) *trckd ldr: wkng whn hmpd ins fnl f* **7/1**2
0464 11 1¾ **James Street (IRE)**27 [696] 5-9-0 42 ....(v) LPKeniry 8 23
(Peter Grayson) *a towards rr* **9/1**
3404 12 ½ **Cantique (IRE)**10 [858] 4-8-8 46 .... RossAtkinson(7) 13 23
(R J Price) *swtchd to ins fr wd draw: a bhd* **14/1**
3600 13 1¾ **Blushing Russian (IRE)**9 [871] 6-9-0 41 ....(p) ChrisCatlin 12 16
(J M Bradley) *a struggling in rr* **25/1**

1m 14.83s (-0.17) **Going Correction** -0.10s/f (Stan) 13 Ran SP% **124.5**
Speed ratings (Par 97): **97,96,94,93,92 90,90,89,87,86 84,83,81**
CSF £40.39 TOTE £9.20: £2.80, £1.10, £1.90; EX 55.20.
Owner P M Sedgwick **Bred** A C M Spalding **Trained** Edwinstowe, Notts

FOCUS
A moderate but competitive classified sprint rated around the placed horses.
Fly Time Official explanation: jockey said filly hung left

973 JOIN THE EASTER PARADE @ PONTIN'S H'CAP 1m 1f 103y(P)
7:50 (7:50) (Class 5) (0-75,74) 4-Y-0+ **£2,730** (£806; £403) **Stalls** Low

Form RPR
-412 1 **Royal Amnesty**16 [811] 5-8-7 63 ....(b) TomEaves 7 78+
(Miss L A Perratt) *mid-div and a gng wl: gd hdwy bef swtchd lft and led appr fnl f: sn clr* **5/2**1
014- 2 3½ **Merrymadcap (IRE)**184 [5568] 6-9-3 73 .... FrancisNorton 3 77
(M Blanshard) *in rr tl hdwy 3f out: kpt on to chse wnr fnl f* **7/1**
1215 3 2 **Morbick**10 [860] 4-9-2 72 .... TGMcLaughlin 2 73
(W M Brisbourne) *a in tch: rdn and fdd ins fnl f* **4/1**2
12-6 4 hd **Moment Of Clarity**73 [104] 6-8-2 65 ....(p) KrishGundowry(7) 9 65
(R C Guest) *hld up: hdwy over 1f out: nvr nr to chal* **20/1**
200- 5 6 **Libre**154 [6342] 8-8-8 64 .... JoeFanning 8 53
(F Jordan) *t.k.h: hld up in rr: rdn and hdwy bef edgd lft over 1f out: sn wknd* **25/1**
5325 6 3¾ **Tancredi (SWE)**8 [879] 6-8-4 63 .... WilliamBuick(3) 4 45
(N B King) *led tl hdd & wknd appr fnl f* **15/2**
530/ 7 2 **Man Of Letters (UAE)**1345 [3915] 7-8-7 63 .... ChrisCatlin 5 41
(M Hill) *trckd ldr tl wknd over 1f out* **25/1**
4261 8 2½ **Saviour Sand (IRE)**10 [860] 4-9-4 74 .... HayleyTurner 6 47
(D R C Elsworth) *trckd ldrs: rdn 3f out: wknd wl over 1f out* **9/2**3
560- 9 1½ **Deadline (UAE)**168 [6021] 4-8-10 66 .... MickyFenton 1 36
(P T Midgley) *in tch: rdn 4f out: wknd over 2f out* **17/2**

1m 59.63s (-2.07) **Going Correction** -0.10s/f (Stan) 9 Ran SP% **114.0**
Speed ratings (Par 103): **105,101,100,99,94 91,89,87,85**
CSF £19.60 CT £66.03 TOTE £3.20: £1.40, £2.40, £2.00; EX 32.10.
Owner Mrs Francesca Mitchell **Bred** Brick Kiln Stud, Mrs L Hicks & Partners **Trained** Carluke, S Lanarks

FOCUS
A modest handicap. The winning time was 2.16 seconds quicker than later 46-60 and the form looks solid and decent for the grade.

974 ANTHONY NUTTALL 50TH BIRTHDAY CELEBRATION MEDIAN AUCTION STKS 1m 141y(P)
8:20 (8:23) (Class 5) 3-Y-0 **£2,730** (£806; £403) **Stalls** Low

Form RPR
1 **House Of Lords (USA)** 3-9-3 0 .... JamieSpencer 7 69+
(M L W Bell) *s.i.s: sn in tch: hdwy to go 2nd over 4f out: led ins fnl f: rdn out* **11/10**1
2 1¼ **Speyside (IRE)** 3-8-12 0 .... PatrickHills(5) 5 67+
(J W Hills) *in rr: rdn 3f out: hdwy and r.o wl fnl f to go 2nd cl home* **40/1**
2-2 3 hd **Two Left Feet**14 [837] 3-9-3 0 .... AdamKirby 3 66+
(W R Swinburn) *trckd ldr to over 3f out: ev ch ins fnl 2f: n.m.r and swtchd rt ins fnl f: kpt on towards fin* **5/4**2
0-4 4 nk **Lawton**26 [698] 3-9-3 0 .... RobertHavlin 4 65
(Miss J R Tooth) *led tl rdn: hdd and fdd ins fnl f* **33/1**
5 2¾ **Themwerethedays** 3-9-3 0 .... LPKeniry 6 59+
(S Kirk) *s.i.s: mid-div: rdn 2f out: swtchd rt over 1f out: no hdwy after* **16/1**
3-22 6 1¾ **Inontime (IRE)**43 [484] 3-8-12 68 .... AndrewElliott 1 50
(K R Burke) *trckd ldrs tl rdn and wknd over 2f out* **10/1**3
0 7 7 **Kijivu**8 [885] 3-8-12 0 .... EdwardCreighton 2 34
(M R Channon) *slowly away: effrt over 1f out: a bhd* **66/1**

1m 51.68s (1.18) **Going Correction** -0.10s/f (Stan) 7 Ran SP% **113.9**
Speed ratings (Par 98): **90,88,88,88,86 84,78**
CSF £46.36 TOTE £2.40: £1.30, £5.30; EX 39.40.
Owner Sheikh Marwan Al Maktoum **Bred** Darley **Trained** Newmarket, Suffolk

FOCUS
An ordinary maiden, but it should still produce some winners. The time was moderate for the type of race, so the form is muddling and hard to be positive about.

975 HAPPY EASTER HOLIDAYS @ PONTIN'S H'CAP 7f 32y(P)
8:50 (8:51) (Class 4) (0-85,81) 3-Y-0 **£4,857** (£1,445; £722; £360) **Stalls** High

Form RPR
1 1 **Underworld**25 [705] 3-9-3 77 .... JoeFanning 1 93+
(M Johnston) *mde all: rdn to go clr appr fnl f: eased nr fin* **4/7**1
-152 2 3¾ **Fathsta (IRE)**24 [723] 3-9-6 80 .... LPKeniry 2 81
(S Kirk) *in tch: hdwy over 2f out: rdn and kpt on to go 2nd ins fnl f* **9/2**2
00-6 3 2¼ **Nawaaff**17 [798] 3-9-3 77 .... ChrisCatlin 6 72
(M R Channon) *t.k.h: chsd wnr: rdn over 1f out and lost 2nd ins fnl f* **33/1**
00-3 4 2 **Monsieur Reynard**61 [244] 3-8-10 70 .... RobertWinston 8 60
(B J Meehan) *t.k.h: hdwy on outside to chal for 2nd 2f out: nt run on and fdd ins fnl f* **14/1**
1-14 5 1 **Bookish**52 [355] 3-9-1 75 .... JohnEgan 5 62
(Jamie Poulton) *chsd ldrs tl wknd over 1f out* **16/1**
1- 6 4 **Desert Clover (USA)**121 [6903] 3-9-7 81 .... TQuinn 7 57
(P F I Cole) *slowly away: outpcd thrght* **13/2**3
14-0 U **Ten Pole Tudor**24 [723] 3-9-2 79 ....(p) KevinGhunowa(3) 4 —
(R A Harris) *uns rdr leaving stalls* **25/1**

1m 28.77s (-0.83) **Going Correction** -0.10s/f (Stan) 7 Ran SP% **114.5**
Speed ratings (Par 100): **100,95,93,90,89 85,—**
CSF £3.53 CT £37.24 TOTE £1.60: £1.70, £1.90; EX 3.50.
Owner Sheikh Hamdan Bin Mohammed Al Maktoum **Bred** St Clare Hall Stud **Trained** Middleham Moor, N Yorks

FOCUS
A fair handicap and an easy success for the well-treated winner with the consistent runner-up setting the standard.
Desert Clover(USA) Official explanation: jockey said colt reared at the start

976 HAVE A HAPPY EASTER @ PONTIN'S H'CAP 1m 1f 103y(P)
9:20 (9:21) (Class 6) (0-60,60) 3-Y-0 **£2,218** (£654; £327) **Stalls** Low

Form RPR
1342 1 **Novestar (IRE)**2 [950] 3-8-7 52 .... KevinGhunowa(3) 10 56+
(G J Smith) *mde all: rdn and edgd rt appr 1f out: r.o wl ins fnl f* **13/2**2
000- 2 2½ **Supporting Role (IRE)**136 [6725] 3-9-2 58 .... GrahamGibbons 5 57
(E S McMahon) *t.k.h: a in tch: rdn 2f out: edgd lft appr 1f out but r.o to go 2nd ins fnl f* **5/1**1
06-3 3 hd **Persistent (IRE)**17 [803] 3-9-1 57 .... MickyFenton 2 56
(P T Midgley) *in rr: rdn and hdwy over 1f out: edgd lft but r.o: nvr nrr* **5/1**1
600- 4 ½ **Gunnadoit (USA)**150 [6417] 3-8-13 55 .... JamieSpencer 7 53
(M L W Bell) *s.i.s: in rr: hdwy and swtchd rt over 1f out: r.o: nvr nrr* **7/1**3
00-3 5 2¾ **Jemiliah**38 [547] 3-9-0 56 ....(b) RobertHavlin 11 48
(B J Meehan) *trckd wnr rdn over 2f out: hung lft over 1f out and wknd ins fnl f* **16/1**
600- 6 1½ **Moon Spray (USA)**210 [4818] 3-8-9 51 .... PaulMulrennan 4 40
(K A Ryan) *trckd ldrs: rdn over 2f out: wkng whn sltly hmpd ins fnl f* **25/1**
6446 7 hd **Tapas Lad (IRE)**15 [820] 3-8-12 57 ....(v) RussellKennemore(3) 1 45
(G J Smith) *hld up: sltly hmpd over 4f out: effrt whn n.m.r ent fnl f* **16/1**
050- 8 ¾ **Trip The Light**192 [5328] 3-8-7 49 .... PaulHanagan 9 36+
(R A Fahey) *a in rr* **5/1**1
4522 9 4 **John Potts**17 [803] 3-9-4 60 .... AndrewElliott 8 38
(B P J Baugh) *mid-div: rdn over 2f out: wkng whn hmpd over 1f out* **13/2**2
-632 10 3 **Dickie Valentine**10 [853] 3-8-6 48 ....(b) ChrisCatlin 6 20
(M R Bosley) *hld up in tch: wknd 3f out* **14/1**
-505 11 7 **Sunley Smiles**8 [885] 3-8-13 55 .... AlanMunro 3 12
(D R C Elsworth) *a bhd* **14/1**

2m 1.79s (0.09) **Going Correction** -0.10s/f (Stan) 11 Ran SP% **118.1**
Speed ratings (Par 96): **95,92,92,92,89 88,88,87,83,81 75**
CSF £39.20 CT £178.57 TOTE £6.90: £2.20, £2.60, £2.10; EX 67.40 Place 6 £ 19.09, Place 5 £ 4.84.
Owner Graham Smith **Bred** Mrs Eithne Thompson **Trained** Six Hills, Leics

FOCUS
A moderate handicap, but some of these from the bigger stables appeared quite interesting beforehand. The winning time was 2.16 seconds slower than the earlier 61-75 and the form is modest but sound enough, rated around the placed horses.
T/Plt: £71.20 to a £1 stake. Pool: £82,633.85. 847.10 winning tickets. T/Qpdt: £8.10 to a £1 stake. Pool: £6,616.70. 600.60 winning tickets. JS

MUSSELBURGH (R-H)

Sunday, March 23

OFFICIAL GOING: Good (good to firm in places on round course)

Wind: Strong against Weather: Overcast

977 TOTEPLACEPOT H'CAP 5f

2:20 (2:21) (Class 5) (0-75,74) 3-Y-O **£3,238** (£963; £481; £240) **Stalls** Low

Form RPR

45-3 **1** **Barraland**[18] 798 3-9-5 **72** JoeFanning 3 77+
(M R Channon) *cl up: led after 1f: rdn over 1f out: kpt on wl u.p ins fnl f* **5/2**[2]

350- **2** 1 1/4 **Kinout (IRE)**[169] 6017 3-9-6 **73** NCallan 1 74+
(K A Ryan) *trckd ldrs: hdwy to chse wnr wl over 1f out: rdn and edgd lft ent fnl f: kpt on same pce* **2/1**[1]

6034 **3** 5 **Andrasta**[47] 444 3-8-4 **62** DanielleMcCreery(5) 5 45
(A Berry) *towards rr: hdwy 2f out: swtchd rt and rdn over 1f out: styd on ins fnl f: nrst fin* **28/1**

320- **4** 1 3/4 **Our Sunnie**[235] 4065 3-8-13 **66** AdrianTNicholls 4 42
(D Nicholls) *chsd ldrs: rdn along 2f out: sn drvn: carried hd high and no imp* **12/1**

000- **5** 2 3/4 **Miss Sunshine**[156] 6306 3-7-12 **56** oh6 ow1 KellyHarrison(5) 7 22
(J S Goldie) *a in rr* **50/1**

022- **6** *hd* **Paddy Jack**[166] 6072 3-9-2 **69** PhillipMakin 2 35
(J R Weymes) *wnt bdly rt s: led 1f: sn rdn along: lost pl 1/2-way and sn bhd* **11/2**

2-21 **7** 12 **Chivola (IRE)**[73] 114 3-9-7 **74** PaulMulrennan 6 —
(B Smart) *chsd ldng pair on outer: rdn along over 2f out: sn wknd* **7/2**[3]

62.08 secs (1.68) **Going Correction** +0.375s/f (Good) **7 Ran SP% 112.6**

Speed ratings (Par 98): **101,99,91,88,83 83,64**

CSF £7.66 TOTE £3.30: £1.10, £2.00; EX 10.00.

Owner Box 41 **Bred** Tattersalls Scoundrels & Trickledown Stud **Trained** West Ilsley, Berks

FOCUS

Modest sprint handicap form.

Chivola(IRE) Official explanation: jockey said colt was unsuied by the good going

978 TOTECOURSE TO COURSE (S) STKS 1m 1f

2:50 (2:51) (Class 6) 3-Y-O+ **£1,943** (£578; £288; £144) **Stalls** High

Form RPR

11-6 **1** **Friends Hope**[24] 47 7-9-9 75 StephenDonohoe 9 69+
(P A Blockley) *dwlt: sn in tch: hdwy to chse ldrs wl over 2f out: rdn to chal wl over 1f out: led ent fnl f: drvn out* **4/1**[2]

036- **2** 2 3/4 **Top Jaro (FR)**[172] 5905 5-9-10 60 TonyHamilton 5 64
(D W Barker) *a.p: hdwy to chal 3f out: rdn to ld wl over 1f out: drvn and hdd ent fnl f: kpt on same pce* **3/1**[1]

1520 **3** *nk* **Pianoforte (USA)**[15] 841 6-9-10 56 (b) JimmyQuinn 1 63
(E J Alston) *hld up in midfield: hdwy on inner 4f out: swtchd outside and gd hdwy over 2f out: rdn to chal and ev ch over 1f out tl hung lft and one pce ins fnl f* **11/1**

3104 **4** 1 **Sparky Vixen**[10] 872 4-9-0 50 KellyHarrison(5) 12 56
(C J Teague) *cl up: rdn along 3f out: drvn and kpt on same pce fnl 2f* **14/1**

305/ **5** 2 3/4 **Truly Fruitful (IRE)**[130] 5599 5-9-7 71 JamieMoriarty(3) 3 55
(R A Fahey) *in tch: rdn along 1/2-way: drvn 3f out: kpt on same pce fnl 2f* **3/1**[1]

24-3 **6** 2 **Defi (IRE)**[50] 408 6-10-0 64 (b) PhillipMakin 11 55
(Miss L A Perratt) *led: rdn along 3f out: sn edgd lft and drvn: hdd wl over 1f out and grad wknd* **7/1**[3]

005- **7** 5 **Scotty's Future (IRE)**[141] 6637 10-9-5 50 DanielleMcCreery(5) 6 40
(A Berry) *sn outpcd and bhd* **50/1**

8 4 1/2 **Slivovic (IRE)**[41] 4-9-2 0 PJMcDonald(3) 7 25
(J S Wainwright) *a towards rr* **80/1**

000- **9** 2 3/4 **Nevinstown (IRE)**[12] 6311 8-9-10 43 JoeFanning 2 24
(C Grant) *a in rr* **28/1**

10 2 **Karaburan (GER)**[22] 4-9-10 55 (v[1]) PaulMulrennan 8 19
(P Monteith) *chsd ldrs: rdn along over 4f out: sn wknd* **40/1**

650- **11** 5 **Lago D'Orta (IRE)**[136] 6732 8-9-10 62 (bt[1]) AdrianTNicholls 10 8
(D Nicholls) *s.i.s: a bhd* **8/1**

1m 55.68s (0.98) **Going Correction** +0.20s/f (Good) **11 Ran SP% 117.7**

Speed ratings (Par 101): **103,100,100,99,96 95,90,86,84,82 78**

CSF £16.10 TOTE £4.60: £1.50, £1.40, £2.80; EX 20.70.There was no bid for the winner.

Owner Mrs Joanna Hughes **Bred** Huish Bloodstock **Trained** Lambourn, Berks

FOCUS

Ordinary selling-grade form rated around the placed horses.

Sparky Vixen Official explanation: trainer said filly lost right front shoe

Lago D'Orta(IRE) Official explanation: jockey said gelding hung left and had no more to give

979 TOTEPOOL EASTER H'CAP 7f 30y

3:20 (3:20) (Class 4) (0-85,85) 4-Y-O+ **£6,477** (£1,927; £963; £481) **Stalls** High

Form RPR

5-33 **1** **Cha Cha Cha**[66] 192 4-8-8 **75** NCallan 5 88+
(K A Ryan) *trckd ldrs on inner gng wl: effrt and nt clr run over 2f out: swtchd lft and qcknd to ld wl over 1f out: clr ins fnl f* **4/1**[2]

0/2- **2** 2 1/4 **Pure Imagination (IRE)**[342] 1060 7-8-5 **72** (b) SilvestreDeSousa 6 77
(D Nicholls) *hld up in rr: swtchd lft and hdwy 2f out: rdn to chse wnr ins fnl f: kpt on* **9/2**[3]

600- **3** 1 1/4 **Kabis Amigos**[204] 5035 6-8-4 **71** (t) AdrianTNicholls 4 73
(D Nicholls) *led: rdn along 3f out: hdd over 2f out: sn drvn and kpt on same pce* **7/1**

0-00 **4** *nk* **Jamieson Gold (IRE)**[15] 833 5-9-1 **82** PhillipMakin 7 83
(Miss L A Perratt) *hld up in rr: hdwy on inner over 2f out: rdn to chse ldrs over 1f out: kpt on ins fnl f* **10/1**

100- **5** 1 1/4 **Handsome Falcon**[183] 5635 4-8-7 **74** DaleGibson 2 72
(R A Fahey) *t.k.h: cl up: rdn to ld briefly over 2f out: sn hdd and drvn: wknd appr fnl f* **10/1**

400- **6** *shd* **Frank Crow**[22] 6021 5-8-4 **71** JoeFanning 9 69
(J S Goldie) *hld up in rr: hdwy on outer 3f out: rdn along 2f out and sn no imp* **11/4**[1]

240- **7** 3 **Byron Bay**[9] 846 6-8-6 **73** PaulFessey 3 64
(R C Guest) *chsd ldrs: rdn along 3f out: sn wknd* **16/1**

006- **8** 5 **Ravi River (IRE)**[242] 3857 4-8-13 **80** PatCosgrave 1 58
(J R Boyle) *chsd ldrs: rdn along over 3f out: sn wknd* **11/2**

1m 30.13s (-0.17) **Going Correction** +0.20s/f (Good) **8 Ran SP% 116.8**

Speed ratings (Par 105): **108,105,104,103,102 102,98,92**

CSF £22.90 CT £122.67 TOTE £3.70: £1.10, £1.80, £2.60; EX 23.30.

Owner Guy Reed **Bred** G Reed **Trained** Hambleton, N Yorks

FOCUS

A fair handicap in which the early pace was fairly steady. The winner looks progressive on turf, though.

980 TOTESPORT 0800 221 221 MAIDEN STKS 7f 30y

3:55 (3:57) (Class 5) 3-Y-O+ **£2,590** (£770; £385; £192) **Stalls** High

Form RPR

0- **1** **Nortune (USA)**[149] 6468 3-8-12 0 PaulMulrennan 9 70
(B Smart) *chsd ldr: rdn along and sltly outpcd over 2f out: styd on u.p ins fnl f: rn green and edgd lft towards fin: kpt on to ld nr line* **10/1**

244- **2** *nk* **Prince Kalamoun (IRE)**[194] 5294 3-8-12 72 NCallan 3 69
(G A Swinbank) *prom: hdwy 3f out: rdn to take slt ld wl over 1f out: drvn and edgd rt and lft ins fnl f: hdd and nt qckn nr line* **6/4**[1]

3-24 **3** 2 1/2 **Ace Of Spies (IRE)**[43] 500 3-8-12 72 JoeFanning 2 63
(M Johnston) *trckd ldrs: hdwy over 2f out: challenegd wl over 1f out and ev ch tl rdn and one pce ins fnl f* **11/4**[2]

40- **4** 5 **Almost Married (IRE)**[268] 3062 4-9-8 0 GaryBartley(5) 8 54
(J S Goldie) *in rr: rdn along 1/2-way: plugged on fnl 2f: n.d* **20/1**

-550 **5** 1 **Afton View (IRE)**[18] 803 3-8-12 62 (b[1]) DarrenWilliams 5 46
(S Parr) *led: rdn along 3f out: drvn and hdd wl over 1f out: sn wknd* **8/1**

00- **6** 1/2 **Bourse (IRE)**[289] 2424 3-8-9 0 PJMcDonald(3) 1 45
(J S Wainwright) *a towards rr* **40/1**

33- **7** 5 **Binario Uno**[277] 2758 3-8-12 0 AdrianTNicholls 4 31
(D Nicholls) *midfield: rdn along 1/2-way: nvr a factor* **6/1**[3]

000- **8** 13 **Senora Lenorah**[170] 5970 4-9-8 35 (t) GregFairley 7 —
(D A Nolan) *a in rr* **150/1**

0 **9** 5 **Amber May**[31] 634 5-9-1 0 BMcHugh(7) 10 —
(J P L Ewart) *dwlt: hdwy into midfield 1/2-way: rdn along 3f out and sn wknd* **66/1**

10 *shd* **Ducal Damsel** 3-8-9 0 ow2 PhillipMakin 6 —
(J R Weymes) *a outpcd and bhd* **40/1**

1m 31.48s (1.18) **Going Correction** +0.20s/f (Good)

WFA 3 from 4yo+ 15lb **10 Ran SP% 112.9**

Speed ratings (Par 103): **101,100,97,92,90 90,84,69,64,63**

CSF £24.09 TOTE £5.70: £1.70, £1.80, £1.60; EX 25.20.

Owner Prime Equestrian **Bred** Clovelly Farms **Trained** Hambleton, N Yorks

FOCUS

Fairly ordinary maiden form rated around the third.

Bourse(IRE) Official explanation: jockey said gelding ran very green

981 TOTESPORT.COM MUSSELBURGH GOLD CUP (A H'CAP STKS) 1m 6f

4:30 (4:30) (Class 4) (0-85,85) 4-Y-O+

£12,464 (£3,732; £1,866; £934; £466; £234) **Stalls** High

Form RPR

5564 **1** **Pass The Port**[15] 838 7-9-7 **78** NCallan 14 85
(D Haydn Jones) *hld up in rr: gd hdwy 4f out: chsd ldrs 2f out: sn rdn and led ent fnl f: drvn and hung rt ins fnl f: jst hld on* **10/1**

114/ **2** *shd* **Souffleur**[36] 3981 5-9-9 **80** JimCrowley 4 87+
(P Bowen) *hld up towards rr: hdwy on outer 3f out: rdn wl over 1f out: str run ins fnl f: jst failed* **5/1**[1]

-162 **3** 1/2 **Casual Affair**[15] 838 5-9-0 **71** JimmyQuinn 2 77+
(J D Bethell) *hld up and bhd: gd hdwy on inner 3f out: effrt and nt clr run 2f out: sn rdn and styd on wl fnl f* **8/1**[3]

443- **4** 3/4 **Smugglers Bay (IRE)**[8] 5296 4-8-10 **71** RobertWinston 13 76
(T D Easterby) *hld up in midfield: hdwy to chse ldrs over 3f out: rdn 2f out: ev ch over 1f out tl drvn and one pce ins fnl f* **8/1**[3]

-152 **5** 1 1/2 **Clear Reef**[31] 638 4-9-6 **81** TGMcLaughlin 10 84
(Jane Chapple-Hyam) *t.k.h: trckd ldrs on inner: hdwy 3f out: swtchd lft and effrt 2f out: sn rdn and ev ch tl drvn and one pce ent fnl f* **8/1**[3]

41-2 **6** 1/2 **Salute (IRE)**[11] 859 9-9-6 **77** RobertHavlin 1 79
(P G Murphy) *hld up in midfield: gd hdwy on outer 5f out: led 3f out: rdn over 2f out: drvn and hdd over 1f out: wknd ins fnl f* **12/1**

221- **7** 2 **Gordonsville**[167] 6070 5-9-9 **80** DanielTudhope 3 79
(J S Goldie) *hld up in rr tl styd on fnl 3f: nrst fin* **12/1**

210- **8** 5 **Sadler's Kingdom (IRE)**[154] 6366 4-9-10 **85** TonyHamilton 5 77
(R A Fahey) *hld: a towards rr* **9/1**

426- **9** 1 1/4 **Cotton Eyed Joe (IRE)**[181] 5677 7-8-13 **73** PJMcDonald(3) 6 64
(G A Swinbank) *trckd ldrs: hdwy over 3f out: sn rdn and wknd over 1f out* **16/1**

45/4 **10** 1 1/2 **Rehearsal**[12] 561 7-9-9 **80** (p) JoeFanning 11 69
(L Lungo) *led: rdn along over 3f out: sn hdd & wknd* **14/1**

063- **11** 5 **Los Nadis (GER)**[22] 6733 4-8-12 **73** PaulMulrennan 7 55
(P Monteith) *chsd ldrs on outer: rdn along 5f out: wknd over 3f out* **7/1**[2]

25-2 **12** 5 **Cybersnow (USA)**[16] 823 4-8-11 **75** AndrewMullen(3) 12 50
(Barry Potts, Ire) *trckd ldng pair on inner: hdwy over 3f out: sn cl up and ev ch tl rdn and wknd 2f out* **20/1**

05-0 **13** 16 **Red Lancer**[41] 525 7-9-6 **77** AdrianTNicholls 9 29+
(D Nicholls) *t.k.h: hld up: a in rr* **33/1**

404- **14** 1 1/2 **Nelsons Column (IRE)**[21] 5968 5-9-0 **71** AndrewElliott 8 21+
(G M Moore) *chsd ldr: rdn along 6f out: drvn and wknd over 3f out* **16/1**

3m 6.28s (0.98) **Going Correction** +0.20s/f (Good)

WFA 4 from 5yo+ 4lb **14 Ran SP% 123.1**

Speed ratings (Par 105): **105,104,104,104,103 103,101,99,98,97 94,91,82,81**

CSF £60.65 CT £434.22 TOTE £10.90: £3.00, £1.90, £4.00; EX 68.80 Trifecta £216.40 Part won. Pool £304.80 - 0.10 winning units..

Owner The Porters **Bred** Meon Valley Stud **Trained** Efail Isaf, Rhondda C Taff

■ Stewards' Enquiry : N Callan caution: used whip with excessive frequency

FOCUS

They went a decent gallop here and the first three all came from well off the pace.

Red Lancer Official explanation: jockey said gelding had no more to give

982 TOTEEXACTA MAIDEN STKS 1m 4f

5:00 (5:01) (Class 5) 3-Y-O+ **£2,590** (£770; £385; £192) **Stalls** High

Form RPR

1 **Tourism (IRE)** 3-8-6 0 GregFairley 12 74+
(M Johnston) *prom: hdwy to chse ldr over 4f out: effrt to chal 2f out: sn rdn and styd on to ld over 1f out: rn green and drvn ins fnl f: kpt on* **7/2**[2]

2 2 1/2 **Evelith Regent (IRE)**[21] 5-9-11 0 PJMcDonald(3) 10 72
(G A Swinbank) *led: rdn along 3f out: drvn 2f out: hdd over 1f out: kpt on same pce u.p ins fnl f* **9/2**[3]

25-4 **3** 1 1/2 **Clovis**[46] 454 3-8-6 75 JoeFanning 6 67
(M Johnston) *prom: effrt 3f out: rdn to chal 2f out and ev ch tl drvn and one pce fnl f* **11/4**[1]

4/- **4** 2 3/4 **Flamed Amazement**[22] 5565 4-9-12 0 (p) RobertWinston 8 65
(L Lungo) *midfield: hdwy 3f out: rdn to chse ldrs 2f out: sn drvn and no imp* **5/1**

03 **5** *hd* **Ella**[48] [435] 4-9-7 0 .... NCallan 9 59+
(G A Swinbank) *plld hrd: trckd ldrs: effrt 3f out: rdn 2f out and sn one pce* **7/2**[2]

005- **6** *19* **Stravonian**[104] [6728] 8-10-0 37 .... JimmyQuinn 7 34
(D A Nolan) *a in rr* **150/1**

5- **7** *17* **Giant Star (USA)**[204] [5036] 5-10-0 58 .... DanielTudhope 1 7
(J S Goldie) *in tch: rdn along to chse ldr 3f out: drvn over 2f out and sn wknd* **22/1**

003- **8** *5* **Sierras Future**[214] [4713] 4-9-12 57 .... (b) PaulFessey 2 —
(Miss L A Perratt) *v.s.a: a bhd* **18/1**

00- **9** *37* **Asrar**[299] [1804] 6-9-6 0 .... AndrewMullen(3) 11 —
(Miss Lucinda V Russell) *s.i.s: a bhd* **50/1**

2m 41.96s (2.26) **Going Correction** +0.20s/f (Good)
WFA 3 from 4yo 22lb 4 from 5yo+ 2lb **9** Ran SP% **118.2**
Speed ratings (Par 103): **100,98,97,95,95 82,71,68,43**
CSF £20.01 TOTE £4.80: £1.80, £2.20, £1.30; EX 22.40.
Owner Sheikh Hamdan Bin Mohammed Al Maktoum **Bred** Victor Stud Bloodstock Ltd **Trained** Middleham Moor, N Yorks

FOCUS
No more than fair maiden form, but the winner showed signs of inexperience and is open to further improvement. They went an ordinary gallop.
Ella ◆ Official explanation: jockey said filly hung right and lost its action in final furlong
Sierras Future Official explanation: jockey said gelding virtually refused to race

983 TOTESPORTCASINO.COM H'CAP 5f
5:30 (5:31) (Class 4) (0-85,85) 4-Y-0+ **£6,477** (£1,927; £963; £481) **Stalls** Low

Form RPR

630- **1** **Blue Tomato**[288] [2466] 7-9-2 80 .... AdrianTNicholls 8 93+
(D Nicholls) *trckd ldrs: hdwy over 1f out: rdn and qcknd to ld ent fnl f: kpt on* **16/1**

000- **2** *1 ¼* **Caribbean Coral**[148] [6487] 9-9-2 80 .... GrahamGibbons 9 89
(J J Quinn) *hld up in tch: effrt and nt clr run over 1f out: swtchd rt and hdwy over 1f out: sn ev ch tl rdn and nt qckn wl ins fnl f* **11/1**

31-4 **3** *½* **First Order**[50] [411] 7-9-7 85 .... (v) PhillipMakin 6 92
(Miss L A Perratt) *in tch: hdwy 1/2-way: chal over 1f out and ev ch tl rdn and nt qckn ins fnl f* **7/1**[2]

0500 **4** *¾* **Tartatartufata**[8] [907] 6-8-2 73 .... (v) PatrickDonaghy(7) 3 77
(D Shaw) *led: rdn along wl over 1f out: drvn and hdd ent fnl f: kpt on same pce* **14/1**

004- **5** *¾* **Geojimali**[134] [6753] 6-9-0 78 .... DanielTudhope 1 80
(J S Goldie) *bhd: hdwy wl over 1f out: swtchd rt and rdn 1f out: kpt on ins fnl f: nrst fin* **7/2**[1]

040- **6** *4 ½* **Circuit Dancer (IRE)**[153] [6381] 8-8-12 76 .... SilvestreDeSousa 11 61
(D Nicholls) *in rr: swtchd outside and rdn wl over 1f out: styd on ins fnl f: nrst fin* **25/1**

003- **7** *hd* **Steelcut**[178] [5747] 4-8-12 76 .... TonyHamilton 4 61
(R A Fahey) *midfield: rdn along 2f out: no imp ent fnl f* **12/1**

030- **8** *shd* **Rasaman (IRE)**[176] [5806] 4-9-4 82 .... NCallan 10 66
(K A Ryan) *prom: effrt and ev ch 2f out: sn rdn and wknd appr fnl f* **7/1**[2]

500- **9** *1 ¼* **Mr Wolf**[184] [5584] 7-9-2 80 .... (p) FergalLynch 2 60
(D W Barker) *cl up: rdn along 2f out: sn drvn and wknd* **10/1**

010- **10** *½* **Blazing Heights**[125] [6876] 5-9-0 83 .... GaryBartley(5) 12 61+
(J S Goldie) *hld up in rr: hdwy on bit 2f out: nt clr run and swtchd lft over 1f out: n.d* **9/1**[3]

2253 **11** *nk* **Bo McGinty (IRE)**[10] [866] 7-9-3 84 .... (b) JamieMoriarty(3) 14 61
(R A Fahey) *chsd ldrs on outer: rdn along 2f out and sn wknd* **7/1**[2]

2005 **12** *2 ¼* **Yungaburra (IRE)**[16] [824] 4-8-11 78 .... DNolan(3) 13 47
(S Parr) *chsd ldrs: rdn along 2f out and sn wknd* **14/1**

500- **13** *nk* **Melalchrist**[153] [6381] 6-9-5 83 .... (p) PaulMulrennan 5 51
(K A Ryan) *cl up: rdn 2f out: sn drvn and wknd* **14/1**

61.60 secs (1.20) **Going Correction** +0.375s/f (Good) **13** Ran SP% **124.6**
Speed ratings (Par 105): **105,103,102,101,99 92,92,92,90,89 88,85,84**
CSF £189.15 CT £1368.26 TOTE £21.10: £5.20, £3.50, £3.10; EX 228.90 Place 6 £16.61, Place 5 £11.68..
Owner Dab Hand Racing **Bred** Bearstone Stud **Trained** Sessay, N Yorks

FOCUS
A competitive, strongly run sprint handicap.
Rasaman(IRE) Official explanation: jockey said gelding lost its action
T/Jkpt: Not won. T/Plt: £27.00 to a £1 stake. Pool: £68,831.60. 1,855.85 winning tickets. T/Qpdt: £7.90 to a £1 stake. Pool: £3,440.50. 319.60 winning tickets. JR

984 - 986a (Foreign Racing) - See Raceform Interactive

REDCAR (L-H)
Monday, March 24

OFFICIAL GOING: Good to soft (7.6)
Wind: Moderate, against Weather: Ovecast and cold with wintry showers

987 MARKET CROSS JEWELLERS FILLIES' H'CAP 5f
2:00 (2:00) (Class 5) (0-70,70) 4-Y-0+ **£2,331** (£693; £346; £173) **Stalls** Centre

Form RPR

152- **1** **Feelin Foxy**[146] [6559] 4-9-7 70 .... JimmyFortune 7 81
(J G Given) *trckd ldrs: swtchd rt and hdwy over 1f out: rdn to ld ins fnl f: edgd lft and drvn out* **8/1**[3]

324- **2** *2* **Miss Daawe**[173] [5908] 4-8-4 53 .... JoeFanning 10 57
(B Ellison) *led: rdn and qcknd over 1f out: drvn and hdd ins fnl f: kpt on same pce* **11/2**[2]

043- **3** *½* **Dorn Dancer (IRE)**[150] [6467] 6-8-9 58 .... RobertWinston 1 60
(D W Barker) *hld up towards rr: pushed along 1/2-way: hdwy on outer wlover 1f out: sn rdn and kpt on ins fnl f* **9/2**[1]

530- **4** *1* **Lambency (IRE)**[186] [5552] 5-8-7 56 .... FergalLynch 13 54
(J S Goldie) *in tch: hdwy on outer to chse ldrs over 2f out: sn rdn and kpt on same pce ins fnl f* **8/1**[3]

146- **5** *½* **Comptonspirit**[191] [5401] 4-9-4 67 .... PaulMulrennan 3 64
(B P J Baugh) *wnt lft s: cl up: rdn wl over 1f out: drvn and wknd ent fnl f* **12/1**

55-3 **6** *1* **Silly Gilly (IRE)**[12] [856] 4-8-6 55 .... AndrewElliott 8 48+
(R E Barr) *prom: rdn along 2f out: wkng whn n.m.r appr fnl f* **9/1**

000- **7** *hd* **Rothesay Dancer**[142] [6639] 5-8-8 62 .... KellyHarrison(5) 4 54
(J S Goldie) *in tch: swtchd lft and gd hdwy 2f out: cl up and ev ch over 1f out: sn rdn and wknd ins fnl f* **8/1**[3]

500- **8** *1 ¾* **Gap Princess (IRE)**[173] [5907] 4-8-10 62 .... JamieMoriarty(3) 9 48+
(R A Fahey) *hld up in tch: effrt whn n.m.r and hmpd 2f out: sn rdn and no hdwy* **9/1**

000- **9** *5* **Darcy's Pride (IRE)**[179] [5747] 4-9-5 68 .... TonyHamilton 5 36
(D W Barker) *cl up: rdn along wl over 1f out and wknd appr fnl f* **9/1**

00-0 **10** *3 ¾* **Beechside (IRE)**[12] [857] 4-8-0 52 oh5 ow1 .... AndrewMullen(3) 6 6
(W A Murphy, Ire) *dwlt: a towards rr* **50/1**

051- **11** *1* **Morristown Music (IRE)**[150] [6466] 4-8-11 63 .... PJMcDonald(3) 11 14
(J S Wainwright) *s.i.s: a in rr* **14/1**

3213 **12** *2 ¼* **Ducal Regancy Red**[12] [857] 4-7-13 51 oh6 .... DuranFentiman(3) 12 —
(C J Teague) *cl up on outer: rdn along over 2f out and sn wknd* **25/1**

600- **13** *17* **Just Joey**[198] [5232] 4-9-7 70 .... PhillipMakin 2 —
(J R Weymes) *hmpd s: a towards rr* **28/1**

62.81 secs (4.21) **Going Correction** +0.85s/f (Soft) **13** Ran SP% **120.5**
Speed ratings (Par 100): **100,96,96,94,93 92,91,88,80,74 73,69,42**
CSF £51.19 CT £234.53 TOTE £5.10: £2.10, £2.00, £2.30; EX 60.50.
Owner Danethorpe Racing Partnership **Bred** Bearstone Stud **Trained** Willoughton, Lincs

FOCUS
A modest fillies' sprint handicap and the field bunched together down the centre of the track as they normally do here. The winning time was 2.87 seconds quicker than the later three-year-old handicap, but that was a very poor contest.

988 BECOME AN ANNUAL BADGE HOLDER TODAY H'CAP 2m 4y
2:35 (2:35) (Class 6) (0-65,62) 4-Y-0+ **£1,943** (£578; £288; £144) **Stalls** Low

Form RPR

336- **1** **Hue**[16] [6077] 7-9-11 61 .... JimmyFortune 7 79+
(B Ellison) *hld up and bhd: stdy hdwy on inner 6f out: in tch 4f out: swtchd rt and effrt 2f out: sn chsng ldr: rdn to ld 1f out: drvn and edgd lft wl ins fnl f: kpt on* **3/1**[1]

0/0- **2** *nk* **Accordello (IRE)**[37] [913] 7-9-5 55 .... PhillipMakin 1 72+
(K G Reveley) *hld up towards rr: pushed along over 6f out: hdwy on outer over 4f out: rdn to chal 2f out: drvn and ev ch ent fnl f: sn edgd lft: kpt on u.p towards fin* **11/2**[3]

4321 **3** *2* **Grizebeck (IRE)**[11] [869] 6-9-9 59 .... NCallan 6 74
(R F Fisher) *mde most to 1/2-way: cl up tl led again over 4f out: rdn clr over 2f out: drvn and hdd 1f out: hld in 3rd whn n.m.r towards fin* **4/1**[2]

3003 **4** *14* **Haatmey**[11] [869] 6-9-0 50 .... (bt) DanielTudhope 10 48
(N Wilson) *chsd ldrs: rdn along over 3f out: drvn over 2f out and plugged on same pce* **13/2**

46/ **5** *1 ¾* **Sun Quest**[24] [5146] 4-8-4 45 .... AndrewElliott 14 41
(I W McInnes) *in tch: hdwy on outer to chse ldrs 1/2-way: rdn along 4f out: drvn 3f out and plugged on same pce* **16/1**

-302 **6** *nse* **Young Scotton**[26] [722] 8-9-12 62 .... RobertWinston 8 58
(J D Bethell) *in tch: hdwy on inner over 4f out and sn chsng ldrs: rdn wl over 2f out and sn one pce* **10/1**

0-36 **7** *2 ¾* **Just Waz (USA)**[36] [600] 6-8-11 50 .... MichaelJStainton(3) 3 43
(R M Whitaker) *hld up towards rr: hdwy over 4f out: rdn along over 3f out: no imp fnl 2f* **14/1**

506- **8** *5* **Kyber**[176] [5839] 7-9-2 57 .... GaryBartley(5) 11 44
(J S Goldie) *hld up towards rr: hdwy over 4f out: in tch whn rdn and wnt lft wl over 2f out: sn no imp* **18/1**

000- **9** *¾* **Into Action**[118] [6271] 4-8-10 54 .... (p) DominicFox(3) 12 40
(W Storey) *in midfield: hdwy to chse ldrs 1/2-way: rdn along over 4f out and sn wknd* **25/1**

600- **10** *1* **Caraman (IRE)**[22] [4003] 10-9-5 58 .... JamieMoriarty(3) 9 43
(J J Quinn) *chsd ldrs: rdn along over 3f out and sn wknd* **18/1**

/00- **11** *47* **Kinfayre Boy**[11] [3638] 6-8-2 45 .... KrishGundowry(7) 13 —
(K W Hogg) *a towards rr* **100/1**

400- **12** *12* **Brabazon (IRE)**[33] [4096] 5-9-5 55 .... (v) PaulMulrennan 4 —
(Barry Potts, Ire) *chsd ldrs: rdn along 4f out and grad wknd* **66/1**

560 **13** *29* **Spellman**[24] [758] 4-8-7 48 .... JoeFanning 2 —
(N P Littmoden) *a in rr: wl bhd fr 1/2-way* **25/1**

300- **14** *½* **Hugs Destiny (IRE)**[168] [6056] 7-9-5 55 .... (t) DeanMcKeown 5 —
(M A Barnes) *cl up tl rdn along over 5f out and sn wknd* **25/1**

600- **15** *18* **Malguru**[124] [3159] 4-8-13 54 .... RobertHavlin 15 —
(A G Foster) *chsd ldng pair: hdwy to ld 1/2-way: rdn along and hdd over 4f out: sn wknd* **40/1**

3m 46.35s (14.95) **Going Correction** +1.05s/f (Soft)
WFA 4 from 5yo+ 5lb **15** Ran SP% **122.3**
Speed ratings (Par 101): **104,103,102,95,94 94,93,91,90,90 66,60,46,45,36**
CSF £18.07 CT £69.28 TOTE £4.00: £1.30, £2.30, £1.90; EX 18.10.
Owner Mike Ashton **Bred** Juddmonte Farms **Trained** Norton, N Yorks
■ Stewards' Enquiry : Jimmy Fortune one day ban: careless riding (Apr 7)

FOCUS
Several in this field were fit from the All-Weather or had been jumping, but this was not as competitive as the numbers might suggest with only four starting at less than 10-1 and they were the first four home. They went a very decent pace in the conditions though, and this became a true test of stamina. The front three pulled miles clear of the others and the form looks solid.
Malguru Official explanation: jockey said gelding had no more to give

989 RACING UK CHANNEL 432 (S) STKS 1m 2f
3:10 (3:12) (Class 6) 4-Y-0+ **£1,684** (£501; £250; £125) **Stalls** Low

Form RPR

/62- **1** **Bedouin Blue (IRE)**[100] [7150] 5-8-9 72 .... (b) PatrickDonaghy(7) 3 66+
(P C Haslam) *hld up in midfield: stdy hdwy 4f out: chsd ldrs over 2f out: rdn to ld wl over 1f out: sn clr* **11/4**[1]

640- **2** *2 ¼* **Coronado's Gold (USA)**[89] [4820] 7-8-9 53 .... LanceBetts(7) 10 62
(B Ellison) *towards rr: hdwy on outer wl over 2f out: sn rdn and styd on strly ins fnl f* **16/1**

040- **3** *2* **Tizzy May (FR)**[176] [5838] 8-9-2 65 .... JimmyFortune 4 58
(B Ellison) *chsd ldrs: hdwy 3f out: rdn 2f out: drvn over 1f out and kpt on same pce* **7/2**[2]

212/ **4** *1 ¾* **Basinet**[19] [586] 10-9-2 0 .... PaulMulrennan 6 54
(J J Quinn) *in tch: hdwy 1/2-way: chsd ldrs 3f out: sn rdn and kpt on same pce fr wl over 1f out* **7/1**

350- **5** *5* **Skye But N Ben**[23] [6019] 4-9-2 53 .... (v[1]) PaulFessey 14 44
(G A Harker) *chsd ldrs: hdwy to ld wl over 2f out and sn rdn: drvn and hdd wl over 1f out: sn one pce* **25/1**

/44- **6** *4* **Riverhill (IRE)**[39] [2714] 5-9-2 49 .... RobertWinston 1 36
(J Howard Johnson) *chsd ldrs on inner: rdn along 3f out: sn edgd rt and wknd 2f out* **14/1**

-506 **7** *2 ¼* **Besi**[34] [613] 6-8-11 43 .... DanielleMcCreery(5) 12 32
(A Berry) *chsd ldrs: rdn along 3f out: sn drvn and wknd fnl 2f* **40/1**

00-0 **8** *2 ½* **Rotuma (IRE)**[46] [468] 9-8-9 46 .... (b) JohnCavanagh(7) 11 27
(M Dods) *led: rdn along 3f out: sn hdd & wknd* **33/1**

300/ **9** *16* **Donna's Double**[374] [5955] 13-9-2 43 .... (p) TonyHamilton 15 —
(Karen McLintock) *stdd s: a in rr* **33/1**

1501 **10** *3 ¾* **Sawwaah (IRE)**[21] [781] 11-9-8 74 .... (v) DanielTudhope 13 —
(D Carroll) *hld up towards rr: hdwy on outer 4f out: rdn 3f out and sn btn* **5/1**[3]

11 5 **Brutus Maximus**[42] 5-9-2 0 (b[1]) PatrickMathers 5 —
(I W McInnes) *a towards rr* **125/1**

3-41 12 18 **Ming Vase**[20] 788 6-9-5 49 JamieMoriarty(3) 2 —
(P T Midgley) *t.k.h: hld up in midfield: effrt on inner over 4f out: sn rdn along and nvr a factor* **12/1**

50-0 13 3 1/4 **Lago D'Orta (IRE)**[1] 978 8-9-2 62 (bt) AdrianTNicholls 8 —
(D Nicholls) *trckd ldrs: hdwy to chse ldr 1/2-way: rdn along 4f out and sn wknd* **20/1**

-634 14 21 **Blue Opal**[31] 654 6-8-11 40 (p) NCallan 9 —
(Miss S E Hall) *chsd ldrs: rdn along over 4f out: sn wknd* **16/1**

2m 17.31s (10.21) **Going Correction** +1.05s/f (Soft) **14** Ran SP% **121.9**
Speed ratings (Par 101): **101,99,97,96,92 89,87,85,72,69 65,51,48,31**
CSF £46.81 TOTE £3.50: £1.50, £6.00, £1.90; EX 64.50.There was no bid for the winner.
Owner Blue Lion Racing VII **Bred** John Weld **Trained** Middleham Moor, N Yorks

FOCUS
A routine seller comfortably won by the horse best treated at the weights. The form will not mean a lot outside of this level.
Riverhill(IRE) Official explanation: jockey said gelding hung left handed throughout
Lago D'Orta(IRE) Official explanation: jockey said gelding had no more to give

990 BECK'S VIER H'CAP 7f
3:45 (3:46) (Class 5) (0-70,68) 4-Y-0+ **£2,331** (£693; £346; £173) **Stalls** Centre

Form RPR

620- 1 **Nok Twice (IRE)**[136] 6749 7-8-10 **60** DanielTudhope 11 69
(D Carroll) *dwlt and in rr: hdwy 3f out: rdn to chal over 1f out: drvn ins fnl f: styd on to ld last 50yds* **50/1**

403- 2 hd **Grand Opera (IRE)**[40] 5035 5-9-3 **67** RobertWinston 13 76
(J Howard Johnson) *towards rr: gd hdwy 1/2-way: led wl over 1f out: sn rdn: drvn: and edgd lft ins fnl f: hdd and no ex towards fin* **12/1**

101- 3 5 **Maia**[257] 3413 4-9-1 **65** SilvestreDeSousa 4 61
(D Nicholls) *in midfield: hdwy 3f out: rdn to chse ldrs wl over 1f out: kpt on same pce ins fnl f* **17/2**[3]

4031 4 3/4 **Avontuur (FR)**[23] 766 6-7-13 **56** (p) MCGeran(7) 12 50
(Mrs R A Carr) *led: rdn along over 2f out: drvn and hdd wl over 1f out: kpt on same pce* **16/1**

510- 5 2 1/4 **Chin Wag (IRE)**[137] 6731 4-8-10 **60** FergalLynch 17 49+
(J S Goldie) *in rr: hdwy 2f out: styd on strly ins fnl f: nrst fin* **16/1**

620- 6 nk **Tyrannosaurus Rex (IRE)**[95] 7207 4-8-8 **58** (v) AndrewElliott 16 46
(K R Burke) *chsd ldrs: hdwy 3f out: rdn and ch 2f out: sn drvn and wknd over 1f out* **12/1**

004- 7 hd **Messiah Garvey**[99] 7164 4-8-9 **59** AdrianTNicholls 6 46
(D Nicholls) *in rr tl styd on fnl 2f: nrst fin* **20/1**

100- 8 2 **Double Carpet (IRE)**[104] 7107 5-8-9 **59** MartinDwyer 10 41
(R C Guest) *cl up: rdn along 3f out: drvn 2f out and grad wknd* **20/1**

332- 9 hd **Aussie Blue (IRE)**[143] 6623 4-8-10 **63** MichaelJStainton(3) 9 45
(R M Whitaker) *chsd ldrs: rdn over 2f out: drvn and one pce appr fnl f* **6/1**[1]

260- 10 nk **Violent Velocity (IRE)**[160] 6258 5-9-3 **67** PaulMulrennan 14 48
(J J Quinn) *in tch: hdwy to chse ldrs 1/2-way: rdn over 2f out and grad wknd* **14/1**

150- 11 nse **Kirkby's Treasure**[170] 6021 10-8-12 **65** PJMcDonald(3) 19 46
(G A Swinbank) *in rr: hdwy 3f out: in tch 2f out: sn rdn and wknd* **12/1**

60-0 12 3 3/4 **Dressed To Dance (IRE)**[12] 856 4-8-10 **60** NCallan 5 32
(N Tinkler) *dwlt: sn in tch: rdn along over 2f out and grad wknd* **16/1**

000- 13 1/2 **Stoic Leader (IRE)**[86] 7024 8-9-4 **68** PhillipMakin 3 38
(R F Fisher) *chsd ldrs: rdn along 1/2-way: sn wknd* **20/1**

100/ 14 3/4 **Woodsley House (IRE)**[470] 6781 6-9-2 **66** RobertHavlin 18 34
(A G Foster) *in tch: rdn along 1/2-way and sn wknd* **66/1**

460- 15 2 **A Big Sky Brewing (USA)**[236] 4078 4-8-7 **57** PaulFessey 2 20
(T D Barron) *chsd ldrs: rdn along 3f out: wknd over 2f out* **20/1**

0-06 16 3/4 **Boy Dancer (IRE)**[24] 749 5-8-7 **57** JoeFanning 1 19
(J J Quinn) *in tch: rdn along 1/2-way and sn wknd* **9/1**

650- 17 nse **Sands Of Barra (IRE)**[150] 6463 5-9-3 **67** PatrickMathers 8 28
(I W McInnes) *prom: rdn along 3f out and sn wknd* **20/1**

300- 18 nse **Ghafeer (USA)**[157] 6310 4-9-1 **65** JimmyFortune 15 26
(B Ellison) *in tch: rdn along after 3f and sn wknd* **22/1**

306- 19 19 **Cheery Cat (USA)**[181] 5701 4-8-13 **63** (p) TonyHamilton 7 —
(D W Barker) *cl up: rdn along 3f out and sn wknd* **8/1**[2]

000- 20 29 **Valdan (IRE)**[173] 5905 4-9-1 **65** (t) DeanMcKeown 20 —
(M A Barnes) *racd alone stands' side: a outpcd and wl bhd fr 1/2-way* **16/1**

1m 33.21s (8.71) **Going Correction** +0.85s/f (Soft) **20** Ran SP% **130.8**
Speed ratings (Par 103): **84,83,78,77,74 74,74,71,71,71 71,66,66,65,63 62,62,62,40,7**
CSF £548.75 CT £5677.12 TOTE £91.70: £14.00, £3.20, £2.30, £4.20; EX 1606.50.
Owner J M Walsh **Bred** Simon H K Wu And Richard K L Yip **Trained** Sledmere, E Yorks

FOCUS
This was run in a blizzard and conditions were awful, which makes the very slow time rather more understandable. The main bulk of the field raced down the middle whilst one raced alone stands' side, and he finished tailed-off last.

991 STELLA ARTOIS MAIDEN STKS 1m 1f
4:20 (4:22) (Class 5) 3-Y-0+ **£2,331** (£693; £346; £173) **Stalls** Low

Form RPR

566- 1 **Albaqaa**[151] 6449 3-8-9 72 TonyHamilton 9 85
(R A Fahey) *in tch: smooth hdwy over 3f out: led wl over 2f: rdn: hung bdly rt and hdd 2f out: led again over 1f out and sn rdn clr* **6/1**[3]

03- 2 4 **Tajweed (IRE)**[145] 6592 3-8-9 0 MartinDwyer 5 77
(M Johnston) *led: rdn along 3f out and sn hdd: led again 2f out tl drvn and hdd over 1f out: kpt on same pce* **6/4**[1]

3 17 **Platoche (IRE)** 3-8-9 0 NCallan 10 43
(P W Chapple-Hyam) *trckd ldrs: hdwy 3f out and sn ev ch tl rdn 2f out and kpt on same pce* **2/1**[2]

06- 4 3 1/2 **Caffari (GER)**[160] 6254 3-8-4 0 AndrewElliott 3 31
(K R Burke) *chsd ldrs: rdn along over 3f out: sn drvn and outpcd over 2f out* **40/1**

5 5 **Key Decision (IRE)**[22] 4-10-0 0 RobertWinston 7 26
(G A Swinbank) *s.i.s and bhd tl styd on fnl 2f: nvr a factor* **20/1**

56-6 6 3/4 **Ros Cuire (IRE)**[17] 826 3-8-9 0 PaulFessey 11 25
(W A Murphy, Ire) *n.d* **66/1**

3-0 7 3/4 **Baaher (USA)**[16] 837 4-10-0 0 RobertHavlin 8 23
(T J Pitt) *a in midfield* **9/1**

540- 8 3 1/2 **Zabougg**[219] 4612 3-8-9 70 FergalLynch 1 16
(D W Barker) *dwlt: a in rr* **20/1**

/245 9 5 **Red Fama**[39] 552 4-9-11 50 MarkLawson(3) 6 6
(N Bycroft) *trckd ldrs: hdwy to chse ldr over 5f out: rdn along over 3f out and sn wknd* **80/1**

10 5 **Miss Understanding** 3-8-5 0 ow1 JoeFanning 12 —
(J R Weymes) *s.i.s: a bhd* **50/1**

11 2 1/2 **My Mate Mal**[58] 4-9-7 0 LanceBetts(7) 13 —
(B Ellison) *in tch: rdn along over 4f out and sn wknd* **100/1**

400- 12 5 **Rivington Pike (IRE)**[177] 5813 3-8-9 68 PaulMulrennan 2 —
(J J Quinn) *in tch tl rdn along 4f out and sn wknd* **16/1**

13 49 **Monte Pattino (USA)** 4-10-0 0 (t) DavidAllan 4 —
(C J Teague) *a bhd* **50/1**

2m 2.90s (9.90) **Going Correction** +1.05s/f (Soft)
WFA 3 from 4yo 19lb **13** Ran SP% **123.1**
Speed ratings (Par 103): **98,94,79,76,71 71,70,67,62,58 56,51,8**
CSF £15.07 TOTE £7.10: £1.90, £1.40, £1.30; EX 18.90.
Owner J H Tattersall **Bred** C Eddington And Partners **Trained** Musley Bank, N Yorks

FOCUS
Plenty of these had no chance and the way they finished so spread out was more akin to a 3m chase than a 1m1f maiden. The form may be a little suspect given the conditions and the front pair handled them much better than their rivals.
Red Fama Official explanation: jockey said gelding was unsuited by the good to soft ground

992 BODDINGTONS REDCAR STRAIGHT-MILE CHAMPIONSHIP (H'CAP) (QUALIFIER) 1m
4:55 (4:57) (Class 4) (0-85,81) 4-Y-0+ **£4,210** (£1,252; £625; £312) **Stalls** Centre

Form RPR

350- 1 **The Osteopath (IRE)**[156] 6331 5-8-8 **71** TonyHamilton 12 89
(M Dods) *in midfield: gd hdwy over 3f out: led 2f out: rdn clr ent fnl f* **22/1**

141- 2 5 **Spinning**[129] 6838 5-8-9 **72** (b) PhillipMakin 17 78
(T D Barron) *hld up towards rr: gd hdwy 3f out: chsd wnr wl: over 1f out: sn rdn and kpt on same pce ins fnl f* **17/2**[3]

103- 3 hd **Tsaroxy (IRE)**[41] 4497 6-8-12 **75** RobertWinston 14 81
(J Howard Johnson) *in rr: rdn along 1/2-way: hdwy 3f out: rdn 2f out: styd on u.p appr fnl f* **14/1**

110- 4 5 **Middlemarch (IRE)**[170] 6016 8-8-13 **81** (v) GaryBartley(5) 18 76
(J S Goldie) *hld up in rr: hdwy 1/2-way: sn pushed along: rdn 2f out: styd on ins fnl f: nrst fin* **25/1**

6301 5 nk **Boundless Prospect (USA)**[11] 864 9-8-10 **78** NicolPolli(5) 13 72
(Miss Gay Kelleway) *hld up on stands' rail: hdwy over 2f out: sn rdn and kpt on ins fnl f: nrst fin* **14/1**

030- 6 3 1/2 **Shot To Fame (USA)**[147] 6539 9-9-0 **77** SilvestreDeSousa 7 63
(D Nicholls) *in tch: hdwy to chse ldrs over 2f out: sn rdn and no imp appr fnl f* **12/1**

404- 7 2 1/4 **Osteopathic Remedy (IRE)**[142] 6637 4-8-11 **77** PJMcDonald(3) 19 58
(M Dods) *prom: cl up 1/2-way: rdn along 3f out: wknd over 2f out* **8/1**[2]

206- 8 1 1/2 **Tencendur (IRE)**[205] 5043 4-8-4 **74** AdeleRothery(7) 6 51
(D Nicholls) *prom: led 1/2-way: hdd 2f out and grad wknd* **40/1**

-242 9 2 **Inside Story (IRE)**[23] 768 6-8-6 **69** (b) DaleGibson 3 42
(M W Easterby) *towards rr: pushed along over 3f out: rdn over 2f out: kpt on appr fnl f: n.d* **11/1**

004- 10 5 **Moheebb (IRE)**[95] 7200 4-8-9 **72** JoeFanning 9 33
(Mrs R A Carr) *in rr: rdn along 1/2-way: nvr a factor* **18/1**

154- 11 5 **Chicken George (IRE)**[149] 6492 4-8-10 **73** AdrianTNicholls 11 23
(D Nicholls) *chsd ldrs: rdn along over 2f out and sn wknd* **13/2**[1]

6-66 12 5 **King Of The Moors (USA)**[12] 852 5-8-8 **71** PaulFessey 15 9
(T D Barron) *led 2f: cl up tl rdn along and wknd over 3f out* **16/1**

310- 13 5 **Nuit Sombre (IRE)**[109] 7045 8-8-13 **81** NataliaGemelova(5) 16 8
(G A Harker) *cl up: led after 2f: hdd 1/2-way: rdn along and wknd wl over 2f out* **20/1**

23-6 14 nk **Kingsholm**[28] 697 6-8-5 **68** AndrewElliott 4 —
(I W McInnes) *hmpd s: sn prom: rdn along 1/2-way and sn wknd* **22/1**

300- 15 1 1/2 **Bid For Gold**[135] 6753 4-8-9 **72** PaulMulrennan 1 —
(Jedd O'Keeffe) *in tch: pushed along 1/2-way: sn rdn and wknd* **28/1**

600- 16 1 1/4 **Wovoka (IRE)**[199] 5196 5-9-3 **80** FergalLynch 10 —
(D W Barker) *prom tl rdn along over 3f out and sn wknd* **14/1**

4-24 17 5 **Westport**[38] 574 5-9-1 **78** NCallan 2 —
(K A Ryan) *prom: rdn along 1/2-way: sn wknd* **17/2**[3]

040- 18 5 **Daaweitza**[168] 6067 5-9-2 **79** JimmyFortune 5 —
(B Ellison) *a in rr* **10/1**

1m 43.83s (5.83) **Going Correction** +0.85s/f (Soft) **18** Ran SP% **125.0**
Speed ratings (Par 105): **104,99,98,93,93 90,87,86,84,79 74,69,64,63,62 61,56,51**
CSF £187.47 CT £2747.29 TOTE £25.00: £4.80, £2.40, £3.90, £8.70; EX 250.10 TRIFECTA Not won..
Owner Kevin Kirkup **Bred** Joe Rogers **Trained** Denton, Co Durham

FOCUS
A wide-open handicap and they went a fair pace in the conditions. The runners all stayed together down the centre of the track this time and there were some decent margins separating the front four at the line.
Chicken George(IRE) ◆ Official explanation: jockey said gelding was unsuited by the good to soft ground
Wovoka(IRE) Official explanation: jockey said gelding ran too free
Daaweitza Official explanation: jockey said gelding was never travelling

993 THE COMMITMENTS ARE HERE IN AUGUST H'CAP 5f
5:30 (5:33) (Class 6) (0-60,60) 3-Y-0 **£1,943** (£578; £288; £144) **Stalls** Centre

Form RPR

000- 1 **Killer Class**[150] 6462 3-8-8 **50** FergalLynch 1 53
(J S Goldie) *hld up: hdwy 2f out: rdn ent fnl f: styd on wl to ld nr fin* **10/1**

050- 2 1/2 **Straight (IRE)**[173] 5902 3-9-1 **60** MarkLawson(3) 9 61
(M Brittain) *chsd ldrs: hdwy to ld 2f out: rdn and hung rt over 1f out: drvn ins fnl f: hdd and nt qckn nr fin* **16/1**

5602 3 shd **Golden Dane (IRE)**[7] 917 3-9-4 **60** (p) PaulMulrennan 11 61
(C R Dore) *trckd ldrs: hdwy 2f out: rdn to chal over 1f out and ev ch tl drvn and nt qckn last 50yds* **10/3**[1]

00-0 4 1 1/2 **Bellas Chicas (IRE)**[23] 767 3-8-8 **53** ow3 JamieMoriarty(3) 8 49
(P T Midgley) *towards rr: rdn along and hdwy 2f out: styd on wl fnl f: nrst fin* **40/1**

003- 5 5 **Mchepple**[137] 6729 3-8-7 **52** DominicFox(3) 2 30
(W Storey) *towards rr and rdn along 1/2-way: styd on u.p appr fnl f: n.d* **28/1**

400- 6 1 1/2 **Madame Rio (IRE)**[154] 6388 3-9-1 **57** AndrewElliott 6 29
(K R Burke) *chsd ldrs: rdn along 1/2-way: sn wknd* **9/1**

636- 7 nk **Curio**[114] 7000 3-9-0 **56** DeanMcKeown 5 27
(R M Whitaker) *led: rdn and hdd 2f out: sn wknd* **15/2**[3]

-041 8 shd **Mujinda**[21] 780 3-8-8 **50** (b) TWilliams 7 21+
(M Brittain) *sn rdn along: a in rr* **6/1**[2]

000- 9 4 **Captain Turbot (IRE)**[167] 6072 3-8-4 **46** oh1 JoeFanning 4 —
(D W Barker) *chsd ldr: rdn along 2f out: sn wknd* **16/1**

035- **10** *16* **Next Best**[207] 4970 3-8-6 **53**................................ DanielleMcCreery(5) 10 —
(A Berry) *chsd ldrs to 1/2-way: sn wknd* **16/1**
65.68 secs (7.08) **Going Correction** +0.85s/f (Soft) **10** Ran SP% **91.8**
Speed ratings (Par 96): **77,76,76,73,65 63,62,62,56,30**
CSF £94.01 CT £297.22 TOTE £14.00: £2.90, £3.20, £1.30; EX 181.30 Place 6 £111.10, Place 5 £56.85..
Owner Frank Brady **Bred** Jonayro Investments **Trained** Uplawmoor, E Renfrews
■ Rich James was withdrawn after bolting before the start (11/4F, deduct 25p in the £ under Rule 4).
FOCUS
An extremely slow time for a sprint handicap, 2.87 seconds slower than the opener, and something of a slow-motion finish. The conditions proved too much for the majority of the field and the front four pulled a long way clear. The late withdrawal of the favourite weakened the contest still further and the form looks very moderate.
Killer Class Official explanation: trainer said, regarding apparent improvement in form, that the filly had matured over the winter.
Next Best Official explanation: jockey said filly hung right handed in final 2f
T/Jkpt: Not won. T/Plt: £89.10 to a £1 stake. Pool: £70,416.25. 576.30 winning tickets. T/Qpdt: £34.60 to a £1 stake. Pool: £2,796.50. 59.80 winning tickets. JR

WARWICK (L-H)
Monday, March 24

OFFICIAL GOING: Good to soft (good in places on round course) changing to soft (good to soft in places) after race 3 (3.30)
Wind: Light across Weather: Wintry showers

994 WARWICK RACECOURSE FOR CONFERENCES H'CAP 5f 110y
2:20 (2:21) (Class 5) (0-75,74) 4-Y-0+ **£3,071** (£906; £453) **Stalls** Low

Form RPR
3550 **1** **After The Show**[10] 875 7-8-4 **60** oh2................................ ChrisCatlin 12 76
(Rae Guest) *in midfield: effrt and hdwy to ld over 1f out: edgd lft ins fnl f: won gng away* **11/1**
615- **2** *3 1/4* **El Potro**[128] 6860 6-8-1 **60**.. WilliamBuick(3) 4 65
(J R Holt) *w ldr: rdn whn upsides over 1f out: nt pce of wnr ins fnl f* **8/1**[3]
4205 **3** *3/4* **Chatshow (USA)**[9] 896 7-8-2 **61**................................. LukeMorris(3) 5 63
(A W Carroll) *in tch: effrt 2f out: nt qckn over 1f out: styd on towards fin* **17/2**
050- **4** *nk* **Dualagi**[161] 6239 4-8-9 **65**... LPKeniry 13 66
(M R Bosley) *racd keenly: hld up in rr: rdn over 1f out: prog ent fnl f: fin wl: nrst fin* **28/1**
400- **5** *nse* **Highland Warrior**[164] 6157 9-9-2 **72**................................. MickyFenton 3 73
(P T Midgley) *in rr: rdn and hdwy over 1f out: sn chsd ldrs: one pce towards fin* **12/1**
112- **6** *hd* **Spirit Of Coniston**[136] 6752 5-8-10 **66**.............................. PatDobbs 6 67
(D Nicholls) *led: rdn and hdd over 1f out: kpt on same pce fnl f* **7/1**[2]
1363 **7** *1 1/4* **Lord Of The Reins (IRE)**[10] 875 4-8-9 **65**................ FrancisNorton 7 61+
(D Shaw) *squeezed s: in rr: nt clr run 2f out: swtchd lft and hdwy over 1f out: kpt on ins fnl f: nt pce to trble ldrs towards fin* **8/1**[3]
-000 **8** *1* **Imperial Echo (USA)**[16] 833 7-8-13 **72**..................... TolleyDean(3) 9 65
(D Shaw) *in midfield: rdn and outpcd 3f out: edgd lft fr over 1f out: kpt on: nvr able to chal* **14/1**
000- **9** *3/4* **Tender Process (IRE)**[179] 5747 5-8-9 **65**............... StephenDonohoe 1 55
(E S McMahon) *racd in midfield on inner: effrt to chse ldrs over 1f out: wknd ins fnl f* **7/2**[1]
00-0 **10** *nk* **Namir (IRE)**[9] 901 6-9-4 **74**.......................................(vt) JimCrowley 2 63
(D Shaw) *racd keenly: in tch: rdn over 1f out: wknd ins fnl f* **14/1**
0351 **11** *4* **Methaaly (IRE)**[19] 801 5-8-5 **68**............................ RossAtkinson(7) 11 44
(M Mullineaux) *racd on outside: w ldrs: rdn over 1f out: sn wknd* **8/1**[3]
01-0 **12** *nse* **Brut**[36] 596 6-9-0 **70**...(p) JimmyQuinn 8 46
(D W Barker) *bmpd s: pressed ldrs: pushed along over 2f out: losing pl whn n.m.r and hmpd over 1f out* **14/1**
1m 10.19s (4.29) **Going Correction** +0.80s/f (Soft) **12** Ran SP% **118.1**
Speed ratings (Par 103): **103,98,97,97,97 96,95,93,92,92 87,87**
CSF £95.86 CT £804.76 TOTE £12.30: £4.10, £3.70, £3.90; EX 130.80.
Owner Miss L Thompson **Bred** Michael Ng **Trained** Newmarket, Suffolk
FOCUS
A modest sprint handicap. There was not much strength in depth but the winner is rated back to last year's best turf form. As is often the case when the ground is on the soft side at Warwick, they raced middle to stands' side in the straight.

995 SPONSOR AT WARWICK RACECOURSE MAIDEN FILLIES' STKS 5f
2:55 (3:00) (Class 5) 2-Y-0 **£3,071** (£906; £453) **Stalls** Low

Form RPR
1 **She's A Shaw Thing** 2-9-0 0.................................. TGMcLaughlin 13 83+
(P D Evans) *pressed ldrs: rdn to ld over 1f out: dashed clr ins fnl f* **8/1**[3]
2 *4 1/2* **Percolator** 2-9-0 0.. TQuinn 11 65
(P F I Cole) *led: rdn and hung rt wl over 1f out: sn hdd: nt pce of wnr fnl f* **3/1**[1]
3 *2 1/4* **Meg Jicaro** 2-8-11 0...................................... TolleyDean(3) 3 56
(Mrs L Williamson) *sn pushed along to chse ldrs: hung rt ins fnl f: kpt on: nt pce to chal* **33/1**
4 *nk* **Transcentral** 2-9-0 0.. LiamJones 1 55+
(W M Brisbourne) *pushed along in rr div after 1f: hdwy over 1f out: rn geen: r.o ins fnl f: nt rch ldrs* **20/1**
5 *1 1/4* **Dancing Wave** 2-8-7 0.. JackDean(7) 2 50
(W G M Turner) *in midfield: rdn 2f out: no imp on ldrs* **14/1**
6 *1 1/4* **Joli Haven (IRE)** 2-9-0 0.. SaleemGolam 5 45+
(W G M Turner) *chsd ldrs: pushed along 2f out: rdn and rn green over 1f out: checked whn nt clr run ent fnl f: one pce after* **8/1**[3]
7 *1/2* **Alphabeth** 2-9-0 0.. SamHitchcott 8 43
(M R Channon) *chsd ldrs: rdn and edgd lft over 1f out: wknd ins fnl f* **10/1**
8 *2 1/4* **Lois Darlin (IRE)** 2-9-0 0.. LPKeniry 10 34
(J S Moore) *s.s: racd in midfield: rdn over 1f out: nvr able to chal* **9/2**[2]
9 *3 1/4* **Shes Billie** 2-9-0 0... FergusSweeney 12 21+
(J G M O'Shea) *dwlt: towards rr: pushed along 1/2-way: nvr trbld ldrs* **14/1**
10 *1 1/4* **Dispol Toba** 2-9-0 0.. MickyFenton 6 16
(P T Midgley) *in tch to 2f out: rdn and wknd over 1f out* **25/1**
11 *1 1/4* **Cecilia's Lass** 2-9-0 0.. AlanMunro 9 11
(D H Brown) *s.s: a outpcd* **8/1**[3]
12 *1* **Miss Belle Eve** 2-9-0 0.. NeilChalmers 14 7
(T M Jones) *wnt rt s: racd on outside in midfield: outpcd 2f out* **50/1**
13 *4* **Percys Corismatic** 2-9-0 0...................................... JimCrowley 4 —
(J Gallagher) *s.s: a outpcd* **33/1**
14 *5* **Tarawa Atoll** 2-9-0 0.. ChrisCatlin 7 —
(M R Channon) *a bhd* **10/1**
64.72 secs (5.12) **Going Correction** +0.80s/f (Soft) **14** Ran SP% **124.5**
Speed ratings (Par 89): **91,83,80,79,77 75,74,71,66,64 62,60,54,46**
CSF £31.50 TOTE £10.10: £2.60, £1.60, £12.80; EX 35.60.
Owner R Cave **Bred** M Pennell **Trained** Pandy, Monmouths
FOCUS
Impossible to be sure of the level of this fillies' maiden given the entire field were making their racecourse debuts, but She's A Shaw Thing did it well and the race should produce some winners. They raced all over the place in the straight.
NOTEBOOK
She's A Shaw Thing, a 5,000gns daughter of Reel Buddy, sister to 7f juvenile winner Reel Buddy Star, knew her job and took this in good style. Soon showing bags of early speed to dispute the lead, she stayed on much stronger than one might have expected to draw clear inside the final furlong. It will be no surprise if she is kept busy and she might be able to add to this. (op 15-2 tchd 13-2)
Percolator, a Kheleyf filly, half-sister to dual 7f three-year-old winner Mocha Java, and 7f juvenile winner Carte Noir, out of a dual 7f-1m winner at two to three, was well backed on course but found one too good. Like the winner she was soon showing good speed, but she could not live with that one in that last furlong. (op 13-2)
Meg Jicaro ◆, another daughter of Reel Buddy, is out of a mare who was unplaced on the Flat and over hurdles. She was soon outpaced and running green, but there was plenty to like about the way she finished her race and she looks a nice enough type. This should have taught her plenty and she ought to pick up a similar event.
Transcentral ◆, a 2,000gns daughter of Kheleyf, first foal of a mare who was placed over 7f at three, could not go the early pace but she gradually got the hang of things and finished nicely. She should come on a bundle for the experience and might be able to find a similar race.
Dancing Wave, a daughter of top-class Australian miler Baryshnikov, first foal of a mare who was placed over 1m at four, made only a short-lived effort from off the pace in the straight. (op 11-1)
Joli Haven(IRE), a 2,600euros daughter of Indian Haven, out of a 5f winner at two, showed early speed to chase the leaders, but she took a while to pick up when asked for her challenge in the straight. She was held when hampered around a furlong out, but she ought to know more next time. (op 7-1)
Lois Darlin(IRE), a 7,000euros Indian Haven filly, out of a mare who was unplaced over 1m4f and over hurdles, was not without support but she was too green to get in a blow. (op 13-2 tchd 8-1)

996 WARWICKRACECOURSE.CO.UK H'CAP 1m 22y
3:30 (3:30) (Class 5) (0-70,70) 4-Y-0+ **£3,238** (£963; £481; £240) **Stalls** Low

Form RPR
2111 **1** **Rebellious Spirit**[18] 811 5-9-3 **69**................................ PaulDoe 3 81+
(S Curran) *a.p: led after 3f: rdn over 1f out: sn drew clr: eased towards fin* **3/1**[1]
4160 **2** *4* **Waterline Twenty (IRE)**[5] 941 5-9-2 **68**................... TGMcLaughlin 4 71
(P D Evans) *led for 2f: remained handy: pushed along and outpcd 3f out: styd on to take 2nd jst over 1f out: no ch w wnr fnl f* **13/2**
4600 **3** *1/2* **Latif (USA)**[18] 811 7-8-5 **57** ow1.................................. NeilChalmers 2 59
(Paul Green) *hld up: rdn and hdwy to chse ldrs 2f out: styd on same pce ins fnl f* **14/1**
44-5 **4** *1/2* **Superior Star**[31] 659 5-9-1 **67**..................................(b) JimmyQuinn 1 68
(N Wilson) *trckd ldrs: effrt 2f out: kpt on same pce fnl f* **9/2**[2]
0406 **5** *1 1/4* **Tina's Ridge (IRE)**[13] 844 4-8-8 **60**............................(p) JimCrowley 5 58
(R Hollinshead) *bhd: hdwy on inner 3f out: rdn to chse ldrs 2f out: one pce fnl f* **9/1**
1136 **6** *5* **Under Fire (IRE)**[10] 879 5-8-9 **64**............................ LukeMorris(3) 6 50
(A W Carroll) *prom: led after 2f: hdd after 3f: remained prom: rdn over 3f out: wknd over 1f out* **8/1**
-026 **7** *3/4* **Music Note (IRE)**[20] 791 5-9-4 **70**.............................. HayleyTurner 9 55+
(Miss Gay Kelleway) *handy on outside: rdn and nt clr run over 2f out: sn lost pl: bhd after* **6/1**[3]
300- **8** *5* **The Grey One (IRE)**[151] 6447 5-8-8 **60**.......................(p) ChrisCatlin 7 33
(J M Bradley) *hld up: rdn over 2f out: sn outpcd* **13/2**
1m 44.75s (3.75) **Going Correction** +0.55s/f (Yiel) **8** Ran SP% **111.9**
Speed ratings (Par 103): **103,99,98,98,96 91,91,86**
CSF £21.68 CT £229.05 TOTE £2.90: £1.30, £2.10, £3.60; EX 20.20.
Owner Colin Hill **Bred** Car Colston Hall Stud **Trained** Hatford, Oxon
FOCUS
A modest handicap. They raced stands' side in the straight.

997 EASTER FAMILY FUN DAY MAIDEN STKS 7f 26y
4:05 (4:08) (Class 5) 3-Y-0 **£3,412** (£1,007; £504) **Stalls** Low

Form RPR
1 **Magnitude** 3-9-3 0.. MichaelHills 2 82+
(W J Haggas) *in tch: clsd 4f out: chsd ldr over 2f out: rdn and upsides 1f out: led wl ins fnl f: r.o and in command fnl strides* **5/2**[2]
32- **2** *1/2* **Tawzeea (IRE)**[184] 5621 3-9-3 0.................................. RHills 4 81
(M Johnston) *led: rdn and edgd lft whn pressed 1f out: hdd wl ins fnl f: hld fnl strides* **1/1**[1]
60- **3** *5* **Koraleva Tectona (IRE)**[160] 6248 3-8-12 0................ PaulEddery 3 64
(Pat Eddery) *j. awkwardly fr stalls: trckd ldrs after 1f: sn wnt 2nd: rdn and lost 2nd over 2f out: outpcd by front pair over 1f out* **20/1**
4 *2 1/2* **Spotty Muldoon (IRE)** 3-9-3 0.................................. GeorgeBaker 10 63+
(R M Beckett) *in midfield: lost pl after 2f: kpt on fr 2f out wout troubling ldrs* **16/1**
5- **5** *2 1/2* **Chief Eric**[213] 4764 3-9-0 0.................................. WilliamBuick(3) 7 57
(B I Case) *racd keenly: prom: lost pl 4f out: n.d after* **15/2**[3]
6- **6** *3/4* **Never Catcher (IRE)**[147] 6535 3-8-12 0.................. StephenDonohoe 5 50
(P A Blockley) *in midfield: pushed along 3f out: nvr able to chal* **12/1**
04 **7** *6* **Ramprakash**[21] 773 3-9-3 0.. HayleyTurner 1 40+
(M L W Bell) *towards rr: hdwy on inner 4f out: no imp on ldrs: wknd wl over 1f out* **28/1**
8 *7* **Glitz (IRE)** 3-8-12 0.. JimCrowley 13 18
(M L W Bell) *a towards rr* **16/1**
0 **9** *nk* **Profumo Affair**[11] 867 3-9-0 0.................................. LukeMorris(3) 9 22
(M L W Bell) *in midfield: wknd 4f out* **50/1**
6 **10** *7* **Marysedge**[12] 855 3-8-12 0...................................... J-PGuillambert 8 —
(R Brotherton) *prom tl wknd 4f out* **100/1**
11 *8* **Little Rococoa** 3-9-0 0.. TolleyDean(3) 12 —
(R J Price) *wnt rt s: a bhd* **100/1**
1m 28.7s (4.10) **Going Correction** +0.55s/f (Yiel) **11** Ran SP% **121.9**
Speed ratings (Par 98): **98,97,91,88,86 85,78,70,69,61 52**
CSF £5.36 TOTE £3.20: £1.30, £1.10, £4.70; EX 5.50.
Owner Cheveley Park Stud **Bred** Cheveley Park Stud Ltd **Trained** Newmarket, Suffolk
■ Stewards' Enquiry : J-P Guillambert caution: used whip when out of contention
FOCUS
An ordinary maiden in which the first two finished clear. The winning time was 1.95 seconds quicker than following 46-60 three-year-old handicap. Again, they all raced towards the stands' rail in the straight.

Koraleva Tectona(IRE) Official explanation: jockey said filly stumbled leaving stalls
Chief Eric Official explanation: trainer said colt lost a front shoe

998 TURFTV H'CAP 7f 26y
4:40 (4:51) (Class 6) (0-60,60) 3-Y-O **£2,047** (£604; £302) **Stalls** Low

Form RPR

604- **1** **Lowry's Art**[177] 5818 3-9-4 **60**.............................. GeorgeBaker 10 63
(R M Beckett) *mde all: rdn whn pressed over 1f out: edgd rt ins fnl f: battled gamely* **5/1**[2]

0160 **2** *hd* **Magical Song**[11] 873 3-8-11 **53**.............................. StephenDonohoe 5 56
(P A Blockley) *a.p: moved upsides 2f out: rdn over 1f out whn chalng strly: r.o* **7/2**[1]

400- **3** *hd* **Yakama (IRE)**[147] 6530 3-8-4 **46** oh1.............................. RichardThomas 8 48
(D J S Ffrench Davis) *s.i.s: in midfield: hdwy over 1f out: running on to chal whn swtchd lft ins fnl f: gaining cl home* **16/1**

-444 **4** *1 1/4* **One Called Alice**[11] 873 3-9-1 **60**.............................. JerryO'Dwyer(3) 6 59
(A W Carroll) *s.i.s: in midfield: hdwy to trck ldrs 1/2-way: rdn and styd on over 1f out: nt qckn nr fin* **11/2**[3]

050- **5** *5* **Zaplamation (IRE)**[150] 6462 3-8-4 **46** oh1.............................. JimmyQuinn 12 33
(D W Barker) *swtchd lft s: in rr: rdn and prog over 1f out: styd on wout troubling ldrs fnl f* **11/2**[3]

-560 **6** *shd* **Mad Man Will (IRE)**[11] 873 3-8-10 **52**..............................(t) SaleemGolam 4 38
(S C Williams) *prom: rdn over 1f out: wknd fnl f* **10/1**

004- **7** *1/2* **Tenth Night (IRE)**[157] 6305 3-8-9 **51** ow4.............................. MickyFenton 3 36
(P T Midgley) *hld up: effrt over 1f out: no imp on ldrs* **10/1**

000- **8** *3 1/4* **Just Jimmy (IRE)**[150] 6478 3-9-4 **60**.............................. TGMcLaughlin 1 37
(P D Evans) *plld hrd: hld up: pushed along over 1f out: nvr a danger* **5/1**[2]

654- **9** *5* **Amber Ridge**[182] 5675 3-9-4 **60**.............................. PatDobbs 11 25
(B P J Baugh) *racd keenly in midfield: wknd 3f out* **8/1**

000- **10** *1* **New Minerton (IRE)**[219] 4593 3-8-8 **50**.............................. AlanMunro 9 13
(B R Millman) *prom on outside: wknd 3f out* **18/1**

1m 30.65s (6.05) **Going Correction** +0.55s/f (Yiel) **10** Ran SP% **126.8**
Speed ratings (Par 96): **87,86,86,85,79 79,78,75,69,68**
CSF £25.11 CT £276.04 TOTE £6.20: £2.10, £1.60, £5.80; EX 19.20.
Owner Matthew Green **Bred** Fern Hill Stud & M Green **Trained** Whitsbury, Hants
■ Grand Value was withdrawn after getting loose before the start. Deduct 15p in the £ under Rule 4. New market formed.
■ Stewards' Enquiry : George Baker caution: used whip down the shoulder in the forehand position

FOCUS
A moderate but competitive handicap. The winning time was 1.95 seconds slower than the previous three-year-old maiden. They raced stands' side in the straight.
Tenth Night(IRE) Official explanation: jockey said colt hung left
New Minerton(IRE) Official explanation: jockey said filly hung

999 RACING UK H'CAP 1m 2f 188y
5:15 (5:19) (Class 6) (0-60,59) 4-Y-0+ **£2,047** (£604; £302) **Stalls** Low

Form RPR

350- **1** **Snake Skin**[42] 5132 5-9-2 **56**.............................. JimCrowley 14 66
(J Gallagher) *in tch: rdn to ld over 1f out: r.o and hld on wl* **12/1**

1232 **2** *shd* **Trysting Grove (IRE)**[19] 802 7-8-13 **53**.............................. SaleemGolam 17 63
(E G Bevan) *sn dropped to midfield: hdwy 2f out: str chal ins fnl f: r.o* **12/1**

006- **3** *2* **General Flumpa**[174] 5886 7-8-8 **55**.............................. SoniaEaton(7) 9 61
(Miss Tor Sturgis) *missed break: towards rr: hdwy 2f out: styd on to chse ldng duo ent fnl f: sn edgd rt: no imp cl home* **16/1**

44-2 **4** *1 1/4* **Ryan's Future (IRE)**[79] 57 8-9-2 **56**.............................. LPKeniry 11 62+
(J S Moore) *racd keenly in midfield: rdn and hdwy over 1f out: styd on ins fnl f: nt pce to rch ldrs* **9/1**

000- **5** *nse* **April The Second**[291] 2402 4-8-9 **53**.............................. TolleyDean(3) 8 56
(R J Price) *racd keenly in midfield: rdn 3f out: hdwy over 2f out: rdn and chsd ldrs over 1f out: styd on same pce ins fnl f* **33/1**

1-01 **6** *2 1/4* **Noah Jameel**[40] 541 6-9-1 **55**.............................. FergusSweeney 6 54
(A G Newcombe) *trckd ldrs: rdn to chal over 1f out: no ex ins fnl f* **13/2**[2]

125- **7** *shd* **Brastar Jelois (FR)**[178] 5774 5-9-1 **58**.............................. RussellKennemore(3) 4 57+
(R Hollinshead) *missed break: hld up: hdwy over 2f out: nt clr run over 1f out: sn rdn: kpt on ins fnl f nt pce to trble ldrs* **8/1**[3]

8 *1/2* **Sir Rique (FR)**[14] 5-9-1 **55**.............................. VinceSlattery 16 53
(P J Hobbs) *towards rr: rdn 3f out: kpt on fnl f: nvr able to chal* **20/1**

-6 **9** *1/2* **Top Seed (IRE)**[32] 646 7-8-11 **51**.............................. StephenDonohoe 1 48
(Ian Williams) *s.i.s: in rr: struggling over 2f out: kpt on fnl f: n.d* **8/1**[3]

052- **10** *shd* **David's Cavalier**[338] 1154 4-9-2 **57**.............................. GeorgeBaker 15 54
(R Hollinshead) *missed break: in rr: pushed along 5f out: edgd lft over 1f out: nvr on terms w ldrs* **20/1**

532- **11** *1/2* **Desert Hawk**[121] 6937 7-9-0 **54**.............................. LiamJones 5 50
(W M Brisbourne) *racd keenly: trckd ldrs: rdn 3f out: outpcd over 1f out* **12/1**

05-0 **12** *hd* **King Of Connacht**[78] 67 5-9-1 **55**..............................(p) JimmyQuinn 7 51
(M Wellings) *prom: rdn to chal over 2f out: wknd jst over 1f out* **33/1**

023- **13** *5* **Zain (IRE)**[142] 6640 4-9-1 **56**.............................. J-PGuillambert 2 43
(J G Given) *prom: rdn to chal over 1f out: wknd ent fnl f* **4/1**[1]

010- **14** *2* **Icannshift (IRE)**[194] 5341 8-9-5 **59**.............................. NeilChalmers 3 42
(T M Jones) *sn led: rdn and hdd over 1f out: sn wknd* **14/1**

0213 **15** *3/4* **Ben Bacchus (IRE)**[13] 843 6-8-11 **51**.............................. ChrisCatlin 12 33
(P W Hiatt) *prom: rdn over 2f out: sn wknd* **10/1**

100- **16** *21* **Orphina (IRE)**[82] 5709 5-8-10 **50**..............................(t) TQuinn 10 —
(B G Powell) *a bhd* **20/1**

2m 28.87s (7.77) **Going Correction** +0.55s/f (Yiel)
WFA 4 from 5yo+ 1lb **16** Ran SP% **130.4**
Speed ratings (Par 101): **93,92,91,90,90 88,88,88,87,87 87,87,83,82,81 66**
CSF £148.00 CT £2344.35 TOTE £14.70: £3.60, £2.00, £5.90, £2.30; EX 194.90 Place 6 £204.67, Place £35.73..
Owner Adweb Ltd **Bred** The C H F Partnership **Trained** Moreton-in-Marsh, Gloucs

FOCUS
A moderate handicap. They raced middle to stands' side in the straight.
Brastar Jelois(FR) Official explanation: jockey said mare was denied a clear run
T/Plt: £150.80 to a £1 stake. Pool: £55,897.15. 270.50 winning tickets. T/Qpdt: £4.10 to a £1 stake. Pool: £3,013.60. 532.70 winning tickets. DO

YARMOUTH (L-H)
Monday, March 24

1000 Meeting Abandoned - Snow

An informal boycott by trainers unhappy with the level of prizemoney at Yarmouth would have meant a controversial walkover had racing gone ahead.

1006 - 1013a (Foreign Racing) - See Raceform Interactive

PONTEFRACT (L-H)
Tuesday, March 25

OFFICIAL GOING: Good to soft (5.7)
Wind: Moderate, behind Weather: Changeable

1014 HIGH-RISE MEDIAN AUCTION MAIDEN STKS 1m 2f 6y
2:10 (2:12) (Class 4) 3-Y-0 **£4,533** (£1,348; £674; £336) **Stalls** Low

Form RPR

043- **1** **Bouguereau**[192] 5417 3-9-3 104.............................. AlanMunro 3 91+
(P W Chapple-Hyam) *trckd ldr: smooth hdwy to ld 2f out: clr appr fnl f* **4/9**[1]

402- **2** *6* **St Jean Cap Ferrat**[146] 6592 3-9-3 73.............................. SteveDrowne 7 75
(G Wragg) *hld up in tch: hdwy 3f out: rdn to chse wnr wl over 1f out: sn rdn and no imp* **15/2**[3]

3 *nk* **Sphere (IRE)** 3-8-12 0.............................. RobertWinston 5 69+
(J R Fanshawe) *dwlt: hld up in rr: hdwy over 3f out: rdn wl over 1f out: styd on ins fnl f: nrst fin* **20/1**

6 **4** *1 1/2* **Murcar**[12] 867 3-9-3 0.............................. PhilipRobinson 6 71
(C G Cox) *chsd ldrs: hdwy 3f out: rdn along wl over 1f out and sn one pce* **20/1**

0-2 **5** *5* **Pentathlon (IRE)**[12] 867 3-9-3 0.............................. JoeFanning 9 61
(M Johnston) *led: rdn along and hdd 2f out: sn drvn and wknd* **5/1**[2]

0 **6** *4 1/2* **Capal Dubh Alainn (IRE)**[3] 961 3-9-3 0.............................. GregFairley 8 52
(T J Pitt) *a in rr* **100/1**

0 **7** *22* **Saintsylvadene**[12] 867 3-9-3 0.............................. PaulHanagan 4 8
(T D Walford) *plld hrd: prom tl rdn along and wknd 3f out: sn bhd* **100/1**

2m 20.35s (6.65) **Going Correction** +0.675s/f (Yiel) **7** Ran SP% **109.2**
Speed ratings (Par 100): **100,95,94,93,89 86,68**
CSF £3.65 TOTE £1.40: £1.10, £2.50; EX 3.40.
Owner A Black **Bred** Cheveley Park Stud Ltd **Trained** Newmarket, Suffolk

FOCUS
An ordinary maiden but the winner was different class and is value for more with the runner-up to last year's form. The winning time was 2.19 seconds slower than the later 86-100 handicap.

1015 ANNUAL BADGE HOLDERS H'CAP 6f
2:40 (2:46) (Class 5) (0-70,70) 4-Y-0+ **£3,238** (£963; £481; £240) **Stalls** Low

Form RPR

-266 **1** **Winthorpe (IRE)**[56] 347 8-8-10 **62**.............................. RobertWinston 13 73
(J J Quinn) *hld up in midfield: gd hdwy on outer wl over 1f out: rdn and str run ins fnl f: edgd lft and led nr line* **25/1**

650- **2** *hd* **Swinbrook (USA)**[112] 7026 7-9-4 **70**..............................(v) TonyHamilton 11 80+
(R A Fahey) *in tch: gd hdwy towards outer 2f out: rdn ent fnl f and ev ch tl drvn and nt qckn nr line* **9/2**[1]

43-3 **3** *3/4* **Dorn Dancer (IRE)**[1] 987 6-8-3 **58**.............................. AndrewMullen(3) 5 66
(D W Barker) *dwlt: sn into midfield: gd hdwy 2f out: rdn to ld 1f out: drvn ins fnl f: hdd and no ex towards fin* **5/1**[2]

000- **4** *1* **Varadouro (BRZ)**[143] 6639 6-9-3 **69**.............................. SilvestreDeSousa 15 74
(D Nicholls) *towards rr: hdwy on outer wl over 1f out: sn rdn and kpt on ins fnl f: nrst fin* **10/1**

5110 **5** *3 3/4* **Xpres Maite**[33] 636 5-8-13 **65**..............................(v) PhillipMakin 8 59
(S R Bowring) *chsd ldrs: rdn along 2f out: drvn and kpt on same pce ent fnl f* **9/1**

304- **6** *hd* **Lake Chini (IRE)**[146] 6594 6-9-3 **69**..............................(b) DaleGibson 2 62
(M W Easterby) *chsd ldrs: rdn 2f out: kpt on same pce appr fnl f* **14/1**

-602 **7** *2 1/2* **Gilded Cove**[19] 806 8-8-8 **63**.............................. RussellKennemore(3) 14 49
(R Hollinshead) *hld up in rr tl styd on fnl 2f: nrst fin* **10/1**

440- **8** *1 1/4* **Farefield Lodge (IRE)**[167] 6103 4-9-3 **69**.............................. PhilipRobinson 12 51
(C G Cox) *chsd ldrs: rdn along wl over 1f out and sn wknd* **15/2**[3]

11-0 **9** *nk* **Rabbit Fighter (IRE)**[10] 901 4-9-4 **70**..............................(v) PaulMulrennan 17 51+
(D Shaw) *stdd s: t.k.h and hld up in rr: hdwy whn nt clr run over 1f out: kpt on ins fnl f* **14/1**

220- **10** *4 1/2* **Mr Rooney (IRE)**[159] 6287 5-8-7 **59**.............................. AdrianTNicholls 3 27
(D Nicholls) *chsd ldrs on inner: hdwy 2f out: rdn and ch over 1f out: wknd ins fnl f* **14/1**

3650 **11** *hd* **Social Rhythm**[22] 782 4-8-11 **63**.............................. ChrisCatlin 9 30
(H J Collingridge) *nvr nr ldrs* **14/1**

200- **12** *1/2* **Ronnie Howe**[251] 3637 4-8-12 **64**.............................. TomEaves 6 30
(M Dods) *cl up: ev ch 2f out: sn rdn and wknd ent fnl f* **50/1**

230- **13** *nse* **Steel Blue**[143] 6639 8-8-13 **68**.............................. MichaelJStainton(3) 16 33
(R M Whitaker) *cl up on outer tl rdn along 2f out and sn wknd* **16/1**

20-0 **14** *nk* **Kings College Boy**[17] 840 8-8-13 **65**..............................(b) PaulHanagan 4 30
(R A Fahey) *in tch: rdn along 2f out and sn btn* **33/1**

6226 **15** *1 1/2* **Grimes Faith**[5] 951 5-9-3 **69**..............................(b) NCallan 1 38+
(K A Ryan) *t.k.h: led: rdn 2f out: hdd 1f out and wknd qckly* **16/1**

0-44 **16** *1* **Paddywack (IRE)**[61] 285 11-8-3 **60**..............................(b) DanielleMcCreery(5) 7 17
(Mrs R A Carr) *s.i.s: a in rr* **33/1**

1m 21.38s (4.48) **Going Correction** +0.675s/f (Yiel) **16** Ran SP% **124.9**
Speed ratings (Par 103): **97,96,95,94,89 89,85,84,83,77 77,76,76,76,74 73**
CSF £134.32 CT £710.23 TOTE £40.90: £6.00, £1.60, £1.90, £3.10; EX 257.40.
Owner The New Century Partnership **Bred** M Conaghan **Trained** Settrington, N Yorks

FOCUS
A modest but very competitive sprint handicap with the winner rated to his best. The winning time was 0.71 seconds quicker than the later three-year-old fillies' maiden. The entire field avoided the inside rail on the run to the bend and the majority of these raced towards the middle of the track in the straight.
Gilded Cove Official explanation: trainer's rep said horse had been unsuited by the track
Grimes Faith Official explanation: jockey said gelding had run too freely and had no more to give

1016 DALBY STAND H'CAP 1m 4y
3:10 (3:12) (Class 3) (0-95,93) 4-Y-0+
£7,478 (£2,239; £1,119; £560; £279; £140) **Stalls** Low

Form RPR

600- **1** **Collateral Damage (IRE)**[43] 5327 5-8-3 **81**.............................. DuranFentiman(3) 1 89
(T D Easterby) *hld up towards rr: gd hdwy on inner 3f out: rdn to ld over 1f out: edgd rt and styd on ins fnl f* **9/2**[1]

5-10 **2** *1/2* **Capable Guest (IRE)**[38] 594 6-9-1 **90**..............................(v) ChrisCatlin 3 97
(M R Channon) *trckd ldrs on inner: hdwy to ld 2f out: sn rdn and hdd over 1f out: drvn and kpt on ins fnl f* **5/1**[2]

/21- **3** *3 1/2* **Major Magpie (IRE)**[332] 1287 6-8-5 **80**.............................. DaleGibson 2 79+
(M Dods) *hld up in rr: hdwy over 2f out: sn rdn and styd on ins fnl f: nrst fin* **6/1**[3]

010- **4** 1 **Wigwam Willie (IRE)**[165] 6155 6-8-11 **86**............(p) NCallan 7 83
(K A Ryan) *chsd ldrs: rdn along 2f out: drvn and one pce appr fnl f* **8/1**

1321 **5** ½ **Electric Warrior (IRE)**[18] 829 5-8-11 **93**............ DeclanCannon(7) 10 89
(K R Burke) *chsd ldrs: effrt on wd outside and ev ch 2f out: sn rdn and one pce appr fnl f* **10/1**

634- **6** 5 **Ebert**[182] 5717 5-8-10 **85**............ PaulHanagan 9 70
(R A Fahey) *dwlt: sn in tch: effrt over 2f out: sn rdn and btn* **7/1**

300- **7** 1 ½ **Nevada Desert (IRE)**[148] 6539 8-8-6 **84**............ MichaelJStainton(3) 5 66
(R M Whitaker) *dwlt: in tch: rdn along 3f out and sn outpcd* **12/1**

000/ **8** 5 **Another Bottle (IRE)**[121] 5675 7-9-2 **91**............ RobertWinston 4 62+
(J J Quinn) *hld up: a in rr* **8/1**

3124 **9** 13 **Denbera Dancer (USA)**[11] 888 4-8-6 **81**............ JoeFanning 6 23
(M Johnston) *cl up: rdn along 3f out: hdd over 2f out and sn wknd* **7/1**

040- **10** 2 ¾ **Royal Dignitary (USA)**[185] 5615 8-9-0 **89**............ AdrianTNicholls 8 25
(D Nicholls) *led: rdn along 3f out: hdd 2f out and sn wknd* **28/1**

1m 50.66s (4.76) **Going Correction** +0.675s/f (Yiel) **10** Ran SP% **116.6**
Speed ratings (Par 107): **103,102,99,98,97 92,91,86,73,70**
CSF £26.76 CT £123.27 TOTE £6.90: £2.50, £1.80, £2.10; EX 24.20 Trifecta £169.40 Pool: £357.90 - 1.50 winning units..
Owner Middleham Park Racing Xxv **Bred** Minch Bloodstock And Castletown Stud **Trained** Great Habton, N Yorks

FOCUS
Probably just an ordinary handicap for the grade but the form looks solid and should work out. Just as in the previous race, they avoided the far rail in the straight, racing more towards the middle.

NOTEBOOK
Collateral Damage(IRE) showed himself none the worse for a recent fall over hurdles at Wetherby, taking advantage of having dropped to a winning mark to end a losing run stretching back to May 2006. This was a useful effort, but his overall profile suggests he will struggle to follow up. (op 6-1)
Capable Guest(IRE) is an inconsistent sort but, with the visor re-fitted for the first time in three outings, he returned to the sort of form he showed when winning at Kempton two starts back. He was clear of the remainder, but is no sure thing to repeat this next time. (tchd 11-2)
Major Magpie(IRE), off the track since winning off a 3lb lower mark at Haydock last April, made a pleasing return to action. He looked to be going nowhere at the top of the straight, but eventually ran on and was closing at the finish. He looks to have plenty to offer this season provided he stays sound, although he is a candidate for the bounce factor on his next couple of starts. (op 5-1)
Wigwam Willie(IRE) could only keep on at the one pace in the straight. He is entitled to be sharper next time considering this was his first start in over five months and he might benefit from more severe headgear, just to help him focus a little better. (tchd 17-2)
Electric Warrior(IRE), 6lb higher than when winning on the Polytrack at Dundalk on his most recent outing, did not help his chances by racing keenly through the early stages and he could not sustain his effort after swinging very wide into the straight. (tchd 9-1)
Ebert had the headgear left off on his return from a six-month break and he could make no impression. (op 15-2 tchd 8-1 and 10-1 in a place)

1017 JAMAICAN FLIGHT H'CAP 2m 1f 216y
3:45 (3:45) (Class 5) (0-75,75) 4-Y-0+ **£3,238** (£963; £481; £240) **Stalls** Low

Form RPR

-001 **1** **Bugsy's Boy**[25] 754 4-8-10 **65**............(p) RobertWinston 8 77
(P W D'Arcy) *hld up towards rr: hdwy to trck ldrs after 6f: led 1/2-way: rdn 3f out: drvn clr over 1f out: styd on strly* **13/2**[3]

/5-5 **2** 3 **At The Money**[6] 405 5-9-2 **65**............(b[1]) DaleGibson 12 73
(J M P Eustace) *led to 1/2-way: styd cl up: rdn along 4f out: drvn 2f out: kpt on same pce u.p fnl f* **6/1**[2]

116- **3** 5 **Gallileo Figaro (USA)**[7] 6181 5-9-6 **72**............ JerryO'Dwyer(3) 3 74
(N B King) *hld up in midfield: hdwy 1/2-way: chsd ldrs 6f out: rdn along 4f out: drvn along 2f out: plugged on same pce appr fnl f* **6/1**[2]

1412 **4** 1 ½ **Dreams Jewel**[5] 954 8-8-11 **60**............ NeilChalmers 10 60
(C Roberts) *hld up in rr: stdy hdwy 7f out: chsd ldrs 3f out: rdn along 2f out: sn drvn and no imp appr fnl f* **13/2**[3]

500- **5** 14 **Great As Gold (IRE)**[157] 6335 9-9-12 **75**............ TomEaves 2 62+
(B Ellison) *hld up: hdwy 6f out: chsd ldrs 4f out: sn rdn: drvn over 2f out and no imp* **8/1**

560- **6** 5 **Goldan Jess (IRE)**[11] 4423 4-7-8 **56** oh1............ JamieKyne(7) 1 33
(D Carroll) *plld hrd: in tch on inner: rdn along and outpcd 6f out: no ch after* **50/1**

320- **7** 5 **Sweetheart**[43] 6131 4-8-12 **67**............ IanMongan 9 38
(Jamie Poulton) *hld up in rr: hdwy 1/2-way: chsd ldrs 6f out: sn rdn along and wknd over 3f out* **5/2**[1]

/60- **8** 37 **Helvetio**[304] 1300 6-9-10 **73**............ PaulMulrennan 4 —
(Micky Hammond) *prom: rdn along 6f out and sn wknd* **33/1**

100/ **9** 1 ¼ **Fair Spin**[42] 6178 8-8-7 **56** oh9............(p) PaulHanagan 11 —
(Micky Hammond) *in tch: hdwy 1/2-way: chsd ldrs 6f out: rdn along over 4f out and sn wknd* **66/1**

1061 **10** 1 **Three Boars**[5] 954 6-9-6 **74** 6ex............(b) JamieJones(5) 5 —
(S Gollings) *hld up towards rr: sme hdwy over 6f out: rdn along over 4f out and nvr a factor* **12/1**

/023 **11** 28 **Aqua Pura (GER)**[13] 322 9-8-0 **56** oh5............(v) MHarley(7) 6 —
(A P Stringer) *prom: rdn along over 4f out: drvn over 3f out and sn wknd* **14/1**

660- **12** 42 **Oniz Tiptoes (IRE)**[11] 5300 7-8-7 **56** oh9............(v) ChrisCatlin 7 —
(J S Wainwright) *chsd ldrs: lost pl after 6f: bhd fr 1/2-way* **20/1**

4m 14.95s (11.05) **Going Correction** +0.675s/f (Yiel)
WFA 4 from 5yo+ 6lb **12** Ran SP% **120.4**
Speed ratings (Par 103): **102,100,98,97,91 89,87,70,70,69 57,38**
CSF £44.74 CT £251.62 TOTE £8.80: £2.60, £2.50, £1.90; EX 47.30.
Owner Seaton Stud Limited **Bred** Mrs R S Evans **Trained** Newmarket, Suffolk

FOCUS
A modest staying event run at just an even pace. Although several had a chance entering the last half-mile, the first two home were in those positions well before halfway and this proved too much of a test of stamina for many.
Aqua Pura(GER) Official explanation: jockey said gelding had no more to give

1018 EASTER HOLIDAY H'CAP 1m 2f 6y
4:20 (4:20) (Class 2) (0-100,94) 4-Y-0+
£11,217 (£3,358; £1,679; £840; £419; £210) **Stalls** Low

Form RPR

010- **1** **Flying Clarets (IRE)**[150] 6499 5-9-3 **93**............ PaulHanagan 4 108
(R A Fahey) *mde all: sn clr: stdd 1/2-way: rdn and qcknd 2f out: drvn ent fnl f: styd on gamely* **12/1**

064- **2** 2 ½ **Eradicate (IRE)**[172] 5978 4-9-4 **94**............ JoeFanning 2 104
(M Johnston) *chsd wnr: hdwy and cl up 3f out: rdn 2f out and ev ch tl drvn and one pce ins fnl f* **7/2**[2]

416- **3** 3 ½ **Heaven Knows**[136] 6759 5-9-4 **94**............ RHills 1 98
(W J Haggas) *hld up in rr: gd hdwy on inner over 3f out: chsd ldng pair whn rn wd home turn: sn rdn: edgd lft and no imp appr fnl f* **1/1**[1]

150- **4** 8 **Aureate**[53] 4059 4-8-8 **84**............ TomEaves 3 72
(B Ellison) *chsd ldrs: rdn along over 3f out: sn drvn and wknd wl over 1f out* **16/1**

50/6 **5** 3 **Profit's Reality (IRE)**[25] 757 6-9-2 **92**............ IanMongan 5 75
(P A Blockley) *chsd ldrs: pushed along 3f out: rdn over 2f out and sn outpcd* **14/1**

240- **6** 1 ½ **Mull Of Dubai**[187] 5574 5-9-0 **90**............ MickyFenton 6 70
(T P Tate) *chsd ldng pair: pushed along 1/2-way: rdn 3f out and sn wknd* **11/2**[3]

-406 **7** 41 **Speedy Sam**[38] 592 5-8-9 **85**............ FergusSweeney 7 —
(K R Burke) *hld up in rr: sme hdwy 1/2-way: rdn along 3f out and sn wknd* **20/1**

2m 18.16s (4.46) **Going Correction** +0.675s/f (Yiel) **7** Ran SP% **112.6**
Speed ratings (Par 109): **109,107,104,97,95 94,61**
CSF £51.87 TOTE £13.40: £4.90, £2.20; EX 77.00.
Owner The Matthewman Partnership **Bred** Gabriel Bell **Trained** Musley Bank, N Yorks

FOCUS
A decent-looking handicap run at a fair pace. The form looks sound for the conditions.

NOTEBOOK
Flying Clarets(IRE), who has an excellent record fresh, got an uncontested lead and kept on gamely when strongly pressed by Eradicate in the latter stages. She had not won two races in succession in 32 previous starts, so is not one to follow at a short price next time despite her obvious toughness. Connections are hoping to run her in a Listed event at Dundalk next week; the race Anna Pavlova won last season when the race was run at Navan. (op 16-1)
Eradicate(IRE), gelded since last season, looked all set to make a winning reappearance as he drew alongside Flying Clarets, but was unable to get past the winner. It was a good effort and he can build on it, despite being only fairly handicapped (tchd 4-1)
Heaven Knows, who had been aimed at the Lincoln but failed to get a run, travelled nicely behind the pace but could not raise an effort when asked to quicken up the home straight. Gelded since last season, he looks to be more effective when handicapped under a mark of 90. (tchd 10-11 and 11-10 in places)
Aureate, who has been showing a bit of promise over hurdles during the winter, got outpaced about three furlongs from home and steadily weakened. His sole victory in handicap company came off a 5lb lower mark. (op 14-1)
Profit's Reality(IRE) is not really up to this grade (all of his wins have come in class 3 races or below) and was readily left behind when the race took shape. (op 8-1)
Mull Of Dubai, having his first start for a new trainer, is not well handicapped and ran accordingly. He needs to come down the weights quite a bit before being of serious interest. (op 8-1)

1019 AUNTIE MARGARET'S 75TH BIRTHDAY MAIDEN FILLIES' STKS 6f
4:50 (4:51) (Class 5) 3-Y-O **£3,238** (£963; £481; £240) **Stalls** Low

Form RPR

1 **Khazina (USA)** 3-9-0 0............ LiamJones 1 66+
(C E Brittain) *in tch on inner: gd hdwy over 2f out: rdn to chal enetering fnl f: sn led: drvn and kpt on towards fin ish* **5/1**[3]

443- **2** nk **Everything**[210] 4923 3-9-0 70............ MickyFenton 14 65
(P T Midgley) *cl up: led 1/2-way: rdn and hung lft over 1f out and again ins fnl f: sn hdd: kpt on wl u.p towards fin* **9/2**[2]

0-53 **3** 1 **Precipice**[5] 953 3-9-0 78............ DanielTudhope 5 62
(D Carroll) *hld up in tch: hdwy and n.m.r 2f out: sn rdn and styd on ins fnl f* **4/1**[1]

4 ½ **Deep Winter** 3-9-0 0............ PaulHanagan 10 61
(R A Fahey) *midfield: hdwy on outer 1/2-way: rdn and edgd lft over 1f out: kpt on wl fnl f: nrst fin* **8/1**

5 shd **Leonid Glow** 3-8-7 0............ JohnCavanagh(7) 9 60+
(M Dods) *s.i.s and bhd: hdwy 2f out: swtchd lft and styd on strly ins fnl f: nrst fin* **66/1**

- **6** ¾ **Milton Of Campsie** 3-9-0 0............ ChrisCatlin 12 58+
(S Parr) *trckd ldrs: effrt whn rn green and outpcd 2f out: sn rdn and kpt on ins fnl f* **5/1**[3]

7 2 ¾ **Offshore Anna (IRE)** 3-9-0 0............ PaulMulrennan 4 50+
(J J Quinn) *rr: hdwy 2f out: styd on ins fnl f: nrst fin* **25/1**

50- **8** nse **Piverina (IRE)**[158] 6306 3-9-0 0............ PaulFessey 2 50+
(T D Barron) *s.i.s: a in rr* **14/1**

-324 **9** 5 **Jazenio**[27] 721 3-9-0 61............ NCallan 8 35
(K A Ryan) *t.k.h: chsd ldrs: effrt and ev ch whn edgd rt 2f out: sn rdn and wknd over 1f out* **10/1**

0- **10** 2 ¼ **Bahamian Princess**[186] 5603 3-8-11 0............ RussellKennemore(3) 7 28
(R Hollinshead) *t.k.h: in tch: rdn along over 2f out and sn wknd* **40/1**

11 14 **Lovely Lilling** 3-8-11 0............ JamieMoriarty(3) 3 —
(P T Midgley) *a towards rr* **80/1**

540- **12** 5 **Musical Charm (IRE)**[225] 4459 3-9-0 68............ RobertWinston 16 —
(T D Easterby) *chsd ldrs: rdn along 3f out: wkng whn hmpd 2f out* **11/1**

4 **13** 1 ¼ **Wildcat Island (IRE)**[35] 616 3-9-0 0............ DavidAllan 6 —
(T D Easterby) *in rr: rdn along 1/2-way: a bhd* **28/1**

0- **14** 5 **Fizzy Lover**[342] 1087 3-8-11 0............ DuranFentiman(3) 13 —
(T D Easterby) *t.k.h: a towards rr* **66/1**

5 **15** 5 **Many Welcomes**[27] 721 3-9-0 0............ AndrewElliott 15 —
(B P J Baugh) *a in rr: bhd fr 1/2-way* **50/1**

0 **16** 5 **Notforloveormoney**[29] 700 3-9-0 0............ RobertHavlin 11 —
(A G Foster) *led to 1/2-way: rdn along and wkng whn hmpd 2f out and sn bhd* **100/1**

1m 22.09s (5.19) **Going Correction** +0.675s/f (Yiel) **16** Ran SP% **123.6**
Speed ratings (Par 95): **92,91,90,89,89 88,84,84,78,75 56,49,48,41,34 28**
CSF £26.88 TOTE £7.20: £3.10, £2.30, £1.70; EX 28.00.
Owner Saeed Manana **Bred** Jayeff 'B' Stables **Trained** Newmarket, Suffolk

FOCUS
A real mixed bunch. The runner-up and third do not look up to their official marks, but set the standard and quite a few in the race shaped with promise. The winning time was 0.71 seconds slower than the earlier older-horse 56-70 handicap.
Lovely Lilling Official explanation: jockey said filly had run green
Musical Charm(IRE) Official explanation: jockey said filly had no more to give

1020 PONTEFRACT APPRENTICE SERIES (ROUND ONE) H'CAP 1m 4f 8y
5:20 (5:20) (Class 5) (0-75,75) 4-Y-O+ **£3,238** (£963; £481; £240) **Stalls** Low

Form RPR

4331 **1** **Red Wine**[3] 963 9-9-0 **68** 6ex............ StacyRenwick 7 75
(A J McCabe) *hld up in rr: hdwy over 2f out: str run ent fnl f: styd on wl to ld nr fin* **9/4**[2]

613- **2** ½ **Riguez Dancer**[2] 5197 4-9-0 **70**............ DeanHeslop 4 76
(P C Haslam) *trckd ldng pair: hdwy and cl up 3f out: rdn to ld 1 1/2f out: sn jnd and drvn ins fnl f: hdd and no ex towards fin* **11/10**[1]

126- **3** 2 ¼ **Charlotte Vale**[73] 3719 7-9-4 **75**............ BMcHugh(3) 2 78
(Micky Hammond) *sn led: hdd 1/2-way: styd cl up: rdn to chal over 1f out and ev ch tl drvn and wknd wl ins fnl f* **13/2**[3]

-042 **4** *5* **Kylkenny**[14] 847 13-8-0 **61** oh7.......................................(t) RyanClark(7) 3 56
(H Morrison) *trckd ldr: led 1/2-way: rdn over 2f out: hdd 1 1/2f out and sn wknd* **9/1**

20/6 **5** *5* **Nessen Dorma (IRE)**[33] 638 7-8-8 **65**....................(v) JamesRogers(3) 6 53
(J S Wainwright) *a towards rr* **16/1**

0515 **6** *1 1/2* **Atlantic Gamble (IRE)**[13] 859 8-8-7 **61** oh4.............(p) DeclanCannon 1 46
(K R Burke) *trckd ldrs: effrt 3f out: sn rdn and wknd* **20/1**

2m 52.17s (11.37) **Going Correction** +0.675s/f (Yiel)
WFA 4 from 7yo+ 2lb **6** Ran SP% **112.4**
Speed ratings (Par 103): **89,88,87,83,80 79**
CSF £5.10 TOTE £3.00: £1.70, £1.20; EX 5.60 Place 6 £51.76, Place 5 £40.90.
Owner Paul J Dixon **Bred** Genesis Green Stud Ltd **Trained** Babworth, Notts

FOCUS
Restricted to apprentices who had not ridden more than ten winners. A moderate winning time for the class of contest. The runner-up has been in good form and looks to uphold the form which looks solid at this level.
T/Jkpt: Not won. T/Plt: £83.10 to a £1 stake. Pool: £77,396.55. 679.80 winning tickets. T/Qpdt: £33.00 to a £1 stake. Pool: £3,783.10. 84.65 winning tickets. JR

949 SOUTHWELL (L-H)
Wednesday, March 26

OFFICIAL GOING: Standard
Wind: virtually nil Weather: dull and overcast

1021 RACEHORSE OWNERSHIP WITH HAMBLETON RACING FILLIES' H'CAP 5f (F)
2:20 (2:20) (Class 5) (0-70,70) 4-Y-O+ **£3,238** (£963; £481; £240) **Stalls** High

Form RPR

3134 **1** **Cerebus**[14] 850 6-9-1 **70**.........................(bt) WilliamBuick(3) 5 83
(A J McCabe) *w ldr tl rdn to ld wl over 1f out: clr ins fnl f: comf* **2/1**[1]

610- **2** *1 1/4* **Tilly's Dream**[107] 7105 5-9-4 **70**.............................. AdamKirby 2 78
(G C Bravery) *trckd ldng pair: rdn and effrt over 1f out: chsd wnr ins fnl f: kpt on but nt pce to trble wnr* **4/1**[3]

30-1 **3** *2 1/4* **Rann Na Cille (IRE)**[28] 719 4-8-8 **60**.................... MickyFenton 4 60
(P T Midgley) *short of room sn after s: in tch: rdn 1/2-way: kpt on to go 3rd ins fnl f: nt trble ldng pair* **5/1**

020- **4** *1 1/4* **Coconut Moon**[179] 5806 6-9-1 **67**.............................. NCallan 3 62
(E J Alston) *led: rdn over 2f out: hdd wl over 1f out: wknd ins fnl f* **9/4**[2]

0451 **5** *shd* **Wibbadune (IRE)**[12] 883 4-8-0 **59** oh6 ow3......(v[1]) PatrickDonaghy(7) 1 54
(D Shaw) *a in last pair: rdn 1/2-way: no imp whn rdr dropped whip 1f out* **12/1**

60.02 secs (0.32) **Going Correction** +0.075s/f (Slow) **5** Ran SP% **108.5**
Speed ratings (Par 100): **100,98,94,92,92**
CSF £9.87 TOTE £2.90: £1.60, £3.20; EX 8.40.
Owner Paul J Dixon **Bred** Rookley Holdings **Trained** Babworth, Notts

FOCUS
A modest-looking event, in which the winner dominated from halfway. However, less than 5l covered the whole field and, although the race could be rated higher, the fourth is the best guide for now.
Wibbadune(IRE) Official explanation: jockey said filly hung left

1022 SMALL & FRIENDLY SYNDICATES WITH HAMBLETON CLAIMING STKS 5f (F)
2:50 (2:50) (Class 5) 4-Y-O+ **£3,238** (£963; £481; £240) **Stalls** High

Form RPR

500- **1** **Fire Up The Band**[190] 5505 9-9-5 83........................ AdrianTNicholls 4 72+
(D Nicholls) *mde all: pushed clr over 1f out: easily* **7/4**[2]

0306 **2** *1 3/4* **Regal Royale**[7] 933 5-9-0 53..............................(v) AdamKirby 2 61
(Peter Grayson) *sn drvn along: in tch: chsd wnr 1/2-way: one pce* **25/1**

1322 **3** *2* **Savile's Delight (IRE)**[6] 951 9-8-11 70.................. RichardKingscote 3 51+
(Tom Dascombe) *bhd: shkn up over 2f out: sn hung lft: kpt on to go 3rd nr fin: n.d* **1/1**[1]

0126 **4** *1/2* **Guto**[22] 786 5-8-8 64.. KellyHarrison(5) 1 51
(W J H Ratcliffe) *chsd wnr tl 1/2-way: sn rdn: wknd over 1f out* **9/2**[3]

59.32 secs (-0.38) **Going Correction** +0.075s/f (Slow) **4** Ran SP% **108.4**
Speed ratings (Par 103): **106,103,100,99**
CSF £23.90 TOTE £2.00; EX 21.30.
Owner A Barker D Nicholls & S A Short **Bred** Miss A J Rawding And P M Crane **Trained** Sessay, N Yorks

FOCUS
The race was as good as over from halfway, as the winner always held a clear lead advantage as his rivals toiled. The form looks uninformative as Fire Up The Band is different class to this lot at his best and did not run up to his mark.
Savile's Delight(IRE) Official explanation: jockey had no explanation for the poor form shown

1023 HAMBLETONRACING.CO.UK H'CAP 6f (F)
3:25 (3:25) (Class 4) (0-85,82) 4-Y-O+ **£4,533** (£1,348; £674; £336) **Stalls** Low

Form RPR

3111 **1** **Came Back (IRE)**[12] 887 5-9-4 **82**.............................. NCallan 5 98+
(K A Ryan) *t.k.h: chsd ldr tl led 2f out: sn rdn clr: edgd rt fnl f: readily* **1/1**[1]

122 **2** *2 3/4* **Dickie Le Davoir**[21] 801 4-8-10 **74**........................... ChrisCatlin 3 79
(John A Harris) *chsd ldrs: rdn 3f out: kpt on u.p to chse wnr ins fnl f: nvr pce to chal* **11/4**[2]

6250 **3** *3/4* **Memphis Man**[19] 824 5-8-6 **70**.............................. SaleemGolam 2 73
(P D Evans) *taken down early: s.i.s: hld up in rr: rdn and effrt jst over 2f out: kpt on to go 3rd wl ins fnl f: nvr nr wnr* **15/2**[3]

000- **4** *3/4* **Total Impact**[204] 5119 5-8-13 **77**.............................. PaulHanagan 6 78
(R A Fahey) *led: rdn and hdd 2f out: outpcd by wnr over 1f out: kpt on* **10/1**

400- **5** *1 1/2* **Mandarin Spirit (IRE)**[121] 6949 8-8-6 **70**..................... TomEaves 4 66
(G C H Chung) *chsd ldrs: rdn over 2f out: outpcd wl over 1f out: no ch after* **12/1**

5336 **6** *8* **Chjimes (IRE)**[21] 801 4-8-10 **74**........................... RobertWinston 1 46
(C R Dore) *in tch: rdn over 3f out: wknd 2f out: eased whn no ch ins fnl f* **12/1**

1m 15.27s (-1.23) **Going Correction** -0.075s/f (Stan) **6** Ran SP% **112.9**
Speed ratings (Par 105): **105,101,100,99,97 86**
CSF £3.96 TOTE £1.80: £1.40, £1.60; EX 4.00.
Owner Mrs Ger O'Driscoll **Bred** Yeomanstown Stud **Trained** Hambleton, N Yorks

FOCUS
In-form Came Back won nicely, but probably did not need to run to his official mark to win. The runner-up sets the standard.

1024 OWN A RACEHORSE WITH HAMBLETON RACING H'CAP 7f (F)
4:00 (4:00) (Class 6) (0-60,59) 4-Y-O+ **£1,943** (£578; £288; £144) **Stalls** Low

Form RPR

3206 **1** **Elusive Warrior (USA)**[13] 868 5-8-9 **50**....................(p) NeilPollard 9 65+
(A J McCabe) *chsd ldr tl led 3f out: clr and rdn over 2f out: styd on wl* **16/1**

6413 **2** *1 3/4* **The Geester**[14] 858 4-9-0 **55**..............................(b) PhillipMakin 8 65
(S R Bowring) *plld hrd: hld up in tch: rdn and effrt over 2f out: chsd wnr 1f out: kpt on but nvr able to chal* **3/1**[1]

0433 **3** *1 1/4* **Owed**[15] 846 6-9-4 **59**...(tp) PatCosgrave 3 66
(R Bastiman) *racd in midfield: rdn and outpcd 4f out: hdwy 2f out: wnt 3rd ins fnl f: kpt on: nvr able to chal* **4/1**[2]

-514 **4** *5* **Magic Amour**[36] 615 10-9-1 **56**..................(b) StephenDonohoe 10 49
(P A Blockley) *taken down early: s.i.s: sn rcvrd and chsd ldrs: rdn to chse wnr wl over 2f out: no imp: lost 2 pls fnl f* **10/1**

5-55 **5** *hd* **Tour D'Amour (IRE)**[47] 478 5-8-5 **51**..................(b) KellyHarrison(5) 11 44
(R Craggs) *sn bhd: rdn 4f out: styd on fnl f: nvr nr ldrs* **8/1**

4054 **6** *shd* **Imperial Sword**[22] 790 5-8-6 **47**.............................. PaulFessey 6 39
(T D Barron) *bhd and sn rdn along: styd on fnl f: nvr nr ldrs* **12/1**

4310 **7** *1 1/4* **Guadaloup**[14] 861 6-8-9 **53**.............................. MarkLawson(3) 7 42
(M Brittain) *a bhd: effrt u.p on inner over 2f out: nvr on terms* **15/2**

6212 **8** *2 1/2* **Sion Hill (IRE)**[21] 795 7-9-0 **55**..............................(p) MickyFenton 1 37
(John A Harris) *led tl 3f out: sn wanting to hang rt and btn* **10/1**

5630 **9** *1 1/2* **Buzzin'Boyzee (IRE)**[14] 861 5-8-7 **55**................. RichardEvans(7) 4 33
(P D Evans) *s.i.s: a bhd* **22/1**

5405 **10** *1 1/4* **Johnston's Glory (IRE)**[18] 837 4-8-13 **54**....................... NCallan 2 29
(E J Alston) *t.k.h: chsd ldrs tl 3f out: rdn 2f out: sn wknd* **6/1**[3]

000- **11** *33* **Vibrato (USA)**[239] 4042 6-8-8 **49**.............................. DavidAllan 5 —
(C J Teague) *v.s.a: a t.o* **40/1**

1m 29.52s (-0.78) **Going Correction** -0.075s/f (Stan) **11** Ran SP% **120.7**
Speed ratings (Par 101): **101,99,97,91,91 91,90,87,85,84 46**
CSF £65.43 CT £243.89 TOTE £22.80: £9.30, £1.10, £2.20; EX 125.40 Trifecta £253.10 Pool: £499.09, 1.40 winning units.
Owner Paul J Dixon & Brian Morton **Bred** Steve Peskoff **Trained** Babworth, Notts

FOCUS
A moderate handicap, run at a fair pace. The form is set by the second and third and looks solid.
Guadaloup Official explanation: jockey said mare was unsuited by the kick-back
Sion Hill(IRE) Official explanation: jockey said gelding hung right

1025 CALL HAMBLETON RACING ON 0800 321 3271 CLASSIFIED STKS 1m (F)
4:35 (4:36) (Class 7) 4-Y-O+ **£1,295** (£385; £192; £96) **Stalls** Low

Form RPR

065- **1** **Bert's Memory**[26] 7201 4-9-0 45..............................(p) NCallan 13 49
(J Mackie) *sn bustled along to chse ldr tl 3f out and again over 2f out: kpt on wl u.p to ld towards fin* **8/1**

6223 **2** *nk* **Keon (IRE)**[4] 972 6-8-11 43..................(p) RussellKennemore(3) 7 48
(R Hollinshead) *taken down early: hld up in bhd ldrs: hdwy to ld 3f out: sn drvn: kpt on tl hdd and no ex towards fin* **11/4**[1]

0305 **3** *1/2* **Shifty**[13] 863 9-9-0 43.. DanielTudhope 11 47
(Jedd O'Keeffe) *in tch: hdwy on outer over 3f out: kpt on u.p fr over 1f out: nvr quite getting to ldng pair* **5/1**[2]

644 **4** *3/4* **Cape Dancer (IRE)**[21] 804 4-8-11 41.................. PJMcDonald(3) 12 45
(J S Wainwright) *chsd ldrs tl lost pl 4f out: rallied u.p over 1f out: kpt on but nt able to chal* **9/1**

/000 **5** *1/2* **Tribiani (IRE)**[40] 578 4-9-0 40.............................. StephenDonohoe 14 44
(P A Blockley) *taken down early: s.i.s: rdn and hdwy over 3f out: kpt on u.p but nt pce to chal* **14/1**

0053 **6** *3/4* **Moorside Diamond**[19] 821 4-9-0 37.............................. AndrewElliott 4 43
(A D Brown) *in tch in midfield: hdwy to chse ldrs 3f out: kpt on same pce u.p fr over 1f out* **25/1**

6/00 **7** *hd* **Shami**[9] 916 9-8-7 40...(bt) DeanHeslop(7) 6 42+
(Mrs R A Carr) *s.i.s: wl bhd tl r.o fr over 1f out: nvr able to chal* **33/1**

00-6 **8** *3 1/4* **Beamsley Beacon**[14] 857 7-9-0 45..........................(b) RobertWinston 5 35
(Miss Tracy Waggott) *t.k.h: led tl 3f out: wknd over 2f out* **20/1**

0/00 **9** *3 1/2* **Art Historian (IRE)**[60] 323 5-9-0 43.............................. PaulFitzsimons 2 27
(E G Bevan) *chsd ldrs: rdn and struggling 3f out: no ch last 2f* **20/1**

00-4 **10** *nk* **Rawaabet (IRE)**[55] 299 6-9-0 43.............................. ChrisCatlin 1 27
(P W Hiatt) *s.i.s: sn swtchd to outer: n.d* **11/2**[3]

00-0 **11** *1/2* **The London Gang**[25] 770 5-9-0 42..........................(b) HayleyTurner 8 25
(W M Brisbourne) *racd in midfield: rdn 4f out: sme hdwy wl over 2f out: wknd wl over 1f out* **14/1**

53-0 **12** *2* **Falimar**[13] 863 4-8-9 45.. KellyHarrison(5) 9 21
(C W Fairhurst) *bhd: rdn 4f out: nvr on terms* **8/1**

13 *20* **Conrendelo (IRE)**[168] 6111 6-8-11 37.................. JerryO'Dwyer(3) 10 —
(Adrian Sexton, Ire) *s.i.s: sn rdn and wl bhd: t.o last 2f* **16/1**

000- **14** *19* **Flaming Cat (IRE)**[182] 5739 5-9-0 45.............................. PaulHanagan 3 —
(F Watson) *chsd ldrs for over 1f: sn struggling: t.o last 2f* **33/1**

1m 44.19s (0.49) **Going Correction** -0.075s/f (Stan) **14** Ran SP% **129.4**
Speed ratings (Par 97): **94,93,93,92,91 91,91,87,84,83 83,81,61,42**
CSF £30.45 TOTE £12.00: £2.60, £1.60, £3.00; EX 37.00 Trifecta £125.20 Pool: £294.52, 1.67 winning units.
Owner D Fower & N J Titterton **Bred** D Fower And N J Titterton **Trained** Church Broughton , Derbys

FOCUS
A typically very weak affair for the class. The first seven were fairly closely covered at the finish and the principals set the level.
Rawaabet(IRE) Official explanation: jockey said gelding missed the break
Conrendelo(IRE) Official explanation: jockey said mare never travelled

1026 ENJOY HAMBLETON RACING'S SOLE OWNER SERVICE H'CAP 1m 4f (F)
5:10 (5:10) (Class 4) (0-85,83) 4-Y-O+ **£4,533** (£1,348; £674; £336) **Stalls** Low

Form RPR

1-30 **1** **Tartan Tie**[60] 315 4-9-4 **83**.............................. JoeFanning 8 93+
(M Johnston) *mde all: jnd 3f out: rdn and edgd rt wl over 1f out: drew clr fnl f: styd on strly* **4/1**[2]

1310 **2** *2 3/4* **Bentley Brook (IRE)**[18] 838 6-9-2 **79**.................. StephenDonohoe 2 83
(P A Blockley) *hld up wl in tch: hdwy to chse ldng pair 3f out: chsd wnr u.p 1f out: no imp* **8/1**

032- **3** *2 3/4* **Putra Square**[164] 6211 4-8-10 **75**.............................. NCallan 5 75
(P F I Cole) *t.k.h: chsd ldrs: upsides 3f out: rdn and carried rt briefly wl over 1f out: wknd fnl f* **6/1**[3]

-241 **4** *4* **Jackie Kiely**[55] 368 7-8-12 **75**....................(t) J-PGuillambert 4 69
(R Brotherton) *stdd s: hld up in tch: rdn and effrt over 3f out: no hdwy last 2f* **16/1**

100- **5** *¾* **Rock 'N' Roller (FR)**[167] 6131 4-8-9 **74**.................... HayleyTurner 1 67
(W R Muir) *chsd ldrs: rdn over 4f out: wknd wl over 2f out* **20/1**

-311 **6** *5* **They All Laughed**[14] 854 5-8-13 **76**.................... ChrisCatlin 3 61
(P W Hiatt) *hld up in tch: rdn and effrt on outer over 3f out: wl hld last 2f* **13/2**

003- **7** *9* **Sahrati**[179] 5805 4-8-8 **73**.................... RobertWinston 7 45
(C E Brittain) *hld up in tch: rdn and lost pl 4f out: no ch last 3f* **13/8**[1]

354- **8** *3 ¼* **Shape Up (IRE)**[281] 2743 8-8-9 **72**....................(b) PaulMulrennan 6 39
(R Craggs) *t.k.h: trckd ldrs: rdn 3f out: sn btn: t.o* **33/1**

600- **9** *5* **Vacation (IRE)**[212] 4888 5-9-6 **83**.................... PaulDoe 9 42
(S Curran) *a last: lost tch over 3f out: t.o* **14/1**

2m 38.38s (-2.62) **Going Correction** -0.075s/f (Stan)
WFA 4 from 5yo+ 2lb **9** Ran SP% **117.1**
Speed ratings (Par 105): **105,103,101,98,98 94,88,86,83**
CSF £36.48 CT £191.65 TOTE £5.50: £1.50, £3.10, £2.60; EX 29.20 Trifecta £287.10 Pool: £, winning units.
Owner Mrs I Bird **Bred** D G Hardisty Bloodstock & Marston Stud **Trained** Middleham Moor, N Yorks

FOCUS
A decent middle-distance handicap featuring several course winners and the pace was an even one. This looks solid and reliable Fibresand form, rated through the runner-up.
Sahrati Official explanation: jockey said colt never travelled

1027 REGISTER YOUR INTEREST @ HAMBLETONRACING.CO.UK MAIDEN STKS 5f (F)
5:40 (5:40) (Class 5) 3-Y-O+ **£2,914** (£867; £433; £216) **Stalls** High

Form RPR

1 **Little Eden (IRE)** 3-9-0 0.................... PhillipMakin 4 67+
(T D Barron) *in tch: rdn and hdwy over 1f out: qckna to ld ins fnl f: sn clr: readily* **11/2**[2]

225- **2** *2 ¼* **Tugalu (IRE)**[174] 5931 3-9-0 75.................... NCallan 1 56+
(K A Ryan) *wnt lft s: t.k.h: chsd ldrs: wnt 2nd over 3f out: ev ch 2f out: sn drvn: nt pce of wnr ins fnl f* **1/2**[1]

-500 **3** *¾* **Princess Charlmane (IRE)**[13] 871 5-9-7 37....................(t) MickyFenton 6 46
(C J Teague) *led: rdn wl over 1f out: hdd ins fnl f: outpcd by wnr* **40/1**

0- **4** *1 ¼* **Millie's Rock (IRE)**[140] 6723 3-8-9 0.................... PaulMulrennan 2 37+
(M J Wallace) *s.i.s: sn bustled along: chsd ldrs: rdn wl over 1f out: outpcd over 1f out* **9/1**

0 **5** *1* **Big Boom**[29] 706 3-9-0 0.................... PatCosgrave 5 38+
(M J Wallace) *v.s.a: rn green and sn bhd: rdn and edgd lft last 2f: kpt on but nvr able to chal* **20/1**

056- **6** *3 ½* **My Kaiser Chief**[90] 7243 3-8-11 62.................... AndrewMullen(3) 3 26
(W J H Ratcliffe) *chsd ldr tl over 3f out: sn rdn: wknd wl over 1f out* **13/2**[3]

60.60 secs (0.90) **Going Correction** +0.075s/f (Slow)
WFA 3 from 5yo 12lb **6** Ran SP% **112.6**
Speed ratings (Par 103): **95,91,90,88,86 81**
CSF £8.78 TOTE £6.30: £2.90, £1.20; EX 16.40 Place 6 £ 40.13, Place 5 £ 21.34.
Owner Clive Washbourn **Bred** Harrowgate Bloodstock Ltd **Trained** Maunby, N Yorks

FOCUS
A moderate sprint maiden. The debutant winner is value for a little further, but the 37-rated third puts the form into perspective.
T/Plt: £72.20 to a £1 stake. Pool: £55,497.20. 561.10 winning tickets. T/Qpdt: £19.00 to a £1 stake. Pool: £3,434.50. 133.55 winning tickets. SP

971 WOLVERHAMPTON (A.W) (L-H)
Wednesday, March 26

OFFICIAL GOING: Standard
Wind: Nil Weather: Fine

1028 BE BESIDE THE SEASIDE @ PONTIN'S H'CAP 5f 20y(P)
6:50 (6:51) (Class 6) (0-55,60) 4-Y-O+ **£2,047** (£604; £302) **Stalls** Low

Form RPR

3544 **1** **Taboor (IRE)**[14] 857 10-8-3 **47**....................(p) KirstyMilczarek(3) 2 61
(R M H Cowell) *hld up: hdwy wl over 1f out: rdn to ld ins fnl f: edgd lft: r.o wl* **10/1**

0463 **2** *2 ¼* **Bentley**[4] 971 4-8-9 **53**....................(v) TolleyDean(3) 1 59
(D Shaw) *led 1f: a.p: rdn and wnt 2nd 2f out: r.o one pce fnl f* **4/1**[3]

-242 **3** *nk* **Twinned (IRE)**[31] 690 5-8-12 **53**.................... AdamKirby 3 58
(Mike Murphy) *a.p: rdn and ev ch ins fnl f: nt qckn* **3/1**[2]

1151 **4** *shd* **Blackheath (IRE)**[4] 971 12-9-0 **60** 6ex.................... KellyHarrison(5) 7 65
(S T Mason) *hld up: hdwy on outside 2f out: rdn over 1f out: kpt on same pce fnl f* **7/4**[1]

4241 **5** *1 ½* **Now You See Me**[14] 857 4-8-11 **52**.................... AlanMunro 4 51
(K McAuliffe) *hung rt thrght: plld hrd in rr: r.o ins fnl f: nrst fin* **7/1**

0205 **6** *¾* **Monashee Brave (IRE)**[12] 884 5-9-0 **55**....................(tp) AmirQuinn 5 51
(M A Allen) *led after 1f: rdn wl over 1f out: hdd & wknd ins fnl f* **14/1**

0202 **7** *1* **White Ledger (IRE)**[14] 857 9-8-9 **50**.................... TomEaves 6 43
(R E Peacock) *prom tl wknd 2f out* **16/1**

0060 **8** *3 ½* **Ace Club**[51] 437 7-8-11 **52**....................(b) FergalLynch 9 32+
(Garry Moss) *w ldrs over 2f: wkng whn n.m.r wl over 1f out* **25/1**

00-0 **9** *¾* **Lithaam (IRE)**[4] 971 4-8-13 **54**.................... PaulFitzsimons 8 32
(J M Bradley) *s.i.s: a in rr* **50/1**

61.84 secs (-0.46) **Going Correction** -0.075s/f (Stan) **9** Ran SP% **121.3**
Speed ratings (Par 101): **100,96,95,95,93 92,90,84,83**
CSF £52.41 CT £146.59 TOTE £7.70: £2.70, £1.30, £1.50; EX 39.60.
Owner T W Morley **Bred** Rathasker Stud **Trained** Six Mile Bottom, Cambs
■ Stewards' Enquiry : Kelly Harrison one-day ban: careless riding (Apr 9); further caution: careless riding

FOCUS
Ordinary handicap form rated around the third.
Now You See Me Official explanation: jockey said, regarding running and riding, his orders were to get a lead into the straight and to go on and win, adding that the filly raced keenly early and then hung badly right all the way round the bend being unable to ride out in the straight until the furlong mark, when he had been able to pull out, taking it off the heels of the other runners; trainer confirmed, adding that the filly is very tricky at home and is ponied everywhere

1029 SPONSOR A RACE BY CALLING 01902 390009 H'CAP 7f 32y(P)
7:20 (7:21) (Class 6) (0-52,52) 4-Y-O+ **£2,047** (£604; £302) **Stalls** High

Form RPR

00-1 **1** **Playtotheaudience**[14] 861 5-8-12 **52**....................(v) PaulHanagan 4 68+
(R A Fahey) *hld up in mid-div: hdwy over 3f out: rdn to ld ins fnl f: r.o wl* **11/4**[1]

000- **2** *3 ¼* **Optical Illusion (USA)**[184] 5678 4-8-12 **52**.................... TomEaves 11 59
(Miss L A Perratt) *hld up in mid-div: hdwy over 2f out: hung lft fr wl over 1f out: sn rdn: r.o to take 2nd last strides* **14/1**

6112 **3** *nk* **Marmooq**[11] 898 5-8-10 **50**....................(e) IanMongan 8 56
(M J Attwater) *chsd ldrs: led wl over 1f out: sn rdn: hdd and no ex ins fnl f* **11/4**[1]

0-02 **4** *2 ¼* **Silidan**[23] 781 5-8-5 **52**.................... AdamCarter(7) 2 52
(M Brittain) *led after 1f: rdn and hdd wl over 1f out: wknd wl ins fnl f* **16/1**

235- **4** *dht* **Al Rayanah**[135] 6796 5-9-0 **52**.................... WilliamBuick(3) 9 52
(G Prodromou) *s.i.s: in rr: c v wd st: hdwy fnl f: nrst fin* **8/1**[2]

0040 **6** *3* **Zorn**[7] 933 9-8-8 **48**.................... HayleyTurner 1 40
(P Howling) *led 1f: prom tl wknd over 2f out* **18/1**

00-0 **7** *hd* **Bodden Bay**[43] 528 6-8-10 **50**.................... DanielTudhope 6 41
(I W McInnes) *prom: lost pl over 3f out: n.d after* **18/1**

3360 **8** *¾* **Plateau**[14] 858 9-8-10 **50**.................... RobertWinston 5 39+
(C R Dore) *t.k.h in rr: rdn over 2f out: n.m.r 1f out: n.d* **8/1**[2]

304- **9** *2 ¼* **Rapid Flow**[107] 7103 6-8-9 **49**.................... TGMcLaughlin 3 32
(J W Unett) *s.i.s: nt clr run on ins over 2f out: hdwy on ins wl over 1f out: wknd fnl f* **14/1**

0-05 **10** *½* **Just Spike**[28] 718 5-8-10 **50**.................... AndrewElliott 7 32
(B P J Baugh) *hld up in mid-div: hdwy over 2f out: rdn and wknd over 1f out* **14/1**

460- **11** *2 ¼* **Just Oscar (GER)**[148] 6567 4-8-12 **52**.................... DavidAllan 10 28
(W M Brisbourne) *t.k.h in rr: rdn over 2f out: no rspnse* **10/1**[3]

20-0 **12** *1* **Prince Of Gold**[83] 32 8-8-12 **52**....................(b) FergusSweeney 12 25
(Ms N M Hugo) *s.i.s: rdn over 2f out: a bhd* **20/1**

1m 28.87s (-0.73) **Going Correction** -0.075s/f (Stan) **12** Ran SP% **125.8**
Speed ratings (Par 101): **101,97,96,94,94 90,90,89,87,86 84,83**
CSF £50.13 CT £123.86 TOTE £3.80: £1.20, £5.40, £1.60; EX 47.00.
Owner David M Knaggs & Mel Roberts **Bred** Dunchurch Lodge Stud Co **Trained** Musley Bank, N Yorks
■ Stewards' Enquiry : Adam Carter three-day ban: failed to ride out four outright fourth place (Apr 9-11)

FOCUS
Solid form rated through the third, fourth and fifth. Playtotheaudience built on the level of his recent win.

1030 ROCK AROUND THE CROC @ PONTIN'S H'CAP 1m 141y(P)
7:50 (7:50) (Class 5) (0-75,73) 4-Y-O+ **£2,730** (£806; £403) **Stalls** Low

Form RPR

4315 **1** **Justcallmehandsome**[27] 730 6-8-7 **69**....................(v) BillyCray(7) 5 79
(D J S Ffrench Davis) *sn chsng ldr: led over 2f out: clr wl over 1f out: rdn out* **7/1**[3]

6-13 **2** *1 ¾* **Yes One (IRE)**[14] 852 4-9-2 **71**.................... FergalLynch 1 77
(K A Ryan) *hld up in mid-div: hdwy over 2f out: chsd wnr jst over 1f out: edgd lft ins fnl f: kpt on: nt trble wnr* **7/4**[1]

50-0 **3** *1 ¼* **Harare**[18] 833 7-9-4 **73**....................(v) GeorgeBaker 2 76
(R J Price) *hld up and bhd: hdwy 1f out: sn hung lft: kpt on towards fin* **15/2**

35-0 **4** *2* **Timber Treasure (USA)**[14] 860 4-9-1 **70**.................... ChrisCatlin 3 69
(Paul Green) *hld up in tch: hmpd after 1f: rdn wl over 1f out: one pce* **20/1**

6-04 **5** *2 ½* **Zennerman (IRE)**[9] 914 5-8-5 **65**....................(v[1]) KellyHarrison(5) 6 59
(Miss J E Foster) *sn led: hdd over 2f out: wknd ins fnl f* **33/1**

0-43 **6** *2 ¼* **Not Another Cat (USA)**[21] 805 4-8-12 **67**....................(t) FergusSweeney 4 56
(K R Burke) *prom: rdn over 3f out: wknd 2f out* **14/1**

5441 **7** *3 ¼* **High 'n Dry (IRE)**[7] 938 4-8-11 **66** 6ex....................(p) PaulDoe 8 48
(M A Allen) *hld up in mid-div: rdn over 3f out: sn struggling* **15/8**[2]

206- **8** *15* **Mystical Ayr (IRE)**[144] 6638 6-8-11 **66**.................... TomEaves 7 17
(Miss L A Perratt) *bhd: hmpd after 1f: rdn over 4f out: lost tch 3f out* **14/1**

1m 49.77s (-0.73) **Going Correction** -0.075s/f (Stan) **8** Ran SP% **116.4**
Speed ratings (Par 103): **100,98,97,95,93 91,88,75**
CSF £20.10 CT £97.33 TOTE £9.00: £1.90, £1.10, £2.30; EX 27.00.
Owner Mrs J E Taylor **Bred** Mrs J E Taylor **Trained** Lambourn, Berks
■ Stewards' Enquiry : Billy Cray three-day ban: careless riding (Apr 12-14)

FOCUS
Justcallmehandsome continues to progress. This looks sound, reliable form which should work out.

1031 CHECK IN @ PONTIN'S & CHECK OUT THE FUN CLASSIFIED STKS 1m 1f 103y(P)
8:20 (8:20) (Class 7) 4-Y-O+ **£1,365** (£403; £201) **Stalls** Low

Form RPR

-232 **1** **Faraday (IRE)**[7] 930 5-8-7 45.................... MHarley(7) 3 55+
(A P Stringer) *mde all: shkn up over 1f out: r.o wl* **9/4**[2]

1006 **2** *3* **Tabulate**[25] 769 5-9-0 45.................... RobertWinston 4 49
(P Howling) *hld up in tch: chsd wnr 2f out: rdn and no imp fnl f* **16/1**

5045 **3** *nk* **Bobering**[19] 822 8-8-7 45.................... SoniaEaton(7) 9 49
(B P J Baugh) *hld up in mid-div: hdwy on ins over 2f out: one pce fnl f* **16/1**

3644 **4** *1 ½* **Castle Frome (IRE)**[14] 862 9-9-0 43....................(p) PaulFitzsimons 12 47+
(A E Price) *n.m.r s: hld up and bhd: hdwy and edgd lft fnl f: nvr nrr* **25/1**

000- **5** *1 ½* **King Of Knight (IRE)**[193] 5421 7-9-0 45....................(t) J-PGuillambert 11 43
(G Prodromou) *hld up in rr: hdwy on ins over 2f out: rdn over 1f out: no imp fnl f* **20/1**

6205 **6** *1* **Candy Anchor (FR)**[25] 770 9-9-0 42.................... TomEaves 5 41
(R E Peacock) *s.i.s: hld up towards rr: hdwy on ins over 1f out: no further prog fnl f* **33/1**

0-03 **7** *2* **Nanosecond (USA)**[7] 930 5-9-0 45.................... JimCrowley 2 37
(S A Callaghan) *prom: rdn over 3f out: wknd over 1f out* **5/4**[1]

520 **8** *hd* **Sorbiesharry (IRE)**[53] 400 9-8-11 45....................(p) KirstyMilczarek(3) 7 37
(Mrs N Macauley) *s.i.s: nvr nr ldrs* **14/1**

05-6 **9** *shd* **Almowj**[14] 862 5-9-0 43.................... ChrisCatlin 8 37
(G H Jones) *plld hrd: sn chsng wnr: wknd over 2f out* **50/1**

The Form Book, Raceform Ltd, Compton, RG20 6NL

3-30 **10** *1* **Veneer (IRE)**[74] 145 6-9-0 45 StephenDonohoe 13 35
(Mrs N S Evans) *hld up in mid-div: rdn over 3f out: sn bhd* **28/1**

- **11** *3 ¾* **Breezy Heights (IRE)**[144] 6660 6-8-11 42 TravisBlock(3) 1 28
(Miss Tor Sturgis) *prom: rdn over 3f out: wknd wl over 1f out* **16/1**

000- **12** *31* **Three Half Crowns (IRE)**[265] 3244 4-9-0 45 (p) FergusSweeney 10 —
(M S Saunders) *hld up in tch: rdn over 3f out: wknd over 2f out: t.o* **25/1**

-034 **U** **Over Ice**[19] 822 5-8-11 45 JerryO'Dwyer(3) 6 —
(Karen George) *v awkward and uns rdr leaving stalls* **10/1**[3]

2m 1.38s (-0.32) **Going Correction** -0.075s/f (Stan) **13** Ran SP% **129.4**
Speed ratings (Par 97): **98,95,95,93,92 91,89,89,89,88 85,57,—**
CSF £38.29 TOTE £3.30: £1.70, £2.10, £5.50; EX 57.90.
Owner Curley Leisure **Bred** K Nercessian **Trained** Newmarket, Suffolk

FOCUS
Faraday made all to beat some poor opposition and is rated back to something like his best.
Nanosecond(USA) Official explanation: jockey said gelding emptied in home straight

1032 STAY AT THE WOLVERHAMPTON HOLIDAY INN H'CAP 1m 1f 103y(P)
8:50 (8:50) (Class 6) (0-60,60) 4-Y-0+ **£2,047** (£604; £302) **Stalls** Low

Form RPR

0452 **1** **Casablanca Minx (IRE)**[9] 915 5-8-5 **54** (v) RichardEvans(7) 8 62+
(P D Evans) *hld up and bhd: hdwy on ins wl over 1f out: sn rdn: nt clr run and swtchd rt wl ins fnl f: r.o wl to ld post* **13/2**[3]

2133 **2** *shd* **My Mirasol**[13] 874 4-9-4 **60** (p) ChrisCatlin 2 68
(D E Cantillon) *led: hdd over 6f out: led over 4f out: hrd rdn and edgd lft ins fnl f: hdd post* **3/1**[1]

06-3 **3** *2* **Time To Regret**[9] 916 8-9-1 **57** (p) DanielTudhope 4 61
(I W McInnes) *hld up in tch: rdn over 1f out: kpt on one pce fnl f* **7/1**

6003 **4** *1* **Latif (USA)**[2] 996 7-8-7 **56** AndrewHeffernan(7) 6 58
(Paul Green) *s.i.s: hld up and bhd: hdwy on ins over 2f out: rdn over 1f out: one pce fnl f* **10/1**

0030 **5** *2 ¼* **Krakatau (FR)**[14] 861 4-8-9 **51** VinceSlattery 5 49
(D J Wintle) *hld up towards rr: rdn and hung lft wl over 1f out: styd on fnl f: nvr trbld ldrs* **16/1**

1661 **6** *¾* **General Feeling (IRE)**[13] 872 7-8-9 **58** (p) DeclanCannon(7) 10 55
(S T Mason) *hld up in mid-div: hdwy over 3f out: hung rt ent st: rdn and wknd over 1f out* **17/2**

1166 **7** *¾* **Joe Jo Star**[18] 841 6-8-10 **52** AndrewElliott 9 47
(B P J Baugh) *prom tl wknd 2f out* **14/1**

-202 **8** *1 ¾* **Convallaria (FR)**[30] 703 5-9-2 **58** (t) SteveDrowne 1 50
(G Wragg) *hld up in tch: hung rt and wnt 2nd over 2f out: rdn and wknd over 1f out* **7/2**[2]

3255 **9** *9* **Gifted Heir (IRE)**[18] 841 4-8-11 **53** NeilChalmers 7 28
(A Bailey) *hld up and bhd: rdn 3f out: sn struggling* **15/2**

0300 **10** *13* **Steel Grey**[34] 640 7-8-5 **47** TWilliams 3 —
(M Brittain) *w ldr: led over 6f out: rdn and hdd over 4f out: wknd 3f out* **33/1**

2m 0.97s (-0.73) **Going Correction** -0.075s/f (Stan) **10** Ran SP% **119.9**
Speed ratings (Par 101): **100,99,98,97,95 94,93,92,84,72**
CSF £27.12 CT £145.06 TOTE £6.40: £1.90, £1.20, £2.70; EX 19.00.
Owner J E Abbey **Bred** Airlie Stud And Widden Stud **Trained** Pandy, Monmouths
■ Stewards' Enquiry : Chris Catlin one-day ban: careless riding (Apr 9)

FOCUS
A moderate handicap, run at a sound pace. The form looks solid enough for the class.
Convallaria(FR) Official explanation: jockey said mare hung left-handed throughout
Gifted Heir(IRE) Official explanation: jockey said colt hung right-handed throughout

1033 PONTIN'S GREAT FUN, GREAT TIMES H'CAP 5f 20y(P)
9:20 (9:20) (Class 4) (0-85,83) 4-Y-0+ **£4,857** (£1,445; £722; £360) **Stalls** Low

Form RPR

405- **1** **Bookiesindex Boy**[174] 5942 4-8-5 **73** (v) WilliamBuick(3) 4 79
(J R Jenkins) *mde all: shkn up 1f out: pushed out* **16/1**

-113 **2** *hd* **Distant Sun (USA)**[19] 824 4-9-4 **83** TomEaves 1 88+
(Miss L A Perratt) *hld up: hdwy on ins over 2f out: hrd rdn fnl f: r.o* **5/4**[1]

3013 **3** *2* **Almaty Express**[18] 840 6-9-2 **81** (b) ChrisCatlin 2 79
(J R Weymes) *chsd wnr: rdn and no ex wl ins fnl f* **5/2**[2]

0222 **4** *3* **Spoof Master (IRE)**[27] 726 4-8-7 **72** LPKeniry 5 59
(C R Dore) *prom: rdn and wknd wl over 1f out* **15/2**

55-0 **5** *1 ½* **New York Oscar (IRE)**[78] 84 4-8-12 **77** (p) AndrewElliott 3 59
(A J McCabe) *hmpd after 1f: sn bhd: n.d after* **5/1**[3]

-616 **6** *½* **Drifting Gold**[30] 699 4-8-10 **75** (b) AdamKirby 7 55
(C G Cox) *hld up: wknd wl over 1f out* **10/1**

000- **7** *4* **Loyal Royal (IRE)**[157] 6355 5-8-3 **75** PietroRomeo(7) 6 41
(J M Bradley) *bhd fnl 2f* **50/1**

61.16 secs (-1.14) **Going Correction** -0.075s/f (Stan) **7** Ran SP% **118.4**
Speed ratings (Par 105): **106,105,102,97,95 94,88**
CSF £38.59 CT £73.13 TOTE £19.10: £4.30, £1.20; EX 81.90 Place 6 £51.69, Place 5 £17.86.
Owner Robin Stevens **Bred** D R Tucker **Trained** Royston, Herts

FOCUS
A fair sprint which saw the first pair come clear. Straightforward enough form, the winner back to his best.
New York Oscar(IRE) Official explanation: jockey said gelding suffered interference in running
T/Plt: £34.70 to a £1 stake. Pool: £89,510.75. 1,879.30 winning tickets. T/Qpdt: £7.40 to a £1 stake. Pool: £6,612.90. 652.80 winning tickets. KH

935 LINGFIELD (L-H)
Thursday, March 27

OFFICIAL GOING: Standard
Wind: Light, half against Weather: Fine

1034 GO PONTIN'S FOR GREAT VALUE HOLIDAYS CLAIMING STKS 1m 2f (P)
2:30 (2:30) (Class 6) 3-Y-O **£2,047** (£604; £302) **Stalls** Low

Form RPR

3114 **1** **Bridge Of Fermoy (IRE)**[12] 900 3-9-6 73 (bt) GeorgeBaker 3 74
(Miss Gay Kelleway) *hld up in tch: effrt over 2f out: rdn and r.o to ld last 100yds* **15/8**[1]

1341 **2** *1 ¼* **Home**[14] 865 3-9-3 72 (p) PatCosgrave 1 69
(J R Boyle) *hld up bhd ldrs: effrt 2f out: got through on inner 1f out: styd on to take 2nd nr fin: nt pce of wnr* **3/1**[2]

6-54 **3** *nk* **Agglestone Rock**[20] 820 3-8-5 60 JackDean(7) 2 63+
(W G M Turner) *hld up in last: prog whn stopped in his trcks wl over 1f out: styd on ins fnl f to take 3rd last stride* **16/1**

4-30 **4** *nse* **Mujahope**[30] 704 3-8-5 65 KirstyMilczarek(3) 4 59
(M Botti) *t.k.h: pressed ldr: led on inner over 2f out: hdd and outpcd last 100yds* **13/2**

3-06 **5** *3 ¾* **Henry James (IRE)**[56] 366 3-8-11 63 OscarUrbina 7 55
(M Botti) *led at mod pce to over 2f out: lost 2nd and wknd fnl f* **22/1**

-214 **6** *1* **Little Firecracker**[22] 803 3-8-7 62 (b[1]) JoeFanning 6 50
(Miss M E Rowland) *wl in tch on outer: rdn 2f out: hanging and nt qckn over 1f out: btn after* **9/2**[3]

2126 **7** *2 ¼* **Coral Shores**[8] 940 3-8-5 59 (v) ChrisCatlin 5 44
(P W Hiatt) *in tch: rdn over 2f out: sn wknd* **9/1**

2m 7.01s (0.41) **Going Correction** -0.025s/f (Stan) **7** Ran SP% **111.5**
Speed ratings (Par 96): **97,96,95,95,92 91,90**
CSF £7.19 TOTE £2.30: £1.90, £1.40; EX 6.90.
Owner T & Z Racing Club **Bred** Tally-Ho Stud **Trained** Exning, Suffolk

FOCUS
A reasonable claimer and, with just 9lb separating the entire field at the weights, it was competitive enough. The pace, though, was typically ordinary and the winning time was 1.53 seconds slower than the later 56-70 older-horse handicap.

1035 LINGFIELDPARK.CO.UK (S) STKS 6f (P)
3:00 (3:01) (Class 6) 4-Y-0+ **£2,047** (£604; £302) **Stalls** Low

Form RPR

0443 **1** **Best One**[28] 731 4-8-12 67 SebSanders 2 67+
(C E Brittain) *hld up in last pair: prog on inner 2f out: got through to ld jst ins fnl f: r.o wl* **11/10**[1]

5-26 **2** *1 ¼* **Punching**[13] 884 4-9-3 57 GeorgeBaker 3 68
(Miss Gay Kelleway) *trckd ldrs: smooth prog over 2f out: led jst over 1f out: hdd and outpcd jst ins fnl f* **6/1**[3]

0-42 **3** *1 ½* **Night Prospector**[13] 884 8-8-12 63 (p) AlanMunro 7 58
(R A Harris) *w ldr: led 1/2-way: drvn and hdd jst over 1f out: outpcd* **9/2**[2]

3556 **4** *4* **Prettilini**[5] 972 5-8-4 44 (v[1]) LukeMorris(3) 6 40
(A W Carroll) *led to 1/2-way: pressed ldrs u.p tl wknd jst over 1f out* **14/1**

5240 **5** *1 ¾* **Monashee Prince (IRE)**[28] 729 6-9-3 62 (v) JimCrowley 5 45
(J R Best) *racd wd towards rr: lost grnd whn wdst of all bnd 2f out: hanging over 1f out: plugged on fnl f* **6/1**[3]

4640 **6** *2* **James Street (IRE)**[5] 972 5-8-12 42 (v) LPKeniry 9 33
(Peter Grayson) *w ldrs: drvn fr over 3f out: wknd over 1f out* **25/1**

2540 **7** *1* **Tang**[35] 642 4-8-0 42 JackDean(7) 4 28+
(W G M Turner) *nvr bttr than midfield: struggling 2f out: wknd* **40/1**

0100 **8** *3 ¼* **Mulberry Lad (IRE)**[13] 884 6-9-3 50 (p) ChrisCatlin 10 25
(P W Hiatt) *a in last pair: struggling in last fr 1/2-way* **20/1**

46 **9** *nk* **Yurchenko**[32] 690 4-8-7 38 (b) NeilChalmers 8 14
(M Wellings) *plld hrd: sn trckd ldrs: wd bnd 2f out: wknd* **50/1**

1m 11.58s (-0.32) **Going Correction** -0.025s/f (Stan) **9** Ran SP% **114.0**
Speed ratings (Par 101): **101,99,97,92,89 87,85,81,80**
CSF £7.54 TOTE £1.90: £1.20, £1.60, £1.50; EX 7.00 Trifecta £30.40 Pool: £564.03, 13.14 winning units.The winner was sold to Mr R. Harris for 11,600gns.
Owner Saeed Manana **Bred** Darley **Trained** Newmarket, Suffolk

FOCUS
A reasonable seller run in a time 0.40 seconds quicker than the following maiden. The runner-up limits the form, but the winner won quite well.
Monashee Prince(IRE) Official explanation: jockey said gelding suffered interference after start
Yurchenko Official explanation: jockey said filly ran too free early

1036 CAPTAIN CROC SAYS IT'S PONTIN'S TIME MAIDEN STKS 6f (P)
3:35 (3:36) (Class 5) 3-Y-0+ **£2,331** (£693; £346; £173) **Stalls** Low

Form RPR

1 **Yamal (IRE)** 3-9-0 0 JoeFanning 3 75+
(M Johnston) *s.s: in tch in last pair: effrt on outer wl over 1f out: drvn and r.o to dispute ld last 150yds: asserted nr fin* **9/4**[2]

4- **2** *nk* **Spin Again (IRE)**[175] 5937 3-9-0 0 SebSanders 2 73
(R M Beckett) *trckd ldrs: effrt 2f out: drvn and r.o to dispute ld last 150yds: no ex last strides* **7/4**[1]

-042 **3** *1* **Interactive (IRE)**[24] 777 5-9-13 69 AlanDaly 8 74
(Andrew Turnell) *pressed ldng pair: effrt on outer over 2f out: led wl over 1f out but hanging bdly: hdd and outpcd last 150yds* **10/3**[3]

4 *4* **Elzain (IRE)** 3-8-9 0 ChrisCatlin 6 52
(M R Channon) *pressed ldr: led jst over 2f out to wl over 1f out: sn wknd* **7/1**

0/ **5** *6* **Zayyir (IRE)**[582] 4716 4-9-10 0 KevinGhunowa(3) 5 38
(R A Harris) *led to jst over 2f out: wknd rapidly wl over 1f out* **16/1**

00 **6** *2 ¾* **Estella Mai**[12] 897 3-8-9 0 NeilChalmers 1 24
(J J Bridger) *in tch: rdn 1/2-way: wknd 2f out* **100/1**

0- **7** *22* **Pasta Prayer**[255] 3592 3-9-0 0 VinceSlattery 7 —
(S A Callaghan) *lost tch after 2f: t.o* **50/1**

1m 11.98s (0.08) **Going Correction** -0.025s/f (Stan)
WFA 3 from 4yo+ 13lb **7** Ran SP% **111.5**
Speed ratings (Par 103): **98,97,96,90,82 79,49**
CSF £6.23 TOTE £3.30: £1.90, £1.40; EX 7.80 Trifecta £15.80 Pool: £579.37, 25.92 winning units.
Owner Sheikh Hamdan Bin Mohammed Al Maktoum **Bred** Gainsborough Stud Management Ltd **Trained** Middleham Moor, N Yorks

FOCUS
A reasonable sprint maiden on paper, and the right horses were involved in the finish, although the winning time was 0.40 seconds slower than the previous seller.

1037 PLAY GOLF AT LINGFIELD PARK H'CAP 5f (P)
4:05 (4:06) (Class 6) (0-65,65) 4-Y-0+ **£2,047** (£604; £302) **Stalls** High

Form RPR

6112 **1** **Dodaa (USA)**[5] 971 5-8-4 **56** AshleyHamblett(5) 5 81
(N Wilson) *v fast away: mde all and sn clr: drew rt away fr over 1f out: r.o strly* **9/2**[3]

025- **2** *7* **Azygous**[106] 7116 5-9-1 **62** AlanMunro 3 62
(J Akehurst) *chsd ldng pair: wnt 2nd 2f out: no imp at all on wnr* **3/1**[2]

0-20 **3** *1* **Rocker**[13] 875 4-9-1 **62** (v) NeilPollard 2 58
(B R Johnson) *dwlt: rousted early to rch midfield: drvn and kpt on to take 3rd ins fnl f: n.d* **9/1**

1053 **4** *1 ¾* **Triskaidekaphobia**[8] 939 5-9-3 **64** (t) PaulFitzsimons 4 54
(Miss J R Tooth) *chsd wnr to 2f out: one pce after* **16/1**

3526 **5** *½* **Music Box Express**[21] 806 4-9-0 **61** (t) SebSanders 7 49
(George Baker) *s.i.s: rousted along to rch midfield: wd bnd 2f out and no prog* **11/4**[1]

6-00 **6** *1* **George The Second**[13] 887 5-9-4 **65** RichardKingscote 1 50
(Mrs H Sweeting) *chsd ldrs but nvr on terms: one pce and no prog fnl 2f* **15/2**

400- **7** *2* **Billy Red**[156] 6413 4-9-2 **63** (b) JimCrowley 6 41
(J R Jenkins) *s.s: nvr able to rcvr and a in last trio: no imp fnl 2f* **16/1**

4302 **8** *2 ¼* **Kempsey**[8] 939 6-8-11 **58** (v) ChrisCatlin 8 27
(J J Bridger) *a in last trio: bhd after 2f* **8/1**

-065 9 1/2 **Stoneacre Boy (IRE)**[36] 620 5-8-10 **57**....................(b) LPKeniry 9 21
(Peter Grayson) *racd wd: hld up: a last: shuffled along fnl 2f* **25/1**

57.89 secs (-0.91) **Going Correction** -0.025s/f (Stan) 9 Ran SP% **118.3**
Speed ratings (Par 101): **106,94,93,90,89 88,84,81,78**
CSF £18.93 CT £118.21 TOTE £4.70: £1.60, £1.70, £2.80; EX 17.00 Trifecta £329.50 Part won. Pool: £464.09 - 0.79 winning units..
Owner Paul & Linda Dixon **Bred** Silverleaf Farm Inc **Trained** Flaxton, N Yorks

FOCUS
An extraordinary performance from the seemingly fairly exposed Dodaa, but no apparent fluke. A massive step up from him even with the form rated conservatively, and it will be interesting to see how he fares when reassessed.

1038 SAND, SEA & SUN @ PONTIN'S H'CAP 7f (P)
4:40 (4:41) (Class 5) (0-70,68) 4-Y-O+ £2,331 (£693; £346; £173) **Stalls Low**

Form RPR
-616 1 **Ever Cheerful**[27] 755 7-9-2 **66**....................(p) SteveDrowne 9 72
(A B Haynes) *mde all: hrd pressed 2f out: jnd on all sides fnl f: hld on* **15/2**
1310 2 hd **Joy And Pain**[13] 879 7-8-12 **62**....................(p) IanMongan 5 67
(M J Attwater) *chsd ldng pair: drvn and nt qckn over 1f out: styd on ins fnl f: jst hld* **4/1**[2]
0053 3 hd **Zazous**[8] 937 7-8-5 **55**.................... ChrisCatlin 6 60
(J J Bridger) *towards rr: rdn over 2f out: prog u.str.p over 1f out: styd on: jst hld* **15/2**
-600 4 hd **Corlough Mountain**[38] 609 4-8-11 **68**.................... DeclanCannon(7) 3 72
(M J McGrath) *t.k.h: trckd wnr: urged along to chal 2f out: upsides ins fnl f: jst hld and lost 2 pls nr fin* **12/1**
3215 5 hd **Double Valentine**[8] 937 5-8-2 **55**.................... KirstyMilczarek(3) 2 59
(R Ingram) *stdd s: hld up in rr: stl there 2f out: prog on inner over 1f out: pressed ldrs ins fnl f: nt qckn last 50yds* **3/1**[1]
6166 6 1 3/4 **Fine Ruler (IRE)**[20] 819 4-9-4 **68**.................... GeorgeBaker 8 67
(M R Bosley) *stdd s: hld up in last: prog on outer fr 3f out to chse ldrs 2f out: shkn up and nt qckn after* **10/1**
0040 7 3/4 **Trivia (IRE)**[12] 899 4-9-3 **67**.................... TGMcLaughlin 7 64
(Ms J S Doyle) *a towards rr: rdn over 2f out: struggling after: kpt on ins fnl f* **16/1**
120- 8 1/2 **Quantum Leap**[89] 7269 11-8-6 **63**....................(v) ThomasBubb(7) 4 59
(S Dow) *settled towards rr: bmpd along and no prog fnl 2f* **14/1**
1024 9 5 **Emma Jean Lad (IRE)**[28] 730 4-9-3 **67**.................... LPKeniry 1 51
(J S Moore) *chsd ldrs: u.p 3f out: wknd rapidly over 1f out* **9/2**[3]

1m 24.58s (-0.22) **Going Correction** -0.025s/f (Stan) 9 Ran SP% **116.0**
Speed ratings (Par 103): **100,99,99,99,99 97,96,95,89**
CSF £37.78 CT £236.92 TOTE £8.80: £2.90, £1.70, £1.80; EX 40.70 Trifecta £135.20 Pool: £567.67, 2.98 winning units.
Owner Abacus Employment Services Ltd **Bred** Southill Stud **Trained** Limpley Stoke, Bath

FOCUS
A modest handicap and the first five finished in a bunch.

1039 PONTIN'S SUMMER HOLIDAYS ARE THE BEST APPRENTICE H'CAP 1m 2f (P)
5:10 (5:10) (Class 5) (0-70,70) 4-Y-O+ £2,590 (£770; £385; £96; £96) **Stalls Low**

Form RPR
225- 1 **Trifti**[167] 6145 7-9-1 **66**.................... TravisBlock 3 74
(Miss Jo Crowley) *trckd ldrs: gng easily over 2f out: led over 1f out: rdn and styd on wl* **12/1**
660- 2 2 **Compton Falcon**[117] 6991 4-9-0 **65**.................... LukeMorris 2 69
(G A Butler) *hld up in rr: prog on inner 2f out: tried to chal fnl f: outpcd* **12/1**
300- 3 1 1/4 **Kings Topic (USA)**[129] 6867 8-8-0 **58**.................... PNolan(7) 1 62+
(A B Haynes) *snatched up after 1f: last after tl effrt 2f out: n.m.r briefly sn after: styd on fnl f to take 3rd nr fin* **25/1**
2252 4 hd **Ermine Grey**[19] 841 7-8-0 **56** oh1.................... PatrickDonaghy(5) 4 57
(A W Carroll) *dwlt: hld up in rr: hrd rdn 3f out: kpt on fr over 1f out: n.d* **8/1**
-124 4 dht **Wind Flow**[28] 728 4-8-7 **63**.................... JPHamblett(5) 6 64
(C A Dwyer) *hld up in rr: effrt on outer over 2f out: nt clr run wl over 1f out: kpt on fnl f* **4/1**[3]
41-0 6 1/2 **Dream Of Fortune (IRE)**[5] 963 4-9-2 **70**....................(bt[1]) JamieJones(3) 7 70
(M G Quinlan) *trckd ldrs: gng strly 3f out: rdn wl over 1f out: no rspnse* **11/4**[1]
05-3 7 5 **Keidas (FR)**[28] 736 4-9-0 **68**.................... JackMitchell(3) 8 59
(C F Wall) *led and sn clr: stdd and hdd over 7f out: led over 5f out: kicked on 3f out: hdd & wknd rapidly over 1f out* **6/1**
1633 8 3 3/4 **Watchmaker**[15] 860 5-9-0 **68**.................... PatrickHills(3) 5 52
(Miss Tor Sturgis) *prom: led over 7f out to over 5f out: drvn to chal 2f out: sn wknd: heavily eased* **3/1**[2]

2m 5.48s (-1.12) **Going Correction** -0.025s/f (Stan) 8 Ran SP% **116.3**
Speed ratings (Par 103): **103,101,100,100,100 99,95,92**
CSF £144.53 CT £3500.04 TOTE £17.40: £3.40, £3.20, £4.20; EX 80.50 Trifecta £275.30 Part won. Pool: £387.80 - 0.30 winning units. Place 6 £147.27, Place 5 £104.12.
Owner Mrs Liz Nelson **Bred** C A Cyzer **Trained** Whitcombe, Dorset

FOCUS
A modest apprentice handicap, but it was run at a good pace in a time 1.53 seconds quicker than the earlier three-year-old claimer.
T/Plt: £311.40 to a £1 stake. Pool: £60,561.85. 141.95 winning tickets. T/Qpdt: £165.80 to a £1 stake. Pool: £2,980.20. 13.30 winning tickets. JN

1028 WOLVERHAMPTON (A.W) (L-H)
Thursday, March 27

OFFICIAL GOING: Standard
Wind: virtually nil Weather: partly cloudy

1040 HOTEL & CONFERENCING AT WOLVERHAMPTON H'CAP 5f 216y(P)
6:50 (6:50) (Class 5) (0-70,70) 4-Y-O+ £3,238 (£963; £481; £240) **Stalls Low**

Form RPR
625- 1 **Hammer Of The Gods (IRE)**[323] 1589 8-9-3 **69**....(bt) RobertWinston 8 82+
(G C Bravery) *mde all: clr 2f out: r.o wl: unchal* **14/1**
1461 2 2 1/4 **Doubtful Sound (USA)**[22] 800 4-8-10 **69**.................... MarkCoumbe(7) 4 74
(John A Harris) *in tch: hdwy and rdn 2f out: kpt on to chse wnr ins fnl f: nvr able to chal* **8/1**[3]
0-44 3 nk **Royal Challenge**[22] 801 7-9-4 **70**.................... DanielTudhope 6 74
(I W McInnes) *taken down early: in tch in midfield: hdwy 3f out: sn drvn: chsd wnr jst over 1f out: no imp: lost 2nd ins fnl f* **9/1**
3534 4 1/2 **Obe Royal**[19] 840 4-8-11 **70**....................(b) RichardEvans(7) 3 73
(P D Evans) *s.i.s: hld up bhd: sltly hmpd 4f out: c wd over 1f out: r.o wl but nvr able to chal* **4/1**[1]
1430 5 1 3/4 **Star Strider**[43] 539 4-9-2 **68**.................... MickyFenton 11 66
(Miss Gay Kelleway) *hld up in rr: rdn and rn fr wl over 1f out: nvr nr ldrs* **12/1**
3510 6 nk **Methaaly (IRE)**[3] 994 5-9-2 **68**.................... HayleyTurner 5 66+
(M Mullineaux) *in tch tl lost pl 4f out: kpt on u.p last 2f but nvr able to chal* **17/2**
05-6 7 nse **Sun Catcher (IRE)**[12] 901 5-9-0 **66**.................... PaulHanagan 9 63
(P G Murphy) *sn pushed along and outpcd: n.d* **11/1**
1361 8 3 1/4 **Royal Envoy (IRE)**[12] 901 5-8-10 **65**.................... TolleyDean(3) 2 52+
(D Shaw) *towards rr: hmpd 4f out: effrt and nt clr run jst over 1f out: no ch* **4/1**[1]
50-5 9 3/4 **Bobby Rose**[28] 729 5-9-4 **70**.................... RobertHavlin 10 55
(D K Ivory) *chsd ldrs on outer: hdwy to chse wnr 3f out: sn rdn: wknd qckly jst over 1f out* **10/1**
-126 10 hd **Tag Team (IRE)**[42] 554 7-9-0 **66**.................... StephenDonohoe 1 55+
(John A Harris) *chse wnr for 2f out: sn rdn wknd over 2f out* **13/2**[2]
300- 11 3 1/4 **Hamaasy**[191] 5507 7-8-9 **61**.................... AdrianTNicholls 7 35
(D Nicholls) *chsd ldrs: wnt 2nd 4f out tl 3f out: sn rdn: wknd wl over 1f out* **25/1**

1m 13.94s (-1.06) **Going Correction** -0.05s/f (Stan) 11 Ran SP% **120.6**
Speed ratings (Par 103): **105,102,101,100,98 98,98,93,92,92 88**
CSF £124.58 CT £1081.91 TOTE £23.30: £4.30, £4.30, £2.90; EX 238.10.
Owner Graham Newton & Russell Reed **Bred** Kilfrush Stud Ltd **Trained** Cowlinge, Suffolk

FOCUS
A modest handicap. The form is rated around the second and third and looks solid.
Star Strider Official explanation: jockey said gelding was denied a clear run
Royal Envoy(IRE) Official explanation: jockey said gelding was denied a clear run throughout

1041 NAME A RACE TO ENHANCE YOUR BRAND CLAIMING STKS 1m 1f 103y(P)
7:20 (7:20) (Class 5) 4-Y-O+ £2,590 (£770; £385; £192) **Stalls Low**

Form RPR
00-0 1 **Lucayan Dancer**[5] 962 8-9-10 **78**.................... AdrianTNicholls 4 77+
(D Nicholls) *t.k.h: hld up in last pair: hdwy 3f out: gd hdwy on inner 1f out: led ins fnl f: readily* **10/1**
4314 2 2 1/2 **Princess Cocoa (IRE)**[36] 626 5-9-5 **77**.................... PaulHanagan 2 67
(R A Fahey) *wnt rt s: hld up in midfield: hdwy to trck ldrs 3f out: rdn to ld wl over 1f out: edgd rt over 1f out: hdd ins fnl f: nt pce of wnr* **6/4**[1]
4662 3 nk **Sweet World**[34] 653 4-9-2 **58**.................... AndrewElliott 6 64
(A P Jarvis) *led tl rdn and hdd wl over 1f out: hung rt after: kpt on* **20/1**
16-1 4 2 3/4 **Blue Sky Thinking (IRE)**[10] 915 9-9-2 **74**.................... DarrenWilliams 5 58+
(K R Burke) *hld up in midfield: hdwy to chse ldr and rdn 2f out: hit on nose by rivals whip over 1f out: wl hld after* **13/8**[2]
4410 5 1/2 **Imperial Amber**[8] 935 6-7-13 **51**....................(p) WilliamBuick(3) 1 44
(Karen George) *trckd ldrs: wnt 2nd 4f out: rdn 3f out: sn lost 2nd and outpcd: wl hld after* **20/1**
5010 6 2 1/4 **Sawwaah (IRE)**[3] 989 11-9-2 **74**....................(v) DanielTudhope 3 53
(D Carroll) *hld up in last pair: hdwy on outer over 3f out: rdn and no prog fom 2f out* **5/1**[3]
-000 7 12 **Chart Express**[24] 776 4-8-8 **33**.................... HayleyTurner 7 22
(P Howling) *chsd ldr tl 4f out: sn struggling and bhd* **100/1**

2m 0.75s (-0.95) **Going Correction** -0.05s/f (Stan) 7 Ran SP% **114.4**
Speed ratings (Par 103): **102,99,99,97,96 94,83**
CSF £25.56 TOTE £12.90: £7.10, £1.70; EX 19.90.
Owner James E Greaves **Bred** The National Stud Owner Breeders Club Ltd **Trained** Sessay, N Yorks

FOCUS
Not a bad claimer. The form is set by the runner-up, but the third limits the strength somewhat.

1042 SPONSOR A RACE BY CALLING 01902 390009 MAIDEN FILLIES' STKS 1m 1f 103y(P)
7:50 (7:50) (Class 5) 3-Y-O+ £3,238 (£963; £481; £240) **Stalls Low**

Form RPR
3- 1 **Dancing Abbie (USA)**[156] 6414 3-8-7 0.................... HayleyTurner 6 77+
(M L W Bell) *t.k.h: w ldr tl led 2f out: sn in command: eased towards fin* **4/5**[1]
00- 2 2 1/4 **Kayflaa (IRE)**[156] 6411 3-8-7 0.................... EdwardCreighton 3 68
(M R Channon) *t.k.h: chsd ldrs: rdn 3f out: chsd wnr over 1f out: kpt on but n.d to wnr* **25/1**
3- 3 shd **Try Me (UAE)**[194] 5399 3-8-7 0.................... PaulHanagan 4 68
(C E Brittain) *s.i.s: t.k.h: hld up wl in tch: rdn over 3f out: outpcd over 2f out: kpt on u.p fnl f: nrly snatched 2nd: no ch w wnr* **4/1**[2]
2-3 4 3 **Georgie The Fourth (IRE)**[64] 265 3-8-7 0.................... ChrisCatlin 1 62
(E J O'Neill) *trckd ldrs on inner: rdn over 3f out: outpcd over 2f out: n.d after* **4/1**[2]
5 5 1 **Music Party (USA)**[8] 931 3-8-7 0.................... GregFairley 2 60
(M Johnston) *s.i.s: sn rcvrd to ld: rdn and hdd 2f out: wknd jst over 1f out* **20/1**
40- 6 2 3/4 **Dramatic Solo**[195] 5395 3-8-7 0.................... AndrewElliott 8 55
(K R Burke) *chsd ldrs: rdn 3f out: outpcd over 2f out: no ch fr over 1f out* **20/1**
4 7 3 1/4 **Princess Raya**[32] 694 3-8-9 0 ow2.................... MickyFenton 7 51
(M Botti) *s.i.s: a in last pair: rdn 5f out: nvr on terms* **9/1**[3]
00 8 10 **Hatter's Way**[20] 823 3-8-4 0.................... WilliamBuick(3) 5 30
(R A Farrant) *s.i.s: t.k.h: hld up in rr: rdn and lost tch wl over 3f out: t.o* **200/1**

2m 1.38s (-0.32) **Going Correction** -0.05s/f (Stan) 8 Ran SP% **119.4**
Speed ratings (Par 100): **99,97,96,94,93 90,88,79**
CSF £32.01 TOTE £2.10: £1.70, £6.50, £1.80; EX 44.40.
Owner Sheikh Marwan Al Maktoum **Bred** Ttee Of Hines Family Trust **Trained** Newmarket, Suffolk

FOCUS
This should work out to be fair fillies' maiden. The first three can all rate higher and the cosy winner is value for further with the placed horses dictating the level.

1043 DINE IN STYLE IN HORIZONS H'CAP 1m 1f 103y(P)
8:20 (8:20) (Class 3) (0-95,86) 3-Y-O £7,124 (£2,119; £1,059; £529) **Stalls Low**

Form RPR
1 1 **Dream Desert (IRE)**[35] 645 3-8-13 **78**.................... EdwardCreighton 5 85+
(M R Channon) *hld up in last: hdwy on outer 3f out: rdn to ld over 1f out: r.o strly* **7/1**
2-21 2 2 **Segal (IRE)**[40] 595 3-8-11 **79**.................... WilliamBuick(3) 3 82
(J Noseda) *dictated stdy gallop: rdn and qcknd 3f out: hdd over 1f out: kpt on same pce* **3/1**[3]

4-11 **3** ¾ **Grand Strategy (IRE)**[56] 376 3-9-3 **82** PhilipRobinson 1 84
(M A Jarvis) *stdd after s: hld up in bhd ldng pair: rdn and effrt wl over 1f out: kpt on same pce fnl f* **2/1**[2]

26-1 **4** 1 **Greylami (IRE)**[28] 727 3-9-2 **81** JimCrowley 4 81
(T G Mills) *trckd ldr: rdn and unable qckn jst over 2f out: kpt on same pce* **6/4**[1]

2m 5.67s (3.97) **Going Correction** -0.05s/f (Stan) **4** Ran SP% **110.8**
Speed ratings (Par 102): **80,78,77,76**
CSF £26.43 TOTE £7.50; EX 12.10.
Owner Jaber Abdullah **Bred** Gainsborough Stud Management Ltd **Trained** West Ilsley, Berks

FOCUS
An interesting three-year-old handicap, but it was run at an uneven pace. The form is rated around the runner-up.

NOTEBOOK
Dream Desert(IRE), a debutant winner at the track 35 days previously, showed himself to be a progressive colt and followed up with a ready effort on this handicap bow. He did well to defy the lack of early pace and there was a fair bit to like about the way in which he disposed of his rivals in the home straight, so it will now be fascinating to see how he copes with a likely rise in the weights. (op 8-1)
Segal(IRE) had very much the run of the race out in front, setting an uneven pace. He had every chance in the home straight but the winner simply proved too strong at the business end, and he can have no excuses.
Grand Strategy(IRE), bidding for a hat-trick from a 4lb higher mark, may well have enjoyed a stronger early pace. He is far from one to be writing off yet.
Greylami(IRE) would not really have enjoyed the uneven pace on this slight drop back in trip and, while this could be deemed as disappointing, he is another who should not be fully judged on the back of this effort. (tchd 13-8)

1044 BUY TICKETS ONLINE H'CAP 1m 4f 50y(P)
8:50 (8:50) (Class 6) (0-65,64) 4-Y-0+ **£1,943** (£578; £288; £144) **Stalls** Low

Form RPR

3164 **1** **King's Fable (USA)**[13] 881 5-9-6 **59** (p) TGMcLaughlin 3 65
(Karen George) *v.s.a: bhd: rdn and hdwy 3f out: chsd ldr jst over 1f out: kpt on wl to ld last stride* **5/1**

3235 **2** *shd* **Most Definitely (IRE)**[8] 941 8-9-11 **64** AdamKirby 1 70
(R M Stronge) *hld up wl bhd: stdy hdwy over 3f out: trckd ldr on bit 2f out: shkn up to ld over 1f out: rdn fnl f: hdd last stride* **9/2**[3]

2-50 **3** 1 ¾ **Shandelight (IRE)**[28] 728 4-8-3 **47** (p) AndrewMullen(3) 4 50
(Mrs A Duffield) *led: jnd over 3f out: rdn 3f out: hdd over 1f out: kpt on same pce* **12/1**

0-31 **4** 3 ¾ **Terminate (GER)**[26] 771 6-9-6 **59** StephenDonohoe 7 57
(Ian Williams) *hld up in tch: hdwy over 5f out: chsd ldrs and rdn over 2f out: wknd 1f out* **5/2**[1]

3124 **5** 13 **Buscador (USA)**[15] 859 9-9-4 **57** RichardKingscote 5 35
(W M Brisbourne) *chsd ldr: upsides ldr and rdn over 3f out: wknd 2f out: wl btn and eased ins fnl f* **8/1**

2040 **6** 18 **Lascelles**[13] 881 4-9-6 **61** JimCrowley 2 12
(J A Osborne) *hld up in rr: rdn and lost tch 3f out: eased fnl f: t.o* **3/1**[2]

5305 **7** 7 **Swift Cut (IRE)**[10] 914 4-8-12 **53** SebSanders 8 —
(A P Jarvis) *t.k.h: chsd ldng pair tl wknd qckly over 2f out: eased fnl f: t.o* **9/1**

00/4 **8** 2 **Meohmy**[8] 934 5-7-13 **45** MCGeran(7) 6 —
(M R Channon) *hld up in midfield: rdn over 4f out: sn bhd: eased fnl f: t.o* **16/1**

2m 38.57s (-2.53) **Going Correction** -0.05s/f (Stan)
WFA 4 from 5yo+ 2lb **8** Ran SP% **123.1**
Speed ratings (Par 101): **106,105,104,102,93 81,76,75**
CSF £30.07 CT £265.64 TOTE £10.90: £2.80, £2.10, £5.10; EX 44.00.
Owner Mrs Frank George **Bred** Karen Suzanne Farrar **Trained** Higher Easington, Devon
■ Stewards' Enquiry : Adam Kirby two-day ban: used whip with excessive frequency without giving gelding time to respond (April 10-11)

FOCUS
A moderate handicap, run at a fair pace. The first pair came clear in a bobbing finish and the runner-up and third set the level.

1045 WOLVERHAMPTON-RACECOURSE.CO.UK H'CAP 7f 32y(P)
9:20 (9:21) (Class 2) (0-100,98) 4-Y-0+
£9,971 (£2,985; £1,492; £747; £372; £187) **Stalls** High

Form RPR

1333 **1** **Monkey Glas (IRE)**[12] 904 4-8-10 **90** (v) AndrewElliott 3 97
(K R Burke) *mde all: rdn over 2f out: hld on gamely u.p* **4/1**[2]

6110 **2** *hd* **Buxton**[5] 969 4-8-6 **86** ow2 (t) RobertHavlin 5 93
(R Ingram) *chsd ldng pair: rdn to chal 2f out: r.o u.p but a jst hld* **14/1**

-222 **3** 2 ½ **Gallantry**[12] 904 6-8-8 **91** TolleyDean(3) 7 91
(D Shaw) *stdd and dropped in bhd after s: hdwy over 4f out: drvn to chse ldng pair over 1f out: kpt on* **3/1**[1]

1110 **4** 1 ¼ **Ninth House (USA)**[12] 910 6-8-8 **88** (bt) JimCrowley 2 85
(N P Littmoden) *hld up in midfield: hdwy 4f out: rdn and effrt jst over 2f out: wknd 1f out* **6/1**

5-00 **5** 2 ½ **Councellor (FR)**[19] 832 6-8-8 **88** ow2 (t) MickyFenton 6 79
(Stef Liddiard) *awkward leaving stalls: racd wd: a in rr: n.d* **8/1**

356- **6** *nse* **Mesbaah (IRE)**[165] 6198 4-9-2 **96** PaulHanagan 1 87
(R A Fahey) *a bhd: rdn wl over 3f out: n.d* **9/2**[3]

000- **7** 2 **Party Boss**[124] 6932 6-9-4 **98** SebSanders 4 84
(C E Brittain) *w wnr: rdn over 2f out: wknd 2f out* **3/1**[1]

1m 27.5s (-2.10) **Going Correction** -0.05s/f (Stan) **7** Ran SP% **120.2**
Speed ratings (Par 109): **110,109,106,105,102 102,100**
CSF £58.44 TOTE £5.20: £2.50, £12.10; EX 104.80 Place 6 £ 2,379.10, Place 5 £ 373.24.
Owner Denis Fehan **Bred** D Bourke And Yuriy Meduedyev **Trained** Middleham Moor, N Yorks

FOCUS
A decent, competitive handicap run at a very good gallop throughout. The winner is rated to form and is a good yardstick.

NOTEBOOK
Monkey Glas(IRE) has improved tremendously since being fitted with a visor and being ridden positively from the front. He set a strong gallop here, seeing off fellow pace-setter Party Boss turning into the straight, and despite facing several serious challengers in the closing stages, he fought them all off to record another gutsy success. He certainly has a most admirable attitude. (tchd 9-2)
Buxton, who was racing from 2lb out of the weights, was always well placed tracking the strong pace set by the eventual winner, and he came through with a strong challenge in the straight. Karl Burke's colt would just not be denied, though, and was always just holding him. This was a sound effort from this former course and distance winner, and it went to show that his recent Kempton run was an aberration. (tchd 16-1)
Gallantry finished ahead of Monkey Glas on two separate occasions earlier in the month, but those runs were at Lingfield, and his late-running style just did not get him into contention this time. (op 11-4 tchd 7-2)
Ninth House(USA) is on a stiff mark now and he was another who could just never get in a blow at the positively ridden winner despite coming to have some sort of chance entering the straight. (op 8-1 tchd 5-1)
Councellor(FR), outclassed in Listed company last time, looked to have a better chance here, but he never threatened after a slow start. (op 11-1)
Mesbaah(IRE), debuting for the Fahey yard, was entitled to need his seasonal reappearance on an unfamiliar surface. (op 7-1)
Party Boss hailed from a stable in fine form, but he had been off the track for 124 days, and trying to match the strong gallop set by the race-fit Monkey Glas took its toll in the latter stages. Following a couple of ordinary efforts last backend and this down-the-field performance, he has a bit to prove now. (op 11-4)
T/Plt: £891.60 to a £1 stake. Pool: £103,088.75. 84.40 winning tickets. T/Qpdt: £189.60 to a £1 stake. Pool: £6,969.80. 27.20 winning tickets. SP

964 KEMPTON (A.W) (R-H)
Friday, March 28

OFFICIAL GOING: Standard
Wind: Strong, across Weather: Fine early, showers from race 3

1047 INTERCASINO.CO.UK H'CAP 5f (P)
6:20 (6:21) (Class 5) (0-75,75) 4-Y-0+ **£2,590** (£770; £385; £192) **Stalls** High

Form RPR

455- **1** **Holbeck Ghyll (IRE)**[168] 6141 6-9-1 **75** WilliamBuick(3) 3 89+
(A M Balding) *hld up in 6th: nt clr run on inner tl ins fnl f: pushed along and r.o to ld last 50yds* **4/1**[3]

130- **2** ¾ **Digital**[168] 6157 11-9-2 **73** ChrisCatlin 7 80
(M R Channon) *sn bdly outpcd in last: stl last ent fnl f: str run to take 2nd last strides* **12/1**

-450 **3** *nk* **What Do You Know**[34] 676 5-8-8 **70** (b) JamieJones(5) 6 76
(A M Hales) *sn won battle for ld: drvn over 1f out: holding immediate chalrs ent fnl f: swamped last 50yds* **10/3**[1]

00-0 **4** 1 ¼ **Gleaming Spirit (IRE)**[13] 901 4-8-8 **65** NeilPollard 4 66
(A P Jarvis) *pressed ldng pair but wd bnd over 3f out: wnt 2nd wl over 1f out: hld ent fnl f: one pce* **15/2**

2630 **5** *hd* **Diminuto**[34] 676 4-9-1 **72** RichardSmith 1 73
(M D I Usher) *chsd ldrs: rdn 2f out: no imp over 1f out: plugged on ins fnl f* **11/1**

0-10 **6** 1 **Fast Freddie**[20] 840 4-8-11 **71** ow2 (e) DNolan(3) 9 68
(S Parr) *fored to trck ldrs: effrt wl over 1f out: sn nt qckn: fdd ins fnl f* **9/2**

12-6 **7** 3 ¼ **Spirit Of Coniston**[4] 994 5-8-9 **66** AdrianTNicholls 5 51
(D Nicholls) *mostly chsd ldr to wl over 1f out: wknd* **7/2**[2]

60.36 secs (-0.14) **Going Correction** +0.125s/f (Slow) **7** Ran SP% **111.3**
Speed ratings (Par 103): **106,104,104,102,102 100,95**
CSF £45.84 CT £170.09 TOTE £5.50: £2.20, £4.80; EX 38.90.
Owner Halsall Nicholson Partnership **Bred** David Brickley **Trained** Kingsclere, Hants
■ Stewards' Enquiry : William Buick one-day ban: careless riding (Apr 11)
Jamie Jones one-day ban: used whip with excessive force down shoulder in forehand position (Apr 11)

FOCUS
A modest sprint, run at a strong early pace, which favoured finishers. Holbeck Ghyll has been rated value for 2l but is not the most reliable.

1048 PLAY BLACKJACK AT INTERCASINO.CO.UK H'CAP 1m 2f (P)
6:50 (6:51) (Class 5) (0-75,75) 4-Y-0+ **£2,730** (£806; £403) **Stalls** High

Form RPR

530- **1** **Haarth Sovereign (IRE)**[194] 5454 4-9-1 **72** SaleemGolam 3 85
(W R Swinburn) *mostly in 4th or 5th: drvn and prog wl over 1f out to ld jst ins fnl f: edgd rt but styd on wl* **8/1**

2-21 **2** 1 ¼ **Emperor Court (IRE)**[48] 504 4-9-0 **71** SebSanders 10 82+
(P J Makin) *mostly in 4th or 5th: effrt over 1f out and followed wnr through: sltly checked ins fnl f: styd on same pce* **9/4**[1]

-402 **3** 2 **Lord Theo**[28] 747 4-9-4 **75** JamesDoyle 8 81
(N P Littmoden) *chsd ldr to over 3f out: styd cl up and disp 2nd again over 1f out: styd on same pce* **7/1**[3]

600- **4** 1 **Trans Sonic**[42] 7017 5-9-3 **74** JimmyFortune 1 78
(A P Jarvis) *led: urged along over 1f out: hdd & wknd jst ins fnl f* **12/1**

0-01 **5** ¾ **Dinner Date**[14] 879 6-8-6 **63** J-PGuillambert 2 66
(T Keddy) *settled in midfield: effrt wl over 1f out: styd on steadily: no ch of troubling ldrs* **12/1**

3425 **6** 2 **Steig (IRE)**[16] 852 5-8-5 **62** ChrisCatlin 7 61
(Carl Llewellyn) *t.k.h: racd in 3rd tl chsd ldr over 3f out: tried to chal over 1f out: wknd fnl f* **9/1**

-153 **7** *shd* **Chia (IRE)**[60] 340 5-8-11 **68** (p) HayleyTurner 5 66
(D Haydn Jones) *stdd s: hld up in midfield: rdn over 2f out: no prog and nvr nr ldrs* **10/1**

21-0 **8** 1 ¼ **Sarwin (USA)**[28] 747 5-8-7 **64** NickyMackay 4 60
(W J Musson) *stdd s: hld up wl in rr: shkn up 2f out: no ch* **12/1**

1224 **9** 1 ½ **Given A Choice (IRE)**[16] 860 6-8-11 **75** (p) SimonPearce(7) 6 68
(J Pearce) *stdd s: hld up in detached last: brief prog 3f out: sn no hdwy and btn* **11/2**[2]

00-1 **10** 10 **Steely Dan**[77] 122 9-8-13 **70** (p) NeilPollard 9 43
(Mrs L C Jewell) *dwlt: t.k.h: hld up: last 3f out: no prog: eased* **11/1**

2m 6.79s (-1.21) **Going Correction** +0.125s/f (Slow) **10** Ran SP% **120.3**
Speed ratings (Par 103): **109,108,106,105,105 103,103,102,101,93**
CSF £27.20 CT £138.36 TOTE £13.00: £3.40, £1.10, £2.70; EX 36.60.
Owner The Kingship **Bred** Hardys Of Kilkeel Ltd **Trained** Aldbury, Herts

FOCUS
A fair handicap for the grade. It was run at a sound pace, but nothing got into it from off the pace. Clear personal bests from both the first two.

1049 INTERCASINO.CO.UK CLAIMING STKS 1m (P)
7:20 (7:21) (Class 6) 4-Y-0+ **£2,047** (£604; £302) **Stalls** High

Form RPR

060- **1** **Cactus King**[111] 7075 5-9-11 **75** IanMongan 7 81
(P M Phelan) *t.k.h: hld up in midfield: effrt over 2f out: rdn and prog to ld jst over 1f out: styd on wl* **9/1**

-000 **2** 1 ½ **Apache Dawn**[13] 910 4-9-1 **80** GeorgeBaker 2 68
(G L Moore) *trckd ldr after 2f: led on bit over 2f out: rdn over 1f out: sn hdd and nt qckn: kpt on* **11/4**[2]

-161 **3** *nk* **Dushstorm (IRE)**[55] 408 7-8-6 **67** (p) WilliamBuick(3) 3 61
(M Botti) *racd on outer: trckd ldng pair after 2f: rdn to chal over 1f out: nt qckn and hld ins fnl f* **2/1**[1]

0113 **4** 1 1/4 **Not Now Lewis (IRE)**[14] 879 4-8-10 60 ChrisCatlin 5 59
(J A Osborne) *t.k.h: hld up bhd ldrs: nt qckn wl over 1f out: styd on ins fnl f* **7/2**[3]
4200 **5** 3/4 **Film Queen (IRE)**[14] 885 4-8-4 55 HayleyTurner 9 51
(B G Powell) *hld up in last trio: effrt on inner 2f out: kpt on one pce* **33/1**
30-5 **6** 1/2 **Bed Fellow (IRE)**[37] 622 4-9-5 70 JimmyFortune 6 65
(A P Jarvis) *trckd ldrs: poised to chal 2f out: shuffled along and nt qckn: wknd ins fnl f* **16/1**
-305 **7** 1 **Shouldntbethere (IRE)**[28] 750 4-8-10 57 RobertHavlin 4 54
(Mrs P N Dutfield) *s.i.s: sme prog fr last 1/2-way: rdn and no hdwy 2f out: fdd* **20/1**
/6-0 **8** 3/4 **Victor Trumper**[70] 218 4-9-5 72 (bt) SteveDrowne 8 61
(Jim Best) *led: set stdy pce tl kicked on 3f out: hdd over 2f out: wknd over 1f out* **20/1**
2-56 **9** hd **Barry Island**[44] 546 9-9-1 54 TQuinn 1 57
(D R C Elsworth) *dwlt: hld up in last trio: outpcd whn r sed in earnest over 2f out* **14/1**

1m 43.73s (3.93) **Going Correction** +0.125s/f (Slow) **9** Ran SP% **117.2**
Speed ratings (Par 101): **85,83,83,81,81 80,79,78,78**
CSF £33.74 TOTE £10.30: £3.00, £1.60, £1.10; EX 39.40.Not Now Lewis was claimed by Gay Kelleway for £7,500.
Owner Tony Smith **Bred** Hascombe And Valiant Studs **Trained** Epsom, Surrey

FOCUS
A modest claimer, run at a steady early pace. Not form to take too literally.

1050 INTERCASINO.CO.UK MAIDEN FILLIES' STKS 7f (P)
7:50 (7:50) (Class 5) 3-Y-O+ **£2,590** (£770; £385; £192) **Stalls** High

Form RPR
04- **1** **Frivolous (IRE)**[223] 4602 3-8-7 0 RobertHavlin 8 71
(J H M Gosden) *racd keenly early: mde all: shkn up wl over 1f out: styd on wl* **7/4**[1]
4- **2** 1 1/4 **Viscountess (IRE)**[150] 6571 3-8-7 0 JoeFanning 4 67
(M Johnston) *racd freely early: trckd wnr: rdn to chal 2f out: kpt on fnl 2f but readily hld* **9/4**[2]
03- **3** 3/4 **Moonlight Angel**[260] 3453 3-8-7 0 SaleemGolam 7 65+
(W R Swinburn) *chsd ldng trio: rdn to go 3rd wl over 1f out: styd on but nvr quite able to chal* **4/1**[3]
4 2 1/2 **Mignonette (IRE)** 3-8-7 0 StephenDonohoe 1 58+
(E A L Dunlop) *s.v.s: mostly last tl sme prog on inner 2f out: pushed along and kpt on steadily: n.d* **14/1**
5 1 1/2 **Elzeeza (USA)** 3-8-7 0 TGMcLaughlin 2 54+
(E A L Dunlop) *mostly in same pl: outpcd and rn green 2f out: no ch after: plugged on* **8/1**
0 **6** 2 **Sweet Refrain**[25] 772 3-8-7 0 PaulDoe 9 49
(J Akehurst) *t.k.h: chsd ldng pair tl wknd wl over 1f out* **40/1**
7 5 **Handbags At Dawn (IRE)** 3-8-7 0 LPKeniry 5 35
(S Kirk) *dwlt: t.k.h: a in last trio: wknd over 1f out* **25/1**
8 1 1/4 **Highland Venture (IRE)** 3-8-7 0 HayleyTurner 3 32
(D R C Elsworth) *s.v.s: plld hrd and hld up: wknd 2f out* **12/1**

1m 27.32s (1.32) **Going Correction** +0.125s/f (Slow) **8** Ran SP% **118.9**
Speed ratings (Par 100): **97,95,94,91,90 87,82,80**
CSF £6.17 TOTE £2.60: £1.40, £1.30, £1.60; EX 6.40.
Owner H R H Princess Haya Of Jordan **Bred** Darley **Trained** Newmarket, Suffolk

FOCUS
A fair fillies' maiden. The time was slow and the form might not be the most reliable, but there were several in the field who may well do better.

1051 BIG JACKPOTS AT INTERCASINO.CO.UK H'CAP 7f (P)
8:20 (8:20) (Class 6) (0-60,60) 3-Y-O **£2,047** (£604; £302) **Stalls** High

Form RPR
55-0 **1** **Oceana Blue**[54] 419 3-8-11 **60** (t) DavidProbert(7) 5 71+
(A M Balding) *hld up in midfield on outer: smooth prog to ld jst over 1f out: pushed clr* **14/1**
4625 **2** 3 1/4 **Too Grand**[14] 876 3-8-9 **51** NeilChalmers 12 52
(J J Bridger) *hld up wl in rr: threaded through fr 2f out: styd on to take 2nd last 100yds: no ch w wnr* **7/1**[3]
6023 **3** 1 **Kamal**[14] 876 3-9-4 **60** SebSanders 13 58
(W R Muir) *trckd ldrs: nt qckn 2f out: n.m.r sn after: chsd wnr briefly ins fnl f: one pce* **2/1**[1]
5223 **4** 3/4 **Llab Nala**[29] 732 3-9-1 **57** ChrisCatlin 9 53
(M R Channon) *hld up towards rr: nt keen and no prog 2f out: styd on fnl f: nrst fin* **5/1**[2]
000- **5** 1 1/4 **Follow Your Spirit**[164] 6246 3-9-4 **60** CatherineGannon 1 53
(B Palling) *mostly chsd ldr to over 1f out: fdd* **20/1**
416 **6** 3/4 **Snow Bounty**[29] 737 3-9-4 **60** (p) LPKeniry 4 51
(J S Moore) *t.k.h: hld up in midfield: bmpd after 1f: effrt on inner 2f out: nt qckn and no prog whn n.m.r 1f out* **9/1**
000- **7** nse **Bahia Palace**[142] 6722 3-7-11 **46** oh1 AmyBaker(7) 11 37
(M D I Usher) *hld up in last trio: pushed along fr 2f out: kpt on steadily: n.d* **50/1**
0443 **8** 1 **Shabnaam**[13] 897 3-8-10 **52** HayleyTurner 6 40
(P Howling) *t.k.h: bmpd after 1f: trckd ldrs: nt qckn over 1f out: fdd* **12/1**
0030 **9** shd **Marquis De Louvois (IRE)**[30] 714 3-9-1 **60** AndrewMullen(3) 10 48
(Mrs A Duffield) *mde most to jst over 1f out: fly-jmpd jst ins fnl f: wknd* **14/1**
0605 **10** 4 **Miss Tilen**[35] 665 3-8-1 **46** (p) WilliamBuick(3) 8 23
(V Smith) *a wl in rr: no prog 2f out* **16/1**
0400 **11** 1/2 **Herrbee (IRE)**[23] 797 3-8-8 **50** IanMongan 7 26
(S Dow) *s.i.s: a in rr: wknd over 1f out* **16/1**
6-40 **P** **Lady Sandicliffe (IRE)**[72] 184 3-8-11 **53** AdamKirby 2 —
(Miss Jo Crowley) *prom: disp 2nd over 1f out: losing pl whn p.u jst ins fnl f: broke down* **7/1**[3]

1m 27.53s (1.53) **Going Correction** +0.125s/f (Slow) **12** Ran SP% **124.5**
Speed ratings (Par 96): **96,92,91,90,88 88,87,86,86,82 81,—**
CSF £114.28 CT £291.44 TOTE £16.60: £3.50, £1.80, £1.60; EX 93.50.
Owner J Spence **Bred** The C H F Partnership **Trained** Kingsclere, Hants

FOCUS
A moderate handicap. It was won in good style by Oceana Blue, but most of the field were exposed or regressive.

1052 PLAY ROULETTE AT INTERCASINO.CO.UK H'CAP 2m (P)
8:50 (8:52) (Class 5) (0-70,69) 4-Y-O+ **£2,590** (£770; £385; £192) **Stalls** High

Form RPR
0-13 **1** **Coda Agency**[24] 789 5-8-12 **53** JimCrowley 7 64
(D W P Arbuthnot) *trckd ldrs: prog on outer to ld jst over 2f out: drvn clr fnl f* **7/2**[1]
6-04 **2** 2 3/4 **Featherlight**[14] 880 4-9-8 **68** (b) RobertHavlin 12 75
(Jamie Poulton) *hld up in rr: smooth prog fr 3f out: tried to chal 2f out: chsd wnr fnl f: jst hld on for 2nd* **6/1**[2]
0-46 **3** nk **Best Selection**[14] 881 4-9-2 **62** IanMongan 10 69
(Mrs L J Mongan) *towards rr: rdn and prog on outer over 2f out: nt qckn over 1f out: kpt on again ins fnl f* **12/1**
0-60 **4** 1 1/4 **Arabian Sun**[28] 754 4-8-9 **55** (v) ChrisCatlin 9 61
(M J Attwater) *disp ld to jst over 2f out: kpt on over 1f out: no ex ins fnl f* **7/1**[3]
6322 **5** 1 **Lorikeet**[14] 880 9-10-0 **69** GeorgeBaker 11 73
(G L Moore) *trckd ldrs: effrt to chal jst over 2f out: nt qckn over 1f out: fdd ins fnl f* **7/2**[1]
-163 **6** 1 1/4 **Mister Completely (IRE)**[14] 880 7-9-12 **67** (v) JamesDoyle 5 72+
(Ms J S Doyle) *hld up and sn last: prog on inner over 2f out: tried for rail run but nowhere to go wl over 1f out: nt rcvr* **8/1**
355- **7** 1 **Follow On**[116] 5573 6-8-9 **50** NeilPollard 1 52
(A P Jarvis) *settled wl in rr: rdn over 2f out: kpt on fr over 1f out: nvr rchd ldrs* **8/1**
050- **8** 6 **Brigadore (USA)**[19] 3273 5-9-10 **65** StephenDonohoe 3 59
(Ian Williams) *settled midfield: rdn and effrt 3f out: chsd ldrs and cl enough over 1f out: wknd fnl f* **16/1**
1/0- **9** 4 1/2 **Kick And Prance**[85] 6797 5-9-1 **56** FergusSweeney 4 45
(G L Moore) *disp ld tl wknd over 2f out* **11/1**
00-4 **10** 2 1/2 **Lysander's Quest (IRE)**[44] 544 10-8-9 **50** oh5 (v) CatherineGannon 6 36
(R Ingram) *t.k.h early: prom tl wknd 3f out* **20/1**
0-00 **11** 1 3/4 **Lay The Cash (USA)**[14] 881 4-8-5 **51** (tp) HayleyTurner 2 35
(B G Powell) *a in rr: struggling fr 3f out: sn bhd* **66/1**
600- **12** 6 **Princess Aimee**[131] 5187 8-9-0 **55** (p) VinceSlattery 8 32
(D Burchell) *in tch tl wknd over 4f out: t.o* **66/1**

3m 30.96s (0.86) **Going Correction** +0.125s/f (Slow)
WFA 4 from 5yo+ 5lb **12** Ran SP% **123.1**
Speed ratings (Par 103): **102,100,100,99,99 98,98,95,92,91 90,87**
CSF £24.97 CT £233.99 TOTE £5.20: £1.80, £2.50, £3.30; EX 32.30.
Owner Banfield, Thompson **Bred** Baydon House Stud **Trained** Compton, Berks

FOCUS
An ordinary staying handicap, run at a modest early pace, but the form looks sound enough.
Lorikeet Official explanation: jockey said gelding hung right under pressure

1053 INTERCASINO.CO.UK CLASSIFIED STKS 7f (P)
9:20 (9:21) (Class 7) 4-Y-O+ **£1,365** (£403; £201) **Stalls** High

Form RPR
0021 **1** **Straight Face (IRE)**[10] 922 4-9-6 45 GeorgeBaker 10 58
(Miss Gay Kelleway) *pressed ldr: led 3f out: drvn 2f out: jnd 1f out: battled on wl and jst hld on* **5/2**[1]
5634 **2** nk **Only If I Laugh**[10] 922 7-9-0 44 IanMongan 7 51
(M J Attwater) *hld up in midfield: effrt but hanging fr 2f out: r.o fnl f to take 2nd and gaining on wnr fin* **9/1**
16-2 **3** shd **Prince Valentine**[10] 922 7-9-0 45 (p) FergusSweeney 2 51
(G L Moore) *hld up in rr: prog fr 2f out: drvn and styd on fnl f: jst hld* **5/1**[3]
2252 **4** 3/4 **Suhayl Star (IRE)**[6] 972 4-9-0 45 TQuinn 4 49
(P Burgoyne) *plld hrd early: hld up: smooth prog to trck wnr 2f out: chal and upsides 1f out: fnd nil: lost 2 pls nr fin* **5/1**[3]
05-0 **5** 5 **Raise Again (IRE)**[10] 922 5-9-0 45 RobertHavlin 6 35
(Mrs P N Dutfield) *trckd ldrs: cl enough 2f out: wknd jst over 1f out* **20/1**
4020 **6** 1/2 **A Teen**[10] 922 10-9-0 45 HayleyTurner 14 34
(P Howling) *cl up: rdn and n.m.r 2f out: sn outpcd and btn* **14/1**
-000 **7** 2 **Pajada**[30] 711 4-8-7 39 (p) GabrielHannon(7) 8 29
(M D I Usher) *trckd ldrs: losing pl whn snatched up wl over 1f out: n.d after* **66/1**
6540 **8** 3/4 **Doctor Ned**[10] 922 4-9-0 43 (p) NeilChalmers 11 27
(Miss Sheena West) *nvr on terms w ldrs: outpcd over 2f out: n.d after* **25/1**
-604 **9** 1 1/4 **Cyfrwys (IRE)**[15] 870 7-9-0 45 (p) CatherineGannon 3 23
(B Palling) *led to 3f out: wknd 2f out* **25/1**
000- **10** 1 3/4 **Canary Girl**[23] 4336 5-9-0 41 DMylonas 12 19
(Miss Diana Weeden) *a in rr: struggling fr over 2f out* **28/1**
0603 **11** 3 1/2 **Northstar Express (IRE)**[14] 878 5-9-0 45 AdamKirby 9 9
(J L Spearing) *a in last trio: struggling 3f out* **25/1**
12 1 1/4 **Tvara**[286] 4-9-0 39 PatCosgrave 5 6
(M J Wallace) *s.s: tried to rcvr on wd outside: rdn 1/2-way: wl btn whn hmpd over 2f out* **7/2**[2]
P566 **13** 1 1/4 **Mtoto Girl**[14] 877 4-8-11 41 TolleyDean(3) 1 2
(J J Bridger) *racd on outer in midfield: rdn bef 1/2-way: sn wknd* **40/1**

1m 26.59s (0.59) **Going Correction** +0.125s/f (Slow) **13** Ran SP% **124.5**
Speed ratings (Par 97): **101,100,100,99,93 93,91,90,88,86 82,81,79**
CSF £25.23 TOTE £3.00: £1.40, £2.40, £2.20; EX 26.30 Place 6 £33.17, Place 5 £5.29.
Owner T & Z Racing Club **Bred** P J Towell **Trained** Exning, Suffolk

FOCUS
Low-grade fare, but solid enough form of its type. The first four came clear and the form looks fair for the grade.
Northstar Express(IRE) Official explanation: jockey said mare never travelled
T/Plt: £83.10 to a £1 stake. Pool: £87,050.25. 764.25 winning tickets. T/Qpdt: £7.00 to a £1 stake. Pool: £7,590.30. 799.10 winning tickets. JN

1034 LINGFIELD (L-H)
Friday, March 28

OFFICIAL GOING: Standard
Wind: Fresh, half behind

1054 TIME TO UNWIND - THAT'S PONTIN'S TIME MAIDEN STKS 1m (P)
2:00 (2:01) (Class 5) 3-Y-O **£2,331** (£693; £346; £173) **Stalls** High

Form RPR
0- **1** **Indian Skipper (IRE)**[161] 6294 3-9-3 0 PaulMulrennan 4 79+
(M H Tompkins) *a in tch: wnt 2nd over 2f out: led over 1f out but wnt bdly rt towards stands: clr whn r.o ins fnl f* **4/1**[3]
0- **2** 4 **Riqaab (IRE)**[154] 6469 3-9-3 0 StephenDonohoe 5 70
(E A L Dunlop) *trckd ldrs: led over 2f out: hdd over 1f out: kpt on but nt pce of wnr* **11/2**
3 1/2 **Gulch's Rose (USA)** 3-8-9 0 WilliamBuick(3) 6 63+
(J Noseda) *a in tch on outside: wnt 3rd 2f out: rdn and styd on one pce fnl f* **7/4**[1]
0-6 **4** 4 1/2 **Arniecoco**[13] 897 3-9-3 0 OscarUrbina 8 58
(Miss J R Gibney) *towards rr: rdn and hdwy over 1f out: r.o fnl f: nvr nrr* **66/1**

03 5 hd **Thankuforthemusic (IRE)**[31] 704 3-9-3 0................ FergusSweeney 9 58
(C Tinkler) *hld up in rr: mde sme late hdwy* **25/1**
0-U0 6 1 1/2 **Malt Empress (IRE)**[13] 903 3-8-12 0.................... WandersonD'Avila 3 49
(B W Duke) *slowly away: sn mid-div: effrt 2f out: wknd fnl f* **100/1**
7 3/4 **Buck Cannon (IRE)** 3-9-3 0.................................. IanMongan 10 52
(P M Phelan) *mid-div: rdn over 2f out: sn btn* **66/1**
8 3 1/4 **Blur** 3-8-12 0.. PatDobbs 11 40
(R Hannon) *a in rr* **16/1**
9 15 **Nightjar (USA)** 3-9-3 0.. JoeFanning 1 10
(M Johnston) *trckd ldrs to over 3f out: wknd wl over 2f out* **9/4**[2]
0 10 4 **Too Much To Do**[69] 223 3-9-3 0.......................... J-PGuillambert 2 —
(T D McCarthy) *slowly away: sn mid-div: wknd 2f out* **100/1**
42- 11 13 **Wicksy Creek**[249] 3801 3-9-3 0.......................... SaleemGolam 7 —
(G C H Chung) *sn led: hdd over 2f out: wknd qckly* **33/1**

1m 37.71s (-0.49) **Going Correction** +0.05s/f (Slow) 11 Ran SP% **120.2**
Speed ratings (Par 98): **104,100,99,95,94 93,92,89,74,70 57**
CSF £25.98 TOTE £5.60: £1.80, £1.70, £1.50; EX 26.40 Trifecta £151.30 Pool £483.76 - 2.27 winning units..
Owner Roalco Limited **Bred** Calley House Syndicate **Trained** Newmarket, Suffolk

FOCUS
A modest maiden, but the first three can all rate a bit higher and the winner rates value for further. The fourth and fifth set the standard.
Thankuforthemusic(IRE) Official explanation: jockey said gelding hung left
Buck Cannon(IRE) Official explanation: jockey said gelding suffered interference closing stages

1055 GET A GREAT DEAL @ PONTINS.COM CLAIMING STKS 7f (P)
2:30 (2:30) (Class 6) 4-Y-0+ **£1,774** (£523; £262) **Stalls** Low

Form RPR
6212 1 **Desert Dreamer (IRE)**[15] 870 7-9-13 78..............(t) RichardKingscote 1 87
(Tom Dascombe) *trckd ldr: rdn and r.o to ld ins fnl f: kpt up to work* **3/1**[2]
4421 2 1 1/4 **Danetime Lord (IRE)**[22] 807 5-9-13 82.......................(p) SebSanders 2 84
(J R Gask) *led: rdn over 1f out: hdd ins fnl f: nt qckn* **10/11**[1]
5160 3 1 1/2 **Satyricon**[29] 730 4-9-1 69.................................(b) OscarUrbina 4 68
(M Botti) *a same pl: rdn over 1f out: kpt on fnl f* **7/1**[3]
0-34 4 2 3/4 **Moayed**[13] 896 9-9-1 69..(b) JimCrowley 6 60
(N P Littmoden) *hld up: hdwy on outside over 1f out but nvr nr to chal* **8/1**
3310 5 nk **Arctic Desert**[11] 914 8-8-9 64.................................(t) HayleyTurner 5 53
(Miss Gay Kelleway) *stdd s: a bhd* **10/1**

1m 25.73s (0.93) **Going Correction** +0.05s/f (Slow) 5 Ran SP% **110.1**
Speed ratings (Par 101): **96,94,92,89,89**
CSF £6.17 TOTE £3.70: £1.30, £1.20; EX 5.70.
Owner ONEWAY Partners **Bred** Gainsborough Stud Management Ltd **Trained** Lambourn, Berks

FOCUS
Not a bad little claimer, but they went no early pace. The third puts the form into perspective and not form to take seriously.

1056 ARENALEISUREPLC.COM H'CAP 1m 4f (P)
3:05 (3:05) (Class 5) (0-70,69) 4-Y-0+ **£2,331** (£693; £346; £173) **Stalls** Low

Form RPR
2-11 1 **Bridgewater Boys**[63] 300 7-9-3 66.............................. GeorgeBaker 1 72
(G L Moore) *hld up in tch: rdn to ld 1f out: r.o wl* **5/2**[2]
4311 2 1 **Capitalise (IRE)**[14] 886 5-8-6 58........................... WilliamBuick(3) 6 62
(V Smith) *hld up in rr: gd hdwy on ins over 1f out to chse wnr fnl f* **13/8**[1]
5663 3 nk **Play Up Pompey**[23] 795 6-8-6 55 oh4........................ HayleyTurner 7 59
(J J Bridger) *stdd in rr: plld hrd: pushed along over 4f out: hdwy on outside over 2f out: r.o fnl f* **9/1**
662 4 4 **Site Sentry (IRE)**[25] 773 5-9-4 67.............................. SteveDrowne 3 64
(M F Harris) *led: rdn and hdd 1f out: wknd ins fnl f* **16/1**
56/1 5 7 **Saraba (FR)**[14] 881 7-9-3 66.................................... IanMongan 8 52
(Mrs L J Mongan) *trckd ldrs: wnt 2nd briefly over 2f out: wknd over 1f out* **13/2**[3]
0-60 6 3 3/4 **Sir Liam (USA)**[22] 546 4-9-1 66................................ JimCrowley 5 46
(R A Teal) *trckd ldr tl rdn over 2f out: wknd over 1f out* **13/2**[3]

2m 32.56s (-0.44) **Going Correction** +0.05s/f (Slow)
WFA 4 from 5yo+ 2lb 6 Ran SP% **109.2**
Speed ratings (Par 103): **103,102,102,99,94 92**
CSF £6.56 CT £24.51 TOTE £3.10: £1.70, £1.40; EX 6.20 Trifecta £31.10 Pool £523.89 - 11.95 winning units..
Owner Matthew Green & Richard Green **Bred** Southill Stud **Trained** Woodingdean, E Sussex

FOCUS
A moderate handicap, run at at average pace but sound enough rated around the winner and third.

1057 LINGFIELDPARK.CO.UK H'CAP 1m (P)
3:40 (3:40) (Class 5) (0-75,75) 3-Y-0 **£2,331** (£693; £346; £173) **Stalls** High

Form RPR
563 1 **Canary Islands**[13] 909 3-9-4 75.................................. TGMcLaughlin 2 80+
(E A L Dunlop) *trckd ldrs: shkn up to ld appr fnl f: sn clr* **6/4**[1]
216- 2 2 1/2 **Last Of The Line**[119] 6973 3-9-4 75............................ SteveDrowne 8 75
(H J L Dunlop) *hld up: hdwy on ins over 1f out: r.o to chse wnr ins fnl f* **16/1**
052- 3 nk **Locum**[177] 5895 3-8-10 67.. PaulMulrennan 7 66
(M H Tompkins) *mid-div: rdn and hdwy over 1f out: r.o fnl f: nvr nrr* **20/1**
25-0 4 3/4 **Randama Bay (IRE)**[13] 902 3-9-3 74............................ GeorgeBaker 5 71
(I A Wood) *w ldr: led narrowly 3f out: hdd appr fnl f: kpt on one pce* **22/1**
351- 5 nse **Just Like A Woman**[160] 6329 3-9-4 75.......................... HayleyTurner 6 72
(M L W Bell) *racd on outside in tch: rdn over 1f out: no ex ins fnl f* **8/1**
552- 6 hd **Feasible**[200] 5268 3-8-13 70................................ RichardKingscote 1 67
(J G Portman) *sn led: rdn and hdd narrowly 3f out: ev ch ent fnl f but no ex after* **14/1**
4-35 7 shd **Atheer Dubai (IRE)**[13] 909 3-8-13 70......................(b) SebSanders 10 66+
(C E Brittain) *slowly away: hdwy whn short of room and swtchd rt over 1f out: kpt on but n.d after* **9/2**[3]
3-1 8 1/2 **General Blucher (IRE)**[39] 610 3-9-4 75........................ AlanMunro 9 70
(P W Chapple-Hyam) *t.k.h: hld up: rdn over 2f out: nvr on terms after* **7/2**[2]
23-0 9 6 **It's Josr**[13] 900 3-8-9 66... RichardThomas 3 48
(I A Wood) *hld up: a struggling in rr* **40/1**
3-36 10 3 1/4 **Hollow Point (IRE)**[51] 458 3-8-5 62............................ JoeFanning 4 36
(M Johnston) *slowly away: in rr: rdn 2f out and c wd into st: nvr on terms* **16/1**

1m 40.03s (1.83) **Going Correction** +0.05s/f (Slow) 10 Ran SP% **121.5**
Speed ratings (Par 98): **92,89,89,88,88 88,88,87,81,78**
CSF £30.66 CT £378.86 TOTE £2.50: £1.40, £4.90, £3.90; EX 38.30 Trifecta £375.20 Pool £734.73 - 1.39 winning units..
Owner Gainsborough **Bred** Gainsborough Stud Management Ltd **Trained** Newmarket, Suffolk

FOCUS
A fair handicap three-year-old handicap for the class. The form makes sense rated around the third to sixth.

1058 PLAY GOLF AT LINGFIELD PARK H'CAP 1m (P)
4:15 (4:15) (Class 5) (0-70,70) 4-Y-0+ **£2,590** (£770; £385; £192) **Stalls** High

Form RPR
0223 1 **Millfield (IRE)**[25] 775 5-9-2 68................................... JimCrowley 5 77+
(P R Chamings) *slowly away: in rr on ins: rdn and gd hdwy to ld wl ins fnl f* **9/2**[2]
03-0 2 1/2 **Scarlet Flyer (USA)**[25] 775 5-9-4 70........................... GeorgeBaker 7 78
(G L Moore) *hld up: hdwy 2f out: strly rdn to snatch 2nd last stride* **5/1**[3]
1312 3 shd **Follow The Flag (IRE)**[28] 755 4-8-12 69.................... JackMitchell(5) 4 77
(C F Wall) *in tch: rdn and hdwy to ld ins fnl f: u.p whn headed and lost 2nd towards fin* **7/2**[1]
6653 4 2 1/2 **Binnion Bay (IRE)**[9] 938 7-8-4 59 ow3.....................(b) TolleyDean(3) 3 61
(J J Bridger) *towards rr: c wd into st: rdn and r.o strly fnl f: nvr nrr* **9/2**[2]
0452 5 2 3/4 **Seneschal**[29] 731 7-8-9 68.. PNolan(7) 1 64
(A B Haynes) *led tl rdn and hdd ins fnl f: wknd fnl 100yds* **13/2**
54-6 6 3/4 **Thermidor (USA)**[39] 608 5-9-1 67.............................. SebSanders 6 61
(Lady Herries) *trckd ldr: rdn over 3f out: wknd over 1f out* **5/1**[3]
6-64 7 1 1/4 **Coloso**[51] 448 4-8-6 58.. SimonWhitworth 2 49
(P D Cundell) *s.i.s: sn trckd ldrs: rdn 2f out: wknd fnl f* **10/1**

1m 37.68s (-0.52) **Going Correction** +0.05s/f (Slow) 7 Ran SP% **114.3**
Speed ratings (Par 103): **104,103,103,100,98 97,96**
CSF £26.96 CT £86.80 TOTE £5.60: £2.40, £3.20; EX 29.00 Trifecta £196.70 Pool £467.53 - 1.68 winning units..
Owner Inhurst Players **Bred** Limestone Stud **Trained** Baughurst, Hants

FOCUS
A modest handicap, run at a decent pace. The second and third give the form a sound look.

1059 TIME OF YOUR LIFE AT PONTIN'S MAIDEN STKS 1m 4f (P)
4:50 (4:50) (Class 5) 3-Y-0 **£2,457** (£725; £362) **Stalls** Low

Form RPR
223 1 **Maadraa (IRE)**[20] 837 3-9-3 73................................ PhilipRobinson 3 81
(M A Jarvis) *mde all: rdn over 1f out: kpt on u.p: all out* **11/4**[2]
42-4 2 shd **Flash Of Colour**[83] 58 3-9-3 70................................... JimCrowley 5 81
(Mrs A J Perrett) *trckd wnr thrght: chal ins fnl f and only jst failed* **9/1**
0- 3 4 1/2 **Special Reserve (IRE)**[161] 6296 3-9-3 0............................ PatDobbs 2 74
(R Hannon) *t.k.h: in tch: rdn to go 3rd 2f out: no imp fnl f* **12/1**
0-3 4 hd **Dubai's Wonder (IRE)**[34] 674 3-9-3 0.......................... MichaelHills 1 73
(B W Hills) *in tch tl outpcd 2f out: n.d after* **6/1**
-4 5 1 **Vice Consul**[13] 903 3-9-3 0...................................... JoeFanning 9 72
(M Johnston) *stdd s: sn trckd ldrs: rdn over 2f out: wknd over 1f out* **2/1**[1]
0-3 6 2 1/2 **Allied Powers (IRE)**[15] 867 3-9-3 0.............................. SebSanders 8 68
(M L W Bell) *in rr: effrt 4f out: nvr on terms* **4/1**[3]
00- 7 6 **Sonny Sam (IRE)**[189] 5599 3-9-3 0........................... PaulMulrennan 4 58
(M H Tompkins) *hld up: lost tch over 2f out* **50/1**
00- 8 14 **Golddigging (IRE)**[242] 4028 3-8-12 0..................... RichardKingscote 6 31
(J G Portman) *a in rr: lost tch over 2f out* **100/1**
9 3 1/4 **Persian Wish (IRE)** 3-9-3 0...................................... GeorgeBaker 7 31
(J W Mullins) *a bhd* **66/1**

2m 32.5s (-0.50) **Going Correction** +0.05s/f (Slow) 9 Ran SP% **116.4**
Speed ratings (Par 98): **103,102,99,99,99 97,93,84,81**
CSF £27.79 TOTE £3.20: £1.40, £3.20, £2.70; EX 27.70 Trifecta £254.50 Pool £881.86 - 2.46 winning units..
Owner Sheikh Ahmed Al Maktoum **Bred** Darley **Trained** Newmarket, Suffolk

FOCUS
A fair three-year-old maiden, run at a fair pace. The form should work out.

1060 RACE THE FAMILY TO PONTIN'S TODAY H'CAP 7f (P)
5:20 (5:21) (Class 5) (0-70,70) 3-Y-0 **£2,331** (£693; £346; £86; £86) **Stalls** Low

Form RPR
050- 1 **Benedetto**[139] 6755 3-9-0 66....................................... JimCrowley 3 69+
(Mrs A J Perrett) *t.k.h: a in tch: hdwy to ld ins fnl f: hld on wl* **7/1**
0-13 2 nk **Johnny Friendly**[11] 918 3-8-9 61............................. PaulMulrennan 2 63
(K R Burke) *sn led: racd keenly: rdn and hdd ins fnl f but kpt on wl* **11/4**[1]
1230 3 1/2 **Wee Buns**[10] 924 3-8-9 68....................................... RossAtkinson(7) 1 69
(P Burgoyne) *trckd ldrs: effrt on ins appr fnl f: r.o* **11/1**
44-1 4 1 **Top Draw (USA)**[44] 543 3-9-1 70............................... LukeMorris(3) 9 68+
(M L W Bell) *hld up: hdwy whn checked over 1f out: r.o wl ins fnl f* **7/1**
-462 4 dht **Tiepie**[23] 797 3-8-9 61...(p) TQuinn 4 59
(J Akehurst) *prom on outside: rdn over 2f out: kpt on ins fnl f* **7/2**[2]
06-3 6 1/2 **Terracos Do Pinhal**[74] 157 3-8-12 64............................ JoeFanning 6 61
(M Johnston) *w ldr: rdn 3f out: wknd appr fnl f* **11/2**[3]
-460 7 1/2 **Easy Wonder (GER)**[13] 899 3-9-1 67.......................... RichardThomas 5 62
(I A Wood) *towards rr: effrt on ins over 1f out: one pce ins fnl f* **20/1**
60-0 8 5 **Ruby Delta**[31] 705 3-9-2 68.................................... SimonWhitworth 7 50
(P D Cundell) *a in rr* **20/1**
000- 9 2 **Reel Man**[177] 5895 3-9-2 68....................................... GeorgeBaker 8 45
(D K Ivory) *hld up: a bhd* **12/1**

1m 25.64s (0.84) **Going Correction** +0.05s/f (Slow) 9 Ran SP% **114.8**
Speed ratings (Par 98): **97,96,96,94,94 94,93,88,85**
CSF £26.42 CT £184.98 TOTE £8.60: £2.70, £1.70, £3.90; EX 32.20 Trifecta £175.10 Pool £562.36 - 2.28 winning units. Place 6 £36.58, Place 5 £24.16..
Owner Woodcote Stud Ltd **Bred** Woodcote Stud Ltd **Trained** Pulborough, W Sussex

FOCUS
A modest handicap, run at a steady early pace. The form is rated around the runner-up.
Benedetto Official explanation: trainer's rep said, regarding apparent improvement in form, that the colt had strengthened up over the winter.
Tiepie Official explanation: jockey said colt hung both ways
T/Plt: £76.20 to a £1 stake. Pool: £60,243.85. 576.85 winning tickets. T/Qpdt: £41.20 to a £1 stake. Pool: £3,321.90. 59.60 winning tickets. JS

1040 WOLVERHAMPTON (A.W) (L-H)
Friday, March 28

OFFICIAL GOING: Standard
Wind: Fresh behind Weather: Fine

1061 VISIT PONTIN'S FOR GREAT SHORT BREAKS H'CAP 5f 216y(P)
2:20 (2:20) (Class 6) (0-65,65) 4-Y-0+ **£2,047** (£604; £302) **Stalls** Low

Form RPR
5265 1 **Music Box Express**[1] 1037 4-8-7 61.......................(t) MatthewDavies(7) 7 69
(George Baker) *mde all: clr whn rdn over 1f out: r.o* **4/1**[2]

0314 **2** 1 1/2 **Avontuur (FR)**[4] 990 6-8-2 **56**......(p) MCGeran(7) 6 59
(Mrs R A Carr) *s.i.s: in rr: rdn and hdwy on ins whn swtchd rt over 1f out: r.o wl to take 2nd towards fin: nt rch wnr* **4/1**[2]
-503 **3** 1 1/4 **Wicked Uncle**[69] 230 9-8-7 **59** ow1......(v) JamieJones(5) 1 58
(S Gollings) *chsd wnr over 1f: wnt 2nd again 3f out: rdn wl over 1f out: one pce* **7/1**
0-01 **4** 1 **Marko Jadeo (IRE)**[14] 884 10-9-4 **65**...... NCallan 3 61
(R A Harris) *hld up: hdwy on ins over 2f out: rdn over 1f out: one pce fnl f* **11/2**[3]
3302 **5** 4 **Mr Rev**[10] 923 5-9-1 **62**...... PaulFitzsimons 8 45
(J M Bradley) *hld up: hdwy on outside over 2f out: wknd wl over 1f out* **25/1**
6331 **6** 4 1/2 **Green Pirate**[25] 783 6-9-2 **63**......(p) RobertWinston 4 32
(C R Dore) *prom: chsd wnr over 4f out tl rdn 3f out: sn wknd* **3/1**[1]
1024 **7** 1 **Compton Classic**[9] 939 6-8-11 **65**......(v) PatrickDonaghy(7) 5 31
(J R Boyle) *s.i.s: hld up: rdn over 2f out: no rspnse* **4/1**[2]

1m 14.72s (-0.28) **Going Correction** -0.025s/f (Stan) **7 Ran SP% 116.7**
Speed ratings (Par 101): **100,98,96,95,89 83,82**
CSF £21.06 CT £108.90 TOTE £4.50: £3.00, £5.20; EX 26.80.
Owner Mrs C E S Baker **Bred** Dachel Stud **Trained** Moreton Morrell, Warwicks
■ A first winner for trainer George Baker.
FOCUS
Ordinary sprint handicap form and the pattern for prominent racers dominating continued. The winner improved by 5lb.

1062 COME EVENING RACING TOMORROW NIGHT H'CAP 1m 5f 194y(P)
2:50 (2:50) (Class 6) (0-65,59) 4-Y-0+ **£2,047** (£604; £302) **Stalls** Low

Form RPR
5422 **1** **Little Richard (IRE)**[9] 934 9-9-10 **58**......(p) AdamKirby 4 68
(M Wellings) *led 2f: a.p: rdn to ld over 1f out: styd on* **5/2**[1]
-103 **2** 1 1/2 **Opera Writer (IRE)**[30] 722 5-9-9 **57**...... RobertWinston 6 65
(R Hollinshead) *chsd ldr: chal over 2f out: rdn and ev ch over 1f out: nt qckn ins fnl f* **7/2**[2]
2-56 **3** 3 1/2 **Easibet Dot Net**[28] 754 8-9-3 **51**......(b) TomEaves 5 54
(Miss L A Perratt) *s.i.s: hdwy to ld after 2f: rdn and hdd over 1f out: wknd ins fnl f* **13/2**
6644 **4** 3 3/4 **Reminiscent (IRE)**[15] 869 9-8-4 **45**......(v) DeclanCannon(7) 7 43
(B P J Baugh) *hld up: sltly hmpd over 3f out: sn rdn: no real prog fnl 2f* **12/1**
0202 **5** 1 3/4 **Ronsard (IRE)**[15] 869 6-8-6 **47**...... RichardEvans(7) 2 42
(P D Evans) *hld up and bhd: hmpd over 3f out: n.d* **7/1**
U546 **6** 8 **Saint Eric (FR)**[15] 869 6-8-11 **45**...... VinceSlattery 8 29
(Noel T Chance) *hld up towards rr: rdn over 3f out: sn struggling* **9/1**
005/ **7** 1/2 **Viscount Rossini**[19] 5127 6-8-8 **45**...... KirstyMilczarek(3) 3 28
(A W Carroll) *hld up in tch: rdn and hung lft over 3f out: wknd over 2f out* **33/1**
00-5 **8** 21 **Synonymy**[59] 212 5-9-11 **59**......(b) NCallan 1 13
(M Blanshard) *hld up in tch: rdn over 4f out: wknd and eased over 3f out* **5/1**[3]

3m 5.05s (-0.95) **Going Correction** -0.025s/f (Stan) **8 Ran SP% 113.9**
Speed ratings (Par 101): **101,100,98,96,95 90,90,78**
CSF £11.18 CT £49.04 TOTE £3.10: £1.10, £2.00, £2.20; EX 14.10.
Owner Mark Wellings Racing **Bred** Rathbarry Stud **Trained** Six Ashes, Shropshire
■ Stewards' Enquiry : Adam Kirby three-day ban: careless riding (Apr 12-14)
FOCUS
An ordinary handicap run at a steady early pace and dominated by those who raced prominently. The form is rated around the first two.
Ronsard(IRE) Official explanation: jockey said gelding suffered interference
Viscount Rossini Official explanation: jockey said gelding hung left-handed on bend turn out back straight
Synonymy Official explanation: jockey said gelding was hampered twice in running

1063 STAY AT THE WOLVERHAMPTON HOLIDAY INN CLAIMING STKS 7f 32y(P)
3:25 (3:25) (Class 5) 3-Y-O **£2,730** (£806; £403) **Stalls** High

Form RPR
3411 **1** **Dhhamaan (IRE)**[9] 932 3-8-12 **80**......(b) DebraEngland(7) 1 79
(C E Brittain) *mde all: rdn over 1f out: edgd lft ent fnl f: r.o wl* **11/10**[1]
-360 **2** 1 1/2 **Rockfield Lodge (IRE)**[10] 924 3-9-1 **75**...... JerryO'Dwyer(3) 4 74
(J A Osborne) *hld up: hdwy on ins to chse wnr 2f out: rdn whn swtchd rt 1f out: nt qckn* **5/2**[2]
-403 **3** 5 **Little Knickers**[13] 899 3-8-9 **68**...... KellyHarrison(5) 6 57
(Andrew Reid) *prom: lost pl over 2f out: edgd lft and lft 3rd wl ins fnl f* **10/1**
0-20 **4** 4 **Montefiore (IRE)**[13] 900 3-8-13 **68**......(t) NCallan 5 45
(M Botti) *hld up: rdn over 2f out: sn struggling* **4/1**[3]
-654 **5** 1 1/4 **Flemish Art (IRE)**[25] 780 3-8-13 **65**......(p) RobertWinston 3 57+
(R A Harris) *chsd wnr tl rdn 2f out: wkng whn lost action and eased wl ins fnl f* **16/1**

1m 30.91s (1.31) **Going Correction** -0.025s/f (Stan) **5 Ran SP% 111.2**
Speed ratings (Par 98): **91,89,83,79,77**
CSF £4.15 TOTE £2.10: £1.10, £1.50; EX 3.50.The winner was claimed by S B Clark for £16,000.
Owner C E Brittain **Bred** D Veitch And Musagd Abo Salim **Trained** Newmarket, Suffolk
FOCUS
A straightforward claimer to rate, with the first two running to form.
Flemish Art(IRE) Official explanation: jockey said colt lost its action

1064 PACKED FULL OF FUN - THAT'S PONTIN'S H'CAP 1m 141y(P)
4:00 (4:02) (Class 6) (0-55,55) 4-Y-0+ **£2,047** (£604; £302) **Stalls** Low

Form RPR
-324 **1** **Shunkawakhan (IRE)**[28] 749 5-8-9 **50**......(p) PhillipMakin 2 60
(Miss L A Perratt) *hld up in tch: swtchd rt over 2f out: rdn to ld wl over 1f out: drvn out* **4/1**[2]
-050 **2** nk **Grenane (IRE)**[30] 724 5-8-6 **54** ow2...... RichardEvans(7) 11 63
(P D Evans) *hld up and bhd: hdwy on ins wl over 1f out: rdn and ev ch ins fnl f: kpt on* **12/1**
20-4 **3** 1 **Bivouac (UAE)**[22] 809 4-8-12 **53**...... RobertWinston 4 60
(G A Swinbank) *a.p: nt clr run over 2f out: rdn over 1f out: nt qckn ins fnl f* **7/2**[1]
301 **4** 1 1/2 **Hi Spec (IRE)**[34] 684 5-8-3 **47**......(p) KirstyMilczarek(3) 1 50
(Miss M E Rowland) *t.k.h: prom: lost pl 5f out: hdwy whn nt clr run briefly over 2f out: rdn and no ex ins fnl f* **14/1**
3200 **5** 2 1/4 **Silver Blue (IRE)**[17] 844 5-8-6 **47**......(b) GregFairley 10 45
(C R Dore) *hld up and bhd: rdn over 3f out: hdwy on ins over 2f out: no imp fnl f* **12/1**
4450 **6** 2 1/2 **Circus Polka (USA)**[11] 915 4-8-8 **54**......(t) AshleyHamblett(5) 7 46
(W M Brisbourne) *prom: led over 5f out: rdn and hdd 3f out: led over 2f out tl wl over 1f out: hung lft and wknd ins fnl f* **17/2**
0-00 **7** 1 **Oakbridge (IRE)**[35] 654 6-8-9 **50**...... VinceSlattery 9 40
(R Brotherton) *hld up towards rr: hdwy over 3f out: wknd over 2f out* **28/1**
0164 **8** 3 **Anduril**[17] 844 7-8-11 **52**......(e[1]) FergalLynch 13 35
(I W McInnes) *hld up and bhd: hung rt over 4f out: swtchd lft wl over 1f out: nvr nr ldrs* **12/1**
233- **9** 16 **Cadwell**[92] 7201 4-9-0 **55**...... NCallan 12 —
(T J Pitt) *hld up in mid-div: hdwy over 5f out: rdn over 3f out: wknd wl over 1f out* **9/2**[3]
0434 **10** 8 **Newgate (UAE)**[58] 362 4-8-12 **53**...... AdrianMcCarthy 6 —
(Mrs R A Carr) *hld up in mid-div: rdn over 4f out: sn bhd* **18/1**
0/04 **11** 1 1/4 **Boluisce (IRE)**[14] 878 5-8-0 **48**...... MCGeran(7) 3 —
(P W Hiatt) *led: hdd over 5f out: wknd 4f out* **66/1**
6-43 **12** 16 **Karma Llama (IRE)**[15] 872 4-8-5 **53**......(v) MatthewDavies(7) 8 —
(George Baker) *prom: led 3f out tl over 2f out: wkng whn lost action wl over 1f out: sn eased: fin lame* **4/1**[2]

1m 50.15s (-0.35) **Going Correction** -0.025s/f (Stan) **12 Ran SP% 130.9**
Speed ratings (Par 101): **100,99,98,97,95 93,92,89,75,68 67,53**
CSF £57.79 CT £197.46 TOTE £7.60: £2.60, £6.20, £1.80; EX 54.30.
Owner Partick Thistle Racing Club **Bred** Matthew Duffy **Trained** Carluke, S Lanarks
■ Stewards' Enquiry : Matthew Davies ten-day ban: continuing when filly had gone lame (Apr 11-20)
FOCUS
A very moderate handicap, but the pace was reasonable and the form looks sound for the grade.
Bivouac(UAE) Official explanation: jockey said gelding was denied a clear run

1065 SUPER FAMILY GETAWAYS @ PONTINS.COM H'CAP 1m 1f 103y(P)
4:35 (4:35) (Class 4) (0-80,80) 4-Y-0+ **£4,857** (£1,445; £722; £360) **Stalls** Low

Form RPR
5520 **1** **Bee Stinger**[13] 910 6-9-4 **80**...... NCallan 5 88
(I A Wood) *hld up in tch: rdn to ld ins fnl f: r.o* **4/1**[2]
5164 **2** 1/2 **Moonlight Man**[28] 747 7-9-2 **78**...... RobertWinston 4 85
(C R Dore) *t.k.h early: chsd ldr after 1f: led over 2f out tl wl over 1f out: rdn and ev ch ins fnl f: nt qckn* **4/1**[2]
50-2 **3** 3/4 **Urban Warrior**[18] 660 4-8-4 **69**...... KirstyMilczarek(3) 1 74
(Ian Williams) *hld up: rdn and hdwy 1f out: edgd lft ins fnl f: r.o* **4/1**[2]
1533 **4** 3/4 **Blacktoft (USA)**[14] 888 5-8-6 **75**......(e) WilliamCarson(7) 3 79
(S C Williams) *sn led: hdd over 2f out: rdn to ld wl over 1f out: hdd and no ex ins fnl f* **12/1**
2153 **5** 1/2 **Morbick**[6] 973 4-8-5 **72**...... AshleyHamblett(5) 2 75
(W M Brisbourne) *led early: prom: rdn wl over 1f out: one pce fnl f* **7/2**[1]
50-6 **6** 1/2 **Final Tune (IRE)**[16] 860 5-8-11 **73**...... PhillipMakin 6 75
(Miss M E Rowland) *hld up: rdn over 2f out: nvr nr to chal* **9/1**
3256 **7** 3 **Oakley Heffert (IRE)**[20] 838 4-8-7 **74**......(b) NataliaGemelova(5) 7 69
(R Hannon) *swtchd lft after s: hld up in rr: rdn over 2f out: no rspnse* **7/1**[3]

2m 0.15s (-1.55) **Going Correction** -0.025s/f (Stan) **7 Ran SP% 112.4**
Speed ratings (Par 105): **105,104,103,103,102 102,99**
CSF £19.57 TOTE £5.50: £2.20, £2.10; EX 17.70.
Owner Sporting Occasions No 11 **Bred** Templeton Stud **Trained** Upper Lambourn, Berks
FOCUS
A fair handicap and the form seems sound enough.

1066 RACE THE FAMILY TO PONTIN'S H'CAP 5f 20y(P)
5:10 (5:11) (Class 5) (0-75,75) 3-Y-O **£2,730** (£806; £403) **Stalls** Low

Form RPR
50-2 **1** **Kinout (IRE)**[5] 977 3-9-2 **73**...... NCallan 5 78
(K A Ryan) *mde all: rdn over 1f out: drvn out* **3/1**[2]
3242 **2** 3/4 **Valhillen**[10] 924 3-8-9 **71**...... PatrickHills(5) 6 73
(M D I Usher) *chsd wnr: rdn over 1f out: kpt on ins fnl f* **7/1**
00-3 **3** shd **Artistic License (IRE)**[6] 967 3-8-7 **71**...... MatthewDavies(7) 3 73
(M R Channon) *hld up and bhd: rdn and hdwy over 1f out: r.o ins fnl f* **11/2**
0-31 **4** 1/2 **Baunagain (IRE)**[16] 855 3-9-4 **75**...... PatCosgrave 4 75+
(M J Wallace) *wnt lft and n.m.r s: hdwy over 3f out: rdn over 1f out: edgd lft ins fnl f: kpt on* **7/4**[1]
-156 **5** 4 **Stoneacre Pat (IRE)**[8] 952 3-7-11 **61** oh1...... PatrickDonaghy(7) 1 47
(Peter Grayson) *t.k.h: prom tl rdn and wknd over 1f out* **33/1**
3131 **6** 3 **Orpen's Art (IRE)**[14] 882 3-9-0 **74**...... KirstyMilczarek(3) 2 49
(S A Callaghan) *s.i.s: hld up and bhd: rdn wl over 1f out: no rspnse* **4/1**[3]

62.02 secs (-0.28) **Going Correction** -0.025s/f (Stan) **6 Ran SP% 112.2**
Speed ratings (Par 98): **101,99,99,98,92 87**
CSF £23.29 TOTE £4.50: £2.60, £2.80; EX 17.30 Place 6 £55.23, Place 5 £21.78.
Owner B T McDonald **Bred** M Parola **Trained** Hambleton, N Yorks
FOCUS
A small field and a modest sprint handicap. The winner was the third on the card to make all and the form looks solid.
Orpen's Art(IRE) Official explanation: jockey said colt ran flat
T/Plt: £110.90 to a £1 stake. Pool: £63,267.30. 416.35 winning tickets. T/Qpdt: £18.00 to a £1 stake. Pool: £3,731.20. 153.10 winning tickets. KH

957 DONCASTER (L-H)
Saturday, March 29

OFFICIAL GOING: Soft (5.6)
The ground was described as 'very testing' and conditions became progressively worse during the afternoon.
Wind: Fresh, half-against Weather: overcast, wet and windy

1067 BOOK ONLINE H'CAP 1m (S)
2:00 (2:00) (Class 3) (0-90,90) 4-Y-0+ **£6,800** (£2,023; £1,011; £505) **Stalls** High

Form RPR
6-11 **1** **Mia's Boy**[24] 805 4-8-7 **79**...... JimmyQuinn 1 92
(C A Dwyer) *trckd ldrs: shkn up to ld over 1f out: r.o strly: readily* **11/4**[1]
-102 **2** 3 1/4 **Capable Guest (IRE)**[4] 1016 6-9-4 **90**......(v) RobertWinston 6 96
(M R Channon) *in rr: edgd lft and hdwy 2f out: wnt 2nd jst ins fnl f: no imp* **11/4**[1]
611- **3** 4 **Oddsmaker (IRE)**[276] 2987 7-8-11 **83**......(t) DavidAllan 9 81
(M A Barnes) *w ldr: kpt on same pce fnl 2f* **20/1**
0-50 **4** 3/4 **Freeloader (IRE)**[15] 592 8-8-4 **76**...... DaleGibson 2 72
(R A Fahey) *led tl over 1f out: kpt on same pce* **11/1**
221- **5** 7 **Red Somerset (USA)**[150] 6596 5-8-10 **82**...... TQuinn 11 63
(R J Hodges) *midfield: effrt over 2f out: wknd over 1f out* **10/1**

The Form Book, Raceform Ltd, Compton, RG20 6NL

223- **6** *1/2* **Crocodile Bay (IRE)**[141] 6746 5-8-7 **79**........................ AdrianTNicholls 5 59
(D Nicholls) *chsd ldrs: wknd over 1f out* **11/2**[2]

120- **7** *9* **Fever**[282] 2790 4-8-6 **85**........................ NSLawes(7) 10 46
(M W Easterby) *in rr: hdwy on outer 4f out: hung lft and lost pl over 2f out* **25/1**

2-60 **8** *nse* **Northern Spy (USA)**[7] 962 4-8-9 **81**........................ TPQueally 8 42
(S Dow) *t.k.h in midfield: wknd 2f out* **7/1**[3]

5/1- **9** *25* **Provost**[355] 977 4-9-3 **89**........................ PaulMulrennan 3 —
(M W Easterby) *dwlt: hdwy on wd outside 4f out: sn lost pl and bhd: virtually p.u* **16/1**

1m 46.94s (7.64) **Going Correction** +1.225s/f (Soft) **9** Ran SP% **113.1**
Speed ratings (Par 107): **110,106,102,102,95 94,85,85,60**
CSF £9.42 CT £120.25 TOTE £3.10: £1.50, £1.70, £3.50; EX 12.50 Trifecta £146.00 Pool £637.88 - 3.10 winning units..
Owner Iraj Parvizi **Bred** Sir Eric Parker **Trained** Burrough Green, Cambs

FOCUS
An improved affort from the winner and the race has been rated round the race-fit runner-up.

NOTEBOOK
Mia's Boy, 6lb higher than his two Polytrack wins, is relatively unexposed and still on the up. He travelled strongly, and in the testing conditions had only to be kept up to his work. He may not be finished yet. (op 9-4)
Capable Guest(IRE), with the visor retained, was in one of his less co-operative moods. His rider was at his most determined but he was never going to seriously trouble the progressive winner. (op 3-1)
Oddsmaker(IRE), 8lb higher than his win on his latest outing at Carlisle in June, is a natural front-runner but this trip is half a mile short of his optimum. (op 33-1)
Freeloader(IRE), who aquitted himself well over hurdles at the Cheltenham Festival, cut out the running but this trip is short of his best. (op 10-1)
Red Somerset(USA), 8lb higher than when signing off with success at Nottingham in October, is not at home on ground as soft as he encountered here. (op 8-1)
Crocodile Bay(IRE), 9lb higher than his last winning mark, ended last season in fine form but he ran here as if this return was more than needed. (op 6-1 tchd 13- 2 in a place)
Northern Spy(USA) Official explanation: jockey said colt was unsuited by the soft ground

1068 DONCASTER RACECOURSE FOR CONFERENCES MAIDEN STKS (DIV I) 7f
2:35 (2:35) (Class 4) 3-Y-O **£4,048** (£1,204; £601; £300) **Stalls** High

Form RPR

1 **Savannah Poppy (IRE)** 3-8-12 0........................ TPQueally 11 78+
(M L W Bell) *stdd s: t.k.h in rr: stdy hdwy on inner over 2f out: led appr fnl f: hld on towards fin* **33/1**

434- **2** *1/2* **Harrison George (IRE)**[158] 6403 3-9-0 79........................ JamieMoriarty(3) 9 82
(R A Fahey) *led: hdd appr fnl f: kpt on: no ex towards fin* **2/1**[1]

05- **3** *nse* **Centenerola (USA)**[152] 6535 3-8-12 0........................ MichaelHills 5 77
(B W Hills) *trckd ldrs: t.k.h: effrt appr fnl f: no ex wl ins fnl f* **33/1**

4 *8* **Game Hunt** 3-9-3 0........................ JimmyFortune 10 62+
(J H M Gosden) *hld up in mid-div: hdwy over 2f out: chsng ldrs 1f out: hung rt and sn wknd* **10/1**

0- **5** *3 3/4* **Spirit Of A Nation (IRE)**[169] 6156 3-9-3 0........................ DarrenWilliams 1 53
(S Parr) *trckd ldrs on outer: wknd over 1f out* **80/1**

6 *7* **Carpe Diem** 3-9-3 0........................ PaulMulrennan 6 35
(W J Haggas) *mid-div: drvn over 3f out: wknd 2f out* **12/1**

7 *7* **Your Golf Travel** 3-8-12 0........................ TonyHamilton 7 13
(J S Wainwright) *dwlt: in rr: sme hdwy 2f out: nvr on terms* **100/1**

00- **8** *3 3/4* **Bilboa**[278] 2941 3-9-3 0........................ GrahamGibbons 12 8
(B R Millman) *t.k.h: dropped bk after 2f: no ch after* **100/1**

244- **9** *3 1/2* **Brave Prospector**[154] 6495 3-9-3 101........................ AlanMunro 4 —
(P W Chapple-Hyam) *trckd ldrs: t.k.h: drvn over 2f out: wknd and eased over 1f out* **8/15**[1]

3- **10** *13* **Moothir (USA)**[133] 6850 3-9-3 0........................ JoeFanning 2 —
(M Johnston) *chsd ldrs on outer: lost pl over 2f out* **8/1**[2]

11 *64* **Grey Command (USA)** 3-9-0 0........................ MarkLawson(3) 3 —
(M Brittain) *dwlt: hdwy on wd outside 4f out: lost pl over 2f out: sn bhd: t.o* **100/1**

2- **12** *11* **Louis Seffens (USA)**[155] 6469 3-9-3 0........................ RobertWinston 8 —
(G A Swinbank) *chsd ldrs: lost pl 2f out: eased and sn bhd: t.o* **9/1**[3]

1m 35.76s (9.46) **Going Correction** +1.225s/f (Soft) **12** Ran SP% **119.1**
Speed ratings (Par 100): **94,93,93,84,79 71,63,59,55,40 —,—**
CSF £472.38 TOTE £27.10: £8.40, £3.90, £9.50; EX 676.00 TRIFECTA Not won..
Owner Christopher Wright **Bred** W Maxwell Ervine **Trained** Newmarket, Suffolk

FOCUS
The 79-rated runner-up looks the best guide to the level of this form, which is quite fluid overall.
Bilboa Official explanation: jockey said gelding was unsuited by the soft ground
Brave Prospector Official explanation: jockey said colt was unsuited by the soft ground
Louis Seffens(USA) Official explanation: jockey said colt had no more to give

1069 CORAL.CO.UK H'CAP 7f
3:05 (3:06) (Class 4) (0-85,85) 4-Y-O+ **£4,533** (£1,348; £674; £336) **Stalls** High

Form RPR

300/ **1** **Against The Grain**[610] 3889 5-8-11 **78**........................ JoeFanning 1 89
(L Lungo) *w ldrs: led over 2f out: jnd ins fnl f: all out* **25/1**

3040 **2** *shd* **Cornus**[22] 824 6-8-9 **76**........................(be) JamesDoyle 11 87
(A J McCabe) *chsd ldrs: wnt 2nd 1f out: upsides fnl 100yds: jst hld* **16/1**

-331 **3** *2 1/4* **Cha Cha Cha**[6] 979 4-8-7 **81** 6ex........................ BMcHugh(7) 2 86
(K A Ryan) *s.s: hdwy on outer over 3f out: wnt 2nd 2f out: kpt on same pce fnl f* **5/1**[1]

200- **4** *9* **Kenmore**[161] 6331 6-8-6 **73**........................ GrahamGibbons 8 56
(J G Given) *hld up in mid-div: hdwy 2f out: nvr nr ldrs* **8/1**

000- **5** *2* **Hiccups**[151] 6560 8-8-9 **76**........................ PhillipMakin 3 54
(M Dods) *sn chsng ldrs: wknd over 1f out* **8/1**

206- **6** *1 1/2* **Mezuzah**[152] 6539 8-8-11 **78**........................ PaulMulrennan 4 52
(M W Easterby) *w ldrs: led over 3f out tl over 2f out: wknd over 1f out* **6/1**[2]

6-65 **7** *3/4* **Stevie Gee (IRE)**[25] 791 4-9-1 **82**........................ RobertWinston 5 54
(G A Swinbank) *sn trcking ldrs: wknd over 1f out* **8/1**

302- **8** *3 1/2* **Valery Borzov (IRE)**[193] 5506 4-8-13 **80**........................ AdrianTNicholls 10 44
(D Nicholls) *t.k.h in rr: swtchd lft over 1f out: nvr nr ldrs* **11/1**

060- **9** *1* **Starlight Gazer**[140] 6753 5-8-10 **80**........................ TravisBlock(3) 7 41
(J A Geake) *in rr: drvn over 3f out: nvr a factor* **8/1**

114- **10** *22* **Gunfighter (IRE)**[113] 7061 5-9-1 **85**........................ PJMcDonald(3) 9 —
(J S Wainwright) *s.i.s: sme hdwy on outside 3f out: sn lost pl: bhd whn eased fnl f* **7/1**[3]

10-0 **11** *6* **Nuit Sombre (IRE)**[5] 992 8-9-0 **81**........................ SilvestreDeSousa 12 —
(G A Harker) *chsd ldrs: drvn over 3f out: sn lost pl: bhd whn eased fnl f* **20/1**

1-14 **12** *12* **Red Romeo**[67] 259 7-9-4 **85**........................ JimmyQuinn 6 —
(N Wilson) *led tl over 3f out: sn wknd: eased whn bhd fnl f* **10/1**

1m 34.9s (8.60) **Going Correction** +1.225s/f (Soft) **12** Ran SP% **119.8**
Speed ratings (Par 105): **99,98,96,86,83 82,81,77,76,50 44,30**
CSF £381.62 CT £2365.09 TOTE £38.70: £7.80, £3.80, £2.00; EX 435.00 TRIFECTA Not won..
Owner Len Lungo Racing Limited **Bred** Mrs C F Van Straubeenzee And Miss A G **Trained** Carrutherstown, D'fries & G'way

FOCUS
The first three finished clear and the long absent winner deserves full marks.
Gunfighter(IRE) Official explanation: jockey said horse never travelled

1070 DBS CLASSIC BREEZE UP DONCASTER SHIELD (CONDITIONS STKS) 1m 4f
3:35 (3:36) (Class 2) 4-Y-O+ **£16,192** (£4,817; £2,407; £1,202) **Stalls** Low

Form RPR

230- **1** **Soapy Danger**[153] 6526 5-9-0 109........................ JoeFanning 6 104+
(M Johnston) *chsd ldr: led over 3f out: styd on in dour fashion* **15/8**[1]

301- **2** *1 3/4* **Furmigadelagiusta**[35] 6389 4-8-12 92........................ DarrenWilliams 1 102
(K R Burke) *trckd ldrs: wnt 2nd over 2f out: styd on same pce fnl f* **10/1**

120/ **3** *1 3/4* **Carte Diamond (USA)**[896] 5914 7-9-0 100........................ TomEaves 4 99
(B Ellison) *tardy break: hld up: hdwy over 3f out: plld outside 2f out: kpt on same pce fnl f* **14/1**

100/ **4** *6* **Come On Jonny (IRE)**[39] 6336 6-9-0 0........................ JamesDoyle 3 91
(R M Beckett) *led tl over 3f out: fdd over 1f out* **7/1**

022- **5** *107* **Munsef**[176] 5976 6-9-4 108........................ JimmyFortune 5 —
(J L Dunlop) *in rr: drvn over 3f out: sn lost tch: eased and virtually p.u over 1f out* **11/4**[2]

P00- **P** **The Last Drop (IRE)**[239] 4117 5-9-0 102........................ RobertWinston 2 —
(B W Hills) *trckd ldrs: drvn 4f out: wknd qckly and eased: p.u over 2f out* **10/3**[3]

2m 45.19s (10.09) **Going Correction** +1.15s/f (Soft)
WFA 4 from 5yo+ 2lb **6** Ran SP% **112.8**
Speed ratings (Par 109): **112,110,109,105,— —**
CSF £21.17 TOTE £2.60: £1.30, £4.50; EX 23.60.
Owner Mrs R J Jacobs **Bred** Newsells Park Stud Limited **Trained** Middleham Moor, N Yorks
■ This race was formerly run at Doncaster's opening fixture.

FOCUS
A sound gallop and a very worthy winner, but the the runner-up is rated just 92 and the third and fourth had no recent form, so a big question mark over the overall value of the race.

NOTEBOOK
Soapy Danger, who fractured a pastern at three, had just three outings last term. Looking in really good nick, he went on early in the straight and kept up the gallop all the way to the line. He has already shown he stays 2m and he has plenty of options now. (op 11-8 tchd 9-4 and 5-2 in a place)
Furmigadelagiusta, a useful juvenile hurdler, had 17lb to find with the winner on official ratings. He went in pursuit of the winner but was always going to come off second best. This was almost certainly improved form, but not quite as good as first impressions might suggest. (op 14-1)
Carte Diamond(USA) did remarkably well considering he had been off the track 896 days after suffering two life-threatening injuries in Australia, including getting a metal stake through his thigh when crashing through a rail while being prepared for the 2005 Melbourne Cup. Looking full of beans, he stuck on all the way to the line and the big pot on the horizon is the Nortumberland Plate. (op 11-1)
Come On Jonny(IRE), who looked very wintry in his coat, has only appeared infrequently since his 2005 November Handicap victory here. Despite having 9lb to find with the winner on official figures he came in for plenty of support, but after making the running he dropped away in the closing stages. (op 16-1)
Munsef looked the main danger to the winner on form, but he was a first runner of the season for his stable and looked backward in his coat. Flat out once in line for home and his case was soon a hopeless one. Official explanation: trainer had no explanation for the poor form shown (tchd 5-2 and 3-1)
The Last Drop(IRE), out of sorts after being pulled up in the Yorkshire Cup last May, looked in fine fettle but he suddenly came under pressure and dropped right out in a matter of strides. He has an awful lot to prove now. Official explanation: jockey said horse lost its action (op 7-2)

1071 CORALPOKER.COM H'CAP 6f
4:10 (4:10) (Class 2) (0-100,96) 4-Y-O+ **£10,363** (£3,083; £1,540; £769) **Stalls** High

Form RPR

400- **1** **Pusey Street Lady**[190] 5584 4-8-5 **83** oh2 ow1........................ JoeFanning 1 98
(J Gallagher) *chsd ldrs far side: led and overall ldr over 2f out: clr over 1f out: unchal* **40/1**

400- **2** *5* **High Curragh**[155] 6472 5-8-8 **86**........................ FergalLynch 6 86
(K A Ryan) *chsd ldrs centre: edgd lft and styd on to take 2nd ins fnl f* **25/1**

0-00 **3** *3 1/4* **King Orchisios (IRE)**[14] 907 5-8-11 **96**........................(p) BMcHugh(7) 4 86
(K A Ryan) *overall ldr in centre: hdd over 2f out: edgd lft and kpt on fnl f* **25/1**

054- **4** *nk* **Burning Incense (IRE)**[167] 6205 5-8-13 **91**........................ PhillipMakin 3 80
(M Dods) *chsd ldrs centre: kpt on same pce fnl 2f* **10/1**

140- **5** *1/2* **Masai Moon**[155] 6472 4-8-9 **87**........................ AlanMunro 5 75
(B R Millman) *chsd ldrs centre: one pce fnl 2f* **11/1**

51-1 **6** *nk* **Ingleby Arch (USA)**[53] 442 5-8-12 **90**........................ PaulFessey 2 77
(T D Barron) *led far side: hdd over 2f out: kpt on same pce* **8/1**[3]

050- **7** *hd* **Gift Horse**[155] 6472 8-8-12 **90**........................ StephenDonohoe 9 76
(D Nicholls) *hld up in rr centre: styd on fnl 2f: nvr nr ldrs* **14/1**

640- **8** *nk* **River Falcon**[155] 6472 8-9-2 **94**........................ DanielTudhope 17 79
(J S Goldie) *in rr towards stands' side: kpt on fnl 2f: nvr nrr* **8/1**[3]

30-1 **9** *1 3/4* **Blue Tomato**[6] 983 7-8-8 **86** 6ex........................ AdrianTNicholls 14 66
(D Nicholls) *s.i.s: t.k.h in rr towards stands' side: nvr a factor* **7/1**[2]

165- **10** *4 1/2* **Obe Gold**[155] 6472 6-8-8 **86**........................ SilvestreDeSousa 7 53
(D Nicholls) *a in rr towards centre* **14/1**

14-0 **11** *1 1/2* **Red Cape (FR)**[77] 137 5-8-8 **89**........................ AndrewMullen(3) 15 51
(Mrs R A Carr) *dwlt: sn chsng ldrs towards stands' side: wknd 2f out* **28/1**

200- **12** *nse* **Off The Record**[183] 5765 4-9-4 **96**........................ TPQueally 8 58
(J G Given) *chsd ldrs towards stands' side: lost pl 2f out* **10/1**

000- **13** *1* **Zomerlust**[155] 6472 6-9-2 **94**........................ GrahamGibbons 16 53
(J J Quinn) *a in rr towards stands' side* **9/1**

/000 **14** *1 3/4* **Baby Strange**[11] 925 4-8-12 **90**........................ PaulMulrennan 12 44
(D Shaw) *dwlt: sn chsng ldrs in centre: wknd 2f out* **18/1**

006- **15** *1 1/2* **Green Park (IRE)**[182] 5810 5-8-9 **90**........................ JamieMoriarty(3) 18 39
(R A Fahey) *a in rr towards stands' side* **13/2**[1]

00- **16** *1/2* **Extraterrestrial**[176] 5991 4-8-9 **87**........................ TonyHamilton 10 35
(R A Fahey) *chsd ldrs centre: lost pl over 2f out* **20/1**

0050 **17** *39* **Yungaburra (IRE)**[6] 983 4-7-11 **82** oh4.................. CharlesEddery(7) 13 —
(S Parr) *in rr centre: sme hdwy over 3f out: sn lost pl: virtually p.u: t.o*
40/1

1m 19.46s (5.86) **Going Correction** +1.225s/f (Soft) **17 Ran SP% 123.9**
Speed ratings (Par 109): **109,102,98,97,96 96,96,95,93,87 85,85,84,81,79 79,27**
CSF £809.38 CT £10842.41 TOTE £34.60: £5.40, £5.70, £6.50, £2.90; EX 951.30 TRIFECTA Not won..
Owner C R Marks (banbury) **Bred** S R Hope **Trained** Moreton-in-Marsh, Gloucs

FOCUS
A tricky early-season handicap in which low drawn horses dominated and the winner was one of just two to stick to the far side. Very few got into it.

NOTEBOOK
Pusey Street Lady, in effect 3lb 'wrong', had just one other with which to race on the far side. She had this in the bag the minute she struck for home.
High Curragh, who ended last season on a flat note, is now just 1lb higher than his last winning mark.
King Orchisios(IRE), happy to be back on turf, took them along in the centre but he struggles to last out 6f in conditions as testing as he encountered here. (op 33-1)
Burning Incense(IRE), who has always threatened plenty, changed hands for 85,000gns. With no headgear, he made a pleasing return and the ability is definitely there. (op 11-1)
Masai Moon, who improved a fair bit at four, made a highly satisfactory return. (op 20-1 tchd 10-1)
Ingleby Arch(USA), 5lb higher than when last seen on turf, give the winner a lead on the far side. (op 15-2)
Gift Horse, tried unsuccessfully in a visor on his final five starts last term, starts this campaign a stone lower than at this stage last year. He is no back number.
River Falcon, just 2lb higher than his last success, made a pleasing return. (op 15-2 tchd 9-1)
Blue Tomato, making a quick return, found the ground had turned against him. (op 6-1)

1072 DONCASTER-RACECOURSE.CO.UK H'CAP — 1m 2f 60y
4:45 (4:45) (Class 4) (0-85,85) 4-Y-0+ **£4,533** (£1,348; £674; £336) **Stalls** Low

Form RPR
130- **1** **Best Prospect (IRE)**[14] 6499 6-9-4 **85**..........................(t) PhillipMakin 1 99+
(M Dods) *stall opened early: sn hdd and steadily dropped to rr: stdy hdwy over 2f out: led on bit last 75yds: shkn up and wnt clr* **9/2**[2]
100- **2** *2* **Veiled Applause**[14] 6145 5-8-10 **77**............................ GrahamGibbons 5 87
(J J Quinn) *chsd ldrs: wnt 2nd over 2f out: led 1f out: hdd and no ch w wnr wl ins fnl f* **11/1**
04-0 **3** *2 1/4* **Moheebb (IRE)**[5] 992 4-8-2 **72**............................(b[1]) AndrewMullen(3) 2 78
(Mrs R A Carr) *s.i.s: sn chsng ldrs: led over 3f out: hdd 1f out: no ex* **33/1**
500- **4** *1 1/4* **Rosbay (IRE)**[57] 5805 4-9-1 **82**................................... DavidAllan 16 85
(T D Easterby) *in rr: hdwy on ins over 2f out: styd on fnl f* **8/1**
540- **5** *1/2* **Inchloch**[43] 6759 6-8-13 **80**.. MichaelHills 4 82
(B G Powell) *in rr-div: hdwy over 2f out: nvr rchd ldrs* **14/1**
/1-0 **6** *1 3/4* **Lunar Promise (IRE)**[7] 962 6-8-7 **74** ow1............ StephenDonohoe 12 73
(Ian Williams) *s.i.s: kpt on fnl 3f: nvr nrr* **25/1**
00-3 **7** *2 1/4* **Quince (IRE)**[7] 962 5-8-13 **80**..................................(v) JimmyQuinn 13 75
(J Pearce) *mid-div: kpt on fnl 2f: nvr nr ldrs* **15/2**
11-4 **8** *13* **Suits Me**[7] 962 5-9-4 **85**.. MickyFenton 10 55
(T P Tate) *sn led: hdd over 3f out: wknd over 1f out* **7/2**[1]
364- **9** *4* **Eglevski (IRE)**[185] 5724 4-9-3 **84**.............................. JimmyFortune 6 47
(J L Dunlop) *chsd ldrs: effrt 3f out: lost pl over 1f out* **7/1**[3]
424- **10** *1/2* **Sunisa (IRE)**[17] 6129 7-8-8 **75**...........................(t) AdrianTNicholls 14 37
(J Mackie) *prom: wknd 3f out* **20/1**
06-0 **11** *5* **Shabahar (IRE)**[29] 747 4-8-7 **74**.............................. DavidKinsella 7 26
(M J McGrath) *hld up in rr: hdwy on outside over 3f out: sn wknd* **11/1**
204- **12** *11* **Folio (IRE)**[151] 6576 8-8-11 **78**................................... NickyMackay 8 9
(W J Musson) *mid-div: hdwy to chal over 3f out: wknd 2f out* **16/1**
200- **13** *1* **Ahlawy (IRE)**[147] 6636 5-8-6 **80**................................. NSLawes(7) 15 9
(M W Easterby) *s.i.s: in rr: bhd fnl 3f* **33/1**
000- **14** *4* **Golden Dagger (IRE)**[14] 6185 4-8-12 **79**................(p) PaulMulrennan 11 —
(K A Ryan) *prom: hrd rdn and lost pl over 3f out* **25/1**
421- **15** *13* **Fantastic Morning**[19] 3365 4-9-1 **82**............................ TomEaves 9 —
(F Jordan) *in tch: lost pl over 3f out: sn bhd* **25/1**

2m 22.14s (10.94) **Going Correction** +1.15s/f (Soft) **15 Ran SP% 127.2**
Speed ratings (Par 105): **102,100,98,97,97 95,94,83,80,80 76,67,66,63,52**
CSF £51.09 CT £1496.08 TOTE £6.20: £2.70, £4.70, £7.00; EX 85.30 TRIFECTA Not won..
Owner D Neale **Bred** Farmers Hill Stud **Trained** Denton, Co Durham

FOCUS
The winner was handed a marginal advantage at the start, but for a confirmed hold-up horse that was no advantage. He came there on the bridle and is useful in this grade when he turns his mind to it. The form makes a fair bit of sense.
Folio(IRE) Official explanation: jockey said gelding was unsuited by the soft ground

1073 DONCASTER RACECOURSE FOR CONFERENCES MAIDEN STKS (DIV II) — 7f
5:15 (5:15) (Class 4) 3-Y-0 **£4,048** (£1,204; £601; £300) **Stalls** High

Form RPR
1 **Charm School** 3-9-3 0.. JimmyFortune 6 86+
(J H M Gosden) *hld up: smooth hdwy over 2f out: shkn up to ld over 1f out: sn drew clr* **11/8**[1]
2 *7* **Kargan (IRE)**[160] 6365 3-9-3 0.................................... TomEaves 10 65
(J S Wainwright) *s.i.s: hdwy over 2f out: chal over 1f out: kpt on: outclassed by wnr* **40/1**
3 *3 3/4* **Devinius (IRE)** 3-8-9 0.. PJMcDonald(3) 12 51
(G A Swinbank) *chsd ldrs: led over 2f out: hdd over 1f out: one pce* **33/1**
4 *2 3/4* **Star Choice** 3-9-3 0... TPQueally 2 49+
(M L W Bell) *trckd ldrs: outpcd 2f out: kpt on ins fnl f* **14/1**
0- **5** *nk* **Rockellio (IRE)**[260] 3507 3-8-12 0............................. MichaelHills 8 43
(B W Hills) *dwlt: sn mid-div: kpt on fnl 2f: nvr a threat* **7/1**[3]
0- **6** *8* **Riverside**[191] 5550 3-8-12 0..................................... TWilliams 5 23
(M Brittain) *s.i.s: swtchd lft and chsng ldrs after 1f: lost pl over 1f out* **100/1**
054- **7** *2 1/4* **Royal Acclamation (IRE)**[140] 6755 3-9-3 70........... SilvestreDeSousa 3 22
(G A Harker) *mid-div: wknd 2f out* **15/2**
8 *1/2* **Onceaponatime (IRE)** 3-9-3 0................................ AlanMunro 1 21
(P W Chapple-Hyam) *chsd ldrs on outside: bmpd after 1f: lost pl over 1f out* **4/1**[2]
35 **9** *2 1/2* **Hot Bertie**[9] 953 3-9-0 0... TravisBlock(3) 9 15
(Jedd O'Keeffe) *t.k.h in midfield: lost pl over 2f out* **22/1**
P- **10** *5* **Templetuohy Max (IRE)**[234] 4279 3-9-3 0.................. JimmyQuinn 11 2
(J D Bethell) *in rr: bhd fnl 3f* **40/1**
11 *21* **Tartan Gigha (IRE)** 3-9-3 0.................................... JoeFanning 4 —
(M Johnston) *led tl over 2f out: sn lost pl and bhd* **10/1**

00- **12** *1 1/4* **Lavender And Lace**[200] 5308 3-8-12 0.......................... MickyFenton 7 —
(T Keddy) *in rr: bhd fnl 3f* **33/1**

1m 37.22s (10.92) **Going Correction** +1.225s/f (Soft) **12 Ran SP% 118.2**
Speed ratings (Par 100): **86,78,73,70,70 61,58,57,55,49 25,23**
CSF £85.56 TOTE £2.20: £1.30, £7.80, £6.70; EX 98.50 Trifecta £444.20 Part won. Pool £625.73 - 0.40 winning units. Place 6 £14,203.65, Place 5 £8,902.69.
Owner H R H Princess Haya Of Jordan **Bred** Highclere Stud **Trained** Newmarket, Suffolk

FOCUS
Probably a weak maiden but the heavily backed winner could hardly have done it better in the ground which was heavy by now.
T/Plt: £11,503.50 to a £1 stake. Pool: £81,155.30. 5.15 winning tickets. T/Qpdt: £128.90 to a £1 stake. Pool: £5,627.00. 32.30 winning tickets. WG

1047 KEMPTON (A.W) (R-H)
Saturday, March 29

OFFICIAL GOING: Standard
A cracking day's racing, and superb advertisement for the All-Weather, characterised by a series of breathtakingly close finishes.
Wind: Fresh, half behind

1074 INTERCASINO.CO.UK H'CAP (LONDON MILE QUALIFIER) — 1m (P)
2:05 (2:06) (Class 3) (0-90,87) 3-Y-0
£6,855 (£2,052; £1,026; £513; £256; £128) **Stalls** High

Form RPR
015- **1** **Red Rumour (IRE)**[148] 6621 3-9-4 **87**............................. SebSanders 9 93
(R M Beckett) *towards rr: rdn over 2f out: hdwy over 1f out and kpt on u.str.p to ld post* **12/1**
602- **2** *nse* **Elna Bright**[186] 5705 3-9-2 **85**.. PJSmullen 7 91
(B J Meehan) *hld up in mid-div: hdwy and rdn to ld over 1f out: ct post* **25/1**
1-41 **3** *hd* **Upper Class (IRE)**[31] 723 3-9-0 **83**............................... GregFairley 13 93+
(M Johnston) *s.i.s: sn mid-div: hrd rdn over 1f out and clsng fast on first 2 nr fin* **11/4**[1]
21-2 **4** *1 3/4* **Formation (USA)**[7] 966 3-9-0 **83**................................. SteveDrowne 5 84
(E A L Dunlop) *sn trckd ldr: led 2f out: rdn and hdd over 1f out: no ex towards fin* **7/1**[3]
20-1 **5** *1/2* **Always Ready**[11] 926 3-9-1 **84**................................ J-PGuillambert 12 84
(C E Brittain) *trckd ldrs: rdn over 1f out: fdd wl ins fnl f* **15/2**
416- **6** *1 1/2* **Mujaadel (USA)**[190] 5590 3-9-2 **85**............................... JimCrowley 2 82+
(E A L Dunlop) *towards rr: not clr rn and swtchd rt 2f out: kpt on fnl f: nvr nrr* **10/1**
142- **7** *3 3/4* **Palmerin**[172] 6092 3-8-13 **82**.. PatDobbs 10 70
(R Hannon) *trckd ldr early: wknd over 1f out* **14/1**
165- **8** *1/2* **Legislation**[147] 6644 3-9-3 **86**................................. RobertHavlin 3 73
(J H M Gosden) *hld up: rdn over 2f out: sn btn* **12/1**
105- **9** *2 1/4* **Bere Davis (FR)**[271] 3157 3-8-10 **79**........................... TGMcLaughlin 1 61
(P D Evans) *a in rr* **50/1**
210- **10** *1 1/4* **Errigal Lad**[176] 5974 3-8-13 **82**....................................... NCallan 6 61
(K A Ryan) *stdd s: in rr: outpcd fnl 2f* **14/1**
100- **11** *2 1/4* **Tamara Moon (IRE)**[147] 6644 3-8-7 **76**........................... ChrisCatlin 11 50
(M R Channon) *led tl hdd 2f out: wknd qckly* **50/1**
51- **12** *5* **Elysee Palace (IRE)**[157] 6434 3-8-9 **78**..................... PhilipRobinson 8 40
(M A Jarvis) *trckd ldrs tl short of room and wknd qckly 2f out* **10/3**[2]

1m 38.8s (-1.00) **Going Correction** -0.025s/f (Stan) **12 Ran SP% 119.6**
Speed ratings (Par 102): **104,103,103,102,101 100,96,95,93,92 90,85**
CSF £280.33 CT £1078.48 TOTE £10.90: £2.70, £7.10, £1.40; EX 190.30 Trifecta £297.10 Part won. Pool £418.49 - 0.10 winning units..
Owner R Roberts **Bred** Tally-Ho Stud **Trained** Whitsbury, Hants

FOCUS
A decent enough race for the All-Weather, and although it was run at a routine tempo it looks one to be positive about, with the unexposed winner up 10lb and the second up 6lb.

NOTEBOOK
Red Rumour(IRE), a 6f horse last year, looked likely to get 7f this season but there had to be some doubt about him staying 1m. However, he needed every yard to get his nose in front right on the line. Conceding weight all round, this was a smart performance on his All-Weather debut and connections say he is a likely Britannia Handicap contender at Royal Ascot. (op 16-1)
Elna Bright made an excellent All-Weather debut, looking likely to score throughout the final furlong until being nabbed right on the line. He has obviously trained on well, and this former 6f and 7f performer has also now proved he stays 1m. (op 33-1)
Upper Class(IRE) soon recovered from a stuttering start, but he was in trouble 2f out and only a remarkable late rally between the first two home got him as close as he was. He might have won in another 25 yards, and should be suited by at least 1m from now on. (op 3-1)
Formation(USA) again ran a sound-enough race, but he was cantering when taking the lead 2f out and did not find as much as looked likely. In addition, the tail swishing remains a worry. (tchd 15-2)
Always Ready, a winner over 7f here 11 days earlier, proved he stays this trip on turf last season, so in all probability he was not quite good enough at the weights from a 3lb higher mark. (op 9-1)
Mujaadel(USA), gelded following his last run, may stay a bit farther than a mile this year. He got no run early in the straight, so this was a satisfactory seasonal debut from which improvement is likely. (op 11-1)
Palmerin was easily shaken off when coming under pressure, and now has something to prove next time. (op 16-1)
Legislation, making his handicap debut, never managed to get competitive but is worth keeping an eye on next time for signs of improvement. (op 11-1 tchd 10-1)
Elysee Palace(IRE) should stay a mile better this season, but his chance was ended by interference early in the straight. Official explanation: jockey said filly had been struck into (op 5-2 tchd 7-2)

1075 PLAY BLACKJACK AT INTERCASINO.CO.UK H'CAP — 6f (P)
2:40 (2:40) (Class 2) (0-105,103) 3-Y-0
£9,971 (£2,985; £1,492; £747; £372; £187) **Stalls** High

Form RPR
200- **1** **Vhujon (IRE)**[154] 6488 3-8-8 **90**................................. TGMcLaughlin 9 96
(P D Evans) *stdd s: in rr tl rdn and str hdwy on ins fr 2f out: led u.p post* **16/1**
50-1 **2** *shd* **Soopacal (IRE)**[51] 470 3-8-5 **87**.............................. SaleemGolam 8 92
(B Smart) *trckd ldrs: wnt 2nd 2f out: led ins fnl f: hdd post* **7/1**
140- **3** *2* **Hammadi (IRE)**[148] 6631 3-9-7 **103**.................................. NCallan 7 102
(K A Ryan) *t.k.h: led: hung lft fr 2f out: hdd ins fnl f: no ex* **8/1**
04-3 **4** *1 1/4* **Tia Mia**[11] 926 3-8-10 **92**.. OscarUrbina 10 87
(M Botti) *broke wl: restrained in mid-div: kpt on one pce fnl f* **9/2**[2]

01- **5** *1 1/2* **Chartist**[150] 6595 3-8-1 **86**.............................. WilliamBuick(3) 5 76
(R Hannon) *squeezed out s and hmpd sn after: t.k.h: one pce ins fnl 2f* **4/1**[1]
050- **6** *1* **Mister Hardy**[168] 6182 3-8-11 **93**.............................. PaulHanagan 2 80
(R A Fahey) *c towards centre fr wd draw sn after s: in tch but no hdwy fnl 2f* **12/1**
511- **7** *2* **Miesko (USA)**[167] 6195 3-8-4 **86**.............................. GregFairley 6 67
(M Johnston) *trckd ldr tl hung lft 2f out: wknd over 1f out* **12/1**
1-56 **8** *2 1/4* **Gross Prophet**[11] 926 3-7-12 **87**.............................. DavidProbert(7) 1 60
(Tom Dascombe) *mid-div: wknd 2f out* **25/1**
510- **9** *nk* **Seeking Star (IRE)**[154] 6495 3-8-11 **93**.............................. ChrisCatlin 3 65
(M R Channon) *a towards rr: no ch fr over 2f out* **11/2**[3]
003- **10** *62* **Pelican Prince**[175] 6017 3-8-4 **86**.............................. AndrewElliott 4 —
(K R Burke) *a bhd: wnt lame over 2f out and eased: t.o* **9/2**[2]

1m 12.36s (-0.74) **Going Correction** -0.025s/f (Stan) **10** Ran SP% **120.5**
Speed ratings (Par 104): **103,102,100,98,96 95,92,89,89,6**
CSF £127.55 CT £712.52 TOTE £24.10: £5.30, £2.60, £3.00; EX 204.20 Trifecta £341.70 Part won. Pool £481.40 - 0.10 winning units..
Owner Nick Shutts **Bred** Robert Berns **Trained** Pandy, Monmouths
■ Stewards' Enquiry : Saleem Golam one-day ban: careless riding (Apr 12)

FOCUS
A good handicap for the track, run at a decent pace. The form looks sound enough.

NOTEBOOK
Vhujon(IRE) only got there in the nick of time, but it proved he has trained on and - having won on his juvenile debut last season - he obviously goes well fresh. He may well stay 7f this year, and has the ability to have a good season if he can sustain his form better. (op 20-1)
Soopacal(IRE), raised 9lb for his win last time, made a splendid attempt to defy the rise only to be mown down in the final stride. Apparently more effective since being gelded, he still looks competitive on this sort of mark if he can keep up the good recent work. (op 6-1 tchd 11-2)
Hammadi(IRE) ran well in Group 3 company last season, and he made a good fist of it here conceding 10lb and more to all his rivals. This was a fine All-Weather debut, and his class should stand him in good stead this year if his trainer can find him the right opportunities. (op 12-1 tchd 7-1)
Tia Mia, returned to 6f, again ran a solid race, but looks a few pounds too high in the weights. (op 11-2)
Chartist looks a very keen sort, but the attempt to restrain him back over this extra furlong came to nothing. He may be happier if allowed to use his speed back at 5f. (tchd 9-2)
Mister Hardy won his first two races as a juvenile, and ran some decent races thereafter without success. This was his first run in handicap company, and he needs to improve a bit on this seasonal debut to justify his mark. (op 25-1)
Miesko(USA) has run well at this trip in the past, but ought to be at least as effective back at 5f. (op 9-1)
Pelican Prince went badly wrong turning for home and had to be eased down with what was reported to be a pelvic injury. Official explanation: jockey said colt lost its action (op 7-2)

1076 INTERCASINO.CO.UK ROSEBERY STKS (HERITAGE H'CAP) 1m 3f (P)

3:10 (3:11) (Class 2) (0-105,103) 4-Y-0+

£21,812 (£6,531; £3,265; £1,634; £815; £409) **Stalls** High

Form RPR
5-10 **1** **Philatelist (USA)**[14] 906 4-9-1 **94**.............................. NCallan 6 107+
(M A Jarvis) *mid-div: hdwy over 2f out: rdn and r.o to ld jst ins fnl f* **5/2**[1]
30-1 **2** *1/2* **Mr Aviator (USA)**[10] 929 4-8-11 **95**.............................. HaddenFrost(5) 10 106
(R Hannon) *trckd ldr: led wl over 1f out: rdn and hdd jst ins fnl f: r.o* **13/2**[3]
0-14 **3** *3/4* **John Terry (IRE)**[14] 908 5-8-13 **91**.............................. JimCrowley 5 100
(Mrs A J Perrett) *in tch: r.o u.p to go 3rd ins fnl f* **12/1**
5-00 **4** *2 3/4* **Charlie Tokyo (IRE)**[14] 906 5-9-2 **94**..............................(v) PaulHanagan 9 99
(R A Fahey) *in rr: rdn and hdwy over 1f out: nvr nrr* **33/1**
540- **5** *nk* **Bahar Shumaal (IRE)**[196] 5419 6-9-3 **95**.............................. J-PGuillambert 13 99
(C E Brittain) *led tl hdd wl over 1f out: wknd ins fnl f* **25/1**
140- **6** *1 1/4* **Mustajed**[181] 5830 7-8-2 **80**.............................. ChrisCatlin 7 82
(B R Millman) *in rr: rdn and hdwy over 2f out: nt rch ldrs* **20/1**
024- **7** *nse* **Pinch Of Salt (IRE)**[106] 7147 5-8-11 **92**.............................. WilliamBuick(3) 12 99+
(A M Balding) *t.k.h: mid-div: short of room 2f out: styng on whn hmpd ins fnl f* **15/2**
000- **8** *1* **Heron Bay**[140] 6759 4-9-10 **103**.............................. SteveDrowne 3 103
(G Wragg) *in rr: sme hdwy fr 2f out: short of room over 1f out and nvr nr to chal* **12/1**
054- **9** *shd* **Gold Prospect**[203] 5218 4-8-1 **83**.............................. LukeMorris(3) 11 83
(M L W Bell) *slowly away: in rr: hdwy 3f out: sn rdn and no prog after* **14/1**
251- **10** *1 1/4* **Watamu (IRE)**[378] 701 7-9-5 **97**..............................(v) SebSanders 15 95
(P J Makin) *trckd ldrs tl wknd over 2f out* **11/2**[2]
3341 **11** *nk* **Sgt Schultz (IRE)**[14] 908 5-8-12 **93**.............................. TolleyDean(3) 2 90
(J S Moore) *stdd s: in rr: rdn over 2f out: nvr on terms* **10/1**
1600 **12** *10* **Smokey The Bear**[29] 747 6-8-4 **82** ow3.............................. NeilChalmers 4 62
(Miss Sheena West) *mid-div: wknd 2f out* **40/1**
103- **13** *7* **Players Please (USA)**[168] 6169 4-9-5 **98**.............................. GregFairley 8 67
(M Johnston) *slowly away: sn mid-div: wknd 2f out* **10/1**
01/4 **14** *17* **Permanent Way (IRE)**[29] 757 5-8-10 **88**..............................(b1) PJSmullen 14 28
(B J Meehan) *a towards rr: lost tch over 2f out* **16/1**

2m 18.19s (-3.71) **Going Correction** -0.025s/f (Stan) **14** Ran SP% **129.2**
WFA 4 from 5yo+ 1lb
Speed ratings (Par 109): **112,111,111,109,108 107,107,107,107,106 106,98,93,81**
CSF £18.76 CT £179.41 TOTE £2.90: £1.60, £2.80, £4.20; EX 23.70 Trifecta £591.50 Pool £25,077.48 - 30.10 winning units..
Owner Gary A Tanaka **Bred** Darley **Trained** Newmarket, Suffolk
■ Stewards' Enquiry : J-P Guillambert four-day ban: careless riding (Apr 12-15)

FOCUS
A very competitive All-Weather contest, run at just a medium pace until the tempo quickened noticeably off the home turn, 3f from home. Top form of its type, and the progressive winner has been rated as having improved 7lb, and the second 5lb.

NOTEBOOK
Philatelist(USA) was heavily backed and had no problem up the inside this time, his rider heading for the cutaway rail 2f from home and quickly putting his stamp on the race. Though Mr Aviator reduced the margin in the last 100yds, he was always in charge and remains a very smart sort in quality events on Polytrack. (op 7-2)
Mr Aviator(USA),who lost a shoe in the race, ran a fine race in defeat from a 6lb higher mark, proving that he stays 1m3f in the process with a game effort. He has started the season in flying form and, though he will probably have to defy the Handicapper again after this, it is not out of the question. Official explanation: trainer said colt lost a shoe (tchd 6-1)
John Terry(IRE) again did not look the most enthusiastic of finishers but he stayed on all the way home without quite ever looking likely to win. Ridden from just behind the leaders, at least he saw his race out better than he had at Lingfield last time.
Charlie Tokyo(IRE) had been disappointing in previous attempts on Polytrack, but there can be no doubt now that he acts on it. Giving notice that he is coming back to form after a quiet start to season, he must have every chance of finding a suitable opportunity in the coming months.
Bahar Shumaal(IRE) has been lightly raced in the last year, but this was a spirited effort from a stable bang in form. He is reasonably handicapped if he can step up on this.
Mustajed made an encouraging seasonal debut, and is effective on both turf and Polytrack. He looks as good as ever, even at the age of seven. (op 33-1)
Pinch Of Salt(IRE) was too headstrong early on, and did not get a clear passage in the straight. Though much higher in the weights these days, he has improved greatly and this promising seasonal debut should give connections every hope of defying the Handicapper. (op 8-1)
Heron Bay, patiently ridden from last place, hit traffic problems in the straight and can do better. He will have to concede weight even in good handicaps like this, but he has a touch of class and his trainer will be hoping to find a suitable opportunity. (op 14-1)
Gold Prospect
Watamu(IRE) found disappointingly little when it came to the crunch, but can surely improve on this, even though he has a stiffer task at the weights these days. (op 6-1)
Players Please(USA) developed into a useful sort last year, and was gelded after his final run last season. He ran poorly but should not be discounted yet, as it may just have been an off-day. (op 15-2)

1077 INTERCASINO.CO.UK MAGNOLIA STKS (LISTED RACE) 1m 2f (P)

3:45 (3:46) (Class 1) 4-Y-0+

£14,762 (£5,595; £2,800; £1,396; £699; £351) **Stalls** High

Form RPR
0-2U **1** **Kandidate**[23] 817 6-8-13 0..............................(t) NCallan 6 110
(C E Brittain) *mde all: rdn and hung lft ins fnl f: jst hld on* **9/4**[2]
-260 **2** *hd* **Illustrious Blue**[23] 816 5-8-13 0.............................. RichardKingscote 4 110
(W J Knight) *stdd s: in rr tl gd hdwy over 1f out: r.o strly fnl f: jst failed* **12/1**
466- **3** *1/2* **Spice Route**[189] 5618 4-8-13 107.............................. JimCrowley 8 109
(M L W Bell) *trckd wnr: rdn and edgd lft ins fnl f: lost 2nd towards fin* **14/1**
04-3 **4** *3/4* **Great Hawk (USA)**[14] 906 5-8-13 105..............................(v) SebSanders 1 107
(Sir Michael Stoute) *towards rr: rdn and styd on fr over 1f out: nt rch ldrs* **3/1**[3]
5 *3/4* **Pur Sucre (FR)**[21] 842 4-8-13 0.............................. ChrisCatlin 3 106
(R Pritchard-Gordon, France) *mid-div: rdn and one pce fr over 1f out* **20/1**
2-05 **6** *nk* **Grand Passion (IRE)**[14] 906 8-9-2 104.............................. SteveDrowne 7 108
(G Wragg) *trckd ldrs: rdn 2f out: fdd ins fnl f* **16/1**
-300 **7** *1 1/2* **Impeller (IRE)**[51] 477 9-8-13 92.............................. TGMcLaughlin 5 102
(Jane Chapple-Hyam) *hld up in rr: one pce fnl 2f* **50/1**
/10- **8** *9* **Diamond Tycoon (USA)**[329] 1473 4-8-13 107.............................. PJSmullen 2 84
(B J Meehan) *trckd ldrs tl wknd qckly wl over 1f out* **15/8**[1]

2m 3.77s (-4.23) **Going Correction** -0.025s/f (Stan) **8** Ran SP% **117.5**
Speed ratings (Par 111): **115,114,114,113,113 113,111,104**
CSF £30.20 TOTE £3.20: £1.60, £2.70, £3.20; EX 34.40 Trifecta £322.10 Part won. Pool £453.68 - 0.80 winning units..
Owner Exors of the late A J Richards **Bred** Proton Partnership **Trained** Newmarket, Suffolk
■ Stewards' Enquiry : N Callan one-day ban: careless riding (Apr 12)

FOCUS
A classy contest, with the winner having been a possible runner in the World Cup run on the same day. The pace looked only fair, with Callan judging it well, but it resulted in a course record. It paid to be handy, so the runner-up did particularly well.

NOTEBOOK
Kandidate loves this track and made it three from three here on Polytrack, smashing the course record in the process. Callan judged the pace to perfection and, although not helped by his mount's tendency to edge badly left in the straight, he kept him going just long enough. (op 11-4)
Illustrious Blue was stone last, seven lengths off the leader and going nowhere, a furlong and a half from home, only to rocket home and just fail to get up. His style of running means he would have been suited by a stronger pace, but there is no doubt he can be very useful on his day.
Spice Route has been gelded since last year. He put in a game performance at his first attempt on Polytrack, and should have a good season if he can be found the right races.
Great Hawk(USA) never stopped staying on under pressure to reach his best position at the finish, but he is not always entirely convincing and this was one of those occasions. While talented enough, he still has his quirks. (op 7-2)
Pur Sucre(FR), a French raider, ran well without being quite good enough. He has been beaten on both his forays into Listed Class but deserves a few more chances at this level. (op 16-1 tchd 25-1)
Grand Passion(IRE) had a tricky task with his 3lb Listed penalty, but ran respectably, having raced more prominently than he often does.
Impeller(IRE) was about a stone behind many of these on paper, so did as well as could have been expected. (op 40-1)
Diamond Tycoon(USA) was forced to race three wide all the way, but that cannot explain why he ran so poorly. He returned sore after running ninth in the 2000 Guineas last year, and this first run since was hardly encouraging. Official explanation: jockey said colt ran too free (op 7-4 tchd 13-8 tchd 9-4 in a place)

1078 INTERCASINO.CO.UK E B F MAIDEN STKS 5f (P)

4:15 (4:16) (Class 4) 2-Y-0 **£4,857** (£1,445; £722; £360) **Stalls** High

Form RPR
1 **Asaint Needs Brass (USA)** 2-9-3 0.............................. SebSanders 3 64+
(R M Beckett) *trckd ldr: led over 1f out: no ex nr fin and jst hld on* **15/8**[1]
2 *shd* **Sub Prime (IRE)** 2-9-3 0.............................. SteveDrowne 9 64
(J A Osborne) *s.i.s and towards rr tl str burst ins fnl f: jst failed* **7/2**[2]
3 *shd* **Imperial Skylight** 2-9-3 0.............................. ChrisCatlin 6 64
(M R Channon) *led tl hdd over 1f out: kpt on u.p: lost 2nd post* **5/1**[3]
4 *nk* **Dr Wintringham (IRE)** 2-8-12 0.............................. LPKeniry 5 57
(J S Moore) *s.i.s: sn trckd ldrs: kpt on fnl f* **16/1**
5 *hd* **Grand Honour (IRE)** 2-9-3 0.............................. TGMcLaughlin 7 62+
(P Howling) *in rr tl r.o strly fnl f: nvr nrr* **14/1**
6 *shd* **Gone Hunting** 2-8-10 0.............................. JackDean(7) 2 61
(W G M Turner) *in tch on outside: effrt over 1f out: nt qckn ins fnl f* **7/1**
7 *1 1/4* **Multi Tasker** 2-9-0 0.............................. WilliamBuick(3) 8 56
(V Smith) *in tch tl hung rt over 1f out: fdd ins fnl f* **8/1**
8 *8* **Buckle Up** 2-9-3 0.............................. JimCrowley 1 24+
(D K Ivory) *wnt lft leaving stalls: a bhd* **20/1**
9 *1* **Comanche Trail (FR)** 2-9-3 0.............................. DeanMcKeown 10 20
(R M Whitaker) *slowly away: outpcd thrght* **16/1**

62.01 secs (1.51) **Going Correction** -0.025s/f (Stan) **9** Ran SP% **120.5**
Speed ratings (Par 94): **86,85,85,85,84 84,82,69,68**
CSF £8.80 TOTE £2.60: £1.30, £1.30, £2.00; EX 11.30.
Owner Tony Perkins, J Cameron & Wendy Smith **Bred** Fred Seitz **Trained** Whitsbury, Hants

FOCUS
All debutants, so impossible to rate with any confidence, but producing an amazing finish, with the winner folding up late on and the first six covered by less than a length. The pace was good, but these juveniles showed their inexperience by being all over the place around the bend.

NOTEBOOK
Asaint Needs Brass(USA) showed plenty of pace and looked set to win by a couple of lengths just inside the final furlong, but he tied up near the finish and was nearly caught by five others. This 24,000gns half-brother to juvenile winner Crumb Of Comfort should last longer next time, and this January foal - with this experience behind him - should be able to finish his race off rather better than he did here. (op 9-4 tchd 5-2 tchd 11-4 in places)
Sub Prime(IRE), an 18,000gns foal, is related to a smart 7f performer in Aeroplane, and should stay at least another furlong when those races become available. Finding his stride just too late after a hesitant start, he has the ability to get off the mark in routine maiden company. (op 9-2 tchd 5-1 in a place)
Imperial Skylight, the only one to match the winner for speed throught the race, was coming back at the finish after looking held a furlong from home. A late foal, he is a half-brother to the juvenile winner Splitthedifference, and his natural pace will stand him in good stead in the coming weeks. (op 7-1)
Dr Wintringham(IRE), the first runner for smart sprinter Monsieur Bond, is out of a winless but well-related dam. Very green for this debut, she had trouble rounding the home turn but finished off in a style which suggest that improvement is likely with experience. (op 20-1)
Grand Honour(IRE) has plenty of winners in the family, though it is discouraging that his purchase price dropped from 36,000gns as a foal to 16,000gns as a yearling. He looked set to make an unspectacular debut for most of the race, but suddenly took off in the final furlong and finished best of all. The way the race was run makes it hard to assess the merit of the performace, but he should improve for the run and must be considered in similar company for the time being.
Gone Hunting, whose dam Arasong won twice at 5f as a juvenile, has other winners in the family at a modest level. Beaten less than a length despite finishing sixth, he can be found a suitable opening by his trainer, who continues to do particularly well with two-year-olds. (op 4-1)
Multi Tasker cost only £2,000 as a yearling, so it was a surprise when he turned up in the paddock with all four legs. His dam, though moderate herself, is related to many winners, so it not impossible that this debutant could defy his price tag and follow in their footsteps, but the competition will get stronger as the season progresses. Official explanation: jockey said colt hung right (tchd 15-2)

1079 INTERCASINO.CO.UK CONDITIONS STKS — 6f (P)
4:50 (4:51) (Class 3) 3-Y-0+
£6,543 (£1,959; £979; £490; £244; £122) **Stalls** High

Form				RPR
110-	**1**		**Edge Closer**[183] 5765 4-9-4 97 ... PatDobbs 7	111
			(R Hannon) *chsd ldrs: wnt 2nd wl over 1f out: r.o to ld wl ins fnl f: pushed out* **2/1**[2]	
1-24	**2**	½	**Ceremonial Jade (UAE)**[14] 904 5-9-4 102 ... (t) SebSanders 6	109
			(M Botti) *in rr tl gd hdwy to ld on ins wl over 1f out: hdd wl ins fnl f: nt pce of wnr* **11/8**[1]	
-520	**3**	6	**Machinist (IRE)**[36] 670 8-9-4 0 ... PaulHanagan 5	90
			(D Nicholls) *hld up in tch: rdn and styd on fnl f: no ch w first 2* **7/1**	
-102	**4**	1	**Ajigolo**[11] 925 5-9-4 95 ... EdwardCreighton 3	87
			(M R Channon) *stdd s: hld up: rdn 2f out: nvr on terms* **9/2**[3]	
00-0	**5**	3	**Lucky Kyllachy (USA)**[67] 259 4-9-4 95 ... NCallan 4	77
			(Jane Chapple-Hyam) *led for 1f: trckd ldr tl carried lft wl over 1f out: no ch after* **20/1**	
400-	**6**	4½	**Garstang**[199] 5332 5-9-4 77 ... (b) LPKeniry 1	63
			(Peter Grayson) *led after 1f: hung lft and hdd wl over 1f out: sn btn* **50/1**	

1m 11.11s (-1.99) **Going Correction** -0.025s/f (Stan) **6 Ran SP% 112.8**
Speed ratings (Par 107): **112,111,103,102,98 92**
CSF £5.19 TOTE £2.90: £1.80, £1.70; EX 5.00.
Owner Lady Whent And Friends **Bred** Caroline Wilson **Trained** East Everleigh, Wilts

FOCUS
Quite a classy conditions race. The first two could develop into Listed or Group 3 sprinters.

NOTEBOOK
Edge Closer ◆ had a fine time in handicaps last year, and this was a good start to the new campaign. He should develop into a Listed or even Pattern-class performer if he continues to improve. (op 5-2)
Ceremonial Jade(UAE), a high-class handicapper these days, quickened well to lead on the inside but then just lost out in a good scrap with the winner. Though just held near the finish, he finished a long way clear of the rest. His handicap mark makes things a bit tricky, but he has enough class to give it a good shot in Listed or Group 3 company, and the fact that he stays 1m does give him plenty of options. (op 6-4 tchd 13-8)
Machinist(IRE), who has been running with credit in Dubai, was no match for the first two. He is higher in the weights these days following some good performances last season, which theoretically made him best-in in official figures here, but it is possible he is more effective on turf. (op 6-1)
Ajigolo had a little to do at the weights, and is more exposed than the winner. He should have every chance back in good handicap company. (op 4-1)
Lucky Kyllachy(USA) is very inconsistent and, though needing to find a bit to win this, produced one of his less inspiring performances. (op 16-1)
Garstang, a 77-rated handicapper, looked a bit out of place in this field, and so it proved. There will be many more suitable races for him. (op 66-1)

1080 INTERCASINO.CO.UK QUEEN'S PRIZE (H'CAP) — 2m (P)
5:25 (5:25) (Class 2) (0-105,95) 4-Y-0+
£9,971 (£2,985; £1,492; £747; £372; £187) **Stalls** High

Form				RPR
2321	**1**		**Calculating (IRE)**[23] 810 4-8-9 **83** ... NCallan 7	91
			(M D I Usher) *trckd ldrs: led over 1f out: rdn out fnl f* **10/3**[3]	
/3-1	**2**	¾	**Buster Hyvonen (IRE)**[15] 561 6-8-12 **81** ... OscarUrbina 3	88
			(J R Fanshawe) *hld up: rdn and hdwy 2f out to chse wnr ent fnl f: no imp towards fin* **5/2**[2]	
030-	**3**	1½	**Som Tala**[161] 6335 5-9-6 **89** ... ChrisCatlin 5	94
			(M R Channon) *towards rr tl hdwy to go 2nd 1/2-way: led briefly 2f out: lost 2nd ent fnl f: nt qckn* **2/1**[1]	
16-3	**4**	1¾	**Gallileo Figaro (USA)**[4] 1017 5-8-4 76 oh4 ... (b[1]) LukeMorris[(3)] 2	79
			(N B King) *trckd ldr to 1/2-way: rdn over 2f out: nt qckn appr fnl f* **10/1**	
1-54	**5**	3¼	**St Savarin (FR)**[7] 968 7-9-11 **94** ... NeilPollard 1	93
			(B R Johnson) *t.k.h: in rr: rdn 2f out: sn outpcd* **12/1**	
106-	**6**	nse	**Corum (IRE)**[9] 4786 5-9-1 **87** ... (p) WilliamBuick[(3)] 8	86
			(Mrs K Waldron) *led tl hdd 2f out: sn wknd* **16/1**	
0-20	**7**	5	**Moon Mix (FR)**[27] 630 5-9-0 **83** ... J-PGuillambert 4	76
			(J R Jenkins) *hld up in rr: brief effrt 2f out: nvr on terms* **8/1**	

3m 33.62s (3.52) **Going Correction** -0.025s/f (Stan)
WFA 4 from 5yo+ 5lb **7 Ran SP% 118.8**
Speed ratings (Par 109): **90,89,88,88,86 86,83**
CSF £12.86 CT £20.71 TOTE £4.60: £1.70, £2.00; EX 10.70 Place 6 £104.45, Place 5 £41.19.
Owner Brian Rogan **Bred** Darley **Trained** Upper Lambourn, Berks

FOCUS
Not as competitive as in its glory days, but this traditional race still attracted a decent field if a bit disappointing in quantity. The pace was sedate until halfway, and moderate thereafter until stepping up turning for home. Probably not form to take to literally.

NOTEBOOK
Calculating(IRE) reversed February form at Wolverhampton with the runner-up, but again there was not much between the two. He has had a cracking run in recent months, and it shows no signs of stopping. (op 4-1)
Buster Hyvonen(IRE), whose last race was a winning one over hurdles at Fakenham a fortnight earlier, ran game race in defeat, closing on the winner throughout the final furlong if never quite looking likely to get up. He has now proved he stays 2m, and should have a good season. (op 15-8)
Som Tala, gelded at the end of last season, tried to encourage an increase in the tempo from halfway but this was never going to be a stiff enough to bring out the best in him. That said, he ran a fine race in defeat and will really come into his own given a severe test of stamina. (op 10-3)
Gallileo Figaro(USA), blinkered for the first time, ran a sound race considering that her stamina was not fully tested here. Though a little higher in the weights these days, she remains in good form and cannot be ruled out in races at 2m and beyond, with soft ground appearing to be a bonus on turf. (op 8-1)
St Savarin(FR), trying a longer trip, was ridden accordingly and never became really competitive. Though this race was not run at a breakneck gallop, his effectiveness at this trip has yet to be proven. (op 10-1 tchd 14-1 in a place)
Corum(IRE) has not been at his best of late, and merely did the donkey-work for the others here. However, there were signs that he may be on the way back. (op 20-1)
Moon Mix(FR) needs a stronger end-to-end gallop to bring out the best in him. (op 9-1)
T/Plt: £133.90 to a £1 stake. Pool: £86,004.45. 468.85 winning tickets. T/Qpdt: £10.00 to a £1 stake. Pool: £4,152.10. 304.50 winning tickets. JS

1061 WOLVERHAMPTON (A.W) (L-H)
Saturday, March 29

OFFICIAL GOING: Standard
Wind: Strong behind Weather: Raining

1081 LADBROKES.COM (S) STKS — 5f 216y(P)
6:50 (6:50) (Class 6) 3-Y-0
£1,774 (£523; £262) **Stalls** Low

Form				RPR
0263	**1**		**Bahamarama (IRE)**[12] 917 3-8-12 50 ... (p) AdamKirby 4	56
			(R A Harris) *mde all: rdn clr fr over 1f out* **8/1**	
0004	**2**	2¼	**Stoneacre Ma**[10] 932 3-8-0 50 ... (b[1]) PatrickDonaghy[(7)] 3	44
			(Peter Grayson) *s.i.s: hdwy over 1f out: rdn and hung lft ins fnl f: nt rch wnr* **14/1**	
20-4	**3**	½	**Our Sunnie**[6] 977 3-8-12 66 ... AdrianTNicholls 7	47
			(D Nicholls) *chsd ldrs: rdn over 2f out: styd on same pce appr fnl f* **5/2**[1]	
5-66	**4**	nk	**Countrywide Comet (IRE)**[24] 797 3-9-3 55 ... (b) RobertWinston 1	51
			(P Howling) *a.p: rdn to chse wnr 2f out: styd on same pce appr fnl f* **6/1**	
02-0	**5**	½	**Just Puddie**[18] 845 3-8-4 40 ... (p) TolleyDean[(3)] 2	40
			(W G M Turner) *hld up in tch: plld hrd: rdn 2f out: styd on same pce appr fnl f* **20/1**	
4043	**6**	1	**Mileaminutemurphy**[10] 932 3-8-7 58 ... PatrickHills[(5)] 6	42
			(R Hannon) *prom: rdn over 2f out: styng on same pce whn hmpd ins fnl f: eased whn btn towards fin* **3/1**[2]	
4-00	**7**	8	**Santa Clara**[50] 480 3-8-7 59 ... TGMcLaughlin 5	11
			(Jane Chapple-Hyam) *hld up in tch: lost pl 1/2-way: rdn and wknd over 2f out* **7/2**[3]	
-400	**8**	16	**Miss Bronte**[12] 917 3-8-6 45 ow2 ... RussellKennemore[(3)] 8	—
			(R Hollinshead) *chsd wnr tl rdn 1/2-way: wknd 2f out* **25/1**	

1m 17.49s (2.49) **Going Correction** +0.20s/f (Slow) **8 Ran SP% 116.5**
Speed ratings (Par 96): **91,88,87,86,86 84,74,52**
CSF £111.41 TOTE £6.40: £1.90, £5.20, £1.10; EX 96.10.There was no bid for the winner
Owner Mrs Ruth M Serrell **Bred** Hyde Park Stud & Stephen Hillen **Trained** Earlswood, Monmouths

FOCUS
A moderate seller but the form looks reasonably sound, with the first two plus the fourth and fifth close to previous marks.
Miss Bronte Official explanation: vet said filly finished lame left-fore

1082 ERNIE & PHYLLIS HOUGH GOLDEN WEDDING CELEBRATION MAIDEN STKS — 1m 1f 103y(P)
7:20 (7:21) (Class 5) 3-Y-0+
£2,457 (£725; £362) **Stalls** Low

Form				RPR
6-2	**1**		**Irish Artist (FR)**[14] 900 3-8-4 70 ... PatrickHills[(5)] 2	78
			(R Hannon) *trckd ldrs: led wl over 1f out: sn rdn: all out* **5/2**[2]	
6022	**2**	hd	**Brave Hawk**[12] 920 3-8-9 74 ... (b) PhilipRobinson 4	78
			(M A Jarvis) *hld up in tch: chsd ldr over 2f out: rdn and hung lft fr over 1f out: r.o* **11/10**[1]	
	3	hd	**Bushman** 4-10-0 0 ... LPKeniry 8	82
			(D M Simcock) *hld up: hdwy over 2f out: rdn over 1f out: edgd lft: r.o* **33/1**	
-243	**4**	10	**Ace Of Spies (IRE)**[6] 980 3-8-9 72 ... JoeFanning 6	57
			(M Johnston) *sn led: hung rt fr over 3f out: hdd wl over 1f out: wknd fnl f* **5/1**[3]	
400-	**5**	12	**Landikhaya (IRE)**[129] 6899 3-8-9 68 ... JimCrowley 3	31
			(D K Ivory) *led early: plld hrd and prom: rdn 2f out: sn wknd* **20/1**	
2	**6**	8	**Crystal Spirit (IRE)**[33] 698 3-8-4 0 ... CDHayes 7	10
			(Enda Kelly, Ire) *chsd ldr tl rdn over 3f out: wknd over 2f out: eased* **13/2**	
00	**7**	4	**Camera Shy (IRE)**[14] 909 4-10-0 0 ... JamesDoyle 1	6
			(K A Morgan) *sn pushed along in rr: wknd over 3f out* **80/1**	
	8	21	**Cheveton** 4-9-11 0 ... TolleyDean[(3)] 5	—
			(R J Price) *s.i.s: plld hrd: hdwy 7f out: rdn and wknd over 3f out* **100/1**	

2m 2.29s (0.59) **Going Correction** +0.20s/f (Slow)
WFA 3 from 4yo 19lb **8 Ran SP% 116.1**
Speed ratings (Par 103): **105,104,104,95,85 77,74,55**
CSF £5.62 TOTE £3.50: £1.20, £1.10, £5.60; EX 7.00.
Owner Matthew Green **Bred** Le Thenney S A **Trained** East Everleigh, Wilts

FOCUS
A fair maiden in which the first three finished well clear. The runner-up is rated close to recent course and distance form.
Ace Of Spies(IRE) Official explanation: jockey said colt hung right-handed throughout

1083 LADBROKES - HOME OF FOOTBALL (S) STKS — 1m 141y(P)
7:50 (7:51) (Class 6) 4-Y-0+
£1,774 (£523; £262) **Stalls** Low

Form				RPR
4325	**1**		**One Night In Paris (IRE)**[29] 753 5-8-7 72 ... TGMcLaughlin 2	61
			(P D Evans) *hld up: rdn over 1f out: r.o* **10/11**[1]	
1620	**2**	1¼	**Climate (IRE)**[10] 938 9-8-11 60 ... RichardEvans[(7)] 5	69
			(P D Evans) *a.p: chsd wnr over 2f out: rdn and ev ch ins fnl f: no ex towards fin* **9/2**[3]	

The Form Book, Raceform Ltd, Compton, RG20 6NL

046 **3** *8* **Personify**[61] 341 6-8-12 52..............................(p) AdamKirby 6 45
(R A Harris) *hld up: rdn over 3f out: wnt mod 3rd wl over 1f out: no imp* **10/1**

5034 **4** *1 1/2* **Royal Embrace**[12] 915 5-8-12 53..............................(v) DeanMcKeown 1 41
(D Shaw) *hld up: effrt over 2f out: hung lft over 1f out: n.d* **8/1**

21/6 **5** *1* **Babieca (USA)**[36] 659 4-8-12 65.............................. PhillipMakin 4 39
(T D Barron) *dwlt: sn pushed along and prom: rdn 5f out: wknd wl over 2f out* **4/1**[2]

-504 **6** *16* **Far Seeking**[46] 530 4-8-12 45.............................. LPKeniry 3 —
(R A Harris) *s.i.s: sn chsng wnr: rdn and wknd over 2f out* **33/1**

1m 52.25s (1.75) **Going Correction** +0.20s/f (Slow) **6** Ran SP% **113.7**
Speed ratings (Par 101): **100,98,91,90,89 75**
CSF £5.57 TOTE £1.80: £1.20, £1.90; EX 4.70.
Owner Diamond Racing Ltd **Bred** Ken Carroll **Trained** Pandy, Monmouths
■ Stewards' Enquiry : Phillip Makin one-day ban: careless riding (Apr 12)

FOCUS
A moderate seller rated through the runner-up to his recent best.
Personify Official explanation: jockey said gelding ran too free early

1084 LADBROKES - SERIOUS ABOUT SERVICES H'CAP 7f 32y(P)
8:20 (8:20) (Class 5) (0-75,74) 4-Y-0+ **£2,730** (£806; £403) **Stalls** High

Form RPR

5402 **1** **Divertimenti (IRE)**[17] 850 4-9-3 73.............................. RobertWinston 2 83
(C R Dore) *mde all: shkn up over 1f out: unchal* **9/2**[2]

1322 **2** *2 1/4* **Count Ceprano (IRE)**[7] 969 4-8-11 74.............................. GabrielHannon(7) 6 78+
(M D I Usher) *s.i.s and hmpd s: hld up: hdwy over 1f out: r.o: nt rch wnr* **4/1**[1]

222 **3** *shd* **Dickie Le Davoir**[3] 1023 4-8-11 74.............................. MarkCoumbe(7) 8 78
(John A Harris) *chsd wnr: rdn over 2f out: styd on same pce fnl f* **4/1**[1]

-014 **4** *2 1/2* **Chief Exec**[22] 819 6-8-10 73..............................(b) DavidProbert(7) 7 70
(J R Gask) *hld up in tch: rdn over 1f out: styd on same pce fnl f* **8/1**

5-01 **5** *hd* **Golden Prospect**[49] 506 4-8-13 74.............................. PatrickHills(5) 1 71
(J W Hills) *chsd ldrs: rdn over 2f out: no ex fnl f: eased last strides* **11/2**[3]

5344 **6** *4* **Obe Royal**[2] 1040 4-8-7 70..............................(b) RichardEvans(7) 3 56
(P D Evans) *hld up: rdn over 1f out: n.d* **9/2**[2]

13-0 **7** *3 1/2* **Sedge (USA)**[29] 755 8-9-0 70..............................(b) MickyFenton 4 46
(P T Midgley) *edgd rt s: racd keenly and prom: rdn over 2f out: sn wknd* **12/1**

0330 **8** *1 1/4* **Parkview Love (USA)**[29] 755 7-8-10 66..............................(v) DeanMcKeown 9 39
(D Shaw) *hld up: rdn and wknd 2f out* **16/1**

1m 30.67s (1.07) **Going Correction** +0.20s/f (Slow) **8** Ran SP% **116.4**
Speed ratings (Par 103): **101,98,98,95,95 90,86,85**
CSF £23.32 CT £78.49 TOTE £5.80: £2.20, £1.60, £1.80; EX 21.20.
Owner Page, Ward, Marsh **Bred** Airlie Stud **Trained** West Pinchbeck, Lincs
■ Stewards' Enquiry : Patrick Hills four-day ban: dropped hands before line and lost fourth place (Apr 12-15)

FOCUS
Divertimenti enjoyed the run of the race in front in this fair handicap and is rated to his recent best with the form backed up by the third.

1085 EVERYONE'S GOT AN OPINION WITH LADBROKES H'CAP 1m 141y(P)
8:50 (8:50) (Class 5) (0-70,68) 4-Y-0+ **£2,730** (£806; £403) **Stalls** Low

Form RPR

6333 **1** **Machinate (USA)**[12] 914 6-8-13 63.............................. TGMcLaughlin 2 72
(W M Brisbourne) *hld up: hdwy to chse ldr over 2f out: led over 1f out: drvn out* **8/1**

0-62 **2** *1 1/4* **Juzilla (IRE)**[35] 685 4-8-13 63.............................. AdamKirby 1 69+
(W R Swinburn) *disp ld tl led 4f out: rdn and hdd over 1f out: styd on same pce ins fnl f* **15/8**[1]

0633 **3** *2 1/4* **Sovereignty (JPN)**[22] 819 6-8-11 61.............................. JimCrowley 5 62
(D K Ivory) *hld up in tch: plld hrd: chsd ldr over 2f out: sn outpcd: styd on ins fnl f* **7/1**[3]

4634 **4** *2 1/4* **Putra Laju (IRE)**[24] 805 4-8-11 66..............................(p) PatrickHills(5) 6 62
(J W Hills) *s.i.s: hld up: hdwy whn hmpd wl over 1f out: sn rdn: nt trble ldrs* **17/2**

-212 **5** *1/2* **Wisdom's Kiss**[16] 872 4-8-7 57..............................(p) JimmyQuinn 4 52
(J D Bethell) *chsd ldrs: rdn over 2f out: sn outpcd* **3/1**[2]

30-2 **6** *15* **Billy One Punch**[15] 879 6-9-1 68.............................. TolleyDean(3) 3 28
(D Shaw) *chsd ldrs: rdn over 2f out: wknd over 1f out* **8/1**

2-64 **7** *16* **Moment Of Clarity**[7] 973 6-8-8 65..............................(p) KrishGundowry(7) 7 —
(R C Guest) *disp ld over 4f: rdn and wknd over 2f out* **12/1**

1m 51.39s (0.89) **Going Correction** +0.20s/f (Slow) **7** Ran SP% **112.7**
Speed ratings (Par 103): **104,102,100,98,98 85,70**
CSF £22.80 TOTE £8.10: £3.00, £1.80; EX 24.20.
Owner D Slingsby **Bred** Gaines-Gentry Thoroughbreds & William Condren **Trained** Great Ness, Shropshire
■ Stewards' Enquiry : T G McLaughlin caution: used whip with excessive frequency

FOCUS
A moderate handicap run at a decent pace. The winner is rated to form although the runner-up is better than this at her best.
Putra Laju(IRE) Official explanation: jockey said colt was denied a clear run

1086 LADBROKES IN THE COMMUNITY CHARITABLE TRUST H'CAP 1m 4f 50y(P)
9:20 (9:20) (Class 6) (0-60,60) 4-Y-0+ **£2,047** (£604; £302) **Stalls** Low

Form RPR

1245 **1** **Buscador (USA)**[2] 1044 9-9-4 57.............................. RichardKingscote 1 67
(W M Brisbourne) *mde all: rdn clr over 1f out: eased nr fin* **5/2**[1]

5445 **2** *1 3/4* **Punta Galera (IRE)**[29] 752 5-9-6 59.............................. NeilChalmers 5 66+
(Paul Green) *hld up: hdwy and nt clr run over 1f out: r.o: no ch w wnr* **10/3**[2]

1224 **3** *4* **Still Dreaming**[28] 771 4-9-1 56..............................(b) DaleGibson 3 57
(R J Price) *trckd ldrs: rdn over 2f out: styd on same pce appr fnl f* **9/2**[3]

4 *1 1/2* **Masking Baldini (IRE)**[322] 1686 4-8-8 49.............................. JimmyQuinn 7 47
(P T Midgley) *chsd ldrs: rdn over 3f out: styd on same pce fnl 2f* **16/1**

600/ **5** *nk* **Working Late**[101] 2515 6-8-4 46 ow1..............................(t) TolleyDean(3) 9 44
(Mike Hammond) *s.i.s: hld up: rdn over 6f out: hdwy 5f out: outpcd over 2f out: styd on ins fnl f* **40/1**

000- **6** *2 1/4* **Thorny Mandate**[173] 6068 6-9-6 59.............................. TGMcLaughlin 2 53
(W M Brisbourne) *s.i.s: hld up: hdwy over 2f out: wknd over 1f out: sn hung lft* **17/2**

0002 **7** *5* **Satindra (IRE)**[16] 863 4-9-5 60..............................(tp) MickyFenton 8 46
(John A Harris) *chsd wnr: rdn over 3f out: wknd over 1f out* **6/1**

0340 **8** *13* **Sir Bond (IRE)**[16] 872 7-8-10 54.............................. SladeO'Hara(5) 4 19
(G R Oldroyd) *s.s: hld up: rdn and wknd over 3f out* **8/1**

2m 42.89s (1.79) **Going Correction** +0.20s/f (Slow)
WFA 4 from 5yo+ 2lb **8** Ran SP% **114.1**
Speed ratings (Par 101): **102,100,98,97,96 95,92,83**
CSF £10.85 CT £34.21 TOTE £3.70: £1.20, £1.90, £1.20; EX 8.40 Place 6 £7.99, Place 5 £3.39.
Owner David Robson **Bred** William H Floyd **Trained** Great Ness, Shropshire

FOCUS
A low-grade handicap in which Buscador was another winner on the night to make all. He sets the standard.
Satindra(IRE) Official explanation: jockey said gelding hung left-handed latter stages
T/Plt: £12.20 to a £1 stake. Pool: £87,017.05. 5,167.00 winning tickets. T/Qpdt: £4.20 to a £1 stake. Pool: £7,560.90. 1,318.70 winning tickets. CR

812 NAD AL SHEBA (L-H)
Saturday, March 29

OFFICIAL GOING: Dirt course - fast; turf course - good

1087a GODOLPHIN MILE (SPONSORED BY ETISALAT) (GROUP 2) (DIRT) 1m (D)
1:40 (1:40) 3-Y-0+
£301,507 (£100,502; £50,251; £25,125; £15,075; £10,050)

RPR

1 **Diamond Stripes (USA)**[63] 5-9-0 111..............................(bt) EPrado 8 115
(R Dutrow Jr, U.S.A) *disp ld: hdd 2f out: r.o and led cl home* **3/1**[2]

2 *1 1/4* **Elusive Warning (USA)**[23] 815 4-9-0 111.............................. KerrinMcEvoy 13 112
(Saeed Bin Suroor) *settled in rr: r.o wl fnl 7f: ev ch fnl f: nrst fin* **5/2**[1]

3 *1 1/4* **Don Renato (CHI)**[22] 5-9-0 107..............................(bt) WRamos 1 109
(Stephane Chevalier, UAE) *slowly away: racd in last: r.o wl fnl 2f: nrst fin* **100/1**

4 *nse* **Zakocity (USA)**[29] 7-9-0 108.............................. RAlbarado 11 109
(J Smith Jr, Saudi Arabia) *settled in rr: stl in rr 3f out: r.o wl: nrst fin* **25/1**

5 *3/4* **Rosberg (USA)**[37] 648 7-9-0 107..............................(bt) TPO'Shea 14 107
(E Charpy, UAE) *trckd ldrs: led 2f out: hdd & wknd ins fnl f* **33/1**

6 *7 1/4* **Blackat Blackitten (IRE)**[23] 815 4-9-0 110.............................. LDettori 3 92
(Saeed Bin Suroor) *slowly away: racd in rr: nvr able to chal* **3/1**[2]

7 *1/2* **Jet Express (SAF)**[23] 815 6-9-0 104.............................. RoystonFfrench 12 90
(A Al Raihe, UAE) *mid-div: hrd rdn 3f out: sn btn* **50/1**

8 *hd* **Brave Tin Soldier (USA)**[23] 815 4-9-0 102..............................(e) KShea 6 90
(M F De Kock, South Africa) *prom: ev ch 3f out: wknd fnl f* **50/1**

9 *1/4* **Green Coast (IRE)**[23] 815 5-9-0 102.............................. AGryder 4 89
(Doug Watson, UAE) *trckd ldrs on rail: rdn 3f out: wknd fnl 1 1/2f* **33/1**

10 *1* **Halkin (USA)**[23] 815 6-9-0 104.............................. WayneSmith 5 87
(F Nass, Bahrain) *stmbld after 1f: mid-div: chsd ldrs to 4f out* **50/1**

11 *3 3/4* **Watch What Happens (FR)**[23] 815 5-9-0 104.............................. DBeadman 2 79
(S P C Woods, Hong Kong) *nvr able to chal* **100/1**

12 *3/4* **Barcola (USA)**[112] 5-9-0 106..............................(t) GKGomez 15 77
(M Hennig, U.S.A) *disp ld tl 3f out: sn btn* **14/1**

13 *6 1/2* **Golden Arrow (IRE)**[30] 745 5-9-0 104..............................(bt) MJKinane 9 63
(E Charpy, UAE) *nvr nr to chal* **12/1**

14 *dist* **Baharah (USA)**[55] 418 4-8-9 109.............................. JamieSpencer 10 —
(G A Butler) *hmpd after 1f: mid-div: nvr able to chal* **11/1**[3]

1m 36.96s (0.26) **Going Correction** +0.375s/f (Slow) **14** Ran SP% **118.9**
Speed ratings: **113,111,110,110,109 102,101,101,101,100 96,96,89,—**
CSF: £10.14..
Owner Four Roses Thoroughbreds **Bred** Mr & Mrs Samuel H Rogers Jr **Trained** USA

FOCUS
The weakest race on the card and, while it carries Group 2 status, the race was made up mainly of Group 3/Listed class animals. The one possible exception was the winner Diamond Stripes, who had form in Grade 1 company last year.

NOTEBOOK
Diamond Stripes(USA) placed in three Grade 1s last year and won the Grade 2 Meadowlands Cup in October. While he was subsequently down the field in the Breeders' Cup Classic, an unlucky-in-running third to World Cup hope A P Arrow in the Clark Handicap confirmed his ability, and he could easily be excused a below-par effort on the synthetic surface at Santa Anita last time. He was dropping back in distance here, but broke well from stall eight and was soon prominent. Although he looked in trouble when left behind by Rosberg early in the straight, he simply kept galloping away and in the end his stamina for further, coupled with his rider's excellent judge of pace, saw him claw back the advantage at the 200m pole. The form is nothing to get carried away with, but the winner's success was a timely boost for his younger stable-companion and Kentucky Derby hope Big Brown, who was due to contest the Florida Derby later in the day. He apparently worked all over Diamond Stripes during the winter.
Elusive Warning(USA)'s stable has won this race twice since it became a Group 2 in 2002, and there is a strong argument to be made that he should have notched them a third success. He was squeezed up soon after the start when trying to get an early position and that put him on the back foot with a lot of work to do entering the straight. He ran on really well down the outside but just could not overhaul the winner, who had enjoyed a much better trip throughout. A progressive sort who has had just the five starts, he can go on to better things back in the US later this year.
Don Renato(CHI) finished third to World Cup hope Premium Tap over this trip in Saudi Arabia last time and his price probably underestimated his chance. He made a lot of late ground from off the pace, not enjoying the clearest of runs either, and posted a solid effort in defeat.
Zakocity(USA), another with form in Saudi Arabia, where he had won his last two starts in allowance company, battled for the minor placing with Don Renato and just came off worst in the photo.
Rosberg(USA) has only won in handicap company, but he did score easily last time out. It was something of a surprise to see him cruising at the top of the straight, though, and when he quickened up with two furlongs to run he looked to have stolen a march. But as it happens his rider had gone for home too soon and his mount hit the wall with a furlong to run.
Blackat Blackitten(IRE) was closely matched with Elusive Warning on their running in the Burj Nahaar last time, but he was perhaps open to less improvement than his stablemate. He raced in mid-division here, taking in plenty of kickback, and never really threatened. (op 11-4)
Jet Express(SAF) merely plugged on past beaten horses.
Barcola(USA), who likes to make the running, was never given much peace out in front.

Baharah(USA) struggled throughout after being severely hampered early on in the same incident which caused Elusive Warning to lose his position. She has developed into a smart performer on Polytrack, but this was an altogether different ball game, and she will be of much more interest back on turf in Europe. (op 12-1)

1088a UAE DERBY (SPONSORED BY AL NABOODAH) (GROUP 2) (DIRT) 1m 1f (D)
2:15 (2:15) 3-Y-O

£603,015 (£201,005; £100,502; £50,251; £30,150; £20,100)

RPR

1 **Honour Devil (ARG)**[23] [813] 4-9-4 115 JMurtagh 9 121
(M F De Kock, South Africa) *trckd ldrs: rdn 4f out: disp ld 2f out: r.o wl* **15/8**[1]

2 4 1/4 **Royal Vintage (SAF)**[23] [813] 4-9-4 116 KShea 8 112
(M F De Kock, South Africa) *mid-div: trckd ldrs: ev ch 2f out: nt pce of wnr* **5/2**[2]

3 3 3/4 **Cocoa Beach (CHI)**[30] [744] 4-9-0 110 (v) TedDurcan 1 100
(Saeed Bin Suroor) *settled in rr: prog into mid-div 4 1/2f out: r.o wl fnl 1 1/2f: nrst fin* **5/1**[3]

4 1/4 **Light Green (BRZ)**[36] [672] 4-9-0 110 MJKinane 7 100
(P Nickel Filho, Brazil) *mid-div for 1f: dropped to rr: stl in rr 3f out: r.o wl fnl 1 1/2f: nrst fin* **25/1**

5 1 1/4 **Strike The Deal (USA)**[155] [6484] 3-8-9 112 RyanMoore 11 106
(J Noseda) *mid-div: trckd ldrs 4 1/2f out: led 2f out: wknd fnl f* **14/1**

6 3 1/2 **My Indy (ARG)**[44] [567] 4-9-4 106 LDettori 3 94
(Saeed Bin Suroor) *slowly away: mid-div: rdn 4 1/2f out: n.d* **10/1**

7 1/4 **Ukrainian (BRZ)**[23] [812] 4-9-4 102 RichardMullen 6 93
(A Cintra Pereira, Brazil) *racd in rr: nvr able to chal* **50/1**

8 4 **Iide Kenshin (JPN)**[47] 3-8-9 106 SFujita 12 90
(Mitsugi Kon, Japan) *rdn to ld: hdd & wknd 3f out* **33/1**

9 dist **Massive Drama (USA)**[48] 3-8-9 111 (bt) GKGomez 4 —
(Dale Romans, U.S.A) *trckd ldr: led 3f out: sn hdd & wknd* **12/1**

10 dist **Numaany (USA)**[23] [813] 3-8-9 109 KerrinMcEvoy 2 —
(Saeed Bin Suroor) *racd in rr: nvr nr to chal* **16/1**

1m 49.6s (-0.20) **Going Correction** +0.375s/f (Slow)
WFA 3 from 4yo 19lb 10 Ran SP% **118.1**
Speed ratings: **115,111,107,107,106 103,103,99,—,—**
CSF: £6.54..
Owner Sheikh Mohammed Bin Khalifa Al Maktoum **Bred** Firmamento **Trained** South Africa
■ Mike de Kock saddled the first two home, just as he did in the first two legs of the UAE Triple Crown.

FOCUS
A competitive Group 2 contest, the third leg of the Triple Crown. The first four home were bred in the Southern Hemisphere. Between them Saeed Bin Suroor and Mike de Kock had won all eight previous runnings, and the pair saddled five runners between them in this year's renewal.

NOTEBOOK
Honour Devil(ARG), having beaten his stablemate Royal Vintage into second in the Guineas, looked an unlucky loser when the placings were reversed in the Al Bastakiya, but he made no mistake this time, settling the score in no uncertain terms. After chasing the furious pace from the outset, he was off the bridle much sooner than Royal Vintage, well before the final bend, but he picked up once in line for home. It briefly looked as though he might have a battle on his hands when ranging upsides both Strike The Deal and Royal Vintage at the 400m pole, but the British challenger soon dropped away and he had his stable companion covered in another half furlong or so. His effort is particularly creditable considering he appeared to have had an extremely hard race when beaten over this course and distance three weeks earlier, and he's clearly a very tough colt. It remains to be seen where he will go next, but his trainer is keen to run him in a race at the Breeders' Cup meeting, and mentioned the Mile as a possible target. (op 7-4)
Royal Vintage(SAF) travelled better than the winner and looked as though he might take a bit of beating when still on the bridle and getting a run against the inside rail at the top of the straight, but he was ultimately worn down. Like the winner, he had a very hard race just three weeks earlier and his trainer was of the opinion afterwards that his earlier exertions probably left their mark, as he is considered the more immature of the pair. However, he is regarded by his trainer as a tremendous long-term prospect and it is also considered he might be a little better on turf.
Cocoa Beach(CHI) earned her place in this company after landing both the UAE 1000 Guineas and Oaks and she acquitted herself with real credit. What she lacks is early speed, so she could not have been worse drawn in stall one and, after being squeezed out soon after the start, she was rightly switched to the outside, away from the kickback. She was well enough placed all things considered, but came off the bridle before the turn for home and, although staying on, she could not go with the front two. She is a nice prospect for fillies and mares races in the US and will have no problem staying further, but she will probably want to avoid some of the tighter tracks in the States. (tchd 11-2)
Light Green(BRZ) could not go the early pace and was soon last, but she eventually ran on past beaten horses, confirming the ability she showed when third in a turf Listed race on her debut in Dubai.
Strike The Deal(USA) ran a terrific race on his first start since finishing fourth in the Breeders' Cup Juvenile Turf last October and is better than his placing indicates. Having raced on the strong pace throughout, he looked booked for third once the de Kock pair went on inside the final two furlongs, but he understandably got very tired late on. He looked well suited to the surface and will have plenty of options this year, but a drop back in trip is probably needed.
My Indy(ARG) recovered from being a little short of room soon after the start to sit just off the leaders and he seemed to travel okay, but he was left behind once the field turned for home. (op 12-1)
Numaany(USA) was only a length and a half behind today's winner on his previous start, but he was allowed the run of the race that day. He got worked up beforehand this time and, having been slightly squeezed at the start, he was never going. (op 20-1)

1089a DUBAI GOLDEN SHAHEEN (SPONSORED BY GULF NEWS) (GROUP 1) (DIRT) 6f (D)
2:55 (2:56) 3-Y-0+

£603,015 (£201,005; £100,502; £50,251; £30,150; £20,100)

RPR

1 **Benny The Bull (USA)**[63] 5-9-0 115 (t) EPrado 10 120
(R Dutrow Jr, U.S.A) *mid-div: hrd rdn 2 1/2f out: r.o fnl 1 1/2f: led nr line* **7/4**[1]

2 1 3/4 **Idiot Proof (USA)**[42] 4-9-0 115 (vt) DFlores 14 115
(Clifford Sise Jr, U.S.A) *disp ld: led 1f out: hdd cl home* **5/1**[3]

3 2 1/4 **Star Crowned (USA)**[23] [814] 5-9-0 104 (t) MJKinane 13 108
(R Bouresly, Kuwait) *prom: ev ch whn n.m.r 1f out: r.o* **50/1**

4 1 **Barbecue Eddie (USA)**[68] 4-9-0 113 (bt) AGryder 2 105
(B Koriner, U.S.A) *prom far side: nt qckn fnl f* **14/1**

5 1 3/4 **New Freedom (BRZ)**[23] [814] 7-9-0 105 TPO'Shea 7 100
(A Selvaratnam, UAE) *chsd ldrs: r.o fnl 2f* **33/1**

6 nse **Esperamos (USA)**[50] 4-9-0 105 (t) GKGomez 6 100
(Wesley A Ward, U.S.A) *prom in centre: ev ch 2f out: nt qckn* **16/1**

7 3/4 **Diabolical (USA)**[23] [814] 5-9-0 117 LDettori 5 98
(Saeed Bin Suroor) *mid-div: rdn 3f out: sn btn* **11/4**[2]

8 1 **Drift Ice (SAF)**[15] 7-9-0 102 (b) KShea 8 95
(M F De Kock, South Africa) *nvr bttr than mid-div on far rail* **40/1**

9 1 **Narc (SAF)**[188] 6-9-0 113 JMurtagh 9 92
(M F De Kock, South Africa) *nvr nr to chal* **22/1**

10 1/4 **Mutamarres**[30] [738] 5-9-0 105 RHills 4 91
(Doug Watson, UAE) *trckd ldrs tl 3f out: wknd* **25/1**

11 nse **Sarissa (BRZ)**[23] [814] 5-8-9 102 C-PLemaire 12 86
(P Bary, France) *nvr nr to chal* **50/1**

12 1 1/2 **Cobalt Blue (USA)**[63] 4-9-0 106 (bt) TedDurcan 1 86
(S Seemar, UAE) *a struggling* **33/1**

13 3 **Bushwacker (USA)**[63] 6-9-0 110 (t) JTalamo 3 77
(W Currin, U.S.A) *chsd ldrs for 3f* **16/1**

14 9 1/2 **Calrissian (GER)**[15] 4-9-0 101 RyanMoore 11 49
(L Kelp, Denmark) *nvr able to chal* **50/1**

15 9 **Munaddam (USA)**[30] [741] 6-9-0 110 MartinDwyer 15 22
(E Charpy, UAE) *nvr nr to chal* **25/1**

69.70 secs (-0.50) **Going Correction** +0.375s/f (Slow) **15** Ran SP% **124.4**
Speed ratings: **118,115,112,111,109 108,107,106,105,104 104,102,98,86,74**
CSF: £9.72.
Owner IEAH Stables et al **Bred** Tamoka Farms Inc **Trained** USA

FOCUS
Over the years American-trained runners have dominated the Golden Shaheen, and the pattern continued this time in a race that looked well up to standard. The pace was strong throughout and the draw played little part.

NOTEBOOK
Benny The Bull(USA) completed a double on the card for trainer Richard Dutrow Jr, following the success of Diamond Stripes in the Godolphin Mile, and reversed Breeders' Cup Sprint form with Idiot Proof, who finished two places in front of him at Monmouth Park last November. He has improved since then, winning a Grade 1 at Laurel Park before bolting up in the Sunshine Millions Sprint at Gulfstream Park, and the way this race was run suited him down to the ground as he is at his best being held up for a late run. As the leaders hit the wall he stayed on strongly to get up well inside the last and win a shade comfortably. This success means he can lay genuine claim to currently being the best sprinter in the world. (op 15-8)
Idiot Proof(USA), who likes to race prominently, was fitted with a visor in order to try and keep him concentrated up this long straight, but the headgear did not work at all, for while he was drawn in stall 14, he hung all the way over to the far-side rail. The all-round pace he showed was terrific, but on this evidence he will be a lot happier back in the US, where he gets to race around a left-handed turn.
Star Crowned(USA) has done nothing but improve since being switched to dirt and dropped back in trip, and he posted another personal best here, having been up there with the strong gallop throughout. He was done few favours by Idiot Proof, who carried him over to the far side as he hung, but it probably made no great difference to the final result. Finishing third to two top-class American sprinters was a fine effort.
Barbecue Eddie(USA) is another who likes to be up with the pace. He stayed pretty straight from his draw in stall two and kept on stoutly for fourth. He had finished in front of Idiot Proof on the cushion track at Santa Anita on New Year's Day, but that was over slightly shorter, and he received 6lb from his rival on that occasion, whereas they raced off levels here.
New Freedom(BRZ) struggled in the mid part of the race but was staying on again late. He and Star Crowned had filled the places when well beaten by Diabolical in the Group 3 Mahab Al Shimaal here last time, and they both received 4lb from the Godolphin horse that day. Their performances off levels here suggest that Diabolical was well below form.
Esperamos(USA) was one of the more interesting runners in the line-up, having clocked fast times while winning in lesser company, but he was taking a big step up in class this time. He showed good early speed, but did not see the trip out as strongly as some more battle-hardened rivals.
Diabolical(USA), who gave weight and a beating to Benny The Bull at Saratoga last summer, should have gone close had he been at his best, but that was clearly not the case, as he was not even able to confirm recent course and distance form with Star Crowned and New Freedom, whom he gave weight and a thrashing to in the Mahab Al Shimaal. While he was squeezed up a little at the start, he was otherwise well enough placed throughout to have every chance, but for some reason he was unable to pick up in the latter stages. Having seen American-trained sprinters take this prize on a regular basis Godolphin had bought one of the best from the US to try and keep the prize at home this year, but things did not work out for them.
Drift Ice(SAF), who hung over to the far rail, came out on top against Narc in the battle of the two Mike de Kock runners, but neither was ever a threat to the principals. (op 33-1)
Mutamarres has had a very successful carnival, but his improvement through handicaps and Listed company has come on turf.

1090a DUBAI DUTY FREE (SPONSORED BY DUBAI DUTY FREE) (GROUP 1) (TURF) 1m 194y(T)
3:55 (3:58) 3-Y-0+

£1,507,537 (£502,512; £251,256; £125,628; £75,376; £50,251)

RPR

1 **Jay Peg (SAF)**[23] [818] 5-9-0 116 (b) AMarcus 14 123
(H J Brown, South Africa) *led: hdd 2f out: 5th 1f out: r.o to ld nr line* **50/1**

2 1/2 **Darjina (FR)**[111] [7091] 4-8-9 122 CSoumillon 11 117
(A De Royer-Dupre, France) *mid-div: rdn to chse ldrs 2f out: led 1f out: hdd cl home* **5/1**[2]

3 nse **Archipenko (USA)**[37] [651] 4-9-0 116 (bt) KShea 7 122+
(M F De Kock, South Africa) *mid-div: trckd ldrs 3f out: ev ch whn no room 2f out: r.o once clr* **16/1**

4 1 1/4 **Vodka (JPN)**[35] 4-8-9 117 YTake 12 114
(Katsuhiko Sumii, Japan) *mid-div: chsd ldrs 2 1/2f out: nt qckn fnl f* **10/1**

5 1/2 **Finsceal Beo (IRE)**[174] [6042] 4-8-9 119 KJManning 6 113
(J S Bolger, Ire) *mid-div: rdn 2 1/2f out: nt qckn* **9/1**[3]

6 nse **Seachange (NZ)**[23] [818] 6-8-9 112 TedDurcan 4 113
(R Manning, New Zealand) *trckd ldrs: led briefly 1 1/2f out: wknd fnl 110yds* **25/1**

7 1/4 **Floral Pegasus (AUS)**[34] 5-9-0 115 (t) GMosse 3 118
(A S Cruz, Hong Kong) *trckd ldrs: t.k.h: ev ch 2f out: nt qckn fnl f* **14/1**

8 1/2 **Creachadoir (IRE)**[111] [7091] 4-9-0 118 KerrinMcEvoy 9 117
(Saeed Bin Suroor) *in rr of mid-div: nvr able to chal* **5/1**[2]

9 1/2 **Admire Aura (JPN)**[35] 4-9-0 115 KAndo 5 116
(H Matsuda, Japan) *in rr of mid-div: nvr able to chal* **9/1**[3]

10 1/2 **Lord Admiral (USA)**[23] [818] 7-9-0 112 (b) MJKinane 15 114
(Charles O'Brien, Ire) *settled in rr: nvr nr to chal but r.o fnl 2 1/2f* **40/1**

11 1 1/4 **Niconero (AUS)**[28] 7-9-0 115 (e) CraigAWilliams 8 112
(David Hayes, Australia) *in rr of mid-div: nvr able to chal* **25/1**

12 3/4 **Literato (FR)**[161] [6334] 4-9-0 123 LDettori 10 110
(Saeed Bin Suroor) *mid-div: rdn to chse ldrs 2 1/2f out: nt qckn fnl 1 1/2f* **3/1**[1]

13 1/2 **Bullish Luck (USA)**[34] 9-9-0 115 (b) BPrebble 13 109
(A S Cruz, Hong Kong) *in rr of mid-div: chsd ldrs 2 1/2f out: nt qckn fnl 1 1/2f* **22/1**

14 shd **Linngari (IRE)**[37] [651] 6-9-0 121 RyanMoore 16 109
(H J Brown, South Africa) *settled in rr: nvr nr to chal* **16/1**

15 3 1/4 **Majestic Roi (USA)**[175] 6010 4-8-9 116......................... DarryllHolland 2 97
(M R Channon) *settled in rr: nvr nr to chal* **25/1**
16 19 **Notional (USA)**[41] 4-9-0 113..(b) GKGomez 1 62
(Doug O'Neill, U.S.A) *mid-div: rdn 3f out: wknd* **50/1**
1m 47.2s (-2.80) **Going Correction** +0.125s/f (Good) **16** Ran SP% **128.1**
Speed ratings: **117,116,116,115,114 114,114,114,113,113 112,111,111,111,108 91**
CSF: £287.18.
Owner M Shirtliff,E Braun, P Loomes, S Marcus **Bred** High Season Stud **Trained** South Africa

FOCUS
A maximum field of 16 lined up for just the third time since the Dubai Duty Free Stakes was given Group 1 status back in 2002, and it featured winners of Group/Graded races in 12 different countries, so this was a truly international contest. The eventual winner dictated a stop-start gallop, and the form needs to be treated with caution.

NOTEBOOK
Jay Peg(SAF) was poorly drawn out wide in stall 14 but, with nothing else particularly keen to go on, he was able to get across and take a clear lead soon after the start. From then on he was able to dictate the fractions to suit and went a very sensible pace. Despite having stepped up the tempo and moved a good two lengths clear rounding the final bend, he quickly looked vulnerable when joined on both sides early in the straight and was passed by Vodka on his outside, but he battled on most gamely to get back in front near the finish. This effort is particularly creditable considering his saddle slipped in the straight and his rider very nearly went out the side door just after crossing the line. Indeed, after the race jockey Anton Marcus said he felt the saddle go in the last 250m, so this success owes plenty to a fantastic bit of horsemanship from the jockey. The winner, who landed the 2007 Cape Guineas and Derby, had not been at his best on his first two starts in Dubai, but he ran well with the blinkers fitted when a length second to Lord Admiral conceding 6lb in the Group 2 Jebel Hatta Stakes on his previous start and stepped forward again to land this valuable prize.
Darjina(FR) ◆, last seen finishing third (Creachadoir second) in the Hong Kong Mile in December, ran a mighty race in defeat, stepped up to her furthest trip to date. Settled in mid-division, she showed a good turn of foot to get upsides Jay Peg in the straight, but that one had enjoyed the run of the race and she ultimately had to give second best. A top-class individual, well up to taking on the colts, she should win her share at this level this year.
Archipenko(USA) caused a bit of a surprise when returning to form with victory in the Al Fahidi Fort on his most recent start, but he confirmed that was no fluke with a fine effort in defeat on his first start at the top level since finishing fifth behind Darjina in last year's Prix du Moulin. He could even be considered a little unlucky as he was closing fast at the finish once switched off heels and into the clear well inside the final furlong, but it was his lack of pace early in the straight that got him into that pocket. He gives the impression he will be suited by a return to 1m2f and this ex-Aidan O'Brien-trained colt looks a high-class recruit to the de Kock camp.
Vodka(JPN), a dual Grade-1 winner in Japan, was reasonably placed considering the lack of pace and she looked a big threat when briefly hitting the front halfway up the straight, but she could not sustain her effort.
Finsceal Beo(IRE) ◆, last year's English and Irish 1,000 Guineas winner, had plenty to prove after losing her way in the second half of last season, but she showed she is back to something like her best with a very creditable effort in defeat. She is even better than the bare form indicates, as she found herself much further back than ideal after being a little short of room soon after the start, and the way she picked up late on off just a modest pace, albeit all too late, confirms all her old ability remains intact. (op 10-1)
Seachange(NZ), a prolific winner in New Zealand, was not quite at her best when only sixth on her debut in Dubai in the Jebel Hatta, but this was a decent effort. Having been well placed just off the modest pace, she had every chance against the far rail in the straight, but just found a few too strong. She might be even better on easier ground.
Floral Pegasus(AUS) jumped the path soon after the start and raced keenly in behind the eventual winner, so he did well to finish so close.
Creachadoir(IRE) could make little impression from off the pace and was unsuited by the modest gallop. He was held when short of room against the rail late on, but can do better when getting the race run to suit. (op 9-2)
Admire Aura(JPN) was in an unpromising position at the top of the straight and was never going to peg back the leaders. (op 10-1)
Lord Admiral(USA) needs a strong pace to run at and, last of all for much of the way, he was never going to get involved.
Niconero(AUS), a Group 1 winner in Australia at the beginning of the month, was never seen with a chance.
Literato(FR), last year's Champion Stakes winner making his debut for Godolphin, raced a little keenly out wide with no cover down the back straight and was always going to struggle to get involved. He can do better back over further in a stronger-run race (op 4-1)
Bullish Luck(USA) was far too keen.
Linngari(IRE) was never involved after being dropped in from the widest stall of all.
Majestic Roi(USA), last year's Sun Chariot winner, was keen early on under restraint and never a threat.

1091a DUBAI SHEEMA CLASSIC (SPONSORED BY NAKHEEL) (GROUP 1) (TURF) 1m 4f (T)
4:40 (4:40) 4-Y-0+
£1,507,537 (£502,512; £251,256; £125,628; £75,376; £50,251)

RPR
1 **Sun Classique (AUS)**[36] 672 5-8-7 115.................................... KShea 3 122
(M F De Kock, South Africa) *trckd ldng gp: led 2 1/2f out: r.o wl: comf* **15/2**[3]
2 2 3/4 **Viva Pataca**[34] 6-8-11 122.. DBeadman 12 121
(J Moore, Hong Kong) *mid-div: r.o wl fnl 2f: nrst fin* **9/4**[1]
3 3/4 **Doctor Dino (FR)**[111] 7090 6-8-11 119.. OPeslier 15 120
(R Gibson, France) *settled in rr: rdn 3f out: r.o fnl 1 1/2f: nrst fin* **8/1**
4 shd **Quijano (GER)**[23] 816 6-8-11 119.. AStarke 2 120
(P Schiergen, Germany) *mid-div on rail: swtchd out 3 1/2f out: r.o fnl 2 1/2f: nvr able to chal* **10/1**
5 1/4 **Youmzain (IRE)**[174] 6043 5-8-11 123........................... RichardHughes 5 119
(M R Channon) *mid-div: trckd wnr 2 1/2f out: wknd fnl 110yds* **5/1**[2]
6 hd **Sushisan (AUS)**[30] 739 6-8-11 115................................(t) RyanMoore 7 119
(H J Brown, South Africa) *mid-div: nvr able to chal but r.o fnl 2f: nrst fin* **40/1**
7 2 1/2 **Gower Song**[23] 816 5-8-7 112... TedDurcan 16 111
(D R C Elsworth) *settled in last: nvr able to chal* **16/1**
8 nse **Mourilyan (IRE)**[23] 816 4-8-11 115.. MJKinane 13 117
(John M Oxx, Ire) *settled in rr: rdn 3f out: nvr nr to chal* **14/1**
9 2 1/4 **Better Talk Now (USA)**[49] 9-8-11 119........................(bt) RADominguez 6 111
(H G Motion, U.S.A) *settled in rr: nvr nr to chal* **33/1**
10 1/4 **Spring House (USA)**[35] 6-8-11 116..................................(bt) GKGomez 11 111
(J Canani, U.S.A) *led: rdn 3f out: hdd 2 1/2f out: wknd* **33/1**
11 1 1/4 **Latency (ARG)**[23] 817 7-8-11 113.. JCMendez 1 109
(J B Udaondo, Argentina) *mid-div: n.d* **25/1**
12 1 1/2 **Gravitas**[23] 816 5-8-11 113.. LDettori 8 107
(Saeed Bin Suroor) *mid-div: rdn 3f out: kpt on same pce* **25/1**
13 hd **Oracle West (SAF)**[23] 816 7-8-11 119.................................. JMurtagh 10 106
(M F De Kock, South Africa) *trckd ldrs: chsd wnr 2 1/2f out: no room 1 1/2f out: wknd* **18/1**
14 2 **Yellowstone (IRE)**[174] 6043 4-8-11 117...................................(p) JohnEgan 9 105
(Jane Chapple-Hyam) *mid-div: rdn 4f out: sn btn* **40/1**
15 3/4 **West Wind**[195] 5465 4-8-7 116.. KerrinMcEvoy 4 100
(Saeed Bin Suroor) *trckd ldrs: rdn 2 1/2f out: sn wknd* **12/1**
16 9 1/2 **Dansant**[35] 678 4-8-11 113.. JamieSpencer 14 89
(G A Butler) *in rr of mid-div: n.d* **25/1**
2m 28.45s (-2.55) **Going Correction** +0.125s/f (Good)
WFA 4 from 5yo+ 2lb **16** Ran SP% **127.2**
Speed ratings: **113,111,110,110,110 110,108,108,107,106 106,105,104,103,103 96**
CSF: £23.85.
Owner L Cohen & W V Rippon **Bred** L Cohen **Trained** South Africa

FOCUS
A high-quality and competitive Group 1, featuring eight individual winners at the same level from all around the world. Four of the last eight winners of this particular race were drawn in stall 11 or higher, but a low draw has consistently been an advantage in races on turf at this track, including at this distance.

NOTEBOOK
Sun Classique(AUS) clearly benefited from her low draw as she was always well placed tracking the pace in a race run at a fair gallop. She had impressed in overcoming trouble to win the Balanchine Stakes last time over a trip short of her best, and things went far more smoothly for her this time. Sent to the front at the 400m pole, she soon put a gap between herself and the chasing pack, and kept galloping on strongly to the line. While she undoubtedly had the run of the race, she won fairly comfortably in the end, and it is exciting to think that she will be heading to Britain this summer, although first of all she will go to Hong Kong for the Queen Elizabeth II Cup. Having beaten the colts here, connections have every right to believe that she will be able to hold her own against the best in Europe, and the Prince Of Wales's Stakes at Royal Ascot has already been mentioned as a possible target, with the Arlington Million another possibility. (op 7-1)
Viva Pataca was representing Hong Kong, who took this race last year with Vengeance Of Rain, and he was considered by many to be an even stronger contender. However, he was drawn out wide and, unlike the winner, was forced to take a position towards the back of the field. Pushed wide rounding the turn into the straight, he finished to great effect, passing most of his rivals, only to find the winner had gone beyond recall. Considering the way the race was run it was a sound effort, and one could easily imagine that had the pace been stronger this multiple Group 1 scorer might have run out a clear winner himself.
Doctor Dino(FR) was similarly positioned out the back for most of the race having also been drawn out wide. A supremely consistent, globe-trotting multiple Group 1 winner, he never lets his connections down, and this was another fine performance given the way the race was run. He had last been seen beating Quijano in the Hong Kong Vase in December, and the old rivals ran close to that form again, matching strides as they made up ground from the rear in the straight.
Quijano(GER), who was seventh in this race last year, did not make the most of his favourable draw in stall two, and found himself shuffled back into midfield early on, resulting in him having to be switched at the top of the straight before getting a clear run at the line.
Youmzain(IRE) did best of the hold-up horses when third in this race in 2007 from a wide draw, and having been allotted a more favourable stall this time, there were plenty expecting a bold show from the Arc runner-up. However, while he was well placed turning into the straight and was the first to go in pursuit of the eventual winner, he could never cut down her advantage and in fact weakened in the closing stages. Given the way things panned out it was a slightly disappointing performance.
Sushisan(AUS) probably ran to a similar level in this year's race as he did when fifth to Vengeance Of Rain last year. He is a reliable performer but lacks that bit of class at the top level.
Gower Song impressed with her turn of foot in a Group 3 over this course and distance last time, but the opposition was a lot tougher this time. Again ridden with a late challenge in mind, she did not get the best of luck when going for a gap up the rail in the straight, but she would not have troubled the principals even with a dream run. (op 25-1)
Mourilyan(IRE) looked to have prospects of reversing Dubai City Of Gold form with Gower Song, but he again came out second best in that sideshow. He has made great strides over the course of the carnival and, while well held on this step up in class, he remains open to further improvement, especially when he gets some dig in the ground.
Better Talk Now(USA)'s best days are behind him.
Spring House(USA) found dominating some of the world's best middle-distance turf horses a tougher assignment than he is usually set.
Latency(ARG), a multiple Argentinian Grade 1 winner, was well beaten by Jalil on his debut in Dubai earlier in the month, but the switch to turf from dirt promised to suit. He found the competition here too hot, though, and was never a real threat.
Gravitas, who had a lot to find at this level, was ridden by Frankie Dettori only because he could not do the weight on stablemate West Wind.
Oracle West(SAF) was runner-up at a big price in this race last year but he could not repeat the trick this time around. He kept his winning stable-companion company for much of the race but weakened when the pace picked up in the straight. (op 14-1)
Yellowstone(IRE), who was debuting for a new stable having left Ballydoyle, was reported to have suffered an interrupted preparation, so it is not too difficult to excuse him this below-par effort.
West Wind, last year's Prix de Diane winner, was disappointing on her debut for Godolphin as she looked to have plenty in her favour and had apparently been working well. She weakened very tamely having entered the straight just ahead of the eventual winner.
Dansant, who has progressed from a handicapper to a pattern-class horse on Polytrack this winter, failed to translate that improvement back to turf, although of course the competition he faced here was much hotter than that which he has been encountering in Listed races at Lingfield and Kempton.

1092a DUBAI WORLD CUP (SPONSORED BY EMIRATES AIRLINE) (GROUP 1) (DIRT) 1m 2f (D)
5:30 (5:30) 3-Y-0+
£1,809,045 (£603,015; £301,507; £150,753; £90,452; £60,301)

RPR
1 **Curlin (USA)**[30] 742 4-9-0 129..(t) RAlbarado 12 131+
(S Asmussen, U.S.A) *trckd ldrs: gng wl 3f out: led 2f out: easily* **4/11**[1]
2 7 3/4 **Asiatic Boy (ARG)**[23] 815 5-9-0 117.. JMurtagh 9 116
(M F De Kock, South Africa) *trckd ldrs: rdn to chse wnr 2 1/2f out: r.o: no ch w wnr* **10/1**[3]
3 1/4 **Well Armed (USA)**[49] 5-9-0 116..(t) AGryder 2 115
(E G Harty, U.S.A) *led on rail: hdd 2f out: kpt on same pce* **66/1**
4 3/4 **A P Arrow (USA)**[56] 6-9-0 115...................................(v) RADominguez 13 114
(T Pletcher, U.S.A) *mid-div: r.o fnl 3f: nvr nr to chal* **33/1**
5 1 **Great Hunter (USA)**[28] 4-9-0 110..(bt) GKGomez 5 112
(Doug O'Neill, U.S.A) *settled in rr: nvr nr to chal: r.o fnl 2f: nrst fin* **100/1**
6 1/2 **Lucky Find (SAF)**[23] 817 5-9-0 115.. KShea 10 111
(M F De Kock, South Africa) *in rr of mid-div: styd on one pce fnl 2f* **66/1**
7 5 1/4 **Jalil (USA)**[23] 817 4-9-0 118... LDettori 8 100
(Saeed Bin Suroor) *slowly away: nvr nr to chal* **5/1**[2]
8 1 **Gloria De Campeao (BRZ)**[23] 817 5-9-0 115.............. C-PLemaire 11 98
(P Bary, France) *nvr able to chal* **50/1**
9 12 **Premium Tap (USA)**[22] 6-9-0 115..(b) SMadrid 6 74
(J Gardel, Saudi Arabia) *trckd ldrs: checked 5f out: sn btn* **25/1**
10 4 1/2 **Sway Yed (KSA)**[22] 7-9-0 110..(t) OPeslier 1 65
(Saud Saad Alkahtani, Saudi Arabia) *slowly away: nvr nr to chal* **150/1**

11 2 **Kocab**22 6-9-0 113 SPasquier 4 61
(A Fabre, France) *settled in rr: nvr able to chal* **40/1**
12 4½ **Vermilion (JPN)**34 6-9-0 118 (t) YTake 7 52
(S Ishizaka, Japan) *nvr nr to chal* **10/1**3
2m 1.15s (-1.15) **Going Correction** +0.375s/f (Slow) **12** Ran SP% **124.0**
Speed ratings: **119,112,112,112,111 110,106,105,96,92 91,87**
CSF: £5.48. PLACEPOT: £23.30 to a £1 stake. Pool: £18,146.20. 567.95 winning tickets.
QUADPOT: £18.90 to a £1 stake. Pool: £458.60. 17.90 winning tickets..
Owner Stonestreet Stables LLC & Midnight Cry Stables **Bred** Fares Farm Inc **Trained** USA
■ The seventh US-trained winner of the Dubai World Cup in 13 runnings.

FOCUS
A good turnout numerically for the richest horserace in the world, with a field of 12 topped only once in the race's 12-year history, but in truth this lacked strength in depth, and last year's Breeders' Cup Classic winner Curlin was always going to prove in a different league if turning up at his best.

NOTEBOOK
Curlin(USA) had been cut significantly after he sauntered home in a course-and-distance handicap off a mark of 129 in his prep for this last month, and he shortened again after Asiatic Boy was beaten a week later. As it turned out, the supporters of this powerful chestnut never had a moment's worry, as he was always travelling enthusiastically and was still hard on the bridle at the top of the straight. Once asked for his effort approaching the 400m pole, he immediately swept past early leader Well Armed and, kept up to his work, he gradually drew clear of the staying-on Asiatic Boy. The opposition was not as strong as one might have hoped for such a prestigious race, but Curlin once again proved himself a genuine top-class colt, with his winning margin the biggest in the history of the race. Provided he stays sound, he will no doubt be aimed at a repeat bid in the Breeders' Cup Classic, although Santa Anita's synthetic surface will provide a different test.
Asiatic Boy(ARG), last year's UAE Triple Crown winner, looked good when winning a 6f Group 3 on his reappearance, but he was disappointing when only third at that level over 1m on his most recent start and came into this with plenty to prove. He was no match for the top-class winner, but returned to something like his best to take second. Having lacked Curlin's pace when that one was sent on early in the straight, he had to work to get past Well Armed and only mastered that rival inside the final furlong.
Well Armed(USA) did not look up to anywhere near this level when trained by Clive Brittain in 2005/06, but he has improved considerably since returning from an absence and switching to the US, as he showed when winning a Grade 2 at Santa Anita last month, and this was a terrific effort pitched into Group 1 company for the first time. Ridden from the front as usual, he was kept honest by the eventual winner and second, but was in a good rhythm throughout and stuck to his task gamely when passed in the straight. (op 50-1)
A P Arrow(USA), who had the Godolphin Mile winner Diamond Stripes behind when winning a Grade 2 at Churchill Downs last November, stayed on after getting outpaced rounding the final bend and this was a decent showing in defeat.
Great Hunter(USA) had plenty to find in this company and was never seen with a winning a chance, but he stayed on from well back in the straight to take fifth.
Lucky Find(SAF) looks better over shorter and probably would have been better off in the Godolphin Mile.
Jalil(USA) has made great strides this winter, but even his recent Group 2 success in the third round of the Maktoum Challenge left him with plenty to find with Curlin and he was never involved. A late developer, he still looks an immature type and this probably came a bit too soon in his career. He might be able to continue to improve given the benefit of time, but he will need to toughen up if he is to seriously complete at this sort of level. (op 13-2)
Premium Tap(USA) was well beaten, but in fairness he suddenly got lit up down the back straight and almost got caught on heels, so perhaps there was an excuse.

1093 - 1102a (Foreign Racing) - See Raceform Interactive

CURRAGH (R-H)
Sunday, March 30

OFFICIAL GOING: Heavy

1103a LADBROKES 1800 777 888 H'CAP 6f
3:25 (3:27) 3-Y-0+ **£16,035** (£4,704; £2,241; £763)

RPR
1 **Snaefell (IRE)**182 5842 4-9-13 106 JMurtagh 5 113
(M Halford, Ire) *chsd ldrs: 4th 2f out: chal u.p and led ins fnl f: jst hld on* **11/2**3
2 shd **Raptor (GER)**8 960 5-9-5 98 FergusSweeney 1 105
(K R Burke) *chsd ldrs: clsd u.p into 3rd ins fnl f: sn 2nd and chal: styd on wl: jst failed* **4/1**2
3 1¾ **Northern Dare (IRE)**191 5584 4-8-9 88 AdrianTNicholls 6 90
(D Nicholls) *prom: led 2f out: strly pressed and hdd ins fnl f: sn dropped to 3rd and kpt on same pce* **2/1**1
4 2½ **Alone He Stands (IRE)**161 6363 8-8-4 83 JimmyQuinn 10 77
(J C Hayden, Ire) *towards rr: kpt on wout threatening u.p fr under 2f out* **6/1**
5 ¾ **Kingsdale Ocean (IRE)**234 4346 5-8-11 90 PJSmullen 9 82
(D K Weld, Ire) *in rr of mid-div: kpt on wout threatening u.p fr under 2f out* **9/1**
6 4 **Toberogan (IRE)**110 7111 7-7-11 83 oh32 JPFahy(7) 7 63?
(W A Murphy, Ire) *towards rr: kpt on wout threatening u.p fr under 2f out* **100/1**
7 1½ **Braddock (IRE)**160 6391 5-7-11 83 oh6 MHarley(7) 4 59
(S Donohoe, Ire) *led: strly pressed and hdd 2f out: sn no ex* **16/1**
8 4 **Infinite Charm (IRE)**23 829 5-8-6 85 (b) WMLordan 12 49
(M J P O'Brien, Ire) *towards rr for most: nvr a factor* **12/1**
9 ½ **Senor Benny (USA)**30 765 9-9-4 107 MPFahy(10) 3 69
(M McDonagh, Ire) *sn chsd ldrs: clsr in 3rd and sltly short of room 2f out: sn wknd* **14/1**
10 17 **Controvento (IRE)**61 349 6-8-4 83 oh18 (b) MCHussey 8 —
(Eamon Tyrrell, Ire) *prom: lost pl and wknd fr under 2f out* **50/1**
11 2½ **Fit The Cove (IRE)**128 6918 8-8-11 90 CDHayes 11 —
(H Rogers, Ire) *in rr of mid-div: 9th 1/2-way: no imp u.p fr under 2f out: eased ins fnl f* **10/1**
12 3 **College Scholar (GER)**188 5684 4-8-1 83 oh3 DJMoran(3) 2 —
(Liam McAteer, Ire) *cl up: lost pl u.p fr 2f out: eased wl over 1f out* **25/1**
1m 23.0s (8.50) **Going Correction** +1.625s/f (Heav) **12** Ran SP% **129.1**
Speed ratings: **110,109,107,104,103 97,95,90,89,67 63,59**
CSF £30.26 CT £63.20 TOTE £6.40: £2.90, £2.00, £1.50; DF 36.30.
Owner Lady Clague **Bred** Newberry Stud Farm **Trained** the Curragh, Co Kildare

NOTEBOOK
Snaefell(IRE), whose two previous wins, one of them in a Listed event on soft ground here last season, were achieved over the minimum trip, just shaded the verdict here, hanging on after hitting the front 150 yards from the finish. It had been a three-horse battle from over a furlong out and all three involved appeared to tire in the testing conditions. He is expected to come on for the run and his trainer will now look to find a Listed race for him. (op 13/2 tchd 7/1)
Raptor(GER), a three-time winner - twice over this trip and once over 7f - in Germany two years ago, showed then that he handled soft and heavy ground. He has not won since and had been placed a couple of times on the all-weather before finishing in midfield in the Lincoln at Doncaster on his previous start. He began his effort next to the stands'-side rail over two furlongs out and arrived with every chance over the final furlong, only just losing out. (op 7/2)
Northern Dare(IRE), his stable's representative here from six entries, was a three-time winner last year on ground ranging from good to firm to heavy. He was also placed several times last season and was always in the front rank. He went on a furlong and a half out but began to struggle early in the final furlong and soon gave best. (op 5/2)

1104a LODGE PARK STUD EUROPEAN BREEDERS FUND PARK EXPRESS STKS (FILLIES) (GROUP 3) 1m
3:55 (3:55) 3-Y-0+ **£47,867** (£14,044; £6,691; £2,279)

RPR
1 **Marjalina (IRE)**148 6658 3-8-9 DPMcDonogh 11 108+
(Kevin Prendergast, Ire) *dwlt: towards rr: prog on inner into 4th under 2f out: rdn to go mod 2nd 1f out: wandered arnd ins fnl f: styd on wl to ld nr line* **20/1**
2 nk **Savethisdanceforme (IRE)**161 6364 3-8-11 112 ow2 JMurtagh 2 109
(A P O'Brien, Ire) *mid-div: gd hdwy to ld under 2f out and sn clr: kpt on same pce cl home and hdd nr line* **3/1**1
3 5 **Deauville Vision (IRE)**153 6554 5-9-10 107 RPCleary 7 100
(M Halford, Ire) *cl up: 3rd fr over 3f out: no imp u.p and kpt on same pce fr over 1f out* **4/1**3
4 1¾ **Jalmira (IRE)**16 893 7-9-10 107 WJLee 8 97
(C F Swan, Ire) *towards rr: clsr in 6th over 3f out: no imp u.p and kpt on same pce fr over 1f out* **9/1**
5 nk **Indiana Gal (IRE)**16 893 3-8-9 93 CDHayes 9 93
(Patrick Martin, Ire) *sn led: strly pressed and hdd under 2f out: no ex fr over 1f out* **14/1**
6 8 **Ice Queen (IRE)**148 6657 3-8-10 ow1 JAHeffernan 5 78
(A P O'Brien, Ire) *towards rr: rdn over 3f out: sn no imp* **33/1**
7 shd **Lush Lashes**198 5395 3-8-10 ow1 KJManning 4 78
(J S Bolger, Ire) *t.k.h and led early: trckd ldr after: lost pl and wknd fr under 2f out* **7/2**2
8 6 **Danehill Music (IRE)**162 6349 5-9-10 104 WMLordan 1 68
(David Wachman, Ire) *chsd ldrs: 7th over 3f out: no ex fr under 2f out* **9/2**
9 1 **Truly Mine (IRE)**177 5998 4-9-10 103 (b1) PJSmullen 10 66
(D K Weld, Ire) *trckd ldrs: btn whn sltly hmpd under 2f out: no ex and wknd* **16/1**
1m 55.9s (14.00) **Going Correction** +2.00s/f (Heav)
WFA 3 from 4yo+ 17lb **11** Ran SP% **115.7**
Speed ratings: **110,109,104,102,102 94,94,88,87**
CSF £79.72 TOTE £33.10: £5.20, £1.70, £1.70; DF 110.40.
Owner J Vasicek **Bred** Kenilworth House Stud **Trained** Friarstown, Co Kildare

FOCUS
The front pair came clear in a race that has a very mixed history.

NOTEBOOK
Marjalina(IRE), winner of a 7f maiden at Leopardstown on her only start last year, just prevailed over the much more experienced Savethisdanceforme, with the pair of three-year-olds finishing clear of the rest. The winner, who was held up in rear early on, had won her maiden on fast ground and it was probably a combination of the very different conditions here and her relative inexperience which caused her to hang badly left after being switched from the inside to deliver her challenge a furlong out. She ran about a bit before getting up near the finish, to the slight surprise of trainer Kevin Prendergast, who expects her to need middle distances in time. She is in the Juddmonte Oaks.
Savethisdanceforme(IRE), who carried 2lb overweight, had a very different profile to the winner. She raced six times last year for two wins, including a nine-length victory in a Listed event over this course and trip on her final start, having previously run fourth in the Prix Marcel Boussac. Held up off an ordinary enough pace, she hit the front under two furlongs out and was soon clear. She looked all set to score before tiring and being collared late on. She will be more effective on better ground and is expected to take her chance in the 1000 Guineas at Newmarket.
Deauville Vision(IRE), winner of the Irish Lincolnshire on this card a year ago and also a Listed winner over the trip, relishes these conditions. Soon tracking the leaders, she was unable to improve her position or make any impression on the first two from over a furlong out.
Lush Lashes, winner of the Goffs Fillies Million here over 7f on her only start last season, was encountering very different ground on this occasion. Soon prominent, she raced quite keenly before dropping away from two furlongs out. Her performance did nothing to advertise her Classic claims but it will be a surprise if she does not leave this performance well behind her when she gets decent ground. (op 5/2)
Truly Mine(IRE) Official explanation: jockey said filly received slight interference 2f out

1105a LADBROKES.COM IRISH LINCOLNSHIRE (PREMIER H'CAP) 1m
4:30 (4:31) 4-Y-0+ **£47,867** (£14,044; £6,691; £2,279)

RPR
1 **Crooked Throw (IRE)**23 829 9-9-9 102 WJLee 1 108
(C F Swan, Ire) *towards rr: stdy hdwy into 3rd 1f out: sn chal u.p and led: strly pressed and kpt on wl ins fnl f: all out* **20/1**
2 hd **Vaqueras (FR)**5 6000 5-7-12 84 oh4 ow1 EJMcNamara(7) 2 90
(Mrs John Harrington, Ire) *towards rr: hdwy 1/2-way: led 2f out: strly pressed and narrowly hdd ins fnl f: kpt on wl: jst failed* **25/1**
3 2 **Victram (IRE)**16 7039 8-8-6 85 CDHayes 23 87
(Adrian McGuinness, Ire) *towards rr: rdn and styd on wout threatening fr 2f out: 3rd and no imp ins fnl f: kpt on same pce* **16/1**
4 hd **Alarazi (IRE)**358 948 4-9-9 102 MJKinane 11 103
(John M Oxx, Ire) *towards rr: r.o u.p on outer wout threatening fr under 2f out* **12/1**
5 1½ **Estrela Brage (USA)**22 842 5-9-4 97 DPMcDonogh 12 95
(J E Hammond, France) *mid-div: hdwy to trck ldrs and rdn 1f out: sn no imp: kpt on same pce* **11/2**1
6 nk **Dul Ar An Ol (IRE)**39 6217 7-8-1 83 oh1 DJMoran(3) 10 81
(Peter Henley, Ire) *towards rr: kpt on wout threatening u.p fr under 2f out* **33/1**
7 ½ **Royal Island (IRE)**23 829 6-8-6 85 RPCleary 22 82
(Michael Cunningham, Ire) *chsd ldrs: kpt on same pce u.p fr under 2f out* **14/1**
8 ½ **Celtic Dane (IRE)**147 6685 4-8-9 95 MPSnee(7) 9 91
(Kevin Prendergast, Ire) *mid-div: kpt on wout threatening u.p fr under 2f out* **20/1**
9 1¼ **Indian Pace (IRE)**6 1008 7-7-11 83 oh1 JPFahy(7) 19 76
(John E Kiely, Ire) *towards rr: hdwy to trck ldrs 2f out: sn no imp u.p: kpt on same pce* **7/1**2
10 1½ **Head Of The River (IRE)**161 6368 4-8-4 83 oh2 JimmyQuinn 6 73
(Daniel Mark Loughnane, Ire) *sn towards rr: n.d and kpt on same pce fr under 2f out* **16/1**

11 7 **Propinquity**95 5846 6-7-13 83 oh3 MACleere(5) 13 59
(Liam McAteer, Ire) *towards rr: n.d and kpt on same pce fr 2f out* **50/1**
12 1/2 **Moody Tunes**8 958 5-8-4 83 WJSupple 25 58
(K R Burke) *cl up: no ex u.p fr under 2f out* **14/1**
13 hd **Tis Mighty (IRE)**274 3116 5-8-9 88 NGMcCullagh 26 63
(P J Prendergast, Ire) *mid-div: impr and on terms 2f out: sn no imp u.p: no ex fr over 1f out* **9/1**3
14 1/2 **Akua'Ba (IRE)**147 6681 4-8-13 92 (t) KJManning 3 66
(J S Bolger, Ire) *trckd ldrs: wknd u.p fr 1f out* **20/1**
15 3 1/2 **Ginger Princess (IRE)**16 893 6-7-11 83 oh23.(t) JamesPSullivan(7) 16 50
(Oliver McKiernan, Ire) *nvr a factor* **66/1**
16 hd **Shayrazan (IRE)**210 5074 7-8-4 83 (t) MCHussey 20 49
(James Leavy, Ire) *towards rr: hdwy on inner whn nt clr run over 2f out: sn no imp* **33/1**
17 5 **Little White Lie (IRE)**8 960 4-9-4 97 JMurtagh 14 53
(G M Lyons, Ire) *nvr bttr than mid-div* **12/1**
18 4 1/2 **Hard Rock City (USA)**162 6349 8-10-2 109 JAHeffernan 7 56
(M J Grassick, Ire) *prom: 5th 1/2-way: lost pl under 2f out: sn wknd* **20/1**
19 1 3/4 **Cashel Bay (USA)**337 1053 10-7-11 83 oh24 BACurtis(7) 17 27
(Luke Comer, Ire) *prom early: dropped towards rr and no imp u.p fr bef 1/2-way* **100/1**
20 3/4 **Takestan (IRE)**46 2337 5-8-4 83 oh2 MAPhillips 4 25
(Patrick O Brady, Ire) *mid-div: no ex fr 2f out* **33/1**
21 4 1/2 **Monthly Medal**7 986 5-8-0 86 MHarley(7) 5 19
(Anthony Mullins, Ire) *sn cl up: wknd u.p fr under 2f out* **25/1**
22 1 1/2 **Giant Slalom**23 829 4-7-11 83 oh3 (p) AmyKathleenParsons(7) 27 13
(T G McCourt, Ire) *sn led: hdd 2f out: wknd* **33/1**
23 1 **Fremen (USA)**8 960 8-9-1 94 AdrianTNicholls 15 22
(D Nicholls) *towards rr for most: no ex fr under 2f out* **12/1**
24 5 **Sciatin (IRE)**6 1008 5-8-4 86 PBBeggy(3) 18 —
(David P Myerscough, Ire) *chsd ldrs: wknd u.p fr under 2f out* **10/1**
25 2 1/2 **Green Tobasco**16 894 5-8-12 91 WMLordan 21 —
(M J P O'Brien, Ire) *mid-div best: wknd fr under 2f out* **16/1**
26 10 **Incline (IRE)**23 829 9-8-10 99 CPHarrison(10) 8 —
(R McGlinchey, Ire) *prom: rdn and wknd qckly fr over 3f out* **25/1**

1m 55.6s (13.70) **Going Correction** +2.00s/f (Heav) **27** Ran SP% **147.8**
Speed ratings: **111,110,108,108,107 106,106,105,104,103 96,95,95,94,91 91,86,81,79,79 74,73,72,67,64 54**
CSF £464.39 CT £8073.74 TOTE £28.20: £6.80, £4.60, £3.90, £3.40; DF 1028.80.
Owner Hogan Wood Whelan Syndicate **Bred** Andrew Prendergast **Trained** Cloughjordan, Co Tipperary

FOCUS
An ultra-competitive handicap rated around the third to his latest all-weather mark, and the runner-up to his old French form.

NOTEBOOK
Crooked Throw(IRE), runner-up to Deauville Vision in this a year ago, came from off the pace to lead inside the final furlong. He survived a stewards' enquiry after coming across and interfering with French raider Estrela Brage, and his trainer believes this very testing ground helped. He showed a fine attitude and it will be interesting to see where he heads next. (op 20/1 tchd 25/1)
Vaqueras(FR) carried 1lb over and ran a cracker under this light-weight. Fit from hurdling, he travelled smoothly to take up the running passing the two-furlong marker but just found one too good.
Victram(IRE) had won this race three years ago and this tough competitor, who has failed to recapture his best hurdling form of late, was another to appreciate these conditions.
Alarazi(IRE) came from a long way back to get into the frame and would have gone close to winning had he been put in the race earlier. The Spectrum colt landed a 1m maiden in similar conditions here last March and he looks capable of better on this evidence. Official explanation: jockey said colt met with intereference before marker poles, effectively costing it a clear run in race (op 10/1)
Estrela Brage(USA) looked to have plenty going for him at declaration on Friday until adjusted to shoulder 9lb more when his second place in a Listed race just over three weeks ago was taken into account. This ultimately made the difference, although he was not helped when the winner caused him to lose some momentum at a crucial stage. (op 6/1)
Moody Tunes, well beaten by Don't Panic in the Spring Mile, ran well for a long way in the testing ground.
Fremen(USA), who ran respectably in the Lincoln, was expected to be suited by this soft ground, but he never really looked like picking up from his midfield position. (op 10/1)

1106 - 1107a (Foreign Racing) - See Raceform Interactive

1046 SAINT-CLOUD (L-H)
Sunday, March 30

OFFICIAL GOING: Heavy

1108a PRIX EDMOND BLANC (GROUP 3) 1m
2:45 (2:48) 3-Y-0+ £29,412 (£11,765; £8,824; £5,882; £2,941)

RPR
1 **Konig Turf (GER)**189 5670 6-9-2 SPasquier 5 113
(C Sprengel, Germany) *racd in 2nd tl led 5f out: brought field wd ent st: hrd rdn in narrow ld over 2f out: hdd 100yds out: rallied to ld post* **37/10**3
2 nse **Gris De Gris (IRE)**22 842 4-8-12 TThulliez 2 109
(J-M Capitte, France) *racd in 3rd: rdn to press ldr 2f out: led narrowly against outside hedge 100yds out: hdd on the nod on line* **5/2**2
3 3 **Spirito Del Vento (FR)**112 7091 5-9-2 OPeslier 6 107
(J-M Beguigne, France) *sltly outpcd in last and niggled along early: wnt 5th 4f out: rdn 2 1/2f out: wnt 3rd 1 1/2f out: eased whn hld clsng stages* **13/10**1
4 2 **Runaway**113 6-8-12 TJarnet 4 99
(R Pritchard-Gordon, France) *racd in 4th: hrd rdn in 3rd whn ducked lft over 1 1/2f out: one pce* **21/1**
5 8 **Chopastair (FR)**150 6614 7-9-0 J-BEyquem 3 85
(T Lerner, France) *racd in 5th tl dropped bk to last 4f out: effrt and lost tch over 2f out* **13/2**
6 10 **Air Bag (FR)**87 35 4-8-8 FBlondel 1 59
(Mme C Barande-Barbe, France) *set str pce to 5f out: 2nd st: sn wknd* **19/1**

1m 52.2s (4.70) **Going Correction** +0.925s/f (Soft) **6** Ran SP% **116.2**
Speed ratings: **113,112,109,107,99 89**
PARI-MUTUEL: WIN 4.70; PL 2.50, 2.00; SF 14.80.
Owner Stall Route 66 **Bred** Gestut Elsetal **Trained** Germany

NOTEBOOK
Konig Turf(GER), a real mudlark, was tucked in just behind the leader early on, then started his run from two furlongs out and had a battle royal with the runner-up throughout the final furlong. His nose was in the right place at the post and it was a gutsy victory. A consistent horse, this was winning his fourth Group race win, and will now come back to the same course and distance for the Prix de Muguet on May 1.
Gris De Gris(IRE) pulled out all the stops in the final stages. He came up the stands' side and had a slight lead with 20 yards left to run, before losing it on the nod. He was initially announced the winner but it was a mistake as the photograph showed the German visitor had won. He lost nothing in defeat and will now be rested for five to six weeks.
Spirito Del Vento(FR) has to be described as a little disappointing. He was the favourite for this race but never seemed to be enjoying himself while back in last position. Niggled along before the straight, he was given every chance but could not produce his normal finishing burst. Connections will stick with their original programme of the Prix Muguet, Prix d'Isapahan and Queen Anne Stakes at Ascot, and he should be a different proposition next time out.
Runaway put up a fair performance and battled throughout the straight after being held up early on. He did hang slightly left when challenging, but it made little difference to his final place. He was probably not suited by the deep ground.

1054 LINGFIELD (L-H)
Monday, March 31

OFFICIAL GOING: Standard
Wind: Light, behind Weather: Cloudy

1109 THERE'S NO PLACE QUITE LIKE PONTIN'S (S) STKS 1m (P)
2:10 (2:11) (Class 6) 3-Y-0+ £1,774 (£523; £262) Stalls High

Form RPR
1540 1 **Samuel Charles**24 819 10-10-0 68 (b) RyanMoore 1 68
(C R Dore) *mde all: set mod pce: qcknd over 2f out: hung rt and carried hd high over 1f out: drvn out* **11/10**1
6-00 2 3 1/2 **Victor Trumper**3 1049 4-9-8 72 (bt) SteveDrowne 6 54
(Jim Best) *t.k.h: sn stdd towards rr: hdwy over 2f out: chsd wnr fnl f: edgd lft: a hld* **11/2**3
0-66 3 3/4 **Hansomelle (IRE)**8 935 6-9-3 60 (p) NeilChalmers 7 47
(Miss Sheena West) *hld up in rr: rdn 3f out: gd hdwy over 1f out: one pce fnl f* **7/2**2
600 4 1 3/4 **Bandits Pistol (NZ)**26 611 8-9-8 47 (v1) J-PGuillambert 5 48
(M Madgwick) *hld up in tch: rdn over 2f out: styd on same pce* **14/1**
-500 5 1 3/4 **Valart**28 776 5-9-3 32 (b1) ChrisCatlin 8 39
(C Tinkler) *t.k.h: chsd wnr tl wknd 1f out* **16/1**
00-6 6 shd **Cumae (USA)**83 83 4-9-3 31 (v1) RobertHavlin 4 39
(J Pearce) *t.k.h: chsd ldrs: hrd rdn over 1f out: wknd fnl f* **25/1**
0605 7 1/2 **Golden Spectrum (IRE)**14 916 9-9-8 50 (b) AlanMunro 10 43
(R A Harris) *bhd: rdn 3f out: nvr rchd ldrs* **11/1**
00-0 8 13 **Feelin Irie (IRE)**20 844 5-9-8 45 (v1) SamHitchcott 2 13
(M J Gingell) *dwlt and hmpd s: plld hrd and sn prom: wknd qckly over 2f out* **33/1**
-006 9 4 **Cavallo Di Ferro (IRE)**19 851 4-9-5 48 (b1) RussellKennemore(3) 3 4
(M J Gingell) *chsd ldrs on rail: hrd rdn over 3f out: sn wknd* **25/1**

1m 38.99s (0.79) **Going Correction** 0.0s/f (Stan) **9** Ran SP% **116.7**
Speed ratings (Par 101): **96,92,91,90,88 88,87,74,70**
CSF £7.42 TOTE £2.00: £1.10, £1.40, £1.50; EX 7.70 Trifecta £11.70 Pool: £375.07 - 22.58 winning units..There was no bid for the winner.
Owner Chris Marsh **Bred** Sheikh Mohammed Obaid Al Maktoum **Trained** West Pinchbeck, Lincs

FOCUS
A dire affair, even for this grade. The winner did not have to improve to score and the fourth to sixth set the standard.

1110 GO COMPLETELY PONTIN'S THIS SUMMER H'CAP 6f (P)
2:40 (2:41) (Class 5) (0-75,75) 3-Y-O £2,590 (£770; £385; £192) Stalls Low

Form RPR
112- 1 **What Katie Did (IRE)**115 7052 3-9-3 74 RyanMoore 8 78
(P F I Cole) *sn chsng ldrs: rdn to ld ins fnl f: hld on wl* **10/3**1
654- 2 1/2 **Hobson**177 6004 3-9-3 74 StephenCarson 7 76
(Eve Johnson Houghton) *dwlt: t.k.h in rr: hung lft ent st: gd late hdwy: jst hld* **8/1**
0220 3 1/2 **Maggie Kate**16 899 3-8-6 63 (p) RobertHavlin 2 63
(R Ingram) *led: hrd rdn and hdd ins fnl f: nt qckn* **13/2**
535- 4 1/2 **Cracking Nick (IRE)**235 4328 3-9-0 71 AdamKirby 4 70
(W R Swinburn) *hld up in rr: rdn and hdwy over 1f out: styd on same pce fnl f* **7/2**2
1122 5 hd **Seductive Witch**17 882 3-8-3 63 ow2 TolleyDean(3) 1 61
(J Balding) *chsd ldrs: drvn to chal fnl f: no ex fnl 100yds* **12/1**
011- 6 2 1/4 **We Have A Dream**165 6282 3-8-13 70 MartinDwyer 5 61
(W R Muir) *chsd ldrs: rdn over 2f out: wknd over 1f out* **11/2**3
2-10 7 1/2 **Young Ivanhoe**13 924 3-9-1 72 SteveDrowne 3 61
(C A Dwyer) *hld up in 6th: rdn over 2f out: sn outpcd* **8/1**
100- 8 3/4 **Our Acquaintance**175 6059 3-9-4 75 SebSanders 6 62
(W R Muir) *in tch on outside tl rdn and wknd over 1f out* **9/1**

1m 12.32s (0.42) **Going Correction** 0.0s/f (Stan) **8** Ran SP% **113.9**
Speed ratings (Par 98): **97,96,95,95,94 91,91,90**
CSF £29.89 CT £164.70 TOTE £4.30: £1.90, £2.20, £1.90; EX 26.50 TRIFECTA Not won..
Owner Bernard Gover Bloodstock Trading Ltd **Bred** Brian Williamson **Trained** Whatcombe, Oxon

FOCUS
A modest three-year-old handicap, run at a fair pace. The first five came clear and the form is set by the third and fifth.

1111 WISH YOU WERE HERE @ PONTIN'S MAIDEN AUCTION FILLIES' STKS 5f (P)
3:10 (3:10) (Class 6) 2-Y-O £2,047 (£604; £302) Stalls High

Form RPR
2 1 **Percolator**7 995 2-8-4 0 JoeFanning 5 70+
(P F I Cole) *broke wl and showed gd early pce: mde all: green and wd on bnd into st: rdn clr ins fnl f: eased nr fin* **1/1**1
2 2 1/2 **Grand Plan (USA)** 2-8-7 0 ChrisCatlin 4 57
(J A Osborne) *chsd wnr: rdn 2f out: one pce appr fnl f: regained 2nd fnl 100yds* **5/2**2
0 3 1/2 **Lois Darlin (IRE)**7 995 2-8-3 0 ow1 TolleyDean(3) 1 54
(J S Moore) *dwlt: racd in 5th: rdn 3f out: styd on appr fnl f: tk 3rd nr fin* **5/1**3
4 1 1/4 **Missy Que (IRE)** 2-8-4 0 MartinDwyer 2 47
(W R Muir) *chsd ldng pair: rdn to chal on rail over 1f out: wknd and lost 2nd fnl 100yds* **33/1**

5 2 1/4 **Dedante** 2-8-7 0 ow1 .... RobertHavlin 3 41
(D K Ivory) *travelled wl in 4th: rn green and cornered bdly into st: sn rdn and btn* **20/1**

6 6 1 1/2 **Joli Haven (IRE)**[7] 995 2-7-12 0 .... MCGeran(7) 6 33
(W G M Turner) *s.s: a last: rdn and n.d fnl 3f* **12/1**

60.47 secs (1.67) **Going Correction** 0.0s/f (Stan) 6 Ran SP% **110.6**
Speed ratings (Par 87): **86,82,81,79,75 73**
CSF £3.54 TOTE £2.00: £1.10, £1.60; EX 4.30.
Owner A H Robinson **Bred** A H And C E Robinson Partnership **Trained** Whatcombe, Oxon

FOCUS
An ordinary juvenile fillies' maiden. The winner - the clear form pick - is value for around treble her winning margin.

NOTEBOOK
Percolator, runner-up on debut at Warwick a week previously, showed the clear benefit of that experience and ran out a taking winner from the front. She clearly has plenty of speed and should be rated value for a good deal further than the bare margin, as she still looked green. She was also eased towards the finish and ought to be high on confidence after this. (op 8-11)
Grand Plan(USA), a $30,000 purchase, proved popular in the betting ring yet never looked like getting to the more experienced eased-down winner. She ought to learn from this and has a little race in her, but another furlong may be more up her street in due course. (op 7-2)
Lois Darlin(IRE), as was the case when well behind the winner at Warwick on debut a week previously, fluffed the start and never seriously threatened. This was still a step in the right direction and she did leave the impression a stiffer test will suit her more in due course. (op 8-1)
Missy Que(IRE), a cheap purchase, showed some early pace on this racecourse bow and should be able to last longer next time out. (op 25-1)

1112 DINE IN TRACKSIDE CARVERY H'CAP 1m (P)
3:40 (3:41) (Class 5) (0-75,75) 4-Y-0+ £2,590 (£770; £385; £192) Stalls High

Form RPR
3110 1 **King's Ransom**[27] 789 5-9-1 72 .... ChrisCatlin 4 82
(S Gollings) *mde all: rdn over 2f out: hld on wl fnl f* **11/2**[3]

000- 2 1 1/2 **Murrin (IRE)**[168] 6236 4-9-4 75 .... JimCrowley 1 82
(T G Mills) *in tch: drvn to press ldrs over 1f out: wnt 2nd ins fnl f: nt qckn* **9/2**[2]

-125 3 hd **Paradise Dancer (IRE)**[28] 775 4-9-3 74 .... GeorgeBaker 5 80
(J A R Toller) *in tch: effrt and wd st: kpt on to dispute 2nd fnl 50yds* **7/2**[1]

006- 4 1 1/4 **Art Market (CAN)**[161] 6293 5-8-11 68 ow2 .... AdamKirby 6 71
(Miss Jo Crowley) *hld up in 6th: effrt over 2f out: styd on: nt pce to chal* **6/1**

-356 5 hd **Happy As Larry (USA)**[74] 196 6-9-0 71 ....(t) MartinDwyer 2 74
(J S Moore) *chsd ldrs: rdn 3f out: chal over 1f out: no ex ins fnl f* **9/2**[2]

60-0 6 1 **Teen Ager (FR)**[17] 887 4-9-2 73 .... RobertHavlin 3 74
(P Burgoyne) *stdd s: plld hrd and difficult to settle in rr early: rdn over 2f out: n.d* **16/1**

-425 7 1 1/2 **Convivial Spirit**[24] 819 4-8-6 63 ....(t) RichardKingscote 7 60
(E F Vaughan) *chsd wnr tl wknd ent st* **9/2**[2]

1m 37.54s (-0.66) **Going Correction** 0.0s/f (Stan) 7 Ran SP% **112.3**
Speed ratings (Par 103): **103,101,101,100,99 98,97**
CSF £29.06 TOTE £4.70: £2.50, £2.30; EX 29.10.
Owner Mrs D Dukes **Bred** Darley **Trained** Scamblesby, Lincs

FOCUS
A fair little handicap, run at a sound pace. The winner set a personal-best and the form is rated through the third.
Teen Ager(FR) Official explanation: jockey said gelding was denied a clear run

1113 HBLB H'CAP 7f (P)
4:10 (4:10) (Class 4) (0-85,83) 3-Y-0 £4,100 (£1,227; £613; £306; £152) Stalls Low

Form RPR
314- 1 **Hustle (IRE)**[192] 5597 3-9-0 79 .... RichardHughes 2 86
(R Hannon) *t.k.h: chsd ldr: rdn to ld over 1f out: a holding runner-up* **10/3**[2]

21 2 1 **Maslaha**[17] 885 3-9-1 80 .... PhilipRobinson 4 84
(M A Jarvis) *covered up in 4th: effrt 2f out: kpt on to take 2nd ins fnl f: a hld* **10/11**[1]

-350 3 1 1/2 **Atheer Dubai (IRE)**[3] 1057 3-8-5 70 ....(b) ChrisCatlin 1 70
(C E Brittain) *sn led: hdd and hrd rdn over 1f out: no ex fnl f* **4/1**[3]

10- 4 nk **Keep Discovering (IRE)**[175] 6052 3-9-4 83 .... JoeFanning 5 82
(M Johnston) *t.k.h: chsd ldrs: effrt and hung lft ent st: sltly outpcd: kpt on again nr fin* **16/1**

246- 5 nse **Artsu**[185] 5773 3-9-0 79 .... RyanMoore 6 78
(M L W Bell) *hld up in rr: rdn over 2f out: styd on fnl f* **12/1**

031- 6 1 1/2 **My Mate Pete (IRE)**[93] 7264 3-8-12 77 .... TomEaves 3 72
(Mrs L Stubbs) *hld up in 5th: rdn over 2f out: no imp over 1f out* **20/1**

1m 24.47s (-0.33) **Going Correction** 0.0s/f (Stan) 6 Ran SP% **113.8**
Speed ratings (Par 100): **101,99,98,97,97 96**
CSF £6.93 TOTE £3.70: £2.00, £1.10; EX 8.90.
Owner Highclere Thoroughbred Racing (Tamarisk) **Bred** Gigginstown House Stud **Trained** East Everleigh, Wilts

FOCUS
A fair handicap that can be treated positively with the frirst two unexposed and progressive.

1114 BOOK YOUR PONTIN'S FAMILY HOLIDAY NOW MAIDEN STKS 1m 2f (P)
4:40 (4:40) (Class 5) 3-Y-0 £2,331 (£693; £346; £173) Stalls Low

Form RPR
03- 1 **Monterrico**[167] 6252 3-9-3 0 .... RyanMoore 4 79+
(G Wragg) *trckd ldng pair: led ent st: rdn and hld on wl fnl f* **1/1**[1]

0 2 1 **Always Cruising (USA)**[9] 961 3-9-3 0 .... JoeFanning 5 77
(M Johnston) *led tl ent st: kpt on wl u.p* **10/1**[3]

052 3 1 1/2 **Silver Waters**[32] 727 3-9-3 68 .... AlanMunro 1 74
(D R C Elsworth) *chsd wnr tl over 2f out: kpt on again fnl f* **10/1**[3]

4- 4 1/2 **Rock Peak (IRE)**[200] 5361 3-9-3 0 .... SteveDrowne 2 73
(H Morrison) *s.s: hld up in 5th: hdwy to chse ldng pair 2f out: one pce fnl f* **15/8**[2]

5 6 **Montevetro** 3-9-3 0 .... RichardHughes 3 61
(R Hannon) *hld up in 4th: rdn over 2f out: sn wknd* **14/1**

6 4 1/2 **Persian Flyer (IRE)** 3-9-3 0 .... JamesDoyle 6 52
(J W Mullins) *hld up in rr: hung rt thrght: rdn and n.d fnl 2f* **66/1**

2m 6.77s (0.17) **Going Correction** 0.0s/f (Stan) 6 Ran SP% **111.1**
Speed ratings (Par 98): **99,98,97,96,91 88**
CSF £11.93 TOTE £2.10: £1.10, £4.10; EX 11.40.
Owner Mrs R Philipps **Bred** Mrs Rebecca Philipps **Trained** Newmarket, Suffolk

FOCUS
An ordinary maiden but tricky to rate, with the third the best guide.
Persian Flyer(IRE) Official explanation: jockey said colt hung right throughout

1115 GOLF AND RACING DAYS OUT H'CAP 1m (P)
5:10 (5:10) (Class 6) (0-65,65) 3-Y-0 £2,047 (£604; £302) Stalls High

Form RPR
-220 1 **My Shadow**[16] 909 3-9-4 65 .... IanMongan 9 77+
(S Dow) *hld up towards rr: rdn 3f out: str run to ld fnl 100yds* **8/1**

-043 2 2 3/4 **Desiderio**[16] 900 3-8-13 60 ....(p) RichardHughes 1 64
(R Hannon) *led: rdn and kpt on fnl 2f: hdd and nt pce of wnr fnl 100yds* **9/4**[1]

000- 3 1/2 **Saafend Geezer**[164] 6295 3-8-13 60 .... ChrisCatlin 7 63
(B J Meehan) *patiently rdn fr rr: promising hdwy ent st: ch 1f out: nt qckn ins fnl f* **8/1**

2115 4 3/4 **What's For Tea**[32] 737 3-9-2 63 .... RichardKingscote 6 64
(P Butler) *chsd ldr tl 2f out: kpt on same pce* **11/2**[3]

-162 5 2 1/4 **Ledgerwood**[24] 820 3-9-4 65 ....(p) JamesDoyle 3 61
(J W Hills) *in tch: drvn to chse ldrs over 1f out: no ex fnl f* **5/1**[2]

056- 6 3/4 **Chanteuse De Rue (IRE)**[157] 6461 3-8-5 52 .... JoeFanning 8 46
(M Johnston) *chsd ldrs tl wknd wl over 1f out* **12/1**

000- 7 3/4 **Coloratura (IRE)**[149] 6649 3-9-3 64 .... TGMcLaughlin 4 57
(E A L Dunlop) *towards rr: hdwy to chal over 1f out: wknd qckly fnl f* **14/1**

040- 8 7 **Elizabeth's Quest**[187] 5729 3-8-8 62 .... SophieDoyle(7) 2 38
(R Simpson) *dwlt: sn rcvrd and racd in 5th: rdn 3f out: sn wknd* **50/1**

660- 9 5 **Darley Star**[189] 5682 3-9-4 65 .... SebSanders 5 30
(C E Brittain) *hld up in 6th: rdn 3f out: wknd qckly 2f out* **13/2**

1m 38.75s (0.55) **Going Correction** 0.0s/f (Stan) 9 Ran SP% **114.7**
Speed ratings (Par 96): **97,94,93,93,90 90,89,82,77**
CSF £26.17 CT £151.70 TOTE £10.70: £3.50, £1.30, £2.80; EX 32.80 Trifecta £205.50 Pool: £457.42 - 1.58 winning units. Place 6 £13.46, Place 5 £11.92.
Owner T G Parker **Bred** Millsec Limited **Trained** Epsom, Surrey

FOCUS
A modest handicap, but sound form rated through the runner-up and the race should produce some winners.
T/Plt: £17.40 to a £1 stake. Pool: £57,175.95. 2,396.10 winning tickets. T/Qpdt: £10.10 to a £1 stake. Pool: £2,679.60. 195.70 winning tickets. LM

1021 SOUTHWELL (L-H)
Monday, March 31

OFFICIAL GOING: Standard
Wind: Nil Weather: Dry and fine

1116 SOUTHWELL-RACECOURSE.CO.UK AMATEUR RIDERS' H'CAP 1m (F)
2:30 (2:30) (Class 6) (0-60,58) 4-Y-0+ £1,714 (£527; £263) Stalls Low

Form RPR
3342 1 **Wodhill Schnaps**[39] 640 7-10-10 52 ....(b) MrBMMorris(5) 12 69
(D Morris) *dwlt: hld up in rr: gd hdwy over 2f out: str run to ld jst ins fnl f: sn clr* **9/2**[2]

13-0 2 8 **Penel (IRE)**[39] 639 7-10-10 52 ....(p) MissWGibson(5) 2 50
(P T Midgley) *hld up in tch: hdwy wl over 2f out: rdn over 1f out: kpt on wl fnl f* **12/1**

4-00 3 hd **Cheonmado (USA)**[17] 879 4-11-4 58 ....(tp) MrDavidTurner(3) 3 56
(J R Gask) *chsd ldrs: rdn along and outpcd over 2f out: styd on u.p ins fnl f* **16/1**

-004 4 1 **Cabourg (IRE)**[19] 861 5-11-0 56 .... MissRBastiman(5) 10 52
(R Bastiman) *trckd ldrs: hdwy to ld 3f out: pushed clr wl over 1f out: rdn: wknd and hdd ins fnl f* **11/1**

-114 5 1 1/4 **Blue Empire (IRE)**[18] 864 7-11-6 57 ....(p) MrSWalker 8 50
(John A Harris) *trckd ldrs: hdwy to chse ldr wl over 2f out: rdn wl over 1f out: sn drvn and wknd* **4/1**[1]

1044 6 1 **Sparky Vixen**[8] 978 4-10-10 50 .... MissARyan(3) 7 41
(C J Teague) *midfield: hdwy on outer over 2f out: sn rdn and no imp appr fnl f* **13/2**[3]

440- 7 3/4 **Mycenean Prince (USA)**[16] 6956 5-10-1 45 ....(v) MrCAHarris(7) 1 34
(R C Guest) *chsd ldrs on inner: hdwy 3f out: rdn along 2f out: grad wknd appr fnl f* **25/1**

1640 8 1/2 **Anduril**[3] 1064 7-11-1 52 ....(p) MrSDobson 6 40
(I W McInnes) *cl up: rdn along 3f out: wknd 2f out: b.b.v* **13/2**[3]

0155 9 1 3/4 **Ruffie (IRE)**[14] 915 5-10-8 50 .... MrRBirkett(5) 5 34
(Miss J Feilden) *sn outpcd and bhd tl sme late hdwy* **7/1**

000- 10 6 **Crafty Fox**[167] 6247 5-10-8 50 ....(v) MrKJames(5) 11 20
(John A Harris) *a towards rr* **20/1**

600- 11 3 3/4 **Wee Ellie Coburn**[210] 5084 4-10-12 54 .... MissMMullineaux(5) 14 15
(M Mullineaux) *a in midfield* **25/1**

02/0 12 2 1/4 **Royal Lustre**[19] 862 7-10-8 45 .... MissSBrotherton 9 —
(Miss Tracy Waggott) *led: rdn along and hdd 3f out: wknd 2f out* **33/1**

20/0 13 8 **Naughty Girl (IRE)**[14] 914 8-10-8 45 .... MrsMMorris 4 —
(John A Harris) *a in rr* **25/1**

000- 14 hd **Psycho Cat**[173] 2656 5-10-10 52 .... MrBenBrisbourne(5) 13 —
(W M Brisbourne) *sn outpcd and a bhd* **10/1**

1m 45.68s (1.98) **Going Correction** +0.30s/f (Slow) 14 Ran SP% **127.6**
Speed ratings (Par 101): **102,94,93,92,91 90,89,89,87,81 77,75,67,67**
CSF £57.06 CT £850.12 TOTE £5.30: £1.90, £4.30, £7.10; EX 73.10.
Owner Miss S Graham **Bred** Wodhill Stud **Trained** Newmarket, Suffolk

FOCUS
A moderate contest though the pace was a reasonable. The winner absolutely bolted up, but the overall form is probably very modest.
Anduril Official explanation: trainer said gelding bled from the nose

1117 CAPTAIN CROC'S SNAPPY HAPPY @ PONTIN'S CLAIMING STKS 6f (F)
3:00 (3:01) (Class 6) 3-Y-0 £1,774 (£523; £262) Stalls Low

Form RPR
321 1 **Copperbottomed (IRE)**[20] 845 3-9-6 67 ....(e) FergusSweeney 4 69
(J R Boyle) *cl up: led over 3f out: rdn wl over 1f out: kpt on strly appr fnl f* **1/1**[1]

4444 2 3 3/4 **One Called Alice**[7] 998 3-8-10 60 .... JerryO'Dwyer(3) 3 50
(A W Carroll) *chsd ldrs: hdwy over 2f out and sn rdn: drvn over 1f out: kpt on same pce ins fnl f: tk 2nd nr line* **11/4**[2]

0-43 3 1/2 **Our Sunnie**[2] 1081 3-9-4 66 .... AdrianTNicholls 5 53
(D Nicholls) *sn led: pushed along and hdd over 3f out: rdn 2f out: sn drvn and wknd appr fnl f* **9/2**[3]

-435 4 nse **Indecision**[20] 845 3-8-12 52 .... PaulMulrennan 1 47
(M W Easterby) *hld up in tch: hdwy on inner over 2f out: sn rdn: drvn and kpt on ins fnl f: nrst fin* **20/1**

The Form Book, Raceform Ltd, Compton, RG20 6NL

0155 **5** *1 1/2* **Her Name Is Rio (IRE)**[48] 534 3-8-9 56 .... RobertWinston 2 39
(Mrs S Lamyman) *trckd ldrs: pushed along 1/2-way: rdn and hung lft wl over 1f out: swtchd rt and drvn ent fnl f: one pce* **8/1**

1m 18.72s (2.22) **Going Correction** +0.30s/f (Slow) **5** Ran SP% **110.7**
Speed ratings (Par 96): **97,92,91,91,89**
CSF £4.02 TOTE £2.00: £1.10, £1.80; EX 4.00.
Owner M Khan X2 **Bred** Paul McEnery **Trained** Epsom, Surrey

FOCUS
A moderate but closely matched claimer with the top four in the market within 1lb of each other on adjusted official ratings. The favourite eventually won easily, but there is nothing solid about those behind the winner and the form will mean little outside of this level.

1118 TAKE A BREAK - TAKE A PONTIN'S BREAK MEDIAN AUCTION MAIDEN STKS 5f (F)
3:30 (3:30) (Class 6) 2-Y-O **£1,774** (£523; £262) **Stalls** High

Form RPR

0 **1** **Bad Beat**[9] 957 2-9-0 0 .... JerryO'Dwyer(3) 4 75+
(V Smith) *mde all: rdn along wl over 1f out: styd on strly* **7/1**

2 *2 3/4* **Dispol Mulofky (IRE)** 2-8-9 0 .... JamieMoriarty(3) 1 57
(P T Midgley) *hung lft thrght: chsd ldrs: rdn along 2f out: kpt on to take 2nd ins fnl f* **25/1**

3 *hd* **Count Almaviva (USA)** 2-9-3 0 .... NCallan 2 61+
(K A Ryan) *awkward fr stalls: sn trcking ldrs: chsd wnr 1/2-way: rdn wl over 1f out: kpt on same pce* **6/4**[1]

5 **4** *6* **Dancing Wave**[7] 995 2-8-5 0 .... JackDean(7) 3 32
(W G M Turner) *chsd wnr to 1/2-way: sn rdn along and wknd* **4/1**[3]

5 *4 1/2* **Handcuff** 2-9-3 0 .... TPQueally 5 19
(J A Osborne) *in tch: rdn along after 1f: sn outpcd and bhd* **15/8**[2]

61.94 secs (2.24) **Going Correction** +0.20s/f (Slow) **5** Ran SP% **111.1**
Speed ratings (Par 90): **90,85,85,75,68**
CSF £105.57 TOTE £9.50: £3.70, £7.50; EX 59.40.
Owner R West **Bred** R J H West **Trained** Exning, Suffolk

FOCUS
A moderate maiden and this surface would have been a stiff test for two-year-olds at this stage of their career. Therefore it was probably no surprise that previous experience counted for so much.

NOTEBOOK
Bad Beat, 13th of the 19 runners in the Brocklesby, utilised that experience to maximum effect and he never saw another rival. The form is moderate, but his experience will continue to be an asset until some better juveniles start to appear. (op 8-1 tchd 9-1)
Dispol Mulofky(IRE), a 2,000gns half-sister to a winning juvenile, came down the centre of the track and did show a bit of ability. She should improve and there ought to be a small race in her. (op 20-1 tchd 33-1)
Count Almaviva(USA), a half-brother to five winners in the US and very much bred for speed, did his chances little good with a very awkward start and, though he tried to get on terms with the winner, he could never really do so. The market suggested he was thought capable of better. (op 15-8)
Dancing Wave did not build on her Warwick debut effort though her stamina-laden pedigree does not suggest this sort of trip would suit in any case. (op 9-2)
Handcuff, an 18,000gns half-brother to Mac Gille Eoin, was always struggling to go the pace from the rails draw. He may not have liked the surface and should not be written off just yet. (op 6-4 tchd 11-8 in places)

1119 FOREST LODGE HOTEL MEDIAN AUCTION MAIDEN STKS 1m 4f (F)
4:00 (4:00) (Class 5) 3-5-Y-O **£2,457** (£725; £362) **Stalls** Low

Form RPR

400- **1** **An Scaribh**[185] 5771 3-8-5 60 .... PaulHanagan 4 70
(P D Evans) *hld up in rr: hdwy over 3f out: chal on outer 2f out: rdn to ld ent fnl f: edgd lft and kpt on* **8/1**[3]

304 **2** *1 1/4* **Azabu Juban (IRE)**[9] 961 3-7-12 0 ow1 .... LukeMorris(3) 7 64
(J Jay) *trckd ldrs: pushed along over 3f out: led 2f out and sn rdn: drvn and hdd ent fnl f: one pce* **8/13**[1]

553- **3** *1 3/4* **Dinarius**[96] 7234 3-8-2 68 .... WilliamBuick(3) 3 65
(K J Burke) *trckd ldr: effrt on inner 2f out: sn rdn and one pce ent fnl f* **7/2**[2]

5 **4** *1 1/4* **Night Orbit**[14] 919 4-9-4 0 .... AmyBaker(7) 6 64
(Miss J Feilden) *chsd ldrs: effrt and cl up 3f out: ev ch tl rdn 2f out and wknd appr fnl f* **9/1**

5 *14* **La Cortezana**[25] 4-9-6 0 .... DavidKinsella 5 36
(P G Murphy) *hld up: hdwy 1/2-way: cl up 4f out: rdn along 3f out and sn wknd* **25/1**

0 **6** *3/4* **Mollie Blackburn**[24] 823 4-9-6 0 .... SilvestreDeSousa 2 35
(A D Brown) *led: jnd and rdn along 4f out: drvn and hdd 2f out: sn wknd* **66/1**

2m 46.77s (5.77) **Going Correction** +0.30s/f (Slow)
WFA 3 from 4yo 22lb **6** Ran SP% **110.6**
Speed ratings (Par 103): **92,91,90,89,79 79**
CSF £13.14 TOTE £7.70: £2.80, £1.40; EX 11.00.
Owner John P Jones **Bred** P Young **Trained** Pandy, Monmouths

FOCUS
A moderate maiden in which the pace was modest and the time was slow. As a result the form may not be totally reliable with the principals' previous form not that solid.

1120 AND THEY'RE OFF TO PONTIN'S H'CAP 5f (F)
4:30 (4:30) (Class 6) (0-60,60) 3-Y-O **£1,774** (£523; £262) **Stalls** High

Form RPR

50-2 **1** **Straight (IRE)**[7] 993 3-9-1 60 .... MarkLawson(3) 4 62
(M Brittain) *cl up: rdn 2f out: drvn to ld jst ins fnl f: hld on gamely* **9/2**[3]

0-65 **2** *nk* **Swallow Forest**[14] 917 3-8-8 50 ....(b) PaulFessey 5 51
(T D Barron) *in rr and sn pushed along: rdn wl over 1f out: styd on strly ins fnl f: jst failed* **8/1**

5363 **3** *hd* **Planet Paradise (IRE)**[11] 952 3-7-13 46 .... KellyHarrison(5) 1 46
(D Shaw) *chsd ldrs on outer: hdwy 1/2-way: rdn to ld wl over 1f out: edgd lft and hdd jst ins fnl f: drvn and no ex towards fin* **9/2**[3]

-002 **4** *12* **Admirals Way**[17] 876 3-9-0 56 .... TPQueally 6 13
(C N Kellett) *led to 1/2-way: sn rdn along and wknd wl over 1f out* **2/1**[1]

226 **5** *1/2* **Stoneacre Chris (USA)**[12] 928 3-8-12 54 ....(b[1]) LPKeniry 2 9
(Peter Grayson) *cl up: led 1/2-way: sn rdn and hdd wl over 1f out: sn wknd: b.b.v* **8/1**

-634 **6** *7* **Heron (IRE)**[14] 917 3-8-10 52 ....(b) AndrewElliott 3 —
(A M Hales) *dwlt: sn rdn along and a in rr* **4/1**[2]

61.30 secs (1.60) **Going Correction** +0.20s/f (Slow) **6** Ran SP% **111.9**
Speed ratings (Par 96): **95,94,94,75,74 63**
CSF £37.58 TOTE £6.20: £2.50, £5.20; EX 49.80.
Owner Northgate Poker **Bred** P Moyles **Trained** Warthill, N Yorks
■ Stewards' Enquiry : Paul Fessey three-day ban: used whip with excessive frequency (Apr 14-16)

FOCUS
A moderate sprint handicap in which the front three pulled miles clear of the other trio who included the first two in the market. The winning time was 0.64 seconds faster than the two-year-old maiden, which is about what you would expect.
Admirals Way Official explanation: trainer said gelding was unsuited by the fibresand surface
Stoneacre Chris(USA) Official explanation: vet said filly bled from the nose
Heron(IRE) Official explanation: trainer said gelding did not handle the track

1121 CALL PONTIN'S NOW ON 0844 8153648 H'CAP 1m 6f (F)
5:00 (5:01) (Class 6) (0-65,60) 4-Y-0+ **£1,774** (£523; £262) **Stalls** Low

Form RPR

1411 **1** **Zaffeu**[27] 787 7-9-11 60 .... VinceSlattery 8 69
(A G Juckes) *trckd ldrs: hdwy over 3f out: rdn to chse ldr over 1f out: drvn and styd on ins fnl f to ld nr fin* **4/1**[2]

54 **2** *hd* **Leyte Gulf (USA)**[11] 954 5-9-6 55 .... LPKeniry 3 63
(C C Bealby) *trckd ldrs: hdwy 1/2-way: led 5f out: rdn clr 2f out: drvn ins fnl f: wknd and hdd towards fin* **6/1**[3]

46/5 **3** *6* **Sun Quest**[7] 988 4-8-6 45 .... AndrewElliott 9 45
(I W McInnes) *chsd ldrs: rdn along and outpcd over 3f out: hdwy 2f out: kpt on u.p ins fnl f* **7/1**

2025 **4** *1* **Ronsard (IRE)**[3] 1062 6-8-9 47 .... JamieMoriarty(3) 5 46
(P D Evans) *dwlt: in rr tl hdwy on outer 3f out: rdn wl over 1f out: kpt on ins fnl f: nrst fin* **8/1**

4-06 **5** *1* **Muntami (IRE)**[17] 789 7-9-6 55 .... StephenDonohoe 1 52
(John A Harris) *chsd ldrs: rdn along and outpcd over 4f out: kpt on u.p fnl 2f* **10/1**

-131 **6** *1* **Cragganmore Creek**[55] 438 5-9-5 54 ....(v) NCallan 2 50
(D Morris) *trckd ldr: effrt 3f out: rdn along over 2f out: sn drvn and wknd* **9/4**[1]

5023 **7** *9* **Matinee Idol**[27] 787 5-8-10 45 ....(b) RobertWinston 4 28
(Mrs S Lamyman) *hld up towards rr: sme hdwy over 3f out: rdn along wl over 2f out and n.d* **14/1**

006/ **8** *14* **Only For Sue**[485] 2099 9-8-12 47 .... FergusSweeney 6 11
(W S Kittow) *led: pushed along and hdd 5f out: sn rdn and wknd 3f out* **17/2**

3m 12.22s (3.92) **Going Correction** +0.30s/f (Slow)
WFA 4 from 5yo+ 4lb **8** Ran SP% **114.9**
Speed ratings (Par 101): **100,99,96,95,95 94,89,81**
CSF £28.29 CT £162.21 TOTE £5.20: £1.50, £2.10, £2.40; EX 25.80 Place 6 £966.11, Place 5 £246.74.
Owner Whispering Winds **Bred** Patrick Eddery Ltd **Trained** Abberley, Worcs
■ Stewards' Enquiry : Andrew Elliott one-day ban: careless riding (Apr 14)

FOCUS
A moderate staying event run at a modest early pace and the front pair pulled right away. The form looks sound rated through the runner-up.
T/Jkpt: Part won. £52,050.80 to a £1 stake. Pool: £73,311.10. 0.50 winning tickets. T/Plt: £2,256.80 to a £1 stake. Pool: £62,140.85. 20.10 winning tickets. T/Qpdt: £272.70 to a £1 stake. Pool: £3,133.40. 8.50 winning tickets. JR

FOLKESTONE (R-H)
Tuesday, April 1

OFFICIAL GOING: Soft (heavy in places)
Wind: Moderate, behind Weather: Fine

1122 EBF BETDAQ.CO.UK MAIDEN STKS 5f
2:20 (2:20) (Class 5) 2-Y-O **£3,561** (£1,059; £529; £264) **Stalls** Low

Form RPR

1 **Doughnut** 2-8-12 0 .... RichardHughes 4 71
(R Hannon) *trckd ldrs: effrt and got through against rail to chal fnl f: drvn and styd on to ld on the nod* **9/2**[3]

5 **2** *shd* **Riflessione**[10] 957 2-9-3 0 .... LPKeniry 5 76
(J S Moore) *pressed ldr: drvn to ld ent fnl f: hdd on the nod last stride* **7/4**[1]

3 *3 1/4* **Just The Lady** 2-8-5 0 .... JackDean(7) 1 58
(W G M Turner) *led: hdd & wknd ent fnl f* **12/1**

4 *1 1/4* **Raimond Ridge (IRE)** 2-9-3 0 .... ChrisCatlin 3 58+
(M R Channon) *s.i.s: sn in tch: effrt on outer 2f out: wknd jst over 1f out* **2/1**[2]

5 *1 1/4* **Call Me Courageous (IRE)** 2-9-3 0 .... SebSanders 2 53+
(A B Haynes) *s.s: a last: no imp 2f out: wknd fnl f* **11/2**

63.00 secs (3.00) **Going Correction** +0.40s/f (Good) **5** Ran SP% **111.0**
Speed ratings (Par 92): **92,91,86,84,82**
CSF £12.95 TOTE £5.30: £1.80, £1.40; EX 13.60.
Owner Simon Leech **Bred** R F And S D Knipe **Trained** East Everleigh, Wilts

FOCUS
A moderate juvenile maiden, run at a fair pace. The first pair came clear and the form is rated around the second.

NOTEBOOK
Doughnut, the first foal of a 7f juvenile winner, is the first two-year-old to be seen out from her stable and she just did enough to make a winning start to her career. She showed a good attitude when the gap appeared against the rail nearing the final furlong and, with the aid of that to race against, eventually stuck her head out where it mattered most. She went on this ground, but will probably prefer a sounder surface in due course and her connections were quick after the race to nominate the Newbury Super Sprint (a race in which they have a great record) as her big target. (op 5-2)
Riflessione, the only runner with any previous form, showed the benefit of her debut fifth in the Brocklesby and was only denied right at the death. He finished clear of the remainder and can be pretty much considered a winner without a penalty ahead of his next assignment. (op 15-8 tchd 2-1)
Just The Lady is a half-sister to two early juvenile winners from her stable and she showed up well enough from the front until tiring soon after passing the final furlong marker. Better ground will be more in her favour. (op 16-1)
Raimond Ridge(IRE), by far the most expensive of these at 70,000euros, did not help his chances on this racecourse bow by missing the break. He still showed some ability and ought to prove a deal sharper for the experience. (op 3-1)

Call Me Courageous(IRE), whose dam was a multiple winner in Italy, was another who was always playing catch-up after a sluggish start. He should really know a lot more next time. (op 8-1 tchd 5-1)

1123 BET CHAMPIONS LEAGUE - BETDAQ MEDIAN AUCTION MAIDEN STKS 6f
2:50 (2:50) (Class 6) 3-Y-O £2,266 (£674; £337; £168) Stalls Low

Form RPR

6-6 **1** **Never Catcher (IRE)**[8] 997 3-8-5 0 SophieDoyle(7) 1 69
(P A Blockley) *racd against nr side rail: pressed ldr: led over 3f out: rdn 1f out: gng away at fin* 4/1[3]

200- **2** 2 1/4 **Magical Speedfit (IRE)**[179] 5974 3-9-3 74 JimmyQuinn 4 67
(G G Margarson) *swtchd to r nr side after 1f and settled in last: shkn up sn after 1/2-way: got through 2f out: hrd rdn to chal over 1f out: nt qckn* 8/13[1]

500- **3** 2 3/4 **Midnite Blews (IRE)**[196] 5498 3-9-3 63 DavidKinsella 3 58
(A B Haynes) *racd on outer: cl up: ch 2f out: wknd jst over 1f out* 3/1[2]

4 27 **Heroic Fool** 3-9-3 0 SamHitchcott 2 —
(Miss Z C Davison) *led to over 3f out: wknd rapidly jst over 2f out: t.o* 25/1

1m 16.98s (4.28) **Going Correction** +0.625s/f (Yiel) 4 Ran SP% **110.8**
Speed ratings (Par 96): **96,93,89,53**
CSF £7.25 TOTE £4.60; EX 9.10.
Owner Mrs Joanna Hughes **Bred** Patrick Hayes **Trained** Lambourn, Berks

FOCUS
A weak maiden. The winner scored readily, but 74-rated runner-up looks regressive.

1124 BETDAQPOKER.CO.UK (S) STKS 7f (S)
3:25 (3:25) (Class 6) 3-Y-O £1,774 (£523; £262) Stalls Low

Form RPR

4123 **1** **Tiger's Rocket (IRE)**[34] 712 3-9-3 70 RichardSmith 5 66
(R Hannon) *pressed ldng pair and racd towards outer: led jst over 2f out and sn crossed to nr side rail: rdn and styd on wl fr over 1f out* 3/1[2]

3 **2** 1 1/2 **Zeffirelli**[19] 864 3-8-12 0 SteveDrowne 2 57
(J L Spearing) *t.k.h early: trckd ldr: chal over 2f out: chsd wnr after: kpt on but no imp fnl f* 9/2[3]

333- **3** nk **Rub Of The Relic (IRE)**[159] 6448 3-8-12 67 StephenDonohoe 1 56
(P A Blockley) *trckd ldrs: shkn up over 2f out: effrt u.p over 1f out: disp 2nd fnl f: kpt on* 9/4[1]

2405 **4** 1/2 **Coole Dodger (IRE)**[17] 897 3-8-7 62 ow2 KylieManser(7) 7 57
(B G Powell) *hld up in last pair: stdy prog fr jst over 2f out and edgd towards outer: rdn over 1f out: kpt on same pce* 14/1

0-01 **5** 3 1/4 **Secret Meaning**[20] 853 3-8-5 58 (p) JackDean(7) 4 46
(W G M Turner) *racd on wd outside: cl up: wl on terms w wnr 2f out: wknd jst over 1f out* 5/1

5606 **6** 5 **Mad Man Will (IRE)**[8] 998 3-8-5 52 (t) WilliamCarson(7) 6 33
(S C Williams) *led and sn crossed to nr side rail: hdd jst over 2f out: sn wknd* 12/1

0-06 **7** 2 3/4 **Hero Heart**[56] 439 3-8-12 53 TGMcLaughlin 3 26
(Jane Chapple-Hyam) *hld up in last pair: pushed along and no prog over 2f out: wknd over 1f out* 16/1

000- **8** 4 **Una Auroraborealis**[211] 5089 3-8-7 49 (v[1]) JimmyQuinn 8 11
(J Ryan) *a in rr: wknd over 2f out* 25/1

1m 33.1s (5.80) **Going Correction** +0.625s/f (Yiel) 8 Ran SP% **114.7**
Speed ratings (Par 96): **91,89,88,88,84 78,75,71**
CSF £17.03 TOTE £3.00: £1.60, £1.20, £1.60; EX 17.80 Trifecta £30.30 Pool: £460.06, 10.76 winning units.The winner was sold to Steve Gollings 7,400gns. Coole Dodger was claimed by R. H. Brookes for £6,000. Zeffirelli was claimed by M. Quinn for £6,000
Owner Michael Mulholland **Bred** Bryan Ryan **Trained** East Everleigh, Wilts
■ Stewards' Enquiry : Richard Smith one-day ban: used whip above shoulder height (Apr 15)

FOCUS
Not a bad seller, but it was a modest winning time for the type of race and the slowest of the three contests over the trip at the meeting. The form does not look that sound.

1125 DAVID PACY BIRTHDAY MAIDEN STKS 7f (S)
4:00 (4:01) (Class 5) 3-Y-O+ £2,590 (£770; £385; £192) Stalls Low

Form RPR

2- **1** **Pravda Street**[137] 6827 3-8-12 0 TQuinn 1 91
(P F I Cole) *mde all and racd against nr side rail: sn clr: pressed briefly over 1f out: styd on wl fnl f* 4/1[3]

42- **2** 5 **Glorious Gift (IRE)**[207] 5194 3-8-12 0 AlanMunro 4 78
(P W Chapple-Hyam) *chsd clr ldrs: no prog tl styd on fr over 1f out to take 2nd last 100yds: no ch w wnr* 2/1[2]

2- **3** 3 **Oarsman**[202] 5337 3-8-12 0 SteveDrowne 13 70+
(R Charlton) *crossed fr wd draw and sn chsd wnr: pushed along to cl 2f out: no imp over 1f out: wknd and lost 2nd ins fnl f* 7/4[1]

36 **4** 1/2 **Bartercard (USA)**[17] 909 7-9-7 0 JackMitchell(5) 2 74
(Stef Liddiard) *chsd ldrs but nvr on terms: kpt on fnl f and nrly snatched 3rd* 20/1

6-0 **5** 4 **Polychrome**[48] 543 3-8-4 0 KirstyMilczarek(3) 10 54
(John Berry) *sn struggling and wl in rr: kpt on fnl 2f: no ch* 66/1

0- **6** 1 3/4 **Contrada**[173] 6127 3-8-12 0 RichardHughes 5 54+
(R Charlton) *hld up wl off the pce: wl in rr 3f out: shuffled along and sme prog over 2f out: shkn up and kpt on: nvr a factor* 16/1

5 **7** 1 **Sunny Spells**[13] 936 3-8-5 0 WilliamCarson(7) 3 51+
(S C Williams) *dwlt: hld up in last and sn long way bhd: taken to outer and stdy prog fr 3f out: nvr nr ldrs* 100/1

04- **8** 4 **Mick's Dancer**[116] 7051 3-8-12 0 MartinDwyer 8 41
(W R Muir) *chsd clr ldrs and nvr on terms: no prog fnl 2f* 16/1

0 **9** 15 **La Zarza**[17] 909 3-8-7 0 RichardKingscote 6 —
(S C Williams) *sn struggling and wl in rr: t.o* 100/1

-00 **10** 1/2 **Running Supreme**[35] 705 4-9-7 0 JimCrowley 7 —
(Mrs N Smith) *dwlt: sn struggling and wl bhd: t.o* 100/1

11 9 **Valdemar Victory**[164] 4-9-12 0 SilvestreDeSousa 9 —
(D Nicholls) *nvr on terms w ldrs: struggling by 1/2-way: wknd: t.o* 66/1

3- **12** 9 **Street Devil (USA)**[175] 6079 3-8-12 0 StephenDonohoe 14 —
(P A Blockley) *carried across to far side by rival: sn bhd: hung lft fnl 3f: t.o* 14/1

0 **13** 49 **Hibou De Nuit (IRE)**[10] 965 3-8-12 0 (b[1]) FergusSweeney 12 —
(J R Boyle) *racd far side: t.o after 3f* 100/1

1m 30.94s (3.64) **Going Correction** +0.625s/f (Yiel)
WFA 3 from 4yo+ 14lb 13 Ran SP% **119.8**
Speed ratings (Par 103): **104,98,94,94,89 87,86,82,64,64 54,43,—**
CSF £12.20 TOTE £5.40: £1.70, £1.60, £1.50; EX 16.80 Trifecta £33.70 Pool: £469.56, 9.87 winning units.
Owner R A Instone **Bred** R A Instone **Trained** Whatcombe, Oxon

FOCUS
A decent maiden for the track, which saw those drawn low at an advantage. The winner was impressive but the fourth and fifth limit the form to some extent.
La Zarza Official explanation: jockey said filly had no more to give
Valdemar Victory Official explanation: jockey said gelding lost its action 2f out
Hibou De Nuit(IRE) Official explanation: jockey said gelding lost its action after 3 1/2f

1126 BET GRAND NATIONAL - BETDAQ H'CAP 7f (S)
4:35 (4:35) (Class 5) (0-75,74) 4-Y-O+ £2,590 (£770; £385; £192) Stalls Low

Form RPR

41/ **1** **Benfleet Boy**[573] 5106 4-9-4 74 RyanMoore 4 83+
(B G Powell) *trckd ldr: clsd to ld wl over 1f out: drvn and styd on fnl f* 10/3[2]

-404 **2** 2 **Proud Killer**[47] 554 5-8-7 63 MartinDwyer 5 67
(J R Jenkins) *led: crossed to nr side but racd off the rail: rdn and hdd wl over 1f out: edgd rt but kpt on* 5/1

414- **3** 3 1/4 **Poppets Sweetlove**[170] 6199 4-8-9 65 DavidKinsella 7 60
(A B Haynes) *racd on outer: trckd ldrs: effrt over 2f out: easily outpcd fr over 1f out* 7/2[3]

0-00 **4** 1 1/2 **Mick Is Back**[45] 587 4-8-4 60 (p) JimmyQuinn 2 51
(G G Margarson) *t.k.h: hld up bhd ldng pair against nr side pair: drvn and nt qckn 2f out: btn after* 10/1

201- **5** 3 **Mugeba**[150] 6638 7-8-4 60 oh1 (t) ChrisCatlin 3 44
(Miss Gay Kelleway) *hld up in last pair: pushed along and effrt on outer over 2f out: sn no prog and btn* 13/2

/2-2 **6** 1 **Pure Imagination (IRE)**[9] 979 7-9-2 72 (b) SilvestreDeSousa 1 53
(D Nicholls) *hld up in last pair: pushed along 3f out: struggling sn after* 11/4[1]

1m 32.23s (4.93) **Going Correction** +0.625s/f (Yiel) 6 Ran SP% **111.1**
Speed ratings (Par 103): **96,93,90,88,84 83**
CSF £19.46 TOTE £4.10: £2.10, £2.00; EX 28.00.
Owner Miss J Semple **Bred** Crandon Park Stud **Trained** Upper Lambourn, Berks

FOCUS
A modest handicap but the winner is unexposed, although the poor effort of the favourite weakened the form.
Pure Imagination(IRE) Official explanation: jockey said gelding never travelled

1127 BETDAQ THE BETTING EXCHANGE FILLIES' H'CAP 1m 4f
5:05 (5:05) (Class 5) (0-70,69) 4-Y-O+ £2,331 (£693; £346; £173) Stalls Low

Form RPR

-000 **1** **Royal Audition**[29] 776 7-8-4 56 oh9 ow2 (p) KirstyMilczarek(3) 8 58
(T T Clement) *cl up: rdn to chse ldr wl over 2f out: led jst over 1f out: all out and jst hld on* 66/1

50-1 **2** shd **Snake Skin**[8] 999 5-8-13 62 6ex JimCrowley 5 64
(J Gallagher) *cl up: prog to go 2nd 4f out: led and kicked on 3f out: hung lft over 1f out: sn hdd: rallied nr fin: jst failed* 5/1[2]

-411 **3** 2 **Naughty Thoughts (IRE)**[24] 841 4-8-11 61 RichardKingscote 7 66+
(Tom Dascombe) *hld up in last pair: nowhere to go on inner wl over 3f out: plld wd and last into st: rdn and prog 2f out to take 3rd ins fnl f: hopeless task* 5/2[1]

140- **4** 7 **Magdalene**[169] 6245 4-9-5 69 ChrisCatlin 3 58
(Rae Guest) *hld up in 5th/6th: rdn over 3f out: chsd ldng pair 2f out: no imp: lost 3rd ins fnl f* 8/1

643- **5** 4 1/2 **Lapina (IRE)**[181] 5924 4-9-1 65 (b) PatDobbs 6 48
(Pat Eddery) *hld up in 5th/6th: nt clr run wl over 3f out: sn rdn: no prog fr over 2f out* 7/1

4332 **6** 3 3/4 **Phone Call**[29] 779 5-8-8 57 (p) TQuinn 2 35
(Mouse Hamilton-Fairley) *led to 3f out: sn wknd* 10/1

3-20 **7** 2 **Raquel White**[45] 586 4-8-11 64 KevinGhunowa(3) 4 39
(J L Flint) *chsd ldr to 4f out: sn lost pl and btn* 13/2[3]

-236 **8** 2 3/4 **Aphrodisia**[33] 736 4-8-12 62 RyanMoore 1 33
(S C Williams) *hld up in last pair: drvn over 3f out: no prog: sn bhd* 5/1[2]

2m 58.65s (17.75) **Going Correction** +1.45s/f (Soft)
WFA 4 from 5yo+ 1lb 8 Ran SP% **109.4**
Speed ratings (Par 100): **98,97,96,91,88 86,85,83**
CSF £339.89 CT £1076.09 TOTE £71.70: £7.00, £1.60, £1.50; EX 365.40 Trifecta £392.50 Part won. Pool: £552.88 - 0.10 winning units..
Owner Mrs C Clement **Bred** Summertree Stud **Trained** Newmarket, Suffolk

FOCUS
The first race on the round course and the ground seemed testing. Royal Audition caused a shock but would probably have finished third had things gone right for the placed horses and the form is rated around the runner-up.
Naughty Thoughts(IRE) Official explanation: jockey said filly stumbled on 1st bend
Aphrodisia Official explanation: jockey said filly stopped quickly 4f out

1128 BET MULTIPLES - BETDAQ H'CAP 1m 1f 149y
5:35 (5:36) (Class 5) (0-70,68) 3-Y-O £2,331 (£693; £346; £173) Stalls Centre

Form RPR

600- **1** **Air Chief**[209] 5127 3-8-12 62 IanMongan 9 69
(H J L Dunlop) *trckd ldr after 2f: led over 2f out and kicked on: hrd pressed ins fnl f: jst hld on* 12/1

040- **2** nse **Zen Factor**[181] 5918 3-8-12 62 JamesDoyle 1 69
(J G Portman) *hld up in last pair: prog 3f out: chsd wnr wl over 1f out: clsd grad fnl f: jst failed* 25/1

206- **3** 10 **Tamrai Dancer**[183] 5871 3-9-3 67 SebSanders 7 56
(R M Beckett) *led at decent pce: rdn and hdd over 2f out: lft bhd by ldng pair over 1f out* 7/2[2]

15-5 **4** 11 **Mganga**[27] 799 3-9-2 66 CatherineGannon 4 35
(M R Channon) *s.i.s: settled in last pair: rdn over 3f out: sn wknd: wl bhd fnl 2f* 5/1[3]

065- **5** 11 **General Tufto**[174] 6106 3-9-4 68 SteveDrowne 8 17
(R Charlton) *trckd ldr 2f: rdn over 3f out: sn wknd: t.o* 5/2[1]

060- **6** 1 3/4 **Morestead (IRE)**[182] 5883 3-9-1 65 TQuinn 3 11
(B G Powell) *dropped to last after 2f: rdn wl over 3f out: sn btn: t.o* 7/1

-31P **7** 34 **Ten Spot (IRE)**[40] 644 3-8-7 62 (vt) JackMitchell(5) 6 —
(Stef Liddiard) *cl up on outer tl wknd rapidly over 3f out: wl t.o* 10/1

2m 19.4s (14.50) **Going Correction** +1.45s/f (Soft) 7 Ran SP% **111.7**
Speed ratings (Par 98): **100,99,91,83,74 72,45**
CSF £183.35 CT £873.46 TOTE £12.00: £5.10, £6.00; EX 61.00 Trifecta £265.40 Part won. Pool: £373.89 - 0.80 winning units. Place 6 £56.95, Place 5 £34.29.
Owner Chris Craig-Wood & Tina Blockley **Bred** Biddestone Stud **Trained** Lambourn, Berks
■ Boss Hog was withdrawn on vet's advice (8/1, deduct 10p in the £ under Rule 4).

FOCUS
The front two apart, runners came home at long intervals in what was clearly sapping ground. The form is rather guessy as a result.
Air Chief Official explanation: trainer's rep said, regarding the apparent improvement in form, that gelding had benefited from the step up in trip and the soft ground.

Morestead(IRE) Official explanation: jockey said gelding was unsuited by the soft (heavy in places) ground
Ten Spot(IRE) Official explanation: jockey said filly had breathing problems
T/Plt: £79.10 to a £1 stake. Pool: £54,238.50. 500.25 winning tickets. T/Qpdt: £15.10 to a £1 stake. Pool: £4,003.60. 196.10 winning tickets. JN

1116 SOUTHWELL (L-H)

Tuesday, April 1

OFFICIAL GOING: Standard
Wind: Strong, half behind Weather: Dry and sunny

1129 SOUTHWELL-RACECOURSE.CO.UK H'CAP — 5f (F)

2:30 (2:30) (Class 5) (0-70,69) 4-Y-O+ — **£2,456** (£725; £362) **Stalls** High

Form	Pos	Dist	Horse	Jockey	RPR
335-	1		**Rebel Duke (IRE)**[131] 6905 4-9-4 **69**	FergalLynch 5	84
			(D W Barker) *cl up: led 1/2-way: rdn clr over 1f out: kpt on*	**4/1**[3]	
1226	2	2 1/4	**Strathmore (IRE)**[54] 466 4-9-1 **66**	PaulHanagan 3	73
			(R A Fahey) *chsd ldrs: rdn along and outpcd 1/2-way: hdwy u.p over 1f out: drvn and edgd lft ins fnl f: kpt on*	**3/1**[1]	
1264	3	hd	**Guto**[6] 1022 5-8-10 **64**	AndrewMullen(3) 8	70
			(W J H Ratcliffe) *cl up: rdn along 2f out: drvn and one pce ent fnl f*	**12/1**	
20-0	4	1 3/4	**Mr Rooney (IRE)**[7] 1015 5-8-8 **59**	AdrianTNicholls 4	59
			(D Nicholls) *cl up: rdn along 1/2-way: grad wknd*	**8/1**	
00-0	5	shd	**Tender Process (IRE)**[8] 994 5-9-0 **65**	(v[1]) GrahamGibbons 6	65
			(E S McMahon) *s.i.s and sn rdn along in rr: hdwy and drvn whn hung lft over 1f out: no imp ins fnl f*	**7/2**[2]	
1140	6	3/4	**Sherjawy (IRE)**[13] 933 4-8-1 **55**	(b) WilliamBuick(3) 1	52
			(Miss Z C Davison) *wnt lft s: in tch on outer: rdn along 1/2-way: sn btn*	**9/2**	
50-4	7	3 1/4	**Twosheetstothewind**[89] 29 4-8-12 **63**	RobertWinston 7	48
			(C R Dore) *led to 1/2-way: sn rdn along and wknd wl over 1f out*	**8/1**	
3-05	8	2	**No Time (IRE)**[83] 94 8-8-11 **62**	NeilPollard 2	40
			(A J McCabe) *a outpcd in rr*	**20/1**	

57.83 secs (-1.87) **Going Correction** -0.275s/f (Stan) — 8 Ran SP% **120.1**
Speed ratings (Par 103): **103,99,99,96,96 94,89,86**
CSF £17.41 CT £136.33 TOTE £3.70: £1.60, £1.30, £3.70; EX 16.60.
Owner Ian Bishop **Bred** Rathbarry Stud **Trained** Scorton, N Yorks

FOCUS
An ordinary sprint won by a well-handicapped horse and the form looks solid rated around the placed horses.

1130 PLAY GOLF AT SOUTHWELL GOLF COURSE MEDIAN AUCTION MAIDEN STKS — 1m (F)

3:05 (3:05) (Class 5) 3-5-Y-0 — **£2,456** (£725; £362) **Stalls** Low

Form	Pos	Dist	Horse	Jockey	RPR
335-	1		**Golden Penny**[162] 6379 3-8-8 71	TravisBlock(3) 3	67
			(H Morrison) *mde virtually all: rdn along 2f out: sn jnd and drvn ins fnl f: styd on gamely towards fin*	**11/8**[1]	
00-	2	hd	**Ogmore Junction (IRE)**[153] 6578 3-8-11 0	TPQueally 4	67
			(Mrs S Leech) *trckd ldrs: smooth hdwy over 2f out: chal wl over 1f out: sn rdn and ev ch tl drvn and nt qckn wl ins fnl f*	**12/1**	
5	3	3	**Director's Chair**[32] 748 3-8-8 0	JerryO'Dwyer(3) 1	60
			(Miss J Feilden) *cl up: rdn along 3f out: drvn over 2f out and sn one pce*	**5/1**[3]	
662-	4	5	**Ivestar (IRE)**[194] 5551 3-8-11 82	AdrianTNicholls 5	49
			(D Nicholls) *cl up: rdn along wl over 2f out: drvn and wknd wl over 1f out*	**13/8**[2]	
0	5	nk	**Sharp Indian**[53] 483 4-9-4 0	AndrewMullen(3) 6	43?
			(W J H Ratcliffe) *cl up on outer: rdn along over 4f out: drvn 3f out and sn wknd*	**40/1**	
6320	6	4 1/2	**Dickie Valentine**[10] 976 3-8-13 46 ow2	(b) AmirQuinn 2	39?
			(M R Bosley) *a in rr*	**25/1**	

1m 45.55s (1.85) **Going Correction** +0.05s/f (Slow)
WFA 3 from 4yo 15lb — 6 Ran SP% **110.8**
Speed ratings (Par 103): **92,91,88,83,83 79**
CSF £17.78 TOTE £2.40: £1.40, £5.00; EX 17.70.
Owner Mrs B Oppenheimer **Bred** Mrs B D Oppenheimer **Trained** East Ilsley, Berks

FOCUS
A modest maiden run in a moderate time for a race of this type, 3.61 seconds slower than the later Class 2 handicap. The form is rated through the third for now.
Director's Chair Official explanation: jockey said colt hung right in home straight

1131 BOOK A CONFERENCE AT SOUTHWELL H'CAP — 1m 3f (F)

3:40 (3:40) (Class 4) (0-85,83) 4-Y-O+ — **£4,209** (£1,252; £625; £312) **Stalls** Low

Form	Pos	Dist	Horse	Jockey	RPR
103-	1		**Robustian**[187] 5748 5-8-6 **78**	(v[1]) MatthewDavies(7) 6	93+
			(George Baker) *plld hrd: trckd ldrs: hdwy to ld wl over 2f out: rdn clr and hung lft wl over 1f out: comf*	**4/1**[2]	
2414	2	6	**Jackie Kiely**[6] 1026 7-8-10 **75**	(t) J-PGuillambert 1	79
			(R Brotherton) *hld up in rr: hdwy on outer over 2f out: rdn to chse wnr over 1f out: sn drvn and no imp*	**7/2**[1]	
502-	3	3 1/4	**First To Call**[172] 6144 4-9-4 **83**	AmirQuinn 5	82
			(P J Makin) *cl up: effrt over 2f out: sn rdn and kpt on same pce fr wl over 1f out*	**4/1**[2]	
0424	4	nk	**Kylkenny**[7] 1020 13-8-7 **75** ow1	(t) TravisBlock(3) 2	73
			(H Morrison) *set stdy pce: rdn along over 3f out: hdd wl over 2f out: wknd wl over 1f out*	**13/2**	
223-	5	1 3/4	**Rudry Dragon (IRE)**[150] 6636 4-8-8 **73**	RobertWinston 3	68
			(P A Blockley) *t.k.h: trckd ldrs on inner: effrt 3f out: swtchd rt and rdn to chse wnr over 2f out: sn drvn and wknd wl over 1f out*	**7/2**[1]	
0/	6	9	**Fly Free**[123] 6989 4-9-3 **82**	TPQueally 4	62
			(M L W Bell) *cl up: effrt 3f out: sn rdn and wknd 2f out*	**6/1**[3]	

2m 29.71s (1.71) **Going Correction** +0.05s/f (Slow) — 6 Ran SP% **112.1**
Speed ratings (Par 105): **95,90,88,88,86 80**
CSF £18.14 TOTE £6.20: £2.60, £1.90; EX 24.70.
Owner James, Dean & Partners **Bred** T J Cooper **Trained** Moreton Morrell, Warwicks

FOCUS
A fair handicap, but the early pace was ordinary, resulting in a moderate winning time for the class. The runner-up is the best guide to the level.

1132 RACEHORSE OWNERSHIP WITH HAMBLETON RACING MAIDEN FILLIES' STKS — 6f (F)

4:15 (4:15) (Class 5) 3-Y-O+ — **£2,456** (£725; £362) **Stalls** Low

Form	Pos	Dist	Horse	Jockey	RPR
204-	1		**Crying Aloud (USA)**[158] 6461 3-8-12 80	FrankieMcDonald 2	85+
			(P A Blockley) *mde all: pushed clr wl over 1f out: easily*	**5/4**[1]	
3	2	5	**Orpenella**[42] 616 3-8-12 0	NCallan 1	66
			(K A Ryan) *cl up: rdn along over 2f out: drvn wl over 1f out and sn one pce*	**9/4**[2]	
000-	3	9	**Sweet Mind**[176] 6065 3-8-12 60	PaulHanagan 4	37
			(R A Fahey) *chsd ldrs: rdn along and outpcd over 3f out: kpt on u.p appr last: n.d*	**9/1**	
326-	4	3 1/4	**Kyllis**[158] 6477 3-8-12 67	TomEaves 5	27
			(B Smart) *prom: rdn along 3f out: drvn 2f out and sn wknd*	**4/1**[3]	
	5	1 1/4	**Kai Mer (IRE)** 3-8-5 0	DawnRankin(7) 3	23
			(Miss J A Camacho) *in tch: rdn along over 3f out and sn outpcd*	**33/1**	
0-0	6	4	**The Dragon (IRE)**[18] 885 3-8-12 0	TPQueally 6	10
			(M Quinn) *a in rr: bhd fnl 3f*	**20/1**	

1m 15.72s (-0.78) **Going Correction** +0.05s/f (Slow) — 6 Ran SP% **112.9**
Speed ratings (Par 100): **107,100,88,84,82 77**
CSF £4.35 TOTE £2.00: £1.40, £1.40; EX 4.10.
Owner M J Wiley **Bred** Eric Heitzmann & Darley **Trained** Lambourn, Berks

FOCUS
This did not a particularly competitive maiden and very few ever got into it, but they finished very well spread out and the winning time was 0.19 seconds faster than the later 0-80 handicap over the same trip. The winner is rated to the best of her juvenile form.
Kai Mer(IRE) Official explanation: jockey said saddle slipped

1133 ARENALEISUREPLC.COM H'CAP — 1m (F)

4:45 (4:48) (Class 2) (0-100,100) 4-Y-O+ **£10,361** (£3,083; £1,540; £769) **Stalls** Low

Form	Pos	Dist	Horse	Jockey	RPR
00-2	1		**Benandonner (USA)**[10] 958 5-8-4 **86** oh2	PaulHanagan 7	98
			(R A Fahey) *cl up: led after 2f: rdn 2f out: drvn and edgd rt ins fnl f: hld on wl*	**6/4**[1]	
40-5	2	nk	**Regal Parade**[10] 958 4-8-4 **86** oh1	AdrianTNicholls 3	97+
			(D Nicholls) *trckd ldrs: hdwy on outer over 2f out: rdn over 1f out: styng on whn edgd lft ins fnl f: drvn and kpt on wl towards fin*	**9/1**	
00-0	3	4 1/2	**Party Boss**[5] 1045 6-9-2 **98**	NCallan 2	99
			(C E Brittain) *led 2f: cl up tl rdn along 2f out: sn drvn and one pce appr fnl f*	**8/1**	
00-4	4	1/2	**Rio Riva**[10] 960 6-9-4 **100**	TomEaves 5	100
			(Miss J A Camacho) *hld up in rr: hdwy over 2f out: rdn and styd on ins fnl f: nrst fin*	**7/1**	
2300	5	nse	**Kabeer**[32] 757 10-8-2 **89**	(t) NataliaGemelova(5) 6	88
			(A J McCabe) *hld up: gd hdwy on outer 3f out: chal 2f out and ev ch tl rdn and wknd ent fnl f*	**12/1**	
4-00	6	8	**Red Cape (FR)**[3] 1071 5-8-12 **97**	AndrewMullen(3) 1	78
			(Mrs R A Carr) *chsd ldrs on inner: rdn along 3f out and grad wknd*	**33/1**	
1311	7	3/4	**Silver Hotspur**[20] 850 4-8-4 **89**	WilliamBuick(3) 8	68
			(V Smith) *chsd ldrs: rdn along 3f out and sn wknd*	**9/2**[2]	
00-0	8	13	**Very Wise**[10] 960 6-8-13 **95**	JimmyFortune 4	44
			(W J Haggas) *in tch: effrt to chse ldrs 3f out: sn rdn and wknd: bhd and eased over 1f out*	**6/1**[3]	

1m 41.94s (-1.76) **Going Correction** +0.05s/f (Slow) — 8 Ran SP% **116.7**
Speed ratings (Par 109): **110,109,105,104,104 96,95,82**
CSF £16.76 CT £85.16 TOTE £2.10: £1.20, £3.30, £2.10; EX 20.40.
Owner J C Parsons & Sinead Parsons **Bred** Gainsborough Farm Llc **Trained** Musley Bank, N Yorks

FOCUS
A very decent handicap for the track and there was no hanging about. This proved a big boost to the form of the William Hill Spring Mile with the second and fifth in the Doncaster event filling the first two places here. The pair pulled a long way clear of the rest.

NOTEBOOK
Benandonner(USA) ◆ had failed to win in five previous starts on sand though he had been placed in four of those, but he is a much-improved performer now and came into this off the back of a cracking effort in the William Hill Spring Mile. In front after a couple of furlongs, he kept on finding a bit more when challenged and never really looked like being overhauled. This was a fine effort from 2lb wrong and he looks set for a good season. (tchd 13-8)
Regal Parade ◆, unbeaten in two previous outings on sand including one here, had finishing eighth lengths behind Benandonner in the William Hill Spring Mile last month and was meeting him on 3lb worse terms. Putting in a power-packed finish down the outside from off the pace, he could never quite get there but this was still a good effort and he looks to be on a winnable mark now. (op 10-1 tchd 12-1)
Party Boss, unbeaten in two previous tries here, had put in a rather tame effort on his return to action at Wolverhampton five days earlier when unable to gain an uncontested lead and the presence of Benandonner meant that he was unable to get his own way out in front here either. He was making hard work of it from some way out, so under the circumstances he probably did well to keep battling away for third place at a respectful distance.
Rio Riva, a fine fourth in the Lincoln, had only shown reasonable form in two previous tries on Polytrack and he did not get going until it was too late on this Fibresand debut. This surface does not really suit his come-from-behind style. (tchd 15-2)
Kabeer, back on his favourite surface after a couple of tame efforts on Polytrack, was given a patient ride this time but he raced very wide around the home bend as he made progress and that probably told against him late on. (op 10-1)
Red Cape(FR) had every chance on the inside, but this trip on a slow surface appeared to find him out.
Silver Hotspur, up another 8lb, has been in cracking form here this winter but he was up in class this time and he found things far too hot at this level. (op 5-1)
Very Wise is rather inclined to blow hot and cold, and this was very much a case of cold on a surface he is yet to really prove himself on. (tchd 13-2)

1134 GOLF MEMBERSHIP AT SOUTHWELL GOLF COURSE H'CAP — 6f (F)

5:15 (5:17) (Class 4) (0-85,88) 4-Y-O+ — **£4,209** (£1,252; £625; £312) **Stalls** Low

Form	Pos	Dist	Horse	Jockey	RPR
50-2	1		**Swinbrook (USA)**[7] 1015 7-8-6 **70**	(v) PaulHanagan 4	83
			(R A Fahey) *chsd ldrs: hdwy 2f out and sn rdn: drvn ins fnl f and styd on to ld last 75yds*	**7/4**[1]	
4054	2	3/4	**Lethal**[24] 839 5-8-8 **75** ow1	JamieMoriarty(3) 6	86
			(R A Fahey) *chsd ldr: hdwy to ld 2f out: sn rdn: drvn ins fnl f: hdd and no ex last 75yds*	**12/1**	
1341	3	1 3/4	**Cerebus**[6] 1021 6-8-9 **76** 6ex	(bt) WilliamBuick(3) 2	81
			(A J McCabe) *dwlt and sn rdn along in rr: hdwy over 2f out: kpt on u.p ins fnl f: nrst fin*	**5/1**[3]	

0060 **4** 2 1/4 **Qadar (IRE)**[10] 969 6-8-13 **80**........................(p) LukeMorris(3) 7 78
(N P Littmoden) *in tch: rdn along wl over 2f out and sn one pce* **11/2**

606- **5** 3 1/4 **Makshoof (IRE)**[143] 6753 4-9-2 **80**........................ NCallan 5 67
(K A Ryan) *chsd ldng pair: hdwy over 2f out: sn rdn and wknd wl over 1f out* **5/2**[2]

010- **6** 10 **Count Cougar (USA)**[102] 7215 8-8-8 **75**............... MichaelJStainton(3) 1 30
(S P Griffiths) *led: rdn along and hdd 2f out: sn wknd* **10/1**

1m 15.91s (-0.59) **Going Correction** +0.05s/f (Slow) **6** Ran SP% **113.8**
Speed ratings (Par 105): **105,104,101,98,94 81**
CSF £23.41 TOTE £2.20: £1.60, £6.00; EX 21.60 Place 6 £ 17.98, Place 5 £ 9.02.
Owner Mark A Leatham **Bred** Bill Bronstad **Trained** Musley Bank, N Yorks

FOCUS
Just a fair sprint handicap and the time was slightly slower than the earlier maiden, though still an acceptable one for the class. The race provided a one-two for trainer Richard Fahey with the third the best guide to the form.
T/Plt: £22.30 to a £1 stake. Pool: £59,997.45. 1,960.20 winning tickets. T/Qpdt: £7.30 to a £1 stake. Pool: £3,566.50. 358.50 winning tickets. JR

CATTERICK (L-H)
Wednesday, April 2

OFFICIAL GOING: Good to soft (good in places)
Wind: Virtually nil Weather: Dry, sunny periods

1135 GO RACING AT DONCASTER NEXT FRIDAY (S) STKS 7f
2:20 (2:20) (Class 6) 3-4-Y-O £2,047 (£604; £302) **Stalls** Low

Form RPR

00-0 **1** **Ghafeer (USA)**[9] 990 4-9-5 65........................(p) TomEaves 11 63
(B Ellison) *cl up: led 2f out: sn rdn and kpt on wl fnl f* **9/2**[3]

000- **2** 1/2 **Polish Priory (IRE)**[120] 7021 3-7-11 46........................ LukeMorris(3) 10 52
(P D Evans) *hld up: swtchd rt and hdwy over 2f out: rdn to chse wnr over 1f out: drvn and edgd lft ins fnl f: kpt on* **5/1**

3 5 **Gioacchino (IRE)** 3-8-5 0........................ PaulHanagan 9 43
(D W Barker) *s.i.s and bhd: hdwy 1/2-way: rdn to chse ldrs 2f out: drvn and edgd lft over 1f out: kpt on same pce* **6/1**

3025 **4** hd **Whitcombe Flyer (USA)**[13] 950 3-8-5 50..............(b) RoystonFfrench 7 42
(Miss M E Rowland) *trckd ldrs: effrt over 2f out: sn rdn and one pce* **4/1**[2]

00-0 **5** 1 1/2 **Millenium Sun (IRE)**[38] 690 4-9-5 45........................ PaulMulrennan 3 44
(E J Creighton) *in tch: effrt over 2f out: swtchd rt and rdn wl over 1f out: sn drvn and no imp* **20/1**

000- **6** 1/2 **Only A Splash**[254] 3786 4-9-5 40........................ JoeFanning 8 42
(Mrs R A Carr) *led: rdn along 3f out: hdd 2f out and grad wknd* **16/1**

0-00 **7** 2 1/4 **Scar Tissue**[38] 693 4-8-11 45........................ DNolan(3) 6 31
(E J Creighton) *a in rr* **14/1**

500- **8** 1 **Heidi Hi**[113] 7108 4-8-11 38........................ AndrewMullen(3) 4 28
(J R Turner) *dwlt and in rr: sme hdwy on outer 2f out: sn rdn and nvr a factor* **25/1**

0-00 **9** 4 **Josama**[28] 804 4-8-11 33........................(b[1]) MarkLawson(3) 1 18
(R Bastiman) *chsd ldng pair: rdn along rdn along over 2f out and sn wknd* **50/1**

-040 **10** 1 1/2 **Mister Always**[51] 521 4-9-11 47........................(v) FergalLynch 2 25
(I W McInnes) *in rr: effrt over 2f out: sn rdn and nvr a factor* **10/3**[1]

1m 31.02s (4.02) **Going Correction** +0.45s/f (Yiel)
WFA 3 from 4yo 14lb **10** Ran SP% **115.3**
Speed ratings (Par 101): **95,94,88,88,86 86,83,82,77,76**
CSF £26.34 TOTE £3.50: £1.10, £2.30, £2.70; EX 32.70.There was no bid for the winner. Gioacchino was claimed by R A Harris for £6,000.
Owner Mrs Andrea M Mallinson **Bred** Shadwell Farm LLC **Trained** Norton, N Yorks
■ Stewards' Enquiry : Luke Morris two-day ban: used whip with excessive frequency (Apr 16-17)

FOCUS
A very weak race won by the highest-rated horse in the race (he was 15lb clear of the next highest) who ran below his best. The form looks very limited.
Mister Always Official explanation: trainer had no explanation for the poor form shown

1136 GORACING.CO.UK H'CAP 1m 7f 177y
2:50 (2:51) (Class 6) (0-65,67) 4-Y-O+ £2,047 (£604; £302) **Stalls** Low

Form RPR

3213 **1** **Grizebeck (IRE)**[9] 988 6-9-5 59........................(p) PaulHanagan 12 71
(R F Fisher) *mde all: qcknd 4f out: rdn along 2f out: drvn ins fnl f and styd on strly* **10/3**[1]

021- **2** 1 **Toboggan Lady**[163] 6383 4-9-1 59........................ RoystonFfrench 15 70
(Mrs A Duffield) *hld up in midfield: stdy hdwy 1/2-way: chsd wnr over 2f out and sn rdn: drvn ent fnl f: kpt on* **11/2**[3]

36-1 **3** nk **Hue**[9] 988 7-9-6 67 6ex........................ LanceBetts(7) 11 77+
(B Ellison) *hld up and bhd: hdwy 3f out: styng on whn swtchd rt over 1f out: rdn and edgd lft ins fnl f: fin wl* **9/2**[2]

3230 **4** 5 **Sand Repeal (IRE)**[30] 779 6-9-0 61........................(v) AmyBaker(7) 2 65
(Miss J Feilden) *trckd ldrs: hdwy 1/2-way: rdn along to chse ldng pair over 2f out: sn drvn and kpt on same pce appr fnl f* **18/1**

0355 **5** 6 **Flame Creek (IRE)**[11] 963 12-9-9 63........................ GregFairley 3 60
(E J Creighton) *in tch: hdwy to chse ldrs 6f out: rdn along wl over 2f out and kpt on same pce* **20/1**

0034 **6** 1 1/2 **Haatmey**[9] 988 6-8-6 51 ow1........................(bt) AshleyHamblett(5) 7 46
(N Wilson) *prom: cl up 1/2-way: rdn along 4f out: drvn and wknd wl over 2f out* **9/1**

4-14 **7** 2 1/4 **Snowberry Hill (USA)**[30] 779 5-9-4 58........................ NeilChalmers 5 51
(Lucinda Featherstone) *hld up: hdwy 6f out: rdn along and in tch over 3f out: sn wknd* **11/1**

530- **8** 19 **Blue Jet (USA)**[165] 6330 4-8-8 55........................ MichaelJStainton(3) 6 25
(R M Whitaker) *prom: rdn along 6f out and sn wknd* **25/1**

625/ **9** 3/4 **Patxaran (IRE)**[33] 3396 6-9-4 65........................(t) PatrickDonaghy(7) 14 34
(P C Haslam) *midfield: effrt and sme hdwy over 4f out: rdn along 3f out and sn btn* **33/1**

600- **10** 8 **Vice Admiral**[176] 6076 5-8-9 49........................ PaulMulrennan 4 8
(M W Easterby) *hld up towards rr: hdwy 1/2-way: in tch over 4f out: sn rdn along and wknd* **10/1**

00-5 **11** 1 3/4 **Pheidias (IRE)**[13] 954 4-8-9 53........................ AdrianTNicholls 13 10
(Mrs P Sly) *sn rdn along and alwy in rr* **20/1**

265- **12** 11 **Rocknest Island (IRE)**[127] 4638 5-9-2 59............... AndrewMullen(3) 10 3
(P D Niven) *s.i.s: a bhd* **16/1**

1042 **13** 3 1/2 **George Henson (IRE)**[58] 436 4-8-10 54........................ FergalLynch 1 —
(Garry Moss) *a bhd* **14/1**

00-0 **14** 8 **Into Action**[9] 988 4-8-7 54........................(p) DominicFox(3) 8 —
(W Storey) *chsd ldrs: rdn along 1/2-way: sn wknd* **50/1**

210- **15** 15 **Lady Pickpocket**[153] 6259 4-8-0 47........................(b[1]) LukeMorris(3) 9 —
(F P Murtagh) *chsd ldrs: rdn along over 5f out and sn wknd* **40/1**

3m 36.5s (4.50) **Going Correction** +0.45s/f (Yiel)
WFA 4 from 5yo+ 4lb **15** Ran SP% **122.6**
Speed ratings (Par 101): **106,105,105,102,99 99,97,88,88,84 83,77,75,71,64**
CSF £19.22 CT £86.28 TOTE £4.30: £1.70, £2.30, £2.30; EX 26.00.
Owner Sporting Occasions **Bred** John Killeen **Trained** Ulverston, Cumbria
■ Stewards' Enquiry : Lance Betts 10-day ban: breach of Rule 156 - asked for an effort too late (Apr 16-25)

FOCUS
A fair winning time for the class of contest. Hue probably would have won had his jockey started his run earlier, but the overall level looks sound for the class.
Hue Official explanation: jockey said, regarding running and riding, that his orders were to settle the gelding; trainer said that the orders were to settle mid-division, but the gelding was too far back in the field and was not asked for an effort early enough.
Rocknest Island(IRE) Official explanation: jockey said mare never travelled
Into Action Official explanation: trainer said colt finished distressed

1137 CATTERICKBRIDGE.CO.UK H'CAP 1m 5f 175y
3:20 (3:20) (Class 4) (0-85,84) 4-Y-O+ £4,209 (£1,252; £625; £312) **Stalls** Low

Form RPR

60-2 **1** **Puy D'Arnac (FR)**[11] 963 5-8-8 65........................ RobertWinston 1 77+
(G A Swinbank) *hld up in tch: smooth hdwy over 3f out: led over 1f out: pushed out* **5/2**[1]

50-4 **2** 2 1/4 **Aureate**[8] 1018 4-9-10 84........................ TomEaves 8 90
(B Ellison) *hld up in rr: hdwy on bit 3f out: effrt over 1f out: rdn to chse wnr ins fnl f: no imp* **4/1**[3]

/30- **3** 1 1/2 **Aleron (IRE)**[32] 1532 10-8-8 65........................(p) RoystonFfrench 2 69
(J J Quinn) *trckd ldrs: hdwy on inner over 3f out: rdn along 2f out: kpt on same pce appr fnl f* **7/1**

/01- **4** 3/4 **Hernando's Boy**[51] 6703 7-8-13 70........................ PaulHanagan 5 73
(K G Reveley) *trckd ldrs: smooth hdwy 4f out: led over 2f out: sn rdn and hdd wl over 1f out: drvn and kpt on same pce ins fnl f* **10/3**[2]

100- **5** 11 **Mister Arjay (USA)**[159] 6473 8-9-3 74........................ PaulMulrennan 6 62
(B Ellison) *led: rdn along 4f out: hdd over 2f out and grad wknd* **16/1**

205- **6** 3/4 **Thewhirlingdervish (IRE)**[219] 4893 10-9-4 78........ DuranFentiman(3) 4 65
(T D Easterby) *hld up towards rr: hdwy 4f out: chsd ldrs wl over 2f out: sn rdn and wknd over 1f out* **14/1**

00-0 **7** 5 **Hugs Destiny (IRE)**[9] 988 7-8-2 62 oh7........................(t) LukeMorris(3) 7 42
(M A Barnes) *prom: effrt and cl up over 3f out: sn rdn and wknd over 2f out* **50/1**

5016 **8** 44 **Kames Park (IRE)**[11] 968 6-8-8 70........................ NeilBrown(5) 3 —
(R C Guest) *s.i.s: a in rr* **10/1**

11-0 **9** 28 **Wild Fell Hall (IRE)**[38] 692 5-9-10 81........................ PhillipMakin 9 —
(A D Brown) *cl up: rdn along over 5f out: sn lost pl and bhd* **20/1**

3m 11.54s (7.94) **Going Correction** +0.45s/f (Yiel)
WFA 4 from 5yo+ 3lb **9** Ran SP% **112.5**
Speed ratings (Par 105): **95,93,92,92,86 85,82,57,41**
CSF £12.11 CT £59.35 TOTE £2.80: £1.20, £1.70, £2.50; EX 14.20.
Owner Barrow Brook Racing **Bred** Mrs Axelle Du Verdier **Trained** Melsonby, N Yorks

FOCUS
A competitive staying event and the winner looks to have more to offer. The form is rated around the placed horses.
Wild Fell Hall(IRE) Official explanation: trainer said gelding was unsuited by the good to soft (good in places) ground

1138 GODS SOLUTION H'CAP 7f
3:50 (3:51) (Class 5) (0-75,74) 4-Y-O+ £2,590 (£770; £385; £192) **Stalls** Low

Form RPR

06-0 **1** **Tencendur (IRE)**[9] 992 4-9-1 74........................ AndrewMullen(3) 7 85
(D Nicholls) *trckd ldrs: hdwy to ld 2f out and sn rdn: drvn ins fnl f and hld on gamely* **14/1**

00-0 **2** 1/2 **Stoic Leader (IRE)**[9] 990 8-8-12 68........................ PaulHanagan 9 77
(R F Fisher) *midfield: hdwy on outer 2f out and sn rdn along: styd on to chal ins fnl f and ev ch tl edgd lft and nt qckn towards fin* **14/1**

2503 **3** 1/2 **Memphis Man**[7] 1023 5-8-7 70........................ RichardEvans(7) 3 78
(P D Evans) *dwlt: hdwy on inner and in tch 1/2-way: swtchd rt over 2f out: effrt and nt clr run over 1f out: swtchd rt and rdn ent fnl f: kpt on wl* **13/2**[2]

200- **4** 1 1/4 **King Harson**[148] 6701 9-8-6 69........................ BMcHugh(7) 13 74
(J D Bethell) *cl up on outer: effrt over 2f out and sn ev ch tl rdn over 1f out and kpt on same pce ins fnl f* **12/1**

40-0 **5** nk **Byron Bay**[10] 979 6-8-12 73........................ NeilBrown(5) 6 77
(R C Guest) *in rr: hdwy 2f out: sn rdn and styd on wl fnl f: nrst fin* **20/1**

03-2 **6** 1 1/2 **Grand Opera (IRE)**[9] 990 5-8-11 67........................ RobertWinston 5 69
(J Howard Johnson) *chsd ldrs: rdn along 1/2-way: effrt and n.m.r 2f out and again over 1f out: sn one pce* **2/1**[1]

00-0 **7** 1 **Valdan (IRE)**[9] 990 4-8-9 65........................(t) DavidAllan 12 62
(M A Barnes) *towards rr: pushed along 1/2-way: rdn and hdwy wl over 1f out: kpt on ins fnl f: nrst fin* **50/1**

060- **8** 1 1/2 **Crux**[269] 3345 6-7-13 60 oh6........................ DanielleMcCreery(5) 10 53
(R E Barr) *in rr tl sme late hdwy* **80/1**

030- **9** nk **Wind Shuffle (GER)**[159] 6463 5-8-5 61........................ RoystonFfrench 8 53
(J S Goldie) *chsd ldrs: rdn along 3f out and grad wknd* **11/1**

200- **10** 4 1/2 **Guest Connections**[165] 6331 5-9-3 73........................(v) JoeFanning 2 53
(D Nicholls) *cl up: ev ch over 2f out: sn rdn and edgd lft: wknd over 1f out* **7/1**[3]

310- **11** 4 1/2 **Malinsa Blue (IRE)**[183] 5885 6-8-10 66........................ TomEaves 1 34
(B Ellison) *led: rdn along 3f out: drvn and hdd 2f out: sn wknd* **25/1**

0V0- **12** 18 **Kamanda Laugh**[97] 7241 7-8-11 67........................ PaulMulrennan 11 —
(K A Ryan) *a in rr* **11/1**

00-3 **13** 3 **Kabis Amigos**[10] 979 6-9-1 71........................(t) AdrianTNicholls 4 —
(D Nicholls) *stmbld s: hdwy and in tch after 2f: rdn along over 2f out and sn wknd* **8/1**

1m 29.6s (2.60) **Going Correction** +0.45s/f (Yiel) **13** Ran SP% **119.8**
Speed ratings (Par 103): **103,102,101,100,100 98,97,95,95,90 84,64,60**
CSF £190.02 CT £1448.24 TOTE £18.10: £5.90, £5.10, £2.20; EX 280.70.
Owner Mrs L Scaife, Mrs S Radford **Bred** Michael O'Mahony **Trained** Sessay, N Yorks

FOCUS
A fair, competitive handicap run at a reasonable pace and the form looks pretty sound.

Kabis Amigos Official explanation: jockey said gelding stumbled at start and lost its action

1139 TOYTOP MAIDEN STKS 5f 212y
4:20 (4:26) (Class 5) 3-Y-0+ **£2,590** (£770; £385; £192) **Stalls** Low

Form RPR

1 **Marvellous Value (IRE)** 3-8-13 0 .... PhillipMakin 11 71+
(M Dods) *midfield: hdwy and in tch 3f out: rdn along 2f out: styd on wl u.p ent fnl f: edgd lft and led last 50yds* **15/2**[3]

0- 2 ¾ **Ancient Cross**[279] 3015 4-9-11 0 .... PaulMulrennan 9 71
(M W Easterby) *chsd ldrs: hdwy 2f out: rdn to ld and hung lft appr fnl f: sn drvn: hdd and no ex last 50yds* **66/1**

5-2 3 1 ½ **Flying Sommelier (USA)**[43] 616 3-8-13 0 .... PaulFessey 1 64
(T D Barron) *midfield: hdwy on inner over 2f out: sn rdn and styd on u.p ent fnl f* **12/1**

33-0 4 ½ **Binario Uno**[10] 980 3-8-13 0 .... AdrianTNicholls 7 62
(D Nicholls) *led: rdn along over 2f out: drvn and hdd wl over 1f out: kpt on same pce ent fnl f* **8/1**

5 ½ **Dnata Flyer (USA)** 3-8-13 0 .... GregFairley 4 63+
(M Johnston) *in rr: pushed along and hdwy over 2f out: swtchd lft and rdn over 1f out: hdwy whn nt clr run and swtchd rt ent fnl f: styd on wl towards fin* **9/4**[1]

6 1 ¼ **Atlantic Beach** 3-8-13 0 .... PaulHanagan 6 56
(R A Fahey) *hld up in tch: hdwy 3f out: effrt and ev ch 2f out: rdn and edging lft whn n.m.r appr fnl f: kpt on same pce* **11/4**[2]

040- 7 1 **Miss Taboo (IRE)**[181] 5946 4-9-6 49 .... RobertWinston 3 51
(P T Midgley) *towards rr: rdn along 3f out: styd on u.p fnl 2f* **12/1**

62 8 ¾ **Moonage Daydream (IRE)**[13] 953 3-8-13 0 .... DavidAllan 10 57+
(T D Easterby) *chsd ldrs: hdwy 1/2-way: rdn to ld wl over 1f out: drvn and hdd whn n.m.r ent fnl f: eased* **12/1**

0- 9 2 ¼ **Ursus**[190] 5702 3-8-10 0 .... AndrewMullen(3) 5 53+
(C R Wilson) *rn loose bef s: cl up: rdn along wl over 2f out: drvn and wknd wl over 1f out: hmpd ent fnl f* **250/1**

04 10 2 ½ **Chevaliers Dream (IRE)**[13] 953 3-8-13 0 .... FergalLynch 2 36
(T D Easterby) *towards rr: hdwy on inner over 2f out: sn rdn along and btn* **16/1**

5 11 1 ¾ **Foxy Jane**[54] 486 3-8-8 0 .... TWilliams 8 25
(M Brittain) *a in rr* **66/1**

0300 12 shd **Marquis De Louvois (IRE)**[5] 1051 3-8-13 60 .... RoystonFfrench 12 30
(Mrs A Duffield) *wnt rt s: racd wd: a in rr* **25/1**

1m 17.64s (4.04) **Going Correction** +0.45s/f (Yiel)
WFA 3 from 4yo 12lb 12 Ran SP% **116.5**
Speed ratings (Par 103): **91,90,88,87,86 85,83,82,79,76 74,73**
CSF £428.03 TOTE £8.40: £2.60, £12.50, £2.50; EX 443.10.
Owner A J Henderson **Bred** John Cullinan **Trained** Denton, Co Durham
■ Stewards' Enquiry : Adrian T Nicholls three-day ban: careless riding (Apr 16-18)
Greg Fairley two-day ban: careless riding (Apr 16-17)

FOCUS
A modest winning time, but this looked a reasonable sprint maiden and, with the form sound rated around the third, fourth and seventh, the race should produce a few winners.

1140 YARM H'CAP 1m 3f 214y
4:50 (4:50) (Class 5) (0-75,71) 3-Y-O **£2,590** (£770; £385; £192) **Stalls** Low

Form RPR

-024 1 **Forsyte Saga**[16] 920 3-9-3 70 .... GregFairley 5 78
(M Johnston) *mde all: rdn along 3f out: drvn over 1f out: styd on strly ins fnl f* **5/1**[3]

006- 2 2 **Kiribati King (IRE)**[140] 6805 3-8-5 65 .... MatthewDavies(7) 1 69
(M R Channon) *s.i.s: rdn early: recovered to trck ldrs after 3f: rdn along 3f out: drvn 2f out: kpt on wl u.p* **9/2**[2]

00-2 3 2 ¾ **Pepper's Ghost**[30] 784 3-8-10 63 .... DMylonas 4 63
(Miss J Feilden) *towards rr: hdwy 4f out: sn rdn along: styd on u.p fnl 2f: nrst fin* **5/1**[3]

040- 4 3 ¼ **Crimson Mitre**[128] 6952 3-8-13 69 .... LukeMorris(3) 7 64
(J Jay) *chsd wnr: rdn along 3f out: drvn 2f out and sn wknd* **13/2**

41-1 5 ½ **Sheer Fantastic**[77] 184 3-8-11 71 .... (b) PatrickDonaghy(7) 3 65
(P C Haslam) *chsd ldrs: rdn along 3f out: sn outpcd* **3/1**[1]

-255 6 2 ¼ **Roundthetwist (IRE)**[16] 920 3-8-8 68 .... DeclanCannon(7) 6 58
(K R Burke) *plld hrd: trckd ldrs: stmbld after 2f: sddle slipped after 4f: remained prom tl wknd fnl 2f* **14/1**

00-0 7 72 **Sabre Light**[11] 961 3-8-12 65 .... RobertWinston 2 —
(P T Midgley) *a in rr: outpcd and bhd fnl 4f* **5/1**[3]

2m 47.46s (8.56) **Going Correction** +0.45s/f (Yiel) 7 Ran SP% **113.2**
Speed ratings (Par 98): **89,87,85,83,83 81,33**
CSF £26.93 TOTE £5.40: £1.80, £3.80; EX 30.90.
Owner Sheikh Hamdan Bin Mohammed Al Maktoum **Bred** Gainsborough Stud Management Ltd **Trained** Middleham Moor, N Yorks

FOCUS
A modest handicap and, with the early pace steady, the winning time was ordinary. The third is rated to his latest All-Weather mark.
Roundthetwist(IRE) Official explanation: jockey said saddle slipped
Sabre Light Official explanation: jockey said gelding was unsuited by the good to soft (good in places) ground

1141 GIANT SCREEN IS HERE EVERY DAY H'CAP 5f
5:20 (5:21) (Class 6) (0-60,66) 3-Y-O **£2,047** (£604; £302) **Stalls** Low

Form RPR

00-1 1 **Killer Class**[9] 993 3-9-0 56 6ex .... FergalLynch 3 59+
(J S Goldie) *trckd ldrs: hdwy 2f out: effoirt whn nt clr run over 1f out: rdn to ld ins fnl f: drvn and hung bdly lft towards fin* **11/4**[2]

000- 2 nk **Maahe (IRE)**[197] 5502 3-8-7 49 .... PaulHanagan 1 51
(R A Fahey) *in tch: hdwy on inner wl over 1f out: drvn and ev ch ins fnl f: kpt on* **11/2**[3]

00-0 3 1 ¾ **Captain Turbot (IRE)**[9] 993 3-8-4 46 oh1 .... PaulQuinn 4 46+
(D W Barker) *cl up: rdn to ld and edgd rt appr last: sn drvn and hdd ins fnl f: hld whn bdly hmpd towards fin* **33/1**

6656 4 nk **Rightcar Hull (IRE)**[19] 882 3-7-12 47 .... (b[1]) PatrickDonaghy(7) 2 42
(Peter Grayson) *sn rdn along and outpcd in rr: hdwy wl over 1f out: styd on wl fnl f: hmpd and swtchd towards fin* **14/1**

000- 5 ½ **Kyzer Chief**[176] 6073 3-8-5 47 .... RoystonFfrench 6 40
(R E Barr) *cl up: led 2f out: sn rdn: hung lft and hdd appr fnl f: sn drvn and one pce* **12/1**

03-5 6 7 **Mchepple**[9] 993 3-8-7 52 .... DominicFox(3) 8 20
(W Storey) *chsd ldrs on outer: rdn along over 2f out and sn wknd* **16/1**

6023 7 6 **Golden Dane (IRE)**[9] 993 3-9-2 58 .... (p) RobertWinston 5 4
(C R Dore) *led: rdn along and hdd 2f out: sn wknd* **10/11**[1]

64.97 secs (5.17) **Going Correction** +0.95s/f (Soft) 7 Ran SP% **117.6**
Speed ratings (Par 96): **96,95,92,92,91 80,70**
CSF £19.08 CT £411.11 TOTE £3.70: £1.10, £5.40; EX 23.10 Place 6 £297.07, Place 5 £142.69.

Owner Frank Brady **Bred** Jonayro Investments **Trained** Uplawmoor, E Renfrews
■ Stewards' Enquiry : Fergal Lynch five-day ban: careless riding (Apr 16-20)

FOCUS
A moderate sprint handicap and the form looks weak.
Golden Dane(IRE) Official explanation: jockey said gelding became unbalanced by the undulations
T/Jkpt: Not won. T/Plt: £730.80 to a £1 stake. Pool: £65,524.80. 65.45 winning tickets. T/Qpdt: £111.70 to a £1 stake. Pool: £3,592.60. 23.80 winning tickets. JR

1074 KEMPTON (A.W) (R-H)
Wednesday, April 2

OFFICIAL GOING: Standard
Wind: Almost nil Weather: Overcast

1142 PANORAMIC BAR & RESTAURANT H'CAP 1m (P)
6:20 (6:22) (Class 6) (0-55,55) 4-Y-0+ **£2,047** (£604; £302) **Stalls** High

Form RPR

2252 1 **Having A Ball**[22] 844 4-8-12 53 .... MartinDwyer 4 60
(P D Cundell) *trckd ldng pair: rdn to chse ldr over 1f out: styd on wl to ld last 75yds: readily* **4/1**[1]

655- 2 1 **Fairy Festival (IRE)**[166] 6315 4-8-13 54 .... LPKeniry 2 59
(J S Moore) *pressed ldr: led 2f out and kicked on: kpt on fnl f: hdd last 75yds* **16/1**

20-6 3 1 ¼ **Ready To Crown (USA)**[51] 524 4-8-12 53 .... AlanDaly 1 55
(Andrew Turnell) *hld up in midfield: rdn and nt qckn 2f out: nt on terms after: styd on fnl f to take 3rd nr fin* **9/1**

5461 4 ½ **Alucica**[18] 898 5-8-9 53 .... (v) TolleyDean(3) 9 54
(D Shaw) *hld up in midfield: effrt and prog to chse ldrs over 1f out: kpt on: nt pce to chal* **8/1**

5360 5 shd **Postmaster**[28] 795 6-8-8 49 .... RobertHavlin 7 50
(R Ingram) *hld up in rr on inner: effrt over 2f out: styng on whn swtchd lft over 1f out: kpt on fnl f* **15/2**

0406 6 1 **Zorn**[7] 1029 9-8-6 47 .... HayleyTurner 12 45
(P Howling) *t.k.h: led: drvn and hdd 2f out: wknd fnl f* **18/1**

5303 7 ½ **Kinsman (IRE)**[35] 711 11-8-5 46 .... (p) J-PGuillambert 10 43
(T D McCarthy) *t.k.h: trckd ldng pair: lost pl 2f out: one pce and no imp fr over 1f out* **16/1**

2005 8 1 **Silver Blue (IRE)**[5] 1064 5-8-3 47 .... (b) WilliamBuick(3) 14 42
(C R Dore) *hld up: last over 3f out: rdn and no prog over 2f out: modest late hdwy* **9/2**[2]

2025 9 1 ¼ **Winged Farasi**[22] 844 4-8-8 52 .... (p) KevinGhunowa(3) 6 44
(R A Harris) *s.i.s: hld up in rr: effrt on outer over 2f out: sn no prog and btn* **8/1**

4500 10 1 ¼ **Grey Gurkha**[33] 749 7-9-0 55 .... PatrickMathers 5 44
(I W McInnes) *slowest away: t.k.h and rchd midfield 1/2-way: rdn and steadily wknd fr over 2f out* **6/1**[3]

6/0- 11 26 **Butlers Best**[224] 4718 4-8-11 55 .... JerryO'Dwyer(3) 8 —
(M R Hoad) *s.i.s: a in rr: brief effrt on outer over 2f out: sn wknd rapidly and eased: t.o* **33/1**

1m 43.22s (3.42) **Going Correction** +0.25s/f (Slow) 11 Ran SP% **116.4**
Speed ratings (Par 101): **92,91,89,89,89 88,87,86,85,84 58**
CSF £68.26 CT £425.06 TOTE £5.00: £1.50, £4.80, £3.80; EX 106.50.
Owner Miss M C Fraser **Bred** R G Percival **Trained** Compton, Berks
■ Stewards' Enquiry : Kevin Ghunowa two-day ban: used whip from above shoulder height (Apr 16-17)

FOCUS
A weak handicap and a moderate winning time for the class, so not a race to be positive about.
Butlers Best Official explanation: jockey said gelding hung left in straight

1143 KEMPTON.CO.UK CLAIMING STKS 7f (P)
6:50 (6:50) (Class 6) 4-Y-0+ **£2,047** (£604; £302) **Stalls** High

Form RPR

2121 1 **Desert Dreamer (IRE)**[5] 1055 7-9-7 78 .... (t) RichardKingscote 8 80
(Tom Dascombe) *hld up in midfield: prog to trck ldr 2f out: clsd to ld 1f out: shkn up and a holding on* **15/8**[1]

6421 2 ½ **Teasing**[20] 870 4-9-4 77 .... (p) RobertHavlin 9 76
(J Pearce) *stdd s: hld up in last pair: prog fr 2f out: styd on to chse wnr last 100yds: clsng at fin but nvr really threatened* **9/2**[3]

1603 3 1 **Satyricon**[5] 1055 4-8-7 69 .... (b) AndreaAtzeni(7) 6 69
(M Botti) *trckd ldrs: wd bnd 3f out: tried to cl fr 2f out: bmpd along furiously and kpt on* **13/2**

-022 4 ½ **The Jailer**[47] 571 5-8-2 57 .... (p) MCGeran(7) 7 63
(J G M O'Shea) *led: drvn 2f out: hdd 1f out: one pce* **14/1**

3015 5 1 ½ **Landucci**[27] 807 7-9-3 75 .... (p) PatrickHills(5) 5 72
(J W Hills) *sn trckd ldng pair: rdn 2f out: nt qckn over 1f out: one pce after* **13/2**

0002 6 2 ¼ **Apache Dawn**[5] 1049 4-9-1 80 .... GeorgeBaker 3 59
(G L Moore) *stdd s: hld up in last pair: gng wl 3f out: rdn and no rspnse wl over 1f out* **7/2**[2]

460 7 1 ¼ **Sir Douglas**[30] 783 5-9-3 68 .... (p) LPKeniry 4 57
(R A Harris) *t.k.h: pressed ldr to 2f out: wknd u.p* **25/1**

/3-0 8 25 **Zeeuw (IRE)**[30] 777 4-9-6 63 .... AdamKirby 2 —
(D J Coakley) *prom 3f: sn rdn and lost pl: t.o* **50/1**

1m 27.09s (1.09) **Going Correction** +0.25s/f (Slow) 8 Ran SP% **114.3**
Speed ratings (Par 101): **103,102,101,100,99 96,95,66**
CSF £10.57 TOTE £2.90: £1.30, £1.60, £2.50; EX 10.50.
Owner ONEWAY Partners **Bred** Gainsborough Stud Management Ltd **Trained** Lambourn, Berks

FOCUS
Most of these have been in good heart recently so, for the grade, this form should be fairly sound with the third to recent form. With a couple of horses well known for setting the pace, it was not surprising that the winning time was reasonably respectable.
Apache Dawn Official explanation: jockey said gelding ran flat

1144 DIGIBET MAIDEN FILLIES' STKS 7f (P)
7:20 (7:20) (Class 5) 3-Y-0+ **£2,456** (£725; £362) **Stalls** High

Form RPR

42-6 1 **Tathkaar**[18] 905 3-8-12 79 .... NCallan 6 76
(C E Brittain) *sweating: trckd ldrs: wnt 2nd on inner over 2f out: narrow ld over 1f out: hrd rdn and jst hld on* **6/4**[1]

-2 **2** hd **Erlydors (IRE)**[18] 897 3-8-12 0 .... AdamKirby 4 75
(W R Swinburn) *plld hrd early: sn led: narrowly hdd over 1f out: drvn and kpt trying: jst hld* **13/8**[2]

33- **3** 3 **Ivory Silk**[95] 7266 3-8-12 0 .... MartinDwyer 9 67
(D K Ivory) *s.s: prog fr rr 3f out: c wd in st: shuffled along and styd on to take 3rd ins fnl f* **14/1**

22-5 **4** 3/4 **Nice Wee Girl (IRE)**[91] 17 3-8-12 67 .... LPKeniry 2 65
(S Kirk) *v keen early: hld up: clsd on ldrs 3f out: wnt 3rd over 1f out to ins fnl f: one pce* **25/1**

5 nse **Plum Asset (USA)** 3-8-12 0 .... SebSanders 5 65+
(R M Beckett) *s.v.s: sn in tch in rr: c wd st: prog 2f out: kpt on same pce over 1f out* **16/1**

6 2 1/2 **Passionforfashion (IRE)** 3-8-12 0 .... RichardHughes 7 58
(R Hannon) *s.s: sn rcvrd into midfield: tried to cl on ldrs over 2f out: shkn up and fdd fnl f* **9/2**[3]

00- **7** 1 1/4 **Moluccella**[137] 6857 3-8-12 0 .... SteveDrowne 3 55
(H Morrison) *hld up in midfield: rdn over 2f out: sn lost tch w ldrs* **80/1**

003- **8** 7 **Pennyspider (IRE)**[251] 3867 3-8-9 52 .... KevinGhunowa(3) 10 36
(M S Saunders) *t.k.h: pressed ldr to over 2f out: sn wknd: t.o* **66/1**

00 **9** 1 1/2 **Hold Fire**[14] 931 4-9-9 0 .... KirstyMilczarek(3) 8 32
(A W Carroll) *sn last: struggling fr 1/2-way: t.o* **100/1**

10 9 **Good News Too** 3-8-12 0 .... RobertHavlin 11 7
(D K Ivory) *a towards rr: wknd rapidly fnl 2f: t.o* **33/1**

1m 28.55s (2.55) **Going Correction** +0.25s/f (Slow)
WFA 3 from 4yo 14lb **10** Ran SP% **119.3**
Speed ratings (Par 100): **95,94,91,90,90 87,86,78,76,66**
CSF £4.20 TOTE £2.40: £1.20, £1.30, £2.20; EX 5.10.
Owner Saeed Manana **Bred** Sir Gordon Brunton **Trained** Newmarket, Suffolk
■ Stewards' Enquiry : Adam Kirby one-day ban: used whip in incorrect place (Apr 16)

FOCUS
Some strong stables were represented, so the two who fought out the finish may be worth following with the third and fourth close to recent form. The winning time was, however, slower than the claimer on the card.
Pennyspider(IRE) Official explanation: jockey said filly ran too free

1145 DIGIBET.COM H'CAP 6f (P)
7:50 (7:51) (Class 6) (0-58,58) 4-Y-0+ **£2,047** (£604; £302) **Stalls** High

Form RPR

5-04 **1** **Duke Of Milan (IRE)**[19] 883 5-8-6 48 .... HayleyTurner 2 60
(G C Bravery) *hld up in last: scythed through on inner fr 2f out gng easily: led ent fnl f: hung fire in front and drvn out* **10/1**

4615 **2** 1 1/4 **Guildenstern (IRE)**[40] 663 6-9-1 57 .... JimmyQuinn 12 65
(P Howling) *t.k.h early: hld up in midfield: prog 2f out: tried to chal 1f out: styd on to snatch 2nd last strides* **11/2**[2]

-600 **3** hd **Is It Time (IRE)**[76] 191 4-8-6 53 .... JackMitchell(5) 11 60
(Mrs P N Dutfield) *sn pressed ldr: drvn to ld jst over 1f out: hdd and one pce ent fnl f* **33/1**

4644 **4** shd **Hart Of Gold**[30] 782 4-9-0 56 .... AdamKirby 4 63
(R A Harris) *hld up in rr: pushed along and prog fr jst over 2f out: upsides 1f out: kpt on same pce* **12/1**

50-4 **5** 2 **Greenwood**[14] 933 10-8-11 53 .... RobertHavlin 3 53
(P G Murphy) *stmbld s: wl in rr: stdy prog fr 2f out: chsd ldrs 1f out: one pce and no imp after* **8/1**

2155 **6** 1 **Double Valentine**[6] 1038 5-8-10 55 .... KirstyMilczarek(3) 6 61+
(R Ingram) *hld up in rr: prog on inner 2f out: n.m.r over 1f out: nt rcvr* **11/2**[2]

0-65 **7** 1/2 **Nightstrike (IRE)**[19] 875 5-8-11 56 ....(b) JerryO'Dwyer(3) 9 51
(Luke Comer, Ire) *led at str pce to jst over 1f out: wknd* **16/1**

506- **8** 1/2 **Bollin Franny**[210] 5139 4-8-10 57 .... NataliaGemelova(5) 10 51
(J E Long) *chsd ldrs: lost pl sn after 1/2-way: tried to rally on outer 2f out: one pce* **20/1**

4163 **9** 1 3/4 **Simpsons Gamble (IRE)**[14] 933 5-8-11 53 ....(p) SebSanders 8 41
(R A Teal) *nvr beyond midfield: drvn on wd outside 2f out: nt qckn and no prog* **7/2**[1]

0641 **10** 1 1/4 **Desert Light (IRE)**[14] 933 7-8-7 52 ....(v) TolleyDean(3) 7 36
(D Shaw) *pressed ldrs: grad lost pl u.p fnl 2f* **15/2**[3]

050- **11** 1/2 **Barbar**[154] 6581 5-9-0 56 .... StephenCarson 1 39
(Eve Johnson Houghton) *fast away fr wd draw to press ldrs: lost pl and struggling over 2f out* **16/1**

500- **12** 2 1/2 **Stamford Blue**[182] 5923 7-8-13 58 ....(b) KevinGhunowa(3) 5 33
(R A Harris) *prog fr midfield 1/2-way: drvn to chal 2f out: immediately gave up u.p* **14/1**

1m 14.04s (0.94) **Going Correction** +0.25s/f (Slow) **12** Ran SP% **118.8**
Speed ratings (Par 101): **103,101,101,100,98 96,96,95,93,91 90,87**
CSF £64.29 CT £1796.84 TOTE £11.80: £3.80, £2.30, £10.50; EX 86.10.
Owner T W Morley **Bred** Irish National Stud **Trained** Cowlinge, Suffolk
■ Stewards' Enquiry : Adam Kirby caution: careless riding

FOCUS
A moderate sprint full of frustrating characters with the runner-up the best guide. It got very tight at the end, and there was an exciting finish.

1146 DIGIBET CASINO H'CAP 6f (P)
8:20 (8:22) (Class 4) (0-80,78) 4-Y-0+ **£4,209** (£1,252; £625; £312) **Stalls** High

Form RPR

10/ **1** **Jake The Snake (IRE)**[691] 1651 7-8-4 67 .... KirstyMilczarek(3) 6 84+
(A W Carroll) *hld up in last pair: taken to outer and prog 2f out: stl only 5th 1f out: pushed along and r.o wl to ld last strides* **11/2**[2]

-151 **2** 3/4 **Diriculous**[34] 729 4-8-12 72 .... JimCrowley 7 83
(T G Mills) *hld up in midfield: prog to chse ldr 2f out: clsd grad: rdn to ld ins fnl f: swamped nr fin* **11/8**[1]

-534 **3** hd **Misaro (GER)**[26] 824 7-9-0 77 ....(b) KevinGhunowa(3) 1 87
(R A Harris) *fast away fr wd draw: racd freely and led at str pce: over 2l clr 2f out: worn down ins fnl f* **13/2**[3]

010- **4** 3 1/4 **Hereford Boy**[154] 6589 4-9-2 76 .... RobertHavlin 8 76
(D K Ivory) *off the pce in midfield: prog but hanging 2f out: chsd ldrs over 1f out: one pce* **14/1**

14-5 **5** shd **Cativo Cavallino**[19] 887 5-8-13 78 .... NataliaGemelova(5) 2 78
(J E Long) *chsd ldr to 2f out: fdd over 1f out* **9/1**

5504 **6** 3/4 **Resplendent Alpha**[19] 887 4-9-0 74 ....(b) JimmyQuinn 4 71
(P Howling) *wl in rr: checked sltly over 2f out: drvn and kpt on one pce fr over 1f out: n.d* **7/1**

50-6 **7** 3 **Impromptu**[19] 887 4-8-13 73 .... SteveDrowne 3 61
(P G Murphy) *pushed along in last pair bef 1/2-way: n.d: shuffled along and modest late prog* **18/1**

320- **8** 2 1/4 **Minaash (USA)**[133] 6900 4-8-9 76 .... ChrisHough(7) 9 56
(D M Simcock) *t.k.h in midfield: struggling and btn jst over 2f out* **16/1**

500- **9** 2 1/4 **H Harrison (IRE)**[171] 6209 8-8-6 73 .... DonnaCaldwell(7) 5 46
(I W McInnes) *chsd ldng trio to over 2f out: wknd* **28/1**

3641 **10** hd **Love On Sight**[18] 896 4-8-10 70 ....(v) NeilPollard 10 43
(A P Jarvis) *plld hrd: chsd ldng pair to over 2f out: wknd rapidly* **7/1**

1m 13.47s (0.37) **Going Correction** +0.25s/f (Slow) **10** Ran SP% **127.1**
Speed ratings (Par 105): **107,106,105,101,101 100,96,93,90,90**
CSF £14.74 CT £56.70 TOTE £7.70: £2.60, £1.20, £1.90; EX 15.20.
Owner David Miller **Bred** J F Tuthill **Trained** Cropthorne, Worcs
■ Stewards' Enquiry : Natalia Gemelova four-day ban: used whip with excessive frequency without giving gelding time to respond (Apr 16-19)

FOCUS
A solid-looking race for the grade, although a few had something to prove or were a little high in the weights. The pace was very generous, the first two are progressive and the third is on a good mark.

1147 MPR SOLICITORS LLP H'CAP 1m 4f (P)
8:50 (8:52) (Class 6) (0-60,60) 3-Y-0 **£2,047** (£604; £302) **Stalls** Centre

Form RPR

0-60 **1** **Cape Colony**[25] 837 3-9-3 59 .... RichardHughes 5 71+
(R Hannon) *sn in tch in midfield: effrt and pushed along over 3f out: prog over 2f out: drvn to cl on ldr 1f out: led last 100yds* **13/8**[1]

00-4 **2** 1/2 **Gunnadoit (USA)**[11] 976 3-8-13 55 .... HayleyTurner 14 66
(M L W Bell) *sweating: wl in tch in midfield: prog on inner over 2f out: drvn to ld over 1f out: hdd and hld last 100yds* **5/1**[2]

3421 **3** 3 **Novestar (IRE)**[11] 976 3-9-0 59 .... KevinGhunowa(3) 7 65
(G J Smith) *led: hanging and rdn bnd over 9f out: drvn and hdd over 1f out: one pce* **15/2**

000- **4** 1 1/2 **Okafranca (IRE)**[167] 6274 3-9-3 59 .... MartinDwyer 12 63
(W R Muir) *sn chsd ldng pair: rdn over 3f out: stl cl enough over 1f out: fdd* **25/1**

000- **5** 5 **Io (IRE)**[158] 6494 3-9-3 59 .... SebSanders 10 55+
(J L Dunlop) *stdd s: buried away on inner in midfield: chsng ldrs over 2f out: shkn up sn after: pushed along and outpcd* **14/1**

004- **6** 3/4 **Captain Mainwaring**[167] 6285 3-9-2 58 .... JimCrowley 11 53+
(N P Littmoden) *mostly in last pair: rdn over 2f out: kpt on but nvr trbld ldrs* **33/1**

6-00 **7** 1 1/2 **Asmodea**[33] 748 3-9-4 60 .... JimmyQuinn 13 52
(D J Coakley) *mostly in midfield on inner: effrt over 2f out: one pce and no imp on ldrs* **22/1**

20-2 **8** 2 1/2 **Lord's Bidding**[14] 940 3-9-3 59 ....(v[1]) RobertHavlin 2 47
(R Ingram) *dwlt and reminders s: sme prog into midfield 1/2-way: no hdwy u.p over 2f out* **9/1**

06-0 **9** 1/2 **Black Heart**[77] 184 3-9-0 59 .... JerryO'Dwyer(3) 8 46
(M Botti) *a towards rr on outer: drvn wl over 3f out: nvr on terms* **33/1**

3-00 **10** 3/4 **Dawn Wind**[14] 940 3-9-1 57 ....(p) NCallan 3 43
(I A Wood) *trckd ldrs on outer after 4f: rdn over 3f out: wknd over 2f out* **25/1**

00-6 **11** 3 1/4 **Lady Florence**[13] 953 3-8-10 52 .... SteveDrowne 4 33
(A B Coogan) *wl in tch tl wknd over 3f out: no ch whn n.m.r over 2f out* **40/1**

446- **12** 1 1/4 **Poppy Dean (IRE)**[159] 6478 3-9-4 60 ....(t) JamesDoyle 9 39
(J G Portman) *snatched up after 2f and wl in rr: rdn over 3f out: no prog* **14/1**

004- **13** 2 3/4 **Yes Meg**[205] 5268 3-8-12 54 .... TQuinn 6 29
(P F I Cole) *chsd ldr tl wknd rapidly over 2f out* **7/1**[3]

0445 **14** 10 **I Certainly May**[14] 940 3-9-1 57 .... IanMongan 1 16
(S Dow) *prom tl wknd u.p wl over 3f out* **20/1**

2m 38.23s (3.73) **Going Correction** +0.25s/f (Slow) **14** Ran SP% **127.5**
Speed ratings (Par 96): **97,96,94,93,90 89,88,87,86,86 84,83,81,74**
CSF £8.85 CT £53.54 TOTE £3.00: £1.70, £2.30, £1.90; EX 14.70.
Owner A F Merritt **Bred** Allan Merritt **Trained** East Everleigh, Wilts

FOCUS
A moderate handicap in which those with proven ability took on some darker types making their handicap debuts. A couple of those really caught the eye before the off, and it was little surprise to see one of them win with the third a preety good yardstick. The winning time was nothing special, however.
Cape Colony ◆ Official explanation: trainer's rep said, regarding the apparent improvement in form, that colt had benefited from the step up in trip.
Poppy Dean(IRE) Official explanation: jockey said filly suffered interference in running

1148 MIX BUSINESS WITH PLEASURE H'CAP 1m 3f (P)
9:20 (9:22) (Class 6) (0-60,60) 4-Y-0+ **£2,047** (£604; £302) **Stalls** High

Form RPR

624- **1** **Susie May**[168] 6271 4-9-2 58 .... GeorgeBaker 4 69+
(G L Moore) *hld up in last trio: prog over 2f out: rdn to cl over 1f out: led last 150yds: styd on wl* **7/2**[1]

3-22 **2** 1 3/4 **Wee Charlie Castle (IRE)**[19] 541 5-9-0 56 .... MartinDwyer 5 64
(G C H Chung) *trckd ldng trio: smooth prog to ld 2f out: rdn over 1f out: hdd and one pce last 150yds* **7/2**[1]

2625 **3** 1 1/2 **Megalala (IRE)**[19] 881 7-9-3 59 .... NeilChalmers 7 64
(J J Bridger) *trckd ldng pair: led over 2f out to 2f out: one pce fr over 1f out* **12/1**

2322 **4** shd **Trysting Grove (IRE)**[9] 999 7-8-11 53 .... SaleemGolam 6 58
(E G Bevan) *hld up in midfield: prog on inner and cl up 2f out: nt qckn over 1f out: kpt on* **4/1**[2]

060- **5** hd **Bowl Of Cherries**[19] 7115 5-8-10 52 ....(bt) NCallan 3 57
(I A Wood) *hld up in midfield: effrt over 2f out: sn drvn and nt qckn: styd on again ins fnl f* **10/1**

060- **6** 1 1/4 **Scutch Mill (IRE)**[32] 6883 6-9-1 60 ....(t) JerryO'Dwyer(3) 11 63
(P C Haslam) *stdd s: hld up in detached last: effrt 3f out: hrd rdn and nt qckn 2f out: kpt on* **16/1**

4331 **7** 2 **Granary Girl**[14] 934 6-8-8 50 .... JimmyQuinn 9 49
(J Pearce) *hld up in midfield: clsd on ldrs over 2f out: stl wl there over 1f out: wknd ins fnl f* **8/1**

506/ **8** 5 **Robbie Can Can**[508] 6435 9-8-4 49 .... KirstyMilczarek(3) 10 40
(A W Carroll) *stdd s: hld up in last pair: no prog fnl 2f* **14/1**

201/ **9** 4 1/2 **Irish Ballad**[548] 5736 6-8-11 53 ow1 ....(t) SebSanders 2 36
(S Dow) *t.k.h: mostly chsd ldr tl wknd over 2f out* **7/1**[3]

00-0 **10** 21 **Three Half Crowns (IRE)**[7] 1031 4-8-5 50 oh1 ow4(b[1])
KevinGhunowa(3) 1 —
(M S Saunders) *dwlt: keen and sn led: hdd & wknd rapidly over 2f out: t.o* **66/1**

00/6 **P** **Love Academy**[26] [821] 13-7-13 **46** oh1 NicolPolli(5) 8 —
(Luke Comer, Ire) *in tch tl broke down and p.u 5f out* **66/1**

2m 24.28s (2.38) **Going Correction** +0.25s/f (Slow) 11 Ran SP% **120.4**
Speed ratings (Par 101): **101,99,98,98,98 97,96,92,89,73** —
CSF £15.99 CT £133.96 TOTE £4.30: £1.80, £1.70, £3.50; EX 14.70 Place 6 £27.86, Place 5 £8.74.
Owner Mrs Charles Cyzer **Bred** Bottisham Heath Stud **Trained** Woodingdean, E Sussex

FOCUS
A low-grade event, with question marks against many for varying reasons, so it would be surprising if too many winners emerged from the race although the race looks sound enough rated around the placed horses.
T/Plt: £45.70 to a £1 stake. Pool: £80,133.95. 1,277.45 winning tickets. T/Qpdt: £14.60 to a £1 stake. Pool: £6,788.90. 343.60 winning tickets. JN

1109 LINGFIELD (L-H)
Wednesday, April 2

OFFICIAL GOING: Standard
Wind: medium across Weather: overcast

1149 SCOTS GROUP QUAICH MAIDEN STKS — 7f (P)
2:30 (2:32) (Class 5) 3-Y-0 **£2,331** (£693; £346; £173) **Stalls** Low

Form — RPR

50- **1** **Bombardier Wells**[174] [6125] 3-9-3 0 StephenCarson 6 74+
(Eve Johnson Houghton) *chsd ldrs: rdn to ld ins fnl f: fnd ex last 50yds* **11/1**

2 *nk* **Maghya (IRE)** 3-8-12 0 RHills 11 68+
(W J Haggas) *stdd and dropped in after s: hdwy jst over 2f out: rdn and str run 1f out: sn chsng wnr: hld last 50yds* **6/1**[2]

-2 **3** *1 ½* **Christophers Quest**[14] [936] 3-9-3 0 RobertHavlin 3 69
(R Simpson) *t.k.h: hld up in bhd ldrs: swtchd rt and hdwy over 1f out: kpt on* **9/1**[3]

242- **4** *2* **Andaman Sunset**[158] [6493] 3-9-3 83 SebSanders 5 64
(G Wragg) *towards rr: rdn over 4f out: styd on over 1f out: nvr pce to chal ldrs* **4/7**[1]

0-0 **5** *1 ¼* **Pasta Prayer**[6] [1036] 3-9-3 0 StephenDonohoe 4 60
(S A Callaghan) *led: rdn over 2f out: hdd ins fnl f: wknd last 100yds* **66/1**

60- **6** *2 ¾* **Dynamo Dave (USA)**[95] [7266] 3-9-3 0 PaulEddery 2 53
(B J Meehan) *w ldr: ev ch and rdn jst over 2f out: wknd 1f out: eased last 100yds* **12/1**

0-44 **7** *¾* **Evenstorm (USA)**[53] [498] 3-8-12 58 NCallan 9 46
(B Gubby) *racd in midfield: rdn 3f out: keeping on same pce whn hmpd over 1f out: no imp after* **16/1**

8 *3 ¾* **Cape Tycoon (IRE)** 3-9-3 0 VinceSlattery 1 41
(S A Callaghan) *s.i.s: a bhd* **33/1**

00- **9** *hd* **Sarah's Boy**[166] [6294] 3-9-3 0 IanMongan 10 40
(S Dow) *stdd and dropped in after s: a bhd* **40/1**

10 *4* **Borrowdale** 3-9-0 0 JerryO'Dwyer(3) 7 30
(J A Osborne) *wnt lft s: racd wd: towards rr: rdn over 3f out: hung rt and rn wd bnd over 2f out: wl bhd after* **20/1**

1m 25.58s (0.78) **Going Correction** +0.05s/f (Slow) 10 Ran SP% **121.5**
Speed ratings (Par 98): **97,96,94,92,91 88,87,82,82,78**
CSF £76.08 TOTE £17.10: £3.50, £2.50, £2.30; EX 127.90 TRIFECTA Not won..
Owner G C Stevens **Bred** Brick Kiln Stud & Miss E Wright **Trained** Blewbury, Oxon
■ Stewards' Enquiry : Robert Havlin one-day ban: careless riding (Apr 16)

FOCUS
A fair-looking maiden but dominated by unexposed sorts, the form is not sure to prove reliable.
Borrowdale Official explanation: jockey said gelding hung right

1150 TAGWORLDWIDE.COM (S) STKS — 6f (P)
3:00 (3:01) (Class 6) 3-Y-0+ **£1,774** (£523; £262) **Stalls** Low

Form — RPR

6560 **1** **Majestical (IRE)**[46] [584] 6-9-5 50 (p) WilliamBuick(3) 2 63
(V Smith) *mounted on crse: hld up in tch: hdwy 2f out: rdn to chse ldr 1f out: led ins fnl f: sn in command* **14/1**

-262 **2** *1 ¼* **Punching**[6] [1035] 4-9-13 57 GeorgeBaker 5 64
(Miss Gay Kelleway) *trckd ldrs: rdn to ld over 1f out: hdd and nt pce of wnr ins fnl f* **9/4**[1]

14-0 **3** *½* **Scarlett Heart (IRE)**[27] [806] 4-9-5 55 KirstyMilczarek(3) 4 58
(S Curran) *bhd: hdwy 2f out: swtchd rt ins fnl f: r.o wl to go 3rd towards fin: nvr able to chal* **7/2**[3]

-014 **4** *hd* **Marko Jadeo (IRE)**[5] [1061] 10-9-10 65 KevinGhunowa(3) 1 62
(R A Harris) *hld up in tch: hdwy to chse ldrs over 1f out: kpt on same pce u.p fnl f* **7/1**

4460 **5** *2 ¼* **Lawdy Miss Clawdy**[19] [884] 4-9-3 43 JamesDoyle 8 45
(D W P Arbuthnot) *t.k.h: trckd ldrs: lost pl and nt clr run wl over 1f out: no imp fnl f* **40/1**

-350 **6** *½* **Compulsion**[14] [937] 5-9-3 52 PaulEddery 9 43
(Pat Eddery) *awkward leaving stalls and slowly away: bhd: rdn and hdwy on inner wl over 1f out: wknd last 100yds* **10/1**

0205 **7** *¾* **Calloff The Search**[14] [933] 4-9-13 50 (p) MickyFenton 7 51
(Stef Liddiard) *led tl rdn and hdd over 1f out: chsd ldr after tl wknd 1f out* **25/1**

-423 **8** *1 ½* **Night Prospector**[6] [1035] 8-9-8 63 (p) SebSanders 6 41
(R A Harris) *t.k.h: chsd ldr: rdn and ev ch 2f out: wknd jst over 1f out* **11/4**[2]

1m 11.71s (-0.19) **Going Correction** +0.05s/f (Slow) 8 Ran SP% **114.2**
Speed ratings (Par 101): **103,101,100,100,97 96,95,93**
CSF £45.73 TOTE £17.00: £4.40, £1.10, £1.90; EX 61.00 Trifecta £462.80 Part won. Pool £651.95 - 0.79 winning units..There was no bid for the winner.
Owner V Smith **Bred** Sean Beston **Trained** Exning, Suffolk

FOCUS
A fairly competitive seller judged on official ratings with the winner rated to his winter best.

1151 PREMIER SHOWFREIGHT H'CAP — 1m 4f (P)
3:30 (3:31) (Class 5) (0-75,75) 4-Y-0+ **£2,590** (£770; £385; £192) **Stalls** Low

Form — RPR

262- **1** **Apache Fort**[18] [6902] 5-8-12 68 NCallan 6 74
(T Keddy) *in tch: hdwy and rdn over 2f out: ev ch wl over 1f out: led ins fnl f: hld on gamely* **6/1**[3]

-122 **2** *nk* **War Of The Roses (IRE)**[42] [630] 5-9-5 75 J-PGuillambert 3 81
(R Brotherton) *hld up in tch: hdwy to trck ldrs wl over 1f out: r.o u.p to chal ins fnl f: no ex nr fin* **15/8**[1]

453 **3** *½* **Bassinet (USA)**[14] [941] 4-8-8 68 KirstyMilczarek(3) 9 73
(J A R Toller) *t.k.h: hld up bhd: hdwy over 2f out: rdn over 1f out: r.o to go 3rd wl ins fnl f: no imp last 50yds* **8/1**

306- **4** *1* **Ross Moor**[170] [6241] 6-8-10 66 TQuinn 8 70
(Mike Murphy) *chsd ldr 8f out: led gng wl over 2f out: rdn wl over 1f out: hdd ins fnl f: fdd nr fin* **11/1**

-253 **5** *½* **Wait For The Will (USA)**[19] [886] 12-8-11 67 (b) AdamKirby 7 70
(G L Moore) *hld up in tch: rdn and effrt wl over 1f out: kpt on fnl f but nvr pce to chal* **10/1**

-455 **6** *1* **Savannah**[19] [880] 5-8-10 69 JerryO'Dwyer(3) 4 70
(Luke Comer, Ire) *chsd ldr for 4f: styd handy tl shuffled bk and lost pl jst over 2f out: swtchd rt and rdn over 1f out: plugged on but nvr pce to chal* **16/1**

056- **7** *4 ½* **Kings Story (IRE)**[64] [4687] 4-8-9 66 MickyFenton 1 60
(Mrs S Leech) *led: rdn 5f out: hdd over 2f out: wknd 2f out* **33/1**

4251 **8** *12* **My Mentor (IRE)**[22] [847] 4-9-0 71 SebSanders 5 46
(Sir Mark Prescott) *hld up towards rr: hdwy 7f out: reminders over 4f out: rdn and wknd over 2f out: sn wl bhd* **10/3**[2]

2m 34.71s (1.71) **Going Correction** +0.05s/f (Slow)
WFA 4 from 5yo+ 1lb 8 Ran SP% **109.5**
Speed ratings (Par 103): **96,95,95,94,94 93,90,82**
CSF £16.19 CT £77.12 TOTE £6.80: £1.70, £1.10, £2.90; EX 16.60 Trifecta £94.40 Pool £661.46 - 4.97 winning units..
Owner Andrew Duffield **Bred** Juddmonte Farms Ltd **Trained** Newmarket, Suffolk
■ Nothingtodeclaire was withdrawn after refusing to enter the stalls (12/1, deduct 5p in the £ under rule 4).

FOCUS
A modest handicap run at a moderate gallop and producing a close finish. The form makes enough sense to think the race is sound.

1152 ASHFORD ENVIRONMENTAL H'CAP — 1m 2f (P)
4:00 (4:00) (Class 6) (0-60,60) 4-Y-0+ **£2,047** (£604; £302) **Stalls** Low

Form — RPR

5325 **1** **Siena Star (IRE)**[35] [716] 10-8-13 55 MickyFenton 7 64
(Stef Liddiard) *in tch: chsd ldr over 7f out: upsides ldr over 5f out: led over 2f out: rdn wl over 1f out: hld on gamely u.p fnl f* **9/2**

00-3 **2** *hd* **Kings Topic (USA)**[6] [1039] 8-9-2 58 SebSanders 5 67
(A B Haynes) *in tch in rr on outer: hdwy and rdn wl over 2f out: ev ch jst ins fnl f: unable qckn last 100yds* **4/1**[3]

6633 **3** *2 ½* **Play Up Pompey**[5] [1056] 6-8-9 51 HayleyTurner 4 55
(J J Bridger) *t.k.h: hld up in tch: rdn over 4f out: hdwy to chse ldrs 2f out: wnt 3rd ins fnl f: no imp on ldrs after* **11/4**[2]

2222 **4** *3 ¾* **Dawson Creek (IRE)**[14] [938] 4-9-4 60 NCallan 6 57
(B Gubby) *led: hdd and rdn over 2f out: wknd wl over 1f out* **2/1**[1]

3436 **5** *2 ½* **Bramcote Lorne**[18] [822] 5-8-9 51 (p) DarryllHolland 3 43
(R C Guest) *chsd ldr tl over 7f out: styd chsng ldrs tl rdn and wknd over 2f out* **12/1**

00-0 **6** *7* **Love Angel (USA)**[14] [934] 6-7-11 46 oh1 DavidProbert(7) 1 24
(J J Bridger) *sn rdn: hdwy and in tch 6f out: rdn and droped out over 3f out: sn wl bhd* **25/1**

2m 5.46s (-1.14) **Going Correction** +0.05s/f (Slow) 6 Ran SP% **109.7**
Speed ratings (Par 101): **106,105,103,100,98 93**
CSF £21.41 TOTE £5.20: £2.70, £2.40; EX 13.50.
Owner ownaracehorse.co.uk (Shefford) **Bred** Mrs T Brudenell **Trained** Great Shefford, Berks

FOCUS
A modest handicap though the early pace was stronger than many races over this trip, but despite that a couple of these were inclined to race keenly. The winner is rated slightly above recent efforts with the runner-up to his best. The runners gave the inside rail a wide berth once into the straight and came down the centre.

1153 NICHOLAS HALL H'CAP — 7f (P)
4:30 (4:31) (Class 5) (0-70,70) 4-Y-0+ **£2,331** (£693; £346; £173) **Stalls** Low

Form — RPR

3142 **1** **Dvinsky (USA)**[18] [901] 7-9-4 70 (b) DarryllHolland 1 81
(P Howling) *mde all: sn clr: rdn over 1f out: eased nr fin: unchal* **4/1**[2]

022- **2** *2* **Prince Of Delphi**[174] [6122] 5-9-3 69 SebSanders 4 75
(R M Beckett) *t.k.h: chsd ldrs: rdn to chse wnr wl over 1f out: kpt on but no imp* **11/8**[1]

20-0 **3** *1* **Quantum Leap**[6] [1038] 11-8-11 63 (v) TQuinn 5 66
(S Dow) *bhd: hdwy jst over 2f out: styd on fnl f: nvr nr wnr* **14/1**

20-2 **4** *nk* **Anthill**[18] [899] 4-8-11 63 NCallan 3 65
(I A Wood) *t.k.h: chsd wnr: rdn over 2f out: kpt on same pce u.p* **11/2**

1666 **5** *1 ¾* **Fine Ruler (IRE)**[6] [1038] 4-9-2 68 GeorgeBaker 6 65
(M R Bosley) *t.k.h: dropped in after s: hld up bhd: hdwy into midfield 4f out: rdn and no hdwy wl over 1f out* **16/1**

4405 **6** *¾* **Cool Sands (IRE)**[11] [964] 6-8-11 63 (v) AdamKirby 8 58
(D Shaw) *t.k.h: hld up in tch in rr: rdn wl over 2f out: nvr nr to chal* **12/1**

3204 **7** *2 ¾* **Gimme Some Lovin (IRE)**[18] [899] 4-8-7 62 (p) WilliamBuick(3) 7 50
(D W P Arbuthnot) *in tch in midfield: rdn over 3f out: bhd last 2f* **5/1**[3]

1m 24.29s (-0.51) **Going Correction** +0.05s/f (Slow) 7 Ran SP% **114.4**
Speed ratings (Par 103): **104,101,100,100,98 97,94**
CSF £9.94 CT £67.18 TOTE £5.50: £2.50, £1.10; EX 11.70 Trifecta £98.70 Pool £567.29 - 4.08 winning units..
Owner Richard Berenson **Bred** Eclipse Bloodstock & Tipperary Bloodstock **Trained** Newmarket, Suffolk

FOCUS
An ordinary handicap, but the winner set a decent pace and the winning time was 1.29 seconds faster than the opening maiden. The winner is rated to last year's turf best with the runner-up to form.
Cool Sands(IRE) Official explanation: jockey said gelding ran too free

1154 OYSTER PARTNERSHIP H'CAP — 7f (P)
5:00 (5:00) (Class 6) (0-65,65) 4-Y-0+ **£2,047** (£604; £302) **Stalls** Low

Form — RPR

220- **1** **Hazytoo**[177] [6062] 4-9-4 65 StephenDonohoe 1 73
(S A Callaghan) *t.k.h: trckd ldr: chal over 1f out: hld hd high and drvn to ld jst ins fnl f: drvn out* **7/4**[1]

1243 **2** *½* **Over To You Bert**[33] [749] 9-8-7 59 ow2 HaddenFrost(5) 2 66
(R J Hodges) *led: jnd and rdn over 1f out: hdd jst ins fnl f: kpt on same pce* **6/1**[3]

0434 **3** *1* **Imperium**[19] [879] 7-8-11 58 (p) StephenCarson 3 62
(Jean-Rene Auvray) *dwlt: t.k.h: sn chsng ldrs: rdn wl over 1f out: kpt on same pce* **12/1**

-502 **4** *1 ¼* **Metropolitan Chief**[14] [937] 4-8-9 56 TQuinn 4 57
(P Burgoyne) *plld hrd: chsd ldrs: rdn and nt qckn over 1f out: kpt on same pce* **8/1**

0603 **5** ½ **Mind Alert**[11] 964 7-8-13 **60**....(v) JamesDoyle 6 60+
(D Shaw) *hld up in midfield on inner: rdn and effrt wl over 1f out: nvr pce to chal* **12/1**

0-55 **6** 1½ **Game Lady**[14] 939 4-9-2 **63**.... RichardThomas 5 59
(I A Wood) *t.k.h: hld up towards rr: rdn over 2f out: nvr nr to chal* **25/1**

5461 **7** ¾ **Napoletano (GER)**[14] 937 7-8-11 **58** ow1....(p) SebSanders 8 52
(S Dow) *dropped in after s: plld hrd: hld up in rr: hdwy on outer over 2f out: no hdwy fr wl over 1f out* **6/1**[3]

0533 **8** nk **Zazous**[6] 1038 7-8-9 **56** ow1.... NCallan 9 49
(J J Bridger) *t.k.h: hld up in tch: hdwy 4f out: rdn and outpcd jst over 2f out: n.d after* **9/2**[2]

2154 **9** 2¼ **Stargazy**[40] 663 4-7-11 **51** oh3.... MCGeran(7) 7 38
(W G M Turner) *t.k.h: hld up in last: rdn and outpcd 2f out: no ch after* **20/1**

1m 25.84s (1.04) **Going Correction** +0.05s/f (Slow) **9** Ran SP% **118.2**
Speed ratings (Par 101): **96,95,94,92,92 90,89,89,86**
CSF £12.91 CT £97.56 TOTE £2.50: £1.20, £2.60, £3.10; EX 20.40 Trifecta £322.20 Pool £862.49 - 1.90 winning units. Place 6 £61.83, Place 5 £14.27.
Owner T Mohan,M Walsh & Allan McNamee **Bred** Mrs Liza Judd **Trained** Newmarket, Suffolk

FOCUS
This race was spoiled rather by a pedestrian early pace and several threw their chances away by pulling. As a result, those that raced prominently were at a big advantage and the first two home were at the sharp end thoughout. The winning time was 1.55 seconds slower than the preceding handicap over the same trip and 0.26 seconds slower than the opening three-year-old maiden. The form is rated around the winner and third.
T/Plt: £133.10 to a £1 stake. Pool: £64,617.45. 354.25 winning tickets. T/Qpdt: £22.50 to a £1 stake. Pool: £5,302.50. 174.10 winning tickets. SP

NOTTINGHAM (L-H)
Wednesday, April 2

OFFICIAL GOING: Soft (good to soft in places; 6.2)
Wind: Light across Weather: Overcast

1155 WEATHERBYS BLOODSTOCK SERVICES H'CAP 5f 13y
2:10 (2:10) (Class 5) (0-70,70) 3-Y-O **£2,590** (£770; £385; £192) **Stalls** High

Form RPR

214- **1** **Mission Impossible**[103] 7210 3-9-4 **70**.... LeeEnstone 13 81+
(P C Haslam) *hld up: hdwy over 1f out: r.o to ld last strides* **8/1**

0-34 **2** nk **Monsieur Reynard**[11] 975 3-9-2 **68**.... RyanMoore 7 76
(B J Meehan) *hld up: hdwy to ld over 1f out: hdd last strides* **4/1**[1]

134 **3** 2¾ **The Little Fizzer (IRE)**[61] 397 3-8-11 **63**.... FergusSweeney 9 61
(K R Burke) *s.i.s: hld up: r.o ins fnl f: nt trble ldrs* **9/1**

300- **4** nk **Select Committee**[229] 4560 3-9-0 **66**.... GrahamGibbons 11 63
(J J Quinn) *hung lft thrght: chsd ldrs: rdn over 1f out: styd on same pce ins fnl f* **5/1**[2]

155- **5** ¾ **Speedy Senorita (IRE)**[145] 6741 3-8-13 **65**.... AndrewElliott 6 59
(K R Burke) *w ldr: rdn and ev ch over 1f out: no ex ins fnl f* **16/1**

500- **6** ½ **Rio Sands**[165] 6326 3-9-0 **66**.... DeanMcKeown 1 58+
(R M Whitaker) *chsd ldrs: rdn 1/2-way: ev ch over 1f out: no ex ins fnl f* **20/1**

0-41 **7** 1½ **Thomas Malory (IRE)**[19] 876 3-8-8 **65** ow2.... SCreighton(5) 4 52
(Miss V Haigh) *sn pushed along in rr: hdwy over 1f out: wknd ins fnl f* **14/1**

556- **8** shd **Dalarossie**[242] 4175 3-8-12 **64**.... JimmyQuinn 12 51
(E J Alston) *led: rdn and hdd over 1f out: wknd ins fnl f* **7/1**

134- **9** ¾ **Leading Edge (IRE)**[133] 6892 3-9-3 **69**.... ChrisCatlin 5 53
(M R Channon) *s.i.s: sn mid-div: rdn 1/2-way: wknd over 1f out* **10/1**

010- **10** 1 **Handsinthemist (IRE)**[165] 6326 3-8-4 **56** oh1....(p) FrankieMcDonald 2 36
(P T Midgley) *chsd ldrs: rdn over 1f out: wknd fnl f* **50/1**

000- **11** ½ **Sandy Par**[175] 6098 3-8-13 **65**.... PaulFitzsimons 10 44
(J M Bradley) *plld hrd and prom: rdn over 1f out: sn wknd* **33/1**

3232 **12** 2¼ **Diademas (USA)**[13] 952 3-8-12 **64**....(v) SimonWhitworth 8 33
(V Smith) *chsd ldrs over 3f* **6/1**[3]

63.83 secs (3.13) **Going Correction** +0.65s/f (Yiel) **12** Ran SP% **115.9**
Speed ratings (Par 98): **100,99,95,94,93 92,90,90,88,87 86,82**
CSF £38.29 CT £301.98 TOTE £9.40: £3.20, £1.10, £3.00; EX 46.80.
Owner Vyas Ltd & M T Buckley **Bred** Rodney Meredith **Trained** Middleham Moor, N Yorks
■ Stewards' Enquiry : Graham Gibbons caution: careless riding.

FOCUS
A competitive sprint-handicap that went to the highest-drawn runner. the front pair were clear but neither has a totally convincing profile.
The Little Fizzer(IRE) Official explanation: jockey said filly was denied a clear run

1156 EUROPEAN BREEDERS' FUND NOVICE STKS 5f 13y
2:40 (2:41) (Class 4) 2-Y-O **£4,695** (£1,397; £698; £348) **Stalls** High

Form RPR

1 **1** **She's A Shaw Thing**[9] 995 2-9-0 0.... TGMcLaughlin 4 87
(P D Evans) *mde all: clr 1/2-way: rdn and hung lft over 1f out: edgd rt wl ins fnl f: eased nr fin* **13/8**[2]

1 **2** 6 **Sally's Dilemma**[11] 957 2-8-7 0.... JackDean(7) 1 65
(W G M Turner) *wnt lft s: chsd wnr: rdn 3f out: sn outpcd* **4/5**[1]

3 12 **Lady Kingston** 2-8-7 0.... AndrewElliott 2 15
(K R Burke) *sn outpcd* **16/1**

4 7 **Mr Clearview** 2-8-12 0.... AlanMunro 3 —
(B R Millman) *s.i.s: sn outpcd* **10/1**[3]

64.56 secs (3.86) **Going Correction** +0.65s/f (Yiel) **4** Ran SP% **108.6**
Speed ratings (Par 94): **95,85,66,55**
CSF £3.31 TOTE £3.10; EX 3.40.
Owner R Cave **Bred** M Pennell **Trained** Pandy, Monmouths

FOCUS
This looked a straight match on paper between the two previous winners Sally's Dilemma and She's A Shaw Thing, and it was the latter who romped away with it. The winner is rated an improver with the runner-up well below her Brocklesby form.

NOTEBOOK
She's A Shaw Thing, a quite impressive winner on her debut at Warwick (runner-up scored next time) is clearly all about speed and it was hard not to be taken with the manner of her victory over Brocklesby winner Sally's Dilemma. Soon in front, she had them all struggling after about a furlong and a half and gradually drew clear before being eased close home. Her stable had a similarly speedy type in Vhujon quite early last term and, although she is not that big, she would seem a likely winner of Chester's Lily Agnes Stakes next month, her next intended target. (op 6-5 tchd 7-4)
Sally's Dilemma, whose Brocklesby win had already received a form boost, looked the one to beat with her rider claiming a valuable 7lb, but she was soon on the back foot as the winner went about her business. She slowly fell further and further behind and, although doing her best to close the gap inside the final furlong, she could never get anywhere near. There was a huge gap back to the remainder and it is likely she bumped into a smart sort for the time of year, so deserves another chance back on better ground. (op 11-10)
Lady Kingston, a 10,000gns daughter of Kyllachy, was always likely to struggle against the two previous winners and was quickly in trouble. She readily beat the other debutant and it is likely she will require 6f in time. (op 14-1 tchd 20-1)
Mr Clearview, a son of Makbul whose dam was very speedy, comes from a yard that can ready one to win first time up, but he was always going to struggle and did not show much. He can be given another chance. (op 17-2)

1157 WEATHERBYS BLOODSTOCK INSURANCE CONDITIONS STKS 5f 13y
3:10 (3:10) (Class 3) 3-Y-O+ **£6,799** (£2,023; £1,011; £505) **Stalls** High

Form RPR

00-2 **1** **Sonny Red (IRE)**[11] 959 4-9-1 108.... RichardHughes 7 109
(R Hannon) *trckd ldrs: rdn to ld 1f out: r.o* **4/5**[1]

20-0 **2** hd **Hoh Hoh Hoh**[11] 959 6-9-1 102.... TPQueally 2 108
(R J Price) *s.i.s: racd keenly: hdwy over 3f out: rdn and ev ch ins fnl f: r.o* **20/1**

213- **3** 2 **Angus Newz**[166] 6300 5-8-10 89....(v) ChrisCatlin 3 96
(M Quinn) *chsd ldrs: rdn over 1f out: styd on same pce ins fnl f* **12/1**[3]

50-0 **4** 1½ **Strike Up The Band**[11] 959 5-9-1 97.... SilvestreDeSousa 4 95
(D Nicholls) *chsd ldr tl led over 3f out: hdd 1/2-way: led wl over 1f out: rdn and hdd 1f out: no ex* **16/1**

560- **5** 2 **Reverence**[223] 4746 7-9-1 109.... JimmyQuinn 1 88
(E J Alston) *trckd ldrs: led 1/2-way: hdd wl over 1f out: wknd ins fnl f* **15/8**[2]

620- **6** 1 **Prigsnov Dancer (IRE)**[144] 6756 3-8-4 74....(p) AndrewElliott 6 85?
(J O'Reilly) *sn outpcd* **100/1**

15-2 **7** 3¼ **El Potro**[9] 994 6-9-1 60.... GrahamGibbons 5 73?
(J R Holt) *led: hdd over 3f out: outpcd fr 1/2-way* **80/1**

63.05 secs (2.35) **Going Correction** +0.65s/f (Yiel)
WFA 3 from 4yo+ 11lb **7** Ran SP% **110.9**
Speed ratings (Par 107): **107,106,103,101,97 96,91**
CSF £18.75 TOTE £2.00: £2.00, £3.80; EX 13.40.
Owner Michael Pescod & J A Leek **Bred** Denis Bergin **Trained** East Everleigh, Wilts

FOCUS
These small-field conditions races can often produce the odd shock result and Hoh Hoh Hoh very nearly pulled it off, but Sonny Red's extra stamina got him out of trouble. The form may not be entirely trustworthy with the sixth not beaten far.

NOTEBOOK
Sonny Red(IRE), narrowly denied in the 6f Listed Cammidge Trophy at Doncaster on his seasonal debut, is just as effective at this shorter distance and it was that extra stamina that dug him out of trouble. He rallied gamely under pressure to deny the speedy Hoh Hoh Hoh and now has Newmarket's Abernant Stakes on his agenda. His rider thinks he will improve again for this run. (op 5-6 tchd Evens)
Hoh Hoh Hoh, tailed off behind Sonny Red at Doncaster, showed that running to be all wrong and bounced right back to his best, looking the likely winner inside the final furlong only to be denied. This soft ground is not to his liking and he remains capable of further progress back on a fast surface. (op 14-1)
Angus Newz, placed in a Listed contest at Newmarket last backend, had it on at the weights, but often runs above herself in these races and she stuck on best of the rest for third. (tchd 10-1 and 14-1)
Strike Up The Band, another who finished well down the field in the Cammidge, had clearly benefited from that run but he still shaped as though the outing was needed. (op 22-1 tchd 14-1)
Reverence, the class act of the field, being a dual Group 1 winner two seasons back, won this contest in 2006, but he was always likely to need the run here having been off since August. He showed plenty of speed towards the outer and edged ahead at past halfway, but that lack of a run soon started to tell and he faded out of it. This was a satisfactory return and he should be a lot sharper next time, but will probably struggle to recapture his best form, having had an interrupted campaign last season. (op 7-4 tchd 13-8)

1158 WEATHERBYS BANK "FURTHER FLIGHT" STKS (LISTED RACE) 1m 6f 15y
3:40 (3:40) (Class 1) 4-Y-O+
£14,760 (£5,595; £2,800; £1,396; £699; £351) **Stalls** Low

Form RPR

145- **1** **Gull Wing (IRE)**[144] 6757 4-8-6 92.... RichardMullen 3 104
(M L W Bell) *hld up: hdwy over 3f out: chal over 1f out: styd on to ld towards fin* **6/1**

216/ **2** nse **Shipmaster**[53] 2804 5-9-0 0.... RichardHughes 6 109
(A King) *sn chsng ldr: reminders 6f out: led over 3f out: hdd over 2f out: rallied to ld over 1f out: hdd towards fin* **9/1**

210- **3** 4½ **Spanish Hidalgo (IRE)**[136] 6863 4-9-0 106.... JimmyFortune 5 106+
(J L Dunlop) *chsd ldrs: led over 2f out: rdn and hdd over 1f out: edgd rt and wknd ins fnl f* **2/1**[1]

210/ **4** ¾ **Frank Sonata**[528] 6119 7-9-0 0.... TPQueally 7 102
(M G Quinlan) *sn led: hdd over 3f out: rdn whn n.m.r over 2f out: edgd rt and wknd over 1f out* **11/4**[2]

402- **5** 2 **Bogside Theatre (IRE)**[186] 5808 4-8-6 86.... AndrewElliott 2 94
(G M Moore) *prom: rdn over 2f out: wknd over 1f out* **33/1**

406- **6** 5 **Hawridge Prince**[165] 6337 8-9-0 97.... JimCrowley 4 92
(B R Millman) *s.i.s: hld up in tch: rdn over 3f out: wknd over 2f out* **20/1**

433- **7** 9 **Veenwouden**[165] 6337 4-8-8 106 ow2.... RyanMoore 8 76
(E F Vaughan) *hld up: rdn over 4f out: wknd over 2f out: eased over 1f out* **9/2**[3]

3m 12.65s (5.35) **Going Correction** +0.55s/f (Yiel)
WFA 4 from 5yo+ 3lb **7** Ran SP% **110.2**
Speed ratings (Par 111): **106,105,103,102,101 98,93**
CSF £52.47 TOTE £8.10: £2.50, £2.90; EX 36.00.
Owner Lady Bamford **Bred** Lady Bamford **Trained** Newmarket, Suffolk
■ Stewards' Enquiry : Richard Hughes one-day ban (reduced from three days on appeal): used whip with excessive frequency in incorrect place (Apr 16)

FOCUS
This looked an average race for the grade and the winning time was slow. The form is rated around the winner and fifth to their form.

NOTEBOOK
Gull Wing(IRE), a progressive handicapper at three, had always looked worth a try at this sort of distance and she relished every yard of it, sticking on gamely against the rail despite having the much larger Shipmaster leaning in towards her. This soft ground posed no problem for the daughter of In The Wings and connections are now eyeing a crack at Ascot's Sagaro Stakes. (op 7-1)

Shipmaster, largely disappointing in three starts over hurdles this winter, had last been seen on the Flat when beaten four lengths in the 2006 Queen's Vase, so had the class to get involved if on his game. He was ridden positively and took it up early in the straight but, despite willingly battling on under pressure, he could not repel the equally determined winner. Clear of the third, he looks an interesting prospect for the season ahead as this was only the seventh Flat start of his career. It would come as no surprise to see him win in this grade at some point, and he may reoppose the winner at Ascot. (op 10-1 tchd 8-1)

Spanish Hidalgo(IRE), a progressive type last season who won a Listed prize at San Siro, comes from a yard that has made a quiet start to the season and he very much ran as though this outing was needed. He came with a strong-looking challenge to lead over two out, but could find no extra inside the final furlong and should strip a lot fitter next time. (op 7-2 tchd 4-1)

Frank Sonata, winner of this two seasons back, missed the whole of 2007 with a problem, but was quite solid in the market and was clearly expected to put up a bold show on this return. However, having led early, he started to look vulnerable from the turn in and ended up getting tired. He is not going to be easy to place this season, although should at least come on for the run. (op 5-2 tchd 9-4)

Bogside Theatre(IRE), second off a mark of 85 over this distance towards the end of last season, had plenty on at the weights here and ran about as well as could have been expected. (op 25-1)

Hawridge Prince remains unable to recapture his best form from a couple of seasons back. (op 16-1)

Veenwouden, racing from 2lb out of the weights, was a progressive type towards the end of last season and looked a player if straight for this reappearance. She was very weak in the market though and never picked up in the straight, producing a rather laboured effort. This was obviously not her form, but she has it to prove now. Official explanation: jockey said filly failed to pick up (op 5-2)

1159 WEATHERBYS PRINTING H'CAP — 1m 1f 213y

4:10 (4:11) (Class 5) (0-70,75) 4-Y-O+ — **£2,590** (£770; £385; £192) **Stalls** Low

Form	Pos	Dist	Horse / details	Jockey	RPR
-060	**1**		**Street Life (IRE)**[27] 811 10-8-4 **56** oh2 (W J Musson) *hld up: hdwy u.p over 1f out: r.o to ld towards fin* **7/1**	ChrisCatlin 12	67
4-24	**2**	*hd*	**Ryan's Future (IRE)**[9] 999 8-8-4 **56** (J S Moore) *hld up: hdwy u.p over 1f out: ev ch wl ins fnl f: r.o* **11/2**	JimmyQuinn 2	67
414-	**3**	*¾*	**Nutkin**[189] 5738 4-9-3 **69** (J R Fanshawe) *chsd ldrs: rdn and hung lft over 3f out: led over 1f out: edgd rt ins fnl f: hdd towards fin* **3/1**[1]	RyanMoore 14	79+
442-	**4**	*2 ¾*	**Trouble Mountain (USA)**[147] 6727 11-9-0 **66** (M W Easterby) *hld up in tch: rdn over 3f out: styd on same pce ins fnl f* **25/1**	(t) DaleGibson 15	70
1111	**5**	*¾*	**Rebellious Spirit**[9] 996 5-9-9 **75** 6ex (S Curran) *chsd ldr: led over 2f out: rdn and hdd over 1f out: wknd towards fin* **5/1**[3]	PaulDoe 16	78
416/	**6**	*1*	**Wednesdays Boy (IRE)**[576] 5064 5-8-5 **57** (P D Niven) *chsd ldrs: rdn over 2f out: wknd ins fnl f* **50/1**	AdrianMcCarthy 5	58
3311	**7**	*2*	**Red Wine**[8] 1020 9-9-4 **70** (A J McCabe) *hld up in tch: rdn over 1f out: wknd fnl f* **9/2**[2]	NeilPollard 1	67
0-34	**8**	*¾*	**Sforzando**[65] 340 7-8-10 **69** (Mrs L Stubbs) *mid-div: effrt over 3f out: edgd rt fnl f: nt trble ldrs* **33/1**	KristinStubbs(7) 9	64
3-00	**9**	*1*	**Prince Rossi (IRE)**[41] 640 4-7-13 **56** oh6 (A E Price) *sn led: hdd over 2f out: wknd over 1f out* **66/1**	(p) NataliaGemelova(5) 10	49
52-0	**10**	*½*	**David's Cavalier**[9] 999 4-8-5 **57** (R Hollinshead) *prom over 7f* **28/1**	AndrewElliott 11	49
23-0	**11**	*¾*	**John Dillon (IRE)**[4] 963 4-9-1 **67** (P C Haslam) *hld up: rdn over 4f out: n.d* **16/1**	LeeEnstone 13	58
000-	**12**	*2 ¾*	**Joshua's Gold (IRE)**[114] 6423 7-9-2 **68** (D Carroll) *hld up: rdn over 4f out: n.d* **50/1**	DanielTudhope 3	53
	13	*1 ¾*	**Bogside Dancer**[273] 3225 6-8-9 **68** (John A Harris) *s.i.s: hld up: rdn 1/2-way: sn bhd* **100/1**	MarkCoumbe(7) 8	50
200-	**14**	*2*	**Holiday Cocktail**[137] 6380 6-8-8 **60** (J J Quinn) *s.s: hld up: a in rr* **25/1**	GrahamGibbons 6	38
612-	**15**	*22*	**Gala Sunday (USA)**[154] 6598 8-8-9 **61** (M W Easterby) *hld up: a in rr: bhd fnl 3f* **28/1**	(bt) TonyHamilton 4	—

2m 16.06s (5.36) **Going Correction** +0.55s/f (Yiel) — **15** Ran SP% **117.5**

Speed ratings (Par 103): **100,99,99,97,96 95,94,93,92,92 91,89,88,86,68**

CSF £39.94 CT £141.72 TOTE £9.40: £2.90, £1.90, £1.60; EX 44.00.

Owner W J Musson **Bred** Derek Veitch **Trained** Newmarket, Suffolk

FOCUS

A moderate handicap, run at a fair pace. The first three came clear and the form looks sound for the class.

1160 WEATHERBYS FINANCE H'CAP — 1m 54y

4:40 (4:41) (Class 6) (0-65,65) 4-Y-O+ — **£1,942** (£578; £288; £144) **Stalls** Centre

Form	Pos	Dist	Horse / details	Jockey	RPR
-552	**1**		**Carlitos Spirit (IRE)**[34] 730 4-9-4 **65** (B R Millman) *hld up: hdwy 2f out: rdn to ld 1f out: edgd rt: r.o* **7/1**[3]	AlanMunro 4	78
250/	**2**	*1*	**Prince Egor (IRE)**[662] 2441 5-8-12 **62** (M Dods) *s.s: hld up: hdwy over 1f out: rdn and hung lft ins fnl f: r.o* **25/1**	PJMcDonald(3) 7	73
/000	**3**	*1 ¾*	**Princelywallywogan**[27] 811 6-8-4 **51** (John A Harris) *hld up: rdn over 4f out: hdwy and nt clr run over 1f out: swtchd rt ins fnl f: nt trble ldrs* **50/1**	AdrianMcCarthy 11	58+
550-	**4**	*½*	**Semi Detached (IRE)**[132] 6904 5-8-10 **57** (J W Unett) *chsd ldrs: led over 2f out: rdn and hdd 1f out: styd on same pce* **28/1**	GrahamGibbons 12	63
36-2	**5**	*2 ½*	**Top Jaro (FR)**[10] 978 5-8-13 **60** (D W Barker) *prom: racd keenly: rdn and ev ch over 1f out: no ex ins fnl f* **6/1**[1]	TonyHamilton 16	60
6642	**6**	*1 ¼*	**Jord (IRE)**[13] 949 4-8-6 **53** (A J McCabe) *led: rdn and hdd over 2f out: wknd ins fnl f* **13/2**[2]	AndrewElliott 2	50
50-5	**7**	*1*	**Skye But N Ben**[9] 989 4-8-6 **53** (G A Harker) *chsd ldrs: rdn over 3f out: wknd fnl f* **12/1**	(v) SilvestreDeSousa 10	48
4065	**8**	*½*	**Tina's Ridge (IRE)**[9] 996 4-8-13 **60** (R Hollinshead) *s.i.s: hld up: rdn over 2f out: nt trble ldrs* **15/2**	(p) RyanMoore 14	54
00-0	**9**	*hd*	**The Grey One (IRE)**[9] 996 5-8-13 **60** (J M Bradley) *mid-div: hdwy over 3f out: rdn 2f out: wknd fnl f* **14/1**	(p) TedDurcan 8	53
3104	**10**	*½*	**Josr's Magic (IRE)**[14] 938 4-8-6 **53** (H J Collingridge) *chsd ldrs: lost pl after 1f: hdwy over 3f out: sn rdn: wknd fnl f* **12/1**	JimmyQuinn 13	45
200-	**11**	*2 ¼*	**Apache Nation (IRE)**[151] 6640 5-8-11 **58** (M Dods) *mid-div: rdn over 3f out: wknd over 2f out* **8/1**	DaleGibson 3	45
000-	**12**	*¾*	**Outer Hebrides**[171] 6199 7-9-3 **64** (J M Bradley) *hld up in tch: rdn over 2f out: wknd over 1f out* **40/1**	(v) PaulFitzsimons 15	49
00-5	**13**	*5*	**Libre**[11] 973 8-9-1 **62** (F Jordan) *s.s: a in rr* **14/1**	TGMcLaughlin 17	36
060-	**14**	*½*	**Rowan Lodge (IRE)**[28] 6710 6-8-13 **63** (Ollie Pears) *hmpd and lost pl sn after s: sn mid-div: wknd over 2f out* **16/1**	(b) JamieMoriarty(3) 5	36
400-	**15**	*3 ½*	**Bidable**[184] 5860 4-8-13 **60** (B Palling) *s.i.s: sn pushed along and prom: rdn over 2f out: sn wknd* **20/1**	CatherineGannon 1	25
-566	**16**	*½*	**Cornerstone**[40] 663 4-8-10 **57** (S C Williams) *chsd ldr: rdn over 2f out: sn wknd* **12/1**	(v) ChrisCatlin 9	20
200-	**17**	*2 ½*	**Djalalabad (FR)**[160] 6447 4-8-10 **57** (Mrs C A Dunnett) *hld up: sme hdwy over 2f out: sn rdn and wknd* **20/1**	JohnEgan 6	15

1m 49.27s (3.67) **Going Correction** +0.55s/f (Yiel) — **17** Ran SP% **126.5**

Speed ratings (Par 101): **103,102,100,99,97 96,95,94,94,93 91,90,85,85,81 81,78**

CSF £186.11 CT £8202.40 TOTE £7.50: £1.80, £8.10, £12.90, £7.50; EX 180.30.

Owner Karmaa Racing Limited **Bred** Tally-Ho Stud **Trained** Kentisbeare, Devon

■ Stewards' Enquiry : Alan Munro one-day ban: careless riding (Apr 16)

FOCUS

Another moderate handicap, but it was run at a good pace and the form should work out.

Rowan Lodge(IRE) Official explanation: jockey said gelding became unbalanced in straight

1161 WEATHERBYS MESSAGING SERVICE H'CAP — 1m 54y

5:10 (5:18) (Class 5) (0-70,70) 3-Y-O — **£2,590** (£770; £385; £192) **Stalls** Centre

Form	Pos	Dist	Horse / details	Jockey	RPR
001-	**1**		**Jaser**[128] 6944 3-9-4 **70** (P W Chapple-Hyam) *hld up in tch: racd keenly: led over 1f out: drvn out* **7/4**[1]	AlanMunro 10	87+
13-	**2**	*1*	**Stevie Thunder**[160] 6454 3-8-11 **66** (G A Swinbank) *chsd ldrs: chal over 1f out: sn rdn: unable qckn wl ins fnl f* **12/1**[3]	PJMcDonald(3) 9	80
-151	**3**	*4 ½*	**Bookiebasher Babe (IRE)**[30] 785 3-9-2 **68** (M Quinn) *led: rdn and hdd over 1f out: no ex ins fnl f* **16/1**	ChrisCatlin 4	72
034-	**4**	*2*	**Highland Love**[202] 5363 3-8-13 **65** (Jedd O'Keeffe) *prom: rdn over 2f out: styd on same pce* **33/1**	TonyHamilton 14	64
00-2	**5**	*1 ¼*	**Black Dahlia**[21] 855 3-8-13 **65** (A J McCabe) *hld up: rdn over 3f out: hdwy over 2f out: hung lft and wknd over 1f out* **16/1**	NeilPollard 17	62
06-4	**6**	*1 ¾*	**Rossini's Dancer**[41] 634 3-8-8 **63** (R A Fahey) *broke wl: hmpd and lost pl after 1f: hdwy over 2f out: wknd over 1f out* **8/1**[2]	JamieMoriarty(3) 11	56+
056-	**7**	*1 ½*	**Looter (FR)**[177] 6058 3-8-10 **62** (J L Dunlop) *hld up: pushed along 1/2-way: nt clr run 3f out: n.d* **8/1**[2]	TedDurcan 7	51+
002-	**8**	*2 ½*	**Double On Red**[155] 6571 3-9-3 **69** (J M P Eustace) *s.i.s: hld up: rdn over 3f out: n.d* **16/1**	RichardMullen 3	52
054-	**9**	*2 ¼*	**Great Charm (IRE)**[134] 6884 3-9-2 **68** (M L W Bell) *s.i.s: plld hrd and sn prom: rdn over 2f out: hung rt and wknd sn after* **14/1**	TPQueally 6	46
1602	**10**	*3*	**Magical Song**[9] 998 3-8-4 **56** oh3 (P A Blockley) *chsd ldrs: rdn over 2f out: wknd over 1f out* **12/1**[3]	FrankieMcDonald 5	27
603-	**11**	*hd*	**Mr Lu**[193] 5621 3-8-8 **60** (G A Swinbank) *chsd ldrs over 5f* **50/1**	AndrewElliott 2	31
54-0	**12**	*shd*	**Royal Acclamation (IRE)**[4] 1073 3-9-4 **70** (G A Harker) *hld up: rdn 1/2-way: a in rr* **33/1**	SilvestreDeSousa 16	41
041-	**13**	*nk*	**Didana (IRE)**[104] 7196 3-9-2 **68** (M G Quinlan) *hld up: rdn over 3f out: a in rr* **8/1**[2]	RyanMoore 8	38
600-	**14**	*nk*	**Infinite Patience**[155] 6572 3-8-12 **64** (J S Moore) *hld up: hdwy over 3f out: rdn and wknd over 2f out* **25/1**	SimonWhitworth 1	33
000-	**15**	*½*	**Intersky Melody (USA)**[194] 5601 3-8-10 **62** (R M Whitaker) *hld up: rdn 1/2-way: a in rr* **100/1**	DeanMcKeown 12	30
4-45	**16**	*nk*	**Natural Rhythm (IRE)**[62] 366 3-8-13 **65** (Mrs R A Carr) *hld up: a in rr* **66/1**	DanielTudhope 15	32
020-	**17**	*1*	**Townkab (IRE)**[182] 5914 3-9-0 **66** (N P Littmoden) *hld up: rdn over 3f out: wknd sn after* **20/1**	TGMcLaughlin 13	31

1m 49.08s (3.48) **Going Correction** +0.55s/f (Yiel) — **17** Ran SP% **128.3**

Speed ratings (Par 98): **104,103,98,96,95 93,92,89,87,84 84,83,83,83,82 82,81**

CSF £23.65 CT £285.69 TOTE £2.80: £1.40, £3.60, £3.40, £6.20; EX 38.70 Place 6 £1,271.02, Place 5 £502.54.

Owner Ziad A Galadari **Bred** Galadari Sons Stud Company Limited **Trained** Newmarket, Suffolk

FOCUS

A modest handicap, but the form looks solid with the first pair coming clear and the third to recent All-Weather form. The winner is progressive and posted a fair time for a race like this, 0.19 seconds faster than the preceding older-horse handicap.

T/Plt: £772.60 to a £1 stake. Pool: £59,006.95. 55.75 winning tickets. T/Qpdt: £126.10 to a £1 stake. Pool: £4,245.70. 24.90 winning tickets. CR

1142 KEMPTON (A.W) (R-H)

Thursday, April 3

OFFICIAL GOING: Standard

Wind: Almost nil Weather: Overcast

1162 KEMPTON.CO.UK MEDIAN AUCTION MAIDEN STKS — 5f (P)

6:50 (6:51) (Class 5) 3-5-Y-O — **£2,456** (£725; £362) **Stalls** High

Form	Pos	Dist	Horse / details	Jockey	RPR
-403	**1**		**Ben**[15] 928 3-9-0 65 (P G Murphy) *chsd ldrs: rdn to ld ins fnl f: hld on wl nr fin* **4/1**[3]	(v) TQuinn 5	56
55	**2**	*½*	**Walragnek**[15] 928 4-9-11 (J G M O'Shea) *dwlt: hld up disputing 5th: rdn to chse ldrs over 1f out: kpt on fnl f* **25/1**	AndrewElliott 7	59
5	**3**	*½*	**Espy**[12] 965 3-9-0 (S Kirk) *dwlt: t.k.h and bhd: hdwy and nt clr rn 1f out: swtchd lft: r.o wl fnl f* **11/4**[1]	LPKeniry 4	59+
0-33	**4**	*½*	**Firespin (USA)**[16] 923 3-8-9 60 (M Botti) *hld up disputing 5th: rdn to chse ldrs over 1f out: one pce fnl f* **7/2**[2]	(t) OscarUrbina 8	46
-522	**5**	*1 ¾*	**Honest Value (IRE)**[15] 928 3-9-0 59 (Mrs L C Jewell) *disp ld: led over 3f out tl wknd ins fnl f* **7/1**	(p) NeilPollard 3	44
53-	**6**	*½*	**All In The Red (IRE)**[214] 5065 3-9-0 (Miss Gay Kelleway) *chsd ldrs: nt clr run on ins rail from over 1f out: rcvr* **4/1**[3]	HayleyTurner 6	54+
6000	**7**	*1 ¼*	**Joe Rich**[20] 877 4-9-8 37 (Mrs L C Jewell) *disp ld over 1f: w ldr tl wknd over 1f out* **66/1**	(p) JerryO'Dwyer(3) 1	43
04	**8**	*nk*	**Bonne**[20] 885 3-8-9 (M L W Bell) *dwlt: bhd: pushed along over 2f out: n.d* **10/1**	JamieSpencer 2	32

61.48 secs (0.98) **Going Correction** +0.125s/f (Slow)

WFA 3 from 4yo 11lb — **8** Ran SP% **115.8**

Speed ratings (Par 103): **97,96,95,94,91 91,89,88**

CSF £92.39 TOTE £3.70: £1.10, £9.60, £2.00; EX 102.70.

Owner K W Anidjah **Bred** North Farm Stud **Trained** East Garston, Berks

■ Stewards' Enquiry : Neil Pollard three-day ban: careless riding (April 17-19)

FOCUS
A modest maiden rated around the first two, but some improvement is likely from the more inexperienced contestants.

1163 DAY TIME, NIGHT TIME, GREAT TIME H'CAP — 1m 2f (P)
7:20 (7:20) (Class 6) (0-65,65) 3-Y-O — **£2,047** (£604; £302) **Stalls** High

Form — RPR
000- **1** **Mista Rossa**[162] 6417 3-9-0 **64** .... TravisBlock(3) 9 — 71
(H Morrison) *prom: wnt 2nd and pushed along briefly 6f out: led 3f out: hld on gamely fnl f* **9/2**[2]
0-33 **2** *1* **Calistos Quest**[31] 784 3-9-4 **65** ....(t) SebSanders 5 — 70+
(M Botti) *hld up in rr of midfield: rdn and hdwy 2f out: pressed wnr fnl f: r.o: jst hld* **2/1**[1]
-502 **3** *2* **Si Belle (IRE)**[21] 873 3-9-3 **64** .... ChrisCatlin 10 — 65
(Rae Guest) *in tch: rdn to chse ldrs 2f out: styd on same pce* **8/1**[3]
00-2 **4** *¾* **Milanollo**[39] 694 3-9-4 **65** .... JamieSpencer 3 — 64
(M L W Bell) *hld up towards rr: pushed along 3f out: styd on fnl 2f: nvr nrr* **9/2**[2]
31-6 **5** *2* **Alfredtheordinary**[17] 920 3-8-11 **65** .... MatthewDavies(7) 6 — 60
(M R Channon) *in tch: effrt over 2f out: one pce appr fnl f* **12/1**
100- **6** *1½* **King Supreme (IRE)**[148] 6715 3-9-4 **65** .... RichardHughes 2 — 57
(R Hannon) *prom: rdn 3f out: wknd over 1f out* **8/1**[3]
0-53 **7** *½* **Soxy Doxy (IRE)**[34] 758 3-8-8 **55** .... GregFairley 1 — 46
(M Johnston) *bhd: mod effrt 2f out: nvr trbld ldrs* **12/1**
000- **8** *6* **Romford Car Two**[156] 6571 3-8-7 **54** .... DMylonas 4 — 33
(Miss J Feilden) *a bhd: rdn and no ch over 2f out* **50/1**
4056 **9** *1* **Bon Ton Roulet**[29] 803 3-8-8 **60** .... HaddenFrost(5) 8 — 37
(R Hannon) *racd freely: sn led: uncomfortable on bnds: hdd 3f out: wknd wl over 1f out* **16/1**
000 **10** *30* **Ten Hour Lunch**[21] 867 3-8-4 **51** oh3........ HayleyTurner 7 — —
(B J Meehan) *chsd ldrs 3f: drvn and wknd 5f out: t.o fnl 3f* **40/1**

2m 9.64s (1.64) **Going Correction** +0.125s/f (Slow) — **10** Ran SP% **117.6**
Speed ratings (Par 96): **98,97,95,95,93 92,91,87,86,62**
CSF £14.00 CT £70.53 TOTE £4.90: £1.40, £1.20, £3.50; EX 18.40.
Owner Wood Street Syndicate IV **Bred** The National Stud **Trained** East Ilsley, Berks

FOCUS
A moderate handicap, but several were relatively lightly-raced and can improve a bit and the form is rated slightly positively around the third and fourth.
Mista Rossa Official explanation: trainer said, regarding the apparent improvement in form, that gelding had improved physically since its previous run in October 2007.
Milanollo Official explanation: jockey said filly hung left
Bon Ton Roulet Official explanation: jockey said filly ran too free and failed to handle the bends

1164 SUNBURY CLAIMING STKS — 1m 4f (P)
7:50 (7:50) (Class 6) 4-Y-O+ — **£2,047** (£604; £302) **Stalls** High

Form — RPR
605- **1** **Bull Market (IRE)**[24] 4976 5-9-1 78........ RichardSmith 1 — 76
(J A Osborne) *trckd ldr: led wl over 1f out: rdn and r.o wl* **7/2**[3]
-013 **2** *3* **Turner's Touch**[16] 921 6-9-3 67........(b) GeorgeBaker 3 — 76+
(G L Moore) *stdd s: plld hrd and patiently rdn fr bhd: hdwy whn nt clr run ins fnl 2f: swtchd wd: r.o to take 2nd fnl 75yds* **2/1**[1]
0-01 **3** *1* **Lucayan Dancer**[7] 1041 8-9-8 76........ AdrianTNicholls 5 — 77
(D Nicholls) *stdd s: hld up in 4th: hdwy to chse wnr over 1f out: nt qckn fnl f: lost 2nd fnl 75yds* **9/4**[2]
0-10 **4** *5* **Steely Dan**[6] 1048 9-9-1 70........(p) NeilPollard 6 — 62
(Mrs L C Jewell) *hld up in 3rd: effrt over 2f out: wknd over 1f out* **8/1**
50-0 **5** *3¼* **Brigadore (USA)**[6] 1052 5-9-3 65........(b[1]) StephenDonohoe 2 — 58
(Ian Williams) *led and sn had field stretched out: rdn and qcknd over 3f out: hdd wl over 1f out: sn wknd* **13/2**

2m 36.93s (2.43) **Going Correction** +0.125s/f (Slow) — **5** Ran SP% **110.8**
Speed ratings (Par 101): **96,94,93,90,87**
CSF £10.99 TOTE £4.10: £2.10, £1.10; EX 11.60.The winner was claimed by Ian Williams for £10,000.
Owner Fergus Jones **Bred** King Bloodstock **Trained** Upper Lambourn, Berks

FOCUS
A fair claimer, but Brigadore was allowed an uncontested lead and the field were soon stretched out by 15 lengths even though the tempo was nothing special. The form does not look that solid but makes some sort of sense.

1165 KEMPTON FOR CONFERENCES H'CAP — 1m 4f (P)
8:20 (8:22) (Class 6) (0-65,65) 4-Y-O+ — **£2,047** (£604; £302) **Stalls** High

Form — RPR
4452 **1** **Punta Galera (IRE)**[5] 1086 5-8-11 **59**........ JamieSpencer 3 — 70
(Paul Green) *patiently rdn fr rr: hdwy 2f out: styd on strly under wl-judged ride to ld fnl 75yds* **11/4**[2]
0-00 **2** *1¼* **One To Follow**[20] 880 4-9-0 **63**........ AdamKirby 5 — 72
(C G Cox) *chsd ldr: led 5f out: rdn 4l clr 2f out: hdd and no ex fnl 75yds* **9/1**
54-0 **3** *2½* **Rose Bien**[50] 544 6-8-8 **56**........(p) AmirQuinn 7 — 61
(P J McBride) *hld up in 6th: rdn over 4f out: styd on u.p fnl 2f* **25/1**
1244 **4** *¾* **Wind Flow**[7] 1039 4-9-0 **63**........ AdrianMcCarthy 6 — 67
(C A Dwyer) *chsd ldrs tl 4f out: losing pl towards rr whn hmpd 3f out: styd on again appr fnl f* **11/2**[3]
5-32 **5** *9* **Rose Row**[54] 510 4-8-12 **61**........ HayleyTurner 2 — 50
(Mrs Mary Hambro) *chsd ldrs: hrd rdn over 2f out: sn outpcd* **5/2**[1]
3256 **6** *18* **Tancredi (SWE)**[12] 973 6-8-10 **61**........(t) JerryO'Dwyer(3) 4 — 22
(N B King) *in tch: disputed 2nd 3f out: rdn and wknd wl over 1f out: eased wn btn fnl f* **8/1**
-421 **7** *14* **Just Intersky (USA)**[31] 248 5-8-10 **65**........(e) AshleyMorgan(7) 1 — 3
(V Smith) *hld up in rr: hdwy on outside 5f out: wknd 4f out* **7/1**
1-45 **8** *3¼* **Summerofsixtynine**[71] 272 5-8-4 **52**........(v[1]) AndrewElliott 8 — —
(J G M O'Shea) *led at str pce tl 5f out: wknd over 3f out: fin lame* **14/1**

2m 34.4s (-0.10) **Going Correction** +0.125s/f (Slow)
WFA 4 from 5yo+ 1lb — **8** Ran SP% **114.7**
Speed ratings (Par 101): **105,104,102,102,96 84,74,72**
CSF £27.68 CT £508.30 TOTE £3.90: £1.40, £3.80, £6.90; EX 37.60.
Owner Derek A Howard **Bred** Bill Dwan **Trained** Lydiate, Merseyside

FOCUS
A modest race, but solid enough at its level rated around those in the frame behind the winner. The pace was good, allowing the winner to be patiently ridden from behind.
Summerofsixtynine Official explanation: jockey said horse finished lame

1166 KEMPTON FOR OUTDOOR EVENTS H'CAP — 1m (P)
8:50 (8:51) (Class 6) (0-60,60) 3-Y-O — **£2,047** (£604; £302) **Stalls** High

Form — RPR
0432 **1** **Desiderio**[3] 1115 3-9-4 **60**........(p) RichardHughes 13 — 67
(R Hannon) *disp ld 3f: w ldrs: hrd rdn over 2f out: led ins fnl f: rdn out* **5/4**[1]
03-4 **2** *1½* **Fools Gold**[23] 848 3-9-4 **60**........ PaulEddery 7 — 63
(G D Blake) *prom: slt ld 1f out tl ins fnl f: nt qckn* **7/1**[3]
2234 **3** *½* **Llab Nala**[6] 1051 3-8-8 **57**........ MatthewDavies(7) 14 — 59
(M R Channon) *in tch: effrt over 2f out: chal over 1f out: one pce ins fnl f* **8/1**
-505 **4** *1¼* **Miss Bouggy Wouggy**[29] 803 3-8-8 **50**........(b) JamesDoyle 12 — 49
(M Blanshard) *disp ld 3f: w ldrs after: no ex fnl f* **25/1**
03-0 **5** *hd* **Minwir (IRE)**[23] 849 3-9-4 **60**........ MartinDwyer 2 — 59
(M Quinn) *towards rr: hdwy over 2f out: chsd ldng gp over 1f out: kpt on fnl f* **10/1**
000- **6** *¾* **Payne Relief (IRE)**[162] 6432 3-8-13 **58**........ LukeMorris(3) 10 — 55+
(M L W Bell) *mid-div: rdn and outpcd 3f out: sme hdwy whn hmpd 2f out: styd on strly fnl f* **20/1**
6656 **7** *½* **Scots W'Hae**[21] 873 3-8-11 **53**........(t) AmirQuinn 1 — 49
(P J McBride) *plld hrd: led after 3f tl 1f out: wknd fnl f* **25/1**
30-4 **8** *¾* **Ile Royale**[15] 931 3-9-4 **60**........ NeilPollard 3 — 54
(B R Johnson) *s.s: bhd tl hdwy 2f out: no further prog over 1f out* **11/1**
00-4 **9** *1* **Dear Will**[79] 163 3-9-1 **57**........ JamieSpencer 9 — 49+
(J R Fanshawe) *hmpd s: bhd: effrt 2f out: nt pce to chal* **5/1**[2]
066- **10** *1½* **Nathan Dee**[190] 5721 3-8-4 **53** ow1........ GabrielHannon(7) 6 — 41
(Mrs H Sweeting) *mid-div: effrt on outside 3f out: sn btn* **33/1**
00-0 **11** *hd* **New Minerton (IRE)**[10] 998 3-8-8 **50**........ RobertHavlin 4 — 38
(B R Millman) *s.s: wl bhd tl sme late hdwy* **40/1**
-000 **12** *¾* **Elegant Step**[20] 876 3-8-8 **53**........ KirstyMilczarek(3) 5 — 39
(A W Carroll) *chsd ldrs 5f* **33/1**
000- **13** *3¾* **Aim**[106] 7182 3-8-12 **54**........ JimCrowley 11 — 32
(J R Jenkins) *in tch 4f* **40/1**
0-00 **14** *6* **Honest Yankee (USA)**[40] 674 3-8-4 **46** oh1........(v) FrankieMcDonald 8 — 10
(Mrs L C Jewell) *hmpd s: sn rdn along towards rr: wl bhd fnl 3f* **66/1**

1m 41.94s (2.14) **Going Correction** +0.125s/f (Slow) — **14** Ran SP% **126.9**
Speed ratings (Par 96): **94,92,92,90,90 89,89,88,87,86 85,85,81,75**
CSF £9.87 CT £59.37 TOTE £2.10: £1.20, £3.20, £1.50; EX 13.90.
Owner Exors of the late Cathal M Ryan **Bred** Keith Freeman **Trained** East Everleigh, Wilts

FOCUS
A modest but competitive race in which the early pace was ordinary and as a result five were in a line at the furlong pole. The form is rated around the third and fourth.
Dear Will Official explanation: jockey said gelding suffered interference at the start
New Minerton(IRE) Official explanation: jockey said filly missed the break

1167 PANORAMIC BAR & RESTAURANT H'CAP — 6f (P)
9:20 (9:22) (Class 4) (0-85,85) 3-Y-O — **£4,209** (£1,252; £625; £312) **Stalls** High

Form — RPR
1522 **1** **Fathsta (IRE)**[12] 975 3-9-2 **80**........ LPKeniry 9 — 86
(S Kirk) *chsd ldrs: drvn to ld 1f out: r.o strly* **11/2**[3]
1035 **2** *1¼* **Asian Power (IRE)**[12] 967 3-8-10 **74**........ DarryllHolland 8 — 76
(P J O'Gorman) *prom: rdn over 2f out: chsd wnr ins fnl f: kpt on same pce* **12/1**
000- **3** *¾* **Enodoc**[180] 6004 3-8-10 **74**........ MartinDwyer 10 — 74
(W R Muir) *led: hrd rdn and hdd 1f out: one pce* **25/1**
02-1 **4** *1½* **Emperors Jade**[16] 923 3-8-12 **76**........ JamieSpencer 1 — 71
(A P Jarvis) *hld up towards rr: rdn and r.o fnl 2f: nrst fin* **8/1**
521- **5** *½* **Incomparable**[145] 6754 3-9-3 **81**........ SebSanders 4 — 74
(A J McCabe) *prom: rdn over 2f out: one pce appr fnl f* **13/2**
235- **6** *hd* **Balata**[162] 6419 3-8-9 **73**........ SimonWhitworth 6 — 66
(B R Millman) *mid-div: effrt over 2f out: styd on same pce* **20/1**
21- **7** *¾* **Premier Danseur (IRE)**[145] 6755 3-8-13 **77**........ GregFairley 11 — 67
(M Johnston) *dwlt: sn prom: rdn 3f out: wknd 2f out* **3/1**[1]
04-6 **8** *¾* **Sofia's Star**[12] 967 3-9-2 **80**........ JimCrowley 3 — 68
(P Winkworth) *bhd: rdn 3f out: nvr rchd ldrs* **11/1**
45-5 **9** *1* **Tadalavil**[16] 926 3-8-12 **83**........ MatthewDavies(7) 5 — 68
(M R Channon) *s.s: bhd: sme hdwy into midfield 3f out: wknd 2f out* **7/1**
01- **10** *nk* **Northern Bolt**[196] 5550 3-9-7 **85**........ AdrianTNicholls 2 — 69
(D Nicholls) *in tch on outside: rdn 3f out: wknd over 2f out* **9/2**[2]

1m 13.19s (0.09) **Going Correction** +0.125s/f (Slow) — **10** Ran SP% **120.1**
Speed ratings (Par 100): **104,102,101,99,98 98,97,96,95,94**
CSF £71.63 CT £1079.19 TOTE £6.80: £2.00, £2.90, £6.20; EX 45.60 Place 6 £89.55, Place 5 £47.46.
Owner Speedlith Group **Bred** Brian Miller **Trained** Upper Lambourn, Berks

FOCUS
A fair handicap rated through the runner-up backed up by the fourth to course form.
T/Plt: £173.60 to a £1 stake. Pool: £73,943.12. 310.84 winning tickets. T/Qpdt: £29.10 to a £1 stake. Pool: £6,269.42. 159.10 winning tickets. LM

LEICESTER (R-H)
Thursday, April 3

OFFICIAL GOING: Soft (good to soft in places; 6.0)
Wind: overcast Weather: virtually nil

1168 LADBROKES.COM MEDIAN AUCTION MAIDEN STKS — 5f 2y
2:10 (2:10) (Class 6) 2-Y-O — **£1,942** (£578; £288; £144) **Stalls** Low

Form — RPR
1 **Art Connoisseur (IRE)** 2-9-3 0........ JamieSpencer 1 — 83+
(M L W Bell) *chsd ldr: hung rt fr 1/2-way: led wl over 1f out: clr 1f out: pushed out* **10/3**[2]
2 *3¼* **Joe Caster** 2-9-3 0........ RyanMoore 3 — 67
(J M P Eustace) *chsd ldrs: hung rt fr 1/2-way: outpcd over 1f out: kpt on to snatch 2nd nr fin* **85/40**[1]
4 **3** *hd* **Transcentral**[10] 995 2-8-12 0........ NCallan 4 — 61
(W M Brisbourne) *led: hung rt fr 1/2-way: hdd wl over 1f out: sn outpcd by wnr: lost 2nd nr fin* **7/2**[3]
4 *3¼* **Come On Buckers (IRE)** 2-9-3 0........ TGMcLaughlin 2 — 53
(P D Evans) *sn rdn and outpcd: wl bhd tl styd on fnl f: nvr on terms* **16/1**
5 *½* **Fyelehk (IRE)** 2-9-3 0........ AlanMunro 5 — 51
(B R Millman) *chsd ldrs: rdn and outpcd 1/2-way: n.d after* **14/1**

6 *21* **Rhydian** 2-9-3 0.. SebSanders 6 —
(R M Beckett) *racd awkwardly: in tch: rdn and hung lft 1/2-way: sn wl bhd* **7/2**[3]

63.64 secs (3.64) **Going Correction** +0.525s/f (Yiel) **6** Ran SP% **112.1**
Speed ratings (Par 90): **91,85,85,80,79 45**
CSF £10.82 TOTE £3.60: £2.00, £1.60; EX 10.60.
Owner R A Green **Bred** D McDonnell **Trained** Newmarket, Suffolk

FOCUS
This looked a reasonable two-year-old maiden for the time of year best rated through the third. They all ended up towards the far rail in the closing stages.

NOTEBOOK
Art Connoisseur(IRE) ◆, a 55,000gns son of Lucky Story, first foal of a 7f two-year-old winner, proved good enough to make a winning debut. He showed signs of inexperience, drifting over to the far rail under pressure, but he was basically too good for this lot and will be worth his place in better company. (op 3-1 tchd 4-1)
Joe Caster, by Makbul, first foal of an unraced half-sister to smart sprinter If Paradise, had Ryan Moore booked and a big run was seemingly expected. He lacked the sharpness of the winner, but stuck on for pressure to claim second and will know more next time. (op 5-2 tchd 11-4 and 2-1)
Transcentral, fourth first time up at Warwick, showed plenty of early dash and has clearly learnt from her debut. She was eventually put in her place, but showed enough to suggest she can pick up a modest contest. (op 11-4)
Come On Buckers(IRE), an 8,000euros gelded son of Fath, half-brother to among others dual 5f two-year-old winner Secret Index, who was later a triple winner in the US, was outpaced for much of the way and only found his stride very late. He seemed badly in need of the experience and this should bring him on. (op 12-1)
Fyelehk(IRE), a 30,000gns son of Kheleyf, first foal of an unraced half-sister to among others high-class Polar Force, a prolific 5f-6f winner at two to seven, was easy to back on his debut and finished up well held. (tchd 16-1)
Rhydian, a 10,000euros son of Monsieur Bond, out of a multiple 5f-6f winner at four, raced very awkwardly throughout, carrying his head at an angle, and looked a difficult ride. (op 5-1)

1169 LADBROKES.COM (S) STKS 5f 218y
2:45 (2:46) (Class 6) 3-Y-O **£1,942** (£578; £288; £144) **Stalls** Low

Form RPR
3240 **1** **Jazenio**[9] 1019 3-8-9 61.. NCallan 2 61
(K A Ryan) *bhd: rdn and hdwy over 3f out: chsd ldr 2f out: led ins fnl f: sn clr* **5/2**[2]
-433 **2** *3* **Our Sunnie**[3] 1117 3-9-0 66........................(v[1]) AdrianTNicholls 4 56
(D Nicholls) *chsd ldr tl led over 2f out: rdn and nt run on 1f out: sn hdd and btn* **7/2**[3]
4442 **3** *2* **One Called Alice**[3] 1117 3-8-9 60 ow3..................... JerryO'Dwyer[(3)] 1 48
(A W Carroll) *s.i.s: bhd: rdn and hdwy 3f out: chsd ldng pair and hung rt 2f out: wknd fnl f* **6/4**[1]
0042 **4** *9* **Stoneacre Ma**[5] 1081 3-8-9 50.....................................(b) LPKeniry 5 16
(Peter Grayson) *outpcd in midfield: n.d* **10/1**
0260 **5** *2 1/4* **Tilly Ann (IRE)**[31] 780 3-8-2 42.......................... PatrickDonaghy[(7)] 3 9
(Peter Grayson) *awkward leaving stalls: a bhd* **40/1**
04-0 **6** *1/2* **Tenth Night (IRE)**[10] 998 3-9-0 47...........................(b[1]) MickyFenton 6 12
(P T Midgley) *led and sn clr: hdd over 2f out: wknd qckly 2f out* **12/1**
0-40 **7** *8* **Avian Flew**[31] 780 3-8-2 41.. StacyRenwick[(7)] 7 —
(J A Pickering) *chsd ldrs for 3f: sn struggling* **50/1**

1m 17.23s (4.23) **Going Correction** +0.525s/f (Yiel) **7** Ran SP% **112.0**
Speed ratings (Par 96): **92,88,85,73,70 69,59**
CSF £11.19 TOTE £3.80: £1.70, £1.80; EX 12.40.There was no bid for the winner.
Owner Zen Racing **Bred** Kingwood Bloodstock **Trained** Hambleton, N Yorks
■ Stewards' Enquiry : Adrian T Nicholls caution: careless riding

FOCUS
A standard seller run at a very strong early pace and rated around the first two. The winning time was 1.38 seconds slower than the following three-year-old conditions contest. As in the first race, they edged towards the far rail in the second half of the contest.
Tenth Night(IRE) Official explanation: jockey said colt hung right-handed

1170 LADBROKESCASINO.COM CONDITIONS STKS 5f 218y
3:20 (3:21) (Class 3) 3-Y-O **£6,799** (£2,023; £1,011; £505) **Stalls** Low

Form RPR
1- **1** **Quiet Elegance**[176] 6105 3-8-9 76.. JimmyQuinn 8 96+
(E J Alston) *stdd s: hld up towards rr: hdwy 3f out: rdn to chal ins fnl f: rn green but r.o to ld nr fin* **22/1**
1- **2** *1/2* **Inxile (IRE)**[209] 5192 3-9-0 89.. AdrianTNicholls 6 99+
(D Nicholls) *taken down early: stdd s: hdwy to ld over 4f out: rdn jst over 2f out: hdd and no ex nr fin* **10/1**
106- **3** *1 3/4* **Irish Pearl (IRE)**[153] 6619 3-8-9 90........................... FergusSweeney 5 89
(K R Burke) *chsd ldrs: wnt 2nd over 2f out: sn rdn: unable qck u.p fnl f* **10/1**
150- **4** *1 1/2* **Victorian Bounty**[200] 5456 3-8-12 87........................... MickyFenton 3 87
(Stef Liddiard) *chsd ldr tl led after 1f: sn hdd: chsd ldrs after: rdn 2f out: kpt on same pce* **25/1**
263- **5** *1 1/4* **Oasis Wind**[183] 5922 3-9-0 98.. RyanMoore 2 85
(P F I Cole) *hung rt thrght: t.k.h: chsd ldrs: rdn over 2f out: no hdwy fr over 1f out* **8/11**[1]
221- **6** *3 1/4* **Ramatni**[149] 6699 3-8-5 88.. JoeFanning 1 66
(M Johnston) *led for 1f: sn struggling in rr* **8/1**[3]
12- **7** *1* **Eternal Luck (IRE)**[280] 3025 3-8-12 83........................... PhilipRobinson 4 69
(M A Jarvis) *a bhd: rdn after 1f: n.d* **6/1**[2]

1m 15.85s (2.85) **Going Correction** +0.525s/f (Yiel) **7** Ran SP% **109.7**
Speed ratings (Par 102): **102,101,99,97,95 91,89**
CSF £197.23 TOTE £19.60: £7.20, £3.40; EX 155.10 Trifecta £356.20 Part won. Pool £501.76 - 0.39 winning units..
Owner Mr & Mrs G Middlebrook **Bred** G And Mrs Middlebrook **Trained** Longton, Lancs

FOCUS
A good conditions contest on paper, and the form looks pretty solid around the fourth but the winner had the lowest official rating of this lot and the winning time was only 1.38 seconds quicker than the previous three-year-old seller. Unlike in the first two races, they stayed stands' side this time, and that might help explain the ordinary time.

NOTEBOOK
Quiet Elegance's debut success at Nottingham last year represented just fair form and she had plenty to find stepped up in grade off the back of a six-month break, but she proved up to the task. Dropped in from the widest stall of all, she travelled well in behind the pace and stayed on steadily once switched out with her effort. It would be unwise to get too carried away, as the winning time was nothing special and several of her rivals ran below form, but she if from a family that improves with age and she should continue to progress. A half-sister to the stable's Group 1 winning sprinter Reverence, the objective now will surely be to pick up some black type. (op 14-1)
Inxile(IRE), a 33/1 winner on his debut in a 5f maiden at Haydock last September, ran well on his return to action. He showed good speed for much of the way, but the soft ground probably blunted him somewhat late on and he was just pegged back. He looks a very useful sprinter in the making. (op 6-1)
Irish Pearl(IRE) won her maiden on soft ground and this was a reasonable effort on her return from five months off. (op 11-1 tchd 9-1)
Victorian Bounty, making his debut for Stef Liddiard off the back of a 200-day break, ran a creditable race and can build on this. He was a little short of room around 3f out, but was not unlucky and is basically going to want a better surface. (op 33-1)
Oasis Wind, returning from six months off, seemed to be hanging a touch to his right almost from the off and never looked happy. He was the pick of the weights but was nowhere near his two-year-old form and this ground might have been softer than he would have liked. Official explanation: jockey said colt hung right-handed (op Evens)
Ramatni was well beaten after five months off and she needs quick ground. (tchd 9-1)
Eternal Luck(IRE) had a little bit to find in this company and had not been seen since last June. (tchd 11-2)

1171 LADBROKES.COM KIBWORTH H'CAP 1m 1f 218y
3:55 (3:55) (Class 3) (0-95,95) 3-Y-O **£6,623** (£1,982; £991; £495; £246) **Stalls** High

Form RPR
1- **1** **Captain Webb**[168] 6274 3-8-4 **78**.. JoeFanning 3 84+
(M Johnston) *w ldr tl led 3f out: sn rdn: jnd 2f out: hung lft ins fnl f: forged ahd last 100yds* **7/4**[1]
210- **2** *2 1/4* **Ballochroy (IRE)**[160] 6471 3-8-7 **81**.. MichaelHills 6 85+
(B W Hills) *chsd ldrs: hdwy to join wnr 2f out: 1/2l down and keeping on same pce whn hmpd and swtchd rt ins fnl f: no ch after* **10/1**
2-01 **3** *2 1/4* **No To Trident**[12] 961 3-8-11 **85**.. TGMcLaughlin 5 82
(P D Evans) *t.k.h: hld up in last trio: effrt on inner 3f out: no imp u.p fnl f* **12/1**
-212 **4** *hd* **Segal (IRE)**[7] 1043 3-8-2 **79**.. WilliamBuick[(3)] 1 76
(J Noseda) *t.k.h: chsd ldrs: hdwy over 3f out: rdn over 2f out: outpcd and hung rt 1f out* **7/2**[2]
1- **5** *6* **Bright Falcon**[173] 6184 3-9-0 **88**.. JamieSpencer 2 73
(S Parr) *rrd leaving stalls: a bhd: rdn and effrt over 3f out: btn whn hung rt 2f out* **4/1**[3]
210- **6** *1 1/4* **Quam Celerrime**[153] 6631 3-9-7 **95**.. StephenDonohoe 4 77
(P A Blockley) *hld up in last trio: rdn and lost tch 3f out* **25/1**
214- **7** *1 1/2* **Shannersburg (IRE)**[232] 4495 3-8-10 **84**.. ChrisCatlin 7 63
(E J O'Neill) *led tl 3f out: sn wknd* **7/1**

2m 13.02s (5.12) **Going Correction** +0.30s/f (Good) **7** Ran SP% **111.7**
Speed ratings (Par 102): **91,89,87,87,82 81,80**
CSF £19.50 CT £156.05 TOTE £2.70: £1.30, £4.10; EX 21.00 Trifecta £80.40 Pool £471.64 - 4.16 winning units..
Owner Sheikh Hamdan Bin Mohammed Al Maktoum **Bred** Gainsborough Stud Management Ltd **Trained** Middleham Moor, N Yorks

FOCUS
A good handicap run in a time 1.70 seconds quicker than the following maiden rated around the third and fourth.

NOTEBOOK
Captain Webb ◆ left the bare form of last year's Brighton maiden success over 1m well behind with a likable effort on his three-year-old bow and is now two from two. He was unable to dominate as he had when winning on his debut, but he responded to pressure to take over in the straight and galloped on strongly, despite still looking green. He is open to a good deal more improvement and could be one for something like the King George V Handicap at Royal Ascot later in the year. (op 5-2)
Ballochroy(IRE) ◆, stepped up in trip on his return from over five months off, had the ground to suit and made the potentially useful Captain Webb work hard enough. He seemed to shy away from the winning rider's whip around a furlong out and, although held at the time, that probably exaggerated the margin of defeat. He can win a similar event. (op 12-1 tchd 14-1)
No To Trident, a surprise winner of a Doncaster maiden on his previous start, ran a creditable race in this tougher contest. (op 9-1)
Segal(IRE) travelled reasonably well and loomed up with every chance in the straight, but he found little for pressure. He looked to be paddling a bit on this ground and he will probably appreciate a quicker surface. (tchd 4-1)
Bright Falcon looked a nice prospect when winning a 1m maiden on his debut at York for Declan Murphy last year and he has been given an entry in both the Dante and the Derby, so this was bitterly disappointing. He was no sure thing to stay this trip on breeding, but he was basically never going and was beaten well before stamina became an issue. (op 3-1)

1172 LADBROKES.COM MAIDEN STKS 1m 1f 218y
4:30 (4:32) (Class 5) 3-Y-O+ **£2,590** (£770; £385; £192) **Stalls** High

Form RPR
222- **1** **Downhiller (IRE)**[161] 6451 3-8-8 81.. RyanMoore 12 87
(J L Dunlop) *chsd ldr: rdn to ld over 1f out: styd on wl* **3/1**[2]
2 *1 1/4* **Meshtri (IRE)** 3-8-8 0.. PhilipRobinson 7 85
(M A Jarvis) *s.i.s: hld up in midfield: rdn over 3f out: styd on to go modest 3rd over 1f out: kpt on wl to chse wnr ins fnl f: nvr able to chal* **3/1**[2]
035 **3** *2 1/2* **Ella**[11] 982 4-9-8 0.. NCallan 13 79
(G A Swinbank) *led: clr 4f out: rdn over 2f out: hdd over 1f out: one pce* **16/1**
4 *9* **Empowered (IRE)** 3-8-8 0.. AlanMunro 4 62+
(P W Chapple-Hyam) *t.k.h: hld up in midfield: hdwy on outer over 5f out: rdn wl over 3f out: no imp after* **5/2**[1]
0/4 **5** *2 1/4* **Songmaster (USA)**[35] 727 5-9-13 0.. FergusSweeney 6 61
(A King) *chsd ldrs: rdn and outpcd 4f out: no ch after* **50/1**
0- **6** *nk* **Asian Classic (IRE)**[155] 6593 3-8-8 0.. SteveDrowne 10 56
(R Charlton) *racd in midfield: outpcd 4f out: nvr nr ldrs* **40/1**
0- **7** *nk* **Star Pattern (USA)**[153] 6616 3-8-8 0.. RobertHavlin 14 56
(J H M Gosden) *s.i.s: t.k.h: sn chsng ldrs: rdn and outpcd 3f out: no ch after* **9/1**[3]
00- **8** *5* **Mount Lavinia (IRE)**[176] 6106 3-8-0 0.. WilliamBuick[(3)] 3 41
(R M Beckett) *sn bhd and pushed along: sme modest late hdwy: nvr on terms* **33/1**
00 **9** *1/2* **El Masir**[12] 961 3-8-8 0.. JoeFanning 9 45
(M Johnston) *t.k.h: chsd ldrs tl wknd 4f out* **16/1**
10 *4 1/2* **Golden Bishop** 3-8-8 0.. JimCrowley 15 36
(M L W Bell) *rn green in midfield: rdn and struggling over 4f out: t.o* **33/1**
0/2- **11** *11* **Saloon (USA)**[168] 6275 4-9-13 0.. PaulDoe 11 18
(S Curran) *s.i.s: a bhd: t.o* **18/1**
00- **12** *1 1/2* **Splinter Group**[314] 2005 4-9-10 0.. KirstyMilczarek[(3)] 1 15
(S A Callaghan) *dropped in after s: a bhd: lost tch over 4f out: t.o* **50/1**
13 *9* **Just Olive**[123] 7-9-8 0.. AlanDaly 2 —
(G Fierro) *s.i.s: a bhd: lost tch 5f out: t.o* **250/1**
0 **14** *40* **Come On Molly**[26] 837 4-9-8 0.. J-PGuillambert 8 —
(R Brotherton) *bhd: lost tch over 4f out: virtually p.u fnl f: t.o* **250/1**

2m 11.32s (3.42) **Going Correction** +0.30s/f (Good)
WFA 3 from 4yo+ 19lb **14** Ran SP% **118.6**
Speed ratings (Par 103): **98,97,95,87,86 85,85,81,81,77 68,67,60,28**
CSF £11.84 TOTE £3.40: £1.70, £1.50, £3.20; EX 13.00 Trifecta £102.00 Pool £485.68 - 3.38 winning units..

Owner Windflower Overseas Holdings Inc **Bred** Windflower Overseas Holdings Inc **Trained** Arundel, W Sussex

FOCUS

A fair maiden on paper, but they finished strung out and the form is a bit guessy. The winning time was 1.70 seconds slower than the previous 76-95 handicap for three-year-olds.

1173 LADBROKESCASINO.COM MAIDEN STKS — 1m 3f 183y

5:05 (5:05) (Class 5) 3-4-Y-O — **£2,590** (£770; £385; £192) **Stalls** High

Form				RPR
054-	1		**Enroller (IRE)**[175] 6130 3-8-7 77 MartinDwyer 4 (W R Muir) *chsd ldng pair: hdwy to ld over 2f out: sn wl clr: eased ins fnl f* **11/10**[1]	80+
56-	2	2 1/4	**Spiritonthemount (USA)**[162] 6417 3-8-7 0 MichaelHills 3 (B W Hills) *bhd and pushed along early: hdwy over 4f out: hung rt over 2f out: chsd wnr 2f out: kpt on: flattered by proximity to wnr* **4/1**[3]	68
564-	3	4 1/2	**Al Azy (IRE)**[185] 5858 3-8-7 73 RHills 6 (J L Dunlop) *led for 1f: chsd ldr after tl led again over 3f out: hdd over 2f out: sn btn* **9/4**[2]	61
00	4	1/2	**Brave Boogie**[17] 919 3-8-2 0 JimmyQuinn 1 (H J L Dunlop) *racd in midfield: rdn wl over 3f out: nvr gng pce to threaten ldrs* **33/1**	55
0-	5	18	**Damascus Gold**[29] 2726 4-9-13 0 (b) SamHitchcott 5 (Miss Z C Davison) *s.i.s: a bhd: t.o last 2f* **150/1**	31
00-	6	5	**Arrewig Lissome (USA)**[97] 7252 3-8-4 0 (v[1]) WilliamBuick(3) 2 (A M Balding) *t.k.h: led after 1f: hdd over 3f out: sn wknd: t.o* **14/1**	23
6/0-	7	4	**Just Chrissie**[87] 1012 4-9-8 0 AlanDaly 7 (G Fierro) *a bhd: t.o last 2f* **200/1**	12

2m 41.71s (7.81) **Going Correction** +0.30s/f (Good)
WFA 3 from 4yo 21lb — 7 Ran SP% **109.2**
Speed ratings (Par 103): **85,83,80,80,68 64,62**
CSF £5.35 TOTE £2.00: £1.10, £2.00; EX 7.00.
Owner D G Clarke & C L A Edginton **Bred** Mrs Denise Brophy **Trained** Lambourn, Berks

FOCUS

An ordinary maiden, but an impressive performance from Enroller, who is rated to his juvenile firm.

1174 LEVY BOARD H'CAP — 7f 9y

5:40 (5:41) (Class 4) (0-85,85) 4-Y-O+ — **£4,209** (£1,252; £625; £312) **Stalls** Low

Form				RPR
50-1	1		**The Osteopath (IRE)**[10] 992 5-8-10 77 6ex PhillipMakin 10 (M Dods) *t.k.h: hld up in tch: hung rt thrght: hdwy 1/2-way: led over 1f out: pushed out* **2/1**[1]	88
000-	2	2	**Guilded Warrior**[154] 6606 5-8-11 85 TimothyMeadows(7) 11 (W S Kittow) *t.k.h: chsd ldrs tl led over 2f out: rdn and hdd over 1f out: nt pce of wnr: eased and nrly lost 2nd nr fin* **9/1**	91
105-	3	nse	**Fifty Cents**[194] 5617 4-8-13 80 SteveDrowne 1 (R Charlton) *stdd s: hld up in rr: swtchd rt after 2f out: hdwy 2f out: kpt on u.p fr over 1f out: nrly snatched 2nd but nvr pce to threaten wnr* **12/1**	86
1-33	4	1 3/4	**Den's Gift (IRE)**[60] 417 4-8-13 80 PhilipRobinson 4 (C G Cox) *led for 2f: chsd ldrs after tl hung rt and outpcd jst over 2f out: kpt on u.p fnl f* **5/1**[3]	81
000-	5	2 1/2	**Bustan (IRE)**[141] 6806 9-8-11 78 RobertWinston 12 (G C Bravery) *in tch: rdn and hdwy 1/2-way: no imp over 1f out* **12/1**	73
310-	6	3/4	**Gilded Youth**[197] 5532 4-8-7 74 FergusSweeney 5 (H Candy) *t.k.h: chsd ldr untl led 5f out: rdn and hdd over 2f out: edgd rt and wknd over 1f out* **25/1**	67
06-4	7	1/2	**Kyle (IRE)**[12] 969 4-8-13 80 RyanMoore 2 (R Hannon) *hld up in tch in rr: rdn and effrt 2f out: no imp* **4/1**[2]	72
-106	8	1	**Sailor King (IRE)**[36] 717 6-9-1 82 JimCrowley 9 (D K Ivory) *in tch: hdwy 3f out: rdn and btn wl over 1f out* **14/1**	71
40-0	9	1 3/4	**Heywood**[12] 958 4-9-3 84 SilvestreDeSousa 3 (D Nicholls) *in tch: rdn 4f out: wknd wl over 2f out* **28/1**	69
133-	10	9	**Dakota Rain (IRE)**[198] 5505 6-8-6 80 JackDean(7) 13 (Jennie Candlish) *t.k.h: chsd ldrs tl rdn and wknd over 2f out: eased ins fnl f* **16/1**	41
020-	11	1/2	**Thabaat**[167] 6301 4-9-1 82 NCallan 7 (J M Bradley) *s.i.s: a bhd* **25/1**	42
5-56	P		**Secret Liaison**[70] 280 5-8-13 80 PaulEddery 8 (Garry Moss) *midfield tl rdn and lost pl qckly 1/2-way: p.u after 2f out: collapsed* **40/1**	—

1m 28.59s (2.39) **Going Correction** +0.525s/f (Yiel) — 12 Ran SP% **121.5**
Speed ratings (Par 105): **107,104,104,102,99 98,98,97,95,84 84,—**
CSF £20.78 CT £183.66 TOTE £2.70: £1.60, £2.80, £2.70; EX 38.30 Trifecta £170.60 Part won. Pool £240.34 - 0.90 winning units. Place 6 £337.56, Place 5 £204.73..
Owner Kevin Kirkup **Bred** Joe Rogers **Trained** Denton, Co Durham

FOCUS

A fair handicap run at a sound gallop with the winner setting the level. They ended up racing middle to far side.

T/Plt: £342.20 to a £1 stake. Pool: £45,120.36. 96.25 winning tickets. T/Qpdt: £66.70 to a £1 stake. Pool: £2,731.72. 30.30 winning tickets. SP

1149 LINGFIELD (L-H)

Friday, April 4

OFFICIAL GOING: Standard

Wind: fresh across Weather: bright partly cloudy

1176 DERBY TRIAL HERE MAY 10TH MAIDEN FILLIES' STKS — 1m 2f (P)

2:10 (2:10) (Class 5) 3-Y-O+ — **£2,590** (£770; £385; £192) **Stalls** Low

Form				RPR
032	1		**Emshabb**[20] 903 3-8-8 0 ow1 RyanMoore 6 (W J Haggas) *s.i.s: hld up in last pair: hdwy over 3f out: chsd ldng pair and wd bnd 2f out: r.o u.p to ld ins fnl f* **11/8**[1]	67+
	2	3/4	**Beautiful Lady (IRE)** 3-8-7 0 TQuinn 5 (P F I Cole) *chsd ldr: rdn wl over 2f out: chal wl over 1f out: kpt on u.p* **11/2**[3]	64
43-2	3	nk	**Dream Sea**[16] 931 3-8-7 67 DarryllHolland 3 (M R Channon) *led at stdy gallop: rdn and qcknd 2f out: hdd ins fnl f: kpt on same pce* **5/2**[2]	64
	4	2 1/2	**Ever Rigg** 3-8-7 0 StephenDonohoe 7 (E A L Dunlop) *s.i.s: hld up in last: effrt and rdn wl over 2f out: styd on fnl f: nt pce to threaten ldrs* **7/1**	59+
40	5	1 1/4	**Princess Raya**[8] 1042 3-8-4 0 KirstyMilczarek(3) 1 (M Botti) *s.i.s: in tch: rdn jst over 2f out: outpcd over 1f out: kpt on same pce* **16/1**	56
6	6	3/4	**Code Violation**[49] 570 3-8-7 0 FrankieMcDonald 4 (Jean-Rene Auvray) *in tch: rdn jst over 2f out: outpcd wl over 1f out: n.d after* **50/1**	55
30	7	1 1/4	**Queen Macha (IRE)**[16] 931 3-8-7 0 HayleyTurner 2 (A M Hales) *trckd ldrs on inner: rdn jst over 2f out: sn outpcd: wknd over 1f out* **20/1**	52

2m 11.58s (4.98) **Going Correction** +0.25s/f (Slow) — 7 Ran SP% **111.2**
Speed ratings (Par 100): **90,89,89,87,86 85,84**
CSF £8.95 TOTE £1.90: £1.10, £5.10; EX 6.80.
Owner W J Haggas **Bred** Darley **Trained** Newmarket, Suffolk

FOCUS

A modest fillies' maiden with a couple of interesting debutantes taking on fillies with experience. The pace was funereal until picking up on the run down to the straight and the time was 6.74secs slower than the later handicap. The winner did not have to improve to score.

1177 EUROPEAN BREEDERS' FUND MAIDEN FILLIES' STKS — 5f (P)

2:45 (2:45) (Class 5) 2-Y-O — **£4,209** (£1,252; £625; £312) **Stalls** High

Form				RPR
	1		**Kate The Great** 2-9-0 0 EddieAhern 6 (M J Wallace) *w'like: lw: on toes: hld up in tch: rdn wl over 1f out: str run to ld on post* **11/4**[3]	73+
	2	nse	**Raggle Taggle (IRE)** 2-9-0 0 SebSanders 4 (R M Beckett) *small: w ldrs: rdn to ld wl over 1f out: kpt on wl tl hdd on post* **9/4**[2]	73
4	3	1 1/4	**Dr Wintringham (IRE)**[6] 1078 2-9-0 0 LPKeniry 5 (J S Moore) *unf: hung rt thrght: w ldr for 1f: lost pl and racd awkwardly bnd jst over 2f out: rallied and swtchd lft jst ins fnl f: styd on: nt pce to rch ldrs* **7/4**[1]	68+
0	4	1	**Amosite**[13] 957 2-9-0 0 JimCrowley 2 (J R Jenkins) *tall: w ldrs on inner: led narrowly jst over 2f out: hdd wl over 1f out: hung rt fnl f: fdd last 50yds* **33/1**	64
0	5	1 3/4	**Alphabeth**[11] 995 2-9-0 0 SamHitchcott 3 (M R Channon) *unf: led tl jst over 2f out: wkng whn sltly hmpd 1f out* **7/1**	57
	6	18	**Maybe Blue** 2-9-0 0 IanMongan 1 (Mrs L J Mongan) *unf: lt-f: sn outpcd: t.o fr 1/2-way* **20/1**	—

59.71 secs (0.91) **Going Correction** +0.25s/f (Slow) — 6 Ran SP% **114.0**
Speed ratings (Par 89): **102,101,99,98,95 66**
CSF £9.63 TOTE £3.20: £1.70, £2.00; EX 10.50.
Owner Anthony Rogers **Bred** Lord Harrington **Trained** Newmarket, Suffolk

■ Kate The Great was Eddie Ahern's first ride since returning from a three-month whip ban.
■ Stewards' Enquiry : Eddie Ahern caution: used whip with excessive frequency

FOCUS

An ordinary juvenile fillies' race run at a decent gallop that produced a very close finish. The form is fairly decent for the time of year.

NOTEBOOK

Kate The Great, who cost 56,000euros as a foal, is out of a mare who won over 7f and 1m as a three-year-old but is clearly much sharper than her dam and, after being held up having been drawn on the outside, responded to strong pressure to get there on the post. Her trainer does well with similar sorts and, open to some improvement, she should be able to win again providing this hard race does not set her back. (op 4-1)

Raggle Taggle(IRE) is a small sprinting type and clearly knew her job. She looked sure to score when going on turning in, lost little in being caught on the post, and should not be long in getting off the mark. (op 15-8)

Dr Wintringham(IRE) was drawn wide and her rider appeared to try to get to the front early. However, that manoeuvre failed and she was forced to sit in behind. She tended to hang right and did not negotiate the home bend that well either but ran on in the straight without getting a clear passage. She too can find another opportunity before long, and possibly a straight track may suit her better. Official explanation: jockey said filly hung right (op 5-2 tchd 11-4)

Amosite is a tall filly who is related to juvenile winners and showed good pace from her inside draw before fading late on. She looks the sort for nurseries later in the season.

Alphabeth, who still looked woolly in her coat, improved on her debut but was fading when short of room in the final furlong. (op 9-2 tchd 8-1)

1178 BACK HERE TOMORROW FILLIES' H'CAP — 6f (P)

3:20 (3:20) (Class 5) (0-95,76) 3-Y-O+ — **£2,590** (£770; £385; £192) **Stalls** Low

Form				RPR
425-	1		**Cinnamon Hill**[158] 6546 4-9-10 68 StephenCarson 4 (Eve Johnson Houghton) *hld up in tch: rdn 2f out: hld hd awkwardly over 1f out: str run ins fnl f to ld fnl 50yds* **5/1**[2]	76
-660	2	nk	**Linda Green**[13] 964 7-8-9 60 MatthewDavies(7) 1 (M R Channon) *hld up in last: rdn and effrt on outer 2f out: r.o wl to press wnr fnl 50yds: hld nr fin* **6/1**[3]	67
52-1	3	1/2	**Feelin Foxy**[11] 987 4-10-4 76 6ex TPQueally 7 (J G Given) *t.k.h: chsd ldr: rdn and led narrowly over 1f out: hdd and no ex fnl 50yds* **9/4**[1]	81
2203	4	3/4	**Maggie Kate**[4] 1110 3-8-7 63 (p) RobertHavlin 2 (R Ingram) *trckd ldrs on inner: rdn and effrt over 1f out: ev ch ins fnl f: no ex fnl 100yds* **13/2**	63
046-	5	3/4	**Forever Changes**[141] 6820 3-8-2 58 HayleyTurner 3 (L Montague Hall) *sn led: rdn and hdd over 1f out: ev ch tl fdd fnl 100yds* **25/1**	55
000-	6	hd	**Penrice Castle**[169] 6282 3-8-10 66 RichardHughes 5 (R Hannon) *t.k.h: stdd s: hld up in tch: nt clr run briefly jst over 1f out: sn rdn and chsng ldrs: no imp fnl 100yds* **9/4**[1]	63

1m 13.71s (1.81) **Going Correction** +0.25s/f (Slow)
WFA 3 from 4yo+ 12lb — 6 Ran SP% **109.7**
Speed ratings (Par 100): **97,96,95,94,93 93**
CSF £32.05 TOTE £6.70: £2.80, £3.30; EX 31.20.
Owner Mrs C J Hue Williams & J C Nowell Smith **Bred** Mrs C J Hue Williams **Trained** Blewbury, Oxon

FOCUS

A modest fillies' sprint handicap that was run at a relatively steady early pace and all six were still in with a chance halfway up the straight. In the end the older filles came out best while the third and fourth set the level.

Penrice Castle Official explanation: jockey said filly suffered interference going into first bend

1179 LINGFIELD PARK FOR WEDDINGS H'CAP — 2m (P)

3:55 (3:55) (Class 2) (0-100,77) 4-Y-O+ — **£10,361** (£3,083; £1,540) **Stalls** Low

Form				RPR
520-	1		**Noddies Way**[165] 6383 5-8-8 60 JimCrowley 3 (J F Panvert) *mde all: reminder sn after s: rdn 4f out: hrd pressed and drvn 2f out: styd on wl* **5/1**[3]	67
0111	2	1 1/4	**Rollin 'n Tumblin**[21] 880 4-8-13 72 KirstyMilczarek(3) 1 (W Jarvis) *stdd s: hld up in last: hdwy on outer jst over 2f out: drvn 1f out: kpt on to go 2nd nr fin: nt pce to chal wnr* **1/2**[1]	78+

1-26 **3** *nk* **Salute (IRE)**[12] 981 9-9-11 77 .... RobertHavlin 4 82
(P G Murphy) *chsd ldr: rdn to chal jst over 2f out: drifted wd and lost grnd bnd 2f out: kpt on same pce u.p* **3/1**[2]

3m 28.68s (2.98) **Going Correction** +0.25s/f (Slow)
WFA 4 from 5yo+ 4lb 3 Ran SP% **108.3**
Speed ratings (Par 109): **102,101,101**
CSF £8.32 TOTE £4.50; EX 9.30.
Owner W Cox **Bred** W Cox **Trained** Stoodleigh, Devon
■ A first Flat winner for trainer John Panvert.

FOCUS
A poor turnout for some decent prizemoney in this Class 2 contest with the top weight rated just 77. The form looks suspect.

NOTEBOOK
Noddies Way, finally lost his maiden tag by making all the running. Given a fine tactical ride by Crowley, he wound up the pace from the top turn and was the first under pressure, but the rider had kept a little up his sleeve and his mount found more to hold off the odds-on favourite. His trainer, for whom this was a first Flat winner, is keen to run the gelding over hurdles again. (op 6-1 tchd 9-2)
Rollin 'n Tumblin had won four of his last five starts, as a result of which his rating has risen 25lb. He got rather lit up under restraint around the halfway mark and, although he appeared to be still going well turning in, he could not pick up enough to reel in the winner. (op 4-7 tchd 4-6 in a place)
Salute(IRE), who has been racing over shorter trips for the last nine months, was on the heels of the leader throughout. However, after looking to be travelling best of all on the run to the straight, failed to pick up as well as looked likely. (op 5-2)

1180 LINGFIELDPARK.CO.UK H'CAP 1m 2f (P)
4:30 (4:30) (Class 2) (0-100,98) 4-Y-0+
£12,462 (£3,732; £1,866; £934; £466; £234) **Stalls** Low

Form RPR
0-12 **1** **Mr Aviator (USA)**[6] 1076 4-9-1 95 .... RichardHughes 6 103+
(R Hannon) *trckd ldrs: shkn up and hdwy over 1f out: rdn to ld ins fnl f: readily* **4/6**[1]
000- **2** *1* **Luberon**[216] 5049 5-9-4 98 .... JoeFanning 1 104
(M Johnston) *led: rdn and hung rt fr over 1f out: hdd ins fnl f: kpt on same pce* **10/1**
1113 **3** *1/2* **Scamperdale**[16] 929 6-8-7 87 .... TPQueally 4 92
(B P J Baugh) *stdd s: hld up in last: hdwy on outer jst over 2f out: ev ch 1f out: sn one pce* **16/1**
/41- **4** *1/2* **Celtic Spirit (IRE)**[15] 3002 5-8-10 90 .... (b[1]) RyanMoore 3 94
(G L Moore) *hld up in tch: rdn 2f out: styd on same pce fnl f* **11/2**[2]
120- **5** *2 1/2* **Jeer (IRE)**[307] 2231 4-8-6 86 .... AlanMunro 2 85
(E A L Dunlop) *hld up in tch: rdn and effrt 2f out: no prog fnl f* **8/1**
05-2 **6** *shd* **Ballinteni**[16] 929 6-8-8 88 .... HayleyTurner 7 87
(Miss Gay Kelleway) *chsd ldr: rdn wl over 2f out: wknd jst over 1f out* **13/2**[3]

2m 4.84s (-1.76) **Going Correction** +0.25s/f (Slow) 6 Ran SP% **114.8**
Speed ratings (Par 109): **117,116,115,115,113 113**
CSF £8.91 TOTE £1.80: £3.00, £2.40; EX 6.60.
Owner Mrs Sue Brendish **Bred** Dr Tom Keenan & Dr H G White Jr **Trained** East Everleigh, Wilts

FOCUS
A decent handicap run at good gallop and the time was 6.74secs faster than the earlier fillies' maiden. The winner did not need to run up to his Kempton form to score and the form is not the most solid.

NOTEBOOK
Mr Aviator(USA) had few problems confirming the impression of a sound effort behind the progressive Philatelist in the Rosebery at Kempton six days earlier after losing a shoe. He was due to go up 3lb for that effort and was always travelling well before being asked to hit the front just inside the final furlong. He handled this track well enough, appears on the upgrade and connections believe he will be up to winning at Listed level on this surface. (op 4-5 tchd 10-11)
Luberon ◆, winner of the Rosebery off this mark last year, ran well on his first outing since September and was soon bowling along in front. He had little problem confirming that Kempton form with the fourth on 7lb better terms but was no match for the winner. He should come on for the run and is on a mark from which he can win. (op 8-1)
Scamperdale was held up in the early stages and brought wide with his effort from the home turn. He is a consistent sort and ran close to Kempton form with the winner from early last month on 6lb better terms. He could well find another race off his current mark. (op 12-1)
Celtic Spirit(IRE), wearing blinkers for the first time, had run well over hurdles on his latest start at Wincanton 15 days earlier and was held up just off the pace. He tried to mount his challenge in the final two furlongs but could only keep on at the same pace and the Handicapper probably just has his measure. (op 9-2 tchd 4-1)
Jeer(IRE) was having his first outing since June of last year and should improve for the run and could do better back on the turf when there is some cut in the ground. (tchd 10-1)
Ballinteni was a little disappointing because he had run well behind the winner at Kempton - with today's third behind - and was 4lb better off for a length and threequarters. He faded in the closing stages and possibly is better going right-handed. (op 15-2 tchd 8-1)

1181 LINGFIELD PARK FOR CONFERENCES H'CAP 1m 5f (P)
5:05 (5:05) (Class 6) (0-65,65) 4-Y-0+ **£2,266** (£674; £337; £168) **Stalls** Low

Form RPR
00-0 **1** **Cavallini (USA)**[92] 28 6-9-9 65 .... RyanMoore 7 71
(G L Moore) *trckd ldrs: drvn to ld wl over 1f out: styd on wl u.p fnl f* **10/3**[2]
-463 **2** *1 1/4* **Best Selection**[7] 1052 4-9-4 62 .... IanMongan 3 66+
(Mrs L J Mongan) *w.w in tch in midfield: shuffled bk and lost pl over 2f out: rallied u.p fnl f: wnt 2nd nr fin: unable to chal wnr* **7/1**
602- **3** *nk* **Bob's Your Uncle**[162] 6453 5-9-2 58 .... JamesDoyle 1 61
(J G Portman) *w.w in tch in midfield: hdwy to chse ldrs over 2f out: chsd wnr u.p ins fnl f: no imp: lost 2nd nr fin* **11/2**[3]
3112 **4** *nk* **Capitalise (IRE)**[7] 1056 5-9-2 58 .... GeorgeBaker 12 61
(V Smith) *stdd s: hld up in rr: hdwy 4f out: chsd ldrs and rdn 2f out: hung lft over 1f out: kpt on but nvr pce to chal wnr* **9/4**[1]
-610 **5** *shd* **Whaxaar (IRE)**[21] 881 4-8-12 56 .... RobertHavlin 9 59
(R Ingram) *stdd after s: t.k.h: hld up towards rr: hdwy 5f out: drvn and ev ch 2f out: unable qckn 1f out: lost 3 pls ins fnl f* **14/1**
166- **6** *1/2* **Adage**[170] 6271 5-9-4 60 .... (t) NeilChalmers 11 62+
(David Pinder) *stdd after s: hld up towards rr: shuffled bk and lost pl over 2f out: hdwy over 1f out: r.o u.p fnl f: nt rch ldrs* **11/1**
5600 **7** *nk* **Spellman**[11] 988 4-8-4 48 .... (b[1]) JoeFanning 5 50
(N P Littmoden) *awkward and slowly away: hld up bhd: c wd and hdwy over 2f out: styd on fnl f: nt trble ldrs* **33/1**
400- **8** *shd* **Great View (IRE)**[191] 5725 9-9-7 63 .... (p) EddieAhern 10 65
(Mrs A L M King) *hld up in tch: lost pl 3f out: styd on steadily u.p fnl f: nvr trbld ldrs* **16/1**
460- **9** *1 1/2* **Bobsleigh**[269] 3397 9-8-4 46 oh1 .... HayleyTurner 8 45
(H S Howe) *sn pushed into ld: rdn and hdd over 2f out: outpcd 2f out: plugged on* **40/1**

0-03 **10** *3/4* **Montosari**[58] 455 9-9-1 57 .... JimCrowley 6 55
(R A Teal) *chsd ldr tl led over 2f out: rdn and jnd 2f out: sn hdd: wknd fnl f* **20/1**
/403 **11** *1 1/4* **Barnbrook Empire (IRE)**[26] 776 6-8-4 46 oh1 .... PaulDoe 2 42
(L A Dace) *stdd s: hld up bhd: n.d* **25/1**
22-6 **12** *1 1/4* **Party Palace**[25] 14 4-8-2 46 oh1 .... AdrianMcCarthy 4 40
(H S Howe) *chsd ldrs: rdn over 2f out: wknd 2f out* **16/1**

2m 48.3s (2.30) **Going Correction** +0.25s/f (Slow)
WFA 4 from 5yo+ 2lb 12 Ran SP% **122.5**
Speed ratings (Par 101): **102,101,101,100,100 100,100,100,99,98 98,97**
CSF £26.87 CT £129.70 TOTE £4.50: £1.40, £2.50, £2.20; EX 38.10.
Owner G L Moore **Bred** Newbiggin Ltd **Trained** Woodingdean, E Sussex

FOCUS
A modest event but a battling performance by the winner with a blanket finish for the places. The form is rated negatively as a result.

1182 ARENALEISUREPLC.COM H'CAP 1m (P)
5:40 (5:40) (Class 5) (0-70,70) 4-Y-0+ **£2,590** (£770; £385; £192) **Stalls** High

Form RPR
4/-2 **1** **Tinnarinka**[36] 736 4-9-3 69 .... RichardHughes 2 77
(R Hannon) *t.k.h: chsd ldr: drifted wd over 1f out: rdn to ld over 1f out: hdd wl ins fnl f: rallied gamely to ld again on post* **9/4**[2]
000- **2** *shd* **Daniel Thomas (IRE)**[179] 6063 6-8-10 62 .... EddieAhern 1 70
(Mrs A L M King) *s.i.s: sn chsng ldrs: rdn and hdwy over 1f out: led wl ins fnl f: hdd on post* **10/1**
3-02 **3** *1 1/4* **Scarlet Flyer (USA)**[7] 1058 5-9-4 70 .... (b) RyanMoore 4 75
(G L Moore) *stdd s: t.k.h: hld up in last: swtchd rt over 1f out: r.o u.p fnl f: nvr pce to threaten ldrs* **11/10**[1]
3102 **4** *6* **Joy And Pain**[8] 1038 7-8-10 62 .... (p) IanMongan 5 53
(M J Attwater) *t.k.h: hld up in tch in last pair: rdn and effrt jst over 2f out: wknd 1f out* **4/1**[3]
-606 **5** *hd* **Sir Liam (USA)**[7] 1056 4-9-0 66 .... (b[1]) JimCrowley 6 57
(R A Teal) *led: rdn 2f out: hdd over 1f out: wknd fnl f* **14/1**

1m 38.8s (0.60) **Going Correction** +0.25s/f (Slow) 5 Ran SP% **114.1**
Speed ratings (Par 103): **107,106,105,99,99**
CSF £22.76 TOTE £2.20: £1.10, £4.20; EX 18.30 Place 6 £ 223.66, Place 5 £ 144.93.
Owner Denis J Barry **Bred** Dr J M Leigh **Trained** East Everleigh, Wilts

FOCUS
They went a decent gallop in this modest handicap but ultimately it took little winning.
T/Plt: £342.90 to a £1 stake. Pool: £41,128.82. 87.55 winning tickets. T/Qpdt: £159.80 to a £1 stake. Pool: £2,484.00. 11.50 winning tickets. SP

[1129] SOUTHWELL (L-H)
Friday, April 4

OFFICIAL GOING: All-weather - standard, turf course - good (7.7)
Wind: Light, behind Weather: Overcast

1183 BETDAQ THE BETTING EXCHANGE MAIDEN AUCTION STKS 5f (F)
2:20 (2:24) (Class 6) 2-Y-0 **£1,774** (£523; £262) **Stalls** High

Form RPR
1 **Bahamian Babe** 2-8-8 0 ow1 .... JamieSpencer 4 78+
(M L W Bell) *a gng best: mde all: shkn up: edgd lft and qcknd clr ins fnl f: readily* **5/4**[1]
2 *5* **Red Cell (IRE)** 2-9-1 0 .... ChrisCatlin 1 59
(E J O'Neill) *w wnr: drvn fr 1/2-way: kpt on u.p fnl f: no imp* **6/4**[2]
3 *1 1/2* **Kings House** 2-8-9 0 .... PaulMulrennan 2 47
(M W Easterby) *dwlt and wnt lft s: sn w ldrs: rdn and no ex over 1f out* **22/1**
4 *11* **Hartshead Flyer (IRE)** 2-8-12 0 .... PatCosgrave 3 6
(M J Wallace) *chsd ldrs: rn green and sn pushed along: lost tch fr 1/2-way* **6/1**[3]

59.39 secs (-0.31) **Going Correction** -0.25s/f (Stan) 4 Ran SP% **103.1**
Speed ratings (Par 90): **92,84,81,64**
CSF £3.08 TOTE £1.60; EX 3.30.
Owner Mrs P D Gray And H J P Farr **Bred** Mrs P D Gray And H Farr **Trained** Newmarket, Suffolk
■ Dispol Bertie (14/1) was withdrawn (very unruly at the start). R4 applies, deduct 5p in the £.

FOCUS
In all probability just ordinary form behind the ready winner, who appeals as the sort to win more races. The pace was sound.

NOTEBOOK
Bahamian Babe ◆, a sister to last year's dual sprint turf winner Victorian Bounty, justified the market support when creating a good impression on her debut. Her stable is going well, she should stay 6f and is the sort to win again. (op 10-11 tchd 7-4)
Red Cell(IRE), out of a mare who won over 7f on turf in Ireland, attracted support and was not disgraced on this racecourse debut. He left the strong impression that the step up to 6f would suit and he is sure to win a race. (op 2-1 tchd 5-4)
Kings House, a cheap purchase as a yearling, was very easy to back but showed ability at a modest level on this racecourse debut. He is entitled to improve for the experience and is sure to be placed to best advantage in due course. (op 14-1)
Hartshead Flyer(IRE), first foal of a half-sister to several winners up to middle distances, was too green to do himself justice on this racecourse debut and was soundly beaten. He should improve for the experience, though. (op 7-1 tchd 15-2)

1184 BET FA CUP - BETDAQ AMATEUR RIDERS' CLAIMING STKS 1m 4f
2:55 (2:57) (Class 6) 4-Y-0+ **£1,714** (£527; £263) **Stalls** Low

Form RPR
000 **1** **Shenandoah Girl**[15] 953 5-10-2 50 .... MrLeeNewnes 8 57
(M D I Usher) *in tch: reminders and rdn briefly 1/2-way: rallied 4f out: effrt over 2f out: led ins fnl f: r.o* **33/1**
62-1 **2** *3/4* **Bedouin Blue (IRE)**[11] 989 5-10-12 72 .... (b) MrSWalker 11 65
(P C Haslam) *hld up: hdwy 4f out: rdn to ld over 1f out: edgd rt and hdd ins fnl f: kpt on u.p* **5/4**[1]
266- **3** *2 3/4* **Court Of Appeal**[219] 4941 11-10-9 66 .... (tp) MissLEllison 12 58
(B Ellison) *prom: hdwy to press ldr after 4f: effrt and disp ld over 1f out: one pce fnl f* **7/2**[2]
450- **4** *nk* **York Cliff**[151] 6697 10-10-4 51 .... MrBenBrisbourne[(5)] 5 58
(W M Brisbourne) *prom: effrt over 2f out: kpt on u.p fnl f* **14/1**
20-6 **5** *3/4* **Ilviz (FR)**[35] 485 6-10-4 52 .... (v[1]) MissVCoates[(7)] 1 58
(Ollie Pears) *t.k.h: led to over 1f out: sn one pce* **28/1**
-650 **6** *5* **Good Cause (IRE)**[57] 461 7-10-11 54 .... MrsMMorris 4 51+
(Mrs S Lamyman) *hld up: hdwy over 4f out: rdn and no imp fr 2f out* **40/1**
3432 **7** *2 1/4* **Starcross Maid**[23] 851 6-10-1 45 .... MrBMMorris[(5)] 7 42
(J F Coupland) *hld up: stdy hdwy 1/2-way: in tch over 3f out: rdn and wkng whn n.m.r briefly over 1f out* **8/1**

0/ 8 5 **Polished**[25] 4593 9-10-2 0 .... MrMDeady(5) 13 35
(K J Burke) *reluctant to enter stalls: bhd: pushed along 5f out: nvr on terms* **33/1**

2500 9 4½ **Ndola**[18] 914 9-11-0 48 ....(v) MissMBryant(7) 2 42
(P Butler) *sn wl bhd: nvr on terms* **50/1**

004- 10 1¼ **Dancewiththestars (USA)**[149] 4516 4-10-0 44 ....(t) MrRBirkett(5) 9 25
(Miss J Feilden) *cl up tl lost pl 5f out: sn btn* **33/1**

400- 11 1 **Next Flight (IRE)**[220] 4925 9-10-6 44 .... MissVBarr(7) 3 30
(R E Barr) *hld up: outpcd over 5f out: n.d* **100/1**

2202 12 2½ **Kanisorn (SWE)**[31] 787 6-10-13 65 ....(bt) MissSBrotherton 14 26
(Mrs R A Carr) *in tch: drvn and outpcd over 4f out: hung lft 3f out: sn btn* **9/2**[3]

2m 41.64s (-0.06) **Going Correction** +0.025s/f (Good)
WFA 4 from 5yo+ 1lb 12 Ran SP% **120.3**
Speed ratings (Par 101): **101,100,98,98,97 94,93,89,86,85 85,83**
CSF £74.12 TOTE £54.90: £9.70, £1.20, £1.40; EX 193.20 Trifecta £221.90 Part won. Pool: £312.64 - 0.20 winning units..The winner was claimed by Gay Kelleway for £5,000. Bedouin Blue was claimed by A Lidderdale for £7,500
Owner M D I Usher **Bred** Julian Czerpak And Robert Cole **Trained** Upper Lambourn, Berks
■ Stewards' Enquiry : Mr Lee Newnes three-day ban: used whip in incorrect place (Apr 26, May 12,19)

FOCUS
The usual mixed bag of ability and a race that was run at just an ordinary gallop but the form looks sound enough rated around the fifth and sixth.

1185 TRY BETDAQ FOR AN EXCHANGE H'CAP 5f (F)
3:30 (3:33) (Class 6) (0-60,62) 4-Y-0+ **£1,774** (£523; £262) **Stalls** High

Form RPR

-430 1 **Jilly Why (IRE)**[29] 806 7-8-12 54 ....(b) JamieSpencer 3 66
(Paul Green) *swtchd lft (out of kickbk) s: hld up in tch: hdwy 2f out: kpt on to ld cl home* **7/1**[3]

4632 2 nse **Bentley**[9] 1028 4-8-10 52 ....(v) DeanMcKeown 8 64
(D Shaw) *w ldr: sn rdn along: led ins fnl f: kpt on: hdd cl home* **8/1**

1121 3 1¾ **Dodaa (USA)**[8] 1037 5-9-1 62 6ex .... AshleyHamblett(5) 5 68
(N Wilson) *slt ld to ins fnl f: kpt on same pce u.p* **6/4**[1]

-222 4 2 **Limonia (GER)**[23] 856 6-8-7 49 .... FergalLynch 13 47+
(Mike Murphy) *dwlt: bhd tl hdwy over 1f out: kpt on fnl f: nrst fin* **12/1**

0510 5 ½ **Montzando**[13] 972 5-8-6 48 ow2 ....(v) GrahamGibbons 1 45
(B R Millman) *prom: drvn along fr 1/2-way: one pce fnl f* **16/1**

2130 6 ½ **Ducal Regancy Red**[11] 987 4-8-2 49 .... KellyHarrison(5) 9 44
(C J Teague) *midfield: drvn and outpcd 1/2-way: rallied over 1f out: no imp* **33/1**

0-13 7 shd **Rann Na Cille (IRE)**[9] 1021 4-9-4 60 .... MickyFenton 12 54
(P T Midgley) *midfield: drvn and outpcd 1/2-way: no imp fr over 1f out* **25/1**

20-1 8 1¼ **Russian Rocket (IRE)**[15] 951 6-9-4 60 .... ChrisCatlin 7 50
(Mrs C A Dunnett) *prom: hrd drvn fr 1/2-way: btn fnl f* **13/2**[2]

0-06 9 ¾ **Polar Force**[44] 625 8-8-8 50 .... DMylonas 10 37
(Mrs C A Dunnett) *sn outpcd and drvn along: no imp fr 1/2-way* **33/1**

2235 10 1½ **Maktavish**[15] 951 9-8-4 46 oh1 ....(b) AndrewElliott 2 28
(R Brotherton) *chsd ldrs tl rdn and wknd over 1f out* **12/1**

060- 11 1 **Missus Molly Brown**[183] 5935 4-8-6 48 ....(b) DaleGibson 4 26
(R A Fahey) *s.s: a outpcd* **40/1**

5441 12 nk **Taboor (IRE)**[9] 1028 10-8-11 53 6ex ....(p) RobertWinston 14 30
(R M H Cowell) *hld up on stands' side: drvn 1/2-way: nvr on terms* **14/1**

045- 13 1¼ **City For Conquest (IRE)**[254] 3853 5-8-4 46 oh1 .... JimmyQuinn 11 19
(John A Harris) *dwlt: a bhd* **66/1**

58.57 secs (-1.13) **Going Correction** -0.25s/f (Stan) 13 Ran SP% **118.5**
Speed ratings (Par 101): **99,98,96,92,92 91,91,89,87,85 83,83,81**
CSF £58.74 CT £128.90 TOTE £8.20: £2.40, £2.20, £1.20; EX 54.50 Trifecta £213.90 Part won. Pool: £301.31 - 0.39 winning units..
Owner Oaklea Racing **Bred** K And Mrs Cullen **Trained** Lydiate, Merseyside
■ Stewards' Enquiry : Dean McKeown two-day ban: used whip with excessive frequency (Apr 18-19)

FOCUS
An ordinary but truly run race in which the principals raced centre to far side. This form should stand up with the winner rated to her winter best.

1186 BETDAQPOKER.CO.UK H'CAP 1m 3f
4:05 (4:06) (Class 6) (0-60,60) 3-Y-0 **£1,774** (£523; £262) **Stalls** Low

Form RPR

4213 1 **Novestar (IRE)**[2] 1147 3-9-0 59 .... KevinGhunowa(3) 8 68
(G J Smith) *mde all: rdn over 2f out: hld on gamely fnl f* **10/3**[1]

000- 2 ¾ **Fantastic Lass**[212] 5140 3-8-5 47 .... RoystonFfrench 10 55
(R A Fahey) *prom: effrt and chsd wnr over 2f out: kpt on fnl f* **18/1**

005- 3 2½ **Graylyn Ruby (FR)**[191] 5736 3-8-13 58 .... LukeMorris(3) 14 61
(J Jay) *hld up: stdy hdwy 1/2-way: effrt over 2f out: edgd lft over 1f out: kpt on fnl f* **6/1**[3]

00-0 4 3 **Ba Dreamflight**[68] 325 3-8-8 50 .... ChrisCatlin 9 48
(H Morrison) *trckd ldrs: effrt over 2f out: no ex over 1f out* **14/1**

50-0 5 2½ **Trip The Light**[13] 976 3-8-3 52 ow5 .... BMcHugh(7) 2 46
(R A Fahey) *hld up: pushed along 5f out: sn outpcd: kpt on fnl f: no imp* **10/1**

004- 6 ¾ **Saturday Boy**[122] 7022 3-8-6 55 .... AndrewHeffernan(7) 13 48
(Paul Green) *cl up tl rdn and wknd wl over 1f out* **16/1**

000- 7 nse **Dance Easily**[162] 6451 3-8-4 46 oh1 .... JimmyQuinn 3 39
(J L Dunlop) *bmpd s: sn midfield: effrt and shkn up over 2f out: sn no imp* **10/1**

000- 8 5 **Pure Scandal**[193] 5680 3-8-12 54 .... DaleGibson 7 38
(M W Easterby) *dwlt: bhd: rdn 4f out: n.d* **20/1**

000- 9 ½ **Illusionary**[252] 3902 3-8-5 47 .... NickyMackay 4 30
(J G Portman) *bmpd s: sn midfield: pushed along over 2f out: sn outpcd* **12/1**

6-33 10 7 **Persistent (IRE)**[13] 976 3-9-1 57 .... MickyFenton 11 29
(P T Midgley) *hld up: drvn over 3f out: hung lft over 2f out: n.d* **4/1**[2]

000- 11 10 **Agon Eyes (USA)**[145] 6776 3-8-5 47 .... TPO'Shea 12 —
(D J Coakley) *hld up: shortlived effrt on outside 4f out: sn btn* **16/1**

00-6 12 ¾ **Moon Spray (USA)**[13] 976 3-8-7 49 .... PaulMulrennan 5 —
(K A Ryan) *midfield: drvn over 3f out: wknd over 2f out* **25/1**

00-6 13 14 **Mr Fantozzi (IRE)**[20] 900 3-9-4 60 .... DMylonas 1 —
(Miss J Feilden) *t.k.h: cl up: hmpd bnd after 2f and n.m.r bnd 4f out: sn wknd* **16/1**

2m 27.81s (0.01) **Going Correction** +0.025s/f (Good) 13 Ran SP% **121.4**
Speed ratings (Par 96): **100,99,97,95,93 93,93,89,89,83 76,76,65**
CSF £67.43 CT £357.34 TOTE £3.80: £1.90, £7.10, £2.30; EX 83.90 Trifecta £154.10 Pool £234.42. 1.08 winning units.
Owner Graham Smith **Bred** Mrs Eithne Thompson **Trained** Six Hills, Leics
■ Stewards' Enquiry : Paul Mulrennan caution: prematurely eased unplaced gelding

FOCUS
A moderate handicap run at an ordinary gallop and those racing prominently held the edge.
Persistent(IRE) Official explanation: jockey said gelding hung left
Mr Fantozzi(IRE) Official explanation: jockey said colt could not handle bends

1187 BET "GRAND NATIONAL" - BETDAQ H'CAP 6f
4:40 (4:42) (Class 6) (0-60,60) 3-Y-0 **£1,774** (£523; £262) **Stalls** Low

Form RPR

660- 1 **Berrymead**[158] 6536 3-8-11 60 .... NSLawes(7) 7 63
(M W Easterby) *hld up bhd ldng gp: effrt and hdwy over 1f out: led and edgd lft ins fnl f: r.o* **15/2**

404- 2 ½ **Piccolo Pete**[184] 5903 3-9-0 56 .... MickyFenton 1 61+
(T P Tate) *trckd ldrs: effrt 2f out: styng on whn nt clr run and swtchd ins fnl f: r.o strly to take 2nd towards fin* **4/1**[3]

000- 3 1¼ **Kingstyle (IRE)**[198] 5526 3-8-8 53 ow1 ....(b[1]) MarkLawson(3) 6 50
(M Brittain) *chsd ldrs: led over 1f out to ins fnl f: kpt on same pce* **14/1**

3143 4 1 **Note Perfect**[24] 849 3-8-11 53 ....(b) DaleGibson 3 47
(M W Easterby) *t.k.h: w ldr: led over 2f out to over 1f out: no ex ins fnl f* **5/2**[1]

0-04 5 hd **Bellas Chicas (IRE)**[11] 993 3-8-8 53 ow3 .... JamieMoriarty(3) 9 46
(P T Midgley) *towards rr: hdwy and hung lft 2f out: kpt on fnl f: nrst fin* **10/1**

-555 6 3¾ **Hold That Call (USA)**[53] 523 3-8-13 55 .... JimmyQuinn 4 36
(A J Chamberlain) *dwlt: bhd: pushed along 1/2-way: no imp fr 2f out* **14/1**

002- 7 5 **Bonny's Babe**[168] 6305 3-8-11 53 ....(t) PaulEddery 5 18
(G D Blake) *t.k.h: prom tl rdn and wknd over 1f out* **7/2**[2]

000- 8 1¾ **Lucky Stream**[198] 5521 3-8-4 46 .... TWilliams 8 6
(M Brittain) *bhd: rdn along 1/2-way: nvr on terms* **25/1**

40-0 9 5 **Nestor Protector (IRE)**[21] 876 3-9-2 58 .... SteveDrowne 2 2
(A B Haynes) *led to over 2f out: wknd over 1f out* **10/1**

1m 17.03s (1.23) **Going Correction** +0.025s/f (Good) 9 Ran SP% **117.9**
Speed ratings (Par 96): **92,91,89,88,88 83,76,74,67**
CSF £38.43 CT £420.74 TOTE £9.20: £2.50, £1.90, £4.50; EX 54.30 Trifecta £329.30 Part won. Pool: £463.87 - 0.39 winning units..
Owner W T Allgood **Bred** W T Allgood And M W Easterby **Trained** Sheriff Hutton, N Yorks

FOCUS
Another moderate handicap and one in which the pace was fair. The form is rated through the third backed up by the fifth.
Hold That Call(USA) Official explanation: jockey said gelding was upset in the stalls and missed the break

1188 TQ.COM 50TH ANNIVERSARY H'CAP 7f
5:15 (5:15) (Class 5) (0-70,70) 4-Y-0+ **£2,456** (£725; £362) **Stalls** Low

Form RPR

1105 1 **Xpres Maite**[10] 1015 5-8-13 65 ....(v) PhillipMakin 11 74
(S R Bowring) *mde all: rdn 2f out: hld on wl fnl f* **9/2**[2]

04-0 2 nk **Messiah Garvey**[11] 990 4-8-7 59 .... SilvestreDeSousa 9 67
(D Nicholls) *t.k.h to post: in tch: effrt over 2f out: hung lft and chsd wnr ins fnl f: kpt on* **4/1**[1]

50-0 3 1 **Sands Of Barra (IRE)**[11] 990 5-8-8 67 .... DonnaCaldwell(7) 2 72+
(I W McInnes) *hld up: hdwy 2f out: r.o strly fnl f: nrst fin* **20/1**

526- 4 ¾ **Poppy's Rose**[178] 6089 4-8-12 64 .... RoystonFfrench 4 67
(I W McInnes) *prom: effrt 2f out: one pce fnl f* **9/1**

000- 5 hd **Five Wishes**[183] 5935 4-8-4 56 oh2 ....(be[1]) AndrewElliott 1 59
(M Dods) *in tch: rdn and outpcd over 2f out: r.o fnl f* **17/2**

2661 6 nk **Winthorpe (IRE)**[10] 1015 8-8-9 68 6ex .... BMcHugh(7) 5 70
(J J Quinn) *in tch: drvn and outpcd over 2f out: kpt on fnl f: nrst fin* **9/1**

602- 7 2½ **Sedgwick**[171] 6258 6-9-1 67 .... PaulEddery 13 65+
(Ian Williams) *stmbld s: bhd tl edgd lft and hdwy fr over 1f out: nvr nrr* **12/1**

1234 8 ½ **Louisiade (IRE)**[31] 791 7-9-1 70 ....(p) RussellKennemore(3) 8 64
(M C Chapman) *hld up on outside: drvn 3f out: nvr rchd ldrs* **16/1**

2061 9 4½ **Elusive Warrior (USA)**[9] 1024 5-8-4 56 6ex ....(p) NeilPollard 3 38
(A J McCabe) *t.k.h: chsd wnr tl wknd over 1f out* **11/2**[3]

3100 10 1½ **Guadaloup**[9] 1024 6-8-4 56 oh3 .... TWilliams 10 34
(M Brittain) *chsd ldrs tl rdn and wknd wl over 1f out* **25/1**

400- 11 10 **Gracie's Gift (IRE)**[184] 5917 6-8-4 56 .... ChrisCatlin 6 7
(A G Newcombe) *bhd: drvn over 2f out: nvr on terms* **6/1**

000- 12 3 **Fan Club**[142] 6816 4-8-4 56 oh1 ....(b) DaleGibson 7 —
(Mrs R A Carr) *s.i.s: t.k.h and sn midfield: hung lft and wknd over 2f out* **40/1**

1m 28.92s (-0.48) **Going Correction** +0.025s/f (Good) 12 Ran SP% **123.0**
Speed ratings (Par 103): **103,102,101,100,100 100,97,96,91,89 78,74**
CSF £23.28 CT £342.86 TOTE £5.10: £2.20, £2.00, £6.20; EX 30.90 TRIFECTA Not won..
Owner Charterhouse Holdings Plc **Bred** S R Bowring **Trained** Edwinstowe, Notts

FOCUS
A run-of-the-mill handicap in which the pace was just fair. The form is rated around the winner and the runner-up backed up by the fourth and fifth.
Sedgwick ◆ Official explanation: jockey said gelding pulled up lame
Guadaloup Official explanation: trainer said mare finished distressed

1189 POCHIN@LONGEATONPLUMBERSCLUB H'CAP 6f
5:50 (5:52) (Class 6) (0-60,64) 4-Y-0+ **£1,774** (£523; £262) **Stalls** Low

Form RPR

5501 1 **After The Show**[11] 994 7-9-8 64 6ex .... ChrisCatlin 10 76
(Rae Guest) *hld up: hdwy 2f out: led ins fnl f: drvn and r.o strly* **8/1**

6161 2 1 **Ever Cheerful**[8] 1038 7-9-0 56 6ex ....(p) SteveDrowne 1 65
(A B Haynes) *prom: effrt over 2f out: kpt on to chse wnr ins fnl f: r.o* **7/2**[2]

2120 3 ½ **Sion Hill (IRE)**[9] 1024 7-8-8 55 ....(p) KellyHarrison(5) 5 62
(John A Harris) *led: rdn over 2f out: hdd ins fnl f: kpt on same pce* **16/1**

2450 4 2¼ **Epidaurian King (IRE)**[13] 964 5-9-4 60 ....(v) DeanMcKeown 6 60
(D Shaw) *hld up: effrt and hdwy over 2f out: no imp ins fnl f* **22/1**

4132 5 hd **The Geester**[9] 1024 4-8-9 51 ow1 ....(b) PhillipMakin 3 51
(S R Bowring) *w ldr: rdn over 2f out: no ex ins fnl f* **3/1**[1]

00-1 6 hd **Invincible Lad (IRE)**[39] 700 4-9-2 58 .... JimmyQuinn 4 57
(E J Alston) *hld up in tch: effrt and hdwy over 1f out: one pce fnl f* **6/1**[3]

6513 7 4 **Wiltshire (IRE)**[37] 718 6-9-1 57 .... MickyFenton 9 43
(P T Midgley) *stdd s: hld up: pushed along over 2f out: n.d* **8/1**

455- 8 1¼ **Soto**[161] 6467 5-9-4 60 .... PaulMulrennan 14 42
(M W Easterby) *bhd: rdn over 2f out: nvr rchd ldrs* **8/1**

06-0 9 3 **Norcroft**[90] 55 6-8-12 54 ....(p) DMylonas 11 27
(Mrs C A Dunnett) *prom tl lost pl wl over 2f out: sn btn* **20/1**

/554 10 1¼ **Ela Aleka Mou**[50] 558 4-9-4 60 ....(b[1]) SaleemGolam 2 29
(Miss D Mountain) *prom: outpcd over 2f out: n.d after* **25/1**

5-36 **11** *1* **Silly Gilly (IRE)**[11] 987 4-8-13 55 AndrewElliott 7 20
(R E Barr) *chsd ldrs tl lost pl over 3f out: sn btn* **25/1**
000- **12** *1 1/2* **Vesuvio**[126] 6979 4-8-8 50 TomEaves 13 11
(C W Thornton) *sn towards rr and drvn along: nvr on terms* **18/1**
1m 15.21s (-0.59) **Going Correction** +0.025s/f (Good) **12 Ran SP% 122.8**
Speed ratings (Par 101): **104,102,102,99,98 98,93,91,87,85 84,82**
CSF £35.56 CT £453.19 TOTE £6.00: £2.80, £2.40, £6.20; EX 35.30 Trifecta £315.80 Part won.
Pool: £444.87 - 0.50 winning units. Place 6 £38.34, Place 5 £18.33.
Owner Miss L Thompson **Bred** Michael Ng **Trained** Newmarket, Suffolk

FOCUS
Mainly exposed performers in this ordinary handicap but a truly run race and this form should stand up despite being limited by the third.
T/Plt: £87.80 to a £1 stake. Pool: £45,358.38. 376.75 winning tickets. T/Qpdt: £181.80 to a £1 stake. Pool: £3,071.65. 12.50 winning tickets. RY

1081 WOLVERHAMPTON (A.W) (L-H)
Friday, April 4

OFFICIAL GOING: Standard
Wind: Light half behind Weather: Fine

1190 BET FA CUP - BETDAQ CLAIMING STKS 5f 20y(P)
6:50 (6:51) (Class 6) 4-Y-0+ **£1,774** (£523; £262) **Stalls Low**

Form RPR
00-1 **1** **Fire Up The Band**[9] 1022 9-9-7 83 AdrianTNicholls 1 92
(D Nicholls) *mde all: clr wl over 1f out: pushed out* **6/5**[1]
345- **2** *6* **Funfair Wane**[169] 6283 9-8-11 66 PaulQuinn 5 61
(D Nicholls) *hld up: hdwy and hung lft over 1f out: tk 2nd cl home: no ch w wnr* **14/1**
300- **3** *nk* **Desperate Dan**[114] 7126 7-9-6 80 (b) SebSanders 4 69
(A B Haynes) *chsd wnr: rdn over 1f out: no imp* **3/1**[2]
4612 **4** *1/2* **Doubtful Sound (USA)**[8] 1040 4-9-0 69 MarkCoumbe(7) 7 68
(John A Harris) *bhd: rdn wl over 1f out: kpt on towards fin* **9/2**
2260 **5** *3 3/4* **Grimes Faith**[10] 1015 5-9-1 68 (b) JamieSpencer 3 49
(K A Ryan) *prom: hung lft fr over 2f out: eased whn btn ins fnl f* **10/3**[3]
61.96 secs (-0.34) **Going Correction** +0.075s/f (Slow) **5 Ran SP% 118.4**
Speed ratings (Par 101): **105,95,94,94,88**
CSF £19.60 TOTE £1.50: £1.10, £9.00; EX 13.90.Fire Up The Band and Funfair Wane were the subjects of friendly claims.
Owner A Barker D Nicholls & S A Short **Bred** Miss A J Rawding And P M Crane **Trained** Sessay, N Yorks

FOCUS
A reasonable claimer, but nothing could go with Fire Up The Band and the time was decent. That said, there are doubts about the placed horses.
Doubtful Sound(USA) Official explanation: jockey said colt hung right
Grimes Faith Official explanation: jockey said gelding hung left

1191 BACK OR LAY AT BETDAQ H'CAP 5f 216y(P)
7:20 (7:20) (Class 5) (0-70,75) 4-Y-0+ **£2,456** (£725; £362) **Stalls Low**

Form RPR
3610 **1** **Royal Envoy (IRE)**[8] 1040 5-8-10 65 TolleyDean(3) 2 82
(D Shaw) *a.p: led wl over 1f out: sn rdn and edgd rt: r.o wl* **6/1**
3446 **2** *3 1/2* **Obe Royal**[6] 1084 4-8-11 70 (b) RichardEvans(7) 8 76
(P D Evans) *s.i.s: hld up: hdwy on ins over 2f out: chsd wnr over 1f out: rdn and edgd lft ins fnl f: no imp* **6/1**
25-1 **3** *4 1/2* **Hammer Of The Gods (IRE)**[8] 1040 8-9-9 75 6ex (bt) RobertWinston 6 66
(G C Bravery) *led: rdn and hdd wl over 1f out: wknd ins fnl f* **6/4**[1]
5106 **4** *2 3/4* **Methaaly (IRE)**[8] 1040 5-9-2 68 (e[1]) SebSanders 5 51
(M Mullineaux) *sn prom: rdn 2f out: wknd wl over 1f out* **10/1**
2651 **5** *nse* **Music Box Express**[7] 1061 4-8-10 67 6ex (t) DanielleMcCreery(5) 4 49
(George Baker) *s.i.s: t.k.h: shortlived effrt on outside over 2f out* **9/2**[3]
3142 **6** *2* **Avontuur (FR)**[7] 1061 6-7-11 56 (p) MCGeran(7) 1 32
(Mrs R A Carr) *s.i.s: hld up: nt clr run wl over 2f out: sn rdn and bhd* **4/1**[2]
004- **7** *7* **Jakeini (IRE)**[222] 4857 5-8-12 64 GrahamGibbons 3 18
(E S McMahon) *sn chsng ldr: wknd over 2f out* **33/1**
-006 **8** *hd* **George The Second**[8] 1037 5-8-6 65 KylieManser(7) 7 18
(Mrs H Sweeting) *hld up in tch: lost pl and swtchd lft over 3f out: sn struggling* **28/1**
1m 14.79s (-0.21) **Going Correction** +0.075s/f (Slow) **8 Ran SP% 122.2**
Speed ratings (Par 103): **104,99,93,89,89 86,77,77**
CSF £44.60 CT £83.32 TOTE £6.30: £2.30, £1.70, £1.10; EX 35.50.
Owner The Circle Bloodstock I Limited **Bred** Northern Lights Bloodstock **Trained** Danethorpe, Notts

FOCUS
A reasonable sprint handicap for the grade, but they finished surprisingly strung out. The winner is better than ever with the runner-up to his recent best.

1192 BETDAQ.CO.UK CLAIMING STKS 1m 1f 103y(P)
7:50 (7:50) (Class 5) 4-Y-0+ **£2,456** (£725; £362) **Stalls Low**

Form RPR
6202 **1** **Climate (IRE)**[6] 1083 9-8-6 60 RichardEvans(7) 3 56+
(P D Evans) *t.k.h: chsd ldr: led wl over 1f out: rdn ins fnl f: eased nr fin* **4/7**[1]
6444 **2** *1 1/4* **Castle Frome (IRE)**[9] 1031 9-8-12 43 (p) PaulFitzsimons 4 49
(A E Price) *hld up: rdn and outpcd wl over 2f out: hdwy over 1f out: kpt on ins fnl f: nt trble wnr* **14/1**
33-0 **3** *nse* **Cadwell**[7] 1064 4-8-7 55 DanielleMcCreery(5) 5 49
(T J Pitt) *hld up in rr: outpcd wl over 2f out: reminder jst over 1f out: hdwy fnl f: nvr nrr* **7/1**[3]
02-0 **4** *6* **Crow's Nest Lad**[78] 190 4-9-0 59 AdamKirby 1 38
(J O'Reilly) *set slow pce: qcknd over 3f out: hdd wl over 1f out: sn rdn: edgd rt ent fnl f: sn wknd* **10/3**[2]
2m 12.47s (10.77) **Going Correction** +0.075s/f (Slow) **4 Ran SP% 105.9**
Speed ratings (Par 103): **55,53,53,48**
CSF £8.25 TOTE £1.40; EX 5.80.
Owner J E Abbey **Bred** Mrs A Naughton **Trained** Pandy, Monmouths

FOCUS
An uncompetitive claimer run at a steady pace and limited by the proximity of the runner-up.
Crow's Nest Lad Official explanation: jockey said gelding moved poorly

1193 BETDAQ THE BETTING EXCHANGE H'CAP 1m 141y(P)
8:20 (8:20) (Class 6) (0-60,66) 3-Y-0 **£2,047** (£604; £302) **Stalls Low**

Form RPR
00-3 **1** **Fujin Dancer (FR)**[24] 848 3-9-1 60 JamieMoriarty(3) 1 76+
(R A Fahey) *a.p: slipped through narrow gap on ins to ld ins fnl f: r.o wl* **5/4**[1]
4460 **2** *4* **Tapas Lad (IRE)**[13] 976 3-8-10 55 (v) KevinGhunowa(3) 3 54
(G J Smith) *led: rdn wl over 1f out: hdd and no ex ins fnl f* **11/1**
5-01 **3** *3/4* **Oceana Blue**[7] 1051 3-9-3 66 6ex (t) DavidProbert(7) 2 64
(A M Balding) *hld up in tch: ev ch over 2f out: rdn over 1f out: one pce* **5/2**[2]
00-3 **4** *nk* **Yakama (IRE)**[11] 998 3-8-4 46 oh1 RichardThomas 9 43
(D J S Ffrench Davis) *hld up and bhd: rdn over 1f out: hdwy fnl f: nrst fin* **6/1**[3]
5645 **5** *nk* **Scientific**[22] 873 3-8-11 53 (v) J-PGuillambert 5 49
(G Prodromou) *hld up towards rr: hdwy on ins over 2f out: rdn over 1f out: kpt on same pce* **9/1**
006- **6** *3 3/4* **Holden Caulfield (IRE)**[162] 6448 3-8-4 46 oh1 ChrisCatlin 4 34
(Mouse Hamilton-Fairley) *hld up towards rr: hdwy over 2f out: rdn wl over 1f out: wknd fnl f* **100/1**
000- **7** *14* **Bahamian Blue (IRE)**[191] 5729 3-9-4 60 JamieSpencer 10 15
(H J L Dunlop) *stdd s: hld up in rr: shortlived effrt on ins wl over 1f out* **12/1**
000- **8** *12* **Love Cat (USA)**[161] 6469 3-8-13 55 FergalLynch 6 —
(K A Ryan) *chsd ldr 2f: wknd over 3f out* **20/1**
00-0 **9** *9* **Whodouthinkur (IRE)**[15] 950 3-8-4 46 oh1 (b[1]) JimmyQuinn 7 —
(Mrs C A Dunnett) *prom: chsd ldr over 6f out tl over 3f out: sn lost pl* **66/1**
0-01 **10** *14* **Ricci De Mare**[15] 950 3-9-4 60 SebSanders 8 —
(A B Haynes) *hld up: hdwy 6f out: chsd ldr over 3f out tl hung rt bnd over 2f out: sn lost pl and eased* **11/1**
1m 52.34s (1.84) **Going Correction** +0.075s/f (Slow) **10 Ran SP% 128.9**
Speed ratings (Par 96): **94,90,89,89,89 85,73,62,54,42**
CSF £19.87 CT £36.56 TOTE £2.70: £1.50, £1.80, £1.70; EX 27.30.
Owner Aidan J Ryan Racing **Bred** Loughtown Stud Ltd **Trained** Musley Bank, N Yorks

FOCUS
A moderate handicap, but it was won in good style by Fujin Dancer, who looks to have a future. The form looks pretty weak, though.
Ricci De Mare Official explanation: jockey said filly never travelled

1194 TRY BETDAQ FOR AN EXCHANGE MEDIAN AUCTION MAIDEN STKS 7f 32y(P)
8:50 (8:53) (Class 6) 3-Y-O **£2,047** (£604; £302) **Stalls High**

Form RPR
1 **Rehabilitation** 3-9-3 0 AdamKirby 7 72+
(W R Swinburn) *hld up in rr: hdwy on ins 2f out: rdn to ld ins fnl f: edgd rt nr fin: r.o* **4/1**[3]
230- **2** *1* **Ink Spot**[195] 5613 3-9-3 78 JamieSpencer 3 69
(M L W Bell) *reminders after s: sn chsng ldr: led 2f out: rdn and edgd lft whn hdd ins fnl f: nt qckn* **10/11**[1]
3 *1 1/2* **Times Vital (IRE)** 3-9-3 0 ChrisCatlin 6 65
(E J O'Neill) *s.i.s: hld up in tch: wnt 2nd over 1f out: rdn and no ex ins fnl f* **8/1**
0-0 **4** *3/4* **Yes Eighteen (IRE)**[20] 909 3-8-12 0 PatrickHills(5) 4 63
(J W Hills) *hld up and bhd: rdn over 2f out: hdwy over 1f out: kpt on ins fnl f: nvr able to chal* **12/1**
24- **5** *11* **Sunny Sprite**[206] 5313 3-9-3 0 AlanMunro 5 33
(J M P Eustace) *prom: lost pl over 2f out: sn bhd* **11/4**[2]
00- **6** *12* **Southwark Newsboy (IRE)**[249] 4028 3-9-3 0 NeilPollard 1 1
(Mrs C A Dunnett) *led: hdd 2f out: sn rdn and wknd* **100/1**
1m 30.8s (1.20) **Going Correction** +0.075s/f (Slow) **6 Ran SP% 118.8**
Speed ratings (Par 96): **96,94,93,92,79 66**
CSF £8.70 TOTE £5.90: £2.20, £1.40; EX 9.00.
Owner Mrs Sue French **Bred** Southill Stud **Trained** Aldbury, Herts
■ Stewards' Enquiry : Adam Kirby one-day ban: careless riding (Apr 18)

FOCUS
A weak maiden rated around the runner-up, but not to his best juvenile form.
Sunny Sprite Official explanation: trainer's rep said gelding moved poorly

1195 BET GRAND NATIONAL - BETDAQ H'CAP 5f 20y(P)
9:20 (9:20) (Class 4) (0-85,85) 4-Y-0+ **£4,209** (£1,252; £625; £312) **Stalls Low**

Form RPR
2201 **1** **Harry Up**[36] 726 7-8-12 79 (p) JamieSpencer 9 89
(K A Ryan) *led after 1f: rdn fnl f: hld on wl* **6/1**
026 **2** *3/4* **Stolt (IRE)**[49] 580 4-8-8 75 JimmyQuinn 6 82
(N Wilson) *t.k.h: a.p: rdn and kpt on ins fnl f* **9/1**
0133 **3** *nk* **Almaty Express**[9] 1033 6-8-11 81 (b) WilliamBuick(3) 4 87
(J R Weymes) *led 1f: chsd wnr: rdn and ev ch 1f out: nt qckn towards fin* **15/2**
5511 **4** *1/2* **Sands Crooner (IRE)**[16] 939 5-8-7 77 (v) TolleyDean(3) 5 81
(D Shaw) *s.i.s: outpcd: swtchd rt wl over 1f out: sn rdn: hdwy fnl f: r.o* **11/1**
1433 **5** *nk* **Distinctly Game**[17] 925 6-9-3 84 FergalLynch 8 87
(K A Ryan) *outpcd: hdwy jst over 1f out: sn rdn: kpt on ins fnl f* **5/1**[3]
1-43 **6** *1 3/4* **First Order**[12] 983 7-9-4 85 (v) TomEaves 7 82
(Miss L A Perratt) *hld up: lost pl 3f out: shortlived effrt 2f out* **7/2**[2]
/33- **7** *1/2* **Jimmy The Guesser**[437] 227 5-8-11 81 (p) KirstyMilczarek(3) 3 76
(N P Littmoden) *t.k.h: hdwy 2f out: fdd fnl f* **7/1**
5343 **8** *nse* **Misaro (GER)**[2] 1146 7-8-7 77 (b) KevinGhunowa(3) 1 72
(R A Harris) *prom tl wknd wl over 1f out* **10/3**[1]
61.89 secs (-0.41) **Going Correction** +0.075s/f (Slow) **8 Ran SP% 118.9**
Speed ratings (Par 105): **106,104,104,103,103 100,99,99**
CSF £60.22 CT £417.54 TOTE £6.30: £1.90, £1.70, £2.30; EX 134.60 Place 6 £ 35.23, Place 5 £ 17.60.
Owner The Fishermen **Bred** J E Rose **Trained** Hambleton, N Yorks

FOCUS
A competitive handicap run at a good pace. The first three were prominent throughout and the form looks solid rated around those in the frame behind the winner.
T/Plt: £19.30 to a £1 stake. Pool: £72,595.73. 2,738.80 winning tickets. T/Qpdt: £13.50 to a £1 stake. Pool: £5,669.50. 310.34 winning tickets. KH

1196 - 1197a (Foreign Racing) - See Raceform Interactive

[1094]DUNDALK (A.W) (L-H)

Friday, April 4

OFFICIAL GOING: Standard

1198a MARSHES SHOPPING CENTRE RACE — 5f
7:40 (7:41) 3-Y-O+ **£10,052** (£2,949; £1,405; £478)

RPR

1 **An Tadh (IRE)**[28] 829 5-9-9 106 .... JMurtagh 2 104
(G M Lyons, Ire) *trckd ldrs in 3rd: rdn to chal and ld ins fnl f: styd on wl* **3/1**[2]

2 *1* **Knot In Wood (IRE)**[13] 959 6-9-9 .... (p) PaulHanagan 5 100
(R A Fahey) *trckd ldr in 2nd: rdn to chal and on terms fr over 1f out: hdd and kpt on same pce ins fnl f* **2/1**[1]

3 *2 ½* **Flash McGahon (IRE)**[166] 6363 4-9-9 97 .... (b) MJKinane 1 91
(John M Oxx, Ire) *sn led: strly pressed and jnd fr over 1f out: hdd and dropped to 3rd ins fnl f: no ex* **3/1**[2]

4 *1 ½* **Johnstown Lad (IRE)**[16] 943 4-9-2 89 .... (t) MHarley(7) 6 86
(Niall Moran, Ire) *chsd ldrs in 4th: no ex u.p fr over 1f out* **4/1**[3]

5 *3 ½* **Parc Aux Boules**[637] 5975 7-9-9 .... FMBerry 4 71
(John C McConnell, Ire) *in tch in rr: no ex u.p fr over 1f out* **50/1**

59.10 secs (59.10)
WFA 3 from 4yo+ 11lb — 6 Ran SP% **105.3**
CSF £8.53 TOTE £4.00: £2.10, £1.30; DF 7.10.

Owner Vincent Gaul **Bred** Gainsborough Stud Management L **Trained** Dunsany, Co. Meath

FOCUS
A decent little sprint. The form makes sense.

NOTEBOOK
An Tadh(IRE), who failed to stay over 1m on his seasonal bow in March, showed his true colours on this drop back to the minimum trip - the shortest distance he has raced over - and did the job readily. He is best kept to sprint distances this year and, a Group 3 winner at 7f, will prove worthy of respect when stepping back into Group races in due course.

Knot In Wood(IRE), who has been campaigned in Group and Listed races of late, had the cheekpieces left off for this drop back a furlong and return to the All-Weather in this lower-grade event. He showed much-improved form in defeat and finished a clear second best, but simply found the winner too good. (op 7/4)

Flash McGahon(IRE) was not disgraced on this seasonal bow and should come on a good deal for the outing. He probably needs another furlong to be at his very best, however.

1199a IRISH STALLION FARMS EUROPEAN BREEDERS FUND SALSABIL STKS (LISTED RACE) — 1m 2f 150y
8:10 (8:11) 3-Y-O+ **£33,507** (£9,830; £4,683; £1,595)

RPR

1 **Truly Mine (IRE)**[5] 1104 4-9-11 103 .... PJSmullen 1 97
(D K Weld, Ire) *trckd ldr in 2nd: rdn to chal and ld 1 1/2f out: styd on wl* **8/1**[3]

2 *nk* **Allicansayis Wow (USA)**[189] 5784 3-8-7 98 .... DJMoran 4 98
(J S Bolger, Ire) *towards rr: clsr in 4th bef st: 2nd and styd on wl u.p fr under 1f out: nt rch wnr* **11/1**

3 *½* **Queen Of France (USA)**[182] 5998 4-9-11 93 .... JMurtagh 3 95
(David Wachman, Ire) *in rr: 5th 2f out: rdn to go 3rd under 1f out: kpt on wout threatening* **11/1**

4 *1 ½* **Flying Clarets (IRE)**[10] 1018 5-9-11 .... PaulHanagan 5 92
(R A Fahey) *sn led: rdn bef st: hdd 1 1/2f out: dropped to 4th and no ex ins fnl f* **2/1**[2]

5 *nk* **Simawa (IRE)**[153] 6657 3-8-7 .... MJKinane 6 94
(John M Oxx, Ire) *trckd ldrs: 3rd bef st: swtchd to outer and briefly short of room under 2f out: sn no imp u.p: kpt on same pce* **11/10**[1]

6 *8* **Via Mantua**[34] 5959 4-9-11 78 .... (b[1]) DPMcDonogh 2 76
(P J Rothwell, Ire) *sn settled towards rr: rdn appr st: no ex fr under 2f out* **20/1**

7 *3* **Nora Chrissie (IRE)**[7] 1099 6-9-11 70 .... (b) MHarley 7 71
(Niall Moran, Ire) *trckd ldrs: 3rd appr st: sn lost pl u.p: no ex fr under 2f out* **25/1**

2m 14.5s (134.50)
WFA 3 from 4yo+ 20lb — 7 Ran SP% **117.3**
CSF £90.50 TOTE £7.90: £3.60, £5.30; DF 71.40.

Owner Mrs C L Weld **Bred** Sir E J Loder **Trained** The Curragh, Co Kildare

FOCUS
A fair renewal of this fillies' Listed prize, which had been run in previous years at Navan. The form is rated around the runner-up.

NOTEBOOK
Truly Mine(IRE), with the blinkers abandoned, bounced back from her lacklustre effort on heavy ground at the Curragh five days previously and just did enough to get up. The decent pace over this longer trip proved very much to her liking and she is a smart filly on her day, but she will need to improve on this again if she is to strike in Group company this year. This will have boosted her potential paddock value nicely as she is currently in-foal. Official explanation: trainers' rep said, regarding the improved form, filly ran free with blinkers and did not last home on the testing ground on her last run, but returned to form today and enjoyed the different surface (op 13/2)

Allicansayis Wow(USA), taking a big step up in trip, was racing without any headgear on this first outing since September. She turned in a very pleasing effort, staying the distance without fuss, and should come on a deal for the run. (op 10/1)

Queen Of France(USA), given a very patient ride, ultimately left the impression she would benefit for this seasonal return and should prove a good bit sharper next time out. (op 12/1)

Flying Clarets(IRE), stepping up from handicaps on this All-Weather debut, set off at a brisk pace in front and not that surprisingly paid the price at the business end. She has been held in all three attempts in this class, but she still performed below her recent level. (op 7/4)

Simawa(IRE), well backed, was having her first outing since winning her maiden back in November last year. She failed to make a serious impact in the race and has to rate as somewhat disappointing, although it would be unwise to write her off just yet as her stable has yet to hit top gear. (op 6/4)

1200 - 1202a (Foreign Racing) - See Raceform Interactive

[1162]KEMPTON (A.W) (R-H)

Saturday, April 5

OFFICIAL GOING: Standard
Wind: Moderate, acoss Weather: showery, chilly

1203 SUNBURY CLAIMING STKS — 7f (P)
6:20 (6:22) (Class 6) 3-Y-O **£2,047** (£604; £302) **Stalls** High

Form — RPR

4111 1 **Dhhamaan (IRE)**[8] 1063 3-9-7 80 .... (b) SebSanders 6 79
(Mrs R A Carr) *mde all at ordinary gallop: qcknd over 1f out: hrd pressed ins fnl f: hld on wl u.p* **2/1**[1]

3602 2 *1* **Rockfield Lodge (IRE)**[8] 1063 3-9-1 75 .... JerryO'Dwyer(3) 1 73
(J A Osborne) *stdd in tch: hdwy 2f out: rdn and ev ch ins fnl f: edgd rt: no ex towards fin* **11/4**[2]

4033 3 *5* **Little Knickers**[8] 1063 3-8-11 68 .... HayleyTurner 3 53
(Andrew Reid) *hld up in tch: outpcd over 2f out: swtchd lft and rallied over 1f out: no imp fnl f* **11/1**[3]

36-2 4 *2 ¾* **Clifton Four (USA)**[33] 772 3-8-9 65 .... RyanMoore 2 43
(R Hannon) *cl up: rdn and hung lft 2f out: sn wknd* **2/1**[1]

4166 5 *6* **Snow Bounty**[8] 1051 3-9-0 60 .... (p) LPKeniry 4 32
(J S Moore) *rrd s: t.k.h: trckd ldrs tl rdn and wknd fr 2f out* **16/1**

1m 27.94s (1.94) **Going Correction** +0.225s/f (Slow) — 5 Ran SP% **107.5**
Speed ratings (Par 96): **97,95,90,87,80**
CSF £7.39 TOTE £3.00: £1.40, £2.00; EX 6.70.Rockfield Lodge was claimed by Michael Wigham for £14,000.

Owner S B Clark **Bred** D Veitch And Musagd Abo Salim **Trained** Stillington, N Yorks

FOCUS
This was a virtual re-run of a race run at Wolverhampton in late March, as the first three finished in the same order then. The form could go a bit higher but there is nothing solid about the others.

1204 MICHAEL SMALL 21ST BIRTHDAY CLAIMING STKS — 6f (P)
6:50 (6:50) (Class 6) 3-Y-O+ **£2,047** (£604; £302) **Stalls** High

Form — RPR

4223 1 **Red Rudy**[19] 915 6-9-8 70 .... SebSanders 4 77+
(A W Carroll) *awkward leaving stalls and slowly away: t.k.h: hld up in last: hdwy 3f out: pushed along and gd hdwy 2f out: led 1f out: rdn out* **6/4**[1]

006- 2 *¾* **Honey Monster (IRE)**[161] 6502 3-8-9 68 .... SCreighton(5) 5 76
(Miss V Haigh) *racd in 3rd pl tl dropped to last and outpcd wl over 2f out: rdn and hdwy wl over 1f out: wnt 2nd ins fnl f: nt trble wnr* **10/1**[3]

0535 3 *2 ½* **Goodbye Cash (IRE)**[28] 839 4-9-1 60 .... TGMcLaughlin 1 60
(P D Evans) *t.k.h: chsd ldr: rdn over 2f out: kpt on same pce* **4/1**[2]

5230 4 *1 ½* **Angel Voices (IRE)**[22] 887 5-8-10 66 .... (p) DeclanCannon(7) 3 57
(K R Burke) *led: rdn and qcknd over 2f out: hdd 1f out: wknd ins fnl f* **6/4**[1]

1m 13.9s (0.80) **Going Correction** +0.225s/f (Slow)
WFA 3 from 4yo+ 12lb — 4 Ran SP% **109.1**
Speed ratings (Par 101): **103,102,98,96**
CSF £14.51 TOTE £2.30; EX 11.90.

Owner Winding Wheel Partnership **Bred** Mrs C J Tribe **Trained** Cropthorne, Worcs

FOCUS
A modest claimer run at a modest early pace but the time was decent. The runner-up is the best guide but it is hard to have the race any higher.

1205 DIGIBET MAIDEN STKS — 1m 4f (P)
7:20 (7:20) (Class 5) 3-Y-O+ **£2,456** (£725; £362) **Stalls** Centre

Form — RPR

2-42 1 **Flash Of Colour**[8] 1059 3-8-7 77 .... JimCrowley 1 79+
(Mrs A J Perrett) *wnt lft s and slowly away: hdwy to chse ldr after 1f: shkn up to ld over 2f out: sn rdn clr: eased ins fnl f* **6/5**[1]

2 *4 ½* **Victoria Montoya** 3-7-13 0 .... WilliamBuick(3) 4 64+
(A M Balding) *dwlt and v.s.a: rn green in rr: hdwy and in tch 3f out: outpcd over 2f out: kpt on to chse wnr ins fnl f: nvr able to chal* **14/1**

00- 3 *6* **Hampton Court**[161] 6494 3-8-7 0 .... JoeFanning 2 59
(M Johnston) *chsd ldrs: rdn over 2f out: chsd clr wnr jst over 2f out: no imp: lost 2nd ins fnl f* **4/1**[3]

25-2 4 *5* **Spanish Diva**[19] 919 4-9-8 70 .... JamieSpencer 5 46
(S C Williams) *led tl rdn and hdd over 2f out: sn outpcd and btn* **2/1**[2]

00- 5 *4* **Pay The Grey**[187] 5858 3-7-9 0 .... CharlesEddery(7) 6 40
(R Hannon) *a bhd: lost tch 4f out: t.o* **33/1**

/00- 6 *109* **Garrya**[148] 6751 4-9-13 28 .... (v[1]) TGMcLaughlin 3 —
(B P J Baugh) *chsd ldrs: rdn 1/2-way: lost pl 6f out: t.o last 3f* **100/1**

2m 36.46s (1.96) **Going Correction** +0.225s/f (Slow)
WFA 3 from 4yo 21lb — 6 Ran SP% **109.4**
Speed ratings (Par 103): **102,99,95,91,89** —
CSF £18.08 TOTE £2.00: £1.40, £3.20; EX 17.20.

Owner S Barnett, J Deer, R Doel and T Wellard **Bred** D J And Mrs Deer **Trained** Pulborough, W Sussex

FOCUS
A fair maiden won by a progressive sort who was value for seven lengths and his previous form is sound.

1206 DIGIBET CASINO H'CAP — 1m 4f (P)
7:50 (7:50) (Class 6) (0-55,54) 4-Y-O+ **£2,047** (£604; £302) **Stalls** Centre

Form — RPR

1144 1 **Lough Beg (IRE)**[23] 874 5-9-0 **54** .... (t) DaneO'Neill 10 65
(Miss Tor Sturgis) *trckd ldrs: hdwy to chse ldr gng wl 2f out: rdn to ld over 1f out: clr ins fnl f: eased towards fin* **13/2**

-030 2 *3* **Nanosecond (USA)**[10] 1031 5-8-8 **48** .... (p) JamieSpencer 12 54
(S A Callaghan) *hld up in midfield: hdwy over 2f out: swtchd rt jst over 1f out: chsd wnr ins fnl f: no imp* **7/2**[1]

0336 3 *½* **Amwell Brave**[38] 720 7-8-11 **54** .... WilliamBuick(3) 2 59
(J R Jenkins) *stdd stat: hld up bhd: hdwy on outer over 3f out: rdn over 2f out: styd on to chse ldng pair ins fnl f: nvr trbld wnr* **13/2**

46-0 4 *1 ¼* **Summer Bounty**[17] 934 12-8-12 **52** .... TGMcLaughlin 1 55
(F Jordan) *stdd s and dropped in bhd: hld up towards rr: hdwy over 2f out: kpt on u.p fnl f: nvr gng pce to rch ldrs* **22/1**

2130 5 *shd* **Ben Bacchus (IRE)**[12] 999 6-8-10 **50** .... ChrisCatlin 6 53
(P W Hiatt) *t.k.h: rdn and unable qckn wl over 2f out: sn swtchd lft: kpt on u.p but nvr gng pce to threaten ldrs* **10/1**

-000 6 *¾* **Lay The Cash (USA)**[8] 1052 4-8-7 **48** .... (vt[1]) JamesDoyle 11 50
(B G Powell) *led for 1f: chsd ldr after: ev ch and drvn over 2f out: outpcd over 1f out* **33/1**

05-0 **7** ¾ **Laurentian Lad**[21] 909 4-8-9 **50**.................................... SaleemGolam 3 51
(Rae Guest) *in tch: rdn and lost pl over 3f out: kpt on again u.p ins fnl f* **20/1**

1254 **8** *nse* **Sahf London**[41] 695 5-9-0 **54**............................(b) FergusSweeney 5 55
(G L Moore) *t.k.h: hld up in tch in midfield: hdwy to chse ldrs over 4f out: led over 2f out: sn rdn: hdd over 1f out: fdd fnl f* **4/1**[2]

/000 **9** 1¼ **Shami**[10] 1025 9-8-5 **45**...(bt) JoeFanning 9 44
(Mrs R A Carr) *stdd s: t.k.h: hld up bhd: detached last wl over 3f out: kpt on u.p fnl f: n.d* **25/1**

-326 **10** *nk* **Niqaab**[70] 317 4-8-12 **53**.. RichardHughes 7 51
(W J Musson) *hld up in midfield: rdn 4f out: nvr able to chal* **6/1**[3]

44-1 **11** 2½ **Tiegs (IRE)**[24] 269 6-8-9 **49**.. JimCrowley 4 43
(P W Hiatt) *dwlt: hdwy to ld after 1f: rdn and hdd over 2f out: wknd over 1f out* **9/1**

2m 39.28s (4.78) **Going Correction** +0.225s/f (Slow)
WFA 4 from 5yo+ 1lb **11** Ran SP% **118.2**
Speed ratings (Par 101): **93,91,90,89,89 89,88,88,87,87 86**
CSF £28.16 CT £156.91 TOTE £9.40: £2.70, £1.70, £2.40; EX 33.30.
Owner M M McGrogan **Bred** Joe Fogarty **Trained** Lambourn, Berks
■ Stewards' Enquiry : James Doyle caution: careless riding.

FOCUS
A very moderate handicap but the form looks fairly sound with the four immediately behind the winner close to recent form.
Sahf London Official explanation: jockey said gelding ran too free

1207 DIGIBET SPORTS BETTING H'CAP 1m (P)
8:20 (8:20) (Class 6) (0-52,59) 4-Y-0+ **£2,047** (£604; £302) **Stalls** High

Form RPR

6340 **1** **Jomus**[37] 728 7-8-9 **49**.. PatDobbs 12 59
(L Montague Hall) *taken down early: stdd s: hld up in rr: hdwy 2f out: swtchd lft and shkn up wl over 1f out: qckdn to ld 1f out: sn in command: pushed out* **9/1**

3605 **2** 1½ **Postmaster**[3] 1142 6-8-9 **49**.. RobertHavlin 7 56+
(R Ingram) *hld up towards rr: hdwy and nt clr run over 2f out: rdn and hdwy over 1f out: chsd wnr ins fnl f: nt trble wnr* **5/1**[2]

02-0 **3** ¾ **Bold Phoenix (IRE)**[31] 795 7-8-6 **46**..........................(b) JamieSpencer 3 51+
(A P Stringer) *hld up in rr: plld out and rdn 2f out: r.o to go 3rd ins fnl f: nvr gng pce to threaten wnr* **10/3**[1]

030/ **4** ¾ **Shropshirelass**[37] 6700 5-8-9 **49**.................................... JimCrowley 2 52
(Norma Twomey) *in tch: hdwy to chse ldrs over 2f out: rdn 2f out: one pce u.p fnl f* **33/1**

006- **5** *hd* **The Graig**[247] 4106 4-8-3 **50**.. StacyRenwick(7) 5 53
(J R Holt) *chsd ldr tl over 5f out and again over 2f out: one pce u.p fnl f* **100/1**

6050 **6** *nse* **Mister Benji**[23] 872 9-8-6 **46**...................................(p) JoeFanning 14 49
(B P J Baugh) *led: rdn over 2f out: hdd 1f out: one pce after* **14/1**

0502 **7** ½ **Grenane (IRE)**[8] 1064 5-9-5 **59**................................ TGMcLaughlin 10 61
(P D Evans) *hld up in midfield: hdwy on inner and nt clr run over 2f out: swtchd rt and effrt 2f out: chsd ldrs over 1f out: no ex fnl f* **5/1**[2]

40-4 **8** ¾ **Da Bookie (IRE)**[31] 795 8-8-9 **49**..............................(tp) LPKeniry 13 49+
(Jean-Rene Auvray) *stdd s: hld up in rr: hdwy on inner and nt clr run jst over 2f out: rdn over 1f out: kpt on: nvr able to chal* **10/1**

0-00 **9** 3 **Bodden Bay**[10] 1029 6-8-10 **50**..................................... PatrickMathers 11 43
(I W McInnes) *taken down early: chsd ldrs: rdn over 2f out: wknd over 1f out* **50/1**

000- **10** 2½ **Edgefour (IRE)**[228] 4684 4-8-10 **50**........................... RichardKingscote 9 37
(B I Case) *chsd ldrs: rdn over 2f out: wknd wl over 1f out* **66/1**

500- **11** *nk* **Major League (USA)**[207] 5303 6-8-12 **52**.................(t) FergusSweeney 6 38
(W S Kittow) *hld up in midfield: rdn and effrt jst over 2f out: no imp* **12/1**

-006 **12** 1¾ **Korty**[31] 795 4-8-7 **47**...(t) ChrisCatlin 8 29
(W J Musson) *in tch: rdn 2f out: wknd over 1f out* **16/1**

/006 **13** 5 **King Of Diamonds**[68] 332 7-8-8 **48**............................ JamesDoyle 4 19
(Norma Twomey) *chsd ldrs: wnt 2nd over 5f out tl over 2f out: sn wknd* **12/1**

003- **14** *dist* **Foreign Edition (IRE)**[157] 6582 6-8-12 **52**................... JimmyQuinn 1 —
(Miss J A Camacho) *racd in midfield on outer tl lost pl 1/2-way: wl bhd and virtually p.u last 2f* **8/1**[3]

1m 41.2s (1.40) **Going Correction** +0.225s/f (Slow) **14** Ran SP% **121.9**
Speed ratings (Par 101): **102,100,99,99,98 98,98,97,94,92 91,89,84,—**
CSF £53.70 CT £190.91 TOTE £12.70: £3.10, £2.20, £1.70; EX 52.40.
Owner B H Page **Bred** W And R Barnett Ltd **Trained** Epsom, Surrey

FOCUS
A very moderate handicap won by a horse who had previously made a habit of losing. The form looks questionable.
Bold Phoenix(IRE) Official explanation: jockey said gelding hung both ways
Edgefour(IRE) Official explanation: jockey said filly was denied a clear run
King Of Diamonds Official explanation: jockey said gelding hung right
Foreign Edition(IRE) Official explanation: vet said gelding finished distressed

1208 PANORAMIC BAR & RESTAURANT LOYALTY SCHEME H'CAP 1m (P)
8:50 (8:52) (Class 4) (0-80,82) 3-Y-0 **£4,209** (£1,252; £625; £312) **Stalls** High

Form RPR

50-1 **1** **Commander Cave (USA)**[31] 796 3-9-7 **80**.................. RichardHughes 1 89+
(R Hannon) *mde all: shkn up and qcknd clr 2f out: in n.d after* **15/2**

055- **2** 1¾ **Totally Focussed (IRE)**[240] 4323 3-8-9 **68**....................... IanMongan 8 72
(S Dow) *t.k.h: hld up in rr: c wd and gd hdwy over 2f out: chsd wnr and edgd rt fr over 1f out: r.o: nt trble wnr* **66/1**

1- **3** 3¼ **Crosstar**[120] 7051 3-9-7 **80**.. JimmyQuinn 9 77
(M Botti) *stdd s: hld up towards rr: hdwy into midfield over 3f out: rdn over 2f out: wnt 3rd ins fnl f: nvr gng pce to trble ldng pair* **9/1**

120- **4** 2 **Mizooka**[196] 5613 3-8-13 **72**... JamesDoyle 7 64
(R M Beckett) *chsd ldrs: rdn to chse wnr briefly 2f out: sn wl outpcd* **6/1**[3]

0-11 **5** ½ **Gallic Charm (IRE)**[37] 737 3-9-4 **77**............................ JamieSpencer 10 68
(D R C Elsworth) *stdd s: plld hrd: hld up in rr: swtchd lft and rdn over 2f out: no rspnse* **3/1**[2]

436- **6** 1¼ **Summon Up Theblood (IRE)**[191] 5749 3-9-4 **77**.... CatherineGannon 5 65
(M R Channon) *stdd s: t.k.h: hdwy to chse ldrs 1/2-way: rdn over 2f out: sn wl outpcd* **20/1**

003- **7** 1 **Black Or Red (IRE)**[127] 6980 3-8-12 **71**........................ JimCrowley 11 57
(I A Wood) *hld up in rr: rdn over 2f out: no hdwy* **18/1**

5631 **8** ½ **Canary Islands**[8] 1057 3-9-9 **82**................................... TGMcLaughlin 4 67
(E A L Dunlop) *in tch: rdn 2f out: sn wl outpcd and wl btn* **2/1**[1]

460- **9** 3¾ **Always Brave**[183] 5984 3-8-9 **68**.................................. JoeFanning 6 44
(M Johnston) *t.k.h: plld hrd: sn chsng ldr: rdn and wknd qckly 2f out* **20/1**

1m 40.52s (0.72) **Going Correction** +0.225s/f (Slow) **9** Ran SP% **110.7**
Speed ratings (Par 100): **105,103,100,98,97 96,95,94,91**
CSF £402.59 CT £4258.40 TOTE £6.70: £1.90, £11.10, £2.20; EX 617.60.
Owner Sir David Seale **Bred** R D Hubbard **Trained** East Everleigh, Wilts

FOCUS
A fair maiden won in good style by Commander Cave. The form should be fairly solid despite a couple of well-fancied horses running below par and the placed horses showing some improvement.
Always Brave Official explanation: jockey said gelding ran too free

1209 KEMPTON FOR WEDDINGS H'CAP 7f (P)
9:20 (9:20) (Class 6) (0-60,60) 4-Y-0+ **£2,047** (£604; £302) **Stalls** High

Form RPR

1610 **1** **Jessica Wigmo**[17] 937 5-8-5 **54**................................ MarkCoumbe(7) 14 62
(A W Carroll) *hld up towards rr on inner: hdwy over 2f out: swtchd lft over 1f out: rdn and qcknd to ld wl ins fnl f: pushed out* **10/1**

000- **2** ¾ **Forced Upon Us**[105] 7227 4-9-3 **59**.....................(b) RichardHughes 11 65
(P J McBride) *chsd ldrs: rdn 2f out: led jst ins fnl f: hdd and unable qckn wl ins fnl f* **7/1**

00-4 **3** *nk* **Franksalot (IRE)**[19] 916 8-9-0 **56**.......................... PatrickMathers 3 61
(I W McInnes) *dropped in after s: hld up in rr: rdn and effrt over 2f out: r.o wl to go 3rd wl ins fnl f: nt rch ldng pair* **14/1**

4136 **4** ¾ **Aggbag**[24] 861 4-8-7 **56**...................................... DeclanCannon(7) 12 59
(B P J Baugh) *chsd ldrs: rdn and unable qck jst over 2f out: rallied fnl f: kpt on* **12/1**

2005 **5** ½ **Film Queen (IRE)**[8] 1049 4-8-10 **52**................................ JamesDoyle 8 54
(B G Powell) *in tch: hdwy 4f out: rdn 3f out: ev ch over 1f out: unable qckn ins fnl f* **20/1**

-060 **6** ½ **Tamino (IRE)**[44] 639 5-9-4 **60**..(t) JimmyQuinn 7 60
(P Howling) *sn led: hrd pressed and rdn over 2f out: hhd jst ins fnl f: one pce* **12/1**

2314 **7** *hd* **Solicitude**[50] 571 5-9-2 **58**..(p) RobertHavlin 13 58
(D Haydn Jones) *hld up in midfield on inner: hdwy on inner over 2f out: chsd ldrs over 1f out: no ex fnl f* **9/2**[2]

65-6 **8** 1½ **Wadnagin (IRE)**[47] 609 4-9-4 **60**...................................... JimCrowley 2 59+
(I A Wood) *dropped in after s: hld up in rr: rdn and hdwy over 2f out: no imp fnl f* **20/1**

30/0 **9** *nse* **Man Of Letters (UAE)**[14] 973 7-9-2 **58**........................... ChrisCatlin 4 54
(M Hill) *chsd ldr tl over 2f out: struggling whn short of room over 1f out: one pce after* **12/1**

20-6 **10** *nse* **Tyrannosaurus Rex (IRE)**[12] 990 4-9-1 **57**..........(v) FergusSweeney 6 53
(K R Burke) *chsd ldrs: rdn to chse ldr over 2f out: sn ev ch tl fdd jst ins fnl f* **11/2**[3]

244- **11** 1½ **Sintenis Mac (GER)**[100] 7239 5-9-3 **59**............................ AlanMunro 1 51
(P J O'Gorman) *hld up towards rr on outer: rdn 3f out: no hdwy* **4/1**[1]

-640 **12** 1¾ **Coloso**[8] 1058 4-8-13 **55**.. SimonWhitworth 10 42
(P D Cundell) *s.i.s: a towards rr: n.d* **16/1**

6300 **13** 1¾ **Buzzin'Boyzee (IRE)**[10] 1024 5-8-11 **53**.................... TGMcLaughlin 5 35
(P D Evans) *t.k.h: hld up in midfield tl lost pl 4f out: n.d after* **28/1**

360- **14** 3¾ **Namibian Pink (IRE)**[26] 6882 4-8-4 **53**........................ SimonPearce(7) 9 25
(R H York) *sn outpcd in last* **66/1**

1m 27.81s (1.81) **Going Correction** +0.225s/f (Slow) **14** Ran SP% **125.2**
Speed ratings (Par 101): **98,97,96,95,95 94,94,92,92,92 91,89,87,82**
CSF £78.36 CT £1031.58 TOTE £11.30: £3.90, £3.40, £2.00; EX 91.60 Place 6 £107.32, Place 5 £62.12..
Owner J Wigmore Racing Partnership **Bred** J Wigmore **Trained** Cropthorne, Worcs

FOCUS
A very weak handicap but the form appears sound enough rated around the runner-up, fourth and fifth.
T/Plt: £159.30 to a £1 stake. Pool: £73,086.43. 334.75 winning tickets. T/Qpdt: £38.40 to a £1 stake. Pool: £6,020.88. 116.00 winning tickets. SP

1176 LINGFIELD (L-H)
Saturday, April 5

OFFICIAL GOING: Standard
Wind: medium against Weather: overcast

1210 MARION AND MARK ADAMS BIRTHDAY H'CAP 1m 2f (P)
1:35 (1:37) (Class 6) (0-65,65) 4-Y-0+ **£2,047** (£604; £302) **Stalls** Low

Form RPR

-214 **1** **Blue Eyed Eloise**[44] 646 6-9-1 **62**................................ StephenCarson 2 70
(B J McMath) *hld up in tch: gd hdwy jst over 2f out: led 1f out: r.o wl* **4/1**[3]

0-32 **2** 1¾ **Kings Topic (USA)**[3] 1152 8-8-11 **58**............................ SteveDrowne 1 63
(A B Haynes) *chsd ldrs: rdn to chal 2f out: ev ch tl outpcd by wnr ins fnl f* **11/8**[1]

53-5 **3** *nk* **Wheelavit (IRE)**[14] 970 5-8-13 **60**.. TQuinn 5 64
(B G Powell) *t.k.h: chsd ldr tl led over 2f out: hdd 1f out: kpt on same pce* **8/1**

6534 **4** *hd* **Binnion Bay (IRE)**[8] 1058 7-8-9 **56**.................................(b) ChrisCatlin 3 60
(J J Bridger) *stdd s: hld up in rr: hdwy 3f out: sn rdn and ev ch: one pce fnl f* **8/1**

5660 **5** 2 **Mtoto Girl**[8] 1053 4-8-6 **53** oh6 ow2.. NeilChalmers 8 53?
(J J Bridger) *hld up in rr: rdn over 2f out: no hdwy* **66/1**

0121 **6** 1¾ **Competitor**[17] 935 7-9-1 **65**...................................(v) KirstyMilczarek(3) 4 61
(J Akehurst) *led at stdy gallop: hdd over 2f out: wknd over 1f out* **3/1**[2]

2m 8.71s (2.11) **Going Correction** +0.025s/f (Slow) **6** Ran SP% **110.8**
Speed ratings (Par 101): **92,90,90,90,88 87**
CSF £9.69 CT £37.30 TOTE £4.40: £1.80, £1.60; EX 10.60.
Owner G D Newton **Bred** Miss M E Steele **Trained** Newmarket, Suffolk

FOCUS
A moderate handicap run at a steady gallop until the last half-mile. The form looks dubious with the out-of-the-handicap fifth limiting things.

1211 HEART OF THE SOUTH SHOWJUMPING PARTNERSHIP H'CAP 7f (P)
2:10 (2:11) (Class 3) (0-90,90) 4-Y-0+
£6,542 (£1,959; £979; £490; £244; £122) **Stalls** Low

Form RPR

2-1 **1** **King Of Dixie (USA)**[80] 175 4-9-4 **90**.................................... PaulDoe 4 101+
(W J Knight) *sn led: pressed and rdn 2f out: edgd rt u.p: styd on wl* **9/4**[1]

4-55 **2** ¾ **Yarqus**[28] 834 5-9-3 **89**..(bt[1]) RyanMoore 9 98
(C E Brittain) *hld up in rr: swtchd rt and hdwy over 1f out: r.o wl: nt rch wnr* **11/2**[3]

6/5- **3** *nk* **Farley Star**[347] 1228 4-8-8 **80**.. SteveDrowne 2 88
(R Charlton) *in tch: rdn and hdwy 2f out: chal u.p over 1f out: one pce* **4/1**[2]

-005 **4** *hd* **Councellor (FR)**[9] [1045] 6-8-13 **85**....................................(t) TPQueally 8 92
(Stef Liddiard) *in tch: rdn and hdwy 2f out: chsd ldrs 1f out: kpt on same pce* **20/1**

0-01 **5** *3/4* **Secret Night**[37] [733] 5-8-10 **82**....................... AlanMunro 3 87
(J A R Toller) *bhd: hdwy over 1f out: r.o but nvr able to chal* **14/1**

030- **6** *hd* **Lunces Lad (IRE)**[205] [5360] 4-8-2 **81**....................... MatthewDavies(7) 14 86
(M R Channon) *wnt rt s: prom: rdn to chal 2f out: wknd fnl f* **25/1**

0646 **7** *1* **Carcinetto (IRE)**[28] [833] 6-8-11 **83**....................... TGMcLaughlin 11 85
(P D Evans) *in tch: rdn and effrt over 2f out: kpt on same pce* **28/1**

200- **8** *1* **Forest Dane**[136] [6900] 8-8-7 **82**....................... KirstyMilczarek(3) 13 81
(Mrs N Smith) *a towards rr: n.d* **20/1**

6664 **9** *nk* **Lucayos**[39] [707] 5-8-5 **84** ow1....................... KylieManser(7) 7 83
(Mrs H Sweeting) *w ldr: rdn over 2f out: wknd wl over 1f out* **33/1**

51-5 **10** *1 1/4* **Purus (IRE)**[21] [904] 6-8-13 **85**....................... ChrisCatlin 1 80
(R A Teal) *chsd ldrs tl lost pl over 2f out: n.d after* **10/1**

1211 **11** *hd* **Desert Dreamer (IRE)**[3] [1143] 7-9-3 **89** 6ex.........(t) RichardKingscote 10 84
(Tom Dascombe) *hld up in rr: nvr nr ldrs* **10/1**

1102 **12** *hd* **Buxton**[9] [1045] 4-9-4 **90**....................................(t) RobertHavlin 5 84
(R Ingram) *in tch in midfield: rdn 2f out: no imp* **14/1**

4212 **13** *1 1/4* **Danetime Lord (IRE)**[8] [1055] 5-8-10 **82**....................(p) RichardHughes 6 73
(J R Gask) *a bhd* **12/1**

1m 23.07s (-1.73) **Going Correction** +0.025s/f (Slow) **13** Ran SP% **125.1**
Speed ratings (Par 107): **110,109,108,108,107 107,106,105,104,103 103,102,101**
CSF £13.87 CT £51.60 TOTE £3.00: £1.60, £2.30, £2.20; EX 14.50 Trifecta £143.50 Pool: £262.81, 1.30 w/u.

Owner Hesmonds Stud **Bred** Bee Zee LLC **Trained** Patching, W Sussex

FOCUS

A decent handicap for the money run at a good gallop throughout. The form is rated at face value with the runner-up rated to his Cambridgeshire form.

NOTEBOOK

King Of Dixie(USA) ◆, a lightly-raced colt who took well to this surface when winning his maiden at Kempton in January, was facing a much stiffer task against these battle-hardened handicappers. Nevertheless, he set off in front and then resisted several challengers in the straight to make all. He looks a horse with plenty of potential and could be the sort for some of the big handicaps on turf this summer, with the Victoria Cup next month a possible starting point. (op 2-1 tchd 5-2)

Yarqus had run decent races in the Winter Derby Trial and the Lincoln Trial on his last two starts and had blinkers on for the first time. Taking a drop in trip, this was one of his best efforts on sand and he may be ready to score back on turf. (op 7-1 tchd 5-1 in places)

Farley Star, absent for almost a year following her three-year-old debut, showed she has lost none of her ability with a fine effort. She won her maiden on easy ground and, providing she remains in one piece after this, can score before long, although the 'bounce' factor will have to be considered. (op 7-2 tchd 5-1)

Councellor(FR), who had a good spell on this surface in the autumn, has slipped to a pound below his last winning mark and this looked like a return to form. (op 16-1)

Secret Night, who won a slightly lower-grade fillies' race over course and distance last time, improved fractionally on that form on a line through Carcinetto without ever landing a blow. (op 16-1)

Lunces Lad(IRE) ◆, who has had only one previous outing on the All-Weather and was running for the first time since September, missed the break and then was rushed up to race prominently on the outside. In the circumstances he did well to finish so close, as he did a lot of early running, and with this outing behind him could well take his chance in the Victoria Cup, having run well over that course and distance before. (tchd 28-1)

Carcinetto(IRE) has put up some fair efforts at this trip on Polytrack of ate, but her recent wins have been at shorter and off lower marks. She is slipping in the handicap but may need a bit more help before winning again. (op 33-1)

1212 HEARTOFTHESOUTH.NET H'CAP 1m 4f (P)

2:45 (2:45) (Class 2) (0-100,94) 4-Y-0+

£9,969 (£2,985; £1,492; £560; £560; £187) **Stalls** Low

Form RPR

51-0 **1** **Watamu (IRE)**[7] [1076] 7-9-5 **94**....................................(v) SebSanders 5 102
(P J Makin) *t.k.h: hld up in last pair: hdwy on outer 3f out: rdn to ld 1f out: r.o strly* **5/1**[3]

300- **2** *1 1/4* **Paktolos (FR)**[53] [3105] 5-8-13 **88**....................... JamieSpencer 1 94
(A King) *stdd s: hld up in rr: swtchd rt and bmpd rival over 2f out: sn hrd rdn: hung lft fr over 1f out: r.o to chse wnr ins fnl f: no imp last 100yds* **9/1**

5111 **3** *1* **Motarjm (USA)**[28] [838] 4-8-9 **85**....................................(t) ChrisCatlin 4 89
(H J Collingridge) *hld up in tch in midfield: hdwy to chse ldrs over 2f out: styd on u.p fnl f* **7/1**

40-5 **4** *1 3/4* **Bahar Shumaal (IRE)**[7] [1076] 6-9-5 **94**....................... J-PGuillambert 9 96
(C E Brittain) *t.k.h: led: hrd pressed over 2f out: hdd 1f out: outpcd fnl f* **11/1**

656- **4** *dht* **Prince Sabaah (IRE)**[162] [6473] 4-8-11 **87**....................... RichardHughes 3 89
(R Hannon) *trckd ldrs: rdn and sltly outpcd 2f out: kpt on u.p fnl f* **10/3**[2]

130- **6** *shd* **Zero Cool (USA)**[97] [7281] 4-8-4 **80**....................... RichardMullen 2 81
(G L Moore) *hld up towards rr: hdwy over 2f out: n.m.r fr over 1f out: kpt on same pce* **33/1**

-143 **7** *nk* **John Terry (IRE)**[7] [1076] 5-9-4 **93**....................... JimCrowley 8 94
(Mrs A J Perrett) *chsd ldr: chal jst over 2f out: one pce fnl f* **3/1**[1]

-301 **8** *12* **Tartan Tie**[10] [1026] 4-8-13 **89**....................... JoeFanning 6 71
(M Johnston) *s.i.s: sn in tch: rdn 4f out: wkng whn bmpd over 2f out: no ch after* **5/1**[3]

2m 30.53s (-2.47) **Going Correction** +0.025s/f (Slow)
WFA 4 from 5yo+ 1lb **8** Ran SP% **115.2**
Speed ratings (Par 109): **109,108,107,106,106 106,106,98**
CSF £48.97 CT £315.12 TOTE £6.10: £1.20, £3.30, £2.90; EX 44.60 Trifecta £101.40 Part won. Pool: £142.93, 0.10 w/u..

Owner R A Henley **Bred** Crandon Park Stud **Trained** Ogbourne Maisey, Wilts

FOCUS

Another good handicap and a decisive winner with the form best rated through the runner-up.

NOTEBOOK

Watamu(IRE) ◆, who had shown his best form over 1m2f, had dropped out in the closing stages in the Rosebery Handicap at Kempton seven days earlier on his first outing in over year, but the run had brought him on and he was always travelling nicely off the pace. He was asked to make his progress running down to the turn for home and quickened up nicely to score authoritatively. He is relatively lightly raced and could well add to this despite a likely rise. Official explanation: trainer said, regarding apparent improvement in form, that the gelding appeared suited by a return to a course in which it had shown good form previously. (op 13-2 tchd 9-2)

Paktolos(FR) put up a reasonable effort on his first outing on the Flat in 280 days, having raced over hurdles during the winter. He followed the winner through but did not have the pace to challenge. He gained his only success over course and distance and all his best form has been on sand. (op 11-1 tchd 8-1)

Motarjm(USA) had won his last three races at Wolverhampton and was racing off a 5lb higher mark than when scoring last month, but acquitted himself well against this tougher opposition. He was soon chasing the leader and kept on well enough in the final furlong to suggest he could be winning again back at his favourite track, although his current mark limits opportunities. (op 13-2)

Bahar Shumaal(IRE) made the running until headed by the winner and ran pretty well considering he was quite keen early. (tchd 10-1 and 12-1)

Prince Sabaah(IRE), whose sole success was on his only previous try on the All-Weather, was always close up on the inside and kept on in the closing stages without suggesting he was going to win. He has some decent form on turf and this should put him right for a return to that surface. (tchd 10-1 and 12-1)

Zero Cool(USA) never really got involved but was not beaten far and should come on for his first outing in three months.

John Terry(IRE) was soon tracking the leader and travelling quite well but proved a little disappointing when asked for his effort in the final furlong, as he failed to find an extra gear. (op 11-4 tchd 7-2)

Tartan Tie failed to run his race after he missed the break and, although bumped going into the turn, was already on the retreat at that point. He has been well beaten here before and Fibresand seems to suit him better. (op 4-1)

1213 HEART OF THE SOUTH RACING INTERNATIONAL TRIAL STKS (LISTED RACE) 1m (P)

3:20 (3:21) (Class 1) 3-Y-O

£14,760 (£5,595; £2,800; £1,396; £699; £351) **Stalls** High

Form RPR

110- **1** **Sharp Nephew**[189] [5795] 3-9-0 101....................... RichardHughes 3 94
(B J Meehan) *hld up in tch: rdn wl over 1f out: str run 1f out: led ins fnl f: r.o wl* **5/2**[2]

2-1 **2** *nk* **Orientalist Art**[47] [608] 3-9-0 94....................... AlanMunro 8 93+
(P W Chapple-Hyam) *dwlt: hld up bhd on inner: rdn and hdwy jst over 1f out: burst through horses ins fnl f: wnt 2nd nr fin* **9/2**[3]

111- **3** *hd* **Traphalgar (IRE)**[123] [7027] 3-9-0 91....................... TQuinn 6 93
(P F I Cole) *w ldrs tl led 5f out: hrd pressed and rdn 2f out: kpt on wl tl no ex towards fin* **7/1**

023- **4** *shd* **Redolent (IRE)**[156] [6615] 3-9-0 110....................... RyanMoore 2 93
(R Hannon) *led tl 5f out: w ldr after: drvn 2f out: kpt on same pce u.p fnl f* **15/8**[1]

1-13 **5** *1/2* **Geezers Colours**[21] [905] 3-9-0 92....................... FergusSweeney 5 92
(K R Burke) *t.k.h: chsd ldrs: chal 2f out: ev ch tl unable qckn last 100yds* **10/1**

566- **6** *hd* **Solent Ridge (IRE)**[176] [6161] 3-9-0 92....................... LPKeniry 1 91
(J S Moore) *t.k.h: trckd ldrs on inner: rdn and effrt over 1f out: ev ch ins fnl f: no ex last 100yds* **50/1**

320- **7** *nk* **Mut'Ab (USA)**[228] [4694] 3-9-0 85....................... SebSanders 4 90
(C E Brittain) *stdd s: t.k.h: hld up in rr: outpcd 2f out: rallied over 1f out: swtchd rt ins fnl f: r.o but nvr able to chal* **14/1**

12-5 **8** *2 1/2* **King Hafhafah**[21] [905] 3-9-0 87....................... JoeFanning 7 85
(I A Wood) *hld up in last trio: rdn and effrt over 2f out: no imp* **25/1**

1m 37.24s (-0.96) **Going Correction** +0.025s/f (Slow) **8** Ran SP% **115.6**
Speed ratings (Par 106): **105,104,104,104,103 103,103,100**
CSF £14.48 TOTE £3.50: £1.10, £1.50, £2.50; EX 16.70 Trifecta £69.80 Pool: £274.50, 2.79 w/u.

Owner Saleh Al Homaizi & Imad Al Sagar **Bred** Keith Wills **Trained** Manton, Wilts

FOCUS

An ordinary renewal of this Listed race with just two of the runners rated above 100. The pace was modest early but it produced a good finish with the first seven covered by just a length and a half and the form looks somewhat messy.

NOTEBOOK

Sharp Nephew, who won a Listed race at Newbury on his second juvenile start before finishing well beaten on soft ground in the Royal Lodge, bounced back with a determined effort on this first try on Polytrack. Connections are considering a Classic and Group campaign now - he is currently 40/1 for the 2000 Guineas - and although that may be aiming a bit high he has a good attitude and should win his share of decent races. (op 7-2 tchd 9-4)

Orientalist Art, who got off the mark over 7f here in February, missed the break and was switched inside to over come his high draw, but was close enough turning in before producing a late surge that only just failed. He could go for the Greenham or another race at the same meeting next, although he is likely to need decent ground. (op 10-3)

Traphalgar(IRE), who completed a hat-trick on this surface before Christmas, was given a positive ride and responded gamely, losing nothing in defeat. He is consistent and progressive and helps set the level of the form. (op 10-1)

Redolent(IRE) had the highest official rating in the race following second to subsequent Racing Post Trophy winner Ibn Khaldun and third in a Group 1 in France last November. He was another who appeared to run his race under a positive ride on this debut on sand, but he will be suited by a return to turf and the outing should bring him on. (op 6-4 tchd 2-1)

Geezers Colours is a likeable individual who has performed with credit since stepped up to this level and he is probably the best guide to the form. He ran well, only being run out of the placings late on, and in the process paid a compliment to Paco Boy, who beat him further in the Spring Cup here last month. (op 12-1 tchd 9-1)

Solent Ridge(IRE) had previous form on this surface at a lower level and ran pretty well considering he was quite keen early. (op 66-1)

Mut'Ab(USA), still a maiden and offically the lowest rated in the field, was having his first outing since the Acomb Stakes in August and did not help his chance by pulling early. In the circumstances it was not a bad effort. (op 16-1)

King Hafhafah, who finished two lengths behind Geezers Colours in the Spring Cup here last time, ran slightly below that form and never got in a blow. He does not quite look up to this class but has yet to race on turf and may have more to offer on that surface. (op 33-1 tchd 20-1)

1214 MARY AND ARTHUR PERCHARD MEMORIAL MAIDEN AUCTION STKS 5f (P)

3:55 (3:55) (Class 6) 2-Y-O **£2,266** (£674; £337; £168) **Stalls** High

Form RPR

6 **1** **Gone Hunting**[7] [1078] 2-8-2 0....................... JackDean(7) 6 70
(W G M Turner) *chsd ldrs on outer: rdn over 2f out: hung lft fr over 1f out: led ins fnl f: hld on* **9/4**[2]

2 *nse* **Firth Of Fifth (IRE)** 2-8-9 0....................... RichardKingscote 2 70+
(Tom Dascombe) *s.i.s: sn outpcd: hdwy over 2f out: r.o wl to chse wnr ins fnl f: jst hld* **12/1**

3 *1 1/2* **Smalljohn** 2-8-11 0....................... TGMcLaughlin 1 66
(P D Evans) *led: hung rt and c wd bnd 2f out: hdd ins fnl f: wknd last 100yds* **12/1**

2 **4** *3 1/2* **Grand Plan (USA)**[5] [1111] 2-8-6 0....................... TPQueally 3 47+
(J A Osborne) *chsd ldr: carried wd bnd 2f out: wknd 1f out* **6/5**[1]

0 **5** *2* **Shadow Bay (IRE)**[14] [957] 2-8-13 0....................... ChrisCatlin 4 46
(M R Channon) *chsd ldrs tl 1/2-way: sn struggling* **7/2**[3]

59.94 secs (1.14) **Going Correction** +0.025s/f (Slow) **5** Ran SP% **113.8**
Speed ratings (Par 90): **91,90,88,82,79**
CSF £25.72 TOTE £4.00: £2.00, £4.70; EX 35.70.

Owner M W Easterby **Bred** Norman Court Stud **Trained** Sigwells, Somerset

FOCUS

An ordinary maiden but another close finish but the form could work out a little better than rated.

The Form Book, Raceform Ltd, Compton, RG20 6NL

NOTEBOOK

Gone Hunting, who ran with plenty of promise when a close fifth on his debut, was well backed against the favourite and put that experience to good use to claim a narrow victory. He does not look anything special but may win again before the better juveniles appear. (op 7-2)

Firth Of Fifth(IRE), whose yearling price was much lower than when he was sold as a foal, fell out of the stalls and was slowly into his stride on this debut. However, he went in pursuit of the rest and, as the remainder of the field came wide around the bend, cut to the inside and got upsides only to run green and prick an ear near the finish, which resulted in him losing out narrowly. He will know a lot more next time and should soon gain compensation. (op 10-1)

Smalljohn, a speedily-bred gelding related to several winning juveniles including The Crooked Ring, showed plenty of pace on this debut and, although run out of it late on, looks capable of emulating his relatives. (op 7-1)

Grand Plan(USA), favourite on the strength of a promising debut behind Percolator earlier in the week, showed pace from the start but got carried wide on the bend and did not appear to relish being short of room between the winner and third halfway up the straight, quickly backing out of it. To be fair, the race may have come too soon. (op 5-6 tchd 8-11)

Shadow Bay(IRE) was third favourite when out the back in the Brocklesby and again failed to show much in this first try on Polytrack. (op 6-1 tchd 7-1)

1215 PLAY GOLF @ LINGFIELD PARK MAIDEN STKS — 6f (P)

4:40 (4:43) (Class 5) 3-Y-O — £2,331 (£693; £346; £173) Stalls Low

Form — RPR

20- **1** **Sir George (IRE)**[224] 4832 3-9-3 0 .... AlanMunro 8 — 78
(P W Chapple-Hyam) *chsd ldr: outpcd over 1f out: rallied u.p ins fnl f: r.o strly to ld last 50yds* — 13/8[1]

200- **2** nk **Pha Mai Blue**[171] 6270 3-9-3 75 .... RichardKingscote 2 — 77
(W J Knight) *sn led: rdn and wnt clr over 1f out: hdd and no ex last 50yds* — 6/1[3]

0- **3** 1 ½ **Asian Lady**[147] 6755 3-8-12 0 .... SteveDrowne 11 — 67+
(R Charlton) *hld up towards rr: hdwy over 2f out: r.o fr over 1f out: wnt 3rd ins fnl f: nt rch ldng pair* — 8/1

03- **4** 2 ¼ **Candida's Beau**[150] 6714 3-9-3 0 .... SebSanders 4 — 65
(R M Beckett) *chsd ldng pair: rdn jst over 2f out: outpcd over 1f out: one pce after* — 7/4[2]

40- **5** 1 ½ **Second Opinion (IRE)**[225] 4756 3-8-12 0 .... RichardHughes 7 — 55
(J M P Eustace) *chsd ldrs on inner: rdn jst over 2f out: kpt on same pce* — 20/1

00- **6** ½ **Expediter**[170] 6281 3-8-12 0 .... DaneO'Neill 9 — 54
(H Candy) *chsd ldrs on outer: rdn and outpcd 2f out: n.d after* — 20/1

7 ½ **Beat The Bell** 3-9-3 0 .... RichardMullen 6 — 57
(A Bailey) *s.i.s: sn in tch in midfield: rdn and struggling jst over 2f out: n.d after* — 50/1

0 **8** ½ **Borrowdale**[3] 1149 3-9-3 0 .... TPQueally 10 — 55+
(J A Osborne) *hld up towards rr: nvr on terms* — 50/1

9 12 **Cherries On Top (IRE)** 3-9-3 0 .... JoeFanning 1 — 17
(I A Wood) *s.i.s: t.k.h: hld up in midfield: rdn and struggling over 2f out: t.o* — 10/1

0- **10** 4 **Milloaks (IRE)**[207] 5313 3-8-12 0 .... EdwardCreighton 3 — —
(E J Creighton) *s.i.s: a bhd: t.o* — 100/1

1m 12.44s (0.54) **Going Correction** +0.025s/f (Slow) — **10** Ran SP% **123.4**
Speed ratings (Par 98): **97,96,94,91,89 88,88,87,71,66**
CSF £12.38 TOTE £2.00: £1.10, £2.20, £2.40; EX 9.40.

Owner Diamond Racing Ltd **Bred** Bernard Colclough **Trained** Newmarket, Suffolk

■ Stewards' Enquiry : Alan Munro one-day ban: used whip without giving colt sufficient time time to respond (Apr 19)

FOCUS
Probably a decent little race with the runner-up rated 75 and the form looks sound despite the time being moderate.

1216 ARENALEISUREPLC.COM H'CAP — 7f (P)

5:20 (5:20) (Class 5) (0-70,69) 3-Y-O — £2,331 (£693; £346; £173) Stalls Low

Form — RPR

021- **1** **Chrystal Venture (IRE)**[149] 6736 3-9-3 68 .... (p) NeilPollard 1 — 74
(A J McCabe) *awkward leaving stalls: sn led: wl clr 1/2-way: 8l up 1f out: edgd rt and tired after: hld on* — 11/1

4-14 **2** nk **Top Draw (USA)**[8] 1060 3-9-4 69 .... JamieSpencer 5 — 74
(M L W Bell) *led main gp: allowed wnr to go clr 1/2-way: rdn wl over 1f out: r.o fnl f: nt quite rch wnr: too much to do* — 2/1[1]

50-1 **3** 1 ¼ **Benedetto**[8] 1060 3-9-4 69 .... JimCrowley 2 — 71
(Mrs A J Perrett) *t.k.h: hld up in rr: rdn and hdwy on inner over 1f out: r.o to go 3rd nr fin: nt rch wnr: too much to do* — 7/2[2]

2343 **4** shd **Llab Nala**[2] 1166 3-7-12 56 ow1 .... MatthewDavies(7) 3 — 58
(M R Channon) *t.k.h: racd in 3rd pl: allowed wnr to go clr 1/2-way: rdn wl over 1f out: kpt on: nt rch wnr* — 7/1

506- **5** 1 **Seeking The Star (CAN)**[248] 4065 3-9-2 67 .... RichardMullen 6 — 66
(D M Simcock) *bhd: pushed along 4f out: kpt on u.p: nvr able to chal* — 14/1

645- **6** hd **High Plains (FR)**[138] 6868 3-9-4 69 .... RichardHughes 7 — 67+
(R Hannon) *hld up in rr: c wd and rdn bnd 2f out: styd on: nt rch wnr* — 4/1[3]

2303 **7** 1 ½ **Wee Buns**[8] 1060 3-8-11 69 .... DavidProbert(7) 4 — 63
(P Burgoyne) *racd in midfield: rdn and kpt on fr over 1f out: nvr able to challenege* — 9/1

400- **8** 6 **Allahor**[233] 4524 3-9-0 65 .... TPQueally 8 — 43
(J A Osborne) *sn bhd: rdn along 5f out: no ch fr 1/2-way* — 8/1

1m 25.48s (0.68) **Going Correction** +0.025s/f (Slow) — **8** Ran SP% **124.2**
Speed ratings (Par 98): **97,96,95,95,93 93,92,85**
CSF £36.44 CT £101.23 TOTE £15.00: £2.50, £1.70, £1.10; EX 56.20 Place 6 £59.91, Place 5 £36.46..

Owner Paul J Dixon And The Chrystal Maze Ptn **Bred** Gestut Gorlsdorf **Trained** Babworth, Notts

FOCUS
A modest handicap in which the winner stole the race from the front but the race is rated at face value.

High Plains(FR) Official explanation: jockey said colt hung right in early stages

T/Plt: £292.30 to a £1 stake. Pool: £54,686.90. 136.54 winning tickets. T/Qpdt: £72.50 to a £1 stake. Pool: £2,461.38. 25.10 winning tickets. SP

NEWCASTLE (L-H)

Saturday, April 5

OFFICIAL GOING: Good to soft (soft in places) (6.4)
Wind: Fresh, half behind Weather: Overcast

1217 BET365 BEST ODDS GUARANTEED ON EVERY RACE H'CAP — 1m 3y(S)

2:05 (2:06) (Class 4) (0-80,80) 4-Y-O+ **£4,415** (£1,321; £660; £330; £164) Stalls High

Form — RPR

0-12 **1** **Exit Smiling**[31] 805 6-8-10 72 .... MickyFenton 2 — 79
(P T Midgley) *hld up in tch on far side: hdwy to ld that gp ent fnl f: hung rt ins fnl f: hld on wl* — 8/1

4-03 **2** nk **Moheebb (IRE)**[7] 1072 4-8-7 72 .... (b) AndrewMullen(3) 13 — 78
(Mrs R A Carr) *hld up stands' side: hdwy to ld that gp ins fnl f: kpt on fin: 1st of 9 in gp* — 8/1

120- **3** 2 ½ **Celtic Change (IRE)**[178] 6110 4-9-2 78 .... DarryllHolland 11 — 78+
(M Dods) *prom stands' side: effrt over 2f out: kpt on ins fnl f: bttr for r: 2nd of 9 in gp* — 11/2[1]

00-0 **4** ½ **Wovoka (IRE)**[12] 992 5-9-2 78 .... FergalLynch 14 — 77
(D W Barker) *hld up stands' side: hdwy 2f out: rdn and hung to far side gp ins fnl f: one pce: 3rd of 9 in gp* — 20/1

622/ **5** nk **Polish Corridor**[1069] 1408 9-8-13 75 .... DaleGibson 10 — 73
(M Dods) *prom stands' side: led that gp over 2f out to ins fnl f: no ex: 4th of 9 in gp* — 22/1

40-0 **6** 2 ½ **Daaweitza**[12] 992 5-9-3 79 .... TomEaves 1 — 72
(B Ellison) *cl up far side: led that gp 2f out to ent fnl f: sn no ex: 2nd of 7 in gp* — 28/1

055- **7** 5 **Baileborough (IRE)**[109] 7175 9-8-8 77 .... LanceBetts(7) 16 — 58
(B Ellison) *in tch stands' side: rdn over 2f out: sn no imp: 5th of 9 in gp* — 18/1

06-6 **8** 2 ¾ **Mezuzah**[7] 1069 8-9-0 76 .... PaulMulrennan 4 — 51
(M W Easterby) *cl up far side tl rdn and outpcd fr 2f out: 3rd of 7 in gp* — 14/1

000- **9** ½ **Bold Marc (IRE)**[197] 5585 6-9-4 80 .... AndrewElliott 3 — 54
(K R Burke) *led far side gp to 2f out: sn wknd: 4th of 7 in gp* — 10/1

60-5 **10** 4 ½ **Dancing Lyra**[40] 697 7-8-11 73 .... PaulHanagan 12 — 36
(R A Fahey) *hld up stands' side: drvn over 2f out: n.d: 6th of 9 in gp* — 13/2[3]

00-0 **11** 2 **Bid For Gold**[12] 992 4-8-8 70 .... TonyHamilton 6 — 29
(Jedd O'Keeffe) *in tch far side tl rdn and wknd fr over 2f out: 5th of 7 in gp* — 66/1

20-1 **12** 8 **Nok Twice (IRE)**[12] 990 7-7-12 67 .... JamieKyne(7) 5 — 7
(D Carroll) *hld up far side: rdn 3f out: sn btn: 6th of 7 in gp* — 12/1

236- **13** 1 **Dechiper (IRE)**[172] 6258 6-7-12 67 oh3 ow1 .... PatrickDonaghy(7) 15 — 5
(R Johnson) *in tch stands' side tl wknd over 2f out: 7th of 9 in gp* — 16/1

-660 **14** hd **King Of The Moors (USA)**[12] 992 5-8-7 69 .... PaulFessey 9 — 7
(T D Barron) *prom stands' side tl wknd over 2f out: 8th of 9 in gp* — 33/1

04-0 **15** 8 **Osteopathic Remedy (IRE)**[12] 992 4-8-13 75 .... PhillipMakin 8 — —
(M Dods) *led stands' side tl hdd over 2f out: sn wknd: last of 9 in gp* — 6/1[2]

320- **16** 56 **Rodeo**[249] 4039 5-8-12 74 .... (b) RobertWinston 7 — —
(C W Thornton) *hld up in tch far side: drvn over 3f out: sn lost tch: last of 7 in gp* — 28/1

1m 48.38s (4.98) **Going Correction** +0.60s/f (Yiel) — **16** Ran SP% **120.3**
Speed ratings (Par 105): **100,99,97,96,96 93,88,86,85,81 79,71,70,69,61 5**
CSF £63.73 CT £403.66 TOTE £8.10: £1.80, £2.10, £2.20, £5.70; EX 78.40 Trifecta £150.70 Part won. Pool: £212.28. 0.39 w/u..

Owner Peter Mee **Bred** Mrs D O Joly **Trained** Westow, N Yorks

FOCUS
An ordinary handicap in which the field split into two groups and, on this occasion, there was little in the draw. The pace was sound and the first four were all held up. Exit Smiling, who also won this last year, could have been rated a bit higher than the bare form.

Osteopathic Remedy(IRE) Official explanation: jockey said gelding hung left-handed throughout

1218 BET365 CALL 08000 322 365 H'CAP — 7f

2:35 (2:35) (Class 2) (0-100,96) 4-Y-O+

£9,969 (£2,985; £1,492; £747; £372; £93) Stalls High

Form — RPR

-061 **1** **Markab**[14] 969 5-8-8 86 .... PatCosgrave 15 — 99
(K A Morgan) *mde all stands' rail: rdn and r.o strly fnl f* — 9/2[1]

040- **2** 2 ½ **Fishforcompliments**[289] 2789 4-9-3 95 .... PaulHanagan 14 — 101
(R A Fahey) *prom: effrt and chsd wnr over 2f out: kpt on u.p fnl f* — 10/1

10-4 **3** 3 ½ **Wigwam Willie (IRE)**[11] 1016 6-8-7 85 .... (p) FergalLynch 8 — 82
(K A Ryan) *prom: effrt over 2f out: edgd rt over 1f out: kpt on same pce* — 17/2

3215 **4** 2 ¾ **Electric Warrior (IRE)**[11] 1016 5-8-12 90 .... DarrenWilliams 9 — 79
(K R Burke) *midfield: effrt over 2f out: one pce fnl f* — 8/1[3]

00-0 **5** 2 ¼ **Dhaular Dhar (IRE)**[14] 960 6-9-1 93 .... DanielTudhope 6 — 76+
(J S Goldie) *hld up: n.m.r over 2f out: hdwy over 1f out: nvr nrr* — 10/1

-004 **6** shd **Jamieson Gold (IRE)**[13] 979 5-8-1 82 oh2 .... AndrewMullen(3) 13 — 65
(Miss L A Perratt) *in tch: rdn and outpcd over 2f out: n.d after* — 12/1

560- **6** dht **Overrule (USA)**[189] 5805 4-8-10 88 .... TomEaves 12 — 71
(B Ellison) *midfield: rdn over 2f out: no imp over 1f out* — 12/1

00-0 **8** 5 **White Deer (USA)**[14] 958 4-8-12 90 .... SilvestreDeSousa 1 — 59
(D Nicholls) *chsd ldrs tl rdn and wknd over 1f out* — 25/1

0-10 **9** 1 ¼ **Partners In Jazz (USA)**[14] 958 7-8-12 90 .... PhillipMakin 5 — 56
(T D Barron) *hld up: pushed along over 2f out: nvr rchd ldrs* — 11/2[2]

06-6 **10** ½ **Skhilling Spirit**[14] 958 5-8-13 91 .... PaulFessey 3 — 56
(T D Barron) *missed break: bhd: rdn whn hmpd over 2f out: n.d* — 8/1[3]

/1-0 **11** 2 ¼ **Provost**[7] 1067 4-8-7 85 .... DaleGibson 10 — 43
(M W Easterby) *towards rr: drvn over 2f out: nvr on terms* — 33/1

2223 **12** ½ **Gallantry**[9] 1045 6-8-9 90 .... TolleyDean(3) 7 — 47
(D Shaw) *hld up in midfield on outside: pushed along 3f out: sn btn* — 12/1

30-0 **13** 6 **Minority Report**[14] 958 8-9-0 92 .... AdrianTNicholls 4 — 33
(D Nicholls) *hld up: rdn 3f out: n.d* — 25/1

106/ **14** 14 **Gramm**[525] 6219 5-8-7 85 .... PaulMulrennan 11 — —
(M W Easterby) *cl up: rdn and wkng whn hmpd over 2f out* — 25/1

1m 31.29s (3.89) **Going Correction** +0.60s/f (Yiel) — **14** Ran SP% **122.1**
Speed ratings (Par 109): **110,107,103,100,97 97,97,91,90,89 87,86,79,63**
CSF £47.87 CT £388.54 TOTE £6.20: £2.60, £3.30, £2.70; EX 61.50 Trifecta £141.40 Part won. Pool: £199.24, 0.79 w/u..

Owner Tight Lines Partnership **Bred** Shadwell Estate Company Limited **Trained** Little Marcle, H'fords

■ Stewards' Enquiry : Silvestre De Sousa caution: careless riding.

FOCUS
A fair handicap in which the whole field raced stands' side. The lower drawn horses were at a disadvantage. A step up from the winner, who made all, but not many of these showed their form.

NOTEBOOK

Markab, a winner on Polytrack on his previous start, again had the run of the race from the front and turned in his best effort from this 4lb higher mark. There will be no problems with the return to 1m and he appeals as the sort to win again when allowed to dominate. (op 13-2)

Fishforcompliments, who has found life tough in Listed and Group company since his maiden win in 2006, shaped with plenty of promise on this reappearance run. Although he has little margin for error from this mark, he will be suited by the return to 1m and is likely to be placed to best advantage. (op 8-1)

Wigwam Willie(IRE), ideally suited by 1m and plenty of cut in the ground, shaped well on this second start of the year and left the strong impression that the return to the longer trip would be very much to his liking. (op 10-1)

Electric Warrior(IRE), closely matched with Wigwam Willie on a recent Pontefract run, was not far off that form over a trip that is on the sharp side. The return to 1m will suit but he is likely to remain vulnerable in competitive handicaps from this mark. (op 9-1 tchd 10-1)

Dhaular Dhar(IRE), whose best form is on left-handed turning tracks, was far from disgraced on only this second start of the year. He should be spot on now and will be of interest if returned to Chester next month. (op 9-1 tchd 11-1)

Overrule(USA), who showed fair form in five starts for Jeremy Noseda, was not disgraced over this inadequate trip on this first start for Brian Ellison. He is one to keep an eye returned to further. (op 10-1)

Jamieson Gold(IRE), a capable but inconsistent performer for Barry Hills, was not totally disgraced on this fourth start for a yard that is among the winners but he is going to have to show more before he is a worth a bet. (op 10-1)

Partners In Jazz(USA), well beaten at Doncaster on his previous start, was not at his best from a low draw in a race where the leaders did not come back to the field. He is worth another chance in similar company. Official explanation: jockey said gelding was denied a clear run

Skilling Spirit Official explanation: jockey said gelding missed the break

1219 BET365.COM H'CAP — 1m 4f 93y

3:05 (3:05) (Class 5) (0-70,70) 4-Y-O+ — **£3,238** (£963; £481; £240) **Stalls** Centre

Form	Pos	Dist	Horse / details	Jockey	RPR
02-	1		**Pertemps Networks**[21] 7211 4-8-4 **56** oh1 (M W Easterby) *chsd ldrs: drvn to ld over 2f out: styd on strly to forge clr fnl f* **9/4**[1]	DaleGibson 5	77+
450-	2	8	**Nero West (FR)**[149] 6733 7-9-1 **66** (Miss L A Perratt) *led and sn clr: hdd over 2f out: kpt on: no ch w wnr* **16/1**	(p) TomEaves 4	75
050-	3	hd	**Bijou Dan**[29] 7146 7-8-6 **57** (G M Moore) *hld up: rdn over 3f out: rallied over 1f out: nrst fin* **10/1**	(p) GregFairley 2	65
562-	4	2	**Thunderwing (IRE)**[53] 6640 6-8-7 **58** (James Moffatt) *midfield: effrt over 2f out: sn one pce* **9/1**	RoystonFfrench 6	63
014/	5	½	**Hill Billy Rock (IRE)**[570] 5284 5-8-13 **67** (G A Swinbank) *hld up: shkn up and hdwy over 2f out: edgd lft over 1f out: nvr nrr* **9/2**[2]	PJMcDonald(3) 8	71+
3136	6	1 ½	**Karmest**[14] 963 4-8-8 **60** (A D Brown) *prom: effrt 3f out: no ex over 1f out* **7/1**	SilvestreDeSousa 10	62
052/	7	10	**Calcutta Cup (UAE)**[462] 6317 5-8-7 **58** ow1 (Karen McLintock) *chsd clr ldr: effrt and chal over 2f out: wknd over 1f out* **20/1**	TonyHamilton 7	44
450-	8	16	**Saluscraggie**[260] 3719 6-8-2 **56** oh5 (R E Barr) *hld up in midfield on outside: effrt u.p 3f out: sn btn* **28/1**	DuranFentiman(3) 12	16
003/	9	1 ¼	**Find Me (USA)**[28] 6145 4-8-10 **62** (L Lungo) *midfield: drvn and outpcd 5f out: shortlived effrt over 2f out: sn btn* **33/1**	PaulHanagan 3	20
51-3	10	5	**Calzaghe (IRE)**[14] 963 4-9-4 **70** (K R Burke) *hld up: rdn fr 1/2-way: shortlived effrt over 3f out: sn btn* **5/1**[3]	(v) AndrewElliott 1	20
401-	11	15	**Mayadeen (IRE)**[117] 7102 6-8-5 **56** oh7 (Miss L A Perratt) *missed break: bhd: struggling 1/2-way: nvr on terms* **16/1**	(b) PaulFessey 11	—

2m 51.76s (6.16) **Going Correction** +0.60s/f (Yiel)
WFA 4 from 5yo+ 1lb — **11** Ran SP% **120.1**
Speed ratings (Par 103): **103,97,97,96,95 94,88,77,76,73 63**
CSF £42.90 CT £313.78 TOTE £3.20: £1.60, £5.90, £3.70; EX 48.60 TRIFECTA Not won..
Owner Derek Pearson **Bred** H G Llewellyn **Trained** Sheriff Hutton, N Yorks

FOCUS

A modest handicap but a sound pace throughout and one in which the winner turned in a much improved effort. He was well in on his hurdles form and was value for a bit further too.

Calzaghe(IRE) Official explanation: jockey said gelding never travelled

Mayadeen(IRE) Official explanation: jockey said gelding had a breathing problem

1220 E.B.F./TARMAC NOVICE STKS — 5f

3:45 (3:46) (Class 4) 2-Y-O — **£4,630** (£1,377; £688; £343) **Stalls** High

Form	Pos	Dist	Horse / details	Jockey	RPR
0	1		**Saxford**[14] 957 2-8-12 0 (Mrs L Stubbs) *mde all: rdn and edgd lft ins fnl f: hld on wl* **6/1**[3]	TomEaves 2	70
4	2	1	**Raimond Ridge (IRE)**[4] 1122 2-8-12 0 (M R Channon) *prom: effrt and ev ch over 1f out: edgd lft: kpt on: hld towards fin* **3/1**[2]	DarryllHolland 5	66
3	3	½	**Knavesmire (IRE)**[14] 957 2-8-7 0 (M Brittain) *wnt lft s: cl up: effrt over 2f out: edgd lft over 1f out: kpt on same pce fnl f* **6/4**[1]	TWilliams 8	59+
0	4	¾	**Another Luke (IRE)**[14] 957 2-8-9 0 (T J Etherington) *in tch: hdwy 2f out: rdn and one pce fnl f* **33/1**	PJMcDonald(3) 1	61
	5	2 ¾	**Dotty's Brother** 2-8-12 0 (Mrs A Duffield) *in tch: outpcd 1/2-way: no imp fr over 1f out* **12/1**	RoystonFfrench 6	50
	6	3	**Oriental Rose** 2-8-7 0 (G M Moore) *w wnr tl wknd over 1f out* **14/1**	AndrewElliott 3	33+
	7	14	**Mosspaul** 2-8-7 0 (A C Whillans) *hmpd s: a bhd: lost tch fr 1/2-way* **50/1**	DaleGibson 7	—
	8	1 ¼	**Compton Ford** 2-8-12 0 (M Dods) *wnt lft s: plld hrd in rr: rdn and struggling fr 1/2-way* **13/2**	PhillipMakin 4	—

66.01 secs (5.31) **Going Correction** +0.60s/f (Yiel) — **8** Ran SP% **111.9**
Speed ratings (Par 94): **81,79,78,77,73 68,45,43**
CSF £23.27 TOTE £8.00: £2.30, £1.50, £1.10; EX 33.50 Trifecta £117.80 Pool: £526.38, 3.17 w/u.
Owner D Arundale **Bred** Malih L Al Basti **Trained** Norton, N Yorks

FOCUS

A race lacking quality or strength but the pace was fair and the field raced stands' side. Just fair form, the winner improving on his showing in the Brocklesby.

NOTEBOOK

Saxford, not well drawn in the Brocklesby, attracted plenty of support and turned in a much improved effort. He will have no problems with 6f, has physical scope and may be capable of further improvement. (op 10-1 tchd 12-1)

Raimond Ridge(IRE), who shaped with a degree of promise at Folkestone earlier in the week, bettered that form. He will stay 6f and looks capable of picking up a similarly ordinary event in due course. (tchd 11-4)

Knavesmire(IRE), who shaped well when third in the Brocklesby, ran creditably in terms of form but failed to build on that promise. She does not have much in the way of physical scope but she may improve a little over 6f. (tchd 11-8 and 13-8)

Another Luke(IRE), soundly beaten in the Brocklesby, turned in a much improved effort this time and left the impression that the step up to 6f would be in his favour. He may be capable of picking up a minor event. (op 20-1)

Dotty's Brother, an 8,000 brother to the stable's Dotty's Daughter, showed ability at a modest level on this racecourse debut and can be expected to improve for the experience. (op 10-1 tchd 14-1)

Oriental Rose, a half-sister to winners from 1m to 1m2f, showed up well for a long way on this racecourse debut. She should be better for this experience but is going to have to fare a good deal better to win a race in this grade. (op 8-1)

1221 ST JAMES SECURITY MAIDEN STKS — 1m 2f 32y

4:30 (4:32) (Class 5) 3-Y-O+ — **£2,914** (£867; £433; £216) **Stalls** Centre

Form	Pos	Dist	Horse / details	Jockey	RPR
320-	1		**Drill Sergeant**[162] 6468 3-8-7 86 (M Johnston) *mde all: drew clr over 2f out: eased ins fnl f* **5/4**[1]	GregFairley 7	96
	2	10	**Art Trend (IRE)** 3-8-7 0 (P W Chapple-Hyam) *prom: effrt over 3f out: kpt on fnl f: no ch w wnr* **7/1**[3]	AdrianMcCarthy 4	76
00-3	3	nk	**Internationaldebut (IRE)**[14] 961 3-8-7 92 (S Parr) *t.k.h early: trckd ldrs: effrt over 2f out: one pce over 1f out* **6/4**[2]	DarrenWilliams 1	75
	4	12	**Prince Rhyddarch** 3-8-8 0 ow1 (Miss L A Perratt) *plld hrd: hld up outside: hung bdly rt to outside rail after 3f: struggling 1/2-way: styd on fnl 2f: n.d* **33/1**	TomEaves 6	52
4/-4	5	½	**Flamed Amazement**[13] 982 4-9-12 0 (L Lungo) *hld up: hdwy over 3f out: outpcd fr over 2f out* **10/1**	(p) RobertWinston 2	54
000-	6	20	**Talon (IRE)**[165] 6410 3-8-7 53 (G A Swinbank) *hld up on ins: drvn over 3f out: sn btn* **25/1**	DaleGibson 3	10
000-	7	5	**College Land Boy**[31] 5041 4-9-12 50 (A Kirtley) *chsd ldrs tl wknd fr 4f out* **100/1**	PaulMulrennan 8	—
0	8	45	**Ducal Damsel**[13] 980 3-8-2 0 (J R Weymes) *cl up tl lost pl 1/2-way: hung rt and sn btn* **100/1**	PaulHanagan 5	—

2m 19.24s (7.34) **Going Correction** +0.60s/f (Yiel)
WFA 3 from 4yo 19lb — **8** Ran SP% **114.8**
Speed ratings (Par 103): **101,93,92,83,82 66,62,26**
CSF £10.65 TOTE £2.30: £1.30, £1.50, £1.20; EX 10.00 Trifecta £19.00 Pool: £412.56, 15.39 w/u.
Owner J Barson **Bred** D G Hardisty Bloodstock **Trained** Middleham Moor, N Yorks

FOCUS

An uncompetitive maiden in which the market leader was allowed his own way in front. He looks useful but the race did lack strength in depth. The pace was just fair.

1222 PETER CAMPBELL MAIDEN FILLIES' STKS — 1m 3y(S)

5:10 (5:10) (Class 5) 3-Y-O+ — **£2,914** (£867; £433; £216) **Stalls** High

Form	Pos	Dist	Horse / details	Jockey	RPR
50/-	1		**Twilight Dawn**[557] 5596 4-9-10 0 (L Lungo) *hld up in tch stands' side: hdwy over 2f out: led wl ins fnl f: styd on wl* **25/1**	PaulHanagan 9	72
00-	2	nk	**Midnight Mystique (IRE)**[225] 4782 3-8-9 0 (T D Barron) *chsd stands' side ldrs: led that gp over 2f out to wl ins fnl f: r.o: 2nd of 8 in gp* **14/1**	PaulFessey 12	67
	3	7	**Mazloma (USA)** 3-8-9 0 (M R Channon) *missed break: bhd on stands' side: kpt on fr 2f out: no ch w first 2: 3rd of 8 in gp* **5/2**[1]	DarryllHolland 11	51+
-6	4	3 ½	**Milton Of Campsie**[11] 1019 3-8-9 0 (S Parr) *cl up far side: led that gp over 2f out: kpt on u.p fnl f: no ch w stands' side: 1st of 5 in gp* **11/2**[3]	DarrenWilliams 1	43
60-	5	1 ¾	**Lady In Chief**[162] 6470 3-8-9 0 (Miss J A Camacho) *trckd ldrs far side: outpcd over 3f out: rallied 2f out: no imp fnl f: 2nd of 5 in gp* **25/1**	TonyHamilton 4	39
0-	6	1 ½	**Twiglet (IRE)**[248] 4061 3-8-6 0 (George Baker) *cl up far side: disp ld over 2f out: wknd ins fnl f: 3rd of 5 in gp* **7/2**[2]	TolleyDean(3) 2	35
0-20	7	14	**Park Royal (UAE)**[36] 748 3-8-9 68 (D E Cantillon) *bhd stands' side: drvn 1/2-way: n.d: 4th of 8 in gp* **7/2**[2]	PatCosgrave 13	3
0-	8	8	**Forrest Star**[198] 5550 3-8-9 0 (Miss L A Perratt) *led far side to over 2f out: sn wknd: 4th of 5 in gp* **25/1**	TomEaves 5	—
00-	9	1 ½	**Boppys Diamond**[157] 6597 4-9-10 0 (P T Midgley) *hld up in tch stands' side: drvn over 2f out: sn btn: 5th of 8 in gp* **40/1**	MickyFenton 10	—
	10	2 ¾	**Springfield Lass** 3-8-9 0 (Mrs A Duffield) *led stands' side to over 2f out: sn wknd: 6th of 8 in gp* **12/1**	RoystonFfrench 8	—
-226	11	1	**Inontime (IRE)**[14] 974 3-8-9 66 (K R Burke) *chsd stands' side ldrs: drvn over 3f out: wknd over 2f out: 7th of 8 in gp* **15/2**	(p) AndrewElliott 7	—
	12	¾	**Fluoree (FR)**[40] 4-9-10 0 (D W Thompson) *dwlt: sn struggling far side: t.o after 3f: last of 5 in gp* **66/1**	DaleGibson 3	—
000-	13	2 ½	**Motherwell**[258] 3760 3-8-9 43 (M Brittain) *dwlt: sn in tch stands' side: rdn 1/2-way: sn wknd: last of 8 in gp* **80/1**	TWilliams 6	—

1m 49.67s (6.27) **Going Correction** +0.60s/f (Yiel)
WFA 3 from 4yo 15lb — **13** Ran SP% **131.2**
Speed ratings (Par 100): **94,93,86,83,81 79,65,57,56,53 52,51,49**
CSF £349.93 TOTE £39.60: £8.00, £5.20, £1.60; EX 481.10 TRIFECTA Not won. Place 6 £26.05, Place 5 £10.52..
Owner Len Lungo Racing Limited **Bred** Greenland Park Ltd **Trained** Carrutherstown, D'fries & G'way

FOCUS

A modest event in which the group that raced far side were at a disadvantage. It was run on the worst ground of the day. The first two finished clear and the form is somewhat guessy.

Mazloma(USA) Official explanation: jockey said filly missed the break

Park Royal(UAE) Official explanation: jockey said filly was unsuited by the good to soft (soft in places) ground

Forrest Star Official explanation: jockey said filly had no more to give

T/Plt: £15.80 to a £1 stake. Pool: £60,192.80. 2,763.90 winning tickets. T/Qpdt: £5.00 to a £1 stake. Pool: £2,456.76. 361.70 winning tickets. RY

1223 - 1229a (Foreign Racing) - See Raceform Interactive

LEOPARDSTOWN (L-H)

Sunday, April 6

OFFICIAL GOING: Yielding (yielding to soft in places)

1230a LEOPARDSTOWN 1,000 GUINEAS TRIAL STKS (GROUP 3) (FILLIES) 7f

3:15 (3:15) 3-Y-0 **£33,507** (£9,830; £4,683; £1,595)

RPR

1 **Carribean Sunset (IRE)**[13] 1009 3-9-0 93 .... PJSmullen 3 102
(D K Weld, Ire) *led: hdd after 1f: 3rd 1/2-way: impr to chal under 2f out: narrow ld over 1f out: kpt on wl: all out* **12/1**

2 *hd* **Halfway To Heaven (IRE)**[154] 6678 3-9-0 90 .... JAHeffernan 7 102
(A P O'Brien, Ire) *chsd ldrs: impr to dispute after 2f: cl 2nd 1/2-way: rdn to ld 2f out: narrowly hdd over 1f out: kpt on wl: jst hld* **7/1**[3]

3 *2 1/2* **Saoirse Abu (USA)**[190] 5796 3-9-3 111 ....(b) KJManning 2 98
(J S Bolger, Ire) *chsd ldrs: 4th 1/2-way: rdn over 2f out: 3rd 1 1/2f out: no imp on ldrs fr 1f out: kpt on* **2/1**[2]

4 *1 1/2* **Yali (IRE)**[160] 6549 3-9-0 86 .... RPCleary 8 91
(Francis Ennis, Ire) *hld up: rdn into 5th 2f out: styd on to 4th 1 1/2f out: no imp on ldrs fr over 1f out: kpt on same pce* **25/1**

5 *4 1/2* **Dash Back (USA)**[351] 1170 3-9-0 .... DPMcDonogh 9 79
(Kevin Prendergast, Ire) *mid-div: 6th 1/2-way: rdn in 5th 3f out: no imp over 2f out: kpt on same pce* **12/1**

6 *3/4* **Queen Jock (USA)**[58] 496 3-9-0 95 .... PShanahan 4 77
(Tracey Collins, Ire) *chsd ldrs: 5th 1/2-way: rdn in 6th and no ex bef st: kpt on one pce* **16/1**

7 *7* **Psalm (IRE)**[175] 6214 3-9-0 .... JMurtagh 5 58
(A P O'Brien, Ire) *mid-div: sddled slipped after 2f: sn in rr and n.d* **5/4**[1]

8 *1/2* **Miss Red Eye (IRE)**[7] 1106 3-9-0 58 .... FFDaSilva 6 57
(Luke Comer, Ire) *a towards rr* **100/1**

9 *2* **Valentine Hill (IRE)**[13] 1009 3-9-0 80 .... MJKinane 1 51
(Adrian Maguire, Ire) *chsd ldrs: impr to ld after 1f: rdn and hdd 2f out: sn wknd* **16/1**

1m 28.9s (-1.40) **Going Correction** +0.125s/f (Good) 9 Ran SP% **122.3**
Speed ratings: **113,112,109,108,103 102,94,93,91**
CSF £98.32 TOTE £17.50: £3.40, £2.20, £1.30; DF 95.80.
Owner Dr R Lambe **Bred** Barronstown Stud **Trained** The Curragh, Co Kildare

FOCUS

The first pair came clear in this Group 3 1,000 trial. The form may not be totally reliable, but both still look capable of rating higher.

NOTEBOOK

Carribean Sunset(IRE), disappointing at Cork on her seasonal bow 13 days previously, put up a greatly-improved display and narrowly got up to record her first win at the sixth time of asking. This better ground was evidently much more to her liking and she showed a very game attitude inside the final furlong to get the better of the runner-up. She now most likely heads for the Irish 1000 Guineas next month and, while she will need to step up again a good deal to play a part in that, she is in very good hands. (op 10/1)

Halfway To Heaven(IRE) ◆, last seen winning her maiden over course and distance back in November, was the stable's second string on jockey bookings and ran a blinder in defeat. She looks to have done well physically during her time off the track and it would be a surprise were she not to go one better at this sort of level before long. It remains to be seen whether she will re-oppose the winner in the 1000 Guineas at the Curragh next month as the extra furlong could well find her out at this stage of her career, being as she has plenty of speed in her pedigree. (op 8/1)

Saoirse Abu(USA), shouldering a Group 1 penalty, set the standard on her juvenile form and had the blinkers back on for this three-year-old debut. She proved easy to back, however, and never looked like getting to the first pair inside the final furlong. It is fair to expect her to be all the better for the outing, but she does have to prove she has trained on. (op 7/4)

Psalm(IRE), just pipped by her stable companion Kitty Matcham over 6f on her sole outing last term, has clearly been doing something right in her home work as she was all the rage in the betting for this seasonal bow. Her saddle soon after the start, however, and her chance was quickly gone. Official explanation: jockey said saddle slipped (op 11/8 tchd 6/4)

1232a LEOPARDSTOWN 2,000 GUINEAS TRIAL STKS (GROUP 3) (C&G) 1m

4:15 (4:17) 3-Y-0 **£33,507** (£9,830; £4,683; £1,595)

RPR

1 **Famous Name**[160] 6549 3-9-0 105 .... PJSmullen 5 113+
(D K Weld, Ire) *trckd ldr in 2nd: impr to chal bef st: led over 2f out: rdn clr fnl f: impressive* **4/6**[1]

2 *4* **Moiqen (IRE)**[179] 6115 3-9-0 .... DPMcDonogh 2 102
(Kevin Prendergast, Ire) *hld up: rdn in 3rd 1 1/2f out: styd on to go 2nd ins fnl f: no ch w wnr* **4/1**[3]

3 *1 1/4* **Hebridean (IRE)**[154] 6680 3-9-0 85 .... JAHeffernan 4 99
(A P O'Brien, Ire) *racd 3rd: rdn to 2nd 1 1/2f out: no imp wnr fr 1f out: sn lost 2nd: kpt on same pce* **16/1**

4 *8* **Greek Mythology (USA)**[292] 2732 3-9-0 93 .... JMurtagh 1 81
(A P O'Brien, Ire) *led: rdn and chal bef st: hdd over 2f out: sn wknd* **3/1**[2]

1m 43.9s (2.70) **Going Correction** +0.125s/f (Good) 5 Ran SP% **110.9**
Speed ratings: **91,87,85,77**
CSF £3.78 TOTE £1.40; DF 3.00.
Owner K Abdulla **Bred** Juddmonte Farms Ltd **Trained** The Curragh, Co Kildare
■ Great Rumpuscat (12/1) was withdrawn after refusing to enter the stalls. Deduct 5p in the £ under rule 4.

FOCUS

A slightly disappointing turnout for this Group 3 Guineas trial. The winner was entitled to win on previous form and duly did the job in taking fashion. The form is set by the third, who ran up to his best.

NOTEBOOK

Famous Name ◆, who has physically developed during the winter, ran out a taking winner on this three-year-old bow. He could have been called the winner nearing the 2f pole and did not have to be fully extended to go clear. This looks to be his ideal trip at present, despite the likelihood of him being able to handle 1m2f in due course, and a bit of cut in the ground is really ideal for him. His leading trainer now intends to aim him at one of the Guineas and no doubt he has more to offer this year. (op 8/11 tchd 4/7)

Moiqen(IRE), a Navan maiden winner over this trip on his final outing last year, was patiently ridden early on and took time to find his full stride. He was never going to get to the winner, but he has scope and left the impression he would enjoy stepping up in trip now. (op 4/1 tchd 7/2)

Hebridean(IRE), having his first run for Aidan O'Brien, found just the same pace when it mattered and was readily beaten off in the end. This was still a sound-enough effort, however, and a drop back down in class can see him find another race.

Greek Mythology(USA) was given a very positive ride on this return to the track and, while dropping right out after the 2f pole, he should really come on a deal for the run. (op 7/2 tchd 5/1)

1233a FOXROCK (C & G) RACE 1m 2f

4:45 (4:45) 3-Y-0 **£9,573** (£2,808; £1,338; £455)

RPR

1 **Unwritten Rule (IRE)**[246] 4189 3-9-4 97 .... PJSmullen 3 96+
(D K Weld, Ire) *trckd ldrs in 4th: impr to chal over 1f out: sn led: jnd last 150yds: jst hld on* **9/2**[2]

2 *shd* **Washington Irving (IRE)**[167] 6394 3-9-0 .... JMurtagh 2 91+
(A P O'Brien, Ire) *hld up in 5th: swtchd to chal 1f out: r.o to join ldr last 150yds: drifted lft cl home: jst failed* **8/13**[1]

3 *1 3/4* **Houston Dynimo (IRE)**[154] 6682 3-9-4 91 .... DPMcDonogh 5 92
(Kevin Prendergast, Ire) *chsd ldrs in 3rd: rdn to ld over 1f out: sn hdd: kpt on same pce* **10/1**

4 *2 1/2* **Hindu Kush (IRE)**[154] 6682 3-9-0 .... JAHeffernan 4 83
(A P O'Brien, Ire) *chsd ldr in 2nd: chal 3f out: rdn in 2nd and no ex 1 1/2f out: 4th over 1f out: kpt on same pce* **10/1**

5 *3/4* **Dirar (IRE)**[30] 827 3-9-4 91 .... MJKinane 6 86
(M Halford, Ire) *led: rdn and hdd over 1f out: sn no ex* **6/1**[3]

6 *7* **Chevie (IRE)**[184] 5990 3-9-0 .... FMBerry 1 69
(T Hogan, Ire) *a in rr* **25/1**

2m 11.9s (3.70) **Going Correction** +0.125s/f (Good) 6 Ran SP% **116.4**
Speed ratings: **90,89,88,86,85 80**
CSF £8.09 TOTE £6.00: £2.80, £1.10; DF 11.70.
Owner Moyglare Stud Farm **Bred** Moyglare Stud Farm Ltd **Trained** The Curragh, Co Kildare

1231 - 1236a (Foreign Racing) - See Raceform Interactive

COLOGNE (R-H)

Sunday, April 6

OFFICIAL GOING: Heavy

1237a WWW.GERMANTOTE.DE GRAND PRIX AUFGALOPP (GROUP 3) 1m 3f

4:10 (4:18) 4-Y-0+ **£23,529** (£7,353; £3,676; £2,206)

RPR

1 **Oriental Tiger (GER)**[259] 3778 5-8-13 ....(b) THellier 6 102
(U Ostmann, Germany) *led after 3f: 3l clr ent st: comf* **29/10**[2]

2 *2* **Dwilano (GER)**[219] 5-8-11 .... JiriPalik 1 97
(P Remmert, Germany) *in midfield: 3rd st: tk 2nd 1f out: no ch w wnr* **16/1**

3 *3* **White Lightning (GER)**[147] 6781 6-8-11 .... JBojko 2 92
(U Stech, Norway) *racd in 4th: impr over 3f out: 2nd st: no ex and lost 2nd 1f out* **57/1**

4 *5* **Eiswind**[140] 4-8-11 .... AStarke 3 83
(P Schiergen, Germany) *led 3f: 4th st: sn wknd* **93/10**

5 *4* **Sereth (IRE)**[196] 5-8-11 .... TPQueally 8 77
(J Hirschberger, Germany) *2nd early: wknd steadily fr 3f out* **6/1**

6 *12* **Waldvogel (IRE)**[189] 5849 4-8-13 .... EPedroza 4 58
(A Wohler, Germany) *in midfield: btn 3f out* **82/10**

7 *6* **Egerton (GER)**[119] 7090 7-9-1 .... TMundry 5 50
(P Rau, Germany) *hld up in rr: nvr a factor* **14/10**[1]

8 *3/4* **Poseidon Adventure (IRE)**[169] 6353 5-8-13 ....(b) ASuborics 9 47
(W Figge, Germany) *a in rr* **47/10**[3]

9 *22* **Blushing King (FR)**[231] 4655 6-8-11 .... LennartHammer-Hansen 7 7
(Frau E Mader, Germany) *last thrght: t.o fr over 2f out* **23/1**

2m 33.39s (12.59) 9 Ran SP% **131.5**
(including 10 Euro stake): WIN 39; PL 22, 36, 70; SF 602.
Owner Gestut Auenquelle **Bred** Gestut Auenquelle **Trained** Germany

1175 LONGCHAMP (R-H)

Sunday, April 6

OFFICIAL GOING: Heavy

1239a PRIX NOAILLES (GROUP 2) (C&F) 1m 2f 110y

3:20 (3:27) 3-Y-0 **£54,412** (£21,030; £10,037; £6,691; £3,346)

RPR

1 **Full Of Gold (FR)**[147] 6782 3-9-2 .... TGillet 3 105
(Mme C Head-Maarek, France) *racd in 3rd: wnt 2nd 2f out: rdn over 1f out: led 100yds out: pushed out clsng stages: jst hld on* **4/5**[1]

2 *hd* **Court Canibal**[22] 913 3-9-2 .... OPeslier 5 105
(M Delzangles, France) *last early: 5th st: styd on down outside to take 2nd fnl 50yds: jst failed* **73/10**

3 *3/4* **Blue Bresil (FR)**[16] 3-9-2 .... OTrigodet 6 104
(Mlle B Halley des Fontaines, France) *set gd pce: 2 l clr 2f out: sn rdn: hdd 100yds out: kpt on* **22/1**

4 *nk* **Mount Helicon**[26] 3-9-2 .... SPasquier 2 103
(A Fabre, France) *racd in 5th: 4th st: styd on wl towards outside fr 2f out tl sltly short of room and no ex last 100yds* **51/10**[2]

5 *6* **Mayweather**[24] 3-9-2 .... C-PLemaire 4 92
(J-C Rouget, France) *racd in 2nd to 2f out: wknd* **62/10**

6 *dist* **Chirango (FR)**[12] 3-9-2 .... CSoumillon 1 —
(P Demercastel, France) *4th early: last st: t.o fnl 2f* **11/2**[3]

2m 22.5s (9.50) **Going Correction** +1.10s/f (Soft) 6 Ran SP% **117.6**
Speed ratings: **109,108,108,108,103** —
PARI-MUTUEL: WIN 1.80; PL 1.30, 2.30; SF 7.80.
Owner Alec Head **Bred** A & Mme A Head **Trained** Chantilly, France

NOTEBOOK

Full Of Gold(FR) produced a much better performance than the bare result suggests as he was making his seasonal debut on very heavy ground against five others who had all had the advantage of a previous outing this season. He looked in fine condition while parading in the paddock and, settled in third place in the early part of the race, he made a rather laboured challenge starting one and a half out but kept on pulling out just that little bit extra. If anything he won with something in hand and he has to come on enormously for the outing. This colt will not be going for the Vodafone Derby and the intention now is to run him in the Prix Hocquart before a tilt at the Prix du Jockey Club.

Court Canibal looked the winner running into the final furlong but, although he battled on well, he could not hold first place inside the final 50 yards. Still relatively inexperienced, he was given a waiting ride and accelerated well considering the state of the ground. He was beaten by a better horse on the day but may have a chance for revenge in the Hocquart.

Blue Bresil(FR)'s breeding suggested that he would revel in the testing ground and this provincially trained colt did just that. He took the field along at a sensible pace from the very start and still had a lead of several lengths coming into the straight, but he eventually had to give best. He was running for the first time at a Paris track and will now be aimed at the Jockey Club, with a probable run in a Listed race at Bordeaux beforehand.
Mount Helicon looked rather one-paced at the end of this race but is certainly a decent colt in the making. In fourth place early on, he made a forward move running into the final two furlongs and then could not quicken as the race came to an end. He should be suited by a longer distance and is worth keeping an eye on in the future.

1240a PRIX D'HARCOURT (GROUP 2) 1m 2f
3:50 (3:58) 4-Y-O+ **£54,486** (£21,030; £10,037; £6,691; £3,346)

RPR
1 **Loup Breton (IRE)**^{183} [6032] 4-8-12 .... C-PLemaire 1 117
(E Lellouche, France) *hld up in 6th: hdwy on ins fr 2f out to ld 75yds out: drvn out* **84/10**
2 ½ **Spirit One (FR)**^{22} [912] 4-8-12 .... CSoumillon 5 116
(P Demercastel, France) *set str pce: rdn over 1 1/2f out: hdd 75yds out: kpt on to hold 2nd* **9/10^1**
3 ½ **Boris De Deauville (IRE)**^{154} [6689] 5-9-1 .... TThulliez 4 118
(S Wattel, France) *racd in 3rd: wnt 2nd jst over 1f out: lost 2nd 150yds out: kpt on at one pce* **63/10^3**
4 ¾ **Balius (IRE)**^{22} [912] 5-8-12 ....(b) MBlancpain 7 114
(C Laffon-Parias, France) *hld up in 7th: hdwy down outside fr over 2f out to take 4th 150yds out: kpt on* **19/1**
5 2½ **Aspectus (IRE)**^{22} [912] 5-8-12 .... JVictoire 6 109
(A Fabre, France) *chsd ldr to jst over 1f out: wknd* **33/1**
6 4 **Persian Storm (GER)**^{203} [5464] 4-8-12 .... SPasquier 8 102
(A Fabre, France) *hld up in last: nvr a factor* **84/10**
7 6 **Quest For Honor**^{232} [4627] 4-9-1 .... OPeslier 3 94
(A Fabre, France) *racd in 4th tl wknd 2f out* **11/1**
8 1½ **Musical Way (FR)**^{30} 6-8-12 .... RonanThomas 2 89
(P Van De Poele, France) *racd in 5th: brief effrt 2f out: sn btn* **56/10^2**

2m 14.6s (7.70) **Going Correction** +1.10s/f (Soft) **8** Ran SP% **119.0**
Speed ratings: **113,112,112,111,109 106,101,100**
PARI-MUTUEL: WIN 9.40; PL 1.90, 1.20, 1.70; DF 8.10.
Owner Ecurie Wildenstein **Bred** Dayton Investments Ltd **Trained** Lamorlaye, France

NOTEBOOK
Loup Breton(IRE) was given a highly professional waiting ride and is a colt who may well go on to win a Group 1 event later in the season as he appears to be getting better with age. He still had plenty to do coming into the straight but came with a progressive run up the far rail to take the lead with under 50 yards left to run. He appeared to appreciate the heavy ground and this would appear to be his perfect distance. Connections will now look at either the Ganay or the Prix d'Ispahan. One of his main targets now will be the Prince of Wales's Stakes at Royal Ascot.
Spirit One(FR) made a game effort to go from pillar to post. He appeared to be going well for much of the race and came under strong pressure halfway up the straight. He still had a narrow lead running into the final furlong but guts alone were not sufficient to hold off the winner. His trainer felt that having to make all in such terrible conditions played a role in his defeat. Connections will now decide between the Prix Ganay, d'Ispahan or both.
Boris De Deauville(IRE), making his seasonal debut and conceding 3lb to the front pair, produced a fine effort. Third early on, he went in pursuit of the leader halfway up the straight but could not keep up the tempo until the line. His target is now the Prix d'Ispahan and it was a brave effort to try and land back-to-back wins in this Group 2 event.
Balius(IRE), held up early on, was one but last coming into the straight. He came with a late run and was putting in his best work at the finish. This was probably not the best ground for this five-year-old and his trainer is hoping to receive an invitation for the Queen Elizabeth II Cup in Hong Kong.

1203 KEMPTON (A.W) (R-H)
Monday, April 7

OFFICIAL GOING: Standard
Wind: modest half against Weather: overcast, chilly

1242 PANORAMIC BAR & RESTAURANT H'CAP 5f (P)
2:10 (2:10) (Class 5) (0-70,70) 4-Y-O+ **£2,590** (£770; £385; £192) **Stalls** High

Form RPR
3630 **1** **Lord Of The Reins (IRE)**^{14} [994] 4-8-12 **64** .... AdamKirby 8 75
(D Shaw) *trckd ldrs on inner: rdn wl over 1f out: squeezed through on rail to ld ins fnl f: r.o wl* **4/1^2**
2224 **2** ¾ **Spoof Master (IRE)**^{12} [1033] 4-9-4 **70** .... RobertWinston 7 78
(C R Dore) *sn led: rdn over 1f out: rdr dropped whip jst ins fnl f: sn hdd: kpt on same pce* **7/2^1**
25-2 **3** hd **Azygous**^{11} [1037] 5-8-10 **62** .... AlanMunro 6 69
(J Akehurst) *w ldr: drvn wl over 1f out: unable qck u.p fnl f* **4/1^2**
003- **4** ¾ **The Fisio**^{145} [6810] 8-8-10 **62** ....(b^1) PaulEddery 4 67
(G D Blake) *dwlt: bhd: hdwy on inner wl over 1f out: r.o but nvr able to chal* **14/1**
2115 **5** hd **Decider (USA)**^{16} [971] 5-8-12 **67** .... KevinGhunowa$^{(3)}$ 1 71
(R A Harris) *awkward leaving stalls: in tch: rdn wl over 1f out: kpt on same pce fnl f* **5/1^3**
6133 **6** 1 **Hollow Jo**^{23} [901] 8-9-1 **67** .... MickyFenton 2 67
(J R Jenkins) *a in last pair: rdn 1/2-way: c wd over 1f out: kpt on but nvr pce to chal* **7/2^1**
302 **7** ½ **Overstayed (IRE)**^{24} [875] 5-8-5 **57** ....(be) RichardMullen 5 55
(M Mullineaux) *chsd ldrs: rdn 2f out: outpcd fnl f* **8/1**

60.26 secs (-0.24) **Going Correction** +0.125s/f (Slow) **7** Ran SP% **118.9**
Speed ratings (Par 103): **106,104,104,103,102 101,100**
CSF £19.46 CT £60.33 TOTE £5.80: £3.40, £2.20; EX 25.50.
Owner Danethorpe Racing Partnership **Bred** C Farrell **Trained** Danethorpe, Notts

FOCUS
A modest sprint handicap, but pretty sound form.

1243 KEMPTON.CO.UK MEDIAN AUCTION MAIDEN STKS 1m 2f (P)
2:40 (2:40) (Class 5) 3-4-Y-O **£2,590** (£770; £385; £192) **Stalls** High

Form RPR
053- **1** **Title Role**^{150} [6750] 3-8-6 72 .... TolleyDean$^{(3)}$ 6 77
(P F I Cole) *sn led: mde rest: hrd pressed and rdn wl over 1f out: edgd lft ins fnl f: hld on: all out* **11/4^2**
2 hd **Sweet Lightning** 3-8-9 0 .... MartinDwyer 9 77+
(W R Muir) *hld up in rr: gd hdwy on inner 2f out: chsd ldng pair over 1f out: pushed along jst over 1f out: r.o wl: wnt 2nd towards fin: jst hld* **33/1**
02-2 **3** nk **St Jean Cap Ferrat**^{13} [1014] 3-8-9 73 .... RyanMoore 5 76
(G Wragg) *chsd wnr: rdn to chal wl over 1f out: hrd rdn and unable qck fnl f* **5/4^1**
4 9 **Qui Moi (CAN)** 3-8-1 0 .... WilliamBuick$^{(3)}$ 4 53
(J R Fanshawe) *s.i.s: in rr: pushed along after 3f out: hdwy on outer 2f out: plugged on to go modest 4th ins fnl f: nvr threatened ldrs* **12/1**
5 1¾ **Hi Hopes** 3-8-9 0 .... JamieSpencer 7 55
(T G Mills) *chsd ldrs: rdn over 2f out: wknd wl over 1f out* **7/2^3**
0-2 **6** ¾ **Poppy Red**^{41} [704] 3-8-5 0 ow1 .... PaulFitzsimons 3 49
(Miss J R Tooth) *in tch: rdn 3f out: wknd 2f out* **25/1**
430- **7** 1½ **Havanavich**^{159} [6585] 3-8-9 73 .... LPKeniry 2 50
(S Kirk) *in tch: hdwy to chse ldrs over 3f out: rdn and wknd 2f out* **16/1**
445- **8** 4½ **Split The Wind (USA)**^{180} [6097] 4-9-9 57 .... StephenCarson 1 36
(Eve Johnson Houghton) *racd in midfield: rdn and struggling over 3f out: sn bhd* **25/1**
0 **9** 7 **Handbags At Dawn (IRE)**^{10} [1050] 3-8-4 0 .... ChrisCatlin 8 22
(S Kirk) *rrd in stalls and slowly away: a bhd* **66/1**

2m 7.55s (-0.45) **Going Correction** +0.125s/f (Slow)
WFA 3 from 4yo 19lb **9** Ran SP% **119.0**
Speed ratings (Par 103): **106,105,105,98,97 96,95,91,86**
CSF £94.26 TOTE £3.70: £1.50, £6.20, £1.10; EX 141.80.
Owner Axom (IX) **Bred** Mrs S E Barclay **Trained** Whatcombe, Oxon

FOCUS
An ordinary maiden, but the winning time was 1.71 seconds quicker than the following 61-75 handicap. The first three came clear and the form could be rated a bit higher.

1244 KEMPTON FOR WEDDINGS H'CAP 1m 2f (P)
3:10 (3:10) (Class 5) (0-75,75) 3-Y-O **£2,590** (£770; £385; £192) **Stalls** High

Form RPR
541- **1** **Animator**^{129} [6978] 3-9-3 **74** .... TQuinn 6 78+
(P F I Cole) *t.k.h: chsd ldr tl led 8f out: mde rest: rdn wl over 1f out: r.o gamely* **5/2^1**
0-1 **2** 1 **Summer Winds**^{23} [903] 3-9-4 **75** .... JamieSpencer 2 77
(T G Mills) *sn led: hdd 8f out: chsd wnr after: rdn 3f out: ev ch and hrd rdn over 1f out: edgd rt and unable qck fnl f* **3/1^3**
30-4 **3** shd **Jollyhockeysticks**^{16} [966] 3-9-1 **72** .... CatherineGannon 3 74
(M R Channon) *hld up in tch: hdwy 3f out: n.m.r omn inner fr wl over 1f out: styd on nr fin* **5/1**
025- **4** ½ **Higgy's Boy (IRE)**^{159} [6585] 3-8-11 **73** .... PatrickHills$^{(5)}$ 5 74
(R Hannon) *hld up in tch: rdn wl over 1f out: r.o ins fnl f: unable to challenge* **6/1**
33-1 **5** 1 **Warming Up (IRE)**^{19} [940] 3-8-11 **68** .... SebSanders 1 67
(C E Brittain) *chsd ldrs: rdn and effrt over 2f out: no imp fnl f* **11/4^2**

2m 9.26s (1.26) **Going Correction** +0.125s/f (Slow) **5** Ran SP% **111.2**
Speed ratings (Par 98): **99,98,98,97,96**
CSF £10.37 TOTE £3.00: £1.40, £1.90; EX 9.50.
Owner Strategic Thoroughbred Racing **Bred** Stowell Park Stud **Trained** Whatcombe, Oxon

FOCUS
A fair handicap on paper, but the pace was steady, resulting in a time 1.71 seconds slower than the previous maiden, and the form wants treating with caution. The winner has improvement in him.

1245 KEMPTON FOR OUTDOOR EVENTS CLAIMING STKS 1m (P)
3:40 (3:42) (Class 6) 3-Y-O **£2,047** (£604; £302) **Stalls** High

Form RPR
1 **Lizzie Wiggins** 3-8-12 0 .... JohnEgan 3 69
(M Botti) *hld up in 3rd pl: hdwy on inner over 2f out: rdn to ld 1f out: r.o wl* **12/1**
1141 **2** 1 **Bridge Of Fermoy (IRE)**^{11} [1034] 3-9-7 76 ....(bt) GeorgeBaker 2 76
(Miss Gay Kelleway) *led for 1f: chsd ldr after tl led 2f out: sn rdn: hdd 1f out: nt qckn* **4/6^1**
5231 **3** 5 **Days Of Pleasure (IRE)**^{18} [953] 3-9-4 69 .... TPQueally 1 62
(J A Osborne) *chsd ldr tl led after 1f: rdn and hdd 2f out: btn and hung lft fnl f* **5/2^2**
-204 **4** 2 **Montefiore (IRE)**^{10} [1063] 3-8-4 65 ....(bt^1) AntiocoMurgia$^{(7)}$ 4 50
(M Botti) *stdd s: hld up in last: hdwy over 2f out: chsd ldrs over 1f out: sn shuffled along and fnd little* **13/2^3**

1m 42.17s (2.37) **Going Correction** +0.125s/f (Slow) **4** Ran SP% **109.6**
Speed ratings (Par 96): **93,92,87,85**
CSF £21.53 TOTE £11.30; EX 16.10.The winner was claimed by R A Green for £11,000.
Owner Dachel Stud **Bred** Dachel Stud **Trained** Newmarket, Suffolk

FOCUS
Just the four runners, and probably a moderate claimer. The winning time was 0.64 seconds quicker than the later 51-65 handicap.

1246 OPTICHROME PRINTERS H'CAP 2m (P)
4:10 (4:10) (Class 6) (0-55,55) 4-Y-O+ **£2,047** (£604; £302) **Stalls** High

Form RPR
604- **1** **Lady Dedlock**^{166} [6421] 4-8-13 **55** .... RobertHavlin 9 67+
(Jamie Poulton) *in tch: hdwy to chse ldr over 3f out: rdn to ld 2f out: drew clr fnl f: eased towards fin* **15/2**
042 **2** 3½ **Salut Saint Cloud**^{54} [544] 7-8-12 **50** ....(p) SimonWhitworth 7 58
(G L Moore) *s.i.s: hld up in midfield: hdwy over 4f out: rdn 3f out: chsd ldng pair over 2f out: r.o to chse wnr ins fnl f: nvr nr wnr* **7/2^1**
410 **3** 2¾ **Starstruck Peter (IRE)**^{15} [544] 4-8-11 **53** ....(t) PaulDoe 11 58
(S Curran) *chsd ldr tl led 4f out: clr w wnr and rdn over 2f out: hdd 2f out: wknd fnl f* **8/1**
/400 **4** nk **Ocean Rock**^{19} [934] 7-8-10 **48** .... DarryllHolland 2 52+
(C A Horgan) *hld up wl bhd: hdwy over 3f out: styd on fr over 2f out: nvr nr ldrs* **20/1**
00/1 **5** nse **Fade To Grey (IRE)**^{83} [166] 4-8-11 **53** ....(t) LPKeniry 3 57
(S Lycett) *hld up in midfield: reminders 5f out: hdwy 4f out: rdn over 3f out: plugged on u.p press but nvr threatened ldrs* **7/1^3**
3246 **6** 1¼ **Ernmoor**^{19} [934] 6-8-5 **46** oh1 .... WilliamBuick$^{(3)}$ 8 49
(J R Jenkins) *hld up wl bhd: hdwy 6f out: effrt and gd hdwy on outer 4f out: kpt on same pce fr over 1f out* **10/1**
0/00 **7** 14 **Taxman (IRE)**^{54} [540] 6-9-3 **55** ....(p) DaneO'Neill 5 41
(A G Newcombe) *hld up wl in tch: rdn and effrt wl over 3f out: btn wl over 2f out* **7/2^1**
4400 **8** 5 **Vanishing Dancer (SWI)**^{43} [695] 11-8-8 **46** oh1..(v) CatherineGannon 1 26
(Mrs D Thomas) *a bhd: no ch last 3f* **50/1**
-604 **9** hd **Arabian Sun**^{10} [1052] 4-8-12 **54** ....(v) ChrisCatlin 14 34
(M J Attwater) *chsd ldrs: rdn wl over 3f out: sn wl btn* **5/1^2**
0/05 **10** 27 **Tetragon (IRE)**^{8} [930] 8-8-8 **46** oh1 ....(b) OscarUrbina 12 —
(A M Hales) *in tch: rdn and wknd 4f out: wl btn whn short of room over 3f out: eased fnl f: t.o* **50/1**

500- **11** *15* **Nod's Star**[215] 5138 7-8-9 **47**....(t) RichardThomas 4 —
(Jim Best) *chsd ldrs tl rdn and wknd over 3f out: eased fnl f: t.o* **14/1**
/250 **12** *6* **Huggle**[19] 930 5-8-8 **46** oh1.... DavidKinsella 10 —
(P Leech) *led tl 4f out: sn wknd: t.o and eased fnl f* **18/1**
00/5 **13** *1* **Working Late**[9] 1086 6-8-5 **46** oh1....(t) TolleyDean(3) 6 —
(Mike Hammond) *a bhd: rdn 6f out: t.o last 2f* **50/1**
605- **14** *31* **Finished Article (IRE)**[327] 891 11-8-11 **49**.... RobertWinston 13 —
(Mrs D Thomas) *hld up towards rr: lost tch 5f out: t.o and eased wl over 1f out* **50/1**

3m 29.7s (-0.40) **Going Correction** +0.125s/f (Slow)
WFA 4 from 5yo+ 4lb **14** Ran SP% **130.1**
Speed ratings (Par 101): **106,104,102,102,102 102,95,92,92,78 71,68,67,52**
CSF £35.67 CT £226.19 TOTE £11.80: £4.30, £1.60, £3.50; EX 44.50.
Owner Oceana racing **Bred** C A Cyzer **Trained** Lewes, E Sussex
FOCUS
A moderate staying handicap run at a good pace. Sound form, best rated through the runner-up.

1247 SUNBURY H'CAP 1m (P)
4:40 (4:40) (Class 6) (0-65,71) 3-Y-O £2,047 (£604; £302) **Stalls** High

Form RPR
2201 **1** **My Shadow**[7] 1115 3-9-10 **71** 6ex.... IanMongan 5 83+
(S Dow) *sn nudged along in rr: pushed along over 3f out: plld out and rdn wl over 2f out: str run to ld jst over 1f out: sn clr: readily* **13/8**[1]
200- **2** *3 ¾* **Kashmina**[160] 6572 3-9-4 **65**.... DarryllHolland 6 67+
(M R Channon) *hld up in rr: hdwy over 3f out: nt clr run over 2f out: swtchd lft wl over 1f out: r.o wl to snatch 2nd nr fin: no ch w wnr* **14/1**
500- **3** *hd* **Pantherii (USA)**[193] 5746 3-9-1 **62**.... RyanMoore 7 60
(P F I Cole) *s.i.s: hld up in tch on inner: swtchd rt and rdn jst over 2f out: ev ch over 1f out: chsd wnr but wl outpcd fnl f: lost 2nd nr fin* **8/1**
000- **4** *¾* **Peas In A Pod**[199] 5595 3-8-6 **53** ow1.... JamieSpencer 9 49+
(J R Fanshawe) *trckd ldrs: plld out and rdn to ld over 1f out: sn hdd and outpcd by wnr: kpt on* **3/1**[2]
00-3 **5** *¾* **Saafend Geezer**[7] 1115 3-8-13 **60**.... ChrisCatlin 1 55
(B J Meehan) *hld up bhd: hdwy on outer over 3f out: rdn wl over 2f out: outpcd over 1f out: kpt on* **5/1**[3]
-304 **6** *1 ¼* **Mujahope**[11] 1034 3-9-2 **63**.... JohnEgan 8 55
(M Botti) *t.k.h: hld up in tch: nt clr run briefly jst over 2f out: sn rdn and unable qck: kpt on same pce* **8/1**
00-0 **7** *hd* **Hla Tun (USA)**[33] 796 3-8-12 **62**.... WilliamBuick(3) 4 53
(W R Swinburn) *led: rdn jst over 2f out: hdd over 1f out: wknd fnl f* **12/1**
056- **8** *1 ¼* **Sarah's First**[158] 6601 3-9-2 **63**.... StephenDonohoe 3 51
(E A L Dunlop) *hld up in tch: rdn and effrt 3f out: outpcd 2f out* **12/1**
00-0 **9** *7* **Tell Me What (FR)**[19] 931 3-8-3 **55**.... PatrickHills(5) 2 27
(R Hannon) *chsd ldr: rdn over 2f out: wknd wl over 1f out* **25/1**

1m 42.81s (3.01) **Going Correction** +0.125s/f (Slow) **9** Ran SP% **127.9**
Speed ratings (Par 96): **89,85,85,84,83 82,82,80,73**
CSF £31.48 CT £161.62 TOTE £2.50: £1.30, £3.70, £3.00; EX 29.80.
Owner T G Parker **Bred** Millsec Limited **Trained** Epsom, Surrey
■ Stewards' Enquiry : Darryll Holland caution: used whip above shoulder height
FOCUS
A good handicap for the grade, but the pace was ordinary and the winning time was 0.64 seconds slower than earlier claimer. The form has been rated through the third and My Shadow can rate higher still.
Mujahope Official explanation: jockey said gelding suffered interference in running

1248 KEMPTON PARK PUNTERS CLUB APPRENTICE H'CAP 7f (P)
5:10 (5:11) (Class 6) (0-52,52) 4-Y-O+ £2,047 (£604; £302) **Stalls** High

Form RPR
0211 **1** **Straight Face (IRE)**[10] 1053 4-8-12 **52**....(p) AshleyHamblett 7 60
(Miss Gay Kelleway) *mde all: rdn over 2f out: edgd rt 1f out: hld on* **15/8**[1]
5360 **2** *shd* **Balerno**[19] 937 9-8-5 **48**.... SophieDoyle(3) 2 56
(Mrs L J Mongan) *hld up towards rr: hdwy on inner over 2f out: swtchd lft ins fnl f: r.o wl: jst failed* **8/1**
1540 **3** *¾* **Stargazy**[5] 1154 4-8-5 **48**.... MatthewDavies(3) 1 54
(W G M Turner) *in tch: rdn to chse wnr over 1f out: kpt on u.p: lost 2nd ins fnl f* **11/1**
6302 **4** *5* **Shosolosa (IRE)**[40] 724 6-8-3 **48**.... KrishGundowry(5) 5 41
(R C Guest) *hld up bhd: hdwy jst over 2f out: chsd ldng trio jst over 1f out: no imp* **8/1**
-213 **5** *½* **Fun In The Sun**[20] 922 4-8-10 **50**.... JackMitchell 6 41
(A B Haynes) *t.k.h: chsd ldrs: rdn over 2f out: wknd over 1f out* **11/4**[2]
000- **6** *2 ½* **Border Artist**[132] 6956 9-8-5 **50**....(v) SimonPearce(5) 8 34
(J Pearce) *chsd ldrs: wnt 2nd over 2f out: sn pushed along: lost 2nd over 1f out: wknd* **12/1**
-43P **7** *1 ¾* **Chasing Memories (IRE)**[57] 516 4-8-9 **49**.... JamieJones 9 29
(A M Hales) *rrd in stalls and slowly away: rdn and hdwy 4f out: no hdwy whn short of room and snatched up jst over 2f out* **14/1**
3066 **8** *nse* **Tuning Fork**[19] 937 8-8-1 **46**.... StacyRenwick(5) 3 26
(M J Attwater) *t.k.h: chsd ldr tl over 2f out: sn wknd* **13/2**[3]

1m 27.76s (1.76) **Going Correction** +0.125s/f (Slow) **8** Ran SP% **119.7**
Speed ratings (Par 101): **94,93,93,87,86 83,81,81**
CSF £18.95 CT £136.87 TOTE £2.50: £1.10, £3.40, £3.10; EX 13.30 Place 6 £248.18, Place 5 £123.70..
Owner T & Z Racing Club **Bred** P J Towell **Trained** Exning, Suffolk
■ Stewards' Enquiry : Stacy Renwick one-day ban: careless riding (Apr 21)
FOCUS
A moderate sprint handicap restricted to apprentices who had not ridden more than 50 winners. The winning time was modest. This is weak form, with Straight Face showing ony marginal improvement on his recent classified wins.
T/Plt: £206.60 to a £1 stake. Pool: £57,451.87. 202.93 winning tickets. T/Qpdt: £58.10 to a £1 stake. Pool: £2,571.39. 32.70 winning tickets. SP

1249 - 1250a (Foreign Racing) - See Raceform Interactive

1210 LINGFIELD (L-H)
Tuesday, April 8

OFFICIAL GOING: Standard
Wind: Light, across Weather: Fine but cloudy

1251 RON GILBEY'S 60TH BIRTHDAY (S) STKS 1m 2f (P)
2:10 (2:11) (Class 6) 3-Y-O £1,774 (£523; £262) **Stalls** Low

Form RPR
2-00 **1** **Rosy Dawn**[20] 940 3-8-6 50....(be) SophieDoyle(7) 9 52
(Ms J S Doyle) *racd keenly: mde all at mod pce: drew 3l clr 2 out: shkn up over 1f out: unchal* **14/1**
4000 **2** *3 ½* **Herrbee (IRE)**[11] 1051 3-8-12 48.... IanMongan 6 44
(S Dow) *hld up in rr: rdn and effrt on outer over 2f out: prog over 1f out: styd on to take 2nd nr fin* **14/1**
6-65 **3** *¾* **Lancaster Lad (IRE)**[42] 704 3-8-12 54....(p) DaneO'Neill 8 43
(A B Haynes) *hld up towards rr: prog wl over 2f out: drvn to chse wnr over 1f out: no imp: lost 2nd nr fin* **3/1**[2]
-424 **4** *1 ½* **Arabesque Dancer**[47] 644 3-8-7 57....(b) EddieAhern 4 38
(M Botti) *settled in midfield: pushed along as wnr wnt clr 2f out: effrt over 1f out: keeping on to chal for pl whn no room and snatched up 50yds out* **8/11**[1]
000- **5** *3 ½* **Cobbold Point**[261] 3761 3-8-12 42.... TGMcLaughlin 7 33
(S W Hall) *s.s: mostly in last pair: rdn over 3f out: modest late prog* **50/1**
606- **6** *shd* **Rubytwosox (IRE)**[176] 6242 3-8-7 53.... RichardMullen 3 27
(W R Muir) *mostly chsd wnr: drvn over 2f out: wknd over 1f out* **10/1**[3]
2605 **7** *3* **Tilly Ann (IRE)**[5] 1169 3-8-7 42.... LPKeniry 5 21
(Peter Grayson) *s.i.s: a in rr: struggling 3f out* **25/1**
006- **8** *¾* **Alannah (IRE)**[136] 6928 3-8-7 45.... JamesDoyle 2 20
(Mrs P N Dutfield) *disp 2nd to wl over 1f out: wknd rapidly* **33/1**
000- **9** *2 ¼* **Dome Blonde**[136] 6933 3-8-7 36....(b) NickyMackay 1 15
(W J Musson) *nvr beyond midfield w tail swirling furiously: wknd over 3f out* **66/1**

2m 9.20s (2.60) **Going Correction** +0.025s/f (Slow) **9** Ran SP% **115.6**
Speed ratings (Par 96): **90,87,86,85,82 82,80,79,77**
CSF £176.60 TOTE £14.20: £4.40, £4.40, £1.60; EX 306.60 Trifecta £409.60 Part won. Pool: £577.03 - 0.10 winning units..The winner was bought in for 3,600gns. Herrbee was claimed by P. Butler for £6,000.
Owner W Wood **Bred** Overbury Stallions Ltd **Trained** Eastbury, Berks
FOCUS
A very weak three-year-old seller, run at an uneven pace. The winner sets the level with nothing solid behind.
Lancaster Lad(IRE) Official explanation: jockey said colt hung right
Arabesque Dancer Official explanation: jockey said filly was denied a clear run

1252 RACING AT FOLKESTONE THIS THURSDAY MEDIAN AUCTION MAIDEN STKS 1m (P)
2:40 (2:43) (Class 6) 3-4-Y-O £2,388 (£705; £352) **Stalls** High

Form RPR
3 **1** **Sir Billy Nick**[17] 965 3-8-12 0.... TPQueally 8 74+
(J Noseda) *sn trckd ldrs: effrt and green 2f out: rdn to ld over 1f out: sn clr* **2/1**[1]
5 **2** *2* **Themwerethedays**[17] 974 3-8-12 0.... LPKeniry 9 69
(S Kirk) *sn trckd ldrs: effrt 2f out: clsd 1f out: r.o to take 2nd last 75yds: no ch w wnr* **20/1**
0- **3** *shd* **Mexican Venture**[200] 5595 3-8-12 0.... J-PGuillambert 6 72+
(W Jarvis) *t.k.h: hld up bhd ldrs: effrt over 1f out: nt clr run sn after and swtchd: r.o wl last 100yds and nrly snatched 2nd* **66/1**
6- **4** *½* **Moksi**[190] 5872 3-8-12 0.... AlanMunro 10 68
(P W Chapple-Hyam) *dwlt: rapid prog to press ldr after 2f: narrow ld over 1f out: sn hdd: lost 2 pls last 75yds* **7/2**[2]
03- **5** *hd* **Mezzanisi (IRE)**[173] 6285 3-8-12 0.... JamieSpencer 11 67+
(M L W Bell) *rn v green in rr: hanging bdly whn asked for effrt 2f out: gd prog fnl f: nrst fin* **9/2**[3]
2 **6** *1* **Speyside (IRE)**[17] 974 3-8-12 0.... EddieAhern 1 65
(J W Hills) *trckd ldrs on inner: shkn up 2f out: trying to cl over 1f out: n.m.r briefly: nudged along after* **10/1**
7 *1 ½* **Scorched (IRE)** 4-9-8 0.... OscarUrbina 12 57+
(J R Fanshawe) *rrd s: rn green towards rr on outer: effrt 2f out: sme prog over 1f out: no hdwy fnl f* **33/1**
8 *1 ¼* **Clearing House** 3-8-12 0.... StephenDonohoe 5 59+
(E A L Dunlop) *dwlt: a wl in rr: outpcd and n.d fnl 2f* **12/1**
05- **9** *2 ¼* **No Rules**[161] 6571 3-8-12 0.... JimmyQuinn 2 54
(M H Tompkins) *nvr beyond midfield: struggling and outpcd over 2f out* **16/1**
32 **10** *nk* **Turtle Dove**[20] 931 3-8-7 0.... JohnEgan 3 48
(M Botti) *mde most to over 1f out: wknd rapidly* **15/2**
- **11** *1 ½* **Looping The Loop (USA)** 3-8-12 0.... JamesDoyle 4 49
(J G Portman) *dwlt: wl in rr: rdn over 2f out: sn btn* **66/1**
12 *14* **Mary Dunsmore** 4-9-8 0.... StephenCarson 7 12
(B J McMath) *chsd ldr 2f: styd prom: wkng whn n.m.r on inner over 2f out: t.o* **100/1**

1m 38.71s (0.51) **Going Correction** +0.025s/f (Slow)
WFA 3 from 4yo 15lb **12** Ran SP% **119.8**
Speed ratings (Par 101): **98,96,95,95,95 94,92,91,89,88 87,73**
CSF £50.59 TOTE £3.40: £1.50, £3.00, £18.60; EX 54.50 TRIFECTA Not won..
Owner N17 Partnership **Bred** Roan Rocket Partners **Trained** Newmarket, Suffolk
FOCUS
This could work out to be a fair maiden but the form is somewhat messy with the fifth and sixth the best guides for now.
Mexican Venture ◆ Official explanation: jockey said colt was denied a clear run

1253 WEATHERBYS BANK FILLIES' H'CAP 7f (P)
3:10 (3:11) (Class 5) (0-70,70) 4-Y-O+ £2,331 (£693; £346; £173) **Stalls** Low

Form RPR
0-60 **1** **Hessian (IRE)**[17] 969 4-9-4 **70**.... JamieSpencer 6 77+
(M D Squance) *hld up in last: stdy prog over 2f out: rdn and hanging over 1f out: drvn and r.o fnl f to ld last 75yds* **7/1**
4410 **2** *½* **High 'n Dry (IRE)**[13] 1030 4-9-0 **66**....(p) PaulDoe 5 71
(M A Allen) *cl up: wnt 2nd 3f out: led wl over 1f out gng strly: sn rdn and limited rspnse: hdd last 75yds* **4/1**[2]
021- **3** *¾* **Oat Cuisine**[176] 6229 4-8-10 **62**.... HayleyTurner 7 65
(M L W Bell) *chsd ldr to 3f out: sn shkn up: lost pl over 2f out: rallied on inner over 1f out: kpt on fnl f* **11/4**[1]
0400 **4** *nse* **Trivia (IRE)**[12] 1038 4-8-13 **65**.... JamesDoyle 4 68
(Ms J S Doyle) *hld up in last trio: prog over 2f out: chsd ldr jst over 1f out to ins fnl f: one pce* **9/1**
1556 **5** *½* **Double Valentine**[6] 1145 5-8-4 **56** oh1.... JimmyQuinn 3 57
(R Ingram) *stdd s: hld up in last trio: dropped to last 1/2-way: no ch 2f out: drvn and r.o fnl f* **11/2**[3]
2040 **6** *2 ¼* **Gimme Some Lovin (IRE)**[6] 1153 4-8-10 **62**....(b[1]) ChrisCatlin 2 57
(D W P Arbuthnot) *t.k.h: trckd ldrs: lost pl fr 3f out: struggling in rr over 1f out* **13/2**
030- **7** *½* **Mango Music**[144] 6826 5-9-4 **70**.... TPQueally 1 64
(M Quinn) *led to wl over 1f out: wknd rapidly fnl f* **6/1**

1m 25.4s (0.60) **Going Correction** +0.025s/f (Slow) **7** Ran SP% **112.2**
Speed ratings (Par 100): **97,96,95,95,94 92,91**
CSF £33.51 TOTE £7.80: £3.40, £2.70; EX 52.60.

Owner Miss T J Fitzgerald **Bred** Rathbarry Stud **Trained** Newmarket, Suffolk

■ A first winner for trainer Michael Squance.

FOCUS

A modest fillies-only handicap, run at an average pace. The first four were closely covered at the finish and the runner-up helps to set the level.

1254 PLAY GOLF @ LINGFIELD PARK H'CAP — 6f (P)

3:40 (3:42) (Class 6) (0-55,55) 4-Y-0+ — **£2,047** (£604; £302) **Stalls** Low

Form — RPR

1630 **1** **Simpsons Gamble (IRE)**[6] 1145 5-8-11 53....................(p) EddieAhern 6 63
(R A Teal) *prom: chsd ldr over 2f out: led over 1f out: drvn and hld on nr fin* **8/1**[3]

/00- **2** *½* **Espartano**[190] 5877 4-8-13 55.................................... TPO'Shea 4 63
(P A Blockley) *hld up in midfield: effrt over 2f out: drvn and nt qckn over 1f out: styd on wl fnl f and gaining on wnr fin* **6/4**[1]

-041 **3** *1 ¼* **Duke Of Milan (IRE)**[6] 1145 5-8-12 54 6ex.................... HayleyTurner 3 58
(G C Bravery) *hld up in last: coaxed along and prog on inner over 1f out: styd on fnl f but nt pce to rch ldng pair* **9/4**[2]

4605 **4** *1* **Lawdy Miss Clawdy**[6] 1150 4-8-4 46 oh1.......................... ChrisCatlin 9 47
(D W P Arbuthnot) *led at str pce: rdn and hdd over 1f out: fdd ins fnl f* **20/1**

5-03 **5** *1 ¾* **Camissa**[25] 884 4-8-13 55.................................... DaneO'Neill 2 50
(D K Ivory) *dwlt: hld up in last pair: angled to outer over 2f out: sn drvn: kpt on same pce* **9/1**

564 **6** *hd* **Prettilini**[12] 1035 5-8-1 46 oh1.................................... LukeMorris(3) 8 41
(A W Carroll) *chsd ldr to over 2f out: sn lost pl and btn* **20/1**

000- **7** *1* **Exit Strategy (IRE)**[146] 6818 4-8-13 55.................................... LPKeniry 7 46
(R A Harris) *bdly bmpd by rival sn after s: nvr beyond midfield: no prog over 1f out: fdd* **33/1**

3062 **8** *1 ¾* **Regal Royale**[13] 1022 5-8-11 53 ow1..............................(v) AdamKirby 1 39
(Peter Grayson) *chsd ldrs: shkn up 1/2-way: wknd over 1f out: eased* **8/1**[3]

9 *2 ¼* **New York Prince (IRE)**[25] 892 4-8-4 46 oh1..........(b[1]) RichardMullen 5 25
(R J Osborne, Ire) *wnt rt s and collided w rival: racd wd: nvr on terms: struggling fnl 2f* **40/1**

1m 11.59s (-0.31) **Going Correction** +0.025s/f (Slow) — **9** Ran SP% **117.9**

Speed ratings (Par 101): **103,102,100,99,97 96,95,93,90**

CSF £20.13 CT £37.52 TOTE £10.70: £2.30, £1.10, £1.10; EX 34.30 Trifecta £146.50 Pool: £390.16 - 1.89 winning units..

Owner Chris Simpson **Bred** D And Mrs D Veitch **Trained** Ashtead, Surrey

FOCUS

A moderate handicap, run at a fair pace. The penalised third sets the level and the form appears sound.

Simpsons Gamble(IRE) Official explanation: trainer said, regarding apparent improvement in form, previous race, gelding failed to settle and despite having a good draw, ran wide.

1255 LINGFIELD PARK DERBY TRIAL ON MAY 10TH MAIDEN STKS — 5f (P)

4:10 (4:11) (Class 5) 3-Y-0+ — **£2,331** (£693; £346; £173) **Stalls** High

Form — RPR

20- **1** **Befortyfour**[294] 2737 3-9-0 0.................................... PhilipRobinson 4 86+
(M A Jarvis) *mde all: shkn up and drew rt away over 1f out: eased nr fin* **30/100**[1]

-U46 **2** *6* **Spic 'n Span**[17] 965 3-9-0 65.................................... AdamKirby 5 58
(R A Harris) *chsd ldng pair: wnt 2nd 1/2-way: easily lft bhd by wnr fnl f* **8/1**[2]

0-4 **3** *6* **Millie's Rock (IRE)**[13] 1027 3-8-9 0.................................... EddieAhern 6 31
(M J Wallace) *in tch: outpcd fr 2f out* **8/1**[2]

05 **4** *3* **Gelert (IRE)**[40] 734 3-9-0 0.................................... LPKeniry 1 25
(Peter Grayson) *chsd wnr to 1/2-way: wknd* **25/1**

05 **5** *19* **Big Boom**[13] 1027 3-9-0 0.................................... PatCosgrave 3 —
(M J Wallace) *s.s: outpcd and sn t.o* **14/1**[3]

58.00 secs (-0.80) **Going Correction** +0.025s/f (Slow)

WFA 3 from 4yo 11lb — **5** Ran SP% **109.7**

Speed ratings (Par 103): **107,97,87,83,52**

CSF £3.33 TOTE £1.30: £1.02, £2.80; EX 2.90.

Owner M F Bailey **Bred** Slatch Farm Stud **Trained** Newmarket, Suffolk

FOCUS

This was somewhat weakened by the withdrawal of Doric Lady, but the winner still scored easily in a decent time and looks capable of rating much higher this term. The runner-up is rated to this year's form and sets the level.

1256 ARENALEISUREPLC.COM APPRENTICE H'CAP — 1m 2f (P)

4:40 (4:40) (Class 5) (0-75,78) 4-Y-0+ — **£2,590** (£770; £385; £192) **Stalls** Low

Form — RPR

2240 **1** **Given A Choice (IRE)**[11] 1048 6-9-0 73..................(p) SimonPearce(3) 6 86
(J Pearce) *hld up: prog 3f out: bmpd over 2f out: sn chsd ldr: led wl over 1f out: edgd rt but pushed clr* **8/1**

32-3 **2** *7* **Putra Square**[13] 1026 4-9-5 75.................................... GaryBartley 1 74
(P F I Cole) *chsd ldr: clsd 4f out: u.p whn bmpd over 2f out: sn outpcd: plugged on to take 2nd last strides* **11/4**[2]

1101 **3** *½* **King's Ransom**[8] 1112 5-9-8 78 6ex.................... PatrickDonaghy 3 76
(S Gollings) *led at str pce: c bk to field 4f out: hdd and outpcd over 1f out: lost 2nd last strides* **5/1**[3]

3-53 **4** *4 ½* **Wheelavit (IRE)**[3] 1210 5-8-5 61 oh1.................................... KMay 2 50
(B G Powell) *chsd ldng pair 4f: dropped to last 4f out: outpcd over 2f out: n.d after* **11/2**

-122 **5** *2 ½* **Sun Of The Sea**[25] 888 4-9-4 74..............................(b[1]) HarryPoulton 5 58
(N P Littmoden) *s.i.s: trckd ldrs fr 1/2-way: cl up over 2f out: wknd tamely* **2/1**[1]

0060 **6** *9* **Smokin Joe**[36] 775 7-8-9 72..............................(b) KierenFox(7) 4 38
(J R Best) *t.k.h: hld up in tch: rdn 3f out: sn lost tch and btn* **12/1**

2m 4.85s (-1.75) **Going Correction** +0.025s/f (Slow) — **6** Ran SP% **110.9**

Speed ratings (Par 103): **108,102,102,98,96 89**

CSF £29.36 TOTE £10.70: £4.20, £1.70 Place 6 £84.16, Place 5 £29.02.

Owner Mrs E M Clarke **Bred** Rathasker Stud **Trained** Newmarket, Suffolk

FOCUS

A fair little handicap, run at a sound pace and the winner is rated back to his form from early in the year.

T/Plt: £293.00 to a £1 stake. Pool: £54,688.87. 136.25 winning tickets. T/Qpdt: £26.90 to a £1 stake. Pool: £3,896.10. 106.80 winning tickets. JN

1183 SOUTHWELL (L-H)

Tuesday, April 8

OFFICIAL GOING: Standard

Wind: Light, across Weather: Overcast with the odd shower

1257 SOUTHWELL GOLF CLUB H'CAP — 5f (F)

2:30 (2:30) (Class 6) (0-65,64) 3-Y-0 — **£3,070** (£906; £453) **Stalls** High

Form — RPR

-652 **1** **Swallow Forest**[8] 1120 3-8-4 50..............................(b) PaulFessey 4 57
(T D Barron) *s.i.s: hdwy 2f out: led over 1f out: rdn out* **6/1**[3]

-313 **2** *2 ¼* **Lujiana**[54] 557 3-9-0 63.................................... MarkLawson(3) 2 62
(M Brittain) *sn pushed along and prom: outpcd over 3f out: rallied 2f out: styd on same pce ins fnl f* **9/4**[2]

2631 **3** *1* **Bahamarama (IRE)**[10] 1081 3-8-6 55..................(p) KevinGhunowa(3) 6 50
(R A Harris) *chsd ldrs: rdn 1/2-way: styd on same pce fnl f* **14/1**

2320 **4** *½* **Diademas (USA)**[6] 1155 3-9-4 64..............................(v) NCallan 1 58
(V Smith) *led: rdn: edgd lft and hdd over 1f out: wknd ins fnl f* **7/4**[1]

3633 **5** *½* **Planet Paradise (IRE)**[8] 1120 3-7-13 50 oh4............ KellyHarrison(5) 3 42
(D Shaw) *chsd ldrs: outpcd over 3f out: rallied over 1f out: wknd ins fnl f* **9/1**

003- **6** *1 ¾* **Lekin Sedona (IRE)**[169] 6388 3-8-4 50.................................... PaulHanagan 5 36
(Joss Saville) *chsd ldrs: rdn 1/2-way: wknd fnl f* **13/2**

61.71 secs (2.01) **Going Correction** +0.325s/f (Slow) — **6** Ran SP% **111.4**

Speed ratings (Par 96): **96,92,90,90,89 86**

CSF £19.60 TOTE £4.60: £3.30, £2.40; EX 17.00.

Owner Laurence O'Kane **Bred** Foreneish Bloodstock **Trained** Maunby, N Yorks

FOCUS

A moderate but competitive little sprint with the form rated around the winner and fifth.

1258 BOOK YOUR HOSPITALITY PACKAGES H'CAP — 1m (F)

3:00 (3:01) (Class 6) (0-60,59) 4-Y-0+ — **£2,729** (£806; £403) **Stalls** Low

Form — RPR

3421 **1** **Wodhill Schnaps**[8] 1116 7-9-3 58 6ex..............................(b) NCallan 2 68
(D Morris) *dwlt: hld up in tch: edgd rt and led over 1f out: shkn up and r.o wl* **11/10**[1]

35-4 **2** *2* **Al Rayanah**[13] 1029 5-8-8 52.................................... KirstyMilczarek(3) 4 57
(G Prodromou) *s.s: hld up: nt clr run over 3f out: hdwy over 2f out: rdn to chse wnr over 1f out: styd on* **7/1**[3]

024- **3** *¾* **Moonstreaker**[118] 7127 5-9-0 58.................................... MichaelJStainton(3) 3 61
(R M Whitaker) *s.i.s: sn prom: rdn over 2f out: styd on same pce ins fnl f* **17/2**

-500 **4** *7* **Preskani**[35] 792 6-7-13 45.................................... KellyHarrison(5) 7 32
(Mrs N Macauley) *chsd ldrs: led 7f out: rdn: edgd rt and hdd over 1f out: wknd fnl f* **66/1**

-141 **5** *6* **Montemayorprincess (IRE)**[22] 916 4-8-13 54.........(p) AndrewElliott 9 27
(D Haydn Jones) *chsd ldrs: hung lft thrght: rdn over 2f out: sn wknd* **5/2**[2]

500- **6** *nk* **Kadia**[220] 5035 5-8-4 45.................................... FrankieMcDonald 6 18
(P T Midgley) *led 1f: chsd ldrs: rdn and wknd over 2f out: bhd whn hmpd ins fnl f* **40/1**

4340 **7** *1* **Newgate (UAE)**[11] 1664 4-8-10 51..............................(p) LiamJones 1 21
(Mrs R A Carr) *hld up in tch: rdn and wknd over 2f out* **40/1**

2-04 **8** *12* **Crow's Nest Lad**[4] 1192 4-9-1 59.................................... WilliamBuick(3) 8 2
(J O'Reilly) *chsd ldrs: lost pl over 4f out: rdn and wknd over 2f out* **20/1**

400- **9** *¾* **Murdoch**[312] 2196 4-9-3 58..............................(t) GrahamGibbons 5 —
(E S McMahon) *chsd ldrs: rdn over 2f out: sn wknd* **16/1**

1m 46.51s (2.81) **Going Correction** +0.375s/f (Slow) — **9** Ran SP% **116.2**

Speed ratings (Par 101): **100,98,97,90,84 83,82,70,70**

CSF £9.48 CT £45.48 TOTE £2.20: £1.10, £2.00, £2.50; EX 7.10.

Owner Miss S Graham **Bred** Wodhill Stud **Trained** Newmarket, Suffolk

FOCUS

A moderate handicap but the winner had little to beat with his main rival running poorly.

Montemayorprincess(IRE) Official explanation: jockey said filly hung left

1259 DINE IN THE QUEEN MOTHER RESTAURANT MEDIAN AUCTION MAIDEN STKS — 6f (F)

3:30 (3:30) (Class 5) 4-6-Y-0 — **£3,399** (£1,011; £505; £252) **Stalls** Low

Form — RPR

/405 **1** **Welcome Releaf**[35] 790 5-8-10 49.................................... MarkCoumbe(7) 8 61
(P Leech) *hld up: hdwy u.p over 2f out: led and edgd lft over 1f out: r.o: eased nr fin* **9/2**

552 **2** *2* **Walragnek**[5] 1162 4-9-3 0.................................... AndrewElliott 2 55
(J G M O'Shea) *led: rdn and hdd over 1f out: styd on same pce ins fnl f* **9/4**[1]

45- **3** *1* **Irish Conection (IRE)**[103] 7239 5-9-3 0.................................... FergalLynch 6 51
(Thomas McLaughlin, Ire) *chsd ldrs: rdn over 2f out: styd on same pce fnl f* **11/4**[2]

0060 **4** *3* **Fly Time**[17] 972 4-8-9 40..............................(p) TolleyDean(3) 7 37
(Mrs L Williamson) *hld up: hdwy u.p over 1f out: wknd ins fnl f* **33/1**

064 **5** *4* **Takeanoteofthat (IRE)**[41] 715 6-9-3 23.................................... VinceSlattery 3 29
(D Burchell) *prom: rdn over 4f out: wknd over 2f out* **14/1**

30-0 **6** *3* **White's Ruby**[27] 858 4-8-12 45..............................(b) PaulEddery 5 14
(G D Blake) *chsd ldr: rdn over 2f out: wknd over 1f out* **10/3**[3]

0-40 **7** *8* **Eastern Princess**[57] 522 4-8-9 42..............................(b) KevinGhunowa(3) 1 —
(G H Yardley) *chsd ldrs: rdn 1/2-way: wknd 2f out* **25/1**

-000 **8** *16* **Josama**[6] 1135 4-8-9 33..............................(b) MarkLawson(3) 4 —
(R Bastiman) *sn outpcd* **66/1**

1m 19.29s (2.79) **Going Correction** +0.375s/f (Slow) — **8** Ran SP% **113.6**

Speed ratings: **96,93,92,88,82 78,68,46**

CSF £14.78 TOTE £5.40: £1.60, £1.20, £1.10; EX 19.10.

Owner Russell Reed & Danny Berry **Bred** Mrs H M Shaw **Trained** Newmarket, Suffolk

■ The first winner as a trainer for Pat Leech, a former successful jump jockey in Ireland.

FOCUS

A poor maiden with the winner rated to his old form backed up by the third to his debut form.

Josama Official explanation: jockey said filly wouldn't face the kick-back

1260 SOUTHWELL-RACECOURSE.CO.UK H'CAP — 7f (F)

4:00 (4:00) (Class 5) (0-70,70) 4-Y-0+ — **£3,399** (£1,011; £505; £252) **Stalls** Low

Form — RPR

0610 **1** **Elusive Warrior (USA)**[4] 1188 5-8-4 56..............................(p) NeilPollard 1 68
(A J McCabe) *mde virtually all: clr over 2f out: rdn out* **8/1**

5-60 **2** *1 ¾* **Sun Catcher (IRE)**[12] 1040 5-8-11 63.................................... RobertWinston 3 70
(P G Murphy) *a.p: rdn to chse wnr 3f out: styd on* **15/2**[3]

-333 3 *nk* **Dasheena**[19] 949 5-8-8 **65**..............................(be) DanielleMcCreery(5) 8 71
(A J McCabe) *dwlt: bhd whn swtchd lft 5f out: styd on appr fnl f: nt rch ldrs* **4/1**[2]

0-11 4 *3* **Playtotheaudience**[13] 1029 5-8-8 **60**..........................(v) PaulHanagan 6 58
(R A Fahey) *chsd ldrs: rdn over 2f out: edgd rt over 1f out: no ex fnl f* **2/1**[1]

4066 5 *1 3/4* **Zorn**[6] 1142 9-8-4 **56** oh9.. LiamJones 2 49
(P Howling) *sn rdn along: chsd ldr 4f: styd on same pce fnl 2f* **28/1**

2340 6 *2 1/4* **Louisiade (IRE)**[4] 1188 7-8-11 **70**..........................(p) MarkCoumbe(7) 7 57
(M C Chapman) *chsd ldrs: lost pl over 5f out: n.d after* **11/1**

3140 7 *6* **Solicitude**[3] 1209 5-8-6 **58**..........................(p) RobertHavlin 4 29
(D Haydn Jones) *chsd ldrs: rdn 1/2-way: wknd over 1f out* **4/1**[2]

-002 8 *29* **Victor Trumper**[8] 1109 4-8-13 **65**..........................(bt) NCallan 5 —
(Jim Best) *hld up: rdn 1/2-way: bhd fnl 3f* **10/1**

1m 31.7s (1.40) **Going Correction** +0.375s/f (Slow) **8** Ran SP% **117.1**
Speed ratings (Par 103): **107,105,104,101,99 96,89,56**
CSF £67.35 CT £280.29 TOTE £11.00: £2.60, £1.30, £1.70; EX 90.90.
Owner Paul J Dixon & Brian Morton **Bred** Steve Peskoff **Trained** Babworth, Notts

FOCUS
A modest handicap run at a good gallop. The form looks sound with the third to recent form and the winner back to near his best.
Victor Trumper Official explanation: jockey said gelding never travelled

1261 BOOK YOUR TICKETS ONLINE H'CAP 6f (F)
4:30 (4:31) (Class 5) (0-75,75) 4-Y-0+ **£3,561** (£1,059; £529; £264) **Stalls** Low

Form RPR

1512 1 **Diriculous**[6] 1146 4-9-1 **72**.. JimCrowley 7 85+
(T G Mills) *chsd ldrs: shkn up over 3f out: led 2f out: sn rdn and hung lft: r.o* **6/4**[1]

0542 2 *1/2* **Lethal**[7] 1134 5-9-3 **74**.. PaulHanagan 6 85
(R A Fahey) *in tch: sn drvn along: hdwy over 2f out: rdn and edgd lft fr over 1f out: r.o* **9/4**[2]

3413 3 *1 1/4* **Cerebus**[7] 1134 6-9-0 **74**..........................(bt) WilliamBuick(3) 8 81
(A J McCabe) *chsd ldrs: rdn over 1f out: styd on same pce ins fnl f* **10/1**

4056 4 *3* **Cool Sands (IRE)**[6] 1153 6-8-4 **64** ow1..........................(v) TolleyDean(3) 4 61
(D Shaw) *sn outpcd: hdwy u.p over 1f out: wknd ins fnl f* **10/1**

4111 5 *1 1/2* **Toms Laughter**[17] 964 4-8-12 **72**........................ KevinGhunowa(3) 3 65
(R A Harris) *disp ld 4f: wknd fnl f* **6/1**[3]

30-0 6 *1/2* **Steel Blue**[14] 1015 8-7-13 **61** oh4........................ KellyHarrison(5) 1 52
(R M Whitaker) *hld up: rdn over 2f out: n.d* **22/1**

000- 7 *8* **The Bear**[318] 2025 5-8-10 **70**........................ PJMcDonald(3) 2 35
(R Johnson) *chsd ldrs to 1/2-way* **33/1**

10-6 8 *1* **Count Cougar (USA)**[7] 1134 8-9-1 **75**........................ MichaelJStainton(3) 5 37
(S P Griffiths) *disp ld tl rdn 2f out: wknd over 1f out* **16/1**

1m 18.25s (1.75) **Going Correction** +0.375s/f (Slow) **8** Ran SP% **116.4**
Speed ratings (Par 103): **103,102,100,96,94 94,83,82**
CSF £5.09 CT £23.00 TOTE £2.50: £1.40, £1.30, £1.40; EX 5.80.
Owner Sherwoods Transport Ltd **Bred** Sherwoods Transport Ltd **Trained** Headley, Surrey

FOCUS
A fair handicap featuring two or three in-form and improving horses. The form looks solid for the grade with the [placed horses close to their latest marks.
Toms Laughter Official explanation: trainer's rep said gelding was unsuited by the fibresand surface

1262 SOUTHWELL RACECOURSE FOR CONFERENCES H'CAP 1m 3f (F)
5:00 (5:01) (Class 6) (0-52,52) 4-Y-0+ **£2,729** (£806; £403) **Stalls** Low

Form RPR

53-0 1 **Pegasus Prince (USA)**[32] 822 4-8-10 **48**........................ TomEaves 4 57
(Miss J A Camacho) *hld up in tch: rdn over 3f out: led over 1f out: edgd rt: styd on* **8/1**

-410 2 *2 1/2* **Ming Vase**[15] 989 6-8-10 **48**........................ MickyFenton 11 53
(P T Midgley) *a.p: chsd ldr 8f out: ev ch over 2f out: sn rdn and hung lft: carried rt ins fnl f: styd on same pce* **10/1**

0446 3 *3/4* **Sparky Vixen**[8] 1116 4-8-9 **52**........................ KellyHarrison(5) 9 56
(C J Teague) *chsd ldrs: led 2f out: rdn: hung lft and hdd over 1f out: hung rt ins fnl f: no ex* **20/1**

510- 4 *1/2* **Living On A Prayer**[127] 7004 5-8-12 **50**........................ FergalLynch 7 53
(Thomas McLaughlin, Ire) *hld up: rdn over 2f out: sn hung lft: styd on ins fnl f: nt rch ldrs* **11/1**

-503 5 *1* **Shandelight (IRE)**[12] 1044 4-8-9 **47**..........................(p) RoystonFfrench 10 48
(Mrs A Duffield) *led: rdn and hdd 2f out: edgd rt and no ex fnl f* **11/2**[2]

60-5 6 *1 1/4* **Bowl Of Cherries**[6] 1148 5-9-0 **52**..........................(bt) NCallan 13 51
(I A Wood) *sn pushed along in mid-div: hdwy 8f out: rdn 4f out: wknd fnl f* **5/1**[1]

0-00 7 *2* **Sir Jake**[20] 934 4-8-7 **48**........................ TolleyDean(3) 12 44
(T T Clement) *hld up: sme hdwy over 1f out: n.d* **12/1**

0-52 8 *nk* **Kentucky Bullet (USA)**[49] 613 12-8-8 **46** oh1........................ SimonWhitworth 6 41
(A G Newcombe) *hld up: hdwy over 3f out: shkn up and hung lft over 1f out: wknd ins fnl f* **12/1**

6/53 9 *2 1/4* **Sun Quest**[8] 1121 4-8-8 **46** oh1........................ AndrewElliott 5 37
(I W McInnes) *hld up: n.d* **15/2**

4222 10 *8* **On Every Street**[36] 776 7-8-8 **46**..........................(p) RobertWinston 3 24
(R Bastiman) *w ldr 3f: rdn over 5f out: wkng whn swtchd rt 2f out* **13/2**[3]

0-04 11 *4* **Itsy Bitsy**[15] 613 6-8-8 **46** oh1........................ NeilPollard 2 17
(W J Musson) *s.i.s: a in rr* **33/1**

0001 12 *3* **Royal Auditon**[7] 1127 7-8-10 **51** 6ex..........................(p) KirstyMilczarek(3) 1 17
(T T Clement) *hld up: rdn 1/2-way: sn wknd* **10/1**

200 13 *1/2* **Sorbiesharry (IRE)**[13] 1031 9-8-5 **46** oh1........................ DuranFentiman(3) 14 11
(Mrs N Macauley) *s.i.s: hld up: hdwy 1/2-way: wknd over 3f out* **25/1**

20-0 14 *13* **Giovanni D'Oro (IRE)**[26] 872 4-9-0 **52**..........................(b[1]) FergusSweeney 8 —
(Miss M E Rowland) *hld up: plld hrd: rdn over 3f out: sn wknd* **40/1**

2m 31.66s (3.66) **Going Correction** +0.375s/f (Slow) **14** Ran SP% **124.1**
Speed ratings (Par 101): **101,99,98,98,97 96,95,94,93,87 84,82,82,72**
CSF £84.91 CT £1572.54 TOTE £7.60: £2.80, £3.80, £10.00; EX 105.30 Place 6 £74.75, Place 5 £36.40.
Owner David W Armstrong **Bred** Liberty Road Stables **Trained** Norton, N Yorks

FOCUS
A moderate but competitive handicap and sound form for the grade, rated around the placed horses.
Living On A Prayer ◆ Official explanation: jockey said mare wouldn't face kick-back early on
Royal Auditon Official explanation: jockey said mare never travelled
Giovanni D'Oro(IRE) Official explanation: jockey said gelding ran too freely
T/Plt: £82.20 to a £1 stake. Pool: £55,705.66. 494.40 winning tickets. T/Qpdt: £27.00 to a £1 stake. Pool: £3,573.20. 97.60 winning tickets. CR

BATH (L-H)
Wednesday, April 9

OFFICIAL GOING: Good (good to soft in places; 7.5)
The official going was an accurate reflection of the ground conditions according to the jockeys.
Wind: Light, against Weather: Fine but chilly

1263 LINDLEY CATERING MAIDEN STKS 5f 11y
2:10 (2:11) (Class 5) 2-Y-O **£2,460** (£732; £365; £182) **Stalls** Centre

Form RPR

1 **April Pride** 2-8-12 0.. RichardHughes 10 71
(R Hannon) *a.p: swtchd rt and rdn 1f out: r.o to ld post* **3/1**[2]

2 *nse* **Musical Bridge** 2-9-0 0.. TolleyDean(3) 9 76
(Mrs L Williamson) *w ldrs: led over 1f out: rdn ins fnl f: hdd post* **17/2**

3 *1 1/4* **Kingswinford (IRE)** 2-9-3 0.. TGMcLaughlin 6 71
(P D Evans) *led: rdn and hdd over 1f out: ev ch ins fnl f: no ex cl home* **11/2**

3 4 *3 1/2* **Imperial Skylight**[11] 1078 2-9-3 0........................ EdwardCreighton 4 57
(M R Channon) *trckd ldrs: wknd ins fnl f* **5/2**[1]

4 5 *2 1/2* **Lagan Handout**[18] 957 2-9-3 0........................ FergusSweeney 3 47
(Dr J R J Naylor) *w ldr: rdn over 1f out: wknd fnl f* **4/1**[3]

6 *1 1/4* **Dazzling Dust (IRE)** 2-8-10 0........................ JackDean(7) 2 42
(W G M Turner) *prom: rdn and wknd 2f out* **12/1**

7 *2* **Proper Tool (IRE)** 2-9-0 0........................ KevinGhunowa(3) 8 34
(R A Harris) *s.i.s: outpcd: rdn and short-lived effrt 2f out* **20/1**

0 8 *1/2* **Percys Corismatic**[16] 995 2-8-12 0........................ JimCrowley 11 27
(J Gallagher) *bhd fnl 3f* **40/1**

9 *1/2* **Saunton Sands** 2-9-3 0........................ DaneO'Neill 5 30
(A G Newcombe) *s.i.s: a bhd* **33/1**

10 *4 1/2* **Sharp Discovery** 2-8-12 0........................ PaulFitzsimons 7 7
(J M Bradley) *bhd fnl 3f* **80/1**

65.88 secs (3.38) **Going Correction** +0.70s/f (Yiel) **10** Ran SP% **118.6**
Speed ratings (Par 92): **100,99,97,92,88 86,83,82,81,74**
CSF £28.17 TOTE £4.10: £1.80, £2.00, £2.10; EX 32.70 Trifecta £156.50 Pool £352.84 - 1.60 winning units..
Owner R E Greatorex **Bred** Sir Eric Parker **Trained** East Everleigh, Wilts

FOCUS
Quite an interesting maiden which should throw up a few early season winners. The time compared favourably with both the following seller and the older-horse handicap. There was very little form to go on but a positive view has been taken of the race.

NOTEBOOK
April Pride, out of a mare who won at 6f in the US and a half-sister to a couple of winners, broke well before chasing the leaders and, noticeably more professional on her debut than the runner-up, forced her head in front on the nod. She is likely to be given a break now and there are no plans for her yet. (op 7-4 tchd 7-2)
Musical Bridge's yard is not noted for its success with juveniles, but cost 24,000gns and is out of a likeable mare who won nine races at 6f-7f. He looked rather green and carried his head a little high, but still looked sure to prevail only to be caught on the nod. Almost sure to improve for the experience, he has a bit of scope and can get off the mark before long. (op 33-1 tchd 8-1)
Kingswinford(IRE), whose connections landed this race last year with the very useful Vhujon, is the first foal of a fairly useful 6f winner. He had every chance and only gave best well inside the last. A sprinting type, he should find a race in the coming weeks. (op 17-2 tchd 9-2)
Imperial Skylight made a promising debut on the Kempton Polytrack, but he was unable to build on that on this turf debut. He may prefer a quicker surface. (tchd 11-4)
Lagan Handout set the standard on his debut fourth behind Sally's Dilemma in the Brocklesby at Doncaster and was a little disappointing on this second start, fading inside the last furlong. (tchd 7-2)
Dazzling Dust(IRE) is the first foal of a multiple winning sprinter for the Turner yard who won by 11 lengths on her juvenile debut. Quite a late foal, he looked and ran as if in need of the outing, but should pay his way, perhaps over 6f. (op 11-1 tchd 10-1 and 14-1)

1264 LINDLEY CATERING (S) STKS 5f 11y
2:40 (2:43) (Class 6) 2-Y-O **£1,683** (£501; £250; £125) **Stalls** Centre

Form RPR

1 **Heaven Or Hell (IRE)** 2-8-11 0........................ TGMcLaughlin 2 55
(P D Evans) *mde all: rdn fnl f: bmpd cl home: r.o* **3/1**[1]

0 2 *1/2* **Tarawa Atoll**[16] 995 2-8-6 0........................ TPO'Shea 6 48
(M R Channon) *a.p: ev ch whn rdn and edgd lft towards fin: r.o* **5/1**

3 *1 1/4* **Syrup (IRE)** 2-8-6 0........................ JamesDoyle 7 43+
(P D Evans) *hld up: hdwy and swtchd rt jst over 1f out: ev ch whn hmpd and snatched up cl home: nt rcvr* **10/3**[2]

0 4 *2 1/2* **Shes Billie**[16] 995 2-8-7 0 ow1........................ FergusSweeney 4 34
(J G M O'Shea) *a.p: rdn over 1f out: wknd wl ins fnl f* **4/1**[3]

5 *2 1/2* **In The Moment** 2-8-4 0 ow1........................ TolleyDean(3) 5 24+
(W G M Turner) *w wnr: rdn and fading whn n.m.r over 1f out* **9/1**

6 *30* **Talulah Bells** 2-8-3 0........................ LukeMorris(3) 3 —
(A W Carroll) *unruly and uns rdr whn mounted in paddock: hung lft sn after s: nvr gng wl in rr: lost tch 2f out: eased jst over 1f out* **20/1**

68.04 secs (5.54) **Going Correction** +0.70s/f (Yiel) **6** Ran SP% **99.5**
Speed ratings (Par 90): **83,82,80,76,72 24**
CSF £13.91 TOTE £2.30: £1.40, £2.40; EX 10.90.The winner was bought in for 4,200gns.
Owner J R B Williams **Bred** Miss Jane Hogan **Trained** Pandy, Monmouths
■ Joli Haven was withdrawn (9/2, refused to enter stalls). R4 applies, deduct 15p in the £.
■ Stewards' Enquiry : T P O'Shea four-day ban: careless riding (Apr 23-26)

FOCUS
A pretty modest seller, run in a time more than two seconds slower than the opening maiden. The winner might do a bit better but it is hard to be enthusiastic about the form.

NOTEBOOK
Heaven Or Hell(IRE) knew what was required on this debut and made just about all of the running, although he only scrambled home in the end. He edged away from the rail when his rider switched his stick close home, helping to squeeze up the second and receiving a bump himself, but he kept the race after an enquiry. (op 4-1)
Tarawa Atoll finished behind Shes Billie when last on her debut in a maiden at Warwick, but showed she has a bit of ability on this drop in grade. Tracking the pace on the outside, she could not quite quicken up inside the last and contributed to hampering the third when edging across. (op 10-1)
Syrup(IRE) is a half-sister to the one-time decent 6f-7f performer Chin Wag. She was keeping on between the first two, but appeared just held, when she was squeezed out badly near the finish. She would have finished closer than she did but for the interference. (op 6-1 tchd 10-3)

Shes Billie, quickly dropped into a seller, had finished ahead of Tarawa Atoll at Warwick, but could not confirm that superiority, although she was not disgraced. (tchd 9-2)

1265 WEATHERBYS BANK MAIDEN STKS — 1m 5y
3:10 (3:16) (Class 5) 3-Y-0+ — **£2,460** (£732; £365; £182) **Stalls** Low

Form / RPR

246- **1** **Sugar Mint (IRE)**[193] 5796 3-8-7 104 ow1 .... MichaelHills 13 — 81+
(B W Hills) *hld up in tch: led over 1f out: rdn and edgd lft ins fnl f: r.o* — **8/13**[1]

00- **2** 1 1/4 **Duntulm**[158] 6650 3-8-11 0 .... DaneO'Neill 14 — 82
(H Candy) *prom: lft 2nd over 6f out: led over 2f out: hdd over 1f out: swtchd rt ins fnl f: nt qckn* — **7/1**[3]

5- **3** 4 1/2 **Colorado Blue (IRE)**[166] 6468 3-8-11 0 .... SteveDrowne 12 — 72
(R Charlton) *chsd ldrs: rdn over 1f out: one pce* — **5/2**[2]

0 **4** 6 **Blur**[12] 1054 3-8-6 0 .... RichardSmith 9 — 53
(R Hannon) *hld up in mid-div: rdn 3f out: no hdwy fnl 2f* — **33/1**

06- **5** 1/2 **Hawk Flight (IRE)**[144] 6855 3-8-11 0 .... MartinDwyer 8 — 57
(W R Muir) *towards rr: pushed along and hdwy 3f out: no real prog fnl 2f* — **16/1**

06- **6** 1/2 **Highland Homestead**[291] 2876 3-8-11 0 .... FergusSweeney 11 — 56
(B R Millman) *mid-div: lost pl over 5f out: hdwy 3f out: no imp fnl 2f* — **40/1**

7 5 **Milldown Bay** 3-8-6 0 .... TPO'Shea 7 — 39
(B R Millman) *s.s: a bhd* — **100/1**

00/0 **8** nk **Old Time Dancing**[63] 445 5-9-7 45 .... GeorgeBaker 4 — 42
(J F Panvert) *a in rr* — **100/1**

0/5 **9** 1 3/4 **Zayyir (IRE)**[13] 1036 4-9-9 0 .... KevinGhunowa(3) 10 — 43
(R A Harris) *led: rdn and hdd over 2f out: wknd wl over 1f out* — **66/1**

00- **10** 4 **Tiger Trail (GER)**[217] 5129 4-9-12 0 .... HayleyTurner 6 — 34
(Mrs N Smith) *a bhd* — **100/1**

403- **11** 11 **Parliamentary (JPN)**[172] 6329 3-8-11 73 .... JimCrowley 1 — —
(Mrs A L M King) *hld up in mid-div: wknd 3f out* — **25/1**

2/0- **P** **Sabre's Edge (IRE)**[293] 2799 7-9-12 50 .... StephenDonohoe 3 — —
(G A Ham) *w ldr tl p.u lame over 6f out* — **100/1**

1m 44.38s (3.58) **Going Correction** +0.475s/f (Yiel)
WFA 3 from 4yo+ 15lb — **12** Ran SP% **123.6**
Speed ratings (Par 103): **101,99,95,89,88 88,83,82,81,77 66,—**
CSF £6.32 TOTE £1.70: £1.02, £2.00, £1.30; EX 7.80 Trifecta £10.80 Pool £327.78 - 21.36 winning units..
Owner Rick Barnes **Bred** Grangecon Stud **Trained** Lambourn, Berks

FOCUS
Little strength in depth in this maiden and they went 16/1 bar three. Those three pulled clear and the form is rated around the placed horses. Sugar Mint was 20lb off her May Hill form.

1266 WEATHERBYS FINANCE H'CAP — 1m 2f 46y
3:40 (3:44) (Class 6) (0-65,65) 4-Y-0+ — **£1,942** (£578; £288; £144) **Stalls** Low

Form / RPR

-242 **1** **Ryan's Future (IRE)**[7] 1159 8-8-9 56 .... LPKeniry 8 — 71
(J S Moore) *s.i.s: hld up towards rr: hdwy over 2f out: rdn to ld jst ins fnl f: r.o* — **11/4**[1]

640- **2** 1 1/2 **Gracechurch (IRE)**[129] 6911 5-8-6 53 .... HayleyTurner 10 — 65
(R J Hodges) *hld up in tch: led on bit wl over 2f out: rdn and hdd jst ins fnl f: nt qckn* — **15/2**

14-2 **3** 4 1/2 **Merrymadcap (IRE)**[18] 973 6-9-4 65 .... SteveDrowne 11 — 68
(M Blanshard) *hld up in mid-div: hdwy over 2f out: rdn and one pce fnl f* — **5/1**[3]

030- **4** 6 **Lunar River (FR)**[187] 5983 5-9-0 61 .... (t) NeilChalmers 13 — 52
(David Pinder) *hld up in mid-div: hdwy over 3f out: ev ch wl over 1f out: sn rdn: wknd fnl f* — **25/1**

5313 **5** 1 1/2 **Our Kes (IRE)**[18] 970 6-9-1 62 .... TPQueally 6 — 50
(P Howling) *hld up in mid-div: swtchd rt and hdwy over 1f out: sn rdn: no imp* — **9/2**[2]

00-5 **6** 1/2 **April The Second**[16] 999 4-8-4 54 ow1 .... TolleyDean(3) 4 — 41
(R J Price) *s.i.s: in rr: pushed along over 3f out: swtchd rt to wd outside and sme hdwy over 1f out: nvr nr ldrs* — **14/1**

-000 **7** 1 **Prince Rossi (IRE)**[7] 1159 4-8-4 51 oh1 .... (p) PaulFitzsimons 7 — 36
(A E Price) *t.k.h in mid-div: hdwy over 2f out: rdn and wknd over 1f out* — **25/1**

6130 **8** 1 1/4 **Altos Reales**[32] 841 4-8-10 57 .... DaneO'Neill 2 — 40
(D Shaw) *hld up towards rr: rdn over 1f out: n.d* — **20/1**

4-14 **9** 1 1/4 **Mandalay Prince**[35] 802 4-8-10 62 .... JamieJones(5) 15 — 42
(W J Musson) *bhd: rdn over 2f out: nvr nr ldrs* — **8/1**

4-00 **10** 10 **Gouranga**[6] 317 5-8-1 51 oh1 .... (b) LukeMorris(3) 1 — 11
(A W Carroll) *s.i.s: sn rcvrd: hld up in tch: rdn over 3f out: wknd over 2f out* — **50/1**

050- **11** 2 **Stroppi Poppi**[15] 6821 4-8-4 51 oh6 .... CatherineGannon 5 — 7
(Jean-Rene Auvray) *chsd ldr: led over 5f out: rdn and hdd over 2f out: sn wknd* — **66/1**

-003 **12** 2 **Cheonmado (USA)**[9] 1116 4-8-11 58 .... (tp) MartinDwyer 9 — 10
(J R Gask) *led: hdd over 5f out: prom tl rdn and wknd wl over 1f out* — **10/1**

-100 **13** 1 1/2 **Ugenius**[27] 864 4-8-4 54 ow3 .... KevinGhunowa(3) 14 — —
(P A Blockley) *prom: rdn over 2f out: wknd wl over 1f out* — **16/1**

2m 15.26s (4.26) **Going Correction** +0.475s/f (Yiel) — **13** Ran SP% **121.9**
Speed ratings (Par 101): **101,99,96,91,90 89,89,88,87,79 77,75,74**
CSF £22.85 CT £102.30 TOTE £3.20: £1.50, £2.90, £2.00; EX 27.40 Trifecta £74.70 Pool £337.01 - 3.20 winning units..
Owner Vimal Khosla **Bred** A F O'Callaghan **Trained** Upper Lambourn, Berks

FOCUS
A modest handicap in which most of the field were fit from recent outings either on sand or over hurdles. The pace was initially sound before slowing markedly before the end of the back straight. There is little solid form to go on and it is best rated through the fourth to last year's turf mark.

1267 EDWARD CHARLES INVESTMENTS LTD H'CAP — 2m 1f 34y
4:10 (4:11) (Class 5) (0-75,75) 4-Y-0+ — **£2,590** (£770; £385; £192) **Stalls** Low

Form / RPR

1 **Lupita (IRE)**[48] 5697 4-8-1 56 .... WilliamBuick(3) 7 — 63
(B G Powell) *hld up in mid-div: hdwy over 3f out: led jst over 2f out: rdn over 1f out: styd on wl* — **13/2**[3]

0011 **2** 1 3/4 **Bugsy's Boy**[15] 1017 4-9-6 72 .... (p) TPQueally 11 — 77
(P W D'Arcy) *hld up in tch: led briefly over 2f out: edgd lft and rdn over 1f out: styd on one pce* — **1/1**[1]

0-50 **3** 1/2 **Synonymy**[12] 1062 5-8-8 56 oh5 .... (b) JamesDoyle 6 — 61
(M Blanshard) *hld up in tch: rdn wl over 1f out: styd on towards fin* — **10/1**

000- **4** 8 **Madam Vouvray**[98] 4877 4-8-4 58 ow2 .... TolleyDean(3) 13 — 55
(B G Powell) *hld up towards rr: rdn over 2f out: hdwy over 1f out: sn no imp* — **33/1**

240- **5** 2 1/2 **Cantabilly (IRE)**[16] 5924 5-9-12 74 .... RichardHughes 12 — 67
(R J Hodges) *hld up in mid-div: rdn over 2f out: wknd over 1f out* — **11/2**[2]

60-0 **6** 3/4 **Bobsleigh**[5] 1181 9-8-8 56 oh11 .... CatherineGannon 10 — 48
(H S Howe) *hld up in mid-div: rdn over 2f out: sn wknd* — **40/1**

305- **7** hd **Sister Agnes (IRE)**[188] 5938 4-9-2 68 .... SteveDrowne 3 — 60
(M F Harris) *hld up in tch: rdn over 2f out: wknd wl over 1f out* — **18/1**

-403 **8** 3 **Stoop To Conquer**[34] 810 8-9-7 72 .... JerryO'Dwyer(3) 2 — 61
(A W Carroll) *led: hdd over 2f out: sn wknd* — **10/1**

/36- **9** 1 3/4 **Go Free**[143] 2764 7-8-8 56 oh10 .... FergusSweeney 1 — 43
(J G M O'Shea) *a in rr* — **16/1**

004- **10** dist **Altenburg (FR)**[143] 6622 6-9-7 69 .... HayleyTurner 4 — —
(Mrs N Smith) *a bhd: lost tch 4f out: eased fnl 2f* — **8/1**

3m 59.63s (7.73) **Going Correction** +0.475s/f (Yiel)
WFA 4 from 5yo+ 4lb — **10** Ran SP% **124.5**
Speed ratings (Par 103): **100,99,98,95,94 93,93,92,91,—**
CSF £14.30 CT £72.39 TOTE £8.30: £2.10, £1.10, £2.70; EX 19.20 Trifecta £273.70 Pool £424.19 - 1.10 winning units..
Owner K Rhatigan **Bred** Roland H Alder **Trained** Upper Lambourn, Berks

FOCUS
An ordinary staying handicap, which was run at just a fair pace. The runner-up is rated to his latest form with the third rated to his All-weather mark.
Altenburg(FR) Official explanation: jockey said gelding had bled from the nose

1268 ASSET PROPERTY BROKERS H'CAP — 5f 11y
4:40 (4:40) (Class 5) (0-75,73) 4-Y-0+ — **£2,590** (£770; £385; £192) **Stalls** Centre

Form / RPR

30-2 **1** **Digital**[12] 1047 11-8-11 73 .... ThomasO'Brien(7) 2 — 84
(M R Channon) *sn outpcd in rr: plld out 2f out: gd hdwy on wd outside over 1f out: led jst ins fnl f: r.o wl* — **9/2**[3]

0-00 **2** 2 3/4 **Namir (IRE)**[16] 994 6-9-3 72 .... (vt) DaneO'Neill 3 — 73
(D Shaw) *stdd s: hld up: swtchd rt and hdwy over 1f out: ev ch ent fnl f: nt qckn* — **17/2**

6444 **3** 1 1/4 **Hart Of Gold**[7] 1145 4-8-5 63 .... KevinGhunowa(3) 6 — 60
(R A Harris) *w ldr: rdn to ld and bmpd over 1f out: hdd jst ins fnl f: one pce* — **13/2**

620 **4** 4 1/2 **Monte Major (IRE)**[32] 840 7-8-4 62 oh2 ow3 .... TolleyDean(3) 8 — 42
(D Shaw) *w ldrs: rdn and ev ch 1f out: wknd ins fnl f* — **10/3**[1]

6305 **5** 2 1/4 **Diminuto**[12] 1047 4-8-10 70 .... PatrickHills(5) 5 — 42
(M D I Usher) *led: rdn and hdd over 1f out: wknd fnl f* — **10/3**[1]

5624 **6** 1/2 **Figaro Flyer (IRE)**[18] 964 5-8-10 65 .... TPQueally 4 — 36
(P Howling) *hld up: rdn over 1f out: no rspnse* — **7/2**[2]

400- **7** 1 3/4 **Harrison's Flyer (IRE)**[234] 4634 7-9-1 70 .... (p) JimCrowley 7 — 34
(J M Bradley) *w ldrs: ev ch whn rdn and edgd lft over 1f out: wknd fnl f* — **12/1**

65.54 secs (3.04) **Going Correction** +0.70s/f (Yiel) — **7** Ran SP% **118.1**
Speed ratings (Par 103): **103,98,96,89,85 85,82**
CSF £43.06 CT £250.72 TOTE £4.30: £2.20, £3.50; EX 37.70 Trifecta £59.00 Pool £549.16 - 6.60 winning units. Place 6 £65.73, Place 5 £21.42..
Owner W G R Wightman **Bred** W G R Wightman **Trained** West Ilsley, Berks

FOCUS
A routine sprint handicap which was run at a strong pace and was set up for the winner, so not form to take too literally.
T/Plt: £19.70 to a £1 stake. Pool: £56,645.32. 2,097.70 winning tickets. T/Qpdt: £3.10 to a £1 stake. Pool: £3,684.86. 861.28 winning tickets. KH

1242 KEMPTON (A.W) (R-H)
Wednesday, April 9

OFFICIAL GOING: Standard
Wind: Almost nil.

1269 KEMPTON.CO.UK CLASSIFIED STKS — 1m (P)
6:20 (6:21) (Class 7) 4-Y-0+ — **£1,364** (£403; £201) **Stalls** High

Form / RPR

0-46 **1** **Hey Presto**[68] 392 8-9-0 43 .... MickyFenton 3 — 51
(R Rowe) *mde all: hrd drvn fr over 1f out: all out* — **20/1**

0050 **2** nk **Silver Blue (IRE)**[7] 1142 5-9-0 45 .... (b) LiamJones 1 — 50
(C R Dore) *in rr: n.m.r over 2f out and edgd rt: swtchd lft and hdwy over 1f out: str run ins fnl f: fin wl: jst failed* — **15/2**[3]

5206 **3** hd **Club Captain (USA)**[45] 693 5-9-0 43 .... J-PGuillambert 12 — 50
(T D McCarthy) *chsd ldrs: rdn to go 2nd 2f out: styd on u.p to cl on wnr thrght fnl f but nvr quite gng pce to get up* — **12/1**

6342 **4** 1 **Only If I Laugh**[12] 1053 7-9-0 45 .... IanMongan 9 — 47
(M J Attwater) *in tch: chsd ldrs on ins fr 3f out: kpt on ins fnl f but nvr gng pce to chal* — **7/2**[2]

6-23 **5** 3/4 **Prince Valentine**[12] 1053 7-9-0 45 .... (p) JimmyFortune 4 — 46
(G L Moore) *hld up in rr: hdwy over 2f out: styd on fnl f but nvr gng pce to chal* — **2/1**[1]

0000 **6** nse **Pajada**[12] 1053 4-8-7 39 .... (p) GabrielHannon(7) 8 — 45
(M D I Usher) *chsd ldrs: rdn 3f out: wknd ins fnl f* — **33/1**

0-04 **7** shd **Hester Brook (IRE)**[59] 513 4-9-0 42 .... AndrewElliott 14 — 45
(J G M O'Shea) *in rr: hdwy on ins over 2f out: kpt on same pce ins fnl f* — **20/1**

500/ **8** 4 1/2 **Mutared (IRE)**[779] 467 10-9-0 40 .... RichardThomas 11 — 35
(N P Littmoden) *in rr: styd on fnl 2f: nvr in contention* — **12/1**

0555 **9** 1 1/4 **Batchworth Blaise**[25] 898 5-9-0 45 .... StephenCarson 13 — 32
(E A Wheeler) *chsd ldrs: rdn over 2f out: wknd ins fnl f* — **15/2**[3]

0-00 **10** 1/2 **Old Etonian (UAE)**[51] 611 4-9-0 44 .... AdamKirby 6 — 31
(Peter Grayson) *s.i.s: rdn 3f out: nvr in contention* — **16/1**

000- **11** 1 1/4 **Goodwood Spirit**[180] 6152 6-9-0 42 .... (v) NCallan 10 — 28
(J M Bradley) *in tch: sme hdwy 3f out: nvr in contention* — **12/1**

0-00 **12** 1 **The London Gang**[14] 1025 5-9-0 40 .... (b) PatCosgrave 7 — 26
(W M Brisbourne) *in tch 5f* — **33/1**

/040 **13** 8 **Boluisce (IRE)**[12] 1064 5-9-0 45 .... SaleemGolam 2 — 7
(P W Hiatt) *chsd ldrs 5f: sn bhd* — **50/1**

00-0 **14** 4 **Canary Girl**[12] 1053 5-9-0 39 .... DMylonas 5 — —
(Miss Diana Weeden) *chsd ldrs 5f: sn wknd* — **80/1**

1m 41.73s (1.93) **Going Correction** +0.10s/f (Slow) — **14** Ran SP% **126.6**
Speed ratings (Par 97): **94,93,93,92,91 91,91,87,85,85 84,83,75,71**
CSF £162.94 TOTE £16.60: £6.30, £2.70, £3.80; EX 272.50.
Owner Richard Rowe **Bred** Michael Edwards And John Parsons **Trained** Sullington, W Sussex

FOCUS
An ordinary race for the lowly grade, in which first seven finished within a couple of lengths of each other.

1270 KEMPTON FOR WEDDINGS MAIDEN FILLIES' STKS 1m (P)
6:50 (6:52) (Class 5) 3-Y-O+ **£2,456** (£725; £362) **Stalls High**

Form RPR
6- **1** **Ada River**[158] 6649 3-8-9 0 .... WilliamBuick(3) 10 82
(A M Balding) *stdd s and hld up in rr: stdy hdwy on outside over 2f out: str run fr over 1f out: qcknd ins fnl f to ld fnl 75yds: comf* **15/8**[1]
243- **2** *1* **Dubai Power**[181] 6126 3-8-12 85 .... NCallan 8 79
(C E Brittain) *chsd ldrs: rdn to ld over 1f out: styd on tl hdd and outpcd fnl 75yds* **2/1**[2]
0- **3** *1* **Hepburn Bell (IRE)**[188] 5937 3-8-12 0 .... JamieSpencer 11 77
(J R Fanshawe) *in tch: hdwy to trck ldrs and swtchd lft over 1f out: styng on again whn swtchd lft wl ins fnl f: nt rcvr and nvr any ch w easy wnr* **12/1**
5- **4** *2 1/2* **Queen's Speech (IRE)**[160] 6611 3-8-12 0 .... JimmyFortune 4 71
(J H M Gosden) *in tch: lost position 3f out: shkn up over 2f out: r.o strly fnl f but nvr gng pce to be competitive* **6/1**[3]
240- **5** *1/2* **Spiritofthestorm (USA)**[150] 6777 3-8-12 70 .... EddieAhern 5 70
(R A Teal) *in tch rdn to chse ldrs 2f out: styd on same pce fr over 1f out* **16/1**
0- **6** *2 1/2* **Loveinanelevator**[327] 1814 3-8-12 0 .... HayleyTurner 3 64
(M L W Bell) *t.k.h: sn led: rdn over 2f out: hdd over 1f out: sn wknd* **25/1**
25- **7** *1* **Mrs Summersby (IRE)**[103] 7252 3-8-12 0 .... SteveDrowne 1 62
(H Morrison) *chsd ldr: rdn 3f out: wknd ins fnl 2f* **7/1**
0 **8** *3 1/4* **Glitz (IRE)**[16] 997 3-8-12 0 .... RichardMullen 6 54
(M L W Bell) *in rr: rdn 3f out: nvr in contention* **66/1**
5 **9** *6* **Elzeeza (USA)**[12] 1050 3-8-12 0 .... RHills 2 41
(E A L Dunlop) *chsd ldrs: rdn 3f out: wknd qckly 2f out* **14/1**
06 **10** *12* **Sweet Refrain**[12] 1050 3-8-12 0 .... PaulDoe 9 13
(M J Attwater) *a in rr* **100/1**

1m 40.15s (0.35) **Going Correction** +0.10s/f (Slow) 10 Ran SP% **121.5**
Speed ratings (Par 100): **102,101,100,97,97 94,93,90,84,72**
CSF £6.12 TOTE £3.00: £1.30, £1.20, £4.20; EX 6.40.
Owner G B Russell **Bred** G Russell **Trained** Kingsclere, Hants

FOCUS
The winning time was 1.58 seconds faster than the Class 7 classified stakes and this looked a fair race of its type. Rated through the fifth for now, it should produce winners.

1271 DIGIBET FILLIES' H'CAP 7f (P)
7:20 (7:21) (Class 6) (0-65,65) 3-Y-O **£2,047** (£604; £302) **Stalls High**

Form RPR
400- **1** **Binfield (IRE)**[162] 6572 3-9-3 64 .... JamieSpencer 12 77
(B G Powell) *trckd ldrs: drvn to ld over 1f out: styd on strly* **9/2**[2]
2-54 **2** *3 3/4* **Nice Wee Girl (IRE)**[7] 1144 3-9-4 65 .... LPKeniry 3 68
(S Kirk) *t.k.h: in tch: rdn and hdwy over 2f out: styd on u.p to go 2nd wl ins fnl f but nvr any ch w wnr* **7/2**[1]
-644 **3** *2 1/4* **Bye Baby Bunting**[35] 796 3-9-1 62 .... DaneO'Neill 4 59
(B R Johnson) *towards rr: hdwy on outside 3f out: styd on wl fnl f but nvr gng pce to trble ldng duo* **6/1**[3]
420- **4** *nk* **Red Amaryllis**[133] 6964 3-9-4 65 .... RichardKingscote 11 61
(H J L Dunlop) *led: rdn over 2f out: hdd over 1f out: wknd ins fnl f* **10/1**
000- **5** *1 3/4* **Oriental Girl**[144] 6847 3-8-13 60 .... RichardThomas 9 51
(J A Geake) *in tch: hdwy to chse ldrs over 2f out but sn hung rt: outpcd fnl f* **16/1**
440- **6** *hd* **Solo River**[168] 6425 3-8-13 60 .... RichardSmith 7 51
(P J Makin) *s.i.s: plld hrd in rr: hdwy fr 2f out: kpt on ins fnl f but nvr in contention* **20/1**
000- **7** *1 1/2* **Tenraninthemist (IRE)**[137] 6928 3-8-4 51 oh6 .... NeilPollard 8 38
(B R Johnson) *in rr but in tch: rdn along 3f out: nvr gng pce to be competitive* **33/1**
000- **8** *2 1/4* **Miss Okaloosa**[160] 6601 3-8-12 59 .... RichardMullen 6 40
(D M Simcock) *unruly and uns rdr bef s: slowly away: mod late prog* **16/1**
04-1 **9** *hd* **Lowry's Art**[16] 998 3-9-2 63 .... SebSanders 5 43
(R M Beckett) *chsd ldr tl rdn 2f out: sn wknd* **7/2**[1]
02-0 **10** *2 1/4* **Bonny's Babe**[5] 1187 3-8-6 53 .... PaulEddery 2 27
(G D Blake) *in rr: drvn and effrt over 3f out: nvr in contention and towards rr fnl 2f* **16/1**
06-0 **11** *shd* **River Gleam (IRE)**[25] 899 3-9-1 62 .... JimmyFortune 10 36
(A P Jarvis) *chsd ldrs: rdn 3f out: sn wknd* **11/1**

1m 27.34s (1.34) **Going Correction** +0.10s/f (Slow) 11 Ran SP% **119.7**
Speed ratings (Par 93): **96,91,89,88,86 86,84,82,82,79 79**
CSF £21.03 CT £98.52 TOTE £5.30: £2.30, £1.90, £1.30; EX 23.50.
Owner N J Hitchins **Bred** Miss Annette McMahon **Trained** Upper Lambourn, Berks

FOCUS
An ordinary fillies' handicap and the time was acceptable for the type of race, but the winner did it very nicely. The form looks sound rated through the runner-up.
Oriental Girl Official explanation: jockey said filly hung right
Lowry's Art Official explanation: trainer's rep had no explanation for the poor form shown
River Gleam(IRE) Official explanation: jockey said filly ran too free early

1272 DIGIBET.COM MAIDEN STKS 1m 3f (P)
7:50 (7:50) (Class 5) 3-Y-O **£2,456** (£725; £362) **Stalls High**

Form RPR
1 **Top Lock** 3-9-3 0 .... MartinDwyer 8 77+
(A M Balding) *in rr: hdwy on outside 3f out: stl plenty to do over 2f out: rapid hdwy to ld appr fnl f: styd on wl u.p* **9/1**
2 *nk* **Touchdown** 3-9-3 0 .... GregFairley 6 76+
(M Johnston) *chsd ldrs: rdn and one pce whn edgd lft 2f out: styd on u.p to chse wnr ins fnl f but a jst hld* **9/4**[2]
3 *2* **Dance The Star (USA)** 3-9-3 0 .... RichardMullen 4 73
(D M Simcock) *towards rr: rdn along 1/2-way: styd on fr 2f out but nvr gng pce to rch ldng duo* **25/1**
00-4 **4** *3/4* **Mahadee (IRE)**[23] 918 3-9-3 67 .... NCallan 3 75+
(C E Brittain) *chsd ldrs: one pce whn hmpd 2f out: rallied and r.o fnl f but nt trble ldrs* **5/1**[3]
600- **5** *1/2* **Hadron Collider (FR)**[184] 6058 3-9-3 68 .... RichardHughes 5 71
(R Hannon) *led: narrowly hdd 3f out but styd chalng tl over 1f out: wknd ins fnl f* **7/1**
0-2 **6** *1* **Riqaab (IRE)**[12] 1054 3-9-3 0 .... RHills 2 69
(E A L Dunlop) *hld up in rr: stdy hdwy on outside fr 4f out to take slt ld 3f out: rdn 2f out: hdd & wknd appr fnl f* **7/4**[1]
0-0 **7** *14* **Amphibalus (IRE)**[25] 903 3-9-3 0 .... HayleyTurner 1 45?
(D K Ivory) *w ldr: rdn 3f out: wknd over 2f out* **66/1**

2m 26.32s (4.42) **Going Correction** +0.10s/f (Slow) 7 Ran SP% **111.6**
Speed ratings (Par 98): **87,86,85,84,84 83,73**
CSF £28.23 TOTE £11.50: £1.70, £2.00; EX 22.40.
Owner David Brownlow **Bred** Bishop Wilton Stud **Trained** Kingsclere, Hants
■ Stewards' Enquiry : Greg Fairley three-day ban: careless riding (Apr 23-25)
Martin Dwyer caution: careless riding

FOCUS
A modest maiden with a couple of horses officially rated in the 60s. The early pace was very modest and it developed into something of a sprint down the home straight, but the first three were newcomers so at least they are open to improvement, while the fourth sets the level for the form.

1273 DIGIBET CASINO H'CAP 1m 3f (P)
8:20 (8:21) (Class 4) (0-80,79) 4-Y-O+ **£4,209** (£1,252; £625; £312) **Stalls High**

Form RPR
452- **1** **Proper (IRE)**[167] 6455 4-8-1 65 oh1 .... WilliamBuick(3) 7 76
(C J Mann) *hld up in rr: stl last and plenty to do over 2f out: rdn and rapid hdwy to ld over 1f out: c clr ins fnl f: readily* **14/1**
00 **2** *3* **Dakiyah (IRE)**[45] 692 4-9-2 77 .... IanMongan 8 83
(Mrs L J Mongan) *in tch: rdn and styd on to chal 2f out: kpt on to chse wnr wl ins fnl f but no ch* **20/1**
111- **3** *nk* **Boz**[153] 6739 4-9-4 79 .... JamieSpencer 2 84
(L M Cumani) *trckd ldng duo: rdn to take slt ld appr fnl 2f: hdd and outpcd appr fnl f* **11/8**[1]
04-0 **4** *1 1/2* **Folio (IRE)**[11] 1072 8-8-9 77 .... DebraEngland(7) 4 79
(W J Musson) *in rr: t.k.h: hdwy over 2f out: styd on ins fnl f: nt trble ldng trio* **25/1**
431- **5** *3* **Garafena**[130] 6430 5-8-11 72 .... RichardHughes 6 69
(B G Powell) *chsd ldr: rdn over 2f out: wknd appr fnl f* **12/1**
4023 **6** *3 1/4* **Lord Theo**[12] 1048 4-9-0 75 .... JamesDoyle 9 67
(N P Littmoden) *led: narrowly hdd but ev ch appr fnl 2f: wknd fnl f* **5/1**[3]
1121 **7** *1* **Safari Sundowner (IRE)**[26] 888 4-9-4 79 .... JimCrowley 3 69
(P Winkworth) *rdn 3f out: towards rr most of way* **5/2**[2]
41-0 **8** *2 1/2* **Pearl (IRE)**[15] 309 4-8-9 70 .... (p) TedDurcan 5 56
(I A Wood) *sn rdn in rr: nvr in contention* **20/1**

2m 19.65s (-2.25) **Going Correction** +0.10s/f (Slow) 8 Ran SP% **115.1**
Speed ratings (Par 105): **112,109,109,108,106 103,103,101**
CSF £245.20 CT £633.55 TOTE £17.10: £3.30, £5.30, £1.10; EX 380.50.
Owner CGA Racing Partnership 1 **Bred** Sean Finnegan **Trained** Upper Lambourn, Berks

FOCUS
A fair handicap run at a strong pace and the form looks very solid.

1274 AUTOTRADER H'CAP 7f (P)
8:50 (8:50) (Class 6) (0-65,65) 3-Y-O **£2,047** (£604; £302) **Stalls High**

Form RPR
20-2 **1** **Greystoke Prince**[23] 918 3-9-4 65 .... AdamKirby 6 72
(W R Swinburn) *mde all: drvn along 2f out: forged clr fnl f: readily* **1/1**[1]
-410 **2** *2* **Thomas Malory (IRE)**[7] 1155 3-8-11 63 .... SCreighton(5) 2 65
(Miss V Haigh) *hld up towards rr: hdwy to trck ldng gp of five 3f out: qcknd to chse wnr ins fnl 2f but a wl hld* **10/1**
4600 **3** *1* **Easy Wonder (GER)**[12] 1060 3-9-4 65 .... NCallan 8 64
(I A Wood) *chsd ldrs: rdn 3f out: chsd wnr over 2f out but no imp: styd on same pce and dropped to 3rd ins fnl quarter m* **11/1**
050- **4** *shd* **Maddy**[161] 6584 3-9-2 63 .... (p) TedDurcan 4 62
(George Baker) *sn chsd along: rdn to chse ldrs 3f out: one pce fnl 2f* **15/2**[3]
00-5 **5** *3 1/2* **Never Sold Out (IRE)**[83] 195 3-8-4 51 oh1 .... (v[1]) AndrewElliott 3 41
(J G M O'Shea) *chsd ldrs: rdn 3f out: wknd ins fnl 2f* **33/1**
00-0 **6** *1 3/4* **Bahia Palace**[12] 1051 3-8-1 51 oh6 .... WilliamBuick(3) 1 36
(M D I Usher) *sn pushed along: a in rr* **25/1**
40-3 **7** *nk* **Little Toto**[37] 785 3-9-1 62 .... EddieAhern 5 46
(C G Cox) *chsd ldrs: rdn over 3f out: wknd fr 2f out* **7/2**[2]

1m 27.11s (1.11) **Going Correction** +0.10s/f (Slow) 7 Ran SP% **108.2**
Speed ratings (Par 96): **97,94,93,93,89 87,87**
CSF £10.82 CT £52.33 TOTE £1.80: £1.20, £3.50; EX 9.20.
Owner The Pendley Royals **Bred** New Hall Stud **Trained** Aldbury, Herts
■ Too Grand (9/1) was withdrawn after rearing up in the stalls. R4 applies, deduct 10p in the £.

FOCUS
A modest handicap run at an ordinary pace but the form looks solid rated through the runner-up.
Little Toto Official explanation: trainer said colt had bled from the nose

1275 PANORAMIC BAR & RESTAURANT H'CAP 6f (P)
9:20 (9:20) (Class 6) (0-52,53) 4-Y-O+ **£2,047** (£604; £151; £151) **Stalls High**

Form RPR
1123 **1** **Marmooq**[14] 1029 5-8-10 50 .... (e) IanMongan 1 58
(M J Attwater) *in rr: stl last and plenty to do over 2f out: rapid hdwy over 1f out: str run ins fnl f to ld last stride* **9/2**[2]
0620 **2** *nse* **Regal Royale**[1] 1254 5-8-13 53 ow1 .... (v) AdamKirby 11 61
(Peter Grayson) *drvn to ld s: rdn over 2f out: hdd over 1f out: rallied ins fnl f and led nr fin: ct last stride* **5/1**[3]
-213 **3** *shd* **High Reach**[47] 655 8-8-12 52 .... AndrewElliott 7 60
(J G M O'Shea) *chsd ldrs: rdn over 2f out: styd on wl thrght fnl f and chal last stride: jst failed* **12/1**
-414 **3** *dht* **Davids Mark**[49] 625 8-8-12 52 .... EddieAhern 12 60
(J R Jenkins) *chsd ldrs: rdn to ld over 1f out: hdd cl home* **4/1**[1]
1000 **5** *1* **Mulberry Lad (IRE)**[13] 1035 6-8-8 48 .... JimCrowley 8 52
(P W Hiatt) *in rr: hdwy over 1f out: styd on wl fnl f: gng on cl home* **20/1**
365- **6** *1* **Razzano (IRE)**[163] 6542 4-8-6 51 .... JamieJones(5) 3 52
(A M Hales) *in rr: hdwy over 1f out: fin wl but nt rch ldrs* **16/1**
0130 **7** *1 1/2* **Piccostar**[21] 933 5-8-5 52 ow3 .... GihanArnolda(7) 10 48
(A B Haynes) *chsd ldrs: rdn over 2f out: wknd fnl f* **9/1**
6410 **8** *1 1/4* **Desert Light (IRE)**[7] 1145 7-8-12 52 .... (v) NCallan 2 44
(D Shaw) *outpcd: rdn and sme prog fr over 1f out* **8/1**
000- **9** *3* **Fervent**[182] 6100 4-8-7 47 .... PaulFitzsimons 5 30
(J M Bradley) *a outpcd* **50/1**
2524 **10** *2 1/2* **Suhayl Star (IRE)**[12] 1053 4-8-7 47 .... LPKeniry 4 22
(P Burgoyne) *a towards rr* **13/2**
2050 **11** *1 1/2* **Calloff The Search**[7] 1150 4-8-10 50 .... (p) MickyFenton 6 20
(Stef Liddiard) *chsd ldrs: rdn: hung rt and wknd 2f out* **11/1**
0600 **12** *3 3/4* **Ace Club**[14] 1028 7-8-10 50 .... (b) DaneO'Neill 9 8
(Garry Moss) *chsd ldrs over 3f* **33/1**

1m 13.14s (0.04) **Going Correction** +0.10s/f (Slow) 12 Ran SP% **120.9**
Speed ratings (Par 101): **103,102,102,102,101 100,98,96,92,89 87,82**
Place High Reach £2.30, Davids Mark £1.20. Tricast: M/RR/HR £130.90, M/RR/DM £50.38. CSF £27.38 TOTE £5.30: £2.20, £2.00; EX 32.60 Place 6 £80.44, Place 5 £11.50. .
Owner The Attwater Partnership **Bred** Matthews Breeding And Racing Ltd **Trained** Epsom, Surrey

FOCUS
A moderate sprint handicap run at a strong pace. It produced a cracking finish and the form seems sound.
T/Plt: £226.60 to a £1 stake. Pool: £82,219.03. 264.85 winning tickets. T/Qpdt: £17.10 to a £1 stake. Pool: £8,034.99. 347.08 winning tickets. ST

1122 FOLKESTONE (R-H)
Thursday, April 10

OFFICIAL GOING: Good to soft
On the straight course the stands'-side rail was a big advantage, just as it had been at Folkestone's first Flat meeting of the year the previous week.
Wind: virtually nil Weather: overcast

1276 KMFM MEDIAN AUCTION MAIDEN STKS 5f
2:10 (2:10) (Class 6) 2-Y-O £2,388 (£705; £352) Stalls Low

Form RPR
6 1 **Northern Tour**[19] 957 2-9-3 0 TQuinn 6 75+
(P F I Cole) *mde all: pushed along 2f out: comf* **4/6**[1]
2 *1* **Soul Sista (IRE)** 2-8-12 0 LiamJones 4 62+
(J L Spearing) *awkward leaving stalls: sn bustled along: chsd wnr after 1f: rdn wl over 1f out: kpt on same pce fnl f* **7/1**[3]
3 *6* **Sorrel Ridge (IRE)** 2-9-3 0 EddieAhern 2 43+
(M G Quinlan) *chsd wnr for 1f: rdn wl over 1f out: wknd fnl f* **10/3**[2]
4 *14* **Strictly Royal** 2-9-3 0 (v[1]) TPO'Shea 1 —
(M R Channon) *a bhd: lost tch 1/2-way: t.o* **8/1**
63.21 secs (3.21) **Going Correction** +0.35s/f (Good) 4 Ran SP% 106.7
Speed ratings (Par 90): **88,86,76,54**
CSF £5.50 TOTE £1.60; EX 5.50.
Owner Hunter, Maynard, Ward **Bred** Arbib Bloodstock Partnership **Trained** Whatcombe, Oxon

FOCUS
Just the four runners and this looked an ordinary juvenile maiden.

NOTEBOOK
Northern Tour, sixth of 19 on his debut in the Brocklesby, found this easier and got off the mark in workmanlike fashion. Having been quickly into his stride, he was able to grab the favoured stands' rail and, although having to be shaken up, his rider never had to resort to the whip. (op 8-11 tchd 8-13)
Soul Sista(IRE), a daughter of 1999 July Stakes winner City On A Hill, first foal of a multiple 6f-1m winner at five to seven, made a pleasing introduction. Having been slow to find her stride, she quickly recovered to chase the winner, but that one had the benefit of the rail and she was always just held. She should benefit from this experience and looks up to winning a similar contest. (op 9-1 tchd 10-1)
Sorrel Ridge(IRE), a 10,000euros son of Namid, first foal of a mare who was placed over 1m2f, showed some early speed but was soon put in his place. Like the runner-up, this should bring him on. (op 11-4 tchd 7-2)
Strictly Royal, a son of Imperial Dancer, first foal of a mare who was unplaced over 6f-1m1f, had a visor on for his racecourse debut and showed very little. (op 7-1 tchd 5-1)

1277 ALEX AND PETER HATFIELD H'CAP 6f
2:40 (2:40) (Class 5) (0-75,75) 3-Y-O £2,331 (£693; £346; £173) Stalls Low

Form RPR
11-6 1 **We Have A Dream**[10] 1110 3-8-13 70 MartinDwyer 4 83
(W R Muir) *prom: rdn to ld jst over 1f out: styd on wl* **9/2**[3]
-314 2 *¾* **Baunagain (IRE)**[13] 1066 3-9-4 75 PatCosgrave 2 85+
(M J Wallace) *taken down early: hld up in tch on stands' rail: lost pl over 2f out: hdwy and wanting to hang rt fr 2f out: chsd wnr last 100yds: styd on but nt able to chal* **4/1**[2]
00-0 3 *3* **Our Acquaintance**[10] 1110 3-9-1 72 SebSanders 5 73
(W R Muir) *t.k.h: in tch: hdwy to ld over 1f out: hdd jst over 1f out: kpt on same pce u.p fnl f* **12/1**
134- 4 *4* **Blue Jack**[125] 7052 3-9-4 75 (t) RichardMullen 6 63+
(W R Muir) *in tch: hdwy and rdn 2f out: ev ch wl over 1f out: wknd fnl f* **7/2**[1]
000- 5 *shd* **Party In The Park**[207] 5452 3-8-11 68 RyanMoore 9 56+
(R Hannon) *cl up: rdn to ld narrowly 2f out: hdd over 1f out: fdd fnl f* **9/2**[3]
416- 6 *1 ¾* **Whiteoak Lady (IRE)**[200] 5665 3-9-1 72 LiamJones 3 54
(J L Spearing) *t.k.h: hld up towards rr: rdn and effrt over 2f out: no imp fr over 1f out* **10/1**
5-66 7 *1 ¼* **Copperwood**[38] 777 3-9-1 72 NCallan 10 50
(M Blanshard) *dropped in after s: t.k.h: hld up in rr: rdn 1/2-way: n.d* **12/1**
254- 8 *½* **Kalligal**[169] 6425 3-9-2 73 RobertHavlin 8 49
(R Ingram) *led tl 2f out: sn rdn: wknd over 1f out* **20/1**
516 9 *3 ¾* **Helping Hand (IRE)**[62] 489 3-8-13 73 RussellKennemore(3) 7 37
(R Hollinshead) *stdd s: t.k.h: hld up in rr: rdn 1/2-way: n.d* **12/1**
-100 10 *12* **Young Ivanhoe**[10] 1110 3-9-1 72 JimmyQuinn 11 —
(C A Dwyer) *in tch on outer: rdn and struggling 1/2-way: no ch and eased ins fnl f* **20/1**
1m 15.07s (2.37) **Going Correction** +0.35s/f (Good) 10 Ran SP% 120.3
Speed ratings (Par 98): **98,97,93,87,87 85,83,82,77,61**
CSF £23.71 CT £175.90 TOTE £4.50: £1.40, £1.40, £4.30; EX 25.10 TRIFECTA Not won..
Owner The Dreaming Squires **Bred** Whitsbury Manor Stud **Trained** Lambourn, Berks

FOCUS
A good result for the William Muir stable, which sent out three of the first four home. The first two home raced against the stands' rail throughout, which looked the place to be. The winning time was 1.19 seconds slower than following older-horse 71-85, but a reasonably positive view has been taken of the form.

1278 WEATHERBYS BANK H'CAP 6f
3:15 (3:15) (Class 4) (0-85,85) 4-Y-O+ £4,209 (£1,252; £625; £312) Stalls Low

Form RPR
-160 1 **Bonnie Prince Blue**[65] 442 5-8-10 77 (b) MichaelHills 6 91+
(B W Hills) *chsd ldrs: rdn to chse ldr wl over 1f out: led 1f out: styd on wl last 100yds* **9/1**
020- 2 *2* **Nobilissima (IRE)**[187] 6006 4-8-12 79 LiamJones 5 86
(J L Spearing) *led: rdn jst over 2f out: hdd 1f out: outpcd by wnr last 100yds* **6/1**
200- 3 *¾* **Mujood**[168] 6450 5-9-2 83 (v) StephenCarson 3 88
(Eve Johnson Houghton) *in tch: rdn over 2f out: hdwy over 1f out: edgd rt but styd on u.p fnl f: nt pce to trble wnr* **5/1**[3]
1213 4 *½* **Hits Only Jude (IRE)**[33] 833 5-8-13 80 DeanMcKeown 4 83
(P A Blockley) *chsd ldr: rdn over 2f out: lost 2nd wl over 1f out: onpced fnl f* **7/1**
5-05 5 *1 ¾* **Andronikos**[65] 442 6-9-1 82 RyanMoore 9 80+
(P F I Cole) *dropped in and grad crossed to stands' rail: hld up bhd: hdwy and rdn wl over 1f out: styd on but nvr threatened ldrs* **4/1**[1]
223 6 *1 ½* **Dickie Le Davoir**[12] 1084 4-8-7 74 ChrisCatlin 2 67
(John A Harris) *s.i.s: sn in tch in midfield: rdn over 2f out: no imp last 2f* **8/1**
00-0 7 *4 ½* **Stamford Blue**[8] 1145 7-8-11 81 (b) KevinGhunowa(3) 1 60
(R A Harris) *a in rr: rdn and no hdwy over 2f out: no ch fnl f* **16/1**
136- 8 *2 ¾* **Don Pele (IRE)**[180] 6173 6-9-4 85 (p) AlanMunro 10 55
(R A Harris) *racd on outer: in tch tl rdn 2f out: sn outpcd* **20/1**
040- 9 *2 ½* **Shes Minnie**[189] 5954 5-9-1 82 FergusSweeney 8 44
(J G M O'Shea) *s.i.s: a bhd* **25/1**
341- 10 *1 ½* **Golden Desert (IRE)**[141] 6900 4-8-13 80 JimCrowley 7 37
(T G Mills) *chsd ldrs: rdn wl over 2f out: wknd 2f out and sn bhd* **9/2**[2]
1m 13.88s (1.18) **Going Correction** +0.35s/f (Good) 10 Ran SP% 117.2
Speed ratings (Par 105): **106,103,102,101,99 97,91,87,84,82**
CSF £62.49 CT £304.24 TOTE £10.50: £3.30, £2.80, £1.80; EX 91.40 TRIFECTA Not won..
Owner G J Hicks **Bred** George Joseph Hicks **Trained** Lambourn, Berks

FOCUS
Most of these were pretty well exposed and this looked like an ordinary sprint handicap for the grade, but the winning time was 1.19 seconds quicker than the previous 61-75 three-year-old handicap. It paid to be handy, as nothing came from far back.

1279 FOLKESTONE RACECOURSE FOR WEDDINGS MAIDEN FILLIES' STKS 1m 1f 149y
3:50 (3:51) (Class 5) 3-Y-O £2,590 (£770; £385; £192) Stalls Centre

Form RPR
325- 1 **Riverscape (IRE)**[170] 6411 3-9-0 75 JimCrowley 4 69
(Mrs A J Perrett) *in tch: hdwy to chse ldr 8f out: upsides 2f out: rdn to ld wl ins fnl f: pushed out cl home* **13/8**[1]
2 *½* **Valferno (IRE)** 3-9-0 0 MickyFenton 7 68
(Mrs P Sly) *chsd ldrs: rdn and unable qck 2f out: r.o strly last 100yds: wnt 2nd nr fin* **8/1**
32- 3 *hd* **Pharaohs Queen (IRE)**[143] 6868 3-9-0 0 RyanMoore 1 68
(E A L Dunlop) *led at stdy gallop: rdn 2f out: sn jnd: edgd lft u.p fr over 1f out: headed and no ex last 100yds* **2/1**[2]
6 4 *6* **Barring Decree (IRE)**[26] 903 3-9-0 0 ChrisCatlin 8 55
(E J O'Neill) *in tch in midfield: rdn 3f out: outpcd by ldng trio fr wl over 1f out* **5/1**[3]
000- 5 *3 ¾* **L'Orage**[230] 4774 3-8-9 46 JamieJones(5) 5 48
(M G Quinlan) *hld up in last pair: rdn and effrt 2f out: sn outpcd* **66/1**
000- 6 *¾* **The Hoofer (IRE)**[164] 6536 3-9-0 56 TedDurcan 3 46
(J L Dunlop) *hld up in last pair: rdn and effrt on outer 2f out: sn no imp* **12/1**
0- 7 *11* **Dancing Ellie**[179] 6202 3-9-0 0 IanMongan 2 23
(P M Phelan) *t.k.h: in tch rdn 3f out: wknd 2f out* **40/1**
2m 12.1s (7.20) **Going Correction** +0.675s/f (Yiel) 7 Ran SP% 110.8
Speed ratings (Par 95): **98,97,97,92,89 89,80**
CSF £14.44 TOTE £2.40: £1.60, £3.90; EX 12.70 Trifecta £42.20 Pool: £506.72, 8.51 winning units.
Owner Lady Clague **Bred** Newberry Stud Farm Ltd **Trained** Pulborough, W Sussex

FOCUS
A weakish fillies' maiden run at a modest gallop. The winning time was 0.71 seconds slower than the following 46-60 older-horse handicap, and the 46-rated fifth was plenty close enough for comfort.

1280 INVICTA MOTORS H'CAP 1m 1f 149y
4:25 (4:28) (Class 6) (0-60,60) 4-Y-O+ £2,047 (£604; £302) Stalls Centre

Form RPR
0003 1 **Princelywallywogan**[8] 1160 6-8-9 51 PatCosgrave 1 57
(John A Harris) *broke wl but sn stdd and hld up in tch: hdwy over 2f out: rdn to ld over 1f out: drvn out* **6/1**[2]
2356 2 *1* **Flight Dream (FR)**[35] 811 5-9-4 60 NCallan 9 64
(M G Quinlan) *chsd ldrs: shkn up and hdwy jst over 2f out: rdn to ld wl over 1f out: sn hung lft and hdd: unable qck u.p fnl f* **10/1**
0/22 3 *shd* **Ruling Reef**[5] 843 6-8-5 47 HayleyTurner 3 51
(M D I Usher) *hld up towards rr: hdwy over 3f out: rdn and effrt on inner 2f out: chsd ldrs 1f out: kpt on u.p* **9/2**[1]
5-00 4 *shd* **King Of Connacht**[17] 999 5-8-10 52 (p) LiamJones 8 56
(M Wellings) *t.k.h: hld up in tch: rdn and effrt on inner 2f out: chsd ldrs fnl f: kpt on u.p* **33/1**
3020 5 *1 ¾* **Earl Kraul (IRE)**[42] 728 5-9-1 57 StephenDonohoe 2 57+
(P A Blockley) *s.i.s: hld up in rr: plld out and rdn over 1f out: r.o but nvr able to chal* **14/1**
5264 6 *½* **Amical Risks (FR)**[19] 963 4-9-1 57 NeilPollard 10 59+
(W J Musson) *hld up in rr: gd hdwy on inner 2f out: short of room and snatched up over 1f out: kpt on same pce after* **9/2**[1]
000/ 7 *½* **Muskatsturm (GER)**[1320] 5159 9-8-1 50 MHarley(7) 6 51+
(Shaun Harley, Ire) *hld up wl in tch: stl gng wl over 2f out: nt clr run and shuffled bk over 1f out: styd on last 100yds* **8/1**
020- 8 *3 ½* **Forfeiter (USA)**[18] 7168 6-8-10 52 JimCrowley 12 42
(C Gordon) *led after 1f: rdn over 2f out: hdd wl over 1f out: wknd fnl f* **6/1**[2]
2500 9 *1 ¾* **Copper King**[27] 879 4-9-1 57 ChrisCatlin 11 44
(Miss Tor Sturgis) *hld up towards rr: rdn and effrt jst over 2f out: n.d* **16/1**
463 10 *nk* **Personify**[12] 1083 6-8-5 50 (p) KevinGhunowa(3) 4 36
(R A Harris) *t.k.h: chsd ldrs on outer: rdn 2f out: sn wknd* **25/1**
621- 11 *2 ¾* **Etoile D'Or (IRE)**[17] 6408 4-9-1 57 JimmyQuinn 7 37
(M J Gingell) *t.k.h: hld up towards rr: hdwy on outer 3f out: rdn and no imp 2f out* **20/1**
45-0 12 *1 ½* **The Dagger**[43] 716 4-9-2 58 RyanMoore 5 35
(G L Moore) *led for 1f: chsd ldr after: ev ch and rdn jst over 2f out: wknd over 1f out* **7/1**[3]
0PP- 13 *52* **Istibian (IRE)**[150] 6804 4-8-8 50 (v[1]) RichardKingscote 13 —
(Mrs H Sweeting) *v.s.a: a last: t.o last 2f* **100/1**
2m 11.39s (6.49) **Going Correction** +0.675s/f (Yiel) 13 Ran SP% 122.7
Speed ratings (Par 101): **101,100,100,100,98 98,97,95,93,93 91,90,48**
CSF £64.32 CT £302.55 TOTE £8.00: £2.70, £3.40, £1.70; EX 114.50 Trifecta £157.10 Part won. Pool: £221.34 - 0.50 winning units..
Owner Mrs A E Harris **Bred** Mrs J A Gawthorpe **Trained** Eastwell, Leics

FOCUS
A moderate handicap. It was slowly run, but the winning time was still 0.71 seconds quicker than the steadily run three-year-old fillies' maiden. It was a bit messy and did not produce much of interest.

1281 BETFAIR APPRENTICE TRAINING SERIES H'CAP 1m 4f
5:00 (5:00) (Class 6) (0-60,60) 4-Y-0+ **£2,047** (£604; £302) **Stalls** Low

Form RPR
002- **1** **Compton Charlie**[269] 3593 4-8-13 **52** .... JackDean 10 57
(J G Portman) *t.k.h: in tch: hdwy to ld over 1f out: sn hung bdly lft: hld on wl* **20/1**
0601 **2** *1* **Street Life (IRE)**[8] 1159 10-9-0 **60** 6ex .... DebraEngland[(8)] 9 63+
(W J Musson) *hld up bhd: stl last 2f out: hdwy over 1f out: r.o to chse wnr ins fnl f: no imp towards fin* **3/1**[1]
-253 **3** *hd* **Berry Hill Lass (IRE)**[55] 575 4-9-5 **58** .... (p) MCGeran 6 61
(J G M O'Shea) *chsd ldr: rdn and ev ch over 1f out: sn hung lft u.p: kpt on same pce last 100yds* **8/1**
000/ **4** *1* **Ardglass (IRE)**[451] 1769 6-9-4 **56** .... HarryPoulton 2 57
(Mrs P Townsley) *s.i.s: t.k.h: sn chsng ldrs: rdn and carried lft over 1f out: kpt on same pce fnl f* **40/1**
0/40 **5** *½* **Meohmy**[14] 1044 5-8-4 **45** .... MatthewDavies[(3)] 11 45
(M R Channon) *led tl rdn and hdd over 1f out: sn hung lft: one pce fnl f* **8/1**
0043 **6** *shd* **Ashmolian (IRE)**[38] 778 5-8-9 **47** .... ThomasO'Brien 4 47
(Miss Z C Davison) *t.k.h: hld up towards rr: pushed along and hdwy over 3f out: chsd ldrs u.p over 1f out: unable qck* **7/1**[3]
06-3 **7** *2* **General Flumpa**[17] 999 7-9-1 **58** .... SoniaEaton[(5)] 7 55
(Miss Tor Sturgis) *hld up towards rr: rdn and effrt on inner wl over 1f out: plugged on but nvr pce to chal* **5/1**[2]
-640 **8** *1* **Top Spec (IRE)**[19] 963 7-9-0 **55** .... SimonPearce[(3)] 1 50
(J Pearce) *s.i.s: hld up in tch on outer: hdwy over 3f out: c wd bnd over 2f out: sn rdn and no hdwy* **3/1**[1]
000/ **9** *2¼* **Sandokan (GER)**[1169] 6524 7-8-4 **45** .... (t) MHarley[(3)] 5 37
(Shaun Harley, Ire) *t.k.h: hld up in tch: rdn jst over 2f out: wknd over 1f out* **14/1**

2m 54.14s (13.24) **Going Correction** +0.675s/f (Yiel)
WFA 4 from 5yo+ 1lb **9** Ran SP% **115.3**
Speed ratings (Par 101): **82,81,81,80,80 80,78,78,76**
CSF £79.44 CT £536.54 TOTE £23.30: £5.20, £1.40, £2.50; EX 132.80 TRIFECTA Not won. Place 6 £ 108.35, Place 5 £ 64.74 .
Owner A S B Portman **Bred** The Hon Mrs R Pease **Trained** Compton, Berks

FOCUS
A moderate handicap restricted to apprentices who, at the start of the current Flat turf season, had not ridden more than 20 winners. They went no pace at all through the early stages and, unsurprisingly, the winning time was slow. The majority ended up towards the stands' rail in the straight, and the form is weak.
Top Spec(IRE) Official explanation: jockey said gelding hung left in straight
T/Plt: £126.30 to a £1 stake. Pool: £48,814.54. 282.10 winning tickets. T/Qpdt: £41.80 to a £1 stake. Pool: £2,439.00. 43.10 winning tickets. SP

1269 KEMPTON (A.W) (R-H)
Thursday, April 10

OFFICIAL GOING: Standard
Wind: Almost nil Weather: Fine

1282 KEMPTON.CO.UK H'CAP 1m 2f (P)
6:50 (6:50) (Class 6) (0-55,61) 4-Y-0+ **£2,266** (£674; £337; £168) **Stalls** High

Form RPR
0056 **1** **Western Roots**[41] 753 7-8-4 **52** .... DavidProbert[(7)] 9 63
(A M Balding) *mde all: nudged along and styd on wl fr over 1f out: unchal* **8/1**
3251 **2** *3* **Siena Star (IRE)**[8] 1152 10-9-6 **61** 6ex .... MickyFenton 11 66
(Stef Liddiard) *pressed ldrs: wnt 2nd over 3f out: drvn and no imp on wnr fnl 2f* **11/2**[2]
2365 **3** *nk* **Patavium Prince (IRE)**[36] 795 5-8-3 **47** .... KevinGhunowa[(3)] 1 51+
(Miss Jo Crowley) *stdd s: hld up in last: prog on outer fr 3f out: rchd 3rd over 1f out: kpt on but no ch w wnr* **9/1**
0-56 **4** *1½* **Bowl Of Cherries**[2] 1262 5-8-11 **52** .... (bt) NCallan 10 53
(I A Wood) *dwlt: sn in midfield: prog to trck ldrs 3f out and gng wl: rdn and nt qckn 2f out* **9/2**[1]
03-2 **5** *¾* **Magic Amigo**[32] 420 7-8-3 **47** .... WilliamBuick[(3)] 6 47
(J R Jenkins) *wl in tch: rdn on outer over 3f out: no imp 2f out: kpt on* **6/1**[3]
0062 **6** *nse* **Tabulate**[15] 1031 5-8-5 **46** .... JimmyQuinn 5 46
(P Howling) *hld up wl in rr: gng wl enough over 2f out: nt clr run wl over 1f out tl fnl f: kpt on one pce* **10/1**
6333 **7** *2* **Play Up Pompey**[8] 1152 6-9-0 **55** .... SebSanders 7 51
(J J Bridger) *hld up in midfield: effrt 3f out: rdn and nt qckn 2f out: n.d after* **7/1**
0305 **8** *½* **Krakatau (FR)**[15] 1032 4-8-8 **49** .... (p) EdwardCreighton 4 44
(D J Wintle) *hld up wl in rr: shkn up on outer 2f out: no prog: one pce* **11/2**[2]
440- **9** *1¾* **Weet Yer Tern (IRE)**[129] 7009 6-8-9 **50** .... (p) JamieSpencer 2 45
(W M Brisbourne) *stdd s: hld up in rr: pushed along on inner 3f out: no real prog* **6/1**[3]
4360 **10** *9* **Shaheer (IRE)**[14] 541 6-8-6 **47** .... (v) GregFairley 3 20
(J Gallagher) *prom: chsd wnr over 4f out to over 3f out: wknd rapidly fnl 2f* **20/1**
400- **11** *8* **Tykie Two**[261] 3825 4-8-11 **52** .... ChrisCatlin 8 9
(S Wynne) *mostly chsd wnr to over 4f out: wknd rapidly: t.o* **33/1**

2m 7.14s (-0.86) **Going Correction** -0.05s/f (Stan) **11** Ran SP% **127.9**
Speed ratings (Par 101): **101,98,98,97,96 96,94,94,93,85 79**
CSF £56.40 CT £422.73 TOTE £15.60: £5.00, £2.60, £4.30; EX 78.30.
Owner I A Balding **Bred** Stratford Place Stud **Trained** Kingsclere, Hants
■ Stewards' Enquiry : Kevin Ghunowa caution: used whip with arm above shoulder height

FOCUS
A routinely modest handicap of its type and the pace was ordinary, though the winning time was about what you would expect despite being slightly slower than the following maiden. The winner is rated back to last year's best form.
Weet Yer Tern(IRE) Official explanation: jockey said gelding had no more to give

1283 DAY TIME, NIGHT TIME, GREAT TIME MAIDEN STKS 1m 2f (P)
7:20 (7:20) (Class 5) 3-Y-0+ **£2,590** (£770; £385; £192) **Stalls** High

Form RPR
333- **1** **Judgethemoment (USA)**[162] 6585 3-8-9 75 .... JohnEgan 6 80
(Jane Chapple-Hyam) *mde virtually all: rdn 3f out: styd on wl u.p: gng away at fin* **11/4**[3]
2 *4½* **Ben Ami** 3-8-9 0 .... OscarUrbina 1 71
(Miss J R Gibney) *hld up in last: prog over 3f out: rdn to go 2nd jst over 1f out: no imp on wnr* **14/1**
03-5 **3** *1½* **Tharawaat (IRE)**[19] 961 3-8-9 78 .... RHills 3 68
(B W Hills) *pressed wnr after 2f: pushed along 3f out: rdn and nt qckn wl over 1f out: fdd* **1/1**[1]
044- **4** *12* **Talayeb**[202] 5590 3-8-9 87 .... MartinDwyer 4 47
(M P Tregoning) *w wnr 2f: settled in bhd after: rdn over 3f out: sn wknd* **13/8**[2]
5 *98* **Quws Vision (IRE)** 5-9-9 0 .... LPKeniry 5 —
(Mrs L C Jewell) *s.s: in tch to 1/2-way: wknd rapidly: btn over a f* **50/1**

2m 6.82s (-1.18) **Going Correction** -0.05s/f (Stan)
WFA 3 from 5yo 19lb **5** Ran SP% **123.4**
Speed ratings (Par 103): **102,98,97,87,9**
CSF £36.26 TOTE £4.50: £2.90, £12.30; EX 28.50.
Owner Gordon Li **Bred** Todd Graves & Michele Graves **Trained** Lambourn, Berks

FOCUS
A reasonable maiden in which they went a decent pace, producing a time that was slightly faster than the preceding handicap. The winner is rated close to his best 2yo form.

1284 DIGIBET.COM H'CAP 5f (P)
7:50 (7:50) (Class 4) (0-85,79) 3-Y-0 **£4,533** (£1,348; £674; £336) **Stalls** High

Form RPR
1-00 **1** **Storey Hill (USA)**[23] 924 3-8-12 **70** .... DeanMcKeown 7 81
(D Shaw) *mde virtually all: jnd and rdn over 1f out: hld on wl: won on the nod* **4/1**[3]
01-0 **2** *nse* **Van Bossed (CAN)**[19] 967 3-9-5 **77** .... AdrianTNicholls 2 88
(D Nicholls) *hld up bhd ldrs: rapid prog on wd outside to join wnr over 1f out: upsides after and hanging rt: nt qckn nr fin* **6/1**
2422 **3** *5* **Valhillen**[13] 1066 3-9-0 **72** .... HayleyTurner 6 65
(M D I Usher) *in tch in rr of main gp: shkn up 2f out: styd on fnl f to take 3rd nr fin: no ch* **10/3**[2]
615- **4** *1* **Wavertree Princess (IRE)**[124] 7072 3-9-0 **72** .... NCallan 3 61
(N P Littmoden) *missed the break: rcvrd to chse ldrs on inner over 3f out: effrt over 1f out: sn outpcd* **13/2**
300- **5** *1½* **Brassini**[201] 5629 3-9-7 **79** .... AlanMunro 5 63
(B R Millman) *outpcd in last and sn wl adrift: styd on fnl f: no ch* **11/1**
31- **6** *½* **Your Pleasure (USA)**[192] 5856 3-9-3 **75** .... MartinDwyer 4 57
(A M Balding) *t.k.h: hld up bhd ldrs: cl up over 1f out: sn outpcd: fdd* **5/2**[1]
00-3 **7** *5* **Enodoc**[7] 1167 3-9-2 **74** .... RichardMullen 1 38
(W R Muir) *w wnr to 2f out: wknd rapidly over 1f out* **13/2**

60.14 secs (-0.36) **Going Correction** -0.05s/f (Stan) **7** Ran SP% **120.9**
Speed ratings (Par 100): **100,99,91,90,87 87,79**
CSF £29.97 TOTE £4.60: £2.60, £4.70; EX 50.20.
Owner Jim Goose **Bred** And Mrs Richard S Kaster **Trained** Danethorpe, Notts

FOCUS
A fair little sprint handicap and they went a good pace. The front pair pulled right away over the last furlong or so. A tricky race to rate, neither of the first two having shown anything in handicaps previously and the favourite disappointing.
Brassini Official explanation: jockey said gelding did not face the kickback

1285 DIGIBET FILLIES' H'CAP 6f (P)
8:20 (8:20) (Class 5) (0-70,70) 4-Y-0+ **£2,590** (£770; £385; £192) **Stalls** High

Form RPR
6003 **1** **Is It Time (IRE)**[8] 1145 4-8-4 **56** oh3 .... JimmyQuinn 4 66
(Mrs P N Dutfield) *trckd ldr and clr of rest: clsd over 1f out: rdn to ld ins fnl f: kpt on wl* **10/1**
130- **2** *nk* **Expensive Art (IRE)**[138] 6930 4-9-2 **68** .... JamieSpencer 1 77
(S A Callaghan) *dwlt: hld up in 3rd and off the pce: rdn to cl fr 2f out: styd on to take 2nd nr fin: too much to do* **4/5**[1]
0224 **3** *¾* **The Jailer**[8] 1143 5-7-12 **57** .... (p) MCGeran[(7)] 6 64
(J G M O'Shea) *led at decent pce: rdn over 2f out: hdd and one pce ins fnl f* **5/1**[3]
3055 **4** *7* **Diminuto**[1] 1268 4-8-13 **70** .... PatrickHills[(5)] 3 54
(M D I Usher) *taken down early: dwlt: hld up in last pair and wl off the pce: rdn 2f out: no prog* **13/2**
6602 **5** *1* **Linda Green**[6] 1178 7-8-1 **60** .... MatthewDavies[(7)] 2 41
(M R Channon) *hld up off the pce in last pair: rdn over 2f out: no prog* **4/1**[2]

1m 12.29s (-0.81) **Going Correction** -0.05s/f (Stan) **5** Ran SP% **114.6**
Speed ratings (Par 100): **103,102,101,92,90**
CSF £19.75 TOTE £8.40: £5.20, £1.10; EX 22.00.
Owner Mrs Nerys Dutfield **Bred** Century Bloodstock **Trained** Axmouth, Devon

FOCUS
An uncompetitive fillies' handicap, but The Jailer made sure the pace was decent and the form looks reliable enough. The winner is rated up 5lb.
Linda Green Official explanation: jockey said mare ran flat

1286 DIGIBET CLAIMING STKS 1m (P)
8:50 (8:50) (Class 6) 4-Y-0+ **£2,266** (£674; £337; £168) **Stalls** High

Form RPR
1613 **1** **Dushstorm (IRE)**[13] 1049 7-8-7 67 .... (p) KirstyMilczarek[(3)] 1 75
(M Botti) *hld up: effrt on inner over 2f out: rdn to ld jst over 1f out: styd on wl* **5/2**[3]
40-0 **2** *1* **Royal Dignitary (USA)**[16] 1016 8-9-8 87 .... AdrianTNicholls 5 85
(D Nicholls) *racd freely: led: rdn 2f out: hdd jst over 1f out: one pce* **15/8**[2]
4212 **3** *1* **Teasing**[8] 1143 4-9-3 77 .... (p) RobertHavlin 2 77
(J Pearce) *stdd s: hld up: trckd ldr over 3f out: rdn to chal wl over 1f out: fnd nil* **5/4**[1]
10-0 **4** *33* **Sekula Pata (NZ)**[22] 935 9-8-10 50 .... (v) EdwardCreighton 4 —
(E J Creighton) *chsd ldr to over 3f out: wknd and sn t.o* **16/1**

1m 40.64s (0.84) **Going Correction** -0.05s/f (Stan) **4** Ran SP% **113.7**
Speed ratings (Par 101): **93,92,91,58**
CSF £7.92 TOTE £3.20; EX 8.00.The winner was claimed by D. Nicholls for £6,000
Owner Giuliano Manfredini **Bred** M Fahy **Trained** Newmarket, Suffolk

FOCUS
Ony four runners, but a wide variety of abilities with 25lb between the best and worst in. The pace was ordinary, the time was moderate, and the form looks dubious, the winner up 3lb.

Sekula Pata(NZ) Official explanation: jockey said gelding had no more to give

1287 SUNBURY FILLIES' H'CAP — 1m (P)

9:20 (9:21) (Class 5) (0-75,75) 4-Y-0+ — £2,590 (£770; £385; £192) — Stalls High

Form — RPR

2 **1** **Miss Marauder**[27] 878 4-8-4 **61** .... JimmyQuinn 1 — 71
(M Botti) *reluctant to enter stalls: dwlt: hld up in last: gd prog over 2f out: led over 1f out: drvn and styd on wl* — **8/1**

456- **2** *1* **Montrachet**[159] 6637 4-9-4 **75** .... JamieSpencer 4 — 83
(M L W Bell) *t.k.h: hld up in tch: effrt and hanging over 2f out: drvn to chal over 1f out: pressed wnr after: hld fnl 100yds* — **9/4**[2]

100- **3** *7* **Rowan River**[197] 5725 4-8-13 **70** .... RichardKingscote 5 — 62
(Tom Dascombe) *pressed ldr: led over 2f out: hanging lft and fnd little in front: hdd & wknd over 1f out* — **9/4**[2]

210- **4** *2 1/4* **Apple Blossom (IRE)**[228] 4848 4-9-2 **73** .... TedDurcan 6 — 60
(G Wragg) *hld up: prog on inner over 2f out: cl up over 1f out: wknd* — **11/1**

0-61 **5** *3 3/4* **Indian's Feather (IRE)**[21] 949 7-8-11 **73** .... HaddenFrost(5) 3 — 51
(N Tinkler) *chsd ldrs: lost pl and rdn 1/2-way: sn struggling* — **6/1**[3]

4/1- **6** *5* **Power Ballad**[197] 5728 4-9-0 **71** .... SebSanders 2 — 38
(W J Knight) *led to over 2f out: wknd rapidly* — **2/1**[1]

1m 38.88s (-0.92) **Going Correction** -0.05s/f (Stan) — **6** Ran SP% **128.6**
Speed ratings (Par 100): **102,101,94,91,88 83**
CSF £30.51 TOTE £4.70: £3.00, £1.60; EX 22.00 Place 6 £1,101.11, Place 5 £ 283.72.
Owner Mrs Sally Doyle **Bred** Mrs Sally Doyle **Trained** Newmarket, Suffolk

FOCUS
A modest fillies' handicap, but the pace was a fair one and the front pair pulled miles clear of the others. The winner is up 12lb on the bare form of her maiden win.

1288 - 1294a (Foreign Racing) - See Raceform Interactive

[1067] DONCASTER (L-H)

Friday, April 11

OFFICIAL GOING: Good to soft (soft in places; 8.3)
The ground was described as 'genuinely soft'. There was a running rail in place 4 metres wide from the 10 furlong start to the home turn.
Wind: Fresh, half-against Weather: overcast, windy and heavy showers

1295 BOOK TICKETS ONLINE MAIDEN STKS (DIV I) — 7f

1:40 (1:40) (Class 4) 3-Y-O — £4,047 (£1,204; £601; £300) — Stalls High

Form — RPR

5- **1** **Royalist (IRE)**[255] 4048 3-9-3 0 .... PhilipRobinson 7 — 88+
(M A Jarvis) *trckd ldrs: plld hrd: led over 4f out: shkn up over 1f out: edgd rt ins fnl f: r.o wl* — **2/1**[1]

224- **2** *3 3/4* **Alwaabel**[153] 6754 3-9-3 81 .... RHills 1 — 75
(J L Dunlop) *a.p: chsd wnr 3f out: rdn and carried hd to one side over 1f out: no ex ins fnl f* — **7/2**[3]

0- **3** *3/4* **Bowder Stone (IRE)**[252] 4125 3-9-3 0 .... JimmyQuinn 11 — 73+
(M H Tompkins) *s.i.s: hld up in tch: swtchd lft over 2f out: sn rdn: hung lft and outpcd: r.o ins fnl f* — **40/1**

02- **4** *hd* **Ninefineirishmen (IRE)**[160] 6634 3-9-3 0 .... AndrewElliott 10 — 72
(K R Burke) *w ldrs: rdn over 2f out: styd on same pce fnl f* — **12/1**

0-5 **5** *nse* **Spirit Of A Nation (IRE)**[13] 1068 3-9-3 0 .... DarrenWilliams 5 — 72
(S Parr) *hld up in tch: rdn over 2f out: styd on same pce fnl f* — **40/1**

4 **6** *6* **Game Hunt**[13] 1068 3-9-3 0 .... JimmyFortune 3 — 56
(J H M Gosden) *trckd ldrs: rdn and hung rt over 1f out: wknd fnl f* — **13/2**

0 **7** *1/2* **Grey Command (USA)**[13] 1068 3-9-3 0 .... TWilliams 2 — 54
(M Brittain) *hld up: racd keenly: rdn over 2f out: wknd over 1f out* — **200/1**

65 **8** *8* **Szaba**[62] 498 3-8-9 0 .... LukeMorris(3) 4 — 28
(J M P Eustace) *hld up: plld hrd: rdn over 2f out: wkng whn hung rt wl over 1f out* — **100/1**

0- **9** *2* **Castlebury (IRE)**[266] 3718 3-9-3 0 .... RobertWinston 8 — 27
(G A Swinbank) *chsd ldrs 5f* — **100/1**

00 **10** *1/2* **Profumo Affair**[18] 997 3-9-3 0 .... HayleyTurner 9 — 26
(M L W Bell) *prom: rdn 1/2-way: wknd over 2f out* — **100/1**

2 **11** *11* **August Gale (USA)**[37] 796 3-9-3 0 .... JoeFanning 6 — —
(M Johnston) *n.m.r s: sn led: hdd over 4f out: wknd over 2f out* — **9/4**[2]

1m 30.29s (3.99) **Going Correction** +0.55s/f (Yiel) — **11** Ran SP% **115.7**
Speed ratings (Par 100): **99,94,93,93,93 86,86,77,74,74 61**
CSF £9.15 TOTE £2.50: £1.10, £1.40, £7.80; EX 9.50 Trifecta £225.60 Part won. Pool £317.77 - 0.40 winning units..
Owner Sheikh Ahmed Al Maktoum **Bred** Irish National Stud **Trained** Newmarket, Suffolk

FOCUS
A decent maiden, with the exposed runner-up rated 81, although the fourth may prove a better guide to the overall value of the form. It was the clear pick of three races over the distance on time, but the value of the form is undermined by the runner-up almost certainly below his best and the second favourite running very poorly.
Bowder Stone(IRE) Official explanation: jockey said colt hung left from halfway
Game Hunt Official explanation: jockey said colt hung right
August Gale(USA) Official explanation: trainer had no explanation for the poor form shown

1296 AMATEUR JOCKEYS' ASSOCIATION LADY AMATEUR RIDERS' H'CAP — 1m 2f 60y

2:10 (2:12) (Class 5) (0-70,70) 4-Y-O+ — £3,123 (£968; £484; £242) — Stalls Low

Form — RPR

005- **1** **Blue Spinnaker (IRE)**[160] 6636 9-10-2 **65** .... MissJCoward(3) 2 — 88
(M W Easterby) *trckd ldrs: wnt 2nd over 3f out: shkn up to ld appr fnl f: sn wnt clr* — **9/4**[1]

0-43 **2** *10* **Bivouac (UAE)**[14] 1064 4-9-11 **57** .... MissSBrotherton 12 — 61
(G A Swinbank) *chsd ldng pair: led 4f out: hdd appr fnl f: no ch w wnr* — **7/1**[2]

-102 **3** *6* **Resplendent Ace (IRE)**[28] 881 4-9-13 **64** .... MissAWallace(5) 13 — 57
(P Howling) *mid-div: hdwy 3f out: kpt on: nvr nr 1st 2* — **16/1**

-111 **4** *5* **Bridgewater Boys**[14] 1056 7-10-5 **70** ....(b) MissHayleyMoore(5) 15 — 53
(G L Moore) *s.i.s: hdwy over 3f out: nvr nr ldrs* — **7/1**[2]

3214 **5** *1 1/2* **Hucking Heat (IRE)**[49] 658 4-9-4 **57** .... MissRKneller(7) 11 — 37
(R Hollinshead) *hld up in rr: kpt on fnl 3f: nvr nr ldrs* — **20/1**

40-2 **6** *3/4* **Coronado's Gold (USA)**[18] 989 7-10-5 **65** .... MissLEllison 9 — 44
(B Ellison) *in rr: kpt on fnl 2f: nvr nr ldrs* — **8/1**[3]

6624 **7** *3* **Site Sentry (IRE)**[14] 1056 5-10-2 **65** ....(t) MissGDGracey-Davison(3) 7 — 38
(M F Harris) *chsd ldrs: wknd over 2f out* — **25/1**

45-6 **8** *7* **Active Asset (IRE)**[31] 847 6-10-4 **67** .... MissARyan(3) 10 — 27
(A J McCabe) *hld up in rr: effrt on wd outside over 3f out: hung lft: wknd 2f out* — **12/1**

00-0 **9** *5* **Royal Rainbow**[25] 919 4-9-7 **56** oh3 .... MrsMarieKing(3) 6 — 6
(P W Hiatt) *uns rdr gng to s: mid-div: nvr a factor* — **40/1**

000- **10** *2* **Emperor's Well**[163] 6598 9-9-6 **57** .... MissJoannaMason(5) 4 — 4
(M W Easterby) *led early: jnd ldrs over 8f out: lost pl over 3f out: sn bhd* — **28/1**

6506 **11** *6* **Good Cause (IRE)**[7] 1184 7-9-10 **56** oh2 .... MrsMMorris 8 — —
(Mrs S Lamyman) *s.i.s: a in rr* — **33/1**

/113 **12** *7* **Schinken Otto (IRE)**[16] 438 7-9-7 **56** .... MissNJefferson(3) 5 — —
(J M Jefferson) *mid-div: lost pl over 3f out* — **7/1**[2]

600- **13** *23* **Resaass (USA)**[184] 6109 5-9-5 **58** .... MissAColley(7) 14 — —
(J O'Reilly) *sn bhd: t.o 3f out* — **100/1**

00-0 **14** *66* **Old Romney**[20] 962 4-10-2 **67** .... MissKellyBurke(5) 1 — —
(M W Easterby) *sn led: hdd 4f out: wknd qckly: sn t.o: virtually p.u* — **28/1**

2m 15.73s (4.53) **Going Correction** +0.55s/f (Yiel) — **14** Ran SP% **114.8**
Speed ratings (Par 103): **103,95,90,86,85 84,82,76,72,70 66,60,42,—**
CSF £14.76 CT £201.51 TOTE £3.30: £1.60, £2.30, £4.30; EX 18.60 TRIFECTA Not won..
Owner G Sparkes G Hart S Curtis & T Dewhirst **Bred** M3 Elevage And Haras D'Etreham **Trained** Sheriff Hutton, N Yorks

FOCUS
The winner's two stablemates set a very strong pace and they came home strung out like jumpers. Having won off 90 two seasons ago Blue Spinnaker was entitled to take this by a wide-margin, and he landed a real gamble in the process, having been out of sorts last term.
Old Romney Official explanation: jockey said gelding had a breathing problem

1297 LEGER WAY H'CAP — 1m (S)

2:40 (2:42) (Class 4) (0-85,85) 3-Y-O — £4,533 (£1,348; £674; £336) — Stalls High

Form — RPR

004- **1** **Perks (IRE)**[203] 5598 3-8-6 **73** .... JimmyQuinn 4 — 91
(J L Dunlop) *hld up in tch: led over 1f out: rdn clr* — **20/1**

041- **2** *6* **Silver Rime (FR)**[198] 5720 3-9-0 **81** .... RichardHughes 3 — 84
(R Hannon) *trckd ldrs: led 3f out: rdn and hdd over 1f out: no ex ins fnl f* — **5/1**[3]

331- **3** *1 1/4* **Pinkindie (USA)**[204] 5570 3-9-4 **85** .... RyanMoore 7 — 85
(E A L Dunlop) *hld up: hdwy over 2f out: sn rdn: styd on ins fnl f* — **10/1**

1- **4** *hd* **Mukhber**[175] 6296 3-9-2 **83** .... RHills 16 — 83
(J H M Gosden) *hld up: hdwy 2f out: rdn and hung lft over 1f out: styd on same pce* — **7/2**[2]

404- **5** *hd* **Dubai Petal (IRE)**[153] 6756 3-8-4 **71** .... JohnEgan 9 — 70
(J S Moore) *hld up: outpcd over 3f out: styd on fnl f* — **20/1**

21- **6** *1 1/4* **Collection (IRE)**[178] 6255 3-8-13 **80** .... SebSanders 6 — 76
(W J Haggas) *trckd ldrs: racd keenly: rdn over 1f out: wknd fnl f* — **10/3**[1]

31- **7** *1 1/2* **Prince Hamlet (IRE)**[118] 7152 3-8-10 **77** .... TedDurcan 1 — 70
(B Smart) *hld up: hdwy 1/2-way: rdn over 1f out: sn wknd* — **20/1**

034- **8** *2 3/4* **Ellemujie**[168] 6471 3-9-3 **84** .... HayleyTurner 12 — 70
(D K Ivory) *hld up: hdwy and edgd lft over 2f out: rdn and wknd over 1f out* — **25/1**

500- **9** *2* **Flight Plan**[183] 6120 3-8-13 **83** .... JamieMoriarty(3) 8 — 65
(R A Fahey) *plld hrd and prom: rdn and ev ch over 2f out: wknd over 1f out* — **50/1**

521- **10** *3/4* **Boy Blue**[203] 5580 3-9-3 **84** .... SilvestreDeSousa 2 — 64
(D Nicholls) *hld up: rdn over 2f out: sn wknd* — **16/1**

1- **11** *21* **Bigfanofthat (IRE)**[316] 2166 3-8-13 **80** .... FergusSweeney 15 — 12
(K R Burke) *trckd ldrs: rdn over 2f out: sn edgd lft and wknd: eased fnl f* — **16/1**

1 **12** *1 1/4* **Khazina (USA)**[17] 1019 3-8-5 **72** .... LiamJones 5 — 1
(C E Brittain) *chsd ldrs over 5f* — **14/1**

201- **13** *1 3/4* **Doon Haymer (IRE)**[160] 6634 3-8-13 **80** ....(v) RobertWinston 11 — 5
(Miss L A Perratt) *sn led: hdd 3f out: wknd over 2f out: eased over 1f out* — **20/1**

042- **14** *3 1/4* **Castles In The Air**[163] 6588 3-8-5 **72** .... PaulEddery 14 — —
(Pat Eddery) *hld up in tch: rdn and wknd over 2f out* — **40/1**

02-0 **15** *4* **Averoo**[20] 966 3-8-8 **75** .... TGMcLaughlin 13 — —
(M D Squance) *sn pushed along in rr: wknd over 3f out* — **100/1**

046- **16** *5* **Horatio Carter**[153] 6754 3-8-9 **76** .... JamieSpencer 10 — —
(K A Ryan) *s.i.s: hld up: rdn and wknd over 3f out* — **33/1**

1m 43.04s (3.74) **Going Correction** +0.55s/f (Yiel) — **16** Ran SP% **120.7**
Speed ratings (Par 100): **103,97,95,95,95 94,92,89,87,87 66,64,63,59,55 50**
CSF £105.52 CT £1089.61 TOTE £26.70: £3.80, £1.60, £2.30, £2.00; EX 185.60 TRIFECTA Not won..
Owner Benny Andersson **Bred** Chess Racing Ab **Trained** Arundel, W Sussex

FOCUS
A competitive three-year-old handicap with plenty of unexposed types and handicap debutants, but in the end a wide margin winner. No apparent fluke behind his success, and there should be plenty of winners emerging from further back too.
Horatio Carter Official explanation: jockey said colt had no more to give

1298 BOOK TICKETS ONLINE MAIDEN STKS (DIV II) — 7f

3:15 (3:15) (Class 4) 3-Y-O — £4,047 (£1,204; £601; £300) — Stalls High

Form — RPR

2- **1** **The Oil Magnate**[264] 3760 3-9-3 0 .... PhillipMakin 3 — 85+
(M Dods) *trckd ldrs: effrt over 2f out: led over 1f out: wnt clr: easily* — **9/4**[2]

50- **2** *7* **Tactical Move**[247] 4293 3-8-12 0 .... SCreighton(5) 6 — 58
(Miss V Haigh) *led tl over 3f out: kpt on to take 2nd last 75yds: no ch w wnr* — **150/1**

2- **3** *1 1/2* **Adab (IRE)**[336] 1631 3-9-3 0 .... RHills 8 — 54
(J H M Gosden) *t.k.h: w ldr: led over 3f out: hdd over 1f out: fdd ins fnl f* — **9/2**[3]

4 *1 1/2* **Plenilune (IRE)** 3-9-3 0 .... TWilliams 4 — 50
(M Brittain) *chsd ldrs: outpcd over 2f out: kpt on fnl f* — **66/1**

5 *6* **Bahamian Kid** 3-9-0 0 .... RussellKennemore(3) 11 — 34
(R Hollinshead) *sn w ldrs: edgd lft and lost pl over 1f out* — **33/1**

6 *1* **Threecheersforanby (IRE)** 3-9-0 0 ....(t) DNolan(3) 5 — 31
(S Parr) *swvd rt s: nvr a factor* — **100/1**

06- **7** *1 1/4* **Bertie Vista**[223] 5042 3-9-3 0 .... DavidAllan 10 — 28
(T D Easterby) *hld up in rr: hdwy over 2f out: wknd fnl f* — **25/1**

8 *3/4* **Zeeran** 3-9-3 0 .... SebSanders 1 — 26
(C E Brittain) *mid-div: rdn and wknd 2f out* — **14/1**

00- **9** *nk* **Topazes**[191] 5910 3-9-3 0 .... JamieSpencer 2 — 25
(M L W Bell) *hld up in rr: hdwy on outside over 3f out: sn chsng ldrs: wknd 2f out* — **10/1**

4 **10** *1 1/2* **Star Choice**[13] 1073 3-9-3 0 .... HayleyTurner 9 — 21
(M L W Bell) *in rr and sn drvn along: nvr on terms* — **14/1**

5 **11** *5* **Dnata Flyer (USA)**[9] 1139 3-9-3 0 .... JoeFanning 7 — 7
(M Johnston) *prom: drvn over 3f out: lost pl over 2f out: eased* — **2/1**[1]

1m 31.96s (5.66) **Going Correction** +0.75s/f (Yiel) — **11** Ran SP% **114.6**
Speed ratings (Par 100): **97,89,87,85,78 77,76,75,74,73 67**
CSF £336.72 TOTE £3.40: £1.40, £15.10, £1.70; EX 252.70 Trifecta £279.00 Part won. Pool £392.98 - 0.40 winning units..
Owner Smith & Allan Racing **Bred** Wheelersland Stud **Trained** Denton, Co Durham

FOCUS
The weaker division and much the slower time, but a facile winner. Exactly what the form is worth is open to doubt.
Dnata Flyer(USA) Official explanation: trainer had no explanation for the poor form shown

1299 DONCASTER-RACECOURSE.CO.UK H'CAP 1m 6f 132y
3:50 (3:50) (Class 4) (0-80,80) 4-Y-0+ £4,533 (£1,348; £674; £336) Stalls Low

Form RPR
0-21 1 **Puy D'Arnac (FR)**[9] 1137 5-9-4 72 6ex........................ RobertWinston 5 86+
(G A Swinbank) *chsd ldrs: nt clr run over 1f out: swtchd rt: styd on to ld wl ins fnl f* 3/1[1]
1623 2 1 1/2 **Casual Affair**[19] 981 5-9-4 72........................ JimmyQuinn 10 79+
(J D Bethell) *hld up in tch: plld hrd: rdn and ev ch ins fnl f: unable qck towards fin* 3/1[1]
3/2- 3 hd **Pee Jay's Dream**[127] 1178 6-8-5 62........................ AndrewMullen(3) 8 69
(M W Easterby) *chsd ldrs: led over 3f out: hdd over 2f out: rdn to ld ins fnl f: sn hdd and unable qck* 13/2[3]
013- 4 1 3/4 **Fourth Dimension (IRE)**[238] 4576 9-9-2 70........................ JimCrowley 4 76+
(Miss T Spearing) *s.i.s: hld up: hdwy over 1f out: styng on whn nt clr run towards fin: nvr able to chal* 18/1
26-3 5 nk **Charlotte Vale**[17] 1020 7-9-7 75........................ SebSanders 7 79
(Micky Hammond) *chsd ldr: rdn to ld over 2f out: hdd over 1f out: ev ch ins fnl f: no ex towards fin* 16/1
3110 6 3 1/2 **Red Wine**[9] 1159 9-9-6 74........................ JamieSpencer 1 73
(A J McCabe) *hld up: hdwy over 2f out: led over 1f out: rdn: edgd lft and hdd ins fnl f: wknd towards fin* 5/1[2]
0/ 7 1 3/4 **Euro American (GER)**[48] 8-9-7 75........................ PhillipMakin 9 72
(E W Tuer) *hld up: hdwy over 5f out: rdn over 2f out: wknd over 1f out* 40/1
21-0 8 13 **Gordonsville**[19] 981 5-9-10 78........................ DanielTudhope 2 58
(J S Goldie) *chsd ldrs: rdn over 4f out: wknd over 2f out* 8/1
3116 9 1 1/4 **They All Laughed**[16] 1026 5-9-8 76........................ DarrenWilliams 3 55
(P W Hiatt) *hld up: rdn over 3f out: sn wknd* 18/1
00-5 10 nk **Mister Arjay (USA)**[9] 1137 8-9-6 74........................ JimmyFortune 11 52
(B Ellison) *led: rdn and hdd over 3f out: wknd over 2f out* 20/1
-200 11 2 3/4 **Moon Mix (FR)**[13] 1080 5-9-12 80........................ EddieAhern 6 55
(J R Jenkins) *hld up: rcd keenly: effrt over 3f out: wknd over 2f out* 40/1

3m 26.87s (20.17) **Going Correction** +0.75s/f (Yiel) 11 Ran SP% 117.2
Speed ratings (Par 105): **76,75,75,74,74 72,71,64,63,63 61**
CSF £10.97 CT £52.94 TOTE £4.10: £1.80, £1.90, £2.50; EX 14.90 Trifecta £158.20 Pool £289.68 - 1.30 winning units..
Owner Barrow Brook Racing **Bred** Mrs Axelle Du Verdier **Trained** Melsonby, N Yorks
■ Stewards' Enquiry : Andrew Mullen two-day ban: used whip down shoulder in forehand position (Apr 25-26)

FOCUS
Just a very steady gallop resulting in a pedestrian winning time. The winner overcame traffic problems and is value for much further. The runner-up, like several others, could have done with a stronger pace.
Fourth Dimension(IRE) Official explanation: jockey said gelding was denied a clear run

1300 FIRST TRANSPENNINE EXPRESS H'CAP 6f
4:25 (4:25) (Class 3) (0-95,95) 4-Y-0+ £6,799 (£2,023; £1,011; £505) Stalls High

Form RPR
04- 1 **Cape**[175] 6300 5-8-11 88........................ JamieSpencer 18 97+
(P Howling) *s.i.s: swtchd lft after s: hdwy and nt clr run over 2f out: str run to ld last 100yds: hld on towards fin* 7/1[2]
0000 2 nk **Baby Strange**[13] 1071 4-8-8 85........................ FergusSweeney 15 93
(D Shaw) *hld up towards rr: hdwy and nt clr run over 1f out: styd on wl ins fnl f: jst hld* 25/1
000- 3 nk **Tajneed (IRE)**[173] 6363 5-7-11 81........................ OliveGaule(7) 12 88
(D Nicholls) *trckd ldrs: led over 1f out: hdd ins fnl f: no ex* 50/1
610- 4 1/2 **Damika (IRE)**[160] 6654 5-9-1 95........................ MichaelJStainton(3) 13 105+
(R M Whitaker) *hld up in mid-div: hdwy over 1f out: styd on wl towards fin* 25/1
2136 5 nk **Bel Cantor**[35] 824 5-8-1 81 oh1........................ AndrewMullen(3) 5 86+
(W J H Ratcliffe) *chsd ldrs: kpt on same pce fnl f* 20/1
000- 6 hd **Turnkey**[181] 6183 6-8-7 91........................ AdeleRothery(7) 16 95
(D Nicholls) *in rr: hdwy on outer 2f out: styd on ins fnl f* 16/1
00-1 7 2 **Pusey Street Lady**[13] 1071 4-9-2 93........................ JimCrowley 3 90
(J Gallagher) *w ldr: led over 2f out tl over 1f out: fdd* 5/1[1]
061- 8 shd **Tudor Prince (IRE)**[164] 6575 4-8-1 81 oh1........................ LukeMorris(3) 14 78
(A W Carroll) *prom on outer: kpt on same pce over 1f out* 16/1
404- 9 nse **Ice Planet**[223] 5044 7-8-13 90........................ SilvestreDeSousa 4 87+
(D Nicholls) *in rr: hdwy 2f out: kpt on fnl f* 10/1[3]
054- 10 nse **Southandwest (IRE)**[244] 4374 4-8-10 87........................ LPKeniry 17 84
(J S Moore) *trckd ldrs on outer: kpt on same pce fnl 2f* 20/1
610- 11 1 3/4 **Barney McGrew (IRE)**[168] 6472 5-9-1 92........................ PhillipMakin 7 83+
(M Dods) *hld up towards rr: hdwy 2f out: kpt on steadily ins fnl f* 7/1[2]
200- 12 1 **Special Day**[190] 5954 4-8-13 90........................ MichaelHills 10 78
(B W Hills) *s.i.s: hdwy over 2f out: wknd fnl f* 11/1
000- 13 3 **He's A Humbug (IRE)**[200] 5684 4-8-4 81 oh1........................ CatherineGannon 8 59
(K A Ryan) *t.k.h: sn trcking ldrs: lost pl over 1f out* 18/1
4025 14 1 **Fyodor (IRE)**[29] 866 7-9-4 95........................ LiamJones 6 70
(W J Haggas) *chsd ldrs: lost pl over 1f out* 16/1
510- 15 1/2 **Ellens Academy (IRE)**[202] 5638 13-8-4 81........................ JimmyQuinn 9 55
(E J Alston) *s.s: hld up: a towards rr* 33/1
000- 16 3 1/2 **Charles Darwin (IRE)**[211] 5356 5-8-4 81 oh1........................ HayleyTurner 1 43
(M Blanshard) *chsd ldrs far side: hmpd over 2f out: sn wknd* 14/1
2530 17 1 1/4 **Bo McGinty (IRE)**[19] 983 7-8-5 82........................(v) JoeFanning 11 40
(R A Fahey) *mid-div and drvn along: lost pl 2f out* 14/1
00-0 18 shd **Mr Wolf**[19] 983 7-8-4 81 oh3........................ AndrewElliott 2 39
(D W Barker) *led racing far side: edgd lft and hdd over 2f out: sn wknd* 28/1

1m 17.11s (3.51) **Going Correction** +0.75s/f (Yiel) 18 Ran SP% 120.9
Speed ratings (Par 107): **106,105,105,104,104 103,101,101,101,100 98,97,93,91,91 86,84,84**
CSF £176.93 CT £7892.28 TOTE £4.60: £1.50, £8.80, £13.00, £7.10; EX 253.30 TRIFECTA Not won..
Owner Wyck Hall Stud **Bred** Wyck Hall Stud Ltd **Trained** Newmarket, Suffolk

FOCUS
They avoided the stands' side. Overall the form has a sound look about it, with the winner having threatened to be better than this at times, the runner-up racing from a very lenient mark, and the third well in on last year's Irish form.

NOTEBOOK
Cape, a winner three times at three, drew a blank last year. Highest drawn, she was switched soon after the start and came from last to first under a typical Jamie Spencer ride. She has the ability to make her mark in Listed company. (op 9-2)
Baby Strange, out of sorts and tumbling down the ratings, stuck on after meeting traffic problems and can surely end his drought from this sort of mark. (op 22-1)
Tajneed(IRE), winner twice in Ireland, was picked up for just 4,000gns. Ridden by an inexperienced apprentice he went on but was picked off by the winner near the line. This was a sound effort from a horse that stays a mile.
Damika(IRE), who made further progress at four, starts the year 5lb higher than for his last success. Backward in his coat, he was putting in some solid work at the finish and should add to his record this time. (tchd 28-1)
Bel Cantor, at his best when able to dominate, did best of those who raced exclusively towards the far side running rail.
Turnkey, just 1lb higher than when ending his drought under this rider last year, stuck on in good style down the wide outside. He prefers even more testing conditions. (op 20-1)
Pusey Street Lady, 10lb higher, had plenty of company on the far side this time. (op 11-2)
Barney McGrew(IRE), who changed hands for 87,000gns, was given a considerate return. He is just the quirky type his yard does so well with. (op 8-1)
Special Day Official explanation: jockey said filly was unsuited by the good to soft (soft in places) ground

1301 DONCASTER EXHIBITION CENTRE CLAIMING STKS 1m (S)
5:00 (5:00) (Class 5) 4-Y-0+ £2,729 (£806; £403) Stalls High

Form RPR
3015 1 **Boundless Prospect (USA)**[18] 992 9-8-11 77............ HayleyTurner 6 67+
(Miss Gay Kelleway) *stdd s: stdy hdwy over 3f out: led over 1f out: pushed out* 11/8[1]
5203 2 3/4 **Pianoforte (USA)**[19] 978 6-9-0 60........................(b) JimmyQuinn 9 66
(E J Alston) *hld up in rr: hdwy and nt clr run over 2f out: swtchd lft and chsd wnr over 1f out: kpt on same pce ins fnl f* 8/1[3]
1505 3 11 **Alexander Guru**[36] 811 4-9-7 57........................ JamesDoyle 8 48
(M Blanshard) *trckd ldrs: kpt on same pce fnl 2f* 12/1
30-6 4 nk **Shot To Fame (USA)**[18] 992 9-9-9 75........................(t) SilvestreDeSousa 4 49
(D Nicholls) *mde most: drvn 3f out: hdd over 1f out: sn wknd* 7/4[2]
5 14 **Jayne Dean** 4-8-6 0 ow3........................ MichaelJStainton(3) 2 3
(A Crook) *dwlt: sn chsng ldrs: drvn over 3f out: edgd lft and lost pl 2f out* 66/1
06/0 6 3/4 **Gramm**[6] 1218 5-9-4 85........................ NSLawes(7) 1 17
(M W Easterby) *w ldr racing wd: drvn 3f out: lost pl over 1f out* 10/1

1m 46.81s (7.51) **Going Correction** +0.95s/f (Soft) 6 Ran SP% 107.9
Speed ratings (Par 103): **100,99,88,87,73 73**
CSF £11.85 TOTE £2.10: £1.60, £2.00; EX 10.80 Trifecta £34.20 Pool: £393.52 - 8.15 winning units..The winner was claimed by Ollie Pears for £6,000
Owner M M Foulger A Maclennan **Bred** Mrs Edgar Scott Jr & Mrs Lawrence Macelree **Trained** Exning, Suffolk

FOCUS
A weak claimer. The winner did not need to be anywhere his best and he was always containing the runner-up's challenge.

1302 BAWTRY MAIDEN FILLIES' STKS 7f
5:35 (5:36) (Class 4) 3-Y-0+ £4,533 (£1,348; £674; £336) Stalls High

Form RPR
05-3 1 **Centenerola (USA)**[13] 1068 3-8-12 74........................ MichaelHills 3 85+
(B W Hills) *hld up wl in tch: smooth hdwy to ld over 2f out: rdn wl clr fnl f* 11/4[2]
026- 2 9 **Amylee (IRE)**[210] 5395 3-8-12 88........................ PhilipRobinson 4 69+
(C G Cox) *led 1f: w ldrs: wnt 2nd over 2f out: kpt on: no ch w wnr* 11/10[1]
0- 3 3 3/4 **Nice Dream**[311] 2344 3-8-12 0........................ HayleyTurner 1 51
(C E Brittain) *w ldrs: kpt on same pce fnl 2f* 12/1
062- 4 3 **Hasty Lady**[175] 6306 3-8-12 72........................ RobertWinston 10 42
(K A Ryan) *w ldrs: t.k.h: outpcd over 2f out: edgd lft and kpt on fnl f* 10/1
4-2 5 nk **Viscountess (IRE)**[14] 1050 3-8-12 0........................ JoeFanning 11 42
(M Johnston) *w ldrs: drvn 3f out: wknd fnl f* 6/1[3]
05 6 1 1/4 **Sharp Indian**[10] 1130 4-9-9 0........................ AndrewMullen(3) 6 43
(W J H Ratcliffe) *t.k.h: led after 1f tl over 2f out: sn wknd* 100/1
0-6 7 hd **Riverside**[13] 1073 3-8-12 0........................ TWilliams 5 38
(M Brittain) *s.i.s sn in tch: drvn over 3f out: kpt on fnl f* 50/1
0 8 10 **Your Golf Travel**[13] 1068 3-8-12 0........................ JimmyQuinn 7 11
(J S Wainwright) *in tch: hung lft and lost pl over 2f out* 80/1
9 7 **Ma Mirage (IRE)** 3-8-12 0........................ TedDurcan 9 —
(S C Williams) *racd in last: drvn over 3f out: sn bhd* 22/1
10 11 **Cherrytree Ella (IRE)** 3-8-12 0........................ LeeEnstone 2 —
(K R Burke) *w ldrs: drvn over 3f out: lost pl over 2f out* 22/1

1m 31.85s (5.55) **Going Correction** +0.95s/f (Soft)
WFA 3 from 4yo 14lb 10 Ran SP% 118.2
Speed ratings (Par 102): **106,95,91,88,87 86,86,74,66,54**
CSF £5.99 TOTE £4.20: £1.10, £1.10, £3.90; EX 7.30 Trifecta £77.20 Pool £435.13 - 4.00 winning units. Place 6 £115.53, Place 5 £64.75..
Owner Paul Moulton **Bred** Arbaway Ventures **Trained** Lambourn, Berks

FOCUS
A wide-margin success from the improved winner. The runner-up has an official rating of 88 but ran nowhere near that mark in a race tricky to rate with any confidence.
T/Plt: £58.60 to a £1 stake. Pool: £66,366.96. 825.60 winning tickets. T/Qpdt: £13.50 to a £1 stake. Pool: £4,146.40. 227.10 winning tickets. WG

977 MUSSELBURGH (R-H)
Friday, April 11

OFFICIAL GOING: Soft
Wind: Virtually nil Weather: Overcast with heavy showers

1303 EUROPEAN BREEDERS' FUND MAIDEN STKS 5f
2:00 (2:00) (Class 5) 2-Y-O £3,885 (£1,156; £577; £288) Stalls Low

Form RPR
1 **Polish Pride** 2-8-9 0........................ MarkLawson(3) 1 67
(M Brittain) *towards rr: pushed along and hdwy over 2f out: swtchd rt and rdn over 1f out: styd on wl u.p ins fnl f to ld nr fin* 11/1
3 2 nk **Count Almaviva (USA)**[11] 1118 2-9-3 0........................ NCallan 3 71
(K A Ryan) *dwlt: sn trcking ldrs: swtchd rt and hdwy over 1f out: rdn to chal ins fnl f: drvn and nt qckn nr fin* 11/4[1]
3 3 nse **Just The Lady**[10] 1122 2-8-9 0........................ TolleyDean(3) 7 66
(W G M Turner) *led: rdn along and edgd rt over 1f out: drvn ins fnl f: hdd and no ex last 50yds* 10/3[2]
4 1 3/4 **Russet Reward** 2-9-3 0........................ TomEaves 4 64
(Mrs L Stubbs) *cl up: rdn and sltly outpcd over 1f out: kpt on ins fnl f* 7/2[3]
2 5 3/4 **Dispol Mulofky (IRE)**[11] 1118 2-8-12 0........................ MickyFenton 5 56
(P T Midgley) *chsd ldrs: rdn along and hung rt over 1f out: sn one pce* 10/1

6 2 **Lady Fantasie** 2-8-12 0 ... RoystonFfrench 2 48
(Mrs A Duffield) *chsd ldrs: rdn along 2f out: wkng whn n.m.r over 1f out*
16/1

7 10 **Especially For You (IRE)** 2-8-12 0 ... ChrisCatlin 8 8
(E J O'Neill) *prom: rdn along wl over 1f out and sn wknd*
15/2

8 4 ½ **Maigh Eo (IRE)** 2-9-3 0 ... PatCosgrave 6 —
(D J G Murray Smith) *sn outpcd and a bhd*
16/1

63.85 secs (3.45) **Going Correction** +0.475s/f (Yiel) 8 Ran SP% 112.9
Speed ratings (Par 92): **91,90,90,87,86 83,67,60**
CSF £40.43 TOTE £14.30: £3.10, £1.20, £1.40; EX 39.30.
Owner Mel Brittain **Bred** Darley **Trained** Warthill, N Yorks

FOCUS
Probably just an ordinary juvenile maiden, but a race that should produce winners. The second and third both improved on their debut form. The first three home raced up the centre of the track in the closing stages.

NOTEBOOK
Polish Pride, a daughter of Polish Precedent, first foal of an unraced half-sister to high-class triple 1m winner Notability, showed a good attitude to make a winning debut. She raced off the pace through the early stages, but responded well to strong pressure to get the call in a three-way battle. This was a pleasing start, but the bare form looks just ordinary and she probably had a hard enough race. (op 12-1 tchd 10-1)
Count Almaviva(USA), behind Dispol Mulofky when beaten at 6/4F on his debut on the Fibresand at Southwell, improved on that form and was just held. He had to be switched right with his challenge inside the final two furlongs having been caught behind the early leader, Just The Lady, but he was probably in the clear for long enough if good enough. (op 9-2)
Just The Lady, just as when third on her debut at Folkestone, showed good early speed but she again just found a couple too strong. She is probably only modest, but she has enough early pace to nick a similar event in the coming weeks. (op 11-4 tchd 7-2)
Russet Reward, a 10,000gns gelded son of Bahamian Bounty, out of a triple 7f-1m4f winner, showed good speed on his racecourse debut but he could not quite sustain his challenge. He raced tight against the near-side rail for much of the way, but the first three ended up more towards the middle of the track and he found that trio too strong. He is entitled to come on for this and looks up to winning a minor maiden. (op 4-1 tchd 9-2 in a place)
Dispol Mulofky(IRE) could not confirm Southwell form with Count Almaviva and this was an unconvincing effort. She was already going right when bumped in that direction in the closing stages and she ended up extremely wide, pretty much on the far side of the track. (op 8-1)

1304 WEATHERBYS BLOODSTOCK INSURANCE H'CAP 2m
2:30 (2:33) (Class 5) (0-70,68) 4-Y-0+ £3,238 (£963; £481; £240) Stalls Low

Form RPR

2131 1 **Grizebeck (IRE)**[9] 1136 6-10-1 68 6ex ... (p) PaulHanagan 7 76
(R F Fisher) *mde all: qcknd 3f out: rdn and edgd lft 2f out: sn drvn and styd on gamely ins fnl f*
6/4[1]

602- 2 2 **Danzatrice**[155] 6733 6-9-3 59 ... PJMcDonald(3) 4 65
(C W Thornton) *hld up in rr: stdy hdwy 4f out: rdn to chse ldrs over 2f out: drvn to chse wnr ins fnl f: one pce towards fin*
6/1[3]

446- 3 1 ½ **Categorical**[17] 6308 5-9-13 66 ... TonyHamilton 5 70
(K G Reveley) *a chsng wnr: rdn along over 3f out: drvn 2f out: kpt on same pce u.p ent fnl f*
11/2[2]

-563 4 3 ½ **Easibet Dot Net**[14] 1062 8-9-2 55 ... (b) TomEaves 6 55
(Miss L A Perratt) *hld up in tch: hdwy over 3f out: rdn along over 2f out and sn no imp*
16/1

046- 5 9 **Dance Sauvage**[164] 6561 5-8-11 50 ... NCallan 1 39
(C W Thornton) *hld up in tch: hdwy 4f out: rdn along 3f out and sn btn*
11/2[2]

00-0 6 29 **Asrar**[19] 982 6-8-8 47 oh2 ... PaulMulrennan 8 1
(Miss Lucinda V Russell) *prom: rdn along over 4f out: wknd 3f out* 66/1

4 7 1 ½ **Masking Baldini (IRE)**[13] 1086 4-8-1 47 ... DuranFentiman(3) 2 —
(P T Midgley) *a towards rr*
18/1

000- 8 27 **Grey Outlook**[203] 5586 5-8-8 47 oh2 ... RoystonFfrench 3 —
(Miss L A Perratt) *trckd ldrs: effrt over 4f out: sn rdn along and wknd* 6/1[3]

3m 44.86s (8.76) **Going Correction** +0.625s/f (Yiel)
WFA 4 from 5yo+ 4lb 8 Ran SP% 112.0
Speed ratings (Par 103): **103,102,101,99,95 80,79,66**
CSF £10.38 CT £37.65 TOTE £2.20: £1.10, £1.80, £2.10; EX 9.50.
Owner Sporting Occasions **Bred** John Killeen **Trained** Ulverston, Cumbria

FOCUS
A modest staying handicap and, despite the pace appearing steady, rain had got into the ground and they finished reasonably strung out. The winner was 4lb wrong and there are doubts whether anything else was at their best.

1305 TURFTV (S) STKS 1m 4f
3:05 (3:05) (Class 6) 4-Y-0+ £1,942 (£578; £288; £144) Stalls High

Form RPR

66-3 1 **Court Of Appeal**[7] 1184 11-9-0 66 ... (tp) TomEaves 12 71
(B Ellison) *trckd ldr: hdwy to ld over 3f out and sn rdn: drvn and hung rt over 1f out: kpt on gamely*
4/1[2]

05/5 2 nk **Truly Fruitful (IRE)**[19] 978 5-9-0 68 ... PaulHanagan 2 71
(R A Fahey) *trckd ldrs gng wl: smooth hdwy to join ldng pair 3f out: chal over 2f out and sn rdn: ev ch tl drvn ins fnl f and no ex towards fin* 5/1[3]

1-61 3 1 ¾ **Friends Hope**[19] 978 7-8-2 70 ... SophieDoyle(7) 7 65+
(P A Blockley) *hld up in tch: smooth hdwy on inner 4f out: clsng on ldng pair whn nt clr run on inner over 1f out: swtchd lft and rdn ent fnl f: no imp towards fin*
3/1[1]

060/ 4 10 **Perez (IRE)**[29] 5510 6-8-11 52 ... (v) MickyFenton 5 49
(W Storey) *led: rdn along 4f out: hdd 3f out: sn drvn and grad wknd* 80/1

-013 5 4 **Lucayan Dancer**[8] 1164 8-9-5 80 ... AdrianTNicholls 8 51
(D Nicholls) *hld up in rr: hdwy 3f out: sn rdn and no imp fnl 2f* 3/1[1]

065- 6 hd **Trance (IRE)**[154] 6744 8-9-0 73 ... (p) PaulFessey 6 45
(T D Barron) *midfield: rdn along 4f out: drvn and plugged on same pce fnl 2f*
11/2

00-0 7 7 **Malguru**[18] 988 4-8-10 50 ... (p) PJMcDonald(3) 1 34
(A G Foster) *chsd ldrs: rdn along over 4f out: drvn over 3f out and grad wknd*
100/1

00/0 8 ½ **Donna's Double**[18] 989 13-9-0 40 ... (p) RoystonFfrench 9 33
(Karen McLintock) *towards rr: sme hdwy 3f out: sn rdn nvr a factor* 33/1

0 9 7 **Karaburan (GER)**[19] 978 4-8-13 50 ... (v) PaulMulrennan 11 22
(P Monteith) *a in rr*
40/1

10 20 **Vie A Deux (FR)**[10] 5-8-9 0 ... TonyHamilton 4 —
(W Storey) *a in rr*
150/1

000- 11 19 **Fardi (IRE)**[352] 1239 6-8-7 30 ... KrishGundowry(7) 10 —
(K W Hogg) *a towards rr*
150/1

400- 12 ½ **Roman History (IRE)**[188] 6019 5-9-0 50 ... (p) NCallan 3 —
(Miss Tracy Waggott) *a towards rr*
28/1

00/0 13 25 **Time Dancer (IRE)**[35] 821 4-8-13 30 ... PatrickMathers 14 —
(H A McWilliams) *chsd ldrs on inner: rdn along over 5f out and sn wknd*
150/1

2m 48.75s (9.05) **Going Correction** +0.625s/f (Yiel)
WFA 4 from 5yo+ 1lb 13 Ran SP% 115.1
Speed ratings (Par 101): **94,93,92,85,83 83,78,78,73,60 47,47,30**
CSF £22.72 TOTE £5.40: £1.80, £2.00, £1.50; EX 32.60.There was no bid for the winner.
Owner Spring Cottage Syndicate No 2 **Bred** John And Susan Davis **Trained** Norton, N Yorks

FOCUS
A good seller, with a minimum claiming price of £20,000 for those beaten attracting a better class of horse than is usually the case in this grade. The first three finished well clear and the winner is the best guide.
Roman History(IRE) Official explanation: jockey said gelding hung left-handed in back straight and right-handed in straight
Time Dancer(IRE) Official explanation: jockey said gelding lost its action

1306 EDINBURGH EVENING NEWS H'CAP 7f 30y
3:40 (3:48) (Class 5) (0-70,69) 3-Y-O £2,914 (£867; £433; £216) Stalls High

Form RPR

13-2 1 **Stevie Thunder**[9] 1161 3-9-1 66 ... PJMcDonald(3) 1 80+
(G A Swinbank) *hld up in tch: smooth hdwy 3f out: rdn to ld over 1f out: styd on wl*
4/5[1]

562- 2 2 ¾ **Grand Value (USA)**[216] 5226 3-8-8 56 ... PaulFessey 6 63
(T D Barron) *uns rdr and rn loose bef s: cl up tl led 3f out: rdn 2f out: drvn and hdd appr fnl f: kpt on same pce*
11/1

-364 3 2 ¾ **Splash The Cash**[51] 629 3-9-0 62 ... NCallan 8 62
(K A Ryan) *chsd ldrs: hdwy over 3f out: rdn and ev ch 2f out tl drvn: edgd rt and wknd appr fnl f*
10/1[3]

00-6 4 8 **Bourse (IRE)**[19] 980 3-9-3 65 ... TomEaves 2 44
(J S Wainwright) *hld up and bhd: hdwy over 3f out: rdn 2f out: styd on ins fnl f: nrst fin*
25/1

300- 5 ½ **Willyn (IRE)**[168] 6462 3-8-9 62 ... GaryBartley(5) 10 40
(J S Goldie) *in rr tl styd on fnl 2f: nvr a factor*
20/1

1415 6 hd **Fulford**[42] 756 3-8-13 64 ... MarkLawson(3) 12 41
(M Brittain) *midfield: effrt and hdwy 3f out: rdn 2f out and sn no imp* 9/1[2]

6-24 7 shd **Always Certain (USA)**[23] 936 3-9-7 69 ... GregFairley 4 46
(M Johnston) *a midfield*
12/1

55-4 8 3 ½ **Carnival Dream**[80] 257 3-8-12 60 ... PatrickMathers 3 28
(H A McWilliams) *in tch: rdn along over 3f out and sn btn*
66/1

2-30 9 5 **Complete Frontline (GER)**[39] 777 3-8-7 60 ... KellyHarrison(5) 11 15
(K R Burke) *a towards rr*
25/1

35-0 10 6 **Turn And River (IRE)**[31] 849 3-8-7 55 ... AdrianTNicholls 9 —
(M Brittain) *chsd ldrs: rdn along over 3f out and sn wknd*
50/1

226- 11 13 **Hurstpierpoint (IRE)**[139] 6933 3-8-12 60 ... PaulHanagan 5 —
(R A Fahey) *a towards rr*
16/1

455- 12 2 ¼ **Legendary Guest**[176] 6282 3-9-7 69 ... TonyHamilton 7 —
(D W Barker) *led: rdn along and hdd 3f out: sn drvn and wknd*
14/1

1m 34.3s (4.00) **Going Correction** +0.625s/f (Yiel) 12 Ran SP% 119.1
Speed ratings (Par 98): **102,98,95,86,86 85,85,81,75,69 54,51**
CSF £9.67 CT £59.53 TOTE £1.60: £1.10, £4.00, £2.10; EX 15.70.
Owner Steve Gray **Bred** Sir Eric Parker **Trained** Melsonby, N Yorks

FOCUS
A modest handicap and very few got involved. The early pace was steady, yet the front three still finished well clear. The form is best rated around the third, with a slight step up from the winner.
Fulford Official explanation: jockey said gelding was unsuited by the soft going
Turn And River(IRE) Official explanation: trainer later said filly had not been suited by the rain-softened ground
Hurstpierpoint(IRE) Official explanation: jockey said filly was unsuited by the soft going

1307 CORE CHAMPAGNE CHARLIE MAIDEN STKS 1m 1f
4:15 (4:15) (Class 5) 3-Y-O+ £2,590 (£770; £385; £192) Stalls High

Form RPR

03-2 1 **Tajweed (IRE)**[18] 991 3-8-9 71 ... GregFairley 5 77+
(M Johnston) *cl up: led 3f out: rdn and hdd over 1f out: rallied to ld ent fnl f: drvn out*
1/1[1]

44-2 2 3 **Prince Kalamoun (IRE)**[19] 980 3-8-9 72 ... NCallan 1 71
(G A Swinbank) *trckd ldng pair: hdwy 3f out: rdn to ld over 1f out: sn drvn: hdd ent fnl f and sn one pce*
9/4[2]

340- 3 10 **Flagstone (USA)**[283] 3183 4-9-12 58 ... AdrianTNicholls 8 54
(D Nicholls) *led: rdn along and hdd 3f out: sn drvn and wknd fnl 2f* 18/1

03- 4 2 ¼ **Legion D'Honneur (UAE)**[184] 6106 3-8-9 0 ... PaulMulrennan 9 45
(L Lungo) *chsd ldng pair: rdn along 3f out: sn drvn and outpcd fnl 2f* 6/1[3]

3- 5 8 **Bretwalda (IRE)**[207] 5488 5-9-12 0 ... MickyFenton 7 32
(P T Midgley) *chsd ldrs: rdn along over 3f out: sn one pce*
14/1

0/ 6 2 **Nelson Vettori**[595] 4774 4-9-12 0 ... TomEaves 3 28
(Miss L A Perratt) *a in rr*
66/1

0/ 7 10 **Never Cross (IRE)**[550] 5859 4-9-4 0 ... PJMcDonald(3) 4 2
(M A Barnes) *a bhd*
100/1

8 29 **Notnowrosie (IRE)** 3-8-4 0 ... PaulHanagan 2 —
(A G Foster) *a bhd*
50/1

2m 1.38s (6.68) **Going Correction** +0.625s/f (Yiel)
WFA 3 from 4yo+ 17lb 8 Ran SP% 111.4
Speed ratings (Par 103): **95,92,83,81,74 72,63,37**
CSF £3.13 TOTE £2.10: £1.02, £1.50, £4.50; EX 3.30.
Owner Hamdan Al Maktoum **Bred** Kilboy Estate **Trained** Middleham Moor, N Yorks

FOCUS
An ordinary maiden and very little strength in depth. The winner is progressing nicely and the runner-up is the best guide, the first two finishing clear.

1308 DM HALL H'CAP 1m
4:50 (4:50) (Class 4) (0-85,85) 4-Y-0+ £5,504 (£1,637; £818; £408) Stalls High

Form RPR

01-2 1 **Ansells Pride (IRE)**[30] 852 5-8-8 75 ... TomEaves 8 91
(B Smart) *mde all: rdn and qcknd over 2f out: drvn and edgd lft ent fnl f: styd on wl*
5/1[2]

0-52 2 ¾ **Regal Parade**[10] 1133 4-9-4 85 ... AdrianTNicholls 5 99
(D Nicholls) *hld up in tch: hdwy 3f out: chsd ldrs over 1f out: sn rdn and styd on wl fnl f*
11/4[1]

3313 3 5 **Cha Cha Cha**[13] 1069 4-9-1 82 ... NCallan 3 86
(K A Ryan) *trckd ldng pair: smooth hdwy 3f out: rdn and ev ch wl over 1f out: sn drvn and kpt on same pce*
6/1[3]

260- 4 1 ¼ **Rubenstar (IRE)**[170] 6435 5-8-4 71 oh1 ... DaleGibson 10 72
(D J G Murray Smith) *plld hrd: chsd wnr: rdn along 3f out: kpt on same pce fnl 2f*
33/1

500- 5 2 ½ **Bajan Pride**[180] 6203 4-8-8 75 ... PaulHanagan 2 71
(R A Fahey) *trckd ldrs: effrt 3f out: rdn along 2f out and sn btn* 11/4[1]

The Form Book, Raceform Ltd, Compton, RG20 6NL

0-04 **6** *2½* **Wovoka (IRE)**[6] 1217 5-8-11 **78**... FergalLynch 9 68
(D W Barker) *a in rr* **13/2**
00-6 **7** *6* **Frank Crow**[7] 979 5-8-4 **71** oh1... NickyMackay 1 49
(J S Goldie) *hld up: a in rr* **8/1**
8 *3* **Solis (GER)**[82] 5-9-2 **83**... PaulMulrennan 6 54
(P Monteith) *dwlt: a towards rr* **40/1**

1m 46.49s (5.29) **Going Correction** +0.625s/f (Yiel) **8** Ran SP% **114.1**
Speed ratings (Par 105): **98,97,92,91,88 86,80,77**
CSF £19.08 CT £83.40 TOTE £6.70: £2.10, £1.10, £2.40; EX 23.10.
Owner Ansells Of Watford **Bred** E Lonergan **Trained** Hambleton, N Yorks

FOCUS
A good handicap. The winner is progressive and this form looks sound.
Bajan Pride Official explanation: jockey said gelding was unsuited by the soft going

1309 SCOTTISH RACING H'CAP — 5f
5:25 (5:26) (Class 5) (0-70,75) 4-Y-O+ **£2,914** (£867; £433; £216) **Stalls** Low

Form RPR
35-1 **1** **Rebel Duke (IRE)**[10] 1129 4-9-9 **75** 6ex... FergalLynch 11 94
(D W Barker) *cl up: effrt to chal over 1f out: sn rdn: led ent fnl f: kpt on* **3/1**[2]
1212 **2** *1¼* **Alexander Huricane (IRE)**[31] 846 4-9-1 **67**... NCallan 3 81
(K A Ryan) *cl up: led 2f out and sn rdn: drvn and hdd ent fnl f: kpt on* **9/4**[1]
00-0 **3** *5* **Rothesay Dancer**[18] 987 5-8-4 **61**... KellyHarrison(5) 10 57
(J S Goldie) *in tch: hdwy wl over 1f out: sn rdn and kpt on ins fnl f* **9/1**
2-60 **4** *2¼* **Spirit Of Coniston**[14] 1047 5-8-12 **64**... AdrianTNicholls 9 52
(D Nicholls) *chsd ldrs: rdn wl over 1f out: kpt on u.p ins fnl f* **12/1**
046- **5** *1* **Argentine (IRE)**[155] 6731 4-9-4 **70**... PaulMulrennan 7 54
(L Lungo) *towards rr: hdwy wl over 1f out: sn rdn and n.d* **11/1**
0-00 **6** *1¼* **Kings College Boy**[17] 1015 8-8-11 **63**...(b) PaulHanagan 5 43
(R A Fahey) *chsd ldrs: rdn along wl over 1f out: sn btn* **12/1**
30-4 **7** *1¼* **Lambency (IRE)**[18] 987 5-8-4 **56** oh1... NickyMackay 6 31
(J S Goldie) *a towards rr* **13/2**[3]
414- **8** *½* **Whinhill House**[254] 4083 8-8-11 **63**... TonyHamilton 1 37
(D W Barker) *led: rdn along and hdd 2f out: sn wknd* **20/1**
005- **9** *1* **Sea Land (FR)**[252] 4141 4-8-13 **65**... TomEaves 8 35
(B Ellison) *a outpcd towards rr* **12/1**
000- **10** *7* **Miacarla**[176] 6287 5-8-4 **56**... PatrickMathers 12 —
(H A McWilliams) *in tch: rdn along over 2f out and sn wknd* **20/1**
500- **11** *2½* **Mutayam**[201] 5667 8-8-6 **58** oh11 ow2...(t) GregFairley 2 —
(D A Nolan) *a towards rr* **100/1**
000- **12** *31* **Sokoke**[224] 4996 7-8-1 **56** oh11... DuranFentiman(3) 13 —
(D A Nolan) *chsd ldrs to 1/2-way: wknd qckly and sn bhd* **100/1**

62.25 secs (1.85) **Going Correction** +0.475s/f (Yiel) **12** Ran SP% **122.0**
Speed ratings (Par 103): **104,102,94,90,88 86,84,84,82,71 67,17**
CSF £10.15 CT £56.31 TOTE £3.70: £1.60, £1.20, £3.00; EX 10.30 Place 6 £4.37, Place 5 £2.72.
Owner Ian Bishop **Bred** Rathbarry Stud **Trained** Scorton, N Yorks

FOCUS
A decent sprint handicap for the grade, and the progressive front pair came clear. The form looks sound. The majority of these raced a little way off the stands' rail.
Miacarla Official explanation: jockey said mare was unsuited by the soft going
T/Plt: £4.10 to a £1 stake. Pool: £54,112.02. 9,418.35 winning tickets. T/Qpdt: £2.20 to a £1 stake. Pool: £2,767.60. 908.80 winning tickets. JR

1190 WOLVERHAMPTON (A.W) (L-H)
Friday, April 11

OFFICIAL GOING: Standard
Wind: Fresh, behind Weather: Cloudy

1310 BOOK TICKETS ONLINE CLAIMING STKS — 1m 4f 50y(P)
6:50 (6:50) (Class 6) 4-Y-O+ **£2,047** (£604; £302) **Stalls** Low

Form RPR
11-2 **1** **Nawamees (IRE)**[86] 182 10-9-8 76...(p) GeorgeBaker 4 74
(G L Moore) *chsd ldrs: pushed along over 3f out: led over 1f out: styd on wl* **4/9**[1]
0333 **2** *5* **Looks The Business (IRE)**[30] 859 7-8-10 59... JackDean(7) 7 61
(W G M Turner) *trckd ldr: racd keenly: rdn and ev ch over 1f out: edgd lft: styd on same pce* **8/1**[3]
25-0 **3** *shd* **Brastar Jelois (FR)**[18] 999 5-9-0 58... RussellKennemore(3) 3 61
(R Hollinshead) *hld up: hdwy over 2f out: rdn over 1f out: styd on same pce fnl f* **11/2**[2]
0420 **4** *7* **George Henson (IRE)**[9] 1136 4-9-2 54... DanielTudhope 8 50
(Garry Moss) *led: shkn up 7f out: rdn and hdd over 1f out: wknd fnl f* **33/1**
4442 **5** *7* **Castle Frome (IRE)**[7] 1192 9-9-0 42...(p) PaulFitzsimons 5 35
(A E Price) *hld up: racd keenly: rdn and wknd over 2f out* **20/1**
-366 **6** *6* **Treetops Hotel (IRE)**[71] 373 9-8-13 56... TPQueally 2 25
(R Hollinshead) *hld up: rdn and wknd 3f out* **12/1**

2m 41.5s (0.40) **Going Correction** +0.075s/f (Slow)
WFA 4 from 5yo+ 1lb **6** Ran SP% **111.1**
Speed ratings (Par 101): **101,97,97,92,88 84**
CSF £4.65 TOTE £1.40: £1.10, £2.40; EX 3.90.
Owner Paul Stamp **Bred** Kilfrush Stud Ltd **Trained** Woodingdean, E Sussex

FOCUS
A very uncompetitive claimer run at a modest early pace and the favourite duly bolted up. The second and third ran close to their marks.

1311 RINGSIDE SUITE CONFERENCE VENUE MAIDEN STKS — 5f 216y(P)
7:20 (7:21) (Class 5) 3-Y-O+ **£2,456** (£725; £362) **Stalls** Low

Form RPR
4-2 **1** **Spin Again (IRE)**[15] 1036 3-9-0 0... SebSanders 9 70+
(R M Beckett) *hld up: hdwy over 2f out: rdn to ld over 1f out: r.o* **10/11**[1]
0 **2** *¾* **Cheveton**[13] 1082 4-9-12 0... SaleemGolam 6 70
(R J Price) *chsd ldrs: led 4f out: rdn and hdd over 1f out: styd on* **150/1**
3 *shd* **Great Knight (IRE)** 3-9-0 0... LiamJones 2 67+
(W J Haggas) *chsd ldrs: rdn and ev ch ins fnl f: styd on* **2/1**[2]
00 **4** *4* **Borrowdale**[6] 1215 3-9-0 0... TPQueally 3 54+
(J A Osborne) *hld up: hdwy and hung lft over 1f out: nvr nr to chal* **25/1**
5 *1* **Near The Front** 3-9-0 0... SamHitchcott 4 51+
(J L Spearing) *s.s: outpcd: swtchd rt over 1f out: r.o ins fnl f: nrst fin* **40/1**
6 *hd* **Focail Eile** 3-9-0 0... GrahamGibbons 8 50
(E S McMahon) *trckd ldr: plld hrd: led 5f out: hdd 4f out: rdn and n.m.r over 1f out: wknd ins fnl f* **12/1**
0-0 **7** *6* **Bahamian Princess**[17] 1019 3-8-6 0... RussellKennemore(3) 11 26
(R Hollinshead) *in rr: rdn over 3f out: n.d* **50/1**
03- **8** *nk* **Solemn**[168] 6477 3-9-0 0... PaulFitzsimons 12 30
(J M Bradley) *led 1f: chsd ldrs: rdn: hung lft and wknd over 1f out* **28/1**
00- **9** *1¼* **Womaniser (IRE)**[340] 1523 4-9-12 0... J-PGuillambert 10 29
(T Keddy) *s.i.s: outpcd* **66/1**
5- **10** *½* **Watch This Place**[292] 2911 3-9-0 0... AndrewElliott 7 25
(K R Burke) *broke wl: lost pl 5f out: hung rt over 3f out: sn bhd* **25/1**
03-0 **11** *½* **Pennyspider (IRE)**[9] 1144 3-8-9 52... FergusSweeney 1 18
(M S Saunders) *mid-div: rdn over 2f out: wknd wl over 1f out* **33/1**
5- **12** *1¼* **Scanno (IRE)**[269] 3606 3-9-0 0... AlanDaly 5 19
(M Mullineaux) *chsd ldrs over 3f* **8/1**[3]

1m 15.48s (0.48) **Going Correction** +0.075s/f (Slow)
WFA 3 from 4yo 12lb **12** Ran SP% **125.2**
Speed ratings (Par 103): **99,98,97,92,91 90,82,82,80,80 79,77**
CSF £272.24 TOTE £2.00: £1.10, £24.00, £1.10; EX 95.20.
Owner Richard Morecombe **Bred** Barry Lyons **Trained** Whitsbury, Hants

FOCUS
A moderate-looking maiden, and with Cheveton - who had been beaten 55l on his debut over 1m1f here last month - running so prominently, questions have to be asked as to the value of the form.
Great Knight(IRE) ◆ Official explanation: jockey said colt suffered interference in running
Borrowdale Official explanation: jockey said gelding hung left-handed
Pennyspider(IRE) Official explanation: jockey said filly had no more to give

1312 STAY AT THE WOLVERHAMPTON HOLIDAY INN H'CAP — 5f 216y(P)
7:50 (7:51) (Class 5) (0-70,70) 4-Y-O+ **£2,456** (£725; £362) **Stalls** Low

Form RPR
1-00 **1** **Rabbit Fighter (IRE)**[17] 1015 4-9-2 **68**...(v) PhillipMakin 6 76
(D Shaw) *prom: rdn 1/2-way: edgd lft over 1f out: r.o to ld wl ins fnl f* **7/2**[1]
1064 **2** *nk* **Methaaly (IRE)**[7] 1191 5-9-1 **67**...(be1) SebSanders 4 74
(M Mullineaux) *hld up in tch: rdn 1/2-way: r.o wl ins fnl f* **8/1**
03-4 **3** *½* **The Fisio**[4] 1242 8-8-10 **62**...(b) PaulEddery 1 67
(G D Blake) *s.i.s: hld up: hdwy u.p over 1f out: r.o wl* **11/1**
0423 **4** *nk* **Interactive (IRE)**[15] 1036 5-9-3 **69**... AlanDaly 7 73
(Andrew Turnell) *led: rdn over 1f out: hdd wl ins fnl f* **8/1**
4462 **5** *½* **Obe Royal**[7] 1191 4-8-10 **69**...(b) RichardEvans(7) 8 72
(P D Evans) *dwlt: hld up: hdwy u.p over 1f out: r.o* **7/2**[1]
4305 **6** *1¼* **Star Strider**[15] 1040 4-9-1 **67**... JamieSpencer 2 66
(Miss Gay Kelleway) *hld up in tch: rdn and nt clr run over 1f out: nt trble ldrs* **4/1**[2]
2114 **7** *hd* **Crimson Fern (IRE)**[63] 488 4-9-1 **67**... FergusSweeney 9 65
(M S Saunders) *trckd ldrs: racd keenly: wnt 2nd 2f out: sn rdn: hung lft and no ex ins fnl f* **11/1**
430- **8** *½* **Briery Lane (IRE)**[154] 6752 7-8-5 **57**... PaulFitzsimons 3 54
(J M Bradley) *chsd ldrs: rdn 2f out: no ex fnl f* **40/1**
-443 **9** *1¼* **Royal Challenge**[15] 1040 7-9-4 **70**... DanielTudhope 5 63
(I W McInnes) *trckd ldr tl rdn 2f out: no ex ins fnl f* **6/1**[3]

1m 15.38s (0.38) **Going Correction** +0.075s/f (Slow) **9** Ran SP% **120.1**
Speed ratings (Par 103): **100,99,98,98,97 96,95,95,93**
CSF £33.55 CT £287.60 TOTE £4.70: £2.00, £3.60, £4.10; EX 52.90.
Owner Market Avenue Racing Club Ltd **Bred** Hawthorn Villa Stud **Trained** Danethorpe, Notts
■ Stewards' Enquiry : Paul Eddery caution: careless riding

FOCUS
A competitive little sprint, but just over 3l separated the first eight home. Ordinary form, best rated through the fourth.
Star Strider Official explanation: jockey said gelding hung right-handed

1313 DINE IN THE HORIZONS RESTAURANT H'CAP — 7f 32y(P)
8:20 (8:21) (Class 6) (0-55,55) 4-Y-O+ **£2,047** (£604; £302) **Stalls** High

Form RPR
60-0 **1** **A Big Sky Brewing (USA)**[18] 990 4-8-9 **55**...(b1) NeilBrown(5) 12 66
(T D Barron) *hld up: hdwy and hung lft over 1f out: styd on u.p to ld wl ins fnl f* **14/1**
2111 **2** *¾* **Straight Face (IRE)**[4] 1248 4-8-11 **52**...(b) JamieSpencer 4 61
(Miss Gay Kelleway) *a.p: rdn to chse ldr over 2f out: hung lft fr over 1f out: ev ch ins fnl f: nt qckn nr fin* **9/4**[1]
00-2 **3** *nk* **Optical Illusion (USA)**[16] 1029 4-8-12 **53**...(p) PhillipMakin 10 61
(Miss L A Perratt) *chsd ldr tl led over 2f out: rdn and hung lft fr over 1f out: hdd wl ins fnl f* **7/2**[2]
0-45 **4** *2¾* **Greenwood**[9] 1145 10-8-12 **53**... RobertHavlin 3 54
(P G Murphy) *hld up: hdwy over 2f out: rdn and edgd lft over 1f out: no ex ins fnl f* **7/1**
4614 **5** *3½* **Alucica**[9] 1142 5-8-12 **53**...(v) RobertWinston 5 44
(D Shaw) *dwlt: hld up: hdwy u.p and hung lft over 1f out: nt trble ldrs* **10/1**
/60- **6** *1¾* **Vanatina (IRE)**[233] 4714 4-8-9 **50**... LiamJones 7 37
(W M Brisbourne) *hld up in tch: racd keenly: lost pl wl over 3f out: n.d after* **40/1**
00-0 **7** *¾* **Shaftesbury Avenue (USA)**[98] 42 5-9-0 **55**...(b) DanielTudhope 2 40
(I W McInnes) *s.s: nvr nrr* **9/2**[3]
450- **8** *5* **Moon Forest (IRE)**[217] 5190 6-8-3 **47**...(p) KevinGhunowa(3) 9 18
(J M Bradley) *prom over 4f* **28/1**
000/ **9** *2½* **Amongst Amigos (IRE)**[512] 6503 7-8-6 **47**...(b) GrahamGibbons 8 11
(C Moore, Ire) *led over 4f: rdn and wknd over 1f out* **16/1**
3014 **10** *1¼* **Hi Spec (IRE)**[14] 1064 5-8-6 **47**...(p) AndrewElliott 11 8
(Miss M E Rowland) *s.i.s: sn prom: rdn and wknd over 2f out* **9/1**

1m 30.03s (0.43) **Going Correction** +0.075s/f (Slow) **10** Ran SP% **121.2**
Speed ratings (Par 101): **100,99,98,95,91 89,88,83,80,78**
CSF £47.56 CT £145.51 TOTE £23.30: £4.20, £1.40, £1.90; EX 72.90.
Owner Trevor Boanas **Bred** Braeburn Farm Corp **Trained** Maunby, N Yorks

FOCUS
A moderate contest which produced a good finish. Sound form.

1314 WOLVERHAMPTON-RACECOURSE.CO.UK H'CAP — 1m 1f 103y(P)
8:50 (8:50) (Class 4) (0-85,83) 4-Y-O+ **£4,209** (£1,252; £625; £312) **Stalls** Low

Form RPR
54-0 **1** **Gold Prospect**[13] 1076 4-9-0 **79**... JamieSpencer 5 89+
(M L W Bell) *dwlt: hld up: hdwy over 1f out: r.o to ld wl ins fnl f* **13/8**[1]
4060 **2** *¾* **Speedy Sam**[17] 1018 5-9-4 **83**... FergusSweeney 4 91
(K R Burke) *sn led: rdn over 1f out: edgd rt and hdd wl ins fnl f* **5/1**
4121 **3** *2* **Royal Amnesty**[20] 973 5-8-8 **73**...(b) PhillipMakin 2 77
(Miss L A Perratt) *prom: rdn over 2f out: styd on* **2/1**[2]
010- **4** *1½* **General Knowledge (USA)**[149] 6806 5-8-5 **70**...(t) PaulEddery 1 71
(G D Blake) *trckd ldr: rdn and ev ch fr over 2f out: hung lft over 1f out: wknd ins fnl f* **28/1**
1642 **5** *3¾* **Moonlight Man**[14] 1065 7-9-0 **79**... RobertWinston 3 72
(C R Dore) *trckd ldrs: rdn over 3f out: hung lft and wknd over 1f out* **4/1**[3]

2m 0.56s (-1.14) **Going Correction** +0.075s/f (Slow) **5** Ran SP% **111.5**
Speed ratings (Par 105): **108,107,105,104,100**
CSF £10.21 TOTE £2.70: £1.20, £2.70; EX 9.90.

Owner B J Warren **Bred** W And R Barnett Ltd **Trained** Newmarket, Suffolk

FOCUS

A small field, but the pace was sound and the winning time was very sound. The form is perhaps not the most solid but the winner looks capable of better.

1315 SPONSOR A RACE BY CALLING 01902 390009 H'CAP — 5f 216y(P)

9:20 (9:22) (Class 6) (0-65,65) 3-Y-O — **£2,047** (£604; £302) **Stalls** Low

Form — RPR

-542 **1** **Nice Wee Girl (IRE)**[2] 1271 3-8-13 **65** .... HaddenFrost[(5)] 8 — 72
(S Kirk) *hld up: hdwy over 2f out: rdn to ld ins fnl f: r.o* **7/2**[2]

0230 **2** *2* **Golden Dane (IRE)**[9] 1141 3-8-13 **60** .... (p) RobertWinston 7 — 61
(C R Dore) *hld up: rdn 1/2-way: hdwy and nt clr run over 1f out: r.o* **14/1**

200- **3** *3/4* **Towy Boy (IRE)**[133] 6973 3-9-2 **63** .... SebSanders 1 — 62
(I A Wood) *chsd ldrs: led over 1f out: sn rdn and edgd rt: hdd and no ex ins fnl f* **11/2**[3]

00-0 **4** *1/2* **Wave Hill (IRE)**[24] 924 3-9-1 **62** .... RobertHavlin 5 — 59
(B J Meehan) *hld up: hdwy over 1f out: styd on* **8/1**

506- **5** *1/2* **Charmel's Lad**[178] 6252 3-9-4 **65** .... SaleemGolam 6 — 60+
(W R Swinburn) *s.i.s: hld up: rdn over 2f out: r.o ins fnl f: nrst fin* **3/1**[1]

642- **6** *1/2* **Richardthesecond (IRE)**[170] 6426 3-9-0 **61** .... TGMcLaughlin 2 — 55
(W M Brisbourne) *chsd ldr: led 4f out: hung rt over 2f out: hdd over 1f out: styd on same pce fnl f* **8/1**

1225 **7** *1* **Seductive Witch**[11] 1110 3-8-13 **60** .... JamesDoyle 12 — 51
(J Balding) *chsd ldrs: rdn and ev ch over 1f out: wknd ins fnl f* **9/1**

-533 **8** *3/4* **Precipice**[17] 1019 3-9-2 **63** .... DanielTudhope 9 — 51
(D Carroll) *mid-div: rdn over 2f out: styd on ins fnl f: nvr nrr* **9/1**

300- **9** *nse* **Keeparryappy (IRE)**[217] 5199 3-9-1 **62** .... AndrewElliott 13 — 50
(K R Burke) *bhd and rdn 1/2-way: nvr trbld ldrs* **66/1**

54-0 **10** *2 1/2* **Amber Ridge**[18] 998 3-8-11 **58** .... TPQueally 11 — 38
(B P J Baugh) *hld up: rdn over 3f out: a in rr* **33/1**

0024 **11** *1 1/2* **Admirals Way**[11] 1120 3-8-9 **56** .... PhillipMakin 4 — 31
(C N Kellett) *led: hdd 4f out: chsd ldrs tl rdn and wknd over 1f out* **12/1**

-022 **12** *5* **Rich James (IRE)**[39] 780 3-8-4 **51** oh1 .... JimmyQuinn 10 — 10
(J D Bethell) *mid-div: rdn over 3f out: wknd 2f out* **7/1**

1m 15.76s (0.76) **Going Correction** +0.075s/f (Slow) — **12 Ran** SP% **136.1**

Speed ratings (Par 96): **97,94,93,92,92 91,90,89,88,85 83,76**

CSF £61.19 CT £293.08 TOTE £4.20: £2.00, £6.20, £2.40; EX 107.70 Place 6 £21.18, Place 5 £16.96 .

Owner Family Amusements Ltd **Bred** John McLoughlin **Trained** Upper Lambourn, Berks

FOCUS

A wide-open affair, run at a strong pace. Just ordinary form, with little progressive, but sound enough.

T/Plt: £49.40 to a £1 stake. Pool: £89,724.02. 1,324.30 winning tickets. T/Qpdt: £73.10 to a £1 stake. Pool: £5,266.70. 53.30 winning tickets. CR

1316 - 1322a (Foreign Racing) - See Raceform Interactive

1108 SAINT-CLOUD (L-H)

Friday, April 11

OFFICIAL GOING: Heavy

1323a PRIX PENELOPE (GROUP 3) (FILLIES) — 1m 2f 110y

2:20 (2:27) 3-Y-O — **£29,412** (£11,765; £8,824; £5,882; £2,941)

RPR

1 **Gagnoa (IRE)**[171] 6416 3-9-0 .... SPasquier 1 — 111
(A Fabre, France) *racd in 2nd: led 2f out: drvn and r.o 1 1/2f out: r.o gamely fnl f to hold chal of 2nd* **21/10**[2]

2 *nk* **Top Toss (IRE)**[27] 911 3-9-0 .... TThulliez 6 — 110
(Y De Nicolay, France) *racd in 3rd: pushed along to chse ldrs over 2f out: 2nd and ev ch 1 1/2f out: styd on u.p fnl f: nrest at fin* **18/10**[1]

3 *1/2* **Sanjida (IRE)**[173] 6377 3-9-0 .... CSoumillon 5 — 109
(A De Royer-Dupre, France) *racd in 4th: pushed along on ins and wnt 3rd 2f out: rdn and r.o over 1f out: disputing 2nd 100yds out: styd on* **28/10**[3]

4 *3* **Quarayed (USA)**[31] 3-9-0 .... C-PLemaire 4 — 104
(J-C Rouget, France) *racd in 5th: last 1/2-way: styd on fr over 1f out to go 4th: no imp on ldrs* **42/10**

5 *2 1/2* **La Fresca**[12] 3-9-0 .... AlainBadel 2 — 99
(Mme M Bollack-Badel, France) *racd in last: 5th 1/2-way: rdn 1 1/2f out: n.d* **24/1**

6 *4* **Vadsalina (IRE)**[27] 911 3-9-0 .... OPeslier 3 — 92
(A De Royer-Dupre, France) *led to 2f out: rdn and wknd wl over 1f out* **28/10**[3]

2m 23.1s (3.50) **Going Correction** +0.45s/f (Yiel) — **6 Ran** SP% **143.8**

Speed ratings: **105,104,104,102,100 97**

PARI-MUTUEL: WIN 3.10; PL 1.60, 1.30; SF 9.20.

Owner D Smith, M Tabor & Mrs J Magnier **Bred** Quay Bloodstock **Trained** Chantilly, France

NOTEBOOK

Gagnoa(IRE) looked splendid in the paddock and, judging by the way she ran on to win this Group 3 event, she will soon be racing with the best this season. She fended off the challenges of the runner-up and third to win with just a little bit in hand. This was the perfect seasonal debut for a filly who has all the top engagements, including the Oaks at Epsom. Judging by her breeding, she will definitely stay 1m4f, and she will now head for the Prix Saint-Alary before a tilt at either the Prix de Diane or the Oaks at Epsom. The Irish Oaks is also definitely on the cards in July.

Top Toss(IRE), like the winner, was the only other filly in the race with a previous Group success. She pulled out all the stops but could never quite get to the head of affairs, even though she had had the benefit of a previous race this season. She will now probably go directly for the Prix de Diane.

Sanjida(IRE) began her challenge from two out but seemed reluctant to go between the winner and runner-up inside the final furlong. It will be interesting to see her next time out with a clear run. She may be seen out next in the Prix Vanteaux.

Quarayed(USA), last in the early part of the race, still had plenty to do in the straight, but she did make up late ground, which augurs well for the future. This outing will have certainly done her some good.

1295 DONCASTER (L-H)

Saturday, April 12

OFFICIAL GOING: Soft

Wind: Virtually nil Weather: Cloudy

1324 BOOK TICKETS ONLINE MAIDEN STKS — 5f

2:30 (2:30) (Class 4) 2-Y-O — **£3,885** (£1,156; £577; £288) **Stalls** High

Form — RPR

1 **Dispol Kylie (IRE)** 2-8-9 0 .... JamieMoriarty[(3)] 3 — 73+
(P T Midgley) *mde virtually all: rdn clr appr last: styd on wl* **15/2**

2 *2 3/4* **Eilean Eeve** 2-8-12 0 .... NeilPollard 7 — 62+
(A J McCabe) *s.i.s: hld up in rr: hdwy 1/2-way: chsd ldrs wl over 1f out: sn rdn and kpt on ins fnl f: tk 2nd nr fin* **7/2**[2]

3 *nk* **Marygate (IRE)** 2-8-9 0 .... MarkLawson[(3)] 8 — 61
(M Brittain) *trckd ldrs: hdwy 2f out and sn ev ch tl rdn and one pce ent fnl f: lost 2nd nr line* **7/2**[2]

4 **4** *3 1/4* **Come On Buckers (IRE)**[9] 1168 2-9-3 0 .... TGMcLaughlin 1 — 53
(P D Evans) *cl up: effrt over 2f out: sn rdn and ev ch tl wknd over 1f out* **3/1**[1]

5 *1/2* **Monsieur Jourdain (IRE)** 2-9-3 0 .... DavidAllan 4 — 51
(T D Easterby) *chsd ldrs: rdn along 1/2-way: sn wknd* **5/1**[3]

6 *2* **Adozen Dreams** 2-8-7 0 .... SladeO'Hara[(5)] 2 — 38
(G R Oldroyd) *s.i.s: sn prom: rdn along and hung lft over 2f out: sn wknd* **13/2**

7 *5* **Moon Warrior** 2-9-3 0 .... DeanMcKeown 5 — 23
(C Smith) *hung lft thrght: a in rr* **20/1**

64.12 secs (3.62) **Going Correction** +0.475s/f (Yiel) — **7 Ran** SP% **116.0**

Speed ratings (Par 94): **90,85,85,79,79 75,67**

CSF £34.73 TOTE £9.40: £4.10, £2.60; EX 44.40 TRIFECTA Not won..

Owner W B Imison **Bred** Century Farms **Trained** Westow, N Yorks

FOCUS

Probably just an ordinary juvenile maiden, based on pedigrees and the time. The race has been tentatively rated through the fourth, the only runner with a previous outing.

NOTEBOOK

Dispol Kylie(IRE), a 3,200euros daughter of Kheleyf, closely related to dual 5f three-year-old winner Rosie Cross, knew her job and made a winning debut in quite good style. Quickly into her stride, she soon bagged the stands' rail and ran on strongly to the line. This was probably just an ordinary contest and she might not be open to as much improvement as some of these, but she clearly has a fair amount of ability. (tchd 7-1)

Eilean Eeve, a daughter of 2001 Queen's Vase winner And Beyond, out of a 7f juvenile winner who was later placed over 1m4f at three, would appear to be a surprisingly precocious type. She ran green in behind the eventual winner, continually having to be niggled along, but she kept on nicely enough to take second. She will surely require further before long. (op 8-1)

Marygate(IRE), a 3,000euros daughter of Spartacus, half-sister to dual 5f juvenile winner Monashee Rose, showed good speed but she was caught a little wider than the first two home and could not quite sustain her challenge. She finished clear of the remainder and might be able to find a similar contest. (op 9-2)

Come On Buckers(IRE) showed much more early speed than on his debut at Leicester, but he failed to see out his race. This was disappointing and he has something to prove now. (op 9-4 tchd 7-2)

Monsieur Jourdain(IRE), a gelded son of Royal Applause, first foal of a mare who was unplaced over 1m in a light career at three in France, seemed to run very green and he will know a lot more next time. (tchd 11-2)

Moon Warrior Official explanation: jockey said gelding ran green

1325 URBAN-I H'CAP — 5f

3:05 (3:05) (Class 2) (0-100,96) 4-Y-O+

£10,904 (£3,265; £1,632; £817; £407; £204) **Stalls** High

Form — RPR

010- **1** **Northern Fling**[204] 5584 4-9-4 **96** .... SilvestreDeSousa 3 — 110
(D Nicholls) *trckd ldrs in centre: hdwy 2f out: rdn to chal and edgd rt over 1f out: led ins fnl f: kpt on wl* **20/1**

/41- **2** *1/2* **Chief Editor**[160] 6676 4-8-13 **91** .... JamieSpencer 4 — 103+
(M J Wallace) *trckd ldrs in centre: headway 2f out: led 1 1/2f out and immediately hung rt: sn rdn: hdd ins fnl f: kpt on u.p* **9/4**[1]

40-0 **3** *3/4* **River Falcon**[14] 1071 8-9-1 **93** .... DanielTudhope 5 — 102
(J S Goldie) *hld up in rr: hdwy 2f out: rdn to chse ldng pair ent fnl f: kpt on u.p* **4/1**[2]

06-0 **4** *1 3/4* **Green Park (IRE)**[14] 1071 5-8-11 **89** .... PaulHanagan 12 — 95+
(R A Fahey) *hld up towards rr: hdwy whn nt clr run wl over 1f out: styd on ins fnl f: nrst fin* **6/1**[3]

200- **5** *2* **Bond City (IRE)**[175] 6327 6-8-11 **94** .... SladeO'Hara[(5)] 13 — 90
(G R Oldroyd) *chsd ldrs in centre: effrt 2f out: sn rdn and kpt on same pce appr fnl f* **15/2**

000- **6** *shd* **Fantasy Believer**[169] 6472 10-8-13 **91** .... JimmyQuinn 10 — 86
(J J Quinn) *towards rr: effrt 2f out: sn rdn and kpt on same pce appr fnl f* **12/1**

0001 **7** *1* **Canadian Danehill (IRE)**[30] 866 6-9-3 **95** .... (p) AlanMunro 6 — 87
(R M H Cowell) *cl up in centre: effrt and ev ch 2f out: sn rdn and wknd* **14/1**

00-0 **8** *4* **Cape Royal**[30] 866 8-8-9 **90** .... (bt) KevinGhunowa[(3)] 9 — 67
(J M Bradley) *racd alone stands' rail: led: rdn along and hdd 1 1/2f out: sn wknd* **20/1**

1111 **9** *3/4* **Came Back (IRE)**[17] 1023 5-8-12 **90** .... FergalLynch 11 — 64
(K A Ryan) *trckd ldrs in centre: effrt 2f out: sn rdn and wknd over 1f out* **8/1**

600- **10** *7* **Bigalos Bandit**[315] 2234 6-8-8 **86** .... AdrianTNicholls 8 — 35
(D Nicholls) *hmpd s: sn led centre gp: rdn along 2f out: sn hdd & wknd* **28/1**

61.90 secs (1.40) **Going Correction** +0.475s/f (Yiel) — **10 Ran** SP% **115.3**

Speed ratings (Par 109): **107,106,105,102,99 98,97,90,89,78**

CSF £62.88 CT £217.05 TOTE £21.20: £5.50, £1.30, £2.00; EX 85.20 Trifecta £412.20 Part won. Pool: £580.63 - 0.60 winning tickets..

Owner Jim Dale/Jason Berry **Bred** Lady Juliet Tadgell **Trained** Sessay, N Yorks

FOCUS

A good sprint handicap, and a race to take a positive view of with the first two on the up. All bar Cape Royal, who stayed tight against the near-side rail throughout, raced up the middle of the track early on, but the majority edged towards the stands' rail under pressure.

NOTEBOOK

Northern Fling was said to have run flat when failing to beat a rival in the Ayr Silver Cup on his final start last year, but he has clearly benefited from a near seven-month break and he returned to the action with a career-best effort. A rise in the weights will make things a lot tougher, but he is clearly improving and this was close to Listed class. (tchd 22-1)

Chief Editor narrowly failed to defy a 4lb rise in the weights for his success at Wolverhampton when last seen over five months previously. He edged right under pressure, but still ran on to the line and can have few excuses. He still seems to be improving, but a bit of ease in the ground would appear to be a must for him when racing on turf. (op 5-2)

River Falcon, just 1lb higher than when winning at York last August, stepped up on the form he showed over 6f here on his reappearance and this was a solid effort. (op 5-1 tchd 11-2)

Green Park(IRE) ◆ did not have much room when trying to make his move and he probably would have finished a length or two closer with a better trip. This was a big improvement on the form he showed on his reappearance, and just 1lb higher than when last winning, he appeals as one to keep on side. (op 15-2 tchd 8-1)

Bond City(IRE), without the cheekpieces, ran with credit on his return from around six months off the track. He is entitled to come on for this. Official explanation: jockey said gelding hung right (op 7-1 tchd 8-1)

Fantasy Believer was another having his first run of the year and he might improve for the outing. (op 20-1 tchd 8-1)

Came Back(IRE) Official explanation: trainer later said horse was found to be lame

1326 DONCASTER MILE STKS (LISTED RACE) 1m (R)

3:35 (3:36) (Class 1) 4-Y-O+ £17,778 (£6,723; £3,360; £1,680) Stalls High

Form RPR

61-1 **1** **Medicine Path**[69] 418 4-9-1 110 .... JamieSpencer 8 116+
(P W Chapple-Hyam) *dwlt: hld up in rr: smooth hdwy 3f out: qcknd down outer to ld ent fnl f: sn rdn and edgd lft: styd on wl* **9/2**[2]

51-1 **2** *1* **Don't Panic (IRE)**[21] 958 4-8-12 104 .... AlanMunro 7 111
(P W Chapple-Hyam) *trckd ldrs: hdwy 3f out: led 1 1/2f out: sn rdn and hdd ent fnl f: one pce* **6/4**[1]

60-3 **3** *2* **Babodana**[21] 960 8-8-12 98 .... JimmyQuinn 6 106+
(M H Tompkins) *hld up towards rr: hdwy 3f out: rdn wl over 1f out: kpt on ins fnl f: nrst fin* **22/1**

30-2 **4** *1 1/4* **Blythe Knight (IRE)**[21] 960 8-9-3 112 .... GrahamGibbons 4 108
(J J Quinn) *trckd ldrs: hdwy 3f out: effrt 2f out and sn ev ch: rdn wl over 1f out and one pce ent fnl f* **6/1**

242- **5** *5* **Tell**[161] 6655 5-8-12 110 ....(b) RHills 5 92
(J L Dunlop) *cl up: led 2f out: sn rdn and hdd 1 1/2f out: wknd* **5/1**[3]

016- **6** *9* **Smart Enough**[161] 6655 5-8-12 105 .... FergusSweeney 1 71
(M A Magnusson) *led: rdn along and hdd 2f out: sn wknd* **14/1**

4-24 **7** *2 1/4* **Dubai's Touch**[28] 906 4-9-1 107 .... JoeFanning 2 69
(M Johnston) *in tch: rdn along and lost pl over 3f out: sn bhd* **12/1**

/041 **8** *29* **Re Barolo (IRE)**[35] 834 5-8-12 105 ....(t) TedDurcan 3 —
(M Botti) *chsd ldng pair: rdn along over 3f out and sn wknd* **16/1**

1m 41.27s (0.27) **Going Correction** +0.325s/f (Good) **8** Ran SP% **113.7**
Speed ratings (Par 111): **111,110,108,106,101 92,90,61**
CSF £11.52 TOTE £6.10: £1.60, £1.20, £2.80; EX 8.20 Trifecta £139.60 Pool: £1,573.66 - 8.00 winning tickets..

Owner J C Fretwell **Bred** Jenny Hall Bloodstock Ltd **Trained** Newmarket, Suffolk

■ This race was back at Doncaster after a couple of runnings on the Polytrack at Lingfield. A 1-2 for Peter Chapple-Hyam.

FOCUS

A good renewal of the Doncaster Mile, although the early pace seemed just ordinary. Decent form for the grade, with the winner fulfilling his juvenile potential with a stylish performance and the runner-up and third close to their recent handicap form.

NOTEBOOK

Medicine Path ◆ has left Eoghan O'Neill since recording a two-length success in an ordinary Listed contest at Kempton in February, but the change of scenery would not appear to have done him any harm and he followed up in quite good style in this tougher contest. Having been held up last early on, he probably would have appreciated a stronger gallop, but he still travelled easily and picked up in decent style once pulled out with his challenge, sweeping by his new stablemate, who was in receipt of 3lb, without much hesitation. He wandered around once in front and gave the impression he was just idling a touch, so he could be considered even better than the bare form. He was unsuited by racing at around 1m2f for much of last year, but he has rediscovered his form since being returned to 1m and his form figures at this trip now read 23111, with the two defeats coming when second in the Royal Lodge and third to Authorized in the Racing Post Trophy. A conditions success late last season and two Listed wins this term show he is finally fulfilling his potential and he looks ready for a return to Group company. The Sandown Mile is now on the agenda and he should go well. (tchd 4-1 and 5-1)

Don't Panic(IRE) was seriously impressive when winning the Spring Mile off a mark of 92 on the straight course here on his reappearance, recording a time almost a second quicker than the Lincoln itself, but this provided a different test. Unlike in the big-field handicap he contested last time, the early pace was just ordinary and he raced a touch keenly without any cover on the outside of horses. He would probably have been much better off dropping in and not seeing any daylight, just as the winner was ridden, and it is to his credit he stuck on for a clear second. He seemed to be coming back at Medicine Path close home, but that one was probably just idling. He gives the impression he can do better again off a stronger pace and he could join his stablemate in the Sandown Mile, although a bit of give underfoot seems crucial. (op 13-8)

Babodana has not won since landing the 2004 Lincoln, but he showed he retains plenty of ability when third in this year's renewal on his reappearance and this was another decent effort in defeat. He deserves to win another race and might be worth another try in a conditions contest. (op 25-1)

Blythe Knight(IRE) could not confirm Lincoln form with Babodana and was a little way below his best back in fourth. (op 7-1)

Tell did not offer a great deal on his return from over five months off, but this ground might have been a little softer than he really wants. Official explanation: jockey said horse was unsuited by the soft ground (op 9-2)

Smart Enough, returning from 161 days off, set a sensible pace but weakened very tamely in the straight. (op 16-1 tchd 20-1)

Dubai's Touch has been in good form in a couple of starts on the Polytrack so far this year, including when fourth in the Winter Derby, but he was beaten at the top of the straight this time. He might want better ground, but this was still disappointing. (tchd 11-1)

Re Barolo(IRE) has won on heavy ground in Italy, so he should not have minded the conditions, but he ran really poorly and was unable to add to his success in the Lincoln Trial at Wolverhampton. (op 22-1)

1327 DONCASTER EXHIBITION CENTRE H'CAP 7f

4:10 (4:11) (Class 4) (0-80,80) 4-Y-O+ £5,180 (£1,541; £770; £384) Stalls High

Form RPR

-650 **1** **Stevie Gee (IRE)**[14] 1069 4-9-1 80 .... PJMcDonald[(3)] 8 93+
(G A Swinbank) *trckd ldrs: hdwy 2f out: rdn over 1f out: drvn and styd on ins fnl f to ld nr line* **14/1**

551- **2** *shd* **King's Bastion (IRE)**[176] 6310 4-8-11 73 .... JamieSpencer 7 86
(M L W Bell) *hld up in rr: hdwy wl over 2f out: rdn to ld over 1f out: drvn ins fnl f: edgd rt: hdd nr line* **15/2**[2]

452- **3** *3 1/2* **Charlie Tipple**[156] 6731 4-8-13 75 .... TedDurcan 3 79
(T D Easterby) *in rr: hdwy over 2f out and sn rdn: styd on u.p ins fnl f: nrst fin* **10/1**

0-21 **4** *nk* **Swinbrook (USA)**[11] 1134 7-8-11 73 ....(v) PaulHanagan 2 76
(R A Fahey) *midfield: rdn along 3f out: styd on u.p appr fnl f: nrst fin* **4/1**[1]

500- **5** *1* **Eau Good**[91] 4847 4-8-11 80 .... MarkCoumbe[(7)] 9 81
(M C Chapman) *chsd ldrs: hdwy over 2f out: rdn to ld 2f out: sn rdn and hdd over 1f out: wknd ins fnl f* **40/1**

3366 **6** *3/4* **Chjimes (IRE)**[17] 1023 4-9-4 80 .... FergusSweeney 20 79
(C R Dore) *hld up: hdwy over 2f out: swtchd lft and rdn over 1f out: styd on wl fnl f: nrst fin* **22/1**

214- **7** *1 1/4* **Society Music (IRE)**[201] 5674 6-8-11 73 .... TonyHamilton 5 68
(M Dods) *chsd ldrs: rdn along 2f out: sn drvn and kpt on same pce appr fnl f* **16/1**

6-60 **8** *1/2* **Mezuzah**[7] 1217 8-8-11 73 .... PaulMulrennan 6 67+
(M W Easterby) *hld up and bhd: n.m.r 3f out: pushed along and hdwy 2f out: styd on ins fnl f: nrst fin* **12/1**

160- **9** *2 1/2* **Neon Blue**[161] 6651 7-8-5 70 .... MichaelJStainton[(3)] 1 58
(R M Whitaker) *chsd ldrs on outer: rdn along over 2f out and grad wknd* **25/1**

0402 **10** *1 1/4* **Cornus**[14] 1069 6-9-4 80 ....(be) JamesDoyle 15 64
(A J McCabe) *chsd ldrs: rdn along over 2f out: grad wknd* **8/1**[3]

6-01 **11** *4* **Tencendur (IRE)**[10] 1138 4-9-1 77 .... AdrianTNicholls 10 51
(D Nicholls) *led: hdd over 4f out: cl up tl rdn along over 2f out and sn wknd* **10/1**

400- **12** *2 1/4* **Balakiref**[154] 6753 9-8-8 77 .... JohnCavanagh[(7)] 14 45
(M Dods) *cl up: led over 4f out: rdn along and hdd 2f out: sn wknd* **14/1**

00-4 **13** *3 1/2* **Kenmore**[14] 1069 6-8-10 72 .... TPQueally 13 31
(J G Given) *dwlt: a towards rr* **10/1**

00-4 **14** *2 3/4* **Varadouro (BRZ)**[18] 1015 6-8-7 69 .... SilvestreDeSousa 12 21
(D Nicholls) *chsd ldrs: rdn along wl over 2f out: sn drvn and wknd* **8/1**[3]

-140 **15** *hd* **Red Romeo**[14] 1069 7-8-11 80 .... SamuelDrury[(7)] 18 31
(N Wilson) *racd alone stands' side: prom: edgd across to join main gp in centre over 2f out: sn rdn and wknd* **28/1**

004- **16** *5* **Prospect Court**[161] 6639 6-8-13 78 .... AndrewMullen[(3)] 17 16
(A C Whillans) *in tch: rdn along over 2f out and sn wknd* **16/1**

1m 28.64s (2.34) **Going Correction** +0.475s/f (Yiel) **16** Ran SP% **128.1**
Speed ratings (Par 105): **105,104,100,100,99 98,97,96,93,92 87,85,81,77,77 72**
CSF £116.59 CT £1131.80 TOTE £14.60: £3.10, £2.30, £2.20, £1.80; EX 191.70 TRIFECTA Not won..

Owner Steve Gray **Bred** Irish National Stud **Trained** Melsonby, N Yorks

■ Stewards' Enquiry : Paul Hanagan one-day ban: careless riding (Apr 26)
Jamie Spencer caution: used whip down shoulder in forehand position

FOCUS

A good, competitive handicap run in a time 1.12 seconds quicker than the following three-year-old conditions contest. All bar Red Romeo, who was kept on his own against the near-side rail early on, raced up the centre of the track, although the first two home ended up against the stands' rail. Solid form, with the second and third to their marks and the winner travelling well and looking more the horse he was at two, after a disappointing second season.

Stevie Gee(IRE) Official explanation: trainer had no explanation for the apparent improvement in form

Red Romeo Official explanation: jockey said gelding was unsuited by the soft ground

1328 BAWTRY CONDITIONS STKS 7f

4:45 (4:46) (Class 2) 3-Y-O £12,952 (£3,854; £1,926; £962) Stalls High

Form RPR

10-2 **1** **Tasdeer (USA)**[28] 905 3-8-12 93 .... RHills 4 95+
(M A Jarvis) *cl up: shkn up to ld wl over 1f out: rdn clr appr fnl f: styd on strly* **1/1**[1]

104- **2** *1 3/4* **Spitfire**[168] 6488 3-9-1 99 .... EddieAhern 5 93
(J R Jenkins) *hld up: effrt and n.m.r 2f out: swtchd rt and hdwy over 1f out: rdn to chse wnr ins fnl f: kpt on* **7/2**[2]

225- **3** *1 1/4* **Silver Wind**[197] 5773 3-8-12 87 ....(v) TGMcLaughlin 2 87
(P D Evans) *hld up: pushed along and outpcd 1/2-way: hdwy 2f out: sn drvn and kpt on u.p fnl f* **9/1**[3]

0-46 **4** *5* **Kalhan Sands (IRE)**[72] 376 3-8-12 80 .... PJMcDonald 1 74
(G A Swinbank) *chsd ldrs: hdwy over 2f out: rdn wl over 1f out and sn one pce* **18/1**

50-6 **5** *1/2* **Mister Hardy**[14] 1075 3-8-12 90 .... PaulHanagan 6 72
(R A Fahey) *led: rdn along over 2f out: hdd wl over 1f out and sn wknd* **7/2**[2]

210- **6** *5* **Baronovici (IRE)**[232] 4775 3-8-12 78 .... TonyHamilton 7 59
(D W Barker) *t.k.h: prom: rdn along wl over 2f out and sn wknd* **25/1**

1m 29.76s (3.46) **Going Correction** +0.475s/f (Yiel) **6** Ran SP% **113.6**
Speed ratings (Par 104): **99,97,95,89,89 83**
CSF £4.92 TOTE £1.80: £1.10, £2.40; EX 3.70.

Owner Hamdan Al Maktoum **Bred** Shadwell Farm LLC **Trained** Newmarket, Suffolk

FOCUS

An ordinary conditions contest. The early pace was just steady and the winning time was 1.12 seconds slower than the older-horse 66-80 handicap. They all seemed happy to avoid the stands' rail, racing more towards the centre of the track throughout.

NOTEBOOK

Tasdeer(USA) confirmed the promise he showed when second on the Polytrack in the Listed Spring Cup on his reappearance with a straightforward success, despite not looking totally comfortable on the soft ground. He settled much better this time, despite the lack of pace, and found enough for pressure when asked, but his action suggests he will be better suited by a quicker surface. (tchd 10-11 and 5-4 tchd 11-8 in places)

Spitfire, a very useful juvenile over 6f last year, showed he has trained on with a good effort on his return from 168 days off. He saw this longer trip out okay, but the way he travelled suggests he will have more than enough speed to cope with a return to sprinting. (tchd 4-1)

Silver Wind, returning from 197 days off the track, looked the first beaten, needing stern reminders to stay interested, but he eventually responded to take a respectable third. This should bring him on and he might be the type to do better in big fields, although he may not be easy to place. (op 10-1 tchd 11-1)

Kalhan Sands(IRE) seemed to travel okay, but he was left behind when it mattered. He might do better on quicker ground in handicaps. (op 12-1 tchd 11-1)

Mister Hardy is another who is likely to be difficult to place this year. (op 5-1)

Baronovici(IRE), gelded since leaving Richard Hannon's yard last year, appeared to get a little warm and he was too keen for his own good in the race itself. (op 22-1)

1329 DONCASTER CONFERENCE VENUE FILLIES' H'CAP 1m 2f 60y

5:15 (5:15) (Class 4) (0-85,82) 4-Y-O+ £5,180 (£1,541; £770; £384) Stalls Low

Form RPR

510- **1** **Honorable Love**[217] 5218 4-8-8 72 .... TomEaves 4 80
(M Dods) *hld up: hdwy over 3f out: rdn to chal and ev ch 2f out: edgd lft over 1f out: drvn and styd on to ld ins fnl f* **9/1**

000- **2** *1* **She's Our Lass (IRE)**[157] 6727 7-8-7 71 .... DavidAllan 5 77
(D Carroll) *hld up: hdwy 3f out: rdn to ld wl over 1f out: drvn: hdd and no ex ins fnl f* **12/1**

236- **3** *1 ¼* **Lady Friend**[196] 5814 6-8-13 **77** .... RHills 7 81
(J W Hills) *hld up: hdwy over 2f out: sn rdn and styd on ins fnl f: nrst fin* **10/1**

/01- **4** *¾* **Valrhona (IRE)**[214] 5311 4-9-2 **80** .... TPQueally 8 83
(J Noseda) *trckd ldrs: hdwy to ld wl over 2f out: rdn: hung lft and hdd wl over 1f out: wknd ent fnl f* **7/2**[3]

026- **5** *3 ¼* **Magic Echo**[184] 6129 4-8-13 **77** .... JamieSpencer 1 73
(M Dods) *led: rdn along 3f out: sn hdd & wknd over 2f out* **9/4**[1]

6420 **6** *6* **Fusili (IRE)**[28] 908 5-9-3 **81** .... (b) JamesDoyle 2 66
(N P Littmoden) *trckd ldr: rdn along wl over 3f out and sn wknd* **8/1**

/-21 **7** *11* **Tinnarinka**[8] 1182 4-8-4 **68** .... RichardSmith 6 32
(R Hannon) *trckd ldrs: rdn along 4f out and sn wknd* **10/3**[2]

2m 16.22s (5.02) **Going Correction** +0.325s/f (Good) **7** Ran SP% **114.0**
Speed ratings (Par 102): **92,91,90,89,87 82,73**
CSF £103.72 CT £1096.73 TOTE £12.20: £4.40, £3.90; EX 72.80 TRIFECTA Not won..
Owner P Taylor **Bred** Gem Sas Di Giulia Montanari Ec **Trained** Denton, Co Durham

FOCUS
Ordinary form, but marginal improvement from the winner. The pace was good early on, but slowed rounding the final bend and the field were well bunched until about the three-furlong pole. The muddling gallop resulted in a moderate winning time. They all avoided the far rail in the straight and raced more towards the middle of the track.
Valrhona(IRE) ◆ Official explanation: jockey said filly was unsuited by the soft ground
Magic Echo Official explanation: jockey said filly ran too free early
Tinnarinka Official explanation: jockey said filly was unsuited by the soft ground

1330 DONCASTER-RACECOURSE.CO.UK MAIDEN STKS 1m 4f
5:50 (5:50) (Class 4) 3-Y-O **£4,857** (£1,445; £722; £360) **Stalls** Low

Form RPR

2-2 **1** **Fiulin**[21] 961 3-9-3 0 .... TedDurcan 6 90+
(M Botti) *hld up in tch: effrt to chse ldrs 3f out: rdn along over 2f out: hdwy to ld over 1f out and sn clr* **4/5**[1]

0-3 **2** *4* **Special Reserve (IRE)**[15] 1059 3-9-3 0 .... PatDobbs 2 83
(R Hannon) *led: rdn along over 2f out: drvn and hdd over 1f out: sn one pce* **3/1**[2]

025- **3** *3 ¼* **Full Speed (GER)**[176] 6307 3-9-0 76 .... PJMcDonald(3) 4 78
(G A Swinbank) *trckd ldr: hdwy on bit and cl up 3f out: shkn up wl over 1f out and sn one pce* **8/1**

-45 **4** *9* **Vice Consul**[15] 1059 3-9-3 0 .... JoeFanning 5 64
(M Johnston) *trckd ldng pair: hdwy and cl up 4f out: rdn along 3f out and sn wknd* **5/1**[3]

06 **5** *1 ½* **Capal Dubh Alainn (IRE)**[18] 1014 3-9-3 0 .... PaulHanagan 1 61
(T J Pitt) *hld up: effrt 4f out: sn rdn along and outpcd 3f out* **50/1**

2m 40.52s (5.42) **Going Correction** +0.325s/f (Good) **5** Ran SP% **110.3**
Speed ratings (Par 100): **94,91,89,83,82**
CSF £3.48 TOTE £1.70: £1.20, £1.80; EX 3.10 Place 6 £691.97, Place 5 £146.76.
Owner Scuderia Rencati Srl **Bred** Azienda Agricola Francesca **Trained** Newmarket, Suffolk

FOCUS
Only four counted on paper, but this was still a reasonable little maiden. The gallop was just ordinary, resulting in a modest winning time for the type of race, but the form looks sound enough, with the winner up 8lb on his reappearance effort and the runner-up improving too. The majority of these raced a little way off the far rail in the straight.
T/Plt: £376.20 to a £1 stake. Pool: £97,444.09. 189.05 winning tickets. T/Qpdt: £116.80 to a £1 stake. Pool: £5,480.20. 34.70 winning tickets. JR

1282 KEMPTON (A.W) (R-H)
Saturday, April 12

OFFICIAL GOING: Standard
The stallion Pivotal sired the winners of all three Listed races, including a 1-2 in the first of them.
Wind: Moderate, across Weather: Sunshine and heavy showers

1331 COMPARE ODDS AT ODDSCHECKER.COM SNOWDROP FILLIES' STKS (LISTED RACE) 1m (P)
2:10 (2:13) (Class 1) 4-Y-O+
£14,760 (£5,595; £2,800; £1,396; £699; £351) **Stalls** High

Form RPR

623- **1** **Heaven Sent**[189] 6009 5-8-12 106 .... RyanMoore 1 103+
(Sir Michael Stoute) *racd wd in midfield: shkn up and prog over 2f out: led over 1f out: styd on wl and drew clr fnl f* **4/6**[1]

004- **2** *2 ¼* **Chantilly Tiffany**[179] 6249 4-8-12 90 .... JimmyFortune 2 98
(E A L Dunlop) *lw: mostly trckd ldr: clsd to ld briefly wl over 1f out: chsd wnr after but outpcd fnl f* **33/1**

142- **3** *2 ¾* **Nans Joy (IRE)**[293] 2914 4-8-12 96 .... ChrisCatlin 8 92
(E J O'Neill) *led: kicked on over 3f out: rdn and hdd wl over 1f out: outpcd u.p* **12/1**[3]

200- **4** *nk* **Folly Lodge**[168] 6497 4-8-12 85 .... SteveDrowne 7 91
(G Wragg) *lw: hld up in last: outpcd over 2f out: kpt on fr over 1f out: n.d* **20/1**

110- **5** *1 ¼* **Cosmodrome (USA)**[296] 2786 4-8-12 103 .... SebSanders 3 88
(L M Cumani) *settled in midfield: rdn over 2f out: sn outpcd: fdd ins fnl f* **9/2**[2]

01-0 **6** *1* **Pelican Waters (IRE)**[21] 958 4-8-12 85 .... LPKeniry 6 86
(E F Vaughan) *disp 2nd to 3f out: wknd 2f out* **33/1**

520- **7** *9* **Our Faye**[196] 5799 5-8-12 86 .... RichardHughes 9 81
(S Kirk) *stdd s: hld up: shkn up and no prog over 2f out: eased whn btn fnl f* **14/1**

1m 39.05s (-0.75) **Going Correction** +0.10s/f (Slow) **7** Ran SP% **103.2**
Speed ratings (Par 108): **107,104,102,101,100 99,90**
CSF £24.75 TOTE £1.40: £1.10, £12.00; EX 17.80 Trifecta £157.50 Pool: £221.90 - 1.00 winning ticket..
Owner Cheveley Park Stud **Bred** Cheveley Park Stud Ltd **Trained** Newmarket, Suffolk
■ Heaven Sent was Ryan Moore's first ride in his new position as stable jockey to Sir Michael Stoute.

FOCUS
A weakish race by Listed standards, and an opportunity for black type seized upon by connections of several fillies who on previous form did not look up to this level. Heaven Sent did not have a great deal to beat and did it comfortably. The runner-up showed improved form but the next two give the race a sound look. Once Upon A Grace was withdrawn after becoming upset in the stalls (8/1, deduct 10p in the £ under Rule 4).

NOTEBOOK
Heaven Sent was making her debut on this surface but stood out on form, having improved considerably after winning a handicap off 87 early last season and ended up placed in a Group 3. Although she had to come round the outside from stall 1, she was always well enough placed and was driven out for a convincing win after leading over a furlong from home. Her stable's first winner of the year, she did not need to be at her best, but this was a pleasing reappearance from a mare whose family tend to get better with age. The Dahlia Stakes and the Princess Elizabeth are possibilities now. (tchd 8-13)
Chantilly Tiffany, making her sand debut, had plenty to find. She led briefly and ran really well, but she was at her best early on at three and is from a stable that usually has them ready first time out. (tchd 25-1)
Nans Joy(IRE), who was on her toes beforehand, looked the field's obvious front-runner, but they never let her get too far away and the writing was on the wall for her two furlongs out. (op 14-1)
Folly Lodge, making her debut for a new stable, was an impressive handicap winner first time out last year, so it was no surprise to see her go so well first time out despite her stiff task. However, having been held up in last she never threatened to challenge for any more than a place. (op 25-1)
Cosmodrome(USA), the only one in the field who had already won at this level, had been off the track since injuring herself in the Ribblesdale at Royal Ascot and was always liable to find this trip on the sharp side. (op 5-1 tchd 11-2)
Pelican Waters(IRE), who had not come in her coat, had a stiff task and dropped away after chasing the leader. (tchd 25-1)
Our Faye, edgy beforehand, was another who had it to do and was not sure to stay. She was heavily eased when beaten. (op 16-1 tchd 20-1)

1332 ODDSCHECKER.COM MASAKA STKS (LISTED RACE) (FILLIES) 1m (P)
2:45 (2:48) (Class 1) 3-Y-O
£14,760 (£5,595; £2,800; £1,396; £699; £351) **Stalls** High

Form RPR

312- **1** **Jazz Jam**[161] 6652 3-8-12 90 .... TQuinn 8 89
(P F I Cole) *lw: trckd ldrs: effrt over 2f out: prog to ld over 1f out: rdn and styd on wl* **5/1**[3]

15- **2** *½* **Comeback Queen**[161] 6652 3-8-12 89 .... MartinDwyer 5 88+
(S Kirk) *hld up in last pair: effrt over 2f out: prog over 1f out: got through fnl f and r.o to take 2nd last 50yds* **8/1**

522- **3** *½* **Madame Hoi (IRE)**[169] 6461 3-8-12 77 .... ChrisCatlin 4 87
(M R Channon) *lw: racd freely: led to over 2f out: rallied to dispute 2nd 1f out: kpt on* **14/1**

22-1 **4** *¾* **Elizabeth Swann**[28] 897 3-8-12 82 .... RichardHughes 1 85
(R Hannon) *t.k.h: hld up in last trio: prog on outer over 2f out: rdn to chal over 1f out: nt qckn: one pce fnl f* **12/1**

04-1 **5** *1 ¼* **Frivolous (IRE)**[15] 1050 3-8-12 85 .... JimmyFortune 3 82
(J H M Gosden) *lw: trckd ldr: led over 2f out: rdn and hdd over 1f out: wknd ins fnl f* **10/1**

-632 **6** *hd* **Love Of Dubai (USA)**[44] 744 3-8-12 0 .... RyanMoore 9 84+
(C E Brittain) *hld up in midfield: rdn to chse ldrs over 1f out: wl hld whn squeezed out last 100yds* **5/2**[1]

31- **7** *¾* **Jeninsky (USA)**[182] 6177 3-8-12 84 .... SebSanders 2 83+
(P J McBride) *sn restrained in last: nt clr run on inner wl over 1f out and swtchd: shkn up ins fnl f: r.o: nvr nr ldrs* **14/1**

021- **8** *1 ½* **Honky Tonk Sally**[196] 5801 3-8-12 86 .... HayleyTurner 10 76
(M L W Bell) *taken down early: hld up in midfield on inner: rdn over 2f out: wknd over 1f out* **16/1**

055- **9** *1 ¼* **Kay Es Jay (FR)**[175] 6336 3-8-12 99 .... MichaelHills 7 74
(B W Hills) *t.k.h: trckd ldrs on outer: rdn to chal over 2f out: wknd over 1f out* **11/4**[2]

1m 40.28s (0.48) **Going Correction** +0.10s/f (Slow) **9** Ran SP% **119.0**
Speed ratings (Par 103): **101,100,100,99,98 97,97,95,94**
CSF £45.97 TOTE £4.90: £2.10, £2.80, £3.30; EX 37.00 Trifecta £324.30 Part won. Pool: £456.80 - 0.70 winning tickets..
Owner Faisal Salman **Bred** Belgrave Bloodstock Ltd **Trained** Whatcombe, Oxon
■ Stewards' Enquiry : Martin Dwyer three-day ban; careless riding (April 26-28)

FOCUS
A race that seldom has much bearing on the Classics, and although three of these had entries, only one was in the 1,000 Guineas. The pace was only steady, and in a bunch finish the winning time was well over a second slower than that recorded by the older fillies half an hour earlier. The form is rated around the front pair and does not look up to much.

NOTEBOOK
Jazz Jam won her nursery off only 72, but a subsequent Listed second over this trip gave her a chance and she represented a stable that has made a blinding start to the turf season. There were plenty with chances 2f out, but once she got to the front she was always going to win. The Premio Regina Elena (Italian 1000 Guineas) is on the agenda now. (op 7-2 tchd 10-3)
Comeback Queen, fifth in the Listed race at Newmarket in which the winner was second, has an Oaks entry, which suggested that 1m round here would be sharp enough unless they went very quick, which they didn't. Held up in rear, she had to weave her way through the pack and gave Love Of Dubai a bump before running on strongly to close the winner down inside the final furlong. She is going to be very well suited by further. (op 12-1 tchd 16-1)
Madame Hoi(IRE) is still a maiden, but Irish Classic entries suggested she is well regarded and she made a pleasing sand debut. While she admittedly had the run of the race and was allowed to dictate her own pace, she kept on well when headed. (op 16-1)
Elizabeth Swann had not needed to run to her best when a maiden winner here last month, and this was more in line with her juvenile form. She looked dangerous on the outside halfway up the straight. (op 10-1 tchd 8-1)
Frivolous(IRE), another who had already won round here this year, was reluctant to go in the stalls but got to the front briefly in the straight and seemed to run her race. (op 9-1)
Love Of Dubai(USA), who had good form in Dubai, would have been a bit closer but for being squeezed up between Comeback Queen and Elizabeth Swann inside the final furlong. (op 3-1)
Jeninsky(USA) landed a 6f auction maiden here on the second of her two runs as a juvenile. She ran better than her finishing position suggests, for she was going on well at the finish, with something left in the tank, having been held up last in a slowly run race and then denied a run when trying to nose up the inner at the intersection. (op 16-1 tchd 12-1)
Kay Es Jay(FR), who was dropped in class for this seasonal return, was very disappointing, having been quite keen early on. (op 7-2 tchd 4-1)

1333 ODDSCHECKER.COM EASTER STKS (LISTED RACE) (C&G) 1m (P)
3:20 (3:20) (Class 1) 3-Y-O
£14,760 (£5,595; £2,800; £1,396; £699; £351) **Stalls** High

Form RPR

616- **1** **Il Warrd (IRE)**[255] 4057 3-8-12 95 .... MartinDwyer 3 108+
(M P Tregoning) *lw: disp ld tl def advantage over 3f out: shkn up 2f out: drew away fnl f* **13/2**[3]

036- **2** *4 ½* **Gaspar Van Wittel (USA)**[190] 5974 3-8-12 99 .... SebSanders 5 98
(S A Callaghan) *hld up: rdn and prog to chse ldng pair over 1f out: no ch w wnr but kpt on to take 2nd last 100yds* **7/2**[2]

122- **3** *nk* **Latin Lad**[173] 6382 3-8-12 100 .... RichardHughes 7 97
(R Hannon) *disp ld to over 3f out: chsd wnr after: no ch ent fnl f: lost 2nd last 100yds* **7/4**[1]

415- **4** *3 1/4* **Fool's Wildcat (USA)**[190] 5972 3-8-12 93 .... (b) JimmyFortune 8 90
(B J Meehan) *hld up: effrt on inner over 2f out: no imp on ldrs over 1f out: wl outpcd after* **16/1**

-135 **5** *1/2* **Geezers Colours**[7] 1213 3-8-12 92 .... AndrewElliott 6 89
(K R Burke) *lw: trckd ldrs: rdn 2f out: sn no prog: fdd ins fnl f* **12/1**

61- **6** *1* **Speedy Dollar (USA)**[169] 6468 3-8-12 90 .... PhilipRobinson 2 86
(M A Jarvis) *bit bkwd: racd wd: in tch: lost pl and btn over 2f out: plugged on* **7/2**[2]

16-2 **7** *3 1/2* **Last Of The Line**[15] 1057 3-8-12 75 .... SteveDrowne 4 78
(H J L Dunlop) *a in last pair: struggling over 2f out* **40/1**

044- **8** *6* **Eastern Gift**[134] 6974 3-8-12 90 .... RyanMoore 1 65
(R Hannon) *racd wd: w ldrs to over 3f out: sn wknd and bhd* **16/1**

1m 38.56s (-1.24) **Going Correction** +0.10s/f (Slow) **8** Ran SP% **116.0**
Speed ratings (Par 106): **110,105,105,101,101 100,96,90**
CSF £29.98 TOTE £7.70: £2.30, £1.80, £1.40; EX 26.80 Trifecta £38.20 Pool: £419.80 - 7.80 winning tickets..
Owner Sheikh Ahmed Al Maktoum **Bred** Castleton Group **Trained** Lambourn, Berks

FOCUS
A respectable winning time, even for a race like this, and the fastest of the four races over the trip at the meeting. This looked the strongest of the card's three Listed races over the trip. Il Warrd impressed and can rate higher.

NOTEBOOK
Il Warrd(IRE) ◆ impressed at Ascot last year before running too keen and finishing down the field in the Group 2 Vintage Stakes at Goodwood. A 2000 Guineas and Dante entry, he was to the fore throughout and forged well clear in the final furlong to win impressively, from the two market leaders, which suggests the form should be all right. He was said to be Marcus Tregoning's best juvenile last year and Goodwood was simply too bad to be true. Only his stable's second runner of the year, he won in a style which suggests he is worth his chance in the Guineas, but Tregoning is wary of running him on quick ground and he is more likely to run in the French version. (op 9-2)
Gaspar Van Wittel(USA) was more patiently ridden over this longer trip. He took second from Latin Lad near the finish, but he was not closing on the winner. Probably a decent run nevertheless, for Latin Lad was the form choice and the pair were both clear of the rest. (op 4-1)
Latin Lad was a good second in two similar races last year and represented a stable with a terrific record in this race, but he is by strong middle-distance influence Hernando and is entered in the Derby, which suggested he would find 1m on the sharp side this year. He went with the winner at the head of affairs but was unsurprisingly outspeeded in the straight. A step up in trip looks in order now. (op 9-4 tchd 5-2 in places)
Fool's Wildcat(USA), upped in trip for this reappearance, reverted to hold-up tactics and just got the better of Geezers Colours for fourth. (op 20-1)
Geezers Colours ran a little below the level to which he has been performing at Lingfield this spring. (tchd 14-1)
Speedy Dollar(USA), who looked the part but was not sure to get this longer distance, saw plenty of daylight from his outside draw and ended up well held. (tchd 4-1)
Eastern Gift, the Hannon second string looked fit enough beforehand for this seasonal reappearance. He does not seem to act on Polytrack. (op 25-1)

1334 ODDSCHECKER.COM CASINO AND POKER H'CAP 7f (P)
3:55 (3:56) (Class 2) (0-100,97) 4-Y-0+
£9,969 (£2,985; £1,492; £747; £372; £187) **Stalls** High

Form RPR

42-0 **1** **Vitznau (IRE)**[21] 960 4-9-4 97 .... RichardHughes 5 108+
(R Hannon) *lw: hld up bhd ldrs: clsd smoothly fr wl over 1f out to dispute ld ent fnl f: rdn to assert last 100yds* **3/1**[1]

30-0 **2** *1/2* **Esteem Machine (USA)**[28] 907 4-8-8 87 .... RyanMoore 8 96
(R A Teal) *lw: stdd s: hld up towards rr: shkn up and gd prog fr 2f out: disp ld ent fnl f: jst outpcd nr fin* **10/1**

-003 **3** *1/2* **Resplendent Nova**[21] 969 6-8-5 84 .... ChrisCatlin 10 92
(P Howling) *b: chsd clr ldr: clsd to ld over 2f out: hdd ent fnl f: battled on but hld last 100yds* **9/2**[2]

324- **4** *2 1/2* **Presumptive (IRE)**[196] 5797 8-9-3 96 .... SteveDrowne 6 97+
(R Charlton) *stdd s: hld up in last and wl off the pce: prog and swtchd several times fr 2f out: one reminder over 1f out: styd on to take 4th nr fin: do bttr* **6/1**

030- **5** *1 1/4* **Hazzard County (USA)**[161] 6654 4-8-8 87 .... RichardMullen 9 85
(D M Simcock) *bit bkwd: trckd ldrs: disp 2nd 3f out: sn nt qckn: renewed effrt to press ldrs over 1f out: wknd ins fnl f* **15/2**

-006 **6** *1 3/4* **Red Cape (FR)**[11] 1133 5-9-0 93 .... (p) SebSanders 4 86
(Mrs R A Carr) *hld up in rr: effrt over 2f out: cajoled along and plugged on one pce: n.d* **25/1**

3331 **7** *1 1/4* **Monkey Glas (IRE)**[16] 1045 4-9-2 95 .... (v) AndrewElliott 7 85
(K R Burke) *led at str pce and sn clr: hdd over 2f out: wknd fnl f* **11/2**[3]

/20- **8** *3* **Mr Garston**[324] 1962 5-8-3 85 .... WilliamBuick(3) 2 67
(J R Boyle) *a wl in rr: struggling fr 3f out* **14/1**

0-03 **9** *11* **Party Boss**[11] 1133 6-9-3 96 .... JimmyFortune 1 48
(C E Brittain) *nvr beyond midfield: struggling 3f out: wknd and t.o* **9/1**

000- **10** *2* **El Bosque (IRE)**[212] 5355 4-9-2 95 .... DarryllHolland 3 42
(B R Millman) *stmbld s: sn chsd ldrs: wknd rapidly over 2f out: t.o* **16/1**

1m 25.0s (-1.00) **Going Correction** +0.10s/f (Slow) **10** Ran SP% **120.1**
Speed ratings (Par 109): **109,108,107,105,103 101,100,96,84,81**
CSF £35.55 CT £140.84 TOTE £3.50: £2.00, £3.00, £1.80; EX 41.20 Trifecta £372.70 Part won. Pool: £525.00 - 0.70 winning tickets..
Owner Louis Stalder **Bred** John McLoughlin **Trained** East Everleigh, Wilts

FOCUS
No hanging around here, but the pace rather collapsed turning in. Vitznau continues to progress and this form looks pretty solid.

NOTEBOOK
Vitznau(IRE) was ideally suited by the strong pace. Much improved last year following two Polytrack seconds off much lower marks, he was clearly going best approaching the 2f marker but Richard Hughes hung on to him until launching him between horses approaching the furlong marker. It was a three-way battle through the final furlong, but Hughes always looked to have matters in hand and the colt won a shade comfortably without him getting at all serious. He is better at this trip than the 1m of the Lincoln and he has done all his winning on a turning track, although he has decent form at Newmarket. The Victoria Cup would seem an obvious target, although it wasn't mentioned. (tchd 5-2 and 10-3)
Esteem Machine(USA), slightly on his toes beforehand, was all the better for last month's pipe-opener over 5f. He came from the rear but got there in plenty of time, and this was a good effort in defeat. (op 14-1 tchd 16-1)
Resplendent Nova back to form here last time, ran another excellent race. He chased clear leader Monkey Glas until taking it up over 2f out, and he battled hard when headed. (op 13-2)
Presumptive(IRE) ◆, who had not come in his coat, was running off his highest ever mark at the age of eight, but shaped really well in fourth, coming much too late after being held up in last place. The Victoria Cup is reportedly his target again (his bridle broke at the start last year) and while he will be vulnerable to less exposed runners he ought to give a good account of himself, having run two cracking races over the course and distance in 2007. (op 5-1 tchd 15-2)
Hazzard County(USA), having his first run here but proven on the Polytrack at Lingfield, made a more than satisfactory reappearance in fifth. (op 10-1)
Red Cape(FR) is nicely treated nowadays but not running particularly well. (op 20-1)
Monkey Glas(IRE) is probably too high in the handicap now, but he was never going to be able to maintain such a strong pace in any case. (op 5-1)

1335 COMPARE POKER/CASINO ROOMS AT ODDSCHECKER.COM H'CAP (LONDON MILE QUALIFIER) 1m (P)
4:30 (4:31) (Class 4) (0-85,87) 4-Y-0+ **£4,209** (£1,252; £625; £312) **Stalls** High

Form RPR

414- **1** **Cape Hawk (IRE)**[217] 5221 4-9-4 85 .... RichardHughes 16 102+
(R Hannon) *w ldr: led over 2f out: swtchd to rail over 1f out: sn qcknd clr: comf* **15/8**[1]

164- **2** *1 1/2* **Nice To Know (FR)**[140] 6929 4-8-9 76 .... RyanMoore 15 89+
(G L Moore) *trckd ldrs on inner: drvn to chal whn hmpd by wnr over 1f out: kpt on to take 2nd again 1f out: no real ch* **12/1**

3-52 **3** *2 1/2* **Dichoh**[28] 910 5-9-1 82 .... (v[1]) PhilipRobinson 14 87
(M A Jarvis) *lw: dwlt: t.k.h and sn trckd ldrs: effrt 2f out: disp 2nd 1f out: fdd nr fin* **8/1**[3]

040- **4** *3/4* **Danski**[138] 6949 5-8-13 80 .... SebSanders 2 83
(P J Makin) *pressed ldng pair: rdn over 2f out: outpcd fr over 1f out: kpt on* **25/1**

060- **5** *nk* **Cross The Line (IRE)**[171] 6437 6-9-4 85 .... RichardMullen 9 88+
(A P Jarvis) *hld up in midfield: shkn up 2f out: styd on fnl f: nrst fin* **22/1**

314- **6** *1 1/4* **Rambling Light**[276] 3420 4-8-9 79 .... WilliamBuick(3) 1 79
(A M Balding) *racd on outer: wl in tch: cl enough 2f out: sn outpcd u.p: fdd nr fin* **12/1**

0054 **7** *1/2* **Councellor (FR)**[7] 1211 6-9-6 87 .... (t) MickyFenton 12 86
(Stef Liddiard) *mde most to over 2f out: wknd fnl f* **14/1**

610- **8** *1* **Mount Hermon (IRE)**[197] 5768 4-8-11 78 .... SteveDrowne 4 74
(H Morrison) *trckd ldrs: u.p over 2f out: lost pl sn after: n.d over 1f out* **14/1**

612- **9** *nk* **Pendulum Star**[161] 6646 4-8-12 79 .... (t) DarryllHolland 7 75
(W R Swinburn) *hld up in last trio: rdn and kpt on same pce fnl 2f: no ch* **8/1**[3]

000- **10** *1 1/4* **Fiefdom (IRE)**[118] 7165 6-8-11 78 .... JimCrowley 3 71
(I W McInnes) *lw: hld up wl in rr: sme prog fr 2f out: no hdwy 1f out: fdd* **33/1**

00-0 **11** *nse* **Bold Marc (IRE)**[7] 1217 6-8-11 78 .... AndrewElliott 8 71
(K R Burke) *hld up wl in rr: rdn and no significant hdwy fnl 2f* **33/1**

35-0 **12** *hd* **Mcnairobi**[21] 969 5-8-13 80 .... JimmyFortune 11 72
(P D Cundell) *dwlt: t.k.h: hld up in midfield: no imp on ldrs over 1f out: fdd fnl f* **6/1**[2]

5-04 **13** *1* **Master Pegasus**[60] 531 5-8-13 80 .... IanMongan 10 70+
(C F Wall) *hld up in last trio: prog on inner whn nt clr run over 1f out: no ch after* **25/1**

5201 **14** *8* **Bee Stinger**[15] 1065 6-9-1 82 .... (p) RobertWinston 6 53
(I A Wood) *hld up in rr: rdn over 3f out: sn struggling* **20/1**

2351 **15** *6* **Dudley Docker (IRE)**[28] 910 6-8-13 80 .... (b) LiamJones 5 38
(C R Dore) *dwlt: plld hrd in rr: rapid prog on wd outside over 3f out: wknd rapidly over 2f out* **20/1**

1m 39.74s (-0.06) **Going Correction** +0.10s/f (Slow) **15** Ran SP% **127.5**
Speed ratings (Par 105): **104,102,100,99,98 97,97,96,95,94 94,94,93,85,79**
CSF £24.50 CT £149.39 TOTE £2.60: £1.50, £4.10, £3.60; EX 38.30.
Owner Thurloe Thoroughbreds XVII **Bred** John And Leslie Young **Trained** East Everleigh, Wilts

FOCUS
The pace was not that strong for the size of the field, and although these were decent handicappers the time was only the third best of four races over the trip. It paid to race handily, and none of the first four came from far back. The first two are progressive.
Pendulum Star Official explanation: jockey said filly was bumped on bend
Dudley Docker(IRE) Official explanation: jockey said gelding ran too free

1336 ODDSCHECKER.COM - THE ODDS COMPARISON SITE H'CAP 7f (P)
5:05 (5:05) (Class 4) (0-85,84) 3-Y-O **£4,209** (£1,252; £625; £312) **Stalls** High

Form RPR

561- **1** **Meydan Princess (IRE)**[180] 6228 3-8-12 78 .... RyanMoore 4 89+
(J Noseda) *hld up in last: rapid prog on outer fr 2f out: drvn to ld last 100yds: r.o wl* **5/1**[3]

30-2 **2** *1 1/4* **Wigram's Turn (USA)**[21] 967 3-8-13 82 .... WilliamBuick(3) 1 87
(A M Balding) *lw: trckd ldrs: prog to ld 2f out: rdn and styd on fr over 1f out: hdd and outpcd last 100yds* **15/8**[1]

532- **3** *3* **Bailey (IRE)**[191] 5937 3-8-13 79 .... RobertWinston 6 76
(B J Meehan) *hld up in last trio: effrt on outer over 2f out: nt qckn over 1f out: kpt on to snatch 3rd last stride* **9/1**

2301 **4** *nse* **Miss Mujanna**[28] 899 3-8-8 74 .... ChrisCatlin 10 71
(J Akehurst) *hld up towards rr: prog on inner 2f out: nt pce to trble ldng pair 1f out: lost 3rd last stride* **10/1**

100- **5** *1 1/2* **King's Icon (IRE)**[252] 4152 3-9-1 81 .... MartinDwyer 2 74
(M P Tregoning) *prom: rdn to dispute 2nd briefly wl over 1f out: sn outpcd and btn* **8/1**

204- **6** *nk* **Farthermost (IRE)**[232] 4764 3-8-8 74 .... RichardHughes 8 66
(R Hannon) *wnt lft s: hld up in midfield: swtchd lft 2f out: nt clr run sn after: no prog* **4/1**[2]

14-0 **7** *2* **Lady Sorcerer**[21] 966 3-8-10 76 .... RichardMullen 9 63
(A P Jarvis) *trckd ldrs: rdn and grad wknd fr 2f out* **40/1**

4140 **8** *nk* **Southwest Star (IRE)**[21] 967 3-8-6 72 ow1 .... LPKeniry 7 58
(J S Moore) *dwlt: wl in rr: hmpd 2f out: no ch after* **16/1**

-560 **9** *1 1/4* **Gross Prophet**[14] 1075 3-8-11 84 .... DavidProbert(7) 5 66
(Tom Dascombe) *drvn in rr sn after 1/2-way: struggling after* **25/1**

310- **10** *2 1/2* **Feisty Royale**[168] 6486 3-9-2 82 .... GregFairley 3 58
(M Johnston) *mde most to 2f out: wknd rapidly* **16/1**

1m 26.54s (0.54) **Going Correction** +0.10s/f (Slow) **10** Ran SP% **119.7**
Speed ratings (Par 100): **100,98,95,95,93 93,90,90,88,86**
CSF £15.17 CT £86.21 TOTE £6.20: £1.80, £1.60, £2.20; EX 16.50.
Owner Franconson Partners **Bred** J Costello **Trained** Newmarket, Suffolk
■ Stewards' Enquiry : Greg Fairley caution: used whip with arm above shoulder height

FOCUS
The winning time was much slower than for the earlier older-horse 7f race, but this was not a bad contest, and the pair that finished clear both look well ahead of the handicapper. Sound form, the winner value for a bit extra.

1337 FIND THE BEST ODDS AT ODDSCHECKER.COM H'CAP — 2m (P)
5:35 (5:36) (Class 4) (0-85,81) 4-Y-0+ **£4,209** (£1,252; £625; £312) **Stalls** High

Form — RPR

/10- **1** **Gala Evening**[49] 1794 6-9-11 **77** .... RichardHughes 2 — 92+
(J A B Old) *hld up in midfield: prog to go 2nd jst over 2f out: clsd to ld 1f out gng easily: pushed clr* **20/1**

-115 **2** 3 1/4 **Legend Erry (IRE)**[80] 268 4-9-9 **79** .... JohnEgan 6 — 87
(Jane Chapple-Hyam) *trckd ldng trio: prog on outer to ld wl over 2f out and kicked on: styd on but hdd and outpcd 1f out* **8/1**[3]

-042 **3** 8 **Featherlight**[15] 1052 4-8-12 **68** ....(b) RobertHavlin 4 — 66
(Jamie Poulton) *rdr lost an iron briefly after s: hld up in rr: effrt but outpcd over 2f out: wnt modest 3rd over 1f out* **11/1**

1636 **4** nk **Mister Completely (IRE)**[15] 1052 7-9-1 **67** ....(v) GeorgeBaker 5 — 65
(Ms J S Doyle) *stdd s: hld up in last: outpcd over 2f out: plugged on* **22/1**

-131 **5** 1 3/4 **Coda Agency**[15] 1052 5-8-6 **58** oh1 .... JimCrowley 3 — 54
(D W P Arbuthnot) *lw: led to wl over 2f out: wknd wl over 1f out* **2/1**[2]

200- **6** 1/2 **Dhehdaah**[29] 6473 7-9-6 **72** .... MickyFenton 7 — 67
(Mrs P Sly) *hld up in midfield: effrt on inner over 2f out: sn outpcd and btn* **22/1**

3225 **7** 9 **Lorikeet**[15] 1052 9-9-2 **68** .... RyanMoore 1 — 53
(G L Moore) *trckd ldr to over 3f out: wknd over 2f out* **12/1**

120- **8** 1 **Irish Quest (IRE)**[191] 5955 4-9-11 **81** .... PhilipRobinson 8 — 64
(M A Jarvis) *lw: trckd ldng pair: shkn up wl over 2f out: lost pl and wknd tamely* **1/1**[1]

3m 27.1s (-3.00) **Going Correction** +0.10s/f (Slow)
WFA 4 from 5yo+ 4lb — **8** Ran SP% **123.9**
Speed ratings (Par 105): **111,109,105,105,104 104,99,99**
CSF £176.56 CT £1871.76 TOTE £25.20: £5.30, £2.40, £2.30; EX 385.40 Place 6 £22.62, Place 5 £15.76.
Owner W E Sturt **Bred** Juddmonte Farms **Trained** Barbury Castle, Wilts

FOCUS
A decent winning time for the grade, although it was the only truly run race on the card. Sound form, the first pair finishing clear and the winner value for a bit extra.
Irish Quest(IRE) Official explanation: jockey said colt became very tired
T/Plt: £24.70 to a £1 stake. Pool: £100,706.01. 2,975.29 winning tickets. T/Qpdt: £7.50 to a £1 stake. Pool: £3,998.40. 390.20 winning tickets. JN

1310 WOLVERHAMPTON (A.W) (L-H)
Saturday, April 12

OFFICIAL GOING: Standard
Wind: modest behind Weather: bright partly cloudy

1338 BOOK TICKETS ONLINE H'CAP — 5f 216y(P)
6:50 (6:51) (Class 6) (0-60,60) 4-Y-0+ **£2,266** (£674; £337; £168) **Stalls** Low

Form — RPR

500- **1** **Jun Fan (USA)**[227] 4939 6-8-4 **46** oh1 .... RoystonFfrench 4 — 61
(B Ellison) *chsd ldng trio: wnt 2nd travelling wl over 2f out: led wl over 1f out: sn clr: easily* **20/1**

2053 **2** 2 3/4 **Chatshow (USA)**[19] 994 7-8-11 **60** .... MarkCoumbe(7) 8 — 66+
(A W Carroll) *hld up towards rr: hdwy over 3f out: rdn wl over 1f out: r.o to chse wnr fnl f: nvr able to chal* **8/1**[3]

5033 **3** 4 1/2 **Wicked Uncle**[15] 1061 9-8-10 **57** ....(v) JamieJones(5) 12 — 49
(S Gollings) *sn outpcd in rr: styd on u.p fr over 1f out: wnt 3rd nr fin: nvr nr ldrs* **8/1**[3]

04-0 **4** 3/4 **Rapid Flow**[17] 1029 6-8-5 **47** .... SimonWhitworth 7 — 36
(J W Unett) *off the pce in midfield: hdwy over 3f out: chsd ldng pair wl over 1f out: no imp u.p after* **16/1**

1426 **5** 1 **Avontuur (FR)**[8] 1191 6-8-7 **56** ....(p) MCGeran(7) 5 — 42
(Mrs R A Carr) *s.i.s: wl bhd tl styd on fr over 1f out: n.d* **9/2**[2]

0330 **6** 3/4 **Mambazo**[29] 875 6-9-1 **60** ....(e) LukeMorris(3) 1 — 44
(S C Williams) *disp ld tl led over 3f out: rdn over 2f out: hdd wl over 1f out: wknd fnl f* **4/1**[1]

3060 **7** 3/4 **Stormburst (IRE)**[24] 933 4-8-4 **53** ow3 .... WilliamCarson(7) 10 — 34
(A J Chamberlain) *off the pce in midfield: hdwy over 3f out: short of room briefly over 2f out: sn rdn and no hdwy* **28/1**

00-0 **8** 6 **Wilford Maverick (IRE)**[72] 365 6-8-4 **46** oh1 .... PaulEddery 3 — 8
(Garry Moss) *s.i.s: a struggling towards rr* **66/1**

00- **9** 1 1/4 **Law Maker**[217] 5234 8-9-4 **60** ....(v) NeilChalmers 13 — 18
(A Bailey) *a bhd: n.d* **33/1**

0-00 **10** 4 1/2 **Stir Crazy (IRE)**[37] 806 4-8-7 **49** .... JimmyQuinn 11 — —
(D W Barker) *off the pce in midfield: rdn and hdwy on outer over 3f otu: no hdwy fr 2f out* **14/1**

4333 **11** 1/2 **Owed**[17] 1024 6-9-2 **58** ....(tp) PatCosgrave 2 — —
(R Bastiman) *disp ld tl over 3f out: sn rdn: wknd qckly 2f out: eased ins fnl f* **4/1**[1]

2104 **12** 1 1/2 **Tenancy (IRE)**[23] 951 4-8-6 **48** ....(be) NeilPollard 9 — —
(A J McCabe) *pressed ldrs tl over 3f out: sn wknd* **11/1**

0400 **13** 53 **Mister Always**[10] 1135 4-8-0 **49** ow2 ....(b) DonnaCaldwell(7) 6 — —
(I W McInnes) *s.i.s: sn detached in last: t.o* **9/1**

1m 14.76s (-0.24) **Going Correction** +0.10s/f (Slow) — **13** Ran SP% **123.9**
Speed ratings (Par 101): **105,101,95,94,93 92,91,83,81,75 74,72,2**
CSF £173.73 CT £1459.25 TOTE £27.00: £10.90, £3.20, £3.90; EX 425.10.
Owner The Lucky Magpies **Bred** Pacific Heritage Farms Llc **Trained** Norton, N Yorks

FOCUS
A big field, but a routine Wolverhampton sprint handicap full of the usual suspects. A three-way battle for the early lead ensured there was plenty of pace on though, which took its toll on those that set it, and the winning time was not bad at all. Jun Fan is rated back to something like his best.
Avontuur(FR) Official explanation: jockey said gelding missed the break

1339 HOTEL AND CONFERENCING CLAIMING STKS — 5f 216y(P)
7:20 (7:21) (Class 6) 3-Y-0 **£2,266** (£674; £337; £168) **Stalls** Low

Form — RPR

06-2 **1** **Honey Monster (IRE)**[7] 1204 3-8-13 **70** .... SCreighton(5) 3 — 79
(Miss V Haigh) *hld up in last pair: hedaway 3f out: led jst ins fnl f: sn clr: readily* **7/2**[3]

3331 **2** 3 1/2 **Ballycroy Boy (IRE)**[51] 635 3-8-13 **75** .... NeilChalmers 4 — 63
(A Bailey) *w ldr tl rdn to ld 2f out: hdd jst ins fnl f: sn outpcd by wnr* **15/8**[2]

-060 **3** 6 **Hero Heart**[11] 1124 3-8-9 **47** .... TGMcLaughlin 2 — 40
(Jane Chapple-Hyam) *led tl rdn and hdd 2f out: wknd over 1f out* **33/1**

1111 **4** 3 **Dhhamaan (IRE)**[7] 1203 3-9-7 **80** ....(b) SebSanders 6 — 42
(Mrs R A Carr) *chsd ldrs on outer: rdn 1/2-way: wknd 2f out: sn wl btn* **11/10**[1]

030- **5** 18 **Little Angel (IRE)**[301] 2663 3-8-4 **53** .... EdwardCreighton 5 — —
(Miss V Haigh) *in tch in rr: rdn over 3f out: sn wknd: t.o* **66/1**

1m 15.29s (0.29) **Going Correction** +0.10s/f (Slow) — **5** Ran SP% **109.1**
Speed ratings (Par 96): **102,97,89,85,61**
CSF £10.28 TOTE £5.50: £1.80, £1.10; EX 12.50.The winner was claimed by A J McCabe for £15,000.
Owner R J Budge **Bred** Michael O'Mahony **Trained** Wiseton, Notts

FOCUS
Not a bad little claimer on paper with the favourite rated 80 and the pace was sound. They finished very well spread out and the form is tricky to rate with the favourite disappointing, although the winner showed improvement.
Dhhamaan(IRE) Official explanation: trainer said, regarding running, that the colt was unsuited by the 6f trip.

1340 WOLVERHAMPTON-RACECOURSE.CO.UK H'CAP — 1m 5f 194y(P)
7:50 (7:50) (Class 5) (0-75,75) 4-Y-0+ **£2,590** (£770; £385; £192) **Stalls** Low

Form — RPR

2444 **1** **Wind Flow**[9] 1165 4-8-10 **62** .... JimmyQuinn 3 — 71
(C A Dwyer) *hld up in tch: rdn to chse ldr over 3f out: led over 1f out: hdd last 100yds: rallied gamely to ld again on post* **2/1**[1]

435- **2** shd **Strong Survivor (USA)**[115] 6314 5-9-1 **64** .... SebSanders 5 — 73
(P R Webber) *s.i.s: hld up in last: rdn and hdwy over 3f out: swtchd to inner 2f out: ev ch 1f out: led last 100yds tl hdd on post* **10/3**[3]

-660 **3** 6 **Bazart**[35] 838 6-9-12 **75** .... FergusSweeney 6 — 76
(K R Burke) *t.k.h: chsd ldr tl led 5f out: rdn over 2f out: hdd over 1f out: outpcd fnl f* **10/1**

26-0 **4** 3 1/2 **Cotton Eyed Joe (IRE)**[20] 981 7-9-5 **68** .... RobertWinston 4 — 64
(G A Swinbank) *hld up in tch: rdn and hdwy over 3f out: wknd 2f out* **9/4**[2]

110- **5** 7 **Merrymaker**[126] 7081 8-9-11 **74** .... TGMcLaughlin 1 — 60
(W M Brisbourne) *hld up in last pair: rdn wl over 3f out: outpcd 3f out: no ch after* **13/2**

0-00 **6** 21 **Hugs Destiny (IRE)**[10] 1137 7-8-4 **56** oh6 ....(t) LukeMorris(3) 2 — 13
(M A Barnes) *t.k.h: led at stdy pce tl qcknd 8f out: rdn and hdd 5f out: wknd 3f out: t.o and eased ins fnl f* **22/1**

3m 7.84s (1.84) **Going Correction** +0.10s/f (Slow)
WFA 4 from 5yo+ 3lb — **6** Ran SP% **114.0**
Speed ratings (Par 103): **98,97,94,92,88 76**
CSF £9.30 TOTE £2.50: £2.00, £1.70; EX 9.10.
Owner Super Six Partnership **Bred** Lord Halifax **Trained** Burrough Green, Cambs
■ Stewards' Enquiry : Jimmy Quinn caution: used whip with excessive frequency

FOCUS
The pace on the first circuit was very slow and although things quickened up significantly on the second, the winning time was still ordinary. This was therefore by no means the test of stamina it might have been, but despite that the front pair still came from off the pace. Pretty weak form, with only marginal improvement from the first pair.

1341 STAY AT THE WOLVERHAMPTON HOLIDAY INN MAIDEN STKS — 5f 20y(P)
8:20 (8:21) (Class 5) 2-Y-0 **£2,590** (£770; £385; £192) **Stalls** Low

Form — RPR

5 **1** **Grand Honour (IRE)**[14] 1078 2-9-3 **0** .... JimmyQuinn 2 — 71+
(P Howling) *chsd ldrs: rdn 1/2-way: chsd ldr wl over 1f out: led last 100yds: r.o strly* **5/2**[2]

5 **2** 2 1/4 **Dedante**[12] 1111 2-8-12 **0** .... SebSanders 3 — 57+
(D K Ivory) *led: rdn wl over 1f out: hdd and no ex last 100yds* **16/1**

5 **3** 1 1/2 **Dotty's Brother**[7] 1220 2-9-3 **0** .... RoystonFfrench 4 — 56
(Mrs A Duffield) *sn chsd ldr: rdn wl over 2f out: lost 2nd wl over 1f out: onepced fnl f* **12/1**[3]

2 **4** nk **Sub Prime (IRE)**[14] 1078 2-9-3 **0** .... TPQueally 1 — 55
(J A Osborne) *bhd: rdn wl over 3f out: hdwy on outer 1/2-way: hung rt u.p 1f out: onepced after* **8/13**[1]

5 8 **Kuwinda** 2-8-12 **0** .... EdwardCreighton 5 — 18
(M R Channon) *in tch in rr on outer: rdn wl over 2f out: sn struggling and bhd* **16/1**

63.40 secs (1.10) **Going Correction** +0.10s/f (Slow) — **5** Ran SP% **109.9**
Speed ratings (Par 92): **95,91,89,88,75**
CSF £32.86 TOTE £2.90: £1.10, £3.30; EX 56.50.
Owner Ajaz Ahmed **Bred** Mrs E Kent **Trained** Newmarket, Suffolk

FOCUS
An ordinary maiden and not form to go overboard about.

NOTEBOOK
Grand Honour(IRE), who shaped with promise when involved in a bunch finish at Kempton on his debut, ran out a clear-cut winner in the end. With the favourite disappointing there is a question mark over the value of the form, but he is going the right way and shaped as though he will stay another furlong in time. His trainer has a conditions race at Ascot in mind for him next. (op 9-4 tchd 2-1)
Dedante shaped better than her finishing position suggests on her debut when greenness was her undoing, but she had clearly benefited from that run and tried to make every yard here. Showing great speed from the gate, she was only worn down inside the last. (op 22-1 tchd 25-1)
Dotty's Brother probably did not achieve any more than on his debut, but he might be of interest in a modest race on the Fibresand as his sire has a better record there than on Polytrack. (op 10-1 tchd 14-1)
Sub Prime(IRE), who finished ahead of Grand Honour in the bunch finish at Kempton a fortnight earlier, was well backed but proved disappointing. He was not the quickest away, hung right on the bend and simply failed to land a blow. A return to Kempton might help him. (op 5-6)
Kuwinda, a sister to 7f juvenile winner Mwindaji, out of a high-class sprinter, was the only newcomer in the field, and she was too green to do herself justice on her debut. (op 10-1)

1342 SPONSOR A RACE BY CALLING 01902-390009 MEDIAN AUCTION MAIDEN STKS — 1m 1f 103y(P)
8:50 (8:50) (Class 5) 3-5-Y-0 **£2,590** (£770; £385; £192) **Stalls** Low

Form — RPR

0-25 **1** **Pentathlon (IRE)**[18] 1014 3-8-11 **71** .... JoeFanning 3 — 78
(M Johnston) *mde all: rdn clr 2f out: in n.d fnl f: eased towards fin* **9/4**[2]

33- **2** 5 **Top Ticket (IRE)**[179] 6248 3-8-11 **0** .... RichardMullen 1 — 69
(D M Simcock) *in tch: rdn over 3f out: chsd wnr wl over 1f out: no imp* **6/5**[1]

600- **3** 1 1/2 **Nikolaievich (IRE)**[194] 5858 3-8-11 **69** .... NelsonDeSouza 2 — 64
(P F I Cole) *in tch in rr: rdn over 3f out: hung rt bnd 3f out: plugged on into modest 3rd ins fnl f* **15/2**

334- **4** 2 1/4 **Stop On**[212] 5344 3-8-11 **76** .... EdwardCreighton 4 — 60
(M R Channon) *in tch: chsd wnr 3f out: outpcd 2f out: wknd over 1f out* **7/2**[3]

0-00 **5** *7* **Ticking**[38] [804] 5-9-7 35 .... AshleyMorgan(7) 5 49+
(T Keddy) *chsd wnr tl 3f out: wknd 2f out: eased ins fnl f* **200/1**

2m 3.51s (1.81) **Going Correction** +0.10s/f (Slow)
WFA 3 from 5yo 17lb 5 Ran SP% **110.7**
Speed ratings (Par 103): **95,90,89,87,81**
CSF £5.40 TOTE £2.70: £2.20, £1.40; EX 6.40.
Owner Sheikh Hamdan Bin Mohammed Al Maktoum **Bred** Gainsborough Stud Management Ltd **Trained** Middleham Moor, N Yorks

FOCUS
The winner dictated a modest pace and even the lowly rated fifth was still in touch turning into the straight. The race has been rated through the third.
Stop On Official explanation: vet said gelding finished distressed

1343 DINE IN HORIZONS H'CAP 1m 1f 103y(P)
9:20 (9:20) (Class 6) (0-60,59) 3-Y-O **£2,266** (£674; £337; £168) **Stalls** Low

Form RPR

56-6 **1** **Chanteuse De Rue (IRE)**[12] [1115] 3-8-8 **49** .... JoeFanning 8 51
(M Johnston) *chsd ldrs tl led over 7f out: mde rest: rdn over 2f out: styd on gamely* **14/1**

0-00 **2** *¾* **Art Exhibition (IRE)**[43] [748] 3-9-2 **57** .... SebSanders 7 57
(J Noseda) *hld up in tch: hdwy 5f out: chsd ldr and drvn over 2f out: kpt on u.p fnl f: wnt 2nd towards fin: nt pce to chal wnr* **3/1**[2]

0-64 **3** *shd* **Arniecoco**[15] [1054] 3-9-4 **59** .... TPQueally 3 59+
(Miss J R Gibney) *bmpd s: hld up in rr: hdwy on outer bnd over 3f out: kpt on u.p fr over 1f out: wnt 3rd nr fin* **7/1**[3]

035 **4** *nk* **Thankuforthemusic (IRE)**[15] [1054] 3-9-4 **59** .... FergusSweeney 4 58
(C Tinkler) *chsd ldrs: rdn and effrt 3f out: kpt on u.p fnl f* **10/1**

00-2 **5** *¾* **Supporting Role (IRE)**[21] [976] 3-9-3 **58** .... RichardMullen 6 56
(E S McMahon) *chsd ldrs: wnt 2nd 6f out: rdn over 2f out: unable qck under presssure over 1f out: fdd towards fin* **5/4**[1]

50-5 **6** *1 ½* **Zaplamation (IRE)**[19] [998] 3-8-4 **45** .... JimmyQuinn 5 40
(D W Barker) *t.k.h: hld up towards rr: hdwy over 4f out: rdn and no imp over 2f out* **8/1**

000- **7** *4 ½* **Jevington Star (IRE)**[207] [5498] 3-8-4 **45** .... RoystonFfrench 1 30
(B Ellison) *wnt rt s: chsd ldr for 2f: lost pl 6f out: rdn and struggling over 3f out: no ch last 2f* **16/1**

00-4 **8** *10* **Moss Way**[23] [950] 3-8-4 **45** .... NeilPollard 9 9
(W J Musson) *t.k.h: sn led: hdd over 7f out: rdn and lost pl 4f out: wl bhd last 2f: t.o* **22/1**

2m 4.33s (2.63) **Going Correction** +0.10s/f (Slow) 8 Ran SP% **119.0**
Speed ratings (Par 96): **92,91,91,90,90 88,84,76**
CSF £58.29 CT £332.17 TOTE £12.40: £3.70, £1.70, £2.80; EX 84.80 Place 6 £153.56, Place 5 £31.98..
Owner J S Morrison **Bred** Mark Johnston Racing Ltd **Trained** Middleham Moor, N Yorks

FOCUS
A weak handicap and a moderate winning time for the type of race, 0.82sec slower than the previous maiden, which was dominated at a steady pace throughout. It has been rated around the third and fourth.
Chanteuse De Rue(IRE) Official explanation: trainer's rep said, regarding the apparent improvement in form, that filly may have benefited from front-running.
T/Plt: £170.00 to a £1 stake. Pool: £82,179.15. 352.75 winning tickets. T/Qpdt: £31.30 to a £1 stake. Pool: £6,752.00. 159.30 winning tickets. SP

BRIGHTON (L-H)
Sunday, April 13

OFFICIAL GOING: Good to soft (good in places; 7.0)
Wind: Virtually nil Weather: bright partly cloudy

1344 WHOLE LOTTA RACIN' GOIN' ON MEDIAN AUCTION MAIDEN STKS 7f 214y
2:10 (2:11) (Class 5) 3-4-Y-O **£2,914** (£867; £433; £216) **Stalls** Low

Form RPR

1 **The Galloping Shoe** 3-8-9 0 .... SebSanders 1 80+
(J Noseda) *chsd ldrs tl wnt 2nd over 4f out: rdn and ev ch over 2f out: led 1f out: drew clr last 100yds: styd on wl* **1/1**[1]

2 *4* **Lady Longcroft** 3-8-4 0 .... ChrisCatlin 2 61
(J Pearce) *t.k.h: in tch: hdwy on outer 3f out: rdn and outpcd 2f out: kpt on fnl f to go 2nd wl ins fnl f: nvr trbld wnr* **33/1**

03-2 **3** *1* **North South Divide (IRE)**[95] [95] 4-9-10 73 .... GeorgeBaker 3 68
(R A Teal) *chsd ldr after 2f: led over 4f out: rdn over 1f out: hdd 1f out: fdd last 100yds* **9/4**[2]

4 *2 ¾* **Zaarmit (IRE)** 3-8-9 0 .... RichardMullen 5 58
(D M Simcock) *t.k.h: chsd ldr for 2f: styd in tch: rdn over 2f out: rn green and no hdwy after* **12/1**

5 *hd* **Benhego** 3-8-9 0 .... SaleemGolam 4 57
(S C Williams) *s.i.s: bhd: rdn over 3f out: kpt on fnl f: nvr nr ldrs* **33/1**

51 **6** *3 ½* **Kitto Katsu**[30] [878] 4-9-5 0 .... JimmyQuinn 6 48
(D J Coakley) *t.k.h: led for 2f: chsd ldrs after: rdn 2f out: wknd jst over 1f out* **9/2**[3]

1m 39.37s (3.37) **Going Correction** +0.45s/f (Yiel)
WFA 3 from 4yo 15lb 6 Ran SP% **112.5**
Speed ratings (Par 103): **101,97,96,93,93 89**
CSF £34.67 TOTE £2.00: £1.60, £6.70; EX 21.20.
Owner Arashan Ali **Bred** Wood Hall Stud Limited **Trained** Newmarket, Suffolk

FOCUS
An ordinary maiden run in a time 0.82 seconds slower than the following 65-70 handicap. Little previous form to go on, with the third perhaps the best guide.

1345 GREGGI G'S CRAZY GG'S H'CAP 7f 214y
2:40 (2:40) (Class 5) (0-70,70) 4-Y-O+ **£2,590** (£770; £385; £192) **Stalls** Low

Form RPR

4256 **1** **Steig (IRE)**[16] [1048] 5-9-0 66 .... JamesDoyle 5 74
(Carl Llewellyn) *chsd ldr: rdn to ld narrowly 2f out: forged ahd towards fin* **15/2**

500- **2** *¾* **Winning Show**[188] [6070] 4-8-4 56 .... MartinDwyer 1 62
(A M Balding) *stmbld s: sn led: rdn over 2f out: narrowly hdd 2f out: no ex last 50yds* **11/4**[1]

615- **3** *1 ½* **Support Fund (IRE)**[171] [6447] 4-8-12 64 .... StephenCarson 7 67
(Eve Johnson Houghton) *racd in midfield: rdn over 3f out: chsd ldng pair over 2f out: kpt on u.p fnl f: nt rch ldng pair* **9/2**[3]

5-00 **4** *hd* **The Dagger**[3] [1280] 4-8-6 58 .... RichardMullen 6 61
(G L Moore) *hld up in rr: angled out and hdwy 2f out: kpt on steadily fnl f: nt rch ldrs* **20/1**

2231 **5** *1* **Millfield (IRE)**[16] [1058] 5-9-4 70 .... JimCrowley 8 70
(P R Chamings) *taken down early: stdd s: t.k.h: hld up in midfield: rdn and effrt over 2f out: kpt on same pce u.p fnl f* **7/2**[2]

-663 **6** *1 ¾* **Hansomelle (IRE)**[6] [1109] 6-8-10 62 .... (p) NeilChalmers 3 58
(Miss Sheena West) *s.i.s: a bhd: rdn and effrt on outer over 2f out: no real hdwy* **9/1**

4525 **7** *4 ½* **Seneschal**[16] [1058] 7-9-1 67 .... TPQueally 4 53
(A B Haynes) *chsd ldrs: rdn over 2f out: hung lft and wknd fnl f: eased towards fin* **10/1**

4-66 **8** *3 ¼* **Thermidor (USA)**[16] [1058] 5-8-11 63 .... (p) SebSanders 2 41
(Lady Herries) *hld up in last pair: rdn and effrt 3f out: no hdwy: eased towards fin* **6/1**

1m 38.55s (2.55) **Going Correction** +0.45s/f (Yiel) 8 Ran SP% **117.0**
Speed ratings (Par 103): **105,104,102,102,101 99,95,92**
CSF £29.18 CT £106.38 TOTE £8.50: £2.70, £1.40, £2.10; EX 37.80 Trifecta £224.10 Pool: £315.64, 1.00 w/u.
Owner Something In The City 2 **Bred** Elisabeth And Neil Draper **Trained** Upper Lambourn, Berks

FOCUS
A modest handicap run in a time 0.82 seconds quicker than the opening maiden. The winner is rated back to something like his 3yo Irish form.
Thermidor(USA) Official explanation: trainer later said gelding had not been suited by the tacky ground

1346 JUKEBOX SHOWDOWN H'CAP 5f 213y
3:10 (3:10) (Class 2) (0-105,99) 4-Y-O **£9,969** (£2,985; £1,492; £747; £372) **Stalls** Low

Form RPR

000- **1** **Bentong (IRE)**[253] [4150] 5-9-4 99 .... TQuinn 6 108
(P F I Cole) *chsd ldr: ev ch 2f out: rdn to ld jst over 1f out: forged ahd last 50yds* **2/1**[1]

13-3 **2** *1 ½* **Angus Newz**[11] [1157] 5-8-8 89 .... (v) ChrisCatlin 5 93
(M Quinn) *led: rdn 2f out: hdd jst over 1f out: no ex last 50yds* **5/2**[2]

003- **3** *3 ¾* **Woodcote (IRE)**[230] [4886] 6-8-7 88 .... (b) PaulDoe 1 80
(P R Chamings) *taken down early: s.i.s: t.k.h: trckd ldng pair: plld out and rdn over 1f out: kpt on same pce* **9/2**[3]

3323 **4** *4 ½* **Sand Cat**[30] [887] 5-8-4 85 .... (b) RichardMullen 4 63
(G L Moore) *hld up in tch: hdwy on outer 3f out: rdn over 2f out: wknd fnl f* **6/1**

1024 **5** *4* **Ajigolo**[15] [1079] 5-9-1 96 .... DarryllHolland 2 61
(M R Channon) *taken down early: hld up in tch: rdn over 2f out: no imp: eased ins fnl f* **5/1**

1m 11.98s (1.78) **Going Correction** +0.45s/f (Yiel) 5 Ran SP% **111.0**
Speed ratings (Par 109): **106,104,99,93,87**
CSF £7.35 TOTE £2.60: £1.40, £1.90; EX 8.20.
Owner H R H Sultan Ahmad Shah **Bred** J Egan, J Corcoran And J Judd **Trained** Whatcombe, Oxon

FOCUS
A disappointing turnout numerically for the grade and the form is ordinary, rated through the runner-up. Only the first two showed anything like their form.

NOTEBOOK
Bentong(IRE) had a disappointing season last year, but he had the tongue-tie left off for his first start in 253 days, so whatever was troubling him last year has presumably been ironed out, and he took this in workmanlike fashion. He took a while to see off the persistent challenge of Angus Newz, but was well on top at the line. Things will be tougher from now on, but he has always promised to progress into a smart sort and is back on track now. (op 9-4 tchd 5-2 and 15-8)
Angus Newz, a good third in a conditions contest at Nottingham on her reappearance, stuck on well when headed by Bentong and finished a clear second. (op 9-4 tchd 3-1)
Woodcote(IRE), without the eye-shields on his first start since leaving Clive Cox, did not help his chances by racing keenly, but this was his first start in 230 days and it will have to be hoped this takes the freshness out of him. (op 5-1)
Sand Cat, back on turf, made his move widest of all and he struggled to land a blow. (op 9-2 tchd 13-2)
Ajigolo ran no sort of race on his first start at Brighton and the track might not have suited. (op 7-1 tchd 9-2)

1347 FANTASTIC FIFTIES FURLONGS MEDIAN AUCTION MAIDEN STKS 5f 213y
3:40 (3:40) (Class 5) 3-4-Y-O **£2,914** (£867; £433; £216) **Stalls** Low

Form RPR

0- **1** **Restless Genius (IRE)**[272] [3592] 3-9-1 0 .... (t) MartinDwyer 7 78+
(A M Balding) *stdd s: t.k.h: sn in midfield: hdwy to ld jst over 1f out: briefly edgd lft: sn clr: readily* **9/1**[3]

53 **2** *3 ¼* **Espy**[10] [1162] 3-9-1 0 .... SebSanders 6 68
(S Kirk) *stdd s: hld up in last: hdwy 3f out: nt clr run briefly jst over 1f out: chsd wnr ins fnl f: nt threaten wnr* **15/8**[2]

00-2 **3** *1 ¾* **Pha Mai Blue**[8] [1215] 3-9-1 78 .... RichardKingscote 4 62
(W J Knight) *chsd ldr untl led 2f out: sn rdn: hdd jst over 1f out: edgd lft ins fnl f: sn outpcd* **4/5**[1]

00-3 **4** *1 ¾* **Midnite Blews (IRE)**[12] [1123] 3-9-1 63 .... DavidKinsella 5 58+
(A B Haynes) *led tl hdd 2f out: unbalanced and btn jst over 1f out* **16/1**

4430 **5** *2 ¾* **Shabnaam**[16] [1051] 3-8-10 50 .... JimmyQuinn 3 43
(P Howling) *in tch tl lost pl over 2f out: no ch last 2f* **20/1**

0000 **6** *4* **Joe Rich**[10] [1162] 4-9-10 40 .... (p) JerryO'Dwyer(3) 8 38
(Mrs L C Jewell) *in tch on outer tl lost pl 3f out: bhd last 2f* **66/1**

1m 12.56s (2.36) **Going Correction** +0.45s/f (Yiel)
WFA 3 from 4yo 12lb 6 Ran SP% **112.5**
Speed ratings (Par 103): **102,97,95,93,89 84**
CSF £26.49 TOTE £10.80: £3.40, £1.50; EX 21.40 Trifecta £36.50 Pool: £268.79, 5.22 w/u.
Owner Favourites Racing IV **Bred** Sunland Holdings Sc **Trained** Kingsclere, Hants

FOCUS
An ordinary maiden. The favourite disappointed and the form is weak behind the placed horses.
Pha Mai Blue Official explanation: trainer said colt was unsuited by the good to soft (good in places) ground
Midnite Blews(IRE) Official explanation: jockey said gelding hung right

1348 KINGS GOLDEN DISC DERBY H'CAP 1m 1f 209y
4:10 (4:10) (Class 3) (0-95,89) 3-Y-O **£6,938** (£2,076; £1,038; £519) **Stalls** High

Form RPR

1-1 **1** **Captain Webb**[10] [1171] 3-9-4 86 .... JoeFanning 5 103+
(M Johnston) *hld up in 3rd: hdwy to ld 4f out: clr 2f out: eased ins fnl f: v easily* **4/9**[1]

100- **2** *20* **Maximus Aurelius (IRE)**[181] [6233] 3-8-2 73 .... LukeMorris(3) 2 48
(J Jay) *chsd ldr tl 4f out: chsd wnr after: rdn and outpcd over 2f out: no ch after: jst hld on for 2nd* **20/1**

00-2 **3** *hd* **Kayflaa (IRE)**[17] [1042] 3-8-3 71 .... EdwardCreighton 1 46
(M R Channon) *hld up in last: rdn over 3f out: sn wl outpcd: plugged on and nrly snatched 2nd* **9/1**[3]

521- 4 34 **Benhavis**177 6307 3-9-0 82 ....(t) SebSanders 3 —
(J L Dunlop) *led tl 4f out: rdn and wknd 3f out: t.o and eased ins fnl f* **3/1**2

2m 5.17s (1.57) **Going Correction** +0.45s/f (Yiel) **4** Ran SP% **109.0**
Speed ratings (Par 102): **111,95,94,67**
CSF £9.79 TOTE £1.40; EX 9.10.
Owner Sheikh Hamdan Bin Mohammed Al Maktoum **Bred** Gainsborough Stud Management Ltd **Trained** Middleham Moor, N Yorks

FOCUS
He might not have beaten much, but Captain Webb could hardly have won any easier, and he recorded a fine time in the process, 1.90 seconds quicker than the following 61-75 older-horse handicap, and 2.75 seconds faster than the closing 0-55 classified event. He might have won by further and looks a smart prospect.

NOTEBOOK
Captain Webb ♦, a winner here on his only start at two and successful on his reappearance off a mark of 78 over this trip at Leicester, made it three from three in terrific style. His main danger according to the market, Benhavis, ran below form, but he fairly bolted up, recording a very good time in the process, and it is hard not to get carried away. The 1m2f three-year-old handicap at Epsom on Derby day looks made for him, but that race is not until June and it might be handicaps are off the agenda by then. If that's the case, it would be no surprise to see him take his chance in a Derby Trial and the Blue Riband at Nottingham would be an option, but considering he has already proven himself on an undulating track, races such as the Dee Stakes and the Lingfield Derby Trial could be suitable targets. This imposing son of Storming Home still has to prove himself on quicker ground, however. (op 8-15)
Maximus Aurelius(IRE), trying his furthest trip to date off the back of a six-month break, won the separate race for second but, with Benhavis running below form, he probably didn't achieve a great deal. (op 12-1)
Kayflaa(IRE) just missed second on her handicap debut but she was still beaten a mile. (op 7-1)
Benhavis managed to get off the mark at Redcar on his final start at two, but he ran no sort of race on his return to action. (op 7-2)

1349 CHANTILLY RACE H'CAP — 1m 1f 209y
4:40 (4:40) (Class 5) (0-75,75) 4-Y-0+ **£2,590** (£770; £385; £192) **Stalls** High

Form RPR

650- 1 **Harvest Joy (IRE)**207 5539 4-8-13 70 .... JimCrowley 5 79
(J Gallagher) *s.i.s: racd in last: hdwy 4f out: rdn over 2f out: chsd ldr wl over 1f out: led last 100yds: sn clr* **12/1**

6014 2 4½ **Prime Number (IRE)**26 927 6-9-0 71 .... TPQueally 6 71
(J Akehurst) *chsd ldrs: wnt 2nd over 3f out: led 2f out: sn rdn: hdd last 100yds: sn btn* **11/8**1

/002 3 21 **Arturius (IRE)**27 914 6-8-10 70 ....(p) KevinGhunowa(3) 1 28
(R A Harris) *sn led and clr: rdn and hdd 2f out: sn wknd* **5/1**3

140- 4 5 **The Flying Cowboy (IRE)**181 6235 4-8-9 66 .... TGMcLaughlin 4 14
(Jane Chapple-Hyam) *chsd ldr tl over 3f out: sn rdn and btn: t.o* **9/4**2

100- 5 32 **Sonny Parkin**172 6439 6-8-11 75 ....(v) JosephineBruning(7) 3 —
(J Pearce) *t.k.h: hld up in tch: rdn 4f out: wknd over 3f out: virtually p.u ins fnl f* **8/1**

2m 7.07s (3.47) **Going Correction** +0.45s/f (Yiel) **5** Ran SP% **108.3**
Speed ratings (Par 103): **104,100,83,79,54**
CSF £28.38 TOTE £11.20: £4.00, £1.40; EX 22.70.
Owner R S Jeffery **Bred** John Hutchinson **Trained** Moreton-in-Marsh, Gloucs

FOCUS
A weak race for the grade, the form best rated around the runner-up. The winning time was 1.90 seconds slower than the 76-95 three-year-old handicap, but 0.85 seconds faster than the closing 0-55 classified event.
Arturius(IRE) Official explanation: jockey said gelding ran too free early

1350 KOMEDIA BRIGHTON CLASSIFIED STKS — 1m 1f 209y
5:10 (5:12) (Class 6) 3-Y-0+ **£1,683** (£501; £250; £125) **Stalls** High

Form RPR

0-42 1 **Gunnadoit (USA)**11 1147 3-8-11 61 .... HayleyTurner 4 62
(M L W Bell) *hld up in last pair: pushed along and hdwy over 4f out: drvn to chse ldng pair over 2f out: styd on u.p to ld towards fin* **8/11**1

0-50 2 1¼ **Floodlight Fantasy**35 468 5-9-10 46 ....(b) JimCrowley 6 57
(Dr R D P Newland) *chsd ldr tl over 6f out and again over 3f out: rdn and hung rt wl over 1f out: led ins fnl f: sn hdd and no ex* **16/1**

060- 3 1½ **Fairly Honest**206 5557 4-9-10 52 .... ChrisCatlin 2 54
(P W Hiatt) *led: rdn over 1f out: hdd ins fnl f: wknd towards fin* **7/1**3

0400 4 5 **Bollywood (IRE)**6 415 5-9-10 42 .... SebSanders 1 44
(J J Bridger) *in tch: lost pl over 3f out: swtchd rt and rdn over 2f out: no hdwy* **20/1**

6605 5 4 **Mtoto Girl**8 1210 4-9-10 45 .... NeilChalmers 8 36
(J J Bridger) *hld up in rr: rdn over 3f out: no prog* **33/1**

605- 6 5 **Rock Haven (IRE)**171 6452 6-9-10 51 .... TGMcLaughlin 5 26
(W M Brisbourne) *stdd s: t.k.h: hld up in tch: rdn wl over 2f out: sn btn* **5/1**2

0014 7 16 **Paul The Carpet (UAE)**41 784 3-8-5 47 ....(b) SimonWhitworth 7 —
(G L Moore) *t.k.h: chsd ldr over 6f out tl over 3f out: sn wknd: eased ins fnl f: t.o* **7/1**3

2m 7.92s (4.32) **Going Correction** +0.45s/f (Yiel)
WFA 3 from 4yo+ 19lb **7** Ran SP% **113.2**
Speed ratings (Par 101): **100,99,97,93,90 86,73**
CSF £14.50 TOTE £1.60: £1.30, £5.50; EX 17.20 Trifecta £63.70 Pool: £422.58, 4.71 w/u, Place 6 £ 17.49, Place 5 £ 9.51.
Owner One Carat Partnership **Bred** Harry McCalmont,Hugo Lascelles, & Angus Gold **Trained** Newmarket, Suffolk

FOCUS
A moderate contest and the form is rated around the third. The winning time was 2.75 seconds slower than the 76-95 three-year-old handicap, and 0.85 seconds slower than the older-horse 61-75 handicap.
T/Plt: £49.60 to a £1 stake. Pool: £60,281.23. 886.95 winning tickets. T/Qpdt: £6.80 to a £1 stake. Pool: £3,061.31. 329.00 winning tickets. SP

1351 - 1352a (Foreign Racing) - See Raceform Interactive

1101 CURRAGH (R-H)
Sunday, April 13

OFFICIAL GOING: Round course - soft; straight course - heavy

1353a ASCON ROHCON ALLEGED STKS (LISTED RACE) — 1m 2f
3:15 (3:17) 4-Y-0+ **£23,933** (£7,022; £3,345; £1,139)

RPR

1 **Red Moloney (USA)**29 906 4-9-4 110 .... DPMcDonogh 7 109+
(Kevin Prendergast, Ire) *mod 3rd: tk clsr order appr st: travelling best 2f out: qckn d to ld 1f out: sn clr: kpt on u.p cl home* **9/2**3

2 1¼ **Alarazi (IRE)**14 1105 4-9-1 104 .... MJKinane 3 104
(John M Oxx, Ire) *mod 4th: clsr 5th and rdn 2f out: no imp tl styd on wl ins fnl f* **5/2**2

3 shd **Profound Beauty (IRE)**273 3576 4-8-12 106 .... PJSmullen 5 101
(D K Weld, Ire) *mod 2nd: tk clsr order appr st: rdn 2f out: kpt on ins fnl f* **13/2**

4 nk **Deauville Vision (IRE)**14 1104 5-9-1 107 .... RPCleary 8 103
(M Halford, Ire) *mod 5th: prog on inner early st: 2nd and chal under 1 1/2f out: 3rd under 1f out: kpt on* **7/1**

5 3 **Arkadina (IRE)**238 4649 4-8-12 91 .... WMLordan 6 95
(David Wachman, Ire) *hld up: 6th st: rdn and kpt on fr 2f out* **25/1**

6 4½ **Baron De'L (IRE)**175 6367 5-9-1 94 ....(b) FMBerry 4 90
(Edward P Harty, Ire) *led and clr: reduced advantage appr st: sn rdn: hdd 1f out: no ex and wknd* **20/1**

7 4½ **Macarthur**211 5408 4-9-1 112 .... JMurtagh 1 82
(A P O'Brien, Ire) *hld up: 7th st: no imp fr 2f out* **9/4**1

8 4 **Mooretown Lady (IRE)**149 6843 5-8-12 99 .... CDHayes 2 72
(H Rogers, Ire) *a in rr* **25/1**

2m 31.82s (22.32) **Going Correction** +2.55s/f (Heav) **8** Ran SP% **115.8**
Speed ratings: **112,111,110,109,109 107,103,100**
CSF £15.99 TOTE £6.60: £1.80, £1.50, £1.90; DF 18.90.
Owner Norman Ormiston **Bred** Linda Clough **Trained** Friarstown, Co Kildare

FOCUS
Ordinary Listed form rated through the runner-up and fifth.

NOTEBOOK
Red Moloney(USA) was recording a fifth career success, and a third at Listed level. He had run poorly in the Winter Derby at Lingfield on his previous start but was happier back on home soil and ground out a gutsy victory. He has won on fast ground, and on the Polytrack at Dundalk, but he seems to handle soft ground well and, as he is adaptable trip-wise, there will be plenty of options for him without having to travel. Official explanation: trainer said, regarding the improvement in form, gelding did not act on the track at Lingfield (polytrack) and did not travel well to the UK (op 4/1)
Alarazi(IRE) needs testing conditions and, following his run in the Irish Lincoln in which he finished well for fourth, he was stepping up in trip and grade here. He stayed on steadily for pressure over the last two furlongs and was again doing his best work in the closing stages, getting up to snatch second in the last couple of strides. (op 5/2 tchd 9/4)
Profound Beauty(IRE), making her first appearance since finishing fifth in the Irish Oaks in July, raced in second for most of the journey and tired somewhat only in the closing stages. She should come on for the run and do better on quicker ground. (op 6/1 tchd 7/1)
Deauville Vision(IRE), tackling this trip for only the second time, had finished third in a Group 3 event over 1m here on her reappearance last month. Another suited by the ground conditions, she went second under two furlongs out and had every chance before finding no extra in the closing stages. She probably gets the trip but gives the impression that a bit shorter suits her better. (op 13/2)
Macarthur, who failed to win in four attempts last year, finished sixth in the St Leger at Doncaster on his final outing last season. He never counted at any stage here and, while he is obviously capable of better, the ground was no help to his cause. (op 2/1 tchd 11/4)

1355a CASTLEMARTIN & LA LOUVIERE STUDS GLADNESS STKS (GROUP 3) — 7f
4:15 (4:16) 4-Y-0+ **£33,455** (£9,779; £4,632; £1,544)

RPR

1 **Jumbajukiba**190 6009 5-9-3 111 ....(b) FMBerry 3 115
(Mrs John Harrington, Ire) *mde all: rdn clr over 1f out: styd on wl ins fnl f: comf* **12/1**

2 3½ **Major Cadeaux**252 4214 4-9-3 .... RichardHughes 8 109
(R Hannon) *trckd ldrs in 3rd: mod 2nd and rdn under 1 1/2f out: no imp: kpt on u.p* **9/4**2

3 ¾ **US Ranger (USA)**190 6029 4-9-0 114 .... JMurtagh 7 101+
(A P O'Brien, Ire) *trckd ldrs: 5th 1/2-way: prog into mod 4th over 1f out: kpt on* **4/5**1

4 1¾ **Crooked Throw (IRE)**14 1105 9-9-0 109 .... WJLee 2 96
(C F Swan, Ire) *hld up towards rr: 8th 1/2-way: styd on fr over 1f out* **16/1**

5 1¾ **Captain Marvelous (IRE)**176 6332 4-9-0 .... MichaelHills 9 92
(B W Hills) *trckd ldrs: 4th 1/2-way: rdn over 2f out: kpt on same pce* **20/1**

6 4 **Lady Grace (IRE)**22 959 4-8-11 .... MJKinane 6 78
(W J Haggas) *trckd ldr in 2nd: rdn 2f out: no imp: wknd fr over 1f out* **16/1**

7 3½ **Excelerate (IRE)**161 6681 5-9-0 107 .... CDHayes 5 71+
(Edward Lynam, Ire) *a towards rr* **33/1**

8 1¾ **Grecian Dancer**101 35 5-8-11 100 .... PJSmullen 1 64+
(Charles O'Brien, Ire) *hld up: 6th 2f out: sn no ex* **25/1**

9 dist **Honoured Guest (IRE)**336 1703 4-9-0 114 .... JAHeffernan 4 63+
(A P O'Brien, Ire) *hld up: 6th and rdn 1/2-way: sn wknd: t.o* **10/1**3

1m 36.61s (9.51) **Going Correction** +1.70s/f (Heav) **9** Ran SP% **126.4**
Speed ratings: **113,109,105,104,102 100,95,91,89**
CSF £42.40 TOTE £10.80: £1.80, £1.70, £1.30; DF 30.50.
Owner J P O'Flaherty **Bred** Woodcote Stud Ltd **Trained** Moone, Co Kildare

FOCUS
The winner was flattered by the way the race was run and as a result the race has been rated through the sixth.

NOTEBOOK
Jumbajukiba, who was successful at this level of competition over 1m on good ground at this track last season, is well suited by plenty of give, and the decision to make all with him over this shorter trip paid off handsomely. He was quite keen early on, but was about three lengths clear at halfway and, from two furlongs out, he never looked in real danger, although he did appear to tire a bit in the closing stages. He apparently has bad joints so will be kept away from firm ground.
Major Cadeaux, successful at this level over the same trip in the Greenham Stakes at Newbury a year ago, subsequently finished sixth in the 2000 Guineas and fourth in a Group 1 over 1m at Deauville. This was his first start since that French race and he performed well, disputing second for much of the journey and keeping on best of the rest, without troubling the winner, in the closing stages.
US Ranger(USA), a smart performer with four wins in France to his credit, ran second in the Jersey Stakes in June before joining Aidan O'Brien, for whom he won a 6f Listed event here. Fourth in the Prix de la Foret on his final start last season, he could never get in a serious challenge on this reappearance, and made little impression after going fourth well over a furlong out. (op 10/11 tchd 1/1)
Crooked Throw(IRE), raised 7lb to a rating of 109 for his Irish Lincoln win here last month, ran on quite well in the closing stages, having been one of the backmarkers for most of the journey. The run was good enough to warrant another try in this type of event or at Listed level.
Captain Marvelous(IRE), a Group 2 winner over 6f in France as a two-year-old, failed to win last season. Soon chasing the leaders, he could make no real impression from under two furlongs out. (op 16/1)
Lady Grace(IRE), who finished in mid-division in the Cammidge Trophy last time out, probably ran to a similar level in defeat here. She will be of more interest when back racing against her own sex.

Honoured Guest(IRE), off the track since finishing third in the Poule d'Essai des Poulains a year ago, was being ridden along at halfway and was never in contention. His rider reported that his mount made a respiratory noise in running. Official explanation: jockey said colt made a respiratory noise in running (op 8/1)

1356a BANK OF IRELAND LOUGHBROWN STKS (LISTED RACE) 7f

4:45 (4:45) 3-Y-O **£23,933** (£7,022; £3,345; £1,139)

RPR

1 **Georgebernardshaw (IRE)**[14] 1102 3-9-1 93 JMurtagh 6 113
(A P O'Brien, Ire) *settled 2nd: led fr 1/2-way: edgd clr travelling easily fr 2f out: r.o wl fnl f: nt extended* **15/8**[2]

2 *7* **Croi Mo Ri (IRE)**[20] 1007 3-9-1 97 WJSupple 7 94
(P D Deegan, Ire) *prom: 4th 1/2-way: rdn 2f out: 3rd and no imp 1f out: kpt on* **9/1**

3 *shd* **Capt Chaos (IRE)**[167] 6549 3-9-1 101 CDHayes 3 94
(Edward Lynam, Ire) *hld up in rr: rdn over 2f out: styd on ins fnl f* **10/1**

4 *1 1/2* **Badger Or Bust (IRE)**[14] 1106 3-9-1 89 MHarley 5 90
(Liam Roche, Ire) *hld up in tch: prog on far side 2 1/2f out: sn rdn: mod 2nd over 1f out: no imp* **16/1**

5 *3 1/2* **Mr Medici (IRE)**[8] 1225 3-9-1 106 DPMcDonogh 4 80
(Kevin Prendergast, Ire) *trckd ldrs in 5th: rdn under 2f out: no imp: eased cl home* **6/4**[1]

6 *1 1/2* **Teacht An Earraig (USA)**[174] 6394 3-8-12 90 KJManning 1 73
(J S Bolger, Ire) *chsd ldrs in 3rd: 2nd briefly over 2f out: sn wknd: eased ins fnl f* **10/1**

6 *dht* **Rock Of Rochelle (USA)**[191] 5975 3-9-1 101 (t) VRDeSouza 2 76
(A Kinsella, Ire) *led: restrained and hdd 1/2-way: wknd fr 2f out* **8/1**[3]

1m 38.89s (11.79) **Going Correction** +1.70s/f (Heav) **7 Ran SP% 120.0**
Speed ratings: **101,93,92,91,87 85,85**
CSF £20.52 TOTE £2.00: £1.70, £3.40; DF 20.70.
Owner Mrs John Magnier **Bred** Quay Bloodstock **Trained** Ballydoyle, Co Tipperary

FOCUS
An impressive win from Georgebernardshaw and sound form rated through the runner-up and sixth.

NOTEBOOK
Georgebernardshaw(IRE) ended last season as a maiden after four attempts and only one first-three placing. However, he has clearly gone the right way over the winter and, following his three-length maiden win over 6f here last month, he stepped up in grade and trip in fine style, drawing clear of his rivals from well over a furlong out, having led from halfway. Both his wins have been achieved on heavy or soft ground, but his trainer sees no reason why the colt will not be equally as effective on better going, and he expects him to stay a mile. This might not have been the strongest of Listed races, but he could hardly have won it more easily, and the French or Irish Guineas may now come into calculations. (op 7/4)
Croi Mo Ri(IRE), rated 97 since winning a handicap at Cork on his previous start, proved no match for the winner but performed creditably nonetheless, and kept on gamely to edge the battle for second.
Capt Chaos(IRE), a maiden winner over 6f on testing ground last season and rated 101, stayed on from behind over the last two furlongs but was never in serious contention.
Badger Or Bust(IRE), rated 89, having got off the mark in a handicap over this course and trip last time, looked up against it here and was far from disgraced, although he was unable to make any impression inside the final furlong having made a forward move over a furlong out.
Mr Medici(IRE), an easy winner on his reappearance at Limerick, was reported by his rider to have raced keenly and to have failed to quicken in the closing stages. The colt was reported to be clinically abnormal following veterinary examination. Official explanation: jockey said colt ran keen and did not quicken in the latter stages; vet said colt was clinically abnormal post race (op 2/1)

1354 - 1359a (Foreign Racing) - See Raceform Interactive

1238 LONGCHAMP (R-H)

Sunday, April 13

OFFICIAL GOING: Heavy

1360a SG PRIVATE BANKING - PRIX DE LA GROTTE (GROUP 3) (FILLIES) 1m

2:45 (2:47) 3-Y-O **£29,412** (£11,765; £8,824; £5,882; £2,941)

RPR

1 **Zarkava (IRE)**[189] 6040 3-9-0 CSoumillon 7 114+
(A De Royer-Dupre, France) *racd in 5th: hdwy and 3rd st: pushed along 1 1/2f out: qcknd to ld appr fnl f: sn clr: easily* **7/10**[1]

2 *2 1/2* **Conference Call**[189] 6040 3-9-0 SPasquier 4 106
(P Bary, France) *racd in 2nd to st: ev ch 1 1/2f out: one pce* **29/10**[2]

3 *hd* **Lessing (FR)**[23] 956 3-9-0 OPeslier 1 106
(R Gibson, France) *trckd ldr on ins: cl 4th st: swtchd lft 1 1/2f out: r.o u.p to jst miss 2nd* **12/1**

4 *nk* **Mousse Au Chocolat (USA)**[155] 6769 3-9-0 IMendizabal 5 105
(J-C Rouget, France) *hld up: 6th st: hdwy wl over 1f out: hrd rdn and r.o ins fnl f: nrst fin* **46/10**[3]

5 *nk* **Gipson Dessert (USA)**[173] 6416 3-9-0 C-PLemaire 3 104
(J-C Rouget, France) *led to appr fnl f: one pce* **46/10**[3]

6 *2 1/2* **Nera Divine (FR)**[10] 3-9-0 DBoeuf 2 99
(M Boutin, France) *5th st: sn btn* **22/1**

7 *2 1/2* **Luna Royale (IRE)**[23] 956 3-9-0 JVictoire 6 94
(H-A Pantall, France) *s.i.s: last thrght* **40/1**

1m 44.7s (5.90) **Going Correction** +0.925s/f (Soft) **7 Ran SP% 134.7**
Speed ratings: **107,104,104,104,103 101,98**
PARI-MUTUEL: WIN 1.70; PL 1.20, 1.40; SF 2.50.
Owner H H Aga Khan **Bred** His Highness The Aga Khan's Studs S C **Trained** Chantilly, France

NOTEBOOK
Zarkava(IRE) proved that a top-class performer can act on any ground. The prevailing surface did not make the slightest difference to this brilliant filly. She settled from the start and raced in fourth position before making gradual progress in the straight. A furlong out her jockey pressed the button and she quickened like a class act. She is an exceptional filly and the Pouliches looks at her mercy. She will be entered in the Coronation Stakes and her trainer is convinced a longer trip will be no problem, so an entry in the Arc de Triomphe is also on the cards.
Conference Call did her very best but was beaten by her old rival exactly the same distance that was posted after the Marcel Boussac. Always well placed, she made a forward move early in the straight to lead a furlong and a half out. When the winner came along shortly afterwards, she once again did not have the legs to fend off the challenge. There are no plans for her at the moment.
Lessing(FR) was the fittest of the first three past the post and given every possible chance. Third for the early part of the mile, she stayed on throughout the final two furlongs and battled gamely to keep third place. There are no definite plans, but the Prix de Sandringham is being talked about as a target for this ex-Spanish filly.
Mousse Au Chocolat(USA) was not seen for much of the early part of the race but was brought with a progressive run from a furlong and a half out. She ran on really well in the final stages and this was a perfect reappearance. She may well be in the line-up for the Pouliches.

1361a SG PRIVATE BANKING - PRIX DE FONTAINEBLEAU (GROUP 3) (COLTS) 1m

3:15 (3:17) 3-Y-O **£29,412** (£11,765; £8,824; £5,882; £2,941)

RPR

1 **Tamayuz**[188] 3-9-2 DBonilla 6 109
(F Head, France) *hld up in cl 4th to st: trcking ldr 2f out: swtchd out over 1f out: qcknd to ld 100yds out: drvn out* **22/10**[3]

2 *hd* **Murcielago (FR)**[30] 3-9-2 TCastanheira 4 108
(R Le Gal, France) *hld up: 5th st: hdwy wl over 1f out: ev ch 100yds out: r.o same pce* **30/1**

3 *1* **Hello Morning (FR)**[20] 1011 3-9-2 SPasquier 5 106
(Mme C Head-Maarek, France) *first to show: trckd ldr and pulling early: led 2f out: hrd rdn over 1f out: hdd 100yds out: one pce* **21/10**[2]

4 *1* **Arcadia's Angle (USA)**[20] 1011 3-9-2 C-PLemaire 2 104
(P Bary, France) *a cl up: 3rd on ins st: nt clr run over 1f out: styd on one pce to take 4th cl home* **17/10**[1]

5 *1* **Lucifer Sam (USA)**[196] 5845 3-9-2 CSoumillon 1 102
(A P O'Brien, Ire) *led after 1f: set stdy pce: qcknd 1/2-way: hdd 2f out: stl 2nd ins fnl f: one pce* **17/10**[1]

6 *3* **Blue Chagall (FR)**[164] 6615 3-9-2 JVictoire 7 96
(H-A Pantall, France) *last to st: effrt on outside wl over 1f out: btn 1f out* **13/2**

7 *3/4* **One Great Cat (USA)**[211] 5406 3-9-2 DavidMcCabe 3 94
(A P O'Brien, Ire) *a towards rr: 6th on ins st: sn btn* **17/10**[1]

1m 48.3s (9.50) **Going Correction** +0.925s/f (Soft) **7 Ran SP% 191.2**
Speed ratings: **89,88,87,86,85 82,82**
PARI-MUTUEL: WIN 3.20; PL 2.50, 5.90; DF 41.80.
Owner Hamdan Al Maktoum **Bred** Shadwell Estate Company Limited **Trained** France

NOTEBOOK
Tamayuz put up an excellent performance considering the total lack of early pace, and he is now unbeaten in three outings. Raced just behind the leaders, he was completely outpaced when things quickened suddenly in the straight, but once balanced he began his run to the line and had his head in the right place at exactly the right time. Described as rather a tense individual, he is getting better with every race, and he was the only one in the first four not to have had a previous outing. His target now is the Poule d'Essai des Poulains.
Murcielago(FR), ignored in the betting, looked the likely winner half a furlong out. He had been given a waiting race and still had plenty to do halfway up the straight, but he came with a sweeping late run up the centre of the track and was just run out of things in the final 50 yards. He will have a chance to take his revenge in the Poulains.
Hello Morning(FR) followed the leader for much of the early part of the mile before taking the advantage a furlong and a half from the line. At the furlong marker he was level with the winner and runner-up but he just could not quicken in the same way. Another not suited by the lack of early pace, he is programmed to be in the line-up for the Poulains.
Arcadia's Angle(USA), another not suited by the crawl early on and the sudden injection of pace early in the straight, did not get the best of runs, but he finished well and connections still feel he deserves a chance to be in the line-up for the Poulians.
Lucifer Sam(USA) had it all to prove in the ground and, having set the early pace, was readily brushed aside.
One Great Cat(USA) was never going to be seen to best effect in this ground and never threatened to get involved. He deserves another chance.

1362a SG PRIVATE BANKING - PRIX LA FORCE (GROUP 3) 1m 2f

3:45 (3:47) 3-Y-O **£29,412** (£11,765; £8,824; £5,882; £2,941)

RPR

1 **High Rock (IRE)**[175] 6377 3-9-2 C-PLemaire 4 115+
(J-C Rouget, France) *plld hrd: a cl up 3rd st: led over 2f out: sn clr: easily* **22/10**[2]

2 *6* **Salsalavie (FR)**[175] 6377 3-9-2 OPeslier 6 99
(P Demercastel, France) *hld up: last st: rdn and hdwy wl over 1f out: mod 2nd fr dist* **22/1**

3 *2 1/2* **Watar (IRE)**[24] 3-9-2 DBonilla 1 90
(F Head, France) *a cl up: 5th st on ins: wnt for gap on rails 1 1/2f out: hmpd appr fnl f: swtchd out and rallied for 3rd* **88/10**

4 *1 1/2* **Sligo**[191] 5990 3-9-2 DavidMcCabe 7 87
(A P O'Brien, Ire) *set mod pce: hung lft ent st: sn rdn: hdd over 2f out: hung lft 1 1/2f out: one pce* **6/4**[1]

5 *2* **Mess Around (FR)**[33] 3-9-2 IMendizabal 3 84
(J-C Rouget, France) *trckd ldr: clsd up on outside after 4f: 2nd st: rdn and one pce wl over 1f out* **9/1**

6 *4* **Achill Island (IRE)**[170] 6484 3-9-2 CSoumillon 5 77
(A P O'Brien, Ire) *hld up: clsd up to dispute 3rd 1/2-way: 4th st: one pce fr 1 1/2f out* **6/4**[1]

7 *20* **Putney Bridge (USA)**[154] 6782 3-9-2 SPasquier 2 41
(Mme C Head-Maarek, France) *hld up in rr: 6th st: cl up whn nt clr run and squeezed up wl over 1f out: nt rcvr: eased* **38/10**[3]

2m 12.9s (6.00) **Going Correction** +0.925s/f (Soft) **7 Ran SP% 156.6**
Speed ratings: **113,108,106,105,103 100,84**
PARI-MUTUEL: WIN 3.20; PL 2.10, 6.20; SF 51.40.
Owner R Bousquet **Bred** Ecurie Skymarc Farm **Trained** Pau, France

NOTEBOOK
High Rock(IRE) ◆ produced an awesome performance, especially considering he pulled so hard. He was almost impossible to restrain early on but, when given his head at the entrance to the straight around two and a half furlongs out, the result was astonishing. Instead of running out of steam he quickened impressively and totally outclassed his six rivals. Clearly a high-class colt, he now rates as a live Classic prospect but, seeing as the Prix Lupin has stupidly been removed from the French programme, he has no alternative but to go straight to the Prix du Jockey-Club on June 1. He should be hard to beat at Chantilly.
Salsalavie(FR), who raced in last place for much of the way, stayed on well for second after racing a little freely, but he was never going to get to the winner.
Watar(IRE) looked unlucky not to finish closer as he was continually denied a clear run in the straight. He might have been second with a better trip.
Sligo soon led at just a steady pace, but he was passed by the winner early in the straight and finished well held in fourth.
Achill Island(IRE) was nowhere near the form he showed when second in the Breeders' Cup Juvenile Turf on his final start at two.

WINDSOR (R-H)

Monday, April 14

OFFICIAL GOING: Good to soft (8.1)

Wind: Moderate, behind Weather: Unsettled, showers

1363 READING EVENING POST MAIDEN STKS 5f 10y

2:30 (2:30) (Class 5) 2-Y-O £2,729 (£806; £403) Stalls High

Form RPR

1 **Bonnie Charlie** 2-9-3 0 RichardHughes 2 92+
(R Hannon) *wnt lft s: sn trckd ldrs on outer: cruised up to ld 1f out: shkn up and wl in command nr fin* **4/1[2]**

2 *2* **Miss Chamanda (IRE)** 2-8-12 0 TGMcLaughlin 7 77
(P D Evans) *chsd ldr: rdn and hanging 1/2-way: clsd to chal over 1f out: chsd wnr fnl f: readily hld* **8/1**

52 3 *1* **Riflessione**[13] 1122 2-9-3 0 LPKeniry 10 78
(J S Moore) *led: gng easily 2f out: rdn and hdd 1f out: one pce* **7/4[1]**

4 *3 ¾* **Smokey Storm** 2-9-3 0 AlanMunro 6 63+
(W Jarvis) *nt on terms w ldrs in midfield: rdn 2f out: kpt on fnl f to take 4th nr fin* **16/1**

5 *hd* **Sharav** 2-9-3 0 StephenCarson 5 62+
(Eve Johnson Houghton) *chsd ldrs: outpcd fr over 1f out: lost 4th nr fin* **10/1**

42 6 *2 ¾* **Raimond Ridge (IRE)**[9] 1220 2-9-3 0 DarryllHolland 8 51
(M R Channon) *chsd ldrs: steadily wknd fnl 2f* **5/1[3]**

7 *3 ½* **Maria Milena** 2-8-12 0 EddieAhern 11 32
(M J Wallace) *nvr on terms w ldrs: struggling 2f out* **20/1**

8 *3 ¼* **Rich Red (IRE)** 2-9-3 0 RyanMoore 9 24+
(R Hannon) *dwlt: a wl in rr: lost tch over 1f out* **8/1**

9 *1* **Twos And Eights (IRE)** 2-9-3 0 PaulEddery 4 20
(G D Blake) *chsd ldrs to 1/2-way: sn wknd* **25/1**

10 *6* **Noworneva** 2-9-3 0 SebSanders 1 —
(S Kirk) *dwlt and bmpd s: a in rr: wknd 2f out: heavily eased fnl f* **40/1**

62.05 secs (1.75) **Going Correction** +0.175s/f (Good) 10 Ran SP% 121.3
Speed ratings (Par 92): **93,89,88,82,81 77,71,66,65,55**
CSF £36.73 TOTE £5.40: £2.10, £1.90, £1.20; EX 49.00 Trifecta £214.20 Pool £452.68 - 1.50 winning units..

Owner Thurloe Thoroughbreds XXII **Bred** C D S Bryce And Mrs M Bryce **Trained** East Everleigh, Wilts

FOCUS
A fair juvenile maiden likely to produce winners, and sound form. Bonnie Charlie impressed and is the type to rate higher.They all came stands' side.

NOTEBOOK
Bonnie Charlie, a 46,000gns son of Intikhab, was the shorter of the Richard Hannon-trained pair in the betting and he continued the yard's fine start to the season with a tidy victory. Always going strongly, he had things well under control once in front and looks a useful prospect. He is not overly big, but can win again. (op 10-3)
Miss Chamanda(IRE), a 20,000euros daughter of Choisir, comes from a yard who have made a bright start with their juveniles and it was no surprise to see her show up well. This February foal knew her job and, although no match for the winner this time, she can go one better in a similar contest. (tchd 10-1)
Riflessione, a promising fifth in the Brocklesby before just losing to another Hannon inmate at Folkestone, had no ground worries, but this looked a stronger event and it was no surprise to see him come up short. He was far enough clear of the remainder to suggest a small race will come his way eventually. (op 9-4)
Smokey Storm ◆, a son of One Cool Cat who is bred to need further in time, comes from a yard who can ready the odd newcomer and he made a satisfactory debut, keeping on for fourth under considerate riding. The experience should not be lost on him and he can win a maiden. (op 14-1)
Sharav, a half-brother to smart sprinter Bygone Days, seemed to know his job, but could not quicken when the principals upped the tempo. He will require 6f in time and should learn from this outing. (op 8-1)
Raimond Ridge(IRE), a few lengths behind Riflessione at Folkestone, improved on that effort to finish second at Newcastle, but was unable to make any further progress here, fading out tamely. He has a bit to prove now. (op 6-1)
Maria Milena, a daughter of Stravinsky, is bred to get further than this and she was always struggling to stay on terms.
Rich Red(IRE), a stablemate of the winner, was always struggling following a tardy start and showed little. He is presumably thought capable of a good deal better and is worth giving another chance to. (op 9-1 tchd 10-1)
Noworneva Official explanation: jockey said bit slipped through gelding's mouth

1364 GOLDRING SECURITY SERVICES CLAIMING STKS 1m 2f 7y

3:00 (3:00) (Class 5) 3-Y-O £2,593 (£765; £383) Stalls Low

Form RPR

1 **Silver Spruce** 3-9-0 0 SebSanders 7 65
(E S McMahon) *s.i.s and reminder after s: sn midfield: hmpd 1/2-way: prog 4f out: rdn to ld over 2f out: kpt on wl* **16/1**

00-6 2 *1* **King Supreme (IRE)**[11] 1163 3-9-6 64 RichardHughes 12 69
(R Hannon) *prom: rdn over 3f out: nt qckn over 2f out: styd on u.p to take 2nd nr fin* **8/1**

4450 3 *½* **Carry On Cleo**[52] 665 3-8-5 53 (v) JamesDoyle 1 53
(P D Evans) *hld up wl in rr: prog over 3f out: chal over 2f out: hld ins fnl f: lost 2nd nr fin* **16/1**

-543 4 *1* **Agglestone Rock**[18] 1034 3-8-7 65 JackDean(7) 4 60
(W G M Turner) *hld up: plld way through bnd 1/2-way: c wd in st and wl on terms 2f out: one pce fnl f* **15/2[3]**

00-5 5 *4* **Landikhaya (IRE)**[16] 1082 3-9-5 68 JerryO'Dwyer(3) 5 60
(D K Ivory) *hld up in last: rdn 3f out: kpt on u.p fnl 2f: nvr rchd ldrs* **16/1**

046- 6 *½* **Sergeant Sharpe**[201] 5735 3-9-1 70 NicolPolli(5) 10 57
(M H Tompkins) *hld up in rr: prog on wd outside 3f out: cl enough 2f out: wknd over 1f out* **11/2[2]**

3412 7 *1 ¼* **Home**[18] 1034 3-9-5 70 (p) PatCosgrave 9 54
(J R Boyle) *sn in midfield: rdn and struggling over 4f out: effrt u.p and in tch over 2f out: sn btn* **3/1[1]**

0560 8 *shd* **Bon Ton Roulet**[11] 1163 3-8-7 57 RichardSmith 11 41
(R Hannon) *dwlt: hld up in rr: gng wl enough 4f out: effrt 3f out: sn drvn and no prog* **14/1**

41-0 9 *10* **Didana (IRE)**[12] 1161 3-8-11 65 RyanMoore 3 25
(M G Quinlan) *led to over 2f out: wknd rapidly* **3/1[1]**

500- 10 *13* **Border Defence (IRE)**[175] 6388 3-8-12 54 FrankieMcDonald 6 —
(P A Blockley) *t.k.h: mostly chsd ldr to 3f out: wknd rapidly: t.o* **33/1**

00-0 11 *9* **Una Auroraborealis**[13] 1124 3-8-4 45 (p) ChrisCatlin 8 —
(J Ryan) *t.k.h: prom to 1/2-way: wknd rapidly sn after: t.o* **100/1**

0002 P **Herrbee (IRE)**[6] 1251 3-8-12 48 RichardKingscote 2 —
(P Butler) *in tch whn sddle slipped and rn wd bnd 1/2-way: sn p.u* **25/1**

2m 11.87s (3.17) **Going Correction** +0.175s/f (Good) 12 Ran SP% 120.4
Speed ratings (Par 98): **94,93,92,92,88 88,87,87,79,68 61,—**
CSF £138.94 TOTE £16.00: £3.60, £3.30, £5.40; EX 131.60 TRIFECTA Not won..Agglestone Rock was claimed by Mr P. Kirby for £10,000. Silver Spruce was claimed by Mr I. W. McInnes for £10,000.

Owner Mrs J McMahon **Bred** T Trafford **Trained** Lichfield, Staffs

■ Stewards' Enquiry : Frankie McDonald one-day ban: used whip when out of contention (Apr 28)

FOCUS
A competitive enough claimer on paper, but several of the fancied runners flopped and it went the way of newcomer Silver Spruce. Modest form, rated through the third's turf form.
Herrbee(IRE) Official explanation: jockey said saddle slipped

1365 AT THE RACES H'CAP 1m 67y

3:30 (3:32) (Class 4) (0-85,85) 4-Y-O+ £5,180 (£1,541; £770; £384) Stalls High

Form RPR

005- 1 **Look So**[263] 3889 4-8-10 77 SebSanders 5 87
(R M Beckett) *uns rdr and bolted to post: hld up in last: reminder 1/2-way: prog on wd outside 2f out: drvn and styd on wl to ld nr fin* **11/1**

01- 2 *nk* **Trans Siberian**[294] 2951 4-8-6 76 TolleyDean(3) 3 85
(P F I Cole) *t.k.h: prom: chsd ldr 2f out: drvn to chal fnl f: jst hld* **8/1**

1314 3 *shd* **Highland Harvest**[30] 910 4-8-9 76 HayleyTurner 8 85
(D R C Elsworth) *trckd ldr: t.k.h and led wl over 3f out: taken to nr side rail over 2f out: drvn over 1f out: hdd nr fin* **15/2[3]**

400- 4 *shd* **Full Victory (IRE)**[135] 7002 6-8-9 76 SteveDrowne 2 85
(R A Farrant) *hld up towards rr: stdy prog on outer 3f out: gng strly over 2f out: rdn to chal over 1f out: one pce* **12/1**

23-5 5 *1 ½* **Rudry Dragon (IRE)**[13] 1131 4-8-11 78 StephenDonohoe 9 84
(P A Blockley) *chsd ldrs: pushed along fr 1/2-way: kpt on u.p fnl 2f but nvr pce to chal* **8/1**

21-5 6 *½* **Red Somerset (USA)**[16] 1067 5-9-1 82 RichardHughes 4 86
(R J Hodges) *hld up in rr: prog on outer over 2f out: chsd ldrs over 1f out: one pce after* **15/2[3]**

102- 7 *2* **Gazboolou**[121] 7158 4-8-7 74 NeilChalmers 10 74
(David Pinder) *trckd ldrs: cl enough 2f out: fdd over 1f out* **33/1**

1200 8 *nk* **Alfresco**[30] 906 4-9-4 85 GeorgeBaker 6 84
(I A Wood) *hld up in last: sme prog over 2f out: shkn up 1f out: kpt on but nvr nr ldrs* **12/1**

160- 9 *5* **Wester Ross (IRE)**[290] 3058 4-8-9 76 RyanMoore 13 64
(J M P Eustace) *trckd ldrs tl wknd over 2f out* **15/2[3]**

0-40 10 *2 ½* **Zafonical Storm (USA)**[30] 910 4-8-11 78 (bt[1]) DaneO'Neill 12 60
(B W Duke) *led to 3f out: wknd wl over 1f out* **33/1**

41-5 11 *11* **Twilight Star (IRE)**[30] 910 4-8-13 80 ChrisCatlin 14 37
(R A Teal) *t.k.h: trckd ldng pair to 1/2-way: wknd over 2f out: t.o* **13/2[2]**

125- 12 *nk* **Novikov**[240] 4603 4-9-3 84 JimmyFortune 11 40
(J H M Gosden) *s.i.s: sn midfield: wknd over 2f out: eased over 1f out: t.o* **7/2[1]**

1m 44.77s (0.07) **Going Correction** +0.175s/f (Good) 12 Ran SP% 122.7
Speed ratings (Par 105): **106,105,105,105,104 103,101,101,96,93 82,82**
CSF £99.66 CT £713.14 TOTE £16.10: £4.00, £3.60, £3.00; EX 116.50 TRIFECTA Not won..

Owner J H Richmond-Watson **Bred** Lawn Stud **Trained** Whitsbury, Hants

FOCUS
An ultra-competitive handicap and the first four were separated by half a length. Pretty solid form with the first pair less exposed than most.
Novikov Official explanation: trainer's rep had no explanation for the poor form shown

1366 GRANT THORNTON H'CAP 5f 10y

4:00 (4:02) (Class 4) (0-80,80) 4-Y-O+ £4,533 (£1,348; £674; £336) Stalls High

Form RPR

5011 1 **After The Show**[10] 1189 7-8-6 68 ChrisCatlin 8 80
(Rae Guest) *hld up: rdn and prog fr 2f out: hung lft fnl f: drvn and r.o to ld last strides* **15/8[1]**

10-4 2 *hd* **Hereford Boy**[12] 1146 4-8-13 75 RobertHavlin 6 86
(D K Ivory) *stdd s: hld up in rr: prog 2f out: hrd rdn to ld ins fnl f: hdd last strides* **13/2[3]**

5004 3 *1 ½* **Tartatartufata**[22] 983 6-8-10 72 (v) DaneO'Neill 4 78
(D Shaw) *trckd ldrs: effrt to ld 2f out: edgd lft fr over 1f out: hdd and no ex ins fnl f* **4/1[2]**

550- 4 *3 ½* **Corridor Creeper (FR)**[184] 6173 11-9-3 79 (p) RyanMoore 5 72
(J M Bradley) *led 1f: pressed ldr: rdn and stl ch jst over 1f out: hanging lft and nt qckn* **9/1**

151- 5 *1 ¼* **Ocean Blaze**[191] 6020 4-9-1 77 AlanMunro 2 66
(B R Millman) *plld hrd: led after 1f to 2f out: fdd fnl f* **7/1**

3606 6 *1* **Silver Prelude**[30] 907 7-9-4 80 SebSanders 1 65
(D K Ivory) *prom: wl on terms 2f out: pushed along over 1f out: steadily wknd* **9/1**

00-6 7 *4 ½* **Garstang**[16] 1079 5-8-8 70 (b) LPKeniry 3 39
(Peter Grayson) *stdd s: hld up in rr: rdn and no prog 2f out: sn wknd* **11/1**

154- 8 *4 ½* **Nordic Light (USA)**[321] 2114 4-9-1 77 JimCrowley 7 30
(J M Bradley) *struggling in rr fr 1/2-way: sn bhd* **20/1**

61.05 secs (0.75) **Going Correction** +0.175s/f (Good) 8 Ran SP% 113.7
Speed ratings (Par 105): **101,100,98,92,90 89,81,74**
CSF £14.33 CT £43.50 TOTE £2.70: £1.10, £2.10, £1.80; EX 15.50 Trifecta £35.40 Pool £726.25 - 14.53 winning units..

Owner Miss L Thompson **Bred** Michael Ng **Trained** Newmarket, Suffolk

FOCUS
A tight sprint handicap. Pretty sound form, the winner back to his best.

1367 HSBC INVESTMENT MAIDEN STKS 1m 2f 7y

4:30 (4:32) (Class 5) 3-Y-O £2,729 (£806; £403) Stalls Low

Form RPR

45- 1 **By Command**[275] 3552 3-9-3 0 SebSanders 11 93+
(J L Dunlop) *trckd ldrs: led over 2f out: drew clr over 1f out: easily* **13/8[1]**

04- 2 *6* **Criterion**[173] 6418 3-9-3 0 RyanMoore 3 76
(Sir Michael Stoute) *a in ldng trio: upsides over 2f out: sn no ch w wnr: jst hld on for 2nd* **6/1[3]**

0- 3 *nse* **Crazy About You (IRE)**[234] 4774 3-8-9 0 WilliamBuick(3) 10 71
(B W Hills) *hld up wl in rr: prog fr 4f out: nrly upsides jst over 2f out: sn outpcd: styd on* **20/1**

4 *¾* **Stock Market (USA)** 3-9-3 0 TGMcLaughlin 6 74
(E A L Dunlop) *hld up towards rr: prog 3f out: shkn up to cl on ldrs 2f out: sn outpcd: kpt on* **16/1**

4-4 5 *½* **Rock Peak (IRE)**[14] 1114 3-9-3 0 SteveDrowne 7 73
(H Morrison) *trckd ldrs: effrt and cl up 3f out: shkn up and outpcd fnl 2f* **10/3[2]**

0-0 **6** 7 **Star Pattern (USA)**[11] 1172 3-9-3 0 JimmyFortune 2 59+
(J H M Gosden) *hld up in midfield: prog to press ldrs over 2f out: wknd over 1f out* **16/1**
7 9 **Force Tradition (IRE)** 3-9-3 0 JimmyQuinn 4 41
(M H Tompkins) *dwlt: wl in rr: shkn up and lost tch 4f out: no ch after* **66/1**
04- **8** 1/2 **Emerald Crystal (IRE)**[164] 6618 3-9-3 0 RobertHavlin 12 43
(B J Meehan) *mde most to over 2f out: wknd rapidly and eased* **14/1**
33- **9** 3/4 **Hasty Retreat**[123] 7130 3-9-3 0 AlanMunro 14 39+
(E A L Dunlop) *lost midfield pl on bnd over 5f out: lost tch 4f out: bhd after* **15/2**
5 **10** 3/4 **Montevetro**[14] 1114 3-9-3 0 RichardHughes 9 37
(R Hannon) *pressed ldrs: reminders 4f out: wknd rapidly wl over 2f out* **20/1**
0 **11** hd **Persian Wish (IRE)**[17] 1059 3-9-3 0 LPKeniry 1 37
(J W Mullins) *cl up: rdn 3f out: wknd rapidly over 2f out* **100/1**
12 1 1/4 **Sleeping Dragon** 3-9-3 0 StephenDonohoe 8 35
(P A Blockley) *dwlt: a wl in rr: lost tch 4f out* **100/1**
00- **13** 3/4 **Shoot Pontoon (IRE)**[122] 7140 3-9-3 0 ChrisCatlin 15 33
(S A Callaghan) *a wl in rr: bhd fr 4f out* **100/1**
0 **14** 19 **Buck Cannon (IRE)**[17] 1054 3-9-3 0 EddieAhern 5 —
(P M Phelan) *a in last pair: wl bhd fr 4f out: t.o* **66/1**

2m 9.83s (1.13) **Going Correction** +0.175s/f (Good) **14** Ran SP% **121.1**
Speed ratings (Par 98): **102,97,97,96,96 90,83,82,82,81 81,80,80,64**
CSF £11.16 TOTE £2.90: £1.10, £2.60, £6.60; EX 13.50 TRIFECTA Not won..
Owner Prince A A Faisal **Bred** Nawara Stud Co Ltd **Trained** Arundel, W Sussex

FOCUS
Not much of a maiden, but it was hard not to be impressed with the ease in which By Command won. He looks a useful prospect. The form has been rated around the runner-up and fifth.
Hasty Retreat Official explanation: jockey said gelding was hampered on bend

1368 MONDAY NIGHT RACING RETURNS 21ST APRIL H'CAP 6f
5:00 (5:01) (Class 5) (0-75,75) 4-Y-0+ **£3,070** (£906; £453) **Stalls** High

Form RPR
2110 **1** **Kensington (IRE)**[45] 755 7-8-12 **69** (p) StephenDonohoe 2 82
(P D Evans) *pressed ldr and sn clr of rest: narrow ld over 1f out: jst hld on* **20/1**
3223 **2** shd **Savile's Delight (IRE)**[19] 1022 9-8-11 **68** RichardKingscote 6 81
(Tom Dascombe) *led and sn clr w wnr: narrowly hdd over 1f out: upsides but hung lft fnl f: jst hld* **11/1**
060- **3** 3 1/4 **Cheap Street**[201] 5722 4-9-3 **74** RyanMoore 7 76
(J G Portman) *chsd ldrs: rdn to go 3rd 2f out: no imp on ldng pair: kpt on* **15/2**[3]
5033 **4** hd **Memphis Man**[12] 1138 5-9-1 **72** TGMcLaughlin 12 74
(P D Evans) *dwlt: t.k.h: hld up wl in rr: swtchd to far rail and prog over 2f out: kpt on fnl f: nvr able to chal* **5/1**[1]
50-4 **5** 2 1/4 **Dualagi**[21] 994 4-8-7 **64** LPKeniry 8 58
(M R Bosley) *s.s: wl in rr: rdn 2f out: prog over 1f out: kpt on but nvr a threat* **12/1**
4042 **6** 1 **Proud Killer**[13] 1126 5-8-7 **64** ow1 EddieAhern 9 55
(J R Jenkins) *prom in chsng gp: no imp 2f out: fdd over 1f out* **17/2**
3/3- **7** 1 1/2 **Blue Charm**[378] 885 4-9-4 **75** RichardHughes 14 61+
(S Kirk) *hld up in last: nudged along and stdy prog fr 2f out: nvr nr ldrs* **14/1**
044- **8** nk **Equuleus Pictor**[167] 6575 4-8-5 **65** WilliamBuick[(3)] 3 50
(J L Spearing) *dwlt: towards rr: prog 1/2-way: chsng ldrs 2f out: n.m.r sn after: fdd* **10/1**
33-0 **9** 2 **Jimmy The Guesser**[10] 1195 5-9-4 **75** (p) HayleyTurner 13 54
(N P Littmoden) *nvr beyond midfield: nt on terms fr 2f out: no ch after* **16/1**
0-55 **10** 3/4 **Hits Only Cash**[51] 685 6-8-6 **63** (p) JimmyQuinn 11 40
(J Pearce) *dwlt: a wl in rr: no prog fnl 2f* **11/1**
25-1 **11** 2 3/4 **Cinnamon Hill**[10] 1178 4-9-0 **71** StephenCarson 1 39
(Eve Johnson Houghton) *prom in chsng gp tl wknd wl over 1f out* **8/1**
020- **12** 2 1/2 **Makabul**[180] 6273 5-9-2 **73** AlanMunro 5 33
(B R Millman) *t.k.h: hld up in rr: nvr on terms: rdn and no prog 2f out* **7/1**[2]
0/2- **13** 3 1/2 **Valentino Swing (IRE)**[301] 2719 5-8-13 **70** JimCrowley 10 19
(Miss T Spearing) *sn towards rr: struggling over 2f out: sn bhd* **15/2**[3]

1m 13.67s (0.67) **Going Correction** +0.175s/f (Good) **13** Ran SP% **125.1**
Speed ratings (Par 103): **102,101,97,97,94 92,90,90,87,86 83,79,75**
CSF £235.06 CT £1827.87 TOTE £25.40: £5.40, £4.00, £3.60; EX 477.60 TRIFECTA Not won.
Place 6 £417.48, Place 5 £283.76..
Owner Derek Buckley **Bred** Mountarmstrong Stud **Trained** Pandy, Monmouths

FOCUS
A moderate sprint that produced a cracking finish. This was an unusual race in that the front pair were always in control and a downbeat view has been taken of the form, which might have been rated higher.
T/Jkpt: Not won. T/Plt: £1,015.00 to a £1 stake. Pool: £73,627.15. 52.95 winning tickets. T/Qpdt: £57.40 to a £1 stake. Pool: £4,649.84. 59.90 winning tickets. JN

1338 WOLVERHAMPTON (A.W) (L-H)
Monday, April 14

OFFICIAL GOING: Standard
Wind: Moderate across Weather: Mainly sunny

1369 HORIZONS RESTAURANT APPRENTICE CLAIMING STKS 1m 141y(P)
2:20 (2:20) (Class 6) 4-Y-0+ **£2,729** (£806; £403) **Stalls** Low

Form RPR
2021 **1** **Climate (IRE)**[10] 1192 9-8-9 68 RichardEvans[(5)] 4 68
(P D Evans) *hld up in mid-div: hdwy 3f out: led 1f out: rdn and edgd lft ins fnl f: drvn out* **9/4**[1]
-344 **2** nk **Moayed**[17] 1055 9-9-2 67 (b) KirstyMilczarek 3 70
(N P Littmoden) *s.i.s: hld up in rr: hdwy 2f out: edgd lft ins fnl f: r.o wl towards fin: nt rch wnr* **9/2**[3]
400- **3** 2 3/4 **Dark Charm (FR)**[203] 5674 9-8-13 66 (p) FrederikTylicki[(7)] 5 67
(R A Fahey) *sn chsng ldr: led over 2f out: rdn and hdd 1f out: one pce* **10/1**
3331 **4** 4 **Machinate (USA)**[16] 1085 6-9-1 68 AshleyHamblett[(3)] 9 56
(W M Brisbourne) *hld up in tch: rdn wl over 1f out: wknd fnl f* **5/2**[2]
5-61 **5** 2 3/4 **Mountain Pass (USA)**[28] 914 6-8-9 65 (p) DavidProbert[(7)] 6 48
(B J Llewellyn) *dwlt: hld up and bhd: n.m.r and stmbld over 4f out: hdwy over 1f out: sn edgd lft: wknd ent fnl f* **9/1**
3-03 **6** 2 3/4 **Cadwell**[10] 1192 4-8-7 50 DanielleMcCreery[(5)] 7 37
(T J Pitt) *hld up and bhd: nvr trbld ldrs* **16/1**
00-3 **7** 1 1/2 **Boulevin (IRE)**[7] 215 8-8-5 41 RossAtkinson[(5)] 1 32
(R J Price) *t.k.h in tch: lost pl on ins 3f out: n.d after* **33/1**
500- **8** 3 **Soldiers Quest**[219] 5235 4-8-5 80 PatrickDonaghy[(5)] 8 25
(Peter Grayson) *sn led: hdd over 2f out: rdn and wknd wl over 1f out* **12/1**
/000 **9** 2 3/4 **Tiara Boom De Ay (IRE)**[33] 857 4-8-8 45 JamieJones[(3)] 2 20
(D J Wintle) *led early: prom: rdn over 2f out: sn wknd* **66/1**

1m 52.11s (1.61) **Going Correction** +0.175s/f (Slow) **9** Ran SP% **114.6**
Speed ratings (Par 101): **99,98,96,92,90 87,86,83,81**
CSF £12.67 TOTE £3.40: £1.10, £1.80, £6.00; EX 10.90.The winner was the subject of a friendly claim.
Owner J E Abbey **Bred** Mrs A Naughton **Trained** Pandy, Monmouths

FOCUS
A moderate claimer despite the presence of a horse rated 80 and the first three home were all nine-year-olds. They went no pace early. The form is rated through the runner-up.

1370 SPONSOR A RACE BY CALLING 0870 220 2442 (S) STKS 5f 20y(P)
2:50 (2:51) (Class 6) 3-Y-0+ **£1,774** (£523; £262) **Stalls** Low

Form RPR
5105 **1** **Montzando**[10] 1185 5-9-6 46 (v) JamesMillman[(5)] 5 61
(B R Millman) *a.p: rdn over 2f out: swtchd rt over 1f out: led ins fnl f: r.o* **10/1**
04-4 **2** nk **Shatter Resistant (IRE)**[26] 928 3-8-9 63 LiamJones 10 50
(J R Gask) *hld up and bhd: stdy hdwy over 2f out: swtchd rt over 1f out: sn rdn: r.o wl ins fnl f: nt rch wnr* **11/2**[3]
646 **3** 1 **Prettilini**[6] 1254 5-8-12 43 (v) LukeMorris[(3)] 4 46
(A W Carroll) *chsd ldrs: rdn and n.m.r briefly jst over 1f out: kpt on ins fnl f* **8/1**
2622 **4** 1 1/4 **Punching**[12] 1150 4-9-11 59 JamieSpencer 8 52
(Miss Gay Kelleway) *a.p: wnt 2nd 3f out: rdn and hung lft over 1f out: one pce* **11/10**[1]
4230 **5** 3 1/2 **Night Prospector**[12] 1150 8-9-6 58 (p) PaulHanagan 11 34
(R A Harris) *racd wd: hld up towards rr: rdn wl over 1f out: nvr trbld ldrs* **4/1**[2]
6346 **6** nk **Heron (IRE)**[14] 1120 3-8-2 52 (b) PatrickDonaghy[(7)] 3 28
(A M Hales) *s.i.s: sn rcvrd: led after 1f: hrd rdn and hdd ins fnl f: wknd* **16/1**
0060 **7** 4 1/2 **Vlasta Weiner**[32] 871 8-9-6 40 (b) PaulFitzsimons 2 17
(J M Bradley) *s.i.s: outpcd: rdn over 2f out: short-lived effrt on ins wl over 1f out* **20/1**
0-00 **8** nk **Lithaam (IRE)**[19] 1028 4-8-13 45 (p) PietroRomeo[(7)] 6 16
(J M Bradley) *led 1f: prom tl wknd over 2f out* **40/1**
2-05 **9** 3/4 **Just Puddie**[16] 1081 3-7-11 41 RossAtkinson[(7)] 1 —
(W G M Turner) *outpcd: n.m.r on ins wl over 3f out: a in rr* **25/1**
000- **10** 10 **Ballybunion (IRE)**[214] 5349 9-9-6 45 RichardThomas 7 —
(B J Llewellyn) *bhd fnl 3f* **33/1**

63.11 secs (0.81) **Going Correction** +0.175s/f (Slow)
WFA 3 from 4yo+ 11lb **10** Ran SP% **123.1**
Speed ratings (Par 101): **100,99,97,95,90 89,82,82,80,64**
CSF £64.93 TOTE £15.20: £3.20, £2.40, £2.70; EX 96.50.There was no bid for the winner. Shatter Resistant was claimed by Mr M. Squance for £6,000.
Owner The Links Partnership **Bred** Peter Baldwin **Trained** Kentisbeare, Devon

FOCUS
They went a decent pace, but this was still a poor seller with the winner officially rated 46. The form is none too solid.

1371 WEATHERBYS PRINTING H'CAP 7f 32y(P)
3:20 (3:22) (Class 6) (0-60,60) 4-Y-0+ **£2,388** (£705; £352) **Stalls** Low

Form RPR
1043 **1** **Mineral Rights (USA)**[33] 861 4-9-2 **58** (v[1]) TomEaves 3 70
(Miss L A Perratt) *sn led: rdn over 1f out: hdd ins fnl f: sn led again: drvn out* **5/1**[2]
123 **2** nk **Cape Of Storms**[39] 806 5-9-3 **59** PaulMulrennan 2 70
(R Brotherton) *a.p: wnt 2nd over 2f out: rdn over 1f out: led and edgd lft ins fnl f: sn hdd: nt qckn* **7/1**[3]
1364 **3** 2 3/4 **Aggbag**[9] 1209 4-8-6 **55** DeclanCannon[(7)] 9 59
(B P J Baugh) *s.i.s: bhd: pushed along 3f out: hdwy wl over 1f out: kpt on ins fnl f* **16/1**
6152 **4** nse **Guildenstern (IRE)**[12] 1145 6-9-1 **57** RobertWinston 1 60+
(P Howling) *hld up in mid-div: pushed along over 3f out: swtchd rt 2f out: hdwy over 1f out: edgd lft ent fnl f: kpt on* **7/1**[3]
0-00 **5** 5 **Valdan (IRE)**[12] 1138 4-9-4 **60** (t) DeanMcKeown 6 50
(M A Barnes) *s.i.s: sn in tch: rdn over 2f out: wknd over 1f out* **12/1**
-045 **6** 1 1/2 **Zennerman (IRE)**[19] 1030 5-8-13 **60** (b) KellyHarrison[(5)] 11 46
(Miss J E Foster) *hld up in rr: nvr nr ldrs* **25/1**
33-2 **7** 1 3/4 **Cap St Jean (IRE)**[33] 861 4-9-1 **60** RussellKennemore[(3)] 7 41
(R Hollinshead) *prom: rdn over 2f out: wknd wl over 1f out* **4/1**[1]
5024 **8** 3 1/4 **Metropolitan Chief**[12] 1154 4-8-13 **55** TQuinn 8 27
(P Burgoyne) *mid-div: rdn 3f out: sn wknd* **8/1**
-211 **9** 1 1/2 **High Five Society**[33] 862 4-9-0 **56** (bt) PhillipMakin 12 24
(S R Bowring) *rdn over 3f out: a bhd* **5/1**[2]
46-0 **10** nk **Empire Dancer (IRE)**[49] 703 5-9-0 **56** DanielTudhope 4 24
(I W McInnes) *led early: chsd ldr tl rdn over 2f out: wknd wl over 1f out* **25/1**
0044 **11** 7 **Cabourg (IRE)**[14] 1116 5-8-13 **55** TPQueally 10 4
(R Bastiman) *t.k.h: sn mid-div: bhd fnl 3f* **8/1**

1m 29.56s (-0.04) **Going Correction** +0.175s/f (Slow) **11** Ran SP% **121.8**
Speed ratings (Par 101): **107,106,103,103,97 96,94,90,88,88 80**
CSF £41.60 CT £535.73 TOTE £7.60: £2.40, £3.20, £3.50; EX 34.90.
Owner Belstane Park Racing **Bred** Budget Stable **Trained** Carluke, S Lanarks

FOCUS
A modest handicap, but they went a very decent pace and the winning time was a good one for a race at this level. Not many got into it and the front pair were always handy. The winner is rated up 6lb.
Cap St Jean(IRE) Official explanation: jockey said gelding bolted to post

1372 WOLVERHAMPTON-RACECOURSE.CO.UK MAIDEN FILLIES' STKS 1m 141y(P)
3:50 (3:52) (Class 5) 3-Y-0+ **£2,456** (£725; £362) **Stalls** Low

Form RPR
1 **Saphira's Fire (IRE)** 3-8-8 0 MartinDwyer 8 79
(W R Muir) *hld up and bhd: hdwy 3f out: rdn to ld wl ins fnl f: r.o wl* **33/1**
3- **2** 1 1/2 **Wood Chorus**[174] 6411 3-8-8 0 JamieSpencer 9 76
(M L W Bell) *sn led: rdn and hdd wl ins fnl f: nt qckn* **4/5**[1]
3 1 **Tableau Vivant (IRE)** 3-8-8 0 RobertWinston 7 74+
(Sir Michael Stoute) *rn green: hld up in mid-div: hdwy over 3f out: rdn and ev ch over 1f out: nt qckn ins fnl f* **2/1**[2]

05- **4** 1 ¾ **Idesia (IRE)**[280] 3387 4-9-6 0 .... JamieJones(5) 3 74
(W R Swinburn) *a.p: wnt 2nd briefly 2f out: one pce ins fnl f* **11/1**[3]

05- **5** 9 **Arabian Art (USA)**[149] 6847 3-8-8 0 .... TPQueally 5 49
(H R A Cecil) *prom: wnt 2nd 6f out: rdn and ev ch over 2f out: wknd wl over 1f out* **14/1**

00- **6** 6 **Pennygee**[109] 7239 4-9-11 0 .... PhillipMakin 2 39
(S R Bowring) *hld up in mid-div: rdn and wknd over 2f out* **100/1**

520- **7** 3 ¾ **Duty Doctor**[168] 6535 3-8-8 70 .... TQuinn 10 27
(S Kirk) *chsd ldrs: pushed along 3f out: sn wknd* **12/1**

0 **8** 9 **Fluoree (FR)**[9] 1222 4-9-11 0 .... TomEaves 1 10
(D W Thompson) *a in rr* **150/1**

00 **9** dist **Come On Molly**[11] 1172 4-9-11 0 .... PaulMulrennan 4 —
(R Brotherton) *led early: prom tl wknd over 4f out: t.o* **250/1**

1m 51.22s (0.72) **Going Correction** +0.175s/f (Slow)
WFA 3 from 4yo 17lb **9** Ran SP% **116.6**
Speed ratings (Par 100): **103,101,100,99,91 85,82,74,—**
CSF £61.76 TOTE £45.70: £7.30, £1.02, £1.40; EX 126.10.
Owner M J Caddy **Bred** Gainsborough Stud Management Ltd **Trained** Lambourn, Berks
■ Stewards' Enquiry : Jamie Spencer caution: careless riding

FOCUS
This was probably a fair maiden with some very big stables represented and the time stacks up well when compared with the earlier claimer. The first four finished clear but the form has been rated fairly negatively with the winner and third both unknown quantities.

1373 WEATHERBYS BLOODSTOCK INSURANCE FILLIES' H'CAP 5f 20y(P)
4:20 (4:20) (Class 5) (0-75,72) 3-Y-0+ £2,914 (£867; £433; £216) Stalls Low

Form RPR

204- **1** **Valley Of The Moon (IRE)**[144] 6905 4-9-13 71 .... PaulHanagan 1 80
(R A Fahey) *led 1f: prom: led wl over 1f out: rdn ins fnl f: r.o wl* **3/1**[2]

1003 **2** 1 ¾ **Baileys Outshine**[46] 726 4-9-10 68 .... TPQueally 2 71
(J G Given) *stmbld s: hld up: hdwy on ins 2f out: sn ev ch: rdn over 1f out: nt qckn ins fnl f* **15/2**

-630 **3** 1 **Nigella**[37] 840 5-10-0 72 .... GrahamGibbons 3 71+
(E S McMahon) *s.i.s: plld hrd: clipped heels over 3f out: hdwy over 1f out: one pce fnl f* **11/4**[1]

46-5 **4** 1 ½ **Comptonspirit**[21] 987 4-9-8 66 .... PaulMulrennan 5 60
(B P J Baugh) *a.p: one pce fnl f* **10/1**

411- **5** 5 **Contentious (IRE)**[264] 3853 4-8-11 58 .... KirstyMilczarek(3) 4 34
(D M Simcock) *plld hrd: led after 1f: hung rt fr over 2f out: rn wd and hdd wl over 1f out: sn wknd* **3/1**[2]

0-40 **6** 1 ½ **Twosheetstothewind**[13] 1129 4-9-2 60 .... RobertWinston 7 31
(C R Dore) *plld hrd: prom: ev ch 2f out: hung rt to stands' side wl over 1f out: sn wknd* **13/2**[3]

62.79 secs (0.49) **Going Correction** +0.175s/f (Slow) **6** Ran SP% **110.9**
Speed ratings (Par 100): **103,100,98,96,88 85**
CSF £23.95 TOTE £3.40: £2.80, £4.90; EX 26.00.
Owner T Elsey,S A Elsey,R Mustill,J Tunstall **Bred** Mrs P Grubb **Trained** Musley Bank, N Yorks

FOCUS
A modest handicap in which the time was slightly faster than the seller, as would be expected. Although the field were spread right out across the track passing the furlong pole, the sextet were still within a couple of lengths of each other though two basically hung their chances away. A career best from the winner at face value.
Baileys Outshine Official explanation: jockey said filly stumbled on leaving stalls
Contentious(IRE) Official explanation: jockey said filly hung right
Twosheetstothewind Official explanation: jockey said filly hung right

1374 STAY AT WOLVERHAMPTON HOLIDAY INN H'CAP 1m 1f 103y(P)
4:50 (4:50) (Class 6) (0-65,63) 4-Y-0+ £2,047 (£604; £302) Stalls Low

Form RPR

1040 **1** **Josr's Magic (IRE)**[12] 1160 4-8-4 52 .... KirstyMilczarek(3) 6 61
(H J Collingridge) *hld up: hdwy over 2f out: led over 1f out: pushed out* **9/2**[3]

-314 **2** 2 **Terminate (GER)**[18] 1044 6-8-12 57 .... RobertWinston 1 62
(Ian Williams) *set slow pl: rdn and hdd over 1f out: nt qckn* **11/4**[1]

0034 **3** ¾ **Latif (USA)**[19] 1032 7-8-11 56 .... JamieSpencer 5 59
(Paul Green) *stdd s: hld up and bhd: nt clr run whn swtchd rt and hdwy wl over 1f out: kpt on same pce ins fnl f* **9/2**[3]

4445 **4** 2 **Norwegian**[65] 508 7-8-4 49 oh1 ....(p) PaulHanagan 4 48
(Ian Williams) *chsd ldr tl wl over 1f out: no ex fnl f* **9/1**

2524 **5** ½ **Ermine Grey**[18] 1039 7-8-6 54 .... LukeMorris(3) 7 52
(A W Carroll) *hld up: rdn 3f out: no hdwy fnl 2f* **7/2**[2]

4521 **6** ½ **Casablanca Minx (IRE)**[19] 1032 5-8-7 59 ....(v) RichardEvans(7) 2 56
(P D Evans) *s.i.s: hld up and bhd: rdn wl over 1f out: no rspnse* **11/2**

50-5 **7** 3 **Ruwain**[90] 161 4-8-4 49 oh1 .... NeilPollard 3 39
(W J Musson) *t.k.h: sn prom: rdn over 1f out: wknd fnl f* **20/1**

2m 4.53s (2.83) **Going Correction** +0.175s/f (Slow) **7** Ran SP% **115.4**
Speed ratings (Par 101): **94,92,91,89,89 88,86**
CSF £17.64 CT £58.42 TOTE £4.70: £2.20, £2.10; EX 18.30 Place 6 £120.46, Place 5 £69.77..
Owner Ken Tyre & Lee Tyre **Bred** Bryan Ryan **Trained** Exning, Suffolk

FOCUS
This was run at an early dawdle which would not have suited a few and it was also noticeable that all bar Casablanca Minx made for the centre of the track after turning in. The winning time was moderate. Weak form.
T/Plt: £549.00 to a £1 stake. Pool: £56,295.70. 74.85 winning tickets. T/Qpdt: £35.30 to a £1 stake. Pool: £4,488.70. 93.90 winning tickets. KH

1249 MAISONS-LAFFITTE (R-H)
Monday, April 14

OFFICIAL GOING: Heavy

1375a PRIX IMPRUDENCE (LISTED RACE) (FILLIES) (STRAIGHT COURSE) 7f (S)
1:20 (1:23) 3-Y-0 £20,221 (£8,088; £6,066; £4,044; £2,022)

RPR

1 **Natagora (FR)**[192] 5973 3-9-0 .... C-PLemaire 7 115+
(P Bary, France) *racd in 2nd: led over 1f out: pushed out* **4/5**[1]

2 1 ½ **Modern Look**[164] 6630 3-9-0 .... SPasquier 3 107
(D Smaga, France) *racd in 5th: wnt 3rd over 2f out: kpt on to take 2nd on line* **23/10**[2]

3 shd **Blue Cayenne (FR)**[21] 3-9-0 .... TJarnet 6 107
(Mlle S-V Tarrou, France) *led to over 1f out: lost 2nd on line* **20/1**

4 4 **Silent Sunday (IRE)**[31] 3-9-0 .... MGuyon 4 96
(H-A Pantall, France) *racd in 6th on outside: wnt 4th over 1 1/2f out: one pce* **30/1**

5 1 ½ **Rainbow Crossing**[200] 5760 3-9-0 .... OPeslier 2 92
(F Rohaut, France) *hld up in last: hdwy on ins to go 5th over 1 1/2f out: sn one pce* **17/1**

6 3 **Lips Arrow (GER)**[164] 6630 3-9-0 ....(b) IMendizabal 1 84
(Andreas Lowe, Germany) *racd in 7th: a in rr* **25/1**

7 2 **Roscoff (IRE)**[21] 1012 3-9-0 ....(b) DBoeuf 10 79
(Robert Collet, France) *racd in 4th on outside: wknd over 1 1/2f out* **11/1**[3]

8 8 **Saga D'Or (FR)**[21] 1012 3-9-0 .... DBonilla 5 57
(F Head, France) *racd in 3rd: wknd 2f out* **19/1**

1m 29.9s (1.60) **Going Correction** +0.50s/f (Yiel) **8** Ran SP% **116.6**
Speed ratings: **110,108,108,103,101 98,96,87**
PARI-MUTUEL: WIN 1.80; PL 1.10, 1.10, 1.70; DF 1.80.
Owner Stefan Friborg **Bred** Bertrand Gouin & Georges Duca **Trained** Chantilly, France

FOCUS
A taking 1000 Guineas trial from last year's Cheveley Park winner Natagora.

NOTEBOOK
Natagora(FR) has not only trained on after a lengthy and successful juvenile career at the highest level but may even have improved, judging by her faultless trial in this race. She relaxed in second place until the furlong marker and then lengthened her stride to win with great authority. She was in a totally different class to the others, and the fact that she was very relaxed throughout the 7f bodes well for her first try over a mile in the 1000 Guineas next month. Her trainer certainly believes she will stay the trip, and she looks a very serious contender to give the English Classic to the French for the first time since Hatoof in 1992. She acts on all sorts of going.
Modern Look was given every possible chance. She started her challenge from a furlong and a half out but never looked like getting in a blow at the winner. Her trainer felt she was unsuited by the lack of early pace, and that a mile will suit her much better. She has now been marked down for the Pouliches at Longchamp on May 11.
Blue Cayenne(FR) made a brave effort to make every yard of the running and was still going well a furlong and a half out, but she could do nothing when the winner sailed past her at the furlong marker. She ran on to the line with courage and just failed to hold second place in the dying stages. The Pouliches remains her objective.
Silent Sunday(IRE), behind early on, made some late progress up the centre of the track but never looked like troubling the first three past the post. She was a little bit out of her depth here.

1376a PRIX DJEBEL (LISTED RACE) (C&G) (STRAIGHT COURSE) 7f (S)
1:50 (1:52) 3-Y-0 £20,221 (£8,088; £6,066; £4,044; £2,022)

RPR

1 **Salut L'Africain (FR)**[24] 955 3-9-2 .... IMendizabal 4 104
(Robert Collet, France) *racd in 4th: hrd rdn to chal 1f out: led 100yds out: drvn out: jst hld on* **53/10**

2 nse **Elusif (FR)**[211] 3-9-2 .... OPeslier 1 104
(A Fabre, France) *hld up in last on ins: swtchd outside and hdwy 2f out: r.o wl fnl f: jst failed* **24/10**[2]

3 ½ **Indigo Blue (FR)**[21] 1011 3-9-2 .... TThulliez 2 103
(J-P Gallorini, France) *set stdy pce: hdd 100yds out: one pce* **15/1**

4 ½ **Sceptre Rouge (IRE)**[165] 6615 3-9-2 .... CSoumillon 5 102
(A De Royer-Dupre, France) *hld up in 5th: hdwy on outside 2f out: pressing ldrs and ev ch ins fnl f: one pce last 100yds* **17/10**[1]

5 snk **Konig Concorde (GER)**[183] 6219 3-9-2 .... SPasquier 7 101
(C Sprengel, Germany) *pressed ldr in 2nd: hrd rdn over 1f out: stl ev ch tl one pce last 200yds* **12/1**

6 hd **Bermuda Rye (IRE)**[142] 3-9-2 .... JVictoire 3 101
(M Delzangles, France) *trckd ldr in 3rd on ins: trcking ldrs but no room fr 1 1/2f out tl wl ins fnl f: unlucky* **37/10**[3]

1m 31.9s (3.60) **Going Correction** +0.50s/f (Yiel) **6** Ran SP% **117.5**
Speed ratings: **99,98,98,97,97 97**
PARI-MUTUEL: WIN 6.30; PL 2.40, 2.10; SF 26.90.
Owner Mme D Ricard **Bred** S A R L Classic Breeding & E Gonfray & M Hassan **Trained** Chantilly, France
■ Stewards' Enquiry : I Mendizabal €500 fine: whip abuse

FOCUS
The six runners were separated by around a length and a half at the line.

NOTEBOOK
Salut L'Africain(FR), who was running in his 17th race in just under a year and has never been out of the money, held on by inches in a desperate drive to the line in a race that lacked any pace. This heavy-ground specialist will now be allowed to take his chance in the Poulains next month.
Elusif(FR), totally unsuited by the lack of early pace, failed by a nose to keep his unbeaten record, and he is the one in this field most likely to make a name for himself in the future. Last early on and slightly outpaced when things quickened, he did not get into the race until well inside the final furlong. With another stride he would have been declared the winner. He will probably be allowed to take his chance in the Poulains, and is certain to have greatly benefited from this outing.
Indigo Blue(FR), smartly away, led from the start and battled courageously to the line. He was challenged for the lead halfway through the final furlong but did not give up his advantage without a battle.
Sceptre Rouge(IRE) lost his unbeaten record as a juvenile last year when encountering testing ground, so conditions were far from ideal. He tried to make a forward move a furlong and a half out but was slightly one-paced when things warmed up. He should certainly not be written off, and will be a different proposition on a better surface later in the season.

1155 NOTTINGHAM (L-H)
Tuesday, April 15

OFFICIAL GOING: Soft (good to soft in places) changing to soft after race 3 (3.20)
Wind: Moderate, half against Weather: Overcast and raining

1377 EUROPEAN BREEDERS' FUND MAIDEN STKS 5f 13y
2:20 (2:21) (Class 5) 2-Y-0 £3,626 (£1,079; £539; £269) Stalls High

Form RPR

0 **1** **Calypso Girl (IRE)**[24] 957 2-8-12 0 .... StephenDonohoe 6 76
(P D Evans) *mde all: rdn over 1f out: styd on wl* **3/1**[3]

2 ½ **Shampagne** 2-9-3 0 .... TQuinn 2 79
(P F I Cole) *cl up: effrt 2f out and sn ev ch: rdn and wandered over 1f out: kpt on u.p ins fnl f* **2/1**[1]

2 **3** 7 **Eilean Eeve**[3] 1324 2-8-12 0 .... SebSanders 1 49
(A J McCabe) *s.i.s: t.k.h and sn chsng ldng pair on outer: effrt 2f out: sn rdn and one pce* **11/4**[2]

4 2 ½ **Ridgeway Silver** 2-8-5 0 .... GabrielHannon(7) 4 40
(M D I Usher) *s.i.s: in rr tl styd on fnl 2f: nvr a factor* **18/1**

5 3 ¾ **Amorachy** 2-9-3 0 .... NCallan 5 32
(K A Ryan) *dwlt: sn chsng ldrs: rdn along over 2f out and sn wknd* **4/1**

4 **6** *7* **Strictly Royal**[5] 1276 2-9-3 0 ChrisCatlin 3 —
(M R Channon) *chsd ldrs: rdn along after 2f: sn outpcd and bhd* **33/1**

65.38 secs (4.68) **Going Correction** +0.80s/f (Soft) **6** Ran SP% **113.2**
Speed ratings (Par 92): **94,93,82,78,72 60**
CSF £9.61 TOTE £3.80: £2.00, £1.50; EX 13.10.
Owner M D Jones **Bred** Yeomanstown Stud **Trained** Pandy, Monmouths

FOCUS
A moderate-looking contest. The bad ground makes the form unreliable for the near future, with the first two coping with it better than the rest.

NOTEBOOK
Calypso Girl(IRE), who had ran well in the Brocklesby, used her experience to see off newcomer Shampagne's late challenge. She handled the ground well, but there is no reason why she should not improve again on a better surface. (op 9-2)
Shampagne ◆, who was much bigger in stature than the winner, showed plenty of speed throughout and only just lost out in a driving finish. He will improve for this experience and can collect next time. (op 13-8 tchd 11-8)
Eilean Eeve, who was also slowly away at Doncaster three days earlier, tried to get on terms at the halfway point but could not sustain her challenge in the closing stages. She will obviously need to learn to break much quicker to have a chance. (op 2-1 tchd 3-1)
Ridgeway Silver could not pick up in the easy ground and will be better judged after an effort on quicker ground. (op 50-1)
Amorachy, wearing a noseband on this debut, managed to get prominent after missing the break but failed to get home. (op 8-1 tchd 9-1)

1378 LYFAB ENTERPRISES H'CAP 5f 13y
2:50 (2:50) (Class 5) (0-70,70) 4-Y-0+ **£2,590** (£770; £385; £192) **Stalls** High

Form RPR

3-33 **1** **Dorn Dancer (IRE)**[21] 1015 6-8-7 **59** FergalLynch 3 71+
(D W Barker) *in rr and pushed along after 1f: swtchd rt and hdwy 2f out: nt clr run on stands' rails wl over 1f out: sn rdn and styd on strly to ld wl ins fnl f* **4/1**[1]

04-0 **2** *1 1/4* **Jakeini (IRE)**[11] 1191 5-8-8 **60** GrahamGibbons 7 63
(E S McMahon) *towards rr: hdwy over 2f out: rdn to chse ldng pair over 1f out: kpt on u.p ins fnl f* **10/1**

1411 **3** *1 1/4* **Garlogs**[42] 786 5-8-13 **68** RussellKennemore(3) 11 67+
(R Hollinshead) *led: qckng clr 1/2-way: rdn wl over 1f out: wknd and hdd ins fnl f* **6/1**[3]

05-1 **4** *1/2* **Bookiesindex Boy**[20] 1033 4-9-3 **69** (v) RyanMoore 8 66
(J R Jenkins) *towards rr: swtchd lft over 3f out: gd hdwy over 2f out: rdn to chse ldr wl over 1f out: wknd ins fnl f* **6/1**[3]

5-20 **5** *3 3/4* **El Potro**[13] 1157 6-8-8 **60** SteveDrowne 4 44
(J R Holt) *chsd ldrs: effrt 2f out: sn rdn and no imp fr over 1f out* **5/1**[2]

6456 **6** *hd* **Desert Opal**[38] 840 8-9-4 **70** (b) PhilipRobinson 9 53
(C R Dore) *chsd ldrs: effrt 2f out: sn rdn and edgd rt: no imp appr fnl f* **6/1**[3]

6322 **7** *1/2* **Bentley**[11] 1185 4-8-4 **56** oh1 (v) JimmyQuinn 6 37
(D Shaw) *chsd ldrs: rdn along 2f out: grad wknd* **14/1**

-050 **8** *2* **No Time (IRE)**[14] 1129 8-8-8 **60** PatCosgrave 10 34
(A J McCabe) *chsd ldrs: rdn along over 2f out and sn wknd* **12/1**

1040 **9** *3 1/4* **Tenancy (IRE)**[3] 1338 4-8-4 **56** oh8 (p) ChrisCatlin 5 18
(A J McCabe) *rrd s: sn chsng ldrs: rdn along over 2f out and sn wknd* **28/1**

105- **10** *5* **Sofinella (IRE)**[158] 6752 5-8-4 **59** LukeMorris(3) 2 —
(A W Carroll) *prom: rdn along over 2f out: sn wknd* **33/1**

040- **11** *1 3/4* **Toy Top (USA)**[195] 5908 5-8-7 **59** (b) TomEaves 12 —
(M Dods) *chsd ldrs: rdn along over 2f out and sn wknd* **14/1**

100- **12** *3 3/4* **Viewforth**[196] 5879 10-8-5 **57** (b) MartinDwyer 1 —
(M A Buckley) *prom: rdn along over 2f out and sn wknd* **33/1**

64.74 secs (4.04) **Going Correction** +0.80s/f (Soft) **12** Ran SP% **119.0**
Speed ratings (Par 103): **99,97,95,94,88 87,87,83,78,70 67,61**
CSF £44.07 CT £241.53 TOTE £6.50: £1.30, £3.90, £2.40; EX 33.20.
Owner The Ebor Partnership **Bred** Timothy Coughlan **Trained** Scorton, N Yorks

FOCUS
An average handicap in which Garlogs set a strong pace. However, he went too fast and set the race up for a couple of strong finishers. The form is rated through the winner.

1379 SHOWSEC MAIDEN STKS (DIV I) 1m 54y
3:20 (3:21) (Class 5) 3-Y-0 **£2,104** (£626; £312; £156) **Stalls** Centre

Form RPR

1 **Born Tobouggie (GER)** 3-8-12 0 TedDurcan 11 75
(H R A Cecil) *prom: cl up 1/2-way: led wl over 2f out: rdn: rn green and hdd over 1f out: rallied ins fnl f to ld last 50yds* **7/1**

2 *nk* **Fosool (IRE)** 3-8-12 0 RHills 8 75
(M Johnston) *dwlt: hdwy on inner to trck ldrs 1/2-way: effrt to chal wl over 2f out: rdn to ld appr fnl f: drvn: hdd and no ex last 50yds* **11/1**

5- **3** *3 1/2* **Sir Royal (USA)**[207] 5580 3-9-0 0 PJMcDonald(3) 1 71
(G A Swinbank) *prom: rdn along to chse ldng pair over 2f out: drvn and rdr dropped whip over 1f out: kpt on same pce* **22/1**

6- **4** *3* **Master Spy**[150] 6850 3-9-3 0 JimmyFortune 4 65
(J H M Gosden) *prom: rdn along over 2f out: drvn wl over 1f out and one pce* **17/2**

42-4 **5** *nk* **Andaman Sunset**[13] 1149 3-9-3 83 SebSanders 6 64+
(G Wragg) *in tch: hdwy to chse ldrs over 2f out: sn rdn and no imp* **15/8**[1]

0- **6** *2* **King's Alchemist**[187] 6130 3-9-3 0 HayleyTurner 2 59+
(M D I Usher) *towards rr: sme hdwy on inner over 2f out: sn no imp* **20/1**

0-60 **7** *1* **Lady Florence**[13] 1147 3-8-9 49 LukeMorris(3) 10 52?
(A B Coogan) *chsd ldrs: rdn along over 3f out: sn outpcd* **150/1**

5- **8** *8* **Staten (USA)**[164] 6634 3-9-3 0 PhillipMakin 7 39
(T D Barron) *a towards rr* **33/1**

9 *1 1/4* **Modernist** 3-9-3 0 RyanMoore 3 36
(Sir Michael Stoute) *s.i.s: a in rr* **5/1**[3]

40- **10** *3/4* **Azeer (USA)**[297] 2855 3-9-3 0 AlanMunro 5 34
(P W Chapple-Hyam) *sn led: rdn along and hdd 3f out: sn wknd* **10/3**[2]

11 *6* **Jordi Roper (IRE)** 3-9-3 0 DarrenWilliams 9 20
(S Parr) *wnt rt s: in rr tl sme hdwy 3f out: sn rdn and wknd* **100/1**

1m 51.47s (5.87) **Going Correction** +0.80s/f (Soft) **11** Ran SP% **119.6**
Speed ratings (Par 98): **102,101,98,95,94 92,91,83,82,81 75**
CSF £77.56 TOTE £7.70: £2.70, £2.70, £6.60; EX 70.00.
Owner The Sticky Wicket Syndicate **Bred** Graf Und Grafin Von Stauffenberg **Trained** Newmarket, Suffolk

FOCUS
A moderate-looking maiden and, with the first two being debutantes, only time will tell what the form amounts to. The third and fourth look the best guide. The winning time was a fraction quicker than the second division.
Azeer(USA) Official explanation: jockey said colt was unsuited by the soft ground

1380 SHOWSEC MAIDEN STKS (DIV II) 1m 54y
3:50 (3:51) (Class 5) 3-Y-0 **£2,104** (£626; £312; £156) **Stalls** Centre

Form RPR

42-2 **1** **Glorious Gift (IRE)**[14] 1125 3-9-3 80 AlanMunro 8 87
(P W Chapple-Hyam) *prom: hdwy over 3f out: led wl over 2f out: rdn clr wl over 1f out: comf* **8/11**[1]

3- **2** *6* **Barricado (FR)**[182] 6246 3-9-3 0 SteveDrowne 7 73
(R Charlton) *t.k.h: hld up in tch: hdwy to trck ldrs over 3f out: rdn to chse wnr wl over 1f out: kpt on same pce* **7/2**[2]

42- **3** *2* **King Kenny**[140] 6960 3-9-0 0 DNolan(3) 5 68
(S Parr) *in rr: stdy hdwy on outer 3f out: rdn to chse ldrs 2f out: sn drvn and one pce* **11/1**

4 *4 1/2* **Reine De Violette** 3-8-12 0 TedDurcan 3 53+
(H R A Cecil) *t.k.h: hld up in tch: hdwy 3f out: swtchd lft wl over 1f out: kpt on same pce* **16/1**

0- **5** *1/2* **Trenchant**[168] 6574 3-9-3 0 JamieSpencer 9 57+
(J R Fanshawe) *hld up in tch: hdwy to join ldrs over 3f out: rdn and edgd lft over 2f out: sn wknd* **11/1**

00- **6** *6* **Mouse White**[265] 3842 3-9-3 0 DaneO'Neill 10 43
(H Candy) *in tch: rdn along wl over 3f out and sn wknd* **100/1**

7 *1 1/4* **Pick Of The Day (IRE)** 3-9-3 0 TPQueally 6 40
(J G Given) *chsd ldng pair: rdn along over 3f out and sn wknd* **40/1**

5- **8** *1* **Top Man Dan (IRE)**[185] 6184 3-9-3 0 DanielTudhope 4 38
(D Carroll) *led: rdn along over 3f out: hdd wl over 2f out and grad wknd* **8/1**[3]

0-0 **9** *28* **Milloaks (IRE)**[10] 1215 3-8-7 0 SCreighton(5) 1 —
(E J Creighton) *chsd ldr: rdn along on inner 1/2-way: sn wknd* **200/1**

1m 51.59s (5.99) **Going Correction** +0.80s/f (Soft) **9** Ran SP% **117.7**
Speed ratings (Par 98): **102,96,94,89,89 83,81,80,52**
CSF £3.54 TOTE £1.70: £1.10, £1.30, £2.40; EX 3.60.
Owner Jaber Abdullah **Bred** Gainsborough Stud Management Ltd **Trained** Newmarket, Suffolk

FOCUS
A moderate affair, but with a clear-cut winner. The form has been rated around the second. It was run in a slightly slower time than the first division.

1381 BEST RACECOURSES ON TURFTV H'CAP 1m 54y
4:20 (4:22) (Class 4) (0-80,80) 3-Y-0 **£4,857** (£1,445; £722; £360) **Stalls** Centre

Form RPR

01-1 **1** **Jaser**[13] 1161 3-9-2 **78** AlanMunro 9 96+
(P W Chapple-Hyam) *dwlt and towards rr: hdwy 1/2-way: effrt on outer over 2f out: rdn to ld and hung lft wl over 1f out: drvn out* **6/4**[1]

060- **2** *2 3/4* **Conquisto**[193] 5977 3-8-12 **74** AdamKirby 2 84
(C G Cox) *prom: effrt 3f out: rdn to ld over 2f out sn: drvn and hdd wl over 1f out: kpt on u.p ins fnl f* **40/1**

221- **3** *7* **Bermacha**[173] 6456 3-8-13 **75** MartinDwyer 4 69
(W R Muir) *prom: effrt to ld briefly wl over 2f out: sn rdn and hdd: drvn and one pce fr over 1f out* **28/1**

034- **4** *1 1/4* **Dr Livingstone (IRE)**[200] 5780 3-9-0 **76** SteveDrowne 3 67
(C R Egerton) *led: rdn along 3f out: sn hdd and grad wknd* **50/1**

6-61 **5** *nk* **Never Catcher (IRE)**[14] 1123 3-8-7 **69** StephenDonohoe 11 59
(P A Blockley) *in rr: hdwy 3f out: rdn and styd on fnl 2f: nt rch ldrs* **40/1**

051- **6** *5* **Brave Mave**[189] 6093 3-8-12 **74** NCallan 7 53
(W Jarvis) *a towards rr* **28/1**

51-0 **7** *1/2* **Elysee Palace (IRE)**[17] 1074 3-9-2 **78** PhilipRobinson 6 55
(M A Jarvis) *trckd ldrs: pushed along 3f out: wknd 2f out* **11/1**[3]

030- **8** *7* **Farsighted**[187] 6128 3-8-9 **71** DaleGibson 10 32
(J M P Eustace) *a in rr* **100/1**

516- **9** *3 1/2* **Kiwi Bay**[171] 6486 3-9-3 **79** PhillipMakin 8 32
(M Dods) *plld hrd: a towards rr* **8/1**[2]

1-3 **10** *4* **Crosstar**[10] 1208 3-9-4 **80** SebSanders 12 24
(M Botti) *prom: rdn along over 3f out: wkng whn eased wl over 1f out* **20/1**

61- **11** *55* **Sky Dive**[210] 5498 3-9-2 **78** JamieSpencer 1 —
(L M Cumani) *in tch: pushed along over 3f out: sn wknd and eased fnl 2f* **6/4**[1]

1m 50.93s (5.33) **Going Correction** +0.80s/f (Soft) **11** Ran SP% **118.9**
Speed ratings (Par 100): **105,102,95,94,93 88,88,81,77,73 18**
CSF £88.70 CT £1281.70 TOTE £2.20: £1.10, £6.70, £4.40; EX 66.90.
Owner Ziad A Galadari **Bred** Galadari Sons Stud Company Limited **Trained** Newmarket, Suffolk

FOCUS
This looked an interesting race on paper, but with several of the horses failing to handle the soft ground and running well below form, it took less winning than it might have done. That said, the first two came clear and Jaser continues on the up.
Crosstar Official explanation: jockey said colt was unsuited by the soft ground
Sky Dive Official explanation: trainer's rep said colt was unsuited by the soft ground

1382 WILDGOOSECONSTRUCTION.CO.UK MAIDEN STKS 1m 1f 213y
4:50 (4:50) (Class 5) 3-Y-0+ **£2,590** (£770; £385; £192) **Stalls** Low

Form RPR

204- **1** **Bold Choice (IRE)**[176] 6382 3-8-9 96 PhilipRobinson 6 92+
(M A Jarvis) *mde all: qckng clr wl over 2f out: heavily eased ins fnl f: unchal* **8/11**[1]

2 *2 3/4* **Coin Of The Realm (IRE)** 3-8-9 0 TPQueally 4 71+
(E A L Dunlop) *in rr: hdwy on inner over 2f out: sn rdn and styd on ins fnl f: no ch w wnr* **18/1**

3 *1/2* **Sea Chorus** 3-8-4 0 HayleyTurner 3 65
(M L W Bell) *in tch: hdwy 3f out: rdn to chse wnr over 2f out: sn drvn: lost 2nd ins fnl f* **40/1**

4 *4 1/2* **World Time** 3-8-9 0 RobertHavlin 5 61+
(J H M Gosden) *s.i.s and bhd: hdwy wl over 2f out: sn rdn and kpt on: nrst fin* **7/1**[2]

5 *1/2* **Danesman** 3-8-9 0 ChrisCatlin 1 60+
(E J O'Neill) *towards rr: swtchd outside and hdwy 3f out: rdn 2f out: kpt on: nrst fin* **33/1**

66- **6** *3 1/4* **Lady Killer Queen**[188] 6109 4-9-9 0 DanielTudhope 11 52
(D Carroll) *in rr: hdwy 3f out: styd on fnl 2f: nrst fin* **150/1**

7 *4 1/2* **Haldibari (IRE)**[17] 4-10-0 0 DaneO'Neill 8 48
(A King) *prom on inner: rdn along over 3f out: sn drvn and wknd* **8/1**

5 **8** *1 3/4* **Key Decision (IRE)**[22] 991 4-9-11 0 PJMcDonald(3) 9 45
(G A Swinbank) *chsd ldrs: rdn along 3f out: wknd 2f out* **40/1**

5 **9** *1/2* **Coco L'Escargot**[32] 878 4-9-9 0 StephenCarson 16 39
(J R Jenkins) *prom: rdn along over 3f out: sn drvn and wknd over 2f out* **150/1**

10 nk **Goldrenched (IRE)** 3-8-4 0 .... JimmyQuinn 12 34
(M L W Bell) *a towards rr* **14/1**
11 3 1/2 **Freedom Flying**[111] 5-9-6 0 .... (p) JamieMoriarty(3) 15 31
(Joss Saville) *racd wd: midfield tl rdn along 1/2-way and sn outpcd* **125/1**
12 hd **Heartsanddiamonds**[50] 4-9-6 0 .... JerryO'Dwyer(3) 2 31
(A W Carroll) *a towards rr* **150/1**
- 13 4 1/2 **Missycomelightly**[132] 5-9-9 0 .... TomEaves 10 22
(W J H Ratcliffe) *s.i.s: a bhd* **150/1**
- 14 2 **Factotum** 4-10-0 0 .... PatCosgrave 7 23
(L M Cumani) *dwlt: rdn along in rr 1/2-way: a bhd* **25/1**
6 15 9 **Emerging Light**[55] 633 6-9-7 0 .... ThomasBubb(7) 13 5
(S Dow) *a bhd* **200/1**
16 7 **Mytexie (FR)** 3-8-9 0 .... JoeFanning 14 —
(M Johnston) *chsd ldrs: rdn along over 3f out: sn wknd* **15/2[3]**

2m 17.2s (6.50) **Going Correction** +0.80s/f (Soft)
WFA 3 from 4yo+ 19lb **16** Ran SP% **120.8**
Speed ratings (Par 103): **106,103,103,99,99 96,93,91,91,91 88,88,84,83,75 70**
CSF £16.64 TOTE £1.90: £1.10, £5.40, £9.80; EX 22.30.
Owner B E Nielsen **Bred** Max Morris **Trained** Newmarket, Suffolk

FOCUS
Bold Choice won easily and was value for around 10l, but his form stood out beforehand and the race had little strength in depth.

1383 PADDOCKS CONFERENCE CENTRE AT NOTTINGHAM RACECOURSE H'CAP 1m 1f 213y
5:20 (5:21) (Class 5) (0-70,70) 4-Y-0+ **£2,590** (£770; £385; £192) **Stalls** Low

Form RPR
000/ 1 **Penny Island (IRE)**[19] 3752 6-8-10 **65** .... TravisBlock(3) 13 72
(A King) *trckd ldrs: hdwy 3f out: rdn to ld wl over 1f out: drvn ins fnl f and hld on gamely* **14/1**
053- 2 hd **Effigy**[176] 6380 4-8-12 **64** .... DaneO'Neill 1 71
(H Candy) *trckd ldrs on inner: swtchd rt and hdwy 3f out: rdn to chse wnr over 1f out: drvn and kpt on ins fnl f: jst hld* **6/1[3]**
156- 3 1 1/4 **Mae Cigan (FR)**[40] 6422 5-8-11 **63** .... NCallan 2 68+
(M Blanshard) *trckd ldrs on inner: hdwy over 2f out: rdn to chse ldrs over 1f out: drvn and kpt on ins fnl f* **4/1[1]**
40-4 4 3/4 **Magdalene**[14] 1127 4-9-1 **67** .... ChrisCatlin 7 70
(Rae Guest) *prom: chsd ldr 1/2-way: rdn over 2f out: drvn and one pce appr fnl f* **13/2**
150- 5 2 3/4 **King Of Rhythm (IRE)**[185] 6180 5-9-4 **70** .... DanielTudhope 14 68
(D Carroll) *hld up in rr: hdwy 3f out: rdn along 2f out: kpt on ins fnl f: nrst fin* **16/1**
42-4 6 1/2 **Trouble Mountain (USA)**[13] 1159 11-8-13 **65** .... (t) DaleGibson 9 62
(M W Easterby) *chsd ldrs: rdn along and outpcd over 3f out: plugged on appr fnl f* **13/2**
3224 7 3/4 **Trysting Grove (IRE)**[13] 1148 7-8-6 **58** .... SaleemGolam 12 53
(E G Bevan) *dwlt: towards rr: hdwy 3f out: rdn to chse ldrs 2f out: sn drvn and no imp appr fnl f* **10/1**
350- 8 4 **Willow Dancer (IRE)**[207] 5604 4-9-2 **68** .... AdamKirby 5 55
(W R Swinburn) *led: rdn along 3f out: drvn and hdd wl over 1f out: wknd* **10/1**
00-0 9 2 1/4 **Joshua's Gold (IRE)**[13] 1159 7-8-8 **67** .... PaulPickard(7) 10 50
(D Carroll) *chsd ldrs: rdn along over 2f out: grad wknd* **50/1**
10 2 1/4 **Never Pink (FR)**[149] 4-8-13 **65** .... StephenDonohoe 11 43
(Ian Williams) *hld up towards rr: hdwy on outer over 2f out: sn rdn and wknd* **33/1**
053- 11 1 **Stalking Tiger (IRE)**[183] 6238 4-9-1 **67** .... SteveDrowne 6 43
(R Charlton) *trckd ldng pair: effrt wl over 2f out: sn rdn and wknd* **5/1[2]**
1/65 12 2 1/2 **Babieca (USA)**[17] 1083 4-8-8 **65** .... (b[1]) NeilBrown(5) 3 36
(T D Barron) *s.i.s: a bhd* **33/1**
0- 13 13 **Out Of Nothing**[137] 6987 5-9-1 **67** .... PatCosgrave 8 12
(K M Prendergast) *a in rr* **66/1**

2m 18.68s (7.98) **Going Correction** +0.80s/f (Soft) **13** Ran SP% **117.7**
Speed ratings (Par 103): **100,99,98,98,96 95,95,91,90,88 87,85,75**
CSF £92.58 CT £406.45 TOTE £21.40: £5.70, £2.30, £1.80; EX 135.20 Place 6 £75.11, Place 5 £49.36.
Owner Alan King **Bred** Calley House Syndicate **Trained** Barbury Castle, Wilts

FOCUS
A fairly weak handicap but at least the first two were relatively unexposed. The first four home were nicely clear and the from appears solid.
Stalking Tiger(IRE) Official explanation: jockey said gelding was unsuited by the soft ground
T/Plt: £48.30 to a £1 stake. Pool: £54,229.97. 818.04 winning tickets. T/Qpdt: £13.50 to a £1 stake. Pool: £3,449.40. 188.50 winning tickets. JR

994 WARWICK (L-H)
Tuesday, April 15

OFFICIAL GOING: Soft (good to soft in places; 6.0)
Wind: Light across for the 1st, changing to fresh against Weather: Overcast, turning to light rain race for races 2 and 3, becoming heavier for race 4, then easing off

1384 MERCIA RADIO FOR COVENTRY AND WARWICKSHIRE (S) STKS 5f
2:30 (2:30) (Class 6) 2-Y-0 **£2,047** (£604; £302) **Stalls** Centre

Form RPR
1 **Fuaigh Mor (IRE)** 2-8-6 0 .... PaulHanagan 8 61+
(A Bailey) *a.p: led and hung lft fr over 1f out: rdn out* **4/1[2]**
54 2 nk **Dancing Wave**[15] 1118 2-8-4 0 ow1 .... TolleyDean(3) 5 61+
(W G M Turner) *chsd ldr: rdn and ev ch fr over 1f out: edgd lft: r.o* **10/3[1]**
1 3 3 **Heaven Or Hell (IRE)**[6] 1264 2-8-9 0 .... RichardEvans(7) 4 59
(P D Evans) *s.i.s: sn chsng ldrs: rdn and edgd rt over 1f out: styng on same pce whn edgd lft fnl f* **4/1[2]**
02 4 3 1/4 **Tarawa Atoll**[6] 1264 2-8-6 0 .... TPO'Shea 6 37
(M R Channon) *chsd ldrs: rdn over 1f out: sn wknd* **4/1[2]**
6 5 1/2 **Talulah Bells**[6] 1264 2-8-7 0 ow8 .... MarkCoumbe(7) 2 44
(A W Carroll) *wnt lft s: sn hung lft and outpcd: nvr nrr* **50/1**
6 1 1/2 **Kheley (IRE)** 2-8-6 0 .... JohnEgan 1 30
(W M Brisbourne) *dwlt: outpcd: rdn 1/2-way: hung lft 2f out: wkng whn hung rt over 1f out* **8/1[3]**
7 1 1/4 **Makaluna** 2-8-4 0 .... JackDean(7) 3 31
(W G M Turner) *led: rdn and hdd over 1f out: sn wknd* **14/1**
8 shd **Champagne Leader** 2-8-4 0 ow5 .... GihanArnolda(7) 7 30
(A B Haynes) *hung rt thrght: sn outpcd* **9/1**

64.53 secs (4.93) **Going Correction** +0.90s/f (Soft) **8** Ran SP% **112.8**
Speed ratings (Par 90): **96,95,90,85,84 82,80,80**
CSF £17.25 TOTE £5.40: £1.50, £2.30, £1.70; EX 20.80.The winner was bought in for 7,600gns. Dancing Wave was claimed by M. C. Chapman for £6,000.
Owner Phil Buchanan **Bred** Anamoine Ltd **Trained** Newmarket, Suffolk

FOCUS
A reasonable juvenile seller for the time of year. The third ran close to his Bath form. The winning time was 0.47 seconds quicker than the following maiden, but the wind changed and they were running into a headwind in the following contest. They tended to race up the middle of the track in the straight.

NOTEBOOK
Fuaigh Mor(IRE), a 6,000euros daughter of Dubai Destination, half-sister to among others smart 6f-7f winner Medley, out of a 5f juvenile winner, was supported on course and she justified the money with a game success on her racecourse debut. Having raced just off the pace through the early stages, she responded well when asked for her effort early in the straight and just proved good enough. She has some size about her and, bought in for 7,600gns, it will be a little surprising if she can not add to this in similarly moderate company at some point. (op 6-1)
Dancing Wave, who showed ability on her debut here but was well beaten next time on the Fibresand at Southwell, benefited from the drop in grade and was just held. After showing plenty of speed, she found the well-backed Fuaigh Mor too strong inside the final furlong but stuck on once headed and, clear of the remainder, she should find a similar race. She carried 1lb overweight. (op 7-2 tchd 3-1)
Heaven Or Hell(IRE), whose trainer won this race with Wizby in 2005, was bought in for 4,200gns after winning on his debut in this grade at Bath, but he found this tougher under his penalty, despite a 7lb claimer taking over. He will probably continue to be vulnerable, although he should be able to find weaker races at some point. (op 7-2 tchd 10-3)
Tarawa Atoll was 5lb better off with Heaven Or Hell for a half-length beating at Bath, but she failed to pick up for pressure and was unable to reverse form. (op 7-2)
Talulah Bells was beaten 37 lengths on her debut at Bath behind Heaven Or Hell and Tarawa Atoll, but this was better, especially considering she carried 8lb overweight and, although clearly only moderate, at least she is going the right way.
Kheley(IRE), a 5,400gns daughter of Kheleyf, first foal of an unraced mare, gave trouble in the paddock and was very green in the race itself, missing the break and then hanging in the straight. Despite all that, she showed some ability and, not a bad type for the grade, she might be capable of better if growing up. (op 10-1)
Makaluna, a gelded son of Makbul, half-brother to multiple sprint winner Emilio, and to four others winners, including a couple of quite useful sprinters in the US, out of a juvenile winner in France, showed good speed but could not sustain his effort. He should come on for this and better ground might help. (op 12-1)
Champagne Leader, a daughter of Monsieur Bond, half-sister to smart sprinter Fantasy Believer, was representing last year's winning trainer, but there is not much of her and she showed little. She carried 5lb overweight. (op 17-2 tchd 8-1)

1385 EUROPEAN BREEDERS' FUND MAIDEN FILLIES' STKS 5f
3:00 (3:06) (Class 5) 2-Y-0 **£3,626** (£1,079; £539; £269) **Stalls** Centre

Form RPR
1 **Aspen Darlin (IRE)** 2-9-0 0 .... PaulHanagan 7 73
(A Bailey) *a.p: rdn over 1f out: r.o to ld nr fin* **15/2**
2 1/2 **Miss Hollybell** 2-9-0 0 .... JimCrowley 3 71
(J Gallagher) *chsd ldrs: rdn to ld ins fnl f: hdd nr fin* **8/1**
3 4 **Moss Likely (IRE)** 2-9-0 0 .... EdwardCreighton 5 57
(M R Channon) *led: rdn: hdd & wknd ins fnl f* **13/8[1]**
4 1 1/4 **Bethie** 2-9-0 0 .... PaulMulrennan 1 52
(R Brotherton) *chsd ldr tl rdn over 1f out: wknd fnl f* **40/1**
5 2 3/4 **Premier Krug (IRE)** 2-9-0 0 .... TGMcLaughlin 2 49+
(P D Evans) *s.s: outpcd: r.o ins fnl f: nvr nrr* **6/1[3]**
6 2 1/2 **Kyllorien** 2-9-0 0 .... MichaelHills 8 33
(B W Hills) *swvd rt s: outpcd* **10/3[2]**
7 17 **Right Price** 2-9-0 0 .... NeilPollard 4 —
(A P Jarvis) *s.s: outpcd* **20/1**
8 15 **Agnes Love** 2-9-0 0 .... EddieAhern 6 —
(Mrs H Sweeting) *s.i.s: outpcd* **11/1**

65.00 secs (5.40) **Going Correction** +0.90s/f (Soft) **8** Ran SP% **113.9**
Speed ratings (Par 89): **92,91,84,82,78 74,47,23**
CSF £64.54 TOTE £8.60: £2.30, £2.20, £1.30; EX 74.10.
Owner Indian Haven Syndicate **Bred** Miss Annmarie Burke **Trained** Newmarket, Suffolk

FOCUS
A field of newcomers for this fillies' maiden, so impossible to be sure of the level, but it looked a fair contest. The leaders looked to go off a little too fast and set the race up for the closers. The winning time was 0.47 seconds slower than the previous seller but, unlike in the opener, they were racing into a headwind and comparisons are likely to prove misleading. The majority tended to race up the middle of the track.

NOTEBOOK
Aspen Darlin(IRE), a 10,000euros daughter of Indian Haven, first foal of an unraced sister to a dual 6f winner, justified market support with a winning debut. She struggled a touch to lay up with the furious early pace, but really found her stride as the leaders began to come back early in the straight and she stayed on strongest of all to get up close home and win going away. Her trainer is of the opinion she will be better suited by good ground, but thinks she is probably just a nursery type for later in the season. (op 14-1)
Miss Hollybell, by Umistim, out of a multiple sprint winner, looked the winner early inside the final furlong, but she was collared close home. This was a pleasing debut and she might be able to find a similar race for her bang in-form yard. (op 14-1)
Moss Likely(IRE), a 24,000euros daughter of Clodovil, out of a dual 1m1f winner, was extremely well backed on her racecourse debut but found a couple too strong. She knew her job and showed bags of early speed, but if anything she probably went off a touch too fast and she had little left for the last furlong. She looks up to winning a similar race, but she might want slightly better ground. (op 6-4 tchd 2-1)
Bethie, by Bold Edge, half-sister to 5f juvenile winner Baytown Valentina, out of a triple 6f-7f three-year-old winner, showed loads of early speed to match strides with the favourite, but she could not sustain her challenge after sticking more towards the far rail. She is entitled to come on for this and has the natural speed to win a similar contest. (tchd 33-1)
Premier Krug(IRE), a 24,000euros Xaar filly, half-sister to very smart dual 1m winner Kilworth, and 6f scorer Vigano, out of a 6f juvenile scorer, missed the break and was too green to do herself justice, but she was noted doing some good late work. She should have learnt plenty and can improve. (op 7-2)
Kyllorien, a daughter of Kyllachy, first foal of a 7f three-year-old winner, was green to post and looked in need of the experience in the race itself. (tchd 9-4 and 7-2)

1386 MERCIA'S BREAKFAST WITH JOHN AND ROISIN H'CAP 5f
3:30 (3:31) (Class 5) (0-75,79) 4-Y-0+ **£3,070** (£906; £453) **Stalls** Centre

Form RPR
3164 1 **Judge 'n Jury**[50] 699 4-9-1 **72** .... (t) PaulHanagan 8 81
(R A Harris) *chsd ldrs: led over 1f out: rdn whn rdr dropped reins ins fnl f: r.o* **12/1**

2242 **2** *hd* **Spoof Master (IRE)**[8] 1242 4-8-13 **70** RobertWinston 5 78
(C R Dore) *chsd ldrs: outpcd: rallied and swtchd lft over 1f out: r.o* **9/2**[2]

00-5 **3** *nk* **Highland Warrior**[22] 994 9-9-0 **71** MickyFenton 9 78
(P T Midgley) *s.i.s: hdwy over 1f out: rdn and edgd lft ins fnl f: r.o* **9/2**[2]

10-2 **4** *nse* **Tilly's Dream**[20] 1021 5-8-13 **70** EddieAhern 7 77
(G C Bravery) *mid-div: hdwy over 1f out: sn rdn and hung lft: r.o* **8/1**

4133 **5** *nk* **Cerebus**[7] 1261 6-8-12 **72** (bt) WilliamBuick(3) 6 78
(A J McCabe) *chsd ldrs: rdn over 1f out: r.o* **9/1**

-002 **6** *1 3/4* **Namir (IRE)**[6] 1268 6-9-1 **72** (vt) JimCrowley 4 71
(D Shaw) *dwlt: outpcd: hdwy over 1f out: swtchd rt ins fnl f: nt rch ldrs* **6/1**[3]

110- **7** *3 1/4* **Princess Ellis**[171] 6487 4-9-4 **75** DavidAllan 1 63
(E J Alston) *led over 3f: wknd ins fnl f* **11/1**

0-21 **8** *1/2* **Digital**[6] 1268 11-9-1 **79** 6ex ThomasO'Brien(7) 3 65
(M R Channon) *sn outpcd* **4/1**[1]

6515 **9** *nk* **Music Box Express**[11] 1191 4-8-5 **65** (t) TolleyDean(3) 2 50
(George Baker) *prom: rdn 1/2-way: wknd fnl f* **12/1**

63.83 secs (4.23) **Going Correction** +0.90s/f (Soft) **9** Ran SP% **115.5**
Speed ratings (Par 103): **102,101,101,101,100 97,92,91,91**
CSF £65.25 CT £286.33 TOTE £18.40: £4.60, £2.20, £2.20; EX 97.00.

Owner Mrs Ruth M Serrell **Bred** C A Cyzer **Trained** Earlswood, Monmouths

FOCUS
A reasonable sprint handicap and certainly quite competitive, with the first five separated by less than a length. The winning time was much quicker than the two two-year-old races, despite them running into a headwind once again. They raced middle to stands' side in the straight.

Digital Official explanation: vet said gelding had an irregular heartbeat following post-race examination

Music Box Express Official explanation: jockey & trainer said gelding was unsuited by the soft, good to soft in places ground

1387 TAYLOR WIMPEY AND PPS GROUP CONDITIONS STKS 7f 26y
4:00 (4:01) (Class 3) 4-Y-0+ **£6,799** (£2,023; £1,011; £505) **Stalls** Low

Form RPR

160- **1** **Dabbers Ridge (IRE)**[171] 6491 6-8-8 **102** MichaelHills 1 107
(B W Hills) *chsd ldrs: rdn to ld 1f out: edgd rt: r.o* **5/2**[2]

621- **2** *1 1/4* **Welsh Emperor (IRE)**[169] 6541 9-9-2 **113** MickyFenton 4 112
(T P Tate) *sn led: rdn: edgd rt and hdd whn rdr dropped reins 1f out: styd on same pce* **6/5**[1]

310- **3** *1/2* **Vanderlin**[177] 6370 9-8-5 **102** WilliamBuick(3) 2 104+
(A M Balding) *chsd ldr: rdn and nt clr run over 1f out: swtchd lft ins fnl f: styd on* **10/3**[3]

/3-0 **4** *2* **Prince Forever (IRE)**[24] 960 4-8-8 **104** EddieAhern 5 97
(M A Jarvis) *hld up: rdn over 1f out: nt trble ldrs* **8/1**

1m 26.97s (2.37) **Going Correction** +0.525s/f (Yiel) **4** Ran SP% **108.2**
Speed ratings (Par 107): **107,105,105,102**
CSF £5.93 TOTE £2.60; EX 6.00.

Owner Maurice Mogg **Bred** Franco Castelfranci **Trained** Lambourn, Berks

FOCUS
Just the four runners, but some sort of case could be made for all of these - they were all rated over 100 - and this looked like a decent conditions contest, although the form may not prove too solid. The race was run in driving rain and they went a decent pace considering the conditions. They all raced against the stands' rail in the straight.

NOTEBOOK
Dabbers Ridge(IRE), whose trainer won this race in 2004 with Pablo and in 2006 with Etlaala, returned from a near six-month break at the top of his game and was a convincing winner. He managed just one win last season, showing very patchy form, but he was never right according to Charlie Hills and is clearly over whatever was troubling him. He had to work hard to get past Welsh Emperor, who had the benefit of the rail in the straight, but he was well on top at the line and there was a lot to like about this effort. He could now go for a Listed race at Haydock on May 10th, or for the Victoria Cup on the same day, and he also has an entry in the Duke Of York Stakes over 6f. He would not be inconvenienced by a drop back in trip if taking his chance at York but, wherever he goes, he will probably appreciate a bit of ease in the ground. (tchd 9-4 and 11-4)

Welsh Emperor(IRE) set a reasonable pace considering the conditions but, despite grabbing the often favoured stands' rail in the straight, he ultimately found one too strong. To be fair he kept on once headed, despite his rider briefly dropping his reins, and he was able to keep Vanderlin at bay back in third after that one had to be switched. This was a smart effort considering he was conceding 8lb to the rejuvenated winner and he is entitled to come on for this first run in 169 days. (tchd 11-10 and 5-4 in a place)

Vanderlin, returning from six months off, travelled well just in behind Welsh Emperor for much of the way, but could find only the one pace. He would have been closer had he not been squeezed up against the rail at the furlong pole, and he had to be switched, but he was not unlucky. (op 9-2)

Prince Forever(IRE) was well held by the front three, but he still showed a lot more than in the Lincoln on his reappearance and he might be able to build on this. (op 6-1)

1388 MERCIA'S RICHARD NEALE 10AM TO 2PM H'CAP 1m 2f 188y
4:30 (4:30) (Class 4) (0-80,79) 4-Y-0+ **£4,533** (£1,348; £674; £336) **Stalls** Low

Form RPR

-212 **1** **Inspirina (IRE)**[50] 701 4-8-8 **69** JimCrowley 8 77
(R Ford) *a.p: rdn to chse ldr over 1f out: led ins fnl f: styd on* **13/2**

054- **2** *1/2* **Dove Cottage (IRE)**[182] 6253 6-8-7 **68** FergusSweeney 1 75
(W S Kittow) *led: rdn and hdd ins fnl f: styd on* **7/2**[3]

-032 **3** *1/2* **Moheebb (IRE)**[10] 1217 4-8-11 **75** (b) AndrewMullen(3) 5 81
(Mrs R A Carr) *hld up: hdwy over 1f out: sn rdn: unable qck towards fin* **10/3**[2]

440- **4** *4 1/2* **Snowed Under**[182] 6253 7-8-12 **73** RobertWinston 3 71
(J D Bethell) *prom: chsd ldr 3f out tl rdn over 1f out: wknd ins fnl f* **15/2**

2352 **5** *1 1/2* **Most Definitely (IRE)**[19] 1044 8-8-7 **68** ow1 RichardHughes 2 63
(R M Stronge) *hld up: hdwy over 1f out: swtchd rt ent fnl f: sn hung lft and wknd* **3/1**[1]

311- **6** *1 1/2* **Cheshire Prince**[236] 4735 4-8-12 **73** LiamJones 7 66
(W M Brisbourne) *hld up: effrt over 2f out: wknd over 1f out* **9/1**

4252 **7** *54* **Prince Charlemagne (IRE)**[27] 935 5-8-7 **68** (p) SimonWhitworth 6 —
(R M Stronge) *chsd ldr tl rdn over 3f out: wknd wl over 2f out* **16/1**

2m 28.65s (7.55) **Going Correction** +0.75s/f (Yiel) **7** Ran SP% **111.3**
Speed ratings (Par 105): **102,101,101,98,96 95,56**
CSF £27.77 CT £85.90 TOTE £7.40: £2.70, £2.40; EX 57.00.

Owner Miss Gill Quincey **Bred** Mohammad Al-Qatami **Trained** Cotebrook, Cheshire

FOCUS
Just a fair handicap, but quite competitive. The form is rated through the runner-up. The pace was fair considering the conditions, with Prince Charlemagne putting some pressure on Dove Cottage up front, and the winning time was 1.18 seconds quicker the following three-year-old 61-75 handicap. They raced towards the stands' side in the straight.

1389 MERCIA'S DRIVE TIME WITH HELEN KNOTT H'CAP 1m 2f 188y
5:00 (5:01) (Class 5) (0-75,71) 3-Y-0 **£3,238** (£963; £481; £240) **Stalls** Low

Form RPR

000- **1** **Black Tor Figarro (IRE)**[141] 6944 3-8-5 **58** LiamJones 3 65
(B W Duke) *s.i.s: sn pushed along in rr: hdwy 2f out: rdn to ld ins fnl f: r.o* **11/1**

0-33 **2** *1 3/4* **Shaftesbury (IRE)**[71] 434 3-8-11 **64** LPKeniry 7 67
(Jane Southcombe) *hld up: hdwy to ld over 1f out: hdd and unable qck ins fnl f* **33/1**

455- **3** *3* **King Bathwick (IRE)**[197] 5858 3-9-0 **67** JohnEgan 1 65
(B R Millman) *prom: chsd ldr 3f out: rdn and ev ch over 1f out: wknd ins fnl f* **5/1**[3]

001- **4** *1 1/4* **Tasheba**[168] 6571 3-9-4 **71** AdrianMcCarthy 11 67
(P W Chapple-Hyam) *chsd ldrs: rdn over 2f out: wknd fnl f* **6/1**

02-0 **5** *4* **Double On Red**[13] 1161 3-8-13 **66** RichardMullen 4 55
(J M P Eustace) *led: rdn and hdd over 1f out: wknd ins fnl f* **8/1**

005- **6** *7* **Dusk**[183] 6233 3-8-12 **65** EddieAhern 9 41
(J L Dunlop) *mid-div: rdn over 3f out: wknd 2f out* **3/1**[1]

-450 **7** *3* **Natural Rhythm (IRE)**[13] 1161 3-8-8 **61** ow1 (v) PaulMulrennan 6 32
(Mrs R A Carr) *prom: racd keenly: rdn over 4f out: n.m.r and wknd over 3f out* **50/1**

001- **8** *10* **Any Given Day (IRE)**[174] 6427 3-8-12 **65** FergusSweeney 8 18
(D M Simcock) *s.i.s and wnt rt s: hld up: rdn over 4f out: wknd over 3f out* **15/2**

4321 **9** *20* **Desiderio**[12] 1166 3-8-12 **65** (b[1]) RichardHughes 5 —
(R Hannon) *racd keenly: trckd ldr tl rdn over 3f out: wknd over 2f out* **4/1**[2]

00-2 **10** *1* **Ogmore Junction (IRE)**[14] 1130 3-9-3 **70** EdwardCreighton 10 —
(Mrs S Leech) *hld up: rdn over 4f out: wknd over 3f out* **16/1**

2m 29.83s (8.73) **Going Correction** +0.75s/f (Yiel) **10** Ran SP% **117.9**
Speed ratings (Par 98): **98,96,94,93,90 85,83,76,61,60**
CSF £313.22 CT £2038.69 TOTE £12.70: £3.10, £5.80, £2.50; EX 350.70 Place 6 £246.61, Place 5 £162.97.

Owner B W Duke Racing Ms R E Tupper T H Fletcher **Bred** Sweetmans Bloodstock **Trained** Lambourn, Berks

FOCUS
A modest handicap and, with the pace fair, this proved quite a test for these three-year-olds. Improvement from the winner, but the form does not look all that solid. The winning time was 1.18 seconds slower than the previous older-horse 66-80 handicap. They tended to race middle to stands' side in the straight.

Black Tor Figarro(IRE) Official explanation: trainer said, regarding the apparent improvement in form, that colt had benefited from the step up in trip to 1m 2f and the soft ground.
Any Given Day(IRE) Official explanation: jockey said gelding never travelled
Desiderio Official explanation: jockey said colt had no more to give
T/Plt: £4,024.50 to a £1 stake. Pool: £53,477.45. 9.70 winning tickets. T/Qpdt: £695.30 to a £1 stake. Pool: £3,570.80. 3.80 winning tickets. CR

BEVERLEY (R-H)
Wednesday, April 16

OFFICIAL GOING: Good to soft (soft in places; 7.9)
Wind: fresh half-behind Weather: overcast, cold and breezy

1390 ALEC AND DICK 174 NOT OUT MAIDEN AUCTION STKS (DIV I) 5f
1:40 (1:41) (Class 5) 2-Y-0 **£2,428** (£722; £361; £180) **Stalls** High

Form RPR

1 **Vintage Steps (IRE)** 2-8-4 0 PaulHanagan 10 75
(R A Fahey) *trckd ldrs: hdwy over 1f out: led jst ins fnl f: sn rdn and kpt on* **7/2**[2]

2 *3/4* **Woteva** 2-8-6 0 GrahamGibbons 11 74
(J J Quinn) *in tch: switchd lft and hdwy 2f out: rdn over 1f out: styd on wl fnl f* **9/2**[3]

3 *5* **Favourite Girl (IRE)** 2-8-8 0 DavidAllan 4 56
(T D Easterby) *wnt bdly lft s and bhd: hdwy 2f out: rdn and styd on ins fnl f: nrst fin* **12/1**

04 **4** *3/4* **Another Luke (IRE)**[11] 1220 2-8-9 0 NickyMackay 8 54
(T J Etherington) *chsd ldrs: rdn along 2f out: sn one pce* **11/4**[1]

3 **5** *4 1/2* **Kings House**[12] 1183 2-8-9 0 PaulMulrennan 3 36
(M W Easterby) *led: rdn wl over 1f out: hdd jst ins fnl f: wknd* **11/1**

6 *2 1/2* **Queen Of Dalyan (IRE)** 2-7-11 0 PatrickDonaghy(7) 6 21+
(P C Haslam) *chsd ldrs: rdn along 1/2-way: sn wknd* **12/1**

7 *1/2* **Scarlet Blade** 2-8-11 0 RoystonFfrench 7 26
(Mrs A Duffield) *dwlt: a in rr* **5/1**

8 *1 3/4* **Lucky Buddha** 2-8-9 0 TPQueally 1 17
(Jedd O'Keeffe) *cl up: rdn along 2f out: sn wknd* **16/1**

9 *2 1/4* **Madame Jourdain (IRE)** 2-8-1 0 DuranFentiman(3) 5 3+
(T D Easterby) *towards rr: effrt and sme hdwy on outer 1/2-way: sn rdn and wknd* **33/1**

66.78 secs (3.28) **Going Correction** +0.475s/f (Yiel) **9** Ran SP% **116.3**
Speed ratings (Par 92): **92,90,82,81,74 70,69,66,63**
CSF £19.86 TOTE £4.40: £1.50, £2.20, £3.90; EX 15.90.

Owner J C Parsons & J J Gilmartin **Bred** J Browne & J Cullinan **Trained** Musley Bank, N Yorks
■ Stewards' Enquiry : T P Queally caution: careless riding

FOCUS
An average juvenile event which saw the two drawn highest come clear. The form can be rated through the fourth.

NOTEBOOK
Vintage Steps(IRE), a 7,500gns purchase, got her career off to a perfect start and did the job with a little left up her sleeve at the finish. She acted well on the easy ground, will improve for the experience, and could prove a useful early-season juvenile. Another furlong will also be within her compass in due course. (op 11-4)

Woteva ◆, who cost 13,500gns, posted a very pleasing debut effort and finished nicely clear of the remainder in second. Granted she had the best of the draw against the rail, but juveniles from this stable normally always improve for their debut runs and she could soon be placed to go one better. (op 4-1 tchd 11-2)

Favourite Girl(IRE), bred to want a longer trip in time, did little to help her cause by going left on coming out of the stalls and had ground to make up thereafter. The manner in which she kept on in the last two furlongs was encouraging, however, and she eventually did best of those drawn low.

Another Luke(IRE) failed to build on his previous effort at Newcastle, but still ran close enough to that form and helps to set the level here. It remains to be seen how much more he has to offer. (op 3-1 tchd 10-3)

Lucky Buddha Official explanation: jockey said colt hung left throughout

1391 WELCOME BACK TO BEVERLEY (S) STKS — 1m 100y
2:10 (2:13) (Class 5) 3-Y-O+ — **£2,331** (£693; £346; £173) **Stalls** High

Form — RPR

60-0 **1** **Rowan Lodge (IRE)**[14] 1160 6-9-9 61..................(b) JamieMoriarty(3) 16 — 62
(Ollie Pears) *trckd ldrs: led over 2f out: clr over 1f out: jst hld on* **12/1**

3-02 **2** *½* **Penel (IRE)**[16] 1116 7-9-12 50..............................(p) LeeEnstone 12 — 61
(P T Midgley) *prom: effrt over 2f out: wnt 2nd ins fnl f: styd on towards fin: jst hld* **15/2**

12/4 **3** *2 ¾* **Basinet**[23] 989 10-9-6 58.. GrahamGibbons 4 — 49
(J J Quinn) *s.i.s: hdwy over 3f out: wnt 2nd over 1f out: kpt on same pce* **7/1**[3]

2022 **4** *3 ½* **Tidy (IRE)**[40] 822 8-9-6 52..(v) DeanMcKeown 9 — 40
(Micky Hammond) *mid-div: nt clr run over 3f out: styd on fnl 2f: nvr nr ldrs* **15/2**

0 **5** *2 ¾* **Brutus Maximus**[23] 989 5-9-6 0..............................(b) PatrickMathers 5 — 34
(I W McInnes) *in rr: kpt on fnl 2f: nvr on terms* **50/1**

0650 **6** *shd* **Tina's Ridge (IRE)**[14] 1160 4-9-5 56...................(p) DavidProbert(7) 6 — 40
(R Hollinshead) *in rr: hdwy over 2f out: kpt on: nvr nr ldrs* **7/1**[3]

4354 **7** *nk* **Indecision**[16] 1117 3-8-12 52.. PaulMulrennan 8 — 35
(M W Easterby) *mid-div: kpt on fnl 2f: nvr a factor* **14/1**

600- **8** *1 ½* **Blazing Mask (IRE)**[202] 5746 3-8-1 51........................ RoystonFfrench 2 — 21
(Mrs A Duffield) *in rr: kpt on fnl 2f: nvr a factor* **25/1**

50-5 **9** *2 ¾* **Lauro**[27] 949 8-9-0 57.. DawnRankin(7) 17 — 24
(Miss J A Camacho) *s.v.s: kpt on fnl 3f: nvr a factor* **6/1**[2]

1555 **10** *3 ¾* **Her Name Is Rio (IRE)**[16] 1117 3-8-7 65..................(b[1]) PaulHanagan 3 — 12
(Mrs S Lamyman) *chsd ldrs: wknd over 2f out* **16/1**

0-65 **11** *2 ¼* **Grey Vision**[46] 768 5-8-12 45..............................(b) MarkLawson(3) 14 — 5
(M Brittain) *led: edgd lft and hdd over 2f out: sn wknd* **25/1**

05-0 **12** *3 ¼* **Scotty's Future (IRE)**[24] 978 10-9-7 47........... DanielleMcCreery(5) 15 — 8
(A Berry) *s.s: a in rr* **22/1**

5155 **13** *3* **Todwick Owl**[34] 868 4-9-12 56.. TPQueally 10 — 1
(J G Given) *chsd ldrs: wknd 2f out* **5/1**[1]

6-33 **14** *2 ½* **Time To Regret**[21] 1032 8-9-5 57...........................(p) DonnaCaldwell(7) 7 — —
(I W McInnes) *chsd ldrs: c stands' side to r alone over 3f out: sn lost pl* **9/1**

0 **15** *25* **Slivovic (IRE)**[24] 978 4-9-1 0.. PhillipMakin 1 — —
(J S Wainwright) *in rr: bhd fnl 3f: sn t.o* **66/1**

0/0- **16** *18* **Brave Hiawatha (FR)**[275] 3598 6-9-6 60.......................... ChrisCatlin 11 — —
(G J Smith) *chsd ldrs: lost pl over 3f out: t.o 2f out* **33/1**

1m 52.86s (5.26) **Going Correction** +0.775s/f (Yiel)
WFA 3 from 4yo+ 14lb — **16** Ran SP% **128.2**
Speed ratings (Par 103): **104,103,100,97,94 94,94,92,89,86 83,80,77,75,50 32**
CSF £97.92 TOTE £17.10: £4.90, £2.70, £2.40; EX 103.80.There was no bid for the winner.
Owner F K Baxter **Bred** M P B Bloodstock Ltd **Trained** Norton, N Yorks

FOCUS
A typically moderate seller. The first pair had it to themselves in the last two furlongs and the runner-up is the best guide to the form.
Tidy(IRE) Official explanation: jockey said, regarding the running and riding, that his instructions were to sit as handy as possible and make his best way up the hill, but after being denied a clear run turning in the horse could only stay on at the one pace

1392 ALEC AND DICK 174 NOT OUT MAIDEN AUCTION STKS (DIV II) — 5f
2:45 (2:48) (Class 5) 2-Y-O — **£2,428** (£722; £361; £180) **Stalls** High

Form — RPR

2 **1** **Soul Sista (IRE)**[6] 1276 2-8-4 0.. LiamJones 8 — 70
(J L Spearing) *sn prom: rdn along to chal 2f out: led appr fnl f: drvn out* **11/8**[1]

2 *4 ½* **Veronicas Boy** 2-8-9 0.. AndrewElliott 4 — 57
(G M Moore) *chsd ldrs: rdn along over 2f out: styd on u.p ins fnl f: tk 2nd towards fin* **14/1**

3 *4 ½* **Rioja Ruby (IRE)** 2-7-11 0.................................... PatrickDonaghy(7) 10 — 34
(P C Haslam) *led: rdn along 2f out: hdd appr fnl f: sn wknd* **9/2**[2]

4 *4* **Flog It** 2-8-9 0.. DavidAllan 2 — 23
(T D Easterby) *dwlt: hdwy and in tch 1/2-way: sn rdn along and kpt on same pce* **9/1**

5 *1* **Quadrifolio** 2-8-9 0.. HayleyTurner 3 — 19+
(N Tinkler) *chsd ldrs: rdn along and outpcd 1/2-way: styd on u.p appr fnl f* **18/1**

6 *6* **Falbrina (IRE)** 2-8-6 0.. TWilliams 6 — —
(M Brittain) *chsd ldrs: rdn along over 2f out and sn wknd* **11/2**[3]

7 *5* **Holst (IRE)** 2-8-6 0.. DuranFentiman(3) 7 — —
(T D Easterby) *s.i.s: a bhd* **14/1**

8 *2 ¾* **Tyler** 2-8-9 0.. RobertWinston 5 — —
(W M Brisbourne) *unruly and led to s: s.i.s: a bhd* **7/1**

67.52 secs (4.02) **Going Correction** +0.475s/f (Yiel) — **8** Ran SP% **116.8**
Speed ratings (Par 92): **86,78,71,65,63 54,46,41**
CSF £24.08 TOTE £2.00: £1.10, £3.40, £2.30; EX 25.50.
Owner Living In The Saddle Syndicate **Bred** T Berwanger & Aaron Quinn **Trained** Kinnersley, Worcs

FOCUS
This was the weaker of the two juvenile divisions although there was little previous form to go on. The winner rates value for a little further.

NOTEBOOK
Soul Sista(IRE), second on her debut at Folkestone six days previously, put that experience to great use and came away from her rivals late on to score comfortably. She did well to win as she did considering she got upset in the stalls, a bit of cut underfoot looks ideal for her, and she ought to still have something left to offer yet. A step up to novice company now looks on the cards. (op 6-4 tchd 2-1)
Veronicas Boy, a half-brother to multiple 6-9f winner Arctic Desert among others, was firmly put in his place when the winner asserted for home. He still showed ability and finished nicely clear of the rest in second, so can be expected to last longer next time out.
Rioja Ruby(IRE), a 7,000euros April foal, showed good speed on this racecourse bow before fading nearing the furlong marker. She should come on a deal for the run. (op 7-2 tchd 3-1)
Flog It, related to juvenile sprint winners, was never a serious factor after a sluggish start and clearly needed the race. (op 8-1)

1393 YORK HOUSE CONSTRUCTION H'CAP — 5f
3:20 (3:21) (Class 3) (0-95,93) 4-Y-O+ — **£6,799** (£2,023; £1,011; £505) **Stalls** High

Form — RPR

60-6 **1** **Luscivious**[34] 866 4-8-4 79..(b) ChrisCatlin 12 — 93
(A J McCabe) *chsd ldrs: led jst ins fnl f: styd on wl* **4/1**[1]

046- **2** *2* **Malapropism**[159] 6743 8-8-7 82.............................. EdwardCreighton 4 — 89
(M R Channon) *w ldr: led over 2f out tl jst ins fnl f: no ex* **18/1**

1000 **3** *1 ¾* **Come Out Fighting**[39] 836 5-9-4 93..................... FrankieMcDonald 10 — 94
(P A Blockley) *dwlt and sltly hmpd s: sn drvn along: hdwy to chse ldrs over 3f out: kpt on fnl f* **14/1**

160- **4** *5* **Glasshoughton**[186] 6173 5-8-8 83.............................. PhillipMakin 8 — 66
(M Dods) *hmpd s: chsd ldrs: wknd appr fnl f* **17/2**

0-11 **5** *¾* **Fire Up The Band**[12] 1190 9-8-10 85.................. SilvestreDeSousa 9 — 65
(D Nicholls) *hmpd s: mid-div: kpt on fnl 2f: nvr nr ldrs* **4/1**[1]

330- **6** *1 ¼* **Wyatt Earp (IRE)**[164] 6668 7-8-12 87.............................. PaulHanagan 6 — 62+
(R A Fahey) *in rr: kpt on fnl f: nvr on terms* **11/2**[3]

00-0 **7** *nse* **Melalchrist**[24] 983 6-8-7 82..(b) PaulMulrennan 11 — 57
(K A Ryan) *stmbld and wnt lft s: led tl over 2f out: wknd 1f out* **5/1**[2]

405- **8** *¾* **Tabaret**[204] 5700 5-9-1 90.. DeanMcKeown 2 — 62
(R M Whitaker) *a in rr* **16/1**

00-2 **9** *7* **Caribbean Coral**[24] 983 9-8-6 81.............................. GrahamGibbons 7 — 28
(J J Quinn) *sn in rr* **5/1**[2]

105- **10** *¾* **Inter Vision (USA)**[197] 5891 8-9-0 89.............................. DanielTudhope 3 — 34
(A Dickman) *hld up: a in rr* **40/1**

65.07 secs (1.57) **Going Correction** +0.475s/f (Yiel) — **10** Ran SP% **119.5**
Speed ratings (Par 107): **106,102,100,92,90 88,88,87,76,75**
CSF £80.71 CT £953.13 TOTE £4.80: £1.70, £5.70, £4.00; EX 107.00.
Owner Paul J Dixon And Keith Barratt **Bred** R J Turner **Trained** Babworth, Notts

FOCUS
A decent sprint, run at a solid pace. Nothing got into this from the rear. The winner is rated back to his best, albeit from a favourable draw.

NOTEBOOK
Luscivious ◆, fit from a spin on the All-Weather, had the best of the draw and came home to score comfortably in the end. He has fallen in the weights as a result of not winning since his juvenile campagin, but this still rates his best effort to date and the easy ground proved right up his street. The handicapper will no doubt raise him back up for this, but he would have to be given serious respect if bidding to follow up under a penalty now. (op 9-2)
Malapropism had a decent time of it last term and looks set for another fruitful campaign on the evidence of this seasonal return. He had the visor off for this, but that will probably be back on next time and improvement should be expected. (op 20-1 tchd 16-1)
Come Out Fighting, with the blinkers abandoned for this return to turf, appreciated the drop in class and ran very close to his official mark in defeat. This was a sound effort under top weight. (op 10-1)
Glasshoughton was certainly not at his best on this seasonal debut and looks high enough in the weights now, but he should really come on a deal for the run. (op 7-1)
Fire Up The Band, back to form with consecutive wins on the All-Weather, was unable to get on the early pace after being hampered at the start and ran well below expectations. He is better than this, but evidently needs things his own way now. Official explanation: jockey said gelding suffered interference at start (op 5-1)
Caribbean Coral Official explanation: jockey said gelding was unsuited by the soft ground

1394 RAPID LAD STKS (H'CAP) — 1m 1f 207y
3:55 (3:55) (Class 5) (0-70,71) 4-Y-O+ — **£2,590** (£770; £385; £192) **Stalls** High

Form — RPR

321- **1** **Harry The Hawk**[183] 6259 4-9-0 64.............................. GrahamGibbons 8 — 76+
(T D Walford) *hld up in tch: hdwy 3f out: rdn and edgd rt over 1f out: led jst ins fnl f: drvn out* **4/1**[2]

05-1 **2** *1 ¼* **Blue Spinnaker (IRE)**[5] 1296 9-9-7 71 6ex.............. PaulMulrennan 14 — 84+
(M W Easterby) *hld up: smooth hdwy on inner 3f out: cl up whn effrt and nt clr run wl over 1f out: sn swtchd lft and rdn: styd on ins fnl f* **1/1**[1]

04-0 **3** *1 ¼* **Nelsons Column (IRE)**[24] 981 5-9-4 68.............................. TPQueally 11 — 75
(G M Moore) *hld up in tch: hdwy whn nt clr run 3f out: swtchd lft over 1f out: rdn and styd on wl fnl f* **12/1**

1366 **4** *1* **Karmest**[11] 1219 4-8-9 59..(b[1]) SilvestreDeSousa 4 — 64
(A D Brown) *trckd ldrs: hdwy 3f out: led and hung rt wl over 1f out: sn drvn: hdd & wknd ins fnl f* **16/1**

16/6 **5** *5* **Wednesdays Boy (IRE)**[14] 1159 5-8-2 55.............(p) AndrewMullen(3) 5 — 50
(P D Niven) *in tch: effrt wl over 2f out: sn rdn and kpt on same pce fr over 1f out* **15/2**[3]

230- **6** *¾* **Keisha Kayleigh (IRE)**[111] 7249 5-8-9 62............(b) JamieMoriarty(3) 12 — 56
(B Ellison) *s.i.s and towards rr: hdwy over 3f out: rdn 2f out: kpt on ins fnl f: nrst fin* **14/1**

000/ **7** *1* **Capped For Victory (USA)**[687] 2108 7-8-5 55.................. DaleGibson 2 — 47
(G A Swinbank) *sn led: rdn along 3f out: hdd wl over 1f out and sn wknd* **20/1**

23-0 **8** *½* **Zain (IRE)**[23] 999 4-8-6 56..(t) RoystonFfrench 1 — 47
(J G Given) *chsd ldr: rdn along 3f out: drvn 2f out and sn wknd* **25/1**

106- **9** *3 ¼* **Amanda Carter**[229] 4993 4-9-2 66.............................. PaulHanagan 13 — 50
(R A Fahey) *s.i.s: a in rr* **20/1**

12-0 **10** *3 ½* **Gala Sunday (USA)**[14] 1159 8-8-10 60..........................(bt) DavidAllan 7 — 37
(M W Easterby) *midfield: rdn along on outer 1/2-way and sn wknd* **40/1**

010- **11** *2 ¾* **Grethel (IRE)**[165] 6638 4-8-1 56.......................... DanielleMcCreery(5) 3 — 28
(A Berry) *prom: rdn along over 3f out: sn wknd* **50/1**

056- **12** *hd* **Intavac Boy**[117] 7219 7-8-4 54 oh5.............................. ChrisCatlin 10 — 25
(S P Griffiths) *chsd ldrs: rdn along 3f out: sn wknd* **25/1**

2m 14.86s (7.86) **Going Correction** +0.775s/f (Yiel) — **12** Ran SP% **123.6**
Speed ratings (Par 103): **99,98,97,96,92 91,90,90,87,85 82,82**
CSF £7.96 CT £47.26 TOTE £4.70: £1.70, £1.30, £3.20; EX 12.20.
Owner David Dickson **Bred** Robe Farm Stud **Trained** Sheriff Hutton, N Yorks

FOCUS
A modest handicap in which the pace was somewhat steady. The form looks fair for the class with the runner-up rated as finishing upsides the winner.
Capped For Victory(USA) Official explanation: jockey said gelding hung left

1395 HEARING DOGS FOR DEAF PEOPLE H'CAP — 1m 1f 207y
4:30 (4:31) (Class 4) (0-80,80) 3-Y-O — **£4,533** (£1,348; £674; £336) **Stalls** High

Form — RPR

11 **1** **William Blake**[42] 799 3-9-4 80.............................. RobertWinston 3 — 92+
(M Johnston) *led after 1f: qcknd over 5f out: clr over 1f out: styd on strly* **5/6**[1]

04-5 **2** *3 ¾* **Dubai Petal (IRE)**[5] 1297 3-8-9 71.............................. SimonWhitworth 6 — 73+
(J S Moore) *hld up towards rr: effrt and nt clr run over 2f out: styd on fnl f: tk 2nd nr fin* **11/4**[2]

014- **3** *hd* **Flying Time**[190] 6092 3-8-6 68.............................. EdwardCreighton 2 — 67
(M R Channon) *hld up in rr: effrt 4f out: styd on to go 2nd ins fnl f: no ex* **20/1**

1231 **4** *1 ½* **Tiger's Rocket (IRE)**[15] 1124 3-8-8 70.............................. ChrisCatlin 5 — 66
(S Gollings) *reluctant ldr for 1f; t.k.h: trckd wnr: one pce fnl 2f* **10/1**

541- **5** *7* **Thunderstruck**[210] 5526 3-9-4 80.............................. NCallan 1 — 62
(K A Ryan) *trckd ldrs: effrt over 3f out: wknd over 1f out* **6/1**[3]

200- **6** *8* **Welcome Return (IRE)**[207] 5613 3-8-9 **71** .... DavidAllan 7 37
(T D Easterby) *chsd ldrs: pushed along over 5f out: lost pl over 2f out: sn bhd* **20/1**

2m 16.22s (9.22) **Going Correction** +0.775s/f (Yiel) **6** Ran SP% **114.1**
Speed ratings (Par 100): **94,91,90,89,84 77**
CSF £3.44 TOTE £1.60: £1.10, £2.80; EX 3.70.

Owner Sheikh Hamdan Bin Mohammed Al Maktoum **Bred** Gainsborough Stud Management Ltd **Trained** Middleham Moor, N Yorks

FOCUS
A tactical race and dominated throughout by the front-running William Blake. He looks better than the bare form, and the second and third were close to their marks.

1396 JENNIE PARVIN BIRTHDAY STKS (H'CAP) 7f 100y

5:05 (5:05) (Class 5) (0-70,70) 3-Y-O **£2,590** (£770; £385; £192) **Stalls** High

Form RPR

64-4 **1** **Duke Of Touraine (IRE)**[76] 366 3-8-9 **68** .... PatrickDonaghy(7) 12 81
(P C Haslam) *trckd ldng pair: smooth hdwy 3f out: led wl over 1f out: rdn clr* **11/2**[3]

6-46 **2** *5* **Rossini's Dancer**[14] 1161 3-8-8 **60** .... PaulHanagan 1 64+
(R A Fahey) *bhd: riddern along over 2f out: swtchd outside over 1f out: styd on strly ins fnl f: tk 2nd towards fin* **3/1**[1]

004- **3** *½* **Jafra (IRE)**[194] 5965 3-8-7 **59** .... DeanMcKeown 6 58
(R M Whitaker) *in tch: hdwy 3f out and sn rdn along and edgd lft over 1f out: chsd wnr ent fnl f: lost 2nd towards fin* **28/1**

23-4 **4** *4* **Tamasou (IRE)**[68] 484 3-9-2 **68** .... PaulEddery 7 57
(Garry Moss) *chsd ldng pair: rdn along over 2f out: sn drvn and kpt on same pce* **20/1**

000- **5** *2 ¼* **Ride A White Swan**[236] 4764 3-9-3 **69** .... DarrenWilliams 8 52
(K R Burke) *dwlt: t.k.h: sn in tch: posuehd along 3f out: rdn 2f out and kpt on same pce* **25/1**

100- **6** *1 ¼* **Veronicas Way**[170] 6536 3-8-5 **57** .... RoystonFfrench 15 37
(G M Moore) *led: rdn along 3f out: hdd wl over 1f out: sn drvn and grad wknd* **8/1**

430 **7** *1 ¼* **Boss Hog**[34] 867 3-8-13 **65** .... FrankieMcDonald 16 42+
(P A Blockley) *towards rr: rdn along on inner 3f out: no real hdwy* **10/1**

52-2 **8** *1* **Caltire (GER)**[105] 20 3-8-10 **67** .... JamieJones(5) 14 41
(M G Quinlan) *s.i.s: a in rr* **6/1**

050- **9** *1 ½* **Marlena (IRE)**[220] 5251 3-8-2 **57** .... DuranFentiman(3) 5 28
(T D Easterby) *chsd ldrs: rdn along 3f out: drvn 2f out: wknd over 1f out* **12/1**

602- **10** *2 ¾* **The Last Bottle (IRE)**[144] 6936 3-9-0 **66** .... LiamJones 13 30
(W M Brisbourne) *chsd ldrs: rdn along 3f out: sn drvn and wknd* **9/2**[2]

4-00 **11** *2* **Royal Acclamation (IRE)**[14] 1161 3-8-13 **65** .... SilvestreDeSousa 3 24
(G A Harker) *a towards rr* **20/1**

40-0 **12** *4 ½* **Musical Charm (IRE)**[22] 1019 3-8-13 **65** .... PaulMulrennan 4 13
(T D Easterby) *midfield: rdn along over 3f out and sn wknd* **20/1**

55-5 **13** *6* **Speedy Senorita (IRE)**[14] 1155 3-8-12 **64** .... AndrewElliott 9 —
(K R Burke) *cl up: rdn along 3f out: sn drvn and wknd 2f out* **16/1**

1m 39.53s (5.73) **Going Correction** +0.775s/f (Yiel) **13** Ran SP% **128.2**
Speed ratings (Par 98): **98,92,91,87,84 83,81,80,78,75 73,68,61**
CSF £22.17 CT £465.15 TOTE £8.70: £2.40, £1.70, £9.50; EX 35.10.

Owner Middleham Park Racing & John J Maguire **Bred** F Bayrou&haras De Son Altesse L'Aga Khan **Trained** Middleham Moor, N Yorks

■ Stewards' Enquiry : Darren Williams two-day ban: careless riding (Apr 30-May 1)

FOCUS
A modest handicap run at a steady pace. The winner was always well placed, unlike the runner-up who shaped better than the bare form.

Jafra(IRE) Official explanation: jockey said gelding hung badly right in closing stages

Ride A White Swan Official explanation: jockey said gelding ran too free

1397 RACING HERE AGAIN NEXT THURSDAY H'CAP 1m 4f 16y

5:40 (5:40) (Class 5) (0-70,70) 3-Y-O **£2,590** (£770; £385; £192) **Stalls** High

Form RPR

06-2 **1** **Kiribati King (IRE)**[14] 1140 3-9-1 **67** .... EdwardCreighton 8 73
(M R Channon) *in rr: sn pushed along: hdwy on outer over 2f out: styd on to ld ins fnl f* **9/2**[3]

066- **2** *¾* **Bouggler**[180] 6307 3-8-4 **56** oh2 .... RoystonFfrench 4 60
(Miss J A Camacho) *trckd ldrs: nt clr run on inbner over 1f out: led 1f out: hdd and no ex ins fnl f* **8/1**

2-34 **3** *3 ¾* **Georgie The Fourth (IRE)**[20] 1042 3-9-2 **68** .... ChrisCatlin 6 66
(E J O'Neill) *hld up in mid-div: effrt over 3f out: kpt on one pce fnl 2f* **6/1**

00-0 **4** *1 ½* **Pure Scandal**[12] 1186 3-8-1 **56** oh4 .... AndrewMullen(3) 3 52
(M W Easterby) *dwlt: sn trcking ldrs: chal over 2f out: wknd appr fnl f* **10/1**

040- **5** *4 ½* **Italian Goddess**[175] 6434 3-9-4 **70** .... HayleyTurner 2 59
(M L W Bell) *trckd ldrs: hmpd path after 2f: wknd over 1f out* **4/1**[2]

004 **6** *2 ¼* **Brave Boogie**[13] 1173 3-8-8 **60** .... TPQueally 7 45
(H J L Dunlop) *hld up in rr: drvn along over 5f out: lost pl 2f out* **6/1**

2131 **7** *4 ½* **Novestar (IRE)**[12] 1186 3-9-0 **66** .... NCallan 5 44
(G J Smith) *led: ducked lft path after 2f: qcknd over 3f out: hdd & wknd 1f out* **11/4**[1]

000- **8** *27* **Viscount Monty**[180] 6307 3-7-11 **56** oh11 .... MarzenaJeziorek(7) 1 —
(N Tinkler) *trckd ldrs: rn wd bnd after 1f: lost pl over 2f out: sn bhd* **100/1**

2m 53.34s (12.44) **Going Correction** +0.775s/f (Yiel) **8** Ran SP% **114.6**
Speed ratings (Par 98): **89,88,86,85,82 80,77,59**
CSF £39.95 CT £216.85 TOTE £4.40: £1.60, £2.80, £2.20; EX 46.70 Place 6 £54.54, Place 5 £18.02..

Owner Box 41 **Bred** Noel Finnegan **Trained** West Ilsley, Berks

FOCUS
A modest handicap run at a steady early pace. The form is not too solid but has been rated at face value.

T/Plt: £62.40 to a £1 stake. Pool: £45,495.24. 532.00 winning tickets. T/Qpdt: £12.80 to a £1 stake. Pool: £3,564.60. 205.50 winning tickets. JR

NEWMARKET (Rowley) (R-H)

Wednesday, April 16

OFFICIAL GOING: Good (7.9)

Wind: Light against Weather: Overcast conditions giving way to sunny spells after race 2

1398 FEDERATION OF BLOODSTOCK AGENTS MAIDEN STKS 1m 2f

2:00 (2:04) (Class 4) 3-Y-O **£5,180** (£1,541; £770; £384) **Stalls** High

Form RPR

1 **Pampas Cat (USA)** 3-9-3 0 .... JimmyFortune 11 100+
(J H M Gosden) *gd sort: trckd ldrs: led over 1f out: rdn clr fnl f* **20/1**

0- **2** *5* **Daraahem (IRE)**[173] 6468 3-9-3 0 .... MartinDwyer 5 90
(B W Hills) *chsd ldr tl led over 2f out: rdn and hdd over 1f out: styd on same pce fnl f* **5/1**[2]

3 *1 ½* **Checklow (USA)** 3-9-3 0 .... LDettori 1 87+
(J Noseda) *wl grwn: hld up: hdwy 1/2-way: rdn over 1f out: no ex fnl f* **7/2**[1]

4 *nk* **King O'The Gypsies (IRE)** 3-9-3 0 .... SteveDrowne 14 87+
(R Charlton) *neat: scope: hld up: hdwy 2f out: styd on: nt trble ldrs* **20/1**

5 *½* **Maraased** 3-9-3 0 .... MichaelHills 2 86+
(M A Jarvis) *w'like: bit bkwd: hld up: hdwy over 1f out: nvr nr to chal* **25/1**

44- **6** *3 ¼* **Savarain**[172] 6493 3-9-3 0 .... SebSanders 3 79
(L M Cumani) *bit bkwd: s.i.s: hld up: hdwy over 4f out: rdn over 1f out: sn wknd* **5/1**[2]

6- **7** *¾* **Tale Of Two Cities (IRE)**[157] 6782 3-9-3 0 .... JMurtagh 4 78
(A P O'Brien, Ire) *lw: chsd ldrs: rdn over 2f out: wknd over 1f out* **11/2**[3]

8 *½* **Nisaal (IRE)** 3-9-3 0 .... RHills 6 77
(J L Dunlop) *w'like: unf: hld up: hdwy over 3f out: rdn over 2f out: wknd over 1f out* **6/1**

9 *3* **Byblos** 3-9-3 0 .... RyanMoore 12 71
(B J Meehan) *w'like: scope: hld up: nvr nrr* **40/1**

22- **10** *2 ½* **Seattle Storm (IRE)**[119] 7181 3-9-3 0 .... TQuinn 13 66
(D R C Elsworth) *lw: hld up in tch: plld hrd: rdn and wknd over 1f out* **16/1**

00- **11** *nk* **Blimey O'Riley (IRE)**[169] 6574 3-9-3 0 .... JimmyQuinn 15 65
(M H Tompkins) *hld up in tch: lost pl over 7f out: hdwy 4f out: wknd over 2f out* **66/1**

12 *1 ¼* **Swingkeel (IRE)** 3-9-3 0 .... EddieAhern 8 62
(J L Dunlop) *leggy: scope: hld up: n.d* **66/1**

13 *3* **Monaadi (IRE)** 3-9-3 0 .... PhilipRobinson 9 56
(M A Jarvis) *gd sort: hld up: shkn up 1/2-way: a in rr* **14/1**

03- **14** *2* **Zhebe**[141] 6960 3-9-3 0 ....(t) AmirQuinn 7 52
(P J McBride) *lw: led over 7f: wknd over 1f out* **100/1**

15 *17* **Yellow Thunder (IRE)** 3-9-0 0 .... JerryO'Dwyer(3) 10 18
(Luke Comer, Ire) *w'like: scope: prom over 6f* **100/1**

2m 9.03s (3.23) **Going Correction** +0.45s/f (Yiel) **15** Ran SP% **118.5**
Speed ratings (Par 100): **105,101,99,99,99 96,95,95,93,91 90,89,87,85,72**
CSF £110.04 TOTE £23.60: £4.40, £2.50, £1.60; EX 249.90.

Owner Carwell Equities Ltd **Bred** Carwell Equities Ltd **Trained** Newmarket, Suffolk

FOCUS
An interesting maiden, full of unknown quantities, and the pace was sound. The field stayed on the far side, which is where the stalls were. The winner was impressive and there was no fluke about it. He looked to have plenty of future winners behind him, and this looks strong form.

Seattle Storm(IRE) Official explanation: jockey said colt ran too free

Yellow Thunder(IRE) Official explanation: jockey said colt hung left

1399 CALL GEOFF HUFFER RACING ON 0871 2464925 CONDITIONS STKS 5f

2:35 (2:37) (Class 3) 2-Y-O **£6,476** (£1,927; £963; £481) **Stalls** High

Form RPR

1 **1** **Art Connoisseur (IRE)**[13] 1168 2-8-12 0 .... JamieSpencer 3 99+
(M L W Bell) *hld up in tch: led and hung rt fr over 1f out: r.o wl* **11/10**[1]

2 *2 ¼* **Servoca (CAN)** 2-8-6 0 .... WilliamBuick(3) 8 83+
(B W Hills) *w'like: bit bkwd: trckd ldrs: nt clr run and lost pl over 1f out: r.o ins fnl f* **33/1**

3 *¾* **Ouqba** 2-8-9 0 .... RHills 12 84+
(B W Hills) *w'like: scope: s.i.s: hld up: hdwy and nt clr run fnl f: r.o: nt rch ldrs* **7/1**[3]

4 *nk* **Brenin Taran** 2-8-9 0 .... MartinDwyer 9 78+
(D M Simcock) *lt-f: leggy: s.s: hld up: nt clr run 1/2-way: swtchd lft 2f out: hdwy over 1f out: r.o* **66/1**

5 *nk* **Senatorial** 2-8-9 0 .... MichaelHills 4 77+
(B W Hills) *w'like: hld up: hdwy over 1f out: r.o* **8/1**

6 *½* **Rayvin Mad (IRE)** 2-8-9 0 .... KerrinMcEvoy 11 75
(P W Chapple-Hyam) *neat: w ldr: rdn and ev ch over 1f out: edgd rt and no ex ins fnl f* **11/2**[2]

1 **7** *nk* **Asaint Needs Brass (USA)**[18] 1078 2-9-4 0 .... SebSanders 6 83
(R M Beckett) *chsd ldrs: rdn and n.m.r over 1f out: no ex fnl f* **11/1**

01 **8** *1* **Bad Beat**[16] 1118 2-8-9 0 .... JerryO'Dwyer(3) 7 73
(V Smith) *led over 3f: no ex ins fnl f* **22/1**

9 *hd* **Icesolator (IRE)** 2-8-9 0 .... RyanMoore 10 75+
(R Hannon) *leggy: unf: prom: n.m.r fr over 1f out: styd on same pce* **8/1**

10 *8* **Swingfire (USA)** 2-8-9 0 .... RichardMullen 5 37
(R M H Cowell) *cmpt: bkwd: s.i.s: sn pushed along into mid-div: rdn over 3f out: wknd 1/2-way* **66/1**

11 *nk* **Persian Tomcat (IRE)** 2-8-2 0 .... AmyBaker(7) 2 36
(Miss J Feilden) *small: mid-div: rdn 1/2-way: wknd 2f out* **80/1**

12 *1* **Free To Choose (IRE)** 2-8-9 0 .... NeilPollard 1 32
(A P Jarvis) *cmpt: bkwd: s.i.s: sn pushed along in rr: bhd fr 1/2-way* **66/1**

61.59 secs (2.49) **Going Correction** +0.45s/f (Yiel) **12** Ran SP% **119.1**
Speed ratings (Par 96): **98,94,93,92,92 91,90,89,89,76 75,74**
CSF £57.21 TOTE £2.20: £1.10, £8.80, £2.50; EX 57.80.

Owner R A Green **Bred** D McDonnell **Trained** Newmarket, Suffolk

FOCUS
Probably the best two-year-old race of the season so far and an impressive winner. The form looks strong and winners should emerge from this contest.

NOTEBOOK
Art Connoisseur(IRE) ◆, carrying a 3lb penalty for his easy win in a modest Leicester maiden, put up an even better performance here against a much stronger field. He was inclined to hang over to the far rail under pressure, but the turn of speed he showed was still impressive and he put daylight between himself and his rivals very quickly. He is likely to have one more run before a crack at the Norfolk and at this stage nothing has better credentials. (op 5-4 tchd 11-8 in a place)

Servoca(CAN) ◆, a 130,000euros colt out of a half-sister to winners in Peru and Canada, looked to be the Hills third-string on jockey bookings but emerged the best of the trio. He had to switch left in order to get a run a furlong out before finishing very nicely and it should not be long before he goes one better.

Ouqba ◆, a 140,000gns half-brother to four winners including the smart Foxhaven, stayed on nicely in the second-half of the contest despite not having much room to play with. He should not be hard to place, but there is plenty of stamina on the dam's side of his pedigree so he may prove better over an extra furlong or two in due course. (op 9-1 tchd 10-1)

Brenin Taran ◆, out of a dual winner over 6f, cost just 800gns and should not have any trouble recouping that with plenty of interest if this debut is anything to go by. He walked out of the stalls and was last early, but he finished in fine style even though he met plenty of traffic late on. He has a speedy pedigree and if building on this he should be able to find a maiden before too long.

Senatorial, out of a winning half-sister to Insinuate and the dam of Stronghold and Imroz, stayed on pleasingly in the closing stages and there should be better to come with this outing under his belt. Although by a top-class sprinter, the dam's side of his pedigree suggests he will get a bit further. (tchd 7-1 and 17-2)

Rayvin Mad(IRE), a 20,000gns colt out of a winning half-sister to Kyllachy, showed decent pace for a long way. His pedigree is all speed and he can be expected to last longer next time. (op 9-2 tchd 6-1)

Asaint Needs Brass(USA), carrying a 9lb penalty for his debut victory in a Polytrack maiden that has given mixed signals in the meantime, raced close to the pace but looked to have run his race when getting short of room. (op 12-1 tchd 14-1)

Bad Beat, penalised 3lb for his victory in a very modest Fibresand maiden, tried to make the most of his experience with a positive ride but he found this company much too classy for him. (op 25-1 tchd 20-1)

Icesolator(IRE), a 65,000euros half-brother to two winners at up to 1m1f, would have been closer had he not run out of room against the far rail over the last furlong or so and can be expected to come on from this. (op 7-1 tchd 9-1)

1400 MAKING BETTING BETTER ON NEWMARKET HIGH STREET EUROPEAN FREE H'CAP (LISTED RACE) 7f

3:10 (3:11) (Class 1) 3-Y-O

£17,031 (£6,456; £3,231; £1,611; £807; £405) **Stalls** High

Form				RPR
122-	**1**		**Stimulation (IRE)**[172] 6495 3-9-3 **106** ... SteveDrowne 1	111+
			(H Morrison) *h.d.w: hld up in touch: hdwy 1/2-way: rdn and edgd rt over 1f out: r.o to ld post* **15/8**[1]	
121-	**2**	*nse*	**Fat Boy (IRE)**[233] 4899 3-9-6 **109** ... LDettori 7	114
			(P W Chapple-Hyam) *bit bkwd: led: rdn over 1f out: hdd post* **5/1**[2]	
143-	**3**	*nk*	**Royal Confidence**[179] 6336 3-8-13 **102** ... MichaelHills 4	106
			(B W Hills) *trckd ldrs: rdn and ev ch fr over 1f out: r.o* **12/1**	
303-	**4**	*2*	**Nacho Libre**[172] 6488 3-8-12 **101** ... WilliamBuick 5	100
			(B W Hills) *hld up: outpcd over 1f out: r.o ins fnl f* **22/1**	
020-	**5**	*2*	**Maze (IRE)**[172] 6488 3-8-13 **102** ... TomEaves 8	95
			(B Smart) *b.hind: hld up: racd keenly: effrt and nt clr run over 1f out: swtchd lft: styd on: nt trble ldrs* **12/1**	
511-	**6**	*nse*	**Exclamation**[194] 5974 3-8-13 **102** ... JamieSpencer 10	95
			(B J Meehan) *hld up: hdwy u.p over 1f out: wknd wl ins fnl f* **7/1**[3]	
014-	**7**	*nk*	**Philario (IRE)**[207] 5630 3-9-4 **107** ... FergusSweeney 2	99
			(K R Burke) *bit bkwd: chsd ldr: rdn and edgd rt over 1f out: wknd ins fnl f* **14/1**	
620-	**8**	*1*	**Spirit Of Sharjah (IRE)**[186] 6167 3-9-7 **110** ... JMurtagh 11	100+
			(P W Chapple-Hyam) *lw: hld up: rdn over 1f out: nt trble ldrs* **12/1**	
432-	**9**	*½*	**Berbice (IRE)**[196] 5922 3-9-4 **107** ... RyanMoore 9	95
			(R Hannon) *h.d.w: prom: rdn over 2f out: wknd fnl f* **11/1**	
203-	**10**	*9*	**Cake (IRE)**[186] 6167 3-8-13 **102** ... PatDobbs 3	66
			(R Hannon) *lw: s.s: hld up: wknd 2f out* **33/1**	
44-0	**11**	*¾*	**Brave Prospector**[18] 1068 3-8-12 **101** ... JimmyFortune 6	63
			(P W Chapple-Hyam) *lw: chsd ldrs: rdn over 2f out: wknd over 1f out* **12/1**	

1m 27.17s (1.77) **Going Correction** +0.45s/f (Yiel) **11** Ran SP% **117.0**
Speed ratings (Par 106): **107,106,106,104,102 101,101,100,99,89 88**
CSF £10.45 CT £89.74 TOTE £2.80: £1.50, £2.30, £2.80; EX 13.80.

Owner Michael Kerr-Dineen **Bred** Illuminatus Investments **Trained** East Ilsley, Berks

FOCUS

A reasonable renewal of the Free Handicap and certainly quite competitive, although a number had stamina doubts. Stimulation, who was less exposed than most, was value for more than the bare form in a race rated around the third and fourth. They went just an ordinary pace and it paid to race close up. The winning time was 0.02 seconds slower than the following Nell Gwyn. The first two home were sired by Choisir, who although a sprinter himself, is producing a nice mix of horses from 5f to around 1m.

NOTEBOOK

Stimulation(IRE), a winner on his debut at Newbury before finishing runner-up to Confront in a conditions contest at Ascot and a close second in the Group 3 Horris Hill on his third and final start of the campaign, looked well treated off a mark of just 106 on his return from almost six months off. He was never too far away from the ordinary early gallop, but took a while to pick up when first coming under pressure and only grabbed Fat Boy on the line. On this evidence he will be well suited by a step up to 1m and he will now be aimed at the Guineas but, in truth, he is unlikely to be playing anything other than a supporting role. (op 15-8 tchd 7-4 and 2-1 in places)

Fat Boy(IRE), off the track since winning a weak 6f Listed race for Richard Hannon at Ripon last August, was just held on his debut for the Chapple-Hyam yard. Trying this trip for the first time, he was allowed the run of the race at just an ordinary pace and very nearly made every yard. He should take his racing well this year and can remain competitive in similar events from 5f-7f. His trainer is considering the French Guineas, where he hopes the turning track will help him get the 1m but, on this evidence, he will have to be considered an unlikely stayer. (tchd 11-2)

Royal Confidence, third in the Rockfel over course and distance on her final start last season, ran well against the colts on her return from six months off the track. She seems to get this trip okay, but her pedigree is all speed and she gives the impression she will be seen at her best when dropped back to sprinting later in the year. Barry Hills, who thinks she will be suited by faster ground, is considering bringing her back here for the 1000 Guineas, but the 1m is likely to stretch her stamina. (op 10-1)

Nacho Libre, returning from nearly six months off, was under pressure sooner than some of these and was outpaced when the leader increased the tempo, but he saw his race out well. He is very much sprint bred, but ran like a horse who needed every yard of this trip and he might get even further. He should be sharper next time and a stronger-run race is also likely to suit. (op 25-1)

Maze(IRE), returning from almost six months off the track, can be keen so he was held up, but as a result he was poorly positioned considering how the race was run. He did not enjoy the best of runs when trying to stay on, but he was not unlucky. (op 11-1)

Exclamation shaped as though he would get this trip when winning both his maiden on testing ground at Haydock, and a valuable sales race over 6f here on his final start at two, but he was well held after 194 days off. (op 6-1)

Philario(IRE) was well held after 207 days off the track and he might be better suited by easier ground back over sprint trips. (op 16-1)

Spirit Of Sharjah(IRE) Official explanation: jockey said colt became unbalanced

Brave Prospector Official explanation: jockey said colt lost its action

1401 LESLIE HARRISON MEMORIAL NELL GWYN STKS (GROUP 3) (FILLIES) 7f

3:45 (3:46) (Class 1) 3-Y-O

£28,385 (£10,760; £5,385; £2,685; £1,345; £675) **Stalls** High

Form				RPR
1-	**1**		**Infallible**[165] 6649 3-8-12 0 ... JimmyFortune 3	111+
			(J H M Gosden) *lw: s.i.s: hld up: hdwy and edgd rt fr over 1f out: led 1f out: r.o wl* **7/2**[1]	
501-	**2**	*3 ½*	**Kylayne**[182] 6270 3-8-12 93 ... JohnEgan 6	98
			(P W D'Arcy) *led: rdn and hdd 1f out: styde on same pce* **66/1**	
615-	**3**	*3*	**Festivale (IRE)**[166] 6619 3-8-12 92 ... KerrinMcEvoy 14	90+
			(J L Dunlop) *lw: hld up: hdwy over 1f out: nt rch ldrs* **10/1**	
140-	**4**	*1*	**Rosaleen (IRE)**[193] 6012 3-8-12 95 ... LDettori 12	92+
			(B J Meehan) *s.i.s: hld up: rdn over 2f out: nt clr run over 1f out: r.o ins fnl f* **33/1**	
311-	**5**	*½*	**Spinning Lucy (IRE)**[166] 6619 3-8-12 101 ... MichaelHills 11	86
			(B W Hills) *chsd ldrs: rdn and ev ch over 1f out: wknd ins fnl f* **11/2**[3]	
231-	**6**	*1 ¼*	**Nijoom Dubai**[299] 2812 3-8-12 105 ... DarryllHolland 1	82+
			(M R Channon) *hld up: rdn over 2f out: nvr nrr* **15/2**	
412-	**7**	*hd*	**Rinterval (IRE)**[215] 5395 3-8-12 94 ... RyanMoore 5	82
			(R Hannon) *lw: trckd ldrs: rdn over 2f out: wknd fnl f* **4/1**[2]	
303-	**8**	*½*	**Highland Daughter (IRE)**[207] 5614 3-8-12 99 ... PhilipRobinson 13	81
			(C G Cox) *hld up: hdwy over 2f out: rdn over 1f out: wknd fnl f* **16/1**	
21-	**9**	*1 ¾*	**Shabiba (USA)**[195] 5949 3-8-12 84 ... RHills 10	76
			(M P Tregoning) *chsd ldr: rdn over 1f out: wknd fnl f* **6/1**	
600-	**10**	*nk*	**Gone Fast (USA)**[194] 5973 3-8-12 95 ... RichardMullen 7	75
			(D M Simcock) *bit bkwd: prom: rdn over 2f out: wknd over 1f out* **100/1**	
40-0	**11**	*3*	**Albabilia (IRE)**[48] 745 3-8-12 0 ...(t) SebSanders 9	67
			(C E Brittain) *h.d.w: hld up in tch: rdn and wknd over 1f out* **14/1**	
1-1	**12**	*7*	**Quiet Elegance**[13] 1170 3-8-12 94 ... JimmyQuinn 4	48
			(E J Alston) *lw: hld up: rdn over 2f out: sn wknd* **16/1**	
052-	**13**	*shd*	**Anosti**[194] 5974 3-8-12 89 ... JamieSpencer 2	48
			(K A Ryan) *lw: hld up: hdwy 1/2-way: rdn: hung rt and wknd over 1f out* **25/1**	
04-1	**14**	*2 ¾*	**Crying Aloud (USA)**[15] 1132 3-8-12 80 ... StephenDonohoe 8	40
			(P A Blockley) *h.d.w: plld hrd and prom: rdn and wknd over 2f out* **50/1**	

1m 27.15s (1.75) **Going Correction** +0.45s/f (Yiel) **14** Ran SP% **122.4**
Speed ratings (Par 105): **108,104,100,99,98 97,97,96,94,94 90,82,82,79**
CSF £268.57 TOTE £4.40: £2.00, £14.20, £3.20; EX 198.90.

Owner Cheveley Park Stud **Bred** Cheveley Park Stud Ltd **Trained** Newmarket, Suffolk

FOCUS

A weakish renewal of the Nell Gwyn - they were all available beforehand at upwards of 20-1 for the 1000 Guineas and the second, third and fourth came into this rated in the 90s - but Infallible was very impressive. On RPRs the bare form still leaves her 6lb to find with Natagora in the Guineas, however. The winning time was 0.02 seconds quicker than the Free Handicap.

NOTEBOOK

Infallible, the winner of a backend maiden over course and distance last November, was a mightily impressive winner on her return to action. Held up last of all early on, she was always travelling very easily and, once produced with her challenge towards the outside, she made good headway to join the leader, Kylayne, still on the bridle, although she did show her inexperience by edging right. She bounded away once shaken up and marked herself down as a very smart filly. She was made favourite at around 4/1 for the 1000 Guineas following this but, as good and as promising as she obviously is, that race will provide a different test altogether. For a start the opposition will be significantly tougher and, by Pivotal out of a triple 5f-6f winner, she is not even guaranteed to get 1m, particularly considering the speed she showed on the bridle this time. Quicker ground will also be a concern. (tchd 4-1 and 9-2 in places)

Kylayne, a useful two-year-old last year who rounded off her campaign with a win in a 6f conditions contest on the Polytrack at Lingfield, ran surprisingly well on her return from six months off, belying her big odds in second. Always bang on the speed, she kept on for pressure but was no match for Infallible who, to put it simply, is just a much better horse. She should prove most effective at around 6f-7f and might be able to pick up some more black type as the season progresses. (tchd 100-1)

Festivale(IRE), third in a Listed race over 6f here last November on her final start at two, ran a respectable race on her return to action. Trying 7f for the first time, she kept on for third having been waited with, but she was still beaten quite a way into third and had a rival rated just 93 three lengths in front. (tchd 9-1)

Rosaleen(IRE) ran a creditable race after 193 days off the track and probably would have finished a little closer with a better run.

Spinning Lucy(IRE), three and a half lengths in front of Festivale when winning a 6f Listed race here last November, failed to see out her race stepped back up in trip on her reappearance. (op 5-1)

Nijoom Dubai stepped up markedly on her two previous efforts when winning the Albany at Royal Ascot last June, but she had not been seen since. There was not a great deal of promise in this effort, but she is entitled to come on considering she had been off for so long. (op 7-1 tchd 8-1)

Rinterval(IRE), returning from 215 days off, could not match the form she showed when second in the Goffs Fillies Million at the Curragh. (op 9-2 tchd 5-1 in a place)

Shabiba(USA)'s dam, Misterah, won this in 2002, but she only had a Newmarket maiden win last October to her name and was well beaten on her return. (op 15-2)

Anosti Official explanation: jockey said filly hung right

1402 TUDDENHAM MILL FEILDEN STKS (LISTED RACE) 1m 1f

4:20 (4:21) (Class 1) 3-Y-O

£17,031 (£6,456; £3,231; £1,611; £807; £405) **Stalls** High

Form				RPR
10-1	**1**		**Campanologist (USA)**[32] 902 3-8-13 95 ... JoeFanning 3	109
			(M Johnston) *lw: chsd ldrs: led over 3f out: rdn over 1f out: styd on* **9/2**[3]	
211-	**2**	*½*	**Kandahar Run**[180] 6297 3-8-13 105 ... TedDurcan 2	108
			(H R A Cecil) *h.d.w: hld up: plld hrd: hdwy over 2f out: rdn and ev ch fr over 1f out: styd on* **5/4**[1]	
	3	*4 ½*	**Poet**[17] 1107 3-8-13 0 ... JMurtagh 6	99
			(A P O'Brien, Ire) *chsd ldr 3f: rdn over 2f out: wknd ins fnl f* **4/1**[2]	
23-4	**4**	*1 ¼*	**Redolent (IRE)**[11] 1213 3-8-13 108 ... RyanMoore 1	96
			(R Hannon) *b: hld up in tch: rdn over 2f out: edgd rt over 1f out: wknd fnl f* **9/2**[3]	
3-05	**5**	*1*	**Yahrab (IRE)**[48] 743 3-8-13 0 ... KerrinMcEvoy 4	94
			(C E Brittain) *led over 5f: rdn and wknd over 1f out* **12/1**	
15-5	**6**	*1 ¼*	**Pegasus Again (USA)**[32] 902 3-8-13 95 ... LDettori 5	91
			(T G Mills) *lw: hld up: rdn over 2f out: wknd over 1f out* **16/1**	

1m 54.15s (3.55) **Going Correction** +0.45s/f (Yiel) **6** Ran SP% **114.4**
Speed ratings (Par 106): **102,101,97,96,95 94**
CSF £10.92 TOTE £5.60: £2.30, £1.20; EX 11.30.

Owner Sheikh Hamdan Bin Mohammed Al Maktoum **Bred** Darley **Trained** Middleham Moor, N Yorks

FOCUS
A good renewal of the Feilden Stakes, run in a decent time despite what looked an ordinary pace. Solid form, the first two finishing clear. Both can rate higher.

NOTEBOOK
Campanologist(USA) did not cut much ice in the Royal Lodge on his final start at two, but he created a good impression when winning a 1m1f conditions contest on the Polytrack at Kempton on his reappearance and took another significant step forward with a battling success from the well-touted Kandahar Run. He was transferred to Godolphin afterwards. (tchd 5-1)
Kandahar Run looked good when winning his maiden at Doncaster last year and again when following up in a conditions event over 1m here on his final start of the campaign. He always promised to make an even nicer three-year-old, and has done well physically over the winter, but he was just held. His rider was not over hard on him in the finish, so he should step forward again. (tchd 6-4 and 13-8 in places)
Poet created a good impression when winning a 1m maiden at the Curragh on his reappearance, and the form has already been boosted, so this could be considered as disappointing. A long-striding type, he seemed to change his legs a few times once coming off the bridle and might have been happy on this undulating track. (op 9-2 tchd 5-1)
Redolent(IRE), a close fourth in a bunch finish to the International Trial Stakes on the Polytrack at Lingfield on his reappearance, found this tougher. (op 6-1 tchd 4-1)
Yahrab(IRE), back in the UK after a couple of unsuccessul spins in Dubai, was put in his place when it mattered.
Pegasus Again(USA) was reported to have a breathing problem. Official explanation: jockey said colt had a breathing problem on pulling up (op 12-1)

1403 ALEX SCOTT MAIDEN STKS (C&G) 7f
4:55 (4:58) (Class 4) 3-Y-O **£5,180** (£1,541; £770; £384) **Stalls** High

Form RPR
22- **1** **Virtual**[194] 5977 3-9-0 0 JimmyFortune 10 92+
(J H M Gosden) *mde all: rdn over 1f out: r.o* **11/10**[1]
6- **2** *1 ½* **Otaared**[238] 4725 3-9-0 0 PhilipRobinson 8 88+
(M A Jarvis) *lw: chsd wnr: rdn over 1f out: styd on* **9/2**[3]
2- **3** *1 ½* **Masaalek**[333] 1832 3-9-0 0 RHills 1 84+
(M P Tregoning) *h.d.w: dwlt: hdwy 1/2-way: rdn over 1f out: styd on same pce* **15/8**[2]
0- **4** *¾* **Slugger O'Toole**[196] 5910 3-9-0 0 MichaelHills 2 82
(B W Hills) *hld up: swtchd lft over 2f out: hdwy over 1f out: nt trble ldrs* **25/1**
56- **5** *6* **El Duende (USA)**[183] 6251 3-9-0 0 JamieSpencer 3 65+
(W Jarvis) *hld up: shkn up over 2f out: nvr nr to chal* **33/1**
65- **6** *1 ¼* **Timbalier (USA)**[158] 6763 3-9-0 0 RichardMullen 4 62
(D M Simcock) *chsd ldrs: rdn over 2f out: sn wknd* **100/1**
7 *shd* **Style Icon** 3-9-0 0 TQuinn 9 62
(D R C Elsworth) *gd sort: s.i.s: sn chsng ldrs: rdn over 2f out: wknd over 1f out* **25/1**
6- **8** *shd* **Brother Barry (USA)**[166] 6617 3-9-0 0 RyanMoore 6 65+
(W J Musson) *bkwd: hld up: hdwy and nt clr run over 1f out: nt rcvr* **16/1**
0-0 **9** *4 ½* **Kuriyama (IRE)**[25] 961 3-9-0 0 JimmyQuinn 5 49
(M H Tompkins) *hld up in tch: rdn over 2f out: sn wknd* **66/1**
1m 28.51s (3.11) **Going Correction** +0.45s/f (Yiel) **9** Ran SP% **119.6**
Speed ratings (Par 100): **100,98,96,95,88 87,87,87,82**
CSF £6.72 TOTE £2.00: £1.10, £1.70, £1.10; EX 7.40.
Owner Cheveley Park Stud **Bred** Cheveley Park Stud Ltd **Trained** Newmarket, Suffolk

FOCUS
An ordinary maiden, with the market going 16-1 bar three and the front four pulled a long way clear of the others. The winning time was about what you would expect when compared with the earlier Pattern races, and a couple of these probably have futures. The form seems sound enough.
Brother Barry(USA) ◆ Official explanation: jockey said gelding was denied a clear run

1404 VOUTE SALES STKS (H'CAP) 6f
5:30 (5:31) (Class 2) (0-100,96) 3-Y-O **£11,656** (£3,468; £1,733; £865) **Stalls** High

Form RPR
261- **1** **Prohibit**[196] 5910 3-8-13 **86** JimmyFortune 10 94+
(J H M Gosden) *h.d.w: b.hind: racd stands' side: hld up: hdwy over 2f out: rdn to ld ins fnl f: r.o* **8/1**[3]
131- **2** *½* **Kaldoun Kingdom (IRE)**[173] 6462 3-9-0 **87** TonyHamilton 11 94
(R A Fahey) *racd stands' side: hld up: hdwy over 1f out: sn rdn: r.o: 2nd of 10 in gp* **16/1**
161- **3** *hd* **Fol Hollow (IRE)**[232] 4921 3-9-8 **95** LDettori 19 101
(D Nicholls) *lw: led far side: rdn over 1f out: r.o: 1st of 7 in gp* **11/1**
512- **4** *nk* **Crystany (IRE)**[217] 5322 3-9-5 **92** TedDurcan 20 97+
(H R A Cecil) *lw: racd far side: s.i.s: hld up: hdwy and nt clr run over 1f out: swtchd lft: r.o wl: 2nd of 7 in gp* **11/2**[2]
5221 **5** *1* **Fathsta (IRE)**[13] 1167 3-8-12 **85** LPKeniry 17 87
(S Kirk) *racd far side: trckd ldrs: rdn and ev ch that gp 1f out: styd in same pce towards fin: 3rd of 7 in gp* **20/1**
512- **6** *nk* **Striking Spirit**[187] 6154 3-9-3 **90** MichaelHills 18 91+
(B W Hills) *racd far side: hld up in tch: rdn over 1f out: hmpd ins fnl f: styd on: 4th of 7 in gp* **4/1**[1]
50-4 **7** *nk* **Victorian Bounty**[13] 1170 3-9-0 **87** MickyFenton 7 87
(Stef Liddiard) *led stands' side: edgd rt over 2f out: hdd over 1f out: styd on: 3rd of 10 in gp* **33/1**
01-5 **8** *nk* **Chartist**[18] 1075 3-8-13 **86** RyanMoore 6 85
(R Hannon) *lw: racd stands' side: chsd ldrs: led that gp over 1f out: hdd and unable qck ins fnl f: 4th of 10 in gp* **9/1**
004- **9** *1 ½* **Johar Jamal (IRE)**[199] 5837 3-8-9 **82** TPO'Shea 2 76+
(M R Channon) *racd stands' side: hld up: r.o ins fnl f: nvr trbld ldrs: 5th of 10 in gp* **25/1**
150- **10** *1 ¼* **Calmdownmate (IRE)**[215] 5397 3-9-8 **95** FergusSweeney 4 85
(K R Burke) *lw: racd stands' side: chsd ldrs: rdn and ev ch that side over 1f out: no ex fnl f: 6th of 10 in gp* **66/1**
011- **11** *hd* **Hadaf (IRE)**[193] 6004 3-8-13 **86** MartinDwyer 13 76
(M P Tregoning) *racd far side: hld up in tch: rdn and hung lft over 1f out: no ex: 5th of 7 in gp* **14/1**
360- **12** *1* **Carleton**[186] 6167 3-9-6 **93** PhilipRobinson 5 79
(W J Musson) *h.d.w: racd stands' side: hld up: n.d: 7th of 10 in gp* **50/1**
1- **13** *nk* **Kashimin (IRE)**[177] 6384 3-8-9 **85** PJMcDonald[(3)] 1 71
(G A Swinbank) *b.hind: racd stands' side: s.i.s: sn prom: rdn and wknd over 1f out: 8th of 10 in gp* **12/1**
00-1 **14** *½* **Vhujon (IRE)**[18] 1075 3-9-9 **96** TGMcLaughlin 9 80
(P D Evans) *s.i.s: swtchd to r far side sn after s: hld up: rdn over 1f out: n.d: 6th of 7 in gp* **20/1**
600- **15** *2 ¾* **Spanish Bounty**[221] 5219 3-9-3 **90** EddieAhern 16 77+
(J G Portman) *racd far side: chsd ldr: rdn over 1f out: wkng whn hmpd ins fnl f: last of 7 in gp* **33/1**
103- **16** *1 ¾* **Mister Fips (IRE)**[193] 6004 3-8-11 **84** JohnEgan 8 54
(Jane Chapple-Hyam) *racd stands' side: chsd ldrs: rdn over 2f out: wknd over 1f out: 9th of 10 in gp* **50/1**
1- **17** *10* **Mookhlesa**[363] 1101 3-8-9 **82** RHills 3 20
(B W Hills) *racd stands' side: s.i.s: sn chsng ldrs: wknd wl over 1f out: eased fnl f: last of 10 in gp* **11/2**[2]
1m 14.68s (2.48) **Going Correction** +0.45s/f (Yiel) **17** Ran SP% **125.1**
Speed ratings (Par 104): **101,100,100,99,98 97,97,97,95,93 93,91,91,90,87 84,71**
CSF £120.50 CT £1435.39 TOTE £8.30: £2.40, £4.00, £2.70, £2.10; EX 187.30 Place 6 £10.61, Place 5 £5.58..
Owner K Abdulla **Bred** Juddmonte Farms Ltd **Trained** Newmarket, Suffolk
■ Prohibit completed a 1,785-1 four-timer for John Gosden and Jimmy Fortune.
■ Stewards' Enquiry : Ted Durcan two-day ban: careless riding (Apr 30-May 1)

FOCUS
A competitive sprint handicap that has been won by some decent sorts over the years, not least Sakhee's Secret in 2007. The field split into two, with ten coming stands' side and seven staying far side, but there was nothing between the two groups with two each coming from each flank amongst the quartet that fought out the finish. Plenty of winners should emerge from the race.

NOTEBOOK
Prohibit ◆, making his handicap debut after more than six months off, travelled well in the stands'-side group and when asked for his effort starting up the final climb, produced a telling turn of foot to complete a four-timer for his in-form trainer/jockey combination. He should not have a problem returning to 7f and ought to be able to build on this. (op 10-1)
Kaldoun Kingdom(IRE) ◆, another returning from around six months off but more experienced than the winner, was produced with his effort in plenty of time and went down with all guns blazing. This effort shows that the 15lb rise for his romp in an Ayr nursery on his final start at two was not excessive and he should have another good season.
Fol Hollow(IRE), returning from eight months off, led the smaller far-side group and battled on really well to win the race on his side, but the front pair racing on the opposite flank mugged him in the very closing stages. He has quite a bit of experience, but this was an encouraging return and he will not mind if the ground starts to firm up. (op 14-1)
Crystany(IRE) ◆, absent for seven months, gave herself quite a bit to do in the far-side group after fluffing the start, so she did extremely well to get as close as she did. She should not take long in finding another opportunity.
Fathsta(IRE), a four-time winner on Polytrack this winter, has gained all his wins around a bend and was 15lb higher than when last on turf. He ran well against the far rail having been prominent from the start, and although he enjoyed a fitness advantage over the quartet that beat him, this was still a fair effort off such an inflated mark.
Striking Spirit, returning from six months off and 5lb higher than when runner-up in a York nursery on his final start at two, seemed to have every chance in the far-side group but he is still open to a bit of improvement. (tchd 7-2 and 9-2)
Chartist looked happier being allowed to race up with the pace and comprehensively turned Kempton form around with Vhujon. He still looks worth dropping back to the minimum. (op 10-1)
Vhujon(IRE), raised 6lb for his Kempton win, was switched dramatically across to join the far-side group after the runners had gone a few strides, but it did not help his chance.
T/Plt: £17.00 to a £1 stake. Pool: £99,629.32. 4,267.00 winning tickets. T/Qpdt: £4.70 to a £1 stake. Pool: £4,754.50. 746.70 winning tickets. CR

1369 WOLVERHAMPTON (A.W) (L-H)
Wednesday, April 16

OFFICIAL GOING: Standard
Wind: Almost nil Weather: Fine

1405 PARADE RESTAURANT APPRENTICE (S) STKS 1m 4f 50y(P)
6:50 (6:51) (Class 6) 4-Y-O+ **£2,047** (£604; £302) **Stalls** Low

Form RPR
2535 **1** **Wait For The Will (USA)**[14] 1151 12-8-11 66 (b) JemmaMarshall[(3)] 9 72
(G L Moore) *hld up in tch: wnt 2nd 3f out: led on bit 2f out: rdn towards fin: jst hld on* **5/2**[2]
5/52 **2** *nse* **Truly Fruitful (IRE)**[5] 1305 5-8-8 68 BMcHugh[(6)] 3 72
(R A Fahey) *a.p: swtchd rt and chsd wnr wl over 1f out: rdn to chal ins fnl f: jst failed* **5/6**[1]
3310 **3** *13* **Granary Girl**[14] 1148 6-9-1 50 SimonPearce 10 52
(J Pearce) *hld up in tch: wknd over 1f out* **20/1**
060- **4** *4 ½* **Fiddlers Creek (IRE)**[112] 4713 9-9-0 53 (v) DeclanCannon 1 44
(R Allan) *led: rdn and hdd 2f out: wknd over 1f out* **40/1**
-35P **5** *nk* **Kofi**[44] 776 6-8-9 43 TimothyMeadows[(5)] 7 43
(Karen George) *hld up and bhd: rdn 3f out: nvr nr ldrs* **40/1**
6 *¾* **Skyler**[29] 7-8-9 0 AshleyMorgan[(5)] 6 42
(J L Flint) *hld up towards rr: rdn over 2f out: n.d* **16/1**
0001 **7** *½* **Shenandoah Girl**[12] 1184 5-8-10 53 RosieJessop[(5)] 8 42
(Miss Gay Kelleway) *hld up in mid-div: wknd 2f out* **8/1**[3]
8 *¾* **Paperboy**[13] 4-8-13 0 RossAtkinson 5 40
(Karen George) *pushed along 7f out: a in rr* **100/1**
205/ **9** *6* **Countrywide Luck**[557] 521 7-8-9 70 NBazeley[(5)] 2 31
(B N Pollock) *chsd ldr to 3f out: wknd 2f out* **14/1**
2m 43.95s (2.85) **Going Correction** +0.275s/f (Slow)
WFA 4 from 5yo+ 1lb **9** Ran SP% **117.4**
Speed ratings (Par 101): **101,100,92,89,89 88,88,87,83**
CSF £4.86 TOTE £3.70: £1.10, £1.10, £1.70; EX 8.50.There was no bid for the winner. Truly Fruitful was claimed by R Trow for £6,000.
Owner Rdm Racing **Bred** Paul Mellon **Trained** Woodingdean, E Sussex

FOCUS
The two at the head of the market came well clear in this slowly-run, poor seller. They are both rated close to their recent marks.

1406 HORIZONS RESTAURANT H'CAP 1m 141y(P)
7:20 (7:21) (Class 6) (0-65,65) 4-Y-O+ **£2,047** (£604; £302) **Stalls** Low

Form RPR
3241 **1** **Shunkawakhan (IRE)**[19] 1064 5-8-8 **55** (p) TomEaves 3 62
(Miss L A Perratt) *t.k.h in tch: rdn to ld towards fin: r.o* **7/2**[2]
000- **2** *nk* **Uig**[167] 6603 7-8-7 **59** ow1 HaddenFrost[(5)] 9 65
(H S Howe) *sn chsng ldr: rdn 2f out: led ins fnl f: hdd towards fin* **14/1**
5216 **3** *1 ¼* **Casablanca Minx (IRE)**[2] 1374 5-8-6 **60** ow1 (v) RichardEvans[(7)] 8 63
(P D Evans) *hld up towards rr: swtchd lft and hdwy on ins wl over 1f out: ev ch ins fnl f: nt qckn* **7/1**[3]
3024 **4** *½* **Shosolosa (IRE)**[9] 1248 6-7-11 **51** oh3 StacyRenwick[(7)] 7 53
(R C Guest) *s.i.s: hld up in rr: edgd lft over 1f out: hdwy fnl f: nrst fin* **40/1**
-622 **5** *1 ½* **Juzilla (IRE)**[18] 1085 4-9-4 **65** SaleemGolam 10 64
(W R Swinburn) *sn led: edgd rt over 1f out: hdd ins fnl f: fdd* **5/2**[1]
140- **6** *1* **Grandad Bill (IRE)**[180] 6304 5-7-13 **51** oh1 KellyHarrison[(5)] 1 47
(J S Goldie) *led early: a.p: rdn wl over 1f out: wknd wl ins fnl f* **9/1**

301- **7** *hd* **Golden Brown (IRE)**[175] 6431 4-8-11 **58** .... NeilChalmers 4 54
(David Pinder) *hld up in mid-div: hdwy over 2f out: rdn wl over 1f out: wknd fnl f* **11/1**

34- **8** *5* **Marquee (IRE)**[237] 4429 4-8-9 **63** .... RyanRaftery(7) 2 47
(P A Blockley) *a towards rr* **7/1**[3]

0-50 **9** *2 3/4* **Libre**[14] 1160 8-8-13 **60** .... JamesDoyle 6 38
(F Jordan) *a towards rr* **16/1**

450- **10** *5* **Papa's Princess**[194] 5967 4-8-1 **51** oh1 .... WilliamBuick(3) 5 17
(J S Goldie) *s.i.s: rdn over 3f out: a bhd* **11/1**

1m 53.64s (3.14) **Going Correction** +0.275s/f (Slow) **10** Ran SP% **117.4**
Speed ratings (Par 101): **97,96,95,95,93 92,92,88,85,81**
CSF £52.10 CT £336.04 TOTE £5.10: £1.40, £5.50, £2.60; EX 63.90.
Owner Partick Thistle Racing Club **Bred** Matthew Duffy **Trained** Carluke, S Lanarks
■ Stewards' Enquiry : Saleem Golam one-day ban: failed to keep straight from the stalls (Apr 30)

FOCUS
A slowly-run, weak handicap. The form is rated around the third and fourth.

1407 HOTEL & CONFERENCING CLAIMING STKS 1m 141y(P)
7:50 (7:50) (Class 6) 3-Y-O **£2,047** (£604; £302) **Stalls** Low

Form RPR

4503 **1** **Carry On Cleo**[2] 1364 3-8-8 **53** ow1 .... (v) TomEaves 6 56
(P D Evans) *a.p: rdn and wnt 2nd wl over 1f out: r.o u.p to ld last strides* **9/1**

1412 **2** *hd* **Bridge Of Fermoy (IRE)**[9] 1245 3-9-7 **76** .... (bt) GeorgeBaker 5 69
(Miss Gay Kelleway) *chsd ldr: led over 3f out: clr wl over 1f out: rdn and edgd lft jst ins fnl f: ct last strides* **8/15**[1]

3046 **3** *1/2* **Mujahope**[9] 1247 3-8-3 **63** .... AndreaAtzeni(7) 3 56
(M Botti) *t.k.h in rr: swtchd rt 2f out: rdn and hdwy over 1f out: r.o ins fnl f* **6/1**[2]

4054 **4** *4* **Coole Dodger (IRE)**[15] 1124 3-8-8 **62** .... GabrielHannon(7) 4 52
(M D I Usher) *s.i.s: t.k.h: hdwy over 5f out: hung rt fr over 3f out: rn v wd ent st: n.d after* **25/1**

1625 **5** *1/2* **Ledgerwood**[16] 1115 3-9-2 **64** .... (p) JamesDoyle 7 52
(J W Hills) *set stdy pce: hdd over 3f out: rdn over 2f out: wknd over 1f out* **7/1**[3]

-015 **6** *4 1/2* **Secret Meaning**[15] 1124 3-8-2 **55** .... (p) JackDean(7) 2 35
(W G M Turner) *awkward leaving stalls: hld up: pushed along over 3f out: bhd fnl 2f* **25/1**

1m 58.18s (7.68) **Going Correction** +0.275s/f (Slow) **6** Ran SP% **109.7**
Speed ratings (Par 96): **76,75,75,71,71 67**
CSF £13.80 TOTE £7.20: £4.40, £1.10; EX 17.20.The winner was claimed by E Nisbet for £6,000. Mujahope was claimed by C Teague for £4,000.
Owner J E Abbey **Bred** J E Abbey **Trained** Pandy, Monmouths

FOCUS
A pedestrian winning time for this falsely-run claimer which developed into a sprint in the final half a mile. Weak form.
Coole Dodger(IRE) Official explanation: jockey said colt hung right-handed throughout

1408 BOOK TICKETS ONLINE H'CAP 2m 119y(P)
8:20 (8:20) (Class 6) (0-65,63) 4-Y-0+ **£2,047** (£604; £302) **Stalls** Low

Form RPR

-503 **1** **Synonymy**[7] 1267 5-9-5 **57** .... (b) JamesDoyle 5 66
(M Blanshard) *a.p: led 3f out to 2f out: rdn to ld and edgd lft ins fnl f: styd on* **4/1**[1]

-140 **2** *nk* **Snowberry Hill (USA)**[14] 1136 5-9-3 **55** .... NeilChalmers 12 64
(Lucinda Featherstone) *hld up in tch: led 2f out: rdn and hung rt over 1f out: hdd ins fnl f: styd on* **7/1**

530/ **3** *3* **Zeloso**[519] 1883 10-8-7 **45** .... (v) J-PGuillambert 11 50
(M F Harris) *hld up in mid-div: rdn and hdwy over 2f out: styd on to take 3rd last strides* **50/1**

0-60 **4** *1/2* **Archimboldo (USA)**[25] 778 5-9-7 **59** .... (b) DaneO'Neill 7 64
(T Wall) *s.i.s: sn hld up in mid-div: rdn and hdwy over 2f out: one pce fnl f* **25/1**

3130 **5** *nk* **Champagne Shadow (IRE)**[34] 869 7-9-3 **62** .... SimonPearce(7) 6 66
(J Pearce) *hld up in rr: hdwy wl over 1f out: rdn and edgd lft ent fnl f: one pce* **6/1**[3]

/2-0 **6** *13* **Saloon (USA)**[13] 1172 4-9-7 **63** .... PaulDoe 3 52
(S Curran) *hld up towards rr: rdn and hdwy on outside over 2f out: wknd wl over 1f out* **12/1**

1032 **7** *1* **Opera Writer (IRE)**[19] 1062 5-9-7 **59** .... (v) JimCrowley 1 47
(R Hollinshead) *led early: prom tl rdn and wknd 2f out* **9/2**[2]

440 **8** *8* **Right You Are (IRE)**[47] 758 8-9-0 **52** .... TomEaves 4 30
(Paul Green) *hld up in tch: reminders over 4f out: wknd wl over 1f out* **33/1**

1641 **9** *9* **King's Fable (USA)**[20] 1044 5-9-11 **63** .... (p) TGMcLaughlin 10 30+
(Karen George) *dwlt: sn swtchd lft: hld up in rr: gng wl whn bdly hmpd on ins over 2f out: sn eased* **9/2**[2]

0006 **10** *4* **Lay The Cash (USA)**[11] 1206 4-8-1 **46** .... (bt) WilliamBuick(3) 8 8
(B G Powell) *sn led: rdn and hdd 3f out: wkng whn n.m.r on ins over 2f out* **14/1**

63-6 **11** *nse* **Berbatov**[46] 771 4-7-11 **46** ow1 .... AndrewHeffernan(7) 2 8
(Paul Green) *hld up in mid-div: rdn over 4f out: sn struggling* **25/1**

2243 **12** *4* **Still Dreaming**[18] 1086 4-8-5 **54** .... (b) RossAtkinson(7) 9 12
(R J Price) *t.k.h: chsd ldr after 1f tl rdn over 3f out: wknd over 2f out* **14/1**

6315 **13** *1 1/4* **Piano Key**[34] 869 4-8-5 **47** .... RichardSmith 13 3
(M D I Usher) *a bhd* **12/1**

3m 44.98s (3.18) **Going Correction** +0.275s/f (Slow)
WFA 4 from 5yo+ 4lb **13** Ran SP% **124.5**
Speed ratings (Par 101): **103,102,101,101,101 94,94,90,86,84 84,82,82**
CSF £32.39 CT £1257.93 TOTE £5.70: £1.90, £3.20, £8.20; EX 32.20.
Owner G H Phillips,J M Beever & D G Chambers **Bred** Biddestone Stud **Trained** Upper Lambourn, Berks

FOCUS
This minor staying handicap was run at an even pace. The form seems sound.
Right You Are(IRE) Official explanation: jockey said gelding ran too free early on

1409 WOLVERHAMPTON-RACECOURSE.CO.UK H'CAP 7f 32y(P)
8:50 (8:51) (Class 4) (0-85,85) 4-Y-0+ **£4,209** (£1,252; £625; £312) **Stalls** High

Form RPR

3222 **1** **Count Ceprano (IRE)**[18] 1084 4-8-7 **74** .... RichardSmith 7 86+
(M D I Usher) *hld up: hdwy 3f out: rdn to ld ins fnl f: r.o wl* **7/4**[1]

1400 **2** *3 1/2* **Red Romeo**[4] 1327 7-9-4 **85** .... DanielTudhope 3 88
(N Wilson) *led early: a.p: led 2f out: rdn and hdd ins fnl f: one pce* **7/1**

0-03 **3** *3 3/4* **Harare**[21] 1030 7-8-6 **73** .... (v) JamesDoyle 9 65
(R J Price) *hld up: stdy hdwy over 5f out: rdn wl over 1f out: hung lft ins fnl f: one pce* **12/1**

-240 **4** *1/2* **Westport**[23] 992 5-8-9 **76** .... PaulMulrennan 4 67
(K A Ryan) *hld up: rdn and hdwy over 1f out: one pce fnl f* **8/1**

0-06 **5** *1* **Teen Ager (FR)**[16] 1112 4-8-1 **71** .... WilliamBuick(3) 2 59
(P Burgoyne) *hld up in rr: rdn and hdwy on outside wl over 1f out: one pce fnl f* **17/2**

00-0 **6** *7* **H Harrison (IRE)**[14] 1146 8-8-0 **74** oh2 ow3 .... DonnaCaldwell(7) 6 43
(I W McInnes) *sn led: rdn and hdd 2f out: wknd over 1f out* **33/1**

0-50 **7** *5* **Inch Lodge**[56] 626 6-8-5 **72** .... PaulEddery 8 28
(Miss D Mountain) *sn prom: rdn and wknd over 3f out* **13/2**[3]

0-05 **8** *1/2* **Byron Bay**[14] 1138 6-8-13 **80** .... (p) TomEaves 1 35
(R C Guest) *sn chsng ldr: wknd 3f out* **10/1**

4021 **9** *6* **Divertimenti (IRE)**[18] 1084 4-8-11 **78** .... RobertWinston 5 16
(C R Dore) *hld up: short-lived effrt over 2f out: eased over 1f out* **10/3**[2]

1m 29.38s (-0.22) **Going Correction** +0.275s/f (Slow) **9** Ran SP% **126.6**
Speed ratings (Par 105): **112,108,103,103,102 94,88,87,80**
CSF £16.81 CT £125.67 TOTE £4.00: £1.10, £2.90, £1.90; EX 37.00.
Owner G A Summers **Bred** Pendley Farm **Trained** Upper Lambourn, Berks

FOCUS
An ordinary event but a smart winning time, 1.75 seconds faster than the maiden. The winner looks at least as good as ever.
Divertimenti(IRE) Official explanation: trainer had no explanation for the poor form shown

1410 RINGSIDE CONFERENCE SUITE MAIDEN STKS 7f 32y(P)
9:20 (9:21) (Class 5) 3-Y-0+ **£2,456** (£725; £362) **Stalls** High

Form RPR

32 **1** **Always A Rock (IRE)**[32] 909 3-9-0 0 .... RobertWinston 2 78+
(M Johnston) *mde all: shkn up ins fnl f: r.o wl* **8/13**[1]

00- **2** *2* **Opera Prince**[166] 6617 3-9-0 0 .... LPKeniry 5 73
(S Kirk) *hld up in tch: rdn to chse wnr and hung lft 1f out: no imp* **28/1**

26- **3** *1* **Agente Romano (USA)**[131] 7051 3-8-11 0 .... WilliamBuick(3) 12 70+
(G A Butler) *hld up and bhd: hdwy on wd outside over 2f out: c wd st: kpt on same pce fnl f* **3/1**[2]

0- **4** *2* **St Michael's Mount**[222] 5200 3-9-0 0 .... PatDobbs 4 65
(M P Tregoning) *t.k.h: chsd wnr: wknd fnl f* **9/1**

5- **5** *3/4* **Tantris (IRE)**[178] 6358 3-9-0 0 .... DaneO'Neill 7 68+
(J A Osborne) *s.i.s: sn hld up in mid-div: hdwy over 2f out: n.m.r on ins jst ins fnl f: one pce* **22/1**

24 **6** *1/2* **Key News (IRE)**[34] 867 3-8-9 0 .... MatthewHenry 11 56
(M A Jarvis) *hld up in mid-div: hdwy on outside over 2f out: wknd wl over 1f out* **8/1**[3]

7 *14* **Tallest Peak (USA)** 3-8-11 0 .... JerryO'Dwyer(3) 6 23
(M G Quinlan) *a bhd* **40/1**

- **8** *6* **Annawanna**[147] 4-9-8 0 .... LeeEnstone 1 2
(S Wynne) *s.i.s: prom tl rdn and wknd over 2f out* **150/1**

06 **9** *hd* **Lucky Character**[55] 645 3-9-0 0 .... (t) SamHitchcott 9 7
(N J Vaughan) *prom: rdn over 3f out: wknd 2f out* **33/1**

10 *1 1/2* **Bombay Dreams**[13] 5-9-1 0 .... GihanArnolda(7) 3 —
(Karen George) *s.s: a in rr* **150/1**

1m 31.13s (1.53) **Going Correction** +0.275s/f (Slow)
WFA 3 from 4yo+ 13lb **10** Ran SP% **122.5**
Speed ratings (Par 103): **102,99,98,96,95 94,78,72,71,70**
CSF £33.09 TOTE £1.90: £1.10, £4.90, £1.10; EX 29.20.
Owner Always Trying Partnership IV **Bred** Ascagnano S P A **Trained** Middleham Moor, N Yorks

FOCUS
A moderate maiden. The form seems sound, with the first six coming well clear, and the winner can rate higher.
T/Plt: £24.70 to a £1 stake. Pool: £92,487.38. 2,728.67 winning tickets. T/Qpdt: £7.60 to a £1 stake. Pool: £6,182.60. 595.00 winning tickets. KH

1331 KEMPTON (A.W) (R-H)
Thursday, April 17

OFFICIAL GOING: Standard
Wind: fresh behind Weather: bright and breezy

1411 KEMPTON.CO.UK CLAIMING STKS 1m 2f (P)
6:50 (6:50) (Class 6) 4-Y-0+ **£2,266** (£674; £337; £168) **Stalls** High

Form RPR

6131 **1** **Dushstorm (IRE)**[7] 1286 7-8-13 **67** .... JamieSpencer 7 71+
(D Nicholls) *hld up in tch: hdwy to ld wl over 1f out: clr 1f out: comf* **10/11**[1]

-104 **2** *1 1/2* **Steely Dan**[14] 1164 9-9-3 **66** .... (p) GeorgeBaker 3 69
(Mrs L C Jewell) *stdd s: t.k.h: hld up in tch: rdn and hdwy over 2f out: chsd wnr fnl f: kpt on but nt pce to threaten wnr* **16/1**

4210 **3** *3/4* **Just Intersky (USA)**[14] 1165 5-8-11 **64** .... (e) WilliamBuick(3) 5 65
(V Smith) *stdd s: hld up in tch in rr: rdn 3f out: kpt on fom over 1f out: nvr pce to trble wnr* **8/1**[3]

500- **4** *3 1/2* **Title Deed (USA)**[62] 6848 4-9-5 **63** .... RichardThomas 2 63
(A P Jarvis) *chsd ldr tl 2f out: outpcd u.p over 1f out* **20/1**

6000 **5** *1 3/4* **Smokey The Bear**[19] 1076 6-9-6 **79** .... NeilChalmers 1 60
(Miss Sheena West) *t.k.h: chsd ldrs: rdn and outpcd over 2f out: n.d after* **13/8**[2]

5400 **6** *1/2* **Doctor Ned**[20] 1053 4-8-2 **42** .... DavidProbert(7) 4 48?
(Miss Sheena West) *led tl wl over 1f out: wknd u.p fnl f* **33/1**

2m 11.54s (3.54) **Going Correction** +0.025s/f (Slow) **6** Ran SP% **115.2**
Speed ratings (Par 101): **86,84,84,81,80 79**
CSF £17.99 TOTE £1.70: £1.30, £4.70; EX 15.40.
Owner The Untouchable Partnership **Bred** M Fahy **Trained** Sessay, N Yorks

FOCUS
A moderate claimer and there was no pace on at all early which caused a couple to race keenly. The winning time was exactly two seconds slower than the following three-year-old fillies' handicap. The winner had little to beat with his market rival off the boil and the sixth finished too close for comfort.

1412 PANORAMIC BAR & RESTAURANT FILLIES' H'CAP 1m 2f (P)
7:20 (7:20) (Class 5) (0-75,77) 3-Y-O **£2,590** (£770; £385; £192) **Stalls** High

Form RPR

63-0 **1** **Amanjena**[26] 961 3-9-0 **74** .... WilliamBuick(3) 12 86+
(A M Balding) *trckd ldng pair: led on inner wl over 1f out: sn wl clr: easily* **8/1**

51- **2** *6* **Bushy Dell (IRE)**[195] 5984 3-8-9 **73** .... AmyBaker(7) 8 73
(Miss J Feilden) *t.k.h: hld up wl in tch: rdn and hdwy 2f out: chsd wnr over 1f out: no imp* **25/1**

61 **3** *1 1/4* **Moon Crystal**[29] 931 3-8-13 **70**..............................(t) StephenDonohoe 6 77+
(E A L Dunlop) *stdd s: t.k.h: hld up in rr: hdwy 2f out: edgd lft but r.o fr over 1f out: wnt 3rd ins fnl f: nvr nr wnr* **9/2**[2]

404- **4** *2* **Geestring (IRE)**[194] 6012 3-9-4 **75**.............................. RichardHughes 3 69
(R Hannon) *chsd ldr: rdn 3f out: outpcd wl over 1f out: no ch w wnr after* **5/2**[1]

00-2 **5** *nse* **Kashmina**[10] 1247 3-8-8 **65**.. JamieSpencer 10 58
(M R Channon) *t.k.h: hld up in tch: rdn and effrt jst over 2f out: wl outpcd over 1f out* **9/1**

40-5 **6** *1/2* **Spiritofthestorm (USA)**[8] 1270 3-8-13 **70**....................... EddieAhern 1 62
(R A Teal) *stdd s: hld up in midfield: hdwy 4f out: c wd bnd 2f out: sn rdn and wl outpcd* **25/1**

0321 **7** *1 1/2* **Emshabb**[13] 1176 3-8-13 **70**.. LiamJones 5 59
(W J Haggas) *towards rr: rdn over 3f out: hdwy on inner 2f out: sn wl outpcd* **12/1**

1154 **8** *1/2* **What's For Tea**[17] 1115 3-8-5 **62**............................. RichardKingscote 9 50
(P Butler) *chsd ldrs: rdn 3f out: wknd 2f out: sn bhd* **8/1**

431- **9** *2 1/4* **Trinkila (USA)**[209] 5605 3-9-1 **75**............................... TolleyDean(3) 7 59
(P F I Cole) *w.w in midfield: hdwy over 3f out: rdn over 2f out: sn struggling and no ch after* **11/2**[3]

10 **10** *1/2* **Mrs Jefferson (IRE)**[33] 899 3-8-11 **68**........................... JamesDoyle 2 51
(J G Portman) *stdd s: hld up bhd: sme hdwy 3f out: carried wd bnd 2f out: no ch after* **16/1**

-000 **11** *1 3/4* **Asmodea**[15] 1147 3-8-4 **61** oh3.. TPO'Shea 11 40
(D J Coakley) *led tl wl over 1f out: sn wknd* **20/1**

60-0 **12** *4* **Feeling Proud (USA)**[48] 756 3-9-1 **77** ow2............ JamesMillman(5) 4 48
(Jane Chapple-Hyam) *a towards rr: rdn 4f out: wl bhd last 2f* **33/1**

2m 9.54s (1.54) **Going Correction** +0.025s/f (Slow) **12** Ran SP% **123.3**
Speed ratings (Par 95): **94,89,88,86,86 86,84,84,82,82 80,77**
CSF £202.26 CT £1024.27 TOTE £12.50: £3.30, £5.40, £1.90; EX 355.20.
Owner Mrs M R Wates **Bred** M E Wates **Trained** Kingsclere, Hants

FOCUS
The early pace was much more solid than the preceding claimer and the winning time was two seconds quicker, but still nothing to write home about. The winner was still very impressive though. The form is rated through the runner-up.

1413 DIGIBET MAIDEN AUCTION STKS 5f (P)
7:50 (7:52) (Class 5) 2-Y-O **£2,729** (£806; £403) **Stalls** High

Form RPR

1 **Mullionmileanhour (IRE)** 2-9-1 0....................................... LPKeniry 4 89+
(J R Best) *sn crossed over to chse ldrs on inner: gd hdwy to ld 2f out: sn rdn clr: r.o strly: eased towards fin* **10/1**

2 *3* **The Dial House** 2-9-1 0.. TPQueally 10 73+
(J A Osborne) *racd in midfield: rdn and hdwy on inner 2f out: chsd wnr 1f out: r.o but no imp* **9/2**[2]

2 **3** *nse* **Firth Of Fifth (IRE)**[12] 1214 2-8-10 0....................... RichardKingscote 2 68
(Tom Dascombe) *s.i.s: bhd: hdwy over 2f out: styd on fr over 1f out: wnt 3rd ins fnl f: nrly snatched 2nd but nvr nr wnr* **3/1**[1]

4 *2* **Spring Tale (USA)** 2-8-9 0.. JamieSpencer 3 59+
(M J Wallace) *s.i.s: dropped in after s: hdwy on inner 2f out: styd on steadily but nvr nr wnr* **7/1**

0 **5** *1/2* **Multi Tasker**[19] 1078 2-8-9 0.. NCallan 6 57
(V Smith) *pressed ldrs: chsd wnr 2f out tl 1f out: fdd fnl f* **6/1**[3]

3 **6** *1/2* **Smalljohn**[12] 1214 2-8-11 0.. TGMcLaughlin 8 61+
(P D Evans) *led: awkward bnd over 3f out: hung lft and hdd 2f out: hmpd sn after and lost pl: no ch after but styd on again fnl f* **10/1**

7 *2* **Hay Fever (IRE)** 2-8-12 0.. StephenCarson 9 50
(Eve Johnson Houghton) *s.i.s: bhd: kpt on fr over 1f out: nvr on terms* **33/1**

8 *1 3/4* **Fasalee (IRE)** 2-8-11 0.. RichardThomas 11 42
(A P Jarvis) *s.i.s: a bhd* **66/1**

04 **9** *1/2* **Amosite**[13] 1177 2-8-1 0.. WilliamBuick(3) 5 33
(J R Jenkins) *in tch: carried wd and lost pl bnd 2f out: hung rt and n.d after* **16/1**

4 **10** *2 1/2* **Missy Que (IRE)**[17] 1111 2-8-4 0.................................... RichardMullen 1 23
(W R Muir) *wnt rt s: towards rr: hdwy on outer 3f out: n.d* **33/1**

11 *4 1/2* **Anacaona (IRE)** 2-8-7 0 ow2....................................... RichardHughes 7 —
(R Hannon) *w ldr tl over 2f out: sn rdn and wknd: eased ins fnl f* **3/1**[1]

60.48 secs (-0.02) **Going Correction** +0.025s/f (Slow) **11** Ran SP% **126.4**
Speed ratings (Par 92): **101,96,96,92,92 91,88,85,84,80 73**
CSF £58.35 TOTE £12.50: £4.00, £1.90, £1.60; EX 101.00.
Owner Kent Bloodstock **Bred** L Fox **Trained** Hucking, Kent

FOCUS
An ordinary event of its type but the time was decent, 0.45 seconds faster than the following three-year-old handicap. The winner did it nicely, whilst a couple of the others also hinted at ability. The form seems sound through the third and fifth.

NOTEBOOK
Mullionmileanhour(IRE) ◆, a 26,000gns colt out of a half-sister to Creative Mind, travelled really well and his cause was helped no end by getting a dream run through on the inside turning for home. He made very good use of it though and strode clear in quite impressive fashion. The form is hard to evaluate, but the time suggests this was a good effort. (op 20-1)

The Dial House, a 27,000gns half-brother to two winners at up to 7f, travelled equally as well as the winner but could not match his finishing pace over the last furlong or so. He should be up to winning an ordinary race. (op 6-1)

Firth Of Fifth(IRE), as on his debut, gave away valuable ground at the start and over this 5f track it is especially hard to make up lost ground. He finished strongly and under the circumstances he got as close as could have been expected. He did have the edge in experience over the pair that beat him, but he will probably appreciate another furlong in due course. Official explanation: jockey said colt missed the break and was slowly away (op 4-1)

Spring Tale(USA) ◆, resold for 34,000euros as a yearling, is out of a half-sister to a couple of winners in the US plus the dam of Carry On Katie. She did her chances no good by falling out of the stalls on this debut and her final position was as close as she got. She is almost certainly capable of a lot better. (op 5-1 tchd 15-2 a place)

Multi Tasker ran fast for a long way and probably improved a little from his debut. He may need a bit more time in order to see out the trip. (op 7-1 tchd 15-2)

Smalljohn ◆ again finished adrift of Firth Of Fifth just as on his debut, but that does not tell the whole story as he had terrible trouble negotiating the bend and the way he stayed on again late suggests he had a bit more energy left. He can probably do better on a more regular track. Official explanation: jockey said gelding hung left (op 8-1 tchd 12-1)

Hay Fever(IRE) Official explanation: jockey said colt was very slowly away

Anacaona(IRE) Official explanation: trainer had no explanation for the poor form shown

1414 DIGIBET.COM H'CAP 5f (P)
8:20 (8:21) (Class 5) (0-70,67) 3-Y-O **£2,590** (£770; £385; £192) **Stalls** High

Form RPR

031- **1** **Joss Stick**[131] 7071 3-9-3 **66**...(p) EddieAhern 4 71
(P J Makin) *hld up in tch: rdn and hdwy jst over 1f out: led ins fnl f: pushed out* **6/1**

3204 **2** *1 1/4* **Diademas (USA)**[9] 1257 3-9-1 **64**..................................(v) NCallan 6 64
(V Smith) *chsd ldng pair: rdn and swtchd rt jst over 1f out: r.o u.p to go 2nd nr fin* **11/2**[3]

6-32 **3** *hd* **Irish Music (IRE)**[26] 965 3-9-4 **67**.............................. JamieSpencer 1 67
(A P Jarvis) *stdd after s: t.k.h: hld up in last pair: plld out and rdn over 1f out: r.o u.p: nt quite rch ldrs* **4/5**[1]

00-6 **4** *nk* **Penrice Castle**[13] 1178 3-9-1 **64**.................................. RichardHughes 5 63
(R Hannon) *t.k.h: led: rdn wl over 1f out: hdd ins fnl f: no ex last 100yds* **7/2**[2]

000- **5** *1 1/4* **Our Kally**[217] 5357 3-7-11 **53** oh3...................................... AmyBaker(7) 3 47
(M D I Usher) *a in last pair: in tch: rdn 2f out: kpt on but nvr pce to chal* **33/1**

0-30 **6** *nk* **Lady Vibeeka**[59] 612 3-8-9 **58**................................. RichardKingscote 2 51
(Mrs H Sweeting) *chsd ldr: rdn 2f out: wkng whn short of room ins fnl f* **28/1**

60.93 secs (0.43) **Going Correction** +0.025s/f (Slow) **6** Ran SP% **113.8**
Speed ratings (Par 98): **97,95,94,94,92 91**
CSF £38.29 TOTE £6.80: £2.80, £2.10; EX 20.80.
Owner Lady Davis J P Carrington D M Ahier **Bred** K W Green **Trained** Ogbourne Maisey, Wilts

FOCUS
A weakish sprint handicap in which the winner improved by 5lb, the form rated around the runner-up. The time was around par, despite being 0.45 seconds slower than the two-year-old maiden auction.

1415 DIGIBET CASINO H'CAP 6f (P)
8:50 (8:51) (Class 4) (0-80,81) 4-Y-O+ **£4,533** (£1,348; £674; £336) **Stalls** High

Form RPR

55-1 **1** **Holbeck Ghyll (IRE)**[20] 1047 6-9-0 **79**......................... WilliamBuick(3) 8 97
(A M Balding) *t.k.h: trckd ldrs: hdwy to chse ldr over 2f out: rdn to ld ins fnl f: rdn out* **5/2**[1]

02-0 **2** *1 1/2* **Valery Borzov (IRE)**[19] 1069 4-9-4 **80**.......................(v[1]) JamieSpencer 4 93
(D Nicholls) *t.k.h: hld up bhd: rdn and hdwy on inner over 2f out: chsd ldng pair 2f out: r.o to go 2nd wl ins fnl f: nt rch wnr* **5/2**[1]

1421 **3** *3/4* **Dvinsky (USA)**[15] 1153 7-8-13 **75**.................................(b) JimmyQuinn 7 86
(P Howling) *led: rdn jst over 2f out: jnd 2f out: hdd ins fnl f: no ex last 100yds* **5/1**[2]

6101 **4** *1 3/4* **Royal Envoy (IRE)**[13] 1191 5-8-8 **73**.............................. TolleyDean(3) 1 78
(D Shaw) *hld up in tch in midfield: hdwy and rdn over 2f out: carried lft 2f out: styd on: nvr able to chal* **7/1**[3]

00-5 **5** *3 1/2* **Mandarin Spirit (IRE)**[22] 1023 8-8-6 **68**.........................(b) ChrisCatlin 3 62
(G C H Chung) *restless in stalls: hld up bhd: rdn and effrt over 2f out: nvr pce to chal* **12/1**

0- **6** *3/4* **Double Bill (USA)**[244] 4574 4-8-10 **72**.. TQuinn 6 63
(P F I Cole) *in tch in midfield: rdn and effrt whn carried lft 2f out: n.d after* **8/1**

30-0 **7** *6* **Our Blessing (IRE)**[26] 969 4-9-0 **76**.. NCallan 5 48
(A P Jarvis) *chsd ldrs: rdn over 2f out: hung bdly lft 2f out: nt rcvr* **15/2**

150- **8** *2 1/4* **Whitbarrow (IRE)**[127] 7126 9-9-0 **81** ow2..............(b) JamesMillman(5) 2 46
(B R Millman) *chsd ldr tl c wd bnd wl over 2f out: n.d after* **33/1**

1m 11.62s (-1.48) **Going Correction** +0.025s/f (Slow) **8** Ran SP% **119.8**
Speed ratings (Par 105): **110,108,107,104,100 99,91,88**
CSF £8.98 CT £29.53 TOTE £3.40: £1.30, £1.40, £1.60; EX 13.10.
Owner Halsall Nicholson Partnership **Bred** David Brickley **Trained** Kingsclere, Hants

FOCUS
A fair sprint handicap run at a strong pace and the winning time was decent, 1.51 seconds faster than the following Class 6 classified event. The thirs sets the standard and the winner was better than ever.

1416 KEMPTON FOR SUMMER WEDDINGS CLASSIFIED STKS 6f (P)
9:20 (9:20) (Class 6) 3-Y-O+ **£1,683** (£501; £250; £125) **Stalls** High

Form RPR

0604 **1** **Perlachy**[26] 971 4-9-6 53.....................................(v) KirstyMilczarek(3) 11 60
(Mrs N Macauley) *in tch: rdn and hdwy over 2f out: led ins fnl f: hld on wl last 100yds* **4/1**[2]

000/ **2** *1/2* **Stamford Street (IRE)**[736] 982 5-9-9 50..........................(t) LiamJones 10 58
(J R Gask) *in tch: hdwy over 2f out: rdn over 1f out: chsd wnr ins fnl f: hld last 100yds* **33/1**

65-6 **3** *2* **Razzano (IRE)**[8] 1275 4-9-4 51.................................... JamieJones(5) 12 52
(A M Hales) *chsd ldrs: swtchd rt and rdn 2f out: led 1f out: sn hdd and one pce* **9/2**[3]

0-60 **4** *1 1/4* **Buzbury Rings**[33] 898 4-9-9 50.. LPKeniry 7 48
(A M Balding) *squeezed out at s: t.k.h: hld up towards rr: styd on u.p last 2f: nt rch ldrs* **6/1**

000- **5** *3/4* **Diksie Dancer**[195] 5982 4-9-9 53.. NCallan 4 45
(K A Ryan) *awkward leaving stalls: sn chsng ldr: rdn over 2f out: carried sltly lft 2f out: wknd fnl f* **12/1**

-500 **6** *1 1/2* **Elusive Dreams (USA)**[36] 861 4-9-6 55............................. TolleyDean(3) 2 40
(D Shaw) *towards rr: hdwy on outer over 3f out: carried wd on bnd wl over 2f out: sn hrd drvn and no imp* **13/2**

0/0- **7** *1 1/2* **Indian Lady (IRE)**[355] 1309 5-9-9 52........................ RichardKingscote 6 36
(Mrs A L M King) *wnt rt s: sn led: rdn over 2f out: hung lft briefly 2f out: hdd 1f out: wknd* **33/1**

0-00 **8** *2 1/2* **Tell Me What (FR)**[10] 1247 3-8-7 55................................ PatrickHills(5) 8 28
(R Hannon) *squeezed out s: a bhd: rdn and effrt over 2f out: n.d* **25/1**

0-60 **9** *4* **Tyrannosaurus Rex (IRE)**[12] 1209 4-9-9 55...........(v) FergusSweeney 3 15
(K R Burke) *chsd ldrs on outer: rn wd bnd wl over 2f out and lost pl: no ch after* **5/2**[1]

0254 **10** *7* **Whitcombe Flyer (USA)**[15] 1135 3-8-12 48...................(bt) ChrisCatlin 9 —
(Miss M E Rowland) *bmpd s: sn bhd: lost tch 3f out* **14/1**

1m 13.13s (0.03) **Going Correction** +0.025s/f (Slow)
WFA 3 from 4yo+ 11lb **10** Ran SP% **118.5**
Speed ratings (Par 101): **100,99,96,95,94 92,90,86,81,72**
CSF £132.07 TOTE £4.80: £1.50, £9.40, £1.60; EX 141.00 Place 6 £ 158.91, Place 5 £ 87.77.
Owner Mrs N Macauley **Bred** J James **Trained** Sproxton, Leics

FOCUS
A moderate race, run in a time 1.51 seconds slower than the Class 4 handicap. The draw played its part with the front trio starting from the three highest stalls, but the form is unlikely to amount to much. The winner was 5lb off his winter best.

Tell Me What(FR) Official explanation: jockey said filly suffered interference at start

Tyrannosaurus Rex(IRE) Official explanation: jockey said gelding hung left

1398
NEWMARKET (Rowley) (R-H)
Thursday, April 17

OFFICIAL GOING: Good (8.5)
Wind: Light half-against Weather: Cloudy with sunny spells

1417 IRISH THOROUGHBRED MARKETING WOOD DITTON STKS (DIV I) 1m
1:30 (1:33) (Class 4) Unraced 3-Y-O **£5,990** (£1,782; £890; £444) Stalls Low

Form RPR
1 **Tri Nations (UAE)** 3-9-3 0... SebSanders 8 82
(J W Hills) *neat: hld up: hdwy over 2f out: chsd ldr over 1f out: r.o to ld nr fin* **40/1**
2 *shd* **Tryst** 3-9-3 0... RyanMoore 10 82
(Sir Michael Stoute) *wl grwn: hld up in tch: led over 1f out: sn rdn: hdd nr fin* **4/1**[2]
3 *2¼* **Crown Choice** 3-9-3 0... AdamKirby 5 77
(W R Swinburn) *w'like: scope: b: hld up in tch: rdn ins fnl f: styd on same pce* **25/1**
4 *½* **King's Charm (FR)** 3-9-3 0... EddieAhern 2 80+
(J Noseda) *leggy: scope: lw: hld up: hdwy over 3f out: swtchd rt over 2f out: outpcd over 1f out: r.o towards fin* **8/1**[3]
5 *shd* **Never Ending Tale** 3-9-3 0... TedDurcan 6 75
(W Jarvis) *gd sort: hld up: hdwy over 1f out: nt trble ldrs* **66/1**
6 *½* **Moonquake (USA)** 3-9-3 0... JimmyFortune 9 74
(J H M Gosden) *w'like: chsd ldrs: led over 2f out: hdd over 1f out: no ex ins fnl f* **9/4**[1]
7 *6* **Promise Maker (USA)** 3-9-3 0... MichaelHills 4 60
(B W Hills) *w'like: trckd ldr: rdn and ev ch over 2f: hung rt and wknd over 1f out* **12/1**
8 *nk* **Closertobelieving** 3-9-3 0... TQuinn 1 60
(D R C Elsworth) *w'like: leggy: prom over 5f* **14/1**
9 *9* **Confederate** 3-9-3 0... SteveDrowne 3 39
(R Charlton) *gd sort: lw: dwlt: hld up: rdn over 2f out: sn wknd* **8/1**[3]
10 *10* **Hapi** 3-8-10 0... WilliamCarson(7) 7 16
(S C Williams) *cmpt: led over 5f: sn wknd* **100/1**

1m 41.77s (3.17) **Going Correction** +0.375s/f (Good) **10 Ran SP% 96.1**
Speed ratings (Par 100): **99,98,96,96,96 95,89,89,80,70**
CSF £128.60 TOTE £47.70: £6.90, £1.50, £3.10; EX 172.90.
Owner Donald M Kerr **Bred** Darley **Trained** Upper Lambourn, Berks
■ Amaakin (7/2) was withdrawn at the start. R4 applies, deduct 20p in the £.

FOCUS
The pace was only steady and the winning time was just fractionally faster than the second division. With none of the runners having raced before it is hard to pin down the form, but there were plenty of encouraging efforts.

1418 IRISH THOROUGHBRED MARKETING WOOD DITTON STKS (DIV II) 1m
2:00 (2:06) (Class 4) Unraced 3-Y-O **£5,990** (£1,782; £890; £444) Stalls Low

Form RPR
1 **Fanjura (IRE)** 3-9-3 0... LDettori 11 85
(J Noseda) *cmpt: b: chsd ldrs: rdn over 1f out: led ins fnl f: r.o* **4/1**[2]
2 *nk* **Khateeb (IRE)** 3-9-3 0...(t) RHills 2 84
(M A Jarvis) *neat: led: hdd over 6f out: chsd ldr tl led again over 2f out: rdn and hdd ins fnl f: r.o* **4/1**[2]
3 *2½* **Zulu Chief (USA)** 3-9-3 0... JMurtagh 3 79
(A P O'Brien, Ire) *gd sort: tall: chsd ldrs: rdn over 2f out: styd on same pce fnl f* **11/4**[1]
4 *2* **Mr Hichens** 3-9-3 0... RobertHavlin 4 74
(B J Meehan) *str: scope: bit bkwd: hld up: rdn over 1f out: r.o ins fnl f: nt trble ldrs* **50/1**
5 *2* **Unbiased (IRE)** 3-9-3 0... KerrinMcEvoy 6 69
(J L Dunlop) *w'like: scope: prom: lost pl over 6f out: styd on ins fnl f* **16/1**
6 *¾* **Stone Of Scone** 3-9-3 0... RyanMoore 9 68
(E A L Dunlop) *leggy: scope: lw: rn green in rr: hdwy on outside 1/2-way: rdn over 2f out: wknd over 1f out* **5/1**[3]
7 *hd* **Effortless** 3-8-12 0... MichaelHills 8 62
(B W Hills) *w'like: chsd ldr tl led over 6f out: rdn and hdd over 2f out: wknd over 1f out* **16/1**
8 *6* **De Facto** 3-9-3 0... JimmyFortune 1 53
(J H M Gosden) *gd sort: hld up: effrt over 2f out: wkng whn n.m.r over 1f out* **12/1**
9 *9* **Nefaf (IRE)** 3-9-3 0... NCallan 10 33
(C E Brittain) *neat: hld up in tch: rdn over 2f out: wknd over 1f out* **33/1**
10 *1¼* **Abstract Colours (IRE)** 3-9-0 0... WilliamBuick(3) 7 30
(A M Balding) *w'like: scope: s.i.s: outpcd* **33/1**

1m 41.85s (3.25) **Going Correction** +0.375s/f (Good) **10 Ran SP% 110.6**
Speed ratings (Par 100): **98,97,95,93,91 90,90,84,75,74**
CSF £18.17 TOTE £4.80: £1.60, £1.60, £1.60; EX 20.70.
Owner Terry Benson **Bred** Patrick F Kelly **Trained** Newmarket, Suffolk
■ Schopenhauer was withdrawn (12/1, refused to enter stalls.) R4 applies, deduct 5p in the £.

FOCUS
This looked the stronger of the two divisions despite the fact that the winning time was fractionally slower, and it should produce its share of winners.

1419 WYCK HALL STUD MAIDEN FILLIES' STKS 5f
2:35 (2:36) (Class 4) 2-Y-O **£4,533** (£1,348; £674; £336) **Stalls** Low

Form RPR
1 **Danehill Destiny** 2-9-0 0... RyanMoore 7 83+
(W J Haggas) *cmpt: hld up: hdwy over 1f out: led ins fnl f: r.o wl* **3/1**[1]
2 *2* **Art Princess (USA)** 2-9-0 0... MichaelHills 10 75
(B W Hills) *w'like: hld up in tch: rdn over 1f out: styd on same pce ins fnl f* **14/1**
3 *¾* **Mambo Light (USA)** 2-9-0 0... TQuinn 9 72
(P F I Cole) *w'like: lw: chsd ldrs: rdn and ev ch over 1f out: styd on same pce ins fnl f* **7/2**[2]
4 *nk* **Beat Seven** 2-9-0 0... MickyFenton 1 71+
(Miss Gay Kelleway) *w'like: scope: dwlt: hld up: plld hrd: hdwy 3f out: outpcd over 1f out: r.o ins fnl f* **25/1**
5 *¾* **River Rye (IRE)** 2-9-0 0... RichardHughes 5 68
(R Hannon) *lt-f: unf: w ldr tl led over 1f out: hdd and no ex ins fnl f* **6/1**[3]
6 *½* **Fasliyanne (IRE)** 2-9-0 0... NCallan 3 66
(K A Ryan) *cmpt: bit bkwd: s.i.s: sn chsng ldrs: rdn over 1f out: styd on same pce* **7/1**
7 *1¼* **Misdaqeya** 2-9-0 0... RHills 8 61+
(B W Hills) *leggy: scope: lw: s.s: hld up: racd keenly: n.d* **13/2**
43 8 *½* **Dr Wintringham (IRE)**[13] 1177 2-9-0 0... LPKeniry 4 59
(J S Moore) *neat: led over 3f: wknd ins fnl f* **16/1**
9 *2¼* **Danidh Dubai (IRE)** 2-9-0 0... ChrisCatlin 2 50+
(M R Channon) *cmpt: hld up: wknd 1/2-way* **20/1**
10 *3¾* **Yaldas Girl (USA)** 2-9-0 0... JamieSpencer 6 35
(J R Best) *neat: prom to 1/2-way* **8/1**

62.07 secs (2.97) **Going Correction** +0.375s/f (Good) **10 Ran SP% 119.6**
Speed ratings (Par 91): **91,87,86,86,84 84,82,81,77,71**
CSF £47.95 TOTE £3.70: £1.50, £4.30, £1.80; EX 45.30.
Owner Cheveley Park Stud **Bred** T G Mills And Mr J Humphreys **Trained** Newmarket, Suffolk

FOCUS
Danehill Destiny was an impressive winner of this maiden in which only one of the field had previously run. There is better to come from her.

NOTEBOOK
Danehill Destiny ◆, whose sale price almost doubled to 120,000gns as a yearling, is the first foal of her dam, a 6f winner who is a half-sister to Queen Elizabeth II Stakes winner Where Or When. Dropped in at the start and last at halfway, she was switched to the outer but ran green and wanted to hang when first asked to improve. She really found her stride in the final furlong, though, and swept past her rivals to win impressively. Even at this early stage she looks a Royal Ascot filly. (tchd 7-2)
Art Princess(USA), the longer priced of the Hills duo, ran a pleasing debut, keeping on to get the best of a bunch finish for second but no match for the impressive winner. Bred to go well on an artificial surface, she has plenty of speed in her pedigree but should get further than this. (op 9-1)
Mambo Light(USA), a half-sister to smart sprinter Dietrich, cost 325,000gns as a yearling. She knew her job and showed bright pace, only giving best to the winner inside the last. A maiden should certainly come her way. (op 11-2)
Beat Seven, a relatively cheap buy at 10,000gns, made a pleasing debut, running on against the rail in the latter stages having raced rather keenly. (op 22-1)
River Rye(IRE) is the first foal of her dam, who notched her only win, in a 1m Polytrack maiden, in a controversial race in which Kieren Fallon eased the clear leader prematurely. She showed plenty of pace and briefly looked like holding on inside the last, only to be swallowed up. (op 9-2 tchd 7-2)
Fasliyanne(IRE) is a half-sister to the smart 6-7f runner Instant Recall. She ran creditably and is entitled to improve. (op 12-1)
Misdaqeya ◆, whose stable companion finished second, is bred to come into her own over a bit further later on this year. She certainly shaped with promise, not given a hard introduction following a slow start and only really getting the hang of things when it was all over. There should be plenty of improvement in her. (op 7-1)

1420 CONNAUGHT ACCESS FLOORING ABERNANT STKS (LISTED RACE) 6f
3:10 (3:12) (Class 1) 3-Y-O+
£17,031 (£6,456; £3,231; £1,611; £807; £405) **Stalls** Low

Form RPR
400- 1 **Zidane**[159] 6758 6-9-4 106... JamieSpencer 14 113+
(J R Fanshawe) *lw: racd stands' side: hld up: hdwy over 1f out: r.o to ld nr fin* **17/2**
330- 2 *shd* **Assertive**[180] 6338 5-9-8 109... RyanMoore 11 117
(R Hannon) *racd stands' side: hld up: hdwy over 1f out: rdn and ev ch ins fnl f: r.o: 2nd of 14 in gp* **9/1**
220- 3 *nse* **Dark Missile**[179] 6375 5-8-13 107... WilliamBuick 12 108
(A M Balding) *racd stands' side: hld up: hdwy over 2f out: rdn to ld ins fnl f: hdd nr fin: 3rd of 14 in gp* **8/1**[3]
0-21 4 *nk* **Sonny Red (IRE)**[15] 1157 4-9-4 108... RichardHughes 8 112
(R Hannon) *racd stands' side: chsd ldrs: led overall over 1f out: rdn and hdd ins fnl f: styd on: 4th of 14 in gp* **7/1**[2]
20-0 5 *2¼* **Advanced**[26] 959 5-9-4 110... NCallan 20 105
(K A Ryan) *lw: racd far side: chsd ldrs: rdn to ld that gp ins fnl f: r.o: 1st of 6 in gp* **16/1**
2 6 *2¼* **War Artist (AUS)**[40] 832 5-10-0 111... KerrinMcEvoy 3 116+
(J M P Eustace) *racd stands' side: hld up: hdwy over 1f out: r.o: nrst fin: 5th of 14 in gp* **18/1**
30-4 7 *nk* **Prime Defender**[26] 959 4-9-4 108... MichaelHills 18 97
(B W Hills) *racd far side: chsd ldrs: led that gp over 1f out: rdn and hdd ins fnl f: styd on same pce: 2nd of 6 in gp* **5/1**[1]
2105 8 *shd* **Evens And Odds (IRE)**[40] 832 4-9-4 104...(b) TedDurcan 6 96
(K A Ryan) *racd stands' side: chsd ldr: led overall over 2f out: rdn and hdd over 1f out: no ex fnl f: 6th of 14 in gp* **66/1**
/10- 9 *nk* **Abraham Lincoln (IRE)**[188] 6160 4-9-4 0... JMurtagh 10 95+
(A P O'Brien, Ire) *racd stands' side: hld up: hdwy over 1f out: styd on: 7th of 14 in gp* **16/1**
0/0- 10 *3* **Aeroplane**[215] 5416 5-9-4 104... AlanMunro 1 86+
(P W Chapple-Hyam) *lw: racd stands' side: hld up: rdn over 1f out: n.d: 8th of 14 in gp* **12/1**
5203 11 *nse* **Machinist (IRE)**[19] 1079 8-9-4 100... TPO'Shea 13 85
(D Nicholls) *racd stands' side: hld up: rdn and hung lft over 2f out: n.d: 9th of 14 in gp* **33/1**
-640 12 *2* **Indian Trail**[55] 666 8-9-4 0...(v) JoeFanning 4 79
(D Nicholls) *lw: racd stands' side: racd stands' side: hld up: effrt over 1f out: n.d: 10th of 14 in gp* **33/1**
0030 13 *½* **Beckermet (IRE)**[42] 815 6-9-8 0... ChrisCatlin 7 81
(R F Fisher) *racd stands' side: overall ldr over 3f: wknd over 1f out: 11th of 14 in gp* **25/1**
304- 14 *2½* **Balthazaar's Gift (IRE)**[180] 6332 5-9-10 113... JimmyFortune 16 75
(L M Cumani) *lw: racd far side: hld up: wknd over 1f out: 3rd of 6 in gp* **10/1**
01-0 15 *1¼* **Kostar**[54] 677 7-9-4 102... PhilipRobinson 15 65
(C G Cox) *racd far side: led that side over 4f: sn wknd: 4th of 6 in gp* **33/1**
160- 16 *nk* **Per Incanto (USA)**[222] 5214 4-9-4 108... RHills 2 65
(J L Dunlop) *racd stands' side: chsd ldrs 4f: 12th of 14 in gp* **14/1**
40-1 17 *2¼* **Aahayson**[26] 959 4-9-8 109... FergusSweeney 5 61
(K R Burke) *racd stands' side: chsd ldrs: rdn over 2f out: wknd over 1f out: 13th of 14 in gp* **16/1**
0-14 18 *hd* **Excusez Moi (USA)**[33] 907 6-9-8 106... LiamJones 19 61
(C E Brittain) *lw: racd far side: hld up: wknd over 1f out: 5th of 6 in gp* **18/1**
636- 19 *1½* **Bertoliver**[173] 6487 4-9-4 88... SebSanders 9 52
(D K Ivory) *racd stands' side: chsd ldrs: rdn over 2f out: sn wknd: last of 14 in gp* **100/1**

120- **20** *40* **Prior Warning**[325] 2100 4-9-4 105.. LDettori 17 —
(Miss D Mountain) *bit bkwd: racd far side: hld up: wknd 2f out: last of 6 in gp* **33/1**

1m 12.56s (0.36) **Going Correction** +0.375s/f (Good) **20** Ran SP% **130.5**
Speed ratings (Par 111): **112,111,111,111,108 105,105,104,104,100 100,97,97,93,92 91,88,88,86,33**
CSF £82.35 TOTE £10.00: £3.40, £4.50, £3.80; EX 145.10.

Owner Jan and Peter Hopper **Bred** Mrs J P Hopper And Mrs E M Grundy **Trained** Newmarket, Suffolk

FOCUS
Early-season form, but this looked a good race for the grade. The form is rated through the fourth. The field split into two unequal groups, with half a dozen racing down the far side. The larger group held the advantage.

NOTEBOOK
Zidane, successful in last year's Stewards' Cup but held in Listed and Group races subsequently, was well suited by this big field. Held up as usual by Spencer, he was brought through to deliver his challenge on the outside of the larger stands'-side group and put his head in front close home. From a family which improves with age - his half-sister Frizzante won the July Cup at five - he is well capable of making his mark at Group level granted a race run to suit. The Golden Jubilee Stakes looks a suitable target. (op 8-1 tchd 9-1)

Assertive, also runner-up in this race on his reappearance a year ago, was slow to leave the stalls but soon recovered. He came through to hold every chance but was just denied. This was a fine effort under his 4lb penalty and he ran close to last autumn's Diadem Stakes form with Zidane. (op 12-1)

Dark Missile, last season's Wokingham winner, ran a cracker on this return to action but, after putting her head in front inside the last, she was just caught. A big mare who is not easy to get fit, she is set for a crack at the Golden Jubilee at Ascot, a track at which she excels. (op 7-1)

Sonny Red(IRE) came here in good form having finished second in a Listed race at Doncaster prior to picking up a 5f conditions event at Nottingham. A stablemate of the runner-up, he was always in the front rank and nosed ahead briefly before having to give best inside the last. (op 8-1 tchd 10-1 in a place)

Advanced, sharper for his return to action at Doncaster, ran a good race to finish clear of the other five who raced on the far side, but never threatened the much larger near-side bunch.

War Artist(AUS) ◆, runner-up over 7f at Wolverhampton on his British debut, gave away weight all round under the penalty for his Grade 1 win in South Africa last July. Running on very nicely at the end after finding himself stuck behind the weakening Beckermet, he will be suited by a return to 7f on this evidence and is clearly a smart recruit to the Eustace yard. Official explanation: jockey said gelding was denied a clear run (op 20-1 tchd 25-1 in places)

Prime Defender ran respectably to finish second on his side, but the horse that finished in front of him, Advanced, had been a long way behind when they made their respective seasonal debuts at Doncaster. (op 6-1 tchd 13-2)

Evens And Odds(IRE), held in this grade on the two most recent starts of a busy sand campaign, showed plenty of dash on this return to turf but may not be easy to place this season.

Abraham Lincoln(IRE), not seen since winning on the artificial surface at Dundalk in October, lacked the pace to get to the principals but was going on quite nicely at the end. A step up to 7f might suit him.

1421 BANSHAHOUSESTABLES.COM CRAVEN STKS (GROUP 3) (C&G) 1m
3:45 (3:46) (Class 1) 3-Y-O

£28,385 (£10,760; £5,385; £2,685; £1,345; £675) **Stalls** Low

Form RPR

11- **1** **Twice Over**[166] 6650 3-8-12 94.. TedDurcan 9 121
(H R A Cecil) *h.d.w: trckd ldrs: led over 1f out: sn rdn and hdd: hung rt ins fnl f: rallied to ld nr fin* **9/4**[2]

113- **2** *shd* **Raven's Pass (USA)**[180] 6333 3-8-12 120.................. JimmyFortune 12 121
(J H M Gosden) *h.d.w: hld up: hdwy 2f out: led 1f out: sn rdn and hung rt: hdd nr fin* **11/8**[1]

0- **3** *6* **The Bogberry (USA)**[299] 2855 3-8-12 0.............................. JMurtagh 2 107
(A P O'Brien, Ire) *h.d.w: hld up: hdwy over 1f out: r.o: nt trble ldrs* **28/1**

010- **4** *1 1/2* **River Proud (USA)**[173] 6489 3-8-12 110.................................. TQuinn 6 104
(P F I Cole) *lw: led: rdn and hdd over 1f out: wknd ins fnl f* **14/1**

12- **5** *6* **Alexander Castle (USA)**[215] 5406 3-8-12 109...................... NCallan 7 90
(K A Ryan) *h.d.w: lw: hld up: hdwy u.p 2f out: edgd rt and wknd over 1f out* **15/2**[3]

212- **6** *3 1/2* **City Leader (IRE)**[173] 6489 3-9-1 111........................ JamieSpencer 3 85
(B J Meehan) *hld up: hdwy over 3f out: rdn over 2f out: hung rt and wknd over 1f out* **12/1**

226- **7** *2* **Declaration Of War (IRE)**[173] 6489 3-8-12 115........... RobertHavlin 10 78
(P W Chapple-Hyam) *prom: rdn over 3f out: wknd 2f out* **14/1**

0-1 **8** *6* **Indian Skipper (IRE)**[20] 1054 3-8-12 80......................... JimmyQuinn 1 64
(M H Tompkins) *hld up: wknd over 2f out* **100/1**

231- **9** *2 1/2* **Scintillo**[186] 6222 3-9-1 114.. RichardHughes 5 61
(R Hannon) *lw: chsd ldrs: rdn over 2f out: wknd over 1f out* **25/1**

60- **10** *28* **Great Rumpuscat (USA)**[171] 6549 3-8-12 0.............. DavidMcCabe 11 —
(A P O'Brien, Ire) *gd sort: wl grwn: chsd ldrs over 5f: eased over 1f out* **100/1**

1m 38.54s (-0.06) **Going Correction** +0.375s/f (Good) **10** Ran SP% **114.9**
Speed ratings (Par 108): **115,114,108,107,101 97,95,89,87,59**
CSF £5.44 TOTE £3.40: £1.40, £1.10, £5.10; EX 6.00.

Owner K Abdulla **Bred** Juddmonte Farms Ltd **Trained** Newmarket, Suffolk

FOCUS
This looked a strong renewal of the Craven, even after the Sir Michael Stoute-trained Perfect Stride was taken out at the last minute as a result of a swollen hock. The winning time was very smart, even for a race like this, and the form looks extremely solid for a Group 3 contest. A reproduction of the RPRs recorded by the first two in this trial would be good enough to have won four of the last nine 2000 Guineas. One hopes they have not left the Guineas behind in the trial.

NOTEBOOK
Twice Over came into the race hyped as a serious Classic contender but with plenty to prove still, his two wins at two having been more style than substance. Despite winning over 1m2f at two, his pedigree raised doubts about his stamina for 1m4f, and it became apparent through the winter that connections were wondering if he might be more of a Guineas horse than a Derby contender. In the event, having travelled strongly throughout, he was headed by Raven's Pass running out of the Dip, but then found his stronger stamina seeing him narrowly home. This was high class form and he would be a very serious Guineas contender, but despite being cut to a best price of 6-1 connections were reluctant to commit. The Dante is the alternative, and if he heads that way a decision on whether he goes to Chantilly (where the 1m2f might prove his optimum trip) or Epsom for his Derby would be taken after that. A point in favour of the latter option is that it would give him more time to recover, for both the principals here must have had hardish races in finishing so far clear in such a fast time. (op 5-2 tchd 11-4 in a place)

Raven's Pass(USA), in contrast to Twice Over, who was being tested to see if he had the speed for a mile, had his stamina for the Classic distance to prove, having not got home on easy ground in the Dewhurst last autumn. The good pace ensured a proper test and he travelled very strongly buried in the pack. However, after quickening to the front with over a furlong to run, he was rejoined by Twice Over and could not shake him off, edging to his right on the climb to the line. He was only narrowly edged out and certainly got the trip, but one still cannot help but think that he will ultimately prove at his very best over shorter. He has now been beaten twice here having travelled best, and he will probably find one or two too strong once again on Guineas day. He has the potential to come on for the run – his trainer had warned beforehand that he was not fully wound up – but it is a worry for both him and the winner that they had a hard race, recording a fast time and high RPRs, in their supposed trial. He is now a best-priced 5-1 for the Guineas, but the St James's Palace Stakes, run on a turning track and usually on quick ground, might give him a better shot at Group 1 glory over a mile. Longer term, he looks the type to thrive if dropped back to sprinting, with the July Cup an obvious target.

The Bogberry(USA), who had been off the track since finishing lame in the Chesham last season, had a good deal to prove at this level and was predictably a big price beforehand. Held up, he couldn't go with the first two when they quickened things up, but he stayed on well, while still running a bit green, and the impression left was that he will do better with this run under his belt. One would imagine that he is a little way down the pecking order at Ballydoyle, so his performance will no doubt give supporters of the stable's main Guineas contenders Henrythenavigator and Jupiter Pluvius some cheer. (op 22-1)

River Proud(USA), who won the Somerville Tattersall Stakes over 7f here last autumn, was below form over 1m in the Racing Post Trophy subsequently, so he still had his stamina to prove for this distance. Having burst out of the stalls he set a solid gallop and made it a true test, and it is to his credit that despite weakening into fourth late on he still finished six lengths clear of the rest. It is possible that this day was the day for him and connections were trying to nick a Group 3 from less-fit rivals. If that was the case then he may prove difficult to place for the remainder of the season, but it is too early to say for sure. (op 16-1)

Alexander Castle(USA) had not been seen since finishing a highly creditable second in the Champagne Stakes on only his second start, but his trainer had been very bullish in the press, suggesting the son of Lemon Drop Kid was his first proper chance of winning a Classic. In the event he was a bit laboured - he looked like finishing fourth at one point but did not really see his race out. This has to go down as a disappointing effort, but perhaps he needs proper fast ground to be seen at his best. (op 8-1 tchd 10-1 in a place)

City Leader(IRE), one of two colts in the line-up saddled with a 3lb penalty for winning above Group 3 level at two, looked to have a stiff task considering he had not been able to live with Raven's Pass in last year's Solario Stakes. He should have done better than this, but his trainer has not hit form this year yet - he has saddled just one winner so far - and it is too early to write this well-related colt off. (tchd 11-1)

Declaration Of War(IRE), whose best run at two came when runner-up to Rio De La Plata on easy ground in the Grand Criterium, could have done with more testing conditions. The chances are that he will struggle to win at this level in this country this season, but he may find success on the continent. (op 12-1)

Indian Skipper(IRE) looked a useful prospect when winning on the Polytrack last month, but this was a case of flying too high too soon. He was predictably outclassed. (op 66-1)

Scintillo, who won an Italian Group 1 on his final start at two, was another who had a 3lb penalty to carry, and his previous efforts when beaten in Listed company and by City Leader in the Royal Lodge suggested he lacked the ability to defy it. He was well beaten in the end and is another who will probably have to go on his travels in search of further Pattern success. Official explanation: jockey said colt stopped very quickly

Great Rumpuscat(USA), a half-brother to his stable's former top-class juvenile Rumplestiltskin, was beating a retreat three furlongs out. He had finished down the field behind Jupiter Pluvius on his final start at two and looks no great shakes.

1422 WEATHERBYS EARL OF SEFTON STKS (GROUP 3) 1m 1f
4:20 (4:21) (Class 1) 4-Y-O+

£28,385 (£10,760; £5,385; £2,685; £1,345; £675) **Stalls** Low

Form RPR

/11- **1** **Phoenix Tower (USA)**[346] 1544 4-8-12 100......................... TPQueally 1 117+
(H R A Cecil) *lw: plld hrd: trckd ldr over 5f: nt clr run over 1f out: r.o to ld nr fin* **8/1**[3]

5403 **2** *hd* **Traffic Guard (USA)**[42] 818 4-8-12 109.............................. JohnEgan 3 115
(Jane Chapple-Hyam) *a.p: chsd ldr over 3f out: rdn to ld over 1f out: hdd nr fin* **14/1**

411- **3** *nk* **Pipedreamer**[194] 6011 4-8-12 110.................................. JimmyFortune 6 114+
(J H M Gosden) *h.d.w: hld up: hdwy over 1f out: rdn and edgd lft ins fnl f: sn ev ch: r.o* **6/4**[1]

/15- **4** *2 3/4* **Multidimensional (IRE)**[180] 6334 5-8-12 111.................. TedDurcan 7 109+
(H R A Cecil) *lw: hld up in tch: rdn and ev ch over 1f out: styng on same pce whn hmpd ins fnl f* **2/1**[2]

031- **5** *1* **Stotsfold**[214] 5451 5-9-1 110... AdamKirby 2 109
(W R Swinburn) *s.i.s: hld up: rdn over 1f out: r.o ins fnl f: nvr able to chal* **33/1**

51-1 **6** *1 1/2* **Smokey Oakey (IRE)**[26] 960 4-8-12 101......................... JimmyQuinn 5 103
(M H Tompkins) *lw: prom: rdn over 1f out: styd on same pce* **16/1**

-450 **7** *hd* **Halicarnassus (IRE)**[42] 816 4-9-1 0.................................. TPO'Shea 8 106
(M R Channon) *lw: hld up: hdwy over 2f out: wknd ins fnl f* **20/1**

-2U1 **8** *1 1/2* **Kandidate**[19] 1077 6-8-12 110..(t) RyanMoore 4 100
(C E Brittain) *led: rdn and hdd over 1f out: wknd ins fnl f* **10/1**

1m 54.11s (3.51) **Going Correction** +0.375s/f (Good) **13** Ran SP% **113.8**
Speed ratings (Par 113): **99,98,98,96,95 93,93,92**
CSF £108.38 TOTE £9.60: £2.40, £3.20, £1.10; EX 122.90.

Owner K Abdulla **Bred** Juddmonte Farms Inc **Trained** Newmarket, Suffolk

■ Stewards' Enquiry : Jimmy Fortune caution: careless riding

FOCUS
The pace was only steady, leading to a somewhat messy race and a very moderate winning time indeed for an older-horse Group 3. Phoenix Tower showed big improvement on his previous form and Traffic Guard confirmed his improved Dubai form was no fluke. Messy form however, with circumstances preventing several of the principals from being seen to full advantage.

NOTEBOOK
Phoenix Tower(USA), off the track for almost a year after fracturing his pelvis and racing for only the fourth time, narrowly retained his unbeaten status. He failed to settle as he tracked the very moderate pace and was trapped in behind horses with nowhere to go approaching the final furlong, before a path opened for him next to the rail and he quickened up to score a shade readily. There is further improvement in him. (op 9-1)

Traffic Guard(USA), who raced for two other trainers during his campaign in Dubai, was still without the cheekpieces on this debut for his new yard. Always well placed in this steadily run contest, he got to the front going to the final furlong and seemed set to prevail, only to be cut down in the last few strides. This was a good effort, especially as his trainer reported he had bruised a foot in the build-up to the race. (op 16-1)

Pipedreamer ◆ progressed into a smart colt last season, slamming his field to land the Cambridgeshire over course and distance on his final start. Upped in class, he took time to pick up when the pace finally lifted but was running on strongly at the end. This was a pleasing return in a race not run to suit his style, but a step up to 1m2f will see him in an even better light and he looks sure to make his mark at this sort of level this season. A bit of cut in the ground may suit him. (tchd 7-4)

Multidimensional(IRE), a stablemate of the winner, was restricted to just two runs last term. Although unable to get much cover from his draw, he had his chance if good enough, but was unable to quicken and was held in fourth place when slightly hampered inside the last. He is worth another chance. (op 7-4 tchd 13-8)
Stotsfold carried a penalty for his win at this level at Goodwood on his final appearance last season. Taken to post early and held up after a slow start, he was not best suited by this slowly run affair but was keeping on nicely at the end.
Smokey Oakey(IRE), winner of the Lincoln first time out, faced a stiff task at the weights on this rise in grade. He was not disgraced in a race not run to suit him and on ground faster than he would have liked. (tchd 14-1, 20-1 in places)
Halicarnassus(IRE), twice a winner in this Grade last season, and penalised as a result, was found out by the lack of a true gallop on this drop in trip.
Kandidate made all in a Listed race on Polytrack at Kempton last time and attempted a repeat of those tactics. Setting a pretty modest pace, he quickened things up with around three to run but was headed going to the final furlong before back-pedalling fairly rapidly. (op 12-1)

1423 ROSSDALES MAIDEN FILLIES' STKS — 7f
4:55 (4:56) (Class 4) 3-Y-O — **£5,180** (£1,541; £770; £384) **Stalls** Low

Form — RPR
5- **1** **Danae**[166] 6648 3-9-0 0 ... DaneO'Neill 10 — 87
(H Candy) *b.bhd: mde all: rdn and hung rt fr over 1f out: r.o* **16/1**
4- **2** *hd* **Melodramatic (IRE)**[243] 4598 3-9-0 0 ... SteveDrowne 13 — 86
(R Charlton) *chsd wnr: rdn and ev ch fr over 1f out: carried rt ins fnl f: r.o* **1/1**[1]
3 *4 1/2* **Miss Brown To You (IRE)** 3-9-0 0 ... NCallan 16 — 74
(M L W Bell) *lt-f: leggy: hld up: hdwy 1/2-way: rdn over 1f out: styd on same pce* **20/1**
35- **4** *1 1/4* **Lush (IRE)**[296] 2969 3-9-0 0 ... RyanMoore 17 — 70
(R Hannon) *s.i.s: hld up: hdwy over 1f out: nt trble ldrs* **12/1**
3- **5** *1* **Portodora (USA)**[191] 6093 3-9-0 0 ... TedDurcan 1 — 68+
(H R A Cecil) *h.d.w: s.i.s: hld up: hdwy 3f out: rdn over 1f out: styd on same pce* **7/1**[3]
6 *hd* **Gulf Stream Lady (IRE)** 3-9-0 0 ... MichaelHills 2 — 67+
(B W Hills) *w'like: scope: s.s: styd on ins fnl f: nvr nrr* **33/1**
0 **7** *hd* **Star Acclaim**[29] 931 3-9-0 0 ... AlanMunro 15 — 67
(T Keddy) *prom: rdn over 2f out: no ex fr over 1f out* **80/1**
6- **8** *1 3/4* **Alseraaj (USA)**[191] 6087 3-9-0 0 ... RHills 8 — 62
(Sir Michael Stoute) *hld up: sme hdwy over 1f out: n.d* **11/2**[2]
33-3 **9** *hd* **Ivory Silk**[15] 1144 3-9-0 72 ... ChrisCatlin 11 — 61
(D K Ivory) *lw: mid-div: hdwy 3f out: wknd over 1f out* **33/1**
10 *nk* **Kelowna (IRE)** 3-9-0 0 ... JimmyFortune 6 — 61+
(J L Dunlop) *w'like: unf: hld up: nvr trbld ldrs* **25/1**
11 *shd* **Light Hearted** 3-9-0 0 ... TPQueally 9 — 60
(J Noseda) *cmpt: hld up in tch: lost pl over 2f out: hung rt fr over 1f out: n.d after* **14/1**
563- **12** *2 1/4* **Pampas (USA)**[158] 6777 3-9-0 74 ... JimmyQuinn 14 — 54
(Jane Chapple-Hyam) *wl grwn: chsd ldrs over 4f* **33/1**
13 *1* **Miss Clarice (USA)** 3-9-0 0 ... LDettori 3 — 52
(B J Meehan) *w'like: leggy: s.i.s: sn prom: wknd wl over 1f out* **20/1**
00- **14** *5* **Cheviot Red**[224] 5162 3-9-0 0 ... RobertHavlin 12 — 38
(B J Meehan) *chsd ldrs over 4f* **100/1**
15 *1 1/2* **Toon Army** 3-9-0 0 ... OscarUrbina 4 — 34
(Miss D Mountain) *a in rr* **100/1**
0- **16** *2 1/4* **Ice Bellini**[166] 6648 3-9-0 0 ... HayleyTurner 7 — 28
(J M P Eustace) *hld up: rdn 1/2-way: sn wknd* **66/1**

1m 28.98s (3.58) **Going Correction** +0.375s/f (Good) **16** Ran SP% **125.0**
Speed ratings (Par 97): **94,93,88,87,86 85,85,83,83,83 82,80,79,73,71 69**
CSF £30.78 TOTE £18.20: £4.00, £1.40, £4.30; EX 46.70.
Owner Girsonfield Ltd **Bred** Girsonfield Ltd **Trained** Kingston Warren, Oxon
■ Stewards' Enquiry : Dane O'Neill one-day ban: careless riding (May 1)

FOCUS
The winning time was modest for this maiden, and the form may not prove that solid, with the front pair prominent throughout. It has been rated through the runner-up and fourth.
Lush(IRE) Official explanation: jockey said filly was slowly away

1424 CURRAGH "HOME OF THE IRISH CLASSICS" H'CAP — 1m 2f
5:30 (5:33) (Class 3) (0-95,87) 3-Y-O — **£9,066** (£2,697; £1,348; £673) **Stalls** Low

Form — RPR
011- **1** **Bronze Cannon (USA)**[189] 6120 3-9-1 **84** ... JimmyFortune 13 — 104+
(J H M Gosden) *lw: a.p: led over 2f out: rdr dropped rein ins fnl f: edgd lft: drvn out* **8/1**[3]
221- **2** *nk* **Doctor Fremantle**[169] 6592 3-9-1 **84** ... RyanMoore 3 — 103+
(Sir Michael Stoute) *lw: hld up: hdwy over 2f out: ev ch fr over 1f out: sn rdn: r.o* **11/8**[1]
11 **3** *5* **Dream Desert (IRE)**[21] 1043 3-9-0 **83** ... EdwardCreighton 5 — 92
(M R Channon) *lw: hld up: hdwy over 2f out: rdn and ev ch wl over 1f out: styd on same pce* **12/1**
031- **4** *5* **Ragamuffin Man (IRE)**[176] 6418 3-8-10 **79** ... PaulDoe 14 — 78
(W J Knight) *chsd ldrs: rdn over 2f out: edgd lft and wknd over 1f out* **33/1**
10-2 **5** *1/2* **Ballochroy (IRE)**[14] 1171 3-9-2 **85** ... MichaelHills 10 — 83
(B W Hills) *hld up: hdwy over 2f out: rdn and wknd over 1f out* **16/1**
032- **6** *1 3/4* **Irish Mayhem (USA)**[181] 6296 3-8-13 **82** ... LDettori 8 — 81+
(B J Meehan) *hld up: racd keenly: rdn over 2f out: sn wknd* **14/1**
41- **7** *1* **Prime Exhibit**[184] 6252 3-9-1 **84** ... SteveDrowne 1 — 77+
(R Charlton) *hld up: hdwy over 2f out: edgd rt and wknd over 1f out* **4/1**[2]
210- **8** *1/2* **Presbyterian Nun (IRE)**[194] 6012 3-9-4 **87** ... SebSanders 7 — 79
(J L Dunlop) *lw: hld up: rdn over 1f out: n.d* **20/1**
100- **9** *2 3/4* **Giant Love (USA)**[186] 6201 3-8-12 **81** ... JoeFanning 12 — 67
(M Johnston) *lw: led: rdn and hdd over 2f out: wknd over 1f out* **16/1**
231- **10** *4* **Mystery Star (IRE)**[159] 6763 3-9-1 **84** ... JimmyQuinn 2 — 62
(M H Tompkins) *hld up: hdwy over 2f out: sn wknd* **50/1**
443- **11** *3/4* **The Betchworth Kid**[174] 6471 3-9-2 **85** ... HayleyTurner 4 — 62
(M L W Bell) *hld up: rdn 3f out: wkng whn nt clr run over 2f out* **16/1**
-113 **12** *9* **Grand Strategy (IRE)**[21] 1043 3-8-13 **82** ... PhilipRobinson 11 — 41
(M A Jarvis) *prom: wknd wl over 1f out: eased* **25/1**
11- **13** *2 1/4* **Goodwood Starlight (IRE)**[226] 5109 3-8-11 **80** ... KerrinMcEvoy 9 — 34
(J L Dunlop) *lw: racd alone: w ldrs tl wknd over 2f out* **14/1**
032- **14** *1 1/4* **Black Rain**[167] 6616 3-8-13 **82** ... (t) TedDurcan 6 — 34
(P J McBride) *prom over 7f* **50/1**

2m 6.35s (0.55) **Going Correction** +0.375s/f (Good) **14** Ran SP% **127.4**
Speed ratings (Par 102): **112,111,107,103,103 101,101,100,98,95 94,87,85,84**
CSF £19.47 CT £145.71 TOTE £9.70: £2.60, £1.40, £4.30; EX 24.30 Place 6 £ 55.30, Place 5 £ 11.31.
Owner A E Oppenheimer **Bred** Hascombe And Valiant Studs **Trained** Newmarket, Suffolk

FOCUS
A quality-looking three-year-old handicap contested by a number of horses holding Group-race entries, and run in an outstanding winning time for a race of its type. It should produce plenty of winners, for the form looks very solid, rated through the fourth and fifth.
NOTEBOOK
Bronze Cannon(USA) ◆, chasing a hat-trick following a couple of wins on the Polytrack last autumn, has a marvellous attitude, and that will stand him in good stead as he progresses through the ranks. Despite the fact that his rider dropped a rein in the closing stages, he ran on well to edge out another well-handicapped rival, and on this evidence it will be a surprise if he does not end up contesting pattern races later in the season. However, in the shorter term a valuable handicap such as the one over this trip at Epsom on Derby day looks an attractive option.
Doctor Fremantle ◆, who impressed in winning his maiden on his final start at two, looked favourably rated on his first start in handicap company and, unsurprisingly, was very popular in the market for stable that won this race in 2006 with Papal Bull, a colt who went on to win a Group 3 race on his next start. He was just edged out at the finish, but finished well clear of the third and was a little unlucky to run into a rival as well handicapped as himself. The valuable handicap over this trip at Epsom on Derby day could be on his agenda as well - it is a race in which his trainer has a good record - but no doubt his connections will be eying up pattern races for him at some stage, too. (op 5-4 tchd 6-5 and 6-4 in places)
Dream Desert(IRE) ◆, winner of his first two starts this season, both on Polytrack, had more to do here, but the Handicapper had not been too harsh on him in raising him only 5lb for his handicap win three weeks earlier and he was one of a number who came here unexposed and open to further improvement. He was well held by the first two but he finished equally clear of the rest, and would be unlucky to run into such favourably treated rivals again. He will be of plenty of interest in similar company, even if raised a few pounds for this effort. (op 14-1 tchd 11-1)
Ragamuffin Man(IRE), who shaped very much like a horse who would appreciate stepping up to middle distances this season when winning his maiden over a mile at Bath last autumn, shaped well for a stable whose few runners so far this season have run with a deal of credit.
Ballochroy(IRE), runner-up to the progressive Captain Webb on his reappearance, had the benefit of that run and his performance helps set the level of the form. It is possible, however, that he needs softer ground to be seen at his vey best. (op 33-1)
Irish Mayhem(USA), who improved with every outing at two, was running in a handicap for the first time and did not shape too badly for a stable that has yet to really hit form. (op 20-1)
Prime Exhibit ◆, a Leicester maiden winner last October, was solid in the market and travelled quite well out the back for a long way. He threatened to throw down a challenge up the centre of the track but the action developed away from him towards the far side and his effort petered out somewhat. He looks capable of better than this bare form suggests. (tchd 9-2, 5-1 and 11-2 in places)
Presbyterian Nun(IRE), who raced exclusively over 7f at two, should have been suited by the step up to 1m2f, but she never really got competitive. (op 33-1)
Goodwood Starlight(IRE), who won both his starts at two despite hanging left, raced away from the main pack and the impression left was that he is probably a bit tricky.
T/Plt: £64.40 to a £1 stake. Pool: £87,932.32. 996.00 winning tickets. T/Qpdt: £12.30 to a £1 stake. Pool: £6,393.74. 383.20 winning tickets. CR

RIPON (R-H)
Thursday, April 17

OFFICIAL GOING: Good to soft (7.0)
The ground was good to soft but after the rain was nearer soft by the end of the day.
Wind: moderate 1/2 against Weather: fine and sunny, overcast and light rain race 3, heavier ran race 5 onwards

1425 E B F EAT SLEEP & DRINK AT NAGS HEAD PICKHILL MAIDEN STKS — 5f
2:10 (2:10) (Class 5) 2-Y-O — **£4,209** (£1,252; £625; £312) **Stalls** Low

Form — RPR
1 **Anglezarke (IRE)** 2-8-12 0 ... DavidAllan 4 — 74+
(T D Easterby) *mde all: hung rt and styd on fnl 2f: hld on wl towards fin* **10/3**[2]
2 *1/2* **Caranbola** 2-8-9 0 ... MarkLawson(3) 7 — 72
(M Brittain) *sn chsng ldrs on outer: kpt on wl ins fnl f: no ex towards fin* **12/1**
3 *2 1/4* **Faraway Sound (IRE)** 2-9-3 0 ... LeeEnstone 3 — 68
(P C Haslam) *prom: sn drvn along: edgd rt and kpt on fnl f* **2/1**[1]
05 **4** *nk* **Shadow Bay (IRE)**[12] 1214 2-9-3 0 ... DarryllHolland 1 — 67+
(M R Channon) *sn trcking ldrs: effrt over 1f out: kpt on same pce* **9/2**[3]
5 *hd* **Crewezando** 2-9-3 0 ... TGMcLaughlin 2 — 66
(P D Evans) *prom: outpcd over 2f out: kpt on fnl f* **13/2**
6 *12* **Dispol Diva** 2-8-9 0 ... JamieMoriarty(3) 6 — 13
(P T Midgley) *s.s: sn detached in last* **20/1**
7 *3 1/2* **Dougie Peel** 2-9-3 0 ... PaulMulrennan 5 — 4
(K A Ryan) *chsd ldrs: lost pl over 2f out: sn bhd* **7/1**

65.37 secs (4.67) **Going Correction** +1.00s/f (Soft) **7** Ran SP% **112.9**
Speed ratings (Par 92): **102,101,97,97,96 77,72**
CSF £39.80 TOTE £4.50: £2.50, £4.20; EX 32.10.
Owner David W Armstrong **Bred** Mount Coote Stud **Trained** Great Habton, N Yorks
■ Trainer Tim Easterby's third successive win in this event.

FOCUS
Almost certainly a weak event but the winner has the potential to go on from here. The winning time was decent, 0.41 seconds quicker than the later 0-70 handicap for older horses.
NOTEBOOK
Anglezarke(IRE), an April foal, is still on the weak side and showed her inexperience going to the start. She tended to hang right but always looked in command, though the margin was slim at the line. Her trainer has his eye on the Hilary Needler at Beverley and the track there will suit her better. (op 7-2 tchd 4-1)
Caranbola, a March foal, is on the leg and narrow. Drawn widest of all, she stuck on but in truth was always going to come off second best. (op 11-1 tchd 10-1)
Faraway Sound(IRE), a February foal, is an active type. Soon driven along, in the end he came up well short. (op 9-4 tchd 5-2)
Shadow Bay(IRE), having his third run, is still backward in his coat. He stuck on without ever threateing to enter the argument. (op 9-1)
Crewezando, a January foal, is a close-coupled type. Backward in his coat, he stuck on after being run off his feet. (op 9-2)
Dougie Peel, who gave real problems in the paddock and on the way down, was on the retreat before the halfway mark and this was hardly an auspicious debut. (tchd 5-1)

1426 COPT HEWICK H'CAP — 6f
2:45 (2:45) (Class 4) (0-85,85) 3-Y-O — **£4,209** (£1,252; £625; £312) **Stalls** Low

Form — RPR
1-02 **1** **Van Bossed (CAN)**[7] 1284 3-8-10 **77** ... SilvestreDeSousa 11 — 91
(D Nicholls) *swtchd lft s and racd stands' side: chsd ldrs: led over 1f out: r.o strly: readily* **8/1**[2]

30-2 **2** *3* **Ink Spot**[13] 1194 3-8-9 **76**........ JimCrowley 4 81
(M L W Bell) *racd stands' side: in rr: hdwy 2f out: styd on wl ins fnl f* **14/1**

001- **3** *hd* **The Twelve Steps**[125] 7139 3-8-6 **73**........ MartinDwyer 13 77+
(P F I Cole) *racd far side: chsd ldr: edgd bdly lft over 1f out: kpt on same pce ins fnl f* **8/1**[2]

0-61 **4** *nk* **Harbour Blues**[80] 339 3-8-12 **79**........(t) CatherineGannon 3 82
(A W Carroll) *racd stands' side: in rr: styd on fnl 2f: kpt on wl ins fnl f* **40/1**

1-6 **5** *2 1/2* **Desert Clover (USA)**[26] 975 3-9-0 **81**........ NelsonDeSouza 16 76
(P F I Cole) *red far side: chsd ldrs: kpt on to ld that side nr fin* **16/1**

543- **6** *nk* **Jonny Lesters Hair (IRE)**[237] 4784 3-8-7 **74**........ DavidAllan 12 68
(T D Easterby) *swtchd rt s and led far side: hdd that gp nr fin* **16/1**

104- **7** *1 3/4* **Irving Place**[192] 6052 3-8-11 **78**........ PaulHanagan 10 66+
(R A Fahey) *racd stands' side: hld up in rr: kpt on fnl 2f* **16/1**

5-11 **8** *1/2* **Lieutenant Pigeon**[30] 924 3-8-8 **75**........ PaulEddery 7 62
(G D Blake) *led stands' side tl over 1f out: grad wknd* **9/1**[3]

0-63 **9** *1/2* **Nawaaff**[26] 975 3-8-1 **75**........ MCGeran(7) 2 60
(M R Channon) *racd stands' side: in tch: hung rt and one pce fnl 2f* **18/1**

500- **10** *nk* **Lindoro**[187] 6167 3-9-4 **85**........ SaleemGolam 14 69
(W R Swinburn) *stdd s: racd far side: hdwy over 2f out: kpt on: nvr rchd ldrs* **16/1**

143- **11** *1/2* **Captain Dunne (IRE)**[278] 3562 3-9-0 **81**........ PaulMulrennan 1 64+
(T D Easterby) *racd stands' side: towards rr: kpt on fnl 2f: nvr nr ldrs* **28/1**

21 **12** *2* **Opus Maximus (IRE)**[45] 777 3-8-6 **73**........ DeanMcKeown 9 49
(M Johnston) *racd stands' side: chsd ldrs: lost pl over 1f out* **8/1**[2]

01- **13** *1 1/2* **Flashy Photon**[245] 4537 3-8-11 **78**........ FrankieMcDonald 5 49
(H Candy) *racd stands' side: in tch: wkng whn hmpd ins fnl f* **14/1**

020- **14** *2* **Rubirosa (IRE)**[188] 6154 3-9-4 **85**........ PhillipMakin 19 50
(M Dods) *swvd rt s: racd far side: hdwy over 2f out: wknd over 1f out* **9/2**[1]

321- **15** *8* **Revue Princess (IRE)**[261] 4041 3-8-2 **72**........ DuranFentiman(3) 8 11
(T D Easterby) *racd stands' side: chsd ldr: lost pl 2f out: bhd and eased ins fnl f* **66/1**

31-6 **16** *14* **My Mate Pete (IRE)**[17] 1113 3-8-10 **77**........ TomEaves 15 —
(Mrs L Stubbs) *racd far side: chsd ldrs: lost pl wl over 1f out: eased* **28/1**

20-6 **17** *2* **Prigsnov Dancer (IRE)**[15] 1157 3-8-8 **75** ow1........ RobertWinston 17 —
(J O'Reilly) *racd far side: mid-div: lost pl 2f out: eased* **20/1**

020- **18** *2 3/4* **The Real Guru**[153] 6834 3-8-5 **72**........ RoystonFfrench 20 —
(Mrs A Duffield) *racd far side: in rr: bhd fnl 2f: eased* **25/1**

21-1 **19** *3 1/4* **Chrystal Venture (IRE)**[12] 1216 3-8-5 **72**........(p) AndrewElliott 6 —
(A J McCabe) *s.s: racd far side: sn chsng ldrs: lost pl over 2f out: eased and sn bhd* **12/1**

1m 18.51s (5.51) **Going Correction** +1.00s/f (Soft) **19** Ran SP% **130.8**
Speed ratings (Par 100): **103,99,98,98,95 94,92,91,90,90 89,87,85,82,71 53,50,46,42**
CSF £112.98 CT £978.23 TOTE £11.50: £2.60, £3.80, £2.50, £9.60; EX 116.20 TRIFECTA Not won..
Owner Mike & Maureen Browne **Bred** Bernard And Karen McCormack **Trained** Sessay, N Yorks
■ Baldemar (14/1) was withdrawn after spreading a plate. R4 applies, deduct 5p in the £. New market formed.

FOCUS
Eight went to the far side. The Twelve Steps was first of them home but he drifted left and ended up with the stands' side group. The winner was able to race from the same mark as Kempton but was raised 6lb for that improved effort. The form looks sound rated through the second and fourth.
My Mate Pete(IRE) Official explanation: jockey said gelding was unsuited by the course
Prigsnov Dancer(IRE) Official explanation: jockey said gelding was unsuited by the course

1427 RIPON SILVER BOWL CONDITIONS STKS 1m 1f 170y
3:20 (3:21) (Class 3) 4-Y-0+
£6,542 (£1,959; £979; £490; £244; £122) **Stalls** High

Form RPR

-050 **1** **Championship Point (IRE)**[49] 739 5-9-0 105........ DarryllHolland 4 102
(M R Channon) *led: qckn 4f out: styd on strly fnl f: won gng away* **3/1**[2]

66-3 **2** *1 1/2* **Spice Route**[19] 1077 4-9-3 106........ JimCrowley 7 101
(M L W Bell) *trckd ldrs: chal over 1f out: sn rdn and no ex* **15/8**[1]

514- **3** *shd* **Bid For Glory**[123] 7163 4-9-0 91........ RobertWinston 6 98
(H J Collingridge) *trckd ldrs effrt 4f out: chalng 1st 2 2f out: styd on same pce ins fnl f* **14/1**

-004 **4** *11* **Charlie Tokyo (IRE)**[19] 1076 5-9-0 103........(v) PaulHanagan 5 74
(R A Fahey) *trckd ldrs: effrt over 2f out: wknd over 1f out* **10/3**[3]

212- **5** *2 3/4* **Ronaldsay**[181] 6299 4-8-9 101........ PatDobbs 3 63
(R Hannon) *hld up in rr: effrt 4f out: sn chsng ldrs: lost pl over 1f out* **7/2**

211/ **6** *13* **Numero Due**[579] 5383 6-9-0 84........ TomEaves 8 39
(G M Moore) *s.i.s: racd in last: detached 3f out* **33/1**

2m 11.36s (5.96) **Going Correction** +0.775s/f (Yiel) **6** Ran SP% **114.7**
Speed ratings (Par 107): **107,105,105,96,94 84**
CSF £9.37 TOTE £4.00: £1.90, £1.60; EX 9.50 Trifecta £72.40 Pool: £586.86 - 5.75 winning units..
Owner John Livock **Bred** Mount Coote Stud **Trained** West Ilsley, Berks

FOCUS
A tactical affair and Darryll Holland deserves full marks. The level of the form is a bit shaky with Championship Point not having been at his best in Dubai and the third showing much-improved form.

NOTEBOOK
Championship Point(IRE), who looked in fine trim after his stint in Dubai, is usually held up but his rider seized the initiative. Winding up the pace once in line for home, in the end he won going away. (op 10-3 tchd 7-2)
Spice Route, back on turf, worked his way upsides but near the finish the winner proved much the stronger. The race was not run to suit him. (tchd 7-4 and 2-1)
Bid For Glory, who had almost a stone to find with the first two, seemed to run out of his skin but as a result his handicap mark will shoot up. (tchd 18-1)
Charlie Tokyo(IRE), suited by the soft ground, was disappointing. (op 5-1)
Ronaldsay, best in on offical figures, was a long way below her best on her return. (op 3-1 tchd 4-1)

1428 BETFAIR RIPON "COCK O' THE NORTH" H'CAP 1m
3:55 (3:56) (Class 3) (0-95,92) 3-Y-0 **£8,756** (£2,645; £1,338; £686; £358) **Stalls** High

Form RPR

101- **1** **Cobo Bay**[208] 5613 3-9-7 **92**........ DarryllHolland 5 104
(K A Ryan) *mde all: drvn and styd on strly fnl 2f: clr appr fnl f: unchal* **10/1**[3]

66-1 **2** *3 1/2* **Albaqaa**[24] 991 3-8-7 **78**........ PaulHanagan 1 82+
(R A Fahey) *t.k.h: hdwy and plld outside over 2f out: wnt 2nd and hung rt over 1f out: no imp* **4/1**[2]

62-4 **3** *7* **Ivestar (IRE)**[16] 1130 3-8-7 **78**........ SilvestreDeSousa 7 66
(D Nicholls) *sn chsng ldrs: hung lft 2f out: one pce fnl 2f* **25/1**

21- **4** *1 1/4* **Robby Bobby**[189] 6130 3-9-4 **89**........ RobertWinston 4 74
(M Johnston) *trckd ldrs: effrt over 2f out: wknd appr fnl f* **11/10**[1]

343- **5** *12* **Upton Grey (IRE)**[173] 6486 3-9-2 **87**........ DavidKinsella 2 44
(J H M Gosden) *hld up: hdwy to trck ldrs over 6f out: wnt 2nd over 3f out: wknd 2f out: eased ins fnl f* **4/1**[2]

140- **P** **Runswick Bay**[236] 4812 3-8-13 **84**........ TomEaves 6 —
(G M Moore) *sn pushed along and detached in rr: t.o whn p.u after 2f: lame bhd* **33/1**

1m 46.94s (5.54) **Going Correction** +0.775s/f (Yiel) **6** Ran SP% **103.5**
Speed ratings (Par 102): **103,99,92,91,79** —
CSF £40.75 CT £713.05 TOTE £10.70: £2.50, £2.00; EX 42.10 Trifecta £403.00 Part won. Pool: £567.72 - 0.91 winning units..
Owner The C H F Partnership **Bred** The C H F Partnership **Trained** Hambleton, N Yorks
■ American Art was withdrawn on vet's advice (11/1, deduct 5p in the £ under Rule 4).

FOCUS
Cobo Bay was given his own way out in front but he scored in most convincing fashion in the end. This was a considerable step up from him but no fluke.

NOTEBOOK
Cobo Bay, 8lb higher than his success at Ayr in September on his final start at two, looked to have done himself well over the winter. His rider repeated the tactics used on Championship Point in the previous race and he had this won coming to the final furlong.
Albaqaa, 4lb higher than his final try in nursery company, is still much too keen. He went in pursuit of the winner but hung in behind him and was never going to get anywhere near him. (op 7-2)
Ivestar(IRE), who is not that big, was the first to come under serious pressure and he could do no more than plug away in his own time. (tchd 20-1 and 28-1)
Robby Bobby, who won his second and final back-end start at two at Newbury in October, seemed to roll about and never really threatened. Despite his soft-ground success at Newbury he may need better ground and a much more galloping track. He will definitely prove a lot better than he showed on this day. Official explanation: jockey said, regarding running and riding, that his orders were to sit handy and that the colt was a straightforward ride, adding that he was happy with his position and held it together in the final furlong as it had become tired and began changing its legs, adding that he kept pushing his mount to the line. (op 10-11 tchd 6-5 in places)
Upton Grey(IRE), still on the narrow side, went in pursuit of the winner but emptied badly two furlongs from home. This trip may have proved beyond him. (op 8-1)

1429 RON & ELSIE HOPPER MEMORIAL MAIDEN STKS 1m
4:30 (4:30) (Class 5) 3-Y-0 **£2,914** (£867; £433; £216) **Stalls** High

Form RPR

1 **City Bonus (IRE)** 3-9-3 0........ DavidKinsella 12 77+
(J H M Gosden) *s.i.s: hdwy and plld outside 3f out: styd on to ld towards fin* **15/8**[1]

2 *1 1/4* **Al Wasef (USA)** 3-9-3 0........ MartinDwyer 3 69+
(M Johnston) *trckd ldrs: chal 3f out: hung rt and led over 1f out: hdd last 50yds* **2/1**[2]

4 **3** *3/4* **Plenilune (IRE)**[6] 1298 3-9-3 0........ TWilliams 11 64
(M Brittain) *sn trcking ldrs: led over 3f out until over 1f out: kpt on ins fnl f* **7/1**[3]

4- **4** *3 1/2* **Salerosa (IRE)**[160] 6742 3-8-12 0........ RoystonFfrench 8 51
(Mrs A Duffield) *t.k.h: trckd ldrs: one pce fnl 2f* **11/1**

5 *nk* **Merrion Tiger (IRE)** 3-9-3 0........ AndrewElliott 6 55
(K R Burke) *chsd ldrs: outpcd 3f out: kpt on fnl f* **20/1**

6 *1 3/4* **Cheers For Thea (IRE)** 3-8-12 0........ DavidAllan 10 46
(T D Easterby) *mid-div: outpcd 4f out: styd on fnl 2f* **10/1**

06- **7** *10* **Harrison's Star**[181] 6303 3-9-3 0........ PhillipMakin 2 28
(G M Moore) *mid-div: effrt over 3f out: sn btn* **20/1**

0 **8** *hd* **Tartan Gigha (IRE)**[19] 1073 3-9-3 0........ RobertWinston 1 28
(M Johnston) *hld up in rr: nvr a factor* **16/1**

00- **9** *7* **Monte Cassino (IRE)**[162] 6721 3-9-3 0........ TonyHamilton 7 12
(J O'Reilly) *t.k.h: led: hdd over 3f out: wknd over 1f out* **33/1**

P-0 **10** *nse* **Templetuohy Max (IRE)**[19] 1073 3-9-3 0........ GrahamGibbons 9 12
(J D Bethell) *chsd ldrs: drvn 3f out: sn wknd* **66/1**

11 *18* **Victorias** 3-8-12 0........ TomEaves 4 —
(A Crook) *s.i.s: t.k.h in rr: bhd fnl 4f: sn t.o* **40/1**

1m 52.46s (11.06) **Going Correction** +0.775s/f (Yiel) **11** Ran SP% **120.3**
Speed ratings (Par 98): **75,73,73,69,69 67,57,57,50,50 32**
CSF £5.58 TOTE £2.80: £1.30, £1.40, £2.10; EX 6.00 Trifecta £49.60 Pool: £331.55 - 4.74 winning units..
Owner H R H Princess Haya Of Jordan **Bred** David John Brown **Trained** Newmarket, Suffolk

FOCUS
A pedestrian winning time, 5.52 seconds slower than the preceding handicap. Modest maiden form but the first two will both progress. The race has been rated through the fourth for the time being.
Monte Cassino(IRE) Official explanation: jockey said colt ran too free

1430 LEVY BOARD H'CAP 6f
5:05 (5:05) (Class 4) (0-85,85) 4-Y-0+ **£4,209** (£1,252; £625; £312) **Stalls** Low

Form RPR

00-3 **1** **Tajneed (IRE)**[6] 1300 5-9-0 81........ SilvestreDeSousa 5 98
(D Nicholls) *chsd ldrs: led 2f out: rdn clr fnl f* **11/4**[1]

0334 **2** *4 1/2* **Memphis Man**[3] 1368 5-8-5 72........ SaleemGolam 8 75
(P D Evans) *chsd ldrs: styd on to take 2nd wl ins fnl f* **6/1**[3]

1365 **3** *1/2* **Bel Cantor**[6] 1300 5-8-10 80........(p) AndrewMullen(3) 4 81
(W J H Ratcliffe) *led tl 2f out: kpt on same pce* **5/1**[2]

06-5 **4** *1 1/4* **Makshoof (IRE)**[16] 1134 4-8-11 78........ PaulMulrennan 9 75
(K A Ryan) *chsd ldrs: kpt on same pce fnl 2f* **11/1**

300- **5** *hd* **Compton's Eleven**[186] 6205 7-8-11 85........ MCGeran(7) 1 81
(M R Channon) *s.i.s: hdwy and plld wd appr fnl f: nvr nr ldrs* **25/1**

65-0 **6** *3 3/4* **Obe Gold**[19] 1071 6-9-4 85........ PaulQuinn 11 69
(D Nicholls) *in tch: wknd over 1f out* **20/1**

061- **7** *hd* **Paris Bell**[166] 6639 6-8-10 77........ DavidAllan 10 69+
(T D Easterby) *s.s: hmpd after 1f: hld up in rr: sme hdwy whn hmpd on ins over 1f out: nvr nr ldrs* **8/1**

050- **8** *1 3/4* **Yorkshire Blue**[159] 6753 9-8-4 71 oh1........ PaulHanagan 6 49
(J S Goldie) *hld up towards rr: kpt on fnl 2f: nvr nr ldrs* **25/1**

640- **9** *1/2* **Viva Volta**[170] 6560 5-8-6 76........ DuranFentiman(3) 2 53
(T D Easterby) *chsd ldrs: wknd over 1f out* **40/1**

112- **10** *1/2* **Swift Princess (IRE)**[209] 5581 4-9-0 81........(v) AndrewElliott 7 56
(K R Burke) *chsd ldrs: edgd rt over 1f out: wkng whn edgd lft ins fnl f* **10/1**

530- **11** *3* **Misphire**[186] 6205 5-8-11 78........(v[1]) PhillipMakin 12 43
(M Dods) *hld up in mid-div: sme hdwy over 2f out: wkng whn hmpd ins fnl f* **25/1**

000- **12** *2 3/4* **Sadeek**[174] 6472 4-9-1 82........ TomEaves 3 60+
(B Smart) *dwlt: sn chsng ldrs: lost pl over 2f out: hmpd ins fnl f* **20/1**

005- **13** *2* **Prince Namid**[163] 6701 6-8-10 77........ RoystonFfrench 14 27
(Mrs A Duffield) *racd wd: swtchd lft after 1f: sn mid-div: lost pl over 1f out* **14/1**

4020 **14** *2* **Cornus**[5] 1327 6-8-13 80 ....(be) RobertWinston 13 24
(A J McCabe) *s.i.s: swtchd lft after s: hmpd after 1f: nvr on terms* **12/1**
1m 18.88s (5.88) **Going Correction** +1.00s/f (Soft) **14** Ran SP% **124.0**
Speed ratings (Par 105): **100,94,93,91,91 86,86,83,83,82 78,74,72,69**
CSF £17.07 CT £82.78 TOTE £3.70: £1.70, £2.70, £2.30; EX 25.60 Trifecta £264.50 Pool: £562.74, 1.51 winning units.
Owner AlexNichollsRobertGilmartinFinolaDevaney **Bred** R Hodgins **Trained** Sessay, N Yorks
FOCUS
They all raced towards the stands' side. The winner stepped up on his Doncaster effort and scored with plenty in hand. He is rated back to his best but the others probably didn't run their races in the testing ground.
Cornus Official explanation: jockey said gelding lost its action

1431 NEWBY APPRENTICE H'CAP 5f
5:40 (5:40) (Class 5) (0-70,70) 4-Y-0+ **£2,914** (£867; £433; £216) **Stalls** Low

Form RPR
016- **1** **Baybshambles (IRE)**[170] 6562 4-8-1 **57** .... AshleyMorgan(5) 5 65
(R E Barr) *rrd s: hdwy on wd outside over 2f out: sn chsng ldrs: styd on to ld towards fin* **10/1**
4625 **2** *½* **Obe Royal**[6] 1312 4-9-2 **70** ....(b) RichardEvans(3) 9 76
(P D Evans) *swvd rt s: sn chsng ldrs on outer: no ex wl ins fnl f* **7/2**[2]
1-00 **3** *hd* **Brut**[24] 994 6-9-1 **69** ....(p) NSLawes(3) 6 74
(D W Barker) *led: edgd rt over 1f out: hdd and no ex towards fin* **9/1**
406- **4** *3* **Woqoodd**[167] 6625 4-8-7 **66** .... FrederikTylicki(8) 1 60
(R A Fahey) *chsd ldrs: one pce fnl f* **12/1**
350- **5** *hd* **Colorus (IRE)**[188] 6157 5-8-9 **67** .... PaulPickard(7) 2 61
(W J H Ratcliffe) *swvd rt s: sn chsng ldrs: fdd fnl 100yds* **13/2**
0-03 **6** *2 ¼* **Rothesay Dancer**[6] 1309 5-8-10 **61** .... DeclanCannon 3 47
(J S Goldie) *hld up: effrt on ins over 1f out: nvr trbld ldrs* **4/1**[3]
00-0 **7** *1* **Ronnie Howe**[23] 1015 4-8-3 **62** .... JohnCavanagh(8) 8 44
(M Dods) *chsd ldrs: wknd fnl f* **10/1**
6616 **8** *½* **Winthorpe (IRE)**[13] 1188 8-8-12 **66** .... BMcHugh(3) 4 46
(J J Quinn) *chsd ldrs: wknd over 1f out* **3/1**[1]
-440 **9** *3 ½* **Paddywack (IRE)**[23] 1015 11-8-7 **58** ....(b) DeanHeslop 7 26
(Mrs R A Carr) *sn outpcd in last: nvr a factor* **16/1**
65.78 secs (5.08) **Going Correction** +1.00s/f (Soft) **9** Ran SP% **122.3**
Speed ratings (Par 103): **99,98,97,93,92 89,87,86,81**
CSF £47.77 CT £342.36 TOTE £12.20: £3.20, £1.30, £3.80; EX 53.70 TRIFECTA Not won. Place 6 £110.26, Place 5 £34.52.
Owner Miss S Haykin **Bred** Mrs H F Mahr **Trained** Seamer, N Yorks
FOCUS
A low-grade apprentice riders' sprint handicap but the winner is bred to improve with age and he can surely work his way up the ratings from such a low starting point. The race has been rated through the back-to-his best third.
Ronnie Howe Official explanation: jockey said gelding was unsuited by the good to soft ground
T/Plt: £78.20 to a £1 stake. Pool: £56,722.80. 528.90 winning tickets. T/Qpdt: £5.50 to a £1 stake. Pool: £4,223.30. 559.55 winning tickets. WG

1432 - 1438a (Foreign Racing) - See Raceform Interactive

NEWBURY (L-H)
Friday, April 18

OFFICIAL GOING: Good to soft (6.0)
Wind: strong behind

1439 EUROPEAN BREEDERS' FUND MAIDEN STKS 5f 34y
1:10 (1:12) (Class 4) 2-Y-0 **£5,828** (£1,734; £866; £432) **Stalls** High

Form RPR
1 **Baycat (IRE)** 2-9-3 0 .... JamesDoyle 5 78+
(J G Portman) *leggy: trckd ldrs: shkn up and qcknd over 1f out to ld fnl 110yds: sn edgd rt: comf* **33/1**
2 *¾* **Skid Solo (IRE)** 2-9-3 0 .... AlanMunro 7 75
(P W Chapple-Hyam) *leggy: neat: pressed ldr tl drvn to take slt advantage over 1f out styd on tl hdd and outpcd fnl 110yds* **10/11**[1]
3 *1* **Sun Ship (IRE)** 2-9-3 0 .... RichardHughes 1 71+
(R Hannon) *w'like: bit bkwd: slt ld tl shkn up and hdd over 1f out: styd chalng tl outpcd fnl 110yds* **11/2**[3]
4 *2 ½* **Entrancer (IRE)** 2-9-3 0 .... RichardMullen 2 61+
(W R Muir) *str: bit bkwd: chsd ldrs: rdn 2f out: outpcd appr fnl f* **12/1**
5 *5* **Dabbers Chief (USA)** 2-9-3 0 .... MichaelHills 3 41+
(B W Hills) *w'like: scope: wnt lft s and s.i.s: sn rcvrd to chse ldrs but hanging lft: rdn 2f out: sn wknd* **9/2**[2]
6 *7* **Klynch** 2-9-3 0 .... LDettori 6 13+
(B J Meehan) *w'like: scope: bit bkwd: s.i.s: in rr and rn greenly thrght* **11/2**[3]
64.71 secs (3.31) **Going Correction** +0.25s/f (Good) **6** Ran SP% **112.0**
Speed ratings (Par 94): **83,81,80,76,68 57**
CSF £64.53 TOTE £47.90: £6.30, £1.30; EX 90.50.
Owner A S B Portman **Bred** D Couper Snr **Trained** Compton, Berks
FOCUS
Drying ground for the opening day of the Newbury 2008 turf season, although it was still on the slow side of good. This was probably nothing more than a fair contest and, though it should produce winners, it would be a surprise were any of them to prove up to Pattern class. The winner was a big price but it was no fluke.
NOTEBOOK
Baycat(IRE) sprang something of a surprise, winning with a bit to spare. Providing One Cool Cat with his first winner in Britain, he showed plenty of speed, quickening quite well when given a slap, and was nicely on top at the line, despite edging both ways under pressure. His relatively small yard is hardly renowned for its success with juveniles, although it does have winners, and it will be fascinating to see where he turns up next. Connections, who admitted they expected him to win a maiden but not at somewhere like Newbury, reportedly have no specific plans. (op 25-1)
Skid Solo(IRE), whose yard chose this race to launch the career of star two-year-old Winker Watson last term, has a Group 1 Phoenix Stakes entry and was understandably made favourite, sporting the same colours as last term's victor. Though having stamina in his pedigree (half-brother to 1m2f performer Tadabul and 1m6f winner Duroob) his dam won over 5f and this late foal looked well forward for his debut. It was soon clear he knew his job, grabbing the assistance of the rail, but things did not pan out as expected and he simply failed to match the pace of the winner. A race will certainly come his way, but he is no Winker Watson. (op 5-6 tchd 11-10)
Sun Ship(IRE), a January foal whose dam stayed 1m, travelled strongly throughout, but as with the runner-up, he could not match the winner in the final 100 yards. This was a pleasing start and he looks capable of winning an ordinary maiden. (op 5-1 tchd 9-2)
Entrancer(IRE) ◆, a brother to speedy juvenile winner Siena Gold, comes from a yard that has made a bright start to the season and he shaped with plenty of promise in fourth, finishing well clear of the other two. He was under pressure quite early, showing signs of inexperience, but his trainer's juveniles often improve for a run and it was pleasing to see him keep on right the way to the line. Winning an ordinary maiden should prove a formality. (op 14-1)
Dabbers Chief(USA), a US-bred who cost 120,000euros, was representing the yard that took this race in 2005, but he went left coming out of the gate and never looked at ease, running very green. A fine, big sort, he was not given a hard time and can be expected to step up markedly next time. (op 4-1)
Klynch, the first juvenile runner of the season for the yard, will want a little further than this in time and he was struggling from the word go, being slow out of the gate and running green. (op 8-1)

1440 ROBERT SANGSTER MEMORIAL MAIDEN FILLIES' STKS (DIV I) 1m 2f 6y
1:40 (1:41) (Class 4) 3-Y-O **£5,342** (£1,589; £794; £396) **Stalls** Centre

Form RPR
4- **1** **Clowance**[190] 6127 3-9-0 0 .... SteveDrowne 5 96+
(R Charlton) *s.i.s: in rr: nudged along 5f out: hdwy fr 3f out: slt ld ins fnl 2f: pushed out fnl f: readily* **9/2**[2]
4- **2** *1 ¼* **Montbretia**[178] 6414 3-9-0 0 .... TedDurcan 3 94
(H R A Cecil) *chsd ldrs: shkn up 2f out: styd on to chse wnr appr fnl f but no imp* **9/2**[2]
23- **3** *2 ¼* **Miracle Seeker**[175] 6470 3-9-0 0 .... PhilipRobinson 6 89
(C G Cox) *lw: led: pushed along fr 3f out: hdd ins fnl 2f: lost 2nd over 1f out but kpt on same pce to hold 3rd* **11/4**[1]
4 *1 ¼* **Classic Remark (IRE)** 3-9-0 0 .... EddieAhern 7 87+
(H J L Dunlop) *unf: bit bkwd: in rr: stl last 5f out: swtchd rt and hdwy over 2f out: styd on wl fr over 1f out to take 4th ins fnl f: fin wl* **40/1**
2- **5** *3 ½* **Elmaleeha**[167] 6649 3-9-0 0 .... RHills 9 80
(J L Dunlop) *chsd ldr: rdn and effrt 3f out: nvr quite on terms: wknd over 1f out* **11/4**[1]
0- **6** *9* **Cinerama (IRE)**[177] 6434 3-9-0 0 .... PatDobbs 8 62
(M P Tregoning) *in rr: pushed along and styd on fr over 2f out but nvr in contention* **33/1**
7 *3 ¼* **Dunedin Star** 3-9-0 0 .... JimmyFortune 10 55
(J H M Gosden) *w'like: lw: in tch: pushed along and outpcd over 4f out: nvr in contention after* **12/1**[3]
0- **8** *nse* **Rabeera**[210] 5596 3-8-7 0 .... DavidProbert(7) 1 55
(A M Balding) *chsd ldrs: rdn 4f out and sn wknd* **12/1**[3]
0- **9** *1 ¼* **Light Sea (IRE)**[178] 6414 3-9-0 0 .... DarryllHolland 2 52
(M R Channon) *chsd ldrs: rdn along over 3f out: sn wknd* **50/1**
0- **10** *2 ¼* **Marie Tempest**[167] 6648 3-9-0 0 .... MichaelHills 4 48
(B W Hills) *a in rr* **33/1**
2m 12.7s (3.90) **Going Correction** +0.40s/f (Good) **10** Ran SP% **115.4**
Speed ratings (Par 97): **100,99,97,96,93 86,83,83,82,80**
CSF £24.10 TOTE £5.40: £1.70, £1.70, £1.60; EX 28.80.
Owner Seasons Holidays **Bred** B Hurley **Trained** Beckhampton, Wilts
FOCUS
A maiden won by the likes of Islington and Eswarah and there were plenty of Oaks entrants in this year's line-up. This was undoubtedly the stronger of the two divisions and the time was much the quicker. The form looks decent and has been rated around the third and fifth.

1441 DUBAI DUTY FREE FINEST SURPRISE H'CAP 7f (S)
2:10 (2:13) (Class 3) (0-95,95) 3-Y-O
£8,723 (£2,612; £1,306; £653; £326; £163) **Stalls** High

Form RPR
134- **1** **Huzzah (IRE)**[174] 6486 3-8-9 **86** .... MichaelHills 3 103
(B W Hills) *chsd ldrs: drvn to ld over 1f out: narrowly hdd fnl 100yds: rallied to ld again last stride* **14/1**
311- **2** *shd* **Generous Thought**[160] 6756 3-8-11 **88** .... JamieSpencer 6 105+
(P Howling) *s.i.s: in rr: hdwy fr 3f out: qcknd to chse wnr fnl f and slt ld fnl 100yds: ct last stride* **7/2**[2]
10-4 **3** *4* **Keep Discovering (IRE)**[18] 1113 3-8-6 **83** .... GregFairley 1 89
(M Johnston) *chsd ldrs: rdn to chal 2f out: outpcd fnl f* **25/1**
U00- **4** *nk* **Ramona Chase**[174] 6495 3-9-1 **92** .... JimmyFortune 11 98
(S Kirk) *s.i.s: hld up in rr: rdn and hdwy fr 2f out: r.o wl fr over 1f out to take 4th ins fnl f but nvr gng pce to be competitive* **50/1**
100- **5** *hd* **Clifton Dancer**[174] 6498 3-8-4 **81** .... RichardKingscote 9 86
(Tom Dascombe) *led: rdn over 2f out: hdd over 1f out: wknd ins fnl f* **66/1**
131- **6** *¾* **Kal Barg**[174] 6486 3-8-12 **89** .... PhilipRobinson 5 92+
(M A Jarvis) *lw: chsd ldrs: shkn up over 2f out and kpt on same pce* **11/2**[3]
2-1 **7** *2* **Pravda Street**[17] 1125 3-8-8 **85** .... TQuinn 12 83
(P F I Cole) *lw: chsd ldrs: drvn along 3f out: wknd over 1f out: edgd rt ins fnl f* **10/3**[1]
131- **8** *1 ¼* **Choose Your Moment**[222] 5251 3-9-2 **93** .... RyanMoore 13 100+
(P C Haslam) *lw: in rr: hdwy on ins over 2f out: styng on whn hmpd ins fnl f: nt rcvr* **7/1**
135- **9** *4* **Aye Aye Digby (IRE)**[189] 6154 3-8-8 **85** .... DaneO'Neill 10 68
(H Candy) *in tch: sn chsng ldrs: pushed along over 2f out: wknd over 1f out* **12/1**
451- **10** *3 ¾* **Almoutaz (USA)**[168] 6617 3-8-7 **84** .... RHills 15 57
(B W Hills) *in tch: trckd ldrs 3f out: wknd 2f out* **25/1**
254- **11** *¾* **Perfect Act**[174] 6498 3-8-11 **88** .... KerrinMcEvoy 7 59
(C G Cox) *bhd fr 1/2-way* **17/2**
110- **12** *7* **Fifteen Love (USA)**[174] 6495 3-9-4 **95** .... SteveDrowne 8 47
(R Charlton) *towards rr: effrt into mid-div 3f out: sn wknd: nvr in contention* **20/1**
14-1 **13** *11* **Hustle (IRE)**[18] 1113 3-8-8 **85** .... RichardHughes 2 8
(R Hannon) *chsd ldrs: rdn over 2f out: sn wknd* **20/1**
10-0 **14** *8* **Seeking Star (IRE)**[20] 1075 3-9-2 **93** .... DarryllHolland 16 —
(M R Channon) *sn bhd* **33/1**
1m 26.09s (0.39) **Going Correction** +0.25s/f (Good) **14** Ran SP% **121.7**
Speed ratings (Par 102): **107,106,102,101,101 100,98,97,92,88 87,79,66,57**
CSF £58.68 CT £921.81 TOTE £15.40: £4.70, £1.90, £5.80; EX 137.60 Trifecta £449.00 Part won. Pool £632.40 - 0.10 winning units..
Owner J Gale,J Finch,D Cole,R Dollar,D Powell **Bred** S And S Hubbard Rodwell **Trained** Lambourn, Berks
FOCUS
A warm handicap with several progressive and unexposed three-year-olds facing off. The winner is progressive and this is form to be positive about.
NOTEBOOK
Huzzah(IRE), kept busy as a two-year-old, stays further than this and that assured stamina saw him through. Soon prominent, he edged his way towards the stands' rail and showed a fine attitude. He reportedly does not want the ground too fast and will head to Chester's May meeting for an extended 7f handicap. His trainer traditionally does well there and he should be capable of going close if the draw is kind to him, even off a higher mark. (op 28-1)
Generous Thought ◆, who shaped as though he may get further when signing off with a ready nursery win over 6f at Doncaster last backend (under this rider), was reappearing off an 8lb higher mark and did have to prove his effectiveness on this slower ground. Neither of those presented a problem and, despite being slowly away, he came with what looked a winning challenge over a furlong out. However, he seemed to get a little tired and was just run out of it, with Jamie Spencer evidently having the future in mind, as he did not resort to the whip. He may well have won had he received a slap or two with the whip.

Keep Discovering(IRE) ran really well off what looked a stiff mark. A 6f Folkestone maiden winner for Godolphin as a juvenile, he never got involved behind Hustle at Lingfield on his recent reappearance, but the return to turf suited and he should get 1m.

Ramona Chase ◆ gave the impression of better to come. Highly thought of as a juvenile, he would have found this 7f on the sharp side and it was pleasing to see him come home nicely in fourth, giving the impression he could have been even closer had things gone his way. He would not want to be going up much more in the handicap, though.

Clifton Dancer did a lot better than expected, showing up well from an early stage and keeping on to just be run out of the places. This was a promising effort and she can win in lower grade.

Kal Barg progressed with racing as a juvenile, showing useful handicap form after winning his maiden, but needed to have made further progress over the winter, as he was reappearing off an 11lb higher mark than when scoring at Doncaster in October. He ran well without suggesting he is a winner waiting to happen. (tchd 5-1)

Pravda Street, who had the favoured stands' rail when winning easily at Folkestone on his seasonal debut, received a tidy form boost when the runner-up Glorious Gift won just as well at Nottingham and looked fairly well handicapped off a mark of 85. His stable has made a blistering start to the season, but he never looked happy and was beaten at halfway. Official explanation: jockey said colt hung left (op 5-2 tchd 7-2)

Choose Your Moment ◆, a 2000 Guineas entrant, would have needed to win well to earn his place in the season's opening Classic, and even then it would have been stretching the imagination to see him figuring. He ran a lot better than his finishing position suggests, keeping on under a considerate ride and finding himself short of room inside the final furlong. He is an interesting one for next time. Official explanation: jockey said colt was denied a clear run (op 13-2)

Aye Aye Digby(IRE), a son of mudlark Captain Rio whose only win as a juvenile came when getting some cut in the ground, was reappearing in a warm heat and needed to have made strides over the winter to get involved off a mark of 85. He ran well to a point and the way he faded suggests the outing may have been needed. (op 25-1)

Fifteen Love(USA) needed to have made progress over the winter to defy a mark of 95. His form as a juvenile was pretty useful until he flopped on soft ground in the Horris Hill over course and distance in October and he again seemed to find conditions against him.

Hustle(IRE) looked the type to make a better three-year-old and confirmed that impression when quickening up well off a steady gallop to make a winning reappearance at Lingfield. Though 6lb higher for this return to turf, there was every chance he had progressed again and he looked to hold a chance as long as the ground was not too slow. He ran poorly, though, and perhaps a sound surface is required for him to show his best form. Official explanation: jockey said colt stopped quickly (tchd 16-1)

1442 DUBAI DUTY FREE FULL OF SURPRISES H'CAP — 5f 34y

2:40 (2:42) (Class 2) (0-110,102) 4-Y-0+

£9,969 (£2,985; £1,492; £747; £372; £187) **Stalls** High

Form				RPR
012-	**1**		**Oldjoesaid**[181] 6327 4-9-4 **102**........ DaneO'Neill 1 (H Candy) *trckd ldr towards centre: drvn to ld appr fnl f: hld on all out* **2/1**[1]	113+
256-	**2**	*nk*	**The Trader (IRE)**[206] 5700 10-8-13 **97**........(b) TedDurcan 7 (M Blanshard) *lw: hld up in rr: swtchd lft 2f out and str run fnl f: fin wl: nt quite get up* **25/1**	104
100-	**3**	*1*	**Fullandby (IRE)**[181] 6338 6-9-0 **101**........ PJMcDonald(3) 5 (T J Etherington) *hld up in rr: hdwy 2f out: n.m.r over 1f out: styd on wl but nt pce of ldng duo* **8/1**	104
-003	**4**	*3/4*	**King Orchisios (IRE)**[20] 1071 5-8-12 **96**........(p) JamieSpencer 2 (K A Ryan) *led towards centre: rdn 2f out: hdd appr fnl f: kpt on same pce ins fnl f* **4/1**[2]	97
000-	**5**	*3 1/4*	**Hogmaneigh (IRE)**[194] 6039 5-9-4 **102**........ SaleemGolam 3 (S C Williams) *t.k.h early: trckd ldrs: drvn to challenege over 1f out: wknd ins fnl f* **13/2**	91
006-	**6**	*4*	**Elhamri**[172] 6541 4-8-6 **90**........ ChrisCatlin 4 (S Kirk) *led principal gp on stands' side: rdn 2f out: wknd fnl f* **12/1**	65
006-	**7**	*1/2*	**Dazed And Amazed**[187] 6197 4-8-8 **92**........ RichardHughes 8 (R Hannon) *chsd ldrs: rdn 2f out: wknd over 1f out* **18/1**	65
00-1	**8**	*2 3/4*	**Conquest (IRE)**[34] 907 4-9-4 **102**........(v) JimmyFortune 6 (W J Haggas) *lw: plld hrd in tch: shkn up 2f out: little rspnse* **6/1**[3]	65
10-3	**9**	*3 1/2*	**Stoneacre Lad (IRE)**[34] 907 5-8-11 **95**........(b) LPKeniry 9 (Peter Grayson) *sn outpcd* **10/1**	45

62.24 secs (0.84) **Going Correction** +0.25s/f (Good) — **9** Ran SP% **118.0**
Speed ratings (Par 109): **103,102,100,99,94 88,87,82,77**
CSF £60.16 CT £346.42 TOTE £3.10: £1.30, £5.70, £3.00; EX 54.10.

Owner J J Byrne **Bred** Mrs R D Peacock **Trained** Kingston Warren, Oxon

FOCUS

A useful sprint handicap. The winner was always in control and is a smart performer now. The runner-up lends slight doubts to the form.

NOTEBOOK

Oldjoesaid ◆, is with a trainer who has won this contest twice in recent years, perhaps most notably with subsequent Nunthorpe winner Kyllachy, and although the son of Royal Applause may not go on to reach those heights, he could develop into a Pattern-class performer. Having just the ninth start of his career, he tracked King Orchisios wide of the rest for the first couple of furlongs and showed a nice change of pace to lead a furlong out. He handles most ground, has an uncomplicated way of racing and looks a sprinter to keep onside. (op 9-4 tchd 5-2 in a place)

The Trader(IRE) is used to plying his trade at a higher level and looked potentially interesting on this first run in a handicap in almost seven years. There were few going better at halfway and having been switched to the outside, he looked set to claim the winner, but as has often been the case, he was unable to go by. He has not won enough for a horse of his ability, but evidently still has the ability. (op 20-1)

Fullandby(IRE) remains 4lb higher than when last winning, but doesn't mind some cut in the ground and it was no surprise to see him run well. He usually needs a run, so this was a good start. (op 12-1)

King Orchisios(IRE) gave the winner a nice tow towards the centre of the track and had every chance, but could just keep on at the one pace once headed. (op 11-2)

Hogmaneigh(IRE) struggled a bit last season after winning the 'Dash' at Epsom on Derby Day and could make no impact when upped markedly in grade on his final start last season in the Prix de l'Abbaye. He would have needed this run. (op 15-2 tchd 8-1)

Elhamri took them along in the main group, but needs a sound surface and will soon become of interest, as he is becoming well handicapped. (op 16-1)

Conquest(IRE) has always been very talented, as his victory in the 2006 Gimcrack showed, but with that talent he brings a certain level of temperament and it took a first-time visor to get him back to winning ways in a minor Listed event at Lingfield on his seasonal reappearance. His one previous run in a handicap ended disappointingly and, having refused to settle, he decided he did not fancy it once asked for his effort. He is hardly a horse to follow. Official explanation: jockey said gelding ran too free (op 4-1)

1443 DUBAI DUTY FREE GOLF WORLD CUP CONDITIONS STKS — 1m 2f 6y

3:15 (3:15) (Class 3) 3-Y-0

£6,854 (£2,052; £1,026; £513; £256; £128) **Stalls** Centre

Form				RPR
222-	**1**		**Unnefer (FR)**[225] 5161 3-8-13 94........ TedDurcan 4 (H R A Cecil) *trckd ldrs: wnt 2nd 4f out: chal over 2f out tl slt advantage appr fnl f: styd on strly and a jst gng best* **9/2**[2]	109
43-1	**2**	*nk*	**Bouguereau**[24] 1014 3-8-13 104........ AlanMunro 5 (P W Chapple-Hyam) *lw: led: rdn whn strly chal fr over 2f out: narrowly hdd appr fnl f: styd on gamely but a jst hld* **11/4**[1]	108
61-	**3**	*10*	**Patkai (IRE)**[191] 6107 3-8-13 0........ RyanMoore 2 (Sir Michael Stoute) *hld up in rr but in tch: pushed along 3f out: styd on fr 2f out: gng on ins fnl f but nvr a threat to ldng duo* **5/1**[3]	88+
1-	**4**	*3 1/2*	**Staying On (IRE)**[180] 6358 3-8-13 88........ SaleemGolam 1 (W R Swinburn) *chsd ldr: t.k.h: lost 2nd 4f out: wknd over 2f out* **12/1**	81
351-	**5**	*9*	**Mountain Pride (IRE)**[185] 6248 3-8-13 84........ LDettori 7 (J L Dunlop) *lw: in rr: hdwy on outside to chse ldrs 4f out: rdn 3f out and sn wknd* **11/4**[1]	63
210-	**6**	*2 1/2*	**Better Hand (IRE)**[244] 4598 3-8-13 99........ ChrisCatlin 3 (M R Channon) *a towards rr* **13/2**	58
01-4	**7**	*3 1/2*	**Straight And Level (CAN)**[44] 799 3-8-13 77........ DaneO'Neill 6 (Miss Jo Crowley) *in tch: rdn 4f out: wknd 3f out* **50/1**	51

2m 11.24s (2.44) **Going Correction** +0.40s/f (Good) — **7** Ran SP% **111.2**
Speed ratings (Par 102): **106,105,97,94,87 85,82**
CSF £16.28 TOTE £5.30: £2.70, £2.00; EX 16.60.

Owner Niarchos Family **Bred** S Niarchos **Trained** Newmarket, Suffolk

FOCUS

A race that has produced two Epsom Classic winners over the past eight years - Oath, second in this race in 1999 before winning the Derby, and Oaks winner Light Shift a year ago (both trained by Henry Cecil) and it was encouraging to see that a few of these hold Dante entries. The time was quicker than both of the fillies' maidens over the same distance. The form is tricky to pin down, but the first two were big improvers and finished clear.

NOTEBOOK

Unnefer(FR), representing the connections of last year's victor Light Shift, stepped up on his two-year-old form to get the better of Bouguereau. He lacks the potential to develop into a serious Classic contender but posted several fair efforts at two, notably when second to Raven's Pass in an Ascot Listed event, and would be worthy of his place in something like the Dee Stakes at Chester next month - Cecil won that race with Oath en route to Epsom. (tchd 5-1)

Bouguereau, whose best form as a juvenile came when fourth in a 1m Listed race at Deauville, broke his maiden at the fourth attempt when upped to 1m2f at Pontefract on his reappearance and looked well worth his place in this better contest, having won so easily. The Italian Derby had been cited as his big target and he ran really well in second, attempting to make all and battling on gamely right the way to the line. He ended up well clear of the remainder and is evidently still progressing. (op 6-4 tchd 3-1 in a place)

Patkai(IRE), from the well-known family of Islington and Greek Dance, seemed to appreciate the ease in the ground when winning his maiden at the second attempt in October and the step up to middle distances this season was always going to coax improvement. A Dante entrant, on this evidence he is going to fall short of Group-race level, this season at least, as he could keep on at only one pace back in third, having taken an age to pick up. He was not given a hard time, though, and it would be no surprise if he took the handicap route, with the step up to 1m4f and perhaps further likely to suit. (op 11-2 tchd 9-2)

Staying On(IRE) is bred to appreciate this trip and more on the dam's side of the pedigree, although his sire is more about speed. He faced a much stiffer task than when winning at Wolverhampton on his sole start at two and on this evidence he will find life easier in handicaps. (op 16-1)

Mountain Pride(IRE), whose trainer has taken this race twice in recent times, notably with Derby third Let The Lion Roar, improved for the step up to 1m when winning an ordinary Leicester maiden last backend and the son of High Chaparral looked open to further improvement as a three-year-old. Backed as though a big run was expected, he moved into a challenging position rounding for home, but carried his head quite high under pressure and dropped out tamely inside the final two furlongs. He is evidently thought to be capable of a good deal better and perhaps there was something amiss. (op 7-2 tchd 5-2)

Better Hand(IRE), a disappointment in the Washington Singer at this course on his final start at two, had shown useful form in winning a Sandown maiden, but he produced little on this seasonal return. He has plenty to prove. (op 11-1)

1444 ROBERT SANGSTER MEMORIAL MAIDEN FILLIES' STKS (DIV II) — 1m 2f 6y

3:50 (3:50) (Class 4) 3-Y-0 — **£5,342** (£1,589; £794; £396) **Stalls** Centre

Form				RPR
543-	**1**		**Burn The Breeze (IRE)**[198] 5912 3-9-0 75........ TedDurcan 9 (H R A Cecil) *lw: mde all: shkn up over 2f out: qcknd over 1f out: readily* **3/1**[2]	82
3-	**2**	*1 1/4*	**Changing Skies (IRE)**[190] 6127 3-9-0 0........ LDettori 8 (B J Meehan) *lw: sn chsng wnr: rdn over 2f out: no ch w wnr fnl f but r.o wl to hold clr 2nd* **15/8**[1]	79
5-	**3**	*1 1/4*	**Arthur's Girl**[186] 6225 3-9-0 0........ JimmyFortune 10 (G Wragg) *chsd ldrs in 3rd thrght: one pce fnl 2f* **7/1**	77
	4	*2 1/2*	**Dolly Penrose** 3-9-0 0........ EdwardCreighton 4 (M R Channon) *w'like: towards rr: rdn and styd on fr 2f out: chsd ldng trio fnl f but nvr any ch* **33/1**	72
	5	*1 1/4*	**Gravitation** 3-9-0 0........ AlanMunro 6 (W Jarvis) *w'like: bit bkwd: chsd ldrs: rdn 3f out: wknd fr 2f out* **20/1**	69
4-	**6**	*1 1/2*	**Belotto (IRE)**[153] 6849 3-9-0 0........ SteveDrowne 3 (R Charlton) *t.k.h in rr: rdn and sme prog fr over 2f out: nvr in contention* **11/1**	66
	7	*1/2*	**Pure Song** 3-9-0 0........ KerrinMcEvoy 5 (J L Dunlop) *leggy: bit bkwd: stdd towards rr 5f out: sn pushed along and nvr in contention after* **12/1**	65
0-	**8**	*6*	**Certain Promise (USA)**[167] 6648 3-9-0 0........ RyanMoore 1 (Sir Michael Stoute) *chsd ldrs tl wknd fr 3f out* **4/1**[3]	53
60-	**9**	*9*	**Garland**[197] 5949 3-9-0 0........ RichardHughes 2 (R Hannon) *stdd s: t.k.h: a in rr* **28/1**	35

2m 14.25s (5.45) **Going Correction** +0.40s/f (Good) — **9** Ran SP% **119.5**
Speed ratings (Par 97): **94,93,92,90,89 87,87,82,75**
CSF £9.19 TOTE £4.10: £1.50, £1.30, £2.60; EX 9.20.

Owner Bloomsbury Stud **Bred** Bloomsbury Stud **Trained** Newmarket, Suffolk

FOCUS
Much the weaker of the two divisions and connections of beaten favourite Changing Skies will no doubt be disappointed they failed to win, as she finished one place ahead of the winner of the first division on her debut in October. The times confirmed the initial impression. The first three raced in that order throughout.

1445 BRIDGET MAIDEN FILLIES' STKS — 7f (S)
4:25 (4:26) (Class 4) 3-Y-O — £5,828 (£1,734; £866; £432) Stalls High

Form — RPR

1 **Musical Bar (IRE)** 3-9-0 0 .... MichaelHills 2 — 88+
(B W Hills) *unf: scope: mde all: pushed along 2f out: in command thrght fnl f* **5/1**[2]

2 1 1/4 **Bramaputra (IRE)** 3-9-0 0 .... AlanMunro 1 — 81+
(B R Millman) *unf: s.i.s: sn in tch: pushed along 3f out: chsd wnr ins fnl 2f: styd on ins fnl f but a readily hld* **8/1**

3 1 1/2 **Rio Guru (IRE)** 3-9-0 0 .... ChrisCatlin 3 — 77
(M R Channon) *unf: chsd ldrs: rdn over 2f out: styd on to go 3rd fnl f but a hld by ldng duo* **16/1**

4 2 1/4 **Badweia (USA)** 3-9-0 0 .... RHills 7 — 71+
(J L Dunlop) *w'like: atheltic: in tch: pushed along and sme hdwy over 2f out: sn one pce* **7/2**[1]

5 1 **Sir Kyffin's Folly** 3-9-0 0 .... RichardThomas 5 — 68
(J A Geake) *unf: in rr: sn pushed along: styd on u.p fnl 2f but nvr in contention* **33/1**

6 2 1/2 **Profitability (USA)** 3-9-0 0 .... JimmyFortune 4 — 64+
(J H M Gosden) *w'like: scope: in tch: shkn up 1/2-way: n.d after* **7/2**[1]

7 2 1/2 **Travelling Light (USA)** 3-9-0 0 .... SteveDrowne 8 — 54
(R Charlton) *w'like: scope: in rr: pushed along and sme hdwy 1/2-way: nvr in contention* **10/1**

8 1 **Priti Fabulous (IRE)** 3-9-0 0 .... JamieSpencer 10 — 52
(W J Haggas) *w'like: scope: a towards rr* **11/2**[3]

9 1 1/4 **Dhahab (USA)** 3-8-9 0 .... AhmedAjtebi(5) 11 — 48
(C E Brittain) *leggy: chsd ldrs: hrd rdn over 2f out: sn edgd rt and wknd* **20/1**

10 16 **Krasavitsa** 3-9-0 0 .... EddieAhern 9 — 5
(J L Dunlop) *leggy: angular: chsd ldrs to 1/2-way* **16/1**

11 7 **True And Fair (IRE)** 3-9-0 0 .... RichardKingscote 12 — —
(Tom Dascombe) *w'like: tall: bit bkwd: chsd ldrs over 3f* **16/1**

1m 27.5s (1.80) **Going Correction** +0.25s/f (Good) — **11** Ran SP% **122.0**
Speed ratings (Par 97): **99,97,95,93,92 89,86,85,83,65 57**
CSF £46.70 TOTE £5.10: £1.60, £3.30, £5.60; EX 50.10.
Owner Martin S Schwartz **Bred** Rathbarry Stud **Trained** Lambourn, Berks

FOCUS
A fair maiden likely to produce winners, although the form is guessy as the race was confined to unraced fillies.

1446 PETER SMITH MEMORIAL MAIDEN STKS — 1m 3f 5y
4:55 (5:00) (Class 4) 3-Y-O — £5,828 (£1,734; £866; £432) Stalls Centre

Form — RPR

62- 1 **Tighnabruaich (IRE)**[161] 6740 3-9-3 0 .... MichaelHills 9 — 88
(M A Jarvis) *hld up in rr: drvn along 3f out: hdwy over 2f out: r.o to ld appr fnl f: kpt on wl* **4/1**[2]

5- 2 1/2 **Manyriverstocross (IRE)**[198] 5919 3-9-3 0 .... JamieSpencer 8 — 87
(A King) *chsd ldrs in 3rd: rdn 3f out: styd on u.p to chse wnr fnl f: gng on cl home but a jst hld* **7/1**[3]

2 3 2 1/2 **Art Trend (IRE)**[13] 1221 3-9-3 0 .... AlanMunro 5 — 83
(P W Chapple-Hyam) *lw: sn led: rdn over 2f out: hdd appr fnl f: no ex ins fnl f* **8/1**

0- 4 11 **Houghton (IRE)**[218] 5361 3-9-3 0 .... RyanMoore 2 — 64
(Sir Michael Stoute) *chsd ldrs: pushed along 3f out: no imp: wknd 2f out* **2/1**[1]

0- 5 7 **Dalhaan (USA)**[258] 4151 3-9-3 0 .... RHills 6 — 52
(J L Dunlop) *bit bkwd: hld up in rr: hdwy to chse ldrs over 2f out: wknd sn after* **16/1**

0- 6 3/4 **Ballisodare**[174] 6494 3-9-3 0 .... JimmyFortune 1 — 51
(P W Chapple-Hyam) *chsd ldrs: rdn 3f out: sn wknd* **25/1**

3 7 1 1/4 **Deer Daylami (IRE)**[50] 727 3-9-3 0 .... EdwardCreighton 10 — 49
(M R Channon) *rdn 4f out: a in rr* **7/1**[3]

0- 8 1 3/4 **Eddie Dowling**[174] 6493 3-9-3 0 .... DarryllHolland 7 — 46
(M R Channon) *in rr but in tch: rdn over 4f out: sn wknd* **66/1**

2m 28.12s (6.92) **Going Correction** +0.40s/f (Good) — **8** Ran SP% **100.7**
Speed ratings (Par 100): **90,89,87,79,74 74,73,72**
CSF £23.94 TOTE £4.70: £1.40, £1.70, £2.00; EX 30.60 Place 6 £32.65, Place 5 £18.68..
Owner Thomas Barr **Bred** Gerrardstown House Stud **Trained** Newmarket, Suffolk
■ Nemo Spirit (9/2, uns rdr at s) & In Close (22/1, ref to enter stalls) were withdrawn. R4 applies, deduct 15p in the £.

FOCUS
A maiden that often produces its share of winners, with St Leger hero Millenary and Derby fourth Hala Bek the most high-profile victors in recent years. This did not look a strong renewal pre-race but has been rated slightly positively.
Eddie Dowling Official explanation: jockey said gelding hung left
T/Jkpt: Not won. T/Plt: £92.80 to a £1 stake. Pool: £62,705.73. 492.75 winning tickets. T/Qpdt: £22.80 to a £1 stake. Pool: £4,424.50. 143.60 winning tickets. ST

THIRSK (L-H)
Friday, April 18

OFFICIAL GOING: Good to soft (7.8)
The ground was described as 'mainly dead'.
Wind: fresh half-against Weather: overcast, breezy and cold

1447 E B F HABTON NOVICE STKS — 5f
2:00 (2:00) (Class 4) 2-Y-O — £5,180 (£1,541; £770; £384) Stalls High

Form — RPR

1 1 **Bahamian Babe**[14] 1183 2-8-9 0 .... HayleyTurner 10 — 78
(M L W Bell) *mde all: rdn over 1f out: qcknd clr ent fnl f: hung bdly lft: kpt on* **4/6**[1]

61 2 1/2 **Gone Hunting**[13] 1214 2-8-7 0 .... JackDean(7) 6 — 81
(W G M Turner) *trckd ldrs: pushed along 2f out: swtchd lft and hdwy over 1f out: sn rdn and styd on wl fnl f* **15/2**[3]

3 nse **Lord Shanakill (USA)** 2-8-12 0 .... FergusSweeney 2 — 82+
(K R Burke) *chsd ldrs on outer: rdn and edgd lft over 1f out: kpt on u.p ins fnl f* **20/1**

4 2 1/2 **Majuba (USA)** 2-8-12 0 .... NCallan 1 — 74+
(K A Ryan) *s.i.s and bhd: swtchd rt after 1f: smooth hdwy to trck ldrs over 2f out: swtchd lft and rdn to chal over 1f out: wknd ent fnl f* **6/1**[2]

5 4 1/2 **Tagula Sunset (IRE)** 2-8-8 0 ow1 .... MickyFenton 5 — 50
(P T Midgley) *s.i.s and bhd: hdwy wl over 1f out: kpt on ins fnl f: nrst fin* **28/1**

01 6 1/2 **Saxford**[13] 1220 2-8-12 0 .... KristinStubbs(7) 3 — 59
(Mrs L Stubbs) *cl up: rdn along 2f out: wknd over 1f out* **12/1**

7 6 **Pokfulham (IRE)** 2-8-12 0 .... DavidAllan 7 — 30
(T D Easterby) *sn outpcd and bhd* **22/1**

6 8 4 **Oriental Rose**[13] 1220 2-8-7 0 .... AndrewElliott 4 — 11
(G M Moore) *prom: rdn along after 1f: sn lost pl and bhd* **33/1**

3 9 6 **Marygate (IRE)**[6] 1324 2-8-7 0 .... TWilliams 8 — —
(M Brittain) *cl up: rdn along 2f out: sn wknd* **10/1**

64.06 secs (4.46) **Going Correction** +0.75s/f (Yiel) — **9** Ran SP% **118.3**
Speed ratings (Par 94): **94,93,93,89,81 81,71,65,55**
CSF £6.04 TOTE £1.70: £1.10, £2.50, £4.30; EX 7.40.
Owner Mrs P D Gray And H J P Farr **Bred** Mrs P D Gray And H Farr **Trained** Newmarket, Suffolk

FOCUS
It is hard to rate the form too highly given the slow time and the first two having already posted figures in the 70s. The third and fourth may prove the best prospects from the race.

NOTEBOOK
Bahamian Babe probably did not have to improve on her debut Fibresand win to follow up. She had the advantage of the stands' rail for most of the race, quickened up well and appeared to put the race to bed from a furlong out, but she hung left in the closing stages and things got a bit tight towards the finish. She would be far from sure to confirm the form with the newcomers in third and fourth if they meet again. (op 5-6 tchd 10-11 in a place)
Gone Hunting, another who had the benefit of previous racing experience having won at Lingfield last time, stayed on well late but could not quite get to the winner. He should get another furlong, but in the short term he may well find others improving past him. (op 8-1 tchd 9-1)
Lord Shanakill(USA), who cost $110,000, is by Breeders' Cup Sprint winner Speightstown out of an unraced half-sister to Spanish Fern, a top-class dual 7f winner in the UK and later winner of the 1m1f Grade 1 Yellow Ribbon Stakes in the US. He was making his debut at a realistic level but was unfancied in the market. He ran well from a poor draw and should not be long in winning. (op 16-1)
Majuba(USA), who cost $110,000, is a half-brother to Preferred Yield, a triple sprint winner, including on turf, in the US. He had the worst of the draw but was switched to race near the favoured stands' rail. He seemed to get tired in the testing ground late on but shaped with promise and should come on for the run. (tchd 5-1)
Tagula Sunset(IRE), a cheap purchase, took a while to get the hang of what was required but she was staying on at the finish. (op 20-1)
Saxford, weak in the market, had plenty to do under his penalty and found the task beyond him. (op 9-1)

1448 ROSEDALE H'CAP — 1m
2:30 (2:30) (Class 5) (0-75,80) 3-Y-O — £3,885 (£1,156; £577; £288) Stalls Low

Form — RPR

60-0 1 **Always Brave**[13] 1208 3-8-8 64 .... RobertWinston 11 — 71
(M Johnston) *chsd ldrs: pushed along 3f out: swtchd lft and hdwy 2f out: rdn on inner to ld ent fnl f: sn drvn and edgd rt: hld on* **20/1**

35- 2 1/2 **Marning Star**[227] 5109 3-9-2 72 .... SilvestreDeSousa 9 — 78
(D Nicholls) *chsd ldng pair: hdwy 3f out: rdn to chal 2f out and sn ev ch tl drvn ins fnl f and no ex towards fin* **14/1**

065- 3 nk **Society Venue**[199] 5883 3-9-0 70 .... PaulHanagan 10 — 75
(Jedd O'Keeffe) *hld up towards rr: gd hdwy on outer over 2f out: rdn to chse ldrs over 1f out: styd on u.p ins fnl f* **16/1**

0-23 4 3/4 **Cathedral Walk (USA)**[42] 826 3-9-2 72 .... AndrewElliott 6 — 75
(K R Burke) *cl up: led over 2f out and sn rdn: drvn and hdd ent fnl f: hld whn n.m.r towards fin* **16/1**

1-2 5 1 1/2 **My Mate Max**[99] 116 3-9-0 73 .... RussellKennemore(3) 4 — 76+
(R Hollinshead) *hld up in rr: hdwy over 2f out and sn rdn along: edgd lft over 1f out: styd on ins fnl f: nrst fin* **14/1**

540- 6 1 1/4 **Morocchius (USA)**[177] 6436 3-9-0 70 .... PaulMulrennan 2 — 67
(Miss J A Camacho) *hld up in rr: stdy hdwy over 2f out: rdn and n.m.r wl over 1f out: kpt on same pce* **40/1**

0-1 7 2 1/2 **Nortune (USA)**[26] 980 3-9-3 73 .... TomEaves 8 — 64
(B Smart) *trckd ldrs: effrt 3f out: sn rdn and wknd over 1f out* **9/1**[2]

4500 8 1 3/4 **Natural Rhythm (IRE)**[3] 1389 3-8-1 60 .... AndrewMullen(3) 5 — 47
(Mrs R A Carr) *in rr: hdwy whn n.m.r 2f out: sn rdn and kpt on ins fnl f: nt rch ldrs* **28/1**

40-0 9 3/4 **Zabougg**[25] 991 3-8-10 66 .... TonyHamilton 14 — 52
(D W Barker) *hld up in tch: hdwy wl over 2f out: rdn and wknd wl over 1f out* **22/1**

5-31 10 nse **Centenerola (USA)**[7] 1302 3-9-10 80 6ex .... MartinDwyer 12 — 65
(B W Hills) *towards rr: rdn along on outer over 2f out: n.d* **5/4**[1]

510- 11 1 **Writingonthewall (IRE)**[189] 6154 3-9-4 74 .... HayleyTurner 13 — 57
(M L W Bell) *stdd s: hld up in rr: hdwy whn n.m.r 2f out: nvr a factor* **11/1**[3]

1 12 9 **So Sublime**[87] 257 3-8-10 66 .... NCallan 1 — 28
(M C Chapman) *led: rdn along over 2f out: sn hdd & wknd* **14/1**

410- 13 1/2 **Coffee Cup (IRE)**[225] 5153 3-8-7 63 .... DaleGibson 7 — 24
(G A Swinbank) *s.i.s: a in rr* **12/1**

320- 14 17 **Daring Dream (GER)**[179] 6379 3-9-4 74 .... DavidAllan 3 — —
(T D Easterby) *chsd ldrs on inner: rdn along 3f out: sn wknd* **14/1**

1m 44.89s (4.79) **Going Correction** +0.65s/f (Yiel) — **14** Ran SP% **123.9**
Speed ratings (Par 98): **102,101,101,100,98 97,95,93,92,92 91,82,82,65**
CSF £274.04 CT £4560.61 TOTE £21.20: £4.00, £3.50, £6.20; EX 464.70.
Owner Always Trying Partnership V **Bred** D J G Murray Smith **Trained** Middleham Moor, N Yorks

FOCUS
Modest handicap form, particularly with the well-in favourite disappointing. The form has been rated around the fourth and sixth.
My Mate Max Official explanation: jockey said gelding ran green around the bend
Centenerola(USA) Official explanation: trainer's rep had no explanation for the poor form shown

1449 BARRIE SULLIVAN H'CAP — 1m
3:05 (3:05) (Class 5) (0-70,71) 4-Y-O+ — £3,885 (£1,156; £577; £288) Stalls Low

Form — RPR

5-12 1 **Blue Spinnaker (IRE)**[2] 1394 9-9-6 71 6ex .... PaulMulrennan 13 — 89+
(M W Easterby) *hld up in rr: hdwy on outer over 3f out: led over 1f out: drew clr: v readily* **13/8**[1]

054- 2 6 **Surwaki (USA)**[236] 4850 6-9-2 67 .... NCallan 6 — 71
(R M H Cowell) *led 2f: chsd ldr: led over 2f out tl over 1f out: kpt on: no ch w wnr* **14/1**

050- 3 1 1/4 **Hula Ballew**[199] 5885 8-9-4 69 .... PhillipMakin 5 — 73+
(M Dods) *mid-div: hdwy over 2f out: styd on to take 3rd ins fnl f* **12/1**

206- **4** 1 3/4 **Getrah**[167] 6636 4-9-4 69.....(b[1]) GrahamGibbons 18 66
(N Wilson) *in tch: swtchd lft after 1f: hrd rdn and hung lft over 1f out: kpt on same pce* **20/1**

3300 **5** 3/4 **Parkview Love (USA)**[20] 1084 7-8-13 64.....(v) HayleyTurner 12 59
(D Shaw) *chsd ldrs: kpt on same pce fnl 2f* **33/1**

4-02 **6** 3 1/4 **Messiah Garvey**[14] 1188 4-8-11 62..... SilvestreDeSousa 3 50
(D Nicholls) *chsd ldrs: wknd over 1f out* **13/2**[2]

0-10 **7** 2 1/4 **Nok Twice (IRE)**[13] 1217 7-9-0 65..... DanielTudhope 7 48
(D Carroll) *hld up in rr: hdwy on outer 2f out: nvr nr ldrs* **20/1**

105- **8** 2 **Dee Jay Wells**[229] 4287 4-8-11 62.....(t) TonyHamilton 14 40
(D W Thompson) *prom: wknd fnl 2f* **33/1**

26-4 **9** hd **Poppy's Rose**[14] 1188 4-8-13 64..... RoystonFfrench 15 42
(I W McInnes) *in rr: styd on fnl 2f: nvr nr ldrs* **14/1**

060- **10** 3 **Tough Love**[211] 5559 9-8-12 63.....(p) DavidAllan 10 34
(T D Easterby) *in rr: sme hdwy over 2f out: nvr on terms* **14/1**

2213 **11** 1 1/4 **Supercast (IRE)**[43] 811 5-9-2 67..... SamHitchcott 2 35
(N J Vaughan) *prom: effrt over 2f out: wknd over 1f out* **8/1**[3]

50-0 **12** 3/4 **Kirkby's Treasure**[25] 990 10-8-12 63..... RobertWinston 1 29
(G A Swinbank) *s.i.s: hdwy on outer 2f out: nvr on terms* **12/1**

6600 **13** 2 **King Of The Moors (USA)**[13] 1217 5-8-8 66..... DeanHeslop(7) 11 28
(T D Barron) *in rr and sn drvn along: hung lft 2f out* **33/1**

140/ **14** 1 1/4 **Apres Ski (IRE)**[548] 6054 5-8-13 64..... MickyFenton 4 23
(J F Coupland) *swvd rt s: t.k.h: hdwy to ld after 2f: hdd over 2f out: wkng whn hmpd over 2f out* **33/1**

404- **15** 5 **Marieschi (USA)**[263] 4018 4-8-11 62..... PaulHanagan 16 9
(R F Fisher) *mid-div on outer: lost pl 3f out* **40/1**

0-01 **16** 3/4 **Ghafeer (USA)**[16] 1135 4-8-11 62.....(p) TomEaves 9 7
(B Ellison) *prom: lost pl over 2f out* **14/1**

3406 **17** 8 **Louisiade (IRE)**[10] 1260 7-8-11 65.....(p) RussellKennemore(3) 17 —
(M C Chapman) *mid-div: reminders bnd over 4f out: lost pl over 2f out* **33/1**

030- **18** 13 **Mujma**[299] 2915 4-9-2 67..... DarrenWilliams 8 —
(S Parr) *hld up in rr: brief effrt 3f out: sn lost pl: bhd whn eased over 1f out* **50/1**

1m 43.85s (3.75) **Going Correction** +0.65s/f (Yiel) **18 Ran SP% 133.2**
Speed ratings (Par 103): **107,101,99,98,97 94,91,89,89,86 85,84,82,81,76 75,67,54**
CSF £25.56 CT £247.99 TOTE £2.30: £1.10, £4.00, £2.60, £3.30; EX 38.50.
Owner G Sparkes G Hart S Curtis & T Dewhirst **Bred** M3 Elevage And Haras D'Etreham **Trained** Sheriff Hutton, N Yorks Supercast subs. disq. (prohibited substance); Vaughan fined £1,250

FOCUS
They went a good gallop here and that suited the favourite, who ended up winning with plenty in hand. He looks back to last year's best at least.
Apres Ski(IRE) Official explanation: jockey said gelding ran too free

1450 HAWNBY H'CAP 7f
3:40 (3:40) (Class 5) (0-75,74) 4-Y-0+ **£3,885** (£1,156; £577; £288) **Stalls** Low

Form RPR

41-2 **1** **Spinning**[25] 992 5-8-11 72.....(b) NeilBrown(5) 8 84
(T D Barron) *stdd s: hld up and bhd: hdwy over 2f out: rdn and n.m.r over 1f out: styd on strly ins fnl f to ld last 50yds* **7/2**[1]

-132 **2** 1 1/4 **Yes One (IRE)**[23] 1030 4-9-3 73..... NCallan 16 82+
(K A Ryan) *chsd ldrs: hdwy over 2f out: rdn to ld 1f out: hung rt ins fnl f: hdd and nt qckn last 50yds* **17/2**[3]

60-0 **3** 3/4 **Violent Velocity (IRE)**[25] 990 5-8-10 66..... GrahamGibbons 15 73
(J J Quinn) *hld up towards rr: gd hdwy on inner 2f out: rdn over 1f out: kpt on ins fnl f* **20/1**

00-5 **4** 3/4 **Hiccups**[20] 1069 8-9-4 74..... TomEaves 7 79
(M Dods) *in tch: hdwy wl over 2f out: rdn to chse ldrs over 1f out: kpt on same pce ins fnl f* **7/1**[2]

0-03 **5** nse **Sands Of Barra (IRE)**[14] 1188 5-8-5 68..... DonnaCaldwell(7) 9 73
(I W McInnes) *chsd ldr: led over 2f out: sn rdn: drvn and hdd 1f out: kpt on same pce* **14/1**

00-4 **6** 2 3/4 **King Harson**[16] 1138 9-8-13 69..... RobertWinston 11 66
(J D Bethell) *chsd ldrs: hdwy over 2f out: rdn and ch over 1f out: drvn and wknd ins fnl f* **10/1**

10-6 **7** 1 1/4 **Gilded Youth**[15] 1174 4-9-2 72..... FergusSweeney 13 66
(H Candy) *hld up towards rr: hdxway over 2f out: sn rdn and kpt on ins fnl f: nt rch ldrs* **14/1**

00-5 **8** shd **Handsome Falcon**[26] 979 4-9-3 73..... PaulHanagan 1 67
(R A Fahey) *in tch on inner: hdwy 2f out: sn rdn and edgd rt over 1f out: wknd ins fnl f* **9/1**

0-00 **9** nk **Bid For Gold**[13] 1217 4-8-11 67.....(b[1]) PaulMulrennan 3 60
(Jedd O'Keeffe) *towards rr: hdwy over 2f out: sn rdn and no imp* **25/1**

10-5 **10** 1 1/2 **Chin Wag (IRE)**[25] 990 4-8-4 60..... RoystonFfrench 12 49
(J S Goldie) *hld up towards rr: hdwy over 2f out: swtchd lft and rdn wl over 1f out: n.d* **10/1**

4-00 **11** 1/2 **Osteopathic Remedy (IRE)**[13] 1217 4-9-2 72..... PhillipMakin 14 60
(M Dods) *midfield: hdwy on outer wl over 2f out: rdn and wknd over 1f out* **16/1**

340- **12** 3 3/4 **Kunte Kinteh**[211] 5555 4-8-9 65..... MartinDwyer 2 42
(D Nicholls) *chsd ldng pair: rdn along over 2f out and sn wknd* **14/1**

0-30 **13** 16 **Kabis Amigos**[16] 1138 6-9-0 70.....(t) PaulQuinn 4 4
(D Nicholls) *led: rdn along and hdd over 2f out: grad wknd* **25/1**

01-3 **14** 9 **Maia**[25] 990 4-8-9 65..... SilvestreDeSousa 6 —
(D Nicholls) *midfield whn bdly hmpd bnd over 4f out: sn lost pl and bhd: eased wl over 2f out* **7/1**[2]

364 **P** **Bartercard (USA)**[17] 1125 7-9-0 70..... MickyFenton 10 —
(Stef Liddiard) *midfield whn hung lft bnd over 4f out: sn lost action and p.u 3f out: struck into* **11/1**

1m 31.18s (3.98) **Going Correction** +0.65s/f (Yiel) **15 Ran SP% 132.6**
Speed ratings (Par 103): **103,101,100,99,99 96,95,95,94,93 92,88,69,59,—**
CSF £34.92 CT £564.60 TOTE £4.80: £1.70, £2.60, £8.00; EX 30.30.
Owner Mrs J Hazell **Bred** Cheveley Park Stud **Trained** Maunby, N Yorks
■ Stewards' Enquiry : Paul Quinn two-day ban: careless riding (May 2nd & 5th)

FOCUS
They went a strong gallop here and the winner and third came from well off the pace as the leaders hit the wall. A best-ever figure from Spinning.
Gilded Youth Official explanation: jockey said gelding reared at start
Maia Official explanation: jockey said filly hung right round bottom bend
Bartercard(USA) Official explanation: vet said gelding had been struck into

1451 BETFAIR BETTING AS IT SHOULD BE H'CAP 5f
4:15 (4:15) (Class 4) (0-80,81) 4-Y-0+ **£5,180** (£1,541; £577; £577) **Stalls** High

Form RPR

262 **1** **Stolt (IRE)**[14] 1195 4-8-9 76..... AshleyHamblett(5) 14 84
(N Wilson) *mde all: styd on wl fnl f* **7/1**[3]

2643 **2** 1 1/4 **Guto**[17] 1129 5-8-5 70..... AndrewMullen(3) 15 74
(W J H Ratcliffe) *chsd ldrs: kpt on to take 2nd ins fnl f* **10/1**

0-53 **3** 3/4 **Highland Warrior**[3] 1386 9-8-9 71..... MickyFenton 2 72+
(P T Midgley) *dwlt: hdwy on outer 2f out styd on ins fnl f* **13/2**[2]

06-6 **3** dht **River Thames**[101] 85 5-9-4 80..... PaulMulrennan 12 81+
(K A Ryan) *dwlt: hld up in rr: stdy hdwy over 1f out: shkn up and kpt on ins fnl f* **16/1**

5-11 **5** 1 1/4 **Rebel Duke (IRE)**[7] 1309 4-9-5 81 6ex..... TonyHamilton 7 77
(D W Barker) *chsd ldrs: kpt on same pce fnl f* **9/4**[1]

33-0 **6** 1 **Dakota Rain (IRE)**[15] 1174 6-9-4 80..... TPO'Shea 11 73+
(Jennie Candlish) *in rr: n.m.r over 1f out: kpt on wl ins fnl f* **18/1**

006- **7** nk **Mormeatmic**[342] 1669 5-8-4 66..... DaleGibson 13 58
(M W Easterby) *trckd ldrs: kpt on fnl f* **40/1**

20-4 **8** nk **Coconut Moon**[23] 1021 6-9-4 80..... DavidAllan 10 71
(E J Alston) *chsd wnr: kpt on same pce appr fnl f* **16/1**

40-6 **9** 1/2 **Circuit Dancer (IRE)**[26] 983 8-8-13 75..... SilvestreDeSousa 5 64
(D Nicholls) *mid-div: effrt on outer over 2f out: nvr rchd ldrs* **20/1**

03-0 **10** 1 3/4 **Steelcut**[26] 983 4-8-13 75..... PaulHanagan 4 57+
(R A Fahey) *swtchd rt after s: in rr: styd on fnl f* **7/1**[3]

305- **11** 2 1/4 **Rainbow Fox**[156] 6818 4-8-6 68..... RoystonFfrench 8 42
(R A Fahey) *mid-div: lost pl over 1f out* **18/1**

255- **12** 1/2 **Sea Rover (IRE)**[311] 2534 4-8-7 69..... TWilliams 6 42
(M Brittain) *chsd ldrs: lost pl over 1f out* **10/1**

30-0 **13** 8 **Rasaman (IRE)**[26] 983 4-9-4 80.....(p) NCallan 3 24
(K A Ryan) *w ldrs: lost pl over 1f out* **14/1**

120- **14** 5 **Mandurah (IRE)**[208] 5662 4-8-10 72..... PaulQuinn 1 —
(D Nicholls) *in rr: bhd fnl 2f* **25/1**

62.71 secs (3.11) **Going Correction** +0.75s/f (Yiel) **14 Ran SP% 127.3**
Speed ratings (Par 105): **105,103,101,101,99 98,97,97,96,93 90,89,76,68**
PL: River Thames £2.80, Highland Warrior £1.30; TRI: Stolt/Guto/RT £379.46, S/G/HW£253.35 CSF £78.25 CT £253.35 TOTE £8.30: £2.50, £3.60; EX 73.70.
Owner Dixon, McIntyre, Tobin **Bred** Seamus Phelan **Trained** Flaxton, N Yorks

FOCUS
One for the draw bores, with the stands' rail proving a big advantage and the top two stalls completing an exacta. The winner is rated back to his best and several others shaped better than the bare form.

1452 HAMBLETON INN MEDIAN AUCTION MAIDEN STKS (DIV I) 6f
4:45 (4:45) (Class 5) 3-4-Y-0 **£3,399** (£1,011; £505; £252) **Stalls** High

Form RPR

56-6 **1** **My Kaiser Chief**[23] 1027 3-8-11 62..... AndrewMullen(3) 15 72
(W J H Ratcliffe) *hld up in rr: n.m.r on stands' rail 1/2-way: swtchd lft and hdwy wl over 1f out: rdn and styd on to ld wl ins fnl f* **20/1**

00-6 **2** 2 **Rio Sands**[16] 1155 3-8-11 64..... MichaelJStainton(3) 9 65
(R M Whitaker) *a.p: rdn to ld 2f out: drvn over 1f out: hdd and no ex wl ins fnl f* **14/1**

43-2 **3** nk **Everything**[24] 1019 3-8-9 70..... MickyFenton 1 59+
(P T Midgley) *wnt lft s and bhd: pushed along 1/2-way: swtchd rt and hdwy wl over 1f out: rdn and styd on strly ins fnl f* **6/1**[3]

0-0 **4** 1 **Castlebury (IRE)**[7] 1295 3-9-0 0..... PaulMulrennan 10 61+
(G A Swinbank) *midfield: hdwy 2f out: rdn to chse ldrs over 1f out: kpt on ins fnl f* **33/1**

5 **5** 1 **Leonid Glow**[24] 1019 3-8-2 0..... JohnCavanagh(7) 16 53+
(M Dods) *s.i.s and towards rr: hdwy 1/2-way: swtchd towards outer and ch wl over 1f out: sn rdn and wknd ent fnl f* **11/2**[2]

3- **6** 3/4 **Pay Parade**[349] 1478 3-8-9 0..... RobertWinston 13 50+
(T D Easterby) *midfield: gd hdwy to chse ldrs wl over 1f out: rdn and hung lft ent fnl f: sn one pce* **11/1**

7 2 1/2 **Tangerine Trees** 3-9-0 0..... TomEaves 14 47
(B Smart) *trckd ldrs on stands' rail: effrt over 2f out: sn rdn and no imp appr fnl f* **7/2**[1]

040- **8** nk **Tanley**[158] 6799 3-9-0 61..... SamHitchcott 12 46
(J F Coupland) *led: rdn along over 2f out: sn hdd and grad wknd* **40/1**

3- **9** hd **Portrush Storm**[384] 845 3-8-9 0..... DanielTudhope 4 41
(D Carroll) *prom o0n outer: rdn along over 2f out: sn drvn and grad wknd* **17/2**

0-0 **10** 3 1/2 **Lady Aviator**[29] 953 3-8-9 0..... DavidAllan 2 30
(T D Easterby) *hld up and bhd: hdwy over 2f out: rdn to chse ldrs over 1f out: sn drvn and wknd* **50/1**

002- **11** 2 3/4 **Dolly No Hair**[198] 5901 3-9-0 73..... TonyHamilton 11 26
(D W Barker) *cl up: rdn along 2f out and sn wknd* **8/1**

12 2 3/4 **Fair Fact (IRE)** 3-8-9 0..... TWilliams 8 12
(M Brittain) *nvr bttr than midfield* **25/1**

00 **13** 5 **Saintsylvadene**[24] 1014 3-9-0 0..... GrahamGibbons 7 —
(T D Walford) *chsd ldrs: rdn along and hung lft over 2f out: sn wknd* **33/1**

32 **14** 15 **Orpenella**[17] 1132 3-8-9 0..... NCallan 6 —
(K A Ryan) *in tch towards outer: rdn along over 2f out and sn wknd* **6/1**[3]

345- **15** 4 **First Valentini**[193] 6057 4-9-6 45..... AndrewElliott 3 —
(N Bycroft) *a towards rr* **66/1**

50-0 **P** **Meathop (IRE)**[56] 663 4-9-11 45..... PaulHanagan 5 —
(R F Fisher) *towards rr: sddle slipped and bhd whn p.u 1/2-way* **50/1**

1m 18.55s (5.85) **Going Correction** +0.75s/f (Yiel)
WFA 3 from 4yo 11lb **16 Ran SP% 125.2**
Speed ratings (Par 103): **91,88,87,86,85 84,80,80,80,75 71,68,61,41,36 —**
CSF £268.50 TOTE £29.40: £7.80, £3.50, £2.40; EX 299.80.
Owner Camela Racing Limited **Bred** John Watson **Trained** Wensley, N Yorks

FOCUS
A modest maiden and the slower of the two divisions by 1.07sec. Not straightforward to rate, but this is probably modest form.
Pay Parade Official explanation: jockey said filly ran green in closing stages
Meathop(IRE) Official explanation: jockey said saddle slipped

1453 HAMBLETON INN MEDIAN AUCTION MAIDEN STKS (DIV II) 6f
5:15 (5:16) (Class 5) 3-4-Y-0 **£3,399** (£1,011; £505; £252) **Stalls** High

Form RPR

1 **Hazelrigg (IRE)** 3-9-0 0..... DavidAllan 7 83+
(T D Easterby) *dwlt: racd stands' side: sn trcking ldrs: led 2f out: r.o strly: v readily* **4/1**[2]

53-6 **2** 4 **All In The Red (IRE)**[15] 1162 3-9-0 65..... HayleyTurner 2 70
(Miss Gay Kelleway) *mde most far side: kpt on fnl 2f: no ch w wnr* **11/1**

3 3/4 **Celtic Lynn (IRE)** 3-8-9 0..... PhillipMakin 5 63+
(M Dods) *racd stands' side: mid-div: effrt over 2f out: kpt on fnl f* **16/1**

4 4 **Marchingontogether (IRE)** 3-8-9 0..... DanielTudhope 6 50+
(D Carroll) *racd stands' side: trckd ldrs: edgd lft over 1f out: one pce* **28/1**

5 3 1/4 **Nabeeda** 3-8-7 0 AdamCarter(7) 15 44
(M Brittain) *racd stands' side: w ldrs: hung bdly lft over 2f out: wknd over 1f out* **20/1**

643- 6 1/2 **Capone (IRE)**[160] 6761 3-9-0 72 NCallan 4 43
(Garry Moss) *trckd ldrs far side: chal and hung bdly rt 2f out: sn wknd* **7/1**[3]

5 7 2 **Kai Mer (IRE)**[17] 1132 3-8-9 0 TomEaves 13 31
(Miss J A Camacho) *racd stands' side: mid-div: kpt on fnl 2f: nvr trbld ldrs* **25/1**

8 3/4 **Isabella's Fancy** 3-8-9 0 OscarUrbina 12 29
(J R Fanshawe) *dwlt: racd stands' side: sn chsng ldrs: lost pl over 1f out* **10/1**

5400 9 3 1/4 **Avoncreek**[27] 972 4-9-11 39 DarrenWilliams 16 27
(B P J Baugh) *racd stands' side: trckd ldrs: effrt 2f out: sn wknd* **16/1**

0-0 10 nk **Ursus**[16] 1139 3-8-11 0 AndrewMullen(3) 1 23
(C R Wilson) *racd far side: w ldr: wknd 2f out* **66/1**

11 1 1/4 **Paris Hall** 3-9-0 0 PatrickMathers 10 19
(I W McInnes) *racd stands' side: mid-div: outpcd fnl 2f* **25/1**

00-0 12 9 **Sultan Of The Sand**[41] 837 3-9-0 47 SamHitchcott 11 —
(C C Bealby) *racd stands' side: chsd ldrs: lost pl 2f out* **33/1**

00-6 13 1 1/4 **Madame Rio (IRE)**[25] 993 3-8-9 54 (v[1]) AndrewElliott 8 —
(K R Burke) *led stands' side: hdd 2f out: sn lost pl and bhd* **33/1**

14 3/4 **Stormin Heart (USA)** 3-8-9 0 NeilBrown(5) 9 —
(T D Barron) *racd stands' side: chsd ldrs on outer: lost pl over 2f out* **15/2**

06- 15 shd **Eseej (USA)**[220] 5313 3-9-0 0 MartinDwyer 3 —
(B W Hills) *racd far side: trckd ldrs: effrt 2f out: edgd rt and sn wknd: eased* **15/8**[1]

1m 17.48s (4.78) **Going Correction** +0.75s/f (Yiel)
WFA 3 from 4yo 11lb 15 Ran SP% 131.5
Speed ratings (Par 103): **98,92,91,86,82 81,78,77,73,72 71,59,57,56,56**
CSF £48.35 TOTE £7.10: £2.10, £3.50, £5.00; EX 60.00 Place 6 £883.72, Place 5 £658.48.
Owner Duncan & Sarah Davidson **Bred** Rathbarry Stud **Trained** Great Habton, N Yorks

FOCUS
An ordinary maiden but the quicker of the two divisions by 1.07sec, and the winner won in good style and looks to have a future. The field split in two with four horses electing to race up the far-side rail, and there looked no bias between the two sides.
Isabella's Fancy Official explanation: jockey said filly lost a right-fore shoe
Eseej(USA) Official explanation: trainer's rep had no explanation for the poor form shown
T/Plt: £2,297.30 to a £1 stake. Pool: £50,982.94. 16.20 winning tickets. T/Qpdt: £75.40 to a £1 stake. Pool: £4,386.24. 43.00 winning tickets. JR

YARMOUTH (L-H)
Friday, April 18

OFFICIAL GOING: Good (good to soft in places; 7.5)
Wind: Strong, across Weather: bright and breezy

1454 FIRSTBET.COM ONLINE BLACKJACK ROOM MEDIAN AUCTION MAIDEN STKS 5f 43y
5:05 (5:07) (Class 5) 3-5-Y-O **£2,590** (£770; £385; £192) **Stalls High**

Form RPR

400- 1 **Dragon Flame (IRE)**[172] 6537 5-9-10 54 (v) SebSanders 2 66
(M Quinn) *chsd ldrs: hdwy to ld jst over 1f out: hung lft ins fnl f: r.o strly: comf* **9/1**

2034 2 2 1/4 **Maggie Kate**[14] 1178 3-8-9 63 (p) RobertHavlin 3 49
(R Ingram) *prom: led 2f out: sn rdn: hdd jst over 1f out: nt pce of wnr* **11/2**

3 2 **Steel Mask (IRE)** 3-8-11 0 MarkLawson(3) 1 47
(M Brittain) *s.i.s: hdwy and in tch on outer after 2f: rdn 2f out: kpt on one pce* **14/1**

350- 4 3/4 **Jaconet (USA)**[203] 5780 3-8-9 65 PaulFessey 9 39
(T D Barron) *hld up in tch: rdn over 2f out: styd on steadily u.p fnl f: nvr able to chal* **7/1**

5003 5 1 **Princess Charlmane (IRE)**[23] 1027 5-9-0 43 (t) KellyHarrison(5) 8 39
(C J Teague) *led tl 2f out: sn rdn and wanting to hang lft: fdd fnl f* **14/1**

00-2 6 1/2 **Magical Speedfit (IRE)**[17] 1123 3-9-0 69 (b[1]) JimmyQuinn 6 39
(G G Margarson) *pushed along early: bhd: rdn wl over 2f out: sme late hdwy: nvr on terms* **11/4**[1]

4- 7 5 **Hurricane Harriet**[261] 4077 3-8-9 0 PatCosgrave 5 16
(R M H Cowell) *hld up in tch: rdn over 2f out: no imp* **3/1**[2]

25-2 8 nk **Tugalu (IRE)**[23] 1027 3-9-0 72 (p) CatherineGannon 7 20
(K A Ryan) *pressed ldr tl 1/2-way: sn rdn and wknd* **5/1**[3]

00-6 9 8 **Southwark Newsboy (IRE)**[14] 1194 3-9-0 30 StephenDonohoe 4 —
(Mrs C A Dunnett) *sn rdn along: in tch tl 1/2-way: sn lost tch* **100/1**

62.58 secs (0.38) **Going Correction** +0.05s/f (Good)
WFA 3 from 5yo 10lb 9 Ran SP% 120.5
Speed ratings (Par 103): **98,94,91,90,88 87,79,79,66**
CSF £60.34 TOTE £14.40: £4.50, £1.60, £4.50; EX 147.50.
Owner A Newby **Bred** Denis Hackett **Trained** Newmarket, Suffolk

FOCUS
A weak sprint maiden, although the race could have rated higher on time.

1455 CLIFF HOTEL FOR FINE DINING H'CAP 6f 3y
5:30 (5:33) (Class 6) (0-50,55) 4-Y-0+ **£2,266** (£674; £337; £168) **Stalls High**

Form RPR

-060 1 **Polar Force**[14] 1185 8-8-9 47 DMylonas 12 61
(Mrs C A Dunnett) *chsd ldr on stands' side: pushed along and r.o wl fnl f to ld towards fin* **17/2**

0546 2 1/2 **Imperial Sword**[23] 1024 5-8-8 46 oh1 (b) PaulFessey 10 58
(T D Barron) *in tch on far side: hdwy over 2f out: rdn to ld ins fnl f: hdd and no ex towards fin* **8/1**

4051 3 1 **Welcome Releaf**[10] 1259 5-8-10 55 6ex MarkCoumbe(7) 7 64
(P Leech) *racd in midfield on far side: hdwy and rdn over 2f out: kpt on u.p fnl f* **11/1**

3602 4 hd **Balerno**[11] 1248 9-8-10 48 IanMongan 11 56
(Mrs L J Mongan) *stdd s: hld up in rr on far side gp: hdwy over 2f out: kpt on u.p fnl f: nt rch ldrs* **13/2**[2]

2224 5 2 **Limonia (GER)**[14] 1185 6-8-10 48 PatCosgrave 14 50
(Mike Murphy) *led stands' side trio: led overall over 2f out tl wl over 1f out: sn drvn: fdd ins fnl f* **7/1**[3]

060- 6 1 1/4 **Falmassim**[196] 5966 5-8-10 48 SebSanders 2 46
(Miss J A Camacho) *in tch on far side: hdwy to chse overall ldr 3f out: led wl over 1f out: rdn and hdd ins fnl f: wknd last 100yds* **8/1**

0564 7 nk **Cool Sands (IRE)**[10] 1261 6-8-8 46 oh1 (v) JimmyQuinn 5 56+
(D Shaw) *in tch on far side: hdwy over 2f out: nt clr run over 1f out: nvr able to chal* **6/1**[1]

00-6 8 1 1/2 **Charming Ballet (IRE)**[35] 883 5-8-9 47 SimonWhitworth 1 39
(G L Moore) *hld up towards rr on far side: hdwy over 2f out: chsd ldrs and rdn over 1f out: wknd fnl f* **14/1**

9 nk **Sceilin (IRE)**[167] 6659 4-8-5 46 oh1 KirstyMilczarek(3) 6 37
(Miss D Mountain) *s.i.s: a bhd on far side: sme modest late hdwy* **25/1**

5665 10 1/2 **Gone'N'Dunnett (IRE)**[58] 625 9-8-10 48 (v) CatherineGannon 4 38
(Mrs C A Dunnett) *chsd ldrs on far side: rdn 2f out: wknd jst over 1f out* **10/1**

2010 11 7 **Bahamian Bay**[35] 877 6-8-9 50 ow3 MarkLawson(3) 3 17
(M Brittain) *chsd ldrs on far side: rdn over 2f out: wknd qckly over 1f out* **14/1**

1306 12 6 **Ducal Regancy Red**[14] 1185 4-8-3 46 oh1 KellyHarrison(5) 9 —
(C J Teague) *led on far side for 1f: chsd overall ldr after tl 1/2-way: sn rdn: wknd jst over 2f out* **33/1**

3316 13 2 **Green Pirate**[21] 1061 6-8-10 48 (p) LiamJones 13 —
(C R Dore) *s.i.s: a bhd: hung bdly rt to stands' side over 3f out: nvr on terms* **10/1**

5044 14 3 1/4 **Orchestration (IRE)**[27] 972 7-8-8 46 oh1 (v) PaulEddery 15 —
(Garry Moss) *a bhd on stands' side: no ch and eased ins fnl f* **33/1**

0-06 15 2 **Oh Gracious Me (IRE)**[37] 858 4-8-12 50 (b) StephenDonohoe 8 —
(P A Blockley) *s.i.s: sn rcvrd: led far side and overall after 1f: hdd over 2f out: sn wknd: eased ins fnl f* **20/1**

1m 13.35s (-1.05) **Going Correction** +0.05s/f (Good) 15 Ran SP% 127.2
Speed ratings (Par 101): **109,108,107,106,104 102,102,100,99,98 89,81,78,74,71**
CSF £75.59 CT £772.75 TOTE £11.60: £2.90, £2.70, £4.40; EX 66.70.
Owner Mrs Christine Dunnett **Bred** Cheveley Park Stud Ltd **Trained** Hingham, Norfolk

FOCUS
A very moderate sprint handicap but the form seems sound enough. They raced all over the place, but there seemed no great bias.
Orchestration(IRE) Official explanation: jockey said gelding moved poorly

1456 GREAT YARMOUTH GLASS H'CAP 1m 3y
6:05 (6:05) (Class 3) (0-90,87) 4-Y-0+ **£6,854** (£2,052; £1,026; £513; £256; £128) **Stalls Low**

Form RPR

-111 1 **Mia's Boy**[20] 1067 4-9-4 87 JimmyQuinn 1 95+
(C A Dwyer) *stdd s: hld up and bhd: hdwy 3f out: rdn to chal over 1f out: hrd drvn to ld last 100yds: r.o wl* **10/11**[1]

0236 2 shd **Lord Theo**[9] 1273 4-8-6 75 JamesDoyle 7 83
(N P Littmoden) *hld up in tch: hdwy to chse ldr 3f out: rdn to ld wl over 1f out: sn hrd pressed: hdd last 100yds: kpt on jst hld* **14/1**

0- 3 3 **Northern Jem**[202] 5805 4-9-0 83 SebSanders 3 84
(G G Margarson) *hld up in last pair: hdwy 3f out: chsd ldng pair over 1f out: kpt on same pce u.p fnl f* **13/2**[3]

56-2 4 2 1/2 **Montrachet**[8] 1287 4-8-3 75 LukeMorris(3) 5 70
(M L W Bell) *in tch in midfield tl lost pl over 3f out: bhd and rdn 3f out: hdwy u.p over 1f out: wnt 4th ins fnl f: nvr trbld ldrs* **4/1**[2]

004- 5 2 3/4 **Rain Stops Play (IRE)**[156] 6816 6-8-4 73 LiamJones 6 62
(M Quinn) *led tl 2f out: rdn and hdd wl over 1f out: wknd fnl f* **14/1**

-000 6 2 1/2 **Moody Tunes**[19] 1105 5-8-12 81 FergusSweeney 2 64
(K R Burke) *rn wout declared tongue strap: chsd ldr for 2f out: lost pl over 3f out: rdn over 2f out: no ch last 2f* **10/1**

000- 7 11 **Glencalvie (IRE)**[192] 6081 7-8-4 73 (p) JoeFanning 4 31
(J Akehurst) *stdd s: plld hrd: chsd ldr after 2f tl 3f out: sn wknd* **25/1**

1m 39.38s (-1.22) **Going Correction** +0.05s/f (Good) 7 Ran SP% 112.0
Speed ratings (Par 107): **108,107,104,102,99 97,86**
CSF £14.99 TOTE £1.90: £1.40, £6.60; EX 20.10.
Owner Iraj Parvizi **Bred** Sir Eric Parker **Trained** Burrough Green, Cambs

FOCUS
An ordinary handicap for the grade, but Mia's Boy is probably a little better than the bare form suggests. The race has been rated around the second and third. The pace was just modest, yet the winning time was 0.67 seconds quicker than the following conditions event.

NOTEBOOK
Mia's Boy ◆ only narrowly defied an 8lb rise in the weights for an impressive success at Doncaster to complete the four-timer, but he is probably better than the bare results. He was on and off the bridle pretty much throughout and was hardly ideally placed considering the ordinary gallop, but he eventually made headway on the outside of horses quite easily and battled on well to get the better of the persistent Lord Theo, who had the benefit of the rail. He can do even better in a stronger-run race and might even stay a little further. His trainer is eyeing a Listed handicap at York. (op 6-5 tchd 5-6)
Lord Theo, due to be dropped 1lb, benefited from the drop back in trip after going off too fast over 1m3f at Kempton on his previous start and he battled on well when challenged. (tchd 16-1)
Northern Jem ran with credit on his return from 202 days off the track and can improve when stepped back up in trip. (op 7-1 tchd 9-1)
Montrachet was 4lb lower than in future following her recent second at Kempton, but this was tougher and she was unable to take advantage. She probably wants even easier ground. Official explanation: jockey said filly hung right (op 7-2)
Rain Stops Play(IRE) has not won since October 2006 and he was well held after five months off. (op 16-1 tchd 12-1)

1457 FIRSTBET.COM ONLINE POKER ROOM CONDITIONS STKS 1m 3y
6:35 (6:35) (Class 3) 4-Y-0+ **£6,542** (£1,959; £979) **Stalls Low**

Form RPR

2-02 1 **Raptor (GER)**[19] 1103 5-8-12 100 FergusSweeney 3 106
(K R Burke) *hld up in 3rd: plld out over 2f out: ev ch over 1f out: rdn ins fnl f: led on post* **7/2**[3]

142- 2 nse **Mutajarred**[188] 6172 4-8-12 100 LiamJones 2 106
(W J Haggas) *led: rdn 2f out: hld hd high and edgd lft fnl f: hdd on post* **5/4**[1]

/2F- 3 6 **Drumfire (IRE)**[259] 4119 4-8-12 104 JoeFanning 1 92
(M Johnston) *w ldr: rdn jst over 2f out: wknd jst over 1f out* **6/4**[2]

1m 40.05s (-0.55) **Going Correction** +0.05s/f (Good) 3 Ran SP% 106.7
Speed ratings (Par 107): **104,103,97**
CSF £7.86 TOTE £4.60; EX 7.00.
Owner Mark T Gittins **Bred** Gestut Rheinberg Ag **Trained** Middleham Moor, N Yorks

FOCUS
Just the three runners, but a reasonable conditions contest. The winning time was 0.67 seconds slower than the 76-90 handicap. The form is rated around the first two.

NOTEBOOK
Raptor(GER), runner-up off a mark of 98 over 6f at the Curragh on his previous start, coped just fine with the step back up to 1m and just got the call. He did well to pick up from last off the modest pace and basically just wanted it more than the favourite. He should continue to go well in big handicaps and Listed races. (op 3-1)

Mutajarred, very progressive last year, was allowed the run of the race, but he could not shake off the attentions of Raptor, carrying his head a touch high, and was just denied. He can be expected to come on a little for this first run in over six months. (tchd 11-10)

Drumfire(IRE), off the track since falling at Goodwood last August, made a respectable return to action and this should have helped his confidence. (op 7-4)

1458 FIRSTBET 0800 230 0800 TELE-BETTING H'CAP 1m 2f 21y
7:10 (7:11) (Class 4) (0-80,77) 4-Y-0+ £4,533 (£1,348; £674; £336) Stalls Low

Form				RPR
0431	1		**Shogun Prince (IRE)**[30] 941 5-9-0 73 SebSanders 1 (W Jarvis) *trckd ldrs: shkn up to ld 2f out: rdn and styd on wl fr over 1f out* 3/1[2]	82
002	2	¾	**Dakiyah (IRE)**[9] 1273 4-9-4 77 IanMongan 3 (Mrs L J Mongan) *hld up in tch: rdn over 3f out: hdwy to press wnr over 1f out: unable qck u.p fnl f* 5/1	84
01/	3	½	**Marvo**[556] 5900 4-8-8 72 NicolPolli(5) 6 (M H Tompkins) *s.i.s: hld up in rr: stl last over 2f out: hdwy and rdn wl over 1f out: chsd ldng pair over 1f out: one pce ins fnl f* 15/8[1]	78
032-	4	5	**Coyote Creek**[227] 5113 4-9-3 76 JoeFanning 5 (E F Vaughan) *led tl rdn and hdd 2f out: wknd jst over 1f out* 7/2[3]	72
050-	5	11	**New Star (UAE)**[175] 6474 4-9-1 74 LiamJones 7 (W M Brisbourne) *t.k.h: hld up in tch: hdwy to chse ldr 4f out tl 2f out: sn wknd* 20/1	48
506-	6	54	**To The Max (IRE)**[209] 5641 4-9-2 75 DMylonas 2 (Mrs C A Dunnett) *plld hrd: chsd ldr tl 4f out: bhd last 2f: virtually p.u fr wl over 1f out: t.o* 33/1	—

2m 9.94s (-0.56) **Going Correction** +0.05s/f (Good) 6 Ran SP% **106.4**
Speed ratings (Par 105): **104,103,103,99,90 47**
CSF £15.97 TOTE £3.20: £1.30, £3.00; EX 11.40.

Owner M C Banks **Bred** Forenaghts Stud Co Ltd **Trained** Newmarket, Suffolk

■ Spirit Of The Mist was withdrawn (11/1, refused to enter stalls). R4 applies, deduct 5p in the £.

FOCUS
A fair handicap run at just a steady pace. Ordinary form, the winner rated to last year's best.

Coyote Creek Official explanation: jockey said gelding hung right

1459 FIRSTBET.COM ONLINE SPORTS BOOK H'CAP 1m 6f 17y
7:45 (7:45) (Class 6) (0-55,55) 4-Y-0+ £2,266 (£674; £337; £168) Stalls Low

Form				RPR
6-00	1		**Cavendish**[19] 771 4-8-8 54 (b) LukeMorris(3) 14 (J M P Eustace) *s.i.s: reminder sn after s: hdwy to chse ldr after 2f: rdn to ld 3f out: clr 1f out: styd on strly* 25/1	68
422	2	4 ½	**Salut Saint Cloud**[11] 1246 7-8-9 50 (p) SimonWhitworth 13 (G L Moore) *t.k.h: hld up wl in tch: hdwy to chse wnr and rdn over 2f out: no imp fnl f* 5/2[1]	58
6105	3	2 ½	**Whaxaar (IRE)**[14] 1181 4-8-12 55 RobertHavlin 6 (R Ingram) *in tch: rdn to chse ldrs jst over 2f out: kpt on same pce fr over 1f out* 14/1	59
3363	4	1	**Amwell Brave**[13] 1206 7-8-5 46 NickyMackay 15 (J R Jenkins) *t.k.h: chsd ldrs: wnt 2nd 6f out: led jst over 3f out: sn hdd and rdn: outpcd over 1f out* 11/1	49
0230	5	hd	**Aqua Pura (GER)**[24] 1017 9-8-9 50 StephenDonohoe 1 (A P Stringer) *led tl rdn and hdd jst over 3f out: outpcd fr wl over 1f out* 12/1	53
6123	6	2 ¼	**Medieval Maiden**[30] 934 5-8-12 53 IanMongan 9 (Mrs L J Mongan) *hld up in rr: hdwy 4f out: rdn over 2f out: plugged on but nvr pce to chal* 11/2[2]	52
50-4	7	shd	**York Cliff**[14] 1184 10-8-13 54 LiamJones 7 (W M Brisbourne) *hld up in midfield: pushed along and hdwy 5f out: no imp fr wl over 2f out* 14/1	53
0/10	8	hd	**Wizard Looking**[30] 934 7-9-0 55 PatCosgrave 16 (D E Cantillon) *taken down early: stdd and dropped in after s: hld up in rr: smooth hdwy on outer 4f out: rdn 3f out: wknd over 2f out* 7/1[3]	54
-000	9	10	**Sir Jake**[10] 1262 4-8-3 49 ow1 KirstyMilczarek(3) 11 (T T Clement) *hld up in rr: rdn over 3f out: sn wl btn* 14/1	34
6-04	10	5	**Summer Bounty**[13] 1206 12-8-10 51 SebSanders 10 (F Jordan) *stdd s: hld up in rr: sme hdwy 4f out: sn no imp* 16/1	29
6000	11	1 ¾	**Spellman**[14] 1181 4-8-4 47 ow1 (b) JoeFanning 2 (N P Littmoden) *chsd ldr for 2f: styd prom tl rdn and wknd over 3f out* 18/1	23
4204	12	5	**George Henson (IRE)**[7] 1310 4-8-9 52 (v[1]) PaulEddery 4 (Garry Moss) *s.i.s: t.k.h: hld up towards rr: rdn over 3f out: no imp: no ch last 2f: t.o* 40/1	21
5-00	13	½	**Laurentian Lad**[13] 1206 4-8-5 48 JimmyQuinn 12 (Rae Guest) *bustled along early: in tch: rdn over 4f out: wknd 4f out: t.o* 14/1	16
40-0	14	6	**Scaramoushca**[103] 67 5-8-6 47 J-PGuillambert 3 (G C Bravery) *hld up in tch in midfield: lost pl 4f out: sn wl bhd: t.o* 20/1	6
450-	15	81	**Lawyer To World**[182] 6315 4-7-12 46 oh1 (p) NicolPolli(5) 8 (Mrs C A Dunnett) *t.k.h: hld up wl in tch: wknd 4f out: t.o whn veered lft ins fnl f* 28/1	—

3m 7.28s (-0.32) **Going Correction** +0.05s/f (Good)
WFA 4 from 5yo+ 2lb 15 Ran SP% **124.8**
Speed ratings (Par 101): **102,99,98,97,97 96,95,95,90,87 86,83,83,79,33**
CSF £86.43 CT £975.17 TOTE £23.40: £9.40, £1.50, £7.10; EX 149.60 Place 6 £1,349.05, Place 5 £218.41.

Owner The Cavendish Partnership **Bred** Mrs S Clifford **Trained** Newmarket, Suffolk

FOCUS
A very moderate staying handicap. It was run at a steady pace and prominent racers were to the fore. The form has been rated through the second.

Summer Bounty Official explanation: jockey said saddle slipped

Scaramoushca Official explanation: jockey said gelding was struck into

T/Plt: £988.90 to a £1 stake. Pool: £42,334.38. 31.25 winning tickets. T/Qpdt: £39.60 to a £1 stake. Pool: £3,421.67. 63.90 winning tickets. SP

1460 - 1466a (Foreign Racing) - See Raceform Interactive

1439 NEWBURY (L-H)
Saturday, April 19

OFFICIAL GOING: Good to soft (soft in places) changing to soft after race 1 (1.40)
Wind: Brisk, behind

1467 DUBAI INTERNATIONAL AIRPORT MAIDEN STKS 1m (S)
1:40 (1:46) (Class 4) 3-Y-0 £5,828 (£1,734; £866; £432) Stalls Centre

Form				RPR
4-	1		**Moyenne Corniche**[171] 6593 3-9-3 0 RyanMoore 12 (G Wragg) *lw: rangy: trckd ldrs: led over 2f out: drvn clr fnl f* 6/1[3]	94+
5-	2	4	**French Art**[198] 5951 3-9-3 0 SebSanders 15 (D R C Elsworth) *plld hrd: chsd ldrs: rdn over 2f out: chsd wnr fr over 1f out but nvr any ch* 9/2[1]	84
4	3	3 ¾	**Arts Guild (USA)**[50] 748 3-9-3 0 JimmyFortune 10 (W J Musson) *b.hind: chsd ldrs: pushed along and styd on same pce fnl 2f* 20/1	76
00-	4	2 ¾	**Longevity**[176] 6468 3-9-3 0 KerrinMcEvoy 11 (W Jarvis) *slt ld tl narrowly hdd 4f out: led again 3f out: hdd over 2f out: wknd over 1f out* 66/1	69
	5	3 ¾	**Eqbaal** 3-9-3 0 RHills 6 (J L Dunlop) *unf: scope: bit bkwd: trckd ldrs: pushed along 1/2-way: styd on same pce fnl 2f* 10/1	61
	6	¾	**Mooted (UAE)** 3-9-3 0 RichardKingscote 9 (R Charlton) *leggy: w'like: chsd ldrs: pushed along 3f out: wknd fr 2f out* 33/1	59
	7	¾	**Blue Spartan (IRE)** 3-9-3 0 RobertWinston 20 (B J Meehan) *w'like: scope: bit bkwd: in rr: pushed along 3f out: styd on wl fnl 2f but nvr in contention* 12/1	57+
	8	1	**East Drive (IRE)** 3-9-3 0 PhilipRobinson 17 (M A Jarvis) *w'like: in tch: pushed along over 3f out: styd on fr over 2f out: no further prog fr over 1f out* 8/1	55
6-	9	1 ¼	**Kiho**[178] 6418 3-9-3 0 StephenCarson 13 (Eve Johnson Houghton) *chsd ldrs: rdn over 3f out: wknd qckly 2f out* 25/1	52
	10	1 ½	**Carbon Print (USA)** 3-9-3 0 SteveDrowne 18 (R Charlton) *w'like: scope: s.i.s: bhd tl styd on fnl 2f* 14/1	49
6-	11	¾	**Forget It**[175] 6494 3-9-3 0 RichardHughes 1 (R Hannon) *scope: bit bkwd: pressed ldrs tl wknd over 2f out* 5/1[2]	47
	12	¾	**Mohathab (IRE)** 3-9-3 0 MartinDwyer 19 (J H M Gosden) *w'like: scope: bit bkwd: in rr tl sme late prog* 9/1	45
5-5	13	2 ¾	**Chief Eric**[26] 997 3-9-3 0 NCallan 7 (B I Case) *bhd tl sme prog fnl 2f* 14/1	39
50-	14	1	**Daddy's Boy**[199] 5918 3-9-3 0 JimCrowley 21 (Mrs A J Perrett) *bit bkwd: in rr and nvr in contention* 20/1	37
-23	15	1 ¼	**Christophers Quest**[17] 1149 3-8-10 0 SophieDoyle(7) 3 (R Simpson) *lw: w ldr: slt advantage 4f out to 3f out: sn wknd* 25/1	34
04	16	1 ½	**Blur**[10] 1265 3-8-7 0 HaddenFrost(5) 16 (R Hannon) *chsd ldrs 5f* 50/1	25
-0	17	1 ¼	**Looping The Loop (USA)**[11] 1252 3-9-3 0 TPQueally 8 (J G Portman) *a towards rr* 100/1	27
	18	5	**Grit (IRE)** 3-8-10 0 MCGeran(7) 14 (M R Channon) *w'like: bit bkwd: s.i.s: a in rr* 50/1	16
0-	19	½	**Rettorical Lad**[191] 6127 3-9-3 0 JohnEgan 2 (Jamie Poulton) *str: bit bkwd: rdn 1/2-way: a towards rr* 66/1	15
04-	20	32	**Rowaad**[173] 6530 3-9-3 0 PatDobbs 4 (M P Tregoning) *sn bhd: t.o* 20/1	—

1m 42.67s (2.97) **Going Correction** +0.45s/f (Yiel) **20** Ran SP% **133.2**
Speed ratings (Par 100): **103,99,95,92,88 88,87,86,85,83 82,82,79,78,77 75,74,69,68,36**
CSF £31.34 TOTE £8.10: £2.80, £2.40, £8.20; EX 25.80.

Owner J L C Pearce **Bred** J L C Pearce **Trained** Newmarket, Suffolk

FOCUS
Light rain in the run-up to racing after just 1mm overnight saw soft initially added to the official going, before it was changed to soft in the straight after this race. Despite a strong breeze behind up the straight, the ground was clearly testing. They went a sensible pace in the conditions, so the big distances at the front of this finish strongly suggest some useful performers in a maiden which has a rich tradition - last year's winner, Diamond Tycoon, was ninth in the Guineas, runner-up Lucarno went on to win the St Leger and the sixth, Pipedreamer, won the Cambridgeshire off a mark of 102. This might not be such a strong race in depth, at least, with the form of the third and fourth casting doubt over the overall form, although there were others behind who can improve past them.

1468 DUBAI TENNIS CHAMPIONSHIPS STKS (REGISTERED AS THE JOHN PORTER STAKES) (GROUP 3) 1m 4f 5y
2:15 (2:15) (Class 1) 4-Y-0+
£26,681 (£10,114; £5,061; £2,523; £1,264; £634) Stalls Centre

Form				RPR
331-	1		**Royal And Regal (IRE)**[182] 6337 4-9-0 0 NCallan 10 (M A Jarvis) *lw: mid-div: tk clsr order over 4f out: rdn to chse ldr over 2f out: sn hung lft: led ins fnl f: styd on wl: rdn out* 13/2[3]	119+
22-0	2	nk	**Zaham (USA)**[35] 906 4-8-11 113 RHills 4 (M Johnston) *trckd ldrs: rdn whn sltly hmpd 2f out and lost pl: styd on wl fnl 100yds: wnt 2nd towards fin* 7/1	116+
110-	3	¾	**Tempelstern (GER)**[240] 4749 4-8-11 98 (b) TPQueally 3 (H R A Cecil) *led: rdn over 2f out: edgd lft and hdd ins fnl f: no ex: lost 2nd towards fin* 25/1	112
432-	4	½	**Ivy Creek (USA)**[175] 6496 5-8-12 111 SteveDrowne 8 (G Wragg) *lw: in tch: effrt 3f out: hung lft u.p over 1f out: styd on* 7/1	112
155-	5	3 ½	**Red Gala**[175] 6496 5-8-12 102 RyanMoore 5 (Sir Michael Stoute) *lw: mid-div: rdn and hdwy over 3f out: hld in 5th whn squeezed up ent fnl f* 9/1	106
2410	6	shd	**Gower Song**[21] 1091 5-8-12 0 TQuinn 14 (D R C Elsworth) *mid-div: rdn over 3f out: no imp tl styd on fnl f* 14/1	106
533-	7	1 ¼	**Regime (IRE)**[175] 6496 4-8-11 112 JamieSpencer 1 (M L W Bell) *lw: s.i.s: bhd: rdn and swtchd lft over 2f out: stdy prog to chse ldrs over 1f out: fdd ins fnl f* 15/2	104
606-	8	nk	**Big Robert**[219] 5351 4-8-11 107 RichardMullen 15 (W R Muir) *s.i.s: swtchd lft sn after s: towards rr: rdn and sme hdwy over 2f out: one pce fr over 1f out* 50/1	104
216-	9	1 ¼	**Bauer (IRE)**[211] 5589 5-8-12 104 DaneO'Neill 13 (L M Cumani) *bit bkwd: hld up towards rr: sme prog u.p whn nt clr run and swtchd rt over 2f out: no further imp fr over 1f out* 40/1	102

11-1 **10** *2 ½* **Malt Or Mash (USA)**[28] 968 4-8-11 111 .... RichardHughes 12 98
(R Hannon) *lw: rdn 3f out: a mid-div* **6/1**[2]

122- **11** *1 ½* **Ajhar (USA)**[175] 6499 4-8-11 92 .... MartinDwyer 7 96
(M P Tregoning) *chsd ldrs: rdn over 3f out: grad fdd fr 2f* **20/1**

065- **12** *9* **Sergeant Cecil**[242] 4691 9-8-12 112 .... DarryllHolland 2 83
(B R Millman) *broke wl: sn restrained towards rr: wknd 3f out* **33/1**

100- **13** *3 ¾* **Petara Bay (IRE)**[322] 2235 4-8-11 105 .... JimCrowley 11 77
(T G Mills) *mid-div: rdn 4f out: wknd 2f out* **40/1**

014- **14** *3 ½* **Tranquil Tiger**[198] 5952 4-8-11 112 .... TedDurcan 9 72
(H R A Cecil) *in tch: effrt 3f out: wknd 2f out* **9/2**[1]

2m 43.19s (7.69) **Going Correction** +0.75s/f (Yiel)
WFA 4 from 5yo+ 1lb 14 Ran SP% **117.6**
Speed ratings (Par 113): **104,103,103,102,100 100,99,99,98,97 96,90,87,85**
CSF £46.52 TOTE £8.20: £2.30, £2.70, £7.60; EX 69.90 Trifecta £506.60 Part won. Pool £713.44 - 0.20 winning units..
Owner P D Savill **Bred** P D Savill **Trained** Newmarket, Suffolk
■ Stewards' Enquiry : Steve Drowne caution: careless riding

FOCUS
The bottom bend on the round course had been pushed out 2.5m overnight. This was an unusually big field for the John Porter. Few could be entirely ruled out, although there were fitness question marks over many of them with only three having raced previously this season, and there were worries over the ground with some of the principals, too. They raced up the centre of the track in the straight, although in the closing stages the principals had all drifted back towards the far rail. It was probably a decent renewal and the winner looks a high-class stayer, but the third does hold down the form somewhat.

NOTEBOOK
Royal And Regal(IRE) ◆, one of only two with a penalty and having his first race for Michael Jarvis, was racing over what is likely to be his minimum trip this year, but conditions made this a fair test of stamina and he confirmed the class he had shown at three in last year's Jockey Club Cup for Andre Fabre with a good effort, marred only by the incident two furlongs out when he hung left and did Zaham no favours. He will have a Cup campaign, but his owner reportedly has reservations about him as an Ascot Gold Cup horse this year owing to his age group's dismal record in the race. The Yorkshire Cup is next on the agenda. (op 8-1)
Zaham(USA) ◆, who suffered an overreach in the Winter Derby, resumed the upwards curve he was on at the end of last year with another excellent effort. What's more, he was arguably unlucky, for he lost ground and momentum when hampered by the winner two furlongs out and must have made up the best part of three lengths on him when coming back strongly in the final furlong. He ought to be able to land a similar race this year. (op 15-2 tchd 8-1)
Tempelstern(GER), who has done well over the winter, won his handicap last year off only 82, albeit by eight lengths, and his proximity here does hold down the form. However, he was very progressive in blinkers last year until disappointing in the Melrose, he represented a stable in blinding form this week, and on top of that he had the run of the race here, allowed an easy lead. He may well have been flattered.
Ivy Creek(USA) was closing at the finish and was nicely clear of the rest. Although he has yet to win above Listed class he has plenty of form that entitled him to run well and he is another from a stable in great form. (op 15-2 tchd 8-1 in a place)
Red Gala won the 1m2f handicap on this card last year off a mark of only 84, but he was most progressive afterwards and looks the sort to make his mark in this company one day. He was held when squeezed just inside the final furlong, but did not run at all badly. His stable has been slow getting into top gear and he just got tired. (tchd 8-1)
Gower Song, penalised for her Group 3 win in Dubai, wasn't disgraced, but she never got in a blow. (op 12-1)
Regime(IRE) ran well to a point after a slow start, but he was going nowhere in the closing stages and may well have found this stretching his stamina. (op 13-2 tchd 8-1)
Big Robert, whose trainer was on record as expecting a big run, having reportedly sorted out a few things that weren't right at the end of last year, didn't run badly after his slow start and Muir was more than pleased. He insists the colt needed this, and that we will see a different horse on quicker ground in the Jockey Club Stakes at Newmarket next time.
Malt Or Mash(USA) has been highly progressive and can be forgiven this as the ground had gone against him completely. He is a different proposition on fast going or Polytrack and will be well worth another chance in this sort of grade. Official explanation: jockey said colt was unsuited by the soft ground (op 5-1)
Sergeant Cecil had been fourth in this race for the last two years, but the vibes had been negative through the week and he was the first beaten, just passing a couple of stragglers before the finish.

Tranquil Tiger had been the subject of highly encouraging reports, but was another who was not sure to appreciate the ground. His rider confirmed that the ground was the problem, and so he ought to be worth another chance on better going. Official explanation: jockey said colt was unsuited by the soft ground (op 5-1 tchd 4-1)

1469 BLOOR HOMES SPRING CUP (HERITAGE H'CAP) 1m (S)
2:50 (2:51) (Class 2) 4-Y-0+

£21,808 (£6,531; £3,265; £1,634; £815; £409) **Stalls** Centre

Form RPR

126- **1** **Lang Shining (IRE)**[204] 5764 4-8-11 89 .... RyanMoore 11 104+
(Sir Michael Stoute) *lw: chsd ldrs: rdn 2f out: styd on u.p to ld fnl 75yds* **9/2**[1]

0-21 **2** *nk* **Benandonner (USA)**[18] 1133 5-8-7 92 .... BMcHugh(7) 10 106
(R A Fahey) *chsd ldrs: rdn to ld over 1f out: hdd fnl 75yds: no ex cl home* **13/2**[3]

13-4 **3** *3 ¼* **Zaahid (IRE)**[28] 958 4-9-0 92 .... RHills 7 99+
(B W Hills) *lw: s.i.s: in rr: hdwy 3f out: styd on over 1f out: kpt on ins fnl f but no ch w ldng duo* **11/2**[2]

046- **4** *¾* **Proponent (IRE)**[210] 5615 4-8-12 90 .... SteveDrowne 14 95
(R Charlton) *lw: chsd ldrs: rdn over 2f out: kpt on fnl f but nvr gng pce to be competitive* **14/1**

0611 **5** *2* **Markab**[14] 1218 5-9-1 93 .... PatCosgrave 12 94
(K A Morgan) *led: rdn over 2f out: hdd over 1f out: wknd ins fnl f* **9/1**

00- **6** *1 ½* **Kingsdale Orion (IRE)**[244] 4646 4-8-12 90 .... RobertWinston 2 88
(B Ellison) *w'like: bit bkwd: in rr: hrd drvn over 2f out: styd on fnl f but nvr in contention* **20/1**

1022 **7** *¾* **Capable Guest (IRE)**[21] 1067 6-9-0 92 .... (v) ChrisCatlin 4 88
(M R Channon) *chsd ldrs: rdn 3f out: wknd appr fnl f* **20/1**

00-3 **8** *nk* **Trafalgar Square**[28] 958 6-8-9 87 .... PaulDoe 13 82
(M J Attwater) *lw: t.k.h early: mid-div: hdwy over 2f out: styd on same pce fr over 1f out* **16/1**

-520 **9** *½* **Plum Pudding (IRE)**[28] 958 5-8-10 93 .... PatrickHills(5) 15 87
(R Hannon) *in tch: rdn 3f out: styd on same pce fnl 2f* **20/1**

000- **10** *1* **South Cape**[168] 6654 5-8-5 90 .... MCGeran(7) 17 82
(M R Channon) *in tch: rdn over 2f out: nvr gng pce to be competitive and wknd appr fnl f* **33/1**

0-43 **11** *4 ½* **Wigwam Willie (IRE)**[14] 1218 6-8-5 83 .... (p) JoeFanning 3 65
(K A Ryan) *s.i.s: rdn towards rr 1/2-way: nvr in contention* **16/1**

-260 **12** *nse* **Orchard Supreme**[28] 958 5-8-9 87 .... RichardHughes 5 69
(R Hannon) *s.i.s: hld up in rr: hdwy to get in bhd ldrs 3f out: sn fdd* **33/1**

60-6 **13** *10* **Mine (IRE)**[28] 960 10-9-10 102 .... (v) DarryllHolland 1 62
(J D Bethell) *s.i.s: a in rr* **25/1**

020- **14** *3* **Formax (FR)**[198] 5950 6-8-8 86 .... MartinDwyer 6 39
(M P Tregoning) *in tch: rdn 3f out: sn wknd* **20/1**

250- **15** *2 ½* **Heroes**[72] 6301 4-8-9 87 .... EddieAhern 8 35
(C F Wall) *swtg: a towards rr* **22/1**

56-6 **16** *2* **Mesbaah (IRE)**[23] 1045 4-8-13 94 .... JamieMoriarty(3) 16 37
(R A Fahey) *s.i.s: a towards rr* **40/1**

131- **17** *22* **Sound Of Nature (USA)**[333] 1922 5-8-11 89 .... TedDurcan 19 —
(H R A Cecil) *swtg: a in rr: wl bhd fnl 3f* **9/2**[1]

1m 41.48s (1.78) **Going Correction** +0.45s/f (Yiel) 17 Ran SP% **129.1**
Speed ratings (Par 109): **109,108,105,104,102 101,100,100,99,98 94,94,84,81,78 76,54**
CSF £29.44 CT £173.99 TOTE £5.60: £1.80, £2.00, £1.60, £4.30; EX 41.40 Trifecta £198.90 Pool £1,060.20 - 3.80 winning units..
Owner Ballymacoll Stud **Bred** Ballymacoll Stud Farm Ltd **Trained** Newmarket, Suffolk

FOCUS
Traditionally a strong handicap and a signpost to further heritage handicap winners with the principals often going on to a Pattern-race future. This renewal looks no different with two unexposed four-year-olds taking the eye and the runner-up in top form already this season. It strengthened further the form of the Spring Mile at Doncaster. This is solid form which has been rated positively, with Lang Shining up 8lb and Benandonner producing a career best.

NOTEBOOK
Lang Shining(IRE) ◆ became the eighth four-year-old to win the Spring Cup in the last ten runnings, gaining ample consolation for missing out on the cut for the Lincoln, for which he had been fancied. As such, he was well prepared for this but, apart from a non-staying effort over 1m2f at the end of last season, he has a most progressive profile with his form working out well, suggesting he could be well treated. He took time to pick up when asked against race-fitter rivals, but impressed in coming clear with Benandonner through the final furlong, although he needed almost all of it to assert. Connections are likely to stick at 1m, but did not rule out another try at 1m2f later. He may prefer a bit of cut in the ground, which tempers enthusiasm for faster-ground handicaps like the Hunt Cup. (op 5-1)
Benandonner(USA), runner-up in Doncaster's Spring Mile, scored at Southwell last time and was racing off a 6lb higher mark. He went down fighting and must surely win soon on turf as he did nothing wrong again here in adding another placing off a mark that is naturally creeping up. (op 9-1)
Zaahid(IRE) ◆, fourth in the Spring Mile on his reappearance, again sat well back off the pace and deserves plenty of credit for getting as close as he did, especially as he hung badly left when first put under pressure. Straightened out, he stayed on strongly and looks to have more to offer on better ground this summer in similar races. (op 13-2 tchd 7-1 in places)
Proponent(IRE), who was gelded over the winter, travelled well with the pace, but he became outpaced before plugging on to suggest he might prefer further nowadays. (op 12-1)
Markab excelled himself, setting a sound gallop in the conditions and only giving best into the final furlong. He had won over 7f last time and has been edging up the handicap, but on this showing can get back to winning ways over a furlong shorter. (op 8-1 tchd 10-1)
Kingsdale Orion(IRE), who was gelded over the winter, took the eye on this seasonal return. Despite being a 7f winner, he was doing his best work at the finish, never threatening to get competitive, but leaving the impression his new stable will be winning with him soon. (op 25-1)
Capable Guest(IRE) is fully exposed, but he gives the form a solid look even if the ground was probably soft enough for him. (op 28-1)
Trafalgar Square was unable to repeat his Spring Mile form with the second and has always gone best fresh before losing his form. It could be the case again for this lightly raced gelding.
Plum Pudding(IRE) is better on better ground and he travelled well enough in the pack before getting tired in the last two furlongs in these conditions. (op 16-1)
South Cape ended nearest the stands' rail and plugged on, and he can improve on the bare form of this seasonal return.
Mine(IRE), bringing Lincoln form to the race, was held up travelling well as usual, but he was another who got bogged down on this ground under his big weight.
Formax(FR) ran far too freely early to get home in these conditions.
Sound Of Nature(USA) had not run for 11 months, having been injured in the horsebox on his way to Ascot for the Royal Hunt Cup, for which he was well fancied. He trailed in well beaten. Official explanation: jockey said horse was unsuited by the soft ground (tchd 4-1, 5-1 in places)

1470 DUBAI DUTY FREE STKS (REGISTERED AS THE FRED DARLING STAKES) (GROUP 3) (FILLIES) 7f (S)
3:25 (3:25) (Class 1) 3-Y-O

£26,681 (£10,114; £5,061; £2,523; £1,264; £634) **Stalls** Centre

Form RPR

11- **1** **Muthabara (IRE)**[268] 3880 3-9-0 103 .... RHills 10 109+
(J L Dunlop) *mid-div on stands' side: sme prog over 2f out: sn rdn: chsd ldrs over 1f out: r.o strly to ld but edgd lft ins fnl f: readily* **9/4**[1]

126- **2** *1 ¼* **Dream Day**[196] 6008 3-9-0 96 .... RyanMoore 7 100
(R Hannon) *chsd ldrs in centre: rdn over 2f out: led jst over 1f out: hdd ins fnl f: nt pce of wnr* **20/1**

121- **3** *¾* **Lady Deauville (FR)**[151] 6888 3-9-0 105 .... StephenDonohoe 2 98
(P A Blockley) *wnt lft s: chsd ldrs in centre: rdn over 2f out: r.o fnl f: wnt 3rd nr fin* **13/2**

2-14 **4** *nk* **Elizabeth Swann**[7] 1332 3-9-0 82 .... EddieAhern 3 97
(R Hannon) *hld up towards rr of centre gp: hdwy over 2f out: sn rdn: kpt on ins fnl f* **25/1**

154- **5** *nk* **Edge Of Light**[246] 4573 3-9-0 99 .... CatherineGannon 9 96
(B Palling) *led centre gp: rdn and hdd over 2f out: rallied and ev ch ent fnl f: no ex* **50/1**

205- **6** *1* **Don't Forget Faith (USA)**[195] 6040 3-9-0 103 .... PhilipRobinson 12 100
(C G Cox) *led stands' side trio but overall chsd ldrs: outpcd over 2f out: styd on ins fnl f* **11/1**

2-61 **7** *¾* **Tathkaar**[17] 1144 3-9-0 79 .... NCallan 8 92
(C E Brittain) *trckd ldr in centre gp: rdn to ld jst over 2f out: hdd over 1f out: kpt on same pce* **33/1**

132- **8** *2 ¼* **Annie Skates (USA)**[176] 6482 3-9-0 104 .... JohnEgan 4 86
(Jane Chapple-Hyam) *broke wl: sn restrained in mid-div of centre gp: hdwy over 3f out: sn rdn: one pce fnl 2f* **10/1**

1- **9** *1 ¼* **Michita (USA)**[179] 6414 3-9-0 0 .... JimmyFortune 6 83
(J H M Gosden) *swtg: prom in centre: rdn 3f out: one pce fnl 2f* **6/1**[3]

031- **10** *3 ½* **Nahoodh (IRE)**[240] 4744 3-9-0 110 .... RichardHughes 11 80
(M R Channon) *lw: hld up on stands' side: swtchd lft and rdn over 2f out: no imp* **5/1**[2]

1 **11** *6* **Savannah Poppy (IRE)**[21] 1068 3-9-0 76 .... TPQueally 13 58
(M L W Bell) *lw: strong: awkward leaving stalls: swtchd to centre gp sn after s: a towards rr* **14/1**

6326 **12** *shd* **Love Of Dubai (USA)**[7] 1332 3-9-0 0 .... KerrinMcEvoy 5 58
(C E Brittain) *hld up towards rr of centre gp: hdwy u.p over 2f out: wknd over 1f out* **25/1**

201- **13** ½ **Lille Ida**[176] 6477 3-9-0 78 MartinDwyer 1 57
(M P Tregoning) *lw: wnt lft s: a towards rr of centre gp* **25/1**

1m 28.69s (2.99) **Going Correction** +0.45s/f (Yiel) **13** Ran SP% **120.3**
Speed ratings (Par 105): **100,98,97,97,97 95,95,92,91,87 80,80,79**
CSF £57.74 TOTE £2.60: £1.40, £5.50, £2.40; EX 61.30 Trifecta £513.40 Part won. Pool £723.20 - 0.50 winning units..
Owner Hamdan Al Maktoum **Bred** Shadwell Estate Company Limited **Trained** Arundel, W Sussex
■ Stewards' Enquiry : Eddie Ahern three-day ban: excessive use of the whip (May 5-7)

FOCUS
A biggish field, but not a prepossessing bunch and not much strength in depth so far as previous form was concerned. Several fillies who were hard to fancy finished too close for comfort, which undermines the strength of the form, as does the time, which was a second and a half slower than that taken by Paco Boy in the Greenham. The form is guessy, but Muthabara did it well and can be rated better than the bare form.

NOTEBOOK
Muthabara(IRE) ◆ was unbeaten in her two starts last year before being ruled out of the big autumn races by injury and had been the subject of a major ante-post gamble for the 1000 Guineas following a well publicised racecourse gallop at Goodwood. She did not disappoint, but it was only in the final furlong that she began to look a Classic prospect, and they were in a bit of a heap behind her. This was not as impressive a trial as either Natagora's or Infallible's earlier in the week, and bookmakers were divided afterwards. She was one of three to race on what her rider felt was better ground towards the stands' side, where she was led by Don't Forget Faith, but her chance did not look bright when being ridden approaching two furlongs out, and having drifted left to join the main group she had four or five ahead of her and a couple of lengths to make up going into the final furlong. To her credit, when she found top gear she picked up quite impressively, and having led well inside the final furlong she was comfortably on top at the finish. The extra furlong at Newmarket is going to suit her admirably, and if she enjoys a bit of sunshine in the meantime so much the better, for she clearly hadn't come to herself here. (op 5-2)
Dream Day proved something of a surprise package in second, appearing to leave her juvenile form well behind. She had not been back in long and so her connections were thrilled with her, especially as they feel she will be much better next time. She will probably go to Newmarket, although she is also entered in France. (op 25-1)
Lady Deauville(FR) was a good second too Muthabara at Sandown last summer and had shown herself well suited by the ground. She ran a big race in third, but was one of the sharper members of the field and one suspects this may have been her Guineas. (op 8-1)
Elizabeth Swann, a stablemate of Dream Day, is not entered at Newmarket. Fit from the Polytrack, having persuaded connections she was a non stayer when fourth in the Masaka, she was another who seemingly showed improved form in fourth, so her proximity is another negative. She had a hard race in the process, too. (tchd 22-1)
Edge Of Light led the main group up the middle of the track and was still there going to the furlong marker. This trip may well stretch her stamina, and to be only just edged out of the placings was a cracking effort from a filly who had been off the track eight months.
Don't Forget Faith(USA), fifth to Zarkava in the Prix Marcel Boussac, looked one of the better types in the preliminaries and led the stands'-side trio until Muthabara took over. Her stable is not really firing yet and she should do better. (op 14-1)
Tathkaar only scrambled home in a Kempton maiden earlier this month, and she had a mountain to climb on form. She was beaten little more than four lengths and is another who was too close for comfort. (op 40-1)
Annie Skates(USA), second on soft in the US in the autumn, was on her toes beforehand. She raced handily and had her chance, but was not good enough. (op 12-1 tchd 9-1)
Michita(USA) represented the stable responsible for Nell Gwyn winner Infallible as well as the sidelined Sense Of Joy, and there was no suggestion beforehand she was top flight. She got warm in the preliminaries and never really figured. (op 7-1 tchd 15-2)
Nahoodh(IRE)'s Lowther win was the best juvenile form, but Mick Channon, who has such a good record in this race, made no secret of the fact that she was more backward than he would have liked. She raced with Muthabara in the stands'-side trio, but was very disappointing, even making allowance for her having not come to herself yet. (op 3-1 tchd 11-2)
Love Of Dubai(USA) was only just behind Elizabeth Swann at Kempton but ran nowhere near that form this time.

1471 BATHWICK TYRES GREENHAM STKS (GROUP 3) (C&G) 7f (S)
4:00 (4:02) (Class 1) 3-Y-O
£26,681 (£10,114; £5,061; £2,523; £1,264; £634) **Stalls** Centre

Form RPR
11-1 **1** **Paco Boy (IRE)**[35] 905 3-9-0 100 RichardHughes 8 110
(R Hannon) *lw: trckd ldrs: shkn up and qcknd to trck ldr over 1f out: led fnl 100yds: readily* **6/1**[3]
050- **2** ¾ **Bobs Surprise**[260] 4120 3-9-0 101 MichaelHills 7 108
(B W Hills) *led: rdn and kpt on fr over 1f out: hdd fnl 100yds: kpt on wl but nt pce of wnr* **33/1**
224- **3** 4 **Red Alert Day**[197] 5975 3-9-0 107 LDettori 5 97
(S A Callaghan) *in tch: hdwy 3f out: rdn to chse ldrs 2f out: outpcd ins fnl f* **15/2**
31- **4** ½ **Shallal**[263] 4048 3-9-0 95 JimmyFortune 4 96
(P W Chapple-Hyam) *b.hind: chsd ldr: rdn over 2f out: wknd fnl f* **16/1**
21- **5** 3 ¼ **Confront**[189] 6171 3-9-0 108 RyanMoore 2 88
(Sir Michael Stoute) *lw: chsd ldrs: rdn over 2f out: sn btn* **11/8**[1]
211- **6** 1 ½ **Beacon Lodge (IRE)**[175] 6495 3-9-0 107 PhilipRobinson 3 84
(C G Cox) *lw: in rr but in tch: rdn and effrt 3f out: nvr rchd ldrs and wknd 2f out* **4/1**[2]
410- **7** 2 ¼ **Sir Gerry (USA)**[197] 5975 3-9-0 111 JamieSpencer 1 78
(J R Fanshawe) *lw: hld up in rr: rdn and little rspnse over 2f out* **13/2**
213- **8** 16 **Without A Prayer (IRE)**[242] 4694 3-9-0 96 SebSanders 6 36
(R M Beckett) *stmbld stalls: sn in tch: rdn 3f out: sn wknd* **16/1**

1m 27.14s (1.44) **Going Correction** +0.45s/f (Yiel) **8** Ran SP% **116.2**
Speed ratings (Par 108): **109,108,103,103,99 97,95,76**
CSF £165.99 TOTE £7.30: £1.70, £4.70, £2.20; EX 147.50 Trifecta £374.20 Pool £579.80 - 1.10 winning units..
Owner The Calvera Partnership No 2 **Bred** Mrs Joan Browne **Trained** East Everleigh, Wilts

FOCUS
No Guineas winner has come from this since Wollow in 1976 and that trend looks sure to continue after this renewal, which looked a long way removed from the Craven earlier in the week. The principals are not even entered in the Classic, although Paco Boy is set to be supplemented. The fifth, sixth and seventh failed to run their races which devalues the form even further. It may still turn out to be up to its Group 3 status, but is more likely to throw up a Jersey winner than a Group 1 and many shaped like sprinters in the making. On the plus side the time compared favourably with the Fred Darling, and the progressive Paco Boy improved by 13lb on his impressive polytrack win.

NOTEBOOK
Paco Boy(IRE) put his race fitness to full use - all the others were making their seasonal returns - and maintains his most progressive profile. His Listed win on the Polytrack at Lingfield last time was impressive and this was comfortable enough, and the way he quickened on the softest ground he has encountered was decent. He remains an unexposed horse, admirably adaptable to all conditions, and the way he went to the line suggests 1m should be within his scope. He is likely to be supplemented for the Guineas. (op 5-1 tchd 7-1)
Bobs Surprise looked perhaps the fittest of the returning runners and ran accordingly. He set a steady early pace, but left the rest behind comprehensively in his private battle with the winner, which saw them record a much quicker time than the fillies in the Fred Darling. Off longer than the rest since his beating in the Richmond at Goodwood, he deserves plenty of credit, but shapes more like a sprinter in the making.
Red Alert Day, not disgraced in the Middle Park on his last start at two, is another who looks more sprinting material. He was readily left behind before the final furlong, but gamely held off the stragglers. Better ground should also suit him better, but he has what looks a high rating on this showing and he may prove just shy of Group class. (op 14-1)
Shallal, who has not developed much over the winter, showed pace, but dropped away on unsuitable ground and looks a pure sprinter in the making. Official explanation: jockey said colt hung right-handed (tchd 14-1)
Confront, who beat this week's Free Handicap winner Stimulation at Ascot last September, seemed to blow up with two furlongs to run after moving into contention. He has plenty to prove after this tame effort as he has handled ease in the ground in his win last backend. (op 13-8 tchd 7-4 in a place)
Beacon Lodge(IRE) was quite keen early under hold-up tactics and found disappointingly little when let down. He has plenty to prove on this showing. (op 6-1)
Sir Gerry(USA), winner of the Gimcrack last year, was settled well off the pace, but when asked to creep closer, there was only a brief response and he was beating a retreat before the final furlong. He is another who has not developed much over the winter and could be a pure sprinter. Official explanation: trainer had no explanation for the poor form shown (op 7-2)

1472 PERTEMPS H'CAP 2m
4:30 (4:31) (Class 4) (0-85,85) 4-Y-O+ **£6,476** (£1,927; £963; £481) **Stalls** Centre

Form RPR
3555 **1** **Flame Creek (IRE)**[17] 1136 12-7-13 62 oh1 MCGeran(7) 11 70
(E J Creighton) *mid-div: hdwy 3f out: led 2f out: edgd lft and styd on wl fnl f: rdn out* **25/1**
064- **2** 1 ¼ **Winged D'Argent (IRE)**[184] 6284 7-9-6 76 (b) NCallan 4 82
(B J Llewellyn) *trckd ldrs: rdn to chal fr 3f out: kpt on but a hld ins fnl f* **14/1**
400- **3** ½ **Ned Ludd (IRE)**[28] 6760 5-9-9 79 EddieAhern 12 84
(J G Portman) *mid-div: tk clsr order 5f out: rdn 3f out: ev ch 2 out: kpt on same pce* **10/1**
40-5 **4** ½ **Inchloch**[21] 1072 6-9-8 78 RyanMoore 10 83
(B G Powell) *hld up towards rr: rdn and hdwy fr 3f out: styd on fnl f* **8/1**
1152 **5** 4 ½ **Legend Erry (IRE)**[7] 1337 4-9-7 81 JohnEgan 2 80
(Jane Chapple-Hyam) *trckd ldrs: rdn 3f out: led sn after: hdd 2f out: fdd ins fnl f* **8/1**
10-0 **6** hd **Sadler's Kingdom (IRE)**[27] 981 4-9-5 82 JamieMoriarty(3) 7 81
(R A Fahey) *lw: trckd ldrs: rdn 3f out: one pce fnl 2f* **4/1**[1]
541- **7** 2 ½ **Plane Painter (IRE)**[201] 5857 4-9-2 76 JoeFanning 3 72
(M Johnston) *led: rdn and hdd over 2f out: fdd fnl f* **7/1**[3]
0-42 **8** 4 **Aureate**[17] 1137 4-9-11 85 JimmyFortune 6 76
(B Ellison) *lw: mid-div: rdn and effrt over 2f out: wknd over 1f out* **4/1**[1]
4030 **9** ¾ **Stoop To Conquer**[10] 1267 8-9-0 70 RobertWinston 5 60
(A W Carroll) *trckd ldr: rdn to chal 3f out: wknd over 1f out* **33/1**
000- **10** 3 **Fascinatin Rhythm**[259] 4147 4-9-2 76 EdwardCreighton 1 63
(M R Channon) *rrd leaving stalls: bhd: short-lived effrt over 2f out* **50/1**
313- **11** 28 **Aphorism**[184] 6284 5-9-3 73 JamieSpencer 9 26
(J R Fanshawe) *s.i.s: rdn over 2f out: a bhd: eased fnl f* **5/1**[2]
100- **12** 21 **Mickmacmagoole (IRE)**[47] 6422 6-9-7 77 LDettori 8 5
(Evan Williams) *lw: rdn 4f out: a towards rr: eased fnl f* **11/1**

3m 49.33s (12.43) **Going Correction** +0.75s/f (Yiel)
WFA 4 from 5yo+ 4lb **12** Ran SP% **124.2**
Speed ratings (Par 105): **98,97,97,96,94 94,93,91,90,89 75,64**
CSF £349.62 CT £3731.10 TOTE £50.20: £10.70, £4.90, £3.70; EX 401.50.
Owner E J Creighton **Bred** Kilcornan Stables **Trained** Mill Hill, London NW7

FOCUS
A moderate staying handicap in which the runners again spread out off the home turn looking for better ground away from the inside rail. The pace was also muddling with a good early gallop looking to be slowed down the back straight, with a few pulling for their head. The relevance of the form in this bad ground is questionable. The third looks the best guide.
Mickmacmagoole(IRE) Official explanation: jockey said gelding moved poorly throughout

1473 DUBAI DUTY FREE MILLENNIUM MILLIONAIRE H'CAP 1m 2f 6y
5:05 (5:05) (Class 4) (0-85,85) 4-Y-O+ **£5,180** (£1,541; £770; £384) **Stalls** Centre

Form RPR
013- **1** **Ezdiyaad (IRE)**[206] 5724 4-9-1 82 RHills 14 98
(M P Tregoning) *t.k.h: trckd ldr: led 3f out: pushed out and r.o wl fnl f* **7/1**[3]
64-0 **2** 2 ½ **Eglevski (IRE)**[21] 1072 4-9-1 82 EddieAhern 10 93
(J L Dunlop) *lw: in tch: hdwy 3f out: ev ch 2f out tl chsd wnr appr fnl f: kpt on but a hld* **11/1**
03-2 **3** 1 ¼ **Curzon Prince (IRE)**[92] 218 4-9-1 82 GeorgeBaker 11 91
(C F Wall) *hld up in rr: stdy hdwy over 3f out: drvn to dispute 2nd ins fnl 2f: kpt on one pce ins fnl f* **14/1**
20-5 **4** 6 **Jeer (IRE)**[15] 1180 4-9-3 84 JimmyFortune 15 81
(E A L Dunlop) *hld up in rr: hdwy over 3f out: styd on fr 2f out but nvr gng pce to rch ldrs* **11/1**
510- **5** 2 ¾ **Dzesmin (POL)**[161] 6759 6-9-1 82 DarryllHolland 13 73+
(R C Guest) *in rr: hdwy over 2f out: edgd rt over 1f out: kpt on ins fnl f but nvr in contention* **20/1**
-061 **6** ½ **Granston (IRE)**[28] 962 7-9-3 84 RobertWinston 4 74
(J D Bethell) *lw: chsd ldrs: chal 3f out: sn rdn and hung lft: wknd 2f out* **10/1**
30-6 **7** nk **Zero Cool (USA)**[14] 1212 4-9-2 83 RyanMoore 2 72
(G L Moore) *chsd ldrs: rdn and effrt 3f out: wknd fr 2f out* **12/1**
000- **8** 1 ½ **Ascalon**[176] 6474 4-9-2 83 PaulEddery 6 69
(Pat Eddery) *towards rr: rdn 3f out but nvr gng pce to get into contention* **16/1**
231- **9** 2 ¾ **Kavachi (IRE)**[172] 6576 5-8-2 76 RossAtkinson(7) 16 57
(G L Moore) *hdwy on outside to chse ldrs 5f out: wknd over 2f out* **20/1**
051- **10** 1 **Bee Sting**[294] 3079 4-9-4 85 AdamKirby 7 64
(W R Swinburn) *in tch: rdn over 3f out: sn btn* **5/1**[2]
100/ **11** 1 **Alfie Noakes**[644] 3533 6-9-4 85 JimCrowley 8 62
(Mrs A J Perrett) *bit bkwd: sn bhd* **20/1**
20-3 **12** hd **Celtic Change (IRE)**[14] 1217 4-8-11 78 JamieSpencer 12 55
(M Dods) *stdd s: hld up in rr: rdn over 3f out and brief effrt: nvr bttr than mid-div and sn wknd* **4/1**[1]
02-3 **13** 5 **First To Call**[18] 1131 4-9-0 81 AmirQuinn 5 48
(P J Makin) *lw: in tch: rdn to chse ldrs over 3f out: wknd sn after* **33/1**
616- **14** 6 **Nur Tau (IRE)**[210] 5639 4-9-4 85 SteveDrowne 3 40
(H Morrison) *led tl hdd 3f out: rdn: sddle slipped and bhd sn after* **16/1**
2-32 **15** 3 **Putra Square**[11] 1256 4-9-0 81 (b) TQuinn 1 30
(P F I Cole) *lw: chsd ldrs: rdn over 3f out: sn btn* **16/1**

40-6 16 ¾ **Mustajed**[21] 1076 7-8-13 **85**........................ JamesMillman(5) 9 32
(B R Millman) *in tch to 1/2-way* **14/1**

2m 14.68s (5.88) **Going Correction** +0.75s/f (Yiel) **16** Ran SP% **130.8**
Speed ratings (Par 105): **106,104,103,98,96 95,95,94,91,91 90,90,86,81,79 78**
CSF £83.56 CT £1088.84 TOTE £7.50: £1.90, £3.30, £3.50, £3.20; EX 82.60 Place 6 £1,994.92, Place 5 £634.40.
Owner Hamdan Al Maktoum **Bred** Shadwell Estate Co Ltd **Trained** Lambourn, Berks

FOCUS
A big field, but not many that one could seriously fancy. They finished so well strung out that all those out of the frame were beaten upwards of 12 lengths, which tempers enthusiasm for their immediate prospects. This is decent form for the grade and there is more to come from the progressive Ezdiyaad.
Bee Sting Official explanation: jockey said gelding never travelled
Putra Square Official explanation: jockey said gelding was unsuited by the soft ground
T/Jkpt: Not won. T/Plt: £5,944.00 to a £1 stake. Pool: £130,687.39. 16.05 winning tickets. T/Qpdt: £447.60 to a £1 stake. Pool: £6,412.60. 10.60 winning tickets. ST

1377 NOTTINGHAM (L-H)
Saturday, April 19

OFFICIAL GOING: Soft (good to soft in places)
Wind: Fresh behind Weather: Overcast

1474 HENSON FRANKLYN MAIDEN STKS — 5f 13y
5:30 (5:30) (Class 5) 2-Y-O **£2,590** (£770; £385; £192) **Stalls** High

Form RPR
1 **Lisburn (IRE)** 2-8-9 0........................ MarkLawson(3) 3 72
(M Brittain) *mde virtually all: rdn and edgd lft fr over 1f out: r.o* **25/1**
2 hd **Harwalla (IRE)** 2-9-3 0........................ GregFairley 2 76
(M Johnston) *chsd ldrs: rdn and ev ch fr over 1f out: r.o* **5/1**[2]
2 3 ¾ **Raggle Taggle (IRE)**[15] 1177 2-8-12 0........................ JamesDoyle 4 69+
(R M Beckett) *s.i.s: hld up: hdwy over 1f out: swtchd rt ins fnl f: r.o wl: nt rch ldrs* **15/8**[1]
3 4 ½ **Kingswinford (IRE)**[10] 1263 2-9-3 0........................ TGMcLaughlin 1 72
(P D Evans) *chsd ldrs: rdn along thrght: styd on same pce ins fnl f* **5/1**[2]
5 nk **Voulez Vous** 2-8-12 0........................ ChrisCatlin 6 66
(E J O'Neill) *w wnr: rdn and hung lft fr over 1f out: no ex ins fnl f* **9/1**
5 6 2 ¾ **Call Me Courageous (IRE)**[18] 1122 2-9-3 0........................ DaneO'Neill 5 61
(A B Haynes) *hld up in tch: rdn 1/2-way: wkng whn hmpd ins fnl f* **11/2**[3]
7 5 **Johnmanderville** 2-9-3 0........................ DarrenWilliams 7 43
(K R Burke) *dwlt: hdwy 1/2-way: wknd over 1f out* **11/2**[3]

63.03 secs (2.33) **Going Correction** +0.275s/f (Good) **7** Ran SP% **112.7**
Speed ratings (Par 92): **92,91,90,89,89 84,76**
CSF £138.81 TOTE £32.60: £15.60, £3.20; EX 118.60.
Owner Mel Brittain **Bred** Chevington Stud **Trained** Warthill, N Yorks
■ Stewards' Enquiry : James Doyle one-day ban: careless riding (May 5)

FOCUS
This was just an average juvenile maiden. The first five finished closely covered and the third/fourth set the level.

NOTEBOOK
Lisburn(IRE), a half-sister to winners over further including the useful Along The Nile, showed decent early speed to bag the lead and eventually had enough left in the locker to hold off her rivals at the death. She has a decent attitude and should have no trouble with another furlong in due course. (op 33-1)
Harwalla(IRE) ◆, a half-brother to five winners in Italy, had seen his purchase price double as a yearling and was the first juvenile runner to be sent out by his leading trainer. He only just failed to make a winning debut, showing a deal of ability, and will very likely prove hard to stop next time out. (op 13-2)
Raggle Taggle(IRE), second on her debut at Lingfield 15 days previously, would have given the first pair more to think about with a better leap from the stalls. She can win a maiden, but really now looks as though a sixth furlong will be ideal. Official explanation: jockey said filly was denied a clear run (op 2-1 tchd 7-4)
Kingswinford(IRE), third on his debut at Bath ten days previously, was never going that smoothly yet still showed up well enough in defeat. He is another who helps to set the level and may just have found this coming a little too soon. (op 5-2)

1475 HECTOR CROWHURST 4TH BIRTHDAY FILLIES' H'CAP — 5f 13y
6:00 (6:02) (Class 5) (0-70,68) 3-Y-O **£2,590** (£770; £385; £192) **Stalls** High

Form RPR
0-11 1 **Killer Class**[17] 1141 3-8-8 **58**........................ ChrisCatlin 3 65
(J S Goldie) *a.p: led over 1f out: rdn out* **8/1**
400- 2 2 **Linnet Park**[164] 6722 3-8-7 **57**........................ J-PGuillambert 6 56+
(J G Given) *plld hrd and prom: hmpd wl over 3f out: rdn over 1f out: styd on* **7/1**
40-5 3 1 ½ **Second Opinion (IRE)**[14] 1215 3-9-4 **68**........................ HayleyTurner 11 62
(J M P Eustace) *hld up in tch: rdn and edgd lft 1f out: styd on same pce* **16/1**
1343 4 hd **The Little Fizzer (IRE)**[17] 1155 3-8-13 **63**........................ FergusSweeney 1 56
(K R Burke) *led: rdn and hdd over 1f out: edgd lft and no ex ins fnl f* **6/1**[3]
3132 5 1 ¾ **Lujiana**[11] 1257 3-8-11 **64**........................ MarkLawson(3) 12 51
(M Brittain) *chsd ldrs: rdn and ev ch over 1f out: wknd ins fnl f* **5/1**[1]
2254 6 nk **Alabama Spirit (USA)**[52] 714 3-8-10 **65**........................ PatrickHills(5) 2 51
(J Balding) *chsd ldrs: rdn over 1f out: wknd ins fnl f* **15/2**
6003 7 2 ¼ **Easy Wonder (GER)**[10] 1274 3-8-13 **63**........................(p) LiamJones 13 41
(I A Wood) *sn pushed along in rr: wknd over 1f out* **8/1**
-334 8 1 ¼ **Firespin (USA)**[16] 1162 3-8-8 **58**........................(t) TedDurcan 7 31
(M Botti) *s.i.s: hld up: hdwy u.p over 1f out: wkng whn hmpd 1f out* **14/1**
6521 9 1 ½ **Swallow Forest**[11] 1257 3-8-7 **57**........................(b) PaulFessey 8 25
(T D Barron) *s.s: outpcd* **11/2**[2]
060- 10 2 ½ **Klarity**[140] 7000 3-8-3 **60**........................ JosephineBruning(7) 10 19
(J Pearce) *s.i.s and wnt lft s: sn pushed along in rr: wknd 2f out* **25/1**

62.06 secs (1.36) **Going Correction** +0.275s/f (Good) **10** Ran SP% **109.2**
Speed ratings (Par 95): **100,96,94,94,91 90,87,85,82,78**
CSF £56.15 CT £765.33 TOTE £5.30: £2.60, £2.60, £5.10; EX 55.50.
Owner Frank Brady **Bred** Jonayro Investments **Trained** Uplawmoor, E Renfrews
■ Stewards' Enquiry : Ted Durcan caution: allowed filly to coast home

FOCUS
A modest sprint handicap for fillies, won by the progressive Killer Class. The draw held no real advantage and the form is rated through the fourth. This was the pick of the three C/D times.

1476 MARK CLARK MEMORIAL H'CAP — 5f 13y
6:30 (6:32) (Class 6) (0-65,63) 4-Y-O+ **£2,047** (£604; £302) **Stalls** High

Form RPR
00-0 1 **Black Moma (IRE)**[36] 875 4-8-12 **57**........................ DaneO'Neill 3 66
(A B Haynes) *led 2f: rdn to ld and edgd rt over 1f out: r.o* **14/1**
-406 2 hd **Twosheetstothewind**[5] 1373 4-9-1 **60**........................ LiamJones 8 69
(C R Dore) *trckd ldrs: plld hrd: led 3f out: rdn and hdd over 1f out: r.o* **12/1**
500- 3 1 ¼ **Steel City Boy (IRE)**[169] 6625 5-9-2 **61**........................ DanielTudhope 6 65
(D Carroll) *hld up: hdwy over 1f out: r.o* **9/1**
30-0 4 1 **Briery Lane (IRE)**[8] 1312 7-8-11 **56**........................ StephenDonohoe 4 56
(J M Bradley) *chsd ldrs: rdn over 1f out: styd on same pce ins fnl f* **16/1**
0426 5 1 ½ **Proud Killer**[5] 1368 5-9-4 **63**........................ ChrisCatlin 2 58
(J R Jenkins) *bmpd s: chsd ldrs: rdn over 1f out: no ex ins fnl f* **4/1**[2]
204 6 ¾ **Monte Major (IRE)**[10] 1268 7-8-7 **57**........................ PatrickHills(5) 13 49
(D Shaw) *prom: rdn 1/2-way: styd on same pce fnl f* **5/2**[1]
435- 7 ½ **Niteowl Lad (IRE)**[171] 6594 6-9-1 **60**........................(b[1]) PaulMulrennan 9 51
(J Balding) *chsd ldrs: rdn 1/2-way: wknd ins fnl f* **9/1**
310- 8 shd **Registrar**[148] 6910 6-8-11 **56**........................ SaleemGolam 10 46+
(Mrs C A Dunnett) *dwlt: nvr nrr* **8/1**[3]
51-0 9 ½ **Morristown Music (IRE)**[26] 987 4-8-11 **63**........................ JamesRogers(7) 1 51
(J S Wainwright) *wnt rt and bmpd rival s: outpcd* **20/1**
1406 10 nk **Sherjawy (IRE)**[18] 1129 4-8-9 **54**........................(b) SamHitchcott 14 41
(Miss Z C Davison) *prom: rdn 1/2-way: wknd fnl f* **10/1**
000- 11 ¾ **Mr Forthright**[140] 7003 4-8-6 **51**........................ GregFairley 12 36
(J M Bradley) *mid-div: rdn 1/2-way: sn lost pl* **28/1**
05-0 12 nk **Sea Land (FR)**[8] 1309 4-9-4 **63**........................ J-PGuillambert 5 46
(B Ellison) *s.i.s: a in rr* **20/1**

62.71 secs (2.01) **Going Correction** +0.275s/f (Good) **12** Ran SP% **122.0**
Speed ratings (Par 101): **94,93,91,90,87 86,85,85,84,84 83,82**
CSF £171.52 CT £1613.63 TOTE £6.80: £3.30, £3.40, £4.00; EX 208.30.
Owner Alan Moore **Bred** Poulton Farm Stud **Trained** Limpley Stoke, Bath

FOCUS
A moderate sprint which saw the first pair fight out the finish. Ordinary form, rated through the second and third.

1477 HENSON FRANKLYN MEDIAN AUCTION MAIDEN STKS — 1m 1f 213y
7:00 (7:01) (Class 6) 3-Y-O **£2,047** (£604; £302) **Stalls** Low

Form RPR
2-23 1 **St Jean Cap Ferrat**[12] 1243 3-9-3 73........................(v[1]) SebSanders 3 77
(G Wragg) *trckd ldrs: rdn to ld and hung lft fr over 1f out: styd on u.p* **1/1**[1]
3-3 2 2 ¾ **Princess Lomi (IRE)**[35] 903 3-8-12 0........................ ChrisCatlin 1 67
(E J O'Neill) *chsd ldr tl led 7f out: rdn and hdd over 1f out: styd on same pce* **2/1**[2]
0- 3 3 **Dancing Sword**[219] 5344 3-9-3 0........................ DaneO'Neill 4 66
(H J L Dunlop) *hld up in tch: rdn over 2f out: styd on same pce appr fnl f* **20/1**
5- 4 3 ½ **Loveofmylife**[162] 6748 3-8-12 0........................ JamesDoyle 2 54
(R M Beckett) *sn led: hdd 7f out: chsd ldr: rdn over 4f out: wknd over 1f out* **10/1**[3]
5 10 **Solas Alainn (IRE)** 3-9-3 0........................ OscarUrbina 8 39
(J R Fanshawe) *s.i.s: hld up: rdn: hung lft and outpcd over 4f out: n.d after* **12/1**
6 2 ¾ **Enderby Princess (IRE)** 3-8-12 0........................ DanielTudhope 6 28
(D Carroll) *s.s: hld up: hdwy 1/2-way: rdn over 3f out: wknd over 2f out* **20/1**
00- 7 5 **Great Future**[176] 6470 3-8-12 0........................ StephenDonohoe 7 18
(J R Holt) *chsd ldrs over 6f* **50/1**
0- 8 1 ½ **River Kent**[192] 6107 3-9-3 0........................ RoystonFfrench 5 20
(Mrs A Duffield) *hld up: plld hrd: rdn and wknd over 3f out* **16/1**

2m 17.99s (7.29) **Going Correction** +0.675s/f (Yiel) **8** Ran SP% **117.5**
Speed ratings (Par 96): **97,94,92,89,81 79,75,74**
CSF £3.14 TOTE £2.10: £1.10, £1.10, £4.60; EX 3.10.
Owner J L C Pearce **Bred** J L C Pearce **Trained** Newmarket, Suffolk

FOCUS
A moderate maiden, run at a modest pace. The form, which makes sense, is rated around the winner and runner-up.

1478 EQUINE2U.COM H'CAP — 1m 1f 213y
7:30 (7:31) (Class 6) (0-60,60) 3-Y-O **£2,047** (£604; £302) **Stalls** Low

Form RPR
00-2 1 **Fantastic Lass**[15] 1186 3-8-11 **53**........................ PaulHanagan 5 61
(R A Fahey) *hld up in tch: rdn over 3f out: swtchd rt over 1f out: led 1f out: styd on u.p* **6/1**[1]
00-4 2 3 ¼ **Okafranca (IRE)**[17] 1147 3-9-3 **59**........................ HayleyTurner 12 61
(W R Muir) *trckd ldrs: rdn over 3f out: styd on* **6/1**[1]
0-34 3 nk **Yakama (IRE)**[15] 1193 3-8-5 **47**........................(p) RichardThomas 7 48
(D J S Ffrench Davis) *chsd ldrs: led over 3f out: rdn and hdd 1f out: styd on same pce* **7/1**[3]
000- 4 ½ **Kalokairi (IRE)**[192] 6106 3-9-3 **59**........................ SebSanders 11 59+
(J L Dunlop) *s.i.s: hld up: styd on u.p fr over 2f out: styd on* **9/1**
000- 5 2 ¾ **Flower Appeal**[246] 4578 3-8-7 **49** ow1........................ TomEaves 1 44
(M W Easterby) *prom: rdn over 2f out: wknd fnl f* **8/1**
030- 6 3 **Titfer (IRE)**[162] 6750 3-8-11 **56**........................ LukeMorris(3) 2 45
(A W Carroll) *led over 6f: sn rdn: wknd fnl f* **14/1**
050- 7 nk **Paddy Rielly (IRE)**[236] 4876 3-9-4 **60**........................ TGMcLaughlin 10 48+
(P D Evans) *dwlt: hld up: styd on appr fnl f: nvr nrr* **12/1**
000- 8 shd **Patthepainter (GER)**[186] 6255 3-8-11 **53**........................ FergusSweeney 3 41
(K R Burke) *hld up in tch: rdn over 3f out: wknd over 1f out* **13/2**[2]
304- 9 nk **Pequeno Dinero (IRE)**[206] 5736 3-8-11 **58**........................ KellyHarrison(5) 14 45
(C W Fairhurst) *hld up: rdn over 3f out: n.d* **16/1**
-000 10 4 **Dawn Wind**[17] 1147 3-8-11 **53**........................(p) LiamJones 13 32
(I A Wood) *hld up: rdn 1/2-way: sme hdwy and hung lft over 3f out: sn wknd* **25/1**
000- 11 ¾ **Promised Gold**[171] 6592 3-8-13 **58**........................ TravisBlock(3) 8 36
(J A Geake) *plld hrd and prom: rdn 1/2-way: wknd over 1f out* **20/1**
0-00 12 2 **New Minerton (IRE)**[16] 1166 3-8-7 **49** ow1........................ RobertHavlin 9 23
(B R Millman) *hld up: plld hrd: a in rr* **40/1**
6-61 13 shd **Chanteuse De Rue (IRE)**[7] 1343 3-8-11 **53**........................ GregFairley 4 26
(M Johnston) *hld up: rdn over 4f out: wknd 2f out* **8/1**
000- 14 11 **Eighty Twenty**[246] 4565 3-8-4 **46** oh1........................ RoystonFfrench 15 —
(M W Easterby) *hld up: rdn 1/2-way: hung lft over 4f out: sn wknd* **40/1**
506- 15 23 **Bewdley**[170] 6611 3-9-1 **57**........................ SaleemGolam 16 —
(Mrs K Waldron) *prom to 1/2-way* **66/1**
0354 16 nk **Thankforthemusic (IRE)**[7] 1343 3-9-3 **59**........................(b[1]) ChrisCatlin 6 —
(C Tinkler) *prom: lost pl 8f out: bhd fr 1/2-way* **16/1**

2m 18.28s (7.58) **Going Correction** +0.675s/f (Yiel) **16** Ran SP% **127.7**
Speed ratings (Par 96): **96,93,93,92,90 88,87,87,87,84 83,82,82,73,54 54**
CSF £40.82 CT £269.96 TOTE £6.30: £1.50, £1.70, £2.30, £3.70; EX 36.60.
Owner Mel Roberts and Ms Nicola Meese **Bred** Paradime Ltd **Trained** Musley Bank, N Yorks

FOCUS
A moderate handicap. The form still looks sound enough for the class, however, and the winner is progressive.

1479 RACING UK THE UK'S BEST RACECOURSES H'CAP — 1m 54y
8:00 (8:01) (Class 6) (0-65,65) 3-Y-O — **£2,047** (£604; £302) **Stalls** Centre

Form — RPR

00-0 **1** **Buddy Holly**[45] 796 3-8-13 **60** .... PatDobbs 9 — 68
(Pat Eddery) *chsd ldr over 6f out: led over 2f out: drvn out* — **16/1**

050- **2** ½ **Xtravaganza (IRE)**[178] 6427 3-8-12 **59** .... JamesDoyle 5 — 65
(J W Hills) *chsd ldrs: rdn over 2f out: ev ch fr over 1f out: r.o* — **12/1**

50-4 **3** 3¼ **Maddy**[10] 1274 3-9-0 **61** .... (p) TedDurcan 2 — 60
(George Baker) *a.p: rdn over 2f out: styd on same pce fnl f* — **6/1**[3]

005- **4** 1½ **Aquarian Dancer**[207] 5702 3-8-7 **54** ow1 .... TomEaves 6 — 49
(Jedd O'Keeffe) *plld hrd: led 1f: trckd ldrs: rdn over 2f out: no ex fnl f* **25/1**

0333 **5** 1¾ **Little Knickers**[14] 1203 3-9-4 **65** .... HayleyTurner 1 — 56
(Andrew Reid) *dwlt: hld up: hdwy over 3f out: sn rdn: wknd over 1f out* — **10/1**

33-3 **6** nse **Rub Of The Relic (IRE)**[18] 1124 3-9-3 **64** .... StephenDonohoe 3 — 55
(P A Blockley) *led 7f out: rdn and hdd over 2f out: wknd fnl f* — **13/2**

5000 **7** 1 **Marino Prince (FR)**[45] 803 3-8-11 **58** .... DaneO'Neill 8 — 47
(T Wall) *hld up: hdwy 1/2-way: rdn and wknd over 1f out* — **25/1**

053- **8** nse **Bid Art (IRE)**[164] 6715 3-9-4 **65** .... SebSanders 4 — 54
(A M Balding) *hld up in tch: rdn over 2f out: n.m.r over 1f out: sn wknd* — **3/1**[1]

600- **9** nk **Redarsene**[169] 6618 3-8-13 **60** .... SamHitchcott 7 — 48
(M G Quinlan) *s.s: hld up: rdn over 3f out: n.d* — **14/1**

000- **10** 1¼ **Orbital Orchid**[219] 5344 3-8-5 **52** .... ChrisCatlin 12 — 37
(W S Kittow) *hld up: bhd fr 1/2-way* — **25/1**

3-05 **11** ½ **Minwir (IRE)**[16] 1166 3-9-4 **65** .... RobertHavlin 13 — 49
(M Quinn) *hld up: rdn over 2f out: wknd over 1f out* — **18/1**

045- **12** ½ **Kristal Glory (IRE)**[222] 5268 3-8-10 **57** .... PaulHanagan 10 — 46
(J L Dunlop) *hld up: rdn and nt clr run over 1f out: hmpd and eased ins fnl f* — **7/2**[2]

1m 52.41s (6.81) **Going Correction** +0.675s/f (Yiel) — **12 Ran SP% 121.0**
Speed ratings (Par 96): **92,91,88,86,85 84,83,83,83,82 81,81**
CSF £194.12 CT £1297.00 TOTE £14.20: £4.40, £3.30, £2.90; EX 308.10 Place 6 £1,799.96 Place 5 £350.85 ..
Owner Hayman, Pearson, Phillips & McGuinness **Bred** R J & S A Carter **Trained** Nether Winchendon, Bucks

FOCUS
An ordinary three-year-old handicap which saw the first pair come clear. The third sets the level.
Buddy Holly Official explanation: trainer's rep said, regarding the apparent improvement in form, colt had benefited from the soft ground and step up in trip
Kristal Glory(IRE) Official explanation: trainer's rep said colt had suffered a breathing problem
T/Plt: £4,144.00 to a £1 stake. Pool: £41,440.30. 7.30 winning tickets. T/Qpdt: £84.30 to a £1 stake. Pool: £5,216.40. 45.75 winning tickets. CR

[1447] THIRSK (L-H)
Saturday, April 19
OFFICIAL GOING: Good (good to soft in places)
Wind: Moderate, half-against Weather: Overcast

1480 DAVID CHAPMAN "CAPPUCCINO" CLAIMING STKS — 5f
2:05 (2:07) (Class 5) 2-Y-O — **£3,885** (£1,156; £577; £288) **Stalls** High

Form — RPR

1 **Fangfoss Girls** 2-8-7 0 .... PJMcDonald(3) 4 — 58
(G R Oldroyd) *trckd ldrs: effrt over 1f out: rdn to ld jst ins fnl f: styd on* — **33/1**

2 2¼ **Gaborone** 2-8-6 0 .... TPO'Shea 9 — 45+
(M R Channon) *s.i.s and bhd: hdwy wl over 1f out: sn rdn and styd on strly ins fnl f* — **9/2**

3 ¾ **Rose Of Coma (IRE)** 2-8-8 0 .... PaulHanagan 10 — 44+
(R A Fahey) *dwlt: sn chsng ldrs: effrt 2f out: sn rdn and edgd lft appr fnl f: kpt on u.p* — **11/4**[1]

6 **4** ¾ **Dazzling Dust (IRE)**[10] 1263 2-8-10 0 .... JackDean(7) 6 — 50
(W G M Turner) *led: rdn wl over 1f out: drvn and hung lft ent fnl f: sn hdd & wknd* — **10/3**[2]

3 **5** hd **Syrup (IRE)**[10] 1264 2-8-1 0 .... LukeMorris(3) 5 — 36
(P D Evans) *chsd ldrs: rdn along and outpcd 1/2-way: swtchd rt over 1f out: kpt on u.p ins fnl f* — **4/1**[3]

6 nk **Kneesy Earsy Nosey** 2-8-12 0 .... KimTinkler 2 — 43
(N Tinkler) *chsd ldrs on outer: effrt 2f out: sn rdn: edgd rt and wknd ent fnl f* — **22/1**

7 2 **Naughty Natz** 2-8-8 0 .... MickyFenton 3 — 31
(P T Midgley) *dwlt: a outpcd in rr* — **12/1**

13 **8** 1¼ **Heaven Or Hell (IRE)**[4] 1384 2-8-11 0 .... TGMcLaughlin 1 — 29+
(P D Evans) *wnt lft s: sn prom: cl up 1/2-way: rdn and ev ch over 1f out: edgd lft and wkng whn n.m.r ent fnl f* — **6/1**

64.81 secs (5.21) **Going Correction** +0.675s/f (Yiel) — **8 Ran SP% 117.2**
Speed ratings (Par 92): **85,81,80,79,78 78,75,73**
CSF £179.05 TOTE £56.10: £11.60, £1.80, £1.50; EX 417.90.Fangfoss Girls was claimed by P. D. Evans for £9,000. Gaborone was claimed by E. Wilmott for £7,000.
Owner R C Bond **Bred** Bond Thoroughbred Corporation **Trained** Brawby, N Yorks

FOCUS
Low-grade stuff. The form horse finished last.

NOTEBOOK
Fangfoss Girls, who lacks scope, was very professional on her debut and belied her long odds. She should hold her own at a low level and was claimed by David Evans.
Gaborone, who is related to 2yo winners, got behind when the tempo increased and also ran green under pressure but, once straightened out, she stayed on well to be gaining at the finish. She should improve for the run. (op 7-2 tchd 5-1)
Rose Of Coma(IRE), from a stable that has already had a debut juvenile winner, looked to have the ideal draw to make a winning debut but lack of experience counted against her at the end. She looks up to winning a small race at some stage. (op 4-1 tchd 9-2)
Dazzling Dust(IRE) broke quickly and led his rivals until looking very one-paced inside the final furlong. A drop to selling company might help his cause. (op 7-2)
Syrup(IRE), who was behind stablemate Heaven Or Hell last time, proved she is going in the right direction but looks in need of a stiffer test. (op 5-1 tchd 11-2)
Kneesy Earsy Nosey was not disgraced but never looked like winning. (op 25-1 tchd 20-1)
Heaven Or Hell(IRE), beaten in a seller last time after landing one on his debut, did not get away too sharply from the lowest stall and proved very disappointing when placed under pressure. He was beaten fully 2f from home. (op 4-1)

1481 CONSTANT SECURITY H'CAP — 7f
2:40 (2:40) (Class 3) (0-90,90) 4-Y-O+ — **£7,771** (£2,312; £1,155; £577) **Stalls** Low

Form — RPR

201- **1** **Transcend**[177] 6450 4-9-0 **86** .... RobertHavlin 7 — 103+
(J H M Gosden) *trckd ldr: led over 2f out: rdn clr over 1f out: kpt on* — **2/1**[1]

00-0 **2** 1¼ **Extraterrestrial**[21] 1071 4-8-12 **84** .... PaulHanagan 11 — 95
(R A Fahey) *hld up in midfield: hdwy over 2f out: swtchd lft and rdn over 1f out: styd on wl fnl f* — **25/1**

601- **3** 3¾ **Signor Peltro**[267] 3911 5-9-3 **89** .... FergusSweeney 10 — 90
(H Candy) *trckd ldrs: hdwy on outer 3f out: rdn to chse wnr over 1f out: kpt on same pce ins fnl f* — **7/1**[3]

6-60 **4** ¾ **Skhilling Spirit**[14] 1218 5-8-12 **89** .... NeilBrown(5) 5 — 88+
(T D Barron) *dwlt and towards rr: rdn along and hdwy over 2f out: kpt on ins fnl f: nrst fin* — **12/1**

200- **5** 1½ **Malcheek (IRE)**[176] 6472 6-9-1 **90** .... DuranFentiman(3) 2 — 85
(T D Easterby) *in tch: hdwy 3f out: rdn along over 2f out: drvn over 1f out and kpt on same pce* — **16/1**

0-00 **6** ½ **White Deer (USA)**[14] 1218 4-9-1 **87** .... SilvestreDeSousa 9 — 80
(D Nicholls) *chsd ldrs: rdn along 3f out: drvn 2f out: one pce fr over 1f out* — **12/1**

0-11 **7** ¾ **The Osteopath (IRE)**[16] 1174 5-8-12 **84** .... PhillipMakin 13 — 75
(M Dods) *hld up towards rr: hdwy on outer wl over 2f out: sn rdn and no imp appr fnl f* — **5/1**[2]

00-0 **8** 5 **Nevada Desert (IRE)**[25] 1016 8-8-7 **82** .... MichaelJStainton(3) 14 — 60
(R M Whitaker) *hld up towards rr: effrt and sme hdwy 2f out: sn rdn and nvr nr ldrs* — **28/1**

1132 **9** nk **Distant Sun (USA)**[24] 1033 4-8-13 **85** .... TomEaves 4 — 62
(Miss L A Perratt) *chsd ldrs on inner: rdn along wl over 2f out: grad wknd* — **12/1**

14-0 **10** 2½ **Lap Of Honour (IRE)**[28] 958 4-8-12 **84** .... (p) TPO'Shea 6 — 54
(Jennie Candlish) *led: rdn along 3f out: sn hdd and grad wknd* — **25/1**

60-6 **11** 1 **Overrule (USA)**[14] 1218 4-9-0 **86** .... RoystonFfrench 8 — 54
(B Ellison) *a midfield* — **25/1**

00/0 **12** nk **Another Bottle (IRE)**[25] 1016 7-9-1 **87** .... GrahamGibbons 1 — 54
(J J Quinn) *towards rr: rdn along over 3f out: n.d* — **25/1**

000- **12** dht **Countdown**[210] 5617 6-8-11 **83** .... DavidAllan 3 — 50
(T D Easterby) *in tch on inner: rdn along over 2f out: sn wknd* — **20/1**

0-00 **14** 3½ **Minority Report**[14] 1218 8-9-4 **90** .... PaulFessey 16 — 47
(D Nicholls) *a in rr* — **33/1**

2230 **15** ½ **Gallantry**[14] 1218 6-8-12 **87** .... TolleyDean(3) 15 — 43
(D Shaw) *hld up: a in rr* — **28/1**

051- **16** nk **Captain Jacksparra (IRE)**[229] 5092 4-9-2 **88** .... DO'Donohoe 12 — 43
(K A Ryan) *chsd ldrs: rdn along 3f out: sn wknd* — **10/1**

1m 28.83s (1.63) **Going Correction** +0.425s/f (Yiel) — **16 Ran SP% 130.5**
Speed ratings (Par 107): **107,105,101,100,98 98,97,91,91,88 87,86,86,82,82 81**
CSF £69.89 CT £331.86 TOTE £3.20: £1.30, £6.00, £2.00, £2.60; EX 117.70.
Owner H R H Princess Haya Of Jordan **Bred** Keith Freeman **Trained** Newmarket, Suffolk

FOCUS
Quite a competitive handicap, won in good style by the unexposed Transcend whose stable is in such good form. This is strong form for the grade.

NOTEBOOK
Transcend ◆, running without any headgear this time, took a nice lead from Lap Of Honour until hitting the front over 2f out. He stayed on too strongly for his rivals from that point and was never in any danger of being caught. With more improvement to come, he looks a step in front of the handicapper. (op 15-8 tchd 9-4 in places)
Extraterrestrial, who was always going well, had a bit to do as they turned in but, once moved to the inside rail, kept on strongly, threading his way through the field. The winner had already flown but he beat the rest nicely.
Signor Peltro, without the blinkers he wore when last seen, had every chance down the centre of the track but could not get on terms. It was a good effort after such a long absence and he should be able to build on the effort.
Skhilling Spirit, who has some sound form figures at this distance, finished very nicely from off the pace. Well handicapped on his winning form, he is not one to trust completely until proving he can get his head in front after some quirky behaviour last season. (tchd 14-1)
Malcheek(IRE) has a superb record at the track and did not shape too badly after pulling very hard on his seasonal debut.
White Deer(USA), back on some better ground, is steadily coming down the weights and it would be no surprise to see his trainer land a nice handicap with him during the summer. (op 18-1)
The Osteopath(IRE), given a patient ride at the rear of the pack, was produced to have every chance but ran as though firmly in the grip of the handicapper after two recent wins. (op 13-2 tchd 9-2)
Minority Report was not given a positive ride (although he has been held up in the past) and should ease in the weights again as a result. (op 66-1)
Captain Jacksparra(IRE) was well supported before the race but weakened tamely under pressure. (op 25-1)

1482 SQUIRE FREDERICK BELL H'CAP — 1m 4f
3:15 (3:15) (Class 5) (0-75,75) 4-Y-O+ — **£3,885** (£1,156; £577; £288) **Stalls** Low

Form — RPR

/2-3 **1** **Pee Jay's Dream**[8] 1299 6-8-7 **62** .... DaleGibson 1 — 72
(M W Easterby) *a.p: hdwy to ld wl over 2f out: rdn wl over 1f out and sn hdd: drvn and rallied to ld ins fnl f: kpt on gamely* — **11/4**[1]

060- **2** nk **Maneki Neko (IRE)**[149] 5807 6-8-7 **62** .... RoystonFfrench 2 — 72
(E W Tuer) *a.p: hdwy over 2f out: rdn to ld wl over 1f out: drvn and hdd ins fnl f: no ex towards fin* — **14/1**

203- **3** 1¾ **Sporting Gesture**[165] 6703 11-9-1 **70** .... PhillipMakin 8 — 77
(M W Easterby) *hld up towards rr: pushed along and hdwy 3f out: rdn wl over 1f out: kpt on u.p ins fnl f* — **20/1**

540- **4** 1½ **Pretty Demanding (IRE)**[173] 6555 4-9-3 **73** .... TPO'Shea 14 — 78
(M G Quinlan) *hld up in rr: hdwy 3f out: rdn wl over 1f out: kpt on ins fnl f: nrst fin* — **14/1**

14/5 **5** ½ **Hill Billy Rock (IRE)**[14] 1219 5-8-9 **67** .... PJMcDonald(3) 4 — 71
(G A Swinbank) *trckd ldrs: hdwy and pushed along over 2f out: sn drvn and kpt on same pce* — **3/1**[2]

0-26 **6** 7 **Coronado's Gold (USA)**[8] 1296 7-8-5 **60** .... TWilliams 10 — 53
(B Ellison) *hld up in rr: hdwy over 3f out and sn pushed along: rdn 2f out: sn no imp* — **20/1**

562- **7** hd **Dan Tucker**[187] 6235 4-8-13 **69** .... PaulHanagan 7 — 61
(N Tinkler) *midfield: hdwy to chse ldrs 4f out: rdn along 2f out: kpt on same pce* — **9/1**

-340 **8** hd **Sforzando**[17] 1159 7-8-6 **68** .... KristinStubbs(7) 12 — 60
(Mrs L Stubbs) *in rr tl styd on fnl 2f: nvr a factor* — **25/1**

0-00 **9** *1 1/4* **Turn Of Phrase (IRE)**[28] 963 9-8-10 **65**....................(b) TonyHamilton 5 55
(N Wilson) *prom: cl up 5f out: rdn along over 2f out: sn drvn and grad wknd* **33/1**

62-1 **10** *1 1/4* **Apache Fort**[17] 1151 5-9-1 **70**.. MickyFenton 15 58
(T Keddy) *hld up towards in midfield: effrt and sme hdwy on outer over 3f out: rdn along 2f and wknd appr fnl f* **15/2**[3]

40-3 **11** *1/2* **Flagstone (USA)**[8] 1307 4-8-4 **60** oh2..................... SilvestreDeSousa 13 47
(D Nicholls) *led: rdn along over 3f out: hdd wl over 2f out and sn wknd* **20/1**

000- **12** *1 1/4* **Moonwalking**[190] 6158 4-8-12 **68**... TomEaves 9 53
(Jedd O'Keeffe) *chsd ldrs: hdwy and prom 4f out: rdn along over 3f out and sn wknd* **22/1**

65-6 **13** *3/4* **Trance (IRE)**[8] 1305 8-9-1 **70**...(p) PaulFessey 3 54
(T D Barron) *a in rr* **16/1**

60-0 **14** *2 1/4* **Helvetio**[25] 1017 6-9-2 **71**.. PaulMulrennan 6 52
(Micky Hammond) *hld up: a towards rr* **50/1**

322- **15** *10* **Kalasam**[176] 6481 4-8-12 **75**... NSLawes(7) 11 40
(M W Easterby) *chsd ldrs on outer: rdn along over 3f out: sn wknd* **16/1**

2m 43.1s (6.90) **Going Correction** +0.425s/f (Yiel)
WFA 4 from 5yo+ 1lb **15** Ran SP% **125.9**
Speed ratings (Par 103): **94,93,92,91,91 86,86,86,85,84 84,83,83,81,74**
CSF £39.65 CT £682.53 TOTE £3.80: £1.40, £3.90, £6.60; EX 42.30.
Owner P Bown & R Edmonds **Bred** Downfield Cottage Stud **Trained** Sheriff Hutton, N Yorks

FOCUS
Sound-looking form for the grade with the first five finishing clear. The race should work out.
Moonwalking Official explanation: jockey said gelding hung left in closing stages

1483 MICHAEL FOSTER MEMORIAL CONDITIONS STKS 6f
3:50 (3:51) (Class 3) 4-Y-O+

£7,477 (£2,239; £1,119; £560; £279; £140) **Stalls** High

Form RPR

310- **1** **Utmost Respect**[203] 5797 4-9-0 103.................................. PaulHanagan 1 114+
(R A Fahey) *trckd ldrs: smooth hdwy on outer to ld over 1f out: shkn up ins fnl f: comf* **15/8**[2]

3002 **2** *1 3/4* **Big Timer (USA)**[51] 738 4-9-0 0.. TomEaves 5 108
(Miss L A Perratt) *trckd ldrs: effrt and nt clr run wl over 1f out: swtchd rt and rdn ent fnl f: sn chsng wnr: drvn and no imp towards fin* **8/1**[3]

2136 **3** *4 1/2* **Ebraam (USA)**[56] 677 5-8-11 99..................................... TolleyDean(3) 3 94
(D Shaw) *hld up: swtchd lft and hdwy wl over 1f out: sn rdn and kpt on ins fnl f* **14/1**

20-0 **4** *3* **Hinton Admiral**[28] 959 4-9-7 103....................................... DaleGibson 2 91
(R A Fahey) *dwlt: sn cl up: rdn along 2f out and grad wknd* **33/1**

50-3 **5** *hd* **Wi Dud**[28] 959 4-9-0 109... DO'Donohoe 4 83
(K A Ryan) *led: rdn along 2f out: drvn: edgd lft and hdd over 1f out: sn wknd* **5/6**[1]

100- **6** *16* **Celtic Mill**[240] 4746 10-9-5 103.....................................(p) TonyHamilton 6 37
(D W Barker) *cl up: rdn along over 2f out and sn wknd* **16/1**

1m 15.59s (2.89) **Going Correction** +0.675s/f (Yiel) **6** Ran SP% **115.9**
Speed ratings (Par 107): **107,104,98,94,94 73**
CSF £17.61 TOTE £3.00: £1.50, £4.20; EX 21.70.
Owner The Rumpole Partnership **Bred** Heather Raw **Trained** Musley Bank, N Yorks

FOCUS
Quite a competitive conditions sprint won in good style by the progressive-looking Utmost Respect. There is more to come from him but overall this form is a bit shaky.

NOTEBOOK
Utmost Respect ◆ looks firmly on the upgrade after a smooth success. Having his first run since September, he was value for more than the winning distance and is ready for a step up in grade. (op 9-4 tchd 11-4)
Big Timer(USA), who has been running respectably in Dubai this year, was definitely the second-best horse in the race on the day but got a little lucky, as he had nowhere to go up the rail for much of the race after being covered up. However, the weakening Wi Dud edged to his left and allowed him up his inside. He should hold his own in these sort of races. (op 11-2 tchd 9-1 in a place)
Ebraam(USA) did not run too badly considering he was the lowest-rated of these on official figures. He has never won on a straight course and will be better suited by a left-handed track, as he has only ever won that way round.
Hinton Admiral, who had a 7lb penalty, showed good speed until faltering inside the final furlong. There are races to be won with him this year. (op 28-1 tchd 25-1)
Wi Dud was most disappointing after showing good pace. He looked ill at ease in the final furlong and something may have been amiss. Official explanation: trainer had no explanation for the poor form shown (op Evens)
Celtic Mill was beaten a long way from home after showing a bit of early speed. (tchd 14-1)

1484 THOMAS LORD STKS (H'CAP) 5f
4:25 (4:30) (Class 3) (0-90,88) 3-Y-O **£7,771** (£2,312; £1,155; £577) **Stalls** High

Form RPR

060- **1** **Mey Blossom**[169] 6619 3-9-1 **85**.......................... MichaelJStainton(3) 4 92
(R M Whitaker) *trckd ldr far side: hdwy to ld that gp and overall ldr appr fnl f: sn rdn and hung rt: kpt on* **40/1**

221- **2** *1/2* **Hamish McGonagall**[163] 6729 3-9-0 **81**........................... DavidAllan 11 86
(T D Easterby) *trckd ldrs stands' side: hdwy to ld that gp 2f out and sn rdn: drvn ins fnl f and styd on wl towards fin* **12/1**

213- **3** *1 1/4* **Rose Siog**[239] 4775 3-8-12 **79**... PaulHanagan 12 80+
(R A Fahey) *trckd ldrs stands' side: hdwy 2f out: rdn ent fnl f and kpt on* **11/2**[3]

11- **4** *3/4* **Cape Vale (IRE)**[211] 5582 3-9-2 **83**........................... SilvestreDeSousa 6 81+
(D Nicholls) *chsd ldrs stands' side: rdn wl over 1f out: kpt on u.p ins fnl f* **5/2**[1]

623- **5** *nk* **President Elect (IRE)**[182] 6326 3-8-9 **76**........................ PhillipMakin 16 73+
(T D Barron) *towards rr stands' side: hdwy 2f out: sn rdn and kpt on ins fnl f: nrst fin* **5/1**[2]

31-1 **6** *1 3/4* **Style Award**[45] 798 3-9-1 **85**............................... AndrewMullen(3) 17 79+
(W J H Ratcliffe) *in rr stands' side: effrt and nt clr run over 2f out: swtchd rt and lft and hdwy over 1f out: sn rdn and styd on ins fnl f: nrst fin* **7/1**

0-21 **7** *hd* **Kinout (IRE)**[22] 1066 3-8-10 **77**.................................... DO'Donohoe 3 67
(K A Ryan) *overall ldr far side: rdn along 2f out: hdd appr fnl f: wknd* **20/1**

061- **8** *1/2* **Firenza Bond**[182] 6326 3-8-9 **81**.................................. SladeO'Hara(5) 13 69
(G R Oldroyd) *chsd ldrs stands' side: rdn along wl over 1f out: drvn and wknd ent fnl f* **25/1**

006- **9** *1 3/4* **Bespoke Boy**[215] 5480 3-9-7 **88**... LeeEnstone 2 70
(P C Haslam) *chsd ldrs far side: rdn along over 2f out: sn wknd* **16/1**

21-5 **10** *hd* **Incomparable**[16] 1167 3-8-13 **80**...................................... MickyFenton 14 61
(A J McCabe) *cl up stands' rail: rdn along 2f out: drvn and wknd appr fnl f* **14/1**

10-6 **11** *1/2* **Baronovici (IRE)**[7] 1328 3-8-11 **78**................................ TonyHamilton 15 57
(D W Barker) *a towards rr stands' side* **16/1**

606- **12** *1* **Not My Choice (IRE)**[182] 6326 3-8-13 **80**.................. GrahamGibbons 5 56
(S Parr) *a towards rr stands' side* **33/1**

6221 **13** *2* **Loose Caboose (IRE)**[30] 952 3-8-5 **72**.....................(p) AndrewElliott 10 40
(A J McCabe) *led stands' side gp: rdn along and hdd 2f out: sn wknd* **25/1**

11-0 **14** *3 1/2* **Miesko (USA)**[21] 1075 3-9-5 **86**................................... RoystonFfrench 7 42
(M Johnston) *a towards rr stands' side* **12/1**

-210 **15** *1 1/2* **Chivola (IRE)**[27] 977 3-8-7 **74** ow2................................. TomEaves 1 24
(B Smart) *chsd ldng pair far side: rdn along over 2f out: sn wknd* **33/1**

5-31 **16** *7* **Barraland**[27] 977 3-8-11 **78**.. TPO'Shea 9 3
(M R Channon) *cl up stands' side: rdn along 1/2-way: sn wknd* **12/1**

62.70 secs (3.10) **Going Correction** +0.675s/f (Yiel) **16** Ran SP% **135.4**
Speed ratings (Par 102): **102,101,99,98,97 94,94,93,90,90 89,88,84,79,76 65**
CSF £483.25 CT £3200.46 TOTE £60.90: £9.60, £2.00, £2.20, £1.40; EX 460.20.
Owner Waz Developments Ltd **Bred** Hellwood Stud Farm **Trained** Scarcroft, W Yorks

FOCUS
Mey Blossom won at a big price but this was no fluke. A race that should throw up some winners and, although they split into two groups, the evidence of this race and the following contest suggests there was no significant bias.

NOTEBOOK
Mey Blossom stayed on the far side of the track before finishing strongly down the middle of the course. She had some fair form at two and probably did not deserve to go off at such long odds, even allowing for the negative-looking draw she had. (op 50-1)
Hamish McGonagall ◆ showed good pace throughout and was a clear winner down the near-side rail. Very consistent last season, he looks set for a decent year at this trip. (op 20-1)
Rose Siog ◆ made a highly satisfactory return to the track. Given a light campaign at two, she has the scope to improve again this season and can find an opportunity before too long. (op 5-1 tchd 9-2)
Cape Vale(IRE) ◆, dropping to 5f for the first time, kept towards the middle of the track and stayed on well for pressure. Unbeaten in two runs last season, he is probably capable of better, especially over another furlong. (op 4-1 tchd 9-2)
President Elect(IRE) ◆ went nicely right up the stands' rail before getting slightly outpaced when the tempo increased. To his credit, he kept on well for pressure, and should shed his maiden tag soon. (op 7-1)
Style Award was by far the most unlucky horse in the race and would have gone a lot closer with a clearer passage. Official explanation: jockey said filly was denied a clear run (op 6-1)
Firenza Bond ran a lot better than his final position suggests and could pop up at a nice price soon.

1485 PINDER DALE H'CAP 6f
5:00 (5:00) (Class 5) (0-75,75) 4-Y-O+ **£3,885** (£1,156; £577; £288) **Stalls** High

Form RPR

0000 **1** **Imperial Echo (USA)**[26] 994 7-8-10 **70**....................... TolleyDean(3) 17 79
(D Shaw) *hld up towards rr stands' side: effrt and n.m.r wl over 1f out: sn rdn and hdwy ent fnl f: swtchd rt ins fnl f: styd on strly to ld on line* **7/1**[3]

55-0 **2** *hd* **Soto**[15] 1189 5-8-4 **61** oh1.. DaleGibson 6 69
(M W Easterby) *cl up far side: hdwy to ld that gp and overall ldr wl over 2f out: rdn over 1f out: drvn ins fnl f: hdd on line* **14/1**

-331 **3** *shd* **Dorn Dancer (IRE)**[4] 1378 6-8-8 **65** 6ex........................ TonyHamilton 2 73
(D W Barker) *trckd ldrs far side: hdwy over 2f out: rdn to chal over 1f out: drvn ins fnl f and ev ch tl no ex nr line* **7/2**[1]

200- **4** *1 1/4* **Dark Champion**[196] 6020 8-8-4 **61** oh1........................ FrankieMcDonald 15 68+
(R E Barr) *towards rr stands' side: hdwy and nt clr run 2f out and again over 1f out: sn rdn and styd on ins fnl f: nrst fin* **20/1**

00-0 **5** *2 1/4* **Double Carpet (IRE)**[26] 990 5-8-1 **61** oh3............ AndrewMullen(3) 10 58
(R C Guest) *prom stands' side: led that gp over 2f out and sn rdn: drvn ent fnl f and kpt on same pce* **14/1**

5353 **6** *shd* **Goodbye Cash (IRE)**[14] 1204 4-8-5 **65**........................ LukeMorris(3) 1 61
(P D Evans) *chsd ldrs far side: rdn along over 2f out: sn drvn and one pce appr fnl f* **16/1**

0255 **7** *1 1/4* **Inca Soldier (FR)**[45] 801 5-8-5 **62**......................... SilvestreDeSousa 20 54+
(R C Guest) *hld up and bhd stands' side: swtchd lft and hdwy whn n.m.r wl over 1f out: sn rdn and styd on ins fnl f: nrst fin* **12/1**

4430 **8** *shd* **Royal Challenge**[8] 1312 7-8-12 **69**............................... PatrickMathers 8 61+
(I W McInnes) *in tch stands' side: hdwy 2f out: rdn wl over 1f out: kpt on same pce ins fnl f* **25/1**

14-0 **9** *2* **Society Music (IRE)**[7] 1327 6-9-2 **73**............................... PhillipMakin 3 59
(M Dods) *chsd ldrs far side: rdn along 2f out: sn wknd* **14/1**

-364 **10** *shd* **Coleorton Dancer**[58] 636 6-9-0 **71**................................. DO'Donohoe 13 56
(K A Ryan) *chsd ldrs stands' side: rdn 2f out: drvn over 1f out: wknd ent fnl f* **17/2**

0-06 **11** *hd* **Steel Blue**[11] 1261 8-8-7 **67**.................................. MichaelJStainton(3) 11 52
(R M Whitaker) *cl up stands' side: rdn along over 2f out and grad wknd* **12/1**

000- **12** *1* **Danum Dancer**[213] 5522 4-9-1 **72**................................. RobertHavlin 4 54
(N Bycroft) *overall ldr far side: rdn along and hdd wl over 2f out: grad wknd* **16/1**

2262 **13** *1 1/4* **Strathmore (IRE)**[18] 1129 4-8-8 **65**.............................. PaulHanagan 7 43
(R A Fahey) *in tch far side: rdn along wl over 2f out and sn wknd* **13/2**[2]

000- **14** *1/2* **Windjammer**[186] 6256 4-8-8 **65**... DavidAllan 16 41
(T D Easterby) *trckd ldrs stands' side: effrt over 2f out: sn rdn and btn* **12/1**

260- **15** *3/4* **Oranmore Castle (IRE)**[206] 5722 6-8-10 **74**........... FrederikTylicki(7) 18 48
(R A Fahey) *chsd ldrs stands' side: effrt 2f out: sn rdn and wknd* **10/1**

00-0 **16** *1 1/4* **The Bear**[11] 1261 5-8-7 **67** ow2.................................... PJMcDonald(3) 12 37
(R Johnson) *led stands' side gp: rdn along over 2f out: sn hdd & wknd* **25/1**

130- **17** *16* **Ryedane (IRE)**[183] 6313 6-8-7 **67**............................. DuranFentiman(3) 9 —
(T D Easterby) *prom stands' side: rdn along 1/2-way: sn lost pl and bhd* **20/1**

1m 17.32s (4.62) **Going Correction** +0.675s/f (Yiel) **17** Ran SP% **139.7**
Speed ratings (Par 103): **96,95,95,93,90 90,89,89,86,86 85,84,82,82,81 79,58**
CSF £110.51 CT £431.55 TOTE £9.80: £3.00, £4.10, £1.30, £6.60; EX 168.40 Place 6 £91.38, Place 5 £42.18.
Owner The Circle Bloodstock I Limited **Bred** Derby Lane Farm **Trained** Danethorpe, Notts

FOCUS
One of the most interesting aspects of this race was the time, which was more than 1.7 seconds slower than the conditions sprint won by Utmost Respect. As in the previous event on the straight course, they split into two groups, but just a head separated the two sides at the line. Ordinary form, rated around the second and third.
Danum Dancer Official explanation: jockey said colt hung right throughout
Windjammer Official explanation: jockey said gelding was denied a clear run
T/Plt: £98.60 to a £1 stake. Pool: £61,540.21. 455.49 winning tickets. T/Qpdt: £26.70 to a £1 stake. Pool: £2,875.90. 79.50 winning tickets. JR

[1405]WOLVERHAMPTON (A.W) (L-H)

Saturday, April 19

OFFICIAL GOING: Standard

Wind: Fresh, half against

1486 WOLVERHAMPTON-RACECOURSE.CO.UK APPRENTICE H'CAP 1m 141y(P)

6:45 (6:45) (Class 5) (0-70,69) 4-Y-O+ £2,729 (£806; £403) Stalls Low

Form RPR

03-0 1 **Don Pietro**[60] 443 5-8-12 65 SophieDoyle(3) 2 74
(P A Blockley) *led for 1f: led again over 4f out: responded wl to chal fr over 1f out* **9/2[2]**

3565 2 hd **Happy As Larry (USA)**[19] 1112 6-9-5 69 (t) HaddenFrost 3 78
(J S Moore) *trckd ldrs: chal wnr and ev ch fr over 1f out: no ex nr fin* **6/1[3]**

6344 3 2 1/4 **Putra Laju (IRE)**[21] 1085 4-9-1 65 (v1) JamieJones 4 68
(J W Hills) *stdd s: hld: hdwy over 3f out: sn rdn: kpt on fnl f* **8/1**

3314 4 1/2 **Machinate (USA)**[5] 1369 6-9-4 68 AshleyHamblett 8 70
(W M Brisbourne) *in rr: hdwy on outside over 2f out: kpt on one pce fr over 1f out* **7/1**

1134 5 1 1/2 **Not Now Lewis (IRE)**[22] 1049 4-8-9 59 NicolPolli 6 58
(Miss Gay Kelleway) *hld up: rdn over 1f out: n.d* **16/1**

616- 6 hd **Pitbull**[152] 6878 5-8-4 61 (p) IanCraven(7) 5 59
(Mrs G S Rees) *slowly away: hld up: effrt on ins over 1f out: nvr on terms* **16/1**

2163 7 2 3/4 **Casablanca Minx (IRE)**[3] 1406 5-8-6 61 ow2 (v) RichardEvans(5) 1 53
(P D Evans) *in tch tl rdn and lost pl over 2f out* **9/2[2]**

6-52 8 3 **Scripted (USA)**[31] 941 4-9-4 68 (t) JackMitchell 7 53
(C F Wall) *led after 1f: hdd over 4f out: wknd qckly over 1f out* **5/2[1]**

1m 52.66s (2.16) **Going Correction** +0.175s/f (Slow) **8 Ran SP% 114.6**
Speed ratings (Par 103): **97,96,94,94,93 92,90,87**
CSF £31.56 CT £208.77 TOTE £5.90: £2.00, £2.40, £2.40; EX 43.80.
Owner Mighty Fine Partnership **Bred** B N And Mrs Toye **Trained** Lambourn, Berks
■ Stewards' Enquiry : Hadden Frost one-day ban: used whip with excessive frequency (May 5)

FOCUS
Ordinary handicap form, with the race slowly run and the favourite disappointing.

1487 RINGSIDE SUITE CLAIMING STKS 7f 32y(P)

7:15 (7:15) (Class 6) 3-Y-O £2,047 (£604; £302) Stalls High

Form RPR

4122 1 **Bridge Of Fermoy (IRE)**[3] 1407 3-9-6 76 (vt) NCallan 6 75
(Miss Gay Kelleway) *t.k.h: in tch on outside: wnt 2nd wl over 1f out: led ins fnl f and hld on wl* **5/6[1]**

242 2 3/4 **Caprio (IRE)**[31] 932 3-9-6 70 PatCosgrave 8 73
(J R Boyle) *trckd ldr: led over 2f out: hung lft and wandered u.p: hdd ins fnl f and no ex* **7/2[2]**

00-2 3 11 **Polish Priory (IRE)**[17] 1135 3-8-7 49 RichardMullen 3 30
(P D Evans) *in rr: carried wd 3f out: kpt on fnl f but no ch w first 2* **14/1**

0424 4 3 3/4 **Stoneacre Ma**[16] 1169 3-7-12 46 (v1) PatrickDonaghy(7) 4 18
(Peter Grayson) *hld up in rr: carried wd 3f out: nvr on terms* **50/1**

0603 5 3 1/2 **Hero Heart**[7] 1339 3-8-9 45 KirstyMilczarek(3) 2 16
(Jane Chapple-Hyam) *led tl hdd over 2f out: wknd qckly over 1f out* **14/1**

2540 6 1 **Whitcombe Flyer (USA)**[2] 1416 3-8-11 48 (bt) LPKeniry 5 12
(Miss M E Rowland) *in tch tl rdn and hung rt 3f out: sn btn* **28/1**

2313 7 1 1/2 **Days Of Pleasure (IRE)**[12] 1245 3-9-0 69 JerryO'Dwyer(3) 9 14
(J A Osborne) *t.k.h: in tch: rdn 3f out: wknd over 2f out* **13/2[3]**

-360 8 13 **Hollow Point (IRE)**[22] 1057 3-9-0 59 MickyFenton 7 —
(P T Midgley) *slowly away: racd wd: a bhd* **28/1**

1m 30.94s (1.34) **Going Correction** +0.175s/f (Slow) **8 Ran SP% 112.3**
Speed ratings (Par 96): **99,98,85,81,77 76,74,59**
CSF £3.62 TOTE £1.70: £1.10, £1.40, £2.00; EX 4.20.
Owner T & Z Racing Club **Bred** Tally-Ho Stud **Trained** Exning, Suffolk

FOCUS
A modest claimer and the two principals stamped their authority and came well clear in the closing stages. Bridge of Fermoy was just a shade off his best.
Whitcombe Flyer(USA) Official explanation: jockey said gelding hung right on final bend

1488 FIVE PROFITABLE YEARS AT EQUINEINVESTMENTS.CO.UK H'CAP 5f 216y(P)

7:45 (7:45) (Class 5) (0-70,70) 4-Y-O+ £2,914 (£867; £433; £216) Stalls Low

Form RPR

30-2 1 **Expensive Art (IRE)**[9] 1285 4-9-4 70 NCallan 3 86
(S A Callaghan) *a in tch and gng wl: led over 1f out: pushed clr: comf* **2/1[1]**

22-2 2 2 1/4 **Prince Of Delphi**[17] 1153 5-9-3 69 (p) GeorgeBaker 5 78
(R M Beckett) *in tch tl lost pl 1/2-way: rdn and hdwy over 1f out to chse wnr fnl f* **9/4[2]**

0642 3 2 1/4 **Methaaly (IRE)**[8] 1312 5-9-3 69 (be) RichardMullen 7 71
(M Mullineaux) *mid-div: styd on to go 3rd fnl f* **9/1**

-556 4 3 **Game Lady**[17] 1154 4-8-2 61 SophieDoyle(7) 2 53
(I A Wood) *trckd ldrs: rdn to ld over 2f out: hdd over 1f out: wknd ins fnl f* **14/1**

6246 5 1 1/4 **Figaro Flyer (IRE)**[10] 1268 5-8-13 65 PatCosgrave 6 53
(P Howling) *s.i.s: sn prom on outside: ev ch 2f out: sn wknd* **5/1[3]**

4301 6 3/4 **Jilly Why (IRE)**[15] 1185 7-8-7 59 ow1 (b) NeilChalmers 4 45
(Paul Green) *a struggling in rr* **13/2**

430- 7 21 **Millfields Dreams**[184] 6288 9-8-4 63 ow1 WilliamCarson(7) 1 —
(G C H Chung) *led tl hdd over 2f out: wknd qckly: sn eased* **28/1**

1m 15.03s (0.03) **Going Correction** +0.175s/f (Slow) **7 Ran SP% 114.2**
Speed ratings (Par 103): **106,103,100,96,94 93,65**
CSF £6.75 TOTE £2.40: £1.80, £1.80; EX 5.70.
Owner Matthew Green **Bred** Stone Ridge Farm **Trained** Newmarket, Suffolk

FOCUS
A modest handicap but won in great style by Expensive Art, who looks most progressive. The third is a good guide and the form has been taken at face value.

1489 RACINGFINEART.CO.UK CLAIMING STKS 5f 20y(P)

8:15 (8:16) (Class 6) 3-Y-O+ £2,388 (£705; £352) Stalls Low

Form RPR

00-3 1 **Desperate Dan**[15] 1190 7-10-0 78 (b) NCallan 6 78+
(A B Haynes) *mde all: rdn clr over 1f out: easily* **2/5[1]**

0600 2 5 **Stormburst (IRE)**[7] 1338 4-9-5 50 NeilChalmers 4 51
(A J Chamberlain) *in rr: rdn and hdwy on ins over 1f out to chse wnr fnl f* **7/1[3]**

50 3 2 1/4 **Many Welcomes**[25] 1019 3-8-9 0 PaulMulrennan 1 39
(B P J Baugh) *chsd ldng pair: wnt 2nd briefly appr fnl f: one pce* **28/1**

00-0 4 1/2 **Barbossa**[39] 845 3-7-13 35 DanielleMcCreery(5) 7 32
(A J McCabe) *trckd wnr tl wknd appr fnl f* **33/1**

2442 5 3/4 **Lady Hopeful (IRE)**[37] 871 6-8-9 45 (b) LPKeniry 5 28
(Peter Grayson) *racd on outside: brief effrt over 1f out: nvr on terms* **9/2[2]**

63.15 secs (0.85) **Going Correction** +0.175s/f (Slow)
WFA 3 from 4yo+ 10lb **5 Ran SP% 108.5**
Speed ratings (Par 101): **100,92,88,87,86**
CSF £3.67 TOTE £1.30: £1.10, £2.40; EX 4.00.
Owner Joe McCarthy **Bred** Sheikh Amin Dahlawi **Trained** Limpley Stoke, Bath

FOCUS
A weak claimer in which the winner did not have to run anywhere near his best to score.

1490 GWEN STAFFORD GOOD 70TH BIRTHDAY MAIDEN STKS 1m 141y(P)

8:45 (8:45) (Class 5) 3-Y-O+ £2,456 (£725; £362) Stalls Low

Form RPR

1 **Hollander (IRE)** 3-8-11 0 TPO'Shea 7 84+
(D J Coakley) *slowly away: sn in tch: wnt 2nd 4f out: led briefly 1f out: rallied to ld again last strides* **13/2[3]**

35- 2 shd **Military Power**[227] 5140 3-8-11 0 EddieAhern 5 84+
(J W Hills) *in tch: hdwy and swtchd lft to ld 1f out: rdn and hdd last strides* **5/2[2]**

536- 3 2 1/4 **King's Wonder**[197] 5977 3-8-11 79 RichardMullen 1 79
(W R Muir) *trckd ldrs: r.o one pce ins fnl 2f* **2/1[1]**

4 1 **Blow Hole (USA)** 3-8-11 0 NCallan 6 77+
(J Noseda) *in rr: effrt on outside over 2f out: kpt on one pce* **5/2[2]**

0-2 5 4 1/2 **Ancient Cross**[17] 1139 4-9-5 0 NSLawes(7) 2 69
(M W Easterby) *led tl rdn and hdd 1f out: wknd ins fnl f* **20/1**

65 6 12 **Royal Soverin**[61] 610 3-8-11 0 PatCosgrave 4 39
(M J Wallace) *trckd ldrs to over 3f out: sn wknd* **28/1**

00- 7 2 1/4 **Insured**[311] 2569 3-8-6 0 DanielleMcCreery(5) 11 34
(A J McCabe) *in tch tl lost pl over 3f out* **50/1**

8 1 1/4 **St Johns Wood** 3-8-11 0 PaulMulrennan 8 31
(M W Easterby) *outpcd and a bhd* **20/1**

0 9 8 **Springfield Lass**[14] 1222 3-8-3 0 AndrewMullen(3) 10 7
(Mrs A Duffield) *t.k.h on outside: hung rt and a bhd* **66/1**

1m 52.38s (1.88) **Going Correction** +0.175s/f (Slow)
WFA 3 from 4yo 15lb **9 Ran SP% 120.2**
Speed ratings (Par 103): **98,97,95,95,91 80,78,77,70**
CSF £22.95 TOTE £6.50: £1.40, £1.50, £1.50; EX 38.70.
Owner Chris Van Hoorn **Bred** Tower Bloodstock **Trained** West Ilsley, Berks

FOCUS
A fair maiden, with the second, third and fourth all giving the form a solid look.
Springfield Lass Official explanation: jockey said filly hung right throughout

1491 DINE IN THE HORIZONS RESTAURANT H'CAP 7f 32y(P)

9:15 (9:16) (Class 6) (0-65,65) 4-Y-O+ £2,047 (£604; £302) Stalls High

Form RPR

3400 1 **Newgate (UAE)**[11] 1258 4-7-13 51 oh6 (b1) DanielleMcCreery(5) 4 60
(Mrs R A Carr) *hld up: hdwy and swtchd rt over 1f out: r.o strly to ld ins fnl f* **50/1**

6333 2 2 1/4 **Sovereignty (JPN)**[21] 1085 6-8-9 61 PatrickHills(5) 10 64
(D K Ivory) *mid-div: hdwy on outside 2f out: edgd lft but kpt on to go 2nd ins fnl f* **7/1**

510- 3 hd **Affrettando (IRE)**[113] 7253 4-9-4 65 EddieAhern 1 67
(J A R Toller) *mid-div: rdn 3f out: swtchd rt 1f out: r.o fnl f* **7/1**

00-6 4 3/4 **It's A Dream (FR)**[37] 872 5-8-12 59 DaleGibson 11 59
(M W Easterby) *trckd ldrs: ev ch fr 2f out tl one pce ins fnl f* **6/1[3]**

1232 5 3/4 **Cape Of Storms**[5] 1371 5-8-12 59 (b1) PaulMulrennan 7 57
(R Brotherton) *trckd ldrs: rdn and led briefly 1f out: no ex ins fnl f* **11/4[1]**

0506 6 nk **Mister Benji**[14] 1207 9-7-11 51 oh6 (p) SoniaEaton(7) 5 49
(B P J Baugh) *mid-div: rdn over 1f out: outpcd ins fnl f* **20/1**

6101 7 1 1/4 **Elusive Warrior (USA)**[11] 1260 5-9-0 61 (p) NCallan 2 55
(A J McCabe) *led tl rdn and hdd 1f out: wknd ins fnl f* **9/2[2]**

6665 8 nk **Fine Ruler (IRE)**[17] 1153 4-9-4 65 GeorgeBaker 3 58
(M R Bosley) *in rr: rdn 2f out: hung lft and no hdwy after* **8/1**

5150 9 2 3/4 **Music Box Express**[4] 1386 4-9-1 65 (t) TolleyDean(3) 9 51
(George Baker) *trckd ldr: ev ch over 2f out: swtchd lft over 1f out: wknd* **11/1**

61-0 10 7 **Hollywood George**[35] 901 4-9-4 65 LPKeniry 6 32
(Miss M E Rowland) *a towards rr* **25/1**

3000 11 6 **Buzzin'Boyzee (IRE)**[14] 1209 5-8-6 53 ow2 RichardMullen 8 4
(P D Evans) *a bhd* **28/1**

1m 30.35s (0.75) **Going Correction** +0.175s/f (Slow) **11 Ran SP% 117.6**
Speed ratings (Par 101): **102,99,99,98,97 97,95,95,92,84 77**
CSF £359.95 CT £2829.51 TOTE £81.20: £12.50, £1.50, £2.00; EX 290.70 Place 6 £38.22, Place 5 £9.26..
Owner Michael Hill **Bred** Darley **Trained** Stillington, N Yorks

FOCUS
No more than moderate handicap form, and not a race to be with, the winner scoring from 6lb wrong and the favourite disapppointing.
T/Plt: £34.00 to a £1 stake. Pool: £62,555.13. 1,339.50 winning tickets. T/Qpdt: £6.00 to a £1 stake. Pool: £4,890.40. 601.40 winning tickets. JS

1492 - 1494a (Foreign Racing) - See Raceform Interactive

NAAS (L-H)

Saturday, April 19

OFFICIAL GOING: Yielding (yielding to soft in places on round course)

1495a WOODLANDS STKS (LISTED RACE) 5f

4:10 (4:11) 3-Y-O+ £23,933 (£7,022; £3,345; £1,139)

RPR

1 **Snaefell (IRE)**[20] 1103 4-9-12 110 JMurtagh 4 116
(M Halford, Ire) *trckd ldr: chal fr 2f out: disp ld wl ins fnl f: styd on wl to ld cl home* **7/2[2]**

2 hd **Tax Free (IRE)**[28] 959 6-9-12 AdrianTNicholls 8 115+
(D Nicholls) *led: jnd briefly 1 1/2f out: narrow advantage 1f out: jnd wl ins fnl f: hdd cl home* **11/8[1]**

3 1 1/2 **Reverence**[17] 1157 7-9-9 JimmyQuinn 10 107
(E J Alston) *prom: chal and disp ld briefly 1 1/2f out: no ex ins fnl f: kpt on* **9/2[3]**

4 2 **Senor Benny (USA)**[20] 1103 9-9-12 102............ PJSmullen 9 103
(M McDonagh, Ire) *5th on outer: 4th fr 1/2-way: no ex fr over 1f out: kpt on* **16/1**

5 ½ **Peak District (IRE)**[230] 5075 4-9-9 92............ WMLordan 5 98
(David Wachman, Ire) *chsd ldrs in 5th: no ex fr over 1f out: kpt on* **20/1**

6 ½ **Dedo (IRE)**[20] 1106 3-8-13 93............ DPMcDonogh 2 92
(Kevin Prendergast, Ire) *towards rr: kpt on one pce u.p fr over 1f out wout rching ldrs* **16/1**

7 1 **Age Of Chivalry (IRE)**[180] 6392 3-8-10 99............ MJKinane 7 86
(John M Oxx, Ire) *racd keenly early and hld up on outer: 6th 2f out: no ex fr over 1f out* **5/1**

8 nk **Benwilt Breeze (IRE)**[181] 6363 6-9-9 100............(t) KLatham 1 92
(G M Lyons, Ire) *trckd ldrs on inner: 7th 2f out: no imp fr over 1f out* **20/1**

9 4 **Fly By Magic (IRE)**[31] 943 4-9-6 81............ WJLee 6 74
(Patrick Carey, Ire) *a towards rr: no imp fr 1 1/2f out* **33/1**

10 2 **Prize Spirit (USA)**[318] 2378 3-8-13 83............ CDHayes 3 66
(Joseph G Murphy, Ire) *a in rr: no threat fnl 2f* **50/1**

62.01 secs (0.01)
WFA 3 from 4yo+ 10lb **10** Ran SP% **125.4**
CSF £9.07 TOTE £3.90: £1.70, £1.10, £2.10; DF 11.00.

Owner Lady Clague **Bred** Newberry Stud Farm **Trained** the Curragh, Co Kildare

FOCUS
This Listed sprint was not the fastest-run race, resulting in just a modest time. Ther form still looks solid, however, with the first pair coming clear.

NOTEBOOK
Snaefell(IRE), who just defied a mark of 106 when landning a handicap over 6f at the Curragh last time, followed up with another narrow success on this step up in class. He had beaten Tax Free last year in handicap company, when getting 10lb, but this performance at level weights is a clear indication of how he has progressed in the meantime. Soft ground is important to his cause, he is just as good over this trip as he is 6f, and a crack at the Group 3 Greenlands Stakes back at the Curragh next month now looks on the cards. (op 7/2 tchd 4/1)

Tax Free(IRE) was always on the pace and had every chance, but just went down towards the line. This was still much more like his true self, however, having not run to par over an extra furlong at Doncaster last time. He still looks set for another profitable season at this sort of level and it should be noted he is really happiest on a sounder surface. (op 6/4 tchd 7/4)

Reverence showed the clear benefit of his seasonal return at Nottingham earlier in the month and ran a much-improved race in defeat. This former champion sprinter of 2006 may well be past his peak, but there is no doubt his enthusiasm remains and he should more than pay his way this season. (op 9/2 tchd 5/1)

1497a SUMMER BARBEQUE EVENINGS H'CAP 7f
5:15 (5:17) (60-100,92) 3-Y-O+ £11,966 (£3,511; £1,672; £569)

RPR

1 **Russian Empress (IRE)**[162] 6785 4-8-10 77............ PBBeggy(3) 15 94+
(David P Myerscough, Ire) *prom: 2nd 2f out: sn chal: led ins fnl f: styd on wl* **16/1**

2 1 ½ **My Girl Sophie (USA)**[26] 1007 3-8-4 84............ DJMoran(3) 6 90
(J S Bolger, Ire) *led: strly pressed and edgd lft over 1f out: hdd ins fnl f: no ex* **12/1**

3 2 **Inwood (IRE)**[6] 1354 5-8-5 69............(bt) CDHayes 13 75+
(Paul Magnier, Ire) *bhd: 13th and rdn over 2f out: swtchd lft and gd hdwy into 7th 1f out: styd on wl fnl f* **25/1**

4 ¾ **Ginger Princess (IRE)**[1] 1462 6-7-13 70............(t) JPFahy(7) 4 74
(Oliver McKiernan, Ire) *in rr on inner: hdwy on far side early st: wnt 4th 1 1/2f out: kpt on one pce u.p* **8/1**

5 1 **Fremen (USA)**[20] 1105 8-10-0 92............ AdrianTNicholls 7 93
(D Nicholls) *mid-div: 9th over 2f out: 5th 1f out: kpt on* **9/1**

6 shd **Royal Island (IRE)**[20] 1105 6-9-7 85............ PJSmullen 10 86
(Michael Cunningham, Ire) *in rr: sme hdwy on outer early st: kpt on wl fr over 1f out* **10/1**

7 ¾ **Alhabeeb (IRE)**[13] 1231 3-8-12 89............(b) DPMcDonogh 3 83
(Kevin Prendergast, Ire) *trckd ldrs: 4th over 2f out: no ex fr over 1f out* **13/2**[3]

8 1 ½ **Port Of Spain (USA)**[168] 6656 4-9-7 85............ JMurtagh 1 80
(A P O'Brien, Ire) *trckd ldrs on inner: 3rd 2f out: sn no ex: wknd fnl f* **5/1**[2]

9 nk **Sinsational**[14] 1227 4-8-4 68............(t) DMGrant 8 62
(Edward Lynam, Ire) *nvr bttr than mid-div* **12/1**

10 ½ **Insiyaabi (USA)**[26] 1006 4-8-13 84............ JamesPSullivan(7) 2 77
(J G Burns, Ire) *t.k.h on inner in mid-div: 8th over 2f out: no imp fr over 1f out* **8/1**

11 1 ½ **Fit The Cove (IRE)**[20] 1103 8-9-2 90............ SMMcGuinness(10) 5 79
(H Rogers, Ire) *trckd ldrs: 7th over 2f out: sn no ex* **20/1**

12 4 **Master Marvel (IRE)**[202] 5846 7-8-10 74............ WMLordan 14 52
(T J O'Mara, Ire) *nvr a factor* **25/1**

13 8 **Dont Cross Tina (IRE)**[14] 1227 4-7-13 70............ MHarley(7) 12 26
(Seamus Fahey, Ire) *mid-div on outer: 6th ent st: no ex fr 2f out: wknd* **12/1**

14 3 **Alone He Stands (IRE)**[13] 1231 8-9-8 86............ FMBerry 9 34
(J C Hayden, Ire) *prom: 5th over 2f out: sn no ex: wknd* **15/2**

15 3 ½ **Cuilaphuca (IRE)**[13] 1231 4-9-10 88............ PShanahan 11 27
(Tracey Collins, Ire) *mid-div: rdn ent st: no ex over 2f out: wknd and eased* **7/2**[1]

16 9 **Dallool**[30] 7-9-4 82............ JAHeffernan 16 —
(John Queally, Ire) *mid-div on outer: wknd fr 2f out* **33/1**

1m 27.77s (0.27)
WFA 3 from 4yo+ 13lb **16** Ran SP% **149.7**
CSF £229.57 CT £5021.98 TOTE £38.40: £9.50, £2.40, £4.50, £2.80; DF 312.20.

Owner Mrs P Myerscough **Bred** Lodge Park Stud **Trained** Newbridge, Co Kildare

■ Stewards' Enquiry : J P Fahy severe caution: excessive use of the whip

NOTEBOOK
Fremen(USA) showed his lastest effort at the Curragh to be all wrong and posted a perfectly respectable effort, running right up to his mark. (op 8/1)

Cuilaphuca(IRE) Official explanation: jockey said filly never travelled

1496 - 1498a (Foreign Racing) - See Raceform Interactive

GREAT LEIGHS (A.W) (L-H)
Sunday, April 20

OFFICIAL GOING: Standard
Great Leighs became Britain's first new racecourse since Taunton opened in 1927. The Essex track was originally scheduled to open in June 2006.
Wind: Moderate, against. Weather: Sunny.

1499 STAN JAMES AT GREAT LEIGHS MAIDEN FILLIES' STKS 6f (P)
2:10 (2:14) (Class 5) 3-4-Y-0 £2,331 (£693; £346; £173) Stalls Centre

Form RPR

32- 1 **Temple Of Thebes (IRE)**[284] 3417 3-8-12 0............ StephenDonohoe 7 80+
(E A L Dunlop) *hld up in tch: hdwy to chse ldr over 2f out: led jst over 1f out: sn clr: easily* **7/4**[1]

0-3 2 4 **Nice Dream**[9] 1302 3-8-12 0............ HayleyTurner 6 64
(C E Brittain) *racd in midfield: rdn and hdwy jst over 2f out: chsd ldng pair over 1f out: wnt 2nd ins fnl f: no ch w wnr* **13/2**

430- 3 3 **Mollyatti**[209] 5692 3-8-7 74............ SCreighton(5) 4 54
(Miss V Haigh) *led: clr over 2f out: rdn over 1f out: hdd jst over 1f out: sn wknd* **15/2**

655- 4 2 ¼ **Pixie's Blue (IRE)**[251] 4453 3-8-12 72............ JimmyFortune 1 47
(J H M Gosden) *chsd ldr for 1f: chsd ldng pair after: rdn 2f out: sn no imp* **5/2**[2]

5 2 **Little Cee (IRE)** 3-8-12 0............ SebSanders 5 41
(D R C Elsworth) *v s.i.s: sme hdwy bnd 3f out: n.d* **6/1**[3]

-000 6 4 **Running Supreme**[19] 1125 4-9-9 38............(b[1]) RoystonFfrench 8 31
(Mrs N Smith) *sn rdn and struggling: nvr on terms* **66/1**

0- 7 4 ½ **Amicable Terms**[170] 6617 3-8-12 0............ ChrisCatlin 3 14
(Rae Guest) *s.i.s: a behiind: t.o 2f out* **14/1**

0- 8 9 **Sue's Hawk (IRE)**[222] 5308 3-8-12 0............ NeilPollard 2 —
(A P Jarvis) *s.i.s: sn rcvrd and chsd ldr after 1f: rdn 3f out: wknd qckly 2f out: t.o* **25/1**

1m 13.68s (-0.02) **Going Correction** +0.025s/f (Slow)
WFA 3 from 4yo 11lb **8** Ran SP% **116.3**
Speed ratings (Par 100): **101,95,91,88,86 80,74,62**
CSF £14.27 TOTE £2.20: £1.10, £1.90, £2.10; EX 16.80 Trifecta £35.30 Pool £109.50 - 2.20 winning units..

Owner Cliveden Stud **Bred** Cliveden Stud Ltd **Trained** Newmarket, Suffolk

■ Temple Of Thebes became the first horse to win at Britain's newest track.

FOCUS
Probably an ordinary maiden, but impossible to assess the winning time with no historical data to go on. The pace seemed solid enough though and not many got into it. The winner was up 11lb on her 2yo best, but the sixth holds down the form to an extent.

1500 CHELMSFORD "RETURN OF RACING" H'CAP (SPONSORED BY STAN JAMES) 6f (P)
2:40 (2:40) (Class 3) (0-90,89) 4-Y-0 £6,938 (£2,076; £1,038; £519; £258) Stalls Centre

Form RPR

0-02 1 **Esteem Machine (USA)**[8] 1334 4-9-4 **89**............ RyanMoore 5 99+
(R A Teal) *racd in midfield: hdwy jst over 2f out: rdn wl over 1f out: led ins fnl f: r.o strly* **6/4**[1]

000- 2 ¾ **Manchurian**[191] 6143 4-9-3 **88**............ JamieSpencer 3 96
(M J Wallace) *in tch: rdn over 2f out: swtchd rt wl over 1f out: ev ch 1f out: kpt on same pce u.p last 100yds* **4/1**[2]

1335 3 1 ¼ **Cerebus**[5] 1386 6-8-4 **75** oh1............(bt) NeilPollard 2 79
(A J McCabe) *t.k.h: led: hrd pressed and rdn over 1f out: hdd ins fnl f: no ex last 100yds* **10/1**

1-25 4 1 ½ **Crimson King (IRE)**[68] 532 7-8-12 **83**............ AdamKirby 1 82
(R W Price) *s.i.s: bhd: rdn over 2f out: hdwy on inner over 1f out: kpt on fnl f: nt pce to rch ldrs* **13/2**[3]

300/ 5 3 ¼ **Banjo Patterson**[617] 4372 6-8-4 **75** oh1............(b) ChrisCatlin 7 64
(M G Quinlan) *sn pushed along in last trio: kpt on u.p fnl f: nvr nr ldrs* **20/1**

0-00 6 nk **Our Blessing (IRE)**[3] 1415 4-8-5 **76**............(v[1]) AndrewElliott 6 64
(A P Jarvis) *pressed ldrs on outer: rdn over 2f out: wknd jst over 1f out* **20/1**

6640 7 nk **Lucayos**[15] 1211 5-8-10 **81**............ HayleyTurner 4 68
(Mrs H Sweeting) *w ldr tl rdn jst over 2f out: wknd jst over 1f out* **7/1**

00-0 8 6 **Forest Dane**[15] 1211 8-8-9 **80**............ RoystonFfrench 8 48
(Mrs N Smith) *a last trio: rdn over 2f out: n.d* **11/1**

1m 12.46s (-1.24) **Going Correction** +0.025s/f (Slow) **8** Ran SP% **112.8**
Speed ratings (Par 107): **109,108,106,104,100 99,99,91**
CSF £7.15 CT £41.04 TOTE £2.10: £1.30, £1.30, £3.50; EX 6.40 Trifecta £9.60 Pool £94.10 - 6.90 winning units..

Owner M Vickers **Bred** Mindy Hodges Powell **Trained** Ashtead, Surrey

FOCUS
A decent little sprint handicap run at a strong pace thanks to Cerebus and the time was 1.22 seconds faster than the fillies' maiden.

NOTEBOOK
Esteem Machine(USA), raised 2lb for his narrow defeat at Kempton eight days earlier, got stronger as the race progressed and after being brought widest in order to make his effort, stayed on strongly down the outside to claim the prize. It may be significant that he gets 7f so well as the ability to see out every yard of the trip seemed important here. (op 10-11)

Manchurian, having his first outing over a trip this short since his racecourse debut, was always in a good position behind the leaders on the inside and he made his effort at just the right time, but the favourite had the greater impetus on the run to the line. The way the track seems to be riding just now appears to be helping those who stay further such as him. (op 8-1)

Cerebus, 1lb wrong, was given her usual positive ride and, hugging the rail throughout, made a good fist of it. She battled on gamely once headed, but a couple of stronger stayers proved too good for her. (op 8-1 tchd 11-1)

Crimson King(IRE), whose only poor effort to date came in his only previous try on Polytrack, has been performing well on Fibresand otherwise and there was a question as to how this surface would suit. As things turned out he ran as though the trip was inadequate and it appears that he needs 7f on Polytrack. (op 6-1 tchd 7-1)

Banjo Patterson ◆, making his debut for the yard off the back of a 20-month absence and on sand for the first time, was never in the race but showed enough to suggest that he retains some ability. Off a mark 8lb lower than when last seen but still 1lb wrong, he should strip fitter next time. (op 16-1)

Lucayos raced up with the pace for much of the way, but did not see out the trip on this surface.

1501 GREATLEIGHS.COM H'CAP (SPONSORED BY STAN JAMES) 2m (P)
3:15 (3:15) (Class 2) (0-100,93) 4-Y-0+

£9,969 (£2,985; £1,492; £747; £372; £187) Stalls Low

Form RPR

-411 1 **Pocket Too**[8] 268 5-8-3 **74** oh3..............................(p) KirstyMilczarek(3) 6 82
(M Salaman) *led: rdn wl over 1f out: hdd 1f out: leaned on fnl f: rallied to gamely to ld again on post* **13/2**

3-12 2 *nse* **Buster Hyvonen (IRE)**[22] 1080 6-9-1 **83**........................ JamieSpencer 1 91
(J R Fanshawe) *t.k.h: hld up wl in tch in rr: nt clr run briefly jst over 2f out: shkn up to ld 1f out: sn rdn and edgd lft: hdd on post* **2/1**[1]

3211 3 1 ½ **Calculating (IRE)**[22] 1080 4-9-1 **87**........................ HayleyTurner 3 93
(M D I Usher) *trckd ldrs on inner: wnt 2nd over 2f out: sn swtchd rt and chalng: keeping on same pce whn short of room ins fnl f: one pce after* **9/2**[3]

465- 4 *hd* **Velvet Heights (IRE)**[184] 6302 6-9-11 **93**........................ SebSanders 2 99
(J L Dunlop) *hld up wl in tch in rr: c wd 2f out: chsng ldrs and rdn over 1f out: nudged along and kpt on same pce fnl f* **5/1**

-263 5 10 **Salute (IRE)**[16] 1179 9-8-9 **77**........................ RobertHavlin 4 71
(P G Murphy) *chsd ldr tl 3f out: sn rdn: wknd wl over 1f out* **14/1**

1112 6 4 ½ **Rollin 'n Tumblin**[16] 1179 4-8-2 **74** oh2........................ ChrisCatlin 5 63
(W Jarvis) *in tch on outer: hdwy to chse ldr 3f out tl over 2f out: wknd wl over 1f out* **7/2**[2]

3m 32.2s (2.20) **Going Correction** +0.125s/f (Slow)
WFA 4 from 5yo+ 4lb **6** Ran SP% **110.4**
Speed ratings (Par 109): **99,98,98,98,93 90**
CSF £19.29 TOTE £8.30: £2.90, £1.60; EX 22.70.
Owner Oaktree Racing **Bred** M J Lewin **Trained** Baydon, Wilts
■ Stewards' Enquiry : Jamie Spencer 1st incident; two-day ban; allowing gelding to drift left under pressure and causing interference (May 5-6); 2nd incident; caution, careless riding
Kirsty Milczarek caution: used whip down shoulder in forehand position

FOCUS
A decent staying handicap, but the pace was very ordinary and the race developed into something of a sprint. The form seems reasonably sound based around the second and third.

NOTEBOOK
Pocket Too, back on the Flat after a spell over hurdles, was racing from 3lb wrong but he is a confirmed front-runner and he very much had the run of the race here as he was able to enjoy a soft lead. Strongly pressed in the home straight, he showed real guts and determination despite the runner-up leaning into him throughout the last furlong. (op 8-1 tchd 6-1)
Buster Hyvonen(IRE), 2lb better off with Calculating for a threequarter-length beating at Kempton, was switched off out the back for most of the journey, but the gaps opened up for him at just the right time turning for home and he looked sure to collect. However, he found the winner very determined and despite pressing his rival against the rail, which earned his rider a two-day ban, he was just worried out of it. (op 9-4 tchd 5-2 in places)
Calculating(IRE), bidding for a hat-trick off a 4lb higher mark, raced quite keenly behind the leaders but had every chance down the straight despite getting a bit short of room and was third best on merit. (op 10-3)
Velvet Heights(IRE), returning from six months off, ran a very strange race. He was forced to make his effort widest turning for home, but he hung right out into the centre of the track for no obvious reason and his rider appeared to give up before riding him out under hands and heels near the line when there was still a chance of him finishing third. He has won on Polytrack, but may be a better horse on Fibresand. (op 4-1)
Salute(IRE) raced prominently for much of the trip, but found very little off the bridle and seems to have lost his way. (op 12-1)
Rollin 'n Tumblin, in great form on Polytrack this year but off a 9lb higher mark than for his last win including being 2lb wrong, had his chance but had nothing more to offer in the straight and the handicapper seems to have him now. (op 4-1 tchd 10-3)

1502 STANJAMESUK.COM H'CAP 1m 2f (P)
3:50 (3:50) (Class 3) (0-90,87) 4-Y-0 £6,938 (£2,076; £1,038; £519; £258) Stalls Low

Form RPR

-366 1 **Basra (IRE)**[29] 962 5-8-8 **80**........................ TravisBlock(3) 7 90
(Miss Jo Crowley) *in tch: hdwy to chse ldng pair over 2f out: rdn to ld jst over 2f out: r.o gamely fnl f* **13/2**[3]

2104 2 *nk* **Mataram (USA)**[32] 929 5-8-12 **81**........................ KerrinMcEvoy 5 91
(W Jarvis) *stdd s: t.k.h: hld up in rr: gd hdwy wl over 1f out: r.o to chse wnr ins fnl f: r.o wl* **8/1**

40-5 3 1 ¾ **Rapid City**[32] 929 5-8-12 **84**........................ JerryO'Dwyer(3) 6 90
(Miss J Feilden) *hld up in midfield: hdwy 4f out: chsd ldrs over 2f out: rdn to chse wnr over 1f out: kpt on same pce: lost 2nd ins fnl f* **8/1**

30-1 4 1 ½ **Haarth Sovereign (IRE)**[23] 1048 4-8-11 **80**........................ AdamKirby 2 83
(W R Swinburn) *chsd ldrs: edgd out off rail over 2f out: sn rdn: swtchd lft over 1f out: chsd ldrs 1f out: kpt on same pce u.p fnl f* **11/2**[2]

313- 5 2 ¾ **Shela House**[193] 6110 4-9-1 **84**........................ JamieSpencer 1 82
(J R Fanshawe) *stdd s: hld up in rr: hdwy and rdn 2f out: edgd rt jst over 1f out: kpt on but nvr nr ldrs* **8/1**

60-5 6 1 ½ **Cross The Line (IRE)**[8] 1335 6-9-1 **84**........................ SebSanders 3 79
(A P Jarvis) *hld up in midfield on inner: rdn and effrt 2f out: no imp over 1f out* **15/2**

2010 7 *nk* **Bee Stinger**[8] 1335 6-8-13 **82**........................ NCallan 9 76
(I A Wood) *hld up towards rr: rdn over 3f out: sme hdwy whn short of room jst over 1f out: nvr trbld ldrs* **20/1**

03-1 8 1 **Robustian**[19] 1131 5-9-1 **87**........................(v) TolleyDean(3) 8 79
(George Baker) *plld hrd: chsd ldrs tl led 4f out: rdn and hdd jst over 2f out: lost 2nd over 1f out: sn wknd* **4/1**[1]

0-56 9 1 ¼ **Crossbow Creek**[33] 927 10-9-0 **83**........................ ChrisCatlin 10 72
(M G Rimell) *stdd s: hld up in last trio: hdwy over 3f out: rdn 2f out: wknd over 1f out* **20/1**

014- 10 6 **Fongs Gazelle**[260] 4147 4-9-1 **84**........................ JoeFanning 4 61
(M Johnston) *led for 1f: chsd ldr after tl over 2f out: rdn and hld hd high wl over 1f out: sn btn* **7/1**

116- 11 7 **Lobengula (IRE)**[111] 7287 6-9-1 **84**........................ DanielTudhope 11 47
(I W McInnes) *led after 1f: hdd and wd bnd 4f out: sn wknd: wl bhd last 2f* **20/1**

2m 7.56s (-1.04) **Going Correction** +0.125s/f (Slow) **11** Ran SP% **120.6**
Speed ratings (Par 107): **109,108,107,106,103 102,102,101,100,95 90**
CSF £57.28 CT £417.71 TOTE £7.50: £2.30, £3.20, £3.20; EX 50.90 TRIFECTA Not won..
Owner Mrs Liz Nelson **Bred** Redmondstown Stud **Trained** Whitcombe, Dorset

FOCUS
A decent handicap run at a good pace and the winning time was 1.37 seconds faster than the Class 2 handicap that followed and 0.83 seconds faster than the later Class 6 handicap. Probably only ordinary form for the grade, but pretty solid.

NOTEBOOK
Basra(IRE), closely matched with a couple of these on Lingfield running back in February, was tackling Listed company the last time he raced on Polytrack but found this level much more to his liking. Never far away, he was sent for home after turning for home and ran on very gamely to hold on all-out. This was his first win since his second start at two, but he has been consistent on Polytrack this winter and there is no doubting his attitude. (op 9-1)
Mataram(USA) again raced keenly out the back despite the generous pace but finished with a rare rattle down the wide outside once into the straight and would have prevailed with a bit further to go. He is another that has been consistent on Polytrack this winter and there will be another day. (op 9-1)
Rapid City, closely matched with Mataram on recent Kempton running, had every chance over the last couple of furlongs and seems to have returned from his lengthy layoff as good as ever.
Haarth Sovereign(IRE), hiked up 8lb for his successful return to action at Kempton last month, was one of four almost in a line passing the furlong pole but then had little more to offer. He will need to find improvement from somewhere to defy this mark. (op 6-1)
Shela House, making his sand debut off the back of a six-month absence, took time to find his stride and was doing his best work late. He should come on for this. (op 11-2)
Cross The Line(IRE), trying his longest trip so far in his 30th outing, never really got involved and his stamina was not really proved one way or the other. (op 7-1)
Bee Stinger did not have much room to play with in the straight as he tried to get closer and was reportedly struck into. Official explanation: jockey said gelding was struck into (tchd 16-1)
Robustian, raised 9lb for his Southwell romp, raced up there for a long way but weakened very tamely. The higher mark and different surface may well have conspired against him. (op 9-2 tchd 11-2)
Lobengula(IRE) Official explanation: jockey said gelding hung right

1503 GREAT LEIGHS "ONLY IN ESSEX" H'CAP (SPONSORED BY STAN JAMES) 1m 2f (P)
4:20 (4:22) (Class 2) (0-105,100) 4-Y-£9,969 (£2,985; £1,492; £747; £372) Stalls Low

Form RPR

6405 1 **Escape Route (USA)**[29] 960 4-8-11 **93**....................(p) JimmyFortune 5 102
(J H M Gosden) *chsd ldng pair: wnt 2nd wl over 3f out: rdn to ld ins fnl f: cosily* **5/4**[1]

00-2 2 1 ¼ **Luberon**[16] 1180 5-9-3 **99**........................ JoeFanning 3 106
(M Johnston) *led: rdn 2f out: hdd ins fnl f: nt pce of wnr last 100yds* **4/1**[3]

054- 3 2 ¾ **Rayhani (USA)**[218] 5411 5-8-13 **95**........................ MartinDwyer 1 96
(M P Tregoning) *t.k.h: hld up in last pair: shkn up 3f out: rdn and hung lft over 1f out: kpt on to go 3rd ins fnl f: nvr trbld ldng pair* **4/1**[3]

-506 4 2 **Snoqualmie Boy**[52] 739 5-9-4 **100**........................ JohnEgan 2 97
(Jane Chapple-Hyam) *chsd ldr tl wl over 3f out: rdn 2f out: wknd 1f out* **10/3**[2]

10/0 5 14 **Clipperdown (IRE)**[29] 960 7-9-4 **100**....................(t) EdwardCreighton 4 69
(E J Creighton) *stdd s: hld up in tch: hdwy to chse ldrs on outer 5f out: rdn over 2f out: wknd wl over 1f out* **18/1**

2m 8.93s (0.33) **Going Correction** +0.125s/f (Slow) **5** Ran SP% **112.8**
Speed ratings (Par 109): **103,102,99,98,87**
CSF £6.85 TOTE £2.60: £1.40, £1.80; EX 7.90.
Owner H R H Princess Haya Of Jordan **Bred** Robert N Clay & Serengeti Stable **Trained** Newmarket, Suffolk

FOCUS
A good-quality handicap, but the pace was moderate and the winning time was the slowest of the three races over this trip on the day despite being the highest class of the trio. The lack of pace means there are question marks over the form.

NOTEBOOK
Escape Route(USA), fifth in the Lincoln but still with questions to answer over this trip, settled nicely in the main group before moving on to the shoulder of the leader turning for home. He had to battle very hard to get on top of Luberon in the home straight, but did it very gamely. The way the race was run still did not prove his stamina conclusively however. (op 2-1)
Luberon, an established front-runner, could hardly have had the race go better as he was allowed to dictate at his own pace and tried to quicken from the front turning for home. He battled back in typically game style when headed, but probably ran into a fair sort. (op 11-4)
Rayhani(USA), returning from seven months off but successful after an even longer layoff on his return last year, stays further than this so he really needed a stronger pace over this trip. Pulling hard out the back, he got outpaced on the home turn as the pace quickened from the front and his final position was as close as he was able to get. (op 11-4)
Snoqualmie Boy, who has been running adequately in Dubai, was making his debut for the yard and having his first run on sand since his second start at two. He led the main group for a long way, but found very little once off the bridle. (op 11-2 tchd 3-1)
Clipperdown(IRE), having his second start since returning from the US, pulled too hard and was inclined to hang right rounding the home bend as he came under pressure. His last win in this country came off a 19lb lower mark, so he could continue to find life tough for a while. (op 16-1 tchd 20-1 and 33-1)

1504 RACING IN A NEW LIGHT MEDIAN AUCTION MAIDEN STKS (SPONSORED BY STAN JAMES) 1m (P)
4:50 (4:53) (Class 6) 3-5-Y-0 £2,590 (£770; £385; £192) Stalls Low

Form RPR

0/5- 1 **Mumbleswerve (IRE)**[463] 114 4-9-12 69.................. J-PGuillambert 10 76+
(W Jarvis) *hld up in rr: stl plenty to do 2f out: grad edgd out rt over 1f out: str run fnl f to ld towards fin* **14/1**

0- 2 ½ **Indy Driver**[261] 4130 3-8-12 0........................ JamieSpencer 8 71
(J R Fanshawe) *stdd s: hld up in rr: hmpd and stmbld over 6f out: hdwy over 2f out: rdn wl over 1f out: hrd rdn to ld ins fnl f: hdd and no ex towards fin* **16/1**

0-3 3 ¾ **Mexican Venture**[12] 1252 3-8-12 0........................ KerrinMcEvoy 11 74+
(W Jarvis) *t.k.h: hld up in midfield on inner: hdwy and swtchd rt wl over 1f out: chsng ldrs whn short of room briefly and swtchd rt again ins fnl f: r.o to go 3rd towards fin* **5/4**[1]

52 4 1 **Themwerethedays**[12] 1252 3-8-12 0........................ JimmyFortune 5 67
(S Kirk) *chsd ldrs: rdn and effrt 2f out: led over 1f out: sn edgd lft: hdd ins fnl f: outpcd last 100yds* **9/4**[2]

5 2 ¼ **Sir John Lilley (USA)** 3-8-12 0........................ JoeFanning 6 62
(M Johnston) *hld up in tch on outer: hdwy over 2f out: ev ch and rdn over 1f out: sn edgd lft: outpcd fnl f* **7/1**

0 6 2 ¼ **Clearing House**[12] 1252 3-8-12 0........................ RyanMoore 3 57
(E A L Dunlop) *led tl over 2f out: rdn 2f out: wknd over 1f out* **4/1**[3]

7 ¾ **Quinzey's Best (IRE)** 3-8-7 0........................ PaulDoe 1 50
(W J Knight) *prom: led over 2f out: rdn and hdd over 1f out: wknd over 1f out* **33/1**

8 *shd* **Silver Willow** 3-8-7 0........................ StephenDonohoe 9 50
(Miss Gay Kelleway) *led to s and mounted at s: s.i.s: bhd: pushed along 3f out: sme hdwy ins fnl f: n.d* **50/1**

-005 9 ½ **Ticking**[8] 1342 5-9-5 35........................ AshleyMorgan(7) 2 58
(T Keddy) *chsd ldrs: rdn and effrt on inner 2f out: sn outpcd* **100/1**

0- **10** *4 1/2* **Sun In Splendour (USA)**[316] 2447 3-8-12 0 .... NeilPollard 4 43
(A P Jarvis) *plld hrd: hld up in midfield: hung rt bnd 4f out: wknd over 2f out* **28/1**

1m 41.75s (1.85) **Going Correction** +0.125s/f (Slow)
WFA 3 from 4yo+ 14lb 10 Ran SP% **129.6**
Speed ratings (Par 101): **95,94,93,92,90 88,87,87,86,82**
CSF £224.61 TOTE £17.70: £3.50, £3.60, £1.30; EX 200.60 TRIFECTA Not won..
Owner The XPY Partnership **Bred** Arthur S Phelan **Trained** Newmarket, Suffolk

FOCUS
Probably an ordinary maiden and with the pace not that strong there was plenty of trouble. Improvement from the winner but this form is not that solid.
Mexican Venture ◆ Official explanation: jockey said colt was denied a clear run

1505 FIRST SINCE 1927 H'CAP (SPONSORED BY STAN JAMES) 1m 2f (P)
5:20 (5:22) (Class 6) (0-60,62) 4-Y-0+ **£2,266** (£674; £337; £168) **Stalls** Low

Form RPR
341- **1** **Sir Duke (IRE)**[191] 6147 4-9-2 **58** .... JohnEgan 3 75+
(P W D'Arcy) *hld up in tch: hdwy to chse ldr wl over 1f out: rdn to ld over 1f out: sn clr: eased towards fin* **5/1**[2]
-322 **2** *4* **Kings Topic (USA)**[15] 1210 8-9-4 **60** .... SebSanders 7 69
(A B Haynes) *hld up towards rr: hdwy on outer 4f out: rdn over 2f out: styd on to go 2nd towards fin: nvr nr wnr* **3/1**[1]
3-25 **3** *1/2* **Magic Amigo**[10] 1282 7-7-11 **46** ....(b[1]) DavidProbert(7) 6 54
(J R Jenkins) *t.k.h: chsd ldr tl led 6f out: clr over 2f out: rdn over 1f out: sn hdd: no ch w wnr after: lost 2nd towards fin* **14/1**
4046 **4** *2 1/2* **Bienheureux**[40] 843 7-8-2 **49** ....(t) NicolPolli(5) 1 52
(Miss Gay Kelleway) *hld up towards rr on inner: lost pl over 3f out: swtchd rt over 2f out: hdwy over 1f out: kpt on but n.d* **9/1**
0626 **5** *1 1/2* **Tabulate**[10] 1282 5-8-4 **46** oh1 .... AndrewElliott 12 46
(P Howling) *in tch in midfield: hdwy on outer over 3f out: chsd ldrs and rdn 2f out: sn hung lft: wl hld fnl f* **14/1**
000 **6** *1 1/4* **Sorbiesharry (IRE)**[12] 1262 9-8-3 **48** oh1 ow2.....(p) KirstyMilczarek(3) 4 46
(Mrs N Macauley) *hld up towards rr: hdwy 4f out: chsd ldrs and rdn over 2f out: wknd over 1f out* **20/1**
04- **7** *2* **Blockley (USA)**[249] 4518 4-8-12 **54** .... StephenDonohoe 11 48
(Ian Williams) *hld up in rr: struggling and rdn over 3f out: sme modest hdwy fr over 1f out: n.d* **16/1**
2512 **8** *hd* **Siena Star (IRE)**[10] 1282 10-9-6 **62** .... MickyFenton 9 55
(Stef Liddiard) *chsd ldrs: wnt 2nd over 3f: rdn over 2f out: lost 2nd wl over 1f out: wl btn whn sltly hmpd over 1f out* **9/1**
/223 **9** *shd* **Ruling Reef**[10] 1280 6-8-5 **47** .... HayleyTurner 5 40
(M D I Usher) *hld up in tch: rdn and effrt 4f out: wknd 2f out* **6/1**[3]
420/ **10** *26* **Senor Set (GER)**[631] 3935 7-8-11 **53** ....(v[1]) EdwardCreighton 10 —
(D Shaw) *awkward leaving stalls and slowly away: a bhd: lost tch 4f out: t.o and virtually p.u fnl f* **20/1**
00-0 **11** *5* **Djalalabad (FR)**[18] 1160 4-8-13 **55** .... ChrisCatlin 8 —
(Mrs C A Dunnett) *sn led: hdd 6f out: chsd ldr tl over 3f out: sn dropped out: virtually p.u fnl f: t.o* **25/1**
4111 **12** *4* **Bahhmirage (IRE)**[50] 770 5-8-9 **51** ....(p) TGMcLaughlin 2 —
(C N Kellett) *chsd ldrs on inner: rdn over 3f out: wknd over 2f out: virtually p.u fnl f: t.o* **12/1**
0344 **13** *12* **Royal Embrace**[22] 1083 5-8-9 **51** ow1 ....(v) NCallan 13 —
(D Shaw) *stdd s: hld up in rr: lost tch over 3f out: virtually p.u fr over 1f out: t.o* **7/1**

2m 8.39s (-0.21) **Going Correction** +0.125s/f (Slow) 13 Ran SP% **128.7**
Speed ratings (Par 101): **105,101,101,99,98 97,95,95,95,74 70,67,57**
CSF £21.43 CT £211.77 TOTE £4.70: £2.40, £1.30, £4.40; EX 23.00 TRIFECTA Not won. Place 6 £41.76, Place 5 £22.35..
Owner Mrs Jan Harris **Bred** Southern Bloodstock **Trained** Newmarket, Suffolk

FOCUS
A modest handicap and although the winning time appeared to compare well with the two much higher-class handicaps earlier on the card, the size of the field always made a decent pace likely. Solid form for the grade.
Bahhmirage(IRE) Official explanation: jockey said mare had no more to give
T/Plt: £102.80 to a £1 stake. Pool: £47,158.12. 334.87 winning tickets. T/Qpdt: £40.10 to a £1 stake. Pool: £46.40. 2,516.00 winning tickets. SP

1506 - 1508a (Foreign Racing) - See Raceform Interactive

1229 LEOPARDSTOWN (L-H)
Sunday, April 20

OFFICIAL GOING: Good to yielding

1509a P.W.MCGRATH MEMORIAL BALLYSAX STKS (GROUP 3) 1m 2f
4:05 (4:06) 3-Y-O **£33,507** (£9,830; £4,683; £1,595)

RPR
1 **Moiqen (IRE)**[14] 1232 3-9-1 95 .... DPMcDonogh 3 102+
(Kevin Prendergast, Ire) *trckd ldrs: cl 3rd on outer ent st: disp ld under 2f out: led over 1f out: kpt on wl u.p* **9/2**[3]
2 *1* **Hebridean (IRE)**[14] 1232 3-9-1 92 .... JAHeffernan 4 101+
(A P O'Brien, Ire) *racd in 6th: rdn and sme hdwy ent st: cl 4th 1 1/2f out: 2nd and chal ins fnl f: no ex fnl 100yds* **14/1**
3 *1* **Unwritten Rule (IRE)**[14] 1233 3-9-1 100 .... PJSmullen 7 99+
(D K Weld, Ire) *racd in 5th: tk clsr order over 2f out: sn rdn and kpt on to go 3rd ins fnl f* **2/1**[2]
4 *3* **Alessandro Volta**[168] 6682 3-9-1 99 .... JMurtagh 1 93
(A P O'Brien, Ire) *trckd ldr: hdwy on inner to dispute ld appr st: hdd over 1f out: 4th and no ex ins fnl f: eased cl home* **6/4**[1]
5 *1/2* **King Of Rome (IRE)**[176] 6489 3-9-1 95 .... CO'Donoghue 5 92
(A P O'Brien, Ire) *led: qcknd pce over 4f out: jnd appr st: hdd 1 1/2f out: sn no ex and wknd* **14/1**
6 *1/2* **Dirar (IRE)**[14] 1233 3-9-1 91 .... RPCleary 2 91
(M Halford, Ire) *chsd ldrs in 4th: clsr and rdn 2f out: no ex 1f out* **20/1**
7 *16* **Solas Na Greine (IRE)**[203] 5843 3-8-12 90 .... KJManning 6 58
(J S Bolger, Ire) *a towards rr: no ex fr 2f out: sn wknd: eased fnl f* **16/1**

2m 13.6s (5.40) **Going Correction** +0.575s/f (Yiel) 7 Ran SP% **115.5**
Speed ratings: **101,100,99,97,96 96,83**
CSF £62.39 TOTE £4.80: £2.50, £3.80; DF 88.10.
Owner Hamdan Al Maktoum **Bred** Shadwell Estate Company Ltd **Trained** Friarstown, Co Kildare

FOCUS
Just an average renewal of this Group 3 and well-known Derby trial. The form looks to make sense, rated through the fifth. The first two both boosted the form of Famous Name's win in the 2,000 Guineas Trial here.

NOTEBOOK
Moiqen(IRE), second over 1m to Famous Name here on his seasonal debut a fortnight previously, relished the step up to this trip and did the job in resolute fashion. He did not obviously have to improve on that form to win this, but there is no doubt he is a colt on the up and it is likely the best of him has still to be seen. A return to faster ground should also suit him better and his next port of call is likely to be in the Derrinstown back at this venue next month in a bid to further test his Derby credentials. (op 5/1)
Hebridean(IRE), behind the winner in the 2,000 Guineas Trial last time, showed improved form over this extra distance and is clearly going the right way. He was a clear second best and looks well up to striking in Listed company at the least on this evidence. (op 12/1)
Unwritten Rule(IRE), a winner on his return over course and distance a fortnight previously, stepped up on that effort without ever seriously threatening. He now looks in need of further and, in good hands, is another of whom the best has probably yet to be seen. (op 13/8)
Alessandro Volta, who broke his duck in Listed company on his final outing at two, was the leading candidate from his powerful stable who have a good past history in this event. He was unable to land a serious blow, however, and basically looked very one-paced. His rider was later very keen to report that his saddle had slipped not long after the start and that the colt should be given another chance, so his next outing really ought to reveal a lot more about his potential. It should also be noted his yard have certainly not yet hit top gear this season. Official explanation: jockey said saddle slipped slightly late on (op 2/1)

1510 - 1512a (Foreign Racing) - See Raceform Interactive

CAPANNELLE (R-H)
Sunday, April 20

OFFICIAL GOING: Good

1513a PREMIO PARIOLI (GROUP 3) (COLTS) 1m
4:05 (4:13) 3-Y-O **£70,313** (£30,938; £16,875; £8,438)

RPR
1 **Senlis (IRE)**[14] 1241 3-9-2 .... ASanna 9 111
(E Borromeo, Italy) *racd in 5th: led over 1f out: sn 3 l clr: rdn out* **106/10**
2 *1 1/2* **Eustachione (IRE)**[21] 3-9-2 .... NMurru 12 108
(M Gasparini, Italy) *racd in 6th: hrd rdn on outside 2f out: styd on strly fnl f* **116/10**
3 *2 1/2* **Eldest (IRE)**[21] 3-9-2 .... MDemuro 2 102
(V Caruso, Italy) *hld up in rr: 12th st: hdwy towards ins fr 2f out: styd on wl fnl f to take 3rd last strides* **47/10**[3]
4 *nk* **Touch Of Mida** 3-9-2 .... MPasquale 10 101
(G Pucciatti, Italy) *chsd clr ldrs in 3rd: clsd up 3f out: ev ch over 1f out: one pce: lost 3rd cl home* **23/1**
5 *1/2* **Farrel (IRE)**[14] 1241 3-9-2 .... DVargiu 4 100
(B Grizzetti, Italy) *hld up in rr: 11th st: styd on steadily fnl 2f: nrst fin* **11/20**[1]
6 *1* **Amaldi (ITY)**[21] 3-9-2 .... SLandi 3 98
(A Renzoni, Italy) *racd in 7th on ins: kpt on steadily fnl 2f* **37/1**
7 *hd* **Calciobalilla (ITY)**[21] 3-9-2 .... MEsposito 8 98
(F & S Brogi, Italy) *pressed ldr in 2nd: 5 l clr of remainder after 3f: reduced advantage 3f out: hrd rdn wl over 2f out: wknd 1f out* **62/1**
8 *2* **Remarque (IRE)**[14] 1236 3-9-2 .... FBranca 5 93
(L Riccardi, Italy) *set gd pce: 5 l clr w one other after 3f: reduced advantage 3f out: hdd over 1f out: wknd* **23/1**
9 *1 1/2* **Orientalist Art**[15] 1213 3-9-2 .... AlanMunro 13 90
(P W Chapple-Hyam) *s.s and sn pushed along: last to over 2f out: nvr a factor* **41/10**[2]
10 *nk* **Sampeyre (ITY)**[21] 3-9-2 .... CColombi 7 89
(Laura Grizzetti, Italy) *a in rr* **43/1**
11 *2* **Dimmi Di Su (IRE)**[14] 1241 3-9-2 .... EBotti 1 85
(G Miliani, Italy) *racd in 4th: outpcd fnl 2f* **24/1**
12 *1* **Tenson (IRE)**[14] 1236 3-9-2 .... GBietolini 11 83
(R Brogi, Italy) *a in rr* **61/1**
13 *hd* **Black Mambazo (IRE)**[309] 2684 3-9-2 .... GMarcelli 6 82
(L Riccardi, Italy) *midfield: wknd 2f out* **36/1**

1m 38.1s (-1.70) 13 Ran SP% **141.4**
PARI-MUTUEL: WIN 11.56; PL 2.96, 3.51, 2.67; DF 40.77.
Owner Scuderia Pieffegi **Bred** Compagnia Generale Srl **Trained** Italy

NOTEBOOK
Orientalist Art, drawn out wide, was slowly away and pushed along to try and remain competitive. Still in last position turning into the straight, he never got in a blow.

KREFELD (R-H)
Sunday, April 20

OFFICIAL GOING: Soft

1514a DR BUSCH MEMORIAL (GROUP 3) 1m 110y
3:25 (3:53) 3-Y-O **£23,529** (£7,353; £3,676; £2,206)

RPR
1 **Liang Kay (GER)**[189] 6219 3-9-2 .... THellier 1 100
(U Ostmann, Germany) *trckd ldr on ins in 3rd: travelling wl but no room 1 1/2f out: sn swtchd outside and hdwy: hrd rdn 100yds out: led fnl strides* **26/10**[2]
2 *shd* **Precious Boy (GER)**[189] 6219 3-9-2 .... ADeVries 5 100
(W Hickst, Germany) *re-shod bef s: racd in 2nd: pushed along 3f out: hrd rdn 1 1/2f out: led 1f out: hdd fnl strides* **4/5**[1]
3 *3/4* **Schutzenjunker (GER)**[184] 6324 3-9-2 .... LHammerHansen 2 98
(U Ostmann, Germany) *set gd pce: hdd 1f out: kpt on* **33/10**[3]
4 *7* **Let's Rock (GER)**[184] 6324 3-9-2 .... TMundry 4 84
(P Rau, Germany) *4th thrght: outpcd fnl 2f* **69/10**
5 *6* **Balios (GER)**[147] 3-9-2 .... EPedroza 3 72
(A Wohler, Germany) *last thrght* **66/10**

1m 48.0s (1.40) 5 Ran SP% **132.4**
PARI-MUTUEL (including 10 euro stake): WIN 36; PL 14, 11; SF 68.
Owner Stall Emina **Bred** Frau I Zimmermann **Trained** Germany

[1014] PONTEFRACT (L-H)

Monday, April 21

OFFICIAL GOING: Good to soft (5.9)

Wind: Moderate against Weather: Suny spells

1515 DEM WINDOW SOLUTIONS MEDIAN AUCTION MAIDEN FILLIES' STKS 5f

2:10 (2:11) (Class 5) 2-Y-0 **£3,238** (£963; £481; £240) **Stalls** Low

Form				RPR
	1		**Clumber Place** 2-9-0 0 .... DeanMcKeown 6 (R C Guest) *mde all: rdn over 1f out: edgd rt and styd on wl fnl f* **16/1**	69+
	2	3/4	**Camelot Communion (IRE)** 2-9-0 0 .... RoystonFfrench 1 (Mrs A Duffield) *trckd ldng pair: hdwy to chal over 1f out: rdn and ev ch ins fnl f tl drvn and no ex last 75yds* **7/2[2]**	66
	3	2 1/4	**Asian Tale (IRE)** 2-9-0 0 .... LeeEnstone 4 (P C Haslam) *dwlt and towards rr: gd hdwy on outer wl over 1f out: rdn ent fnl f: kpt on same pce* **9/2[3]**	57
43	4	2 1/4	**Transcentral**[18] 1168 2-9-0 0 .... LiamJones 8 (W M Brisbourne) *wnt rt s: t.k.h and sn cl up: ev ch 2f out: sn rdn and wknd over 1f out* **10/3[1]**	48
	5	*nk*	**Rosabee (IRE)** 2-8-9 0 .... SCreighton(5) 2 (Miss V Haigh) *in tch: rdn along over 2f out: sn one pce* **8/1**	47
	6	11	**Sale Or Return (IRE)** 2-9-0 0 .... RobertWinston 5 (T D Easterby) *chsd ldrs: rdn along 2f out: wknd over 1f out* **9/2[3]**	3
	7	8	**Orphaned Annie** 2-9-0 0 .... TomEaves 3 (B Ellison) *s.i.s: a in rr* **6/1**	—

69.67 secs (6.37) **Going Correction** +0.725s/f (Yiel) 7 Ran SP% **112.9**

Speed ratings (Par 89): **78,76,73,69,69 51,38**

CSF £69.20 TOTE £22.70: £6.70, £2.50; EX 83.90.

Owner The Clumber Park Syndicate **Bred** Worksop Manor Stud **Trained** Carburton, Notts

FOCUS

A modest fillies' maiden, in which only the fourth had previous experience. Clumber Place did it well and was arguably value for at least a length more.

NOTEBOOK

Clumber Place, bred to want further than this, comes from a yard hardly renowned for their success with juveniles and she led throughout for a surprise success. She clearly knew her job and always seemed to be in control down the straight, her rider not really having to get too serious. This was a pleasing start to her career and her trainer, who believes she is "all class", intends on letting her take her chance in either the Lily Agnes or the Hilary Needler. The latter would seem the better option. (op 18-1 tchd 20-1)

Camelot Communion(IRE), a 65,000euros daughter of Elusive City, is another likely to require further in time, but she seemed to know her job and kept on well in second. She was always being held by the winner, but should come on for the run and find a small race. (op 3-1 tchd 4-1)

Asian Tale(IRE), an 8,000gns daughter of Namid, is a half-sister to a 1m4f winner and she was immediately on the back foot following a slow start. She recovered to keep on well in the straight though and should learn from the experience. (op 5-1 tchd 11-2)

Transcentral set the standard having been the only one to have previously seen a racecourse. Third behind the smart-looking Art Connoisseur at Leicester last time, she raced a shade keenly and could find no extra in the straight. This was disappointing. (op 5-2 tchd 7-2)

Rosabee(IRE) is related to sprint winners and she showed enough on this racecourse debut to suggest she should find a small race. (op 14-1)

Sale Or Return(IRE), whose trainer introduced a debut winner the other day, failed to show anything on this racecourse debut, but should learn from the experience. (op 7-2)

1516 CORNMARKET H'CAP 1m 4f 8y

2:40 (2:41) (Class 5) (0-70,70) 3-Y-0 **£3,238** (£963; £481; £240) **Stalls** Low

Form				RPR
0523	1		**Silver Waters**[21] 1114 3-9-2 **68** .... AlanMunro 4 (D R C Elsworth) *trckd ldrs: pushed along over 3f out: rdn and hdwy on outer wl over 1f out: led ent fnl f: styd on strly* **4/1[2]**	79
006-	2	5	**Stealth Project**[166] 6725 3-8-10 **62** .... HayleyTurner 5 (A M Hales) *t.k.h: trckd ldng pair on inner: effrt over 2f out: rdn and ev ch 1f out: sn drvn and kpt on same pce* **16/1**	65
643-	3	3 1/4	**Stow**[156] 6857 3-9-2 **68** .... SteveDrowne 7 (H Morrison) *hld up in tch: hdwy on outer over 3f out: rdn to ld over 1f out: hdd and drvn ent fnl f: sn one pce* **7/4[1]**	66
64-3	4	1 1/2	**Al Azy (IRE)**[18] 1173 3-9-4 **70** .... RHills 8 (J L Dunlop) *led: rdn along over 2f out: drvn and hdd over 1f out: wknd* **11/2**	66
00-0	5	8	**Intersky Melody (USA)**[19] 1161 3-8-5 **57** .... DeanMcKeown 2 (R M Whitaker) *hld up in rr: sme hdwy wl 2f out: sn rdn and nvr a factor* **25/1**	40
500-	6	7	**Prince's Decree**[271] 3833 3-8-11 **63** .... GregFairley 9 (G M Moore) *chsd ldr: rdn along over 3f out: wknd over 2f out* **12/1**	35
-231	7	21	**Oberlin (USA)**[59] 657 3-9-2 **68** .... J-PGuillambert 1 (T Keddy) *chsd ldrs: rdn along 3f out: sn wknd* **5/1[3]**	6
0-00	8	5	**Sabre Light**[19] 1140 3-8-11 **63** .... LeeEnstone 6 (P T Midgley) *a in rr* **33/1**	—
000-	9	11	**Generous Boy**[167] 6698 3-8-6 **58** .... DavidAllan 3 (T D Easterby) *a towards rr: bhd fnl 3f* **12/1**	—

2m 47.94s (7.14) **Going Correction** +0.725s/f (Yiel) 9 Ran SP% **116.5**

Speed ratings (Par 98): **105,101,99,98,93 88,74,71,63**

CSF £65.51 CT £150.52 TOTE £5.00: £1.80, £4.60, £1.20; EX 77.10.

Owner D R C Elsworth **Bred** Natton House Thoroughbreds **Trained** Newmarket, Suffolk

FOCUS

A fair handicap and quite a test for the 3yos in the ground. The form looks pretty solid with the winner ip 10lb.

1517 RIU PALACE MELONERAS H'CAP 6f

3:10 (3:11) (Class 2) (0-100,100) 4-Y-0+

£11,215 (£3,358; £1,679; £840; £419; £210) **Stalls** Low

Form				RPR
00-6	1		**Turnkey**[10] 1300 6-8-1 **90** .... AdeleRothery(7) 5 (D Nicholls) *hld up in rr: hdwy on wd outside wl over 1f out: rdn ent fnl f: styd on to ld on line* **8/1**	100
10-4	2	*hd*	**Damika (IRE)**[10] 1300 5-8-10 **95** .... MichaelJStainton(3) 12 (R M Whitaker) *hld up: hdwy 2f out: rdn ent fnl f: styd on to ld nr fin: hdd on line* **7/1[3]**	105
6501	3	*hd*	**Stevie Gee (IRE)**[9] 1327 4-8-4 **86** .... PaulHanagan 13 (G A Swinbank) *trckd ldrs: hdwy wl over 1f out: rdn to chal whn hmpd jst ins fnl f: sn drvn and led fnl 50yds: hdd and nt qckn towards fin* **5/1[1]**	95
121-	4	3/4	**Genki (IRE)**[206] 5765 4-9-3 **99** .... SteveDrowne 1 (R Charlton) *trckd ldrs on inner: swtchd rt and hdwy wl over 1f out: rdn to chal and hung rt ent fnl f: drvn to ld wl ins fnl f: hdd and no ex last 50yds* **6/1[2]**	106
1-16	5	3/4	**Ingleby Arch (USA)**[23] 1071 5-8-7 **89** .... PaulFessey 14 (T D Barron) *hmpd s: sn chsng ldrs: rdn over 1f out: stayintg on whn n.m.r wl ins fnl f* **9/1**	93
4335	6	1 1/4	**Distinctly Game**[17] 1195 6-8-4 **86** oh2 .... HayleyTurner 16 (K A Ryan) *cl up: rdn to ld over 1f out: drvn and hdd wl ins fnl f: one pce* **25/1**	86
06-0	7	1 3/4	**Rising Shadow (IRE)**[30] 959 7-9-2 **98** .... AlanMunro 3 (N Wilson) *towards rr tl styd on fnl 2f: n.d* **12/1**	93
000-	8	*nk*	**Steenberg (IRE)**[205] 5797 9-8-4 **91** .... NicolPolli(5) 10 (M H Tompkins) *midfield: pushed along over 2f out: sn drvn and no imp* **20/1**	85
00-2	9	*nk*	**High Curragh**[23] 1071 5-8-4 **86** .... DO'Donohoe 8 (K A Ryan) *led: rdn along 2f out: hdd over 1f out and sn wknd* **12/1**	79
5-02	10	3 1/2	**Knot In Wood (IRE)**[17] 1198 6-9-1 **100** .... JamieMoriarty(3) 2 (R A Fahey) *a towards rr* **7/1[3]**	81
00-0	11	1/2	**Zomerlust**[23] 1071 6-8-11 **93** .... (p) GrahamGibbons 4 (J J Quinn) *a towards rr* **8/1**	73
04-0	12	3/4	**Ice Planet**[10] 1300 7-8-7 **89** .... AdrianTNicholls 15 (D Nicholls) *chsd ldrs: rdn wl over 1f out and sn wknd* **16/1**	66

1m 20.56s (3.66) **Going Correction** +0.725s/f (Yiel) 12 Ran SP% **118.0**

Speed ratings (Par 109): **104,103,103,102,101 99,97,97,96,92 91,90**

CSF £62.80 CT £312.69 TOTE £10.00: £3.50, £2.70, £1.80; EX 50.20 Trifecta £321.30 Part won. Pool £452.60 - 0.40 winning units..

Owner Middleham Park Racing Xxiii **Bred** Mrs E M Charlton **Trained** Sessay, N Yorks

■ Fayr Jag, winner of the 2004 Golden Jubilee Stakes, was fatally injured entering the stalls (25/1, no R4).

■ Stewards' Enquiry : Steve Drowne caution: careless riding

FOCUS

A highly competitive sprint handicap that produced a tight finish. Sound form, and decent for the grade.

NOTEBOOK

Turnkey, beaten just over a length on his reappearance at Doncaster, had been dropped 1lb and he came late and wide with a winning challenge, just getting there under Adele Rothery. He is a horse who likes a bit of dig in the ground and should remain competitive off this sort of mark.

Damika(IRE), just ahead of the winner at Doncaster, held obvious claims and he only just lost out in a driving finish. He remains 5lb higher than when last winning, but is clearly capable of winning off this mark. (tchd 6-1)

Stevie Gee(IRE), 6lb higher than when narrowly prevailing over 7f on his reappearance at Doncaster, again had the ground in his favour and he coped well enough with the drop in trip. However, he was done no favours when slightly impeded inside the final furlong and, having hit the front, was unable to repel the front pair. (tchd 9-2 and 11-2)

Genki(IRE) developed into a consistent sprinter last season, but all his winning has been done on a sound surface and he ran really well considering, just getting run out of it close home. This was a highly promising return and he can continue his progression back on better ground. (tchd 13-2)

Ingleby Arch(USA), a winner at Southwell in February, has since run creditably at Doncaster and this was another fair effort. He is probably too high in the weights to win again. (tchd 10-1)

Distinctly Game, 9lb higher on turf than the All-Weather, ran well for a long way and could be of interest once receiving some help from the handicapper. (op 20-1)

Knot In Wood(IRE) Official explanation: jockey said gelding was denied a clear run

1518 PONTEFRACT MARATHON H'CAP 2m 5f 122y

3:40 (3:40) (Class 5) (0-75,73) 4-Y-0+ **£3,885** (£1,156; £577; £288) **Stalls** Low

Form				RPR
1311	1		**Grizebeck (IRE)**[10] 1304 6-9-13 **73** .... (p) PaulHanagan 2 (R F Fisher) *mde all: pushed along over 3f out: rdn 2f out: drvn over 1f out: styd on gamely fnl f* **7/1**	88
130-	2	5	**Go Amwell**[9] 6561 5-8-8 **54** .... LiamJones 3 (J R Jenkins) *hld up in tch: stdy hdwy over 4f out: rdn to chal 2f out and ev ch tl drvn and one pce ent fnl f* **5/1[3]**	64
5-52	3	11	**At The Money**[27] 1017 5-9-7 **67** .... (b) DaleGibson 7 (J M P Eustace) *cl up: effrt and ev ch over 3f out: sn rdn and outpcd fnl 2f* **11/2**	66
21-2	4	3/4	**Toboggan Lady**[19] 1136 4-8-12 **64** .... RoystonFfrench 8 (Mrs A Duffield) *trckd ldrs: hdwy over 5f out: rdn along wl over 2f out: sn drvn and outpcd* **9/4[1]**	62
65-0	5	11	**Rocknest Island (IRE)**[19] 1136 5-8-11 **57** .... (p) RobertWinston 4 (P D Niven) *chsd ldrs: rdn along over 3f out and sn wknd* **14/1**	44
656-	6	9	**Toni Alcala**[38] 2204 9-8-3 **54** oh8 .... NicolPolli(5) 9 (N B King) *hld up in rr: hdwy 6f out: rdn to chse ldrs over 3f out: sn wknd* **25/1**	32
00-5	7	1 3/4	**Great As Gold (IRE)**[27] 1017 9-9-13 **73** .... TomEaves 5 (B Ellison) *trckd ldrs: hdwy 5f out: rdn 3f out and sn btn* **3/1[2]**	50
-640	8	78	**Topwell**[26] 843 7-8-3 **54** oh9 .... NataliaGemelova(5) 1 (R C Guest) *a bhd* **50/1**	—
30-6	9	61	**Welcome Cat (USA)**[93] 229 4-8-2 **54** oh1 .... (t) SilvestreDeSousa 6 (A D Brown) *a bhd* **33/1**	—

5m 11.23s (2.43) **Going Correction** +0.725s/f (Yiel)

WFA 4 from 5yo+ 6lb 9 Ran SP% **115.7**

Speed ratings (Par 103): **103,101,97,96,92 89,89,60,38**

CSF £41.22 CT £208.01 TOTE £7.10: £2.10, £1.90, £2.10; EX 45.50.

Owner Sporting Occasions **Bred** John Killeen **Trained** Ulverston, Cumbria

FOCUS

A competitive marathon event and a real test of stamina. An improved run form all-the-way winner Grizebeck, although this form may not prove too relevant in more conventinal races.

Great As Gold(IRE) Official explanation: trainer said gelding was unsuited by the good to soft ground

Welcome Cat(USA) Official explanation: vet said gelding finished lame

1519 SUBSCRIBE ONLINE @ RACINGUK.TV MAIDEN STKS 6f

4:10 (4:11) (Class 5) 3-Y-0+ **£3,238** (£963; £481; £240) **Stalls** Low

Form				RPR
2-	1		**Solar Spirit (IRE)**[188] 6255 3-8-11 0 .... PJMcDonald(3) 1 (G A Swinbank) *trckd ldrs on inner: smooth hdwy to ld 1/2-way: clr wl over 1f out: shkn up and swished tail ins fnl f: easily* **2/1[1]**	85
	2	4 1/2	**Strawberry Moon (IRE)** 3-8-9 0 .... TomEaves 12 (B Smart) *towards rr: hdwy over 2f out: rdn over 1f out: styd on ins fnl f: no ch w wnr* **10/1[3]**	66+
	3	2 1/4	**Mark Of Meydan** 3-9-0 0 .... PhillipMakin 4 (M Dods) *trckd ldrs: hdwy to chse wnr wl over 1f out: sn rdn and one pce* **6/1[2]**	63

6 **4** *13* **Atlantic Beach**[19] [1139] 3-9-0 0 PaulHanagan 11 22
(R A Fahey) *dwlt and towards rr: hdwy 1/2-way: rdn wl over 1f out: kpt on ins fnl f: n.d* **10/1**[3]

40-0 **5** *nk* **Miss Taboo (IRE)**[19] [1139] 4-9-6 49 MickyFenton 10 16
(P T Midgley) *racd wd: led: rdn along and hdd 1/2-way: drvn and one pce fnl 2f* **28/1**

6 *4 1/2* **Sosostris Pitch (FR)** 3-9-0 0 J-PGuillambert 2 —
(P C Haslam) *chsd ldrs: rdn along over 2f out: sn drvn and wknd* **20/1**

7 *hd* **Take It Easee (IRE)** 3-8-9 0 RobertWinston 14 —
(G A Swinbank) *in tch on outer: effrt: edgd lft and n.m.r wl over 1f out: sn no imp* **18/1**

4324 **8** *nk* **Extreme North (USA)**[38] [882] 3-8-9 64 (b) SCreighton[(5)] 6 —
(Miss V Haigh) *plld hrd: prom tl rdn over 2f out and sn wknd* **16/1**

60- **9** *2 1/2* **Bunny Hug**[248] [4565] 3-8-9 0 DavidAllan 9 —
(T D Easterby) *midfeild: rdn along 1/2-way and sn outpcd* **66/1**

2-3 **10** *3/4* **Adab (IRE)**[10] [1298] 3-9-0 0 RHills 13 —
(J H M Gosden) *chsd ldrs: rdn along over 2f out: sn wknd* **2/1**[1]

11 *6* **Sleeping** 3-8-9 0 PaulMulrennan 15 —
(M H Tompkins) *s.i.s: a in rr* **40/1**

00 **12** *25* **Notforloveormoney**[27] [1019] 3-8-9 0 GregFairley 7 —
(A G Foster) *chsd ldrs: riudden along over 2f out and sn wknd* **100/1**

0000 **13** *11* **Josama**[13] [1259] 4-9-6 30 (b) DaneO'Neill 5 —
(R Bastiman) *cl up: rdn along over 3f out and sn wknd* **250/1**

14 *8* **White Rose George** 3-9-0 0 LiamJones 3 —
(J O'Reilly) *s.i.s: a bhd* **40/1**

1m 20.6s (3.70) **Going Correction** +0.725s/f (Yiel)
WFA 3 from 4yo 11lb **14** Ran SP% **126.2**
Speed ratings (Par 103): **104,98,95,77,77 71,71,70,67,66 58,24,10,—**
CSF £26.09 TOTE £3.20: £1.40, £3.10, £2.90; EX 38.40.
Owner Christopher James Allan **Bred** Paul Hensey **Trained** Melsonby, N Yorks

FOCUS
A typically moderate sprint maiden for older horses. The first three finished well clear and the time was decent, but overall this is not form to get carried away with.
Take It Easee(IRE) Official explanation: jockey said filly ran very green and became unbalanced

1520 CATTERICK RACES ON 23RD APRIL H'CAP 1m 4y
4:40 (4:45) (Class 5) (0-75,75) 4-Y-0+ £3,238 (£963; £481; £240) Stalls Low

Form RPR

1/0- **1** **Ben Chorley**[333] [1978] 4-9-1 72 TedDurcan 8 85
(D R Lanigan) *in tch: hdwy over 2f out: led wl over 1f out: rdn and hung rt ins fnl f: drvn out* **7/1**[2]

42-1 **2** *4* **Granary**[103] [95] 4-8-12 69 DaneO'Neill 11 73
(H Candy) *hld up: hdwy over 2f out: chsd ldrs over 1f out: rdn to chse wnr ins fnl f: drvn and no imp last 100yds* **8/1**[3]

50/2 **3** *1 1/4* **Prince Egor (IRE)**[19] [1160] 5-8-10 67 ow2 (p) PhillipMakin 14 68
(M Dods) *in rr: swtchd oustdie and hdwy over 1f out: sn rdn and styd on strly ins fnl f: nrst fin* **7/1**[2]

116- **4** *3 1/2* **Young Bertie**[180] [6423] 5-8-12 72 TravisBlock[(3)] 5 65
(H Morrison) *chsd ldrs: rdn 2f out: drvn over 1f out: kpt on same pce* **7/2**[1]

656- **5** *nk* **Demolition**[196] [6055] 4-9-3 74 GrahamGibbons 7 66
(N Wilson) *midfield: hdwy 2f out and sn rdn along: drvn over 1f out: kpt on ins fnl f: nrst fin* **8/1**[3]

400- **6** *3 1/2* **Distant Pleasure**[235] [4971] 4-8-4 61 DaleGibson 4 45
(M Dods) *towards rr: hdwy wl over 1f out: sn rdn and styd on ins fnl f: nrst fin* **25/1**

32-0 **7** *3/4* **Aussie Blue (IRE)**[28] [990] 4-8-6 63 DeanMcKeown 2 45
(R M Whitaker) *chsd ldrs on inner: rdn along wl over 1f out: drvn and one pce appr fnl f* **8/1**[3]

310/ **8** *6* **Cote D'Argent**[20] [1115] 5-9-4 75 PaulHanagan 9 44
(L Lungo) *a towards rr* **28/1**

306- **9** *nk* **San Antonio**[308] [2722] 8-9-0 71 (b) MickyFenton 10 39+
(Mrs P Sly) *led and sn clr: rdn along over 2f out: hdd wl over 1f out: wknd* **14/1**

2610 **10** *1 1/4* **Saviour Sand (IRE)**[30] [973] 4-9-2 73 HayleyTurner 3 38
(D R C Elsworth) *chsd ldrs: rdn along ocer 2f out: drvn over 1f out and sn wknd* **12/1**

060- **11** *2* **Prince Golan (IRE)**[142] [6999] 4-9-2 73 RobertWinston 12 34
(J W Unett) *a towards rr* **28/1**

5412 **12** *18* **Kildare Sun (IRE)**[40] [860] 6-8-13 70 RoystonFfrench 6 —
(J Mackie) *c hased ldrs: rdn along over 3f out: sn wknd* **17/2**

10-0 **13** *3 3/4* **Malinsa Blue (IRE)**[19] [1138] 6-8-8 65 TomEaves 13 —
(B Ellison) *a towards rr* **22/1**

20-0 **14** *5* **Rodeo**[16] [1217] 5-9-1 72 (b) J-PGuillambert 15 —
(C W Thornton) *sn rdn along and a in rr* **40/1**

050- **15** *43* **Wahoo Sam (USA)**[153] [6882] 8-8-4 61 oh3 (p) TWilliams 1 —
(D W Barker) *chsd ldr: rdn along 3f out and sn wknd* **40/1**

1m 50.26s (4.36) **Going Correction** +0.725s/f (Yiel) **15** Ran SP% **125.4**
Speed ratings (Par 103): **107,103,101,98,97 94,93,87,87,86 84,66,62,57,14**
CSF £59.42 CT £425.96 TOTE £8.30: £3.20, £3.70, £3.10; EX 74.40.
Owner Diamond Racing Ltd **Bred** Mrs A Yearley **Trained** Newmarket, Suffolk
■ A first winner at the first attempt for former Henry Cecil assistant David Lanigan.
■ Stewards' Enquiry : Ted Durcan one-day ban: used whip with excessive frequency in incorrect place (May 5)

FOCUS
A moderate handicap in which San Antonio set a fast pace. None of the first three were fully exposed and this form could have been underrated.

1521 PONTEFRACT APPRENTICE SERIES (ROUND 2) H'CAP 1m 2f 6y
5:10 (5:12) (Class 5) (0-70,70) 4-Y-0+ £3,238 (£963; £481; £240) Stalls Low

Form RPR

/26- **1** **Force Group (IRE)**[339] [1827] 4-9-0 68 AshleyMorgan[(3)] 8 81+
(M H Tompkins) *trckd ldrs: swtchd ins and hdwy over 1f out: styd on to ld wl ins fnl f: kpt on strly* **7/1**

0135 **2** *1 1/4* **Lucayan Dancer**[10] [1305] 8-9-2 70 AdeleRothery[(3)] 1 75
(D Nicholls) *trckd ldrs: hdwy over 2f out: rdn to chse ldr over 1f out: drvn and ev ch ins fnl f: kpt on* **9/2**[2]

205/ **3** *nk* **Three Strings (USA)**[594] [5082] 5-8-0 58 oh2 ow2 PaulPickard[(7)] 2 62
(P D Niven) *led: pushed along over 2f out: rdn over 1f out: edgd rt and hdd wl ins fnl f: kpt on towards fin* **16/1**

6012 **4** *5* **Street Life (IRE)**[11] [1281] 10-8-7 61 DebraEngland[(3)] 11 55
(W J Musson) *hld up towards rr: hdwy over 2f out: rdn along wl over 1f out: kpt on same pce u.p fnl f: nvr rch ldrs* **7/2**[1]

544- **5** *5* **Wulimaster (USA)**[153] [6883] 5-8-5 56 oh2 MatthewDavies 4 40
(D W Barker) *hld up: gd hdwy on outer over 3f out: chal 2f out: sn rdn: hung lft and wknd over 1f out* **15/2**

-561 **6** *4* **Sol Rojo**[34] [921] 6-8-12 63 (v) SimonPearce 6 39
(J Pearce) *hld up towards rr: hdwy over 2f out: rdn wl over 1f out and no imp* **6/1**[3]

03/0 **7** *1 1/4* **Find Me (USA)**[16] [1219] 4-8-6 60 NSLawes[(3)] 5 34
(L Lungo) *midfield: rdn along 2f out: swtchd lft over 1f out: nvr nr ldrs* **50/1**

40-3 **8** *6* **Tizzy May (FR)**[28] [989] 8-8-5 63 AnthonyBetts[(7)] 12 25
(B Ellison) *prom: rdn along 3f out and sn wknd* **10/1**

/650 **9** *9* **Babieca (USA)**[6] [1383] 4-9-0 65 DeanHeslop 3 9
(T D Barron) *a towards rr* **33/1**

0224 **10** *2 3/4* **Tidy (IRE)**[5] [1391] 8-8-5 56 oh4 (v) JemmaMarshall 10 —
(Micky Hammond) *chsd ldrs: rdn along wl over 2f out: grad wknd* **16/1**

3-00 **11** *1 1/2* **Baaher (USA)**[28] [991] 4-8-11 65 BMcHugh[(3)] 9 —
(T J Pitt) *sn pushed along in rr: bhd fr 1/2-way* **8/1**

-436 **12** *16* **Not Another Cat (USA)**[26] [1030] 4-9-0 65 DeclanCannon 7 —
(K R Burke) *chsd ldrs: rdn along over 3f out: sn lost pl and bhd* **20/1**

2m 20.25s (6.55) **Going Correction** +0.725s/f (Yiel) **12** Ran SP% **120.6**
Speed ratings (Par 103): **102,101,100,96,92 89,88,83,76,74 73,60**
CSF £38.53 CT £498.82 TOTE £8.60: £2.40, £2.00, £4.30; EX 41.60 Place 6 £129.85, Place 5 £38.58.
Owner The Force Group **Bred** Airlie Stud And Sir Thomas Pilkington **Trained** Newmarket, Suffolk

FOCUS
A race low on quality and restricted to apprentices who had not ridden more than ten winners prior to the start of the turf season. Ordinary form, held down by the third, with the unexposed winner likely to rate higher.
T/Jkpt: Not won. T/Plt: £258.20 to a £1 stake. Pool: £73,893.61. 208.85 winning tickets. T/Qpdt: £39.40 to a £1 stake. Pool: £4,453.80. 83.60 winning tickets. JR

1363 WINDSOR (R-H)
Monday, April 21

OFFICIAL GOING: Good (8.4)
Wind: Moderate, against Weather: Cloudy

1522 GET ON WITH WILLIAM HILL 0800 44 40 40 APPRENTICE H'CAP 6f
5:25 (5:26) (Class 5) (0-75,74) 4-Y-0+ £3,070 (£906; £453) Stalls High

Form RPR

2232 **1** **Savile's Delight (IRE)**[7] [1368] 9-9-8 68 RossAtkinson[(5)] 8 78
(Tom Dascombe) *awkward s: sn trckd ldrs: prog to ld on outer over 1f out: shkn up and kpt on wl* **7/2**[1]

004- **2** *1/2* **Adantino**[203] [5874] 9-9-5 74 (b) JamesMillman 3 82
(B R Millman) *hld up in last quartet: rdn and prog on outer over 1f out: r.o fnl f to take 2nd last strides* **14/1**

5341 **3** *nk* **Kelamon**[45] [819] 4-9-2 71 PatrickHills 7 78
(M D I Usher) *trckd ldrs and racd on outer: effrt to press wnr fnl f: hld last 100yds and lost 2nd nr fin* **15/2**

6025 **4** *nse* **Linda Green**[11] [1285] 7-8-4 62 ThomasO'Brien[(3)] 12 69
(M R Channon) *hld up in last quartet: rdn 2f out: prog on outer fnl f: nvr quite able to chal* **12/1**

0532 **5** *hd* **Chatshow (USA)**[9] [1338] 7-8-5 60 KellyHarrison 9 66
(A W Carroll) *hld up wl in rr: shkn up and effrt over 1f out: styd on fnl f: nrst fin* **8/1**

44-0 **6** *1 3/4* **Equuleus Pictor**[7] [1368] 4-8-7 65 JackDean[(3)] 5 66
(J L Spearing) *pressed ldrs: rdn and upsides over 1f out: fdd fnl f* **10/1**

010- **7** *1* **Rydal Mount (IRE)**[163] [6753] 5-8-12 72 TimothyMeadows[(5)] 13 69+
(W S Kittow) *hld up in last quartet against nr side rail: nt clr run over 1f out and swtchd sharply lft: styd on fnl f: nrst fin* **16/1**

0606 **8** *shd* **Tamino (IRE)**[16] [1209] 5-9-1 70 (t) JamieJones 6 67
(P Howling) *hld up in midfield: rdn and no real prog over 1f out: kpt on* **16/1**

3342 **9** *1/2* **Memphis Man**[4] [1430] 5-8-12 72 RichardEvans[(5)] 14 67
(P D Evans) *hld up in last quartet: effrt 2f out: no real prog 1f out: plugged on* **5/1**[2]

050- **10** *1/2* **Grey Boy (GER)**[201] [5909] 7-8-7 65 MarkCoumbe[(3)] 4 59
(A W Carroll) *prom on outer: rdn 2f out: wknd jst over 1f out* **40/1**

000- **11** *1 1/4* **Ken's Girl**[164] [6747] 4-8-12 70 WilliamCarson[(3)] 11 60
(W S Kittow) *prom against nr side rail tl wknd over 1f out* **25/1**

320- **12** *1/2* **Gwilym (GER)**[208] [5722] 5-9-5 74 AshleyHamblett 1 62
(D Haydn Jones) *fast away fr low draw: led and crossed to nr side rail: hdd & wknd over 1f out* **7/1**[3]

3020 **13** *1 1/4* **Kempsey**[25] [1037] 6-8-0 60 oh2 (b) DavidProbert[(5)] 10 44
(J J Bridger) *nvr bttr than midfield: wknd over 1f out* **40/1**

131/ **14** *1/2* **Tadlil**[599] [4957] 6-8-11 69 MCGeran[(3)] 2 52
(J M Bradley) *nvr beyond midfield on outer: lost pl and struggling in rr wl over 1f out* **22/1**

1m 13.56s (0.56) **Going Correction** +0.175s/f (Good) **14** Ran SP% **122.6**
Speed ratings (Par 103): **103,102,101,101,101 99,97,97,97,96 94,94,92,91**
CSF £53.81 CT £354.63 TOTE £5.10: £1.70, £4.00, £2.90; EX 77.70.
Owner ONEWAY Partners **Bred** Romany Investments Ltd **Trained** Lambourn, Berks

FOCUS
A modest handicap, confined to apprentice riders, which saw the field race stands-to-middle side of the straight. The first five were closely covered at the finish. Ordinary form, but sound.

1523 GET A BONUS @ WILLIAMHILLCASINO.COM MAIDEN STKS 5f 10y
5:55 (5:56) (Class 5) 2-Y-O £2,729 (£806; £403) Stalls High

Form RPR

2 **1** **Miss Chamanda (IRE)**[7] [1363] 2-8-12 0 TGMcLaughlin 11 75
(P D Evans) *mde all: racd against nr side rail: rdn and hung bdly lft fr over 1f out: clr fnl f* **9/4**[1]

2 *1 1/4* **Heliodor (USA)** 2-9-3 0 RichardHughes 2 76+
(R Hannon) *hld up in rr: sme prog over 1f out: shkn up and styd on wl fnl f to take 2nd last strides* **11/2**[3]

3 *nk* **Flashmans Papers** 2-9-3 0 LPKeniry 10 74+
(J R Best) *trckd ldrs: chsd wnr 2f out: no imp fnl f: lost 2nd last strides* **9/1**

6 **4** *1 3/4* **Klynch**[3] [1439] 2-9-3 0 RobertHavlin 4 67
(B J Meehan) *rn green in midfield on outer: outpcd over 1f out: kpt on* **20/1**

5 *2 1/4* **Duke Of Aquitaine (USA)** 2-9-3 0 TQuinn 1 58+
(P F I Cole) *v green in last pair and reminder after 1f: modest prog on outer fnl 2f: nvr a threat* **10/3**[2]

6 *shd* **Buddy Marvellous (IRE)** 2-9-3 0 RyanMoore 3 57
(R Hannon) *trckd ldrs and racd against nr side rail: outpcd fr over 1f out* **13/2**

7 2 1/4 **Blushing Maid** 2-8-8 0 ow1 HaddenFrost(5) 7 44
(H S Howe) *mostly chsd wnr to 2f out: wknd over 1f out* **33/1**

8 1 1/2 **Striding Edge (IRE)** 2-9-3 0 MartinDwyer 6 42
(W R Muir) *chsd ldrs: rdn 2f out: steadily wknd over 1f out* **8/1**

0 9 2 **Buckle Up**23 1078 2-9-3 0 JimCrowley 8 34+
(D K Ivory) *cl up to 1/2-way: steadily wknd fr over 1f out* **20/1**

0 10 1/2 **Sharp Discovery**12 1263 2-8-12 0 PaulFitzsimons 5 27
(J M Bradley) *prom 3f: sn wknd* **100/1**

11 8 **The Beat Is On** 2-8-9 0 TolleyDean(3) 9 —
(J M Bradley) *a in last pair: t.o* **66/1**

62.13 secs (1.83) **Going Correction** +0.175s/f (Good) **11 Ran SP% 118.6**
Speed ratings (Par 92): **92,90,89,86,83 82,79,76,73,72 60**
CSF £14.26 TOTE £3.60: £1.30, £1.90, £2.60; EX 16.40.
Owner E A R Morgans **Bred** T Molan **Trained** Pandy, Monmouths

FOCUS
Not much previous form to go on but this could work out to be a fair juvenile maiden. The winner rates value for a bit further than her winning margin.

NOTEBOOK
Miss Chamanda(IRE), runner-up on her debut over course and distance a week previously, made all to go one better. She had the benefit of the stands' rail draw, but ended up drifting markedly left across the track inside the final furlong and would have won by further had she kept straight. A filly with some scope, from a yard which have made a bright start with its juveniles, she is reportedly being aimed at the Queen Mary at Royal Ascot. (tchd 5-2)
Heliodor(USA) ◆, the first foal of a multiple 1m plus winner in the US, ran green when asked for maximum effort on this racecourse bow. He stayed on nicely inside the final furlong, however, and should prove hard to beat next time now he has this experience under his belt. (op 3-1)
Flashmans Papers, whose dam was a triple 7f-1m winner in Germany, showed up nicely under a prominent ride and did more than enough to suggest he has a similar race within his compass. (op 8-1)
Klynch, last of sixth on his debut just three days previously, ran a much improved race on this quick reappearance despite again looking distinctly green. He will appreciate a stiffer test in due course and is one to keep an eye on. (tchd 22-1)
Duke Of Aquitaine(USA), half-brother to a multiple sprint winner in the US, lost any chance he may have held by blowing the start and then proving too green. The penny dropped with him late on, however, and the support he received in the betting ring would indicate he is thought capable of deal better than this. (op 6-1 tchd 3-1)
Buddy Marvellous(IRE), whose dam was a dual 5-6f winner at two, hit a flat spot before keeping on again without posing a threat. It is fair to expect a good deal of improvement from this debut experience. (op 6-1 tchd 15-2)
Blushing Maid Official explanation: jockey said filly lost its action

1524 NEW PLAYER BONUS @ WILLIAMHILLPOKER.COM H'CAP 1m 67y
6:25 (6:26) (Class 4) (0-85,85) 3-Y-O **£5,180** (£1,541; £770; £384) **Stalls High**

Form RPR

41-2 1 **Silver Rime (FR)**10 1297 3-9-2 83 RichardHughes 1 89+
(R Hannon) *mde all: hrd pressed fr over 2f out: styd on wl and in command fnl f* **11/4**1

21- 2 1 1/2 **Adversity**175 6530 3-9-1 82 RyanMoore 3 84+
(Sir Michael Stoute) *trckd wnr: effrt to chal over 2f out: pressed wnr after tl btn off fnl f: jst hld on for 2nd* **5/1**2

21- 3 hd **The Which Doctor**192 6139 3-8-11 78 TPQueally 2 80+
(J Noseda) *s.i.s: hld up in midfield: rdn over 2f out: styd on fr over 1f out to take 3rd fnl f: nrst fin* **13/2**3

65-0 4 nk **Legislation**23 1074 3-9-3 84 JimmyFortune 6 85+
(J H M Gosden) *chsd ldrs: rdn over 2f out: styd on fnl f: nvr able to chal* **20/1**

510- 5 1 3/4 **Bencoolen (IRE)**212 5613 3-9-3 84 MartinDwyer 5 81+
(R Charlton) *hld up in midfield: lost pl and in last trio 1/2-way: nudged along and styd on steadily fnl 2f: nvr nr ldrs: do bttr* **16/1**

0-33 6 shd **Internationaldebut (IRE)**16 1221 3-9-4 85 JohnEgan 12 82
(S Parr) *cl up: chsd ldng pair over 3f out: rdn and no imp 2f out: fdd fnl f* **12/1**

3-1 7 5 **Sundowner (IRE)**37 909 3-8-13 80 JamieSpencer 8 66
(G A Butler) *hld up in midfield: rdn over 2f out: no prog and btn wl over 1f out* **11/4**1

2011 8 1/2 **My Shadow**14 1247 3-8-13 80 IanMongan 7 64
(S Dow) *hld up in rr: rdn wl over 2f out: no real prog* **14/1**

10- 9 1 **Dusty Moon**240 4804 3-9-3 84 PaulDoe 11 66
(W J Knight) *dwlt: hld up in last and wl adrift: pushed along 3f out: sme prog on inner over 2f out: sn no hdwy* **40/1**

04-0 10 1/2 **Mick's Dancer**20 1125 3-8-5 72 RichardMullen 4 53
(W R Muir) *prom to 3f out: steadily wknd* **66/1**

210- 11 16 **Bonny Rose**177 6486 3-8-9 76 JoeFanning 10 20
(M Johnston) *a wl in rr: t.o* **33/1**

46-5 12 30 **Artsu**21 1113 3-8-12 79 JimCrowley 9 —
(M L W Bell) *sddle slipped and rapid prog on wd outside bnd 6f out: wknd over 2f out: virtually p.u* **22/1**

1m 42.99s (-1.71) **Going Correction** -0.075s/f (Good) **12 Ran SP% 119.6**
Speed ratings (Par 100): **105,103,103,103,101 101,96,95,94,94 78,48**
CSF £15.58 CT £80.95 TOTE £3.70: £1.90, £2.30, £3.00; EX 20.90.
Owner Fieldspring Racing **Bred** Jean-Philippe Dubois **Trained** East Everleigh, Wilts

FOCUS
A good three-year-old handicap for the class. The first pair were always prominent. The form looks sound and, rated positively, should work out.
Bonny Rose Official explanation: jockey said filly was hampered at the start
Artsu Official explanation: jockey said saddle slipped

1525 ARENA LEISURE CATERING MAIDEN FILLIES' STKS 1m 67y
6:55 (6:56) (Class 5) 3-Y-O **£2,729** (£806; £403) **Stalls High**

Form RPR

24- 1 **Katimont (IRE)**185 6296 3-9-0 0 MichaelHills 3 71+
(B W Hills) *sn trckd ldrs: wnt 2nd 2f out: rdn to ld jst over 1f out: styd on* **5/2**1

26 2 1/2 **Mekong Melody (IRE)**30 961 3-9-0 0 PhilipRobinson 7 70
(C G Cox) *trckd ldrs: rdn and nt qckn 2f out: effrt again over 1f out: wnt 2nd ins fnl f and pressed wnr nr fin* **8/1**

03- 3 1/2 **Bikini**202 5882 3-9-0 0 ChrisCatlin 9 69
(H Candy) *led after 1f: rn green bnd 5f out: rdn over 2f out: hdd jst over 1f out: kpt on but lost 2nd ins fnl f* **15/2**

06- 4 1 1/4 **Where's Susie**193 6119 3-9-0 0 RobertHavlin 14 66
(D K Ivory) *sn in midfield on inner: rdn and effrt over 2f out: styd on: nt pce to chal* **50/1**

5 1 **Casilda (IRE)** 3-9-0 0 PaulDoe 6 64
(W J Knight) *rousted along in rr early: prog on wd outside fr 3f out: chsd ldrs over 1f out: one pce after* **16/1**

4- 6 2 1/4 **Diamond Royal (IRE)**195 6087 3-9-0 0 TPQueally 8 59+
(E A L Dunlop) *hld up in rr: stdy prog on outer over 2f out: rdn wl over 1f out: fdd fnl f* **7/1**3

0- 7 1/2 **Sabancaya**170 6648 3-9-0 0 MartinDwyer 13 58
(W J Haggas) *nvr bttr than midfield: u.p and struggling over 2f out: plugged on* **16/1**

8 nk **Janshe Gold** 3-9-0 0 JamesDoyle 11 57
(J G Portman) *dwlt: rchd midfield on inner over 3f out: no hdwy fnl 2f* **50/1**

9 hd **Finney Hill** 3-9-0 0 FergusSweeney 5 56+
(H Candy) *sn in last trio: shkn up over 2f out: kpt on fnl 2f: nrst fin* **12/1**

10 1 **Ci Vediamo (IRE)** 3-9-0 0 SebSanders 12 54
(R M Beckett) *hld up in midfield: pulling hrd and hanging bnd over 5f out: rdn and effrt over 2f out: no imp wl over 1f out: wknd* **8/1**

5-4 11 nk **Queen's Speech (IRE)**12 1270 3-9-0 0 JimmyFortune 4 53
(J H M Gosden) *trckd ldr after 1f to 2f out: pushed along and wknd* **6/1**2

0- 12 3/4 **Charming Tale (USA)**170 6649 3-9-0 0 RichardHughes 1 52
(B J Meehan) *led 1f: styd prom: reminders and green over 3f out: lost pl fr over 2f out* **25/1**

13 3/4 **Shayera** 3-9-0 0 NeilPollard 2 50
(B R Johnson) *dwlt: a wl in rr: struggling over 3f out* **33/1**

00 14 27 **Glitz (IRE)**12 1270 3-9-0 0 JamieSpencer 10 50
(M L W Bell) *a wl in rr: t.o over 1f out* **40/1**

1m 45.04s (0.34) **Going Correction** -0.075s/f (Good) **14 Ran SP% 121.9**
Speed ratings (Par 95): **95,94,94,92,91 89,89,88,88,87 87,86,85,58**
CSF £21.79 TOTE £3.30: £1.80, £3.00, £2.00; EX 27.40.
Owner Martin S Schwartz **Bred** Lynch-Bages Ltd **Trained** Lambourn, Berks

FOCUS
An average fillies' maiden, run at an uneven pace. The winner can rate higher and the form is rated around the placed horses.
Charming Tale(USA) Official explanation: jockey said filly was denied a clear run

1526 8 EVENTS AT ROYAL WINDSOR RACECOURSE MAIDEN STKS 1m 2f 7y
7:25 (7:27) (Class 5) 3-Y-O+ **£2,729** (£806; £403) **Stalls Centre**

Form RPR

3 1 **Bushman**23 1082 4-10-0 0 RichardMullen 3 95+
(D M Simcock) *trckd ldrs: lost pl sltly over 3f out: prog again over 2f out: led over 1f out: bounded clr fnl f* **10/1**3

205- 2 4 1/2 **Woolfall Treasure**222 5323 3-8-11 90 NCallan 11 80
(G G Margarson) *trckd ldrs: rdn on inner over 2f out: outpcd over 1f out: styd on wl to take 2nd nr fin* **11/1**

2- 3 1 3/4 **French Riviera**166 6725 3-8-11 0 RyanMoore 9 77
(Sir Michael Stoute) *trckd ldrs: effrt to ld over 2f out: hdd and outpcd over 1f out: lost 2nd nr fin* **4/6**1

4 3/4 **Eureka Moment** 3-8-3 0 LukeMorris(3) 4 70+
(E A L Dunlop) *rn green in midfield: dropped to rr by 1/2-way: shkn up and styd on wl fnl 2f: nrst fin* **50/1**

23- 5 1 **Polmaily**185 6294 3-8-11 0 RichardHughes 5 73
(B J Meehan) *led for 3f: pressed ldr after: upsides over 2f out: sn shkn up and btn* **7/2**2

55- 6 nse **Prairie Storm**166 6725 3-8-11 0 LPKeniry 8 73
(A M Balding) *trckd ldrs: outpcd over 2f out: shuffled along and kpt on one pce fr over 1f out* **20/1**

7 shd **Dr Brass** 3-8-11 0 EddieAhern 14 73+
(H J L Dunlop) *dwlt: mostly in last trio: pushed along over 3f out: no prog tl picked up wl jst over 1f out: running on strly at fin* **66/1**

00- 8 2 **Fiume**177 6493 3-8-11 0 PatDobbs 6 69
(R Hannon) *w ldr: led after 3f to over 2f out: wknd over 1f out* **50/1**

5- 9 nk **Danse The Blues**159 6805 3-8-6 0 StephenDonohoe 13 63
(E A L Dunlop) *nvr beyond midfield: dropped to rr and rdn over 3f out: kpt on again fnl 2f* **16/1**

10 3 **Sarando** 3-8-11 0 SteveDrowne 12 62
(R Charlton) *hld up in midfield: no prog over 2f out: wknd over 1f out* **16/1**

0-6 11 1 1/2 **Asian Classic (IRE)**18 1172 3-8-11 0 RichardKingscote 2 59
(R Charlton) *hld up wl in rr: no prog 3f out: bhd fnl 2f* **66/1**

12 7 **Road To Hucking (GER)** 3-8-11 0 JimCrowley 1 45
(J R Best) *a in last trio: no ch fnl 3f* **50/1**

13 3 1/2 **Princess Flame (GER)**11 6-9-9 0 TQuinn 10 36
(B G Powell) *s.s: wl in rr: brief effrt on outer 4f out: sn wknd: bhd fnl 2f* **33/1**

14 5 **Deep Waters (IRE)** 3-8-11 0 IanMongan 7 28
(S Dow) *s.s: wl in rr: prog to chse ldrs 4f out: sn wknd rapidly and bhd* **50/1**

2m 7.11s (-1.59) **Going Correction** -0.075s/f (Good)
WFA 3 from 4yo+ 17lb **14 Ran SP% 129.9**
Speed ratings (Par 103): **103,99,98,97,96 96,96,94,94,92 91,85,82,78**
CSF £117.42 TOTE £11.80: £2.40, £2.60, £1.10; EX 148.40.
Owner Khalifa Dasmal **Bred** Darley **Trained** Newmarket, Suffolk

FOCUS
A good maiden, but the pace was not all that strong. The winner readily defied his weight-for-age concession and looks potentially very useful. The form is best rated through the runner-up.
Asian Classic(IRE) Official explanation: jockey said, regarding running and riding, that his orders were to get across to the rail, get cover and then come through the field in home straight, adding that he met trouble on the bend as the pace slowed, and was then one paced up the straight

1527 WINDSOR CLUB H'CAP 1m 3f 135y
7:55 (7:56) (Class 5) (0-75,75) 3-Y-O **£3,070** (£906; £453) **Stalls Centre**

Form RPR

-601 1 **Cape Colony**19 1147 3-8-11 68 RichardHughes 3 71
(R Hannon) *hld up in midfield: prog 3f out: hrd rdn to ld ent fnl f: asserted last 100yds* **3/1**2

422- 2 1 1/4 **Heritage Coast (USA)**156 6857 3-9-2 73 RyanMoore 1 74
(Sir Michael Stoute) *hld up in midfield: clsd on ldrs over 2f out: hrd rdn to chal fnl f: hld last 100yds* **9/4**1

25-1 3 1/2 **Riverscape (IRE)**11 1279 3-9-4 75 JimCrowley 9 76
(Mrs A J Perrett) *led 1f: led again 1/2-way: drvn over 2f out: hdd ent fnl f: kpt on wl* **11/2**

53-1 4 nk **Title Role**14 1243 3-9-1 75 TolleyDean(3) 2 75
(P F I Cole) *dwlt: hld up in last trio: prog over 2f out: drvn to chal 1f out: one pce fnl f* **9/1**

0-55 5 3 1/4 **Landikhaya (IRE)**7 1364 3-8-11 68 SebSanders 5 63
(D K Ivory) *t.k.h: hld up in midfield: rdn to cl on ldrs 2f out: no imp 1f out: fdd* **16/1**

40-2 6 3/4 **Zen Factor**20 1128 3-8-9 66 JamesDoyle 7 60
(J G Portman) *t.k.h: led after 3f to 1/2-way: w ldr 5f out to over 2f out: wknd over 1f out* **9/1**

00-5 **7** *nk* **Io (IRE)**[19] 1147 3-8-4 **61** oh3 ChrisCatlin 8 54
(J L Dunlop) *hld up in last trio: rdn wl over 2f out: nt pce to make inroads on ldrs fnl 2f* **16/1**

653- **8** *3 1/2* **Wannarock (IRE)**[166] 6723 3-9-1 **72** JimmyFortune 4 65+
(E A L Dunlop) *t.k.h: led after 1f to after 3f: drvn over 2f out: looked hld whn hmpd over 1f out: hanging: wknd and eased after* **9/2**[3]

055- **9** *4* **House Of Tudor**[196] 6051 3-8-10 **67** NeilChalmers 6 48
(David Pinder) *a in last pair: rdn and struggling 4f out* **50/1**

00-1 **10** *9* **An Scaribh**[21] 1119 3-8-9 **73** RichardEvans(7) 10 40
(P D Evans) *t.k.h: sddle slipped sn after s: prom to 3f out* **33/1**

2m 29.34s (-0.16) **Going Correction** -0.075s/f (Good) **10 Ran SP% 126.0**
Speed ratings (Par 98): **97,96,95,95,93 92,92,90,87,81**
CSF £11.17 CT £37.75 TOTE £3.90: £1.40, £1.50, £2.80; EX 11.30 Place 6 £12.76, Place 5 £5.19.
Owner A F Merritt **Bred** Allan Merritt **Trained** East Everleigh, Wilts

FOCUS
A fair three-year-old handicap, run at a fair pace. The form should work out and might have been rated a bit higher.
Zen Factor Official explanation: jockey said gelding had run too free and hung left-handed in straight
Wannarock(IRE) Official explanation: jockey said gelding hung right-handed
An Scaribh Official explanation: jockey said saddle slipped
T/Plt: £8.10 to a £1 stake. Pool: £73,231.89. 6,564.22 winning tickets. T/Qpdt: £4.90 to a £1 stake. Pool: £5,795.87. 863.63 winning tickets. JN

1263 BATH (L-H)
Tuesday, April 22

OFFICIAL GOING: Good (good to soft in places; 7.6)
Wind: Almost nil Weather: Fine

1528 PREMIER CONSERVATORY ROOFS AND K2 H'CAP — 1m 2f 46y
5:10 (5:13) (Class 6) (0-55,55) 4-Y-0+ **£2,719** (£809; £404; £202) **Stalls** Low

Form RPR

-60 **1** **Top Seed (IRE)**[29] 999 7-8-9 **50** StephenDonohoe 5 68+
(Ian Williams) *stdd s: hld up and bhd: hdwy on ins over 3f out: swtchd rt 2f out: rdn to ld over 1f out: sn clr: eased cl home* **7/1**[3]

0031 **2** *3 3/4* **Princelywallywogan**[12] 1280 6-8-12 **53** SebSanders 6 64
(John A Harris) *hld up and bhd: hdwy on ins 3f out: swtchd rt 2f out: r.o to take 2nd last strides: nt trble wnr* **7/2**[2]

600- **3** *nk* **Monda**[154] 6886 6-8-1 **49** SophieDoyle(7) 1 59
(M Hill) *chsd ldr: led 2f out: rdn and hdd over 1f out: one pce* **16/1**

-004 **4** *4 1/2* **King Of Connacht**[12] 1280 5-8-11 **52** (p) JimmyQuinn 9 53
(M Wellings) *hld up in tch: rdn and wknd over 1f out* **16/1**

0-63 **5** *3/4* **Ready To Crown (USA)**[20] 1142 4-8-13 **54** AlanDaly 2 54+
(Andrew Turnell) *hld up in mid-div: rdn over 2f out: swtchd lft wl over 1f out: kpt on same pce* **10/1**

0000 **6** *3/4* **Prince Rossi (IRE)**[13] 1266 4-8-7 **48** (p) PaulFitzsimons 11 46
(A E Price) *led: rdn 3f out: hdd 2f out: sn wknd* **66/1**

630 **7** *1 3/4* **Personify**[12] 1280 6-8-3 **47** (p) KevinGhunowa(3) 7 42
(R A Harris) *t.k.h in tch: swtchd rt 2f out: sn wknd* **25/1**

-016 **8** *2 1/4* **Noah Jameel**[29] 999 6-8-13 **54** DaneO'Neill 13 44
(A G Newcombe) *mid-div: rdn over 2f out: wknd over 1f out* **14/1**

1660 **9** *nk* **Joe Jo Star**[27] 1032 6-8-2 **50** MatthewDavies(7) 12 39
(B P J Baugh) *prom: rdn over 2f out: wknd over 1f out* **25/1**

000- **10** *1 1/2* **Barbirolli**[158] 6837 6-8-8 **54** PatrickHills(5) 16 40
(W M Brisbourne) *hld up towards rr: rdn 3f out: btn whn edgd lft over 1f out* **16/1**

3653 **11** *3/4* **Patavium Prince (IRE)**[12] 1282 5-8-7 **53** JamieJones(5) 3 38
(Miss Jo Crowley) *stdd s: hld up in rr: rdn and struggling over 2f out* **16/1**

502- **12** *3 1/4* **Bruhaha**[201] 5945 4-8-11 **52** TQuinn 10 30
(B J McMath) *prom: rdn over 2f out: wknd wl over 1f out* **11/4**[1]

2540 **13** *1 1/2* **Sahf London**[17] 1206 5-8-11 **52** PatDobbs 17 27
(G L Moore) *s.s: a in rr* **16/1**

/00- **14** *20* **Cosimo Primo**[232] 5095 4-8-6 **47** FrankieMcDonald 4 —
(J A Geake) *t.k.h: rdn over 3f out: a in rr: t.o* **66/1**

-320 **15** *7* **Mix N Match**[24] 587 4-8-11 **52** SimonWhitworth 8 —
(R M Stronge) *plld hrd in mid-div: lost pl after 2f: t.o* **40/1**

-300 **16** *1 1/4* **Fateful Attraction**[69] 546 5-8-7 **48** (b) JamesDoyle 14 —
(I A Wood) *a towards rr: t.o* **20/1**

2m 15.02s (4.02) **Going Correction** +0.45s/f (Yiel) **16 Ran SP% 124.4**
Speed ratings (Par 101): **101,98,97,94,93 92,91,89,89,88 87,85,83,67,62 61**
CSF £30.14 CT £393.87 TOTE £8.70: £1.50, £1.50, £3.40, £2.60; EX 22.20.
Owner Paternosters & Tredwell **Bred** Hugo Merry And Jack Dorrian **Trained** Portway, Worcs
■ Stewards' Enquiry : Matthew Davies one-day ban: used whip above shoulder height (May 6)

FOCUS
A moderate handicap in which the winning time was 2.87 seconds quicker than the later 56-70 three-year-old handicap. The runner-up and fourth are rated close to their recent Folkestone form.
Mix N Match Official explanation: jockey said gelding ran too free

1529 KENT PLASTICS AND CELSIUS GLASS MAIDEN STKS — 5f 11y
5:40 (5:42) (Class 5) 3-Y-0+ **£3,238** (£963; £481; £240) **Stalls** Centre

Form RPR

342- **1** **Dunn'o (IRE)**[181] 6419 3-9-0 81 SebSanders 13 83+
(C G Cox) *hld up in mid-div: hdwy 2f out: rdn to ld and edgd lft 1f out: r.o wl* **6/4**[1]

230- **2** *4 1/2* **Rathmolyon**[197] 6059 3-8-9 68 TQuinn 7 62
(D Haydn Jones) *w ldr: led 2f out: hdd 1f out: one pce* **9/1**

0-3 **3** *1/2* **Asian Lady**[17] 1215 3-8-9 0 SteveDrowne 6 60
(R Charlton) *trckd ldrs: kpt on same pce fnl f* **11/4**[2]

0- **4** *1* **Billy Hot Rocks (IRE)**[283] 3550 3-9-0 0 JamesDoyle 10 61+
(R M Beckett) *s.i.s: sn hld up in mid-div: rdn 2f out: kpt on ins fnl f* **20/1**

0/2- **5** *nk* **Whiskey Junction**[351] 1520 4-9-10 73 LPKeniry 9 64
(A M Balding) *trckd ldrs: hrd rdn over 1f out: one pce* **11/2**[3]

U462 **6** *1* **Spic 'n Span**[14] 1255 3-9-0 65 PatDobbs 11 57
(R A Harris) *hld up in mid-div: rdn over 1f out: no hdwy fnl f* **16/1**

3-00 **7** *3/4* **Pennyspider (IRE)**[11] 1311 3-8-9 48 JimCrowley 2 49
(M S Saunders) *led: hdd 2f out: rdn and wknd fnl f* **50/1**

8 *5* **Acclimate** 3-8-9 0 DaneO'Neill 1 31
(W S Kittow) *s.i.s: outpcd early: nvr trbld ldrs* **14/1**

3-25 **9** *3 1/4* **Maraagel (USA)**[69] 535 5-9-10 45 J-PGuillambert 12 28
(G A Ham) *outpcd: n.d* **25/1**

-000 **10** *1/2* **Lithaam (IRE)**[8] 1370 4-9-10 45 (p) StephenDonohoe 8 27
(J M Bradley) *w ldrs: rdn over 2f out: wknd over 1f out* **80/1**

0604 **11** *4 1/2* **Fly Time**[14] 1259 4-9-5 40 (p) PatrickMathers 5 —
(Mrs L Williamson) *a bhd* **40/1**

6 **12** *4 1/2* **Opening Hand**[84] 350 3-8-9 0 JamieJones(5) 3 —
(Evan Williams) *a bhd* **66/1**

0/0- **13** *19* **Tatillius (IRE)**[248] 4616 5-9-10 25 PaulFitzsimons 4 —
(J M Bradley) *trckd ldrs: rdn and wknd 2f out: eased fnl f* **80/1**

64.76 secs (2.26) **Going Correction** +0.45s/f (Yiel)
WFA 3 from 4yo+ 10lb **13 Ran SP% 121.6**
Speed ratings (Par 103): **99,91,91,89,88 87,86,78,72,72 64,57,27**
CSF £16.04 TOTE £2.10: £1.20, £3.00, £1.40; EX 21.90.
Owner Dennis Shaw **Bred** R Hodgins **Trained** Lambourn, Berks

FOCUS
Just an ordinary sprint maiden, but an above-average winner, although the proximity of the seventh tends to limit the form. They raced far side in the straight, although the winner made his move wide of horses, more towards the middle of the track.

1530 WEATHERBYS BLOODSTOCK INSURANCE H'CAP — 1m 2f 46y
6:15 (6:16) (Class 5) (0-70,70) 3-Y-0 **£3,399** (£1,011; £505; £252) **Stalls** Low

Form RPR

00-1 **1** **Air Chief**[21] 1128 3-9-1 **67** JimmyQuinn 11 76
(H J L Dunlop) *chsd ldr: led over 2f out: reminder 1f out: sn clr: comf* **6/1**[2]

06-1 **2** *7* **Kyrie Eleison (IRE)**[50] 773 3-8-9 **66** PatrickHills(5) 10 61
(R Hannon) *a.p: rdn over 1f out: tk 2nd wl ins fnl f: no ch w wnr* **9/2**[1]

15-0 **3** *1 1/4* **Spinning Ridge (IRE)**[36] 918 3-8-13 **68** KevinGhunowa(3) 1 61
(R A Harris) *t.k.h early: in tch: chsd wnr over 1f out: no imp* **33/1**

006- **4** *1 3/4* **Dancing Dik**[178] 6493 3-9-2 **68** JimCrowley 8 57
(Mrs A J Perrett) *hld up in mid-div: rdn and hdwy over 2f out: kpt on one pce* **9/2**[1]

-332 **5** *1 1/4* **Shaftesbury (IRE)**[7] 1389 3-8-12 **64** LPKeniry 9 51
(Jane Southcombe) *hld up in tch: rdn over 1f out: wknd fnl f* **7/1**

060- **6** *2 3/4* **Love And Glory (FR)**[159] 6820 3-8-11 **63** DaneO'Neill 3 44
(G L Moore) *hld up and bhd: sme hdwy over 1f out: n.d* **14/1**

0-54 **7** *3* **Samurai Warrior**[88] 310 3-9-4 **70** SebSanders 6 45
(P J Makin) *a bhd* **8/1**

-001 **8** *2* **Rosy Dawn**[14] 1251 3-7-13 **58** ow1 (be) SophieDoyle(7) 4 29
(Ms J S Doyle) *led: hdd over 2f out: rdn over 1f out: wknd fnl f* **25/1**

5-54 **9** *2* **Mganga**[21] 1128 3-8-5 **64** MatthewDavies(7) 7 31
(M R Channon) *a bhd* **13/2**[3]

06-3 **10** *7* **Tamrai Dancer**[21] 1128 3-8-6 **65** RichardFelton(7) 2 18
(R M Beckett) *t.k.h in mid-div: sddle slipped over 5f out: bhd fnl 2f* **20/1**

-351 **11** *6* **Kryptonite (IRE)**[50] 784 3-9-2 **68** JamesDoyle 5 9
(J W Hills) *hld up and bhd: swtchd rt and short-lived effrt on outside over 3f out* **7/1**

2m 17.89s (6.89) **Going Correction** +0.45s/f (Yiel) **11 Ran SP% 118.3**
Speed ratings (Par 98): **90,84,83,82,81 78,76,74,73,67 62**
CSF £32.57 CT £832.21 TOTE £6.50: £2.20, £2.00, £11.20; EX 30.00.
Owner Chris Craig-Wood & Tina Blockley **Bred** Biddestone Stud **Trained** Lambourn, Berks

FOCUS
Just a modest three-year-old handicap and they went a steady pace. The winning time was 2.87 seconds slower than the earlier older-horse 46-55 handicap.
Tamrai Dancer Official explanation: jockey said saddle slipped

1531 WEATHERBYS BANK H'CAP — 1m 3f 144y
6:45 (6:46) (Class 4) (0-85,85) 4-Y-0+ **£5,180** (£1,541; £770; £384) **Stalls** Low

Form RPR

123- **1** **Sugar Ray (IRE)**[196] 6091 4-9-4 **85** RyanMoore 1 96+
(Sir Michael Stoute) *set slow pce: qcknd over 2f out: pushed out* **1/1**[1]

014- **2** *3 3/4* **Mister Right (IRE)**[180] 5415 7-8-1 **74** BillyCray(7) 7 79
(D J S Ffrench Davis) *hld up in rr: hdwy over 2f out: rdn jst over 1f out: kpt on same pce* **14/1**

125- **3** *nk* **Ollie George (IRE)**[339] 1844 5-9-5 **85** LPKeniry 2 89
(A M Balding) *chsd wnr: rdn and edgd lft 1f out: one pce* **9/4**[2]

5-64 **4** *1 3/4* **Resonate (IRE)**[76] 450 10-9-0 **80** DaneO'Neill 6 81
(A G Newcombe) *hld up in tch: rdn over 1f out: one pce* **11/2**[3]

420- **5** *hd* **Hawridge King**[194] 6131 6-8-6 **79** TimothyMeadows(7) 5 80
(W S Kittow) *hld up in tch: wknd wl ins fnl f* **14/1**

2m 42.39s (11.79) **Going Correction** +0.45s/f (Yiel)
WFA 4 from 5yo+ 1lb **5 Ran SP% 109.5**
Speed ratings (Par 105): **78,75,75,74,74**
CSF £15.07 TOTE £1.70: £1.20, £4.40; EX 13.30.
Owner Philip Newton **Bred** Barronstown Stud And Pacelco S A **Trained** Newmarket, Suffolk

FOCUS
Just the five runners and this looked an ordinary handicap for the grade, but the winner has the potential to be decent. They went no pace.

1532 MB FRAMES AND CELSIUS GLASS H'CAP — 1m 5y
7:15 (7:15) (Class 4) (0-85,80) 4-Y-0+ **£5,180** (£1,541; £770; £384) **Stalls** Low

Form RPR

503- **1** **The Snatcher (IRE)**[171] 6646 5-8-9 **76** PatrickHills(5) 2 94
(R Hannon) *a.p: led over 2f out: hrd rdn over 1f out: sn clr: r.o wl* **9/1**

00-4 **2** *5* **Full Victory (IRE)**[8] 1365 6-9-0 **76** SteveDrowne 3 82
(R A Farrant) *hld up in mid-div: hdwy over 2f out: chsd wnr jst over 1f out: sn rdn: no imp* **5/2**[1]

-334 **3** *6* **Den's Gift (IRE)**[19] 1174 4-9-4 **80** (b[1]) AdamKirby 1 72
(C G Cox) *sn led: rdn and hdd over 2f out: wknd over 1f out* **7/1**[3]

55-0 **4** *1 1/4* **Davenport (IRE)**[31] 962 6-8-10 **72** TPO'Shea 5 61
(B R Millman) *hld up towards rr: hdwy on outside over 2f out: hrd rdn over 1f out: one pce* **11/1**

40-4 **5** *3 1/4* **Danski**[10] 1335 5-9-3 **79** SebSanders 9 61
(P J Makin) *hld up in tch: rdn 3f out: sn hung lft and wknd* **5/1**[2]

530/ **6** *shd* **Master Mahogany**[33] 6502 7-8-12 **74** RyanMoore 10 56
(R J Hodges) *led early: w ldr: rdn over 2f out: wknd wl over 1f out* **11/1**

3151 **7** *1/2* **Justcallmehandsome**[27] 1030 6-8-1 **70** (v) BillyCray(7) 7 50
(D J S Ffrench Davis) *a.p: ev ch over 2f out: wknd over 1f out* **12/1**

-033 **8** *1/2* **Harare**[6] 1409 7-8-11 **73** (v) JamesDoyle 6 52
(R J Price) *hld up and bhd: rdn 2f out: nt run on* **16/1**

052- **9** *5* **Roodolph**[197] 6063 4-8-10 **72** (b) StephenCarson 4 40
(Eve Johnson Houghton) *s.i.s: hld up and bhd: hrd rdn 3f out: nt run on* **10/1**

315- **10** *9* **Optimus (USA)**[157] 6853 6-9-4 **80** TQuinn 8 27
(B G Powell) *rel to r: sn lost tch* **17/2**

1m 43.61s (2.81) **Going Correction** +0.45s/f (Yiel) **10 Ran SP% 117.6**
Speed ratings (Par 105): **103,98,92,90,87 87,86,86,81,72**
CSF £32.05 CT £158.24 TOTE £12.60: £2.30, £1.50, £2.50; EX 44.80.
Owner Mrs R Ablett **Bred** Miss Eileen Grealish **Trained** East Everleigh, Wilts

FOCUS
A fair handicap and it looked quite competitive beforehand, but they finished surprisingly strung out. The winning time was 3.55 seconds quicker than the following 0-55 classified event and the winner is rated to the best of last year's form.
Danski Official explanation: jockey said horse hung left-handed

1533 WINDOW FACTORY AND K2 CLASSIFIED STKS 1m 5y
7:45 (7:46) (Class 6) 3-Y-0+ £1,942 (£578; £288; £144) Stalls Low

Form RPR
200- 1 **Turkish Sultan (IRE)**[33] 4807 5-9-7 54....(p) DaneO'Neill 4 55
(J M Bradley) *led early: a.p: led wl over 1f out: sn hrd rdn: hld on wl towards fin* 7/1
5000 2 *nk* **Grey Gurkha**[20] 1142 7-9-7 55.... PatrickMathers 12 54
(I W McInnes) *s.i.s: hld up and bhd: plld out over 3f out: gd hdwy on outside over 2f out: sn hrd rdn: ev ch ins fnl f: r.o* 6/1[2]
00/0 3 *hd* **Capped For Victory (USA)**[6] 1394 7-9-4 55.... PJMcDonald(3) 3 54
(G A Swinbank) *hld up in tch: rdn over 1f out: chal ins fnl f: r.o* 4/1[1]
0055 4 *shd* **Film Queen (IRE)**[17] 1209 4-9-7 51.... TQuinn 10 54
(B G Powell) *hld up in mid-div: hdwy over 2f out: hrd rdn and ev ch ins fnl f: r.o* 15/2
602 5 1 3/4 **Tapas Lad (IRE)**[18] 1193 3-8-7 55....(v) SimonWhitworth 14 49+
(G J Smith) *s.i.s: hld up and bhd: nt clr run fr 3f out tl swtchd lft and hdwy on ins over 1f out: sn rdn: kpt on ins fnl f* 13/2[3]
06-6 6 1 1/2 **Holden Caulfield (IRE)**[18] 1193 3-8-7 39.... JamesDoyle 6 42
(Mouse Hamilton-Fairley) *hld up: sn bhd: rdn and hdwy over 2f out: one pce fnl f* 33/1
0-05 7 *nk* **Brigadore (USA)**[19] 1164 5-9-7 55.... StephenDonohoe 5 45
(Ian Williams) *s.i.s: bhd: pushed along over 3f out: rdn and hdwy 2f out: one pce fnl f* 8/1
000/ 8 2 **African Blues**[496] 6801 5-9-0 5.... BillyCray(7) 15 41
(D J S Ffrench Davis) *plld hrd: led over 6f out: hung bdly rt and hdd wl over 1f out: nt rcvr* 100/1
3320 9 2 1/4 **Strut The Stage (IRE)**[34] 937 4-9-0 53....(tp) GabrielHannon(7) 1 36
(B W Duke) *hld up in tch: pushed along over 2f out: eased whn btn wl ins fnl f* 9/1
000- 10 2 3/4 **Charlie Be (IRE)**[182] 6401 3-8-7 52.... AdrianMcCarthy 13 25
(Mrs P N Dutfield) *bhd: pushed along over 3f out: nvr trbld ldrs* 33/1
66-0 11 15 **Nathan Dee**[19] 1166 3-8-7 51.... LPKeniry 8 —
(Mrs H Sweeting) *prom tl wknd over 2f out: eased ins fnl f* 22/1
0/50 12 1 3/4 **Zayyir (IRE)**[13] 1265 4-9-4 52.... KevinGhunowa(3) 7 —
(R A Harris) *plld hrd: sn led: hdd over 6f out: rdn over 2f out: wknd over 1f out: eased fnl f* 18/1
6560 13 4 1/2 **Scots W'Hae**[19] 1166 3-8-7 52....(t) J-PGuillambert 2 —
(P J McBride) *plld hrd towards rr: rdn and hdwy over 2f out: wknd wl over 1f out: eased fnl f* 12/1
000- 14 9 **April's Quest (IRE)**[214] 5603 3-8-7 49.... NeilChalmers 9 —
(David Pinder) *prom tl rdn and wknd over 2f out: eased fnl f* 66/1
000 15 14 **Hatter's Way**[26] 1042 3-8-0 36.... SophieDoyle(7) 11 —
(R A Farrant) *hld up in tch: wknd 3f out: eased over 1f out* 80/1
5556 16 7 **Hold That Call (USA)**[18] 1187 3-8-7 52.... TPO'Shea 16 —
(A J Chamberlain) *hld up and bhd: short-lived effrt on outside over 3f out: eased whn no ch fnl 2f* 20/1

1m 47.16s (6.36) **Going Correction** +0.45s/f (Yiel)
WFA 3 from 4yo+ 14lb 16 Ran SP% 124.7
Speed ratings (Par 101): **86,85,85,85,83 82,81,79,77,74 59,58,53,44,30 23**
CSF £47.09 TOTE £8.90: £2.40, £3.10, £1.80; EX 84.50 Place 6 £32.02, Place 5 £9.62.
Owner The Lovely Jubbly's **Bred** Sir Tatton Skyes And Lady Legard **Trained** Sedbury, Gloucs

FOCUS
A moderate classified contest, but plenty of runners and very competitive with the fifth offering the best guide to the level. A very moderate winning time, 3.55 seconds slower than the preceding handicap. They were spread all over the track in the straight, with the main action taking place up the middle.
Brigadore(USA) Official explanation: jockey said gelding had no more to give
T/Plt: £48.70 to a £1 stake. Pool: £50,149.70. 750.20 winning tickets. T/Qpdt: £20.10 to a £1 stake. Pool: £4,731.00. 173.90 winning tickets. KH

1276 FOLKESTONE (R-H)
Tuesday, April 22

OFFICIAL GOING: Good to soft (6.0)
Wind: Modest, across Weather: Bright and sunny

1534 FOLKESTONE-RACECOURSE.CO.UK APPRENTICE H'CAP 6f
1:45 (1:45) (Class 6) (0-60,60) 4-Y-0+ £2,047 (£604; £302) Stalls Low

Form RPR
0/0- 1 **Miltons Choice**[395] 750 5-9-0 **54**.... BillyCray 1 64
(J M Bradley) *led after 1f: mde rest: clr jst over 1f out: styd on wl* 20/1
2166 2 2 **Reigning Monarch (USA)**[31] 964 5-9-3 **57**.... AshleyMorgan 3 61
(Miss Z C Davison) *chsd ldrs: w wnr 1/2-way: rdn and sltly outpcd wl over 1f out: kpt on same pce fnl f* 3/1[2]
/2-0 3 2 1/2 **Ali Bruce**[34] 938 8-8-9 **49**.... NBazeley 2 45
(M R Hoad) *s.i.s: hld up bhd: hdwy and rdn wl over 2f out: kpt on u.p to go 3rd wl ins fnl f: nt trble ldng pair* 16/1
01-5 4 3/4 **Mugeba**[21] 1126 7-9-5 **59**....(t) RosieJessop 4 52
(Miss Gay Kelleway) *s.i.s: hld up towards rr: hdwy 3f out: chsd ldng pair and rdn wl over 1f out: outpcd fnl f* 9/1
1612 5 1 3/4 **Ever Cheerful**[18] 1189 7-9-0 **57**....(p) PNolan(3) 5 45
(A B Haynes) *chsd ldrs rdn wl over 2f out: wknd jst over 1f out* 5/2[1]
3562 6 4 **Flight Dream (FR)**[12] 1280 5-9-1 **60**....(b) AndreaAtzeni(5) 8 35
(M G Quinlan) *wnt lft s: a towards rr: rdn over 3f out: no ch last 2f* 9/2[3]
063- 7 2 1/4 **Thomas Lawrence (USA)**[233] 5062 7-8-9 **57** ow7...(p) RyanRaftery(8) 7 25
(P A Blockley) *bmpd s: a bhd: rdn over 3f out: no ch last 2f* 8/1
000- 8 3 3/4 **Exponential (IRE)**[193] 6149 6-8-5 **48**.... PietroRomeo(3) 6 4
(J M Bradley) *led for 1f out: rdn and lost pl over 3f out: sn wknd: no ch last 2f* 12/1
4400 9 1/2 **Arfinnit (IRE)**[31] 964 7-9-0 **54**....(v) DavidProbert 9 8
(Mrs A L M King) *chsd ldrs tl lost pl and rdn 3f out: no ch last 2f* 18/1

1m 15.06s (2.36) **Going Correction** +0.25s/f (Good) 9 Ran SP% 116.5
Speed ratings (Par 101): **94,91,88,87,84 79,76,71,70**
CSF £80.27 CT £797.79 TOTE £33.60: £6.60, £1.50, £5.20; EX 140.40 TRIFECTA Not won..
Owner racingshares.co.uk **Bred** G C Neate **Trained** Sedbury, Gloucs

FOCUS
A weak sprint and the stands' rail once again proved imperative. The race is rated around the first two.

1535 RICHARD FLOWER MAIDEN STKS 7f (S)
2:15 (2:15) (Class 5) 3-Y-0+ £2,590 (£770; £385; £192) Stalls Low

Form RPR
42- 1 **Thannaan (USA)**[194] 6125 3-8-13 0.... RHills 5 82+
(B W Hills) *mde all: clr over 1f out: 5l clr 100yds out: eased wl ins fnl f and nrly ct* 9/4[2]
03- 2 *nk* **Mega Watt (IRE)**[253] 4448 3-8-13 0.... AlanMunro 10 78
(W Jarvis) *dropped in after s: hld up wl in rr: stl modest 12th 3f out: hdwy over 1f out: styd on to chse wnr ins fnl f: nrly ct wnr napping* 16/1[3]
26 3 6 **Speyside (IRE)**[14] 1252 3-8-13 0.... MichaelHills 3 62+
(J W Hills) *hld up in midfield: outpcd 3f out: swtchd to centre and hdwy 2f out: styd on steadily to go 3rd ins fnl f: nvr nr enough to chal* 20/1
4 1 3/4 **Simarian (IRE)**[200] 5996 3-8-13 0.... RobertHavlin 9 57
(Evan Williams) *s.i.s: sn chsng ldrs: outpcd 3f out: kpt on same pce last 2f* 33/1
2-3 5 1 **Oarsman**[21] 1125 3-8-13 0.... SteveDrowne 4 54
(R Charlton) *chsd ldng pair: chse wnr and clr of remainder wl over 2f out: wknd over 1f out: lost 3 pls ins fnl f* 5/6[1]
0- 6 1/2 **Kannon**[148] 6948 3-8-8 0.... PaulDoe 8 48
(W J Knight) *s.i.s: sn chsng wnr tl wl over 2f out: sn outpcd: plugged on* 80/1
0- 7 1/2 **Carmela Maria**[194] 6125 3-8-8 0.... TedDurcan 14 47+
(C F Wall) *dropped in after s: hld up wl bhd: swtchd rt wl over 1f out: kpt on: nvr nr ldrs* 25/1
6- 8 1 3/4 **Earlsmedic**[223] 5337 3-8-6 0.... WilliamCarson(7) 13 47+
(S C Williams) *in tch on outer: outpcd 3f out: kpt on same pce after* 40/1
0-6 9 *nk* **Contrada**[21] 1125 3-8-13 0.... FergusSweeney 11 46+
(R Charlton) *hld up bhd: rdn and struggling 3f out: sme modest late hdwy* 25/1
10 1 **Royal Bloom (IRE)** 3-8-8 0.... OscarUrbina 6 38
(J R Fanshawe) *bhd: outpcd 3f out: sme hdwy wl over 1f out: nvr on terms* 33/1
11 8 **Poulaine Bleue** 3-8-8 0.... HayleyTurner 2 17
(M L W Bell) *chsd ldrs: rdn and outpcd over 3f out: no ch last 2f* 33/1
40 12 1/2 **Star Choice**[11] 1298 3-8-13 0.... DarryllHolland 7 20
(M L W Bell) *chsd ldrs tl rdn and outpcd 3f out: no ch last 2f: t.o* 50/1
60 13 9 **Emerging Light**[7] 1382 6-9-12 0.... JohnEgan 1 —
(S Dow) *a bhd: lost tch 3f out: t.o* 100/1
00- 14 3 1/4 **Bakers Boy**[139] 7029 4-9-7 0.... NataliaGemelova(5) 12 —
(J E Long) *bhd: rdn and hung rt over 3f out: sn lost tch: t.o* 100/1

1m 29.25s (1.95) **Going Correction** +0.25s/f (Good)
WFA 3 from 4yo+ 13lb 14 Ran SP% 120.1
Speed ratings (Par 103): **98,97,90,88,87 87,86,84,84,83 73,73,63,59**
CSF £32.06 TOTE £3.80: £1.20, £3.20, £3.40; EX 30.50 Trifecta £261.70 Part won. Pool: £368.62 - 0.50 winning units..
Owner Hamdan Al Maktoum **Bred** Walton Breeders **Trained** Lambourn, Berks

FOCUS
A modest maiden with little strength in depth. The winner was eased and is value for further with the third the best guide for now.
Oarsman Official explanation: trainer later said gelding returned distressed

1536 T DENNE & SONS (HOLDINGS) LTD CLAIMING STKS 5f
2:50 (2:50) (Class 6) 3-Y-0 £2,047 (£604; £302) Stalls Low

Form RPR
36-0 1 **Swindon Town Flyer (IRE)**[42] 848 3-9-5 65....(b) DavidKinsella 1 64
(A B Haynes) *w ldr tl led 1/2-way: sn u.p: battled on gamely fnl f* 4/1[3]
3211 2 *nk* **Copperbottomed (IRE)**[22] 1117 3-9-2 68....(e) FergusSweeney 5 60
(J R Boyle) *chsd ldng pair tl wnt 2nd over 2f out: sn ev ch: shkn up and edgd lft wl over 1f out: rdn over 1f out: unable qckn fnl f* 10/11[1]
6324 3 3 1/4 **Regal Veil**[39] 876 3-8-2 46.... NickyMackay 2 34
(S C Williams) *led narrowly tl 1/2-way: 3rd and swtchd rt over 1f out: outpcd fnl f* 3/1[2]
4 4 1 1/4 **Heroic Fool**[21] 1123 3-8-11 0.... SamHitchcott 3 39
(Miss Z C Davison) *s.i.s: hld up in tch: rdn and effrt over 1f out: outpcd fnl f* 28/1
-050 5 6 **Just Puddie**[8] 1370 3-8-4 47....(p) JohnEgan 4 10
(W G M Turner) *sn rdn along in last: no ch last 2f* 12/1

62.04 secs (2.04) **Going Correction** +0.25s/f (Good) 5 Ran SP% 108.5
Speed ratings (Par 96): **93,92,87,85,75**
CSF £7.91 TOTE £4.20: £2.00, £1.20; EX 8.30.
Owner WCR IV The County Ground Syndicate **Bred** Patrick Doyle **Trained** Limpley Stoke, Bath

FOCUS
This was not a strong contest and two pulled clear. They are rated 7lb below their recent All-Weather marks

1537 TEMPLE LIFTS LTD H'CAP 5f
3:25 (3:26) (Class 4) (0-80,80) 4-Y-0+ £4,209 (£1,252; £625; £312) Stalls Low

Form RPR
0-42 1 **Hereford Boy**[8] 1366 4-8-13 **75**.... RobertHavlin 3 87+
(D K Ivory) *hld up in tch: swtchd rt jst over 1f out: pushed along and qcknd to ld last 100yds: sn in command: readily* 15/8[1]
50-4 2 2 **Corridor Creeper (FR)**[8] 1366 11-9-3 **79**....(p) AlanMunro 2 84
(J M Bradley) *led for 1f: led again wl over 1f out: rdn 1f otu: hdd last 100yds: nt pce of wnr* 15/2
326- 3 *hd* **Pretty Miss**[213] 5642 4-8-10 **72**.... FergusSweeney 7 76
(H Candy) *dropped in bhd after s: n.m.r fr over 1f out: hdwy jst ins fnl f: r.o but nvr able to chal* 4/1[2]
303- 4 1 3/4 **Idle Power (IRE)**[170] 6667 10-9-4 **80**.... AmirQuinn 5 78
(J R Boyle) *hld up in tch in rr: swtchd rt and effrt over 1f out: no imp fnl f* 16/1
111- 5 *hd* **For Life (IRE)**[188] 6273 6-8-9 **76**.... NataliaGemelova(5) 1 73
(J E Long) *chsd ldr tl led after 1f: rdn and hdd wl over 1f out: one pce fnl f* 9/2[3]
440- 6 3/4 **Zowington**[291] 3268 6-9-4 **80**.... GeorgeBaker 4 74
(C F Wall) *chsd ldng pair: rdn and effrt over 1f out: outpcd fnl f* 15/2
000- 7 7 **Spanish Ace**[191] 6197 7-8-13 **75**.... TedDurcan 6 44
(J M Bradley) *a bhd: rdn over 2f out: no ch over 1f out: eased wl ins fnl f* 12/1

60.46 secs (0.46) **Going Correction** +0.25s/f (Good) 7 Ran SP% 110.1
Speed ratings (Par 105): **106,102,102,99,99 98,86**
CSF £15.27 TOTE £2.40: £1.40, £2.90; EX 12.60.
Owner Recycled Products Limited **Bred** Mrs L R Burrage **Trained** Radlett, Herts
■ Stewards' Enquiry : Robert Havlin caution: careless riding

FOCUS
A fair handicap sprint that was run in a decent time and should produce winners.

1538 FOLKESTONE RACECOURSE GIRLS' NIGHT OUT JULY 24TH H'CAP — 1m 7f 92y
4:00 (4:00) (Class 5) (0-75,71) 4-Y-O+ **£2,331** (£693; £346; £173) **Stalls** Low

Form RPR
00-5 **1** **Rock 'N' Roller (FR)**[27] 1026 4-9-9 **71**.................... GeorgeBaker 3 76
(W R Muir) *hld up towards rr: hdwy 7f out: shkn up to chse ldr wl over 1f out: led and hung rt briefly over 1f out: kpt on fnl f* **7/2**[3]
0436 **2** *1 ½* **Ashmolian (IRE)**[12] 1281 5-8-7 **52** oh7.................... SamHitchcott 7 55
(Miss Z C Davison) *hld up in last pair: hdwy on outer 3f out: rdn jst over 2f out: chsd wnr ins fnl f: kpt on but a hld* **16/1**
05-0 **3** *5* **Sister Agnes (IRE)**[13] 1267 4-9-3 **65**....................(v[1]) RobertHavlin 2 62
(M F Harris) *chsd ldr tl 6f out and again over 2f out: rdn and tried to chal jst over 2f out: outpcd fnl f* **28/1**
4632 **4** *1 ¾* **Best Selection**[18] 1181 4-9-0 **62**.................... TGMcLaughlin 5 56
(Mrs L J Mongan) *bhd: rdn over 3f out: kpt on u.p to go 4th ins fnl f: nvr trbld ldrs* **5/2**[2]
10-0 **5** *1 ¾* **Icannshift (IRE)**[29] 999 8-8-12 **57**.................... FergusSweeney 8 49
(T M Jones) *led: rdn and hdd over 1f out: sn wknd* **8/1**
00-4 **6** *1* **Madam Vouvray**[13] 1267 4-8-7 **55**.................... TedDurcan 6 46
(B G Powell) *in tch in midfield: rdn over 4f out: no hdwy 2f out: btn and eased fnl f* **12/1**
00-0 **7** *½* **Great View (IRE)**[18] 1181 9-9-12 **71**....................(p) AlanMunro 1 61
(Mrs A L M King) *in tch tl dropped to rr 5f out: n.d after* **20/1**
1 **8** *49* **Lupita (IRE)**[13] 1267 4-8-11 **59**.................... MichaelHills 4 —
(B G Powell) *in tch: chsd ldr 6f out tl over 2f out: sn rdn and immediately btn: virtually p.u fnl f* **9/4**[1]

3m 36.08s (6.38) **Going Correction** +0.40s/f (Good)
WFA 4 from 5yo+ 3lb **8** Ran SP% **114.5**
Speed ratings (Par 103): **98,97,94,93,92 92,91,65**
CSF £56.08 CT £1341.30 TOTE £3.90: £1.20, £4.40, £5.10; EX 62.50 TRIFECTA Not won..
Owner D G Clarke & C L A Edginton **Bred** Eric Puerari, Oceanic Bloodstock Et Al **Trained** Lambourn, Berks

FOCUS
A modest staying handicap and weakish form.
Lupita(IRE) Official explanation: trainer had no explanation for the poor form shown; vet said filly was distressed

1539 FOLKESTONE RACECOURSE FOR EXHIBITIONS MAIDEN STKS — 1m 4f
4:35 (4:35) (Class 5) 3-Y-O+ **£2,590** (£770; £385; £192) **Stalls** Low

Form RPR
56 **1** **Precision Break (USA)**[87] 311 3-8-7 0.................... JohnEgan 10 61
(P F I Cole) *chsd ldrs: pushed along whn bmpd and forced wd bnd wl over 4f out: hdwy on outer 3f out: lft 2nd over 1f out: led 1f out: all out* **14/1**
2 *¾* **Harlestone Gold** 3-8-7 0.................... TedDurcan 2 60+
(J L Dunlop) *stdd s: hld up in rr: stdy hdwy 4f out: shkn up 2f out: lft 5th over 1f out: r.o fnl f: wnt 2nd nr fin: nt rch wnr* **11/1**
0-20 **3** *½* **Lord's Bidding**[20] 1147 3-8-7 57....................(v) RobertHavlin 5 59
(R Ingram) *t.k.h: chsd ldrs: chsd ldr over 4f out: looked btn whn lft in ld over 1f out: hdd 1f out: unable qckn last 100yds* **16/1**
0-5 **4** *hd* **Damascus Gold**[19] 1173 4-9-12 0....................(b) SamHitchcott 7 61
(Miss Z C Davison) *t.k.h: hld up in midfield: hdwy to chse ldrs over 3f out: rdn and lft 4th over 1f out: kpt on u.p: last 100yds* **125/1**
2 **5** *1 ½* **Touchdown**[13] 1272 3-8-7 0.................... GregFairley 9 64+
(M Johnston) *t.k.h: chsd ldr tl led over 4f out: 3 l clr whn hung bdly lft and hdd over 1f out: stl hanging and hit rail ins fnl f: nt rcvr* **7/4**[1]
6 *15* **Karashar (IRE)** 3-8-8 0 ow1.................... FergusSweeney 8 33
(Evan Williams) *s.i.s: hld up bhd: hdwy over 6f out: chsd ldrs 3f out: rdn over 2f out: lft 3rd over 1f out: sn wknd* **20/1**
7 *7* **Arthurian (IRE)** 3-8-4 0....................(b[1]) DominicFox[(3)] 4 21
(J Jay) *s.i.s: a bhd: rdn 5f out: no ch last 3f: sme modest late hdwy* **20/1**
44-4 **8** *1* **Talayeb**[12] 1283 3-8-7 76.................... RHills 11 19
(M P Tregoning) *chsd ldrs: swtchd lft and bmpd rival over 4f out: rdn over 2f out: sn btn* **9/2**[3]
9 *1 ¼* **Black Cloud**[43] 5-9-6 0.................... HarryPoulton[(7)] 3 19
(A Ennis) *in tch in midfield: rdn 3f out: sn wknd* **125/1**
3 **10** *3* **Platoche (IRE)**[29] 991 3-8-7 0.................... AlanMunro 12 13
(P W Chapple-Hyam) *led tl over 3f out: sn wknd: wl bhd last 2f* **5/2**[2]
11 *14* **Pharly Green**[58] 6-9-1 0.................... JemmaMarshall[(7)] 6 —
(G P Enright) *s.i.s: a bhd: t.o last 3f* **125/1**
0- **12** *49* **Double R**[134] 7097 3-8-2 0.................... DavidKinsella 1 —
(A B Haynes) *hld up towards rr: bhd last 5f: t.o last 3f* **50/1**

2m 44.73s (3.83) **Going Correction** +0.40s/f (Good)
WFA 3 from 4yo 20lb 4 from 5yo+ 1lb **12** Ran SP% **117.9**
Speed ratings (Par 103): **103,102,102,102,101 91,86,85,84,82 73,40**
CSF £148.32 CT £97.20 TOTE £16.30: £2.80, £3.20, £3.70; EX 97.20 TRIFECTA Not won..
Owner JMH Lifestyle Ltd **Bred** Gainesway Thoroughbreds Ltd **Trained** Whatcombe, Oxon

FOCUS
A weak maiden that would have been won by Touchdown had he not hung violently left in the straight. The exposed third limits the form and the proximity of the fourth raises further doubts.
Touchdown Official explanation: jockey said colt hung badly left in straight
Talayeb Official explanation: jockey said gelding suffered breathing problems
Double R Official explanation: jockey said filly hung left

1540 NEXT MEETING MAY 1ST H'CAP — 1m 1f 149y
5:05 (5:05) (Class 5) (0-75,75) 3-Y-O **£2,331** (£693; £346; £173) **Stalls** Centre

Form RPR
060- **1** **Classical Rhythm (IRE)**[209] 5736 3-8-5 **62**.................... DavidKinsella 6 66
(J R Boyle) *hld up in last trio: rdn 3f out: c wd ent st 2f out: str run fnl f to ld nr fin* **8/1**
-321 **2** *½* **Ocean Legend (IRE)**[40] 867 3-9-1 **72**.................... JohnEgan 8 75
(Miss J Feilden) *chsd ldr tl 5f out and again 3f out: rdn to ld over 1f out: kpt on u.p tl hdd nr fin* **7/2**[2]
00-2 **3** *2 ¾* **Maximus Aurelius (IRE)**[9] 1348 3-9-2 **73**.................... RobertHavlin 5 70
(J Jay) *set str gallop: rdn over 2f out: hdd over 1f out: kpt on trying tl no ex last 100yds* **12/1**
61- **4** *3 ½* **Astrodonna**[172] 6626 3-9-2 **73**.................... MichaelHills 1 63
(M H Tompkins) *t.k.h: hld up in tch: hdwy to chse ldr over 4f out: rdn 2f out: fnd little and one pce after* **4/1**[3]
130- **5** *14* **Dancer's Legacy**[204] 5871 3-9-4 **75**....................(t) TGMcLaughlin 2 35
(E A L Dunlop) *in tch in midfield: rdn and effrt 3f out: sn outpcd: eased whn wl btn fnl f* **9/1**
025- **6** *1 ¼* **Spectrana**[163] 6777 3-8-11 **68**.................... DarryllHolland 4 26
(Mrs A J Perrett) *s.i.s: hld up in rr: rdn over 3f out: sn lost tch: no ch last 2f* **14/1**
230 **7** *1 ¼* **West Lorne (USA)**[39] 885 3-8-5 **62**.................... GregFairley 7 17
(M Johnston) *s.i.s: a in last pair: rdn over 3f out: no imp* **10/1**
-332 **8** *5* **Calistos Quest**[19] 1163 3-8-12 **69**....................(t) TedDurcan 3 14
(M Botti) *chsd ldng pair tl wnt 2nd 5f out tl 3f out: sn btn: virtually p.u fnl f* **9/4**[1]

2m 8.11s (3.21) **Going Correction** +0.40s/f (Good) **8** Ran SP% **117.6**
Speed ratings (Par 98): **103,102,100,97,86 85,84,80**
CSF £37.22 CT £341.11 TOTE £12.70: £3.10, £1.30, £3.50; EX 49.50 TRIFECTA Not won. Place 6 £605.63, Place 5 £181.92.
Owner Inside Track Racing Club **Bred** Denis And Mrs Teresa Bergin **Trained** Epsom, Surrey

FOCUS
They went a decent gallop for what was a modest handicap and the form makes sense with the third to form.
Classical Rhythm(IRE) Official explanation: trainer said, regarding the apparent improvement in form, that gelding had matured over the winter and benefited from step up in trip to 1m 1f.
Calistos Quest Official explanation: trainer said colt was unsuited by the good to soft ground
T/Plt: £6,565.50 to a £1 stake. Pool: £41,372.15. 4.60 winning tickets. T/Qpdt: £314.80 to a £1 stake. Pool: £3,445.80. 8.10 winning tickets. SP

[1411] KEMPTON (A.W) (R-H)
Tuesday, April 22

OFFICIAL GOING: Standard
Wind: Brisk, behind

1541 KERRY LONDON H'CAP — 6f (P)
1:55 (1:55) (Class 5) (0-70,69) 4-Y-O+ **£2,590** (£770; £385; £192) **Stalls** High

Form RPR
015- **1** **Vintage (IRE)**[195] 6100 4-8-11 **62**.................... IanMongan 3 72
(J Akehurst) *chsd ldrs: drvn along over 2f out: styd on u.p to ld fnl 100yds* **12/1**
62-6 **2** *½* **Rhapsilian**[108] 54 4-8-6 **57**.................... ChrisCatlin 7 65
(J A Geake) *hld up in rr: rapid hdwy on ins fr 2f out: r.o strly ins fnl f to take 2nd fnl 75yds but a hld by wnr* **4/1**[1]
0-04 **3** *1 ¼* **Gleaming Spirit (IRE)**[25] 1047 4-8-13 **64**.................... JamieSpencer 4 68
(A P Jarvis) *led: rdn 2f out: styd on tl hdd fnl 100yds: wknd nr fin* **5/1**[2]
0031 **4** *shd* **Is It Time (IRE)**[12] 1285 4-8-8 **59**.................... JimmyQuinn 6 63
(Mrs P N Dutfield) *in tch: rdn over 2f out: styd on u.p fnl f but nt pce to be competitive* **5/1**[2]
40-0 **5** *¾* **Farefield Lodge (IRE)**[28] 1015 4-9-3 **68**.................... PhilipRobinson 10 69
(C G Cox) *towards rr: rdn over 2f out: hanging rt but styd on fr over 1f out: nvr in contention* **6/1**[3]
4234 **6** *1 ¼* **Interactive (IRE)**[11] 1312 5-9-4 **69**.................... AlanDaly 8 66
(Andrew Turnell) *t.k.h: chsd ldrs: rdn over 2f out: wknd ins fnl f* **7/1**
3230 **7** *nse* **Lindbergh**[31] 964 6-8-4 **60**....................(v) JackMitchell[(5)] 2 57
(J Ryan) *pressed ldrs: chal over 2f out tl over 1f out: wknd ins fnl f* **14/1**
00-2 **8** *4* **Bertie Swift**[31] 964 4-8-10 **61**.................... JimCrowley 1 45
(J Gallagher) *a in rr* **10/1**
6-00 **9** *hd* **Trees Of Green (USA)**[50] 777 4-9-0 **65**.................... TQuinn 9 49
(M Wigham) *a in rr* **10/1**
1336 **10** *hd* **Hollow Jo**[15] 1242 8-9-2 **67**.................... EddieAhern 5 50
(J R Jenkins) *in tch: rdn over 2f out: sn btn* **13/2**

1m 11.87s (-1.23) **Going Correction** +0.10s/f (Slow) **10** Ran SP% **126.0**
Speed ratings (Par 103): **112,111,109,109,108 106,106,101,101,100**
CSF £64.52 CT £285.37 TOTE £14.30: £4.30, £2.00, £2.00; EX 126.20.
Owner Sheldon Homes Ltd **Bred** Mountarmstrong Stud **Trained** Epsom, Surrey

FOCUS
No messing about in this sprint handicap and a very decent winning time for the class. Not many ever got into it and the race is rated through the second backed up by the fourth.

1542 SWINTON MAIDEN FILLIES' STKS — 1m 4f (P)
2:25 (2:25) (Class 5) 3-Y-O+ **£2,590** (£770; £385; £192) **Stalls** Centre

Form RPR
4 **1** **Ever Rigg**[18] 1176 3-8-8 0.................... StephenDonohoe 3 75
(E A L Dunlop) *hld up in tch: hdwy on ins fr 3f out to ld ins fnl 2f: rdn and hld on wl thrght fnl f* **15/2**
3-3 **2** *hd* **Try Me (UAE)**[26] 1042 3-8-8 0.................... RyanMoore 6 75
(C E Brittain) *led: kpt on whn chal fr.5f out: rdn and edgd lft over 2f out: hdd ins fnl 2f: rallied fnl f and styd pressing wnr: no ex cl home* **5/2**[2]
2 **3** *2 ¾* **Victoria Montoya**[17] 1205 3-8-8 0.................... LPKeniry 2 71
(A M Balding) *chsd ldrs: drvn along over 2f out: styd on same pce fr over 1f out* **5/2**[2]
2 **4** *2 ½* **Beautiful Lady (IRE)**[18] 1176 3-8-8 0.................... TQuinn 4 67
(P F I Cole) *trckd ldrs: drvn and qcknd to chal on bnd 3f out: bmpd and veered lft sn after and one pce fnl 2f* **9/4**[1]
50 **5** *24* **Coco L'Escargot**[7] 1382 4-9-13 0.................... EddieAhern 5 28
(J R Jenkins) *trckd ldr: chal fr 5f out to 3f out: wknd sn after* **20/1**
6 *27* **Sindanna**[16] 4-9-13 0.................... ChrisCatlin 1 —
(A King) *sn rdn along in rr: lost tch fnl 5f* **13/2**[3]

2m 36.81s (2.31) **Going Correction** +0.10s/f (Slow)
WFA 3 from 4yo 20lb **6** Ran SP% **117.8**
Speed ratings (Par 100): **96,95,94,92,76 58**
CSF £28.07 TOTE £8.20: £3.00, £2.00; EX 33.00.
Owner St Albans Bloodstock LLP **Bred** Palm Tree Thoroughbreds **Trained** Newmarket, Suffolk

FOCUS
A modest fillies' maiden and the early pace was ordinary. The race developed into something of a sprint down the home straight and the runner-up is the best guide to the form, which is basically modest.

1543 DAS LEGAL EXPENSES INSURANCE COMPANY H'CAP — 1m 3f (P)
3:00 (3:00) (Class 4) (0-80,80) 3-Y-O **£4,209** (£1,252; £625; £312) **Stalls** High

Form RPR
1- **1** **Relative Strength (IRE)**[132] 7114 3-8-11 **73**.................... LPKeniry 8 78
(A M Balding) *sn trcking ldr: drvn to ld ins fnl 2f: hld on wl thrght fnl f* **9/1**
25-4 **2** *1 ¼* **Higgy's Boy (IRE)**[15] 1244 3-8-11 **73**.................... RichardHughes 10 76
(R Hannon) *trckd ldrs: rdn and qcknd fr 2f out to press wnr ins fnl f: kpt on but a hld* **14/1**
6-14 **3** *½* **Greylami (IRE)**[26] 1043 3-9-4 **80**.................... JimmyFortune 5 83+
(T G Mills) *in tch: rdn over 2f out: styd on and edgd lft appr fnl f: r.o ins fnl f but nt pce to trble ldng duo* **7/2**[1]

2124 **4** *nk* **Segal (IRE)**[19] 1171 3-9-3 **79** TPQueally 3 81
(J Noseda) *towards rr: hdwy 4f out: chsd ldrs and hung lft over 1f out: styd on again cl home* **8/1**

1 **5** *3/4* **House Of Lords (USA)**[31] 974 3-9-3 **79** JamieSpencer 2 80+
(M L W Bell) *in rr: hdwy 4f out: chsd ldrs and hung lft over 1f out: styd on again ins fnl f* **6/1**

106- **6** *1 1/2* **It's My Day (IRE)**[147] 6960 3-8-3 **68** ow2 KirstyMilczarek(3) 6 66
(Jane Chapple-Hyam) *in rr: hdwy and wd fr 3f out: hung lft fr 2f out: styd on ins fnl f but nvr in contention* **16/1**

-421 **7** *hd* **Flash Of Colour**[17] 1205 3-9-1 **77** JimCrowley 9 75
(Mrs A J Perrett) *led: rdn 3f out: hdd ins fnl 2f: wknd ins fnl f* **5/1**[3]

0-44 **8** *hd* **Mahadee (IRE)**[13] 1272 3-8-8 **70** RyanMoore 1 67
(C E Brittain) *in rr and sn pushed along: styd on and hung lft over 1f out: swtchd lft and kpt on again ins fnl f* **20/1**

420- **9** *1 1/4* **Miss Jolyon (USA)**[190] 6233 3-8-7 **69** PhilipRobinson 11 64
(M A Jarvis) *in rr: rdn and sme hdwy over 2f out: nvr gng pce to be competitive* **25/1**

461- **10** *3* **Resplendent Light**[183] 6379 3-9-3 **79** MartinDwyer 4 69
(W R Muir) *chsd ldrs: rdn 3f out: wknd fr 2f out* **4/1**[2]

2441 **11** *1* **Boy On A Swing (USA)**[36] 919 3-9-4 **80** (t) ChrisCatlin 7 69
(J A Osborne) *chsd ldrs tl rdn 3f out: wknd over 2f out* **8/1**

2m 23.61s (1.71) **Going Correction** +0.10s/f (Slow) **11** Ran SP% **126.6**
Speed ratings (Par 100): **97,96,95,95,94 93,93,93,92,90 89**
CSF £137.49 CT £538.52 TOTE £11.10: £4.00, £4.30, £1.60; EX 158.00.
Owner D H Caslon **Bred** Holborn Trust Co **Trained** Kingsclere, Hants

FOCUS
A fair but quite interesting handicap and they went no pace at all early which would not have suited the stayers. As a result the race has not been rated positively, with the runner-up the best guide.
It's My Day(IRE) Official explanation: jockey said colt hung left

1544 APC UNDERWRITING H'CAP 1m 4f (P)
3:35 (3:35) (Class 2) (0-105,94) 4-Y-0+
£9,969 (£2,985; £1,492; £747; £372; £187) **Stalls** Centre

Form RPR

41-4 **1** **Celtic Spirit (IRE)**[18] 1180 5-9-1 **89** RyanMoore 6 100+
(G L Moore) *hld up in rr: hdwy whn hmpd and lost pl 2f out: plenty to do whn str run fnl f: led fnl 25yds: won gng away* **3/1**[3]

24-0 **2** *3/4* **Pinch Of Salt (IRE)**[24] 1076 5-9-3 **91** MartinDwyer 1 99+
(A M Balding) *trckd ldrs: hdwy on outside and hung rt 2f out: sn led: hrd drvn ct fnl 25yds* **5/2**[2]

1-32 **3** *1 1/2* **Grande Caiman (IRE)**[38] 908 4-9-5 **94** RichardHughes 4 100
(R Hannon) *chsd ldrs: drvn to chal ins fnl 2f: styd on same pce ins fnl f* **6/4**[1]

3010 **4** *4* **Tartan Tie**[17] 1212 4-9-0 **89** JoeFanning 5 88
(M Johnston) *led and kpt narrow advantage tl hdd ins fnl 2f: wknd appr fnl f* **9/1**

-545 **5** *3/4* **St Savarin (FR)**[24] 1080 7-9-4 **92** EddieAhern 3 90
(B R Johnson) *trckd ldr: rdn and upsides 5f out tl wknd ins fnl 2f* **16/1**

000- **6** *3 3/4* **Athenian Way (IRE)**[192] 6168 4-9-2 **91** JamieSpencer 2 83
(J R Fanshawe) *chsd ldrs: rdn and bmpd over 2f out: sn hung rt: wknd wl over 1f out* **10/1**

2m 33.35s (-1.15) **Going Correction** +0.10s/f (Slow)
WFA 4 from 5yo+ 1lb **6** Ran SP% **118.5**
Speed ratings (Par 109): **107,106,105,102,102 99**
CSF £11.75 TOTE £4.10: £1.80, £2.20; EX 13.20.
Owner Miss S Bowles **Bred** Genesis Green Stud Ltd **Trained** Woodingdean, E Sussex
■ Stewards' Enquiry : Martin Dwyer caution: careless riding

FOCUS
Another race in which they did not go very quick early, but they were travelling towards the end and the winning time was 3.46 seconds faster than the earlier maiden fillies' contest over the same trip. Despite the modest early pace, the first two home occupied the last two places for most of the way and the third is the best guide to the level.

NOTEBOOK
Celtic Spirit(IRE), trying this trip for the first time on the Flat, did well to win this as he was held up off the modest early pace and became short of room at a crucial stage halfway up the home straight. After managing to find his stride again, he found an impressive turn of speed and maintained his effort down the middle of the track to mow down the runner-up. He has shown some ability in a few tries over hurdles and could be just the type of useful dual-purpose performer the stable does so well with. (op 7-2 tchd 11-4)
Pinch Of Salt(IRE), seventh in the Rosebery here last time, did well to find cover early as he threatened to take a hold. The race looked his when he was produced between horses passing the intersection and put daylight between himself and his rivals, but despite doing little wrong he had the prize snatched from him. He deserves compensation, but is now 16lb higher than for his last win so has very little room for manoeuvre. (op 9-4)
Grande Caiman(IRE) has been very consistent on Polytrack this winter, but he has not covered himself in glory in two previous tries here. Sent off favourite nonetheless, he had every chance when diving for the inside rail after the intersection but failed to match the finish pace of the front pair. He stays further than this and probably needs a stronger all-round gallop. (op 11-8 tchd 13-8)
Tartan Tie managed to get the early lead this time and set just a modest early pace, but when the dash for the line started up the home straight he was found wanting. He is much better off grinding his rivals into submission on the Southwell Fibresand. (op 10-1)
St Savarin(FR), back over a more suitable trip, raced on the shoulder of the leader for much of the way but was comfortably left behind when the pace quickened. He still looks to be on a stiff mark.
Athenian Way(IRE), making her sand debut, had her chance but appeared to have run her race by the time she got squeezed out passing the two-furlong pole. She is still to truly convince over this trip. (op 12-1)

1545 BLUECYCLE SALVAGE H'CAP 1m (P)
4:10 (4:11) (Class 3) (0-95,93) 4-Y-0+
£6,854 (£2,052; £1,026; £513; £192; £192) **Stalls** High

Form RPR

131- **1** **Russki (IRE)**[184] 6359 4-8-11 **86** (b) RichardMullen 2 96
(D M Simcock) *mde virtually all: drvn and qcknd over 2f out: styd on strly fnl f* **20/1**

051- **2** *2* **Kay Gee Be (IRE)**[199] 6002 4-9-4 **93** JamieSpencer 5 98
(M J Wallace) *chsd ldrs: wnt narrow 2nd 3f out: rdn 2f out: styd on same pce and no imp on wnr ins fnl f* **2/1**[1]

5200 **3** *2 1/4* **Plum Pudding (IRE)**[3] 1469 5-8-13 **93** (p) HaddenFrost(5) 7 93
(R Hannon) *chsd wnr to 3f out: rdn to stay disputing 2nd but no imp: wknd ins fnl f* **4/1**[2]

2154 **4** *1/2* **Electric Warrior (IRE)**[17] 1218 5-9-4 **93** DarrenWilliams 6 92
(K R Burke) *chsd ldrs: rdn 3f out: wknd ins fnl f* **14/1**

1104 **5** *1* **Ninth House (USA)**[26] 1045 6-8-8 **86** (b) KirstyMilczarek(3) 9 83
(N P Littmoden) *in rr: rdn and styd on same fnl 2f* **20/1**

-552 **5** *dht* **Yarqus**[17] 1211 5-9-3 **92** (bt) RyanMoore 4 89
(C E Brittain) *in rr: hdwy to cl on ldrs 4f out: rdn 3f out: wknd fr 2f out* **5/1**[3]

/5-3 **7** *1 3/4* **Farley Star**[17] 1211 4-8-7 **82** ChrisCatlin 1 75
(R Charlton) *rdn 3f out: a in rr* **11/2**

-523 **8** *3 1/2* **Dichoh**[10] 1335 5-8-7 **82** (v) PhilipRobinson 3 67
(M A Jarvis) *shkn up fr 3f out: a in rr* **10/1**

1m 39.46s (-0.34) **Going Correction** +0.10s/f (Slow) **8** Ran SP% **110.7**
Speed ratings (Par 107): **105,103,100,100,99 99,97,94**
CSF £48.75 CT £115.79 TOTE £10.20: £3.40, £1.30, £1.70; EX 28.60.
Owner DXB Bloodstock Ltd **Bred** Mark Commins **Trained** Newmarket, Suffolk
■ Overturn (4/1) was withdrawn after refusing to enter the stalls. Deduct 20p in the £ under rule 4.
■ Stewards' Enquiry : Jamie Spencer caution: used whip down shoulder in forehand position

FOCUS
A decent handicap on paper, but a strange race in that the early pace was moderate and the order hardly changed throughout the contest. Although not form to take too literally, the winner is progressive and the third ran to course form.

NOTEBOOK
Russki(IRE), returning from a six-month absence and off a 6lb higher mark than when last seen, was sent straight to the front and was given a skillfully executed ride to make every yard. The way the race was run does place a question mark against the form, but he has now won four of his last five starts and you cannot argue with that. (op 16-1)
Kay Gee Be(IRE), another returning from six months off and off a 5lb higher mark, came into this unbeaten in two starts on sand. Always in about the same place, he tried his best to get to the winner, but was always being held. He will need to improve in order to defy this mark, but should at least come on for this. (op 9-4 tchd 5-2)
Plum Pudding(IRE), 5lb higher than when finishing runner-up in the Lincoln Trial in his last outing on sand, tracked the pace throughout and had every chance on the inside, but failed to find the necessary turn of foot. His last win came off this mark on turf almost a year ago, but recent efforts suggest he is not well handicapped at present. (op 11-2 tchd 6-1)
Electric Warrior(IRE), 6lb higher than when winning a valuable handicap at Dundalk in his most recent start on sand, travelled well throughout and tried to get on terms with the leaders in the straight, but everything was quickening at the same time and he was never doing enough.
Ninth House(USA) had been dropped 2lb since his last start, but was still 9lb higher than when completing his four-timer last month. Being held up in a race run at a modest early pace was not ideal, but his current mark still looks his biggest problem. (op 6-1)
Yarqus, up 3lb, was off his highest mark in a year despite not having won for two years. He tried to get into the race at halfway, but it came to little and he will continue to struggle until the Handicapper shows some leniency. (op 6-1)
Farley Star was not helped by being held up out the back in a race dominated by those that raced handily, but still ran very close to form with Yarqus on recent Lingfield running. (op 9-2 tchd 4-1)

1546 INSURANCEJOBS.CO.UK H'CAP 7f (P)
4:45 (4:48) (Class 4) (0-80,80) 3-Y-O £4,209 (£1,252; £625; £312) **Stalls** High

Form RPR

330- **1** **Fervent Prince**[191] 6201 3-8-8 **73** TravisBlock(3) 6 82+
(H Morrison) *trckd ldrs: rdn and veered lft over 2f out: rdn to ld over 1f out and hung lft again: styd on wl and edgd rt cl home* **14/1**

55-2 **2** *1 3/4* **Totally Focussed (IRE)**[17] 1208 3-8-10 **72** IanMongan 11 76
(S Dow) *in tch: nt clr run on ins over 2f out: gd hdwy and rdn sn after: chal over 1f out: chsd wnr ins fnl f but a hld* **5/1**[3]

6-40 **3** *nk* **Naughty Frida (IRE)**[38] 905 3-8-12 **77** KirstyMilczarek(3) 12 80
(M Botti) *rr: hdwy 3f out: rdn and styd on wl fnl f but nvr quite gng pce to chal* **8/1**

3-25 **4** *3/4* **Hansinger (IRE)**[31] 966 3-9-3 **79** (v[1]) ChrisCatlin 5 80
(B I Case) *chsd ldr: chal fr 4f out: led over 2f out: sn hrd rdn: hdd over 1f out and kpt on same pce* **9/2**[2]

1 **5** *1/2* **Yamal (IRE)**[26] 1036 3-8-13 **75** JoeFanning 7 75
(M Johnston) *s.i.s: sn in tch: wd bnd 3f out and hung lft sn after: kpt on but nvr gng pce to be competitive* **2/1**[1]

51-5 **6** *3 1/4* **Just Like A Woman**[25] 1057 3-8-12 **74** HayleyTurner 4 65+
(M L W Bell) *s.i.s: rr: n.m.r over 2f out and swtchd rt: styd on fnl f but nvr in contention* **12/1**

1 **7** *1* **Rehabilitation**[18] 1194 3-9-2 **78** AdamKirby 3 66+
(W R Swinburn) *in rr: rdn 3f out: sme prog fr over 1f out* **8/1**

4-60 **8** *3/4* **Sofia's Star**[19] 1167 3-8-12 **77** TolleyDean(3) 10 63
(P Winkworth) *in rr tl sme late prog* **12/1**

410- **9** *2* **Hunt The Bottle (IRE)**[194] 6128 3-9-1 **77** JamieSpencer 13 58
(B W Hills) *rdn and hung lft over 2f out: a in rr* **7/1**

2-14 **10** *1 3/4* **Emperors Jade**[19] 1167 3-8-13 **75** RichardHughes 2 51+
(A P Jarvis) *chsd ldrs tl bdly hmpd over 2f out: nt rcvr* **20/1**

5600 **11** *1/2* **Gross Prophet**[10] 1336 3-9-4 **80** RichardKingscote 8 55
(Tom Dascombe) *slt advantage tl hdd over 2f out and wknd qckly* **16/1**

534- **12** *5* **Acquifer**[157] 6847 3-8-12 **74** EddieAhern 1 35+
(J L Dunlop) *chsd ldrs tl bdly hmpd and wknd over 2f out* **33/1**

50-1 **13** *1 1/4* **Bombardier Wells**[20] 1149 3-9-0 **76** StephenCarson 14 34+
(Eve Johnson Houghton) *chsd ldrs tl hmpd on rails and dropped to rr 4f out: nvr in contention after* **10/1**

1m 25.96s (-0.04) **Going Correction** +0.10s/f (Slow) **13** Ran SP% **147.6**
Speed ratings (Par 100): **104,102,101,100,100 96,95,94,92,90 89,83,82**
CSF £102.04 CT £648.79 TOTE £23.50: £5.00, £2.00, £3.60; EX 194.50.
Owner Thurloe Finsbury II **Bred** Fonthill Stud **Trained** East Ilsley, Berks
■ Stewards' Enquiry : Travis Block five-day ban: careless riding (May 6-10)

FOCUS
A competitive handicap and they went a decent pace too. The front five pulled nicely clear and the form looks pretty solid.
Yamal(IRE) Official explanation: jockey said colt missed the break
Bombardier Wells Official explanation: jockey said colt suffered interference in running

1547 TRAVELERS H'CAP 2m (P)
5:15 (5:15) (Class 4) (0-85,84) 4-Y-0+ £4,209 (£1,252; £625; £312) **Stalls** High

Form RPR

10-1 **1** **Gala Evening**[10] 1337 6-9-11 **84** RichardHughes 5 99+
(J A B Old) *trckd ldrs in 3rd: rdn over 2f out: wnt 2nd over 1f out and drvn to ld jst ins fnl f: r.o strly* **2/1**[2]

/1-1 **2** *1* **The Carlton Cannes**[31] 970 4-9-4 **81** JimmyFortune 3 93+
(G Wragg) *hld up in cl 4th: drvn and qcknd over 2f out to ld over 1f out: hdd jst ins fnl f and sn outpcd by wnr* **4/5**[1]

5-35 **3** *4 1/2* **Jagger**[45] 838 8-9-11 **84** (p) EddieAhern 2 91
(G A Butler) *sn led: rdn over 2f out: hdd over 1f out and sn wknd* **6/1**[3]

1-00 **4** *16* **Pearl (IRE)**[13] 1273 4-8-3 **66** (p) ChrisCatlin 4 54
(I A Wood) *chsd ldr: pushed along fr 6f out: rdn 4f out: wknd over 2f out* **14/1**

6364 **5** *nse* **Mister Completely (IRE)**[10] 1337 7-8-6 **65** oh1....(v) EdwardCreighton 1 53
(Ms J S Doyle) *towards rr but in tch: hdwy to cl up 4f out: rdn 3f out: sn wknd* **12/1**

3m 28.35s (-1.75) **Going Correction** +0.10s/f (Slow)
WFA 4 from 6yo+ 4lb **5** Ran SP% **117.5**
Speed ratings (Par 105): **108,107,105,97,97**
CSF £4.32 TOTE £2.20: £1.20, £1.30; EX 4.30 Place 6 £238.99, Place 5 £121.54.
Owner W E Sturt **Bred** Juddmonte Farms **Trained** Barbury Castle, Wilts

FOCUS
A small field, but this was run at quite a decent pace under the circumstances and stamina was crucial. The third sets the standard.
T/Plt: £348.40 to a £1 stake. Pool: £94.80. 45,252.00 winning tickets. T/Qpdt: £88.40 to a £1 stake. Pool: £25.10. 2,999.40 winning tickets. ST

1257 SOUTHWELL (L-H)
Tuesday, April 22

OFFICIAL GOING: Good to firm (good in places; 9.0)
Wind: Slight, across Weather: Dry and sunny

1548 DINE IN THE QUEEN MOTHER RESTAURANT H'CAP 6f
1:35 (1:36) (Class 5) (0-70,70) 3-Y-O **£2,456** (£725; £362) **Stalls** Low

Form RPR

55-0 **1** **Legendary Guest**[11] 1306 3-8-13 **65**.................. TonyHamilton 9 71
(D W Barker) *chsd ldrs: hdwy 2f out: rdn to ld ent fnl f: drvn out* **16/1**

34-0 **2** *1/2* **Leading Edge (IRE)**[20] 1155 3-8-9 **68**.................. ThomasO'Brien(7) 13 73+
(M R Channon) *towards rr: hdwy 2f out: rdn and styd on ins fnl f: nrst fin* **16/1**

35-4 **3** *1 1/2* **Cracking Nick (IRE)**[22] 1110 3-9-4 **70**.................. SaleemGolam 2 70
(W R Swinburn) *led: rdn along wl over 1f out: drvn and hdd ent fnl f: kpt on same pce* **5/1**[2]

306- **4** *1* **Discanti (IRE)**[253] 4447 3-8-11 **63**.................. DavidAllan 4 60
(T D Easterby) *chsd ldrs: rdn along and outpcd over 2f out: rdn and styd on appr fnl f* **18/1**

4102 **5** *1* **Thomas Malory (IRE)**[13] 1274 3-8-6 **63**.................. SCreighton(5) 5 57
(Miss V Haigh) *towards rr: hdwy on outer wl over 1f out: drvn and kpt on ins fnl f: nrst fin* **7/1**[3]

0-21 **6** *1 1/2* **Straight (IRE)**[22] 1120 3-8-8 **63** ow2.................. MarkLawson(3) 11 52
(M Brittain) *in tch on outer: hdwy over 2f out: rdn wl over 1f out: no imp ent fnl f* **9/1**

04-2 **7** *1* **Piccolo Pete**[18] 1187 3-8-9 **61** ow1.................. MickyFenton 6 47
(T P Tate) *towards rr: effrt over 2f out: sn rdn and sme late hdwy* **9/2**[1]

60-1 **8** *hd* **Berrymead**[18] 1187 3-8-12 **64**.................. PaulMulrennan 14 49
(M W Easterby) *midfield: effrt and sme hdwy 2f out: sn rdn and n.d* **10/1**

00-3 **9** *hd* **Towy Boy (IRE)**[11] 1315 3-8-13 **65**.................. NCallan 1 49
(I A Wood) *chsd ldrs on inner: hdwy 2f out: sn rdn and wknd appr fnl f* **8/1**

5160 **10** *nse* **Helping Hand (IRE)**[12] 1277 3-9-1 **70**.................. RussellKennemore(3) 7 54
(R Hollinshead) *cl up: rdn along wl over 1f out: drvn and wknd appr fnl f* **25/1**

006- **11** *1 1/4* **Wooden King (IRE)**[209] 5729 3-8-4 **56**.................. PaulHanagan 3 36
(P D Evans) *cl up: rdn along over 2f out: sn drvn and wknd* **9/2**[1]

10 **12** *4 1/2* **So Sublime**[4] 1448 3-8-9 **68** ow2.................. MarkCoumbe(7) 12 34
(M C Chapman) *sn outpcd and a bhd* **33/1**

1m 14.94s (-0.86) **Going Correction** -0.175s/f (Firm) **12** Ran SP% **119.5**
Speed ratings (Par 98): **98,97,95,94,92 90,89,89,88,88 87,81**
CSF £250.99 CT £1496.47 TOTE £18.30: £5.70, £7.20, £1.90; EX 156.30.
Owner Stef Stefanou **Bred** J H And J M Wall **Trained** Scorton, N Yorks

FOCUS
A modest handicap with the third the best guide to the form.
Legendary Guest ◆ Official explanation: trainer said, regarding apparent improvement in form, that the gelding may have benefited from the good to firm (good in places) ground.

1549 BOOK YOUR HOSPITALITY PACKAGES MEDIAN AUCTION MAIDEN STKS 1m 3f
2:05 (2:06) (Class 6) 3-Y-O **£1,774** (£523; £262) **Stalls** Low

Form RPR

40-4 **1** **Crimson Mitre**[20] 1140 3-9-3 **67**.................. NCallan 4 68
(J Jay) *led 3f: cl up tl led again 5f out: rdn clr wl over 1f out* **2/1**[1]

53 **2** *5* **Director's Chair**[21] 1130 3-9-0 **0**.................. JerryO'Dwyer(3) 8 60
(Miss J Feilden) *a.p: rdn along on outer over 3f out: drvn fnl 2f and kpt on same pce* **7/2**[2]

04- **3** *2 1/4* **Orkney (IRE)**[157] 6857 3-9-3 **0**.................. TomEaves 1 56
(Miss J A Camacho) *hld up in tch: hdwy on inner over 3f out: rdn over 2f out: sn drvn and kpt on same pce* **5/1**[3]

4 *1 1/4* **Miss Mactango** 3-8-12 **0**.................. LiamJones 5 49
(W M Brisbourne) *chsd ldrs: rdn along and outpcd 5f out: styd on u.p fnl 2f* **16/1**

00-5 **5** *1/2* **L'Orage**[12] 1279 3-8-12 **52**.................. SaleemGolam 3 48
(M G Quinlan) *chsd ldrs: rdn along 3f out: drvn 2f out and grad wknd* **18/1**

6 *3* **Heroic Lad** 3-8-10 **0**.................. GihanArnolda(7) 7 48
(A B Haynes) *hld up: hdwy over 4f out: rdn along wl over 2f out and sn btn* **16/1**

00- **7** *2 3/4* **Hotel Felix**[186] 6294 3-9-3 **0**.................. MickyFenton 6 43
(Miss Gay Kelleway) *chsd ldrs tl led after 3f: hdd 5f out and sn rdn along: drvn wl over 2f out and sn wknd* **17/2**

50-0 **8** *5* **Whatalotofbuts**[54] 727 3-9-3 **48**.................. PaulHanagan 9 35
(B De Haan) *t.k.h: hld up: hdwy on outer over 5f out: chsd ldrs over 3f out: sn rdn and wknd wl over 2f out* **25/1**

9 *10* **Fielder (IRE)** 3-9-3 **0**.................. PatCosgrave 2 18
(J G Portman) *s.i.s: a in rr* **15/2**

2m 27.43s (-0.37) **Going Correction** -0.175s/f (Firm) **9** Ran SP% **115.4**
Speed ratings (Par 96): **94,90,88,87,87 85,83,79,72**
CSF £8.83 TOTE £3.40: £1.10, £1.50, £2.20; EX 6.80.
Owner The Bubbly Bishops **Bred** R Withers **Trained** Newmarket, Suffolk

FOCUS
An uncompetitive maiden and pretty moderate form. It is doubtful if the winner had to improve.

1550 SPONSOR A RACE AT SOUTHWELL (S) STKS 7f
2:40 (2:40) (Class 6) 3-Y-O+ **£1,774** (£523; £262) **Stalls** Low

Form RPR

1145 **1** **Blue Empire (IRE)**[22] 1116 7-9-5 **60**..................(p) MarkCoumbe(7) 2 67
(John A Harris) *midfield: effrt over 2f out and sn rdn: hdwy ent fnl f: styd on strly to ld nr fin* **8/1**

0-64 **2** *3/4* **Shot To Fame (USA)**[11] 1301 9-9-7 **70**.................. AdrianTNicholls 14 60
(D Nicholls) *prom: rdn to ld over 1f out: drvn ins fnl f: hdd and no ex towards fin* **11/4**[1]

6040 **3** *1* **Cyfrwys (IRE)**[25] 1053 7-9-2 **48**..................(p) CatherineGannon 5 52
(B Palling) *cl up: led over 2f out and sn rdn: hdd over 1f out: ev ch tl drvn and no ex wl ins fnl f* **20/1**

00-5 **4** *hd* **Oi Vay Joe (IRE)**[41] 850 4-9-7 **73**..................(b[1]) RobertWinston 6 56
(W Jarvis) *prom: effrt to chal over 2f out: sn rdn and ev ch tl drvn and hld whn n.m.r ins fnl f* **7/1**[3]

000- **5** *2* **Capistrano**[16] 4272 5-9-7 **57**.................. MickyFenton 8 51
(Mrs P Sly) *bhd: hdwy over 2f: rdn over 1f out: kpt on ins fnl f: nrst fin* **14/1**

3-20 **6** *nk* **Cap St Jean (IRE)**[8] 1371 4-9-4 **60**.................. RussellKennemore(3) 3 50
(R Hollinshead) *chsd ldrs: rdn along 2f out: grad wknd* **9/2**[2]

3405 **7** *3/4* **Temtation (IRE)**[31] 972 4-8-9 **42**.................. StacyRenwick(7) 1 43
(J A Pickering) *sn led: rdn along and hdd over 2f out: grad wknd* **33/1**

030- **8** *1* **Bolton Hall (IRE)**[143] 6997 6-9-0 **63**..................(p) BMcHugh(7) 9 46
(R A Fahey) *s.i.s and bhd tl styd on fnl 2f* **15/2**

-000 **9** *1/2* **Bodden Bay**[17] 1207 6-9-7 **48**.................. RoystonFfrench 11 44
(I W McInnes) *a in rr* **12/1**

0-00 **10** *2* **Nestor Protector (IRE)**[18] 1187 3-8-8 **55**..................(b[1]) PatCosgrave 10 34
(A B Haynes) *a in rr* **28/1**

00-0 **11** *3/4* **Boppys Diamond**[17] 1222 4-8-13 **40**.................. JamieMoriarty(3) 13 32
(P T Midgley) *a in rr* **66/1**

0000 **12** *2* **Shadow Jumper (IRE)**[49] 792 7-9-2 **41**..................(v) AhmedAjtebi(5) 7 31
(J T Stimpson) *a towards rr* **18/1**

0-23 **13** *1/2* **Polish Priory (IRE)**[3] 1487 3-8-3 **49**.................. PaulHanagan 12 20
(P D Evans) *midfield: rdn along on outer 3f out: sn wknd* **7/1**[3]

1m 28.71s (-0.69) **Going Correction** -0.175s/f (Firm)
WFA 3 from 4yo+ 13lb **13** Ran SP% **125.0**
Speed ratings (Par 101): **96,95,94,93,91 91,90,89,88,86 85,83,82**
CSF £30.63 TOTE £11.30: £1.60, £1.70, £6.00; EX 34.90.There was no bid for the winner.
Owner Shaun Taylor **Bred** Yeomanstown Stud **Trained** Eastwell, Leics

FOCUS
A modest seller with the third the best guide. The winner was close to his sand form.
Polish Priory(IRE) Official explanation: vet said filly returned lame

1551 SOUTHWELL RACECOURSE FOR CONFERENCES H'CAP 2m
3:15 (3:15) (Class 6) (0-65,62) 4-Y-O+ **£1,774** (£523; £262) **Stalls** Low

Form RPR

/25- **1** **Dansilver**[13] 4809 4-8-12 **53**.................. NCallan 12 67
(D J Wintle) *in tch: hdwy over 4f out: rdn to ld 2f out: sn hung bdly rt and jockey dropped whip over 1f out: styd on* **9/1**

30-0 **2** *6* **Blue Jet (USA)**[20] 1136 4-8-11 **52**.................. DeanMcKeown 14 59
(R M Whitaker) *trckd ldrs: hdwy 4f out: effrt and ev ch whn bdly hmpd 2f out: sn rdn to chse wnr: no imp ins fnl f* **12/1**

111- **3** *2* **Lady Pilot**[29] 1032 6-9-6 **57**.................. RichardThomas 4 62+
(Jim Best) *dwlt: hld up towards rr: stdy hdwy 6f out: rdn to chse ldrs over 2f out: sn drvn and kpt on same pce* **2/1**[1]

2304 **4** *4 1/2* **Sand Repeal (IRE)**[20] 1136 6-9-3 **61**..................(v) AmyBaker(7) 3 60
(Miss J Feilden) *dwlt and in rr: hdwy after 6f: cl up 1/2-way: led 6f out: rdn along over 3f out: drvn: hung lft and hdd 2f out: sn wknd* **9/2**[2]

5035 **5** *hd* **Shandelight (IRE)**[14] 1262 4-8-5 **46**..................(p) RoystonFfrench 8 45
(Mrs A Duffield) *led 6f: cl up: effrt 4f out and sn ev ch tl rdn and edgd rt 2f out: sn drvn and wknd* **17/2**

401/ **6** *3* **Skit**[603] 4868 5-8-8 **45**.................. LiamJones 6 40
(W M Brisbourne) *midfield: effrt over 6f out: sn rdn along and nvr a factor* **20/1**

00-0 **7** *2* **Next Flight (IRE)**[18] 1184 9-8-8 **45**.................. TomEaves 7 38
(R E Barr) *s.i.s: a in rr* **40/1**

-360 **8** *4 1/2* **Just Waz (USA)**[29] 988 6-8-5 **45**.................. MichaelJStainton(3) 1 33
(R M Whitaker) *trckd ldrs: pushed along 5f out: rdn along 4f out and sn wknd* **8/1**

0230 **9** *1* **Matinee Idol**[22] 1121 5-8-8 **45**..................(b) PaulHanagan 11 31
(Mrs S Lamyman) *a towards rr* **33/1**

4124 **10** *3 1/4* **Dreams Jewel**[28] 1017 8-9-11 **62**.................. NeilChalmers 13 44
(C Roberts) *trckd ldrs: rdn along over 4f out and sn btn* **15/2**[3]

-025 **11** *8* **Feeling Peckish (USA)**[44] 345 4-8-4 **45**..................(t) DMylonas 5 18
(M C Chapman) *in tch: pushed along and lost pl bef 1/2-way: sn in rr* **50/1**

500- **12** *37* **Ellies Faith**[210] 5698 4-8-4 **45**.................. PaulFessey 9 —
(L R James) *chsd ldrs tl led after 6f: rdn along and hdd 6f out: sn wknd* **50/1**

3m 35.7s (-2.90) **Going Correction** -0.175s/f (Firm)
WFA 4 from 5yo+ 4lb **12** Ran SP% **116.7**
Speed ratings (Par 101): **100,97,96,93,93 92,91,88,88,86 82,64**
CSF £103.92 CT £300.81 TOTE £10.60: £3.30, £4.20, £1.70; EX 88.00.
Owner Mrs Joan L Egan **Bred** Mrs J L Egan **Trained** Naunton, Gloucs
■ Stewards' Enquiry : Amy Baker one-day ban: careless riding (May 6)

FOCUS
A moderate handicap run at just a steady pace. The form looks decent for the grade, with a career best from Dansilver and the fourth a solid marker.
Matinee Idol Official explanation: trainer later said filly was found to be in season after race

1552 SOUTHWELL-RACECOURSE.CO.UK H'CAP 7f
3:50 (3:50) (Class 4) (0-80,80) 4-Y-O+ **£4,209** (£1,252; £625; £312) **Stalls** Low

Form RPR

3510 **1** **Dudley Docker (IRE)**[10] 1335 6-8-8 **70**..................(b) LiamJones 5 78
(C R Dore) *s.i.s and bhd: gd hdwy over 2f out: swtchd lft and rdn ent fnl f: qcknd wl to ld last 100yds* **10/3**[2]

-010 **2** *1 1/4* **Tencendur (IRE)**[10] 1327 4-9-1 **77**.................. AdrianTNicholls 4 82
(D Nicholls) *trckd ldrs: hdwy 3f out: rdn to ld over 1f out: drvn ins fnl f: hdd and nt qckn last 100yds* **9/4**[1]

000- **3** *3 1/4* **Thunderousapplause**[186] 6300 4-9-4 **80**.................. NeilPollard 2 76
(A J McCabe) *trckd ldr: hdwy 3f out: effrt and led briefly 2f out: sn rdn and hdd over 1f out: sn drvn and one pce ins fnl f* **8/1**

1101 **4** *2 1/4* **Kensington (IRE)**[8] 1368 7-8-13 **75** 6ex..................(p) NCallan 1 65+
(P D Evans) *trckd ldng pair: effrt whn n.m.r on inner wl over 1f out: sn rdn and btn* **9/4**[1]

0-00 **5** *nk* **Mr Wolf**[11] 1300 7-8-13 **75**..................(p) FergalLynch 6 64
(D W Barker) *led: rdn along and hdd 2f out: sn drvn and wknd over 1f out* **11/2**[3]

1m 26.82s (-2.58) **Going Correction** -0.175s/f (Firm) **5** Ran SP% **111.1**
Speed ratings (Par 105): **107,105,101,99,98**
CSF £11.32 TOTE £3.50: £2.00, £2.20; EX 13.20.
Owner Sean J Murphy **Bred** Nuri Fuat Basak **Trained** West Pinchbeck, Lincs
■ Stewards' Enquiry : Fergal Lynch two-day ban: careless riding (May 6-7)

FOCUS
Ordinary handicap form, rated through the runner-up. The winner was close to his recent sand form.

1553 SOUTHWELL GOLF CLUB H'CAP — 1m 3f
4:25 (4:25) (Class 6) (0-60,60) 3-Y-O — **£1,774** (£523; £262) **Stalls** Low

Form RPR
040- **1** **Ovthenight (IRE)**[181] 6427 3-9-2 **58** MickyFenton 6 68
(Mrs P Sly) *led 3f: prom: led 2f out and sn rdn: drvn over 1f out: edgd rt ins fnl f: hld on wl* **15/2**
05-3 **2** *hd* **Graylyn Ruby (FR)**[18] 1186 3-9-1 **60** LukeMorris(3) 3 70
(J Jay) *hld up in tch: hdwy to trck ldrs over 4f out: chal 2f out and sn rdn: drvn over 1f out and ev ch whn carried rt ins fnl f: no ex nr fin* **9/2**[1]
06-0 **3** *12* **Balais Folly (FR)**[111] 20 3-8-9 **51** CatherineGannon 9 41
(B Palling) *towards rr: hdwy 3f out: rdn over 2f out: styd on u.p appr fnl f* **16/1**
04-6 **4** *2 3/4* **Captain Mainwaring**[20] 1147 3-9-1 **57** RichardThomas 4 42
(N P Littmoden) *prom: led over 3f out: rdn and hdd 2f out: grad wknd* **12/1**
000- **5** *1 1/4* **Teadancer (IRE)**[201] 5944 3-9-0 **56** PatCosgrave 14 39
(J G Portman) *stdd s: hld up and bhd: hdwy 3f out: rdn over 2f out: kpt on u.p: nvr a factor* **28/1**
0-04 **6** *1 3/4* **Ba Dreamflight**[18] 1186 3-8-7 **49** (v[1]) AdrianTNicholls 12 29
(H Morrison) *hld up: hdwy and in tch 5f out: rdn along over 3f out and sn no imp* **7/1**[3]
-530 **7** *5* **Soxy Doxy (IRE)**[19] 1163 3-8-11 **53** RobertWinston 8 24
(M Johnston) *towards rr: hdwy on outer 3f out: rdn along over 2f out and no prog* **6/1**[2]
0000 **8** *6* **Dawn Wind**[3] 1478 3-8-11 **53** (p) NCallan 1 14
(I A Wood) *chsd ldrs on inner: rdn along 4f out: sn wknd* **11/1**
056- **9** *1 3/4* **Sand Maiden (IRE)**[224] 5298 3-9-2 **58** (b[1]) DavidAllan 11 16
(T D Easterby) *a towards rr* **12/1**
0-30 **10** *3 1/2* **Scruffy Skip (IRE)**[50] 785 3-9-2 **58** LiamJones 10 10
(C R Dore) *prom: rdn along 4f out: drvn 3f out and sn wknd* **11/1**
6-00 **11** *16* **Fortunes Maid (IRE)**[94] 223 3-8-8 **50** PaulMulrennan 5 —
(M H Tompkins) *bhd fr 1/2-way* **40/1**
040- **12** *6* **Social Spirit (IRE)**[202] 5904 3-9-0 **56** DO'Donohoe 2 —
(J R Weymes) *a in rr* **66/1**
60-5 **13** *2* **Lady In Chief**[17] 1222 3-8-12 **54** TomEaves 13 —
(Miss J A Camacho) *chsd ldrs: rdn along 1/2-way: sn wknd* **10/1**
-653 **14** *49* **Lancaster Lad (IRE)**[14] 1251 3-8-8 **50** (b[1]) PaulHanagan 7 —
(A B Haynes) *chsd ldrs: led after 3f: hdd over 3f out and sn wknd* **9/1**

2m 24.58s (-3.22) **Going Correction** -0.175s/f (Firm) **14** Ran SP% **121.1**
Speed ratings (Par 96): **104,103,95,93,92 90,87,82,81,79 67,63,61,26**
CSF £40.92 CT £538.93 TOTE £9.50: £3.00, £1.50, £5.20; EX 43.70.
Owner D Bayliss, T Davies, G Libson & P Sly **Bred** Derek Veitch And Mark Tong **Trained** Thorney, Cambs

FOCUS
No previous winners in this very moderate handicap but the first two finished a long way clear in a decent time and have clearly both improved.
Scruffy Skip(IRE) Official explanation: jockey said gelding ran too free
Lady In Chief Official explanation: trainer said filly was found to be lame on off-hind
Lancaster Lad(IRE) Official explanation: jockey said colt ran too free

1554 PERTEMPS PEOPLE DEVELOPMENT "HANDS AND HEELS" APPRENTICE H'CAP — 1m 4f
5:00 (5:00) (Class 5) (0-70,70) 4-Y-O+ — **£2,456** (£725; £362) **Stalls** Low

Form RPR
1-30 **1** **Calzaghe (IRE)**[17] 1219 4-9-6 **70** (v) DeclanCannon 1 75
(K R Burke) *trckd ldrs: hdwy over 2f out: chal over 1f out: led jst ins fnl f: kpt on* **7/2**[3]
6400 **2** *1* **Top Spec (IRE)**[12] 1281 7-8-6 **55** oh2 SimonPearce 5 59
(J Pearce) *hld up: hdwy 3f out: swtchd lft wl over 1f out: effrt on inner ins fnl f: sn rdn and kpt on: nt rch wnr* **5/2**[2]
05-4 **3** *1 3/4* **Black Falcon (IRE)**[77] 443 8-8-11 **60** DeanHeslop 2 61
(M A Peill) *t.k.h: trckd ldrs tl led 1/2-way: rdn 2f out: hdd jst ins fnl f: lost 2nd nr fin* **4/1**
2103 **4** *5* **Just Intersky (USA)**[5] 1411 5-8-12 **64** (e) BMcHugh(3) 6 57
(V Smith) *led 4f: cl up: rdn along 3f out: wknd 2f out* **2/1**[1]
000- **5** *5* **Sularno**[214] 5604 4-8-7 **62** (v[1]) RyanClark(5) 7 47
(H Morrison) *cl up: led after 4f: hdd 1/2-way: cl up and ev ch tl rdn and wknd wl over 1f out* **9/1**

2m 39.94s (-1.76) **Going Correction** -0.175s/f (Firm)
WFA 4 from 5yo+ 1lb **5** Ran SP% **114.1**
Speed ratings (Par 103): **98,97,96,92,89**
CSF £13.07 TOTE £4.90: £2.50, £1.60; EX 12.30 Place 6 £78.75, Place 5 £15.74.
Owner Mrs Maura Gittins **Bred** Wentworth Racing Pty Ltd **Trained** Middleham Moor, N Yorks
■ Stewards' Enquiry : Dean Heslop seven-day ban: used whip intentionally contrary to restrictions (May 9-10, 13,15,17,19,21)
Ryan Clark one-day ban: careless riding (May 5)

FOCUS
A modest event for riders who had ridden no more than ten winners under rules. The pace was pretty steady and all five were in with some sort of chance turning for home. It was a bit of a messy race and the form does not amount to much.
T/Jkpt: Not won. T/Plt: £72.20 to a £1 stake. Pool: £64,354.04. 649.90 winning tickets. T/Qpdt: £11.00 to a £1 stake. Pool: £2,770.90. 185.70 winning tickets. JR

1135 CATTERICK (L-H)
Wednesday, April 23

OFFICIAL GOING: Good to soft (good in places)
The ground was described as 'tacky, on the soft side'.
Wind: Almost nil Weather: Fine, sunny and warm

1555 MELROSE AVENUE (S) STKS — 5f
2:00 (2:01) (Class 6) 2-Y-O — **£2,047** (£604; £302) **Stalls** Low

Form RPR
1 **Ykikamoocow** 2-8-6 0 SilvestreDeSousa 3 66+
(G A Harker) *w ldrs: led 3f out: drvn clr over 1f out: rdn out* **7/1**[3]
35 **2** *10* **Syrup (IRE)**[4] 1480 2-8-8 0 ow2 TGMcLaughlin 4 28
(P D Evans) *swvd rt s: led tl 3f out: kpt on: no ch w wnr* **7/2**[2]
5 **3** *1* **In The Moment**[14] 1264 2-7-13 0 AshleyMorgan(7) 6 26+
(W G M Turner) *hmpd and taken rt s: sn chsng ldrs: kpt on same pce fnl 2f* **11/1**
4 *nk* **Forzando Bloom** 2-8-11 0 RobertHavlin 2 26+
(R A Harris) *dwlt: in tch: hdwy over 1f out: kpt on* **7/2**[2]
5 *6* **Sweet Mujahid** 2-8-11 0 ChrisCatlin 1 2+
(R A Harris) *sn chsng ldrs: wknd over 1f out* **11/4**[1]
6 *2 1/2* **Keiser Blue** 2-8-11 0 LeeEnstone 5 —
(P C Haslam) *dwlt and carried rt s: sn chsng ldrs: wknd 1f out: sn eased* **7/2**[2]

62.99 secs (3.19) **Going Correction** +0.375s/f (Good) **6** Ran SP% **114.2**
Speed ratings (Par 90): **89,73,71,70,61 57**
CSF £32.04 TOTE £10.20: £6.70, £1.90; EX 45.80.The winner was bought in for 8,500gns.
Owner G A Harker **Bred** Mrs Karen Heath **Trained** Thirkleby, N Yorks

FOCUS
A weak seller but a wide-margin first-time out winner and the time compared favourably with the later low-grade sprint handicap. The winner was retained and should be able to follow up in a claimer.

NOTEBOOK
Ykikamoocow, a March foal, is out of a mare that won three times in sprints. Tall and unfurnished, she was very green to post but she soon grasped the nettle coming back and came right away coming to the final furlong. She was retained at the auction and a claimer is probably the next logical step. (op 11-1)
Syrup(IRE), having her third run, ducked sideways leaving the traps, knocking over the two on her outside. She set the pace but in the end had but a distant view of the winner. (op 15-8)
In The Moment, five lengths behind Syrup at Bath, was knocked sideways at the start by her. (op 9-1 tchd 8-1)
Forzando Bloom, a close-coupled April foal, stuck on in his own time after missing a beat the the start. This will have taught him a fair bit. (op 6-1)
Sweet Mujahid, an April foal, proved disappointing and dropped right away coming to the final furlong. (op 4-1)
Keiser Blue, a close-coupled March foal, was very green going down. Pushed sideways at the start, he stopped to nothing a furlong out and was heavily eased. (op 4-1)

1556 YOUMZAIN MAIDEN STKS — 7f
2:35 (2:36) (Class 5) 3-Y-O — **£2,331** (£693; £346; £173) **Stalls** Low

Form RPR
04- **1** **Blindspin**[224] 5328 3-9-3 0 TonyHamilton 3 73
(M Dods) *trckd ldrs: led 2f out: kpt on wl* **8/1**
40 **2** *1 1/2* **Eastern Hills**[55] 727 3-9-3 0 RobertWinston 5 69
(M Johnston) *prom: effrt 3f out: chsd wnr over 1f out: lugged lft: kpt on same pce* **9/2**[1]
3 *1 1/4* **Imperial Djay (IRE)** 3-9-3 0 DavidAllan 6 66
(D Carroll) *s.i.s: hdwy over 4f out: sn chsng ldrs: kpt on same pce fnl f* **25/1**
300- **4** *5* **Dream Express (IRE)**[216] 5550 3-8-12 70 NeilBrown(5) 1 68+
(M Dods) *t.k.h: trckd ldrs: nt clr run on ins 2f out: swtchd rt: kpt on* **11/2**[2]
0 **5** *2 3/4* **Great Destination**[71] 529 3-9-3 0 RoystonFfrench 12 45
(B Smart) *chsd ldrs: drvn over 2f out: lost pl over 1f out* **16/1**
40- **6** *2 1/2* **Highland Laddie**[236] 5011 3-9-3 0 RobertHavlin 13 46+
(C R Egerton) *mid-div: outpcd over 3f out: one pce whn sltly hmpd over 1f out* **13/2**[3]
7 *nk* **Ceduna Roadhouse (IRE)**[185] 6365 3-8-12 0 PatrickMathers 7 32
(A M Crow) *s.i.s: in rr: swtchd rt over 1f out: styd on wl towards fin* **50/1**
60- **8** *3/4* **Desert Lark**[228] 5227 3-9-3 0 PaulMulrennan 10 35
(G A Swinbank) *w ldrs: lost pl over 1f out* **14/1**
5-23 **9** *3/4* **Flying Sommelier (USA)**[21] 1139 3-9-3 66 PaulFessey 14 33
(T D Barron) *trckd ldrs: effrt 3f out: lost pl over 1f out* **13/2**[3]
10 *2* **King Fingal (IRE)** 3-9-0 0 JamieMoriarty(3) 11 28
(J J Quinn) *s.s: a in rr* **25/1**
5- **11** *3/4* **Jakam (IRE)**[131] 7139 3-9-3 0 ChrisCatlin 8 26
(E J O'Neill) *hld up in rr: nvr on terms* **11/2**[2]
46-0 **12** *3/4* **Horatio Carter**[12] 1297 3-9-0 73 AndrewMullen(3) 9 24
(K A Ryan) *stdd s: a in rr* **12/1**
22-6 **13** *6* **Paddy Jack**[31] 977 3-9-3 68 DO'Donohoe 2 7
(J R Weymes) *led tl 2f out: wknd* **14/1**

1m 30.02s (3.02) **Going Correction** +0.375s/f (Good) **13** Ran SP% **123.3**
Speed ratings (Par 98): **97,95,93,88,85 82,81,80,80,77 76,76,69**
CSF £44.54 TOTE £10.30: £3.00, £2.20, £9.70; EX 51.80.
Owner A Mallen **Bred** Mrs Dare Wigan **Trained** Denton, Co Durham
■ Stewards' Enquiry : Neil Brown two-day ban: careless riding (May 7-8)

FOCUS
An average maiden for this track, the first three clear. The form looks sound.
Ceduna Roadhouse(IRE) Official explanation: jockey said filly ran green
Jakam(IRE) Official explanation: trainer had no explanation for the poor form shown

1557 RICHMOND CONDITIONS STKS — 1m 3f 214y
3:10 (3:10) (Class 3) 3-Y-O — **£6,542** (£1,959; £979) **Stalls** Low

Form RPR
5211 **1** **Mischief Making (USA)**[37] 920 3-8-7 81 TGMcLaughlin 1 91+
(E A L Dunlop) *trckd ldrs: drvn 3f out: hdwy on ins to ld over 1f out: styd on strly: eased towards fin* **9/4**[2]
615- **2** *1 1/2* **Silk Affair (IRE)**[151] 6939 3-8-10 89 JerryO'Dwyer(3) 4 91
(M G Quinlan) *trckd ldr: effrt over 2f out: kpt on same pce appr fnl f* **5/1**[3]
212- **3** *8* **Planetarium**[172] 6650 3-9-4 86 RobertWinston 2 83+
(M Johnston) *led: shkn up over 2f out: hdd and wnt lft over 1f out: sn btn: eased ins fnl f* **8/13**[1]

2m 48.64s (9.74) **Going Correction** +0.375s/f (Good) **3** Ran SP% **109.4**
Speed ratings (Par 102): **82,81,75**
CSF £9.71 TOTE £3.40; EX 9.10.
Owner Cliveden Stud **Bred** Clivedon Stud Ltd **Trained** Newmarket, Suffolk

FOCUS
Just a steady pace and the winning time was 5.16 seconds slower than the later handicap. The winner, making her turf debut, improved a good deal on her last two victories in modest handicap company. The favourite flopped in the end

NOTEBOOK
Mischief Making(USA), making her turf debut, had taken handicaps from marks of 67 and 75 on her last two starts. With plenty to find, she was the first to feel the strain but she really knuckled down and was able to take things easily in the end. The step up in trip clearly suited her and she will get even further. (op 10-3)
Silk Affair(IRE), fifth in a Listed race in Italy on her third and final start at two, had the leader covered but in the end she was very much second best. (op 4-1)

Planetarium, runner-up to Twice Over on his third and final start at two, set just a modest pace. He hung out on the paddock bend and then dived left when headed. In the end allowed to complete in his own time, a line is best put through this. The undulating track seemed totally against him. (tchd 4-6 and 8-11 in places)

1558 BOOK NOW FOR 6TH MAY H'CAP 7f
3:45 (3:47) (Class 6) (0-65,65) 3-Y-O £2,047 (£604; £302) Stalls Low

Form RPR
4254 1 **Montiboli (IRE)**[34] 952 3-9-2 **63** FergalLynch 7 74
(K A Ryan) *chsd ldrs: led over 2f out: styd on wl* **11/1**
500- 2 2 1/4 **Just Sam (IRE)**[217] 5520 3-8-8 **55** ChrisCatlin 14 60
(D Carroll) *in rr-div: hdwy on outside over 2f out: styd on to go 2nd ins fnl f: no imp* **33/1**
26-4 3 2 **Kyllis**[22] 1132 3-9-3 **64** RoystonFfrench 6 64
(B Smart) *w ldr: led 4f out tl over 2f out: kpt on same pce* **20/1**
050- 4 3/4 **Medici Time**[240] 4892 3-8-10 **57** DavidAllan 8 55
(T D Easterby) *s.i.s: hdwy on ins over 2f out: kpt on: nt rch ldrs* **13/2**[2]
00-6 5 hd **Talon (IRE)**[18] 1221 3-8-4 **51** PaulQuinn 1 48
(G A Swinbank) *chsd ldrs: kpt on same pce fnl 2f* **10/1**
62-2 6 1 1/2 **Grand Value (USA)**[12] 1306 3-8-11 **58** PaulFessey 2 51
(T D Barron) *wnt rt s: trckd ldrs: effrt over 2f out: kpt on same pce* **13/8**[1]
000- 7 2 **Caught In Paradise (IRE)**[242] 4824 3-8-13 **60** AndrewElliott 4 48
(D W Thompson) *led tl 4f out: wknd over 1f out* **25/1**
0-64 8 3/4 **Bourse (IRE)**[12] 1306 3-9-1 **62** RobertWinston 5 48
(J S Wainwright) *hld up in rr: kpt on fnl 2f: nvr nr ldrs* **11/1**
621- 9 2 **Paint Stripper**[172] 6635 3-8-11 **61** DominicFox(3) 9 41
(W Storey) *mid-div: effrt 3f out: nvr nr ldrs* **11/1**
-000 10 nk **Royal Acclamation (IRE)**[7] 1396 3-9-4 **65** SilvestreDeSousa 15 44
(G A Harker) *in rr: sme hdwy 2f out: nvr a factor* **22/1**
2401 11 4 1/2 **Jazenio**[20] 1169 3-8-13 **60** DO'Donohoe 10 27
(K A Ryan) *chsd ldrs: wknd 2f out* **12/1**
-540 12 1 **Mujada**[40] 876 3-8-4 **51** oh1 TWilliams 13 16
(M Brittain) *s.i.s: sn chsng ldrs: lost pl 2f out* **16/1**
06-0 13 2 **Wooden King (IRE)**[1] 1548 3-8-9 **56** TGMcLaughlin 3 15
(P D Evans) *hmpd s: s.i.s: in rr and sn drvn along* **9/1**[3]
000- 14 10 **Bollin Guil**[267] 4037 3-8-5 **55** DuranFentiman(3) 12 —
(T D Easterby) *sn chsng ldrs on outer: sn drvn along: lost pl over 2f out* **40/1**

1m 30.05s (3.05) **Going Correction** +0.375s/f (Good) **14** Ran SP% **127.4**
Speed ratings (Par 96): **97,94,92,91,91 89,87,86,83,83 78,77,75,63**
CSF £352.92 CT £7181.73 TOTE £15.80: £4.50, £14.60, £6.10; EX 665.80.
Owner Dales Homes Ltd **Bred** Amanda Brudenell, James Boughey And Tric **Trained** Hambleton, N Yorks

FOCUS
A low-grade handicap taken in decisive fashion by the maiden Montiboli. The runner-up did well from her outside draw but the form could go either way.
Wooden King(IRE) Official explanation: jockey said gelding suffered interference in running

1559 MOONAX H'CAP 1m 3f 214y
4:20 (4:21) (Class 5) (0-70,70) 4-Y-O+ £2,331 (£693; £346; £173) Stalls Low

Form RPR
50-0 1 **Saluscraggie**[18] 1219 6-8-0 **56** oh6 DanielleMcCreery(5) 7 66
(R E Barr) *dwlt: hld up towards rr: hdwy 4f out: led over 1f out: styd on strly: readily* **25/1**
140- 2 3 **Collette's Choice**[209] 5750 5-8-8 **62** (p) JamieMoriarty(3) 11 67
(R A Fahey) *hld up in rr: hdwy 6f out: sn chsng ldrs: styd on to take 2nd ins fnl f: no ch w wnr* **11/1**
542 3 2 1/2 **Leyte Gulf (USA)**[23] 1121 5-8-9 **60** ChrisCatlin 10 61
(C C Bealby) *chsd ldrs: drvn 4f out: one pce fnl 2f* **7/1**
-000 4 2 1/4 **Turn Of Phrase (IRE)**[4] 1482 9-9-0 **65** (b) TonyHamilton 12 63
(N Wilson) *drvn along to chse ldrs: rdn 4f out: one pce fnl 2f* **14/1**
00-4 5 2 3/4 **Trans Sonic**[26] 1048 5-8-13 **64** PaulMulrennan 6 57
(A J Lockwood) *led: hung rt and reminders over 5f out: hdd over 2f out: wknd over 1f out* **6/1**[3]
4/4- 6 1 1/4 **San Deng**[322] 1239 6-8-9 **60** DO'Donohoe 4 51
(Micky Hammond) *mid-div: sn pushed along: one pce fnl 3f* **22/1**
44-5 7 1 1/2 **Wulimaster (USA)**[2] 1521 5-8-5 **56** oh2 AndrewElliott 3 45
(D W Barker) *prom: effrt over 3f out: fdd over 1f out* **9/2**[2]
464- 8 7 **Vincenzio (IRE)**[247] 4667 4-9-4 **70** RobertHavlin 1 48
(C R Egerton) *t.k.h: trckd ldr: led over 2f out: hdd over 1f out: sn lost pl* **13/2**
60/4 9 8 **Perez (IRE)**[10] 1305 6-8-2 **56** oh6 (v) DominicFox(3) 8 21
(W Storey) *hld up in rr: bhd fnl 2f* **40/1**
400/ 10 14 **Toss The Caber (IRE)**[577] 4570 6-8-5 **56** oh6 RoystonFfrench 5 —
(K G Reveley) *in rr: bhd and eased 2f out* **14/1**
00-6 11 3 **Kadia**[15] 1258 5-8-5 **56** oh11 PaulFessey 2 —
(P T Midgley) *chsd ldrs: lost pl over 3f out: sn wl bhd* **80/1**
01-4 P **Hernando's Boy**[21] 1137 7-9-5 **70** RobertWinston 9 —
(K G Reveley) *hld up in mid-div: eased and lost pl over 3f out: p.u over 2f out* **5/2**[1]

2m 43.48s (4.58) **Going Correction** +0.375s/f (Good)
WFA 4 from 5yo+ 1lb **12** Ran SP% **120.4**
Speed ratings (Par 103): **99,97,95,93,92 91,90,85,80,70 68,—**
CSF £274.53 CT £2149.51 TOTE £34.80: £8.30, £3.10, £2.40; EX 359.10.
Owner Brian Morton **Bred** Hilborough Stud Farm Ltd **Trained** Seamer, N Yorks
■ Stewards' Enquiry : Paul Mulrennan caution: used whip down shoulder in forehand position

FOCUS
A modest handicap run at a sound pace. The winner was out of the handicap but she took it in some style and it was certainly no fluke. The form looks fairly sound at this low level.
Saluscraggie Official explanation: trainer said, regarding apparent improvement in form, that the mare had returned to form following a long lay-off.
Trans Sonic Official explanation: jockey said gelding hung right
Kadia Official explanation: trainer said mare failed to stay
Hernando's Boy Official explanation: trainer said gelding finished distressed

1560 WHITE MUZZLE H'CAP 5f
4:55 (4:55) (Class 6) (0-60,64) 3-Y-O £2,047 (£604; £302) Stalls Low

Form RPR
000- 1 **Big Slick (IRE)**[203] 5901 3-8-4 **46** TWilliams 12 58
(M Brittain) *mde all stands' side: tk overall ld ins fnl f: 1st of 6 that gp* **33/1**
00-5 2 1 3/4 **Kyzer Chief**[21] 1141 3-8-4 **46** oh1 RoystonFfrench 1 52+
(R E Barr) *racd far side: w ldr: led that side over 2f out: hdd overall ins fnl f: no ex: 1st of 8 that gp* **8/1**[3]
-111 3 3/4 **Killer Class**[4] 1475 3-9-8 **64** 6ex FergalLynch 14 67
(J S Goldie) *racd stands' side: chsd ldrs: styd on same pce fnl f: 2nd of 6 that gp* **7/4**[1]
300- 4 2 3/4 **Myriola**[184] 6388 3-8-8 **55** JamieJones(5) 3 48
(S Gollings) *racd far side: in tch: kpt on fnl 2f: 2nd of 8 that gp* **12/1**
054 5 1/2 **Gelert (IRE)**[15] 1255 3-8-12 **54** PatrickMathers 10 46
(Peter Grayson) *racd stands' side: chsd ldrs: one pce fnl 2f: 3rd of 6 that gp* **50/1**
6313 6 nk **Bahamarama (IRE)**[15] 1257 3-8-13 **55** (p) ChrisCatlin 9 46
(R A Harris) *racd stands' side: chsd ldrs: kpt on same pce fnl 2f: 4th of 6 that gp* **12/1**
3-56 7 3/4 **Mchepple**[21] 1141 3-8-3 **48** DominicFox(3) 8 36
(W Storey) *racd far side: w ldrs: one pce fnl 2f: 3rd of 8 that gp* **40/1**
000- 8 3 **Emir Bagatelle**[196] 6105 3-8-4 **46** oh1 EdwardCreighton 15 23
(H Morrison) *s.i.s: racd stands' side: nvr a factor: 5th of 6 that gp* **18/1**
0-60 9 3/4 **Moon Spray (USA)**[19] 1186 3-8-4 **46** (b[1]) DO'Donohoe 7 20
(K A Ryan) *racd far side: sn outpcd: kpt on fnl 2f: nvr nr ldrs: 4th of 8 that gp* **16/1**
03-0 10 hd **Mr Lu**[21] 1161 3-9-1 **57** RobertWinston 6 31
(G A Swinbank) *racd far side: chsd ldrs: hung lft and one pce fnl 2f: 5th of 8 that gp* **6/1**[2]
6564 11 1/2 **Rightcar Hull (IRE)**[21] 1141 3-7-11 **46** (b) PatrickDonaghy(7) 13 18
(Peter Grayson) *racd stands' side: sn chsng ldrs: lost pl over 1f out: last of 6 that gp* **22/1**
0-03 12 hd **Captain Turbot (IRE)**[21] 1141 3-8-4 **46** oh1 (p) PaulQuinn 2 17
(D W Barker) *led far side: hdd over 2f out: wknd over 1f out: 6th of 8 that gp* **9/1**
000- 13 1 **Kiowa Princess**[216] 5550 3-8-2 **47** AndrewMullen(3) 4 14
(M Dods) *racd far side: sn outpcd and drvn along: hdwy 3f out: nvr a factor: 7th of 8 that gp* **12/1**
300- 14 7 **Stormy Journey**[197] 6074 3-9-4 **60** PaulMulrennan 5 —
(Mrs K Walton) *racd far side: w ldrs: lost pl over 2f out: sn bhd: last of 8 that gp* **8/1**[3]

63.12 secs (3.32) **Going Correction** +0.375s/f (Good) **14** Ran SP% **128.8**
Speed ratings (Par 96): **88,85,84,79,78 78,77,72,71,70 70,69,68,56**
CSF £291.30 CT £746.98 TOTE £55.00: £9.50, £3.00, £1.40; EX 331.50.
Owner Northgate Poker **Bred** John Murphy **Trained** Warthill, N Yorks
■ A first winner under rules for three years for Tyrone Williams, who has renewed his licence this year.

FOCUS
A moderate winning time, 0.13 seconds slower than the earlier two-year-old seller and not easy form to rate. Six raced on the stands' side but there seemed very little between the two wings.
Big Slick(IRE) Official explanation: trainer's rep said, regarding the apparent improvement in form, that colt had lost its action on its previous start and the yard had come back into form having had a bad season last year.
Mr Lu Official explanation: jockey said gelding hung left

1561 GO RACING AT BEVERLEY TOMORROW APPRENTICE H'CAP 5f 212y
5:30 (5:30) (Class 6) (0-65,65) 4-Y-O+ £2,047 (£604; £302) Stalls Low

Form RPR
4443 1 **Hart Of Gold**[14] 1268 4-8-11 **62** DavidProbert(5) 12 69
(R A Harris) *w ldrs on outside: led over 3f out: edgd lft over 1f out: hld on towards fin* **8/1**
30-0 2 1/2 **Campo Bueno (FR)**[110] 41 6-8-9 **55** DanielleMcCreery 6 60
(A Berry) *chsd ldrs: no ex wl ins fnl f* **16/1**
3313 3 1 1/4 **Dorn Dancer (IRE)**[4] 1485 6-9-0 **65** 6ex BMcHugh(5) 4 66
(D W Barker) *hld up towards rr: effrt over 3f out: hdwy on outside to chse ldrs over 1f out: kpt on same pce* **7/4**[1]
2620 4 3/4 **Strathmore (IRE)**[4] 1485 4-9-0 **65** (p) FrederikTylicki(5) 8 64
(R A Fahey) *mid-div: hdwy on outer over 2f out: styd on same pce appr fnl f* **8/1**
056 5 3 3/4 **Sharp Indian**[12] 1302 4-8-13 **62** DeclanCannon(3) 10 49
(W J H Ratcliffe) *led tl over 3f out: edgd lft and fdd fnl f* **25/1**
0-40 6 3/4 **Lambency (IRE)**[12] 1309 5-8-8 **54** GaryBartley 2 39
(J S Goldie) *in rr: kpt on fnl 2f: nvr nr ldrs* **13/2**[3]
3536 7 2 **Goodbye Cash (IRE)**[4] 1485 4-9-2 **65** RichardEvans(3) 5 43
(P D Evans) *s.s: hdwy over 2f out: styd on fnl f: nvr nrr* **17/2**
106- 8 1/2 **Orotund**[190] 6256 4-8-9 **55** RobbieEgan 7 32
(T D Easterby) *trckd ldrs: fdd over 1f out* **5/1**[2]
050- 9 4 1/2 **Greek Secret**[192] 6210 5-8-10 **56** PatrickDonaghy 1 18
(J O'Reilly) *in rr: bhd fnl 2f* **20/1**
050- 10 1/2 **Summer Gift**[204] 5890 5-8-0 **51** oh2 JamesRogers(5) 11 12
(J O'Reilly) *chsd ldrs: wknd over 1f out* **20/1**
520- 11 7 **Rue Soleil**[176] 6562 4-8-6 **57** AshleyMorgan(5) 3 —
(J R Weymes) *hld up in rr: bhd fnl 2f* **25/1**

1m 16.38s (2.78) **Going Correction** +0.375s/f (Good) **11** Ran SP% **122.2**
Speed ratings (Par 101): **96,95,93,92,87 86,84,83,77,76 67**
CSF £123.51 CT £331.53 TOTE £11.50: £2.80, £3.90, £1.40; EX 201.30 Place 6 £6,723.57, Place 5 £1,747.94..
Owner Leeway Group Limited **Bred** Bearstone Stud **Trained** Earlswood, Monmouths

FOCUS
A low-grade apprentices' sprint handicap and they all stuck to the far side in the home straight. The runner-up is rated to his form from late last year.
Goodbye Cash(IRE) Official explanation: jockey said filly missed the break
T/Plt: £966.50 to a £1 stake. Pool: £36,609.75. 27.65 winning tickets. T/Qpdt: £122.10 to a £1 stake. Pool: £2,393.40. 14.50 winning tickets. WG

1541 KEMPTON (A.W) (R-H)
Wednesday, April 23

OFFICIAL GOING: Standard
Wind: Almost nil Weather: Fine, mild

1562 OLIVE COMMUNICATIONS H'CAP 1m 4f (P)
6:50 (6:52) (Class 6) (0-55,55) 4-Y-O+ £2,047 (£604; £302) Stalls Centre

Form RPR
-502 1 **Floodlight Fantasy**[10] 1350 5-8-5 **46** (b) HayleyTurner 11 61+
(Dr R D P Newland) *t.k.h early: trckd ldrs: wnt 2nd 2f out: clsd on bit to ld jst over 1f out: sn clr: easily* **16/1**
1230 2 4 **Mixing**[32] 963 6-8-11 **55** KirstyMilczarek(3) 5 60
(M J Attwater) *hld up in midfield: prog over 2f out: drvn and styd on to take 2nd last 100yds: no ch w wnr* **9/2**[2]
-040 3 3/4 **Artzola (IRE)**[56] 716 8-8-11 **52** TQuinn 12 56
(C A Horgan) *s.s: hld up in last trio: rdn and prog fr 2f out: r.o fnl f to take 3rd nr fin* **14/1**
2343 4 1/2 **Bethanys Boy (IRE)**[41] 863 7-9-0 **55** LPKeniry 8 58
(A M Hales) *swtg: led after 2f: kicked on wl over 2f out: hdd jst over 1f out: fdd ins fnl f* **9/1**

-221 **5** *nk* **Classic Blue (IRE)**[82] 387 4-8-8 **50** PaulEddery 7 53
(Ian Williams) *hld up in midfield: prog over 2f out: styd on to chse ldng pair over 1f out: kpt on one pce after* **11/2**[3]

6 *4 1/2* **Joleahs Star (IRE)**[35] 948 4-8-4 **46** oh1 JimmyQuinn 10 41
(Paul Nolan, Ire) *prom: chsd ldr wl over 2f out to 2f out: wknd rapidly fnl f* **8/1**

440- **7** *1* **Chalice Welcome**[24] 1206 5-8-4 **50** oh1 ow4 JackMitchell(5) 3 44
(N B King) *rdn in last trio after 4f: nvr really gng: plugged on u.str.p fnl 2f: no ch* **50/1**

3050 **8** *hd* **Krakatau (FR)**[13] 1282 4-8-5 **47** SimonWhitworth 14 40
(D J Wintle) *trckd ldrs: effrt over 2f out: rdn and nrly disputing 3rd over 1f out: sn wknd rapidly* **10/1**

01/0 **9** *2* **Irish Ballad**[21] 1148 6-8-9 **50** (t) IanMongan 4 40
(S Dow) *settled in midfield: rdn and lost pl 3f out: brief rally 2f out: n.d and sn fdd* **20/1**

5000 **10** *2* **Ndola**[19] 1184 9-8-6 **47** oh1 ow1 (v) JohnEgan 6 34
(P Butler) *a towards rr: rdn and no prog wl over 2f out* **25/1**

1305 **11** *7* **Ben Bacchus (IRE)**[18] 1206 6-8-8 **49** JimCrowley 13 25
(P W Hiatt) *led 2f: chsd ldr: rdn 4f out: wknd wl over 2f out: eased* **4/1**[1]

455- **12** *6* **Dubai Shadow (IRE)**[252] 4518 4-8-13 **55** SebSanders 9 21
(C E Brittain) *chsd ldrs: pushed along wl over 2f out: sn lost pl and bhd* **13/2**

00/4 **13** *1 3/4* **Ardglass (IRE)**[13] 1281 6-8-5 **53** MatthewDavies(7) 1 16
(Mrs P Townsley) *s.v.s: last tl brief effrt 4f out: u.p and btn 3f out* **33/1**

2m 33.59s (-0.91) **Going Correction** 0.0s/f (Stan)
WFA 4 from 5yo+ 1lb **13** Ran SP% **123.2**
Speed ratings (Par 101): **103,100,99,99,99 96,95,95,94,92 88,84,83**
CSF £86.26 CT £1069.26 TOTE £20.30: £6.80, £2.20, £4.70; EX 127.40.
Owner Dr R D P And Mrs L J Newland **Bred** Freynestown Stud **Trained** Claines, Worcs

FOCUS
An ordinary event but Floodlight Fantasy won in the manner of a gelding who is well ahead of the Handicapper. The form looks sound rated through the runner-up.

1563 DIGIBET MEDIAN AUCTION MAIDEN STKS 1m 3f (P)
7:20 (7:22) (Class 6) 3-5-Y-O £2,590 (£770; £385; £192) Stalls High

Form RPR

2 **1** **Sweet Lightning**[16] 1243 3-8-9 0 MartinDwyer 8 76+
(W R Muir) *t.k.h: trckd ldng trio: hung briefly bnd over 9f out: prog to ld 2f out: pushed clr* **8/11**[1]

6- **2** *4 1/2* **Everybody Knows**[232] 5116 3-8-9 0 NCallan 4 69
(M L W Bell) *led: drvn and hdd 2f out: plugged on wl to hold on for 2nd* **10/1**

4533 **3** *1/2* **Bassinet (USA)**[21] 1151 4-9-6 68 KirstyMilczarek(3) 5 66
(J A R Toller) *hld up in midfield: rdn and prog on inner to press ldrs 2f out: nt qckn and sn outpcd* **9/2**[2]

4 *1* **Bell Island**[187] 4-10-0 0 SebSanders 6 69
(Lady Herries) *pressed ldr: rdn to chal over 2f out: nt qckn and sn outpcd: one pce after* **14/1**

423- **5** *shd* **Power Player**[145] 6975 4-10-0 70 EddieAhern 3 69
(D J Coakley) *trckd ldng pair: clsd and tried to chal 2f out: nt qckn and sn one pce* **9/1**[3]

00-3 **6** *4 1/2* **Nikolaievich (IRE)**[11] 1342 3-8-9 68 NelsonDeSouza 1 58
(P F I Cole) *hld up in midfield: hanging bnd over 3f out: outpcd over 2f out: one pce after* **16/1**

7 *3 1/2* **Don't Stop Me Now (IRE)** 3-8-4 0 MatthewHenry 9 47
(J W Hills) *dwlt: mostly in last trio: pushed along and lost tch 3f out: kpt on fnl f* **33/1**

8 *1/2* **Bonzo** 3-8-9 0 JimmyQuinn 2 52
(P Howling) *reluctant to enter stalls: s.i.s: a in last quartet: lft bhd fr over 2f out* **33/1**

/60- **9** *11* **Hawk Gold (IRE)**[128] 6277 4-10-0 40 RichardKingscote 7 36
(P Butler) *a towards rr: pushed along 5f out: wknd and bhd fr over 2f out* **100/1**

10 *35* **Smart Artist** 3-8-9 0 LPKeniry 10 —
(S Kirk) *s.s: a in last pair and rn green: t.o* **40/1**

2m 21.04s (-0.86) **Going Correction** 0.0s/f (Stan)
WFA 3 from 4yo 19lb **10** Ran SP% **117.0**
Speed ratings (Par 101): **103,99,99,98,98 95,92,92,84,58**
CSF £9.04 TOTE £1.70: £1.10, £2.00, £1.80; EX 10.90.
Owner A J De V Patrick & M J Caddy **Bred** Mrs M Lavell **Trained** Lambourn, Berks

FOCUS
No more than a fair maiden, best rated through the reliable third and fifth.

1564 DIGIBET.COM H'CAP 1m 3f (P)
7:50 (7:52) (Class 5) (0-70,70) 4-Y-O+ £2,590 (£770; £385; £192) Stalls High

Form RPR

1023 **1** **Resplendent Ace (IRE)**[12] 1296 4-9-1 **67** JimmyQuinn 10 73
(P Howling) *trckd ldng pair: effrt to ld 2f out: drvn fnl f: hld on all out* **4/1**[2]

0132 **2** *hd* **Turner's Touch**[20] 1164 6-9-4 **70** (b) GeorgeBaker 6 76
(G L Moore) *stdd s: hld up in last: stdy prog through rivals to trck wnr over 1f out: cajoled along to chal fnl f: nvr finding quite enough* **13/2**[3]

41-1 **3** *1* **Sir Duke (IRE)**[3] 1505 4-8-12 **64** 6ex JohnEgan 1 68
(P W D'Arcy) *settled in 6th: pushed along fr 4f out: drvn and effrt on inner to dispute 2nd over 1f out: nt qckn and hld fnl f* **1/1**[1]

6/15 **4** *1 1/2* **Saraba (FR)**[26] 1056 7-8-13 **65** IanMongan 2 67+
(Mrs L J Mongan) *hld up in last trio: prog whn nt clr run 2f out: rdn and styd on one pce fr over 1f out* **12/1**

6253 **5** *3/4* **Megalala (IRE)**[21] 1148 7-8-7 **59** NeilChalmers 3 59
(J J Bridger) *led at mod pce: rdn and hdd 2f out: grad outpcd* **11/1**

1042 **6** *1 3/4* **Steely Dan**[6] 1411 9-9-0 **66** (p) MartinDwyer 5 64
(Mrs L C Jewell) *hld up in 5th: coaxed along fr over 2f out: fnd nil and no imp on ldrs* **20/1**

110- **7** *3/4* **Bold Adventure**[167] 6739 4-9-0 **66** NeilPollard 9 62
(W J Musson) *a in last trio: struggling in last over 2f out: one pce after* **9/1**

636- **8** *nk* **Kokkokila**[160] 6821 4-8-7 **62** KirstyMilczarek(3) 7 58
(Lady Herries) *t.k.h: trckd ldr to over 2f out: lost pl qckly* **14/1**

00-0 **9** *7* **Classic Hall (IRE)**[56] 365 5-8-4 **56** oh11 SimonWhitworth 11 40
(J Akehurst) *t.k.h: trckd ldng pair: losing pl whn hmpd 2f out: sn bhd* **100/1**

2m 21.48s (-0.42) **Going Correction** 0.0s/f (Stan) **9** Ran SP% **121.8**
Speed ratings (Par 103): **101,100,100,99,98 97,96,96,91**
CSF £32.08 CT £45.52 TOTE £6.30: £1.90, £1.80, £1.10; EX 25.50.
Owner Resplendent Racing Limited **Bred** Newlands House Stud **Trained** Newmarket, Suffolk
■ Stewards' Enquiry : Jimmy Quinn one-day ban: used whip with excessive frequency (May 7)

FOCUS
A modest handicap run at an ordinary pace and in a time 0.44sec slower than the earlier maiden. The first two were close to recent form backed up by the fourth.

1565 DIGIBET SPORTS BETTING H'CAP 1m (P)
8:20 (8:21) (Class 6) (0-65,65) 4-Y-O+ £2,047 (£604; £302) Stalls High

Form RPR

-015 **1** **Dinner Date**[26] 1048 6-9-1 **62** J-PGuillambert 9 71
(T Keddy) *trckd ldrs: pushed along and prog to ld over 1f out: drvn fnl f: a holding on* **8/1**

21-3 **2** *1/2* **Oat Cuisine**[15] 1253 4-9-1 **62** HayleyTurner 10 70
(M L W Bell) *trckd ldr: rdn over 2f out: chal wl over 1f out but sn outpcd by wnr: clsd grad fnl f: a hld* **4/1**[1]

6101 **3** *1* **Jessica Wigmo**[18] 1209 5-8-7 **57** LukeMorris(3) 3 63
(A W Carroll) *hld up in last trio: brought wd and gd prog fr over 2f out: drvn to dispute 2nd ent fnl f: no ex last 100yds* **12/1**

3263 **4** *shd* **Pab Special (IRE)**[35] 935 5-8-11 **58** NeilPollard 5 64
(B R Johnson) *hld up at rr of midfield: prog fr over 2f out: chsd ldrs u.p 1f out: kpt on* **5/1**[3]

0-24 **5** *1/2* **Anthill**[21] 1153 4-9-1 **62** NCallan 14 67
(I A Wood) *led and racd freely: drvn and hdd over 1f out: one pce* **7/1**

00-2 **6** *hd* **Daniel Thomas (IRE)**[19] 1182 6-9-3 **64** EddieAhern 6 73+
(Mrs A L M King) *dwlt: hld up wl in rr: effrt on inner whn no room and snatched up over 2f out: styd on fr over 1f out: nrst fin* **7/1**

0-03 **7** *1 3/4* **Quantum Leap**[21] 1153 11-8-8 **62** (v) ThomasBubb(7) 12 62
(S Dow) *t.k.h in midfield: bmpd along and no real imp on inner fnl 2f* **25/1**

4004 **8** *shd* **Trivia (IRE)**[15] 1253 4-8-11 **65** SophieDoyle(7) 1 65
(Ms J S Doyle) *dropped in fr wd draw and hld up in last pair: effrt on outer over 2f out: nt pce to threaten* **25/1**

55-2 **9** *nk* **Fairy Festival (IRE)**[21] 1142 4-8-10 **57** LPKeniry 8 56
(J S Moore) *trckd ldrs: rdn and lost pl jst over 2f out: n.d over 1f out* **14/1**

2521 **10** *1/2* **Having A Ball**[21] 1142 4-8-12 **59** MartinDwyer 4 57
(P D Cundell) *hld up in rr: taken to outer over 2f out: already btn whn shkn up over 1f out* **9/2**[2]

600- **11** *8* **Royal Choir**[183] 6413 4-8-12 **59** SebSanders 11 39
(C E Brittain) *prom tl wknd rapidly fnl 2f* **16/1**

1366 **12** *2 1/2* **Under Fire (IRE)**[30] 996 5-8-8 **62** MarkCoumbe(7) 2 36
(A W Carroll) *missed break bdly and lft 15l: latched on to rr after 3f: wknd over 2f out* **16/1**

1m 40.43s (0.63) **Going Correction** 0.0s/f (Stan) **12** Ran SP% **124.8**
Speed ratings (Par 101): **96,95,94,94,93 93,91,91,91,91 83,80**
CSF £42.19 CT £399.37 TOTE £11.40: £3.10, £1.90, £3.20; EX 54.70.
Owner Mrs H Keddy **Bred** J M Greetham **Trained** Newmarket, Suffolk

FOCUS
A moderate handicap and a messy contest with a couple getting into trouble. The form looks modest and is not sure to prove reliable.
Under Fire(IRE) Official explanation: jockey said gelding missed the break

1566 AZURE H'CAP 7f (P)
8:50 (8:50) (Class 3) (0-90,89) 4-Y-O+
£6,854 (£2,052; £1,026; £513; £256; £128) Stalls High

Form RPR

130- **1** **Al Khaleej (IRE)**[194] 6143 4-9-4 **89** SebSanders 8 107+
(E A L Dunlop) *t.k.h: hld up in last: sliced through field fr over 2f out to ld over 1f out: rdn clr hands and heels* **5/2**[1]

00-2 **2** *3 1/4* **Guilded Warrior**[20] 1174 5-9-2 **87** FergusSweeney 2 96
(W S Kittow) *t.k.h: trckd ldng trio: effrt 2f out: prog to take 2nd last 150yds: styd on but no ch w wnr* **9/1**

0033 **3** *2 1/2* **Resplendent Nova**[11] 1334 6-9-0 **85** JamieSpencer 7 87
(P Howling) *hld up in 6th: pushed along over 2f out: outpcd and rdn over 1f out: styd on to snatch 3rd last stride* **5/2**[1]

30-6 **4** *shd* **Lunces Lad (IRE)**[18] 1211 4-8-3 **81** MatthewDavies(7) 3 83
(M R Channon) *t.k.h: trckd ldr: narrow ld 2f out to over 1f out: wknd ins fnl f* **7/1**[3]

133- **5** *2 1/2* **Titan Triumph**[136] 7087 4-8-8 **79** (t) PaulDoe 1 74
(W J Knight) *t.k.h: hld up in last pair: shkn up over 2f out: kpt on one pce fr over 1f out: n.d* **5/1**[2]

060- **6** *1 1/2* **Phluke**[200] 6006 7-7-13 **77** DanielBlackett(7) 9 68
(Eve Johnson Houghton) *trckd ldng pair: pushed along and easily outpcd fnl 2f* **20/1**

2210 **7** *1* **Super Frank (IRE)**[32] 969 5-8-9 **80** TQuinn 4 68
(J Akehurst) *led to 2f out: wknd rapidly fnl f* **8/1**

3234 **8** *1* **Sand Cat**[10] 1346 5-8-6 **80** (b) MichaelJStainton(3) 5 66
(G L Moore) *racd wd: hld up in 5th: shkn up over 2f out: no rspnse* **14/1**

1m 24.56s (-1.44) **Going Correction** 0.0s/f (Stan) **8** Ran SP% **118.8**
Speed ratings (Par 107): **108,104,101,101,98 96,95,94**
CSF £27.98 CT £63.12 TOTE £3.70: £1.60, £3.20, £1.30; EX 25.70.
Owner Mayoof Sultan **Bred** A Stroud And J Hanly **Trained** Newmarket, Suffolk

FOCUS
A good handicap and an impressive winner. The form is rated fairly positively rated around the placed horses.

NOTEBOOK
Al Khaleej(IRE) ◆ returned from over six months off with the track with a most impressive display, bursting clear when produced with his challenge from off the pace. He is reportedly very buzzy, which is why connections opted to start him off over 7f, but he is smart prospect if his head can be kept right. He is likely to be targeted at some big handicaps this season and the Royal Hunt Cup could be on the agenda. (op 11-4 tchd 7-2)
Guilded Warrior, 2lb higher than when second at Leicester on his reappearance, showed himself every bit as effective on Polytrack as he on soft turf with a decent effort behind the very useful winner. (op 10-1 tchd 12-1)
Resplendent Nova was off the same mark as when winning over this course and distance last August and he ran with credit. (op 3-1 tchd 10-3)
Lunces Lad(IRE) was a little too keen for his own good but this still a reasonable effort. (tchd 6-1)
Titan Triumph was another who raced a little keenly and he can be expected to come on for this first run in 136 days. Official explanation: jockey said colt hung left (tchd 4-1)

1567 KEMPTON FOR SUMMER WEDDINGS H'CAP 6f (P)
9:20 (9:20) (Class 4) (0-80,80) 4-Y-O+ £4,209 (£1,252; £625; £312) Stalls High

Form RPR

2-02 **1** **Valery Borzov (IRE)**[6] 1415 4-9-4 **80** (v) AdrianTNicholls 3 91
(D Nicholls) *plld hrd early and chsd ldr over 4f out: drvn over 2f out: clsd grad u.p over 1f out: edgd ahd last 75yds* **11/8**[1]

4213 **2** *1/2* **Dvinsky (USA)**[6] 1415 7-8-13 **75** (b) JimmyQuinn 1 84
(P Howling) *drvn fr s and led after 100yds: hrd pressed fr over 1f out: hdd last 75yds* **7/2**[2]

1014 **3** *1* **Royal Envoy (IRE)**[6] 1415 5-8-8 **73** .... TolleyDean(3) 4 79
(D Shaw) *in tch: effrt on outer over 2f out: hanging and nt qckn sn after: kpt on fnl f* **7/2**[2]
4-55 **4** *1 1/4* **Cativo Cavallino**[21] 1146 5-8-9 **76** .... NataliaGemelova(5) 6 78
(J E Long) *n.m.r on inner after 1f: chsd ldng pair over 3f out: rdn and no imp over 1f out* **8/1**
-420 **5** *5* **Louphole**[87] 329 6-8-12 **74** .... SebSanders 5 60
(P J Makin) *dwlt: hld up in last pair: effrt over 2f out: rdn and fnd nil over 1f out: wknd* **11/2**[3]
5/ **6** *8* **Chiltai (IRE)**[241] 6380 7-8-7 **69** oh21 ow3 .... NeilChalmers 2 26
(J J Bridger) *led 100yds: last and losing tch sn after 1/2-way* **50/1**

1m 12.41s (-0.69) **Going Correction** 0.0s/f (Stan) **6** Ran SP% **115.0**
Speed ratings (Par 105): **104,103,102,100,93 83**
CSF £6.77 TOTE £2.70: £2.00, £1.80; EX 4.80 Place 6 £21.50, Place 5 £4.15..
Owner D Kilburn/I Hewitson/D Nicholls **Bred** Vincent Harrington **Trained** Sessay, N Yorks
■ Stewards' Enquiry : Adrian T Nicholls two-day ban: used whip with excessive frequency (May 7-8)

FOCUS
A fair sprint run at a good pace. It is a straightforward race to rate, with the winner and runner-up running close to their recent course and distance form.
T/Plt: £25.70 to a £1 stake. Pool: £63,461.92. 1,802.36 winning tickets. T/Qpdt: £2.30 to a £1 stake. Pool: £5,483.00. 1,728.50 winning tickets. JN

1474 NOTTINGHAM (L-H)
Wednesday, April 23

OFFICIAL GOING: Good to soft (soft in places; 6.8)
This meeting was transferred from Epsom whilst redevelopment goes on at the Surrey track.
Wind: Light across Weather: Overcast

1568 INTERCASINO.CO.UK H'CAP — 1m 6f 15y
2:20 (2:21) (Class 3) (0-95,95) 4-Y-0+
£9,346 (£2,799; £1,399; £700; £349; £175) **Stalls** Low

Form RPR
112- **1** **Double Banded (IRE)**[166] 6744 4-9-0 **86** .... KerrinMcEvoy 5 97+
(J L Dunlop) *chsd ldrs: led over 1f out: rdn out* **8/1**[2]
344- **2** *1 3/4* **Tilt**[212] 5677 6-9-3 **87** .... (p) TomEaves 4 93
(B Ellison) *trckd ldrs: racd keenly: rdn over 1f out: styd on* **8/1**[2]
5/ **3** *1 1/2* **Talenti (IRE)**[26] 5-9-8 **92** .... AlanMunro 8 96
(Miss E C Lavelle) *sn led: rdn and hdd over 1f out: styd on same pce ins fnl f* **33/1**
5641 **4** *2 1/4* **Pass The Port**[31] 981 7-8-10 **80** .... NCallan 14 81
(D Haydn Jones) *hld up: hdwy over 2f out: rdn over 1f out: styng on same pce whn edgd lft fnl f* **16/1**
03-0 **5** *3/4* **Sahrati**[28] 1026 4-9-4 **90** .... RyanMoore 1 90
(C E Brittain) *hld up: rdn over 3f out: nt clr run over 1f out: nt rch ldrs* **12/1**
1413 **6** *1/2* **Millville**[32] 968 8-9-6 **90** .... PhilipRobinson 9 91+
(M A Jarvis) *prom: nt clr run and lost pl over 1f out: styd on ins fnl f* **12/1**
-211 **7** *1/2* **Puy D'Arnac (FR)**[12] 1299 5-8-5 **78** .... PJMcDonald(3) 11 76+
(G A Swinbank) *trckd ldrs: rdn over 2f out: hung lft and wknd ins fnl f* **2/1**[1]
56-4 **8** *nk* **Prince Sabaah (IRE)**[18] 1212 4-8-13 **85** .... RichardHughes 13 83
(R Hannon) *hld up: rdn over 2f out: nvr nrr* **10/1**[3]
051- **9** *3/4* **Inchnadamph**[165] 6760 8-9-7 **91** .... (t) PaulHanagan 10 88+
(T J Fitzgerald) *hld up: racd keenly: rdn over 2f out: n.d* **22/1**
462- **10** *3/4* **Kasthari (IRE)**[165] 6760 9-9-11 **95** .... TedDurcan 7 91
(J D Bethell) *chsd ldrs: rdn over 2f out: wknd fnl f: eased nr fin* **28/1**
500- **11** *nse* **Odiham**[85] 6335 7-9-4 **88** .... SteveDrowne 12 84
(Dr R D P Newland) *chsd ldr tl rdn over 2f out: wknd over 1f out* **25/1**
0-12 **12** *3/4* **Man Of Gwent (UAE)**[63] 626 4-8-10 **82** .... JimCrowley 2 77
(P D Evans) *hld up: racd keenly: hmpd over 6f out: rdn over 2f out: wknd over 1f out* **11/1**
424- **13** *1* **Lets Roll**[180] 6473 7-9-1 **85** .... JimmyFortune 6 78
(C W Thornton) *hld up: edgd lft over 6f out: rdn and wknd over 2f out* **14/1**
110- **14** *5* **Polish Red**[269] 3993 4-8-8 **80** .... JohnEgan 3 66
(G G Margarson) *hld up: plld hrd: hdwy over 3f out: wknd 2f out* **11/1**

3m 11.99s (4.69) **Going Correction** +0.225s/f (Good)
WFA 4 from 5yo+ 2lb **14** Ran SP% **123.8**
Speed ratings (Par 107): **95,94,93,91,91 91,90,90,90,89 89,89,88,85**
CSF £69.68 CT £2036.34 TOTE £8.50: £2.70, £2.90, £12.60; EX 61.80 TRIFECTA Not won..
Owner Sir Thomas Pilkington **Bred** Sir Thomas Pilkington **Trained** Arundel, W Sussex

FOCUS
This race was the equivalent of the Great Metropolitan Handicap when it is run at Epsom, but over an extra 2f making it closer to its traditional distance of 2m2f. However, despite looking a competitive event on paper, the pace was very moderate for most of the journey which meant that it was not the test of stamina it might have been. Those that raced handily were therefore at an advantage and the form may not prove that solid.

NOTEBOOK
Double Banded(IRE), making his seasonal reappearance off a 4lb higher mark than when last seen, was given a very intelligent ride in a steadily run race as his rider had him stalking the leaders throughout. His only problem came when it looked as though he might not be able to get out with Kasthari holding him in, but he was extricated in plenty of time and quickly put the race to bed. This was his fifth win from his last seven starts and the yard have done extremely well with staying handicappers over the years, so there is probably more to come. (op 7-1 tchd 17-2)
Tilt, returning from seven months off, was another that was helped by being ridden handily in a steadily run race and despite racing with plenty of enthusiasm never gave up trying. His consistency is a problem though, as he is currently off his highest mark for 18 months despite not having won for two years. (op 11-1)
Talenti(IRE), having his first run on the Flat for two years but fit from hurdling, very much had the run of the race out in front and set his own modest tempo. That enabled him to battle on for a place in the frame even after the winner had swooped past him and although this was a creditable effort, the way the race was run might mean this performance flatters him.
Pass The Port, raised 2lb for his narrow Musselburgh victory, did not get the race run to suit him this time but he stayed on really well down the wide outside in the home straight and fared much the best of the hold-up performers. (tchd 18-1)
Sahrati, back on turf after a miserable return to action on Fibresand, would have finished a bit closer had he not taken so long to get around the weakening Kasthari but would never have won.
Millville, off a 17lb lower mark than on sand, had fitness on his side and was going the right way round this time. He got caught in traffic halfway up the home straight, but lacked the pace to get himself out of trouble straight away and by the time he did all he could do was stay on at one pace. A proper gallop would have suited him better, but that would have been the case with several of his rivals too. (op 11-1 tchd 14-1)
Puy D'Arnac(FR), bidding for a hat-trick off a 6lb higher mark, could never get cover and saw too much daylight as a result. He had his chance up the home straight, but was making hard work of it from some way out and was beaten fair and square. (op 11-4)

1569 INTERCASINO.CO.UK STKS (HERITAGE H'CAP) — 1m 2f 50y
2:55 (2:56) (Class 2) (0-105,100) 4-Y-0+
£21,808 (£6,531; £3,265; £1,634; £815; £409) **Stalls** Low

Form RPR
142- **1** **Cabinet (IRE)**[207] 5805 4-9-3 **93** .... RyanMoore 13 107+
(Sir Michael Stoute) *trckd ldrs: rdn over 1f out: hung lft ins fnl f: styd on to ld nr fin* **6/4**[1]
64-2 **2** *nk* **Eradicate (IRE)**[29] 1018 4-9-5 **95** .... JoeFanning 8 108
(M Johnston) *chsd ldrs: led over 2f out: rdn over 1f out: hdd nr fin* **15/2**[3]
16-3 **3** *2 1/2* **Heaven Knows**[29] 1018 5-9-4 **94** .... RHills 12 102
(W J Haggas) *s.i.s: hld up: hdwy over 2f out: rdn and hung lft over 1f out: nt rch ldrs* **11/2**[2]
163- **4** *2* **Night Crescendo (USA)**[165] 6759 5-9-8 **98** .... JimCrowley 1 102+
(Mrs A J Perrett) *hld up: hdwy over 2f out: rdn over 1f out: styd on* **12/1**
103- **5** *6* **Tears Of A Clown (IRE)**[208] 5764 5-8-13 **89** .... TPQueally 10 81
(J A Osborne) *hld up: hdwy 3f out: sn rdn: wknd over 1f out* **9/1**
1-40 **6** *nk* **Suits Me**[25] 1072 5-8-8 **84** .... MickyFenton 14 75
(T P Tate) *led over 7f: wknd fnl f* **25/1**
40-6 **7** *1 1/2* **Mull Of Dubai**[29] 1018 5-8-12 **88** .... JohnEgan 5 76
(T P Tate) *hld up: rdn over 2f out: nvr nrr* **25/1**
200- **8** *nk* **Peruvian Prince (USA)**[193] 6169 6-8-13 **89** .... PaulHanagan 2 79+
(R A Fahey) *hld up in tch: rdn over 2f out: wknd fnl f* **40/1**
0-3 **9** *1 1/4* **Northern Jem**[5] 1456 4-8-7 **83** .... RichardHughes 7 69+
(G G Margarson) *plld hrd and prom: rdn over 2f out: wknd over 1f out* **18/1**
050- **10** *1 1/4* **Pevensey (IRE)**[18] 6169 6-9-4 **94** .... GrahamGibbons 4 77
(J J Quinn) *hld up: rdn over 3f out: n.d* **33/1**
0-44 **11** *hd* **Rio Riva**[22] 1133 6-9-10 **100** .... JimmyFortune 11 82
(Miss J A Camacho) *hld up: hdwy over 2f out: wkng whn n.m.r 2f out* **20/1**
30-1 **12** *6* **Best Prospect (IRE)**[25] 1072 6-9-3 **93** .... (t) JamieSpencer 16 63
(M Dods) *hld up: rdn and hung lft over 2f out: n.d* **11/1**
22-0 **13** *2* **Ella Woodcock (IRE)**[32] 958 4-8-12 **88** .... TedDurcan 9 54
(E J Alston) *chsd ldrs: rdn over 2f out: wknd over 1f out* **40/1**
321- **14** *3 1/2* **Longspur**[238] 4948 4-8-7 **83** .... TomEaves 6 42
(M W Easterby) *hld up: rdn over 3f out: sn wknd* **33/1**
6425 **15** *1* **Moonlight Man**[12] 1314 7-8-11 **87** .... LiamJones 3 44
(C R Dore) *hld up in tch: rdn over 3f out: wknd 2f out* **80/1**
1311 **16** *nk* **Maslak (IRE)**[55] 735 4-9-0 **90** .... DarrenWilliams 15 47
(P W Hiatt) *chsd ldrs: rdn over 3f out: wknd wl over 1f out* **40/1**

2m 13.96s (1.46) **Going Correction** +0.225s/f (Good) **16** Ran SP% **125.3**
Speed ratings (Par 109): **109,108,106,105,100 100,98,98,97,96 96,91,90,87,86 86**
CSF £11.44 CT £55.19 TOTE £2.50: £1.30, £1.70, £1.90, £3.10; EX 17.90 Trifecta £46.20 Pool £514.10 - 7.90 winning units..
Owner The Royal Ascot Racing Club **Bred** Hascombe And Valiant Studs **Trained** Newmarket, Suffolk

FOCUS
This race was the equivalent of Epsom's City And Suburban Handicap and unlike the previous contest, this was run at a better pace. The front four pulled a long way clear of the others and the race could be rated a little higher.

NOTEBOOK
Cabinet(IRE), returning from a seven-month absence off a 4lb higher mark, was all the rage in the market. He settled well behind the leaders, but took a long time to organise himself when asked to go after the leader coming to the last furlong and also tended to hang. He got the job done though, if only just, and probably still has some improvement in him. He gave the impression here that he will get further which would bring races like Royal Ascot's Duke Of Edinburgh Handicap into the equation. (op 15-8 tchd 2-1)
Eradicate(IRE), who had the advantage of a recent run, was given a canny ride as, with his stamina not in doubt, he was sent to the front a fair way from home and tried to steal it. He very nearly succeeded too, and was only cut down late by a rival who may go on to better things but there should be a nice handicap or two to be won with him as well. (op 13-2)
Heaven Knows, suited by this ground, had finished over three lengths behind Eradicate on his Pontefract reappearance, but was only 1lb better off. Given plenty to do, he was forced to make his effort wide and stayed on strongly late despite edging left as he did so. He is 6lb higher than for his last win, but looks capable of winning off it given his ground and when things go his way. (op 5-1 tchd 6-1)
Night Crescendo(USA), having his first start since finishing third in the November Handicap and now 4lb higher, was doing all his best work late and pulled a long way clear of the others. The ground would have suited, but this performance suggests he needs the extra 2f now.
Tears Of A Clown(IRE), reappearing from seven months off, has won after a similar layoff in the past so it is debatable how much he needed it. He saw plenty of daylight on the outside and that may have been a bigger problem, so he probably ran his race under the circumstances. (op 10-1 tchd 17-2)
Suits Me, given his usual positive ride, tried hard to make all but looked rather awkward after he was headed and eventually fell away. (op 50-1)
Mull Of Dubai, a long way behind Eradicate and Heaven Knows on his debut for the yard at Pontefract last month, made some late progress without being able to land a blow. He is still 7lb above his last winning mark, but seems to retain some ability which will be handy for when he is more feasibly handicapped. (op 22-1 tchd 20-1)
Northern Jem Official explanation: jockey said gelding lost its action

1570 INTERCASINO.CO.UK CONDITIONS STKS — 1m 2f 50y
3:30 (3:30) (Class 2) 3-Y-O **£12,462** (£3,732; £1,866) **Stalls** Low

Form RPR
215- **1** **Curtain Call (FR)**[179] 6489 3-9-5 0 .... JamieSpencer 1 113+
(L M Cumani) *hld up: hdwy 3f out: led over 1f out: shkn up and r.o wl* **8/11**[1]
20-1 **2** *6* **Drill Sergeant**[18] 1221 3-9-1 95 .... JoeFanning 4 97
(M Johnston) *chsd ldr: rdn over 2f out: styd on same pce appr fnl f* **3/1**[2]
04-1 **3** *1 1/2* **Bold Choice (IRE)**[8] 1382 3-9-1 96 .... PhilipRobinson 2 94
(M A Jarvis) *led: rdn and hdd over 1f out: no ex* **3/1**[2]

2m 14.44s (1.94) **Going Correction** +0.225s/f (Good) **3** Ran SP% **107.9**
Speed ratings (Par 104): **107,102,101**
CSF £3.13 TOTE £1.50; EX 2.50.
Owner Mrs P K Cooper and Partners **Bred** Famille Niarchos **Trained** Newmarket, Suffolk

FOCUS
The equivalent of Epsom's Blue Riband Trial Stakes, but still a small field for a race that has failed to attract more than five runners in the past ten years. The winning time was nearly half a second slower than the preceding older-horse handicap, but considering the size of the field and the age of those taking part the time was not bad at all and that was purely down to the decent pace set by Bold Choice. The winner was impressive and the form looks sound rated around the other two.

NOTEBOOK

Curtain Call(FR) ◆, winner of the Group 2 Beresford Stakes last season for Jessica Harrington, was second-favourite for the Derby prior to this debut for his new yard and this performance did nothing to undermine that. Always travelling like a dream adrift of his two rivals, he eventually moved up outside on the bridle and when finally asked to quicken, he had little difficulty in scooting clear in impressive style. He had no problem with this longer trip in a race run at a true gallop, though admittedly he had the ground in his favour, and he will stay further. He will now head for the Lingfield Derby Trial in which his trainer was successful with the subsequent Derby-winners Kahyasi and High-Rise. (op 4-5 tchd 4-6)

Drill Sergeant, impressive under similar conditions in a Newcastle maiden on his return to action, was unable to get his own way out in front this time thanks to Bold Choice, but despite being totally outclassed by the winner he stayed on to win the separate race for second. He still has a bit of scope, but will need to improve in order to defy a mark of 95 in handicap company. (op 11-4 tchd 7-2)

Bold Choice(IRE), easy winner of a maiden over a similar trip here on his return to action and suited by soft ground, tried to make every yard once again but he found these rivals a totally different kettle of fish. He is another that will probably need to find improvement in order to be effective in handicap company off this sort of mark. (op 7-2 tchd 11-4)

1571 PLAY BLACKJACK AT INTERCASINO.CO.UK H'CAP 5f 13y

4:05 (4:05) (Class 3) (0-95,95) 4-Y-0+

£6,542 (£1,959; £979; £490; £244; £122) **Stalls** High

Form				RPR
41-2	1		**Chief Editor**[11] 1325 4-9-3 **94** JamieSpencer 6 (M J Wallace) *hld up: rdn and r.o ins fnl f: led nr fin* **5/4**[1]	105+
0010	2	¾	**Canadian Danehill (IRE)**[11] 1325 6-9-4 **95** (p) NCallan 9 (R M H Cowell) *chsd ldr: rdn over 1f out: led ins fnl f: hdd nr fin* **22/1**	99
00-5	3	nk	**Bond City (IRE)**[11] 1325 6-8-12 **92** PJMcDonald(3) 4 (G R Oldroyd) *chsd ldrs: rdn and ev ch ins fnl f: unable qckn towards fin* **14/1**	95
0-00	4	nk	**Cape Royal**[11] 1325 8-8-7 **87** (bt) KevinGhunowa(3) 5 (J M Bradley) *led: rdn and edgd lft fr over 1f out: hdd and unable qckn ins fnl f* **12/1**	89
030-	5	hd	**How's She Cuttin' (IRE)**[179] 6487 5-8-9 **86** PhillipMakin 8 (T D Barron) *chsd ldrs: rdn 1/2-way: edgd lft fnl f: no ex nr fin* **9/1**	87
0002	6	1 ¾	**Baby Strange**[12] 1300 4-8-10 **87** PaulHanagan 1 (D Shaw) *sn pushed along in rr: rdn over 1f out: nvr trbld ldrs* **8/1**[3]	82
0-61	7	shd	**Luscivious**[7] 1393 4-8-9 **86** 6ex ow1 (b) StephenDonohoe 2 (A J McCabe) *s.i.s: hld up: hdwy u.p over 1f out: no ex ins fnl f* **4/1**[2]	80
0250	8	shd	**Fyodor (IRE)**[12] 1300 7-9-2 **93** LiamJones 7 (W J Haggas) *trckd ldrs: rdn and ev ch whn hung lft fr over 1f out: wknd wl ins fnl f* **20/1**	87
/60-	9	nk	**Fantasy Explorer**[326] 2234 5-8-9 **86** RyanMoore 3 (J J Quinn) *hld up: hdwy over 1f out: sn rdn: wknd wl ins fnl f* **16/1**	79

62.67 secs (1.97) **Going Correction** +0.575s/f (Yiel) **9** Ran SP% **114.9**
Speed ratings (Par 107): **107,105,105,104,104 101,101,101,100**
CSF £34.19 CT £276.03 TOTE £1.80: £1.02, £5.00, £3.00; EX 23.60.
Owner Mrs P Good **Bred** J R And Mrs P Good **Trained** Newmarket, Suffolk

FOCUS
A good, competitive sprint handicap. They raced towards the stands' rail, but spread out towards the middle of the track.

NOTEBOOK

Chief Editor ◆ defied a 3lb rise in the weights for his second at Doncaster on his reappearance under a fine ride from the joint champion. Although just about last a furlong out, he was travelling noticeably strongly close enough to the leaders and picked up well when Spencer found a gap between Canadian Danehill and Cape Royal, just off the stands' rail. He is very useful and should continue to progress, although he does seem to need easy ground. (tchd 11-8)

Canadian Danehill(IRE) had every chance against the stands' rail and ran much better than at Doncaster on his previous start, getting much closer to Chief Editor this time. (op 20-1 tchd 25-1)

Bond City(IRE) improved on the form he showed at Doncaster on his reappearance, although he was unable to confirm form with Canadian Danehill. He raced more towards the middle of the track than the front two, but seemed to have his chance. (op 18-1 tchd 12-1)

Cape Royal ◆ has dropped to a good mark, 3lb lower than when last winning, and this was an encouraging effort. His stable seem to be emerging from a bit of a lean spell and he appeals as one to have on-side in similar events in the coming weeks. (op 14-1 tchd 11-1)

How's She Cuttin'(IRE) ◆ ran with credit after six months off and she can improve on this. (tchd 17-2 and 10-1, 8-1 in a place)

Baby Strange lacked the pace of some of these and will probably do better back over 6f. (op 6-1)

Luscivious was 1lb well-in under the penalty he picked up for his recent Beverley success, but he was stuck out widest of all and never looked a real threat. Official explanation: jockey said gelding banged its head on leaving stalls (tchd 9-2 in places)

1572 PLAY ROULETTE AT INTERCASINO.CO.UK H'CAP 1m 75y

4:40 (4:40) (Class 5) (0-75,74) 3-Y-0 **£2,914** (£867; £433; £216) **Stalls** Centre

Form				RPR
1-	1		**Wasan**[158] 6850 3-9-4 **74** RHills 6 (E A L Dunlop) *chsd ldrs: led 2f out: rdn clr fr over 1f out* **5/4**[1]	93+
5-04	2	6	**Randama Bay (IRE)**[26] 1057 3-9-3 **73** RyanMoore 4 (I A Wood) *chsd ldrs: lost pl over 5f out: outpcd 3f out: swtchd rt and hdwy u.p over 1f out: no ch w wnr* **16/1**	73
003-	3	½	**Nino Cochise (IRE)**[131] 7140 3-9-1 **71** SteveDrowne 5 (C R Egerton) *chsd ldrs: rdn over 2f out: wknd ins fnl f* **14/1**	70
45-6	4	2 ½	**High Plains (FR)**[18] 1216 3-9-2 **72** RichardHughes 7 (R Hannon) *led: hdd over 6f out: chsd ldrs: rdn over 1f out: wknd fnl f* **6/1**[3]	65
350-	5	1 ½	**Transmission (IRE)**[223] 5350 3-9-4 **74** TomEaves 9 (B Smart) *led over 6f out: rdn and hdd 2f out: wknd fnl f* **5/1**[2]	64
03-3	6	1	**Moonlight Angel**[26] 1050 3-9-4 **74** AdamKirby 1 (W R Swinburn) *hld up in tch: rdn over 2f out: wknd over 1f out* **10/1**	61
620	7	¾	**Moonage Daydream (IRE)**[21] 1139 3-8-9 **65** GrahamGibbons 8 (T D Easterby) *plld hrd and prom: stdd and lost pl over 6f out: rdn and hung lft fr over 2f out: n.d* **25/1**	51
330-	8	nk	**Mon Plaisir (USA)**[196] 6107 3-9-3 **73** TedDurcan 2 (J L Dunlop) *hld up: rdn over 2f out: wknd over 1f out* **8/1**	58
2-00	9	12	**Averoo**[12] 1297 3-9-0 **70** TPQueally 3 (M D Squance) *hld up: rdn over 3f out: wknd wl over 1f out* **33/1**	27

1m 49.62s (4.22) **Going Correction** +0.225s/f (Good) **9** Ran SP% **114.9**
Speed ratings (Par 98): **95,89,88,86,84 83,82,82,70**
CSF £24.56 CT £197.69 TOTE £1.90: £1.40, £3.00, £3.30; EX 25.10.
Owner Hamdan Al Maktoum **Bred** Belgrave Bloodstock **Trained** Newmarket, Suffolk

FOCUS
A fair handicap, but the winner was in a different league with the form rated around the placed horses. The pace was modest and the winning time was 0.51 seconds slower than the following maiden.

Moonlight Angel Official explanation: jockey said filly had no more to give

1573 INTERCASINO.CO.UK MAIDEN STKS 1m 75y

5:15 (5:17) (Class 5) 3-Y-0+ **£2,914** (£867; £433; £216) **Stalls** Centre

Form				RPR
30-	1		**Tarkheena Prince (USA)**[267] 4037 3-8-9 0 PJMcDonald(3) 12 (G A Swinbank) *trckd ldrs: led over 1f out: edgd lft: rdn out* **7/1**	84
4-	2	nk	**Hawk Island (IRE)**[174] 6602 3-8-12 0 SteveDrowne 10 (G Wragg) *hld up in tch: racd keenly: rdn and ev ch fr over 1f out: edgd lft: unable qckn towards fin* **13/2**[3]	83
	3	4 ½	**Light From Mars** 3-8-12 0 AlanMunro 15 (B R Millman) *hld up: hdwy over 2f out: rdn and edgd lft over 1f out: no ex fnl f* **33/1**	73
32-	4	shd	**Just Rob**[175] 6593 3-8-9 0 RussellKennemore(3) 7 (R Hollinshead) *hld up: hdwy over 2f out: nt clr run over 1f out: nt rch ldrs* **17/2**	73+
6-	5	2 ¼	**Ascot Lime**[224] 5323 3-8-12 0 RyanMoore 9 (Sir Michael Stoute) *hld up: rdn over 3f out: swtchd rt over 1f out: nvr trbld ldrs* **13/8**[1]	68
50-2	6	2 ¾	**Tactical Move**[12] 1298 3-8-7 74 SCreighton(5) 11 (Miss V Haigh) *chsd ldr: led 2f out: sn rdn: hung lft and hdd: wknd fnl f* **25/1**	61
060-	7	nk	**Seventh Hill**[203] 5919 3-8-12 77 JamesDoyle 1 (M Blanshard) *hld up in tch: rdn over 2f out: wknd fnl f* **22/1**	61
05/-	8	2 ¾	**Bold Bobby Be (IRE)**[559] 5918 4-9-12 0 KerrinMcEvoy 6 (J L Dunlop) *hld up: rdn over 1f out: nvr nrr* **16/1**	54
5-	9	2	**Totoman**[258] 4325 3-8-12 0 JoeFanning 2 (G G Margarson) *chsd ldrs tl rdn and wknd over 1f out* **25/1**	50
50-	10	½	**Defies Logic**[209] 5749 3-8-12 0 TPQueally 14 (J G Given) *hld up: rdn over 3f out: sn hung rt: n.d* **100/1**	48
	11	1 ½	**Rye Rocket** 3-8-12 0 FergusSweeney 3 (K R Burke) *sn pushed along in rr: effrt over 3f out: wknd over 2f out* **50/1**	45
0-	12	4 ½	**Ejeed (USA)**[168] 6724 3-8-12 0 RHills 5 (J H M Gosden) *sn led: rdn and hdd 2f out: sn wknd* **9/2**[2]	35
	13	¾	**Capucci** 3-8-12 0 JimmyFortune 13 (J H M Gosden) *hld up: rdn over 3f out: wknd 2f out* **12/1**	33
00-	14	½	**Rosentraub**[182] 6436 3-8-12 0 TedDurcan 4 (H J L Dunlop) *plld hrd and prom: wknd over 1f out* **18/1**	32

1m 49.11s (3.71) **Going Correction** +0.225s/f (Good)
WFA 3 from 4yo 14lb **14** Ran SP% **129.4**
Speed ratings (Par 103): **97,96,92,92,89 87,86,84,82,81 80,75,74,74**
CSF £52.83 TOTE £8.30: £2.70, £2.30, £9.50; EX 62.00 Place 6 £98.51, Place 5 £18.86..
Owner G H Bell **Bred** Whitewood Stable Inc **Trained** Melsonby, N Yorks

FOCUS
A fair maiden and the winning time was 0.51 seconds quicker than the previous 61-75 handicap. The form makes sense.

Just Rob ◆ Official explanation: jockey said colt was denied a clear run
Defies Logic Official explanation: jockey said gelding hung right
T/Jkpt: £4,714.10 to a £1 stake. Pool: £1,645,295.50. 247.80 winning tickets. T/Plt: £85.00 to a £1 stake. Pool: £102,854.11. 883.30 winning tickets. T/Qpdt: £16.20 to a £1 stake. Pool: £3,486.30. 158.40 winning tickets. CR

1390 BEVERLEY (R-H)

Thursday, April 24

OFFICIAL GOING: Good to soft (good in places) changing to good to soft (soft in places) after race 3 (3.15)
Wind: Virtually nil Weather: Overcast and showers

1574 NEW T-MOBILE BEVERLEY STORE CLAIMING STKS 5f

2:00 (2:02) (Class 5) 2-Y-0 **£2,428** (£722; £361; £180) **Stalls** High

Form				RPR
6	1		**Dispol Diva**[7] 1425 2-8-7 0 JamieMoriarty(3) 6 (P T Midgley) *in tch: hdwy 1/2-way: rdn wl over 1f out: styd on to ld ins fnl f* **17/2**	55
64	2	4	**Dazzling Dust (IRE)**[5] 1480 2-9-0 0 (p) AshleyMorgan(7) 5 (W G M Turner) *cl up: led over 2f out: rdn clr over 1f out: drvn and hdd ins fnl f: one pce* **11/4**[1]	50
6	3	3 ¼	**Kheley (IRE)**[9] 1384 2-8-8 0 LiamJones 1 (W M Brisbourne) *wnt lft s: sn led: rdn: hung bdly lft and hdd over 2f out: sn drvn and wknd* **9/2**[2]	24
65	4	½	**Talulah Bells**[9] 1384 2-8-1 0 LukeMorris(3) 4 (A W Carroll) *rr: hdwy 1/2-way: sn rdn and no imp* **7/1**	18
	5	2	**Ron's Princess (IRE)** 2-8-1 0 PatrickDonaghy(7) 3 (P C Haslam) *towards rr: rdn along after 2f and nvr a factor* **11/4**[1]	14
5	6	½	**Quadrifolio**[8] 1392 2-8-13 0 KimTinkler 2 (N Tinkler) *chsd ldng pair: rdn along 1/2-way: sn wknd* **5/1**[3]	17

1m 10.83s (7.33) **Going Correction** +1.275s/f (Soft) **6** Ran SP% **111.2**
Speed ratings (Par 92): **92,85,80,79,76 75**
CSF £31.36 TOTE £15.40: £4.40, £1.20; EX 36.10.
Owner W B Imison **Bred** P C Hunt **Trained** Westow, N Yorks
■ Stewards' Enquiry : Jamie Moriarty six-day ban: used whip with excessive frequency in the incorrect position (May 8-10, 12-14)

FOCUS
Weak form and not a race to dwell on.

NOTEBOOK

Dispol Diva, a cheap purchase whose dam placed over 1m4f in Germany, showed little on her debut, but she was dropping in grade and she came home well as her stamina kicked in. She will get further than this but the form is nothing to write home about. (op 11-1)

Dazzling Dust(IRE), fourth in similar company at Thirsk last time, was wearing cheekpieces for the first time and showed good speed. He just did not see the trip out as well as the winner. (tchd 5-2 and 3-1)

Kheley(IRE), too green to do herself justice on her debut, again showed signs of inexperience by veering left leaving the stalls. She also hung left when beginning to tire. Quicker ground might help her. (tchd 4-1 and 5-1)

Talulah Bells, well held in sellers on her first two starts, failed to show any improvement. (op 4-1)

Ron's Princess(IRE), whose dam won over 5f at four, ran a bit green and never got in a blow. She will appreciate further in time. (tchd 7-2)

Quadrifolio, whose dam won between 1m1f and 1m2f, is bred to want a good deal further in time. (op 10-1 tchd 11-1)

1575 BRYAN DUNN AND JOHN WADE H'CAP — 1m 1f 207y

2:35 (2:36) (Class 5) (0-70,74) 3-Y-O — £2,590 (£770; £385; £192) Stalls High

Form				RPR
4-41	1		**Duke Of Touraine (IRE)**[8] 1396 3-9-1 **74** 6ex......... PatrickDonaghy(7) 5	80
			(P C Haslam) *hld up in tch: hdwy 3f out: effrt and nt clr run wl over 1f out: rdn to chal on inner appr last: styd on to ld last 100yds* **11/8**[1]	
34-4	2	3/4	**Highland Love**[22] 1161 3-8-13 **65**................................ PaulMulrennan 1	69
			(Jedd O'Keeffe) *cl up: led wl over 1f out and sn rdn: drvn ent fnl f: hdd and no ex last 100yds* **3/1**[2]	
5000	3	3 1/4	**Natural Rhythm (IRE)**[6] 1448 3-8-5 **60**.................... AndrewMullen(3) 3	58
			(Mrs R A Carr) *dwlt: hld up in rr: hdwy on outer 3f out: rdn and ch wl over 1f out: edgd rt and wknd ent fnl f* **22/1**	
500	4	1 1/2	**Fairfield Flame (GER)**[40] 903 3-8-9 **61**........................... AlanMunro 2	56
			(D R C Elsworth) *chsd ldrs: pushed along over 4f out: rdn along 3f out: kpt on same pce fnl 2f* **9/1**	
263-	5	15	**Azure Mist**[167] 6740 3-9-4 **70**... JimmyQuinn 6	35
			(M H Tompkins) *trckd ldng pair: effrt 3f out: rdn along 2f out and sn wknd* **5/1**[3]	
054-	6	5	**Chaenomeles (USA)**[183] 6432 3-9-2 **68**........................... JoeFanning 4	23
			(M Johnston) *led: rdn along over 2f out: hdd wl over 1f out and sn wknd* **7/1**	

2m 16.49s (9.49) **Going Correction** +0.75s/f (Yiel) — **6** Ran SP% **110.6**
Speed ratings (Par 98): **92,91,88,87,75 71**
CSF £5.47 TOTE £2.00: £1.40, £1.90; EX 6.50.
Owner Middleham Park Racing & John J Maguire **Bred** F Bayrou&haras De Son Altesse L'Aga Khan **Trained** Middleham Moor, N Yorks
■ Stewards' Enquiry : Patrick Donaghy one-day ban: careless riding (May 8)

FOCUS
An ordinary handicap which cannot be rated too favourably with the out of form Natural Rhythm finishing third. The winning time was moderate but the winner is rated to his latest mark.

1576 DADIE'S BIRTHDAY CELEBRATION STKS (H'CAP) — 7f 100y

3:10 (3:10) (Class 3) (0-90,84) 3-Y-O — £6,799 (£2,023; £1,011; £505) Stalls High

Form				RPR
6-12	1		**Albaqaa**[7] 1428 3-8-12 **78**.. PaulHanagan 8	87
			(R A Fahey) *hld up in tch: hdwy on inner over 2f out: rdn to chal over 1f out: styd on u.p to ld last 150yds* **15/8**[1]	
R41-	2	2	**Toto Skyllachy**[294] 3238 3-9-4 **84**.. MickyFenton 7	87
			(T P Tate) *trckd ldrs: hdwy on inner 1/2-way: led 3f out: rdn wl over 1f out: drvn ent fnl f: edgd lft: hdd and no ex last 150yds* **13/2**[3]	
21-3	3	1 1/4	**Atabaas Pride**[33] 966 3-9-0 **80**.. JoeFanning 4	80
			(M Johnston) *trckd ldrs: hdwy over 2f out: rdn to chse ldng pair over 1f out: edgd rt and one pce ent fnl f* **2/1**[2]	
104-	4	5	**Joinedupwriting**[193] 6194 3-8-11 **77**........................... DeanMcKeown 2	64
			(R M Whitaker) *hld up towards rr: hdwy over 2f out: rdn and kpt on ins fnl f: nrst fin* **20/1**	
41-5	5	nk	**Thunderstruck**[8] 1395 3-9-0 **80**.. JamieSpencer 1	66
			(K A Ryan) *hld up in tch on outer: hdwy whn hung lft home to stands' rail home turn: rdn wl over 1f out: kpt on same pce* **15/2**	
1114	6	3 1/4	**Dhhamaan (IRE)**[12] 1339 3-8-11 **80**......................(b) AndrewMullen(3) 6	58
			(Mrs R A Carr) *led: hung lft and hdd 3f out: sn rdn and wknd* **25/1**	
510-	7	4	**Peter's Storm (USA)**[166] 6756 3-8-11 **77**...................... PaulMulrennan 5	45
			(K A Ryan) *chsd ldr: rdn along 3f out: sn wknd* **14/1**	
-133	8	7	**Royal Applord**[78] 458 3-8-9 **75**.. FergalLynch 3	24
			(K A Ryan) *hld up: a in rr* **16/1**	

1m 38.63s (4.83) **Going Correction** +0.75s/f (Yiel) — **8** Ran SP% **114.4**
Speed ratings (Par 102): **102,99,98,92,92 88,83,75**
CSF £14.76 CT £26.33 TOTE £2.70: £1.10, £2.00, £1.10; EX 15.30.
Owner J H Tattersall **Bred** C Eddington And Partners **Trained** Musley Bank, N Yorks

FOCUS
A fair handicap and sound form for the grade rated through the third.

NOTEBOOK
Albaqaa, who is inclined to be keen in his races, settled a bit better than at Ripon and, when asked to challenge next to the far rail, ran on well. He clearly appreciates a bit of give in the ground and, because he is difficult to settle, he will always be seen at his best in a strongly run race. (tchd 7-4, 2-1 in places)
Toto Skyllachy, off the track since winning a soft-ground Warwick maiden last July, did well against the race-fit winner and, should he improve as expected for the run, will take plenty of beating in similar company. (op 5-1)
Atabaas Pride was a bit disappointing, failing to improve on his reappearance effort, but he was clear of the rest and gives the form a solid look. (op 11-4)
Joinedupwriting, another making his seasonal reappearance, kept on from off the pace without threatening the principals. Quicker ground probably suits him better. (tchd 25-1)
Thunderstruck, back down to a more suitable trip, hung over to the stands'-side rail entering the straight, which cost him a shot at a place. He is another who probably needs better ground to be seen at his best. (op 8-1 tchd 13-2)
Dhhamaan(IRE), who has been mopping up in Polytrack claimers lately, found things tougher back in handicap company against more progressive rivals on a different surface. (op 22-1)
Peter's Storm(USA), who did not run beyond 6f at two, was much too keen in the early stages of this seasonal reappearance. Hopefully this will have taken the freshness out of him. (op 12-1)

1577 BEVERLEY BELLES FILLIES' H'CAP — 1m 1f 207y

3:45 (3:45) (Class 5) (0-70,70) 4-Y-O+ — £2,428 (£722; £361; £180) Stalls High

Form				RPR
3664	1		**Karmest**[8] 1394 4-8-7 **59**..(b) SilvestreDeSousa 9	73
			(A D Brown) *reminders in rr after s: hdwy into midfield after 2f: smooth hdwy over 2f out: led on bit appr last: edgd rt and sn rdn clr* **3/1**[1]	
03-0	2	5	**Stringsofmyheart**[113] 14 4-8-10 **62**............................ DarryllHolland 6	66
			(Miss Gay Kelleway) *racd wd: led: rdn along over 2f out: drvn over 1f out: hdd appr last and kpt on same pce* **5/1**[3]	
522-	3	2	**Lady Valentino**[234] 5084 4-8-4 **56** oh6.................................. DaleGibson 5	56
			(M Dods) *hld up towards rr: hdwy over 2f out: sn rdn and kpt on ins fnl f: nrst fin* **15/2**	
0-50	4	4	**Lauro**[8] 1391 8-8-7 **59** ow2.. TomEaves 8	51
			(Miss J A Camacho) *hld up: hdwy on inner 2f out: sn ridden and kpt on same pce u.p* **8/1**	
30-4	5	3 1/2	**Lunar River (FR)**[15] 1266 5-8-6 **58**.........................(t) NeilChalmers 3	43
			(David Pinder) *trckd ldrs: hdwy 3f out: rdn to chse ldr wl over 1f out: drvn and wknd appr fnl f* **9/1**	
10-0	6	2 1/4	**Grethel (IRE)**[8] 1394 4-7-13 **56**........................... DanielleMcCreery(5) 10	37
			(A Berry) *in rr: hdwy on outer wl over 2f out: sn rdn and no imp fr wl over 1f out* **20/1**	
154-	7	6	**Prelude**[208] 5807 7-9-4 **70**... LiamJones 7	39
			(W M Brisbourne) *chsd ldrs: rdn along 3f out: sn wknd* **17/2**	
00-3	8	7	**Rowan River**[14] 1287 4-9-4 **70**...............................(p) RichardKingscote 1	25
			(Tom Dascombe) *prom: effrt to chse ldr over 2f out: sn rdn and wkng whn n.m.r wl over 1f out* **7/2**[2]	
54/0	9	22	**Mozayada (USA)**[73] 526 4-8-6 **58**.. TWilliams 2	—
			(M Brittain) *cl up: rdn along 3f out and sn wknd* **25/1**	

2m 14.44s (7.44) **Going Correction** +0.75s/f (Yiel) — **9** Ran SP% **115.9**
Speed ratings (Par 100): **100,96,94,91,88 86,81,76,58**
CSF £18.29 CT £102.44 TOTE £3.70: £1.60, £2.10, £1.90; EX 19.70.
Owner David Logan **Bred** Charles B B Booth **Trained** Pickering, York
■ Stewards' Enquiry : Silvestre De Sousa one-day ban: careless riding (May 8)

FOCUS
A modest fillies' handicap and the placed horses are the best guides to the form.
Rowan River Official explanation: jockey said filly was unsuited by the good to soft (soft in places) ground
Mozayada(USA) Official explanation: trainer later said filly had been unsuited by the rain softened ground

1578 NORFOLK STREET H'CAP — 7f 100y

4:20 (4:23) (Class 6) (0-60,60) 4-Y-O+ — £1,942 (£578; £288; £144) Stalls High

Form				RPR
24-3	1		**Moonstreaker**[16] 1258 5-8-8 **53**.............................. MichaelJStainton(3) 9	66
			(R M Whitaker) *in tch: effrt on outer over 2f out: sn rdn along and sltly outpcd: drvn and hdwy over 1f out: styd on u.p to ld wl ins fnl f: sn clr* **7/1**[3]	
0-01	2	3 1/4	**A Big Sky Brewing (USA)**[13] 1313 4-8-13 **60**............(b) NeilBrown(5) 10	65
			(T D Barron) *a.p: led wl over 2f out: rdn and edgd rt over 1f out: drvn and hdd wl ins fnl f: one pce* **6/1**[2]	
00-0	3	1	**Emperor's Well**[13] 1296 9-8-8 **57**.. NSLawes(7) 4	59
			(M W Easterby) *midfield: hdwy 3f out: rdn to chse ldrs wl over 1f out: kpt on same pce u.p ent fnl f* **16/1**	
000-	4	1 1/4	**Ensign's Trick**[215] 5627 4-8-13 **55**.. LiamJones 5	54
			(W M Brisbourne) *midfield: gd hdwy on outer over 2f out: rdn to chse ldr over 1f out: sn drvn and one pce* **50/1**	
00-0	5	3 3/4	**Apache Nation (IRE)**[22] 1160 5-9-1 **57**................................ TomEaves 2	46+
			(M Dods) *bhd: hdwy 2f out: sn rdn and kpt on ins fnl f: nrst fin* **10/1**	
504-	6	1/2	**Nufoudh (IRE)**[202] 5966 4-8-13 **55**................................ DeanMcKeown 1	43+
			(Miss Tracy Waggott) *dwlt and bhd: hdwy on outer over 2f out: edgd rt and kpt on ins fnl f: nrst fin* **25/1**	
65-1	7	3 3/4	**Bert's Memory**[29] 1025 4-8-10 **52**..................................(p) JoeFanning 8	30
			(J Mackie) *prom: rdn along 3f out: grad wknd fnl 2f* **20/1**	
2125	8	nk	**Wisdom's Kiss**[26] 1085 4-9-1 **57**...............................(p) JimmyQuinn 14	34
			(J D Bethell) *nvr bttr than midfield* **7/1**[3]	
60-6	9	1 1/4	**Scutch Mill (IRE)**[22] 1148 6-9-3 **59**................................(t) LeeEnstone 11	33
			(P C Haslam) *a bhd* **10/1**	
004-	10	2 1/2	**Regal Dream (IRE)**[198] 6088 6-9-0 **56**........................... RobertWinston 7	24
			(J W Unett) *in tch: rdn along 2f out: sn drvn and wknd wl over 1f out* **20/1**	
0002	11	1 1/2	**Grey Gurkha**[2] 1533 7-8-13 **55**................................... RoystonFfrench 6	19
			(I W McInnes) *s.i.s: a in rr* **4/1**[1]	
0-00	12	4 1/2	**Shaftesbury Avenue (USA)**[13] 1313 5-8-11 **53**....(b) PatrickMathers 13	5
			(I W McInnes) *chsd ldrs: rdn along over 2f out and grad wknd* **18/1**	
2326	13	4	**Only A Grand**[35] 949 4-8-12 **54**...................................(b) FergalLynch 12	—
			(R Bastiman) *led: rdn along 3f out: sn hdd and grad wknd fnl 2f* **14/1**	
5660	14	8	**Cornerstone**[22] 1160 4-8-10 **52**...................................(v) PaulHanagan 15	—
			(S C Williams) *chsd ldrs on inner: rdn along 3f out and sn wknd* **9/1**	
-040	15	8	**Crow's Nest Lad**[16] 1258 4-9-3 **59**.. DavidAllan 16	—
			(J O'Reilly) *a towards rr* **20/1**	

1m 39.44s (5.64) **Going Correction** +0.75s/f (Yiel) — **15** Ran SP% **125.4**
Speed ratings (Par 101): **97,93,92,90,86 85,81,81,79,76 75,70,65,56,47**
CSF £46.63 CT £685.89 TOTE £6.30: £2.00, £2.90, £5.60; EX 51.40.
Owner Ian B Ender **Bred** Hellwood Stud Farm **Trained** Scarcroft, W Yorks

FOCUS
A moderate handicap with the runner-up strictly to form and pretty solid overall.
Grey Gurkha Official explanation: jockey said horse missed the break

1579 CONSTANT SECURITY MAIDEN STKS — 1m 100y

4:55 (4:57) (Class 5) 3-Y-O+ — £2,428 (£722; £361; £180) Stalls High

Form				RPR
0-3	1		**Hepburn Bell (IRE)**[15] 1270 3-8-7 0 ow1........................ JamieSpencer 4	74
			(J R Fanshawe) *trckd ldrs: hdwy over 2f out: rdn to ld ent fnl f: sn drvn clr and styd on wl* **2/1**[1]	
0-3	2	2 1/4	**Bowder Stone (IRE)**[13] 1295 3-8-11 0........................... JimmyQuinn 10	73
			(M H Tompkins) *prom: led 3f out: rdn along wl over 1f out: drvn and hdd ent fnl f: kpt on same pce* **2/1**[1]	
34	3	2 3/4	**Shadowtime**[64] 633 3-8-11 0.. DeanMcKeown 7	67
			(Miss Tracy Waggott) *in tch on inner: pushed along over 2f out: kpt on appr fnl f* **18/1**	
	4	2 1/4	**Sirvino** 3-8-11 0.. PaulFessey 13	62+
			(T D Barron) *hld up in rr: hdwy over 2f out: rdn and styd on appr fnl f: nrst fin* **50/1**	
2-	5	1/2	**Salsa Time**[211] 5734 3-8-7 0 ow1...................................... TomEaves 2	57
			(Miss J A Camacho) *t.k.h: hdwy to chse ldrs over 2f out: rdn and edgd rt over 1f out: kpt on same pce* **11/1**	
3-	6	1/2	**E Major**[171] 6694 3-8-11 0.. RobertWinston 3	63+
			(Sir Michael Stoute) *s.i.s and towards rr: hdwy over 3f out: effrt and nt clr run 2f out: sn swtchd rt and styd on fnl f: nt rch ldrs* **13/2**[3]	
200-	7	3 1/4	**Jiminor Mack**[191] 6250 5-9-3 43.................................(p) AndrewMullen(3) 8	51
			(W J H Ratcliffe) *s.i.s and bhd tl styd on fnl 2f* **50/1**	
3-5	8	6	**Bretwalda (IRE)**[13] 1307 5-9-11 0.. LeeEnstone 6	42
			(P T Midgley) *chsd ldrs: rdn along whn n.m.r on inner wl over 2f out: grad wknd* **40/1**	
650	9	2 1/4	**Able Dara**[36] 369 5-9-8 44... MarkLawson(3) 12	37
			(N Bycroft) *a in rr* **66/1**	
522-	10	1/2	**Bavarian Nordic (USA)**[184] 6410 3-8-11 77............ RoystonFfrench 11	32
			(Mrs A Duffield) *prom: effrt to chse ldng pair over 2f out: sn rdn and wknd over 1f out* **9/2**[2]	
	11	17	**Orangina Wood (GER)**[153] 6921 5-9-1 40........... DanielleMcCreery(5) 9	—
			(A Berry) *led: rdn along and hdd 3f out: sn wknd* **200/1**	
000/	12	nk	**Frogs' Gift (IRE)**[565] 4154 6-9-6 0................................ DanielTudhope 14	—
			(G M Moore) *a in rr* **100/1**	
06	13	29	**Mollie Blackburn**[24] 1119 4-9-6 0................................ SilvestreDeSousa 1	—
			(A D Brown) *a in rr* **150/1**	

1m 55.15s (7.55) **Going Correction** +0.75s/f (Yiel)
WFA 3 from 4yo+ 14lb — **13** Ran SP% **121.8**
Speed ratings (Par 103): **92,89,87,84,84 83,80,74,72,71 54,54,25**
CSF £5.61 TOTE £3.30: £1.30, £1.40, £3.70; EX 6.60.

Owner Mr & Mrs Duncan Davidson **Bred** Forenaghts Stud And Dermot Cantillon **Trained** Newmarket, Suffolk

FOCUS

An ordinary miaden and a modest winning time with the proximity of the seventh limiting the form.

Sirvino Official explanation: jockey said gelding was denied a clear run

1580 LEVY BOARD H'CAP — 1m 4f 16y

5:30 (5:30) (Class 4) (0-85,83) 4-Y-0+ **£4,209** (£1,252; £625; £312) **Stalls** High

Form RPR

511- **1** **Greyfriars Abbey**[241] 4902 4-8-10 75 ... JoeFanning 1 90+
(M Johnston) *trckd ldr: hdwy 3f out: rdn to ld wl over 1f out: sn hung rt: drvn clr appr fnl f and styd on strly* **3/1**[3]

402- **2** *5* **Mighty Moon**[170] 6703 5-8-6 70 ... PaulHanagan 3 77
(R A Fahey) *trckd ldng pair: effrt 2f out: swtchd lft and rdn over 1f out: no imp* **6/4**[1]

00-4 **3** *3 1/2* **Rosbay (IRE)**[26] 1072 4-9-2 81 ... DavidAllan 4 82
(T D Easterby) *hld up in tch: hdwy 3f out: rdn wl over 1f out: kpt on same pce* **7/4**[2]

0/0- **4** *4 1/2* **Ursis (FR)**[104] 6153 7-9-5 83 ... DarrylHolland 2 77
(S Gollings) *racd wd: led: rdn along 3f out: hdd and n.m.r wl over 1f out: sn drvn and wknd appr fnl f* **10/1**

2m 50.86s (9.96) **Going Correction** +0.75s/f (Yiel)
WFA 4 from 5yo+ 1lb **4** Ran SP% **110.5**
Speed ratings (Par 105): **96,92,90,87**
CSF £8.06 TOTE £2.80; EX 6.50 Place 6 £ 17.66, Place 5 £ 6.31.
Owner Greyfriars And White Rose Poultry **Bred** Itchen Valley Stud **Trained** Middleham Moor, N Yorks
■ Stewards' Enquiry : Joe Fanning caution: used whip down shoulder in forehand position

FOCUS

The fair handicap but the winning time was moderate for the class. The winner looks progressive.
T/Plt: £33.20 to a £1 stake. Pool: £46,532.16. 1,020.08 winning tickets. T/Qpdt: £13.30 to a £1 stake. Pool: £3,314.30. 183.95 winning tickets. JR

[1499] GREAT LEIGHS (A.W) (L-H)

Thursday, April 24

OFFICIAL GOING: Standard

Wind: modest across Weather: sunny, showers threatening

1581 BILLERICAY MAIDEN STKS — 6f (P)

5:20 (5:21) (Class 5) 3-Y-0+ **£2,590** (£770; £385; £192) **Stalls** Centre

Form RPR

3-62 **1** **All In The Red (IRE)**[6] 1453 3-9-0 65 ... JimmyFortune 5 72
(Miss Gay Kelleway) *chsd ldr tl over 4f out: rdn over 2f out: swtchd rt over 1f out: led ins fnl f: r.o wl* **5/2**[2]

50 **2** *1 1/2* **Dnata Flyer (USA)**[13] 1298 3-9-0 0 ... J-PGuillambert 6 67
(M Johnston) *chsd ldrs tl jnd ldr over 4f out: rdn to ld over 1f out: hdd ins fnl f: one pce* **4/1**[3]

0-32 **3** *5* **Nice Dream**[4] 1499 3-8-9 0 ... HayleyTurner 10 46
(C E Brittain) *led: jnd over 4f out: rdn and hdd over 1f out: wknd ins fnl f* **11/8**[1]

4 *1* **In Toto** 3-9-0 0 ... OscarUrbina 9 48
(M Wigham) *s.i.s: sn in tch on outer: hdwy to chse ldng trio over 2f out: hung lft over 1f out: no imp after* **16/1**

0- **5** *3 1/4* **Upstairs**[333] 2059 4-9-8 0 ... MarcHalford(3) 3 41+
(D R C Elsworth) *awkward leaving stalls and slowly away: t.k.h: hld up in tch: outpcd over 3f out: plugged on over 1f out: nt trble ldrs* **14/1**

0- **6** *6* **Warden Fizz**[223] 5380 3-9-0 0 ... TQuinn 2 18
(D R C Elsworth) *t.k.h: chsd ldrs: rdn 4f out: outpcd wl over 2f out: no ch after* **12/1**

055 **7** *3/4* **Big Boom**[16] 1255 3-9-0 0 ... PatCosgrave 8 16
(M J Wallace) *awkward leaving stalls and slowly away: a towards rr: wd and rdn over bnd 3f out: sn lost tch: no ch last 2f* **33/1**

0- **8** *nk* **Embra (IRE)**[153] 6912 3-9-0 0 ... TedDurcan 7 15
(T J Etherington) *t.k.h: hld up in tch in midfield: rdn over 3f out: outpcd over 2f out: no ch after* **20/1**

0 **9** *7* **Cape Tycoon (IRE)**[22] 1149 3-9-0 0 ... VinceSlattery 4 —
(S A Callaghan) *stdd s: a bhd: lost tch 3f out: no ch last 2f: t.o* **25/1**

0 **10** *3 1/4* **Super Al**[59] 700 3-8-7 0 ... TobyAtkinson(7) 1 —
(M Wigham) *s.i.s: a bhd: lost tch 3f out: no ch last 2f: t.o* **33/1**

1m 13.27s (-0.43) **Going Correction** +0.025s/f (Slow)
WFA 3 from 4yo 11lb **10** Ran SP% **125.4**
Speed ratings (Par 103): **103,101,94,93,88 80,79,79,69,65**
CSF £13.62 TOTE £2.70: £1.40, £1.60, £1.50; EX 12.10.
Owner Chris Peach **Bred** John McEnery **Trained** Exning, Suffolk

FOCUS

A moderate maiden with the winner rated just 65 and not many got into it. The winning time was marginally faster than the later three-year-old handicap over the same trip and the winner put up an improved effort.

In Toto Official explanation: jockey said gelding hung left

Super Al Official explanation: jockey said, regarding running and riding, that his orders were to be handy early on and to do his best thereafter, adding that the gelding was upset in the stalls, was keen early stages and hung right in home straight when he dropped his reins while changing hands a furlong out thus causing it to hang; trainer confirmed instructions adding that it was only the jockey's fifth ride in public.

1582 MILL GREEN H'CAP — 5f (P)

5:50 (5:51) (Class 4) (0-85,83) 4-Y-0+ **£4,533** (£1,348; £674; £336) **Stalls** Low

Form RPR

6301 **1** **Lord Of The Reins (IRE)**[17] 1242 4-8-4 69 oh2 ... AndrewElliott 7 81
(D Shaw) *dropped in bhd after 1f: outpcd and hung rt on bnd over 3f out: stl last jst over 1f out: str run after to ld last 50yds* **11/4**[1]

3430 **2** *1 1/4* **Misaro (GER)**[20] 1195 7-8-10 78 ... (b) KevinGhunowa(3) 6 86
(R A Harris) *s.i.s: sn rdn along to chse ldrs: wd on bnd 2f out and sltly outpcd: rallied u.p fnl f: wnt 2nd towards fin* **6/1**

1333 **3** *1 1/4* **Almaty Express**[20] 1195 6-9-2 81 ... (b) ChrisCatlin 2 84
(J R Weymes) *sn rdn along to chse ldr: led 4f out: kpt on wl tl hdd and fdd last 50yds* **11/2**[3]

0-30 **4** *3/4* **Merlin's Dancer**[40] 907 8-9-4 83 ... IanMongan 3 83
(S Dow) *led for 1f: pressed ldr after: ev ch and rdn wl over 1f out: fdd wl ins fnl f* **7/1**

5-05 **5** *1* **New York Oscar (IRE)**[29] 1033 4-8-10 75 ... (p) JamesDoyle 4 72
(A J McCabe) *wnt rt s: in tch: effrt and nt clr run fr wl over 1f out: nvr able to mount a chal* **4/1**[2]

5-14 **6** *1/2* **Bookiesindex Boy**[9] 1378 4-8-5 77 ... (v) DavidProbert(7) 5 72
(J R Jenkins) *bmpd sn after s: in tch: rdn 2f out: wknd ins fnl f* **13/2**

11-4 **7** *1/2* **Smokin Beau**[99] 187 11-8-4 72 ow3 ... KirstyMilczarek(3) 1 65
(N P Littmoden) *chsd ldrs on inner: rdn wl over 1f out: kpt on same pce* **15/2**

59.71 secs (-0.49) **Going Correction** +0.025s/f (Slow) **7** Ran SP% **113.9**
Speed ratings (Par 105): **104,102,100,98,97 96,95**
CSF £19.40 TOTE £4.30: £3.50, £4.40; EX 28.70.
Owner Danethorpe Racing Partnership **Bred** C Farrell **Trained** Danethorpe, Notts

FOCUS

The first race ever run over the minimum trip at the track and, with some established speedsters present, a very strong pace was always likely. The front pair made their efforts widest and that may have been significant. The runner-up sets the standard.

New York Oscar(IRE) Official explanation: jockey said gelding was denied a clear run

1583 HIGH EASTER H'CAP — 1m 6f (P)

6:20 (6:20) (Class 4) (0-85,82) 4-Y-0+ **£4,533** (£1,348; £674; £336) **Stalls** Low

Form RPR

445- **1** **Chocolate Caramel (USA)**[139] 7055 6-9-11 82 ... JimCrowley 2 91
(Mrs A J Perrett) *hld up in tch: hdwy to trck ldrs over 2f out: rdn to chse ldr over 1f out: led ins fnl f: sn in command: rdn out* **10/3**[1]

361- **2** *3* **Nawow**[348] 1668 8-9-8 79 ... DaneO'Neill 5 84
(P D Cundell) *chsd ldr: rdn to ld wl over 1f out: hdd ins fnl f: nt pce of wnr* **9/2**[2]

6410 **3** *3 3/4* **King's Fable (USA)**[8] 1408 5-8-7 64 ow1 ... (p) TGMcLaughlin 4 64
(Karen George) *s.i.s: t.k.h: hld up in rr: hdwy over 4f out: rdn and effrt over 2f out: hung lft over 1f out: kpt on to go 3rd nr fin: nvr threatened ldrs* **9/2**[2]

60-2 **4** *nk* **Compton Falcon**[28] 1039 4-8-3 65 ... LukeMorris(3) 3 64
(G A Butler) *trckd ldrs: rdn over 3f out: hrd rdn over 1f out: wknd fnl f* **10/3**[1]

000- **5** *1 1/4* **Tribe**[257] 4398 6-9-4 75 ... JimmyFortune 1 73
(P R Webber) *wnt rt s: led: rdn over 2f out: hdd wl over 1f out: wknd fnl f* **6/1**[3]

25-1 **P** **Trifti**[28] 1039 7-8-12 72 ... KevinGhunowa(3) 6 —
(Miss Jo Crowley) *t.k.h: hld up in tch: rdn 6f out: sn dropped to last: t.o and p.u 1f out: b.b.v* **6/1**[3]

3m 2.05s (-1.15) **Going Correction** +0.025s/f (Slow)
WFA 4 from 5yo+ 2lb **6** Ran SP% **111.1**
Speed ratings (Par 105): **104,102,100,99,99 —**
CSF £17.97 TOTE £3.70: £1.90, £2.90; EX 36.70.
Owner Mrs Priscilla Graham **Bred** Sierra Thoroughbreds **Trained** Pulborough, W Sussex

FOCUS

Another trip being used for the first time here and the pace in this fair handicap was only ordinary. This was another race where the winner was the one who made his effort widest.

Trifti Official explanation: vet said gelding had bled from the nose

1584 LITTLE BENTLEY H'CAP — 6f (P)

6:50 (6:51) (Class 4) (0-85,82) 3-Y-0 **£4,533** (£1,348; £674; £336) **Stalls** Centre

Form RPR

2210 **1** **Loose Caboose (IRE)**[5] 1484 3-8-8 72 ... (p) PatCosgrave 9 76
(A J McCabe) *mde all: rdn 2f out: hld on gamely fnl f* **12/1**

1-61 **2** *nk* **We Have A Dream**[14] 1277 3-8-12 76 ... MartinDwyer 2 79
(W R Muir) *chsd wnr: rdn to chal fr wl over 1f out: unable qckn fnl f* **4/1**[1]

0352 **3** *3/4* **Asian Power (IRE)**[21] 1167 3-8-11 75 ... OscarUrbina 6 76
(P J O'Gorman) *stdd after s: hld up in rr: hdwy on outer over 2f out: rdn wl over 1f out: r.o wl fnl f to snatch 3rd nr fin: nt rch ldng pair* **9/1**

4223 **4** *hd* **Valhillen**[14] 1284 3-8-8 72 ... HayleyTurner 1 72
(M D I Usher) *trckd ldrs gng wl on inner: rdn and effrt jst over 1f out: unable qck u.p ins fnl f: lost 3rd nr fin* **9/1**

403- **5** *shd* **Zippi Jazzman (USA)**[193] 6195 3-8-13 77 ... JamesDoyle 7 77
(R M Beckett) *hld up in tch: rdn and edgd lft wl over 1f out: unable qckn u.p fnl f: btn whn short of room nr fin* **9/2**[2]

12-0 **6** *hd* **Eternal Luck (IRE)**[21] 1170 3-9-4 82 ... PhilipRobinson 5 81+
(M A Jarvis) *s.i.s: racd wd and bhd: rdn wl over 2f out: styd on wl u.p ins fnl f: nt rch ldrs* **4/1**[1]

1-14 **7** *1* **Ike Quebec (FR)**[33] 967 3-8-9 78 ... HaddenFrost(5) 8 74
(J R Boyle) *hld up in tch: rdn and effrt wl over 1f out: kpt on same pce u.p fnl f* **8/1**

00-6 **8** *2 1/2* **Geoffdaw**[78] 457 3-8-11 75 ... EddieAhern 3 63
(M J Wallace) *s.i.s: a in rr: nvr trbld ldrs* **16/1**

54-2 **9** *3/4* **Hobson**[24] 1110 3-8-11 75 ... StephenCarson 4 61
(Eve Johnson Houghton) *s.i.s: a bhd: rdn wl over 2f out: nvr on terms* **5/1**[3]

30-3 **10** *1 3/4* **Mollyatti**[4] 1499 3-8-5 74 ... SCreighton(5) 10 54
(Miss V Haigh) *in tch in midfield: rdn and hdwy to chse ldrs 2f out: wknd jst over 1f out* **33/1**

1m 13.4s (-0.30) **Going Correction** +0.025s/f (Slow) **10** Ran SP% **122.5**
Speed ratings (Par 100): **103,102,101,101,101 100,99,96,95,92**
CSF £62.68 CT £481.22 TOTE £26.80: £6.80, £1.10, £4.60; EX 114.40.
Owner Dixon, McCabe and Timms **Bred** Paradime Ltd **Trained** Babworth, Notts
■ Stewards' Enquiry : Pat Cosgrave caution: used whip with excessive frequency

FOCUS

A competitive sprint handicap and the majority of the field were still within a couple of lengths of each other in a line across the track passing the furlong pole. The winner bucked the trend by racing closer to the inside rail than the three previous winners on the night. Those in behind the first two were all close to form.

Hobson Official explanation: jockey said gelding ran too free

1585 ALDHAM H'CAP — 1m 2f (P)

7:20 (7:22) (Class 4) (0-80,80) 4-Y-0+ **£4,533** (£1,348; £674; £336) **Stalls** Low

Form RPR

4-04 **1** **Folio (IRE)**[15] 1273 8-9-0 76 ... JimmyFortune 5 86
(W J Musson) *hld up in tch: hdwy 4f out: chsd ldrs gng wl 2f out: rdn over 1f out: led ins fnl f: r.o wl* **11/2**[3]

52-1 **2** *hd* **Proper (IRE)**[15] 1273 4-8-9 71 ... TedDurcan 8 81
(C J Mann) *awkward leaving stalls: dropped in bhd after s: hld up in last pair: hdwy 3f out: rdn to ld narrowly 1f out: hdd ins fnl f: r.o but a hld* **5/4**[1]

6426 **3** *3* **Jord (IRE)**[22] 1160 4-8-10 72 ... AndrewElliott 6 76
(A J McCabe) *awkward leaving stalls and missed break: sn rcvrd and led after 1f: clr 7f out: rdn 2f out: hdd 1f out: outpcd by ldng pair fnl f* **16/1**

06-4 **4** *nk* **Ross Moor**[22] 1151 6-8-4 66 ... ChrisCatlin 4 69
(Mike Murphy) *in tch: lost pl 3f out: rdn and outpcd 2f out: hdwy over 1f out: styd on: nvr pce to rch ldng pair* **8/1**

06-4 **5** *1/2* **Art Market (CAN)**[24] 1112 5-8-4 69 ow3 ... KevinGhunowa(3) 7 71
(Miss Jo Crowley) *chsd ldrs: wnt 2nd 6f out: rdn over 2f out: kpt on same pce u.p fnl f* **12/1**

-040 **6** *5* **Master Pegasus**[12] 1335 5-9-4 **80** .... GeorgeBaker 1 72
(C F Wall) *stdd after s: t.k.h: hld up in tch: swtchd rt and effrt 2f out: wknd fnl f* **4/1**[2]

006 **7** *5* **Obrigado (USA)**[36] 941 8-8-7 **69** ....(t) TGMcLaughlin 2 51
(Karen George) *stdd s: hld up in last: rdn and effrt on outer 3f out: nvr trbld ldrs* **14/1**

1-00 **8** *nk* **Wild Fell Hall (IRE)**[22] 1137 5-9-3 **79** ....(p) DaneO'Neill 3 61
(A D Brown) *t.k.h: led for 1f: chsd ldr tl 7f out: rdn 3f out: wknd wl over 1f out* **20/1**

2m 7.70s (-0.90) **Going Correction** +0.025s/f (Slow) **8** Ran SP% **115.9**
Speed ratings (Par 105): **104,103,101,101,100 96,92,92**
CSF £12.99 CT £104.34 TOTE £8.50: £2.20, £1.30, £2.10; EX 11.70.
Owner Goodey and Broughton **Bred** Lord Rothschild **Trained** Newmarket, Suffolk

FOCUS
A fair handicap and a decent pace set by Jord. The winning time was 1.51 secs faster than the following Class 6 handicap and the form looks sound enough.

1586 HORSEY ISLAND H'CAP 1m 2f (P)
7:50 (7:53) (Class 6) (0-60,60) 3-Y-O **£2,266** (£674; £337; £168) **Stalls** Low

Form RPR

0-25 **1** **Black Dahlia**[22] 1161 3-9-2 **58** .... JamesDoyle 12 71
(A J McCabe) *hld up in midfield: hdwy 3f out: rdn to chal 2f out: led over 1f out: edgd lft but r.o wl to forge clr fnl f* **5/2**[1]

-002 **2** *1 3/4* **Art Exhibition (IRE)**[12] 1343 3-9-2 **58** .... JimmyFortune 5 67
(J Noseda) *chsd ldrs: wnt 2nd over 6f out: rdn to ld 2f out: hdd over 1f out: kpt on u.p but nt pce of wnr: btn whn eased towards fin* **10/3**[2]

-643 **3** *5* **Arniecoco**[12] 1343 3-9-4 **60** .... OscarUrbina 9 59
(Miss J R Gibney) *chsd ldrs: rdn wl over 2f out: wl outpcd by ldng pair fnl f: plugged on steadily* **6/1**[3]

0-00 **4** *1 3/4* **Una Auroraborealis**[10] 1364 3-8-4 **46** oh1 ....(p) DavidKinsella 1 42
(J Ryan) *led: rdn wl over 2f out: hdd 2f out: outpcd over 1f out: plugged on steadily* **66/1**

56-0 **5** *nk* **Sarah's First**[17] 1247 3-9-3 **59** ....(b[1]) TGMcLaughlin 7 54
(E A L Dunlop) *plld hrd: hld up in tch: hdwy to chse ldrs 4f out: rdn over 2f out: outpcd by ldng pair over 1f out: plugged on* **9/1**

00-6 **6** *4* **Payne Relief (IRE)**[21] 1166 3-9-2 **58** .... HayleyTurner 13 45
(M L W Bell) *dropped in bhd after s: hld up in rr: rdn along and sme hdwy 3f out: nvr trbld ldrs: no ch whn swtchd rt wl ins fnl f* **8/1**

-136 **7** *nse* **Duneen Dream (USA)**[62] 665 3-9-3 **59** .... EddieAhern 14 46
(W J Musson) *stdd s: hld up in rr: hdwy 3f out: c wd 2f out: no imp and no ch fnl f* **6/1**[3]

000- **8** *hd* **Amicus**[165] 6777 3-9-4 **60** .... TQuinn 15 46
(D K Ivory) *dropped in after s: t.k.h: hld up towards rr: rdn and sme hdwy 3f out: no hdwy whn hung lft 1f out: wl btn whn bmpd nr fin* **25/1**

002P **9** *nse* **Herrbee (IRE)**[10] 1364 3-8-4 **49** ow1 .... KevinGhunowa[(3)] 4 35
(P Butler) *t.k.h: chsd ldr tl over 6f out: rdn jst over 2f out: wknd qckly over 1f out* **33/1**

00-0 **10** *19* **Sarah's Boy**[22] 1149 3-8-8 **50** .... IanMongan 6 —
(S Dow) *plld hrd: chsd ldrs: rdn over 3f out: wknd over 2f out: sn wl bhd: t.o* **20/1**

000- **11** *nse* **Holy Storm (IRE)**[220] 5470 3-8-10 **52** .... StephenCarson 11 —
(Eve Johnson Houghton) *hld up in midfield: lost pl and rdn wl over 3f out: sn wl bhd: t.o* **25/1**

0-00 **12** *1* **Amphibalus (IRE)**[15] 1272 3-8-8 **50** .... ChrisCatlin 10 —
(D K Ivory) *in tch in midfield: rdn 4f out: wknd wl over 2f out: t.o* **33/1**

00-0 **P** **Tenraninthemist (IRE)**[15] 1271 3-8-4 **46** oh1 .... AndrewElliott 3 —
(B R Johnson) *t.k.h: racd in midfield tl dropped to rr and hung bdly rt fr over 6f out: wl t.o whn p.u ins fnl f* **25/1**

2m 9.21s (0.61) **Going Correction** +0.025s/f (Slow) **13** Ran SP% **125.0**
Speed ratings (Par 96): **98,96,92,91,90 87,87,87,87,72 72,71,—**
CSF £10.19 CT £48.06 TOTE £4.30: £1.30, £1.20, £3.90; EX 10.20 Place 6 £ 15.23, Place 5 £ 13.57.
Owner Paul J Dixon and D Sharp **Bred** Worksop Manor Stud **Trained** Babworth, Notts

FOCUS
A modest handicap though quite a competitive one, but the winning time was 1.51 seconds slower than the preceding handicap which suggests the form is modest, although it might be worth viewing positively.
Amicus Official explanation: jockey said filly hung left in closing stages
Tenraninthemist(IRE) Official explanation: jockey said filly was unrideable
T/Plt: £29.40 to a £1 stake. Pool: £34,334.42. 851.25 winning tickets. T/Qpdt: £12.10 to a £1 stake. Pool: £3,335.50. 203.50 winning tickets. SP

1548 SOUTHWELL (L-H)
Thursday, April 24

OFFICIAL GOING: Standard
Wind: light 1/2 behind Weather: fine and sunny but very heavy shower race 1

1587 BOOK YOUR TICKETS ONLINE MEDIAN AUCTION MAIDEN STKS 7f (F)
5:35 (5:35) (Class 6) 3-4-Y-O **£1,774** (£523; £262) **Stalls** Low

Form RPR

54-0 **1** **Great Charm (IRE)**[22] 1161 3-8-13 66 .... TPQueally 2 82
(M L W Bell) *trckd ldrs: led over 2f out: edgd rt and rdn wl clr appr fnl f: eased ins fnl f* **3/1**[3]

32 **2** *9* **Zeffirelli**[23] 1124 3-8-13 0 .... SebSanders 3 57
(M Quinn) *trckd ldrs: chsd wnr fnl 2f: no ch* **11/2**

33- **3** *4* **Midnight Fling**[319] 2488 3-8-8 0 .... NCallan 5 41
(R Charlton) *trckd ldrs: effrt 3f out: hung lft and wknd 2f out* **15/8**[1]

000- **4** *2 1/2* **Jack Got Even (USA)**[181] 6471 3-8-13 68 ....(b) RichardMullen 4 39
(D M Simcock) *led: edgd rt and hdd over 2f out: sn wknd* **2/1**[2]

000- **5** *27* **Alloro**[177] 6559 4-9-12 42 .... TonyHamilton 1 —
(D W Thompson) *s.i.s: sn drvn along and outpcd: lost tch over 3f out: t.o whn eased over 1f out* **50/1**

1m 29.96s (-0.34) **Going Correction** +0.025s/f (Slow)
WFA 3 from 4yo 13lb **5** Ran SP% **110.5**
Speed ratings (Par 101): **102,91,87,84,53**
CSF £18.69 TOTE £8.00: £1.70, £1.60; EX 30.00.
Owner Mr & Mrs G Middlebrook **Bred** G And Mrs Middlebrook **Trained** Newmarket, Suffolk

FOCUS
A very weak maiden, easy meat for the 66-rated Great Charm with the runner-up close to his plating form.

1588 DINE IN THE QUEEN MOTHER RESTAURANT CLAIMING STKS 6f (F)
6:05 (6:05) (Class 6) 3-Y-O+ **£1,774** (£523; £262) **Stalls** Low

Form RPR

00-0 **1** **Hamaasy**[28] 1040 7-9-2 59 .... PaulMulrennan 7 70
(D Nicholls) *chsd ldr: led over 2f out: kpt on wl* **33/1**

2254 **2** *2 1/4* **Kingsmaite**[84] 365 7-9-1 45 ....(b) PhillipMakin 9 62
(S R Bowring) *chsd ldrs: rdn over 2f out: styd on to take 2nd ins fnl f* **33/1**

-115 **3** *1* **Fire Up The Band**[8] 1393 9-9-11 85 .... AdrianTNicholls 5 69
(D Nicholls) *led tl over 2f out: wknd ins fnl f* **2/1**[1]

2110 **4** *1* **Desert Dreamer (IRE)**[19] 1211 7-9-10 83 ....(t) RichardKingscote 2 64
(Tom Dascombe) *sn outpcd and in rr: hdwy over 2f out: edgd lft: nvr nrr* **7/2**[3]

5422 **5** *2* **Lethal**[16] 1261 5-9-8 76 .... JamieMoriarty[(3)] 1 59
(R A Fahey) *chsd ldrs: sn drvn along: hrd rdn and outpcd 3f out: no threat after* **9/4**[2]

2236 **6** *3 1/4* **Dickie Le Davoir**[14] 1278 4-9-4 74 .... MarkCoumbe[(7)] 6 49
(John A Harris) *s.i.s: outpcd and in rr: nvr a factor* **11/2**

0 **7** *13* **Mary Dunsmore**[16] 1252 4-8-10 0 .... JerryO'Dwyer[(3)] 3 —
(B J McMath) *sn outpcd and in rr: lost tch over 4f out* **100/1**

- **8** *1/2* **Oren Ishi (IRE)**[139] 7063 4-8-12 42 ow2 ....(t) AdamKirby 8 —
(Miss M E Rowland) *chsd ldrs: sn drvn along: lost pl over 3f out: sn bhd* **100/1**

1m 16.81s (0.31) **Going Correction** +0.025s/f (Slow) **8** Ran SP% **109.6**
Speed ratings (Par 101): **98,95,93,92,89 85,68,67**
CSF £600.96 TOTE £23.90: £9.70, £6.10, £1.30; EX 190.90.The winner was claimed R A Harris for £6,000
Owner J P Honeyman **Bred** Shadwell Estate Company Limited **Trained** Sessay, N Yorks

FOCUS
With Fire Up The Band running out of stamina Hamaasy accounted for Kingsmaite who had 13lb to find on official ratings. He is unlikely to have improved but there is a chance this is better than rated.

1589 SPONSOR A RACE AT SOUTHWELL H'CAP 1m 4f (F)
6:35 (6:35) (Class 5) (0-75,74) 4-Y-0+ **£2,456** (£725; £362) **Stalls** Low

Form RPR

6-04 **1** **Cotton Eyed Joe (IRE)**[12] 1340 7-8-8 **66** .... PJMcDonald[(3)] 8 78
(G A Swinbank) *trckd ldrs: chal 3f out: led 2f out: wnt lft 1f out: sn drew clr* **5/1**[3]

02-1 **2** *2 1/4* **Pertemps Networks**[19] 1219 4-8-11 **67** .... DaleGibson 2 75
(M W Easterby) *set mod pce: hdd over 8f out: led over 3f out: hdd 2f out: 1l down whn hmpd 1f out: styd on same pce* **5/4**[1]

4142 **3** *3* **Jackie Kiely**[23] 1131 7-9-5 **74** ....(t) PaulMulrennan 5 78
(R Brotherton) *hld up in rr: hdwy over 3f out: kpt on same pce fnl 2f* **11/1**

2510 **4** *2 3/4* **My Mentor (IRE)**[22] 1151 4-8-13 **69** .... SebSanders 7 68
(Sir Mark Prescott) *hld up in rr: hdwy 8f out: chal 3f out: one pce* **7/2**[2]

4244 **5** *12* **Kylkenny**[23] 1131 13-8-13 **71** ....(t) TravisBlock[(3)] 3 51
(H Morrison) *trckd ldrs: drvn along over 5f out: lost pl 3f out* **16/1**

413- **6** *1* **Mr Mischief**[164] 6802 8-8-5 **67** .... MarkCoumbe[(7)] 1 45
(M C Chapman) *in rr: drvn over 4f out: sn bhd* **14/1**

1132 **7** *4* **Exit To Luck (GER)**[43] 854 7-8-12 **72** ....(b) JamieJones[(5)] 6 44
(S Gollings) *sn trcking ldr: led over 8f out tl over 3f out: lost pl over 2f out* **13/2**

2m 40.3s (-0.70) **Going Correction** +0.025s/f (Slow)
WFA 4 from 7yo+ 1lb **7** Ran SP% **117.5**
Speed ratings (Par 103): **103,101,99,97,89 89,86**
CSF £12.23 CT £66.74 TOTE £5.70: £2.30, £1.70; EX 16.00.
Owner Mrs S Sanbrook **Bred** Tally-Ho Stud **Trained** Melsonby, N Yorks

FOCUS
No gallop and only the first four running anywhere near their pre-race marks. The winner is rated back to his best with the third to form.

1590 SOUTHWELL GOLF CLUB H'CAP 1m (F)
7:05 (7:05) (Class 5) (0-75,73) 4-Y-0+ **£2,456** (£725; £362) **Stalls** Low

Form RPR

1051 **1** **Xpres Maite**[20] 1188 5-9-3 **72** ....(v) PhillipMakin 5 87
(S R Bowring) *trckd ldr: led 3f out: drew clr fnl f: readily* **11/2**[3]

1010 **2** *6* **Elusive Warrior (USA)**[5] 1491 5-8-6 **61** ....(p) NeilPollard 6 63
(A J McCabe) *sn led: hdd 3f out: fdd fnl f* **9/1**

-615 **3** *3 3/4* **Indian's Feather (IRE)**[14] 1287 7-9-4 **73** .... TomEaves 1 66
(N Tinkler) *in rr and sn drvn along: wnt modest 3rd over 2f out: one pce* **20/1**

4211 **4** *15* **Wodhill Schnaps**[16] 1258 7-8-10 **65** ....(b) NCallan 4 24
(D Morris) *s.i.s: sn chsng ldrs: lost pl over 2f out* **9/4**[2]

10-4 **5** *8* **General Knowledge (USA)**[13] 1314 5-8-11 **66** ....(t) PaulEddery 2 6
(G D Blake) *led early: drvn over 4f out: bhd fnl 3f* **8/1**

-121 **6** *42* **Exit Smiling**[19] 1217 6-8-10 **65** .... MickyFenton 3 —
(P T Midgley) *trckd ldrs: drvn 4f out: sn lost pl: bhd and eased 2f out: virtually p.u* **11/8**[1]

1m 44.18s (0.48) **Going Correction** +0.025s/f (Slow) **6** Ran SP% **114.1**
Speed ratings (Par 103): **98,92,88,73,65 23**
CSF £51.12 TOTE £7.70: £3.50, £5.50; EX 17.00.
Owner Charterhouse Holdings Plc **Bred** S R Bowring **Trained** Edwinstowe, Notts

FOCUS
They came home well strung out with only the first three running any sort of race and the form looks dubious. Take nothing away from the improved winner though.
Wodhill Schnaps Official explanation: vet said gelding had an irregular heartbeat
Exit Smiling Official explanation: vet said gelding finished distressed

1591 BOOK YOUR HOSPITALITY PACKAGES H'CAP 7f (F)
7:35 (7:35) (Class 5) (0-70,70) 4-Y-0+ **£2,456** (£725; £362) **Stalls** Low

Form RPR

364P **1** **Bartercard (USA)**[6] 1450 7-9-4 **70** .... MickyFenton 4 76
(Stef Liddiard) *trckd ldrs: led over 1f out: drvn clr ins fnl f* **9/2**[2]

3333 **2** *3 3/4* **Dasheena**[16] 1260 5-8-8 **65** ....(be) DanielleMcCreery[(5)] 2 61
(A J McCabe) *dwlt: racd in last but wl in tch: styd alone far side in home st: hdwy to chse 1st 2 over 2f out: kpt on to take 2nd wl ins fnl f: no threat to wnr* **4/6**[1]

0665 **3** *shd* **Zorn**[16] 1260 9-8-4 **56** oh11 .... JimmyQuinn 3 52?
(P Howling) *led: drvn 3f out: hdd over 1f out: kpt on same pce* **13/2**[3]

250- **4** *7* **Sheriff's Silk**[306] [2881] 4-9-4 **70** .... (b) PaulEddery 1 47
(G D Blake) *trckd ldrs: drvn 3f out: wknd appr fnl f: eased ins fnl f* **9/2**[2]

1m 30.12s (-0.18) **Going Correction** +0.025s/f (Slow) **4** Ran SP% **109.7**
Speed ratings (Par 103): **102,97,97,89**
CSF £8.27 TOTE £6.40; EX 11.00.
Owner Mrs Stef Liddiard **Bred** Red Gate Venture Llc **Trained** Great Shefford, Berks

FOCUS
The winner was clearly none-the-worse after being pulled up at Thirsk just six days earlier. It was a weak handicap though despite the winner being a marginal improver.

1592 SOUTHWELL-RACECOURSE.CO.UK H'CAP — 1m (F)
8:05 (8:06) (Class 6) (0-60,60) 3-Y-O — **£1,774** (£523; £262) **Stalls** Low

Form				RPR
00-0	**1**		**Topazes**[13] [1298] 3-9-2 **58** .... JamieSpencer 9 (M L W Bell) *chsd ldrs: hdwy and hrd rdn over 2f out: led over 1f out: forged clr ins fnl f* **7/4**[1]	69
00-2	**2**	*3 1/2*	**Hennessy Island (USA)**[62] [656] 3-9-2 **58** .... SebSanders 8 (T G Mills) *trckd ldrs: led 3f out: hdd over 1f out: styd on same pce* **7/2**[2]	61
0-00	**3**	*2 3/4*	**Hla Tun (USA)**[17] [1247] 3-9-4 **60** .... AdamKirby 10 (W R Swinburn) *chsd ldrs: effrt 3f out: kpt on same pce over 1f out* **28/1**	57
-330	**4**	*2 1/2*	**Persistent (IRE)**[20] [1186] 3-9-0 **56** .... (p) MickyFenton 2 (P T Midgley) *s.i.s and reminders after s: hdwy to chse ldrs 4f out: one pce fnl 2f* **10/1**	47
50-0	**5**	*shd*	**Arcetri (IRE)**[38] [918] 3-9-4 **60** .... NCallan 6 (K A Ryan) *chsd ldrs: wknd over 1f out* **11/1**	51
1310	**6**	*17*	**Novestar (IRE)**[8] [1397] 3-9-1 **60** .... TravisBlock(3) 7 (G J Smith) *swtchd lft s: led tl 3f out: sn lost pl: eased over 1f out* **9/2**[3]	12
254-	**7**	*1 1/2*	**Little Bones**[164] [6800] 3-8-11 **56** .... PJMcDonald(3) 3 (J F Coupland) *starated slowly: in rr: sme hdwy on ins over 2f out: sn lost pl and bhd* **50/1**	4
-226	**8**	*1*	**Whaston (IRE)**[52] [785] 3-9-2 **58** .... JimmyQuinn 5 (J D Bethell) *mid-div: sn pushed along: lost pl over 4f out: sn bhd* **7/1**	4
00-5	**9**	*9*	**Flower Appeal**[5] [1478] 3-8-7 **49** ow1 .... TomEaves 4 (M W Easterby) *sn drvn along to chse ldrs: lost pl over 4f out: sn bhd* **16/1**	—

1m 43.61s (-0.09) **Going Correction** +0.025s/f (Slow) **9** Ran SP% **118.0**
Speed ratings (Par 96): **101,97,94,92,92 75,73,72,63**
CSF £8.03 CT £124.94 TOTE £2.80: £1.10, £1.20, £5.20; EX 9.00 Place 6 £1142.61, Place 5 £ 290.50.
Owner Baron F C Oppenheim **Bred** Baron F Von Oppenheim **Trained** Newmarket, Suffolk
■ Stewards' Enquiry : Travis Block three-day ban: careless riding (May 12-14)

FOCUS
A moderate handicap but the first three are relatively unexposed types. Topazes made hard work of it but pulled clear in the end. The third sets the level.
Topazes Official explanation: trainer's rep said, regarding the apparent improvement in form, colt was having his first run on the all-weather
T/Plt: £776.00 to a £1 stake. Pool: £41,090.50. 38.65 winning tickets. T/Qpdt: £135.10 to a £1 stake. Pool: £4,711.80. 25.80 winning tickets. WG

SANDOWN (R-H)
Friday, April 25

OFFICIAL GOING: Good to soft (good in back straight)
Wind: Light, against Weather: Fine

1595 BET365.COM ESHER CUP (H'CAP) — 1m 14y
1:15 (1:16) (Class 2) (0-100,98) 3-Y-O
£12,462 (£3,732; £1,866; £934; £466; £234) **Stalls** High

Form				RPR
0-11	**1**		**Commander Cave (USA)**[20] [1208] 3-8-8 **88** .... RichardHughes 2 (R Hannon) *trckd ldng pair tl wnt 2nd over 2f out: pushed into ld over 1f out: drvn and styd on wl fnl f* **17/2**	96
311-	**2**	*1/2*	**Unbreak My Heart (IRE)**[194] [6201] 3-8-9 **89** .... SteveDrowne 7 (R Charlton) *lw: hld up in 7th: rdn and prog 2f out: chsd wnr ent fnl f: nt qckn 100yds out: kpt on but hld* **12/1**	96+
01-1	**3**	*1 1/2*	**Cobo Bay**[8] [1428] 3-9-4 **98** 6ex .... NCallan 1 (K A Ryan) *lw: led at fair pce: rdn over 2f out: hdd over 1f out: one pce fnl f* **9/2**[3]	102
614-	**4**	*1/2*	**Arctic Cape**[237] [5053] 3-8-5 **85** .... JoeFanning 4 (M Johnston) *plld hrd: trckd ldr to over 2f out: lost pl u.p and edgd lft over 1f out: kpt on fnl f* **6/1**	87
213-	**5**	*shd*	**Stubbs Art (IRE)**[174] [6650] 3-8-7 **87** .... AlanMunro 9 (D R C Elsworth) *plld hrd: hld up in 6th: rdn and effrt 2f out: kpt on but nvr pce to chal* **7/2**[2]	89+
155-	**6**	*3*	**Jedediah**[195] [6170] 3-9-4 **98** .... MartinDwyer 6 (A M Balding) *bit bkwd: hld up in 8th: shkn up and effrt on inner 2f out: nt pce to trble ldrs over 1f out: fdd fnl f* **11/1**	93
410-	**7**	*1 1/2*	**Hawaana (IRE)**[224] [5397] 3-8-6 **86** .... RHills 3 (B W Hills) *settled in 5th on outer: shkn up 2f out: no prog: wknd fnl f* **10/3**[1]	78
-660	**8**	*3/4*	**Dalkey Girl (IRE)**[57] [744] 3-8-9 **89** .... RyanMoore 8 (V Smith) *sn stdd and hld up in last: shkn up and no prog 2f out: detached over 1f out: plugged on* **33/1**	79
11-3	**9**	*4*	**Traphalgar (IRE)**[20] [1213] 3-8-13 **93** .... TQuinn 5 (P F I Cole) *trckd ldng trio: rdn wl over 2f out: wknd wl over 1f out* **10/1**	74

1m 45.02s (1.72) **Going Correction** +0.275s/f (Good) **9** Ran SP% **116.4**
Speed ratings (Par 104): **102,101,100,99,99 96,94,94,90**
CSF £104.93 CT £522.47 TOTE £8.40: £3.10, £3.80, £1.60; EX 121.30 Trifecta £210.40 Pool: £592.92, 2.00 winning units.
Owner Sir David Seale **Bred** R D Hubbard **Trained** East Everleigh, Wilts

FOCUS
A good, competitive handicap likely to produce its share of winners. Most of the runners had progressive profiles and a positive view has been taken of the form, with the winner up 9lb on his turf debut, and the runner-up improving a similar amount on his juvenile form.

NOTEBOOK
Commander Cave(USA) has really blossomed as a three-year-old, winning his maiden at Lingfield and bettering that effort with a comfy all the way success off a mark of 80 at Kempton recently. Making his turf debut, he had much more on off an 8lb higher mark against stronger opposition, but proved up to it and held on well close home. He has quickly developed into a very useful handicapper and there is no reason why he cannot continue to progress, even though things will be tougher again next time. (op 8-1 tchd 9-1)
Unbreak My Heart(IRE) really got his act together towards the end of last season, appreciating the ease in the ground to win at Windsor and a handicap at Goodwood off a mark of 83. The surface looked ideal for this return and he ran on really well down the stretch, although never getting past the winner. He was the only one among the principals to come from off the pace and this was a highly satisfactory seasonal debut. He looks capable of further progress. (op 14-1)
Cobo Bay, successful in four of his last five starts, was shouldering a 6lb penalty for last week's comfortable Ripon victory but was still 2lb well in. Soon in front, he tried to kick on over two out, but could never get away from his field and could only keep on at the one pace once headed. This was a good effort off a mark of 98, but things are only going to get tougher. (tchd 5-1 in places)
Arctic Cape, who did not look great in his coat, shaped as though in need of this trip when a keeping-on fourth at the course on his final start at two, but he raced a little freely early on and wandered left under pressure in the final quarter mile, possibly getting tired. He is a fine-looking animal and will be entitled to come on for this, so it would not surprise to see a marked improvement next time. (tchd 5-1 and 7-1)
Stubbs Art(IRE), 15lb higher than when winning at Newmarket in September of last year but third behind Twice Over in the Zetland on his only subsequent outing, looked to have it all to do on this seasonal return but is held in high regard and was well backed. He would have prefered a faster pace and pulled much too hard, but kept plugging away and was going on at the finish. His stable has yet to hit form and he should come on for this, but on racecourse evidence he is hardly well handicapped. (op 4-1)
Jedediah, a progressive juvenile who finished fifth behind Ibn Khaldun in the Autumn Stakes on his final start at two, was making his handicap debut off a stiff mark and his trainer had warned that the run would be needed. In the circumstances this was not too bad a reappearance, for he was only a few lengths off the lead until getting tired in the final furlong. (op 16-1)
Hawaana(IRE), winner of a Leicester maiden before failing to fire in the Goffs Million at two, was well supported throughout the day and evidently expected to prove a bit better than his mark of 86. However, having been held up wide, he failed to pick up in the straight and gave a rather laboured performance. His maiden win came on firm ground and it is possible he needs a quick surface to be seen at his best. (op 3-1 tchd 11-4, 7-2 in places)
Traphalgar(IRE) has shown easily his best form on artificial surfaces.

1596 BET365 GORDON RICHARDS STKS (GROUP 3) — 1m 2f 7y
1:50 (1:50) (Class 1) 4-Y-O+ **£26,681** (£10,114; £5,061; £2,523; £1,264) **Stalls** High

Form				RPR
112-	**1**		**Ask**[187] [6374] 5-9-3 119 .... RyanMoore 4 (Sir Michael Stoute) *trckd ldr: rdn to press new ldr over 2f out: drvn into narrow ld over 1f out: sn jnd: fnd ex to assert ins fnl f* **8/13**[1]	117
40-1	**2**	*1/2*	**Hattan (IRE)**[41] [906] 6-9-3 112 .... SebSanders 3 (C E Brittain) *lw: hld up in last pair: prog over 2f out: jnd wnr jst over 1f out: jst hld ins fnl f* **6/1**[2]	116
-101	**3**	*2 1/2*	**Philatelist (USA)**[27] [1076] 4-9-0 102 .... NCallan 7 (M A Jarvis) *cl 3rd tl led on inner over 2f out: drvn and hdd over 1f out: wknd last 100yds* **10/1**	108
0501	**4**	*3/4*	**Championship Point (IRE)**[8] [1427] 5-9-0 105 .... DarryllHolland 2 (M R Channon) *led: rdn and hdd over 2f out: nt qckn and sn in 4th: kpt on ins fnl f* **8/1**[3]	107
2602	**5**	*3/4*	**Illustrious Blue**[27] [1077] 5-9-0 108 .... LDettori 6 (W J Knight) *hld up in last pair: urged along and nt qckn fr over 2f out: kpt on but no ch* **8/1**[3]	105

2m 10.63s (0.13) **Going Correction** +0.275s/f (Good) **5** Ran SP% **107.5**
Speed ratings (Par 113): **110,109,107,107,106**
CSF £4.41 TOTE £1.60: £1.10, £2.30; EX 4.80.
Owner Patrick J Fahey **Bred** Side Hill Stud **Trained** Newmarket, Suffolk

FOCUS
Often an informative race and, although he did not need to run up to his best and he made hard work of winning, Ask still created a good impression on this seasonal debut. Despite the steady pace, the form looks pretty solid.

NOTEBOOK
Ask, highly progressive in a restricted four-year-old campaign, looked unlucky to be touched-off on unsuitably firm ground in the Canadian International at Woodbine in October, and he had been given plenty of time to recover. Though struggling to hit form with his younger horses, the Stoute older brigade have made a good start to the season and he managed to overcome the drop in trip/steady gallop. Always well positioned, he took a while to hit top stride and looked more likely to finish third racing into the final quarter mile, but the further they went the better he was and he edged ahead of the persistent Hattan close home. This was a highly pleasing return and connections can now set their sights on some of the bigger prizes later in the year, with the King George and Arc likely to be the focal point of his season. In the meantime races such as the Tattersalls Gold Cup, Coronation Cup and Hardwicke are all likely to come under consideration. (op 8-11 tchd 4-5 in places)
Hattan(IRE), back to something like his best when springing a minor surprise in taking the Winter Derby on his seasonal debut, is reportedly a much happier horse this season as a result of some dental work over the winter and he took a further step forward on this return to turf. He looked the likeliest winner when coming alongside over a furlong out, but he was unable to press on and in the end the winner's class told. He could go close if turning up in Huxley Stakes at Chester's May meeting. (op 11-2)
Philatelist(USA) ran much better than his finishing position of 10th suggests behind Hattan in the Winter Derby and had since won the Rosebery at Kempton off a mark of 94, so it was no surprise to see him run above himself in this small-field event. He went on over two out, coming with his challenge against the rail, but could never build much of a lead and in the end faded out of it. This was his best effort yet, and while he may still struggle to win at this level in Britain his new owner Gary Tanaka will no doubt have his eye on suitable targets abroad. (op 8-1)
Championship Point(IRE) received a fine front-running ride from Holland to win a conditions stakes at Ripon last time and again seemed to have conditions in his favour. However, this presented a much stiffer task with a horse of Ask's calibre in the line-up and he was unable to shake them off from the front this time. (op 15-2)
Illustrious Blue, narrowly denied in the Magnolia Stakes at Kempton last time, never threatened to get into it on this return to turf and was plainly unsuited by being held up off a steady pace. He is better than this and is worth another chance in a race in which a stronger gallop is on the cards. (op 7-1 tchd 13-2)

1597 BET365 BEST ODDS GUARANTEED H'CAP — 5f 6y
2:25 (2:26) (Class 2) (0-100,95) 3-Y-O
£9,969 (£2,985; £1,492; £747; £372; £187) **Stalls** High

Form				RPR
21-	**1**		**Corrybrough**[193] [6234] 3-9-4 **90** .... RyanMoore 11 (H Candy) *lw: towards rr: pushed along 1/2-way: prog over 1f out: rdn to ld jst ins fnl f: forged clr* **5/4**[1]	102+
1-50	**2**	*2*	**Chartist**[9] [1404] 3-9-0 **86** .... RichardHughes 3 (R Hannon) *lw: trckd ldng pair: cruising over 1f out: asked to ld 1f out but immediately surprised by wnr: limited rspnse whn rdn* **13/2**[3]	91
102-	**3**	*3/4*	**Rash Judgement**[167] [6756] 3-8-13 **85** .... FergusSweeney 9 (W S Kittow) *hld up in last trio: nt clr run over 1f out: styd on wl fnl f to take 3rd last strides* **13/2**[3]	91+
00-5	**4**	*nk*	**Brassini**[15] [1284] 3-8-5 **77** .... JohnEgan 2 (B R Millman) *racd on outer in midfield: reminders and prog 1/2-way: cl enough 1f out: kpt on one pce* **40/1**	78

244- **5** *nk* **Lesson In Humility (IRE)**[217] 5583 3-9-1 **87**................. AndrewElliott 5 87
(K R Burke) *t.k.h: trckd ldng pair: n.m.r on inner jst over 1f out: kpt on same pce fnl f w tail flashing* **20/1**

302- **6** *1* **Perfect Flight**[197] 6128 3-8-9 **81**................................ TedDurcan 1 78
(M Blanshard) *pushed along in rr after 2f: styd on fnl f: nrst fin* **33/1**

060- **7** *1 3/4* **Lady Avenger (IRE)**[203] 5973 3-9-9 **95**......................... KerrinMcEvoy 6 85
(J M P Eustace) *bit bkwd: t.k.h: hld up bhd ldrs: nt qckn over 1f out: fdd fnl f* **33/1**

002- **8** *nse* **Bosun Breese**[194] 6195 3-8-13 **85**.. LPKeniry 10 75
(P W D'Arcy) *led 1f: led again 2f out: drvn and hdd jst insn fnl f: wknd* **11/1**

0-12 **9** *shd* **Soopacal (IRE)**[27] 1075 3-9-6 **92**................................ TomEaves 8 82
(B Smart) *lw: sn trckd ldrs: rdn whn nt clr run briefly over 1f out: sn btn* **14/1**

043- **10** *hd* **Good Gorsoon (USA)**[179] 6544 3-8-11 **83**...................... MichaelHills 7 72+
(B W Hills) *swtg: hld up in last: effrt and nt clr run over 1f out: repeatedly hmpd ins fnl f whn gng wl: no ch* **16/1**

61-3 **11** *5* **Fol Hollow (IRE)**[9] 1404 3-9-9 **95**......................... AdrianTNicholls 4 66
(D Nicholls) *led after 1f to 2f out: wknd rapidly fnl f* **11/2[2]**

62.22 secs (0.62) **Going Correction** +0.275s/f (Good) **11 Ran SP% 120.5**
Speed ratings (Par 104): **106,102,101,101,100 99,96,96,96,95 87**
CSF £9.48 CT £42.10 TOTE £2.10: £1.20, £2.30, £2.30; EX 12.30.

Owner Thurloe Thoroughbreds XXI **Bred** Mrs Sheila Oakes **Trained** Kingston Warren, Oxon

■ Stewards' Enquiry : Ryan Moore one-day ban: careless riding (May 9)

FOCUS
A really good three-year-old sprint won impressively by the promising Corrybrough from two similarly unexposed types. The race should produce its share of winners.

NOTEBOOK
Corrybrough ◆ is a sprinter going places. Impressive when winning a Windsor maiden on his second and final start at two, he was dropping to 5f for the first time and it was interesting his trainer had chosen this race, having won it with his high-class sire Kyllachy seven years ago. Sporting the same colours as the Nunthorpe winner, he was all the rage in the betting and it was easy to see why, having reportedly been working with last week's Newbury winner Oldjoesaid. Things did not look to be going to plan after a couple of the furlongs, as he was towards the rear and being pushed along, but once hitting top gear he produced a sustained burst worthy of a top-class sprinter, scything through the pack and running away with it in the final 100 yards. This was a highly impressive display first time up, over a new trip and his trainer believes he can turn out to be as good as his sire. There is a chance he may be even better given his size and scope, but he will not be rushed this season. The Listed Scurry Stakes over course and distance in June looks a suitable short-term target, but he will not be rushed this season and the Abbaye is his likely long-term target. An easy surface seems imperative. Official explanation: one-day ban: careless riding (May 9) (tchd 11-8 and 6-4 in places)

Chartistin mid-division in a competitive sprint handicap at the Craven meeting, has been crying out for this drop back down to 5f and he travelled much the best. However, there was little response once he asked for his effort and in the end was over-powered by the winner. This is his trip. (op 6-1 tchd 7-1)

Rash Judgement ◆, a progressive juvenile who finished runner-up to the useful Generous Thought off a mark of 80 on his final start at Doncaster, looked a shade unlucky back in third and may have been second with a cleaner run. He came from a long way back and should benefit from having this run under his belt when returning to 6f. (op 9-1 tchd 10-1)

Brassini has an exposed look to him, but he has been falling in the weights and ran a blinder back in fourth. His draw made life difficult, but he responded well to pressure and stuck on gamely. He can find a less competitive contest.

Lesson In Humility(IRE), a Carlisle maiden winner who went on to twice finish fourth in Listed sprints last year, had made the long journey down from Middleham and she looked one of the more interesting outsiders. She showed plenty of speed, but flashed her tail inside the final furlong and was unable to get any nearer. On the whole this was a pleasing comeback. Official explanation: jockey said filly was denied a clear run.

Perfect Flight showed some fair nursery form as a juvenile and this was a good comeback run, keeping on under pressure having been in rear and outpaced for most of the way.

Lady Avenger(IRE), off since finishing down the field in the Cheveley Park, had it all to do here off a mark of 95 and she struggled to make an impact.

Bosun Breese had a good draw and made the most of it, but could not sustain the gallop. (op 14-1)

Soopacal(IRE), just denied by Vhujon at Kempton last month, was 5lb higher here and could not make any impact on this drop in trip.

Good Gorsoon(USA) ◆ met all the trouble going and this can be completely ignored. He did not have a race. Official explanation: jockey said colt was denied a clear run (op 18-1 tchd 20-1)

Fol Hollow(IRE), not beaten far in a competitive 6f handicap at the Craven meeting, was off the same mark here, but having shown plenty of early speed he dropped away tamely. (tchd 6-1)

1598 CASINO AT BET365.COM CONDITIONS STKS 1m 14y

3:00 (3:02) (Class 3) 3-Y-O **£6,542** (£1,469; £1,469; £490; £244) **Stalls** High

Form RPR

1- **1** **General Eliott (IRE)**[189] 6294 3-9-0 93......................... TQuinn 6 93
(P F I Cole) *trckd ldng pair: shkn up over 2f out: nt clr run on inner over 1f out: drvn and squeezed through fnl f to ld last 75yds* **11/4[3]**

1 **2** *3/4* **Charm School**[27] 1073 3-9-0 0.. JimmyFortune 2 91
(J H M Gosden) *strong: lw: s.s: hld up in last: urged along and green over 2f out: hrd rdn and grad styd on fnl f: nvr quite able to chal* **7/4[1]**

46-1 **2** *dht* **Steele Tango (USA)**[101] 163 3-8-10 73........................... DaneO'Neill 5 87
(R A Teal) *b.hind: in tch in 4th: rdn on outer over 2f out: clsd over 1f out: tried to chal ins fnl f: kpt on* **33/1**

612- **4** *hd* **Zakhaaref**[194] 6194 3-9-0 90.. RHills 1 91
(M Johnston) *led: shkn up and looked in command over 1f out: drvn and hdd last 75yds: lost 2 pls last strides* **2/1[2]**

310- **5** *3* **Manassas (IRE)**[201] 6041 3-9-0 103.......................... LDettori 3 84
(B J Meehan) *trckd ldr: rdn over 2f out: clsd to chal jst over 1f out: hld whn squeezed out last 150yds* **7/1**

1m 45.23s (1.93) **Going Correction** +0.275s/f (Good) **5 Ran SP% 111.8**
Speed ratings (Par 102): **101,100,100,100,97**
PL: £2.10, Charm School £0.60, Steele Tango £1.70. EX: GE/CS £3.90, GE/ST £39.90. CSF: GE/CS £4.08, GE/ST £27.17 TOTE £3.60.

Owner Sir George Meyrick **Bred** Maddenstown Equine Enterprise Ltd **Trained** Whatcombe, Oxon

■ Stewards' Enquiry : Jimmy Fortune four-day ban: used whip with excessive force and down the shoulder in forehand position (May 9-10, 12, 14)

FOCUS
A race that has thrown up the likes of Little Rock and Medicean over the years. This form looks a little suspect as a result of the steady pace, and neither General Eliott nor Charm School were seen to best effect off of it. It has provisionally been rated around the fourth.

NOTEBOOK
General Eliott(IRE) ◆ won with more in hand than the official margin suggests on his sole start at two and is highly regarded by connections. This looked a good starting point to launch his three-year-old career and he overcame trouble in running to score, squeezing through having already been cut off once to get the better of the favourite. A good-looking individual, he looks to be crying out for further and, although the form is a little suspect as they finished well bunched, the steady gallop was against him as much as any of them. Connections are eyeing a crack at the French 2,000 Guineas and he remains a horse to keep on side. (op 7-2 tchd 5-2)

Charm School, who created a strong impression when bolting up in a soft-ground Doncaster maiden last month, was held up in last following a slussigh start and could have done with a stronger gallop. He still came to have a chance, despite running green, but the winner was always doing a bit too much inside the final half a furlong and he was forced to settle with a tie for second. He too can be rated better than the bare form and remains capable of further improvement. (op 50-1)

Steele Tango(USA), narrow winner of a modest Kempton maiden back in January, had it all to do with the best of these and his prominent placing does the form no favours. It is possible he has made a good deal of improvement, but for now it is probably best to assumed he was flattered. (op 50-1)

Zakhaaref, a disappointment on his final start at two, being beaten at short odds at Bath, had the run of things on the front end and still came up short, being swamped inside the final half furlong. Things are going to be tough off his current rating, but he is likely to do better once upped in trip. (op 7-2)

Manassas(IRE), winner of a York maiden then outclassed behind Rio De La Plata in the Jean-Luc Lagardere at Longchamp, had the highest official rating of these, but he was not very popular in the market and was already held when tight for room inside the final furlong. He can be rated a little better than the bare form though and will no doubt benefit from a stronger gallop. (tchd 13-2)

1599 POKER AT BET365.COM MAIDEN FILLIES' STKS 1m 2f 7y

3:35 (3:40) (Class 4) 3-Y-O **£5,180** (£1,541; £770; £384) **Stalls** High

Form RPR

2- **1** **Dar Re Mi**[174] 6648 3-9-0 0.. JimmyFortune 6 93+
(J H M Gosden) *mde all: pushed along and drew rt away fnl 2f* **1/1[1]**

2 *7* **Icon Project (USA)** 3-9-0 0.. RichardHughes 1 75+
(B J Meehan) *strong: bit bkwd: prog fr midfield to trck ldng pair 1/2-way: wnt 2nd over 3f out: kpt on but no ch w wnr fnl 2f* **14/1**

3 *1* **Albarouche** 3-9-0 0.. PhilipRobinson 7 73+
(M A Jarvis) *w'like: scope: bit bkwd: rn green in midfield: effrt over 2f out: disp 3rd fr wl over 1f out: kpt on but no threat* **7/1[3]**

6- **4** *hd* **Sovereign's Honour (USA)**[258] 4402 3-9-0 0................. RyanMoore 8 73+
(Sir Michael Stoute) *lw: settled midfield: shkn up over 2f out: eased out and styd on fr over 1f out to press for 3rd nr fin* **15/2**

04- **5** *nk* **Star Of Gibraltar**[217] 5596 3-9-0 0................................ EddieAhern 9 72
(J L Dunlop) *strong: bit bkwd: t.k.h: hld up bhd ldrs: effrt to dispute 3rd 2f out: shkn up and styd on* **4/1[2]**

0- **6** *hd* **Piano Sonata**[174] 6649 3-9-0 0...................................... MichaelHills 11 72
(B W Hills) *tall: leggy: scope: prom: disp 3rd fr 2f out but no ch: kpt on* **14/1**

7 *2 3/4* **Testimonial** 3-9-0 0... StephenDonohoe 10 66
(E A L Dunlop) *w'like: neat: dwlt: hld up in last: sme prog fr over 2f out but nvr on terms w ldrs* **20/1**

8 *1* **Seedless** 3-9-0 0.. NeilChalmers 2 64
(A M Balding) *w'like: scope: bit bkwd: rn green in rr: last and shkn up wl over 2f out: plugged on* **25/1**

9 *1* **Massiuta (UAE)** 3-9-0 0.. SebSanders 5 62
(C E Brittain) *leggy: a towards rr: shkn up and no prog over 2f out* **25/1**

10 *2 3/4* **Requia** 3-9-0 0.. DaneO'Neill 4 57
(H Candy) *unf: mostly chsd wnr to over 3f out: wknd rapidly* **50/1**

11 *3 3/4* **Keen Eye** 3-9-0 0.. PaulDoe 3 49
(W J Knight) *s.i.s: a in last pair: no ch over 2f out* **28/1**

2m 13.02s (2.52) **Going Correction** +0.275s/f (Good) **11 Ran SP% 125.5**
Speed ratings (Par 97): **100,94,93,93,93 93,90,90,89,87 84**
CSF £18.16 TOTE £2.00: £1.20, £3.00, £2.20; EX 22.90.

Owner Lord Lloyd-Webber **Bred** Watership Down Stud **Trained** Newmarket, Suffolk

FOCUS
A decent fillies' maiden. Difficult to know quite what the form amounts to, but hard not to be impressed by new Oaks favourite Dar Re Mi.

1600 BET365.COM H'CAP 1m 2f 7y

4:10 (4:13) (Class 3) (0-90,92) 3-Y-O

£6,542 (£1,959; £979; £490; £244; £122) **Stalls** High

Form RPR

01- **1** **Colony (IRE)**[184] 6417 3-8-5 **77**........................... KerrinMcEvoy 8 90
(Sir Michael Stoute) *scope: hld up in last pair: prog on outer fr over 2f out: sustained effrt and rdn to ld last 100yds: sn clr* **6/1[3]**

103- **2** *1 3/4* **Midships (USA)**[264] 4199 3-9-1 **87**.............................. JimCrowley 3 96
(Mrs A J Perrett) *lw: led at decent pce: pressed 3f out: styd on wl: hdd and outpcd last 100yds* **25/1**

031- **3** *3/4* **Conduit (IRE)**[216] 5646 3-8-7 **79**................................ RyanMoore 11 87+
(Sir Michael Stoute) *lw: t.k.h early: hld up towards rr: effrt on inner over 2f out: prog and got through over 1f out: tk 3rd nr fin but nt pce to chal* **3/1[2]**

0-12 **4** *hd* **Pacifism (UAE)**[98] 217 3-8-13 **85**......................... PhilipRobinson 4 93
(M A Jarvis) *plld hrd: hld up bhd ldrs: hanging bdly rt fr over 2f out: kpt on despite being hrd to keep st* **16/1**

1-11 **5** *1 1/4* **Captain Webb**[12] 1348 3-9-6 **92** 6ex........................... JoeFanning 9 97
(M Johnston) *lw: t.k.h: prom: wnt 2nd 4f out: rdn to chal 3f out and wandered: nt qckn fnl 2f and steadily lost pl* **5/4[1]**

210- **6** *1/2* **Safari Sunup (IRE)**[182] 6471 3-9-4 **90**.................... StephenCarson 5 94
(P Winkworth) *settled in rr: hrd rdn and effrt 2f out: kpt on but unable to rch ldrs* **33/1**

-536 **7** *3 1/4* **Harry Gee**[51] 799 3-8-8 **80**.. TedDurcan 2 78
(G Wragg) *lw: dropped in to last fr wd draw: pushed along on inner over 2f out: sharp reminder over 1f out: kpt on steadily* **14/1**

621- **8** *1 3/4* **Trenchtown (IRE)**[231] 5186 3-9-1 **87**......................... SteveDrowne 1 81
(R Charlton) *trckd ldr after 2f to 4f out: wknd over 2f out* **20/1**

412- **9** *shd* **Dona Alba (IRE)**[211] 5746 3-8-13 **85**........................ EddieAhern 10 79
(J L Dunlop) *hld up bhd ldrs: prog to chse ldng pair over 2f out to over 1f out: wknd* **17/2**

041- **10** *1* **Cossack Prince**[153] 6934 3-8-9 **81**............................... AlanMunro 7 73
(B J Meehan) *chsd ldr 2f: cl up tl steadily wknd fr over 2f out* **66/1**

411- **11** *14* **City Of The Kings (IRE)**[223] 5400 3-8-13 **85**............. RichardHughes 6 49
(R Hannon) *in tch tl wknd wl over 2f out: t.o* **16/1**

2m 10.44s (-0.06) **Going Correction** +0.275s/f (Good) **11 Ran SP% 125.7**
Speed ratings (Par 102): **111,109,109,108,107 107,104,103,103,102 91**
CSF £155.77 CT £550.97 TOTE £8.70: £2.60, £4.40, £1.60; EX 171.60 Place 6 £ 26.74, Place 5 £ 5.75.

Owner Highclere Thoroughbred Racing (Delilah) **Bred** Barronstown Stud And Orpendale **Trained** Newmarket, Suffolk

FOCUS
A most informative three-year-old handicap, run in a decent time. The first six all looked progressive, and although red-hot favourite Captain Webb failed to meet market expectation, the form looks solid. A race that looks sure to produce winners.

NOTEBOOK
Colony(IRE) ◆, one of two representing Sir Michael Stoute, looked the second-string on jockey bookings, but he had won in taking style at Bath on his second and final start at two and proved good enough to make a winning handicap debut off a mark of 77. Restrained right at the back, he started to come with a promising run inside the final quarter mile and got well on top inside the half a final furlong, proving his yard with their first three-year-old winner of the season. An attractive sort whose dam won over 1m4f, he gave the impression here that trip would be within reach. There should be more to come. (tchd 9-2 and 13-2)
Midships(USA), a winner on his debut over 6f at Newbury at two, failed to progress in two subsequent starts when faced with stiffer company and looked on a stiff enough mark for this seasonal return. However, he is bred to stay this trip and, having been made plenty of use of, he stuck on well under pressure to hold second. There may well be more to come, although quite a few by his sire Mizzen Mast seem best when fresh. (op 20-1)
Conduit(IRE) ◆, the seemingly better fancied of the Stoute pair, improved with racing as a juvenile and wound up winning a Wolverhampton maiden on his third and final start. A mark of 79 looked about right, but he got a bit too far back and, despite running on really well once in the clear, it was too late. He was probably unlucky not to get second and looks to be crying out for 1m4f. A decent race should come his way this season and at this stage, he already looks an obvious one for the King George V Handicap at Royal Ascot. (op 11-4 tchd 10-3 in places)
Pacifism(UAE) showed fair form in winning a 1m2f Lingfield maiden in January and bettered that effort when bumping into a progressive Mark Johnston handicapper at Wolverhampton next time. Up 3lb for this return to turf, he ran a blinder. Refusing to settle early, he gave his rider a torrid time in the straight by hanging badly right and it says a lot for his ability that he still managed to finish so close. He could prove better than this mark if his apparent flaws can be ironed out.
Captain Webb, winner of his sole start at two, has quickly made up into a useful handicapper by winning on his reappearance at Leicester and then destroying a weak field at Brighton easing down by 20 lengths. Officially 8lb well in under the penalty, he was too keen this time, racing just behind the leaders, and having moved into a winning position rounding for home he could never get away from his field and still looked rather green under pressure. This was disappointing, but he is not one to give up on just yet. (op 6-4 tchd 13-8 in places)
Safari Sunup(IRE), a generally progressive type at two, was reappearing off a 9lb higher mark than when last winning and his hopes were pinned on the extra quarter mile bringing about improvement. He ran well, keeping on past beaten horses, but never looked a threat and will need to improve to defy this mark. (op 50-1)
Harry Gee, a close-up sixth in a slowly run race at Lingfield last time, was the most exposed in the field and held slim chances of winning, but he kept on late having been held up right at the back. (op 28-1 tchd 33-1)
Trenchtown(IRE), edgy beforehand, signed off at two by winning a Chepstow maiden, but he needed to have made marked improvement to win off a mark of 87 and in the end dropped away, having been up there early. He is entitled to improve for the run. (op 25-1)
Dona Alba(IRE), on her toes beforehand, had some fair form to her name at two and she shaped as though this first run since September was needed. (op 10-1 tchd 8-1)
Cossack Prince, not far behind the winner at Bath as a juvenile, had not been seen since winning a Wolverhampton maiden in November and he was readily dismissed in the market. His yard have made a slow start to the season and he dropped away under pressure, but this would have been needed and he can find a small race once dropped a few pounds.
City Of The Kings(IRE), winner off a mark of 76 on his final start at two, came into this in search of a hat-trick and his yard have made a great start to the season, but he dropped out tamely in the final quarter mile and there was presumably something amiss. Official explanation: jockey said colt had no more to give. (op 14-1)
T/Jkpt: £2,722.80 to a £1 stake. Pool: £15,340.09. 4.00 winning tickets. T/Plt: £28.00 to a £1 stake. Pool: £82,014.70. 2,131.85 winning tickets. T/Qpdt: £6.30 to a £1 stake. Pool: £3,858.10. 446.50 winning tickets. JN

1486 WOLVERHAMPTON (A.W) (L-H)
Friday, April 25

OFFICIAL GOING: Standard
Wind: Light behind Weather: Overcast with the odd shower

1601 DINE IN THE HORIZONS RESTAURANT MAIDEN STKS 7f 32y(P)
2:15 (2:16) (Class 5) 3-Y-O £3,070 (£906; £453) Stalls High

Form				RPR
0-4	1		**Slugger O'Toole**[9] 1403 3-9-3 0 ChrisCatlin 3 (B W Hills) *trckd ldrs: racd keenly: swtchd lft over 1f out: led ins fnl f: shkn up and r.o wl* 9/4[2]	89
2-	2	¾	**Skadrak (USA)**[271] 3991 3-9-3 0 RobertWinston 8 (B J Meehan) *trckd ldr: racd keenly: rdn and ev ch ins fnl f: unable qck towards fin* 4/6[1]	87
20	3	2 ¾	**August Gale (USA)**[14] 1295 3-9-3 0 RoystonFfrench 4 (M Johnston) *sn led: rdn over 1f out: hdd ins fnl f: styd on same pce* 11/4[3]	80
2-	4	3 ½	**James Dean (IRE)**[210] 5780 3-8-10 0 DTDaSilva(7) 6 (P F I Cole) *prom: racd keenly: rdn over 2f out: hung lft over 1f out: styd on same pce* 9/1	71
6-	5	½	**Novellen Lad (IRE)**[167] 6755 3-9-3 0 JimmyQuinn 7 (E J Alston) *s.i.s: hld up: hdwy 1/2-way: rdn over 2f out: styd on same pce appr fnl f* 20/1	69
	6	2	**Cheney Manor** 3-8-10 0 AshtonByles(7) 9 (B W Hills) *hld up: nvr nr to chal* 20/1	64+
	7	24	**Little Molly (IRE)** 3-8-12 0 EdwardCreighton 2 (E J Creighton) *hld up in tch: wknd 1/2-way* 40/1	—

1m 32.8s (3.20) **Going Correction** +0.20s/f (Slow) **7** Ran SP% **139.4**
Speed ratings (Par 98): **89,88,85,81,80 78,50**
CSF £5.23 TOTE £4.20: £1.80, £1.40; EX 6.30 Trifecta £28.90 Pool: £424.88, 10.43 winning units.
Owner R J Crothers, Phil Cunningham **Bred** Harts Farm And Stud **Trained** Lambourn, Berks

FOCUS
A strong maiden for the track in which they bet 9/1 bar three and those dominated throughout and finished clear. The time was moderate though, being the slowest of the four races over the trip on the day, and how reliable the bare form turns out to be remains to be seen.
Cheney Manor Official explanation: jockey said, regarding running and riding, his instructions were to settle and keep him balanced intitially and do the best he could; he added he was a big leggy gelding with a long stride which became unbalanced leaving back straight; trainer's rep said gelding had lost its action on the bend.

1602 SPONSOR A RACE BY CALLING 01902 390009 H'CAP 7f 32y(P)
2:50 (2:51) (Class 6) (0-55,55) 4-Y-0+ £2,047 (£604; £302) Stalls High

Form				RPR
1203	1		**Sion Hill (IRE)**[21] 1189 7-8-9 55 (p) KellyHarrison(5) 3 (John A Harris) *mde all: edgd lft over 3f out: rdn over 1f out: r.o* 4/1[2]	69
06-4	2	2 ¼	**Willie Ever**[95] 251 4-8-8 49 J-PGuillambert 7 (B Ellison) *plld hrd and prom: rdn over 2f out: r.o: nt rch wnr* 6/1	57
003-	3	1 ¾	**Maison Dieu**[176] 6608 5-9-0 55 JimmyQuinn 8 (E J Alston) *a.p: chsd wnr over 3f out: rdn over 1f out: no ex fnl f* 12/1	58
1231	4	nk	**Marmooq**[16] 1275 5-8-10 51 (e) IanMongan 5 (M J Attwater) *hld up: rdn over 2f out: styd on ins fnl f: nt rch ldrs* 10/3[1]	53
4001	5	½	**Newgate (UAE)**[6] 1491 4-8-5 51 6ex (b) DanielleMcCreery(5) 4 (Mrs R A Carr) *s.i.s: hld up: hdwy on outside over 1f out: nvr nrr* 9/2[3]	52
00-6	6	nse	**Border Artist**[18] 1248 9-8-7 48 ChrisCatlin 12 (J Pearce) *hld up: rdn over 1f out: nrst fin* 20/1	49
60-6	7	nse	**Vanatina (IRE)**[14] 1313 4-8-7 48 LiamJones 6 (W M Brisbourne) *hld up: rdn over 1f out: n.d* 33/1	49
	8	shd	**Chiefofthemowhawks (USA)**[42] 892 5-8-8 52 (v[1]) JerryO'Dwyer(3) 10 (Stephen Michael Cox, Ire) *hld up: hdwy 1/2-way: rdn over 2f out: styd on same pce appr fnl f* 5/1	53
06-5	9	1	**The Graig**[20] 1207 4-8-2 50 StacyRenwick(7) 2 (J R Holt) *s.i.s: sn prom: rdn over 1f out: wknd fnl f* 25/1	48
5066	10	2 ¼	**Mister Benji**[6] 1491 9-7-12 46 oh1 (p) SoniaEaton(7) 1 (B P J Baugh) *chsd wnr tl hmpd and hit rails 1/2-way: rdn and wknd over 1f out* 16/1	38
640-	11	3	**Miss Percy**[235] 5084 4-8-11 52 (p) PatrickMathers 11 (I W McInnes) *hld up: rdn 1/2-way: n.d* 33/1	36
1112	12	5	**Straight Face (IRE)**[14] 1313 4-8-9 55 AshleyHamblett(5) 9 (Miss Gay Kelleway) *chsd ldrs: rdn over 2f out: wknd over 1f out: eased fnl f* 5/1	25

1m 30.14s (0.54) **Going Correction** +0.20s/f (Slow) **12** Ran SP% **136.9**
Speed ratings (Par 101): **104,101,99,99,98 98,98,98,97,94 91,85**
CSF £32.12 CT £291.10 TOTE £10.50: £2.70, £2.70, £3.90; EX 65.40 Trifecta £234.80 Part won. Pool: £330.73, 0.20 winning units..
Owner Peter Taylor Miss Laura Morgan **Bred** Joe Rogers **Trained** Eastwell, Leics
■ Stewards' Enquiry : Kelly Harrison two-day ban: careless riding (May 9-10)

FOCUS
A moderate handicap with an all-the-way winner in a race run at a sound gallop. He was showing his best form since he was a 2yo.
Marmooq Official explanation: jockey said gelding suffered interference in running shortly after the start.
Mister Benji Official explanation: jockey said gelding suffered interference in running.
Straight Face(IRE) Official explanation: jockey said gelding ran flat

1603 HOTEL & CONFERENCING AT WOLVERHAMPTON (S) STKS 7f 32y(P)
3:30 (3:30) (Class 6) 3-Y-O £2,047 (£604; £302) Stalls High

Form				RPR
0156	1		**Secret Meaning**[9] 1407 3-8-5 55 (v[1]) JackDean(7) 2 (W G M Turner) *s.i.s: hld up: rdn over 2f out: hdwy u.p over 1f out: led and hung rt ins fnl f: sn clr* 12/1	63
4423	2	4 ½	**One Called Alice**[22] 1169 3-8-4 58 LukeMorris(3) 7 (A W Carroll) *hld up: pushed along over 4f out: hdwy u.p over 2f out: hung lft over 1f out: styd on same pce ins fnl f* 11/4[2]	46
225	3	¾	**Jal Music**[45] 848 3-8-12 67 (b[1]) AdamKirby 3 (R A Harris) *s.s: hdwy to ld over 5f out: rdn and hung rt over 1f out: hung lft: hdd & wknd ins fnl f* 6/4[1]	49
0-	4	¾	**Rich Harvest (USA)**[118] 7266 3-8-12 0 NeilPollard 5 (A P Jarvis) *chsd ldr: rdn over 2f out: hung lft over 1f out: wknd ins fnl f* 13/2[3]	47
0-06	5	2 ¼	**Bahia Palace**[16] 1274 3-8-7 38 (p) HayleyTurner 9 (M D I Usher) *hld up: rdn 1/2-way: nvr nrr* 16/1	36
4305	6	2	**Shabnaam**[12] 1347 3-8-7 50 JimmyQuinn 8 (P Howling) *chsd ldrs: rdn over 2f out: sn wknd* 8/1	30
-536	7	1 ¼	**Distant Noble**[36] 950 3-8-12 45 (b) PaulMulrennan 1 (R Brotherton) *led: hdd over 5f out: rdn over 2f out: wknd over 1f out* 20/1	32
6545	8	½	**Flemish Art (IRE)**[28] 1063 3-8-9 65 (b[1]) KevinGhunowa(3) 6 (R A Harris) *prom: rdn over 2f out: hung lft and wknd over 1f out* 12/1	31
0	9	1 ½	**Good News Too**[23] 1144 3-8-7 0 RobertHavlin 4 (D K Ivory) *prom: pushed along 5f out: rdn and wknd over 2f out* 20/1	22
00	10	10	**Handbags At Dawn (IRE)**[18] 1243 3-8-7 0 ChrisCatlin 11 (S Kirk) *s.i.s: hld up: rdn and wknd 1/2-way* 16/1	—

1m 31.73s (2.13) **Going Correction** +0.20s/f (Slow) **10** Ran SP% **127.8**
Speed ratings (Par 96): **95,89,89,88,85 83,81,81,79,68**
CSF £49.57 TOTE £18.20: £5.70, £1.30, £1.10; EX 64.90 Trifecta £93.50 Pool: £339.82, 2.58 winning units.There was no bid for the winner
Owner Sparsholt Stud **Bred** P C Hunt **Trained** Sigwells, Somerset

FOCUS
A weak seller won in a time more than a second slower than the previous handicap for horses rated below 55 but faster than the opening maiden. With the third disappointing there is a doubt over the strength of the form.
Jal Music Official explanation: jockey said gelding failed to stay the 7 furlongs

1604 WOLVERHAMPTON-RACECOURSE.CO.UK H'CAP 7f 32y(P)
4:05 (4:05) (Class 5) (0-75,75) 4-Y-0+ £3,238 (£963; £481; £240) Stalls High

Form				RPR
1-12	1		**Arthur's Edge**[100] 177 4-8-13 70 CatherineGannon 1 (B Palling) *mde all: rdn over 1f out: styd on gamely* 5/1	82
0144	2	1 ¾	**Chief Exec**[27] 1084 6-9-1 72 (v) LiamJones 4 (J R Gask) *s.i.s and hmpd s: hld up: hdwy over 2f out: rdn and ev ch ins fnl f: nt qckn towards fin* 3/1[1]	79
-114	3	nk	**Playtotheaudience**[17] 1260 5-8-4 61 oh1 (v) PaulHanagan 6 (R A Fahey) *hld up: hdwy 1/2-way: rdn and hung lft fr over 1f out: r.o* 3/1[1]	67
-601	4	½	**Hessian (IRE)**[17] 1253 4-9-2 73 JimmyQuinn 2 (M D Squance) *a.p: chsd wnr over 2f out: sn rdn: styd on* 4/1[2]	78
3005	5	¾	**Parkview Love (USA)**[7] 1449 7-8-7 64 (v) DeanMcKeown 7 (D Shaw) *hld up: hdwy over 2f out: sn rdn: styd on* 12/1	67
/3-0	6	1	**Blue Charm**[11] 1368 4-8-13 75 HaddenFrost(5) 3 (S Kirk) *prom: lost pl over 4f out: n.d after* 9/2[3]	75
0-06	7	18	**H Harrison (IRE)**[9] 1409 8-8-7 69 NataliaGemelova(5) 8 (I W McInnes) *chsd ldrs: rdn 1/2-way: wknd over 2f out* 18/1	21
0023	8	3 ½	**Arturius (IRE)**[12] 1349 6-8-10 70 (p) KevinGhunowa(3) 5 (R A Harris) *dwlt: hdwy to chse wnr over 5f out: rdn 1/2-way: wknd over 2f out* 10/1	12

1m 29.5s (-0.10) **Going Correction** +0.20s/f (Slow) **8** Ran SP% **126.9**
Speed ratings (Par 103): **108,106,105,105,104 103,82,78**
CSF £22.92 CT £56.33 TOTE £4.60: £1.80, £1.30, £1.40; EX 23.60 Trifecta £74.70 Pool: £356.03, 3.38 winning units.
Owner Mrs Annabelle Mason **Bred** Christopher J Mason **Trained** Tredodridge, Vale Of Glamorgan

FOCUS
A fair handicap run at a good gallop, being much the fastest of the four races over the trip on the day, and the winner made all. Sound form.

1605 HOTEL & CONFERENCING AT WOLVERHAMPTON H'CAP 1m 141y(P)
4:45 (4:46) (Class 6) (0-65,65) 4-Y-0+ £2,388 (£705; £352) Stalls Low

Form RPR
2145 **1** **Hucking Heat (IRE)**[14] 1296 4-9-2 **63**..........................(p) HayleyTurner 1 70
(R Hollinshead) *a.p: rdn to ld and edgd lft ins fnl f: r.o* **11/2**[3]
-550 **2** *nk* **Hits Only Cash**[11] 1368 6-8-9 **63**.............................. SimonPearce(7) 4 69
(J Pearce) *hld up: rdn over 3f out: hdwy over 1f out: r.o* **8/1**
5053 **3** *1 1/4* **Alexander Guru**[14] 1301 4-9-0 **61**.............................. JamesDoyle 5 64
(M Blanshard) *hld up: hdwy over 1f out: rdn and edgd lft ins fnl f: r.o* **7/1**
000- **4** *1 1/4* **Indian Edge**[184] 6423 7-9-1 **62**.............................. CatherineGannon 7 62
(B Palling) *led: rdn and hdd over 2f out: rallied to ld over 1f out: hdd and unable qck ins fnl f* **14/1**
02-6 **5** *1* **He's Mine Too**[90] 240 4-9-1 **65**.............................. DNolan(3) 9 63
(D G Bridgwater) *hld up: rdn over 1f out: nvr trbld ldrs* **14/1**
5020 **6** *3/4* **Grenane (IRE)**[20] 1207 5-8-11 **58**.............................. RobertWinston 2 54
(P D Evans) *hld up: hdwy over 2f out: rdn and nt clr run over 1f out: styd on same pce* **4/1**[2]
500- **7** *shd* **Jalamid (IRE)**[196] 5503 6-8-4 **51** oh6..........................(t) DeanMcKeown 3 47
(M A Barnes) *chsd ldr tl led over 2f out: rdn and hdd over 1f out: hmpd and no ex ins fnl f* **6/1**
3332 **8** *1* **Sovereignty (JPN)**[6] 1491 6-8-9 **61**.............................. PatrickHills(5) 6 55
(D K Ivory) *plld hrd and prom: hung rt over 3f out: sn rdn: wknd over 1f out* **11/4**[1]
-330 **9** *1* **Time To Regret**[9] 1391 8-8-10 **57**..........................(p) RoystonFfrench 8 48
(I W McInnes) *chsd ldrs: rdn over 3f out: edgd lft and wknd over 1f out* **8/1**

1m 51.16s (0.66) **Going Correction** +0.20s/f (Slow) **9** Ran SP% **124.4**
Speed ratings (Par 101): **105,104,103,102,101 100,100,99,99**
CSF £52.79 CT £324.32 TOTE £9.10: £2.70, £3.10, £3.30; EX 69.10 TRIFECTA Not won..
Owner Ed Weetman (haulage & Storage) Ltd **Bred** Thomas J Reid **Trained** Upper Longdon, Staffs

FOCUS
A modest handicap run at a sound gallop. The winner is rated back to his winter best.
Jalamid(IRE) Official explanation: jockey said gelding suffered interference in the home straight.
Sovereignty(JPN) Official explanation: jockey said gelding hung right throughout.

1606 PERTEMPS PEOPLE DEVELOPMENT "HANDS & HEELS" APPRENTICE SERIES H'CAP 1m 1f 103y(P)
5:15 (5:15) (Class 6) (0-55,54) 4-Y-0+ £2,047 (£604; £302) Stalls Low

Form RPR
650- **1** **Treasure Isle**[200] 6069 4-8-2 **45**.............................. BMcHugh(3) 7 54
(R A Fahey) *edgd lft sn after s: prom: chsd ldr 5f out: shkn up to ld 1f out: r.o* **4/1**[2]
0244 **2** *nk* **Shosolosa (IRE)**[9] 1406 6-8-7 **47**.............................. StacyRenwick 9 55
(R C Guest) *s.i.s: hld up: hdwy over 1f out: r.o* **10/1**
5021 **3** *1* **Floodlight Fantasy**[2] 1562 5-8-12 **52** 6ex................(b) JemmaMarshall 8 58
(Dr R D P Newland) *hld up in tch: racd keenly: shkn up over 1f out: styd on* **11/10**[1]
4463 **4** *1/2* **Sparky Vixen**[17] 1262 4-8-11 **51**.............................. DeclanCannon 1 56
(C J Teague) *led 1f: chsd ldrs: shkn up and ev ch 1f out: styd on same pce* **8/1**[3]
0530 **5** *1/2* **Dream Forest (IRE)**[37] 938 5-8-10 **50**.............................. MatthewDavies 4 54
(P W Hiatt) *led over 8f out: shkn up and hdd 1f out: no ex* **14/1**
/0-3 **6** *3/4* **Haoin An Bothar (IRE)**[14] 1320 4-8-9 **54**.............................. AndreaAtzeni(5) 3 56
(Adrian Sexton, Ire) *s.i.s: plld hrd and sn prom: shkn up over 1f out: no ex ins fnl f* **11/1**
0453 **7** *3/4* **Bobering**[30] 1031 8-8-2 **45**.............................. SoniaEaton(3) 5 46
(B P J Baugh) *prom: hmpd and lost pl after 1f: n.d after* **10/1**
6030 **8** *1 1/4* **Northstar Express (IRE)**[28] 1053 5-8-5 **45**.............................. RossAtkinson 6 43
(J L Spearing) *prom: hmpd and lost pl after 1f: hld up: hdwy 2f out: wknd fnl f* **33/1**
5-42 **9** *1* **Al Rayanah**[17] 1258 5-8-9 **54**.............................. DanielNaidu(5) 10 50
(G Prodromou) *hld up: hdwy over 5f out: wknd over 1f out* **9/1**
40-0 **10** *1 1/4* **Weet Yer Tern (IRE)**[15] 1282 6-8-8 **48**..........................(b) DeanHeslop 2 41
(W M Brisbourne) *plld hrd and prom: wknd over 1f out* **12/1**

2m 5.10s (3.40) **Going Correction** +0.20s/f (Slow) **10** Ran SP% **132.5**
Speed ratings (Par 101): **92,91,90,90,89 89,88,87,86,85**
CSF £50.49 CT £76.53 TOTE £6.50: £2.00, £4.00, £1.10; EX 64.30 TRIFECTA Not won. Place 6 £ 32.73, Place 5 £ 27.26.
Owner R A Fahey **Bred** Worksop Manor Stud **Trained** Musley Bank, N Yorks

FOCUS
A poor, steadily run apprentice handicap and the time was moderate. The form is rated through the fourth but might not work out.
T/Plt: £72.90 to a £1 stake. Pool: £43,760.50. 437.90 winning tickets. T/Qpdt: £17.00 to a £1 stake. Pool: £3,017.60. 130.70 winning tickets. CR

1607 - 1609a (Foreign Racing) - See Raceform Interactive

HAYDOCK (L-H)
Saturday, April 26

OFFICIAL GOING: Good to soft (good in places)
Wind: Virtually nil Weather: Overcast, but dry

1610 E B F BET365 MAIDEN FILLIES' STKS 5f
5:50 (5:53) (Class 5) 2-Y-O £3,399 (£1,011; £505; £252) Stalls Centre

Form RPR
1 **Maggie Lou (IRE)** 2-9-0 **0**.............................. FergalLynch 2 73+
(K A Ryan) *prom: hdwy to ld wl over 1f out: rdn and kpt on wl fnl f* **3/1**[2]
2 *3* **Aahaygirl (IRE)** 2-9-0 **0**.............................. FergusSweeney 4 62+
(K R Burke) *cl up: effrt 2f out and ev ch tl rdn: edgd lft and one pce ins fnl f* **5/2**[1]
0 **3** *2* **Cecilia's Lass**[33] 995 2-9-0 **0**.............................. PaulMulrennan 3 55
(D H Brown) *led: rdn along 1/2-way: sn hdd and kpt on same pce* **11/1**
4 *hd* **Bahamian Ceilidh** 2-9-0 **0**.............................. DaneO'Neill 1 54
(B R Millman) *cl up: rdn along 2f out: kpt on same pce appr fnl f* **6/1**
5 *1/2* **Neo's Mate (IRE)** 2-8-7 **0**.............................. AndrewHeffernan(7) 6 36
(Paul Green) *cl up: rdn along bef 1/2-way and sn wknd: fin 6th: plcd 5th* **14/1**
6 *2 1/4* **Wigan Pier** 2-8-11 **0**.............................. DuranFentiman(3) 8 28
(T D Easterby) *wnt rt s: sn chsng ldrs: rdn along over 2f out and sn wknd: fin 7th: plcd 6th* **11/2**[3]
7 *25* **Avonlini** 2-9-0 **0**.............................. DanielTudhope 7 —
(B P J Baugh) *s.i.s: sn outpcd and bhd: fin 8th: plcd 7th* **16/1**
D *4 1/2* **Betws Y Coed (IRE)** 2-8-11 **0**.............................. DominicFox(3) 5 38
(A Bailey) *s.i.s and sn rdn along in rr: sme late hdwy: fin 5th: disq & plcd last* **7/1**

63.51 secs (3.01) **Going Correction** +0.275s/f (Good) **8** Ran SP% **116.6**
Speed ratings (Par 89): **86,81,78,77,69 66,26,70**
CSF £11.22 TOTE £3.50: £1.50, £1.40, £2.70; EX 11.90.
Owner Highbank Syndicate **Bred** Mount Coote Stud, Richard Pegum & M Bell Racing **Trained** Hambleton, N Yorks

FOCUS
Little form to go on but probably just a modest maiden, although the winner did it well and looks one with a future.

NOTEBOOK
Maggie Lou(IRE), who cost 77,000gns, is a half-sister to Listed-race winning sprinter One Putra, 6f winner Lambency, and 1m2f winner Rondelet. Travelling best throughout on her debut, she pulled nicely clear in the closing stages for minimal pressure, and looks a useful prospect. The Lily Agnes and Hilary Needler look the obvious targets. (op 10-3 tchd 4-1)
Aahaygirl(IRE), a half-sister to smart 6f Listed race-winning juvenile Irish Jig, was green and hung left, but she kept on well without having any chance with the easy winner. She should not have too much trouble going one better in similar company. (op 9-2 tchd 9-4)
Cecilia's Lass, whose dam won over 6f at two and is a half-sister to Racing Post Trophy winner Saratoga Springs, showed that she had learnt a lot from her debut at Warwick. This time she knew enough to put the pace to the race. (op 14-1 tchd 10-1)
Bahamian Ceilidh, a half-sister to juvenile winners Cop Hill Lad, Clifton Dancer and Okikoki, and Making Music, a multiple 5f winner, is bred to get going early as a two-year-old. She showed enough to suggest she will continue the family tradition. (op 9-2 tchd 13-2 in places)
Wigan Pier, whos cost 65,000gns, is the first foal of mare who had smart form over 7f at two in Italy and was later third in the Italian 1,000 Guineas. Too green to live up to market expectations on her debut, she should be capable of better in time over further. (op 9-2 tchd 4-1)
Betws Y Coed(IRE) was disqualified after her rider weighed in with the incorrect weight. (op 9-2)

1611 NORTHERNRACINGCLUB.COM H'CAP 5f
6:20 (6:20) (Class 5) (0-75,75) 3-Y-O £2,590 (£770; £385; £192) Stalls Centre

Form RPR
1 **1** **Marvellous Value (IRE)**[24] 1139 3-9-2 **73**.............................. PhillipMakin 3 91+
(M Dods) *hmpd s and bhd: gd hdwy over 2f out: rdn to ld appr fnl f and sn clr* **7/1**
0-62 **2** *3 3/4* **Rio Sands**[8] 1452 3-8-7 **64**.............................. DeanMcKeown 9 67
(R M Whitaker) *cl up: led wl over 1f out: sn rdn and hdd appr fnl f: kpt on same pce* **7/2**[2]
065- **3** *1* **Supermassive Muse (IRE)**[238] 5032 3-9-0 **71**.............................. StephenDonohoe 2 70
(E S McMahon) *midfield: pushed along 1/2-way: sn rdn and styd on fnl f: nrst fin* **10/1**
34-4 **4** *1* **Blue Jack**[16] 1277 3-9-3 **74**..........................(t) RichardMullen 8 70
(W R Muir) *hld up towards rr: hdwy 2f out: sn rdn: edgd lft ins fnl f and no imp* **11/4**[1]
651- **5** *3 1/4* **Outside Edge (IRE)**[337] 1989 3-9-3 **74**.............................. SaleemGolam 5 58
(W R Swinburn) *towards rr: sme hdwy 2f out: sn rdn and no imp* **10/1**
5-50 **6** *1/2* **Speedy Senorita (IRE)**[10] 1396 3-8-5 **62**.............................. AndrewElliott 1 44
(K R Burke) *chsd ldrs: rdn along 2f out and grad wknd* **18/1**
0343 **7** *2 3/4* **Andrasta**[34] 977 3-7-13 **61** oh1.............................. DanielleMcCreery(5) 10 33
(A Berry) *in tch on outer: rdn along over 2f out and sn wknd* **33/1**
00-4 **8** *1 3/4* **Select Committee**[24] 1155 3-8-8 **65**.............................. PaulMulrennan 6 31
(J J Quinn) *prom: rdn along over 2f out and sn wknd* **10/1**
544- **9** *nk* **Le Toreador**[246] 4781 3-9-4 **75**.............................. FergalLynch 7 40
(K A Ryan) *led: rdn along 2f out: sn hdd & wknd* **4/1**[3]
21-0 **10** *1* **Revue Princess (IRE)**[9] 1426 3-8-10 **70**.............................. DuranFentiman(3) 4 31
(T D Easterby) *chsd ldrs: rdn along over 2f out and sn wknd* **33/1**

62.05 secs (1.55) **Going Correction** +0.275s/f (Good) **10** Ran SP% **119.8**
Speed ratings (Par 98): **98,92,90,88,83 82,78,75,75,73**
CSF £32.67 CT £253.49 TOTE £8.60: £3.10, £1.90, £3.30; EX 30.20.
Owner A J Henderson **Bred** John Cullinan **Trained** Denton, Co Durham

FOCUS
A fair handicap won in clear-cut fashion by Marvellous Value who improved markedly on the form of his debut win.

1612 HAYDOCK PARK RAILS AND RING BOOKMAKERS H'CAP 1m 30y
6:50 (6:57) (Class 4) (0-85,83) 4-Y-0+ £4,857 (£1,445; £722; £360) Stalls Low

Form RPR
0-00 **1** **Bold Marc (IRE)**[14] 1335 6-8-11 **76**.............................. AndrewElliott 6 84
(K R Burke) *mde all: sn clr: rdn over 2f out: drvn ent fnl f and styd on gamely* **6/1**
130- **2** *3/4* **Goodbye**[175] 6651 4-8-11 **79**.............................. PJMcDonald(3) 7 85+
(G A Swinbank) *hld up in tch: hdwy 3f out: effrt and nt clr run over 1f out: rdn ins fnl f: styd on wl towards fin* **9/2**[3]
21-3 **3** *nk* **Major Magpie (IRE)**[32] 1016 6-9-1 **80**.............................. PhillipMakin 11 85+
(M Dods) *v.s.a and bhd: hdwy over 2f out and sn rdn: swtchd rt and drvn over 1f out: styd on strly ins fnl f* **9/4**[1]
52-3 **4** *shd* **Charlie Tipple**[14] 1327 4-8-10 **75**.............................. PaulMulrennan 9 80
(T D Easterby) *t.k.h: chsd ldrs: effrt over 2f out: sn rdn and ch tl drvn: edgd lft and one pce wl ins fnl f* **7/2**[2]
0-00 **5** *3 1/2* **Nevada Desert (IRE)**[7] 1481 8-9-1 **80**.............................. DeanMcKeown 5 77
(R M Whitaker) *trckd ldrs: hdwy over 3f out: rdn to chal 2f out: drvn and wkng whn n.m.r wl ins fnl f* **13/2**
20-0 **6** *8* **Fever**[28] 1067 4-8-11 **83**.............................. BradleyRoper(7) 8 62
(M W Easterby) *hld up: a towards rr* **25/1**
05-1 **7** *1 1/2* **Bull Market (IRE)**[23] 1164 5-8-13 **78**.............................. StephenDonohoe 3 53
(Ian Williams) *trckd ldrs: effrt 3f out: rdn along 2f out and sn wknd* **12/1**
000- **8** *nse* **Obezyana (USA)**[319] 2528 6-8-11 **79**.............................. DominicFox(3) 1 54
(A Bailey) *chsd wnr: rdn along 3f out: sn drvn and wknd* **40/1**
1-00 **9** *7* **Provost**[21] 1218 4-9-3 **82**.............................. DaleGibson 4 41
(M W Easterby) *hld up: a in rr* **50/1**
4-00 **10** *3 1/4* **Lap Of Honour (IRE)**[7] 1481 4-9-3 **82**..........................(p) DaneO'Neill 10 33
(Jennie Candlish) *plld hrd: chsd ldrs on outer: rdn along 3f out and sn wknd* **18/1**

1m 47.28s (3.48) **Going Correction** +0.575s/f (Yiel) **10** Ran SP% **120.0**
Speed ratings (Par 105): **105,104,103,103,100 92,90,90,83,80**
CSF £33.77 CT £82.35 TOTE £8.60: £2.40, £2.20, £1.10; EX 47.20.
Owner Market Avenue Racing Club Ltd **Bred** Eamon D Delany **Trained** Middleham Moor, N Yorks
■ Pure Imagination was withdrawn (11/1, uns rdr & bolted bef s.) Deduct 5p in the £ under R4. New market formed.

FOCUS
The winner set a decent gallop here but was still able to hold off the closers. He had slipped to a good mark and did not need to match his best form of last year. The form looks solid for the grade with the fourth the best guide.

Bold Marc(IRE) Official explanation: trainer said, regarding the apparent improvement in form, gelding had been better suited by being allowed to dominate the race.

1613 JOHN DOHERTY MEMORIAL H'CAP — 1m 2f 120y
7:20 (7:23) (Class 4) (0-80,79) 4-Y-0+ — **£4,857** (£1,445; £722; £360) **Stalls** High

Form — RPR

30-2 **1** **First Buddy**[23] 962 4-9-1 **79** .... PJMcDonald(3) 10 97+
(G A Swinbank) *led: qcknd over 3f out: rdn clr over 1f out: easily* **7/4**[1]

105- **2** *8* **Royal Flynn**[12] 4072 6-8-12 **78** .... KellyHarrison(5) 8 81
(Mrs K Walton) *hld up towards rr: hdwy 3f out: rdn wl over 1f out: kpt on ins fnl f: no ch w wnr* **12/1**

56-3 **3** *2 1/4* **Mae Cigan (FR)**[11] 1383 5-8-4 **65** oh1 .... ChrisCatlin 9 64
(M Blanshard) *chsd ldrs: rdn along 3f out: drvn 2f out: kpt on u.p fnl f* **13/2**[3]

05-0 **4** *1 1/2* **Cruise Director**[35] 962 8-9-3 **78** .... StephenDonohoe 2 74
(Ian Williams) *chsd ldrs: rdn along over 2f out: sn drvn and kpt on same pce* **14/1**

4521 **5** *3/4* **Punta Galera (IRE)**[23] 1165 5-8-5 **66** ow1 .... DeanMcKeown 5 60
(Paul Green) *hld up in rr: pushed along 4f out: rdn and hung lft wl over 2f out: styd on ins fnl f: nrst fin* **12/1**

00-0 **6** *hd* **Ahlawy (IRE)**[28] 1072 5-8-10 **78** .... NSLawes(7) 4 72+
(M W Easterby) *dwlt: hld up in rr tl styd on fnl 2f* **40/1**

0323 **7** *7* **Moheebb (IRE)**[11] 1388 4-9-0 **75** ....(b) DaleGibson 3 56
(Mrs R A Carr) *dwlt: hdwy and in tch 1/2-way: rdn along 3f out and sn btn* **13/2**[3]

22/5 **8** *1/2* **Polish Corridor**[21] 1217 9-9-0 **75** .... PhillipMakin 7 55
(M Dods) *dwlt: sn chsng ldng pair: effrt to chse wnr 1/2-way: rdn along 3f out: sn edgd rt and wknd* **7/2**[2]

55-0 **9** *5* **Bailieborough (IRE)**[21] 1217 9-9-0 **75** .... RoystonFfrench 11 45
(B Ellison) *chsd wnr to 1/2-way: sn rdn along and wknd over 3f out* **20/1**

201- **10** *6* **Snow Dancer (IRE)**[201] 6055 4-8-8 **69** .... PatrickMathers 1 28
(H A McWilliams) *dwlt: a in rr* **25/1**

2m 20.19s (3.49) **Going Correction** +0.575s/f (Yiel) — **10** Ran SP% **118.4**
Speed ratings (Par 105): **110,104,102,101,100 100,95,95,91,87**
CSF £24.89 CT £116.56 TOTE £2.70: £1.40, £3.90, £2.30; EX 23.00.

Owner W J Gredley **Bred** Tarworth Bloodstock Investments Ltd **Trained** Melsonby, N Yorks

FOCUS
Run in a time 2.7sec quicker than the following three-year-old handicap, this race was taken to pieces by First Buddy, who made every yard. He was allowed to dictate the pace and it is unclear exactly what he achieved in basically outclassing the opposition.

Polish Corridor Official explanation: jockey said gelding hung right in the final two furlongs

1614 WARRINGTON GUARDIAN H'CAP — 1m 2f 120y
7:50 (7:51) (Class 5) (0-75,78) 3-Y-0 — **£2,590** (£770; £385; £192) **Stalls** High

Form — RPR

60-2 **1** **Conquisto**[11] 1381 3-9-7 **78** .... PhilipRobinson 3 89+
(C G Cox) *plld hrd: hld up in rr: swtchd rt and hdwy 3f out: led 2f out: rdn and hdd jst ins fnl f: drvn and rallied wl to ld nr line* **6/4**[1]

100- **2** *shd* **Indian Days**[183] 6471 3-9-3 **74** .... J-PGuillambert 6 85
(J G Given) *prom: cl up 1/2-way: effrt 2f out and sn rdn: drvn to ld jst ins fnl f: hdd and no ex nr line* **4/1**[3]

0-36 **3** *shd* **Allied Powers (IRE)**[29] 1059 3-8-11 **68** .... RichardMullen 2 79+
(M L W Bell) *plld hrd: chsd ldrs: effrt and nt clr run 2f out: swtchd outside and rdn ent fnl f: fin strly: jst failed* **13/2**

40-6 **4** *7* **Dramatic Solo**[30] 1042 3-8-11 **68** .... FergusSweeney 4 66
(K R Burke) *set stdy pce: pushed along 4f out: rdn 3f out: hdd 2f out and sn one pce* **33/1**

000- **5** *1/2* **Yathreb (USA)**[206] 5918 3-9-2 **73** .... EddieAhern 1 70
(J L Dunlop) *dwlt: t.k.h and sn cl up: stdd 1/2-way: effrt 3f out: rdn 2f out and sn one pce* **5/2**[2]

5031 **6** *2 1/4* **Carry On Cleo**[10] 1407 3-8-4 **61** oh1 .... RoystonFfrench 7 53
(P Monteith) *cl up: rdn along over 3f out and sn wknd* **12/1**

04-6 **7** *1 1/4* **Saturday Boy**[22] 1186 3-7-11 **61** oh8 .... AndrewHeffernan(7) 5 51
(Paul Green) *t.k.h: hld up in tch: effrt over 3f out: sn rdn and wknd* **33/1**

2m 22.89s (6.19) **Going Correction** +0.575s/f (Yiel) — **7** Ran SP% **115.5**
Speed ratings (Par 98): **100,99,99,94,94 92,91**
CSF £8.15 TOTE £2.50: £1.60, £2.90; EX 7.10.

Owner Reid's Racers **Bred** Bricklow Ltd **Trained** Lambourn, Berks

FOCUS
They went a steady pace here and the sprint to the line resulted in a three-way photo. The form is not solid but the winner and third race both shaped better than the bare figures.

1615 ST HELENS STAR MAIDEN STKS — 1m 3f 200y
8:20 (8:20) (Class 5) 3-Y-0 — **£2,590** (£770; £385; £192) **Stalls** High

Form — RPR

2 **1** **Meshtri (IRE)**[23] 1172 3-9-3 0 .... PhilipRobinson 1 85+
(M A Jarvis) *trckd ldr: hdwy to ld over 2f out: rdn over 1f out: drvn ins fnl f and kpt on* **2/5**[1]

32- **2** *1/2* **Nemo Spirit (IRE)**[182] 6494 3-9-3 0 .... RichardMullen 3 82
(W R Muir) *hld up: hdwy over 3f out: pushed along to chse wnr 2f out: rdn over 1f out: drvn and ev ch ins fnl f: no ex towards fin* **10/3**[2]

-22 **3** *10* **Montfjord (IRE)**[61] 702 3-9-3 0 .... ChrisCatlin 4 66
(E J O'Neill) *set stdy pce: qcknd over 3f out: rdn and hdd over 2f out: sn one pce* **7/1**[3]

4 *hd* **Daraiym (IRE)** 3-9-3 0 .... PhillipMakin 2 65
(Paul Green) *dwlt: sn trcking ldng pair: rdn along over 3f out and sn wknd* **20/1**

2m 42.21s (9.01) **Going Correction** +0.575s/f (Yiel) — **4** Ran SP% **111.8**
Speed ratings (Par 98): **92,91,85,84**
CSF £2.22 TOTE £1.50; EX 1.90 Place 6 £17.36, Place 5 £10.77.

Owner Sheikh Ahmed Al Maktoum **Bred** Round Hill Stud **Trained** Newmarket, Suffolk

FOCUS
A steadily run maiden which turned into something of a sprint. The front pair brought fair form to the race and finished clear, with the runner-up the best guide.

T/Plt: £17.70 to a £1 stake. Pool: £62,301.55. 2,568.15 winning tickets. T/Qpdt: £4.70 to a £1 stake. Pool: £4,055.23. 632.95 winning tickets. JR

1168 LEICESTER (R-H)
Saturday, April 26

OFFICIAL GOING: Good to soft (7.1)
Wind: Fresh, behind Weather: Fine

1616 JOHN SMITH'S MEDIAN AUCTION MAIDEN STKS — 5f 2y
2:15 (2:15) (Class 5) 2-Y-0 — **£2,590** (£770; £385; £192) **Stalls** Low

Form — RPR

1 **Waffle (IRE)** 2-9-3 0 .... TPQueally 2 81+
(J Noseda) *chsd ldrs: led over 1f out: rdn out* **4/5**[1]

6 **2** *1 1/4* **Rayvin Mad (IRE)**[10] 1399 2-9-3 0 .... AlanMunro 5 75
(P W Chapple-Hyam) *led: rdn and hdd over 1f out: styd on same pce* **13/8**[2]

0 **3** *2 1/2* **Johnmanderville**[7] 1474 2-9-3 0 .... DarrenWilliams 7 66
(K R Burke) *chsd ldr: rdn 1/2-way: edgd lft over 1f out: styd on same pce* **25/1**

4 *3 3/4* **Classic Blade (IRE)** 2-9-3 0 .... RichardKingscote 1 52
(Tom Dascombe) *s.i.s: outpcd* **14/1**[3]

0 **5** *2 3/4* **Nowornevа**[12] 1363 2-8-12 0 .... HaddenFrost(5) 6 42
(S Kirk) *sn outpcd* **40/1**

6 *18* **Simple Rhythm** 2-8-7 0 .... JamieJones(5) 3 —
(M G Quinlan) *dwlt: bucked and kicked leaving stalls: outpcd* **20/1**

60.98 secs (0.98) **Going Correction** -0.10s/f (Good) — **6** Ran SP% **111.4**
Speed ratings (Par 92): **88,86,82,76,71 42**
CSF £2.22 TOTE £1.70: £1.10, £1.50; EX 2.10.

Owner Mrs Susan Roy **Bred** Mrs M Rogers **Trained** Newmarket, Suffolk

■ Stewards' Enquiry : Jamie Jones three-day ban: used whip when out of contention (May 10-12)

FOCUS
A fair juvenile contest and a nice debut from Waffle. The runner-up looks a fair marker for the form.

NOTEBOOK
Waffle(IRE), a 180,000euros son of Kheleyf, hadn't come in his coat and was a touch burley, but he had a nice look about him and that was reflected in his performance. He broke nicely and was soon tucked in behind the leader in third place and came through to lead approaching the final furlong and only had to be shaken up to assert. He will come on a ton for this outing and can follow up before greater plans are hatched. (op 5-6)
Rayvin Mad(IRE), who had been a little keen when sixth on his debut at Newmarket ten days earlier, was quickly into his stride again and provided the winner with a proper test, but could not propel his challenge. There should be a little race in him, especially on a sharper track. (tchd 15-8)
Johnmanderville, too green to do himself justic on debut at Nottingham, had clearly learnt a good deal from that and was soon chasing the leader. He held his chance until fading in the final furlong, but he clearly has ability and should find a race in due course. (op 28-1 tchd 16-1)
Classic Blade(IRE), a son of Daggers Drawn, was always struggling following a slow start, but this was a fair contest and he can be expected to come on for it. (op 10-1 tchd 9-1)
Nowornevа improved on his debut effort, but is already crying out for six furlongs and appeals as more of a nursery type. (op 66-1)
Simple Rhythm was bucking and kicking soon after leaving the stalls and gave her rider a torrid time. (op 50-1)

1617 JOHN SMITH'S EXTRA COLD H'CAP — 5f 218y
2:45 (2:46) (Class 4) (0-85,85) 4-Y-0+ — **£4,209** (£1,252; £625; £312) **Stalls** Low

Form — RPR

20-2 **1** **Nobilissima (IRE)**[16] 1278 4-8-10 **80** .... TolleyDean(3) 9 88
(J L Spearing) *led: rdn and hdd ins fnl f: rallied to ld nr fin* **8/1**

-214 **2** *hd* **Swinbrook (USA)**[14] 1327 7-8-7 **74** ....(v) TPQueally 4 82
(R A Fahey) *chsd ldrs: lost pl over 4f out: hdwy over 2f out: rdn to ld ins fnl f: hdd nr fin* **10/3**[1]

0200 **3** *nk* **Cornus**[9] 1430 6-8-13 **80** ....(be) JamesDoyle 10 87
(A J McCabe) *hld up: rdn over 1f out: sn swtchd lft: r.o wl towards fin* **25/1**

40-5 **4** *3/4* **Masai Moon**[28] 1071 4-8-13 **85** .... JamesMillman(5) 11 89
(B R Millman) *chsd ldrs: rdn over 2f out: styng on whn edgd rt wl ins fnl f* **7/1**[3]

00-3 **5** *3/4* **Mujood**[16] 1278 5-9-2 **83** ....(v) StephenCarson 6 85
(Eve Johnson Houghton) *mid-div: hdwy u.p over 1f out: nt rch ldrs* **12/1**

61-0 **6** *1* **Tudor Prince (IRE)**[15] 1300 4-8-13 **80** .... PhilipRobinson 12 82+
(A W Carroll) *s.i.s: sn chsng ldrs: rdn and ev ch over 1f out: styng on same pce whn hmpd wl ins fnl f* **8/1**

362- **7** *1 1/4* **Rainbow Mirage (IRE)**[148] 6981 4-9-4 **85** .... StephenDonohoe 1 80
(E S McMahon) *chsd ldrs: rdn over 1f out: no ex ins fnl f* **14/1**

4126 **8** *1 1/2* **Financial Times (USA)**[39] 925 6-9-1 **82** ....(t) HayleyTurner 7 72
(Stef Liddiard) *hld up: rdn over 1f out: nvr trbld ldrs* **20/1**

-055 **9** *shd* **Andronikos**[16] 1278 6-8-13 **80** .... NelsonDeSouza 8 70
(P F I Cole) *mid-div: hdwy 1/2-way: rdn over 1f out: wknd ins fnl f* **7/1**[3]

00-5 **10** *1* **Compton's Eleven**[9] 1430 7-8-10 **84** .... MatthewDavies(7) 2 70
(M R Channon) *hld up: rdn 1/2-way: n.d* **14/1**

1601 **11** *hd* **Bonnie Prince Blue**[16] 1278 5-9-2 **83** ....(b) MichaelHills 5 69
(B W Hills) *chsd ldrs: rdn over 2f out: wkng whn hmpd over 1f out* **5/1**[2]

60-0 **12** *10* **Oranmore Castle (IRE)**[7] 1485 6-8-4 **71** oh1 .... GregFairley 3 25
(R A Fahey) *rrd s: sn chsng ldrs: wknd over 2f out* **18/1**

1m 11.53s (-1.47) **Going Correction** -0.10s/f (Good) — **12** Ran SP% **121.9**
Speed ratings (Par 105): **105,104,104,103,102 101,99,97,97,95 95,82**
CSF £35.76 CT £670.02 TOTE £7.60: £1.50, £1.90, £7.10; EX 54.20 TRIFECTA Not won..

Owner Nine Traders Syndicate **Bred** Sea Syndicate **Trained** Kinnersley, Worcs

■ Stewards' Enquiry : James Millman caution: careless riding

FOCUS
A competitive sprint.

1618 JOHN SMITH'S CLUB AND INSTITUTE UNION H'CAP — 1m 3f 183y
3:15 (3:16) (Class 3) (0-95,85) 3-Y-0
£9,346 (£2,799; £1,399; £700; £349; £175) **Stalls** High

Form — RPR

321- **1** **All The Aces (IRE)**[178] 6585 3-9-4 **82** .... PhilipRobinson 7 102
(M A Jarvis) *trckd ldr: racd keenly: led over 2f out: rdn over 1f out: styd on gamely* **6/1**

54-1 **2** *hd* **Enroller (IRE)**[23] 1173 3-8-13 **77** .... RichardMullen 3 97
(W R Muir) *hld up: hdwy over 3f out: rdn and ev ch fr over 1f out: styd on wl* **9/4**[1]

22-1 **3** *10* **Downhiller (IRE)**[23] 1172 3-9-6 **84** .... EddieAhern 1 88
(J L Dunlop) *trckd ldrs: racd keenly: rdn and ev ch 2f out: wknd fnl f* **4/1**[2]

41-1 **4** *6* **Animator**[19] 1244 3-9-0 **78** .... TQuinn 8 72
(P F I Cole) *hld up in tch: rdn over 2f out: wknd wl over 1f out* **8/1**

1 **5** *1/2* **Tourism (IRE)**[34] 982 3-9-5 **83** .... J-PGuillambert 4 77
(M Johnston) *hld up: bhd fnl 4f* **14/1**

21 **6** ½ **Red Linnet**[63] 674 3-9-0 **78** HayleyTurner 5 71
(M L W Bell) *chsd ldrs over 8f* **12/1**

223- **7** 1¾ **City Stable (IRE)**[184] 6451 3-8-8 **79** JPHamblett(7) 2 69
(Sir Michael Stoute) *hld up: effrt over 2f out: sn wknd* **11/2**[3]

321 **8** 2 **Always Bold (IRE)**[57] 758 3-9-7 **85** GregFairley 6 72
(M Johnston) *led over 9f: wknd wl over 1f out* **12/1**

2m 33.8s (-0.10) **Going Correction** +0.125s/f (Good) **8** Ran SP% **113.6**
Speed ratings (Par 102): **105,104,98,94,93 93,92,91**
CSF £19.65 CT £60.00 TOTE £6.20: £1.80, £1.30, £1.80; EX 23.80 Trifecta £260.30 Part won. Pool: £366.76, 0.59 winning units..
Owner A D Spence **Bred** Jack Ronan And Des Ver Hunt Farm Ltd **Trained** Newmarket, Suffolk

FOCUS
The front two pulled well clear in what was a decent three-year-old handicap.

NOTEBOOK
All The Aces(IRE) made a winning reappearance in game fashion. He had tracked the leader on the inside until taking up the running over two furlongs out and kept on strongly to repel the runner-up. His trainer intimated that he would not want the ground any firmer than he encountered here and he will wait until he is reassessed before making any plans. He looks the sort that well progress further this year. (op 13-2 tchd 8-1)
Enroller(IRE) had an easy task when winning over course and distance on his reappearance and the handicapper had left him on his current mark but he will be having a rethink after this effort. He was held up until making his progress in the final half mile and came there to have every chance from over a furlong out as the pair went clear. He could be one to go with if his trainer can find an opportunity before he is reassessed. (op 11-4 tchd 3-1)
Downhiller(IRE), winner of a 1m2f course maiden on his reappearance, was a little keen on this handicap debut and had every chance entering the final three furlongs. He may be more effective back down in trip. (tchd 10-3)
Animator, on a hat-trick following two handicap wins on the All-Weather, was 4lb higher on this return to turf and failed to last home. Perhaps a drop back down in distance would help. (tchd 15-2 and 9-1)
Tourism(IRE), a ready winner on debut at Musselburgh, had been handed a pretty stiff mark for this handicap debut and he failed to make an impression. (op 12-1)
Red Linnet, winner of a 1m4f Lingfield maiden last time, made no impression on this handicap debut and may prefer a faster surface. (op 11-1)
City Stable(IRE), up half a mile in distance for this handicap debut, showed fair form in three starts at two and it was disappointing he could make no impression on this handicap debut. (op 7-1 tchd 5-1)
Always Bold(IRE), cosy winner of a modest Wolverhampton maiden last time, looked vulnerable off a mark of 85 on this turf debut and he was unable to put up much of a fight. (op 17-2)

1619 TOTESPORT.COM LEICESTERSHIRE STKS (LISTED RACE) 7f 9y
3:50 (3:52) (Class 1) 4-Y-0+
£17,031 (£6,456; £3,231; £1,611; £807; £405) **Stalls** Low

Form RPR

00-5 **1** **Captain Marvelous (IRE)**[13] 1355 4-9-2 107 MichaelHills 3 109
(B W Hills) *chsd ldrs: rdn over 1f out: r.o to ld nr fin* **10/1**

520- **2** hd **Al Qasi (IRE)**[139] 7091 5-9-7 114 AlanMunro 6 113
(P W Chapple-Hyam) *hld up: hdwy u.p over 1f out: r.o* **1/1**[1]

410- **3** nk **Eisteddfod**[189] 6332 7-9-5 106 NelsonDeSouza 4 111
(P F I Cole) *chsd ldr tl led over 1f out: sn rdn: edgd lft ins fnl f: hdd nr fin* **8/1**[3]

0300 **4** ¾ **Beckermet (IRE)**[9] 1420 6-9-5 0 ChrisCatlin 2 109
(R F Fisher) *led: rdn and hdd over 1f out: struck on hd by rivals whip ins fnl f: styd on* **20/1**

-050 **5** 3½ **Appalachian Trail (IRE)**[35] 959 7-9-5 109 (b) PhillipMakin 8 99
(Miss L A Perratt) *chsd ldrs: rdn over 2f out: wknd ins fnl f* **11/1**

150- **6** 4 **Confuchias (IRE)**[189] 6338 4-9-7 109 EddieAhern 7 90
(W R Swinburn) *hld up: hdwy u.p over 1f out: wknd fnl f* **4/1**[2]

-060 **7** 4½ **Hurricane Spirit (IRE)**[58] 741 4-9-2 0 GeorgeBaker 1 73
(J R Best) *hld up: a in rr: wknd over 2f out* **40/1**

010- **8** 4½ **Hotel Du Cap**[177] 6614 5-9-5 103 (t) SteveDrowne 5 64
(G Wragg) *s.i.s: sn prom: rdn 1/2-way: wknd wl over 2f out* **11/1**

1m 24.03s (-2.17) **Going Correction** -0.10s/f (Good) **8** Ran SP% **114.1**
Speed ratings (Par 111): **108,107,107,106,102 98,92,87**
CSF £20.41 TOTE £12.80: £2.80, £1.10, £1.40; EX 27.60 Trifecta £74.20 Pool: £355.65, 3.40 winning units.
Owner R J Arculli **Bred** Duncan A McGregor **Trained** Lambourn, Berks

FOCUS
A trappy contest that saw Captain Marvelous get the better of favourite Al Qasi.

NOTEBOOK
Captain Marvelous(IRE), who had shaped with plenty of encouragement behind Jumbajukiba at the Curragh 13 days earlier, saw that form given a boost by Major Cadeaux in the Sandown Mile and he battled on gamely to win his first race since October 2006. He was a Group 2 winner as two-year-old and the determination he showed here should stand him in good stead at a higher level. (op 17-2 tchd 8-1 and 12-1)
Al Qasi(IRE) was held up in the early stages and made headway over three furlongs out and was staying on well near the finish. He was giving 5lb to the winner and he gave the impression he will come on considerably for this reappearance effort. (tchd 11-10)
Eisteddfod chased the leader until going on over a furlong out and was just touched off in the closing stages. His stable have been in great form and, a listed winner at Sandown last season, he should soon find a race at this level. (op 11-2 tchd 9-2)
Beckermet(IRE) ran a solid race and has shown some of his best form for Chris Catlin and his turn in this grade will come in due course once more. (op 14-1)
Appalachian Trail(IRE) is best with the strong pace he got here and kept on well enough towards the centre. (op 12-1 tchd 10-1)
Confuchias(IRE), winner of a Group 3 at Newcastle last season when trained in Ireland, was well supported on this debut for the Swinburn yard, but he was a shade keen early on and could make no impression this run may do him good. (op 8-1)

1620 JOHN SMITH'S PREMIER CLUB H'CAP 1m 1f 218y
4:25 (4:25) (Class 5) (0-70,76) 4-Y-0+ **£2,590** (£770; £385; £192) **Stalls** High

Form RPR

123- **1** **Smirfy's Silver**[244] 4858 4-8-8 **60** TQuinn 5 69+
(E S McMahon) *chsd ldr tl led over 2f out: rdn over 1f out: r.o: eased nr fin* **7/2**[2]

3P0- **2** 1¾ **Jafaru**[47] 6733 4-8-11 **63** (b) HayleyTurner 2 68
(G A Butler) *a.p: rdn to chse wnr over 1f out: edgd rt: styd on same pce ins fnl f* **14/1**

21-1 **3** nk **Harry The Hawk**[10] 1394 4-8-11 **68** NeilBrown(5) 1 72+
(T D Walford) *hld up: hdwy on bit over 2f out: rdn and edgd rt fnl f: styd on same pce* **10/11**[1]

-100 **4** hd **Nok Twice (IRE)**[8] 1449 7-8-13 **65** AlanMunro 4 69
(D Carroll) *s.i.s: hld up: racd keenly: hdwy and swtchd lft over 1f out: r.o: nt rch ldrs* **14/1**

150- **5** 6 **Princess Lavinia**[219] 5559 5-8-13 **65** SteveDrowne 3 57
(G Wragg) *chsd ldrs: rdn over 2f out: wknd fnl f* **12/1**

0 **6** 1¼ **Never Pink (FR)**[11] 1383 4-8-8 **60** ChrisCatlin 6 50
(Ian Williams) *hld up: rdn over 3f out: a in rr* **22/1**

50-1 **7** 3 **Harvest Joy (IRE)**[13] 1349 4-9-10 **76** JimCrowley 8 60
(J Gallagher) *hld up: rdn over 4f out: wknd 2f out* **7/1**[3]

5 **8** 11 **Sendreni (FR)**[68] 607 4-8-11 **63** OscarUrbina 7 25
(M Wigham) *plld hrd: led: rdn and hdd over 2f out: wknd wl over 1f out* **25/1**

2m 8.27s (0.37) **Going Correction** +0.125s/f (Good) **8** Ran SP% **116.3**
Speed ratings (Par 103): **103,101,101,101,96 95,93,84**
CSF £51.06 CT £78.35 TOTE £4.30: £1.10, £2.30, £1.10; EX 53.70 Trifecta £328.90 Pool: £546.73, 1.18 winning units.
Owner Mrs Dian Plant **Bred** G S Shropshire **Trained** Lichfield, Staffs

FOCUS
Just an ordinary handicap.
Sendreni(FR) Official explanation: jockey said gelding ran too freely

1621 JOHN SMITH'S EXTRA SMOOTH MAIDEN STKS 1m 1f 218y
5:00 (5:02) (Class 5) 3-Y-0+ **£2,590** (£770; £385; £192) **Stalls** High

Form RPR

2- **1** **Tartan Bearer (IRE)**[176] 6618 3-8-10 0 AlanMunro 5 73+
(Sir Michael Stoute) *chsd ldrs: led over 1f out: r.o wl: eased nr fin* **2/5**[1]

6- **2** 2¾ **Warringah**[152] 6944 3-8-10 0 JDSmith 4 68
(Sir Michael Stoute) *chsd ldr tl led 2f out: rdn and hdd over 1f out: styd on same pce ins fnl f* **12/1**[3]

3 1½ **Deadly Silence (USA)** 3-8-10 0 SteveDrowne 16 65+
(Dr J D Scargill) *s.s: hld up: rdn: swtchd lft and hdwy over 2f out: swtchd rt over 1f out: r.o wl towards fin* **50/1**

4 **4** ¾ **Spanish Cruise (IRE)**[40] 919 4-9-13 0 AlanDaly 14 66
(Andrew Turnell) *led 8f: no ex ins fnl f* **33/1**

5 ¾ **Marie Louise** 3-8-7 0 ow2 TPQueally 3 59
(H R A Cecil) *chsd ldrs: rdn over 2f out: hung rt fr over 1f out: styd on same pce* **12/1**[3]

6-05 **6** 1¼ **Zach's Harmoney (USA)**[44] 874 4-9-6 57 WilliamCarson(7) 15 62
(P W Hiatt) *chsd ldrs: rdn over 2f out: wknd over 1f out* **100/1**

00- **7** ½ **Lady Petrus**[175] 6649 3-8-5 0 JamesDoyle 11 53
(H J L Dunlop) *chsd ldrs: rdn over 2f out: wknd over 1f out* **50/1**

4 **8** 1¾ **World Time**[11] 1382 3-8-10 0 RobertHavlin 9 55+
(J H M Gosden) *hld up: shkn up over 3f out: hung rt 2f out: nvr nr to chal* **9/2**[2]

00/ **9** 4 **Dance Hall Diva**[34] 5800 6-9-1 0 GabrielHannon(7) 10 45
(M D I Usher) *hld up in tch: rdn over 3f out: wknd over 2f out* **200/1**

10 1¼ **Sunny Peace** 3-8-5 0 RichardSmith 7 39+
(B G Powell) *s.i.s: hld up: hdwy over 2f out: sn wknd* **100/1**

0 **11** 6 **Princess Flame (GER)**[5] 1526 6-9-8 0 TQuinn 13 30
(B G Powell) *s.i.s: hld up: hdwy over 3f out: wknd over 2f out* **66/1**

0 **12** 1 **Goldrenched (IRE)**[11] 1382 3-8-5 0 HayleyTurner 8 25
(M L W Bell) *hld up: rdn over 3f out: a in rr* **33/1**

0 **13** 6 **Monaadi (IRE)**[10] 1398 3-8-10 0 MatthewHenry 6 18
(M A Jarvis) *mid-div: wknd 1/2-way* **28/1**

- **14** 5 **Kennyboy** 3-8-10 0 MichaelHills 1 8
(Mrs H Sweeting) *s.s: a bhd* **50/1**

15 7 **Fraaedd (USA)** 3-8-10 0 JimCrowley 2 —
(M A Jarvis) *hld up: bhd fr 1/2-way* **16/1**

2m 11.58s (3.68) **Going Correction** +0.125s/f (Good)
WFA 3 from 4yo+ 17lb **15** Ran SP% **130.1**
Speed ratings (Par 103): **90,87,86,86,85 84,84,82,79,78 73,72,68,64,58**
CSF £7.63 TOTE £1.50: £1.10, £2.60, £12.90; EX 8.90 Trifecta £266.60 Part won. Pool: £375.52, 0.99 winning units..
Owner Ballymacoll Stud **Bred** Ballymacoll Stud Farm Ltd **Trained** Newmarket, Suffolk

FOCUS
They went a slow pace in this maiden and the form does not look solid, with a bumper winner in fourth.
Princess Flame(GER) Official explanation: jockey said mare was slowly away

1622 JOHN SMITH'S H'CAP 1m 60y
5:35 (5:37) (Class 5) (0-70,70) 3-Y-0 **£2,590** (£770; £385; £192) **Stalls** High

Form RPR

0544 **1** **Coole Dodger (IRE)**[10] 1407 3-8-4 **63** ow1 GabrielHannon(7) 8 72
(M D I Usher) *s.i.s: hld up: hdwy over 2f out: hung rt and led 1f out: r.o wl* **50/1**

0-01 **2** 3¼ **Always Brave**[8] 1448 3-9-4 **70** GregFairley 3 72
(M Johnston) *led: racd keenly: rdn and hdd 1f out: styd on same pce* **5/1**[2]

60-3 **3** 1¼ **Koraleva Tectona (IRE)**[33] 997 3-9-0 **66** PaulEddery 7 65
(Pat Eddery) *trckd ldrs: plld hrd: rdn over 1f out: styd on same pce* **8/1**

0-06 **4** 1¼ **Star Pattern (USA)**[12] 1367 3-8-13 **65** RobertHavlin 9 61
(J H M Gosden) *hld up: hdwy over 2f out: rdn over 1f out: styd on same pce* **4/1**[1]

0-13 **5** 1¼ **Benedetto**[21] 1216 3-9-3 **69** JimCrowley 6 62
(Mrs A J Perrett) *hld up: plld hrd: hdwy over 2f out: rdn and nt clr run over 1f out: no ex fnl f* **11/1**

2-20 **6** ½ **Caltire (GER)**[10] 1396 3-8-7 **64** (b) JamieJones(5) 10 56
(M G Quinlan) *s.i.s: hld up: hdwy u.p over 1f out: nt rch ldrs* **25/1**

045- **7** nse **Nordic Commander (IRE)**[162] 6827 3-9-1 **67** TGMcLaughlin 11 59
(E A L Dunlop) *prom: hmpd and lost pl over 6f out: hdwy over 2f out: sn rdn: no ex fnl f* **12/1**

52-6 **8** ½ **Feasible**[29] 1057 3-9-3 **69** TPQueally 13 60+
(J G Portman) *prom: rdn whn nt clr run and swtchd lft over 1f out: wknd ins fnl f* **10/1**

660- **9** ½ **Secret Gem (IRE)**[175] 6648 3-9-2 **68** SteveDrowne 14 58
(C G Cox) *chsd ldrs: rdn over 1f out: wknd fnl f* **12/1**

530- **10** ¾ **Danamight (IRE)**[212] 5746 3-9-0 **66** StephenCarson 2 54
(J L Dunlop) *trckd ldrs: plld hrd: rdn over 1f out: wknd ins fnl f* **8/1**

520- **11** 1¾ **Gala Casino Star (IRE)**[209] 5828 3-8-8 **67** BMcHugh(7) 1 51
(R A Fahey) *s.i.s: rdn 1/2-way: a bhd* **20/1**

064- **12** 3½ **Sparkling Montjeu (IRE)**[210] 5811 3-8-13 **65** MichaelHills 12 41
(J W Hills) *chsd ldrs over 6f* **14/1**

040- **13** 16 **Excape (IRE)**[290] 3435 3-9-2 **68** TQuinn 4 7
(D R C Elsworth) *rrd s: a bhd* **11/2**[3]

601- **P** **Distant Diamond (IRE)**[206] 5896 3-9-2 **68** AdamKirby 5 —
(W R Swinburn) *hld up: bhd fr 1/2-way: sn p.u* **14/1**

1m 46.66s (1.56) **Going Correction** +0.125s/f (Good) **14** Ran SP% **131.0**
Speed ratings (Par 98): **97,93,92,91,90 89,89,88,88,87 85,82,66,—**
CSF £306.53 CT £2299.89 TOTE £72.00: £12.50, £2.40, £3.40; EX 316.80 TRIFECTA Not won. Place 6 £4.88, Place 5 £4.65.
Owner R H Brookes **Bred** Hyde Park Stud & Stephen Hillen **Trained** Upper Lambourn, Berks

FOCUS
This has to be a weak handicap as the manner of Coole Dodger's victory does not say a lot for the rest.
Feasible Official explanation: jockey said gelding had been denied a clear run
Danamight(IRE) Official explanation: jockey said filly had run too freely
Sparkling Montjeu(IRE) Official explanation: jockey said filly had lost her action
Distant Diamond(IRE) Official explanation: vet said colt had bled from the nose
T/Plt: £6.00 to a £1 stake. Pool: £45,650.40. 5,468.45 winning tickets. T/Qpdt: £2.20 to a £1 stake. Pool: £2,481.67. 804.59 winning tickets. CR

[1425]RIPON (R-H)
Saturday, April 26

OFFICIAL GOING: Good (7.7)
Wind: Breezy, half behind Weather: Overcast

1623 TOTESCOOP6 H'CAP 6f
2:30 (2:31) (Class 3) (0-95,92) 3-Y-O
£9,346 (£2,799; £1,399; £700; £349; £175) **Stalls** Low

Form RPR
-021 **1** **Van Bossed (CAN)**[9] 1426 3-8-12 **86**........................ AdrianTNicholls 6 100
(D Nicholls) *trckd ldrs: led over 2f out: drvn out fnl f* **11/4**[1]
023- **2** 2 ¾ **Baldemar**[210] 5802 3-8-6 **80**........................ AndrewElliott 8 85
(K R Burke) *in tch: drvn and outpcd over 2f out: rallied to chse wnr ins fnl f: kpt on* **25/1**
32-2 **3** 2 **Tawzeea (IRE)**[33] 997 3-8-6 **80**........................ RHills 5 79
(M Johnston) *cl up gng wl: ev ch over 2f out: sn rdn: no ex over 1f out* **5/1**[3]
0-65 **4** hd **Mister Hardy**[14] 1328 3-9-0 **88**........................ TonyHamilton 10 86
(R A Fahey) *bhd and pushed along stands' side: hdwy on outside 2f out: kpt on fnl f: nrst fin* **14/1**
621- **5** 1 ½ **Lord Sandicliffe (IRE)**[180] 6540 3-8-5 **82**........................ WilliamBuick[(3)] 4 75
(B W Hills) *bhd and sn niggled along: hdwy and edgd rt over 1f out: nrst fin* **9/2**[2]
52-0 **6** 1 ½ **Anosti**[10] 1401 3-8-13 **87**........................ NCallan 12 75+
(K A Ryan) *racd alone far side: rdn over 2f out: nt pce of stands' side ldrs* **11/1**
00-0 **7** 1 **Flight Plan**[15] 1297 3-8-6 **80**........................ DaleGibson 7 65
(R A Fahey) *sn niggled towards rr: edgd rt over 2f out: n.d* **8/1**
43-0 **8** 1 ½ **Captain Dunne (IRE)**[9] 1426 3-8-3 **80**........................ DuranFentiman[(3)] 9 60+
(T D Easterby) *hld up: pushed along 2f out: nt pce to chal* **33/1**
350- **9** 3 ½ **Cristal Clear (IRE)**[203] 6017 3-9-4 **92**........................ DavidAllan 13 61+
(T D Easterby) *carried rt s: sn tacked over to join main stands' side gp: towards rr: drvn 1/2-way: nvr on terms* **20/1**
06-0 **10** 5 **Bespoke Boy**[7] 1484 3-8-5 **86**........................ PatrickDonaghy[(7)] 1 39
(P C Haslam) *led to over 2f out: wknd over 1f out* **8/1**
010- **11** 3 **Fyodorovich (USA)**[227] 5331 3-8-5 **79** ow1...........(v) DeanMcKeown 11 23
(J S Wainwright) *wnt rt s: racd on outside of stands' side gp: hung rt and wknd fr 1/2-way* **50/1**
1-16 **12** ½ **Style Award**[7] 1484 3-8-11 **85**........................ RobertWinston 3 27
(W J H Ratcliffe) *cl up tl rdn and wknd fr 2f out* **10/1**
1m 14.57s (1.57) **Going Correction** +0.10s/f (Good) **12** Ran SP% **121.3**
Speed ratings (Par 102): **93,89,86,86,84 82,81,79,74,67 63,63**
CSF £85.54 CT £341.22 TOTE £3.90: £1.80, £4.40, £2.10; EX 92.80 Trifecta £216.60 Pool: £305.20 - 0.60 winning units..
Owner Mike & Maureen Browne **Bred** Bernard And Karen McCormack **Trained** Sessay, N Yorks

FOCUS
A decent handicap run at an ordinary pace and one in which all bar one raced stands' side. The winner is a progressive sort who is capable of further improvement and the runner-up ran to form.

NOTEBOOK
Van Bossed(CAN) ◆, a fluent winner over course and distance on his previous start, turned in a career best effort. He won in the manner of a progressive sort and, although he will be racing from a mark around the mid-90s next time, he looks the sort to win more races for this yard. (op 10-3 tchd 5-2, 7-2 in a place)
Baldemar looked fit enough to do himself justice on this first start since September and showed he retains at least all his ability. On this evidence he should have no problems with 7f and he looks capable of picking up another race. (tchd 28-1)
Tawzeea(IRE), who looked better than ever over 7f on his reappearance, travelled like the best horse in the race for much of the way on this handicap debut but failed to find as much as anticipated once asked for an effort. The return to 7f may suit and he remains capable of winning a race. (op 4-1 tchd 11-2)
Mister Hardy's form has been patchy since his last win over a year ago but, after failing to stay 7f last time, he shaped as though worth another try over the trip on this occasion. He is likely to remain vulnerable from his current mark against progressive sorts, though.
Lord Sandicliffe(IRE) making his handicap debut on this first start since winning his maiden at Leicester last autumn, was not totally disgraced after appearing ill-at-ease on this track. He should stay 7f and is worth another chance from this mark. (op 4-1)
Anosti, out of her depth in the Group 3 Nell Gwyn, may be better than she was able to show on this occasion as she raced on her own next to the far rail. She is going to have to improve to defy her current mark, though. (tchd 10-1 and 12-1)
Flight Plan, having only his second start for Richard Fahey, fared better than on his reappearance. He will be one to keep a close eye on back over 7f plus, especially if there is any market confidence behind him. (op 14-1)
Cristal Clear(IRE) is better than this bare form suggests but is likely to struggle in handicaps from his current mark. (op 16-1 tchd 14-1)
Fyodorovich(USA) Official explanation: jockey said colt hung right-handed throughout.
Style Award Official explanation: jockey said filly was never travelling from halfway.

1624 STOWE FAMILY LAW LLP H'CAP 5f
3:05 (3:06) (Class 5) (0-75,75) 4-Y-O+ **£2,914** (£867; £433; £216) **Stalls** Low

Form RPR
545- **1** **Sandwith**[145] 7005 5-8-6 **66**........................(p) PJMcDonald[(3)] 19 76
(J S Wainwright) *cl up far side: led that gp 1f out: hld on wl u.p* **22/1**
010- **2** nk **Green Lagonda (AUS)**[129] 7183 6-8-4 **61**........................ RoystonFfrench 8 70
(J G Given) *hld up on outside of stands' side gp: hdwy over 1f out: r.o wl fnl f: jst hld* **28/1**
50-5 **3** ½ **Colorus (IRE)**[9] 1431 5-8-9 **66**........................ RobertWinston 5 73
(W J H Ratcliffe) *chsd stands' side ldrs: swtchd to stands' rail and hdwy over 1f out: rdn and hung rt ins fnl f: r.o* **13/2**[1]
3640 **4** nk **Coleorton Dancer**[7] 1485 6-8-11 **68**........................ NCallan 12 74
(K A Ryan) *chsd far side ldrs: drvn over 2f out: kpt on u.p fnl f* **8/1**[2]
0043 **5** ½ **Tartatartufata**[12] 1366 6-9-1 **72**........................(v) DeanMcKeown 7 76
(D Shaw) *prom far side: effrt and ev ch ins fnl f: edgd rt: r.o same pce* **11/1**
3-00 **6** shd **Steelcut**[8] 1451 4-9-0 **74**........................ JamieMoriarty[(3)] 18 78
(R A Fahey) *prom far side: effrt 2f out: kpt on u.p fnl f* **18/1**
00-3 **7** 1 ¼ **Steel City Boy (IRE)**[7] 1476 5-8-1 **61**........................ WilliamBuick[(3)] 1 62
(D Carroll) *slt ld stands' side tl edgd rt and no ex ins fnl f* **13/2**[1]
00-0 **8** 1 **Windjammer**[7] 1485 4-8-8 **65**........................ DavidAllan 15 61
(T D Easterby) *cl up: led far side gp over 2f out to 1f out: one pce* **14/1**
-533 **9** 1 ¾ **Highland Warrior**[8] 1451 9-9-0 **71**........................ MickyFenton 16 61
(P T Midgley) *dwlt: hld up far side: effrt 2f out: no imp fnl f* **8/1**[2]
20-0 **10** ¾ **Mandurah (IRE)**[8] 1451 4-8-3 **67**........................ OliveGaule[(7)] 17 54
(D Nicholls) *plld hrd: prom far side: effrt over 2f out: no ex fnl f* **33/1**
0-60 **11** nk **Circuit Dancer (IRE)**[8] 1451 8-9-1 **72**........................ SilvestreDeSousa 3 58
(D Nicholls) *in tch stands' side: drvn over 2f out: no ex over 1f out* **20/1**
1641 **12** ½ **Judge 'n Jury**[11] 1386 4-9-1 **75**........................(t) KevinGhunowa[(3)] 2 59
(R A Harris) *cl up stands' side tl no ex over 1f out* **9/1**[3]
0026 **13** ¾ **Namir (IRE)**[11] 1386 6-8-11 **71**........................(vt) DuranFentiman[(3)] 4 52
(D Shaw) *hld up stands' side: drvn over 2f out: no imp over 1f out* **16/1**
-500 **14** hd **Hawaii Prince**[86] 370 4-8-0 **62**........................ KellyHarrison[(5)] 10 43
(S T Mason) *disp ld stands' side tl no ex over 1f out* **66/1**
-006 **15** hd **Kings College Boy**[15] 1309 8-8-4 **61**........................(b) DaleGibson 11 41
(R A Fahey) *bhd stands' side: drvn 1/2-way: nvr rchd ldrs* **40/1**
10-0 **16** nk **Princess Ellis**[11] 1386 4-9-3 **74**........................ TedDurcan 20 53
(E J Alston) *slt ld far side to over 2f out: hung lft and wknd over 1f out* **14/1**
-003 **17** ½ **Brut**[9] 1431 6-8-12 **69**........................(p) TonyHamilton 9 46
(D W Barker) *disp ld stands' side tl wknd over 1f out* **14/1**
-604 **18** 3 ¼ **Spirit Of Coniston**[15] 1309 5-8-5 **62**........................ AdrianTNicholls 13 27
(D Nicholls) *w far side ldr to over 2f out: sn btn and eased* **14/1**
5-00 **19** 1 **Sea Land (FR)**[7] 1476 4-8-4 **61** oh1........................ DO'Donohoe 6 23
(B Ellison) *dwlt: a outpcd stands' side* **33/1**
06-4 **20** 1 **Woqoodd**[9] 1431 4-8-9 **66**........................ TomEaves 14 24
(R A Fahey) *racd far side: sn lost tch: nvr on terms* **33/1**
60.79 secs (0.09) **Going Correction** +0.10s/f (Good) **20** Ran SP% **130.3**
Speed ratings (Par 103): **103,102,101,101,100 100,98,96,93,92 92,91,90,89,89 89,88,83,81,79**
CSF £532.83 CT £4515.21 TOTE £30.90: £6.30, £5.70, £2.50, £2.60; EX 950.10.
Owner M Sawers **Bred** R R Whitton **Trained** Kennythorpe, N Yorks

FOCUS
A big field of ordinary handicappers and a good pace but the field, that split into two fairly even groups, merged in the closing stages and there seemed very little in the draw. The form looks pretty solid.
Princess Ellis Official explanation: jockey said filly hung left throughout.
Spirit Of Coniston Official explanation: jockey said gelding hung badly left throughout.

1625 TOTESPORT BETXTRA H'CAP 2m
3:40 (3:40) (Class 2) (0-100,90) 4-Y-O+
£12,462 (£3,732; £1,866; £934; £466; £234) **Stalls** High

Form RPR
311- **1** **Highland Legacy**[191] 6284 4-9-7 **88**........................ NCallan 1 100+
(M L W Bell) *hld up in tch: checked over 5f out: hdwy to ld 3f out: clr whn edgd rt over 1f out: eased towards fin* **4/5**[1]
02-5 **2** 2 **Bogside Theatre (IRE)**[24] 1158 4-9-5 **86**........................ AndrewElliott 9 91
(G M Moore) *prom: edgd lft over 5f out: hdwy to ld briefly over 3f out: kpt on fr 2f out: no ch w wnr* **9/1**
235- **3** 3 **Sphinx (FR)**[191] 6284 10-9-11 **88**........................ PaulMulrennan 5 89
(E W Tuer) *chsd ldrs: effrt and ev ch over 3f out: one pce fnl 2f* **33/1**
026- **4** 5 **Dr Sharp (IRE)**[168] 6760 8-9-4 **81**........................ MickyFenton 3 76
(T P Tate) *cl up: n.m.r and outpcd 4f out: no imp fnl 2f* **15/2**[3]
11/6 **5** ¾ **Numero Due**[9] 1427 6-9-6 **83**........................ TomEaves 7 78
(G M Moore) *bhd: pushed along 4f out: nvr rchd ldrs* **16/1**
0-06 **6** 4 ½ **Sadler's Kingdom (IRE)**[7] 1472 4-8-13 **80**........................ TonyHamilton 8 69
(R A Fahey) *hld up: rdn and edgd rt over 2f out: nvr on terms* **11/2**[2]
05-6 **7** 4 **Thewhirlingdervish (IRE)**[24] 1137 10-8-13 **76**........................ DavidAllan 10 60
(T D Easterby) *hld up: rdn 4f out: n.d* **20/1**
11-3 **8** 1 ¾ **Oddsmaker (IRE)**[28] 1067 7-9-6 **83**........................(t) DeanMcKeown 6 65
(M A Barnes) *led to over 3f out: sn wknd* **18/1**
340- **9** 54 **Philanthropy**[168] 6759 4-9-9 **90**........................ DO'Donohoe 2 7
(K A Ryan) *cl up: carried lft over 5f out: sn lost pl: t.o* **33/1**
3m 35.78s (3.98) **Going Correction** +0.50s/f (Yiel)
WFA 4 from 6yo+ 4lb **9** Ran SP% **114.5**
Speed ratings (Par 109): **110,109,107,105,104 102,100,99,72**
CSF £8.46 CT £127.86 TOTE £1.90: £1.10, £2.60, £5.20; EX 9.10 Trifecta £29.60 Pool: £233.88, 5.60 winning units.
Owner B J Warren **Bred** Deerfield Farm **Trained** Newmarket, Suffolk
■ Stewards' Enquiry : Andrew Elliott two-day ban: careless riding (May 10, 12)

FOCUS
A fair handicap in which the pace was on the steady side in the first half of the race but the overall time was good. The winner won with more in hand than the official margin suggests and is the type to hold his own in stronger company.

NOTEBOOK
Highland Legacy ◆, a progressive middle-distance stayer last year, looks better than ever this time round and he won with a fair bit more in hand than the winning margin suggested. He travelled strongly before powering clear and will be an interesting runner in the Chester Cup next month, a race in which he is now the market leader. (op Evens)
Bogside Theatre(IRE), who quickly made up into a fairly useful handicapper last term, shaped as though retaining at least all his ability on this reappearance run and first attempt at the trip, despite being flattered by his proximity to the winner. A stronger gallop would have suited and he is the type to win races this term. (op 15-2 tchd 7-1 and 10-1)
Sphinx(FR), a fair stayer for Jamie Poulton who was not at his best behind Highland Legacy on his final run last year, got closer to that eased down rival this time and shaped as though retaining plenty of ability. He is high enough in the weights on the Flat but will be interesting if and when sent over hurdles.
Dr Sharp(IRE) has not won for well over a year but was not disgraced on this reappearance outing. He may be best when allowed to dominate when there is cut in the ground and may be capable of resuming winning ways this year when things conspire in his favour. (op 11-1)
Numero Due, who missed the whole of last year and was well beaten over an inadequate 1m2f on his reappearance, fared better over this more suitable trip in a race not run to suit those held up. However, is going to have to drop in the weights if he is to regain the winning thread. (op 12-1)

Sadler's Kingdom(IRE), a multiple winner up to middle distances last year, has slipped to a fair mark and was not disgraced over a trip he has still to prove conclusively he stays in a race run to suit the prominent racers. He is not one to write off. (tchd 6-1)

1626 TOTESPORT BETXTRA WIN ONLY (S) STKS — 1m 1f 170y

4:15 (4:15) (Class 5) 3-4-Y-O — **£2,590** (£770; £385; £192) **Stalls** High

Form — RPR

614- **1** **Cherri Fosfate**^{200} [6090] 4-9-10 57 .... DavidAllan 5 — 55
(D Carroll) *prom: hdwy to ld over 2f out: clr whn edgd rt over 1f out: r.o wl* **7/2**^{2}

6444 **2** *2* **Cape Dancer (IRE)**^{31} [1025] 4-9-2 42 .... PJMcDonald(3) 9 — 46
(J S Wainwright) *t.k.h: chsd ldrs: ev ch 3f out: rdn and kpt on same pce fr wl over 1f out* **9/1**^{3}

00-0 **3** *3* **Jevington Star (IRE)**^{14} [1343] 3-8-7 42 .... TomEaves 12 — 48
(B Ellison) *trckd ldrs: effrt over 3f out: hung rt over 1f out: kpt on same pce* **10/1**

060- **4** *5* **Buds Dilemma**^{203} [6026] 4-9-5 45 .... TedDurcan 6 — 30
(W M Brisbourne) *cl up: led briefly 3f out: outpcd fnl 2f* **12/1**

6500 **5** *nk* **Babieca (USA)**^{5} [1521] 4-9-10 60 .... NCallan 13 — 34
(T D Barron) *set stdy pce: hdd 3f out: sn outpcd* **3/1**^{1}

4-06 **6** *2¼* **Tenth Night (IRE)**^{23} [1169] 3-8-7 45 .... FrankieMcDonald 1 — 33
(P T Midgley) *bhd: hdwy over 2f out: nvr rchd ldrs* **20/1**

0250 **7** *2¾* **Winged Farasi**^{24} [1142] 4-9-7 50 .... (p) KevinGhunowa(3) 3 — 24
(R A Harris) *s.i.s and early reminders: effrt 3f out: nvr on terms* **7/2**^{2}

5 **8** *5* **Jayne Dean**^{15} [1301] 4-9-2 0 .... MichaelJStainton(3) 10 — 9
(A Crook) *in tch: drvn and outpcd 3f out: sn btn* **40/1**

00-5 **9** *7* **Ingleby Hill (IRE)**^{45} [862] 4-9-10 41 .... (v^{1}) DO'Donohoe 7 — —
(Micky Hammond) *t.k.h: in tch tl outpcd 3f out: sn btn* **20/1**

0536 **10** *2½* **Moorside Diamond**^{31} [1025] 4-9-5 39 .... AndrewElliott 4 — —
(A D Brown) *hld up on wd outside: drvn and wknd over 3f out* **16/1**

00-0 **11** *16* **Viscount Monty**^{10} [1397] 3-8-7 38 .... DaleGibson 2 — —
(N Tinkler) *bhd: drvn 4f out: nvr on terms* **50/1**

3600 **12** *45* **Hollow Point (IRE)**^{7} [1487] 3-8-8 56 ow1 .... (p) MickyFenton 8 — —
(P T Midgley) *bhd: drvn over 4f out: nvr on terms* **10/1**

2m 11.72s (6.32) **Going Correction** +0.50s/f (Yiel)
WFA 3 from 4yo 17lb — **12 Ran SP% 125.1**
Speed ratings (Par 103): **94,92,90,86,85 83,81,77,72,70 57,21**
CSF £35.85 TOTE £3.70: £1.40, £2.90, £3.60; EX 34.40.There was no bid for the winner.
Owner Document Express Ltd **Bred** The Newchange Syndicate **Trained** Sledmere, E Yorks

FOCUS
A low-grade seller in which those racing prominently held the edge. The pace was on the ordinary side and the form looks weak.
Hollow Point(IRE) Official explanation: jockey said gelding had a breathing problem.

1627 TOTESPORT BETXTRA PLACE ONLY MAIDEN AUCTION FILLIES' STKS — 5f

4:50 (4:50) (Class 5) 2-Y-O — **£2,914** (£867; £433; £216) **Stalls** Low

Form — RPR

2 **1** **Caranbola**^{9} [1425] 2-8-4 0 .... TWilliams 7 — 77
(M Brittain) *mde all: rdn and edgd rt fnl f: kpt on strly* **9/2**^{3}

3 **2** *2¼* **Meg Jicaro**^{33} [995] 2-8-4 0 .... SilvestreDeSousa 2 — 69+
(Mrs L Williamson) *cl up: effrt and ch over 1f out: kpt on same pce fnl f* **12/1**

25 **3** *3¼* **Dispol Mulofky (IRE)**^{15} [1303] 2-8-4 0 .... FrankieMcDonald 12 — 57
(P T Midgley) *prom: drvn over 2f out: one pce over 1f out* **40/1**

6 **4** *2* **Fasliyanne (IRE)**^{9} [1419] 2-8-8 0 .... NCallan 5 — 54
(K A Ryan) *chsd ldrs: drvn over 2f out: no ex over 1f out* **9/4**^{2}

5 *2* **The Magic Of Rio** 2-8-10 0 .... LiamJones 8 — 49
(W J Haggas) *in tch: sn pushed along: nt qckn fr 2f out* **9/1**

2 **6** *1½* **Woteva**^{10} [1390] 2-8-8 0 .... RobertWinston 3 — 41+
(J J Quinn) *midfield: drvn after 2f: hung rt and no imp fnl 2f* **15/8**^{1}

7 *2¼* **Brierty (IRE)** 2-8-6 0 .... DO'Donohoe 11 — 31+
(D Carroll) *s.i.s: hld up on outside: hdwy 1/2-way: wknd wl over 1f out* **50/1**

8 *2½* **Fashion Icon (USA)** 2-8-6 0 .... PaulFessey 4 — 22
(T D Barron) *in tch: drvn 1/2-way: wknd wl over 1f out* **22/1**

9 *1½* **Jillolini** 2-8-8 0 .... DavidAllan 6 — 19+
(T D Easterby) *hld up: pushed along 1/2-way: sn outpcd* **18/1**

10 *1¾* **Mousy Mousy (IRE)** 2-8-12 0 .... TedDurcan 9 — 17
(T D Easterby) *dwlt: plld hrd in rr: grad wknd fr 1/2-way* **16/1**

11 *1¾* **French Forest** 2-8-4 0 .... AdrianTNicholls 1 — —
(M Brittain) *bhd: drvn 1/2-way: sn btn* **25/1**

12 *23* **Magical Night** 2-8-7 0 ow1 .... TomEaves 10 — —
(T D Walford) *s.i.s: sn wl bhd* **50/1**

61.91 secs (1.21) **Going Correction** +0.10s/f (Good) — **12 Ran SP% 127.1**
Speed ratings (Par 89): **94,90,85,82,78 76,72,68,66,63 60,24**
CSF £58.61 TOTE £6.50: £1.80, £3.30, £7.80; EX 73.10.
Owner Mel Brittain **Bred** T E Pocock **Trained** Warthill, N Yorks

FOCUS
With the two market leaders disappointing, this did not take as much winning as seemed likely beforehand, but the form is decent with the third setting the level. The pace was sound and the field raced stands' side.

NOTEBOOK
Caranbola, who shaped well at this course on her debut, did not have to improve too much with her two main market rivals disappointing but she went about her business in a pleasing enough manner and may well be capable of a bit better. (op 4-1 tchd 7-1)
Meg Jicaro, who shaped well when third to two subsequent winners on her debut at Warwick, had the run of the race from a favourable draw and bettered that form against a rival who had shown promise first time. She should stay 6f and can pick up a minor event.
Dispol Mulofky(IRE) seems a consistent sort who again ran her race from a double-figure draw and she looks a good guide to the worth of this form. While vulnerable to the more progressive sorts in this grade, she should continue to give it her best shot. (op 22-1)
Fasliyanne(IRE), who shaped pleasingly in a better race than this one on her debut, was a shade disappointing in this lesser event. However, she is in good hands, should stay 6f and is worth another chance in ordinary company. (op 10-3)
The Magic Of Rio, the first foal of a 5f winner and entered in several of the valuable sales races, was relatively easy to back but was not disgraced on this racecourse debut. Six furlongs may suit better in due course and she is entitled to improve for this run. (op 10-1 tchd 11-1)
Woteva, who shaped well from a decent draw at Beverley, failed to build on that promise. She left the impression that a stiffer test of stamina would be in her favour and she is worth another chance in ordinary company. Official explanation: jockey said filly suffered interference at the start and was never travelling thereafter. (op 5-2 tchd 13-8)

1628 TOTESPORT BETXTRA SHOW ONLY MAIDEN STKS — 1m 1f 170y

5:20 (5:20) (Class 5) 3-Y-O — **£2,914** (£867; £433; £216) **Stalls** High

Form — RPR

563- **1** **Jabal Tariq**^{213} [5735] 3-9-3 81 .... NCallan 10 — 90+
(B W Hills) *mde all: qcknd clr over 2f out: eased ins fnl f* **11/10**^{1}

56- **2** *3¾* **Wells Lyrical (IRE)**^{169} [6740] 3-9-3 0 .... TomEaves 9 — 75
(B Smart) *prom: effrt 3f out: chsd wnr over 1f out: kpt on: no imp* **14/1**

50- **3** *2¾* **Pondapie (IRE)**^{196} [6184] 3-9-0 0 .... MichaelJStainton(3) 5 — 70
(R M Whitaker) *midfield: shkn up 3f out: kpt on fnl 2f: nrst fin* **20/1**

4 *2¼* **Maha Dubai (USA)** 3-8-12 0 .... RHills 3 — 60+
(M Johnston) *pressed wnr: rdn and hung rt over 2f out: no ex and lost 2nd over 1f out* **3/1**^{2}

0-0 **5** *10* **River Kent**^{7} [1477] 3-9-3 0 .... PaulFessey 8 — 52
(Mrs A Duffield) *t.k.h: prom tl rdn and wknd fr 3f out* **66/1**

6 *1* **Greyfriarsblessing (IRE)** 3-8-12 0 .... RobertWinston 6 — 38+
(M Johnston) *s.i.s: hmpd after 4f: shkn up 3f out: n.d* **14/1**

43 **7** *11* **Plenilune (IRE)**^{9} [1429] 3-9-3 0 .... TWilliams 2 — 21+
(M Brittain) *towards rr: drvn 3f out: sn btn* **15/2**^{3}

8 *2½* **Waarid** 3-9-3 0 .... LiamJones 7 — 16+
(W J Haggas) *midfield: hmpd after 4f: sn struggling* **9/1**

9 *17* **Royal Avenue (IRE)** 3-9-3 0 .... DavidAllan 1 — —
(T D Easterby) *wnt lft s: hmpd after 4f: n.d* **33/1**

0 **10** *5* **Victorias**^{9} [1429] 3-8-12 0 .... MickyFenton 4 — —
(A Crook) *t.k.h: hld up: hmpd after 4f: sn n.d* **100/1**

0- **F** **Jontobel**^{190} [6307] 3-9-3 0 .... TonyHamilton 11 — —
(Jedd O'Keeffe) *t.k.h: in tch: fell after 4f* **100/1**

2m 9.71s (4.31) **Going Correction** +0.50s/f (Yiel) — **11 Ran SP% 118.9**
Speed ratings (Par 98): **102,99,96,95,87 86,77,75,61,57** —
CSF £19.41 TOTE £2.00: £1.10, £3.40, £4.40; EX 18.80.
Owner Mohamed Obaida **Bred** Gainsborough Stud Management Ltd **Trained** Lambourn, Berks

FOCUS
A race lacking strength in depth and one in which the market leader and most experienced runner was allowed to do his own thing in front. The form is rated around the first two and a couple of these will be worth keeping an eye on in handicaps.
River Kent Official explanation: jockey said gelding hung left in the straight.

1629 HELP ME THRO' CONDITIONS STKS — 1m 4f 10y

5:55 (5:55) (Class 3) 4-Y-O+ — **£6,542** (£1,959; £979; £490; £244) **Stalls** High

Form — RPR

030- **1** **Raincoat**^{224} [5408] 4-8-8 109 .... TedDurcan 4 — 104+
(J H M Gosden) *chsd ldr: rdn to ld 2f out: edgd rt over 1f out: hld on wl fnl f* **10/11**^{1}

200- **2** *½* **Dunaskin (IRE)**^{155} [6645] 8-8-9 107 .... TomEaves 5 — 103
(B Ellison) *led to 2f out: sn drvn: kpt on wl to take 2nd nr fin* **9/1**

215- **3** *1* **Wing Collar**^{248} [4722] 7-8-9 97 .... DavidAllan 1 — 101
(T D Easterby) *hld up in last but in tch: drvn over 3f out: rallied to chse wnr ins fnl f: lost 2nd nr fin* **14/1**

201- **4** *hd* **Greek Envoy**^{190} [6302] 4-8-8 103 .... MickyFenton 3 — 103+
(T P Tate) *prom: hung rt fr over 3f out: effrt whn nt clr run over 2f out: swtchd lft and kpt on fnl f* **6/1**^{3}

00-0 **5** *10* **Heron Bay**^{28} [1076] 4-8-8 101 .... NCallan 2 — 85
(G Wragg) *chsd ldrs: effrt over 2f out: edgd rt and wknd over 1f out: eased whn btn ins fnl f* **5/2**^{2}

2m 40.43s (3.73) **Going Correction** +0.50s/f (Yiel)
WFA 4 from 7yo+ 1lb — **5 Ran SP% 111.9**
Speed ratings (Par 107): **107,106,106,105,99**
CSF £10.10 TOTE £1.80: £1.20, £4.00; EX 7.70 Place 6 £213.01, Place 5 £104.33.
Owner K Abdulla **Bred** Juddmonte Farms Ltd **Trained** Newmarket, Suffolk

FOCUS
A useful field but a modest early gallop renders this an unreliable guide. The third really took the eye beforehand and is better than the bare form which looks slightly messy.

NOTEBOOK
Raincoat, a useful performer last year, is from a yard in tremendous form but did not have to improve too much to win on his reappearance. Always well placed in a muddling event, he showed a fair attitude for pressure and, although things were in his favour this time, he remains the sort to win more races. (op 5-6 tchd 4-5 and Evens)
Dunaskin(IRE), having his first run for this yard, is a fair front runner at best and he showed he retains plenty of ability, despite being allowed the run of the race. Small fields and conditions contests are always likely to see him to best effect and he should be able to win races this term when allowed to dominate. (op 12-1)
Wing Collar, having his first run for over eight months, shaped well in the face of a stiff task, especially as this race was not exactly run to suit. He is a consistent sort who goes on any ground and will be seen to better effect back in handicaps when a better gallop is on the cards. (tchd 12-1 and 16-1)
Greek Envoy ◆, who took the eye in the paddock as a fine big sort with plenty of scope, was not suited by the way this race panned out and was unlucky not to finish closer. A flatter track is going to be in his favour too and he is lightly raced enough to be open to further improvement. He goes well in soft ground and is one to keep an eye on. (op 9-2)
Heron Bay took the eye in the paddock but proved a bit of a disappointment, despite not faring as badly as the distance beaten suggests. A flatter track and a stronger gallop will suit and he is well worth another chance, especially back on quick ground. Official explanation: vet said colt was jarred up. (op 4-1)
T/Plt: £176.70 to a £1 stake. Pool: £72,979.95. 301.35 winning tickets. T/Qpdt: £18.00 to a £1 stake. Pool: £3,134.09. 128.20 winning tickets. RY

1595 SANDOWN (R-H)

Saturday, April 26

OFFICIAL GOING: Good (good to soft in places on flat course; good to firm in places on jumps courses)
Other races run over jumps.
Wind: Light, against Weather: Sunny, warm

1630 BET365.COM FLAT V JUMP JOCKEYS H'CAP — 1m 14y

1:05 (1:07) (Class 4) (0-80,80) 4-Y-O+ — **£7,123** (£2,119; £1,059; £529) **Stalls** High

Form — RPR

00-5 **1** **Bustan (IRE)**^{23} [1174] 9-11-0 76 .... SamThomas 10 — 83
(G C Bravery) *trckd ldrs on inner: effrt 2f out: drvn and squeezed though to chal fnl f: styd on to ld nr fin* **14/1**

The Form Book, Raceform Ltd, Compton, RG20 6NL

01-2 **2** *hd* **Trans Siberian**[12] 1365 4-11-1 77 .... JimmyFortune 7 84
(P F I Cole) *pressed ldr: upsides fr wl over 2f out: stl disputing 1f out: styd on: jst hld* **9/4**[1]

60-1 **3** *nse* **Cactus King**[29] 1049 5-11-4 80 .... IanMongan 8 86
(P M Phelan) *trckd ldrs: effrt 2f out: drvn to ld ent fnl f: nt qckn u.p: hdd nr fin* **25/1**

5334 **4** *hd* **Blacktoft (USA)**[29] 1065 5-10-12 74 .... (e) RyanMoore 11 80+
(S C Williams) *t.k.h in midfield: hrd rdn 3f out: no prog tl over 1f out: clsd on ldrs ins fnl f: nt quite get there* **14/1**

443- **5** *2* **Froissee**[182] 6497 4-11-1 77 .... LDettori 2 78
(S A Callaghan) *hld up in rr: rdn over 2f out: prog over 1f out: styd on fnl f: nt rch ldrs* **7/1**

-015 **6** *nk* **Golden Prospect**[28] 1084 4-10-11 73 .... DarryllHolland 5 74+
(J W Hills) *hld up in last trio: effrt on inner 2f out: styd on fnl f: nrst fin* **20/1**

0-06 **7** *1 3/4* **Daaweitza**[21] 1217 5-11-1 77 .... RichardHughes 6 74
(B Ellison) *led and sharp reminder sn after s: hrd pressed fr 3f out: hdd ent fnl f: fading whn snatched up 100yds out* **11/2**[2]

00-0 **8** *1/2* **Fiefdom (IRE)**[14] 1335 6-11-0 76 .... PJBrennan 1 72
(I W McInnes) *dwlt: hld up in rr: rdn over 2f out: no real prog: kpt on fnl f* **33/1**

1115 **9** *1* **Rebellious Spirit**[24] 1159 5-11-2 78 .... TimmyMurphy 12 71
(S Curran) *pressed ldng pair: rdn and upsides over 2f out tl wknd jst over 1f out* **6/1**[3]

14-6 **10** *3 1/4* **Rambling Light**[14] 1335 4-11-2 78 .... RichardJohnson 3 64
(A M Balding) *trckd ldrs: rdn and cl up over 2f out: wknd over 1f out* **10/1**

3666 **11** *1* **Chjimes (IRE)**[14] 1327 4-11-2 78 .... JamieMoore 9 61
(C R Dore) *hld up and racd on outer: rdn over 2f out: wknd over 1f out* **16/1**

1060 **12** *hd* **Sailor King (IRE)**[23] 1174 6-11-3 79 .... RobertThornton 4 62
(D K Ivory) *t.k.h: hld up and racd wd: rdn over 2f out: wknd wl over 1f out* **20/1**

1m 46.06s (2.76) **Going Correction** +0.125s/f (Good) **12** Ran SP% **117.6**
Speed ratings (Par 105): **91,90,90,90,88 88,86,86,85,81 80,80**
CSF £43.02 CT £812.35 TOTE £18.20: £4.20, £1.40, £6.50; EX 66.00.
Owner Mrs J Morley **Bred** Sean Twomey **Trained** Cowlinge, Suffolk
■ The first winner on the Flat for Sam Thomas.

FOCUS
An ordinary handicap, notable mainly for the rare sight of jump jockeys taking on their Flat counterparts. Pretty ordinary form with Bustan taking advantage of a good mark.

1631 BET365 MILE (GROUP 2) 1m 14y
3:55 (3:59) (Class 1) 4-Y-0+

£45,416 (£17,216; £8,616; £4,296; £2,152; £1,080) **Stalls** High

Form RPR

25-2 **1** **Major Cadeaux**[13] 1355 4-9-0 114 .... RichardHughes 2 115
(R Hannon) *hld up in last pair: stdy prog on inner to trck ldng pair over 1f out: shkn up and clsd to ld last 100yds: readily* **3/1**[3]

625/ **2** *3/4* **Rob Roy (USA)**[279] 6-9-0 0 .... RyanMoore 6 114
(Sir Michael Stoute) *trckd ldng pair: effrt to ld jst over 2f out: rdn and over a l clr 1f out: hdd and outpcd last 100yds* **11/4**[2]

6-52 **3** *shd* **Metropolitan Man**[58] 745 5-9-0 0 .... JoeFanning 1 113
(D M Simcock) *hld up in 6th: nt clr run 2f out and swtchd to inner: prog whn nt clr run and eased out 1f out: r.o and nrly snatched 2nd* **33/1**

42-5 **4** *2* **Tell**[14] 1326 5-9-0 110 .... (b) KerrinMcEvoy 4 109
(J L Dunlop) *led: rdn and hdd jst over 2f out: one pce after* **9/1**

0-24 **5** *2 1/4* **Blythe Knight (IRE)**[14] 1326 8-9-0 112 .... GrahamGibbons 7 104
(J J Quinn) *hld up in 5th: rdn and nt qckn 2f out: one pce after* **12/1**

0-33 **6** *nk* **Babodana**[14] 1326 8-9-0 100 .... JimmyQuinn 5 103
(M H Tompkins) *chsd ldrs: rdn and no imp over 2f out: btn after* **33/1**

1-11 **7** *5* **Medicine Path**[14] 1326 4-9-0 110 .... JamieSpencer 8 92
(P W Chapple-Hyam) *dwlt: hld up in last: rdn and effrt on outer over 2f out: no prog over 1f out: wknd* **15/8**[1]

250- **8** *2 3/4* **Bahia Breeze**[190] 6298 6-8-11 109 .... JimmyFortune 3 82
(Rae Guest) *trckd ldr to 3f out: wknd 2f out* **16/1**

1m 43.23s (-0.07) **Going Correction** +0.125s/f (Good) **8** Ran SP% **115.9**
Speed ratings (Par 115): **105,104,104,102,99 99,94,91**
CSF £11.91 TOTE £3.80: £1.50, £1.50, £5.20; EX 12.70 Trifecta £350.40 Pool: £1,085.93, 2.20 winning units.
Owner N A Woodcock, A C Pickford & David Mort **Bred** Earl Richard Evain **Trained** East Everleigh, Wilts

FOCUS
Rarely the strongest of Group 2 races, and this looked a typical renewal. They went fairly steadily early on and the time was 1sec slower than the limited handicap run later on the card. Not form one could be that confident about, but the winner is rated as having run to his best.

NOTEBOOK
Major Cadeaux shaped with promise on his reappearance in a Group 3 at The Curragh and that form was given a boost when the fifth home, Captain Marvelous, won a Listed race at Leicester just before this race was run. The big question mark for Major Cadeaux to answer was whether he would get home over a mile, and he answered the doubters in style, quickening up well to take Rob Roy's measure inside the last. His rider had earlier wisely held in Metropolitan Man, ensuring he got first run on him, and that may have been crucial. Now that he has proven his stamina the Lockinge is next on his agenda, but the opposition will be a lot tougher at Newbury. (op 10-3 tchd 7-2 in a place)
Rob Roy(USA), whose last win came in this race in 2006, only raced once for Neil Drysdale in America last year and is now back with his original trainer. Always well placed, he ran a solid race on his seasonal return until finding the turn of foot of the race-fit too much to handle in the closing stages. He has never reached the heights some expected of him, but he remains a smart performer at Group 3/Group 2 level. However, connections pointed the way to another crack at the Lockinge, or possibly the Prix d'Ispahan next. (op 10-3 tchd 7-2)
Metropolitan Man, who ran well out in Dubai earlier this year, got no luck in running. He was stuck on the rail and the eventual winner held him there before kicking for home, and by the time he was in the clear he had too much ground to make up in too little time. It would be dangerous to assume that he would have won with a clear run because he is notoriously difficult to win with, but he would have been second at worst.
Tell looked to have a stiff task trying to turn around Doncaster Mile form with Medicine Path, but the better ground made all the difference and he was allowed his own way in front. He is a difficult horse to place but he may find a little conditions race or Listed contest which he can dominate at some point. (op 10-1 tchd 15-2)
Blythe Knight(IRE), fourth in the Doncaster Mile, reversed form with Babodana and Medicine Path but could not confirm positions with Tell. Ideally he would have liked easier conditions, but he is another who is tricky to place. (op 16-1)
Babodana, placed in the Lincoln and Doncaster Mile on his last two starts, found this company just a bit too hot.
Medicine Path, who impressed in winning the Doncaster Mile, was disappointing. He was brought with every chance down the outside but his run flattened out and he dropped away. Each of his four wins have come after breaks of at least two months and perhaps he is the sort who simply needs plenty of time between his races. Official explanation: jockey said colt never travelled (op 6-4 tchd 2-1 in places)
Bahia Breeze, runner-up in her two previous starts over this course and distance, including in this race last year, was unable to replicate that performance this time. (op 12-1)

1632 CASINO AT BET365.COM CLASSIC TRIAL (GROUP 3) 1m 2f 7y
4:30 (4:30) (Class 1) 3-Y-O

£26,681 (£10,114; £5,061; £2,523; £1,264; £634) **Stalls** High

Form RPR

112- **1** **Centennial (IRE)**[196] 6187 3-9-0 105 .... JimmyFortune 3 107+
(J H M Gosden) *led after 1f: kicked on 4f out: drvn 2f out: pressed ins fnl f: hld on* **11/8**[1]

01- **2** *nk* **Whistledownwind**[182] 6493 3-9-0 88 .... LDettori 6 106+
(P W Chapple-Hyam) *hld up in rr: pushed along over 4f out: prog fr 2f out to chse wnr 1f out: clsng nr fin: a jst hld* **5/1**[3]

603- **3** *1 1/4* **Feared In Flight (IRE)**[182] 6489 3-9-0 111 .... DarryllHolland 7 104+
(B W Hills) *hld up in last pair: brought wd and prog wl over 1f out: r.o wl to cl on ldng pair nr fin: no ch to chal* **7/2**[2]

1 **4** *1 1/2* **Top Lock**[17] 1272 3-9-0 80 .... JamieSpencer 8 101+
(A M Balding) *led 1f: chsd ldng pair after: rdn fr 1/2-way: stl cl up 2f out: kpt on wl u.p* **14/1**

20-0 **5** *3 3/4* **Mut'Ab (USA)**[21] 1213 3-9-0 90 .... RyanMoore 5 93
(C E Brittain) *trckd ldrs: rdn and prog to chse wnr 2f out to 1f out: hanging and wknd* **16/1**

22-3 **6** *2 1/4* **Latin Lad**[14] 1333 3-9-0 100 .... RichardHughes 9 89+
(R Hannon) *hld up towards rr: nt clr run briefly over 2f out: no prog and btn whn hmpd over 1f out: plugged on* **8/1**

21- **7** *hd* **Endless Luck (USA)**[169] 6740 3-9-0 90 .... JoeFanning 1 88
(M Johnston) *trckd wnr after 1f to 2f out: sn wknd* **10/1**

41-2 **8** *1 3/4* **Whitcombe Minister (USA)**[42] 902 3-9-0 92 .... JohnEgan 4 85
(Jamie Poulton) *hld up in midfield: rdn over 2f out: no prog: wknd over 1f out* **20/1**

04-0 **9** *2* **Ruff Diamond (USA)**[42] 905 3-9-0 90 .... LPKeniry 2 81
(J R Best) *hld up in last pair: brief effrt 3f out: sn btn* **14/1**

2m 9.61s (-0.89) **Going Correction** +0.125s/f (Good) **9** Ran SP% **125.2**
Speed ratings (Par 108): **108,107,106,105,102 100,100,99,97**
CSF £9.57 TOTE £2.50: £1.10, £1.70, £2.00; EX 10.10.
Owner Michael O'Flynn **Bred** W Lazy T Ltd **Trained** Newmarket, Suffolk
■ Stewards' Enquiry : L Dettori caution: careless riding

FOCUS
A classic trial with a mixed history. This looked no more than a fair race on paper and the lack of a decent gallop means the form is far from solid. Centennial is a nice prospect, but he enjoyed the run of the race. Good efforts too from the second and third, and much improved form from the fourth.

NOTEBOOK
Centennial(IRE), who looked progressive at two, winning the Haynes, Hanson & Clark before chasing home Thewayyouare in a Group 3 race in France, is bred to come into his own this season over middle distances. Soon taken to the front, he was allowed to dictate his own pace and very much got the run of things, but he still showed the right attitude in the final quarter mile and one got the impression that he won a shade cosily in the end despite the narrow winning margin. His trainer, who won this race four times in the 90s and sent out subsequent Derby winner Benny The Dip to finish second in it in 1997, expects improvement for the run from Centennial, and an outing in the Dante or the Lingfield Derby Trial is likely to tell us more about his chances at Epsom. It was no surprise to see his price for the Derby remained largely unchanged at around 12-1. (op 6-4 tchd 7-4)
Whistledownwind, who surprised connections when winning a maiden at Newbury last backend, has no fancy entries and came into the race rated just 88. Clearly handicaps do not interest them as he would have been a good thing on this evidence had he turned up for one. He took a while to hit top gear but was staying on well at the finish and one can see why his trainer does not consider him an Epsom horse, but more of a St Leger candidate. However, unlike his owner's 2006 St Leger winner Sixties Icon, he is far from bred for the job, being by Danehill Dancer out of a mare who won over a mile. (op 6-1 tchd 9-2)
Feared In Flight(IRE), third in the Racing Post Trophy on his final start at two, brought the best juvenile form to the table, and his pedigree gave hope that he would improve between two and three, and for a step up in trip. Like the runner-up he was held up at the back of the field in a race that was run at no more than an ordinary gallop. He had work to do entering the straight and, while he made up plenty of ground late on, one cannot help but think that he would have given the winner more to think about had he been ridden closer to the pace. (op 9-2)
Top Lock achieved little in terms of form when winning a 1m3f Polytrack maiden on his debut 17 days earlier, but he acquitted himself very well on this big step up in class, plugging on for pressure having raced handily throughout. Whether this effort will mean he is difficult to place from now on remains to be seen, though, and connections are apparently already considering options abroad. (op 16-1)
Mut'Ab(USA), last but one in a Listed event on the Polytrack on his reappearance, looked up against it here but had his chance. He settled better this time, but hung when brought to challenge two furlongs out. He does not look straightforward but is likely to remain agresively campaigned.
Latin Lad, done for pace in the closing stages of the Easter Stakes, looked to be crying out for this step up in trip. He endured a nightmare run as his rider sat waiting for a gap to appear on the rail from two and a half furlongs out, only for one not to come, and once switched he got squeezed out when going for a run between horses a furlong later. He is better than his finishing position suggests and deserves another chance to prove himself over this sort of trip. Official explanation: jockey said colt suffered interference in running (tchd 10-1)
Endless Luck(USA), whose backend Musselburgh maiden win had been given a boost when the well-beaten runner-up went in at Newbury earlier this month, was alongside the eventual winner entering the straight but dropped out tamely. He ran as though this outing was needed. (op 8-1)
Whitcombe Minister(USA), who shaped well behind Campanologist on his reappearance, failed to build on that effort and did not see his race out.
Ruff Diamond(USA), backed in from 50-1, was clearly expected to run better than he did. However, despite being out of a dual 1m2f winner, this trip may be beyond him anyway. (op 50-1 tchd 12-1)

1633 POKER AT BET365.COM H'CAP 1m 14y
5:05 (5:07) (Class 2) (0-100,98) 4-Y-0+

£9,969 (£2,985; £1,492; £747; £372; £187) **Stalls** High

Form RPR

022- **1** **Jamboretta (IRE)**[225] 5385 4-8-6 86 ow1 .... RyanMoore 1 100+
(Sir Michael Stoute) *stdd s: hld up in 8th: sustained prog on outer fr over 2f out: led 1f out: styd on wl* **5/2**[2]

030/ **2** *2* **Humble Opinion**[634] 4023 6-8-4 84 oh1 .... NickyMackay 4 93
(B J Meehan) *hld up in 6th: prog jst over 2f out: drvn and w wnr 1f out: styd on same pce fnl f* **12/1**

0-54 **3** 2 ½ **Bahar Shumaal (IRE)**[21] 1212 6-8-2 **87**........................ AhmedAjtebi(5) 7 90
(C E Brittain) *led at str pce: clr over 2f out: hdd 1f out: fdd but hld on for 3rd* **10/1**

360- **4** 1 **Ace Of Hearts**[203] 6011 9-8-8 **93**........................ JackMitchell(5) 8 94
(C F Wall) *hld up in tch: prog to chse ldr 3f out: no imp over 1f out: sn lost pl: one pce fnl f* **14/1**

14-1 **5** 5 **Cape Hawk (IRE)**[14] 1335 4-9-0 **94**........................ RichardHughes 2 83
(R Hannon) *hld up bhd ldrs: shkn up over 2f out: no prog whn sltly hmpd sn after: no ch after* **15/8**[1]

204- **6** nk **Prince Of Thebes (IRE)**[175] 6654 7-8-3 **84** ow2...... KirstyMilczarek(3) 6 75
(M J Attwater) *chsd ldr to 3f out: sn lost pl and struggling* **8/1**

150- **7** nk **Press The Button (GER)**[182] 6499 5-8-5 **85**.................. KerrinMcEvoy 5 73
(J R Boyle) *hld up in 7th: effrt over 2f out: no prog wl over 1f out: wknd sn after* **6/1**[3]

/00- **8** 6 **Birkspiel (GER)**[88] 882 7-9-2 **96**........................(t) IanMongan 3 70
(S Dow) *hld up in last: rdn 3f out: no prog* **50/1**

0-00 **9** 5 **Very Wise**[25] 1133 6-9-4 **98**........................ JimmyFortune 9 61
(W J Haggas) *trckd ldng pair to 3f out: sn wknd and bhd* **11/1**

1m 42.23s (-1.07) **Going Correction** +0.125s/f (Good) **9** Ran SP% **122.5**
Speed ratings (Par 109): **110,108,105,104,99 99,98,92,87**
CSF £35.08 CT £271.18 TOTE £3.50: £1.50, £3.60, £2.60; EX 55.80 Place 6 £316.99, Place 5 £138.31.
Owner Cheveley Park Stud **Bred** Castleton Group **Trained** Newmarket, Suffolk

FOCUS
A decent handicap run at a good gallop and Jamboretta won it in taking style in much the quickest time of three races run over the course and distance. This was much improved form and there should be more to come.

NOTEBOOK
Jamboretta(IRE), who did not race as a juvenile, won her maiden at Goodwood last May and went on to show fair form in defeat in handicaps thereafter. Expected to have progressed over the winter, her yard have made a good start to the season with their older horses and she came with a sweeping run to win in the style of a smart filly. This drop in trip did not pose a problem, but she will prove as effective at 1m2f and can be expected to step into pattern company before long. (op 9-4 tchd 2-1 tchd 11-4 in places)
Humble Opinion, off since August 2006, comes from a yard who have made a pretty slow start to the season and as a result this has to go down as a highly promising reappearance. He was no match for the classy-looking winner, but had some really good handicap form to his name from a couple of seasons ago and it will be interesting to see if he goes the right way from this. (tchd 8-1)
Bahar Shumaal(IRE), down markedly in trip, seemed happy leading at a decent clip and he kept plugging away for third without being able to answer the front pair. He can find a race, but is hardly consistent. (op 12-1 tchd 14-1)
Ace Of Hearts is at the veteran stage of his career, but he managed to win a race at Glorious Goodwood last term and this was a highly satisfactory comeback. He finished clear of the remainder and should remain competitive off this sort of mark. (op 12-1)
Cape Hawk(IRE) has taken a real shine to the Kempton Polytrack, winning three of his last four starts there, but was 9lb higher for this return to turf and he failed to meet with market expectation, already looking beaten when getting slightly hampered. He may deserve one more chance. Official explanation: jockey said gelding lost its action (tchd 9-4)
Prince Of Thebes(IRE) would have needed this first outing since November and can be expected to show improved form next time. (op 10-1)
T/Jkpt: Not won. T/Plt: £238.70 to a £1 stake. Pool: £159,319.77. 487.20 winning tickets. T/Qpdt: £32.40 to a £1 stake. Pool: £10,184.09. 232.09 winning tickets. JN

[1601] WOLVERHAMPTON (A.W) (L-H)
Saturday, April 26

OFFICIAL GOING: Standard
Wind: Almost nil Weather: Fine

1634 CLEANEVENT AMATEUR RIDERS' H'CAP 5f 216y(P)
6:35 (6:35) (Class 6) (0-60,63) 4-Y-0+ **£1,977** (£608; £304) Stalls Low

Form RPR

0-52 **1** **Trinculo (IRE)**[95] 256 11-10-13 **57**........................(b) MrRPFlint(5) 2 67
(R A Harris) *sn led: clr whn rdn over 1f out: r.o* **16/1**

3306 **2** ¾ **Mambazo**[14] 1338 6-11-5 **58**........................(e) MrSWalker 9 66
(S C Williams) *hld up in mid-div: rdn and hdwy over 1f out: r.o wl ins fnl f: nt rch wnr* **5/1**[2]

4265 **3** nk **Avontuur (FR)**[14] 1338 6-11-2 **55**........................(p) MissSBrotherton 7 62
(Mrs R A Carr) *s.i.s: in rr: swtchd rt and hdwy over 1f out: r.o wl ins fnl f* **5/1**[2]

0-42 **4** 1 **Commander Wish**[92] 304 5-11-2 **60**........................ JPFeatherstone(5) 3 64
(Lucinda Featherstone) *s.i.s: bhd tl hdwy on ins wl over 1f out: sn rdn: kpt on ins fnl f* **17/2**

000- **5** 4 **Nusoor (IRE)**[126] 7221 5-10-12 **58**........................ MrCEllingham(7) 6 49
(Peter Grayson) *t.k.h towards rr: hdwy over 2f out: no imp fnl f* **50/1**

0-04 **6** hd **Briery Lane (IRE)**[7] 1476 7-10-9 **55**........................ MissHDavies(7) 13 47
(J M Bradley) *prom: chsd wnr 2f out tl wknd ins fnl f* **20/1**

0333 **7** ½ **Wicked Uncle**[14] 1338 9-10-11 **55**........................(v) MrTFWoodside(5) 12 44
(S Gollings) *racd wd: hld up towards rr: hdwy on outside over 1f out: sn hung lft: no further prog* **10/1**

5325 **8** 2 **Chatshow (USA)**[5] 1522 7-11-4 **60**........................ MrMJJSmith(3) 1 42
(A W Carroll) *prom: rdn over 1f out: wknd qckly ins fnl f* **7/2**[1]

500- **9** ¾ **Roman Quintet (IRE)**[197] 6148 8-11-3 **63** ow3........................ MrSGray(7) 5 43
(A J McCabe) *mid-div: nt clr run and lost pl wl over 1f out: n.d after* **16/1**

000- **10** ½ **No Grouse**[177] 6610 8-10-9 **55**........................ MissSESiddall(7) 10 33
(E J Alston) *a bhd* **33/1**

00-1 **11** 1 ¼ **Jun Fan (USA)**[14] 1338 6-11-1 **54**........................ MissLEllison 4 28
(B Ellison) *prom: wkng whn n.m.r wl over 1f out* **11/2**[3]

62-0 **12** 3 **Mozakhraf (USA)**[111] 64 6-11-1 **57**........................ MissARyan(3) 11 22
(K A Ryan) *t.k.h: prom: n.m.r over 2f out: sn lost pl* **16/1**

6041 **13** 1 ½ **Perlachy**[9] 1416 4-10-10 **56**........................(v) MissKLMorgan(7) 8 16
(Mrs N Macauley) *t.k.h: led early: prom tl wknd wl over 1f out* **14/1**

1m 16.37s (1.37) **Going Correction** +0.175s/f (Slow) **13** Ran SP% **124.5**
Speed ratings (Par 101): **97,96,95,94,88 88,88,85,84,83 82,78,76**
CSF £96.65 CT £490.65 TOTE £21.80: £7.20, £2.80, £2.20; EX 148.70.
Owner Peter A Price **Bred** Humphrey Okeke **Trained** Earlswood, Monmouths
■ The first Flat winner for Rhys Flint.
■ Stewards' Enquiry : Miss K L Morgan two-day ban: careless riding (May 12, 19); caution: careless riding

FOCUS
A weak handicap run at a fair pace with the winner rated to last year's best and the placed horses to recent course form.

1635 LILLESHALL STEEL LTD STRUCTURAL STEEL SPECIALISTS H'CAP 5f 20y(P)
7:05 (7:06) (Class 6) (0-65,65) 3-Y-0 **£2,047** (£604; £302) Stalls Low

Form RPR

5-33 **1** **Jane's Payoff (IRE)**[104] 146 3-9-4 **65**........................ RichardThomas 6 69
(Mrs L C Jewell) *w ldr: led wl over 2f out: rdn jst over 1f out: hld on wl* **14/1**

2302 **2** nk **Golden Dane (IRE)**[15] 1315 3-8-11 **61**........................(p) LukeMorris(3) 7 64
(C R Dore) *wnt rt s: t.k.h: sn prom: hrd rdn over 1f out: chal ins fnl f: kpt on* **9/2**[2]

56-0 **3** 1 ¼ **Dalarossie**[24] 1155 3-9-1 **62**........................ JimmyQuinn 9 61+
(E J Alston) *s.i.s and wnt rt s: bhd tl rdn and gd hdwy on outside fnl f: edgd lft towards fin: r.o* **4/1**[1]

42-6 **4** nk **Richardthesecond (IRE)**[15] 1315 3-8-13 **60**........................ PatCosgrave 4 57
(W M Brisbourne) *s.i.s: t.k.h: sn chsng ldrs: rdn over 1f out: cl 3rd whn n.m.r briefly ins fnl f: nt qckn* **5/1**[3]

00-0 **5** 2 **Just Jimmy (IRE)**[33] 998 3-8-7 **54**........................ CatherineGannon 2 53+
(P D Evans) *hld up towards rr: hdwy whn nt clr run fr wl over 1f out tl ent fnl f: r.o* **8/1**

3136 **6** ½ **Bahamarama (IRE)**[3] 1560 3-8-8 **55**........................(p) SamHitchcott 5 43
(R A Harris) *hld up in mid-div: rdn and hdwy whn swtchd lft wl over 1f out: one pce fnl f* **13/2**

3466 **7** ½ **Heron (IRE)**[12] 1370 3-7-13 **53** oh1 ow2..............(v[1]) PatrickDonaghy(7) 8 40
(A M Hales) *bmpd s: hld up in mid-div: rdn and hdwy over 1f out: no further prog fnl f* **20/1**

3240 **8** 1 ¼ **Extreme North (USA)**[5] 1519 3-8-12 **64**........................(bt) SCreighton(5) 10 46
(Miss V Haigh) *t.k.h: prom: ev ch 2f out: rdn whn hmpd jst over 1f out: wknd ins fnl f* **6/1**

5605 **9** 1 **Sazerac (USA)**[43] 882 3-8-5 **55**........................ TolleyDean(3) 11 34+
(D Shaw) *stdd s: sn swtchd lft: hld up in rr: nt clr run 1f out and ins fnl f: n.d* **16/1**

-306 **10** 3 ¾ **Lady Vibeeka**[9] 1414 3-8-5 **55**........................ RussellKennemore(3) 1 20
(Mrs H Sweeting) *w ldr tl rdn and wknd over 2f out* **20/1**

005- **11** 2 ¼ **Dark Queen**[239] 5017 3-8-1 **51** oh6........................ WilliamBuick(3) 3 8
(D Carroll) *led over 2f: wknd wl over 1f out* **28/1**

1565 **12** 12 **Stoneacre Pat (IRE)**[29] 1066 3-8-10 **57**........................(b[1]) LPKeniry 12 —
(Peter Grayson) *rel to r: a wl in rr* **16/1**

63.63 secs (1.33) **Going Correction** +0.175s/f (Slow) **12** Ran SP% **125.0**
Speed ratings (Par 96): **96,95,93,93,89 89,88,86,84,78 75,55**
CSF £78.18 CT £312.47 TOTE £11.00: £2.50, £2.20, £2.20; EX 47.20.
Owner Keith C Bennett **Bred** Airlie Stud **Trained** Sutton Valence, Kent
■ Stewards' Enquiry : Sam Hitchcott two-day ban: careless riding (May 10-11)

FOCUS
A moderate sprint handicap with the runner-up rated to recent form and the winner up 9lb.
Stoneacre Pat(IRE) Official explanation: jockey said colt failed to face first time blinkers

1636 CLEANDOMAIN (S) STKS 1m 141y(P)
7:35 (7:35) (Class 6) 3-Y-0+ **£1,774** (£392; £392) Stalls Low

Form RPR

3251 **1** **One Night In Paris (IRE)**[28] 1083 5-9-2 70........................ RichardEvans(7) 2 45
(P D Evans) *w ldr: rdn fnl f: led nr fin* **11/10**[2]

-000 **2** nk **The London Gang**[17] 1269 5-9-9 39........................(b) TGMcLaughlin 8 44
(W M Brisbourne) *dwlt: hld up in rr: rdn and hdwy on outside over 2f out: led wl over 1f out: sn rdn: edgd rt wl ins fnl f: hdd nr fin* **20/1**[3]

06-0 **2** dht **Ravi River (IRE)**[34] 979 4-9-9 78........................ PatCosgrave 3 46+
(J R Boyle) *sn led: hung rt bnd over 2f out: rdn whn swvd bdly lft and hdd wl over 1f out: rallied ins fnl f: r.o* **10/11**[1]

5-60 **4** 1 ½ **Almowj**[31] 1031 5-9-6 40........................ JerryO'Dwyer(3) 7 41
(G H Jones) *hld up and bhd: pushed along 4f out: nt clr run on ins over 2f out: squeezed through and hdwy wl over 1f out: rdn fnl f: no ex towards fin* **50/1**

P/0- **5** 3 **Bond Cruz**[13] 2006 5-9-9 37........................ VinceSlattery 4 34
(D Burchell) *hld up in tch: rdn over 2f out: hmpd wl over 1f out: sn wknd* **50/1**

0-00 **6** 9 **Wilford Maverick (IRE)**[14] 1338 6-9-9 39........................ JimmyQuinn 5 13
(Garry Moss) *t.k.h in tch: rdn wl over 2f out: hmpd wl over 1f out: sn wknd* **33/1**

7 38 **Cabb City (IRE)**[226] 3295 5-9-4 37........................ RichardKingscote 6 —
(W M Brisbourne) *led early: prom tl rdn and wknd over 3f out: eased whn no ch fnl 2f* **28/1**

1m 51.94s (1.44) **Going Correction** +0.175s/f (Slow) **7** Ran SP% **115.1**
Speed ratings (Par 101): **100,99,99,98,95 87,53**
WIN: One Night In Paris £2.40. PL: ONIP £1.10, Ravi River £0.60, The London Gang £2.40. EX: ONIP/RR £1.40, ONIP/TLG £5.70. CSF: ONIP/RR £1.17, ONIP/TLG £10.77..There was no bid for the winner.
Owner Diamond Racing Ltd **Bred** Ken Carroll **Trained** Pandy, Monmouths

FOCUS
This eventful seller proved to be more competitive than the betting suggested. The form is very messy with a lowly rated pair too close to the form horses, both of whom were well below their best.

1637 CLEAN CONCIERGE FILLIES' H'CAP 1m 141y(P)
8:05 (8:05) (Class 5) (0-70,69) 3-Y-0 **£2,914** (£867; £433; £216) Stalls Low

Form RPR

12-1 **1** **Longoria (IRE)**[101] 186 3-9-3 **68**........................ NeilChalmers 1 81
(Lucinda Featherstone) *hld up: hdwy on ins 2f out: led jst over 1f out: sn clr: easily* **10/1**

1513 **2** 5 **Bookiebasher Babe (IRE)**[24] 1161 3-9-3 **68**........................ JimmyFortune 2 70
(M Quinn) *led: rdn and hdd jst over 1f out: sn btn* **5/4**[1]

0-43 **3** ¾ **Maddy**[7] 1479 3-8-6 **60**........................(p) TolleyDean(3) 6 60
(George Baker) *a.p: rdn and chsd ldr 3f out tl wl over 1f out: one pce* **7/1**[3]

00-0 **4** 4 **Coloratura (IRE)**[26] 1115 3-8-9 **60**........................ TGMcLaughlin 7 51
(E A L Dunlop) *hld up in rr: rdn over 1f out: edgd lft and wnt mod 4th ins fnl f* **16/1**

505- **5** 2 **Jelly Mo**[178] 6584 3-8-13 **69**........................ PatrickHills(5) 5 55
(J W Hills) *hld up and bhd: rdn wl over 1f out: no rspnse* **8/1**

004- **6** 8 **Karate Queen**[186] 6401 3-8-5 **59**........................ WilliamBuick(3) 4 27
(A M Balding) *plld hrd early: chsd ldr: sltly hmpd by loose horse 4f out: carried sltly wd and lost 2nd 3f out: rdn and wknd wl over 1f out* **15/2**

00-0 **7** 7 **Miss Okaloosa**[17] 1271 3-8-6 **57**........................ SaleemGolam 8 9
(D M Simcock) *t.k.h towards rr: rdn and hung rt bnd over 2f out: sn struggling* **33/1**

The Form Book, Raceform Ltd, Compton, RG20 6NL

006- **U** **Miss Olivia**[230] 5252 3-8-4 **55** oh3 JimmyQuinn 3 —
(H R A Cecil) *rrd and uns rdr stalls* **5/1**[2]

1m 52.12s (1.62) **Going Correction** +0.175s/f (Slow) **8** Ran SP% **114.4**
Speed ratings (Par 95): **99,94,93,90,88 81,75,—**
CSF £23.04 CT £97.76 TOTE £8.20: £2.00, £1.20, £2.10; EX 23.10.
Owner J Roundtree **Bred** Cathal Ryan **Trained** Atlow, Derbyshire

FOCUS
A loose horse raced with the leaders in this modest event. The form is rated at face value with the placed horses having reasonable recent form.

1638 LILLESHALL STEEL LTD SALES NIGHT OUT MAIDEN FILLIES' STKS — 1m 1f 103y(P)
8:35 (8:35) (Class 5) 3-Y-0+ **£2,456** (£725; £362) **Stalls** Low

Form — RPR

203- **1** **Queen Of Naples**[175] 6652 3-8-10 **93** JimmyFortune 3 73+
(J H M Gosden) *chsd ldr: shkn up to ld jst over 1f out: easily* **2/13**[1]

0-6 **2** *5* **Twiglet (IRE)**[21] 1222 3-8-7 0 TolleyDean(3) 1 62
(George Baker) *led: rdn and hdd jst over 1f out: sn btn* **12/1**[3]

3 *3 ¾* **Kimbolton** 3-8-10 0 JimmyQuinn 5 54+
(H R A Cecil) *s.i.s: hld up: stdy hdwy on ins over 4f out: wknd over 2f out* **6/1**[2]

00-0 **4** *9* **Edgefour (IRE)**[21] 1207 4-9-8 **46** WilliamBuick(3) 2 38
(B I Case) *hld up: rdn over 2f out: sn struggling* **33/1**

5 *50* **Partner In Crime**[28] 4-9-11 0 SamHitchcott 4 —
(C E Longsdon) *hld up: reminder 7f out: rdn over 3f out: sn lost tch: t.o* **50/1**

2m 3.14s (1.44) **Going Correction** +0.175s/f (Slow)
WFA 3 from 4yo 15lb **5** Ran SP% **113.5**
Speed ratings (Par 100): **100,95,92,84,39**
CSF £3.64 TOTE £1.10: £1.02, £3.80; EX 3.50.
Owner H R H Princess Haya Of Jordan **Bred** Normandie Stud Ltd **Trained** Newmarket, Suffolk

FOCUS
An open goal for what was one of the best maiden fillies in training. She did not have to be anywhere near her best to score easily in this slowly run event.

1639 CLEAN VU H'CAP — 1m 4f 50y(P)
9:05 (9:05) (Class 6) (0-65,65) 4-Y-0+ **£2,388** (£705; £352) **Stalls** Low

Form — RPR

01-4 **1** **Hatton Flight**[35] 970 4-9-0 **64** (b) WilliamBuick(3) 5 72+
(A M Balding) *a.p: rdn to ld over 1f out: edgd lft towards fin: r.o wl* **11/4**[1]

3142 **2** *1 ½* **Terminate (GER)**[12] 1374 6-8-6 **57** JamieJones(5) 10 63
(Ian Williams) *t.k.h towards rr: hdwy on ins over 2f out: nt clr run and swtchd lft wl over 1f out: sn ev ch: rdn and nt qckn ins fnl f* **5/1**[3]

2240 **3** *1 ½* **Trysting Grove (IRE)**[11] 1383 7-8-10 **56** SaleemGolam 4 60
(E G Bevan) *hld up in mid-div: hdwy 2f out: rdn over 1f out: styd on ins fnl f* **7/1**

1300 **4** *1 ¾* **Altos Reales**[17] 1266 4-8-8 **55** DeanMcKeown 3 56
(D Shaw) *hld up towards rr: c wd st: styd on fnl f: nvr trbld ldrs* **12/1**

00-6 **5** *hd* **Thorny Mandate**[28] 1086 6-8-10 **56** JimmyQuinn 7 56
(W M Brisbourne) *hld up in tch: wnt 2nd wl over 1f out: rdn and wknd ins fnl f* **12/1**

0/5- **6** *2 ¾* **Grooms Affection**[118] 7277 8-9-5 **65** LPKeniry 9 61
(A M Hales) *s.i.s: sn chsng ldr: led over 8f out: rdn over 2f out: hdd over 1f out: wknd fnl f* **20/1**

40-5 **7** *nk* **Desert Leader (IRE)**[108] 104 7-9-3 **63** TGMcLaughlin 6 59
(W M Brisbourne) *s.i.s: hld up in rr: rdn over 2f out: no rspnse* **10/1**

-222 **8** *½* **Wee Charlie Castle (IRE)**[24] 1148 5-8-12 **58** PatCosgrave 8 53
(G C H Chung) *set stdy pce: hdd over 8f out: w ldr: rdn over 2f out: hmpd on ins wl over 1f out: sn wknd* **4/1**[2]

3260 **9** *shd* **Niqaab**[21] 1206 4-8-4 **51** oh1 NickyMackay 1 46
(W J Musson) *hld up in mid-div: rdn over 3f out: bhd fnl 2f* **9/1**

20/0 **10** *4* **Senor Set (GER)**[6] 1505 7-8-4 **53** TolleyDean(3) 2 41
(D Shaw) *t.k.h in rr: pushed along over 3f out: hung lft wl over 1f out: eased whn no ch wl ins fnl f* **33/1**

2m 40.96s (-0.14) **Going Correction** +0.175s/f (Slow)
WFA 4 from 5yo+ 1lb **10** Ran SP% **118.0**
Speed ratings (Par 101): **107,106,105,103,103 101,101,101,101,98**
CSF £16.65 CT £88.14 TOTE £3.90: £1.60, £2.30, £2.70; EX 17.80 Place 6 £9.29, Place 5 £2.84.
Owner David Brownlow **Bred** Fittocks Stud Ltd **Trained** Kingsclere, Hants
■ Stewards' Enquiry : Jamie Jones one-day ban: careless riding (May 14)

FOCUS
This low-grade handicap was run at a modest pace but the form appears sound enough rated around the placed horses.
T/Plt: £20.70 to a £1 stake. Pool: £60,458.19. 2,131.03 winning tickets. T/Qpdt: £1.80 to a £1 stake. Pool: £4,253.88. 1,668.98 winning tickets. KH

1344 BRIGHTON (L-H)
Sunday, April 27

OFFICIAL GOING: Good (good to firm in places)
As the meeting progressed, there may have been an advantage in racing mid-track, with the last two winners both coming wide
Wind: Moderate, half-against Weather: Fair

1640 E B F NEWHAVEN TO LE HAVRE ON TRANSMANCHE FERRIES MAIDEN STKS — 5f 59y
2:10 (2:11) (Class 5) 2-Y-0 **£3,626** (£1,079; £539; £269) **Stalls** Low

Form — RPR

4 **1** **Smokey Storm**[13] 1363 2-9-3 AlanMunro 4 80
(W Jarvis) *hld up in 5th: rdn and hdwy 2f out: chsd ldr 1f out: mde up 2l to ld fnl stride* **9/4**[2]

4 **2** *hd* **Brenin Taran**[11] 1399 2-9-3 RichardMullen 7 79
(D M Simcock) *prom: led 2f out and rdn 2l ahd: no ex fnl 100yds: ct fnl stride* **6/5**[1]

4 **3** *5* **Entrancer (IRE)**[9] 1439 2-9-3 RichardHughes 6 61
(W R Muir) *swvd lft s: racd keenly and sn led: rdn and hdd 2f out: no ex over 1f out* **9/2**[3]

45 **4** *1 ¼* **Lagan Handout**[18] 1263 2-9-3 FergusSweeney 1 57
(Dr J R J Naylor) *hld up in rr of main gp: effrt over 2f out: wandered and no imp over 1f out* **33/1**

5 *1 ¼* **Old Father Zieten** 2-9-3 RichardKingscote 2 52+
(Tom Dascombe) *outpcd and bhd: styd on fnl f: nvr nr ldrs* **10/1**

6 *4* **Piccaso's Sky** 2-9-3 NCallan 8 38
(A B Haynes) *stmbld sltly s: in tch in centre: effrt over 2f out: wknd over 1f out* **12/1**

7 *2 ¼* **Taurus Twins** 2-8-10 JackDean(7) 3 30
(W G M Turner) *prom 2f: sn rdn and lost pl: n.d fnl 2f* **40/1**

8 *19* **Ruby's Song (IRE)** 2-8-12 PaulFitzsimons 5 —
(J M Bradley) *missed break and wnt lft s: sn drvn along and bhd: no ch fr 1/2-way* **100/1**

63.31 secs (1.01) **Going Correction** +0.10s/f (Good) **8** Ran SP% **117.6**
Speed ratings (Par 92): **95,94,86,84,82 76,72,42**
CSF £5.46 TOTE £3.80: £1.20, £1.10, £1.40; EX 8.00 Trifecta £18.50 Pool: £261.70 - 10.01 winning units..
Owner The Bk Partnership **Bred** P V And Mrs J P Jackson **Trained** Newmarket, Suffolk

FOCUS
Probably an above-average juvenile maiden for the track, run at a decent tempo. The first two finished clear.

NOTEBOOK
Smokey Storm took a while to find his stride but really got going up the final climb to snatch it on the line, suggesting that 6f will be no problem. With the first two finishing clear, the form is probably a bit above average for a Brighton juvenile maiden. (op 11-4 tchd 4-1)
Brenin Taran looked set to score readily when taking a two-length lead on the run to the final furlong, but he did not quite see out the final hill and was caught on the line. On the evidence of his first two runs, he has his fair share of ability and it is only a matter of time before he gets off the mark. (op Evens tchd 10-11 and 5-4 in places)
Entrancer(IRE) was a bit keen early on, even when allowed to make the running, and had nothing left for the last furlong and a half. However, he has shown ability in his first two races, and comes from a winning family, so further opportunities will soon come along. (op 5-1 tchd 11-2 and 4-1)
Lagan Handout was never finding enough speed to get involved from behind, and did not look entirely comfortable on the camber, but is now qualified for nurseries and that will be his ideal home from now on, although he will have to wait until July for them to start.
Old Father Zieten, a 17,000gns yearling whose dam won at around 1m2f in France, already looks to need a stiffer test than this. He was quickly taken off his feet and only began to recover too late. (op 12-1 tchd 8-1)
Piccaso's Sky has plenty of speed in his family, but he attracted no bid at the sales and should be most effective when handicapped. (op 28-1)

1641 NEWHAVEN TO DIEPPE ON TRANSMANCHE FERRIES H'CAP — 6f 209y
2:40 (2:40) (Class 6) (0-65,65) 4-Y-0+ **£2,331** (£693; £346; £173) **Stalls** Low

Form — RPR

4610 **1** **Napoletano (GER)**[25] 1154 7-8-10 **57** ow1 (p) NCallan 2 73+
(S Dow) *stdd s: hld up in rr: nt clr run over 2f out: swtchd wd and hdwy over 1f out: styd on to ld fnl 50yds* **9/2**[1]

15-3 **2** *½* **Support Fund (IRE)**[14] 1345 4-9-3 **64** StephenCarson 10 79+
(Eve Johnson Houghton) *mid-div: pushed along 4f out: gd hdwy to ld 1f out: hdd and nt qckn fnl 50yds* **11/2**[2]

5130 **3** *3 ¾* **Wiltshire (IRE)**[23] 1189 6-8-9 **56** (v) MickyFenton 8 61
(P T Midgley) *stdd s: hld up towards rr: rdn 3f out: hung lft and styd on appr fnl f: nvr nrr* **8/1**[3]

0-43 **4** *1 ½* **Franksalot (IRE)**[22] 1209 8-8-11 **58** RoystonFfrench 5 59
(I W McInnes) *bhd: rdn 1/2-way: styd on appr fnl f: nt rch ldrs* **11/2**[2]

50-0 **5** *hd* **Moon Forest (IRE)**[16] 1313 6-8-1 **51** oh6 (b[1]) LukeMorris(3) 12 51
(J M Bradley) *stdd s: sn chsng ldrs: rdn to ld wl over 1f out: hung lft: hdd & wknd 1f out* **16/1**

-065 **6** *½* **Teen Ager (FR)**[11] 1409 4-9-0 **61** LPKeniry 3 60
(P Burgoyne) *in tch: effrt whn n.m.r ins fnl 2f: one pce* **9/1**

6-00 **7** *¾* **Briannsta (IRE)**[36] 964 6-8-10 **62** NataliaGemelova(5) 11 59
(J E Long) *chsd ldrs: effrt over 2f out: hrd rdn: one pce* **18/1**

120- **8** *1* **Magroom**[148] 6997 4-9-4 **65** RichardHughes 1 59+
(R J Hodges) *hld up in midfield on rail: nowhere to go 2f out tl swtchd wd ins fnl f: nvr able to rcvr in time and nt knocked abt* **9/2**[1]

5330 **9** *2* **Zazous**[25] 1154 7-8-8 **55** ChrisCatlin 6 44
(J J Bridger) *towards rr: rdn 1/2-way: n.d* **11/1**

00-0 **10** *¾* **Outer Hebrides**[25] 1160 7-9-2 **63** (v) StephenDonohoe 9 50
(J M Bradley) *w ldrs: carried lft over 1f out: wknd fnl f* **16/1**

3025 **11** *5* **Mr Rev**[30] 1061 5-9-1 **62** PaulFitzsimons 4 35
(J M Bradley) *led tl hdd wl over 1f out: 4th and jst hld whn hmpd on rail appr fnl f: nt rcvr and eased* **16/1**

5/6 **12** *5* **Chiltai (IRE)**[4] 1567 7-8-6 **53** oh6 ow2 NeilChalmers 13 13
(J J Bridger) *in tch on outside: outpcd after 3f: sn lost pl* **50/1**

1m 22.84s (-0.26) **Going Correction** +0.10s/f (Good) **12** Ran SP% **121.4**
Speed ratings (Par 101): **105,104,100,98,98 97,96,95,93,92 86,81**
CSF £29.37 CT £200.45 TOTE £4.60: £1.60, £2.00, £3.90; EX 38.50 Trifecta £188.20 Part won. Pool: £265.08 - 0.50 winning units..
Owner Miss Helen Chamberlain **Bred** Gestut Hof Ittlingen **Trained** Epsom, Surrey
■ Stewards' Enquiry : Luke Morris one-day ban: careless riding (May 12)
Richard Hughes one-day ban; careless riding (May 12)

FOCUS
A modest but competitive handicap, run at a good pace and the first four came from the rear.
Wiltshire(IRE) Official explanation: jockey said gelding was unsuited by the track.
Moon Forest(IRE) Official explanation: jockey said gelding hung left down the hill
Magroom ◆ Official explanation: jockey said gelding was denied a clear run.

1642 TRANSMANCHEFERRIES.CO.UK (S) STKS — 5f 213y
3:15 (3:16) (Class 6) 3-Y-0+ **£1,813** (£539; £269; £134) **Stalls** Low

Form — RPR

6224 **1** **Punching**[13] 1370 4-9-12 59 NCallan 2 70
(Miss Gay Kelleway) *hld up in midfield: hdwy ins fnl 2f: drvn to ld ins fnl f* **4/1**[2]

620- **2** *1 ½* **Kyllachy Storm**[247] 4758 4-9-6 51 RichardHughes 14 59
(R J Hodges) *prom: led over 2f out tl ins fnl f: kpt on same pce* **7/1**

2305 **3** *shd* **Night Prospector**[13] 1370 8-9-6 55 (p) AlanMunro 4 59
(R A Harris) *hld up in rr of midfield: hrd rdn and hdwy over 1f out: r.o to take 3rd ins fnl f: nrly rchd 2nd* **7/1**

-130 **4** *2 ½* **Rann Na Cille (IRE)**[23] 1185 4-9-7 57 MickyFenton 10 52
(P T Midgley) *chsd ldrs: effrt whn sltly short of room over 1f out: one pce* **9/1**

00-0 **5** *1 ¼* **Goodwood Spirit**[18] 1269 6-8-13 40 (v) PietroRomeo(7) 5 47
(J M Bradley) *bhd: shkn up and styd on fnl 2f: nvr nrr* **33/1**

5323 **6** *hd* **Cleveland**[45] 868 6-9-9 50 RussellKennemore(3) 1 57+
(R Hollinshead) *trckd ldrs on rail: nt clr run over 2f out: tried to squeeze through tl no room and snatched up over 1f out: nt rcvr* **7/2**[1]

4-03 **7** *¾* **Scarlett Heart (IRE)**[25] 1150 4-9-7 55 PaulDoe 8 45
(S Curran) *stdd s: sn chsng ldrs on outside: hrd rdn and no ex over 1f out* **11/2**[3]

2056 **8** *nk* **Monashee Brave (IRE)**[32] 1028 5-9-12 58 (p) AmirQuinn 13 49
(M A Allen) *led tl over 2f out: n.m.r and wknd over 1f ut* **14/1**

0005 **9** 2 1/4 **Mulberry Lad (IRE)**[18] 1275 6-9-12 42 ChrisCatlin 6 41
(P W Hiatt) *bhd: mod effrt in centre 2f out: nt pce to chal* **20/1**
0500 **10** 2 1/2 **Calloff The Search**[18] 1275 4-9-9 48 (p) JerryO'Dwyer(3) 11 33
(Stef Liddiard) *stdd s: a towards rr: hrd rdn and n.d fnl 2f* **16/1**
660- **11** 1/2 **Convince (USA)**[197] 6179 7-9-3 49 (p) TolleyDean(3) 3 26
(J M Bradley) *bhd: rdn 3f out: modest hdwy in rr of midfield whn nt clr run 1f out: nt trble ldrs* **14/1**
000- **12** 4 **Boot Strap Bill**[145] 7021 3-8-9 60 PaulFitzsimons 12 13
(Miss J R Tooth) *in tch: outpcd 1/2-way: sn lost pl* **50/1**

1m 10.98s (0.78) **Going Correction** +0.10s/f (Good)
WFA 3 from 4yo+ 11lb 12 Ran SP% **121.5**
Speed ratings (Par 101): **98,96,95,92,90 90,89,89,86,82 82,76**
CSF £32.56 TOTE £4.80: £1.90, £2.40, £2.50; EX 35.80 Trifecta £150.10 Part won. Pool: £211.51 - 0.20 winning units..There was no bid for the winner.
Owner bettingjobs.com **Bred** Cheveley Park Stud Ltd **Trained** Exning, Suffolk

FOCUS
A routine seller, and the early pace was modest for 6f. The winner is probably the best guide on his recent All-Weather form.
Cleveland Official explanation: jockey said gelding was denied a clear run.

1643 TRANSMANCHE FERRIES H'CAP 1m 3f 196y
3:50 (3:52) (Class 6) (0-60,57) 4-Y-0+ **£1,942** (£578; £288; £144) **Stalls** High

Form RPR
0464 **1** **Bienheureux**[7] 1505 7-8-11 49 (t) NCallan 9 61+
(Miss Gay Kelleway) *hld up towards rr: smooth hdwy to ld 2f out: drvn clr over 1f out: comf* **9/2**[2]
1413 **2** 4 1/2 **Blue Hills**[18] 954 7-9-5 57 (b) ChrisCatlin 3 62
(P W Hiatt) *prom: rdn 4f out: kpt on same pce fnl 2f: tk 2nd nr fin* **12/1**
-010 **3** 3/4 **Take A Mile (IRE)**[63] 541 6-9-3 55 JimCrowley 1 59
(C Gordon) *hld up in 5th: drvn to chse wnr 2f out: nt pce of wnr: lost 2nd nr fin* **16/1**
000- **4** 2 1/2 **Makai**[52] 3854 5-8-0 45 RossAtkinson(7) 11 45
(M R Hoad) *mid-div: rdn to chse ldrs 2f out: styd on same pce* **50/1**
05/0 **5** shd **Viscount Rossini**[30] 1062 6-8-4 45 LukeMorris(3) 14 45
(A W Carroll) *chsd ldrs: hrd rdn over 2f out: one pce: disputing 5th and btn whn bmpd ins fnl f* **66/1**
005 **6** 1 1/4 **Tribiani (IRE)**[32] 1025 4-8-3 45 KevinGhunowa(3) 16 43
(P A Blockley) *stdd s: hld up in rr: hdwy on outside 2f out: hung lft: nt rch ldrs* **33/1**
330- **7** 1 **She's So Pretty (IRE)**[190] 6330 4-9-4 57 GeorgeBaker 5 53
(G L Moore) *in tch: rdn and lost pl 4f out: sme late hdwy* **8/1**
02-3 **8** hd **Bob's Your Uncle**[23] 1181 5-9-3 55 SebSanders 8 51
(J G Portman) *hld up in rr of midfield: hrd rdn 3f out: nt pce to chal* **11/4**[1]
50-0 **9** 1 1/4 **Lawyer To World**[9] 1459 4-8-6 45 (p) HayleyTurner 12 39
(Mrs C A Dunnett) *bhd: drvn along and sme hdwy in centre 2f out: n.d* **50/1**
005- **10** 3 3/4 **Mud Monkey**[16] 6453 4-8-11 50 TQuinn 4 44+
(B G Powell) *chsd ldr: hrd rdn 2f out: wknd over 1f out: eased whn btn fnl f* **6/1**
62-0 **11** 2 **Star Of Pompey**[39] 934 4-9-4 57 SamHitchcott 2 53+
(A B Haynes) *mid-div on rail: mod effrt over 2f out: no imp* **33/1**
000- **12** 3 1/2 **Dawn Mystery**[133] 7168 4-8-7 46 MickyFenton 10 25
(Rae Guest) *led tl 2f out: sn wknd* **20/1**
3330 **13** 23 **Play Up Pompey**[17] 1282 6-8-12 50 AmirQuinn 7 —
(J J Bridger) *stdd s: rdn 5f out: a bhd: eased whn no ch over 1f out* **25/1**
00-0 **14** 5 **Orphina (IRE)**[34] 999 5-8-4 49 ow2 (t) GabrielHannon(7) 15 —
(B G Powell) *hrd rdn 3f out: a towards rr: eased whn no ch over 1f out* **40/1**
6306 **15** 5 **Stoneacre Gareth (IRE)**[7] 808 4-8-6 45 NeilPollard 6 —
(J Jay) *chsd ldrs: rdn 4f out: sn wknd: eased whn no ch over 1f out* **25/1**
0302 **16** 27 **Nanosecond (USA)**[22] 1206 5-9-1 53 (p) RichardHughes 13 —
(S A Callaghan) *prom tl wknd qckly 4f out: bhd whn eased heavily fnl 2f* **5/1**[3]

2m 33.31s (0.61) **Going Correction** +0.10s/f (Good)
WFA 4 from 5yo+ 1lb 16 Ran SP% **126.7**
Speed ratings (Par 101): **101,98,97,95,95 94,94,94,93,90 89,87,71,68,65 47**
CSF £53.91 CT £825.16 TOTE £6.10: £1.80, £2.60, £3.10, £8.70; EX 50.70 TRIFECTA Not won..
Owner Mr & Mrs I Henderson **Bred** N R Shields **Trained** Exning, Suffolk

FOCUS
Selling class, with the well-handicapped winner proving far too good for the rest at the weights. The form is rated around the placed horses.
Mud Monkey Official explanation: jockey said gelding was unbalanced in the straight.
Play Up Pompey Official explanation: jockey said gelding was never travelling
Nanosecond(USA) Official explanation: jockey said gelding lost its action.

1644 PORTSMOUTH TO LE HAVRE ON TRANSMANCHE H'CAP 1m 1f 209y
4:25 (4:25) (Class 6) (0-65,62) 4-Y-0+ **£2,201** (£655; £327; £163) **Stalls** High

Form RPR
2360 **1** **Aphrodisia**[26] 1127 4-9-2 60 NCallan 10 72
(S C Williams) *hld up in tch: led over 2f out: drvn clr over 1f out: comf* **17/2**
2535 **2** 5 **Megalala (IRE)**[4] 1564 7-9-1 59 NeilChalmers 6 61
(J J Bridger) *hld up in midfield: hdwy 2f out: rdn to chse wnr jst over 1f out: no imp* **9/1**
0/00 **3** 1 1/4 **Tuscan Treaty**[94] 289 8-8-5 49 oh3 ow1 (t) EdwardCreighton 4 48
(R W Price) *dwlt: hld up in rr: gd hdwy on outside to chse ldrs 3f out: rdn and one pce fnl 2f* **50/1**
0205 **4** nk **Earl Kraul (IRE)**[17] 1280 5-8-12 56 StephenDonohoe 5 54
(P A Blockley) *hld up in rr: rdn and hdwy 2f out: edgd lft and one pce appr fnl f: fin lame* **6/1**[3]
40-2 **5** 1 1/4 **Gracechurch (IRE)**[18] 1266 5-8-13 57 RichardHughes 1 53
(R J Hodges) *chsd ldrs tl wknd over 1f out* **7/4**[1]
20-6 **6** 4 1/2 **Pactolos Way**[55] 430 5-9-4 62 JimCrowley 11 49
(P R Chamings) *chsd ldrs: led 3f out tl over 2f out: wknd wl over 1f out* **5/1**[2]
60-3 **7** 5 **Fairly Honest**[14] 1350 4-8-8 52 ChrisCatlin 2 29
(P W Hiatt) *disp ld tl over 4f out: wknd over 2f out* **6/1**[3]
0-00 **8** 1 3/4 **The Grey One (IRE)**[25] 1160 5-8-9 56 (p) TolleyDean(3) 9 29
(J M Bradley) *hld up towards rr: hdwy over 3f out: wknd over 2f out* **11/1**
0006 **9** 27 **Running Supreme**[7] 1499 4-8-4 48 oh3 (b) RoystonFfrench 8 —
(Mrs N Smith) *stdd s: plld hrd in rr: hdwy into midfield after 3f: wknd 4f out: bhd whn lost action and eased over 2f out* **66/1**
0-06 **10** 1/2 **Sagunt (GER)**[95] 276 5-8-9 60 WilliamCarson(7) 3 —
(S Curran) *disp ld: led over 4f out tl wknd rapidly 3f out: sn bhd: eased whn no ch fnl 2f* **20/1**
0-00 **11** nk **Djalalabad (FR)**[7] 1505 4-8-11 55 SebSanders 7 —
(Mrs C A Dunnett) *a bhd: eased whn no ch fnl 2f* **16/1**

2m 4.79s (1.19) **Going Correction** +0.10s/f (Good) 11 Ran SP% **124.6**
Speed ratings (Par 101): **99,95,94,93,92 89,85,83,62,61 61**
CSF £86.42 CT £3635.87 TOTE £11.40: £3.20, £3.40, £9.30; EX 84.00 TRIFECTA Not won..
Owner bellhouseracing.com **Bred** Theobalds Stud **Trained** Newmarket, Suffolk

FOCUS
A low-grade race, but the comfortable winner is lightly raced and can progress a little. The proximity of the third raises doubts about the form.
Earl Kraul(IRE) Official explanation: jockey said gelding finished lame.
Running Supreme Official explanation: jockey said filly ran too free.

1645 VISITEZ LES SEVEN SISTERS AVEC TRANSMANCHE H'CAP 7f 214y
4:55 (4:56) (Class 5) (0-70,70) 4-Y-0+ **£2,460** (£732; £365; £182) **Stalls** Low

Form RPR
2315 **1** **Millfield (IRE)**[14] 1345 5-9-4 70 JimCrowley 2 79
(P R Chamings) *stdd s: plld hrd in rr: hrd rdn and hdwy over 1f out: r.o to ld fnl 75yds* **10/3**[2]
100- **2** 1/2 **Haasem (USA)**[121] 7257 5-8-11 63 StephenDonohoe 8 71
(J R Jenkins) *hld up in tch: jnd ldr over 3f out: led wl over 1f out: hrd rdn and pricked ears: hdd and no ex fnl 75yds* **15/2**
-113 **3** 1 3/4 **Cape Velvet (IRE)**[52] 809 4-9-4 70 JamesDoyle 9 74
(J W Hills) *bhd: pushed along 4f out: styd on to chse first 2 fnl f* **3/1**[1]
000- **4** 5 **Moyoko (IRE)**[167] 6801 5-7-11 56 oh6 RossAtkinson(7) 4 49
(M Blanshard) *chsd ldrs on rail: outpcd over 2f out: a hld after* **14/1**
130- **5** nk **Goose Green (IRE)**[148] 6993 4-8-13 65 RichardHughes 1 57
(R J Hodges) *prom tl hrd rdn and wknd over 1f out* **6/1**
0240 **6** 2 3/4 **Metropolitan Chief**[13] 1371 4-8-4 56 oh3 DavidKinsella 3 41
(P Burgoyne) *led tl wl over 1f out: sn wknd* **12/1**
306- **7** 5 **Finsbury**[201] 6081 5-9-1 67 NCallan 5 41
(J M Bradley) *hld up in 6th: effrt and hrd rdn 2f out: wknd over 1f out* **7/2**[3]
/1-6 **8** 49 **Power Ballad**[17] 1287 4-9-1 67 SebSanders 6 —
(W J Knight) *prom tl wknd and eased 3f out* **11/1**

1m 37.08s (1.08) **Going Correction** +0.10s/f (Good) 8 Ran SP% **119.0**
Speed ratings (Par 103): **98,97,95,90,90 87,82,33**
CSF £29.74 CT £84.53 TOTE £3.80: £1.70, £2.20, £1.60; EX 33.50 Trifecta £92.50 Pool: £276.36 - 2.12 winning units..
Owner Inhurst Players **Bred** Limestone Stud **Trained** Baughurst, Hants

FOCUS
A moderate to fair race for the track, run at a modest pace until the front-runners quickened it at halfway. The first three home were the only three to race in the centre of the track in the home straight and the third sets the standard.
Power Ballad Official explanation: jockey said filly lost its action.

1646 VISIT THE COTE D'ALBATRE WITH TRANSMANCHE H'CAP 5f 59y
5:25 (5:27) (Class 5) (0-70,71) 4-Y-0+ **£2,460** (£732; £365; £182) **Stalls** Low

Form RPR
4503 **1** **What Do You Know**[30] 1047 5-9-4 70 (v[1]) DavidKinsella 14 82
(A M Hales) *prom: wd of others in centre: led and hung bdly lft towards far rail 1f out: drvn out* **13/2**[3]
-203 **2** 2 1/2 **Rocker**[31] 1037 4-8-10 62 (v) HayleyTurner 15 65
(B R Johnson) *prom: hrd rdn over 1f out: nt pce of wnr fnl f: tk 2nd nr fin* **10/1**
0-31 **3** shd **Desperate Dan**[8] 1489 7-9-4 70 (b) NCallan 11 73
(A B Haynes) *in tch: effrt over 2f out: kpt on fnl f* **6/1**[2]
2124 **4** hd **Thoughtsofstardom**[44] 875 5-8-10 62 SebSanders 4 64
(M Wigham) *prom: hrd rdn over 1f out: one pce* **4/1**[1]
00-0 **5** 2 1/4 **Signor Panettiere**[92] 318 7-8-4 56 oh11 SilvestreDeSousa 2 50
(A D Brown) *led: hrd rdn and hdd 1f out: wknd ins fnl f* **14/1**
460- **6** hd **Jayanjay**[186] 6428 9-8-7 59 PaulDoe 1 52
(B R Johnson) *hld up in midfield: effrt whn swtchd rt and lft ins fnl 2f: no further prog fnl f* **14/1**
24-2 **7** 1/2 **Cosmic Destiny (IRE)**[50] 840 6-9-4 70 LPKeniry 3 61
(E F Vaughan) *stdd s: hld up in rr: sme hdwy 2f out: nvr able to chal* **7/1**
06-0 **8** 1 3/4 **Bollin Franny**[25] 1145 4-7-13 56 oh1 NataliaGemelova(5) 16 41
(J E Long) *chsd ldrs on outside: hrd rdn and btn 2f out* **20/1**
00-0 **9** 4 1/2 **Harrison's Flyer (IRE)**[18] 1268 7-8-13 68 (p) TolleyDean(3) 6 57+
(J M Bradley) *towards rr: styng on but n.d whn nt clr run ins fnl f* **14/1**
000- **10** 3 **Peopleton Brook**[167] 6794 6-8-10 62 JimCrowley 7 47+
(J M Bradley) *in tch: rdn over 2f out: wknd wl over 1f out* **10/1**
1155 **11** 5 **Decider (USA)**[20] 1242 5-8-11 66 KevinGhunowa(3) 10 6
(R A Harris) *sn pushed along in midfield: wknd 1/2-way: sn bhd and eased* **12/1**
0200 **12** 5 **Kempsey**[6] 1522 6-8-6 58 (v) ChrisCatlin 12 —
(J J Bridger) *sn rdn along and a trailing* **33/1**

62.90 secs (0.60) **Going Correction** +0.10s/f (Good) 12 Ran SP% **113.7**
Speed ratings (Par 103): **99,95,94,94,90 90,89,87,79,75 67,59**
CSF £61.03 CT £310.33 TOTE £7.20: £1.50, £4.30, £2.10; EX 79.70 Trifecta £319.20 Part won. Pool: £449.66 - 0.50 winning units. Place 6 £257.58, Place 5 £232.85..
Owner Brick Farm Racing **Bred** C G Reid **Trained** Preston Capes, Northants

FOCUS
A moderate-quality sprint won in surprisingly decisive fashion by the horse racing widest in the straight. The third sets the level but the form is limited by the proximity of the fifth from way out of the handicap.
T/Jkpt: Not won. T/Plt: £177.00 to a £1 stake. Pool: £69,385.63. 286.15 winning tickets. T/Qpdt: £58.40 to a £1 stake. Pool: £3,926.04. 49.69 winning tickets. LM

1647 - 1654a (Foreign Racing) - See Raceform Interactive

NAVAN (L-H)
Sunday, April 27

OFFICIAL GOING: Good to yielding (yielding in back straight)

1655a VINTAGE CROP STKS (LISTED RACE) 1m 5f
4:30 (4:30) 4-Y-0+ **£23,933** (£7,022; £3,345; £1,139)

RPR
1 **Yeats (IRE)**[203] 6044 7-9-8 121 JAHeffernan 1 114
(A P O'Brien, Ire) *settled 2nd: chal fr 2 1/2f out: led 1f out: kpt on wl* **4/6**[1]
2 3/4 **Red Moloney (USA)**[14] 1353 4-9-4 110 DPMcDonogh 6 110
(Kevin Prendergast, Ire) *trckd ldrs in 4th: 3rd after 1/2-way: chal travelling wl 2f out: sn led: hdd 1f out: kpt on u.p* **11/4**[2]
3 1 **Alfie Flits**[302] 3119 6-9-1 RobertWinston 3 105
(G A Swinbank) *trckd ldrs in 3rd: 4th appr st: sn rdn: cl 3rd and chal 1 1/2f out: kpt on* **6/1**[3]

The Form Book, Raceform Ltd, Compton, RG20 6NL

4 nk **Nick's Nikita (IRE)**[252] 4647 5-9-3 103 ...... RPCleary 2 106
(M Halford, Ire) *hld up in 5th: prog early st: 4th and kpt on fnl f* **16/1**

5 5 **Scotch Bonnet (IRE)**[153] 6953 4-8-12 94 ...... (p) FMBerry 7 95
(Edward P Harty, Ire) *hld up in rr: kpt on same pce st* **50/1**

6 2 1/2 **Lounaos (FR)**[22] 6358 5-8-12 ...... (p) PJSmullen 5 90
(Eoin Griffin, Ire) *led: qcknd ent st: hdd under 2f out: sn no ex* **16/1**

2m 54.6s (-5.40)
WFA 4 from 5yo+ 1lb 7 Ran SP% **114.7**
CSF £2.87 TOTE £1.50: £1.10, £1.80; DF 2.30.
Owner Mrs John Magnier **Bred** Barronstown Stud & Orpendale **Trained** Ballydoyle, Co Tipperary

FOCUS
A steadily run Listed contest which developed into something of a sprint.

NOTEBOOK
Yeats(IRE) started off this season the same way as last year, but he was made to battle much harder on this occasion before getting the better of Red Moloney by three-quarters of a length. Under severe pressure from Seamie Heffernan, he had the help of the inside rail as he battled with Red Moloney, and it was not until the last 150 yards that he got his head in front before keeping his opposition at bay. While this victory was nothing like his five-length success 12 months earlier, this was a much better renewal and, according to the winning jockey, Yeats was not as forward as he was at this time last year. (op 4/6 tchd 8/11)
Red Moloney(USA) was bidding to make it two Listed race wins on the trot and he looks up to adding another to his collection following this game effort. He may get the chance later in the season to avenge for this defeat as Kevin Prendergast stated his desire to go for the Irish St Leger with him, a race Yeats won last season. (op 5/2 tchd 9/4)
Alfie Flits, a winner of two Listed races in 2006, looked a big threat to the front two finishers approaching the final furlong, but he was one-paced from there onwards. This was a decent effort and one which could possibly lead to more Irish assaults with Alan Swinbank's charge. (op 7/1)
Nick's Nikita(IRE), winner of last season's Group 3 Noblesse Stakes, ran as though he will be better suited when returning to a longer trip. His connections also indicated the possibility of aiming the son of Machiavellian at the Irish St. Leger later in the year.
Lounaos(FR), running in her second Listed race on her seventh start on the Flat, set the race up for the race principals with her moderate yet steady pace and she dropped off once the tempo increased from two furlongs out. (op 14/1)

1656 - 1658a (Foreign Racing) - See Raceform Interactive

1513 CAPANNELLE (R-H)
Sunday, April 27

OFFICIAL GOING: Good

1659a PREMIO CARLO CHIESA (GROUP 3) (F&M) 6f
4:00 (4:09) 3-Y-0+ **£26,801** (£11,793; £6,432; £3,216)

RPR

1 **Love Intrigue (IRE)**[203] 3-8-5 ...... PAragoni 13 104
(A Peraino, Italy) *outpcd early: hdwy fr 2f out and angled towards outside: led 100yds out: drvn out* **534/10**

2 1/2 **Eastern Romance**[182] 6525 3-8-5 ...... FergalLynch 11 102
(K A Ryan) *pressed ldr on outside: led over 2f out to 100yds out: r.o* **6/5**[1]

3 1 **Docksil**[35] 4-9-2 ...... PConvertino 2 99
(B Grizzetti, Italy) *a.p on rails: hrd rdn and ev ch 1f out: kpt on same pce* **17/1**

4 nk **L'Indiscreta**[182] 3-8-5 ...... DVargiu 7 98
(B Grizzetti, Italy) *a in tch: stvd on same pce fnl f* **3/1**[2]

5 3/4 **Vitamina Plus (ITY)**[350] 1701 4-9-2 ...... GBietolini 5 96
(R Giorgetti, Italy) *mid-div: stvd on fnl 2f: nvr nr to chal* **16/1**

6 hd **Lady Marmelade (ITY)**[37] 5-9-2 ...... FBranca 12 95
(D Ducci, Italy) *trckd ldrs on outside: disp 2nd wl over 1f out: one pce* **10/1**

7 3/4 **White Rose (ITY)**[35] 4-9-2 ...... MDemuro 9 93
(M Bucci, Italy) *in tch on outside to over 1f out* **33/1**

8 2 **Smorova (IRE)** 3-8-5 ...... CFiocchi 6 87
(F Saggiomo, Italy) *chsd ldrs tl wkng wl over 1f out* **96/10**

9 1 **Different Opinion (IRE)**[28] 3-8-5 ...... MMonteriso 10 84
(A Peraino, Italy) *mid-div: rdn and btn wl over 1f out* **73/1**

10 2 **Ekta**[14] 4-9-2 ...... EBotti 3 78
(S Botti, Italy) *mid-div tl btn over 2f out* **17/2**[3]

11 1 **Powerful Speed**[182] 3-8-6 ow1 ...... MPasquale 1 76
(L Brogi, Italy) *cl up on rails to 2f out* **88/10**

12 hd **Velvet Revolver (IRE)**[14] 5-9-2 ...... GMarcelli 8 74
(L Riccardi, Italy) *led to over 2f out: wknd qckly wl over 1f out* **36/1**

13 2 **Shoshiba (IRE)**[338] 5-9-2 ...... PSirigu 4 68
(Mafalda Osthaus, Italy) *a outpcd: in rr fr 1/2-way* **47/1**

14 5 **Vola Vola (IRE)**[371] 4-9-2 ...... (b) DPorcu 14 53
(R Feligioni, Italy) *spd to 1/2-way on outside: eased whn btn* **20/1**

69.20 secs (-1.10)
WFA 3 from 4yo+ 11lb 14 Ran SP% **136.8**
(including one euro stakes): WIN 54.46; PL 8.93, 1.65, 3.66; DF 70.81.
Owner Scuderia Alex **Bred** Loscot S R L **Trained** Italy

NOTEBOOK
Love Intrigue(IRE) runs as though she wants further than 6f, but she still proved good enough to land this Group 3, staying on best having been outpaced.
Eastern Romance, favourite to make a winning reappearance, was in the first three throughout and beat all her fancied opponents, but she could not match the finishing burst of an unconsidered rival who had finished last of nine - in a race in which the first three were all running again - over course and distance four weeks earlier.

1237 COLOGNE (R-H)
Sunday, April 27

OFFICIAL GOING: Soft

1662a GERLING-PREIS (GROUP 2) 1m 4f
4:15 (4:28) 4-Y-0+ **£29,412** (£11,029; £4,412; £2,941)

RPR

1 **Oriental Tiger (GER)**[21] 1237 5-8-11 ...... (b) THellier 10 111
(U Ostmann, Germany) *mde all: drvn fnl stages: comf* **28/10**[2]

2 2 **Dickens (GER)**[190] 6353 5-8-11 ...... ASuborics 7 108
(H Blume, Germany) *hld up towards rr: fin steadily fr 1 1/2f out: tk 2nd cl home* **124/10**

3 nk **Poseidon Adventure (IRE)**[21] 1237 5-8-11 ...... (b) JohnEgan 5 108
(W Figge, Germany) *in tch: running on st: wnt 2nd over 1f out: lost pl cl home* **25/1**

4 2 **Shrek (GER)**[224] 5464 4-8-11 ...... EPedroza 4 106
(A Wohler, Germany) *racd in 2nd: drvn over 2f out: styd on tl no ex fr over 1f out* **3/1**[3]

5 1 1/2 **Eiswind**[21] 1237 4-8-11 ...... FilipMinarik 9 103
(P Schiergen, Germany) *trckd ldrs in mid-div: styd on same pce st* **28/1**

6 shd **First Stream (GER)**[175] 6689 4-8-11 ...... (b) AHelfenbein 3 103
(Mario Hofer, Germany) *trckd ldrs: pushed along over 3f out: nvr able to chal* **62/10**

7 3/4 **Adlerflug (GER)**[238] 5077 4-9-4 ...... TPQueally 6 109
(J Hirschberger, Germany) *prom on outside early: lost pl 4f out: drvn ent st: one pce* **19/10**[1]

8 shd **Appel Au Maitre (FR)**[189] 6376 4-8-11 ...... FJohansson 1 102
(Wido Neuroth, Norway) *hld up: nvr in chalng position* **89/10**

9 8 **Brisant (GER)**[155] 6941 6-8-11 ...... ADeVries 2 89
(M Trybuhl, Germany) *hld up on ins: shkn up st: unable qck* **26/1**

10 2 1/2 **Estima Directa (GER)** 4-8-7 ...... KatharinaWerning 8 82
(P Bradik, Germany) *bhd on ins: nvr in contention* **47/1**

2m 26.44s (-6.46)
WFA 4 from 5yo+ 1lb 10 Ran SP% **130.3**
PARI-MUTUEL (including ten euro stake): WIN 38; PL 21, 33, 50; SF 346.
Owner Gestut Auenquelle **Bred** Gestut Auenquelle **Trained** Germany

1359 LONGCHAMP (R-H)
Sunday, April 27

OFFICIAL GOING: Soft

1663a PRIX DE BARBEVILLE-MTPA (GROUP 3) 1m 7f 110y
2:15 (2:17) 4-Y-0+ **£29,412** (£11,765; £8,824; £5,882; £2,941)

RPR

1 **Coastal Path**[204] 6028 4-9-2 ...... SPasquier 5 114
(A Fabre, France) *settled in 7th: 4th 1/2-way: cl 3rd and running on st: chal 1 1/2f out: led 100yds out: comf* **3/5**[1]

2 1 1/2 **Orion Star (FR)**[17] 6-8-10 ...... JVictoire 7 103
(H-A Pantall, France) *racd in 5th: disputing cl 2nd 1/2-way: led appr st: drvn and r.o 2f out: hdd 100yds out: kpt on* **18/1**

3 2 **Ponte Tresa (FR)**[20] 1250 5-8-10 ...... CSoumillon 2 101
(Y De Nicolay, France) *prom: disputing 4th: 5th 1/2-way: 4th st: drvn to chse ldr over 2f out: disputing 2nd over 1f out: styd on u.p* **10/1**[3]

4 1 1/2 **Incanto Dream**[34] 1013 4-8-11 ...... TThulliez 6 104
(C Lerner, France) *disputing 4th early: 8th on ins st: r.o over 2f out: styd on to go 4th cl home* **20/1**

5 shd **Winter Dream (IRE)**[14] 1359 4-8-8 ...... J-BHamel 4 101
(Robert Collet, France) *hld up in last: 10th st: styd on in centre fr over 1 1/2f out: jst missed 4th* **25/1**

6 2 **Le Miracle (GER)**[182] 6526 7-9-6 ...... DBoeuf 8 107
(W Baltromei, Germany) *hld up: 10th 1/2-way: hdwy over 3f out: 6th and drvn st: wnt 4th briefly 1 1/2f out: styd on same pce* **11/1**

7 1 1/2 **High Maintenance (FR)**[20] 1250 4-8-5 ...... MGuyon 12 95
(A Fabre, France) *towards rr of mid-div: n.d* **58/1**

8 3/4 **Thundering Star (SAF)**[267] 5-9-6 ...... J-BEyquem 11 105
(C Ferland, France) *towards rr: last and rdn st: nvr a factor* **19/1**

9 nk **Latin Mood (FR)**[20] 1250 5-8-13 ...... OPeslier 3 97
(P Demercastel, France) *racd in 6th: 9th st: effrt 2f out: no imp* **23/1**

10 20 **Soledad (IRE)**[14] 8-8-10 ...... AlainBadel 1 74
(G Cherel, France) *led to 1/2-way: cl 5th but u.p st: sn wknd* **71/1**

11 **Art Martial (FR)**[20] 1250 4-8-11 ...... C-PLemaire 9 79
(A De Royer-Dupre, France) *racd in 2nd: led bef 1/2-way: hdd appr st: pushed along over 2f out: wknd* **68/10**[2]

3m 17.8s (-3.70) **Going Correction** -0.10s/f (Good)
WFA 4 from 5yo+ 3lb 11 Ran SP% **118.9**
Speed ratings: **119,118,117,116,116 115,114,114,114,104 104**
PARI-MUTUEL: WIN 1.60; PL 1.10, 2.50, 1.90; DF 20.80.
Owner K Abdulla **Bred** Juddmonte Farms Ltd **Trained** Chantilly, France

NOTEBOOK
Coastal Path was in a different league to his rivals. Always going easily in the early part of the race, he moved up to an attacking position just before the straight and soon took the advantage, only having to be pushed out to win with plenty in hand. This was a fine seasonal debut and he is now unbeaten in five races. He is sure to strip much fitter next time out and his big target is the Ascot Gold Cup. He is likely to be seen next time out in the Prix Vicomtesse Vigier back over the course and distance on May 18.
Orion Star(FR) was always close up and he ran an honest race but, after taking over early in the straight, he found the winner too strong. He will continue to be campaigned in staying events.
Ponte Tresa(FR), another always handy, tried her best but she could only find the one pace.
Incanto Dream stayed on in the straight and just pinched fourth place in the final few strides.

1664a PRIX VANTEAUX-BEACHCOMBER HOTELS LE ROYAL PALM (GROUP 3) (FILLIES) 1m 1f 55y
2:45 (2:46) 3-Y-0 **£29,412** (£11,765; £8,824; £5,882; £2,941)

RPR

1 **Belle Allure (IRE)**[203] 6040 3-9-0 ...... DBonilla 2 103
(R Pritchard-Gordon, France) *hld up in 5th: disputing last st: sn pushed along: r.o fr over 1 1/2f out: qcknd to ld appr fnl f: drvn out* **238/10**

2 1 1/2 **Wait And See (FR)**[17] 3-9-0 ...... DBoeuf 5 100
(Robert Collet, France) *racd in 4th: hdwy 1 1/2f out: ev ch appr fnl f: tk 2nd comf 150yds out: nt pce of wnr* **22/1**

3 2 **Proviso**[211] 5796 3-9-0 ...... SPasquier 3 96
(A Fabre, France) *led: pushed along st: hdd appr fnl f: no ex fnl 100yds* **7/10**[1]

4 2 **Cymbal (IRE)**[28] 3-9-0 ...... JVictoire 1 93
(H-A Pantall, France) *racd in 3rd: drvn over 1 1/2f out: unable qck* **5/2**[2]

5 3/4 **Step Softly**[21] 1238 3-9-0 ...... OPeslier 4 91
(J-C Rouget, France) *hld up in last: 3 l detached 1/2-way: disputing last st: shkn up 2f out: no imp* **16/1**

6 1 1/2 **Trip To Glory (FR)**[34] 1012 3-9-0 ...... C-PLemaire 6 89
(J-C Rouget, France) *racd in 2nd tl wknd over 1f out* **53/10**[3]

1m 54.3s (-2.00) **Going Correction** -0.10s/f (Good) 6 Ran SP% **117.5**
Speed ratings: **104,102,100,99,98 97**
PARI-MUTUEL: WIN 24.80; PL 8.50, 7.30; SF 198.50.
Owner Ronchalon Racing (UK) Ltd **Bred** Paul Nataf **Trained** France

NOTEBOOK

Belle Allure(IRE) caused a big surprise to many but not her connections. A 24/1 chance, she was held up early on and then produced an outstanding turn of foot from one and a half out. She took command at the furlong marker before cruising past the post. This was an impressive performance from the filly who had run last year in the Marcel Boussac after winning a maiden at Deauville. Her trainer believes she may need a little time between races so she could go directly for the Prix de Diane at Chantilly on June 8. If she recovers well the Prix Saint-Alary could also be taken into consideration.

Wait And See(FR), fourth coming into the straight, she went to join the leaders a furlong and a half out and picked up well, but she had no chance with the winner. A longer trip should suit this daughter of Montjeu and she has all the top engagements.

Proviso was asked to make all the running and appeared to be going well coming into the straight but, by the furlong and a half marker the writing was on the wall and her stride shortened as she gradually dropped back. Her connections were at a loss to explain the way the filly ran and are hoping that she just had an off day.

Cymbal(IRE), smartly into her stride, settled behind the leader but was completely outpaced when things quickened up in the straight. She ran on once beaten and looks to need further.

1665a PRIX GANAY-40EME ANNIVERSAIRE AIR MAURITIUS (GROUP 1) 1m 2f 110y

3:20 (3:19) 4-Y-0+ **£126,044** (£50,426; £25,213; £12,596; £6,309)

RPR

1 **Duke Of Marmalade (IRE)**211 5798 4-9-2 .... JMurtagh 3 124
(A P O'Brien, Ire) *racd in 2nd: clsd up to ldr appr st: drvn and chal 2f out: led 1 1/2f out: rdn and r.o fnl f: drvn out* **38/10**3

2 ½ **Saddex**154 6943 5-9-2 .... TThulliez 1 123
(P Rau, Germany) *racd in 3rd: pushed along 1 1/2f out: fin wl and wnt 2nd 100yds out: pressing wnr cl home: styd on* **11/1**

3 2 **Sageburg (IRE)**204 6032 4-9-2 .... CSoumillon 8 119
(A De Royer-Dupre, France) *hld up in last: hdwy 2f out: disputing 3rd 1 1/2f out: styd on to take 3rd 100yds out* **56/10**

4 hd **Spirit One (FR)**21 1240 4-9-2 .... OPeslier 6 119
(P Demercastel, France) *led: clr at 1/2-way: hdd 1 1/2f out: sn rdn: styd on tl lost 3rd 100yds out* **57/10**

5 3 **Mrs Lindsay (USA)**189 6373 4-8-13 .... C-PLemaire 2 110
(F Rohaut, France) *hld up in 5th: rdn on outside 2f out: no imp* **28/10**2

6 ¾ **Zambezi Sun**203 6043 4-9-2 .... SPasquier 7 112
(P Bary, France) *racd in 4th: drvn over 2f out: sn one pce* **21/10**1

2m 8.30s (-4.70) **Going Correction** -0.10s/f (Good) **6 Ran SP% 117.8**
Speed ratings: **113,112,111,111,108 108**
PARI-MUTUEL: WIN 4.80; PL 3.30, 4.90; DF 19.40.
Owner Mrs John Magnier & M Tabor **Bred** Southern Bloodstock **Trained** Ballydoyle, Co Tipperary

NOTEBOOK

Duke Of Marmalade(IRE), an imposing individual, stood out in the paddock and produced a fine performance. Settled in second off a fast pace, he took over shortly after entering the straight and quickened well. He ran consistently well in Group 1 company last year, even though his connections felt that pins in a leg were niggling him, and that problem may well have been corrected. He is now likely to go for the Tattersalls Gold Cup and all being well, the Prince of Wales's Stakes at Royal Ascot. His trainer also believes he will be just as effective over a strongly run 1m.

Saddex missed his intended seasonal debut in German after suffering a setback in training, so this was a fine performance in defeat. After settling in fourth place, he quickened well from one and a half out but could never peg back the winner. It was a very promising performance over a distance that was probably a little short of his best. No decisions have been made about his future but connections are hoping to land another Group 1 race with this beautifully bred five-year-old.

Sageburg(IRE) performed well on his first run for a new trainer. Led down to the start, he got a little warm before the off but relaxed during the early part of the race. He looked dangerous halfway up the straight but his effort soon flattened out. His connections felt the distance stretched him to the limit so he will now come back to 1m and will probably run in the Prix du Chemin de Fer du Nord at Chantilly in June.

Spirit One(FR), who looked very fit, took the field along at a very good pace and, running down the hill to the straight he was clear of his five rivals, but he found a few too strong in the straight. He is a genuine individual but probably not quite up to this class.

SHA TIN (R-H)

Sunday, April 27

OFFICIAL GOING: Good

1666a AUDEMARS PIGUET QE II CUP (GROUP 1) 1m 2f

9:35 (9:35) 3-Y-0+

£515,464 (£193,299; £96,649; £51,546; £28,995; £16,108)

RPR

1 **Archipenko (USA)**29 1090 4-9-0 .... (b) KShea 10 122+
(M F De Kock, South Africa) **138/10**

2 1 ¾ **Balius (IRE)**21 1240 5-9-0 .... (b) ODoleuze 9 119
(C Laffon-Parias, France) **83/1**

3 nk **Viva Pataca**29 1091 6-9-0 .... DBeadman 11 118+
(J Moore, Hong Kong) **11/10**1

4 ½ **Packing Winner (NZ)**34 6-9-0 .... DWhyte 3 117
(L Ho, Hong Kong) **82/1**

5 1 ¼ **Quijano (GER)**29 1091 6-9-0 .... AStarke 2 115
(P Schiergen, Germany) **17/1**

6 shd **Matsurida Gogh (JPN)**29 5-9-0 .... MEbina 7 114
(S Kunieda, Japan) **47/10**3

7 nk **Musical Way (FR)**21 1240 6-8-10 .... RonanThomas 5 110
(P Van De Poele, France) **93/1**

8 1 ¼ **Helene Mascot (IRE)**42 4-9-0 .... FCoetzee 8 111
(A S Cruz, Hong Kong) **2/1**2

9 ½ **Bullish Cash (NZ)**34 6-9-0 .... BPrebble 12 110
(A S Cruz, Hong Kong) **21/1**

10 nk **Viva Macau (FR)**52 818 5-9-0 .... MNunes 4 110
(J Moore, Hong Kong) **98/1**

11 1 **Sir Slick (NZ)**15 7-9-0 .... BHerd 1 108
(G Nicholson & P Albion, New Zealand) **52/1**

2m 0.80s (-0.60) **11 Ran SP% 121.7**
WIN 148.00; PL 30.50, 86.50, 14.50; DF 3208.50.
Owner Sheikh Mohammed Bin Khalifa Al Maktoum **Bred** Eagle Holdings **Trained** South Africa

SAN SIRO (R-H)

Saturday, April 26

OFFICIAL GOING: Good

1667a PREMIO AMBROSIANO (GROUP 3) 1m 2f

4:25 (4:26) 4-Y-0+ **£29,779** (£13,103; £7,147; £3,574)

RPR

1 **Axxos (GER)**206 5929 4-8-11 .... THellier 5 110
(P Schiergen, Germany) *mde all: r.o strly whn strly pressed fr over 1f out: pushed out* **18/10**2

2 ½ **Golden Titus (IRE)**188 6372 4-8-11 .... DVargiu 4 109
(A Renzoni, Italy) *racd in 2nd: 3rd 4f out: shkn up to regain 2nd 1f out: sn pressing wnr and ev ch: no ex clsng stages* **23/10**3

3 3 **Selmis**206 4-8-11 .... MDemuro 2 103
(V Caruso, Italy) *racd in 3rd: 2nd 4f out: rdn to press wnr and ev ch over 1f out: one pce fnl f* **21/20**1

4 ¾ **Subitodopo**237 4-8-11 .... NMurru 6 102
(M Gasparini, Italy) *hld up in last: detached over 3f out: styd on wl fr over 1f out: nvr nr ldrs* **147/10**

5 3 **Davidoff (GER)**42 912 4-8-11 .... FilipMinarik 3 96
(P Schiergen, Germany) *hld up in 5th: effrt on ins over 2f out: sn btn* **22/1**

6 3 **Elleno (IRE)**120 4-8-11 .... PConvertino 1 90
(F & L Camici, Italy) *hld up in 4th: rdn to press for 3rd over 2f out: wknd over 1f out* **19/1**

2m 2.70s (-4.00) **6 Ran SP% 130.5**
(including 1 Euro stake): WIN 2.82; PL 2.11, 2.06; DF 4.24.
Owner Gestut Ittlingen **Bred** Gestut Hof Ittlingen **Trained** Germany

1251 LINGFIELD (L-H)

Monday, April 28

OFFICIAL GOING: Standard

Wind: Fresh, behind Weather: Sunny spells

1668 CELEBRATE YOUR BIRTHDAY AT LINGFIELD PARK CLAIMING STKS 1m 4f (P)

2:20 (2:20) (Class 6) 4-Y-0+ **£1,774** (£523; £262) **Stalls Low**

Form RPR

1-21 1 **Nawamees (IRE)**17 1310 10-9-12 76 .... (p) RyanMoore 2 81
(G L Moore) *mde all: allowed to set modest tempo: rdn and qcknd over 2f out: drvn out* **6/4**1

1311 2 1 ½ **Dushstorm (IRE)**11 1411 7-9-2 71 .... AdrianTNicholls 1 69
(D Nicholls) *hld up in 3rd and 4th: rdn over 2f out: kpt on to take 2nd on line: a hld by wnr* **4/1**3

00-4 3 shd **Zamboozle (IRE)**57 358 6-9-0 69 .... RichardHughes 5 66
(A King) *stdd s: hld up in rr: wnt 3rd over 4f out: chsd wnr over 1f out: one pce: lost 2nd on line* **13/8**2

3332 4 4 ½ **Looks The Business (IRE)**17 1310 7-8-9 58 .... JackDean(7) 4 61
(W G M Turner) *t.k.h: sn pressing wnr: rdn over 2f out: wknd over 1f out* **8/1**

2m 36.69s (3.69) **Going Correction** +0.225s/f (Slow)
WFA 4 from 6yo+ 1lb **4 Ran SP% 109.2**
Speed ratings (Par 101): **96,95,94,91**
CSF £7.57 TOTE £2.30; EX 5.00.Dushstorm was claimed by Mr C.R. Dore for £9,000.
Owner Paul Stamp **Bred** Kilfrush Stud Ltd **Trained** Woodingdean, E Sussex

FOCUS

A fair little claimer. It was a falsely-run affair, however, and the form is not solid despite appearing to make sense.

1669 CONFERENCES AT LINGFIELD PARK MEDIAN AUCTION MAIDEN STKS 1m (P)

2:50 (2:52) (Class 6) 3-Y-O **£2,266** (£674; £337; £168) **Stalls High**

Form RPR

2 1 **Maghya (IRE)**26 1149 3-8-12 0 .... RyanMoore 4 71+
(W J Haggas) *trckd ldrs: effrt over 1f out: str run to ld nr fin* **5/6**1

00- 2 nk **Dark Camellia**202 6093 3-8-12 0 .... EddieAhern 3 66
(H J L Dunlop) *chsd ldrs: wnt 2nd over 2f out: drvn to ld 50yds out: kpt on: hdd nr fin* **25/1**

4 3 ¾ **Reine De Violette**13 1380 3-8-12 0 .... TPQueally 1 64
(H R A Cecil) *sn led: 2l ahd 2f out: rdn over 1f out: hdd and nt qckn fnl 50yds* **7/1**2

4 3 ¾ **Caro George (USA)** 3-8-12 0 .... SteveDrowne 11 55+
(R Charlton) *hld up in midfield: hdwy on rail ent st: rdn and one pce appr fnl f* **15/2**3

5 1 ¾ **Acrostic** 3-9-3 0 .... DaneO'Neill 10 56+
(L M Cumani) *dwlt: hld up in rr: sltly hmpd and swtchd ins wl over 1f out: shkn up and gng on wl at fin* **16/1**

06 6 ½ **Clearing House**8 1504 3-9-3 0 .... TGMcLaughlin 9 55+
(E A L Dunlop) *hld up in midfield: effrt whn sltly hmpd and swtchd wd wl over 1f out: styd on* **14/1**

0-0 7 ½ **Rettorical Lad**9 1467 3-9-3 0 .... JohnEgan 8 54
(Jamie Poulton) *chsd ldrs: rdn along 3f out: outpcd appr fnl f* **25/1**

8 1 ¼ **Scary Movie (IRE)** 3-9-3 0 .... TPO'Shea 5 51+
(D J Coakley) *dwlt: a abt same pl: rdn and no hdwy fnl 2f* **33/1**

0- 9 1 ¼ **Milne Bay (IRE)**319 2604 3-9-3 0 .... RichardMullen 12 52+
(D M Simcock) *broke wl: prom: outpcd over 2f out: disputing 6th and losing pl whn hmpd and stmbld wl over 1f out* **80/1**

10 7 **Upstart (IRE)** 3-9-3 0 .... JimmyQuinn 7 32
(H R A Cecil) *dwlt: a bhd: rdn and no ch fnl 3f* **8/1**

00 11 4 **Too Much To Do**31 1054 3-9-3 0 .... RichardThomas 2 23
(T D McCarthy) *dwlt: sn in tch: rdn over 3f out: sn wknd* **100/1**

12 15 **Tewin Green** 3-8-12 0 .... SebSanders 6 —
(M Botti) *dwlt: sn niggled along: a bhd: no ch fnl 3f* **16/1**

1m 40.73s (2.53) **Going Correction** +0.225s/f (Slow) **12 Ran SP% 121.2**
Speed ratings (Par 96): **96,95,94,91,89 88,88,87,85,78 74,59**
CSF £35.14 TOTE £1.80: £1.10, £5.10, £1.90; EX 27.80.
Owner Hamdan Al Maktoum **Bred** Shadwell Estate Company Limited **Trained** Newmarket, Suffolk
■ Stewards' Enquiry : T P O'Shea caution: careless riding

FOCUS

A modest three-year-old maiden, run at a moderate early pace. The first three came clear with the winner close to his debut form, but not a race to be too positive about.

Acrostic Official explanation: jockey said, regarding the running and riding that having been drawn badly, his instructions were to get the horse covered up and not get stuck on the outside of the field and run on as best he could but that the gelding jumped slowly and ran very green. Coming into the home straight he stayed towards the inside and went for a run up the inner, as he was unable to challenge on the outside, having horses on his outer. He was also aware that the trainer had told him not to go wide in the race.
Rettorical Lad Official explanation: jockey said colt made a noise
Milne Bay(IRE) Official explanation: jockey said gelding clipped heels on final bend

1670 PERFECT WEDDING VENUE AT LINGFIELD PARK (S) STKS 7f (P)
3:20 (3:21) (Class 6) 3-Y-O+ £1,774 (£523; £262) Stalls Low

Form RPR
-642 1 **Shot To Fame (USA)**[6] 1550 9-9-7 70 ... AdrianTNicholls 7 67
(D Nicholls) *prom: rdn 3f out: r.o to ld ins fnl f* 10/3[1]
0026 2 1 **Apache Dawn**[26] 1143 4-9-7 71 ... (be[1]) RyanMoore 5 65
(G L Moore) *hld up in last pl: shkn up over 1f out: gd late hdwy to take 2nd nr fin* 7/2[2]
2243 3 ¾ **The Jailer**[18] 1285 5-8-9 57 ... (p) MCGeran[(7)] 2 58
(J G M O'Shea) *led: hrd rdn over 1f out: hdd and one pce ins fnl f* 8/1
5401 4 ¾ **Samuel Charles**[28] 1109 10-9-13 68 ... (b) LiamJones 10 67
(C R Dore) *s.i.s: hdwy to chse ldrs after 2f: wnt 2nd over 3f out: one pce fnl f* 7/2[2]
0144 5 ¾ **Marko Jadeo (IRE)**[26] 1150 10-9-10 60 ... KevinGhunowa[(3)] 1 65
(R A Harris) *mid-div on rail: effrt over 2f out: kpt on u.p fnl f* 20/1
0-40 6 1 **Da Bookie (IRE)**[23] 1207 8-9-7 48 ... (tp) LPKeniry 9 56
(Jean-Rene Auvray) *hld up in rr: rdn 3f out: styd on appr fnl f* 22/1
4624 7 ½ **Tiepie**[31] 1060 3-8-8 61 ... DaneO'Neill 4 55
(J Akehurst) *chsd ldrs tl wknd 1f out* 6/1[3]
0020 8 1½ **Victor Trumper**[20] 1260 4-9-7 58 ... (bt) SteveDrowne 3 51
(Jim Best) *towards rr: rdn 3f out: n.d* 33/1
5601 9 ¾ **Majestical (IRE)**[26] 1150 6-9-10 58 ... (p) WilliamBuick[(3)] 8 55
(V Smith) *chsd ldrs: rdn over 2f out: wknd wl over 1f out* 14/1
3030 10 9 **Wee Buns**[23] 1216 3-9-0 69 ... TQuinn 6 30
(P Burgoyne) *t.k.h in midfield: effrt on outside over 2f out: wknd wl over 1f out* 14/1

1m 25.91s (1.11) **Going Correction** +0.225s/f (Slow)
WFA 3 from 4yo+ 13lb 10 Ran SP% **118.3**
Speed ratings (Par 101): **102,100,100,99,98 97,96,94,94,83**
CSF £15.02 TOTE £4.30: £1.90, £1.70, £1.60; EX 19.70.There was no bid for the winner
Owner Middleham Park Racing Vii **Bred** Eric Puerari **Trained** Sessay, N Yorks

FOCUS
A typically moderate seller in which the fifth sets the level but the form is anchored by the sixth.
Wee Buns Official explanation: jockey said gelding ran flat

1671 LINGFIELDPARK.CO.UK FILLIES' H'CAP 7f
3:50 (3:51) (Class 5) (0-70,70) 3-Y-O £2,590 (£770; £385; £192) Stalls Low

Form RPR
3335 1 **Little Knickers**[9] 1479 3-8-10 62 ... (b[1]) TPQueally 6 67
(Andrew Reid) *chsd ldrs: rdn 2f out: styd on to ld ins fnl f* 9/1
20-0 2 2 **Duty Doctor**[14] 1372 3-8-10 67 ... HaddenFrost[(5)] 12 67
(S Kirk) *led 1f: prom on rail: rdn 2f out: kpt on to take 2nd nr fin* 16/1
-013 3 shd **Oceana Blue**[24] 1193 3-8-8 67 ... (t) DavidProbert[(7)] 9 66
(A M Balding) *chsd ldrs: sit ld over 1f out: hdd and one pce ins fnl f* 9/2[2]
625- 4 ¾ **Shanzu**[202] 6080 3-9-2 68 ... DaneO'Neill 13 65
(H Candy) *led after 1f tl over 1f out: no ex ins fnl f* 8/1[3]
006- 5 nk **Tea Cake (IRE)**[196] 6228 3-8-11 63 ... SebSanders 8 59+
(H J L Dunlop) *t.k.h in midfield: rdn and r.o fnl 2f: nvr nrr* 8/1[3]
00-3 6 ¾ **Pantherii (USA)**[21] 1247 3-8-10 62 ... RyanMoore 2 56+
(P F I Cole) *hld up in rr of midfield: effrt ent st: n.m.r: styd on same pce* 9/2[2]
00-5 7 nk **Miss Firefly**[56] 777 3-9-1 67 ... ChrisCatlin 1 61
(M R Channon) *dwlt: t.k.h: sn in tch: rdn 2f out: no ex appr fnl f* 16/1
100- 8 1 **Rescue Me**[248] 4776 3-9-3 69 ... RichardHughes 10 63+
(R Hannon) *stdd s: hld up in rr: sme hdwy on rail ent st: no imp over 1f out* 3/1[1]
6443 9 2¼ **Bye Baby Bunting**[19] 1271 3-8-8 60 ... (p) SteveDrowne 3 45
(B R Johnson) *plld hrd: in tch: effrt 2f out: hrd rdn and wknd over 1f out* 10/1
-355 10 1¾ **Affirmatively**[44] 899 3-9-3 69 ... AlanMunro 4 49
(D R C Elsworth) *mid-div: effrt over 2f out: wknd wl over 1f out* 10/1
006 11 ¾ **Estella Mai**[32] 1036 3-8-5 57 oh9 ow1 ... NeilChalmers 7 35
(J J Bridger) *rdn 3f out: a towards rr* 100/1
002- 12 1 **Bobal Girl**[198] 6177 3-8-2 61 ... MCGeran[(7)] 11 36
(E F Vaughan) *rdn 3f out: a bhd* 33/1

1m 27.69s (87.69) **Going Correction** +0.225s/f (Slow) 12 Ran SP% **127.5**
Speed ratings (Par 95): **92,89,89,88,88 87,87,86,83,81 80,79**
CSF £155.02 CT £760.82 TOTE £8.80: £3.50, £6.00, £2.20; EX 212.40.
Owner A S Reid **Bred** A S Reid **Trained** Mill Hill, London NW7
■ Stewards' Enquiry : T P Queally two-day ban: careless riding (May 12-13)

FOCUS
A modest fillies' handicap, run at an average pace. The form looks fair enough despite being rated slightly negatively.
Duty Doctor Official explanation: jockey said filly hung right
Shanzu Official explanation: jockey said filly hung right
Pantherii(USA) Official explanation: jockey said filly was denied a clear run
Rescue Me Official explanation: jockey said filly was denied a clear run

1672 ARENALEISUREPLC.COM H'CAP 6f (P)
4:20 (4:21) (Class 6) (0-60,59) 3-Y-O £2,047 (£604; £302) Stalls Low

Form RPR
000- 1 **King Of Cadeaux (IRE)**[136] 7140 3-8-11 52 ... EddieAhern 5 54+
(M A Magnusson) *stdd s: hld up in rr: gd hdwy on rail over 1f out: str run to ld fnl stride* 6/1
46-5 2 nse **Forever Changes**[24] 1178 3-9-1 56 ... AlanMunro 2 58
(L Montague Hall) *led 2f: pressed ldr tl led again ent st: kpt on u.p: hdd fnl stride* 16/1
356- 3 nse **Filligree (IRE)**[159] 6897 3-9-4 59 ... ChrisCatlin 7 60
(Rae Guest) *prom: hrd rdn fnl f: r.o wl nr fin* 9/2[3]
650 4 nk **Szaba**[17] 1295 3-8-9 50 ... JohnEgan 4 50+
(J M P Eustace) *chsd ldrs: sltly outpcd over 2f out: hrd rdn and rallied fnl f: r.o* 14/1
4-42 5 ¾ **Shatter Resistant (IRE)**[14] 1370 3-9-0 55 ... JimmyQuinn 3 53
(M D Squance) *stdd s: sn trcking ldrs: rdn to chal over 1f out: one pce fnl 100yds* 4/1[2]
40-6 6 nk **Solo River**[19] 1271 3-9-0 58 ... TravisBlock[(3)] 6 55
(P J Makin) *towards rr: pushed along over 3f out: styd on u.p fnl 2f: nvr nrr* 10/1
0-44 6 dht **Night Premiere (IRE)**[37] 965 3-9-3 58 ... RyanMoore 9 55+
(R Hannon) *chsd ldrs: trapped wd and lost pl after 2f: rallied and r.o u.p appr fnl f* 11/4[1]
00-5 8 2¾ **Our Kally**[11] 1414 3-8-9 50 ... DaneO'Neill 10 38
(M D I Usher) *dwlt: bhd: effrt over 1f out: unable to chal* 10/1
00-6 9 nse **Expediter**[23] 1215 3-8-11 59 ... AmyScott[(7)] 8 47
(H Candy) *hld up in tch: promising effrt on outside ent st: shkn up over 1f out: fdd fnl f* 20/1
42-0 10 8 **Wicksy Creek**[31] 1054 3-8-11 52 ... TPQueally 1 14
(G C H Chung) *pressed ldr: led after 2f tl ent st: wknd qckly over 1f out* 12/1

1m 13.3s (1.40) **Going Correction** +0.225s/f (Slow) 10 Ran SP% **122.3**
Speed ratings (Par 96): **99,98,98,98,97 97,97,93,93,82**
CSF £101.49 CT £491.70 TOTE £6.60: £2.30, £4.60, £2.00; EX 133.60.
Owner East Wind Racing Ltd **Bred** Mount Coote Partnership **Trained** Upper Lambourn, Berks

FOCUS
A moderate handicap which saw the first six very closely covered at the finish. A tricky race to assess accurately.

1673 LINGFIELD PARK GOLF CLUB APPRENTICE H'CAP 1m 2f (P)
4:50 (4:50) (Class 6) (0-60,64) 4-Y-O+ £2,047 (£604; £302) Stalls Low

Form RPR
4-33 1 **Formidable Guest**[107] 143 4-8-11 52 ... SimonPearce 8 59
(J Pearce) *in tch: carried wd 1st bnd and dropped in at rr: hdwy to chse ldng pair over 3f out: styd on to ld fnl stride* 4/1[3]
3222 2 nse **Kings Topic (USA)**[8] 1505 8-9-0 60 ... (b[1]) KrishGundowry[(5)] 2 67
(A B Haynes) *dwlt: t.k.h: sn trcking ldrs: led over 2f out and wnt 3l ahd: hrd rdn and hung bdly rt fnl f: ct fnl stride* 5/2[1]
5344 3 ¾ **Binnion Bay (IRE)**[23] 1210 7-9-0 55 ... (b) RossAtkinson 7 60
(J J Bridger) *s.s: t.k.h: in tch after 3f: effrt and drvn along 3f out: styd on wl fnl f: nt rch 1st two* 6/1
0561 4 1¼ **Western Roots**[18] 1282 7-9-2 60 ... DavidProbert[(3)] 1 64
(A M Balding) *led tl over 2f out: carried rt by runner-up ins fnl f: one pce* 3/1[2]
60-4 5 4½ **Ground Patrol**[40] 935 7-8-8 52 ... AshleyMorgan[(3)] 3 46
(N R Mitchell) *s.s: bhd: rdn 4f out: sme late hdwy* 16/1
6055 6 1¾ **Mtoto Girl**[15] 1350 4-8-2 46 oh1 ... BillyCray[(3)] 4 36
(J J Bridger) *chsd ldr tl 1/2-way: outpcd and rdn over 3f out: n.d after* 25/1
14-1 7 4½ **Cherri Fosfate**[2] 1626 4-9-2 64 6ex ... PaulPickard[(7)] 6 45
(D Carroll) *in tch tl wknd over 4f out* 10/1
20-0 8 2¾ **Forfeiter (USA)**[18] 1280 6-8-9 50 ... JemmaMarshall 5 26
(C Gordon) *chsd ldrs tl wknd over 3f out* 8/1
60-0 9 14 **Namibian Pink (IRE)**[17] 1209 4-8-2 48 ... JosephineBruning[(5)] 9 —
(R H York) *in tch: rdn and wknd qckly 5f out: sn wl bhd* 66/1

2m 7.96s (1.36) **Going Correction** +0.225s/f (Slow) 9 Ran SP% **119.3**
Speed ratings (Par 101): **103,102,102,101,97 96,92,90,79**
CSF £14.98 CT £60.43 TOTE £5.10: £1.50, £1.40, £1.80; EX 20.10 Place 6 £84.79, Place 5 £38.20..
Owner Macniler Racing Partnership **Bred** Kingwood Bloodstock **Trained** Newmarket, Suffolk
■ Stewards' Enquiry : Simon Pearce two-day ban: careless riding (May 12-13)

FOCUS
A moderate handicap, confined to apprentice riders, run at a decent pace. The third and fourth are rated to their latest form.
T/Plt: £103.00 to a £1 stake. Pool: £42,244.41. 299.30 winning tickets. T/Qpdt: £33.60 to a £1 stake. Pool: £2,925.74. 64.30 winning tickets. LM

1587 SOUTHWELL (L-H)
Monday, April 28

OFFICIAL GOING: Standard
Wind: Light across Weather: Cloudy

1674 SOUTHWELL GOLF CLUB MEDIAN AUCTION MAIDEN STKS 6f (F)
5:25 (5:28) (Class 5) 3-5-Y-O £3,002 (£886; £443) Stalls Low

Form RPR
332 1 **Young Gladiator (IRE)**[48] 848 3-9-1 62 ... TomEaves 10 64
(Miss J A Camacho) *hld up in tch: rdn to ld and hung lft fr over 1f out: styd on u.p* 13/8[1]
40-0 2 2½ **Tanley**[10] 1452 3-9-1 57 ... FergalLynch 4 56
(J F Coupland) *led: hdd over 4f out: led again over 2f out: sn rdn and hdd: styd on same pce fnl f* 14/1
00- 3 shd **Carmine Rock**[149] 7000 3-8-7 0 ... RussellKennemore[(3)] 6 51
(R Hollinshead) *s.i.s: hdwy over 3f out: led 2f out: rdn and hdd over 1f out: styd on same pce fnl f* 14/1
02 4 3¼ **Cheveton**[17] 1311 4-9-9 0 ... TolleyDean[(3)] 11 48
(R J Price) *s.i.s: outpcd: styd on fr over 1f out: nvr nrr* 3/1[2]
5-0 5 nk **Scanno (IRE)**[17] 1311 3-9-1 0 ... GregFairley 3 44
(M Mullineaux) *prom: rdn over 4f out: outpcd 1/2-way: styd on ins fnl f* 40/1
350 6 ¾ **Hot Bertie**[30] 1073 3-9-1 58 ... PaulMulrennan 7 42
(Jedd O'Keeffe) *chsd ldrs: rdn over 2f out: wknd over 1f out* 12/1
5 7 3½ **Nabeeda**[10] 1453 3-8-12 0 ... MarkLawson[(3)] 1 31
(M Brittain) *chsd ldr tl led over 4f out: rdn and hdd over 2f out: wknd over 1f out* 13/2
300- 8 6 **L'Art Du Silence (IRE)**[285] 3642 3-9-1 68 ... (e[1]) FergusSweeney 8 12
(J R Boyle) *sn outpcd* 6/1[3]
0-00 9 ½ **Cryptic Clue (USA)**[88] 371 4-9-9 40 ... AndrewMullen[(3)] 9 13
(Mrs R A Carr) *chsd ldrs over 3f* 125/1
00-6 10 1 **Only A Splash**[26] 1135 4-9-7 40 ... DanielleMcCreery[(5)] 2 10
(Mrs R A Carr) *s.i.s: bhd fr 1/2-way* 100/1
11 3¼ **Ducal Regancy Duke** 4-9-7 0 ... KellyHarrison[(5)] 5 —
(C J Teague) *dwlt: outpcd* 40/1

1m 18.6s (2.10) **Going Correction** +0.20s/f (Slow)
WFA 3 from 4yo 11lb 11 Ran SP% **118.4**
Speed ratings (Par 103): **94,90,90,86,85 84,80,72,71,70 65**
CSF £27.76 TOTE £2.50: £1.10, £4.40, £2.80; EX 35.10.
Owner Cannon,Grundy,Shaw,Bolingbroke,Hamill **Bred** Edmond And Richard Kent **Trained** Norton, N Yorks

FOCUS
This was a very poor maiden with a 62-rated horse beating a 57-rated horse and that just about sums the race up. The pace was a fair one with the leaders racing five-deep rounding the home bend, but they finished quite well spread out.

1675 SOUTHWELL-RACECOURSE.CO.UK H'CAP 6f (F)
5:55 (5:57) (Class 6) (0-52,50) 4-Y-0+ £2,047 (£604; £302) Stalls Low

Form RPR

2542 **1** **Kingsmaite**[4] 1588 7-8-8 **46** ow1 ....(b) PhillipMakin 2 62
(S R Bowring) *a.p: chsd ldr 1/2-way: led 2f out: rdn out* 5/2[1]

0400 **2** 2 1/4 **Tenancy (IRE)**[13] 1378 4-8-8 **46** ....(p) NeilPollard 3 55
(A J McCabe) *plld hrd and prom: rdn over 1f out: styd on same pce fnl f* 17/2

6243 **3** 3 1/2 **Blakeshall Quest**[55] 790 8-8-9 **47** ....(b) PaulMulrennan 14 45
(R Brotherton) *chsd ldrs: rdn over 1f out: wknd ins fnl f* 10/1

2245 **4** hd **Limonia (GER)**[10] 1455 6-8-9 **47** .... FergalLynch 10 44+
(Mike Murphy) *s.s: hdwy over 1f out: nt rch ldrs* 10/3[2]

6000 **5** 1/2 **Ace Club**[19] 1275 7-8-4 **47** ....(b) AhmedAjtebi[(5)] 7 42
(Garry Moss) *led 4f: wknd fnl f* 40/1

0-00 **6** nk **Spinning Game**[109] 106 4-8-2 **45** ....(b) DanielleMcCreery[(5)] 4 39
(Mrs R A Carr) *s.i.s: r.o ins fnl f: nvr nrr* 80/1

0000 **7** nk **Union Jack Jackson (IRE)**[46] 872 6-8-7 **45** ....(b) DaleGibson 6 38
(John A Harris) *mid-div: hdwy over 2f out: no imp fnl f* 8/1[3]

00-6 **8** 3 1/2 **Piccleyes**[48] 846 7-8-0 **45** ....(b) StacyRenwick[(7)] 8 27
(A J McCabe) *s.i.s: hdwy over 2f out: wknd over 1f out* 16/1

0440 **9** 1 1/2 **Orchestration (IRE)**[10] 1455 7-8-8 **46** ow1 ....(v) TomEaves 5 23
(Garry Moss) *chsd ldrs over 3f* 33/1

330- **10** hd **Mis Chicaf (IRE)**[179] 6609 7-8-7 **45** .... DavidAllan 13 22
(D Carroll) *mid-div: rdn and wknd 1/2-way* 25/1

430- **11** 1 3/4 **The Cube**[160] 6886 4-8-8 **49** .... JasonEdmunds[(3)] 9 20
(J Balding) *mid-div: plld hrd: hmpd and lost pl wl over 4f out: n.d after* 8/1[3]

60-0 **12** 3 **Missus Molly Brown**[24] 1185 4-8-9 **47** ....(v[1]) PaulHanagan 12 9
(R A Fahey) *dwlt: outpcd* 16/1

-650 **13** 11 **Racing Stripes (IRE)**[85] 414 4-8-12 **50** ....(b) NCallan 1 —
(K O Cunningham-Brown) *chsd ldr to 1/2-way: wknd over 2f out: eased over 1f out* 20/1

0-05 **14** 12 **Millenium Sun (IRE)**[26] 1135 4-8-7 **45** .... GregFairley 11 —
(E J Creighton) *bhd fr 1/2-way* 40/1

1m 17.43s (0.93) **Going Correction** +0.20s/f (Slow) 14 Ran SP% **122.9**
Speed ratings (Par 101): **101,98,93,93,92 92,91,86,84,84 82,78,63,47**
CSF £23.28 CT £195.88 TOTE £3.80: £1.40, £4.10, £3.00; EX 24.90.
Owner S R Bowring **Bred** S R Bowring **Trained** Edwinstowe, Notts

FOCUS
A poor handicap full of the usual suspects rated through the runner-up. The pace was solid enough and very few got into it, but although the winning time was 1.17 seconds faster than the earlier maiden it was still only about what you would expect for a race like this.
Limonia(GER) Official explanation: jockey said mare missed the break
Racing Stripes(IRE) Official explanation: jockey said gelding lost its action

1676 AMBITIONS PERSONNEL FILLIES' H'CAP 1m (F)
6:25 (6:25) (Class 4) (0-85,80) 4-Y-0+ £5,180 (£1,541; £770; £384) Stalls Low

Form RPR

26-5 **1** **Magic Echo**[16] 1329 4-9-0 **76** .... PhillipMakin 3 88+
(M Dods) *chsd ldr: outpcd over 3f out: hdwy over 2f out: led over 1f out: sn clr: eased fnl f* 13/8[1]

00-3 **2** 11 **Thunderousapplause**[6] 1552 4-9-4 **80** .... NeilPollard 2 67
(A J McCabe) *led: clr 1/2-way: rdn and hung lft over 2f out: hdd & wknd over 1f out* 9/4[2]

200- **3** 2 1/4 **Bavarica**[234] 5198 6-8-2 **71** ....(e[1]) AmyBaker[(7)] 1 53
(Miss J Feilden) *chsd ldrs to 1/2-way* 3/1[3]

0/0- **4** 42 **Frontline In Focus (IRE)**[190] 6355 4-9-4 **80** ....(be[1]) DeanMcKeown 4 —
(K J Burke) *hld up: bhd fnl 5f* 7/1

1m 45.2s (1.50) **Going Correction** +0.20s/f (Slow) 4 Ran SP% **106.4**
Speed ratings (Par 102): **100,89,86,44**
CSF £5.35 TOTE £2.10; EX 4.20.
Owner D C Batey **Bred** D C Batey **Trained** Denton, Co Durham

FOCUS
A weak and very uncompetitive fillies' handicap and two of the four runners were never going to win, but the pace was a fair one and the favourite eventually hacked up.

1677 BOOK YOUR HOSPITALITY PACKAGES H'CAP 5f (F)
6:55 (6:55) (Class 4) (0-80,80) 4-Y-0+ £4,533 (£1,348; £674; £336) Stalls High

Form RPR

5300 **1** **Bo McGinty (IRE)**[17] 1300 7-9-4 **80** ....(b) PaulHanagan 1 87
(R A Fahey) *s.s: outpcd: hdwy u.p over 1f out: r.o to ld post* 11/4[2]

3-30 **2** shd **Pawan (IRE)**[111] 84 8-8-13 **80** ....(b) AnnStokell[(5)] 4 87
(Miss A Stokell) *dwlt: hdwy over 3f out: rdn to ld ins fnl f: hdd post* 12/1

0-6 **3** 1/2 **Double Bill (USA)**[11] 1415 4-8-8 **70** ow1 .... NCallan 6 75
(P F I Cole) *chsd ldrs: rdn over 1f out: r.o* 7/2[3]

0-30 **4** hd **Steel City Boy (IRE)**[2] 1624 5-8-7 **69** .... DavidAllan 3 73
(D Carroll) *led: rdn over 1f out: hdd ins fnl f: styd on* 2/1[1]

0554 **5** 4 **Diminuto**[18] 1285 4-7-13 **68** .... AmyBaker[(7)] 2 58
(M D I Usher) *chsd ldr: rdn 1/2-way: wknd fnl f* 6/1

000- **6** 4 **The History Man (IRE)**[220] 5581 5-8-5 **67** ....(be) GregFairley 5 42
(M Mullineaux) *chsd ldrs to 1/2-way* 14/1

59.96 secs (0.26) **Going Correction** +0.20s/f (Slow) 6 Ran SP% **110.9**
Speed ratings (Par 105): **105,104,104,103,97 90**
CSF £31.76 TOTE £4.10: £2.20, £2.50; EX 22.80.
Owner Paddy McGinty & Bo Turnbull **Bred** Stephen Breen **Trained** Musley Bank, N Yorks
■ Stewards' Enquiry : Ann Stokell two-day ban: used whip in an incorrect place (May 12-13)

FOCUS
A fair sprint handicap, but quite a dramatic finish and unusually for this straight 5f the principals came from well off the pace. The form is rated around the first two.

1678 NEWARK ADVERTISER H'CAP 1m 4f (F)
7:25 (7:26) (Class 4) (0-80,74) 3-Y-0 £4,533 (£1,348; £674; £336) Stalls Low

Form RPR

0241 **1** **Forsyte Saga**[26] 1140 3-9-4 **71** .... GregFairley 4 83
(M Johnston) *led: rdn and hdd over 2f out: rallied to ld 1f out: edgd rt: styd on* 9/2[3]

04-1 **2** 1/2 **Taikoo**[104] 172 3-9-7 **74** .... NCallan 3 85
(H Morrison) *chsd wnr tl led over 2f out: rdn and hung lft over 1f out: hung rt and hdd 1f out: styd on* 2/1[1]

0-21 **3** 12 **Fantastic Lass**[9] 1478 3-8-8 **61** .... PaulHanagan 6 53
(R A Fahey) *chsd ldrs: rdn over 4f out: wknd over 2f out* 9/4[2]

4120 **4** 1/2 **Home**[14] 1364 3-9-1 **68** ....(p) FergusSweeney 2 59
(J R Boyle) *chsd ldrs: rdn over 3f out: wknd over 1f out* 6/1

0-10 **5** 8 **An Scaribh**[7] 1527 3-9-3 **73** .... JamieMoriarty[(3)] 1 51
(P D Evans) *hld up: rdn and wknd over 3f out* 20/1

0-23 **6** 1 3/4 **Pepper's Ghost**[26] 1140 3-8-9 **62** .... DMylonas 5 38
(Miss J Feilden) *hld up: rdn 5f out: sn wknd* 6/1

2m 41.69s (0.69) **Going Correction** +0.20s/f (Slow) 6 Ran SP% **115.6**
Speed ratings (Par 100): **105,104,96,96,91 89**
CSF £14.53 TOTE £4.90: £1.70, £1.80; EX 9.80.
Owner Sheikh Hamdan Bin Mohammed Al Maktoum **Bred** Gainsborough Stud Management Ltd **Trained** Middleham Moor, N Yorks

FOCUS
A fair handicap, but they went a good pace and the front pair pulled miles clear of the others. Not many ever got into it and the order was the same passing the post first time as it was on the second.

1679 MISS NEWARK AND DISTRICT 2008 H'CAP 1m 3f (F)
7:55 (7:57) (Class 6) (0-60,58) 4-Y-0+ £2,047 (£604; £302) Stalls Low

Form RPR

3-01 **1** **Pegasus Prince (USA)**[20] 1262 4-8-13 **53** .... TomEaves 9 62+
(Miss J A Camacho) *chsd ldrs: led over 1f out: edgd rt: rdn out* 2/1[1]

2-00 **2** 1/2 **David's Cavalier**[26] 1159 4-8-10 **53** ....(p) RussellKennemore[(3)] 2 61
(R Hollinshead) *led: rdn over 2f out: hdd over 1f out: styd on* 16/1

3434 **3** hd **Bethanys Boy (IRE)**[5] 1562 7-9-1 **55** .... AndrewElliott 10 62
(A M Hales) *hdwy over 8f out: rdn over 2f out: edgd lft ins fnl f: styd on* 5/2[2]

0-50 **4** 2 1/4 **Skye But N Ben**[26] 1160 4-8-10 **50** ....(p) SilvestreDeSousa 3 54
(G A Harker) *prom: outpcd over 4f out: hdwy over 2f out: styd on same pce fnl f* 7/1[3]

-555 **5** 3/4 **Tour D'Amour (IRE)**[33] 1024 5-8-4 **49** ....(b) KellyHarrison[(5)] 7 51
(R Craggs) *hld up: hdwy over 3f out: rdn over 2f out: styd on* 25/1

400- **6** 6 **Ja Myford**[195] 6257 4-8-11 **54** .... JamieMoriarty[(3)] 4 46
(P T Midgley) *s.i.s: hld up: hdwy over 3f out: rdn and wknd over 2f out* 16/1

00-0 **7** hd **Noble Edge**[46] 863 5-8-6 **46** ....(p) PaulHanagan 6 38
(Karen McLintock) *hld up: rdn over 3f out: a in rr* 28/1

5-03 **8** 4 **Brastar Jelois (FR)**[17] 1310 5-9-4 **58** ....(p) NCallan 1 43
(R Hollinshead) *hdwy over 8f out: rdn over 2f out: wknd over 1f out* 9/1

0-00 **9** 1 1/2 **Hunting Haze**[34] 863 5-8-6 **46** ow1 ....(p) DeanMcKeown 8 28
(Miss S E Hall) *chsd ldr: rdn over 3f out: wknd wl over 1f out* 50/1

0321 **10** 23 **West End Lad**[48] 844 5-9-0 **54** ....(p) PhillipMakin 5 —
(S R Bowring) *prom: lost pl 8f out: rdn over 4f out: sn wknd: eased over 1f out* 7/1[3]

2m 27.76s (-0.24) **Going Correction** +0.20s/f (Slow) 10 Ran SP% **117.9**
Speed ratings (Par 101): **108,107,107,105,105 100,100,97,96,80**
CSF £36.14 CT £85.44 TOTE £3.10: £1.50, £6.40, £1.70; EX 52.20 Place 6 £ 57.90, Place 5 £29.65..
Owner David W Armstrong **Bred** Liberty Road Stables **Trained** Norton, N Yorks

FOCUS
Probably a fair race of its type, run at an even pace in a decent time for the grade. The form is solid rated around the placed horses.
T/Plt: £46.10 to a £1 stake. Pool: £46,694.57. 738.15 winning tickets. T/Qpdt: £15.20 to a £1 stake. Pool: £3,491.46. 169.18 winning tickets. CR

1522 WINDSOR (R-H)
Monday, April 28

OFFICIAL GOING: Good to firm (9.0)
Wind: Light, behind Weather: Mostly fine

1680 CORAL.CO.UK MAIDEN AUCTION FILLIES STKS 5f 10y
5:40 (5:45) (Class 5) 2-Y-0 £2,729 (£806; £403) Stalls High

Form RPR

4 **1** **Beat Seven**[11] 1419 2-8-7 0 ow1 .... MickyFenton 4 77+
(Miss Gay Kelleway) *mde virtually all: rdn whn jnd 1f out: styd on wl* 11/4[1]

2 1/2 **Fazbee (IRE)** 2-8-8 0 .... DarryllHolland 1 76+
(P W D'Arcy) *trckd ldrs on outer: prog 2f out: drvn to join wnr 1f out: styd on but jst hld last 100yds* 8/1[3]

3 2 1/4 **Daddy's Gift (IRE)** 2-8-7 0 ow1 .... RichardHughes 12 67
(R Hannon) *pressed wnr: shkn up over 1f out: one pce fnl f* 11/4[1]

4 nk **Readily** 2-8-8 0 .... JamesDoyle 15 67
(J G Portman) *pressed ldrs: rdn over 1f out: edgd lft and one pce fnl f* 16/1

5 shd **You've Been Mowed** 2-8-5 0 ow1 .... SaleemGolam 9 64+
(D K Ivory) *chsd ldrs: outpcd 2f out: shkn up over 1f out: hung lft after but styd on fnl f* 50/1

6 1 1/2 **The Saucy Snipe** 2-8-6 0 .... StephenCarson 11 59
(P Winkworth) *chsd ldrs: cl enough 2f out: fdd fnl f* 18/1

7 shd **Souter's Sister (IRE)** 2-8-6 0 .... RichardSmith 6 59+
(R Hannon) *dwlt: off the pce towards rr and rn green: styd on fnl 2f: nrst fin* 25/1

8 1/2 **Meydan Groove** 2-8-8 0 .... TQuinn 8 59
(P F I Cole) *sn chsd ldrs: rdn over 1f out: wknd fnl f* 6/1[2]

9 2 **Shiva Adiva** 2-8-4 0 .... RichardKingscote 5 48+
(Tom Dascombe) *racd on outer: in midfield: no imp on ldrs 2f out: fdd over 1f out* 14/1

10 1/2 **Sienna Lake (IRE)** 2-8-10 0 .... SebSanders 2 52
(S Kirk) *nvr on terms w ldrs: ended up on nr side rail and hanging: no real prog* 20/1

11 hd **Mount Ella** 2-8-13 0 .... ShaneKelly 10 54
(J A Osborne) *s.s: nt on terms towards rr: effrt 1/2-way and n.m.r briefly: no prog over 1f out: fdd* 20/1

12 2 **Happy Anniversary (IRE)** 2-8-3 0 ow2 .... SCreighton[(5)] 13 42
(Miss V Haigh) *s.s: rn green and a wl bhd* 66/1

03 **13** 1/2 **Lois Darlin (IRE)**[28] 1111 2-8-4 0 ....(p) LiamJones 7 36
(J S Moore) *nvr beyond midfield: struggling and off the pce 1/2-way* 14/1

14 6 **Four Green Fields (IRE)** 2-8-4 0 .... WandersonD'Avila 16 15
(B W Duke) *s.i.s: rn green and a bhd* 33/1

15 8 **Premier Demon (IRE)** 2-8-10 0 .... TGMcLaughlin 14 —
(P D Evans) *sn wl bhd: t.o* 14/1

16 17 **Leaf Hollow** 2-8-6 0 .... NeilChalmers 3 —
(M Madgwick) *s.s: v green and sn t.o* 66/1

59.70 secs (-0.60) **Going Correction** -0.30s/f (Firm) 16 Ran SP% **131.1**
Speed ratings (Par 92): **92,91,87,87,86 84,84,83,80,79 79,76,75,65,52 25**
CSF £25.91 TOTE £4.00: £1.50, £4.70, £1.70; EX 48.40.

The Form Book, Raceform Ltd, Compton, RG20 6NL

Owner Holistic Racing, Mullin, Crook, Edwards **Bred** Thoroughbred Farms Ltd **Trained** Exning, Suffolk

FOCUS
Just a fair fillies' maiden and they finished rather in a heap, but plenty of runners from trainers capable with speedy two-year-olds and the race should produce winners.

NOTEBOOK
Beat Seven, carrying 1lb overweight, confirmed the promise she showed when fourth on her debut at Newmarket, although she did not win as well as one might have expected at halfway. She showed good early speed, but if anything was a little keen and, carrying her head at a slight angle, very much showing her inexperience, she struggled to get away from her rivals once coming under pressure. She gives the impression she will come on a fair bit for this, but that will still leave her with plenty to find for her next intended target, the Queen Mary at Royal Ascot. (tchd 9-4)
Fazbee(IRE) ◆, a 15,000gns daughter of Fasliyev, out of a multiple middle-distance winner, was well backed on course and she justified the support with a close second on her racecourse debut. Although she eventually had to give best, she showed good early speed and should be well up to winning a similar event before stepping up in class. (op 12-1 tchd 16-1)
Daddy's Gift(IRE), a 10,000gns daughter of Trans Island, and a half-sister to dual 6f juvenile winner Carrickmacross, out of a dual two-year-old winner at up to 7f, was a short enough price to make a winning debut, but she found a couple too good. She ought to come on for the experience and should make her mark in similar company. (op 2-1 tchd 15-8 and 3-1)
Readily, a 15,000gns half-brother to among others dual 5f-6f three-year-old winner Brioso, out of a 5f winner, is from a stable who recently sent out a first-time out juvenile winner at Newbury, and she shaped nicely on her racecourse debut. Being by Captain Rio she might do even better on easier ground. (op 12-1 tchd 20-1)
You've Been Mowed, an Ishiguru half-sister to among others dual 5f juvenile winner Lucys Lady, out of a 1m winner, only cost 2,000gns but she showed ability.
The Saucy Snipe, by Josr Algarhoud, and sister to The Willowy Widgeon, who was placed over 1m at two, was backed at big prices and made a respectable start. (op 40-1 tchd 50-1 and 16-1)
Meydan Groove, by Reset, half-sister to five winners, including dual 5f-6f juvenile winner Incarvillea, out of a champion three-year-old filly in Europe, winner of four Group 1 races, including the Irish 1000 Guineas, only cost 11,000gns. She was well backed on course, but seemed to run very green and should be all the better for this experience. (op 16-1 tchd 5-1)

1681 CORALPOKER.COM H'CAP — 1m 3f 135y
6:10 (6:12) (Class 5) (0-75,73) 3-Y-O — **£2,729** (£806; £403) **Stalls High**

Form — RPR
4-52 **1** **Dubai Petal (IRE)**[12] 1395 3-9-2 **71** .... RyanMoore 5 — 74
(J S Moore) *hld up in last: effrt 4f out: rdn over 2f out: clsd u.str.p over 1f out: led ins fnl f: all out* **5/4**[1]
00-1 **2** *nk* **Black Tor Figarro (IRE)**[13] 1389 3-8-10 **65** .... LiamJones 7 — 67
(B W Duke) *in tch: pushed along fr 5f out: swtchd lft and effrt 3f out: clsd u.p over 1f out: pressed wnr last 100yds: jst hld* **13/2**
0-62 **3** *nk* **King Supreme (IRE)**[14] 1364 3-8-10 **65** .... RichardHughes 4 — 67
(R Hannon) *cl up: pressed ldr 4f out: rdn to ld narrowly over 2f out: hdd and nt qckn u.p ins fnl f* **10/3**[2]
300- **4** *¾* **Sea Admiral**[187] 6418 3-8-12 **67** .... SteveDrowne 1 — 68
(R Charlton) *cl up: narrow ld 4f out to over 2f out: pressed ldr and upsides ent fnl f: no ex* **6/1**[3]
31-0 **5** *13* **Moment's Notice**[37] 966 3-9-4 **73** .... LPKeniry 2 — 53
(S Kirk) *t.k.h: cl up tl wknd wl over 2f out: sn bhd* **17/2**
60-6 **6** *5* **Morestead (IRE)**[27] 1128 3-8-3 **61** .... WilliamBuick(3) 6 — 33
(B G Powell) *dropped to rr after 5f: rdn and brief effrt over 3f out: sn btn: eased and bhd after* **25/1**
0010 **7** *42* **Rosy Dawn**[6] 1530 3-7-11 **59** oh2 .... (be) SophieDoyle(7) 3 — —
(Ms J S Doyle) *racd freely: led to 4f out: wknd rapidly: wl t.o* **50/1**

2m 27.23s (-2.27) **Going Correction** -0.30s/f (Firm) **7 Ran SP% 111.5**
Speed ratings (Par 98): **95,94,94,94,85 82,54**
CSF £9.53 TOTE £2.20: £1.20, £2.60; EX 9.10.
Owner S A Belton **Bred** Pier House Stud **Trained** Upper Lambourn, Berks

FOCUS
A modest middle-distance handicap run at an ordinary pace with the third to his latest (claimer) form.

1682 D4 & CO H'CAP — 1m 2f 7y
6:40 (6:42) (Class 4) (0-80,80) 4-Y-0+ — **£5,180** (£1,541; £770; £384) **Stalls Low**

Form — RPR
-212 **1** **Emperor Court (IRE)**[31] 1048 4-9-0 **76** .... RyanMoore 1 — 85
(P J Makin) *led to 1/2-way: led again wl over 3f out: hrd pressed fr over 1f out: drifted lft fnl f: hld on* **13/2**[1]
105- **2** *nk* **Shake On It**[225] 5445 4-9-4 **80** .... (t) StephenCarson 14 — 88
(Eve Johnson Houghton) *hld up towards rr: stdy prog and weaved through fr over 2f out: drvn to chal ins fnl f: post c too sn* **20/1**
3-55 **3** *½* **Rudry Dragon (IRE)**[14] 1365 4-9-1 **77** .... SimonWhitworth 12 — 84
(P A Blockley) *hld up in midfield: rdn and prog over 2f out: pressed wnr jst over 1f out: edgd lft fnl f: nt qckn* **9/1**
006- **4** *¾* **Multicultural**[179] 6612 5-8-4 **66** oh1 .... RichardMullen 10 — 72
(D M Simcock) *trckd ldr: led 1/2-way to wl over 3f out: sn rdn: styd pressing ldrs: hung lft and nt qckn fnl f* **17/2**
F-00 **5** *1* **Krugerrand (USA)**[37] 962 9-8-9 **71** .... EddieAhern 3 — 75+
(W J Musson) *hld up in midfield: lost pl 3f out: pushed along and kpt on steadily fnl 2f: nvr nr ldrs* **8/1**[3]
0142 **6** *1* **Prime Number (IRE)**[15] 1349 6-8-6 **68** .... JamesDoyle 7 — 70
(J Akehurst) *prom: pressed wnr over 3f out: nt qckn 2f out: sn lost pl* **13/2**[1]
331/ **7** *1¼* **Show Winner**[551] 6177 5-8-13 **75** .... LPKeniry 9 — 74
(A M Balding) *t.k.h: hld up bhd ldrs: effrt on outer 3f out: nt qckn and btn 2f out* **20/1**
650- **8** *1¼* **Aegean Prince**[201] 6110 4-8-13 **75** .... RichardHughes 2 — 72
(R Hannon) *hld up towards rr: shkn up 3f out: no real prog fnl 2f* **7/1**[2]
416- **9** *¾* **Etain (IRE)**[275] 3964 4-8-9 **71** .... SaleemGolam 11 — 66
(W R Swinburn) *reluctant to go to post: t.k.h: hld up bhd ldrs: drvn 3f out: fdd u.p fnl 2f* **16/1**
10 *nk* **L'Homme De Nuit (GER)**[29] 4-8-4 **66** .... JimmyQuinn 6 — 60
(G L Moore) *nvr gng wl and urged along early: struggling in rr 3f out* **20/1**
01-1 **11** *1¾* **Ryedale Ovation (IRE)**[60] 586 5-8-6 **68** .... ChrisCatlin 4 — 59
(M Hill) *a towards rr: effrt on outer 3f out: sn no prog and btn* **16/1**
0-30 **12** *1½* **Quince (IRE)**[30] 1072 5-9-2 **78** .... (v) SteveDrowne 13 — 66
(J Pearce) *dwlt: a in rr: drvn and no prog 3f out* **7/1**[2]
646- **13** *1* **Just Two Numbers**[181] 6576 4-9-2 **78** .... AlanMunro 8 — 64
(W Jarvis) *t.k.h: hld up: effrt u.p: effrt tl wknd u.p over 2f out* **8/1**[3]
000- **14** *6* **Leptis Magna**[165] 6824 4-8-9 **71** .... SebSanders 5 — 45
(D R C Elsworth) *a wl in rr: brief effrt on wd outside 3f out: sn wknd* **25/1**

2m 5.40s (-3.30) **Going Correction** -0.30s/f (Firm) **14 Ran SP% 124.3**
Speed ratings (Par 105): **101,100,100,99,98 98,97,96,95,95 93,92,91,87**
CSF £141.50 CT £1194.49 TOTE £6.70: £2.70, £4.20, £2.20; EX 176.80.
Owner Four Seasons Racing Ltd **Bred** John O'Connor **Trained** Ogbourne Maisey, Wilts

FOCUS
A fair, competitive handicap that looks pretty sound rated through the third. The winning time was exactly one second quicker than the later three-year-old maiden won by Checklow.
Quince(IRE) Official explanation: jockey said gelding was never travelling

1683 ARENA LEISURE PLC H'CAP — 6f
7:10 (7:11) (Class 4) (0-80,80) 4-Y-0+ — **£4,533** (£1,348; £674; £336) **Stalls High**

Form — RPR
510- **1** **Salsa Steps (USA)**[192] 6300 4-9-4 **80** .... (t) SteveDrowne 5 — 101+
(H Morrison) *t.k.h: trckd ldrs: prog to ld jst over 1f out: sn drew clr: comf* **5/1**[1]
6400 **2** *3¾* **Lucayos**[8] 1500 5-8-7 **76** .... KylieManser(7) 8 — 85
(Mrs H Sweeting) *mde most in centre: rdn 2f out: hdd jst over 1f out: kpt on but no ch w wnr* **33/1**
5121 **3** *1¼* **Diriculous**[20] 1261 4-9-0 **76** .... JimCrowley 2 — 81
(T G Mills) *t.k.h: pressed ldrs on outer: tried to chal over 1f out: sn outpcd* **13/2**[3]
136- **4** *nse* **Fleuret**[207] 5954 4-8-13 **75** .... StephenCarson 14 — 80+
(Eve Johnson Houghton) *racd against nr side rail: on terms w ldr to over 1f out: one pce* **9/1**
545- **5** *hd* **Seamus Shindig**[276] 3911 6-8-7 **76** .... AmyScott(7) 7 — 80
(H Candy) *trckd ldrs: cl up over 1f out: nudged along and nt qckn* **10/1**
00-5 **6** *1¾* **Eau Good**[16] 1327 4-8-11 **80** .... MarkCoumbe(7) 15 — 79
(M C Chapman) *dwlt: wl in rr: outpcd and rdn 1/2-way: styd on fr over 1f out: nrst fin* **16/1**
6-40 **7** *shd* **Kyle (IRE)**[25] 1174 4-9-3 **79** .... RichardHughes 4 — 77
(R Hannon) *stdd s: hld up in last pair: prog 2f out: shkn up and no rspnse over 1f out* **6/1**[2]
1014 **8** *1* **Kensington (IRE)**[6] 1552 7-8-13 **75** .... (p) JamesDoyle 3 — 70
(P D Evans) *towards rr: shkn up 2f out: no imp on ldrs* **9/1**
60-3 **9** *nk* **Cheap Street**[14] 1368 4-8-12 **74** .... RyanMoore 11 — 68
(J G Portman) *hld up in last trio: rdn 2f out: no imp on ldrs* **6/1**[2]
0-00 **10** *½* **Stamford Blue**[18] 1278 7-8-10 **79** .... (b) DavidProbert(7) 13 — 72
(R A Harris) *chsd ldrs: u.p 1/2-way: steadily fdd fnl 2f* **25/1**
3-00 **11** *1¼* **Jimmy The Guesser**[14] 1368 5-8-12 **74** .... RichardThomas 1 — 63
(N P Littmoden) *racd on wd outside in midfield: struggling over 2f out* **33/1**
00-2 **12** *½* **Manchurian**[8] 1500 4-9-4 **80** .... EddieAhern 9 — 67+
(M J Wallace) *nvr beyond midfield: no prog u.p 2f out: n.m.r ent fnl f and eased* **7/1**
54-0 **13** *12* **Nordic Light (USA)**[14] 1366 4-8-5 **74** .... MCGeran(7) 10 — 23
(J M Bradley) *nvr on terms w ldrs: bmpd along and wknd fr 2f out: t.o* **66/1**
0-60 **P** **Impromptu**[26] 1146 4-9-4 **80** .... GeorgeBaker 16 — —
(P G Murphy) *a towards rr: wknd over 2f out: p.u ins fnl f: b.b.v* **22/1**

1m 10.4s (-2.60) **Going Correction** -0.30s/f (Firm) **14 Ran SP% 121.6**
Speed ratings (Par 105): **105,100,98,98,98 95,95,94,93,93 91,90,74,—**
CSF £184.85 CT £1102.03 TOTE £5.90: £2.50, £9.70, £1.70; EX 186.50.
Owner Ben & Sir Martyn Arbib **Bred** Martyn Arbib **Trained** East Ilsley, Berks

FOCUS
A fair sprint handicap and it looked quite competitive, but the winner was in a different league. The form is rated around the runner-up to recent marks.
Impromptu Official explanation: jockey said gelding had bled from the nose

1684 AT THE RACES MAIDEN STKS — 1m 2f 7y
7:40 (7:42) (Class 5) 3-Y-O — **£2,729** (£806; £403) **Stalls Low**

Form — RPR
3 **1** **Checklow (USA)**[12] 1398 3-9-3 0 .... LDettori 2 — 77+
(J Noseda) *pressed ldr: shkn up over 2f out: rdn to ld over 1f out: styd on strly and clr ins fnl f* **4/9**[1]
5- **2** *2¼* **Gaia Prince (USA)**[267] 4201 3-9-3 0 .... JimCrowley 7 — 72
(Mrs A J Perrett) *prom: w ldr 4f out: upsides wl over 1f out: outpcd by wnr fnl f* **12/1**
5-3 **3** *hd* **Colorado Blue (IRE)**[19] 1265 3-9-3 0 .... SteveDrowne 4 — 72
(R Charlton) *trckd ldrs: rdn 3f out: nt qckn 2f out: styd on again fnl f* **5/1**[2]
06- **4** *1¾* **Celt**[217] 5680 3-9-3 0 .... NickyMackay 1 — 68+
(L M Cumani) *settled towards rr: shuffled along and styd on steadily fnl 2f: nrst fin: do bttr* **33/1**
5 *2¾* **Cheeky Download (IRE)** 3-8-12 0 .... SebSanders 8 — 58+
(E A L Dunlop) *hld up towards rr: nt clr run briefly over 2f out: shuffled along and kpt on steadily* **33/1**
00- **6** *¾* **Timber Creek**[193] 6285 3-9-3 0 .... DaneO'Neill 5 — 61
(H Candy) *led: jinked bnd 5f out: hdd & wknd over 1f out* **80/1**
0- **7** *¾* **Teen Spirit (IRE)**[200] 6130 3-9-3 0 .... EddieAhern 6 — 60
(J W Hills) *hld up in midfield: shkn up over 2f out: sn outpcd* **100/1**
6-0 **8** *shd* **Forget It**[9] 1467 3-9-3 0 .... RichardHughes 11 — 59
(R Hannon) *hld up in last pair: rdn and no prog 2f out* **16/1**
9 *2* **Drum Major (IRE)** 3-9-3 0 .... RyanMoore 10 — 55
(Sir Michael Stoute) *s.v.s: rn green in last: kpt on fr over 1f out* **15/2**[3]
00- **10** *7* **Rockjumper**[180] 6592 3-9-0 0 .... TravisBlock(3) 3 — 41
(H Morrison) *hld up in midfield: shkn up 3f out: wknd 2f out* **100/1**
040- **11** *5* **Howe's Jack (IRE)**[132] 7176 3-8-10 **37** .... (t) GihanArnolda(7) 9 — 31
(M C Chapman) *t.k.h: hld up bhd ldrs: wknd over 2f out* **100/1**

2m 6.40s (-2.30) **Going Correction** -0.30s/f (Firm) **11 Ran SP% 121.3**
Speed ratings (Par 98): **97,95,95,93,91 90,90,90,88,82 78**
CSF £7.85 TOTE £1.50: £1.10, £2.90, £1.40; EX 7.90.
Owner Mrs Susan Roy **Bred** William Thomson **Trained** Newmarket, Suffolk

FOCUS
The bare form of this maiden looked just fair, but the winner rates as a serious prospect and there were one or two in behind who shaped as though they can make their mark once handicapped. The winning time was exactly one second slower than the earlier older-horse 66-80 handicap and the form is muddling at this stage.
Forget It Official explanation: jockey said he struck his foot on leaving stalls

1685 HAPPY BIRTHDAY YVONNE AND GEMMA H'CAP — 1m 67y
8:10 (8:11) (Class 5) (0-75,75) 3-Y-O — **£3,070** (£906; £453) **Stalls High**

Form — RPR
36-6 **1** **Summon Up Theblood (IRE)**[23] 1208 3-9-4 **75** .... DarryllHolland 10 — 80
(M R Channon) *prog to trck ldrs 1/2-way: drvn to ld over 1f out: hung lft fnl f: hld on* **12/1**
2-22 **2** *½* **Rich Kid (IRE)**[87] 393 3-8-12 **72** .... KevinGhunowa(3) 12 — 76
(R A Harris) *hld up in midfield: effrt on outer over 2f out: drvn to chal fnl f: hld nr fin* **16/1**
062- **3** *hd* **Pediment**[215] 5727 3-9-1 **72** .... KerrinMcEvoy 13 — 76
(J R Fanshawe) *hld up in midfield: prog towards outer 2f out: rdn to chal 1f out: styd on same pce* **10/1**

640- **4** *2* **Trumpet Lily**[200] 6125 3-9-3 **74**........................ RyanMoore 6 73
(J G Portman) *hld up in rr: stdy prog fr 3f out: rdn over 1f out: kpt on fnl f: nrst fin* **14/1**

35-1 **5** *hd* **Golden Penny**[27] 1130 3-8-11 **71**........................ TravisBlock(3) 9 73+
(H Morrison) *t.k.h: pressed ldr 2f: styd cl up: looked hld whn n.m.r over 1f out: fdd* **9/2[3]**

04-6 **6** *2* **Farthermost (IRE)**[16] 1336 3-9-1 **72**........................ RichardHughes 2 66
(R Hannon) *led: rdn over 2f out: hung lft and hdd over 1f out: fdd* **7/2[2]**

0-44 **7** *1* **Lawton**[37] 974 3-9-0 **71**........................ PaulFitzsimons 14 63
(Miss J R Tooth) *a in midfield: no imp on ldrs 2f out: one pce* **33/1**

21-3 **8** *1* **Bermacha**[13] 1381 3-9-4 **75**........................ RichardMullen 4 64+
(W R Muir) *t.k.h: prom: rdn and looked hld whn n.m.r over 1f out: btn whn hmpd ins fnl f* **12/1**

1- **9** *¾* **Harlem Shuffle (UAE)**[200] 6119 3-9-4 **75**........................ EddieAhern 8 68+
(M Johnston) *free to post: t.k.h: prom: pressed ldr after 2f: edgd lft 2f out: losing pl whn n.m.r over 1f out* **3/1[1]**

06-6 **10** *¾* **Highland Homestead**[19] 1265 3-8-8 **65**........................ AlanMunro 11 51
(B R Millman) *s.i.s: hld up in last pair: wl off the pce 4f out: kpt on steadily fnl 2f: nvr nrr* **25/1**

61-6 **11** *11* **Miss Phoebe (IRE)**[117] 12 3-9-1 **72**........................ LPKeniry 7 33
(S Kirk) *hld up in rr: hanging and no prog over 2f out: wknd: t.o* **50/1**

1221 **12** *4* **Bridge Of Fermoy (IRE)**[9] 1487 3-9-4 **75**........................(vt) GeorgeBaker 5 26
(Miss Gay Kelleway) *stmbld s: hld up in last trio: hrd rdn and no rspnse over 2f out: eased: t.o* **9/1**

040- **13** *hd* **Effingham (IRE)**[203] 6058 3-8-13 **73**........................ WilliamBuick(3) 1 24
(B W Hills) *hld up in last trio: sltly hmpd 5f out: wknd 3f out: t.o* **25/1**

60-6 **U** **Dynamo Dave (USA)**[26] 1149 3-8-8 **65**........................ ChrisCatlin 3 —
(B J Meehan) *racd wd in midfield: stmbld and uns rdr bnd 5f out* **25/1**

1m 42.6s (-2.10) **Going Correction** -0.30s/f (Firm) **14** Ran SP% **128.9**
Speed ratings (Par 98): **98,97,97,95,95 93,92,91,90,89 78,74,74,—**
CSF £192.00 CT £1282.91 TOTE £18.90: £4.70, £5.30, £3.60; EX 224.90 Place 6 £195.19, Place 5 £105.14..
Owner Derek And Jean Clee **Bred** D D And Mrs Jean P Clee **Trained** West Ilsley, Berks

FOCUS
A fair three-year-old handicap rated around the first four but slightly messy form.
Golden Penny ◆ Official explanation: jockey said gelding was denied a clear run
T/Plt: £73.70 to a £1 stake. Pool: £81,466.04. 806.22 winning tickets. T/Qpdt: £26.10 to a £1 stake. Pool: £5,751.29. 163 winning tickets. JN

1454 YARMOUTH (L-H)

Monday, April 28

OFFICIAL GOING: Good to firm (8.5)
Wind: Fresh, against Weather: bright partly cloudy

1686 HEATHCOTES OUTSIDE CATERING H'CAP — 1m 3y
2:00 (2:03) (Class 4) (0-85,84) 3-Y-O — **£4,533** (£1,348; £674; £336) **Stalls** Low

Form RPR

32-6 **1** **Irish Mayhem (USA)**[11] 1424 3-9-2 **82**........................ RobertWinston 3 87
(B J Meehan) *hld up in tch: hdwy 4f out: led 2f out: sn shkn up: rdn 1f out: jst hld on* **14/1**

221- **2** *shd* **Yaddree**[186] 6451 3-9-4 **84**........................ PhilipRobinson 8 89
(M A Jarvis) *chsd ldrs: wnt 2nd over 1f out: clsd steadily u.p last 100yds: jst hld* **10/3[2]**

22-0 **3** *1 ½* **Seattle Storm (IRE)**[12] 1398 3-8-10 **76**........................ JamieSpencer 5 78+
(D R C Elsworth) *stdd after s: hld up last: pushed along over 3f out: sltly hmpd 2f out: styd on 1f out: wnt 2nd wl ins fnl f: nt clr run nr fin* **33/1**

1-4 **4** *½* **Mukhber**[17] 1297 3-9-3 **83**........................ RHills 6 83
(J H M Gosden) *chsd ldr tl led 3f out: hdd 2f out: kpt on same pce fnl f* **6/4[1]**

0-15 **5** *½* **Always Ready**[30] 1074 3-9-4 **84**........................(b[1]) KerrinMcEvoy 7 83
(C E Brittain) *hld up in rr: hdwy jst over 2f out: chsd ldrs and rdn 1f out: one pce* **10/1**

31 **6** *2* **Sir Billy Nick**[20] 1252 3-8-10 **76**........................ ShaneKelly 2 70
(J Noseda) *chsd ldrs: lost pl over 2f out: rdn 2f out: wknd fnl f* **5/1[3]**

5-16 **7** *1 ¼* **Admiral Dundas (IRE)**[37] 966 3-8-7 **73**........................(p) J-PGuillambert 4 65
(W Jarvis) *t.k.h: hld up in tch: rdn over 2f out: no imp fr over 1f out* **18/1**

021- **8** *10* **Flight To Quality**[216] 5702 3-8-13 **79**........................ JoeFanning 1 48
(M Johnston) *led tl 3f out: sn wknd: wl bhd fnl f* **8/1**

1m 39.45s (-1.15) **Going Correction** -0.125s/f (Firm) **8** Ran SP% **114.8**
Speed ratings (Par 100): **100,99,98,97,97 95,94,84**
CSF £60.66 CT £1541.13 TOTE £16.20: £3.10, £1.50, £3.10; EX 75.30 Trifecta £569.90 Part won. Pool: £802.81 - 0.39 winning units..
Owner Dean Fleming **Bred** Heaven Trees Farm **Trained** Manton, Wilts
■ Stewards' Enquiry : Philip Robinson one-day ban: careless riding (May 12)

FOCUS
This was a decent little handicap on paper but there was not much pace on and it remains to be seen how literally this form can be taken. The field edged across from the stands' side to reach the far side with 3f to run.
Seattle Storm(IRE) Official explanation: jockey said colt was denied a clear run

1687 DIGIBET H'CAP — 7f 3y
2:30 (2:31) (Class 6) (0-52,52) 4-Y-O+ — **£1,942** (£578; £288; £144) **Stalls** High

Form RPR

6024 **1** **Balerno**[10] 1455 9-8-10 **50**........................ IanMongan 6 58
(Mrs L J Mongan) *hld up in midfield: hdwy wl over 2f out: rdn to chal 1f out: led ins fnl f: drvn out* **4/1[1]**

00/0 **2** *½* **Moverra (IRE)**[61] 718 4-8-10 **50**........................(p) NickyMackay 1 57
(M Wigham) *racd in midfield: hdwy over 3f out: led wl over 1f out: sn rdn: hrd pressed 1f out: hdd and unable qckn ins fnl f* **10/1[3]**

5462 **3** *nk* **Imperial Sword**[10] 1455 5-8-11 **51** ow2........................(b) JimmyFortune 8 57
(T D Barron) *stdd s: t.k.h: hld up in rr: hdwy jst over 2f out: swtchd lft over 1f out: r.o u.p: nt quite rch ldrs* **6/1[2]**

6-00 **4** *¾* **Norcroft**[24] 1189 6-8-12 **52**........................(p) PatCosgrave 9 56
(Mrs C A Dunnett) *hld up in midfield: hdwy wl over 1f out: kpt on u.p ins fnl f: nt pce to rch ldrs* **14/1**

0-00 **5** *2 ¼* **Gee Ceffyl Bach**[66] 663 4-8-6 **46** oh1........................ SilvestreDeSousa 12 44
(R C Guest) *t.k.h: chsd ldrs tl lost pl 2f out: rallied u.p fnl f: styd on* **14/1**

4143 **6** *shd* **Davids Mark**[19] 1275 8-8-12 **52**........................ HayleyTurner 3 49
(J R Jenkins) *hld up in midfield: hdwy wl over 2f out: chsd ldrs and rdn over 1f out: wknd ins fnl f* **11/1**

00-2 **7** *hd* **Forced Upon Us**[23] 1209 4-8-12 **52**........................(b) JamieSpencer 13 49
(P J McBride) *chsd ldrs tl led after 1f tl 4f out: ev ch and rdn over 1f out: wknd ins fnl f* **6/1[2]**

3010 **8** *½* **Shava**[72] 584 8-8-12 **52**........................ VinceSlattery 10 48
(H J Evans) *t.k.h: hld up towards rr: hdwy over 2f out: chsd ldrs and rdn over 1f out: wknd 1f out* **16/1**

60-0 **9** *½* **Just Oscar (GER)**[33] 1029 4-8-10 **50**........................ TedDurcan 5 44
(W M Brisbourne) *s.i.s: hld up in rr: rdn and effrt 2f out: nvr on terms* **10/1[3]**

2135 **10** *6* **Fun In The Sun**[21] 1248 4-8-8 **48**........................(b) KerrinMcEvoy 14 26
(A B Haynes) *chsd ldrs tl led and racd alone towards stands' side 4f out: sn clr: wknd and hdd wl over 1f out: sn btn* **6/1[2]**

0000 **11** *¾* **Bodden Bay**[6] 1550 6-8-8 **48**........................(p) PatrickMathers 7 24
(I W McInnes) *taken down early: led for 1f: chsd ldrs tl rdn and dropped out: 3f out: sn bhd* **18/1**

000- **12** *3 ¼* **Barley Moon**[263] 4339 4-8-6 **46** oh1........................ J-PGuillambert 4 13
(T Keddy) *chsd ldrs: rdn over 3f out: wknd 3f out: wl bhd last 2f* **40/1**

/50- **13** *1 ½* **Torver**[201] 6100 4-8-10 **50**........................ JoeFanning 2 13
(Dr J D Scargill) *racd in midfield: hdwy 4f out: rdn and wknd 2f out: wl bhd fnl f* **20/1**

1m 27.18s (0.58) **Going Correction** -0.125s/f (Firm) **13** Ran SP% **121.1**
Speed ratings (Par 101): **91,90,90,89,86 86,86,85,85,78 77,73,72**
CSF £45.00 CT £252.42 TOTE £5.80: £1.70, £3.20, £2.20; EX 72.40 Trifecta £231.50 Part won. Pool: £326.15 - 0.79 winning units..
Owner K Santana **Bred** Juddmonte Farms **Trained** Epsom, Surrey
■ Stewards' Enquiry : Nicky Mackay two-day ban: used whip with excessive frequency and without allowing time to respond. (May 12-13)

FOCUS
This is ordinary low-grade form. It was a very moderate winning time despite being over half a second quicker than the following Class 4 handicap for three-year-olds. The field again raced mid-track.
Imperial Sword Official explanation: jockey said gelding ran too free
Gee Ceffyl Bach Official explanation: vet said filly finished lame
Fun In The Sun Official explanation: jockey said gelding ran too free
Barley Moon Official explanation: jockey said filly lost a hind shoe; trainer said filly finished lame

1688 LINDLEY-CATERING.CO.UK H'CAP — 7f 3y
3:00 (3:05) (Class 4) (0-85,83) 3-Y-O — **£4,533** (£1,348; £674; £336) **Stalls** High

Form RPR

1 **1** **Magnitude**[35] 997 3-9-3 **82**........................ MichaelHills 6 84
(W J Haggas) *t.k.h: hld up wl in tch: hdwy 2f out: led 1f out: edgd lft u.p: hdd wl ins fnl f: no ex: fin 2nd, nk: subs awrdd r* **9/4[1]**

43-2 **2** *1 ½* **Dubai Power**[19] 1270 3-9-4 **83**........................ KerrinMcEvoy 5 82
(C E Brittain) *t.k.h: hld up wl in tch: rdn over 1f out: swtchd rt 1f out: kpt on same pce fnl f: fin 3rd, nk & 1¼l: plcd 2nd* **11/2[2]**

00-5 **3** *3* **King's Icon (IRE)**[16] 1336 3-9-0 **79**........................ PatDobbs 2 70
(M P Tregoning) *hld up wl in tch: rdn and effrt over 1f out: outpcd fnl f: fin 4th, nk, 1¼l & 3l: plced 3rd* **10/1**

1-65 **4** *nk* **Desert Clover (USA)**[11] 1426 3-9-2 **81**........................ NelsonDeSouza 3 71
(P F I Cole) *plld hrd: led tl 2f out: sn rdn: outpcd fnl f: fin 5th, plcd 4th* **6/1[3]**

651- **D** **Debonnaire**[179] 6601 3-8-7 **72**........................ JoeFanning 4 75
(M Johnston) *chsd ldr tl led 2f out: sn rdn: hdd 1f out: battled bk gamely to ld again wl ins fnl f: fin 1st, nk: subs disq (prohibited sample)* **9/1**

1m 27.69s (1.09) **Going Correction** -0.125s/f (Firm) **5** Ran SP% **79.5**
Speed ratings (Par 100): **87,86,82,82,88**
CSF £15.18 TOTE £6.30: £2.50, £1.10; EX 13.60 Trifecta £15.90 Pool £250.77 - 11.18 winning units..
Owner Cheveley Park Stud **Bred** Cheveley Park Stud Ltd **Trained** Newmarket, Suffolk
■ High Standing was withdrawn (2/1F, lost shoe at the start). R4 applies, deduct 30p in the £.

FOCUS
They went a steady pace, racing mid-track, and the winning time was very moderate for the type of race. The form is pretty dubious, rated through the third.

1689 LINDLEY CATERING - OFFICIAL RACECOURSE CATERERS - H'CAP — 6f 3y
3:30 (3:31) (Class 2) (0-100,94) 4-Y-O+
£9,969 (£2,985; £1,492; £747; £372; £187) **Stalls** High

Form RPR

116- **1** **Royal Rock**[254] 4607 4-9-4 **94**........................ GeorgeBaker 7 107+
(C F Wall) *hld up towards rr: hdwy over 2f out: led over 1f out: hld on wl fnl f* **4/1[3]**

636- **2** *½* **Orpenindeed (IRE)**[122] 7255 5-8-11 **90**........................(t) KirstyMilczarek(3) 6 99
(M Botti) *t.k.h: chsd clr ldr: clsd 2f out: ev ch fr over 1f out: unable qck wl ins fnl f* **4/1[3]**

2500 **3** *1 ¼* **Fyodor (IRE)**[5] 1571 7-9-3 **93**........................ MichaelHills 4 98
(W J Haggas) *t.k.h: hld up wl in rr: hdwy 2f out: chal jst ins fnl f: sn rdn and fnd little* **10/1**

0-10 **4** *3 ¾* **Blue Tomato**[30] 1071 7-8-9 **85**........................ SilvestreDeSousa 5 78
(D Nicholls) *sn bustled along in rr: rdn and hdwy over 2f out: no hdwy fr over 1f out* **10/3[2]**

0245 **5** *½* **Ajigolo**[15] 1346 5-9-2 **92**........................ EdwardCreighton 1 83
(M R Channon) *stdd s: racd in midfield: rdn over 2f out: n.d last 2f* **16/1**

-165 **6** *4 ½* **Ingleby Arch (USA)**[7] 1517 5-8-13 **89**........................ JimmyFortune 2 66
(T D Barron) *chsd ldrs: drvn over 2f out: wknd wl over 1f out* **5/2[1]**

00-3 **7** *8* **Classic Encounter (IRE)**[46] 866 5-9-0 **90**........................ JoeFanning 3 41
(D M Simcock) *racd freely: led and sn clr: wknd and hdd over 1f out: sn bhd* **16/1**

1m 11.47s (-2.93) **Going Correction** -0.125s/f (Firm) **7** Ran SP% **112.5**
Speed ratings (Par 109): **114,113,111,106,106 100,89**
CSF £19.60 CT £145.65 TOTE £3.80: £2.40, £2.60; EX 22.00 Trifecta £74.70 Pool: £556.01 - 5.28 winning units..
Owner S Fustok **Bred** Deerfield Farm **Trained** Newmarket, Suffolk

FOCUS
A smart winning time for the class and Royal Rock impressed in a race rated through the runner-up. They again raced up the centre of the track.

NOTEBOOK
Royal Rock ◆, a progressive sprinter at three, who was going down with the virus when well beaten on his final start, improved again to make a winning reappearance. He took this with plenty up his sleeve and there are nice handicaps to be won with him this year. (op 3-1)
Orpenindeed(IRE) ran well on this first start on turf in Britain, unable to quite get to the progressive winner but losing nothing in defeat. (op 7-1)
Fyodor(IRE) was produced to have his chance inside the last but did not really go through with his effort. He has become hard to win with. (op 9-1 tchd 11-1)
Blue Tomato had no excuses about the ground this time and the pace was decent despite the small field. Official explanation: trainer's rep said gelding was unsuited by the good to firm going (op 7-2)
Ajigolo, dropped 4lb after a poor run at Brighton, performed better here but still looks a bit high in the weights on turf. (op 9-1)

Classic Encounter(IRE) is one of the fastest sprinters around and it was no surprise that, after blazing the trail as usual, he did not see out the extra furlong. Official explanation: jockey said gelding ran too free

1690 LINDLEY CATERING MAIDEN STKS 1m 3f 101y
4:00 (4:01) (Class 5) 3-4-Y-0 £2,914 (£867; £433; £216) Stalls Low

Form RPR
0- **1** **Amerigo (IRE)**[173] 6724 3-8-9 0 .... PhilipRobinson 2 85
(M A Jarvis) *mde all: jnd 3f out: kpt on to assert nr fin* **10/3**[3]
2 *nk* **Ordination (IRE)** 3-8-9 0 .... RobertWinston 6 84
(B J Meehan) *in tch: chsd wnr after 2f: ev ch 3f out: wanting to hang lft after: rdn 1f out: nt qckn* **6/1**
-0 **3** *7* **Factotum**[13] 1382 4-10-0 0 .... PatCosgrave 5 76
(L M Cumani) *s.i.s: sn bustled along: in tch: rdn 4f out: outpcd over 1f out: plugged on to go modest 3rd ins fnl f* **20/1**
022- **4** *3* **Wraith**[165] 6821 4-10-0 75 .... TedDurcan 7 70
(H R A Cecil) *t.k.h: hld up in tch: rdn over 3f out: wknd over 1f out* **7/4**[1]
3 **5** *shd* **Boy Racer (IRE)**[94] 310 3-8-9 0 .... JoeFanning 1 67
(M Johnston) *chsd wnr for 2f: in tch: rdn and effrt 3f out: wknd over 1f out* **9/4**[2]
6 *72* **Bathwick Penny**[51] 4-9-9 0 .... DavidKinsella 8 —
(A B Haynes) *v.s.a: sn detached in last: t.o last 4f* **100/1**

2m 26.85s (-1.85) **Going Correction** +0.05s/f (Good)
WFA 3 from 4yo 19lb 6 Ran SP% **110.2**
Speed ratings (Par 103): **108,107,102,100,100 48**
CSF £22.01 TOTE £3.50: £2.30, £4.80; EX 26.50 Trifecta £85.50 Pool: £570.19 - 4.73 winning units..
Owner B E Nielsen **Bred** Bjorn Nielsen **Trained** Newmarket, Suffolk
■ Stewards' Enquiry : Robert Winston one day ban: used whip with excessive frequency and down the shoulder in forehand position (May 12)

FOCUS
A decent winning time for a race like this and the fastest of the three races over the trip on the day. Tricky form to pin down, with the favourite clearly not running his race, but slightly above-average efforts from the front pair to pull clear.

1691 LINDLEY HEATHCOTES H'CAP 1m 3f 101y
4:30 (4:30) (Class 4) (0-85,85) 4-Y-0+ £4,533 (£1,348; £674; £336) Stalls Low

Form RPR
1/1- **1** **Abandon (USA)**[362] 1414 5-8-13 80 .... MichaelHills 4 89
(W J Haggas) *hld up wl in tch: hdwy to trck ldrs gng wl 3f out: led over 1f out: sn rdn: r.o wl: eased nr fin* **6/4**[1]
100- **2** *1* **Natural Action**[207] 5955 4-8-1 71 .... LukeMorris(3) 2 79+
(W Jarvis) *s.i.s: sn chsng ldrs: rdn: hld hd high and outpcd over 2f out: rallied and swtchd rt 1f out: edgd lft but r.o wl to go 2nd last 100yds: nt rch wnr* **14/1**
5-23 **3** *¾* **Royal Fantasy (IRE)**[41] 927 5-8-10 77 .... JamieSpencer 6 83
(J R Fanshawe) *stdd after s: hld up in last: crept nrr over 3f out: swtchd rt over 1f out: sn rdn: styd on to go 3rd nr fin: nt pce to threaten wnr* **9/2**[3]
2000 **4** *¾* **Moon Mix (FR)**[17] 1299 5-8-4 71 oh1 .... HayleyTurner 5 76
(J R Jenkins) *t.k.h: hld up in last pair: hdwy 4f out: ev ch and rdn over 1f out: unable qck: lost 2 pls last 100yds* **28/1**
1113 **5** *3 ¼* **Motarjm (USA)**[23] 1212 4-9-4 85 .... (t) TedDurcan 7 84
(H J Collingridge) *chsd ldr: led 3f out: hdd and rdn 2f out: btn whn short of room ins fnl f* **7/1**
11-1 **6** *nk* **Greyfriars Abbey**[4] 1580 4-9-0 81 6ex .... JoeFanning 3 80
(M Johnston) *racd awkwardly and wanting to hang thrght: led tl 3f out: wknd over 2f out: no ch fr over 1f out* **9/4**[2]

2m 30.08s (1.38) **Going Correction** +0.05s/f (Good) 6 Ran SP% **111.6**
Speed ratings (Par 105): **96,95,94,94,91 91**
CSF £22.57 TOTE £2.10: £1.50, £5.70; EX 24.10.
Owner Cheveley Park Stud **Bred** 6 C Stallions Limited **Trained** Newmarket, Suffolk
■ Stewards' Enquiry : Luke Morris three-day ban: careless riding (May 12-14)

FOCUS
The steady pace produced a somewhat messy race and this is not form to take too literally. Abandon is a progressive mare, however.
Greyfriars Abbey Official explanation: jockey said gelding hung badly right throughout

1692 LINDLEY FINE DINING H'CAP 1m 3f 101y
5:00 (5:01) (Class 6) (0-60,60) 4-Y-0+ £1,942 (£578; £288; £144) Stalls Low

Form RPR
01-0 **1** **Royal Premier (IRE)**[45] 881 5-8-13 58 .... (v) JerryO'Dwyer(3) 13 73+
(H J Collingridge) *chsd ldr: led wl over 2f out: sn rdn clr: unchal after: eased towards fin* **8/1**[3]
/00- **2** *2* **Wyeth**[193] 6286 4-9-4 60 .... JamieSpencer 11 68
(J R Fanshawe) *t.k.h: hld up in tch in midfield: rdn wl over 3f out: hdwy u.p over 1f out: styd on to go 2nd ins fnl f: nvr nr wnr* **14/1**
601 **3** *hd* **Top Seed (IRE)**[6] 1528 7-9-0 56 6ex .... StephenDonohoe 5 64
(Ian Williams) *t.k.h: hld up towards rr: swtchd rt and hdwy 3f out: sn rdn: styd on u.p to go 3rd nr fin: nvr nr wnr* **6/4**[1]
041- **4** *shd* **Ashwell Rose**[174] 6700 6-8-5 54 .... (v) GabrielHannon(7) 1 62
(J R Jenkins) *s.i.s: hld up towards rr: hdwy over 2f out: kpt on u.p fnl f: nvr nr wnr* **25/1**
1236 **5** *1* **Medieval Maiden**[10] 1459 5-8-9 51 .... IanMongan 6 57
(Mrs L J Mongan) *chsd ldrs: rdn 3f out: outpcd wl over 2f out: chsd wnr briefly jst ins fnl f: kpt on but nvr pce to threaten wnr* **4/1**[2]
-560 **6** *¾* **Barry Island**[31] 1049 9-8-7 54 .... JackMitchell(5) 9 59
(D R C Elsworth) *stdd s: t.k.h: hld up bhd: hdwy 2f out: styd on u.p fnl f: nvr trbld ldrs* **14/1**
32-0 **7** *1 ¼* **Desert Hawk**[35] 999 7-8-5 52 .... AshleyHamblett(5) 2 55
(W M Brisbourne) *t.k.h: hld up wl in tch: n.m.r and shuffled bk over 2f out: styd on fnl f: nvr able to chal* **11/1**
-040 **8** *1 ½* **Summer Bounty**[10] 1459 12-8-7 49 .... JoeFanning 12 51+
(F Jordan) *s.i.s: t.k.h: hld up in rr: hdwy on inner over 2f out: styd on but nvr nr ldrs: nt clr run and swtchd rt wl ins fnl f* **33/1**
546- **9** *½* **Iceman George**[176] 6673 4-9-4 60 .... (b[1]) TedDurcan 7 59
(D Morris) *sn led: hdd and rdn over 2f out: sn outpcd by wnr: lost 2nd jst ins fnl f: wknd* **18/1**
3151 **10** *nk* **Jarvo**[44] 769 7-8-13 55 .... PatrickMathers 16 54
(I W McInnes) *t.k.h: hld up in rr on outer: rdn and effrt wl over 2f out: n.d* **16/1**
-500 **11** *4 ½* **Inch Lodge**[12] 1409 6-9-4 60 .... PaulEddery 8 51
(Miss D Mountain) *t.k.h: chsd ldrs tl rdn and wknd over 2f out: eased whn wl btn ins fnl f* **16/1**
3103 **12** *6* **Granary Girl**[12] 1405 6-8-7 49 .... RobertHavlin 14 30
(J Pearce) *hld up in midfield: hdwy 4f out: rdn and wknd 3f out: wl bhd fnl f* **16/1**
45-0 **13** *1 ¼* **Split The Wind (USA)**[21] 1243 4-9-0 56 .... HayleyTurner 3 35
(Eve Johnson Houghton) *t.k.h: chsd ldrs: rdn and wknd 3f out* **50/1**
350- **14** *10* **Sibo Baggins (IRE)**[159] 6895 4-8-10 52 .... PatCosgrave 15 14
(Mrs C A Dunnett) *t.k.h: hld up in midfield: rdn and wknd over 3f out: t.o* **50/1**

2m 28.77s (0.07) **Going Correction** +0.05s/f (Good) 14 Ran SP% **126.4**
Speed ratings (Par 101): **101,99,99,99,98 98,97,96,95,95 92,87,86,79**
CSF £117.76 CT £263.22 TOTE £9.40: £2.50, £3.70, £1.10; EX 142.90 Trifecta £297.70 Part won. Pool £419.38 - 0.39 winning units. Place 6 £241.00, Place 5 £64.41..
Owner Maynard Durrant Partnership I **Bred** Mrs Anne Hughes **Trained** Exning, Suffolk

FOCUS
A steadily run handicap and ordinary form. The winner is rated back to his best.
Summer Bounty Official explanation: jockey said gelding was denied a clear run
Inch Lodge Official explanation: jockey said horse lost its action
T/Plt: £248.30 to a £1 stake. Pool: £55,034.27. 161.75 winning tickets. T/Qpdt: £42.60 to a £1 stake. Pool: £3,509.73. 60.85 winning tickets. SP

1528 BATH (L-H)
Tuesday, April 29

OFFICIAL GOING: Good changing to good to soft after race 2 (2.40) changing to soft after race 3 (3.10)
Conditions quickly deteriorated with the rain setting in for the afternoon just before racing.
Wind: Moderate behind Weather: Raining

1693 M J CHURCH MAIDEN AUCTION STKS 5f 11y
2:10 (2:11) (Class 6) 2-Y-O £1,813 (£539; £269; £134) Stalls Centre

Form RPR
1 **Missile Dodger (USA)** 2-8-11 0 .... SebSanders 10 88+
(R M Beckett) *mde all: shkn up over 1f out: r.o wl* **4/1**[2]
2 *3 ¼* **Every Second** 2-8-13 0 .... RichardMullen 8 78+
(E S McMahon) *trckd ldrs: chsd wnr over 1f out: no imp* **4/1**[2]
3 *4 ½* **Mazzola** 2-8-9 0 .... EdwardCreighton 7 58
(M R Channon) *chsd ldrs: rdn over 2f out: one pce fnl f* **14/1**
2 **4** *nk* **Miss Hollybell**[14] 1385 2-8-4 0 .... ChrisCatlin 14 52
(J Gallagher) *w wnr: wknd fnl f* **3/1**[1]
5 *nse* **Abhainn (IRE)** 2-8-11 0 .... CatherineGannon 11 59
(B Palling) *w ldrs tl rdn over 2f out: wknd over 1f out* **25/1**
36 **6** *2 ¼* **Smalljohn**[12] 1413 2-8-9 0 .... TGMcLaughlin 6 49+
(P D Evans) *s.i.s and bmpd s: outpcd: sme hdwy over 1f out: nvr nr ldrs* **10/1**
7 *½* **Caressing** 2-8-7 0 ow1 .... RichardHughes 4 45
(R Hannon) *wnt rt s: nvr nr ldrs* **6/1**[3]
8 *1* **Forster Island** 2-8-9 0 .... JamesDoyle 9 43
(M Blanshard) *s.i.s: sn chsng ldrs: wknd wl over 2f out* **50/1**
9 *2* **Lucky Score (IRE)** 2-8-8 0 .... NeilChalmers 5 35
(Mouse Hamilton-Fairley) *s.i.s and bmpd s: outpcd* **50/1**
10 *1* **Lislin** 2-8-4 0 .... JimmyQuinn 1 28
(S Kirk) *mid-div: wknd over 2f out* **14/1**
11 *1 ¾* **Paymaster In Chief** 2-8-9 0 .... HayleyTurner 12 26
(M D I Usher) *bmpd s: outpcd* **16/1**
12 *1 ½* **Hatchet Man** 2-8-13 0 .... JimCrowley 13 25
(P Winkworth) *outpcd* **8/1**
13 *11* **Calypso Prince** 2-8-9 0 .... RichardSmith 3 —
(M D I Usher) *bhd fnl 3f* **33/1**

63.43 secs (0.93) **Going Correction** -0.05s/f (Good) 13 Ran SP% **129.4**
Speed ratings (Par 90): **90,84,77,77,77 73,72,71,67,66 63,61,43**
CSF £21.80 TOTE £4.50: £1.80, £2.00, £4.50; EX 23.40 Trifecta £189.30 Pool: £314.65 - 1.18 winning units.
Owner R Roberts **Bred** Kim Nardelli, Rodney Nardelli Et Al **Trained** Whitsbury, Hants

FOCUS
Not many got into this modest maiden and the first two had it to themselves in the last quarter-mile.

NOTEBOOK
Missile Dodger(USA) had certainly been taught his job and turned the race into something of a procession. He could be fairly useful and we should find out more about him when he is upgraded next time. (op 9-2 tchd 5-1 and 7-2)
Every Second, a half-brother to mile Polytrack Pendulum Star, has plenty of speed in his pedigree. He proved no match for the winner but could have come up against an above average sort for this grade. (op 5-1)
Mazzola, who only cost 2,000 guineas, just got the better of a three-way battle for third. (op 10-1)
Miss Hollybell did not do a lot for the form of the fillies' maiden in which she was narrowly beaten at Warwick. (op 7-2 tchd 4-1)
Abhainn(IRE), a half-brother to several winners at between 6f and 1m, showed speed to halfway. (op 20-1)

1694 SALTWELL SIGNS (S) STKS 1m 2f 46y
2:40 (2:40) (Class 6) 3-Y-O+ £1,683 (£501; £250; £125) Stalls Low

Form RPR
0-66 **1** **Cumae (USA)**[29] 1109 4-9-4 39 .... SebSanders 11 51
(J Pearce) *hld up in tch: rdn over 2f out: led and edgd lft over 1f out: rdn out* **20/1**
0-00 **2** *2* **Classic Hall (IRE)**[6] 1564 5-9-4 33 .... SimonWhitworth 3 47
(J Akehurst) *s.i.s: sn rcvrd to ld: hdd over 7f out: w ldr: led over 4f out: rdn over 2f out: hdd over 1f out: no ex wl ins fnl f* **28/1**
-050 **3** *4 ½* **Brigadore (USA)**[7] 1533 5-9-9 55 .... StephenDonohoe 4 43
(Ian Williams) *hld up in mid-div: hdwy on ins over 4f out: rdn over 2f out: one pce* **5/2**[1]
6004 **4** *½* **Bandits Pistol (NZ)**[29] 1109 8-9-9 47 .... (v) GeorgeBaker 10 42
(M Madgwick) *hld up and bhd: hdwy on ins over 2f out: sn rdn: styd on one pce fnl f* **16/1**
0/00 **5** *¾* **Old Time Dancing**[20] 1265 5-9-4 45 .... JimCrowley 7 36
(J F Panvert) *prom: led over 7f out tl over 4f out: rdn over 2f out: wknd fnl f* **11/1**
230- **6** *6* **Leprechaun's Gold (IRE)**[176] 6250 4-9-9 44 .... ChrisCatlin 8 29
(B J Llewellyn) *hld up and bhd: hdwy on ins over 3f out: sn rdn: edgd rt over 1f out: wknd ins fnl f* **17/2**
00-0 **7** *¾* **Charlie Be (IRE)**[7] 1533 3-8-6 52 .... RobertHavlin 13 27
(Mrs P N Dutfield) *dwlt: bhd: c wd st: rdn over 2f out: sme hdwy over 1f out: n.d* **25/1**
000- **8** *½* **Art Gallery**[167] 6806 4-9-9 45 .... (b) RyanMoore 12 26
(G L Moore) *stdd s: hld up in rr: rdn over 2f out: sme hdwy whn nt clr run jst over 1f out: n.d after* **7/1**[3]

1216 **9** 1 1/4 **Competitor**[24] 1210 7-9-11 51....(v) KirstyMilczarek(3) 5 29
(J Akehurst) *prom: ev ch wl over 1f out: sn rdn and wknd* **9/2**[2]

0305 **10** 2 **Persian Fox (IRE)**[47] 864 4-9-9 47.... VinceSlattery 9 20
(A G Juckes) *hld up in mid-div: rdn 2f out: no hdwy whn n.m.r jst over 1f out* **10/1**

6050 **11** 1 **Golden Spectrum (IRE)**[29] 1109 9-9-9 44....(p) AdamKirby 2 18
(R A Harris) *led early: prom: rdn over 2f out: sn wknd* **12/1**

000- **12** 1/2 **Pay Pay Pay**[181] 6591 3-8-1 48.... CatherineGannon 6 12
(P D Evans) *hld up in tch: rdn and wknd 3f out* **10/1**

0000 **13** 35 **Tiara Boom De Ay (IRE)**[15] 1369 4-9-4 41.... DaneO'Neill 14 —
(D J Wintle) *sn bhd: eased whn no ch fnl 2f* **66/1**

2m 17.42s (6.42) **Going Correction** +0.60s/f (Yiel)
WFA 3 from 4yo+ 17lb **13** Ran SP% **123.4**
Speed ratings (Par 101): **98,96,92,92,91 87,86,86,85,83 82,82,54**
CSF £487.52 TOTE £26.00: £6.60, £10.20, £1.20; EX 720.60 TRIFECTA Not won..There was no bid for the winner.
Owner S Birdseye **Bred** David M Nash & Elizabeth Nash **Trained** Newmarket, Suffolk

FOCUS
The first two appeared to show much-improved form in this poor seller with the form rated around the third.
Art Gallery Official explanation: jockey said gelding was denied a clear run
Competitor Official explanation: trainer said horse was unsuited by the good to soft ground

1695 BET365 BEST ODDS GUARANTEED ON EVERY RACE MEDIAN AUCTION MAIDEN STKS 1m 2f 46y
3:10 (3:11) (Class 5) 3-Y-O **£2,460** (£732; £365; £182) **Stalls** Low

Form RPR

33-2 **1** **Top Ticket (IRE)**[17] 1342 3-9-3 78.... RichardMullen 5 82+
(D M Simcock) *led 1f: chsd ldr: led over 2f out: rdn over 1f out: drvn out* **7/2**[3]

042- **2** 1 1/4 **Brexca (IRE)**[201] 6130 3-9-3 79.... AdamKirby 3 77
(C G Cox) *hld up in tch: rdn over 2f out: r.o one pce fnl f* **9/4**[1]

0 **3** 3/4 **Byblos**[13] 1398 3-9-3 0.... RyanMoore 9 76+
(B J Meehan) *s.i.s: hld up and bhd: rdn and hdwy over 2f out: sn swtchd rt: styd on ins fnl f* **10/1**

4 1/2 **Calamansac** 3-8-12 0.... JamesDoyle 1 70
(R M Beckett) *led after 1f: hdd over 2f out: rdn over 1f out: no ex wl ins fnl f* **33/1**

00- **5** 6 **Better In Heaven**[200] 6139 3-9-3 0.... DaneO'Neill 6 63+
(H J L Dunlop) *t.k.h in tch: rdn over 2f out: wknd over 1f out* **50/1**

0- **6** 3 3/4 **King Of Pentacles**[185] 6493 3-9-3 0.... SteveDrowne 11 55+
(H Morrison) *mid-div: rdn over 4f out: carried rt 2f out: sn wknd* **33/1**

0-6 **7** 1/2 **King's Alchemist**[14] 1379 3-9-3 0.... HayleyTurner 14 54
(M D I Usher) *mid-div: wknd 2f out: sn hung lft* **25/1**

8 1 **Burry Green** 3-8-12 0.... RichardHughes 8 47+
(R Hannon) *dwlt: swtchd wd over 3f out: nvr nr ldrs* **20/1**

244- **9** 3/4 **Celtic Dragon**[143] 7070 3-9-3 76.... JimCrowley 4 51
(Mrs A J Perrett) *t.k.h in mid-div: rdn over 2f out: sn wknd* **11/4**[2]

00- **10** 1 1/2 **Houri (IRE)**[186] 6470 3-8-12 0.... SebSanders 7 43
(R M Beckett) *a towards rr* **4/1**

11 nse **Poppy Gregg** 3-8-12 0.... FergusSweeney 13 42
(Dr J R J Naylor) *a bhd* **66/1**

00-6 **12** 3 1/2 **Mouse White**[14] 1380 3-8-10 47.... AmyScott(7) 2 40
(H Candy) *prom tl wknd wl over 2f out* **66/1**

0 **13** 26 **Little Rococoa**[36] 997 3-9-3 0.... LiamJones 12 —
(R J Price) *stdd s: sn mid-div: swtchd rt and hdwy on outside over 4f out: rdn and wknd 3f out* **100/1**

2m 18.33s (7.33) **Going Correction** +0.70s/f (Yiel) **13** Ran SP% **129.2**
Speed ratings (Par 98): **98,97,96,96,91 88,87,87,86,85 85,82,61**
CSF £12.18 TOTE £4.90: £1.80, £1.50, £3.40; EX 14.50 Trifecta £83.60 Pool: £268.62 - 2.28 winning units..
Owner Khalifa Dasmal **Bred** Kilcarn Stud **Trained** Newmarket, Suffolk

FOCUS
An ordinary maiden with the rain just starting to get into the ground. The runner-up sets the level.

1696 JOHN SMITH'S H'CAP 1m 2f 46y
3:40 (3:40) (Class 5) (0-70,73) 3-Y-O **£2,914** (£867; £433; £216) **Stalls** Low

Form RPR

0-01 **1** **Buddy Holly**[10] 1479 3-8-13 65.... PatDobbs 2 73+
(Pat Eddery) *led after 1f: hung bdly rt to stands' rail fr wl over 1f out: rdn and r.o wl* **8/1**[3]

55-3 **2** 2 1/2 **King Bathwick (IRE)**[14] 1389 3-9-1 67....(t) DaneO'Neill 3 67
(B R Millman) *hld up in tch: rdn over 2f out: swtchd rt wl over 1f out: r.o wl ins fnl f to take 2nd nr fin* **17/2**

2-05 **3** nk **Double On Red**[14] 1389 3-8-12 64.... ShaneKelly 8 63
(J M P Eustace) *stdd s: hld up towards rr: hdwy on outside 3f out: hrd rdn and r.o one pce fnl f* **16/1**

00-5 **4** hd **Hadron Collider (FR)**[20] 1272 3-9-2 68.... RichardHughes 9 68+
(R Hannon) *hld up in tch: pushed along over 3f out: n.m.r briefly and lost pl over 2f out: rallied fnl f: styng on whn swtchd rt towards fin* **25/1**

0-11 **5** 1/2 **Air Chief**[7] 1530 3-9-7 73 6ex.... JimmyQuinn 15 73+
(H J L Dunlop) *a.p: w wnr whn carried bdly rt over 1f out: rdn and one pce fnl f* **2/1**[1]

0-26 **6** 1 3/4 **Zen Factor**[8] 1527 3-9-0 66.... JimCrowley 4 63+
(J G Portman) *hld up in mid-div: nt clr run over 2f out: rdn over 1f out: styd on ins fnl f* **10/1**

000- **7** hd **Krisnando**[189] 6414 3-8-10 62.... RyanMoore 5 56
(G L Moore) *stdd s: hld up and bhd: rdn and hdwy over 2f out: eased whn btn wl ins fnl f* **16/1**

00-1 **8** 1 1/2 **Mista Rossa**[26] 1163 3-9-1 70.... TravisBlock(3) 6 61
(H Morrison) *prom: rdn over 1f out: wknd wl ins fnl f* **3/1**[2]

006- **9** 1 1/4 **Addwaitya**[186] 6469 3-8-11 63.... IanMongan 14 56+
(C F Wall) *s.i.s: bhd: sme hdwy over 1f out: hrd rdn and no imp whn nt clr run wl ins fnl f* **16/1**

5-03 **10** 8 **Spinning Ridge (IRE)**[7] 1530 3-8-13 68.... KevinGhunowa(3) 13 41
(R A Harris) *plld hrd in mid-div: hdwy over 3f out: rdn over 1f out: wknd ins fnl f* **28/1**

50-0 **11** 1 1/2 **Paddy Rielly (IRE)**[10] 1478 3-8-6 58.... CatherineGannon 7 28
(P D Evans) *s.i.s: a bhd* **20/1**

310- **12** 1 **Blandys Wood**[190] 6379 3-9-0 66.... EdwardCreighton 12 34
(M R Channon) *a bhd* **33/1**

00-0 **13** 9 **Bahamian Blue (IRE)**[25] 1193 3-8-6 58.... JamesDoyle 10 8
(H J L Dunlop) *a towards rr* **33/1**

0-25 **14** 10 **Supporting Role (IRE)**[17] 1343 3-8-6 58....(p) RichardMullen 1 —
(E S McMahon) *prom tl rdn and wknd over 2f out* **20/1**

500- **15** 13 **Beauchamp Warrior**[139] 7114 3-8-8 63.... WilliamBuick(3) 11 —
(G A Butler) *led 1f: chsd ldr tl wknd over 2f out* **14/1**

2m 19.46s (8.46) **Going Correction** +0.80s/f (Soft) **15** Ran SP% **136.1**
Speed ratings (Par 98): **98,96,95,95,95 93,93,92,91,85 83,83,75,67,57**
CSF £77.10 CT £1109.15 TOTE £9.20: £3.50, £3.60, £6.40; EX 72.60 TRIFECTA Not won..
Owner Hayman, Pearson, Phillips & McGuinness **Bred** R J & S A Carter **Trained** Nether Winchendon, Bucks

FOCUS
The rain had really got into the ground by now. Buddy Holly set a trend for the remainder of the meeting by inadvertantly ending up on the stands' side in this ordinary handicap. The form looks sound through the runner-up and fourth.
Bahamian Blue(IRE) Official explanation: trainer's rep said that gelding was unsuited by the soft ground

1697 HSBC FILLIES' H'CAP 1m 3f 144y
4:10 (4:11) (Class 5) (0-75,69) 4-Y-O+ **£2,914** (£867; £433; £216) **Stalls** Low

Form RPR

-325 **1** **Rose Row**[26] 1165 4-8-9 60.... HayleyTurner 4 72
(Mrs Mary Hambro) *t.k.h in tch: led on bit over 2f out: rdn over 1f out: drvn out* **15/2**

340- **2** 1 1/2 **Spring Dream (IRE)**[32] 2887 5-9-1 65.... RichardHughes 5 75
(A King) *a.p: wnt 2nd 5f out: chal over 2f out: rdn and nt qckn ins fnl f* **6/1**[3]

-613 **3** 6 **Friends Hope**[18] 1305 7-9-1 65.... StephenDonohoe 7 65
(P A Blockley) *hld up in rr: hdwy on ins over 3f out: ev ch 2f out: sn rdn: btn over 1f out* **7/1**

051- **4** 1 3/4 **Gamesters Lady**[124] 7249 5-9-2 66.... LiamJones 1 64
(W M Brisbourne) *led: rdn and hdd over 2f out: sn wknd: hung lft 1f out* **16/1**

4113 **5** 1 3/4 **Naughty Thoughts (IRE)**[28] 1127 4-8-11 62.... RichardKingscote 8 57
(Tom Dascombe) *t.k.h: short-lived effrt 3f out* **11/10**[1]

00-2 **6** 4 1/2 **Uig**[13] 1406 7-9-0 69.... HaddenFrost(5) 3 57
(H S Howe) *chsd ldr to 5f out: wknd 3f out* **9/1**

0-12 **7** 4 **Snake Skin**[28] 1127 5-8-13 63.... JimCrowley 6 44
(J Gallagher) *hld up towards rr: rdn 3f out: sn struggling* **5/1**[2]

2m 41.5s (10.90) **Going Correction** +0.90s/f (Soft)
WFA 4 from 5yo+ 1lb **7** Ran SP% **118.7**
Speed ratings (Par 100): **99,98,94,92,91 88,86**
CSF £53.52 CT £334.28 TOTE £9.00: £4.60, £2.90; EX 73.60 Trifecta £436.00 Part won. Pool: £614.10 - 0.89 winning units..
Owner Richard Hambro **Bred** Cotswold Stud **Trained** Bourton-on-the-Hill, Gloucs

FOCUS
A steadily-run typically modest fillies' handicap rated through the runner-up to her old form.
Naughty Thoughts(IRE) Official explanation: jockey said filly ran too free
Uig Official explanation: jockey said mare had no more to give

1698 EUROPEAN BREEDERS' FUND LANSDOWN FILLIES' STKS (LISTED RACE) (F&M) 5f 11y
4:40 (4:40) (Class 1) 3-Y-O+
£14,760 (£5,595; £2,800; £1,396; £699; £351) **Stalls** Centre

Form RPR

400- **1** **Morinqua (IRE)**[219] 5666 4-9-0 94.... TPQueally 9 101
(J G Given) *mde all: c to stands' rail over 2f out: drvn out fnl f* **8/1**[3]

20-3 **2** 2 1/2 **Dark Missile**[12] 1420 5-9-0 107.... WilliamBuick 12 92
(A M Balding) *hld up in mid-div: hdwy over 2f out: rdn and edgd lft over 1f out: chsd wnr ins fnl f: no imp* **4/5**[1]

600- **3** 1 **Sweet Afton (IRE)**[262] 4373 5-9-0 80.... FergusSweeney 7 88
(M S Saunders) *mid-div: pushed along over 2f out: rdn and hdwy over 1f out: kpt on one pce ins fnl f* **66/1**

4266 **4** 1 1/2 **Ripples Maid**[38] 959 5-9-4 97.... RoystonFfrench 10 87
(J A Geake) *prom: rdn whn n.m.r over 1f out: one pce fnl f* **9/2**[2]

110- **5** 3/4 **Edge Of Gold**[201] 6128 3-8-4 79.... CatherineGannon 2 76
(B Palling) *prom: pushed along and lost pl over 2f out: rdn over 1f out: kpt on ins fnl f* **25/1**

250- **6** 3/4 **Day By Day**[193] 6300 4-9-0 88....(b) RyanMoore 4 77
(B J Meehan) *chsd wnr tl rdn over 1f out: wknd wl ins fnl f* **14/1**

0-24 **7** 2 **Tilly's Dream**[14] 1386 5-9-0 70.... AdamKirby 13 70
(G C Bravery) *hld up and bhd: rdn over 1f out: no rspnse* **20/1**

10- **8** 2 **Masada (IRE)**[179] 6619 3-8-4 89.... NickyMackay 1 59
(B J Meehan) *s.i.s: a in rr* **20/1**

400- **9** 1/2 **Reel Gift**[199] 6167 3-8-4 90.... RichardSmith 6 57
(R Hannon) *a in rr* **25/1**

400- **10** nk **Loch Jipp (USA)**[199] 6182 3-8-4 100.... JimmyQuinn 3 56
(J S Wainwright) *prom tl wknd over 2f out* **12/1**

64.00 secs (1.50) **Going Correction** +0.60s/f (Yiel)
WFA 3 from 4yo+ 10lb **10** Ran SP% **117.9**
Speed ratings (Par 108): **112,108,106,104,102 101,98,95,94,93**
CSF £14.12 TOTE £8.80: £2.30, £1.10, £13.30; EX 24.10 Trifecta £335.10 Pool: £556.95 - 1.18 winning units..
Owner J G Given **Bred** Corrin Stud **Trained** Willoughton, Lincs

FOCUS
Several of the runners in this Listed event really want 6f but the ground did put something of an emphasis on stamina. The form is somewhat guessy.

NOTEBOOK
Morinqua(IRE), who has been working nicely at home, did not mind the deteriorating conditions having finished second in heavy ground at Chester last July. Always finding enough after bagging the favoured stands' rail, she does seem at her best when able to dominate. The Group 2 Temple Stakes which is now run at Haydock could be on the agenda. (op 6-1)
Dark Missile had the soft ground to help on what was only her second run over the minimum distance. She had to be content to play second fiddle and confirmed that 6f is her trip. (op 8-11 tchd 4-6 and 5-6 tchd 10-11 in places)
Sweet Afton(IRE) ◆, who is in-foal to Cadeaux Genereux, ran a cracker despite having never previously run on ground worse than good even when she was trained in Ireland. She looks like one of those who is going to do well with the prospect of motherhood around the corner. Official explanation: vet said mare had bled from the nose
Ripples Maid, who may be in-foal to Bahamian Bounty, was rather tightened up by Dark Missile and just like the second she really needs 6f. (op 13-2 tchd 4-1)
Edge Of Gold did not mind the soft ground but is yet another who is more effective over another furlong.

Day By Day was by no means disgraced on ground that seemed to have gone against her. (op 11-1)

1699 LINDLEY CATERING H'CAP 5f 11y
5:10 (5:10) (Class 5) (0-70,70) 3-Y-O **£2,914** (£867; £433; £216) **Stalls** Centre

Form RPR

-000 **1** **Pennyspider (IRE)**[7] 1529 3-8-1 **56** oh8 WilliamBuick(3) 8 57
(M S Saunders) *mde all: rdn 1f out: drvn out* **20/1**

004- **2** *1/2* **Flying Indian**[223] 5529 3-8-10 **62** LPKeniry 9 62
(A M Balding) *a chsng wnr: rdn jst over 1f out: ev ch ins fnl f: kpt on* **5/1**[3]

040- **3** *1* **Saranome (IRE)**[174] 6721 3-9-4 **70** SteveDrowne 1 66
(R Charlton) *sn outpcd: hdwy over 1f out: kpt on same pce fnl f* **4/1**[2]

03-0 **4** *nk* **Solemn**[18] 1311 3-9-0 **66** DaneO'Neill 3 61
(J M Bradley) *prom: outpcd over 2f out: rallied u.p over 1f out: kpt on same pce fnl f* **14/1**

54-0 **5** *8* **Kalligal**[19] 1277 3-9-4 **70** RobertHavlin 2 36
(R Ingram) *prom: rdn over 1f out: wknd fnl f* **6/1**

00-0 **6** *2* **Sandy Par**[27] 1155 3-8-8 **60** PaulFitzsimons 4 19
(J M Bradley) *hld up: hdwy over 2f out: rdn and wknd wl over 1f out* **20/1**

332- **7** *1 1/2* **Capefly**[173] 6729 3-9-4 **70** RyanMoore 7 24
(P F I Cole) *outpcd* **15/8**[1]

0-64 **8** *18* **Penrice Castle**[12] 1414 3-8-11 **63** RichardHughes 5 —
(R Hannon) *hld up: hdwy over 2f out: wknd wl over 1f out: eased whn no ch ins fnl f* **5/1**[3]

66.46 secs (3.96) **Going Correction** +0.70s/f (Yiel) **8** Ran SP% **118.6**
Speed ratings (Par 98): **96,95,93,93,80 77,74,45**
CSF £120.44 CT £491.54 TOTE £21.20: £2.50, £2.30, £1.60; EX 131.80 Trifecta £335.30 Part won. Pool: £472.29 - 0.39 winning units. Place 6 £358.18, £162.43.
Owner Chris Scott **Bred** Tally-Ho Stud **Trained** Green Ore, Somerset
■ Stewards' Enquiry : William Buick two-day ban: used whip with excessive frequency (May 13-14)

FOCUS
There was only one previous winner in this minor sprint handicap which was run on the worst ground on the card. The form looks pretty ordinary rated around the third and fourth.
Capefly Official explanation: trainer's rep said filly was unsuited by the soft ground
Penrice Castle Official explanation: jockey said filly had no more to give
T/Jkpt: Not won. T/Plt: £1,082.30 to a £1 stake. Pool: £61,014.47. 41.15 winning tickets. T/Qpdt: £146.10 to a £1 stake. Pool: £4,108.75. 20.80 winning tickets. KH

1674 SOUTHWELL (L-H)
Tuesday, April 29

OFFICIAL GOING: Standard
Wind: Virtually nil Weather: Dry - sunny periods

1700 SOUTHWELL RACECOURSE FOR CONFERENCES CLAIMING STKS 1m (F)
2:30 (2:30) (Class 6) 4-Y-0+ **£1,774** (£523; £262) **Stalls** Low

Form RPR

-111 **1** **Yakimov (USA)**[48] 851 9-9-7 85 JamieMoriarty(3) 4 89+
(Ollie Pears) *trckd ldrs: effrt on bit and nt clr run over 1f out: swtchd outside and qcknd to ld jst ins fnl f: sn clr* **2/5**[1]

622- **2** *5* **Little Jimbob**[168] 5838 7-9-7 64 PaulHanagan 2 67
(R A Fahey) *led: rdn over 2f out: hdd over 1f out: drvn and kpt on ins fnl f: no ch w wnr* **4/1**[2]

0-21 **3** *3* **Rambling Socks**[38] 972 5-7-13 52 (p) DuranFentiman(3) 7 41
(S R Bowring) *cl up: rdn 2f out: led over 1f out: drvn and hdd jst ins fnl f: one pce* **9/1**[3]

40/0 **4** *4 1/2* **Apres Ski (IRE)**[11] 1449 5-9-7 62 MickyFenton 3 50
(J F Coupland) *dwlt: plld hrd and sn prom: effrt to chal 2f out and ev ch tl rdn: edgd lft and wknd ent fnl f* **16/1**

0140 **5** *1/2* **Hi Spec (IRE)**[18] 1313 5-8-4 46 (p) GregFairley 1 32
(Miss M E Rowland) *dwlt: sn chsng ldrs: effrt on inner and ev ch 2f out: sn rdn and wknd over 1f out* **33/1**

050 **6** *2 1/2* **Art Of Being (IRE)**[56] 788 4-8-9 36 (p) MarkCoumbe(7) 6 38
(M C Chapman) *cl up: rdn along over 2f out: sn drvn and wknd* **100/1**

0050 **7** *12* **Ticking**[9] 1504 5-8-6 35 AshleyMorgan(7) 9 7
(T Keddy) *a in rr: bhd fnl 3f* **80/1**

1m 44.35s (0.65) **Going Correction** +0.125s/f (Slow) **7** Ran SP% **112.5**
Speed ratings (Par 101): **101,96,93,88,88 85,73**
CSF £2.23 TOTE £1.50: £1.10, £1.90; EX 2.40.
Owner Diamond Racing Ltd **Bred** Jane & Jeff Wooder **Trained** Norton, N Yorks

FOCUS
An ordinary claimer run in a time 0.92 seconds slower than the following maiden and the proximity of the sixth limits the form.
Ticking Official explanation: vet said gelding finished lame

1701 BOOK YOUR TICKETS ONLINE MAIDEN STKS 1m (F)
3:00 (3:01) (Class 5) 3-Y-0+ **£2,456** (£725; £362) **Stalls** Low

Form RPR

6-4 **1** **Master Spy**[14] 1379 3-9-0 0 JimmyFortune 11 91+
(J H M Gosden) *prom: led wl over 2f out: clr over 1f out: easily* **3/1**[2]

2 *10* **Deep River Bay (USA)** 4-10-0 0 AdrianMcCarthy 1 67
(P W Chapple-Hyam) *s.i.s: hdwy on inner 1/2-way: rdn to chse ldng pair wl over 2f out: kpt on u.p appr fnl f: no ch w wnr* **20/1**

3 *4 1/2* **Flying Squad (UAE)**[20] 4-9-7 0 JWStevenson(7) 9 57
(D J Wintle) *s.i.s: hdwy over 3f out: rdn wl over 1f out: kpt on ins fnl f: nrst fin* **16/1**

30- **4** *2* **Dubai Meydan (IRE)**[192] 6333 3-9-0 0 DarryllHolland 3 49
(Miss Gay Kelleway) *cl up: led 1/2-way: rdn and hdd wl over 2f out: drvn wl over 1f out and sn wknd* **11/8**[1]

0 **5** *5* **Pick Of The Day (IRE)**[14] 1380 3-9-0 0 J-PGuillambert 5 37
(J G Given) *chsd ldrs: rdn along 3f out: grad wknd* **33/1**

- **6** *7* **Reprieved** 3-8-7 0 MarkCoumbe(7) 10 21
(M C Chapman) *s.i.s: a towards rr* **66/1**

0-4 **7** *8* **St Michael's Mount**[13] 1410 3-9-0 0 DaleGibson 8 3
(M P Tregoning) *in tch: rdn along over 3f out: sn wknd* **12/1**

0 **8** *9* **Tallest Peak (USA)**[13] 1410 3-8-11 0 JerryO'Dwyer(3) 4 —
(M G Quinlan) *a in rr* **66/1**

9 *shd* **Edgbaston (IRE)** 3-9-0 0 GregFairley 2 —
(M Johnston) *sn outpcd and a wl bhd* **8/1**

0 **10** *6* **Valdemar Victory**[28] 1125 4-10-0 0 (v[1]) SilvestreDeSousa 6 —
(D Nicholls) *led: rdn along and hdd 1/2-way: sn wknd* **40/1**

0- **11** *44* **Music In Exile (USA)**[178] 6648 3-8-9 0 NCallan 7 —
(B W Hills) *chsd ldrs: rdn along over 3f out: sn wknd and eased fnl 2f* **13/2**[3]

1m 43.43s (-0.27) **Going Correction** +0.125s/f (Slow)
WFA 3 from 4yo 14lb **11** Ran SP% **118.3**
Speed ratings (Par 103): **106,96,91,89,84 77,69,60,60,54 10**
CSF £66.98 TOTE £4.00: £1.40, £3.00, £4.90; EX 55.90.
Owner H R H Princess Haya Of Jordan **Bred** Darley **Trained** Newmarket, Suffolk

FOCUS
This looked an interesting maiden for the track, but it turned out less competitive as one might have expected. The pace was strong and the winning time was 0.92 seconds quicker than the opening claimer but the form is not easy to assess at this stage.
Edgbaston(IRE) Official explanation: jockey said colt never travelled
Music In Exile(USA) Official explanation: jockey said filly moved poorly

1702 BOOK YOUR HOSPITALITY PACKAGES (S) STKS 1m 4f (F)
3:30 (3:30) (Class 6) 4-Y-0+ **£1,774** (£523; £262) **Stalls** Low

Form RPR

0342 **1** **Key Partners (IRE)**[67] 658 7-8-6 52 SophieDoyle(7) 7 63
(P A Blockley) *hld up in rr: stdy hdwy 4f out: led wl over 1f out: rdn and edgd lft ins fnl f: kpt on* **10/3**[2]

2020 **2** *1 1/4* **Kanisorn (SWE)**[25] 1184 6-9-5 65 (bt) NCallan 4 67
(Mrs R A Carr) *trckd ldng pair: cl up over 4f out: rdn over 3f out: drvn 2f out: rallied u.p ins fnl f: no ex towards fin* **10/11**[1]

500- **3** *1 3/4* **Annibale Caro**[146] 6558 6-8-6 57 DeanHeslop(7) 6 58
(Grant Tuer) *trckd ldrs: hdwy to ld over 4f out: rdn along 3f out: drvn and hdd wl over 1f out: kpt on same pce ins fnl f* **9/1**

-300 **4** *19* **Veneer (IRE)**[34] 1031 6-8-13 42 J-PGuillambert 5 28
(Mrs N S Evans) *chsd ldr: cl up 1/2-way: rdn along over 4f out and kpt on same pce fnl 3f* **40/1**

4102 **5** *2 1/2* **Ming Vase**[21] 1262 6-9-5 48 MickyFenton 1 30
(P T Midgley) *led: rdn along 5f out: sn hdd & wknd over 3f out* **11/2**[3]

6 *18* **Pur Star (FR)**[38] 5-8-10 0 JerryO'Dwyer(3) 2 —
(N B King) *in tch: rdn along over 5f out and sn wknd* **22/1**

05/0 **7** *1/2* **Countrywide Luck**[13] 1405 7-8-10 65 RussellKennemore(3) 3 —
(B N Pollock) *chsd ldrs: rdn along 5f out and sn wknd* **20/1**

2m 42.89s (1.89) **Going Correction** +0.125s/f (Slow) **7** Ran SP% **112.4**
Speed ratings (Par 101): **98,97,96,83,81 69,69**
CSF £6.48 TOTE £3.10: £1.90, £1.10; EX 10.00.The winner was bought in for 4,000gns. Kanisorn was claimed by M P Hammond for £5,000.
Owner John Wardle **Bred** Michael Munnelly **Trained** Lambourn, Berks

FOCUS
A standard seller rated through the winner with the third to last year's form.

1703 SPONSOR A RACE AT SOUTHWELL H'CAP 6f (F)
4:00 (4:01) (Class 5) (0-70,70) 4-Y-0+ **£2,593** (£765; £383) **Stalls** Low

Form RPR

0-40 **1** **Varadouro (BRZ)**[17] 1327 6-9-2 **68** SilvestreDeSousa 9 87+
(D Nicholls) *trckd ldrs: hdwy to ld 2f out: shkn up and qcknd clr appr fnl f: eased towards fin* **5/1**[2]

2325 **2** *3 3/4* **Cape Of Storms**[10] 1491 5-8-10 **62** (b) PaulMulrennan 5 66
(R Brotherton) *wnt lft s: sn prom: effrt and ev ch 2f out: sn rdn: drvn appr fnl f and kpt on same pce* **15/2**[3]

3330 **3** *1/2* **Owed**[17] 1338 6-8-5 **57** (tp) PaulHanagan 8 59
(R Bastiman) *cl up: rdn and ev ch 2f out: drvn and one pce appr fnl f* **9/1**

5640 **4** *shd* **Cool Sands (IRE)**[11] 1455 6-8-6 **61** (v) TolleyDean(3) 1 63
(D Shaw) *in tch: hdwy on inner over 2f out: rdn wl over 1f out: drvn and one pce ins fnl f* **10/1**

1500 **5** *1 3/4* **Music Box Express**[10] 1491 4-8-4 **63** (t) MatthewDavies(7) 6 59
(George Baker) *led: rdn along 3f out: hdd 2f out and grad wknd* **12/1**

231- **6** *3 1/4* **Cape Cobra**[193] 6309 4-9-0 **66** JimmyFortune 7 52
(J H M Gosden) *s.i.s and bhd: rdn along and sme hdwy 3f out: no imp fnl 2f* **15/8**[1]

6035 **7** *shd* **Mind Alert**[27] 1154 7-8-7 **59** (v) AndrewElliott 4 45
(D Shaw) *hmpd s: rr and n.m.r bnd over 4f out: nvr a factor* **20/1**

5-02 **8** *4 1/2* **Soto**[10] 1485 5-8-11 **63** DaleGibson 2 34
(M W Easterby) *chsd ldrs on inner: rdn along wl over 2f out and sn wknd* **17/2**

3-43 **9** *6* **The Fisio**[18] 1312 8-8-11 **63** (v) PaulEddery 3 15
(G D Blake) *wnt rt s: sn rdn along and outpcd: a in rr* **16/1**

146- **10** *26* **Doctor's Cave**[302] 3149 6-9-4 **70** (b) NCallan 10 —
(K O Cunningham-Brown) *racd wd: a in rr* **10/1**

1m 16.19s (-0.31) **Going Correction** +0.125s/f (Slow) **10** Ran SP% **120.3**
Speed ratings (Par 103): **107,102,101,101,98 94,94,88,80,45**
CSF £43.80 CT £335.00 TOTE £5.90: £2.20, £2.60, £2.60; EX 43.30.
Owner Clarke & Harlow Partnership **Bred** Haras Valente **Trained** Sessay, N Yorks

FOCUS
A modest sprint handicap but the time was good and the form looks solid rated around the placed horses.
Cape Cobra Official explanation: jockey said gelding hung left
Mind Alert Official explanation: jockey said, regarding running and riding, that his orders were to jump out and get a position in behind the leaders, keep the gelding out of the kick-back and not to make a move until 1 1/2f out. Having missed the break, and unable to get in behind leaders he manoeuvred to the outside in the straight and made an effort from 1 1/2f out to the line.
Doctor's Cave Official explanation: jockey said gelding never travelled

1704 SOUTHWELL-RACECOURSE.CO.UK H'CAP 1m 3f (F)
4:30 (4:30) (Class 5) (0-70,70) 4-Y-0+ **£2,593** (£765; £383) **Stalls** Low

Form RPR

3-45 **1** **The King And I (IRE)**[64] 701 4-9-4 **70** (b) NCallan 2 81
(Miss E C Lavelle) *trckd ldng pair: smooth hdwy 2f out: shkn up to ld appr fnl f: pushed out* **15/8**[1]

4120 **2** *1 3/4* **Mid Valley**[41] 934 5-7-11 **56** oh3 DavidProbert(7) 3 63
(J R Jenkins) *trckd ldrs: hdwy to ld 2f out: sn rdn and hdd appr 1f out: edgd lft and one pce ins fnl f* **9/4**[2]

4320 **3** *10* **Starcross Maid**[25] 1184 6-8-1 **56** oh1 DuranFentiman(3) 4 46
(J F Coupland) *hld up in rr: hdwy over 3f out: rdn 2f out: sn one pce* **7/1**

325 **4** *2 1/4* **Kingoftheswingers (IRE)**[58] 695 4-8-4 **56** oh4 GregFairley 1 42
(K J Burke) *led: rdn along and hdd 3f out: sn drvn and wknd* **9/1**

00-3 **5** *1 3/4* **Dark Charm (FR)**[15] 1369 9-9-0 **66** (p) PaulHanagan 5 49
(R A Fahey) *trckd ldr: cl up 1/2-way: led 3f out: rdn and hdd 2f out: sn wknd* **7/2**[3]

2m 29.95s (1.95) **Going Correction** +0.125s/f (Slow) **5** Ran SP% **110.3**
Speed ratings (Par 103): **97,95,88,86,85**
CSF £6.41 TOTE £2.80: £1.70, £1.60; EX 6.50.
Owner The Villains **Bred** Lisieux Stud **Trained** Wildhern, Hants

FOCUS
An uncompetitive handicap in which the front two finished clear and little solid behind.

1705 SOUTHWELL GOLF CLUB APPRENTICE H'CAP 7f (F)
5:00 (5:00) (Class 6) (0-60,57) 4-Y-0+ **£1,774** (£523; £262) Stalls Low

Form RPR
0513 **1** **Welcome Releaf**[11] 1455 5-9-0 **55**........................ MarkCoumbe(3) 8 63
(P Leech) *towards rr: rdn along and outpcd 3f out: hdwy wl over 1f out: styd on u.p ins fnl f to ld fnl 50yds* **2/1**[1]
536- **2** ¾ **Scuba (IRE)**[220] 5643 6-8-12 **57**........................(b) RyanClark(7) 6 63
(H Morrison) *chsd ldrs: hdwy to ld wl over 1f out: sn rdn: drvn ins fnl f: hdd and no ex fnl 50yds* **4/1**[2]
-420 **3** ¾ **Al Rayanah**[4] 1606 5-8-13 **54**........................ PatrickDonaghy(3) 1 58
(G Prodromou) *dwlt and rr: hdwy over 2f out: sn rdn and styd on u.p ins fnl f: nrst fin* **5/1**[3]
0006 **4** 2 **Pajada**[20] 1269 4-8-2 **45**........................(be[1]) BillyCray(5) 9 44
(M D I Usher) *prom: led wl over 2f out: sn rdn and hdd wl over 1f out: hung bdly lft and wknd ent fnl f* **14/1**
5000 **5** ¾ **Copper King**[19] 1280 4-8-13 **54**........................ SophieDoyle(3) 3 51
(Miss Tor Sturgis) *towards rr: rdn along wl over 2f out: styd on u.p appr fnl f: nt rch ldrs* **5/1**[3]
6005 **6** 2 **Jabraan (USA)**[47] 871 6-8-2 **45**........................ DeanHeslop(5) 7 37
(Mrs R A Carr) *cl up: led 1/2-way: sn rdn and hdd wl over 2f out: grad wknd* **22/1**
0004 **7** 9 **Cadogen Square**[48] 856 6-8-4 **45**........................(b) DanielleMcCreery(3) 2 12
(Mrs R A Carr) *led to 1/2-way: rdn along and cl up tl drvn 2f out and sn wknd* **33/1**
4420 **8** 14 **Local Poet**[49] 844 7-8-9 **52**........................(b) BMcHugh(5) 4 —
(Ollie Pears) *chsd ldrs: rdn along over 3f out and sn wknd* **7/1**
0-00 **9** 2 **Giovanni D'Oro (IRE)**[21] 1262 4-8-6 **49**........................(b) SimonPearce(5) 5 —
(Miss M E Rowland) *a bhd* **25/1**

1m 31.4s (1.10) **Going Correction** +0.125s/f (Slow) **9** Ran SP% **117.0**
Speed ratings (Par 101): **98,97,96,94,93 90,80,64,62**
CSF £9.87 CT £35.19 TOTE £2.50: £1.40, £1.20, £2.20; EX 11.70 Place 6 £16.58, Place 5 £15.36.
Owner Russell Reed & Danny Berry **Bred** Mrs H M Shaw **Trained** Newmarket, Suffolk

FOCUS
A moderate handicap restricted to apprentices who had not ridden more than 50 winners. The winner is rated a slight improver with the runner-up to his mark.
T/Plt: £71.00 to a £1 stake. Pool: £39,957.16. 410.80 winning tickets. T/Qpdt: £13.90 to a £1 stake. Pool: £2,327.52. 123.70 winning tickets. JR

1634 WOLVERHAMPTON (A.W) (L-H)
Tuesday, April 29

OFFICIAL GOING: Standard
Wind: Light against Weather: Raining

1706 SPONSOR A RACE BY CALLING 01902 390009 H'CAP 5f 20y(P)
6:35 (6:36) (Class 6) (0-55,55) 4-Y-0+ **£2,047** (£604; £302) Stalls Low

Form RPR
2415 **1** **Now You See Me**[34] 1028 4-8-11 **52**........................ RobertWinston 4 64+
(K McAuliffe) *mid-div: hung rt fr 1/2-way: nt clr run over 1f out: r.o wl ins fnl f to ld nr fin* **4/1**[1]
4515 **2** nk **Wibbadune (IRE)**[34] 1021 4-8-6 **50**........................ TolleyDean(3) 11 58
(D Shaw) *prom: pushed along 1/2-way: rdn to ld and edgd lft ins fnl f: hdd nr fin* **20/1**
3242 **3** ½ **Time Share (IRE)**[46] 883 4-8-1 **47**........................ KellyHarrison(5) 9 53
(M Wigham) *s.i.s: hld up: hdwy over 1f out: edgd lft: r.o* **8/1**
3220 **4** ½ **Bentley**[14] 1378 4-9-0 **55**........................(v) DeanMcKeown 12 59
(D Shaw) *led 1f: chsd ldr: rdn over 1f out: led ins fnl f: sn hdd and edgd lft: styd on same pce* **5/1**[3]
3330 **5** 1 **Wicked Uncle**[3] 1634 9-8-9 **55**........................(v) JamieJones(5) 5 56
(S Gollings) *s.i.s: sn pushed along in rr: hdwy and swtchd lft over 1f out: rdn and ev ch ins fnl f: no ex* **4/1**[1]
2423 **6** ¾ **Twinned (IRE)**[34] 1028 5-8-12 **53**........................ FergalLynch 10 51
(Mike Murphy) *chsd ldrs: rdn over 1f out: styd on same pce ins fnl f* **9/2**[2]
4410 **7** 1¼ **Taboor (IRE)**[25] 1185 10-8-9 **53**........................(p) KirstyMilczarek(3) 8 47
(R M H Cowell) *hld up: rdn over 1f out: nvr trbld ldrs* **8/1**
000- **8** 1¾ **Clipper Hoy**[311] 2879 6-8-7 **55**........................ KylieManser(7) 1 42
(Mrs H Sweeting) *led 4f out: rdn and edgd rt over 1f out: hdd & wknd ins fnl f* **33/1**
540- **9** 1¼ **Calypso King**[131] 7206 5-9-0 **55**........................ PatrickMathers 3 38
(Peter Grayson) *s.i.s: sn chsng ldrs: rdn over 1f out: wknd ins fnl f* **8/1**

62.35 secs (0.05) **Going Correction** +0.075s/f (Slow) **9** Ran SP% **115.9**
Speed ratings (Par 101): **102,101,100,99,98 97,95,92,90**
CSF £83.20 CT £617.17 TOTE £4.00: £2.10, £3.80, £3.10; EX 133.60.
Owner K W J McAuliffe **Bred** Gainsborough Stud Management Ltd **Trained** Fernham, Oxon

FOCUS
A routine sprint handicap for the track full of horses that regularly beat each other. They went a decent gallop, but the first three all came from off the pace and the form looks straightforward and solid.
Taboor(IRE) Official explanation: jockey said gelding never travelled
Clipper Hoy Official explanation: vet said gelding returned lame

1707 STAY AT THE WOLVERHAMPTON HOLIDAY INN H'CAP 5f 20y(P)
7:05 (7:05) (Class 4) (0-85,83) 3-Y-0 **£4,209** (£1,252; £625; £312) Stalls Low

Form RPR
-121 **1** **Ten Down**[52] 835 3-9-2 **78**........................ FergalLynch 7 85
(Miss Gay Kelleway) *w ldr tl led wl over 3f out: rdn clr over 1f out: hung rt ins fnl f: all out* **5/1**[3]
200- **2** shd **Piscean (USA)**[171] 6756 3-9-1 **77**........................ MickyFenton 8 84
(T Keddy) *sn outpcd: racd wd: hdwy 1/2-way: rdn over 1f out: r.o wl* **15/2**
3-32 **3** 2¾ **The Game**[82] 470 3-9-7 **83**........................ PatCosgrave 4 80
(J R Boyle) *wnt lft s: prom: rdn over 1f out: styd on same pce fnl f* **9/2**[2]
621- **4** 1½ **Another Socket**[176] 6692 3-8-13 **75**........................ GrahamGibbons 1 66
(E S McMahon) *chsd ldrs: rdn over 1f out: wknd ins fnl f* **10/1**
03-0 **5** nk **Mister Fips (IRE)**[13] 1404 3-9-4 **83**........................ KirstyMilczarek(3) 6 73
(Jane Chapple-Hyam) *led: hdd wl over 3f out: rdn and n.m.r 1/2-way: sn edgd rt: styd on same pce appr fnl f* **9/1**
0-03 **6** ¾ **Our Acquaintance**[19] 1277 3-8-9 **71**........................ MartinDwyer 9 59
(W R Muir) *mid-div: sn pushed along: hdwy and hmpd 1/2-way: rdn and hung lft fr over 1f out: no ex fnl f* **9/1**
-001 **7** 1¼ **Storey Hill (USA)**[19] 1284 3-9-1 **77**........................ DeanMcKeown 2 60
(D Shaw) *chsd ldrs: edgd rt 1/2-way: rdn over 1f out: wknd ins fnl f* **3/1**[1]
4031 **8** 1¾ **Ben**[26] 1162 3-8-3 **65**........................(v) DavidKinsella 5 42
(P G Murphy) *hld up: rdn over 1f out: n.d* **22/1**
31-1 **9** 1¾ **Joss Stick**[12] 1414 3-8-9 **71**........................(p) SebSanders 3 41
(P J Makin) *hmpd s: sn outpcd: rdn over 1f out: wknd fnl f* **13/2**

61.98 secs (-0.32) **Going Correction** +0.075s/f (Slow) **9** Ran SP% **118.4**
Speed ratings (Par 100): **105,104,100,98,97 96,94,91,88**
CSF £43.30 CT £183.86 TOTE £6.50: £1.50, £3.10, £1.30; EX 60.70.
Owner A G MacLennan **Bred** Baydon House Stud **Trained** Exning, Suffolk

FOCUS
This looked quite a decent three-year-old sprint and the winning time was 0.37 seconds faster than the older sprinters in the previous contest. The form looks reliable with the front two clear of the third and fourth. The field fanned right out across the track after turning in, but nothing decided to stick tight to the inside rail.
Mister Fips(IRE) Official explanation: jockey said colt hung right final bend

1708 WOLVERHAMPTON-RACECOURSE.CO.UK H'CAP 7f 32y(P)
7:35 (7:35) (Class 5) (0-75,78) 4-Y-0+ **£2,590** (£770; £385; £192) Stalls High

Form RPR
0511 **1** **Xpres Maite**[5] 1590 5-9-10 **78** 6ex........................(v) PhillipMakin 2 96
(S R Bowring) *led: hdd 6f out: trckd ldr tl led over 2f out: rdn clr over 1f out: eased ins fnl f* **10/11**[1]
321- **2** 9 **Flying Bantam (IRE)**[321] 2550 7-9-2 **70**........................ PaulHanagan 1 64
(R A Fahey) *prom: rdn to chse wnr over 2f out: wknd over 1f out* **6/1**[3]
-205 **3** 1¼ **Tanforan**[68] 395 6-8-9 **63**........................ RobertWinston 5 53
(B P J Baugh) *hld up: effrt over 2f out: wknd over 1f out* **8/1**
-060 **4** 3½ **H Harrison (IRE)**[4] 1604 8-8-13 **67**........................ AndrewElliott 3 48
(I W McInnes) *chsd wnr tl led 6f out: rdn and hdd over 2f out: wknd over 1f out* **14/1**
0055 **5** shd **Parkview Love (USA)**[4] 1604 7-8-8 **62**........................(v) DeanMcKeown 4 43
(D Shaw) *hld up: rdn 1/2-way: wknd over 2f out* **9/2**[2]
5-04 **6** 1¼ **Timber Treasure (USA)**[34] 1030 4-9-0 **68**........................ SebSanders 6 45
(Paul Green) *chsd ldrs: rdn over 2f out: wknd over 1f out* **10/1**

1m 28.34s (-1.26) **Going Correction** +0.075s/f (Slow) **6** Ran SP% **111.7**
Speed ratings (Par 103): **110,99,98,94,94 92**
CSF £6.80 TOTE £2.00: £1.10, £2.50; EX 5.50.
Owner Charterhouse Holdings Plc **Bred** S R Bowring **Trained** Edwinstowe, Notts

FOCUS
Two separate races here - the winner was in one and the rest in the other - and the winning time was smart, 3.76 seconds quicker than the following fillies' maiden. There is some doubt over the opposition though.

1709 HOTEL & CONFERENCING AT WOLVERHAMPTON MEDIAN AUCTION MAIDEN FILLIES' STKS 7f 32y(P)
8:05 (8:05) (Class 6) 3-4-Y-0 **£2,047** (£604; £302) Stalls High

Form RPR
0-00 **1** **Bahamian Princess**[18] 1311 3-8-9 46........................ RussellKennemore(3) 3 56
(R Hollinshead) *hld up: rdn over 2f out: hdwy u.p to ld over 1f out: edgd lft ins fnl f: styd on* **33/1**
52 **2** 1¼ **Bahamian Bliss**[46] 885 3-8-9 0........................ KirstyMilczarek(3) 1 53
(J A R Toller) *chsd ldrs: rdn and hung lft over 1f out: sn ev ch: styng on same pce whn nt clr run ins fnl f* **7/2**[3]
00-6 **3** shd **Pennygee**[15] 1372 4-9-11 45........................ PhillipMakin 2 58
(S R Bowring) *led: hdd 5f out: led again over 3f out: rdn: edgd rt and hdd over 1f out: styd on same pce* **33/1**
53- **4** 2¼ **Lullaby Lady**[188] 6432 3-8-12 0........................ MichaelHills 7 47
(B W Hills) *s.i.s: hdwy 6f out: led 5f out: hdd over 3f out: rdn over 1f out: styd on same pce* **2/1**[2]
0 **5** hd **Martingrange Lass (IRE)**[38] 961 3-8-9 0........................ DNolan(3) 4 46
(S Parr) *chsd ldrs: rdn and hung lft over 1f out: styd on same pce* **33/1**
- **6** 1¼ **Betonart** 3-8-12 0........................ JamesDoyle 8 43
(R M Beckett) *hld up: rdn 1/2-way: nvr trbld ldrs* **14/1**
5 **7** 10 **Plum Asset (USA)**[27] 1144 3-8-12 0........................ SebSanders 5 16
(R M Beckett) *chsd ldrs: rdn over 2f out: wknd wl over 1f out* **5/4**[1]
8 95 **Kintyres Promise (IRE)** 4-9-11 0........................ HayleyTurner 6 —
(Mrs N Macauley) *s.s: outpcd* **50/1**

1m 32.1s (2.50) **Going Correction** +0.075s/f (Slow)
WFA 3 from 4yo 13lb **8** Ran SP% **117.5**
Speed ratings (Par 98): **88,86,86,83,83 82,70,—**
CSF £145.87 TOTE £31.60: £6.60, £1.10, £8.90; EX 41.10.
Owner J D Graham **Bred** J D Graham **Trained** Upper Longdon, Staffs
■ Stewards' Enquiry : Russell Kennemore three-day ban: careless riding (May 13-15); five-day ban: used whip with excessive force and above shoulder height (May 16-20)

FOCUS
A dreadful fillies' maiden with the winner rated 46 and the third 45. The winning time was 3.76 seconds slower than the preceding handicap over the same trip which is a big margin even allowing for the difference in class and the form looks very dubious. The race provided a one-two for the offspring of Bahamian Bounty.

1710 RINGSIDE CONFERENCE SUITE H'CAP 1m 4f 50y(P)
8:35 (8:35) (Class 6) (0-60,60) 3-Y-0 **£2,047** (£604; £302) Stalls Low

Form RPR
0022 **1** **Art Exhibition (IRE)**[5] 1586 3-9-2 **58**........................ SebSanders 1 68
(J Noseda) *led: hdd 10f out: chsd ldr 7f out: rdn to ld and edgd lft fr over 1f out: styd on* **5/4**[1]
0140 **2** 2¼ **Paul The Carpet (UAE)**[16] 1350 3-8-5 **47**........................ GregFairley 7 53
(G L Moore) *s.i.s: hld up: hdwy over 2f out: nt rch wnr* **9/1**
0-42 **3** 2 **Okafranca (IRE)**[10] 1478 3-9-4 **60**........................ MartinDwyer 3 63
(W R Muir) *chsd ldrs: led over 8f out: rdn and hdd over 1f out: no ex ins fnl f* **3/1**[2]
0-05 **4** 9 **Trip The Light**[25] 1186 3-8-5 **47**........................ PaulHanagan 2 35
(R A Fahey) *prom: lost pl 8f out: outpcd 4f out: n.d after* **13/2**[3]
0-55 **5** ½ **Pie O My (IRE)**[83] 454 3-8-13 **55**........................ StephenDonohoe 4 43
(J Jay) *hld up: hdwy 7f out: rdn over 2f out: sn wknd: b.b.v* **13/2**[3]
050- **6** 21 **Lady Jinks**[188] 6427 3-8-11 **53**........................ HayleyTurner 5 7
(M D I Usher) *chsd ldrs: rdn over 5f out: wknd 3f out* **40/1**
1-04 **7** 3¼ **Ostinata (IRE)**[67] 665 3-8-3 **52**........................ GabrielHannon(7) 6 1
(B W Duke) *hld up: a in rr: wknd over 3f out* **20/1**
0-40 **8** 12 **Moss Way**[17] 1343 3-8-4 **46** oh1........................ DavidKinsella 9 —
(W J Musson) *led 10f out: hdd over 8f out: chsd ldrs tl wknd over 3f out* **66/1**
0-26 **9** 51 **Poppy Red**[22] 1243 3-8-13 **55**........................ PaulFitzsimons 8 —
(Miss J R Tooth) *prom 8f* **28/1**

2m 41.88s (0.78) **Going Correction** +0.075s/f (Slow) **9** Ran SP% **118.3**
Speed ratings (Par 96): **100,98,97,91,90 76,74,66,32**
CSF £13.83 CT £30.31 TOTE £2.20: £1.50, £2.80, £1.10; EX 22.60.
Owner Matthew Green **Bred** Jean Brennan And Edward O'Regan **Trained** Newmarket, Suffolk

The Form Book, Raceform Ltd, Compton, RG20 6NL

FOCUS
An ordinary middle-distance handicap for three-year-olds run in heavy rain. The pace was a fair one and made this a true test of stamina, hence some big margins separating the runners at the line and the form looks sound with the first three close to their marks.
Pie O My(IRE) Official explanation: jockey said colt had bled from the nose

1711 HORIZONS RESTAURANT H'CAP — 1m 1f 103y(P)
9:05 (9:05) (Class 3) (0-90,90) 4-Y-0+ **£6,623** (£1,982; £991; £495; £246) **Stalls** Low

Form — RPR
3-23 **1** **Curzon Prince (IRE)**[10] [1473] 4-8-6 **83** .... JackMitchell(5) 6 89+
(C F Wall) *hld up: rdn 3f out: hdwy over 1f out: r.o to ld wl ins fnl f* **15/8**[2]
500- **2** ½ **Boo**[186] [6475] 6-9-4 **90** .... RobertWinston 5 95
(J W Unett) *led over 8f out: rdn and hdd 2f out: ev ch ins fnl f: r.o* **20/1**
3142 **3** ¾ **Princess Cocoa (IRE)**[33] [1041] 5-8-4 **76** oh1 .... PaulHanagan 1 79
(R A Fahey) *led 1f: chsd ldr tl led 2f out: rdn: edgd rt and hdd wl ins fnl f* **11/2**[3]
4-01 **4** 2½ **Gold Prospect**[18] [1314] 4-8-11 **83** .... JamieSpencer 3 81
(M L W Bell) *hld up: hdwy over 2f out: rdn over 1f out: styng on same pce whn hung lft ins fnl f* **5/4**[1]
11-0 **5** 2¾ **Hoh Wotanite**[38] [958] 5-8-11 **86** .... (v) RussellKennemore(3) 4 78
(R Hollinshead) *chsd ldrs: rdn over 2f out: wknd over 1f out* **7/1**

2m 3.50s (1.80) **Going Correction** +0.075s/f (Slow) **5** Ran SP% **111.9**
Speed ratings (Par 107): **95,94,93,91,89**
CSF £30.31 TOTE £3.40: £1.30, £4.50; EX 66.50 Place 6 £126.12, Place 5 £44.17.
Owner H N Alsabah **Bred** Scuderia San Pancrazio **Trained** Newmarket, Suffolk

FOCUS
The best race on the card, despite being the last, and contested by the smallest field on the night. The contest was spoilt to a degree by a moderate early pace though, and it developed into something of a sprint from the home bend. The first and third ran close to January course form.

NOTEBOOK
Curzon Prince(IRE) ◆, trying his longest trip to date on sand, though he did run well in testing ground over slightly further on turf last time, looked the first beaten on the home bend as he was off the bridle in a detached last. However, he rallied in great fashion and maintained his effort up the inside rail to win all-out. His record on sand now reads 4321 and there may be more to come from him. (op 5-2)
Boo, making his debut for the yard and returning from six months off, was off a 5lb lower mark than when last on sand and was allowed to enjoy an uncontested lead. after taking it up with a circuit left. He battled back really well after getting headed, but there must be the possibility that he was flattered due to the way the race was run. (op 16-1)
Princess Cocoa(IRE) was content to get a lead from Boo until taking over turning for home, but she could never stamp her authority on the contest and was run out of it. A stronger pace would have suited her, but she continues to run consistently well. (op 8-1 tchd 7-2)
Gold Prospect, raised 4lb for his recent success over course and distance and unbeaten in two previous starts here, had every chance but did not find anything like as much off the bridle as had looked likely. Perhaps the way the race was run did not suit him as he is much better than he showed here. (op Evens tchd 6-4)
Hoh Wotanite, who only beat one home in the Lincoln, had won his previous four starts, all of them here. Racing off a 4lb higher mark than for his last win, he threatened to pull his chance away early and, for a horse that needs a strong pace, the tempo they went here would have been no help to him at all. He is better than this, but will still need to find plenty more in order to defy this mark. (op 6-1 tchd 8-1)
T/Plt: £162.90 to a £1 stake. Pool: £58,680.39. 262.90 winning tickets. T/Qpdt: £13.20 to a £1 stake. Pool: £4,922.23. 274.28 winning tickets. CR

1593 CHANTILLY (R-H)
Tuesday, April 29

OFFICIAL GOING: Very soft

1712a PRIX SIGY (LISTED RACE) — 6f
1:20 (1:21) 3-Y-0 **£20,221** (£8,088; £6,066; £4,044; £2,022)

RPR
1 **War Officer (USA)**[39] [955] 3-9-1 .... C-PLemaire 2 111
(J-C Rouget, France) **17/10**[2]
2 1 **Elusif (FR)**[15] [1376] 3-8-11 .... OPeslier 8 104
(A Fabre, France) **5/4**[1]
3 1 **Inxile (IRE)**[26] [1170] 3-8-11 .... AdrianTNicholls 5 101
(D Nicholls) *led after 1f: hdd 1f out: kpt on at one pce* **10/1**[3]
4 6 **Trevelez (IRE)**[39] [955] 3-8-11 .... TJarnet 7 83
(F-X de Chevigny, France)
5 1½ **Lettre Spirituelle**[39] [956] 3-8-8 .... TThulliez 3 76
(J E Pease, France)
6 2 **Surething (FR)**[18] 3-8-11 .... MBlancpain 10 73
(M Rolland, France)
7 4 **Ginostra**[189] 3-8-8 .... SPasquier 9 58
(S Wattel, France)
8 15 **Le Baron Jenney (ITY)** 3-8-11 .... IMendizabal 1 16
(L Riccardi, Italy)

1m 14.1s (2.70) **Going Correction** +0.675s/f (Yiel) **8** Ran SP% **90.6**
Speed ratings: **109,107,106,98,96 93,88,68**
PARI-MUTUEL: WIN 2.70; PL 1.10, 1.10, 1.70; DF 2.50.
Owner Joseph Allen **Bred** Joseph Allen **Trained** Pau, France

NOTEBOOK
Inxile(IRE) put up a good performance for an inexperienced colt. None too quickly into his stride, he was soon taken up to lead the field which he did until the furlong marker. He battled well to the line and finally went under to two French colts who are both highly rated. This was a very promising effort and his trainer feels he will be better suited to 5f. He is likely to return to France for another Listed event.

1713a PRIX ALLEZ FRANCE (GROUP 3) (F&M) — 1m 2f
2:50 (2:58) 4-Y-0+ **£29,412** (£11,765; £8,824; £5,882; £2,941)

RPR
1 **Fair Breeze (GER)**[170] [6781] 5-9-0 .... AHelfenbein 3 109
(Mario Hofer, Germany) *racd in 2nd: smooth hdwy bto ld jst over 2f out: sn rdn clr: easily* **152/10**
2 4 **Claire Et Bleu (FR)**[26] [1175] 4-8-7 .... AlexisBadel 4 95
(Mme M Bollack-Badel, France) *led to jst over 2f out: kpt on gamely u.p fnl 1 1/2f to hold 2nd* **83/10**
3 snk **Believe Me (IRE)**[26] [1175] 4-8-9 .... TThulliez 7 97
(J-M Beguigne, France) *hld up towards rr: 8th st: styd on down outside fnl 2f: jst missed 2nd* **36/10**[2]
4 1½ **Avanti Polonia (GER)**[212] [5849] 4-9-0 .... DBonilla 5 99
(F Head, France) *unruly s: racd in 5th on outside: reminder under 2 1/2f out: hrd rdn and edgd rt to ins rail fr over 1f out: kpt on* **26/1**
5 1 **Hapsburg (FR)**[187] [6460] 4-8-7 .... IMendizabal 6 90
(E Libaud, France) *racd in 4th: wnt 3rd over 2f out: lost 3rd ins fnl f* **25/1**
6 ¾ **Diyakalanie (FR)**[205] [6042] 4-8-9 .... C-PLemaire 9 91
(J Boisnard, France) *dropped out in last: 10th st: rdn and kpt on down outside fr over 1 1/2f out* **11/1**
7 ½ **Concentric**[26] [1175] 4-8-9 .... SPasquier 2 90
(A Fabre, France) *hld up in rr: 9th st: n.m.r towards ins over 2f out and again 1 1/2f out: kpt on steadily fnl f* **48/10**[3]
8 4 **Penkinella (FR)**[11] 5-8-7 .... AClement 10 81
(A Couetil, France) *racd in 3rd: wknd 2f out* **59/1**
9 1½ **La Boum (GER)**[187] [6460] 5-9-0 .... CSoumillon 11 85
(Robert Collet, France) *hld up: 7th st: effrt 2f out: nt qckn: eased clsng stages* **26/10**[1]
10 nse **Les Fazzani (IRE)**[177] [6688] 4-8-7 .... EddieAhern 1 78
(M J Wallace) *midfield on ins: pushed along 3 1/2f out: rdn wl over 2f out: nt qckn* **33/1**
11 **Legerete (USA)**[26] [1175] 4-9-2 .... OPeslier 8 87
(A Fabre, France) *hld up in rr: last st: bhd fr over 1 1/2f out* **69/10**

2m 9.00s (4.20) **Going Correction** +0.675s/f (Yiel) **11** Ran SP% **116.8**
Speed ratings: **110,106,106,105,104 104,103,100,99,99 99**
PARI-MUTUEL: WIN 16.20; PL 3.90, 2.70, 1.60; DF 64.80.
Owner Stall Margarethe **Bred** *unknown **Trained** Germany
■ Stewards' Enquiry : T Thulliez €200 fine: whip abuse

NOTEBOOK
Fair Breeze(GER), a German filly, did not deserve to be a 15/1 chance as she had pretty useful form at the backend of last year. Always well placed, she took the race by the scruff of the neck 2f out and went on to win in a canter. She loves to get her toe in and could be back for the Prix Corrida at the end of May, whilst the long-term target is the Prix de L'Opera.
Claire Et Bleu(FR), a very genuine filly, was taken into the lead from the start and set a pretty brisk pace, but had nothing in reverse when passed by the winner early in the straight. She ran on gamely to hold second place in the final stages, but her future plans will be decided by underfoot conditions.
Believe Me(IRE) had plenty to do entering the straight and she was putting in her best work at the finish. Ridden more handily, she would have finished second but would not have beaten the winner. Her jockey was given a €200 fine for excessive use of the whip.
Avanti Polonia(GER), in mid-division for much of the race, did not have the clearest of runs in the straight. Once clear, she ran on really well and may appreciate a slightly longer trip
Les Fazzani(IRE) did not appreciate being shut in the stalls because of a delayed start. Well away, she raced just behind the leaders early on before gradually dropping out of contention in the straight, but she was making her seasonal debut and the ground was testing. She may now head for the Blue Wind Stakes at Naas on May 14th.

ASCOT (R-H)
Wednesday, April 30

OFFICIAL GOING: Straight course - good to soft; round course - soft
Wind: light against Weather: rain before meeting

1714 ASCOT ANNUAL BADGEHOLDERS' CONDITIONS STKS — 5f
2:10 (2:10) (Class 3) 2-Y-0
£6,231 (£1,866; £933; £467; £233; £117) **Stalls** Centre

Form — RPR
1 **1** **Baycat (IRE)**[12] [1439] 2-9-1 0 .... JamesDoyle 8 90
(J G Portman) *hld up bhd ldrs: hung lft and led over 1f out: kpt on wl: rdn out* **11/4**[1]
23 **2** 1¼ **Firth Of Fifth (IRE)**[13] [1413] 2-8-11 0 .... RichardKingscote 7 82
(Tom Dascombe) *unf: bit bkwd: prom: led over 2f out: rdn and hdd over 1f out: kpt on but a hld by wnr* **10/1**
3 **3** 1¼ **Sun Ship (IRE)**[12] [1439] 2-8-11 0 .... RichardHughes 6 77
(R Hannon) *lw: led tl over 2f out: rdn wl over 1f out: kpt on same pce fnl f* **3/1**[2]
51 **4** 3½ **Grand Honour (IRE)**[18] [1341] 2-9-1 0 .... JimmyQuinn 3 68
(P Howling) *hld up bhd ldrs: rdn over 2f out: one pce fr over 1f out* **12/1**
5 shd **Light The Fire (IRE)** 2-8-11 0 .... LDettori 2 64+
(B J Meehan) *s.i.s and wnt lft s: hld up last but in tch: hdwy jst over 2f out and edgd sltly rt: rdn over 1f out: wknd ins fnl f* **11/1**
2 **6** 3¾ **Skid Solo (IRE)**[12] [1439] 2-8-11 0 .... AlanMunro 4 51+
(P W Chapple-Hyam) *awkward leaving stalls: sn prom: rdn and sltly short of room jst over 2f out: wknd over 1f out* **11/4**[1]
7 7 **Pride Of Kings** 2-8-11 0 .... JoeFanning 5 25+
(M Johnston) *prom: rdn over 2f out: sn btn* **8/1**[3]

64.85 secs (4.35) **Going Correction** +0.75s/f (Yiel) **7** Ran SP% **114.6**
Speed ratings (Par 96): **95,93,91,85,85 79,68**
CSF £30.29 TOTE £4.10: £2.00, £4.40; EX 31.50 Trifecta £202.60 Pool £ 713.54 - 2.50 winning units..
Owner A S B Portman **Bred** D Couper Snr **Trained** Compton, Berks

FOCUS
One of the best juvenile races to have been staged this season to date although not the strongest-ever renewal.

NOTEBOOK
Baycat(IRE) followed up his Newbury maiden success 12 days previously with another dogged display, confirming form with the third despite being 4lb worse off. He took longer to find his full stride this time, and still looked distinctly green when asked to make his effort nearing 2f out, but he was always holding sway over his rivals when in front inside the final furlong. A return to the track Royal Meeting in June for something like the Norfolk Stakes will no doubt be tempting his connections now and further improvement still looks on the cards. Whether he is really up to that sort of level is still obviously open to debate, but a step into Listed company now looks his best option. (op 9-2)
Firth Of Fifth(IRE), placed on Polytrack on his previous two outings, was much better away from the gates this time and posted his best effort to date in defeat, keeping the winner up to his work inside the closing stages. He has a maiden well within his compass, but again just left the impression he will ideally benefit more when the 6f races begin. (op 17-2 tchd 8-1)
Sun Ship(IRE) could have been expected to have come on physically for his Newbury debut experience and reverse form with the winner thanks to a 4lb pull in the weights with that rival. He can have no excuses, however, and simply lacked a change of gear when it mattered most. He is another who may do better when sent over another furlong in due course and this still rates an improved effort in defeat. (op 4-1)
Grand Honour(IRE), the only other penalised runner in the field, was patiently ridden on this turf debut and came through to run his race. He is not going to be the easiest to place in the short term, but he still helps to put this form into perspective and has a future. (op 14-1 tchd 16-1)

Light The Fire(IRE) ◆, the most expensive of these at the sales, proved very easy to back ahead of this racecourse debut yet posted a pleasing effort in defeat. He has some scope and looks sure to come on a bundle for the experience, so is one to take from the race with the future in mind. (op 12-1 tchd 14-1)

Skid Solo(IRE) odds-on to get off the mark at the first time of asking when second to Baycat at Newbury last time, never looked likely to get involved here after a tardy start. He now has it all to prove and his Group 1 entry looks most ambitious at this stage. (op 2-1)

Pride Of Kings, an athletic type who holds a Derby entry for next year, has speed in his pedigree and knew his job as he broke well from the gates. He was in trouble from 2f out, however, and is going to need to come on plenty for the race if he is to be getting his head in front at any stage in the near future. (op 7-1)

1715 X FACTOR STKS (CONDITIONS RACE) (FILLIES) 1m (R)

2:45 (2:46) (Class 3) 3-Y-O

£6,854 (£2,052; £1,026; £513; £256; £128) **Stalls** High

Form RPR

40-4 **1** **Rosaleen (IRE)**[14] 1401 3-9-1 93 .... LDettori 6 95+
(B J Meehan) *hld up: wnt cl 4th over 6f out: rdn to ld ent fnl f: kpt on: rdn out* **15/8**[1]

2 **2** ¾ **Bramaputra (IRE)**[12] 1445 3-8-12 0 .... AlanMunro 5 90
(B R Millman) *lw: led: rdn 2f out: hdd ent fnl f: sn hung rt: kpt on* **9/2**[3]

55-0 **3** 5 **Kay Es Jay (FR)**[18] 1332 3-8-12 99 .... WilliamBuick(3) 2 82
(B W Hills) *trckd ldrs: swtchd rt over 6f out: swtchd lft 2f out: sn rdn: nt pce of ldng pair* **5/1**

3- **4** ¾ **My Aunt Fanny**[236] 5202 3-8-12 0 .... LPKeniry 7 77
(A M Balding) *chsd ldrs: n.m.r and snatched up over 6f out: rdn over 3f out: styd on ins fnl f* **15/2**

12-0 **5** 5 **Rinterval (IRE)**[14] 1401 3-9-1 93 .... RichardHughes 1 69
(R Hannon) *trckd ldr: rdn whn sltly short of room 2f out: wknd ent fnl f* **11/4**[2]

6 16 **Applesnap (IRE)**[244] 4988 3-9-1 0 .... (p) JohnEgan 4 32
(Mrs C A Dunnett) *w'like: sn restrained in last: rdn over 3f out: wknd over 2f out: eased whn btn fnl f* **40/1**

1m 49.4s (8.60) **Going Correction** +0.95s/f (Soft) 6 Ran SP% **110.5**
Speed ratings (Par 99): **95,94,89,88,83 67**
CSF £10.33 TOTE £2.70: £1.80, £2.80; EX 12.00.
Owner F C T Wilson **Bred** Alan Dargan **Trained** Manton, Wilts

FOCUS

A race that lost its Listed status, but this looked a strong renewal on paper even after the withdrawal of Makaaseb. It was run at a steady early pace, but the form still looks reasonable with the first pair pulling clear.

NOTEBOOK

Rosaleen(IRE) continued her stable's trend of coming on for a run, although her comeback was in the Group 3 Nell Gwyn. She took time to hit top stride, but was well on top in the final 100yds and left the impression she will get 1m2f in due course. Connections are considering another step up for the Height of Fashion Stakes (formerly Lupe, but still Listed) at Goodwood, which is now at the end of May. (op 2-1 tchd 9-4)

Bramaputra(IRE) ◆ confirmed the good impression of her debut second in what could be a decent Newbury 7f maiden. This big scopey filly pulled well clear of the rest after also taking time to hit top stride early in the straight. She has an optimistic Coronation Stakes entry, but midsummer fast ground may not play to her strengths even if she continues to progress as expected. (op 3-1)

Kay Es Jay(FR) had to squeeze through a narrow gap to challenge into the final 2f, but could not match the speed of the front two into the final furlong. She still gives the form a sound-enough look and is likely to be seen to better effect on a sounder surface. (op 9-2 tchd 11-2)

My Aunt Fanny ◆, another filly with size and scope, was not suited by the steady gallop yet was staying on well in the final furlong to suggest further will bring more improvement. This was still a step up on her only previous start last year and she was meeting race fitter rivals. (op 8-1 tchd 6-1)

Rinterval(IRE), a couple of lengths behind the winner in the Nell Gwyn, could not run to that form and was disappointingly left behind up the straight. (op 7-2)

1716 BRITAIN'S GOT TALENT PARADISE STKS (LISTED RACE) 1m (S)

3:20 (3:21) (Class 1) 4-Y-O+ **£17,031** (£6,456; £3,231; £1,611; £807) **Stalls** Centre

Form RPR

240- **1** **Cesare**[193] 6332 7-9-7 120 .... JamieSpencer 4 123+
(J R Fanshawe) *lw: stalked front four: swtchd rt and cruised upsides ent fnl f: led fnl 75yds: eased ahd: unextended* **11/8**[1]

1-12 **2** 1 **Don't Panic (IRE)**[18] 1326 4-9-0 105 .... AlanMunro 6 106
(P W Chapple-Hyam) *lw: t.k.h trcking ldrs: rdn to chal 2f out: remained pressing ldrs ins fnl f: wnt 2nd fnl 75yds but no ch w wnr* **15/8**[2]

2F-3 **3** shd **Drumfire (IRE)**[12] 1457 4-9-0 100 .... JoeFanning 3 106
(M Johnston) *prom: rdn over 2f out: remained pressing ldrs ins fnl f: kpt on but no ch w wnr fnl 75yds* **25/1**

003- **4** 2¾ **Caldra (IRE)**[179] 6655 4-9-0 108 .... RyanMoore 1 100
(S Kirk) *trckd ldrs: rdn over 2f out: nvr able to mount pce to chal: wnt 4th fnl strides* **17/2**

525- **5** nk **Ordnance Row**[194] 6298 5-9-0 106 .... RichardHughes 5 99
(R Hannon) *bit bkwd: led: rdn 2f out: hld narrow advantage tl hdd by wnr fnl 75yds: fdd and lost 4 pls* **5/1**[3]

1m 46.36s (5.76) **Going Correction** +0.75s/f (Yiel) 5 Ran SP% **107.9**
Speed ratings (Par 111): **101,100,99,97,96**
CSF £4.01 TOTE £2.10: £1.20, £1.40; EX 3.50.
Owner Cheveley Park Stud **Bred** Cheveley Park Stud Ltd **Trained** Newmarket, Suffolk

FOCUS

The late defection of Royal Oath took a fair amount of competitive interest away from this Listed event, but Cesare still ran out an impressive winner under his penalty and rates value for plenty further. It was a very moderate winning time for a Listed race, due to the lack of early pace.

NOTEBOOK

Cesare repeated his comeback win in this race last year, when he also came from last to first to score, despite having to carry a 7lb penalty for his Group 2 success at the track last season. There was little early pace on, but it was clear when the sprint for home began that he was moving best of all and, under the cheekiest of rides from Spencer, he emerged upsides the leaders travelling all over them at the furlong marker. Any surface seems to come alike to the seven-year-old, he is clearly in love with this straight mile, and his form figures here now read 115141. This should now put him spot on for a crack at the Lockinge Stakes at Newbury next month, when he is likely to line up as favourite, as he attempts to find that elusive and deserved first Group 1 success. (op Evens tchd 6-4 in places)

Don't Panic(IRE), very well backed in receipt of 7lb from Cesare, was undone by the lack of early pace and ran far too freely for his own good. He found the winner in a different league, but kept on inside the final furlong and there will surely be other days for this improved four-year-old in Listed company. (op 2-1 tchd 9-4)

Drumfire(IRE) showed the clear benefit of his lacklustre return from a lay-off at Yarmouth 12 days previously and posted a much more encouraging effort in defeat. He likes this sort of ground and, while hard to place successfully nowadays, should come on a little again for the run. Official explanation: jockey said colt hung right (op 20-1)

Caldra(IRE) returning from a 179-day break, was another who would have not ideally enjoyed the steady early pace. He was found wanting from 2f out and left the impression this comeback run was needed, but is another who is not going to prove simple to place this term. (op 9-1 tchd 10-1)

Ordnance Row, another seasonal debutant, would have really found this an insufficient test and he can be expected to last longer now he has this outing under his belt. (op 6-1 tchd 13-2)

1717 WOODCOTE STUD SAGARO STKS (GROUP 3) 2m

3:55 (3:55) (Class 1) 4-Y-O+

£28,385 (£10,760; £5,385; £2,685; £1,345; £675) **Stalls** High

Form RPR

16/2 **1** **Shipmaster**[28] 1158 5-9-1 101 .... RichardHughes 5 111
(A King) *a.p: rdn 3f out: battled gamely ins fnl f u.str.p: led nr fin* **4/1**

165- **2** shd **Peppertree Lane (IRE)**[213] 5849 5-9-4 106 .... JimmyFortune 3 114+
(M Johnston) *t.k.h early: settled in 5th after 3f: prog 5f out: rdn over 2f out: led over 1f out: sn hrd pressed: kpt on: hdd nr fin* **7/2**[3]

414- **3** 5 **Distinction (IRE)**[193] 6337 9-9-1 110 .... RyanMoore 2 105
(Sir Michael Stoute) *bit bkwd: hld up 6th but in tch: prog into 4th 3f out: sn rdn: styd on: wnt 3rd ins fnl f* **5/2**[1]

30-1 **4** ¾ **Soapy Danger**[32] 1070 5-9-1 109 .... JoeFanning 6 104
(M Johnston) *lw: led: rdn 3f out: hdd over 1f out: kpt on same pce: lost 3rd ins fnl f* **3/1**[2]

530- **5** 10 **Baddam**[82] 6335 6-9-1 95 .... IanMongan 4 92
(Ian Williams) *trckd ldrs: rdn 4f out: wknd 2f out* **20/1**

10/4 **6** 6 **Frank Sonata**[28] 1158 7-9-1 105 .... TPO'Shea 7 85
(M G Quinlan) *trckd ldrs: rdn over 3f out: wknd jst over 2f out* **8/1**

3m 42.22s (9.62) **Going Correction** +0.95s/f (Soft) 6 Ran SP% **111.7**
Speed ratings (Par 113): **113,112,110,110,105 102**
CSF £18.01 TOTE £5.20: £2.40, £2.20; EX 20.50.
Owner Nigel Bunter **Bred** Newsells Park Stud Limited **Trained** Barbury Castle, Wilts

FOCUS

The withdrawal of last year's winner and race regular Tungsten Strike as the rain continued to fall and with Distinction not enjoying the softening ground casts doubt over the strength of the form, along with a moderate pace that brought a notably slow time - fully 12secs slower than last year's Group 3 Queen's Vase which was run on comparable ground. The form is rated around the first two.

NOTEBOOK

Shipmaster, so narrowly denied at Nottingham last time, again showed great battling qualities to step up on that form and score in this higher class. He continues to look progressive and, told that he picks up just a 3lb penalty for the Chester Cup (9st 6lb), his trainer will leave him in at the five-day stage and see how he comes out of this race. VCbet cut him to 10-1 from 16-1 and Hills went 12-1 behind 4-1 favourite Highland Legacy, whose trainer Michael Bell has a line to this winner having beaten him at Nottingham. That event will be a completely different experience, but there is plenty to recommend him as he likes to race handily and has a touch of class. (op 9-2 tchd 5-1)

Peppertree Lane(IRE) deserves plenty of credit despite being run out of what looked an assured victory when he went past both stablemate Soapy Danger and the winner. He had conditions in his favour and beat the rest well, but will remain hard to place as he clearly excels with cut in the ground. (op 5-1 tchd 3-1, 11-2 in places)

Distinction(IRE)'s connections were far from dispirited in defeat with the ground having turned against him, especially in the Swinley Bottom section where it was testing. He needed a stronger test as well and another tilt at the Gold Cup remains the aim at the age of nine. (op 3-1)

Soapy Danger may have won on soft on his recent comeback yet that was back at 1m4f and, while he won the Queen's Vase over old the course and distance that was on firm ground. While it can be argued that he has "bounced" here after that first run of the season, it may simply be that the ground found him out. (op 13-8)

Baddam proved most disappointing as he had conditions to suit, but dropped away tamely. (op 33-1)

1718 O'CONNELL LONDON WASPS PAVILION STKS (LISTED RACE) 6f

4:30 (4:31) (Class 1) 3-Y-O

£17,031 (£6,456; £3,231; £1,611; £807; £405) **Stalls** Centre

Form RPR

10-0 **1** **Sir Gerry (USA)**[11] 1471 3-9-4 110 .... JamieSpencer 1 116+
(J R Fanshawe) *lw: slowly away: in last pair: rdn and qcknd up wl 2f out: edgd rt and led ent fnl f: idled briefly but in command: rdn out* **4/1**[2]

143- **2** 2 **Tajdeef (USA)**[208] 5975 3-8-11 111 .... RHills 8 103
(B W Hills) *plld hrd: prom: led over 2f out: rdn and nt pce of wnr whn hdd ent fnl f* **3/1**[1]

61-1 **3** 1¾ **Prohibit**[14] 1404 3-8-11 91 .... JimmyFortune 5 97
(J H M Gosden) *lw: b.hind: squeezed out s: t.k.h in last pair: hdwy 2f out: sn rdn: edgd lft ins fnl f: no ex fnl 75yds* **3/1**[1]

-144 **4** hd **Elizabeth Swann**[11] 1470 3-8-6 98 .... EddieAhern 9 91
(R Hannon) *prom: rdn and outpcd 2f out: kpt on wl ins fnl f* **15/2**[3]

03-0 **5** 1 **Highland Daughter (IRE)**[14] 1401 3-8-7 98 ow1 .... PhilipRobinson 4 89
(C G Cox) *wnt rt s: cl up: rdn over 2f out: kpt on same pce fnl f* **15/2**[3]

634- **6** 2 **Sophie's Girl**[180] 6619 3-8-6 95 .... NickyMackay 3 82
(B J Meehan) *trckd ldrs: rdn 2f out: sn one pce* **8/1**

54-5 **7** nk **Edge Of Light**[11] 1470 3-8-6 99 .... CatherineGannon 2 81
(B Palling) *led: rdn and hdd over 2f out: sn btn* **8/1**

1m 17.22s (2.82) **Going Correction** +0.75s/f (Yiel) 7 Ran SP% **115.8**
Speed ratings (Par 106): **111,108,106,105,104 101,101**
CSF £16.86 TOTE £4.10: £2.50, £1.90; EX 10.90 Trifecta £23.40 Pool £840.70 - 25.47 winning units..
Owner Mrs Gerry Galligan **Bred** Dr Catherine Wills **Trained** Newmarket, Suffolk

FOCUS

This Listed event represents a decent opportunity for three-year-olds about to embark on a tricky sprinting season ahead and Sir Gerry looks well up to par with past winners of the race. Solid enough form, despite the early pace being average.

NOTEBOOK

Sir Gerry(USA) showed his disappointing comeback in the Greenham 11 days previously to be all wrong and defied his 7lb penalty in ready fashion. The drop back in trip proved ideal, he goes well on an easy surface, and is clearly not the finished article. He produced a smart turn of foot to settle the issue nearing the final furlong and showed a willing attitude when out in front, despite idling somewhat. This confirms him as a pure sprinter and he is no doubt Group class, but his opportunities are going to be limited from now on and he will be forced to take on the older sprinters. It is not clear exactly where he will head next, although the Duke Of York next month was not totally ruled out, but it may well transpire that his best chance of further success comes later in the year when he has matured that bit further. As a four-year-old next year, however, he should really develop into a formidable sprinter. (op 5-2)

Tajdeef(USA), who signed off last year with an excellent third in the Group 1 Middle Park when well ahead of a below-par Sir Gerry, was not helped by the lack of early pace and pulled hard through the first two furlongs as a result. He still turned in a very pleasing display in defeat, despite not confirming form with the penalised winner, and confirmed he has trained on from two to three. There will be other days for him. (op 11-4 tchd 4-1)

Prohibit a ready winner on his handicap debut at Newmarket a fortnight previously, came into this with the lowest official rating on 91 yet had the profile of a horse potentially better than that. He was another who proved free early on, but still came there with his chance only to bottom out inside the final furlong. This still rates as an improved effort in defeat, on ground he may just have found easier than ideal, and he left the impression he can make his mark in this grade at some point during the season. (op 10-3 tchd 11-4)
Elizabeth Swann the Fred Darling fourth, got outpaced at a crucial stage on this drop back a furlong before staying on again towards the finish and only just missed out on third place. She helps to set the level of this form. (op 9-1)
Highland Daughter(IRE) showed she has come on since her comeback effort in the Nell Gwyn a fortnight previously, but was still found out on this drop back to 6f and is not going to prove straightforward to place on this evidence. (op 14-1)

1719 KELTBRAY H'CAP 1m (S)
5:05 (5:08) (Class 4) (0-85,85) 4-Y-O+ **£7,123** (£2,119; £1,059; £529) **Stalls** Centre

Form RPR
011- **1** **Bankable (IRE)**[215] 5768 4-9-8 **85** .... LDettori 20 101+
(L M Cumani) *lw: s.i.s: towards rr: hdwy 3f out: sn pushed along: led jst over 1f out: styd on wl: rdn out* **11/8**[1]
6/0- **2** *1 1/2* **Tastahil (IRE)**[377] 1106 4-9-3 **80** .... RHills 13 89
(B W Hills) *trckd ldrs: led 3f out: rdn and hdd over 2f out: styd on ins fnl f but a hld by wnr* **25/1**
1-56 **3** *3/4* **Red Somerset (USA)**[16] 1365 5-9-3 **80** .... RichardHughes 10 87
(R J Hodges) *wnt rt s: t.k.h in mid-div: hdwy over 2f out: rdn wl over 1f out: styd on* **11/1**[3]
154- **4** *nk* **Habshan (USA)**[205] 6067 8-9-7 **84** .... GeorgeBaker 17 90+
(C F Wall) *t.k.h in rr: hdwy over 2f out: rdn over 1f out: styd on fnl f: wnt 4th towards fin* **25/1**
03-1 **5** *1* **The Snatcher (IRE)**[8] 1532 5-9-0 **82** 6ex .... PatrickHills(5) 18 86
(R Hannon) *mid-div: hdwy 3f out: led over 2f out: rdn and hdd over 1f out: edgd lft and kpt on same pce fnl f* **9/2**[2]
00-2 **6** *7* **Murrin (IRE)**[30] 1112 4-8-12 **75** .... JimCrowley 1 63
(T G Mills) *hld up towards rr: rdn wl over 2f out: no imp tl styd on fr over 1f out: nvr trbld ldrs* **20/1**
25-0 **7** *2 1/4* **Novikov**[16] 1365 4-9-7 **84** ....(t) JimmyFortune 5 67
(J H M Gosden) *nvr bttr than mid-div* **14/1**
342- **8** *1/2* **Jawaab (IRE)**[197] 6253 4-8-9 **72** .... MartinDwyer 19 54
(M A Buckley) *t.k.h in mid-div: hdwy 3f out: sn rdn wknd over 1f out* **12/1**
06- **9** *1 1/2* **Kaballero (GER)**[330] 2346 7-8-7 **75** .... JamieJones(5) 4 53
(S Gollings) *mid-div: hdwy to trck ldrs 1/2-way: rdn 3f out: sn hung rt and fdd* **66/1**
50-0 **10** *1 1/4* **Heroes**[11] 1469 4-9-7 **84** .... IanMongan 11 59
(C F Wall) *late removing hood and slowly away: a towards rr* **20/1**
11-2 **11** *2 1/2* **Alpes Maritimes**[95] 315 4-9-8 **85** .... RyanMoore 14 55
(G L Moore) *lw: hld up towards rr: rdn and sme prog over 2f out: wknd over 1f out* **12/1**
105- **12** *1 1/2* **Blue Java**[179] 6651 7-8-9 **72** .... RichardSmith 3 38
(H Morrison) *led tl over 3f out: grad fdd* **20/1**
2362 **13** *8* **Lord Theo**[12] 1456 4-9-2 **79** .... JamesDoyle 7 27
(N P Littmoden) *prom: led briefly over 3f out: sn rdn: wknd jst over 2f out* **14/1**
155- **14** *15* **Ainama (IRE)**[187] 6473 4-9-1 **78** .... NickyMackay 8 —
(M Wigham) *chsd ldrs: rdn over 3f out: wkng whn n.m.r over 2f out* **33/1**
400- **15** *9* **Invention (USA)**[126] 4153 5-9-3 **80** .... GregFairley 16 —
(Miss E C Lavelle) *hung lft thrght: chsd ldrs tl 1/2-way* **33/1**

1m 45.47s (4.87) **Going Correction** +0.75s/f (Yiel) **15** Ran SP% **126.7**
Speed ratings (Par 105): **105,103,102,102,101 94,92,91,90,88 86,84,76,61,52**
CSF £51.59 CT £320.60 TOTE £2.30: £1.40, £7.40, £3.00; EX 66.00 Trifecta £368.40 Pool £1,032.6 - 1.99 winning units. Place 6 £32.44, Place 5 £13.00..
Owner Ronchalon Racing (UK) Ltd **Bred** Barronstown Stud And Cobra **Trained** Newmarket, Suffolk

FOCUS
A competitive handicap, run at a sound pace. The form looks solid with the first five coming clear and the third and fourth setting the level.
T/Jkpt: £1,388.30 to a £1 stake. Pool: £82,127.67. 42.00 winning tickets. T/Plt: £117.30 to a £1 stake. Pool: £98,817.00. 614.75 winning tickets. T/Qpdt: £27.40 to a £1 stake. Pool: £5,339.04. 144.00 winning tickets. TM

1581 GREAT LEIGHS (A.W) (L-H)
Wednesday, April 30

OFFICIAL GOING: Standard
Wind: medium behind Weather: brightening up after rain earlier, rain last 2 races

1721 HOSPITALITY AT GREAT LEIGHS MAIDEN FILLIES' STKS 1m (P)
5:20 (5:23) (Class 5) 3-Y-O+ **£2,590** (£770; £385; £192) **Stalls** Low

Form RPR
34- **1** **Aromatherapy**[207] 6015 3-8-12 0 .... JimmyQuinn 4 83
(H R A Cecil) *chsd ldrs: wnt 2nd over 2f out: chal over 1f out: pushed into ld ins fnl f: r.o wl* **9/4**[1]
3 **2** *1* **Tableau Vivant (IRE)**[16] 1372 3-8-12 0 .... RobertWinston 2 81
(Sir Michael Stoute) *led for 1f: chsd ldr after tl led again over 2f: rdn and hrd pressed over 1f out: hdd ins fnl f: one pce* **9/4**[1]
3 *1 1/4* **Illusion** 3-8-12 0 .... RobertHavlin 8 78
(J H M Gosden) *wnt bdly rt leaving stalls: hung rt thrght and racd wd: hdwy to ld after 1f: hdd over 2f out: kpt on same pce fnl f* **3/1**[2]
06- **4** *3 1/2* **Totem Flower (IRE)**[241] 5063 3-8-12 0 .... SteveDrowne 3 70
(R Charlton) *hld up in midfield: hdwy to chse ldng trio over 2f out: no imp fr over 1f out* **16/1**
5 *1 1/4* **Dolcetto (IRE)** 3-8-12 0 .... OscarUrbina 7 67+
(J R Fanshawe) *hld up in rr: hdwy 4f out: kpt on steadily but n.d* **10/1**[3]
4 **6** *6* **Mignonette (IRE)**[33] 1050 3-8-12 0 .... StephenDonohoe 9 53
(E A L Dunlop) *hmpd s: bhd: sme hdwy last 2f: nvr on terms* **16/1**
0-56 **7** *2* **Spiritofthestorm (USA)**[13] 1412 3-8-12 68 .... ChrisCatlin 10 49
(R A Teal) *t.k.h: chsd ldrs: rdn 3f out: wknd over 2f out* **10/1**[3]
0-0 **8** *4 1/2* **Sabancaya**[9] 1525 3-8-12 0 .... LiamJones 5 38
(W J Haggas) *wnt rt s: racd in midfield: rdn 4f out: lost tch wl over 2f out* **33/1**
9 *1/2* **Let Me Pass (USA)** 3-8-12 0 .... ShaneKelly 11 37
(Jane Chapple-Hyam) *chsd ldrs for 2f: sn dropped towards rr: wl bhd and swished tail 2f out* **25/1**
00- **10** *nk* **Nisbah**[287] 3648 3-8-12 0 .... SebSanders 6 43
(C E Brittain) *bmpd s: a in rr: no ch last 2f: eased ins fnl f* **50/1**
400- **11** *12* **Bunty Malenoir**[301] 3213 3-8-12 49 ....(p) TGMcLaughlin 1 9
(Mrs C A Dunnett) *sn outpcd in last: t.o fr 3f out* **100/1**

1m 38.6s (-1.30) **Going Correction** -0.025s/f (Stan) **11** Ran SP% **126.2**
Speed ratings (Par 100): **105,104,102,99,98 92,90,85,85,84 72**
CSF £7.78 TOTE £3.20: £1.80, £1.10, £4.20; EX 10.30.
Owner K Abdulla **Bred** Juddmonte Farms Ltd **Trained** Newmarket, Suffolk

FOCUS
Plenty of big stables represented, probably the shape of things to come at Great Leighs, and this looked a fair fillies' maiden. The form is rated positively athrough the fourth.
Illusion Official explanation: jockey said filly hung badly right throughout
Nisbah Official explanation: jockey said filly had no more to give

1722 BROOMFIELD MAIDEN STKS 5f (P)
5:50 (5:52) (Class 5) 2-Y-O **£2,914** (£867; £433; £216) **Stalls** Low

Form RPR
1 **White Shift (IRE)** 2-8-12 0 .... RobertWinston 3 74
(P D Evans) *mde all: edgd rt briefly 2f out: hld on gamely ins fnl f* **20/1**[3]
2 **2** *1/2* **The Dial House**[13] 1413 2-9-3 0 .... ShaneKelly 6 77
(J A Osborne) *hld up in tch: hdwy to chse wnr jst over 2f out: swtchd lft wl over 1f out: styd on but nvr quite getting to wnr* **11/10**[1]
3 *4 1/2* **Barbee (IRE)** 2-8-12 0 .... StephenDonohoe 5 59+
(E A L Dunlop) *outpcd and pushed along: hung rt bnd wl over 3f out: gd hdwy 3f out: pressed ldrs jst over 2f out: btn and eased ins fnl f* **12/1**[2]
0 **4** *2 1/4* **Twos And Eights (IRE)**[16] 1363 2-9-3 0 .... PaulEddery 4 53
(G D Blake) *dwlt: sn rcvrd to chsd wnr tl jst over 2f out: sn wknd* **50/1**
5 *5* **Ready To Prime** 2-8-12 0 .... SebSanders 1 30+
(D K Ivory) *v s.i.s: a outpcd in rr* **20/1**[3]
6 *4 1/2* **Lonsdale Lad** 2-9-3 0 ....(e[1]) DeanMcKeown 2 19
(R C Guest) *chsd ldrs tl wknd over 2f out: wl bhd whn hung rt over 1f out* **40/1**

60.80 secs (0.60) **Going Correction** -0.025s/f (Stan) **6** Ran SP% **69.2**
Speed ratings (Par 92): **94,93,86,82,74 67**
CSF £15.10 TOTE £7.50: £4.50, £1.02; EX 17.80.
Owner Premier Cru Racing **Bred** Grange Stud **Trained** Pandy, Monmouths

FOCUS
The late withdrawal of debutant Mrs Kipling took much of the interest from this contest, but White Shift created a strong impression in making a winning debut. The level of the form is fluid with the runner-up the only real guide.

NOTEBOOK
White Shift(IRE) ◆, a 16,000euros daughter of Night Shift, comes from a yard who have made a bright start to the season with their juveniles and she certainly knew her job. Showing tons of early speed, she was brought away from the rail in the straight and found more inside the final furlong to hold The Dial House. The late withdrawal of Mrs Kipling obviously made her task easier, but she impressed with her attitude and her trainer later admitted he had left plenty to work on. She is in a valuable sales race at Ireland and looks capable of further progress.
The Dial House, second behind a useful-looking sort on his debut at Kempton, set a strong standard, but having closed in on the winner he was unable to find any extra and could not go past. He was clear of the third and should find a similar race before long. (tchd 6-4)
Barbee(IRE), another daughter of Night Shift, is bred to want a bit further than this in time and as a result this has to go down as a pleasing debut. She showed enough speed to suggest she could find a race over this trip, but will want 6f in time and should learn a good deal from the experience. (op 11-1)
Twos And Eights(IRE), who managed to beat just one home on his Windsor debut, has clearly learnt a bit from that and fared better here. He appeals as a likely sort for nurseries a bit later in the season and should fare better in that sphere.
Ready To Prime is bred for speed and she was nibbled at in the market before the race. However, she blew it with a very slow start and was never going to recover. She should benefit from the experience. (op 40-1)
Lonsdale Lad, whose yard sent out a debut winner at Pontefract recently, was only a cheap purchase and it was mightily off-putting that he had an eyeshield on for this racecourse debut. He seemed to know his job, but was hanging under pressure and looks to have a bit to prove. Official explanation: jockey said gelding hung right

1723 EPPING FOREST H'CAP 1m (P)
6:20 (6:21) (Class 3) (0-95,93) 4-Y-O+ **£6,623** (£1,982; £991; £495; £246) **Stalls** Low

Form RPR
303- **1** **Emerald Wilderness (IRE)**[71] 5639 4-9-3 **92** .... EddieAhern 2 101
(A King) *s.i.s: hld up wl in tch: rdn to chal and hld hd high wl over 1f out: led 1f out: hld on wl last 100yds* **6/1**
30-5 **2** *1/2* **Hazzard County (USA)**[18] 1334 4-8-10 **85** .... SteveDrowne 5 93
(D M Simcock) *hld up in rr: stl last over 2f out: swtchd lft and hdwy wl over 1f out: pressing ldrs and edgd lft jst ins fnl f: unable qckn towards fin* **5/1**[3]
1111 **3** *shd* **Mia's Boy**[12] 1456 4-9-3 **92** .... JimmyQuinn 3 100
(C A Dwyer) *hld up in midfield: shuffled bk over 4f out: hdwy on outer over 3f out: chal wl over 1f out: drvn over 1f out: unable qckn towards fin* **4/1**[2]
106- **4** *6* **The Kiddykid (IRE)**[158] 6932 8-8-12 **87** .... TGMcLaughlin 6 81
(P D Evans) *chsd ldr tl led after 2f out: rdn 2f out: hdd over 1f out: wknd qckly* **20/1**
51-2 **5** *4 1/2* **Kay Gee Be (IRE)**[8] 1545 4-9-4 **93** .... JamieSpencer 4 76
(M J Wallace) *led for 2f: chsd ldrs tl fdd tamely wl over 1f out: sn wl btn* **7/4**[1]
-654 **6** *1 3/4* **Bahiano (IRE)**[53] 833 7-8-10 **85** .... SebSanders 1 64
(C E Brittain) *t.k.h: chsd ldrs on inner tl dropped to rr over 5f out: rdn 3f out: wknd 2f out* **9/1**
3005 **7** *12* **Kabeer**[29] 1133 10-8-7 **87** ....(t) NataliaGemelova(5) 8 39
(A J McCabe) *hld up in midfield tl hdwy to chse ldr over 4f out: rdn over 2f out: wknd qckly wl over 1f out: virtually p.u ins fnl f: t.o* **20/1**
103- **P** **St Andrews (IRE)**[184] 6539 8-8-6 **88** .... MartinGuest(7) 7 —
(M A Jarvis) *awkward leaving stalls: hld up in tch in rr tl p.u 4f out: lame* **14/1**

1m 38.19s (-1.71) **Going Correction** -0.025s/f (Stan) **8** Ran SP% **113.5**
Speed ratings (Par 107): **107,106,106,100,95 94,82,—**
CSF £35.36 CT £132.53 TOTE £5.10: £2.50, £1.90, £1.60; EX 50.70.
Owner Terry Warner & David Sewell **Bred** Mrs Joan Murphy **Trained** Barbury Castle, Wilts

FOCUS
A decent little handicap rated through the runner-up, despite the favourite not running his race.

NOTEBOOK
Emerald Wilderness(IRE), a generally progressive type for Mick Channon last season, did not really go on as expected over hurdles for his current yard, but he looked a player on this return to the level and, having travelled strongly, found plenty under pressure to hold the runner-up. His yard continues in great form, both Flat and jumps, but more will be required off higher marks in future. (op 7-1)

Hazzard County(USA) shaped as though on his way back to form when fourth at Kempton last time and this extra furlong saw him in an even better light. He stuck on well for pressure and, although unable to get past Emerald Wilderness, looks to be nearing a return to winning ways. (op 11-2)
Mia's Boy, who completed a four-timer when scoring narrowly at Yarmouth last time, was up a further 5lb and obviously had more on his plate. He had claims for being a shade unlucky though as he lost his place at halfway before coming with a challenge in the straight and just missing out. This represented another step forward and he may well be capable of winning off this sort of mark. (op 3-1)
The Kiddykid(IRE), a winner at Lingfield back in October, remained 4lb higher here and there looked a doubt as to whether he would stay the 1m. He raced enthusiastically and was still there over a furlong out, but ended up tiring badly late on. (op 25-1)
Kay Gee Be(IRE) made a pleasing comeback to finish second at Kempton last week and he looked a major player off the same mark. However, having raced handily early on, he found little for pressure stopped quickly. This was obviously disappointing and it leaves him with a bit to prove now. Official explanation: jockey said gelding ran flat (op 2-1)
Bahiano(IRE) is a rare winner for a horse of his ability and he was another to drop out tamely in the final quarter mile. (op 10-1)

1724 OLD HALL MARSHES CONDITIONS STKS — 1m 2f (P)
6:50 (6:50) (Class 3) 4-Y-O+ — **£6,799** (£2,023; £1,011) **Stalls** Low

Form — RPR
0410 **1** — **Re Barolo (IRE)**[18] [1326] 5-9-6 **105**..........(t) SebSanders 2 — 111
(M Botti) *hmpd s: trckd ldr: rdn and effrt over 1f out: led 1f out: r.o strly* **2/1**[2]
5030 **2** *2 1/4* **Troubadour (IRE)**[39] [958] 7-9-0 **99**..........(b) AlanMunro 5 — 101
(W Jarvis) *t.k.h: hld up in 3rd pl: plld out and hdwy 3f out: ev and rdn wl over 1f out: outpcd by wnr fnl f* **11/4**[3]
520- **3** *3 1/4* **Road To Love (IRE)**[313] [2815] 5-9-0 **106**.......... RobertWinston 1 — 94
(M Johnston) *wnt rt s: t.k.h: led rdn over 1f out: hdd 1f out: wknd ins fnl f* **11/10**[1]

2m 7.91s (-0.69) **Going Correction** -0.025s/f (Stan) — **3** Ran SP% **107.6**
Speed ratings (Par 107): **101,99,96**
CSF £6.74 TOTE £2.10; EX 5.20.
Owner Effevi Snc Di Villa Felice & C **Bred** Luciano Bosio **Trained** Newmarket, Suffolk

FOCUS
A poor turnout for this conditions event but still quite a competitive heat on paper, although the favourite appeared not to run his race.

NOTEBOOK
Re Barolo(IRE) goes well on the Polytrack surface and supplemented his Lincoln Trial win with success here. Despite being 4lb worse off with Troubadour for beating him less than two lengths at Wolverhampton, he confirmed the form over this longer trip. The soft surface at Doncaster did not suit him last time and he will be happier on fast ground on turf, but the opening of this track will also hopefully increase opportunities for horses of his calibre on sand. (op 15-8)
Troubadour(IRE) had a 4lb pull in the weights with Re Barolo compared with when they met in the Lincoln Trial, but it was not enough for him to reverse the form. He probably was not as suited by the longer trip as the winner, and he remains a difficult horse to place. (op 3-1)
Road To Love(IRE), having his first run since Royal Ascot last year and debuting on the All-Weather, was allowed to take up his customary front-running role without any opposition. He failed to take advantage, though, and finished up well held. He probably needed the run. (op Evens tchd 5-4)

1725 HARE GREEN H'CAP — 1m 2f (P)
7:20 (7:20) (Class 5) (0-70,68) 4-Y-O+ — **£2,590** (£770; £385; £192) **Stalls** Low

Form — RPR
1-06 **1** — **Dream Of Fortune (IRE)**[34] [1039] 4-9-4 **68**..........(t) JamieSpencer 3 — 76
(M G Quinlan) *mde all: set stdy gallop tl qckned wl over 2f out: edgd rt briefly u.p over 1f out: hld on wl fnl f* **7/2**[2]
0401 **2** *nk* **Josr's Magic (IRE)**[16] [1374] 4-8-3 **56**.......... KirstyMilczarek(3) 7 — 63
(H J Collingridge) *plld hrd: hld up in tch: c wd bnd 2f out: hdwy u.p wl over 1f out: r.o to go 2nd ins fnl f: hld toward fin* **3/1**[1]
3135 **3** *1/2* **Our Kes (IRE)**[21] [1266] 6-9-1 **65**.......... RobertWinston 5 — 71
(P Howling) *stdd s and slowly away: plld hrd: hld up in last pl: stl last jst over 2f out: r.o wl u.p fnl f: nt rch ldrs* **7/2**[2]
6-45 **4** *1 3/4* **Art Market (CAN)**[6] [1585] 5-8-13 **66**.......... KevinGhunowa(3) 6 — 69
(Miss Jo Crowley) *chsd ldrs tl wnt 2nd over 6f out: short of room briefly and sltly outpcd over 2f out: rallied to chse wnr u.p over 1f out: no ex ins fnl f* **4/1**[3]
5-60 **5** *3/4* **Active Asset (IRE)**[19] [1296] 6-9-1 **65**.......... NeilPollard 9 — 66
(A J McCabe) *t.k.h: hld up in tch: hdwy to press ldrs over 3f out: rdn to chse wnr over 2f out tl over 1f out: wknd fnl f* **17/2**
60-0 **6** *1/2* **Nothingtodeclaire**[42] [941] 4-8-11 **61**.......... RobertHavlin 2 — 61
(V Smith) *hld up in tch in rr: rdn and unable qck 3f out: rallied over 1f out: swtchd lft 1f out: kpt on but nvr pce to threaten ldrs* **33/1**
40-4 **7** *1 1/2* **The Flying Cowboy (IRE)**[17] [1349] 4-9-1 **65**.......... TGMcLaughlin 8 — 62
(Jane Chapple-Hyam) *t.k.h: hld up bhd: rdn and unable qck wl over 3f out: swtchd lft over 1f out: no ch w ldrs* **10/1**
06-6 **8** *3* **To The Max (IRE)**[12] [1458] 4-9-2 **66**.......... JohnEgan 4 — 57
(Mrs C A Dunnett) *t.k.h: chsd wnr tl over 6f out: styd chsng ldrs: rdn 2f out: wknd over 1f out* **25/1**

2m 10.73s (2.13) **Going Correction** -0.025s/f (Stan) — **8** Ran SP% **115.8**
Speed ratings (Par 103): **90,89,89,87,87 86,85,83**
CSF £14.69 CT £38.78 TOTE £3.10: £1.70, £1.10, £2.10; EX 24.30.
Owner N J Jones **Bred** Newborough Stud **Trained** Newmarket, Suffolk

FOCUS
An ordinary handicap run at a dawdle and the winning time was 2.82 seconds slower than the preceding three-runner conditions event. The way the race was run caused a few to pull very hard though, and so the form, despite the runner-up and fourth being close to their marks, may not be totally reliable. The bulk of the field seemed very keen to come down the middle of the track in the home straight and they certainly held the advantage here.
Our Kes(IRE) Official explanation: jockey said mare ran too free early

1726 GREAT HOLLAND H'CAP — 2m (P)
7:50 (7:51) (Class 6) (0-55,55) 4-Y-O+ — **£1,942** (£578; £288; £144) **Stalls** Low

Form — RPR
1053 **1** — **Whaxaar (IRE)**[12] [1459] 4-9-1 **55**.......... RobertHavlin 4 — 68
(R Ingram) *t.k.h: hld up in tch: rdn 3f out: led over 1f out: styd on wl* **8/1**
/06- **2** *2 1/2* **Wotchalike (IRE)**[9] [733] 6-9-5 **55**..........(p) RichardThomas 13 — 65
(Jim Best) *hmpd s: bhd: 4f out: kpt on u.p fr 3f out: wnt 2nd last 100yds: nvr nr wnr* **13/2**[3]
6040 **3** *1 1/2* **Arabian Sun**[23] [1246] 4-8-11 **51**..........(v) MickyFenton 12 — 59
(M J Attwater) *wnt rt s: chsd ldr tl wnt 2nd 8f out: rdn over 5f out: clsd on ldr over 4f out: led 3f out: hdd over 2f out: one pce fnl f* **8/1**
4103 **4** *hd* **Starstruck Peter (IRE)**[23] [1246] 4-8-13 **53**..........(t) PaulDoe 14 — 61
(S Curran) *bmpd s: hld up in tch: hdwy over 4f out: rdn to ld narrowly over 2f out: hdd over 1f out: one pce* **7/2**[1]
53-4 **5** *6* **Missie Baileys**[98] [269] 6-8-12 **48** oh1 ow2..........(p) RobertWinston 10 — 49
(Mrs L J Mongan) *t.k.h: hld up in midfield: hdwy over 3f out: chsd ldrs and hrd rdn over 2f out: wknd over 1f out* **20/1**
2305 **6** *1 1/4* **Aqua Pura (GER)**[12] [1459] 9-8-13 **49**.......... JamieSpencer 3 — 50
(A P Stringer) *led: drvn clr over 7f out: 6 l clr 6f out: reduced ld and drvn 4f out: hdd 3f out: wknd over 1f out: eased whn btn ins fnl f* **9/2**[2]
30/3 **7** *1* **Zeloso**[14] [1408] 10-8-10 **46** oh1..........(b) SteveDrowne 8 — 44
(M F Harris) *hld up towards rr: hdwy and rdn over 4f out: chsd ldrs u.p over 2f out: sn no imp and wl btn* **12/1**
510- **8** *19* **Rajayoga**[223] [5573] 7-8-10 **46** oh1.......... JimmyQuinn 5 — 21
(M H Tompkins) *hld up in midfield: rdn and wl over 3f out: no imp whn nt clr run 3f out: t.o* **10/1**
6400 **9** *7* **Topwell**[9] [1518] 7-8-10 **46** oh1..........(be) DeanMcKeown 15 — 13
(R C Guest) *s.i.s: hld up wl bhd: t.o last 4f* **66/1**
0254 **10** *1* **Ronsard (IRE)**[30] [1121] 6-8-10 **46** oh1.......... TGMcLaughlin 6 — 12
(P D Evans) *stdd s: hld up towards rr: rdn and struggling 4f out: t.o* **14/1**
0010 **11** *6* **Shenandoah Girl**[14] [1405] 5-9-1 **51**.......... DarryllHolland 2 — 9
(Miss Gay Kelleway) *hld up in tch: rdn wl over 3f out: wknd 3f out: virtually p.u ins fnl f: t.o* **16/1**
6664 **12** *12* **Only Hope**[58] [776] 4-8-6 **46** oh1..........(p) PaulEddery 9 — —
(Miss Diana Weeden) *s.i.s: hedl up wl bhd: lost tch over 4f out: virtually p.u fnl f: t.o* **20/1**
0-04 **13** *46* **Sadler's Hill (IRE)**[61] [751] 4-8-7 **47** oh1 ow1.......... ShaneKelly 7 — —
(M J McGrath) *t.k.h: hld up towards rr: rdn over 4f out: sn wl bhd: virtually p.u last 2f: t.o* **66/1**
/00- **14** *nk* **Public Eye**[466] [187] 7-8-10 **46** oh1.......... ChrisCatlin 1 — —
(L A Dace) *chsd ldrs tl rdn and lost pl 4f out: virtually p.u last 2f: t.o* **40/1**
000/ **P** — **Money Hills**[411] [871] 6-8-10 **46** oh1.......... JohnEgan 11 — —
(Mrs C A Dunnett) *chsd ldr tl 8f out: sn rdn and dropped to rr: wl t.o fr 5f out: p.u 1f out* **66/1**

3m 28.69s (-1.31) **Going Correction** -0.025s/f (Stan)
WFA 4 from 5yo+ 4lb — **15** Ran SP% **121.7**
Speed ratings (Par 101): **102,100,100,99,96 96,95,86,82,82 79,73,50,50,—**
CSF £56.16 CT £436.51 TOTE £11.10: £2.70, £2.80, £3.80; EX 66.00 Place 6 £36.45, Place 5 £30.65..
Owner G F Chesneaux **Bred** Agricola Del Parco **Trained** Epsom, Surrey

FOCUS
Quite a competitive staying handicap despite nine of the 15 runners being out of the handicap. The sudden quickening of the pace on the final circuit made this a proper test and they finished very well spread out. The form looks sound and has been rated positively.
T/Plt: £26.50 to a £1 stake. Pool: £43,707.06. 1,200.28 winning tickets. T/Qpdt: £24.20 to a £1 stake. Pool: £4,544.72. 138.80 winning tickets. SP

1515 PONTEFRACT (L-H)
Wednesday, April 30

OFFICIAL GOING: Soft (heavy in places; 5.5) changing to heavy after race 3 (3.30)
Wind: Virtually nil Weather: Dry, sunny periods

1727 EUROPEAN BREEDERS' FUND BETDIRECT.COM MAIDEN STKS — 5f
2:20 (2:23) (Class 4) 2-Y-O — **£4,857** (£1,445; £722; £360) **Stalls** Low

Form — RPR
1 — **Toby Tyler** 2-9-0 0.......... JamieMoriarty(3) 3 — 70
(P T Midgley) *chsd ldrs: hdwy 2f out: rdn to ld appr fnl f: styd on wl* **12/1**
2 *1 1/4* **Cutting Comments** 2-9-3 0.......... PhillipMakin 10 — 66
(M Dods) *prom: led 2f out: sn rdn and hdd over 1f out: kpt on* **9/2**[1]
3 *2 1/2* **Fitzolini** 2-9-3 0.......... SilvestreDeSousa 7 — 57
(A D Brown) *towards rr: rdn along 1/2-way: hdwy over 1f out: swtchd lft and styd on wl fnl f: nrst fin* **11/1**
4 *1 1/4* **Tito Gobbi** 2-9-3 0.......... LeeEnstone 12 — 52+
(P C Haslam) *cl up on outer: ev ch whn carried wd home bnd to stands' rail: sn rdn and kpt on: no ch w ins gp* **10/1**
5 *3* **Mullglen** 2-9-3 0.......... DavidAllan 6 — 41
(T D Easterby) *chsd ldrs: effrt and ev ch 2f out: sn rdn and wknd over 1f out* **6/1**[2]
6 *hd* **El Portet** 2-9-3 0.......... AndrewElliott 2 — 40
(G M Moore) *s.i.s and towards rr: hdwy over 2f out: sn rdn and no imp* **10/1**
7 *1 3/4* **Mymateeric** 2-9-3 0.......... PatCosgrave 4 — 34
(J Pearce) *chsd ldrs: swtchd rt to centre 2f out: sn rdn and outpcd* **6/1**[2]
23 **8** *9* **Eilean Eeve**[15] [1377] 2-8-12 0.......... NeilPollard 1 — —
(A J McCabe) *led: hung bdly rt and hdd 2f out: c wd to stands rail and sn wknd* **9/2**[1]
8 *dht* **Sandies Sister** 2-8-9 0.......... MarkLawson(3) 9 — —
(M Brittain) *v.s.a: a bhd* **10/1**
10 *1/2* **Rios Boy (IRE)** 2-9-0 0.......... DuranFentiman(3) 11 — —
(T D Easterby) *in tch: rdn along 1/2-way: sn wknd* **8/1**[3]

69.71 secs (6.41) **Going Correction** +1.15s/f (Soft) — **10** Ran SP% **119.3**
Speed ratings (Par 94): **94,92,88,86,81 80,78,63,63,62**
CSF £66.91 TOTE £17.60: £5.20, £1.60, £3.40; EX 60.70.
Owner Anthony D Copley **Bred** Whitsbury Manor Stud **Trained** Westow, N Yorks

FOCUS
A few of these seemed fancied, but it looked just a modest fillies' maiden and has been rated conservatively for now. A couple raced stands' side, and one came up the middle, but those who stayed towards the far side appeared to be at an advantage.

NOTEBOOK
Toby Tyler, a 2,500gns gelded son of Best Of The Bests, half-brother to useful dual 7f juvenile winner Sister Bluebird, dual 1m4f winner Tifernati, and hurdles winner Fanling Lady, out of a 1m2f winner, made a successful debut in convincing fashion. Having travelled well enough just off the pace, he stayed on strongest of all when asked for his effort in the straight and was well on top at the line. This is probably just modest form, but he looks the type who can improve and he should stay further in time.
Cutting Comments, a 45,000gns son of Acclamation and half-brother to 1m1f juvenile winner Gold Response, out of a 1m2f winner, was sent off joint-favourite on his racecourse debut and ran a pleasing race. He was clear in second and, with the benefit of this outing, he should find a similarly ordinary maiden. (op 7-2 tchd 5-1)
Fitzolini, a gelded son of Bertolini and half-brother to 5f juvenile winner Fitzwarren, showed signs of inexperience, coming under pressure a fair way out, but he responded well and stuck on for a place. He should learn from this. (op 25-1)
Tito Gobbi, a Lomitas half-sister to 5f juvenile winner Bosun Breeze, out of a triple 7f-1m winner, ended up on the stands' side in the straight, but it was unclear whether that was by design, as Eilean Eeve, who was on his inside, pretty much carried him that way when cutting across. He showed plenty of ability. (op 9-1 tchd 8-1)

Mullglen, an 8,000gns son of Mull Of Kintyre and first foal of an unraced sister to Epos, a dual 1m-1m2f winner at two to three in France, was well held on his racecourse bow, running to just a moderate level. (op 8-1 tchd 11-2)

Eilean Eeve was too keen for her own good early on and, one of only two to race stands' side in the straight, the other being Tito Gobbi, she weakened out of contention very tamely. Official explanation: jockey said filly hung badly right-handed (op 5-1 tchd 7-2)

Sandies Sister Official explanation: jockey said filly missed the break (op 5-1 tchd 7-2)

1728 TOTESPORT.COM MAIDEN STKS 1m 2f 6y
2:55 (2:55) (Class 5) 3-Y-O £3,238 (£963; £481; £240)

Form					RPR
0-	1		**Ephorus (USA)**[165] 6855 3-9-3 0 ... J-PGuillambert 5		81
			(Sir Michael Stoute) *led 1f: trckd ldr: chal wl over 1f out: sn rdn: styd on ins fnl f to ld fnl 75yds*	6/1	
5-3	2	1/2	**Sir Royal (USA)**[15] 1379 3-9-0 0 ... PJMcDonald(3) 1		80
			(G A Swinbank) *led after 1f: rdn along wl over 1f out: drvn and edgd rt ent fnl f: hdd and no ex fnl 75yds*	5/2[2]	
3	3	2 1/2	**Sea Chorus**[15] 1382 3-8-12 0 ... HayleyTurner 3		70
			(M L W Bell) *trckd ldng pair: effrt 3f out: rdn along 2f out: drvn and one pce appr fnl f*	9/2[3]	
2	4	3 1/2	**Coin Of The Realm (IRE)**[15] 1382 3-9-3 0 ... TQuinn 7		68
			(E A L Dunlop) *trckd ldrs: pushed along 3f out: rdn wl over 1f out and sn btn*	2/1[1]	
42-3	5	2 1/4	**King Kenny**[15] 1380 3-9-0 78 ... DNolan(3) 4		64
			(S Parr) *hld up: effrt and sme hdwy over 2f out: sn rdn and wknd*	5/1	

2m 24.61s (10.91) **Going Correction** +1.15s/f (Soft) 5 Ran SP% **111.0**
Speed ratings (Par 98): **102,101,99,96,95**
CSF £21.28 TOTE £6.30: £2.90, £1.60; EX 16.70.
Owner D Smith, Mrs J Magnier, M Tabor **Bred** B M Kelley, B P Walden & Aerial Bstk **Trained** Newmarket, Suffolk

FOCUS
A reasonable maiden for the course but not that easy to rate although it has been treated slightly positively. A flip start and, despite the early pace being just steady, the order they jumped off in didn't change much. The action took place up the centre of the track in the straight.

Coin Of The Realm(IRE) Official explanation: jockey said colt was unsuited by the soft (heavy in places) ground

1729 SKYBET.COM H'CAP 1m 4y
3:30 (3:30) (Class 5) (0-70,70) 4-Y-O+ £3,238 (£963; £481; £240) Stalls Low

Form					RPR
100-	1		**Dispol Isle (IRE)**[176] 6701 6-9-2 68 ... PaulFessey 6		78
			(T D Barron) *hld up towards rr: hdwy 3f out: rdn wl over 1f out: styd on strly to ld wl ins fnl f*	14/1	
50-3	2	1 3/4	**Hula Ballew**[12] 1449 8-9-4 70 ... PhillipMakin 4		76
			(M Dods) *chsd ldrs: hdwy and wd st to stands' rail: sn prom and rdn over 1f out: edgd lft and kpt on same pce ins fnl f*	5/1[2]	
00-0	3	1/2	**Holiday Cocktail**[28] 1159 6-8-7 59 ... GrahamGibbons 13		64
			(J J Quinn) *towards rr: pushed along and outpcd 1/2-way: rdn and hdwy 2f out: styd on u.p ins fnl f: nrst fin*	18/1	
0-0	4	1/2	**Out Of Nothing**[15] 1383 5-8-5 62 ... JackMitchell(5) 2		66
			(K M Prendergast) *prom: hdwy to ld wl over 1f out: sn rdn: hdd & wknd wl ins fnl f*	33/1	
54-2	5	6	**Surwaki (USA)**[12] 1449 6-9-2 68 ... NCallan 5		58
			(R M H Cowell) *cl up: effrt over 2f out: sn rdn and ev ch tl drvn wl over 1f out and grad wknd*	7/2[1]	
04-5	6	5	**Rain Stops Play (IRE)**[12] 1456 6-9-4 70 ... PatCosgrave 3		48
			(M Quinn) *led: rdn along over 2f out: hdd wl over 1f out and grad wknd*	7/1[3]	
0-30	7	7	**Tizzy May (FR)**[9] 1521 8-8-11 63 ... TomEaves 17		25
			(B Ellison) *chsd ldrs on outer: rdn along 3f out: sn drvn and outpcd fnl 2f*	12/1	
363-	8	4	**Aggravation**[167] 6824 6-9-4 70 ... TQuinn 1		23
			(D R C Elsworth) *s.i.s: a towards rr*	9/1	
2-00	9	3	**Gala Sunday (USA)**[14] 1394 8-8-6 58 ...(t) DaleGibson 16		4
			(M W Easterby) *a in rr*	28/1	
	10	3/4	**Ornella**[148] 4-9-0 69 ... TravisBlock(3) 10		13
			(H Morrison) *midfield: rdn along over 3f out: nvr a factor*	12/1	
100-	11	11	**Mountain Cat (IRE)**[180] 6623 4-9-4 70 ... NeilPollard 9		—
			(W J Musson) *chsd ldrs on outer: rdn along 3f out and sn wknd*	14/1	
-035	12	4 1/2	**Sands Of Barra (IRE)**[12] 1450 5-9-1 67 ... RoystonFfrench 7		—
			(I W McInnes) *prom: rdn along over 2f out and sn wknd*	7/1[3]	
6616	13	4 1/2	**General Feeling (IRE)**[35] 1032 7-8-0 59 ow2...(p) DeclanCannon(7) 11		—
			(S T Mason) *a towards rr: bhd fnl 3f*	18/1	

1m 56.83s (10.93) **Going Correction** +1.55s/f (Heav) 13 Ran SP% **119.5**
Speed ratings (Par 103): **107,105,104,104,98 93,86,82,79,78 67,63,58**
CSF £82.58 CT £1332.14 TOTE £20.30: £4.10, £2.50, £5.50; EX 138.00.
Owner W B Imison **Bred** Mrs I A Balding **Trained** Maunby, N Yorks

FOCUS
This was still the biggest field on the card despite the four non-runners and they went a decent pace in the conditions. The field came centre to stands' side in the home straight and the front four pulled well clear, with the third and fourth setting the standard.

1730 LADBROKES FILLIES' H'CAP 1m 2f 6y
4:05 (4:05) (Class 3) (0-90,84) 3-Y-O- £9,346 (£2,799; £1,399; £700; £349) Stalls Far side

Form					RPR
0353	1		**Ella**[27] 1172 4-9-4 72 ... NCallan 4		85+
			(G A Swinbank) *t.k.h: mde all: rdn 2f out: edgd lft ent fnl f: styd on wl*	11/4[2]	
1	2	5	**Born Tobouggie (GER)**[15] 1379 3-8-13 84 ... TPQueally 5		89+
			(H R A Cecil) *trckd ldng pair: hdwy to chse wnr over 2f out and sn rdn: drvn and wandered over 1f out: one pce ins fnl f*	7/4[1]	
-115	3	4	**Gallic Charm (IRE)**[25] 1208 3-8-6 77 ... TQuinn 3		72
			(D R C Elsworth) *hld up in rr: hdwy 3f out: rdn to chse ldng pair 2f out: sn drvn and no imp*	12/1	
010-	4	15	**Barawin (IRE)**[187] 6471 3-8-10 81 ... AndrewElliott 1		46
			(K R Burke) *hld up: swtchd wd and hdwy over 4f out: rdn along 3f out: drvn 2f out and sn btn*	6/1	
36-3	5	25	**Lady Friend**[18] 1329 6-9-9 77 ... MichaelHills 7		—
			(J W Hills) *chsd wnr: rdn along 3f out: sn wknd and eased*	7/2[3]	

2m 30.58s (16.88) **Going Correction** +1.55s/f (Heav)
WFA 3 from 4yo+ 17lb 5 Ran SP% **107.2**
Speed ratings (Par 104): **94,90,86,74,54**
CSF £7.54 TOTE £3.80: £1.90, £1.20; EX 8.10.
Owner Guy Reed **Bred** G Reed **Trained** Melsonby, N Yorks

FOCUS
Another race with no stalls and dominated by the horse given a start by her rivals and there os not much solid form to go on. It took a couple of seconds for the horses to jump off - hence the moderate winning time - and not only did they finish well spread out but they also finished legless.

NOTEBOOK
Ella, making her handicap debut after running well on easy ground last time, made every yard and saw it out in game style especially as she was keen enough early, but she was given a couple of lengths start by her rivals so it remains to be seen quite what she achieved. She is still open to further improvement though. (tchd 5-2)

Born Tobouggie(GER), winner of her only previous start on testing ground and therefore a difficult filly for the Handicapper to assess, was keen enough early once again over this extra 2f, but was still the only one to stick with the winner from the home turn before eventually finding it all too much. This was a rather odd race though, and she remains open to further improvement. (op 11-8)

Gallic Charm(IRE), making her turf debut and stepping up 2f in distance, was ridden to get the trip in the conditions but she was making no impression on the front pair from the home turn. She should be given another chance to prove that she stays this trip on better ground. (op 17-2)

Barawin(IRE), whose only previous win came on a soft surface, tried to get into the race approaching the final bend but was soon treading water. There is the strong possibility that she needed these after six months off and any horse can be forgiven a modest effort in these conditions. (op 9-1)

Lady Friend had finished third on easy ground on her Doncaster reappearance, but those conditions were nothing like as testing as these. Beaten before the home bend, she was then allowed to coast home and is a lot better than this. (op 9-2)

1731 CORALBET BY FREEPHONE 0800 242 232 H'CAP 1m 4f 8y
4:40 (4:41) (Class 5) (0-75,74) 3-Y-O £3,238 (£963; £481; £240) Stalls Low

Form					RPR
-363	1		**Allied Powers (IRE)**[4] 1614 3-8-11 68 ... TravisBlock(3) 7		91+
			(M L W Bell) *hld up in rr: gd hdwy on inner 3f out: led over 2f out: sn rdn clr: easily*	5/2[2]	
00-0	2	4	**Blimey O'Riley (IRE)**[14] 1398 3-9-4 72 ... PaulMulrennan 3		82
			(M H Tompkins) *led: rdn along 3f out: hdd over 2f out: sn drvn and kpt on: no ch w wnr*	14/1	
5231	3	7	**Silver Waters**[9] 1516 3-9-6 74 6ex ... TQuinn 6		73
			(D R C Elsworth) *prom: cl up and niggled along 3f out: rdn over 2f out and sn one pce*	15/8[1]	
5-32	4	5	**Graylyn Ruby (FR)**[8] 1553 3-8-3 60 ... LukeMorris(3) 2		51
			(J Jay) *trckd ldrs: effrt 3f out: sn rdn along: drvn 2f out and sn wknd*	11/4[3]	
1	5	3	**Silver Spruce**[16] 1364 3-8-11 65 ... FergalLynch 5		51
			(I W McInnes) *trckd ldrs: hdwy on outer 4f out: rdn along 3f out: drvn and wknd over 2f out*	10/1	
000-	6	3/4	**Flash Of Fire (USA)**[292] 3478 3-8-7 61 ... PaulHanagan 1		46
			(J M P Eustace) *in tch: rdn along 4f out: sn wknd*	20/1	

3m 0.75s (19.95) **Going Correction** +1.95s/f (Heav) 6 Ran SP% **110.5**
Speed ratings (Par 98): **111,108,103,100,98 97**
CSF £32.56 TOTE £3.40: £1.80, £5.10; EX 31.90.
Owner David Fish And Edward Ware **Bred** Saad Bin Mishrif **Trained** Newmarket, Suffolk

FOCUS
A very decent winning time for the type of contest given the conditions and possible to take the race at something close to face value for now.

1732 FRIENDS OF THE NORTHERN RACING COLLEGE H'CAP 1m 2f 6y
5:15 (5:16) (Class 5) (0-75,73) 4-Y-O+ £3,238 (£963; £481; £240) Stalls Far side

Form					RPR
26-1	1		**Force Group (IRE)**[9] 1521 4-8-13 68 ... PaulMulrennan 6		81+
			(M H Tompkins) *trckd ldrs: hdwy over 3f out: led 2f out and sn rdn: drvn over 1f out: kpt on wl u.p ins fnl f*	9/4[1]	
-140	2	3/4	**Mandalay Prince**[21] 1266 4-8-6 61 ... DavidKinsella 2		69
			(W J Musson) *trckd ldrs: effrt 3f out: rdn to chal 2f out and ev ch tl drvn and no ex wl ins fnl f*	12/1	
1352	3	2	**Lucayan Dancer**[9] 1521 8-8-8 70 ... AdeleRothery(7) 9		74
			(D Nicholls) *led: rdn along 3f out and sn hdd: drvn 2f out: kpt on same pce ent fnl f*	6/1[3]	
1106	4	2 3/4	**Red Wine**[19] 1299 9-9-3 72 ... NCallan 7		71
			(A J McCabe) *hld up in rr: hdwy 4f out: chal 2f out: rdn wl over 1f out and ch tl wknd jst ins fnl f*	7/2[2]	
0/-1	5	11	**Twilight Dawn**[25] 1222 4-9-4 73 ... PaulHanagan 4		50
			(L Lungo) *trckd ldrs: effrt on outer 4f out: rdn along 3f: sn wknd*	18/1	
53-2	6	10	**Effigy**[15] 1383 4-8-12 67 ... DaneO'Neill 8		24
			(H Candy) *prom: effrt to ld wl over 2f out: sn rdn and hdd 2f out: sn wknd*	9/4[1]	
22-0	7	8	**Kalasam**[11] 1482 4-8-10 72 ... BradleyRoper(7) 1		13
			(M W Easterby) *trckd ldrs: hdwy on inner 4f out: rdn along 3f out: sn wknd*	25/1	
0-00	8	2 1/4	**Old Romney**[19] 1296 4-8-5 67 ... NSLawes(7) 12		—
			(M W Easterby) *hld up in rr: rapid hdwy to chse ldr 7f out: rdn along over 4f out and sn wknd*	50/1	

2m 34.23s (20.53) **Going Correction** +1.95s/f (Heav) 8 Ran SP% **116.8**
Speed ratings (Par 103): **95,94,92,90,81 73,67,65**
CSF £32.42 CT £146.05 TOTE £2.70: £1.30, £3.00, £1.90; EX 37.70 Place 6 £248.08, Place 5 £70.24..
Owner The Force Group **Bred** Airlie Stud And Sir Thomas Pilkington **Trained** Newmarket, Suffolk

FOCUS
No stalls once again and four came well clear in what was a modest handicap. The form looks sound enough rated around the third and fourth.

Old Romney Official explanation: trainer later said gelding was found to be coughing after the race

T/Plt: £299.80 to a £1 stake. Pool: £55,592.69. 135.35 winning tickets. T/Qpdt: £53.90 to a £1 stake. Pool: £3,494.88. 47.90 winning tickets. JR

1733 - 1735a (Foreign Racing) - See Raceform Interactive

1534 FOLKESTONE (R-H)
Thursday, May 1

OFFICIAL GOING: Good to soft
Wind: Fresh, across

1736 FOLKESTONE-RACECOURSE.CO.UK MAIDEN AUCTION STKS 5f
2:20 (2:22) (Class 6) 2-Y-O £2,266 (£674; £337; £168) Stalls Low

Form					RPR
	1		**Langs Lash (IRE)** 2-8-7 0 ... AlanMunro 5		83+
			(M G Quinlan) *mde all: shkn up and drew clr appr fnl f*	4/1[2]	
0	2	4	**Hay Fever (IRE)**[14] 1413 2-8-12 0 ... StephenCarson 7		74
			(Eve Johnson Houghton) *slowly out of stalls: sn trckd ldr: kpt on but outpcd fr over 1f out*	9/2[3]	
	3	1 3/4	**Sonhador** 2-9-1 0 ... JimCrowley 9		70
			(P Winkworth) *chsd ldrs: one pce ins fnl 2f*	14/1	

4 3 1/2 **Lucky Punt** 2-8-12 0 .... TQuinn 6 55
(B G Powell) *in tch: nt qckn 1/2-way: styd on one pce* **14/1**

05 5 hd **Multi Tasker**[14] 1413 2-8-9 0 .... ChrisCatlin 8 51
(V Smith) *prom on outside: rdn 2f out: wknd fnl f* **7/2**[1]

6 6 **Astroleo** 2-8-11 0 .... JamieSpencer 1 31
(M H Tompkins) *towards rr and a outpcd* **7/1**

0 7 3 **Rich Red (IRE)**[17] 1363 2-9-1 0 .... PatDobbs 4 25
(R Hannon) *broke wl: sn rdn and bhd fr 1/2-way* **4/1**[2]

8 3 **Debbys Boy** 2-8-10 0 .... HayleyTurner 2 9
(Miss Gay Kelleway) *outpcd and a bhd* **10/1**

9 2 1/4 **Tightrope (IRE)** 2-8-11 0 .... FergusSweeney 3 —
(T D McCarthy) *outpcd and sn struggling in rr* **28/1**

61.01 secs (1.01) **Going Correction** +0.10s/f (Good) **9** Ran SP% **118.8**
Speed ratings (Par 91): **95,88,85,80,79 70,65,60,57**
CSF £23.14 TOTE £5.30: £1.60, £1.50, £4.70; EX 30.80 TRIFECTA Not won..
Owner John Hanly **Bred** Cathal Ryan **Trained** Newmarket, Suffolk

FOCUS
Probably only modest maiden form but could be rated higher.

NOTEBOOK
Langs Lash(IRE) is a half-sister to Resonator, a triple winner at 1m4f plus in France, and Sir Echo, a 1m4f winner in France, but her sire is more of an influence for speed. Fast away, she got the all-important rail position and, quickening up approaching the furlong marker, she drew away for an easy win. This was probably not a great heat but she did it well. (tchd 9-2)
Hay Fever(IRE), a half-brother to Ten Spot, a dual 7f-1m winner, was again slowly away, just like on his debut, but he soon overcame it this time and raced upsides the leader. He was left behind by her when she quickened up, but it was still a solid effort, and he reversed Kempton form with Multi Tasker in the process. (op 8-1 tchd 9-1)
Sonhador, a half-brother to Stamford Blue, a prolific winner between 5f and 1m, raced two off the favoured rail and in the circumstances he was not disgraced on his debut. (op 12-1)
Lucky Punt, whose dam was a 6f winner at two, is bred for speed. He stayed on late without being competitive and is entitled to come on for the run. Official explanation: jockey said colt hung left (op 16-1 tchd 10-1)
Multi Tasker, the most experienced runner in the field, could not confirm Kempton form with Hay Fever after racing widest of all throughout. He was hugely disadvantaged by where he raced. (op 11-2 tchd 6-1)
Astroleo had the best draw but was unable to take advantage of it on his debut. (op 4-1)
Tightrope(IRE) Official explanation: jockey said colt hung left

1737 EASTWELL MANOR MAIDEN STKS 5f
2:50 (2:52) (Class 5) 3-Y-O+ **£2,590** (£770; £385; £192) **Stalls** Low

Form RPR

22- 1 **Maimoona (IRE)**[216] 5770 3-8-9 0 .... RHills 9 82+
(W J Haggas) *sn trckd ldr: shkn up to ld wl over 1f out: sn clr* **5/4**[1]

2 4 **Filemot** 3-8-6 0 .... KirstyMilczarek(3) 8 64
(John Berry) *led tl rdn and hdd wl over 1f out: outpcd by wnr: jst hld on for 2nd* **40/1**

5- 3 nk **Compton Rose**[276] 4016 3-8-9 0 .... FergusSweeney 7 63
(H Candy) *prom: rdn and kpt on fnl f* **13/2**

632- 4 1 3/4 **Doric Lady**[176] 6721 3-8-9 73 .... AlanMunro 3 57
(J A R Toller) *slowly away: hld up: styd on fr over 1f out* **4/1**[2]

-323 5 1/2 **Irish Music (IRE)**[14] 1414 3-9-0 67 .... JamieSpencer 1 60
(A P Jarvis) *slowly away: swtchd rt over 1f out: kpt on but nvr on terms* **5/1**[3]

3-0 6 1 1/4 **Portrush Storm**[13] 1452 3-8-9 0 .... PatCosgrave 4 50
(D Carroll) *t.k.h early: chsd ldrs: swtchd rt 1/2-way: sn btn* **16/1**

5-5 7 2 3/4 **Tantris (IRE)**[15] 1410 3-9-0 0 .... JimCrowley 2 46+
(J A Osborne) *slowly away: a in rr* **22/1**

4 8 1 1/4 **Elzain (IRE)**[35] 1036 3-8-9 0 .... ChrisCatlin 5 36
(M R Channon) *prom: rdn 1/2-way: sn wknd* **20/1**

9 3 3/4 **Colour Of Money** 3-9-0 0 .... PatDobbs 10 28
(S A Callaghan) *c over to ins fr wd draw: a bhd* **25/1**

10 3 **Delerios** 3-9-0 0 .... RichardThomas 11 17
(Jim Best) *v.s.a: a struggling in rr* **66/1**

60.33 secs (0.33) **Going Correction** +0.10s/f (Good) **10** Ran SP% **117.2**
Speed ratings (Par 103): **101,94,94,91,90 88,84,82,76,71**
CSF £77.95 TOTE £2.20: £1.20, £14.30, £2.10; EX 83.00 Trifecta £259.30 Part won. Pool: £365.35 - 0.49 winning units..
Owner Hamdan Al Maktoum **Bred** Shadwell Estate Company Limited **Trained** Newmarket, Suffolk

FOCUS
Only a modest maiden and the winner looked a league above the rest, although the form looks modest behind the winner.

1738 HUNTER CHASE EVENING HERE MAY 15TH FILLIES' H'CAP 6f
3:20 (3:20) (Class 5) (0-70,70) 3-Y-O **£2,331** (£693; £346; £173) **Stalls** Low

Form RPR

062- 1 **Luminous Gold**[205] 6082 3-9-2 68 .... AlanMunro 5 83+
(C F Wall) *trckd ldr: led over 2f out: r.o wl: comf* **7/2**[2]

4-02 2 1 1/2 **Leading Edge (IRE)**[9] 1548 3-9-2 68 .... ChrisCatlin 3 75
(M R Channon) *a.p: rdn to go 2nd fnl 100yds* **11/4**[1]

405- 3 1 3/4 **Tina's Best (IRE)**[191] 6404 3-8-12 69 .... HaddenFrost(5) 7 70
(R Hannon) *trckd ldr: rdn and lost 2nd fnl 100yds* **7/2**[2]

3351 4 nse **Little Knickers**[3] 1671 3-9-2 68 6ex .... (b) TPQueally 2 69
(Andrew Reid) *in rr: reminders and swtchd rt over 1f out: kpt on but nvr nr to chal* **7/2**[2]

2546 5 4 **Alabama Spirit (USA)**[12] 1475 3-8-8 63 .... TolleyDean(3) 11 51
(J Balding) *in rr on outside: rdn over 2f out: no ch fr over 1f out* **10/1**[3]

040- 6 1 1/4 **Imperial Decree**[191] 6410 3-9-4 70 .... NeilPollard 6 54
(John Berry) *hld up: on outside: nvr nr to chal* **11/1**

6-00 7 6 **River Gleam (IRE)**[22] 1271 3-8-6 58 .... (v[1]) RichardThomas 9 23
(A P Jarvis) *led tl hdd over 2f out: wknd qckly* **25/1**

1m 13.82s (1.12) **Going Correction** +0.10s/f (Good) **7** Ran SP% **114.6**
Speed ratings (Par 96): **96,94,91,91,86 84,76**
CSF £13.64 CT £35.10 TOTE £4.30: £1.70, £1.40; EX 14.50 Trifecta £64.50 Pool: £253.51 - 2.79 winning units..
Owner Dr Philip Brown **Bred** Darley **Trained** Newmarket, Suffolk

FOCUS
A modest handicap in which the stands' rail once again proved a big advantage. The form is rated around the runner-up and fourth.

1739 INVICTA MOTORS H'CAP 6f
3:50 (3:50) (Class 5) (0-75,73) 4-Y-O+ **£2,331** (£693; £346; £173) **Stalls** Low

Form RPR

30-0 1 **Mango Music**[23] 1253 5-9-1 70 .... TPQueally 2 82
(M Quinn) *mde all: rdn over 1f out: r.o* **11/2**

2321 2 1/2 **Savile's Delight (IRE)**[10] 1522 9-9-4 73 .... RichardKingscote 7 83
(Tom Dascombe) *chsd ldrs: wnt 2nd over 1f out: no imp on wnr ins fnl f* **5/2**[1]

0111 3 1 1/2 **After The Show**[17] 1366 7-9-4 73 .... ChrisCatlin 11 79
(Rae Guest) *stdd s: hdwy over 2f out: kpt on fnl f* **11/4**[2]

00-0 4 1/2 **Billy Red**[35] 1037 4-8-7 62 .... (b) JimCrowley 8 66
(J R Jenkins) *stdd s and swtchd lft: swtchd rt and hdwy over 1f out: nvr nrr* **22/1**

-043 5 2 1/4 **Gleaming Spirit (IRE)**[9] 1541 4-8-9 64 .... JamieSpencer 6 61
(A P Jarvis) *trckd wnr tl wknd over 1f out* **4/1**[3]

0254 6 2 1/4 **Linda Green**[10] 1522 7-8-0 62 .... MatthewDavies(7) 9 52
(M R Channon) *racd on outside: nvr on terms* **15/2**

0554 7 2 **Mine Behind**[87] 427 8-8-12 67 .... HayleyTurner 5 50
(J R Best) *chsd ldrs: rdn 1/2-way: sn bhd* **12/1**

1m 13.94s (1.24) **Going Correction** +0.10s/f (Good) **7** Ran SP% **114.4**
Speed ratings (Par 103): **95,94,92,91,88 85,83**
CSF £19.70 CT £45.47 TOTE £9.10: £3.10, £1.80; EX 22.80 Trifecta £153.50 Pool: £ 279.07 - 1.29 winning units..
Owner Brian Morton **Bred** A G Antoniades **Trained** Newmarket, Suffolk

FOCUS
Modest handicap form and once again the stands' rail proved a huge advantage. The form is ordinary rated around the placed horses.

1740 STAY IN TO WIN WITH H'CAP 7f (S)
4:20 (4:20) (Class 6) (0-60,64) 3-Y-O **£2,047** (£604; £302) **Stalls** Low

Form RPR

0-01 1 **Topazes**[7] 1592 3-9-8 64 6ex .... JamieSpencer 9 79+
(M L W Bell) *hld up: stdy hdwy to ld 2f out: wnt lft over 1f out: all out* **4/5**[1]

000- 2 nk **My Flame**[147] 7042 3-8-8 50 .... JimCrowley 4 61
(J R Jenkins) *a.p: led 1/2-way: hdd 2f out: short of room and swtchd rt over 1f out: kpt on wl ins fnl f* **50/1**

6-05 3 8 **Polychrome**[30] 1125 3-9-0 59 .... KirstyMilczarek(3) 8 48
(John Berry) *hld up: hdwy on outside whn bmpd over 2f: styd on to go 3rd ins fnl f: nvr nr to chal* **8/1**[2]

0-50 4 1 1/2 **Our Kally**[3] 1672 3-8-8 50 .... HayleyTurner 5 35
(M D I Usher) *in tch tl wknd wl over 1f out* **14/1**

5054 5 2 1/4 **Miss Bouggy Wouggy**[28] 1166 3-8-6 48 .... (b) JamesDoyle 3 27
(M Blanshard) *chsd ldrs tl wknd 2f out* **16/1**

040 6 1 3/4 **Blur**[12] 1467 3-9-2 58 .... PatDobbs 2 33
(R Hannon) *chsd ldrs tl wknd over 2f out* **10/1**[3]

06-6 7 3/4 **Rubytwosox (IRE)**[23] 1251 3-8-8 50 .... ChrisCatlin 6 23
(W R Muir) *prom tl wknd and wnt rt over 2f out* **16/1**

1665 8 3 1/4 **Snow Bounty**[26] 1203 3-9-2 58 .... SebSanders 13 22
(J S Moore) *swtchd lft s: a bhd* **10/1**[3]

500- 9 8 **Abfabfong (IRE)**[200] 6207 3-8-8 50 .... (p) FrankieMcDonald 7 —
(Mrs L C Jewell) *a bhd* **22/1**

0-04 10 1/2 **Wave Hill (IRE)**[20] 1315 3-8-11 60 .... KMay(7) 1 —
(B J Meehan) *t.k.h: led tl hdd over 3f out: wknd qckly* **11/1**

040- 11 11 **Libertytyne**[152] 6990 3-8-9 51 .... FergusSweeney 10 —
(S Kirk) *in tch: rdn 3f out: sn wknd* **66/1**

1m 29.9s (2.60) **Going Correction** +0.10s/f (Good) **11** Ran SP% **119.4**
Speed ratings (Par 97): **89,88,79,77,75 73,72,68,59,58 46**
CSF £67.95 CT £232.47 TOTE £1.70: £1.10, £11.00, £1.70; EX 51.20 Trifecta £192.10 Pool: £400.63 - 1.48 winning units..
Owner Baron F C Oppenheim **Bred** Baron F Von Oppenheim **Trained** Newmarket, Suffolk
■ Stewards' Enquiry : Chris Catlin one-day ban: careless riding (May 15)

FOCUS
Moderate form, with little promise shown by those in behind the first two.

1741 LADBROKES FOR INCREASED ODDS MEDIAN AUCTION MAIDEN STKS 1m 1f 149y
4:50 (4:52) (Class 6) 3-4-Y-O **£2,388** (£705; £352) **Stalls** Centre

Form RPR

34-4 1 **Stop On**[19] 1342 3-8-11 75 .... ChrisCatlin 5 69
(M R Channon) *trckd ldrs: wnt 2nd over 4f out kpt on ins to ld fnl 100yds* **10/1**

3- 2 1/2 **Shy**[218] 5727 3-8-6 0 .... StephenCarson 2 63
(P Winkworth) *led for 1f: chsd ldrs hdwy on ins 2f out: kpt on to go 2nd ins fnl f* **9/2**[3]

0-3 3 1/2 **Dancing Sword**[12] 1477 3-8-11 0 .... SebSanders 8 67
(H J L Dunlop) *rdn to ld after 1f: hung lft 2f out: rdn: edgd lft and hdd jst ins fnl f: lost 2nd fnl 100yds* **7/2**[2]

4 7 **First Coming** 4-9-12 0 .... GeorgeBaker 4 53
(B J McMath) *slowly away: mid-div: rdn 4f out: hung lft* **16/1**

3- 5 4 **Foresight**[187] 6494 3-8-11 0 .... JimCrowley 1 44
(Mrs A J Perrett) *sn trckd ldr: rdn and hung bdly lft fr over 2f out: rdn and sn wknd* **5/6**[1]

6 2 3/4 **Fleurs De Censier** 3-8-6 0 .... HayleyTurner 6 33
(D M Simcock) *a bhd* **16/1**

00-5 7 1 **Cobbold Point**[23] 1251 3-8-11 39 .... TGMcLaughlin 3 36
(S W Hall) *a bhd* **100/1**

8 26 **Power Of Speech** 3-8-11 0 .... (t) FergusSweeney 7 —
(J Gallagher) *slowly away: a bhd: t.o* **66/1**

2m 9.69s (4.79) **Going Correction** +0.425s/f (Yiel)
WFA 3 from 4yo 15lb **8** Ran SP% **118.3**
Speed ratings (Par 101): **97,96,96,90,87 85,84,63**
CSF £56.34 TOTE £8.80: £1.80, £1.80, £1.70; EX 56.30 Trifecta £99.10 Pool: £522.31 - 3.74 winning units..
Owner Jaber Abdullah **Bred** Gainsborough Stud Management Ltd **Trained** West Ilsley, Berks

FOCUS
Only a modest maiden and dubious form rated through the fourth and seventh.
First Coming Official explanation: jockey said colt hung left
Foresight Official explanation: trainer had no explanation for the poor form shown

1742 ARENALEISUREPLC.COM H'CAP 1m 1f 149y
5:20 (5:20) (Class 4) (0-80,76) 4-Y-O+ **£4,100** (£1,227; £613; £306) **Stalls** Centre

Form RPR

31-0 1 **Kavachi (IRE)**[12] 1473 5-9-3 75 .... GeorgeBaker 4 82
(G L Moore) *hld up: hdwy to go 2nd 3f out: led appr fnl f: rdn out* **3/1**[2]

14-3 2 3/4 **Nutkin**[29] 1159 4-9-0 72 .... OscarUrbina 1 82+
(J R Fanshawe) *racd 3rd: hdwy on ins whn hmpd on ins over 1f out: swtchd lft: kpt on to go 2nd ins fnl f* **4/7**[1]

040- 3 2 **Bedizen**[48] 5870 5-9-4 76 .... FergusSweeney 5 77
(Mrs P Sly) *led after 1f: rdn and hdd over 1f out: lost 2nd ins fnl f* **20/1**

1253 **4** *13* **Paradise Dancer (IRE)**[31] 1112 4-9-2 **74**.................... PhilipRobinson 3 48
(J A R Toller) *led for 1f: in tch tl rdn and wknd wl over 1f out* **11/2**[3]

2m 7.82s (2.92) **Going Correction** +0.425s/f (Yiel) **4** Ran SP% **108.8**
Speed ratings (Par 105): **105,104,102,92**
CSF £5.25 TOTE £3.10; EX 5.30 Place 6 £59.63, Place 5 £15.20.
Owner Bryan Pennick & Roy Martin **Bred** Gainsborough Stud Management Ltd **Trained** Woodingdean, E Sussex

FOCUS
A bit of a tactical affair and an unsatisfactory result. The form is not sound.
T/Plt: £65.00 to a £1 stake. Pool: £52,406.54. 588.40 winning tickets. T/Qpdt: £7.30 to a £1 stake. Pool: £3,569.59. 358.00 winning tickets. JS

[1721]GREAT LEIGHS (A.W) (L-H)
Thursday, May 1

OFFICIAL GOING: Standard
Wind: Fresh, behind Weather: Bright but showers threatening

1743 SHERRY H'CAP 6f (P)
5:15 (5:16) (Class 6) (0-65,65) 3-Y-O **£2,266** (£674; £337; £168) **Stalls** Low

Form RPR
040- **1** **Rosie Says No**[155] 6964 3-8-11 **58**.. ShaneKelly 8 65
(R M H Cowell) *s.i.s: hld up in midfield: hdwy over 2f out: styd on wl u.p to ld ins fnl f* **10/1**

00-5 **2** *¾* **Party In The Park**[21] 1277 3-8-13 **65**.............................. PatrickHills(5) 9 70
(R Hannon) *chsd ldr: rdn and ev ch 2f out: kpt on wl u.p tl no ex towards fin* **6/1**[3]

000- **3** *hd* **Karky Schultz (GER)**[174] 6750 3-9-1 **62**...................... RobertWinston 6 66
(J M P Eustace) *s.i.s: t.k.h: hld up in rr: hdwy 2f out: r.o u.p fnl f: nt quite rch ldng pair* **8/1**

0342 **4** *1 ¼* **Maggie Kate**[13] 1454 3-9-0 **61**..........................(p) RobertHavlin 3 61
(R Ingram) *led: hrd pressed and rdn over 2f out: kpt on gamely tl hdd ins fnl f: fdd towards fin* **9/2**[2]

06-5 **5** *nse* **Charmel's Lad**[20] 1315 3-9-1 **62**.................................. AdamKirby 10 62
(W R Swinburn) *t.k.h: trckd ldrs: rdn and nt qckn jst over 2f out: hung lft over 1f out: kpt on last 100yds* **7/2**[1]

0240 **6** *¾* **Admirals Way**[20] 1315 3-8-7 **54**...................................... IanMongan 5 52
(C N Kellett) *chsd ldrs: rdn jst over 2f out: keeping on same pce whn swtchd lft jst ins fnl f: nt pce to trble ldrs* **12/1**

0030 **7** *4 ½* **Easy Wonder (GER)**[12] 1475 3-9-1 **62**...................(p) PaulMulrennan 11 45
(I A Wood) *chsd ldrs: rdn over 2f out: wknd fnl f* **10/1**

1025 **8** *¾* **Thomas Malory (IRE)**[9] 1548 3-8-11 **63**........................ SCreighton(5) 4 44
(Miss V Haigh) *hld up in rr: c wd and effrt u.p 2f out: n.d* **9/2**[2]

9 *¾* **Cheeky Try (USA)**[209] 5990 3-8-6 **60**........................ CharlotteKerton(7) 2 39
(G Prodromou) *chsd ldrs on inner: rdn over 2f out: wknd over 1f out* **33/1**

000- **10** *2* **Serious Choice (IRE)**[183] 6578 3-9-3 **64**........................ PatCosgrave 1 36
(J R Boyle) *v.s.a: a bhd* **16/1**

04-5 **11** *hd* **Westwood Dawn**[112] 112 3-8-1 **51** oh6........................ LukeMorris(3) 7 23
(Mrs N Macauley) *racd in midfield tl lost pl over 3f out: n.d last 2f* **66/1**

040- **12** *nk* **Peer Pressure**[185] 6536 3-9-3 **64**................................. SamHitchcott 12 35
(B R Johnson) *hld up in rr: rdn and hdwy on outer 3f out: wknd over 1f out* **33/1**

1m 13.85s (0.15) **Going Correction** +0.075s/f (Slow) **12** Ran SP% **123.1**
Speed ratings (Par 97): **102,101,100,99,99 98,92,91,90,87 87,86**
CSF £70.95 CT £518.76 TOTE £10.50: £3.00, £1.10, £6.00; EX 122.30.
Owner The Hercules Horseracing Syndicate **Bred** C R And Mrs Kennedy **Trained** Six Mile Bottom, Cambs

■ Shane Kelly's first winner since returning from a year-long ban for passing on information for reward.

FOCUS
A modest sprint handicap run at a strong pace. The main action took place just off the inside rail in the straight and the third and fourth are the best guides.
Charmel's Lad Official explanation: jockey said gelding hung left in home straight

1744 MADEIRA H'CAP 1m 6f (P)
5:50 (5:50) (Class 4) (0-80,80) 4-Y-O+ **£4,533** (£1,348; £674; £336) **Stalls** Low

Form RPR
11-3 **1** **Boz**[22] 1273 4-9-3 **79**.. JamieSpencer 5 93+
(L M Cumani) *in tch in midfield: drvn 3f out: hdwy u.p to chal wl over 1f out: led jst ins fnl f: in command last 50yds* **4/5**[1]

0-01 **2** *¾* **Cavallini (USA)**[27] 1181 6-8-7 **68**.. RyanMoore 6 77
(G L Moore) *chsd ldr: rdn to ld 2f out: hdd jst ins fnl f: no ex last 75yds* **15/2**[3]

1160 **3** *3 ¾* **They All Laughed**[20] 1299 5-8-13 **74**.............................. RobertWinston 4 78
(P W Hiatt) *t.k.h: hld up in last trio: hdwy on outer over 3f out: chsd ldrs wl over 1f out: outpcd by ldng pair fnl f but kpt on to go 3rd ins fnl f* **16/1**

4556 **4** *1* **Savannah**[29] 1151 5-8-6 **67**.. EddieAhern 7 69
(Luke Comer, Ire) *hld up in last: rdn wl over 2f out: sme hdwy u.p over 1f out: nvr pce to threaten ldng pair* **18/1**

5/2- **5** *¾* **Tritonville Lodge (IRE)**[359] 192 6-9-5 **80**...................... SamHitchcott 1 81
(Miss E C Lavelle) *s.i.s: sn chsng ldrs: rdn 3f out: wknd over 1f out* **9/1**

1222 **6** *4* **War Of The Roses (IRE)**[29] 1151 5-9-1 **76**...................... PaulMulrennan 3 72
(R Brotherton) *stdd after s: t.k.h: hld up in tch: rdn and effrt 2f out: wknd jst over 1f out* **11/2**[2]

64-4 **7** *1* **Mind How You Go (FR)**[69] 272 10-8-9 **70**............................ LPKeniry 2 64
(J R Best) *stmbld s: sn rcvrd to ld: rdn and hdd 2f out: wknd over 1f out* **16/1**

3m 4.45s (1.25) **Going Correction** +0.075s/f (Slow)
WFA 4 from 5yo+ 1lb **7** Ran SP% **109.7**
Speed ratings (Par 105): **99,98,96,95,95 93,92**
CSF £6.67 TOTE £1.50: £1.20, £2.10; EX 7.90.
Owner Aston House Stud **Bred** Aston House Stud **Trained** Newmarket, Suffolk

FOCUS
A fair staying handicap rated through the runner-up to last year's best. They raced away from the inside rail in the straight.
War Of The Roses(IRE) Official explanation: jockey said gelding hung right throughout

1745 PORT H'CAP 1m (P)
6:20 (6:20) (Class 4) (0-85,82) 3-Y-O **£4,533** (£1,348; £674; £336) **Stalls** Low

Form RPR
0-43 **1** **Keep Discovering (IRE)**[13] 1441 3-9-4 **82**.................... RobertWinston 7 93
(M Johnston) *chsd ldr tl rdn to ld 2f out: hld hd awkwardly but r.o wl u.p: fnd ex whn pressed ins fnl f* **5/1**[3]

61-0 **2** *1 ¼* **Sky Dive**[16] 1381 3-9-0 **78**.. JamieSpencer 1 87
(L M Cumani) *stdd s: t.k.h early: hld up in rr: rdn and hdwy over 2f out: wnt 2nd 1f out: edgd lft u.p: pressed wnr ins fnl f: hld and eased towards fin* **9/4**[1]

56-5 **3** *5* **El Duende (USA)**[15] 1403 3-8-8 **72**.. AlanMunro 6 69
(W Jarvis) *hld up in midfield: hdwy to chse ldrs over 2f out: sn rdn: outpcd by ldng pair fnl f: wnt 3rd ins fnl f* **10/1**

0110 **4** *1* **My Shadow**[10] 1524 3-9-2 **80**.. IanMongan 8 75
(S Dow) *wnt rt s: t.k.h: hld up in rr: rdn 3f out: swtchd rt over 1f out: styd on but nvr nr ldrs* **8/1**

601- **5** *½* **Swanky Lady**[212] 5881 3-9-2 **80**.................................. RichardHughes 5 74
(R Hannon) *t.k.h early: hld up in tch: rdn to chse wnr wl over 1f out: wknd fnl f* **3/1**[2]

010- **6** *1 ¼* **Prince Desire (IRE)**[209] 5974 3-9-4 **82**..................... RichardKingscote 3 73
(Tom Dascombe) *rrng in stalls: led: rdn and hdd 2f out: wknd over 1f out* **16/1**

1-40 **7** *¾* **Straight And Level (CAN)**[13] 1443 3-8-13 **77**.................. AdamKirby 2 66
(Miss Jo Crowley) *chsd ldrs: reminders 5f out: hrd rdn over 2f out: wknd over 1f out* **25/1**

1-30 **8** *9* **Crosstar**[16] 1381 3-9-2 **80**.. JimmyQuinn 9 48
(M Botti) *hmpd s: hung rt thrght: bhd: wd and lost grnd bnd over 3f out: no ch and eased ins fnl f* **9/1**

1m 39.85s (-0.05) **Going Correction** +0.075s/f (Slow) **8** Ran SP% **112.4**
Speed ratings (Par 101): **103,101,96,95,95 94,93,84**
CSF £16.07 CT £106.48 TOTE £4.70: £1.50, £1.40, £2.30; EX 15.60.
Owner Sheikh Hamdan Bin Mohammed Al Maktoum **Bred** Kilfrush Stud **Trained** Middleham Moor, N Yorks

FOCUS
A very good handicap for the grade and the front two, who pulled well clear, look better than this level and the form has been rated positively. The winning time was 0.92 seconds quicker than the later 46-60, but 0.03 seconds slower than the later maiden won by the promising Stone Of Scone.
Crosstar Official explanation: jockey said colt hung right throughout

1746 CLARET H'CAP 1m 2f (P)
6:50 (6:50) (Class 4) (0-85,85) 3-Y-O **£4,533** (£1,348; £674; £336) **Stalls** Low

Form RPR
164- **1** **Mazaaya (USA)**[188] 6471 3-8-11 **78**.............................. RobertWinston 8 86
(M Johnston) *chsd ldrs tl wnt 2nd over 6f out: hrd rdn wl over 1f out: kpt on u.p but looked hld tl ld towards fin* **9/1**

066- **2** *1* **Sheer Bluff (IRE)**[258] 4586 3-8-4 **71**................................ MartinDwyer 3 77
(D R C Elsworth) *t.k.h: led: rdn and hld high awkwardly over 1f out: looked wnr tl hung lft and hdd towards fin* **20/1**

140- **3** *1 ¼* **Winter Bloom (USA)**[208] 6012 3-8-13 **80**.......................... TPQueally 6 84
(H R A Cecil) *t.k.h: hld up in tch: rdn to chse ldrs over 2f out: kpt on same pce u.p fnl f* **8/1**

1-21 **4** *1* **Martyr**[71] 632 3-9-3 **84**.. RichardHughes 9 86
(R Hannon) *hld up in tch: edgd lft 6f out: reminders and lost pl over over 5f out: rdn and hdwy on outer 4f out: chsd ldrs over 1f out: kpt on but nvr able to chal* **4/1**[2]

5-04 **5** *1 ¾* **Legislation**[10] 1524 3-9-3 **84**.. JimmyFortune 10 82
(J H M Gosden) *t.k.h: hld up towards rr: hmpd and clipped heels over 6f out: rdn and hdwy on outer over 3f out: hrd drvn 2f out: keeping on same pce whn hung lft ins fnl f* **11/4**[1]

5-1 **6** *nse* **Haydens Mark**[71] 633 3-9-4 **85**.. LiamJones 4 83
(W J Haggas) *t.k.h: chsd ldr tl over 6f out: styd chsng ldrs: rdn over 2f out: wknd ins fnl f* **7/1**[3]

3-41 **7** *1 ¼* **Benedict Spirit (IRE)**[93] 350 3-8-5 **72**............................... JimmyQuinn 5 67
(M H Tompkins) *t.k.h: hld up wl in tch: rdn over 2f out: wknd ins fnl f* **16/1**

160 **8** *½* **Vettorenjoy**[40] 966 3-8-9 **79**.. KirstyMilczarek(3) 1 73
(M Botti) *wnt rt and stdd s: hld up in rr: rdn and effrt over 2f out: nvr trbld ldrs* **14/1**

26-3 **9** *nk* **Agente Romano (USA)**[15] 1410 3-8-6 **76**..................... WilliamBuick(3) 2 70
(G A Butler) *hld up towards rr on inner: rdn 4f out: no imp last 2f* **12/1**

1- **10** *3 ¾* **Malibu Girl (USA)**[190] 6432 3-9-1 **82**................................ RyanMoore 7 68
(E A L Dunlop) *stdd s: t.k.h: hld up in rr: n.d* **8/1**

2m 8.64s (0.04) **Going Correction** +0.075s/f (Slow) **10** Ran SP% **116.4**
Speed ratings (Par 101): **102,101,100,99,98 97,96,96,96,93**
CSF £171.15 CT £1498.28 TOTE £6.20: £2.80, £7.30, £2.80; EX 252.60.
Owner Saif Ali **Bred** Needham/betz Thoroughbreds & Carl Freeman **Trained** Middleham Moor, N Yorks

FOCUS
A good handicap, but the early pace seemed just ordinary. However, the form looks pretty solid rated around the winner, third and fourth.

1747 BURGUNDY H'CAP 1m (P)
7:20 (7:21) (Class 6) (0-60,59) 4-Y-O+ **£2,266** (£674; £252; £252) **Stalls** Low

Form RPR
/2-5 **1** **Nassar (IRE)**[84] 468 5-8-5 **49**.................................... KirstyMilczarek(3) 15 59
(G Prodromou) *wnt lft s: hld up in midfield: hdwy on outer over 3f out: r.o wl fnl f: edgd lft towards fin: led last strides* **14/1**

00-2 **2** *hd* **Winning Show**[18] 1345 4-9-4 **59**.. MartinDwyer 3 69
(A M Balding) *led: rdn 2f out: styd on wl and looked wnr tl hdd last strides* **5/1**[1]

5430 **3** *nk* **Magic Warrior**[64] 716 8-8-12 **58**.................................. HaddenFrost(5) 5 70+
(J C Fox) *hld up in tch: nt clr run fr 3f out and lost pl tl 2f out: swtchd rt 2f out: gd hdwy to chse ldrs ins fnl f: kpt on* **12/1**

60-5 **3** *dht* **Recalcitrant**[66] 176 5-8-10 **51**.. JamesDoyle 4 60
(S Dow) *chsd ldr: rdn over 2f out: unable qckn over 1f out: kpt on u.p last 100yds* **11/1**

2442 **5** *2* **Shosolosa (IRE)**[6] 1606 6-8-1 **49**..........................(e[1]) StacyRenwick(7) 2 54
(R C Guest) *stdd s: hld up wl bhd: hdwy on outer 3f out: r.o wl fom over 1f out: nt rch ldrs* **10/1**

6052 **6** *¾* **Postmaster**[26] 1207 6-8-10 **51**.. RobertHavlin 1 55+
(R Ingram) *stdd s: hld up wl bhd: hdwy and nt clr run over 1f out: swtchd rt ins fnl f: r.o but no ch* **9/1**

0-50 **7** *½* **Bear Bottom**[110] 143 4-8-9 **50**.. AlanMunro 12 54+
(W J Musson) *hld up in midfield on inner: swtchd rt over 2f out: n.m.r over 1f out: swtchd lft and rdn 1f out: styd on: nvr able to chal* **11/1**

-004 **8** *nse* **Mick Is Back**[30] 1126 4-8-9 **50**...............................(bt) EddieAhern 11 52
(G G Margarson) *hld up in midfield: rdn and nt qckn over 3f out: plugged on u.p fnl f: nvr threatened ldrs* **7/1**[3]

-650 **9** *2 ¼* **Nightstrike (IRE)**[29] 1145 5-8-11 **55**.....................(b) JerryO'Dwyer(3) 7 52
(Luke Comer, Ire) *stdd and awkward leaving stalls: a in rr: rdn and effrt 3f out: wl btn whn sltly hmpd ins fnl f* **20/1**

00-0 **10** *2* **Jalamid (IRE)**[6] 1605 6-8-5 **46** ow1..........................(t) DeanMcKeown 16 38
(M A Barnes) *chsd ldrs: hdwy over 3f out: swtchd ins over 2f out: chsd ldng pair and rdn 2f out: wknd qckly jst over 1f out* **12/1**
5-20 **11** *3/4* **Fairy Festival (IRE)**[8] 1565 4-9-2 **57**.......................... LPKeniry 8 47
(J S Moore) *s.i.s: sn chsng ldrs: rdn 4f out: wknd wl over 2f out* **16/1**
004 **12** *9* **The Dagger**[18] 1345 4-9-3 **58**..........................(b[1]) RyanMoore 13 28
(G L Moore) *s.i.s: dropped in bhd after s: nvr on terms: eased ins fnl f* **11/2**[2]
-461 **13** *3/4* **Hey Presto**[22] 1269 8-8-5 **46**.......................... JimmyQuinn 9 14
(R Rowe) *chsd ldrs: rdn jst over 2f out: wknd qckly: eased ins fnl f* **16/1**
0-50 **14** *26* **Ruwain**[17] 1374 4-8-4 **45**..........................(b[1]) NickyMackay 6 —
(W J Musson) *s.i.s: sn rdn up to chse ldrs tl rdn and wknd qckly 3f out: virtually p.u fnl f: t.o* **16/1**

1m 40.77s (0.87) **Going Correction** +0.075s/f (Slow) **14** Ran SP% **124.8**
Speed ratings (Par 101): **98,97,97,97,95 94,94,94,91,89 89,80,79,53**
PL: Magic Warrior £2.00, Recalcitrant £2.70; TRICAST: Magic Warrior £458.04, Recalcitrant £422.96 CSF £85.51 TOTE £12.80: £2.90, £1.10; EX 70.60.
Owner Faisal Al-Nassar **Bred** Gigginstown House Stud **Trained** East Harling, Norfolk

FOCUS
A very moderate handicap but sound form rated around the runner-up and fifth. The winning time was almost a second slower than both the earlier 71-85 handicap and the following maiden.
Ruwain Official explanation: vet said gelding had been struck into

1748 BRANDY MAIDEN STKS 1m (P)
7:50 (7:52) (Class 5) 3-4-Y-O £2,590 (£770; £385; £192) **Stalls** Low

Form RPR
6 **1** **Stone Of Scone**[14] 1418 3-9-0 0.......................... RyanMoore 9 88+
(E A L Dunlop) *hld up wl in tch: hdwy over 3f out: chsd ldr wl over 1f out: rdn to ld 1f out: pushed clr: readily* **5/2**[1]
2 *2 1/2* **Liberation Spirit (USA)** 3-9-0 0.......................... ShaneKelly 14 82+
(J Noseda) *hld up in tch: hdwy to chse ldrs over 2f out: swtchd rt over 1f out: r.o to snatch 2nd on line: nt pce to trble wnr* **3/1**[2]
00 **3** *shd* **Tartan Gigha (IRE)**[14] 1429 3-9-0 0.......................... RobertWinston 10 82
(M Johnston) *chsd ldr 5f out: rdn to ld 2f out: hdd 1f out: nt pce of wnr fnl f: lost 2nd on line* **10/1**
0 **4** *4 1/2* **Closertobelieving**[14] 1417 3-9-0 0.......................... AlanMunro 13 72
(D R C Elsworth) *in tch in midfield: rdn and sltly outpcd 3f out: rallied to chse ldrs over 1f out: outpcd fnl f* **14/1**
5 *1 3/4* **La Sarrazine (FR)** 3-8-9 0.......................... JamieSpencer 3 63+
(J R Fanshawe) *stdd s: hld up wl bhd: c wd and hdwy 3f out: kpt on steadily: nvr nr ldrs* **8/1**
6 *1 1/2* **Wise Lee** 3-9-0 0.......................... LiamJones 15 64
(W J Haggas) *stdd and dropped in after s: plld hrd: hld up towards rr: hdwy on outer 3f out: rdn and no imp over 1f out* **14/1**
045- **7** *1* **Burnbrake**[145] 7070 3-9-0 67.......................... MartinDwyer 11 62
(J A R Toller) *in tch in midfield: rdn and unable qck 3f out: no ch w ldrs after* **14/1**
5 **8** *3/4* **Benhego**[18] 1344 3-9-0 0.......................... SaleemGolam 8 60
(S C Williams) *s.i.s: bhd: rdn and kpt on past btn horses last 2f: n.d* **50/1**
0 **9** *3* **Yellow Thunder (IRE)**[15] 1398 3-8-11 0.......................... JerryO'Dwyer[(3)] 4 53
(Luke Comer, Ire) *chsd ldr tl 5f out: styd handy: rdn 4f out: wknd wl over 2f out* **66/1**
0 **10** *3/4* **Golden Bishop**[28] 1172 3-9-0 0.......................... HayleyTurner 7 52
(M L W Bell) *t.k.h: hld up towards rr: rdn wl over 3f out: nvr trbld ldrs* **66/1**
11 *1 1/4* **Squire Boldwood (IRE)** 3-9-0 0.......................... SebSanders 12 49
(D R C Elsworth) *s.i.s: rn green and a towards rr* **12/1**
32- **12** *hd* **Cozy Tiger (USA)**[159] 6934 3-9-0 0.......................... NeilPollard 6 48
(W J Musson) *led tl rdn and hdd 2f out: wknd qckly* **11/2**[3]
0 **13** *23* **Hapi**[14] 1417 3-8-7 0.......................... WilliamCarson[(7)] 2 —
(S C Williams) *plld hrd: chsd ldrs tl 1/2-way: wl bhd last 2f: t.o* **33/1**

1m 39.82s (-0.08) **Going Correction** +0.075s/f (Slow) **13** Ran SP% **124.7**
Speed ratings (Par 103): **103,100,100,95,94 92,91,90,87,87 85,85,62**
CSF £10.15 TOTE £3.30: £1.70, £1.10, £5.70; EX 9.30 Place 6 £239.14, Place 5 £46.68.
Owner Cliveden Stud **Bred** Cliveden Stud Ltd **Trained** Newmarket, Suffolk

FOCUS
Some well-bred animals representing top yards gave this maiden a strong look beforehand, and with the winning time faster than both the 1m handicaps run earlier on the card, a few winners should come out of it, although it has been rated slightly cautiously.
T/Plt: £299.00 to a £1 stake. Pool: £43,971.90. 107.35 winning tickets. T/Qpdt: £107.50 to a £1 stake. Pool: £5,016.25. 34.50 winning tickets. SP

987 REDCAR (L-H)
Thursday, May 1

OFFICIAL GOING: Soft (good to soft in places; 6.1)
25 non-runners on account of the changed going since the 48-hour declaration. The ground was described as 'tacky, very gluey'.
Wind: Fresh, half behind Weather: Fine but breezy

1749 REDCAR "A COURSE FOR ALL REASONS" MAIDEN AUCTION STKS 5f
2:30 (2:32) (Class 5) 2-Y-O £2,331 (£693; £346; £173) **Stalls** Centre

Form RPR
33 **1** **Knavesmire (IRE)**[26] 1220 2-8-4 0.......................... TWilliams 9 73
(M Brittain) *mde all: rdn clr 2f out: hld on ins fnl f* **5/2**[1]
2 *1/2* **Sloop Johnb** 2-8-12 0.......................... PaulHanagan 10 79+
(R A Fahey) *chsd ldrs: wnt 2nd over 1f out: kpt on ins fnl f* **5/1**[3]
5 **3** *1 1/4* **Rosabee (IRE)**[10] 1515 2-8-4 0.......................... JoeFanning 4 67+
(Miss V Haigh) *chsd wnr: rdn and hung lft over 2f out: kpt on same pce* **14/1**
4 *9* **Skruton (IRE)** 2-8-4 0.......................... TPO'Shea 2 34
(M G Quinlan) *swvd lft s: hld up towards rr: nvr on fnl 2f: nvr on terms* **9/2**[2]
5 *3* **Gower Valentine** 2-8-7 0.......................... AdrianTNicholls 7 27
(D Nicholls) *swvd lft s: sn chsng ldrs: wknd over 1f out* **5/1**[3]
6 *1* **Reel Bluff** 2-8-9 0.......................... FergalLynch 5 25
(D W Barker) *swvd lft s: mid-div: lost pl 2f out* **15/2**
7 *1/2* **Real Diamond** 2-8-4 0.......................... MichaelJStainton[(3)] 12 21+
(A Dickman) *s.v.s: wl bhd tl sme late hdwy* **11/1**
8 *1 1/4* **El Bobby (IRE)** 2-8-9 0.......................... DO'Donohoe 6 19
(J R Weymes) *in rr-div: sn drvn along: bhd fnl 2f* **33/1**
9 *13* **Flaming Ruby** 2-8-4 0.......................... RoystonFfrench 1 —
(N Tinkler) *mid-div: lost pl and eased over 1f out: sn bhd* **25/1**

61.09 secs (2.49) **Going Correction** +0.325s/f (Good) **9** Ran SP% **113.6**
Speed ratings (Par 93): **93,92,90,75,71 69,68,66,45**
CSF £14.68 TOTE £2.80: £1.10, £2.00, £3.50; EX 10.70.
Owner Mel Brittain **Bred** Michael O'Mahony **Trained** Warthill, N Yorks

FOCUS
Almost certainly a weak event and the winner's experience proved decisive. The placed horses could be of future interest.

NOTEBOOK
Knavesmire(IRE), nothing at all to look at, was having her third start. With everything thrown at her, in the end she did just enough. (op 9-4 tchd 15-8)
Sloop Johnb, a lazy walker, was initially very keen to post. He went in pursuit of the winner and was gradually closing the gap all the way to the line but the post came just too soon. (op 4-1 tchd 11-2)
Rosabee(IRE), having her second outing, raced upsides towards the far side but she gave her rider real problems persisting in wanting to hang left. (op 12-1)
Skruton(IRE), on the leg and narrow, went sideways leaving the stalls. She kept on in her own time from the halfway mark and this will have taught her something. (op 13-2)
Gower Valentine, a January foal, gave problems at the stalls. She ducked leaving them and tired badly with over a furlong left to run. (tchd 4-1 and 11-2)
Reel Bluff, a good-bodied individual, will do better when fitter. (op 8-1)
Flaming Ruby Official explanation: jockey said filly lost her action

1750 BODDINGTONS REDCAR STRAIGHT-MILE CHAMPIONSHIP (H'CAP) (QUALIFIER) 1m
3:00 (3:00) (Class 5) (0-75,74) 3-Y-O £2,331 (£693; £346; £173) **Stalls** Centre

Form RPR
0-55 **1** **Spirit Of A Nation (IRE)**[20] 1295 3-9-4 **74**.......................... KerrinMcEvoy 5 83
(S Parr) *hld up in mid-div: hdwy over 3f out: chal over 1f out: styd on to ld nr fin* **7/1**[2]
3-21 **2** *hd* **Stevie Thunder**[20] 1306 3-9-1 **74**.......................... PJMcDonald[(3)] 7 83
(G A Swinbank) *led 1f: trckd ldr: led over 2f out: shkn up and hdd nr fin* **4/6**[1]
660- **3** *3 1/2* **When Yer Ready (IRE)**[243] 5042 3-8-1 **60**.......................... DuranFentiman[(3)] 10 61
(T D Easterby) *hld up in rr: hdwy 3f out: kpt on to take 3rd ins fnl f* **18/1**
402- **4** *1 3/4* **Hyde Lea Flyer**[204] 6106 3-9-4 **74**.......................... JoeFanning 11 71
(E S McMahon) *t.k.h: led after 1f: hdd over 2f out: hung lft and wknd appr fnl f* **8/1**[3]
2314 **5** *5* **Tiger's Rocket (IRE)**[15] 1395 3-8-9 **70**.......................... JamieJones[(5)] 3 55
(S Gollings) *trckd ldrs: rdn 3f out: lost pl over 1f out* **14/1**
212- **6** *4* **Reel Buddy Star**[194] 6328 3-9-4 **74**.......................... DanielTudhope 8 50
(G M Moore) *hld up in rr: hdwy 3f out: lost pl over 1f out* **8/1**[3]
21-0 **7** *nk* **Paint Stripper**[8] 1558 3-8-2 **61**.......................... DominicFox[(3)] 1 37
(W Storey) *chsd ldrs: drvn over 2f out: wknd over 2f out* **20/1**

1m 43.51s (5.51) **Going Correction** +0.50s/f (Yiel) **7** Ran SP% **111.4**
Speed ratings (Par 99): **92,91,88,86,81 77,77**
CSF £11.49 CT £77.32 TOTE £8.80: £2.70, £1.40; EX 13.70.
Owner Bezwell Fixings Limited **Bred** J P Hardiman **Trained** Bawtry, S Yorks

FOCUS
The much-improved winner proved gritty but it looked very much a case of the second missing out on a winning opportunity. The form is worth taking at face value.

1751 BECOME AN ANNUAL BADGE HOLDER TODAY MEDIAN AUCTION MAIDEN STKS 7f
3:30 (3:31) (Class 5) 3-Y-O £2,331 (£693; £346; £173) **Stalls** Centre

Form RPR
0- **1** **Storyland (USA)**[210] 5949 3-8-12 0.......................... KerrinMcEvoy 14 73+
(W J Haggas) *hld up in mid-div: hdwy over 3f out: led over 1f out: kpt on wl towards fin* **4/5**[1]
2 *1* **Hippolytus** 3-9-3 0.......................... GrahamGibbons 9 71
(J J Quinn) *dwlt: sn chsng ldrs: chal 1f out: edgd lft and no ex wl ins fnl f* **25/1**
02-0 **3** *9* **Dolly No Hair**[13] 1452 3-9-3 69.......................... FergalLynch 12 48
(D W Barker) *w ldrs: one pce fnl 2f* **16/1**
4 *1/2* **Phantom Serenade (IRE)** 3-9-3 0.......................... PhillipMakin 4 47
(M Dods) *mid-div: outpcd over 3f out: hdwy over 1f out: styd on ins fnl f* **15/2**[3]
0- **5** *nk* **Misterisland (IRE)**[252] 4733 3-9-3 0.......................... PaulHanagan 15 46
(A Bailey) *w ldrs: one pce fnl 2f* **16/1**
3-6 **6** *6* **Pay Parade**[13] 1452 3-8-12 0..........................(e[1]) DavidAllan 5 25
(T D Easterby) *led tl over 2f out: lost pl over 1f out* **13/2**[2]
4 **7** *3/4* **Infinity Bond**[111] 130 3-8-12 0.......................... SladeO'Hara[(5)] 8 28
(G R Oldroyd) *w ldrs: led over 2f out tl over 1f out: sn wknd* **14/1**
6 **8** *2* **Threecheersforanby (IRE)**[20] 1298 3-9-0 0..........................(t) DNolan[(3)] 10 23
(S Parr) *hld up in rr: hdwy over 3f out: sn wknd* **33/1**
9 *2 1/2* **Red Rouge** 3-8-12 0.......................... RoystonFfrench 7 12
(N Tinkler) *in rr and sn drvn along: bhd fnl 3f* **28/1**
000- **10** *3 1/4* **Reel Cool**[174] 6742 3-8-12 50.......................... TomEaves 11 3
(B Smart) *in rr: rdn 4f out: sn bhd* **66/1**
11 *14* **Tycoon's Buddy** 3-9-3 0.......................... JoeFanning 6 —
(E J O'Neill) *in rr-div: lost pl 3f out: sn bhd and eased* **12/1**

1m 29.17s (4.67) **Going Correction** +0.50s/f (Yiel) **11** Ran SP% **118.5**
Speed ratings (Par 99): **93,91,81,81,80 73,72,70,67,64 48**
CSF £32.06 TOTE £1.70: £1.10, £6.80, £4.00; EX 25.90.
Owner Mr & Mrs R Scott **Bred** Arthur B Hancock III & James H Stone **Trained** Newmarket, Suffolk

FOCUS
The first two finished some way clear of the 69-rated third. The time was slow and the race has been rated negatively.
Tycoon's Buddy Official explanation: jockey said gelding moved poorly throughout

1752 RACING UK CHANNEL 432 (S) STKS 7f
4:00 (4:00) (Class 6) 3-Y-O+ £1,774 (£523; £262) **Stalls** Centre

Form RPR
060- **1** **Sea Salt**[138] 7158 5-9-4 65.......................... PaulHanagan 14 75
(R A Fahey) *mde all: rdn clr over 1f out: edgd lft: unchal* **7/2**[1]
0456 **2** *4 1/2* **Zennerman (IRE)**[17] 1371 5-9-4 61..........................(b) FergalLynch 16 64
(Miss J E Foster) *chsd ldrs: wnt 2nd over 2f out: no imp* **10/1**
350- **3** *3 1/2* **Efidium**[208] 6016 10-9-1 66.......................... MarkLawson[(3)] 6 55
(N Bycroft) *s.i.s: hdwy over 2f out: kpt on to take 3rd ins fnl f* **9/2**[3]
0-60 **4** *1* **Kadia**[8] 1559 5-8-13 43.......................... PaulFessey 7 47
(P T Midgley) *chsd ldrs: edgd lft and over 1f out: one pce* **40/1**
00-5 **5** *1 1/2* **Five Wishes**[27] 1188 4-8-13 55.......................... PhillipMakin 13 43
(M Dods) *trckd ldrs: rdn over 2f out: one pce* **4/1**[2]
535/ **6** *shd* **Rainbow Zest**[57] 5138 5-9-4 0.......................... JoeFanning 4 48
(W Storey) *in rr: kpt on fnl 3f: nvr nr ldrs* **12/1**
0-00 **7** *1* **Dressed To Dance (IRE)**[38] 990 4-8-13 58..........(v) RoystonFfrench 11 40
(N Tinkler) *in rr: rdn 3f out: wknd over 1f out* **12/1**
050- **8** *3/4* **Frimley's Mattery**[226] 5503 8-8-13 46.......................... DanielleMcCreery[(5)] 5 43
(R E Barr) *chsd ldrs: lost pl 2f out* **50/1**

0-01 **9** 3/4 **Rowan Lodge (IRE)**[15] 1391 6-9-7 64........(b) JamieMoriarty(3) 3 47
(Ollie Pears) *mid-div: effrt 3f out: sn rdn lost pl over 1f out* **5/1**

0-05 **10** *nse* **Obe One**[108] 155 8-9-4 40........ PatrickMathers 9 41
(A Berry) *mid-div: drvn 3f out: sn btn* **50/1**

-006 **11** 1/2 **Pietersen (IRE)**[70] 639 4-8-11 62........(b) DeanHeslop(7) 1 40
(T D Barron) *s.v.s: a bhd* **8/1**

1m 27.66s (3.16) **Going Correction** +0.50s/f (Yiel) **11 Ran SP% 119.0**
Speed ratings (Par 101): **101,95,91,90,89 88,87,86,86,85 85**
CSF £39.65 TOTE £3.60: £1.50, £3.50, £2.60; EX 37.60.There was no bid for the winner. Zennerman was claimed by J. Babb for £6,000.
Owner J H Tattersall **Bred** D R Tucker **Trained** Musley Bank, N Yorks

FOCUS
The one-eyed Sea Salt was backed as if back to his best and he was never in any danger. The proximity of the 43-rated fourth limits the form.

1753 TEES VALLEY H'CAP — 1m 2f
4:30 (4:30) (Class 4) (0-85,84) 3-Y-O — **£4,209** (£1,252; £625; £312) **Stalls** Low

Form — RPR

3-21 **1** **Tajweed (IRE)**[20] 1307 3-8-12 78........ GregFairley 3 91+
(M Johnston) *trckd ldr: led over 2f out: rdn out* **6/5**[1]

25-3 **2** 1 **Full Speed (GER)**[19] 1330 3-8-7 76........ PJMcDonald(3) 2 85
(G A Swinbank) *trckd ldrs: effrt over 2f out: swtchd outside: chal over 1f out: no ex ins fnl f* **9/4**[2]

331- **3** 2 **Laterly (IRE)**[176] 6723 3-9-0 80........ MickyFenton 5 85
(T P Tate) *led: hdd over 2f out: one pce* **4/1**[3]

2-43 **4** 41 **Ivestar (IRE)**[14] 1428 3-8-10 76........ AdrianTNicholls 4 —
(D Nicholls) *a last: reminders over 5f out: lost tch 3f out: bhd whn eased over 1f out* **15/2**

2m 14.17s (7.07) **Going Correction** +0.625s/f (Yiel) **4 Ran SP% 108.0**
Speed ratings (Par 101): **96,95,93,60**
CSF £4.13 TOTE £1.90; EX 3.70.
Owner Hamdan Al Maktoum **Bred** Kilboy Estate **Trained** Middleham Moor, N Yorks

FOCUS
Just a steady pace and the form is not all that strong but the winner seemed to idle in front and there may be even better to come.
Ivestar(IRE) Official explanation: jockey said gelding had a breathing problem

1754 REDCAR CONFERENCE CENTRE APPRENTICE CLAIMING STKS — 6f
5:00 (5:01) (Class 6) 3-4-Y-O — **£2,047** (£604; £302) **Stalls** Centre

Form — RPR

4332 **1** **Our Sunnie**[28] 1169 3-8-5 58........(v) AdeleRothery(5) 8 59
(D Nicholls) *led after 1f: rdn over 1f out and carried hd high: hld on towards fin* **9/2**[3]

5210 **2** 1 **Swallow Forest**[12] 1475 3-8-4 56........(b) DeanHeslop(5) 7 55
(T D Barron) *s.i.s: hdwy over 2f out: styd on to take 2nd ins fnl f: a hld* **7/1**

5-00 **3** 1/2 **Turn And River (IRE)**[20] 1306 3-8-6 55........ AdamCarter(5) 11 55
(M Brittain) *mid-div: hdwy over 2f out: kpt on same pce ins fnl f* **11/1**

4010 **4** *nk* **Jazenio**[8] 1558 3-8-5 60........(p) AndrewMullen 15 48
(K A Ryan) *sn outpcd and drvn along: hdwy over 2f out: kpt on same pce fnl f* **5/2**[1]

0-60 **5** 3 3/4 **Only A Splash**[3] 1674 4-9-4 40........ MichaelJStainton 9 42
(Mrs R A Carr) *led 1f: chsd ldrs: edgd lft and wknd over 1f out* **25/1**

-045 **6** 1 3/4 **Bellas Chicas (IRE)**[27] 1187 3-8-9 50........ JamieMoriarty 3 35
(P T Midgley) *swvd lft s: chsd ldrs: edgd lft and wknd over 1f out* **4/1**[2]

45-0 **7** 4 1/2 **First Valentini**[13] 1452 4-8-8 40........ DanielleMcCreery(5) 1 17
(N Bycroft) *hmpd s: sn chsng ldrs: wknd 2f out* **28/1**

000- **8** 2 1/4 **Lay Down Darling**[248] 4897 3-8-0 26........ MarzenaJeziorek(5) 10 9
(N Tinkler) *prom: lost pl 2f out* **100/1**

-560 **9** 4 1/2 **Mchepple**[8] 1560 3-8-0 48........ SophieDoyle(5) 5 —
(W Storey) *prom early: lost pl over 3f out: sn bhd* **14/1**

50-0 **10** 2 3/4 **Marlena (IRE)**[15] 1396 3-8-9 54........ DuranFentiman 2 —
(T D Easterby) *mid-div: rdn and lost pl over 2f out: sn bhd* **10/1**

40 **11** 15 **Wildcat Island (IRE)**[37] 1019 3-8-6 0........ KellyHarrison(3) 6 —
(T D Easterby) *in rr and rdn 3f out: sn wl bhd* **11/1**

1m 15.88s (4.08) **Going Correction** +0.625s/f (Yiel)
WFA 3 from 4yo 10lb **11 Ran SP% 120.0**
Speed ratings (Par 101): **97,95,95,94,89 87,81,78,72,68 48**
CSF £36.37 TOTE £4.80: £1.90, £2.70, £2.70; EX 31.20.
Owner Mrs Jackie Love & D Nicholls **Bred** Larksborough Stud Limited **Trained** Sessay, N Yorks
■ Stewards' Enquiry : Adele Rothery caution: used whip down shoulder in forehand position
Sophie Doyle three-day ban: used whip when out of contention (May 15-16, 18)

FOCUS
A weak apprentice claimer with little between the first four at the line. The runner-up is rated to her mark but the form is far from solid.

1755 THE COMMITMENTS ARE HERE IN AUGUST FILLIES' H'CAP — 5f
5:30 (5:30) (Class 4) (0-85,85) 3-Y-O+ — **£4,209** (£1,252; £625; £312) **Stalls** Centre

Form — RPR

12-0 **1** **Swift Princess (IRE)**[14] 1430 4-9-13 80........(v) AndrewElliott 6 89+
(K R Burke) *hld up: effrt over 1f out: r.o wl to ld last stride* **3/1**[1]

004- **2** *shd* **Gallery Girl (IRE)**[212] 5891 5-9-10 77........ DavidAllan 3 86
(T D Easterby) *chsd ldrs on wd outside: led over 1f out: jst ct* **7/2**[2]

2-13 **3** 1 **Feelin Foxy**[27] 1178 4-9-9 76........ J-PGuillambert 5 81
(J G Given) *led 1f: w ldrs: kpt on same pce fnl 75yds* **7/2**[2]

103- **4** *nk* **Hypnosis**[347] 1861 5-9-9 76........ TomEaves 8 80
(D W Barker) *sn chsng ldrs: kpt on same pce ins fnl f* **9/2**

04-1 **5** 2 3/4 **Valley Of The Moon (IRE)**[17] 1373 4-9-8 75........ PaulHanagan 4 69
(R A Fahey) *sn chsng ldrs: rdn and outpcd over 2f out: edgd rt and no threat after* **4/1**[3]

331/ **6** 3 1/4 **Wicked Wilma (IRE)**[637] 4089 4-8-8 66 oh6........ DanielleMcCreery(5) 7 48
(A Berry) *swerved rt s: led after 1f: hdd & wknd over 1f out* **20/1**

61.42 secs (2.82) **Going Correction** +0.625s/f (Yiel)
WFA 3 from 4yo+ 9lb **6 Ran SP% 112.4**
Speed ratings (Par 102): **102,101,100,99,95 90**
CSF £13.78 CT £36.52 TOTE £4.10: £2.50, £2.80; EX 16.80 Place 6 £26.00, Place 5 £13.78.
Owner Dennis Fehan & Tweenhills Racing **Bred** Mrs S O'Riordan **Trained** Middleham Moor, N Yorks

FOCUS
A fair handicap although not that easy to pin down, with the third rated to previous course form.
T/Plt: £18.50 to a £1 stake. Pool: £51,498.20. 2,025.65 winning tickets. T/Qpdt: £16.90 to a £1 stake. Pool: £2,285.69. 99.85 winning tickets. WG

1756 - 1759a (Foreign Racing) - See Raceform Interactive

1323 SAINT-CLOUD (L-H)
Thursday, May 1

OFFICIAL GOING: Very soft

1760a PRIX CLEOPATRE (GROUP 3) (FILLIES) — 1m 2f 110y
2:20 (2:20) 3-Y-O — **£29,412** (£11,765; £8,824; £5,882; £2,941)

RPR

1 **Leo's Starlet (IRE)**[41] 3-8-9........ C-PLemaire 4 103
(A De Royer-Dupre, France) *racd in 5th to st: qckly moved up to dispute 2nd on rails 2f out: rdn dist: led 60yds out: r.o wl* **54/10**[3]

2 3/4 **Antiquities**[25] 3-8-9........ SPasquier 1 102
(A Fabre, France) *racd keenly: led 8f out: rdn ins fnl f: unable qck and hdd 60yds out* **9/10**[1]

3 3 **Sanjida (IRE)**[20] 1323 3-8-9........ CSoumillon 6 96
(A De Royer-Dupre, France) *hld up: last st: hdwy on outside 2f out: one pce fnl f* **29/10**[2]

4 3 **Ballerina Blue (IRE)**[20] 3-8-9........ TThulliez 2 91
(Y De Nicolay, France) *a cl up: 3rd st: rdn 2f out: sn one pce* **13/1**

5 1 1/2 **Courageuse (FR)**[42] 3-8-9........ ACrastus 3 88
(E Lellouche, France) *led 2 1/2f: 4th st: one pce fnl 2f* **14/1**

6 10 **Orion Queen (FR)**[25] 1238 3-8-9........ JVictoire 5 70
(H-A Pantall, France) *trckd ldrs: 2nd st: rdn and btn over 2f out: wknd qckly* **24/1**

2m 13.6s (-6.00) **Going Correction** -0.475s/f (Firm) **6 Ran SP% 111.7**
Speed ratings: **102,101,99,97,96 88**
PARI-MUTUEL: WIN 6.40; PL 2.30, 1.50; SF 16.80.
Owner W-J Preston **Bred** Prestonwood Farm Llc **Trained** Chantilly, France

NOTEBOOK
Leo's Starlet(IRE) ♦'s connections were frightened that she might not act on the very soft ground, but they need not have worried and she has now turned into a live Classic prospect. Last but one for most of the way, she began to make progress early in the straight and then collared the long-time leader well inside the final furlong. It was her first run on turf after two victories on the sand at Deauville and she remains unbeaten. She is now likely to go directly for the Prix de Diane, where better ground should be an advantage, and she is definitely one to follow.
Antiquities, having just her second race, ran with great credit. Her jockey decided to try and draw the sting from the others by making the running at a decent pace. She quickened in the straight and looked the winner at the furlong marker before being collared close home. There is certainly further improvement in her and a Group race should come her way before the end of the season.
Sanjida(IRE) was a little disappointing as she looked the winner halfway up the straight. Dropped out in the early stages, she did not really become involved in the race until the straight. Brought with her run up the centre of the track, she looked to have a lot in reserve over a furlong out but failed to go through with her challenge. Better ground will undoubtedly be an advantage for her and she probably is not the easiest of individuals, but nevertheless one with a lot of class.
Ballerina Blue(IRE), a supplementary entry, recovered her entrance fee but never really looked like playing a serious part in the finish. She was in third place for much of the way, but was then one-paced in the straight and is not quite up to this level.

1761a PRIX DU MUGUET (GROUP 2) — 1m
2:50 (2:50) 4-Y-O+ — **£54,485** (£21,029; £10,037; £6,691; £3,346)

RPR

1 **Gris De Gris (IRE)**[32] 1108 4-8-11........ TThulliez 1 112
(J-M Capitte, France) *led 2f: 2nd st: led again over 2f out: sn rdn and wnt 2 l up over 1f out: drvn out and r.o wl* **4/1**[2]

2 2 **Turfrose (GER)**[186] 6524 4-9-0........ JVictoire 4 111
(A Fabre, France) *6th st: rdn 2f out: kpt on u.p to take 2nd last strides* **59/10**

3 *nk* **Spirito Del Vento (FR)**[32] 1108 5-9-0........ OPeslier 3 110
(J-M Beguigne, France) *disp 3rd: 4th st: chsd wnr 1 1/2f out: rdn ins fnl f: one pce and lost 2nd cl home* **13/10**[1]

4 *shd* **Krataios (FR)**[24] 1249 8-8-11........ MBlancpain 2 107
(C Laffon-Parias, France) *disp 3rd: 3rd st: kpt on one pce fr over 1f out* **53/10**[3]

5 2 **Holocene (USA)**[208] 6031 4-8-11........ C-PLemaire 6 103
(P Bary, France) *hld up: 5th st: disp 3rd on rails over 2f out: sn btn: last 1f out: kpt on u.p fnl f* **13/1**

6 *shd* **Persian Storm (GER)**[25] 1240 4-8-11........ SPasquier 7 103
(A Fabre, France) *led after 2f: hdd over 2f out: dropped bk wl over 1f out: one pce and lost 5th last stride* **9/1**

7 2 **King Jock (USA)**[63] 743 7-8-11........ RMBurke 5 99
(R J Osborne, Ire) *last most of way: wnt 6th briefly 1f out* **15/1**

1m 40.6s (-6.90) **Going Correction** -0.475s/f (Firm) **7 Ran SP% 117.2**
Speed ratings: **115,113,112,112,110 110,108**
PARI-MUTUEL: WIN 5.00; PL 2.60, 3.40; SF 26.60.
Owner J C Seroul **Bred** J-C Seroul **Trained** France

NOTEBOOK
Gris De Gris(IRE) gained a thoroughly deserved victory. He had just been touched off by inches over the course and distance the previous month, but made no mistake on this occasion. Well placed throughout, he was taken to the lead early in the straight and never looked like being caught from the furlong marker. A colt who is going from strength to strength, he will now be given a rest with this being his fifth race of the season. His next target now looks like being the Jacques Le Marois at Deauville in August and, if he continues to improve, he might even make his presence felt at Group 1 level.
Turfrose(GER) put in a very promising run having been supplemented. Switched off early, she did not really slip into top gear until the furlong marker, at which point she quickened and was putting in her best work at the finish. Considering this was her seasonal debut and that she was carrying a Group 1 penalty, it was an excellent effort. She now heads for the Prix d'Isapahan later in the month.
Spirito Del Vento(FR) was again a rather disappointing favourite and he might not be at his best on a left-handed track. Given a waiting ride as usual early on, he was close to the winner coming into the straight and did look dangerous 2f out, but did not go through with his run. Better ground may be an advantage and he may go for the Prix d'Isapahan, whilst his longer-term target has always been the Queen Anne at Royal Ascot.
Krataios(FR) was running in this race for the fourth time and once again ran his heart out. Given every possible chance, he was always well up there and tried in vain to catch the winner from over a furlong out before staying on one pace. He still appears to enjoy the game, but this level is probably a little on the high side for him now.

1668 LINGFIELD (L-H)

Friday, May 2

OFFICIAL GOING: Standard

Wind: fresh behind Weather: bright partly cloudy

1762 DERBY TRIAL HERE MAY 10TH MAIDEN FILLIES' STKS — 5f (P)

2:10 (2:11) (Class 5) 2-Y-0 — **£3,885** (£1,156; £577; £288) **Stalls** High

Form — RPR

3 **1** **Moss Likely (IRE)**[17] 1385 2-9-0 0 .... EdwardCreighton 6 83+
(M R Channon) *chsd ldrs: rdn over 2f out: led ins fnl f: hung rt but r.o strly* **3/1**[1]

2 2 **Rebecca De Winter** 2-9-0 0 .... RichardHughes 7 76
(R Hannon) *chsd ldrs: wnt 2nd over 2f out: rdn to ld over 1f out: hdd ins fnl f: no ex* **4/1**[3]

52 **3** 3 1/4 **Dedante**[20] 1341 2-9-0 0 .... SebSanders 2 64
(D K Ivory) *chsd ldr tl led after 1f: rdn 2f out: hdd over 1f out: wknd ins fnl f* **7/1**

4 3/4 **Street Of Hope (USA)** 2-9-0 0 .... EddieAhern 1 61
(J W Hills) *s.i.s: bhd: hdwy over 2f out: styd on steadily fr over 1f out: nvr rchd ldrs* **16/1**

33 **5** shd **Just The Lady**[21] 1303 2-8-7 0 .... JackDean(7) 4 61
(W G M Turner) *led for 1f: chsd ldr after tl over 2f out: rdn and sn outpcd: plugged on ins fnl f* **7/2**[2]

6 nse **Dream City (IRE)** 2-9-0 0 .... MartinDwyer 8 61
(M P Tregoning) *s.i.s: bhd: rdn and sme hdwy on inner 2f out: nvr trbld ldrs* **15/2**

7 7 **Cheap Thrills** 2-9-0 0 .... ShaneKelly 5 36
(J A Osborne) *s.i.s: bhd: rdn 3f out: nvr on terms* **13/2**

8 7 **Amen To That (IRE)** 2-9-0 0 .... JamesDoyle 9 10
(R M Beckett) *s.i.s: a bhd: rdn 3f out: wd bnd 2f out: t.o* **16/1**

59.17 secs (0.37) **Going Correction** +0.075s/f (Slow) **8** Ran SP% **116.6**
Speed ratings (Par 90): **100,96,91,90,90 90,78,67**
CSF £15.56 TOTE £4.90: £1.70, £2.10, £1.10; EX 15.60.
Owner Ridgeway Downs Racing **Bred** Island Syndicate **Trained** West Ilsley, Berks

FOCUS
A fair-looking juvenile contest in which the winning time looked very respectable. The third helps set the level.

NOTEBOOK
Moss Likely(IRE), who was too keen on her debut and hated the soft ground, was ideally positioned to strike from off the pace and came right away from her rivals when asked to quicken. She looks the sort to hold her own in novice company. (op 9-2 tchd 5-1)
Rebecca De Winter ◆ knew her job and ran very well. She only found a more experienced rival too good for her and she looks one to be with next time. (tchd 7-2)
Dedante ◆ showed plenty of pace once again to grab the lead but was not quite good enough to stay there at the business end of the race. She looks sure to pick up a maiden soon. (tchd 11-2)
Street Of Hope(USA) made a most encouraging start to her career. The run will have taught her plenty and she will stay further later in the season. (op 22-1 tchd 25-1)
Just The Lady used her previous experience to jump smartly and be in the firing line throughout. However, she was readily outpaced on the home bend and never looked a threat thereafter. (tchd 10-3 and 4-1)
Dream City(IRE) shaped nicely on her debut and looks sure to improve for the experience. (op 10-1 tchd 11-1)
Cheap Thrills, who was by a long way the most expensive purchase in the race, showed plenty of inexperience and was never a factor. She will need to improve mentally to have any chance next time. (op 7-2)

1763 PLAY GOLF @ LINGFIELD PARK MAIDEN STKS — 7f (P)

2:40 (2:42) (Class 5) 3-4-Y-0 — **£3,885** (£1,156; £577; £288) **Stalls** Low

Form — RPR

2-3 **1** **Masaalek**[16] 1403 3-8-12 0 .... RHills 9 89+
(M P Tregoning) *chsd ldrs: wnt 2nd over 4f out: pushed into ld over 1f out: sn in command: easily* **8/13**[1]

232- **2** 4 **Connor's Choice**[190] 6448 3-8-12 77 .... AlanDaly 6 78
(Andrew Turnell) *sn led: stdd pce over 4f out: qcknd over 2f out: hdd over 1f out: no ch w wnr but kpt on for clr 2nd* **10/1**[3]

0- **3** 2 1/4 **Pride Of India (USA)**[342] 2041 3-8-12 0 .... ShaneKelly 2 72
(J Noseda) *chsd ldr tl over 4f out: chsd ldng pair after: rdn and outpcd jst over 2f out: no ch w ldrs after* **4/1**[2]

0 **4** 3 3/4 **Style Icon**[16] 1403 3-8-12 0 .... TQuinn 10 62+
(D R C Elsworth) *towards rr and pushed along early: hdwy 5f out: chsd ldng trio wl over 2f out: hung rt and wd bnd jst over 2f out: no ch w ldng trio after* **16/1**

60- **5** 2 1/4 **Ma Al Salamah (IRE)**[226] 5540 3-8-7 0 .... HayleyTurner 12 51
(C E Brittain) *hld up wl in tch: rdn and outpcd wl over 2f out: no ch after* **50/1**

0 **6** 1/2 **Nightjar (USA)**[35] 1054 3-8-12 0 .... JoeFanning 5 54+
(M Johnston) *s.i.s: t.k.h: hld up in rr: nvr on terms: sme modest late hdwy* **20/1**

7 1/2 **Thumbs Up** 3-8-12 0 .... JamieSpencer 11 53+
(L M Cumani) *s.i.s: bustled along early: a bhd on outer: wd bnd jst over 2f out: modest late hdwy: nvr on terms* **12/1**

8 1 1/2 **First Tracks (IRE)** 3-8-12 0 .... EddieAhern 4 49
(J W Hills) *chsd ldrs: rdn and outpcd wl over 2f out: no ch after* **20/1**

-504 **9** nk **Ma Ridge**[44] 937 4-9-10 47 .... RichardThomas 3 52
(T D McCarthy) *hld up in tch: clipped heels and stmbld wl over 4f out: rdn and outpcd wl over 2f out: no ch after* **100/1**

3-30 **10** 1/2 **Ivory Silk**[15] 1423 3-8-7 72 .... MartinDwyer 1 42+
(D K Ivory) *in tch in midfield tl bdly hmpd and dropped to rr wl over 4f out: no ch last 3f* **25/1**

00 **11** 1 3/4 **Cape Tycoon (IRE)**[8] 1581 3-8-12 0 .... VinceSlattery 7 42
(S A Callaghan) *t.k.h: hld up in tch: outpcd and dropped to rr 3f out: sn wl bhd* **100/1**

1m 26.13s (1.33) **Going Correction** +0.075s/f (Slow)
WFA 3 from 4yo 12lb **11** Ran SP% **121.9**
Speed ratings (Par 103): **95,90,87,83,81 80,79,78,77,77 75**
CSF £7.77 TOTE £1.60: £1.02, £2.80, £1.70; EX 7.20.
Owner Hamdan Al Maktoum **Bred** Shadwell Estate Company Limited **Trained** Lambourn, Berks
■ Stewards' Enquiry : Eddie Ahern caution: careless riding

FOCUS
A fair-looking maiden rated through the runner-up and, although the winning time was not good, winners should emerge from the race.
Style Icon Official explanation: jockey said colt hung right on final bend

1764 ARENALEISUREPLC.COM H'CAP — 6f (P)

3:10 (3:11) (Class 3) (0-90,86) 3-Y-0 **£6,938** (£2,076; £1,038; £519; £258) **Stalls** Low

Form — RPR

0-23 **1** **Pha Mai Blue**[19] 1347 3-8-13 78 .... RichardKingscote 3 79
(W J Knight) *w.w in midfield: rdn jst over 2f out: hdwy on inner jst over 1f out: r.o wl to ld nr fin* **12/1**

2101 **2** nk **Loose Caboose (IRE)**[8] 1584 3-8-13 78 6ex .... (p) SebSanders 2 78
(A J McCabe) *chsd ldr: rdn over 2f out: led jst over 1f out: kpt on wl tl hdd last strides* **7/1**

260- **3** nk **Shifting Star (IRE)**[255] 4695 3-9-2 81 .... AdamKirby 6 80
(W R Swinburn) *chsd ldrs: rdn and unable qckn over 1f out: styd on u.p ins fnl f: pressed ldrs wl ins fnl f: no ex towards fin* **7/2**[2]

-614 **4** shd **Harbour Blues**[15] 1426 3-9-0 79 .... (t) CatherineGannon 1 78
(A W Carroll) *chsd ldrs: rdn wl over 1f out: ev ch ins fnl f: unable qckn towards fin* **8/1**

210 **5** 1 1/2 **Opus Maximus (IRE)**[15] 1426 3-8-8 73 .... JoeFanning 5 67
(M Johnston) *towards rr: rdn and sltly outpcd over 2f out: styd on u.p fnl f: nt pce to rch ldrs* **3/1**[1]

01-0 **6** nk **Lille Ida**[13] 1470 3-8-13 78 .... MartinDwyer 8 71
(M P Tregoning) *stdd s: dropped in bhd and hld up in last pair: rdn and effrt over 2f out: kpt on u.p fnl f: nvr gng pce to rch ldrs* **13/2**

102- **7** 2 **Blue Eyed Miss (IRE)**[175] 6741 3-9-7 86 .... FrankieMcDonald 4 73
(P A Blockley) *racd keenly: led: rdn jst over 2f out: hdd jst over 1f out: fdd ins fnl f* **14/1**

1- **8** 3 1/4 **Well Informed**[385] 1029 3-9-0 79 .... JamieSpencer 7 55
(K A Ryan) *s.i.s: a bhd: effrt on wd outside bnd jst over 2f out: no imp: eased ins fnl f* **9/2**[3]

1m 11.63s (-0.27) **Going Correction** +0.075s/f (Slow) **8** Ran SP% **116.7**
Speed ratings (Par 103): **104,103,103,103,101 100,98,93**
CSF £94.00 CT £363.75 TOTE £14.20: £3.10, £2.40, £1.10; EX 102.00.
Owner Mr & Mrs I H Bendelow **Bred** Chippenham Lodge Stud Ltd **Trained** Patching, W Sussex

FOCUS
A competitive handicap run at a good pace. The form looks sound although the field finished well bunched so it has not been rated too positively.

NOTEBOOK
Pha Mai Blue, who was still a maiden coming into the race, came out just the strongest in a very tight finish. He reportedly hated the going at Brighton last time and needs a quick surface to race on. (op 14-1 tchd 11-1)
Loose Caboose(IRE), raised 6lb for winning at Great Leighs just over a week ago, was very brave in defeat and is a filly bang in form. She is still on an upward curve on an All-Weather surface. (tchd 8-1)
Shifting Star(IRE), making his seasonal debut, came through to have every chance but was not quite good enough to get his head in front. He is entitled to come on for the run. (op 11-2)
Harbour Blues was never far away and only just missed out in a driving finish. He has been in good form and helps to set the level. (op 10-1)
Opus Maximus(IRE), who was really disappointing on turf last time, could never go the frantic pace and never looked like getting to the leaders. The Handicapper appears to have him about right. (op 4-1)
Lille Ida looks like a horse that reserves her very best for an All-Weather surface. Considering the way she ran, a bit further may suit her better. (op 9-2 tchd 7-1)
Blue Eyed Miss(IRE) ◆ set a very good pace but weakened out of contention inside the final furlong. This run should have done her the world of good and she can go closer next time if given a realistic target. A drop to 5f would not be a problem. (op 9-1 tchd 8-1)
Well Informed missed the break and was always struggling. Spencer eased her noticeably up the home straight. (op 4-1)

1765 LINGFIELD PARK FOR WEDDINGS H'CAP — 7f (P)

3:40 (3:40) (Class 2) (0-105,104) 4-Y-0+
£12,462 (£3,732; £1,866; £934; £466; £234) **Stalls** Low

Form — RPR

-242 **1** **Ceremonial Jade (UAE)**[34] 1079 5-9-2 102 .... (t) SebSanders 5 113
(M Botti) *stdd s: t.k.h: hld up in last pl: hdwy over 2f out: str run fr over 1f out: led wl ins fnl f: sn clr* **11/4**[2]

10-1 **2** 2 1/4 **Edge Closer**[34] 1079 4-9-4 104 .... RichardHughes 7 109
(R Hannon) *chsd ldr: rdn jst over 2f out: ch 1f out: nt pce of wnr last 100yds: snatched 2nd on line* **7/2**[3]

523- **3** hd **Salient**[126] 7254 4-8-2 91 oh3 ow1 .... KirstyMilczarek(3) 1 95
(M J Attwater) *led: rdn 2f out: hdd wl ins fnl f: nt pce of wnr last 100yds: lost 2nd on line* **8/1**

01-1 **4** 1 **Transcend**[13] 1481 4-8-8 94 .... RobertHavlin 4 100+
(J H M Gosden) *chsd ldrs: nt clr run over 1f out: swtchd rt ins fnl f: nvr able to mount a chal* **9/4**[1]

500- **5** shd **Beauchamp Viceroy**[215] 5833 4-8-9 95 .... EddieAhern 2 96
(G A Butler) *t.k.h: hld up in tch: effrt and short of room briefly wl over 1f out: kpt on fnl f* **11/1**

00-1 **6** 4 1/2 **Bentong (IRE)**[19] 1346 5-9-3 103 .... TQuinn 6 92
(P F I Cole) *hld up in tch: rdn over 2f out: outpcd 2f out: bhd after* **6/1**

1m 23.72s (-1.08) **Going Correction** +0.075s/f (Slow) **6** Ran SP% **113.4**
Speed ratings (Par 109): **109,106,106,105,104 99**
CSF £12.98 TOTE £3.80: £1.70, £1.90; EX 9.70.
Owner Giuliano Manfredini **Bred** Darley **Trained** Newmarket, Suffolk

FOCUS
A smart handicap run at a good pace and the form should prove solid rated through the first two.

NOTEBOOK
Ceremonial Jade(UAE), held up early, swept past all of his rivals up the home straight to win impressively in a good time. He is holding his form admirably but will need to improve again to defy a rise in the weights, as this success came off a career-high mark. (op 10-3)
Edge Closer tracked Salient going strongly but lost his position when the pace increased. The winner, who he had finished in front of last time at Kempton, had flown by the time he recovered and he had no chance of challenging again. He appeared to stay the trip well, which should give connections more options. (tchd 4-1)
Salient ◆, who looked half the size of his rivals, was given a positive ride and ran somewhere close to his best. It was a fine effort on his first start for a new trainer (the owners remained the same) and he should improve for this first run since last December. (op 12-1 tchd 14-1 and 15-2)
Transcend ◆, raised 8lb for winning at Thirsk last time, was never far away from the head of affairs but appeared to get a bit short of room when his jockey wanted to make his move. He is better than the bare results suggests and is still one to be interested in. (op 7-4)
Beauchamp Viceroy, having his first run since last September, moved smoothly in midfield in the early stages but could not get to the leaders quickly enough once the tempo lifted. Although a touch high in the handicap on all of his winning form, he is one to have on your side next time. Official explanation: vet said gelding was struck into on near-fore (op 10-1 tchd 12-1)

Bentong(IRE), having his first run on an All-Weather surface since his racecourse debut, never really got into the race and ran very disappointingly. It is probably wise to ignore this effort. (op 7-1 tchd 15-2)

1766 LINGFIELD PARK FOR CONFERENCES H'CAP 1m 2f (P)

4:10 (4:10) (Class 2) (0-105,99) 4-Y-0+

£12,462 (£3,732; £1,866; £934; £466; £234) Stalls Low

Form RPR

1-01 **1** **Watamu (IRE)**[27] [1212] 7-9-4 **99**....(v) SebSanders 4 109
(P J Makin) *hld up in tch: hdwy to chse ldr over 2f out: drvn to ld jst over 1f out: r.o wl* **7/2**[2]

-121 **2** *1* **Mr Aviator (USA)**[28] [1180] 4-9-4 **99**.... RichardHughes 2 107
(R Hannon) *trckd ldrs: rdn and effrt 2f out: drvn to press ldrs 1f out: chsd wnr ins fnl f: btn last 50yds* **11/10**[1]

4-02 **3** *1 1/2* **Pinch Of Salt (IRE)**[10] [1544] 5-8-10 **91**.... MartinDwyer 6 96
(A M Balding) *awkward leaving stalls and slowly away: hld up in last pair: swtchd lft and hdwy wl over 1f out: kpt on u.p: wnt 3rd towards fin: nt pce to threaten ldng pair* **5/1**

4100 **4** *1/2* **Samarinda (USA)**[41] [958] 5-9-0 **95**.... MickyFenton 5 99
(Mrs P Sly) *led tl over 9f out: chsd ldr tl led again 3f out: rdn jst over 2f out: hdd jst over 1f out: wknd last 100yds* **16/1**

320- **5** *10* **Ladies Best**[202] [6169] 4-9-2 **97**.... JamieSpencer 1 81+
(L M Cumani) *hld up in last: rdn and effrt on outer jst over 2f out: edgd lft and no hdwy over 1f out: eased whn btn ins fnl f* **9/2**[3]

-310 **6** *5* **Mafeking (UAE)**[97] [315] 4-8-7 **88**.... JimCrowley 3 62
(M R Hoad) *dwlt: sn pushed up to chse ldr: led over 9f out tl 3f out: sn rdn and wknd: bhd and eased ins fnl f* **25/1**

2m 5.30s (-1.30) **Going Correction** +0.075s/f (Slow) **6** Ran SP% **114.4**
Speed ratings (Par 109): **108,107,106,105,97 93**
CSF £8.02 TOTE £3.90: £1.50, £1.20; EX 8.50.
Owner R A Henley **Bred** Crandon Park Stud **Trained** Ogbourne Maisey, Wilts

FOCUS
A good-quality handicap run at a sound gallop but not the most solid form rated through the fourth.

NOTEBOOK
Watamu(IRE) ◆, ridden closer to the pace than usual, battled on very bravely down the centre of the course to just deny his rivals. He is not over-raced for his age and probably has more to offer, but he will need to find something extra to continue his winning spree as this success came off a career-high handicap mark. (op 4-1)

Mr Aviator(USA), 4lb higher than his win last time, only just lost out to a courageous winner and is still progressing in the right direction. His record on the All-Weather (811212) is very impressive, so he is one to keep on the right side of when faced with it again. (op 6-5 tchd 5-4)

Pinch Of Salt(IRE), having his first run on Lingfield's Polytrack surface, was not ideally positioned for a horse that stays further when the pace increased, so he was always going to find it difficult to throw down a serious challenge. He will do better when given a more positive ride. (tchd 4-1 and 11-2)

Samarinda(USA) chased Mafeking in the early stages before taking up the lead heading into the home straight. Under strong pressure, he only started to wilt inside the final half a furlong and appeared to run up to his best. (op 12-1)

Ladies Best, having his first run for new connections after being purchased from Sir Michael Stoute, could never bridge the gap to the leaders after they quickened away from him up the home straight. He was not given a hard time in the final furlong once his chance had gone but he does have something to prove now. (op 6-1 tchd 7-1)

1767 LINGFIELDPARK.CO.UK CONDITIONS STKS 7f (P)

4:40 (4:40) (Class 3) 3-Y-0+

£9,346 (£2,799; £1,399; £700; £349; £175) Stalls Low

Form RPR

0-55 **1** **Dark Islander (IRE)**[71] [651] 5-9-3 0.... EddieAhern 6 112
(J W Hills) *dropped in after s: hld up in tch: hdwy to chse ldrs on outer over 2f out: wd and lost pl 2f out: hdwy u.p over 1f out: hung lft but r.o wl to ld towards fin* **8/1**

-416 **2** *nk* **Racer Forever (USA)**[64] [738] 5-9-3 110....(b) JimmyFortune 3 111
(J H M Gosden) *hld up wl in tch: hdwy over 2f out: drvn and edgd lft 1f out: led ins fnl f: hdd and no ex towards fin* **7/2**[3]

10-3 **3** *1 1/4* **Vanderlin**[17] [1387] 9-9-0 102.... WilliamBuick[(3)] 1 108
(A M Balding) *chsd ldrs for 1f: trckd ldng pair after: rdn and effrt over 1f out: ev ch 1f out: kpt on same pce last 100yds* **6/1**

0411 **4** *1/2* **Jack Sullivan (USA)**[55] [832] 7-9-13 110....(b) JamieSpencer 5 116
(G A Butler) *chsd ldrs after 1f: drvn and c wd on bnd 2f out: kpt on same pce fnl f* **3/1**[2]

2-01 **5** *shd* **Vitznau (IRE)**[20] [1334] 4-9-3 102.... RichardHughes 2 106
(R Hannon) *hld up in last pair: rdn and effrt over 1f out: kpt on same pce* **11/4**[1]

16-6 **6** *1 1/4* **Smart Enough**[20] [1326] 5-9-7 105....(b[1]) KerrinMcEvoy 4 107
(M A Magnusson) *racd keenly: sn led: rdn over 1f out: hdd ins fnl f: fdd wl ins fnl f* **6/1**

1m 24.11s (-0.69) **Going Correction** +0.075s/f (Slow) **6** Ran SP% **113.6**
Speed ratings (Par 107): **106,105,104,103,103 102**
CSF £36.28 TOTE £9.80: £2.60, £2.40; EX 47.60.
Owner Donald M Kerr **Bred** Addison Racing Ltd Inc **Trained** Upper Lambourn, Berks

FOCUS
A smart conditions race run at a sound pace. The form looks a little muddling and is best rated through the fourth.

NOTEBOOK
Dark Islander(IRE), who had run respectably in Dubai earlier in the year, finished very strongly to steal the victory virtually on the line. The slight drop in trip proved to be no problem (a couple of his previous riders felt that 6f is well within his scope) and he may start to progress again at this sort of distance. He must have fast ground and his trainer is eyeing a race at Baden-Baden at the end of the month before a possible tilt at the Golden Jubilee or Wokingham at Royal Ascot.

Racer Forever(USA), who landed a handicap in Dubai during February, looked to have done just enough to secure victory before being mugged close to the line. He is high in the weights and does not win very often, but looks on good terms with himself this year and should be effective in similar races this season. (op 3-1 tchd 4-1)

Vanderlin is a grand servant to his connections and once again gave his all. This was a good effort and he looks as good as ever. (op 11-2 tchd 9-2)

Jack Sullivan(USA) travelled well for a lot of the race but failed to pick up when asked to quicken. It was reported afterwards that he had gone lame. Official explanation: jockey said gelding returned lame (op 10-3 tchd 7-2)

Vitznau(IRE) ◆ ran far better than the bare result suggests. Held up on the inside early, he was never able to get on terms but was not given a really hard time to do so either. There will be other days for him and he is worth following. (op 3-1 tchd 10-3 and 5-2, 7-2 in a place)

Smart Enough, although not beaten far, did too much in the first-time blinkers and did not have as much left in the locker as his rivals when it came down to a sprint. (op 15-2 tchd 8-1)

1768 THE COMMITMENTS LIVE HERE JUNE 7TH H'CAP 1m 4f (P)

5:10 (5:10) (Class 5) (0-70,70) 4-Y-0+ £3,885 (£1,156; £577; £288) Stalls Low

Form RPR

2-10 **1** **Apache Fort**[13] [1482] 5-9-4 **70**.... ShaneKelly 4 73
(T Keddy) *hld up wl in tch: hdwy to join ldrs 3f out: rdn to ld narrowly 2f out: jst hld on* **3/1**[2]

-21 **2** *nse* **Alonso De Guzman (IRE)**[106] [196] 4-9-0 **66**.... JamieSpencer 1 69+
(J R Boyle) *led: jnd 3f out: rdn and hdd narrowly 2f out: rallied u.p wl ins fnl f: jst hld* **11/4**[1]

4441 **3** *1 1/4* **Wind Flow**[20] [1340] 4-9-2 **68**.... JimmyQuinn 5 69
(C A Dwyer) *chsd ldrs: jnd ldr wl over 3f out: ev ch after tl no ex wl ins fnl f* **7/2**[3]

02-0 **4** *1* **Calming Waters**[44] [941] 5-9-2 **68**.... EddieAhern 3 67
(D W P Arbuthnot) *hld up wl in tch: rdn and nt qckn jst over 2f out: styd on again ins fnl f: nt rch ldrs* **9/1**

013- **5** *14* **Sunset Boulevard (IRE)**[68] [1924] 5-9-3 **69**.... DaneO'Neill 2 46
(Miss Tor Sturgis) *trckd ldrs: rdn wl over 2f out: sn struggling: no ch fr wl over 1f out* **3/1**[2]

2m 32.97s (-0.03) **Going Correction** +0.075s/f (Slow) **5** Ran SP% **108.9**
Speed ratings (Par 103): **103,102,102,101,92**
CSF £11.26 TOTE £3.70: £1.10, £1.30; EX 10.60 Place 6 £ 60.67, Place 5 £ 35.24.
Owner Andrew Duffield **Bred** Juddmonte Farms Ltd **Trained** Newmarket, Suffolk

FOCUS
A strong-looking handicap that turned into a sprint. The form may not be reliable and it is hard to be positive about the form.
T/Plt: £76.00 to a £1 stake. Pool: £65,035.39. 624.45 winning tickets. T/Qpdt: £43.00 to a £1 stake. Pool: £3,103.39. 53.30 winning tickets. SP

1303 MUSSELBURGH (R-H)

Friday, May 2

OFFICIAL GOING: Good to soft (soft in places in home straight; 7.7)
Wind: Light behind Weather: Sunny periods and showers

1769 CALA HOMES H'CAP 5f

2:20 (2:20) (Class 6) (0-65,62) 3-Y-0 £2,266 (£674; £337; £168) Stalls Low

Form RPR

00-1 **1** **Big Slick (IRE)**[9] [1560] 3-8-11 **52** 6ex.... TWilliams 2 62
(M Brittain) *mde all: jnd and rdn over 1f out: styd on strly ins fnl f* **6/1**

1 **2** *2 1/2* **Little Eden (IRE)**[37] [1027] 3-9-3 **58**.... PhillipMakin 1 59
(T D Barron) *chsd ldrs: hdwy over 1f out: rdn and kpt on ins fnl f* **9/4**[1]

00-5 **3** *1/2* **Miss Sunshine**[40] [977] 3-8-8 **49**.... FergalLynch 8 48
(J S Goldie) *towards rr: hdwy 2f out: rdn and kpt on ins fnl f: nrst fin* **25/1**

10-0 **4** *nk* **Handsinthemist (IRE)**[30] [1155] 3-8-10 **54**....(p) JamieMoriarty[(3)] 10 52
(P T Midgley) *chsd ldrs on outer: hdwy 2f out: rdn and ch over 1f out: drvn and one pce ins fnl f* **20/1**

00-2 **5** *1 1/4* **Linnet Park**[13] [1475] 3-9-3 **58**.... J-PGuillambert 6 51
(J G Given) *cl up: rdn wl over 1f out: edgd lft and put and hd in air: wknd ins fnl f* **9/2**[2]

3434 **6** *2 1/2* **The Little Fizzer (IRE)**[13] [1475] 3-9-7 **62**.... AndrewElliott 3 46
(K R Burke) *chsd ldrs: effrt 2f out: sn rdn and wknd* **7/1**

6-03 **7** *3/4* **Dalarossie**[6] [1635] 3-9-7 **62**.... DavidAllan 5 44
(E J Alston) *rrd and bmpd s: swtchd to stands' rail and a in rr* **11/2**[3]

-030 **8** *nk* **Captain Turbot (IRE)**[9] [1560] 3-8-4 **45**.... PaulHanagan 4 26
(D W Barker) *wnt rt s: a towards rr* **14/1**

00-4 **9** *1 3/4* **Myriola**[9] [1560] 3-8-9 **55**.... JamieJones[(5)] 7 29
(S Gollings) *chsd ldrs: rdn along 2f out: sn wknd* **16/1**

300- **10** *7* **La Guancha**[210] [5965] 3-8-5 **46** ow1....(t) GregFairley 9 —
(D A Nolan) *prom: rdn along over 2f out: sn wknd* **100/1**

63.30 secs (2.90) **Going Correction** +0.45s/f (Yiel) **10** Ran SP% **113.3**
Speed ratings (Par 97): **94,90,89,88,86 82,81,78,67**
CSF £18.89 CT £319.41 TOTE £7.60: £3.10, £1.20, £7.30; EX 25.40.
Owner Northgate Poker **Bred** John Murphy **Trained** Warthill, N Yorks

FOCUS
A moderate sprint handicap but a clear-cut winner and the form looks solid rated around the fifth and sixth.
Dalarossie Official explanation: jockey said gelding reared as stalls opened

1770 EUROPEAN BREEDERS FUND MEDIAN AUCTION MAIDEN STKS 5f

2:50 (2:50) (Class 5) 2-Y-0 £3,885 (£1,156; £577; £288) Stalls Low

Form RPR

1 **Go Nani Go** 2-9-3 0.... TomEaves 5 81+
(B Smart) *trckd ldrs: swtchd outside and hdwy over 1f out: rdn to ld: flashed tail and edgd lft ins fnl f: styd on* **13/8**[2]

2 **2** *1 1/4* **Harwalla (IRE)**[13] [1474] 2-9-3 0.... GregFairley 6 76
(M Johnston) *cl up: led wl over 1f out: sn rdn: hdd and drvn ins fnl f: kpt on* **11/8**[1]

3 *1/2* **Peninsular War** 2-9-3 0.... AndrewElliott 1 74+
(K R Burke) *cl up: effrt 2f out: sn rdn and ev ch tl one pce ins fnl f* **12/1**

4 *2 3/4* **Honimiere (IRE)** 2-8-9 0.... PJMcDonald[(3)] 3 59+
(G A Swinbank) *chsd ldrs: rdn along wl over 1f out: kpt on same pce* **8/1**[3]

5 **5** *2* **Amorachy**[17] [1377] 2-9-3 0.... NCallan 2 59+
(K A Ryan) *led: rdn along 2f out: hdd & wknd wl over 1f out* **14/1**

6 *2 1/4* **Glenlini** 2-8-12 0.... DanielTudhope 7 46+
(J S Goldie) *sn outpcd and a in rr* **28/1**

7 *12* **Canclodacancan (IRE)** 2-8-10 0 ow1.... JamieMoriarty[(3)] 4 —
(P T Midgley) *bmpd s: a bhd* **50/1**

63.35 secs (2.95) **Going Correction** +0.45s/f (Yiel) **7** Ran SP% **111.1**
Speed ratings (Par 93): **94,92,91,86,83 80,60**
CSF £3.92 TOTE £3.20: £1.70, £1.10; EX 4.10.
Owner H E Sheikh Rashid Bin Mohammed **Bred** D J And Mrs Deer **Trained** Hambleton, N Yorks
■ Stewards' Enquiry : Greg Fairley caution: careless riding

FOCUS
An uncompetitive juvenile contest in which three dominated the market, and run only 0.05 sec slower than the opening handicap. The runner-up is rated to his debut form and the form could be a little better.

NOTEBOOK
Go Nani Go ◆, solidly backed against the favourite, was travelling well just behind the leaders at halfway, and despite running green when pulled out, showed something of the acceleration of his namesake to score despite swishing his tail in response to the whip. He looks likely to benefit from this and better ground should suit. His trainer will be looking for a conditions race for him next but he could be on course for the Norfolk Stakes at Royal Ascot. (op 7-4 tchd 15-8 tchd 2-1 in places)

Harwalla(IRE), who had been narrowly beaten on his debut at Nottingham, appeared to have every chance and went on 2f out, but had no answer to the winner's challenge. He bumped into a potentially smart colt on this occasion and should be capable of picking up an ordinary maiden before long. (tchd 5-4)
Peninsular War was backed at long prices and ran well from his rail draw despite looking likely to improve for the experience. (op 33-1)
Honimiere(IRE), easy in the market for this debut, was outpaced early before getting to grips with what was required and keeping on in the second half of the contest. He is likely to come on considerably for the run and will appreciate further in time. (op 6-1 tchd 17-2)
Amorachy, backed at long prices to build on his debut, set the early pace but was on the retreat when short of room a furlong out. (op 20-1)

1771 EDMONDS UK 50TH ANNIVERSARY H'CAP — 1m 1f

3:20 (3:21) (Class 4) (0-80,85) 4-Y-0+ **£5,180** (£1,541; £770; £384) **Stalls** High

Form RPR
0-21 **1** **First Buddy**[6] [1613] 4-9-10 **85** 6ex................ NCallan 2 103+
(G A Swinbank) *mde all: qcknd clr 2f out: unchal* **4/9**[1]
3230 **2** *6* **Moheebb (IRE)**[6] [1613] 4-9-0 **75**................ TomEaves 6 79
(Mrs R A Carr) *in tch: hdwy 3f out: rdn to chse wnr wl over 1f out: sn drvn and no imp* **10/1**[3]
02-0 **3** *5* **Prince Samos (IRE)**[41] [962] 6-8-12 **73**................(v) PaulHanagan 9 66
(D Nicholls) *hld up towards rr: hdwy wl over 2f out: sn rdn and kpt on same pce* **11/1**
06-0 **4** *hd* **Mystical Ayr (IRE)**[37] [1030] 6-8-4 **65**................ RoystonFfrench 4 58
(Miss L A Perratt) *trckd ldrs: rdn and hdwy to chse wnr wl over 2f out: sn drvn and one pce* **25/1**
54-0 **5** *4* **Chicken George (IRE)**[39] [992] 4-8-12 **73**................ SilvestreDeSousa 8 57
(D Nicholls) *hld up towards rr: hdwy 3f out: rdn along over 2f out and sn no imp* **8/1**[2]
055- **6** *hd* **Regent's Secret (USA)**[125] [5674] 8-8-9 **70**................ FergalLynch 1 54
(J S Goldie) *stdd s: hld up and bhd tl sme hdwy fnl 2f: nvr a factor* **33/1**
050- **7** *½* **Wilmington**[225] [5555] 4-8-1 **65** oh4................ AndrewMullen(3) 3 48
(Mrs J C McGregor) *chsd wnr: rdn along over 3f out and sn wknd* **100/1**
0-56 **8** *1¼* **Bed Fellow (IRE)**[35] [1049] 4-8-6 **67**................ AndrewElliott 5 47
(Paul Murphy) *chsd ldrs: rdn along 3f out: sn drvn and wknd* **40/1**
00-0 **9** *½* **Trimlestown (IRE)**[48] [910] 5-9-1 **76**................ DO'Donohoe 7 55
(K A Ryan) *stdd s: a in rr* **14/1**

1m 56.08s (1.38) **Going Correction** +0.45s/f (Yiel) **9** Ran SP% **114.7**
Speed ratings (Par 105): **111,105,101,101,97 97,96,95,95**
CSF £5.45 CT £24.04 TOTE £1.20: £1.10, £2.10, £2.50; EX 5.70.
Owner W J Gredley **Bred** Tarworth Bloodstock Investments Ltd **Trained** Melsonby, N Yorks

FOCUS
A fair handicap with a short-priced favourite who ran his rivals ragged and scored in a good time for the grade. The runner-up sets the standard but there is little solid in behind.

1772 POMMERY CHAMPAGNE BAR AT MUSSELBURGH RACECOURSE CONDITIONS STKS — 5f

3:50 (3:51) (Class 2) 3-Y-0+
£12,462 (£3,732; £1,866; £934; £466; £234) **Stalls** Low

Form RPR
422- **1** **Borderlescott**[160] [6930] 6-8-12 109................ RobertWinston 5 113+
(R Bastiman) *trckd ldrs: hdwy 2f out: rdn and qcknd to ld ins fnl f: kpt on* **5/4**[1]
330- **2** *1½* **Desert Lord**[145] [7089] 8-8-12 111................(b) NCallan 8 107
(K A Ryan) *wnt rt s: sn led: rdn along and jnd wl over 1f out: drvn and hdd ins fnl f: kpt on* **11/4**[2]
120- **3** *6* **Fathom Five (IRE)**[254] [4726] 4-8-12 98................ TomEaves 4 86
(B Smart) *chsd ldr: effrt 2f out: sn rdn and one pce appr fnl f* **4/1**[3]
235- **4** *1½* **Look Busy (IRE)**[188] [6488] 3-7-12 93................ DanielleMcCreery 6 71
(A Berry) *swtchd to r wd: in tch: hdwy wl over 1f out: sn rdn and kpt on ins fnl f* **20/1**
0102 **5** *2¼* **Canadian Danehill (IRE)**[9] [1571] 6-8-12 95................(p) FergalLynch 2 72
(R M H Cowell) *chsd ldrs: rdn along 2f out: sn edgd rt and wknd* **6/1**
655- **6** *4½* **Valiant Romeo**[176] [6730] 8-8-12 45................ DanielTudhope 7 56?
(R Bastiman) *chsd ldrs: rdn along 1/2-way: sn wknd* **300/1**
00-0 **7** *3½* **Mutayam**[21] [1309] 8-8-12 45................(t) GregFairley 3 43
(D A Nolan) *a in rr* **400/1**
500- **8** *13* **Alfie Lee (IRE)**[228] [5481] 11-8-12 41................(t) MarkLawson 1 —
(D A Nolan) *a outpcd and bhd* **300/1**

61.43 secs (1.03) **Going Correction** +0.45s/f (Yiel)
WFA 3 from 4yo+ 9lb **8** Ran SP% **111.1**
Speed ratings (Par 109): **109,106,97,94,91 83,78,57**
CSF £4.55 TOTE £2.20: £1.10, £1.10, £1.90; EX 5.50.
Owner James Edgar **Bred** James Clark **Trained** Cowthorpe, N Yorks

FOCUS
A decent conditions event with good prizemoney. The time was 1.87secs faster than the opening handicap but not form to take too literally.

NOTEBOOK
Borderlescott, an admirable sprinter who had a frustrating time last season, being touched off on several occasions including in the Stewards' Cup, got a nice confidence booster on this seasonal return. Despite dropping in back to 5f, he travelled well throughout and, when asked to go past the runner-up, did so with little fuss. His trainer is looking more to this type of event and Listed races rather than the big handicaps and Group races this year. (tchd 6-4)
Desert Lord, another evergreen sprinter, jumped fast from his outside draw and tried to make all, but the winner was always cruising just behind his and he could not respond when challenged. He prefers better ground than this and the outing will bring him on. (op 5-2 tchd 3-1 in places)
Fathom Five(IRE), who had 11lb to find with the winner on official ratings, chased the leader but was left behind by the principals in the latter stages. He should be better for the run but his current mark, 13lb higher than for his last win, means he will not find things easy in handicaps. (op 9-2)
Look Busy(IRE), a diminutive filly who had a fine juvenile campaign in 2007, was up against it even getting a stone from the rest of the field. She ran creditably from her wide draw but is likely to find things difficult this season off her current mark, even in races confined to fillies. Official explanation: jockey said filly anticipated start causing her to lose an iron and hung left in final furlong
Canadian Danehill(IRE) had fitness on his side but found this opposition too hot for him. (op 7-1 tchd 11-2)

1773 BOOGIE IN THE MORNING H'CAP — 1m 6f

4:20 (4:21) (Class 5) (0-70,67) 4-Y-0+ **£3,238** (£963; £481; £240) **Stalls** High

Form RPR
4/55 **1** **Hill Billy Rock (IRE)**[13] [1482] 5-9-6 **66**................ PJMcDonald(3) 5 78+
(G A Swinbank) *trckd ldr: effrt over 2f out and sn rdn: drvn over 1f out: styd on u.p ins fnl f to ld nr fin* **13/8**[1]
02-2 **2** *nk* **Danzatrice**[21] [1304] 6-9-3 **60**................ TomEaves 7 69
(C W Thornton) *hld up in rr: gd hdwy on inner 3f out: swtchd lft and rdn to ld wl over 1f out: drvn ins fnl f: hdd and no ex towards fin* **9/4**[2]
5-60 **3** *3* **Trance (IRE)**[13] [1482] 8-9-10 **67**................(b) PaulFessey 2 72
(T D Barron) *a.p: rdn along and rn in snatches: rdn and outpcd over 2f out: hrd drive: edgd rt and styd on fnl f* **16/1**
003- **4** *3¾* **Forrest Flyer (IRE)**[185] [6561] 4-8-9 **53**................ PhillipMakin 1 53
(Miss L A Perratt) *sn led: rdn along over 2f out: drvn and hdd wl over 1f out: edgd rt and wknd ent fnl f* **5/1**[3]
/-45 **5** *1* **Flamed Amazement**[27] [1221] 4-9-9 **67**................(p) RobertWinston 3 65
(L Lungo) *in rr and rn wd bnd after 2f: hdwy over 3f out: rdn over 2f out: drvn and kpt on same pce appr fnl f* **9/1**
00-0 **6** *5* **Grey Outlook**[21] [1304] 5-8-5 **48** oh3................ RoystonFfrench 6 39
(Miss L A Perratt) *hld up in tch: hdwy over 3f out: sn rdn and btn over 2f out* **16/1**
00-4 **7** *2* **Miss Havisham (IRE)**[52] [843] 4-8-5 **49**................ DeanMcKeown 8 37
(J R Weymes) *trckd ldrs: effrt on inner over 3f out: sn rdn along and wknd* **25/1**
0-00 **8** *3* **Next Flight (IRE)**[10] [1551] 9-8-0 **48** oh3................ DanielleMcCreery(5) 4 32
(R E Barr) *s.i.s: sn chsng ldrs: rdn along over 4f out and sn wknd* **25/1**

3m 10.03s (4.73) **Going Correction** +0.45s/f (Yiel)
WFA 4 from 5yo+ 1lb **8** Ran SP% **115.0**
Speed ratings (Par 103): **104,103,102,99,99 96,95,93**
CSF £5.43 CT £36.86 TOTE £2.80: £1.10, £1.70, £3.00; EX 5.40.
Owner W Powrie And Mrs S Sandbrook **Bred** Darley **Trained** Melsonby, N Yorks

FOCUS
A modest staying contest that produced a close finish between the market principals. The form looks pretty solid.
Next Flight(IRE) Official explanation: jockey said gelding missed the break

1774 TODS MURRAY H'CAP — 7f 30y

4:50 (4:50) (Class 3) (0-90,88) 4-Y-0+
£7,477 (£2,239; £1,119; £560; £279; £140) **Stalls** High

Form RPR
-604 **1** **Skhilling Spirit**[13] [1481] 5-9-2 **88**................ NeilBrown(5) 6 100
(T D Barron) *trckd ldrs: hdwy on outer over 2f out: rdn over 1f out: drvn and edgd rt ins fnl f: styd on to ld last 75yds* **4/1**[3]
000- **2** *1¼* **Il Castagno (IRE)**[185] [6560] 5-8-11 **78**................ TomEaves 3 86
(B Smart) *led: rdn along 2f out: drvn over 1f out: hdd ins fnl f: kpt on wl u.p towards fin* **10/1**
3133 **3** *¾* **Cha Cha Cha**[21] [1308] 4-9-1 **82**................ NCallan 8 88
(K A Ryan) *trckd ldrs: hdwy 3f out: chal wl over 1f out: rdn to ld ins fnl f: hdd and no ex last 75yds* **3/1**[2]
0-02 **4** *½* **Stoic Leader (IRE)**[30] [1138] 8-8-3 **70**................ PaulHanagan 9 75
(R F Fisher) *cl up on inner: rdn along over 2f out: drvn over 1f out: kpt on same pce ins fnl f* **13/2**
5013 **5** *1¼* **Stevie Gee (IRE)**[11] [1517] 4-9-2 **86**................ PJMcDonald(3) 2 88
(G A Swinbank) *trckd ldr: hdwy and cl up 3f out: rdn and ev ch over 1f out: drvn and wknd ins fnl f* **5/2**[1]
-050 **6** *shd* **Byron Bay**[16] [1409] 6-8-5 **72**................ DeanMcKeown 5 73
(R C Guest) *hld up in rr: hdwy 3f out: rdn and kpt on appr fnl f: nrst fin* **28/1**
442- **7** *2½* **Esoterica (IRE)**[175] [6746] 5-8-2 **69**................(b) RoystonFfrench 4 64
(J S Goldie) *hld up: a in rr* **12/1**
000- **8** *½* **Billy Dane (IRE)**[257] [4640] 4-9-0 **84**................ JamieMoriarty(3) 7 77
(R A Fahey) *hld up: a in rr* **33/1**
4002 **9** *5* **Red Romeo**[16] [1409] 7-8-10 **77**................ DanielTudhope 1 57
(N Wilson) *chsd ldrs: effrt to chal on outer over 2f out: sn rdn and ev ch: drvn and wkng whn n.m.r ent fnl f* **16/1**

1m 32.06s (1.76) **Going Correction** +0.45s/f (Yiel) **9** Ran SP% **116.0**
Speed ratings (Par 107): **107,105,104,104,102 102,99,99,93**
CSF £43.61 CT £136.98 TOTE £5.10: £2.00, £3.00, £1.20; EX 70.00.
Owner I Hill **Bred** Pillar To Post Racing **Trained** Maunby, N Yorks

FOCUS
A good, competitive handicap run at a sound gallop and solid form rated around the winner and third.

NOTEBOOK
Skhilling Spirit, who is not the easiest to win with, is very capable on his day and showed it here. Given a good ride, he settled in behind the leading group and, brought with a run down the wide outside, found plenty when asked to win a shade cosily. This was his first success at the trip, he is rated 12lb lower than he was a year ago, so if this signals he is back on song, he could prove well handicapped. (tchd 5-1)
Il Castagno(IRE) ◆ made a fine return to action, soon leading and responding well for pressure when challenged. He should come on for the outing and looks capable of winning at this level on this evidence. (op 11-1)
Cha Cha Cha tracked the leaders throughout and moved up to challenge approaching the quarter-mile mark. However, she could not get past the runner-up and tired inside the last. (op 4-1)
Stoic Leader(IRE) goes well on this track and ran a fine race so is clearly in good heart at the moment. He could be ready to score if dropped to a slightly lower grade and returned to a faster surface. (op 8-1 tchd 11-1)
Stevie Gee(IRE), stepping back up in trip, was prominent throughout but was a little keen. He had every chance halfway up the straight but his effort petered out in the closing stages and he needs to settle better to get home over this distance. (op 15-8)
Red Romeo showed up for a long way but dropped out quickly at the business end. (tchd 14-1)

1775 GILBERTS H'CAP — 7f 30y

5:20 (5:21) (Class 6) (0-65,65) 4-Y-0+ **£2,266** (£674; £337; £168) **Stalls** High

Form RPR
000- **1** **Stellite**[181] [6639] 8-8-12 **59**................ DanielTudhope 11 68
(J S Goldie) *hld up in tch: hdwy over 2f out: rdn to ld appr fnl f: drvn out* **13/2**
00-0 **2** *½* **Vesuvio**[28] [1189] 4-8-1 **51** oh4................ AndrewMullen(3) 7 59
(C W Thornton) *hld up towards rr: hdwy over 2f out: rdn to chse wnr ins fnl f: drvn and nt qckn towards fin* **20/1**
30-0 **3** *1* **Wind Shuffle (GER)**[30] [1138] 5-8-8 **60**................ GaryBartley(5) 10 65
(J S Goldie) *towards rr: hdwy over 2f out: sn rdn and styd on wl fnl f: nrst fin* **12/1**
2411 **4** *hd* **Shunkawakhan (IRE)**[16] [1406] 5-8-10 **57**................(p) TomEaves 9 61
(Miss L A Perratt) *chsd ldrs: effrt over 2f out: swtchd lft and rdn over 1f out: drvn and kpt on ins fnl f* **6/1**[3]
-026 **5** *½* **Messiah Garvey**[14] [1449] 4-9-1 **62**................ SilvestreDeSousa 2 65
(D Nicholls) *led: rdn over 2f out: drvn wl over 1f out: hdd appr fnl f: wknd* **9/2**[2]
-012 **6** *hd* **A Big Sky Brewing (USA)**[8] [1578] 4-8-8 **60**................(b) NeilBrown(5) 5 63
(T D Barron) *prom: effrt and ev ch 2f out: sn rdn and wknd ent fnl f* **7/2**[1]
2550 **7** *¾* **Inca Soldier (FR)**[13] [1485] 5-9-0 **61**................ DeanMcKeown 12 62
(R C Guest) *hld up in rr: hdwy 2f out: rdn and kpt on ins fnl f: nrst fin* **12/1**

00-0 **8** *1* **No Grouse**[6] 1634 8-8-8 **55**........ DavidAllan 6 53
(E J Alston) *towards rr: hdwy over 2f out: sn rdn and kpt on ins fnl f: nrst fin* **14/1**

6204 **9** *1* **Strathmore (IRE)**[9] 1561 4-9-4 **65**........ PaulHanagan 3 60
(R A Fahey) *hld up in rr: sme late hdwy* **12/1**

00/0 **10** *1 1/2* **Woodsley House (IRE)**[39] 990 6-9-3 **64**........ RobertWinston 8 55
(A G Foster) *chsd ldr: rdn along wl over 2f out: wknd over 1f out* **28/1**

04-6 **11** *3 1/4* **Nufoudh (IRE)**[8] 1578 4-8-8 **55**........ RoystonFfrench 4 37
(Miss Tracy Waggott) *chsd ldrs: hdwy on outer over 2f out: sn rdn and wknd appr fnl f* **11/1**

0-30 **12** *4 1/2* **Attacca**[51] 861 7-8-4 **51** oh1........ DO'Donohoe 1 21
(J R Weymes) *a towards rr* **16/1**

240- **13** *1* **Domesday (UAE)**[182] 6629 7-8-4 **51** oh3........ GregFairley 13 18
(W G Harrison) *prom: rdn along 3f out: wknd over 2f out* **28/1**

1m 33.53s (3.23) **Going Correction** +0.45s/f (Yiel) **13 Ran SP% 123.6**
Speed ratings (Par 101): **99,98,97,97,96 96,95,94,93,91 87,82,81**
CSF £136.51 CT £1535.10 TOTE £9.30: £2.80, £10.00, £4.50; EX 209.40 Place 6 £ 4.73, Place 5 £ 2.28.
Owner S Bruce **Bred** Cheveley Park Stud Ltd **Trained** Uplawmoor, E Renfrews

FOCUS
A moderate handicap run 1.47 secs slower than the preceding Class 3 contest but the form looks sound with the third to his mark.
T/Plt: £4.90 to a £1 stake. Pool: £59,135.96. 8,706.45 winning tickets. T/Qpdt: £2.60 to a £1 stake. Pool: £2,876.79. 817.00 winning tickets. JR

1700 SOUTHWELL (L-H)
Friday, May 2

OFFICIAL GOING: Turf course - good (good to soft in places; 6.9); all-weather - standard
The ground was described as 'near perfect'.
Wind: light half-against Weather: fine and sunny

1776 LADBROKES.COM LEADS THE WAY APPRENTICE H'CAP 1m 2f
2:30 (2:30) (Class 6) (0-55,55) 4-Y-0+ **£1,774** (£523; £262) **Stalls** Low

Form RPR

0044 **1** **King Of Connacht**[10] 1528 5-8-11 **52**........(p) SamuelDrury 11 64+
(M Wellings) *mid-div: gd hdwy 2f out: styd on wl to ld nr fin* **10/1**

4365 **2** *1/2* **Bramcote Lorne**[30] 1152 5-8-9 **50**........(p) CharlesEddery 6 61
(R C Guest) *led: clr 7f out: hdd towards fin* **20/1**

4634 **3** *3 3/4* **Sparky Vixen**[7] 1606 4-8-10 **51**........ JamieKyne 1 55
(C J Teague) *dwlt: sn chsng ldrs: kpt on same pce appr fnl f* **7/1**[3]

2-00 **4** *3/4* **Desert Hawk**[4] 1692 7-8-11 **52**........ KrishGundowry 10 54
(W M Brisbourne) *bhd: gd hdwy over 2f out: kpt on same pce fnl f* **9/1**

6/65 **5** *1 3/4* **Wednesdays Boy (IRE)**[16] 1394 5-8-12 **53**........(p) FrederikTylicki 7 52
(P D Niven) *prom: one pce fnl 3f* **4/1**[1]

133- **6** *1 1/2* **Hi Dancer**[29] 5087 5-9-0 **55**........ JamesRogers 13 51
(P C Haslam) *mid-div: drvn over 4f out: styd on: nvr nr ldrs* **11/2**[2]

6506 **7** *12* **Tina's Ridge (IRE)**[16] 1391 4-8-11 **52**........ DavidProbert 14 24
(R Hollinshead) *swtchd lft s: bhd: sme hdwy over 3f out: nvr on terms* **16/1**

-661 **8** *1 1/4* **Cumae (USA)**[3] 1694 4-8-10 **51** 6ex........ JosephineBruning 3 20
(J Pearce) *hmpd appr 1f: mid-div: drvn 7f out: nvr a factor* **12/1**

6400 **9** *hd* **Anduril**[32] 1116 7-8-9 **50**........(p) RosieJessop 12 19
(I W McInnes) *prom: drvn over 4f out: lost pl 3f out* **25/1**

1110 **10** *1 1/4* **Bahhmirage (IRE)**[12] 1505 5-8-10 **51**........(p) BillyCray 8 17
(C N Kellett) *sltly hmpd s: a in rr* **12/1**

00-0 **11** *8* **Fan Club**[28] 1188 4-8-11 **52**........ SoniaEaton 2 2
(Mrs R A Carr) *prom: lost pl over 2f out* **40/1**

-000 **12** *9* **Shaftesbury Avenue (USA)**[8] 1578 5-8-12 **53**........ NSLawes 4 —
(I W McInnes) *chsd ldrs: drvn over 4f out: sn wknd* **16/1**

2m 12.5s (-0.60) **Going Correction** -0.025s/f (Good) **12 Ran SP% 115.2**
Speed ratings (Par 101): **101,100,97,97,95 94,84,83,83,82 76,69**
CSF £192.09 CT £1487.51 TOTE £12.60: £3.20, £7.40, £2.80; EX 290.30 TRIFECTA Not won..
Owner Andre M Gilbert **Bred** B Burrough **Trained** Six Ashes, Shropshire

FOCUS
A low-grade apprentice handicap, a selling race in all but name but the form looks pretty sound at this level.

1777 LADBROKES 24/7 FREEPHONE BETTING 0800 777 888 CLAIMING STKS 6f
3:00 (3:03) (Class 6) 3-Y-0 **£1,774** (£523; £262) **Stalls** Low

Form RPR

253 **1** **Jal Music**[7] 1603 3-8-13 **67**........ ChrisCatlin 4 66
(R A Harris) *mde all: styd on u.p fnl 2f: unchal* **4/1**[3]

5 **2** *1 3/4* **Near The Front**[21] 1311 3-8-7 0........ SamHitchcott 7 54
(J L Spearing) *mid-div: hdwy u.p on outside over 3f out: styd on to take 2nd ins fnl f: no real imp* **7/2**[2]

422 **3** *1 1/4* **Caprio (IRE)**[13] 1487 3-9-7 **70**........ PatCosgrave 6 64
(J R Boyle) *chsd ldrs: wnt 2nd over 2f out: kpt on same pce fnl f* **9/4**[1]

2042 **4** *3* **Diademas (USA)**[15] 1414 3-8-11 **59**........(v) SimonWhitworth 8 45
(V Smith) *s.i.s: styd on fnl 2f: nvr nr ldrs* **6/1**

1-60 **5** *3 1/4* **My Mate Pete (IRE)**[15] 1426 3-9-7 **74**........ DarryllHolland 9 44
(Mrs L Stubbs) *chsd ldrs: wknd 1f out* **4/1**[3]

05-0 **6** *3* **Dark Queen**[6] 1635 3-7-11 **37**........ JamieKyne(7) 5 18
(D Carroll) *unruly at s: mid-div: no imp whn hmpd over 2f out* **66/1**

0-60 **7** *1 3/4* **Madame Rio (IRE)**[14] 1453 3-8-5 **44**........ DeclanCannon(7) 3 20
(K R Burke) *chsd ldrs: wknd over 2f out* **50/1**

50 **8** *2 3/4* **Feeling Pretty**[60] 780 3-8-6 0........ PatrickMathers 2 5
(C Smith) *s.i.s: in rr and drvn over 3f out: nvr on terms* **100/1**

60 **9** *hd* **Marysedge**[39] 997 3-8-8 0........ PaulMulrennan 1 7
(R Brotherton) *s.i.s: a in rr* **100/1**

1m 16.38s (0.58) **Going Correction** -0.025s/f (Good) **9 Ran SP% 112.7**
Speed ratings (Par 97): **95,92,91,87,82 78,76,72,72**
CSF £17.79 TOTE £6.00: £1.10, £1.80, £1.10; EX 23.10 Trifecta £61.90 Pool: £508.07 - 5.82 winning units..Near The Front was claimed by Miss Gay Kelleway for £5,000.
Owner Mrs Ruth M Serrell **Bred** J D And Mrs Knight **Trained** Earlswood, Monmouths

FOCUS
A modest claimer with the majority usually plying their trade on the all-weather surfaces, which means it is a difficult contest to race with certainty.

Marysedge Official explanation: jockey said, regarding running and riding, that his orders were to get a good position and ride the filly with hands and heels to obtain best possible placing, adding that it was slow into stride, shuffled back on 1st bend and, as a result, boxed in on rails until the straight where he asked for an effort with no response; trainer confirmed instructions, adding that filly is of questionable ability and that he's been satisfied with the ride.

1778 BET IN PLAY AT LADBROKES.COM MEDIAN AUCTION MAIDEN STKS 5f (F)
3:30 (3:31) (Class 6) 2-Y-0 **£1,774** (£523; £262) **Stalls** High

Form RPR

1 **Senor Mirasol** 2-9-3 0........ DarryllHolland 6 70+
(K A Ryan) *w ldrs: led 1f out: kpt on wl* **9/4**[2]

2 *1 1/2* **Carmanjoe** 2-9-3 0........ PaulMulrennan 5 64
(M W Easterby) *s.i.s: sn chsng ldrs: chal 1f out: kpt on same pce* **25/1**

3 *3/4* **La Brigitte** 2-8-12 0........ NeilPollard 4 56+
(A J McCabe) *prom: outpcd and lost pl over 2f out: styd on appr fnl f: fin wl* **40/1**

0 **4** *2 1/4* **Especially For You (IRE)**[21] 1303 2-8-12 0........ ChrisCatlin 9 48
(E J O'Neill) *t.k.h: led: hdd & wknd 1f out* **14/1**

5 **5** *4 1/2* **Crewezando**[15] 1425 2-9-3 0........ TGMcLaughlin 1 37
(P D Evans) *w ldrs: rdn over 2f out: wknd over 1f out* **15/8**[1]

4 **6** *nk* **Ridgeway Silver**[17] 1377 2-8-7 0 ow2........ GabrielHannon(7) 3 33
(M D I Usher) *s.s: nvr on terms* **14/1**

0 **7** *1 3/4* **Swingfire (USA)**[16] 1399 2-9-3 0........ AlanMunro 7 30
(R M H Cowell) *sn outpcd and in rr* **11/2**[3]

4 **8** *4 1/2* **Forzando Bloom**[9] 1555 2-9-0 0........ KevinGhunowa(3) 8 14
(R A Harris) *s.i.s: sn bhd* **16/1**

9 *4 1/2* **Transfered (IRE)** 2-8-12 0........ TPO'Shea 2 —
(M G Quinlan) *chsd ldrs: rdn and lost pl over 2f out* **9/1**

60.44 secs (0.74) **Going Correction** -0.075s/f (Stan) **9 Ran SP% 116.4**
Speed ratings (Par 91): **91,88,87,83,76 76,73,66,58**
CSF £56.52 TOTE £2.70: £1.20, £2.90, £9.30; EX 63.70 Trifecta £236.30 Part won. Pool: £332.85 - 0.20 winning units..
Owner Mrs Margaret Forsyth **Bred** P C Hunt **Trained** Hambleton, N Yorks

FOCUS
The first three were newcomers in this very average juvenile median auction maiden event. The winner knew his job and should improve on this.

NOTEBOOK
Senor Mirasol, an April foal, is a close-coupled type. He knew his job and always looked like doing enough. He should go on from here. (op 5-2 tchd 11-4)
Carmanjoe, very much on the leg, is from a stable whose juveniles usually need an outing or two. He was upsides a furlong out but was very much second best at the line. (op 12-1)
La Brigitte, run off her feet at halfway, picked up in fine style late in the day and was seriously cutting back the first two at the line. (op 33-1)
Especially For You(IRE) pulled his way to the front and did not get home. (op 12-1 tchd 11-1)
Crewezando, a lightly-made type, did not improve on his sound debut effort on turf. (op 9-4)

1779 PAM SHAW'S BIRTHDAY CELEBRATIONS H'CAP 1m 4f
4:00 (4:01) (Class 6) (0-65,65) 4-Y-0+ **£1,910** (£564; £282) **Stalls** Low

Form RPR

055- **1** **Colonel Flay**[198] 6271 4-8-11 **63**........ JackMitchell(5) 3 73+
(Mrs P N Dutfield) *hld up in midfield: effrt over 2f out: r.o to ld jst ins fnl f* **5/1**[3]

52/0 **2** *1 3/4* **Calcutta Cup (UAE)**[27] 1219 5-8-8 **55**........ PaulMulrennan 6 62
(Karen McLintock) *sn trcking ldrs, styd on to ld over 1f out, hdd and no ex ins fnl f* **14/1**

4132 **3** *1 1/4* **Blue Hills**[5] 1643 7-8-10 **57**........(b) ChrisCatlin 1 62
(P W Hiatt) *sn trcking ldr: led over 4f out tl over 1f out: kpt on same pce* **4/1**[1]

040- **4** *1 1/4* **Silver Mont (IRE)**[54] 6076 5-8-1 **53**........(b) KellyHarrison(5) 2 56
(S R Bowring) *chsd ldrs: hung lft and one pce fnl 2f* **5/1**[3]

30-3 **5** *3* **Aleron (IRE)**[12] 1137 10-9-3 **64**........ GrahamGibbons 4 62
(J J Quinn) *chsd ldrs: drvn 3f out: sn chalng: wknd appr fnl f* **6/1**

061- **6** *1 1/4* **Ommadawn (IRE)**[212] 5899 4-9-4 **65**........(t) OscarUrbina 8 61
(J R Fanshawe) *hld up in rr: hdwy over 3f out: effrt and hung lft 2f out: nvr nr ldrs* **6/1**

1004 **7** *2 1/4* **Nok Twice (IRE)**[6] 1620 7-9-4 **65**........ AlanMunro 9 58
(D Carroll) *hld up in rr: effrt 3f out: nvr a factor* **9/2**[2]

06/0 **8** *17* **Sir Night (IRE)**[52] 171 8-8-4 **54** oh6 ow3........ KevinGhunowa(3) 5 19
(M Hill) *mid-div: drvn over 5f out: lost pl 3f out: sn bhd* **25/1**

30-0 **9** *dist* **Mujma**[14] 1449 4-9-3 **64**........ DarrenWilliams 7 —
(S Parr) *led: qcknd over 4f out: sn hdd hung lft and lost pl: bhd and eased over 2f out: virtually p.u* **33/1**

2m 41.14s (-0.56) **Going Correction** -0.025s/f (Good) **9 Ran SP% 113.5**
Speed ratings (Par 101): **100,98,98,97,95 94,92,81,—**
CSF £70.23 CT £304.71 TOTE £6.80: £2.20, £3.40, £1.30; EX 100.10 Trifecta £392.20 Part won. Pool: £552.40 - 0.20 winning units..
Owner John Boswell **Bred** Mrs Nerys Dutfield **Trained** Axmouth, Devon

FOCUS
A modest handicap run at just a steady pace but there ought to be better to come from the winner now his dietry problem has been sorted out. The form is best rated around the third and fourth.
Mujma Official explanation: jockey said gelding hung left

1780 LADBROKES.COM LEADS THE WAY H'CAP 7f
4:30 (4:30) (Class 6) (0-60,61) 4-Y-0+ **£1,774** (£523; £262) **Stalls** Low

Form RPR

2031 **1** **Sion Hill (IRE)**[7] 1602 7-9-0 **61** 6ex........(p) KellyHarrison(5) 9 71
(John A Harris) *mde all: hung rt fr over 1f out: hld on wl* **9/1**

1524 **2** *1* **Guildenstern (IRE)**[18] 1371 6-9-1 **57**........ TPQueally 5 64
(P Howling) *hld up towards rr: smooth hdwy over 2f out: carried rt fnl f: no ex last 75yds* **7/1**

4504 **3** *hd* **Epidaurian King (IRE)**[28] 1189 5-9-3 **59**........(v) PaulMulrennan 6 65
(D Shaw) *hld up toward rr: effrt 3f out: styd on fnl f* **14/1**

16-3 **4** *shd* **Dancing Deano (IRE)**[113] 115 6-8-12 **57**........ RussellKennemore(3) 12 63
(R Hollinshead) *chsd ldrs on outer: kpt on wl fnl f* **10/1**

202- **5** *hd* **Navene (IRE)**[196] 6309 4-9-0 **56**........ TedDurcan 3 62
(C F Wall) *stdd s: hld up in rr: hdwy on outside over 2f out: styd on fnl f* **5/1**[2]

5131 **6** *3 1/4* **Welcome Releaf**[3] 1705 5-8-6 **55**........ MarkCoumbe(7) 2 52
(P Leech) *in rr: styd on fnl 2f: nvr nr ldrs* **5/2**[1]

000- **7** *3* **Mister Jingles**[189] 6463 5-9-1 **60**........ MichaelJStainton(3) 10 49
(R M Whitaker) *chsd ldrs: wknd over 1f out* **14/1**

3643 **8** *3/4* **Aggbag**[18] 1371 4-8-6 **55**........ DeclanCannon(7) 4 42
(B P J Baugh) *mid-div: effrt on ins over 2f out: lost pl over 1f out* **16/1**

44-0 **9** *1 3/4* **Sintenis Mac (GER)**[27] 1209 5-9-1 **57**........ DarryllHolland 8 39
(P J O'Gorman) *chsd ldrs: lost pl over 1f out* **6/1**[3]

0/00 **10** *4* **Man Of Letters (UAE)**[27] 1209 7-9-0 56 ChrisCatlin 14 27
(M Hill) *sn w wnr: wknd 2f out* **20/1**
150- **11** *7* **Megalo Maniac**[175] 6747 5-8-8 57 BMcHugh(7) 1 9
(R A Fahey) *hld up in rr: bhd fnl 2f* **16/1**
-213 **12** *6* **Rambling Socks**[3] 1700 5-8-7 52 (p) DuranFentiman(3) 7 —
(S R Bowring) *chsd ldrs: lost pl over 4f out: sn bhd* **11/1**
1m 28.76s (-0.64) **Going Correction** -0.025s/f (Good) **12** Ran SP% **123.2**
Speed ratings (Par 101): **102,100,100,100,100 96,93,92,90,85 77,70**
CSF £73.59 CT £897.33 TOTE £7.80: £1.80, £1.70, £4.10; EX 85.80 Trifecta £261.60 Part won. Pool: £368.58 - 0.39 winning units..
Owner Peter Taylor **Bred** Joe Rogers **Trained** Eastwell, Leics
FOCUS
A modest handicap run at a sound pace. An improved effort from the winner who is clearly in very good heart and the form looks sound rated around the runner-up and fourth.

1781 WEATHERBYS BLOODSTOCK INSURANCE H'CAP 7f
5:00 (5:00) (Class 5) (0-75,74) 3-Y-O **£2,593** (£765; £383) **Stalls** Low

Form RPR
4-01 **1** **Great Charm (IRE)**[8] 1587 3-9-2 72 6ex TPQueally 10 72
(M L W Bell) *sn trcking ldrs on outer: t.k.h: hrd rdn over 1f out: led ins fnl f: all out* **5/4**[1]
2 *nse* **San Jose City (IRE)**[203] 6162 3-9-1 71 AlanMunro 4 71
(D Carroll) *sn trcking ldrs on outer: styd on to chal ins fnl f: jst hld* **25/1**
503- **3** *nk* **Climaxtackledotcom**[174] 6754 3-9-2 72 PaulMulrennan 5 71
(M W Easterby) *hld up: hdwy on ins over 2f out: chal ins fnl f: no ex nr fin* **14/1**
555- **4** *nk* **Game Park (USA)**[198] 6267 3-9-2 72 OscarUrbina 2 70
(J R Fanshawe) *hld up in midfield: hdwy over 2f out: chal ins fnl f: no ex* **13/2**[3]
16-6 **5** *¾* **Whiteoak Lady (IRE)**[22] 1277 3-9-0 70 LiamJones 6 66
(J L Spearing) *led tl 3f out: narrow advantage over 1f out: hdd ins fnl f: wknd towards fin* **20/1**
00-5 **6** *2¼* **Ride A White Swan**[16] 1396 3-8-11 67 DarrenWilliams 3 59
(K R Burke) *sn trcking ldrs on inner: chal 2f out: wknd and eased last 75yds* **4/1**[2]
22-5 **7** *½* **Molly Ann (IRE)**[101] 261 3-8-9 65 TedDurcan 7 54
(T D Easterby) *hld up in rr: effrt over 2f out: nvr a factor* **33/1**
35-6 **8** *1¾* **Balata**[29] 1167 3-9-0 70 SimonWhitworth 8 54
(B R Millman) *charged gates and swvd rt s: in rr: kpt on fnl 2f: nvr nr ldrs* **9/1**
320- **9** *hd* **Bazguy**[124] 7280 3-9-1 71 TGMcLaughlin 9 55
(P D Evans) *trckd ldrs on outer: drvn 3f out: fdd over 1f out* **14/1**
0-26 **10** *3* **Tactical Move**[9] 1573 3-8-13 74 SCreighton(5) 1 50
(Miss V Haigh) *trckd ldrs on inner: led 3f out: hdd & wknd over 1f out* **20/1**
1m 30.15s (0.75) **Going Correction** -0.025s/f (Good) **10** Ran SP% **117.4**
Speed ratings (Par 99): **94,93,93,93,92 89,89,87,87,83**
CSF £45.50 CT £326.65 TOTE £2.30: £1.10, £6.90, £4.80; EX 38.80 Trifecta £365.10 Part won. Pool: £514.31 - 0.59 winning units. Place 6 £382.62, Place 5 £72.78..
Owner Mr & Mrs G Middlebrook **Bred** G And Mrs Middlebrook **Trained** Newmarket, Suffolk
FOCUS
A fair handicap in which five were in line inside the last after a steady pace. The form looks very ordinary.
Balata Official explanation: jockey said gelding anticipated stalls opening and hit its head
T/Plt: £235.40 to a £1 stake. Pool: £53,973.89. 167.35 winning tickets. T/Qpdt: £21.30 to a £1 stake. Pool: £3,759.79. 130.49 winning tickets. WG

1782 - (Foreign Racing) - See Raceform Interactive

1006 CORK (R-H)
Friday, May 2

OFFICIAL GOING: Sprint course - yielding (yielding to soft in places); remainder - good (good to yielding in places)

1783a CORK STKS (LISTED RACE) 6f
5:50 (5:50) 3-Y-O+ **£23,933** (£7,022; £3,345; £1,139)

RPR
1 **Contest (IRE)**[231] 5394 4-9-7 99 JMurtagh 4 108
(David Wachman, Ire) *towards rr: 7th 1/2-way: 5th 1 1/2f out: styd on wl to ld ins fnl f: comf* **10/1**
2 *1¼* **Tax Free (IRE)**[13] 1495 6-9-12 AdrianTNicholls 7 109
(D Nicholls) *led: rdn over 1f out: hdd ins fnl f: no ex cl home* **5/4**[1]
3 *shd* **The Loan Express (IRE)**[22] 1289 3-8-8 103 WMLordan 2 97
(T Stack, Ire) *hld up in rr: last 2f out: hdwy 1 1/2f out: 5th 1f out: kpt on wl wout threatening cl home* **11/1**
4 *¾* **Finicius (USA)**[147] 7063 4-9-7 109 DPMcDonogh 6 101
(Eoin Griffin, Ire) *mid-div: rdn after 1/2-way: kpt on wout threatening fr 1f out* **10/1**
5 *¾* **Senor Benny (USA)**[13] 1495 9-9-10 100 PJSmullen 1 102
(M McDonagh, Ire) *chsd ldrs: rdn 2f out: 5th 1f out: kpt on same pce* **16/1**
6 *½* **An Tadh (IRE)**[28] 1198 5-9-7 106 JAHeffernan 3 97
(G M Lyons, Ire) *chsd ldrs: rdn and no imp fr 2f out* **8/1**[3]
7 *shd* **Croi Mo Ri (IRE)**[19] 1356 3-8-11 97 KJManning 9 94
(P D Deegan, Ire) *prom: rdn and wknd fr 2f out* **14/1**
8 *8* **Pencil Hill (IRE)**[186] 6549 3-9-0 108 PShanahan 5 71
(Tracey Collins, Ire) *prom: rdn and wknd fr 2f out: eased fnl f* **10/1**
9 *15* **Mojito Royale (IRE)**[21] 1317 4-9-7 107 (p) DMGrant 8 23
(Eoin Doyle, Ire) *hld up in tch: rdn after 1/2-way: sn wknd: eased and trailing fnl f* **7/1**[2]
1m 15.3s (2.70)
WFA 3 from 4yo+ 10lb **9** Ran SP% **116.2**
CSF £23.07 TOTE £13.90: £3.40, £1.10, £2.90; DF 27.90.
Owner Derrick Smith **Bred** Mrs D Nagle **Trained** Goolds Cross, Co Tipperary
FOCUS
A well up-to-standard Listed event with the solid yardstick Tax Free finishing in between a colt and a filly who could well be on their way to better things.
NOTEBOOK
Contest(IRE) showed a good turn of foot to score readily from what was originally an unpromising position. Unraced at two, he quickly made up into a smart performer last season, before meeting defeat both as a short-priced favourite for a Listed event at Sandown, and then, after a three-month break, as favourite for a handicap (off an official mark of 102) at The Curragh. He fully deserves a crack at better company now.
Tax Free(IRE), for whom 5f and 6f seem to come alike, ran his usual game race in attempting to make all on ground softer than ideal. He is a model of consistency at this level, but will always be vulnerable to a less exposed improver such as the winner. (op 11/10 tchd 11/8)
The Loan Express(IRE), who kept top-class company as a juvenile, improved markedly on her reappearance effort on desperate ground at Tipperary, albeit in receipt of all the allowances. Official explanation: jockey said filly was accidentally struck on the nose by another rider's whip in the closing stages (op 10/1 tchd 12/1)
Mojito Royale(IRE) Official explanation: jockey said gelding hung badly throughout and was unable to act on today's ground

1324 DONCASTER (L-H)
Saturday, May 3

OFFICIAL GOING: Straight course - good (good to soft in places); round course - good to soft (good in places)
Wind: Moderate, against Weather: Dry, sunny periods

1793 BETFAIR APPRENTICE TRAINING SERIES H'CAP 1m 2f 60y
5:40 (5:40) (Class 4) (0-85,84) 4-Y-O+ **£4,857** (£1,445; £722; £360) **Stalls** Low

Form RPR
2620 **1** **Polish Power (GER)**[49] 908 8-9-0 79 JackDean 7 96+
(J S Moore) *hld up in rr: stdy hdwy 3f out: rdn to ld wl over 1f out and sn clr: styd on strly* **11/2**
0-54 **2** *5* **Jeer (IRE)**[14] 1473 4-9-5 84 WilliamCarson 6 89
(E A L Dunlop) *hld up towards rr: hdwy on outer wl over 2f out: rdn to chse wnr ent fnl f: no imp* **7/2**[2]
113- **3** *3* **Tifernati**[241] 5141 4-9-0 82 BMcHugh(3) 8 81+
(W J Haggas) *trckd ldng pair: smooth hdwy over 3f out: led over 2f out and sn rdn: hdd wl over 1f out and kpt on same pce* **9/4**[1]
/30- **4** *2¼* **Traprain (IRE)**[168] 6473 6-8-5 77 PaulPickard(7) 4 72
(D Carroll) *chsd ldrs: hdwy over 3f out: cl up and rdn over 2f out: sn drvn and one pce* **13/2**
0-06 **5** *2¼* **Ahlawy (IRE)**[7] 1613 5-8-5 75 NSLawes(5) 2 65
(M W Easterby) *s.i.s and in rr: hdwy on inner 3f out: sn rdn along: drvn wl over 1f out and n.d* **5/1**[3]
21-0 **6** *2½* **Longspur**[10] 1569 4-8-11 81 BradleyRoper(5) 1 66
(M W Easterby) *hld up towards rr: effrt and sme hdwy over 3f out: sn rdn and wknd over 2f out* **14/1**
2401 **7** *2¼* **Given A Choice (IRE)**[25] 1256 6-8-10 78 (p) SimonPearce(3) 9 59
(J Pearce) *hld up in tch: effrt 3f out: sn rdn along and btn 2f out* **11/1**
16-0 **8** *nk* **Lobengula (IRE)**[13] 1502 6-9-5 84 DonnaCaldwell 3 64
(I W McInnes) *led and sn clr: rdn along over 3f out: hdd over 2f out and sn wknd* **40/1**
5-10 **9** *1½* **Bull Market (IRE)**[7] 1612 5-8-10 75 MarkCoumbe 5 52
(Ian Williams) *chsd clr ldr: rdn along over 3f out and sn wknd* **20/1**
2m 14.76s (3.56) **Going Correction** +0.50s/f (Yiel) **9** Ran SP% **120.6**
Speed ratings (Par 105): **105,101,98,96,95 93,91,90,89**
CSF £26.32 CT £57.06 TOTE £5.60: £1.70, £1.80, £1.60; EX 40.90.
Owner John Wells **Bred** Gestut Hofgut Mappen **Trained** Upper Lambourn, Berks
FOCUS
Typically few in-form contenders sure to be at home over trip and ground in this apprentice handicap, but they went a good gallop up front and the first two came from off the pace. The form does not look the most solid.

1794 OFFICE DEPOT MAIDEN STKS 5f
6:15 (6:15) (Class 5) 2-Y-O **£3,238** (£963; £481; £240) **Stalls** High

Form RPR
1 **Daisy Moses (IRE)** 2-8-12 0 SilvestreDeSousa 5 73
(D Nicholls) *in tch: hdwy 2f out: rdn over 1f out: styd on strly ins fnl f to ld nr fin* **20/1**
4 **2** *½* **Majuba (USA)**[15] 1447 2-9-3 0 NCallan 4 76+
(K A Ryan) *led: rdn along wl over 1f out: clr ent fnl f: sn drvn and wandered: hdd & wknd nr fin* **8/13**[1]
3 *1¼* **Go Go Green (IRE)** 2-9-3 0 DarrenWilliams 8 72+
(S Parr) *chsd ldr: rdn 2f out: drvn over 1f out: one pce ins fnl f* **10/1**
4 *1¾* **Paquerettza (FR)** 2-8-12 0 J-PGuillambert 3 60
(D H Brown) *s.i.s and in rr: hdwy on outer wl over 1f out: rdn and kpt on ins fnl f: nrst fin* **40/1**
5 **5** *3¾* **Tagula Sunset (IRE)**[15] 1447 2-8-9 0 JamieMoriarty(3) 2 47
(P T Midgley) *chsd ldrs: rdn along over 2f out: sn drvn and wknd over 1f out* **9/1**[3]
6 *¾* **Jethro Bodine (IRE)** 2-9-3 0 PatCosgrave 1 49
(T J Pitt) *chsd ldng pair: rdn along 2f out: sn wknd* **25/1**
7 *4½* **The Kilkenny Kat (IRE)** 2-9-3 0 SebSanders 6 33+
(T D Easterby) *s.i.s: a bhd* **3/1**[2]
62.36 secs (1.86) **Going Correction** +0.275s/f (Good) **7** Ran SP% **117.1**
Speed ratings (Par 93): **96,95,93,90,84 83,76**
CSF £33.93 TOTE £11.20: £4.10, £1.30; EX 38.10.
Owner J Laughton **Bred** Lynn Lodge Stud **Trained** Sessay, N Yorks
FOCUS
Plenty of the newcomers were bred to need further and only one of the two with experience had looked an imminent winner so this may not have been a great race. The second and third took each other on and the winner was the one to benefit.
NOTEBOOK
Daisy Moses(IRE), a half-sister to Spinning and Goodwood Starlight, drifted in the betting and ran slightly green on the outside of the field, but she picked up well inside the final furlong to lead close home. She is likely to have learned plenty from this experience and is bound to improve. She will also get further in time. (op 11-1)
Majuba(USA) set the standard with his debut fourth at Thirsk, but he did not seem to get home that day and again looked to have stamina limitations here, soon in front and grabbing the advantageous stands' rail, looking set to make all for most of the way but tiring late on and getting caught close home. He wants a test of speed rather than stamina and the faster the 5f the better for him at present. (tchd 4-6 tchy 8-11 in places)
Go Go Green(IRE) is speedily bred, being a half-brother to five winners including Cheveley Park Stakes runner-up Dhanyata and Stewards' Cup winner Guinea Hunter. He showed pace to chase the leader until inside the final furlong and should improve for this debut. (op 8-1 tchd 11-1)
Paquerettza(FR) is a half-sister to Sagaro Stakes winner Shipmaster and shaped as though she will be suited by further so was not at all disgraced on this first appearance. (op 16-1)
The Kilkenny Kat(IRE) was backed from 10-1 in to 3-1 for his debut but lost all chance with a very slow start and was never able to get into contention. He has clearly shown something at home and is worth another chance. (op 9-1 tchd 11-4)

1795 CROWNHOTEL-BAWTRY.COM MEDIAN AUCTION MAIDEN STKS 6f
6:45 (6:47) (Class 5) 3-4-Y-O **£3,238** (£963; £481; £240) **Stalls** High

Form RPR
3 **1** **Celtic Lynn (IRE)**[15] 1453 3-8-11 0 PhillipMakin 1 78
(M Dods) *trckd ldrs: swtchd lft and gd hdwy to ld 2f out: rdn over 1f out: drvn ins fnl f and styd on wl* **3/1**[2]

4 **2** *1 1/4* **Marchingontogether (IRE)**[15] 1453 3-8-11 0........................ NCallan 9 74
(D Carroll) *trckd ldrs: gd hdwy over 2f out: chal over 1f out: ev ch whn rdn and hung bdly rt ins fnl f: kpt on* **8/1**[3]

243- **3** *4* **Terry's Tip (IRE)**[198] 6281 3-9-2 87........................ TomEaves 8 67
(Mrs L Stubbs) *chsd ldrs: effrt 2f out: sn rdn and kpt on same pce ins fnl f* **6/4**[1]

06-0 **4** *2 1/2* **Bertie Vista**[22] 1298 3-8-13 66........................ DuranFentiman(3) 7 59
(T D Easterby) *chsd ldrs: rdn 2f out: drvn over 1f out and kpt on same pce* **40/1**

030- **5** *1/2* **Bahamian Ballad**[222] 5692 3-8-11 67........................ PatCosgrave 14 52
(J D Bethell) *chsd ldrs: rdn over 2f out: drvn and one pce appr fnl f* **18/1**

6 *1/2* **Charlie Allnut** 3-9-2 0........................ DarrenWilliams 4 55
(K R Burke) *in tch: hdwy to chse ldrs 2f out: rdn wl over 1f out: kpt on same pce* **25/1**

7 *3/4* **Dalla Finestra** 3-8-11 0........................ IanMongan 3 55+
(C F Wall) *swtchd rt s and bhd tl styd on fnl 2f: nrst fin* **12/1**

0 **8** *1* **Isabella's Fancy**[15] 1453 3-8-11 0........................ OscarUrbina 15 45+
(J R Fanshawe) *towards rr: effrt over 2f out: nvr a factor* **14/1**

360- **9** *1/2* **Foreign Rhythm (IRE)**[198] 6282 3-8-11 68........................ KimTinkler 13 43
(N Tinkler) *midfield: effrt and sme hdwy 2f out: sn rdn and n.d* **16/1**

00- **10** *4 1/2* **Red River Boy**[284] 3812 3-8-11 0........................ KellyHarrison(5) 16 34
(C W Fairhurst) *chsd ldrs: rdn along over 2f out: grad wknd* **50/1**

50 **11** *nk* **Kai Mer (IRE)**[15] 1453 3-8-11 0........................ RoystonFfrench 10 28
(Miss J A Camacho) *in rr fr 1/2-way* **50/1**

0- **12** *1 1/2* **Abitofafath (IRE)**[233] 5363 3-9-2 0........................ J-PGuillambert 6 28
(J G Given) *led: rdn along over 2f out: sn hdd & wknd* **50/1**

05 **13** *5* **Martingrange Lass (IRE)**[4] 1709 3-8-11 0........................ DaneO'Neill 12 7
(S Parr) *a bhd* **40/1**

3-04 **14** *19* **Binario Uno**[31] 1139 3-9-2 66........................(v[1]) AdrianTNicholls 2 —
(D Nicholls) *cl up: rdn along over 2f out: wkng whn n.m.r wl over 1f out: eased* **12/1**

3 **15** *5* **Steel Mask (IRE)**[15] 1454 3-8-13 0........................ MarkLawson(3) 11 —
(M Brittain) *s.i.s: a bhd* **16/1**

1m 14.67s (1.07) **Going Correction** +0.275s/f (Good) **15** Ran SP% **129.8**
Speed ratings (Par 103): **103,101,96,92,92 91,90,89,88,82 81,79,73,47,41**
CSF £28.46 TOTE £4.60: £1.40, £2.40, £1.40; EX 24.40.
Owner P Taylor **Bred** Mrs Miriam O'Donnell **Trained** Denton, Co Durham

FOCUS
Some lightly raced three-year-olds but few obviously up to winning outside modest company in a median auction maiden lacking strength in depth. The fourth looks the best guide to the level of the form.
Binario Uno Official explanation: jockey said gelding hung right-handed
Steel Mask(IRE) Official explanation: trainer later said colt injured itself when rearing in stalls

1796 COME RACING HERE 17TH MAY H'CAP 6f
7:20 (7:21) (Class 3) (0-90,93) 4-Y-0+ **£7,123** (£2,119; £1,059; £529) **Stalls** High

Form RPR

04-5 **1** **Geojimali**[41] 983 6-8-5 77........................ SaleemGolam 10 89
(J S Goldie) *dwlt and towards rr: hdwy over 2f out: rdn to chal ent fnl f: styd on to ld last 100yds* **7/1**[3]

520- **2** *nk* **Joseph Henry**[233] 5356 6-9-3 89........................ SilvestreDeSousa 6 100
(D Nicholls) *trckd ldrs: hdwy over 2f out: rdn to ld ent fnl f: hdd and nt qckn last 100yds* **11/1**

2142 **3** *2 1/4* **Swinbrook (USA)**[7] 1617 7-8-4 76 oh1........................(v) PaulHanagan 3 80
(R A Fahey) *trckd ldrs: hdwy 2f out: rdn to chal ent fnl f and ev ch tl drvn and nt qckn last 100yds* **3/1**[1]

0-61 **4** *nk* **Turnkey**[12] 1517 6-9-0 93........................ AdeleRothery(7) 13 96
(D Nicholls) *towards rr: hdwy over 2f out: rdn to chse ldrs over 1f out: kpt on same pce u.p ins fnl f* **7/1**[3]

2003 **5** *2 1/4* **Cornus**[7] 1617 6-8-8 80........................(be) RobertWinston 15 79+
(A J McCabe) *midfield: hdwy 2f out and sn rdn: styd on ins fnl f: nrst fin* **13/2**[2]

000- **6** *2 1/4* **King Of Swords (IRE)**[216] 5841 4-8-11 83........................ TomEaves 5 71
(N Tinkler) *chsd ldrs: effrt and n.m.r wl over 1f out: sn rdn and kpt on same pce ins fnl f* **100/1**

660- **7** *nse* **Mambo Spirit (IRE)**[204] 6141 4-8-10 82........................ J-PGuillambert 12 70
(J G Given) *in tch: hdwy to chse ldrs 2f out: sn rdn and no imp fnl f* **16/1**

4-00 **8** *hd* **Ice Planet**[12] 1517 7-9-0 86........................ AdrianTNicholls 8 74
(D Nicholls) *in rr tl sme late hdwy* **9/1**

-610 **9** *shd* **Luscivious**[10] 1571 4-9-0 86........................(b) PatCosgrave 11 73
(A J McCabe) *dwlt: sn chsng ldrs: rdn along over 2f out: sn drvn and wknd* **14/1**

3353 **10** *2* **Cerebus**[13] 1500 6-8-4 76 oh5........................(bt) NeilPollard 7 57
(A J McCabe) *led: rdn along and hdd 2f out: sn wknd* **40/1**

0-21 **11** *3/4* **Nobilissima (IRE)**[7] 1617 4-8-7 82........................ TolleyDean(3) 14 61
(J L Spearing) *chsd ldrs: rdn along over 2f out: sn drvn and wknd* **13/2**[2]

61-0 **12** *1 3/4* **Paris Bell**[16] 1430 6-8-2 77........................ DuranFentiman(3) 2 50
(T D Easterby) *dwlt: sn in tch: hdwy on wd outside to ld over 2f out: sn rdn and hdd ent fnl f: wknd* **18/1**

0066 **13** *nk* **Red Cape (FR)**[21] 1334 5-8-10 82........................(p) SebSanders 9 54
(Mrs R A Carr) *chsd ldrs: rdn along over 2f out: sn wknd* **20/1**

05-0 **14** *1 1/4* **Inter Vision (USA)**[17] 1393 8-9-1 87........................ DanielTudhope 4 55
(A Dickman) *cl up: rdn along over 2f out and sn wknd* **50/1**

1m 13.5s (-0.10) **Going Correction** +0.275s/f (Good) **14** Ran SP% **123.0**
Speed ratings (Par 107): **111,110,107,107,104 101,101,100,100,98 97,94,94,92**
CSF £81.67 CT £293.01 TOTE £8.20: £2.60, £3.30, £1.90; EX 125.40.
Owner Fyffees 2 **Bred** Jim Goldie **Trained** Uplawmoor, E Renfrews

FOCUS
A good sprint handicap, run at a strong pace. Solid form with the first pair coming clear.

NOTEBOOK
Geojimali dwelt at the start - as is his wont - but was still able to recover and come through to lead in the final 100 yards. This is decent form for the grade and, though he is not ultra-consistent, he won off a mark 4lb higher than this last year so certainly has fair prospects of following up. (op 13-2 tchd 15-2)
Joseph Henry ◆ is certainly well handicapped at present and he made an encouraging start to his season, leading entering the final furlong until eventually just run out of it by the winner. He was lightly raced last season, but looks to retain plenty of ability and is sure to be placed to advantage by his trainer who has few peers in this type of contest. (op 14-1 tchd 16-1)
Swinbrook(USA) has been revitalised by a change of scenery and ran another fine race in defeat, helping to set the solid level of this form. He will likely go up another few pounds for this, however. (op 5-1)
Turnkey was in rear and still virtually last 2f out, but kept on well in the latter stages to grab fourth place late on. This rates a good effort off a mark 3lb higher than when coming from behind to win at Pontefract and a stiff 6f suits him. (op 11-2 tchd 5-1)
Cornus would have been a little closer at the finish with a slightly better run and clearly remains in form. He is another who sets the level of this form.
King Of Swords(IRE) ◆ ran better than his finishing position suggests as he was short of room over 2f out, but he kept on well and came clear of the others who raced furthest away from the stands' rail. This ex-Irish colt would have finished closer with more company late on, looks potentially well handicapped at present, and is well worth keeping in mind. (op 66-1)
Ice Planet was another to keep on late, although never dangerous, but did much better than on his previous run a fortnight earlier and has got himself well handicapped. (op 14-1 tchd 8-1)

1797 DONCASTER RACECOURSE CONFERENCE CENTRE CONDITIONS STKS 1m (S)
7:50 (7:50) (Class 3) 3-Y-0 **£6,854** (£2,052; £1,026) **Stalls** High

Form RPR

3-44 **1** **Redolent (IRE)**[17] 1402 3-9-0 100........................(p) DaneO'Neill 1 101
(R Hannon) *led: rdn along and hdd 2f out: drvn to rally ent fnl f: sn led and styd on gamely* **11/2**[3]

36-2 **2** *1* **Gaspar Van Wittel (USA)**[21] 1333 3-9-2 100........................ SebSanders 2 101
(S A Callaghan) *hld up: hdwy 2f out: rdn over 1f out: swtchd rt ins fnl f: styd on u.p to take 2nd on line* **5/2**[2]

123- **3** *nk* **Iguazu Falls (USA)**[189] 6495 3-9-0 105........................ LDettori 3 98+
(Saeed Bin Suroor) *trckd ldr: hdwy to ld 2f out: shkn up and edgd lft ent fnl f: sn hdd and rdn: lost 2nd on line* **4/6**[1]

1m 43.53s (4.23) **Going Correction** +0.275s/f (Good) **3** Ran SP% **103.9**
Speed ratings (Par 103): **89,88,87**
CSF £15.40 TOTE £5.50; EX 10.10.
Owner De La Warr Racing **Bred** R O'Callaghan And D Veitch **Trained** East Everleigh, Wilts

FOCUS
This conditions event varies in quality year on year, with recent winners ranging from the top-drawer Dubai Millennium to one or two less distinguished names. Two of this season's trio had been placed in Group company, but the value of the form is open to question with the winner dictating and the favourite disappointing.

NOTEBOOK
Redolent(IRE), in first-time cheekpieces, very much had the run of the race, setting just a fair pace, and after being headed 2f out he rallied to lead again inside the final furlong for a gutsy success. He had managed no better than fourth in a couple of Listed races before this season and had things go his way here so his Irish 2,000 Guineas entry may prove optimistic, but he is clearly very useful. (op 5-1)
Gaspar Van Wittel(USA) looked up against it conceding weight all round and was not at all disgraced, switched to the inside and keeping on to snatch second place close home. This was his best effort to date and, while not easy to place from his official mark, he does deserve another winning turn. (op 11-4 tchd 9-4)
Iguazu Falls(USA) was very disappointing on this seasonal return, racing freely - as he tended to last season - before going on 2f out then edging left and headed inside the final 1f. He now has it to prove, but his leading connections have made just a quiet start to the season and it would be folly to write him off just yet. (op 4-7)

1798 RECTANGLE GROUP H'CAP 1m 6f 132y
8:20 (8:21) (Class 4) (0-85,82) 4-Y-0+ **£4,857** (£1,445; £722; £360) **Stalls** Low

Form RPR

1064 **1** **Red Wine**[3] 1732 9-8-8 72........................ StacyRenwick(7) 3 82
(A J McCabe) *hld up and bhd: stdy hdwy down wd outside fr wl over 2f out: chsd ldr ent fnl f: styd on wl to ld nr fin* **13/2**

234- **2** *hd* **Bukit Tinggi (IRE)**[177] 6733 4-8-12 71........................ NCallan 6 80+
(M A Jarvis) *trckd ldrs: hdwy over 3f out: led over 2f out and sn rdn: drvn and edgd rt ins fnl f: hdd and no ex nr fin* **11/4**[2]

3- **3** *4 1/2* **Command Marshal (FR)**[54] 3496 5-8-9 73........................ JackDean(7) 4 76
(M J Scudamore) *trckd ldrs: hdwy over 2f out: rdn wl over 1f out: kpt on u.p ins fnl f* **22/1**

21-1 **4** *2 1/4* **Birkside**[115] 105 5-9-11 82........................ DavidAllan 5 82
(D Carroll) *in tch: hdwy over 4f out: effrt and ev ch 2f out: sn rdn and one pce appr fnl f* **11/2**[3]

5551 **5** *nk* **Flame Creek (IRE)**[14] 1472 12-8-1 65........................ MCGeran(7) 11 64
(E J Creighton) *hld up in rr: stdy hdwy over 3f out: chsd ldrs 2f out: sn rdn: edgd lft and one pce appr fnl f* **20/1**

0300 **6** *1 1/2* **Stoop To Conquer**[14] 1472 8-8-8 65........................ CatherineGannon 7 62
(A W Carroll) *led after 1f: rdn along 3f out: hdd over 2f out and grad wknd* **33/1**

2110 **7** *4 1/2* **Puy D'Arnac (FR)**[10] 1568 5-9-7 78........................ RobertWinston 2 69
(G A Swinbank) *trckd ldrs on inner: n.m.r and swtchd rt 4f out: rdn wl over 2f out: drvn and btn wl over 1f out* **13/8**[1]

336- **8** *4 1/2* **Abstract Folly (IRE)**[150] 5884 6-8-9 66........................ PatCosgrave 10 51
(J D Bethell) *hld up in rr: effrt and sme hdwy over 3f out: sn rdn and wknd* **40/1**

24-0 **9** *13* **Lets Roll**[10] 1568 7-9-8 82........................ PJMcDonald(3) 9 49
(C W Thornton) *prom: hdwy to chse ldr 1/2-way: rdn along over 4f out and sn wknd* **7/1**

102/ **10** *40* **Stolen Light (IRE)**[511] 6761 7-8-13 70........................ TomEaves 1 —
(A Crook) *led 1f: prom tl rdn 4f out and sn wknd* **33/1**

3m 18.46s (11.76) **Going Correction** +0.50s/f (Yiel)
WFA 4 from 5yo+ 2lb **10** Ran SP% **123.4**
Speed ratings (Par 105): **88,87,85,84,84 83,80,78,71,50**
CSF £24.86 CT £389.37 TOTE £5.80: £2.20, £1.80, £6.20; EX 36.20 Place 6 £103.90, Place 5 £69.57.
Owner Paul J Dixon **Bred** Genesis Green Stud Ltd **Trained** Babworth, Notts

FOCUS
A fair handicap, run at just a steady pace. The first pair pulled clear but there are doubts over the form.
Puy D'Arnac(FR) Official explanation: jockey said gelding ran too freely
T/Plt: £86.30 to a £1 stake. Pool: £61,501.47. 519.83 winning tickets. T/Qpdt: £67.50 to a £1 stake. Pool: £4,455.78. 48.80 winning tickets. JR

GOODWOOD (R-H)
Saturday, May 3

OFFICIAL GOING: Good to soft (good in places; 7.8)
Rail realignment added circa 25yds to advertsied race distances on the races on both round courses.
Wind: Moderate, across (away from stands) Weather: Fine

1799 BETDIRECT.COM STKS (H'CAP) 1m 1f 192y
2:30 (2:30) (Class 3) (0-90,86) 4-Y-0+ **£7,771** (£2,312; £1,155; £577) **Stalls** High

Form RPR

11- **1** **Milne Graden**[190] 6474 4-9-4 86........................ TPQueally 6 104+
(J Noseda) *trckd ldng pair: nt clr run wl over 2f out tl swtchd lft over 1f out: drvn and r.o to ld last 100yds* **1/2**[1]

20-0 **2** ¾ **Formax (FR)**[14] [1469] 6-9-1 **83** .... PatDobbs 3 93
(M P Tregoning) *hld up in last: smooth prog on inner 2f out: led ent fnl f: urged along hands and heels: hdd and nt qckn last 100yds* **15/2**[3]

-560 **3** 4 ½ **Crossbow Creek**[13] [1502] 10-8-13 **81** .... ChrisCatlin 2 82
(M G Rimell) *hld up in 4th: prog on outer over 2f out: led over 1f out: hdd ent fnl f: wknd rapidly* **20/1**

0-60 **4** ¾ **Zero Cool (USA)**[14] [1473] 4-9-0 **82** .... ShaneKelly 8 81
(G L Moore) *hld up in 5th: rdn and no prog over 2f out: struggling after* **20/1**

3-10 **5** 1 ¾ **Robustian**[13] [1502] 5-8-11 **86** ....(v) MatthewDavies(7) 5 82
(George Baker) *hld up in 6th: rdn and effrt on outer over 2f out: no imp over 1f out: wknd* **10/1**

0602 **6** *nse* **Speedy Sam**[22] [1314] 5-9-2 **84** .... FergusSweeney 7 80
(K R Burke) *led: rdn over 2f out: hdd over 1f out: sn wknd* **6/1**[2]

00-0 **7** *shd* **Invention (USA)**[3] [1719] 5-8-12 **80** .... HayleyTurner 4 75
(Miss E C Lavelle) *chsd ldr to over 2f out: sn btn* **50/1**

2m 12.39s (4.39) **Going Correction** +0.475s/f (Yiel) **7** Ran SP% **113.3**
Speed ratings (Par 107): **101,100,96,96,94 94,94**
CSF £4.71 CT £33.91 TOTE £1.50: £1.20, £3.30; EX 5.10 Trifecta £80.10 Pool: £519.52 - 4.60 winning tickets..

Owner Mrs Susan Roy **Bred** Newsells Park Stud Limited **Trained** Newmarket, Suffolk

■ Stewards' Enquiry : T P Queally one-day ban: careless riding (May 18)

FOCUS

Rail realignment added about 25 yards to advertised race distances on the Round course. This was a strong handicap but the winning time was nothing special and the form is not solid, rated around the second. Milne Graden was a class above his rivals and won with plenty in hand.

NOTEBOOK

Milne Graden ◆ maintained his unbeaten record but not before giving his supporters some worrying moments when finding himself trapped behind rivals with nowhere to go well over a furlong out. However, when finding daylight just inside the final furlong he picked up stylishly to grab Formax. The turn of foot he showed when in the clear was most impressive and confirms the four-year-old (who was gelded during the winter) an exciting prospect. Having done this so easily from an 8lb higher mark than his Doncaster win last October, it is not difficult to see why Jeremy Noseda took the trouble to put him in the Hardwicke at Royal Ascot and Irish Leger. (op 4-7 tchd 8-13 in places)

Formax(FR) ran much better than when too free in the Spring Cup last time. Restrained in last up the inside rail, he shot through when the gap opened but could not hold off Milne Graden when challenged. He has not always looked the most straightforward to train but this should have done his confidence some good. (op 8-1)

Crossbow Creek, whose trainer has recently come back into form, put up an encouraging display to get into the money. This dual-purpose performer was switching from three All-Weather runs and did enough to suggest it might be worth keeping him on turf. (op 16-1)

Zero Cool(USA) probably found the soft ground against him when disappointing on his last start. He shaped a little better on this quicker ground but never looked like winning. (op 16-1 tchd 22-1)

Robustian, returning to turf, had the race run more to suit than had been the case at Great Leighs last time but his effort to challenge on the outer was shortlived. (op 8-1)

Speedy Sam dictated the pace but was hard at work a long way out and ultimately came up well short. He has not won for a long time. (op 8-1)

1800 ROYAL SUSSEX REGIMENT STKS (H'CAP) 6f

3:05 (3:05) (Class 4) (0-85,85) 4-Y-0+ **£5,828** (£1,734; £866; £432) **Stalls** Low

Form RPR

0-35 **1** **Mujood**[7] [1617] 5-9-1 **82** ....(b) StephenCarson 3 92
(Eve Johnson Houghton) *rousted along fr s and early reminder: chsd ldrs: u.p fr 1/2-way: clsd over 1f out: r.o fnl f to ld last stride* **7/2**[1]

3212 **2** *shd* **Savile's Delight (IRE)**[2] [1739] 9-7-13 **73** .... RossAtkinson(7) 7 83
(Tom Dascombe) *chsd ldrs: clsd on outer fr 2f out: led jst ins fnl f: urged along: hdd last stride* **4/1**[2]

03-4 **3** ½ **Idle Power (IRE)**[11] [1537] 10-8-12 **79** .... AmirQuinn 2 87
(J R Boyle) *chsd ldrs: hrd rdn fr 2f out: effrt to join ldr ins fnl f: no ex nr fin* **8/1**

444- **4** *nk* **Dingaan (IRE)**[192] [6437] 5-8-10 **80** .... WilliamBuick(3) 5 87
(A M Balding) *stdd s: hld up in last and wl detached: stdy prog on outer fr 1/2-way: drvn to chse ldrs over 1f out: no ex ins fnl f* **7/2**[1]

3413 **5** 1 ¾ **Kelamon**[12] [1522] 4-8-1 **71** .... LukeMorris(3) 4 73
(M D I Usher) *dwlt: nt gng wl and detached in last pair: drvn and prog fr 2f out: chsd ldrs 1f out: no ex* **6/1**[3]

0-64 **6** 3 **Lunces Lad (IRE)**[10] [1566] 4-8-6 **80** .... MatthewDavies(7) 8 72
(M R Channon) *led at str pce: at least a l clr over 1f out: hdd & wknd jst ins fnl f* **8/1**

300- **7** 6 **Mason Ette**[213] [5923] 4-8-10 **77** .... PhilipRobinson 1 50
(C G Cox) *nvr beyond midfield: struggling sn after 1/2-way: hanging and wknd 2f out* **20/1**

20-0 **8** 1 ¾ **Makabul**[19] [1368] 5-8-5 **72** .... ChrisCatlin 9 39
(B R Millman) *pressed ldrs to 1/2-way: wknd rapidly* **22/1**

20-0 **9** 9 **Thabaat**[30] [1174] 4-8-13 **80** .... TPQueally 6 19
(J M Bradley) *chsd ldrs to 1/2-way: wknd rapidly over 2f out* **20/1**

50-0 **10** 3 ¼ **Tony James (IRE)**[46] [925] 6-9-4 **85** ....(b) PatDobbs 10 13
(K O Cunningham-Brown) *pressed ldr to 2f out: wknd alarmingly* **25/1**

1m 12.21s (0.01) **Going Correction** +0.30s/f (Good) **10** Ran SP% **118.7**
Speed ratings (Par 105): **111,110,110,109,107 103,95,93,81,76**
CSF £16.79 CT £108.43 TOTE £5.00: £1.90, £1.60, £2.40; EX 13.60.

Owner Eden Racing **Bred** Bloomsbury Stud & The Hon Sir David Sieff **Trained** Blewbury, Oxon

■ Stewards' Enquiry : Amir Quinn two-day ban; used whip with excessive frequency (May 18-19)
Stephen Carson five-day ban; used whip with excessive frequency (May 17-21)
Luke Morris one-day ban; used whip above shoulder height (May 18)

FOCUS

A strong sprint handicap run at a good pace. The form is very solid and should prove reliable.

Kelamon Official explanation: jockey said gelding missed the break

1801 BETDIRECT.COM E B F CONQUEROR STKS (LISTED RACE) (F&M) 1m

3:40 (3:45) (Class 1) 3-Y-0+

£17,031 (£6,456; £3,231; £1,611; £807; £405) **Stalls** High

Form RPR

654- **1** **Enforce (USA)**[175] [6757] 5-9-4 92 .... WilliamBuick 4 106
(Mrs L Wadham) *trckd ldrs: clsd gng easily 2f out: led 1f out: sn in command: rdn out* **14/1**

221- **2** 2 **Lady Gloria**[165] [6889] 4-9-7 104 .... TPQueally 7 104
(J G Given) *jnd ldr after 3f: disp tl led 2f out: hdd and outpcd 1f out* **3/1**[2]

3-40 **3** 2 ½ **Sweet Lilly**[71] [672] 4-9-7 0 .... TPO'Shea 8 98
(M R Channon) *hld up bhd ldrs: rdn and nt qckn 2f out: kpt on fnl f: nvr able to chal* **6/4**[1]

42-3 **4** 1 ¼ **Nans Joy (IRE)**[21] [1331] 4-9-4 94 .... ChrisCatlin 5 92
(E J O'Neill) *racd freely: led: jnd after 3f: hdd 2f out: wknd fnl f* **13/2**[3]

04-2 **5** ½ **Chantilly Tiffany**[21] [1331] 4-9-4 94 .... StephenDonohoe 1 91
(E A L Dunlop) *dropped in fr wd draw and hld up: shkn up over 2f out: no imp on ldrs after* **17/2**

00-4 **6** *hd* **Folly Lodge**[21] [1331] 4-9-4 87 .... RobertHavlin 6 91
(G Wragg) *a towards rr: rdn over 2f out: no prog* **14/1**

005- **7** ¾ **Miss Bootylishes**[189] [6498] 3-8-5 85 .... KevinGhunowa 9 86?
(A B Haynes) *chsd ldrs: rdn over 3f out: steadily fdd u.p* **50/1**

2-05 **8** ¾ **Rinterval (IRE)**[3] [1715] 3-8-5 93 ....(b[1]) RichardSmith 3 84
(R Hannon) *hld up in last trio: rdn over 2f out: no prog* **14/1**

6-24 **9** 6 **Montrachet**[15] [1456] 4-9-4 75 ....(b[1]) HayleyTurner 2 72
(M L W Bell) *restless in stalls: s.v.s: latched on to bk of gp 1/2-way: wknd 2f out* **33/1**

1m 41.91s (2.01) **Going Correction** +0.475s/f (Yiel)
WFA 3 from 4yo+ 13lb **9** Ran SP% **113.8**
Speed ratings (Par 111): **108,106,103,102,101 101,100,100,94**
CSF £55.12 TOTE £17.60: £3.80, £1.50, £1.30; EX 80.60 Trifecta £467.40 Part won. Pool: £658.44 - 0.40 winning tickets..

Owner Mr And Mrs A E Pakenham **Bred** Juddmonte Farms Inc **Trained** Newmarket, Suffolk

FOCUS

This looked a weakish Listed race. The winner won with plenty of authority and is rated up 8lb, with the second to form.

NOTEBOOK

Enforce(USA), who has been tested in-foal to Sir Percy, was always moving sweetly and bounded clear when asked to quicken. She had shown promise in two Listed fillies' races last autumn for Ed Dunlop and then changed hands at the December mares' sale. Lucy Wadham may look towards the Windsor Forest Stakes at Royal Ascot for her before she has to stop racing. (tchd 16-1)

Lady Gloria did not do a great deal wrong and ran a fine race in defeat. The winner of a 9f Listed contest in France on her final start last year, she had to give 3lb to the winner and would have been a comfortable scorer without that rival. She ought to have a good season in similar events. (op 11-4 tchd 10-3)

Sweet Lilly, who had a couple of runs in Dubai earlier in the year, was a strong favourite but showed signs of temperament again, carrying her head at an awkward angle under pressure when asked to catch Enforce. She will need everything to fall in place for her to return to winning ways. (op 7-4 tchd 15-8)

Nans Joy(IRE) probably went a bit too freely in front and did not get home as a result. She did, however, reverse form with Chantilly Tiffany from when they met last time. (op 7-1 tchd 11-2)

Chantilly Tiffany, whose run last time was enhanced by the winner at Newmarket on the same day, was made to look very one paced under pressure. She probably wants much quicker ground. (op 9-1 tchd 10-1)

Folly Lodge got going far too late but kept on strongly inside the final furlong. (op 12-1)

Rinterval(IRE) did not improve for the application of blinkers for the first time. (tchd 16-1)

Montrachet Official explanation: jockey said filly missed the break

1802 SPOFFORTHS STKS (H'CAP) 5f

4:15 (4:15) (Class 3) (0-90,90) 4-Y-0+ **£7,771** (£2,312; £1,155; £577) **Stalls** Low

Form RPR

534- **1** **Safari Mischief**[204] [6141] 5-8-5 **80** .... LukeMorris(3) 5 94
(P Winkworth) *trckd clr ldng pair: clsd and rdn to ld over 1f out: pressed ins fnl f: styd on wl* **7/1**[3]

3011 **2** ¾ **Lord Of The Reins (IRE)**[9] [1582] 4-8-1 **76** oh3 .... WilliamBuick(3) 8 87
(D Shaw) *trckd clr ldrs in centre: rdn and effrt over 1f out: pressed wnr ins fnl f: readily hld last 75yds* **7/1**[3]

-210 **3** 2 ½ **Digital**[18] [1386] 11-8-6 **78** .... ChrisCatlin 4 80
(M R Channon) *sn outpcd in rr: last 2f out: picked up wl fr over 1f out: r.o to take 3rd last 50yds* **16/1**

06-0 **4** 1 ¼ **Dazed And Amazed**[15] [1442] 4-8-13 **90** .... PatrickHills(5) 6 88
(R Hannon) *sn off the pce towards rr: rdn over 2f out: kpt on one pce: n.d* **14/1**

46-2 **5** *nse* **Malapropism**[17] [1393] 8-8-4 **83** .... MatthewDavies(7) 3 80
(M R Channon) *racd nr side: nvr on terms: u.p and struggling 1/2-way: styd on fnl f* **9/2**[2]

-004 **6** ½ **Cape Royal**[10] [1571] 8-8-11 **86** ....(bt) KevinGhunowa(3) 9 82
(J M Bradley) *disp ld in centre to over 1f out: wknd fnl f* **7/1**[3]

06-6 **7** 1 ½ **Elhamri**[15] [1442] 4-9-2 **88** .... GeorgeBaker 2 78
(S Kirk) *sn outpcd: hanging whn rdn 2f out: no prog* **8/1**

621 **8** ½ **Stolt (IRE)**[15] [1451] 4-8-5 **82** .... AshleyHamblett(5) 10 70
(N Wilson) *disp ld in centre to over 1f out: wknd rapidly* **4/1**[1]

03-3 **9** 2 ½ **Woodcote (IRE)**[20] [1346] 6-9-2 **88** ....(b) PaulDoe 7 67
(P R Chamings) *rrd bdly s: bhd tl effrt into midfield 1/2-way: no prog over 1f out: wknd* **8/1**

0-42 **10** *shd* **Corridor Creeper (FR)**[11] [1537] 11-8-8 **80** ow1 ....(p) StephenDonohoe 1 59
(J M Bradley) *racd nr side: struggling and outpcd after 2f* **9/1**

58.98 secs (0.58) **Going Correction** +0.30s/f (Good) **10** Ran SP% **120.5**
Speed ratings (Par 107): **107,105,101,99,99 98,96,95,91,91**
CSF £57.23 CT £770.05 TOTE £8.50: £2.50, £2.70, £3.90; EX 76.50.

Owner Foxtrot Racing Partnership **Bred** Bearstone Stud **Trained** Chiddingfold, Surrey

■ Stewards' Enquiry : Kevin Ghunowa three-day ban: failed to ride out to line (May 18-20)

FOCUS

A competitive handicap run at a good gallop. This looks solid form with the progressive front pair clear.

NOTEBOOK

Safari Mischief was waited with until his jockey unleashed a powerful run from him inside the final furlong. He has gone well fresh before, so it remains to be seen whether he can build on this career-high effort. (op 10-1)

Lord Of The Reins(IRE) ◆ has been in terrific form on the All Weather and added another good effort to his collection back on turf from 3lb out of the handicap. Although high in the weights, he can win another race on grass soon. (tchd 15-2)

Digital, found to have an irregular heartbeat after his last run, absolutely flew home inside the final furlong but had no hope of catching the leaders. He is still very capable on his day. (op 18-1)

Dazed And Amazed, a Listed winner at Kempton last summer, ran better than he did on his seasonal debut but he did not have much left for the battle under pressure, and the Handicapper probably has his measure for now. (op 16-1)

Malapropism finished well, much like his stablemate Digital, but is another who looks slightly high in the weights. (op 4-1)

Cape Royal went a strong pace in front and could only keep on at the one pace inside the final furlong. Despite being well handicapped for a few runs, he has gone 18 races without a success. (op 6-1)

Elhamri Official explanation: jockey said gelding missed the break

Stolt(IRE), who loves to be up the pace, went much too fast early and paid for it in the latter stages. (op 5-1)

Woodcote(IRE) Official explanation: jockey said gelding reared on leaving stalls

1803 DARREN JENKINS 40TH BIRTHDAY MAIDEN STKS 7f

4:50 (4:50) (Class 5) 3-Y-O £3,238 (£963; £481; £240) **Stalls High**

Form RPR

0 **1** **East Drive (IRE)**[14] 1467 3-9-3 0 PhilipRobinson 3 80
(M A Jarvis) *hld up: smooth prog to ld over 1f out but hanging bdly rt after: hld on* **3/1**[2]

344- **2** *nk* **Strategic Mover (USA)**[231] 5417 3-9-3 100 NelsonDeSouza 1 80
(P F I Cole) *sn trckd ldr: shkn up to chal 2f out: w wnr over 1f out: carried rt and nt qckn fnl f* **6/5**[1]

- **3** *1 1/2* **Siren Sound** 3-8-9 0 TravisBlock(3) 5 70
(H Morrison) *sn hld up: sltly hmpd 5f out: dropped to last 3f out: outpcd 2f out: swtchd out wd and r.o fnl f* **7/1**[3]

35-4 **4** *3 1/2* **Lush (IRE)**[16] 1423 3-8-12 78 PatDobbs 2 61+
(R Hannon) *sn led: shkn up over 2f out: hdd and hmpd over 1f out: wknd* **3/1**[2]

1m 31.11s (3.71) **Going Correction** +0.475s/f (Yiel) **4 Ran SP% 108.0**
Speed ratings (Par 99): **97,96,94,90**
CSF £7.03 TOTE £3.50; EX 5.20.
Owner H R H Sultan Ahmad Shah **Bred** Fin A Co S R L **Trained** Newmarket, Suffolk

FOCUS
This looks muddling form, as the runner-up has only once run close to his official rating and the fourth was hampered.

1804 GOLDRING SECURITY SERVICES MEDIAN AUCTION MAIDEN STKS 5f

5:20 (5:21) (Class 5) 2-Y-O £3,238 (£963; £481) **Stalls Low**

Form RPR

0 **1** **Icesolator (IRE)**[17] 1399 2-9-3 0 PatDobbs 3 81+
(R Hannon) *mde virtually all: shkn up to assert over 1f out: pushed out fnl f* **5/6**[1]

2 *2 1/2* **Rio Royale (IRE)** 2-9-3 0 TPQueally 1 69+
(Mrs A J Perrett) *hld up in 3rd: pushed along 2f out: styd on to take 2nd ins fnl f: no imp on wnr* **11/2**[3]

3 *2 1/4* **Finnegan McCool** 2-9-3 0 GeorgeBaker 2 64+
(R M Beckett) *rn green early: sn w wnr: shkn up over 1f out: wknd* **6/4**[2]

61.96 secs (3.56) **Going Correction** +0.30s/f (Good) **3 Ran SP% 109.9**
Speed ratings (Par 93): **83,79,75**
CSF £5.04 TOTE £1.80; EX 6.10.
Owner B Bull **Bred** Pier House Stud **Trained** East Everleigh, Wilts

FOCUS
A race almost impossible to assess. The winner was entitled to win and did so nicely against two debutants.

NOTEBOOK
Icesolator(IRE), whose trainer Richard Hannon reckons was a shade unlucky not to have finished second instead of ninth on his debut at Newmarket, made his experience count to hold the two newcomers comfortably. It remains to be seen what he is capable of, as he will face much stiffer tasks than this. (op 6-5 tchd 5-4, 11-8 in places)
Rio Royale(IRE), who is bred to enjoy some cut, was the last to have a crack at the winner but with little success. A first juvenile runner for his stable, he shaped with some promise and should improve (op 5-1 tchd 9-2)
Finnegan McCool, who was green to post, hails from a yard whose youngsters are going well. He failed to pick up when asked to quicken but will have benefited for the experience. (op 6-5)

1805 GOODWOOD PARK HOTEL STKS (H'CAP) 1m 3f

5:50 (5:51) (Class 4) (0-80,79) 3-Y-O £4,533 (£1,348; £674; £336) **Stalls Low**

Form RPR

301- **1** **Cool Judgement (IRE)**[202] 6202 3-9-4 79 PhilipRobinson 2 91+
(M A Jarvis) *hld up: t.k.h after 4f: prog to go 2nd over 2f out: rdn to ld over 1f out: kpt on and in command after* **8/11**[1]

5-13 **2** *2 1/2* **Riverscape (IRE)**[12] 1527 3-9-0 75 TPO'Shea 1 78
(Mrs A J Perrett) *trckd ldr: led 3f out: rdn and hdd over 1f out: one pce* **9/2**[2]

6-12 **3** *nk* **Kyrie Eleison (IRE)**[11] 1530 3-8-2 68 ow1 PatrickHills(5) 5 70
(R Hannon) *hld up: rdn and struggling 3f out: kpt on fr 2f out to press for 2nd ins fnl f* **13/2**

20-4 **4** *11* **Mizooka**[28] 1208 3-8-11 72 TPQueally 4 56
(R M Beckett) *trckd ldng pair tl rdn and wknd over 2f out* **5/1**[3]

0-26 **5** *7* **Riqaab (IRE)**[24] 1272 3-8-8 69 StephenDonohoe 3 41
(E A L Dunlop) *racd awkwardly: led to 3f out: sn wknd u.p* **10/1**

2m 33.24s (4.94) **Going Correction** +0.475s/f (Yiel) **5 Ran SP% 115.2**
Speed ratings (Par 101): **101,99,98,90,85**
CSF £4.78 TOTE £1.80: £1.20, £1.50; EX 2.80 Place 6 £68.22, Place 5 £54.19.
Owner H R H Sultan Ahmad Shah **Bred** Crone Stud Farms Ltd **Trained** Newmarket, Suffolk

FOCUS
A fair staying handicap won nicely by Cool Judgement, although the form looks pretty weak.
T/Plt: £307.40 to a £1 stake. Pool: £72,765.99. 172.80 winning tickets. T/Qpdt: £168.60 to a £1 stake. Pool: £2,530.40. 11.10 winning tickets. JN

1417

NEWMARKET (ROWLEY) (R-H)

Saturday, May 3

OFFICIAL GOING: Good
Wind: Fresh, half-against Weather: Cloudy

1806 STAN JAMES 08000 383384 H'CAP 1m

2:10 (2:10) (Class 2) (0-105,93) 3-Y-O £19,428 (£5,781; £2,889; £1,443) **Stalls Low**

Form RPR

00-2 **1** **Duntulm**[24] 1265 3-9-0 84 DaneO'Neill 2 100+
(H Candy) *s.v.s: hdwy and swtchd rt 2f out: led and edgd lft over 1f out: sn rdn: jst hld on* **14/1**

140- **2** *nk* **Flawed Genius**[256] 4695 3-9-3 87 RyanMoore 12 100+
(Sir Michael Stoute) *s.i.s: hld up: hdwy and edgd lft over 1f out: sn rdn: r.o* **5/1**[3]

04-1 **3** *nk* **Perks (IRE)**[22] 1297 3-9-1 85 TedDurcan 7 97+
(J L Dunlop) *s.i.s: hld up: swtchd rt and hdwy over 1f out: sn rdn: r.o* **4/1**[2]

41-0 **4** *5* **Prime Exhibit**[16] 1424 3-9-0 84 SteveDrowne 3 85
(R Charlton) *lw: trckd ldrs: hmpd wl over 1f out: wknd ins fnl f* **7/2**[1]

32- **5** *1/2* **Meydan Dubai (IRE)**[252] 4823 3-9-5 89 JimCrowley 6 91+
(J R Best) *lw: hld up: rdn over 2f out: swtchd rt and hdwy over 1f out: hmpd sn after: r.o towards fin: nvr nrr* **28/1**

61-6 **6** *1* **Speedy Dollar (USA)**[21] 1333 3-9-6 90 NCallan 9 87
(M A Jarvis) *led 2f: chsd ldrs: rdn over 2f out: wknd fnl f* **20/1**

36-3 **7** *1/2* **King's Wonder**[14] 1490 3-8-9 79 MartinDwyer 5 75+
(W R Muir) *trckd ldrs: rdn and edgd lft wl over 1f out: hmpd sn after: wknd fnl f* **25/1**

13-1 **8** *1 3/4* **American Art (IRE)**[108] 178 3-9-4 88 (t) MichaelHills 8 80
(B W Hills) *hld up in tch: rdn whn wkng whn hmpd over 1f out* **12/1**

21-4 **9** *2 1/4* **Robby Bobby**[16] 1428 3-9-5 89 GregFairley 1 76
(M Johnston) *lw: led 6f out: rdn and hdd over 1f out: wknd fnl f* **14/1**

213- **10** *1 1/2* **Harlech Castle**[241] 5135 3-9-2 93 GabrielHannon(7) 13 76
(P F I Cole) *hld up: rdn over 2f out: sn wknd: hung lft over 1f out* **40/1**

14-4 **11** *hd* **Arctic Cape**[8] 1595 3-9-1 85 JoeFanning 10 68
(M Johnston) *chsd ldrs: rdn over 2f out: wknd over 1f out* **15/2**

15-1 **12** *2 3/4* **Red Rumour (IRE)**[35] 1074 3-9-7 91 SebSanders 4 67
(R M Beckett) *lw: prom: rdn over 3f out: wknd 2f out* **8/1**

152- **13** *3/4* **Dixey**[278] 4022 3-9-7 91 AlanMunro 11 66
(M A Jarvis) *prom: lost pl over 2f out: wknd over 1f out* **33/1**

1m 40.58s (1.98) **Going Correction** +0.40s/f (Good) **13 Ran SP% 120.2**
Speed ratings (Par 105): **106,105,105,100,99 98,98,96,94,92 92,89,89**
CSF £78.34 CT £353.26 TOTE £17.60: £3.50, £2.50, £2.00; EX 109.40 Trifecta £687.10 Part won. Pool: £967.76 - 0.90 winning tickets..
Owner Thomas Barr **Bred** W And R Barnett Ltd **Trained** Kingston Warren, Oxon
■ Stewards' Enquiry : Steve Drowne two-day ban; careless riding (May 18-19)

FOCUS
A fresh wind had helped dry out the ground which some jockeys reported after the first race as being on the fast side of good. This looked a strong three-year-old handicap and the time was reasonable for the grade, despite being 1.44secs slower than the 2000 Guineas. The form has been rated positively.

NOTEBOOK
Duntulm ◆, who lost the best part of ten lengths at the start, showed an impressive turn of foot to lose his maiden tag. Runner-up to Sugar Mint on his reappearance at Bath, he played up in the preliminaries and lost ground when standing still as the stalls opened, but by halfway he was going nicely on the heels of the leaders. When asked he picked up really well to lead running down into the Dip and, although inclined to edge left once in front, he was not going to be beaten, although two rivals emerged from the rear to make a race of it. His trainer admits that Duntulm is a bit of a playboy, but he is clearly a talented miler, despite being middle-distance bred by Sakhee out of a daughter of Time Charter. He will now be aimed at the Britannia Handicap at Royal Ascot. He will run in the meantime however, and there is a valuable handicap at Haydock which might be ideal.
Flawed Genius, another who missed the break, had not run for eight months but looked fit and was trying this trip for the first time. He showed he stays it well enough, keeping on well up the hill, and could reoppose the winner at Royal Ascot. (op 6-1 tchd 13-2 tchd 7-1 in a place)
Perks(IRE), who like the first two missed the break, was 12lb higher than when a runaway winner of a soft-ground Doncaster handicap which has worked out well. He looked dull in his coat but travelled well although the winner got first run on him before he found his stride on the rise to the line. He looks likely to continue to hold his own at this level. (op 7-2 tchd 9-2 in a place)
Prime Exhibit, who was well beaten despite running creditably when tried at 1m2f last time, travelled well on this drop back in trip behind pace-setter Robby Bobby, but had nowhere to go when it was time to make a move, and got involved in a barging match with King's Wonder as the winner was going to the front. Disappointingly, he weakened inside the final furlong, and is something of an enigma, but he is not one to give up on yet. (tchd 4-1 in places)
Meydan Dubai(IRE) ◆ was among the pick of the paddock and ran much better than his finishing position suggests, as having been held up in rear he got involved in two separate incidents yet was still going on nicely at the finish. He is still a maiden, but he has been highly tried and looks pretty useful. (op 33-1)
Speedy Dollar(USA) was keen again, despite making the running early on, and did not really see his race out. (op 18-1)
King's Wonder ran better than the bare facts suggest, having got into a barging match running into the Dip, as a result of which he was struck into. He can win a race or two. Official explanation: trainer said colt was struck into (tchd 28-1)
American Art(IRE), a 7f Polytrack winner stepping up in trip, was already beaten when hampered. (op 14-1)
Robby Bobby, who disappointed on his seasonal return, did so again and now has something to prove. (op 12-1)
Harlech Castle, who looked fit, never really got involved having been held up. (op 33-1)
Arctic Cape, who ran so well at Sandown last week on his reappearance, was taken down early and dropped right out after helping force it towards the centre. Maybe this run came came too soon. (op 7-1)

1807 STANJAMESUK.COM DAHLIA STKS (GROUP 3) (F&M) 1m 1f

2:45 (2:46) (Class 1) 4-Y-O+

£28,385 (£10,760; £5,385; £2,685; £1,345; £675) **Stalls Low**

Form RPR

23-1 **1** **Heaven Sent**[21] 1331 5-8-12 106 RyanMoore 6 115
(Sir Michael Stoute) *chsd ldr tl led 6f out: rdn and edgd lft over 1f out: r.o* **6/4**[1]

015- **2** *3* **Harvest Queen (IRE)**[210] 6010 5-8-12 110 SebSanders 4 109
(P J Makin) *hld up in tch: rdn to chse wnr over 1f out: styd on same pce fnl f* **9/2**[3]

006- **3** *1 3/4* **Barshiba (IRE)**[210] 6010 4-8-12 106 TQuinn 1 105+
(D R C Elsworth) *hld up: plld hrd: nt clr run over 2f out: rdn and hung lft over 1f out: r.o ins fnl f: nt trble ldrs* **12/1**

033- **4** *3/4* **Passage Of Time**[189] 6509 4-8-12 115 TedDurcan 3 103
(H R A Cecil) *bit bkwd: prom: chsd wnr over 3f out: rdn and hung rt over 1f out: styd on same pce* **7/4**[2]

-000 **5** *6* **Impetious**[71] 672 4-8-12 95 (be) JMurtagh 2 90
(Eamon Tyrrell, Ire) *prom: rdn over 2f out: wknd over 1f out* **33/1**

10-5 **6** *7* **Cosmodrome (USA)**[21] 1331 4-8-12 103 JamieSpencer 5 75
(L M Cumani) *dull in coat: led 3f: chsd ldrs: rdn over 2f out: sn wknd* **16/1**

1m 55.0s (4.40) **Going Correction** +0.40s/f (Good) **6 Ran SP% 111.1**
Speed ratings (Par 113): **96,93,91,91,85 79**
CSF £8.54 TOTE £2.50: £1.40, £2.60; EX 8.40.
Owner Cheveley Park Stud **Bred** Cheveley Park Stud Ltd **Trained** Newmarket, Suffolk

FOCUS
A fair renewal of this Group 3, but it was run at a very steady gallop and the decisive winner may have been flattered a little following a particularly good ride. The placed horses are rated to their Sun Chariot form.

NOTEBOOK
Heaven Sent, who was placed several times in Group company last season, gained her first success at this level in emphatic style. Moore dictated the pace when he felt the early gallop was too steady and the mare found plenty when asked to draw away up the hill. She appears to be emulating her sister Megahertz, who progressed with age, and she is yet another valuable broodmare prospect for her owners. The Windsor Forest Stakes at Royal Ascot looks a feasible target. (op 13-8)
Harvest Queen(IRE), twice a Listed winner, travelled well and looked likely to score running down into the Dip before finding the winner too strong up the hill. This was the first time she has been placed at Group level in three attempts and she looks capable of scoring in this grade, especially on a flatter track. (tchd 5-1 in places)

Barshiba(IRE), who looked fit for this reappearance, is not that straightforward and did not really settle, but ran almost to the pound with the runner-up compared with their Sun Chariot form. This was also her first Group placing but whether she can build on this remains to be seen. (tchd 11-1)
Passage Of Time, who won the Musidora and started favourite for last season's Oaks, has been placed at the highest level since but did not look great beforehand and was disappointing on this return to action. She was admittedly dropping in trip, but travelled well enough and faded when it could have been expected that she would be running on at the business end. Official explanation: jockey said, regarding riding out, he had made every effort in the race but got no response from filly in closing stages and nursed her home (tchd 2-1 tchd 9-4 in a place)

1808 STANJAMESUK.COM 2000 GUINEAS STKS (THE 200TH RUNNING) (GROUP 1) (ENTIRE COLTS & FILLIES) 1m

3:25 (3:31) (Class 1) 3-Y-O

£212,887 (£80,700; £40,387; £20,137; £10,087; £5,062) **Stalls** Centre

Form RPR
123- **1** **Henrythenavigator (USA)**[252] 4833 3-9-0 0 .... JMurtagh 10 123+
(A P O'Brien, Ire) *swtg: hld up: swtchd rt over 3f out: hdwy over 2f out: chsd ldr over 1f out: rdn to ld wl ins fnl f: r.o* **11/1**
111- **2** *nse* **New Approach (IRE)**[196] 6333 3-9-0 0 .... KJManning 2 123+
(J S Bolger, Ire) *lw: led: rdn over 1f out: hdd wl ins fnl f: r.o* **11/8**[1]
13-5 **3** *4* **Stubbs Art (IRE)**[8] 1595 3-9-0 87 .... SebSanders 7 113
(D R C Elsworth) *lw: hld up: hdwy 1/2-way: swtchd rt over 2f out: rdn and edgd lft over 1f out: no ex fnl f* **100/1**
13-2 **4** *1/2* **Raven's Pass (USA)**[16] 1421 3-9-0 120 .... JimmyFortune 13 111+
(J H M Gosden) *hld up: swtchd rt over 2f out: hdwy over 1f out: sn rdn: edgd lft fnl f: styd on same pce* **4/1**[3]
316- **5** *hd* **Dream Eater (IRE)**[211] 5975 3-9-0 104 ....(t) MartinDwyer 3 111
(A M Balding) *lw: prom: racd keenly: rdn to chse ldr 2f out: sn edgd lft: no ex fnl f* **50/1**
41- **6** *3 1/2* **Moynahan (USA)**[255] 4725 3-9-0 95 .... TQuinn 11 103
(P F I Cole) *edgy: on toes: hld up: rdn over 2f out: sme hdwy over 1f out: edgd lft and no imp fnl f* **40/1**
22-1 **7** *1/2* **Stimulation (IRE)**[17] 1400 3-9-0 110 .... SteveDrowne 12 102
(H Morrison) *lw: hld up: hdwy over 2f out: rdn over 1f out: wknd fnl f* **16/1**
8 *1 1/4* **Plan (USA)**[187] 6550 3-9-0 0 .... MJKinane 1 99
(A P O'Brien, Ire) *w'like: attractive: lw: trckd ldrs: rdn over 2f out: wknd over 1f out* **33/1**
24-5 **9** *2 3/4* **Strike The Deal (USA)**[35] 1088 3-9-0 112 .... EddieAhern 14 93
(J Noseda) *hld up: rdn over 2f out: n.d* **33/1**
111- **10** *2 1/2* **Ibn Khaldun (USA)**[189] 6489 3-9-0 117 .... LDettori 9 87
(Saeed Bin Suroor) *lw: prom: rdn over 2f out: wknd over 1f out* **7/2**[2]
31-0 **11** *2 1/4* **Scintillo**[16] 1421 3-9-0 114 .... RichardHughes 15 82
(R Hannon) *hld up: rdn over 2f out: n.d* **100/1**
12- **12** *1 3/4* **Perfect Stride**[222] 5691 3-9-0 89 .... RyanMoore 5 78
(Sir Michael Stoute) *edgy: on toes: swtg: trckd ldrs: racd keenly: rdn over 3f out: wknd over 2f out* **16/1**
315- **13** *1 3/4* **Alfathaa**[217] 5795 3-9-0 107 .... RHills 4 74
(W J Haggas) *on toes: chsd ldr tl rdn over 2f out: wknd over 1f out* **40/1**
5 **14** *3 1/4* **Bahamian Kid**[22] 1298 3-9-0 0 .... TedDurcan 8 65
(R Hollinshead) *w'like: leggy: hld up: rdn over 2f out: sn wknd* **250/1**
61- **15** *9* **Fireside**[211] 5971 3-9-0 92 .... AlanMunro 6 44
(P W Chapple-Hyam) *lw: prom: rdn over 3f out: sn wknd* **20/1**

1m 39.14s (0.54) **Going Correction** +0.40s/f (Good) **15** Ran SP% **124.3**
Speed ratings (Par 113): **113,112,108,108,108 104,104,103,100,97 95,93,92,88,79**
CSF £25.91 TOTE £11.90: £3.20, £1.10, £15.60; EX 39.80 Trifecta £3880.00 Pool: £13,498.25 - 2.47 winning tickets..
Owner Mrs John Magnier **Bred** Western Bloodstock **Trained** Ballydoyle, Co Tipperary
■ The 200th running of the 2000 Guineas.
■ Stewards' Enquiry : K J Manning four-day ban; used whip with excessive frequency and without giving colt time to respond and after winning post (May 18-21)
J Murtagh two-day ban; used whip with excessive frequency without giving colt time to respond (May 18-19)
Seb Sanders two-day ban: used whip with excessive frequency (May 20-21)

FOCUS

An up-to-scratch renewal of the first Classic dominated by two of the leading juvenile colts from the previous season. The time was well up to standard for the grade, being 1.44 secs faster than the opening handicap. Although the stalls were in the centre the whole field came stands' side. The winner has been raised 8lb, and the runner-up assessed as having run 2lb below his Dewhurst form. There were plenty of improvers behind, notably the third and fifth.

NOTEBOOK

Henrythenavigator(USA) ◆, who looked fit for this return, was given a superb waiting ride by Murtagh, held up before making significant headway to challenge going into the final furlong. He had to fight hard to get past the runner-up, but did so in tenacious fashion to resist the renewed effort of that colt. He had looked a really good prospect on fast ground in the Coventry, and the going had turned against him when he was beaten in two subsequent runs at the Curragh. The drying ground was just right for him and, a miler through and through, the Irish 2000 Guineas - where he could meet the runner-up again - and the St James's Palace Stakes are the obvious races for him. If the ground is on top again he will be the one to beat. (tchd 12-1)
New Approach(IRE) ◆ came here unbeaten and stood out on his Dewhurst form. He had reportedly enjoyed a trouble-free preparation, and while he was ponied to the start again, he was well behaved through the preliminaries. Ideally drawn with front-running tactics in mind, he led the field virtually throughout against the stands' rail and was a good two lengths clear going into the final 2f, and while he just lost the battle with his old rival Henrythenavigator he probably had his nose in front again a stride or two later. One of only a handful in the race likely to appreciate middle distances in due course, he is likely to renew rivalry with the winner in the Irish 2000 Guineas and, if conditions place more emphasis on stamina, he might well reverse placings. All being well, the Irish Derby will be on the agenda after that. (op 7-4 tchd 5-4 in a place)
Stubbs Art(IRE), who had been beaten off 87 in a Sandown handicap eight days previously, has always been highly regarded. Third to Twice Over here over 1m2f last autumn, he gave himself no chance at Sandown because he pulled way too hard, but off this stronger pace he settled well in midfield, racing on the stands' rail until switched right for his effort over 2f out. This was a cracking performance, and connections had no hesitation in nominating the St James's Palace as his next target, although it could be he just excels this course, having won his maiden here as well.
Raven's Pass(USA) had the drying ground connections had been hoping for, but he still had his stamina to prove after snatching defeat from the jaws of victory in both the Dewhurst and the Craven. Fortune clearly had that in mind, but one has to think the waiting tactics might have cost him a place here, for he was dropped out in last from stall 13 and remained there until approaching 2f out, where he was switched to come right around the outside of the field. He made good progress in the wake of the winner, but he was no longer gaining at the finish and this trip may just stretch his stamina. The Jersey Stakes and the July Cup are on the agenda now, and the faster the ground the better. (op 9-2)
Dream Eater(IRE) excelled himself at long odds. Keen to get on with things as usual, he soon pulled himself into a handy position and looked a strong candidate for a place 2f out. He had no more to give though in the final furlong, and dropping to 7f in the Jersey should be perfect for him too. He has clearly trained on well and that Royal Ascot contest is developing into a potentially hot race.
Moynahan(USA) had not enjoyed a smooth preparation and was excitable in the preliminaries, but he ran pretty well and the Dante is on the cards next.
Stimulation(IRE) was just about the pick in the paddock and looked set to appreciate the extra furlong, but the step up in class proved too much for him at this stage and he never really got into it from his wide draw. (tchd 18-1 in a place)
Plan(USA) took the eye beforehand and raced handily on the rail for a long way. He is very inexperienced as yet and will do better in time.
Strike The Deal(USA) was held up to get the trip but looked a non-stayer and is yet another heading for the Jersey.
Ibn Khaldun(USA), the Racing Post Trophy winner, was the disappointment of the contest. Godolphin's first European runner of the year, he had reportedly wintered really well, but he ran very flat and was in trouble before 2f out. Connections could offer no explanation for this effort. Official explanation: jockey said colt ran flat (op 4-1)
Scintillo, winner of Italy's Gran Criterium, showed up on the wide outside but on this year's evidence he is going to struggle. Unfortunately his Group 1 penalty will make it hard for him to drop in class.
Perfect Stride found the occasion all too much as, excitable beforehand, he was in trouble at halfway, having pulled hard through the first couple of furlongs. A handicap mark of 89 might be hard to resist now before he has another crack at a Group race. (op 14-1)
Alfathaa, by Nayef and so one of the likelier middle-distance types, chased the favourite for a long way but weakened over a furlong out. He was evidently rusty for his reappearance and should do better next time when a step up in trip is planned. (op 50-1)
Bahamian Kid, only fifth in a Doncaster maiden on his recent debut, faced an impossible task but looked the part and went well up to a point. He could be interesting when dropped to a more realistic level. (op 300-1)
Fireside had a stiff-enough task based on his maiden success last backend but dropped away when the race began in earnest as if something was amiss. (op 25-1 tchd 16-1)

1809 STANJAMESUK.COM STKS HERITAGE H'CAP 6f

4:00 (4:04) (Class 2) 3-Y-O+

£31,155 (£9,330; £4,665; £2,335; £1,165; £585) **Stalls** Low

Form RPR
00-0 **1** **Off The Record**[35] 1071 4-8-12 **95** .... RichardHughes 13 106
(J G Given) *racd far side: mde virtually all: rdn over 1f out: r.o gamely* **25/1**
0-42 **2** *hd* **Damika (IRE)**[12] 1517 5-8-11 **97** .... MichaelJStainton(3) 14 108
(R M Whitaker) *racd far side: a.p: rdn and ev ch fr over 1f out: r.o* **16/1**
00-3 **3** *1/2* **Fullandby (IRE)**[15] 1442 6-9-4 **101** .... GregFairley 18 110
(T J Etherington) *racd far side: hld up: plld hrd: hdwy over 1f out: r.o* **16/1**
0026 **4** *1/2* **Baby Strange**[10] 1571 4-8-4 **87** .... MartinDwyer 21 94+
(D Shaw) *racd far side: hld up: hdwy over 1f out: r.o* **33/1**
311- **5** *1/2* **King's Apostle (IRE)**[237] 5254 4-9-1 **98** .... LiamJones 20 104+
(W J Haggas) *lw: racd far side: chsd ldrs: rdn over 1f out: styd on* **8/1**[2]
00-5 **6** *1/2* **Hogmaneigh (IRE)**[15] 1442 5-9-4 **101** .... SaleemGolam 22 105
(S C Williams) *racd far side: hld up: rdn over 1f out: r.o: nt rch ldrs* **25/1**
-020 **7** *3/4* **Knot In Wood (IRE)**[12] 1517 6-9-2 **99** .... JoeFanning 5 101+
(R A Fahey) *lw: racd stands' side: hld up: swtchd rt over 2f out: hdwy over 1f out: led that gp ins fnl f: no ch w far side* **25/1**
21-4 **8** *1* **Genki (IRE)**[12] 1517 4-9-2 **99** .... SteveDrowne 15 98
(R Charlton) *racd far side: chsd ldrs: rdn over 2f out: styd on same pce fnl f* **11/2**[1]
060- **9** *1/2* **Mutamared (USA)**[169] 6840 8-9-0 **97** .... TedDurcan 19 99+
(K A Ryan) *racd far side: hld up in tch: nt clr run and lost pl over 1f out: n.d after* **20/1**
00-0 **10** *nk* **Special Day**[22] 1300 4-8-7 **90** .... MichaelHills 8 86+
(B W Hills) *racd centre: hld up: outpcd 2f out: rallied and edgd lft over 1f out: styd on* **33/1**
0-31 **11** *shd* **Tajneed (IRE)**[16] 1430 5-8-11 **94** .... JamieSpencer 10 90+
(D Nicholls) *led centre gp: rdn over 1f out: no ex* **9/1**[3]
32-3 **12** *1* **Northern Dare (IRE)**[34] 1103 4-8-5 **88** .... AdrianTNicholls 25 81
(D Nicholls) *racd far side: chsd ldrs: rdn over 1f out: wknd ins fnl f* **11/2**[1]
-334 **13** *nse* **Beaver Patrol (IRE)**[65] 741 6-9-5 **102** ....(v) MJKinane 4 94+
(Eve Johnson Houghton) *led stands' side: rdn over 1f out: wknd ins fnl f* **10/1**
10-0 **14** *2* **Barney McGrew (IRE)**[22] 1300 5-8-9 **92** .... PhillipMakin 16 78
(M Dods) *racd far side: chsd wnr tl rdn 2f out: wknd fnl f* **16/1**
20-0 **15** *1/2* **Prior Warning**[16] 1420 4-9-3 **103** ....(t) KirstyMilczarek(3) 2 87+
(Miss D Mountain) *racd stands' side: chsd ldrs: rdn and ev ch that gp over 1f out: wknd ins fnl f* **66/1**
6014 **16** *shd* **Hessian (IRE)**[8] 1604 4-7-7 **81** oh16 .... NataliaGemelova(5) 23 65
(M D Squance) *racd far side: hld up: rdn over 2f out: nvr trbld ldrs* **100/1**
6-00 **17** *1* **Rising Shadow (IRE)**[12] 1517 7-8-13 **96** ....(b[1]) JimmyQuinn 17 77
(N Wilson) *racd far side: hld up: rdn whn hmpd 2f out: sn hung rt and wknd* **33/1**
200- **18** *hd* **Viking Spirit**[203] 6183 6-9-3 **100** .... AdamKirby 11 80+
(W R Swinburn) *racd centre: chsd ldrs: rdn over 1f out: sn wknd* **25/1**
50-0 **19** *1 1/4* **Gift Horse**[35] 1071 8-8-5 **88** .... RichardMullen 24 64
(D Nicholls) *on toes: racd far side: hld up in tch: rdn and wknd over 1f out* **20/1**
33-5 **20** *3/4* **Titan Triumph**[10] 1566 4-7-12 **81** oh2 ....(t) NickyMackay 12 55
(W J Knight) *racd far side: prom: rdn and hung lft 2f out: wknd over 1f out* **50/1**
3234 **21** *1 1/4* **Bonus (IRE)**[56] 832 8-8-7 **90** .... EddieAhern 1 60+
(G A Butler) *chsd ldrs stands' side over 4f* **16/1**
0-04 **22** *1/2* **Hinton Admiral**[14] 1483 4-9-4 **101** .... JimmyFortune 3 69+
(R A Fahey) *racd stands' side: w ldr 4f: sn rdn and wknd* **66/1**
031- **23** *2 1/4* **Galeota (IRE)**[175] 6758 6-9-10 **107** .... RyanMoore 7 68+
(R Hannon) *racd centre: chsd ldrs over 4f* **11/1**
00-6 **24** *2 3/4* **Fantasy Believer**[21] 1325 10-8-6 **89** .... LPKeniry 9 41+
(J J Quinn) *s.i.s: racd centre: sn prom: wknd 2f out* **33/1**
20-0 **25** *hd* **Our Faye**[21] 1331 5-8-3 **86** .... DavidKinsella 6 38+
(S Kirk) *racd stands' side: chsd ldrs 4f* **33/1**

1m 13.47s (1.27) **Going Correction** +0.40s/f (Good) **25** Ran SP% **138.4**
Speed ratings (Par 109): **107,106,106,105,104 104,103,101,101,100 100,99,99,96,95 95,94,94,92,91 89,89,86,82,82**
CSF £362.13 CT £6519.78 TOTE £32.90: £7.90, £5.40, £4.20, £8.90; EX 655.60 Trifecta £8621.80 Part won. Pool: £12,143.39 - 0.30 winning tickets..
Owner Peter Onslow & Ian Henderson **Bred** Peter Onslow **Trained** Willoughton, Lincs

FOCUS

A high-class handicap in which they split into two main groups and those racing on the far side dominated the finish. The first three are all progressive and the form looks sound.

NOTEBOOK

Off The Record progressed really well as a three-year-old, completing a four-timer on Fibresand before running well in some high-class handicaps, including two narrow defeats on the July Course. He put a up performance, making all the running and just holding the determined challenge of the runner-up, and he looks the sort who can win more good races if he continues his steady improvement.

Damika(IRE) has become a very useful tool at this sort of level and had won over 7f here last season. He showed up throughout and put in a determined challenge, but he could not quite get past. He is a fair guide to the level of this form. (op 14-1)

Fullandby(IRE), another progressive sprinter, was back up in trip and, despite being keen in the race, was keeping on well at the finish. (op 12-1)

Baby Strange has not done much racing, having missed all of 2007, but he is a Listed winner and is another whose effort here is a guide to the level of the form. He came from well back and is possibly a bit better than the bare form.

King's Apostle(IRE), yet another on the upgrade, put up a decent effort on this return to action and, already a winner over 7f, has options over that distance as well as this. (op 10-1)

Hogmaneigh(IRE), who races mainly at the minimum trip, ran close to recent Newbury form with the third and was going on well at the finish. The drying ground would not have been in his favour.

Knot In Wood(IRE) ◆ did best of those racing on the stands' side, although he had to switch across in the closing stages to give him something to race with. This was a good effort in the circumstances. Official explanation: jockey said gelding suffered interference (op 20-1)

Genki(IRE) was 2lb better off with the runner-up for a length compared with their running at Pontefract, but failed to run to that level. Previously a consistent sort, it looks as if the Handicapper may have caught up with him. (tchd 6-1 tchd 7-1in a place)

Mutamared(USA), who finished runner-up in this race last season, was 1lb lower despite having failed to really build on that performance. He did not get the best of runs and did pretty well to finish so close.

Northern Dare(IRE) has been pretty consistent since winning his maiden early last season but this was a little disappointing. However, he is another for whom the drying ground would not have been ideal. Official explanation: jockey said gelding hung left throughout (op 7-1)

Beaver Patrol(IRE), last year's winner, made the running but was drawn on the unfavoured stands' side, which counted heavily against him. (op 14-1)

Hinton Admiral Official explanation: jockey said gelding hung left

1810 STANJAMESUK.COM/CASINO NEWMARKET STKS (LISTED RACE) (C&G) 1m 2f

4:35 (4:38) (Class 1) 3-Y-O £17,031 (£6,456; £3,231; £1,611) Stalls Low

Form				RPR
11-2	1		**Kandahar Run**[17] 1402 3-8-12 105 TedDurcan 3 (H R A Cecil) *lw: chsd ldr tl led over 1f out: sn rdn clr: eased nr fin* **8/13**[1]	106+
116-	2	2 3/4	**Meeriss (IRE)**[203] 6170 3-9-1 99 DarryllHolland 1 (M R Channon) *lw: led: rdn and hdd over 1f out: styd on same pce* **14/1**	96
10-6	3	1/2	**Better Hand (IRE)**[15] 1443 3-8-12 96 RyanMoore 2 (M R Channon) *hld up: hdwy over 2f out: rdn over 1f out: styd on same pce* **10/1**[3]	92
140-	4	12	**Ridge Dance**[189] 6489 3-8-12 108 JimmyFortune 4 (J H M Gosden) *trckd ldrs: rdn over 2f out: wknd over 1f out* **9/4**[2]	68

2m 10.54s (4.74) **Going Correction** +0.40s/f (Good) **4 Ran SP% 108.4**
Speed ratings (Par 107): **97,94,94,84**
CSF £9.31 TOTE £1.50; EX 7.10.

Owner Gestut Ammerland **Bred** Britton House Stud **Trained** Newmarket, Suffolk

FOCUS

A fair contest despite the small field but the pace was moderate and the time was almost 3 secs slower than the following handicap. The winner was different class to the second and third and looked value for more like six lengths, but he did not need to improve on previous course form.

NOTEBOOK

Kandahar Run is a generally progressive colt and built on his recent effort in the Feilden Stakes, scoring in comfortable fashion. He has some big entries, including the Derby, and connections are undecided as to his next target at this point. (op 4-7 tchd 4-6)

Meeriss(IRE), stepping up a furlong in trip for this seasonal debut, made the running at a steady gallop and, although no match for the winner, battled back up the hill to get the better of the third. He looks the sort for the King Edward VII at Royal Ascot, although his stamina is not guaranteed and connections may opt to stay at this trip. (op 12-1 tchd 16-1)

Better Hand(IRE), who looked dull in his coat, has been held in better company since winning his maiden, seemed to run his race but this appears to be as good as he is. (tchd 9-1)

Ridge Dance, whose best effort last season was when fourth in the Royal Lodge, looked fit but dropped out rather tamely and may need softer ground to produce his best. (op 11-4)

1811 STAN JAMES ON TELETEXT 630 H'CAP 1m 2f

5:10 (5:13) (Class 2) (0-100,99) 3-Y-O

£12,462 (£3,732; £1,866; £934; £466; £234) Stalls Low

Form				RPR
521-	1		**Dr Faustus (IRE)**[238] 5227 3-8-8 89 RyanMoore 2 (Sir Michael Stoute) *lw: chsd ldrs: led 3f out: styd on wl* **5/4**[1]	105+
00-4	2	3	**Ramona Chase**[15] 1441 3-8-11 92 JamieSpencer 11 (S Kirk) *on toes: hld up: plld hrd: hdwy over 2f out: rdn over 1f out: styd on same pce fnl f* **10/1**	99
05-2	3	1/2	**Woolfall Treasure**[12] 1526 3-8-4 85 JohnEgan 1 (G G Margarson) *hld up: racd keenly: hdwy over 2f out: rdn to chse wnr and hung rt over 1f out: styd on same pce* **28/1**	91
5-04	4	3 1/4	**Siberian Tiger (IRE)**[49] 902 3-9-4 99 DarryllHolland 6 (M R Channon) *trckd ldrs: outpcd 3f out: rallied 2f out: wknd ins fnl f* **25/1**	99
0-12	5	5	**Drill Sergeant**[10] 1570 3-9-0 95 JoeFanning 4 (M Johnston) *led tl 3f out: rdn and wknd wl over 1f out* **6/1**[3]	85
215-	6	4 1/2	**Noble Citizen (USA)**[205] 6120 3-8-4 85 oh3 RichardMullen 3 (D M Simcock) *hld up: plld hrd: hdwy over 2f out: rdn: hung rt and wknd over 1f out* **40/1**	66
101-	7	7	**Fitzroy Crossing (USA)**[222] 5691 3-8-7 88 GregFairley 10 (M Johnston) *on toes: chsd ldrs: rdn over 3f out: wknd over 2f out* **16/1**	55
6600	8	1/2	**Dalkey Girl (IRE)**[8] 1595 3-8-4 85 DavidKinsella 9 (V Smith) *hld up: hdwy over 3f out: rdn and wknd over 2f out* **50/1**	51
51-5	9	4	**Mountain Pride (IRE)**[15] 1443 3-8-4 85 oh1 JimmyQuinn 5 (J L Dunlop) *chsd ldrs: rdn over 2f out: wknd over 1f out* **14/1**	43
21-	10	18	**Cuban Missile**[178] 6725 3-8-6 87 SteveDrowne 7 (R Charlton) *lw: trckd ldr: racd keenly: lost pl over 3f out: eased* **8/1**	9
31-3	P		**Pinkindie (USA)**[22] 1297 3-8-4 85 MartinDwyer 8 (E A L Dunlop) *lw: hld up: plld hrd: hung rt 1/2-way: sn p.u and dismntd* **5/1**[2]	—

2m 7.58s (1.78) **Going Correction** +0.40s/f (Good) **11 Ran SP% 119.8**
Speed ratings (Par 105): **108,105,105,102,98 95,89,89,85,71** —
CSF £14.97 CT £249.65 TOTE £2.20: £1.30, £3.80, £4.30; EX 18.40.

Owner Gainsborough **Bred** Gainsborough Stud Management Ltd **Trained** Newmarket, Suffolk

FOCUS

This looked a competitive affair on paper, but the betting was very one-sided and the market proved spot-on. The time was decent for the grade and the runner-up sets the level. Good form.

NOTEBOOK

Dr Faustus(IRE) ◆ came home well clear in a time around three seconds faster than Kandahar Run in the steadily-run Listed race that preceded this. An easy maiden winner after his Leicester second to 1000 Guineas fancy Spacious, he has a middle-distance pedigree and was open to plenty of improvement over this extra 2f. In a race in which several runners pulled much too hard, Dr Faustus chased the pace until going to the front around 3f out. He was soon in charge, and they finished pretty much in single file behind him, which strongly suggests the form is sound. He was no doubt leniently treated here off 89, but he might well turn out a Group horse and so would still be of interest off a new mark in the high-90s. It would be no surprise if the King George V Handicap at Royal Ascot was on the agenda, although he is also entered in the King Edward VII. (tchd 11-8)

Ramona Chase, gelded since last season, was still headstrong and ran really well in the circumstances. Dropped right out early on, he made headway on the far side of the pack to get within a length or two of the winner running into the Dip and, although no match for that rival, he kept on well for second with the rest fairly strung out behind. (op 8-1)

Woolfall Treasure ran into a smart rival when second to Bushman in a Windsor maiden, and he had another stiff enough task here. He ran well and an ordinary maiden would be there for the taking, although there is no reason he cannot win a nice handicap. (op 33-1)

Siberian Tiger(IRE), a Listed winner as a juvenile, ran respectably giving weight all round but in the end was well beaten. He possibly found this longer trip just a bit too far. (op 20-1)

Drill Sergeant led for much of the way but ended up beaten too far to have paid Derby fancy Curtain Call much of a compliment. The ground may have been on the fast side for him. (tchd 5-1)

Noble Citizen(USA), a 7f nursery winner, was not sure to stay this longer trip and did not help himself by racing freely.

Pinkindie(USA) was quite keen under restraint and had to be pulled up soon after halfway with what looked like a leg injury. (op 6-1 tchd 7-1)

1812 STANJAMESUK.COM/CASINO H'CAP 1m 4f

5:45 (5:48) (Class 2) (0-100,97) 4-Y-O+ £12,952 (£3,854; £1,926; £962) Stalls Centre

Form				RPR
114-	1		**Ajaan**[226] 5574 4-8-10 89 (b) TedDurcan 1 (H R A Cecil) *hld up: hdwy over 3f out: led over 1f out: sn swvd rt and bmpd rival: hdd and hung lft ins fnl f: sn swvd rt and barged rival: r.o to ld post* **7/1**	106+
205-	2	hd	**Camps Bay (USA)**[226] 5574 4-8-13 92 JimCrowley 10 (Mrs A J Perrett) *lw: hld up: hdwy over 3f out: rdn, hung lft and bmpd rival 1f out: sn led: hung rt ins fnl f: sn swvd lft and barged rival: hdd post* **13/2**[3]	106
512-	3	2	**Silver Suitor (IRE)**[260] 4572 4-8-8 87 TQuinn 7 (D R C Elsworth) *h.d.w: lw: trckd ldrs: led over 2f out: hdd over 1f out: stl ev ch whn hmpd 1f out: styd on towards fin* **5/1**[2]	102+
54-3	4	4 1/2	**Rayhani (USA)**[13] 1503 5-9-2 95 MartinDwyer 9 (M P Tregoning) *lw: prom: rdn over 2f out: wknd fnl f* **7/1**	99
14-3	5	3 1/2	**Bid For Glory**[16] 1427 4-9-4 97 DarryllHolland 4 (H J Collingridge) *hld up: hdwy over 2f out: rdn and wknd over 1f out* **8/1**	95
215-	6	6	**Pentatonic**[275] 4089 5-9-1 94 JamieSpencer 3 (L M Cumani) *hld up: hdwy over 2f out: rdn and wknd over 1f out* **5/1**[2]	83
126-	7	17	**Generous Jem**[218] 5767 5-8-7 86 JohnEgan 11 (G G Margarson) *swtg: hld up in tch: rdn over 2f out: sn wknd* **20/1**	48
0104	8	nk	**Tartan Tie**[11] 1544 4-8-9 88 JoeFanning 5 (M Johnston) *chsd ldr: hung rt fr 1/2-way: rdn to ld over 3f out: hdd & wknd over 2f out* **14/1**	49
1-40	9	7	**Invasian (IRE)**[91] 410 7-8-11 90 (e) MickyFenton 6 (P W D'Arcy) *led over 8f: sn wknd* **28/1**	40
114-	10	37	**Maid To Believe**[218] 5767 4-9-4 97 EddieAhern 12 (J L Dunlop) *swtg: prom: reminders 1/2-way: wknd over 3f out* **14/1**	—
1-41	11	22	**Celtic Spirit (IRE)**[11] 1544 5-9-2 95 RyanMoore 8 (G L Moore) *b: hld up: wknd wl over 3f out* **4/1**[1]	—

2m 34.38s (0.88) **Going Correction** +0.40s/f (Good) **11 Ran SP% 124.3**
Speed ratings (Par 109): **113,112,111,108,106 102,90,90,86,61 46**
CSF £55.22 CT £256.25 TOTE £9.60: £2.30, £2.80, £2.50; EX 84.70 Place 6 £149.40, Place 5 £44.80.

Owner Niarchos Family **Bred** Miss K Rausing & Course Investment Corporation **Trained** Newmarket, Suffolk

■ Stewards' Enquiry : Jim Crowley four-day ban (reduced to 3 on appeal): careless riding (May 18-20)

Ted Durcan four-day ban: careless riding (May 18-21)

FOCUS

This good handicap was run at a strong pace but produced a rough and unsatisfactory finish that involved three lightly raced and progressive four-year-olds, all of whom have the potential to challenge for big handicaps now.

NOTEBOOK

Ajaan is clearly not straightforward but improved last year for the addition of blinkers. He looked fit for this reappearance and produced a fine turn of foot to come from the back and looked like drawing away going into the final furlong, only to swerve badly right under pressure into Silver Suitor. A switch of the whip caused him to hang left, then he again dived right with the whip switched back . With Camps Bay edging left, there was a collision that did neither horse any favours but Ajaan just got his head in front. He is clearly quirky but there is no doubt about his ability. (tchd 13-2)

Camps Bay(USA), five lengths behind the winner when they met last autumn, was meeting that rival on the same terms. He put in a strong run down the middle of the track and was holding his own when arguably coming out worse in a collision with the winner close to the finish. He enjoys a strong end-to-end gallop and his stable has done well with similar sorts. He has been tried over further but this seems to be his best trip. (op 15-2 tchd 8-1)

Silver Suitor(IRE) ◆, a big individual, showed up from the start, travelling well, and was far from finished when the meat in the sandwich going to the final furlong on this seasonal return. He looks on a nice mark and has a decent handicap in him if connections can resist the temptation to take up more ambitious entries. A return to further will suit and he looks most progressive. (op 4-1 tchd 6-1)

Rayhani(USA) looks an out-and-out galloper. He plugged on better than the rest while still looking in the grip of the Handicapper. (op 15-2 tchd 13-2)

Bid For Glory, who ran well in a conditions race recently, was trying his longest trip to date and seemed to find it a little too far after appearing a big threat. (op 9-1)

Pentatonic can progress for this seasonal return, having briefly looked like getting involved inside the final 3f before weakening. (op 13-2)

Generous Jem ran considerably better than the bare form, as she was allowed to coast the final furlong when beaten, still having been in the firing line going into the final quarter-mile. Official explanation: jockey said mare had no more to give

Maid To Believe Official explanation: jockey said filly hung right on the ground

Celtic Spirit(IRE) was sent off favourite but dropped off the back of the pack as if something was amiss and was allowed to come home in his own time. Official explanation: jockey said gelding lost its action (op 9-2 tchd 7-2)

T/Jkpt: Not won. T/Plt: £190.50 to a £1 stake. Pool: £175,763.62. 673.25 winning tickets. T/Qpdt: £46.70 to a £1 stake. Pool: £7,337.06. 116.05 winning tickets. CR

1480 THIRSK (L-H)
Saturday, May 3

OFFICIAL GOING: Good
The ground was reckoned to be 'mainly on the dead side'.
Wind: Moderate, half against Weather: Fine

1813 TOTESPORT BETXTRA EUROPEAN BREEDERS' FUND NOVICE STKS 5f
2:00 (2:00) (Class 4) 2-Y-O £5,180 (£1,541; £770; £384) Stalls High

Form RPR
1 **1** **Dispol Kylie (IRE)**[21] 1324 2-8-11 0 JamieMoriarty(3) 1 84
(P T Midgley) *w ldrs: led over 1f out: kpt on wl towards fin* **13/2**[3]
1 **2** hd **Polish Pride**[22] 1303 2-8-11 0 MarkLawson(3) 6 83
(M Brittain) *chsd ldrs: swtchd lft over 1f out: chal ins fnl f: no ex nr fin* **7/1**
1 **3** ¾ **Lisburn (IRE)**[14] 1474 2-9-0 0 TWilliams 2 81
(M Brittain) *led tl over 1f out: kpt on wl ins fnl f* **13/2**[3]
1 **4** hd **Fuaigh Mor (IRE)**[18] 1384 2-8-7 0 PaulHanagan 5 73
(A Bailey) *sn outpcd: hdwy 2f out: kpt on fnl f* **10/1**
5 1 ½ **Spin Cycle (IRE)** 2-8-12 0 TomEaves 4 74+
(B Smart) *trckd ldrs: t.k.h: effrt and hung lft over 1f out: kpt on ins fnl f: will improve* **6/4**[1]
1 **6** 8 **Kate The Great**[29] 1177 2-9-0 0 PatCosgrave 3 46
(M J Wallace) *trckd ldrs: t.k.h: edgd lft over 1f out: sn wknd* **4/1**[2]
7 11 **Lunar Romance** 2-8-7 0 RobertWinston 7 —
(T J Pitt) *s.s: in rr: bhd fnl 2f* **22/1**
61.87 secs (2.27) **Going Correction** +0.45s/f (Yiel) **7 Ran SP% 112.6**
Speed ratings (Par 95): **99,98,97,97,94 81,64**
CSF £48.48 TOTE £6.30: £2.60, £3.10; EX 43.40.
Owner W B Imison **Bred** Century Farms **Trained** Westow, N Yorks

FOCUS
A fair novice event with five previous winners in the line-up and rated as high as it is likely to go.

NOTEBOOK
Dispol Kylie(IRE), who had the worst of the draw, travelled strongly but in the end it was a very close call. (op 7-1)
Polish Pride, who gave problems going to the start, had to pulled off the fence to make her final effort. In the end she was only just denied. (tchd 15-2)
Lisburn(IRE), on her toes beforehand, took them along and to her credit stuck on in good style all the way to the end. (op 17-2)
Fuaigh Mor(IRE), without a penalty for her first-time out win in selling company at Warwick, is nothing at all to look at. She struggled to keep up but was closing down the three ahead of her at the line. (op 8-1 tchd 7-1)
Spin Cycle(IRE) ◆, the only colt in the line-up, became upset in the pre-parade ring and was led round the paddock by his trainer. A good-bodied individual, he travelled very strongly but threw away his chance by hanging badly left when called on for a serious effort. This will have taught him plenty and he should be a ready-made winner of a maiden race. (op 7-4 tchd 15-8)
Kate The Great, on the leg and narrow, had a hard race when winning on her debut on the all-weather. She would not settle and edging towards the centre, in the end she dropped right out. (op 7-2)

1814 TOTESPORT 0800 221 221 MAIDEN STKS 1m 4f
2:35 (2:35) (Class 5) 3-Y-O+ £3,885 (£1,156; £577; £288) Stalls Low

Form RPR
04-2 **1** **Criterion**[19] 1367 3-8-8 75 RobertWinston 1 71
(Sir Michael Stoute) *chsd ldrs: hrd rdn and hung lft over 2f out: styd on strly ins fnl f: led nr fin* **2/1**[1]
50 **2** ¾ **Key Decision (IRE)**[18] 1382 4-9-10 0 PJMcDonald(3) 2 71
(G A Swinbank) *t.k.h early: led: hdd over 1f out: led jst ins fnl f: hdd nr fin* **40/1**
56-2 **3** hd **Wells Lyrical (IRE)**[7] 1628 3-8-8 72 TomEaves 6 69
(B Smart) *trckd ldrs: effrt 2f out: hung lft: styd on strly ins fnl f* **4/1**[3]
4 **4** 2 **Stock Market (USA)**[19] 1367 3-8-8 0 TGMcLaughlin 8 66+
(E A L Dunlop) *trckd ldrs: wnt 2nd over 2f out: slt ld over 1f out: hdd jst ins fnl f: wknd towards fin* **9/4**[2]
0-0 **5** ¾ **Eddie Dowling**[15] 1446 3-8-1 0 ThomasO'Brien(7) 5 65
(M R Channon) *sn prom: effrt over 2f out: styd on wl ins fnl f* **80/1**
0 **6** 1 **St Johns Wood**[14] 1490 3-8-8 0 DavidAllan 9 65+
(M W Easterby) *in rr: pushed along over 4f out: hdwy and swtchd ins 2f out: kpt on steadily* **33/1**
7 nk **River Danube**[62] 5-9-13 0 PaulMulrennan 4 65
(T J Fitzgerald) *dwlt: towards rr: kpt on fnl 3f: nvr nr ldrs* **50/1**
3 **8** shd **Sphere (IRE)**[39] 1014 3-8-3 0 PaulHanagan 13 57
(J R Fanshawe) *hld up in mid-div: hdwy over 2f out: kpt on: nvr nr ldrs* **9/2**
9 4 ½ **Osteopathic Care (IRE)** 4-9-8 0 NeilBrown(5) 12 57
(Miss Tracy Waggott) *s.i.s: in rr: sme hdwy over 3f out: nvr on terms* **66/1**
02- **10** 8 **Lyon's Hill**[62] 6700 4-9-13 0 DeanMcKeown 10 44
(M Mullineaux) *tubed: chsd ldrs: drvn along 7f out: lost pl over 2f out* **66/1**
6 **11** nk **Cheers For Thea (IRE)**[16] 1429 3-8-0 0 DuranFentiman(3) 7 37
(T D Easterby) *in rr: lost pl over 2f out: sn bhd* **33/1**
0250 **12** 8 **Feeling Peckish (USA)**[11] 1551 4-9-10 40 (t) LeeVickers(3) 11 31
(M C Chapman) *sn chsng ldrs: lost pl over 3f out: sn bhd* **150/1**
2m 42.3s (6.10) **Going Correction** +0.45s/f (Yiel)
WFA 3 from 4yo+ 19lb **12 Ran SP% 117.4**
Speed ratings (Par 103): **97,96,96,95,94 93,93,93,90,85 85,79**
CSF £90.83 TOTE £3.10: £1.30, £9.90, £1.60; EX 106.80.
Owner The Queen **Bred** The Queen **Trained** Newmarket, Suffolk

FOCUS
A modest maiden run at just a steady pace. The winner snatched thr prize from out of the fire and helps set the standard, but the third is probably the best guide to the level.

1815 TOTESPORT.COM H'CAP 7f
3:10 (3:10) (Class 4) (0-85,83) 4-Y-O+ £5,180 (£1,541; £770; £384) Stalls Low

Form RPR
1322 **1** **Yes One (IRE)**[15] 1450 4-8-9 74 DO'Donohoe 3 87+
(K A Ryan) *drvn along to chse ldrs after 1f: led over 1f out: hld on towards fin* **3/1**[1]
30-2 **2** nk **Goodbye**[7] 1612 4-9-1 80 RobertWinston 14 92+
(G A Swinbank) *hld up in mid-div: smooth hdwy to chal 2f out: hung lft: no ex wl ins fnl f* **7/2**[2]
460- **3** 3 ¾ **Musca (IRE)**[228] 5505 4-8-11 76 PaulHanagan 6 78
(C Grant) *mid-div: hdwy over 1f out: styd on wl ins fnl f* **8/1**
0-25 **4** 2 ¾ **Ancient Cross**[14] 1490 4-8-5 70 DaleGibson 4 65
(M W Easterby) *chsd ldrs: one pce fnl 2f* **12/1**
0-00 **5** nk **Nuit Sombre (IRE)**[35] 1069 8-9-0 79 (p) SilvestreDeSousa 5 73
(G A Harker) *led tl over 2f out: wknd fnl f* **33/1**
0-60 **6** ¾ **Overrule (USA)**[14] 1481 4-9-4 83 TomEaves 1 75+
(B Ellison) *s.i.s: hdwy over 2f out: kpt on wl fnl f* **22/1**
-001 **7** 1 **Bold Marc (IRE)**[7] 1612 6-9-0 79 AndrewElliott 7 68
(K R Burke) *chsd ldrs: wknd fnl f* **11/2**[3]
4-00 **8** 3 **Society Music (IRE)**[14] 1485 6-8-7 72 RoystonFfrench 12 53
(M Dods) *hld up towards rr: kpt on fnl 2f: nvr a factor* **20/1**
00-0 **9** 1 ¾ **Countdown**[14] 1481 6-9-1 80 DavidAllan 8 56
(T D Easterby) *in rr: sme hdwy on wd outside over 2f out: nvr nr ldrs* **14/1**
-000 **10** nk **Provost**[7] 1612 4-8-5 77 NSLawes(7) 2 52
(M W Easterby) *mid-div: effrt over 2f out: wknd over 1f out* **50/1**
5101 **11** 1 **Dudley Docker (IRE)**[11] 1552 6-8-8 73 (b) PaulMulrennan 10 46
(C R Dore) *s.i.s: a in rr* **9/1**
-046 **12** 2 **Wovoka (IRE)**[22] 1308 5-8-11 76 FergalLynch 9 43
(D W Barker) *s.i.s: a in rr* **9/1**
6/06 **13** 11 **Gramm**[22] 1301 5-8-3 75 BradleyRoper(7) 13 13
(M W Easterby) *chsd ldrs: drvn over 4f out: lost pl 3f out: sn bhd* **40/1**
1m 28.67s (1.47) **Going Correction** +0.45s/f (Yiel) **13 Ran SP% 124.5**
Speed ratings (Par 105): **109,108,104,101,100 100,98,95,93,93 91,89,77**
CSF £13.05 CT £82.92 TOTE £3.90: £2.00, £1.80, £2.80; EX 16.00.
Owner Mrs J Ryan **Bred** Carl Holt **Trained** Hambleton, N Yorks

FOCUS
A good handicap for the grade run at a strong pace and solid form, the first two both deserving credit.

1816 TOTESCOOP6 THIRSK HUNT CUP (H'CAP) 1m
3:45 (3:48) (Class 2) (0-100,99) 4-Y-O+ £11,656 (£3,468; £1,733; £865) Stalls Low

Form RPR
0-02 **1** **Extraterrestrial**[14] 1481 4-8-5 86 PaulHanagan 15 101+
(R A Fahey) *hld up in rr: hdwy and n.m.r over 2f out: chal over 1f out: led ins fnl f: edgd lft: kpt on wl* **4/1**[2]
-522 **2** 1 ½ **Regal Parade**[22] 1308 4-8-6 90 PJMcDonald(3) 3 99
(D Nicholls) *in tch: hdwy to chal 2f out: sn hdd: led over 1f out: hdd ins fnl f: no ex whn sltly hmpd wl ins fnl f* **3/1**[1]
0220 **3** 1 ½ **Capable Guest (IRE)**[14] 1469 6-8-11 92 RobertWinston 9 97
(M R Channon) *mid-div: effrt over 2f out: styd on wl ins fnl f* **8/1**
000- **4** ¾ **My Paris**[210] 6011 7-8-7 91 AndrewMullen(3) 4 94
(Ollie Pears) *w ldr: led 2f out: sn hdd and no ex* **11/1**
00-1 **5** ½ **Collateral Damage (IRE)**[39] 1016 5-8-1 85 DuranFentiman(3) 2 87
(T D Easterby) *in rr: hdwy over 2f out: kpt on wl fnl f* **8/1**
0/5- **6** 3 **Scartozz**[69] 6-9-1 99 (t) JerryO'Dwyer(3) 7 94
(M Botti) *led tl 2f out: wknd appr fnl f* **14/1**
-110 **7** ¾ **The Osteopath (IRE)**[14] 1481 5-8-4 85 oh1 DaleGibson 1 79
(M Dods) *in tch: effrt over 2f out: kpt on same pce* **12/1**
130- **8** shd **Vicious Warrior**[154] 7002 9-8-5 86 DeanMcKeown 14 79
(R M Whitaker) *in tch: fdd over 1f out* **33/1**
-006 **9** 1 **White Deer (USA)**[14] 1481 4-8-4 85 SilvestreDeSousa 12 76
(D Nicholls) *in rr: styd on fnl 2f: nvr nr ldrs* **12/1**
-000 **10** 1 ¼ **Very Wise**[7] 1633 6-9-0 95 PaulMulrennan 10 83
(W J Haggas) *in tch: effrt 3f out: wknd over 1f out* **22/1**
000- **11** 3 ½ **Flipando (IRE)**[204] 6155 7-8-10 96 NeilBrown(5) 8 76+
(T D Barron) *in tch: wkng whn n.m.r over 1f out* **20/1**
-440 **12** nk **Rio Riva**[10] 1569 6-9-3 98 TomEaves 6 77
(Miss J A Camacho) *chsd ldrs: drvn over 2f out: lost pl over 1f out* **7/1**[3]
-000 **13** 7 **Minority Report**[14] 1481 8-8-6 87 PaulFessey 5 50
(D Nicholls) *s.i.s: a in rr* **20/1**
42-5 **14** 11 **Orpen Wide (IRE)**[22] 6 6-8-6 87 DavidAllan 11 25
(M C Chapman) *in rr: drvn over 4f out: bhd fnl 2f* **25/1**
1m 42.39s (2.29) **Going Correction** +0.45s/f (Yiel) **14 Ran SP% 130.8**
Speed ratings (Par 109): **106,104,103,102,101 98,97,96,96,95 92,91,84,73**
CSF £16.59 CT £102.29 TOTE £4.80: £2.20, £1.90, £3.30; EX 17.30 Trifecta £89.70 Pool: £429.90 - 3.40 winning tickets..
Owner G J Paver **Bred** Lostford Manor Stud **Trained** Musley Bank, N Yorks
■ Stewards' Enquiry : Paul Hanagan one-day ban; careless riding (May 18)

FOCUS
A strong pace and solid form rated around the third and fifth. There ought to be even better to come from the winner who overcame an outside draw.

NOTEBOOK
Extraterrestrial, having just his third start for this yard, looked a picture of wellbeing. He did well to overcome the worst draw of all and travelling strongly when having to search for racing room, should be capable of even better. (op 3-1 tchd 9-2 in a place)
Regal Parade is at the top of his game but he was safely held when the winner went across his bows inside the last. (op 11-2)
Capable Guest(IRE), 4lb higher than his last winning mark, had the visor left off. He stuck on really strongly inside the last but is not easy to win with. (op 10-1)
My Paris, who took from this same mark a year ago, was having his first outing for his new yard. He was in the firing line throughout and was only found wanting in the closing stages. (op 12-1 tchd 10-1)
Collateral Damage(IRE) stayed on when it was all over and needs either further or more give underfoot. (op 7-1)
Scartozz, a winner eight times in Italy, was having his first outing since February. A grand, big type, he has a pronounced knee action and with him it will be a case of the softer the ground the better. (op 16-1)
The Osteopath(IRE), 1lb out of the handicap, will continue to struggle 8lb higher than his last winning mark. (tchd 14-1)

1817 TOTESPORT BETXTRA WIN ONLY MAIDEN STKS 7f
4:20 (4:22) (Class 4) 3-Y-O £5,180 (£1,541; £770; £384) Stalls Low

Form RPR
43-6 **1** **Jonny Lesters Hair (IRE)**[16] 1426 3-9-3 73 (e[1]) DavidAllan 9 74
(T D Easterby) *mde all: edgd rt fnl f: hld on wl* **4/1**[2]
3 **2** 2 ¾ **Great Knight (IRE)**[22] 1311 3-9-3 0 PaulMulrennan 7 67
(W J Haggas) *trckd ldrs: wnt 2nd over 3f out: kpt on same pce fnl f* **11/4**[1]
3 **3** nk **Devinius (IRE)**[35] 1073 3-8-9 0 PJMcDonald(3) 14 61
(G A Swinbank) *trckd ldrs: kpt on same pce fnl f* **8/1**
0-2 **4** hd **Indy Driver**[13] 1504 3-9-3 0 OscarUrbina 12 66
(J R Fanshawe) *trcking ldrs: effrt 3f out: hung lft and kpt on same pce appr fnl f* **6/1**[3]
3-23 **5** 2 **Everything**[15] 1452 3-8-9 70 JamieMoriarty(3) 6 55
(P T Midgley) *chsd ldrs: one pce fnl 2f* **4/1**[2]
6 2 ½ **Virtuality (USA)** 3-8-12 0 TomEaves 5 49
(B Smart) *hld up in rr: effrt over 2f out: kpt on fnl f* **22/1**
56- **7** 5 **Orpen Bid (IRE)**[182] 6634 3-8-12 0 PatrickMathers 2 35
(A M Crow) *in rr: effrt on wd outside 3f out: nvr a factor* **100/1**

00- 8 shd **Pentandra (IRE)**[182] 6649 3-8-12 0.............................. J-PGuillambert 8 35
(J G Given) *mid-div: drvn over 3f out: nvr on terms* **22/1**

5 9 shd **Merrion Tiger (IRE)**[16] 1429 3-9-3 0.............................. AndrewElliott 13 39+
(K R Burke) *s.i.s: kpt on fnl 2f: nvr on terms* **28/1**

440- 10 nk **Another Decree**[211] 5974 3-9-3 78.............................. RoystonFfrench 3 39
(M Dods) *mid-div: drvn over 4f out: nvr a factor* **66/1**

0- 11 3 1/2 **Willkandoo (USA)**[175] 6763 3-9-3 0.............................. DO'Donohoe 4 29
(K A Ryan) *chsd ldrs: lost pl over 2f out* **33/1**

00- 12 5 **Graze On And On**[179] 6698 3-8-12 0.............................. GrahamGibbons 10 11
(J J Quinn) *chsd ldrs: lost pl 3f out* **100/1**

06- 13 1 1/4 **Fantasy Fighter (IRE)**[210] 6022 3-9-3 0.............................. PatCosgrave 11 12
(J J Quinn) *swvd rt s: a in rr* **100/1**

1m 30.38s (3.18) **Going Correction** +0.45s/f (Yiel) 13 Ran SP% **121.2**
Speed ratings (Par 101): **99,95,95,95,93 90,84,84,84,83 79,74,72**
CSF £14.82 TOTE £6.00: £1.80, £1.80, £2.60; EX 22.40.
Owner Habtons Baggie Rams **Bred** Gary O'Reilly **Trained** Great Habton, N Yorks

FOCUS
A modest maiden with the winner largely given his own way out in front. The first three are all rated as having shown slight improvement.

1818 TOTESPORT BETXTRA SHOW ONLY H'CAP 5f
4:55 (4:56) (Class 4) (0-80,80) 4-Y-0+ **£5,180** (£1,541; £770; £384) **Stalls** High

Form RPR

0143 1 **Royal Envoy (IRE)**[10] 1567 5-8-7 72.............................. TolleyDean(3) 18 86
(D Shaw) *racd stands' side: w ldr: led that gp and overall jst ins fnl f: styd on strly* **11/1**

3133 2 2 1/4 **Dorn Dancer (IRE)**[10] 1561 6-8-5 67.............................. RoystonFfrench 7 73+
(D W Barker) *racd stands' side: in rr: drvn over 2f out: hdwy over 1f out: styd on strly to take 2nd overall nr fin* **4/1**[1]

666- 3 1 **Deserted Dane (USA)**[228] 5506 4-9-0 79.............................. PJMcDonald(3) 5 81
(G A Swinbank) *racd far side: chsd ldr: led that gp 1f out: kpt on wl: 1st of 5 that gp* **9/1**

133- 4 hd **Charles Parnell (IRE)**[182] 6639 5-9-0 76.............................. FergalLynch 1 78
(M Dods) *racd far side: chsd ldrs: tk 2nd that side jst ins fnl f: kpt on wl: 2nd of 5 that gp* **9/1**

054- 5 3/4 **The Nifty Fox**[176] 6743 4-9-2 78.............................. DavidAllan 13 77
(T D Easterby) *racd stands' side: trckd ldrs: kpt on same pce appr fnl f* **10/1**

6432 6 3/4 **Guto**[15] 1451 5-8-7 72.............................. AndrewMullen(3) 12 68
(W J H Ratcliffe) *led stands' side tl jst ins fnl f: no ex* **9/2**[2]

00-6 7 3/4 **The History Man (IRE)**[5] 1677 5-8-5 67..............(be) DeanMcKeown 6 61
(M Mullineaux) *led far side tl 1f out: no ex: 3rd of 5 that gp* **40/1**

04-0 8 hd **Prospect Court**[21] 1327 6-9-0 76.............................. PaulMulrennan 11 69
(A C Whillans) *racd stands' side: chsd ldrs: one pce fnl 2f* **25/1**

00-0 9 nk **He's A Humbug (IRE)**[22] 1300 4-8-12 79.............................. NeilBrown(5) 10 71
(K A Ryan) *racd stands' side: mid-div: hdwy 2f out: edgd lft: nvr trbld ldrs* **16/1**

0-00 10 1/2 **Mandurah (IRE)**[7] 1624 4-7-11 66 oh1.............................. OliveGaule(7) 14 56
(D Nicholls) *racd stands' side: chsd ldrs: wknd over 1f out* **16/1**

00-0 11 1/2 **Balakiref**[21] 1327 9-8-6 75.............................. JohnCavanagh(7) 8 63+
(M Dods) *dwlt: racd stands' side: hdwy and edgd lft 2f out: nvr nr ldrs* **33/1**

0-00 12 1 1/2 **Oranmore Castle (IRE)**[7] 1617 6-8-6 68.............................. PaulHanagan 15 51
(R A Fahey) *rrd s: racd stands' side: a in rr* **10/1**

300- 13 1/2 **Elkhorn**[194] 6381 6-9-4 80.............................. TomEaves 4 61
(Miss J A Camacho) *racd far side: hld up in tch: effrt over 2f out: wknd 1f out: 4th of 5 that gp* **25/1**

0435 14 1 1/2 **Tartatartufata**[7] 1624 6-8-3 72..............................(v) PatrickDonaghy(7) 3 48
(D Shaw) *s.s: racd far side: nvr on terms: last of 5 that gp* **15/2**[3]

00-0 15 1 **Just Joey**[40] 987 4-8-4 66 oh1.............................. DO'Donohoe 9 38
(J R Weymes) *racd stands' side: chsd ldrs on outer: fdd over 1f out* **40/1**

3-06 16 2 3/4 **Dakota Rain (IRE)**[15] 1451 6-9-4 80.............................. RobertWinston 17 42
(Jennie Candlish) *racd stands' side: mid-div: hung lft and lost pl over 1f out* **8/1**

/56- 17 hd **Tom Tower (IRE)**[351] 1802 4-8-4 66 oh1.............................. TWilliams 16 27
(A C Whillans) *racd stands' side: chsd ldrs: lost pl over 1f out* **66/1**

61.10 secs (1.50) **Going Correction** +0.45s/f (Yiel) 17 Ran SP% **136.3**
Speed ratings (Par 105): **106,102,100,100,99 98,96,96,96,95 94,92,91,88,87 82,82**
CSF £57.71 CT £458.10 TOTE £14.20: £3.30, £1.40, £3.20, £2.20; EX 72.90.
Owner The Circle Bloodstock I Limited **Bred** Northern Lights Bloodstock **Trained** Danethorpe, Notts
■ Stewards' Enquiry : Patrick Donaghy one-day ban: used whip down shoulder in forehand position (May 18)

FOCUS
An ordinary sprint handicap with five electing to race on the far side. There did not seem to be a lot between the two groups and a personal best from the winner.
Oranmore Castle(IRE) Official explanation: jockey said gelding reared as stalls opened
Tartatartufata Official explanation: jockey said mare missed the break
Dakota Rain(IRE) Official explanation: jockey said gelding hung left throughout

1819 BET ON US RACING AT TOTESPORT.COM H'CAP 6f
5:30 (5:32) (Class 5) (0-75,75) 3-Y-0 **£3,885** (£1,156; £577; £288) **Stalls** High

Form RPR

43-6 1 **Capone (IRE)**[15] 1453 3-8-8 68.............................. DominicFox(3) 11 74+
(Garry Moss) *racd stands' side: hld up in rr: rapid hdwy and swtchd lft jst ins fnl f: qckng to ld overall last 75yds: v readily* **40/1**

6-61 2 1 1/4 **My Kaiser Chief**[15] 1452 3-8-10 70.............................. AndrewMullen(3) 6 72
(W J H Ratcliffe) *racd far side: trckd ldrs: led that gp over 1f out: hung bdly rt ins fnl f: kpt on: 1st of 8 that gp* **10/1**

4156 3 1 3/4 **Fulford**[22] 1306 3-8-6 63.............................. TWilliams 10 59
(M Brittain) *racd stands' side: w ldr: led that gp over 2f out: hdd and no ex ins fnl f* **16/1**

-300 4 nk **Complete Frontline (GER)**[22] 1306 3-8-4 61 oh3.......... AndrewElliott 8 56
(K R Burke) *led far side 1f: chsd ldrs: kpt on wl fnl f: 2nd of 8 in that group* **33/1**

631- 5 3/4 **Gainshare**[171] 6812 3-8-9 71.............................. NeilBrown(5) 13 64
(T D Barron) *led stands' side tl over 2f out: kpt on same pce appr fnl f* **7/1**[2]

3-44 6 nk **Tamasou (IRE)**[17] 1396 3-8-9 66.............................. DaleGibson 1 58
(Garry Moss) *racd far side: trckd ldrs: kpt on same pce fnl f* **25/1**

5330 7 3/4 **Precipice**[22] 1315 3-8-4 68.............................. JamieKyne(7) 7 58
(D Carroll) *swtchd lft s and racd far side: mid-div: kpt on appr fnl f: 4th of 8 that gp* **25/1**

052- 8 1 **Best Suited**[227] 5520 3-8-6 63.............................. GrahamGibbons 2 49
(J J Quinn) *swvd rt s: racd far side: hdwy to ld that gp after 1f: hdd over 1f out: fdd ins fnl f: 5th of 8 in that group* **50/1**

0-60 9 3/4 **Baronovici (IRE)**[14] 1484 3-9-4 75.............................. FergalLynch 17 59
(D W Barker) *racd stands' side: chsd ldrs: wknd over 1f out* **14/1**

1 10 1 1/4 **Hazelrigg (IRE)**[15] 1453 3-9-4 75.............................. DavidAllan 12 55
(T D Easterby) *upset in stalls: racd stands' side: chsd ldrs on outer: effrt over 2f out: rdn and wknd over 1f out* **6/5**[1]

240- 11 1 **Lady Benjamin**[175] 6756 3-9-4 75.............................. LeeEnstone 14 52
(P C Haslam) *racd stands' side: chsd ldrs: lost pl over 1f out* **28/1**

-630 12 3/4 **Nawaaff**[16] 1426 3-8-9 73.............................. ThomasO'Brien(7) 16 47
(M R Channon) *dwlt: racd stands' side: nvr on terms* **12/1**

1325 13 3/4 **Lujiana**[14] 1475 3-8-6 63.............................. DeanMcKeown 15 35
(M Brittain) *racd stands' side: chsd ldrs: wknd over 1f out* **16/1**

16-6 14 4 **Tobar Suil Lady (IRE)**[46] 924 3-9-0 71.............................. DO'Donohoe 5 30
(K A Ryan) *racd far side: chsd ldrs: lost pl over 1f out: eased ins fnl f: 6th of 8 that gp* **20/1**

540- 15 5 **Red Delight (IRE)**[269] 4279 3-8-4 61.............................. PaulHanagan 9 4
(R A Fahey) *racd stands' side: in rr: bhd fnl 2f* **20/1**

005- 16 5 **Smileforawhile (IRE)**[246] 4995 3-8-11 68.............................. PaulMulrennan 4 —
(K A Ryan) *racd far side: in rr: wknd and eased over 1f out: 7th of 8 that gp* **40/1**

0-33 17 32 **Artistic License (IRE)**[36] 1066 3-9-1 72.............................. RobertWinston 3 —
(M R Channon) *bmpd and slipped s: racd far side: in rr: virtually p.u over 2f out: t.o: last of 8 that gp* **8/1**[3]

1m 15.59s (2.89) **Going Correction** +0.45s/f (Yiel) 17 Ran SP% **134.7**
Speed ratings (Par 99): **98,96,94,93,92 92,91,89,88,87 85,84,83,78,71 65,22**
CSF £403.50 CT £6616.75 TOTE £58.10: £8.10, £2.30, £3.00, £11.00; EX 444.10 Place 6 £71.54, Place 5 £9.11.
Owner Brooklands Racing **Bred** S J Macdonald **Trained** Loughborough, Leics

FOCUS
A modest three-year-old sprint handicap. The favourite had a genuine excuse and the third and fourth set the standard.
Artistic License(IRE) Official explanation: jockey said filly slipped on leaving stalls and never travelled thereafter
T/Plt: £54.90 to a £1 stake. Pool: £62,438.85. 829.25 winning tickets. T/Qpdt: £5.40 to a £1 stake. Pool: £3,658.14. 497.35 winning tickets. WG

CHURCHILL DOWNS (L-H)
Saturday, May 3

OFFICIAL GOING: Dirt course - fast; turf course - firm

1820a KENTUCKY DERBY (PRESENTED BY YUM! BRANDS) (GRADE 1) (3YO) (DIRT) 1m 2f (D)
11:04 (11:15) 3-Y-0 **£623,116** (£201,005; £100,503; £50,251; £30,151)

RPR

1 **Big Brown (USA)**[35] 1093 3-9-0 .... KDesormeaux 20 128
(R Dutrow Jr, U.S.A) *good early pace from outside draw to be 4th on outside after 2f, headway on outside to lead just over 2f out, driven out* **24/10**[1]

2 4 3/4 **Eight Belles (USA)**[27] 3-8-9 .... GSaez 5 114
(J Larry Jones, U.S.A) *close up in 5th, not much room and steadied 3f out, 4th straight, went 2nd 1 1/2f out, hard driven and edged left, no impression, broke down, dead* **131/10**

3 3 1/2 **Denis Of Cork (USA)**[28] 3-9-0 .... CHBorel 16 113
(David M Carroll, U.S.A) *last to over 3f out, headway towards inside to go 9th straight, switched to rail over 1f out, squeezed through on inside to go 3rd 150y out, kept on* **27/1**

4 2 3/4 **Tale Of Ekati (USA)**[28] 3-9-0 .... ECoa 2 108
(B Tagg, U.S.A) *in tight quarters and steadied after 1f, raced in 7th on inside, switched outside 3f out, 5th straight, soon hard ridden and one pace* **372/10**

5 3/4 **Recapturetheglory (USA)**[28] 3-9-0 .... EBaird 18 106
(L Roussel Iii, U.S.A) *raced in 3rd on outside, led over 3f out to just over 2f out, one pace* **49/1**

6 2 1/2 **Colonel John (USA)**[28] 3-9-0 .... CNakatani 10 102
(E G Harty, U.S.A) *steadied early, in rear til headway around outside over 4f out, 7th straight, no further headway* **47/10**[2]

7 3/4 **Anak Nakal (USA)**[28] 3-9-0 .... RBejarano 3 101
(N Zito, U.S.A) *in rear, 17th halfway, kept on steadily down outside final 3f but never a factor* **539/10**

8 nse **Pyro (USA)**[21] 3-9-0 .... SXBridgmohan 9 100
(S Asmussen, U.S.A) *held up in 18th, never a factor* **57/10**[3]

9 3/4 **Cowboy Cal (USA)**[21] 3-9-0 .... JRVelazquez 17 99
(T Pletcher, U.S.A) *raced in 2nd on outside, disputed lead briefly over 3f out, still close 3rd on inside entering straight, weakened* **392/10**

10 3 3/4 **Z Fortune (USA)**[21] 3-9-0 .... RAlbarado 6 92
(S Asmussen, U.S.A) *raced in 8th, 6th straight, soon one pace* **192/10**

11 1 1/2 **Smooth Air (USA)**[35] 1093 3-9-0 .... MCruz 12 90
(B Stutts, U.S.A) *in rear early, went 10th over 2f out, soon beaten* **42/1**

12 1 3/4 **Visionaire (USA)**[21] 3-9-0 .... JLezcano 8 87
(M Matz, U.S.A) *stumbled start, steadied after 1f, held up in 19th, sone late headway* **253/10**

13 1 1/2 **Court Vision (USA)**[28] 3-9-0 ....(b) GKGomez 4 84
(W Mott, U.S.A) *midfield when carried right and bumped after 1f, 13th halfway, never a factor* **177/10**

14 nk **Z Humor (USA)**[28] 3-9-0 .... RRDouglas 11 83
(W Mott, U.S.A) *carried ledt early, snatched up in traffic after 1f, always towards rear* **638/10**

15 7 1/4 **Cool Coal Man (USA)**[21] 3-9-0 .... JRLeparoux 1 70
(N Zito, U.S.A) *tracked leader on inside, 4th halfway, weakened well over 2f out* **44/1**

16 nk **Bob Black Jack (USA)**[28] 3-9-0 ....(b) RMigliore 13 70
(James M Kasparoff, U.S.A) *led to over 3f out, weakened* **294/10**

17 4 3/4 **Gayego (USA)**[21] 3-9-0 .... MESmith 19 61
(P Lobo, U.S.A) *midfield, 9th halfway, weakened well over 2f out* **189/10**

18 12 **Big Truck (USA)**[21] 3-9-0 .... JCastellano 7 40
(B Tagg, U.S.A) *bumped and steadied after 1f, in touch in midfield til weakened over 3f out* **286/10**

19 2 **Adriano (USA)**[42] 3-9-0 .... EPrado 15 36
(H G Motion, U.S.A) *in tight quarters when hampered after 1f, raced in 14th, never a factor* **287/10**

20 8 3/4 **Monba (USA)**[21] 3-9-0 ....(b) RADominguez 14 20
(T Pletcher, U.S.A) *in rear of midfield til dropped to last over 2f out* **315/10**

2m 1.82s (0.63) 20 Ran SP% **119.8**
PARI-MUTUEL: WIN 6.80; PL (1-2) 5.00, 10.60; SHOW (1-2-3) 4.80, 6.40, 11.60; SF 141.60.
Owner IEAH Stables & P Pompa Jr **Bred** Monticule **Trained** USA

NOTEBOOK

Big Brown(USA), unbeaten in his previous three starts and an impressive winner of the Florida Derby on his last outing, was billed by his trainer as a freak, and he certainly confirmed Dutrow's high opinion of him with an imperious display. From the widest draw he showed his customary early pace but that was insufficient to get to the front. His rider appeared happy to track the pace, though, and while he was giving ground away racing on the outside of the pack, he benefited from avoiding kickback and potential trouble in running closer to the rail. When asked to make a forward move leaving the back straight he picked up in great style and once in front early in the straight there was only ever going to be one winner. He drew clear for a decisive success, showing no lack of stamina, despite concerns pedigree-wise beforehand. A drop back in trip for the Preakness will not bother him at all, and the only worry is that the second leg of the Triple Crown will come too soon.

Eight Belles(USA), the only filly in the field and stablemate of Proud Spell, who won the Kentucky Oaks the previous day, ran a fine race but tragically fractured both her fore ankles pulling up after the finish line and had to be put down.

Denis Of Cork(USA), given a hold-up ride by last year's winning rider and track specialist Calvin Borel, made good late headway once switched to the rail in the latter stages. He achieved his best possible placing.

Tale Of Ekati(USA), who saved ground racing on the inside for much of the race, had every chance.

Colonel John(USA) had done all his previous racing on synthetic surfaces, but there were plenty of people prepared to back him on his dirt debut as he is by Tiznow and had been working well on the surface in the build up. He was a bit disappointing in the end but remains a good prospect for the rest of the season, and it is worth bearing in mind that the Breeders' Cup this year is at Santa Anita, where the surface suits him well.

Pyro(USA), the long-time favourite for this race before blowing out in the Blue Grass Stakes last time, was given the benefit of the doubt by many as that defeat came on a synthetic track. He failed to bounce back on his favoured dirt surface, though, never looking like landing a blow.

HAMILTON (R-H)

Sunday, May 4

OFFICIAL GOING: Good to soft (good in places in straight)

Rail realignment added circa 25yards to races on the round course.

Wind: Breezy, behind Weather: Overcast

1821 CANCER RESEARCH UK MAIDEN AUCTION STKS — 5f 4y

2:20 (2:20) (Class 5) 2-Y-O — **£3,238** (£963; £481; £240) **Stalls** Low

Form — RPR

2 **1** **Veronicas Boy**[18] 1392 2-8-9 0 AndrewElliott 2 — 71
(G M Moore) *chsd ldrs: drvn and outpcd 1/2-way: rallied to ld wl ins fnl f: kpt on strly* **4/1**[2]

2 ¾ **Where's Reiley (USA)** 2-8-10 0 PaulFessey 4 — 69
(T D Barron) *t.k.h: cl up: led 2f out: rdn and hdd wl ins fnl f: r.o* **9/2**[3]

3 2 ¼ **Metroland** 2-8-10 0 GregFairley 1 — 61
(M Johnston) *prom: swtchd and hung rt over 3f out: effrt and green over 1f out: no ex ins fnl f* **7/4**[1]

4 **4** ½ **Russet Reward**[23] 1303 2-8-12 0 PaulMulrennan 3 — 61
(Mrs L Stubbs) *led to 2f out: drvn and kpt on same pce* **7/4**[1]

61.26 secs (1.26) **Going Correction** +0.075s/f (Good) **4** Ran SP% **110.9**
Speed ratings (Par 93): **92,90,87,86**
CSF £19.78 TOTE £4.10; EX 18.70.
Owner J Stevenson **Bred** Whatton Manor Stud **Trained** Middleham Moor, N Yorks

FOCUS

In all probability just ordinary form but the pace was sound throughout.

NOTEBOOK

Veronicas Boy, who ran creditably on his debut at Beverley, was tapped for toe when the pace lifted but really found his stride in the closing stages to win going away. The step up to 6f will suit and, although this form is nothing special, he is the type to progress again. (tchd 7-2)

Where's Reiley(USA) ◆, a half-brother to a couple of sprint winners in the US, shaped well on his debut effort against a couple of more experienced performers. He looked the likely winner for a long way, is sure to improve and will be placed to best advantage. (op 5-1)

Metroland, a 20,000gns half-sister to a 1m2f winner in Italy, was not disgraced on this racecourse debut, despite looking the greenest in the field. She will be suited by 6f+ in due course and is capable of picking up a similar event. (op 13-8 tchd 6-4)

Russet Reward, who shaped with a degree of promise on his debut at Musselburgh, was well supported but failed to build on that promise. However he was not disgraced and left the impression that the step up to 6f would suit. (op 2-1 tchd 9-4 in places)

1822 SUNDAY MAIL ANNUAL JUMP JOCKEYS H'CAP (NATIONAL HUNT JOCKEYS) (SERIES QUALIFIER) — 1m 65y

2:55 (2:55) (Class 5) (0-70,66) 4-Y-O+ — **£3,238** (£963; £481; £240) **Stalls** High

Form — RPR

30-6 **1** **Keisha Kayleigh (IRE)**[18] 1394 5-10-12 **60** (v) GLee 3 — 71
(B Ellison) *stdd s: stdy hdwy over 2f out: shkn up fr over 1f out: led wl ins fnl f: r.o* **7/1**[2]

6000 **2** ¾ **King Of The Moors (USA)**[16] 1449 5-11-2 **64** PaddyAspell 11 — 73
(T D Barron) *pressed ldr: led after 2f: rdn over 2f out: hdd wl ins fnl f: r.o* **9/1**

36-0 **3** 7 **Dechiper (IRE)**[29] 1217 6-11-1 **63** KennyJohnson 2 — 56
(R Johnson) *hld up: pushed along over 3f out: kpt on fnl f: no ch w first 2* **16/1**

2032 **4** 1 **Pianoforte (USA)**[23] 1301 6-11-0 **62** (b) DenisO'Regan 8 — 53
(E J Alston) *hld up in tch: stdy hdwy over 2f out: rdn and no ex over 1f out* **8/1**[3]

0- **5** shd **Ergo (FR)**[13] 5906 4-11-2 **64** (v) KeithMercer 4 — 54
(James Moffatt) *hld up on ins: drvn and outpcd 4f out: n.d after* **40/1**

362- **6** shd **Oeuf A La Neige**[178] 6732 8-10-9 **57** GaryBerridge 13 — 47
(Miss L A Perratt) *in tch on ins: effrt over 3f out: no ex over 1f out* **8/1**[3]

640- **7** 2 ¼ **Shy Glance (USA)**[214] 5905 6-11-4 **66** WilsonRenwick 7 — 51
(P Monteith) *hld up on outside: effrt 3f out: no imp fnl 2f* **12/1**

05-0 **8** 2 ¼ **Dee Jay Wells**[16] 1449 4-10-13 **61** (t) BrianHarding 6 — 41
(D W Thompson) *prom: drvn 4f out: outpcd fnl 2f* **12/1**

-432 **9** 1 ¾ **Bivouac (UAE)**[23] 1296 4-10-8 **56** DougieCostello 9 — 32
(G A Swinbank) *cl up: ev ch 4f out: sn rdn and edgd rt: carried hd high and wknd over 1f out* **15/8**[1]

0-06 **10** 1 **Grethel (IRE)**[10] 1577 4-10-4 **52** oh2 JWStevenson 12 — 25
(A Berry) *in tch: drvn over 3f out: wkng whn hmpd over 1f out* **33/1**

440- **11** 6 **Grand Diamond (IRE)**[167] 6874 4-10-12 **60** RichardMcGrath 5 — 20
(J S Goldie) *hld up wd: drvn and outpcd over 3f out: sn btn* **14/1**

0/03 **12** 6 **Capped For Victory (USA)**[12] 1533 7-10-4 **52** (b[1]) BarryKeniry 1 — —
(G A Swinbank) *hld up outside: struggling 4f out: sn btn* **18/1**

006- **13** 17 **Jordans Elect**[294] 3343 8-10-10 **58** PeterBuchanan 10 — —
(P Monteith) *led 2f: cl up tl wknd over 3f out: t.o* **20/1**

1m 50.81s (2.41) **Going Correction** +0.15s/f (Good) **13** Ran SP% **122.8**
Speed ratings (Par 103): **93,92,85,84,84 84,81,79,77,76 70,64,47**
CSF £69.40 CT £1023.44 TOTE £8.50: £1.90, £4.60, £7.50; EX 142.30.
Owner C E Sherry **Bred** Ronnie Boland **Trained** Norton, N Yorks
■ Stewards' Enquiry : Wilson Renwick two-day ban: used whip with excessive force (May 18-19)

FOCUS

An ordinary handicap run at a decent gallop throughout. The first two did well to pull clear of the remainder and the form is rated through the second, with a career best from the winner.

1823 BERNADETTE MURPHY ESTATES (S) STKS — 1m 65y

3:30 (3:31) (Class 6) 3-Y-O — **£1,942** (£578; £288; £144) **Stalls** High

Form — RPR

0U4- **1** **Thompsons Walls (IRE)**[165] 6898 3-8-12 82 (t) LeeEnstone 5 — 74
(P C Haslam) *mde all: qcknd after 2f: rdn over 2f out: r.o wl: unchal* **3/1**[2]

1-34 **2** 1 ¾ **Wiseman's Diamond (USA)**[54] 849 3-8-7 68 FergalLynch 2 — 65
(K A Ryan) *chsd ldng pair: effrt over 2f out: wnt 2nd ent fnl f: nt rch wnr* **5/6**[1]

300- **3** 3 ¾ **Bourbon Highball (IRE)**[221] 5736 3-8-5 60 PatrickDonaghy(7) 6 — 61
(P C Haslam) *chsd wnr: rdn over 2f out: lost 2nd and no ex ent fnl f* **6/1**[3]

3540 **4** 13 **Indecision**[18] 1391 3-8-12 52 PaulMulrennan 1 — 31
(M W Easterby) *towards rr: outpcd 4f out: n.d after* **10/1**

0463 **5** ½ **Mujahope**[18] 1407 3-8-12 60 DavidAllan 3 — 30
(C J Teague) *bhd: drvn over 4f out: nvr on terms* **10/1**

560- **6** 28 **Northwest**[180] 6698 3-8-7 52 DanielleMcCreery(5) 4 — —
(A Berry) *hld up: struggling over 4f out: t.o* **50/1**

1m 51.22s (2.82) **Going Correction** +0.15s/f (Good) **6** Ran SP% **114.0**
Speed ratings (Par 97): **91,89,85,72,72 44**
CSF £6.04 TOTE £4.10: £1.80, £1.30; EX 5.70.The winner was bought in for £7,200
Owner Middleham Park Racing Xi **Bred** Newlands House Stud **Trained** Middleham Moor, N Yorks
■ Stewards' Enquiry : Patrick Donaghy caution: careless riding

FOCUS

An uncompetitive seller in which the winner, who was best in, had things all his own way after increasing the tempo after the first quarter of a mile. The form is rated through the third.

1824 CASH FOR KIDS SILVER BELL NIGHT H'CAP — 1m 5f 9y

4:05 (4:05) (Class 4) (0-80,80) 4-Y-O+ — **£6,476** (£1,927; £963; £481) **Stalls** Centre

Form — RPR

50-2 **1** **Nero West (FR)**[29] 1219 7-8-7 **66** (b) PaulFessey 7 — 77+
(Miss L A Perratt) *pressed ldr: led over 3f out: kpt on wl fr 2f out* **10/1**

2-31 **2** 1 ¼ **Pee Jay's Dream**[15] 1482 6-8-7 **66** DaleGibson 9 — 74
(M W Easterby) *prom: effrt 3f out: kpt on fnl f: nt rch wnr* **13/2**[3]

-041 **3** 1 **Cotton Eyed Joe (IRE)**[10] 1589 7-8-11 **73** PJMcDonald(3) 5 — 79
(G A Swinbank) *hld up in tch: effrt over 3f out: kpt on u.p fnl f* **5/1**[2]

P0-2 **4** ½ **Jafaru**[8] 1620 4-8-6 **65** (b) RoystonFfrench 11 — 70
(G A Butler) *prom: drvn and outpcd over 4f out: rallied over 2f out: edgd rt: kpt on: no imp* **7/2**[1]

2/3- **5** hd **First Look (FR)**[5] 5933 8-8-6 **72** BMcHugh(7) 12 — 77
(P Monteith) *hld up: effrt and hdwy over 2f out: kpt on u.p fnl f: no imp* **15/2**

43-4 **6** nse **Smugglers Bay (IRE)**[42] 981 4-8-12 **71** (b) RobertWinston 6 — 77+
(T D Easterby) *hld up: effrt whn nt clr run over 2f out: sn drvn: effrt over 1f out: no ex towards fin* **7/2**[1]

62-4 **7** 2 **Thunderwing (IRE)**[11] 1219 6-8-1 **63** oh3 ow2 AndrewMullen(3) 4 — 65
(James Moffatt) *hld up: rdn 3f out: effrt 2f out: nvr rchd ldrs* **25/1**

0/0 **8** 4 ½ **Euro American (GER)**[11] 1299 8-8-13 **72** PhillipMakin 3 — 67
(E W Tuer) *hld up: drvn over 3f out: nvr rchd ldrs* **16/1**

1240 **9** nk **Dreams Jewel**[12] 1551 8-7-11 **61** oh1 NataliaGemelova(5) 1 — 56
(C Roberts) *midfield: drvn and outpcd 4f out: n.d after* **22/1**

600- **10** ¾ **Monolith**[7] 6181 10-9-7 **80** (v[1]) PaddyAspell 10 — 74
(L Lungo) *prom: drvn 4f out: wknd 2f out* **20/1**

3-10 **11** 7 **Rare Coincidence**[22] 779 7-8-8 **67** (p) PaulMulrennan 2 — 50
(R F Fisher) *led to over 3f out: sn rdn and wknd over 2f out* **18/1**

/00- **12** 34 **Howards Dream (IRE)**[9] 2764 10-8-6 **65** oh16 ow4 (t) GregFairley 8 — —
(D A Nolan) *s.i.s: bhd: lost tch fnl 4f* **200/1**

2m 54.12s (0.22) **Going Correction** +0.15s/f (Good) **12** Ran SP% **119.9**
Speed ratings (Par 105): **105,104,103,103,103 103,101,99,98,98 94,73**
CSF £71.65 CT £371.35 TOTE £13.60: £2.70, £2.50, £2.20; EX 108.60.
Owner Mr & Mrs Charles Villiers **Bred** Ecurie Pelder **Trained** Carluke, S Lanarks

FOCUS

A competitive handicap, and the form looks really solid for the grade with the fisrt four close to their marks. The gallop seemed debut but those held up were at a disadvantage.

Smugglers Bay(IRE) Official explanation: jockey said gelding hung badly left final furlong

1825 FEEL THE DIFFERENCE AT ESPORTA MEDIAN AUCTION MAIDEN STKS — 1m 3f 16y

4:40 (4:42) (Class 6) 3-5-Y-O — **£2,047** (£604; £302) **Stalls** Centre

Form — RPR

233- **1** **Lochiel**[156] 6745 4-9-12 66 PaulMulrennan 2 — 63
(Mrs S C Bradburne) *prom: drvn over 4f out: rallied to ld over 1f out: styd on wl* **11/4**[2]

065- **2** 1 ¼ **Livvy Inn (USA)**[249] 4930 3-8-9 56 RoystonFfrench 1 — 59
(Miss Lucinda V Russell) *prom: ev ch fr over 3f out to over 1f out: kpt on ins fnl f: nt pce of wnr* **20/1**

4 **3** 1 ¾ **Prince Rhyddarch**[29] 1221 3-8-9 0 PhillipMakin 3 — 56
(Miss L A Perratt) *t.k.h: prom: outpcd over 3f out: rallied over 1f out: nrst fin* **8/1**[3]

2 **4** 3 **Evelith Regent (IRE)**[42] 982 5-9-12 0 RobertWinston 6 — 52
(G A Swinbank) *plld hrd: cl up: led over 3f out to over 1f out: wknd ins fnl f* **8/13**[1]

5 14 **Arch**[220] 5-9-12 0 AdrianTNicholls 4 — 27
(A M Crow) *hld up: outpcd 4f out: n.d after* **40/1**

00-0 **6** 15 **Wee Ellie Coburn**[34] 1116 4-9-7 48 GregFairley 5 — —
(M Mullineaux) *led to over 3f out: wknd over 2f out* **33/1**

7 158 **Deer Park Lord** 4-9-5 0 (t) PaulPickard(7) 7 — —
(D A Nolan) *missed break: bhd: lost tch fr 1/2-way* **50/1**

2m 29.41s (3.81) **Going Correction** +0.15s/f (Good)
WFA 3 from 4yo+ 17lb **7** Ran SP% **111.8**
Speed ratings (Par 101): **92,91,89,87,77 66,—**
CSF £45.88 TOTE £4.20: £1.80, £4.50; EX 36.60.
Owner A Campbell **Bred** D W Barker **Trained** Cunnoquhie, Fife
■ Stewards' Enquiry : Paul Pickard three-day ban: used whip when out of contention (May 18-20)

FOCUS

An uncompetitive race on paper, weakened further by the disappointing run of the odds-on favourite. The winner did not need to improve. The pace was on the steady side and this bare form does not look reliable.

Evelith Regent(IRE) Official explanation: jockey said gelding failed to come down the hill

1826 HAMILTON PARK SUPER SIX H'CAP 6f 5y
5:15 (5:16) (Class 5) (0-70,70) 4-Y-O+ **£2,590** (£770; £385; £192) **Stalls** Low

Form RPR

0-00 **1** **The Bear**[15] 1485 5-8-8 **60**.. GrahamGibbons 8 76
(R Johnson) *mde all: rdn 2f out: kpt on strly* **16/1**

005- **2** 2 1/4 **Ingleby Princess**[187] 6559 4-8-13 **65**................................ PaulFessey 3 74
(T D Barron) *towards rr: rdn and hdwy 2f out: chsd wnr ins fnl f: r.o* **8/1**

425- **3** 1 1/2 **Cross Of Lorraine (IRE)**[280] 3998 5-8-13 **65**...........(b) RobertWinston 5 69
(C Grant) *prom: drvn over 2f out: kpt on u.p fnl f* **5/1[2]**

03-3 **4** 3/4 **Maison Dieu**[9] 1602 5-7-13 **56** oh1.............................. KellyHarrison(5) 12 58
(E J Alston) *trckd ldrs gng wl: effrt and shkn up over 1f out: sn one pce* **7/1[3]**

50-0 **5** 2 1/2 **Yorkshire Blue**[17] 1430 9-9-3 **69**.................................... DanielTudhope 4 63
(J S Goldie) *bhd: drvn 1/2-way: hdwy fnl f: kpt on: nvr rchd ldrs* **4/1[1]**

050- **6** hd **Flying Valentino**[180] 6701 4-9-1 **70**........................ PJMcDonald(3) 10 63
(G A Swinbank) *hld up in tch gng wl: effrt over 1f out: sn no ex* **12/1**

0-10 **7** shd **Howards Tipple**[59] 806 4-8-13 **65**................................(p) PhillipMakin 11 58
(Miss L A Perratt) *towards rr: hdwy over 2f out: no ex over 1f out* **8/1**

-000 **8** 5 **Bid For Gold**[16] 1450 4-8-12 **64**................................(p) PaulMulrennan 2 41
(Jedd O'Keeffe) *bhd: drvn and outpcd after 2f: nvr on terms* **11/1**

0-02 **9** 1 **Campo Bueno (FR)**[11] 1561 6-8-3 **60**.................... DanielleMcCreery(5) 1 34
(A Berry) *midfield: hung rt and outpcd 1/2-way: n.d after* **12/1**

200- **10** 2 3/4 **Borodinsky**[211] 6016 7-8-5 **60**................................ DuranFentiman(3) 7 25
(R E Barr) *missed break: a bhd* **33/1**

000- **11** 26 **Howards Prince**[326] 2561 5-8-6 **58** oh11 ow2..................... GregFairley 6 —
(D A Nolan) *chsd wnr tl wknd over 2f out* **150/1**

1m 12.08s (-0.12) **Going Correction** +0.075s/f (Good) **11** Ran SP% **104.6**
Speed ratings (Par 103): **103,100,98,97,93 93,93,86,85,81 46**
CSF £105.64 CT £477.69 TOTE £17.90: £4.30, £2.30, £1.80; EX 223.10.
Owner M Sawers **Bred** P G Airey And R R Whitton **Trained** Newburn, Tyne & Wear
■ Stewards' Enquiry : Danielle McCreery one-day ban: allowed gelding to coast home with no assistance (May 18)

FOCUS
A modest handicap and one run at just an ordinary gallop. The field raced stands' side and nothing was able to land a blow to the winner. A tricky race to set the level with the first two both well in on old form.
The Bear Official explanation: trainer had no explanation for the apparent improvement in form
Borodinsky Official explanation: jockey said gelding reared as stalls opened

1827 RACING ON FRIDAY H'CAP 5f 4y
5:50 (5:50) (Class 6) (0-60,59) 4-Y-O+ **£2,047** (£604; £302) **Stalls** Low

Form RPR

-036 **1** **Rothesay Dancer**[17] 1431 5-8-13 **59**............................ KellyHarrison(5) 3 72+
(J S Goldie) *hld up in tch on stands' side: smooth hdwy over 1f out: led gng wl ent fnl f: rdn and r.o strly* **5/1[3]**

3256 **2** 1 3/4 **Highland Song (IRE)**[52] 871 5-8-1 **45**..................... AndrewMullen(3) 10 52
(R F Fisher) *led stands' side gp to ent fnl f: kpt on u.p* **10/1**

16-1 **3** 1/2 **Baybshambles (IRE)**[17] 1431 4-9-4 **59**.......................... AndrewElliott 9 64
(R E Barr) *trckd stands' side ldrs: effrt over 1f out: one pce ins fnl f* **3/1[1]**

446- **4** 3/4 **Staked A Claim (IRE)**[191] 6467 4-8-13 **54**...................... PhillipMakin 5 56+
(T D Barron) *bhd in stands' side gp tl hdwy over 1f out: kpt on fnl f: nrst fin* **4/1[2]**

0-05 **5** 3/4 **Double Carpet (IRE)**[15] 1485 5-9-3 **58**............................... PaulFessey 15 58
(R C Guest) *chsd far side ldrs: effrt 2f out: led that quartet nr fin: nt rch stands' side gp* **10/1**

3020 **6** hd **Overstayed (IRE)**[27] 1242 5-9-2 **57**............................(be) GregFairley 13 56
(M Mullineaux) *led far side quartet tl nr fin* **7/1**

0/0- **7** 1 **Angelofthenorth**[256] 4706 6-8-1 **45**......................... DuranFentiman(3) 1 40
(C J Teague) *bhd stands' side gp: hdwy over 1f out: nrst fin* **16/1**

0510 **8** 1 1/4 **Geordie Dancer (IRE)**[73] 641 6-7-13 **45**............. DanielleMcCreery(5) 11 36
(A Berry) *prom in stands' side gp tl rdn and wknd over 1f out* **33/1**

320- **9** nse **Conjecture**[221] 5741 6-9-1 **56**...................................... DarrenWilliams 14 47
(R Bastiman) *w far side ldr tl no ex fnl f* **8/1**

00-0 **10** nk **Alfie Lee (IRE)**[2] 1772 11-8-1 **49** ow4...........................(t) PaulPickard(7) 7 39
(D A Nolan) *prom in stands' side gp tl rdn and no ex wl over 1f out* **150/1**

0-00 **11** 1 **Mutayam**[2] 1772 8-8-1 **49** ow4..........................(t) PatrickDonaghy(7) 6 35
(D A Nolan) *dwlt: bhd in stands' side gp: shortlived effrt 1/2-way: n.d* **40/1**

030- **12** 1/2 **Whozart (IRE)**[178] 6735 5-8-13 **54**................................(p) DaleGibson 8 38
(A Dickman) *prom in stands' side gp tl rdn and wknd over 1f out* **12/1**

20-0 **13** 11 **Rue Soleil**[11] 1561 4-8-11 **55**.................................... JamieMoriarty(3) 12 —
(J R Weymes) *prom on far side: drvn 1/2-way: wknd 2f out* **33/1**

000/ **14** 1 1/2 **Maylea Gold (IRE)**[666] 3306 5-8-4 **45**.............................. RoystonFfrench 2 —
(Mrs S C Bradburne) *bhd in stands' side gp: drvn and outpcd 1/2-way: nvr on terms* **80/1**

60.54 secs (0.54) **Going Correction** +0.075s/f (Good) **14** Ran SP% **127.3**
Speed ratings (Par 101): **98,95,94,93,92 91,90,88,88,87 85,85,67,65**
CSF £56.51 CT £187.55 TOTE £6.50: £2.60, £2.90, £1.90; EX 74.90 Place 6 £ 667.79, Place 5 £ 119.80.
Owner Highland Racing **Bred** Frank Brady **Trained** Uplawmoor, E Renfrews

FOCUS
A low-grade sprint, run at a decent gallop, and the larger stands'-side group held the edge over the four that raced far side. Sound form for the grade, the winner back to her best.
Rothesay Dancer Official explanation: trainer said, regarding apparent improvement in form, that the mare was better suited by a more experienced rider who knows it well
T/Plt: £1,410.50 to a £1 stake. Pool: £54,972.96. 28.45 winning tickets. T/Qpdt: £27.10 to a £1 stake. Pool: £3,498.52. 95.25 winning tickets. RY

1806

NEWMARKET (ROWLEY) (R-H)
Sunday, May 4

OFFICIAL GOING: Good to firm
Wind: Fresh against becoming lighter 3rd race onwards Weather: Overcast

1828 STANJAMESUK.COM/CASINO SUFFOLK STKS (HERITAGE H'CAP) 1m 1f
2:05 (2:10) (Class 2) 3-Y-O+
£31,155 (£9,330; £4,665; £2,335; £1,165; £585) **Stalls** Low

Form RPR

46-4 **1** **Proponent (IRE)**[15] 1469 4-8-11 **90**................................ SteveDrowne 9 104
(R Charlton) *lw: trckd ldrs: rdn over 1f out: r.o to ld wl ins fnl f* **8/1[2]**

142- **2** 1/2 **Oceana Gold**[219] 5768 4-8-1 **83**................................ WilliamBuick(3) 15 96
(A M Balding) *led: rdn over 1f out: edgd rt: hdd wl ins fnl f* **10/1[3]**

1-03 **3** 2 1/4 **King Charles**[72] 673 4-9-3 **96**..................................... JimmyFortune 4 104
(E A L Dunlop) *hld up: hdwy u.p over 1f out: edgd rt: nt rch ldrs* **12/1**

400- **4** 4 1/2 **Supaseus**[211] 6011 5-9-3 **96**.. JohnEgan 5 95
(H Morrison) *on toes: chsd ldr: rdn over 2f out: outpcd wl over 1f out: styd on towards fin* **8/1[2]**

30/2 **5** nse **Humble Opinion**[8] 1633 6-8-7 **86**.............................. RichardHughes 1 84
(B J Meehan) *hld up: rdn over 1f out: r.o ins fnl f: nvr nrr* **8/1[2]**

123- **6** 3/4 **Laa Rayb (USA)**[232] 5431 4-9-6 **99**.................................. JoeFanning 13 96
(M Johnston) *swtg: chsd ldrs: rdn over 2f out: wknd fnl f* **16/1**

31-0 **7** 1 1/4 **Sound Of Nature (USA)**[15] 1469 5-8-10 **89**.................... TPQueally 11 83
(H R A Cecil) *swtg: chsd ldrs: rdn over 2f out: wknd fnl f* **14/1**

40-2 **8** 3/4 **Fishforcompliments**[29] 1218 4-9-4 **97**.......................... PaulHanagan 7 90
(R A Fahey) *lw: hld up: racd keenly: hdwy u.p over 1f out: no ex fnl f* **14/1**

132- **9** 1 1/2 **Free Offer**[212] 5978 4-8-7 **86**.................................... KerrinMcEvoy 2 76
(J L Dunlop) *swtg: trckd ldrs: plld hrd: rdn and hung rt over 1f out: wknd fnl f* **16/1**

6-33 **10** 3/4 **Heaven Knows**[11] 1569 5-9-2 **95**.. RHills 14 83
(W J Haggas) *prom: rdn over 2f out: wknd over 1f out* **8/1[2]**

-041 **11** shd **Folio (IRE)**[10] 1585 8-8-3 **82**.. ChrisCatlin 6 70
(W J Musson) *swtg: hld up: n.d* **40/1**

00-6 **12** 3 1/4 **Kingsdale Orion (IRE)**[15] 1469 4-8-11 **90**...................(b[1]) TomEaves 10 71
(B Ellison) *on toes: hld up: rdn over 2f out: sn wknd* **33/1**

2-00 **13** 2 1/4 **Ella Woodcock (IRE)**[11] 1569 4-8-8 **87** ow1......(b[1]) StephenDonohoe 17 63
(E J Alston) *hld up: rdn over 3f out: wknd over 2f out* **66/1**

211- **14** 6 **Gulf Express (USA)**[220] 5748 4-9-4 **97**.......................... RyanMoore 3 61
(Sir Michael Stoute) *swtg: dwlt: hld up: rdn over 2f out: sn wknd* **3/1[1]**

122- **15** 15 **Many Volumes (USA)**[220] 5748 4-9-10 **103**.................... TedDurcan 16 35
(H R A Cecil) *bit bkwd: hmpd s: hld up: wknd over 3f out* **11/1**

1m 51.73s (1.13) **Going Correction** +0.35s/f (Good) **15** Ran SP% **126.5**
Speed ratings (Par 109): **108,107,105,101,101 100,99,99,97,97 96,94,92,86,73**
CSF £88.84 CT £999.41 TOTE £9.50: £2.60, £4.00, £3.80; EX 120.70 TRIFECTA Not won..
Owner B E Nielsen **Bred** Fortbarrington Stud **Trained** Beckhampton, Wilts

FOCUS
A very good, competitive handicap run at a strong pace. They raced up the middle of the track. The form has been rated positively, with the first three all raised between 8lb and 10lb, and it should work out well.

NOTEBOOK
Proponent(IRE) ◆ improved on the form he showed when fourth over 1m at Newbury on his reappearance with a smart performance. Having been well placed just off the good pace set by the eventual runner-up, he knuckled down well when asked for his effort. His trainer is of the opinion he will be even better over middle-distances - he certainly ran as though that will be the case - and he could be better than a Handicapper in time. He may now be pointed towards Royal Ascot, and something like the Wolferton handicap or the Duke Of Edinburgh could be a suitable target.
Oceana Gold ◆, an improved horse last year, looked fit and showed he is still progressing with a good effort after 219 days off the track. He looked to have gone off plenty quick enough, but he stuck on really well in the closing stages and was only pegged back inside the final furlong. He appeals as a handicapper to keep on side. (tchd 11-1)
King Charles, third in a 1m2f Carnival handicap in Dubai when last seen over two months previously, ran with credit on his return to the UK. He gave the impression he can do even better back over a little further. (op 20-1)
Supaseus, 4lb higher than when winning this race last year, looked fit for this return and was always close up but he could only find the one pace in the closing stages. This was his first run of the season, but he has a good record fresh and might not improve a great deal next time. (tchd 9-1)
Humble Opinion ran well when second at Sandown on his return from a long absence and this was another creditable effort. He was doing all his best work at the finish and gave the impression he will be worth another chance back over further. (op 14-1)
Laa Rayb(USA), trying his furthest trip to date after 232 days off, travelled well for much of the race, but he failed to last home and ran like a non-stayer.
Sound Of Nature(USA), the trainer's second string according to jockey bookings, left his disappointing Newbury effort well behind, appreciating this quicker surface, but he was still well held. (op 10-1)
Gulf Express(USA), who improved to win his final two starts of last year, resumed off a 5lb higher mark on his return from 220 days off. He was well backed but failed to run a race. Official explanation: jockey said colt ran flat (tchd 10-3 and 7-2 in places)
Many Volumes(USA) Official explanation: jockey said colt ran flat

1829 STANJAMESUK.COM JOCKEY CLUB STKS (GROUP 2) 1m 4f
2:40 (2:44) (Class 1) 4-Y-O+
£51,093 (£19,368; £9,693; £4,833; £2,421; £1,215) **Stalls** Centre

Form RPR

124- **1** **Getaway (GER)**[210] 6043 5-9-1 0.. SPasquier 6 127+
(A Fabre, France) *gd sort: str: lw: hld up: hdwy over 2f out: led over 1f out: shkn up and r.o wl* **7/4[1]**

100- **2** 3 3/4 **Sixties Icon**[297] 3461 5-8-12 118.. LDettori 4 118
(J Noseda) *hld up in tch: ev ch over 1f out: sn rdn: styd on same pce fnl f* **7/2[2]**

114- **3** 1/2 **Galactic Star**[190] 6496 5-8-12 110.. RyanMoore 2 117
(Sir Michael Stoute) *swtg: hld up: rdn over 3f out: hdwy over 1f out: r.o: nt rch ldrs* **9/2[3]**

14-0 **4** 1 3/4 **Tranquil Tiger**[15] 1468 4-8-12 112.. TedDurcan 3 114+
(H R A Cecil) *lw: chsd ldr tl led wl over 2f out: rdn and hdd over 1f out: no ex fnl f* **16/1**

4106 **5** 3/4 **Gower Song**[15] 1468 5-8-9 109... TQuinn 1 110+
(D R C Elsworth) *swtg: hld up: plld hrd: hdwy and hung rt over 1f out: r.o: nt trble ldrs* **16/1**

1-10 **6** 2 **Malt Or Mash (USA)**[15] 1468 4-8-12 111..................... RichardHughes 8 110+
(R Hannon) *lw: plld hrd and prom: rdn over 2f out: wknd over 1f out* **8/1**

642- **7** 3/4 **Balkan Knight**[197] 6337 8-8-12 110........................... JimmyFortune 9 109+
(D R C Elsworth) *b.hind: bit bkwd: s.i.s: hld up: swtchd lft over 1f out: styd on ins fnl f: nvr nr to chal* **33/1**

60-0 **8** nk **Yellowstone (IRE)**[36] 1091 4-8-12 113................................ JohnEgan 10 108
(Jane Chapple-Hyam) *chsd ldrs: rdn over 2f out: wknd over 1f out* **12/1**

535- **9** 1 **Under The Rainbow**[197] 6337 5-8-9 104................................. NCallan 7 104
(B W Hills) *hld up in tch: rdn over 2f out: wknd over 1f out* **50/1**

130- **10** 3/4 **Dragon Dancer**[210] 6043 5-8-12 113............................... KerrinMcEvoy 5 106
(G Wragg) *led: rdn and hdd wl over 2f out: wknd over 1f out* **16/1**

2m 35.63s (2.13) **Going Correction** +0.35s/f (Good) **10** Ran SP% **118.1**
Speed ratings (Par 115): **106,103,103,102,101 100,99,99,98,98**
CSF £7.78 TOTE £3.20: £1.10, £1.30, £2.60; EX 7.20 Trifecta £15.20 Pool £5,250.48, 244.18 winning units.
Owner Baron G Von Ullmann **Bred** Baron G Von Ullmann **Trained** Chantilly, France

FOCUS
A strong renewal of this Group 2 contest and a quite outstanding winner, who overcame a steady early pace to win in fine style, stamping himself a major contender for Europe's premier middle-distance races.

NOTEBOOK

Getaway(GER) ◆ had gained his last three wins over 1m7f, but he produced an improved performance when fourth in the Arc on his final start last season and looks to have to progressed again from four to five judged on this demolition job. Conceding upwards of 3lb all round, he was a little keen off the modest gallop, but his rider never seemed too concerned and kept him well covered up. Considering he stays so well he could have been expected to get outpaced when the tempo increased inside the last half mile, but this giant of a horse seemed to be taking three strides to his rivals' one when Pasquier let out a bit of rein and he quickly disposed of last year's winner, Sixties Icon, who had appeared to travel well. He could not have been more impressive and looks another top-class middle-distance performer for Andre Fabre and Baron G Von Ullmann, who have had the likes of Shirocco, winner of this race two years ago, and Manduro over the last couple of years. His trainer suggested races like the Coronation Cup, King George and Arc De Triomphe could be on the agenda and he is likely to prove extremely hard to beat wherever he goes. (op 15-8 tchd 9-4)

Sixties Icon lost his way after winning this race last year and had been off the track since finishing distressed in the Princess Of Wales's Stakes in July, but this was a pleasing return. He was a bit warm beforehand but travelled kindly for much of the way and stayed on when asked, but the winner was simply much too good. (tchd 3-1 and 4-1 in places)

Galactic Star progressed from handicaps to win a Listed race last year, but he was a beaten favourite in the Group 3 St Simon Stakes on his final start last year. Contesting a Group 2 for the first time, he showed he has improved again with a really good run in third. His effort is particularly creditable considering he would have preferred a stronger pace, and there should be more to come. (tchd 4-1 and 5-1)

Tranquil Tiger was unsuited by soft ground when last at Newbury on his reappearance and he showed that running to be all wrong with a respectable fourth back under more suitable conditions. He stays further than this, so he is another who would have preferred a stronger pace. (op 14-1)

Gower Song was too keen for her own good and actually ran quite well in the circumstances, as she is at her best finishing off a strong pace.

Malt Or Mash(USA), unsuited by soft ground at Newbury on his previous start, had conditions to suit this time, but he compromised his chance by pulling hard off the steady pace. (op 10-1)

Balkan Knight made a pleasing reappearance over a trip short of his best and can build on this when returned to staying trips.

Yellowstone(IRE), without the cheekpieces he had fitted when beating only two home in the Sheema Classic at Nad Al Sheba on his debut for this yard, offered little immediate promise on his return to the UK. (op 16-1)

Under The Rainbow had a tough task.

Dragon Dancer is inconsistent and dropped right out once headed.

1830 STANJAMESUK.COM 1000 GUINEAS STKS (GROUP 1) (FILLIES) 1m

3:20 (3:26) (Class 1) 3-Y-O

£212,887 (£80,700; £40,387; £20,137; £10,087; £5,062) **Stalls** Centre

Form				RPR
21-1	**1**		**Natagora (FR)**[20] 1375 3-9-0 0 ... C-PLemaire 13 (P Bary, France) *lw: chsd ldr: led over 6f out: rdn over 1f out: r.o* **11/4**[1]	113+
11-	**2**	½	**Spacious**[234] 5353 3-9-0 108 ... JamieSpencer 9 (J R Fanshawe) *h.d.w: hld up: rdn and hdwy over 1f out: sn hung lft: r.o* **11/2**[3]	112
13-3	**3**	½	**Saoirse Abu (USA)**[28] 1230 3-9-0 0 ... (v) KJManning 5 (J S Bolger, Ire) *hld up in tch: rdn and nt clr run over 1f out: r.o* **20/1**	111
1-1	**4**	*nk*	**Infallible**[18] 1401 3-9-0 110 ... JimmyFortune 14 (J H M Gosden) *lw: trckd ldrs: rdn and edgd lft over 1f out: unable qck nr fin* **7/2**[2]	110
31-0	**5**	*hd*	**Nahoodh (IRE)**[15] 1470 3-9-0 110 ... RichardHughes 6 (M R Channon) *hld up: hdwy over 1f out: sn rdn: running on whn nt clr run ins fnl f: nvr able to chal* **33/1**	114+
1-0	**6**	½	**Lush Lashes**[35] 1104 3-9-0 0 ... KerrinMcEvoy 12 (J S Bolger, Ire) *s.i.s: hld up: swtchd rt over 1f out: r.o ins fnl f: nvr nrr* **40/1**	109+
43-3	**7**	½	**Royal Confidence**[18] 1400 3-9-0 104 ... MichaelHills 3 (B W Hills) *lw: hld up: hdwy 1/2-way: rdn and nt clr run over 1f out: styd on* **66/1**	107
11-1	**8**	¾	**Muthabara (IRE)**[15] 1470 3-9-0 106 ... RHills 11 (J L Dunlop) *b: chsd ldr 6f out: rdn and ev ch over 2f out: hung lft over 1f out: styng on same pce whn hung lft ins fnl f* **8/1**	106
01-	**9**	2½	**Kitty Matcham (IRE)**[197] 6336 3-9-0 0 ... JMurtagh 7 (A P O'Brien, Ire) *lw: hld up: rdn over 1f out: n.d* **8/1**	100+
04-2	**10**	2¾	**Savethisdanceforme (IRE)**[35] 1104 3-9-0 0 ... RyanMoore 8 (A P O'Brien, Ire) *swtg: hld up: rdn over 2f out: hdwy over 1f out: wknd ins fnl f* **12/1**	94
131-	**11**	2	**Max One Two Three (IRE)**[204] 6182 3-9-0 99 ... RichardKingscote 10 (Tom Dascombe) *swtg; edgy: s.i.s: hld up: rdn over 1f out: n.d* **33/1**	89
21-3	**12**	4½	**Lady Deauville (FR)**[15] 1470 3-9-0 105 ... SPasquier 4 (P A Blockley) *chsd ldrs: rdn over 2f out: wkng whn nt clr run over 1f out* **66/1**	79
120-	**13**	2	**Laureldean Gale (USA)**[210] 6040 3-9-0 114 ... LDettori 2 (Saeed Bin Suroor) *edgy: prom: rdn over 2f out: wkng whn hmpd over 1f out* **14/1**	74
11-5	**14**	¾	**Spinning Lucy (IRE)**[18] 1401 3-9-0 101 ... WilliamBuick 15 (B W Hills) *mid-div: wknd over 2f out* **100/1**	72
451-	**15**	9	**Francesca D'Gorgio (USA)**[281] 3962 3-9-0 102 ... (v) TedDurcan 1 (J Noseda) *on edge: unruly in stalls: led: hdd over 6f out: rdn over 3f out: wknd 2f out* **80/1**	52

1m 38.99s (0.39) **Going Correction** +0.35s/f (Good) **15 Ran SP% 119.1**

Speed ratings (Par 110): **112,111,111,110,110 110,109,108,106,103 101,97,95,94,85**

CSF £16.39 TOTE £3.20: £1.30, £3.00, £4.90; EX 17.70 Trifecta £311.40 Pool: £8,698.27, 19.83winning units.

Owner Stefan Friborg **Bred** Bertrand Gouin & Georges Duca **Trained** Chantilly, France

FOCUS

This looked a very good 1000 Guineas beforehand, but it was a muddling race. They raced stands' side throughout, but the pace was just ordinary and the first eight were covered by around three lengths, with a couple looking unlucky in running. There were plenty of smart fillies in the line up and the race should produce some good winners, but the bare form needs treating with caution.

NOTEBOOK

Natagora(FR), last year's Cheveley Park winner, impressed many when easily landing the Prix Imprudence on her reappearance, but this was her first run over 1m and also her first outing on ground with 'firm' in the description. As it turned out, the conditions posed her no problems and she just saw out the trip having enjoyed the run of the race out in front, leading after a couple of furlongs at just an ordinary pace. It could be argued she was a fortunate winner, as the third home, and even more so the fifth, were both unlucky, but it is hard to knock her and she is now a Group 1 winner at two and three. It remains to be seen where she goes next, but her connections think she had a hard race and might give her a little break. On this evidence 1m is as far as she wants to go and she will be every bit as effective back over shorter. (tchd 5-2)

Spacious, off the track since winning the May Hill last September, has reportedly been slow to come to hand, but her connections had been pleased with her in the week leading up to the race, and her regular work companion, Cesare, gave her a boost when landing a Listed race at Ascot four days earlier. This was a cracking effort, but she just lacked the pace of the French filly and was unable to peg that one back. Her connections are apparently keen to stick to 1m, in which case it would be no surprise to see her aimed at the Irish Guineas. She can do even better in a stronger-run race, but she shapes as though she will benefit from a step up in trip, if not now, then most certainly in time. Her trainer said she is not a 1m4f filly, though, which rules out the Oaks. (op 9-2)

Saoirse Abu(USA) was only third in the 1000 Guineas Trial at Leopardstown on her reappearance, but she was a dual Group 1 winner last year and returned to her best in third. She would have finished even closer with a clearer run, as she was forced to switch right with her challenge, although it is worth remembering the fifth home was even more unlucky. (tchd 25-1 in a place)

Infallible was a seriously impressive winner of the Nell Gwyn over 7f here on her reappearance, but this was a lot tougher and she had both her stamina to prove and her ability handle quick ground. She seemed fine on the fast surface, but the trip probably just stretched her. Her trainer said he felt she got lit up after getting bumped at halfway and ended up racing too keenly. Official explanation: jockey said filly ran too keen (op 4-1)

Nahoodh(IRE) ◆ flopped on soft ground in the Fred Darling, but she left that form well behind under these more suitable conditions and might well have won with a clear run. Having travelled well, she took a while to pick up when first asked, but she really found her stride late on and was motoring home when stopped in her run against the rail inside the final furlong. Her rider was unable to push her for the last 50 yards or so and she looked desperately unlucky. She will apparently now head straight for the Coronation Stakes at Royal Ascot and, if the ground comes up quick, she will have a good chance of gaining deserved compensation. (tchd 28-1)

Lush Lashes ◆' debut win in the Goffs Fillies Million, for all that it looked good at the time, didn't really work out as well as one might have expected, and she offered little on her reappearance at the Curragh but, despite looking dull in her coat beforehand, this was a particularly eye-catching effort. She lacked the tactical speed of some of these and McEvoy allowed her to drop back to last at about halfway, leaving her with no chance when the tempo increased. She probably didn't handle the Dip that great either, but she took off in the last two furlongs and finished fastest of all. She has to be considered for the Oaks following this effort.

Royal Confidence ◆, trying 1m for the first time, ran a good race in defeat, confirming the promise she showed when third in the Free Handicap. However, for all that she can clearly be competitive at this trip, she is bred to be a sprinter and she could be very good indeed when dropped back in trip.

Muthabara(IRE) had been well backed for this race in the last couple of months, and she gave her supporters plenty of encouragement when winning the Fred Darling on her reappearance, but she was a late doubt to even run after pulling up sore with a small bruise under the shoe on her near-fore foot after exercise on Friday morning. She was allowed her chance, but failed to shine with the ground, the fastest she has encountered, probably a little quicker than she really wants, especially considering the late injury scare. John Dunlop intends stepping her up in trip now. (op 15-2 tchd 9-1)

Kitty Matcham(IRE) ◆, last year's Rockfel winner, was the choice of Johnny Murtagh, and she finished ahead of her stablemate, but she never landed a blow on the principals. She basically just lacked the speed of some of these and will be suited by a step up to middle-distances. The Oaks will surely now be on the agenda and it is by no means out of the question she could emulate her dam, who won the Epsom Classic in 2001. (op 10-1)

Savethisdanceforme(IRE) has a most progressive profile and there was a lot to like about her reappearance second at the Curragh, where she quickened up smartly in heavy ground before tiring late on, but she was passed over by Johnny Murtagh and failed to run up to her best. She was never really travelling and the ground had probably dried out much more than she would have liked. (tchd 11-1)

Max One Two Three(IRE), a 6f Listed winner on her final start at two, played up beforehand and was never involved after missing the break and being taken wide.

Lady Deauville(FR), third to Muthabara in the Fred Darling, would have finished closer had she not been squeezed out over a furlong out, but she was held at the time. (op 80-1)

Laureldean Gale(USA), rather like Ibn Khaldun in the 2000 Guineas, was a mile below her best. Admittedly she had something to find, but this was still a poor effort. (op 25-1)

Spinning Lucy(IRE) looked fit but was out of her depth and the trip probably stretched her as well.

Francesca D'Gorgio(USA), off the track since winning a 6f maiden last July, looked fit but got very worked up in the stalls and offered little. (tchd 100-1)

1831 STAN JAMES 08000 383384 PALACE HOUSE STKS (GROUP 3) 5f

3:55 (3:57) (Class 1) 3-Y-O+

£28,385 (£10,760; £5,385; £2,685; £1,345; £675) **Stalls** Low

Form				RPR
411-	**1**		**Captain Gerrard (IRE)**[204] 6167 3-8-7 111 ... TomEaves 1 (B Smart) *lw: mde all: rdn and edgd rt over 1f out: r.o* **15/2**	113
115-	**2**	*nk*	**Sakhee's Secret**[239] 5214 4-9-7 120 ... SteveDrowne 4 (H Morrison) *bit bkwd: swtg: chsd ldrs: rdn 1/2-way: edgd rt over 1f out: ev ch ins fnl f: r.o* **11/4**[1]	121+
422-	**3**	1	**Enticing (IRE)**[225] 5632 4-8-10 107 ... JMurtagh 2 (W J Haggas) *chsd ldr: rdn and ev ch ins fnl f: edgd rt: no ex nr fin* **10/3**[2]	107
64-2	**4**	¾	**Matsunosuke**[50] 907 6-8-13 96 ... KerrinMcEvoy 7 (A B Coogan) *hld up: r.o ins fnl f: nvr nrr* **25/1**	107+
00-1	**5**	*shd*	**Zidane**[17] 1420 6-8-13 108 ... JamieSpencer 3 (J R Fanshawe) *s.i.s: hld up: rdn over 1f out: edgd rt and r.o ins fnl f: nt rch ldrs* **7/2**[3]	107+
0-02	**6**	1¾	**Hoh Hoh Hoh**[32] 1157 6-8-13 102 ... RyanMoore 5 (R J Price) *dwlt: hld up: r.o ins fnl f: nvr trbld ldrs* **16/1**	100
0-53	**7**	*hd*	**Reverence**[15] 1495 7-8-13 107 ... JimmyQuinn 6 (E J Alston) *chsd ldrs: rdn 1/2-way: styd on same pce fnl f* **25/1**	100
031-	**8**	2	**Judd Street**[213] 5953 6-8-13 107 ... (v) StephenCarson 11 (Eve Johnson Houghton) *swtg: chsd ldrs: rdn over 1f out: wknd ins fnl f* **10/1**	92
312-	**9**	½	**Rowe Park**[213] 5953 5-9-2 112 ... LPKeniry 9 (Mrs L C Jewell) *swtg: chsd ldrs: rdn over 1f out: wknd fnl f* **16/1**	94
0-10	**10**	3	**Conquest (IRE)**[16] 1442 4-8-13 100 ... (v) JimmyFortune 10 (W J Haggas) *chsd ldrs: rdn and hung rt over 1f out: sn wknd* **33/1**	80

59.00 secs (-0.10) **Going Correction** +0.35s/f (Good)

WFA 3 from 4yo+ 9lb **10 Ran SP% 115.2**

Speed ratings (Par 113): **114,113,111,110,110 107,107,104,103,98**

CSF £27.49 TOTE £8.70: £2.30, £1.30, £1.80; EX 34.10 Trifecta £125.90 Pool: £1,490.54, 8.40 winning units.

Owner R C Bond **Bred** Alan Dargan **Trained** Hambleton, N Yorks

■ Stewards' Enquiry : Tom Eaves four-day ban: used whip with excessive force and frequency (May 18-21)

FOCUS

A decent Group 3 sprint, although the draw played a big part. Captain Gerrard improved again on his progressive 2-y-o form, but Sakhee's Secret comes out of the race as much the best horse under his penalty.

The Form Book, Raceform Ltd, Compton, RG20 6NL

NOTEBOOK

Captain Gerrard(IRE), the only representative of an age group which has now won five of the last 14 runnings of this race, would surely have been better suited by more cut in the ground. Carrying condition as he often does, he handled this quick surface well and, from the best draw, he bagged the stands' rail and made every yard, seeing off the challenge of Enticing before holding off the late challenge of Sakhee's Secret. The Temple Stakes is likely to be next on his agenda, and he was made 16-1 by Coral for the King's Stand. (op 17-2)

Sakhee's Secret, last year's Champion sprinter, had plenty against him on his return to action, not least the drop back to 5f and his Group 1 penalty. He ran a blinder in the circumstances, providing the final challenge to the winner, and he looks set for another fine season. Made 6-1 for the Golden Jubilee and 8-1 for the King's Stand, he makes much more appeal for the former. (op 5-2 tchd 3-1 and 10-3 in places)

Enticing(IRE) had conditions very much to suit as she is at her best over the minimum trip on fast ground. She had also won first time out the previous two seasons, so all looked in place for a big run and it was no surprise to see her well backed. She had every chance and is a good benchmark for the form. (op 4-1 tchd 9-2 in a place)

Matsunosuke, coming here on the back of a personal best on the All-Weather when runner-up in Listed company, stepped up on that form to finish fourth from off the pace. Despite being a six-year-old now, he has never been better, and on this evidence he is good enough to win in Listed company this season. (op 28-1 tchd 33-1)

Zidane, who was given a great ride by Spencer to win over 6f here at the Craven meeting, was one of several who was warm in the preliminaries and was staying on all too late over this shorter distance. He will naturally appreciate a return to 6f. (op 3-1)

Hoh Hoh Hoh, whose best effort last term came when he pinged the gates and almost made all at York, will be of more interest when reverting to those tactics on a speed-favouring track.

Reverence remains out of form, but in fairness he would not have been suited by the drying ground anyway.

Judd Street, who wore the visor which proved so successful over this course and distance on his final start last term, showed speed towards the centre of the track but failed to see it out. He is entitled to come on for this reappearance. (op 12-1)

Rowe Park, narrowly beaten by Judd Street over this course and distance last backend, was below his best on his reappearance. His trainer had warned that he had not come in his coat, though, so there should be improvement in him. (op 14-1)

Conquest(IRE), who was stuck on the outside for most of the race, could have done with getting more cover. When asked for his effort he did not want to know, and he looks a very tricky customer. Official explanation: jockey said gelding moved poorly

1832 STANJAMESUK.COM MAIDEN STKS 5f

4:30 (4:30) (Class 2) 2-Y-O £9,714 (£2,890; £1,444; £721) Stalls Low

Form RPR

1 **Finjaan** 2-9-3 0 MartinDwyer 7 86+
(M P Tregoning) *str: gd-bodied: hld up: hdwy and edgd lft over 1f out: shkn up to ld ins fnl f: r.o* 10/1

3 2 ½ **Ouqba**[18] 1399 2-9-3 0 RHills 2 84
(B W Hills) *lw: sn led: rdn and hdd ins fnl f: r.o* 5/4[1]

3 2 ¼ **Desire To Excel (IRE)** 2-9-3 0 TQuinn 5 76+
(P F I Cole) *str: bit bkwd: w ldr: rdn and ev ch over 1f out: styd on same pce ins fnl f* 12/1

2 4 ¾ **Heliodor (USA)**[13] 1523 2-9-3 0 RichardHughes 1 75+
(R Hannon) *w'like: led early: chsd ldrs: rdn over 1f out: styd on same pce* 3/1[2]

5 ¾ **Cool Art (IRE)** 2-9-3 0 JamieSpencer 4 71
(S A Callaghan) *lengthy: unf: bit bkwd: trckd ldrs: shkn up over 1f out: styd on same pce* 7/2[3]

6 3 ½ **Jazacosta (USA)** 2-9-3 0 JimCrowley 3 58
(Mrs A J Perrett) *tall: lengthy: sn pushed along in rr: wknd over 1f out* 14/1

7 7 **You Avin A Laugh** 2-9-3 0 JimmyQuinn 6 33
(C A Dwyer) *leggy: chsd ldrs: nt clr run 2f out: sn hung rt and wknd* 40/1

61.47 secs (2.37) **Going Correction** +0.35s/f (Good) 7 Ran SP% 117.6
Speed ratings (Par 99): **95,94,90,89,88 82,71**
CSF £24.10 TOTE £12.50: £3.40, £1.60; EX 18.00.

Owner Hamdan Al Maktoum **Bred** Shadwell Estate Company Limited **Trained** Lambourn, Berks

FOCUS

A useful-looking maiden which should produce winners. Finjaan looked Royal Ascot material, and Ouqba advertised the strength of Art Connoisseur's Craven meeting win.

NOTEBOOK

Finjaan, a brother to Fustaan, a 6f winner at three, was the owner's second string and lacked the favourite's previous experience, but he is bred more for speed than him and, challenging down the outside, took his measure inside the last. He is from a stable whose juveniles tend not to be wound up first time so improvement can be expected, and something like the National Stakes or Aubigny Stakes could be on his agenda before a trip to Royal Ascot. (op 8-1)

Ouqba ran well on his debut here at the Craven meeting and looked likely to be difficult to beat, but he ran into a more speedily bred rival in his owner's second colours and was edged out in the final furlong. He still finished clear of the rest and can win a similar race, but another furlong will help. (op 2-1 tchd 9-4 in places)

Desire To Excel(IRE), who cost 150,000gns and is a half-brother to Silver Touch, a high-class, triple 7f-1m winner, ran with plenty of promise on his debut and will surely not be long in winning a maiden. Official explanation: trainer later said colt pulled muscles in its hindquarters (op 14-1 tchd 16-1)

Heliodor(USA), runner-up at Windsor on his debut, was green in the preliminaries and did not get the clearest of runs up the inside rail and was not knocked about, but he would not have troubled the first two even with everything panning out perfectly. (op 9-4)

Cool Art(IRE), whose sales price rose from 58,000euros as a foal to 100,000gns as a yearling, is a half-brother to Fabled Bully, a multiple 6f-1m winner in Italy, and Full Power, a dual winner at three in Italy. Too green to show what he can really do on his debut, he shaped with promise and can win his maiden. (op 10-3 tchd 3-1 and 9-2 in a place)

Jazacosta(USA), who cost $165,000, is a half-brother to five winners in the US including Dyna Del, a multiple winner on turf, Senor Gran Day, a prolific dirt winner at around 6f-9f, and Special Offer, a triple dirt sprint winner. He hails from a stable not known for sending out two-year-old winners first time up, and improvement can be expected. (op 25-1)

You Avin A Laugh, a late May foal and cheap purchase, is a half-brother to Bint Habibi, a triple 7f-1m1f winner, Looking Down, a 7f winner at two, and Wizard Looking, a triple 1m2f-1m3f winner. (tchd 33-1)

1833 STANJAMESUK.COM PRETTY POLLY STKS (LISTED RACE) (FILLIES) 1m 2f

5:05 (5:05) (Class 1) 3-Y-O

£17,031 (£6,456; £3,231; £1,611; £807; £405) Stalls Low

Form RPR

1 1 **Saphira's Fire (IRE)**[20] 1372 3-8-12 83 MartinDwyer 4 92+
(W R Muir) *w'like: attractive: a.p: led over 1f out: rdn out* 7/1

1- 2 1 ½ **Cruel Sea (USA)**[191] 6470 3-8-12 85 MichaelHills 7 89
(B W Hills) *lw: hld up: plld hrd: hdwy over 2f out: rdn and ev ch over 1f out: styd on same pce ins fnl f* 5/2[2]

05-6 3 nk **Don't Forget Faith (USA)**[15] 1470 3-8-12 103 PhilipRobinson 5 88
(C G Cox) *chsd ldr tl led over 2f out: rdn and hdd over 1f out: styd on same pce ins fnl f* 2/1[1]

236- 4 ¾ **Sayyedati Symphony (USA)**[183] 6652 3-8-12 86 JohnEgan 2 87
(C E Brittain) *bit bkwd: chsd ldrs: rdn and edgd lft whn bmpd 2f out: styd on same pce appr fnl f* 12/1

020- 5 hd **Shaker (IRE)**[183] 6652 3-8-12 86 RobertHavlin 1 87+
(M L W Bell) *swtg: hld up: hmpd 2f out: swtchd rt over 1f out: r.o ins fnl f: nt trble ldrs* 16/1

2111 6 nse **Mischief Making (USA)**[11] 1557 3-8-12 81 TGMcLaughlin 6 86
(E A L Dunlop) *chsd ldrs: rdn over 2f out: styd on same pce appr fnl f* 5/1[3]

22-3 7 22 **Madame Hoi (IRE)**[22] 1332 3-8-12 90 ChrisCatlin 3 42
(M R Channon) *led: rdn and hdd over 2f out: hmpd and wknd sn after* 8/1

2m 7.27s (1.47) **Going Correction** +0.35s/f (Good) 7 Ran SP% 115.8
Speed ratings (Par 104): **108,106,106,105,105 105,88**
CSF £25.52 TOTE £10.10: £3.50, £2.00; EX 36.30.

Owner M J Caddy **Bred** Gainsborough Stud Management Ltd **Trained** Lambourn, Berks

FOCUS

This did not look the strongest of Oaks trials beforehand and they went steady early, resulting in a bit of a sprint to the line. The first six finished close up and the form is questionable.

NOTEBOOK

Saphira's Fire(IRE) only had a Wolverhampton maiden win to her name, but she was clearly expected to put up a bold show on this step up in class as she was backed in from 12-1. She picked up well after being switched to the outside, but owing to the steady early pace and sprint to the line they finished in a bit of a heap in behind and the form might not be totally reliable. The Sandringham Stakes, a Listed Handicap at the Royal meeting, was mentioned as a potential target post-race. (op 12-1)

Cruel Sea(USA), who looked a promising filly when winning her maiden at Doncaster last backend, failed to settle off the steady early pace. In the circumstances it was a good effort to keep on for second place, and connections are apparently keen to persevere with Oaks aspirations in the Musidora. (tchd 9-4, 11-4 in places)

Don't Forget Faith(USA), outpaced in the Fred Darling on her reappearance, was expected to appreciate the step up in trip, and her juvenile form did make her the one to beat. However, she proved disappointing. Perhaps the ground was faster than ideal, but in a race that developed into a bit of a sprint, she should have been better equipped than most to deal with that. (tchd 9-4)

Sayyedati Symphony(USA), who showed useful form at two without winning, is not necessarily bred to want further than a mile, but she is only entered in the Irish Oaks and Ribblesdale Stakes, suggesting her trainer sees her very much as a middle-distance filly. She tracked the leader on the rail and had every chance, but has yet to suggest, despite her attractive pedigree, that she is up to this class. (op 14-1)

Shaker(IRE), who finished just behind Sayyedati Symphony when down the field in a 1m Listed contest here last backend, filled a similar position this time, but that does not tell the whole story, as she was unlucky in running. Hampered when going for an ambitious run up the inside, her rider was forced to switch right round the whole field before running on late. She would have finished closer with a clear run and will be suited by a stronger pace in future.

Mischief Making(USA), who was suited by the step up to 1m4f last time, was probably one of those most inconvenienced by the steady pace over this shorter trip. The ground was also quicker than at Catterick, so all in all she had a number of excuses. (op 7-2)

Madame Hoi(IRE), third in the Masaka Stakes on her reappearance, enjoyed the run of the race but was beginning to go backwards when getting badly squeezed out two furlongs out, and she weakened quickly thereafter. (op 11-1 tchd 12-1)

1834 STAN JAMES 08000 383384 H'CAP 7f

5:40 (5:40) (Class 2) (0-100,99) 3-Y-O £12,952 (£3,854; £1,926; £962) Stalls Low

Form RPR

0-41 1 **Slugger O'Toole**[9] 1601 3-8-5 **86** ChrisCatlin 4 90
(B W Hills) *chsd ldrs: led over 1f out: rdn out* 11/1

61-1 2 nk **Meydan Princess (IRE)**[22] 1336 3-8-6 **87** JamieSpencer 1 94+
(J Noseda) *dwlt: hld up: nt clr run over 1f out: swtchd rt: r.o wl ins fnl f* 4/1[2]

341- 3 ¾ **Swift Gift**[156] 6980 3-8-4 **85** oh1 MartinDwyer 8 86+
(B J Meehan) *chsd ldrs: rdn and hmpd over 1f out: r.o wl towards fin* 20/1

211- 4 nk **Billion Dollar Kid**[228] 5536 3-8-8 **89** RichardHughes 2 89
(S A Callaghan) *chsd ldr tl rdn over 1f out: styd on* 5/1[3]

116- 5 1 **Dubai Dynamo**[190] 6495 3-9-1 **96** JohnEgan 6 100+
(P F I Cole) *trckd ldrs: racd keenly: hmpd over 1f out: r.o wl towards fin* 9/1

142- 6 hd **Ancien Regime (IRE)**[209] 6059 3-9-0 **95** PhilipRobinson 11 92
(M A Jarvis) *swtg: hld up in tch: rdn and edgd lft over 1f out: no ex ins fnl f* 9/4[1]

410- 7 ¾ **Insaaf**[184] 6619 3-8-8 **89** RHills 7 90+
(W J Haggas) *hld up: hdwy over 2f out: rdn and hmpd over 1f out: no ex* 16/1

1 8 nse **Throne Of Power (USA)**[85] 500 3-8-4 **85** KerrinMcEvoy 5 80+
(M A Magnusson) *swtg: prom: lost pl 2f out: nt clr run fr over 1f out: nt rcvr* 11/2

04-2 9 ¾ **Spitfire**[22] 1328 3-9-4 **99** PaulHanagan 10 92
(J R Jenkins) *hld up: hdwy over 1f out: wknd ins fnl f* 16/1

210- 10 1 ½ **Bellomi (IRE)**[212] 5972 3-8-8 **89** TPO'Shea 3 78
(W J Haggas) *led: rdn and hdd over 1f out: wknd ins fnl f* 33/1

213- 11 2 ¼ **Just A Dancer (IRE)**[323] 2650 3-8-1 **85** oh2 WilliamBuick(3) 9 68
(B W Hills) *hld up: rdn over 2f out: sn wknd* 40/1

1m 26.34s (0.94) **Going Correction** +0.35s/f (Good) 11 Ran SP% 123.1
Speed ratings (Par 105): **108,107,106,106,105 105,104,104,103,101 99**
CSF £56.35 CT £914.80 TOTE £9.80: £2.70, £2.00, £5.00; EX 41.40 Place 6 £ 59.15, Place 5 £ 9.41.

Owner R J Crothers, Phil Cunningham **Bred** Harts Farm And Stud **Trained** Lambourn, Berks

FOCUS

A decent and competitive handicap likely to throw up plenty of future winners, even allowing for the fact that it was a bit of a messy race.

NOTEBOOK

Slugger O'Toole, who looked quite well handicapped on the form of his last-time-out success at Wolverhampton, was always well placed in a race in which a number of his rivals came back with hard-luck stories. Having tracked the leader, he took over with over a furlong to run and kept on strongly, repelling all challengers in good style. He could well be aimed at the Britannia now and will be worthy of respect at Royal Ascot. (op 8-1)

Meydan Princess(IRE), who looked dull in her coat, struggled to get a clear run and her rider had to switch her out wide. Once in the clear she ran on well and closed the winner right down at the line. Things did not drop right this time but this performance coupled with her impressive win at Kempton last time suggest she remains on the upgrade. (op 7-2)

Swift Gift completed a tricast for last-time-out Polytrack winners, despite racing from 1lb out of the handicap. The meat in the sandwich between Spitfire and Ancien Regime inside the last two furlongs, he overcame that and rallied to finish a good third. He looks capable of better and might appreciate another furlong.

Billion Dollar Kid, who has changed stables, looked dull in his coat but had conditions to suit and was well supported, suggesting he was fit for his reappearance. He was well placed throughout, towards the fore and next to the rail, in a race in which a number of others encountered trouble in running, and can have few excuses. (op 8-1 tchd 9-1)
Dubai Dynamo ◆, looking for room from two furlongs out, got bumped about when going for gaps that were not there, and it was only well inside the last that he eventually got some room and ran on. A Listed sprint winner for his previous stable at two, he looks to have trained on, and will deserve consideration for a similar heat. (op 14-1 tchd 16-1)
Ancien Regime(IRE), who has now been a beaten favourite on his last three starts, was stuck out wide for most of the race and might not quite have stayed in the end, but this was still a bit disappointing. Perhaps the ground was on the quick side for him, but on the back of this his Group 1 entry looks wide of the mark. (tchd 5-2 in a place)
Insaaf, who looked fit for this reappearance, got bumped about and had no luck in running between the two pole and the furlong marker, and her rider was not hard on her once she got in the clear and there was no hope of winning. This run should be forgotten. Official explanation: jockey said filly was denied a clear run (op 20-1)
Throne Of Power(USA) ◆, impressive in winning a 1m Lingfield maiden back in February, had at one stage held a 2000 Guineas entry so had to be of interest off a mark of 85 in this handicap. Racing up the stands' rail, he simply never got a clear run and his rider finished the race having never really had the chance to ask his mount for an effort. It is impossible to know how close he would have gone with a clear run, but he looks well handicapped and can find compensation, possibly back over a mile. Official explanation: jockey said filly was denied a clear run (op 5-1 tchd 6-1)
Spitfire, one of the more exposed runners in the line-up, had work on his plate giving weight all round to more progressive rivals. (op 20-1)
Bellomi(IRE), who was able to dictate an ordinary gallop, dropped out tamely once headed. (op 66-1)
Just A Dancer(IRE), 2lb wrong at the weights, did not run beyond 5f at two and on this evidence she needs to drop back to sprinting. (op 33-1)
T/Jkpt: Not won. T/Plt: £85.60 to a £1 stake. Pool: £175,989.34. 1,499.43 winning tickets. T/Qpdt: £12.70 to a £1 stake. Pool: £7,602.94. 442.58 winning tickets. CR

SALISBURY (R-H)

Sunday, May 4

OFFICIAL GOING: Good (8.6)
Wind: Mild against Weather: Overcast

1835 TOTEPLACEPOT MAIDEN STKS (DIV I) 6f
1:25 (1:26) (Class 5) 3-Y-O+ **£4,047** (£1,204; £601; £300) **Stalls** High

Form RPR
004- **1** **Fifty (IRE)**[202] 6228 3-8-9 77 PatDobbs 11 73
(R Hannon) *chsd ldrs: rdn over 2f out: led jst ins fnl f: r.o wl: rdn out* **9/2**[3]
2 2 ¾ **Palace Moon** 3-8-11 0 TravisBlock(3) 5 69
(H Morrison) *awkward leaving stalls: trckd ldr: led over 2f out: rn green and wandered u.p whn hdd jst ins fnl f: no ex* **2/1**[1]
00-0 **3** 1 ½ **Tiger Trail (GER)**[25] 1265 4-9-10 50 GeorgeBaker 8 67
(Mrs N Smith) *hld up towards rr: rdn over 2f out: styd on fr over 1f out: wnt 3rd ins fnl f* **66/1**
0-4 **4** 1 ½ **Billy Hot Rocks (IRE)**[12] 1529 3-9-0 0 JamesDoyle 9 60
(R M Beckett) *in tch: rdn over 2f out: kpt on fnl f but nt pce to chal* **11/2**
0 **5** 1 ¾ **Acclimate**[12] 1529 3-8-9 0 FergusSweeney 1 49
(W S Kittow) *led: rdn and hdd over 2f out: remained pressing ldrs tl fdd fnl 100yds* **40/1**
6 2 ¼ **Where's Dids** 3-8-9 0 EdwardCreighton 2 42
(M R Channon) *mid-div: rdn over 2f out: sn one pce* **20/1**
46 **7** 4 **Game Hunt**[23] 1295 3-9-0 0 SebSanders 3 34
(J H M Gosden) *trckd ldrs: rdn and ev ch over 2f out: wknd ent fnl f* **9/4**[2]
00 **8** 6 **Minerton Mountain**[91] 416 3-9-0 0 SimonWhitworth 4 15
(B R Millman) *chsd ldrs: rdn 3f out: wknd 2f out* **100/1**
6 **9** ½ **Persian Flyer (IRE)**[34] 1114 3-9-0 0 MickyFenton 6 13
(J W Mullins) *a bhd* **50/1**
10 2 ¾ **Well Styled** 3-9-0 0 AmirQuinn 7 4
(W J Knight) *s.i.s: a towards rr* **8/1**
1m 15.27s (0.47) **Going Correction** +0.175s/f (Good)
WFA 3 from 4yo 10lb **10** Ran SP% **120.4**
Speed ratings (Par 103): **103,99,97,95,93 90,84,76,76,72**
CSF £14.10 TOTE £5.50: £1.60, £1.30, £7.70; EX 18.20.
Owner Alan Franklin & Neville Poole **Bred** Barronstown Stud **Trained** East Everleigh, Wilts
FOCUS
A modest maiden, the form being held down by the third-placed horse, but the race should produce winners at the right level. It was much the quicker of the two divisions.

1836 TOTEPLACEPOT MAIDEN STKS (DIV II) 6f
1:55 (1:59) (Class 5) 3-Y-O+ **£4,047** (£1,204; £601; £300) **Stalls** High

Form RPR
342- **1** **Divine Power**[193] 6432 3-8-9 78 SebSanders 7 74
(R M Beckett) *mid-div: tk clsr order 3f out: swtchd lft jst over 2f out: sn rdn: led fnl 110yds: r.o: rdn out* **2/1**[1]
2- **2** 1 **Orange Pip**[176] 6754 3-8-9 0 DaneO'Neill 10 71
(R Hannon) *trckd ldr: hmpd sn after s: rdn to ld wl over 1f out: hdd fnl 100yds: no ex* **5/2**[2]
0- **3** 1 ¼ **Chelsea Girl**[341] 2122 3-8-9 0 RichardThomas 3 67
(C G Cox) *swtchd rt sn after s: led: rdn and hdd wl over 1f out: kpt on but no ex ins fnl f* **14/1**
0 **4** nk **Priti Fabulous (IRE)**[16] 1445 3-8-9 0 LiamJones 4 66
(W J Haggas) *mid-div: pushed along and hdwy 2f out: styd on fnl f: wnt 4th towards fin* **8/1**
05- **5** nk **Smooth As Silk (IRE)**[245] 5061 3-8-9 0 ShaneKelly 11 65
(C R Egerton) *hmpd sn after s: trckd ldrs: rdn and swtchd lft over 2f out: styd on fnl f* **10/1**
40- **6** 3 **Sir Ike (IRE)**[202] 6234 3-9-0 0 FergusSweeney 2 60
(W S Kittow) *trckd ldrs: rdn and ev ch over 1f out: fdd ins fnl f* **12/1**
03-4 **7** 1 ¾ **Candida's Beau**[29] 1215 3-9-0 75 JamesDoyle 5 55
(R M Beckett) *mid-div: rdn over 2f out: wknd fnl f* **15/2**[3]
8 10 **Owain James** 3-9-0 0 NeilChalmers 9 23
(M Salaman) *dwlt bdly: a bhd* **50/1**
06- **9** 1 **Robbmaa (FR)**[215] 5880 3-9-0 0 CatherineGannon 6 19
(A W Carroll) *trckd ldrs: hmpd sn after s: rdn 3f out: sn edgd rt and wknd* **50/1**
0-00 **10** 6 **Tagula Sands (IRE)**[114] 120 4-9-10 37 RichardSmith 1 —
(J C Fox) *a towards rr* **100/1**
1m 16.13s (1.33) **Going Correction** +0.175s/f (Good)
WFA 3 from 4yo 10lb **10** Ran SP% **113.1**
Speed ratings (Par 103): **98,96,95,94,94 90,87,74,73,65**
CSF £6.69 TOTE £2.40: £1.20, £1.30, £3.20; EX 4.20.
Owner Mill House Stud Racing Partnership **Bred** Mill House Stud **Trained** Whitsbury, Hants
■ Stewards' Enquiry : Richard Thomas four-day ban: careless riding (May 18-21)
FOCUS
Marginally the stronger of the two divisions on paper, even though the time was slightly slower. Ordinary form, rated through the fifth.

1837 BET TOTEPOOL AT TOTESPORT.COM H'CAP 6f
2:25 (2:30) (Class 2) (0-100,98) 3-Y-O
£12,462 (£3,732; £1,866; £934; £466; £234) **Stalls** High

Form RPR
0-40 **1** **Victorian Bounty**[18] 1404 3-8-9 86 MickyFenton 7 91
(Stef Liddiard) *mde all: edgd lft nr fin: kpt on gamely: rdn out* **8/1**
2215 **2** 1 ¼ **Fathsta (IRE)**[18] 1404 3-8-9 86 ow1 DaneO'Neill 5 87
(S Kirk) *in tch: rdn and hdwy 2f out: kpt on ins fnl f: wnt 2nd towards fin* **9/2**[2]
410- **3** nk **C'Mon You Irons (IRE)**[211] 6017 3-8-5 82 AdrianMcCarthy 6 82
(M R Hoad) *trckd wnr: rdn and ev ch over 1f out: no ex ins fnl f: lost 2nd towards fin* **33/1**
410- **4** ¾ **May Day Queen (IRE)**[200] 6270 3-8-2 79 oh1 DavidKinsella 8 77
(R Hannon) *hld up bhd: rdn 2f out: r.o ins fnl f: nrst fin* **22/1**
-612 **5** 1 **We Have A Dream**[10] 1584 3-8-2 79 oh1 HayleyTurner 1 73
(W R Muir) *trckd ldrs: rdn over 2f out: kpt on same pce fnl f* **10/1**
014- **6** 1 ¼ **Royal Intruder**[247] 5008 3-8-10 87 PatDobbs 2 77
(R Hannon) *hld up towards rr: rdn wl over 2f out: styd on fnl f: nvr trbld ldrs* **12/1**
25-3 **7** nk **Silver Wind**[22] 1328 3-8-10 87 (v) ShaneKelly 9 76
(P D Evans) *in tch: bmpd sn after s: rdn over 2f out: kpt on same pce fnl f* **8/1**
63-5 **8** ½ **Oasis Wind**[31] 1170 3-9-7 98 SebSanders 10 86
(P F I Cole) *chsd ldrs: rdn over 2f out: wknd fnl f* **11/2**[3]
42-1 **9** 1 **Dunn'o (IRE)**[12] 1529 3-8-4 81 RichardThomas 11 66
(C G Cox) *hmpd over 5f out: towards rr: rdn and sme prog whn hmpd 2f out: no further imp* **7/2**[1]
0-1 **10** 4 ½ **Restless Genius (IRE)**[21] 1347 3-8-2 79 (t) LiamJones 3 49
(A M Balding) *s.i.s: sn mid-div: rdn over 2f out: wknd over 1f out* **6/1**
50-0 **11** 10 **Calmdownmate (IRE)**[18] 1404 3-9-2 93 FergusSweeney 4 31
(K R Burke) *mid-div: rdn 3f out: wknd over 1f out: eased whn btn* **16/1**
1m 14.75s (-0.05) **Going Correction** +0.175s/f (Good) **11** Ran SP% **122.3**
Speed ratings (Par 105): **107,105,104,103,102 100,100,99,98,92 79**
CSF £45.74 CT £1157.36 TOTE £10.20: £2.80, £2.70, £5.20; EX 53.60 Trifecta £226.10 Part won. Pool: £318.56 - 0.10 winning units..
Owner David Gilbert **Bred** Mrs P D Gray And H Farr **Trained** Great Shefford, Berks
■ Stewards' Enquiry : Dane O'Neill one-day ban: careless riding (May 18); caution: used whip with excessive frequency
FOCUS
A fair sprint handicap with the front pair running pretty much to form, but a race which lacked progressive types. The winner ensured there was a decent pace on.
NOTEBOOK
Victorian Bounty, 1lb lower than when finishing seventh in a highly competitive Newmarket sprint handicap last month, was faced with lesser opposition here and he led throughout for a workmanlike victory. He is evidently progressing and connections will reportedly try to nick a Group 3 abroad with him. (op 11-1 tchd 15-2)
Fathsta(IRE), two places ahead of the winner at Newmarket, was 2lb worse off at the weights this time and he ran pretty much to form, just hitting top gear too late. He continues to take his racing well in this busy spell, but is likely to remain vulnerable to improvers. (op 7-1)
C'Mon You Irons(IRE), a Hamilton maiden winner at two, ran creditably when finishing in midfield in the Redcar Two-Year-Old Trophy on his final start and this was a highly pleasing first run for his new trainer. It is likely he will come on for this outing, although a mark of 82 is not going to make life easy. (op 40-1)
May Day Queen(IRE), racing from 1lb out of the handicap, was generally progressive as a juvenile and she looks to have progressed again over the winter. In rear early, she made some good late headway under pressure and was closing at the line. The run should bring her on. (tchd 12-1)
We Have A Dream has been most progressive and he again looked to have a chance desptite being 9lb higher than when winning at Folkestone two starts back. He had narrowly been beaten at Great Leighs last time and again ran well, but could make no impression inside the final furlong. (op 9-1 tchd 11-1)
Royal Intruder ◆, a 5f Sandown maiden winner last year, had been beaten just half a length back there in a nursery on his final start at two and it was surprising to see him take such a walk in the market. He made some late headway, but never threatened to get involved and the run was clearly needed. There should be more improvement in him this year. (op 9-1 tchd 14-1)
Silver Wind Official explanation: jockey said gelding suffered interference on leaving stalls
Oasis Wind boasted some useful two-year-old form, but he looked set to struggle off a mark of 98 and duly did. (op 7-1 tchd 15-2)
Dunn'o(IRE), easy winner of a 5f maiden at Bath last time, seemed to have the best of the draw and looked set to progress again on this handicap debut, but he got himself a bit behind early and never really saw any daylight on the inside. This was disappointing, but he deserves to be given another chance.
Restless Genius(IRE), winner of a weak maiden at Brighton, could never recover from a sluggish start and dropped right out in the end. (op 9-2)

1838 TOTEQUADPOT FILLIES' CONDITIONS STKS 5f
3:05 (3:10) (Class 3) 2-Y-O **£6,476** (£1,927; £963; £481) **Stalls** High

Form RPR
1 **Foundation Room (IRE)** 2-8-6 0 NeilChalmers 2 86+
(A M Balding) *in tch: hdwy 2f out: sn rdn: edgd lft ent fnl f: led fnl 100yds: r.o wl: comf* **20/1**
1 **2** 2 ¼ **April Pride**[25] 1263 2-8-7 0 HaddenFrost(5) 5 84
(R Hannon) *wnt sltly lft s: chsd ldrs: led 2f out: sn rdn: hdd fnl 100yds: nt pce of wnr* **11/8**[1]
01 **3** 2 ¾ **Calypso Girl (IRE)**[19] 1377 2-8-12 0 ShaneKelly 6 74
(P D Evans) *prom: led 3f out: rdn and hdd 2f out: kpt on same pce* **3/1**[2]
0 **4** 1 ¼ **Blushing Maid**[13] 1523 2-8-9 0 MickyFenton 4 67+
(H S Howe) *sltly hmpd s: sn struggling in rr: stdy prog fr 2f out: wnt 4th ent fnl f: nvr gng pce to threaten ldrs* **33/1**
12 **5** 9 **Sally's Dilemma**[32] 1156 2-8-5 0 JackDean(7) 7 37
(W G M Turner) *led tl 3f out: sn rdn: wknd over 1f out* **4/1**[3]
6 2 ¼ **August Days (IRE)** 2-8-6 0 JamesDoyle 3 23
(R M Beckett) *chsd ldrs: rdn over 3f out: wknd over 1f out* **13/2**
7 ¾ **Flawless Diamond (IRE)** 2-8-6 0 SimonWhitworth 1 20+
(J S Moore) *v.s.a: a outpcd in rr* **20/1**
62.30 secs (1.50) **Going Correction** +0.175s/f (Good) **7** Ran SP% **112.9**
Speed ratings (Par 94): **95,91,87,85,70 67,65**
CSF £47.11 TOTE £21.30: £5.00, £1.50; EX 88.80.
Owner G W Chong **Bred** Garry Chong **Trained** Kingsclere, Hants
FOCUS
This has fallen to some useful fillies over the years and the winner looks a nice type. Slight improvement from the runner-up.

NOTEBOOK

Foundation Room(IRE), a 7,000gns daughter of Saffron Walden, is bred to need further in time, but her stable have made a bright start to the season and she got well on top inside the final half furlong, overcoming greenness in the process. This was a highly promising start to her career and it will be interesting to see how she fares once upped in grade. (op 14-1 tchd 22-1)

April Pride, a daughter of Falbrav who is not bred to be an early two-year-old, scored narrowly on her debut at Bath and was strongly supported at the head of the market to make it two from two. She went on two out, looking the likeliest winner, but in the end Foundation Room had too much for her. This was slightly disappointing, although it is probable she is in need of a sixth furlong now. (op 15-8 tchd 2-1 in a place)

Calypso Girl(IRE), who had the benefit of the rail when winning her maiden at Nottingham last time, faced a stiffer task here giving weight all round and she ran well, just lacking the speed of the front pair. She is likely to stay 6f. (tchd 11-4 and 10-3)

Blushing Maid, reported to have lost her action on her debut, was slightly hampered at the start and soon behind. She began to stay on from over a furlong out though and was closing quite fast at the line. She ended up well clear of the remainder and is another already in need of 6f. (op 25-1 tchd 40-1)

Sally's Dilemma, winner of the Brocklesby, got put in her place by a useful filly at Nottingham last time and, having made the early running, she dropped out tamely. She is evidently going the wrong way and has it all to prove now. (op 11-4 tchd 9-2)

August Days(IRE), whose dam won over 1m, comes from a yard who can ready one to win first time up, but this was a tough introduction and she dropped right out in the final furlong. (op 11-1 tchd 6-1)

Flawless Diamond(IRE), a 20,000gns daughter of Indian Haven, was soon in trouble following a very slow start and should come on for the experience. (op 14-1 tchd 22-1)

1839 TOTEEXACTA H'CAP — 1m 1f 198y

3:40 (3:42) (Class 4) (0-80,78) 3-Y-O — £4,533 (£1,348; £674; £336) Stalls High

Form — RPR

34-4 **1** — **Dr Livingstone (IRE)**[19] 1381 3-9-2 **76** ShaneKelly 10 — 83
(C R Egerton) *mde all: rdn and hung lft fr over 2f out: kpt on gamely: jst hld on* **14/1**

5-42 **2** *hd* **Higgy's Boy (IRE)**[12] 1543 3-8-10 **75** PatrickHills(5) 5 — 82
(R Hannon) *hld up towards rr: rdn and stdy prog fr 3f out: styd on strly fnl 100yds: jst failed* **12/1**

0-12 **3** *nk* **Summer Winds**[27] 1244 3-9-2 **76** DaneO'Neill 1 — 83
(T G Mills) *mid-div: rdn and hdwy fr 3f out: chsd wnr 2f out: styd on fnl f: lost 2nd towards fin* **12/1**

01- **4** *1 3/4* **Trianon**[190] 6494 3-9-4 **78** PatDobbs 3 — 82+
(R Charlton) *mid-div: rdn over 3f out: hdwy 2f out: styd on fnl f: wnt 4th fnl strides* **8/1**[3]

03-1 **5** *hd* **Monterrico**[34] 1114 3-9-1 **75** EddieAhern 4 — 78
(G Wragg) *trckd wnr: rdn whn swtchd rt 2f out: kpt on same pce fnl f* **6/5**[1]

-222 **6** *1 3/4* **Rich Kid (IRE)**[6] 1685 3-8-9 **72** KevinGhunowa(3) 9 — 73+
(R A Harris) *hld up towards rr: snatched up after 2f: rdn 3f out: styd on fr over 1f out: nvr trbld ldrs* **15/2**[2]

2-23 **7** *1* **Mcconnell (USA)**[113] 135 3-9-2 **76** GeorgeBaker 2 — 75
(G L Moore) *restrained in rr: hdwy 3f out: sn rdn: styd on same pce fnl f* **12/1**

446- **8** *3 1/4* **Fearless Warrior**[186] 6593 3-8-7 **67** PatCosgrave 13 — 61
(J L Dunlop) *mid-div: short of room and snatched up 6f out: rdn over 3f out: wknd fnl f* **14/1**

540- **9** *nk* **Silk Hall (UAE)**[206] 6119 3-9-0 **74** AlanMunro 11 — 67
(D W P Arbuthnot) *sme late prog but mainly towards rr* **20/1**

0-43 **10** *1 1/2* **Jollyhockeysticks**[27] 1244 3-8-13 **73** CatherineGannon 7 — 64
(M R Channon) *mid-div: rdn and hdwy 3f out: wknd fnl f* **14/1**

600- **11** *1 1/2* **Leitmotif (USA)**[186] 6592 3-8-7 **67** PaulDoe 8 — 56
(J L Dunlop) *in tch: rdn over 3f out: wknd 1f out* **25/1**

160- **12** *6* **Marchpane**[211] 6012 3-8-13 **73** SebSanders 12 — 52
(R M Beckett) *a towards rr* **12/1**

610- **13** *1 1/2* **The Name Is Frank**[263] 4501 3-8-13 **73** JamesDoyle 6 — 50
(J W Mullins) *racd keenly: trckd ldrs: short of room 3f out: sn rdn: wknd 2f out* **25/1**

2m 12.68s (2.78) **Going Correction** +0.25s/f (Good) — **13** Ran SP% **131.6**
Speed ratings (Par 101): **98,97,97,96,96 94,93,91,91,89 88,83,82**
CSF £184.50 CT £2108.76 TOTE £20.40: £5.50, £3.00, £3.70; EX 222.00.
Owner Exors of the Late Mrs E A Hankinson **Bred** Stone Ridge Farm **Trained** Chaddleworth, Berks
■ Stewards' Enquiry : Alan Munro caution: used whip when out of contention

FOCUS

A fair handicap likely to produce its share of winners. Dr Livingstone dictated an ordinary pace and is rated up 7lb on his previous form.

1840 BET TOTEPOOL ON ALL UK RACING MAIDEN STKS — 1m 4f

4:15 (4:18) (Class 5) 3-Y-O — £4,047 (£1,204; £601; £300) Stalls High

Form — RPR

0- **1** — **Killcara Boy**[160] 6948 3-9-3 0 DaneO'Neill 8 — 83+
(H Candy) *mde virtually all: rdn and hdd briefly over 1f out: styd on wl to assert towards fin* **22/1**

0-32 **2** *nk* **Special Reserve (IRE)**[22] 1330 3-9-3 76 PatDobbs 1 — 83
(R Hannon) *trckd ldrs: cruised upsides wnr 3f out: rdn to ld briefly over 1f out: ev ch ins fnl f: hld towards fin* **3/1**[2]

4 **3** *5* **Dolly Penrose**[16] 1444 3-8-12 0 EdwardCreighton 7 — 70
(M R Channon) *mid-div: hdwy 5f out: rdn to dispute 3rd fr 3f out: kpt on same pce fnl 2f* **7/2**[3]

0 **4** *3/4* **Swingkeel (IRE)**[18] 1398 3-9-3 0 EddieAhern 3 — 74
(J L Dunlop) *trckd wnr: rdn to chal over 3f out: kpt on same pce fnl 2f* **20/1**

06- **5** *1 1/2* **Hamsat Elqamar**[214] 5912 3-8-12 0 SebSanders 9 — 66+
(J H M Gosden) *mid-div: nudged along 6f out: hdwy over 3f out: sn rdn: one pce fnl 2f* **5/1**

00- **6** *1 3/4* **Mazara (IRE)**[214] 5919 3-9-3 0 PatCosgrave 10 — 69
(J L Dunlop) *trckd ldrs: rdn over 5f out: one pce fnl 2f* **33/1**

7 *3 1/2* **Ericarrow (IRE)** 3-8-5 0 DavidProbert(7) 2 — 58
(A M Balding) *mid-div: effrt to chse ldrs over 3f out: wknd ins fnl f* **33/1**

4- **8** *36* **Wine 'n Dine**[198] 6294 3-9-3 0 LiamJones 4 — —
(W J Haggas) *chsd ldrs: rdn 6f out: wknd over 3f out* **6/4**[1]

9 *20* **Haveyouwonyet** 3-8-12 0 (b[1]) PaulDoe 6 — —
(L A Dace) *slowly away: a bhd* **66/1**

0-0 **10** *66* **Light Sea (IRE)**[16] 1440 3-8-12 0 DarryllHolland 5 — —
(M R Channon) *t.k.h early in rr: lost tch fr 5f out: virtually p.u* **33/1**

2m 40.35s (2.35) **Going Correction** +0.25s/f (Good) — **10** Ran SP% **123.3**
Speed ratings (Par 99): **102,101,98,97,96 95,93,69,56,12**
CSF £87.56 TOTE £23.90: £4.80, £1.30, £1.60; EX 117.20.
Owner Miss Julianna Byrne **Bred** Penfold Bloodstock Ltd **Trained** Kingston Warren, Oxon

FOCUS

This was not a strong heat, but the race should produce the odd winner in handicaps. The favourite ran no race and the form has been rated through the second and third.

Wine 'n Dine Official explanation: vet said colt returned lame
Light Sea(IRE) Official explanation: jockey said filly got upset in preliminaries

1841 BET TOTEPOOL ON ALL IRISH RACING H'CAP — 1m 6f 21y

4:50 (4:53) (Class 2) (0-105,105) 4-Y-O+

£9,969 (£2,985; £1,492; £747; £372; £187) Stalls Far side

Form — RPR

412- **1** — **Wing Express (IRE)**[297] 3458 4-9-10 **105** SebSanders 9 — 117+
(L M Cumani) *trckd ldrs: swtchd lft 2f out: led ent fnl f: styd on strly: rdn out* **2/1**[1]

114- **2** *2 1/2* **Tropical Strait (IRE)**[176] 6759 5-8-6 **86** AlanMunro 7 — 92
(D W P Arbuthnot) *hld up bhd ldrs: rdn 4f out: led over 2f out: hdd ent fnl f: kpt on for clr 2nd but sn hld by wnr* **4/1**[2]

120- **3** *5* **Swan Queen**[278] 4047 5-8-12 **92** EddieAhern 8 — 91
(J L Dunlop) *trckd ldr: led over 3f out: rdn and hdd over 2f out: styd on same pce* **11/2**

06-6 **4** *nse* **Hawridge Prince**[32] 1158 8-8-12 **97** ow2 JamesMillman(5) 3 — 96
(B R Millman) *hld up in last pair: rdn 4f out: stdy prog fr over 2f out: styd on same pce* **20/1**

00-2 **5** *2 1/4* **Paktolos (FR)**[29] 1212 5-8-5 **85** oh2 DavidKinsella 10 — 81
(A King) *hld up in last pair: hdwy and effrt 3f out: one pce fnl 2f* **16/1**

6-40 **6** *6* **Prince Sabaah (IRE)**[11] 1568 4-8-4 **85** oh2 RichardSmith 6 — 72
(R Hannon) *in tch tl lost pl over 7f out: smooth hdwy over 3f out: effrt over 2f out: wknd fnl f* **12/1**

032- **7** *7* **Colloquial**[231] 5446 7-9-1 **95** (v) FergusSweeney 4 — 73
(H Candy) *trckd ldrs: rdn 4f out: wknd over 1f out* **10/1**

220/ **8** *10* **Albinus**[14] 3787 7-9-1 **95** DarryllHolland 1 — 59
(A M Balding) *hld up in tch: hdwy 5f out: effrt over 3f out: sn btn* **5/1**[3]

00/4 **9** *1* **Come On Jonny (IRE)**[36] 1070 6-9-2 **96** GeorgeBaker 5 — 58
(R M Beckett) *led tl over 3f out: sn rdn: wknd 2f out* **11/1**

3m 7.75s (0.35) **Going Correction** +0.25s/f (Good)
WFA 4 from 5yo+ 1lb — **9** Ran SP% **121.1**
Speed ratings (Par 109): **109,107,104,104,103 99,95,90,89**
CSF £10.52 CT £39.56 TOTE £2.60: £1.70, £1.80, £1.90; EX 14.10.
Owner Ronchalon Racing (UK) Ltd **Bred** Stonethorn Stud Farms Ltd **Trained** Newmarket, Suffolk

FOCUS

A really decent handicap in which two highly progressive sorts pulled clear of an improving mare and a formerly classy stayer. The form looks good and the front two look destined for better things, particularly Wing Express who does not look far off the better stayers now.

NOTEBOOK

Wing Express(IRE), runner-up to the smart Tranquil Tiger in the Bahrain Trophy on his final start at three, was having to give weight all round on this handicap debut, but he did look open to further progress, what with this being just the fourth start of his career. He had to wait for his run, but once in the clear he quickened up well and was well on top at the line, looking a potential Group performer in the making. He will probably get 2m and it will be interesting to see where he goes next. (op 15-8 tchd 6-4)

Tropical Strait(IRE), a progressive sort on the Polytrack last year who wound up finishing fourth in the November Handicap, was racing off the same mark for this seasonal return and he confirmed himself to still be on the up with a fine effort in second, just finding the classy winner too strong. He was clear of the third and remains one to keep on side for good handicaps. (op 6-1 tchd 7-1)

Swan Queen, another generally progressive type, needed to have made another step forward over the winter to match a couple of these and she ran about as well as could have been expected back in third. She will probably stay 2m. (op 5-1 tchd 6-1)

Hawridge Prince develop into a Group performer two seasons back, but he lost the plot last term and had it to prove on this seasonal reappearance. However, despite carrying 2lb overweight, he plugged on to just miss out on third and this was certainly a step back in the right direction. (op 18-1 tchd 16-1)

Paktolos(FR), racing from 2lb out of the weights, comes from a yard who have carried their good form over to the Flat, but he faced a stiff task against a couple of these and never really threatened. (op 12-1 tchd 10-1)

Prince Sabaah(IRE), another racing from 2lb out, travelled up well towards the outside, but he found little once asked for his effort and faded right out. (op 16-1 tchd 11-1)

Albinus, who has been in decent form over hurdles, has not lived up to expectations on the Flat and this was another disappointing showing. (op 13-2 tchd 15-2)

Come On Jonny(IRE) Official explanation: jockey said gelding ran too free

1842 BATHWICK TYRES LADY RIDERS' SERIES H'CAP — 6f 212y

5:25 (5:30) (Class 6) (0-65,68) 4-Y-O+ — £2,810 (£871; £435; £217) Stalls High

Form — RPR

330- **1** — **Glencal**[206] 6123 4-9-12 **59** MissVCartmel(5) 7 — 71
(H Morrison) *mid-div: rdn and hdwy wl over 1f out: led ent fnl f: r.o wl* **7/1**[3]

000- **2** *2 1/4* **Moves Goodenough**[182] 6677 5-10-6 **62** MissFayeBramley 3 — 68
(Andrew Turnell) *mid-div: hdwy over 2f out: sn rdn: r.o fnl f: snatched 2nd fnl stride* **12/1**

460- **3** *shd* **Vanadium**[167] 6869 6-10-2 **63** MissHayleyMoore(5) 4 — 69
(G L Moore) *hld up towards rr: swtchd lft and hdwy 2f out: sn rdn: chsd wnr jst ins fnl f: eased and lost 2nd fnl strides* **13/2**[2]

3320 **4** *2 3/4* **Sovereignty (JPN)**[9] 1605 6-9-12 **61** MissECrossman(7) 11 — 59
(D K Ivory) *chsd ldrs: rdn and ev ch ent fnl f: no ex* **33/1**

4431 **5** *1 1/4* **Hart Of Gold**[11] 1561 4-10-12 **68** MissSBrotherton 9 — 63
(R A Harris) *chsd ldrs: rdn over 2f out: ev ch over 1f out: kpt on same pce* **8/1**

1630 **6** *3* **Casablanca Minx (IRE)**[15] 1486 5-10-3 **59** (v) MissEFolkes 10 — 46
(P D Evans) *s.i.s: bhd: rdn and stl in last pair 2f out: r.o ins fnl f: nvr a danger* **25/1**

1244 **7** *hd* **Thoughtsofstardom**[7] 1646 5-9-13 **62** MrsLHarris(7) 2 — 48
(M Wigham) *racd alone on stands' side tl joining main gp 4f out: in tch: rdn over 2f out: kpt on same pce* **16/1**

005- **8** *3/4* **My Learned Friend (IRE)**[185] 6610 4-10-9 **65** MissGDGracey-Davison 14 — 49
(A M Balding) *rrd leaving stalls: sn chsng ldrs: rdn and ev ch 2f out: wknd fnl f* **15/2**

-521 **9** *nk* **Trinculo (IRE)**[8] 1634 11-10-1 **60** (b) MissARyan(3) 16 — 43
(R A Harris) *led: rdn and drifted lft fr over 2f out: hdd ent fnl f: wknd* **14/1**

-602 **10** *1 3/4* **Sun Catcher (IRE)**[26] 1260 5-10-8 **64** MrsSMoore 6 — 43
(P G Murphy) *nvr bttr than mid-div* **10/1**

633- **11** *hd* **Bold Cross (IRE)**[188] 6533 5-9-13 **62** MissIPickard(7) 15 — 40
(E G Bevan) *rrd leaving stalls: mid-div: hdwy over 2f out: sn rdn: wknd fnl f* **12/1**

0-00 **12** *1/2* **Outer Hebrides**[7] 1641 7-10-1 **64** ow1 (v) MissHDavies(7) 18 — 41
(J M Bradley) *mid-div: hdwy 3f out: effrt 2f out: wknd fnl f* **20/1**

1442 **13** *hd* **Chief Exec**[9] 1604 6-10-6 **62** (v) MissLEllison 8 — 38
(J R Gask) *in tch: rdn over 2f out: wknd fnl f* **5/1**[1]

5360 **14** *2 3/4* **Goodbye Cash (IRE)**[11] 1561 4-10-3 **62** MrsMarieKing(3) 5 — 31
(P D Evans) *s.i.s: a towards rr* **20/1**

3-00 15 3 1/4 **Strike Force**[102] 270 4-9-11 58......................(p) MissALHutchinson(5) 12 18
(K F Clutterbuck) *mid-div tl 2f out* **40/1**
260- 16 2 1/2 **Looks Could Kill (USA)**[167] 6869 6-10-6 62.................. MissEJJones 1 15
(A B Haynes) *s.i.s: a towards rr* **25/1**
6646 17 1 1/4 **Quality Street**[90] 427 6-10-4 65..............................(p) MissZoeLilly(5) 17 15
(P Butler) *chsd ldrs: rdn and ev ch 2f out: sn wknd* **25/1**
020- 18 7 **Run For Ede'S**[146] 7103 4-10-2 65...............................(p) MissLGray(7) 13 —
(P M Phelan) *dwlt: a bhd* **33/1**

1m 30.6s (1.60) **Going Correction** +0.175s/f (Good) **18** Ran SP% **131.8**
Speed ratings (Par 101): **97,94,94,91,89 86,86,85,84,82 82,82,81,78,75 72,70,62**
CSF £84.48 CT £596.09 TOTE £8.90: £2.50, £3.40, £3.10, £9.20; EX 107.50 Place 6 £ 239.70, Place 5 £ 135.09.
Owner The Caledonian Racing Society **Bred** Fonthill Stud **Trained** East Ilsley, Berks
■ Stewards' Enquiry : Miss Hayley Moore seven-day ban: failed to ride gelding out for second (May 19, 22, 24-25, 27, 30-31)

FOCUS
Quite a competitive handicap, though a poor one and as is the case with most races like this, jockeyship played its part. The field raced centre to far side for most of the journey though they were spread right across the track at the line. Fairly sound form.
T/Plt: £380.00 to a £1 stake. Pool: £56,129.19. 107.80 winning tickets. T/Qpdt: £78.80 to a £1 stake. Pool: £2,899.06. 27.20 winning tickets. TM

1843 - 1846a (Foreign Racing) - See Raceform Interactive

1647 GOWRAN PARK (R-H)
Sunday, May 4

OFFICIAL GOING: Soft (heavy in places)

1847a I.S.F. EUROPEAN BREEDERS' FUND VICTOR MCCALMONT MEMORIAL STKS (LISTED RACE) 1m 1f 100y
4:10 (4:10) 3-Y-O+ £33,507 (£9,830; £4,683; £1,595)

RPR
1 **Chinese White (IRE)**[239] 5239 3-8-9 .... PJSmullen 2 108+
(D K Weld, Ire) *trckd ldrs: chal ent st: led 2f out: clr over 1f out: styd on wl* **5/4**[1]
2 4 1/2 **Zafayra (IRE)**[23] 1318 3-8-9 .... MJKinane 3 99
(John M Oxx, Ire) *trckd ldrs: disp ld over 3f out: advantage briefly ent st: hdd 2f out: no imp on wnr fr over 1f out: kpt on* **5/1**[2]
3 3/4 **Indiana Gal (IRE)**[35] 1104 3-8-10 99 ow1.......................... FMBerry 5 98
(Patrick Martin, Ire) *mid-div: 6th 4f out: hdwy into 3rd under 2f out: no ex fr over 1f out: kpt on* **6/1**[3]
4 3/4 **Beach Bunny (IRE)**[28] 1229 3-8-9 85............................. CDHayes 6 96
(Kevin Prendergast, Ire) *towards rr: swtchd to outer and rdn ent st: 6th under 2f out: kpt on u.p to go 4th fnl f* **10/1**
5 1 3/4 **Yali (IRE)**[28] 1230 3-8-9 92.. RPCleary 8 93
(Francis Ennis, Ire) *towards rr: clsr ent st: rdn to go 5th under 2f out: sn no ex* **9/1**
6 nk **Danehill Music (IRE)**[35] 1104 5-9-12 104......................... DMGrant 12 95
(David Wachman, Ire) *in rr of mid-div on inner: 7th 4f out: rdn in 5th 2f out: no ex fr over 1f out* **17/2**
7 8 **Navajo Moon (IRE)**[233] 5396 4-9-9 103........................... WMLordan 9 77
(David Wachman, Ire) *hld up: clsr in rr ent st: rdn in 7th under 2f out: sn wknd* **9/1**
8 8 **Dani's Girl (IRE)**[28] 1234 5-9-9 90................................ DPMcDonogh 4 62
(P A Fahy, Ire) *chsd ldrs: 4th 4f out: rdn and no ex fr 2f out: wknd* **16/1**
9 1/2 **Juniper Berry (IRE)**[7] 1656 3-8-9 86............................. NGMcCullagh 11 61
(John Joseph Murphy, Ire) *prom: 3rd 4f out: rdn and wknd early st* **33/1**
10 hd **Spanish Cross (IRE)**[35] 1107 3-8-9 .... PShanahan 10 60
(D K Weld, Ire) *led: jnd over 3f out: hdd appr st: sn wknd* **50/1**
11 3 **Soinlovewithyou (USA)**[196] 6364 3-8-9 88......................... JAHeffernan 7 55
(A P O'Brien, Ire) *in rr of mid-div: 8th 4f out: rdn and wknd fr 2f out* **12/1**

2m 7.91s (0.91)
WFA 3 from 4yo+ 14lb **12** Ran SP% **133.5**
CSF £9.05 TOTE £1.90: £1.10, £2.20, £2.10; DF 9.50.
Owner Lady O'Reilly **Bred** Skymarc Farm & Castlemartin St **Trained** The Curragh, Co Kildare

FOCUS
With all eyes focused on the 1000 Guineas at Newmarket it may be that the biggest Oaks clues on show came from this side of the Irish Sea, as the winner routed her opponents in a style that suggested the sky really could be the limit for her.

NOTEBOOK
Chinese White(IRE) produced a most striking display to mark herself out as a potentially top-class filly. Always travelling well just off the pace, she cruised to the front two furlongs out before galloping relentlessly to the line. With Dermot Weld predicting a lot of improvement to come, post-race price quotes for future Classics were, for once, far from fanciful. Out of a winner of the Blandford Stakes, herself a half-sister to the French Oaks winner Rafha, the Oaks trip will pose no problems to Chinese White, with the more galloping nature of The Curragh striking as more suitable than the twists and turns of Epsom at this stage. (op 7/4 tchd 2/1)
Zafayra(IRE), from the family of the smart filly Zafaraniya, tried to stretch the field off the home turn but was simply no match for the winner. (op 12/1)
Indiana Gal(IRE) seems as tough as teak and ran well again, but is now in the twilight world of being uneasily high in the weights for handicaps while at the same time not quite good enough to cope with the bluebloods she encounters at this level. (op 9/2)

1848 - 1849a (Foreign Racing) - See Raceform Interactive

FRANKFURT (L-H)
Sunday, May 4

OFFICIAL GOING: Good

1850a FRUHJAHRSPREIS DES BANKHAUS METZLER (GROUP 3) 1m 2f
4:10 (4:15) 3-Y-O £23,529 (£7,353; £3,676; £2,206)

RPR
1 **Kamsin (GER)** 3-9-0 .... AStarke 2 —
(P Schiergen, Germany) *mde all: rdn out* **30/100**[1]
2 1 1/4 **Lancetto (FR)**[15] 3-9-0 .... AHelfenbein 3 —
(Mario Hofer, Germany) *2nd thrght: rdn fr 1 1/2f out: a hld by wnr* **42/10**[3]
3 2 1/2 **No Pardon (GER)** 3-9-0 .... ADeVries 5 —
(A Trybuhl, Germany) *hld up: hdwy 3f out: 3rd st: sn rdn and one pce* **33/10**[2]
4 2 **Captain Camelot (GER)** 3-9-0 .... MSuerland 4 —
(U Stech, Norway) *hld up in last: nvr a factor* **16/1**
5 6 **Something Stupid (GER)**[35] 3-9-0 .... StefanieHofer 1 —
(Mario Hofer, Germany) *racd in 3rd: 4th st: wknd 1 1/2f out* **114/10**

2m 10.18s (1.61) **5** Ran SP% **133.4**
(including ten euro stakes): WIN 13; PL 12, 17; SF 24.
Owner Stall Blankenese **Bred** Gestut Karlshof **Trained** Germany

1562 KEMPTON (A.W) (R-H)
Monday, May 5

OFFICIAL GOING: Standard
Wind: Fresh, across Weather: Fine and warm

1851 EUROPEAN BREEDERS' FUND MAIDEN STKS 5f (P)
2:00 (2:03) (Class 4) 2-Y-O £4,857 (£1,445; £722; £360) Stalls High

Form RPR
2 1 **Shampagne**[20] 1377 2-9-3 0.. TQuinn 5 82+
(P F I Cole) *mde all: rdn clr ins fnl 2f: readily* **13/8**[1]
2 2 1/4 **The Desert Saint** 2-9-0 0 .... WilliamBuick(3) 10 72
(A M Balding) *prom: rdn 2f out: kpt on to take 2nd fnl 50yds: nt trble wnr* **6/1**[3]
3 3 1 **Flashmans Papers**[14] 1523 2-9-3 0................................ LPKeniry 1 68+
(J R Best) *chsd ldrs: drvn to go 2nd over 1f out: nt qckn fnl f: lost 2nd fnl 50yds* **4/1**[2]
4 1 **Indian Art (IRE)** 2-9-3 0.. RyanMoore 7 65
(R Hannon) *towards rr: pushed along over 3f out: rdn and styd on fnl 2f: nt rch ldrs* **4/1**[2]
5 nk **Ritzy Wildcat (USA)** 2-9-3 0...................................... NCallan 9 64
(S C Williams) *s.s: sn in midfield: effrt 2f out: one pce appr fnl f* **11/1**
5 6 1 **Premier Krug (IRE)**[20] 1385 2-8-12 0........................... JimmyFortune 2 55
(P D Evans) *chsd wnr tl wknd over 1f out* **20/1**
7 2 3/4 **Miss Mojito (IRE)** 2-8-12 0....................................... MartinDwyer 6 45
(J W Hills) *dwlt: rn green and sn bhd: rdn and sme hdwy 2f out: no further prog* **25/1**
34 8 3/4 **Imperial Skylight**[26] 1263 2-9-3 0............................... EdwardCreighton 4 47
(M R Channon) *rrd s: rr gp and wd on bnds: rdn 2f out: n.d* **14/1**
9 3 1/2 **Elusive Ronnie (IRE)** 2-9-3 0.................................... PatCosgrave 8 35
(S A Callaghan) *wd on bnds: a towards rr: rdn and n.d fnl 2f* **25/1**
10 4 1/2 **Josiah Bartlett (IRE)** 2-9-3 0.................................... RHills 3 19
(J W Hills) *mid-div and wd on bnds: nt handle home turn and sn bhd* **40/1**

61.39 secs (0.89) **Going Correction** +0.10s/f (Slow) **10** Ran SP% **122.3**
Speed ratings (Par 95): **96,92,90,89,88 87,82,81,75,68**
CSF £12.05 TOTE £2.50: £1.20, £2.60, £1.60; EX 14.70.
Owner Sisters Syndicate **Bred** Stringston Farm **Trained** Whatcombe, Oxon

FOCUS
A preet solid juvenile race. The winner looks a decent juvenile, and several of those behind should find a race too.

NOTEBOOK
Shampagne ◆ showed the benefit of his debut run with a thoroughly professional performance in which he proved to be overwhelmingly the best of this field on the day. Though he is a good-sized, well-made sort, he handled the sharp bend with aplomb and was always well on top. His speed will stand him in good stead in the coming months, and he should improve again. (op 7-4 tchd 2-1)
The Desert Saint, a 37,000gns Dubai Destination newcomer, has winners in the family up to 1m2f and should settle down around a mile in due course. Though no match for the winner, he made a promising debut and should find a race in his own right. (op 15-2 tchd 8-1)
Flashmans Papers had run well on his racecourse debut, on turf, and this solid effort showed he goes on Polytrack too. There are races to be won with him. (tchd 7-2 and 9-2)
Indian Art(IRE), an 85,000gns Choisir half-brother to the high-class sprinter Perryston View, is obviously bred to be very speedy. Though too green for his own good early on around the tricky 5f bend, he was getting the hang of things in the final furlong and looks an interesting sort with the race under his belt. (op 5-1 tchd 7-2)
Ritzy Wildcat(USA) has a fine US Dirt pedigree, with his sire being a notable speedster in the States and his dam winning a number of races over sprint distances too. Though never looking likely to make a successful debut, he should be sharper for the run and ought to win races, particularly on the All-Weather tracks, if he lives up to his family's record. (op 10-1 tchd 8-1)
Premier Krug(IRE) showed more speed this time, only to fade out of it in the last furlong, and should have a sporting chance in nurseries after one more run. (tchd 22-1)

1852 ODDSCHECKER.COM H'CAP 5f (P)
2:30 (2:30) (Class 4) (0-85,84) 3-Y-O £4,209 (£1,252; £625; £312) Stalls High

Form RPR
532 1 **Espy**[22] 1347 3-8-2 71.. WilliamBuick(3) 6 86
(S Kirk) *trckd ldrs in 4th: led over 1f out: rdn clr: comf* **7/2**[2]
2145 2 3 1/4 **Baytown Blaze**[61] 798 3-8-2 73.................................. KellyHarrison(5) 2 76
(M Wigham) *t.k.h in 3rd: rdn and edgd lft over 1f out: tk 2nd ins fnl f: nt trble wnr* **13/2**
-210 3 2 1/2 **Kinout (IRE)**[16] 1484 3-8-11 77.................................. NCallan 7 71
(K A Ryan) *sn disputing ld: led 2f out: hrd rdn and hdd over 1f out: no ex* **5/2**[1]
-104 4 1/2 **Bertbrand**[82] 538 3-8-4 73.. KirstyMilczarek(3) 4 65
(M Botti) *sn bhd: rdn over 2f out: nrst fin* **15/2**
0-30 5 2 3/4 **Enodoc**[25] 1284 3-8-7 73... MartinDwyer 1 55
(W R Muir) *disp ld tl 2f out: wknd wl over 1f out* **10/1**
02-0 6 1/2 **Bosun Breese**[10] 1597 3-9-4 84.................................. LPKeniry 3 65
(P W D'Arcy) *plld hrd: chsd ldrs early: awkward on bnd and lost pl after 1f: sn rdn along towards rr* **4/1**[3]
1-00 7 2 3/4 **Miesko (USA)**[16] 1484 3-9-2 82.................................. GregFairley 5 53
(M Johnston) *s.i.s: bhd: wnt mod 5th 3f out: rdn and n.d fnl 2f* **15/2**

59.88 secs (-0.62) **Going Correction** +0.10s/f (Slow) **7** Ran SP% **116.7**
Speed ratings (Par 101): **108,102,98,98,93 92,88**
CSF £27.08 TOTE £3.70: £1.60, £4.90; EX 30.60.
Owner P D Merritt J Davies T Sharman **Bred** Miss Brooke Sanders **Trained** Upper Lambourn, Berks

FOCUS
A fair turnout for the track, and a good pace, resulting in a decent winning time for the type of race.
Kinout(IRE) Official explanation: jockey said gelding hung left
Bertbrand Official explanation: jockey said gelding lost a near-fore shoe

1853 AUSTIN GAUGHAN'S 50TH BIRTHDAY CRAIC H'CAP 1m 2f (P)
3:00 (3:02) (Class 6) (0-65,65) 4-Y-O+ £2,047 (£604; £302) Stalls High

Form RPR
1353 1 **Our Kes (IRE)**[5] 1725 6-9-4 65.................................... IanMongan 15 74
(P Howling) *chsd ldrs: effrt and hung rt 2f out: styd on to ld fnl 30yds* **11/2**[3]
0533 2 1/2 **Alexander Guru**[10] 1605 4-9-0 61................................ NCallan 3 69
(M Blanshard) *prom: hrd rdn over 1f out: chal ins fnl f: kpt on* **9/1**

0213 **3** *nk* **Floodlight Fantasy**[10] 1606 5-8-9 **56**....................(b) RyanMoore 6 63
(Dr R D P Newland) *t.k.h: chsd ldr: led over 1f out: hrd rdn fnl f: hdd and nt qckn fnl 30yds* **4/1**[1]
/00- **4** *2* **Follow The Colours (IRE)**[150] 7056 5-8-10 **62**.............. PatrickHills(5) 8 65
(J W Hills) *sn led: hrd rdn and hdd over 1f out: one pce* **28/1**
144- **5** *½* **Constant Cheers (IRE)**[183] 6666 5-9-2 **63**................ SaleemGolam 9 65
(W R Swinburn) *prom: rdn over 2f out: no ex appr fnl f* **15/2**
1034 **6** *1¾* **Just Intersky (USA)**[13] 1554 5-9-1 **62**....................(e) DeanMcKeown 14 61
(V Smith) *mid-div: effrt 3f out: styd on same pce* **12/1**
0151 **7** *hd* **Dinner Date**[12] 1565 6-9-4 **65**.............................. J-PGuillambert 12 64+
(T Keddy) *mid-div: n.m.r and dropped towards rr bnd over 3f out: rdn and styd on fnl 2f* **6/1**
2222 **8** *2¼* **Kings Topic (USA)**[7] 1673 8-9-0 **61**....................(b) JimmyFortune 13 55
(A B Haynes) *towards rr: rdn 1/2-way: nvr rchd ldrs* **5/1**[2]
2020 **9** *½* **Convallaria (FR)**[40] 1032 5-8-10 **57**....................(t) DaneO'Neill 10 50
(G Wragg) *in tch: rdn 1/2-way: btn 3f out* **10/1**
00-0 **10** *10* **Splinter Group**[32] 1172 4-9-1 **62**.......................... PatCosgrave 11 35
(S A Callaghan) *a bhd: drvn along 1/2-way: no ch fnl 3f* **66/1**
554 **11** *1* **Hucking Hill (IRE)**[67] 729 4-9-4 **65**........................ LPKeniry 7 36
(J R Best) *in tch tl hrd rdn and wknd 3f out* **16/1**
01-0 **12** *nk* **Golden Brown (IRE)**[19] 1406 4-8-11 **58**.................... NeilChalmers 4 28
(David Pinder) *towards rr: rdn 4f out: no ch whn rn wd bnd into st* **33/1**
560- **13** *2¾* **Scottish River (USA)**[283] 3907 9-9-0 **61**.................. RichardSmith 5 26
(M D I Usher) *s.s: plld hrd in rr: rdn 3f out: no ch whn rn wd bnd into st* **33/1**

2m 9.31s (1.31) **Going Correction** +0.10s/f (Slow) 13 Ran SP% **121.6**
Speed ratings (Par 101): **98,97,97,95,95 93,93,92,91,83 82,82,80**
CSF £53.87 CT £224.42 TOTE £7.30: £2.70, £3.10, £1.80; EX 70.30.
Owner S J Hammond **Bred** Yeomanstown Stud **Trained** Newmarket, Suffolk

FOCUS
A modest but competitive race, but the pace was steady and it paid to be prominent. The form looks sound rated around the first two.
Convallaria(FR) Official explanation: jockey said mare hung right

1854 CHERYL HUMPHREY'S 50TH BIRTHDAY MAIDEN STKS (DIV I) 1m (P)
3:30 (3:32) (Class 4) 3-Y-O £3,723 (£1,108; £553; £276) Stalls High

Form RPR
42- **1** **Austintatious (USA)**[214] 5951 3-9-3 0.......................... LDettori 3 75+
(B J Meehan) *rrd s: racd wd and hdwy to ld after 2f: rdn and r.o wl fnl 2f: a holding rivals* **4/9**[1]
2 *1¼* **Visions Of Johanna (USA)** 3-9-3 0........................ RyanMoore 7 72+
(J Noseda) *prom: rdn to chse wnr 2f out: a hld but kpt on wl to hold 2nd* **7/1**[2]
03- **3** *½* **Amhooj**[206] 6139 3-8-12 0...................................... RHills 6 66
(M P Tregoning) *hld up in midfield: effrt and drvn along over 2f out: styd on fnl f* **10/1**[3]
05- **4** *¾* **Royal Straight**[194] 6417 3-9-3 0............................ LPKeniry 8 69
(A M Balding) *hld up in midfield: effrt on outside 3f out: hrd rdn 2f out: styd on same pce* **33/1**
0 **5** *4½* **De Facto**[18] 1418 3-9-3 0..............................(b[1]) JimmyFortune 11 59
(J H M Gosden) *bhd: rdn along and sme hdwy over 2f out: nvr rchd ldrs* **16/1**
6 **6** *1¼* **Cheney Manor**[10] 1601 3-8-10 0..................... ChrisGlenister(7) 4 56
(B W Hills) *prom tl wknd 2f out* **50/1**
2-4 **7** *4* **James Dean (IRE)**[10] 1601 3-8-10 0...................... DTDaSilva(7) 9 47
(P F I Cole) *t.k.h: chsd ldrs 3f: stdd bk into midfield: n.m.r and swtchd rt over 2f out: sn rdn and btn* **16/1**
00 **8** *hd* **Tallest Peak (USA)**[6] 1701 3-9-0 0...................... JerryO'Dwyer(3) 5 46
(M G Quinlan) *led 2f: prom tl wknd over 2f out* **100/1**
364- **9** *2¾* **Sainglend**[217] 5871 3-9-3 79.................................... PaulDoe 2 40
(S Curran) *towards rr: shkn up over 2f out: n.d* **16/1**
0 **10** *1½* **Travelling Light (USA)**[17] 1445 3-8-12 0.................. NCallan 10 32
(R Charlton) *s.s: towards rr: sme hdwy on outside and rdn 1/2-way: wknd 3f out* **14/1**
11 *13* **Misselliebee** 3-8-12 0.. MartinDwyer 12 2
(J W Hills) *a bhd: rdn and no ch 3f out* **66/1**

1m 40.56s (0.76) **Going Correction** +0.10s/f (Slow) 11 Ran SP% **122.5**
Speed ratings (Par 101): **100,98,98,97,93 91,87,87,84,83 70**
CSF £4.39 TOTE £1.50: £1.10, £1.50, £2.00; EX 5.80.
Owner Team Valor **Bred** Woodlynn Farm Inc & Brian Hoeweler **Trained** Manton, Wilts

FOCUS
An above-average maiden for the track but not easy to assess with the third and fourth probably the best guides for now.

1855 CHERYL HUMPHREY'S 50TH BIRTHDAY MAIDEN STKS (DIV II) 1m (P)
4:00 (4:03) (Class 4) 3-Y-O £3,723 (£1,108; £553; £276) Stalls High

Form RPR
2 **1** **Khateeb (IRE)**[18] 1418 3-9-3 0..............................(t) RHills 8 92+
(M A Jarvis) *s.i.s: sn in tch and travelled strly: led over 2f out: easily drew clr: impressive* **1/2**[1]
3-2 **2** *8* **Barricado (FR)**[20] 1380 3-9-3 0.............................. NCallan 3 69
(R Charlton) *hld up towards rr: hdwy 3f out: rdn and hung lft 2f out: kpt on to take 2nd fnl 75yds: no ch w wnr* **7/2**[2]
6- **3** *1¾* **Media Stars**[189] 6530 3-9-3 0.......................... JimmyFortune 11 65
(J A Osborne) *mid-div: rdn to take 6l 2nd 2f out: sn no ch w wnr: lost 2nd fnl 75yds* **16/1**
3-0 **4** *2* **Parson's Punch**[92] 416 3-9-3 0............................ DaneO'Neill 2 60+
(P D Cundell) *s.i.s: hld up and bhd: rdn and hdwy into fair 4th 2f out: nt trble ldrs* **25/1**
0-0 **5** *1½* **Ejeed (USA)**[12] 1573 3-9-3 0............................... MartinDwyer 9 57+
(J H M Gosden) *mid-div: rdn and losing grnd over 3f out: styd on same pce fnl 2f: n.d* **14/1**
463- **6** *1¾* **Cotton Reel**[185] 6617 3-9-3 77........................ NelsonDeSouza 6 53
(P F I Cole) *plld hrd early: prom: n.m.r on rail and lost pl home turn: n.d after* **12/1**[3]
7 *10* **Harveys Spirit (IRE)**[197] 6365 3-8-12 0...................... PaulDoe 1 25
(S Curran) *a bhd: rdn and no ch 3f out* **66/1**
00 **8** *hd* **Buck Cannon (IRE)**[21] 1367 3-9-3 0......................... AmirQuinn 5 29
(P M Phelan) *led over 1f: styd prom: rdn along after 3f: wknd over 2f out* **66/1**
00- **9** *¾* **Mellifluous (IRE)**[184] 6649 3-8-7 0.................... PatrickHills(5) 4 23
(J W Hills) *mid-div on outside: rdn and wd bnd into st: sn bhd* **100/1**
0-0 **10** *3½* **Sun In Splendour (USA)**[15] 1504 3-9-3 0.................. NeilPollard 10 20
(A P Jarvis) *prom on rail: led over 6f out tl over 2f out: sn wknd* **100/1**

1m 40.06s (0.26) **Going Correction** +0.10s/f (Slow) 10 Ran SP% **117.9**
Speed ratings (Par 101): **102,94,92,90,88 87,77,76,76,72**
CSF £2.43 TOTE £1.50: £1.10, £1.50, £2.70; EX 2.40.
Owner Hamdan Al Maktoum **Bred** Kilfrush Stud **Trained** Newmarket, Suffolk

FOCUS
Thefaster of the two divisions and the winner looks a very useful sort in the making, but several of the others should also find a race at various levels. The form is rated around the placed horses.

1856 COMPARE ODDS AT ODDSCHECKER.COM H'CAP 2m (P)
4:30 (4:31) (Class 5) (0-75,66) 4-Y-0+ £2,590 (£770; £385; £192) Stalls High

Form RPR
1315 **1** **Coda Agency**[23] 1337 5-8-13 **55**.............................. NCallan 11 65
(D W P Arbuthnot) *chsd ldrs: led 4f out: hrd rdn 2f out: hld on gamely u.p* **10/3**[1]
1326 **2** *¾* **Alnwick**[52] 880 4-9-6 **65**.................................. DaneO'Neill 4 74
(P D Cundell) *hld up in tch: wnt 2l 2nd 3f out: hrd rdn over 2f out: kpt on: a hld* **4/1**[2]
0-06 **3** *nk* **Bobsleigh**[26] 1267 9-8-2 **47** oh2...................... KirstyMilczarek(3) 5 56
(H S Howe) *in tch: rdn to go handy 3rd 3f out: disp 2nd fnl f: kpt on: a hld by wnr* **16/1**
4-03 **4** *9* **Rose Bien**[32] 1165 6-9-0 **56**..............................(p) AmirQuinn 8 54+
(P J McBride) *s.s: hld up and bhd: rdn 3f out: sme hdwy to take modest 4th fnl 2f: n.d* **7/1**
2250 **5** *8* **Lorikeet**[23] 1337 9-9-9 **65**................................... RyanMoore 6 54
(G L Moore) *hld up in rr of midfield: rdn 4f out: wnt remote 5th ins fnl 2f* **11/2**[3]
00-4 **6** *1¾* **Title Deed (USA)**[18] 1411 4-9-4 **63**....................... NeilPollard 10 50
(A P Jarvis) *t.k.h in rr of midfield: drvn to dispute modest 4th over 2f out: nt trble ldrs and sn wknd* **33/1**
3-50 **7** *nk* **High Point (IRE)**[52] 880 10-9-10 **66**................... SimonWhitworth 9 52+
(G P Enright) *bhd: rdn 4f out: nvr nr ldrs* **16/1**
5031 **8** *¾* **Synonymy**[19] 1408 5-9-5 **61**..............................(b) LPKeniry 1 46
(M Blanshard) *prom: hrd rdn 4f out: sn wknd* **8/1**
66P/ **9** *3¼* **Fiddlers Ford (IRE)**[656] 3649 7-9-4 **60**.................. J-PGuillambert 2 41
(T Keddy) *led 4f: chsd ldrs on rail: wknd over 3f out* **25/1**
443 **10** *nse* **Brave Bugsy (IRE)**[59] 823 5-9-1 **57**...................... NeilChalmers 7 38
(A M Balding) *hld up in rr of midfield: hdwy on outside 6f out: rdn over 4f out: sn wknd* **11/2**[3]
5-03 **11** *dist* **Sister Agnes (IRE)**[13] 1538 4-9-3 **62**....................(v) JimmyFortune 3 —
(M F Harris) *stmbld s: sn prom: led after 4f tl 4f out: wknd 3f out: eased whn no ch over 1f out* **16/1**

3m 31.14s (1.04) **Going Correction** +0.10s/f (Slow)
WFA 4 from 5yo+ 3lb 11 Ran SP% **121.9**
Speed ratings (Par 103): **101,100,100,95,91 91,90,90,88,88** —
CSF £17.11 CT £192.94 TOTE £3.60: £1.40, £1.90, £5.90; EX 17.70.
Owner Banfield, Thompson **Bred** Baydon House Stud **Trained** Compton, Berks
■ Stewards' Enquiry : L P Keniry caution: used whip when out of contention

FOCUS
A moderate staying race, and the gallop was not great either so the form may not prove entirely solid, with the close third running from out of the weights.
Lorikeet Official explanation: jockey said gelding hung right

1857 JUBILEE H'CAP (LONDON MILE QUALIFIER) 1m (P)
5:00 (5:01) (Class 3) (0-90,90) 4-Y-0+
£9,346 (£2,799; £1,399; £700; £349; £175) Stalls High

Form RPR
351- **1** **Viva Vettori**[219] 5816 4-8-12 **84**.............................. MartinDwyer 6 95
(D R C Elsworth) *mde all: sn 2l up: rdn and hld on wl fnl 2f* **8/1**
600 **2** *1¼* **Northern Spy (USA)**[37] 1067 4-8-9 **81**....................... DaneO'Neill 2 92+
(S Dow) *hld up and bhd: weaved through and gd hdwy fnl 2f: tk 2nd nr fin* **14/1**
-006 **3** *nk* **Bomber Command (USA)**[44] 969 5-8-6 **83**..........(v) PatrickHills(5) 5 90
(J W Hills) *t.k.h: in tch: effrt and hung rt over 2f out: disp 2nd over 1f out: kpt on same pce* **12/1**
64-2 **4** *nse* **Nice To Know (FR)**[23] 1335 4-8-8 **80**........................ RyanMoore 7 87
(G L Moore) *hld up in tch: wnt 2l 2nd 2f out: nt qckn fnl f: lost 2nd nr fin* **11/4**[1]
0540 **5** *¾* **Councellor (FR)**[23] 1335 6-8-13 **85**........................(t) MickyFenton 8 91
(Stef Liddiard) *mid-div: rdn 4f out: hdwy to dispute 4th pl 2f out: kpt on fnl f* **10/1**
10/1 **6** *½* **Jake The Snake (IRE)**[33] 1146 7-8-2 **77** oh4 ow1... KirstyMilczarek(3) 4 81+
(A W Carroll) *hld up towards rr: hdwy on outside 2f out: rdn and styd on: nt rch ldrs* **11/2**[2]
2221 **7** *2¼* **Count Ceprano (IRE)**[19] 1409 4-8-8 **80**.................. RichardSmith 1 79
(M D I Usher) *mid-div: rdn 3f out: no imp* **10/1**
300- **8** *7* **Jedburgh**[199] 6301 7-9-4 **90**..........................(b) JimmyFortune 10 73
(J L Dunlop) *hld up in rr: rdn over 2f out: n.d* **16/1**
345- **9** *2* **Russian Epic**[277] 4111 4-8-7 **79** ow1......................... NCallan 11 58
(M A Jarvis) *mid-div: drvn along 4f out: sn outpcd* **7/1**[3]
0-56 **10** *½* **Cross The Line (IRE)**[15] 1502 6-8-10 **82**.................. NeilPollard 12 59
(A P Jarvis) *t.k.h: prom tl wknd jst over 2f out* **12/1**
600- **11** *2* **Hopeful Purchase (IRE)**[239] 993 5-9-0 **86**............... NeilChalmers 14 59
(J R Gask) *hld up in tch on rail: shkn up over 2f out: sn wknd* **66/1**
250- **12** *2¾* **Minnis Bay (CAN)**[224] 5685 4-8-6 **78** ow1...................... LPKeniry 13 44
(E F Vaughan) *prom tl hrd rdn and wknd 2f out* **25/1**
001- **13** *16* **Eva Soneva So Fast (IRE)**[15] 6230 6-8-12 **87**.......... DominicFox(3) 9 17
(G F Bridgwater) *s.s: sn drvn along in rr: wl bhd fr 1/2-way* **50/1**
1544 **14** *½* **Electric Warrior (IRE)**[13] 1545 5-8-11 **90**.............. DeclanCannon(7) 3 19
(K R Burke) *prom: wknd over 3f out: 6th and losing pl whn rn wd bnd into st* **12/1**

1m 38.73s (-1.07) **Going Correction** +0.10s/f (Slow) 14 Ran SP% **126.8**
Speed ratings (Par 107): **109,107,107,107,106 106,103,96,94,94 92,89,73,73**
CSF £120.17 CT £1367.10 TOTE £9.90: £2.70, £5.70, £2.50; EX 363.00.
Owner Mike Watson **Bred** Stanley Estate And Stud Co **Trained** Newmarket, Suffolk

FOCUS
A fair race of its type, with a relatively unexposed winner. The form appears sound enough rated around the third and fifth.

NOTEBOOK
Viva Vettori put in a likeable front-running performance and, as a winner of a 1m2f maiden last season, looks capable of winning in handicap company at either trip. He should remain hard to pass for the time being. (op 15-2)
Northern Spy(USA) ◆ made up a lot of ground in the home straight, and would not be inconvenienced by a longer trip. He looks to be on the verge of winning again. (op 16-1)
Bomber Command(USA) has only ever won at 7f, but he has run some good races at this trip, and a win at 1m is still a possibility. (op 14-1)
Nice To Know(FR) travelled really well, so it was something of a disappointment that she could not even hang onto second place in the end. However, the winner was relatively unexposed, and she was not beaten far, so she should not be written off yet off this 4lb higher mark. (op 3-1 tchd 5-2, 9-2, 4-1, 7-2 and 10-3 in places)

Councellor(FR) has been falling just short this season, but he is fairly handicapped at present and two of his last three races have suggested a return to peak form before long.
Jake The Snake(IRE) ◆ should have been suited by the longer trip, but he was given plenty to do and when he reached top gear it was too late. Lightly-raced, and 4lb out of the handicap here, he remains an interesting sort and could yet win a handicap over 1m off a similar mark. (op 9-2)
Count Ceprano(IRE), 6lb higher than last time, drawn in the outside box, and running over an extra furlong, had not ticked enough of the boxes to be a leading hope. (op 11-1)
Eva Soneva So Fast(IRE) Official explanation: jockey said gelding never travelled

1858 FAMILY DAY FILLIES' H'CAP — 6f (P)
5:30 (5:30) (Class 4) (0-85,81) 4-Y-0+ — **£4,209** (£1,252; £625; £312) **Stalls** High

Form — RPR

6460 **1** **Carcinetto (IRE)**[30] 1211 6-9-4 **81** .... JimmyFortune 4 — 86
(P D Evans) *led tl over 1f out: rallied wl: drvn to get bk up last 25yds* **7/2**[2]

0-21 **2** *hd* **Expensive Art (IRE)**[16] 1488 4-8-13 **76** .... NCallan 3 — 80+
(S A Callaghan) *trckd ldr: led over 1f out and wnt a nk up: kpt on u.p: hdd last 25yds* **4/6**[1]

40-0 **3** *2 1/4* **Shes Minnie**[25] 1278 5-9-3 **80** .... RyanMoore 1 — 77
(P A Blockley) *settled in 3rd: rdn over 2f out: one pce* **11/2**[3]

5-10 **4** *2 1/2* **Cinnamon Hill**[21] 1368 4-8-9 **72** ow1 .... DaneO'Neill 5 — 61
(Eve Johnson Houghton) *rrd bdly s and lost 4l: plld hrd in rr: effrt over 2f out: 4th and btn whn hung lft fr over 1f out* **7/1**

1m 15.08s (1.98) **Going Correction** +0.10s/f (Slow) — **4** Ran SP% **110.1**
Speed ratings (Par 102): **90,89,86,83**
CSF £6.52 TOTE £4.10; EX 7.80 Place 6 £12.22, Place 5 £8.74..
Owner Mrs Sally Edwards **Bred** M A Doyle **Trained** Pandy, Monmouths

FOCUS
A fair turnout, though lacking in numbers, and a modest pace for a 6f event, leading to a very slow time for the type of race, so the form cannot be taken literally.
T/Plt: £16.20 to a £1 stake. Pool: £69,672.01. 3,138.75 winning tickets. T/Qpdt: £4.80 to a £1 stake. Pool: £3,536.90. 538.60 winning tickets. LM

1217 NEWCASTLE (L-H)
Monday, May 5
1859 Meeting Abandoned - Waterlogged

1384 WARWICK (L-H)
Monday, May 5

OFFICIAL GOING: Good to soft (soft in places)
Wind: virtually nil Weather: fine

1865 KNOWLE APPRENTICE H'CAP — 6f
2:15 (2:22) (Class 6) (0-55,54) 4-Y-0+ — **£2,047** (£604; £302) **Stalls** Centre

Form — RPR

4623 **1** **Imperial Sword**[7] 1687 5-8-9 **49** ....(b) NeilBrown 11 — 61+
(T D Barron) *hld up and bhd: nt clr run and swtchd lft wl over 1f out: gd hdwy ent fnl f: r.o wl to ld towards fin* **5/1**[1]

20-2 **2** *1 1/4* **Kyllachy Storm**[8] 1642 4-8-11 **51** .... HaddenFrost 10 — 59
(R J Hodges) *a.p: chsd ldr and rdn over 1f out: edgd lft ins fnl f: kpt on* **7/1**

000- **3** *3/4* **Puskas (IRE)**[154] 7011 5-8-5 **50** ....(b[1]) PietroRomeo(5) 8 — 56
(J M Bradley) *t.k.h: w ldr: led over 2f out: hung lft fnl f: hdd towards fin* **22/1**

-425 **4** *3* **Kennington**[78] 596 8-8-10 **53** ....(b) SophieDoyle(3) 13 — 53+
(Mrs C A Dunnett) *hld up in mid-div: lost pl over 2f out: swtchd rt wl over 1f out: hdwy on stands' side: kpt on* **20/1**

-004 **5** *1* **Norcroft**[7] 1687 6-8-7 **52** ....(p) KrishGundowry(5) 3 — 45+
(Mrs C A Dunnett) *n.m.r s: hld up in mid-div: nt clr run wl over 1f out: kpt on fnl f* **12/1**

5-13 **6** *2* **Hammer Of The Gods (IRE)**[31] 1191 8-8-11 **54**(bt) PatrickDonaghy(3) 5 — 40
(G C Bravery) *led: hdd over 2f out: rdn over 1f out: wknd ins fnl f* **15/2**

-454 **7** *2* **Greenwood**[24] 1313 10-8-12 **52** .... JamieJones 1 — 32
(P G Murphy) *wnt rt s: chsd ldrs: rdn 2f out: no hdwy whn rdr dropped whip jst over 1f out* **16/1**

4060 **8** *1/2* **Sherjawy (IRE)**[16] 1476 4-8-7 **52** ....(b) RossAtkinson(5) 7 — 30
(Miss Z C Davison) *hld up and bhd: sme hdwy over 1f out: n.d* **14/1**

-046 **9** *3/4* **Briery Lane (IRE)**[9] 1634 7-8-10 **53** .... SCreighton(3) 16 — 29
(J M Bradley) *chsd ldrs: rdn over 1f out: wknd fnl f* **14/1**

3236 **10** *nk* **Cleveland**[8] 1642 6-8-5 **50** .... NBazeley(5) 2 — 25
(R Hollinshead) *prom: rdn whn edgd lft wl over 1f out: wknd fnl f* **7/1**

000- **11** *2 1/4* **Lady Lorins**[189] 6546 4-8-5 **48** .... ThomasO'Brien(3) 9 — 16
(Andrew Turnell) *mid-div: pushed along over 3f out: rdn whn rdr lost iron wl over 1f out: eased fnl f* **40/1**

0601 **12** *hd* **Polar Force**[17] 1455 8-8-7 **52** .... SimonPearce(5) 12 — 19
(Mrs C A Dunnett) *s.i.s: hld up and bhd: rdn and short-lived effrt over 2f out* **13/2**[3]

/0-0 **13** *7* **Indian Lady (IRE)**[18] 1416 5-8-4 **49** .... AshleyMorgan(5) 15 — —
(Mrs A L M King) *rdn over 2f out: a in rr* **33/1**

00-4 **14** *3 1/4* **Ensign's Trick**[11] 1578 4-9-0 **54** .... AshleyHamblett 14 — —
(W M Brisbourne) *walked to post: half-rrd and s.i.s: racd wd: a bhd* **6/1**[2]

1m 17.2s (5.40) **Going Correction** +0.65s/f (Yiel) — **14** Ran SP% **122.4**
Speed ratings (Par 101): **106,104,103,99,98 95,92,92,91,90 87,87,78,73**
CSF £38.02 CT £724.22 TOTE £4.80: £1.60, £3.10, £6.60; EX 45.80.
Owner Harrowgate Bloodstock Ltd **Bred** David John Brown **Trained** Maunby, N Yorks
■ Stewards' Enquiry : Sophie Doyle two-day ban: used whip with excessive frequency (May 19-20)
Ashley Morgan caution: used whip above shoulder height

FOCUS
A moderate, yet competitive handicap and the form looks sound.
Ensign's Trick Official explanation: jockey said filly reared as gates opened and collided with stalls

1866 EUROPEAN BREEDERS' FUND PRIMROSE MAIDEN FILLIES' STKS — 5f
2:45 (2:50) (Class 5) 2-Y-O — **£3,626** (£1,079; £539; £269) **Stalls** Centre

Form — RPR

1 **To The Point** 2-9-0 0 .... RichardMullen 1 — 82+
(E S McMahon) *chsd ldr: led over 3f out: shkn up over 1f out: r.o wl: eased nr fin* **15/8**[1]

2 *2 1/2* **Forward Feline (IRE)** 2-9-0 0 .... CatherineGannon 2 — 70
(B Palling) *prom: rdn 1/2-way: chsd wnr over 1f out: styd on* **7/1**[3]

3 *6* **Accede** 2-9-0 0 .... JamesDoyle 6 — 48
(J G Portman) *mid-div: hdwy 2f out: wknd ins fnl f* **7/1**[3]

4 *3* **Kerrys Requiem (IRE)** 2-9-0 0 .... ChrisCatlin 10 — 38
(M R Channon) *led: racd keenly: hdd over 3f out: rdn 1/2-way: wknd fnl f* **7/2**[2]

5 *1/2* **Nativity** 2-8-11 0 .... TolleyDean(3) 9 — 36
(J L Spearing) *prom: wkng whn hung lft fr over 1f out* **9/1**

6 *1 1/2* **Dancing Welcome** 2-8-7 0 .... PietroRomeo(7) 4 — 30
(J M Bradley) *dwlt: outpcd* **33/1**

00 **7** *1 1/4* **Sharp Discovery**[14] 1523 2-9-0 0 .... PaulFitzsimons 8 — 26
(J M Bradley) *prom over 3f* **33/1**

8 *6* **Baby Is Here (IRE)** 2-9-0 0 .... RichardThomas 7 — 4
(D J S Ffrench Davis) *sn outpcd* **20/1**

4 **9** *4* **Bethie**[20] 1385 2-9-0 0 .... PaulMulrennan 11 — —
(R Brotherton) *chsd ldrs: rdn 1/2-way: wknd over 1f out* **8/1**

10 *11* **Betoula** 2-8-11 0 .... LukeMorris(3) 3 — —
(Mrs A L M King) *s.s: outpcd* **22/1**

64.68 secs (5.08) **Going Correction** +0.65s/f (Yiel) — **10** Ran SP% **118.1**
Speed ratings (Par 90): **85,81,71,66,65 63,61,51,45,27**
CSF £15.02 TOTE £2.30: £1.30, £1.90, £2.90; EX 17.80.
Owner J C Fretwell **Bred** Mrs Johnny Eddis **Trained** Lichfield, Staffs

FOCUS
A race lacking strength in depth, but To The Point made a highly pleasing start to her career with a dominant display and along with the runner-up could go on from this.

NOTEBOOK
To The Point, whose yard sent out their first juvenile runner to finish second, was strong at the head of the market and she certainly knew her job. In front before halfway, she had it won off the home bend and stayed on strongly under pressure to score with plenty in hand. This was a taking debut from the daughter of Refuse To Bend, who incidentally was having his first winner as a sire, and connections were talking of a possible crack at the Queen Mary afterwards. (op 7-2)
Forward Feline(IRE), a 15,000gns daughter of One Cool Cat, comes from a yard that can ready a debutant and she fared best of the rest in second, keeping on right the way to the line. This was a promising start and winning an ordinary maiden should prove a formality. (op 5-1 tchd 15-2)
Accede, who played up in preliminaries and took some coaxing down to the start, is bred for speed, but she was caught out by inexperience and made just a satisfactory debut back in third. Her yard already has a useful juvenile on their hands in the shape of Baycat and she should improve enough to win races at the right level. (op 5-1 tchd 8-1)
Kerrys Requiem(IRE), a 45,000euros daughter of King's Best, comes from a yard whose juveniles seem to be needing their first runs and she will require further than this in time. (op 10-3 tchd 9-2)
Nativity, a half-sister to numerous winners over further, showed up well to a point, but faded right out in the end and may be in need of more time. (tchd 8-1)
Bethie, a fair fourth on her recent course and distance debut, failed to build on it and ran terribly back in a well-beaten ninth. (tchd 7-1)
Betoula Official explanation: jockey said filly missed the break

1867 RACING UK FILLIES' H'CAP — 7f 26y
3:15 (3:17) (Class 5) (0-70,70) 3-Y-0+ — **£3,238** (£963; £481; £240) **Stalls** Low

Form — RPR

5-32 **1** **Support Fund (IRE)**[8] 1641 4-9-9 **64** .... StephenCarson 5 — 81
(Eve Johnson Houghton) *hld up and bhd: swtchd rt and hdwy wl over 1f out: sn rdn: led ins fnl f: rdn out* **7/2**[1]

14- **2** *1 1/4* **Orpen Fire (IRE)**[160] 6960 3-9-3 **70** .... RichardMullen 3 — 80
(E S McMahon) *hld up in mid-div: hdwy 2f out: led over 1f out: rdn and hdd ins fnl f: nt qckn* **8/1**

6-40 **3** *8* **Poppy's Rose**[17] 1449 4-9-8 **63** .... RoystonFfrench 10 — 55
(I W McInnes) *chsd ldrs: ev ch 2f out: wknd fnl f* **14/1**

20-4 **4** *nk* **Red Amaryllis**[26] 1271 3-9-3 **70** .... RichardKingscote 1 — 57
(H J L Dunlop) *w ldr: led 2f out: rdn and hdd over 1f out: wknd ins fnl f* **14/1**

-615 **5** *hd* **Never Catcher (IRE)**[20] 1381 3-9-2 **69** .... StephenDonohoe 9 — 56
(P A Blockley) *hld up and bhd: rdn and hdwy over 1f out: edgd lft ins fnl f: one pce* **9/1**

1-54 **6** *3/4* **Mugeba**[13] 1534 7-9-3 **58** ....(t) ShaneKelly 8 — 47
(Miss Gay Kelleway) *hld up and bhd: rdn and hdwy on ins 2f out: wknd ins fnl f* **9/1**

3550 **7** *1/2* **Affirmatively**[7] 1671 3-9-2 **69** .... AlanMunro 6 — 52
(D R C Elsworth) *stdd s: hld up in rr: sme hdwy on ins over 1f out: nvr nr ldrs* **25/1**

150- **8** *nk* **Pragmatist**[209] 6089 4-9-6 **61** .... LiamJones 13 — 47
(P Winkworth) *hld up in mid-div: pushed along over 2f out: no hdwy* **18/1**

432- **9** *2 1/4* **Luck Will Come (IRE)**[227] 5602 4-9-5 **60** .... JimmyQuinn 2 — 40
(H J Collingridge) *chsd ldrs tl wknd over 1f out* **7/1**[3]

62-4 **10** *10* **Hasty Lady**[24] 1302 3-9-3 **70** .... PaulMulrennan 14 — 19
(K A Ryan) *bhd fnl 3f* **22/1**

/06- **11** *2 1/2* **Give Her A Whirl**[332] 2435 4-9-5 **60** .... RobertWinston 4 — 7
(G A Swinbank) *led: hdd 2f out: sn n.m.r and wknd* **20/1**

1-32 **12** *2* **Oat Cuisine**[12] 1565 4-9-9 **64** .... HayleyTurner 12 — 5
(M L W Bell) *prom over 3f* **11/2**[2]

0-62 **13** *16* **Twiglet (IRE)**[9] 1638 3-9-0 **70** .... TolleyDean(3) 11 — —
(George Baker) *t.k.h: prom: rdn over 2f out: sn wknd: eased ins fnl f* **9/1**

1m 28.44s (3.84) **Going Correction** +0.65s/f (Yiel)
WFA 3 from 4yo+ 12lb — **13** Ran SP% **122.8**
Speed ratings (Par 100): **104,102,93,93,92 92,91,91,88,77 74,71,53**
CSF £31.16 CT £372.66 TOTE £3.30: £1.50, £2.70, £3.70; EX 33.10.
Owner Betfair Club ROA **Bred** W Maxwell Ervine **Trained** Blewbury, Oxon

FOCUS
Two pulled clear on a modest handicap and the time was good but the form does not look totally solid.

1868 COVENTRY CUP H'CAP — 7f 26y
3:45 (3:48) (Class 4) (0-80,80) 3-Y-O — **£5,828** (£1,734; £866; £432) **Stalls** Low

Form — RPR

410- **1** **Indian Diva (IRE)**[177] 6756 3-9-3 **79** .... StephenDonohoe 1 — 84
(P A Blockley) *s.i.s: sn chsng ldrs: rdn to ld and hung rt over 1f out: r.o* **20/1**

21-0 **2** *1 1/4* **Premier Danseur (IRE)**[32] 1167 3-9-1 **77** .... RobertWinston 6 — 79
(M Johnston) *s.i.s: hdwy 3f out: sn hrd rdn: r.o* **11/2**[2]

4-0U **3** *3/4* **Ten Pole Tudor**[44] 975 3-9-0 **79** .... KevinGhunowa(3) 2 — 79
(R A Harris) *led over 5f out: rdn and hdd over 1f out: styd on same pce ins fnl f* **25/1**

-212 **4** *shd* **Stevie Thunder**[4] 1750 3-8-9 **74** .... PJMcDonald(3) 7 — 74+
(G A Swinbank) *trckd ldrs: lost pl over 4f out: rdn 3f out: hdwy u.p over 1f out: styd on* **10/11**[1]

000- **5** *1* **Shamrock Lady (IRE)**[185] 6621 3-9-1 **77** .... JohnEgan 5 — 74
(J Gallagher) *a.p: rdn over 2f out: styd on same pce fnl f* **20/1**

433- **6** 1 3/4 **Afram Blue**135 7222 3-9-2 78 AlanMunro 12 70
(W J Knight) *mid-div: hdwy over 4f out: rdn over 2f out: styd on* **12/1**
010- **7** 1/2 **The Jostler**226 5629 3-9-1 77 ChrisCatlin 13 68+
(B W Hills) *hld up: hdwy over 1f out: nt rch ldrs* **12/1**
02-4 **8** 1 3/4 **Ninefineirishmen (IRE)**24 1295 3-8-12 74 AndrewElliott 8 60
(K R Burke) *prom: lost pl over 5f out: n.d after* **15/2**3
100- **9** 1 1/2 **Dancing Marabout (IRE)**207 6120 3-8-11 73 ShaneKelly 4 55
(C R Egerton) *chsd ldrs: rdn over 2f out: wknd fnl f* **28/1**
306- **10** 4 1/2 **Semah Harold**163 6936 3-8-12 74 RichardMullen 10 44
(E S McMahon) *led: hdd over 5f out: rdn over 2f out: sn wknd: eased fnl f* **33/1**
6000 **11** 3/4 **Gross Prophet**13 1546 3-9-1 77 RichardKingscote 9 45
(Tom Dascombe) *hld up: a in rr* **16/1**

1m 29.22s (4.62) **Going Correction** +0.65s/f (Yiel) **11 Ran SP% 120.6**
Speed ratings (Par 101): **99,97,96,96,95 93,92,90,89,84 83**
CSF £122.10 CT £2800.77 TOTE £30.80: £5.50, £2.10, £6.70; EX 199.50.
Owner H Downs **Bred** Mountarmstrong Stud **Trained** Lambourn, Berks

FOCUS
This looked a fair handicap and the third looks the best guide to the form backed up by the fifth.

1869 WARWICKRACECOURSE.CO.UK MEDIAN AUCTION MAIDEN FILLIES' STKS 1m 22y
4:15 (4:20) (Class 5) 3-5-Y-O £2,914 (£867; £433; £216) Stalls Low

Form RPR
3- **1** **Diamond Yas (IRE)**229 5540 3-8-12 0 TPQueally 6 81+
(H R A Cecil) *mde all: clr 1f out: easily* **5/4**1
00- **2** 6 **Tara's Garden**191 6494 3-8-12 0 JimmyQuinn 1 63
(M Blanshard) *hld up in mid-div: hdwy on ins over 3f out: wnt 2nd 1f out: rdn and no ch w wnr* **25/1**
50 **3** 5 **Elzeeza (USA)**26 1270 3-8-12 0 StephenDonohoe 2 52
(E A L Dunlop) *hld up and bhd: stdy hdwy on ins over 3f out: swtchd rt 2f out: hrd rdn over 1f out: one pce* **20/1**
0-60 **4** 3 **Vanatina (IRE)**10 1602 4-9-11 47 LiamJones 15 48
(W M Brisbourne) *t.k.h early: sn chsng wnr: wknd ins fnl f* **25/1**
5 hd **Fonda (USA)** 3-8-12 0 PaulMulrennan 8 44+
(J R Fanshawe) *rn green: s.i.s: sn mid-div: lost pl 5f out: hdwy 2f out: styng on whn edgd rt ins fnl f* **10/1**3
0 **6** 1 1/2 **Poulaine Bleue**13 1535 3-8-12 0 HayleyTurner 5 41
(M L W Bell) *prom tl wknd fnl f* **50/1**
7 2 1/2 **Fancy Footsteps (IRE)** 3-8-12 0 SebSanders 7 35+
(C G Cox) *hld up and bhd: hdwy 2f out: no imp fnl f* **9/2**2
0 **8** 1 1/4 **Take It Easee (IRE)**14 1519 3-8-12 0 RobertWinston 3 32+
(G A Swinbank) *t.k.h in mid-div: lost pl over 3f out: n.d after* **14/1**
9 3/4 **Battling Lil (IRE)**150 4-9-8 0 TolleyDean(3) 17 34
(J L Spearing) *mid-div: pushed along over 3f out: rdn over 1f out: no rspnse* **100/1**
0 **10** 1 3/4 **Janshe Gold**14 1525 3-8-12 0 JamesDoyle 14 27
(J G Portman) *hld up in tch: pushed along and lost pl 3f out: n.d after* **16/1**
0 **11** 2 3/4 **Milldown Bay**26 1265 3-8-12 0 AlanMunro 10 20
(B R Millman) *t.k.h in tch: wknd 2f out* **40/1**
12 5 **Bobster** 3-8-12 0 ChrisCatlin 13 9+
(B R Millman) *mid-div: pushed along over 4f out: sn bhd* **10/1**3
13 3 3/4 **Giadiniera** 3-8-7 0 JackMitchell(5) 4 —+
(C F Wall) *s.i.s: a bhd* **25/1**
0 **14** 2 3/4 **Toon Army**18 1423 3-8-12 0 (t) SamHitchcott 9 —
(Miss D Mountain) *a in rr* **50/1**
006- **15** 6 **Magnol**187 6591 3-8-12 51 AndrewElliott 16 —
(J G M O'Shea) *s.i.s: plld hrd: sn prom: rdn and wknd over 3f out* **80/1**

1m 46.03s (5.03) **Going Correction** +0.65s/f (Yiel)
WFA 3 from 4yo 13lb **15 Ran SP% 118.2**
Speed ratings (Par 100): **100,94,89,86,85 84,81,80,79,78 75,70,66,63,57**
CSF £42.76 TOTE £1.90: £1.20, £6.80, £5.40; EX 41.60.
Owner Diamond Racing Ltd **Bred** Mrs A B McDonnell **Trained** Newmarket, Suffolk

FOCUS
A weak maiden but a clear winner with the fourth setting the level for the form.
Take It Easee(IRE) Official explanation: jockey said filly suffered interference in running

1870 TURFTV H'CAP 1m 22y
4:45 (4:49) (Class 6) (0-60,60) 3-Y-O £2,047 (£604; £302) Stalls Low

Form RPR
60-0 **1** **Challow Hills (USA)**92 419 3-9-3 59 AlanMunro 1 68
(B W Hills) *hld up: hdwy over 2f out: rdn over 1f out: sn hung rt: r.o to ld wl ins fnl f* **9/2**2
00-2 **2** 1 1/2 **Just Sam (IRE)**12 1558 3-9-0 56 SebSanders 15 62
(D Carroll) *hld up: hdwy over 2f out: rdn to ld 1f out: hdd wl ins fnl f* **5/1**3
025 **3** 1 3/4 **Tapas Lad (IRE)**13 1533 3-8-10 55 (v) KevinGhunowa(3) 6 57
(G J Smith) *chsd ldrs: rdn to ld over 1f out: sn hung lft and hdd: styd on same pce ins fnl f* **17/2**
-230 **4** 2 3/4 **Rhode Island Red (USA)**53 873 3-8-12 54 RichardKingscote 3 50
(H J L Dunlop) *prom: lost pl over 6f out: hdwy u.p over 1f out: no ex ins fnl f* **16/1**
00-5 **5** 1 **Follow Your Spirit**38 1051 3-9-2 58 CatherineGannon 4 51
(B Palling) *mid-div: hdwy u.p over 3f out: styd on same pce appr fnl f* **20/1**
-433 **6** 2 3/4 **Maddy**9 1637 3-8-10 59 (p) MatthewDavies(7) 5 46
(George Baker) *chsd ldr: led 7f out: hdd 6f out: chsd ldrs tl rdn to ld 2f out: sn hung rt and hdd: wknd ins fnl f* **4/1**1
6-40 **7** nk **Treasure Islands (IRE)**88 464 3-9-4 60 LiamJones 10 46
(S W Hall) *s.i.s: hld up: styd on fnl f: nvr nrr* **50/1**
100 **8** 3/4 **So Sublime**13 1548 3-9-1 60 LeeVickers(3) 2 45
(M C Chapman) *hld up: hdwy over 2f out: sn rdn: hung rt fr over 1f out: wknd ins fnl f* **28/1**
004 **9** 4 1/2 **Borrowdale**24 1311 3-9-1 57 ShaneKelly 7 31
(J A Osborne) *broke wl: lost pl over 6f out: effrt over 2f out: eased whn btn fnl f* **12/1**
6020 **10** nse **Magical Song**33 1161 3-8-12 54 (p) StephenDonohoe 9 28
(P A Blockley) *chsd ldrs: rdn and ev ch over 2f out: wknd fnl f* **7/1**
0-40 **11** 16 **Dear Will**32 1166 3-9-0 56 RobertWinston 13 —
(J R Fanshawe) *hld up: rdn over 2f out: a in rr: eased over 1f out* **11/1**
0-40 **12** 2 **Ile Royale**32 1166 3-9-2 58 (v1) HayleyTurner 14 —
(B R Johnson) *hld up: plld hrd: hdwy to ld 6f out: rdn and hdd 2f out: wknd over 1f out: eased fnl f* **16/1**
00-0 **13** 10 **Moluccella**33 1144 3-9-1 60 TravisBlock(3) 8 —
(H Morrison) *racd keenly: led 1f: chsd ldrs tl rdn and wknd over 2f out: eased over 1f out* **14/1**
03-0 **14** 3 1/2 **Amyann (IRE)**119 74 3-9-2 58 RichardMullen 16 —
(J R Holt) *mid-div: hdwy over 4f out: rdn over 3f out: wknd 3f out: eased over 1f out* **50/1**
030- **15** 3 1/2 **Xaravella (IRE)**214 5944 3-9-1 57 AndrewElliott 17 —
(J G M O'Shea) *sn pushed along in rr: bhd fr 1/2-way: eased fnl 2f* **66/1**

1m 46.93s (5.93) **Going Correction** +0.65s/f (Yiel) **15 Ran SP% 126.0**
Speed ratings (Par 97): **96,94,92,90,89 86,85,85,80,80 64,62,52,49,45**
CSF £27.26 CT £197.70 TOTE £6.20: £2.60, £1.90, £3.20; EX 31.50.
Owner The Athletes **Bred** Luis Bravo Productions Llc **Trained** Lambourn, Berks
■ Stewards' Enquiry : Alan Munro one-day ban: used whip with excessive frequency (May 19)

FOCUS
This was not much of a contest, but the form looks reasonable rated around the placed horses and the race should produce the odd winner at a lowly level.
Dear Will Official explanation: jockey said gelding was unsuited by the good to soft (soft in places) ground

1871 EDGECOTE H'CAP 1m 4f 134y
5:15 (5:20) (Class 5) (0-70,68) 3-Y-O £3,238 (£963; £481; £240) Stalls Low

Form RPR
561 **1** **Precision Break (USA)**13 1539 3-8-9 59 JohnEgan 7 66
(P F I Cole) *hld up towards rr: stdy hdwy over 8f out: rdn over 2f out: led jst over 1f out tl wl ins fnl f: led last strides: all out* **4/1**2
-203 **2** hd **Lord's Bidding**13 1539 3-8-7 57 (v) DavidKinsella 5 64
(R Ingram) *led after 1f: rdn 2f out: hdd jst over 1f out: slt ld wl ins fnl f: hdd last strides* **10/1**
00-4 **3** 2 **Kalokairi (IRE)**16 1478 3-8-9 59 SebSanders 8 63
(J L Dunlop) *hld up towards rr: hdwy over 4f out: rdn 2f out: sn edgd rt: styd on one pce fnl f* **3/1**1
0-12 **4** 5 **Black Tor Figarro (IRE)**7 1681 3-9-1 65 LiamJones 9 61
(B W Duke) *towards rr: hdwy over 6f out: c wd st: rdn over 1f out: sn wknd* **3/1**1
000- **5** 1 **Smetana**145 7121 3-8-8 58 EdwardCreighton 3 53
(H Morrison) *prom: lost pl over 4f out: rdn and hdwy 2f out: wknd 1f out* **16/1**
-206 **6** 2 1/4 **Caltire (GER)**9 1622 3-8-7 62 (b) JamieJones(5) 4 53+
(M G Quinlan) *s.i.s: hld up and bhd: rdn and hdwy over 2f out: wknd 1f out* **10/1**
1360 **7** 2 1/4 **Duneen Dream (USA)**11 1586 3-8-7 57 (t) NickyMackay 6 45
(W J Musson) *hld up in tch: rdn and swtchd rt over 1f out: wknd ins fnl f* **28/1**
6-03 **8** 3/4 **Balais Folly (FR)**13 1553 3-8-4 54 oh4 CatherineGannon 11 41
(B Palling) *s.i.s: hld up towards rr: rdn over 1f out: nvr nr ldrs* **25/1**
3325 **9** 4 **Shaftesbury (IRE)**13 1530 3-9-3 67 RobertWinston 12 48
(Jane Southcombe) *stmbld s: bhd most of way* **17/2**3
50-0 **10** nse **Daddy's Boy**16 1467 3-9-4 68 AlanMunro 2 49
(Mrs A J Perrett) *bhd fnl 5f* **16/1**
-600 **11** 7 **Lady Florence**20 1379 3-8-1 54 oh2 LukeMorris(3) 10 24
(A B Coogan) *prom: chsd ldr 6f out tl over 2f out: sn wknd* **40/1**
00-0 **12** 18 **Holy Storm (IRE)**11 1586 3-8-4 54 oh4 ChrisCatlin 1 —
(Eve Johnson Houghton) *led 1f: chsd ldr to 6f out: pushed along over 4f out: wknd over 3f out* **66/1**

2m 55.0s (10.40) **Going Correction** +0.65s/f (Yiel) **12 Ran SP% 121.7**
Speed ratings (Par 99): **94,93,92,89,88 87,86,85,83,83 78,67**
CSF £43.68 CT £139.83 TOTE £6.00: £2.20, £3.00, £1.60; EX 58.90 Place 6 £204.19, Place 5 £73.87..
Owner JMH Lifestyle Ltd **Bred** Gainesway Thoroughbreds Ltd **Trained** Whatcombe, Oxon
■ Stewards' Enquiry : John Egan three-day ban: excessive use of the whip (May 19-21)

FOCUS
A modest handicap, run at a fair pace. The form makes sense and could be rated a little higher.
Black Tor Figarro(IRE) Official explanation: trainer later said colt was found to be lame on returning home
Shaftesbury(IRE) Official explanation: jockey said gelding slipped on leaving stalls
T/Jkpt: £16,436.60 to a £1 stake. Pool: £34,725.26. 1.50 winning tickets. T/Plt: £313.00 to a £1 stake. Pool: £79,201.14. 184.70 winning tickets. T/Qpdt: £119.70 to a £1 stake. Pool: £3,478.08. 21.50 winning tickets. KH

1680 WINDSOR (R-H)
Monday, May 5

OFFICIAL GOING: Good to soft (good in places) changing to good (good to soft in places) after race 2 (3.05)
Wind: Virtually nil

1872 AT THE RACES APPRENTICE H'CAP 6f
2:35 (2:35) (Class 5) (0-75,75) 4-Y-O+ £2,729 (£806; £403) Stalls High

Form RPR
2241 **1** **Punching**8 1642 4-8-9 65 6ex NicolPolli 11 74
(Miss Gay Kelleway) *chsd ldrs: rdn styd on u.p to chal ins fnl f: led last strides* **7/1**3
10-0 **2** hd **Rydal Mount (IRE)**14 1522 5-8-10 71 TimothyMeadows(5) 4 79
(W S Kittow) *chsd ldrs: rdn 2f out: led fnl 100yds: ct last strides* **15/2**
50-0 **3** nk **Grey Boy (GER)**14 1522 7-8-4 63 MarkCoumbe(3) 13 70
(A W Carroll) *chsd ldrs: rdn to chal ins fnl f: no ex last strides* **20/1**
3420 **4** nk **Memphis Man**14 1522 5-8-13 72 RichardEvans(3) 6 78
(P D Evans) *s.i.s: sn in tch: rdn to chse ldrs whn edgd lft ins fnl 2f: styd on to chal ins fnl f: no ex cl home* **15/2**
4-06 **5** shd **Equuleus Pictor**14 1522 4-8-4 63 JackDean(3) 12 69
(J L Spearing) *slt ld: rdn 2f out: kpt narrow advantage tl hdd and no ex fnl 100yds* **5/1**2
04-2 **6** 1 1/2 **Adantino**14 1522 9-9-5 75 (b) JamesMillman 5 76
(B R Millman) *rdn along to chse ldrs after 2f: styd on fnl f but nvr quite gng pce to chal* **9/2**1
640- **7** nse **Bateleur**220 5768 4-9-0 73 MCGeran(3) 1 74
(M R Channon) *towards rr: rdn and styd on fr 2f out: kpt on cl home but nvr in contention* **16/1**
100- **8** 1 1/4 **Scarlet Oak**194 6423 4-8-3 64 BillyCray(5) 3 61
(D J S Ffrench Davis) *chsd ldrs: rdn to chal whn hung bdly lft ins fnl f: sn wknd* **25/1**
2-62 **9** nk **Rhapsilian**13 1541 4-8-2 61 KMay(3) 2 57
(J A Geake) *t.k.h early: chsd ldrs: drvn to chal over 1f out: wknd ins fnl f* **9/1**
565- **10** 2 **Witchry**384 1080 6-8-5 64 JPHamblett(3) 7 53
(A G Newcombe) *chsd ldrs: rdn 2f out: wknd over 1f out* **20/1**
520- **11** 1/2 **Caustic Wit (IRE)**203 6239 10-7-13 62 JakePayne(7) 9 50
(M S Saunders) *t.k.h: chsd ldrs: rdn and hmpd ins fnl 2f: sn btn* **25/1**

000- 12 nse **Morse (IRE)**[200] 6283 7-8-4 **67**.................... MarieLequarre(7) 10 55
(J A Osborne) *outpcd* **25/1**

0-50 13 8 **Bobby Rose**[39] 1040 5-8-12 **68**.................... SladeO'Hara 14 30
(D K Ivory) *chsd ldrs to 1/2-way* **8/1**

31/0 14 nk **Tadlil**[14] 1522 6-8-8 **67**.................... WilliamCarson(3) 8 28
(J M Bradley) *spd to 1/2-way: sn wknd* **20/1**

1m 14.24s (1.24) **Going Correction** +0.30s/f (Good) **14** Ran SP% **123.7**
Speed ratings (Par 103): **103,102,102,101,101 99,99,98,97,95 94,94,83,83**
CSF £53.56 CT £1025.88 TOTE £9.10: £2.80, £2.70, £5.00; EX 76.50 TRIFECTA Not won..

Owner bettingjobs.com **Bred** Cheveley Park Stud Ltd **Trained** Exning, Suffolk

FOCUS
A modest if competitive apprentice handicap. Several had a chance entering the last furlong and a large blanket would have covered the front five at the line. The form looks solid rated around the runner-up and fourth.

Memphis Man Official explanation: jockey said gelding was denied a clear run

1873 GOLDRING SECURITY MAIDEN STKS 5f 10y
3:05 (3:06) (Class 5) 2-Y-O £2,729 (£806; £403) **Stalls** High

Form RPR

1 **Fault** 2-9-3 0.................... SteveDrowne 4 78+
(R Charlton) *wnt lft s: sn led: shkn up fnl f: a in command* **3/1**[3]

2 2 ¾ **Doc Jones (IRE)** 2-9-3 0.................... TGMcLaughlin 3 68
(P D Evans) *bmpd and wnt lft s: sn rdn to go pce: styd on fnl f and tk 2nd cl home but no ch w wnr* **13/2**

3 nk **Love You Louis** 2-9-3 0.................... KerrinMcEvoy 8 67
(J R Jenkins) *sn chsng wnr: rdn 1/2-way and no imp: wknd and lost 2nd cl home* **17/2**

4 1 ¾ **Imperial Guest** 2-9-3 0.................... AdamKirby 7 61
(G G Margarson) *outpcd and pushed along in rr after 2f: kpt on ins fnl f but nvr gng pce to rch ldng trio* **14/1**

5 1 **Inside Knowledge (USA)** 2-9-3 0.................... JimCrowley 6 57
(Mrs A J Perrett) *chsd ldrs: rdn 1/2-way: no ch fnl 2f* **11/4**[2]

6 5 **Robin The Till** 2-9-3 0.................... RichardHughes 1 39+
(R Hannon) *wnt bdly lft s and veered to r alone far side: possibly upsides to 1/2-way but no ch w main gp fnl 2f: eased ins fnl f* **9/4**[1]

63.61 secs (3.31) **Going Correction** +0.30s/f (Good) **6** Ran SP% **113.0**
Speed ratings (Par 93): **85,80,80,77,75 67**
CSF £22.32 TOTE £3.70: £2.10, £3.00; EX 26.30 Trifecta £181.60 Pool £350.57 - 1.37 winning units..

Owner John Livock **Bred** Mrs A M Vestey **Trained** Beckhampton, Wilts

FOCUS
Not the most competitive maiden, featuring six newcomers, and it may not have taken that much winning after the favourite had swerved his chance away at the start. The winning time was not that great either, so the form may be suspect even though the winner was impressive.

NOTEBOOK
Fault, a 48,000gns half-brother to three winners, made almost every yard against the stands' rail and never looked in much danger. However, with the favourite throwing his chance away early and the winning time so modest, there has to be a question mark against the form. He could not have done much more than he did though, and he could still be anything. (op 7-2 tchd 4-1)

Doc Jones(IRE), a 9,000euros half-brother to a winner in Italy, took a while to get into gear and just got up to snatch second. Given that there is so much stamina on the dam's side of pedigree it was probably no surprise that he found this trip on the sharp side and he should improve over further in due course. (op 11-2 tchd 5-1)

Love You Louis, a 6,500gns colt out of the multiple winning sprinter Maddie's A Jem, showed a fair amount of speed on the stands' side and ought to eventually have a future as a sprinter himself later on. (op 9-1 tchd 11-1 and 8-1)

Imperial Guest, a 20,000gns colt out of a winning miler, showed signs of ability as the race progressed and should improve for a step up in trip. (tchd 20-1)

Inside Knowledge(USA), out of a smart performer at up to 1m in France, attracted market support but never looked like getting involved. He may need more time and a longer trip, but he will need to improve in order to win a race. (op 4-1)

Robin The Till, a 16,000gns colt out of a winning juvenile sprinter, nonetheless has a combination of speed and stamina on the dam's side of his pedigree. Any chance he had went out the window as soon as the stalls opened as he swerved violently to his left and was quickly racing on his own down the far rail. He eventually looked almost unrideable and was allowed to coast home, but he has plenty of questions to answer after this. Official explanation: jockey said colt hung badly left-handed throughout (op 13-8 tchd 5-2 in places)

1874 8 EVENTS AT ROYAL WINDSOR RACECOURSE H'CAP 1m 2f 7y
3:35 (3:35) (Class 4) (0-85,84) 4-Y-O+ £5,180 (£1,541; £770; £384) **Stalls** Centre

Form RPR

1-22 1 **Trans Siberian**[9] 1630 4-8-11 **77**.................... TQuinn 3 87+
(P F I Cole) *in rr but in tch: hdwy fr 3f out: drvn to ld appr 1f out: styd on strly ins fnl f* **7/4**[1]

50-0 2 ¾ **Aegean Prince**[7] 1682 4-8-9 **75**.................... RichardHughes 8 83
(R Hannon) *hld up in rr: hdwy and swtchd lft to outside over 2f out: styd on u.p fnl f to take 2nd cl home but a hld by wnr* **8/1**

215- 3 ½ **Dawn Sky**[261] 4609 4-9-2 **82**.................... PhilipRobinson 2 89+
(M A Jarvis) *chsd ldr: drvn to chal 3 out: led appr fnl 2f: hdd appr 1f out: styd on same pce and lost 2nd cl home* **7/1**[3]

01/3 4 1 ½ **Marvo**[17] 1458 4-8-2 **73**.................... NicolPolli(5) 7 77
(M H Tompkins) *chsd ldrs: n.m.r over 2f out: rallied and kpt on again fr over 1f out but nvr gng pce to be competitive* **8/1**

024- 5 2 ¼ **Sign Of The Cross**[192] 6474 4-9-0 **80**.................... KerrinMcEvoy 5 80
(J R Fanshawe) *chsd ldrs: rdn 2f out: wknd appr fnl f* **7/1**[3]

520- 6 1 ½ **Nightspot**[191] 6500 7-8-6 **72**.................... SteveDrowne 4 69
(Eve Johnson Houghton) *sn led: rdn 3f out: hdd appr fnl 2f: wknd wl over 1f out* **11/2**[2]

6026 7 hd **Speedy Sam**[2] 1799 5-9-4 **84**.................... FergusSweeney 6 80
(K R Burke) *chsd ldrs: rdn over 3f out: wknd 2f out* **12/1**

-644 8 2 ¼ **Resonate (IRE)**[13] 1531 10-8-12 **78**.................... AdamKirby 1 70
(A G Newcombe) *in tch: drvn to chse ldrs 3f out: hrd rdn over 2f out: wknd sn after* **11/1**

2m 6.61s (-2.09) **Going Correction** -0.075s/f (Good) **8** Ran SP% **115.0**
Speed ratings (Par 105): **105,104,104,102,101 99,99,97**
CSF £16.64 CT £79.48 TOTE £2.70: £1.20, £2.80, £1.60; EX 24.00 Trifecta £99.30 Pool £570.98 - 4.08 winning units..

Owner C Shiacolas **Bred** Lordship Stud Limited **Trained** Whatcombe, Oxon

■ Stewards' Enquiry : Adam Kirby one-day ban: used whip with excessive force (May 19)

FOCUS
A fair middle-distance handicap and the pace was decent which helped the hold-up horses. The first two at the line held the last two positions on the turn for home and the form appears sound rated through the runner-up.

1875 ARENA LEISURE PLC H'CAP 1m 67y
4:05 (4:05) (Class 3) (0-90,89) 3-Y-O £7,771 (£2,312; £1,155; £577) **Stalls** High

Form RPR

1-4 1 **Staying On (IRE)**[17] 1443 3-9-1 **86**.................... AdamKirby 9 102+
(W R Swinburn) *sn led: drvn and styd on whn chal fr over 2f out: edgd rt and green fnl f but styd on strly and in control cl home* **9/1**

12- 2 nk **Hurricane Hymnbook (USA)**[218] 5828 3-9-4 **89**.................... RobertHavlin 1 104+
(B J Meehan) *chsd ldrs: rdn to chal fr over 2f out and stl upsides ins fnl f: kpt on but a hld by wnr clsng stages* **7/2**[3]

34-0 3 7 **Ellemujie**[24] 1297 3-8-11 **82**.................... JimCrowley 8 81
(D K Ivory) *towards rr: rdn over 2f out: styd on to take wl hld 3rd ins fnl f* **8/1**

6-50 4 ¾ **Artsu**[14] 1524 3-8-8 **79**.................... FergusSweeney 6 76
(M L W Bell) *chsd ldr: rdn to chal 3f out: wknd 1f out and lost wl hld 3rd ins fnl f* **25/1**

10-5 5 4 **Bencoolen (IRE)**[14] 1524 3-8-13 **84**.................... SteveDrowne 2 72
(R Charlton) *chsd ldrs: rdn 3f out: wknd over 2f out* **3/1**[1]

1 6 1 ½ **Al Samha (USA)**[58] 837 3-9-1 **86**.................... KerrinMcEvoy 5 71
(M Johnston) *chsd ldrs: rdn 3f out: wknd over 2f out* **10/3**[2]

503- 7 1 ¼ **Kinnego Bay (IRE)**[203] 6234 3-8-7 **78** ow1.................... MichaelHills 7 60
(B W Hills) *hld up towards rr: sme hdwy 3f out: sn rdn: wknd over 2f out* **12/1**

-140 8 9 **Ike Quebec (FR)**[11] 1584 3-8-4 **78**.................... WilliamBuick(3) 3 39
(J R Boyle) *a in rr* **18/1**

1m 43.18s (-1.52) **Going Correction** -0.075s/f (Good) **8** Ran SP% **108.2**
Speed ratings (Par 103): **104,103,96,95,91 90,89,80**
CSF £34.96 CT £198.40 TOTE £10.40: £2.70, £1.40, £2.40; EX 43.80 TRIFECTA Not won..

Owner M H Dixon **Bred** M H Dixon **Trained** Aldbury, Herts

■ Stewards' Enquiry : Adam Kirby one-day ban: excessive use of the whip (May 19)

FOCUS
The front pair proved different class in this decent three-year-old handicap and both seem likely to go on to better things. The form is rated fairly positively.

NOTEBOOK
Staying On(IRE) ◆, making his handicap debut and back down in trip, was ridden positively right from the off and the most pleasing aspect of this victory was that he kept battling hard against the stands' rail all the way to the line despite showing distinct signs of greenness. He seems sure to improve further and, once he is the finished article, he could make his mark in decent company. (tchd 10-1)

Hurricane Hymnbook(USA) ◆ had not seen since finishing second to Ibn Khaldun in an Ascot nursery last September, the form of which worked out spectacularly well even without the subsequent exploits of the winner. Never far away, he kept on having a crack at the eventual winner and although he could never quite get to him, this effort should be measured by how far he pulled clear of the others. He remains open to improvement and it is only a matter of time before he wins again. (tchd 9-2)

Ellemujie ran better than on his Doncaster reappearance and plugged on to win the separate race for third. He is quite exposed now, but was up against a couple of potentially useful colts here and there will be easier opportunities. (op 12-1)

Artsu had his chance crossing the intersection, but did not get home. He is still to prove himself over the trip and probably prefers genuinely soft ground. (op 20-1)

Bencoolen(IRE), whose yard appears to be just running into form, did not step up from his reappearance effort here last month as one would have hoped. He may need faster ground, but this was still disappointing. (op 10-3 tchd 11-4 and 7-2 in places)

Al Samha(USA), so impressive on his Wolverhampton debut in a race that has produced its share of winners, proved very disappointing on this switch to turf and was beaten some way out. Either he did not cope with the different surface or he has been harshly handicapped on that maiden victory. (tchd 3-1 and 7-2)

1876 ARENA LEISURE CATERING MEDIAN AUCTION MAIDEN STKS 1m 67y
4:35 (4:36) (Class 5) 3-4-Y-O £2,729 (£806; £403) **Stalls** High

Form RPR

6 1 **Mooted (UAE)**[16] 1467 3-9-1 0.................... SteveDrowne 8 77+
(R Charlton) *in tch: hdwy 3f out: styng on whn hmpd over 1f out and swtchd rt: str run fnl f to ld nr fin* **7/2**[2]

5- 2 nk **Pippbrook Gold**[128] 7266 3-9-1 0.................... FergusSweeney 4 76+
(J R Boyle) *t.k.h: stdd into mid-div after 1f: hdwy whn nt clr run over 1f out: str run ins fnl f: fin wl but nt quite get up* **14/1**

5 3 nk **Acrostic**[7] 1669 3-9-1 0.................... PatCosgrave 5 72+
(L M Cumani) *chsd ldrs: rdn to ld ins fnl 2f: sn hung rt: stl ldng whn hung lft ins fnl f: ct nr fin* **6/1**

06-4 4 ½ **Where's Susie**[14] 1525 3-8-10 69.................... RobertHavlin 9 66
(D K Ivory) *chsd ldrs: lft in ld after 2f: rdn 3 out: kpt slt advantage tl hdd ins fnl 2f: styd upsides tl no ex fnl 100yds* **4/1**[3]

5-0 5 nse **Totoman**[12] 1573 3-9-1 0.................... AdamKirby 11 71
(G G Margarson) *chsd ldrs: rdn over 2f out: styd on thrght fnl f but nvr quite gng pce to chal* **22/1**

0- 6 1 ¾ **Papuan Prince (IRE)**[262] 4571 3-8-10 0.................... HaddenFrost(5) 7 67
(S Kirk) *s.i.s: rr: hdwy towards outside over 2f out: kpt on fr over 1f out: one pce ins fnl f* **20/1**

020- 7 1 **Orchestrator (IRE)**[242] 5175 4-10-0 64.................... JimCrowley 3 68
(T G Mills) *chsd ldrs: rdn and carried lft 1f out: styd on same pce after* **14/1**

0 8 ½ **Sunny Peace**[9] 1621 3-8-10 0.................... TQuinn 6 58
(B G Powell) *in tch tl n.m.r on ins over 2f out: hung lft over 1f out: kpt on wl cl home* **50/1**

0 9 ¾ **Blue Spartan (IRE)**[16] 1467 3-9-1 0.................... RichardHughes 13 62+
(B J Meehan) *led tl rn v wd bnd 6f out: rcvrd to press ldr over 3f out: stl wl there whn hanging lft 2f out: eased whn stl hanging and nt rcvr ins fnl f* **5/2**[1]

4 10 1 ¾ **Zaarmit (IRE)**[22] 1344 3-9-1 0.................... SaleemGolam 2 58+
(D M Simcock) *w ldr whn carried bdly wd bnd 6f out: rcvrd to stay prom: rdn and nt clr run ins fnl 2f: sn wknd* **9/1**

0-0 11 2 ¼ **Dancing Ellie**[25] 1279 3-8-10 0.................... IanMongan 12 47
(P M Phelan) *towards rr: tl mod prog fnl 2f* **100/1**

12 ¾ **Slow Escape (USA)** 4-10-0 0.................... TGMcLaughlin 14 54
(M Wigham) *s.i.s: a towards rr* **50/1**

0 13 4 ½ **Little Molly (IRE)**[10] 1601 3-8-3 0.................... MCGeran(7) 1 35
(E J Creighton) *a in rr* **100/1**

0-0 **14** ¾ **Ice Bellini**[18] 1423 3-8-10 0.. KerrinMcEvoy 10 34
(J M P Eustace) *in rr: effrt and rdn into mid-div 4f out: sn wknd* **20/1**

1m 45.82s (1.12) **Going Correction** -0.075s/f (Good)
WFA 3 from 4yo 13lb **14** Ran SP% **128.2**
Speed ratings (Par 103): **91,90,90,89,89 88,87,86,85,84 81,81,76,75**
CSF £52.20 TOTE £5.10: £1.90, £7.30, £2.40; EX 119.30 TRIFECTA Not won..
Owner Axom (XII) **Bred** Darley **Trained** Beckhampton, Wilts

FOCUS
Quite a dramatic outcome to this maiden and it certainly provided a thrilling finish, but the winning time was moderate, 2.64 seconds slower than the preceding three-year-old handicap, and that does temper enthusiasm somewhat. The form looks muddling despite the fourth and seventh running close to their marks.
Where's Susie Official explanation: jockey said filly hung left-handed
Sunny Peace Official explanation: jockey said filly hung left-handed and was denied a clear run
Blue Spartan(IRE) Official explanation: jockey said bit pulled through colt's mouth
Zaarmit(IRE) Official explanation: jockey said colt was carried left-handed on final bend

1877 WAKE UP TO MONDAYS H'CAP 1m 3f 135y
5:05 (5:05) (Class 4) (0-85,84) 4-Y-0+ **£4,857** (£1,445; £722; £360) **Stalls** Centre

Form RPR
406- **1** **Brief Goodbye**[215] 5924 8-8-4 **70**........................ AdrianMcCarthy 5 81
(John Berry) *in tch: rdn over 2f out: styd on fr over 2f out to ld appr fnl f: drvn out* **16/1**
0221 **2** ½ **Fregate Island (IRE)**[75] 622 5-8-9 **75**........................ RichardHughes 3 85
(A G Newcombe) *chsd ldrs: led ins fnl 3f: hrd drvn and hdd appr 1f out: kpt on same pce ins fnl f* **6/1**[2]
13-5 **3** 1 ¼ **Shela House**[15] 1502 4-9-1 **84**........................ WilliamBuick(3) 9 92
(J R Fanshawe) *trckd ldrs: rdn over 2f out: styd on same pce ins fnl f* **7/2**[1]
0022 **4** 2 ¾ **Dakiyah (IRE)**[17] 1458 4-8-12 **78**........................(p) IanMongan 6 82
(Mrs L J Mongan) *chsd ldrs: rdn and effrt over 2f out: wknd ins fnl f* **15/2**
4311 **5** 1 **Shogun Prince (IRE)**[17] 1458 5-8-11 **77**........................ KerrinMcEvoy 1 79
(W Jarvis) *hld up in rr: drvn and hdwy over 2f out: nvr quite gng pce to rch ldrs: wknd ins fnl f* **7/2**[1]
00/0 **6** 1 ¼ **Alfie Noakes**[16] 1473 6-9-1 **81**........................ JimCrowley 7 81
(Mrs A J Perrett) *chsd ldrs: rdn 3f out: wknd qckly 2f out* **7/1**[3]
20-5 **7** ¾ **Hawridge King**[13] 1531 6-8-11 **77**........................ SteveDrowne 10 76
(W S Kittow) *in rr: sme prog whn nt clr run over 2f out: n.d after* **14/1**
-301 **8** 2 ¼ **Calzaghe (IRE)**[13] 1554 4-8-6 **72**........................(v) FergusSweeney 4 67
(K R Burke) *in tch: rdn to chse ldrs 3f out: wknd over 2f out* **12/1**
10-0 **9** 2 ¾ **Polish Red**[12] 1568 4-8-11 **77**........................ TQuinn 2 68
(G G Margarson) *towards rr most of way* **15/2**
200- **10** 38 **Olimpo (FR)**[198] 6335 7-9-1 **81**........................ DarryllHolland 8 11
(B R Millman) *sn led: hdd & wknd ins fnl 3f: t.o* **10/1**

2m 26.93s (-2.57) **Going Correction** -0.075s/f (Good) **10** Ran SP% **124.1**
Speed ratings (Par 105): **105,104,103,102,101 100,100,98,96,71**
CSF £115.85 CT £426.46 TOTE £27.90: £5.00, £2.40, £1.60; EX 164.00 Trifecta £292.60 Part won. Pool £412.20 - 0.30 winning units. Place 6 £248.73, Place 5 £73.65..
Owner Miss L I McCarthy **Bred** Chippenham Lodge Stud Ltd **Trained** Newmarket, Suffolk

FOCUS
A fair handicap, run at a solid early pace and the form looks sound rated through the runner-up.
T/Plt: £383.60 to a £1 stake. Pool: £83,545.74. 158.95 winning tickets. T/Qpdt: £40.90 to a £1 stake. Pool: £5,772.68. 104.30 winning tickets. ST

1878 - (Foreign Racing) - See Raceform Interactive

1351 CURRAGH (R-H)
Monday, May 5

OFFICIAL GOING: Sprint course - yielding to soft; round course - good to yielding

1879a AUSSIE RULES EUROPEAN BREEDERS FUND TETRARCH STKS (GROUP 3) (ENTIRE COLTS & FILLIES) 7f
2:40 (2:43) 3-Y-0 **£43,080** (£12,639; £6,022; £2,051)

RPR
1 **Capt Chaos (IRE)**[22] 1356 3-9-1 101........................ CDHayes 1 110
(Edward Lynam, Ire) *in rr: clsd travelling wl into 3rd fr 2f out: rdn to chal and ld over 1f out: styd on wl* **9/1**
2 1 ¾ **Great War Eagle (USA)**[189] 6549 3-9-1 106........................(t) JMurtagh 3 105
(David Wachman, Ire) *sn led: strly pressed and jnd 2 1/2f out: hdd over 1f out: kpt on same pce ins fnl f* **5/2**[2]
3 1 ½ **Mr Medici (IRE)**[22] 1356 3-9-1 104........................ DPMcDonogh 6 101
(Kevin Prendergast, Ire) *trckd ldrs in 4th: rdn to go 3rd and no imp fr 1f out: kpt on one pce* **11/2**
4 3 ½ **Hanoverian Baron**[18] 1434 3-9-1 95........................ MJKinane 5 92
(John M Oxx, Ire) *trckd ldr in cl 2nd: chal and disp ld 2 1/2f out: dropped to 4th and wknd u.p fr 1f out* **2/1**[1]
5 2 ½ **Bruges (IRE)**[306] 3221 3-9-1........................(t) WJSupple 4 85
(David P Myerscough, Ire) *sn trckd ldrs in 3rd: dropped to last fr 2f out: no ex u.p and trailing fr over 1f out* **3/1**[3]

1m 32.46s (5.36) **Going Correction** +0.90s/f (Soft) **5** Ran SP% **112.3**
Speed ratings: **105,103,101,97,94**
CSF £31.91 TOTE £13.00: £3.00, £1.60; DF 37.00.
Owner David O'Reilly **Bred** Ballyhane Stud **Trained** Dunshaughlin, Co Meath

FOCUS
A step up from the winner in a race rated through the third.

NOTEBOOK
Capt Chaos(IRE), a well-held third to Georgebernardshaw on his seasonal bow 22 days previously, showed a very willing attitude to seal the issue nearing the final furlong. An easy surface is evidently much to his liking, a trait his sire's progeny are now becoming well known for, and he rates full value for the winning margin. Granted he held a fitness advantage over the runner-up, but he confirmed his reappearance form with the third horse, and now looks worthy of another try in Group company.
Great War Eagle(USA), whose trainer saddled Indesatchel to win this in 2005, was given a positive ride on this return from his winter break and had his chance. He was just done for toe when the winner kicked for home, however, and left the impression he ideally now wants another furlong. A return to quicker ground should also see him back in a better light. (op 9/4)
Mr Medici(IRE) finished a little closer to the winner than had been the case here last time out, but he still never looked like hitting the front. (op 11/2 tchd 6/1)
Hanoverian Baron, an easy maiden winner at Dundalk 18 days previously, simply failed to run up to par on this soft surface. That is not so surprising as he is by Green Desert, predominantly known for producing fast-ground winners, and he should certainly not be fully judged on this display. (op 5/2)
Bruges(IRE), unbeaten in two outings as a juvenile, proved very easy to back ahead of this seasonal return and ran accordingly. He has reportedly had a few problems during his time off the track, so could have badly needed this run, but he still has a good deal now to prove all the same.
Official explanation: trainer said gelding lost its tongue strap during the race; vet said gelding had a nasal discharge post race (op 11/4)

1880a ORATORIO EUROPEAN BREEDERS FUND ATHASI STKS (GROUP 3) (F&M) 7f
3:10 (3:11) 3-Y-0+ **£43,014** (£12,573; £5,955; £1,985)

RPR
1 **Prima Luce (IRE)**[235] 5353 3-8-11 94........................ KJManning 10 100
(J S Bolger, Ire) *sn trckd ldr in 2nd: rdn to chal and dispute ld fr 3f out: led fr 2f out: sn strly pressed: styd on wl ins fnl f* **33/1**
2 ¾ **Emily Blake (IRE)**[29] 1231 4-9-9 82........................ PTownend 5 100
(J C Hayden, Ire) *trckd ldrs: clsr in 2nd travelling wl fr 2f out: rdn fr over 1f out: kpt on wout matching wnr ins fnl f* **33/1**
3 2 ½ **She's Our Mark**[213] 5998 4-9-12 106........................ DMGrant 4 96
(Patrick J Flynn, Ire) *towards rr: rdn to go mod 4th over 1f out: kpt on wout threatening* **7/1**
4 ½ **Sharleez (IRE)**[267] 4440 3-8-11........................ MJKinane 8 90
(John M Oxx, Ire) *towards rr: rdn to go mod 6th over 1f out: styd on wout threatening* **14/1**
5 1 ½ **Grecian Dancer**[22] 1355 5-9-9 100........................ FMBerry 9 88
(Charles O'Brien, Ire) *trckd ldrs: 3rd bef 1/2-way: lost pl and no imp u.p fr 1 1/2f out* **14/1**
6 ½ **Campfire Glow (IRE)**[234] 5395 3-9-2 106........................ PJSmullen 2 90
(D K Weld, Ire) *mid-div: 6th bef 1/2-way: rdn to go mod 3rd over 1f out: sn no imp* **9/2**[2]
7 nk **Mooretown Lady (IRE)**[22] 1353 5-9-9 99........................ WMLordan 1 86
(H Rogers, Ire) *towards rr: no imp u.p and kpt on same pce fr 2f out* **25/1**
8 4 **Silver Touch (IRE)**[218] 5832 5-9-12........................ TPO'Shea 6 78
(M R Channon) *mid-div: clsr in 5th appr 1/2-way: no imp u.p fr under 2f out: no ex fnl f* **11/4**[1]
9 2 ½ **Dimenticata (IRE)**[18] 1436 4-9-9 105........................ CDHayes 11 68
(Kevin Prendergast, Ire) *sn led: jnd fr 3f out: strly pressed and hdd fr 2f out: wknd fr over 1f out* **8/1**
10 2 **Cheyenne Star (IRE)**[171] 6843 5-9-12 108........................ JAHeffernan 3 66
(Ms F M Crowley, Ire) *mid-div: 7th appr 1/2-way: no ex u.p fr under 2f out* **6/1**
11 5 **Elletelle (IRE)**[213] 5973 3-9-2 105........................ JMurtagh 7 52
(G M Lyons, Ire) *chsd ldrs: 8th appr 1/2-way: wknd fr 2f out: eased ins fnl f* **5/1**[3]

1m 31.24s (4.14) **Going Correction** +0.90s/f (Soft)
WFA 3 from 4yo+ 12lb **11** Ran SP% **122.5**
Speed ratings: **112,111,108,107,106 105,105,100,97,95 89**
CSF £854.17 TOTE £25.80: £5.20, £6.10, £2.30; DF 845.20.
Owner Mrs J S Bolger **Bred** John Connaughton **Trained** Coolcullen, Co Carlow

FOCUS
Improved form from the first two.

NOTEBOOK
Prima Luce(IRE), well beaten off in the May Hill on her final outing as a juvenile, showed she has done very well from two to three and ran out a determined winner. She evidently wants easy ground to be at her best and left the impression here that she is now ready to tackle another furlong again. Her trainer later added she would likely be even more of one to look out for next year.
Emily Blake(IRE), placed on all of her three previous outings this term, posted by far her best effort to date in defeat on this step up from handicap company. There was a lot to like about the manner in which she travelled into contention nearing the 2f pole and, while a rise in the ratings is now inevitable, she is worth a chance to prove this was no fluke.
She's Our Mark, progressive last year, met some support in the betting ring for this seasonal debut and ran a fair race in defeat. She ought to benefit a deal for the run and ideally prefers a sounder surface. (op 8/1)
Silver Touch(IRE), officially rated 110 in Britain, was very well backed on this return from a 218-day break. She did not get the best of runs around 3f out, but her response off the bridle when in the clear was disappointing and it is likely she found the dead ground against her. (op 7/2 tchd 4/1)
Elletelle(IRE), last year's Queen Mary heroine, was stepping up in trip for this three-year-old debut and was eventually beaten at the 2f marker. A drop back in trip could prove the answer now, and she is another who really needs faster ground, yet this does rate a very disappointing return.

1882a HIGH CHAPARRAL EUROPEAN BREEDERS FUND MOORESBRIDGE STKS (GROUP 3) 1m 2f
4:10 (4:13) 4-Y-0+ **£43,014** (£12,573; £5,955; £1,985)

RPR
1 **Regime (IRE)**[16] 1468 4-9-1........................ PJSmullen 3 110
(M L W Bell) *chsd ldrs: clsr in 4th bef st: wnt mod 2nd over 2f out: rdn to cl over 1f out: led ins fnl f: styd on wl: all out* **5/1**[3]
2 hd **Alarazi (IRE)**[15] 1508 4-9-1 104........................(b) FMBerry 2 110
(John M Oxx, Ire) *led and disp: in front into st: rdn clr fr over 2f out: reduced ld over 1f out: hdd ins fnl f: rallied: jst failed* **12/1**
3 nk **Mores Wells**[212] 6028 4-9-4 113........................(t) DPMcDonogh 1 112+
(Kevin Prendergast, Ire) *trckd ldrs: 3rd into st: sn rdn: clsd and short of room ins fnl f: kpt on wout threatening* **13/2**
4 shd **Hasanka (IRE)**[238] 5289 4-8-12 102........................ MJKinane 4 106
(John M Oxx, Ire) *chsd ldrs: rdn st: mod 5th over 2f out: kpt on wout threatening fnl f* **7/1**
5 ½ **Ezima (IRE)**[178] 6786 4-8-12 112........................ KJManning 8 105+
(J S Bolger, Ire) *towards rr: rdn st: mod 6th over 2f out: r.o wl wout threatening fnl f* **5/1**[3]
6 4 **Mount Nelson**[198] 6334 4-9-1........................ JMurtagh 6 100
(A P O'Brien, Ire) *racd in mod last: kpt on wout threatening u.p st* **9/4**[1]
7 1 **Ferneley (IRE)**[212] 6009 4-9-1 108........................ WJSupple 7 98
(Francis Ennis, Ire) *t.k.h: sn led and disp: 2nd into st: dropped to mod 4th over 2f out: sn no ex u.p* **25/1**
8 7 **Jumbajukiba**[22] 1355 5-9-4 115........................(b) DJCondon 5 87
(Mrs John Harrington, Ire) *hld up: 7th bef st: sn no imp u.p* **4/1**[2]

2m 17.45s (7.95) **Going Correction** +1.125s/f (Soft) **8** Ran SP% **121.5**
Speed ratings: **113,112,112,112,112 108,108,102**
CSF £65.68 TOTE £6.60: £2.20, £2.60, £1.60; DF 55.10.
Owner Highclere Thoroughbred Racing XL **Bred** Philip Brady **Trained** Newmarket, Suffolk

FOCUS
The form is rated around the second and fourth with Regime still below his 2007 best.

NOTEBOOK
Regime(IRE), back in trip, showed the clear benefit of his seasonal bow at Newbury 16 days previously and proved game in getting his head back in front. This now looks to be his optimum trip and he would have likely found the ground soft enough for him here, so further Group success could still be on the cards this term. (op 6/1)

Alarazi(IRE), reverting to Group company, was given a very positive ride and battled gamely when pressed, eventually only just going down. This rates as just about his best effort to date and he has improved since resuming this term.
Mores Wells rates better than the bare form on this seasonal return and should be all the sharper with this outing now under his belt. He would have also found this trip plenty sharp enough. (op 11/2)
Mount Nelson, whose yard sent out Septimus to capture this on his seasonal return last year, was never in contention from off the pace and proved disappointing. A Group 1 winner at two, he made only the one appearance as a three-year-old and has clearly had his problems, so just how much ability he retains is not simple to gauge. There is a good chance he will come on a bundle for the run, however. (op 9/4 tchd 2/1)
Jumbajukiba, up in trip, never looked like following up his win in the Gladness Stakes at this track 22 days previously and ran as though something was amiss. Official explanation: vet said gelding was post race normal (op 5/1)

1883 - 1885a (Foreign Racing) - See Raceform Interactive

1663 LONGCHAMP (R-H)
Monday, May 5

OFFICIAL GOING: Good to soft

1886a PRIX DE BOIS PREAU (FILLIES) 5f (S)
2:20 (2:20) 2-Y-O **£12,500** (£5,000; £3,750; £2,500; £1,250)

RPR
1 **Percolator**[35] 1111 2-9-0 CSoumillon 6 103+
(P F I Cole) *mde all: pushed clr over 1 1/2f out: unchal* **17/10**[1]
2 *6* **Santabella (FR)** 2-8-7 MSautjeau 7 75
(B Barbier, France)
3 *nk* **Unepetitehistoire (FR)**[11] 2-8-11 SMaillot 5 78
(Robert Collet, France)
4 *1* **Caparroso (FR)**[24] 2-9-0 IMendizabal 1 77
(T Lemer, France)
5 *3* **Charlotte Ki (FR)**[14] 2-9-0 JLermyte 2 66
(M Boutin, France)
6 *4* **Encemille (FR)**[18] 2-9-0 TThulliez 4 52
(S Wattel, France)
57.80 secs (1.10) **Going Correction** +0.125s/f (Good) **6** Ran SP% **37.0**
Speed ratings: **96,86,85,84,79 73**
PARI-MUTUEL: WIN 2.70; PL 2.10, 6.10; SF 37.60.
Owner A H Robinson **Bred** A H And C E Robinson Partnership **Trained** Whatcombe, Oxon

NOTEBOOK
Percolator completely outclassed her five rivals. Smartly away, she had the race sown up at halfway and coasted past the post a long way clear. Her jockey felt she still had plenty in reserve and that she would be helped if she had something to race with in the future. Her trainer is looking for a similar race back in France for her.

1887a PRIX HOCQUART (GROUP 2) (C&F) 1m 3f
2:50 (2:51) 3-Y-O **£54,485** (£21,029; £10,037; £6,691; £3,346)

RPR
1 **Democrate**[22] 3-9-2 SPasquier 4 113
(A Fabre, France) *hld up in 6th: hdwy ent st: chal 1 1/2f out: drvn to ld 100yds out: drvn out* **121/10**
2 *snk* **Starlish (IRE)**[39] 1046 3-9-2 ACrastus 6 113
(E Lellouche, France) *racd in 4th: disputing 3rd st: rdn to ld briefly over 1 1/2f out: wnt lft u.p and hdd 1f out: styd on to take 2nd on line* **13/1**
3 *1* **Blue Bresil (FR)**[29] 1239 3-9-2 WMongil 3 111
(Mlle B Halley des Fontaines, France) *racd in 3rd: disputing 3rd st: effrt to chal 2f out: led 1f out to 100yds out: lost 2nd on line* **28/1**
4 *4* **Full Of Gold (FR)**[29] 1239 3-9-2 TGillet 2 105
(Mme C Head-Maarek, France) *racd in 5th: pushed along 5f out: styd on fnl stages to take 4th but n.d* **11/10**[1]
5 *4* **Court Canibal**[29] 1239 3-9-2 CSoumillon 1 99
(M Delzangles, France) *racd in last: effrt early st: n.d* **7/1**
6 *8* **Celebrissime (IRE)**[36] 3-9-2 OPeslier 5 86
(F Head, France) *racd in 2nd: disputing ld appr st: wknd over 2f out* **49/10**[3]
6 *dht* **Anacarde (FR)**[51] 913 3-9-2 C-PLemaire 7 86
(J-C Rouget, France) *led: jnd appr st: hdd over 1 1/2f out: sn one pce* **33/10**[2]
2m 15.2s (-4.70) **Going Correction** -0.05s/f (Good) **7** Ran SP% **118.5**
Speed ratings: **115,114,114,111,108 102,102**
PARI-MUTUEL: WIN 13.10; PL 4.40, 5.80; SF 74.80.
Owner Skymarc Farm, F De Moussac & N P Gill **Bred** Haras Du Mezeray & Skymarc Farms **Trained** Chantilly, France

NOTEBOOK
Democrate was getting off the mark after a hat-trick of second places. Relaxed in mid division early before coming with a run towards the far rail, he kept straight to the line and held off the renewed challenge of the runner up. He is a nice colt in the making who appreciated the good ground and connections will now be looking at races like the Jockey-Club and Juddmonte Grand Prix de Paris.
Starlish(IRE) would have won if he had not hung left and tried to run out halfway up the straight. Tucked in behind the leaders early on, he was brought up the centre of the track but his young jockey had a job to keep him straight. Once balanced again, he ran on again and was catching the winner at the post. A very good-looking individual, he is still to be aimed at the Jockey-Club.
Blue Bresil(FR), trained in the provinces, once again ran up to expectations and he completely reversed the Noailles form with considerable ease. Smartly away, he then settled behind the leader and was battling for the lead from over a furlong out. He kept up the good work to the finish and also deserves to take his chance in the Jockey-Club.
Full Of Gold(FR) looked in fine condition while strolling around the paddock, but he never seemed to be going well on the changed ground. He was being niggled at before the straight and completely failed to run on in the final stages. Connections were at a total loss to understand this below-par effort, but he is a little one-paced so may need softer ground to show his best. The plan is still to run him in the Jockey-Club

1888a PRIX D'HEDOUVILLE (GROUP 3) 1m 4f
3:20 (3:21) 4-Y-O+ **£29,412** (£11,765; £8,824; £5,882; £2,941)

RPR
1 **Not Just Swing (IRE)**[22] 1359 4-8-9 JVictoire 5 106
(A Fabre, France) *racd in cl 2nd: r.o to ld over 2f out: rdn and fnd more over 1f out: comf* **48/10**[2]
2 *1* **Incanto Dream**[8] 1663 4-8-9 YLerner 6 104
(C Lerner, France) *disp 3rd: 3rd st: rdn and disputing 2nd over 1 1/2f out: styd on to take 2nd fnl strides* **8/1**
3 *nk* **Noble Prince (GER)**[22] 1359 4-8-11 SPasquier 2 106
(A Fabre, France) *disp 3rd: cl 4th st: sn wnt 2nd: disputing 2nd over 1 1/2f out: styd on u.p* **4/5**[1]
4 *1 1/2* **Distalino (FR)**[28] 1250 5-8-9 TThulliez 1 101
(F Doumen, France) *settled in 6th on rail: pushed along 2f out: rdn and styd on to take 4th fnl stages: nvr a threat* **13/1**
5 *1* **Dwilano (GER)**[29] 1237 5-8-11 JiriPalik 3 102
(P Remmert, Germany) *settled in last: drvn in centre over 1 1/2f out: n.d* **14/1**
6 *1/2* **Candy Gift (ARG)**[142] 5-9-4 MGuyon 7 108
(A Fabre, France) *led to over 2f out: wknd fnl f* **6/1**[3]
7 *6* **Fontcia (FR)**[32] 1175 4-8-8 C-PLemaire 4 88
(D Sepulchre, France) *hld up in 5th: pushed along over 2f out: one pce* **20/1**
2m 33.1s (1.90) **Going Correction** -0.05s/f (Good) **7** Ran SP% **116.8**
Speed ratings: **91,90,90,89,88 88,84**
PARI-MUTUEL: WIN 5.80; PL 3.00, 4.40; SF 35.60.
Owner T Storme **Bred** Petra Bloodstock Agency Ltd **Trained** Chantilly, France

NOTEBOOK
Not Just Swing(IRE) certainly appreciated the change in the ground and was given a fine ride by his young jockey. Sat just behind the leader early, he was at the head of affairs in the straight and he then fended off a persistent attack from the runner-up. He is certainly going the right way and his trainer will now be looking at similar events on similar ground.
Incanto Dream put in another good effort and was well placed throughout. He challenged up the middle of the track from over a furlong out, but he could never peg back the winner. His trainer is looking to step him up in trip in which case races like the Prix Kergorlay and Prix du Cadran could become targets later in the season.
Noble Prince(GER), a son of Montjeu, might not have appreciated this faster ground. Given every possible chance, he did not run on as well as might have been hoped in the final stages and this was a rather disappointing effort from the odds-on favourite
Distalino(FR), held up early, was putting in his best work at the finish and runs like a horse who might appreciate a longer trip and a little more cut in the ground

1555 CATTERICK (L-H)
Tuesday, May 6

OFFICIAL GOING: Good (good to soft in places)
The ground had dried right out and was described as 'mainly good, a bit more dead in places on the round course'.
Wind: light 1/2 behind Weather: fine and sunny

1889 CATTERICKBRIDGE.CO.UK MAIDEN AUCTION STKS 5f
6:05 (6:06) (Class 6) 2-Y-O **£2,047** (£604; £302) **Stalls** Low

Form RPR
2 1 **Red Cell (IRE)**[32] 1183 2-8-11 0 ChrisCatlin 6 64+
(E J O'Neill) *chsd ldr: rdn to ld over 1f out: styd on* **6/4**[1]
2 *2 1/2* **Cool Sonata (IRE)** 2-8-6 0 TWilliams 2 45
(M Brittain) *chsd ldrs: sn drvn along: edgd rt over 2f out: kpt on to take 2nd ins fnl f* **9/4**[2]
0 3 *2 1/4* **Dispol Toba**[43] 995 2-8-4 0 PaulFessey 3 35
(P T Midgley) *trckd ldrs: outpcd over 2f out: hung lft and kpt on fnl f* **20/1**
4 *3/4* **Blow Your Mind** 2-8-11 0 PaulHanagan 1 39
(Karen McLintock) *s.s: hdwy 2f out: kpt on fnl f* **10/1**
5 *2 1/4* **Chicken Momo** 2-8-9 0 DarrenWilliams 5 29+
(K R Burke) *led: hdd over 1f out: sn wknd* **3/1**[3]
6 *2 1/2* **Transformation (IRE)** 2-8-4 0 DO'Donohoe 4 15
(J R Weymes) *dwlt: sme hdwy 2f out: sn wknd* **28/1**
61.35 secs (1.55) **Going Correction** +0.175s/f (Good) **6** Ran SP% **113.1**
Speed ratings (Par 91): **94,90,86,85,81 77**
CSF £5.23 TOTE £2.60: £1.30, £2.60; EX 6.30.
Owner Premspace Ltd **Bred** Holborn Trust Co **Trained** Averham Park, Notts

FOCUS
A weak event and the winner's previous experience was a factor.

NOTEBOOK
Red Cell(IRE), beaten by a subsequent winner when runner-up on his all-weather debut, is not that big and looked very fit. In the end he came clear but he was almost certainly doing no more than expected. (op 11-8 tchd 13-8)
Cool Sonata(IRE), a January foal, is narrow. She struggled to keep up but in the end did enough to finish clear second best. (tchd 2-1 and 10-3)
Dispol Toba, having her second outing, was very keen to post. Badly tapped for toe at the halfway mark, she tended to hang and still has something to learn. (op 16-1)
Blow Your Mind, who looked very inexperienced beforehand, had his trainer with him at the start. He lost ground exiting the stalls but was staying on when it was all over and this will certainly have taught him something. (op 9-1 tchd 15-2)
Chicken Momo, easily the biggest in the line-up, took them along but stopped to nothing inside the last. He is surely better than he showed here. (op 11-2 tchd 5-2)
Transformation(IRE), lightly-made and narrow showed plenty of knee action going down. (op 16-1 tchd 33-1)

1890 BOOK RACEDAY HOSPITALITY ON 01748 810165 CLAIMING STKS 1m 3f 214y
6:35 (6:35) (Class 6) 4-Y-O+ **£2,047** (£604; £302) **Stalls** Low

Form RPR
00-3 1 **Annibale Caro**[7] 1702 6-8-7 47 PaulHanagan 2 59
(Grant Tuer) *hld up in rr: stdy hdwy on outside over 4f out: wnt 2nd over 2f out: led over 1f out: styd on strly ins fnl f* **16/1**
50-3 2 *3* **Bijou Dan**[26] 1219 7-9-3 57 GregFairley 6 66+
(G M Moore) *mid-div: effrt over 3f out: styd on fnl 2f: swtchd to outside ins fnl f: tk 2nd nr fin* **9/1**
355- 3 *shd* **Eijaaz (IRE)**[189] 6558 7-8-9 52 RoystonFfrench 12 56
(G A Harker) *mid-div: effrt 3f out: wnt 2nd 1f out: no ex* **9/1**
4 *3/4* **Pendragon (USA)**[42] 5-8-4 0 AndrewMullen(3) 15 53
(Mrs L B Normile) *s.i.s: hdwy over 2f out: edgd lft: kpt on fnl f* **150/1**
6-31 5 *1/2* **Court Of Appeal**[25] 1305 11-8-11 67 (tp) TomEaves 9 56
(B Ellison) *trckd ldrs: led 5f out tl hdd over 1f out: one pce* **11/10**[1]
-030 6 *4 1/2* **Brastar Jelois (FR)**[8] 1679 5-8-3 58 PatrickDonaghy(7) 5 48
(R Hollinshead) *hld up in mid-div: hdwy over 2f out: kpt on fnl f: nvr on terms* **7/1**[2]
-504 7 *5* **Skye But N Ben**[8] 1679 4-8-9 50 (v) SilvestreDeSousa 8 39
(G A Harker) *trckd ldrs: t.k.h: wknd over 1f out* **10/1**
120- 8 *1/2* **Let It Be**[200] 6308 7-9-8 63 PhillipMakin 13 51
(K G Reveley) *hld up in rr: effrt 4f out: sn drvn: nvr nr ldrs* **8/1**[3]

60-6 **9** 1 1/2 **Goldan Jess (IRE)**[11] 1017 4-8-9 53 DavidAllan 11 36
(D Carroll) *mid-div: hdwy 5f out: sn prom: wknd over 1f out* **18/1**

300/ **10** 11 **Channel Crossing**[551] 6305 6-9-3 0 LeeEnstone 3 26
(S Wynne) *t.k.h: led tl 5f out: wknd qckly 2f out* **100/1**

2220 **11** 6 **On Every Street**[28] 1262 7-8-11 48 (vt) DarrenWilliams 14 10
(R Bastiman) *t.k.h: trckd ldrs: lost pl over 2f out* **25/1**

00-0 **12** 4 1/2 **Tykie Two**[26] 1282 4-8-4 53 ChrisCatlin 1 —
(S Wynne) *chsd ldrs: drvn over 3f out: sn lost pl* **100/1**

00-0 **13** 12 **Ellies Faith**[14] 1551 4-8-4 42 (b) PaulFessey 7 —
(L R James) *trckd ldrs: lost pl 4f out: bhd whn eased over 1f out* **100/1**

0 **14** 1 **Vie A Deux (FR)**[9] 1305 5-7-13 0 (v) DominicFox(3) 4 —
(W Storey) *s.i.s: bhd and drvn 6f out: t.o 3f out* **200/1**

0/0 **15** 9 **Never Cross (IRE)**[25] 1307 4-9-3 0 NeilBrown(5) 10 —
(M A Barnes) *trckd ldrs: lost pl over 3f out: sn bhd* **150/1**

2m 37.41s (-1.49) **Going Correction** +0.075s/f (Good) **15** Ran SP% **120.1**
Speed ratings (Par 101): **107,105,104,104,104 101,97,97,96,89 85,82,74,73,67**
CSF £151.74 TOTE £20.70: £3.80, £2.40, £3.30; EX 106.00.
Owner G Tuer **Bred** Cyril Humphris **Trained** Birkby, N Yorks

FOCUS
A decent winning time for a claimer but not rated that positively as there was plenty of dead wood and, with the favourite flopping, it did not take much winning.
Ellies Faith Official explanation: jockey said filly lost its action

1891 WHY NOT TRY A PUNTERS PACKAGE H'CAP 7f
7:05 (7:05) (Class 4) (0-80,80) 4-Y-O+ **£4,209** (£1,252; £625; £312) **Stalls** Low

Form RPR

-060 **1** **Daaweitza**[10] 1630 5-9-0 76 TomEaves 4 88
(B Ellison) *in rr-div: hdwy over 2f out: styd on strly to ld nr fin* **8/1**

0-54 **2** 1/2 **Hiccups**[18] 1450 8-8-11 73 PhillipMakin 1 84
(M Dods) *trckd ldrs: led over 1f out: hdd and no ex nr fin* **7/2**[1]

0102 **3** 2 1/4 **Tencendur (IRE)**[14] 1552 4-9-1 77 AdrianTNicholls 3 82
(D Nicholls) *mid-div: hdwy 3f out: chal over 1f out: kpt on same pce* **5/1**[2]

626- **4** 1 1/2 **Sam's Secret**[230] 5545 6-8-12 77 PJMcDonald(3) 5 78
(G A Swinbank) *s.i.s: hdwy on outside over 2f out: styd on fnl f* **8/1**

134 **5** 1 3/4 **Hits Only Jude (IRE)**[26] 1278 5-9-3 79 DeanMcKeown 6 75
(P A Blockley) *in rr-div: hdwy on inner over 2f out: one pce fnl f* **11/1**

0001 **6** nse **Imperial Echo (USA)**[17] 1485 7-8-9 74 TolleyDean(3) 8 70
(D Shaw) *in rr: hdwy over 2f out: kpt on fnl f* **7/1**[3]

0-46 **7** 4 **King Harson**[18] 1450 9-8-5 67 (v) JoeFanning 11 52
(J D Bethell) *led early: w ldrs: led over 2f out: hdd over 1f out: sn wknd* **14/1**

3653 **8** 2 **Bel Cantor**[19] 1430 5-9-1 80 (p) AndrewMullen(3) 2 60
(W J H Ratcliffe) *sn led: hdd after 2f: lost pl over 1f out* **7/1**[3]

023- **9** 1 1/2 **Champain Sands (IRE)**[182] 6701 9-8-7 69 JimmyQuinn 10 45
(E J Alston) *s.i.s: a in rr* **16/1**

-005 **10** 4 **Nuit Sombre (IRE)**[3] 1815 8-9-3 79 (v) SilvestreDeSousa 12 44
(G A Harker) *w ldrs: led after 2f: hdd over 2f out: wknd over 1f out* **16/1**

100- **11** 2 1/4 **Pay Time**[232] 5476 9-8-4 66 oh4 PaulHanagan 7 25
(R E Barr) *sn chsng ldrs: lost pl over 1f out* **40/1**

524/ **12** 2 **Woody Valentine (USA)**[377] 6332 7-8-13 75 RoystonFfrench 9 29
(Mrs Dianne Sayer) *sn bhd* **50/1**

1m 26.53s (-0.47) **Going Correction** +0.075s/f (Good) **12** Ran SP% **117.3**
Speed ratings (Par 105): **105,104,101,100,98 98,93,91,89,84 82,80**
CSF £35.62 CT £142.58 TOTE £7.60: £3.40, £1.40, £1.80; EX 44.10.
Owner Mrs Andrea M Mallinson **Bred** C Mallinson **Trained** Norton, N Yorks

FOCUS
A strong pace suiting those coming from behind so runner-up Hiccups deserves full marks and the form has a solid look at this level.

1892 GORACING.CO.UK H'CAP 1m 7f 177y
7:35 (7:35) (Class 6) (0-65,65) 4-Y-O+ **£2,047** (£604; £302) **Stalls** Low

Form RPR

-001 **1** **Cavendish**[18] 1459 4-9-4 63 (b) LukeMorris(3) 3 71+
(J M P Eustace) *trckd ldrs: led over 1f out: styd on wl* **5/1**[3]

-266 **2** 1/2 **Coronado's Gold (USA)**[17] 1482 7-8-11 57 LanceBetts(7) 1 63
(B Ellison) *hld up in rr: hdwy on outside over 2f out: chal over 1f out: edgd lft: kpt on same pce ins fnl f* **17/2**

3600 **3** 4 1/2 **Just Waz (USA)**[14] 1551 6-8-7 46 oh1 DeanMcKeown 10 51+
(R M Whitaker) *trckd ldrs: hmpd and dropped bk over 3f out: hdwy over 1f out: styd on wl* **8/1**

/03- **4** 1 1/4 **Aston Lad**[115] 6259 7-8-8 47 PaulHanagan 11 46
(Micky Hammond) *s.i.s: hld up in rr: hdwy on outside over 4f out: led over 2f out: sn hdd: kpt on same pce* **11/2**

300- **5** 1 **Foxxy**[216] 5906 4-8-4 46 oh1 JimmyQuinn 9 44
(J R Norton) *in rr: hdwy over 3f out: one pce fnl 2f* **20/1**

323- **6** 1 1/2 **Chip N Pin**[55] 4718 4-8-8 50 DavidAllan 5 46
(T D Easterby) *prom: shkn up 8f out: sn drvn along: chsng ldrs over 2f out: lost pl appr fnl f* **11/4**[1]

306- **7** 8 **Compton Commander**[140] 4451 10-8-7 46 oh1 PaulMulrennan 7 33
(E W Tuer) *in rr-div: hdwy 8f out: chsng ldrs over 5f out: lost pl over 1f out* **50/1**

00/0 **8** 2 3/4 **Toss The Caber (IRE)**[13] 1559 6-8-9 48 TomEaves 2 31
(K G Reveley) *trckd ldrs: effrt 4f out: led 2f out: sn hdd & wknd* **16/1**

00-0 **9** 8 **Vice Admiral**[34] 1136 5-8-7 46 oh1 DaleGibson 6 20
(M W Easterby) *drvn to ld: hdd over 2f out: sn lost pl* **4/1**[2]

02-0 **10** 35 **Bronze Dancer (IRE)**[118] 105 6-9-9 65 PJMcDonald(3) 8 —
(B Storey) *sn trcking ldrs: drvn 4f out: sn wknd: bhd whn eased over 1f out: t.o* **20/1**

3m 34.42s (2.42) **Going Correction** +0.075s/f (Good)
WFA 4 from 5yo+ 3lb **10** Ran SP% **117.7**
Speed ratings (Par 101): **96,95,93,92,92 91,87,86,82,64**
CSF £46.18 CT £338.19 TOTE £6.60: £1.20, £3.10, £3.50; EX 55.60.
Owner The Cavendish Partnership **Bred** Mrs S Clifford **Trained** Newmarket, Suffolk

FOCUS
A weak handicap and just a steady pace. Cavendish was one of the few to come into this in any sort of form.
Just Waz(USA) Official explanation: jockey said gelding was denied a clear run
Vice Admiral Official explanation: trainer said gelding was found to have a temperature on returning home

1893 DON'T MISS TOTESPORT SATURDAY 24TH MAY H'CAP 5f
8:05 (8:05) (Class 5) (0-70,68) 4-Y-O+ **£2,729** (£806; £403) **Stalls** Low

Form RPR

0030 **1** **Brut**[10] 1624 6-8-11 68 (p) AdeleRothery(7) 3 76
(D W Barker) *w ldrs: hrd rdn to ld jst ins fnl f: edgd lft: hld on towards fin: eased last stride* **9/1**

0-00 **2** hd **Ronnie Howe**[19] 1431 4-8-10 60 PhillipMakin 2 67
(M Dods) *mid-div: hdwy to chse ldrs over 1f out: n.m.r and no ex nr fin* **9/1**

14-0 **3** 1/2 **Whinhill House**[25] 1309 8-8-11 61 (v) TWilliams 5 66
(D W Barker) *mde most: hdd jst ins fnl f: keeping on same pce whn n.m.r nr fin* **8/1**[3]

0-04 **4** 1 **Mr Rooney (IRE)**[35] 1129 5-8-7 57 AdrianTNicholls 6 59
(D Nicholls) *in rr-div: drvn and hdwy over 2f out: chsng ldrs over 1f out: kpt on same pce ins fnl f: hmpd nr fin* **5/1**[1]

405- **5** nk **Mulligan's Gold (IRE)**[187] 6608 5-8-2 55 DuranFentiman(3) 7 56+
(T D Easterby) *hood removed v late: in rr: hdwy over 2f out: styd on wl fnl f* **10/1**

0-05 **6** hd **Signor Panettiere**[9] 1646 7-8-4 54 oh9 SilvestreDeSousa 12 54
(A D Brown) *tubed: chsd ldrs: kpt on same pce fnl f* **16/1**

45-2 **7** 1/2 **Funfair Wane**[32] 1190 9-8-8 65 OliveGaule(7) 1 63
(D Nicholls) *w ldr: kpt on same pce fnl f: n.m.r towards fin* **11/2**[2]

1514 **8** nk **Blackheath (IRE)**[41] 1028 12-8-7 62 KellyHarrison(5) 4 59
(S T Mason) *towards rr: hdwy over 1f out: nvr nr ldrs* **10/1**

0-53 **9** 2 1/4 **Colorus (IRE)**[10] 1624 5-9-1 68 AndrewMullen(3) 10 69+
(W J H Ratcliffe) *sn drvn along in rr: hdwy u.p over 2f out: hung rt: wl hld whn n.m.r wl ins fnl f* **5/1**[1]

000- **10** 2 **Strensall**[155] 7011 11-9-1 65 PaulHanagan 14 47
(R E Barr) *in rr: hdwy on wd outsode 2f out: nvr nr ldrs* **28/1**

40-0 **11** 7 **Toy Top (USA)**[21] 1378 5-8-6 56 (b) TomEaves 13 13
(M Dods) *prom on outer: wknd appr fnl f* **16/1**

06-0 **12** 3 3/4 **Mormeatmic**[18] 1451 5-8-13 63 PaulMulrennan 8 6
(M W Easterby) *outpcd and lost pl over 3f out: sn bhd* **9/1**

0066 **13** 1 1/4 **Percy Douglas**[96] 372 8-7-12 55 oh9 ow1 (b) PatrickDonaghy(7) 11 —
(Miss A Stokell) *outpcd and lost pl over 3f out: sn bhd* **66/1**

60.25 secs (0.45) **Going Correction** +0.175s/f (Good) **13** Ran SP% **124.7**
Speed ratings (Par 103): **103,102,101,100,99 99,98,98,94,91 80,74,72**
CSF £91.64 CT £500.68 TOTE £8.20: £1.80, £3.60, £3.30; EX 195.70.
Owner D W Barker **Bred** Mrs Deborah O'Brien **Trained** Scorton, N Yorks
■ Stewards' Enquiry : Adele Rothery two-day ban: careless riding (May 20-21); three-day ban: used whip with excessive frequency (May 22-24)

FOCUS
A highly competitive low-grade sprint handicap but the eased winner edged in tightening up the four on his inside near the line. The form is modest although the winner is pretty reliable and the race appears sound enough with the placed horses close to their marks.
Mormeatmic Official explanation: jockey said gelding never travelled

1894 SPONSOR A RACE AT CATTERICK MAIDEN STKS 7f
8:35 (8:37) (Class 5) 3-Y-O+ **£2,590** (£770; £385; £192) **Stalls** Low

Form RPR

30-4 **1** **Dubai Meydan (IRE)**[7] 1701 3-9-0 0 PaulHanagan 3 80
(Miss Gay Kelleway) *trckd ldrs: stdd bnd 4f out: kpt on fnl 2f: led nr fin* **10/3**[3]

2- **2** hd **Ramaad**[228] 5595 3-9-0 0 MartinDwyer 13 79
(W J Haggas) *chsd ldrs: led over 1f out: edgd lft ins fnl f: hdd nr fin* **5/2**[2]

35-2 **3** 1 1/2 **Marning Star**[18] 1448 3-9-0 76 AdrianTNicholls 2 78+
(D Nicholls) *w ldrs: kpt on same pce ins fnl f* **7/4**[1]

3 **4** 3 **Imperial Djay (IRE)**[13] 1556 3-9-0 0 DavidAllan 7 67
(D Carroll) *led tl over 1f out: wknd towards fin* **5/1**

0- **5** 8 **Noche De Reyes**[188] 6595 3-9-0 0 JimmyQuinn 15 45
(E J Alston) *sn chsng ldrs: drvn over 3f out: edgd lft and wknd over 1f out* **100/1**

0 **6** 1 3/4 **Miss Understanding**[43] 991 3-8-9 0 DO'Donohoe 6 36
(J R Weymes) *in rr: kpt on fnl 2f: nvr on terms* **100/1**

7 1 1/4 **Carr On Fire (USA)** 3-9-0 0 PaulMulrennan 14 37
(G A Swinbank) *mid-div: drvn over 3f out: sn outpcd* **14/1**

5-0 **8** 1 **Jakam (IRE)**[13] 1556 3-9-0 0 ChrisCatlin 11 35
(E J O'Neill) *in rr: kpt on fnl 2f: nvr nr ldrs* **33/1**

00 **9** 4 **Fluoree (FR)**[22] 1372 4-9-7 0 TomEaves 1 19
(D W Thompson) *s.i.s: in rr-div: bhd fnl 2f* **200/1**

05- **10** 1 **Crossing Bridges**[146] 7121 3-8-9 0 PaulFessey 4 16
(T D Barron) *chsd ldrs over 2f: lost pl over 2f out* **80/1**

0 **11** 7 **Paris Hall**[18] 1453 3-9-0 0 PatrickMathers 9 2
(I W McInnes) *s.s: a in rr* **200/1**

5-0 **12** 3 1/2 **Watch This Place**[25] 1311 3-9-0 0 AndrewElliott 8 —
(K R Burke) *sn chsng ldrs: lost pl over 2f out* **100/1**

13 33 **White Elephant** 4-9-12 0 JoeFanning 5 —
(W Storey) *s.s: in rr: bhd over 2f out: t.o: sddle slipped* **40/1**

1m 28.08s (1.08) **Going Correction** +0.075s/f (Good)
WFA 3 from 4yo+ 12lb **13** Ran SP% **126.7**
Speed ratings (Par 103): **96,95,94,90,81 79,78,76,72,71 63,59,21**
CSF £12.37 TOTE £4.70: £1.60, £1.70, £1.10; EX 12.70 Place 6 £ 172.08, Place 5 £ 139.53.
Owner M K Armitt & N Spence **Bred** Crandon Park Stud **Trained** Exning, Suffolk

FOCUS
An ordinary maiden but the form looks sound rated through the 76-rated third.
White Elephant Official explanation: jockey said saddle slipped
T/Plt: £257.30 to a £1 stake. Pool: £54,410.86. 154.37 winning tickets. T/Qpdt: £23.70 to a £1 stake. Pool: £5,088.25. 158.30 winning tickets. WG

CHEPSTOW (L-H)
Tuesday, May 6

OFFICIAL GOING: Good (good to soft in places; 7.4)
Wind: virtually nil Weather: warm and sunny

1895 DENTS GALLERY AT CHEPSTOW RACECOURSE CLAIMING STKS 1m 2f 36y
2:10 (2:11) (Class 6) 4-Y-O+ **£1,942** (£578; £288; £144) **Stalls** Low

Form RPR

000- **1** **It's No Problem (IRE)**[231] 5497 4-8-0 40 CatherineGannon 11 51
(Mrs N S Evans) *s.i.s: sn chsng ldrs: wnt 2nd over 5f out: led over 3f out: rdn over 2f out: clr 1f out: r.o wl* **66/1**

00/1 **2** 3 3/4 **Penny Island (IRE)**[21] 1383 6-9-5 69 RichardHughes 8 63
(A King) *chsd ldr tl over 5f out: chsd wnr over 3f out: rdn and ev ch 2f out: outpcd by wnr over 1f out: kpt on* **5/2**[1]

300 **3** nk **Personify**[14] 1528 6-8-11 45 (p) TGMcLaughlin 9 54
(R A Harris) *stdd s: t.k.h: hld up wl bhd: hdwy 4f out: nt clr run and swtchd rt over 2f out: edgd lft but r.o wl: nvr nr wnr* **16/1**

00-5 **4** 2 3/4 **Measured Response**[80] 369 6-8-3 47 ow1 (b1) ThomasO'Brien(7) 10 48
(J G M O'Shea) *t.k.h: chsd ldrs: rdn to chse ldng pair 3f out: hung lft over 1f out: wknd fnl f* **25/1**

/00- **5** *7* **Airedale Lad (IRE)**[150] 6999 7-8-2 39.................. NataliaGemelova(5) 12 31
(R M Whitaker) *racd in midfield: rdn 4f out: no ch w ldrs last 2f* **50/1**

4-0 **6** *3/4* **Marquee (IRE)**[20] 1406 4-8-11 63.......................... StephenDonohoe 5 33
(P A Blockley) *s.i.s: towards rr: rdn and effrt over 3f out: no ch last 2f* **4/1**[3]

-604 **7** *2 1/4* **Almowj**[10] 1636 5-8-9 40 ow1.......................... JerryO'Dwyer(3) 6 30
(G H Jones) *t.k.h: hld up in tch in midfield: rdn wl over 3f out: nvr threatened ldrs* **66/1**

-565 **8** *1 1/4* **Bothar Brugha (IRE)**[86] 513 4-8-6 45............ RussellKennemore(3) 4 24
(J G M O'Shea) *rrd and slowly away: bhd: hdwy on outer 4f out: sn rdn: wknd over 2f out* **66/1**

6623 **9** *6* **Sweet World**[40] 1041 4-8-12 62.......................... SteveDrowne 7 15
(B J Llewellyn) *plld hrd: chsd ldrs: rdn and wknd 3f out* **6/1**

5215 **10** *2 1/4* **Lord Of Dreams (IRE)**[48] 935 6-8-6 56.............. JamieJones(5) 3 10
(G L Moore) *hld up bhd: hdwy whn nt clr run over 3f out: nvr on terms* **9/1**

/522 **11** *2 3/4* **Truly Fruitful (IRE)**[20] 1405 5-8-8 66.................. BMcHugh(7) 2 8
(Dr R D P Newland) *s.i.s: hld up in midfield: rdn and lost pl over 3f out: no ch last 2f* **10/3**[2]

0500 **12** *1/2* **Golden Spectrum (IRE)**[7] 1694 9-8-7 44..............(b) LPKeniry 13 —
(R A Harris) *led tl rdn and hdd over 3f out: sn dropped out: no ch and eased ins fnl f* **40/1**

00/ **13** *6* **Lyrical Girl (USA)**[26] 906 7-8-1 0 ow1.............. FrankieMcDonald 1 —
(H J Manners) *a bhd: t.o last 3f* **200/1**

2m 12.99s (2.39) **Going Correction** +0.275s/f (Good) **13** Ran SP% **115.0**
Speed ratings (Par 101): **101,98,97,95,89 89,87,86,81,79 77,77,72**
CSF £98.40: £11.40, £1.40, £3.50; EX 407.60 TRIFECTA Not won..It's No Problem was the subject of a friendly claim.
Owner P T Evans **Bred** M J Lewin And D Grieve **Trained** Pandy, Monmouths

FOCUS
A moderate claimer run at just an ordinary pace. The winning time was 2.39 seconds quicker than the following contest, a slowly run maiden but the form still looks messy.

1896 PONYGURL COUTURE BY D.M. DENT MAIDEN STKS 1m 2f 36y
2:40 (2:42) (Class 5) 3-Y-0+ **£2,590** (£770; £385; £192) **Stalls** Low

Form RPR

64 **1** **Murcar**[42] 1014 3-8-12 0.......................... PhilipRobinson 8 60
(C G Cox) *chsd ldrs: hdwy 4f out: led jst over 2f out: rdn 2f out: styd on wl to forge clr ins fnl f* **11/4**[1]

00 **2** *2* **Persian Wish (IRE)**[22] 1367 3-8-12 0.......................... DaneO'Neill 11 56
(J W Mullins) *chsd ldrs: hdwy over 3f out: ev ch 2f out: no ex ins fnl f* **100/1**

00 **3** *1* **Princess Flame (GER)**[10] 1621 6-9-1 0.................. KylieManser(7) 6 53+
(B G Powell) *v.s.a: wl bhd: stl plenty to do over 2f out: hdwy 2f out: running on whn short of room 1f out: r.o nt rch ldng pair* **100/1**

0 **4** *3/4* **Abstract Colours (IRE)**[19] 1418 3-8-12 0.......................... LPKeniry 9 53
(A M Balding) *hld up in midfield: hdwy 4f out: rdn 2f out: hung lft jst over 1f out: kpt on but nvr pce to rch ldrs* **33/1**

00-0 **5** *2 1/4* **Hill Of Clare (IRE)**[60] 822 6-9-3 32.................. HaddenFrost(5) 12 44
(G H Jones) *t.k.h: chsd ldrs: rdn over 3f out: one pce last 2f* **200/1**

5-4 **6** *2* **Loveofmylife**[17] 1477 3-8-7 0.......................... JamesDoyle 2 39
(R M Beckett) *chsd ldrs: rdn and wknd 2f out* **14/1**

0 **7** *nse* **Heartsanddiamonds**[21] 1382 4-9-5 0.................. JerryO'Dwyer(3) 13 40
(A W Carroll) *led tl rdn and hdd jst over 2f out: sn wknd* **100/1**

0-60 **8** *14* **Asian Classic (IRE)**[15] 1526 3-8-12 0.......................... SteveDrowne 3 16
(R Charlton) *in tch: rdn over 3f out: wknd over 2f out: eased fnl f: t.o* **8/1**

524 **9** *14* **Themwerethedays**[16] 1504 3-8-12 70.......................... RyanMoore 7 —
(S Kirk) *hld up towards rr: rdn and brief effrt 4f out: no ch and eased fr wl over 1f out: t.o* **11/2**[2]

052- **10** *2 1/4* **Border Owl (IRE)**[181] 6714 3-8-12 77.......................... RichardHughes 5 —
(R Hannon) *chsd ldr: ev ch 3f out: rdn over 2f out: wkng whn short of room 1f out: virtually p.u fnl f: t.o* **7/1**[3]

11 *16* **Berry Pomeroy** 3-8-5 0.......................... JackDean(7) 1 —
(A G Newcombe) *uns rdr bef s: sn bhd: t.o last 4f* **50/1**

2m 15.38s (4.78) **Going Correction** +0.275s/f (Good)
WFA 3 from 4yo+ 15lb **11** Ran SP% **80.7**
Speed ratings (Par 103): **91,89,88,88,86 84,84,73,62,60 47**
CSF £158.82 TOTE £2.90: £1.30, £11.70, £12.60; EX 257.70 TRIFECTA Not won..
Owner Peter J Skinner **Bred** John W Ford And Mr Peter J Skinner **Trained** Lambourn, Berks

FOCUS
This looked a very ordinary maiden beforehand and the race was weakened further by the late withdrawal of Nisaal, who had been due to go off favourite. The early pace was just modest, resulting in a winning time 2.39 seconds slower than the opening claimer, and a pair of 100/1 shots chased the winner home suggesting the form is dubious. However, for all that this race lacked strength in depth, there was plenty to like about Murcar.
Princess Flame(GER) ◆ Official explanation: jockey said, regarding running and riding, her orders were to sit mid-division or, if possible, make the running, adding that mare fell out of the stalls and thereafter she niggled it along to join the field, was travelling well and then picked up and ran on through beaten horses, but encountered interference at the furlong pole, possibly denying second place
Asian Classic(IRE) Official explanation: jockey said gelding hung left inside final furlong
Themwerethedays Official explanation: jockey said colt moved poorly
Border Owl(IRE) Official explanation: jockey said gelding suffered interference

1897 DENTS GALLERY H'CAP 6f 16y
3:10 (3:10) (Class 6) (0-65,65) 3-Y-0 **£2,104** (£626; £312; £156) **Stalls** High

Form RPR

0-05 **1** **Just Jimmy (IRE)**[10] 1635 3-8-7 54.......................... CatherineGannon 12 64
(P D Evans) *bhd: rdn and hdwy wl over 2f out: swtchd rt over 1f out: r.o strly to ld wl ins fnl f* **7/1**[3]

56-3 **2** *1/2* **Filligree (IRE)**[8] 1672 3-8-12 59.......................... SaleemGolam 6 67
(Rae Guest) *in tch: rdn and hdwy 2f out: led jst ins fnl f: hdd and no ex wl ins fnl f* **8/1**

054- **3** *3 1/2* **Shakespeare's Son**[138] 7195 3-8-10 57.................. FergusSweeney 1 54
(H J Evans) *chsd ldr: rdn over 2f out: led over 1f out: hdd jst ins fnl f: fdd last 100yds* **12/1**

0-52 **4** *nk* **Party In The Park**[5] 1743 3-8-13 65.................. PatrickHills(5) 5 61
(R Hannon) *chsd ldrs: rdn over 2f out: hrd rdn and one pce fr over 1f out* **2/1**[1]

36-0 **5** *1* **Curio**[43] 993 3-8-2 54.......................... NataliaGemelova(5) 4 47
(R M Whitaker) *chsd ldrs: rdn 2f out: plugged on same pce after* **14/1**

4626 **6** *3 1/4* **Spic 'n Span**[14] 1529 3-9-4 65.......................... AdamKirby 7 47
(R A Harris) *led: rdn and hung lft 2f out: hdd over 1f out: sn wknd* **16/1**

4300 **7** *1 1/4* **Boss Hog**[20] 1396 3-9-1 62.......................... StephenDonohoe 3 40
(P A Blockley) *sn wl out pced in rr: styd on fr over 1f out: n.d* **11/2**[2]

-000 **8** *3 1/4* **New Minerton (IRE)**[7] 1478 3-8-4 51 oh6..........(b[1]) AdrianMcCarthy 10 19
(B R Millman) *chsd ldrs for 2f: sn rdn and struggling: n.d fr 1/2-way* **66/1**

6504 **9** *1/2* **Szaba**[8] 1672 3-8-4 51 oh1..........................(b[1]) JohnEgan 13 17
(J M P Eustace) *a towards rr: rdn 4f out: nvr threatened ldrs* **11/1**

0-05 **10** *1/2* **Pasta Prayer**[34] 1149 3-9-1 62.......................... PatCosgrave 8 27
(S A Callaghan) *v.s.a: a wl bhd* **20/1**

00-0 **11** *2 3/4* **Boot Strap Bill**[9] 1642 3-8-13 60..........................[1] PaulFitzsimons 14 16
(Miss J R Tooth) *racd in midfield: rdn and lost pl 4f out: n.d after* **100/1**

065- **12** *nk* **Operachy**[209] 6104 3-9-4 65.......................... AlanMunro 9 20
(B R Millman) *t.k.h: chsd ldrs tl wknd qckly 2f out* **8/1**

1m 13.28s (0.38) **Going Correction** +0.15s/f (Good) **12** Ran SP% **119.3**
Speed ratings (Par 97): **103,102,97,97,95 91,89,85,84,84 80,80**
CSF £61.73 CT £678.31 TOTE £7.30: £2.40, £2.40, £4.30; EX 42.30 Trifecta £171.30 Pool: £241.38, 1 winning unit.
Owner Richard Edwards Gwynne Williams **Bred** Richard Edwards And Gwynne Williams **Trained** Pandy, Monmouths

FOCUS
A modest but competitive sprint handicap run at a strong pace and solid form for the grade. They tended to race middle to stands' side, but most of these avoided the near rail.
Just Jimmy(IRE) Official explanation: trainer said, regarding the improved form shown, gelding suffered interference on its last run and has matured from two to three years old
Boss Hog ◆ Official explanation: jockey said gelding was unruly in stalls and missed break

1898 JENKINSONS CATERERS H'CAP 1m 14y
3:40 (3:41) (Class 6) (0-65,65) 4-Y-0+ **£2,104** (£626; £312; £156) **Stalls** High

Form RPR

5245 **1** **Ermine Grey**[22] 1374 7-8-2 52.......................... KirstyMilczarek(3) 1 63
(A W Carroll) *hld up towards rr: rdn and hdwy over 2f out: styd on to ld jst over 1f out: rdn out* **5/1**[2]

544- **2** *1 3/4* **Dancing Storm**[186] 6627 5-8-9 56.......................... FergusSweeney 3 63
(W S Kittow) *in tch: hdwy to ld over 2f out: sn rdn: hdd jst over 1f out: kpt on same pce* **9/1**

-500 **3** *3* **Libre**[20] 1406 8-8-11 58.......................... TGMcLaughlin 11 58
(F Jordan) *hld up wl bhd: hdwy over 2f out: swtchd lft over 1f out: styd on to go 3rd ins fnl f: nvr nr ldng pair* **22/1**

000- **4** *1 1/2* **Miss Porcia**[209] 6096 7-8-4 51 oh6.................. FrankieMcDonald 13 48
(P A Blockley) *racd in midfield: rdn 3f out: hdwy over 2f out: kpt on same pce u.p fnl f* **25/1**

4-23 **5** *1* **Merrymadcap (IRE)**[27] 1266 6-9-2 63.......................... RyanMoore 12 58
(M Blanshard) *hld up bhd: hdwy 4f out: chsd ldrs and rdn 2f out: no hdwy jst over 1f out* **2/1**[1]

3050 **6** *3/4* **Swift Cut (IRE)**[27] 1044 4-7-11 51..........(p) DavidProbert(7) 6 44
(D Burchell) *prom: chsd ldr over 4f out: led 3f out: hdd and rdn over 2f out: wknd fnl f* **33/1**

-000 **7** *2 1/2* **The Grey One (IRE)**[9] 1644 5-8-9 56..........(p) TedDurcan 4 43
(J M Bradley) *hld up in midfield: hdwy over 3f out: chsd ldrs and rdn wl over 1f out: wknd fnl f* **10/1**

06-0 **8** *4* **The Gaikwar (IRE)**[69] 724 9-9-0 61..........(b) AdamKirby 5 39
(R A Harris) *s.i.s: wl bhd: rdn over 5f out: plugged on past btn horse last 2f: n.d* **16/1**

00-0 **9** *5* **Bidable**[34] 1160 4-8-12 59.......................... CatherineGannon 14 26
(B Palling) *led for 1f: rdn and lost pl wl over 3f out: n.d after* **14/1**

0230 **10** *nk* **Arturius (IRE)**[11] 1604 6-9-0 64..........(p) KevinGhunowa(3) 8 30
(R A Harris) *chsd ldrs tl led after 1f: hdd 3f out: sn rdn: wknd 2f out* **25/1**

5210 **11** *1 1/4* **Having A Ball**[13] 1565 4-8-11 58.......................... DaneO'Neill 7 21+
(P D Cundell) *hld up in midfield: hdwy 3f out: rdn over 2f out: no imp whn carried lft 1f out* **15/2**[3]

00-0 **12** *nk* **Murdoch**[28] 1258 4-8-10 57 ow2..........(p) StephenDonohoe 10 19
(E S McMahon) *t.k.h: chsd ldrs: rdn over 3f out: wknd qckly 3f out:* **25/1**

100- **13** *7* **Surprise Act**[143] 7155 4-9-4 65.......................... PaulDoe 9 11
(P R Chamings) *chsd ldr tl over 4f out: rdn and wknd over 2f out: wl bhd over 1f out* **16/1**

000- **14** *11* **King's Account (USA)**[131] 5886 6-8-4 51 oh6.................. JohnEgan 2 —
(S Gollings) *hld hd high: prom tl lost pl after 3f: wl bhd fnl 3f: t.o.* **20/1**

1m 37.08s (0.88) **Going Correction** +0.15s/f (Good) **14** Ran SP% **122.9**
Speed ratings (Par 101): **101,99,96,94,93 93,90,86,81,81 79,79,72,61**
CSF £45.32 CT £951.00 TOTE £6.00: £2.20, £2.90, £7.20; EX 64.00 TRIFECTA Not won..
Owner L M Baker **Bred** D Brocklehurst **Trained** Cropthorne, Worcs

FOCUS
A moderate handicap run at a good pace and the runner-up is a solid guide to the form. The winning time was 2.36 seconds quicker than the following three-year-old 66-80 handicap, although that was a modestly run race. They raced middle to stands' side.

1899 MASSIVE SAVINGS AT MERTHYR MOTOR AUCTIONS H'CAP 1m 14y
4:10 (4:11) (Class 4) (0-80,77) 3-Y-0 **£4,533** (£1,348; £674; £336) **Stalls** High

Form RPR

03-2 **1** **Mega Watt (IRE)**[14] 1535 3-9-0 73.......................... AlanMunro 6 78+
(W Jarvis) *hld up in tch: hdwy wl over 2f out: jnd ldr and rdn 2f out: r.o u.p to ld nr fin* **13/8**[1]

05-0 **2** *shd* **Bere Davis (FR)**[38] 1074 3-9-4 77.......................... TGMcLaughlin 1 82
(P D Evans) *restless in stalls: t.k.h: disp ld tl rdn to ld jst over 2f out: jnd 2f out: battled on wl tl hdd nr fin* **16/1**

2226 **3** *2 1/2* **Rich Kid (IRE)**[2] 1839 3-8-10 72.................. KevinGhunowa(3) 5 71
(R A Harris) *in tch in midfield on outer: hdwy to chse ldrs 4f out: rdn wl over 2f out: kpt on same pce fr over 1f out* **5/1**[2]

050- **4** *1 1/4* **Top Vision**[263] 4564 3-9-1 74.......................... EdwardCreighton 9 70
(M R Channon) *stdd s: hld up bhd: hdwy wl over 3f out: edgd lft over 1f out: kpt on same pce fnl f* **14/1**

32-4 **5** *nk* **Just Rob**[13] 1573 3-9-1 74.......................... TedDurcan 2 69
(R Hollinshead) *chsd ldrs: rdn and ev ch wl over 1f out: wknd jst over 1f out* **13/2**[3]

541- **6** *3/4* **Sahaadi**[224] 5707 3-9-3 76.......................... RichardHughes 8 72+
(R Hannon) *stdd s: t.k.h: hld up in rr: hdwy over 2f out: hung lft and no imp and hmpd over 1f out* **7/1**

04-4 **7** *hd* **Joinedupwriting**[12] 1576 3-9-2 75.......................... PatCosgrave 11 68
(R M Whitaker) *chsd ldrs: rdn wl over 2f out: kpt on same pce* **9/1**

030- **8** *2* **Bathwick Man**[227] 5633 3-8-9 68.......................... JohnEgan 4 57
(B R Millman) *disp ld tl jst over 2f out: sn wknd* **50/1**

545- **9** *nse* **Avertitop**[298] 3508 3-8-7 73.................. CharlesEddery(7) 10 62
(R Hannon) *stdd s: hld up bhd: hdwy 3f out: chsd ldrs and rdn over 2f out: sn wknd* **33/1**

6-20 **10** *11* **Last Of The Line**[24] 1333 3-9-2 75.......................... SteveDrowne 7 38
(H J L Dunlop) *a bhd: no ch last 2f* **11/1**

1m 39.44s (3.24) **Going Correction** +0.15s/f (Good) **10** Ran SP% **116.4**
Speed ratings (Par 101): **89,88,86,85,84 84,83,81,81,70**
CSF £31.82 CT £112.01 TOTE £2.50: £1.20, £2.50, £2.20; EX 31.90 Trifecta £167.20 Pool: £442.95, 1.88 winning units.
Owner The Mega Watt Partnership **Bred** Rathbarry Stud **Trained** Newmarket, Suffolk

The Form Book, Raceform Ltd, Compton, RG20 6NL

FOCUS
A fair three-year-old handicap, but they went a modest pace early on and the winning time was 2.36 seconds slower than the previous 51-65 older-horse contest, so the form looks somewhat messy despite the third being a fairly reliable marker. They raced towards the stands' side.
Sahaadi Official explanation: jockey said filly hung left
Last Of The Line Official explanation: jockey said colt hung right

1900 DENTS GALLERY AT CHEPSTOW RACECOURSE H'CAP — 7f 16y
4:40 (4:43) (Class 5) (0-70,70) 4-Y-0+ — **£2,914** (£867; £433; £216) **Stalls** High

Form — RPR
3405 **1** **Unlimited**[48] 938 6-8-2 **57** .... KirstyMilczarek(3) 3 — 72
(A W Carroll) *taken steadily to s: t.k.h: hld up in tch: rdn to chse ldng pair over 2f out: wnt 2nd jst over 1f out: r.o wl u.p to ld wl ins fnl f* **5/1**[1]
0-03 **2** *1 1/4* **Violent Velocity (IRE)**[18] 1450 5-8-7 **66** .... BMcHugh(7) 15 — 78
(J J Quinn) *in tch: hdwy to ld jst over 3f out: clr 2f out: edgd rt u.p 1f out: hdd and no ex wl ins fnl f* **6/1**[3]
0-05 **3** *3* **Farefield Lodge (IRE)**[14] 1541 4-9-1 **67** .... PhilipRobinson 16 — 71
(C G Cox) *disp overall ld on stands rail: chsd wnr 3f out: hung lft u.p fr over 2f out: lost 2nd jst over 1f out: fdd last 100yds* **10/1**
300- **4** *1 1/2* **Isphahan**[188] 6577 5-8-7 **59** .... LPKeniry 7 — 59
(A M Balding) *s.i.s: in tch in midfield: rdn over 3f out: sn outpcd: kpt on u.p fr over 1f out: wnt modest 4th ins fnl f* **9/1**
00-4 **5** *3* **Indian Edge**[11] 1605 7-9-4 **70** .... CatherineGannon 8 — 62
(B Palling) *chsd ldrs: rdn 3f out: outpcd by ldng trio 2f out: no ch after* **11/1**
/2-0 **6** *3 1/2* **Valentino Swing (IRE)**[22] 1368 5-8-12 **69** .... JamesMillman(5) 9 — 51
(Miss T Spearing) *s.i.s: sn rcvrd and chsng ldrs: rdn 3f out: sn outpcd: n.d last 2f* **33/1**
0-05 **7** *2 1/4* **Moon Forest (IRE)**[9] 1641 6-8-4 **56** oh11 ....(p) JohnEgan 11 — 32
(J M Bradley) *hld up in tch: outpcd and rdn over 3f out: no ch after: sme modest late hdwy* **25/1**
60-0 **8** *1 1/4* **Neon Blue**[24] 1327 7-8-11 **68** ....(v) NataliaGemelova(5) 13 — 41
(R M Whitaker) *chsd ldrs: rdn and struggling 4f out: no ch fr wl over 2f out* **14/1**
0-60 **9** *nk* **Gilded Youth**[18] 1450 4-9-4 **70** .... DaneO'Neill 2 — 42
(H Candy) *disp overall ld in centre tl over 3f out: wknd qckly wl over 2f out* **11/2**[2]
00-1 **10** *shd* **Turkish Sultan (IRE)**[14] 1533 5-8-4 **56** oh2 ....(p) DavidKinsella 10 — 28
(J M Bradley) *chsd ldrs tl lost pl over 4f out: n.d after* **16/1**
60-4 **11** *1 1/4* **Rubenstar (IRE)**[25] 1308 5-9-3 **69** .... PatCosgrave 14 — 37
(D J G Murray Smith) *v.s.a: hdwy and in tch over 4f out: sn rdn: wl bhd last 3f* **17/2**
600 **12** *shd* **Sir Douglas**[34] 1143 5-8-8 **60** ow2 ....(p) TGMcLaughlin 6 — 28
(R A Harris) *taken down early: chsd ldrs: rdn over 3f out: wknd wl over 2f out* **20/1**
600- **13** *3 3/4* **Iguacu**[231] 5510 4-8-7 **59** .... PaulFitzsimons 5 — 17
(J L Spearing) *racd in midfield: rdn 3f out: sn outpcd and no ch* **40/1**
030- **14** *4 1/2* **Coup D'Etat**[166] 6024 6-9-1 **70** ....(b) KevinGhunowa(3) 1 — 16
(R A Harris) *chsd ldr for over 2f: sn rdn and lost pl: wl bhd last 2f* **25/1**
20-1 **15** *19* **Hazytoo**[34] 1154 4-9-2 **68** .... StephenDonohoe 12 — —
(S A Callaghan) *in tch tl lost pl and sltly hmpd 4f out: sn detached in last: eased fr over 1f out: t.o* **6/1**[3]

1m 25.45s (2.25) **Going Correction** +0.15s/f (Good) — **15** Ran SP% **129.0**
Speed ratings (Par 103): **93,91,88,86,83 79,76,75,74,74 73,73,68,63,41**
CSF £34.42 CT £310.74 TOTE £6.80: £2.40, £2.50, £2.60; EX 52.30 Trifecta £142.90 Pool: £223.49, 1.11 winning units. Place 6 £ 260.63, Place 5 £ 99.08.
Owner Carnival Quest **Bred** J Wise **Trained** Cropthorne, Worcs
FOCUS
A largish field for this modest handicap and they raced right across the track, but in the end there appeared little advantage as the low-drawn winner beat the two berthed nearest the stands' rail. The time was moderate and the form does not look solid.
Farefield Lodge(IRE) Official explanation: jockey said gelding hung left 3f out
Hazytoo Official explanation: jockey said gelding stopped quickly
T/Jkpt: Not won. T/Plt: £211.80 to a £1 stake. Pool: £65,340.34. 225.13 winning tickets. T/Qpdt: £44.50 to a £1 stake. Pool: £3,639.40. 60.50 winning tickets. SP

1776 SOUTHWELL (L-H)
Tuesday, May 6

OFFICIAL GOING: Standard
Wind: Light against Weather: Cloudy with sunny spells

1901 POLYFLOR.COM H'CAP — 5f (F)
2:30 (2:31) (Class 5) (0-75,73) 4-Y-0+ — **£3,399** (£1,011; £505; £252) **Stalls** High

Form — RPR
2465 **1** **Figaro Flyer (IRE)**[17] 1488 5-8-8 **63** .... ShaneKelly 4 — 74
(P Howling) *chsd ldrs: rdn to ld 1f out: r.o* **17/2**
0-63 **2** *1 1/2* **Double Bill (USA)**[8] 1677 4-9-0 **69** ....(p) NCallan 7 — 75
(P F I Cole) *led: rdn and hdd 1f out: styd on same pce* **11/4**[1]
422 **3** *nk* **Spoof Master (IRE)**[21] 1386 4-9-2 **71** .... RobertWinston 1 — 76
(C R Dore) *w ldr tl rdn 1/2-way: styd on same pce fnl f* **11/4**[1]
6040 **4** *1 1/4* **Spirit Of Coniston**[10] 1624 5-8-7 **62** .... AdrianTNicholls 8 — 62
(D Nicholls) *sn outpcd: hdwy over 1f out: r.o* **12/1**
-240 **5** *nk* **Tilly's Dream**[7] 1698 5-8-12 **70** .... WilliamBuick(3) 3 — 69
(G C Bravery) *chsd ldrs: rdn 1/2-way: styng on same pce whn hung lft fnl f* **11/2**[2]
2366 **6** *2* **Dickie Le Davoir**[12] 1588 4-8-10 **72** .... MarkCoumbe(7) 9 — 64
(John A Harris) *s.i.s: outpcd* **22/1**
4-65 **7** *1/2* **Dancing Mystery**[102] 301 14-8-12 **67** ....(b) StephenCarson 2 — 57
(E A Wheeler) *chsd ldrs: rdn 1/2-way: wknd ins fnl f* **33/1**
0-60 **8** *1* **Count Cougar (USA)**[28] 1261 8-9-1 **73** .... MichaelJStainton(3) 10 — 60
(S P Griffiths) *chsd ldrs: rdn and hung lft fr over 1f out: wknd ins fnl f* **16/1**
-430 **9** *3 3/4* **The Fisio**[7] 1703 8-8-8 **63** ....(b) PaulEddery 5 — 36
(G D Blake) *s.s: outpcd* **16/1**
-205 **10** *1 1/4* **El Potro**[21] 1378 6-7-11 **59** .... StacyRenwick(7) 6 — 28
(J R Holt) *s.i.s: outpcd* **8/1**[3]

59.91 secs (0.21) **Going Correction** +0.125s/f (Slow) — **10** Ran SP% **117.1**
Speed ratings (Par 103): **103,100,100,98,97 94,93,92,86,84**
CSF £32.27 CT £84.63 TOTE £12.00: £3.20, £1.30, £1.40; EX 49.20.
Owner S J Hammond **Bred** Mohammad Al Qatami **Trained** Newmarket, Suffolk
FOCUS
An ordinary Fibresand sprint handicap and as they often do here, the field gradually migrated to the centre of the track as the race progressed. The form looks straightforward rated around the first three.
Tilly's Dream Official explanation: jockey said mare hung left

1902 KARNDEAN.COM CLAIMING STKS — 1m (F)
3:00 (3:00) (Class 6) 4-Y-0+ — **£2,047** (£604; £302) **Stalls** Low

Form — RPR
0-02 **1** **Royal Dignitary (USA)**[26] 1286 8-9-7 **83** .... AdrianTNicholls 2 — 82
(D Nicholls) *mde all: rdn over 1f out: hung lft ins fnl f: all out* **4/1**[2]
1111 **2** *nk* **Yakimov (USA)**[7] 1700 9-9-2 **85** .... JamieMoriarty(3) 8 — 79
(Ollie Pears) *hld up: hdwy over 3f out: chsd wnr over 1f out: shkn up and ev ch whn edgd lft ins fnl f: nt qckn nr fin* **2/5**[1]
451 **3** *5* **Blue Empire (IRE)**[14] 1550 7-8-4 **57** ....(p) MarkCoumbe(7) 6 — 60
(John A Harris) *hld up: racd keenly: hdwy to chse wnr over 5f out: rdn over 2f out: no ex fnl f* **11/1**[3]
500- **4** *4* **The Iron Giant (IRE)**[145] 7069 6-9-2 **42** .... AlanDaly 4 — 56
(Dr J R J Naylor) *chsd ldrs to 1/2-way* **100/1**
300- **5** *shd* **Steel Silk (IRE)**[131] 5604 4-8-9 **63** ....(t) PaulMulrennan 3 — 48
(D H Brown) *chsd ldrs: rdn 1/2-way: wknd over 2f out* **50/1**
4000 **6** *3/4* **Anduril**[4] 1776 7-8-9 **50** ....(p) RobertWinston 5 — 47
(I W McInnes) *hld up: n.d* **22/1**
4-00 **7** *nk* **El Coto**[85] 526 8-8-2 **53** .... StacyRenwick(7) 1 — 46
(J R Holt) *sn pushed along and prom: bhd fr 1/2-way* **50/1**
0000 **8** *9* **Bodden Bay**[6] 1687 6-8-8 **45** .... PatrickMathers 7 — 24
(I W McInnes) *prom over 3f* **50/1**

1m 42.7s (-1.00) **Going Correction** -0.075s/f (Stan) — **8** Ran SP% **111.0**
Speed ratings (Par 101): **102,101,96,92,92 91,91,82**
CSF £5.66 TOTE £3.70: £1.10, £1.02, £1.60; EX 8.70.
Owner Middleham Park Racing XXXVI **Bred** Bentley Smith, J Michael O'Farrell Jr , Joan Thor **Trained** Sessay, N Yorks
FOCUS
An uncompetitive claimer that was a two-horse race according to the market and on adjusted official ratings and the pair duly dominated, but the result was still something of a shock. The winning time was reasonable, despite being 0.63 seconds slower than the following fillies' handicap and the winner is the best guide.

1903 MICHELLE AND STEVE ELLIS HAPPY 1ST ANNIVERSARY FILLIES' H'CAP — 1m (F)
3:30 (3:30) (Class 4) (0-80,82) 4-Y-0+ — **£4,921** (£1,464; £731; £365) **Stalls** Low

Form — RPR
05-1 **1** **Look So**[22] 1365 4-9-3 **79** .... SebSanders 4 — 90+
(R M Beckett) *hld up in tch: pushed along 1/2-way: rdn to chse ldr over 1f out: edgd lft ins fnl f: styd on u.p to ld nr fin* **10/11**[1]
4263 **2** *nk* **Jord (IRE)**[12] 1585 4-8-10 **72** .... AndrewElliott 6 — 82
(A J McCabe) *s.i.s: hdwy to ld 7f out: rdn over 1f out: hdd nr fin* **8/1**[3]
6153 **3** *8* **Indian's Feather (IRE)**[12] 1590 7-8-10 **72** .... TomEaves 1 — 64
(N Tinkler) *led 1f: chsd ldrs tl lost pl over 4f out: n.d after* **9/1**
6-51 **4** *nse* **Magic Echo**[8] 1676 4-9-6 **82** 6ex .... PhillipMakin 5 — 74
(M Dods) *chsd ldrs: rdn over 3f out: sn outpcd* **9/4**[2]
0-32 **5** *9* **Thunderousapplause**[8] 1676 4-9-2 **78** ....(t) NeilPollard 3 — 49
(A J McCabe) *prom: chsd ldr over 4f out: rdn and wknd over 1f out* **14/1**

1m 42.07s (-1.63) **Going Correction** -0.075s/f (Stan) — **5** Ran SP% **110.9**
Speed ratings (Par 102): **105,104,96,96,87**
CSF £8.99 TOTE £1.90: £1.30, £3.30; EX 8.50.
Owner J H Richmond-Watson **Bred** Lawn Stud **Trained** Whitsbury, Hants
FOCUS
A small field for this fillies' handicap, but they went a decent pace and they finished very well spread out. The winning time was 0.63 seconds faster than the preceding claimer.

1904 KARNDEAN FLOORING OF EVESHAM H'CAP — 1m 3f (F)
4:00 (4:00) (Class 4) (0-80,80) 4-Y-0+ — **£4,921** (£1,464; £731; £365) **Stalls** Low

Form — RPR
3102 **1** **Bentley Brook (IRE)**[41] 1026 6-8-11 **80** .... SophieDoyle(7) 9 — 90
(P A Blockley) *chsd ldr over 8f out: rdn to ld over 1f out: edgd rt ins fnl f: eased towards fin* **5/2**[1]
5-43 **2** *nk* **Black Falcon (IRE)**[14] 1554 8-8-7 **69** ow2 .... MickyFenton 2 — 78
(M A Peill) *led: rdn and hdd over 1f out: styd on* **7/1**
1423 **3** *9* **Jackie Kiely**[12] 1589 7-8-10 **72** ....(t) PaulMulrennan 5 — 66
(R Brotherton) *s.i.s: hld up: hdwy u.p over 3f out: sn outpcd* **7/1**
1320 **4** *6* **Exit To Luck (GER)**[12] 1589 7-8-8 **70** ....(b) RobertWinston 1 — 54
(S Gollings) *chsd ldrs: rdn over 5f out: sn bhd* **16/1**
-451 **5** *1* **The King And I (IRE)**[7] 1704 4-9-0 **76** 6ex ....(b) NCallan 8 — 58
(Miss E C Lavelle) *hld up in tch: rdn and wknd over 2f out* **11/4**[2]
46-0 **6** *2 1/4* **Iceman George**[8] 1692 4-8-1 **66** oh6 ....(b) WilliamBuick(3) 7 — 44
(D Morris) *hld up: plld hrd: rdn and wknd over 4f out* **18/1**
00-0 **7** *6* **Moonwalking**[17] 1482 4-8-4 **66** oh1 .... AndrewElliott 3 — 34
(Jedd O'Keeffe) *hld up: rdn 1/2-way: sn wknd* **20/1**
1126 **8** *26* **Sri Kuantan (IRE)**[87] 504 4-9-1 **77** .... TQuinn 6 — 1
(P F I Cole) *trckd ldrs: plld hrd: rdn and wknd over 3f out* **4/1**[3]

2m 25.16s (-2.84) **Going Correction** -0.075s/f (Stan) — **8** Ran SP% **116.1**
Speed ratings (Par 105): **107,106,100,95,95 93,89,70**
CSF £21.01 CT £109.13 TOTE £3.60: £1.10, £2.40, £3.00; EX 27.80.
Owner John Wardle **Bred** Christopher Maye **Trained** Lambourn, Berks
■ Sri Kuantan ran all his previous races under the slightly different name Srikuantan.
■ Stewards' Enquiry : Robert Winston three-day ban: weighed-in 3lb heavier than weighed-out (May 20-22)
FOCUS
They did not hang about in this fair middle-distance handicap, but it paid to race handily and the front pair held those positions throughout. The runner-up is rated to last year's best and with the pair clear the form should prove reasonable.
The King And I(IRE) Official explanation: trainer's rep had no explanation for the poor form shown
Sri Kuantan(IRE) Official explanation: jockey said colt stopped quickly

1905 AXMINSTER CARPETS MAIDEN STKS — 1m 3f (F)
4:30 (4:33) (Class 5) 3-Y-0+ — **£3,399** (£1,011; £505; £252) **Stalls** Low

Form — RPR
3 **1** **Flying Squad (UAE)**[7] 1701 4-9-13 0 .... MickyFenton 1 — 83
(D J Wintle) *hld up: hdwy 1/2-way: shkn up to ld and hung lft fr over 1f out: styd on* **9/1**[2]
3-2 **2** *1/2* **Wood Chorus**[22] 1372 3-8-5 0 .... HayleyTurner 3 — 76
(M L W Bell) *led for 1f: chsd ldr after tl led over 2f out: rdn and hdd over 1f out: edgd lft ins fnl f: styd on same pce* **4/6**[1]
6- **3** *12* **Opening Act**[164] 6934 3-8-10 0 .... TQuinn 7 — 61
(P F I Cole) *sn pushed along and prom: rdn 1/2-way: wknd over 2f out* **16/1**[3]
-6 **4** *4 1/2* **Reprieved**[7] 1701 3-8-4 0 ow1 .... MarkCoumbe(7) 5 — 54
(M C Chapman) *s.i.s: plld hrd: hdwy to ld after 1f: rdn and hdd over 2f out: sn wknd* **100/1**

00-0 **5** *13* **Insured**[17] 1490 3-8-5 54 DanielleMcCreery(5) 4 31
(A J McCabe) *chsd ldrs: hung rt and wknd 1/2-way* **100/1**
0 **6** *29* **Pharly Green**[14] 1539 6-9-1 0 (p) JemmaMarshall(7) 2 —
(G P Enright) *sn pushed along in rr: bhd fnl 7f* **200/1**
2m 26.81s (-1.19) **Going Correction** -0.075s/f (Stan)
WFA 3 from 4yo+ 17lb **6** Ran SP% **78.3**
Speed ratings (Par 103): **101,100,91,88,79 58**
CSF £7.37 TOTE £4.00: £2.40, £1.02; EX 9.30.
Owner Mick Coulson **Bred** Darley **Trained** Naunton, Gloucs
FOCUS
A modest maiden with half the field starting at 100-1 or bigger and the finish was dominated by the front two in the market who pulled miles clear, but this was still a surprise result. The winning time was 1.65 seconds slower than the preceding handicap and that is probably a fair guide to the level.

1906 T & R FLOOR COVERING OF NOTTINGHAM H'CAP 6f (F)
5:00 (5:02) (Class 6) (0-50,50) 4-Y-0+ £2,729 (£806; £403) Stalls Low

Form RPR
2433 **1** **Blakeshall Quest**[8] 1675 8-8-9 47 (b) PaulMulrennan 5 64
(R Brotherton) *mde all: rdn clr fnl f* **15/2**
4002 **2** *2 3/4* **Tenancy (IRE)**[8] 1675 4-8-8 46 (p) NeilPollard 7 54
(A J McCabe) *a.p: chsd wnr over 3f out: rdn and edgd lft over 1f out: styd on same pce* **7/2**[1]
0000 **3** *3 1/2* **Union Jack Jackson (IRE)**[8] 1675 6-8-8 46 oh1 (b) DaleGibson 14 43
(John A Harris) *s.i.s: hdwy u.p over 1f out: nt trble ldrs* **9/1**
-360 **4** *1/2* **Silly Gilly (IRE)**[32] 1189 4-8-12 50 AndrewElliott 10 45
(R E Barr) *hld up in tch: rdn over 2f out: hung lft over 1f out: no imp* **16/1**
6650 **5** *3/4* **Gone'N'Dunnett (IRE)**[18] 1455 9-8-9 47 (p) HayleyTurner 3 40
(Mrs C A Dunnett) *chsd ldrs: rdn over 2f out: styd on same pce* **9/1**
1405 **6** *1* **Hi Spec (IRE)**[7] 1700 5-8-8 46 (v[1]) SamHitchcott 4 36
(Miss M E Rowland) *sn outpcd: nvr nrr* **20/1**
4050 **7** *1* **Temtation (IRE)**[14] 1550 4-8-3 46 oh1 KellyHarrison(5) 9 33
(J A Pickering) *chsd ldrs: rdn over 2f out: wknd over 1f out* **20/1**
0-60 **8** *3/4* **Piccleyes**[8] 1675 7-8-1 46 oh1 (v[1]) StacyRenwick(7) 11 30
(A J McCabe) *mid-div: hdwy over 3f out: rdn over 2f out: sn wknd* **20/1**
5043 **9** *3 1/4* **Pappas Image**[47] 951 4-8-9 47 oh1 ow1 (b) NCallan 12 21
(A J McCabe) *mid-div: rdn 1/2-way: hung lft and wknd over 2f out* **4/1**[2]
4400 **10** *nk* **Orchestration (IRE)**[8] 1675 7-8-3 46 oh1 AhmedAjtebi(5) 2 19
(Garry Moss) *chsd ldrs over 3f* **20/1**
6653 **11** *3 1/2* **Zorn**[12] 1591 9-8-10 48 ShaneKelly 1 10
(P Howling) *sn outpcd* **7/1**[3]
1400 **12** *1/2* **Government (IRE)**[63] 792 7-8-3 46 oh1 DanielleMcCreery(5) 6 6
(M C Chapman) *s.i.s: outpcd* **22/1**
000- **13** *2* **Brean Dot Com (IRE)**[248] 4742 4-8-8 46 (b[1]) RobertHavlin 8 —
(Mrs P N Dutfield) *s.i.s: outpcd* **33/1**
1m 16.28s (-0.22) **Going Correction** -0.075s/f (Stan) **13** Ran SP% **118.7**
Speed ratings (Par 101): **98,94,89,89,87 86,85,84,80,79 74,74,71**
CSF £29.64 CT £253.71 TOTE £8.90: £2.70, £1.40, £3.70; EX 28.70 Place 6 £ 5.08, Place 5 £ 3.53.
Owner Bredon Hill Racing Club **Bred** M P Bishop **Trained** Elmley Castle, Worcs
FOCUS
A distinctly moderate bunch was run ragged by the trail-blazing Blakeshall Quest, who recorded her sixth course success in the process. Apart from the runner-up nothing was able to get into the race but the winner was still reversing previous form with that rival.
T/Plt: £3.70 to a £1 stake. Pool: £49,687.91. 9,637.48 winning tickets. T/Qpdt: £2.90 to a £1 stake. Pool: £2,125.08. 540.30 winning tickets. CR

1574 BEVERLEY (R-H)
Wednesday, May 7

OFFICIAL GOING: Good
Wind: Virtually nil Weather: Sunny

1907 TURFTV MEDIAN AUCTION MAIDEN STKS 5f
2:00 (2:00) (Class 5) 2-Y-0 £2,331 (£693; £346; £173) Stalls High

Form RPR
1 **Deadly Encounter (IRE)** 2-8-10 0 BMcHugh(7) 8 86+
(R A Fahey) *cl up on inner: led 1/2-way: clr over 1f out: easily* **5/2**[1]
03 **2** *9* **Johnmanderville**[11] 1616 2-9-3 0 DarrenWilliams 3 54
(K R Burke) *cl up: effrt 1/2-way: sn rdn and hung rt: drvn over 1f out and sn one pce* **11/4**[2]
3 *7* **Eden Park** 2-8-12 0 PhillipMakin 7 23
(M Dods) *led: rdn along and hdd 1/2-way: drvn and wknd over 1f out* **6/1**
4 *hd* **Svindal (IRE)** 2-9-3 0 NCallan 2 28
(K A Ryan) *chsd ldrs: effrt over 2f out: sn rdn: drvn and edgd rt wl over 1f out: sn wknd* **10/3**[3]
0 **5** *4 1/2* **Sandies Sister**[7] 1727 2-8-9 0 MarkLawson(3) 5 6
(M Brittain) *wnt lft s: in tch and sn rdn along: n.d* **11/1**
6 *11* **Sally Bond (IRE)** 2-8-9 0 DuranFentiman(3) 6 —
(T D Easterby) *s.i.s: sn outpcd and a in rr* **22/1**
7 *7* **Fizzy Friend** 2-8-12 0 DO'Donohoe 4 —
(J R Weymes) *hmpd s: a in rr* **20/1**
8 *2 1/2* **Dispol Bertie** 2-9-3 0 FrankieMcDonald 1 —
(P T Midgley) *wnt lft s: a outpcd in rr* **28/1**
63.34 secs (-0.16) **Going Correction** -0.125s/f (Firm) **8** Ran SP% **113.5**
Speed ratings (Par 93): **96,81,70,70,62 45,34,30**
CSF £9.25 TOTE £2.90: £1.10, £1.50, £1.90; EX 10.30.
Owner J J Staunton **Bred** R A Fahey **Trained** Musley Bank, N Yorks
FOCUS
Probably just a modest maiden, but a really impressive winner in the form of Deadly Encounter, who could be better than rated with the runner-up well below his previous mark.
NOTEBOOK
Deadly Encounter(IRE) ◆, a son of Lend A Hand, and half-brother to dual 5f-6f two-year-old winner Magnolia Blossom, out of a 5f juvenile winner who was later successful over 1m, was well backed on his racecourse debut and justified the support with a taking success. Able to take advantage of the best draw of all after being quickly into his stride, he travelled strongly to the two-furlong marker under his promising 7lb claimer before bounding clear when asked to pick up. He looked green under pressure, but the further he went the better he looked and he crossed the line with plenty left. He deserves his chance in something better now and could come back to Beverley for the Brian Yeardley Two-Year-Old Trophy. A race like that, or something like the Woodcote Stakes at Epsom will tell us whether he is Royal Ascot material. (tchd 11-4)
Johnmanderville, third at Leicester on his previous start, was no match whatsoever for the above-average winner, but he still finished well clear of the remainder. (op 3-1 tchd 7-2)
Eden Park, a 16,000gns daughter of Tobougg, and half-sister to multiple sprint winners Piccolo Prince and Aegean Dancer, out of a dual 5f two-year-old winner, was not without support on her racecourse debut, but she was beaten a long way. The winner looks very useful, so this was no disgrace, and she should improve a fair amount for the run. (tchd 5-1)
Svindal(IRE), a son of Tomba, and brother to 1m winner Deneuve, half-brother to 15-time 5f-6f winner Attorney, out of a useful juvenile over 5f, was another who seemed fancied, but he could only manage a well-beaten fourth. He is entitled to come on for this and easier ground may also suit. (op 7-2 tchd 3-1)
Sandies Sister did not show much on her debut at Pontefract and she was again beaten a long way. (op 12-1)

1908 GO RACING IN YORKSHIRE SUMMER FESTIVAL H'CAP 5f
2:30 (2:31) (Class 4) (0-85,83) 4-Y-0+ £4,209 (£1,252; £625; £312) Stalls High

Form RPR
0260 **1** **Namir (IRE)**[11] 1624 6-8-1 69 (vt) DuranFentiman(3) 11 78
(D Shaw) *hld up in midfield: swtchd lft and hdwy over 1f out: sn rdn and qcknd to ld ins fnl f: drvn out* **7/1**
60-4 **2** *1/2* **Glasshoughton**[21] 1393 5-9-3 82 PhillipMakin 9 89
(M Dods) *trckd ldrs: hdwy wl over 1f out: rdn to chal ent fnl f and ev ch tl drvn and nt qckn fnl 75yds* **10/3**[1]
2103 **3** *shd* **Digital**[4] 1802 11-8-13 78 ChrisCatlin 7 85
(M R Channon) *hld up towards rr: hdwy wl over 1f out: rdn and str run ins fnl f: nrst fin* **13/2**[3]
-302 **4** *1* **Pawan (IRE)**[9] 1677 8-8-9 79 ow1 (b) AnnStokell(5) 10 82
(Miss A Stokell) *chsd ldrs on inner: rdn along wl over 1f out: swtchd lft and drvn ent fnl f: sn n.m.r and kpt on same pce* **8/1**
0-00 **5** *1 1/2* **Melalchrist**[21] 1393 6-9-1 80 (b) NCallan 8 78
(K A Ryan) *wnt rt s: led: rdn along wl over 1f out: drvn and hdd appr fnl f: grad wknd* **7/2**[2]
4300 **6** *1 1/4* **Royal Challenge**[18] 1485 7-8-4 69 oh2 PatrickMathers 4 62
(I W McInnes) *chsd ldrs: rdn along wl over 1f out: sn drvn and kpt on same pce* **20/1**
003- **7** *hd* **Bahamian Ballet**[198] 6381 6-9-1 80 StephenDonohoe 3 72
(E S McMahon) *cl up: hdwy 2f out: rdn to ld over 1f out: sn drvn: hdd ins fnl f and sn wknd* **11/1**
0-50 **8** *nk* **Handsome Falcon**[19] 1450 4-8-5 70 DaleGibson 5 61
(R A Fahey) *a towards rr* **15/2**
3333 **9** *2* **Almaty Express**[13] 1582 6-8-9 74 (b) DarryllHolland 6 58
(J R Weymes) *cl up: rdn along wl over 1f out: wkng whn hmpd ent fnl f* **14/1**
350- **10** *6* **Welcome Approach**[214] 6020 5-8-5 70 DO'Donohoe 1 33
(J R Weymes) *a towards rr* **40/1**
/00- **11** *1 3/4* **Grazeon Gold Blend**[354] 1853 5-9-4 83 (e[1]) GrahamGibbons 2 39
(J J Quinn) *a bhd* **16/1**
62.46 secs (-1.04) **Going Correction** -0.125s/f (Firm) **11** Ran SP% **122.1**
Speed ratings (Par 105): **103,102,102,100,98 96,95,95,92,82 79**
CSF £31.79 CT £165.27 TOTE £10.20: £2.40, £1.80, £2.50; EX 25.30.
Owner ownaracehorse.co.uk (Shakespeare) **Bred** B Kennedy **Trained** Danethorpe, Notts
■ Stewards' Enquiry : Ann Stokell one-day ban: careless riding (May 21)
FOCUS
A fair sprint handicap and very competitive. Not for the first time at Beverley, the high draws dominated and, although the form is ordinary, it looks sound.

1909 JOHN ROBINSON BUILDER RETIREMENT H'CAP 1m 1f 207y
3:05 (3:05) (Class 4) (0-80,80) 4-Y-0+ £4,209 (£1,252; £625; £312) Stalls High

Form RPR
40-4 **1** **Snowed Under**[22] 1388 7-8-10 72 DarryllHolland 2 81
(J D Bethell) *cl up: led after 3f: rdn 2f out: drvn ent fnl f and styd on gamely* **4/1**[3]
0-43 **2** *hd* **Rosbay (IRE)**[13] 1580 4-9-1 80 DuranFentiman(3) 7 89
(T D Easterby) *hld up towards rr: hdwy 2f out: swtchd ins and rdn over 1f out: styd on strly ins fnl f: jst failed* **7/2**[2]
-553 **3** *1 1/4* **Rudry Dragon (IRE)**[9] 1682 4-9-1 77 SimonWhitworth 4 83
(P A Blockley) *t.k.h: hld up in tch: hdwy 2f out: rdn over 1f out: styd on wl fnl f* **5/2**[1]
-245 **4** *2 1/4* **Sudden Impulse**[81] 586 7-8-11 73 AndrewElliott 6 75+
(A D Brown) *hld up and bhd: hdwy over 2f out: swtchd lft and rdn over 1f out: styd on ins fnl f: nrst fin* **12/1**
/0-4 **5** *1/2* **Ursis (FR)**[13] 1580 7-9-3 79 NCallan 1 80
(S Gollings) *trckd ldng pair: hdwy to chal 3f out: rdn along 2f out: drvn and wknd ent fnl f* **16/1**
000- **6** *12* **Rain And Shade**[176] 1415 4-8-6 68 RoystonFfrench 8 45
(E W Tuer) *in tch: effrt 3f out: sn rdn along and n.d* **50/1**
4-03 **7** *1/2* **Nelsons Column (IRE)**[21] 1394 5-8-7 69 ShaneKelly 5 45
(G M Moore) *led 3f: prom tl rdn along 3f out and sn wknd* **5/2**[1]
0-06 **8** *1/2* **Fever**[11] 1612 4-8-11 80 BradleyRoper(7) 3 55
(M W Easterby) *hld up in rr: sme hdwy on outer whn stmbld over 3f out: sn rdn and wknd* **25/1**
2m 7.17s (0.17) **Going Correction** 0.0s/f (Good) **8** Ran SP% **118.7**
Speed ratings (Par 105): **99,98,97,96,95 86,85,85**
CSF £19.25 CT £42.20 TOTE £5.50: £1.70, £1.60, £1.30; EX 20.50.
Owner Mrs G Fane **Bred** Mrs G Fane **Trained** Middleham Moor, N Yorks
■ Stewards' Enquiry : Shane Kelly caution: allowed gelding to coast home with no assistance
FOCUS
A fair handicap, but the pace was ordinary. The winner is rated to last year's best with the third to recent form.

1910 GRAHAM AND ROSEN SOLICITORS H'CAP 1m 100y
3:40 (3:40) (Class 4) (0-85,85) 4-Y-0+ £12,952 (£3,854; £1,926; £962) Stalls High

Form RPR
0-42 **1** **Full Victory (IRE)**[15] 1532 6-9-1 76 DaneO'Neill 1 85
(R A Farrant) *in tch: hdwy on wd outside 2f out: rdn over 1f out: styd on strly to ld wl ins fnl f: kpt on* **12/1**
P60- **2** *hd* **Zero Tolerance (IRE)**[186] 6654 8-9-5 80 ChrisCatlin 13 89
(T D Barron) *hld up in midfield: hdwy 2f out: swtchd lft over 1f out: sn rdn and styd on strly ins fnl f: jst failed* **11/1**
43-5 **3** *nk* **Froissee**[11] 1630 4-9-1 76 StephenDonohoe 16 84
(S A Callaghan) *sltly hmpd s: sn trcking ldrs on inner: hdwy to ld over 2f out: rdn over 1f out: drvn and hdd wl ins fnl f: kpt on* **12/1**
2302 **4** *1* **Moheebb (IRE)**[5] 1771 4-8-11 75 (b) MichaelJStainton(3) 11 81
(Mrs R A Carr) *chsd ldrs: effrt 2f out: rdn over 1f out: drvn and kpt on same pce ins fnl f* **10/1**
2-34 **5** *1 3/4* **Charlie Tipple**[11] 1612 4-9-0 75 (p) PaulMulrennan 6 77
(T D Easterby) *chsd ldrs: rdn along 2f out: drvn over 1f out: kpt on same pce fnl f* **16/1**
00-2 **6** *nk* **Veiled Applause**[39] 1072 5-9-4 79 GrahamGibbons 8 80
(J J Quinn) *in tch: hdwy over 2f out: rdn to chse ldrs whn n.m.r over 1f out: kpt on same pce ins fnl f* **8/1**

651 **7** 1 1/2 **Rock Anthem (IRE)**[56] [852] 4-8-13 **74**............................ PhillipMakin 14 72
(Mike Murphy) *in tch on inner: hdwy over 2f out: rdn whn n.m.r over 1f out: kpt on same pce ins fnl f* **7/1**[3]
550- **8** 1 **Goodbye Mr Bond**[207] [6180] 8-9-8 **83**.............................. ShaneKelly 3 78
(E J Alston) *chsd ldrs on outer: rdn along over 2f out: drvn and hung rt over 1f out: sn wknd* **40/1**
00-5 **9** 1/2 **Bajan Pride**[26] [1308] 4-8-5 **73**.......................................(p) BMcHugh(7) 4 67
(R A Fahey) *in tch on outer: effrt over 2f out: sn rdn along and no imp* **12/1**
4250 **10** nk **Moonlight Man**[14] [1569] 7-9-9 **84**........................ RoystonFfrench 7 77
(C R Dore) *nvr bttr than midfield* **28/1**
000- **11** nk **Hartshead**[214] [6016] 9-9-7 **85**................................ PJMcDonald(3) 5 78
(G A Swinbank) *hld up towards rr: sme hdwy on outer over 2f out: nvr rch ldrs* **40/1**
-430 **12** 1 1/4 **Wigwam Willie (IRE)**[18] [1469] 6-9-7 **82**..............................(p) NCallan 9 76+
(K A Ryan) *a midfield* **12/1**
0-15 **13** 1/2 **Collateral Damage (IRE)**[4] [1816] 5-9-7 **85**............ DuranFentiman(3) 17 74
(T D Easterby) *wnt bdly lft s: a in rr* **6/1**[2]
6-00 **14** 1 1/4 **Lobengula (IRE)**[4] [1793] 6-9-9 **84**............................ DanielTudhope 10 70
(I W McInnes) *led: rdn along and hdd over 2f out: sn drvn and wknd over 1f out* **50/1**
020- **15** 1/2 **Hurlingham**[194] [6474] 4-9-3 **78**.............................. DaleGibson 12 63
(M W Easterby) *midfield: pushed along 1/2-way: sn lost pl and bhd* **33/1**
006- **16** shd **Pagan Belief**[205] [6232] 4-8-6 **67**.............................. OscarUrbina 2 51
(J A R Toller) *stdd s: hld up: a in rr* **40/1**
1-21 **17** 7 **Ansells Pride (IRE)**[26] [1308] 5-9-7 **82**........................ TomEaves 15 50+
(B Smart) *bdly hmpd s: t.k.h and a bhd* **10/3**[1]
1m 45.79s (-1.81) **Going Correction** 0.0s/f (Good) **17** Ran SP% **130.7**
Speed ratings (Par 105): **109,108,108,107,105 105,103,102,102,102 101,100,100,98,98 98,91**
CSF £140.11 CT £1709.51 TOTE £17.70: £3.60, £2.90, £2.50, £3.00; EX 296.70.
Owner Friends of Saunton Sands **Bred** Larry Ryan **Trained** Upper Lambourn, Berks
■ Stewards' Enquiry : B McHugh caution: careless riding
FOCUS
A good, competitive handicap run at a sound gallop with the fifth the best guide to the level.
Lobengula(IRE) Official explanation: jockey said gelding hung left-handed throughout
Ansells Pride(IRE) Official explanation: jockey said gelding was hampered at start

1911 GEORGE AND THE DRAGON DIAMOND H'CAP 5f
4:15 (4:15) (Class 4) (0-85,84) 3-Y-O **£4,209** (£1,252; £625; £312) **Stalls** High

Form RPR
4-44 **1** **Blue Jack**[11] [1611] 3-8-7 **73**.................................... DO'Donohoe 9 82+
(W R Muir) *chsd ldrs: rdn along and sltly outpcd wl over 1f out: n.m.r and swtchd lft and drvn appr fnl f: styd on strly to ld last stride* **4/1**[3]
65-3 **2** nse **Supermassive Muse (IRE)**[11] [1611] 3-8-6 **72** ow1.... GrahamGibbons 2 75
(E S McMahon) *cl up: effrt 2f out and sn rdn: led jst ins fnl f: sn drvn: hdd on line* **6/1**
3-00 **3** nk **Captain Dunne (IRE)**[11] [1623] 3-8-8 **77**.................... DuranFentiman(3) 1 79
(T D Easterby) *wnt lft s: sn chsng ldrs on outer: hdwy to chal wl over 1f out: sn rdn and ev ch tl drvn and no ex nr fin* **18/1**
-160 **4** 1 1/2 **Style Award**[11] [1623] 3-9-1 **84**.............................. AndrewMullen(3) 4 81
(W J H Ratcliffe) *in tch: effrt over 2f out: sn rdn and sltly outpcd over 1f out: kpt on u.p ins fnl f* **17/2**
1452 **5** 1 3/4 **Baytown Blaze**[2] [1852] 3-8-2 **73**.............................. KellyHarrison(5) 7 64
(M Wigham) *led: rdn along 2f out: drvn over 1f out: hdd jst ins fnl f and sn wknd* **7/2**[2]
-464 **6** 1 **Kalhan Sands (IRE)**[25] [1328] 3-8-10 **79**...................... PJMcDonald(3) 3 66
(G A Swinbank) *chsd ldrs: rdn along over 2f out: one pce appr fnl f* **8/1**
23-5 **7** 3 **President Elect (IRE)**[18] [1484] 3-8-10 **76**...................... PhillipMakin 5 52
(T D Barron) *chsd ldr: rdn along 1/2-way: sn drvn and wknd* **2/1**[1]
62.71 secs (-0.79) **Going Correction** -0.125s/f (Firm) **7** Ran SP% **116.7**
Speed ratings (Par 101): **101,100,100,98,95 93,88**
CSF £28.83 CT £388.65 TOTE £5.10: £2.30, £2.20; EX 16.90.
Owner Martin P Graham **Bred** Miss S N Ralphs **Trained** Lambourn, Berks
FOCUS
A fair three-year-old sprint handicap run at a solid pace and a dramatic finish. The form is somewhat fluid though.

1912 WHITE RABBIT H'CAP 7f 100y
4:50 (4:51) (Class 6) (0-60,60) 3-Y-O **£1,683** (£501; £250; £125) **Stalls** High

Form RPR
50-0 **1** **Casino Night**[51] [918] 3-9-4 **60**.................................... DarryllHolland 10 65
(J R Weymes) *mde all: rdn clr wl over 1f out: drvn ins fnl f and styd on wl* **16/1**
26-0 **2** 2 1/4 **Hurstpierpoint (IRE)**[26] [1306] 3-8-6 **55**........................ BMcHugh(7) 3 54
(R A Fahey) *midfield: hdwy 3f out: rdn to chse wnr ent fnl f: sn drvn and kpt on* **16/1**
0-56 **3** hd **Zaplamation (IRE)**[25] [1343] 3-8-4 **46** oh1.................. RoystonFfrench 9 48+
(D W Barker) *hld up in rr: hdwy over 2f out: rdn wl over 1f out: styd on wl u.p ins fnl f: nrst fin* **14/1**
052- **4** nk **Flashy Max**[156] [7007] 3-8-8 **50**.................................... AndrewElliott 13 48
(Jedd O'Keeffe) *a.p: rdn along 2f out: drvn over 1f out: kpt on u.p ins fnl f* **16/1**
-300 **5** 2 1/4 **Scruffy Skip (IRE)**[15] [1553] 3-9-0 **56**...............................(p) TomEaves 5 48
(C R Dore) *in tch: hdwy to chse ldrs 2f out: sn rdn and kpt on same pce appr fnl f* **20/1**
05-4 **6** 3/4 **Aquarian Dancer**[18] [1479] 3-8-11 **53**.............................. PaulMulrennan 8 43
(Jedd O'Keeffe) *prom: hdwy to chse wnr 3f out: rdn wl over 1f out: drvn and wknd ent fnl f* **12/1**
44-3 **7** nk **Dancing Maite**[122] [70] 3-9-3 **59**.................................. PhillipMakin 2 49
(S R Bowring) *midfield: effrt over 2f out: sn rdn and styd on u.p appr fnl f: nt rch ldrs* **16/1**
50-0 **8** 2 1/4 **Piverina (IRE)**[43] [1019] 3-9-2 **58**.................................... NCallan 14 42
(T D Barron) *dwlt and towards rr: hdwy over 2f out and sn rdn: drvn over 1f out and sn no imp* **9/2**[1]
0003 **9** 1/2 **Natural Rhythm (IRE)**[13] [1575] 3-8-10 **55**............ MichaelJStainton(3) 7 38
(Mrs R A Carr) *hld up in rr: swtchd outside and hdwy over 2f out: sn rdn and no imp appr fnl f* **9/1**
000- **10** hd **Princess Maria (USA)**[201] [6306] 3-8-6 **48**........................ DaleGibson 16 30
(R A Fahey) *nvr bttr than midfield* **9/1**
000- **11** nk **Lady Docker (IRE)**[185] [6664] 3-9-1 **57**...................... DarrenWilliams 12 38
(H J L Dunlop) *chsd ldrs: hdwy over 2f out: sn rdn and wknd appr fnl f* **22/1**
405- **12** 1 3/4 **Lu's Woman**[204] [6254] 3-8-8 **57**................................ NSLawes(7) 15 34
(M W Easterby) *s.i.s and bhd: sme hdwy whn n.m.r 2f out: nvr a factor* **16/1**
4-20 **13** nk **Piccolo Pete**[15] [1548] 3-9-2 **58**.................................... MickyFenton 11 34
(T P Tate) *a towards rr* **5/1**[2]
5550 **14** 1 1/4 **Her Name Is Rio (IRE)**[21] [1391] 3-8-9 **54**..................(b) PJMcDonald(3) 6 27
(Mrs S Lamyman) *chsd ldrs: rdn along 3f out and sn wknd* **25/1**
040 **15** 3/4 **Chevaliers Dream (IRE)**[35] [1139] 3-9-0 **59**............. DuranFentiman(3) 4 30
(T D Easterby) *a in rr* **33/1**
434 **16** 4 **Llab Nala**[32] [1216] 3-9-2 **58**.. ChrisCatlin 1 19
(M R Channon) *a towards rr* **15/2**[3]
1m 34.22s (0.42) **Going Correction** 0.0s/f (Good) **16** Ran SP% **126.3**
Speed ratings (Par 97): **97,94,94,93,91 90,90,87,86,86 86,84,84,82,81 77**
CSF £248.01 CT £3812.09 TOTE £19.80: £4.40, £5.90, £4.40, £3.20; EX 457.40.
Owner Barry Robson **Bred** Kingsmead Breeders **Trained** Middleham Moor, N Yorks
■ Stewards' Enquiry : N Callan one-day ban: careless riding (May 21)
FOCUS
A moderate handicap if quite a competitive one due to the size of the field and the form looks pretty sound rated around the placed horses.
Casino Night Official explanation: trainer said, regarding apparent improvement in form, that the filly was better suited by the return to Turf.

1913 GO RACING AT WETHERBY TOMORROW EVENING CLASSIFIED STKS 1m 4f 16y
5:20 (5:20) (Class 6) 3-Y-O+ **£1,774** (£523; £262) **Stalls** High

Form RPR
4-50 **1** **Wulimaster (USA)**[14] [1559] 5-9-6 53.............................. MarkLawson(3) 4 59
(D W Barker) *hld up and bhd: swtchd outside and gd hdwy over 2f out: rdn to ld over 1f out: drvn and hung rt ins fnl f: styd on* **5/1**[3]
2450 **2** 2 **Red Fama**[44] [991] 4-9-9 50.. PhillipMakin 2 56
(N Bycroft) *hld up in tch: hdwy 4f out: led over 2f out: sn rdn and hdd over 1f out: drvn and kpt on same pce ins fnl f* **25/1**
0100 **3** hd **Shenandoah Girl**[7] [1726] 5-9-9 51................................(p) DarryllHolland 8 56
(Miss Gay Kelleway) *hld up and bhd: hdwy over 2f out: swtchd lft: rdn and edgd rt wl over 1f out: styd on u.p ins fnl f: nrst fin* **7/1**
00-0 **4** nk **Caraman (IRE)**[44] [988] 10-9-9 55.............................. GrahamGibbons 7 55
(J J Quinn) *in tch: hdwy to chse ldrs 3f out: rdn along 2f out: drvn and kpt on same pce appr fnl f* **10/1**
02-1 **5** 2 3/4 **Compton Charlie**[27] [1281] 4-9-9 55................................ NCallan 11 51
(J G Portman) *in tch: hdwy to trck ldrs 3f out: effrt over 2f out: sn rdn to chse ldr over 1f out: drvn and wknd ins fnl f* **3/1**[1]
-002 **6** 5 **David's Cavalier**[9] [1679] 4-9-6 53......................(p) RussellKennemore(3) 9 43
(R Hollinshead) *chsd ldrs: rdn along over 3f out: drvn over 2f out and sn wknd* **10/3**[2]
323- **7** 2 1/2 **Fire In Cairo (IRE)**[164] [5980] 4-9-2 51..................(t) PatrickDonaghy(7) 10 39
(P C Haslam) *hld up: a towards rr* **14/1**
005- **8** 2 1/2 **Centenary (IRE)**[173] [6835] 4-9-9 55..............................(p) ChrisCatlin 6 35
(D E Cantillon) *chsd ldrs: rdn along over 3f out: sn wknd* **9/1**
0-00 **9** 8 **Royal Rainbow**[26] [1296] 4-9-9 48.............................. DarrenWilliams 5 22
(P W Hiatt) *a in rr* **22/1**
400- **10** 3/4 **Camerooney**[188] [6613] 5-9-9 46.................................. AndrewElliott 12 21
(A D Brown) *led: rdn along 3f out: sn hdd & wknd* **66/1**
0-04 **11** 7 **Pure Scandal**[21] [1397] 3-8-1 52..............................(b[1]) AndrewMullen(3) 1 10
(M W Easterby) *prom: cl up 1/2-way: rdn along over 3f out and sn wknd* **17/2**
2m 40.56s (-0.34) **Going Correction** 0.0s/f (Good)
WFA 3 from 4yo+ 19lb **11** Ran SP% **123.2**
Speed ratings (Par 101): **101,99,99,99,97 94,92,90,85,85 80**
CSF £129.80 TOTE £7.00: £2.10, £5.10, £2.20; EX 318.60 Place 6 £209.28, Place 5 £158.15.
Owner Andrew Turton & David Barker **Bred** Flaxman Holdings Ltd **Trained** Scorton, N Yorks
■ Stewards' Enquiry : Andrew Mullen caution: allowed gelding to coast home with no assistance
FOCUS
A very moderate race, but at least the pace was sound though those that set it dropped right out and rather set the race up for the closers. The form looks straightforward rated around the placed horses.
David's Cavalier Official explanation: jockey said gelding was unsuited by the good ground
T/Plt: £417.60 to a £1 stake. Pool: £51,143.47. 89.40 winning tickets. T/Qpdt: £114.50 to a £1 stake. Pool: £2,693.46. 17.40 winning tickets. JR

CHESTER (L-H)
Wednesday, May 7

OFFICIAL GOING: Good
Wind: Almost nil Weather: Warm and Sunny

1914 JOSEPH HELER CHEESE LILY AGNES CONDITIONS STKS 5f 16y
1:45 (1:45) (Class 2) 2-Y-O
£13,085 (£3,918; £1,959; £980; £489; £245) **Stalls** Low

Form RPR
2 **1** **Doncaster Rover (USA)**[46] [957] 2-8-12 0.............................. LDettori 2 92+
(S Parr) *unf: scope: trckd ldrs: clsd to go 2nd over 1f out: rdn to ld ins fnl f: pushed out and r.o towards fin* **3/1**[2]
1 **2** 1 1/4 **Aspen Darlin (IRE)**[22] [1385] 2-8-10 0.......................... PaulHanagan 5 86
(A Bailey) *w'like: s.i.s: t.k.h off the pce: rdn and hdwy over 1f out: styd on to take 2nd cl home: nt trble wnr* **11/1**
1 **3** nk **White Shift (IRE)**[7] [1722] 2-8-10 0.......................... RobertWinston 3 84
(P D Evans) *w'like: w ldr: rdn to ld wl over 1f out: hdd ins fnl f: styd on same pce towards fin* **8/1**[3]
11 **4** 3 **She's A Shaw Thing**[35] [1156] 2-8-13 0........................ TGMcLaughlin 4 77
(P D Evans) *leggy: trckd ldrs: rdn 2f out: outpcd over 1f out: nt pce to trble ldrs* **4/5**[1]
335 **5** 1 3/4 **Just The Lady**[5] [1762] 2-8-7 0.................................... JohnEgan 1 64
(W G M Turner) *led: rdn and hdd wl over 1f out: fdd ins fnl f* **9/1**
32 **6** 17 **Meg Jicaro**[11] [1627] 2-8-7 0.................................... TolleyDean 7 —
(Mrs L Williamson) *cmpt: sn pushed along and wl outpcd* **25/1**
61.74 secs (0.74) **Going Correction** +0.225s/f (Good) **6** Ran SP% **113.8**
Speed ratings (Par 99): **103,101,100,95,92 65**
CSF £33.75 TOTE £3.00: £1.80, £3.90; EX 43.30.
Owner P Holling I Raeburn S Halsall S Bolland **Bred** Coffeepot Stable **Trained** Bawtry, S Yorks
FOCUS
A race that often plays host to some of the quickest early-season juveniles around. The pace was frenetic from the outset and Doncaster Rover, the sole male in the race, created a good impression in winning. The winning time was decent and the winner could prove better than rated.

NOTEBOOK

Doncaster Rover(USA), the only male in the line-up, had not been seen since finishing second in the Brocklesby, but he looked to have done well physically and was soon in the ideal stalking position. Always tanking along, he quickly settled it off the final bend and won in taking style. His trainer mentioned the Coventry Stakes at Royal Ascot after the race, but he would not be up to that standard and instead looks best kept to 5f, in which case the Listed Windsor Castle Stakes would make much more sense. (op 10-3 tchd 5-1, 6-1 in places)

Aspen Darlin(IRE), strong at the end of her race when winning in soft ground on her Warwick debut, would have appreciated the strong gallop and seemed to handle this faster ground well. She still looked to have plenty left in the tank turning for home and picked up well to grab second, but the winner was too nippy. She is an attractive filly and there should be further improvement to come at 6f. (op 16-1)

White Shift(IRE) looked all about speed when leading throughout on her recent Great Leighs debut and she provided David Evans with a useful-looking second string. Expected to have improved from that debut, she again showed bags of speed and helped force the pace, but was readily brushed aside by the winner and just run out of second close home. She is not overly big, but managed to beat her stronger-fancied stablemate, and can find another race. (tchd 11-2)

She's A Shaw Thing had created a really strong impression in two previous starts, twice destroying the opposition in soft ground, and looked to have the beating of Doncaster Rover on a line through Brocklesby winner Sally's Dilemma. However, she was forced to race in behind the speed having lacked the early pace and never really looked like winning, possibly finding this trip on quick ground an insufficient test. She will definitely stay further and can be given another chance. (tchd 5-6 and 9-10 in place)

Just The Lady had failed to win in three previous attempts, but her trainer has a decent record in this and she had the best of the draw. Again showing tons of early speed, she was passed by White Shift over a furlong out and quickly retreated. She probably has a small race in her. Official explanation: jockey said filly hung right (op 12-1 tchd 8-1)

Meg Jicaro had placed in a couple of modest maidens and she found this too much of a speed test, being outpaced from the word go. An extra furlong is clearly in order. (op 33-1)

1915 WEATHERBYS BANK CHESHIRE OAKS (FOR THE ROBERT SANGSTER MEMORIAL CUP) (LISTED RACE) 1m 3f 79y

2:15 (2:15) (Class 1) 3-Y-O

£22,708 (£8,608; £4,308; £2,148; £1,076; £540) **Stalls** Low

Form				RPR
	1		**Sail (IRE)**[31] 1229 3-8-12 0 .... JMurtagh 4 (A P O'Brien, Ire) *w'like: str: racd keenly early on: hld up: hdwy 3f out: rdn over 1f out: sn moved up to chal strly: r.o to ld ins fnl 75yds* **9/4**[1]	103+
46-1	**2**	½	**Sugar Mint (IRE)**[28] 1265 3-8-12 104 .... MichaelHills 1 (B W Hills) *lw: midfield: hdwy 5f out: rdn to ld wl over 1f out: hdd ins fnl 75yds* **5/2**[2]	99
3-2	**3**	1 ¾	**Changing Skies (IRE)**[19] 1444 3-8-12 0 .... LDettori 2 (B J Meehan) *racd keenly in midfield: lost pl 5f out: rdn and outpcd over 2f out: styd on and prog fr 1f out: nt pce to trble front pair* **14/1**	96+
03-1	**4**	1 ½	**Queen Of Naples**[11] 1638 3-8-12 93 .... JimmyFortune 8 (J H M Gosden) *lw: sn led: hdd after 2f: continued to chse ldrs: rdn and nt clr run over 1f out: sn edgd rt: kpt on u.p after* **9/1**	93
3-32	**5**	1 ¼	**Try Me (UAE)**[15] 1542 3-8-12 75 .... RobertWinston 9 (C E Brittain) *chsd ldrs: wnt 2nd over 6f out: rdn and upsides 2f out: lost 2nd over 1f out: no ex ins fnl f* **66/1**	91?
15-2	**6**	1	**Silk Affair (IRE)**[14] 1557 3-8-12 89 .... TPO'Shea 5 (M G Quinlan) *hld up: effrt over 1f out: nvr able to chal* **50/1**	90
1-	**7**	1 ¾	**Laughter (IRE)**[211] 6087 3-8-12 85 .... RyanMoore 6 (Sir Michael Stoute) *in tch: pushed along 3f out: sn outpcd: no imp after* **4/1**[3]	87
3	**8**	2	**Rio Guru (IRE)**[19] 1445 3-8-12 0 .... KerrinMcEvoy 7 (M R Channon) *hld up in rr: struggling 2f out: nvr on terms* **20/1**	83?
3-1	**9**	2	**Dancing Abbie (USA)**[41] 1042 3-8-12 85 .... JamieSpencer 3 (M L W Bell) *lw: plld hrd in midfield: hdwy to ld after 2f: rdn and hdd wl over 1f out: sn n.m.r whn losing pl: eased whn btn ins fnl f* **9/1**	85+

2m 27.92s (1.32) **Going Correction** +0.225s/f (Good) **9** Ran SP% **114.2**

Speed ratings (Par 107): **104,103,102,101,100 99,98,96,95**

CSF £7.82 TOTE £3.10: £1.40, £1.50, £2.30; EX 9.10 Trifecta £101.80 Pool: £731.55 - 5.10 winning units..

Owner M Tabor, D Smith & Mrs John Magnier **Bred** Tetsu Nakata **Trained** Ballydoyle, Co Tipperary

FOCUS

This race produced the first and third in last year's Epsom Oaks and, although the bare form of this contest is nothing special and unlikely to prove solid, it would be folly to pay too much attention to those in behind, and instead best to concentrate on the front pair. Sail's win has been rated 7lb below Light Shift last season, but she was still green and looks a highly promising filly.

NOTEBOOK

Sail(IRE) ◆, still green when finishing second in a 1m2f maiden at Leopardstown on her seasonal reappearance (yard won that race with the likes of All Too Beautiful and last year's runner-up in this race All My Loving in recent seasons) looked a significant participant with her trainer having such a fine record in the trials around here. Backed right down from an 11/2 shot in the morning, she did not get off to the best of starts and raced keenly, but Murtagh was happy to bide his time and she went in pursuit of Sugar Mint soon after straightening for home. It briefly looked as though she was going to get done for speed, but she picked up really nicely once gathering herself and was always getting on top close home. She showed guts, having been tapped on the nose with Michael Hills's whip, and will almost certainly improve for a faster pace at a full 1m4f. She looks a definite contender for the Epsom Oaks at this stage, and odds of around 16/1 are still quite generous, but with Ballydoyle having so much strength-in-depth with their middle-distance fillies (Kitty Matcham and Moonstone, who are both as short as 8/1 in the Oaks market, to name but two) it is probable she will be a second-string at best on the day. (op 3-1)

Sugar Mint(IRE) posted several decent efforts without getting her head in front at two, including when fourth behind Spacious in the May Hill, and she had little trouble breaking her maiden with victory over subsequent impressive handicap scorer Duntulm at Bath. Officially the best horse in the race, her trainer has a fine record in this contest and she set the standard. Given a fine ride by Hills, she was sent into the lead over a furlong out and briefly looked to have caught the favourite flat-footed, but soon had that rival bearing down on her and was unable to hold on. This first try over middle distances seemed to suit the daughter of High Chaparral and, although likely to fall short of the top fillies, there is a Pattern race in her. (op 9-4 tchd 11-4)

Changing Skies(IRE) would have been a fitting winner given her connections, but it is impossible not to be pleased with her effort in defeat. A beaten-favourite at Newbury on her seasonal debut, she took a keen grip early on and it was pleasing to see this maiden come home so well, having lost her place and been shuffled back through the field over half a mile out. An extremely well-bred filly, this gives her some important black-type and connections will no doubt be hoping she can win a similar race at some stage this season. Official explanation: jockey said filly was not suited by the track (op 16-1)

Queen Of Naples successfully converted a penalty kick at Wolverhampton last time, scoring at odds of 2/13, and this represented a much stiffer task. She had run well against some smart fillies at two though, being beaten just over seven-lengths by Zarkava in the Marcel Boussac and finishing a close third in a Listed contest in November, so it was no suprise to see her acquit herself wellh. She would have been a shade closer had she got a clear run and, although not that big, she looks capable of gaining more black type. (op 8-1)

Try Me(UAE), third behind Dancing Abbie at Wolverhampton, has since been touched-off in a Kempton maiden, but runners from her yard have a habit of running above themselves in trials, particularly around here, and she ran a fine race back in fifth. She should find a race at some stage, although one suspects this will not be the last time she is asked to run out of her grade.

Silk Affair(IRE) is a generally progressive type and she ran above expectations back in sixth. She would have been flattered to finish so close though and will not find life easy in handicaps. (op 40-1)

Laughter(IRE), winner of a modest 7f Leicester maiden on her sole start at two, is a daughter of Sadler's Wells and she looked the best of the Stoute Oaks entrants coming into the race. However, she was fairly weak in the market and there was no immediate response when asked for her effort. She still looked green and is bound to improve for the run, but it would be a surprise were she to line up at Epsom now. (tchd 9-2)

Rio Guru(IRE), third in a fair 7f Newbury maiden on her recent debut, was up markedly in trip/grade and she never posed a threat. There will be other days for her. (op 16-1)

Dancing Abbie(USA), highly thought-of by her trainer, won her maiden in good style at Wolverhampton and she looked one of the more interesting outsiders. She was allowed to go on after a couple of furlongs, having failed to settle early, but it left her vulnerable as a result and she was readily brushed aside in the straight. Not given a hard time once beaten, she is evidently thought to be capable of much better and will stand more of a chance in handicaps. (tchd 8-1)

1916 TOTESPORT.COM CHESTER CUP HERITAGE H'CAP 2m 2f 147y

2:45 (2:45) (Class 2) 4-Y-0+

£74,772 (£22,392; £11,196; £5,604; £2,796; £1,404) **Stalls** High

Form				RPR
505-	**1**		**Bulwark (IRE)**[33] 6760 6-9-4 **95** .... (v[1]) JimCrowley 11 (Ian Williams) *hld up: nt clr run over 3f out: hdwy wl over 2f out: str run on outside fr over 1f out: edgd lft ins fnl f: led fnl 75yds* **33/1**	108
30-3	**2**	½	**Som Tala**[39] 1080 5-8-12 **89** .... LDettori 13 (M R Channon) *lw: in tch: effrt to chal over 2f out: led over 1f out: hdd narrowly wl ins fnl f: sn edgd rt: r.o u.p* **10/1**	101
44-2	**3**	*nk*	**Tilt**[14] 1568 6-8-10 **87** .... (p) JMurtagh 8 (B Ellison) *midfield: hdwy over 3f out: rdn to chse ldrs over 2f out: r.o to ld briefly wl ins fnl f: n.m.r cl home* **8/1**[3]	99
12-1	**4**	*8*	**Double Banded (IRE)**[14] 1568 4-8-8 **89** 3ex .... KerrinMcEvoy 5 (J L Dunlop) *midfield: hdwy 6f out: effrt 6 wd on bnd over 2f out whn chsng ldrs: wknd ins fnl f* **9/2**[2]	92
11-1	**5**	¾	**Highland Legacy**[11] 1625 4-8-10 **91** 3ex .... JamieSpencer 6 (M L W Bell) *midfield: rdn 4f out: rapid hdwy to chse ldrs over 3f out: nt handle bnd over 2f out: wknd fnl f* **7/2**[1]	93+
15-3	**6**	*4*	**Wing Collar**[11] 1629 7-9-6 **97** .... (p) DavidAllan 4 (T D Easterby) *hld up: pushed along over 3f out: styd on fr over 1f out: nvr able to chal* **14/1**	95+
51-0	**7**	¾	**Inchnadamph**[14] 1568 8-9-0 **91** .... (t) RobertWinston 7 (T J Fitzgerald) *midfield: rdn and hdwy 4f out: chsd ldrs over 2f out: wknd over 1f out* **40/1**	88
00-0	**8**	¾	**Odiham**[14] 1568 7-8-11 **88** .... (v) SteveDrowne 17 (Dr R D P Newland) *midfield: rdn 4f out: no hdwy* **66/1**	84
/23-	**9**	1 ¼	**Fair Along (GER)**[15] 6335 6-9-4 **95** .... (b) RyanMoore 16 (P J Hobbs) *prom: bmpd and forced wd on bnd 6f out: rdn 4f out: wknd 2f out* **14/1**	90
000-	**10**	*2*	**Halla San**[60] 3989 6-8-13 **93** .... JamieMoriarty(3) 2 (R A Fahey) *rdn along s: in rr: rdn over 3f out: nvr rchd chalng position* **25/1**	85
403-	**11**	3 ½	**Greenwich Meantime**[180] 6744 8-9-3 **94** .... PaulHanagan 10 (R A Fahey) *hld up: rdn 4f out: sme hdwy over 3f out: sn hmpd and lost pl: n.d after* **10/1**	83+
011-	**12**	*20*	**Black Rock (IRE)**[228] 5619 4-9-2 **97** .... PhilipRobinson 15 (M A Jarvis) *lw: sn led: jinked twice on bnd 6f out: rdn and hdd over 1f out: sn wknd: eased whn btn fnl f* **11/1**	64
62-0	**13**	4 ½	**Kasthari (IRE)**[14] 1568 9-9-4 **95** .... TedDurcan 3 (J D Bethell) *midfield: rdn over 3f out: no imp: wknd over 1f out* **50/1**	57
141-	**14**	*6*	**Missoula (IRE)**[63] 6181 5-8-8 **85** .... MartinDwyer 9 (Miss Suzy Smith) *trckd ldrs: rdn 4f out: wknd over 2f out* **16/1**	40
/10-	**15**	2 ½	**Sentry Duty (FR)**[11] 3090 6-9-7 **101** .... WilliamBuick(3) 12 (N J Henderson) *in tch: rdn 4f out: sn wknd* **16/1**	53
100-	**P**		**Full House (IRE)**[11] 6335 9-8-12 **89** .... JimmyFortune 1 (P R Webber) *wl bhd: t.o after 4f: p.u after 8f* **18/1**	—
6/21	**P**		**Shipmaster**[7] 1717 5-9-13 **104** 3ex .... RichardHughes 14 (A King) *trckd ldrs: p.u qckly 8f out: dismntd* **16/1**	—

4m 6.57s (1.77) **Going Correction** +0.225s/f (Good)

WFA 4 from 5yo+ 4lb **17** Ran SP% **127.0**

Speed ratings (Par 109): **105,104,104,101,100 99,98,98,98,97 95,87,85,82,81** —,—

CSF £339.00 CT £2931.11 TOTE £49.00: £8.30, £2.00, £2.30, £1.90; EX 441.60 Trifecta £2019.30 Pool: £3128.50 - 1.10 winning units..

Owner Dr Marwan Koukash **Bred** Hesmonds Stud Ltd **Trained** Portway, Worcs

■ Stewards' Enquiry : Jim Crowley caution: careless riding

FOCUS

Traditionally one of the most competitive handicaps of the season and this renewal looked no different, with two highly progressive and unexposed four-year-olds heading up the market. However, three more exposed types managed to pull right away from the pair in the straight and the winner is rated to his best handicap mark.

NOTEBOOK

Bulwark(IRE), a highly progressive handicapper a couple of seasons back who spent most of last term struggling in Group contests, was still 3lb higher than when finishing sixth in this a couple of years ago, but he has clearly benefited from a change of scenery, gelding and a wind operation and the first-time visor enabled him to come right back to his best. A horse who has had his attitude questioned in the past, he can often find trouble in running, but it seems to suit him and, having been briefly blocked over three out, he started to come with a strong charge around the field. With Som Tala and Tilt in his sights a furlong out, he finished strongly and got on top close home. Crowley deserves credit for an excellent ride on this tricky customer and, perhaps having three runs over hurdles earlier in the year just refreshed his enthusiasm. Things will only get tougher from here though and it remains to be seen whether the headgear has the same effect next time.

Som Tala, 4lb higher than when finishing fifth in this last year (ran a lot better than finishing position implies) reappeared with a decent effort at Kempton in March and he ran a blinder, leading over a furlong out and battling back gamely to deny Tilt second. He could do nothing about the winner's late charge, but should remain a challenger in all the big marathon handicaps. (op 16-1)

Tilt, second to Double Banded at Nottingham last time, comprehensively reversed form on 1lb better terms and briefly looked the winner, but he does not seem keen on getting his head in front and lost the battle for second close home. He was clear of the remainder though and, like the runner-up, should remain competitive in marathon handicaps. (op 9-1)

Double Banded(IRE), a highly progressive youngster who came into this having won five of his last seven starts, has improved 37lb since last August and did the job well on his seasonal return at Nottingham, for which he picked up a 3lb penalty. He had a nice berth in five, but was unable to take advantage of it and found himself slipping back to midfield. His rider took no chances and brought him widest of all with his challenge, but having reached a winning position, the manoeuvre took its toll though and he could find no more in the straight. There is a chance this trip proved beyond him and he can be rated a bit better than this. (tchd 10-3)
Highland Legacy improved hugely for the step up to 2m last backend, winning at Newbury and Nottingham, and he shaped as though the run was needed when scoring readily on his reappearance at Ripon. Shouldering a 3lb penalty for that success, he was understandably made favourite, but the drying ground would not have suited the son of Selkirk and he was another who may have made his ground up too quickly, also appearing not to handle the final bend. He could find no more under pressure, but can be given another chance back on slow ground.
Wing Collar, close-up third behind Raincoat at Ripon on his reappearance, was expected to improve for this step back up in trip and he ran well, staying on late having got a bit behind. He should have been closer, but is likely to remain vulnerable to improvers off this sort of mark.
Inchnadamph, well behind Double Banded at Nottingham, briefly threatened to make a play for the places, but he could find no more. This was about as good a run as connections could have hoped for.
Odiham, another to come from the Double Banded Nottingham race, is not the force of old and he never really threatened to get into it.
Fair Along(GER), 10lb higher than when finishign second in the race last year, has not been in as good a form over the jumps this time around and he struggled to sustain the gallop. (op 16-1 tchd 20-1)
Halla San looked an interesting outsider from a low draw, but he was never really going and did not look to be enjoying himself.
Greenwich Meantime, just 1lb higher than when winning this last year, looked to be moving through with a challenge half a mile out, but he soon bumped into trouble and could do no more. His trainer had stated before the race he may not quite be ready, so expect an improved showing next time. (tchd 11-1)
Black Rock(IRE) improved markedly for the step up to middle-distances at three and looked the type who may stay this sort of distance. He had been done no favours with the draw though and was weak in the market as a result. Robinson did well to get him in front, but he failed to settle and did not look at ease on the course, drifting off the rail a couple of times on the final lap. He was eased right off once his chance had gone and deserves another chance to show whether he has progressed from three to four. Official explanation: jockey said colt lost its action
Kasthari(IRE) is not the force of old and he found this all too competitive.
Missoula(IRE), 12lb higher than when bolting up at York last October, enjoyed a recent spin over hurdles and she showed up well for a long way. She could find no more over two out though and ultimately dropped right out. Official explanation: jockey said mare had no more to give; trainer said mare was later found to be in season (op 20-1)
Sentry Duty(FR), a useful novice hurdler who was 8lb higher than when winning at Newmarket around a year ago, never got into it and could have been expected to fare a little better.
Full House(IRE) landed the Ascot Stakes at last year's Royal meeting and was just 3lb higher here. He was another to have enjoyed a recent spin over hurdles and looked potentially interesting from stall one. However, he was soon in trouble and pulled up before halfway. Something was obviously amiss and it could be that he suffered internal haemorrhaging. Official explanation: jockey said he thought there was something amiss with colt; vet said colt pulled up lame (op 16-1)
Shipmaster, a huge tank of a horse shouldering a 3lb penalty for his recent win in the Group 3 Sagaro Stakes, had his share of weight, but is big enough to carry it and it was a shame to see him pulled up and quickly dismounted before halfway. He suffered a serious tendon injury and his career could well be over. Official explanation: jockey said gelding was pulled up lame (op 16-1)

1917 BREITLING WATCHES & WALTONS OF CHESTER H'CAP — 5f 16y

3:15 (3:16) (Class 2) (0-100,100) 4-Y-O+ **£13,246** (£3,964; £1,982; £991; £493) **Stalls** Low

Form / RPR

36-0 **1** **Bertoliver**[20] 1420 4-8-8 **90** ow2 ..... PhilipRobinson 7 101
(D K Ivory) *mde all: qcknd over 1f out: sn rdn: kpt on wl ins fnl f* **12/1**

6-04 **2** *1 1/2* **Green Park (IRE)**[25] 1325 5-8-6 **88** ..... PaulHanagan 2 94
(R A Fahey) *lw: chsd ldrs: rdn 2f out: styd on to take 2nd cl home: nt trble wnr* **10/3**[1]

1363 **3** *1/2* **Ebraam (USA)**[18] 1483 5-8-10 **95** ..... TolleyDean(3) 8 99
(D Shaw) *chsd ldrs: rdn to take 2nd over 1f out: no imp: lost 2nd cl home* **12/1**

0-20 **4** *1 3/4* **Caribbean Coral**[21] 1393 9-8-1 **86** oh5 ..... LukeMorris(3) 6 84
(J J Quinn) *lw: midfield: rdn and hdwy over 1f out: edgd lft ins fnl f: styd on: nt pce to rch ldrs* **9/1**

-035 **5** *nse* **Buachaill Dona (IRE)**[75] 668 5-9-4 **100** ..... SilvestreDeSousa 11 98+
(D Nicholls) *s.i.s: in rr div: forced to switch wd 3f out: rdn over 1f out: r.o wl and gaining fnl f: nrst fin* **20/1**

-115 **6** *1* **Rebel Duke (IRE)**[19] 1451 4-8-1 **86** oh3 ..... WilliamBuick(3) 9 80
(D W Barker) *chsd ldrs: rdn over 1f out: one pce ins fnl f* **14/1**

0-04 **7** *3 3/4* **Strike Up The Band**[35] 1157 5-8-13 **95** ..... TPO'Shea 13 76
(D Nicholls) *chsd wnr: rdn and lost 2nd over 1f out: wknd ins fnl f* **25/1**

2455 **8** *nk* **Ajigolo**[9] 1689 5-8-10 **92** ..... EdwardCreighton 12 72
(M R Channon) *bhd: styd on fnl f: nt pce to trble ldrs* **40/1**

1153 **9** *1* **Fire Up The Band**[13] 1588 9-8-4 **86** oh1 ..... JohnEgan 10 62
(A Berry) *midfield: rdn 2f out: wknd fnl f* **25/1**

030- **10** *nse* **Invincible Force (IRE)**[170] 6876 4-8-12 **94** ..... MartinDwyer 3 70
(Paul Green) *s.i.s: midfield: rdn and outpcd over 2f out* **6/1**[3]

6423 **11** *1* **Methaaly (IRE)**[18] 1488 5-8-4 **86** oh17 ..... LiamJones 5 58
(M Mullineaux) *a towards rr* **28/1**

420- **12** *1/2* **Tournedos (IRE)**[207] 6183 6-9-0 **96** ..... JoeFanning 15 66
(D Nicholls) *midfield: forced to switch wd 3f out: sn lost pl: bhd fnl 2f* **33/1**

4-24 **13** *2 3/4* **Matsunosuke**[3] 1831 6-9-0 **96** ..... KerrinMcEvoy 14 56
(A B Coogan) *in rr: forced to switch wd 3f out: nvr on terms* **8/1**

0034 **P** **King Orchisios (IRE)**[19] 1442 5-8-13 **95** ..... (p) JamieSpencer 4 —
(K A Ryan) *chsd ldrs tl broke down 3f out: p.u qckly: dead* **7/2**[2]

60.98 secs (-0.02) **Going Correction** +0.225s/f (Good) **14** Ran SP% **124.0**
Speed ratings (Par 109): **109,106,105,103,102 101,95,94,93,93 91,90,86,—**
CSF £49.28 CT £527.06 TOTE £16.10: £4.40, £1.80, £3.80; EX 77.20 Trifecta £700.10 Part won. Pool: £490.09 - 0.30 winning units..
Owner Mrs A Shone **Bred** Pillar To Post Racing **Trained** Radlett, Herts

FOCUS

A typical Chester sprint handicap, with a low draw and early speed proving crucial. The form is unlikely to prove reliable when translated to a more conventional track with the runner-up rated to previous course form.

NOTEBOOK

Bertoliver, whose biggest asset has always been speed from the gate, pinged them and was able to cross over to the rail from what was effectively the six box and make all the running. His rider put up 2lb overweight but that was more than made up for by his ability to dictate a pace which left him with enough in reserve to kick on the final bend and have the race won a furlong out. Confirming this form with a few of those in behind on a more conventional track will not be easy, however. (tchd 14-1)
Green Park(IRE), second on his only previous visit to this track two years ago, had the best draw and secured the rail position in the early stages, but he struggled to go the pace, suggesting that the ground was a bit on the quick side for him. Five of his six highest RPRs have been gained on soft or heavy ground. (op 7-2 tchd 4-1)
Ebraam(USA), who adopted a stalking position, was always well enough placed if good enough. He only gave up second place well inside the last.
Caribbean Coral, a winner of his last two starts over this course and distance, had to race from 5lb out of the handicap, albeit off the same mark as when successful in this race last year. The type who needs the breaks when making ground through the pack from off the pace, he ran on well but found the line coming too soon. (tchd 10-1)
Buachaill Dona(IRE) shaped quite well as he was not favourably drawn and had to challenge wide down the outside in the straight. He remains a little high in the handicap but this was a decent effort.
Rebel Duke(IRE), 3lb out of the weights and not drawn particularly well, looked up against it and in the circumstances he ran a fair race. (op 20-1)
Strike Up The Band showed good early pace to cross over from his outside gate and hassle the eventual winner for the lead. That effort coupled with having to race two wide throughout eventually took its toll, though. (op 33-1)
Ajigolo, who last won on turf in September 2005, was poorly drawn and is ideally suited by 6f. He found this far too sharp a test. Official explanation: jockey said horse hung right (op 33-1)
Fire Up The Band, whose recent wins on the All-Weather have come in claimers, is flattered by his current rating. (op 33-1)
Invincible Force(IRE), twice a winner at the track as a juvenile, was making his seasonal reappearance against some race-fit rivals. Slowly away, he failed to take advantage of his good low draw. (op 11-2)
Methaaly(IRE) had a mountain to climb from 17lb out of the handicap. (op 50-1)
Tournedos(IRE) has a good record here having twice won in Listed company over this distance, but he had a nightmare draw to overcome this time and ended up racing wide. (op 40-1)
Matsunosuke had little chance of building on his recent fine fourth in the Palace House Stakes from his car park draw. (op 15-2 tchd 9-1)

1918 BOODLES DIAMOND MAIDEN STKS — 1m 2f 75y

4:00 (4:01) (Class 3) 3-Y-O **£7,123** (£2,119; £1,059; £529) **Stalls** High

Form / RPR

0-2 **1** **Daraahem (IRE)**[21] 1398 3-9-3 0 ..... RHills 2 95+
(B W Hills) *lw: trckd ldrs: led over 1f out: sn edgd lft: r.o and in command after* **11/8**[1]

6 **2** *2* **Moonquake (USA)**[20] 1417 3-9-3 0 ..... JimmyFortune 4 91+
(J H M Gosden) *lw: led: hdd appr fnl f: n.m.r 1f out: sn swtchd rt: styd on same pce after* **3/1**[2]

5 **3** *hd* **Maraased**[21] 1398 3-9-3 0 ..... MartinDwyer 5 91+
(M A Jarvis) *hld up: pushed along and outpcd 3f out: prog to chse ldrs over 1f out: sn lugged lft: sltly intimidated by runner-up ins fnl f: r.o and gaining towards fin* **3/1**[2]

23-5 **4** *11* **Polmaily**[16] 1526 3-9-3 85 ..... RichardHughes 10 69
(B J Meehan) *hld up: pushed along over 3f out: plugged on fnl f wout troubling ldrs* **11/1**[3]

230- **5** *3 1/2* **Crystal Rock (IRE)**[237] 5350 3-9-3 81 ..... MichaelHills 9 62
(B W Hills) *w ldr: u.p but stl ch whn sltly short of room over 1f out: sn wknd* **11/1**[3]

4 **6** *2 1/4* **Miss Mactango**[15] 1549 3-8-12 0 ..... LiamJones 8 52
(W M Brisbourne) *bhd: struggling 3f out: nvr on terms* **66/1**

4 **7** *hd* **Daraiym (IRE)**[11] 1615 3-9-3 0 ..... TPQueally 7 57
(Paul Green) *sltly hmpd s: bhd: struggling 3f out: nvr on terms* **25/1**

6 **8** *1/2* **Greyfriarsblessing (IRE)**[11] 1628 3-8-12 0 ..... GregFairley 1 51
(M Johnston) *rangy: in tch: rdn and wknd 3f out* **25/1**

0-5 **9** *9* **Misterisland (IRE)**[6] 1751 3-9-3 0 ..... PaulHanagan 3 38
(A Bailey) *w'like: plld hrd in midfield: pushed along and wknd over 2f out* **40/1**

2m 14.2s (2.00) **Going Correction** +0.225s/f (Good) **9** Ran SP% **120.4**
Speed ratings (Par 103): **101,99,99,90,87 85,85,85,78**
CSF £5.79 TOTE £2.50: £1.20, £1.50, £1.50; EX 7.00.
Owner Hamdan Al Maktoum **Bred** Shadwell Estate Company Limited **Trained** Lambourn, Berks

FOCUS

Useful maiden form with the first three clear and all look capable of winning decent races.

NOTEBOOK

Daraahem(IRE) ◆, who had run well at Newmarket on his previous start when chasing home Chester Vase hope Pampas Cat, looked to hold sound claims here and the race could not have panned out better for him. He was always well placed tracking the leader on the rail and, pulled out to challenge early in the straight, ran on well to win cosily. He looks a very useful handicapper in the making and Royal Ascot should be on his agenda. (op 9-4)
Moonquake(USA), whose trainer had won this race three times in the previous five years, had improvement to make on his debut effort over a mile. The step up in trip was expected to suit, though, and in theory Gosden had a good line to the level of form required as a result of Pampas Cat winning the maiden at Newmarket in which Daraahem and Maraased were beaten. He enjoyed the run of the race and was beaten on merit, but still did enough to suggest he will not be long in going one better. (op 5-2 tchd 9-4)
Maraased ◆, who was not given such a positive ride as Daraahem when finishing three places behind him at Newmarket, arguably had more improvement in him as that was his racecourse debut whereas Daraahem had run at two. He was not given the best of rides here, though. Held up, he was caught out of his ground when the leading trio quickened things up over two furlongs out, and while he had made up much of the deficit by the time they crossed the line one was left thinking that he would have given his owner's first string more to do with a more positive ride. He clearly has the ability to win a similar race. (op 11-4 tchd 7-2)
Polmaily, who has an official mark of 85, was another caught out when the pace quickened. He stayed on to take a distant fourth and will be suited by a more galloping track. (op 14-1)
Crystal Rock(IRE), who disputed the lead with Moonquake, ended up racing two wide most of the way. He helped wind up the pace from over two furlongs out but weakened from the top of the straight and did not get home. He should be more effective back over 1m. (op 10-1)
Miss Mactango achieved little in finishing sixth in a race dominated by some very useful animals. She will have better chances once eligible to run in moderate handicap company after one more run. (op 50-1)
Daraiym(IRE) Official explanation: jockey said colt was hampered at the start

1919 WALKER SMITH WAY H'CAP — 1m 4f 66y

4:35 (4:35) (Class 3) (0-95,90) 3-Y-O **£10,037** (£2,986; £1,492; £745) **Stalls** Low

Form / RPR

3631 **1** **Allied Powers (IRE)**[7] 1731 3-8-10 **77** 6ex ..... JamieSpencer 3 92+
(M L W Bell) *hld up: gd hdwy over 3f out: str run on outside to ld over 1f out: clr ent fnl f: eased down towards fin* **4/1**[2]

61-3 **2** *2 3/4* **Patkai (IRE)**[19] 1443 3-9-9 **90** ..... RyanMoore 9 101+
(Sir Michael Stoute) *lw: hld up: pushed along over 5f out: hdwy whn nt clr run over 1f out: sn swtchd rt: r.o wl and gd prog ins fnl f: wnt 2nd towards fin wout troubling wnr: promising* **7/2**[1]

43-1 **3** 1 1/4 **Burn The Breeze (IRE)**[19] 1444 3-9-1 **82** .... TedDurcan 2 85
(H R A Cecil) *chsd ldrs: led over 2f out: rdn and hdd over 1f out: styd on same pce ins fnl f* **4/1**[2]

62-1 **4** 2 3/4 **Tighnabruaich (IRE)**[19] 1446 3-9-6 **90** .... WilliamBuick(3) 8 89+
(M A Jarvis) *lw: in tch: rdn 4f out: hung lft whn chsd ldrs fr over 1f out: kpt on same pce ins fnl f* **5/1**[3]

-013 **5** 1 1/2 **No To Trident**[34] 1171 3-8-11 **85** .... RichardEvans(7) 5 82
(P D Evans) *midfield: effrt to chse ldrs over 2f out: nt qckn over 1f out: eased whn no ex wl ins fnl f* **33/1**

1244 **6** 6 **Segal (IRE)**[15] 1543 3-8-12 **79** .... TPQueally 6 66
(J Noseda) *chsd ldrs: wnt 2nd after 3f: led 4f out: hdd over 2f out: wknd 1f out* **16/1**

0-25 **7** 1 **Ballochroy (IRE)**[20] 1424 3-9-4 **85** .... MichaelHills 4 70
(B W Hills) *hld up: pushed along over 3f out: nvr able to trble ldrs* **8/1**

5-41 **8** 26 **Yes Mr President (IRE)**[72] 702 3-9-0 **81** .... JoeFanning 1 25
(M Johnston) *in tch: pushed along and lost pl after 4f: toiling 5f out* **10/1**

-211 **9** 26 **Leamington (USA)**[93] 434 3-9-2 **83** .... RHills 7 —
(M Johnston) *led: hdd 4f out: wknd over 2f out: t.o* **10/1**

2m 39.82s (-0.08) **Going Correction** +0.225s/f (Good) **9** Ran SP% **117.0**
Speed ratings (Par 103): **112,110,109,107,106 102,101,84,67**
CSF £18.71 CT £59.60 TOTE £4.70: £1.90, £2.00, £1.80; EX 18.00 Place 6 £60.37, Place 5 £11.82.
Owner David Fish And Edward Ware **Bred** Saad Bin Mishrif **Trained** Newmarket, Suffolk

FOCUS
A competitive and good-quality handicap run in a smart time which should throw up a number of winners with the runner-up likely to do better on a more conventional track.

NOTEBOOK
Allied Powers(IRE) ◆, who bolted up at Pontefract in heavy ground last time, had different conditions and stiffer competition to deal with here, but he showed himself adaptable and well handicapped under his 6lb penalty. Held up in rear, he made his ground up quickly rounding the turn into the straight and, despite showing signs of inexperience, went clear in ready fashion. For his rider it was soon a case of not winning too far, and he cruised home, scoring with more in hand than the bare margin suggests. He could well be up to contesting something like the King George V Handicap at Royal Ascot next month.
Patkai(IRE) ◆, third in a decent conditions event at Newbury last time, looked to be going nowhere fast for much of the race and struggled when the pace quickened. Going for an adventurous run up the inside early in the straight, he soon found his path blocked, and had to be switched to challenge wide. The bird had flown by the time he got going but the way he stayed on suggests he will come into his own over a longer trip. The Ebor could well be his sort of race later in the year, and he will have two or three options at Royal Ascot. (op 4-1)
Burn The Breeze(IRE), who beat the Cheshire Oaks third into second when winning her maiden at Newbury last time out, ran a solid race behind two very useful colts. She should be able to win off this sort of mark and connections will no doubt be hoping that she will be able to grab some black type somewhere before the season is out. (op 9-2)
Tighnabruaich(IRE), who did not look entirely happy on the track, plugged on well enough but he might need softer ground to be seen at his very best.
No To Trident, more exposed than most in the field, simply came up against some more progressive rivals in what was a decent handicap.
Segal(IRE), stepping up a furlong in distance, is another about whom the Handicapper has a fairly good idea how good he is. He did not get home after racing prominently for a long way. (op 14-1)
Ballochroy(IRE) was expected to improve for this longer trip but he never really threatened. Perhaps the ground was too quick for him.
Yes Mr President(IRE), running on turf for the first time having won his final race on Polytrack back in February, was representing a trainer who had won this race twice in the last three years. Together with his stablemate, who made the running, he finished up well beaten, and this was clearly not his true running. (op 11-1)
Leamington(USA), chasing a hat-trick following two wins on the All-Weather earlier in the year, was returning from a three-month break and was entitled to need the run, but he dropped out very quickly after being headed and proved very disappointing for a stable with a good recent record in this race. Official explanation: jockey said filly lost its action (tchd 9-1)
T/Jkpt: Not won. T/Plt: £54.60 to a £1 stake. Pool: £150,803.02. 2,015.65 winning tickets. T/Qpdt: £12.30 to a £1 stake. Pool: £8,579.41. 512.50 winning tickets. DO

1914 CHESTER (L-H)
Thursday, May 8

OFFICIAL GOING: Good to firm (good in places; 8.4)
Wind: Light, across Weather: Hot and Sunny

1920 BANK OF IRELAND H'CAP 1m 2f 75y
1:45 (1:45) (Class 2) (0-100,100) 4-Y-0+ **£13,246** (£3,964; £1,982; £991; £493) **Stalls** High

Form RPR

0-60 **1** **Mull Of Dubai**[15] 1569 5-8-4 **86** .... JohnEgan 9 97
(T P Tate) *towards rr: niggled along over 3f out: hdwy on outside over 2f out: nt clr run briefly over 1f out: sn swtchd lft: led 1f out: kpt on wl* **13/2**

4051 **2** 1 **Escape Route (USA)**[18] 1503 4-9-1 **97** .... (p) JimmyFortune 7 106
(J H M Gosden) *chsd ldng trio: hdwy 3f out: chalng 2f out: rdn to ld over 1f out: sn hdd: continued to run on u.p ins fnl f* **9/4**[1]

340 **3** 2 1/4 **Vainglory (USA)**[77] 650 4-8-7 **89** .... RichardMullen 8 93
(D M Simcock) *lw: midfield: pushed along 4f out: hdwy 3f out: rdn and upsides 2f out: nt qckn ins fnl f* **14/1**

-543 **4** 3/4 **Bahar Shumaal (IRE)**[12] 1633 6-7-13 **86** .... AhmedAjtebi(5) 5 89+
(C E Brittain) *lw: w ldr helping to set str gallop: led 4f out: rdn and hdd over 1f out: kpt on same pce ins fnl f* **4/1**[2]

3-04 **5** 1 1/4 **Prince Forever (IRE)**[23] 1387 4-9-4 **100** .... PhilipRobinson 4 100
(M A Jarvis) *towards rr: pushed along over 2f out: styd on fnl f: nt pce to trble ldrs* **6/1**[3]

1-05 **6** 2 **Hoh Wotanite**[9] 1711 5-8-4 **86** .... (v) TPO'Shea 6 82
(R Hollinshead) *b.hind: midfield: effrt whn nt clr run over 2f out: one pce fnl f* **33/1**

-000 **7** 1 3/4 **Ella Woodcock (IRE)**[4] 1828 4-8-4 **86** .... PaulHanagan 3 79
(E J Alston) *chsd clr front pair: clsd on ldrs 3f out: rdn whn n.m.r over 2f out: wknd fnl f* **22/1**

40-0 **8** 18 **Philanthropy**[12] 1625 4-8-5 **87** .... (p) DO'Donohoe 1 44
(K A Ryan) *swtg: led at str gallop: hdd 4f out: rdn and wknd over 2f out* **8/1**

10-0 **9** 3 1/4 **Temple Place (IRE)**[13] 960 7-8-10 **92** .... (t) RyanMoore 2 42
(D McCain Jnr) *planted himself in stalls and slowly away: a bhd* **6/1**[3]

2m 10.71s (-1.49) **Going Correction** +0.10s/f (Good) **9** Ran SP% **117.7**
Speed ratings (Par 109): **109,108,106,105,104 103,101,87,84**
CSF £21.97 CT £202.64 TOTE £9.70: £2.70, £1.30, £4.10; EX 37.30 Trifecta £411.00 Part won. Pool: £578.97. 0.40 - winning units..
Owner Mrs Fitri Hay **Bred** B Walters **Trained** Tadcaster, N Yorks

FOCUS
Very few of these looked well handicapped beforehand but the form looks solid with the winner close to his best. It was run at a strong gallop and the first three came from off the pace.

NOTEBOOK
Mull Of Dubai has a style of running which is not normally suited to this track, but on this occasion the race fell into his lap as the leaders set a scorching gallop which allowed him to come through strongly at the finish. Things fell right this time and, while he will probably find it more difficult off a higher mark, he is always worthy of consideration when a good gallop looks assured. (op 9-1)
Escape Route(USA), who won cosily at Great Leighs last time, still looked fairly handicapped off a 4lb higher mark. Well placed in the chasing pack, he was given every chance and had no excuse. (op 2-1 tchd 5-2)
Vainglory(USA), running for the first time since returning from Dubai, where he took part in the Carnival earlier in the year, had the race run to suit but was not good enough and simply looks held off his current mark.
Bahar Shumaal(IRE) would have taken some catching around here had he not been taken on for the lead, but the way things panned out he just ended up setting an unsustainably strong gallop with Philanthropy. He deserves some credit for hanging on to fourth place as his fellow pacemaker was well beaten. (op 9-2 tchd 5-1)
Prince Forever(IRE) was well fancied for the Lincoln, but he ran poorly at Doncaster, and also in a small-field conditions race at Warwick subsequently. Trying something new, he was stepping up in distance here, and given the way the race was run it was set up for a hold-up horse like him. However, he proved very disappointing once again. Perhaps the ground was too fast, but it might be wise not to make too many more excuses for him. (op 13-2 tchd 7-1)
Hoh Wotanite remains high in the handicap and without a win on turf. (op 28-1)
Ella Woodcock(IRE), who led the chasing pack behind the trail-blazing pair up front, is another who needs help from the Handicapper. (op 25-1 tchd 20-1)
Philanthropy, wearing cheekpieces for the first time, was taken on by Bahar Shumaal at the head of affairs and they both paid the price for setting too strong a gallop. (op 11-1 tchd 12-1 in a place)
Temple Place(IRE), a shock winner of this race last year, was only 4lb higher this time around, but he lost several lengths when slowly away from the stalls, and he could never get out of the rear division. Official explanation: jockey said gelding missed the break (op 7-1)

1921 GRANT THORNTON HUXLEY STKS (FOR THE TRADESMAN'S CUP) (GROUP 3) 1m 2f 75y
2:15 (2:16) (Class 1) 4-Y-0+ **£34,224** (£13,074; £6,624; £3,384; £1,776) **Stalls** High

Form RPR

5014 **1** **Championship Point (IRE)**[13] 1596 5-9-0 105 .... DarryllHolland 4 113
(M R Channon) *led: rdn whn pressed over 1f out: hdd narrowly ins fnl f: gamely regained ld towards fin* **12/1**

350- **2** nk **Maraahel (IRE)**[201] 6334 7-9-5 117 .... (b) RHills 1 117
(Sir Michael Stoute) *lw: chsd wnr: rdn to nose ahd ins fnl f: sn edgd lft: hdd towards fin* **5/2**[2]

6-32 **3** 1 1/2 **Spice Route**[21] 1427 4-9-0 106 .... JamieSpencer 5 109
(M L W Bell) *lw: chsd front pair: clsd 3f out: rdn over 1f out: hung lft and nt pce of ldrs ins fnl f* **8/1**

15-4 **4** 1 1/4 **Multidimensional (IRE)**[21] 1422 5-9-0 111 .... TedDurcan 3 107+
(H R A Cecil) *lw: hld up: pushed along and hdwy over 1f out: sn rdn: run flattened out ins fnl f* **5/4**[1]

31-5 **5** 9 **Stotsfold**[21] 1422 5-9-3 110 .... AdamKirby 6 92
(W R Swinburn) *hld up: pushed along and hdwy 3f out: wknd over 1f out* **5/1**[3]

010- **P** **Majounes Song**[214] 6042 4-9-0 106 .... JoeFanning 2 —
(M Johnston) *wore net muzzle: racd keenly: trckd ldrs: wnt wrong and p.u after 1f* **40/1**

2m 11.21s (-0.99) **Going Correction** +0.10s/f (Good) **6** Ran SP% **110.9**
Speed ratings (Par 113): **107,106,105,104,97** —
CSF £41.06 TOTE £11.70: £3.80, £1.80; EX 47.90.
Owner John Livock **Bred** Mount Coote Stud **Trained** West Ilsley, Berks
■ Stewards' Enquiry : Darryll Holland one-day ban: careless riding (May 22)

FOCUS
A modest time for a Group 3, half a second slower than the preceding handicap but the form is best rated through the runner-up to a mark similar to when winning this the previous two years.

NOTEBOOK
Championship Point(IRE) could not make all in the Gordon Richards Stakes against the likes of Ask last time, but this track is kinder to front-runners and, once taking things up and setting a good but not ridiculous gallop up front, he was always going to be tough to pass, as he had previously shown when defeating Spice Route at Ripon. He was headed by Maraahel inside the final furlong, but rallied well under pressure to regain the lead close home, and a change in tactics to front-running has certainly worked well for him. (tchd 10-1)
Maraahel(IRE), winner of this race for the previous three seasons, tracked the leader throughout and at the top of the straight he looked sure to come through and notch a fourth success in this race. Indeed, he hit the front momentarily inside the last, but the winner rallied and denied him close home. In this race last year he rallied after being headed by Blue Bajan well inside the last, but this year it was his turn to be collared, having touched 1.12 in running. Because he carried a 5lb penalty he comes out of the contest as the best horse in the race, and presumably an attempt to win a third Hardwicke Stakes will be next on his agenda. (tchd 11-4)
Spice Route, who had to settle for second behind Championship Point at Ripon last time when that rival got the run of the race out in front, had the same trick played on him again. He could have done with racing handier than he did, but by the time they turned into the straight he had led the chasing pack to close up and in reality he appeared to have every chance. (tchd 9-1 and 10-1 in a place)
Multidimensional(IRE) was expected to have come on for his reappearance at Newmarket and was a hot favourite to get his career back on track. He was very disappointing, though, even allowing for the fairly tactical nature of the race. Perhaps the track did not suit him, but he certainly has a bit to prove now. (op 6-4 tchd 13-8)
Stotsfold, whose previous form figures at the track read 112, surprisingly never looked to be going well despite also having trip and ground to suit. This cannot have been his true form and he deserves another chance. (op 9-2 tchd 4-1)
Majounes Song suffered a career-ending pelvis fracture. (op 28-1)

1922 BANK OF AMERICA CHESTER VASE (GROUP 3) (C&G) 1m 4f 66y
2:45 (2:46) (Class 1) 3-Y-0
£36,900 (£13,988; £7,000; £3,490; £1,748; £877) **Stalls** Low

Form RPR

21-2 **1** **Doctor Fremantle**[21] 1424 3-8-12 93 .... RyanMoore 4 113+
(Sir Michael Stoute) *lw: missed break: sn racd keenly in midfield: clsd over 7f out: qcknd to ld over 1f out: r.o gamely and a on top ins fnl f* **11/8**[1]

21-1 **2** 1/2 **All The Aces (IRE)**[12] 1618 3-8-12 91 .... PhilipRobinson 8 109
(M A Jarvis) *gd sort: lw: a.p: rdn and upsides over 1f out: sn edgd lft: r.o and continued to chal ins fnl f but a looked hld* **10/1**

1 **3** 5 **Pampas Cat (USA)**[22] 1398 3-8-12 103 .... JimmyFortune 1 101+
(J H M Gosden) *sn led: hdd over 6f out: remained prom: regained ld over 2f out: rdn and hdd over 1f out: no ex ins fnl f* **7/2**[2]

03-3 **4** 1/2 **Feared In Flight (IRE)**[12] 1632 3-8-12 111 .... JamieSpencer 5 101
(B W Hills) *lw: racd keenly: hld up: hdwy over 2f out: rdn and hung lft fr over 1f out: styd on same pce ins fnl f* **7/2**[2]

546- **5** 1 **Donegal (USA)**[187] 6650 3-8-12 100 .... DarryllHolland 7 99
(A M Balding) *w ldr: led over 4f out: sn pushed along: hdd over 2f out: wknd ins fnl f* **40/1**

6 nk **Vivaldi (IRE)**[305] 3359 3-8-12 0 ..... JMurtagh 6 99
(A P O'Brien, Ire) *swtg: str: hld up: pushed along over 2f out: rdn 1f out: nvr able to chal* **7/1**[3]

-055 7 3/4 **Yahrab (IRE)**[22] 1402 3-8-12 98 ..... KerrinMcEvoy 3 97
(C E Brittain) *hld up: hdwy over 2f out: rdn over 1f out: no imp on ldrs: wknd ins fnl f* **22/1**

8 50 **Wassily Kandinsky**[216] 5997 3-8-12 0 ..... DavidMcCabe 2 17
(A P O'Brien, Ire) *w'like: swtg: bustled along to chse ldrs: rdn along to take 2nd over 7f out: led over 6f out: hdd over 4f out: wknd qckly over 3f out: t.o* **40/1**

2m 37.39s (-2.51) **Going Correction** +0.10s/f (Good) **8** Ran SP% **117.4**
Speed ratings (Par 109): **116,115,112,112,111 111,110,77**
CSF £17.28 TOTE £2.60: £1.30, £2.70, £1.50; EX 19.00 Trifecta £76.00 Pool: £728.60. 6.80 - winning units..

Owner K Abdulla **Bred** Juddmonte Farms Ltd **Trained** Newmarket, Suffolk

FOCUS
Not a strong Derby trial on paper and none of the first three home are currently entered at Epsom. They went quite steady and the race developed into a bit of a sprint finish, but the winner is the type to go on to better things. The third sets the level, although it is limited somewhat by the proximity of the fifth and seventh.

NOTEBOOK
Doctor Fremantle has clearly always been a well-regarded colt as he has yet to start at bigger than 13-8 for any of his five starts to date. Narrowly beaten by Bronze Cannon in a red-hot handicap at the Craven meeting, he was representing a stable that brought Papal Bull to win this race on the back of success in the very same handicap. Well placed on the rail tracking the pace, he travelled well throughout and, when asked to go and take the gap on the inside as the false rail ran out, he quickened up well. Always holding the runner-up in the closing stages, he won a bit cosier than the winning margin suggests. He is not in the Derby and, with Twice Over being his owner's likeliest representative at Epsom at this stage, he is unlikely to be supplemented. As a result he could well go the King Edward VII and Irish Derby route, with the St Leger an appealing longer-term target - there is certainly no shortage of stamina in his pedigree. (op 13-8)

All The Aces(IRE), who won a handicap off 82 on his reappearance, has no fancy entries but on this evidence he is clearly a smart colt in the making. Picking up well for pressure in the closing stages, he was the only one who could live with the winner and, although always held close home, he finished nicely clear of the rest. There is already talk of the Great Voltigeur for him, and so come September it will not be a surprise to see him renew rivalry with the winner in the final Classic. (op 11-1 tchd 9-1)

Pampas Cat(USA), whose trainer was forced to step him up to Pattern company following the Handicapper's decision to allot him a rating of 103 after winning a Newmarket maiden on his debut, had at least seen the form boosted by the subsequent success of the placed horses, including Daraahem, who won here the previous day. Allowed to dictate a steady enough gallop for much of the race, he was well placed for the sprint to the line but the first two simply proved too strong. He may now drop back to Listed company for the 1m2f Fairway Stakes at Newmarket, a race his stable won last year with Lucarno. (op 10-3)

Feared In Flight(IRE), a running-on third behind Centennial in the Classic Trial at Sandown, once again failed to have the race run to suit. Held up towards the back in what was quite a tactical affair, he raced keenly. He briefly looked threatening at the top of the straight, but his effort flattened out. He has his limitations but is likely to be seen at his best in a strongly run race. (op 9-2)

Donegal(USA), making his seasonal reappearance, has a rating of 100 largely as a result of finishing third to Rio De La Plata in the Vintage Stakes last year. The overall balance of his form suggests he is flattered by that rating and he looks likely to be difficult to place this season. (op 50-1)

Vivaldi(IRE), not seen since winning a Gowran Park maiden last July, was representing the stable that took the race last year with Soldier Of Fortune, but he sweated up beforehand and was weak in the market, being freely available at double-figure prices on Betfair at the off. He had a stablemate in the race seemingly to ensure a good gallop, but the pacemaker could not get to the front and the result was that he ended up held up at the back of the field in a tactical affair. Never seen with a chance, he did not look happy on this continually turning track, and he is surely capable of better than this on a more conventional course. (op 6-1)

Yahrab(IRE), the most experienced runner in the line-up, was stepping up three furlongs in distance. He did not seem to get home, but is another who looks likely to prove difficult to place this season. (op 25-1)

Wassily Kandinsky, fourth in a nursery off 90 on his final start at two, looked to be in the race to ensure a proper gallop for his stable-companion, but he failed miserably in his role as he just could not get to the front. He did lead narrowly for a moment later in the race but it was to no worthwhile effect.

1923 HALIFAX H'CAP 7f 122y

3:15 (3:16) (Class 2) (0-100,93) 3-Y-**£13,246** (£3,964; £1,982; £991; £493) **Stalls** Low

Form RPR

34-1 1 **Huzzah (IRE)**[20] 1441 3-9-4 **93** ..... MichaelHills 6 105
(B W Hills) *trckd ldrs: wnt 2nd over 2f out: led over 1f out: sn rdn: jst hld on whn pressed towards fin* **15/2**[3]

30-1 2 shd **Fervent Prince**[16] 1546 3-8-4 **79** oh1 ..... JohnEgan 9 91
(H Morrison) *racd in rr div: hdwy whn nt clr run over 1f out: sn rdn and hung lft: r.o strly ins fnl f: gaining cl home: jst failed* **20/1**

1-1 3 2 3/4 **Wasan**[15] 1572 3-8-13 **88** ..... RHills 11 96+
(E A L Dunlop) *lw: hld up: nt clr run over 2f out: rdn and hdwy over 1f out: styd on to take 3rd ins fnl f: nt pce to trble front pair* **15/2**[3]

21-0 4 1 1/2 **Boy Blue**[27] 1297 3-8-7 **82** ..... JamieSpencer 10 83
(D Nicholls) *in tch: rdn over 1f out: kpt on same pce ins fnl f* **14/1**

21-2 5 3/4 **Adversity**[17] 1524 3-8-8 **83** ..... RyanMoore 12 93+
(Sir Michael Stoute) *lw: hld up: swtchd rt over 1f out: hdwy ent fnl f: styd on: nrst fin: promising effrt* **5/1**[2]

41-2 6 1 1/2 **Toto Skyllachy**[14] 1576 3-8-11 **86** ..... MickyFenton 4 81
(T P Tate) *niggled along most of way: bhd: styd on ins fnl f: nt pce to trble ldrs* **12/1**

02-2 7 3/4 **Elna Bright**[40] 1074 3-8-13 **88** ..... LDettori 8 82
(B J Meehan) *midfield: rdn and hdwy 2f out: wknd ins fnl f* **12/1**

5-1 8 1/2 **Royalist (IRE)**[27] 1295 3-8-10 **85** ..... PhilipRobinson 1 77+
(M A Jarvis) *broke wl to ld: rdn and hdd over 1f out: wknd ins fnl f* **9/4**[1]

12 9 3/4 **Magnitude**[10] 1688 3-8-7 **82** ..... KerrinMcEvoy 7 72
(W J Haggas) *midfield: nt clr run over 1f out: sn rdn: kpt on but no imp on ldrs* **14/1**

33-4 10 3 **Green Wadi**[54] 909 3-8-5 **80** ..... TPO'Shea 3 63
(M R Channon) *hld up: pushed along and hdwy 2f out: wknd over 1f out* **10/1**

44-0 11 9 **Eastern Gift**[26] 1333 3-9-4 **93** ..... JimmyFortune 2 53
(R Hannon) *chsd ldrs: rdn over 2f out: wknd over 1f out* **28/1**

21-6 12 11 **Ramatni**[35] 1170 3-8-12 **87** ..... JoeFanning 5 20
(M Johnston) *prom: rdn 3f out: losing pl whn n.m.r over 2f out: sn bhd* **25/1**

1m 34.0s (0.20) **Going Correction** +0.10s/f (Good) **12** Ran SP% **120.8**
Speed ratings (Par 105): **103,102,100,98,97 96,95,95,94,91 82,71**
CSF £152.73 CT £1189.42 TOTE £9.00: £3.00, £6.20, £2.90; EX 139.10 Trifecta £862.80 Pool: £1336.88. 1.10 - winning units..

Owner J Gale,J Finch,D Cole,R Dollar,D Powell **Bred** S And S Hubbard Rodwell **Trained** Lambourn, Berks

FOCUS
A good-looking handicap featuring a number of unexposed sorts, and it was run at a strong pace. The form is rated positively with the fourth to his two-year-old form.

NOTEBOOK
Huzzah(IRE), whose Newbury win had been given a boost by the subsequent success of the third and good run of the fourth, looked fairly weighted on a 7lb higher mark. Always well placed to strike in a race in which the leaders went off too quick, he coped well with the quicker conditions, but he was looking for the line somewhat at the end. The Britannia would be the natural target, but he will be rated close to 100 after this and connections could well take their chance in the furlong shorter Jersey Stakes instead. He is certainly progressing well. (op 8-1)

Fervent Prince, who finally got off the mark at Kempton last time, was 1lb wrong at the weights. Given a good waiting ride and sticking to the rail for much of the race, he had to be given a few reminders turning into the straight. He hung left once in line for home but ran on strongly at the finish and almost got up. He is not an easy ride but is talented.

Wasan, unbeaten in his previous two starts, was raised 14lb for his Nottingham win last month. Poorly drawn, he was forced to race two or three off the fence for much of the race and challenged wide in the straight. He ran much better than his finishing position suggests, and he should be able to win a similar race off this sort of mark. (op 7-1)

Boy Blue got himself a good stalking position and was well enough placed turning into the straight if good enough, but he could only keep on one-paced. This was still a big step up on his seasonal reappearance, though. (op 20-1)

Adversity can be rated better than his finishing position as he had the worst draw of all, was held up in last place for much of the race, was still one of the backmarkers entering the straight and did not enjoy the clearest of runs in the closing stages. Lightly raced, he looks capable of defying his current mark. (op 6-1)

Toto Skyllachy did not have the early pace to make use of his low draw, and he ended up racing in rear for much of the race. Still in last place rounding the turn into the straight, he kept on well to be never nearer than at the finish, but perhaps conditions were on the quick side for him. (tchd 10-1)

Elna Bright did not really build on his promising return to action on Polytrack, but not all horses handle this unique track and he should not be written off on the back of this modest effort. (op 14-1)

Royalist(IRE), all the rage having been as big as 5-1 for pennies with some bookmakers in the morning, looked to have been let in lightly off a mark of 85 following his easy maiden win at Doncaster. Ideally drawn to make all the running, he set out to do just that, but strangely he was taken on for the lead by a rival in his owner's second colours. Setting too strong a gallop, he gave himself little chance of getting home, and this run just has to be written off. (op 5-2)

Magnitude got a bump from the eventual runner-up at the point where the false rail came to an end, and he struggled to regain his momentum afterwards. Not beaten up in a lost cause, he should not be given up on. (op 9-1)

Green Wadi, who raced in rear for much of the race, was switched widest of all rounding the bend into the straight and could not muster the pace to challenge. (op 14-1 tchd 9-1)

Eastern Gift always seems to weaken at the end of his races, and a drop back to sprint distances might help. (op 33-1 tchd 20-1)

Ramatni, running beyond a sprint distance for the first time, took on the favourite, who wore his owner's first colours, at the head of affairs. He shaped like a non-stayer even allowing for the strong pace he went.

1924 BOODLES DIAMOND E B F MAIDEN STKS 5f 16y

4:00 (4:01) (Class 2) 2-Y-0 **£8,418** (£2,505; £1,251; £625) **Stalls** Low

Form RPR

2 1 **Rebecca De Winter**[6] 1762 2-8-12 0 ..... RyanMoore 5 83
(R Hannon) *a.p: led over 1f out: rdn and qcknd away ins fnl f: r.o wl* **11/4**[2]

2 2 1/2 **Viva Ronaldo (IRE)** 2-9-3 0 ..... PaulHanagan 9 79+
(R A Fahey) *racd keenly: chsd ldrs: rdn whn n.m.r over 1f out: kpt on to take 2nd ins fnl f: nt pce of wnr* **20/1**

3 2 1/2 **Fivefootnumberone (IRE)** 2-9-3 0 ..... JimmyFortune 2 70+
(J J Quinn) *w'llike: lengthy: b.bkwd: racd keenly: hld up: nt clr run over 2f out: hdwy ent fnl f: styd on: nt pce to chal* **12/1**

5 4 nse **Senatorial**[22] 1399 2-9-3 0 ..... MichaelHills 8 70+
(B W Hills) *missed break: forced wd after 1f: hdwy over 3f out: pushed along on outside to press ldrs 2f out: rdn and hung lft fr over 1f out: one pce ins fnl f* **9/4**[1]

5 3/4 **Rievaulx World** 2-9-3 0 ..... NCallan 1 67+
(K A Ryan) *str: lw: chsd ldrs: rdn 1f out: sn edgd lft: no ex ins fnl f* **6/1**[3]

2 6 5 **Musical Bridge**[29] 1263 2-9-3 0 ..... TolleyDean 3 49+
(Mrs L Williamson) *racd keenly in midfield: n.m.r and hmpd over 3f out: sn rdn and lost pl: n.d after* **11/4**[2]

6 7 1/2 **Neo's Mate (IRE)**[12] 1610 2-8-12 0 ..... AndrewHeffernan 4 42
(Paul Green) *racd keenly: led: rdn and hdd over 1f out: wknd fnl f* **33/1**

0 8 10 **Premier Demon (IRE)**[10] 1680 2-8-12 0 ..... TGMcLaughlin 6 6
(P D Evans) *chsd ldrs: lost pl after 1f: sn outpcd* **66/1**

55 9 4 1/2 **Crewezando**[6] 1778 2-9-3 0 ..... (v1) JohnEgan 7 —
(P D Evans) *w'like: hld up: rdn and outpcd over 2f out* **25/1**

62.52 secs (1.52) **Going Correction** +0.10s/f (Good) **9** Ran SP% **119.1**
Speed ratings (Par 99): **91,87,83,82,81 73,72,56,49**
CSF £59.32 TOTE £3.90: £1.50, £3.20, £2.10; EX 85.70.

Owner Mrs J Wood **Bred** B W Hills & Cavendish Investing Ltd **Trained** East Everleigh, Wilts

FOCUS
A fair maiden that has produced subsequent Group winners in the last two years and this could be better than the average renewal.

NOTEBOOK
Rebecca De Winter, who shaped with plenty of promise on her debut at Lingfield, looked thoroughly professional here and got the job done in good style. She is all speed and could now head to Beverley for the Hilary Needler, or Sandown for the National Stakes, before taking in the Weatherbys' Super Sprint at Newbury. (op 7-2)

Viva Ronaldo(IRE), a half-brother to Kristensen, a multiple winner between 1m4f and 1m6f, is an athletic sort and has a lot more pace than him thanks to his sire Xaar. Wide but never far off the pace, he did not enjoy the best of runs early in the straight and in the circumstances there was plenty to like about his finishing effort behind the more experienced winner. He should have no trouble winning a similar event. (op 14-1)

Fivefootnumberone(IRE), whose dam was fourth in the Phoenix Stakes at two and won over 7f at three, chased the pace and kept on well to take third close home. He is bred for speed and, with this experience under his belt, will be dangerous in similar company next time. (op 9-1)

Senatorial, who shaped with promise in a decent event at Newmarket on his debut, was forced to race wide and hung left in the straight. There was no clear improvement here, but he did not get the best of trips and another furlong will suit him in time. (tchd 5-2 and 11-4)

Rievaulx World, bred to be sharp, showed good early dash but was a bit keen. He did not get home but will have learnt plenty. (op 5-1 tchd 13-2 and 7-1 in a place)

Musical Bridge, only narrowly denied on his debut at Bath, had more to do here and ruined his chance by failing to settle in the early stages. (op 4-1)

1925 CRUISE H'CAP 6f 18y
4:35 (4:37) (Class 3) (0-90,87) 3-Y-O £10,361 (£3,083; £1,540; £769) Stalls Low

Form RPR

06-0 **1** **Not My Choice (IRE)**[19] 1484 3-8-8 77 .... JohnEgan 2 89
(S Parr) *mde all: rdn and dashed away over 1f out: r.o* **6/1**[3]

2152 **2** 1 ½ **Fathsta (IRE)**[4] 1837 3-9-2 85 .... LPKeniry 11 96+
(S Kirk) *lw: racd keenly: hld up: rdn over 1f out: hdwy ent fnl f: sn edgd lft: r.o and gaining towards fin: tk 2nd post* **8/1**

43-0 **3** hd **Good Gorsoon (USA)**[13] 1597 3-9-0 83 .... MichaelHills 3 90
(B W Hills) *racd keenly: in tch: rdn to chse wnr ins fnl f: sn edgd lft: lost 2nd post* **10/3**[1]

10- **4** 1 ¾ **Legal Eagle (IRE)**[261] 4695 3-9-0 83 .... JimmyFortune 6 84
(J H M Gosden) *b.hind: trckd ldrs: rdn to chse wnr over 1f out tl ins fnl f: no ex towards fin* **7/2**[2]

5-30 **5** ¾ **Silver Wind**[4] 1837 3-9-4 87 ....(v) TGMcLaughlin 5 86
(P D Evans) *midfield: lost pl over 2f out: bmpd sltly over 1f out: kpt on wout troubling ldrs ins fnl f* **9/1**

04-0 **6** 2 ¾ **Irving Place**[21] 1426 3-8-9 78 .... PaulHanagan 7 68
(R A Fahey) *lw: midfield: effrt 2f out: no real imp: wknd jst over 1f out* **15/2**

10-0 **7** 1 **Peter's Storm (USA)**[14] 1576 3-8-5 74 .... DO'Donohoe 4 61
(K A Ryan) *prom: pushed along over 3f out: edgd lft wl over 2f out: wknd ent fnl f* **16/1**

160- **8** nk **Danzig Fox**[223] 5773 3-8-5 74 .... TWilliams 13 60
(M Mullineaux) *dwlt: bhd: rdn over 1f out: nvr able to trble ldrs* **50/1**

10- **9** shd **Pearl Dealer (IRE)**[207] 6201 3-8-11 80 .... SamHitchcott 8 65
(N J Vaughan) *s.i.s: racd keenly: hld up: pushed along over 2f out: wnt rt over 1f out: no imp* **33/1**

305- **10** 1 ¾ **Sweet Kiss (USA)**[218] 5910 3-9-0 83 ....(b[1]) TedDurcan 10 63
(B J Meehan) *dwlt: a bhd* **14/1**

6-00 **11** nk **Bespoke Boy**[12] 1623 3-8-13 82 ....(t) LeeEnstone 9 61
(P C Haslam) *racd keenly: hld up: rdn over 2f out: nvr on terms* **16/1**

-323 **12** 2 **The Game**[9] 1707 3-9-0 83 .... KerrinMcEvoy 1 55
(J R Boyle) *broke wl: prom: n.m.r wl over 2f out: rdn and wknd over 1f out* **15/2**

1m 15.13s (1.33) **Going Correction** +0.10s/f (Good) **12** Ran SP% **127.6**
Speed ratings (Par 103): **95,93,92,90,89 85,84,84,83,81 81,78**
CSF £57.88 CT £196.59 TOTE £7.60: £2.20, £3.20, £1.90; EX 67.40 Place 6 £196.73, Place 5 £84.78.
Owner David Kilpatrick **Bred** Alan Dargan **Trained** Bawtry, S Yorks

FOCUS
A competitive sprint handicap on paper, but Not My Choice dominated from the outset under a fine ride from Egan. The third is the best guide to the level.

NOTEBOOK
Not My Choice(IRE), whose only previous win had come at the course last September, was just 1lb higher here and representing a yard already in winning form at the meeting. He had looked a non-stayer on his one try at the distance as a juvenile, but had an ideal draw in stall two and looked almost certain to have come on for his recent Thirsk reppearance. A son of Choisir, there was also a good chance he had strengthened over the winter and, having quickly bagged the rail, he had a chance to steal a march on the other fancied runners. Few ride Chester better than Egan and he sent the three-year-old into a clear lead rounding the final bend. Although tiring a little towards the finish, the hard work had been done and he was always doing enough. This was his big day. (op 7-1 tchd 11-2)
Fathsta(IRE), who got going too late at Salisbury the other day, was 1lb lower here and much depended on how he was going to overcome his wide draw. He had to be dropped in and found himself with too much running to do off the final bend, once again hit top stride too late in the day. He is a progressive sprinter and things look sure to fall his way again before long. (tchd 13-2)
Good Gorsoon(USA), unlucky not to get much closer to potentially high-class sprinter Corrybrough at Sandown the other day, getting repeatedly hampered, is a hold-up performer and was always going to require some luck around here. He got a fairly trouble-free passage, but the winner had flown by the time they straightened up and he was run out of second close home. He deserves to find a race. (tchd 3-1 and 4-1)
Legal Eagle(IRE), well beaten off a 5lb higher mark on his handicap debut last August, showed plenty of early toe and tried to go after the winner off the final bend, but could find no more and got a little tired. This run should bring him on and perhaps a return to slower ground will help (won his maiden in heavy). (op 5-1 tchd 11-2)
Silver Wind, behind Fathsta at Salisbury, managed to close the gap and was a shade unlucky not to finish even closer. He has yet to win a handicap though and is going to remain vulnerable off this sort of mark. Perhaps a return to 7f would help. (op 10-1)
Peter's Storm(USA) showed good early speed, but was outpaced when the winner upped the tempo and ultimately faded.
The Game, who has been proving consistent in All-Weather handicaps, seemed to have the best of the draw and he obtained a good early sit. However, he found himself a bit squeezed for room when the winner was beginning to kick and in the end dropped right out. (op 6-1 tchd 8-1)
T/Jkpt: Not won. T/Plt: £116.20 to a £1 stake. Pool: £135,872.20. 853.16 winning tickets. T/Qpdt: £17.90 to a £1 stake. Pool: £6,251.47. 257.35 winning tickets. DO

[1799]GOODWOOD (R-H)
Thursday, May 8

OFFICIAL GOING: Straight course - good; round course - good to firm (good in places; 8.5)
Wind: Moderate, across

1926 PIONEERPOINT MAIDEN STKS 1m
2:00 (2:04) (Class 5) 3-Y-O+ £3,238 (£963; £481; £240) Stalls High

Form RPR

0 **1** **Kelowna (IRE)**[21] 1423 3-8-9 0 .... TPQueally 16 83+
(J L Dunlop) *hld up in tch: n.m.r 2f out: swtchd lft and smooth hdwy over 1f out to ld ins fnl f: comf* **40/1**

0- **2** 1 **Resurge (IRE)**[216] 5977 3-9-0 0 .... ShaneKelly 11 86
(J Noseda) *t.k.h early: chsd ldrs: drvn and qcknd to chal 1f out: styd on ins fnl f but nt pce of wnr* **6/1**[3]

35-2 **3** 1 **Military Power**[19] 1490 3-9-0 83 .... EddieAhern 13 84
(J W Hills) *chsd ldrs: rdn to take slt ld 1f out: hdd sn after and kpt on same pce* **6/1**[3]

0 **4** 1 ½ **Mohathab (IRE)**[19] 1467 3-9-0 0 .... MartinDwyer 10 80
(J H M Gosden) *chsd ldrs: led appr fnl 2f: rdn and hdd 1f out: wknd ins fnl f* **28/1**

0 **5** 2 ½ **Capucci**[15] 1573 3-9-0 0 .... RobertHavlin 14 75
(J H M Gosden) *led tl hdd appr fnl 2f: styd chsng ldrs tl wknd ins fnl f* **66/1**

24- **6** 1 ½ **Red Icon**[222] 5812 3-8-9 0 .... JamesDoyle 4 66+
(R M Beckett) *hld up towards rr: hdwy and n.m.r 2f out: styd on wl fnl f but nt rch ldrs* **25/1**

4- **7** hd **Dear Maurice**[262] 4666 4-9-13 0 .... SteveDrowne 7 74
(E A L Dunlop) *towards rr: hdwy over 2f out: styd on fnl f but nvr in contention* **25/1**

3 **8** nk **Crown Choice**[21] 1417 3-9-0 0 .... SaleemGolam 9 70
(W R Swinburn) *in tch: hdwy fr 3f out: drvn to chse ldrs and swtchd rt ins fnl 2f: no imp and wknd ins fnl f* **5/1**[2]

0 **9** 5 **Quinzey's Best (IRE)**[18] 1504 3-8-9 0 .... RichardKingscote 8 53
(W J Knight) *t.k.h: in rr: mod prog fnl 2f* **100/1**

4- **10** nse **Rum Jungle**[206] 6238 4-9-13 0 .... DaneO'Neill 2 61+
(H Candy) *a towards rr* **20/1**

5-2 **11** 3 ¼ **French Art**[19] 1467 3-9-0 0 .... SebSanders 6 51
(D R C Elsworth) *chsd ldrs: rdn over 2f out and sn btn* **11/8**[1]

0- **12** 2 ¾ **Colour Trooper (IRE)**[251] 5010 3-9-0 0 .... JimCrowley 12 44
(P Winkworth) *in tch: rdn 3f out: wknd over 2f out* **20/1**

13 1 ¼ **Schopenhauer (USA)** 3-9-0 0 .... PatCosgrave 1 42
(L M Cumani) *a towards rr* **12/1**

0-6 **14** ¾ **Kannon**[16] 1535 3-8-9 0 .... PaulDoe 5 35
(W J Knight) *slowly away: a in rr* **80/1**

0 **15** shd **Grit (IRE)**[19] 1467 3-9-0 0 .... EdwardCreighton 3 40
(M R Channon) *a in rr* **100/1**

0 **16** ¾ **Deep Waters (IRE)**[17] 1526 3-9-0 0 .... IanMongan 15 38
(S Dow) *slowly away: a bhd* **100/1**

1m 39.55s (-0.35) **Going Correction** +0.05s/f (Good)
WFA 3 from 4yo 13lb **16** Ran SP% **123.8**
Speed ratings (Par 103): **103,102,101,99,97 95,95,95,90,89 86,83,82,81,81 81**
CSF £253.62 TOTE £77.30: £12.10, £2.20, £2.00; EX 700.20.
Owner Capt J Macdonald-Buchanan **Bred** The Lavington Stud **Trained** Arundel, W Sussex

FOCUS
A fair maiden run at an ordinary pace and best rated through the third. There were five in a line early in the final furlong and not many got into the race from the rear.
French Art Official explanation: trainer said colt was unsuited by the good (good to firm places) ground

1927 EMPIRE PROPERTY GROUP INTERNATIONAL CONDITIONS STKS 5f
2:30 (2:31) (Class 2) 2-Y-O £9,346 (£2,799; £1,399; £700) Stalls Low

Form RPR

01 **1** **Icesolator (IRE)**[5] 1804 2-8-12 0 .... PatDobbs 4 91
(R Hannon) *trckd ldr: led over 1f out: drvn and hld on wl whn chal thrght fnl f* **5/2**[3]

41 **2** ½ **Smokey Storm**[11] 1640 2-9-1 0 .... AlanMunro 5 92
(W Jarvis) *trckd ldrs: pushed along 1/2-way: styd on to press wnr fnl f but a jst hld* **2/1**[2]

1 **3** 2 ½ **Doughnut**[37] 1122 2-8-10 0 .... RichardHughes 3 78
(R Hannon) *hld up in cl 4th: shkn up and impr on rails over 1f out: sn drvn and nvr quite gng pce to chal: wknd cl home* **6/4**[1]

3 **4** 1 **Mazzola**[9] 1693 2-8-12 0 .... EdwardCreighton 2 76
(M R Channon) *led tl hdd over 1f out: wknd ins fnl f* **12/1**

58.74 secs (0.34) **Going Correction** -0.05s/f (Good) **4** Ran SP% **109.6**
Speed ratings (Par 99): **95,94,90,88**
CSF £7.87 TOTE £3.60; EX 7.50.
Owner B Bull **Bred** Pier House Stud **Trained** East Everleigh, Wilts

FOCUS
An interesting conditions race in which the front three were close to their pre-race marks.

NOTEBOOK
Icesolator(IRE) made all in a maiden over course and distance five days earlier and he followed up on this slightly faster surface. Showing ahead with over a furlong to run, his head carriage was a little awkward but he found enough to hold off the runner-up's persistent challenge. (op 2-1 tchd 7-4 and 3-1 i n places)
Smokey Storm, conceding weight all round under the penalty for his Brighton win, challenged Icesolator with a furlong to run and tried hard, but could not get past. Both he and the winner are sons of first-season sire One Cool Cat. (op 9-4 tchd 11-4)
Doughnut, successful in a Folkestone maiden on her debut, is a stablemate of the winner and looked the first string on jockey bookings. Held up, she was switched to the rails and found herself momentarily short of room when attempting to improve, but she lacked the required turn of foot in any case. (op 2-1)
Mazzola, upped in class for this second start, was found wanting after making the running. (op 10-1 tchd 9-1)

1928 NOVOCAPITAL STKS (H'CAP) 6f
3:00 (3:04) (Class 4) (0-80,80) 4-Y-O+ £4,533 (£1,348; £674; £336) Stalls Low

Form RPR

45-5 **1** **Seamus Shindig**[10] 1683 6-8-7 76 .... AmyScott[(7)] 2 85
(H Candy) *hld up toward rr: stl plenty to do over 1f out: shkn up and str run ins fnl f: qcknd to ld last strides: cosily* **12/1**

3-23 **2** nk **North South Divide (IRE)**[25] 1344 4-8-11 73 ....(p) DaneO'Neill 13 81
(R A Teal) *s.i.s: rr: hdwy fr 2f out: drvn to ld ins fnl f: styd on wl: ct last strides* **14/1**

2122 **3** nk **Savile's Delight (IRE)**[5] 1800 9-8-11 73 .... RichardKingscote 14 80
(Tom Dascombe) *mid-div: rdn and hdwy over 1f out: styd on to press ldr wl ins fnl f: no ex cl home* **4/1**[1]

5046 **4** ½ **Resplendent Alpha**[36] 1146 4-8-10 72 .... ShaneKelly 11 77
(P Howling) *in rr: stl plenty to do over 2f out: styd on wl fnl f but nvr quite gng pce to chal* **12/1**

00-0 **5** ½ **Mason Ette**[5] 1800 4-9-1 77 ....(b[1]) EddieAhern 15 81
(C G Cox) *s.i.s: bhd: hdwy fr 2f out: styd on to chse ldrs ins fnl f but nvr quite gng pce to chal* **20/1**

40-0 **6** 1 **China Cherub**[126] 26 5-9-1 77 ....(b) FergusSweeney 12 78
(S Dow) *led: rdn 2f out: hdd ins fnl f: sn wknd* **25/1**

15-1 **7** ¾ **Vintage (IRE)**[16] 1541 4-8-6 68 .... IanMongan 10 66
(J Akehurst) *s.i.s: rdn 1/2-way: styd wl there tl wknd ins fnl f* **15/2**[2]

4002 **8** nse **Lucayos**[10] 1683 5-8-7 76 .... KylieManser[(7)] 5 74
(Mrs H Sweeting) *chsd ldrs: rdn over 2f out: wknd fnl f* **12/1**

0-00 **9** 1 **Forest Dane**[18] 1500 8-8-9 78 .... SophieDoyle[(7)] 9 73
(Mrs N Smith) *in rr: hdwy fr 2f out: kpt on ins fnl f but nvr gng pce to be competitive* **16/1**

44-4 **10** nk **Dingaan (IRE)**[5] 1800 5-9-1 80 ....(p) WilliamBuick[(3)] 1 74
(A M Balding) *sn outpcd in rr: drvn 1/2-way: styd on fr over 1f out but nvr gng pce to be competitive* **4/1**[1]

20-0 **11** ½ **Gwilym (GER)**[17] 1522 5-8-5 72 .... AshleyHamblett[(5)] 4 64
(D Haydn Jones) *chsd ldrs: rdn 1/2-way: wknd qckly fnl f* **14/1**

340- **12** 2 **Pic Up Sticks**[198] 6405 9-8-9 71 .... TQuinn 3 57
(B G Powell) *chsd ldrs: rdn over 2f out: wknd qckly fnl f* **16/1**

The Form Book, Raceform Ltd, Compton, RG20 6NL

-006 13 ½ **Our Blessing (IRE)**[18] 1500 4-8-9 71 ...(v) SteveDrowne 7 55
(A P Jarvis) in tch: chsd ldrs and rdn 1/2-way: wknd over 1f out 33/1

1-06 14 nse **Tudor Prince (IRE)**[12] 1617 4-9-0 79 LukeMorris(3) 6 63
(A W Carroll) a outpcd 10/1[3]

1335 15 44 **Mogok Ruby**[83] 574 4-9-4 80 RichardHughes 8 —
(L Montague Hall) sn bhd: t.o fnl 2f: b.b.v 16/1

1m 11.12s (-1.08) **Going Correction** -0.05s/f (Good) 15 Ran SP% **126.5**
Speed ratings (Par 105): **105,104,104,103,102 101,100,100,99,98 98,95,94,94,36**
CSF £173.49 CT £824.04 TOTE £15.10: £4.00, £5.10, £1.70; EX 280.50.
Owner Henry Candy **Bred** R S A Urquhart **Trained** Kingston Warren, Oxon

FOCUS
A fair sprint handicap in which the winner defied a low draw, but otherwise those drawn high were to the fore. the form looks straightforward rated around the fourth and fifth.
Mogok Ruby Official explanation: jockey said gelding bled from the nose

1929 GATEWAY PROJECT SERVICES STKS (H'CAP) 1m 3f
3:35 (3:35) (Class 5) (0-70,69) 4-Y-O+ £3,238 (£963; £481; £240) Stalls Low

Form RPR

54-2 1 **Dove Cottage (IRE)**[23] 1388 6-9-4 69 FergusSweeney 10 83
(W S Kittow) led 1f: styd in 2nd and 8l clr of chsng gp: led over 3f out: drvn along over 2f out and nvr in any danger after 9/2[2]

36-0 2 4½ **Kokkokila**[15] 1564 4-8-5 59 KirstyMilczarek(3) 7 65
(Lady Herries) in rr: hdwy fr 4f out: styd on to chse clr wnr over 2f out: nvr any ch but a wl clr of 3rd 18/1

5351 3 4 **Wait For The Will (USA)**[22] 1405 12-8-8 66 ...(b) JemmaMarshall(7) 13 65
(G L Moore) hld up in rr: hdwy 4f out: styd on to take wl hld 3rd over 1f out 10/1

43-5 4 2¼ **Lapina (IRE)**[37] 1127 4-8-12 63 ...(b) ShaneKelly 8 58
(Pat Eddery) in rr: rdn and kpt on fr 3f out: hung rt whn styng on for mod 4th fr over 1f out 12/1

0/45 5 2¾ **Songmaster (USA)**[35] 1172 5-9-1 66 EddieAhern 6 57
(A King) chsd clr ldng duo: rdn over 3f out and no imp: wknd 2f out 11/2

1-01 6 4 **Royal Premier (IRE)**[10] 1692 5-8-10 64 6ex JerryO'Dwyer(3) 11 48
(H J Collingridge) in chsng gp bhd clr ldng duo: rdn and outpcd 6f out: mod prog u.p 4f out: nvr in contention after 11/4[1]

00 7 3 **Ambitious Genes (IRE)**[47] 963 4-9-0 65 TQuinn 4 44
(J W Hills) bhd: rdn 4f out: nvr in contention 20/1

3525 8 9 **Most Definitely (IRE)**[23] 1388 8-9-0 65 JamesDoyle 1 29
(R M Stronge) nvr bttr than mid-div: no ch fr over 3f out 12/1

6-30 9 1 **General Flumpa**[28] 1281 7-8-5 56 MartinDwyer 3 18
(Miss Tor Sturgis) led after 1f and sn 8l clr of 3rd: faltered 6f out: hdd over 3f out: sn wknd 18/1

-002 10 10 **One To Follow**[35] 1165 4-9-0 65 SteveDrowne 9 10
(C G Cox) sn bhd 5/1[3]

060- 11 6 **Silver Surprise**[132] 7256 4-8-5 56 oh10 ow1 NeilChalmers 12 —
(J J Bridger) chsd ldrs: rdn 4f out: wknd 3f out 66/1

2m 27.37s (-0.93) **Going Correction** +0.05s/f (Good) 11 Ran SP% **118.2**
Speed ratings (Par 103): **105,101,98,97,95 92,90,83,82,75 71**
CSF £82.75 CT £777.03 TOTE £5.10: £2.10, £4.10, £2.70; EX 96.40.
Owner Reg Gifford **Bred** D R Tucker **Trained** Blackborough, Devon

FOCUS
A moderate handicap in which two soon went clear, including the eventual winner. Nothing else really got involved and the form is rated at face value.
One To Follow Official explanation: jockey said gelding slipped on first bend

1930 EMPIRE PROPERTY GROUP INTERNATIONAL FILLIES' STKS (H'CAP) 1m
4:10 (4:10) (Class 4) (0-85,82) 3-Y-O £4,533 (£1,348; £674; £336) Stalls High

Form RPR

262 1 **Mekong Melody (IRE)**[17] 1525 3-8-9 73 EddieAhern 1 77+
(C G Cox) hld up in tch: swtchd rt to ins over 1f out and drvn to chal ins fnl f: led fnl 75yds: hld on wl 11/2[3]

221- 2 hd **Badalona**[222] 5811 3-9-2 80 HayleyTurner 9 84
(M L W Bell) led after 2f: rdn over 2f out: kpt advantage u.p tl hdd fnl 75yds: no ex cl home 7/2[1]

04-4 3 2½ **Geestring (IRE)**[21] 1412 3-8-10 74 RichardHughes 11 72
(R Hannon) sn trcking ldrs: rdn and effrt fr 2f out: nvr quite gng pce to chal: outpcd ins fnl f 5/1[2]

062- 4 1 **Marraasi (USA)**[173] 6849 3-8-6 70 DaleGibson 6 66+
(M P Tregoning) slt ld tl hdd after 2f: rdn to chal 3f out: one pce fr 2f out: wknd fnl 100yds 16/1

00-1 5 ½ **Binfield (IRE)**[29] 1271 3-8-10 74 TQuinn 7 69
(B G Powell) chsd ldrs: rdn over 3f out: effrt fr over 2f out: nvr gng pce to chal: wknd ins fnl f 8/1

4-00 6 ¾ **Lady Sorcerer**[26] 1336 3-8-5 72 WilliamBuick(3) 3 65
(A P Jarvis) w ldr 2f: styd front rnk: rdn fr 3f out: styd on same pce fnl 2f 11/1

10-0 7 1 **Dusty Moon**[17] 1524 3-9-4 82 PaulDoe 10 73
(W J Knight) stdd rr after 2f: sme prog 3f out: nvr in contention and no ch fnl 2f 14/1

01- 8 3 **Albaraari**[227] 5682 3-8-10 74 MartinDwyer 4 58
(Sir Michael Stoute) hld up in rr: pushed along 3f out: no rspnse 7/2[1]

51- 9 3¾ **Al Aqabah (IRE)**[186] 6664 3-8-11 75 GregFairley 5 50
(B Gubby) t.k.h: chsd ldrs to 3f out 11/1

1-60 10 nk **Miss Phoebe (IRE)**[10] 1685 3-8-8 72 RichardKingscote 2 47
(S Kirk) a towards rr 33/1

1m 41.19s (1.29) **Going Correction** +0.05s/f (Good) 10 Ran SP% **119.8**
Speed ratings (Par 98): **95,94,92,91,90 90,89,86,82,82**
CSF £25.84 CT £106.82 TOTE £7.60: £1.90, £1.70, £1.80; EX 31.00.
Owner Miss Bridgette Egan **Bred** David C Egan **Trained** Lambourn, Berks
■ Stewards' Enquiry : Hayley Turner two-day ban: used whip in incorrect place (May 22-23)

FOCUS
An informative affair featuring some unexposed fillies. The pace was only steady though, and several were too keen for their own good, so the form is pretty muddling.

1931 WEDLAKE BELL MAIDEN STKS 1m 4f
4:45 (4:45) (Class 5) 3-Y-O+ £3,238 (£963; £481; £240) Stalls Low

Form RPR

44-6 1 **Savarain**[22] 1398 3-8-9 83 DaneO'Neill 7 94+
(L M Cumani) in tch: hdwy and n.m.r over 2f out: hrd drvn and qcknd 1f out to ld fnl 110yds: hld on wl 11/4[2]

0-5 2 ¾ **Dalhaan (USA)**[20] 1446 3-8-9 0 SteveDrowne 6 91+
(J L Dunlop) trckd ldrs: n.m.r and lost position over 2f out: hdwy and swtchd lft over 1f out: edgd lft and r.o strly wl ins fnl f to take 2nd cl home but nt rch wnr 28/1

2- 3 ¾ **Sortita (GER)**[202] 6294 3-8-4 0 MartinDwyer 2 83
(M A Jarvis) t.k.h and hdwy to trck ldrs after 3f: qcknd to ld appr fnl 2f: sn rdn: hdd and no ex fnl 110yds 13/8[1]

5-2 4 ½ **Manyriverstocross (IRE)**[20] 1446 3-8-9 0 EddieAhern 5 87
(A King) chsd ldrs: rdn to disp 2nd over 2f out: kpt on same pce thrght fnl f 7/2[3]

32-2 5 7 **Nemo Spirit (IRE)**[12] 1615 3-8-9 85 RichardHughes 4 76
(W R Muir) chsd ldrs: wnt 2nd 7f out: rdn over 3f out and pressed wnr sn after: wknd fnl f 6/1

6 nk **Cyborg**[63] 4-10-0 0 TQuinn 3 77
(D R C Elsworth) in rr: hdwy and nt clr run whn trying to cl on ldrs over 2f out: wknd over 1f out 14/1

6-2 7 12 **Everybody Knows**[15] 1563 3-8-9 0 TPQueally 9 56
(M L W Bell) plld hrd early: led: hdd over 2f out and sn wknd 33/1

0 8 10 **Arthurian (IRE)**[16] 1539 3-8-9 0 ...(b) IanMongan 1 40
(J Jay) bhd fnl 5f 100/1

0 9 5 **Black Cloud**[16] 1539 5-9-7 0 HarryPoulton(7) 8 32
(A Ennis) bhd fnl 5f 100/1

2m 38.53s (0.13) **Going Correction** +0.05s/f (Good)
WFA 3 from 4yo+ 19lb 9 Ran SP% **116.3**
Speed ratings (Par 103): **101,100,100,99,95 94,86,80,76**
CSF £75.55 TOTE £3.50: £1.20, £3.10, £1.50; EX 99.70.
Owner Ronchalon Racing (UK) Ltd **Bred** Fittocks Stud **Trained** Newmarket, Suffolk

FOCUS
An above-average maiden, featuring three Derby entries and an Oaks entry. It was unfortunately run at a very steady pace, but the four horses who finished clear of the rest all look to be going places. The fourth is rated to its previous mark backed up by the third.
Nemo Spirit(IRE) Official explanation: trainer said colt was unsuited by the good (good to firm) ground

1932 EMPIRE SCHIZOPHRENIA TRUST STKS (H'CAP) 1m 1f
5:20 (5:23) (Class 5) (0-70,70) 4-Y-O+
£3,115 (£933; £466; £233; £116; £58) Stalls High

Form RPR

5-04 1 **Davenport (IRE)**[16] 1532 6-9-4 70 AlanMunro 3 79
(B R Millman) in tch: hdwy fr 3f out: drvn and qcknd to ld fnl 110yds: styd on strly 9/1

3601 2 1 **Aphrodisia**[11] 1644 4-9-0 66 6ex EddieAhern 4 73
(S C Williams) trckd ldrs: qcknd to ld over 1f out: hdd and outpcd fnl 110yds 6/1[2]

50-0 3 ¾ **Willow Dancer (IRE)**[23] 1383 4-8-13 65 SaleemGolam 13 70
(W R Swinburn) in tch: hdwy 3f out: drvn and styd on to chal ins fnl f: no ex cl home 11/1

006- 4 1¾ **Sky Quest (IRE)**[189] 6603 10-9-1 67 AmirQuinn 14 69+
(J R Boyle) mid-div: hdwy over 3f out: styd on fr over 1f out but nvr gng pce to rch ldrs 9/1

260- 5 hd **African Pursuits (USA)**[138] 7224 4-8-12 64 SteveDrowne 6 65
(H Morrison) led tl hdd over 3f out: led again over 2f out: hdd over 1f out: wknd ins fnl f 14/1

5352 6 1¾ **Megalala (IRE)**[11] 1644 7-8-6 58 NeilChalmers 12 55
(J J Bridger) in rr: hdwy on ins over 2f out but nvr gng pce to be competitive 16/1

3443 7 2 **Putra Laju (IRE)**[19] 1486 4-8-4 56 oh2 ...(p) HayleyTurner 16 49
(J W Hills) in rr: sme prog on ins fr over 2f out but n.m.r and nvr in contention 14/1

320- 8 hd **Cormorant Wharf (IRE)**[264] 4597 8-9-3 69 JimCrowley 10 61+
(T E Powell) in rr: sme hdwy and nt clr run over 2f out and over 1f out: nt rcvr but kpt on 20/1

100- 9 nk **Brave Quest (IRE)**[188] 6623 4-8-11 63 IanMongan 9 55
(Mrs L J Mongan) chsd ldrs: rdn and edgd lft over 2f out: sn btn 33/1

-210 10 1 **Tinnarinka**[26] 1329 4-9-2 68 RichardHughes 8 58
(R Hannon) trckd ldrs: n.m.r 2f out: shkn up and wknd sn after 9/2[1]

2520 11 ¾ **Prince Charlemagne (IRE)**[23] 1388 5-8-13 65 ...(p) JamesDoyle 11 53
(R M Stronge) chsd ldrs: rdn 3f out: wknd 2f out 25/1

64 12 1½ **Artreju (GER)**[96] 406 5-9-1 67 DaneO'Neill 1 52
(G L Moore) a towards rr 16/1

0-25 13 1¾ **Gracechurch (IRE)**[11] 1644 5-8-5 57 MartinDwyer 7 47+
(R J Hodges) chsd ldrs: rdn 2f out: hmpd over 1f out: eased whn btn ins fnl f 8/1[3]

3443 14 nk **Binnion Bay (IRE)**[10] 1673 7-7-11 56 oh6 ...(b) RossAtkinson(7) 15 36
(J J Bridger) a in rr 14/1

203- 15 2½ **Jebel Ali (IRE)**[403] 870 5-9-4 70 ...(v) GregFairley 5 45
(B Gubby) t.k.h: chsd ldrs: led over 3f out tl over 2f out: wknd qckly 20/1

4236 16 3¾ **Waqaarr**[50] 938 4-8-2 57 WilliamBuick(3) 2 23
(Lady Herries) a in rr 10/1

1m 57.74s (1.44) **Going Correction** +0.05s/f (Good) 16 Ran SP% **129.1**
Speed ratings (Par 103): **95,94,93,91,91 90,88,88,87,87 86,85,83,83,81 77**
CSF £62.63 CT £651.49 TOTE £12.20: £2.00, £2.10, £3.40, £3.00; EX 78.60 Place 6 £313.44, Place 5 £94.79.
Owner M A Swift and A J Chapman **Bred** M P B Bloodstock Ltd **Trained** Kentisbeare, Devon

FOCUS
This looked a competitive heat beforehand, the field consisting entirely of fully exposed performers. Surprisingly, they went a fairly steady pace for the first half of the race, resulting in a messy and congested finish. Muddling form, despite the third and fifth running to their marks.
Tinnarinka Official explanation: jockey said filly moved poorly throughout
Gracechurch(IRE) Official explanation: jockey said gelding was unsuited by the good (good to firm places) ground
T/Plt: £557.50 to a £1 stake. Pool: £63,884.82. 83.65 winning tickets. T/Qpdt: £34.50 to a £1 stake. Pool: £3,716.88. 79.50 winning tickets. ST

1743 GREAT LEIGHS (A.W) (L-H)
Thursday, May 8

OFFICIAL GOING: Standard
Wind: Virtually nil Weather: Warm and sunny

1933 SMITHFIELD H'CAP 1m 6f (P)
5:40 (5:40) (Class 5) (0-70,70) 4-Y-O+ £2,590 (£770; £385; £192) Stalls Low

Form RPR

4413 1 **Wind Flow**[6] 1768 4-9-5 68 JimmyQuinn 5 78
(C A Dwyer) in tch: chsd ldr over 2f out: rdn to ld over 1f out: styd on wl 4/1[2]

5423 2 1½ **Leyte Gulf (USA)**[15] 1559 5-8-10 58 ChrisCatlin 6 66
(C C Bealby) s.i.s: hld up bhd: hdwy 4f out: chsd ldrs and rdn jst over 2f out: edgd lft ins fnl f: kpt on but nt pce to rch wnr 8/1

-012 **3** *2 ½* **Cavallini (USA)**[7] 1744 6-9-6 68 GeorgeBaker 9 72
(G L Moore) *s.i.s: hld up in tch in rr: hdwy 4f: rdn to chse ldrs over 2f out: hung lft 1f out: no imp fnl f* **15/8**[1]

5104 **4** *3 ¾* **My Mentor (IRE)**[14] 1589 4-9-4 67 SebSanders 7 66
(Sir Mark Prescott) *s.i.s: hdwy to chse ldr after 2f: led 3f out: sn rdn: hdd over 1f out: wknd jst ins fnl f: btn whn sltly hmpd wl ins fnl f* **5/1**[3]

0320 **5** *8* **Opera Writer (IRE)**[22] 1408 5-8-5 58 (p) JackMitchell(5) 1 46
(R Hollinshead) *chsd ldr for 2f: chsd ldrs after rdn over 3f out: wknd 2f out* **14/1**

-004 **6** *5* **Pearl (IRE)**[16] 1547 4-9-0 63 (p) RichardThomas 3 44
(I A Wood) *stdd after s: hld up in rr: rdn 4f out: sn struggling: no ch last 2f* **25/1**

00-5 **7** *1 ¾* **Sularno**[16] 1554 4-9-0 63 (b1) RobertHavlin 8 41
(H Morrison) *sn led: rdn and hdd 3f out: wknd over 2f: sn bhd* **25/1**

35-2 **8** *22* **Strong Survivor (USA)**[26] 1340 5-9-8 70 PatCosgrave 2 17
(P R Webber) *s.i.s: sn in tch in midfield: rdn wl over 5f out: wl bhd last 2f: eased fnl f: t.o* **5/1**[3]

3m 5.67s (2.47) **Going Correction** +0.25s/f (Slow)
WFA 4 from 5yo+ 1lb **8 Ran SP% 113.6**
Speed ratings (Par 103): **102,101,99,97,93 90,89,76**
CSF £35.09 CT £76.74 TOTE £4.10: £1.50, £1.70, £2.20; EX 58.20.
Owner Super Six Partnership **Bred** Lord Halifax **Trained** Burrough Green, Cambs
■ Stewards' Enquiry : Chris Catlin one-day ban: careless riding (May 22)

FOCUS
An ordinary staying handicap with little solid form to go on. The early pace was steady and things did not really pick up until past halfway.
Pearl(IRE) Official explanation: jockey said filly lost near-fore shoe
Strong Survivor(USA) Official explanation: jockey said gelding never travelled

1934 TOWER H'CAP 6f (P)
6:10 (6:11) (Class 4) (0-85,79) 3-Y-O **£4,533** (£1,348; £674; £336) **Stalls** Low

Form RPR
3142 **1** **Baunagain (IRE)**[28] 1277 3-9-3 78 PatCosgrave 4 84+
(M J Wallace) *s.i.s: in tch: trckd ldrs and nt clr run fr wl over 1f out: hit by rival's whip ins fnl f: gap opened wl ins fnl f: pushed along and qckrd to ld nr fin* **11/4**[2]

0-13 **2** *½* **Sparton Duke (IRE)**[90] 489 3-9-4 79 (p) ChrisCatlin 6 83
(K A Ryan) *prom: chsd ldr over 4f out: rdn and ev ch jst over 2f out: led ins fnl f: hdd and no ex nr fin* **13/2**

1012 **3** *nk* **Loose Caboose (IRE)**[6] 1764 3-9-0 75 (p) SebSanders 3 78
(A J McCabe) *led: rdn over 2f out: hdd ins fnl f: no ex last 50yds* **9/4**[1]

2234 **4** *3 ¼* **Valhillen**[14] 1584 3-8-6 72 JackMitchell(5) 1 65
(M D I Usher) *chsd ldrs on inner: rdn 2f out: wknd jst over 1f out* **10/1**

043- **5** *nk* **Arabian Spirit**[192] 6530 3-9-0 75 StephenDonohoe 2 67
(E A L Dunlop) *vey slowly away: a bhd: rdn over 3f out: hdwy 3f out: no imp fr over 1f out* **5/1**[3]

12-1 **6** *13* **What Katie Did (IRE)**[38] 1110 3-8-9 77 GabrielHannon(7) 5 27
(P F I Cole) *chsd ldrs tl lost pl and rdn 3f out: bhd last 2f: eased ins fnl f: t.o* **5/1**[3]

1m 14.72s (1.02) **Going Correction** +0.25s/f (Slow) **6 Ran SP% 113.2**
Speed ratings (Par 101): **103,102,101,97,97 79**
CSF £20.65 TOTE £3.30: £3.00, £3.50; EX 25.80.
Owner P Ransley **Bred** Patrick Doyle **Trained** Newmarket, Suffolk
■ Stewards' Enquiry : Pat Cosgrave one-day ban: careless riding (May 22)

FOCUS
A nice little sprint, despite the small field, run at a strong pace and providing a cracking finish with the front three battling hard over the last furlong or so and none of them giving an inch. The third looks the best guide to the level.

1935 OAK H'CAP 1m 2f (P)
6:40 (6:41) (Class 4) (0-85,85) 4-Y-O+ **£4,533** (£1,348; £674; £336) **Stalls** Low

Form RPR
1251 **1** **Art Man**[51] 927 5-9-0 81 GeorgeBaker 8 93+
(G L Moore) *in tch: c wd bnd 2f out: rdn wl over 1f out: styd on wl to ld wl ins fnl f* **11/4**[1]

2 *½* **Indicible (FR)**[18] 4-9-1 82 FergusSweeney 7 93
(A King) *led for 1f: chsd ldr after: rdn over 3f out: carried wd bnd 2f out: led ins fnl f: hdd and no ex wl ins fnl f* **8/1**

3661 **3** *3 ¼* **Basra (IRE)**[18] 1502 5-9-4 85 RichardMullen 6 89
(Miss Jo Crowley) *trckd ldng pair: rdn to ld over 1f out: hdd ins fnl f: fdd last 50yds* **9/2**[3]

1042 **4** *½* **Mataram (USA)**[18] 1502 5-9-3 84 J-PGuillambert 4 87+
(W Jarvis) *s: plld hrd and hld up wl off the pce in last pair: rdn and effrt 3f out: kpt on fnl f: nvr nr ldrs* **3/1**[2]

0/6 **5** *3 ¼* **Fly Free**[37] 1131 4-8-9 79 (v1) LukeMorris(3) 2 76
(M L W Bell) *chsd ldr tl led after 1f: rdn and c wd bnd 2f out: hdd over 1f out: wknd fnl f* **22/1**

21- **6** *1 ½* **Royal Jasra**[239] 5335 4-8-9 76 SebSanders 3 70
(E A L Dunlop) *t.k.h: hld up in midfield: rdn and effrt over 3f out: outpcd and drvn over 2f out: no hdwy* **3/1**[2]

00-0 **7** *5* **Birkspiel (GER)**[12] 1633 7-9-4 85 (t) JimmyQuinn 5 69
(S Dow) *stdd s: t.k.h: hld up in last: rdn over 3f out: nvr on terms* **33/1**

3112 **8** *8* **Dushstorm (IRE)**[10] 1668 7-8-4 71 LiamJones 1 39
(C R Dore) *hld up in tch: rdn and struggling 3f out: no ch over 1f out* **14/1**

2m 11.92s (3.32) **Going Correction** +0.25s/f (Slow) **8 Ran SP% 119.9**
Speed ratings (Par 105): **96,95,93,92,90 88,84,78**
CSF £26.91 CT £98.84 TOTE £3.90: £1.20, £3.10, £2.10; EX 49.50.
Owner Matthew Green **Bred** Lady Lonsdale **Trained** Woodingdean, E Sussex

FOCUS
A fair handicap, but ruined to an extent by an early dawdle and even though things quickened up later, the winning time was still just under a second slower than the Class 6 classified event and fractionally slower than the claimer. There seemed to be an advantage to those that made their efforts down the centre of the track as the front pair were brought widest. Not the most solid form despite the third being pretty reliable.
Birkspiel(GER) Official explanation: jockey said gelding ran too freely

1936 RAMPARTS H'CAP 1m (P)
7:10 (7:12) (Class 4) (0-85,84) 4-Y-O+ **£4,533** (£1,348; £674; £336) **Stalls** Low

Form RPR
016- **1** **Grand Vizier (IRE)**[227] 5693 4-8-5 76 JackMitchell(5) 7 85+
(C F Wall) *in tch: hdwy to chse ldng pair 4f out: rdn 3f out: chal wl over 1f out: kpt on wl to ld last strides* **16/1**

1- **2** *hd* **Swop (IRE)**[192] 6546 5-9-2 82 SebSanders 1 91+
(L M Cumani) *led: jnd 5f out: rdn over 2f out: kpt on wl tl hdd last strides* **4/5**[1]

1510 **3** *1 ¼* **Justcallmehandsome**[16] 1532 6-8-2 75 (v) BillyCray(7) 3 81
(D J S Ffrench Davis) *chsd ldr tl jnd ldr 2f out: rdn over 2f out: no ex wl ins fnl f* **12/1**

1-50 **4** *shd* **Twilight Star (IRE)**[24] 1365 4-8-12 78 (t) ChrisCatlin 5 84
(R A Teal) *t.k.h: chsd ldrs: rdn 2f out: swtchd rt jst over 1f out: bmpd 1f out: r.o fnl f: nt rch ldrs* **17/2**[3]

/5-1 **5** *shd* **Mumbleswerve (IRE)**[18] 1504 4-8-9 75 J-PGuillambert 4 81
(W Jarvis) *chsd ldrs: nt clr run wl over 1f out: swtchd rt 1f out: r.o ins fnl f: nt rch ldrs* **4/1**[2]

1045 **6** *3* **Ninth House (USA)**[16] 1545 6-9-4 84 (bt) GeorgeBaker 6 83
(N P Littmoden) *hld up in tch in midfield: rdn and effrt over 2f out: kpt on same pce last 2f* **10/1**

00-0 **7** *7* **Obezyana (USA)**[12] 1612 6-8-6 75 DominicFox(3) 2 58
(A Bailey) *hld up bhd: lost tch wl over 2f out* **33/1**

040- **8** *20* **Coeur Courageux (FR)**[194] 6504 6-8-6 72 FergusSweeney 8 9
(G L Moore) *rrd as stalls opened and v.s.a: hdwy and in tch over 4f out: rdn and btn 3f out: t.o and eased fnl f* **11/1**

1m 39.96s (0.06) **Going Correction** +0.25s/f (Slow) **8 Ran SP% 120.0**
Speed ratings (Par 105): **109,108,107,107,107 104,97,77**
CSF £31.02 CT £186.02 TOTE £18.40: £4.50, £1.10, £3.10; EX 70.90.
Owner Hintlesham SP Partners **Bred** Yeomanstown Stud **Trained** Newmarket, Suffolk
■ Stewards' Enquiry : J-P Guillambert three-day ban: careless riding (May 22-24)

FOCUS
A fair handicap, but another race where the early pace was not strong and it suited those that raced handily. The front trio held those positions throughout and the third and fourth are the best guides.
Coeur Courageux(FR) Official explanation: jockey said gelding was slowly away

1937 VICARAGE CLAIMING STKS 1m 2f (P)
7:40 (7:40) (Class 6) 3-Y-O **£2,388** (£705; £352) **Stalls** Low

Form RPR
5-16 **1** **Haydens Mark**[7] 1746 3-9-7 85 LiamJones 3 77+
(W J Haggas) *in tch: smooth hdwy on outer 3f out: led over 1f out: rdn clr: readily* **4/6**[1]

1540 **2** *3 ¾* **What's For Tea**[21] 1412 3-8-10 61 RichardKingscote 4 59
(P Butler) *chsd ldr tl wnt 2nd 6f out: rdn and ev ch 2f out: nt pce of wnr fr over 1f out: kpt on* **8/1**

46-6 **3** *1 ¼* **Sergeant Sharpe**[24] 1364 3-9-4 68 JimmyQuinn 5 64
(M H Tompkins) *s.i.s: hld up in rr: hdwy over 3f out: rdn wl over 2f out: kpt on to go 3rd ins fnl f: no ch w wnr* **3/1**[2]

1-00 **4** *2 ½* **Didana (IRE)**[24] 1364 3-8-6 67 ChrisCatlin 2 47
(M G Quinlan) *chsd ldr tl 6f out: rdn 3f out: wknd over 1f out* **15/2**[3]

0 **5** *nk* **Tewin Green**[10] 1669 3-8-6 0 KirstyMilczarek(3) 1 49
(M Botti) *t.k.h: in tch tl rdn and lost pl 6f out: hdwy 4f out: outpcd over 2f out: plugging on whn swtchd rt ins fnl f* **20/1**

-004 **6** *nse* **Una Auroraborealis**[14] 1586 3-8-2 40 (p) DavidKinsella 6 42
(J Ryan) *led tl rdn and hdd over 1f out: wknd qckly fnl f* **40/1**

4-66 **7** *5* **Hiss And Boo**[88] 514 3-8-13 50 PatCosgrave 7 43
(P Howling) *hld up bhd: rdn over 3f out: n.d* **33/1**

2m 11.84s (3.24) **Going Correction** +0.25s/f (Slow) **7 Ran SP% 118.0**
Speed ratings (Par 97): **97,94,93,91,90 90,86**
CSF £7.45 TOTE £1.80: £1.10, £6.00; EX 6.80.The winner was claimed by D. G. Bridgwater for £18,000.
Owner Mrs J Dye **Bred** A J And Mrs Dye **Trained** Newmarket, Suffolk

FOCUS
An uncompetitive claimer with 27lb covering the seven horses on adjusted official ratings. The pace was ordinary and, although the winning time was fractionally faster than the earlier Class 4 handicap, it was also 0.86 seconds slower than the following Class 6 classified event and the quality of the race time-wise is probably best measured through that.

1938 SHOWGROUND CLASSIFIED STKS 1m 2f (P)
8:10 (8:12) (Class 6) 3-Y-O+ **£1,774** (£523; £262) **Stalls** Low

Form RPR
0253 **1** **Tapas Lad (IRE)**[3] 1870 3-8-4 55 (v) KevinGhunowa(3) 15 58
(G J Smith) *t.k.h: chsd ldrs on outer: rdn to chse ldr wl over 1f out: led over 1f out: r.o wl* **4/1**[1]

0-35 **2** *¾* **Jemiliah**[47] 976 3-8-7 55 RichardKingscote 6 60+
(B G Powell) *dropped in bhd after s: hld up in rr: hdwy over 2f out: r.o fr over 1f out: swtchd lft ins fnl f: snatched 2nd on line* **10/1**

55-0 **3** *nse* **Dubai Shadow (IRE)**[15] 1562 4-9-1 52 DebraEngland(7) 7 57
(C E Brittain) *t.k.h: hld up in midfield: hdwy 3f out: chsd ldrs and rdn 2f out: wnt 2nd ins fnl f: kpt on: lost 2nd last stride* **17/2**

1260 **4** *1 ½* **Coral Shores**[42] 1034 3-8-7 53 (v) ChrisCatlin 14 53
(P W Hiatt) *t.k.h: chsd ldrs: ev ch and rdn jst over 3f out: led over 2f out: hdd over 1f out: nt pce of wnr and lost 2 pls ins fnl f* **10/1**

6000 **5** *2* **Lady Florence**[3] 1871 3-8-4 52 LukeMorris(3) 2 49
(A B Coogan) *in tch: rdn and outpcd over 2f out: rallied and n.m.r over 1f out: styd on fnl f: nt trble ldrs* **40/1**

-520 **6** *1 ¾* **Hayley's Flower (IRE)**[104] 299 4-9-3 50 HaddenFrost(3) 13 47
(J C Fox) *hld up towards rr: hdwy on outer 3f out: chsd ldrs u.p wl over 1f out: no imp fnl f* **20/1**

0-00 **7** *nk* **Whatalotofbuts**[16] 1549 3-8-7 48 JamesDoyle 11 45
(B De Haan) *chsd ldr tl led over 3f out: sn rdn: hdd over 2f out: wknd wl over 1f out* **40/1**

000- **8** *shd* **Madame Bountiful**[192] 6535 3-8-7 55 FergusSweeney 8 45
(A King) *t.k.h: chsd ldrs for 2f out: in tch after: rdn 2f out: kpt on same pce* **10/1**

656 **9** *½* **Royal Soverin**[19] 1490 3-8-8 55 ow1 PatCosgrave 5 45
(M J Wallace) *hld up towards rr: hdwy over 3f out: midfield and no imp whn hmpd over 1f out* **12/1**

4-0 **10** *1* **Blockley (USA)**[18] 1505 4-9-8 52 StephenDonohoe 10 43
(Ian Williams) *v.s.a: bhd: sme late hdwy: n.d* **7/1**[3]

00-0 **11** *¾* **Romford Car Two**[35] 1163 3-8-7 51 (b1) DMylonas 3 41
(Miss J Feilden) *s.i.s: a bhd: rdn wl over 3f out: n.d* **40/1**

00-0 **12** *hd* **Abfabfong (IRE)**[7] 1740 3-8-7 50 (p) FrankieMcDonald 1 40
(Mrs L C Jewell) *led tl rdn and hdd over 3f out: wknd qckly 2f out* **66/1**

-260 **13** *7* **Poppy Red**[9] 1710 3-8-7 55 RichardThomas 12 26
(Miss J R Tooth) *hld up towards rr: rdn and effrt 3f out: wl btn and eased fnl f* **22/1**

00-0 **14** *½* **Amicus**[14] 1586 3-8-4 55 KirstyMilczarek(3) 9 25
(D K Ivory) *in tch in midfield: rdn and hdwy jst over 3f out: chsd ldrs 2f out: wknd over 1f out: eased ins fnl f* **20/1**

6-56 **15** *37* **Espejo (IRE)**[84] 560 4-9-8 53 NickyMackay 4 —
(W J Musson) *s.i.s: hld up in midfield: rdn 3f out: sn wknd: heavily eased fnl f* **4/1**[1]

0554 **16** *17* **Film Queen (IRE)**[16] 1533 4-9-8 52................................ SebSanders 16 —
(B G Powell) *stdd and dropped in bhd after s: rdn over 3f out: no ch 2f out: heavily eased fnl f* **6/1**[2]

2m 10.98s (2.38) **Going Correction** +0.25s/f (Slow)
WFA 3 from 4yo 15lb **16** Ran SP% **135.0**
Speed ratings (Par 101): **100,99,99,98,96 95,94,94,94,93 93,92,87,86,57 43**
CSF £47.12 TOTE £4.50: £1.90, £2.20, £5.40; EX 48.10 Place 6 £43.84, Place 5 £27.67.
Owner Graham Smith **Bred** T F Moorhead **Trained** Six Hills, Leics

FOCUS
A poor race and though the winning time was just under a second faster than both the Class 4 handicap and the claimer, that may have been totally down to the size of the field. The form is sound but limited.
Espejo(IRE) Official explanation: jockey said gelding stopped very quickly
Film Queen(IRE) Official explanation: jockey said filly stopped very quickly
T/Plt: £29.60 to a £1 stake. Pool: £38,108.55. 937.01 winning tickets. T/Qpdt: £7.40 to a £1 stake. Pool: £3,142.22. 312.30 winning tickets. SP

1939 - 1941a (Foreign Racing) - See Raceform Interactive

1920 CHESTER (L-H)
Friday, May 9

OFFICIAL GOING: Good (good to firm in places; 8.6)
Wind: Light, across Weather: Overcast turning fine

1942 WARWICK INTERNATIONAL H'CAP — 7f 122y
1:45 (1:45) (Class 2) (0-100,100) 4-Y-0+ **£13,246** (£3,964; £1,982; £991; £493) **Stalls** Low

Form RPR
314- **1** **Celtic Sultan (IRE)**[195] 6491 4-9-4 **100**........................ MickyFenton 6 109+
(T P Tate) *sn led: rdn over 1f out: sn drifted rt: all out* **7/1**[3]
-021 **2** *nk* **Extraterrestrial**[6] 1816 4-8-10 **92** 6ex.............................. PaulHanagan 4 100+
(R A Fahey) *lw: midfield: nt clr run over 2f out: rdn whn nt clr run again and plenty to do over 1f out: str run fnl f: gaining towards fin: jst failed* **9/2**[2]
2400 **3** *nk* **Dream Lodge (IRE)**[48] 958 4-8-10 **92**........................ TPQueally 1 99
(J G Given) *in tch: pushed along over 3f out: rdn and hdwy over 1f out: r.o towards fin* **11/1**
20-2 **4** *nk* **Joseph Henry**[6] 1796 6-8-7 **89**.................................. SilvestreDeSousa 3 95
(D Nicholls) *chsd ldrs: rdn to chal over 1f out: no ex fnl strides* **9/2**[2]
06-4 **5** *½* **The Kiddykid (IRE)**[9] 1723 8-8-5 **87**............................ JimmyQuinn 10 92
(P D Evans) *chsd ldrs: rdn to chal over 1f out: nt clr run and swtchd lft ins fnl f: nt qckn towards fin* **25/1**
5222 **6** *nk* **Regal Parade**[6] 1816 4-8-8 **90**................................. AdrianTNicholls 8 94
(D Nicholls) *towards rr: hdwy over 3f out: rdn on outside to press ldrs 2f out: styd on same pce towards fin* **15/2**
0-00 **7** *7* **Heywood**[36] 1174 4-8-4 **86** oh4...................................... PaulFessey 7 73
(D Nicholls) *in tch: rdn and hung lft fr over 1f out: sn wknd* **28/1**
0-05 **8** *2 ¼* **Dhaular Dhar (IRE)**[34] 1218 6-8-10 **92**........................ DanielTudhope 2 73
(J S Goldie) *racd keenly: hld up: hmpd over 4f out: rdn and wanted to lugg lft whn btn over 1f out* **4/1**[1]
31-1 **9** *3* **Russki (IRE)**[17] 1545 4-8-10 **92**................................. RichardMullen 5 66
(D M Simcock) *in rr: sn niggled along: nvr on terms* **8/1**
2003 **10** *2* **Plum Pudding (IRE)**[17] 1545 5-8-9 **91**..................(p) RichardHughes 11 60
(R Hannon) *lw: chsd ldr tl pushed along and wknd over 1f out* **20/1**
2300 **11** *2 ¾* **Gallantry**[20] 1481 6-8-1 **86** oh2................................ DuranFentiman(3) 13 48
(D Shaw) *s.s: a bhd* **16/1**

1m 34.51s (0.71) **Going Correction** +0.125s/f (Good) **11** Ran SP% **118.0**
Speed ratings (Par 109): **101,100,100,100,99 99,92,90,87,85 82**
CSF £37.70 CT £354.44 TOTE £8.90: £3.20, £2.10, £3.20; EX 55.30 Trifecta £357.50 Pool £1,208.50 - 2.40 winning units..
Owner Mrs Sylvia Clegg and Louise Worthington **Bred** Miss C Lyons **Trained** Tadcaster, N Yorks
■ Stewards' Enquiry : Micky Fenton caution: careless riding

FOCUS
A very good, competitive handicap and the eventual winner took them along at a decent pace. Unusually for Chester, the principals raced across the track in the straight, but those drawn low still dominated, with the first four emerging from the bottom six stalls. The third is rated to his All-Weather mark and the form is rated as positively as it can be.

NOTEBOOK
Celtic Sultan(IRE), who gained reward for some good efforts in defeat when winning off a mark of 95 on his penultimate start last season, has clearly done well over the winter and was able to defy a break of over six months. Soon in front, he set quite a brisk pace, but crucially the lead was not contested and he ran on strongly when challenged on both sides in the straight, despite continually edging right and ending up more towards the stands' rail. There should be more to come again and he looks another nice prospect for the Tate yard, who have done so well with same Welsh Emperor, a not too dissimilar type who races in the same colours. (op 9-1)
Extraterrestrial, carrying a 6lb penalty for his win in the Thirsk Hunt Cup, finished strongly after initially being denied a clear run when beginning to stay on and this was a fine effort in defeat. Ex-Irish, he has not been with the Fahey yard that long and should continue to improve. (op 4-1)
Dream Lodge(IRE) failed to beat a rival in the Spring Mile on his previous start, but he has been given a short break since then and this was a lot better. He had to be niggled along from some way out to keep his position just off the pace towards the inside, but he kept responding and finished strongly. He is probably better over 1m. (op 14-1)
Joseph Henry, 4lb lower than in future following his recent close second over 6f at Doncaster, proved unable to take advantage, but this was still another solid effort in defeat. He is clearly in great order, but things will be tougher off his higher mark. (op 5-1)
The Kiddykid(IRE) ◆ would have finished closer had he not been short of room and forced to switch inside with under a furlong to run. This was a decent effort from a double-figure stall and, due to be dropped 2lb, he might be of interest if conditions look favourable next time. (op 22-1)
Regal Parade, due to go up 3lb after running second to Extraterrestrial in the Thirsk Hunt Cup on his previous start, was forced to make his move out wide and is better than he showed. (op 8-1)
Dhaular Dhar(IRE) was 2lb lower than when winning this race last year, but he was never involved after being hampered over half a mile out. Official explanation: jockey said horse suffered interference in running (op 9-2)
Russki(IRE), bidding for a hat-trick off a mark 6lb higher than when winning at Kempton on his previous start, had his usual blinkers left off this time, despite having had them fitted for his last four victories, and he had no chance of dominating after being slow to find his stride. The headgear will surely be back on next time. Official explanation: trainer's rep said colt had been struck into (op 9-1)

1943 ADDLESHAW GODDARD DEE STKS (GROUP 3) (C&G) — 1m 2f 75y
2:15 (2:15) (Class 1) 3-Y-O
£36,900 (£13,988; £7,000; £3,490; £1,748; £877) **Stalls** High

Form RPR
10- **1** **Tajaaweed (USA)**[195] 6489 3-8-12 95.. RHills 8 115+
(Sir Michael Stoute) *tall: lw: hld up: hdwy over 1f out: sn rdn to chal: r.o to ld fnl strides* **5/1**[3]
22-1 **2** *shd* **Unnefer (FR)**[21] 1443 3-8-12 105.................................... TedDurcan 4 114
(H R A Cecil) *midfield: rdn and hdwy over 1f out: sn led: hdd fnl strides* **4/1**[2]
22-6 **3** *5* **Achill Island (IRE)**[26] 1362 3-8-12 0................................ JMurtagh 2 105
(A P O'Brien, Ire) *trckd ldrs: rdn to ld over 1f out: sn hdd: wknd fnl 100yds* **2/1**[1]
13- **4** *2 ¼* **Alexandros**[264] 4653 3-8-12 116...................................... LDettori 3 101
(Saeed Bin Suroor) *lw: racd keenly: trckd ldrs: chalng on wd outside whn bmpd over 1f out: sn hung lft and wknd* **4/1**[2]
62- **5** *8* **North Parade**[231] 5590 3-8-12 0..............................(t) JamieSpencer 7 85
(B J Meehan) *lw: hld up: rdn over 3f out: sn hung rt and flashed tail u.p: btn 2f out* **16/1**
4 **6** *13* **Sligo**[26] 1362 3-8-12 0.. DavidMcCabe 5 59
(A P O'Brien, Ire) *str: hdwy to press ldr after 1f: racd keenly: rdn over 3f out: stl chalng whn n.m.r and hmpd over 1f out: sn wl btn* **28/1**
2-36 **7** *1 ¾* **Latin Lad**[13] 1632 3-8-12 100...................................... RichardHughes 1 55
(R Hannon) *swtg: racd keenly: led: hung rt fr over 2f out: hdd over 1f out: sn wknd* **13/2**
31- **8** *37* **Midnight Muse (USA)**[292] 3760 3-8-12 81........................ SebSanders 6 —
(T D Barron) *w'like: leggy: hld up: pushed along over 4f out: lft bhd 3f out: t.o* **28/1**

2m 11.03s (-1.17) **Going Correction** +0.125s/f (Good) **8** Ran SP% **116.1**
Speed ratings (Par 109): **109,108,104,103,96 86,84,55**
CSF £25.74 TOTE £6.90: £2.10, £1.60, £1.40; EX 29.30 Trifecta £66.30 Pool £663.62 - 7.10 winning units..
Owner Hamdan Al Maktoum **Bred** Herman Sarkowsky **Trained** Newmarket, Suffolk

FOCUS
Recent winners of the Dee Stakes include Derby heroes Oath (1999), and Kris Kin (2003). It was difficult to get too excited about this year's renewal beforehand, but the front two, both held up off the strong pace, pulled well clear of a couple proven in Group company and the form looks solid enough.

NOTEBOOK
Tajaaweed(USA) ◆ was tested in the Racing Post Trophy after impressively landing a Nottingham maiden on his debut, but he was too green to do himself justice and beat only two of his 11 rivals. Quite a big horse, he is very much the type to improve with age and, stepped up in trip on his return from over six months off, he justified his connections' high opinion of him with a narrow success. Held up well off the decent gallop, he settled nicely and travelled sweetly in the hands of Richard Hills. Kept towards the inside when the race got serious, he made good headway to move into a challenging position and plugged on for pressure to reel in the speedier, and much nippier Unnefer close home. This performance should not be underestimated for, although he is no sure thing to stay 1m4f on breeding, he already looks in need of the trip, yet he was still able to get the better of a genuine 1m2f horse, whose recent conditions success has worked out really well, and the pair were well clear of a proven Group 2 performer. Sir Michael Stoute won this race with subsequent 2003 Derby winner Kris Kin and, depending on what happens to Tartan Bearer and Twice Over (same owner as Stoute's Vase winner Doctor Fremantle) in the Dante, this one could well end up as his sole representative in the Epsom Classic. Whatever the case, his price is likely to shorten from the current 16/1 on general offer and he goes there with a live chance. (op 7-2 tchd 11-2, 6-1 in a place and 7-1 in a place)
Unnefer(FR)'s reappearance success in a 1m2f conditions race at Newbury has worked out really well, so he deserved this step up in class, and he was just denied. Like the eventual winner, he settled beautifully off the strong pace and came through to have every chance but, after looking the likeliest winner inside the final two furlongs, he was just run out of it by a much stronger stayer. Well clear of the remainder, he proved himself up this sort of level, but he does not want much further. The French Derby, run over an extended 1m2f these days, might appeal to his connections, particularly as he does not seem to want the ground too quick. (op 9-2)
Achill Island(IRE) improved on the form he showed when beating only one home in a Group 3 in France on his reappearance, but he was still well held in third and was below the sort of level he achieved when runner-up in both the Royal Lodge and the Breeders' Cup Juvenile Turf last year. (op 9-4)
Alexandros, successful in both Listed and Group 3 company before running third Prix Morny on his final start at two, ia an athletic colt and has switched to Godolphin from Andre Fabre's yard. Stepped up significantly in trip (he had never previously raced beyond 7f) after 264 days off, he was far too keen for much of the way and gave himself little chance of staying the distance. He was still tanking along turning for home, but he received a bump when Latin Lad hung right off the bend and quickly emptied, with his earlier exertions clearly having taken their toll. He is bred to be effective over middle-distances and it is by no means out of the question he can leave this form behind when his stable return to form, but he will have to learn to settle better to give himself any chance. (op 7-2)
North Parade showed plenty of ability in a couple of 1m conditions races at two, including when second to Sandown Classic Trial winner Centennial at Newbury when last seen 231 days previously, but he was well beaten on his return. Admittedly he was again set a stiff task, but he offered little, hardly convincing with his attitude under pressure, and clearly wants his sights lowered for the time being.
Sligo finished in front of stablemate Achill Island when fourth in a Group 3 in France on his reappearance, but he was allowed to dictate a steady pace that day. He was sacrificed this time, being bustled along to help force a strong pace with Latin Lad, and he was under strong pressure when hampered on the final bend. (op 40-1)
Latin Lad was taken on up front by Sligo and ended up doing too much. He was beaten when hanging badly right off the final bend. Official explanation: jockey said colt hung right (op 14-1)
Midnight Muse(USA), a Redcar maiden winner last July, was well beaten stepped up significantly in class on his return to the track, but his trainer does not usually over-face his horses, so it might be worth giving this one another chance in time. (op 33-1)

1944 BLUE SQUARE ORMONDE STKS (GROUP 3) — 1m 5f 89y
2:45 (2:46) (Class 1) 4-Y-O+
£42,577 (£16,140; £8,077; £4,027; £2,017; £1,012) **Stalls** Low

Form RPR
36-0 **1** **Macarthur**[26] 1353 4-9-0 0.. JMurtagh 3 116+
(A P O'Brien, Ire) *swtg: midfield: hdwy gng wl whn nt clr run 2f out: prog to ld ent fnl f: qcknd clr* **9/4**[1]
240- **2** *4* **Supersonic Dave (USA)**[323] 2789 4-9-0 106............................ RHills 5 108
(B J Meehan) *midfield: pushed along 2f out: hdwy 1f out: r.o to take 2nd towards fin: nt trble wnr* **22/1**
20/3 **3** *nk* **Carte Diamond (USA)**[41] 1070 7-9-0 97........................ PaulHanagan 2 108
(B Ellison) *swtg: led: hung rt most of fnl circ: rdn over 1f out: hdd ent fnl f: kpt on same pce* **14/1**
55-5 **4** *1 ¼* **Red Gala**[20] 1468 5-9-0 105.. JamieSpencer 9 106+
(Sir Michael Stoute) *lw: midfield: nt clr run 2f out: plld out over 1f out: styd on fnl f: nt rch ldrs* **9/2**[3]
/40- **5** *½* **Numide (FR)**[59] 4520 5-9-0 0... GeorgeBaker 8 105
(G L Moore) *dwlt: hld up: nt clr run over 2f out: hdwy over 1f out: styd on ins fnl f: nt pce to trble ldrs* **25/1**
010- **6** *1* **Steppe Dancer (IRE)**[237] 5437 5-9-3 106.............................. TPQueally 1 106
(D J Coakley) *lw: racd keenly: trckd ldrs: wnt 2nd over 2f out tl rdn over 1f out: sn hung lft: wknd fnl 100yds* **12/1**

10-3 **7** 3 1/2 **Tempelstern (GER)**20 1468 4-9-0 111........................(b) TedDurcan 11 98
(H R A Cecil) *trckd ldrs: rdn 2f out: wknd over 1f out* **8/1**

16-0 **8** 3/4 **Bauer (IRE)**20 1468 5-9-0 104.. SebSanders 4 97
(L M Cumani) *midfield: pushed along over 3f out: effrt to chse ldrs 2f out: bmpd over 1f out: sn wknd* **7/1**

30-1 **9** 3 1/2 **Raincoat**13 1629 4-9-0 109.. LDettori 10 110+
(J H M Gosden) *lw: hld up in last pl: nt clr run fr 2f out tl hdwy over 1f out: swtchd lft ent fnl f: gap sn clsd and bdly hmpd: immediately eased* **4/1**2

/05- **10** 30 **Jadalee (IRE)**441 545 5-9-0 108................................. RichardHughes 7 47
(G A Butler) *hld up: pushed along 3f out: rdn on outside over 2f out: dropped away over 1f out* **33/1**

00-P **11** 2 **The Last Drop (IRE)**41 1070 5-9-0 98........................ PhilipRobinson 6 44
(B W Hills) *chsd ldr: rdn 3f out: wknd over 2f out* **33/1**

2m 53.2s (-2.50) **Going Correction** +0.125s/f (Good) **11** Ran SP% **121.0**
Speed ratings (Par 113): **112,109,109,108,108 107,105,105,102,84 83**
CSF £62.96 TOTE £3.40: £1.60, £3.70, £4.00; EX 84.70 Trifecta £717.30 Part won. Pool £1,010.30 - 0.80 winning units..

Owner D Smith, Mrs J Magnier, M Tabor **Bred** Deerfield Farm **Trained** Ballydoyle, Co Tipperary

■ Stewards' Enquiry : T P Queally six-day ban: careless riding (May 23-28)

FOCUS

A decent renewal of the Ormonde Stakes and they went a good, even gallop. The winner is value for slightly more with the runner-up to his debut mark.

NOTEBOOK

Macarthur ◆, an unlucky sixth in last year's St Leger, beat just one horse home in a 1m2f Listed race at the Curragh on his reappearance, but that run clearly brought him on significantly and he took this Group 3 contest in really convincing style. He took a good grip of the bridle for much of the contest, confirming he was a lot more tuned up this time and, once getting a gap in the straight, he bounded well clear. He clearly has plenty of stamina, but as Murtagh pointed out afterwards, he has his fair share of speed as well. There will be endless options for him in the coming months over a range of trips but, with his stable already having such a strong hand in the staying division, this brother to 2005 Derby winner Motivator might be best served trying to prove himself in some of the big middle-distance contests. (tchd 5-2)

Supersonic Dave(USA) is lightly raced but he has always been held in high regard - he raced solely in Listed company last year - and this was his best effort yet after 323 days off the track. Stepped up significantly in trip, he was no match for the comfortable winner, but ran on well to take second. Presumably he has not been the easiest to train, but he looks capable of fulfilling his potential if he can be kept right. (op 25-1 tchd 20-1)

Carte Diamond(USA) was off the track for over two years after suffering two life-threatening injuries in Australia when being trained for the 2005 Melbourne Cup but, remarkably, he seems to retain both his old ability, and his enthusiasm, and he confirmed the promise he showed when third in a Doncaster conditions contest on his return to the track in March. This effort is particularly creditable considering he did not handle the track, continually hanging right and struggling with the sharp turns. It is a credit to his connections that he has come back in such good form and he could do even better again when returned to a more galloping course. Official explanation: jockey said gelding hung right throughout (tchd 12-1)

Red Gala, fifth in the John Porter Stakes at Newbury on his reappearance, can be rated a little better than the bare form as he was denied a clear run around 2f out when trying to stake a claim and had to fight for a gap. (op 5-1 tchd 11-2)

Numide(FR) was last seen finishing down the field over hurdles in the Supreme Novices' at Cheltenham in March, but he was formerly very smart on the Flat in France - he won a Group 2 in 2006 - and this was a very respectable showing. He stuck on well in the straight and gave the impression he might stay further but, whatever the case, he probably wants easier ground.

Steppe Dancer(IRE), conceding 3lb all round, ran well to a point but he got tired in the straight on his return from 237 days off and hung left, with his rider using his whip in his right hand, and badly hampered the staying-on Raincoat against the rail. He should improve a good deal for the run. (op 10-1)

Tempelstern(GER) could not repeat the form he showed when third in the John Porter on his reappearance and probably wants a more galloping track. (op 9-1)

Bauer(IRE)'s biggest win to date was gained over this course and distance when he landed a Listed handicap last September, but he was well held this time. (op 13-2)

Raincoat ◆, successful in a conditions contest at Ripon on his reappearance, was well backed to follow up but he enjoyed no luck at all. Held up last, he was always going to need the splits when the race unfolded, but nothing went his way. Having been short of room and forced to wait turning for home, he was nearly brought down after going for an ambitious gap against the rail a furlong out, with Steppe Dancer coming right across him after hanging under pressure. He almost certainly would have been placed with a clear run and is worth another chance at this level. (op 11-2 tchd 13-2 in a place)

The Last Drop(IRE) Official explanation: jockey said horse had lost its action

1945 HAWKER BEECHCRAFT H'CAP 5f 16y

3:15 (3:23) (Class 2) (0-100,94) 3-Y-O **£13,246** (£3,964; £1,982; £991; £493) **Stalls** Low

Form RPR

35-4 **1** **Look Busy (IRE)**7 1772 3-9-3 **93**.................................... SladeO'Hara(5) 7 104
(A Berry) *hld up: hdwy whn nt clr run over 2f out: rdn over 1f out: prog to ld ins fnl f: r.o* **16/1**

-502 **2** 1 3/4 **Chartist**14 1597 3-9-3 **88**.. RichardHughes 3 93
(R Hannon) *led: rdn and hung lft ins fnl f: sn hdd: nt qckn towards fin* **7/4**1

00-2 **3** 2 3/4 **Piscean (USA)**10 1707 3-8-6 **77**.. JimmyQuinn 9 72
(T Keddy) *missed break: in rr: rdn and hdwy ent fnl f: r.o: nt trble front pair* **12/1**

60-1 **4** nk **Mey Blossom**20 1484 3-9-3 **91**.............................. MichaelJStainton(3) 2 85
(R M Whitaker) *lw: in tch: rdn and outpcd 2f out: styd on ins fnl f: nt pce of ldrs* **13/2**

11-0 **5** 2 3/4 **Hadaf (IRE)**23 1404 3-9-1 **86**.. RHills 1 70
(M P Tregoning) *swtg: chsd ldrs: wnt 2nd briefly over 1f out: rdn and wknd ins fnl f* **3/1**2

113- **6** 1 3/4 **Secret Asset (IRE)**235 5480 3-9-9 **94**................................... TedDurcan 8 72
(W M Brisbourne) *chsd ldrs tl rdn and wknd over 1f out* **14/1**

13-3 **7** 1/2 **Rose Siog**20 1484 3-8-8 **79**.. PaulHanagan 6 55
(R A Fahey) *towards rr: pushed along over 2f out: forced wd on bnd over 1f out: nvr able to chal* **11/2**3

1211 **8** 6 **Ten Down**10 1707 3-8-13 **84** 6ex.. FergalLynch 5 38
(Miss Gay Kelleway) *b: chsd ldr tl rdn over 1f out: sn wknd* **9/1**

61.63 secs (0.63) **Going Correction** +0.125s/f (Good) **8** Ran SP% **120.3**
Speed ratings (Par 105): **99,96,91,91,86 84,83,73**
CSF £46.93 CT £377.79 TOTE £20.00: £3.40, £1.30, £3.00; EX 81.80 Trifecta £629.00 Part won. Pool £886.00 - 0.80 winning units..

Owner A Underwood **Bred** Tom And Hazel Russell **Trained** Cockerham, Lancs

FOCUS

An ordinary sprint handicap for the grade with the top weight rated 6lb below the ceiling of 100 and very few got involved. The runner-up is rated to his Sandown form.

NOTEBOOK

Look Busy(IRE) was actually due to be dropped 3lb, but she had run well for a long way before getting tired in a decent conditions contest at Musselburgh on her reappearance and that run clearly sharpened her up. She is very fast and would often blast off in front last year, but she was ridden with patience from her high draw and was always travelling well. Produced with her effort in the straight, she always looked like reeling in the favourite and did this quite readily. The bare form is nothing special, but she looks to have improved from two to three and it would do her paddock prospects no harm if she could pick up some more black type this year after twice placing in Listed company last season. She apparently may come back to Chester for a Listed race. (op 14-1 tchd 12-1)

Chartist was soon in a good rhythm up front, but he could not quite see out his race and had no answer when Look Busy swept by. He has tons of speed, but very limited stamina. (tchd 2-1)

Piscean(USA) was due to be raised 3lb following his short-head second to Ten Down at Wolverhampton on his reappearance, but he could not take advantage after missing the kick. This was by no means the first time he has given away ground at the start. (tchd 14-1)

Mey Blossom, 6lb higher than when winning at 40/1 on her reappearance at Thirsk, was never really involved but this was still a respectable effort in defeat. (op 11-2 tchd 8-1)

Hadaf(IRE), well held over 6f at Newmarket on his reappearance, seemed to have every chance if good enough but he finished his race tamely. (op 9-2 tchd 11-4)

Secret Asset(IRE) got worked up before the race and can be given another chance. (op 16-1 tchd 12-1)

Rose Siog raced wide for much of the way and struggled to get competitive. (op 5-1)

Ten Down was unable to dominate and he never really looked like defying the 6lb penalty for his recent Wolverhampton success. (op 10-1 tchd 8-1)

1946 ALCHEM MERSEYSIDE CHESHIRE REGIMENT MAIDEN FILLIES' STKS 7f 2y

4:00 (4:00) (Class 3) 3-Y-O **£7,123** (£2,119; £1,059; £529) **Stalls** Low

Form RPR

3-5 **1** **Portodora (USA)**22 1423 3-9-0 0.................................... TedDurcan 10 81+
(H R A Cecil) *lw: hld up: stdy hdwy fr over 2f out: plld out over 1f out: hrd rdn and r.o strly ins fnl f: led post* **14/1**

42- **2** nse **Lindelaan (USA)**179 6799 3-9-0 0.................................... SebSanders 3 78
(Sir Michael Stoute) *str: lw: chsd ldrs: rdn to ld ent fnl f: hdd post* **9/2**2

0- **3** 1/2 **Moon Sister (IRE)**189 6617 3-9-0 0.................................... TPQueally 4 79+
(W Jarvis) *b.bkwd: squeezed out s: midfield: hdwy whn nt clr run and snatched up jst over 1f out: r.o wl towards fin* **33/1**

4- **4** 3/4 **Quirina**188 6648 3-9-0 0.. LDettori 9 75+
(J H M Gosden) *b.bkwd: hld up: hdwy on outside wl over 1f out: styd on to chse ldrs ins fnl f: can improve* **11/4**1

26-2 **5** nk **Amylee (IRE)**28 1302 3-9-0 85...................................... PhilipRobinson 6 74
(C G Cox) *lw: prom: led over 4f out: rdn over 1f out: hdd ent fnl f: nt qckn towards fin* **7/1**

3 **6** 1 1/4 **Mazloma (USA)**34 1222 3-9-0 0.................................. RichardHughes 5 71
(M R Channon) *tall: scope: led: hdd over 4f out: remained prom: rdn over 1f out: one pce ins fnl f* **12/1**

6 **7** shd **Gulf Stream Lady (IRE)**22 1423 3-9-0 0........................ PaulHanagan 2 70
(B W Hills) *b.hind: in tch: lost pl over 4f out: nt clr run over 1f out: kpt on wout threatening ldrs ins fnl f* **9/1**

332- **8** 1 1/2 **Deira Dubai**198 6434 3-9-0 73.. RHills 7 66
(B W Hills) *lw: racd keenly: chsd ldrs: w ldr fr over 4f out: rdn and wknd ins fnl f* **8/1**

3 **9** 4 **Miss Brown To You (IRE)**22 1423 3-9-0 0.................. JamieSpencer 8 56
(M L W Bell) *lw: hld up: rdn and hung lft over 1f out: nvr on term: eased ins fnl f* **8/1**

-22 **10** 54 **Erlydors (IRE)**37 1144 3-9-0 0.. JMurtagh 1 —
(W R Swinburn) *lost iron jst after s: in midfield and sn ironless: taken to outside and chsd ldrs over 5f out: lost pl over 2f out: t.o* **5/1**3

1m 29.39s (2.89) **Going Correction** +0.125s/f (Good) **10** Ran SP% **123.5**
Speed ratings (Par 100): **88,87,87,86,86 84,84,82,78,16**
CSF £80.56 TOTE £21.30: £5.50, £2.10, £5.80; EX 133.60.

Owner K Abdulla **Bred** Juddmonte Farms Inc **Trained** Newmarket, Suffolk

■ Stewards' Enquiry : Ted Durcan one-day ban: used whip without giving filly time to respond (May 23)

FOCUS

All ten of these had already seen a racecourse and, with everyone of them having shown ability, this looked a very good fillies' maiden. They went a decent pace and the first four can go on from this.

NOTEBOOK

Portodora(USA) ◆ was behind Miss Brown To You (only ninth this time) at Newmarket on her reappearance, but she improved significantly on that effort with the narrowest of victories. Having travelled like a very good filly for much of the way, she had to be switched right into the clear at the top of the straight, allowing Lindelaan first run, but she responded gamely to pressure and got up to take this on the nod. She gives the impression she can step forward again and looks Pattern class in the making. Her connections think 7f is her trip, and judging by the speed she showed on the bridle, it is easy to see why, but on breeding she is entitled to get a little further in time. Something like the Sandringham Handicap, a Listed race for three-year-old fillies, could be a suitable target and, although that is 1m, they will probably go a good pace, which would suit her. (op 12-1)

Lindelaan(USA) ◆ was never too far away and stayed on strongly when asked in the straight, but she was just denied. This was a big improvement on the form she showed in two runs as a juvenile, the last being a defeat at 6/4 at Wolverhampton, and she looks like progressing into a very useful filly. She can win a similar event, but also now has the option of handicaps. Like the winner, the Sandringham Handicap at Royal Ascot could be a suitable target if she continues to improve. (op 7-1 tchd 15-2)

Moon Sister(IRE) ◆ improved significantly on the form she showed in a backend 6f maiden at Newmarket last year with a close third and she could even be considered unlucky as she was checked in her run when trying to stay on around a furlong out. This was a cracking effort behind a couple a couple of potentially very useful fillies and she can probably do better again when stepped up further in trip. (op 25-1)

Quirina, fourth in a 7f Newmarket maiden last November on her only previous start, made a pleasing return in fourth and should come on a good deal for the run. (op 10-3 tchd 7-2 in a place and 4-1 in a place)

Amylee(IRE) has some useful form to her name, hence her official mark of 85, but some less-exposed fillies proved too good this time. (op 6-1)

Mazloma(USA), a beaten favourite on her debut over 1m at Newcastle, lost her place after 3f but plugged on for pressure. This was a creditable effort and she will be suited by a return to further. (op 14-1)

Gulf Stream Lady(IRE) was only a head behind today's winner on her debut at Newmarket, but she would appear to be need a little more time. She has ability and is worth another chance when she knows her job. (op 6-1)

Deira Dubai, returning from over six months off, was well beaten after racing keenly out wide. (op 9-1)

Miss Brown To You(IRE) had today's winner and seventh behind when third on her debut at Newmarket, so this was to be considered disappointing. (op 15-2)

Erlydors(IRE) had no chance after Murtagh lost his irons soon after the start. Official explanation: jockey said he had lost his irons (op 11-2)

1947 MANOR HOUSE STABLES LLP H'CAP — 1m 4f 66y

4:35 (4:35) (Class 4) (0-85,85) 4-Y-0+ **£7,123** (£2,119; £1,059; £529) **Stalls** Low

Form — RPR

3110 **1** **Maslak (IRE)**[16] 1569 4-9-4 **85** .... DarrenWilliams 4 — 92
(P W Hiatt) *a.p: wnt 2nd over 3f out: rdn whn pressing ldr over 2f out: led 1f out: jst hld on* **18/1**

5-04 **2** *shd* **Cruise Director**[13] 1613 8-8-8 **75** .... TedDurcan 7 — 86+
(Ian Williams) *midfield: nt clr run fr over 2f out tl wl over 1f out: hdwy ent fnl f: r.o strly: jst failed* **14/1**

55-0 **3** *hd* **Ainama (IRE)**[9] 1719 4-8-11 **78** .... JamieSpencer 12 — 87+
(M Wigham) *s.i.s: hld up: nt clr run wl over 2f out: hdwy and swtchd rt over 1f out: r.o strly ins fnl f: gaining at fin* **4/1**[1]

2121 **4** *¾* **Inspirina (IRE)**[24] 1388 4-7-12 **72** .... MatthewDavies(7) 8 — 77
(R Ford) *s.s: hld up: hdwy 2f out: rdn over 1f out: sn chsd ldrs: styng on whn sltly checked wl ins fnl f* **12/1**

-420 **5** *1* **Aureate**[20] 1472 4-9-3 **84** .... JMurtagh 5 — 88
(B Ellison) *handy: led wl over 7f out: rdn and hdd 1f out: no ex towards fin* **9/2**[2]

-120 **6** *3* **Man Of Gwent (UAE)**[16] 1568 4-8-13 **80** .... TGMcLaughlin 1 — 79
(P D Evans) *midfield: swtchd rt and hdwy over 2f out: sn rdn and chsd ldrs: one pce ins fnl f* **10/1**

/116 **7** *1½* **Basalt (IRE)**[83] 588 4-9-2 **83** .... DanielTudhope 3 — 80
(T J Pitt) *midfield: effrt whn forced wd on bnd over 1f out: no further prog fnl f* **11/2**[3]

3523 **8** *5* **Lucayan Dancer**[9] 1732 8-8-5 **72** .... PaulQuinn 11 — 61
(D Nicholls) *in tch: rdn over 2f out: no imp whn n.m.r and hmpd over 1f out: n.d after* **11/1**

50-5 **9** *hd* **New Star (UAE)**[21] 1458 4-8-2 **72** .... DuranFentiman(3) 2 — 60
(W M Brisbourne) *chsd ldrs: rdn and nt qckn over 2f out: wknd 1f out* **20/1**

066- **10** *½* **Stretton (IRE)**[223] 5807 10-8-4 **71** .... PaulHanagan 10 — 58
(J D Bethell) *hld up: niggled along over 4f out: nvr on terms* **6/1**

2-03 **11** *12* **Prince Samos (IRE)**[7] 1771 6-7-13 **73** ....(v) AdeleRothery(7) 13 — 41
(D Nicholls) *s.i.s: struggling 4f out: a bhd* **25/1**

105- **12** *26* **Bajan Parkes**[228] 5677 5-9-0 **81** .... JimmyQuinn 9 — 8
(E J Alston) *led: hdd wl over 7f out: rdn over 3f out: wknd over 2f out: eased over 1f out* **16/1**

- **13** *19* **Stellino (GER)**[14] 5-9-2 **83** .... RichardHughes 6 — —
(N J Henderson) *prom: rdn over 4f out: wknd 3f out: eased over 1f out* **8/1**

2m 40.71s (0.81) **Going Correction** +0.125s/f (Good) **13** Ran SP% **130.5**
Speed ratings (Par 105): **105,104,104,104,103 101,100,97,97,96 88,71,58**
CSF £271.03 CT £1234.95 TOTE £24.60: £7.00, £3.30, £2.40; EX 543.50 Place 6 £308.76, Place 5 £76.63..
Owner Clive Roberts **Bred** Shadwell Estate Company Limited **Trained** Hook Norton, Oxon
■ Stewards' Enquiry : Jamie Spencer one-day ban: careless riding (May 23)

FOCUS
A fair handicap and very competitive. The winner had the run of the race and the runner-up looked unlucky, but overall the form looks pretty solid.
Stellino(GER) Official explanation: jockey said gelding lost its action
T/Jkpt: Not won. T/Plt: £319.00 to a £1 stake. Pool: £157,703.81. 360.84 winning tickets. T/Qpdt: £77.10 to a £1 stake. Pool: £7,437.18. 71.30 winning tickets. DO

1821 HAMILTON (R-H)

Friday, May 9

OFFICIAL GOING: Good to firm (good in places; 9.2)
Wind: almost nil Weather: overcast

1948 MIGHTY TWO-YEAR-OLD MAIDEN STKS — 5f 4y

6:05 (6:07) (Class 5) 2-Y-0 **£2,590** (£770; £385; £192) **Stalls** Low

Form — RPR

1 **Fathey (IRE)** 2-8-10 0 .... BMcHugh(7) 2 — 76
(R A Fahey) *mde all: rdn and edgd lft ins fnl f: r.o strly* **15/2**

2 *1¾* **Officer Mor (USA)** 2-9-3 0 .... AndrewElliott 4 — 70
(K R Burke) *prom: effrt and ch over 1f out: kpt on u.p fnl f: nt rch wnr* **7/1**

3 *shd* **Bragging Rights (IRE)** 2-9-3 0 .... RichardMullen 5 — 69
(K A Ryan) *cl up: ev ch fr 1/2-way: one pce whn blkd ins fnl f* **2/1**[1]

4 *shd* **Snow Bay** 2-9-3 0 .... TomEaves 1 — 74+
(B Smart) *dwlt: t.k.h and sn w ldrs: ev ch whn nt clr run: swtchd sharply rt and bmpd ins fnl f: no ex* **9/4**[2]

5 *1½* **Going Time (USA)** 2-8-12 0 .... JoeFanning 3 — 64+
(M Johnston) *t.k.h: cl up: rdn and outpcd over 1f out: rallying whn hmpd ins fnl f: nt rcvr* **10/3**[3]

61.28 secs (1.28) **Going Correction** -0.15s/f (Firm) **5** Ran SP% **111.4**
Speed ratings (Par 93): **83,80,80,79,77**
CSF £52.71 TOTE £5.50: £2.70, £2.10; EX 29.20.
Owner R M Jeffs, J Potter & W Walker **Bred** Rathasker Stud **Trained** Musley Bank, N Yorks
■ Stewards' Enquiry : B McHugh two-day ban: careless riding (May 23-24)
Tom Eaves four-day ban: careless riding (May 23-26)

FOCUS
No previous form to go on and just a fair bunch overall on looks. With just over three lengths covering the field, this bare form is messy and almost certainly nothing special but the winner, who looked in need of the run, should progress further.

NOTEBOOK
Fathey(IRE), a 25,000gns half-brother to multiple winning sprinters Kathy Livius and Taboor, looked the one most in need of the run in the paddock and he proved very easy to back on this debut. However, he created a favourable impression in the race itself and looks the type to progress further. (op 7-2)
Officer Mor(USA), a £20,000 half-brother to a couple of US dirt winners, is a neat sort with scope and he shaped with a degree of promise on this debut. The step up to 6f should suit and he looks capable of picking up an ordinary event. (tchd 6-1)
Bragging Rights(IRE), a 31,000gns first foal of a dual 1m1f-1m2f winner, is not a bad sort on looks but, after travelling strongly for much of the way shaped, as his pedigree suggested, that a stiffer test of stamina would have suited. The step up to 6f will be ideal and he is capable of better. (op 3-1)
Snow Bay, who cost 8,000gns and is from a yard that has had juvenile winners this term, looked the fittest in the field and was well supported. He looked unlucky not to finish a good deal closer and, although he may not improve as much as a couple of others in this field, he has the ability to win races on this evidence. (op 3-1)
Going Time(USA), who took the eye on pedigree as a $60,000 half-sister to Group 1 Golden Shaheen winner Saratoga County, is a medium-sized sort with scope and was another to fare better than the distance beaten suggests. The step up to 6f and a flatter track may suit on this evidence and she is well worth another chance in ordinary company. (op 3-1 tchd 4-1)

1949 SITE SERVICES PLANT LTD CONDITIONS STKS — 6f 5y

6:35 (6:35) (Class 3) 3-Y-0 **£8,723** (£2,612; £1,306; £653; £326) **Stalls** Low

Form — RPR

240- **1** **Perfect Polly**[189] 6631 3-8-7 0 .... ShaneKelly 5 — 90
(J Noseda) *mde all: rdn and hung rt fr 2f out: hld on wl fnl f* **7/4**[2]

030- **2** *hd* **Burnwynd Boy**[209] 6182 3-9-5 89 .... TomEaves 6 — 101
(Miss L A Perratt) *w wnr: effrt 2f out: kpt on fnl f: jst hld* **40/1**

0211 **3** *4* **Van Bossed (CAN)**[13] 1623 3-8-9 97 .... AdrianTNicholls 4 — 78
(D Nicholls) *t.k.h: trckd ldrs: effrt and ev ch over 1f out: no ex ins fnl f* **6/4**[1]

313- **4** *½* **Exhibition (IRE)**[280] 4120 3-8-12 104 .... PatDobbs 2 — 80
(S A Callaghan) *t.k.h: trckd ldrs: rdn and outpcd wl over 1f out: n.d after* **10/3**[3]

1- **5** *9* **River Ardeche**[286] 3977 3-8-12 0 .... PaulMulrennan 1 — 51
(P C Haslam) *chsd ldrs tl rdn and wknd fnl 2f* **18/1**

1m 10.69s (-1.51) **Going Correction** -0.15s/f (Firm) **5** Ran SP% **107.1**
Speed ratings (Par 103): **104,103,98,97,85**
CSF £39.93 TOTE £3.00: £1.10, £3.70; EX 27.10.
Owner Red Man Bloodstock **Bred** Old Peartree Stud **Trained** Newmarket, Suffolk

FOCUS
A couple of useful types but not a satisfactory result with two of the three market leaders disappointing and runner-up Burnwynd Boy seeming to excel himself in the face of a stiff task. The pace was just fair.

NOTEBOOK
Perfect Polly looked to have strong claims on the pick of last year's form which saw her finish a fine fourth in the Cheveley Park but she proved relatively easy to back on this reappearance and first run for new connections. With her main rivals disappointing she did not have to be at her best to beat a rival who would have been receiving lumps of weight in a handicap but she had to work hard to score, despite looking ill-at-ease on the track and she would not be guaranteed to build on this in a more competitive event next time. (op 10-11)
Burnwynd Boy, a useful sort, looked to have a very stiff task on these unfavourable terms but he turned in what looked on paper a career best effort. His handicap mark will take a hammering after this but he may be able to pick up a conditions event in the coming weeks. (op 50-1)
Van Bossed(CAN) had a bit to find with the winner strictly at the weights but he looked worth his place in this field as a progressive handicapper. However, after travelling strongly for much of the way he failed to pick up in the anticipated manner and proved a disappointment after attracting plenty of support. He is a lightly raced sort, though, so will be worth another chance back in handicap company. (op 7-4)
Exhibition(IRE), a useful juvenile, looked in good shape for this reappearance run but he failed to settle in the race and he dropped out disappointingly. He is going to have to settle better if he is to progress this year. (op 13-2)
River Ardeche, a heavy-ground winner at York last summer on his only run of 2007, had a stiff task at the weights and was well beaten. He will be seen to better effect in ordinary handicaps, especially back on more testing ground. (op 25-1 tchd 33-1)

1950 BRAVEHEART NIGHT NEXT FRIDAY H'CAP — 1m 4f 17y

7:10 (7:10) (Class 5) (0-70,70) 3-Y-0 **£2,590** (£770; £385; £192) **Stalls** High

Form — RPR

03-4 **1** **Legion D'Honneur (UAE)**[28] 1307 3-9-9 **70** .... PaulMulrennan 7 — 79+
(L Lungo) *mde all: rdn over 2f out: hld on wl fnl f* **8/1**

3-32 **2** *2¼* **Princess Lomi (IRE)**[20] 1477 3-9-6 **67** .... TomEaves 1 — 73
(E J O'Neill) *t.k.h early: cl up: effrt and ev ch over 3f out: kpt on u.p fnl f* **5/2**[1]

1-15 **3** *2* **Sheer Fantastic**[37] 1140 3-8-13 **67** ....(p) PatrickDonaghy(7) 6 — 70
(P C Haslam) *dwlt: t.k.h and sn prom: effrt 3f out: edgd rt over 1f out: kpt on same pce fnl f* **4/1**[3]

-610 **4** *2* **Chanteuse De Rue (IRE)**[20] 1478 3-8-5 **52** .... JoeFanning 5 — 51
(M Johnston) *hld up: outpcd 1/2-way: kpt on fr 2f out: nrst fin* **15/2**

65-2 **5** *nk* **Livvy Inn (USA)**[5] 1825 3-8-9 **56** .... PaulFessey 3 — 55
(Miss Lucinda V Russell) *hld up: effrt 3f out: no imp fnl 2f* **3/1**[2]

5300 **6** *2* **Soxy Doxy (IRE)**[17] 1553 3-8-4 **51** oh1 .... GregFairley 4 — 47
(M Johnston) *chsd ldrs: drvn and outpcd over 2f out: btn whn n.m.r over 1f out* **12/1**

04-0 **7** *15* **Pequeno Dinero (IRE)**[20] 1478 3-8-9 **56** .... AndrewElliott 2 — 28
(C W Fairhurst) *in tch tl rdn and wknd over 3f out* **20/1**

2m 37.67s (-0.93) **Going Correction** -0.10s/f (Good) **7** Ran SP% **108.9**
Speed ratings (Par 99): **99,97,96,94,94 93,83**
CSF £25.64 CT £82.62 TOTE £10.30: £4.70, £1.70; EX 24.60.
Owner Len Lungo Racing Limited **Bred** Darley **Trained** Carrutherstown, D'fries & G'way

FOCUS
A run-of-the-mill handicap in which the gallop was only fair. Those held up were at a disadvantage but the third and fourth make the form look sound based on their All-Weather marks.

1951 RACING UK MAIDEN STKS — 6f 5y

7:40 (7:42) (Class 5) 3-5-Y-0 **£2,590** (£770; £385; £192) **Stalls** Low

Form — RPR

2-23 **1** **Tawzeea (IRE)**[13] 1623 3-9-0 80 .... JoeFanning 12 — 76+
(M Johnston) *prom on outside: smooth hdwy to ld wl over 1f out: rdn and edgd lft: kpt on wl* **10/11**[1]

2 **2** *2¼* **Strawberry Moon (IRE)**[18] 1519 3-8-9 0 .... TomEaves 2 — 65
(B Smart) *cl up: led briefly 2f out: kpt on fnl f: nt pce of wnr* **6/4**[2]

4050 **3** *1¼* **Johnston's Glory (IRE)**[44] 1024 4-9-5 50 ....(b[1]) ShaneKelly 10 — 64
(E J Alston) *cl up: effrt and ev ch over 2f out: one pce fnl f* **33/1**

0-0 **4** *½* **Forrest Star**[34] 1222 3-8-6 0 .... AndrewMullen(3) 5 — 59
(Miss L A Perratt) *led to 2f out: no ex appr fnl f* **50/1**

50/ **5** *¾* **Emirate Isle**[628] 4630 4-9-10 0 .... FergalLynch 7 — 65
(C Grant) *towards rr: drvn and outpcd 1/2-way: kpt on fnl f: n.d* **50/1**

4- **5** *dht* **Howards Way**[397] 952 3-9-0 0 .... PaulFessey 4 — 62
(Miss L A Perratt) *bhd and outpcd: hdwy over 1f out: nrst fin* **15/2**[3]

0 **7** *4* **Ceduna Roadhouse (IRE)**[16] 1556 3-8-9 0 .... AdrianTNicholls 11 — 44
(A M Crow) *bhd and outpcd: no imp fr 1/2-way* **150/1**

0 **8** *5* **Colour Of Money**[8] 1737 3-9-0 0 .... PatDobbs 6 — 33+
(S A Callaghan) *missed break: bhd: shkn up 1/2-way: n.d* **28/1**

0-0P **9** *4½* **Meathop (IRE)**[21] 1452 4-9-5 45 .... NeilBrown(5) 1 — 22
(R F Fisher) *in tch to 1/2-way: sn rdn and btn* **150/1**

00/0 **10** *12* **Maylea Gold (IRE)**[5] 1827 5-9-10 45 .... PaulMulrennan 3 — —
(Mrs S C Bradburne) *chsd ldrs tl rdn and wknd over 2f out* **125/1**

0 **11** *22* **Deer Park Lord**[5] 1825 4-9-7 0 ....(t) MarkLawson(3) 8 — —
(D A Nolan) *missed break: racd wd: hung rt 1/2-way: t.o* **250/1**

1m 10.77s (-1.43) **Going Correction** -0.15s/f (Firm)
WFA 3 from 4yo+ 10lb **11** Ran SP% **117.0**
Speed ratings (Par 103): **103,100,98,97,96 96,91,84,78,62 33**
CSF £2.37 TOTE £2.00: £1.10, £1.10, £4.10; EX 2.90.

Owner Hamdan Al Maktoum **Bred** Shadwell Estate Company Limited **Trained** Middleham Moor, N Yorks

FOCUS

A race lacking strength in depth and one that concerned the two market leaders in the closing stages. The form makes sense rated around those two although the proximity of the next three home casts doubt.

Howards Way ◆ Official explanation: jockey said gelding failed to come down the hill

1952 SHARLES CHARTERED ACCOUNTANTS H'CAP — 6f 5y

8:15 (8:16) (Class 5) (0-75,74) 3-Y-0+ — £3,412 (£1,007; £504) Stalls Low

Form — RPR

06-0 **1** **Cheery Cat (USA)**[46] 990 4-9-0 60 ....(p) MarkLawson(3) 6 — 69
(D W Barker) *prom: drvn to ld ent fnl f: hld on wl* **16/1**

05-0 **2** *nk* **Rainbow Fox**[21] 1451 4-9-1 65 .... FrederikTylicki(7) 7 — 73
(R A Fahey) *towards rr: hdwy 2f out: r.o wl to take 2nd nr fin* **20/1**

0431 **3** *nk* **Mineral Rights (USA)**[25] 1371 4-9-5 62 ....(v) PaulFessey 13 — 69
(Miss L A Perratt) *w ldr: led 1/2-way: edgd lft over 1f out: hdd ent fnl f: r.o* **9/1**

006- **4** *nk* **Opal Noir**[196] 6466 4-9-0 62 .... NeilBrown(5) 11 — 68
(Miss L A Perratt) *hld up: hdwy on outside and cl up over 1f out: kpt on same pce wl ins fnl f* **22/1**

6404 **5** *hd* **Coleorton Dancer**[13] 1624 6-9-12 69 .... FergalLynch 10 — 74
(K A Ryan) *prom: effrt 2f out: kpt on u.p fnl f* **10/1**

00-0 **6** *hd* **Gap Princess (IRE)**[46] 987 4-8-11 61 .... BMcHugh(7) 4 — 66+
(R A Fahey) *towards rr: hdwy whn n.m.r briefly 2f out: nt clr run ins fnl f: r.o fin* **9/2**[2]

0-05 **7** *1 1/2* **Yorkshire Blue**[5] 1826 9-9-7 69 .... GaryBartley(5) 8 — 69
(J S Goldie) *bhd: hdwy over 1f out: nvr able to chal* **15/2**[3]

502 **8** *1 1/4* **Dnata Flyer (USA)**[15] 1581 3-8-13 66 .... GregFairley 9 — 59
(M Johnston) *bhd: hdwy on outside over 1f out: nvr nrr* **12/1**

-060 **9** *4 1/2* **Steel Blue**[20] 1485 8-9-4 64 .... MichaelJStainton(3) 14 — 46
(R M Whitaker) *cl up on outside: effrt and ev ch over 2f out: edgd rt and no ex over 1f out* **16/1**

46-5 **10** *2 1/4* **Argentine (IRE)**[28] 1309 4-9-11 68 .... PaulMulrennan 2 — 42
(L Lungo) *chsd ldrs tl rdn and wknd over 2f out* **10/1**

-401 **11** *1/2* **Varadouro (BRZ)**[10] 1703 6-10-3 74 6ex .... AdrianTNicholls 3 — 47
(D Nicholls) *trckd ldrs: rdn and edgd rt wl over 1f out: sn wknd* **3/1**[1]

005- **12** *nk* **Ulysees (IRE)**[218] 5935 9-8-9 55 oh7 .... AndrewMullen(3) 12 — 27
(J Barclay) *bhd and drvn along: nvr on terms* **66/1**

6-43 **13** *6* **Kyllis**[16] 1558 3-8-11 64 .... TomEaves 1 — 14
(B Smart) *w ldrs to 1/2-way: sn rdn and btn* **33/1**

064- **14** *1/2* **Bahama Baileys**[229] 5665 3-9-3 70 .... JoeFanning 5 — 18
(M Johnston) *slt ld to 1/2-way: wknd wl over 1f out* **14/1**

1m 10.94s (-1.26) **Going Correction** -0.15s/f (Firm)
WFA 3 from 4yo+ 10lb — **14 Ran SP% 122.8**
Speed ratings (Par 103): **102,101,101,100,100 100,98,96,90,87 86,86,78,77**
CSF £312.53 CT £3128.93 TOTE £22.40: £5.60, £7.20, £3.60; EX 305.00.

Owner The Cataractonium Racing Syndicate **Bred** K L Ramsay & Sarah K Ramsay **Trained** Scorton, N Yorks

FOCUS

A modest handicap in which the pace was sound and a bit of a triumph for the Handicapper. The form looks sound with the third to his All-weather mark and the fifth to his latest, while the sixth-placed Gap Princess shaped better than the bare form suggests.

Varadouro(BRZ) Official explanation: trainer had no explanation for the poor form shown

Kyllis Official explanation: jockey said filly hung right-handed throughout

1953 HAMILTON-PARK.CO.UK H'CAP (QUALIFIER) (FOR THE RBS SCOTTISH TROPHY HANDICAP SERIES FINAL) — 1m 1f 36y

8:45 (8:45) (Class 5) (0-70,70) 4-Y-0+ — £2,590 (£770; £385; £192) Stalls High

Form — RPR

1213 **1** **Royal Amnesty**[28] 1314 5-8-8 60 ....(b) TomEaves 1 — 71+
(Miss L A Perratt) *hld up bhd: hdwy over 2f out: led ins fnl f: comf* **15/2**

0324 **2** *3/4* **Pianoforte (USA)**[5] 1822 6-8-10 62 ....(b) ShaneKelly 4 — 68
(E J Alston) *hld up in tch: hung rt and hdwy to ld wl over 1f out: hdd ins fnl f: r.o* **9/1**

4-31 **3** *3* **Moonstreaker**[15] 1578 5-8-5 60 .... MichaelJStainton(3) 7 — 60
(R M Whitaker) *t.k.h: prom: effrt over 2f out: kpt on same pce fnl f* **4/1**[3]

-500 **4** *nk* **Muncaster Castle (IRE)**[72] 724 4-8-1 56 oh4 .... AndrewMullen(3) 10 — 55
(R F Fisher) *pressed ldr: drvn 3f out: one pce over 1f out* **33/1**

0002 **5** *nk* **King Of The Moors (USA)**[5] 1822 5-8-7 64 .... NeilBrown(5) 11 — 62
(T D Barron) *led to wl over 1f out: sn no ex* **5/2**[1]

55-6 **6** *1 1/4* **Regent's Secret (USA)**[7] 1771 8-9-4 70 ....(p) FergalLynch 5 — 66
(J S Goldie) *s.i.s: stdy hdwy 3f out: sn rdn and outpcd: no imp fnl f* **8/1**

026- **7** *3/4* **Farne Island**[168] 5286 5-8-8 60 .... PaulMulrennan 8 — 54
(Micky Hammond) *trckd ldrs tl rdn and wknd fr 2f out* **28/1**

455- **8** *5* **Alberts Story (USA)**[209] 6178 4-8-4 56 .... JoeFanning 6 — 39
(R A Fahey) *hld up: hdwy on outside over 3f out: edgd rt and wknd 2f out* **10/3**[2]

6-04 **9** *1 1/4* **Mystical Ayr (IRE)**[7] 1771 6-8-8 65 .... GaryBartley(5) 3 — 45
(Miss L A Perratt) *bhd: drvn over 3f out: nvr on terms* **12/1**

1m 59.59s (-0.11) **Going Correction** -0.10s/f (Good) — **9 Ran SP% 118.6**
Speed ratings (Par 103): **96,95,92,92,92 91,90,85,84**
CSF £74.57 CT £312.22 TOTE £6.00: £2.80, £1.70, £2.00; EX 36.80 Place 6 £1,415.42, Place 5 £157.87..

Owner Mrs Francesca Mitchell **Bred** Brick Kiln Stud, Mrs L Hicks & Partners **Trained** Carluke, S Lanarks

FOCUS

A modest handicap run at just an ordinary gallop and the form is messy and limited.

T/Plt: £774.10 to a £1 stake. Pool: £42,047.57. 39.65 winning tickets. T/Qpdt: £39.00 to a £1 stake. Pool: £3,803.67. 72.00 winning tickets. RY

1762 LINGFIELD (L-H)

Friday, May 9

OFFICIAL GOING: All-weather - standard; turf course good (good to firm in places) changing to good to firm after race 2 (2.40)

Wind: nil Weather: warm , a little overcast muggy

1954 ASHDOWN FOREST H'CAP — 1m (P)

2:10 (2:11) (Class 5) (0-70,69) 4-Y-0+ — £2,590 (£770; £385; £192) Stalls High

Form — RPR

0-26 **1** **Daniel Thomas (IRE)**[16] 1565 6-8-13 64 .... EddieAhern 9 — 73
(Mrs A L M King) *s.i.s: hld up in rr: stl last over 2f out: hdwy on outer jst over 2f out: chsd ldng pair over 1f out: r.o strly to ld wl ins fnl f* **10/3**[2]

134- **2** *3/4* **Jill Dawson (IRE)**[281] 4112 5-8-8 62 .... KirstyMilczarek(3) 7 — 70
(John Berry) *chsd ldr tl led over 2f out: rdn 2f out: kpt on wl tl hdd and no ex wl ins fnl f* **11/4**[1]

4102 **3** *nk* **High 'n Dry (IRE)**[31] 1253 4-9-3 68 ....(p) PaulDoe 1 — 75
(M A Allen) *hld up in tch in midfield: hdwy over 2f out: chsd ldr wl over 1f out: unable qck u.p fnl f* **8/1**

6660 **4** *4 1/2* **Chjimes (IRE)**[13] 1630 4-9-4 69 .... MartinDwyer 2 — 66
(C R Dore) *t.k.h: hld up in last trio: hdwy on inner over 2f out: no imp u.p fr over 1f out* **6/1**[3]

4325 **5** *1 1/4* **Onenightinlisbon (IRE)**[86] 548 4-9-0 65 .... AmirQuinn 10 — 59
(J R Boyle) *hld up bhd: rdn and wd bnd jst over 2f out: plugged on past btn horses form over 1f out: nvr threatened ldrs* **9/1**

503- **6** *2 3/4* **April Fool**[303] 3429 4-8-7 58 ....(v) DavidKinsella 12 — 45
(J A Geake) *taken down early: bhd tl hdwy to chse ldrs on outer 6f out: rdn over 2f out: wknd wl over 1f out* **28/1**

0-20 **7** *3* **Forced Upon Us**[11] 1687 4-8-2 60 ....(bt) AshleyMorgan(7) 8 — 41
(P J McBride) *towards rr: hdwy over 3f out: rdn over 2f out: wknd qckly wl over 1f out* **10/1**

0656 **8** *1/2* **Teen Ager (FR)**[12] 1641 4-9-4 69 .... LPKeniry 5 — 48
(P Burgoyne) *taken down early: hld up in midfield: rdn 3f out: sn struggling: no ch last 2f* **16/1**

6004 **9** *hd* **Corlough Mountain**[43] 1038 4-9-0 68 ....(p) LukeMorris(3) 11 — 47
(M J McGrath) *chsd ldrs: wnt 2nd and rdn over 2f out: wknd wl over 1f out* **10/1**

0-45 **10** *7* **General Knowledge (USA)**[15] 1590 5-8-13 64 ....(t) PaulEddery 3 — 27
(G D Blake) *led tl hdd over 2f out: wkng whn hmpd jst over 2f out: sn wl bhd: eased fnl f* **14/1**

1m 38.59s (0.39) **Going Correction** +0.125s/f (Slow) — **10 Ran SP% 119.3**
Speed ratings (Par 103): **103,102,101,97,96 93,90,89,89,82**
CSF £13.30 CT £70.55 TOTE £4.20: £1.50, £1.30, £3.00; EX 14.70 Trifecta £20.70 Pool £238.82 - 8.19 winning units..

Owner George Martin **Bred** Lawn Stud **Trained** Wilmcote, Warwicks

■ Stewards' Enquiry : Kirsty Milczarek two-day ban: careless riding (May 23-24)

FOCUS

A modest handicap, but the pace was sound and the form makes plenty of sense with the first three coming clear.

1955 EUROPEAN BREEDERS' FUND MAIDEN STKS — 5f

2:40 (2:41) (Class 5) 2-Y-0 — £3,561 (£1,059; £529; £264) Stalls High

Form — RPR

1 **Mythical Border (USA)** 2-8-9 0 .... WilliamBuick(3) 9 — 86+
(J Noseda) *in tch: hdwy to ld and rn green over 1f out: sn clr: eased towards fin: easily* **5/1**

0 **2** *4* **Souter's Sister (IRE)**[11] 1680 2-8-7 0 .... PatrickHills(5) 3 — 69+
(R Hannon) *chsd ldrs: rdn 2f out: chsd wnr ins fnl f: no ch w wnr* **5/2**[1]

3 *3 1/2* **True Britannia** 2-8-12 0 .... LPKeniry 11 — 57
(S Kirk) *racd in midfield: rdn 1/2-way: styd on to go 3rd wl ins fnl f: nvr nr ldrs* **14/1**

0 **4** *3/4* **Taurus Twins**[12] 1640 2-8-12 0 .... JackDean(5) 8 — 59
(W G M Turner) *led: hung lft fr wl over 1f out: hdd over 1f out: sn outpcd and wl btn* **33/1**

0 **5** *1/2* **Striding Edge (IRE)**[18] 1523 2-9-3 0 .... MartinDwyer 5 — 57+
(W R Muir) *squeezed for room s: racd in midfield on outer: rdn and hanging lft over 2f out: kpt on but nvr on terms* **4/1**[3]

3 **6** *1 1/2* **Sonhador**[8] 1736 2-9-3 0 .... StephenCarson 4 — 52
(P Winkworth) *wnt rt s: sn prom: rdn and swtchd rt over 1f out: sn wknd* **10/3**[2]

0 **7** *hd* **Proper Tool (IRE)**[30] 1263 2-9-0 0 .... KevinGhunowa(3) 7 — 51
(R A Harris) *s.i.s: a towards rr: sme hdwy 1f out: n.d* **33/1**

8 *1 1/2* **Mean Mr Mustard (IRE)** 2-9-3 0 .... EddieAhern 1 — 45+
(J A Osborne) *v.s.a: a wl bhd* **8/1**

0 **9** *2 3/4* **Agnes Love**[24] 1385 2-8-12 0 .... HayleyTurner 2 — 31
(Mrs H Sweeting) *taken down early: wnt lft s: chsd ldr after 1f: rdn 2f out: sn wknd* **22/1**

0 **10** *1 3/4* **Leaf Hollow**[11] 1680 2-8-9 0 .... LukeMorris(3) 6 — 24
(M Madgwick) *sn outpcd inrr: wl bhd fr 1/2-way* **100/1**

0 **11** *1* **Miss Belle Eve**[46] 995 2-8-12 0 .... FergusSweeney 10 — 21
(T M Jones) *sn struggling in rr: wl bhd fr 1/2-way* **66/1**

57.65 secs (-0.55) **Going Correction** -0.225s/f (Firm) — **11 Ran SP% 118.8**
Speed ratings (Par 93): **95,88,83,81,81 78,78,75,71,68 67**
CSF £17.48 TOTE £3.30: £1.60, £1.70, £3.70; EX 17.00 Trifecta £84.10 Pool £187.18 - 1.58 winning units..

Owner Sheikh Mohammed Bin Khalifa Al-Thani **Bred** Crown Bloodstock **Trained** Newmarket, Suffolk

■ Stewards' Enquiry : Jack Dean one-day ban: careless riding (May 23)

FOCUS

Not easy juvenile form to assess, but the winner made an impressive debut and the runner-up finished nicely clear of the remainder, stepping up 9lb on her debut form.

NOTEBOOK

Mythical Border(USA) ◆, whose sales price rose to $500,000 at the Ocala Breeze-Up, got her career off to a perfect start and did the job in the style of a classy filly. She was given time to find her feet early on, but her response when asked to quicken was immediate and, idling when in front, she eventually scored with a deal left up her sleeve. The winning time was particularly noteworthy and it was no surprise when her trainer – who has made a decent start with his juveniles so far – nominated the Queen Mary at Royal Ascot as her target. It remains to be seen if she will have another run beforehand, but she certainly looks a likely sort for that Group 3 event and a sound surface is clearly to her liking. (op 3-1)

Souter's Sister(IRE), seventh on her debut at Windsor last time, met support in the betting ring but simply ran into a superior filly. She finished nicely clear of the remainder, is going the right way, and should not be too long in shedding her maiden tag. (op 3-1 tchd 10-3 in a place)

True Britannia, bred to stay further, posted a creditable debut effort and left the clear impression she would learn from the experience. She will likely prosper from another furlong, however. (op 16-1)

Taurus Twins showed a lot more than had been the case on debut at Brighton and enjoyed the quicker ground. (op 40-1)

Striding Edge(IRE) was the subject of good support in the betting ring, but he got little cover through the race and was never seriously in the hunt on this quicker surface. Official explanation: jockey said colt was unsuited by the good to firm ground (op 10-1)

Sonhador was quickly into his stride, but dropped out tamely when pressure was applied. He has something to prove now. (op 3-1 tchd 7-2)

Proper Tool(IRE) Official explanation: jockey said colt ran very green

Mean Mr Mustard(IRE) Official explanation: jockey said colt missed the break

Agnes Love Official explanation: jockey said filly lost a front shoe

1956 SGMS GROUP H'CAP 5f
3:10 (3:11) (Class 4) (0-85,83) 4-Y-0+ **£4,100** (£1,227; £613; £306; £152) **Stalls** High

Form RPR
40-6 **1** **Zowington**[17] [1537] 6-8-13 **78** .... IanMongan 8 91
(C F Wall) *awkward leaving stalls and slowly away: bhd: hdwy over 1f out: r.o wl u.p to ld nr fin* **4/1**[1]
51-5 **2** *nk* **Ocean Blaze**[25] [1366] 4-8-11 **76** .... DarryllHolland 7 88
(B R Millman) *in tch: swtchd lft and hdwy over 1f out: chsd ldr jst over 1f out: led ins fnl f: hdd and no ex nr fin* **9/2**[2]
-304 **3** *1 1/4* **Merlin's Dancer**[15] [1582] 8-9-0 **82** .... WilliamBuick(3) 2 90
(S Dow) *disp ld tl def advantage over 2f out: rdn 2f out: hdd ins fnl f: wknd last 50yds* **8/1**
4302 **4** *2 3/4* **Misaro (GER)**[15] [1582] 7-8-4 **72** ....(b) KevinGhunowa(3) 1 70
(R A Harris) *wnt sltly lft s: racd wd: chsd ldrs: rdn 1/2-way: outpcd fnl f* **9/2**[2]
1124 **5** *3/4* **Fromsong (IRE)**[52] [925] 10-9-3 **82** .... StephenCarson 5 77
(D K Ivory) *chsd ldrs tl short of room and lost pl after 1f: effrt and swtchd rt wl over 1f out: wknd fnl f* **7/1**[3]
6 *3/4* **Mondovi**[255] 4-9-4 **83** .... EddieAhern 4 75
(N J Vaughan) *in tch in midfield: effrt 2f out: rdn over 1f out: wknd fnl f* **9/2**[2]
2011 **7** *nk* **Harry Up**[35] [1195] 7-9-3 **82** ....(p) DO'Donohoe 3 73
(K A Ryan) *pressed ldrs tl wknd wl over 1f out* **9/1**
6066 **8** *1 1/2* **Silver Prelude**[25] [1366] 7-9-0 **79** .... MartinDwyer 6 65
(D K Ivory) *disp ld tl over 2f out: wknd wl over 1f out* **9/1**

56.21 secs (-1.99) **Going Correction** -0.225s/f (Firm) course record **8** Ran SP% **118.2**
Speed ratings (Par 105): **106,105,103,99,97 96,96,93**
CSF £22.94 CT £140.07 TOTE £7.70: £1.70, £1.90, £2.50; EX 22.90 Trifecta £257.00 Part won. Pool £362.08 - 0.99 winning units..
Owner O Pointing **Bred** O Pointing **Trained** Newmarket, Suffolk

FOCUS
A good sprint handicap, run at a frantic early pace. The first two came from off the speed and it could be that they enjoyed a draw advantage. The winner took 0.03 off the old course record.
Silver Prelude Official explanation: jockey said gelding was unsuited by the good to firm ground

1957 WEATHERBYS BLOODSTOCK INSURANCE MAIDEN STKS 7f
3:45 (3:47) (Class 5) 3-Y-0 **£2,590** (£770; £385; £192) **Stalls** High

Form RPR
2- **1** **Tawaash (USA)**[203] [6295] 3-9-3 0 .... MartinDwyer 15 84+
(M A Jarvis) *mde all on stands rail: pushed along over 1f out: a holding rivals* **4/5**[1]
2 *1 1/4* **Expresso Star (USA)** 3-9-3 0 .... DavidKinsella 4 80+
(J H M Gosden) *stdd s: wl bhd: stdy hdwy in centre over 3f out: chsd wnr over 1f out: sn ev ch and rdn 1f out: kpt on same pce fnl f* **20/1**
3 *1/2* **Grande Annee (USA)** 3-8-12 0 .... EddieAhern 10 74
(J Noseda) *s.i.s: sn in tch: rdn and hdwy over 2f out: chsd ldng pair over 1f out: kpt on* **15/2**[3]
55- **4** *3* **Wise Hawk**[161] [6980] 3-9-3 0 .... LiamJones 17 71
(W J Haggas) *hld up in midfield on stands rail: hdwy over 2f out: kpt on but no imp on ldng trio fnl f* **20/1**
00- **5** *1/2* **Valento**[211] [6126] 3-9-3 0 .... StephenCarson 11 70
(Eve Johnson Houghton) *prom: chsd wnr over 2f tl over 1f out: outpcd fnl f* **50/1**
6 *1 1/4* **Theory** 3-8-12 0 .... DarryllHolland 14 61+
(J H M Gosden) *hld up towards rr on stands' side: nt clr run over 2f out: swtchd lft and hdwy 2f out: edgd lft and no imp fnl f* **14/1**
552- **7** *3 1/4* **Penchesco (IRE)**[171] [6884] 3-9-3 76 .... PaulEddery 3 58
(Pat Eddery) *stdd s: dropped in bhd: hdwy 3f out: sn rdn: kpt on but nvr threatened ldrs* **20/1**
4 **8** *2 1/4* **Mr Hichens**[22] [1418] 3-9-3 0 .... StephenDonohoe 5 51+
(B J Meehan) *racd in midfield: rdn and outpcd 3f out: no ch after* **5/1**[2]
9 *1* **New Havens** 3-8-9 0 .... WilliamBuick(3) 9 44+
(C R Egerton) *bhd: hdwy and hung bdly lft over 3f out: nvr nr ldrs* **33/1**
0-0 **10** *1* **Carmela Maria**[17] [1535] 3-8-12 0 .... IanMongan 7 41+
(C F Wall) *w ldr in centre: rdn 3f out: wknd over 2f out: no ch whn eased ins fnl f* **12/1**
56- **11** *1/2* **Istria (USA)**[169] [6903] 3-8-12 0 .... FergusSweeney 13 40
(R M Beckett) *in tch in midfield: rdn 3f out: sn outpcd and btn* **66/1**
0 **12** *3 3/4* **Delerios**[8] [1737] 3-9-3 0 .... PaulDoe 2 35
(Jim Best) *chsd ldrs in centre: rdn over 2f out: wknd qckly wl over 1f out* **100/1**
50- **13** *11* **Heart Of Dubai (USA)**[233] [5536] 3-8-12 0 .... AhmedAjtebi(5) 6 5
(C E Brittain) *chsd ldrs tl 1/2-way: sn rdn and wknd: no ch fnl 2f: t.o* **40/1**
0 **14** *3/4* **Ma Mirage (IRE)**[28] [1302] 3-8-12 0 .... HayleyTurner 1 —
(S C Williams) *dropped in after s: a bhd* **50/1**
0 **15** *shd* **Krasavitsa**[21] [1445] 3-8-12 0 .... TPO'Shea 12 —
(J L Dunlop) *t.k.h: chsd ldrs tl wknd qckly over 2f out: eased fnl f: t.o* **50/1**
54- **16** *6* **Fantadot**[148] [7129] 3-9-3 0 .... LPKeniry 8 —
(D J S Ffrench Davis) *chsd ldrs: rdn over 3f out: sn struggling: wl bhd last 2f: t.o* **100/1**
0-00 **17** *5* **Milloaks (IRE)**[24] [1380] 3-8-7 0 .... SCreighton(5) 18 —
(E J Creighton) *a bhd: t.o fnl 2f* **100/1**

1m 21.89s (-1.41) **Going Correction** -0.225s/f (Firm) **17** Ran SP% **128.4**
Speed ratings (Par 99): **99,97,97,93,93 91,87,85,84,83 82,78,65,64,64 57,52**
CSF £26.78 TOTE £1.80: £1.20, £5.00, £2.20; EX 25.00 Trifecta £212.60 Pool £326.39 - 1.09 winning units..
Owner Hamdan Al Maktoum **Bred** G Watts Humphrey Jr & Louise I Humphrey **Trained** Newmarket, Suffolk

FOCUS
This looked a reasonable maiden which should produce its share of future winners. The fourth looks the best guide, suggesting Tawaash was 10lb off his debut form. The runner-up did easily best of those drawn low.
Theory Official explanation: jockey said filly ran too free
Carmela Maria Official explanation: jockey said filly was unsuited by the good to firm ground

1958 DLH CENTENARY H'CAP 7f
4:20 (4:20) (Class 5) (0-70,70) 3-Y-0 **£2,914** (£867; £433; £216) **Stalls** High

Form RPR
3210 **1** **Desiderio**[24] [1389] 3-8-6 **65** ....(b) CharlesEddery(7) 11 75
(R Hannon) *wnt lft s: sn edgd rt and led: mde rest: rdn over 1f out: styd on wl fnl 100yds* **10/1**
310- **2** *1* **Danseuse Volante (IRE)**[189] [6619] 3-9-4 **70** .... EddieAhern 14 78
(J W Hills) *t.k.h: hld up in tch: sltly hmpd over 6f out: hdwy to chse wnr wl over 1f out: no imp fnl 100yds* **9/2**[1]
004- **3** *3* **Silky Steps (IRE)**[190] [6601] 3-9-0 **66** .... RichardSmith 10 66
(P J Makin) *stdd s: hld up towards rr: hdwy over 2f out: kpt on u.p to go 3rd wl ins fnl f: nt trble ldng pair* **8/1**
25-0 **4** *1/2* **Mrs Summersby (IRE)**[30] [1270] 3-8-12 **64** .... FergusSweeney 4 62+
(H Morrison) *towards rr: rdn and struggling over 3f out: kpt on u.p fr over 1f out: nvr trbld ldrs* **10/1**
0300 **5** *hd* **Easy Wonder (GER)**[8] [1743] 3-8-7 **62** .... KirstyMilczarek(3) 6 60
(I A Wood) *in tch rdn and effrt wl over 1f out: chsd ldng pair over 1f out: sn wknd* **16/1**
-660 **6** *3 1/4* **Copperwood**[29] [1277] 3-9-1 **67** .... PaulDoe 7 56
(M Blanshard) *chsd ldrs: rdn over 2f out: wknd fnl f* **16/1**
53-0 **7** *1* **Bid Art (IRE)**[20] [1479] 3-8-9 **64** .... WilliamBuick(3) 1 50
(A M Balding) *slowly away and dropped in bhd: hung lft fr over 2f out: n.d* **6/1**[2]
-425 **8** *1 1/4* **Shatter Resistant (IRE)**[11] [1672] 3-7-13 **56** oh1(e[1]) NataliaGemelova(5) 9 39
(M D Squance) *t.k.h: chsd ldrs: wnt 2nd over 3f out tl wl over 1f out: sn hung lft and nt run on* **8/1**
245- **9** *4 1/2* **Gower Belle**[207] [6228] 3-9-1 **67** .... MartinDwyer 12 38
(W R Muir) *t.k.h: hmpd over 6f out: effrt over 2f out: wknd over 1f out* **8/1**
0-35 **10** *3 3/4* **Saafend Geezer**[32] [1247] 3-8-9 **61** .... IanMongan 5 22
(B J Meehan) *s.i.s: a bhd* **7/1**[3]
0-00 **11** *7* **Ruby Delta**[42] [1060] 3-8-12 **64** .... SimonWhitworth 8 6
(P D Cundell) *a struggling towards rr: eased ins fnl f* **16/1**
1400 **12** *3 3/4* **Southwest Star (IRE)**[27] [1336] 3-9-4 **70** .... LPKeniry 3 2
(J S Moore) *prom: rdn over 3f out: sn struggling: bhd last 2f* **9/1**

1m 21.77s (-1.53) **Going Correction** -0.225s/f (Firm) **12** Ran SP% **124.1**
Speed ratings (Par 99): **99,97,94,93,93 89,88,87,82,77 69,65**
CSF £57.23 CT £313.22 TOTE £17.00: £3.60, £2.20, £2.60; EX 44.30 Trifecta £168.50 Part won. Pool £237.33 - 0.10 winning units..
Owner Exors of the late Cathal M Ryan **Bred** Keith Freeman **Trained** East Everleigh, Wilts
■ Stewards' Enquiry : Charles Eddery three-day ban: careless riding (May 23-25)

FOCUS
A modest three-year-old handicap which saw those drawn near the stands' rail at an advantage. The form makes plenty of sense at face value though, rated through the third and fourth.

1959 FOREST ROW FILLIES' H'CAP 1m 2f (P)
4:55 (4:56) (Class 5) (0-70,70) 3-Y-0+ **£2,590** (£770; £385; £192) **Stalls** Low

Form RPR
0-26 **1** **Uig**[10] [1697] 7-9-3 **60** .... HaddenFrost(5) 3 68
(H S Howe) *in tch: chsd ldng pair 3f out: rdn over 2f out: led ins fnl f: hld on* **6/1**[2]
20-0 **2** *1/2* **Miss Jolyon (USA)**[17] [1543] 3-9-0 **67** .... MartinDwyer 8 73
(M A Jarvis) *bhd: bustled along over 4f out: hdwy on outer over 2f out: r.o wl to chse wnr wl ins fnl f: nt quite rch wnr* **14/1**
14-3 **3** *2 1/4* **Flying Time**[23] [1395] 3-9-1 **68** .... TPO'Shea 6 70
(M R Channon) *chsd ldrs: hdwy to ld over 3f out: rdn over 2f out: hdd ins fnl f: fdd fnl 100yds* **6/1**[2]
613 **4** *1 1/4* **Moon Crystal**[22] [1412] 3-9-3 **70** ....(t) StephenDonohoe 9 69
(E A L Dunlop) *s.i.s: sn pushed up into midfield: hdwy to chse ldr over 3f out: rdn over 2f out: wknd jst ins fnl f* **7/4**[1]
1 **5** *nse* **Lizzie Wiggins**[32] [1245] 3-9-3 **70** .... HayleyTurner 5 69
(M L W Bell) *chsd ldrs: rdn over 2f out: wknd jst ins fnl f* **15/2**
/154 **6** *3/4* **Saraba (FR)**[16] [1564] 7-9-13 **65** .... IanMongan 10 63
(Mrs L J Mongan) *in tch in midfield: hdwy 3f out: chsd ldrs and rdn over 2f out: swtchd rt over 1f out: no imp u.p fnl f* **9/1**
660- **7** *1 3/4* **Lindy Lou**[242] [5279] 4-9-9 **61** .... EddieAhern 11 56
(C F Wall) *stdd s: t.k.h: hld up in last pair: hdwy 3f out: nt clr run over 1f out: swtchd rt 1f out: no imp after* **7/1**[3]
400- **8** *2 1/2* **Dream Bee**[219] [5914] 3-8-9 **62** ow1 .... DarryllHolland 2 51
(E A L Dunlop) *chsd ldrs tl lost pl over 4f out: bhd last 2f* **12/1**
365 **9** *hd* **Tripod Molly (IRE)**[65] [796] 3-8-2 **62** ....(t) AshleyMorgan(7) 7 51
(P J McBride) *bhd: hdwy on outer 4f out: rdn wl over 2f out: sn wl btn* **16/1**
050- **10** *21* **Amie Magnificent (IRE)**[218] [5944] 3-8-6 **59** .... StephenCarson 4 6
(P Winkworth) *chsd ldr tl over 3f out: sn wknd: t.o fnl 2f* **66/1**
060 **11** *48* **Sweet Refrain**[30] [1270] 3-8-2 **58** .... KirstyMilczarek(3) 1 —
(M J Attwater) *led tl over 3f out: sn wknd: t.o and virtually p.u over 1f out: t.o* **28/1**

2m 9.14s (2.54) **Going Correction** +0.125s/f (Slow)
WFA 3 from 4yo+ 15lb **11** Ran SP% **124.4**
Speed ratings (Par 100): **94,93,91,90,90 90,88,86,86,69 31**
CSF £92.02 CT £539.69 TOTE £8.20: £1.80, £3.60, £2.00; EX 143.90 TRIFECTA Not won. Place 6 £49.61, Place 5 £32.24.
Owner B P Jones **Bred** Mrs Gillian A R Jones And John Balding **Trained** Oakford, Devon

FOCUS
A modest fillies' only handicap, run at just a steady pace. The form is rated at face value but looks a little shaky.
T/Plt: £64.80 to a £1 stake. Pool: £48,531.30. 546.25 winning tickets. T/Qpdt: £37.00 to a £1 stake. Pool: £2,701.69. 53.90 winning tickets. SP

1568 NOTTINGHAM (L-H)
Friday, May 9

OFFICIAL GOING: Good (good to firm in places)
Wind: Light across Weather: Overcast

1960 TOTEPLACEPOT MEDIAN AUCTION MAIDEN STKS 6f 15y
1:30 (1:30) (Class 5) 3-Y-0 **£2,590** (£770; £385; £192) **Stalls** High

Form RPR
4- **1** **Fabreze**[245] [5194] 3-9-3 0 .... NCallan 6 82+
(P J Makin) *chsd ldrs: led and hung lft over 1f out: rdn out* **7/2**[2]
02- **2** *1* **Choiseau (IRE)**[252] [5003] 3-9-3 0 .... DaneO'Neill 3 79+
(Pat Eddery) *trckd ldrs: rdn over 1f out: swtchd rt: r.o* **8/1**[3]
50- **3** *4* **Sister Moonshine**[207] [6225] 3-8-12 0 .... KerrinMcEvoy 10 61+
(W R Muir) *chsd ldrs: rdn over 2f out: styd on same pce appr fnl f* **22/1**
4 *shd* **This Ones For Eddy** 3-9-3 0 .... JohnEgan 9 66
(S Parr) *disp ld tl rdn and hung lft fr over 1f out: wknd ins fnl f* **20/1**
5 *1 1/4* **Sir Boss (IRE)** 3-9-3 0 .... PatCosgrave 4 62
(D E Cantillon) *s.i.s: hld up: hdwy over 2f out: rdn over 1f out: styd on same pce* **100/1**
432- **6** *2 1/4* **Provence**[193] [6535] 3-8-12 84 .... MichaelHills 8 49
(B W Hills) *w ldr tl rdn and hmpd over 1f out: wknd fnl f* **10/11**[1]

020- **7** 4 **Actabou**[204] 6281 3-9-3 73 .... PhillipMakin 2 42
(M Dods) *hld up: racd keenly: hdwy over 2f: sn rdn: wkng whn hung rt over 1f out* **40/1**
5- **8** 2 **Lady Carollina**[207] 6234 3-8-12 0 .... ChrisCatlin 5 30
(Rae Guest) *hld up: n.d* **50/1**
9 1 ¾ **Master Of Light** 3-9-3 0 .... GrahamGibbons 7 30
(P A Blockley) *s.i.s: hdwy over 3f out: wknd 2f out* **50/1**
60 **10** 1 ¾ **Threecheersforanby (IRE)**[8] 1751 3-9-0 0 ....(t) DNolan(3) 1 24
(S Parr) *mid-div: rdn 1/2-way: wknd 2f out* **150/1**
50 **11** 1 **Sunny Spells**[38] 1125 3-8-10 0 .... WilliamCarson(7) 12 21
(S C Williams) *s.i.s: outpcd* **66/1**
5 **12** 1 ¼ **Little Cee (IRE)**[19] 1499 3-8-9 0 .... MarcHalford(3) 13 12
(D R C Elsworth) *s.i.s: hdwy 4f out: rdn and wknd over 2f out* **50/1**
6- **13** 1 **Croeso Cusan**[207] 6237 3-8-12 0 .... SteveDrowne 11 9
(J L Spearing) *s.s: hdwy over 3f out: rdn and wknd over 2f out* **80/1**
4- **14** 2 **Kenton Street**[189] 6617 3-9-3 0 .... AlanMunro 14 7
(J A R Toller) *sn outpcd* **9/1**

1m 13.52s (-1.58) **Going Correction** -0.25s/f (Firm) **14** Ran SP% **117.5**
Speed ratings (Par 99): **100,98,93,93,91 88,83,80,78,75 74,72,71,68**
CSF £28.55 TOTE £3.60: £1.40, £2.30, £5.80; EX 33.40.
Owner Weldspec Glasgow Limited **Bred** D Brocklehurst **Trained** Ogbourne Maisey, Wilts
■ Stewards' Enquiry : John Egan one-day ban: careless riding (May 23)

FOCUS
A pretty ordinary maiden particularly with the favourite disappointing. That said, the first two came clear and built on their promising juvenile form.
Kenton Street Official explanation: trainer said colt moved badly

1961 E B F TOTEEXACTA MEDIAN AUCTION MAIDEN FILLIES' STKS 5f 13y
2:00 (2:01) (Class 5) 2-Y-O **£3,561** (£1,059; £529; £264) **Stalls** High

Form RPR
2 **1** **Art Princess (USA)**[22] 1419 2-9-0 0 .... MichaelHills 14 77+
(B W Hills) *wnt lft s: chsd ldrs on stands' side: rdn and hung lft fnl f: r.o to ld cl home* **1/1**[1]
040 **2** ½ **Amosite**[22] 1413 2-9-0 0 ....(v[1]) JimCrowley 6 75
(J R Jenkins) *led: clr over 3f out: rdn ins fnl f: hdd cl home* **50/1**
3 ½ **Undaunted Affair (IRE)** 2-9-0 0 .... NCallan 13 73+
(K A Ryan) *hmpd s: bhd: hdwy 3f out: rdn and r.o ins fnl f: bttr for r* **14/1**
5 **4** ¾ **Voulez Vous**[20] 1474 2-9-0 0 .... ChrisCatlin 2 71+
(E J O'Neill) *mid-div: hdwy over 2f out: kpt on ins fnl f* **10/1**
5 2 **Sea Of Leaves (USA)** 2-9-0 0 .... RobertHavlin 12 63+
(J H M Gosden) *wnt rt s: prom: chsd clr ldr 3f out tl rdn and no ex ins fnl f* **11/2**[2]
6 ½ **Ares Choix** 2-9-0 0 .... KerrinMcEvoy 8 62
(P C Haslam) *mid-div: hdwy over 1f out: one pce fnl f* **18/1**
3 **7** 1 ¼ **La Brigitte**[7] 1778 2-9-0 0 .... NeilPollard 1 57
(A J McCabe) *played up in stalls: towards rr: sme hdwy on outside 2f out: no real prog fnl f* **16/1**
8 nk **Jessicas Girl**[12] 1653 2-9-0 0 .... PatCosgrave 7 56
(Eamon Tyrrell, Ire) *prom tl rdn and wknd over 1f out* **40/1**
03 **9** ½ **Cecilia's Lass**[13] 1610 2-9-0 0 .... RobertWinston 15 54
(D H Brown) *s.i.s: sme hdwy on stands' rail 3f out: rdn and wknd over 1f out* **33/1**
4 **10** 1 **Readily**[11] 1680 2-9-0 0 .... JamesDoyle 3 51
(J G Portman) *chsd ldr 2f: wknd over 1f out* **7/1**[3]
40 **11** ¾ **Missy Que (IRE)**[22] 1413 2-9-0 0 .... AlanMunro 5 48
(W R Muir) *chsd ldrs tl wknd wl over 1f out* **40/1**
12 ¾ **Bold Rose** 2-9-0 0 .... TQuinn 9 45
(M D I Usher) *a bhd* **50/1**
13 ½ **Misty Glade** 2-9-0 0 .... SteveDrowne 10 43
(B J Meehan) *dwlt: a in rr* **25/1**
14 ½ **Blusher** 2-9-0 0 .... EdwardCreighton 11 42
(M R Channon) *broke wl: sn mid-div: bhd fnl 3f* **40/1**
0 **15** nk **Sienna Lake (IRE)**[11] 1680 2-9-0 0 .... DaneO'Neill 4 40
(S Kirk) *dwlt: rdn over 1f out: a in rr* **25/1**

60.59 secs (-0.11) **Going Correction** -0.25s/f (Firm) **15** Ran SP% **126.7**
Speed ratings (Par 90): **90,89,88,87,84 83,81,80,79,78 77,75,75,74,73**
CSF £92.34 TOTE £1.70: £1.30, £14.00, £3.90; EX 67.60.
Owner Matthew Green **Bred** Michael Narlinger & Michael Hernon **Trained** Lambourn, Berks

FOCUS
Probably only an ordinary maiden. The winner was close to her pre-race mark but the runner-up showed big improvement and limits the form.

NOTEBOOK
Art Princess(USA), runner-up on her debut at Newmarket last month, confirmed the promise of that race with a workmanlike victory. She did make rather hard work of reeling in Amosite, and was inclined to go left under pressure, but could need a sixth furlong now and she is likely to be targeted at the Albany Stakes at Royal Ascot. (op 6-4)
Amosite, whose best run to date was a fourth of six on Polytrack at Lingfield a month ago, was lit up by a first-time visor and, having been allowed an uncontested lead, she did not give up without a fight on the run to the line. The big question now is whether she can reproduce the form as she gets more accustomed to the headgear. (op 33-1)
Undaunted Affair(IRE) ◆ had plenty to do from halfway after being messed about at the start, but this 47,000gns newcomer was doing some excellent work late on. She is half-sister to Winter Fashion, a Listed winner in France over 7f, and on this evidence could come into her own over that trip later in the summer. (op 11-1 tchd 16-1)
Voulez Vous fifth on her debut over course and distance last month, stepped up just a little on that effort on this slightly better ground. (op 8-1 tchd 7-1)
Sea Of Leaves(USA), whose dam is a half-sister to Kentucky Derby runner-up Aptitude and Kentucky Oaks winner Sleep Easy, travelled well on this racecourse debut and was not given a hard time when she started to tire from the furlong mark. She should come on a lot for this run and can win at this level. (op 6-1 tchd 7-1)
Readily failed to build on the promise of her fourth at Windsor last month and was a beaten horse at the furlong mark. The Windsor ground was riding fast, and perhaps the slightly slower going here was not entirely to her liking. (op 9-1)

1962 TOTEPOOL A BETTER WAY TO BET H'CAP 1m 6f 15y
2:30 (2:31) (Class 5) (0-75,75) 3-Y-O **£4,857** (£1,445; £722; £360) **Stalls** Low

Form RPR
5004 **1** **Fairfield Flame (GER)**[15] 1575 3-8-2 59 ....(b[1]) MarcHalford(3) 5 69+
(D R C Elsworth) *hld up: hdwy over 3f out: rdn to ld and hung lft fr over 1f out: styd on wl: eased nr fin* **33/1**
01-4 **2** 3 **Tasheba**[24] 1389 3-9-3 71 .... AlanMunro 7 77
(P W Chapple-Hyam) *chsd ldrs: rdn over 2f out: swtchd rt over 1f out: styd on* **6/1**[2]
-236 **3** 1 ½ **Pepper's Ghost**[11] 1678 3-8-8 62 ....(b[1]) DMylonas 10 66
(Miss J Feilden) *s.i.s: hld up: hdwy 7f out: rdn over 3f out: hung lft and styd on same pce fnl f* **22/1**
6-21 **4** 2 **Kiribati King (IRE)**[23] 1397 3-9-4 72 .... EdwardCreighton 15 73
(M R Channon) *hld up: rdn over 3f out: styd on appr fnl f: sn edgd lft: nvr nrr* **7/1**[3]
4210 **5** 1 ¼ **Flash Of Colour**[17] 1543 3-9-7 75 .... JimCrowley 17 74+
(Mrs A J Perrett) *prom: lost pl over 7f out: hdwy 5f out: led 2f out: sn rdn and hdd: no ex fnl f* **14/1**
00-4 **6** hd **Sea Admiral**[11] 1681 3-8-13 67 .... RichardKingscote 13 66
(R Charlton) *hld up: rdn over 3f out: styd on appr fnl f: eased towards fin: nvr trbld ldrs* **6/1**[2]
-343 **7** 2 **Georgie The Fourth (IRE)**[23] 1397 3-8-13 67 .... ChrisCatlin 9 63
(E J O'Neill) *chsd ldrs: led over 2f out: sn rdn and hdd: wknd fnl f* **14/1**
4-12 **8** 2 ½ **Taikoo**[11] 1678 3-9-6 74 .... SteveDrowne 4 67
(H Morrison) *hld up in tch: rdn over 3f out: wknd 2f out* **6/1**[2]
0-50 **9** 1 ¼ **Io (IRE)**[18] 1527 3-8-4 58 ow1 .... KerrinMcEvoy 6 49
(J L Dunlop) *hld up: sme hdwy over 2f out: sn rdn: wknd over 1f out* **4/1**[1]
003- **10** 1 ¾ **Rampant Ronnie (USA)**[196] 6478 3-8-9 63 ow1 .... RobertWinston 8 52
(P W D'Arcy) *led after 1f: rdn and hdd over 2f out: wknd over 1f out* **16/1**
-454 **11** 3 ¼ **Vice Consul**[27] 1330 3-9-4 72 .... J-PGuillambert 11 56
(M Johnston) *chsd ldrs: rdn and hung lft over 3f out: wknd and hung lft over 1f out: eased* **14/1**
3510 **12** 12 **Kryptonite (IRE)**[17] 1530 3-9-0 68 .... JamesDoyle 16 35
(J W Hills) *hld up: rdn over 3f out: wknd over 2f out* **33/1**
55-0 **13** 4 ½ **House Of Tudor**[18] 1527 3-8-11 65 .... NeilChalmers 3 26
(David Pinder) *hld up: rdn over 4f out: sn wknd* **66/1**
0-41 **14** 13 **Crimson Mitre**[17] 1549 3-9-5 73 .... NCallan 1 16
(J Jay) *led 1f: chsd ldrs: rdn and wknd over 2f out* **14/1**
06-2 **15** 38 **Stealth Project**[18] 1516 3-8-10 64 .... DaneO'Neill 12 —
(A M Hales) *hld up: racd keenly: wknd over 4f out: eased* **12/1**

3m 4.15s (-3.15) **Going Correction** -0.25s/f (Firm) **15** Ran SP% **127.3**
Speed ratings (Par 99): **99,97,96,95,94 94,93,91,91,90 88,81,78,71,49**
CSF £227.27 CT £4513.66 TOTE £51.40: £8.00, £2.40, £9.20; EX 544.60.
Owner Mrs Anne Coughlan **Bred** Graf Und Grafin Von Stauffenberg **Trained** Newmarket, Suffolk

FOCUS
A modest affair run at a decent pace. The whole field was unexposed at the trip. The winner was up 10lb on her previous form and the fourth looks the best guide.
Vice Consul Official explanation: jockey said colt had no more to give
Stealth Project Official explanation: jockey said colt moved badly

1963 TOTETRIFECTA H'CAP 1m 2f 50y
3:00 (3:00) (Class 5) (0-75,74) 4-Y-O+ **£3,238** (£963; £481; £240) **Stalls** Low

Form RPR
051- **1** **Aypeeyes (IRE)**[50] 5604 4-9-2 72 .... DaneO'Neill 10 84+
(A King) *hld up in mid-div: smooth hdwy on outside over 2f out: shkn up to ld wl over 1f out: sn rdn: drew clr ins fnl f: readily* **15/2**
50-5 **2** 3 **King Of Rhythm (IRE)**[24] 1383 5-9-0 70 .... NCallan 8 76+
(D Carroll) *hld up in mid-div: swtchd rt and hdwy 3f out: rdn and wnt 2nd 1f out: no ch w wnr* **11/2**[1]
5/-0 **3** ¾ **Bold Bobby Be (IRE)**[16] 1573 4-8-9 65 .... KerrinMcEvoy 3 71+
(J L Dunlop) *hld up and bhd: hdwy whn nt clr run and swtchd lft 1f out: r.o ins fnl f* **13/2**[2]
243- **4** hd **Crystal Prince**[277] 4229 4-9-2 72 .... SteveDrowne 14 77
(T P Tate) *hld up in tch: rdn and ev ch wl over 1f out: one pce fnl f* **9/1**
012- **5** ½ **Potentiale (IRE)**[216] 6027 4-9-1 71 .... JamesDoyle 4 77+
(J W Hills) *hld up in mid-div: nt clr run fr over 2f out tl hdwy 1f out: kpt on ins fnl f* **8/1**
3400 **6** ¾ **Sforzando**[20] 1482 7-8-3 66 .... KristinStubbs(7) 15 68
(Mrs L Stubbs) *hld up and bhd: pushed along over 4f out: styd on outside fnl f: n.d* **22/1**
2-46 **7** ½ **Trouble Mountain (USA)**[24] 1383 11-8-8 64 ....(t) DaleGibson 16 65
(M W Easterby) *hld up and bhd: pushed along 4f out: rdn and hdwy over 1f out: no further prog fnl f* **16/1**
6330 **8** 2 ¾ **Watchmaker**[43] 1039 5-8-11 67 .... ChrisCatlin 12 63
(Miss Tor Sturgis) *t.k.h: prom: led briefly wl over 1f out: sn rdn: wknd ins fnl f* **16/1**
520- **9** nk **Mulaazem**[219] 5916 5-8-8 64 ow1 ....(t) J-PGuillambert 9 59
(J Mackie) *hld up in tch: wknd wl over 1f out* **9/1**
60-0 **10** ½ **Wester Ross (IRE)**[25] 1365 4-9-4 74 .... AlanMunro 11 68
(J M P Eustace) *set stdy pce: hdd 3f out: rdn and wknd over 1f out* **15/2**
05-4 **11** nk **Idesia (IRE)**[25] 1372 4-9-1 71 .... AdamKirby 1 64+
(W R Swinburn) *hld up in tch: wknd wl over 1f out* **7/1**[3]
5616 **12** nk **Sol Rojo**[18] 1521 6-7-12 61 .... JosephineBruning(7) 13 54
(J Pearce) *s.i.s: a in rr* **16/1**
00- **13** hd **Bright Sun (IRE)**[294] 3705 7-8-7 63 .... KimTinkler 6 55
(N Tinkler) *plld hrd: w ldr: pushed along to ld 3f out: rdn and hdd wl over 1f out: sn wknd* **40/1**

2m 12.05s (-0.45) **Going Correction** -0.25s/f (Firm) **13** Ran SP% **120.3**
Speed ratings (Par 103): **98,95,95,94,94 93,93,91,91,90 90,90,89**
CSF £48.76 CT £289.14 TOTE £8.40: £3.10, £2.30, £2.90; EX 26.20 Trifecta £84.40 Part won. Pool £118.94 - 0.10 winning units..
Owner D A Wallace **Bred** John Malone **Trained** Barbury Castle, Wilts

FOCUS
A steadily run handicap. Aypeeyes showed improvement and the form seems sound enough.

1964 BET TOTEPOOL ON ALL UK RACING MAIDEN FILLIES' STKS (DIV I) 1m 75y
3:35 (3:36) (Class 5) 3-Y-O **£2,428** (£722; £361; £180) **Stalls** Centre

Form RPR
3- **1** **Scuffle**[195] 6493 3-9-0 0 .... SteveDrowne 2 82+
(R Charlton) *trckd ldr: racd keenly: led and edgd lft over 1f out: r.o wl* **7/4**[1]
2- **2** 2 ½ **Crystal Capella**[174] 6847 3-9-0 0 .... KerrinMcEvoy 13 76+
(Sir Michael Stoute) *hld up in tch: rdn over 2f out: edgd lft and styd on ins fnl f* **2/1**[2]
3 ½ **Persian Sea (UAE)** 3-9-0 0 .... NCallan 8 75
(M A Jarvis) *trckd ldrs: racd keenly: rdn over 2f out: styng on same pce whn edgd lft ins fnl f* **17/2**
4 **4** 2 ¾ **Badweia (USA)**[21] 1445 3-9-0 0 .... DaneO'Neill 3 68
(J L Dunlop) *chsd ldrs: rdn over 2f out: no ex fnl f* **11/2**[3]
5 1 **Soft Shoe Shuffle (IRE)** 3-9-0 0 .... AdamKirby 12 66
(W R Swinburn) *s.i.s: hld up: hdwy over 4f out: rdn over 1f out: wknd ins fnl f* **20/1**
6 nk **Alzaroof (USA)** 3-9-0 0 .... TQuinn 14 65+
(E A L Dunlop) *hld up: styd on appr fnl f: nvr nrr* **33/1**
7 2 **Alutando (IRE)** 3-9-0 0 .... CatherineGannon 9 61?
(B Palling) *led: rdn and hdd over 1f out: wknd fnl f* **100/1**

0-6 **8** nk **Loveinanelevator**[30] 1270 3-9-0 0 JimCrowley 10 60+
(M L W Bell) *s.i.s: hld up: plld hrd: swtchd lft and hdwy over 1f out: nvr nr to chal* **40/1**

9 1 1/2 **Calakanga** 3-9-0 0 JohnEgan 6 57+
(C E Brittain) *hld up: rdn over 3f out: wknd over 1f out: eased* **33/1**

2-5 **10** 2 3/4 **Salsa Time**[15] 1579 3-9-0 0 RobertWinston 5 50
(Miss J A Camacho) *hld up: rdn over 3f out: wkng whn hung lft over 1f out* **22/1**

11 3 3/4 **Digital Dish (IRE)**[12] 1654 3-9-0 0 PatCosgrave 7 42
(Eamon Tyrrell, Ire) *mid-div: rdn 1/2-way: wknd over 2f out: sn hung lft* **66/1**

50- **12** nk **Eastern Pride**[183] 6734 3-8-7 0 SophieDoyle(7) 4 41
(P A Blockley) *s.i.s: sn prom: rdn and wknd over 1f out* **125/1**

5- **13** 3 3/4 **Syvilla**[213] 6087 3-9-0 0 ChrisCatlin 11 32
(Rae Guest) *s.i.s: hld up: rdn over 2f out: sn wknd* **28/1**

1m 45.41s (0.01) **Going Correction** -0.25s/f (Firm) **13** Ran SP% **119.8**
Speed ratings (Par 96): **97,94,94,91,90 89,87,87,86,83 79,79,75**
CSF £4.81 TOTE £2.80: £1.30, £1.40, £2.00; EX 6.80.
Owner K Abdulla **Bred** Juddmonte Farms Ltd **Trained** Beckhampton, Wilts

FOCUS
Several interesting fillies on show in what was the slower of the two divisions by around a second. The bare form seems sound enough with the first two improving on their two-year-old debut form.
Salsa Time Official explanation: jockey said filly hung right

1965 BET TOTEPOOL ON ALL UK RACING MAIDEN FILLIES' STKS (DIV II) 1m 75y
4:10 (4:13) (Class 5) 3-Y-O £2,428 (£722; £361; £180) Stalls Centre

Form RPR

4-2 **1** **Melodramatic (IRE)**[22] 1423 3-9-0 0 SteveDrowne 1 93+
(R Charlton) *chsd ldr: led on bit over 2f out: rdn clr 1f out: easily* **4/9**[1]

32- **2** 7 **Desert Chill (USA)**[196] 6470 3-9-0 0 KerrinMcEvoy 7 74
(Saeed Bin Suroor) *sn led: hdd over 2f out: sn rdn and btn* **11/4**[2]

3 3 1/2 **Flure De Leise (IRE)**[7] 1785 3-9-0 0 PatCosgrave 2 66
(Eamon Tyrrell, Ire) *hld up in tch: rdn and one pce fnl 2f* **28/1**

4 1 1/4 **Haqeeaq (USA)** 3-9-0 0 RobertWinston 6 63
(Sir Michael Stoute) *broke wl: led early: a.p: pushed along 3f out: wknd over 1f out* **9/1**[3]

4-6 **5** 2 **Diamond Royal (IRE)**[18] 1525 3-9-0 0 TQuinn 11 59
(E A L Dunlop) *broke wl: stdd and hld up in tch: hung lft fr over 3f out: hung bdly lft over 1f out: sn wknd* **20/1**

6 2 **April's Daughter** 3-9-0 0 AlanMunro 4 54
(B R Millman) *s.i.s: towards rr: no real prog fnl 2f* **50/1**

5 **7** 2 **Sir Kyffin's Folly**[21] 1445 3-9-0 0 RichardThomas 13 49
(J A Geake) *hld up in mid-div: rdn and wknd over 2f out* **28/1**

0- **8** 1 1/4 **Aura**[188] 6649 3-9-0 0 JimCrowley 8 46
(M L W Bell) *a in rr* **33/1**

- **9** 4 1/2 **Danse De Sioux (IRE)** 3-9-0 0 FrankieMcDonald 12 36
(P A Blockley) *s.i.s: a in rr* **100/1**

00- **10** 1 **The Lady Lapwing**[163] 6964 3-9-0 0 ChrisCatlin 14 34
(G Wragg) *mid-div: wknd over 3f out* **100/1**

00- **11** 8 **Mathool (IRE)**[196] 6461 3-9-0 0 DeanMcKeown 5 15
(C W Thornton) *a in rr* **150/1**

1m 44.41s (-0.99) **Going Correction** -0.25s/f (Firm) **11** Ran SP% **125.1**
Speed ratings (Par 96): **102,95,91,90,88 86,84,83,78,77 69**
CSF £1.94 TOTE £1.50: £1.02, £1.30, £7.20; EX 2.50.
Owner B E Nielsen **Bred** Bjorn E Nielsen **Trained** Beckhampton, Wilts

FOCUS
This was the quicker of the two divisions by around a second but was still steadily run. It is doubtful if Melodramatic had to improve despite the wide-margin win.
Diamond Royal(IRE) Official explanation: jockey said filly hung left

1966 BET TOTEPOOL AT TOTESPORT.COM APPRENTICE H'CAP 6f 15y
4:45 (4:48) (Class 6) (0-60,60) 4-Y-O+ £2,047 (£604; £302) Stalls High

Form RPR

045- **1** **Bold Argument (IRE)**[191] 6582 5-8-11 52 JackMitchell 17 64
(Mrs P N Dutfield) *mid-div: hdwy and hung lft fr over 2f out: styd on u.p to ld wl ins fnl f* **15/2**

2314 **2** nk **Marmooq**[14] 1602 5-8-7 51 (e) MarkCoumbe(3) 11 62
(M J Attwater) *sn outpcd: swtchd rt over 2f out: hdwy u.p over 1f out: hung lft: r.o* **7/2**[1]

5421 **3** 1 1/4 **Kingsmaite**[11] 1675 7-8-5 51 6ex (b) SimonPearce(5) 16 58
(S R Bowring) *chsd ldrs: rdn to ld over 1f out: hdd and no ex wl ins fnl f* **6/1**[3]

0/0- **4** 2 3/4 **Night Rainbow (IRE)**[271] 4416 5-8-5 49 MCGeran(3) 10 47
(Mrs S Leech) *s.i.s: bhd: rdn over 2f out: styd on ins fnl f: nvr nrr* **40/1**

60-6 **5** shd **Falmassim**[21] 1455 5-8-6 47 AshleyHamblett 6 45
(Miss J A Camacho) *prom: rdn and ev ch over 1f out: no ex ins fnl f* **9/2**[2]

0500 **6** nse **No Time (IRE)**[24] 1378 8-9-0 58 DanielleMcCreery(3) 5 56
(A J McCabe) *hld up: hdwy u.p over 1f out: r.o* **16/1**

0-10 **7** hd **Russian Rocket (IRE)**[35] 1185 6-9-0 58 ThomasO'Brien(3) 2 55
(Mrs C A Dunnett) *mid-div: hdwy over 1f out: edgd rt: nt trble ldrs* **12/1**

0-05 **8** 2 **Apache Nation (IRE)**[15] 1578 5-8-10 56 JohnCavanagh(5) 13 47+
(M Dods) *s.i.s: outpcd: r.o ins fnl f* **9/1**

500- **9** 1 1/4 **Edge End**[212] 6101 4-8-11 55 SophieDoyle(3) 15 42
(R A Farrant) *mid-div: rdn 1/2-way: wknd over 1f out* **16/1**

00-0 **10** 1 1/2 **Roman Quintet (IRE)**[13] 1634 8-8-12 58 StacyRenwick(5) 4 40
(A J McCabe) *chsd ldrs: led 1/2-way: hdd over 1f out: wknd ins fnl f* **12/1**

1-00 **11** nk **Hollywood George**[20] 1491 4-9-5 60 JamieJones 3 41
(Miss M E Rowland) *chsd ldrs: rdn over 2f out: wknd fnl f* **33/1**

10-0 **12** 1 **Registrar**[20] 1476 6-8-13 54 NicolPolli 1 32
(Mrs C A Dunnett) *dwlt: n.d* **16/1**

00-0 **13** hd **Royal Choir**[16] 1565 4-8-9 55 DebraEngland(5) 8 32
(C E Brittain) *s.i.s: outpcd* **25/1**

1051 **14** 1/2 **Montzando**[25] 1370 5-9-3 58 (v) JamesMillman 9 33
(B R Millman) *chsd ldrs: rdn over 3f out: wknd over 2f out* **16/1**

00-0 **15** 19 **Viewforth**[24] 1378 10-8-10 54 (b) WilliamCarson(3) 7 —
(M A Buckley) *led to 1/2-way: rdn and wknd over 1f out* **33/1**

1m 14.4s (-0.70) **Going Correction** -0.25s/f (Firm) **15** Ran SP% **127.5**
Speed ratings (Par 101): **94,93,91,88,88 88,87,85,83,81 81,79,79,78,53**
CSF £34.52 CT £157.26 TOTE £8.80: £2.50, £1.50, £2.60; EX 34.90 Place 6 £63.10, Place 5 £17.61..
Owner Simon Dutfield **Bred** K S Lee **Trained** Axmouth, Devon

FOCUS
A very moderate affair. The initial pace was down the centre but the principals came from nearer the stands' rail as the pace collapsed. The form is not solid, rated through the winner to last year's best.
Edge End Official explanation: jockey said gelding never travelled

T/Plt: £57.00 to a £1 stake. Pool: £41,351.92. 529.44 winning tickets. T/Qpdt: £14.80 to a £1 stake. Pool: £3,018.93. 150.40 winning tickets. CR

1623 RIPON (R-H)
Friday, May 9

OFFICIAL GOING: Good (8.5)
Wind: Virtually nil Weather: Warm and overcast

1967 ISIS MAIDEN AUCTION STKS 5f
5:55 (5:57) (Class 5) 2-Y-O £3,238 (£963; £481; £240) Stalls Low

Form RPR

1 **Able Master (IRE)** 2-8-12 0 RoystonFfrench 4 83+
(B Smart) *trckd ldrs: hdwy 2f out: rdn to ld jst ins fnl f: styd on wl* **14/1**

5 **2** 1 1/4 **Mullglen**[9] 1727 2-8-11 0 DavidAllan 3 77
(T D Easterby) *trckd ldrs: hdwy 2f out: rdn to chal and ev ch over 1f out: drvn and one pce ins fnl f* **8/1**[3]

62 **3** 1 1/4 **Rayvin Mad (IRE)**[13] 1616 2-9-1 0 AdrianMcCarthy 11 77
(P W Chapple-Hyam) *hmpd s: sn led: rdn along 2f out: drvn and hdd jst ins fnl f: edgd rt and one pce* **4/5**[1]

4 2 1/2 **Steel Stockholder** 2-8-10 0 TWilliams 9 63+
(M Brittain) *hmpd and wnt rt s: sn prom: cl up 1/2-way: rdn along 2f out: edgd rt and grad wknd* **13/2**[2]

5 3/4 **Coleorton Choice** 2-9-1 0 NCallan 2 65+
(K A Ryan) *chsd ldrs: rdn and sltly outpcd 2f out: swtchd rt over 1f out: kpt on ins fnl f* **10/1**

6 **6** 1 1/2 **El Portet**[9] 1727 2-8-9 0 PJMcDonald(3) 5 56
(G M Moore) *towards rr: pushed along 1/2-way: sn rdn and styd on appr fnl f* **20/1**

7 2 **Dispol Grand (IRE)** 2-8-9 0 SilvestreDeSousa 7 46
(P T Midgley) *hmpd s: chsd ldrs: rdn along 1/2-way: grad wknd* **33/1**

8 1 **Look For Value** 2-8-5 0 KimTinkler 10 39
(N Tinkler) *hmpd and wnt rt s: a bhd* **80/1**

9 3/4 **Sweet Applause (IRE)** 2-8-7 0 NeilPollard 8 38
(A P Jarvis) *sltly hmpd s and s.i.s: a towards rr* **25/1**

0 **10** 2 1/4 **Lucky Buddha**[23] 1390 2-8-11 0 MickyFenton 6 34
(Jedd O'Keeffe) *wnt rt s: a in rr* **40/1**

11 158 **Just Five (IRE)** 2-8-11 0 PhillipMakin 1 —
(M Dods) *s.i.s: outpcd and sn bhd: lost action and t.o fr 1/2-way* **12/1**

60.80 secs (0.10) **Going Correction** +0.025s/f (Good) **11** Ran SP% **118.7**
Speed ratings (Par 93): **100,98,96,92,90 88,85,83,82,78** —
CSF £115.22 TOTE £14.20: £1.70, £1.50, £1.40; EX 11.00.
Owner Ron Hull **Bred** Scuderia Miami Di Sandro Guerra And Co **Trained** Hambleton, N Yorks
■ Stewards' Enquiry : David Allan caution: used whip down shoulder in forehand position

FOCUS
Probably just average maiden form rated through the third.

NOTEBOOK
Able Master(IRE), a half-brother to Sant Jordi, a 6f winner at two, and Tamboril, a dual 1m winner in Italy, showed pace throughout and saw it out well to record a debut win over a couple of more experienced rivals. This was a good effort and there should be improvement to come. (op 9-1 tchd 16-1)
Mullglen, racing on quicker ground, knew more about what was required this time and improved on his debut effort. Being able to race next to the stands'-side rail throughout was a help. (op 10-1)
Rayvin Mad(IRE) was sent off a hot favourite to build on the promise of his first two starts, but he was drawn widest of all and had to do a lot of work early to cross over and get to the lead on the rail. He paid for that effort later in the race. (op Evens tchd 11-10 in a place)
Steel Stockholder, an April foal who cost only 5,000gns, is out of a 6f juvenile winner. Not helping his cause by going right exiting the stalls, he showed a lot of speed to make up the lost ground, but it was no surprise to see him weaken late on having done so much in the early stages. He should know more next time. (op 9-1 tchd 11-2)
Coleorton Choice, a half-brother to multiple winning sprinter Coleorton Dancer, had a good draw but ended up challenging off the rail. It was a promising enough debut. (op 13-2)
El Portet, only just behind Mullglen on his debut at Pontefract, failed to improve on this better ground. (op 14-1)
Look For Value, who is a sister to Estimator, a dual 6f winner at two, and half-sister to 6f juvenile winners Lady Benjamin and Euro Route, and multiple 6f-1m winner Tuscarora, was done no favours when carried right at the start. She looks the type to do better in moderate handicap company down the line. (op 50-1)
Just Five(IRE) Official explanation: jockey said gelding moved poorly throughout

1968 SIS DISPLAY MANAGEMENT SOLUTIONS (S) STKS 1m 1f 170y
6:25 (6:26) (Class 6) 3-4-Y-O £2,590 (£770; £385; £192) Stalls High

Form RPR

4-10 **1** **Cherri Fosfate**[11] 1673 4-10-1 57 DavidAllan 3 71+
(D Carroll) *hld up in tch: smooth hdwy wl over 2f out: chal over 1f out: rdn to ld appr fnl f: sn clr* **11/4**[2]

1345 **2** 5 **Not Now Lewis (IRE)**[20] 1486 4-10-1 58 NCallan 4 60
(Miss Gay Kelleway) *trckd ldrs: hdwy over 2f out: led wl over 1f out: sn rdn and hdd appr fnl f: one pce* **5/2**[1]

00-6 **3** nk **Ja Myford**[11] 1679 4-9-10 54 (p) MickyFenton 10 54
(P T Midgley) *s.i.s and sn rdn along in rr: bhd 1/2-way: hdwy u.p on outer 3f out: sn drvn: styng on whn hung rt ins fnl f: nrst fin* **9/2**[3]

0-03 **4** 5 **Jevington Star (IRE)**[13] 1626 3-8-9 44 RoystonFfrench 5 43
(B Ellison) *cl up: led over 2f out: rdn and hdd wl over 1f out: sn drvn and wknd* **11/2**

4442 **5** 5 **Cape Dancer (IRE)**[13] 1626 4-9-2 44 PJMcDonald(3) 2 28
(J S Wainwright) *prom: rdn along 3f out: grad wknd fnl 2f* **6/1**

-000 **6** 2 1/4 **River Gleam (IRE)**[8] 1738 3-8-4 58 NeilPollard 6 36
(A P Jarvis) *led: rdn along 3f out: sn hdd & wknd* **16/1**

60-4 **7** 4 1/2 **Buds Dilemma**[13] 1626 4-9-5 44 GrahamGibbons 9 23
(W M Brisbourne) *trckd ldrs: pushed along 3f out: rdn 2f out and sn wknd* **16/1**

000- **8** 3 1/4 **Harlequinn Danseur (IRE)**[219] 5904 3-8-9 58 KimTinkler 1 13
(N Tinkler) *chsd ldrs: rdn along over 4f out and sn wknd* **25/1**

00- **9** 57 **Call Of Ktulu (IRE)**[203] 6305 3-8-2 0 (p) JamesRogers(7) 8 —
(J S Wainwright) *s.i.s: a bhd: t.o fr 1/2-way* **80/1**

2m 5.76s (0.36) **Going Correction** +0.10s/f (Good)
WFA 3 from 4yo 15lb **9** Ran SP% **119.9**
Speed ratings (Par 101): **102,98,97,93,89 87,84,81,36**
CSF £10.56 TOTE £4.20: £1.70, £1.50, £1.40; EX 11.00.There was no bid for the winner.
Owner Document Express Ltd **Bred** The Newchange Syndicate **Trained** Sledmere, E Yorks

FOCUS
The highest-rated horses in this seller had a mark of 58 and the form looks distinctly moderate. The time was reasonable and the form is rated at face value through the runner-up.

River Gleam(IRE) Official explanation: jockey said filly hung badly left-handed throughout

1969 SIS PICTURE SERVICES H'CAP 6f
7:00 (7:00) (Class 4) (0-85,85) 4-Y-0+ **£5,504** (£1,637; £818; £408) **Stalls** Low

Form RPR
000- **1** **Pacific Pride**[231] 5584 5-8-10 **77**........ GrahamGibbons 4 85
(J J Quinn) *chsd ldng pair: pushed along 1/2-way: rdn wl over 1f out: styd on u.p to chal ins fnl f: sn drvn and led last strides* **9/2[3]**
2404 **2** *shd* **Westport**[23] 1409 5-8-7 **74**........ NCallan 1 82
(K A Ryan) *cl up: effrt 2f out: rdn to ld appr fnl f: sn drvn: hdd last strides* **3/1[1]**
5-06 **3** *nk* **Obe Gold**[22] 1430 6-9-2 **83**........ SilvestreDeSousa 6 90
(D Nicholls) *dwlt: rr and rdn along 1/2-way: hdwy 2f out: drvn and styd on ent fnl f: sn ev ch tl no ex towards fin* **7/2[2]**
-436 **4** *1 1/2* **First Order**[35] 1195 7-9-4 **85**........(v) PhillipMakin 5 87
(Miss L A Perratt) *sn led: jnd and rdn 2f out: hdd appr fnl f and kpt on same pce* **9/2[3]**
-104 **5** *1 3/4* **Blue Tomato**[11] 1689 7-9-1 **85**........ PJMcDonald(3) 2 81
(D Nicholls) *chsd ldrs: rdn along over 2f out: drvn over 1f out and sn no imp* **7/2[2]**
1-00 **6** *3 1/2* **Paris Bell**[6] 1796 6-8-10 **77**........ DavidAllan 3 62
(T D Easterby) *s.i.s: a in rr* **15/2**

1m 12.32s (-0.68) **Going Correction** +0.025s/f (Good) **6** Ran SP% **117.6**
Speed ratings (Par 105): **105,104,104,102,100 95**
CSF £19.37 TOTE £6.70: £2.90, £1.50; EX 30.40.
Owner Maxilead Limited **Bred** Whitsbury Manor Stud **Trained** Settrington, N Yorks

FOCUS
A tight handicap featuring a number of well-weighted contenders. The race has been rated around the runner-up to his best form over 6f.

1970 SIS OB SERVICES H'CAP 1m 1f 170y
7:30 (7:30) (Class 3) (0-90,88) 4-Y-0+ **£9,066** (£2,697; £1,348; £673) **Stalls** High

Form RPR
5-26 **1** **Ballinteni**[35] 1180 6-9-3 **87**........ NCallan 8 100
(Miss Gay Kelleway) *hld up: hdwy 4f out: chsd ldrs 2f out: rdn and styd on to chal 1f out: drvn to ld wl ins fnl f: kpt on* **7/2[2]**
201- **2** *1* **Jewelled Dagger (IRE)**[209] 6180 4-9-3 **87**........(b) PhillipMakin 12 98
(Miss L A Perratt) *led: rdn along 2f out: drvn over 1f out: hdd and no ex wl ins fnl f* **11/1**
0616 **3** *5* **Granston (IRE)**[20] 1473 7-8-13 **83**........ RobertWinston 7 84
(J D Bethell) *in tch: hdwy 3f out: rdn along 2f out: kpt on same pce appr fnl f* **5/1[3]**
00- **4** *8* **Film Festival (USA)**[31] 4867 5-8-9 **86**........ LanceBetts(7) 9 71
(B Ellison) *chsd ldrs: rdn along and outpcd over 2f out: plugged on same pce u.p fnl f* **25/1**
-406 **5** *3/4* **Suits Me**[16] 1569 5-8-12 **82**........ MickyFenton 6 66
(T P Tate) *prom: rdn along over 3f out: wknd fnl 2f: lost 4th nr fin* **7/2[2]**
200- **6** *nk* **Danish Rebel (IRE)**[69] 3501 4-8-7 **77**........(t) RoystonFfrench 1 60
(G A Charlton) *nvr nr ldrs* **28/1**
062- **7** *2 3/4* **Just Bond (IRE)**[130] 7287 6-8-3 **76**........ DuranFentiman(3) 11 53
(G R Oldroyd) *dwlt and towards rr: hdwy over 3f out: rdn to chse ldrs over 2f out: sn btn* **14/1**
3024 **8** *3 3/4* **Moheebb (IRE)**[2] 1910 4-8-5 **75**........(b) AdrianMcCarthy 10 45
(Mrs R A Carr) *chsd ldr: rdn along 4f out: wknd 3f out* **17/2**
400- **9** *1* **Instructor**[209] 6180 7-8-9 **79**........ PaulHanagan 5 47
(C A Mulhall) *s.i.s: a in rr* **33/1**
4-02 **10** *22* **Eglevski (IRE)**[20] 1473 4-9-1 **85**........ SebSanders 4 9+
(J L Dunlop) *stdd and swtchd rt sn after s: hdwy on inner to trck ldrs whn stmbld bdly and lost pl 6f out: hdwy to chse ldrs over 3f out: sn rdn and wknd* **5/2[1]**

2m 4.01s (-1.39) **Going Correction** +0.10s/f (Good) **10** Ran SP% **125.4**
Speed ratings (Par 107): **109,108,104,97,97 96,94,91,90,73**
CSF £44.27 CT £201.51 TOTE £5.40: £1.40, £4.20, £2.20; EX 44.90.
Owner David Cohen **Bred** Gainsborough Stud Management Ltd **Trained** Exning, Suffolk

FOCUS
A solidly run handicap and sound form for the grade.

NOTEBOOK
Ballinteni, whose stable is in flying form at present and has shown a preferance for going this way round, was taking a drop in grade and stayed on well to get up inside the last. Whether he can cope with a return to better company remains to be seen, though. (op 4-1)
Jewelled Dagger(IRE), making his reappearance off a 9lb higher mark than when winning at York last October, put up a career-best effort in defeat, although he did enjoy the run of the race out in front. Clear of the rest and apparently still improving, the Handicapper may not have his measure yet. (op 9-1)
Granston(IRE), more at home back on a decent surface, posted a solid effort and is a good guide to the level of the form. (op 13-2)
Film Festival(USA), debuting for his new stable following a fruitless campaign over timber, shaped as though finding this trip on the short side now. (op 33-1)
Suits Me looks the type who reserves his best for when able to make his own running. (op 6-1)
Danish Rebel(IRE), another returning from a winter's hurdling, never threatened to take a hand. (op 33-1)
Just Bond(IRE) Official explanation: jockey said gelding hung right-handed
Eglevski(IRE) prefers some ease in the ground so the drying conditions were not in his favour, but he can be excused this as he stumbled going into the far bend and lost his place. (tchd 11-4)

1971 SISLINK MAIDEN STKS 6f
8:05 (8:05) (Class 5) 3-Y-0 **£3,238** (£963; £481; £240) **Stalls** Low

Form RPR
64 **1** **Atlantic Beach**[18] 1519 3-9-3 0........ PaulHanagan 3 75
(R A Fahey) *chsd ldrs: swtchd rt and rdn ent fnl f: styd on to ld last 100yds* **11/1**
0 **2** *3/4* **Tangerine Trees**[21] 1452 3-9-3 0........(v[1]) RoystonFfrench 9 72
(B Smart) *cl up: rdn to ld wl over 1f out: drvn ent fnl f: hdd and no ex last 100yds* **7/1[3]**
6-04 **3** *2* **Bertie Vista**[6] 1795 3-9-3 66........(b[1]) DavidAllan 1 66
(T D Easterby) *prom: effrt 2f out: sn rdn and ev ch ent fnl f: drvn and no ex last 100yds* **5/1[2]**
0 **4** *1 1/4* **Dhahab (USA)**[21] 1445 3-8-12 0........ NCallan 4 57
(C E Brittain) *chsd ldrs: rdn along and outpcd over 2f out: styd on wl appr fnl f: nrst fin* **16/1**
230- **5** *2 3/4* **Alsadeek (IRE)**[219] 5910 3-9-3 75........ SebSanders 7 53
(J L Dunlop) *sn led: rdn 2f out: hdd wl over 1f out: wknd ent fnl f* **8/15[1]**
6 *2* **Mr Rio (IRE)** 3-9-3 0........ NeilPollard 6 47
(A P Jarvis) *sn outpcd and a in rr* **20/1**
7 *1 1/2* **Cabopino (IRE)** 3-8-12 0........ DarrenWilliams 8 37
(K R Burke) *chsd ldrs: effrt on outer over 2f out: sn rdn and btn* **33/1**
00 **8** *2 1/4* **Your Golf Travel**[28] 1302 3-8-12 0........ GrahamGibbons 5 30
(J S Wainwright) *sn outpcd and a in rr* **80/1**
0-0 **9** *6* **Fizzy Lover**[45] 1019 3-8-9 0........ DuranFentiman(3) 2 11
(T D Easterby) *dwlt: a in rr* **66/1**

1m 13.64s (0.64) **Going Correction** +0.025s/f (Good) **9** Ran SP% **119.0**
Speed ratings (Par 99): **96,95,92,90,87 84,82,79,71**
CSF £84.24 TOTE £9.90: £1.80, £2.80, £1.90; EX 54.20.
Owner D R Brotherton **Bred** D R Brotherton **Trained** Musley Bank, N Yorks

FOCUS
Modest maiden form and, with the favourite disappointing, it took little winning and does not look a race to be with.

1972 SIS DATA SERVICES H'CAP 2m
8:35 (8:35) (Class 5) (0-70,70) 4-Y-0+ **£3,238** (£963; £481; £240) **Stalls** Low

Form RPR
2-22 **1** **Danzatrice**[7] 1773 6-9-0 **60**........ RobertWinston 8 70+
(C W Thornton) *hld up in rr: hdwy on inner 3f out: nt clr run wl over 1f out: swtchd lft and rdn ins fnl f: styd on to ld nr fin* **6/4[1]**
0-50 **2** *1/2* **Mister Arjay (USA)**[28] 1299 8-9-6 **69**........ PJMcDonald(3) 7 75
(B Ellison) *led: rdn along 3f out: drvn over 1f out: hdd and no ex nr fin* **4/1[3]**
0-46 **3** *3* **Title Deed (USA)**[4] 1856 4-8-11 **60**........ NeilPollard 3 62
(A P Jarvis) *a.p: effrt 3f out: rdn to chal over 2f out and ev ch tl drvn and one pce ins fnl f* **18/1**
200/ **4** *1 3/4* **Mt Desert**[419] 1690 6-9-10 **70**........ PhillipMakin 5 70
(E W Tuer) *hld up: hdwy over 3f out: sn rdn along and kpt on appr fnl f: nrst fin* **20/1**
0-02 **5** *1 3/4* **Blue Jet (USA)**[17] 1551 4-8-7 **56**........ DeanMcKeown 6 54
(R M Whitaker) *trckd ldrs: hdwy over 3f out: rdn along over 2f out and sn one pce* **3/1[2]**
00-0 **6** *5* **Mystified (IRE)**[45] 374 5-8-6 **52**........(b) PaulHanagan 10 44
(R F Fisher) *prom: rdn along 4f out: wknd 3f out* **12/1**
430- **7** *4 1/2* **Bond Casino**[153] 7081 4-8-9 **58**........ GrahamGibbons 4 44
(G R Oldroyd) *hld up: a towards rr* **9/1**
56- **8** *8* **Double Deputy (IRE)**[163] 4490 7-9-10 **70**........ RoystonFfrench 11 47
(E W Tuer) *chsd ldrs: rdn along over 3f out and sn wknd* **16/1**
500- **9** *34* **Erte**[59] 5626 7-7-13 **52** oh5 ow1........(b[1]) DeclanCannon(7) 2 —
(V Thompson) *chsd ldrs: rdn along 6f out: wknd over 4f out* **40/1**

3m 35.5s (3.70) **Going Correction** +0.10s/f (Good)
WFA 4 from 5yo+ 3lb **9** Ran SP% **121.0**
Speed ratings (Par 103): **94,93,92,91,90 88,85,81,64**
CSF £8.21 CT £80.17 TOTE £2.50: £1.20, £1.70, £4.10; EX 5.50 Place 6 £50.86, Place 5 £37.61..
Owner 980 Racing **Bred** G G A Gregson **Trained** Middleham Moor, N Yorks

FOCUS
Modest form, with the third showing little on the All-Weather of late and the fourth returning from a lengthy absence. The winner is value for four lengths but the form looks weak.
T/Plt: £73.30 to a £1 stake. Pool: £43,785.90. 435.69 winning tickets. T/Qpdt: £46.90 to a £1 stake. Pool: £2,677.75. 42.20 winning tickets. JR

1973 - 1979a (Foreign Racing) - See Raceform Interactive

1714 ASCOT (R-H)
Saturday, May 10

OFFICIAL GOING: Good to firm (str 9.1; rnd 8.9; overall 8.8)
Wind: virtually nil Weather: sunny

1980 JOHN DOYLE BUCKHOUNDS STKS (LISTED RACE) 1m 4f
1:10 (1:11) (Class 1) 4-Y-0+
£17,031 (£6,456; £3,231; £1,611; £807; £405) **Stalls** High

Form RPR
1/6- **1** **Spanish Moon (USA)**[211] 6153 4-8-12 103........ RyanMoore 8 118+
(Sir Michael Stoute) *lw: t.k.h: hld up towards rr: bdly hmpd 4f out: sn rdn: swtchd lft jst under 3f out: plenty to do 2f out: hdwy jst over 1f out: fin v strly: led fnl 40yds* **7/2[3]**
22-5 **2** *1* **Munsef**[42] 1070 6-8-12 108........(b) RHills 3 111
(J L Dunlop) *s.i.s: bhd: gd hdwy on rails fr over 2f out: rdn to ld ent fnl f: ct fnl 40yds* **10/1**
00-0 **3** *nse* **Petara Bay (IRE)**[21] 1468 4-8-12 102........ JimCrowley 1 111
(T G Mills) *chsd ldrs: rdn over 2f out: led over 1f out: hdd ent fnl f: kpt on* **20/1**
610- **4** *2* **Tungsten Strike (USA)**[186] 6712 7-9-1 111........ DarryllHolland 2 111
(Mrs A J Perrett) *led: rdn and edgd lft fr over 2f out: hdd over 1f out: kpt on but no ex fnl 100yds* **10/1**
531- **5** *nk* **Lion Sands**[219] 5952 4-9-1 110........ JamieSpencer 9 110
(L M Cumani) *swtg: mid-div: rdn wl over 2f out: hdwy to chal ent fnl f: no ex fnl 100yds* **11/4[1]**
06-0 **6** *4* **Big Robert**[21] 1468 4-8-12 104........ RichardMullen 7 101
(W R Muir) *slowly away: sn rousted along in rr: rdn and no imp fr over 2f out* **20/1**
200- **7** *3/4* **Classic Punch (IRE)**[223] 5831 5-9-1 110........ TQuinn 5 103
(D R C Elsworth) *swtg: chsd ldr: rdn to chal wl over 2f out: fdd ent fnl f* **17/2**
025- **8** *1 3/4* **Young Mick**[189] 6645 6-8-12 108........(v) RobertWinston 4 97
(G G Margarson) *t.k.h in midfield: hdwy over 3f out: rdn over 2f out: swtchd rt 1f out: fdd fnl f* **14/1**
/12- **9** *14* **Hanella (IRE)**[348] 2082 5-8-7 80........ NickyMackay 11 70
(S C Williams) *chsd ldrs: rdn over 4f out: btn 3f out* **66/1**
32-4 **P** **Ivy Creek (USA)**[21] 1468 5-9-1 110........ SteveDrowne 6 —
(G Wragg) *mid-div whn p.u 4f out: broke leg: dead* **3/1[2]**

2m 30.87s (-4.63) **Going Correction** -0.10s/f (Good) **10** Ran SP% **120.3**
Speed ratings (Par 111): **111,110,110,108,108 106,105,104,95,—**
CSF £38.74 TOTE £4.90: £2.10, £2.70, £7.00; EX 39.50 Trifecta £791.50 Part won. Pool: £1,114.87 - 0.70 winning units..
Owner K Abdulla **Bred** Juddmonte Farms Inc **Trained** Newmarket, Suffolk

FOCUS
Plenty of runners and this was a good, competitive Listed contest producing strong form for the grade. Spanish Moon was value for extra. They went an even gallop courtesy of Tungsten Strike.

The Form Book, Raceform Ltd, Compton, RG20 6NL

NOTEBOOK

Spanish Moon(USA) had been fancied for last year's Derby after landing a 7f Newmarket maiden on his only start at two, but he suffered a non-displaced crack on his pelvis and was restricted to just one run, a fifth placing in a 1m2f conditions contest at Doncaster last October. Stepped up in trip on his return, he travelled well through the early stages, but found himself detached in last place at the top of the straight having lost ground when swerving to avoid the stricken Ivy Creek rounding the final bend, a move which probably cost him around two lengths. He still looked to have no chance passing the two-furlong marker, but he produced a sustained effort down the outside to get up well inside the final furlong and ultimately win going away. This was a terrific effort on just his third racecourse appearance and he looks a nice prospect for the season ahead. He may return to Ascot for the Hardwicke Stakes in June and, considering his trainer's record at improving older horses, he should give a good account, although one gets the impression he may ultimately prove best over a little further. (op 9-2 tchd 11-2)

Munsef had blinkers re-fitted and improved significantly on the form he showed on his reappearance at Doncaster. Listed and conditions races are his sort of level and he should continue to go well when in the mood. (op 17-2)

Petara Bay(IRE) beat just one home in the John Porter Stakes on soft ground at Newbury on his reappearance, but this quicker surface was much more to his liking and he ran a big race in third. This was just his second start since contesting last year's Derby, but he clearly possesses a decent level of ability. (op 40-1)

Tungsten Strike(USA), taken out of the Sagaro Stakes at the last Ascot meeting on account of the softening ground, was making his seasonal reappearance over a trip short of best, so he tried to make this a fair test from the front. Although he found a few too strong, this was a pleasing return from six months off and he can do better when stepped back up in trip. He will surely now be aimed at the Group 2 Henry II Stakes at Sandown, a race he won two years ago. (op 12-1)

Lion Sands, racing for the first time since landing a 1m6f Listed race at Newmarket last October, probably found this trip on the short side and he might just have needed this as well. (op 9-4)

Big Robert did not improve on the form he showed in the John Porter at Newbury on his reappearance.

Classic Punch(IRE) started last year with wins in a Listed event and a conditions race, but he lost his way towards the end of the campaign and was well beaten on this reappearance. Perhaps he needed the run. (op 11-2)

Young Mick, returning from six months off, is another who might have needed this. (op 10-1)

Ivy Creek(USA) was well backed beforehand, but he broke a leg around half a mile from the finish and had to be put down. He was a very smart horse at his best, as he showed when winning back-to-back Listed races last year, and this was a sad end. (op 6-1 tchd 13-2 in a place)

1981 BOVIS HOMES FILLIES' STKS (HERITAGE H'CAP) 1m (S)

1:45 (1:47) (Class 2) 3-Y-0+ **£25,904** (£7,708; £3,852; £1,924) **Stalls** Low

Form				RPR
-120	**1**		**Baharah (USA)**[42] [1087] 4-9-10 **105** RichardHughes 2 (G A Butler) *lw: hld up: tk clsr order 4f out: rdn and swtchd rt over 1f out: qcknd up wl to ld ins fnl f: r.o* **12/1**	115+
134-	**2**	1 1/2	**Kasumi**[209] [6208] 5-8-1 **82** NickyMackay 1 (H Morrison) *trckd ldrs: rdn to ld over 1f out: hdd ins fnl f: nt pce of wnr* **8/1**[3]	89
221-	**3**	nk	**Fragrancy (IRE)**[217] [6016] 4-8-10 **91** JimCrowley 6 (M A Jarvis) *lw: trckd ldr: led 2f out: sn rdn and hdd: remained pressing ldr: no ex fnl 100yds* **5/1**[2]	97
01-4	**4**	3/4	**Valrhona (IRE)**[28] [1329] 4-8-0 **81** ow1 FrancisNorton 4 (J Noseda) *trckd ldrs: nt clr run briefly over 2f out: sn rdn: kpt on fnl 100yds* **8/1**[3]	86
22-1	**5**	2	**Jamboretta (IRE)**[14] [1633] 4-8-12 **93** RyanMoore 3 (Sir Michael Stoute) *hld up: cl enough 2f out: sn rdn: nt pce to chal* **8/11**[1]	93
0-	**6**	1	**Nolas Lolly (IRE)**[308] [3339] 4-9-1 **96** DarryllHolland 8 (M Botti) *hld up 5th: cl enough 2f out: sn rdn: nt pce to chal* **50/1**	94
505-	**7**	1 1/2	**Medicea Sidera**[201] [6391] 4-8-3 **84** KerrinMcEvoy 5 (E F Vaughan) *led: rdn and hdd 2f out: wknd 1f out* **12/1**	78

1m 39.6s (-1.00) **Going Correction** +0.025s/f (Good)
WFA 3 from 4yo+ 13lb 7 Ran SP% **114.1**
Speed ratings (Par 96): **106,104,104,103,101 100,98**
CSF £99.93 CT £545.65 TOTE £12.90: £4.00, £3.20; EX 120.70 Trifecta £759.90 Pool: £1,273.72 - 1.19 winning units..
Owner Erik Penser **Bred** Darley **Trained** Newmarket, Suffolk
■ Stewards' Enquiry : Richard Hughes one-day ban: careless riding (May 24)

FOCUS

A very good fillies' handicap, but the pace was just ordinary and it turned into something of a sprint. The form could be underrated. They raced stands' side, but the main action took place a little way off the rail.

NOTEBOOK

Baharah(USA) ◆ progressed into a smart filly on the Polytrack during the winter, but she was totally unsuited by a fast dirt surface when failing to beat a rival in the Group 2 Godolphin Mile on the dirt at Nad Al Sheba on her latest start. Racing for just the second time on turf, she proved well suited by the conditions and looked to produce a career-best effort in defying a handicap mark of 105, conceding upwards of 9lb all round. Ridden with patience, she was always travelling kindly and produced a neat turn of foot when switched toward the outside. She is now being aimed at the Group 2 Windsor Forest Stakes back over this course and distance at the Royal meeting and she ought to go well, with the likely stronger pace almost sure to suit. (op 10-1 tchd 9-1)

Kasumi ◆ had conditions to suit on her return from seven months and she ran well behind the classy winner. She has a progressive profile and there are races to be won with her this year. (tchd 17-2)

Fragrancy(IRE), 5lb higher than when winning at Redcar last October, was never too far away and this was a satisfactory return. (op 11-2 tchd 4-1)

Valrhona(IRE) ◆, dropped in trip and switched to much quicker ground, was a touch keen off the modest-early gallop and then lacked the pace of some of these inside the final two furlongs. She is going to be suited by a return to 1m2f but, quite a strong traveller, she is likely to need a quiet hold-up ride. (op 9-1)

Jamboretta(IRE) looked a typically progressive Stoute filly beforehand, but she could not defy a 7lb rise in the weights for her reappearance success at Sandown. She might have preferred a stronger pace, but this was still disappointing. (tchd Evens)

Nolas Lolly(IRE), formerly trained in France, was well held on her debut for the Botti yard off the back of a ten-month break, but she is entitled to come on for this and should be capable of better on easier ground. Official explanation: jockey said filly was unsuited by the good to firm ground (op 33-1)

1982 TOTESPORT VICTORIA CUP (HERITAGE H'CAP) 7f

2:20 (2:23) (Class 2) 4-Y-0+
£52,963 (£15,861; £7,930; £3,969; £1,980; £994) **Stalls** Low

Form				RPR
3-43	**1**		**Zaahid (IRE)**[21] [1469] 4-8-11 **92** RHills 14 (B W Hills) *lw: mid-div of centre gp: hdwy 2f out: sn rdn: led ins fnl f: hrd pressed but kpt on gamely: drvn out* **5/1**[1]	107+
30-1	**2**	nk	**Al Khaleej (IRE)**[17] [1566] 4-9-3 **98** RyanMoore 13 (E A L Dunlop) *lw: hld up towards rr in centre: hdwy w wnr 2f out: sn rdn: ev ch ent fnl f: kpt on but a jst hld* **5/1**[1]	112+
-11	**3**	1 1/4	**King Of Dixie (USA)**[35] [1211] 4-9-0 **95** PaulDoe 10 (W J Knight) *swtg: rrd leaving stalls: sn rcvrd to chse ldrs in centre: rdn to ld over 1f out: hdd ins fnl f: kpt on* **8/1**[3]	106+
333-	**4**	1 1/4	**We'll Come**[261] [4745] 4-8-12 **93** DarryllHolland 9 (M A Jarvis) *lw: rrd leaving stalls: hld up bhd on stands' side: rdn and hdwy over 1f out: r.o ins fnl f: nrst fin* **7/1**[2]	100+
0-22	**5**	1 1/4	**Guilded Warrior**[17] [1566] 5-8-6 **87** LPKeniry 4 (W S Kittow) *stmbld leaving stalls: sn chsng ldr on stands' side: rdn and ev ch over 1f out: kpt on same pce fnl f* **33/1**	91
2210	**6**	nk	**Count Ceprano (IRE)**[5] [1857] 4-7-6 **80** DavidProbert(7) 12 (M D I Usher) *swtg: chsd ldrs in centre: rdn over 2f out: kpt on fnl f* **66/1**	83+
0-20	**7**	shd	**Fishforcompliments**[6] [1828] 4-9-2 **97** (p) RichardHughes 16 (R A Fahey) *hld up bhd in centre: rdn and hdwy fr over 1f out: r.o ins fnl f: nt rch ldrs* **14/1**	100
041	**8**	nk	**Skhilling Spirit**[8] [1774] 5-8-7 **93** NeilBrown(5) 6 (T D Barron) *in tch on stands' side: hdwy 2f out: rdn and ev ch over 1f out: no ex ins fnl f* **25/1**	95
1-50	**9**	1/2	**Purus (IRE)**[35] [1211] 6-8-3 **87** LukeMorris(3) 3 (R A Teal) *chsd ldrs on stands' side: rdn over 2f out: kpt on same pce fnl f* **50/1**	88
0-60	**10**	1 1/4	**Mine (IRE)**[21] [1469] 10-9-5 **100** (v) KerrinMcEvoy 20 (J D Bethell) *hld up bhd in centre: styd on fr over 1f out: n.d* **16/1**	97
00-0	**11**	1/2	**South Cape**[21] [1469] 5-8-1 **89** MatthewDavies(7) 8 (M R Channon) *led centre gp: rdn and hdd over 2f out: kpt on same pce* **20/1**	85
403-	**12**	4	**Humungous (IRE)**[196] [6491] 5-9-5 **100** IanMongan 18 (C R Egerton) *bhd on stands' side: struggling 1/2-way: sme late prog: nvr a factor* **10/1**	85
10-4	**13**	nk	**Middlemarch (IRE)**[47] [992] 8-7-13 **80** (v) NickyMackay 5 (J S Goldie) *chsd ldrs on stands' side tl wknd over 1f out* **50/1**	64
0-30	**14**	nk	**Trafalgar Square**[21] [1469] 6-8-5 **86** DavidKinsella 7 (M J Attwater) *mainly towards rr on stands' side* **20/1**	69
24-4	**15**	1/2	**Presumptive (IRE)**[28] [1334] 8-9-1 **96** SteveDrowne 15 (R Charlton) *nvr bttr than mid-div of centre gp* **12/1**	78
2600	**16**	3/4	**Orchard Supreme**[21] [1469] 5-8-4 **85** RichardSmith 11 (R Hannon) *chsd ldrs in centre: led over 2f out: hdd over 1f out: wknd* **33/1**	65
100-	**17**	1 1/2	**Giganticus (USA)**[224] [5797] 5-9-6 **101** TQuinn 19 (B W Hills) *swtg: plld hrd: towards rr in centre: hdwy over 2f out: sn rdn: wknd over 1f out* **16/1**	77
51-0	**18**	1 1/4	**Captain Jacksparra (IRE)**[21] [1481] 4-8-7 **88** ow1 StephenDonohoe 2 (K A Ryan) *overall ldr on stands' side tl over 2f out: sn wknd* **33/1**	61
23-3	**19**	1 3/4	**Salient**[8] [1765] 4-8-4 **88** KirstyMilczarek(3) 21 (M J Attwater) *swtg: nvr bttr than mid-div of centre gp* **25/1**	56
000-	**20**	2 3/4	**Binanti**[175] [6851] 8-8-12 **93** FrancisNorton 26 (P R Chamings) *hmpd by loose horse leaving stalls: towards rr in centre: hdwy 3f out: sn rdn: wknd wl over 1f out* **50/1**	54
60-1	**21**	1	**Dabbers Ridge (IRE)**[25] [1387] 6-9-7 **102** MichaelHills 22 (B W Hills) *lw: hld up towards rr in centre: hdwy 3f out: effrt 2f out: sn wknd* **12/1**	60
23-6	**U**		**Laa Rayb (USA)**[6] [1828] 4-9-4 **99** RobertWinston 25 (M Johnston) *swtg: uns rdr leaving stalls* **12/1**	—

1m 26.08s (-1.92) **Going Correction** +0.025s/f (Good) **22** Ran SP% **141.0**
Speed ratings (Par 109): **111,110,109,107,106 106,105,105,105,103 103,98,98,97,97 96,94,93,91,88 86,—**
CSF £27.40 CT £217.90 TOTE £7.10: £2.20, £2.40, £2.40, £2.70; EX 36.10 Trifecta £661.60 Pool: £33,446.46 - 35.89 winning units.
Owner Hamdan Al Maktoum **Bred** Shadwell Estate Company Limited **Trained** Lambourn, Berks

FOCUS

A typically competitive renewal of the Victoria Cup. Strong handicap form, the first four all on the upgrade. They split into two distinct groups early on, with eight staying stands' side but, although they ended up all over the place in the closing stages, those from the larger group up the middle of the track dominated, filling the first three places. This form will be very important come Royal Ascot, with many of these likely to be engaged in some of the big handicaps.

NOTEBOOK

Zaahid(IRE) was a beaten favourite when fourth in the Spring Mile at Doncaster on his reappearance, and he was given too much to do when third in the Spring Cup at Newbury on his latest start, but he made no mistake this time. Dropped back in trip and faced with much quicker ground than on his first two starts this season, he was never too far away and stayed on strongly to deny the improving Al Khaleej. He is quite stoutly bred, but his sire, Sakhee, has a surprisingly good record with his runners over this sort of trip - he was also responsible for today's runner-up - and he proved well suited by this strongly run 7f. He is now being aimed at the Buckingham Palace handicap back over this course and distance in June. (op 8-1)

Al Khaleej(IRE) only just failed to defy a 9lb rise in the weights for his impressive Kempton success on his reappearance. He is reportedly very buzzy, which is why he has been racing over 7f, but he shapes as though he will be fine back over 1m in a strongly run race and if he is going to Royal Ascot his connections will have to choose between either the Buckingham Palace Stakes, in which he would probably have to re-oppose today's winner, or the Royal Hunt Cup. (op 9-2)

King Of Dixie(USA) ◆, runner-up in a Chepstow maiden last summer before showing very useful form when landing both his starts on Polytrack this year, the latest being a handicap off a mark of 90, ran a big race on his return to turf and can possibly even be considered a little unlucky. He reared as the stalls opened, which left him with ground to make up to move into a challenging position and, although he soon recovered to race handy, he could not quite sustain his challenge late on, with his earlier exertions clearly having taken their toll. He is a 100-plus rated horse in the making and very much appeals as one to keep on-side. Like the first two home, it would be no surprise to see him take his chance in the Buckingham Palace Stakes back over this course and distance in June.

We'll Come ◆ looks the type to make a nice older-horse and this was a very pleasing return from nearly nine months off. He came out on top of the smaller group on the stands' side after travelling well and should be in for a good season, with either the Buckingham Palace or the Royal Hunt Cup surely now on the agenda. (op 8-1)

Guilded Warrior recovered from a stumble at the start and ran surprisingly well considering all of best previous efforts on turf had been saved for a soft surface. His recent second to Al Khaleej on the Polytrack at Kempton had been rated a career-best by RPRs and he is clearly on the up. (op 40-1)

Count Ceprano(IRE), returned to turf for the first time since last July, had a feather weight and ran as well as could have been expected behind some classy sorts.

Fishforcompliments, dropped back from 1m1f, was never able to pose a threat in first-time cheekpieces and would appear to want 1m. (op 16-1)

Skhilling Spirit was 4lb lower than when runner-up in this race last year, but this ground was quicker than he cares for.

Purus(IRE) made his move tight against the stands' rail, which might not have been ideal. (op 66-1)

Mine(IRE) won this race off a mark of 99 in 2004, but he was never a threat this time. (op 20-1)

Dabbers Ridge(IRE) probably needs easier ground.

Laa Rayb(USA)'s rider seemed to be sitting on the side of the stall as the gates opened.

1983 MCGEE GROUP MAIDEN STKS — 5f
2:50 (2:57) (Class 3) 2-Y-O — **£6,476** (£1,927; £963; £481) **Stalls** Low

Form				RPR
1		**Glamorous Spirit (IRE)** 2-8-12 0	RyanMoore 1	80+
		(J Noseda) *scope: plld hrd trcking ldrs: shkn up to ld jst ins fnl f: r.o wl: readily*	**11/8**[1]	
2	*1 ½*	**Agente Parmigiano (IRE)** 2-9-3 0	RobertWinston 5	80
		(G A Butler) *leggy: chsd ldrs: nudged along over 3f out: rdn to ld ent fnl f: sn hdd: nt pce of wnr*	**7/1**[3]	
3	*2 ¼*	**Court Approval (IRE)** 2-9-3 0	JimCrowley 2	72
		(T G Mills) *leggy: lw: led: rdn over 1f out: edgd rt and hdd ent fnl f: one pce after*	**15/2**	
4	*¾*	**Roly Boy** 2-9-3 0	RichardHughes 4	69
		(R Hannon) *w'like: prom: rdn over 1f out: sn one pce*	**11/4**[2]	

61.73 secs (1.23) **Going Correction** +0.025s/f (Good) — **4** Ran SP% **93.0**
Speed ratings (Par 97): **91,88,85,83**
CSF £7.29 TOTE £2.00; EX 8.80.

Owner The Searchers **Bred** Carlo Soria **Trained** Newmarket, Suffolk

FOCUS
Just the four runners, all of them making their debut, but this looked a decent two-year-old maiden. They raced stands' side, but again the action took place away from the rail.

NOTEBOOK
Glamorous Spirit(IRE) ◆, a £105,000 daughter of Invincible Spirit, first foal of a prolific winner at up to 1m in Italy, is an athletic filly and justified a short price on her racecourse debut. She raced quite keenly under restraint early on, which was by no means ideal, but she had enough left when asked to take a gap between rivals around a furlong out and was well on top at the line. She is clearly well regarded and took this in the style of a very talented filly, but she will have to learn to settle better to make the grade when stepping up in class. Unless she learns to drop her head, she will probably be best off avoiding the Albany Stakes and sticking to 5f for the Queen Mary when coming back here for the Royal meeting. She is likely to have another run in the meantime though, and that will tell us how she is progressing mentally. (op 6-4 tchd 15-8)

Agente Parmigiano(IRE), a 26,000gns son of Captain Rio and first foal of a mare who was placed over 6f-1m at two to three, shaped nicely behind a potentially smart filly on his racecourse debut. Having gone with the winner for much of the final furlong, he was eventually worn down, but still finished well clear of the remainder and his rider was unable to pull him up for another six or seven furlongs after the line, eventually coming to a stop by Swinley Bottom. He should be up to winning a similar event and, considering his sire loved soft ground, he might be capable of even better on an easier surface. (op 15-2 tchd 8-1)

Court Approval(IRE), a £25,000 son of Royal Applause out of a 7f two-year-old winner, made a respectable debut in what looked a reasonably hot maiden. He is entitled to come on for this. (op 11-1 tchd 7-1)

Roly Boy, a £57,000 son of Dansili, half-brother to seven winners, including quite useful dual 6f-7f juvenile winner Vikings Bay, out of a smart triple 5f-6f winner at two to three, struggled to land a blow but he should be better for the experience. (op 5-2 tchd 2-1)

1984 EUROPA CORPORATE EVENTS H'CAP — 2m
3:20 (3:25) (Class 3) (0-90,89) 4-Y-O+
£7,477 (£2,239; £1,119; £560; £279; £140) **Stalls** High

Form					RPR
12-3	**1**		**Silver Suitor (IRE)**[7] 1812 4-9-9 **89**	TQuinn 5	100+
			(D R C Elsworth) *lw: t.k.h early: settled after 2f in 3rd: rdn over 2f out: led over 1f out: styd on strly*	**1/1**[1]	
6-13	**2**	*1 ½*	**Hue**[38] 1136 7-8-11 **74**	KerrinMcEvoy 2	84
			(B Ellison) *lw: hld up in last pair: smooth prog over 2f out: rdn and ch over 1f out: styd on but a hld fnl f*	**11/2**[2]	
-122	**3**	*3*	**Buster Hyvonen (IRE)**[20] 1501 6-9-8 **85**	OscarUrbina 3	91
			(J R Fanshawe) *hld up in last trio: smooth prog over 2f out: rdn and wnt 2nd briefly over 1f out: kpt on same pce*	**8/1**[3]	
41-0	**4**	*3*	**Plane Painter (IRE)**[21] 1472 4-8-9 **75**	RobertWinston 1	77
			(M Johnston) *trckd ldr: led over 2f out: sn rdn: hdd over 1f out: one pce fnl f*	**9/1**	
301-	**5**	*1*	**Gee Dee Nen**[183] 6744 5-9-11 **88**	DarryllHolland 9	89
			(M H Tompkins) *in tch: rdn 3f out: one pce fnl 2f*	**10/1**	
00-3	**6**	*1 ¼*	**Ned Ludd (IRE)**[21] 1472 5-9-2 **79**	JimCrowley 7	79
			(J G Portman) *mid-div: hdwy 4f out: rdn and ev ch over 1f out: fdd ins fnl f*	**14/1**	
32-	**7**	*1 ½*	**Gabier**[14] 5800 5-9-5 **82**	RyanMoore 10	80
			(G L Moore) *hld up in last pair: rdn over 2f out: no imp*	**12/1**	
2113	**8**	*1*	**Calculating (IRE)**[20] 1501 4-9-2 **87**	HaddenFrost(5) 6	84
			(M D I Usher) *b: t.k.h in tch: rdn 3f out: edgd rt and wknd over 1f out*	**20/1**	
00-5	**9**	*20*	**Tribe**[16] 1583 6-8-9 **72**	MichaelHills 8	45
			(P R Webber) *led tl over 2f out: sn wknd: eased fnl f*	**25/1**	

3m 26.57s (-6.03) **Going Correction** -0.10s/f (Good)
WFA 4 from 5yo+ 3lb — **9** Ran SP% **118.6**
Speed ratings (Par 107): **111,110,108,107,106 106,105,104,94**
CSF £6.97 CT £30.34 TOTE £2.10: £1.40, £1.90, £1.80; EX 8.80 Trifecta £50.70 Pool: £1,292.05 - 18.07 winning units..

Owner J C Smith **Bred** Tallyho Stud, J Delahooke & P Twoomey **Trained** Newmarket, Suffolk

FOCUS
A good staying handicap and Tribe set a fair pace once going to the front after a furlong or so. The winner was 2lb off his Newmarket form but there is more to come from him.

NOTEBOOK
Silver Suitor(IRE) was a little unlucky when third over 1m4f at Newmarket the previous weekend on his reappearance, but this step up in trip was always going to suit and he gained compensation in workmanlike fashion. He was a little keen early on, but settled fine once Tribe injected some pace after a furlong or and, never too far away, he gradually responded to pressure in the straight. This fine, big horse, an Ascot Gold Cup entry, should be open to more improvement and is a stayer to keep on-side. (op 11-8 tchd 6-4 and 13-8 in a place)

Hue, a winner off 61 at Redcar on his return from a spell hurdling before looking unlucky when third at Catterick, ran a solid race. He just ran into a potentially smart stayer, but was well clear of the remainder. (tchd 5-1 and 6-1)

Buster Hyvonen(IRE), 2lb higher than when just denied at Great Leighs on his previous start, travelled well for a lot of the way but his effort just flattened out a touch late on. This was another respectable effort in defeat. (op 15-2 tchd 7-1)

Plane Painter(IRE) was not asked to try and dominate this time and could only find the one pace in the straight. He might benefit from a return to front-running tactics. (op 8-1)

Gee Dee Nen was well held off a mark 7lb higher than when winning at Musselburgh when last seen in November, but he is entitled to come on for this. (op 14-1 tchd 16-1)

1985 ALFRED FRANKS & BARTLETT SUNGLASSES H'CAP — 6f
3:55 (3:57) (Class 3) (0-95,94) 4-Y-O+ — **£7,771** (£2,312; £1,155; £577) **Stalls** Low

Form					RPR
100-	**1**		**Jimmy Styles**[197] 6472 4-8-12 **88**	RichardHughes 8	101+
			(C G Cox) *lw: racd freely: hld up: smooth hdwy over 2f out: qcknd up wl to ld appr fnl f: sn idled and edgd rt: drvn out*	**7/2**[1]	
466-	**2**	*nk*	**Border Music**[217] 6003 7-8-13 **89**	(b) FrancisNorton 2	98
			(A M Balding) *lw: trckd ldrs: travelling wl ent fnl f: sn rdn: kpt on: nt rch wnr*	**4/1**[2]	
000-	**3**	*¾*	**Phantom Whisper**[209] 6205 5-9-0 **90**	DarryllHolland 5	97
			(B R Millman) *hld up: swtchd lft over 1f out: sn rdn and hdwy: r.o: nrst fin*	**11/1**	
6-04	**4**	*5*	**Dazed And Amazed**[7] 1802 4-8-7 **88**	HaddenFrost(5) 9	79
			(R Hannon) *chsd ldrs: ev ch 2f out: sn rdn: one pce fnl f*	**8/1**[3]	
62-0	**5**	*¾*	**Rainbow Mirage (IRE)**[14] 1617 4-8-8 **84**	TQuinn 7	73
			(E S McMahon) *trckd ldrs: effrt 2f out: wknd ent fnl f*	**9/1**	
54-0	**6**	*nse*	**Southandwest (IRE)**[29] 1300 4-8-9 **85**	LPKeniry 6	73
			(J S Moore) *chsd ldrs: rdn 3f out: wknd ent fnl f*	**8/1**[3]	
-021	**7**	*¾*	**Esteem Machine (USA)**[20] 1500 4-9-4 **94**	RyanMoore 4	80
			(R A Teal) *led after 1f: rdn and edgd rt fr 2f out: hdd appr fnl f: wknd*	**7/2**[1]	
510-	**8**	*¾*	**Mac Gille Eoin**[224] 5797 4-9-4 **94**	JimCrowley 11	78
			(J Gallagher) *hld up: pushed along and hdwy 3f out: rdn 2f out: wkng whn hmpd ent fnl f*	**14/1**	
004-	**9**	*4 ½*	**Golden Dixie (USA)**[188] 6676 9-9-3 **93**	KerrinMcEvoy 1	62
			(R A Harris) *broke wl: led for over 1f: prom: rdn 2f out: sn wknd*	**12/1**	
3-30	**10**	*nk*	**Woodcote (IRE)**[7] 1802 6-8-9 **85**	PaulDoe 3	53
			(P R Chamings) *awkward leaving stalls: sn plld hrd trcking ldrs: rdn and hung rt fr over 2f out: wknd over 1f out*	**20/1**	

1m 12.91s (-1.49) **Going Correction** +0.025s/f (Good) — **10** Ran SP% **124.1**
Speed ratings (Par 107): **110,109,108,101,100 100,99,98,92,92**
CSF £18.80 CT £148.91 TOTE £4.90: £2.00, £1.80, £4.00; EX 18.60 Trifecta £827.90 Part won. Pool: £1,166.07 - 0.89 winning units. Place 6 £255.50, Place 5 £54.25..
Owner Gwyn Powell and Peter Ridgers **Bred** Barry Minty **Trained** Lambourn, Berks

FOCUS
An ordinary sprint handicap for the grade. The first three pulled clear and the form seems sound enough. They raced stands' side early on, but once again nobody wanted to know the rail, and they ended up edging towards the stands' rail.

NOTEBOOK
Jimmy Styles, returning from nearly seven months off, was plenty keen enough early on, but he picked up well when asked, stealing a march on Border Music, and was able to keep that rival at bay. This should have taken the freshness out of him and there ought to be more to in a bigger field, when he can settle better off a strong pace. (tchd 4-1)
Border Music was just held on his return from seven months off. Having travelled well, his rider was reluctant to go too soon, which meant Jimmy Styles nicked a couple of lengths when getting first run but, although he stayed on once asked, it looked as though his run was flattening out a touch late on, and he was probably always being held. (op 9-2)
Phantom Whisper, another back after seven months off, finished strongly and this was a pleasing return. (tchd 12-1)
Dazed And Amazed was well adrift of the front three, who were all making their seasonal reappearance, and there was little promise in this effort. (tchd 15-2)
Rainbow Mirage(IRE) has not won since his two-year-old days. (op 12-1)
Esteem Machine(USA), up 5lb, was well below the form he showed when successful at Great Leighs on his previous start. (tchd 4-1)
T/Jkpt: £28,199.20 to a £1 stake. Pool: £79,434.40. 2.00 winning tickets. T/Plt: £280.70 to a £1 stake. Pool: £120,022.50. 312.10 winning tickets. T/Qpdt: £6.00 to a £1 stake. Pool: £7,574.52. 931.53 winning tickets. TM

1610 HAYDOCK (L-H)
Saturday, May 10

OFFICIAL GOING: Good (jumps courses 6.8; flat course 7.7)
Wind: Almost nil Weather: Overcast

1986 ENTER THE FLAT TOTETENTOFOLLOW CONDITIONS STKS — 6f
3:00 (3:01) (Class 2) 3-Y-O+
£10,904 (£3,265; £1,632; £817; £407; £204) **Stalls** Centre

Form					RPR
-530	**1**		**Reverence**[6] 1831 7-9-0 107	WJSupple 2	108
			(E J Alston) *a.p: led over 2f out: rdn over 1f out: pressed wl ins fnl f: r.o gamley and a doing enough*	**9/2**[3]	
2030	**2**	*½*	**Machinist (IRE)**[23] 1420 8-9-0 100	JoeFanning 5	106
			(D Nicholls) *in rr: niggled along after 2f: rdn and hdwy over 1f out: sn wnt 2nd: moved upsides to chal wl ins fnl f: hld fnl strides*	**8/1**	
0-10	**3**	*2 ½*	**Pusey Street Lady**[29] 1300 4-8-9 92	ChrisCatlin 8	93
			(J Gallagher) *in tch: effrt over 1f out: edgd lft ins fnl f: kpt on same pce fnl 75yds*	**10/1**	
6400	**4**	*4 ½*	**Indian Trail**[23] 1420 8-9-0 106	(v) AdrianTNicholls 1	84
			(D Nicholls) *hld up: rdn and hdwy over 1f out: one pce ins fnl f*	**11/2**	
0-05	**5**	*2*	**Advanced**[23] 1420 5-9-0 109	NCallan 6	77
			(K A Ryan) *trckd ldrs: rdn over 2f out: wknd over 1f out*	**2/1**[1]	
-026	**6**	*1 ¼*	**Hoh Hoh Hoh**[6] 1831 6-9-0 102	SaleemGolam 7	73
			(R J Price) *racd keenly: sn prom: led 4f out: hdd over 2f out: rdn over 1f out: sn wknd*	**7/2**[2]	
00-6	**7**	*2 ½*	**Celtic Mill**[21] 1483 10-9-10 102	(p) FergalLynch 3	75
			(D W Barker) *led: hdd 4f out: rdn and wknd over 1f out*	**16/1**	

1m 12.95s (-1.05) **Going Correction** +0.05s/f (Good)
WFA 3 from 4yo+ 10lb — **7** Ran SP% **115.2**
Speed ratings (Par 109): **109,108,105,99,96 94,91**
CSF £39.72 TOTE £5.20: £2.60, £4.10; EX 38.40.
Owner Mr & Mrs G Middlebrook **Bred** G And Mrs Middlebrook **Trained** Longton, Lancs

FOCUS
A decent conditions sprint. The first pair came clear and the winner has been rated as running to last year's best, but the form still looks worth treating with a little caution.

NOTEBOOK
Reverence registered his first success since landing the Group 1 Betfred Sprint Cup over course and distance back in 2006. He showed real battling qualities to get on top and, considering this ground would have been as fast as he wants it, this was a decent effort. A return to this venue for the Temple Stakes (being run at the track for the first time this year) back over the minimum trip is now probably next for him. (tchd 11-2 tchd 6-1in places)
Machinist(IRE) turned in a vastly improved effort and only lost out to the winner late in the day. Considering that rival is officially rated 7lb his superior this rates as just about his best effort to date in defeat. (tchd 15-2)

Pusey Street Lady posted a better effort and ran very close to her level when winning on her seasonal bow. She is likely to continue to find a few too good in this grade now. (op 12-1 tchd 14-1)
Indian Trail was never in the hunt from off the pace and continues to run well below his official rating at present. It may well prove that he comes good again later in the season, however, as his mark begins to ease. (op 8-1)
Advanced ran miles below the level he showed when fifth in the Abernant last time out and obviously rates bitterly disappointing. (op 7-4)
Hoh Hoh Hoh was closely matched with the winner on their Palace House form, yet he gave himself little chance by refusing to settle on the early pace. (tchd 10-3 and 4-1)

1987 BET TOTEPOOL ON UK RACING MEDIAN AUCTION MAIDEN STKS 6f
3:30 (3:35) (Class 5) 2-Y-O £2,590 (£770; £385; £192) Stalls Centre

Form RPR
0 **1** **Danidh Dubai (IRE)**[23] 1419 2-8-12 0 ChrisCatlin 6 80
(M R Channon) *prom: led after 2f: rdn over 1f out: strly pressed thrght fnl f: r.o* **9/2**[1]
2 *hd* **Seaway** 2-9-3 0 RobertHavlin 5 84
(J H M Gosden) *midfield: rdn and hdwy 2f out: hung lft fr over 1f out: str chal thrght fnl f: r.o* **5/1**[2]
3 *1 3/4* **Tishtar** 2-9-3 0 PatDobbs 9 78
(R Hannon) *a.p: pressed ldrs 1f out: hung lft wl ins fnl f: nt qckn towards fin* **7/1**
4 *5* **Sweet Smile (IRE)** 2-9-3 0 NCallan 10 62
(K A Ryan) *in tch: rdn over 2f out: one pce fnl f* **6/1**[3]
5 **5** *1 1/2* **Old Father Zieten**[13] 1640 2-9-3 0 RichardKingscote 1 58
(Tom Dascombe) *prom: rdn over 1f out: wknd fnl f* **9/2**[1]
6 *1* **Well Of Echoes** 2-8-12 0 NeilPollard 12 49
(A J McCabe) *hld up: rdn 1/2-way: hung lft fr 2f out: nt pce to trble ldrs* **33/1**
7 *2* **Manero** 2-9-3 0 MickyFenton 3 48
(J A Osborne) *midfield: rdn over 2f out: outpcd over 1f out* **20/1**
0 **8** *3/4* **Fasalee (IRE)**[23] 1413 2-9-3 0 FergusSweeney 4 46+
(A P Jarvis) *led for 2f: remained prom: rdn over 2f out: wknd over 1f out* **25/1**
0 **9** *5* **Pokfulham (IRE)**[22] 1447 2-9-3 0 FergalLynch 11 30
(T D Easterby) *midfield: rdn over 2f out: wknd over 1f out* **33/1**
10 *6* **Scrapper Smith (IRE)** 2-9-3 0 JoeFanning 8 10
(E F Vaughan) *s.i.s: a towards rr* **9/2**[1]
11 *7* **Tagalura (IRE)** 2-9-3 0 RoystonFfrench 7 —
(J O'Reilly) *rn green: sn outpcd* **50/1**
12 *12* **Herecomesbella** 2-8-12 0 SimonWhitworth 2 —
(A P Jarvis) *s.i.s: rn green: sn wl bhd* **33/1**

1m 15.09s (1.09) **Going Correction** +0.05s/f (Good) **12** Ran SP% **117.4**
Speed ratings (Par 93): **94,93,91,84,82 81,78,77,71,63 53,37**
CSF £24.49 TOTE £6.00: £2.10, £2.10, £2.40; EX 30.90.
Owner Jaber Abdullah **Bred** Con Harrington **Trained** West Ilsley, Berks

FOCUS
Probably an average juvenile maiden. The form looks fair with the first three coming clear.

NOTEBOOK
Danidh Dubai(IRE) showed the real benefit of her debut at Newmarket 23 days previously and, relishing the extra furlong, proved game in getting off the mark. Her stable has been somewhat unusually slow to find its feet with the juveniles so far this season, but this is a clear indication of how they can improve for the initial outings. A move into novice company now looks her best move. (op 6-1 tchd 4-1)
Seaway ◆, a 160,000gns purchase whose dam was a smart dual 6f winner at two, only just lost out on making a successful debut. He would have prevailed had he not proved green and hung left nearing the final furlong and, granted the normal improvement, he looks sure to make a bold bid for compensation next time out. (op 4-1 tchd 11-2 in places)
Tishtar, a half-brother to his stable's 7f juvenile winner Redsensor, showed up nicely on this racecourse bow yet lacked the pace of the first two when it mattered most. He should learn a good deal from this experience and clearly has a future. (op 13-2 tchd 6-1)
Sweet Smile(IRE), whose brother Kersaint made a winning debut over 5f at two for this stable, was left behind by the principals entering the final furlong. He still showed enough to suggest he has ability and ought to come on for the run. (tchd 9-2 and 13-2)
Old Father Zieten, fifth on his debut at Brighton, failed to see out the extra furlong on this more conventional track. He looks only moderate. (op 7-1 tchd 4-1)
Scrapper Smith(IRE), whose dam was a useful 7f winner at two, proved clueless after missing the break and clearly needs a deal more experience before he comes good. (op 7-1)

1988 TOTESCOOP6 H'CAP 6f
4:00 (4:04) (Class 4) (0-85,83) 3-Y-O £4,857 (£1,445; £722; £360) Stalls Centre

Form RPR
6144 **1** **Harbour Blues**[8] 1764 3-9-0 79 (t) CatherineGannon 8 89
(A W Carroll) *mde all: rdn over 1f out: jst hld on cl home* **14/1**
11-4 **2** *hd* **Cape Vale (IRE)**[21] 1484 3-9-4 83 AdrianTNicholls 15 93+
(D Nicholls) *midfield: hdwy 2f out: rdn over 1f out: r.o to take 2nd wl ins fnl f: jst failed* **3/1**[1]
00-0 **3** *1 1/2* **Lindoro**[23] 1426 3-9-4 83 SaleemGolam 3 88
(W R Swinburn) *midfield: rdn whn n.m.r over 2f out: hdwy over 1f out: r.o ins fnl f: gaining at fin* **18/1**
0-1 **4** *shd* **Mullein**[49] 965 3-8-9 74 JamesDoyle 1 79
(R M Beckett) *prom: rdn and pressing wnr 1f out: no ex towards fin* **8/1**[3]
16-0 **5** *1 3/4* **Kiwi Bay**[25] 1381 3-8-12 77 PhillipMakin 17 76+
(M Dods) *hld up: rdn over 2f out: hdwy over 1f out: edgd lft ins fnl f: r.o: nt rch ldrs* **12/1**
1-02 **6** *nk* **Premier Danseur (IRE)**[5] 1868 3-8-12 77 RoystonFfrench 6 75+
(M Johnston) *s.i.s: sn outpcd: swtchd rt ins fnl f: rapid prog: nrst fin* **10/1**
10-0 **7** *2 3/4* **Hunt The Bottle (IRE)**[18] 1546 3-8-10 75 ChrisCatlin 13 64
(B W Hills) *hld up: rdn over 2f out: hdwy over 1f out: nt pce to rch ldrs* **20/1**
0-22 **8** *3/4* **Ink Spot**[23] 1426 3-8-12 77 JoeFanning 4 76+
(M L W Bell) *midfield: sn rdn along: nt clr run over 2f out and 1f out: kpt on ins fnl f: eased fnl 75yds* **8/1**[3]
5-01 **9** *1* **Legendary Guest**[18] 1548 3-8-5 70 AdrianMcCarthy 10 54
(D W Barker) *chsd ldrs: rdn 2f out: edgd sltly rt over 1f out: sn wknd* **16/1**
-612 **10** *1 1/4* **My Kaiser Chief**[7] 1819 3-8-4 72 AndrewMullen(3) 9 52
(W J H Ratcliffe) *midfield: rdn over 2f out: wknd over 1f out* **10/1**
233- **11** *1* **Lake Sabina**[196] 6502 3-8-9 74 WJSupple 16 51
(E S McMahon) *in tch: rdn 2f out: n.m.r over 1f out: sn wknd* **20/1**
-600 **12** *nse* **Baronovici (IRE)**[7] 1819 3-8-7 72 FergalLynch 12 48
(D W Barker) *chsd ldrs: rdn over 2f out: n.m.r whn wkng ins fnl f* **33/1**
10-6 **13** *nk* **Prince Desire (IRE)**[9] 1745 3-9-1 80 RichardKingscote 11 55
(Tom Dascombe) *midfield: lost pl over 4f out: bhd after* **28/1**
-655 **14** *2* **Desert Clover (USA)**[12] 1688 3-8-13 78 PatDobbs 5 47
(P F I Cole) *s.i.s: a bhd* **28/1**
31-5 **15** *1/2* **Gainshare**[7] 1819 3-8-6 71 PaulFessey 7 38
(T D Barron) *chsd ldrs: rdn over 2f out: wknd over 1f out* **18/1**
02-1 **16** *10* **Minus Fifteen (IRE)**[60] 848 3-8-13 78 NCallan 2 13
(K A Ryan) *chsd ldrs: rdn over 2f out: wknd over 1f out* **13/2**[2]

1m 13.63s (-0.37) **Going Correction** +0.05s/f (Good) **16** Ran SP% **128.9**
Speed ratings (Par 101): **104,103,101,101,99 98,95,94,92,91 89,89,89,86,86 72**
CSF £54.96 CT £841.66 TOTE £18.40: £3.70, £1.50, £6.20, £2.50; EX 89.30 Trifecta £317.50 Pool: £447.23 - 1.00 winning unit..
Owner B Ward **Bred** Ewar Stud Farms **Trained** Cropthorne, Worcs
■ Stewards' Enquiry : Paul Fessey one-day ban: careless riding (May 24)

FOCUS
A decent three-year-old handicap, run at a strong pace. The winner produced a step up and the form should work out.
Ink Spot Official explanation: jockey said gelding jumped right from the stalls
My Kaiser Chief Official explanation: jockey said gelding never travelled
Desert Clover(USA) Official explanation: jockey said colt hung right

1989 TOTESPORT HOME OF POOL BETTING SPRING TROPHY STKS (LISTED RACE) 7f 30y
4:30 (4:32) (Class 1) 3-Y-O+
£18,450 (£6,994; £3,500; £1,745; £874; £438) Stalls Low

Form RPR
0505 **1** **Appalachian Trail (IRE)**[14] 1619 7-9-11 108 (b) FergalLynch 4 115
(Miss L A Perratt) *hld up: nt clr run and swtchd rt over 1f out: sn rapid prog: r.o to ld wl ins fnl f: won gng away* **16/1**
10-0 **2** *3 1/4* **Diamond Tycoon (USA)**[42] 1077 4-9-7 107 NCallan 2 102
(B J Meehan) *chsd ldrs: rdn 2f out: styd on to take 2nd towards fin: nt pce of wnr* **3/1**[1]
/0-0 **3** *1* **Aeroplane**[23] 1420 5-9-7 102 AdrianMcCarthy 5 99+
(P W Chapple-Hyam) *in rr: hdwy on outside over 3f out: led over 2f out: rdn and edgd lft over 1f out and sn qcknd away: hdd wl ins fnl f: no ex* **8/1**
-021 **4** *1* **Raptor (GER)**[22] 1457 5-9-7 101 FergusSweeney 3 97
(K R Burke) *hld up: rdn over 2f out: hdwy over 1f out: styd on ins fnl f: nt pce of ldrs* **6/1**
3004 **5** *1 1/2* **Beckermet (IRE)**[14] 1619 6-9-11 105 ChrisCatlin 6 97
(R F Fisher) *led: hdd over 2f out: sn rdn: wknd ins fnl f* **8/1**
4162 **6** *1* **Racer Forever (USA)**[8] 1767 5-9-7 110 (b) RobertHavlin 7 90
(J H M Gosden) *hld up: rdn over 1f out: no imp* **4/1**[2]
21-2 **7** *1 3/4* **Welsh Emperor (IRE)**[25] 1387 9-9-7 113 MickyFenton 8 85
(T P Tate) *chsd ldr tl rdn over 2f out: wknd ins fnl f* **9/2**[3]
-240 **8** *11* **Dubai's Touch**[28] 1326 4-9-11 105 RoystonFfrench 1 59
(M Johnston) *chsd ldrs: rdn 3f out: wknd over 2f out* **10/1**

1m 28.23s (-1.97) **Going Correction** 0.0s/f (Good) **8** Ran SP% **114.7**
Speed ratings (Par 111): **111,107,106,105,103 102,100,87**
CSF £64.03 TOTE £20.50: £3.50, £1.60, £3.20; EX 67.10 Place 6 £422.46, Place 5 £92.53..
Owner G L S Partnership **Bred** Swettenham Stud **Trained** Carluke, S Lanarks

FOCUS
This Listed event was run at a solid pace and the winner rates full value for the winning margin. That said, the overall form is not that solid.

NOTEBOOK
Appalachian Trail(IRE) came from last to first to put this Listed contest to bed in tremendous style. He turned around last-time-out form with Beckermet and the speed he showed after being switched to the outside was impressive by any standards. He rates full value for his winning margin. (op 14-1)
Diamond Tycoon(USA), back on turf, ran a pleasing race, keeping on for second and suggesting now that 1m may well prove his optimum trip. There will be no easy routes for him with a rating of 107, but he still has the scope to do better. (op 7-2 tchd4-1 in places)
Aeroplane made a dash for victory halfway up the straight, but his stride shortened entering the last furlong and he was put in his place. It was a much more encouraging effort in defeat. (op 7-1)
Raptor(GER) confirmed himself to be in excellent heart and ran right up to his rating in defeat, helping to put this form into perspective. (op 10-1)
Welsh Emperor(IRE) dropped away after failing to dominate on ground he would have probably found against him. (op 7-2 tchd 5-1)
T/Plt: £386.30 to a £1 stake. Pool: £96,173.49. 181.70 winning tickets. T/Qpdt: £66.40 to a £1 stake. Pool: £3,266.77. 36.40 winning tickets. DO

1954 LINGFIELD (L-H)
Saturday, May 10

OFFICIAL GOING: Good to firm (9.4)
Wind: Slight, against

1990 ENTER THE FLAT TOTETENTOFOLLOW CONDITIONS STKS 1m 2f
2:10 (2:11) (Class 2) 4-Y-O+ £12,462 (£3,732; £1,866; £934; £466) Stalls Low

Form RPR
430- **1** **Red Rocks (IRE)**[153] 7090 5-8-12 116 JamieSpencer 5 116
(B J Meehan) *swtg: lw: mde all: responded wl to press fnl f: r.o* **4/6**[1]
22-0 **2** *1/2* **Many Volumes (USA)**[6] 1828 4-8-12 103 EddieAhern 1 115
(H R A Cecil) *hld up in tch: hdwy 3f out: rdn to chse wnr fnl f: a jst hld* **14/1**
20-1 **3** *nk* **Al Shemali**[107] 296 4-8-12 112 (t) LDettori 2 114
(Saeed Bin Suroor) *trckd wnr: hrd rdn over 1f out: lost 2nd ent fnl f: kpt on but no ex ins fnl f* **9/4**[2]
003- **4** *4* **Pinpoint (IRE)**[189] 6653 6-8-12 109 AdamKirby 4 106
(W R Swinburn) *hld up: hdwy to 3rd 6f out: rdn and wknd over 1f out* **8/1**[3]
3035 **5** *8* **Murfreesboro**[49] 968 5-8-12 87 WilliamBuick 3 90?
(K J Burke) *t.k.h in rr: in tch to over 3f out: sn lost all ch* **66/1**

2m 8.38s (-2.12) **Going Correction** 0.0s/f (Good) **5** Ran SP% **110.0**
Speed ratings (Par 109): **108,107,107,104,97**
CSF £11.37 TOTE £1.70: £1.10, £2.10; EX 8.10.
Owner J Paul Reddam **Bred** Ballylinch Stud **Trained** Manton, Wilts

FOCUS
A decent little conditions event, run at a sound pace. The winner was 10lb below his best, with the second up 3lb and the third running to last year's British form.

NOTEBOOK
Red Rocks(IRE), making his seasonal return, showed a decent attitude under pressure late in the day and got his new campaign off to a perfect start. This represented a big drop in class for the 2006 Breeders' Cup Turf hero, and he could have really been expected to have won more comfortably against these rivals, but he is really a happier horse when getting a lead which was not the case here. He should also improve a good deal for the run and the Tattersalls Gold Cup at the Curragh later in the month is now his next likely port of call, but he will have to raise his game a good deal to seriously figure in that. (tchd 8-13 and 4-5)

Many Volumes(USA) turned in a greatly improved effort in defeat on this step up in class and has clearly improved since his lacklustre return at Newmarket six days previously. This was right up to his best and it was a big run at the weights, but his handicap days are now probably over as a result of this display. (op 9-1)

Al Shemali, last seen winning on his debut for current connections in Dubai 107 days previously, did little wrong in defeat and had every chance. He should really come on a good deal for the run and is probably happier when racing in bigger fields. (op 5-2 tchd 11-4 and 2-1)

Pinpoint(IRE) was not disgraced on this seasonal debut and left the clear impression he would improve for the run. He is not simple to place at present from his current mark, however, (op 9-1 tchd 12-1)

Murfreesboro, who refused to settle early on, was eventually predictably outclassed on this return to turf.

1991 TOTESPORT 0800 221 221 OAKS TRIAL STKS (LISTED RACE) (FILLIES) 1m 3f 106y

2:40 (2:40) (Class 1) 3-Y-O

£25,546 (£9,684; £4,846; £2,416; £1,210; £607) Stalls High

Form				RPR
23-3	1		**Miracle Seeker**[22] 1440 3-8-12 80 .... AdamKirby 9 (C G Cox) *mde all: clr 2f out: rdn and styd on wl fnl f* 10/1	100
1-	2	¾	**Look Here**[220] 5918 3-8-12 85 .... SebSanders 8 (R M Beckett) *stdd s: hld up: lost pl over 3f out: swtchd rt and hdwy on ins fr 3f out: wnt 2nd over 1f out: styd on fnl f* 2/1[2]	98+
10-0	3	3 ¼	**Presbyterian Nun (IRE)**[23] 1424 3-8-12 85 .... SPasquier 3 (J L Dunlop) *trckd ldrs: wnt 2nd briefly 2f out: rdn and one pce after* 8/1[3]	93
6	4	½	**Ice Queen (IRE)**[8] 1785 3-8-12 0 .... JMurtagh 1 (A P O'Brien, Ire) *s.i.s: hld up: hdwy on ins over 2f out: sn rdn and fdd fnl f* 13/8[1]	92
4	5	3 ¼	**Classic Remark (IRE)**[22] 1440 3-8-12 0 .... EddieAhern 7 (H J L Dunlop) *w'like: str: t.k.h: hdwy on outside over 3f out: rdn over 2f out: sn btn* 8/1[3]	87+
3-01	6	1 ¼	**Amanjena**[23] 1412 3-8-12 92 .... WilliamBuick 5 (A M Balding) *lw: t.k.h early: trckd wnr tl rdn 2f out: sn wknd* 9/1	85

2m 28.99s (-2.51) **Going Correction** 0.0s/f (Good) **6** Ran SP% **112.7**

Speed ratings (Par 104): **109,108,106,105,103 102**

CSF £30.72 TOTE £12.50: £3.10, £2.20; EX 39.60 Trifecta £161.40 Pool: £272.89 - 1.20 winning units..

Owner D J Burke **Bred** D J Burke **Trained** Lambourn, Berks

FOCUS

This Listed Oaks trial was weakened by three non-runners and no filly came here with an official rating of higher than 92. It is hard to be positive about the form. It was run at an uneven pace and the eventual winner (up 10lb) had the run of things out in front, so it has to be in doubt whether the race will have a serious bearing on proceedings at Epsom. Both the first pair still look likely to take their chances next month, however, and the runner-up holds obvious claims of reversing form there.

NOTEBOOK

Miracle Seeker relished this return to faster ground and, under a canny ride from Kirby, eventually made all to shed her maiden tag in some style. She got the longer trip without fuss and is a filly with a decent attitude, but there is no doubt she had the run of things out in front and she would be far from certain to confirm this form with the runner-up in a more truly-run affair. She is now likely to head to Epsom for the Oaks and is still open to further progression over this sort of distance, although she will obviously need to improve considerably there. (op 17-2 tchd 12-1)

Look Here, a maiden winner from the progressive Doctor Fremantle on her sole start as a juvenile, was representing last year's winning connections of this event and appealed as a big improver as a three-year-old. She ran very well in defeat, but was no doubt undone by the uneven pace set by the eventual winner and has to rate as somewhat unfortunate as she was motoring at the finish. Better than the bare form, she would have obvious prospects of reversing this form with the winner if re-opposing at Epsom next month and should come on a deal for the run. (tchd 9-4)

Presbyterian Nun(IRE), up in trip/class, hails from a stable with a decent past record in this event and, well backed, she duly posted her best effort to date in defeat. She was well held at the finish, but is another who would have enjoyed a stronger pace and appeals as a likely winner in this class before the year is out. (op 14-1)

Ice Queen(IRE), a clear-cut winner of a 1m2f Cork maiden eight days previously, did not help her cause by making a sluggish start and was never a serious threat on this step up in class. She may have fared better off a stronger pace, but she still looks far from one of her powerful connections' brighter fillies at this stage. (op 2-1 tchd 6-4)

Classic Remark(IRE), a half-sister to this race's 2005 winner Cassydora, came here with just a Newbury maiden fourth to her name and she struggled in this better grade on faster ground. She had two handlers in the paddock and looks to need more time. (op 6-1)

Amanjena was taking a massive step up in class, but having run away with a Kempton handicap off only 74 she came here the race's highest-rated runner on 92. She tracked the leader but took quite a keen hold and weakened 2f out. (op 10-1 tchd 8-1)

1992 TOTESPORT.COM DERBY TRIAL STKS (GROUP 3) (C&G) 1m 3f 106y

3:10 (3:11) (Class 1) 3-Y-O £34,062 (£12,912; £6,462; £3,222; £1,614) Stalls High

Form				RPR
4	1		**Alessandro Volta**[20] 1509 3-8-12 0 .... JMurtagh 2 (A P O'Brien, Ire) *rangy: str: scope: mde all: c wd into st: wandered arnd fr 2f out: rdn and kpt on u.p fnl f* 6/4[2]	108+
0-5	2	¾	**King Of Rome (IRE)**[20] 1509 3-8-12 0 .... DavidMcCabe 6 (A P O'Brien, Ire) *str: trckd wd into st: rdn and lost 2nd over 2f out: rallied fnl f to regain 2nd nr fin* 16/1	107
0-11	3	nk	**Campanologist (USA)**[24] 1402 3-8-12 107 .... LDettori 4 (Saeed Bin Suroor) *lw: hld up in tch: hdwy to press wnr 2f out: rdn and lost 2nd nr fin* 6/5[1]	106
223-	4	3 ¼	**Alan Devonshire**[201] 6382 3-8-12 96 .... PaulMulrennan 5 (M H Tompkins) *stdd s: hld up in rr: rdn and hdwy on ins over 2f out: wknd 1f out* 22/1	101
45-1	5	1 ¾	**By Command**[26] 1367 3-8-12 95 .... SebSanders 1 (J L Dunlop) *lw: trckd ldrs: rdn and weakeened over 1f out* 9/2[3]	98

2m 28.91s (-2.59) **Going Correction** 0.0s/f (Good) **5** Ran SP% **113.9**

Speed ratings (Par 109): **109,108,108,105,104**

CSF £22.33 TOTE £2.60: £1.40, £2.90; EX 15.50.

Owner M Tabor, D Smith & Mrs John Magnier **Bred** Meon Valley Stud **Trained** Ballydoyle, Co Tipperary

■ Stewards' Enquiry : J Murtagh caution: careless riding

FOCUS

This Group 3 event featured five colts who all had entries at Epsom, but it was weakened considerably by the withdrawal due to the ground of Derby second favourite Curtain Call and looked a very ordinary renewal. It was run at just a steady early pace, with the winner dictating, and the first three came clear. The exact worth of the form is difficult to gauge and it is doubtful whether the race will have a serious bearing on next month's Classic.

NOTEBOOK

Alessandro Volta, having his first outing over this far, showed his lacklustre seasonal return to Leopardstown to be wrong (when a slipped saddle was given as an excuse) and just did enough to hold off his lesser fancied stable companion in the closing stages. He looked happier on this sounder surface and enjoyed racing more handily, but it has to be noted that he had very much the run of the race from the front. He also looked ill at ease on this track, failing to handle the bend at all well, and hanging both left and right under pressure. This is not at all encouraging with a crack at the Derby in mind and, while he may well learn from the experience, it would be surprising were he to emerge as the leading candidate from his powerful stable at Epsom next month. He was later quoted as short as 10/1 with some bookmakers for the blue riband event, but as big as 20/1 with others and the latter price makes more sense. (op 6-5 tchd 11-10)

King Of Rome(IRE), deployed as a pacemaker for Alessandro Volta in the Ballysax on his seasonal bow last month, was ridden with greater patience here and made his stablemate work all the way to the line. Granted a stronger gallop he may well have prevailed and the extra distance looked more in his favour, with the better ground also helping his cause. He looks capable of going one better in this class before the season's end, but like the winner does not appeal as one of his stable's leading three-year-olds at this stage. (op 33-1)

Campanologist(USA), having his first outing for Godolphin, came into this with much the highest official rating of the domestic trio and not surprisingly was well backed to make it five wins from seven career starts. He emerged to have every chance from 2f out, but he failed to sustain his effort at the business end and was eventually held by the first pair. A drop back in trip now looks on the cards and he should really be able to race more handily again, as he looked a really game sort when holding off Kandahar Run at Newmarket on his previous start. His connections may now send him to the Prix du Jockey Club, run over an extended 1m2f, and the best of him has most likely still to be seen. (op 13-8 tchd 15-8)

Alan Devonshire, progressive as a juvenile and bred to be suited by a step up in trip this season, emerged to have his chance from the top of the home straight yet failed to raise his game when it mattered most. He may have needed the run and probably would have enjoyed a stronger early pace, but it is most likely that this level is just a bit beyond him at this early stage of his career. This trip may also be a little too far for him at present. (op 33-1)

By Command, a taking winner of a Windsor maiden on his comeback last month, was representing a stable with a decent history in this event and had the profile of a horse potentially better than an official mark of 95. His fate was sealed before the final furlong, but this quicker ground may have been against him so he is not one to be writing off yet. (tchd 6-1)

1993 TOTESPORT BETXTRA CHARTWELL FILLIES' STKS (GROUP 3) 7f

3:45 (3:46) (Class 1) 3-Y-O+

£28,385 (£10,760; £5,385; £2,685; £1,345; £675) Stalls High

Form				RPR
031-	1		**Sabana Perdida (IRE)**[244] 5259 5-9-7 0 .... C-PLemaire 3 (A De Royer-Dupre, France) *a in tch on outside: str hdwy over 1f out: led ins fnl f: drew clr* 5/2[1]	111
3-	2	1 ¾	**Verba (FR)**[33] 3-8-5 0 .... SPasquier 6 (R Gibson, France) *led tl hdd 2f out: r.o to regain2nd ins fnl f* 9/2[3]	103
01-2	3	hd	**Kylayne**[24] 1401 3-8-5 100 .... JohnEgan 10 (P W D'Arcy) *trckd ldr: led 2f out: rdn: hdd and lost 2nd ins fnl f* 11/2	98
10-1	4	1	**Salsa Steps (USA)**[12] 1683 4-9-3 80 ....(t) SteveDrowne 5 (H Morrison) *lw: trckd ldrs: rdn and ev ch ent fnl f: nt qckn ins fnl f* 3/1[2]	99
5-	5	1	**Once Upon A Grace (IRE)**[399] 946 4-9-3 0 .... JamieSpencer 8 (B J Meehan) *leggy: stdd s: making hdwy whn hung lft over 1f out: no imp after* 6/1	97
431-	6	1	**Steam Cuisine**[196] 6497 4-9-3 93 .... TPO'Shea 1 (M G Quinlan) *stdd s: rdn over 2f out: one pce after* 12/1	94
-610	7	1 ¾	**Tathkaar**[21] 1470 3-8-5 85 .... RichardMullen 7 (C E Brittain) *in tch tl rdn wl over 2f out: sn btn* 25/1	85
36-4	8	2	**Fleuret**[12] 1683 4-9-3 75 ....(t) StephenCarson 4 (Eve Johnson Houghton) *in tch on outside tl rdn wknd over 1f out* 33/1	84
306-	9	3 ¾	**Daniella**[191] 6604 6-9-3 85 ....(b) AlanMunro 9 (Rae Guest) *slowly away: in rr whn rdn and outpcd over 2f out* 33/1	74

1m 20.51s (-2.79) **Going Correction** 0.0s/f (Good)

WFA 3 from 4yo+ 12lb **9** Ran SP% **118.8**

Speed ratings (Par 110): **115,113,112,111,110 109,107,105,100**

CSF £14.33 TOTE £3.30: £1.40, £2.10, £2.10; EX 10.30 Trifecta £40.80 Pool: £529.42 - 9.20 winning units..

Owner Scuderia Zaro SRL **Bred** Musaed Abo Salim **Trained** Chantilly, France

FOCUS

A fair line-up for this Group 3 fillies' event. It was dominated by the two French raiders and the winner outclassed her rivals despite the penalty. The form looks surprisingly solid for a race of this nature, and the third and fourth have both been rated to their recent efforts.

NOTEBOOK

Sabana Perdida(IRE), having her first outing since winning a Group 3 at Longchamp on Arc weekend last year, got her new season off to a perfect start with a ready success under her penalty. She basically outclassed her rivals and looks a filly who can successfully step up another grade this term. Her third to Nannina in the Windsor Forest last season was her best effort to date and a repeat bid in that event at Royal Ascot next month now looks firmly on the cards. (op 11-4 tchd 3-1 in a place)

Verba(FR) was done for pace when the eventual winner asserted for home, but she kept gamely to her task thereafter and turned in her best effort to date in defeat. She has time on her side, is ideally suited by an easier surface, and has a race of this class within her compass. (op 4-1 tchd 5-1)

Kylayne, a well-held second to Infallible in the Nell Gwyn on her seasonal bow 24 days previously, showed that to be no fluke and again ran very respectably in defeat. As was the case at Newmarket, however, she really left the impression that sprinting will be her game - something her pedigree also backs up. (op 15-2)

Salsa Steps(USA), an impressive handicap winner on her seasonal debut at Windsor 12 days previously, confirmed the improvement shown there in this much more demanding company and got the extra furlong well enough. Her handicap mark may now suffer again, but black type is much more important to her this season and she ought to be placed to gain some on this evidence. (op 11-4)

Once Upon A Grace(IRE), making her British debut for new connections, had not raced since running creditably in last year's 1,000 Guineas Trial at Leopardstown. She met some support in the betting ring and looked a possible player prior to hanging markedly left when under pressure nearing the final furlong marker. This ground may have been plenty fast enough for her and she should come on for the run, but it should be borne in mind that she is clearly quirky as she has a pony to take her to post and had to be withdrawn when upset at the start on her intended reappearance. (op 9-1)

Steam Cuisine left the impression this first run for 196 days was needed and should be sharper next time out.

1994 NIGEL COLLISON FUELS MAIDEN STKS 1m 2f

4:20 (4:21) (Class 5) 3-Y-O+ £3,238 (£963; £481; £240) Stalls Low

Form				RPR
	1		**Vinces**[171] 4-9-12 0 .... LDettori 8 (T D McCarthy) *b: b.hind: t.k.h early: mde all: rdn over 1f out: styd on wl* 4/1[2]	71

6-0 **2** 1 3/4 **Kiho**[21] 1467 3-8-11 0 ...... StephenCarson 1 66
(Eve Johnson Houghton) *hld up: rdn and hdwy on ins over 2f out: styd on to chse wnr over 1f out* **3/1**[1]

0-6 **3** 2 **King Of Pentacles**[11] 1695 3-8-11 0 ...... EddieAhern 6 62
(H Morrison) *lw: racd in 4th pl: rdn 2f out and kpt on to go 3rd appr fnl f* **3/1**[1]

0 **4** 2 3/4 **Modernist**[25] 1379 3-8-8 0 ...... WilliamBuick(3) 5 57
(Sir Michael Stoute) *unf: trckd ldrs: rdn and wnt 2nd 2f out: one pce and no ex appr fnl f* **3/1**[1]

0- **5** 1 3/4 **Ministerofinterior**[224] 5813 3-8-11 0 ...... IanMongan 9 53
(C F Wall) *w'like: trckd wnr tl rdn 2f out: one pce after* **16/1**

0 **6** 3 1/4 **Force Tradition (IRE)**[26] 1367 3-8-11 0 ...... PaulMulrennan 3 47
(M H Tompkins) *w'like: stdd s: a bhd* **16/1**

00- **7** 1 **Hawkstar Express (IRE)**[204] 6296 3-8-11 0 ...... AmirQuinn 4 45
(J R Boyle) *mid-div: rdn over 3f out: sn bhd* **12/1**[3]

0- **8** 17 **Soundbyte**[185] 6723 3-8-11 0 ...... JohnEgan 10 11
(J Gallagher) *w'like: b.bkwd: a bhd: lost tch fnl f: eased 1f out* **33/1**

2m 11.25s (0.75) **Going Correction** 0.0s/f (Good)
WFA 3 from 4yo 15lb **8** Ran SP% **117.4**
Speed ratings (Par 103): **97,95,94,91,90 87,87,73**
CSF £16.96 TOTE £4.90: £1.80, £1.60, £1.30; EX 15.50.
Owner Eastwell Manor Racing Ltd **Bred** Gestut Fahrhof **Trained** Godstone, Surrey

FOCUS
This maiden was weakened notably by the withdrawal of Tatbeeq and the form looks pretty ordinary. Nevertheless, the second, third and fourth have all been rated improvers.

1995 TONY LAWRENCE 50TH BIRTHDAY H'CAP 6f
4:55 (4:56) (Class 4) (0-80,78) 3-Y-O
£6,231 (£1,866; £933; £467; £233; £117) **Stalls** High

Form RPR

0-54 **1** **Brassini**[15] 1597 3-9-3 **77** ...... AlanMunro 12 87
(B R Millman) *a in tch: rdn to ld jst ins fnl f: qcknd clr* **11/2**[3]

3523 **2** 3 1/2 **Asian Power (IRE)**[16] 1584 3-9-2 **76** ...... JMurtagh 5 76
(P J O'Gorman) *a.p: led briefly over 1f out: hdd jst ins fnl f: nt pce of wnr* **7/2**[1]

105- **3** 3/4 **Lodi (IRE)**[196] 6486 3-9-0 **74** ...... IanMongan 4 72
(J Akehurst) *lw: a in tch on outside: kpt on one pce fnl f* **11/2**[3]

-222 **4** 1/2 **Autumn Blades (IRE)**[90] 514 3-9-1 **75** ......(p) EddieAhern 7 71
(J W Hills) *in rr tl hdwy on outside fr 2f out: r.o one pce: nvr nrr* **16/1**

20-0 **5** 1/2 **Bazguy**[8] 1781 3-8-10 **70** ......(b) TGMcLaughlin 9 65
(P D Evans) *led tl rdn and hdd over 1f out: one pce after* **14/1**

01-3 **6** 1 1/2 **The Twelve Steps**[23] 1426 3-8-7 **74** ...... GabrielHannon(7) 8 64
(P F I Cole) *mid-div: rdn 2f out: no imp on ldrs after* **13/2**

344- **7** 2 1/4 **Brazilian Brush (IRE)**[133] 7264 3-8-12 **72** ......(t) SteveDrowne 10 55
(H Morrison) *lw: towards rr though in tch: rdn 2f out: wknd fnl f* **10/1**

40-3 **8** hd **Saranome (IRE)**[11] 1699 3-8-7 **70** ...... WilliamBuick(3) 3 53
(R Charlton) *towards rr on outside: effrt over 2f out: no hdwy fr over 1f out* **5/1**[2]

4-20 **9** 2 3/4 **Hobson**[16] 1584 3-9-1 **75** ...... StephenCarson 6 49
(Eve Johnson Houghton) *c over to stands' side fr s: nvr on terms* **14/1**

300- **10** 4 **First Trim (IRE)**[217] 6004 3-9-4 **78** ...... JamieSpencer 11 40
(B J Meehan) *trckd ldr: rdn over 2f out: wknd over 1f out* **15/2**

500- **11** 16 **Liberty Belle (IRE)**[132] 7280 3-8-12 **72** ...... JohnEgan 1 —
(J R Best) *in tch to 1/2-way: lost tch fnl 2f* **20/1**

69.84 secs (-1.36) **Going Correction** 0.0s/f (Good) **11** Ran SP% **127.8**
Speed ratings (Par 101): **109,104,103,102,102 100,97,96,93,87 66**
CSF £27.47 CT £119.58 TOTE £5.40: £2.20, £1.90, £2.50; EX 36.50.
Owner The Links Partnership **Bred** B N And Mrs Toye **Trained** Kentisbeare, Devon

FOCUS
A fair three-year-old sprint. Those drawn high were again at an advantage, and although the winner looked value for his wide margin he may well have been a bit flattered.
Liberty Belle(IRE) Official explanation: jockey said filly lost her action

1996 OCS GROUP LADIES STKS (H'CAP) (LADY AMATEUR RIDERS) 7f
5:25 (5:25) (Class 5) (0-75,75) 4-Y-O+ **£3,123** (£968; £484; £242) **Stalls** High

Form RPR

5521 **1** **Carlitos Spirit (IRE)**[38] 1160 4-10-3 **71** ...... MissEJJones 16 82
(B R Millman) *a.p: led over 1f out: r.o wl* **11/2**[2]

0-54 **2** 1 1/2 **Oi Vay Joe (IRE)**[18] 1550 4-9-9 **63** ......(b) MissSBrotherton 8 70
(W Jarvis) *t.k.h: chsd ldrs: 2nd and ev ch 1f out but hung bdly lft ins fnl f and nt threaten wnr after* **16/1**

1104 **3** 1 **Desert Dreamer (IRE)**[16] 1588 7-10-4 **75** ...... MissMSowerby(3) 15 79+
(Tom Dascombe) *slowly away: in rr whn swtchd lft over 2f out: r.o fnl f: nvr nrr* **9/2**[1]

4204 **4** 1 3/4 **Memphis Man**[5] 1872 5-10-4 **72** ...... MissEFolkes 10 71
(P D Evans) *in rr: swtchd rt sn after s: in rr: rdn over 2f out: r.o fnl f: nvr nrr* **10/1**

30-1 **5** nk **Glencal**[6] 1842 4-9-6 **65** 6ex ...... MissVCartmel(5) 2 63+
(H Morrison) *in tch on outside: effrt 2f out: kpt on one pce fnl f* **9/1**

4343 **6** 1 **Imperium**[38] 1154 7-9-0 **61** oh4 ......(p) MissJMHindle(7) 12 57
(Jean-Rene Auvray) *s.i.s: in rr: kpt on appr fnl f: n.d* **20/1**

-023 **7** 1/2 **Scarlet Flyer (USA)**[36] 1182 5-9-12 **71** ......(b) MissHayleyMoore(5) 7 65
(G L Moore) *mid-div: hdwy to ld over 2f out: hdd over 1f out: wknd ins fnl f* **9/2**[1]

2440 **8** 1 1/4 **Thoughtsofstardom**[6] 1842 5-9-1 **62** ...... MrsLHarris(7) 5 53
(M Wigham) *mid-div: rdn over 1f out: wknd ins fnl f* **20/1**

1662 **9** 1 1/4 **Reigning Monarch (USA)**[18] 1534 5-9-7 **61** oh4
MissGDGracey-Davison 4 49
(Miss Z C Davison) *swtg: w ldr tl wknd over 2f out* **10/1**

6636 **10** 1 1/4 **Hansomelle (IRE)**[27] 1345 6-9-0 **61** oh3 ......(p) MissTHall(7) 13 45
(Miss Sheena West) *s.i.s: a bhd* **12/1**

2100 **11** 1/2 **Super Frank (IRE)**[17] 1566 5-9-8 **69** ...... MissSSawyer(7) 14 52
(J Akehurst) *led tl rdn and hdd over 2f out: sn wknd* **6/1**[3]

00-0 **12** 21 **Glencalvie (IRE)**[22] 1456 7-9-12 **71** ......(p) MissZoeLilly(5) 1 —
(J Akehurst) *racd alone far side: no ch fr over 4f out: t.o* **20/1**

1m 22.65s (-0.65) **Going Correction** 0.0s/f (Good) **12** Ran SP% **130.3**
Speed ratings (Par 103): **103,101,100,98,97 96,96,94,93,91 91,67**
CSF £96.27 CT £441.07 TOTE £8.20: £2.60, £2.90, £2.60; EX 113.10 Place 6 £32.73, Place 5 £20.66..
Owner Karmaa Racing Limited **Bred** Tally-Ho Stud **Trained** Kentisbeare, Devon

FOCUS
A modest handicap, confined to lady riders, run at a solid pace. The stands' rail was an obvious advantage again.
T/Plt: £52.40 to a £1 stake. Pool: £74,757.21. 1,039.62 winning tickets. T/Qpdt: £15.10 to a £1 stake. Pool: £3,318.17. 161.70 winning tickets. JS

1960 NOTTINGHAM (L-H)
Saturday, May 10

OFFICIAL GOING: Good (good to firm in places; 8.3)
2 1/2mm water had been put on from the three furlong marker to the winning line overnight resulting in good, easy ground the rest on the fast side.
Wind: Almost nil Weather: Fine and sunny

1997 OVER 100 GAMES AT TOTESPORTCASINO.COM H'CAP 5f 13y
1:55 (1:57) (Class 5) (0-70,74) 4-Y-O+ **£3,885** (£1,156; £577; £288) **Stalls** High

Form RPR

016 **1** **Jilly Why (IRE)**[21] 1488 7-8-11 **70** ......(b) AndrewHeffernan(7) 16 83
(Paul Green) *racd stands' side: chsd ldrs: styd on to ld nr fin* **20/1**

5000 **2** 3/4 **Hawaii Prince**[14] 1624 4-8-7 **59** ...... SilvestreDeSousa 17 69
(S T Mason) *led stands' side: edgd lft over 1f out: hdd and no ex nr fin* **28/1**

030- **3** hd **Raccoon (IRE)**[217] 6020 8-8-11 **63** ...... PaulHanagan 4 73
(Mrs R A Carr) *led far side: clr over 1f out: no ex wl ins fnl f: 1st of 5 that gp* **8/1**[2]

6-54 **4** 2 1/2 **Comptonspirit**[26] 1373 4-8-12 **64** ...... J-PGuillambert 13 65
(B P J Baugh) *racd stands' side: chsd ldrs: kpt on same pce appr fnl f* **16/1**

0-00 **5** shd **Harrison's Flyer (IRE)**[13] 1646 7-8-13 **65** ......(p) DaneO'Neill 1 65
(J M Bradley) *chsd ldrs far side: styd on same pce fnl f: 2nd of 5 that gp* **25/1**

00-0 **6** shd **Darcy's Pride (IRE)**[47] 987 4-9-0 **66** ...... TomEaves 14 66
(D W Barker) *racd stands' side: chsd ldrs: hung lft over 1f out: kpt on same pce* **12/1**

-415 **7** 1 1/4 **Multahab**[63] 840 9-9-3 **69** ......(t) JimmyQuinn 15 64
(M Wigham) *mid-div: kpt on fnl 2f: nvr rchd ldrs* **16/1**

4-02 **8** 1/2 **Jakeini (IRE)**[25] 1378 5-8-13 **65** ...... GrahamGibbons 10 59
(E S McMahon) *s.i.s: racd stands' side: in rr tl kpt on fnl 2f* **9/1**[3]

-424 **9** 1/2 **Commander Wish**[14] 1634 5-8-8 **60** ......(p) NeilChalmers 7 52
(Lucinda Featherstone) *dwlt: in rr stands' side: kpt on fnl 2f: nvr on terms* **16/1**

124 **10** nk **Doubtful Sound (USA)**[36] 1190 4-8-10 **69** ...... MarkCoumbe(7) 5 60
(John A Harris) *in rr: kpt on fnl 2f: nvr on terms* **16/1**

00-0 **11** 1 1/2 **Peopleton Brook**[13] 1646 6-8-7 **59** ...... ShaneKelly 8 44
(J M Bradley) *racd stands' side: chsd ldrs: wknd over 1f out* **22/1**

020- **12** nse **Rainbow Bay**[133] 7271 5-8-3 **62** ......(v) MCGeran(7) 3 47
(P D Evans) *racd far side: sn outpcd: 3rd of 5 that gp* **20/1**

0301 **13** 1/2 **Brut**[4] 1893 6-9-1 **74** 6ex ......(p) AdeleRothery(7) 2 57
(D W Barker) *racd far side: chsd ldrs: wknd over 1f out: 4th of 5 that gp* **12/1**

10-2 **14** 1/2 **Green Lagonda (AUS)**[14] 1624 6-8-12 **64** ...... TPQueally 11 46
(J G Given) *racd stands' side: chsd ldrs: lost pl 2f out* **10/3**[1]

1550 **15** nk **Decider (USA)**[13] 1646 5-8-8 **63** ...... KevinGhunowa(3) 9 43
(R A Harris) *racd stands' side: chsd ldrs: lost pl over 1f out* **16/1**

5-23 **16** 3 1/2 **Azygous**[33] 1242 5-8-10 **62** ...... MartinDwyer 12 30
(J Akehurst) *stmbld s: racd stands' side: a in rr* **8/1**[2]

001- **17** 2 **No Worries Yet (IRE)**[289] 3869 4-8-7 **62** ...... TolleyDean(3) 6 23
(J L Spearing) *racd far side: a outpcd and towards rr: last of 5 that gp* **18/1**

59.80 secs (-0.90) **Going Correction** -0.15s/f (Firm) **17** Ran SP% **126.5**
Speed ratings (Par 103): **101,99,99,95,95 95,93,92,91,91 88,88,87,87,86 80,77**
CSF £485.18 CT £4969.62 TOTE £26.30: £5.60, £7.80, £2.60, £3.50; EX 254.50.
Owner Oaklea Racing **Bred** K And Mrs Cullen **Trained** Lydiate, Merseyside

FOCUS
The form looks solid at this level with the winner back to her best. There seemed very little between the two sides.
Hawaii Prince Official explanation: jockey said gelding hung left
Azygous Official explanation: jockey said gelding stumbled coming out of stalls, stumbled mid-race, lost a shoe and finished lame

1998 TOTESPORTCASINO.COM H'CAP 1m 6f 15y
2:25 (2:26) (Class 4) (0-80,80) 4-Y-O+ **£6,476** (£1,927; £963; £481) **Stalls** Low

Form RPR

6414 **1** **Pass The Port**[17] 1568 7-9-9 **79** ...... PaulHanagan 9 85
(D Haydn Jones) *s.i.s: hld up: hdwy over 3f out: led 1f out: r.o* **6/1**[3]

232- **2** 1/2 **Four Miracles**[205] 6276 4-9-4 **75** ...... JimmyQuinn 4 83+
(M H Tompkins) *hld up: hdwy over 3f out: swtchd rt 2f out: sn rdn: r.o* **16/1**

6232 **3** nk **Casual Affair**[29] 1299 5-9-2 **72** ...... HayleyTurner 2 77
(J D Bethell) *led 1f: trckd ldrs: rdn over 2f out: ev ch 1f out: styd on* **10/3**[1]

150/ **4** 1 **Markington**[21] 5284 5-8-11 **67** ......(p) DaneO'Neill 1 70
(P Bowen) *prom: lost pl 8f out: bhd 5f out: r.o ins fnl f* **25/1**

1603 **5** 3/4 **They All Laughed**[9] 1744 5-8-10 **73** ...... WilliamCarson(7) 11 75
(P W Hiatt) *hld up: hdwy over 2f out: rdn over 1f out: edgd lft and no ex ins fnl f* **16/1**

55-1 **6** 2 **Colonel Flay**[8] 1779 4-8-8 **70** ...... JackMitchell(5) 10 70
(Mrs P N Dutfield) *hld up: swtchd rt and hdwy over 3f out: rdn and ev ch 1f out: no ex ins fnl f: eased nr fin* **9/1**

30-4 **7** 1 **Traprain (IRE)**[7] 1793 6-9-6 **76** ...... DavidAllan 5 74
(D Carroll) *chsd ldrs: rdn to ld 2f out: hdd 1f out: wknd wl ins fnl f* **11/2**[2]

0-54 **8** nk **Inchloch**[21] 1472 6-9-7 **77** ...... MartinDwyer 3 75
(B G Powell) *prom: jnd ldr 8f out: led over 3f out: rdn and hdd 2f out: wknd ins fnl f* **7/1**

06-6 **9** 3 1/2 **Corum (IRE)**[13] 1080 5-9-10 **80** ......(p) VinceSlattery 6 73
(Mrs K Waldron) *hld up in tch: racd keenly: rdn over 2f out: sn wknd* **33/1**

22-4 **10** 5 **Wraith**[12] 1690 4-8-11 **68** ...... TedDurcan 8 54
(H R A Cecil) *led after 1f: rdn and hdd over 3f out: wknd over 1f out* **13/2**

-603 **11** 8 **Trance (IRE)**[8] 1773 8-8-10 **66** ......(b) GrahamGibbons 7 41
(T D Barron) *s.i.s: sn prom: rdn over 6f out: wknd 3f out* **8/1**

3m 4.70s (-2.60) **Going Correction** -0.15s/f (Firm)
WFA 4 from 5yo+ 1lb **11** Ran SP% **118.2**
Speed ratings (Par 105): **101,100,100,99,99 98,97,97,95,92 88**
CSF £98.06 CT £375.51 TOTE £5.30: £2.00, £3.20, £1.20; EX 97.90 Trifecta £84.00 Pool: £177.49 - 1.50 winning units..
Owner The Porters **Bred** Meon Valley Stud **Trained** Efail Isaf, Rhondda C Taff

FOCUS
No great gallop and just a modest event but overall sound form at this level.

Wraith Official explanation: jockey said colt had no more to give

1999 TOTESPORTGAMES.COM H'CAP 6f 15y
2:55 (2:56) (Class 3) (0-95,91) 3-Y-O £10,361 (£3,083; £1,540; £769) Stalls High

Form RPR
35-0 1 **Aye Aye Digby (IRE)**[22] 1441 3-8-10 **83**........................ DaneO'Neill 5 89
(H Candy) *sn chsng ldrs: styd on to ld wl ins fnl f* **9/2**[1]
23-2 2 *nk* **Baldemar**[14] 1623 3-8-11 **84**........................ DarrenWilliams 4 89
(K R Burke) *chsd ldrs on inner: led over 1f out: hdd and no ex wl ins fnl f* **13/2**[3]
001- 3 *3* **Quest For Success (IRE)**[219] 5931 3-9-0 **87**............... PatCosgrave 10 82
(D J G Murray Smith) *swvd lft s: hdwy on ins over 2f out: styd on same pce appr fnl f* **17/2**
-120 4 *2 3/4* **Soopacal (IRE)**[15] 1597 3-9-4 **91**........................ TomEaves 2 78
(B Smart) *w ldrs: one pce appr fnl f* **16/1**
20-0 5 *nk* **Rubirosa (IRE)**[23] 1426 3-8-10 **83**........................ DaleGibson 6 69
(M Dods) *prom: sn pushed along: one pce fnl 2f* **16/1**
21-5 6 *nse* **Lord Sandicliffe (IRE)**[14] 1623 3-8-9 **82**........................ TedDurcan 1 67
(B W Hills) *mid-div on wd outside: effrt over 2f out: kpt on: nvr threatened* **12/1**
-654 7 *shd* **Mister Hardy**[14] 1623 3-9-1 **88**........................ PaulHanagan 7 73
(R A Fahey) *chsd ldrs: hmpd and lost pl over 4f out: kpt on fnl 2f* **7/1**
021- 8 *3 1/4* **Kashoof**[239] 5380 3-8-13 **86**........................ MartinDwyer 3 61
(J L Dunlop) *led tl over 1f out: wknd jst ins fnl f: eased towards fin* **7/1**
41- 9 *5* **Wise Melody**[141] 7216 3-8-10 **83**........................ LiamJones 11 42
(W J Haggas) *lost pl over 4f out: hdwy over 2f out: hung lft and lost pl over 1f out* **14/1**
2-06 10 *3/4* **Anosti**[14] 1623 3-8-13 **86**........................ DO'Donohoe 8 42
(K A Ryan) *wnt rt s: in rr and drvn along: bhd fnl 2f* **15/2**
221- 11 *1 1/2* **Street Star (USA)**[234] 5540 3-9-0 **87**........................ TPQueally 9 39
(J R Fanshawe) *hmpd s: in rr: effrt on wd outside over 2f out: sn lost pl* **6/1**[2]

1m 12.9s (-2.20) **Going Correction** -0.15s/f (Firm) **11** Ran SP% **119.2**
Speed ratings (Par 103): **108,107,103,99,99 99,99,95,88,87 85**
CSF £33.65 CT £248.46 TOTE £5.70: £2.20, £2.90, £4.00; EX 40.70 Trifecta £134.10 Part won. Pool: £188.93 - 0.10 winning units..
Owner Trolley Action **Bred** G J King **Trained** Kingston Warren, Oxon

FOCUS
A competitive three-year-old sprint handicap with improved efforts from the first two.

NOTEBOOK
Aye Aye Digby(IRE), who didn't truly stay the seven on his return, was clearly expected to go well and he really knuckled down to show ahead near the line. (op 5-1 tchd 11-2)
Baldemar, 4lb higher, overcame his low draw to lead hard against the stands'-side rail only to just miss out near the line. He has a very willing attitude. (op 7-1 tchd 6-1)
Quest For Success(IRE), off the mark in maiden company on his final start at Ayr in October at two, has joined a new stable. He moved poorly to post and may not want the ground any quicker; from halfway here he was racing on well watered ground. (op 14-1)
Soopacal(IRE), in good form this year after being gelded, is a stone higher than when winning on his return at Wolverhampton in February.
Rubirosa(IRE), who had seven outings at two, is starting to look fully exposed. (tchd 18-1)
Lord Sandicliffe(IRE), drawn one, saw a lot of daylight on the wide outside. He never really entered the argument and may be worth a try over further. (op 17-2 tchd 8-1)
Mister Hardy, who scratched his way to the start, stayed on after being hampered at the start but he would not want conditions any quicker. (op 12-1)
Kashoof doesn't appear to have grown at all from two to three. (op 13-2 tchd 11-2)
Street Star(USA) Official explanation: jockey said filly suffered interference immediately after start and was never travelling thereafter

2000 TOTETENTOFOLLOW.CO.UK KILVINGTON FILLIES' STKS (LISTED RACE) 6f 15y
3:25 (3:27) (Class 1) 3-Y-O+ £17,778 (£6,723; £3,360; £1,680) Stalls High

Form RPR
011- 1 **Cartimandua**[336] 2450 4-9-7 106........................ GrahamGibbons 1 111
(E S McMahon) *racd far side: chsd ldr tl led over 1f out: rdn out* **4/1**[2]
12-4 2 *2* **Crystany (IRE)**[24] 1404 3-8-7 95........................ TedDurcan 7 98+
(H R A Cecil) *racd far side: hld up: hdwy over 2f out: rdn to chse wnr 1f out: r.o: 2nd of 7 in gp* **2/1**[1]
50-6 3 *1 1/2* **Day By Day**[11] 1698 4-9-3 88........................(b) MartinDwyer 13 96
(B J Meehan) *racd stands' side: chsd ldrs: led that gp over 1f out: styd on: no ch w far side: 1st of 5 in gp* **20/1**
062- 4 *hd* **Dubai Princess (IRE)**[190] 6619 3-8-7 98........................ ShaneKelly 8 92
(J A Osborne) *racd far side: chsd ldrs: swtchd lft 4f out: rdn over 1f out: edgd lft and no ex ins fnl f: 3rd of 7 in gp* **8/1**[3]
4-34 5 *3/4* **Tia Mia**[42] 1075 3-8-7 90........................ JimmyQuinn 6 90
(M Botti) *switched to r stands' side: hld up: hdwy over 2f out: nt clr run over 1f out: ev ch that gp ins fnl f: edgd lft and no ex towards fin: 2nd of 6 in gp* **14/1**
000- 6 *3/4* **Manzila (FR)**[215] 6071 5-9-3 98........................ SilvestreDeSousa 10 90
(D Nicholls) *racd stands' side: chsd ldrs: rdn and hung lft fr over 2f out: no ex fnl f: 3rd of 6 in gp* **22/1**
2664 7 *3/4* **Ripples Maid**[11] 1698 5-9-7 97........................ TomEaves 3 92
(J A Geake) *racd far side: in tch: hmpd and lost pl 4f out: n.d after: 4th of 7 in gp* **8/1**[3]
0-55 8 *1 1/4* **Woodnook**[77] 677 5-9-3 80........................ GeorgeBaker 11 84
(J A R Toller) *racd stands' side: chsd ldrs: rdn over 1f out: wknd ins fnl f: 4th of 6 in gp* **28/1**
420- 9 *shd* **Broken Applause (IRE)**[217] 6017 3-8-7 103........................ PatCosgrave 12 81
(D J G Murray Smith) *racd stands' side: dwlt: outpcd: nvr nrr: 5th of 6 in gp* **12/1**
10 *1* **Mocha Java (SAF)**[300] 6-9-3 0........................(b) GregFairley 5 80
(E F Vaughan) *racd far side: hld up in tch: rdn over 2f out: wknd fnl f: 5th of 7 in gp* **25/1**
-133 11 *2* **Feelin Foxy**[9] 1755 4-9-3 76........................ J-PGuillambert 9 74
(J G Given) *led stands' side: over 4f: wknd fnl f: last of 6 in gp* **20/1**
00-0 12 *2 1/4* **Reel Gift**[11] 1698 3-8-8 90 ow1........................ DaneO'Neill 4 65
(R Hannon) *racd far side: a in rr: 6th of 7 in gp* **33/1**
00-1 13 *6* **Morinqua (IRE)**[11] 1698 4-9-7 94........................ TPQueally 2 52
(J G Given) *led far side tl hdd & wknd over 1f out: last of 7 in gp* **8/1**[3]

1m 12.9s (-2.20) **Going Correction** -0.15s/f (Firm)
WFA 3 from 4yo+ 10lb **13** Ran SP% **125.1**
Speed ratings (Par 108): **108,105,103,103,102 101,100,98,98,96 94,91,83**
CSF £11.66 TOTE £5.50: £1.90, £1.20, £7.80; EX 12.60 Trifecta £123.60 Part won. Pool: £174.18 - 0.50 winning units..
Owner Mrs Fiona Williams **Bred** Mrs F S Williams **Trained** Lichfield, Staffs

FOCUS
A decent fillies' Listed race. The winner has come back after injury as good as ever. The first two home raced on the far side andthere was a seemingly much improved effort from the third, first home on the stands' side.

NOTEBOOK
Cartimandua, who chipped a bone in a knee after an impressive success in a similar event at Haydock in June, took this in fine style and now heads for a Group 3 at Leopardstown. (op 3-1)
Crystany(IRE) had 7lb to find with the unexposed winner on official ratings. She went in pursuit of her but was never going to finish anything but second best. She is progressing nicely and deserves to find a similar event. (op 11-4)
Day By Day, who made great strides at three, has struggled at this higher level and had plenty to find with the first two. She was first home on the stands' side but the first two were on the other wing. (op 25-1)
Dubai Princess(IRE), who showed a consistent level of smart form at two, made a highly satisfactory return and should continue to give a good account of herself. (op 15-2)
Tia Mia, back on turf, called wrong at the toss. After running into traffic problems, she passed the post second best of the stands-side group. (op 20-1)
Manzila(FR), a Listed winner in France last year, has won at up to a mile there. (op 33-1)
Broken Applause(IRE), who has changed stables since last year, gave problems going to the start. (op 16-1)

2001 PLAY ROULETTE AT TOTESPORTCASINO.COM H'CAP 1m 2f 50y
4:05 (4:06) (Class 6) (0-60,60) 4-Y-O+ £2,388 (£705; £352) Stalls Low

Form RPR
0312 1 **Princelywallywogan**[18] 1528 6-8-13 **55**........................ PatCosgrave 3 64
(John A Harris) *chsd ldrs: styd on to ld 1f out: hld on wl towards fin* **4/1**[1]
16-6 2 *3/4* **Pitbull**[21] 1486 5-9-4 **60**........................(p) JimmyQuinn 7 68
(Mrs G S Rees) *s.v.s: hdwy 3f out: chal ins fnl f: no ex* **8/1**
0/0- 3 *3/4* **Etoile Russe (IRE)**[58] 913 6-9-2 **58**........................(t) LeeEnstone 4 66+
(P C Haslam) *mid-div: hdwy over 2f out: styd on strly to take 3rd nr line* **16/1**
432 4 *1/2* **Black Falcon (IRE)**[4] 1904 8-9-1 **57**........................ GregFairley 9 62
(M A Peill) *led tl 1f out: kpt on same pce* **9/2**[2]
2/02 5 *1 1/4* **Calcutta Cup (UAE)**[8] 1779 5-9-2 **58**........................ MartinDwyer 12 61
(Karen McLintock) *chsd ldrs: styd on same pce fnl 2f* **15/2**[3]
-056 6 *nk* **Zach's Harmoney (USA)**[14] 1621 4-8-11 **60**........................ WilliamCarson(7) 5 62
(P W Hiatt) *trckd ldrs: effrt 3f out: kpt on same pce* **16/1**
00V- 7 *2 1/2* **L'Oiseau De Feu (USA)**[51] 7100 4-9-1 **57**........................ VinceSlattery 11 54
(Mrs K Waldron) *in rr: kpt on fnl 3f: nvr nr ldrs* **50/1**
0000 8 *1* **The Grey One (IRE)**[4] 1898 5-8-10 **52**........................(p) DaneO'Neill 1 47
(J M Bradley) *s.s: effrt 3f out: edgd lft 1f out: fnl f: nvr nr ldrs* **12/1**
320- 9 *3/4* **Lilac Moon (GER)**[148] 7146 4-9-1 **57**........................ TPQueally 8 50
(N J Vaughan) *in tch: rdn and hung lft over 2f out: sn btn* **12/1**
2133 10 *1 1/4* **Floodlight Fantasy**[5] 1853 5-9-0 **56**........................(b) HayleyTurner 14 47
(Dr R D P Newland) *in tch: rdn and hung lft over 2f out: sn wknd* **8/1**
000- 11 *3 1/4* **Dr Light (IRE)**[315] 3082 4-8-5 **54**........................ JodyWilson(7) 13 38
(M A Peill) *s.i.s: hld up in rr: effrt on wd outside over 3f out: nvr on terms* **50/1**
5626 12 *3/4* **Flight Dream (FR)**[18] 1534 5-9-4 **60**........................ TedDurcan 15 43
(M G Quinlan) *hld up in rr: hdwy on outside over 3f out: wknd 2f out* **14/1**
05/3 13 *3 1/4* **Three Strings (USA)**[19] 1521 5-9-4 **60**........................ TomEaves 6 36
(P D Niven) *trckd ldrs: t.k.h: wknd over 2f out* **10/1**
4/00 14 *10* **Mozayada (USA)**[16] 1577 4-8-12 **57**........................ MarkLawson(3) 10 13
(M Brittain) *chsd ldr: lost pl over 2f out: bhd and eased over 1f out* **40/1**
-000 15 *8* **Gala Sunday (USA)**[10] 1729 8-8-9 **58**........................(bt) NSLawes(7) 16 —
(M W Easterby) *in rr: sn pushed along: bhd fnl 3f* **22/1**
440- 16 *62* **Grafty Green (IRE)**[164] 6969 5-8-13 **55**........................ ShaneKelly 2 —
(W M Brisbourne) *mid-div: lost pl over 5f out: bhd and eased 2f out: virtually p.u* **40/1**

2m 11.2s (-1.30) **Going Correction** -0.15s/f (Firm) **16** Ran SP% **128.2**
Speed ratings (Par 101): **105,104,103,103,102 102,100,99,98,97 95,94,91,83,77 27**
CSF £36.33 CT £484.14 TOTE £5.50: £1.60, £2.30, £5.20, £1.60; EX 36.80.
Owner Mrs A E Harris **Bred** Mrs J A Gawthorpe **Trained** Eastwell, Leics

FOCUS
Ordinary but solid form. The winner is at the top of his form.
Etoile Russe(IRE) Official explanation: jockey said gelding was denied a clear run
Grafty Green(IRE) Official explanation: jockey said gelding lost its action

2002 PLAY BLACKJACK AT TOTESPORTCASINO.COM H'CAP 1m 75y
4:40 (4:41) (Class 5) (0-75,75) 3-Y-O £3,238 (£963; £481; £240) Stalls Centre

Form RPR
30-5 1 **Dancer's Legacy**[18] 1540 3-9-2 **73**........................(t) TedDurcan 12 83
(E A L Dunlop) *mde virtually all: rdn clr and swished tail fr over 1f out* **11/2**[3]
050- 2 *2 3/4* **Sinbad The Sailor**[234] 5538 3-8-13 **70**........................ MartinDwyer 10 74+
(J W Hills) *hld up: hdwy over 1f out: no ch w wnr* **7/1**
0-32 3 *1 1/2* **Bowder Stone (IRE)**[16] 1579 3-9-4 **75**........................ JimmyQuinn 11 76
(M H Tompkins) *hld up: hdwy over 3f out: rdn to chse wnr and hung lft over 1f out: no ex fnl f* **2/1**[1]
2541 4 *2* **Montiboli (IRE)**[17] 1558 3-8-13 **70**........................ DO'Donohoe 6 66
(K A Ryan) *chsd ldrs: rdn over 3f out: wknd ins fnl f* **8/1**
0-25 5 *shd* **Kashmina**[23] 1412 3-8-9 **66**........................ EdwardCreighton 8 62
(M R Channon) *uns rdr and bolted to post: hld up: hdwy over 1f out: sn rdn: edgd lft and wknd ins fnl f* **10/1**
0-00 6 *8* **Zabougg**[22] 1448 3-8-5 **62**........................ GregFairley 2 39
(D W Barker) *plld hrd and prom: rdn over 3f out: wknd over 1f out* **14/1**
0-10 7 *2 3/4* **Nortune (USA)**[22] 1448 3-9-2 **73**........................ TomEaves 9 44
(B Smart) *trckd ldrs: plld hrd: rdn and wknd over 2f out* **5/1**[2]
0-20 8 *4 1/2* **Ogmore Junction (IRE)**[25] 1389 3-8-12 **69**........................ TPQueally 5 30
(Mrs S Leech) *hld up: rdn over 2f out: sn hung lft and wknd* **16/1**
2-44 9 *1/2* **Kool Katie**[92] 487 3-8-2 **66**........................ IanCraven(7) 3 25
(Mrs G S Rees) *chsd wnr: chal 1/2-way: wknd over 2f out* **16/1**
100- 10 *1/2* **Geordie Girl**[188] 6665 3-8-4 **68**........................ StacyRenwick(7) 4 26
(R C Guest) *hld up: rdn over 3f out: sn wknd* **28/1**
5430 11 *7* **Lady Amberlini**[76] 694 3-8-0 **64**........................ RossAtkinson(7) 1 6
(P D Evans) *hld up: hdwy over 4f out: sn rdn and wknd* **33/1**

1m 45.54s (0.14) **Going Correction** -0.15s/f (Firm) **11** Ran SP% **122.9**
Speed ratings (Par 99): **100,97,95,93,93 85,82,78,77,77 70**
CSF £46.03 CT £105.48 TOTE £6.10: £2.00, £3.00, £1.30; EX 61.60.
Owner Miltil Consortium **Bred** Floors Farming **Trained** Newmarket, Suffolk

FOCUS
The winner enjoyed a soft lead and they came home well strung out with no strength in depth at all in just a modest event.

Dancer's Legacy Official explanation: trainer's rep said, regarding the improved form shown, colt is a character who may have been suited by racing on a firmer surface here

2003 PLAY VIDEO POKER AT TOTESPORTCASINO.COM APPRENTICE H'CAP 1m 75y

5:10 (5:12) (Class 5) (0-60,59) 4-Y-O+ **£2,266** (£674; £337; £168) **Stalls** Centre

Form RPR
50-0 **1** **Wahoo Sam (USA)**[19] 1520 8-8-10 **55**........................ RichardEvans(5) 6 68
(P D Evans) *mde all: clr 1/2-way: rdn over 1f out: all out* **12/1**
02-0 **2** *3/4* **Brouhaha**[18] 1528 4-8-9 **52**........................ JackMitchell(3) 3 63
(B J McMath) *a.p: chsd wnr over 3f out: rdn over 1f out: hung lft: styd on* **6/1**[2]
60-0 **3** *shd* **Tough Love**[22] 1449 9-9-5 **59**........................ DuranFentiman 17 70
(T D Easterby) *hld up: plld hrd: hdwy over 2f out: rdn and nt clr run ins fnl f: styd on* **8/1**
5-00 **4** *5* **Split The Wind (USA)**[12] 1692 4-8-9 **52**........................ PatrickHills(3) 9 51
(Eve Johnson Houghton) *hld up: rdn over 3f out: hdwy over 1f out: nt rch ldrs* **14/1**
6343 **5** *1/2* **Sparky Vixen**[8] 1776 4-8-4 **51**........................ JamieKyne(7) 8 49
(C J Teague) *chsd ldrs: rdn over 2f out: hung lft and no ex fnl f* **6/1**[2]
0-10 **6** *1 3/4* **Turkish Sultan (IRE)**[4] 1900 5-8-9 **54**........................(p) RossAtkinson(5) 12 48
(J M Bradley) *chsd ldrs: rdn over 2f out: wknd fnl f* **14/1**
0343 **7** *1 1/2* **Latif (USA)**[26] 1374 7-8-9 **56**........................ AndrewHeffernan(7) 2 47
(Paul Green) *s.s: hld up: rdn over 2f out: nvr nrr* **15/2**[3]
300- **8** *nk* **Bessemer (JPN)**[320] 2947 7-8-13 **58**........................ SimonPearce(5) 4 48
(Miss M E Rowland) *s.s: hdwy 5f out: rdn over 2f out: wknd over 1f out* **25/1**
0241 **9** *1/2* **Balerno**[12] 1687 9-8-8 **53**........................ SophieDoyle(5) 14 42
(Mrs L J Mongan) *hld up: rdn over 2f out: n.d* **11/2**[1]
4203 **10** *nk* **Al Rayanah**[11] 1705 5-8-10 **50**........................ MarcHalford 16 38
(G Prodromou) *hld up: hdwy 1/2-way: sn rdn and hung lft: wknd over 1f out* **6/1**[2]
-000 **11** *3 1/2* **El Coto**[4] 1902 8-8-13 **53**........................(b) MichaelJStainton 5 33
(J R Holt) *chsd ldrs over 5f* **14/1**
6160 **12** *4 1/2* **General Feeling (IRE)**[10] 1729 7-9-3 **57**........................(p) DNolan 15 27
(S T Mason) *s.i.s: hld up: rdn over 2f out: sn hung lft and wknd* **25/1**
000 **13** *7* **Hold Fire**[38] 1144 4-8-5 **50**........................ MarkCoumbe(5) 1 4
(A W Carroll) *hld up: bhd fr 1/2-way* **40/1**
-060 **14** *nk* **Sagunt (GER)**[13] 1644 5-9-0 **59**........................ WilliamCarson(5) 13 12
(S Curran) *chsd ldrs: rdn 1/2-way: wknd over 2f out: eased* **25/1**

1m 45.6s (0.20) **Going Correction** -0.15s/f (Firm) **14** Ran SP% **122.8**
Speed ratings (Par 103): **100,99,99,94,93 91,90,90,89,89 85,81,74,74**
CSF £80.82 CT £644.26 TOTE £17.50: £4.10, £2.40, £3.40; EX 180.20 Place 6 £67.27, Place 5 £10.32..
Owner Premier Cru Racing **Bred** Stonereath Farms Inc **Trained** Pandy, Monmouths

FOCUS
An uncompetitive low-grade handicap with the back-to-form winner running from a career low mark.
T/Plt: £235.70 to a £1 stake. Pool: £61,658.49. 190.90 winning tickets. T/Qpdt: £9.10 to a £1 stake. Pool: £3,193.39. 257.80 winning tickets. WG

1813 THIRSK (L-H)

Saturday, May 10

OFFICIAL GOING: Good to firm (firm in places)
Wind: virtually nil Weather: grey and warm

2004 TURFTV.CO.UK (S) STKS 5f

6:10 (6:11) (Class 5) 2-Y-O **£3,885** (£1,156; £577; £288) **Stalls** High

Form RPR
05 **1** **Alphabeth**[36] 1177 2-7-12 0........................ MCGeran(7) 5 57
(M R Channon) *chsd ldrs: effrt and n.m.r 2f out: rdn to ld appr fnl f: kpt on* **4/1**[2]
3 **2** *2* **Rose Of Coma (IRE)**[21] 1480 2-8-5 0........................ PaulHanagan 2 50
(R A Fahey) *chsd ldrs and sn rdn along: drvn and ch over 1f out: kpt on same pce u.p fnl f* **7/2**[1]
642 **3** *1 1/4* **Dazzling Dust (IRE)**[16] 1574 2-8-5 0........................(p) JackDean(5) 4 50
(W G M Turner) *sn led: rdn along 2f out: drvn and hdd appr fnl f: kpt on same pce* **4/1**[2]
3 **4** *1/2* **Rioja Ruby (IRE)**[24] 1392 2-7-12 0........................ PatrickDonaghy(7) 7 44
(P C Haslam) *chsd ldrs: swtchd lft and hdwy 2f out: rdn over 1f out and sn one pce* **4/1**[2]
35 **5** *1/2* **Kings House**[24] 1390 2-8-10 0........................ DaleGibson 6 47
(M W Easterby) *chsd ldrs: rdn along and outpcd 2f out: kpt on u.p ins fnl f* **7/1**[3]
63 **6** *1* **Kheley (IRE)**[16] 1574 2-8-5 0........................ LiamJones 11 38
(W M Brisbourne) *chsd ldrs: n.m.r 1/2-way: swtchd lft and hdwy wl over 1f out: sn rdn and kpt on same pce* **12/1**
7 *2* **Bold Account (IRE)** 2-8-10 0........................ DarrenWilliams 3 36
(K R Burke) *chsd ldrs: rdn and edgd lft 2f out: sn wknd* **20/1**
0 **8** *1 3/4* **French Forest**[14] 1627 2-8-5 0........................ TWilliams 1 25
(M Brittain) *cl up: rdn and ev ch 2f out: tl wknd appr fnl f* **40/1**
0 **9** *3* **Naughty Natz**[21] 1480 2-8-5 0........................ PaulFessey 10 14
(P T Midgley) *dwlt: effrt and sme hdwy 2f out: sn rdn and wknd* **9/1**
10 *2* **Mimicker** 2-8-1 0 ow3........................ BradleyRoper(7) 8 10
(M W Easterby) *s.i.s: a in rr* **50/1**

61.74 secs (2.14) **Going Correction** +0.175s/f (Good) **10** Ran SP% **121.6**
Speed ratings (Par 93): **89,85,83,83,82 80,77,74,69,66**
CSF £19.03 TOTE £6.70: £2.40, £1.20, £2.00; EX 22.00.The winner was bought in for 5,500gns.
Owner The Lord Ilsley Racing Club **Bred** A C M Spalding **Trained** West Ilsley, Berks

FOCUS
A standard two-year-old seller. The form is rated around the winer and third.

NOTEBOOK
Alphabeth showed just moderate form in a couple of maidens, but she had a feather weight on this drop into selling company with an apprentice taking 7lb off and was a clear-cut winner. (op 7-2 tchd 5-1)
Rose Of Coma(IRE), a beaten favourite when third in course-and-distance claimer on her debut, found one too good on this drop into selling company. (tchd 10-3)
Dazzling Dust(IRE) again showed speed but a couple were too strong late on. (op 15-2)
Rioja Ruby(IRE) showed very moderate form when third on her debut at Beverley and could not take advantage of the drop into selling company. (op 7-2)
Kheley(IRE) Official explanation: jockey said filly hung left

Naughty Natz Official explanation: jockey said filly hung left throughout

2005 DICK PEACOCK SPRINT H'CAP 6f

6:40 (6:40) (Class 5) (0-75,72) 4-Y-O+ **£3,885** (£1,156; £577; £288) **Stalls** High

Form RPR
6160 **1** **Winthorpe (IRE)**[23] 1431 8-8-12 **66**........................ GrahamGibbons 16 75
(J J Quinn) *chsd ldrs stands' side: hdwy wl over 1f out: rdn and styd on strly ins fnl f to ld on line* **25/1**
-046 **2** *hd* **Timber Treasure (USA)**[11] 1708 4-8-11 **65**........................(b[1]) PhillipMakin 1 74
(Paul Green) *trckd ldrs far side: hdwy wl over 1f out: sn rdn and styd on wl to ld last 100yds: hdd on line* **40/1**
2122 **3** *1/2* **Alexander Huricane (IRE)**[29] 1309 4-9-3 **71**........................ NCallan 20 78
(K A Ryan) *cl up stands' side: effrt 2f out: rdn to ld stands' side gp and hung lft ent fnl f: sn drvn: hdd and no ex last 100yds* **7/2**[1]
00-4 **4** *hd* **Dark Champion**[21] 1485 8-8-7 **61**........................ PaulHanagan 5 67
(R E Barr) *led far side 1f: cl up tl rdn to ld and overall ldr ent fnl f: sn drvn: hdd and no ex last 100yds* **14/1**
1332 **5** *2 1/4* **Dorn Dancer (IRE)**[7] 1818 6-9-1 **69**........................ RobertWinston 19 68
(D W Barker) *hld up and towards rr stands' side: hdwy 2f out: sn rdn and kpt on ins fnl f: nrst fin* **9/2**[2]
0-00 **6** *1/2* **Windjammer**[14] 1624 4-8-9 **63**........................ DavidAllan 12 61
(T D Easterby) *prom stands' side: hdwy to ld that gp 2f out: sn rdn and hdd ent fnl f: edgd lft and kpt on same pce* **16/1**
360- **7** *3/4* **Mundo's Magic**[234] 5522 4-8-9 **63**........................ RoystonFfrench 14 58
(G M Moore) *chsd ldrs stands' side: rdn along wl over 1f out: kpt on same pce* **25/1**
-600 **8** *1 1/4* **Circuit Dancer (IRE)**[14] 1624 8-8-13 **70**........................ AndrewMullen(3) 7 61
(D Nicholls) *prom far side: rdn to ld that gp bruiefly and overall ldr over 1f out: drvn and hdd ent fnl f: wknd* **28/1**
1-30 **9** *1/2* **Maia**[22] 1450 4-8-11 **65**........................ SilvestreDeSousa 18 55
(D Nicholls) *hld up and bhd stands' side tl sme late hdwy* **15/2**[3]
0265 **10** *shd* **Messiah Garvey**[8] 1775 4-8-7 **61**........................(b[1]) AdrianTNicholls 17 50
(D Nicholls) *in tch stands' side: rdn along 2f out: sn no imp* **12/1**
-005 **11** *nk* **Mr Wolf**[18] 1552 7-9-4 **72**........................(p) FergalLynch 13 60
(D W Barker) *led stands' side: rdn along and heaqded 2f out: sn drvn and wknd* **11/1**
030- **12** *3/4* **All You Need (IRE)**[205] 6283 4-8-13 **67**........................ DaleGibson 3 53
(R Hollinshead) *in tch far side: rdn along over 2f out and sn wknd* **66/1**
3332 **13** *1/2* **Dasheena**[16] 1591 5-8-6 **65**........................(be) DanielleMcCreery(5) 11 49
(A J McCabe) *a in rr stands' side* **20/1**
40-0 **14** *2 1/4* **Kunte Kinteh**[22] 1450 4-8-9 **63**........................ MickyFenton 15 40
(D Nicholls) *chsd ldrs stands' side: rdn along 2f out: sn wknd* **25/1**
30-0 **15** *hd* **Ryedane (IRE)**[21] 1485 6-8-11 **65**........................ LeeEnstone 6 41
(T D Easterby) *cl up far side: led that gp and overall ldr after 1f tl rdn and hdd wl over 1f out: sn wknd* **50/1**
0-41 **16** *3/4* **Flores Sea (USA)**[121] 111 4-9-1 **69**........................ PaulFessey 9 43
(T D Barron) *a towards rr stands' side* **16/1**
55-0 **17** *2 1/2* **Sea Rover (IRE)**[22] 1451 4-8-11 **65**........................ TWilliams 10 31
(M Brittain) *chsd ldrs stands' side: rdn along over 2f out and sn wknd* **15/2**[3]
100- **18** *1* **John Keats**[204] 6313 5-9-2 **70**........................ DanielTudhope 8 33
(J S Goldie) *in tch far side: rdn along over 2f out and sn wknd* **25/1**

1m 13.21s (0.51) **Going Correction** +0.175s/f (Good) **18** Ran SP% **127.9**
Speed ratings (Par 103): **103,102,102,101,98 98,97,95,94,94 94,93,92,89,89 88,85,83**
CSF £783.07 CT £4442.56 TOTE £31.50: £4.80, £6.70, £1.70, £2.50; EX 1454.90.
Owner The New Century Partnership **Bred** M Conaghan **Trained** Settrington, N Yorks
■ Stewards' Enquiry : Danielle McCreery two-day ban: used whip when out of contention (May 24-25)

FOCUS
A modest sprint handicap. They split into two groups, with six going far side and the majority racing up the middle, but there was little between them. Sound form.
Dorn Dancer(IRE) Official explanation: jockey said mare was unsuited by the good to firm (firm in places) ground
Sea Rover(IRE) Official explanation: trainer later said colt finished lame

2006 CALVERTS CARPETS H'CAP 1m 4f

7:10 (7:10) (Class 5) (0-75,74) 4-Y-O+ **£3,885** (£1,156; £577; £288) **Stalls** Low

Form RPR
60-2 **1** **Maneki Neko (IRE)**[21] 1482 6-8-10 **66** ow1........................ RobertWinston 1 74
(E W Tuer) *trckd ldng pair: hdwy on inner to ld 2f out: rdn over 1f out: drvn ins fnl f: jst hld on* **3/1**[1]
6603 **2** *hd* **Bazart**[28] 1340 6-8-11 **74**........................ DeclanCannon(7) 10 82
(K R Burke) *led: rdn along and hdd 2f out: drvn over 1f out: kpt on gamely u.p ins fnl f: jst hld* **14/1**
40-2 **3** *1* **Collette's Choice**[17] 1559 5-8-8 **64**........................(p) PaulHanagan 9 70
(R A Fahey) *hld up in tch: hdwy 3f out: rdn to chse ldng pair wl over 1f out: ev ch tl drvn and one pce ins fnl f* **4/1**[2]
534- **4** *5* **Its Moon (IRE)**[105] 6077 4-9-1 **71**........................ GrahamGibbons 4 69
(T D Walford) *trckd ldrs: hdwy 3f out: sn rdn and kpt on same pce fr wl over 1f out* **3/1**[1]
5215 **5** *2 1/2* **Punta Galera (IRE)**[14] 1613 5-8-8 **64**........................ PhillipMakin 8 58
(Paul Green) *hld up in rr: hdwy 3f out: rdn along 2f out: kpt on same pce* **7/1**[3]
62-0 **6** *nse* **Dan Tucker**[21] 1482 4-8-11 **67**........................ NCallan 6 61
(N Tinkler) *chsd ldrs: rdn along 3f out: grad wknd fnl 2f* **9/1**
66-6 **7** *4 1/2* **Lady Killer Queen**[25] 1382 4-8-6 **62**........................ DavidAllan 3 49
(D Carroll) *in tch: pushed along and lost pl after 5f: sn in rr* **12/1**
0004 **8** *5* **Turn Of Phrase (IRE)**[17] 1559 9-8-1 **60**........................(b) AndrewMullen(3) 7 39
(N Wilson) *a in rr* **16/1**
303- **9** *2 3/4* **Campli (IRE)**[218] 5968 6-8-7 **63**........................ TomEaves 2 38
(Micky Hammond) *chsd ldr: cl up 1/2-way: rdn along over 3f out and sn wknd* **14/1**

2m 37.52s (1.32) **Going Correction** +0.275s/f (Good) **9** Ran SP% **119.4**
Speed ratings (Par 103): **106,105,105,101,100 100,97,93,92**
CSF £48.88 CT £174.19 TOTE £3.80: £1.30, £3.90, £1.90; EX 62.80.
Owner Mr & Mrs C Tompkins & E Tuer **Bred** Mrs Orlagh Sherry **Trained** Great Smeaton, N Yorks
■ Stewards' Enquiry : Robert Winston three-day ban: used whip with excessive force (May 24-26)

FOCUS
A modest middle-distance handicap run at an ordinary pace. The winner is the best guide to the form.

Turn Of Phrase(IRE) Official explanation: jockey said gelding was unsuited by the good to firm (firm in places) ground

2007 STEVE BOGGETT "CELEBRATION OF LIFE" H'CAP — 1m

7:40 (7:41) (Class 5) (0-75,74) 4-Y-0+ — **£3,885** (£1,156; £577; £288) **Stalls Low**

Form — RPR

-000 **1** **Osteopathic Remedy (IRE)**[22] 1450 4-8-12 **68**.............. PhillipMakin 7 — 78
(M Dods) *chsd ldrs: hdwy over 2f out: rdn to chal appr fnl f: drvn and styd on wl to ld last 50yds* — **15/2**[2]

0-30 **2** *1 1/4* **Celtic Step**[94] 456 4-8-13 **69**.............. RobertWinston 5 — 76
(P D Niven) *led: rdn along over 2f out: drvn over 1f out: hdd ent fnl f: kpt on wl u.p* — **18/1**

034- **3** *1 1/4* **Angaric (IRE)**[131] 7289 5-9-4 **74**..............(t) TomEaves 6 — 78
(B Smart) *t.k.h: cl up: rdn 2f out: led ent fnl f and sn drvn: hdd and no ex last 50yds* — **5/1**[1]

0040 **4** *1 1/4* **Nok Twice (IRE)**[8] 1779 7-8-10 **66**.............. NCallan 1 — 67
(D Carroll) *dwlt and towards rr: hdwy over 3f out: rdn and styng on whn n.m.r ent fnl f: kpt on wl towards fin* — **10/1**

0-00 **5** *1/2* **Malinsa Blue (IRE)**[19] 1520 6-8-7 **63**.............. J-PGuillambert 4 — 63
(B Ellison) *prom: rdn along over 2f out: drvn over 1f out and grad wknd* — **16/1**

00-1 **6** *1 1/4* **Dispol Isle (IRE)**[10] 1729 6-9-2 **72**.............. PaulFessey 10 — 69
(T D Barron) *chsd ldrs: effrt over 2f out: sn rdn: edgd lft and wknd appr fnl f* — **9/1**

06-4 **7** *hd* **Getrah**[22] 1449 4-8-12 **68**..............(b) GrahamGibbons 9 — 65
(N Wilson) *s.i.s and bhd: hdwy on inner over 2f out: swtchd rt and rdn over 1f out: kpt on ins fnl f: nrst fin* — **8/1**[3]

0506 **8** *1/2* **Byron Bay**[8] 1774 6-9-0 **70**.............. DeanMcKeown 14 — 66+
(R C Guest) *hld up in rr tl styd on fnl 2f: nrst fin* — **16/1**

3-60 **9** *3/4* **Kingsholm**[47] 992 6-8-9 **65**.............. FergalLynch 11 — 59+
(I W McInnes) *hld up in rr: hdwy over 2f out: kpt on appr fnl f: nrst fin* **20/1**

60-0 **10** *nk* **Deadline (UAE)**[49] 973 4-8-5 **64**..............(p) AndrewMullen(3) 2 — 57
(P T Midgley) *in tch on inner: hdwy 3f out: rdn along over 2f out and grad wknd* — **16/1**

400- **11** *1/2* **Onatopp (IRE)**[217] 6021 4-8-9 **65**.............. DavidAllan 16 — 57
(T D Easterby) *in tch on outer: effrt 3f out: rdn to chse ldrs over 3f out: sn drvn and wknd over 1f out* — **50/1**

0350 **12** *1/2* **Sands Of Barra (IRE)**[10] 1729 5-8-11 **67**.............. RoystonFfrench 3 — 58
(I W McInnes) *t.k.h: chsd ldrs: effrt over 2f out: sn rdn and wknd* — **12/1**

42-0 **13** *1* **Esoterica (IRE)**[8] 1774 5-8-8 **69**..............(b) GaryBartley(5) 15 — 58
(J S Goldie) *a in rr* — **8/1**[3]

0-00 **14** *nk* **Fiefdom (IRE)**[14] 1630 6-9-3 **73**.............. PatrickMathers 12 — 61
(I W McInnes) *hld up: a in rr* — **11/1**

30-0 **15** *hd* **Bolton Hall (IRE)**[18] 1550 6-8-7 **63**..............(p) PaulHanagan 18 — 50
(R A Fahey) *hld up: a in rr* — **20/1**

50-3 **16** *2 1/2* **Efidium**[9] 1752 10-8-6 **65**.............. MarkLawson(3) 8 — 47
(N Bycroft) *towards rr: swtchd wd and hdwy 3f out: rdn 2f out and sn btn* — **16/1**

23-1 **17** *3 3/4* **Tri Chara (IRE)**[127] 48 4-8-7 **63**.............. MickyFenton 13 — 36
(R Hollinshead) *in tch: rdn along 3f out: sn wknd* — **9/1**

1m 42.25s (2.15) **Going Correction** +0.275s/f (Good) — **17** Ran SP% **136.0**
Speed ratings (Par 103): **100,98,97,96,95 94,94,93,93,92 92,91,90,90,90 87,84**
CSF £147.61 CT £771.36 TOTE £10.70: £2.40, £6.20, £2.10, £3.10; EX 285.40.
Owner Kevin Kirkup **Bred** Airlie Stud **Trained** Denton, Co Durham
■ Stewards' Enquiry : Andrew Mullen one-day ban: used whip down shoulder in forehand position (May 24)

FOCUS
They went a modest pace and it paid to race close up in what was an ordinary handicap. The third looks the best guide.

2008 ARMY BENEVOLENT FUND MAIDEN STKS — 1m

8:10 (8:13) (Class 5) 3-Y-0+ — **£3,885** (£1,156; £577; £288) **Stalls Low**

Form — RPR

222- **1** **Tiger Dream**[197] 6468 3-8-13 **89**.............. NCallan 7 — 71
(K A Ryan) *trckd ldng pair: hdwy 3f out: led over 2f out: rdn over 1f out: drvn and edgd rt ins fnl f: jst hld on* — **4/11**[1]

0 **2** *hd* **King Fingal (IRE)**[17] 1556 3-8-13 0.............. GrahamGibbons 2 — 70
(J J Quinn) *midfield: gd hdwy over 2f out: rdn over 1f out: styd on strly to chal ins fnl f: ev ch tl no ex nr fin* — **66/1**

00 **3** *1 3/4* **Grey Command (USA)**[29] 1295 3-8-10 0.............. MarkLawson(3) 3 — 66
(M Brittain) *a.p: effrt over 2f out: sn rdn and ev ch tl drvn: edgd rt and one pce wl ins fnl f* — **50/1**

6-5 **4** *1 3/4* **Novellen Lad (IRE)**[15] 1601 3-8-13 0.............. AdrianTNicholls 9 — 62
(E J Alston) *in tch: hdwy 3f out: rdn to chse ldrs over 2f out: drvn over 1f out: kpt on same pce* — **25/1**

60 **5** *5* **Cheers For Thea (IRE)**[7] 1814 3-8-8 0.............. DavidAllan 10 — 46+
(T D Easterby) *hld up in rr: hdwy over 2f out: rdn and styd on appr fnl f: nrst fin* — **66/1**

000- **6** *1 3/4* **Flaxton (UAE)**[260] 4782 3-8-13 **45**.............. TWilliams 11 — 46
(M Brittain) *midfield: hdwy 3f out: rdn over 2f out: drvn and edgd rt over 1f out: kpt on ins fnl f* — **100/1**

3- **7** *1* **Ezdeyaad (USA)**[253] 4997 4-9-12 0.............. DougieCostello 18 — 47+
(G A Swinbank) *hld up and bhd: hdwy 3f out: rdn and styd on appr fnl f: nrst fin* — **16/1**

5-0 **8** *hd* **Top Man Dan (IRE)**[25] 1380 3-8-10 0..............(t) DNolan(3) 17 — 44
(D Carroll) *towards rr: hdwy on outer over 2f out: sn rdn and no imp* **20/1**

06 **9** *1 1/4* **Miss Understanding**[4] 1894 3-8-8 0.............. PhillipMakin 13 — 36
(J R Weymes) *hld up in rr tl sme late hdwy* — **66/1**

6 **10** *1/2* **Virtuality (USA)**[7] 1817 3-8-8 0.............. TomEaves 6 — 35
(B Smart) *in tch: effrt on outer over 2f out: sn rdn and wknd* — **10/1**[2]

06 **11** *3/4* **St Johns Wood**[7] 1814 3-8-13 0.............. DaleGibson 5 — 38+
(M W Easterby) *s.i.s and bhd tl sme late hdwy* — **20/1**

045- **12** *1/2* **Cranworth Blaze**[253] 4997 4-9-7 **45**..............(be) GregFairley 12 — 35
(T J Etherington) *a towards rr* — **100/1**

26/ **13** *3/4* **Desert Maze (IRE)**[651] 3940 4-9-12 0.............. PaulHanagan 8 — 38
(J Wade) *chsd ldr: rdn along over 3f out: wknd over 2f out* — **100/1**

0 **14** *4 1/2* **Stormin Heart (USA)**[22] 1453 3-8-13 0..............(b[1]) PaulFessey 14 — 25
(T D Barron) *led: rdn along 3f out: hdd over 2f out and sn wknd* — **40/1**

0 **15** *1/2* **Royal Avenue (IRE)**[14] 1628 3-8-13 0.............. RobertWinston 16 — 24
(T D Easterby) *in tch: hdwy to chse ldrs over 3f out: rdn over 2f out: sn wknd* — **66/1**

05 **16** *1/2* **Pick Of The Day (IRE)**[11] 1701 3-8-13 0.............. J-PGuillambert 4 — 22
(J G Given) *in tch: rdn along over 3f out and sn wknd* — **22/1**

2-0 **17** *7* **Louis Seffens (USA)**[42] 1068 3-8-8 0..............(t) GaryBartley(5) 1 — 6
(G A Swinbank) *a towards rr* — **12/1**[3]

1m 42.95s (2.85) **Going Correction** +0.275s/f (Good)
WFA 3 from 4yo 13lb — **17** Ran SP% **127.0**
Speed ratings (Par 103): **96,95,94,92,87 85,84,84,83,82 81,81,80,76,75 75,68**
CSF £61.37 TOTE £1.30: £1.02, £14.20, £16.90; EX 41.00.
Owner J Duddy A Bailey T Marnane B McDonald **Bred** Grundy Bloodstock Srl **Trained** Hambleton, N Yorks
■ Stewards' Enquiry : Greg Fairley caution: used whip when out of contention

FOCUS
A weak maiden and the winner, Tiger Dream, was made to work hard to justify short odds, running well below his official mark of 89.
Louis Seffens(USA) Official explanation: jockey said colt had a breathing problem

2009 TURFTV.CO.UK H'CAP — 7f

8:40 (8:42) (Class 6) (0-55,55) 4-Y-0+ — **£2,590** (£770; £385; £192) **Stalls Low**

Form — RPR

300- **1** **Zabeel Tower**[135] 7250 5-8-11 **52**..............(p) TomEaves 14 — 59
(R Allan) *prom: hdwy over 2f out: rdn to ld over 1f out: drvn and edgd lft ins fnl f hld on wl* — **20/1**

0-55 **2** *hd* **Five Wishes**[9] 1752 4-9-0 **55**..............(be) PhillipMakin 6 — 61
(M Dods) *midfield: hdwy on outer over 2f out and sn rdn: drvn and edgd rt ent fnl f: styd on wl towards fin* — **9/1**

0-40 **3** *3/4* **Ensign's Trick**[5] 1865 4-8-13 **54**.............. LiamJones 12 — 58
(W M Brisbourne) *in tch: effrt on outer over 2f out and sn rdn: drvn and edgd lft ent fnl f: styd on* — **20/1**

2653 **4** *nk* **Avontuur (FR)**[14] 1634 6-8-10 **51**..............(p) NCallan 8 — 54
(Mrs R A Carr) *cl up: led 1/2-way: rdn 2f out: drvn and hdd over 1f out: kpt on u.p ins fnl f* — **6/1**[2]

-024 **5** *shd* **Silidan**[45] 1029 5-8-8 **52**.............. MarkLawson(3) 11 — 55
(M Brittain) *led to 1/2-way: cl up and rdn along over 2f out: drvn over 1f out: kpt on u.p ins fnl f* — **14/1**

000- **6** *1* **Barataria**[254] 4966 6-8-13 **54**.............. RobertWinston 9 — 61+
(R Bastiman) *rrd s and towards rr: gd hdwy over 2f out: sn rdn and styng on whn hmpd ent fnl f: nt rcvr* — **12/1**

-406 **7** *1 1/2* **Lambency (IRE)**[17] 1561 5-8-6 **52**.............. GaryBartley(5) 5 — 48
(J S Goldie) *towards rr: rdn along 1/2-way: sme late hdwy: nvr trbld ldrs* — **10/1**

-060 **8** *3* **Boy Dancer (IRE)**[47] 990 5-9-0 **55**.............. GrahamGibbons 1 — 43
(J J Quinn) *a towards rr* — **8/1**

3-50 **9** *nk* **Bretwalda (IRE)**[16] 1579 5-8-12 **53**.............. MickyFenton 4 — 40
(P T Midgley) *a towards rr* — **7/1**[3]

600- **10** *nse* **Petite Mac**[193] 6563 8-8-11 **52**.............. PaulHanagan 13 — 39
(N Bycroft) *nvr nr ldrs* — **40/1**

0/02 **11** *nk* **Moverra (IRE)**[12] 1687 4-8-11 **52**..............(p) NickyMackay 10 — 38
(M Wigham) *chsd ldrs: rdn along 3f out: sn wknd* — **8/1**

0-16 **12** *5* **Invincible Lad (IRE)**[36] 1189 4-9-0 **55**.............. DavidAllan 2 — 28
(E J Alston) *chsd ldrs: effrt on inner over 2f out: sn rdn and wknd over 1f out* — **7/2**[1]

0020 **13** *nk* **Grey Gurkha**[16] 1578 7-8-12 **53**.............. PatrickMathers 7 — 25
(I W McInnes) *a in rr* — **16/1**

635- **14** *8* **March Mate**[252] 5045 4-8-5 **53**.............. AnthonyBetts(7) 3 — 3
(B Ellison) *dwlt: a bhd* — **33/1**

1m 28.91s (1.71) **Going Correction** +0.275s/f (Good) — **14** Ran SP% **125.5**
Speed ratings (Par 101): **101,100,99,99,99 98,96,93,92,92 92,86,86,77**
CSF £191.21 CT £3762.55 TOTE £31.60: £7.30, £3.70, £9.10; EX 478.50 Place 6 £213.81, Place 5 £151.19..
Owner R. H. I. Ltd **Bred** Gainsborough Stud Management Ltd **Trained** Duns, Scottish Borders

FOCUS
A moderate handicap in which it paid to race close up. The form is rated through the runner-up.
Bretwalda(IRE) Official explanation: jockey said gelding missed the break; trainer said gelding scoped dirty after race
Moverra(IRE) Official explanation: jockey said filly ran flat
T/Plt: £309.40 to a £1 stake. Pool: £59,476.31. 140.30 winning tickets. T/Qpdt: £65.20 to a £1 stake. Pool: £3,429.08. 38.90 winning tickets. JR

1865 WARWICK (L-H)

Saturday, May 10

OFFICIAL GOING: Good to firm
Wind: virtually nil Weather: Fine and warm

2010 QUANTUM PRECISION TOOLMAKERS WARWICK H'CAP — 6f

5:55 (5:55) (Class 6) (0-65,64) 4-Y-0+ — **£1,942** (£578; £288; £144) **Stalls Centre**

Form — RPR

5210 **1** **Trinculo (IRE)**[6] 1842 11-8-11 **60**..............(b) KevinGhunowa(3) 8 — 71
(R A Harris) *mde all: clr whn rdn over 1f out: sn edgd lft: drvn out* — **10/1**

0-55 **2** *1 1/4* **Mandarin Spirit (IRE)**[23] 1415 8-8-13 **59**..............(b) OscarUrbina 14 — 66
(G C H Chung) *hld up in tch: rdn and chsd wnr over 1f out: edgd rt ent fnl f: kpt on* — **7/1**[2]

2405 **3** *1 1/4* **Monashee Prince (IRE)**[44] 1035 6-8-11 **57**..............(v) SebSanders 12 — 60
(J R Best) *chsd ldrs: rdn wl over 1f out: bmpd jst ins fnl f: nt qckn* — **5/1**[1]

00-0 **4** *1/2* **Gracie's Gift (IRE)**[36] 1188 6-8-8 **54**.............. RichardThomas 4 — 55+
(A G Newcombe) *sn outpcd and bhd: hdwy jst over 1f out: r.o ins fnl f: nrst fin* — **9/1**

2020 **5** *1/2* **White Ledger (IRE)**[45] 1028 9-7-11 **50**..............(p) AmyBaker(7) 10 — 50
(R E Peacock) *hld up and bhd: hdwy on outside fnl f: nvr nrr* — **33/1**

006- **6** *nk* **Currency**[220] 5909 11-8-11 **57**.............. StephenDonohoe 7 — 56
(J M Bradley) *chsd ldrs: rdn 3f out: sn sltly outpcd: kpt on same pce fnl f* — **16/1**

4000 **7** *1* **Arfinnit (IRE)**[18] 1534 7-7-13 **52**..............(p) KMay(7) 5 — 48
(Mrs A L M King) *half-rrd s: bhd: rdn and hdwy over 1f out: no further prog fnl f* — **11/1**

50-0 **8** *shd* **Barbar**[38] 1145 5-8-8 **54**.............. PaulFitzsimons 1 — 49
(Eve Johnson Houghton) *chsd ldrs: rdn over 1f out: sn edgd lft: wknd ins fnl f* — **12/1**

660- **9** *1 1/2* **Lordship (IRE)**[190] 6623 4-8-13 **62**.............. LukeMorris(3) 9 — 53
(A W Carroll) *bhd: rdn over 2f out: nvr trbld ldrs* — **15/2**[3]

4420 **10** *nk* **Chief Exec**[6] 1842 6-9-2 **62**..............(b) FrankieMcDonald 3 — 52
(J R Gask) *chsd ldrs: hmpd on ins and lost pl 1f out: sn rdn: n.d after* — **5/1**[1]

046 **11** *3/4* **Monte Major (IRE)**[21] 1476 7-8-6 **55**.............. TolleyDean(3) 11 — 42
(D Shaw) *bhd: short-lived effrt over 2f out* — **10/1**

000- **12** *5* **Safranine (IRE)**[133] 7265 11-8-9 **60** oh2 ow10.............. AnnStokell(5) 17 — 31
(Miss A Stokell) *chsd ldrs: rdn wl over 1f out: sn wknd* — **33/1**

516 **13** 1 3/4 **Kitto Katsu**[27] 1344 4-9-0 **60** .... AdamKirby 13 26
(D J Coakley) *s.i.s: hld up and bhd: c wd and rdn over 2f out: no rspnse* **10/1**

0250 **14** 9 **Mr Rev**[13] 1641 5-9-0 **60** .... DaneO'Neill 16 —
(J M Bradley) *s.i.s: hdwy on outside over 3f out: rdn over 2f out: wknd wl over 1f out: eased fnl f* **16/1**

1m 11.76s (-0.04) **Going Correction** -0.375s/f (Firm) course record **14** Ran SP% **128.5**
Speed ratings (Par 101): **101,99,97,97,96 95,94,94,92,92 91,84,82,70**
CSF £83.81 CT £414.28 TOTE £9.50: £2.20, £3.00, £2.30; EX 84.10.
Owner Peter A Price **Bred** Humphrey Okeke **Trained** Earlswood, Monmouths

FOCUS
An open-looking sprint handicap. Very modest form, the winner running to his best in the last two years.
Kitto Katsu Official explanation: jockey said filly was unsuited by the good to firm ground

2011 PCA LONG SERVICE AWARDS PRESENTATION MAIDEN AUCTION STKS 5f 110y
6:25 (6:28) (Class 5) 2-Y-0 **£3,070** (£906; £453) **Stalls** Centre

Form RPR
0 **1** **Brierty (IRE)**[14] 1627 2-8-6 0 .... DO'Donohoe 11 68
(D Carroll) *chsd ldr: led over 1f out: rdn and flashed tail ins fnl f: drvn out* **16/1**

2 3/4 **Lesley's Choice** 2-8-9 0 .... FrankieMcDonald 13 68
(P A Blockley) *sn prom: hung rt fr over 3f out: rdn over 1f out: r.o ins fnl f* **12/1**

3 nk **Wing Home (IRE)** 2-8-11 0 .... RichardKingscote 3 69
(Tom Dascombe) *a.p: rdn over 1f out: kpt on one pce fnl f* **7/2**[2]

4 6 **Cocktail Party (IRE)** 2-8-11 0 .... JamesDoyle 2 49+
(J W Hills) *mid-div: rdn over 1f out: no real prog fnl f* **6/1**[3]

6 **5** 3/4 **Buddy Marvellous (IRE)**[19] 1523 2-9-2 0 .... RichardHughes 5 51
(R Hannon) *led: hdd and rdn over 1f out: wknd ins fnl f* **5/2**[1]

6 1/2 **Black N Brew (USA)** 2-8-11 0 .... DaneO'Neill 12 45+
(J R Best) *dwlt: bhd: reminder and rn green jst over 1f out: nvr nrr* **12/1**

0 **7** 2 **Forster Island**[11] 1693 2-8-9 0 .... JimmyQuinn 9 36
(M Blanshard) *chsd ldrs tl rdn and wknd over 1f out* **8/1**

8 1 **Baby Special** 2-8-4 0 .... RichardThomas 4 28
(C G Cox) *outpcd* **9/1**

6 **9** 1 3/4 **Dancing Welcome**[5] 1866 2-8-1 0 .... LukeMorris(3) 8 22
(J M Bradley) *outpcd* **40/1**

10 3/4 **Barcode** 2-8-4 0 .... RichardSmith 14 19
(R Hannon) *dwlt: hld up and bhd: rdn over 2f out: no rspnse* **16/1**

000 **11** 2 1/2 **Sharp Discovery**[5] 1866 2-8-5 0 ow1 .... PaulFitzsimons 15 12
(J M Bradley) *mid-div: pushed along over 2f out: sn wknd* **66/1**

0 **12** 106 **Tyler**[24] 1392 2-8-9 0 .... StephenDonohoe 16 —
(W M Brisbourne) *wnt rt s: sn bdly outpcd and t.o* **33/1**

P **Rigged** 2-8-9 0 .... ShaneKelly 1 —
(J A Osborne) *swvd bdly lft and rdr lost irons s: virtually p.u after 1f: fnlly p.u over 2f out* **12/1**

67.38 secs (1.48) **Going Correction** -0.375s/f (Firm) **13** Ran SP% **127.9**
Speed ratings (Par 93): **75,74,73,65,64 63,61,59,57,56 53,—,—**
CSF £206.86 TOTE £18.00: £3.90, £5.10, £2.00; EX 371.30.
Owner G P Clarke **Bred** Fortbarrington Stud **Trained** Sledmere, E Yorks

FOCUS
The first three finished clear in this minor maiden where there was little previous form to go on. A slightly negative view has been taken of the form.

NOTEBOOK
Brierty(IRE) is a half-sister to 7f juvenile winner Lunces Lad and a two-year-old scorer in Ireland. She apparently proved difficult to break in and did show signs of temperament in the closing stages when in the process of leaving her debut form behind. (op 25-1)
Lesley's Choice ◆, the first juvenile to run from his stable, is a half-brother to a couple of winners abroad. He did not prove an easy ride but should be a useful yardstick and normal improvement can see him take a similar event. (op 18-1 tchd 20-1)
Wing Home(IRE) ◆, a half-brother to 2006 Brocklesby winner Spoof Master, is another who should come on for the outing and there are races to be won with him. (tchd 11-2 in a place)
Cocktail Party(IRE), a 32,000 euros yearling, kept on to finish best of the rest but was never a threat to the three principals. (op 16-1)
Buddy Marvellous(IRE) failed to get home after more use was made of him over this slightly longer trip. (tchd 11-4)
Black N Brew(USA), a $19,000 yearling, should be better for the experience. (tchd 10-1)
Tyler Official explanation: jockey said gelding hung right-handed

2012 TURFTV H'CAP 1m 6f 213y
6:55 (6:56) (Class 5) (0-75,73) 4-Y-0+ **£3,561** (£1,059; £529; £264) **Stalls** Low

Form RPR
0310 **1** **Synonymy**[5] 1856 5-8-9 **57** ....(b) JamesDoyle 1 61
(M Blanshard) *hld up in rr: hdwy on ins over 2f out: sn rdn: swtchd rt wl ins fnl f: led post* **7/1**

3-3 **2** shd **Command Marshal (FR)**[7] 1798 5-9-6 **73** .... PatrickHills(5) 10 77
(M J Scudamore) *led: clr whn rdn over 1f out: edgd lft ins fnl f: ct post* **6/1**[3]

4103 **3** 3/4 **King's Fable (USA)**[16] 1583 5-9-0 **62** ....(p) DarryllHolland 5 65
(Karen George) *dwlt: hld up in rr: hdwy and swtchd rt wl over 1f out: sn rdn: wandered away fr whip fnl f: styd on* **6/1**[3]

0-00 **4** 1 1/4 **Great View (IRE)**[18] 1538 9-9-6 **68** ....(p) TedDurcan 7 69
(Mrs A L M King) *hld up in rr: hdwy whn n.m.r briefly 1f out: styd on towards fin* **14/1**

10-5 **5** nse **Merrymaker**[28] 1340 8-9-5 **67** .... ShaneKelly 11 68
(W M Brisbourne) *s.i.s: sn mid-div: rdn whn n.m.r over 1f out: styd on whn nt clr run wl ins fnl f* **6/1**[3]

25-1 **6** 1 1/4 **Dansilver**[18] 1551 4-8-11 **61** .... VinceSlattery 2 61
(D J Wintle) *prom: wnt 2nd 5f out: rdn over 2f out: wkng whn sltly hmpd wl ins fnl f* **7/2**[1]

31-5 **7** 2 1/4 **Garafena**[31] 1273 5-9-8 **70** .... TQuinn 6 67
(B G Powell) *hld up in tch: rdn wl over 1f out: wknd ins fnl f* **9/2**[2]

10 **8** 12 **Lupita (IRE)**[18] 1538 4-8-8 **58** .... DaneO'Neill 9 39
(B G Powell) *hld up in tch: rdn over 2f out: wknd over 1f out* **9/1**

030- **9** 28 **Icansingarainbow**[213] 6109 4-8-7 **57** .... JoeFanning 8 2
(R Hollinshead) *t.k.h: chsd ldr after 1f to 5f out: wknd 4f out: t.o* **16/1**

3m 21.43s (2.43) **Going Correction** +0.125s/f (Good)
WFA 4 from 5yo+ 2lb **9** Ran SP% **118.3**
Speed ratings (Par 103): **98,97,97,96,96 96,94,88,73**
CSF £49.77 CT £270.93 TOTE £7.80: £2.20, £2.10, £2.20; EX 48.70.
Owner G H Phillips,J M Beever & D G Chambers **Bred** Biddestone Stud **Trained** Upper Lambourn, Berks

FOCUS
This modest staying handicap was run at a stop-start gallop. They finished in a heap and the form is hard to take seriously.

2013 HBG CONSTRUCTION LTD H'CAP 7f 26y
7:25 (7:26) (Class 4) (0-85,87) 4-Y-0+ **£5,180** (£1,541; £770; £384) **Stalls** Low

Form RPR
60-6 **1** **Phluke**[17] 1566 7-8-13 **80** .... StephenCarson 11 88
(Eve Johnson Houghton) *chsd ldr: chal over 1f out: rdn to ld ins fnl f: r.o wl* **6/1**[3]

04-6 **2** 1/2 **Prince Of Thebes (IRE)**[14] 1633 7-9-2 **83** .... PaulDoe 10 89
(M J Attwater) *a.p: rdn to ld 1f out: hdd ins fnl f: r.o* **9/1**

3343 **3** nk **Den's Gift (IRE)**[18] 1532 4-8-12 **79** ....(b) RichardHughes 7 84
(C G Cox) *led: rdn and hdd 1f out: r.o* **10/3**[2]

0-50 **4** 3/4 **Compton's Eleven**[14] 1617 7-9-1 **82** .... DarryllHolland 4 85
(M R Channon) *hld up in mid-div: rdn and carried hd high over 1f out: kpt on ins fnl f* **12/1**

41-0 **5** 1/2 **Golden Desert (IRE)**[30] 1278 4-8-11 **78** .... JoeFanning 13 80
(T G Mills) *stdd s: hld up in mid-div: hdwy over 2f out: rdn over 1f out: nt qckn fnl f* **16/1**

0-22 **6** 3/4 **Goodbye**[7] 1815 4-9-4 **85** .... TedDurcan 1 94+
(G A Swinbank) *a.p: trying to chal whn n.m.r on ins 1f out: nt clr run wl ins fnl f: nt rcvr* **9/4**[1]

4601 **7** 1 1/4 **Carcinetto (IRE)**[5] 1858 6-8-13 **87** 6ex .... RichardEvans(7) 5 84
(P D Evans) *hld up in tch: swtchd rt over 1f out: sn rdn: one pce fnl f* **16/1**

2000 **8** nk **Alfresco**[26] 1365 4-9-1 **82** ....(b) SebSanders 8 78
(I A Wood) *stdd s: hld up in rr: hung lft into ins rail fr 2f out: nvr able to chal* **7/1**

12-0 **9** 1 **Pendulum Star**[28] 1335 4-8-12 **79** ....(t) AdamKirby 12 72
(W R Swinburn) *t.k.h in rr: rdn and hung rt ins fnl f: n.d* **14/1**

0330 **10** shd **Harare**[18] 1532 7-8-1 **71** .... WilliamBuick(3) 9 64
(R J Price) *hld up towards rr: c wd st: rdn and edgd lft fr over 1f out: n.d* **14/1**

0-00 **11** 7 **Thabaat**[7] 1800 4-8-10 **77** .... DaneO'Neill 3 51
(J M Bradley) *t.k.h: sn mid-div: bhd fnl 2f* **40/1**

1m 23.97s (-0.63) **Going Correction** +0.125s/f (Good) **11** Ran SP% **125.9**
Speed ratings (Par 105): **108,107,107,106,105 104,103,103,101,101 93**
CSF £63.57 CT £216.83 TOTE £8.30: £2.50, £3.30, £1.50; EX 67.90.
Owner Mrs R F Johnson Houghton **Bred** Mrs R F Johnson Houghton **Trained** Blewbury, Oxon
■ Stewards' Enquiry : Stephen Carson two-day ban: used whip with excessive frequency and without giving time to respond (May 24-25); caution: careless riding

FOCUS
An ordinary event in which the form seems sound enough among the principals.

2014 PCA LONG SERVICE AWARDS PRESENTATION H'CAP 7f 26y
7:55 (7:56) (Class 5) (0-75,74) 3-Y-0 **£3,238** (£963; £481; £240) **Stalls** Low

Form RPR
00-2 **1** **Opera Prince**[24] 1410 3-9-3 **73** .... RichardHughes 9 78+
(S Kirk) *bmpd s: led over 1f: w ldr: led wl over 1f out: drvn out* **8/1**[3]

040- **2** 1/2 **Sylvias Grove**[211] 6156 3-8-12 **68** .... DO'Donohoe 10 72
(D Carroll) *bmpd s: hld up in tch: rdn and chsd wnr fnl f: kpt on* **20/1**

0-04 **3** 1 1/4 **Castlebury (IRE)**[22] 1452 3-8-8 **64** .... TedDurcan 8 65+
(G A Swinbank) *t.k.h in tch: rdn 1f out: kpt on same pce* **17/2**

60-0 **4** nk **Seventh Hill**[17] 1573 3-9-0 **70** .... JamesDoyle 7 70
(M Blanshard) *wnt rt s: a.p: rdn and nt qckn fnl f* **9/1**

-022 **5** nse **Leading Edge (IRE)**[9] 1738 3-9-2 **72** .... ChrisCatlin 11 72
(M R Channon) *hld up in mid-div: hdwy 1f out: kpt on one pce* **5/1**[2]

4-21 **6** 1 1/2 **Spin Again (IRE)**[29] 1311 3-9-2 **72** .... SebSanders 12 68+
(R M Beckett) *swtchd lft sn after s: t.k.h towards rr: rdn whn n.m.r briefly 1f out: nvr able to chal* **2/1**[1]

310- **7** 1 1/4 **Sawpit Sunshine (IRE)**[219] 5939 3-8-9 **68** .... TolleyDean(3) 6 60
(J L Spearing) *stdd s: hld up and bhd: hung rt bnd over 3f out: nvr trbld ldrs* **20/1**

516 **8** nse **Princess Livius (IRE)**[56] 899 3-8-10 **66** .... StephenDonohoe 2 58
(P A Blockley) *hld up in mid-div: rdn over 1f out: no hdwy* **10/1**

02-0 **9** 1 3/4 **The Last Bottle (IRE)**[24] 1396 3-8-9 **65** .... TGMcLaughlin 3 52
(W M Brisbourne) *s.i.s: a in rr* **14/1**

03-0 **10** 3 1/2 **Black Or Red (IRE)**[35] 1208 3-8-13 **69** .... RichardThomas 5 47
(I A Wood) *a bhd* **20/1**

024- **11** 2 1/4 **Jerry Hamilton (USA)**[168] 6936 3-9-4 **74** .... JoeFanning 4 46
(M Johnston) *led over 5f out tl wl over 1f out: sn rdn: wknd fnl f* **9/1**

1m 25.55s (0.95) **Going Correction** +0.125s/f (Good) **11** Ran SP% **121.7**
Speed ratings (Par 99): **99,98,97,96,96 94,93,93,91,87 84**
CSF £162.66 CT £1380.47 TOTE £7.50: £1.90, £4.90, £3.00; EX 197.90.
Owner J C Smith **Bred** Littleton Stud **Trained** Upper Lambourn, Berks

FOCUS
There were plenty of unexposed sorts in this ordinary handicap. It paid to race prominently.

2015 ALISON FENN 50TH BIRTHDAY MAIDEN FILLIES' STKS 1m 2f 188y
8:25 (8:27) (Class 5) 3-Y-0+ **£3,238** (£963; £481; £240) **Stalls** Low

Form RPR
64 **1** **Barring Decree (IRE)**[30] 1279 3-8-11 0 .... ChrisCatlin 1 70
(E J O'Neill) *led: hdd over 1f out: hrd rdn to ld ins fnl f: all out* **9/1**

020- **2** nk **Baraari (USA)**[224] 5811 3-8-11 76 .... SebSanders 13 70
(J L Dunlop) *chsd wnr: rdn to ld over 1f out: hdd ins fnl f: r.o* **6/1**

00- **3** shd **Ethereal Flame**[200] 6411 3-8-11 0 .... TedDurcan 7 73+
(H R A Cecil) *hld up in mid-div: nt clr run wl over 1f out: hdwy whn nt clr run and swtchd lft ent fnl f: r.o: unlucky* **8/1**

2 **4** 3/4 **Valferno (IRE)**[30] 1279 3-8-11 0 .... AlanMunro 4 68
(Mrs P Sly) *t.k.h: a.p: rdn wl over 1f out: ev ch ins fnl f: nt qckn* **5/1**[3]

00-0 **5** shd **Orbital Orchid**[21] 1479 3-8-11 50 ....(v[1]) DaneO'Neill 15 68?
(W S Kittow) *a.p: ev ch over 1f out: sn rdn: nt qckn ins fnl f* **33/1**

4 **6** 1/2 **Eureka Moment**[19] 1526 3-8-11 0 .... StephenDonohoe 9 67
(E A L Dunlop) *t.k.h in tch: hung lft 2f out: hung lft and swtchd rt ins fnl f: nt qckn* **2/1**[1]

60- **7** nk **Shaama Rose (FR)**[242] 5301 3-8-11 0 .... EdwardCreighton 10 66?
(M R Channon) *stdd s: hld up towards rr: rdn and hdwy 1f out: kpt on one pce* **20/1**

6-0 **8** 2 1/2 **Alseraaj (USA)**[23] 1423 3-8-11 0 .... MartinDwyer 12 62
(Sir Michael Stoute) *hld up in mid-div: swtchd rt wl over 1f out: rdn and no hdwy fnl f* **5/2**[2]

0 **9** 12 **Bombay Dreams**[24] 1410 5-10-0 0 ....(p) TGMcLaughlin 2 41
(Karen George) *s.i.s: bhd: rdn over 3f out: sn toiling* **100/1**

0/ **10** 7 **Topsy Maite**[760] 961 4-10-0 0 .... FrankieMcDonald 3 29
(P A Blockley) *in rr: rdn over 3f out: sn struggling* **100/1**

0U0- **11** *2 1/4* **Amouretta**[204] 6297 3-8-8 0..................................(v) TolleyDean(3) 6 24
(T T Clement) *hld up in rr: rdn over 3f out: sn struggling* **33/1**

2m 22.94s (1.84) **Going Correction** +0.125s/f (Good)
WFA 3 from 4yo+ 17lb **11 Ran SP% 126.6**
Speed ratings (Par 100): **98,97,97,97,97 96,96,94,85,80 79**
CSF £64.57 TOTE £16.10: £3.50, £2.10, £2.70; EX 100.70 Place 6 £861.07, Place 5 £347.90..
Owner Miss A H Marshall **Bred** Frank Dunne **Trained** Averham Park, Notts

FOCUS
The two market leaders disappointed in what was quite an interesting maiden on paper, but which was run at a very steady pace. The form is potentially weak.
T/Plt: £1,500.00 to a £1 stake. Pool: £48,494.39. 23.60 winning tickets. T/Qpdt: £106.90 to a £1 stake. Pool: £4,422.18. 30.60 winning tickets. KH

2016 - 2022a (Foreign Racing) - See Raceform Interactive

1506

LEOPARDSTOWN (L-H)

Sunday, May 11

OFFICIAL GOING: Good

2023a DERRINSTOWN STUD DERBY TRIAL STKS (GROUP 2) 1m 2f
3:55 (3:56) 3-Y-0 **£59,742** (£17,463; £8,272; £2,757)

RPR

1 **Casual Conquest (IRE)**[246] 5245 3-9-1 .... PJSmullen 5 118+
(D K Weld, Ire) *chsd ldrs in 4th: dropped to last 1/2-way: niggled along over 3f out: stdy hdwy on outer to ld u.p over 1 1/2f out: qckly clr: styd on wl: easily* **13/2**[3]

2 *6* **Washington Irving (IRE)**[35] 1233 3-9-1 .... JAHeffernan 6 105
(A P O'Brien, Ire) *in rr: 4th fr 1/2-way: 3rd under 3f out: short of room briefly ent st: no imp u.p fr 1 1/2f out: sn mod 2nd: kpt on same pce* **4/6**[1]

3 *1 1/2* **Moiqen (IRE)**[21] 1509 3-9-1 104.......................... DPMcDonogh 1 102
(Kevin Prendergast, Ire) *trckd ldrs in 3rd: 4th under 3f out: no imp u.p fr over 1 1/2f out: sn kpt on one pce in 3rd* **2/1**[2]

4 *5* **Hindu Kush (IRE)**[35] 1233 3-9-1 88.......................... SMLevey 2 94
(A P O'Brien, Ire) *led: strly pressed and hdd over 1 1/2f out: sn no ex u.p* **50/1**

5 *6* **Matters At Hand (IRE)**[58] 895 3-9-1 .... PShanahan 4 80
(D K Weld, Ire) *trckd ldr in 2nd: dropped to last 2f out: sn no ex: eased ins fnl f* **33/1**

2m 5.35s (-2.85) **Going Correction** +0.05s/f (Good) **5 Ran SP% 111.6**
Speed ratings: **113,108,107,103,98**
CSF £11.71 TOTE £6.00: £2.20, £1.10; DF 11.60.
Owner Moyglare Stud Farm **Bred** Moyglare Stud Farm Ltd **Trained** The Curragh, Co Kildare

FOCUS
A small, select renewal of this well known Derby trial, won in the past by Epsom heroes Galileo and High Chapparal in recent years. It was run at an uneven pace, but the winner was impressive and looks a Group 1 winner in the making.

NOTEBOOK
Casual Conquest(IRE) ◆, a maiden winner over 7f on his sole outing last year, showed himself to be a fast-improving three-year-old and made it two wins from as many starts with an impressive display. He responded strongly when asked to make up his ground from the home turn and once in front he soon put daylight between himself and his rivals. While he holds numerous big race entries, the Epsom Derby is not among them at this stage, and he would have to be supplemented at a cost of £75,000 to take his place next month. No doubt his connections would have to be tempted by to pay the fee, however, as he looks a very classy colt and has now comprehensively won one of the most important trials. Whether that course would suit this imposing colt is uncertain, however, and he may well wait for the Irish equivalent at the end of June. No doubt the extra 2f will be within his range and, wherever he may turn up next, he will be worthy of a great deal of respect. (op 6/1)
Washington Irving(IRE), whose trainer boasts a superb past record in this event, was clearly well fancied to shed his maiden tag and stamp himself a leading Epsom candidate. He was firmly put in his place by the winner in the end, however, and was not surprisingly pushed right out of many ante-post lists for the Derby. He deserves to drop in class in order to gain a confidence booster now and in time he could still well show the potential that his connections believe he has. (op 4/5 tchd 8/13)
Moiqen(IRE), the Ballysax winner, was not that suited by the pace steadying at halfway and was made to look one paced inside the final furlong. He was still not disgraced, running close to his previous level, and looks sure to do better again when faced with a stiffer test. This obviously dents his Epsom aspirations, however. (op 2/1 tchd 15/8)
Hindu Kush(IRE) had finished behind the runner-up on his seasonal bow 35 days previously and was used as a pacemeker for that rival here. He had an easy enough lead and maybe flattered somewhat, but he too is lightly raced and has a future in his own right. Official explanation: jockey said colt ran short of room in straight, was not travelling well at the time and was eased

2024a DERRINSTOWN STUD 1,000 GUINEAS TRIAL (GROUP 3) (FILLIES) 1m
4:25 (4:25) 3-Y-0 **£40,687** (£11,937; £5,687; £1,937)

RPR

1 **Carribean Sunset (IRE)**[35] 1230 3-9-0 102.......................... PJSmullen 3 105
(D K Weld, Ire) *sn trckd ldrs in 3rd: rdn to chal and ld over 1f out: styd on wl* **9/2**[2]

2 *1/2* **Katiyra (IRE)**[266] 4644 3-9-0 .... MJKinane 5 104+
(John M Oxx, Ire) *mid-div: 6th 2f out: rdn to go 4th over 1f out: 2nd ins fnl f: kpt on wout rching wnr* **5/4**[1]

3 *1 1/2* **Indiana Gal (IRE)**[7] 1847 3-9-0 99.......................... FMBerry 4 100
(Patrick Martin, Ire) *trckd ldrs: 4th for much: no imp u.p and kpt on same pce fr 1f out* **16/1**

4 *1/2* **Toirneach (USA)**[238] 5455 3-9-0 92.......................... KJManning 1 99
(J S Bolger, Ire) *sn led and disp: led 2f out: strly pressed and hdd over 1f out: dropped to 4th and kpt on same pce ins fnl f* **6/1**[3]

5 *1 1/2* **Eva's Request (IRE)**[224] 5843 3-9-0 .... DarryllHolland 9 95
(M R Channon) *sn led and disp: 2nd 2f out: u.p whn checked briefly 1f out: sn no imp* **6/1**[3]

6 *1 1/4* **Charlotte Bronte**[22] 1498 3-9-0 100.......................... WMLordan 7 93
(David Wachman, Ire) *towards rr: 7th and rdn fr 2f out: sn no imp* **6/1**[3]

7 *3* **Fikrah**[14] 1656 3-9-0 87.......................... DPMcDonogh 2 86
(Kevin Prendergast, Ire) *towards rr: u.p bef st: no imp sn after* **25/1**

8 *shd* **Valentine Hill (IRE)**[14] 1656 3-9-0 94.......................... JAHeffernan 8 85
(Adrian Maguire, Ire) *chsd ldrs: 5th 2f out: sn no ex u.p* **20/1**

9 *nk* **Amaranda (IRE)**[10] 1758 3-9-0 .... DMGrant 6 85
(David Wachman, Ire) *in rr: rdn bef st: sn no imp* **66/1**

1m 40.48s (-0.72) **Going Correction** +0.05s/f (Good) **9 Ran SP% 121.5**
Speed ratings: **106,105,104,103,102 100,97,97,97**
CSF £10.93 TOTE £5.10: £1.60, £1.10, £3.40; DF 12.30.
Owner Dr R Lambe **Bred** Barronstown Stud **Trained** The Curragh, Co Kildare

NOTEBOOK
Carribean Sunset(IRE) followed up her success over 7f at this track 35 days previously - a race that is working out nicely - and is clearly a filly going places. She relished the longer trip and the sound surface, putting the race to bed with an injection of pace to lead nearing the final furlong. Now a winner of both the domestic 1,000 Guineas trials she obviously deserves to take her place at the Curragh later this month and should make a bold bid for the hat-trick, despite taking on better company again there. (op 5/1)
Katiyra(IRE) ◆, a taking maiden winner on her sole start at two, has been the subject of strong ante-post support for the Juddmonte Oaks at Epsom and was all the rage in the betting to do the job on this seasonal bow. She did not get the best of runs from off the pace, however, and the manner in which she was gaining on the winner late on would suggest she could have prevailed if ridden more prominently. No doubt this copey filly has a touch of class about her and looks sure to relish a step up in trip, so with improvement assured for this outing it would be no surprise to see her show up well at Epsom if turning up next month. (op 11/10 tchd 1/1)
Indiana Gal(IRE), third to the promising Chinese White last time out, lacked a change of pace when it mattered most yet still again ran with credit. She rates the benchmark for this form and deserves another winning turn.
Eva's Request(IRE), last seen taking the C.L.Weld Park Stakes on her final outing last season, was ridden positively on this step up in trip and shaped as though this seasonal bow was needed. She can do better still this year. (op 6/1 tchd 7/1)

2026a AMETHYST STKS (GROUP 3) 1m
5:25 (5:25) 3-Y-0+ **£33,455** (£9,779; £4,632; £1,544)

RPR

1 **Ferneley (IRE)**[6] 1882 4-9-9 108.......................... WJSupple 3 108
(Francis Ennis, Ire) *mde all: rdn clr fr 1 1/2f out: styd on wl: eased nr fin* **8/1**

2 *2* **Lord Admiral (USA)**[43] 1090 7-10-0 112.......................... (b) MJKinane 7 108
(Charles O'Brien, Ire) *towards rr in 5th: wd st: rdn to go mod 2nd over 1f out: kpt on wout threatening* **7/4**[1]

3 *shd* **Excelerate (IRE)**[28] 1355 5-9-9 107.......................... CDHayes 6 103
(Edward Lynam, Ire) *in rr: wnt mod 4th on outer fr 1f out: kpt on wout threatening u.p* **14/1**

4 *3/4* **Summit Surge (IRE)**[30] 1319 4-9-9 104.......................... (t) KLatham 5 101
(G M Lyons, Ire) *trckd ldrs: pushed along in 4th appr st where wd: no imp and kpt on same pce fr over 1f out* **9/1**

5 *4 1/2* **Tian Shan (IRE)**[21] 1508 4-9-9 107.......................... (b) PJSmullen 4 91
(D K Weld, Ire) *trckd ldr in 2nd: rdn ent st: no imp fr 1 1/2f out: no ex fnl f* **5/2**[2]

6 *nk* **Billyford (IRE)**[65] 827 3-8-10 106.......................... FMBerry 1 90
(Liam Roche, Ire) *trckd ldrs: 3rd for much: no imp u.p fr 1 1/2f out: no ex fnl f* **3/1**[3]

1m 40.5s (-0.70) **Going Correction** +0.05s/f (Good)
WFA 3 from 4yo+ 13lb **6 Ran SP% 117.7**
Speed ratings: **105,103,102,102,97 97**
CSF £23.85 TOTE £10.00: £3.60, £1.50; DF 33.90.
Owner Plantation Stud **Bred** Mount Coote Stud & Richard Peg **Trained** the Curragh, Co Kildare

NOTEBOOK
Ferneley(IRE) had finished down the field over 10f on his return six days previously, but that run was obviously well needed and he stepped up greatly on that to score comfortably from the front. He struggled a little last year, but looks as though he is going to have more to give as a four-year-old now and should be rated value for at least double the winning margin.
Lord Admiral(USA), placed in the past two runnings of this event, was returning from an excellent spell out in Dubai. He never seriously looked like getting to the winner, but was still not that far off his previous best here and there will still be other days for him. (op 9/4)
Excelerate(IRE) was another to step up a great deal on the level of his comeback last month and, running close to his mark in defeat, goes some way to helping set the level of this form.
Billyford(IRE) Official explanation: trainer later said colt scoped wrong post-race
T/Jkpt: @2,795.40. Pool of @14,909.00 - 4 winning units. T/Plt: @172.00. Pool of @19,443.00. II

2025 - 2026a (Foreign Racing) - See Raceform Interactive

1659

CAPANNELLE (R-H)

Sunday, May 11

OFFICIAL GOING: Good to firm

2027a PREMIO CARLO D'ALESSIO (GROUP 3) 1m 4f
2:50 (2:53) 4-Y-0+ **£42,188** (£18,563; £10,125; £5,063)

RPR

1 **Gimmy (IRE)**[42] 4-8-9 .... DVargiu 9 111
(B Grizzetti, Italy) *mde all: 4 l clr 3f out: pushed along 2f out to 1f out: easily* **13/20**[1]

2 *4* **Montalegre (IRE)**[8] 6-8-9 .... SMulas 1 105
(A & G Botti, Italy) *disp 5th: 6th st: styd on fr 2f out: tk 2nd 1f out: nvr nr wnr* **5/1**[3]

3 *1/2* **Rockmaster (IRE)**[721] 1872 5-8-9 .... JamieSpencer 3 104
(G Pucciatti, Italy) *hld up in rr: last st: styd on fr 2f out: wnt to rails 1 1/2f out: nt clr run dist: swtchd out: tk 3rd cl home* **113/10**

4 *nk* **Estejo (GER)**[210] 6223 4-8-9 .... DPorcu 5 104
(R Rohne, Germany) *3rd st: 2nd and hrd rdn over 2f out: wknd over 1f out* **96/10**

5 *1* **Subitodopo**[15] 1667 4-8-9 .... NMurru 7 102
(M Gasparini, Italy) *7th st: nvr a factor* **66/10**

6 *1* **Sidereus (IRE)**[175] 6863 4-8-9 .... URispoli 6 101
(F & L Camici, Italy) *5th st: btn 2f out* **113/10**

7 *10* **Cocodrail (IRE)**[42] 7-8-9 .... SLandi 4 85
(F & L Brogi, Italy) *4th st: wknd over 2f out* **22/1**

8 *6* **Go East (GER)**[197] 6519 4-8-6 .... MDemuro 8 72
(V Valiani, Italy) *trckd wnr tl wkng wl over 2f out* **47/10**[2]

2m 30.2s (3.00) **8 Ran SP% 138.0**
(including 1 Euro stake): WIN 1.65; PL 1.15, 1.59, 2.61; DF 4.06.
Owner Lino Scarpellini **Bred** L Scarpellini **Trained** Italy

2028a DERBY ITALIANO (GROUP 1) (C&F) 1m 3f
4:10 (4:25) 3-Y-0 **£334,559** (£147,206; £80,294; £40,147)

RPR

1 **Cima De Triomphe (IRE)**[22] 3-9-2 .... SMulas 6 108
(B Grizzetti, Italy) *midfield: 9th st: hdwy over 3f out: r.o u.p fr 2f out to ld appr fnl f: drvn out*

2 *1/2* **Permesso**[21] 3-9-2 .... URispoli 17 108
(F & L Camici, Italy) *hld up: hdwy on outside 3f out: tk 2nd 100yds out: r.o*

3 1 **Papetti (ITY)** 3-9-2 .... PConvertino 9 106
(B Grizzetti, Italy) *7th st: rdn 4f out: disp 3rd 1f out: one pce*
4 1/2 **Farrel (IRE)**[21] 1513 3-9-2 .... DVargiu 2 105
(B Grizzetti, Italy) *a.p: 3rd st: led wl over 1f out to appr fnl f: one pce*
5 1 1/2 **Voila Ici (IRE)** 3-9-2 .... MDemuro 1 102
(V Caruso, Italy) *last st: hdwy on outside fr over 2f out: nrst fin*
6 3 **Once More Dubai (USA)**[21] 3-9-2 .... GBietolini 18 97
(Gianluca Bietolini, Italy) *bhd to st: nrst fin*
7 nse **Bouguereau**[23] 1443 3-9-2 .... AlanMunro 12 97
(P W Chapple-Hyam) *trckd ldrs: 4th st: 5th and pushed along 3f out: sn one pce*
8 2 1/2 **Fathayer (USA)**[21] 3-9-2 .... RHills 8 93
(P Paciello, Italy) *led to wl over 1f out: one pce*
9 shd **Senlis (IRE)**[21] 1513 3-9-2 .... ASanna 11 93
(E Borromeo, Italy) *replated in paddock: trckd ldr: 2nd st: rdn and ev ch wl over 1f out: sn btn*
10 2 1/2 **Rastignano (IRE)**[183] 6768 3-9-2 .... MMonteriso 5 89
(V Caruso, Italy) *5th st: w ldrs 3f out: sn btn*
11 5 **Sartorio (FR)** 3-9-2 ....(b) AHelfenbein 3 80
(G Dolfi, Italy) *prom: 6th on ins st: btn wl over 2f out*
12 nk **Gibraltar Applied (IRE)** 3-9-2 .... GMarcelli 4 80
(F & L Camici, Italy) *replated at s: racd in midfield: btn 3f out*
13 4 **Sant'Antonio (ITY)** 3-9-2 .... SLandi 10 73
(A & G Botti, Italy) *a bhd*
14 3 1/2 **Lessing (IRE)** 3-9-2 .... MEsposito 13 67
(O Pessi, Italy) *a bhd*
15 2 **Lupo Alberto (ITY)**[22] 3-9-2 .... NPinna 15 63
(R Santini, Italy) *racd in midfield: btn over 2f out*
16 10 **Libero Mercato (IRE)**[22] 3-9-2 .... EBotti 14 46
(A & G Botti, Italy) *midfield on outside st: sn btn*
17 1 1/2 **Clelt Di San Jore (IRE)**[22] 3-9-2 .... JamieSpencer 7 44
(L D'Auria, Italy) *a in rr*
18 5 **Silver Arrow (ITY)**[22] 3-9-2 .... CFiocchi 16 35
(R Menichetti, Italy) *prom: 8th st: btn over 3f out*

2m 14.6s (134.60) **18 Ran**
WIN 9.68; PL 5.69, 3.26, 3.39; DF 146.25.
Owner Scuderia Cocktail **Bred** Sofim Srl **Trained** Italy
■ The Italian Derby was run over a furlong less than previously.

NOTEBOOK
Cima De Triomphe(IRE), a son of Galileo, was the highlight of a terrific day for his trainer, who was also responsible for the third and fourth and two other Group-race winners on the day. The colt will now be trained for the Arc.
Bouguereau, went off favourite having been runner-up in a decent conditions race at Newbury. However, he was one of the first beaten and his rider blamed the fast ground.

2029a PREMIO TUDINI (GROUP 3) 6f
4:50 (5:07) 3-Y-O+ **£21,441** (£21,441; £7,147; £3,574)

RPR
1 **Gesture**[21] 6-9-4 .... SLandi 2 102
(C Di Stasio, Italy) *outpcd early: hrd rdn on rails wl over 1f out: r.o to force dead-heat on line* **32/10**[2]
1 dht **Titus Shadow (IRE)**[22] 4-9-4 .... DVargiu 3 102
(B Grizzetti, Italy) *hdwy 2f out: led ins fnl f: ct on line* **9/2**[3]
3 1 **Black Mambazo (IRE)**[21] 1513 3-8-8 .... MMonteriso 8 99
(L Riccardi, Italy) *a.p: led 1/2-way to ins fnl f: kpt on* **162/10**
4 2 1/2 **Le Cadre Noir (IRE)**[51] 4-9-4 .... EBotti 4 92
(A Renzoni, Italy) *mid-div: hdwy u.p 2f out: no ex fnl f* **2/1**[1]
5 3 **Remarque (IRE)**[21] 1513 3-8-8 ....(b) PConvertino 5 83
(L Riccardi, Italy) *pressed ldrs: 3rd and rdn 2f out: eased whn btn fnl f* **159/10**
6 1 **Golden Joker (IRE)** 4-9-4 .... GChioffi 10 80
(A Renzoni, Italy) *nvr nr to chal* **53/1**
7 3 **Love Intrigue (IRE)**[14] 1659 3-8-5 .... PAragoni 12 68
(A Peraino, Italy) *pressed ldrs to wl over 1f out* **79/10**
8 1 1/2 **Lady Marmelade (ITY)**[14] 1659 5-9-1 .... GBietolini 11 63
(D Ducci, Italy) *effrt on outside 2f out: sn one pce* **22/1**
9 2 **Little Warrior (ITY)** 4-9-4 .... URispoli 9 60
(B Simonaggio, Italy) *led to 1/2-way* **55/1**
10 3/4 **Tony Douglas (IRE)**[21] 4-9-4 .... MDemuro 6 58
(A Di Dio, Italy) *spd to 1/2-way* **118/10**
11 2 **Dream Impact (USA)**[22] 7-9-4 .... GMarcelli 7 52
(L Riccardi, Italy) *prom over 3f* **49/10**
12 1/2 **Polar Wind (ITY)**[22] 4-9-4 .... CFiocchi 1 50
(R Menichetti, Italy) *a outpcd* **148/10**

68.90 secs (-1.40)
WFA 3 from 4yo+ 10lb **12 Ran SP% 137.4**
WIN 2.23 (Gesture), 2.60 (Titus Shadow); PL 1.90, 1.99, 3.68; DF 15.02.
Owner Giordano Grilli **Bred** Cheveley Park Stud Ltd **Trained** Italy
Owner Scuderia Blueberry **Bred** Scuderia Blueberry **Trained** Italy

1885 LONGCHAMP (R-H)
Sunday, May 11

OFFICIAL GOING: Good

2032a POULE D'ESSAI DES POULAINS (GROUP 1) (COLTS) 1m
2:50 (2:56) 3-Y-O **£168,059** (£67,235; £33,618; £16,794; £8,412)

RPR
1 **Falco (USA)**[24] 3-9-2 .... OPeslier 9 122
(C Laffon-Parias, France) *racd in 5th: 4th st: led 2f out: rdn 3 l clr ins fnl f: rdn out* **215/10**
2 3 **Rio De La Plata (USA)**[204] 6333 3-9-2 .... LDettori 16 115
(Saeed Bin Suroor) *hld up: 11th st: hdwy towards ins to go 3rd 1f out: tk 2nd 120yds out: kpt on: jst hld on for 2nd* **7/2**[1]
3 shd **River Proud (USA)**[24] 1421 3-9-2 .... TQuinn 14 115
(P F I Cole) *reluctant to load: re-loaded in outside stall: in rr: pushed along wl over 3f out: 18th st: swtchd ins and hdwy 2f out: fin wl* **46/1**
4 1 **Yorktown (FR)**[58] 3-9-2 .... C-PLemaire 5 113
(J-C Rouget, France) *midfield: 10th st: kpt on steadily fnl 2f* **15/1**
5 hd **Hello Morning (FR)**[28] 1361 3-9-2 .... AlexisBadel 2 112
(Mme C Head-Maarek, France) *led 1f: restrained in 4th: 5th st: one pce fr over 1f out* **12/1**
6 1/2 **Thewayyouare (USA)**[192] 6615 3-9-2 .... SPasquier 15 111
(A Fabre, France) *hld up: 12th st: rdn and styd on down outside fr over 1 1/2f out* **57/10**[3]
7 1/2 **Paco Boy (IRE)**[22] 1471 3-9-2 .... RichardHughes 11 110
(R Hannon) *hld up: 15th st: n.m.r 2f out to 1 1/2f out: kpt on fnl f* **10/1**
8 hd **Bermuda Rye (IRE)**[27] 1376 3-9-2 .... CSoumillon 1 109
(M Delzangles, France) *midfield: 8th st: rdn 2f out: kpt on at one pce* **13/1**
9 1/2 **Tamayuz**[28] 1361 3-9-2 .... DBonilla 17 108
(F Head, France) *hld up in rr: 16th st: swtchd outside over 1 1/2f out: kpt on steadily* **77/10**
10 1 1/2 **Georgebernardshaw (IRE)**[28] 1356 3-9-2 .... JMurtagh 7 105
(A P O'Brien, Ire) *midfield whn bmpd over 4f out: 9th st: effrt towards outside over 1 1/2f out: unable qck* **41/10**[2]
11 shd **Salut L'Africain (FR)**[27] 1376 3-9-2 .... IMendizabal 10 105
(Robert Collet, France) *in tch: 7th st: one pce fr over 1f out* **35/1**
12 nse **Il Warrd (IRE)**[29] 1333 3-9-2 .... KerrinMcEvoy 6 105
(Saeed Bin Suroor) *racd freely early: prom: 3rd st: 2nd 2f out to 120yds out: wknd and eased* **7/2**[1]
13 nse **General Eliott (IRE)**[16] 1598 3-9-2 .... RyanMoore 8 104
(P F I Cole) *racd freely early in 6th: bmpd over 4f out: 6th st: one pce fnl 1 1/2f* **27/1**
14 3/4 **Alexander Castle (USA)**[24] 1421 3-9-2 .... NCallan 12 103
(K A Ryan) *hld up: 13th st: nvr a factor* **60/1**
15 3 **Bon Grain (FR)**[48] 1011 3-9-2 .... TJarnet 18 96
(J J Napoli, France) *hld up: 14th st: nvr a factor* **15/1**
16 6 **Blue Chagall (FR)**[28] 1361 3-9-2 .... JVictoire 19 82
(H-A Pantall, France) *17th st: a in rr* **89/1**
17 2 1/2 **Maille Le Nelois (FR)**[12] 3-9-2 .... TGillet 13 76
(V Greco, France) *last st: a bhd* **130/1**
18 5 **One Great Cat (USA)**[28] 1361 3-9-2 .... TThulliez 3 65
(A P O'Brien, Ire) *led after 1f: hdd after 2f: 2nd st: sn wknd* **41/10**[2]
19 2 **Lucifer Sam (USA)**[28] 1361 3-9-2 .... DavidMcCabe 4 60
(A P O'Brien, Ire) *missed break and given a number of reminders: led after 2f: hdd 2f out: wknd and eased* **41/10**[2]

1m 35.6s (-3.20) **Going Correction** -0.075s/f (Good) **19 Ran SP% 182.5**
Speed ratings: **113,110,109,108,108 108,107,107,107,105 105,105,105,104,101 95,93,88,86**
PARI-MUTUEL: WIN 22.50; PL 6.00, 21.60, 10.70; DF 60.20.
Owner Wertheimer Et Frere **Bred** Wertheimer Et Frere **Trained** Chantilly, France

FOCUS
A messy race and a surprise winner in the shape of Falco.

NOTEBOOK
Falco(USA) was given a superb ride by his jockey who took the initiative early in the straight. Previously only a winner of a Class D race at Longchamp, the colt was settled behind the leaders but moved up to a challenging position early in the straight. When the pacemakers dropped out he quickened in to the lead impressively and the race was wrapped up in a matter of strides. He kept up the gallop and none of the other 19 got in a serious blow. Further improvement can be expected. His next likely target is the St James's Palace Stakes at Royal Ascot.
Rio De La Plata(USA), made favourite for this Classic, lost nothing in defeat. He had a rotten outside draw and the field went quickly from the start. The colt still had plenty to do in the straight but he quickened to take second place running into the final furlong. He then had to pull out all the stops to hold off the third. He looked well in the paddock and certainly looks likely to make it again at the highest level. Has been entered in all the top events from a mile to a mile and a half and connections need a little time before deciding on his next race.
River Proud(USA) has to be considered extremely unlucky. His antics when being loaded delayed the start for six minutes. Equipped with a Monty Roberts rug, he was placed in the number 14 slot but broke the stall. Without the cloth, he was then loaded into the number 20 stall on the wide outside. Still second last coming into the straight, he did not really pick up his bit until two out and then came with a blistering late run up the far rail. He must have made up 20 lengths in the last two furlongs and would have finished second in another stride. If his problems at the start could be overcome, this colt looks sure to win a Group 1 race. All options are being left open and connections are now looking at the Prix du Jockey-Club, Vodafone Derby or the St James's Palace Stakes.
Yorktown(FR) still had plenty to do on the descent before the straight and then came with a run up the centre of the track. He was staying on at the finish but rather one paced. This colt might have been short of a race as his connections did not want to risk him on heavy ground early in the season. He should be watched next time out.
Thewayyouare(USA), a high-class two-year-old, is going to be suited by middle-distances this season and as a result this has to go down as a really good comeback run. He briefly threatened to make a run for it and will be an obvious contender for the Prix Du Jockey Club.
Paco Boy(IRE), supplemented into the race, still had plenty to do coming into the straight. He did not have a totally clear run and was putting in his best work at the finish.
Georgebernardshaw(IRE), impressive in winning two heavy-ground races in Ireland, was faced with quicker conditions here and he failed to prove as effective. He can be given another chance.
Il Warrd(IRE), well up from the very start, led early in the straight and quickly fell out of contention in the last furlong and a half.
General Eliott(IRE) was never seen with a real chance, he just stayed on during the final two furlongs.
Alexander Castle(USA) looked out of his depth in this company and just stayed on in the straight without ever being near the pace.

2033a POULE D'ESSAI DES POULICHES (GROUP 1) (FILLIES) 1m
3:25 (3:35) 3-Y-O **£168,059** (£67,235; £33,618; £16,794; £8,412)

RPR
1 **Zarkava (IRE)**[28] 1360 3-9-0 .... CSoumillon 5 120+
(A De Royer-Dupre, France) *hld up: 8th st: hdwy 2f out: led 1f out: pushed out and r.o wl* **30/100**[1]
2 2 **Goldikova (IRE)**[38] 3-9-0 .... OPeslier 1 112
(F Head, France) *uns rdr at stalls: reluctant load: stmbld s: rcvrd: 5th st: hdwy 2f out: 1 1/2f out: ev ch 1f out: r.o same pce* **9/1**[3]
3 1 1/2 **Halfway To Heaven (IRE)**[35] 1230 3-9-0 .... DavidMcCabe 6 109
(A P O'Brien, Ire) *broke wl: trckd ldr: 2nd st: led 2f out to appr fnl f: r.o same pce* **24/1**
4 3/4 **Modern Look**[27] 1375 3-9-0 .... SPasquier 7 107
(D Smaga, France) *first to show: racd in 3rd: 4th st: 2nd 2f out: led briefly appr fnl f: one pce whn squeezed bk abt 75yds out* **82/10**[2]
5 1/2 **Azabara**[38] 3-9-0 .... LDettori 10 106
(A Fabre, France) *a in tch: 6th and pushed along st: outpcd tl keeping on under driving on outside fr 1 1/2f out: nrest at fin* **16/1**
6 1/2 **Psalm (IRE)**[35] 1230 3-9-0 .... JMurtagh 13 105
(A P O'Brien, Ire) *hld up: last st: hdwy fr wl over 1f out: nrest at fin* **24/1**
7 3/4 **Blue Cayenne (FR)**[27] 1375 3-9-0 .... TJarnet 2 103
(Mlle S-V Tarrou, France) *a.p: 3rd st: one pce fnl 2f* **51/1**
8 3/4 **Nijoom Dubai**[25] 1401 3-9-0 .... RichardHughes 12 101
(M R Channon) *mid-div: one pce fnl 2f* **33/1**

9 4 **Lessing (FR)**[28] 1360 3-9-0 .... JAuge 14 92
(R Gibson, France) *mid-div whn wnt wd st: one pce* **47/1**

10 2 **Kayaba**[30] 3-9-0 .... MBlancpain 3 87
(C Laffon-Parias, France) *prom 5th: rdn and btn 2f out* **9/1**[3]

11 2 **Conference Call**[28] 1360 3-9-0 .... TThulliez 8 83
(P Bary, France) *led after 1f: hdd 2f out: wknd steadily* **82/10**[2]

12 1 **Dream Day**[22] 1470 3-9-0 .... RyanMoore 9 81
(R Hannon) *a bhd* **100/1**

13 ½ **Silent Sunday (IRE)**[27] 1375 3-9-0 .... JVictoire 11 79
(H-A Pantall, France) *a bhd* **115/1**

14 snk **Destare**[19] 3-9-0 .... C-PLemaire 4 79
(J E Pease, France) *7th st: on rails: wknd 1 1/2f out* **38/1**

1m 35.2s (-3.60) **Going Correction** -0.075s/f (Good) **14** Ran SP% **143.9**
Speed ratings: **115,113,111,110,110 109,109,108,104,102 100,99,98,98**
PARI-MUTUEL: WIN 1.30; PL 1.10, 1.60, 3.90; DF 5.40.

Owner H H Aga Khan **Bred** His Highness The Aga Khan's Studs S C **Trained** Chantilly, France

NOTEBOOK

Zarkava(IRE) was given plenty to do on this occasion but she still dominated the final stages and is now unbeaten in four races. Well back for much of the way, she was still only seventh in the straight, but a gap opened up beautifully in front of her and she needed just one slap to put her mind on the job before surging clear. She was much more switched off this time, which no doubt has something to do with her being trained for longer distances and her next target will be the Prix de Diane at Chantilly. On form, she is the best three-year-old filly over a mile in Europe.

Goldikova(IRE) pecked on leaving the stalls but that made little difference to the end result. She began her run from one and a half out and stayed on strongly to the line. A Group race looks sure to come her way in the future and connections are looking at either the Prix de Sandringham or possibly the Coronation Stakes at Royal Ascot.

Halfway To Heaven(IRE), well up from the very start, kept up the good work to the bitter end. She was always in the leading group and came back at the end to re-take third place. Considered a tough individual, this filly will probably now be aimed at the Irish Oaks.

Modern Look, well up from the start, ran a little free and had a narrow advantage halfway up the straight before slightly shortening her stride as the race came to an end. This distance may well be the maximum for this daughter of Zamindar and there are no plans for the moment.

Psalm(IRE) is well regarded, but she was unable to show her best when her saddle slipped on her reappearance. She was given a lot to do - held up behind Zarkava - and her inexperience probably counted against her, but there was a lot like about the way she finished her race. She should improve significantly for this and, along with Zarkava, she is one of the fillies to take from the race. She has plenty of options, including the Irish Guineas and Coronations Stakes, or she could step up in trip for the Prix de Diane. She also still has the option of dropping into maiden company.

Nijoom Dubai was never seen with a real chance after being given a waiting ride. Her jockey reported the filly was never going well

Dream Day, well out of her ground at the bottom of the descent before the straight, she never looked like taking a hand in the finish.

2034a PRIX DE SAINT-GEORGES (GROUP 3) 5f (S)
4:00 (4:05) 3-Y-0+ **£29,412** (£11,765; £8,824; £5,882; £2,941)

RPR

1 **Only Answer**[17] 1593 4-8-11 .... OPeslier 9 105
(A Fabre, France) *a cl up on outside: hrd rdn to ld ins fnl f: rdn out* **64/10**[2]

2 1 **Mood Music**[14] 1660 4-9-0 ....(b) DBoeuf 7 104
(Mario Hofer, Germany) *cl up disputing 2nd: led 1 1/2f out to ins fnl f: jst hld on for 2nd* **27/1**

3 nk **Derison (USA)**[17] 1593 6-9-2 ....(b) TJarnet 1 105
(P Van De Poele, France) *last to 2f out: str run down outside fnl f: fin wl* **10/1**

4 ¾ **Stern Opinion (USA)**[213] 6136 3-8-7 .... SPasquier 4 103
(P Bary, France) *hld up towards rr: kpt on u.p fr over 1f out* **76/10**

5 nse **Calbuco (FR)**[17] 1593 4-9-0 .... WMongil 8 100
(B Dutruel, France) *led to 1 1/2f out: one pce* **7/10**[1]

6 3 **Wilki (FR)**[241] 5373 3-8-4 .... C-PLemaire 2 89
(A De Royer-Dupre, France) *trckd ldr on ins early: lost pl over 3f out: n.d after* **7/1**[3]

7 1 ½ **Garden City (FR)**[34] 3-8-2 .... JVictoire 3 81
(Y De Nicolay, France) *hld up towards rr: nvr a factor* **34/1**

8 ½ **Hammadi (IRE)**[43] 1075 3-8-5 .... DO'Donohoe 6 82
(K A Ryan) *cl up: rdn over 2f out: sn btn* **26/1**

9 15 **Biniou (IRE)**[167] 6954 5-9-0 .... RobertHavlin 5 28
(R M H Cowell) *racd in 8th tl dropped to last 2f out: wknd: t.o* **35/1**

57.00 secs (0.30) **Going Correction** +0.40s/f (Good)
WFA 3 from 4yo+ 9lb **9** Ran SP% **118.5**
Speed ratings: **113,111,110,109,109 104,102,101,77**
PARI-MUTUEL: WIN 7.40; PL 2.00, 4.90, 2.50; DF 68.10.

Owner Wertheimer Et Frere **Bred** Wertheimer Et Frere **Trained** Chantilly, France

NOTEBOOK

Only Answer benefited from a fine ride from Peslier. Smartly away on the wide outside, she settled well before challenging for the lead at the furlong marker and quickened well to settle the race. A very consistent individual, she will now be aimed at the Prix du Gros-Chene and if she runs well in that race her connections might have to consider supplementing her for a sprint in England.

Mood Music, German trained, looked the likely winner at the furlong pole but he could not sustain effort. Certainly a colt who goes well on good ground, he could be back at Chantilly for the Gros-Chene next time out.

Derison(USA) was given an awful lot to do and still had many lengths to make up at the half way stage. He ran on and finished the best of all, but the line came too soon. This was a good performance under top weight.

Stern Opinion(USA) made late progress and this effort suggests that he may well do better of six furlongs.

Calbuco(FR) was three from three so far this year, including a couple of Listed wins, but he was below form this time.

Hammadi(IRE), smartly away in second position early on, was going nowhere from the half way mark.

Biniou(IRE), already beaten at the half way stage, was tailed off and finished last. This ground was a little quicker than he would have liked.

1749 REDCAR (L-H)
Monday, May 12

OFFICIAL GOING: Good to firm (9.3)
Wind: light, half against Weather: sea fret, very cool

2035 WEDDINGS @ MORRITT MEDIAN AUCTION MAIDEN STKS 5f
2:20 (2:21) (Class 6) 2-Y-O **£2,047** (£604; £302) **Stalls** Centre

Form RPR

1 **Lucky Leigh** 2-8-12 0 .... EdwardCreighton 8 77+
(M R Channon) *trckd ldrs: hdwy to ld wl over 1f out: sn clr: comf* **16/1**

0 2 4 ½ **El Bobby (IRE)**[11] 1749 2-9-3 0 .... DO'Donohoe 10 66
(J R Weymes) *a.p: effrt and ev ch 2f out: sn rdn and kpt on appr fnl f: no ch w wnr* **80/1**

5 3 1 **Gower Valentine**[11] 1749 2-8-12 0 .... AdrianTNicholls 7 57
(D Nicholls) *led: rdn along 1/2-way: hdd wl over 1f out and kpt on same pce* **14/1**

4 nk **Verinco** 2-9-3 0 .... TomEaves 3 61+
(B Smart) *dwlt and towards rr: pushed along 1/2-way: gd hdwy over 1f out: styd on wl fnl f: nrst fin* **6/1**[2]

5 ½ **Elaine's Folly** 2-8-12 0 .... GregFairley 4 54
(P C Haslam) *chsd ldrs: rdn along 2f out: hung lft and one pce appr fnl f* **40/1**

2 6 ¾ **Sloop Johnb**[11] 1749 2-9-3 0 .... PaulHanagan 5 57
(R A Fahey) *upset in stalls: s.i.s: sn in tch: effrt to chse ldrs over 2f out: sn rdn and one pce* **13/8**[1]

3 7 nse **Asian Tale (IRE)**[21] 1515 2-8-12 0 .... LeeEnstone 14 51
(P C Haslam) *trckd ldrs: effrt 2f out: sn rdn and one pce* **7/1**[3]

8 1 ½ **Common Diva** 2-8-12 0 .... NeilPollard 6 46
(A J McCabe) *trckd ldrs: rdn along and outpcd 1/2-way: styd on appr fnl f* **33/1**

9 ½ **Tale Of Silver (IRE)** 2-9-3 0 .... TedDurcan 9 52+
(G A Swinbank) *s.i.s: green and bhd tl sme late hdwy* **16/1**

10 shd **Tagula Breeze (IRE)** 2-9-3 0 .... PatrickMathers 1 49
(I W McInnes) *in tch: rdn along 1/2-way: grad wknd* **50/1**

3 11 1 **Fitzolini**[12] 1727 2-9-3 0 .... SilvestreDeSousa 11 45
(A D Brown) *nvr nr ldrs* **6/1**[2]

12 ½ **Approved** 2-8-12 0 .... PaulMulrennan 13 38
(M W Easterby) *a towards rr* **40/1**

13 2 **Drachenfels** 2-9-3 0 .... FergalLynch 16 36
(K A Ryan) *a towards rr* **16/1**

14 2 **Bianca Maria** 2-8-12 0 .... GrahamGibbons 15 24
(T D Easterby) *a towards rr* **33/1**

15 5 **Senora Verde** 2-8-12 0 .... MickyFenton 2 6
(P T Midgley) *chsd ldrs: rdn along and hung lft after 2f: sn lost pl and bhd* **33/1**

59.92 secs (1.32) **Going Correction** +0.175s/f (Good) **15** Ran SP% **120.4**
Speed ratings (Par 91): **96,88,87,86,85 84,84,82,81,81 79,78,75,72,64**
CSF £957.17 TOTE £23.10: £4.00, £8.70, £3.30; EX 825.50.

Owner M Channon **Bred** Norman Court Stud **Trained** West Ilsley, Berks

FOCUS

Probably modest maiden form overall but the winner was impressive enough.

NOTEBOOK

Lucky Leigh won in good style. She travelled well just off the pace, went on over a furlong out and was pushed clear. She is obviously speedy, and did it well enough, but the form is unlikely to be strong.

El Bobby(IRE), well beaten on his debut, improved on that, showing up well and keeping on for second. (op 100-1)

Gower Valentine, racing on quicker ground this time, broke well and showed early speed. (op 16-1)

Verinco, out of a winning sprinter, is a half-brother to six winners. He missed the break but, after taking time for the penny to drop, came home well to finish a closing fourth. He will prove to be a good bit better than this and is the one to take from the race. (op 11-2 tchd 9-2)

Elaine's Folly raced in touch early on, and shaped with a degree of promise on her debut. (op 66-1)

Sloop Johnb, who was second on his debut over course and distance on soft ground, spoiled his chance with a tardy break and never featured. Official explanation: jockey said colt became upset in stalls and missed the break (op 11-8 tchd 5-4)

Senora Verde (tchd 40-1)

2036 MEDICS UK (S) STKS 5f
2:50 (2:51) (Class 6) 3-Y-O+ **£1,774** (£523; £262) **Stalls** Centre

Form RPR

0-40 1 **Kenmore**[30] 1327 6-9-7 70 .... GrahamGibbons 8 65
(J G Given) *w ldrs: styd on to ld wl ins fnl f: jst hld on* **3/1**[2]

5140 2 nse **Blackheath (IRE)**[6] 1893 12-9-2 62 .... KellyHarrison(5) 12 65
(S T Mason) *hld up: hdwy and nt clr run over 1f out: styd on ins fnl f: jst failed* **6/1**

-304 3 ½ **Steel City Boy (IRE)**[14] 1677 5-9-7 61 .... DavidAllan 2 63
(D Carroll) *chsd ldrs: led appr fnl f: hdd and no ex wl ins fnl f* **11/4**[1]

400- 4 1 **Miss Mujahid Times**[193] 6609 5-9-2 43 ....(b) SilvestreDeSousa 5 54
(A D Brown) *mid-div: effrt over 2f out: kpt on wl fnl f* **16/1**

1304 5 ¾ **Rann Na Cille (IRE)**[15] 1642 4-9-2 54 .... MickyFenton 14 52
(P T Midgley) *led tl appr fnl f: no ex* **11/2**[3]

300- 6 1 ¼ **Best Lead**[363] 1753 9-9-7 50 ....(b) DanielTudhope 10 52
(Ian Emmerson) *mid-div: effrt over 2f out: styd on same pce appr fnl f* **25/1**

140/ 7 1 ¾ **Danzili Bay**[555] 6335 6-9-0 0 .... MarkCoumbe(7) 11 46
(A W Carroll) *chsd ldrs: fdd fnl f* **7/1**

-006 8 shd **Spinning Game**[14] 1675 4-8-11 40 ....(b) DanielleMcCreery(5) 4 41
(Mrs R A Carr) *s.i.s: kpt on fnl 2f: nvr trbld ldrs* **50/1**

5-00 9 6 **First Valentini**[11] 1754 4-8-13 38 .... MarkLawson(3) 9 19
(N Bycroft) *sn drvn and outpcd* **66/1**

44- 10 hd **Socceroo**[219] 6022 3-8-7 0 .... PaulHanagan 13 18
(S Parr) *trckd ldrs: lost pl over 1f out* **6/1**

-605 11 2 ¼ **Only A Splash**[11] 1754 4-9-4 44 .... MichaelJStainton(3) 7 15
(Mrs R A Carr) *s.i.s: a in rr* **50/1**

3/00 12 4 **Fiona Fox**[81] 634 4-8-13 45 ....(t) JasonEdmunds(3) 6 —
(J Balding) *chsd ldrs: sn drvn along: wandered and lost pl over 1f out* **80/1**

60.04 secs (1.44) **Going Correction** +0.175s/f (Good)
WFA 3 from 4yo+ 9lb **12** Ran SP% **124.5**
Speed ratings (Par 101): **95,94,94,92,91 89,86,86,76,76 72,66**
CSF £22.22 TOTE £4.60: £2.10, £2.10, £1.50; EX 30.70.There was no bid for the winner. Steel City Boy was claimed by Ann Stokell for £6,000.

Owner Paul Moulton **Bred** Downclose Stud **Trained** Willoughton, Lincs

FOCUS

Most of these were exposed and the winner did not have to run to his best to win. The fourth lends slight doubts to the form.

2037 MARKET CROSS JEWELLERS H'CAP 1m 1f

3:20 (3:20) (Class 5) (0-75,74) 3-Y-O **£2,331** (£693; £346; £173) **Stalls** Low

Form RPR

20-0 **1** **Gala Casino Star (IRE)**[16] [1622] 3-8-8 **64**.......................... PaulHanagan 2 73
(R A Fahey) *trckd ldrs: pushed along 3f out: rdn 2f out: styd on to chal ent fnl f: led fnl 50yds* **8/1**

426- **2** *3/4* **Elk Trail (IRE)**[217] [6051] 3-9-4 **74**.......................... MickyFenton 10 81
(T P Tate) *cl up: led over 3f out: rdn wl over 1f out: drvn ins fnl f: hdd and no ex fnl 50yds* **5/1**[2]

-251 **3** *1 3/4* **Black Dahlia**[18] [1586] 3-8-8 **64**.......................... NeilPollard 5 71+
(A J McCabe) *in tch: hdwy to trck ldrs 3f out: effrt over 1f out: rdn and ev ch whn n.m.r ent fnl f: sn drvn and one pce* **5/2**[1]

634- **4** *1 1/2* **Shaloo Diamond**[234] [5580] 3-9-0 **73**.......................... MichaelJStainton(3) 6 73
(R M Whitaker) *hld up in rr: stdy hdwy on inner over 2f out: nt clr run and swtchd rt ent fnl f: styd on wl towards fin* **18/1**

343 **5** *nk* **Shadowtime**[18] [1579] 3-8-13 **69**.......................... DeanMcKeown 1 68
(Miss Tracy Waggott) *trckd ldrs: hdwy over 2f out: rdn to chal over 1f out and ev ch tl wknd ins fnl f* **7/1**

00-3 **6** *6* **Bourbon Highball (IRE)**[8] [1823] 3-7-11 **60**.......................... PatrickDonaghy(7) 11 46
(P C Haslam) *led: rdn along and hdd over 3f out: drvn over 2f out and grad wknd* **12/1**

2434 **7** *1 3/4* **Ace Of Spies (IRE)**[44] [1082] 3-8-5 **68**.......................... CraigPettigrew(7) 4 50
(M Johnston) *hld up towards rr: hdwy on wd outside over 2f out: sn rdn: edgd lft and wknd* **9/1**

6-36 **8** *2* **Terracos Do Pinhal**[45] [1060] 3-8-6 **62**.......................... GregFairley 8 40
(M Johnston) *in tch: rdn along over 3f out and sn wknd* **8/1**

0-23 **9** *3* **Kayflaa (IRE)**[29] [1348] 3-9-1 **71**.......................... EdwardCreighton 9 42
(M R Channon) *hld up: effrt over 3f out: sn rdn along and btn over 2f out* **13/2**[3]

1m 54.62s (1.62) **Going Correction** +0.275s/f (Good) 9 Ran SP% **116.2**

Speed ratings (Par 99): **103,102,100,99,99 93,92,90,87**

CSF £48.02 CT £130.90 TOTE £9.50: £3.20, £1.70, £1.20; EX 64.80.

Owner The Friar Tuck Racing Club **Bred** Glashare House Stud **Trained** Musley Bank, N Yorks

FOCUS

Just an ordinary gallop and the form may not prove reliable. The winner built slightly on his previous form.

2038 HERALD & POST MAIDEN FILLIES' STKS 6f

3:50 (3:51) (Class 5) 3-Y-O+ **£2,331** (£693; £346; £173) **Stalls** Centre

Form RPR

-64 **1** **Milton Of Campsie**[37] [1222] 3-8-9 0.......................... DNolan(3) 14 69
(S Parr) *trckd ldrs: led jst ins fnl f: styd on wl* **7/1**

05-5 **2** *1 1/4* **Arabian Art (USA)**[28] [1372] 3-8-12 70.......................... TedDurcan 12 65
(H R A Cecil) *mde most tl jst ins fnl f: no ex* **13/2**[3]

00 **3** *1 1/2* **Take It Easee (IRE)**[7] [1869] 3-8-12 0.......................... PaulMulrennan 15 60
(G A Swinbank) *w ldrs: kpt on same pce fnl f* **18/1**

55 **4** *shd* **Leonid Glow**[24] [1452] 3-8-5 0.......................... JohnCavanagh(7) 3 60
(M Dods) *sn chsng ldrs: edgd rt ins fnl f: kpt on* **10/1**

000- **5** *1/2* **Romantic Destiny**[234] [5583] 3-8-12 90.......................... FergalLynch 9 58
(K A Ryan) *stmbld s: hdwy and n.m.r over 1f out: styd on ins fnl f* **8/1**

0- **6** *nk* **Laa Baas (IRE)**[202] [6409] 3-8-12 0.......................... PhilipRobinson 7 57+
(M A Jarvis) *w ldrs on outer: kpt on same pce appr fnl f* **4/1**[2]

326- **7** *1/2* **Recent Times**[187] [6721] 3-8-12 70.......................... DavidAllan 4 55
(T D Easterby) *w ldrs: chal over 1f out: wknd ins fnl f* **15/2**

420- **8** *1* **Slip Star**[233] [5627] 5-9-8 48.......................... GregFairley 8 55
(T J Etherington) *w ldrs: one pce whn n.m.r ins fnl f* **25/1**

605- **9** *1 1/2* **Tumbleweed Di**[160] [7019] 4-9-3 45.......................... SladeO'Hara(5) 13 50
(G R Oldroyd) *w ldrs: wknd appr fnl f: sltly hmpd ins fnl f* **66/1**

4 **10** *3/4* **Deep Winter**[48] [1019] 3-8-12 0.......................... PaulHanagan 10 45
(R A Fahey) *chsd ldrs: keeping on same pce whn n.m.r ins fnl f* **3/1**[1]

40 **11** *nse* **Elzain (IRE)**[11] [1737] 3-8-12 0.......................... EdwardCreighton 16 45
(M R Channon) *in rr: drvn over 3f out: carried rt ins fnl f: nvr nr ldrs* **20/1**

0360 **12** *nk* **Nabra**[61] [858] 4-9-5 44.......................... MarkLawson(3) 6 47
(M Brittain) *mid-div: drvn 4f out: nvr a factor* **100/1**

606/ **13** *4* **Katie's Biscuit**[1288] [6514] 6-9-3 49..........................(v[1]) KellyHarrison(5) 11 34
(Ian Emmerson) *s.s: sn drvn along and in rr* **250/1**

0 **14** *9* **Fair Fact (IRE)**[24] [1452] 3-8-12 0.......................... TWilliams 1 2
(M Brittain) *w ldrs: lost pl over 2f out* **50/1**

15 *nk* **Little Pandora** 4-9-1 0.......................... NSLawes(7) 2 —
(G P Kelly) *s.v.s: hdwy after 2f: lost pl over 3f out: sn bhd* **150/1**

0 **16** *9* **Lovely Lilling**[48] [1019] 3-8-12 0.......................... MickyFenton 5 —
(P T Midgley) *t.k.h: prom: edgd lft and lost pl 3f out: sn bhd* **125/1**

1m 13.47s (1.67) **Going Correction** +0.175s/f (Good)

WFA 3 from 4yo+ 10lb 16 Ran SP% **123.0**

Speed ratings (Par 100): **95,93,91,91,90 90,89,88,86,85 85,84,79,67,66 54**

CSF £50.83 TOTE £11.00: £3.30, £2.40, £6.70; EX 75.00.

Owner Willie McKay **Bred** Slatch Farm Stud **Trained** Bawtry, S Yorks

■ Stewards' Enquiry : John Cavanagh one-day ban: careless riding (May 26)

FOCUS

There didn't appear to be a great deal of strength in this sprint maiden. The form is ordinary and less than solid.

Romantic Destiny Official explanation: jockey said filly stumbled leaving stalls

2039 EVENING GAZETTE FILLIES' H'CAP 7f

4:20 (4:20) (Class 4) (0-85,85) 3-Y-O+ **£4,209** (£1,252; £625; £312) **Stalls** Centre

Form RPR

533- **1** **Island Music (IRE)**[185] [6742] 3-8-2 71 oh1.......................... PaulHanagan 3 69+
(J J Quinn) *trckd ldrs: hdwy 2f out: swtchd rt and qcknd to chal 1f out: rdn and styd on to ld wl ins fnl f* **5/1**[3]

000- **2** *1* **Fantasy Parkes**[219] [6002] 4-9-6 **77**.......................... DavidAllan 7 76
(E J Alston) *led: rdn along 2f out: drvn over 1f out: hdd and nt qckn wl ins fnl f* **9/2**[2]

-403 **3** *1/2* **Poppy's Rose**[7] [1867] 4-9-0 71 oh8.......................... RoystonFfrench 1 69
(I W McInnes) *cl up: effrt and ev ch over 1f out: sn rdn and edgd lft: drvn and nt qckn ins fnl f* **9/2**[2]

330- **4** *3/4* **Cassie's Choice (IRE)**[257] [4934] 4-9-0 71 oh6.......................... TomEaves 5 67
(B Smart) *trckd ldng pair: hdwy 2f out: rdn over 1f out and ev ch tl drvn and nt qckn ins fnl f* **8/1**

10 **5** *1 1/4* **Khazina (USA)**[31] [1297] 3-8-2 71 oh1.......................... SilvestreDeSousa 8 60
(C E Brittain) *chsd ldrs: rdn along 2f out: drvn and one pce appr fnl f* **7/2**[1]

300- **6** *3/4* **Passion Fruit**[219] [6018] 7-10-0 **85**.......................... PaulMulrennan 2 76
(C W Fairhurst) *t.k.h: hld up in rr: swtchd rt and hdwy 2f out: rdn to chse ldrs over 1f out: wknd ins fnl f* **7/1**

1-10 **R** **Chrystal Venture (IRE)**[25] [1426] 3-8-3 **72**..........................(p) NeilPollard 6 —
(A J McCabe) *ref to r* **6/1**

1m 26.82s (2.32) **Going Correction** +0.175s/f (Good)

WFA 3 from 4yo+ 12lb 7 Ran SP% **113.1**

Speed ratings (Par 102): **93,91,91,90,89 88,—**

CSF £26.91 CT £107.07 TOTE £6.40: £2.70, £3.40; EX 38.80.

Owner Robert Miller-Bakewell & Mrs A C Robson **Bred** Andrew W Robson **Trained** Settrington, N Yorks

FOCUS

Weak form, with four of the field out of the handicap. The winner came from off the modest pace and might prove a bit better than the bare form.

2040 PETER & BARBARA'S SILVER CELEBRATION CLAIMING STKS 6f

4:50 (4:51) (Class 6) 3-Y-O+ **£2,047** (£604; £302) **Stalls** Centre

Form RPR

-000 **1** **Dressed To Dance (IRE)**[11] [1752] 4-8-13 55..........................(v) PhillipMakin 4 71
(N Tinkler) *hld up: hdwy wl over 1f out: sn rdn and styd on strly ins fnl f to ld fnl 50yds* **25/1**

4225 **2** *1 1/4* **Lethal**[18] [1588] 5-9-10 76.......................... PaulHanagan 13 78
(R A Fahey) *led: rdn along wl over 1f out: drvn and edgd lft ins fnl f: hdd fnl 50yds* **7/2**[1]

22-3 **3** *3/4* **One More Round (USA)**[124] [103] 10-9-10 87..........................(b) RoystonFfrench 3 76
(Ollie Pears) *in tch: hdwy 2f out: rdn and styd on ins fnl f: n.m.r towards fin* **4/1**[2]

00-0 **4** *1/2* **Guest Connections**[40] [1138] 5-9-10 72..........................(v) AdrianTNicholls 10 74
(D Nicholls) *a.p: cl up 1/2-way: rdn and ev ch over 1f out: drvn and one pce ins fnl f* **9/2**[3]

2231 **5** *1 1/2* **Red Rudy**[37] [1204] 6-9-1 70.......................... MarkCoumbe(7) 15 67
(A W Carroll) *in tch: hdwy wl over 1f out: sn rdn and kpt on same pce ins fnl f* **7/2**[1]

1303 **6** *4* **Wiltshire (IRE)**[15] [1641] 6-9-5 56..........................(v) MickyFenton 2 51
(P T Midgley) *midfield: hdwy and nt clr run over 1f out: swtchd lft and rdn ent fnl f: no imp* **8/1**

/0-0 **7** *1 1/4* **Angelofthenorth**[8] [1827] 6-8-12 45.......................... KellyHarrison(5) 6 45
(C J Teague) *chsd ldrs on outer: hdwy and ch 2f out: sn rdn and wknd over 1f out* **66/1**

0456 **8** *1/2* **Bellas Chicas (IRE)**[11] [1754] 3-7-13 48 ow2.......................... DuranFentiman(3) 1 39
(P T Midgley) *wnt lft s: a towards rr* **40/1**

4-60 **9** *1 3/4* **Nufoudh (IRE)**[10] [1775] 4-9-8 52.......................... DeanMcKeown 7 43
(Miss Tracy Waggott) *cl up: rdn along 2f out: sn drvn and wknd* **20/1**

-453 **10** *3/4* **Jaassey**[62] [844] 5-9-5 44..........................(t) GrahamGibbons 8 38
(J S Wainwright) *s.i.s: a in rr* **16/1**

0000 **11** *1 1/4* **Buzzin'Boyzee (IRE)**[23] [1491] 5-8-12 48..........................(p) TWilliams 12 27
(D W Barker) *a towards rr* **33/1**

-000 **12** *nk* **Stir Crazy (IRE)**[30] [1338] 4-9-4 47.......................... TonyHamilton 9 32
(D W Barker) *prom: rdn along bef 1/2-way and sn wknd* **66/1**

50-0 **13** *33* **Frimley's Matterry**[11] [1752] 8-9-1 46.......................... MarkLawson(3) 14 —
(R E Barr) *chsd ldrs tl lost action 1/2-way and virtually p.u* **33/1**

1m 12.55s (0.75) **Going Correction** +0.175s/f (Good)

WFA 3 from 4yo+ 10lb 13 Ran SP% **119.5**

Speed ratings (Par 101): **102,100,99,98,96 91,89,89,86,85 84,83,39**

CSF £106.71 TOTE £23.30: £6.80, £2.00, £1.70; EX 231.50.

Owner W K Syndicate **Bred** John Doyle **Trained** Langton, N Yorks

FOCUS

Exposed sorts in this ordinary claimer and a surprise winner. It is hard to be confident about the form.

Wiltshire(IRE) Official explanation: jockey said gelding was denied a clear run

Frimley's Matterry Official explanation: jockey said gelding lost its action

2041 BODDINGTONS REDCAR STRAIGHT-MILE CHAMPIONSHIP (HANDICAP QUALIFIER) 1m

5:20 (5:22) (Class 6) (0-60,66) 3-Y-O **£2,047** (£604; £302) **Stalls** Centre

Form RPR

060- **1** **Charlevoix (IRE)**[202] [6411] 3-9-1 **57**.......................... TomEaves 12 69+
(C F Wall) *dwlt: hld up in rr: stdy hdwy 3f out: led over 1f out: pushed out* **16/1**

4-30 **2** *1/2* **Dancing Maite**[5] [1912] 3-9-3 **59**.......................... PhillipMakin 17 70+
(S R Bowring) *hld up in rr: smooth hdwy over 2f out: chal 1f out: no ex ins fnl f* **14/1**

04-3 **3** *3 3/4* **Jafra (IRE)**[26] [1396] 3-9-3 **59**.......................... DeanMcKeown 5 61
(R M Whitaker) *hld up in rr: over 2f out: styd on same pce fnl f* **12/1**

00-5 **4** *1* **Willyn (IRE)**[31] [1306] 3-8-13 **60**.......................... GaryBartley(5) 19 60
(J S Goldie) *hld up in rr: hdwy and swtchd stands' side over 2f out: kpt on: nt rch ldrs* **9/1**[3]

0-01 **5** *4 1/2* **Casino Night**[5] [1912] 3-9-10 **66** 6ex.......................... GrahamGibbons 15 55
(J R Weymes) *led: hdd over 1f out: sn wknd* **8/1**[2]

3005 **6** *1 1/2* **Scruffy Skip (IRE)**[5] [1912] 3-9-0 **56**..........................(p) PaulMulrennan 18 42
(C R Dore) *chsd ldrs: one pce fnl 2f* **20/1**

50-4 **7** *3/4* **Low Flyer (USA)**[80] [656] 3-8-13 **60**.......................... NeilBrown(5) 4 44+
(T D Barron) *mid-div: effrt over 2f out: nvr nr ldrs* **12/1**

60-3 **8** *2 1/2* **When Yer Ready (IRE)**[11] [1750] 3-9-3 **59**.......................... DavidAllan 20 37
(T D Easterby) *mid-div: effrt over 2f out: nvr trbld ldrs* **9/1**[3]

0030 **9** *2 1/4* **Natural Rhythm (IRE)**[5] [1912] 3-8-10 **55**.......................... MichaelJStainton(3) 6 28
(Mrs R A Carr) *dwlt: hdwy on wd outside to chse ldrs over 2f out: hung rt and wknd over 1f out* **14/1**

050- **10** *hd* **Miss Solo**[175] [6865] 3-8-6 **55**.......................... PatrickDonaghy(7) 10 28
(P C Haslam) *mid-div: effrt over 2f out: nvr a factor* **33/1**

2300 **11** *2 1/2* **West Lorne (USA)**[20] [1540] 3-9-3 **59**.......................... GregFairley 1 26
(M Johnston) *chsd ldrs: drvn 3f out: sn fdd* **16/1**

005- **12** *nk* **Umverti**[206] [6303] 3-8-10 **55**.......................... MarkLawson(3) 9 21
(N Bycroft) *w ldrs: t.k.h: wknd over 1f out* **66/1**

0-43 **13** *3/4* **Millie's Rock (IRE)**[34] [1255] 3-9-1 **57**.......................... PaulHanagan 11 22+
(M J Wallace) *hld up in rr: effrt over 2f out: nvr on terms* **8/1**[2]

4635 **14** *1 1/2* **Mujahope**[8] [1823] 3-8-13 **60**.......................... KellyHarrison(5) 3 21
(C J Teague) *w ldrs: wknd 2f out* **33/1**

00-0 **15** *1/2* **Caught In Paradise (IRE)**[19] [1558] 3-8-13 **58**.......................... DuranFentiman(3) 7 18
(D W Thompson) *mid-div: effrt over 2f out: sn wknd* **50/1**

0-60 **16** *19* **Riverside**[31] [1302] 3-9-2 **58**.......................... TWilliams 16 —
(M Brittain) *racd alone stands' side: lost pl over 2f out: sn bhd and eased* **40/1**

5-22 **17** *23* **Waterloo Dock**[124] [98] 3-9-3 **59**.......................... TedDurcan 13 —
(M Quinn) *chsd ldrs: lost pl over 2f out: sn heavily eased* **7/1**[1]

340 **18** *19* **Llab Nala**[5] 1912 3-9-2 58....................................(v) EdwardCreighton 2 —
(M R Channon) *in rr: drvn 3f out: no rspnse: sn bhd: virtually p.u* **16/1**
005- **P** **Admiralcollingwood**[199] 6462 3-9-2 58.............................. MickyFenton 8 —
(T P Tate) *w ldrs: lost pl and p.u over 1f out: dismntd* **9/1[3]**
1m 39.93s (1.93) **Going Correction** +0.175s/f (Good) **19** Ran SP% **127.6**
Speed ratings (Par 97): **97,96,92,91,87 85,85,82,80,80 77,77,76,75,74 55,32,13,—**
CSF £218.35 CT £2870.76 TOTE £19.60: £3.90, £3.20, £1.60, £2.40; EX 609.40 Place 6 £442.24, Place 5 £41.78..
Owner M Sinclair **Bred** Farmers Hill Stud **Trained** Newmarket, Suffolk

FOCUS
A modest handicap low-grade race but some were lightly raced sorts open to improvement. Those included the first pair, who finished clear. The field raced in one group but the best pace ended up nearer the stands' side. The third is the best guide to the form.
Charlevoix(IRE) Official explanation: trainer's rep said, regarding the apparent improvement in form, filly had been weak last year but had matured over the winter.
Waterloo Dock Official explanation: jockey said colt lost its action
Llab Nala Official explanation: jockey said gelding lost its action
Admiralcollingwood Official explanation: jockey said gelding lost its action
T/Jkpt: Not won. T/Plt: £974.40 to a £1 stake. Pool: £50,121.64. 37.55 winning tickets. T/Qpdt: £32.50 to a £1 stake. Pool: £3,642.57. 82.80 winning tickets. JR

1872 WINDSOR (R-H)

Monday, May 12

OFFICIAL GOING: Good to firm (8.8)
Wind: Light, against Weather: Fine, warm

2042 GET ON WITH WILLIAM HILL NOVICE STKS — 5f 10y

5:55 (5:55) (Class 4) 2-Y-O **£3,885** (£1,156; £577; £288) **Stalls** High

Form RPR
5 **1** **River Rye (IRE)**[25] 1419 2-8-7 0.................................. RyanMoore 8 80+
(R Hannon) *chsd ldrs: eased off rail and prog 2f out: rdn to ld 1f out: edgd rt but asserted last 100yds* **7/4[2]**
2 **2** *1 1/4* **Every Second**[13] 1693 2-8-12 0.................................. RichardMullen 1 80
(E S McMahon) *t.k.h: led over 3f out: shkn up and hdd 1f out: nudged by wnr sn after: one pce* **6/4[1]**
3 **3** *1 3/4* **Daddy's Gift (IRE)**[14] 1680 2-8-7 0.................................. DaneO'Neill 6 69
(R Hannon) *chsd ldrs: rdn 2f out: kpt on same pce fnl f: nvr able to chal* **7/1[3]**
34 **4** *1* **Kingswinford (IRE)**[23] 1474 2-8-12 0.................................. TGMcLaughlin 3 70
(P D Evans) *led to over 3f out: pressed ldr to over 1f out: edgd lft and fdd* **8/1**
5 *3 1/2* **Meirig's Dream (IRE)** 2-8-12 0.................................. TQuinn 5 58
(B G Powell) *sn chsd along to stay in tch: no imp on ldrs fr 1/2-way* **50/1**
6 *1/2* **Zezao** 2-8-12 0.................................. AlanMunro 4 56
(B J Meehan) *s.s: rn v green and wl off the pce: modest late prog* **14/1**
7 *2 3/4* **Canadian Rockie (USA)** 2-8-12 0.................................. JimCrowley 7 46
(D K Ivory) *dwlt: rn green and nvr on terms: no prog fnl 2f* **25/1**
5 **8** *9* **Ready To Prime**[12] 1722 2-8-7 0.................................. HayleyTurner 2 8
(D K Ivory) *dwlt: rn v green and sn bhd: t.o* **40/1**
60.88 secs (0.58) **Going Correction** 0.0s/f (Good) **8** Ran SP% **114.9**
Speed ratings (Par 95): **95,93,90,88,83 82,77,63**
CSF £4.69 TOTE £2.90: £1.10, £1.40, £1.30; EX 5.00.
Owner Amblestock Partnership **Bred** Mrs T Brudenell **Trained** East Everleigh, Wilts

FOCUS
This is often a good little event but there were no previous winners in it this year. The right sort of horses were involved in the finish and the form is rated around the runner-up and fourth.

NOTEBOOK
River Rye(IRE) confirmed the promise she showed when fifth in a good fillies' maiden on her debut at Newmarket, but she was made to work hard enough. She was off the bridle much sooner than the favourite, but responded to pressure and, despite showing her inexperience close home, wandering around a bit and bumping the eventual runner-up, she was well on top at the line. This was an ordinary race, but there should be more to come. (op 15-8 tchd 13-8 and 2-1 in places)
Every Second ran his race in second without appearing to improve a great deal on the form he showed when second on his debut. A proper sprinting type on looks, he showed bags of early speed, but could never get away from River Rye once let down and, being a son of Kyllachy, this ground was probably a little quicker than he really wants. (op 13-8 tchd 2-1 in places)
Daddy's Gift(IRE) confirmed the ability she showed when third over course and distance on her debut, but the front two were basically too good. (tchd 13-2)
Kingswinford(IRE) had shown ability on his first two starts, but he was the least appealing of these in the paddock - there is not a lot of him - and he found a few too good. He appeals as one to keep opposing. (op 15-2)
Meirig's Dream(IRE), a son of Golan, out of a triple 1m-1m1f winner at three, was coltish in the paddock, but he showed ability. He should make a fair type over further with the benefit of time.
Zezao, a 36,000gns of Fasliyev, out of a mare who was unplaced over 1m1f-1m4f, ran green throughout and will have learnt plenty. Official explanation: jockey said colt ran green (op 16-1)
Canadian Rockie(USA), a £9,000 gelded son of US Grade 3 winner Canadian Frontier, half-brother to Midnight Tornado, a dirt sprint winner at three in Canada, out of a triple dirt winner at around 6f-1m1f in the US, looked in need of the run in the paddock and was green in the race itself. He should do okay in time.
Ready To Prime did not show much on her debut at Great Leighs, and she was again well held, still looking very inexperienced, but she was one of the nicer types to look at and might be capable of better at some point. Official explanation: jockey said filly hung left-handed throughout

2043 GRAEME LOVE MEMORIAL H'CAP — 1m 2f 7y

6:25 (6:26) (Class 5) (0-75,73) 3-Y-O **£3,070** (£906; £453) **Stalls** Centre

Form RPR
40-0 **1** **Excape (IRE)**[16] 1622 3-8-7 65..................................(b[1]) MarcHalford(3) 12 84+
(D R C Elsworth) *t.k.h: pressed ldng pair: nt clr run and lost pl 3f out: effrt again to chal over 1f out: edgd lft but led wl ins fnl f* **25/1**
03-5 **2** *nk* **Mezzanisi (IRE)**[34] 1252 3-8-13 68.................................. HayleyTurner 14 82
(M L W Bell) *hld up in rr: stdy prog fr 3f out: rdn to ld over 1f out: hung fire in front: hdd wl ins fnl f: jst hld after* **7/1[3]**
01-0 **3** *2* **Any Given Day (IRE)**[27] 1389 3-8-9 64.................................. RichardMullen 8 74
(D M Simcock) *trckd ldrs: rdn 3f out: prog and cl up 2f out: kpt on same pce* **17/2**
5-15 **4** *6* **Golden Penny**[14] 1685 3-9-1 70.................................. SteveDrowne 1 68
(H Morrison) *trckd ldrs: effrt to chal over 2f out: nt qckn over 1f out: wknd* **9/2[1]**
1-05 **5** *1 3/4* **Moment's Notice**[14] 1681 3-8-9 69.................................. HaddenFrost(5) 15 64
(S Kirk) *mostly in midfield: drvn 3f out: edgd towards centre over 2f out: no imp over 1f out: wknd* **12/1**
00-0 **6** *1 1/4* **Houri (IRE)**[13] 1695 3-9-3 72.................................. JamesDoyle 4 64
(R M Beckett) *pressed ldr: rdn wl over 2f out: wknd fr over 1f out* **14/1**
03-3 **7** *2 1/4* **Bikini**[21] 1525 3-9-3 72.................................. DaneO'Neill 5 60
(H Candy) *mde most to over 2f out: wknd rapidly fnl f* **9/2[1]**
60-1 **8** *3/4* **Classical Rhythm (IRE)**[20] 1540 3-8-11 66.................................. DavidKinsella 7 52
(J R Boyle) *hld up towards rr: prog on outer 3f out: rdn and wknd over 1f out* **6/1[2]**
52-3 **9** *1 1/4* **Locum**[45] 1057 3-8-7 67.................................. NicolPolli(5) 13 51
(M H Tompkins) *hld up in midfield: effrt on wd outside 3f out: no prog wl over 1f out: wknd* **8/1**
400- **10** *2 1/4* **Bozeman Trail**[187] 6715 3-8-9 64.................................. TQuinn 16 43
(P F I Cole) *nvr beyond midfield: rdn and wknd over 2f out* **16/1**
00-0 **11** *2 1/2* **Fiume**[21] 1526 3-9-3 72.................................. RyanMoore 9 46
(R Hannon) *dwlt: mostly in last pair: rdn 4f out: struggling after* **8/1**
00-0 **12** *1/2* **Cheviot Red**[25] 1423 3-8-11 66.................................. AlanMunro 2 39
(B J Meehan) *hld up: a in last pair: struggling 3f out* **40/1**
0-36 **13** *3/4* **Nikolaievich (IRE)**[19] 1563 3-8-10 65.................................. NelsonDeSouza 3 37
(P F I Cole) *in tch in midfield tl wknd 3f out* **25/1**
2m 5.20s (-3.50) **Going Correction** -0.375s/f (Firm) **13** Ran SP% **126.3**
Speed ratings (Par 99): **99,98,97,92,90 89,88,87,86,84 82,82,81**
CSF £199.03 CT £1654.09 TOTE £21.80: £4.80, £2.70, £2.60; EX 110.20.
Owner Raymond Tooth **Bred** Kildaragh Stud **Trained** Newmarket, Suffolk

FOCUS
A fair three-year-old handicap and the winning time was good, 1.61 seconds quicker than the later maiden. The first three finished clear and a fairly positive view has been taken of the form.

2044 EXTRABET STKS (REGISTERED AS THE ROYAL WINDSOR STAKES) (LISTED RACE) (C&G) — 1m 67y

6:55 (6:55) (Class 1) 3-Y-O+
£14,760 (£5,595; £2,800; £1,396; £699; £351) **Stalls** High

Form RPR
25-5 **1** **Ordnance Row**[12] 1716 5-9-2 105.................................. RyanMoore 6 110
(R Hannon) *trckd ldr: rdn to cl fr over 2f out: led narrowly ins fnl f: hld on wl* **7/1**
420- **2** *1/2* **Dunelight (IRE)**[219] 6009 5-9-6 109..................................(v) AdamKirby 7 113
(C G Cox) *led: drew 3 l clr over 3f out: pressed over 1f out: hdd ins fnl f: styd on* **10/3[3]**
-523 **3** *1 3/4* **Metropolitan Man**[16] 1631 5-9-2 110.................................. RichardMullen 3 105
(D M Simcock) *hld up in 6th: stdy prog to cl on ldrs 2f out: hanging and nt qckn over 1f out: kpt on* **15/8[1]**
650- **4** *3/4* **Banknote**[170] 6931 6-9-2 108.................................. FrancisNorton 5 103
(A M Balding) *sn t.k.h in 3rd: rdn over 2f out: nt qckn wl over 1f out: one pce* **3/1[2]**
-006 **5** *3/4* **Final Verse**[74] 743 5-9-2 100.................................. JohnEgan 1 102
(Jane Chapple-Hyam) *hld up bhd ldrs: rdn over 2f out: one pce and no imp* **14/1**
40 **6** *1/2* **Classic Port (FR)**[51] 960 4-9-2 100.................................. TGMcLaughlin 2 100
(M Wigham) *dwlt: settled in last: effrt over 2f out: hanging fr over 1f out: kpt on same pce* **33/1**
000- **7** *2* **Levera**[234] 5588 5-9-2 103.................................. DaneO'Neill 4 96
(A King) *hld up bhd ldrs: rdn over 2f out: lost pl sn after: fdd* **12/1**
1m 41.1s (-3.60) **Going Correction** -0.375s/f (Firm) **7** Ran SP% **112.7**
Speed ratings (Par 111): **103,102,100,100,99 98,96**
CSF £29.55 TOTE £6.90: £2.70, £2.40; EX 18.90.
Owner Mrs P Good **Bred** Mrs P Good **Trained** East Everleigh, Wilts

FOCUS
The runner-up is the best guide to the form of this Listed race. The winning time was 2.81 seconds quicker than the later 56-70 handicap despite Dunelight setting only a modest pace. Nothing got into this from off the speed.

NOTEBOOK
Ordnance Row had previously saved his best for an easy surface - his best five RPRs coming into this were gained on ground good to soft or softer - but he handled the quick conditions well and was able to gain his first success at this level. He allowed Dunelight to go off in a clear lead, but was never too far off that rival and stayed on best in the straight. (op 8-1 tchd 13-2)
Dunelight(IRE), returning from seven months off, was allowed his own way in front and enjoyed himself, travelling strongly into the straight having set no more than a fair pace. His lack of a recent run told late on, though, and he was eventually pegged back. (op 7-2)
Metropolitan Man could not repeat the form he showed when third in a Group 2 at Sandown on his previous start and is a difficult horse to win with. (tchd 7-4 and 2-1)
Banknote won a Listed race on the Polytrack and a Group 3 in Germany last year, but he was too keen for his own good after nearly six months off. (op 10-3 tchd 7-2)
Final Verse, having his first start for Jane Chapple-Hyam after over two months off, had conditions to suit, but he has yet to show his best at Windsor and the course probably doesn't suit, as he likes to chase an end-to-end gallop. (op 16-1)
Classic Port(FR) ran a stinker in the Lincoln on his previous start, which was particularly disappointing considering he had shaped so well in the trial for that race at Wolverhampton, but this was a lot better. This was a little surprising, as he had previously looked to be a soft-ground horse. (op 28-1 tchd 50-1)
Levera did not offer a great deal on his return from 234 days off and seems to have lost his way. (op 16-1)

2045 TONY BRETT BIRTHDAY H'CAP — 1m 3f 135y

7:25 (7:25) (Class 5) (0-75,75) 3-Y-O **£3,070** (£906; £453) **Stalls** Centre

Form RPR
001- **1** **Sleepy Hollow**[207] 6285 3-8-11 68.................................. SteveDrowne 7 83+
(H Morrison) *hld up bhd ldrs: got through on inner and led wl over 1f out: sn drew clr: easily* **9/2[1]**
06-6 **2** *2 1/4* **It's My Day (IRE)**[20] 1543 3-8-9 66.................................. JohnEgan 9 72
(Jane Chapple-Hyam) *hld up in last pair: prog on outer and nt clr run briefly over 2f out: chsd wnr over 1f out: styd on wl but no ch* **10/1**
-623 **3** *2 3/4* **King Supreme (IRE)**[14] 1681 3-8-8 65..................................(b[1]) PatDobbs 3 67
(R Hannon) *trckd ldrs: rdn to chal over 2f out: upsides wl over 1f out: sn outpcd* **8/1**
06-4 **4** *1* **Dancing Dik**[20] 1530 3-8-9 66.................................. JimCrowley 8 68+
(Mrs A J Perrett) *trckd ldrs: rdn 3f out: cl up wl over 1f out: sn outpcd* **7/1**
216 **5** *1/2* **Red Linnet**[16] 1618 3-9-4 75.................................. HayleyTurner 1 74
(M L W Bell) *hld up towards rr: rdn and effrt over 2f out: kpt on one pce and n.d* **12/1**
60-6 **6** *nk* **Love And Glory (FR)**[20] 1530 3-8-4 61.................................. TPO'Shea 4 60
(G L Moore) *hld up towards rr: lost pl 3f out and sn last: swtchd to wd outside over 1f out: shuffled along and styd on steadily: nvr nr ldrs* **20/1**
3-15 **7** *3/4* **Warming Up (IRE)**[35] 1244 3-8-9 66.................................. SebSanders 10 64
(C E Brittain) *hld up in rr: effrt against nr side rail over 2f out: outpcd over 1f out* **9/1**
0-54 **8** *1* **Hadron Collider (FR)**[13] 1696 3-8-12 69.................................. RyanMoore 2 65
(R Hannon) *mostly trckd ldr: rdn to chal over 2f out: wknd over 1f out* **5/1[2]**
05-0 **9** *2 1/4* **No Rules**[34] 1252 3-8-0 62.................................. NicolPolli(5) 11 54
(M H Tompkins) *sweating: trckd ldrs: lost pl u.p 2f out: sn btn* **16/1**

1-14 **10** *1 1/4* **Animator**[16] 1618 3-9-4 **75** TQuinn 12 65
(P F I Cole) *mde most to wl over 1f out: sn wknd* **11/2**[3]
-555 **11** *1 1/4* **Landikhaya (IRE)**[21] 1527 3-8-7 **64** AlanMunro 6 52
(D K Ivory) *hld up wl in rr: prog on wd outside over 2f out: cl enough wl over 1f out: sn wknd* **12/1**
540 **12** *nk* **Mganga**[20] 1530 3-8-4 **61** oh1 CatherineGannon 5 49
(M R Channon) *hld up in last: prog on outer 4f out: on terms w ldrs jst over 2f out: wknd over 1f out* **25/1**
2m 25.26s (-4.24) **Going Correction** -0.375s/f (Firm) **12** Ran SP% **122.8**
Speed ratings (Par 99): **99,97,95,95,94 94,93,93,91,90 90,89**
CSF £51.69 CT £360.32 TOTE £4.80: £2.10, £4.30, £3.60; EX 98.90.
Owner Lady Blyth **Bred** Stowell Hill Ltd **Trained** East Ilsley, Berks
FOCUS
A fair handicap. The winner was value for double the actual margin and this is solid form.
Animator Official explanation: jockey said gelding lost its action

2046 GET A BONUS @ WILLIAMHILLPOKER.COM MEDIAN AUCTION MAIDEN STKS 1m 2f 7y
7:55 (7:57) (Class 5) 3-5-Y-O **£2,729** (£806; £403) **Stalls** Centre

Form RPR
2-03 **1** **Seattle Storm (IRE)**[14] 1686 3-8-13 76 SebSanders 9 79+
(D R C Elsworth) *hld up towards rr: stdy prog fr 3f out: rdn to ld 1f out: edgd rt and drvn out* **13/8**[1]
4 **2** *3/4* **Qui Moi (CAN)**[35] 1243 3-8-8 0 JamieSpencer 14 72
(J R Fanshawe) *t.k.h: prom: wandering but led 2f out: hdd 1f out: kpt on wl but hld nr fin* **7/1**
42-2 **3** *nk* **Brexca (IRE)**[13] 1695 3-8-13 79 (b[1]) AdamKirby 7 77
(C G Cox) *led: hung lft 3f out: sn hdd and nt qckn: rallied over 1f out: styd on but a hld* **5/2**[2]
2-35 **4** *1 3/4* **King Kenny**[12] 1728 3-8-13 74 JohnEgan 2 73
(S Parr) *t.k.h: trckd ldr after 2f: hung lft 3f out but sn led: drvn and hdd 2f out: fdd fnl f* **11/2**[3]
5 **5** *3* **Solas Alainn (IRE)**[23] 1477 3-8-13 0 RyanMoore 5 67+
(J R Fanshawe) *dwlt: hld up in last pair: hanging but sme prog fr over 2f out: shkn up and kpt on: nrst fin* **20/1**
00-6 **6** *1/2* **Timber Creek**[14] 1684 3-8-13 68 DaneO'Neill 10 66
(H Candy) *trckd ldrs: shkn up briefly 2f out and sn outpcd: kpt on one pce after* **16/1**
0 **7** *3/4* **Don't Stop Me Now (IRE)**[19] 1563 3-8-8 0 TQuinn 8 60
(J W Hills) *trckd ldr 2f: styd prom and t.k.h: lost pl fr 2f out* **20/1**
8 *1 1/4* **Beau Fighter** 3-8-13 0 IanMongan 6 62
(C F Wall) *dwlt: hld up towards rr: in tch over 2f out: sn outpcd* **22/1**
0 **9** *2 3/4* **Silver Willow**[22] 1504 3-8-3 0 NicolPolli(5) 11 52
(Miss Gay Kelleway) *nvr gng wl: rdn in rr over 4f out: sn btn* **33/1**
-00 **10** *hd* **Looping The Loop (USA)**[23] 1467 3-8-13 0 JimCrowley 13 56
(J G Portman) *hld up wl in rr: brief effrt on outer 3f out: wknd 2f out* **50/1**
11 *6* **Ubiquitous** 3-8-8 0 JamesDoyle 3 39
(S Dow) *trckd ldrs tl wknd over 2f out* **66/1**
00 **12** *30* **Little Rococoa**[13] 1695 3-8-10 0 RussellKennemore(3) 1 —
(R J Price) *a wl in rr: wknd over 2f out: t.o* **150/1**
2m 6.81s (-1.89) **Going Correction** -0.375s/f (Firm) **12** Ran SP% **121.4**
Speed ratings (Par 103): **92,91,91,89,87 86,86,85,83,83 78,54**
CSF £13.25 TOTE £2.90: £1.10, £2.30, £1.60; EX 15.20.
Owner J C Smith **Bred** Littleton Stud **Trained** Newmarket, Suffolk
FOCUS
An ordinary maiden run in a time 1.61 seconds slower than the 61-75 three-year-old handicap. The winner was probably better than the bare result in coming from off the pace but there are reservations about the form.

2047 SPORTING LIFE 10 YEAR ANNIVERSARY H'CAP 1m 67y
8:25 (8:25) (Class 5) (0-70,70) 3-Y-O **£2,729** (£806; £403) **Stalls** High

Form RPR
-011 **1** **Topazes**[11] 1740 3-9-4 **70** JamieSpencer 12 78+
(M L W Bell) *hld up in midfield: trckd ldrs over 2f out: swtchd lft and effrt over 1f out: drvn to ld ent fnl f: hld on* **5/2**[1]
05-3 **2** *1/2* **Tina's Best (IRE)**[11] 1738 3-9-2 **68** RyanMoore 13 75
(R Hannon) *trckd ldrs: effrt 2f out: drvn to press wnr fnl f: styd on but jst hld* **9/2**[3]
2-60 **3** *2* **Feasible**[16] 1622 3-9-1 **67** JamesDoyle 5 69
(J G Portman) *led for 3f: rdn to ld again jst over 1f out: hdd and one pce ent fnl f* **16/1**
30-0 **4** *3 1/4* **Danamight (IRE)**[16] 1622 3-8-12 **64** RichardMullen 1 59+
(J L Dunlop) *s.i.s: hld up in last pair: sme prog 3f out but nt on terms: rdn and styd on fnl 2f: nt pce to rch ldrs* **16/1**
3320 **5** *1 1/2* **Calistos Quest**[20] 1540 3-9-3 **69** (t) SebSanders 3 60
(M Botti) *led after 3f to jst over 2f out: styd on terms tl wknd jst over 1f out* **8/1**
-312 **6** *1 1/4* **Bury Treasure (IRE)**[91] 527 3-9-1 **67** AdamKirby 9 56
(Miss Gay Kelleway) *prom: drvn over 3f out: steadily lost pl fr over 2f out* **4/1**[2]
00-5 **7** *1 3/4* **Better In Heaven**[13] 1695 3-9-1 **67** SteveDrowne 6 58+
(H J L Dunlop) *hld up towards rr: nt clr run and snatched up over 2f out: n.m.r sn after: no ch* **12/1**
000- **8** *3/4* **Presto Levanter**[255] 5008 3-9-1 **67** PatDobbs 14 50
(R Hannon) *hld up in midfield: rdn and effrt over 2f out: no imp over 1f out: wknd fnl f* **16/1**
033- **9** *3 1/4* **Creative (IRE)**[222] 5901 3-8-9 **68** AshleyMorgan(7) 7 43
(M H Tompkins) *hld up in last trio: shkn up 3f out: no real prog* **20/1**
600- **10** *1/2* **Latin Scholar (IRE)**[256] 4964 3-9-2 **68** DaneO'Neill 8 42
(A King) *a towards rr: rdn and no prog wl over 2f out* **12/1**
064- **11** *3/4* **Bainisteoir**[190] 6675 3-8-10 **67** HaddenFrost(5) 10 40
(S Kirk) *chsd ldrs: rdn 3f out: veered rt u.p 2f out: wknd* **20/1**
440- **12** *3 1/2* **Langham House**[195] 6572 3-9-2 **68** JimCrowley 2 32
(J R Jenkins) *hld up in last trio: taken to wd outside 3f out: no prog whn bmpd over 1f out: wknd* **33/1**
1m 43.91s (-0.79) **Going Correction** -0.375s/f (Firm) **12** Ran SP% **123.4**
Speed ratings (Par 99): **88,87,85,82,80 79,77,77,73,73 72,69**
CSF £13.52 CT £158.08 TOTE £3.20: £1.50, £2.20, £4.60; EX 8.60 Place 6 £133.69, Place 5 £118.86..
Owner Baron F C Oppenheim **Bred** Baron F Von Oppenheim **Trained** Newmarket, Suffolk
■ Stewards' Enquiry : Jamie Spencer one-day ban: excessive use of the whip (May 26)
FOCUS
A modest handicap and it is doubtful whether Topazes had to improve. The winning time was 2.81 seconds slower than the earlier Listed race.
Better In Heaven Official explanation: jockey said colt was denied a clear run
T/Plt: £74.30 to a £1 stake. Pool: £75,058.35. 736.82 winning tickets. T/Qpdt: £9.40 to a £1 stake. Pool: £4,394.08. 343.70 winning tickets. JN

1706 WOLVERHAMPTON (A.W) (L-H)
Monday, May 12

OFFICIAL GOING: Standard
Wind: moderate, half against

2048 BOOK ONLINE AT WOLVERHAMPTON-RACECOURSE.CO.UK MAIDEN AUCTION FILLIES' STKS 5f 20y(P)
2:10 (2:11) (Class 5) 2-Y-O **£2,914** (£867; £433; £216) **Stalls** Low

Form RPR
1 **Glorious Dreams (USA)** 2-8-3 0 WilliamBuick(3) 12 72+
(T J Pitt) *mde all: rdn clr over 1f out: unchal* **16/1**
2 *2* **Calahonda** 2-8-6 0 JohnEgan 1 65
(P W D'Arcy) *mid-div: rdn and hdwy on ins over 1f out: r.o to chse wnr ins fnl f* **11/2**[3]
5 **3** *3/4* **The Magic Of Rio**[16] 1627 2-8-12 0 MichaelHills 5 68
(W J Haggas) *in tch: rdn 2f out: kpt on to go 3rd ins fnl f* **9/2**[1]
434 **4** *1 3/4* **Transcentral**[21] 1515 2-8-4 0 TPO'Shea 6 54
(W M Brisbourne) *trckd wnr tl rdn and one pce ins fnl f* **9/2**[1]
0 **5** *1 1/2* **Meydan Groove**[14] 1680 2-8-9 0 TQuinn 10 53
(P F I Cole) *in tch on outside: effrt over 1f out: one pce after* **5/1**[2]
6 *nk* **Hip Hip Hooray** 2-8-8 0 ow1 StephenDonohoe 9 51
(E S McMahon) *slowly away: outpcd: mde sme late hdwy* **9/1**
56 **7** *1 1/4* **Premier Krug (IRE)**[7] 1851 2-8-12 0 TGMcLaughlin 2 51
(P D Evans) *sn outpcd: a bhd* **12/1**
0 **8** *1 3/4* **Lislin**[13] 1693 2-8-7 0 RichardKingscote 8 40
(S Kirk) *chsd ldrs tl rdn and wknd 2f out* **14/1**
0 **9** *2* **Caressing**[13] 1693 2-8-10 0 RyanMoore 11 35
(R Hannon) *outpcd: a bhd* **5/1**[2]
10 *1 1/4* **Peckforton** 2-8-8 0 PatCosgrave 4 29
(D J G Murray Smith) *slowly away: a outpcd* **33/1**
04 **11** *5* **Especially For You (IRE)**[10] 1778 2-8-10 0 ChrisCatlin 3 13
(E J O'Neill) *trckd ldrs tl rdn and wknd wl over 1f out* **10/1**
63.71 secs (1.41) **Going Correction** +0.125s/f (Slow) **11** Ran SP% **127.4**
Speed ratings (Par 90): **93,89,88,85,83 82,80,78,74,72 64**
CSF £110.05 TOTE £21.90: £8.60, £2.50, £2.60; EX 196.90.
Owner Kelly, O'Donnell, Dower & Kelly **Bred** Stewart L Armstrong **Trained** Norton, N Yorks
■ William Buick rode out his claim with this winner.
FOCUS
The fastest time of the three 5f sprints on the card but probably only modest form nonetheless. Two of the four debutantes filled the first two placings.
NOTEBOOK
Glorious Dreams(USA) bounced out of the stalls and didn't see another horse throughout. She looks distinctly speedy and could be a useful prospect. Her sire is not that well known in this country but his progeny do well in the US, where he stands in Kentucky for $7,500. (op 14-1)
Calahonda, by first-season sire Haafhd, did well as her pedigree suggests that she will do better over further. (tchd 6-1)
The Magic Of Rio again ran as though she would appreciate the extra furlong, for all that her pedigree shouts speed. (op 4-1)
Transcentral was having her fourth run and isn't progressing with racing. (op 13-2)
Meydan Groove is surely one of her stable's lesser lights on the evidence of her two starts so far. (op 13-2 tchd 7-1 and 9-2)
Hip Hip Hooray missed the break and ran green but made headway once the penny dropped and can leave this form far behind her next time. (op 15-2)

2049 STAY AT THE WOLVERHAMPTON HOLIDAY INN CLAIMING STKS 5f 20y(P)
2:40 (2:40) (Class 6) 2-Y-O **£2,729** (£806; £403) **Stalls** Low

Form RPR
1 **1** **Fangfoss Girls**[23] 1480 2-8-6 0 CatherineGannon 4 75+
(P D Evans) *mde all: wnt clr over 1f out: easily* **3/1**[2]
24 **2** *7* **Sub Prime (IRE)**[30] 1341 2-9-2 0 ShaneKelly 6 60
(J A Osborne) *trckd ldrs: rdn to chse wnr wl over 1f out but nt pce to chal* **9/4**[1]
0 **3** *5* **Makaluna**[27] 1384 2-8-3 0 JackDean(5) 2 34
(W G M Turner) *chsd wnr tl wl over 1f out: no hdwy after* **12/1**
055 **4** *1/2* **Multi Tasker**[11] 1736 2-8-7 0 ChrisCatlin 3 31
(V Smith) *mid-div: rdn 1/2-way: nvr on terms after* **3/1**[2]
5 **5** *1 1/2* **Sweet Mujahid**[19] 1555 2-8-8 0 JohnEgan 7 27
(R A Harris) *in tch: rdn 1/2-way: wknd over 1f out* **10/1**
6 *1 3/4* **The Wonkey Donkey** 2-7-10 0 ow1 SophieDoyle(7) 5 16
(K J Burke) *s.i.s: wl bhd tl hdwy over 1f out but nvr on terms* **20/1**
40 **7** *nse* **Forzando Bloom**[10] 1778 2-8-5 0 KevinGhunowa(3) 1 20
(R A Harris) *a in rr* **16/1**
8 *1 1/4* **Speak The Truth (IRE)** 2-9-2 0 PatCosgrave 9 24
(J R Boyle) *towards rr: effrt on outside over 2f out: wknd over 1f out* **8/1**[3]
64.12 secs (1.82) **Going Correction** +0.125s/f (Slow) **8** Ran SP% **119.3**
Speed ratings (Par 91): **90,78,70,70,67 64,64,62**
CSF £10.74 TOTE £4.80: £1.90, £1.10, £4.00; EX 9.70.Fangfoss Girls was claimed by Mr D. Hassan for £9,000.
Owner Diamond Racing Ltd **Bred** Bond Thoroughbred Corporation **Trained** Pandy, Monmouths
FOCUS
Just a claimer but the winner clocked a time under half a second slower than the winner of the 2-y-o maiden, which considering the ease of her victory, and the fact that she carried 3lb more, probably makes her worth rating a fair bit better than the average 2-y-o claimer winner, certainly at this track.
NOTEBOOK
Fangfoss Girls ◆ is all speed and turned this contest into a procession. She is well worth supporting next time before the later-maturing types catch up with her. (op 11-4)
Sub Prime(IRE) has now been turned over as favourite on his last two starts, but if one takes the winner away, then he himself has fairly hosed up. He isn't much, but probably deserves to win one of these now. (tchd 2-1 and 5-2)
Makaluna was beaten further here than when only seventh of eight at Warwick on his debut. (op 20-1)
Multi Tasker is beginning to look no better than a plater. (op 11-4 tchd 5-2)
The Wonkey Donkey missed the break and got herself well behind before passing a couple of beaten horses late on. She is sure to learn from this experience. (op 22-1 tchd 25-1)

2050 HORIZONS RESTAURANT CLAIMING STKS 5f 20y(P)
3:10 (3:10) (Class 6) 3-Y-O+ **£2,047** (£604; £302) **Stalls** Low

Form RPR
1213 **1** **Dodaa (USA)**[38] 1185 5-9-7 70 AshleyHamblett(5) 6 73
(N Wilson) *mde all: rdn over 1f out: hld on wl* **2/1**[2]
053 **2** *1/2* **Night Prospector**[15] 1642 8-9-0 51 (p) JohnEgan 5 59
(R A Harris) *chsd ldrs: rdn and edgd lft bef kpt on to go 2nd ins fnl f* **6/1**[3]

211- **3** *hd* **Lady Bahia (IRE)**[413] 787 7-9-3 66 AdamKirby 2 61
(Peter Grayson) *awkward s: rr tl hdwy 1/2-way: hung lft appr fnl f: kpt on* **13/2**

-313 **4** *hd* **Desperate Dan**[15] 1646 7-9-12 78 (b) SebSanders 1 73+
(A B Haynes) *s.i.s: hdwy whn nt clr run on ins fnl f: r.o again towards fin* **6/4**[1]

4425 **5** *2* **Lady Hopeful (IRE)**[23] 1489 6-8-7 45 (b) ChrisCatlin 4 44
(Peter Grayson) *s.i.s: in rr: rdn and swtchd rt over 1f out: nvr on terms* **16/1**

0-01 **6** *4 1/2* **Hamaasy**[18] 1588 7-9-1 59 KevinGhunowa(3) 7 38
(R A Harris) *trckd wnr tl rdn and wknd qckly over 1f out* **8/1**

64.14 secs (1.84) **Going Correction** +0.125s/f (Slow)
WFA 3 from 5yo+ 9lb 6 Ran SP% **117.9**
Speed ratings (Par 101): **90,89,88,88,85 78**
CSF £15.23 TOTE £3.10: £1.60, £1.70; EX 15.60.
Owner Paul & Linda Dixon **Bred** Silverleaf Farm Inc **Trained** Flaxton, N Yorks

FOCUS
Dodaa became the third horse to make all over 5f on the afternoon. The time was relatively slow and he did not need to run to his best.

2051 WOLVERHAMPTON-RACECOURSE.CO.UK H'CAP 1m 5f 194y(P)
3:40 (3:40) (Class 6) (0-65,69) 4-Y-0+ **£2,729** (£806; £403) **Stalls** Low

Form RPR

53-1 **1** **Me Fein**[60] 863 4-9-8 **63** ShaneKelly 7 78+
(A P Stringer) *a in tch: shkn up over 1f out: r.o to ld ins fnl f* **13/8**[1]

-006 **2** *1 1/4* **Hugs Destiny (IRE)**[30] 1340 7-7-12 **45** (t) SophieDoyle(7) 1 54
(M A Barnes) *led: rdn 3f out: hdd ins fnl f: no ex* **20/1**

0341 **3** *2 1/4* **Sovietta (IRE)**[54] 930 7-8-10 **50** (t) StephenDonohoe 12 56
(Ian Williams) *in tch: wnt 2nd 2f out: no ex ins fnl f* **11/1**

66-6 **4** *1 1/2* **Adage**[38] 1181 5-9-6 **60** (t) NeilChalmers 8 64
(David Pinder) *in tch: rdn 4f out: hdwy whn edgd lft ent fnl f: no ex* **6/1**[3]

-063 **5** *2* **Bobsleigh**[7] 1856 9-8-5 **45** TPO'Shea 5 46
(H S Howe) *trckd ldrs: rdn and wknd ent fnl f* **8/1**

0011 **6** *3/4* **Cavendish**[6] 1892 4-9-7 **69** 6ex (b) BMcHugh(7) 3 69
(J M P Eustace) *mid-div: rdn 3f out: sn btn* **7/2**[2]

0000 **7** *3 1/2* **Three Thieves (UAE)**[78] 695 5-8-8 **48** FrancisNorton 10 43
(M S Saunders) *trckd ldrs tl rdn and wknd over 1f out* **12/1**

630- **8** *5* **Swords**[313] 3217 6-8-13 **53** ChrisCatlin 11 41
(R E Peacock) *t.k.h in mid-div: effrt on outside over 2f out: sn wknd* **12/1**

05-0 **9** *2 1/2* **Finished Article (IRE)**[35] 1246 11-8-5 **45** (t) SimonWhitworth 2 30
(Mrs D Thomas) *towards rr: rdn 4f out: nvr on terms* **50/1**

-310 **10** *4* **Tioga Gold (IRE)**[85] 600 9-8-2 **49** MatthewDavies(7) 13 28
(L R James) *slowly away: a towards rr* **20/1**

2-06 **11** *1* **Saloon (USA)**[26] 1408 4-9-5 **60** PaulDoe 6 38
(S Curran) *a bhd* **7/1**

10-0 **12** *21* **Lady Pickpocket**[40] 1136 4-8-2 **46** ow1 (b) AndrewMullen(3) 4 —
(F P Murtagh) *in rr: lost tch over 4f out: t.o* **33/1**

3m 10.35s (4.35) **Going Correction** +0.125s/f (Slow)
WFA 4 from 5yo+ 1lb 12 Ran SP% **136.4**
Speed ratings (Par 101): **92,91,90,89,88 87,85,82,81,79 78,66**
CSF £49.35 CT £326.41 TOTE £3.30: £1.50, £4.30, £3.70; EX 72.20.
Owner Curley Leisure **Bred** Irish National Stud **Trained** Newmarket, Suffolk

FOCUS
There are no shrewder connections in the country than the winner's and with the money down he showed himself to be a cut above these exposed stayers with a comfortable success. This was slowly run and the form is potentially weak, though.
Saloon(USA) Official explanation: jockey said gelding finished distressed

2052 NAME A RACE TO ENHANCE YOUR BRAND FILLIES' H'CAP 1m 141y(P)
4:10 (4:10) (Class 5) (0-70,70) 3-Y-0 **£3,238** (£963; £481; £240) **Stalls** Low

Form RPR

660- **1** **Reclamation (IRE)**[202] 6414 3-8-13 **65** SebSanders 6 76+
(Sir Mark Prescott) *in tch: hdwy to go 2nd 3f out: sn led: hdd briefly 1f out: rallied to ld again ins fnl f* **4/1**[2]

5-40 **2** *nk* **Queen's Speech (IRE)**[21] 1525 3-9-4 **70** RobertHavlin 11 80
(J H M Gosden) *hld up: hdwy on outside 3f out: led briefly 1f out: no ex nr fin* **8/1**

421- **3** *2 3/4* **Ogre (USA)**[152] 7117 3-9-1 **67** PatCosgrave 4 75+
(J R Boyle) *trckd ldrs tl lost pl 3f out: hdwy whn edgd rt over 1f out: kpt on to go 3rd fnl f* **8/1**

004- **4** *4* **Flower**[200] 6448 3-8-9 **61** MichaelHills 2 56+
(W J Haggas) *t.k.h: hld up: hdwy on outside over 2f out: carried rt over 1f out: kpt on one pce fnl f* **3/1**[1]

-053 **5** *shd* **Double On Red**[13] 1696 3-8-9 **61** ShaneKelly 8 56
(J M P Eustace) *in rr: hdwy on outside over 2f out: styd on but nt pce to rch ldrs* **8/1**

32-3 **6** *3 3/4* **Pharaohs Queen (IRE)**[32] 1279 3-9-4 **70** StephenDonohoe 1 56
(E A L Dunlop) *in rr: rdn 3f out: nvr nr to chal* **7/1**[3]

40-5 **7** *1 3/4* **Italian Goddess**[26] 1397 3-9-1 **67** RichardKingscote 13 49
(M L W Bell) *sn led: hdd over 2f out: wknd over 1f out* **14/1**

06-3 **8** *1 1/2* **Star Grazer**[80] 665 3-8-4 **61** JackMitchell(5) 3 39
(C F Wall) *mid-div: rdn 3f out: n.d after* **9/1**

3-23 **9** *1/2* **Dream Sea**[38] 1176 3-9-1 **67** ChrisCatlin 12 44
(M R Channon) *mid-div: hdwy 5f out: rdn and wknd wl over 1f out* **8/1**

42-4 **10** *10* **Sunshine Lady (IRE)**[111] 262 3-8-7 **59** FrancisNorton 9 13
(D Haydn Jones) *in tch: rdn over 3f out: wknd over 2f out* **18/1**

2260 **11** *12* **Inontime (IRE)**[37] 1222 3-9-0 **66** DarrenWilliams 5 —
(K R Burke) *trckd ldr tl rdn over 2f out: sn wknd* **40/1**

1m 52.57s (2.07) **Going Correction** +0.125s/f (Slow) 11 Ran SP% **126.3**
Speed ratings (Par 96): **95,94,92,88,88 85,83,82,81,73 62**
CSF £39.27 CT £260.64 TOTE £5.20: £1.50, £4.00, £3.10; EX 56.00.
Owner Sir Edmund Loder **Bred** Sir E J Loder **Trained** Newmarket, Suffolk

FOCUS
This looked a good race for the grade and the track and four of the first five home have a fair bit of scope for improvement, particularly the winner. They went a good gallop.
Reclamation(IRE) Official explanation: trainer's rep said, regarding the apparent improvement in form, filly was very backward as a 2yo.
Pharaohs Queen(IRE) Official explanation: jockey said filly missed the break

2053 HOTEL & CONFERENCING AT WOLVERHAMPTON RACECOURSE AMATEUR RIDERS' H'CAP 1m 4f 50y(P)
4:40 (4:40) (Class 6) (0-55,55) 4-Y-0+ **£2,307** (£709; £354) **Stalls** Low

Form RPR

100 **1** **Wizard Looking**[24] 1459 7-11-7 **55** MrSWalker 8 69
(D E Cantillon) *mid-div: hdwy 6f out: led 2f out: rdn clr* **3/1**[2]

0-65 **2** *2 1/2* **Thorny Mandate**[16] 1639 6-11-0 **53** MrBenBrisbourne(5) 2 63
(W M Brisbourne) *hld up in mid-div: hdwy over 4f out: styd on to go 2nd ins fnl f* **4/1**[3]

1034 **3** *3 1/4* **Starstruck Peter (IRE)**[12] 1726 4-11-2 **53** (t) MrDRCook(3) 5 58
(S Curran) *chsd ldrs: led 6f out: rdn and hdd 2f out: wknd and lost 2nd ins fnl f* **9/4**[1]

50- **4** *11* **Revolving World (IRE)**[225] 5839 5-10-13 **52** (t) MrKJames(5) 9 39
(L R James) *towards rr: hdwy 5f out: rdn 3f out: no ch w first 3 fnl 2f* **14/1**

0-00 **5** *10* **Prince Of Gold**[47] 1029 8-10-9 **50** (b) MissMHugo(7) 3 21
(Ms N M Hugo) *chsd ldrs: rdn over 2f out: sn wknd* **28/1**

000- **6** *3/4* **Gatecrasher**[17] 7004 5-10-9 **50** MrSeanKerr(7) 12 20
(G F Bridgwater) *in rr: lost tch over 5f out* **66/1**

1316 **7** *6* **Cragganmore Creek**[42] 1121 5-10-13 **52** (v) MrBMMorris(5) 6 12
(D Morris) *trckd ldrs: rdn and wknd 2f out* **8/1**

020- **8** *2* **Monsieur Dumas (IRE)**[219] 6026 4-11-2 **55** MissRBastiman(5) 10 12
(R Bastiman) *a in rr: bhd fnl 5f* **14/1**

3666 **9** *1/2* **Treetops Hotel (IRE)**[31] 1310 9-10-12 **53** (p) MissRKneller(7) 7 9
(R Hollinshead) *a bhd: lost tch over 4f out* **16/1**

1365 **10** *38* **Lordswood (IRE)**[59] 886 4-11-1 **54** MrPCollington(5) 11 —
(J R Best) *a bhd: lost tch 5f out: t.o* **9/1**

0-30 **11** *27* **Fairly Honest**[15] 1644 4-10-13 **50** MrsMarieKing(3) 4 —
(P W Hiatt) *led for 3f: wknd 5f out: t.o* **17/2**

0-06 **12** *1 1/2* **Wee Ellie Coburn**[8] 1825 4-10-13 **52** MissMMullineaux(5) 1 —
(M Mullineaux) *plld hrd: led after 3f: hdd 6f out: wknd qckly: t.o* **33/1**

2m 47.62s (6.52) **Going Correction** +0.125s/f (Slow) 12 Ran SP% **134.5**
Speed ratings (Par 101): **83,81,79,71,65 64,60,59,59,33 15,14**
CSF £17.85 CT £35.21 TOTE £3.80: £1.90, £1.90, £1.20; EX 21.00 Place 6 £72.16, Place 5 £26.43..
Owner T H Heckingbottom **Bred** J G Phillips **Trained** Newmarket, Suffolk

FOCUS
No strength in depth despite the numbers, the first three in the market totally dominant and pulling well clear of some exposed types for whom the prognosis must be awfully bleak. The form seems sound enough.
Cragganmore Creek Official explanation: jockey said gelding lost its action
Fairly Honest Official explanation: jockey said gelding had no more to give
T/Plt: £135.10 to a £1 stake. Pool: £46,989.87. 253.80 winning tickets. T/Qpdt: £43.00 to a £1 stake. Pool: £2,678.98. 46.00 winning tickets. JS

1686 YARMOUTH (L-H)
Monday, May 12

OFFICIAL GOING: Good to firm
Wind: Fresh, across Weather: Fine and sunny

2054 NORFOLK NELSON MUSEUM MAIDEN AUCTION STKS 5f 43y
2:30 (2:32) (Class 5) 2-Y-O **£3,218** (£957; £478; £239) **Stalls** High

Form RPR

42 **1** **Brenin Taran**[15] 1640 2-8-9 0 RichardMullen 4 79+
(D M Simcock) *s.i.s: sn trcking ldrs: racd keenly: swtchd rt over 1f out: shkn up to ld wl ins fnl f* **2/5**[1]

24 **2** *3/4* **Miss Hollybell**[13] 1693 2-8-6 0 JoeFanning 6 71
(J Gallagher) *chsd ldr: rdn to ld over 1f out: hdd wl ins fnl f* **11/1**

64 **3** *3 3/4* **Fasliyanne (IRE)**[16] 1627 2-8-8 0 NCallan 8 60
(K A Ryan) *led: rdn and hdd over 1f out: no ex* **11/2**[2]

4 *nk* **In Transit (IRE)** 2-8-11 0 DarryllHolland 2 62+
(M R Channon) *sn outpcd: r.o ins fnl f: nvr nrr* **10/1**[3]

0 **5** *4 1/2* **Debbys Boy**[11] 1736 2-8-11 0 EddieAhern 3 46
(Miss Gay Kelleway) *chsd ldrs: edgd lft 3f out: rdn over 1f out: wknd fnl f* **40/1**

0 **6** *3 1/4* **Persian Tomcat (IRE)**[26] 1399 2-8-7 0 AmyBaker(7) 1 37
(Miss J Feilden) *chsd ldrs: bmpd 3f out: sn rdn: wknd over 1f out* **33/1**

62.08 secs (-0.12) **Going Correction** -0.325s/f (Firm) 6 Ran SP% **109.6**
Speed ratings (Par 93): **87,85,79,79,72 66**
CSF £5.54 TOTE £1.40: £1.20, £3.20; EX 5.70 Trifecta £9.80 Pool £495.89 - 35.68 winning units..
Owner Mrs Ann Simcock **Bred** D M I Simcock **Trained** Newmarket, Suffolk
■

FOCUS
An uncompetitive maiden.

NOTEBOOK
Brenin Taran had shown a fair level of form in two previous starts, just getting caught late on at Brighton last time, and he proved good enough to score at the third attempt. He was entitled to win this well, but took a while to get on top and it is probable he was a bit below his best. A step up to 6f will suit in time and he remains capable of better. (op 4-7 tchd 8-13 in a place)
Miss Hollybell, a disappointment at Bath last time, had shown fair form when second on her debut and this was a return to that earlier form. She seemed well suited by this faster ground and will be more at home in nurseries. (op 7-1)
Fasliyanne(IRE), sixth in a race that has worked out really well on her debut, failed to build on that when flopping at Ripon last time, but this was a little better. She is another who has it in her to win an ordinary contest, possibly a nursery. (op 9-2 tchd 7-1)
In Transit(IRE), a 7,500gns son of Trans Island, comes from a yard whose juveniles have tended to need their debut run this season and he was too green to do himself justice. An extra furlong will be needed before long and there should be improvement to come. (tchd 15-2)
Debbys Boy, who earned an RPR of 6 on his recent debut, appreciated this better ground and ran a shade better. It may take a drop into claiming/selling level for him to score. (op 33-1)
Persian Tomcat(IRE) is another who is going to require a drop in grade before long. (op 50-1)

2055 GREAT YARMOUTH MERCURY CLASSIFIED STKS 7f 3y
3:00 (3:03) (Class 6) 3-Y-O+ **£2,266** (£674; £337; £168) **Stalls** High

Form RPR

304- **1** **Oh So Saucy**[236] 5546 4-9-8 55 GeorgeBaker 8 69
(C F Wall) *hld up: hdwy over 2f out: rdn to chse ldr over 1f out: r.o to ld nr fin* **7/1**

5006 **2** *nk* **Elusive Dreams (USA)**[25] 1416 4-9-5 55 (v[1]) TolleyDean(3) 7 68
(D Shaw) *chsd ldr: led over 2f out: rdn over 1f out: hdd nr fin* **8/1**

00-4 **3** *5* **Peas In A Pod**[35] 1247 3-8-10 52 JamieSpencer 3 51+
(J R Fanshawe) *s.i.s: hld up: swtchd rt over 2f out: hdwy over 1f out: sn rdn and edgd lft: r.o: nt rch ldrs* **7/1**

-000 **4** *3 1/2* **Djalalabad (FR)**[15] 1644 4-9-8 50 JoeFanning 11 45
(Mrs C A Dunnett) *prom: rdn and hung lft fr over 1f out: nt run on* **33/1**

4202 **5** *2 1/2* **Tilsworth Charlie**[54] 933 5-9-8 55 (b) OscarUrbina 16 38
(J R Jenkins) *hld up: hdwy over 2f out: rdn over 1f out: wknd fnl f* **4/1**[2]

5040 **6** *8* **Ma Ridge**[10] 1763 4-9-8 47 RichardThomas 6 17
(T D McCarthy) *prom: pushed along over 4f out: wknd 2f out* **20/1**

444- **7** *1* **Fair Sailing (IRE)**[188] 6704 4-9-8 55 EddieAhern 4 14
(J W Hills) *hld up in tch: rdn over 2f out: sn wknd* **13/2**[3]

503- **8** *2* **Chalentina**[208] 6268 5-9-3 49 NataliaGemelova(5) 15 9
(J E Long) *hld up: rdn 1/2-way: sn wknd: b.b.v* **9/1**

-000 **9** *nse* **Giovanni D'Oro (IRE)**[13] 1705 4-9-8 45 JimmyQuinn 1 9
(Miss M E Rowland) *a bhd* **50/1**

060- **10** *nk* **Jimmy Dean**[185] 6748 3-8-10 43 (p) LiamJones 12 4
(M Wellings) *mid-div: rdn and wknd over 2f out* **100/1**

0-00 **11** *nk* **On The Map**[105] 338 4-9-8 50 (b1) J-PGuillambert 9 7
(Joss Saville) *led: rdn: hung rt and hdd over 2f out: sn wknd* **28/1**

/30- **12** *½* **Marvin Gardens**[256] 4972 5-9-5 43 KirstyMilczarek(3) 13 6
(M Wigham) *hld up: hdwy 1/2-way: rdn over 2f out: wknd wl over 1f out* **7/2**[1]

50-0 **13** *4½* **Sibo Baggins (IRE)**[14] 1692 4-9-8 50 DMylonas 14 —
(Mrs C A Dunnett) *s.i.s: outpcd* **33/1**

000- **14** *6* **Doubloon**[178] 6828 3-8-10 45 StephenCarson 2 —
(J Gallagher) *prom: lost pl over 4f out: wknd 3f out* **50/1**

1m 23.76s (-2.84) **Going Correction** -0.325s/f (Firm)
WFA 3 from 4yo+ 12lb **14** Ran SP% **120.7**
Speed ratings (Par 101): **103,102,96,92,90 80,79,77,77,77 76,76,71,64**
CSF £58.57 TOTE £8.10: £2.70, £3.70, £2.50; EX 77.90 TRIFECTA Not won..
Owner The Eight Of Diamonds **Bred** Mrs C J Walker **Trained** Newmarket, Suffolk

FOCUS
The front pair drew clear and this is probably fair form for the grade, although there was a lot of dead wood in the race.
Ma Ridge Official explanation: jockey said gelding hung left
Chalentina Official explanation: trainer said mare had bled from the nose
Marvin Gardens Official explanation: jockey said gelding hung left

2056 BBC RADIO NORFOLK MAIDEN STKS 1m 3y
3:30 (3:38) (Class 5) 3-Y-O+ **£3,238** (£963; £481; £240) **Stalls** High

Form RPR

5- **1** **Lazy Days**[220] 5971 3-9-0 0 JamieSpencer 8 88+
(D R C Elsworth) *s.i.s and hmpd s: hld up: hdwy 1/2-way: led over 1f out: rdn out* **7/2**[2]

33- **2** *1* **Missioner (USA)**[282] 4151 3-9-0 0 JoeFanning 1 86
(M Johnston) *w ldr tl led over 2f out: rdn and hdd over 1f out: styd on* **7/4**[1]

3 *hd* **Decameron (USA)** 3-8-7 0 JPHamblett(7) 2 86+
(Sir Michael Stoute) *chsd ldrs: shkn up over 1f out: styd on same pce ins fnl f* **9/2**[3]

4 *hd* **Royal Destination (IRE)** 3-9-0 0 EddieAhern 7 85+
(J Noseda) *hld up: hdwy over 2f out: rdn over 1f out: styd on* **7/2**[2]

60- **5** *5* **Dark Prospect**[195] 6574 3-9-0 0 NCallan 11 74
(M A Jarvis) *hld up in tch: rdn over 2f out: styd on same pce appr fnl f* **10/1**

6 *1¾* **Mont Cervin** 3-9-0 0 LiamJones 5 70+
(W J Haggas) *hld up: rdn over 1f out: n.d* **66/1**

0- **7** *2½* **Spate River**[210] 6237 3-9-0 0 StephenCarson 6 64
(C F Wall) *led over 5f: wknd over 1f out* **50/1**

30 **8** *¾* **Platoche (IRE)**[20] 1539 3-9-0 0 AdrianMcCarthy 10 62
(P W Chapple-Hyam) *chsd ldrs: rdn over 2f out: wknd over 1f out* **20/1**

00 **9** *½* **Grit (IRE)**[4] 1926 3-8-7 0 MCGeran(7) 9 61
(M R Channon) *s.i.s: sn racing keenly and prom: rdn and wknd over 2f out* **150/1**

4450 **10** *shd* **Lady Firecracker (IRE)**[59] 877 4-9-8 40 GeorgeBaker 12 59?
(J R Best) *hld up: a in rr* **100/1**

0 **11** *9* **Road To Hucking (GER)**[21] 1526 3-9-0 0 JimmyQuinn 13 40
(J R Best) *hld up: bhd fr 1/2-way* **150/1**

1m 37.87s (-2.73) **Going Correction** -0.325s/f (Firm)
WFA 3 from 4yo 13lb **11** Ran SP% **118.6**
Speed ratings (Par 103): **100,99,98,98,93 91,89,88,88,88 79**
CSF £9.98 TOTE £4.10: £1.40, £1.10, £2.00; EX 9.00 Trifecta £25.40 Pool £490.98 - 13.71 winning units..
Owner Lordship Stud 3 **Bred** Glebe Stud And Mrs F Woodd **Trained** Newmarket, Suffolk
■

FOCUS
This was steadily run and strictly speaking the ninth and tenth limit the form, but it looked a strong race on paper with the runner-up setting a decent standard and it should produce plenty of winners.

2057 GREAT YARMOUTH ADVERTISER H'CAP 1m 3y
4:00 (4:03) (Class 3) (0-90,85) 4-Y-O+
£7,477 (£2,239; £1,119; £560; £279; £140) **Stalls** High

Form RPR

-351 **1** **Mujood**[9] 1800 5-9-4 85 StephenCarson 5 94
(Eve Johnson Houghton) *led: hdd over 5f out: led again over 2f out: rdn over 1f out: styd on* **5/1**[3]

0-51 **2** *¾* **Bustan (IRE)**[16] 1630 9-8-10 77 NCallan 7 85
(G C Bravery) *chsd ldrs: rdn and edgd lft fr over 1f out: struck by rivals whip ins fnl f: styd on* **7/2**[2]

3620 **3** *nk* **Lord Theo**[12] 1719 4-8-9 79 KirstyMilczarek(3) 1 86
(N P Littmoden) *w ldr tl led over 5f out: rdn and hdd over 2f out: unable qck towards fin* **17/2**

0-53 **4** *6* **Rapid City**[22] 1502 5-8-13 83 JerryO'Dwyer(3) 6 76
(Miss J Feilden) *hld up in tch: rdn over 2f out: sn outpcd* **5/1**[3]

666- **5** *13* **Life's A Whirl**[161] 7009 6-8-4 71 oh19 (p) DMylonas 4 34
(Mrs C A Dunnett) *chsd ldrs: rdn 1/2-way: wknd over 2f out* **66/1**

54-4 **6** *8* **Habshan (USA)**[12] 1719 8-9-4 85 GeorgeBaker 3 30+
(C F Wall) *hld up: hdwy over 2f out: rdn over 1f out: wkng whn virtually p.u ins fnl f: lost three shoes* **5/4**[1]

1m 35.76s (-4.84) **Going Correction** -0.325s/f (Firm) **6** Ran SP% **112.0**
Speed ratings (Par 107): **111,110,109,103,90 82**
CSF £22.47 TOTE £5.00: £2.80, £2.10; EX 18.00.
Owner Eden Racing **Bred** Bloomsbury Stud & The Hon Sir David Sieff **Trained** Blewbury, Oxon

FOCUS
A fair handicap in which the winner, who was granted a fairly easy lead, is rated to something like his best.

NOTEBOOK
Mujood, who was without the usual headgear, has spent the last couple of seasons running at no further than 7f, but he showed himself to be in good form when ending a losing run at Goodwood last time and saw out the extra quarter mile better than expected. Soon in front, he remained up there throughout and picked up best off the front end to score, just doing enough. Small fields like this suit him best and he remains versatile with regards to distance. (tchd 6-1)

Bustan(IRE), up just 1lb for his recent Sandown win in a Flat/jump jockeys' event, would have preferred a faster pace and was closing at the line, but could not get past. Done no favours in getting struck by the winning rider's whip, he should remain competitive off this sort of mark. (tchd 4-1)

Lord Theo, below his best in a competitive handicap at Ascot last time, had earlier finished second over course and distance and he bettered that effort off a 4lb higher mark. He kept finding for pressure, but probably needs to pull out more to win off this mark. (op 15-2 tchd 7-1)

Rapid City failed to cope with the drop in trip and really needs further. His best form has been shown on Polytrack. (op 13-2 tchd 7-1 and 8-1 in a place)

Habshan(USA), a fine fourth at Ascot on his reappearance, has won second time up for the past three seasons and he was rightly made favourite. He travelled well, but having got within striking distance could not quicken and was virtually pulled up inside the final furlong. This was evidently not his form and it emerged he had lost three shoes during the race. Official explanation: jockey said gelding lost three shoes (op 11-8 tchd 6-4)

2058 DIGIBET H'CAP 6f 3y
4:30 (4:30) (Class 4) (0-85,78) 4-Y-O+ **£4,533** (£1,348; £674; £336) **Stalls** High

Form RPR

-212 **1** **Expensive Art (IRE)**[7] 1858 4-9-2 76 NCallan 3 84+
(S A Callaghan) *trckd ldrs: shkn up to ld ins fnl f: edgd lft: r.o* **10/3**[2]

-554 **2** *hd* **Cativo Cavallino**[19] 1567 5-8-9 74 NataliaGemelova(5) 2 81
(J E Long) *chsd ldr: rdn to ld over 1f out: hdd ins fnl f: edgd lft: styd on* **6/1**[3]

-646 **3** *3* **Lunces Lad (IRE)**[9] 1800 4-9-4 78 DarryllHolland 1 75
(M R Channon) *stdd s: hld up: rdn over 2f out: sn edgd lft: no imp fnl f* **9/4**[1]

2132 **4** *shd* **Dvinsky (USA)**[19] 1567 7-8-10 70 (b) JimmyQuinn 5 67
(P Howling) *led: rdn and hdd over 1f out: no ex ins fnl f* **9/4**[1]

0660 **5** *3¼* **Red Cape (FR)**[9] 1796 5-9-1 75 (b1) JoeFanning 4 62
(Mrs R A Carr) *hld up: racd keenly: rdn over 1f out: hung lft and wknd fnl f* **10/1**

1m 11.63s (-2.77) **Going Correction** -0.325s/f (Firm) **5** Ran SP% **108.0**
Speed ratings (Par 105): **105,104,100,100,96**
CSF £20.99 TOTE £3.20: £2.00, £4.00; EX 22.20.
Owner Matthew Green **Bred** Stone Ridge Farm **Trained** Newmarket, Suffolk

FOCUS
A fair handicap which was not strongly run and as such the form does not seem too solid.

2059 SCROBY SANDS WIND FARM H'CAP 1m 3f 101y
5:00 (5:00) (Class 3) (0-90,89) 4-Y-O+ **£6,854** (£2,052; £1,026; £513) **Stalls** Low

Form RPR

6201 **1** **Polish Power (GER)**[9] 1793 8-9-4 89 DarryllHolland 5 96
(J S Moore) *broke wl: stdd to trck ldr: rdn over 3f out: led 2f out: edgd rt ins fnl f: eased nr fin* **13/8**[1]

/20- **2** *1* **Zonergem**[242] 5362 10-9-1 89 (p) KirstyMilczarek(3) 1 94
(Lady Herries) *hld up: racd keenly: hdwy 2f out: sn rdn: carried hd high ins fnl f: styd on* **11/4**[3]

14-0 **3** *3* **Fongs Gazelle**[22] 1502 4-8-12 83 JoeFanning 3 83
(M Johnston) *sn led: rdn and hdd 2f out: no ex ins fnl f* **2/1**[2]

063- **4** *1* **Wild Pitch**[278] 4271 7-8-5 76 (b) JimmyQuinn 2 74
(Stef Liddiard) *trckd ldrs: rdn over 1f out: hung rt and no ex fnl f* **8/1**

2m 28.58s (-0.12) **Going Correction** -0.25s/f (Firm) **4** Ran SP% **109.2**
Speed ratings (Par 107): **90,89,87,86**
CSF £6.37 TOTE £1.90; EX 6.10.
Owner John Wells **Bred** Gestut Hofgut Mappen **Trained** Upper Lambourn, Berks

FOCUS
Potentially weak form with doubts over the winner's three rivals.

NOTEBOOK
Polish Power(GER), who ran away with an apprentice handicap at Doncaster last time, had been stuck up 10lb for that and had faster conditions to deal with here, but he is clearly on great terms with himself and had little trouble following up. He is likely to be aimed at the Ladies' Derby at the Curragh in July, a race he finished fifth in last year. (tchd 7-4)

Zonergem is still capable of fair form on his day and he ran really well on this first start since September. He has not won as many races as he should have over the years though, and it was easy to see why as he held his head high under pressure. (op 4-1)

Fongs Gazelle remains 6lb higher than when last winning and she was beaten out of sight on her reappearance at Great Leighs. This was better, the four-year-old seeming to enjoy herself out in front in a small field, but she was still well held at the line and remains below her best. (op 15-8 tchd 9-4)

Wild Pitch had a bit to find with a couple of these and he quickly backed out of the argument, having travelled up well. (op 13-2 tchd 11-2)

2060 NORFOLK CHAMBER OF COMMERCE H'CAP 1m 2f 21y
5:30 (5:30) (Class 5) (0-70,70) 4-Y-O+ **£3,070** (£906; £453) **Stalls** Low

Form RPR

52-0 **1** **Roodolph**[20] 1532 4-9-4 70 StephenCarson 5 78
(Eve Johnson Houghton) *hld up in tch: led over 2f out: drvn out* **9/2**[2]

06-4 **2** *2* **Multicultural**[14] 1682 5-9-1 67 SaleemGolam 3 71
(D M Simcock) *trckd ldrs: rdn over 2f out: styd on* **11/10**[1]

0040 **3** *3* **Mick Is Back**[11] 1747 4-8-6 58 (vt) JoeFanning 6 56
(G G Margarson) *chsd ldr tl led over 4f out: rdn and hdd over 2f out: wknd ins fnl f* **11/1**

5606 **4** *1¼* **Barry Island**[14] 1692 9-7-11 56 oh2 AmyBaker(7) 2 52
(D R C Elsworth) *s.s: hdwy over 2f out: styd on same pce appr fnl f* **6/1**[3]

0004 **5** *½* **Moon Mix (FR)**[14] 1691 5-9-4 70 NCallan 1 65
(J R Jenkins) *hld up in tch: rdn over 1f out: edgd lft and wknd ins fnl f: eased towards fin* **9/2**[2]

010- **6** *20* **Present**[5] 5899 4-8-1 56 oh4 (vt) DominicFox(3) 4 11
(M J Gingell) *led over 5f: rdn and wknd over 2f out* **25/1**

2m 7.12s (-3.38) **Going Correction** -0.25s/f (Firm) **6** Ran SP% **110.4**
Speed ratings (Par 103): **103,101,99,98,97 81**
CSF £9.59 TOTE £6.20: £2.50, £1.40; EX 12.60 Place 6 £143.20, Place 5 £112.93..
Owner Eden Racing (II) **Bred** Mrs H Johnson Houghton & Mrs R F Johnson Hought **Trained** Blewbury, Oxon
■ Stewards' Enquiry : N Callan three-day ban: failed to ride out for 4th place (May 26-28)

FOCUS
Not much of a race, run at a steady gallop. It is doubtful if the winner had to improve.
T/Plt: £44.40 to a £1 stake. Pool: £52,238.44. 858.25 winning tickets. T/Qpdt: £11.80 to a £1 stake. Pool: £2,398.78. 149.50 winning tickets. CR

1760 SAINT-CLOUD (L-H)
Monday, May 12

OFFICIAL GOING: Good to soft

2064a PRIX GREFFULHE (GROUP 2) (C&F) — 1m 2f
2:50 (2:50) 3-Y-O **£54,485** (£21,029; £10,037; £6,691; £3,346)

RPR

1 **Prospect Wells (FR)**[32] 3-9-2 .... OPeslier 5 104
(A Fabre, France) *hld up in last: pushed along on outside 2f out: rdn and r.o to chal 1f out: led nr fin: pushed out* **18/10**[2]

2 *snk* **Ripple (FR)**[32] 3-9-2 .... CSoumillon 2 103
(J-C Rouget, France) *led: hdd appr st: led again 1 1/2f out: rdn and r.o fnl f: hdd nr fin* **7/2**[3]

3 *snk* **Trois Rois (FR)**[29] 3-9-2 .... DBonilla 3 103
(F Head, France) *racd in 4th: 3rd st: sn pushed along: rdn and 1/2 l bhd ldr 100yds out: styd on same pce* **14/10**[1]

4 *1 1/2* **Salsalavie (FR)**[29] 1362 3-9-2 .... SPasquier 1 100
(P Demercastel, France) *racd in 3rd: 4th st: pushed along 2f out: hrd rdn on rail 1 1/2f out to 100yds out: no ex* **46/10**

5 *1 1/2* **Chirango (FR)**[9] 3-9-2 .... TThulliez 4 97
(P Demercastel, France) *cl 2nd: led appr st: hdd and rdn 1 1/2f out: no ex* **46/10**

2m 11.6s (-4.40) **5 Ran SP% 135.3**
PARI-MUTUEL: WIN 2.80; PL 1.50, 1.90; SF 7.40.
Owner Wertheimer Et Frere **Bred** Wertheimer Et Frere **Trained** Chantilly, France

NOTEBOOK
Prospect Wells(FR), runner-up on his three previous starts, is definitely a Classic prospect in the making. Opening his account in this Group 2 event, he did it in good style despite a lack of early pace. Dropped back last early on, he came with a well timed late run from a furlong and a half out and went on to win with authority. He now goes for the Prix du Jockey Club and his breeding suggests he will easily stay the distance of the Juddmonte Grand Prix de Paris.
Ripple(FR) was taken to the head of the affairs soon after the start but his jockey only set a steady pace early on. Things were quickened up rapidly in the straight and he held on to his lead until well inside the final furlong. He is another possible for the Jockey Club.
Trois Rois(FR) ran a little free in the early stages due to the lack of pace. In a perfect position to challenge for the lead early in the straight, he seemed to hesitate a furlong and a half out before finishing really well. Still a little on the green side, he is another who will take up the challenge again in the Jockey Club.
Salsalavie(FR) was thereabouts for much of the race and in a good position at the entrance to the straight. He tried to challenge up the rail but could not quicken in the same manner as the first three past the post.

1660 COLOGNE (R-H)
Monday, May 12

OFFICIAL GOING: Good

2065a SCHWARZGOLD-RENNEN (GROUP 3) (FILLIES) — 1m
3:05 (3:13) 3-Y-O **£29,412** (£11,029; £4,412; £2,941)

RPR

1 **Peace Royale (GER)**[218] 6040 3-9-0 .... ASuborics 2 102
(A Wohler, Germany) *a cl up: stmbld and lost a shoe on bnd 3f out: sn rcvrd to be 3rd st: led over 1f out: rdn out* **27/10**[2]

2 *1/2* **Love Academy (GER)**[204] 6371 3-9-0 .... AStarke 5 101
(P Schiergen, Germany) *racd in 2nd: led narrowly 2f out to over 1f out: kpt on* **11/10**[1]

3 *1/2* **Rosenreihe (IRE)**[194] 6599 3-9-0 .... FilipMinarik 6 100
(P Schiergen, Germany) *hld up towards rr: hdwy 2f out: styd on down outside fnl 1 1/2f* **143/10**

4 *3/4* **Diamantgottin (GER)**[204] 6371 3-9-0 .... TMundry 9 98
(P Rau, Germany) *midfield: kpt on at same pce fnl 2f* **17/2**

5 *hd* **Themelie Island (IRE)**[222] 3-9-0 .... ADeVries 4 98
(A Trybuhl, Germany) *hld up in 7th: styd on down ins fnl 2f* **132/10**

6 *1 3/4* **Manipura (GER)**[23] 3-9-0 .... THellier 3 94
(A Wohler, Germany) *midfield: rdn and unable qck over 1 1/2f out* **59/10**[3]

7 *3* **Zaya (GER)**[204] 6371 3-9-0 .... WPanov 8 87
(A Wohler, Germany) *hld up in rr: last st: nvr a factor* **45/1**

8 *2 1/2* **Soledad (GER)** 3-9-0 .... PVanDeKeere 7 81
(U Stech, Norway) *in rr: 8th st: nvr a factor* **46/1**

9 *3* **Idonea (CAN)**[239] 5463 3-9-0 .... AHelfenbein 1 74
(Mario Hofer, Germany) *led to 2f out: wknd* **59/10**[3]

1m 37.79s (-0.60) **9 Ran SP% 132.0**
(including 10 Euro stake): WIN 37; PL 14, 13, 23; SF 67.
Owner Filly Syndicate **Bred** Gestut Etzean **Trained** Germany

2066a MEHL-MULHENS-RENNEN GERMAN 2000 GUINEAS (GROUP 2) (C&F) — 1m
4:15 (4:27) 3-Y-O **£73,529** (£27,941; £13,235; £6,618)

RPR

1 **Precious Boy (GER)**[22] 1514 3-9-2 .... ADeVries 5 104
(W Hickst, Germany) *reluctant to load and unruly bef s: a cl up in 3rd or 4th: rdn to ld jst ins fnl f: rdn out* **18/10**[2]

2 *1 1/2* **Konig Concorde (GER)**[28] 1376 3-9-2 .... WPanov 7 101
(C Sprengel, Germany) *hld up in 6th: swtchd outside ent st: styd on down outside to take 2nd cl home* **154/10**

3 *nk* **Liang Kay (GER)**[22] 1514 3-9-2 .... THellier 4 100
(U Ostmann, Germany) *racd in 5th: hdwy to ld narrowly 2f out: rdn 1 1/2f out: hdd jst ins fnl f: lost 2nd cl home* **11/10**[1]

4 *1 1/4* **Balios (GER)**[22] 1514 3-9-2 .... AHelfenbein 6 97
(A Wohler, Germany) *dropped out in last: styd on towards ins fr over 1f out to take 4th cl home* **20/1**

5 *1/2* **Abbashiva (GER)**[43] 3-9-2 .... TMundry 3 96
(P Rau, Germany) *racd in 2nd: ev ch 2f out tl one pce fr 1f out* **67/10**

6 *hd* **Sehrezad (IRE)**[25] 3-9-2 .... ASuborics 2 96
(Andreas Lowe, Germany) *racd in 3rd or 4th: rdn to chal on ins 2f out: one pce fnl f* **46/10**[3]

7 *1 1/2* **Solent Ridge (IRE)**[37] 1213 3-9-2 .... LPKeniry 1 92
(J S Moore) *led to 2f out: wknd* **138/10**

1m 37.13s (-1.26) **7 Ran SP% 131.8**
WIN 28; PL 12, 16, 11; SF 465.
Owner Gestut Park Wiedingen **Bred** Gestut Park Wiedingen **Trained** Germany

NOTEBOOK
Precious Boy(GER) had beaten today's favourite Liang Kay half a length in last year's Preis der Winterfavoriten, Germany's top juvenile event, but that rival gained his revenge three weeks ago at Krefeld. He played up behind the stalls, but did nothing wrong in the race and swept through for a stylish win.
Solent Ridge(IRE), who likes to be up there, made much of the running, but his pedigree gave some concern about his stamina and, having led to two furlongs out, he dropped right out.

1640 BRIGHTON (L-H)
Tuesday, May 13

OFFICIAL GOING: Good to firm (firm in places)
Wind: Strong, behind

2067 CHANTREY VELLACOTT DFK MAIDEN STKS — 5f 213y
2:10 (2:14) (Class 5) 3-Y-O+ **£2,590** (£770; £385; £192) **Stalls Low**

Form RPR

0 1 **Light Hearted**[26] 1423 3-8-9 0 .... ShaneKelly 6 89+
(J Noseda) *mde all: drew clr appr fnl f: v easily* **10/11**[1]

32 2 *8* **Great Knight (IRE)**[10] 1817 3-9-0 0 .... RyanMoore 3 68
(W J Haggas) *chsd ldrs: wnt 2nd ent fnl f: no ch w wnr* **7/4**[2]

540- 3 *1/2* **Superduper**[215] 6128 3-8-9 71 .... RichardHughes 7 61
(R Hannon) *trckd wnr tl rdn and outpcd ent fnl f* **10/1**[3]

0- 4 *1/2* **Senorita Parkes**[302] 3582 3-8-9 0 .... LPKeniry 5 60
(E F Vaughan) *in tch: no hdwy fr over 1f out* **33/1**

30- 5 *8* **The Lady Granuaile (USA)**[223] 5910 3-8-9 0 .... NCallan 2 34
(K A Ryan) *outpcd thrght* **16/1**

0-0 6 *3 3/4* **Amicable Terms**[23] 1499 3-8-9 0 .... ChrisCatlin 8 22
(Rae Guest) *outpcd thrght* **66/1**

600- 7 *3 1/2* **She Wont Wait**[246] 5276 4-9-5 42 .... (b) FrankieMcDonald 1 11
(T M Jones) *bdly outpcd fr s* **100/1**

67.47 secs (-2.73) **Going Correction** -0.40s/f (Firm)
WFA 3 from 4yo 10lb **7 Ran SP% 109.1**
Speed ratings (Par 103): **102,91,90,90,79 74,69**
CSF £2.36 TOTE £2.00: £1.20, £1.30; EX 2.60.
Owner Cheveley Park Stud **Bred** Cheveley Park Stud Ltd **Trained** Newmarket, Suffolk

FOCUS
A following wind coupled with quick ground led to a fast time, 0.17sec outside the track record. The winner impressed in a race best rated around the runner-up.

2068 WEATHERBYS FINANCE H'CAP — 5f 59y
2:40 (2:40) (Class 5) (0-75,73) 3-Y-O **£2,784** (£828; £414; £206) **Stalls Low**

Form RPR

0-26 1 **Magical Speedfit (IRE)**[25] 1454 3-9-0 69 .... RyanMoore 6 76
(G G Margarson) *trckd ldrs on outside: str run to ld ins fnl f: won gng away* **10/3**[2]

0310 2 *3 3/4* **Ben**[14] 1707 3-8-9 64 .... (v) TQuinn 2 58
(P G Murphy) *chsd ldr: rdn to chse wnr ins fnl f: no ex* **9/2**[3]

000- 3 *1* **Only In Jest**[212] 6195 3-8-13 68 .... FergusSweeney 1 59
(J Gallagher) *broke wl: led tl wknd: hdd and lost 2nd ins fnl f* **17/2**

3111 4 *8* **Wynberg (IRE)**[99] 425 3-9-1 70 .... JimCrowley 4 34
(S A Callaghan) *s.i.s: hung lft fr 1/2-way: nvr nr to chal* **6/1**

6-01 5 *1 1/2* **Swindon Town Flyer (IRE)**[21] 1536 3-9-4 73 .... (b) DavidKinsella 3 32
(A B Haynes) *s.i.s: lost all ch whn hmpd on ins 1/2-way* **11/2**

4525 6 *8* **Baytown Blaze**[6] 1911 3-9-4 73 .... ChrisCatlin 7 4
(M Wigham) *racd on outside: outpcd over 2f out* **11/4**[1]

0-06 7 *3* **Sandy Par**[14] 1699 3-7-11 59 oh4 .... RossAtkinson(7) 5 —
(J M Bradley) *a outpcd* **16/1**

60.54 secs (-1.76) **Going Correction** -0.40s/f (Firm) **7 Ran SP% 114.0**
Speed ratings (Par 99): **98,92,90,77,75 62,57**
CSF £18.53 TOTE £3.70: £2.50, £2.80; EX 13.60.
Owner John Guest **Bred** John Malone **Trained** Newmarket, Suffolk

FOCUS
A modest sprint handicap run at a strong gallop from the outset, which set things up for the winner.
Wynberg(IRE) Official explanation: jockey said gelding hung left
Baytown Blaze Official explanation: jockey said filly was unsuited by the good to firm (firm in places) ground

2069 PREMIER FOOD COURT (S) STKS — 6f 209y
3:10 (3:12) (Class 6) 3-Y-O+ **£1,683** (£501; £250; £125) **Stalls Low**

Form RPR

2433 1 **The Jailer**[15] 1670 5-8-3 57 .... (p) MCGeran(7) 11 67
(J G M O'Shea) *mde all: clr over 1f out: pushed out: easily* **7/2**[1]

5-63 2 *6* **Razzano (IRE)**[26] 1416 4-8-10 50 .... TQuinn 4 51
(A M Hales) *sn trckd wnr: no ch whn hung lft ins fnl f* **7/2**[1]

0403 3 *4 1/2* **Mick Is Back**[1] 2060 4-9-1 58 .... (vt) RichardHughes 3 44
(G G Margarson) *a chsng ldrs: no hdwy fr over 1f out* **9/2**[2]

040 4 *1 3/4* **The Dagger**[12] 1747 4-9-1 58 .... (b) RyanMoore 9 39
(G L Moore) *outpcd in rr: styd on on outside ins fnl 2f: nvr nr to chal* **7/1**

0200 5 *hd* **Victor Trumper**[15] 1670 4-9-1 55 .... (p) FergusSweeney 1 39
(Jim Best) *mid-div on ins: one pce fnl 2f* **20/1**

3105 6 *3 1/4* **Arctic Desert**[46] 1055 8-9-7 64 .... (t) NCallan 7 36
(Miss Gay Kelleway) *awkward leaving stalls: towards rr: swtchd rt and effrt over 2f out: sn hung lft and one pce* **13/2**[3]

000- 7 *hd* **Madame Montom (USA)**[181] 6814 3-7-9 44 ow4 .... RossAtkinson(7) 2 24
(S W Hall) *slowly away: outpcd in rr: rdn 1/2-way and nvr on terms* **100/1**

6240 8 *2 1/2* **Tiepie**[15] 1670 3-8-3 60 .... (b[1]) ChrisCatlin 6 19
(J Akehurst) *a in rr* **9/1**

60-0 9 *nk* **Convince (USA)**[16] 1642 7-9-1 45 .... (b[1]) JimCrowley 10 22
(J M Bradley) *mid-div on outside: rdn and wknd 2f out* **25/1**

-050 10 *hd* **Moon Forest (IRE)**[7] 1900 6-9-1 45 .... (b) ShaneKelly 8 21
(J M Bradley) *chsd ldrs tl wknd over 2f out* **14/1**

-050 11 *29* **Millenium Sun (IRE)**[15] 1675 4-9-1 40 .... EdwardCreighton 5 —
(E J Creighton) *mid-div: rdn 1/2-way: sn wl bhd: t.o* **100/1**

1m 20.2s (-2.90) **Going Correction** -0.40s/f (Firm)
WFA 3 from 4yo+ 12lb **11 Ran SP% 115.7**
Speed ratings (Par 101): **100,93,88,86,85 82,81,78,78,78 45**
CSF £14.69 TOTE £4.50: £1.70, £1.50, £2.20; EX 13.70.The winner was bought in for 7,000gns.
Owner N M Lowe **Bred** D R Tucker **Trained** Elton, Gloucs

FOCUS
An ordinary if competitive seller on paper but they went no gallop and the winner was able to dictate things.
The Dagger Official explanation: jockey said gelding was unsuited by the course
Tiepie Official explanation: jockey said colt was hampered at start

2070 WEATHERBYS PRINTING H'CAP — 7f 214y
3:40 (3:40) (Class 6) (0-60,60) 4-Y-O+ **£2,266** (£674; £337; £168) **Stalls** Low

Form — RPR

0502 **1** **Silver Blue (IRE)**[34] 1269 5-8-4 **46** oh1 .... LiamJones 10 — 56
(W K Goldsworthy) *slowly away: hld up: stdy hdwy fr over 2f out: r.o to ld nr fin* **11/2**[3]

0-53 **2** ¾ **Recalcitrant**[12] 1747 5-8-4 **53** .... WilliamCarson(7) 3 — 61
(S Dow) *prom: led wl over 2f out: rdn and kpt on: hdd nr fin* **7/1**

2634 **3** 1¼ **Pab Special (IRE)**[20] 1565 5-9-2 **58** .... SamHitchcott 8 — 63
(B R Johnson) *hld up: hdwy on outside 2f out: rdn and ev ch ins fnl f: no ex towards fin* **6/1**

345- **4** ¾ **Astroangel**[153] 7127 4-9-1 **57** .... NCallan 2 — 60+
(M H Tompkins) *chsd ldrs: short of room on ins ent fnl f: r.o ins fnl f* **8/1**

606- **5** 1¾ **Dancing Jest (IRE)**[236] 5563 4-9-4 **60** .... ChrisCatlin 11 — 59
(Rae Guest) *chsd ldrs: rdn over 1f out: hung lft and one pce ins fnl f* **12/1**

1350 **6** 2½ **Fun In The Sun**[15] 1687 4-8-6 **48** .... DavidKinsella 6 — 42
(A B Haynes) *mid-div: wkng whn n.m.r over 1f out* **14/1**

-235 **7** 3 **Prince Valentine**[34] 1269 7-8-11 **53** .... (p) RyanMoore 4 — 40
(G L Moore) *mid-div: hung lft and no hdwy ins fnl 2f* **7/2**[1]

00-0 **8** 1 **Art Gallery**[14] 1694 4-7-11 **46** oh1 .... (b) MatthewDavies(7) 5 — 30
(G L Moore) *led tl hdd wl over 2f out: wknd over 1f out* **16/1**

0-66 **9** hd **Pactolos Way**[16] 1644 5-9-4 **60** .... (v[1]) JimCrowley 7 — 44
(P R Chamings) *s.i.s: a bhd* **5/1**[2]

43P0 **10** 7 **Chasing Memories (IRE)**[36] 1248 4-8-7 **49** ow1 .... TQuinn 1 — 17
(A M Hales) *a towards rr* **14/1**

0300 **11** 2½ **Northstar Express (IRE)**[18] 1606 5-7-11 **46** oh1 ..... RossAtkinson(7) 12 — 8
(J L Spearing) *hld up: a towards rr* **28/1**

00-0 **12** 13 **Fervent**[34] 1275 4-8-7 **49** oh1 ow3 .... (b[1]) ShaneKelly 9 — —
(J M Bradley) *t.k.h: trckd ldr: n.m.r whn wknd wl over 2f out: eased 1f out* **40/1**

1m 32.56s (-3.44) **Going Correction** -0.40s/f (Firm) **12** Ran SP% **125.0**
Speed ratings (Par 101): **101,100,99,98,96 94,91,90,89,82 80,67**
CSF £46.48 CT £250.98 TOTE £5.50: £2.00, £2.80, £2.40; EX 59.10.
Owner Mrs L A Goldsworthy **Bred** Mrs T V Ryan **Trained** Yerbeston, Pembrokes
■ Keith Goldsworthy's first winner on the Flat.

FOCUS
Run-of-the-mill stuff, but the winner looks as though the move to west Wales could have rejuvenated him. Solid if limited form.
Fervent Official explanation: jockey said gelding hung left and was unsuited by the track

2071 WEATHERBYS BANK H'CAP — 1m 3f 196y
4:10 (4:12) (Class 5) (0-70,70) 4-Y-O+ **£2,784** (£828; £414; £206) **Stalls** High

Form — RPR

436- **1** **Summer Of Love (IRE)**[21] 3351 4-8-8 **60** .... (b) FergusSweeney 2 — 67
(A King) *trckd ldr to over 5f out: styd cl 3rd: rdn on ins to ld 1f out: pushed out* **5/2**[1]

-120 **2** 2 **Snake Skin**[14] 1697 5-8-10 **62** .... JimCrowley 3 — 66
(J Gallagher) *trckd ldrs: wnt 2nd over 5f out to over 1f out: r.o fnl f to go 2nd nr fin* **8/1**

1426 **3** nk **Prime Number (IRE)**[15] 1682 6-9-1 **67** .... TQuinn 6 — 71
(J Akehurst) *sn led: rdn and hdd 1f out: one pce and lost 2nd nr fin* **3/1**[3]

4641 **4** 7 **Bienheureux**[16] 1643 7-8-7 **59** ow2 .... (t) NCallan 7 — 51
(Miss Gay Kelleway) *hld up in tch: rdn and outpcd 2f out* **11/4**[2]

4444 **5** 18 **Generous Lad (IRE)**[56] 921 5-9-4 **70** .... (p) DavidKinsella 4 — 34
(A B Haynes) *s.i.s: hld up in tch: outpcd over 2f out: eased fnl f* **15/2**

6 18 **Sayago (GER)**[182] 6-8-9 **61** ow1 .... RichardHughes 1 — —
(C J Mann) *hld up in tch: effrt on outside over 2f out: sn btn and eased* **12/1**

2m 34.71s (2.01) **Going Correction** -0.40s/f (Firm) **6** Ran SP% **110.8**
Speed ratings (Par 103): **77,75,75,70,58 46**
CSF £21.59 TOTE £3.70: £2.00, £3.40; EX 26.70.
Owner A Sheppard, A Windle & K Hix **Bred** Stratford Place Stud **Trained** Barbury Castle, Wilts

FOCUS
They went an absolute crawl in this handicap, and as is so often the case, the three horses who sat on the pace were best placed when the sprint started, the three hold-up horses getting left well behind. Weak form.

2072 PERTEMPS PEOPLE DEVELOPMENT "HANDS AND HEELS" APPRENTICE H'CAP — 1m 1f 209y
4:40 (4:40) (Class 6) (0-60,55) 4-Y-O+ **£2,137** (£635; £317; £158) **Stalls** High

Form — RPR

020- **1** **Chapter (IRE)**[210] 6259 6-8-10 **46** .... (p) KylieManser 2 — 52
(Mrs A L M King) *hld up: hdwy to trck ldrs 1/2-way: led 2f out: hdd narrowly ins fnl f: fought bk to ld again cl home* **9/2**[2]

340- **2** hd **Astrolibra**[197] 6529 4-8-11 **50** .... AshleyMorgan(3) 5 — 56
(M H Tompkins) *hld up: hdwy on ins to chal wl over 1f out: led ins fnl f: hdd cl home* **3/1**[1]

3324 **3** 2½ **Looks The Business (IRE)**[15] 1668 7-9-5 **55** .... (t) RossAtkinson 7 — 56
(W G M Turner) *in tch: rdn and chsd first two fnl 2f: no ex* **3/1**[1]

00-4 **4** 2¾ **The Iron Giant (IRE)**[7] 1902 6-8-1 **45** .... MatthewCosham(8) 4 — 41
(Dr J R J Naylor) *led tl hdd 2f out: rdn and one pce after* **7/1**

0-06 **5** 3¼ **Love Angel (USA)**[41] 1152 6-8-9 **45** .... (v) BillyCray 1 — 34
(J J Bridger) *s.i.s: sn trckd ldrs: wknd over 2f out* **12/1**

000/ **6** 7 **Sayrianna**[1245] 6900 7-8-1 **45** .... SeanPalmer(8) 6 — 20
(M D I Usher) *prom tl wknd over 2f out* **40/1**

/003 **7** 1 **Tuscan Treaty**[16] 1644 8-8-10 **46** .... (t) MatthewDavies 3 — 19
(R W Price) *in rr on outside: lost tch 2f out* **5/1**[3]

2m 2.03s (-1.57) **Going Correction** -0.40s/f (Firm) **7** Ran SP% **107.5**
Speed ratings (Par 101): **90,89,87,85,83 77,76**
CSF £16.11 TOTE £4.30: £2.40, £1.90; EX 17.10 Place 6 £34.25, Place 5 £31.81.
Owner Richard Mapp **Bred** Paradime Ltd **Trained** Wilmcote, Warwicks

FOCUS
A poor bunch, but providing good experience for their inexperienced partners. The form, as in all hands-and-heels races, should be treated with caution.
T/Plt: £54.50 to a £1 stake. Pool: £54,223.61. 725.15 winning tickets. T/Qpdt: £19.90 to a £1 stake. Pool: £2,756.38. 102.45 winning tickets. JS

1933 GREAT LEIGHS (A.W) (L-H)
Tuesday, May 13

OFFICIAL GOING: Standard
Wind: Medium, against Weather: sunny but breezy

2073 CHAUCER CLAIMING STKS — 1m 2f (P)
5:20 (5:20) (Class 6) 4-Y-O+ **£2,266** (£674; £337; £168) **Stalls** Low

Form — RPR

5614 **1** **Western Roots**[15] 1673 7-8-5 60 .... DavidProbert(7) 7 — 74
(A M Balding) *s.i.s: sn chsng ldr clr of remainder: led over 6f out: mde rest: 6 l clr 3f out: easily* **10/1**

4010 **2** 4½ **Given A Choice (IRE)**[10] 1793 6-9-6 81 .... (p) SebSanders 2 — 73
(J Pearce) *racd in midfield wl off the pce: wnt 3rd over 5f out: rdn to chse wnr over 2f out: no imp* **10/11**[1]

3442 **3** 9 **Moayed**[29] 1369 9-8-10 67 .... (b) SteveDrowne 6 — 45
(N P Littmoden) *hld up wl bhd: hdwy over 4f out: wnt modest 3rd over 1f out: nvr nr ldrs* **5/1**[2]

22-2 **4** 4 **Little Jimbob**[14] 1700 7-9-0 64 .... TonyHamilton 5 — 41
(R A Fahey) *taken down early: led tl over 6f out: chsd wnr after: rdn over 3f out: sn wknd* **8/1**

0426 **5** 14 **Steely Dan**[20] 1564 9-9-0 66 .... (p) NeilPollard 4 — 13
(Mrs L C Jewell) *a wl bhd: no ch last 3f: t.o* **20/1**

6 2¼ **Pepito Collonges (FR)**[14] 5-9-3 0 .... IanMongan 1 — 12
(Mrs L J Mongan) *chsd clr ldng pair tl over 5f out: wl bhd and rdn over 4f out: t.o* **33/1**

00/ **P** **Donatessa (GER)**[5] 5-8-11 75 .... (t) TedDurcan 3 — —
(C J Mann) *rrd as stalls opened: virtually ref to r: p.u* **6/1**[3]

2m 8.97s (0.37) **Going Correction** +0.125s/f (Slow) **7** Ran SP% **111.2**
Speed ratings (Par 101): **103,99,92,89,77 76,—**
CSF £18.61 TOTE £17.20: £7.10, £1.10; EX 49.50.
Owner I A Balding **Bred** Stratford Place Stud **Trained** Kingsclere, Hants

FOCUS
A messy contest and the in-form Western Roots dominated in the straight, getting a pretty easy lead. This was a much improved effort from him at face value.

2074 LIVINGSTONE H'CAP — 5f (P)
5:50 (5:51) (Class 6) (0-60,60) 3-Y-O **£2,047** (£604; £302) **Stalls** Low

Form — RPR

3424 **1** **Maggie Kate**[12] 1743 3-9-4 **60** .... SteveDrowne 7 — 66
(R Ingram) *chsd ldrs: wnt 2nd over 2f out: chal u.p over 1f out: led ins fnl f: kpt on* **11/4**[1]

3340 **2** 1¼ **Firespin (USA)**[24] 1475 3-9-0 **56** .... (t) JohnEgan 6 — 58
(M Botti) *stdd s: dropped in towards rr: hdwy and swtchd rt wl over 1f out: r.o wl fnl f: wnt 2nd nr fin: nt rch wnr* **9/1**

5145 **3** nk **Mac Dalia**[54] 952 3-9-4 **60** .... (p) SebSanders 12 — 60
(A J McCabe) *led: rdn jst over 2f out: hdd ins fnl f: no ex last 100yds* **8/1**

6050 **4** ¾ **Sazerac (USA)**[17] 1635 3-8-10 **55** .... TolleyDean(3) 5 — 53
(D Shaw) *racd in midfield: hdwy wl over 2f out: rdn 2f out: chsd ldrs 1f out: keeping on same pce whn swtchd rt wl ins fnl f* **8/1**

2-00 **5** 6 **Wicky Creek**[15] 1672 3-8-7 **49** ow1 .... OscarUrbina 9 — 25
(G C H Chung) *t.k.h: in tch in midfield on outer: rdn 2f out: outpcd over 1f out* **20/1**

6335 **6** ¾ **Planet Paradise (IRE)**[35] 1257 3-8-4 **46** .... FrancisNorton 3 — 19
(D Shaw) *towards rr: rdn and effrt 2f out: kpt on but nvr pce to rch ldrs* **7/1**

6-52 **7** 2¼ **Forever Changes**[15] 1672 3-9-1 **57** .... DarryllHolland 1 — 22
(L Montague Hall) *in tch in midfield: rdn wl over 2f out: sn outpcd and btn* **5/1**[2]

00-2 **8** nk **Maahe (IRE)**[41] 1141 3-8-7 **49** .... DaleGibson 10 — 13
(R A Fahey) *a towards rr: rdn over 3f out: n.d* **11/2**[3]

5225 **9** 1¼ **Honest Value (IRE)**[40] 1162 3-9-1 **57** .... (p) NeilPollard 4 — 17
(Mrs L C Jewell) *chsd ldr tl over 2f out: sn drvn: wknd wl over 1f out* **14/1**

5650 **10** 3 **Stoneacre Pat (IRE)**[17] 1635 3-9-1 **57** .... LPKeniry 2 — 6
(Peter Grayson) *v.s.a: a bhd* **25/1**

61.27 secs (1.07) **Going Correction** +0.125s/f (Slow) **10** Ran SP% **118.7**
Speed ratings (Par 97): **96,94,93,92,82 81,77,77,75,70**
CSF £29.17 CT £180.75 TOTE £4.00: £1.50, £3.40, £2.80; EX 36.10.
Owner Tommy Tighe **Bred** F L Mallaghan **Trained** Epsom, Surrey

FOCUS
A moderate sprint handicap, and much the slowest of the three 5f races run so far at Great Leighs. The winner did not have to improve much.
Stoneacre Pat(IRE) Official explanation: jockey said colt missed the break

2075 MILTON H'CAP — 6f (P)
6:20 (6:24) (Class 6) (0-55,54) 4-Y-O+ **£2,266** (£674; £337; £168) **Stalls** Low

Form — RPR

6505 **1** **Gone'N'Dunnett (IRE)**[7] 1906 9-8-7 **47** .... (v) FrancisNorton 15 — 59
(Mrs C A Dunnett) *chsd ldrs tl wnt 2nd over 4f out: rdn 2f out: led fnl 100yds: styd on wl* **12/1**

0022 **2** ¾ **Tenancy (IRE)**[7] 1906 4-8-8 **48** .... (p) NeilPollard 6 — 58
(A J McCabe) *sn led: rdn 2f out: hdd and no ex fnl 100yds* **13/2**[3]

6010 **3** 1¾ **Polar Force**[8] 1865 8-8-12 **52** .... DMylonas 8 — 56
(Mrs C A Dunnett) *in tch: sltly hmpd and lost pl after 1f: hdwy 4f out: chsd ldrs over 1f out: kpt on but nt pce to rch ldrs* **14/1**

2406 **4** nk **Metropolitan Chief**[16] 1645 4-8-13 **53** .... CatherineGannon 2 — 56+
(P Burgoyne) *stdd s: hld up in rr: hdwy over 2f out: n.m.r over 1f out: grad edgd out rt: r.o ins fnl f: nt rch ldrs* **16/1**

60-6 **5** 1 **Jayanjay**[16] 1646 9-9-0 **54** .... SebSanders 13 — 54
(B R Johnson) *racd in midfield: rdn and hdwy jst over 2f out: chsd ldrs 1f out: wknd fnl 100yds* **13/2**[3]

-604 **6** nk **Buzbury Rings**[26] 1416 4-8-10 **50** .... LPKeniry 11 — 49
(A M Balding) *rrd as stalls opened and slowly away: t.k.h: hld up in rr: hdwy into midfield 3f out: kpt on u.p but nvr rchd ldrs* **10/1**

400- **7** shd **Inwaan (IRE)**[194] 6607 5-8-13 **53** .... (t) SteveDrowne 10 — 52
(P R Webber) *chsd ldrs: edgd sltly lft after 1f: rdn over 3f out: kpt on same pce fnl 2f* **6/1**[2]

4100 **8** 1 **Taboor (IRE)**[14] 1706 10-8-12 **52** .... (p) DarryllHolland 3 — 47
(R M H Cowell) *hld up in tch: hdwy gng wl 3f out: rdn over 1f out: fnd little and no imp after* **14/1**

6530 **9** ½ **Zorn**[7] 1906 9-8-8 **48** .... IanMongan 4 — 42
(P Howling) *chsd ldr tl over 4f out: sn rdn: steadily lost pl* **25/1**

6-00 **10** nk **Bollin Franny**[16] 1646 4-8-8 **53** .... NataliaGemelova(5) 16 — 46
(J E Long) *hld up towards rr on outer: bhd and rdn 3f out: n.d* **16/1**

0600 **11** ½ **Sherjawy (IRE)**[8] 1865 4-8-12 **52**....................(b) SamHitchcott 5 43
(Miss Z C Davison) *stdd after s: hld up in rr: rdn and effrt over 1f out: n.d* **14/1**

3424 **12** ½ **Only If I Laugh**[34] 1269 7-8-5 **45**.................... JohnEgan 14 35
(M J Attwater) *a bhd* **5/1**[1]

3460 **13** 5 **Macademy Royal (USA)**[60] 884 5-8-3 **50**..........(t) TobyAtkinson(7) 9 24
(M Wigham) *slowly itno stride: a bhd* **16/1**

4100 **14** 14 **Desert Light (IRE)**[34] 1275 7-8-8 **51**....................(v) TolleyDean(3) 1 —
(D Shaw) *stdd after s: hld up in rr: effrt on inner wl over 1f out: btn over 1f out: virtually p.u ins fnl f* **15/2**

1m 14.64s (0.94) **Going Correction** +0.125s/f (Slow) **14** Ran SP% **127.7**
Speed ratings (Par 101): **98,97,94,94,92 92,92,91,90,90 89,88,82,63**
CSF £89.13 CT £1017.44 TOTE £12.00: £3.50, £1.40, £3.90; EX 114.40.
Owner Christine Dunnett Racing **Bred** Ocal Bloodstock **Trained** Hingham, Norfolk

FOCUS
A weak handicap and ordinary form for the grade. The first two were always prominent.
Macademy Royal(USA) Official explanation: jockey said gelding lost its near-fore shoe

2076 HUNTER VALLEY H'CAP — 1m 6f (P)
6:50 (6:52) (Class 4) (0-85,86) 4-Y-0+ **£4,533** (£1,348; £674; £336) **Stalls** Low

Form

113- **1** **Alleviate (IRE)**[263] 4758 4-8-9 **73**.................... SebSanders 9 87+
(Sir Mark Prescott) *hld up in midfield on outer: hdwy to chse ldrs over 6f out: wnt 2nd and qcknd clr w ldr over 2f out: led wl over 1f out: sn clr: rdn out* **5/1**[2]

10-0 **2** 3 **Bold Adventure**[20] 1564 4-8-2 **66** oh1.................... DavidKinsella 7 76
(W J Musson) *stdd s: bhd: rdn over 3f out: hdwy over 1f out: r.o wl to go 2nd ins fnl f: nvr trbld wnr* **8/1**

20-5 **3** 3 ¼ **Cleaver**[52] 962 7-9-0 **77**.................... JohnEgan 8 82
(Lady Herries) *in tch tl dropped to rr after 2f: hdwy 4f out: c wd bnd 2f out: hung lft fr over 1f out: styd on to go 3rd nr fin: nvr trbld ldrs* **15/2**[3]

1135 **4** 1 ¼ **Motarjm (USA)**[15] 1691 4-9-7 **85**....................(t) ChrisCatlin 4 88
(H J Collingridge) *t.k.h: chsd ldrs tl wnt 2nd 7f out: led wl over 3f out: rdn and qcknd clr w wnr over 2f out: hdd wl over 1f out: wknd: lost 2 pls fnl f* **10/1**

1021 **5** hd **Bentley Brook (IRE)**[7] 1904 6-9-2 **86** 6ex.................... SophieDoyle(7) 3 89
(P A Blockley) *t.k.h: hld up towards rr: short of room over 8f out: rdn and effrt wl over 1f out: nvr threatened ldrs* **12/1**

010/ **6** 6 **Tashkandi (IRE)**[24] 3255 8-8-7 **75**.................... NicolPolli(5) 10 70
(Mrs S J Humphrey) *in tch in midfield: bustled along 8f out: rdn over 4f out: chsd clr ldng pair over 2f out: wknd over 1f out* **66/1**

2-12 **7** 2 ¾ **Proper (IRE)**[19] 1585 4-8-12 **76**.................... TedDurcan 6 70+
(C J Mann) *s.i.s: hld up: hdwy on outer over 3f out: rdn over 2f out: wknd wl over 1f out* **15/2**[3]

1-31 **8** 1 ¼ **Boz**[12] 1744 4-9-6 **84**.................... JamieSpencer 5 78+
(L M Cumani) *hld up in midfield: boxed in over 4f out: swtchd rt and drvn 3f out: chsd clr ldrs 2f out: sn no imp: eased ins fnl f* **13/8**[1]

42-0 **9** 3 ¼ **Eumene (IRE)**[72] 410 5-9-8 **85**.................... LPKeniry 11 69
(C C Bealby) *hld up towards rr: hdwy on outer over 7f out: rdn over 3f out: wknd 2f out* **33/1**

-523 **10** 2 **At The Money**[22] 1518 5-8-3 **66**....................(b) FrancisNorton 2 48
(J M P Eustace) *sn led: rdn and hdd over 3f out: wknd qckly over 2f out* **11/1**

61-2 **11** 21 **Nawow**[19] 1583 8-9-3 **80**.................... NCallan 1 32
(P D Cundell) *chsd ldr tl over 7f out: rdn and wknd over 4f out: wl bhd 2f out: eased fnl f* **20/1**

3m 2.09s (-1.11) **Going Correction** +0.125s/f (Slow)
WFA 4 from 5yo+ 1lb **11** Ran SP% **123.7**
Speed ratings (Par 105): **108,106,104,103,103 100,98,97,96,94 82**
CSF £46.52 CT £307.59 TOTE £6.30: £1.50, £4.80, £3.80; EX 73.90.
Owner Mrs Sonia Rogers **Bred** Miss K Rausing And Airlie Stud **Trained** Newmarket, Suffolk

FOCUS
A decent handicap won in good style by the highly progressive Alleviate, but the favourite disappointed. The form seems sound enough.
Proper(IRE) Official explanation: jockey said gelding had no more to give
Nawow Official explanation: jockey said gelding had no more to give

2077 JAKE FILLIES' H'CAP — 6f (P)
7:20 (7:23) (Class 4) (0-85,80) 3-Y-0+ **£4,533** (£1,348; £674; £336) **Stalls** Low

Form RPR

3530 **1** **Cerebus**[10] 1796 6-9-6 **74**....................(b) NCallan 4 83
(A J McCabe) *mde all: sn clr: rdn wl over 1f out: r.o strly* **5/2**[1]

0-03 **2** 3 ¾ **Shes Minnie**[8] 1858 5-9-12 **80**....................(b[1]) FergusSweeney 5 77
(P A Blockley) *racd in 3rd pl: rdn and hdwy over 2f out: chsd wnr 2f out: no imp* **7/1**[2]

6 **3** 1 ½ **Applesnap (IRE)**[13] 1715 3-9-2 **80**.................... JohnEgan 1 69
(Mrs C A Dunnett) *chsd wnr: rdn over 2f out: lost 2nd 2f out: one pce* **25/1**

004- **4** 4 ½ **Piece Of My Heart**[145] 7202 3-8-11 **75**.................... JamieSpencer 6 50
(M J Wallace) *a last: rdn and racd awkwardly over 2f out: no ch after* **12/1**[3]

1m 13.72s (0.02) **Going Correction** +0.125s/f (Slow)
WFA 3 from 5yo+ 10lb **4** Ran SP% **52.6**
Speed ratings (Par 102): **104,99,97,91**
CSF £3.46 TOTE £1.50; EX 3.10.
Owner Paul J Dixon **Bred** Rookley Holdings **Trained** Babworth, Notts

FOCUS
An uncompetitive race that was robbed of much of its interest when Temple Of Thebes failed to enter the stalls. This made it easy for the winner, who ran to form.
Piece Of My Heart Official explanation: jockey said filly hung badly left

2078 SHAKESPEARE FILLIES' H'CAP — 1m 2f (P)
7:50 (7:50) (Class 5) (0-70,72) 4-Y-0+ **£2,590** (£770; £385; £192) **Stalls** Low

Form RPR

3-02 **1** **Stringsofmyheart**[19] 1577 4-8-13 **61**.................... DarryllHolland 4 68
(Miss Gay Kelleway) *s.i.s: sn rcvrd and led: mde rest: rdn over 2f out: hrd pressed ins fnl f: fnd ex and forged ahd fnl 100yds* **7/2**[1]

3531 **2** 1 ¼ **Our Kes (IRE)**[8] 1853 6-9-10 **72** 6ex.................... IanMongan 7 77
(P Howling) *t.k.h: hld up in tch in rr: hdwy 4f out: rdn over 2f out: chsd wnr over 1f out: ev ch ins fnl f: no ex fnl 100yds* **7/2**[1]

440- **3** 5 **Golden Wave (IRE)**[191] 6672 4-8-9 **62**.................... AhmedAjtebi(5) 5 57
(D M Simcock) *chsd ldrs: rdn over 2f out: edgd sltly lft 2f out: chsd ldng pair over 1f out: outpcd fnl f* **8/1**

00-3 **4** 3 ½ **Bavarica**[15] 1676 6-9-0 **69**.................... AmyBaker(7) 6 57
(Miss J Feilden) *stdd s: t.k.h: hld up in tch: hdwy on outer 5f out: chsd ldr over 3f out: ev ch over 2f out: bmpd along and wknd qckly over 1f out* **8/1**

50-1 **5** ½ **Treasure Isle**[18] 1606 4-8-2 **50** oh1.................... DaleGibson 8 37
(R A Fahey) *in tch on outer: bmpd bnd over 8f out: rdn and struggling over 3f out: no ch after* **6/1**

6265 **6** 4 ½ **Tabulate**[23] 1505 5-8-2 **50** oh5.................... JimmyQuinn 3 28
(P Howling) *t.k.h: chsd ldr tl over 3f out: sn rdn: wkng whn short of room briefly 2f out* **9/2**[3]

21 **7** 1 ¾ **Miss Marauder**[33] 1287 4-9-5 **67**.................... OscarUrbina 2 41
(M Botti) *t.k.h: hld up in midfield: lost pl and rdn over 4f out: wl bhd fnl 3f* **4/1**[2]

2600 **8** 2 ¼ **Niqaab**[17] 1639 4-8-2 **50** oh1....................(e[1]) ChrisCatlin 1 20
(W J Musson) *in tch in midfiled: dropped to rr and rdn over 4f out: wl bhd fnl 3f* **12/1**

2m 10.48s (1.88) **Going Correction** +0.125s/f (Slow) **8** Ran SP% **126.8**
Speed ratings (Par 100): **97,96,92,89,88 85,83,82**
CSF £17.97 CT £97.61 TOTE £4.70: £1.80, £1.60, £4.30; EX 23.60.
Owner bettingjobs.com **Bred** Wretham Stud **Trained** Exning, Suffolk

FOCUS
Two came clear in what was a moderate handicap. Weak form, the winner rated to her best for this yard.
Miss Marauder Official explanation: trainer said, regarding running and riding, filly was unsuited by the left-handed track

2079 STANLEY MEDIAN AUCTION MAIDEN STKS — 1m (P)
8:20 (8:22) (Class 5) 3-5-Y-0 **£2,590** (£770; £385; £192) **Stalls** Low

Form RPR

223- **1** **Slam**[200] 6468 3-8-7 91.................... MichaelHills 6 90+
(B W Hills) *mde all: rdn jst over 1f out: r.o wl* **4/9**[1]

2 2 ¾ **Once A Gulch (USA)** 3-8-8 0 ow1.................... SebSanders 7 84
(J Noseda) *sn chsng wnr: rdn and tried to chal over 1f out: drvn and hung lft 1f out: one pce* **5/1**[2]

224- **3** 6 **Barliffey (IRE)**[243] 5343 3-8-7 78.................... TPO'Shea 1 70
(D J Coakley) *in tch in midfield: rdn 3f out: chsd ldng pair 2f out: sn swtchd rt: wl outpcd over 1f out* **5/1**[2]

0- **4** 5 **Paint The Town Red**[216] 6106 3-8-7 0.................... ChrisCatlin 5 58
(H J Collingridge) *stdd after s: t.k.h: hld up in rr: outpcd over 3f out: wl bhd fnl 2f* **33/1**

5 shd **Ainia** 3-8-2 0.................... JimmyQuinn 2 53
(D M Simcock) *stdd s: hld up in rr: outpcd over 3f out: no ch fnl 2f* **28/1**

00- **6** 1 ¾ **Augmentation**[208] 6285 3-8-7 0.................... JohnEgan 4 54
(P W D'Arcy) *chsd ldng pair tl 2f out: sn wknd* **25/1**[3]

0-0 **7** 11 **Milne Bay (IRE)**[15] 1669 3-8-7 0.................... RichardMullen 3 28
(D M Simcock) *t.k.h: hld up in tch: rdn and outpcd over 3f out: no ch after: t.o* **50/1**

1m 39.66s (-0.24) **Going Correction** +0.125s/f (Slow) **7** Ran SP% **114.8**
Speed ratings (Par 103): **106,103,97,92,92 90,79**
CSF £3.02 TOTE £1.30: £1.02, £3.50; EX 3.80 Place 6 £123.29, Place 5 £80.42.
Owner K Abdulla **Bred** Juddmonte Farms Ltd **Trained** Lambourn, Berks

FOCUS
An uncompetitive maiden in which the winner Slam set a high standard and probably ran close to form.
T/Plt: £282.50 to a £1 stake. Pool: £42,405.81. 109.55 winning tickets. T/Qpdt: £42.30 to a £1 stake. Pool: £3,658.10. 63.90 winning tickets. SP

1901 SOUTHWELL (L-H)
Tuesday, May 13

OFFICIAL GOING: Standard
Wind: Fresh, half against Weather: fine and dry but breezy

2080 BOOK YOUR HOSPITALITY PACKAGES AT SOUTHWELL CLAIMING STKS — 1m 3f (F)
2:20 (2:20) (Class 5) 3-Y-0 **£2,100** (£2,100; £481; £240) **Stalls** Low

Form RPR

-105 **1** **An Scaribh**[15] 1678 3-8-7 71.................... RichardEvans(7) 2 67
(P D Evans) *trckd ldrs: nt clr run over 2f out: chal 1f out: edgd lft: dead-heated on line* **11/4**[3]

1204 **1** dht **Home**[15] 1678 3-9-0 67....................(p) PatCosgrave 4 67
(J R Boyle) *trckd ldrs: effrt 3f out: led over 1f out: jnd on line* **9/4**[1]

-64 **3** 8 **Reprieved**[7] 1905 3-8-12 0.................... MarkCoumbe(7) 3 58
(M C Chapman) *t.k.h: trckd ldr: led 3f out: edgd rt: hdd over 1f out: sn wknd* **25/1**

5404 **4** 3 ¾ **Indecision**[9] 1823 3-8-8 52.................... PaulMulrennan 6 41
(M W Easterby) *hld up: drvn over 5f out: hdwy to chse ldrs 3f out: wknd over 1f out* **8/1**

0-55 **5** 11 **L'Orage**[21] 1549 3-8-3 53.................... DominicFox(3) 5 20
(M G Quinlan) *s.s: in rr: nvr on terms* **16/1**

40-0 **6** 6 **Howe's Jack (IRE)**[15] 1684 3-8-4 40....................(t) NBazeley(7) 8 15
(M C Chapman) *led tl 3f out: sn wknd* **100/1**

15 **7** 5 **Silver Spruce**[13] 1731 3-9-2 62.................... FergalLynch 7 12
(I W McInnes) *chsd ldrs: drvn over 4f out: lost pl 3f out* **5/2**[2]

40-0 **8** 11 **Social Spirit (IRE)**[21] 1553 3-8-4 54....................(b[1]) DO'Donohoe 9 —
(J R Weymes) *s.s: reluctant and sn bhd* **40/1**

50-6 **9** ¾ **Lady Jinks**[14] 1710 3-8-4 50....................(be[1]) RichardSmith 1 —
(M D I Usher) *sn chsng ldrs: lost pl over 4f out: sn bhd* **28/1**

2m 29.88s (1.88) **Going Correction** +0.025s/f (Slow) **9** Ran SP% **113.7**
Speed ratings (Par 99): **94,94,88,85,77 73,69,61,60**
TRIFECTA Win: Home £1.50 An Scaribh £1.60. PL: H £1.20 AS £1.30 R £4.70 EX: H/AS £5.00 AS/H £3.00 CSF: H/AS £4.15 AS/H £4.46.Home was claimed by C Gordon for £10,000.
Owner John P Jones **Bred** P Young **Trained** Pandy, Monmouths
Owner M Khan X2 **Bred** A T Macdonald **Trained** Epsom, Surrey
■ Stewards' Enquiry : Fergal Lynch caution: careless riding

FOCUS
A moderate claimer run at a snail's pace. The dead-heaters were pretty much to form.

2081 ARENALEISUREPLC.COM H'CAP — 6f (F)
2:50 (2:50) (Class 5) (0-70,66) 4-Y-0+ **£3,238** (£963; £481; £240) **Stalls** Low

Form RPR

4213 **1** **Kingsmaite**[4] 1966 7-8-8 **56** ow2....................(b) PhillipMakin 3 68
(S R Bowring) *mid-div: drvn over 3f out: styd on to ld wl ins fnl f* **10/3**[1]

3303 **2** 1 ¼ **Owed**[14] 1703 6-8-8 **56**....................(tp) RobertWinston 12 64
(R Bastiman) *swtchd lft after s: led tl hdd and no ex fnl 75yds* **5/1**[3]

3252 **3** 1 ¼ **Cape Of Storms**[14] 1703 5-9-0 **62**....................(b) PaulMulrennan 8 66
(R Brotherton) *chsd ldrs: chal over 1f out: kpt on same pce* **4/1**[2]

06-0 **4** 3 ¼ **Orotund**[20] 1561 4-8-1 **52**.................... DuranFentiman(3) 1 46
(T D Easterby) *w ldrs: wknd fnl 150yds* **8/1**

1260 **5** *2 1/4* **Tag Team (IRE)**47 1040 7-8-10 **65**.......................... MarkCoumbe(7) 10 51
(John A Harris) *chsd ldrs: rdn over 2f out: fdd fnl f* **10/1**
0102 **6** *hd* **Elusive Warrior (USA)**19 1590 5-8-13 **61**......................(p) NeilPollard 2 47
(A J McCabe) *chsd ldrs: edgd lft over 2f out: wknd fnl f* **15/2**
000 **7** *2 1/2* **Trees Of Green (USA)**21 1541 4-9-1 **63**......................... OscarUrbina 4 41
(M Wigham) *sn bhd and drvn along: sme hdwy 2f out: nvr on terms* **11/1**
50-0 **8** *1 1/4* **Megalo Maniac**11 1780 5-8-8 **63**.......................... FrederikTylicki(7) 6 37
(R A Fahey) *s.i.s: nvr on terms* **14/1**
060- **9** *2 1/4* **Tipsy Prince**211 6239 4-9-4 **66**.. NeilChalmers 7 33
(David Pinder) *sn outpcd and bhd* **11/1**
335- **10** *1/2* **Branston Tiger**364 1755 9-9-2 **64**..............................(v) DanielTudhope 5 29
(Ian Emmerson) *mid-div and sn drvn along: outpcd over 4f out: wknd over 2f out* **11/1**

1m 16.12s (-0.38) **Going Correction** +0.025s/f (Slow) **10** Ran SP% **123.4**
Speed ratings (Par 103): **103,101,99,95,92 92,88,87,84,83**
CSF £21.37 CT £72.87 TOTE £5.20: £1.70, £2.20, £1.50; EX 17.00.
Owner S R Bowring **Bred** S R Bowring **Trained** Edwinstowe, Notts

FOCUS
A low-grade handicap but fairly solid form from the first three home.
Trees Of Green(USA) Official explanation: jockey said gelding was unsuited by the kick-back

2082 NSPCC FULL STOP H'CAP 5f (F)
3:20 (3:20) (Class 3) (0-90,90) 4-Y-O+ **£9,066** (£2,697; £1,348; £673) **Stalls** High

Form RPR
6100 **1** **Luscivious**10 1796 4-8-13 **85**...............................(b) PatCosgrave 4 94
(A J McCabe) *chsd ldr: led over 1f out: kpt on wl* **9/2**2
5111 **2** *1* **Xpres Maite**14 1708 5-9-4 **90**..(v) PhillipMakin 7 95+
(S R Bowring) *chsd ldrs: drvn over 2f out: swtchd lft jst ins fnl f: styd on to take 2nd nr fin* **9/2**2
4350 **3** *3/4* **Tartatartufata**10 1818 6-9-1 **87**......................................(v) DaneO'Neill 5 90
(D Shaw) *rrd s: led tl over 1f out: kpt on same pce* **15/2**
-421 **4** *2* **Hereford Boy**21 1537 4-8-9 **81**.. RobertHavlin 3 77
(D K Ivory) *swtchd outside over 3f out: hdwy to chse ldrs 2f out: kpt on same pce* **4/1**1
04-2 **5** *2 3/4* **Gallery Girl (IRE)**12 1755 5-8-8 **80**...................................... DavidAllan 6 66
(T D Easterby) *chsd ldrs: fdd appr fnl f* **6/1**3
3001 **6** *nk* **Bo McGinty (IRE)**15 1677 7-8-10 **82**............................(b) PaulHanagan 8 67
(R A Fahey) *in tch: rdn over 2f out: hung rt: nvr nr to chal* **4/1**1
455- **7** *10* **Tous Les Deux**143 7221 5-7-13 **78** oh13 ow2........... PatrickDonaghy(7) 2 27
(Peter Grayson) *chsd ldrs: drvn over 3f out: sn lost pl: bhd fnl 2f* **28/1**
0-60 **8** *1 1/2* **Garstang**29 1366 5-8-3 **78** oh2 ow2.......................(b) KirstyMilczarek(3) 1 21
(Peter Grayson) *w ldrs: t.k.h: lost pl over 1f out: sn bhd* **16/1**

59.65 secs (-0.05) **Going Correction** +0.175s/f (Slow) **8** Ran SP% **111.7**
Speed ratings (Par 107): **107,105,104,101,96 96,80,77**
CSF £23.82 CT £144.17 TOTE £5.30: £1.80, £1.40, £2.50; EX 29.30.
Owner Paul J Dixon And Keith Barratt **Bred** R J Turner **Trained** Babworth, Notts

FOCUS
A good prize for the Fibresand. The form seems sound at face value but these 5f races rarely are.

NOTEBOOK
Luscivious, 6lb higher than Beverley, is in the form of his life and simply would not be denied. He needs soft ground on turf so is likely to be back here this summer. (op 6-1)
Xpres Maite, 12lb higher, was running over this much shorter trip due to a lack of opportunities now he is rated 90. Never far away, he stuck to his guns but in truth was never going to quite get to grips with the winner. (op 11-2)
Tartatartufata exited from the stalls on her back legs. She took them along and fought back all the way to the line. (tchd 7-1)
Hereford Boy, 6lb higher, made his effort on the outer and never landed a telling blow. (op 11-4)
Gallery Girl(IRE), 3lb higher, was having just her second taste of the All-Weather. (op 13-2)
Bo McGinty(IRE), drawn hard against the rail, wanted to do nothing but hang into the fence and this was not one of his better days. Official explanation: jockey said gelding hung right-handed throughout (op 9-2 tchd 7-2)

2083 ROSELAND GROUP SUPPORTING NSPCC H'CAP 1m (F)
3:50 (3:50) (Class 4) (0-85,85) 4-Y-O+ **£5,504** (£1,637; £818; £408) **Stalls** Low

Form RPR
1-13 **1** **Dado Mush**105 351 5-8-3 **73**.................................(p) KirstyMilczarek(3) 1 81
(T T Clement) *trckd ldrs: drvn and outpcd 4f out: hdwy on ins over 2f out: styd on to ld towards fin* **6/1**3
1112 **2** *nk* **Yakimov (USA)**7 1902 9-8-11 **85**............................. PatrickDonaghy(7) 3 92
(Ollie Pears) *trckd ldrs: effrt over 3f out: styd on to ld ins fnl f: hdd nr fin* **11/4**1
5405 **3** *3/4* **Councellor (FR)**8 1857 6-9-4 **85**..................................(t) MickyFenton 5 90
(Stef Liddiard) *led tl ins fnl f: no ex* **3/1**2
-421 **4** *1* **Full Victory (IRE)**6 1910 6-9-1 **82** 6ex................................ DaneO'Neill 2 85
(R A Farrant) *trckd ldrs: effrt 3f out: sn chalng: kpt on same pce fnl f* **11/4**1
0020 **5** *2 1/4* **Red Romeo**11 1774 7-9-3 **84**.. DanielTudhope 4 82
(N Wilson) *trckd ldrs: drvn 3f out: wknd fnl f* **9/1**
0210 **6** *10* **Divertimenti (IRE)**27 1409 4-8-11 **78**.............................. RobertWinston 6 53
(C R Dore) *chsd ldrs: lost pl over 1f out* **10/1**

1m 43.52s (-0.18) **Going Correction** +0.025s/f (Slow) **6** Ran SP% **111.7**
Speed ratings (Par 105): **101,100,99,98,96 86**
CSF £22.53 TOTE £7.30: £2.80, £1.50; EX 16.90.
Owner Dr M Edres **Bred** Bellow Hill Stud **Trained** Newmarket, Suffolk

FOCUS
A tight handicap run at a modest pace, with the first three stretched right across the track at the finish.

2084 SOUTHWELL-RACECOURSE.CO.UK MEDIAN AUCTION MAIDEN STKS 7f (F)
4:20 (4:21) (Class 5) 3-5-Y-O **£3,561** (£1,059; £529; £264) **Stalls** Low

Form RPR
00-4 **1** **Longevity**24 1467 3-9-0 70...................................... KerrinMcEvoy 4 78+
(W Jarvis) *chsd ldrs: hung lft over 1f out: styd on to ld nr fin* **4/6**1
0-66 **2** *nk* **To Bubbles**81 662 3-8-9 58... PhillipMakin 2 71
(T D Barron) *mde most: hdd towards fin* **11/1**
00-0 **3** *13* **Reel Man**46 1060 3-9-0 64... SaleemGolam 12 41
(D K Ivory) *mid-div: outpcd and lost pl over 3f out: hdwy 2f out: kpt on to take modest 3rd nr fin* **14/1**
0-60 **4** *nk* **Mouse White**14 1695 3-8-7 52....................................... AmyScott(7) 11 40
(H Candy) *chsd ldrs: drvn and outpcd over 3f out: kpt on fnl 2f* **12/1**
5 *3/4* **Bertha** 3-8-9 0.. PatCosgrave 6 33
(J A Osborne) *chsd ldrs: one pce fnl 2f* **9/1**3
6 *1/2* **Cheeky Chilli** 3-8-9 0.. DanielTudhope 5 32
(A J McCabe) *s.s: hdwy over 4f out: nvr nr ldrs* **25/1**
7 *1* **Coup De Torchon (FR)** 3-8-9 0.. DaneO'Neill 8 29
(J A Osborne) *chsd ldrs: outpcd over 2f out: n.d after* **15/2**2
600 **8** *1/2* **Marysedge**11 1777 3-8-9 32.. PaulMulrennan 10 28
(R Brotherton) *chsd ldrs: hung bdly rt over 1f out: one pce* **100/1**
00 **9** *8* **Hapi**12 1748 3-9-0 0..(t) PaulHanagan 7 11
(S C Williams) *chsd ldrs: lost pl over 1f out* **40/1**
6 **10** *9* **Champagne Lawn (USA)**82 634 3-8-9 0............................. PaulFessey 3 —
(T D Barron) *prom: lost pl over 3f out: sn bhd* **12/1**
00-0 **11** *1* **Patsymartin**69 796 3-8-11 48.. DominicFox(3) 9 —
(M G Quinlan) *sn outpcd and in rr: bhd fnl 4f* **40/1**

1m 30.11s (-0.19) **Going Correction** +0.025s/f (Slow) **11** Ran SP% **121.9**
Speed ratings (Par 103): **102,101,86,86,85 85,83,83,74,63 62**
CSF £9.61 TOTE £1.50: £1.20, £2.20, £2.60; EX 8.60.
Owner Gillian, Lady Howard De Walden **Bred** Plantation Stud **Trained** Newmarket, Suffolk

FOCUS
Little strength in depth to this maiden, but the first two both showed improved form in pulling well clear.

2085 BOOK YOUR TICKETS ONLINE AT SOUTHWELL-RACECOURSE.CO.UK H'CAP 7f (F)
4:50 (4:51) (Class 4) (0-85,85) 4-Y-O+ **£5,180** (£1,541; £770; £384) **Stalls** Low

Form RPR
0-54 **1** **Masai Moon**17 1617 4-8-13 **85**.................................... JamesMillman(5) 3 97+
(B R Millman) *hld up: effrt over 2f out: sn rdn: led appr fnl f: forged clr: v readily* **11/4**1
64P1 **2** *4* **Bartercard (USA)**19 1591 7-8-8 **75**..................................... MickyFenton 5 76
(Stef Liddiard) *t.k.h: w ldr: led over 3f out: hdd appr fnl f: no ch w wnr* **7/2**2
21-2 **3** *2 1/4* **Flying Bantam (IRE)**14 1708 7-8-4 **71** oh1........................ PaulHanagan 6 66
(R A Fahey) *w ldrs: chal over 1f out: kpt on same pce* **7/2**2
4135 **4** *4 1/2* **Kelamon**10 1800 4-8-4 **71**.. RichardSmith 2 54
(M D I Usher) *mde most tl over 3f out: wknd over 1f out* **5/1**
0050 **5** *hd* **Kabeer**13 1723 10-8-11 **85**....................................(t) StacyRenwick(7) 1 67
(A J McCabe) *dwlt: effrt on outer over 2f out: nvr a factor* **9/2**3
0600 **6** *3 3/4* **Sailor King (IRE)**17 1630 6-9-1 **82**................................. SaleemGolam 4 54
(D K Ivory) *trckd ldrs: effrt 3f out: sn rdn and btn* **11/1**

1m 29.45s (-0.85) **Going Correction** +0.025s/f (Slow) **6** Ran SP% **114.3**
Speed ratings (Par 105): **105,100,97,92,92 88**
CSF £12.97 TOTE £3.10: £1.70, £1.60; EX 11.30 Place 6 £18.97, Place 5 £11.39.
Owner C Roper **Bred** Mrs B A Matthews **Trained** Kentisbeare, Devon

FOCUS
Not a strong handicap with doubts over most of these. The winner is rated up 5lb.
T/Jkpt: £5,344.90 to a £1 stake. Pool: £15,056.23. 2.00 winning tickets. T/Plt: £21.20 to a £1 stake. Pool: £47,365.47. 1,626.35 winning tickets. T/Qpdt: £15.80 to a £1 stake. Pool: £2,124.18. 99.00 winning tickets. WG

2054 YARMOUTH (L-H)
Tuesday, May 13

OFFICIAL GOING: Good to firm
Wind: Fresh, across Weather: Sea fret clearing after race 1

2086 EUROPEAN BREEDERS' FUND MAIDEN STKS 6f 3y
2:30 (2:31) (Class 5) 2-Y-O **£3,784** (£1,132; £424; £424; £141) **Stalls** High

Form RPR
5 **1** **Cool Art (IRE)**9 1832 2-9-3 0.. JamieSpencer 2 66+
(S A Callaghan) *mde all: rdn over 1f out: r.o* **4/11**1
2 *1 1/4* **Yokozuna** 2-9-3 0.. StephenDonohoe 5 62+
(E A L Dunlop) *hld up in tch: outpcd over 2f out: swtchd rt over 1f out: r.o wl ins fnl f: nt rch wnr* **20/1**3
3 *1 1/4* **Olaudah Equiano** 2-9-3 0... JimmyQuinn 4 59
(M H Tompkins) *hld up in tch: rdn over 1f out: styd on* **40/1**
0 **3** *dht* **Mymateeric**13 1727 2-9-3 0.. EddieAhern 1 59
(J Pearce) *chsd wnr to 1/2-way: rdn and edgd rt over 1f out: styd on* **20/1**3
5 *3/4* **Kings Troop** 2-9-3 0.. TedDurcan 6 56
(H R A Cecil) *dwlt: hdwy over 4f out: chsd wnr 1/2-way: rdn over 1f out: no ex ins fnl f* **10/3**2

1m 14.29s (-0.11) **Going Correction** -0.325s/f (Firm) **5** Ran SP% **108.4**
Speed ratings (Par 93): **87,85,83,83,82**
CSF £9.95 TOTE £1.40: £1.10, £2.90; EX 6.90.
Owner Matthew Green **Bred** Azienda Agricola Robiati Angelo **Trained** Newmarket, Suffolk

FOCUS
An average juvenile maiden. The form is not easy to assess, but is rated around the winner who is a nice enough type.

NOTEBOOK
Cool Art(IRE), fifth on his debut at Newmarket nine days previously, was all the rage to open his account and he rewarded his supporters with a workmanlike success from the front. He is still very much learning his trade, but has an engine and the extra obviously furlong suited. It will be interesting to see where he is pitched in next. (op 4-7 tchd 8-13 in a place)
Yokozuna ◆, who cost 12,500gns, motored home inside the final furlong after hitting a flat spot nearing the 2f pole. He should improve a bundle for the run and clearly has one of these within his compass. (op 14-1)
Olaudah Equiano, a 22,000gns purchase whose dam was a useful winner over 5f at two, proved one-paced on this racecourse debut yet still showed ability. He will do better when able to race more positively over this trip and should really learn a good deal from the experience. (op 28-1 tchd 33-1)
Mymateeric showed the benefit of his debut experience and posted a much-improved effort over this extra furlong. He is going the right way. (op 28-1 tchd 33-1)
Kings Troop, a 25,000gns purchase, travelled nicely enough through the first half of the race but his response when asked to improve from 2f out was limited. He is entitled to come on for the experience and may just be better off dropping to 5f for the short term. (op 9-4 tchd 7-2)

2087 EASTERN DAILY PRESS H'CAP 7f 3y
3:00 (3:01) (Class 5) (0-75,75) 4-Y-O+ **£2,590** (£770; £385; £192) **Stalls** High

Form RPR
1- **1** **Musaalem (USA)**260 4908 4-9-4 **75**.. RHills 8 95+
(W J Haggas) *s.i.s: hld up: plld hrd: hdwy over 2f out: led over 1f out: rdn out* **11/4**2
-032 **2** *2 1/2* **Violent Velocity (IRE)**7 1900 5-8-9 **66**............................ GrahamGibbons 4 73
(J J Quinn) *hld up: hdwy over 2f out: nt clr run over 1f out: sn rdn: r.o* **9/4**1
2114 **3** *3/4* **Wodhill Schnaps**19 1590 7-8-4 **61** oh3..............................(b) HayleyTurner 5 66
(D Morris) *hld up: hdwy over 1f out: edgd rt ins fnl f: r.o* **22/1**

062- 4 2 **Im Ova Ere Dad (IRE)**[151] 7141 5-8-13 **70** JamieSpencer 9 70
(D E Cantillon) *stdd s: hld up: swtchd lft and hdwy over 2f out: rdn over 1f out: no ex fnl f* **8/1**

-000 5 1 1/4 **Fiefdom (IRE)**[3] 2007 6-9-2 **73** RoystonFfrench 1 69
(I W McInnes) *prom: sn pushed along: rdn over 2f out: wknd ins fnl f* **12/1**

6-00 6 5 **Empire Dancer (IRE)**[29] 1371 5-8-4 **61** oh5 PatrickMathers 10 44
(I W McInnes) *chsd ldrs: rdn over 2f out: wknd over 1f out* **50/1**

5502 7 1 1/4 **Hits Only Cash**[18] 1605 6-8-8 **65** JimmyQuinn 7 44
(J Pearce) *hld up: outpcd 1/2-way: n.d* **12/1**

5460 8 2 3/4 **Bertie Southstreet**[75] 729 5-8-12 **69** JoeFanning 2 41
(J R Best) *led: hdd over 5f out: rdn over 2f out: wknd fnl f* **25/1**

0/04 9 6 **Apres Ski (IRE)**[14] 1700 5-8-3 **63** oh1 ow2 KevinGhunowa(3) 3 19
(J F Coupland) *s.i.s: sn prom: rdn over 2f out: sn wknd* **33/1**

00/5 10 16 **Banjo Patterson**[23] 1500 6-8-13 **73** (b) JerryO'Dwyer(3) 11 —
(M G Quinlan) *hld up: rdn and wknd over 2f out* **18/1**

0-03 11 2 1/4 **Grey Boy (GER)**[8] 1872 7-8-6 **63** CatherineGannon 6 —
(A W Carroll) *w ldr tl led over 5f out: rdn whn wnt lame and hdd over 1f out: virtually p.u* **7/1**[3]

1m 23.72s (-2.88) **Going Correction** -0.325s/f (Firm) **11** Ran SP% **114.8**
Speed ratings (Par 103): **103,100,99,97,95 89,88,85,78,60 57**
CSF £8.64 CT £107.49 TOTE £3.20: £1.40, £1.10, £4.40; EX 9.70 Trifecta £178.40 Part won. Pool: £251.29 - 0.50 winning units..
Owner Hamdan Al Maktoum **Bred** Shadwell Farm LLC **Trained** Newmarket, Suffolk

FOCUS
A modest handicap won by a progressive sort who looked a class above these. The runner-up sets the level and the form seems solid.
Im Ova Ere Dad(IRE) Official explanation: jockey said gelding hung right
Grey Boy(GER) Official explanation: jockey said gelding lost its action

2088 NELSON COUNTY FILLIES' H'CAP 5f 43y
3:30 (3:33) (Class 6) (0-65,65) 3-Y-O+ **£1,942** (£578; £288; £144) **Stalls** High

Form RPR

5152 1 **Wibbadune (IRE)**[14] 1706 4-8-13 **51** AdamKirby 5 63
(D Shaw) *edgd lft s: trckd ldrs: led 2f out: r.o* **4/1**[3]

0-01 2 1 1/4 **Black Moma (IRE)**[24] 1476 4-9-9 **61** JamieSpencer 1 69
(A B Haynes) *hld up in tch: rdn to chse wnr over 1f out: unable qck ins fnl f* **11/4**[1]

05-0 3 shd **Sofinella (IRE)**[28] 1378 5-9-4 **56** CatherineGannon 2 63
(A W Carroll) *w ldr: rdn over 1f out: styd on* **12/1**

54-0 4 1 **Little Bones**[19] 1592 3-8-4 **54** KevinGhunowa(3) 3 54
(J F Coupland) *prom: lost pl over 3f out: hdwy u.p over 1f out: edgd lft ins fnl f: styd on same pce* **25/1**

2423 5 3/4 **Time Share (IRE)**[14] 1706 4-8-8 **51** oh4 KellyHarrison(5) 7 52
(M Wigham) *hld up: shkn up over 1f out: edgd rt ins fnl f: nvr nr to chal* **6/1**

-420 6 hd **Blackmalkin (USA)**[59] 899 4-9-13 **65** EddieAhern 8 65
(M Quinn) *chsd ldrs: rdn and hung lft 1/2-way: styd on same pce appr fnl f* **10/3**[2]

11-5 7 1 1/4 **Contentious (IRE)**[29] 1373 4-9-6 **58** RichardMullen 4 54
(D M Simcock) *bmpd s: sn led: rdn and hdd 2f out: sn edgd lft: wknd fnl f* **7/1**

030- 8 2 1/2 **Violet's Pride**[196] 6565 4-8-13 **51** oh6 KimTinkler 6 38
(N Tinkler) *sn pushed along in rr: hung lft 1/2-way: wknd over 1f out* **16/1**

61.76 secs (-0.44) **Going Correction** -0.325s/f (Firm)
WFA 3 from 4yo+ 9lb **8** Ran SP% **114.0**
Speed ratings (Par 98): **90,88,87,86,85 84,82,78**
CSF £15.32 CT £119.61 TOTE £5.40: £1.50, £1.40, £3.40; EX 16.10 Trifecta £73.60 Pool: £313.06 - 3.02 winning units..
Owner Simon Mapletoft Racing I **Bred** Ballyhane Stud **Trained** Danethorpe, Notts

FOCUS
A moderate fillies' sprint handicap won by the progressive Wibbadune. The form looks solid, rated through the runner-up.

2089 GREAT YARMOUTH TOURIST AUTHORITY (S) STKS 1m 1f
4:00 (4:01) (Class 6) 3-Y-O **£1,683** (£501; £250; £125) **Stalls** Low

Form RPR

6255 1 **Ledgerwood**[27] 1407 3-9-3 63 (p) JamesDoyle 5 54
(J W Hills) *trckd ldrs: rdn over 1f out: styd on to ld wl ins fnl f* **1/1**[1]

0046 2 3/4 **Una Auroraborealis**[5] 1937 3-8-7 41 (p) AlanMunro 1 42
(J Ryan) *led: rdn over 1f out: hdd wl ins fnl f* **9/2**[2]

6530 3 2 **Lancaster Lad (IRE)**[21] 1553 3-8-12 47 (p) EddieAhern 7 43
(A B Haynes) *hld up: hdwy over 1f out: sn rdn: styd on* **11/2**[3]

-000 4 3/4 **Fortunes Maid (IRE)**[21] 1553 3-8-7 46 (b[1]) JimmyQuinn 2 36
(M H Tompkins) *prom: rdn over 2f out: styd on* **16/1**

0 5 1 1/2 **Cheeky Try (USA)**[12] 1743 3-8-5 55 (t) CharlotteKerton(7) 3 38
(G Prodromou) *trckd ldr: racd keenly: slipped bnd 5f out: rdn 3f out: wknd ins fnl f* **9/1**

6 6 1 **Pure Inspiration**[56] 923 3-8-7 0 RichardMullen 6 31
(P Howling) *dwlt: hld up: rdn over 2f out: sn outpcd* **25/1**

-034 7 23 **Adam Eterno (IRE)**[83] 623 3-9-0 48 KevinGhunowa(3) 4 —
(A B Haynes) *chsd ldrs: rdn over 5f out: wknd over 2f out: eased ins fnl f* **9/1**

1m 55.81s (0.01) **7** Ran SP% **113.3**
CSF £5.63 TOTE £2.00: £1.50, £2.20; EX 6.80.There was no bid for the winner.
Owner Gary & Linnet Woodward and Neil Ledger **Bred** Shutford Stud And O F Waller **Trained** Upper Lambourn, Berks
■ Stewards' Enquiry : Charlotte Kerton two-day ban: used whip with excessive frequency (May 27-28)

FOCUS
A dire affair. The 61-rated winner obviously did not run near to that mark in winning.
Adam Eterno(IRE) Official explanation: jockey said gelding had a breathing problem

2090 EASTERN EVENING NEWS MEDIAN AUCTION MAIDEN STKS 1m 2f 21y
4:30 (4:30) (Class 6) 3-Y-O **£1,942** (£578; £288; £144) **Stalls** Low

Form RPR

5-05 1 **Totoman**[8] 1876 3-9-3 0 AdamKirby 1 78+
(G G Margarson) *chsd ldr: led over 3f out: rdn clr fr over 1f out* **7/2**[3]

532 2 8 **Director's Chair**[21] 1549 3-9-0 64 (b[1]) JerryO'Dwyer(3) 4 62
(Miss J Feilden) *sn rdn to ld: hdd over 3f out: styd on same pce appr fnl f* **10/1**

020- 3 3 **Colorado Springs**[169] 6944 3-8-12 68 AlanMunro 6 51
(W Jarvis) *s.i.s: hld up: hdwy 1/2-way: rdn over 3f out: wkng whn hung lft over 1f out* **5/1**

60- 4 1 **Blue Admiral**[221] 5977 3-9-3 0 JimmyQuinn 2 54+
(M H Tompkins) *s.i.s: hld up: shkn up over 2f out: nvr nr to chal* **3/1**[2]

320 5 2 3/4 **Turtle Dove**[35] 1252 3-8-5 63 AndreaAtzeni(7) 3 51+
(M Botti) *hld up in tch: racd keenly: nt clr run over 2f out: sn hmpd and lost pl: nt rcvr* **10/1**

0 6 14 **Bonzo**[20] 1563 3-9-3 0 RichardMullen 5 21
(P Howling) *hld up: a in rr: wknd over 2f out* **40/1**

263 7 38 **Speyside (IRE)**[21] 1535 3-9-3 72 MichaelHills 7 —
(J W Hills) *prom: rdn over 3f out: hung lft over 2f out: sn lost action and eased* **11/4**[1]

2m 9.26s (-1.24) **Going Correction** -0.175s/f (Firm) **7** Ran SP% **111.2**
Speed ratings (Par 97): **97,90,88,87,85 74,43**
CSF £34.81 TOTE £4.80: £2.00, £2.60; EX 38.90 Trifecta £294.50 Part won. Pool: £414.81 - 0.79 winning units..
Owner Norcroft Park Stud **Bred** Norcroft Park Stud **Trained** Newmarket, Suffolk

FOCUS
A weak maiden even before the favourite lost his action. The winner rates full value for the winning margin but there is some doubt over what he achieved.
Speyside(IRE) Official explanation: jockey said gelding lost its action twice

2091 DIGIBET H'CAP 2m
5:00 (5:00) (Class 5) (0-70,70) 4-Y-O+ **£2,590** (£770; £385; £192) **Stalls** High

Form RPR

1124 1 **Capitalise (IRE)**[39] 1181 5-9-0 **58** AlanMunro 6 65+
(V Smith) *hld up: hdwy over 2f out: led 1f out: hung lft: styd on wl* **5/2**[2]

10-0 2 3 **Rajayoga**[13] 1726 7-8-7 **51** oh2 JimmyQuinn 4 54
(M H Tompkins) *led: rdn over 2f out: hdd 1f out: styd on same pce* **6/1**

13-4 3 shd **Fourth Dimension (IRE)**[32] 1299 9-9-12 **70** AdamKirby 3 73
(Miss T Spearing) *s.s: hld up: hdwy over 2f out: sn rdn: ev ch over 1f out: styd on same pce* **13/8**[1]

-500 4 1/2 **High Point (IRE)**[8] 1856 10-9-1 **66** JemmaMarshall(7) 5 68
(G P Enright) *a.p: chsd ldr after 3f: rdn over 3f out: no ex ins fnl f* **7/1**

41-4 5 2 1/2 **Ashwell Rose**[15] 1692 6-8-13 **57** (v) EddieAhern 1 56
(J R Jenkins) *chsd ldr 3f: remained handy: rdn over 1f out: wknd ins fnl f* **11/2**[3]

3m 34.14s (-0.46) **Going Correction** -0.175s/f (Firm)
WFA 4 from 5yo+ 3lb **5** Ran SP% **108.8**
Speed ratings (Par 103): **94,92,92,92,90**
CSF £16.34 TOTE £3.10: £1.50, £3.10; EX 18.40 Place 6 £38.98, Place 5 £29.19.
Owner Tilen Electrics Ltd **Bred** Dan Daly **Trained** Exning, Suffolk

FOCUS
A very moderate staying handicap, run at just a modest early pace. The form should be treated with a little caution, with the runner-up the best guide.
T/Plt: £51.00 to a £1 stake. Pool: £41,352.15. 590.80 winning tickets. T/Qpdt: £21.10 to a £1 stake. Pool: £2,171.78. 76.00 winning tickets. CR

2092 - 2095a (Foreign Racing) - See Raceform Interactive

1712 CHANTILLY (R-H)
Tuesday, May 13

OFFICIAL GOING: Good

2096a PRIX DE GUICHE (GROUP 3) (COLTS) 1m 1f
2:50 (2:57) 3-Y-O **£29,412** (£11,765; £8,824; £5,882; £2,941)

RPR

1 **Trincot (FR)**[32] 3-9-2 CSoumillon 3 101
(P Demercastel, France) *hld up in 4th to st: trcking 2nd fr 2f out: swtchd out 1f out: rdn to ld 50yds out: r.o* **22/10**[1]

2 nk **In Chambers**[21] 3-9-2 OPeslier 4 100
(M Delzangles, France) *racd in 3rd: rdn to ld narrowly appr fnl f: hdd 50yds out: r.o* **9/2**

3 1 **Mayweather**[37] 1239 3-9-2 C-PLemaire 2 98
(J-C Rouget, France) *pressed ldr: led after 3f: hdd appr fnl f: one pce last 100yds* **49/10**

4 2 **Putney Bridge (USA)**[19] 1594 3-9-2 (b) SPasquier 5 94
(Mme C Head-Maarek, France) *hld up in rr: swtchd out 2f out: rdn over 1f out: tk 4th cl home* **33/10**[3]

5 1/2 **In Seclusion (USA)**[40] 3-9-2 JVictoire 1 93
(A Fabre, France) *led 3f: 2nd st: rdn and btn 2f out* **27/10**[2]

1m 52.3s (1.20) **5** Ran SP% **116.7**
PARI-MUTUEL: WIN 3.20; PL 1.70, 2.50; SF 10.70.
Owner Ecurie Bader SCEA **Bred** Scea Ecurie Bader **Trained** France

NOTEBOOK
Trincot(FR) had form which pointed to him winning this Group 3 Classic trial and was brought with a well-timed late challenge after racing in fourth place for much of the race. Although he only won by a neck, the official distance does not do the colt justice. He is now unbeaten in three races this season and further improvement can be expected. His connections are not sure he will stay the extended 1m2f of the Prix du Jockey Club but he may well still take his chance.
In Chambers took control of the race halfway up the straight but could not hold the winner in the final 50 yards. It was a good effort from this colt who to all intents and purposes is still a maiden as he was awarded a race at Saint-Cloud by the Stewards. He appears to be improving for every outing and connections have no firm plans for the moment.
Mayweather went to the head of affairs early in the straight and then battled on well to the line. A longer trip may be an advantage in the future.
Putney Bridge(USA) wore blinkers for the first time but they did not have a positive effect. He was last for much of the race and completely failed to quicken in the straight. His form is better than this but he seems to have fallen out of love with the sport.
In Seclusion(USA) finished lame.

1693 BATH (L-H)
Wednesday, May 14

OFFICIAL GOING: Good to firm (9.4)
Wind: moderate, behind

2097 SBW ADVERTISING H'CAP 1m 2f 46y
6:00 (6:00) (Class 6) (0-65,69) 4-Y-O+ **£2,047** (£604; £302) **Stalls** Low

Form RPR

521- 1 **Auntie Mame**[147] 7185 4-8-7 **54** TPO'Shea 7 65
(D J Coakley) *trckd ldrs: rdn to ld fnl 110yds: drvn out* **25/1**

6133 2 1 **Friends Hope**[9] 7-9-1 **69** 6ex SophieDoyle(7) 15 78
(P A Blockley) *chsd ldrs: led ins fnl 2f: rdn: hdd and no ex fnl 110yds* **13/2**[3]

5021 **3** *1 3/4* **Silver Blue (IRE)**[1] 2070 5-8-4 51 6ex................................ LiamJones 5 60+
(W K Goldsworthy) *in rr: hdwy and n.m.r 2f out: swtchd rt to outside and stl nt clr run over 1f out: styd on strly ins fnl f but nt rch ldrs* **4/1**[2]

3660 **4** *3/4* **Under Fire (IRE)**[21] 1565 5-8-8 62.. MarkCoumbe(7) 9 66
(A W Carroll) *sn led: rdn 3f out: hdd ins fnl 2f: wknd ins fnl f* **50/1**

2421 **5** *nk* **Ryan's Future (IRE)**[35] 1266 8-9-4 65................................ LPKeniry 11 68
(J S Moore) *s.i.s: in rr: hdwy over 2f out: styd on fnl f but nvr gng pce to be competitive* **7/2**[1]

/16- **6** *nk* **Jacaranda (IRE)**[230] 4909 8-8-13 65........................ JamesMillman(5) 10 68
(B R Millman) *s.i.s: in rr: shkn up 3f out: hdwy on outside fr over 2f out: kpt on ins fnl f but nt rch ldrs* **8/1**

5120 **7** *5* **Siena Star (IRE)**[24] 1505 10-9-1 62................................ MickyFenton 13 55
(Stef Liddiard) *in tch rdn to chse ldrs over 2f out: one pce fnl f* **10/1**

3155 **8** *1* **King Of Charm (IRE)**[93] 522 5-8-4 51 oh4............... RichardThomas 4 42
(M Hill) *chsd ldrs: rdn over 3f out: wknd ins fnl 2f* **28/1**

1530 **9** *3/4* **Chia (IRE)**[47] 1048 5-9-3 64..................................(p) RobertHavlin 14 53
(D Haydn Jones) *chsd ldrs: wnt 2nd 6f out to 3f out: wknd 2f out* **16/1**

6306 **10** *1/2* **Casablanca Minx (IRE)**[10] 1842 5-8-6 60 ow1.......(v) RichardEvans(7) 2 48
(P D Evans) *s.i.s: nvr in contention* **22/1**

14-3 **11** *1/2* **Poppets Sweetlove**[43] 1126 4-9-4 65.............................. DavidKinsella 12 52
(A B Haynes) *chsd ldrs: rdn 3f out: wknd 2f out: eased whn no ch* **12/1**

1451 **12** *4* **Hucking Heat (IRE)**[19] 1605 4-8-11 58..........................(p) HayleyTurner 3 37
(R Hollinshead) *in rr: rdn 3f out: no ch whn hung bdly lft 1f out* **10/1**

0-00 **13** *5* **Bidable**[8] 1898 4-8-12 59.. CatherineGannon 8 28
(B Palling) *in rr: sme hdwy 3f out: sn wknd* **66/1**

00-4 **14** *1 1/4* **Moyoko (IRE)**[17] 1645 5-8-4 51 oh1................................ FrancisNorton 1 18
(M Blanshard) *chsd ldrs: rdn and wknd 2f out: no ch whn bdly hmpd on ins appr fnl f* **14/1**

2m 9.50s (-1.50) **Going Correction** -0.125s/f (Firm) **14** Ran SP% **120.2**
Speed ratings (Par 101): **101,100,98,98,97 97,93,92,92,91 91,88,84,83**
CSF £173.91 CT £806.18 TOTE £30.40: £9.00, £3.80, £2.20; EX 249.40.
Owner Finders Keepers Partnership **Bred** Eclipse-Rogers Partnership **Trained** West Ilsley, Berks
■ Stewards' Enquiry : David Kinsella caution: careless riding

FOCUS
A modest handicap, run at a fair pace. The form looks moderate but sound for the class.
Silver Blue(IRE) Official explanation: jockey said gelding was denied a clear run
King Of Charm(IRE) Official explanation: jockey said gelding ran too free

2098 E B F / LEONARD CHESHIRE MEDIAN AUCTION MAIDEN STKS 5f 11y
6:30 (6:33) (Class 5) 2-Y-O £3,626 (£1,079; £539; £269) Stalls Centre

Form RPR

1 **Cerito** 2-9-3 0.. DarryllHolland 6 89+
(M R Channon) *trckd ldr: led over 2f out: qcknd clr over 1f out: easily* **2/1**[1]

2 *6* **Master Of Disguise** 2-9-3 0.. AdamKirby 2 67
(C G Cox) *chsd ldrs: wnt 2nd ins fnl 2f: drvn and kpt on wl but no ch w wnr* **6/1**[3]

3 *1 3/4* **Burning Flute** 2-8-10 0.. KMay(7) 10 61
(B J Meehan) *in tch: drvn over 2f out: styd on wl fnl f but nvr gng pce to trble ldng duo* **33/1**

4 **4** *1 1/2* **Lucky Punt**[13] 1736 2-9-3 0.. TQuinn 7 56
(B G Powell) *in rr: sn pushed along: hdwy over 1f out: styd on wl fnl f but nvr in contention* **28/1**

5 **5** *nk* **Sharav**[30] 1363 2-9-3 0.. StephenCarson 8 55
(Eve Johnson Houghton) *towards rr: pushed along over 2f out: styd on fnl f but nvr gng pce to be competitive* **11/4**[2]

6 *nse* **Liturgical (USA)** 2-9-3 0.. FergusSweeney 11 54+
(M A Magnusson) *awkward stalls: towards rr: pushed along 1/2-way: styd on fr over 1f: gng on cl home* **16/1**

454 **7** *1* **Lagan Handout**[17] 1640 2-9-0 0................................ KevinGhunowa(3) 1 51
(Dr J R J Naylor) *wnt lft s: sn in tch: rdn over 2f out: one pce fnl f* **20/1**

8 *2 1/2* **Flute Magic** 2-9-3 0.. LPKeniry 12 42
(W S Kittow) *chsd ldrs: rdn over 2f out: wknd over 1f out* **16/1**

9 *1/2* **Indian Blade (IRE)** 2-9-3 0.. HayleyTurner 5 40+
(M D I Usher) *outpcd fr 1/2-way* **66/1**

5 **10** *1* **Abhainn (IRE)**[15] 1693 2-9-3 0................................ CatherineGannon 3 36
(B Palling) *wnt rt s: slt ld tl hdd over 2f out: sn btn* **11/1**

0 **11** *shd* **Saunton Sands**[35] 1263 2-9-3 0.. DaneO'Neill 9 36
(A G Newcombe) *a in rr* **66/1**

43 **12** *2 3/4* **Entrancer (IRE)**[17] 1640 2-9-3 0.. GeorgeBaker 4 26
(W R Muir) *plld hrd: chsd ldrs to 1/2-way: wknd qckly* **15/2**

61.85 secs (-0.65) **Going Correction** -0.025s/f (Good) **12** Ran SP% **120.3**
Speed ratings (Par 93): **104,94,91,89,88 88,87,83,82,80 80,76**
CSF £13.96 TOTE £3.10: £1.90, £2.80, £5.20; EX 19.40.
Owner Mrs M Findlay **Bred** Nicola And Eleanor Kent **Trained** West Ilsley, Berks

FOCUS
An ordinary juvenile maiden, but the winner was impressive and rates value for around double the winning margin. the form looks solid and could be worth a little more.

NOTEBOOK
Cerito, a 63,000euros purchase whose dam was a 6f winner at three, was all the rage in the betting ring and duly got off the mark at the first attempt with a taking display. He knew his job as he broke well and, after moving up to the leaders travelling easily, he soon put the race to bed when moving to the front. A quick surface looked right up his street and not that surprisingly his connections are now planning to raid Royal Ascot with him next month. The Norfolk or the Windsor Castle Stakes look likely targets there. (op 7-2)
Master Of Disguise, whose dam was a 1m winner at three, lacked anything like the turn of foot displayed by the winner. He still kept on to show ability and will likely be all the better for this debut experience. (op 9-2)
Burning Flute, a 58,000gns purchase, posted a fair debut effort and left the impression he would learn a great deal for the run. He ought to prove a lot sharper next time out. (op 28-1)
Lucky Punt, fourth on debut at Folkestone 13 days previously, again lacked the early pace to get serious and still looks green. He kept on inside the closing stages and did enough to suggest another furlong can see him get closer. (op 20-1)
Sharav was outpaced nearing the home turn and may not have enjoyed this faster ground, but this was disappointing. (tchd 5-2 and 7-2 in places)

2099 LEONARD CHESHIRE DISABILITY CLAIMING STKS 5f 161y
7:00 (7:03) (Class 6) 3-Y-O £1,813 (£539; £269; £134) Stalls Centre

Form RPR

04-2 **1** **Flying Indian**[15] 1699 3-8-10 64.. LPKeniry 11 65
(A M Balding) *trckd ldr: led over 2f out: rdn jst ins fnl f: hld on wl* **5/2**[1]

2344 **2** *1/2* **Valhillen**[6] 1934 3-9-5 72..(p) HayleyTurner 2 72
(M D I Usher) *chsd ldrs: rdn and outpcd over 2f out: styd on u.p to chse wnr appr fnl f: kpt on but a hld* **6/1**

0-50 **3** *2 1/4* **Miss Firefly**[16] 1671 3-8-1 65.. MCGeran(7) 13 54
(M R Channon) *chsd ldrs: rdn over 2f out: hung lft and no ex fnl f* **3/1**[2]

410- **4** *3* **Blue Zenith (IRE)**[186] 6756 3-8-9 69........................ NataliaGemelova(5) 4 49
(J S Moore) *in rr: styd on wl fr over 1f out: gng on cl home but nvr in contention* **15/2**

6266 **5** *hd* **Spic 'n Span**[8] 1897 3-9-5 65.. AdamKirby 3 54
(R A Harris) *stmbld stalls: sn chsng ldrs: rdn 3f out: wknd over 1f out* **16/1**

-000 **6** *6* **Nestor Protector (IRE)**[22] 1550 3-8-9 50.......................... DaneO'Neill 1 23
(A B Haynes) *in tch: rdn over 2f out: sn btn* **22/1**

000- **7** *nk* **Didntcomeback**[184] 6799 3-8-11 48........................ FergusSweeney 5 24
(M S Saunders) *s.i.s: a outpcd* **50/1**

0 **8** *3 1/4* **Flying Seasons**[112] 265 3-9-0 0................................ JamesMillman(5) 9 21
(B R Millman) *led tl hdd over 2f out: sn wknd* **20/1**

2112 **9** *1* **Copperbottomed (IRE)**[22] 1536 3-8-13 68..................(e) JimCrowley 10 12
(J R Boyle) *rdn 3f out: nvr nrr than mid-div* **5/1**[3]

0-34 **10** *1 3/4* **Midnite Blews (IRE)**[31] 1347 3-9-5 63........................(b[1]) DavidKinsella 6 12
(A B Haynes) *a in rr* **25/1**

200- **11** *1 1/2* **No Point (IRE)**[176] 6881 3-8-0 50 ow5........................ SophieDoyle(7) 12 —
(P A Blockley) *slowly away: a in rr* **25/1**

5450 **12** *6* **Flemish Art (IRE)**[19] 1603 3-8-2 60........................(b) KevinGhunowa(3) 8 —
(R A Harris) *early spd: sn wknd* **33/1**

1m 11.39s (0.19) **Going Correction** -0.025s/f (Good) **12** Ran SP% **123.9**
Speed ratings (Par 97): **97,96,93,89,89 81,80,76,75,72 70,62**
CSF £17.12 TOTE £4.40: £2.50, £1.10, £2.10; EX 21.20.The winner was claimed by John Balding for £10,000.
Owner D H Caslon **Bred** C C And Mrs D J Buckley **Trained** Kingsclere, Hants

FOCUS
A moderate claimer which saw the first pair come clear. The form is rated around the runner-up but is not that solid.
Flemish Art(IRE) Official explanation: jockey said colt lost its action

2100 BYGOTT H'CAP 1m 3f 144y
7:30 (7:33) (Class 6) (0-65,65) 4-Y-O+ £1,942 (£578; £288; £144) Stalls Low

Form RPR

1422 **1** **Terminate (GER)**[18] 1639 6-8-11 58........................ StephenDonohoe 10 66
(Ian Williams) *t.k.h: hld up in rr: gd hdwy over 2f out: rdn to ld fnl 75yds: sn in command: comf* **7/2**[1]

2-30 **2** *1/2* **Bob's Your Uncle**[17] 1643 5-8-7 54.. JamesDoyle 7 61
(J G Portman) *hld up in rr: gd hdwy fr 2f out: str run fnl f to chse wnr fnl 50yds: kpt on but a hld* **5/1**[2]

-635 **3** *1* **Ready To Crown (USA)**[22] 1528 4-8-6 53........................ JimCrowley 9 58
(Andrew Turnell) *chsd ldrs: impr on outside fr 3f out to ld 2f out: rdn over 1f out: hdd fnl 75yds and styd on same pce* **7/2**[1]

00-0 **4** *1 1/4* **King Of The Beers (USA)**[72] 778 4-8-4 51 oh3............(p) LiamJones 3 54
(W K Goldsworthy) *in tch: rdn to chse ldrs over 2f out: kpt on fnl f but nvr gng pce to be competitive* **18/1**

000- **5** *2 1/2* **Moonshine Creek**[259] 4945 6-8-4 51 oh6........................ NickyMackay 4 50
(P W Hiatt) *chsd ldrs: led over 2f out: sn hdd: wknd fnl f* **18/1**

0-24 **6** *shd* **Compton Falcon**[20] 1583 4-9-3 64.. HayleyTurner 11 63
(G A Butler) *in rr: rdn over 2f out and sme prog on outside over 1f out: nvr in contention* **5/1**[2]

056- **7** *2 1/2* **Looktheotherway (IRE)**[256] 5040 4-8-12 59............. FergusSweeney 5 54
(J G M O'Shea) *chsd ldrs: drvn along and lost pl over 4f out: nvr a factor after* **22/1**

5/05 **8** *1 1/2* **Viscount Rossini**[17] 1643 6-8-3 53 oh6 ow2............ KirstyMilczarek(3) 2 45
(A W Carroll) *chsd ldrs: rdn 3f out: wknd 2f out* **14/1**

3421 **9** *2 3/4* **Key Partners (IRE)**[15] 1702 7-8-4 58........................ SophieDoyle(7) 12 46
(P A Blockley) *in rr: sme hdwy 3f out: nvr rchd ldrs and sn wknd* **8/1**[3]

5/0- **10** *10* **Risk Challenge (USA)**[12] 1995 6-8-4 51 oh4.................... PaulEddery 8 22
(C J Price) *chsd ldr tl wknd over 3f out* **33/1**

600- **11** *1 1/4* **El Dottore**[210] 6260 4-8-8 55.. CatherineGannon 1 24
(A W Carroll) *sn led: hdd & wknd qckly over 2f out* **33/1**

2m 32.26s (1.66) **Going Correction** -0.125s/f (Firm) **11** Ran SP% **116.3**
Speed ratings (Par 101): **89,88,88,87,85 85,83,82,80,74 73**
CSF £20.01 CT £64.17 TOTE £5.30: £1.90, £1.50, £2.30; EX 20.40.
Owner Dr Marwan Koukash **Bred** Gestut Hofgut Mappen **Trained** Portway, Worcs
■ Stewards' Enquiry : Jim Crowley one-day ban: careless riding (May 28)

FOCUS
A very moderate event, where there was no pace early. The form is modest with the fourth to his turf best.
Viscount Rossini Official explanation: jockey said gelding was denied a clear run

2101 MICHAEL GOODYEAR BE HOPEFUL H'CAP 1m 5y
8:00 (8:00) (Class 5) (0-75,74) 4-Y-O+ £3,885 (£1,156; £577; £288) Stalls Low

Form RPR

250- **1** **Cool Ebony**[214] 6180 5-9-2 72.. DarryllHolland 10 83
(P J Makin) *led 1f: styd trcking ldrs: wnt 2nd and hrd drvn over 1f out: str chal u.p ins fnl f: led fnl 50yds: hld on wl* **15/2**

4051 **2** *1/2* **Unlimited**[8] 1900 6-8-4 63 6ex........................ KirstyMilczarek(3) 5 73
(A W Carroll) *chsd ldrs: led over 2f out: sn hrd drvn: kpt narrow advantage ins fnl f until hdd and no ex fnl 50yds* **9/2**[1]

000- **3** *5* **Royal Storm (IRE)**[253] 5115 9-8-11 72........................ JamesMillman(5) 13 70
(B R Millman) *led after 1f: hdd over 2f out: wknd fnl f* **14/1**

-235 **4** *1* **Merrymadcap (IRE)**[8] 1898 6-8-7 63........................ FrancisNorton 8 59
(M Blanshard) *chsd ldrs: carried wd bnd over 4f out: rdn and sme prog over 2f out: nvr gng pce to be competitive* **11/2**[2]

3-01 **5** *2 3/4* **Don Pietro**[9] 5-9-4 74 6ex.. FrankieMcDonald 7 64
(P A Blockley) *t.k.h: chsd ldrs and rn wd bnd 4f out: hdwy 3f out: chsd ldrs 2f out: sn btn* **7/1**

-454 **6** *nk* **Art Market (CAN)**[14] 1725 5-8-10 66.. DaneO'Neill 1 55
(Miss Jo Crowley) *in rr: rdn and sme hdwy fr over 2f out: nvr gng pce to be competitive* **11/1**

3151 **7** *nse* **Millfield (IRE)**[17] 1645 5-9-3 73.. JimCrowley 2 62
(P R Chamings) *in rr: rdn over 2f out: sme hdwy fr over 1f out but nvr in contention* **13/2**[3]

30/6 **8** *2* **Master Mahogany**[22] 1532 7-8-11 72........................ HaddenFrost(5) 3 56
(R J Hodges) *a towards rr* **15/2**

6020 **9** *2* **Sun Catcher (IRE)**[10] 1842 5-8-8 64.. SteveDrowne 4 44
(P G Murphy) *a towards rr* **12/1**

02-0 **10** *3 1/4* **Gazboolou**[30] 1365 4-9-2 72.. NeilChalmers 9 44
(David Pinder) *in tch whn carried wd bnd 4f out: sn bhd* **17/2**

6-00 **11** *nse* **The Gaikwar (IRE)**[8] 1898 9-8-2 61........................(b) KevinGhunowa(3) 6 33
(R A Harris) *s.i.s: a struggling in rr* **28/1**

30-0 **12** *33* **Coup D'Etat**[8] 1900 6-9-0 **70**....(b) AdamKirby 12 —
(R A Harris) *chsd ldrs tl wknd over 3f out: eased whn no ch over 1f out: t.o* **33/1**

1m 39.53s (-1.27) **Going Correction** -0.125s/f (Firm) **12** Ran SP% **122.5**
Speed ratings (Par 103): **101,100,95,94,91 91,91,89,87,84 84,51**
CSF £42.65 CT £485.00 TOTE £8.70: £2.20, £2.20, £5.10; EX 60.50.
Owner Wedgewood Estates **Bred** Wedgewood Estates **Trained** Ogbourne Maisey, Wilts

FOCUS
A sound race for the class run at a very good pace. The first two drew clear so, despite them not being especially well treated, the form is solid and should be reliable.
Sun Catcher(IRE) Official explanation: jockey said gelding slipped on the bend
Coup D'Etat Official explanation: jockey said gelding ran too free

2102 METEOR FILLIES' H'CAP 5f 161y

8:30 (8:30) (Class 5) (0-70,70) 3-Y-0+ **£2,590** (£770; £385; £192) **Stalls** Centre

Form RPR

0-45 **1** **Dualagi**[30] 1368 4-9-5 **63**.... GeorgeBaker 2 71
(M R Bosley) *stdd s: t.k.h in rr: stl plenty to do whn swtchd rt 1f out: str run to ld cl home* **12/1**

640- **2** *3/4* **Matterofact (IRE)**[163] 7005 5-8-12 **56** oh3.... FrancisNorton 12 61
(M S Saunders) *chsd ldrs: rdn and str run ins fnl f: tk 2nd last strides but a hld by wnr* **16/1**

631- **3** *shd* **Heaven**[247] 5267 3-8-13 **67**.... DarryllHolland 3 69
(P J Makin) *chsd ldrs: led 1f out: hrd drvn: hdd and no ex cl home* **13/2**

3005 **4** *1/2* **Easy Wonder (GER)**[5] 1958 3-8-3 **60**.... KirstyMilczarek(3) 11 60
(I A Wood) *in rr: hdwy on outside whn bmpd 1f out: styd on ins fnl f but nt rch ldng trio* **16/1**

0-33 **5** *shd* **Asian Lady**[22] 1529 3-9-0 **68**.... SteveDrowne 7 68
(R Charlton) *in rr: hdwy on outside whn bmpd 1f out: kpt on but nvr gng pce to chal* **3/1**[1]

2546 **6** *1* **Linda Green**[13] 1739 7-8-11 **62**.... MCGeran(7) 9 62
(M R Channon) *bmpd bnd over 4f out and bhd: rapid hdwy appr fnl f: nt rch ldrs* **6/1**[3]

5545 **7** *1/2* **Diminuto**[16] 1677 4-9-3 **66**.... PatrickHills(5) 5 64
(M D I Usher) *chsd ldrs: led ins fnl 2f: hdd 1f out: wknd ins fnl f* **20/1**

0314 **8** *3/4* **Is It Time (IRE)**[22] 1541 4-8-10 **59**.... JackMitchell(5) 4 54
(Mrs P N Dutfield) *chsd ldrs: rdn 1/2-way: styd on same pce fnl f* **7/1**

30-2 **9** *1/2* **Rathmolyon**[22] 1529 3-9-0 **68**.... RobertHavlin 10 59
(D Haydn Jones) *led tl hdd ins fnl 2f: wknd fnl f* **9/1**

1140 **10** *12* **Crimson Fern (IRE)**[33] 1312 4-9-7 **65**.... FergusSweeney 1 18+
(M S Saunders) *plld hrd: chsng ldrs whn faltered and stmbld bdly 1f out: nt rcvr and eased* **20/1**

4-20 **11** *2 1/4* **Cosmic Destiny (IRE)**[17] 1646 6-9-12 **70**.... LPKeniry 8 15
(E F Vaughan) *plld hrd early: bhd fr 1/2-way* **12/1**

36- **12** *1 3/4* **Edie Superstar (USA)**[179] 6849 3-9-2 **70**.... DaneO'Neill 6 6
(M A Magnusson) *slowly away: sme hdwy into mid-div over 2f out: sn wknd* **11/2**[2]

1m 11.37s (0.17) **Going Correction** -0.025s/f (Good)
WFA 3 from 4yo+ 10lb **12** Ran SP% **127.2**
Speed ratings (Par 100): **97,96,95,95,95 93,93,92,91,75 72,70**
CSF £202.88 CT £1391.77 TOTE £18.30: £5.00, £7.20, £3.30; EX 359.40 Place 6 £139.56, Place 5 £40.80..
Owner Inca Financial Services **Bred** B Burrough **Trained** Lockeridge, Wilts
■ Stewards' Enquiry : Patrick Hills one-day ban: used whip down shoulder in forehand position (May 28)

FOCUS
A competitive handicap that was run at a fair pace. The form looks solid for the class, but a couple were unlucky in-running and can be rated a bit better than the bare result suggests. The runner-up is rated to last year's course form with the fourth to her recent level.
Is It Time(IRE) Official explanation: jockey said filly was denied a clear run
Crimson Fern(IRE) Official explanation: jockey said filly hung badly left and clipped heels
Edie Superstar(USA) Official explanation: jockey said filly slipped on leaving stalls
T/Plt: £270.20 to a £1 stake. Pool: £53,477.06. 144.45 winning tickets. T/Qpdt: £29.10 to a £1 stake. Pool: £4,711.89. 119.50 winning tickets. ST

YORK (L-H)

Wednesday, May 14

OFFICIAL GOING: Good to firm (9.7)

5mm watering two days erlier and the rail from the 9f marker to the home turn moved out a metre on ground decsribed as 'genuine good to firm, good cover'.
Wind: light, half against Weather: fine and sunny

2103 WILLIAM BIRCH AND SONS CONSTRUCTION STKS (H'CAP) 1m 2f 88y

1:40 (1:41) (Class 2) (0-100,97) 4-Y-0+ **£16,513** (£4,913; £2,455; £1,226) **Stalls** Low

Form RPR

/13- **1** **Folk Opera (IRE)**[368] 1663 4-9-4 **94**.... LDettori 8 106
(Saeed Bin Suroor) *lw: set stdy pce: qcknd 1/2-way: pushed along and qcknd 3f out: rdn wl over 1f out: hld on wl fnl f* **6/1**[3]

/0-2 **2** *3/4* **Tastahil (IRE)**[14] 1719 4-8-7 **83**.... RHills 10 94
(B W Hills) *trckd ldrs: effrt on outer over 3f out: sn pushed along and outpcd over 2f out: rdn and styd on wl fnl f* **9/2**[1]

00-4 **3** *shd* **Supaseus**[10] 1828 5-9-6 **96**.... SteveDrowne 4 107
(H Morrison) *trckd wnr: effrt over 2f out: sn rdn and ev ch tl drvn ins fnl f and nt qckn last 100yds* **9/1**

006- **4** *1 3/4* **Smart Instinct (USA)**[228] 5805 4-9-3 **93**.... PaulHanagan 2 100
(R A Fahey) *trckd ldrs: hdwy on inner over 3f out: rdn 2f out: styng on same pce whn n.m.r ins fnl f* **17/2**

033 **5** *1/2* **King Charles**[10] 1828 4-9-6 **96**.... JimmyFortune 9 102
(E A L Dunlop) *lw: cl up: effrt 3f out: sn rdn along and grad wknd appr fnl f* **9/2**[1]

3000 **6** *2* **Impeller (IRE)**[46] 1077 9-9-4 **94**.... JohnEgan 3 96
(Jane Chapple-Hyam) *trckd ldrs: hdwy 3f out: rdn along 2f out: drvn and wknd over 1f out* **16/1**

11-0 **7** *3/4* **Gulf Express (USA)**[10] 1828 4-9-7 **97**.... RyanMoore 1 100+
(Sir Michael Stoute) *lw: dwlt and towards rr: sme hdwy 3f out: sn rdn along and no imp fnl 2f* **11/2**[2]

20-5 **8** *nk* **Ladies Best**[12] 1766 4-9-7 **97**.... JamieSpencer 6 97
(L M Cumani) *hld up on inner towards rr: effrt and swtchd rt over 2f out: sn rdn: hung lft and no imp* **16/1**

-121 **9** *2* **Blue Spinnaker (IRE)**[26] 1449 9-8-8 **84**.... PaulMulrennan 12 81
(M W Easterby) *hld up in tch: hdwy over 4f out: rdn along over 3f out: sn wknd* **14/1**

1U0- **10** *1/2* **Fort Amhurst (IRE)**[73] 3960 4-8-7 **83** oh1.... DaleGibson 11 79?
(M W Easterby) *a in rr* **100/1**

6-60 **11** *2 1/4* **Mesbaah (IRE)**[25] 1469 4-9-1 **91**.... TonyHamilton 5 82
(R A Fahey) *a in rr* **28/1**

2203 **12** *6* **Capable Guest (IRE)**[11] 1816 6-9-2 **92**.... ChrisCatlin 7 72
(M R Channon) *a in rr* **18/1**

2m 10.43s (-2.07) **Going Correction** +0.025s/f (Good) **12** Ran SP% **114.7**
Speed ratings (Par 109): **109,108,108,106,106 104,104,104,102,102 100,95**
CSF £31.93 CT £241.42 TOTE £6.90: £2.50, £2.20, £3.10; EX 34.80 Trifecta £369.10 Pool: £779.79 - 1.50 winning units..
Owner Godolphin **Bred** Abbeville And Meadow Court Partners **Trained** Newmarket, Suffolk

FOCUS
A decent handicap but slightly questionable form due to a steady early pace that the winner set. That said, she does not look flattered. The form is rated through the third.

NOTEBOOK
Folk Opera(IRE) provided Godolphin with their first winner of the year in this country. It is often an advantage to race up with the pace at this track and she was given a good front-running ride by Dettori, who set a fairly ordinary pace and had plenty in hand at the finish to push her out for a comfortable success. She had been off the track since finishing third in the Lingfield Oaks Trial last year and on this evidence will soon be back contesting Pattern races. (tchd 13-2 and 7-1 in a place)
Tastahil(IRE), raised only 3lb for finishing runner-up at Ascot last time, was stepping up in distance. Brought to challenge on the outside, he took a while to pick up but was closing the winner down at the finish. He would have been suited by a stronger pace. (op 11-2)
Supaseus, trying this trip for the first time, has run his best races when fresh so it was a bit of a concern that he was running here just ten days after his seasonal reappearance. Racing prominently in a race lacking much pace, he was well placed for the sprint to the line.
Smart Instinct(USA), representing the stable that has sent out the most winners at this track since 2004, has gone well fresh before and was well backed to do so again. Running off a mark 5lb lower than at this meeting last year, he looked well weighted. Never too far off the pace in a race lacking a strong gallop, he ran a solid race, but a better all-round gallop would undoubtedly have suited him better. (op 14-1)
King Charles had every chance given the way the race was run and the prominent position he held throughout. He just seems held by the Handicapper off his current mark. (op 4-1)
Impeller(IRE) did win narrowly off this mark at Sandown last September, but he generally struggles when up against one or two less exposed rivals. (op 20-1)
Gulf Express(USA) let his supporters down badly at Newmarket on his reappearance but there were plenty of people prepared to give him another chance. Held up towards the back in a steadily run affair, he was not well placed the way things turned out, but there was still some promise in this performance. (op 4-1 tchd 6-1)
Ladies Best, who has steadily crept up the handicap despite not winning since October 2006, was another hold-up performer not suited by the rather tactical nature of this race. Official explanation: jockey said colt got its tongue over the bit and hung left-handed
Blue Spinnaker(IRE), who won this race two years ago off a 6lb higher mark, prefers easier ground. (op 11-1 tchd 10-1)

2104 BLUE SQUARE PREMIER GOES TO WEMBLEY STKS (H'CAP) 7f

2:10 (2:14) (Class 2) (0-100,96) 3-Y-0 **£16,190** (£4,817; £2,407; £1,202) **Stalls** Low

Form RPR

1522 **1** **Fathsta (IRE)**[6] 1925 3-8-10 **85**.... RichardHughes 8 101
(S Kirk) *midfield: smooth hdwy over 2f out: led over 1f out: rdn ins fnl f and styd on wl* **12/1**

11-2 **2** *2* **Generous Thought**[26] 1441 3-9-5 **94**.... JamieSpencer 12 105+
(P Howling) *swtg: stdd s: hld up and bhd: hdwy and pushed along over 2f out: str run on outer over 1f out: rdn and ev ch whn edgd lft ins fnl f: sn one pce* **7/2**[1]

1-12 **3** *2 1/4* **Meydan Princess (IRE)**[10] 1834 3-8-12 **87**.... JMurtagh 3 92
(J Noseda) *lw: dwlt: hdwy on inner 1/2-way: swtchd rt and rdn over 1f out: kpt on ins fnl f: nrst fin* **7/2**[1]

41-3 **4** *1 1/4* **Swift Gift**[10] 1834 3-8-9 **84**.... AlanMunro 6 85
(B J Meehan) *chsd ldrs: hdwy 3f out: ev ch 2f out: sn rdn and kpt on same pce ent fnl f* **12/1**

0-22 **5** *1 3/4* **Wigram's Turn (USA)**[32] 1336 3-8-11 **86**.... LDettori 14 82
(A M Balding) *hld up towards rr: hdwy over 2f out: sn rdn and kpt on same pce ent fnl f* **12/1**

15- **6** *3/4* **Tanweer (USA)**[242] 5414 3-9-4 **93**.... MartinDwyer 2 87
(Sir Michael Stoute) *hld up towards rr: hdwy 3f out: rdn along 2f out: no imp fr over 1f out* **25/1**

16-5 **7** *hd* **Dubai Dynamo**[10] 1834 3-9-7 **96**.... JohnEgan 10 90
(P F I Cole) *chsd ldrs: rdn along wl over 2f out: hung lft and kpt on same pce* **9/1**[3]

12- **8** *3/4* **Seasider**[193] 6644 3-8-12 **87**.... RyanMoore 4 79
(Sir Michael Stoute) *led: rdn along 2f out: hdd over 12f out and sn wknd* **11/2**[2]

-431 **9** *nse* **Keep Discovering (IRE)**[13] 1745 3-9-0 **89**.... RobertWinston 13 81
(M Johnston) *prom: effrt 3f out and sn ev ch tl rdn 2f out and grad wknd* **28/1**

50-0 **10** *nse* **Cristal Clear (IRE)**[18] 1623 3-9-0 **89**.... DavidAllan 5 81
(T D Easterby) *towards rr: hdwy wl over 2f out: sn rdn and n.d* **50/1**

1355 **11** *1 3/4* **Geezers Colours**[32] 1333 3-9-3 **92**.... AndrewElliott 9 79
(K R Burke) *prom: rdn along 3f out: drvn over 2f out and sn wknd* **50/1**

31-2 **12** *nk* **Kaldoun Kingdom (IRE)**[28] 1404 3-9-2 **91**.... PaulHanagan 1 77
(R A Fahey) *lw: chsd ldrs on inner: rdn along 3f out: wkng whn n.m.r 2f out* **16/1**

10-0 **13** *1 3/4* **Hawaana (IRE)**[19] 1595 3-8-9 **84**.... RHills 15 65
(B W Hills) *hld up: a in rr* **12/1**

5-10 **14** *2 1/4* **Red Rumour (IRE)**[11] 1806 3-8-13 **88**.... SebSanders 7 63
(R M Beckett) *lw: prom: rdn along 3f out and sn wknd* **33/1**

1m 24.05s (-1.25) **Going Correction** +0.025s/f (Good) **14** Ran SP% **120.6**
Speed ratings (Par 105): **108,105,103,101,99 98,98,97,97,97 95,95,93,90**
CSF £51.61 CT £188.10 TOTE £13.80: £4.20, £2.00, £1.90; EX 77.50 Trifecta £202.80 Pool: £202.80 - 3.10 winning units..
Owner Speedlith Group **Bred** Brian Miller **Trained** Upper Lambourn, Berks

FOCUS
A strongly run handicap and very solid form for the grade with the first four all officially ahead of the handicapper. The winner is better than ever.

NOTEBOOK
Fathsta(IRE), who ran a blinder from a wide draw over 6f at Chester six days earlier, showed himself to be a well-handicapped and improving three-year-old with a decisive win from two other progressive rivals. He travelled and quickened up well, suggesting there is even better to come from him. (op 20-1 tchd 22-1)
Generous Thought still looked well handicapped despite being raised 6lb for finishing second to Huzzah at Newbury, because the winner had gone in again since at Chester, the third and ninth had won handicaps next time, and the fourth had finished second to handicap good thing Dr Faustus at Newmarket. He did not travel as well as some but appreciated the strong pace and came home well down the outside having been given plenty to do. On this evidence he has a similar race in him. (op 10-3)

Meydan Princess(IRE), running off the same mark as when an unlucky-in-running second at Newmarket last time, looked to hold strong claims. Well placed on the inner, she quickened up well between horses once switched, but the first two finished even stronger on her outer. She is likely to remain dangerous in similar company off this sort of mark.

Swift Gift again finished a place behind Meydan Princess, just like he did at Newmarket on his reappearance. He ran a solid race but could not match the winner's change of gear in the closing stages, and again hinted that he might be worth trying over a mile. (op 11-1)

Wigram's Turn(USA), runner-up to Meydan Princess on the Polytrack last month, challenged from off the pace and kept on well. He was another to help give the form a solid look. Official explanation: jockey said colt lost its action (op 20-1)

Tanweer(USA), last of five when stepped up to Listed company on his second and final start at two, was friendless in the market on his seasonal reappearance having been gelded over the winter. He ran with some promise, not enjoying he clearest of runs, and looks capable of better with this outing under his belt. (op 22-1)

Dubai Dynamo had a stiff task under top weight and was not disgraced in the circumstances. Official explanation: jockey said colt hung left (op 10-1 tchd 7-1)

Seasider ran better than his finishing position suggests as he simply did not get home having set a strong pace. It may turn out that he is more effective over sprint distances. (op 5-1 tchd 6-1)

Keep Discovering(IRE), four lengths behind Generous Thought at Newbury and a winner himself on the Polytrack subsequently, failed to get any closer to his old rival back on turf. His stable is not in the best of form at present. (tchd 33-1)

Cristal Clear(IRE) needs help from the Handicapper. (op 66-1)

Kaldoun Kingdom(IRE), who ran well on his reappearance at Newmarket, was running over a furlong longer trip and is arguably better on easier ground. He is also now on a mark 19lb higher than when last successful. (op 14-1)

2105 TATTERSALLS MUSIDORA STKS (GROUP 3) (FILLIES) 1m 2f 88y

2:40 (2:43) (Class 1) 3-Y-O

£34,062 (£12,912; £6,462; £3,222; £1,614; £810) **Stalls** Low

Form RPR

1-06 **1** **Lush Lashes**[10] 1830 3-8-12 0 .... KJManning 2 113+
(J S Bolger, Ire) *lw: hld up in tch: smooth hdwy 4f out: cl up 3f out: led 2f out and sn qcknd clr: easily* **2/1**[1]

1- **2** *5* **Cape Amber (IRE)**[277] 4402 3-8-12 86 .... JamieSpencer 7 103
(P W Chapple-Hyam) *hld up in rr: hdwy over 2f out: rdn over 1f out: styd on to chse wnr ins fnl f: no imp* **9/1**

2-1 **3** *1 ¾* **Dar Re Mi**[19] 1599 3-8-12 93 .... JimmyFortune 1 100
(J H M Gosden) *trckd ldng pair: hdwy whn bmpd over 4f out: sn cl up: ev ch 2f out: sn rdn and kpt on same pce* **10/3**[3]

4 *hd* **Moonstone**[24] 1510 3-8-12 0 .... JMurtagh 8 99
(A P O'Brien, Ire) *w'like: str: trckd ldrs: hdwy over 4f out and sn cl up: rdn and ev ch 2f out: drvn and outpcd over 1f out: kpt on u.p ins fnl f* **5/2**[2]

6-4 **5** *2 ¼* **Sovereign's Honour (USA)**[19] 1599 3-8-12 0 .... RyanMoore 4 95
(Sir Michael Stoute) *lw: hld up towards rr: hdwy over 3f out: rdn along to chse ldrs over 2f out: sn drvn and one pce* **12/1**

1-2 **6** *1 ¼* **Cruel Sea (USA)**[10] 1833 3-8-12 85 .... MichaelHills 6 92
(B W Hills) *lw: led after 1f: rdn along and qcknd 3f out: hdd 2f out grad wknd* **14/1**

15-2 **7** *7* **Comeback Queen**[32] 1332 3-8-12 91 .... MartinDwyer 5 78
(S Kirk) *lw: t.k.h: hld up towards rr: hdwy 3f out: rdn to chse wnr 2f out: drvn and hld whn hmpd and wknd wl over 1f out* **33/1**

36-4 **8** *33* **Sayyedati Symphony (USA)**[10] 1833 3-8-12 86 .... JohnEgan 3 12
(C E Brittain) *led 1f: chsd ldr: edgd rt on bnd over 4f out: sn rdn and wknd over 3f out: bhd and eased fnl 2f* **50/1**

2m 9.78s (-2.72) **Going Correction** +0.025s/f (Good) **8** Ran SP% **114.2**
Speed ratings (Par 106): **111,107,105,105,103 102,97,70**
CSF £21.10 TOTE £2.60: £1.30, £2.00, £1.60; EX 19.00 Trifecta £74.30 Pool: £74.30 - 7.70 winning units..

Owner Mrs J S Bolger **Bred** Mrs A M Jenkins **Trained** Coolcullen, Co Carlow

FOCUS

On paper this looked the key trial for this year's Oaks, with four of the first six in the betting for Epsom taking each other on. Lush Lashes impressed and looks the one to beat whichever Oaks she goes for. The next four all showed improvement.

NOTEBOOK

Lush Lashes, a running-on sixth in the 1,000 Guineas, is a daughter of Galileo and promised to be very much suited by the step up to 1m2f. Swinging away three furlongs out, she quickened up well to go clear from a furlong and a half out and then maintained her advantage to the line. This was a top-class effort and, with her pedigree suggesting another two furlongs should pose her few problems, she was immediately made favourite for the Oaks. However, her trainer was apparently noncommittal about taking her to Epsom, with the Irish Oaks seemingly taking precedence in his mind, so it might be worth hanging back before taking any 11/4. (op 9-4 tchd 5-2 in places)

Cape Amber(IRE), who won her only start at two in good style and had been talked up by her trainer earlier in the year as his best Classic hope this season, came in for some late support having initially drifted out to big prices on the exchanges. She was given a waiting ride out the back and the winner, who had the advantage of race-fitness, got first run on her, but she stayed on pleasingly past the rest of the field to take second, and had Lush Lashes not been in the race she would have been a good winner. Although she looked fit enough for this reappearance, she is entitled to improve for the run and, while her pedigree does not guarantee stamina for 1m4f, she runs as though she will get it. In the absence of Lush Lashes she will hold sound claims at Epsom. (op 12-1 tchd 14-1)

Dar Re Mi, 7/1 for the Oaks on the back of getting the run of the race in a Sandown maiden, had a good deal more to do in this company. Content to take a lead this time, she had her chance two furlongs out, but the winner's turn of foot left her for dead. She kept on reasonably well but appeared to have her limitations exposed here and will struggle to reverse the form in the Oaks. (op 7-2)

Moonstone ◆, a 700,000gns half-sister to Irish Oaks/Filly and Mare Turf runner-up L'Ancresse, and Prix Saint-Alary winner Cerulean Sky, had only finished second in a Leopardstown maiden on her debut last month, but she had clearly been showing the right signs at home since for she had been backed in from 33/1 to 7/1 for the Oaks in anticipation of a bold showing here. Bumped by Dar Re Mi rounding the turn into the straight, she went for home three furlongs out but could not match the winner's speed. To her credit, having looked as though she was going to weaken right out, she rallied and almost took third place back on the line. The Oaks may come too soon for her, but she is just the type who is likely to keep improving as she gains experience throughout the summer, and it will not come as a surprise to see her develop into a top-class filly later in the season. (tchd 11-4 and 3-1 in places)

Sovereign's Honour(USA), sixth behind Cape Amber on her debut at two and fourth behind Dar Re Mi at Sandown on her reappearance, had quite a bit to find with those fillies, but she did not go unsupported and there were clearly some people out there expecting improvement from her. She was a bit tight for room a furlong and a half out but did not really make any impression once in the clear, and a drop in class now looks on the cards. (op 8-1)

Cruel Sea(USA), who did not settle when runner-up in the Pretty Polly Stakes, was soon taken to the front. This is a track that often favours front-running tactics, but she was not good enough to pull them off in this company. It is also possible that a mile might prove her optimum trip. (op 16-1 tchd 12-1)

Comeback Queen, runner-up in the Masaka Stakes on Polytrack last time out, raced a bit keenly, but she was out of her depth in this class.

Sayyedati Symphony(USA), whose rider was looking down as he eased her up inside the final two furlongs, was another who was out of her depth. Official explanation: jockey said filly lost its action (op 66-1)

2106 DUKE OF YORK HEARTHSTEAD HOMES STKS (GROUP 2) 6f

3:10 (3:14) (Class 1) 3-Y-O+

£56,770 (£21,520; £10,770; £5,370; £2,020; £2,020) **Stalls** High

Form RPR

30-2 **1** **Assertive**[27] 1420 5-9-7 111 .... RyanMoore 6 116
(R Hannon) *lw: racd far side: chsd ldrs: led over 1f out: hld on towards fin* **15/2**[2]

26 **2** *nk* **War Artist (AUS)**[27] 1420 5-9-12 111 .... KerrinMcEvoy 1 120
(J M P Eustace) *lw: racd far side: chsd ldrs: kpt on wl ins fnl f* **11/1**

0045 **3** *nk* **Beckermet (IRE)**[4] 1989 6-9-7 105 .... ChrisCatlin 7 114
(R F Fisher) *led far side tl over 1f out: kpt on wl ins fnl f* **40/1**

14-3 **4** *¾* **US Ranger (USA)**[31] 1355 4-9-7 0 .... JMurtagh 17 112+
(A P O'Brien, Ire) *lw: racd stands' side: in rr: hdwy 2f out: styd on strly ins fnl f: nt rch ldrs* **9/4**[1]

160- **5** *nk* **Hoh Mike (IRE)**[220] 6039 4-9-7 109 .... JamieSpencer 3 111
(M L W Bell) *racd far side: hld up: hdwy over 1f out: kpt on wl: nt rch ldrs* **16/1**

131- **5** *dht* **Haatef (USA)**[227] 5832 4-9-10 0 .... DPMcDonogh 4 114
(Kevin Prendergast, Ire) *racd far side: hld up: hdwy over 2f out: kpt on fnl f* **8/1**[3]

0-40 **7** *1 ¼* **Prime Defender**[27] 1420 4-9-7 106 .... MichaelHills 2 107
(B W Hills) *racd far side: in rr: hdwy over 2f out: sn chsng ldrs: kpt on same pce fnl f* **12/1**

04-0 **8** *½* **Balthazaar's Gift (IRE)**[27] 1420 5-9-7 112 .... JimmyFortune 11 105+
(L M Cumani) *hld up: swtchd rt after 1f and racd stands' side: hdwy and nt clr run over 1f out: nvr rchd ldrs* **14/1**

10-1 **9** *2* **Utmost Respect**[25] 1483 4-9-7 107 .... PaulHanagan 10 99
(R A Fahey) *swtchd rt after 1f and racd stands' side: trckd ldrs: effrt over 2f out: fdd over 1f out* **9/1**

31-0 **10** *1 ¾* **Galeota (IRE)**[11] 1809 6-9-7 107 .... PatDobbs 15 93
(R Hannon) *racd stands' side: w ldr: led that gp over 1f out tl ins fnl f: no ex* **40/1**

13-0 **11** *¾* **Honoured Guest (IRE)**[31] 1355 4-9-7 0 .... JAHeffernan 14 91
(A P O'Brien, Ire) *racd stands' side: in rr and pushed along: nvr nr ldrs* **25/1**

3340 **12** *1* **Beaver Patrol (IRE)**[11] 1809 6-9-7 102 .... (v) RHills 5 88
(Eve Johnson Houghton) *racd far side: w ldrs: wknd over 1f out* **28/1**

0022 **13** *½* **Big Timer (USA)**[25] 1483 4-9-7 101 .... TomEaves 9 86
(Miss L A Perratt) *racd far side: chsd ldrs: effrt over 2f out: sn outpcd* **33/1**

0-35 **14** *1 ½* **Wi Dud**[25] 1483 4-9-7 107 .... NCallan 12 81
(K A Ryan) *racd stands' side: chsd ldrs: wknd over 1f out* **16/1**

-000 **15** *½* **Rising Shadow (IRE)**[11] 1809 7-9-7 98 .... JimmyQuinn 8 80
(N Wilson) *dwlt: racd far side: nvr a factor* **100/1**

410- **16** *1 ¾* **Garnica (FR)**[221] 6029 5-9-7 0 .... AdrianTNicholls 18 74
(D Nicholls) *racd stands' side: trckd ldrs: effrt over 2f out: lost pl over 1f out* **20/1**

-214 **17** *1 ½* **Sonny Red (IRE)**[27] 1420 4-9-7 108 .... (p) RichardHughes 16 69
(R Hannon) *led stands' side tl over 1f out: sn wknd* **20/1**

1m 10.71s (-1.19) **Going Correction** +0.125s/f (Good) **17** Ran SP% **123.7**
Speed ratings (Par 115): **112,111,111,110,109 109,108,107,104,102 101,100,99,97,96 94,92**
CSF £79.87 TOTE £7.20: £2.60, £4.20, £10.10; EX 101.90 Trifecta £1128.60 Part won. Pool: £1,589.70 - 0.30 winning units..

Owner Lady Whent **Bred** Raffin Bloodstock **Trained** East Everleigh, Wilts

FOCUS

As is often the case over sprint distances here, the place to be was up the middle of the track. The previous ten winners of this race had been drawn in single figures, and six of the first seven home on this occasion were drawn in single figures and raced up the centre after the field split into two groups early in the race. This was a competitive renewal and the form is solid among the centre-track group, but the stands' side group were at a disadvantage.

NOTEBOOK

Assertive finished fifth in this race last year from stall 15 in a race in which the only other horse drawn in double figures to make the first seven was subsequent Golden Jubilee Stakes winner Soldier's Tale. He fared much better with the draw this time and took full advantage, taking over approaching the furlong marker and holding off his rivals in gutsy fashion. He deserved this first Group-race win, but it must be stressed that he had everything in his favour on this occasion, not least the draw. (op 13-2 tchd 8-1 in a place)

War Artist(AUS) finished a lot closer to Assertive this time than he did at Newmarket in the Abernant Stakes. One would imagine that this speed-favouring track would not be his ideal course as he likes to be held up for a late run, and the Golden Jubilee at Ascot is likely to suit him better, where he will also be 5lb better off with the likes of Assertive. (op 14-1)

Beckermet(IRE), who seems to thrive on racing and was back over his ideal trip on a track that favours the handy type, took up his usual front-running role and proved a tough horse to pass. He held on well for third and clearly retains enough ability to pick up another Listed race on a similarly speed-favouring track.

US Ranger(USA) ◆, who began last season's campaign as a Guineas contender (second home on the wrong side at Newmarket), recorded his only win of the year after that when dropped back to 6f for a Listed race at the Curragh. Third over 7f on his reappearance in heavy ground, much better was clearly expected dropped back to sprinting on quicker ground and he was very well backed. Unfortunately for him and his supporters, he was poorly drawn in stall 17 and raced with the group up the stands' side, which was not the place to be. He quickened up well from off the pace to win the race on his side by a clear margin, but the principals from the centre group always had his measure. Had he raced up the centre he would have taken a lot of beating and he will have every chance of finishing in front of this lot at Ascot if reopposing in the Golden Jubilee. (op 10-3 tchd 7-2)

Haatef(USA), another who started last year as a Guineas candidate but concluded his campaign by winning the Group 2 Diadem Stakes over 6f, had conditions to suit but lacked a recent run, so his fitness had to be taken on trust. Drawn well to race with the group up the centre, he had every chance, and perhaps a lack of race fitness, coupled with his 3lb penalty, just found him out. (op 10-1)

Hoh Mike(IRE), who has done the majority of his running and winning over the minimum trip, was another making his seasonal reappearance. A strong traveller, he was held up as usual before being asked to quicken with a furlong and a half to run. His run flattened out inside the last, but he showed he retains his ability, and arguably he will be happier back over 5f. (op 10-1)

Prime Defender appreciated the quicker conditions, but he only beat three home from his group so it would be dangerous to overrate the performance.

Balthazaar's Gift(IRE) is not the most consistent of sprinters but he does boast some high-class form and on his day he can mix it with the best. Drawn on the wrong side in the Abernant on his reappearance, he again found himself racing on the wrong side of the track, but he came through well to chase US Ranger home on the stands' side, and it was clearly a better effort than the bare form suggests. (op 12-1)

Utmost Respect, a most progressive sprinter last term, got off to a winning start at Thirsk last month, but this was the first time he had been asked to race on ground officially described as quicker than good, and he came up a bit short. He was still third from the stands'-side group, though, and remains one to be interested in when he can get his toe in. (op 10-1)
Galeota(IRE) set the pace on the unfavoured stands' side before dropping away inside the last. (op 33-1)
Honoured Guest(IRE) struggled to go the pace on his first start over a distance this short.
Beaver Patrol(IRE) is something of a twilight horse now and is likely to remain difficult to place. (op 33-1)
Wi Dud won twice at this track as a juvenile, including the Flying Childers, but he has failed to get on the scoresheet since and, after getting beaten at odds-on last time, this was another tame effort.
Garnica(FR), making his debut for his new stable having won twice in Group 3 company in France last term, had never run on ground this quick before and perhaps it did not suit him. (op 25-1 tchd 18-1)
Sonny Red(IRE) Official explanation: jockey said colt lost its action

2107 BLUE SQUARE KICK FOR £100,000 AT WEMBLEY STKS (H'CAP) 1m 4f
3:45 (3:45) (Class 4) (0-85,84) 4-Y-O+ £7,123 (£2,119; £1,059; £529) **Stalls** Centre

Form RPR
1-14 **1** **Birkside**[11] 1798 5-9-1 **78** DavidAllan 2 88
(D Carroll) *hld up in rr: hdwy over 2f out: swtchd outside over 1f out: led ins fnl f: jst hld on* **7/1**
-406 **2** *nse* **Prince Sabaah (IRE)**[10] 1841 4-9-6 **83** RichardHughes 3 93
(R Hannon) *lw: trckd ldrs: led over 1f out tl ins fnl f: kpt on wl: jst hld* **9/2**[2]
0-23 **3** *6* **Collette's Choice**[4] 2006 5-8-7 **70** oh6 (p) PaulHanagan 6 70
(R A Fahey) *led tl over 1f out: kpt on one pce* **18/1**
03-3 **4** *nk* **Sporting Gesture**[25] 1482 11-8-7 **70** PaulMulrennan 9 70
(M W Easterby) *trckd ldrs: chal over 2f out: one pce fnl f* **14/1**
556- **5** *3 1/2* **Zaif (IRE)**[88] 6169 5-9-2 **79** MartinDwyer 12 73
(Simon Earle) *lw: trckd ldrs: effrt 3f out: wknd ins fnl f* **11/1**
3- **6** *1 1/4* **Rajeh (IRE)**[172] 4690 5-9-7 **84** SebSanders 8 76
(J L Spearing) *chsd ldrs: effrt over 3f out: wknd fnl f* **13/2**[3]
10-5 **7** *3 1/4* **Dzesmin (POL)**[25] 1473 6-9-5 **82** (p) ChrisCatlin 14 69
(R C Guest) *hld up in rr: effrt over 3f out: nvr nr ldrs* **14/1**
5-03 **8** *1 1/4* **Ainama (IRE)**[5] 1947 4-9-1 **78** JamieSpencer 7 63+
(M Wigham) *hld up towards rr: nt clr run over 2f out: eased over 1f out* **2/1**[1]
1-06 **9** *shd* **Longspur**[11] 1793 4-8-8 **78** BradleyRoper[(7)] 10 63
(M W Easterby) *hld up in rr: nvr on terms* **50/1**
5-00 **10** *1 1/4* **Bailieborough (IRE)**[18] 1613 9-8-0 **70** LanceBetts[(7)] 1 53
(B Ellison) *chsd ldrs: lost pl over 2f out* **25/1**
500- **11** *1 1/2* **Tcherina (IRE)**[194] 6620 6-8-6 **72** DuranFentiman[(3)] 5 53
(T D Easterby) *prom: drvn over 4f out: sn btn* **16/1**
0641 **12** *7* **Red Wine**[11] 1798 9-8-8 **78** StacyRenwick[(7)] 11 47
(A J McCabe) *hld up in last: rdn 3f out: no rspnse* **16/1**

2m 31.27s (-1.93) **Going Correction** +0.025s/f (Good) **12** Ran SP% **121.8**
Speed ratings (Par 105): **107,106,102,102,100 99,97,96,96,95 94,90**
CSF £39.64 CT £559.98 TOTE £8.40: £2.60, £1.80, £3.60; EX 47.10.
Owner J M Walsh & R Glynn **Bred** Pendley Farm **Trained** Sledmere, E Yorks

FOCUS
Just a steady gallop until the turn for home. The first two pulled clear in the end in this fair handicap. The third limits the form.
Ainama(IRE) Official explanation: jockey said gelding was unsuited by the good to firm ground
Longspur Official explanation: jockey said gelding had a breathing problem
Red Wine Official explanation: jockey said gelding was unsuited by the good to firm ground

2108 HAPPY BIRTHDAY TO BLUE SQUARE PRICES E B F NOVICE STKS 5f
4:20 (4:20) (Class 3) 2-Y-O £8,418 (£2,505; £1,251; £625) **Stalls** High

Form RPR
1 **Masamah (IRE)** 2-8-12 0 (b[1]) RHills 2 87+
(E A L Dunlop) *w'like: scope: str: trckd ldrs: hung lft over 2f out: led over 1f out: ended up on far side rail* **3/1**[3]
21 **2** *1 3/4* **Caranbola**[18] 1627 2-8-8 0 MarkLawson[(3)] 3 78
(M Brittain) *leggy: w ldr: led over 2f out tl over 1f out: kpt on same pce* **11/4**[2]
42 **3** *2 1/4* **Majuba (USA)**[11] 1794 2-8-12 0 NCallan 1 71
(K A Ryan) *neat: stdd s: t.k.h in rr: effrt over 1f out: rdn and little rspnse ins fnl f* **7/4**[1]
514 **4** *1/2* **Grand Honour (IRE)**[14] 1714 2-9-5 0 JimmyQuinn 4 76
(P Howling) *trckd ldrs: effrt 2f out: sn rdn: edgd lft and wknd* **7/1**
4 **5** *1 1/2* **Steel Stockholder**[5] 1967 2-8-12 0 TWilliams 5 64
(M Brittain) *leggy: led tl over 2f out: wknd over 1f out* **11/1**

60.01 secs (0.71) **Going Correction** +0.125s/f (Good) **5** Ran SP% **108.9**
Speed ratings (Par 97): **99,96,92,91,89**
CSF £11.25 TOTE £4.10: £1.70, £1.90; EX 13.20.
Owner Hamdan Al Maktoum **Bred** Stanley Estate & Stud Co & Mount Coote Stud **Trained** Newmarket, Suffolk

FOCUS
A poor turn-out but a blinkered first-time winner of some potential if he can be kept on the right lines.

NOTEBOOK
Masamah(IRE), a well-made newcomer with plenty of size about him, wore one-cup blinkers. He got loose in the paddock beforehand and once underway soon showed a marked tendency to hang left. He ended up on the far-side rail but still scored with a fair bit in hand. He has a good engine if his steering can be ironed out. (op 4-1 tchd 11-4)
Caranbola saw off her stablemate and stuck on to finish a highly creditable second best. (op 9-4 tchd 3-1 in a place)
Majuba(USA), uptight, became very upset when the winner ran loose and hassled him in the paddock beforehand. Dropped in at the start, he was very free and when popped the question the response was negligible. He is his own worst enemy at present. (tchd 13-8, 15-8 and 2-1 in a place)
Grand Honour(IRE) travelled strongly but when asked to join issue he edged left and faded. He might not have appreciated the quick ground. (tchd 15-2)
Steel Stockholder, on his toes beforehand, diced with his stablemate for the lead but dropped away coming to the final furlong. (tchd 12-1)

2109 STRATFORD PLACE BREEDS BLACK TYPE WINNERS STKS (H'CAP) 1m 2f 88y
4:55 (4:56) (Class 4) (0-85,84) 3-Y-O £7,123 (£2,119; £1,059; £529) **Stalls** Low

Form RPR
21-6 **1** **Collection (IRE)**[33] 1297 3-9-3 **80** KerrinMcEvoy 13 100+
(W J Haggas) *lw: hld up towards rr: hdwy and nt clr run fr 3f out tl swtchd outside over 1f out: qcknd to ld ins fnl f: pushed out* **11/4**[1]
00-2 **2** *2 1/2* **Indian Days**[18] 1614 3-8-13 **76** TPQueally 9 84
(J G Given) *lw: tk fierce hold: sn trcking ldrs: led over 1f out: hdd and no ex ins fnl f* **9/2**[2]
31-0 **3** *nk* **Mystery Star (IRE)**[27] 1424 3-9-5 **82** PaulMulrennan 14 89
(M H Tompkins) *hld up in rr: hdwy over 4f out: chsng ldrs 2f out: kpt on same pce ins fnl f* **20/1**
0-31 **4** *3/4* **Fujin Dancer (FR)**[40] 1193 3-8-7 **70** oh2 PaulHanagan 4 76
(R A Fahey) *mid-div: hdwy on ins over 3f out: chsng ldrs over 1f out: kpt on same pce* **6/1**[3]
431- **5** *1 1/2* **Dandy Erin (IRE)**[179] 6857 3-9-4 **81** ShaneKelly 7 84
(J A Osborne) *led: qcknd over 4f out: hdd over 1f out: wknd ins fnl f* **16/1**
1-25 **6** *1 3/4* **My Mate Max**[26] 1448 3-8-10 **73** GrahamGibbons 5 72
(R Hollinshead) *mid-div: effrt over 3f out: one pce fnl 2f* **16/1**
512- **7** *hd* **Step This Way (USA)**[209] 6291 3-9-5 **82** JoeFanning 10 81
(M Johnston) *chsd ldrs: effrt over 3f out: one pce appr fnl f* **20/1**
546- **8** *2 1/2* **Tomorrow's World (IRE)**[204] 6414 3-8-9 **72** RyanMoore 11 66
(Sir Michael Stoute) *trckd ldrs: drvn over 3f out: lost pl and eased over 1f out* **7/1**
21 **9** *3/4* **Sweet Lightning**[21] 1563 3-9-7 **84** MartinDwyer 6 81+
(W R Muir) *hld up towards rr: effrt: edgd lft and hmpd 2f out: nvr nr ldrs* **8/1**
-336 **10** *1 1/4* **Internationaldebut (IRE)**[23] 1524 3-9-5 **82** (t) JohnEgan 12 72
(Jane Chapple-Hyam) *t.k.h in rr: hdwy whn nt clr run and bmpd 2f out: nvr on terms* **8/1**
010- **11** *1* **Casa Catalina (IRE)**[243] 5395 3-9-7 **84** RobertWinston 1 72
(M Johnston) *trckd ldrs: effrt 4f out: wkng whn n.m.r over 1f out* **20/1**
016- **12** *7* **Port Quin**[166] 6974 3-9-1 **78** TedDurcan 2 52
(G Wragg) *lw: in rr: detached last fr 4f out* **16/1**

2m 10.87s (-1.63) **Going Correction** +0.025s/f (Good) **12** Ran SP% **125.8**
Speed ratings (Par 101): **107,105,104,104,102 101,101,99,98,97 97,91**
CSF £14.98 CT £204.89 TOTE £4.10: £1.70, £2.10, £4.60; EX 19.30 Place 6 £119.44, Place 5 £78.93.
Owner Highclere Thoroughbred Racing (Brunel) **Bred** P D Savill **Trained** Newmarket, Suffolk

FOCUS
Again just a steady gallop until turning in in this decent handicap. The winner is a lot better than the bare form which overall looks fairly solid.
Tomorrow's World(IRE) Official explanation: jockey said filly was unsuited by the good to firm ground
Sweet Lightning Official explanation: jockey said gelding lost its action
Internationaldebut(IRE) Official explanation: jockey said colt ran too free early
T/Jkpt: Not won. T/Plt: £219.90 to a £1 stake. Pool: £169,287.77. 561.81 winning tickets. T/Qpdt: £55.40 to a £1 stake. Pool: £6,933.86. 92.50 winning tickets. JR

2110 - 2112a (Foreign Racing) - See Raceform Interactive

1492 NAAS (L-H)
Wednesday, May 14

OFFICIAL GOING: Good (good to firm in places)

2113a BLUE WIND STKS (GROUP 3) (F&M) 1m 2f
7:20 (7:20) 3-Y-O+ £43,014 (£12,573; £5,955; £1,985)

RPR
1 **Adored (IRE)**[10] 1848 3-8-10 ow1 JMurtagh 3 104+
(A P O'Brien, Ire) *mde all: rdn 2f out: kpt on wl fnl f* **9/2**[3]
2 *1 1/4* **Tiffany Diamond (IRE)**[2] 2061 3-8-9 70 JAHeffernan 2 100+
(A P O'Brien, Ire) *hld up bhd ldrs: 6th 1/2-way: hdwy in 4th 4f out: cl 3rd 2f out: sn short of room: 2nd 1f out: kpt on fnl f: nt rch wnr* **33/1**
3 *2* **Profound Beauty (IRE)**[31] 1353 4-9-9 106 PJSmullen 4 95
(D K Weld, Ire) *chsd ldr: cl 2nd 1/2-way: rdn 2f out: no ex in 3rd 1f out: kpt on same pce* **4/7**[1]
4 *7* **Allicansayis Wow (USA)**[40] 1199 3-8-9 101 KJManning 1 82
(J S Bolger, Ire) *chsd ldrs: 3rd 1/2-way: rdn in 4th 2f out: no ex: kpt on one pce* **14/1**
5 *2 1/2* **Sweet Sixteen (IRE)** 3-8-9 CO'Donoghue 5 77
(A P O'Brien, Ire) *hld up in rr: rdn 4f out: kpt on to mod 5th 2f out: no imp* **25/1**
6 *4 1/2* **Arkadina (IRE)**[31] 1353 4-9-9 96 WMLordan 7 67
(David Wachman, Ire) *hld up bhd ldrs: 5th 1/2-way: rdn and no ex 4f out* **12/1**
7 *24* **Marjalina (IRE)**[45] 1104 3-8-12 DPMcDonogh 6 23
(Kevin Prendergast, Ire) *chsd ldrs in 4th: rdn and wknd 4f out: trailing fnl f* **11/4**[2]

2m 9.24s (-6.36)
WFA 3 from 4yo 15lb **7** Ran SP% **129.6**
CSF £135.12 TOTE £4.40: £1.50, £6.90; DF 43.50.
Owner Mrs John Magnier **Bred** Whisperview Trading Ltd **Trained** Ballydoyle, Co Tipperary
■ Stewards' Enquiry : J A Heffernan two-day ban: careless riding (May 28 & 30)

FOCUS
The race has been rated through the fourth. The performance of the runner-up was a shock but she has plenty of big-race entries and there looked no fluke about this effort.

NOTEBOOK
Adored(IRE) benefited from front-running tactics to record her second career victory. She kept pulling out more when required under a strong ride from Johnny Murtagh, who put up a pound over on the daughter of Galileo. The winning rider said afterwards she had improved a lot since her maiden win at Gowran Park and galloped well to the line on this surface. (op 4/1)
Tiffany Diamond(IRE) had been beaten in a 50-75 handicap at Killarney earlier in the week, and this was without doubt a career-best display. She did not enjoy the clearest of passages when appearing to be travelling better than her two rivals on the inner. Pat Smullen on the well-backed favourite Profound Beauty rightly kept his racing line as Seamie Heffernan was looking for the gap to open. When the gap eventually did come she did not pick up on this surface.
Profound Beauty(IRE), a wide-margin course-and-distance maiden winner last June, was well backed and had every chance turning for home, but she could not raise her game. Her trainer said afterwards that he felt she just did not pick up on this ground as much as he had hoped. He intends stepping last season's Irish Oaks fifth back up to 1m4f now, with the Group 3 Noblesse Stakes at Cork the likely target. (op 11/10)
Allicansayis Wow(USA), fifth in last season's Moyglare Stud Stakes, also had the benefit of a previous run, but she was unable to quicken in the straight to keep in touch. (op 12/1)
Sweet Sixteen(IRE), the outsider of the Ballydoyle trio, plugged on without ever threatening.
Arkadina(IRE) was also held up, but she was unable to make any impression when let down on this surface.
Marjalina(IRE) was the big disappointment of the race. She was one of the first beaten and eventually trailed home a long way adrift, with her trainer saying afterwards that she was in season. Official explanation: vet said filly suffered an overreach and was found to be in season (op 2/1)

2114 - 2116a (Foreign Racing) - See Raceform Interactive

1828 **NEWMARKET (ROWLEY)** (R-H)

Thursday, May 15

OFFICIAL GOING: Good to firm

Wind: Fresh, across Weather: Overcast with the odd light shower

2117 ELMS CAMBRIDGE MEDIAN AUCTION MAIDEN STKS 5f

5:50 (5:53) (Class 5) 2-Y-0 £3,238 (£963; £481; £240) Stalls Low

Form RPR

1 **Prolific (IRE)** 2-9-3 0 RichardHughes 8 90+
(R Hannon) *trckd ldrs: led over 1f out: shkn up and r.o wl* 7/4[1]

2 3 1/4 **Brae Hill (IRE)** 2-9-3 0 HayleyTurner 4 78
(M L W Bell) *led over 3f: styd on same pce ins fnl f* 11/2[3]

3 3 1 3/4 **Barbee (IRE)**[15] 1722 2-8-12 0 SebSanders 5 67
(E A L Dunlop) *chsd ldrs: rdn over 1f out: no ex fnl f* 6/1

4 2 1/4 **Countrywide City (IRE)** 2-9-3 0 AdrianMcCarthy 2 64
(P W Chapple-Hyam) *bmpd s: sn chsng ldrs: rdn over 1f out: wknd fnl f* 3/1[2]

5 4 **Bold Hawk** 2-9-3 0 JohnEgan 7 50
(Mrs C A Dunnett) *sn outpcd* 66/1

6 3 3/4 **Herring Senior (IRE)** 2-9-3 0 TQuinn 3 36
(P F I Cole) *bmpd s: outpcd* 7/1

7 3/4 **Balladiene (IRE)** 2-8-12 0 JimmyQuinn 6 28
(M H Tompkins) *sn outpcd* 33/1

0 8 1/2 **Elusive Ronnie (IRE)**[10] 1851 2-9-3 0 PatCosgrave 1 32
(S A Callaghan) *sn chsng ldrs: rdn: hung rt and wknd over 1f out* 25/1

60.75 secs (1.65) **Going Correction** +0.20s/f (Good) **8 Ran SP% 111.8**

Speed ratings (Par 93): **94,88,86,82,76 70,68,68**

CSF £11.22 TOTE £2.20: £1.30, £2.10, £1.50; EX 10.10.

Owner Highclere Thoroughbred Racing (Stubbs) **Bred** David Jamison Bloodstock **Trained** East Everleigh, Wilts

FOCUS

A fair juvenile maiden, run at an average pace. The debutant winner rates value for further and the form is rated around the third.

NOTEBOOK

Prolific(IRE) ◆, a £52,000 breeze-up purchase bred to make his mark over sprint distances this year, was the subject of decent market support and ran out an impressive debutant winner. He was settled on the outside of the pack just off the pace early on and ran green when entering the Dip nearing 2f out. His reponse when meeting the rising ground was very pleasing, however, and it was clear shortly afterwards that he was going to do the business. A trip to Royal Ascot will now surely be on his agenda, where the likely sound surface will suit him, and improvement looks assured from this experience. The Norfolk Stakes appeals as his most viable target there, but he did shape as though another furlong will suit before that long, and so the Coventry Stakes also may come into the equation. (op 9-4 tchd 13-8)

Brae Hill(IRE), another bred to be suited by sprinting this year, showed up nicely from the front yet was firmly put in his place when the winner kicked for home. He should learn a good deal mentally from this debut experience and has a future. (op 5-1 tchd 9-2)

Barbee(IRE), third on debut at Great Leighs 15 days previously, travelled kindly on the early pace yet found just the one pace when the race became really serious after 2f out. This was still probably an improved effort in defeat, she went on the quick surface, and the switch to a sharper 5f can see her off the mark. (op 8-1)

Countrywide City(IRE), yet another bred for sprinting, was not helped by being bumped soon after the start yet still travelled with the early pace. He was not able to go with the principals when it mattered, however, and will need to come on a bundle for this if he is to be winning a maiden in the coming weeks. (op 9-4 tchd 4-1)

Herring Senior(IRE) is a half-brother to 1m2f three-year-old winner Zain and a good-looking colt. He was never in this after being bumped at the start, however, and looked decidedly short of pace. (op 5-1)

2118 BEDFORD LODGE HOTEL FILLIES' H'CAP 1m

6:20 (6:22) (Class 5) (0-75,75) 3-Y-0 £3,885 (£1,156; £577; £288) Stalls Low

Form RPR

21 1 **Maghya (IRE)**[17] 1669 3-9-3 74 RHills 8 89+
(W J Haggas) *s.i.s: hld up: hdwy over 2f out: rdn to ld ins fnl f: hung lft: r.o* 7/2[2]

431- 2 1 1/4 **Suzi's Decision**[241] 5470 3-8-12 69 JohnEgan 9 81+
(P W D'Arcy) *a.p: rdn over 2f out: hung rt over 1f out: hung lft and r.o ins fnl f* 10/3[1]

0-33 3 1 3/4 **Koraleva Tectona (IRE)**[19] 1622 3-8-8 65 PaulEddery 7 73
(Pat Eddery) *sn w ldr: led 3f out: rdn over 1f out: hung lft and hdd ins fnl f: no ex* 11/1

-430 4 6 **Jollyhockeysticks**[11] 1839 3-9-2 73 DarryllHolland 11 67
(M R Channon) *hld up: hdwy 2f out: sn rdn and hung lft: nt trble ldrs* 20/1

1-30 5 3 **Bermacha**[17] 1685 3-9-1 72 RichardMullen 13 59
(W R Muir) *hld up: rdn over 3f out: nvr trbld ldrs* 20/1

00-0 6 3 1/2 **Lavender And Lace**[47] 1073 3-8-1 61 oh3 WilliamBuick(3) 12 40
(T Keddy) *in rr: hdwy over 3f out: rdn and hung lft over 1f out: wknd fnl f* 50/1

05-5 7 nk **Jelly Mo**[19] 1637 3-8-10 67 EddieAhern 15 45
(J W Hills) *mid-div: rdn over 2f out: styd on appr fnl f: nvr nrr* 50/1

60-0 8 1 3/4 **Garland**[27] 1444 3-8-11 68 RichardHughes 16 42
(R Hannon) *led 5f: rdn and wknd over 1f out* 20/1

40-4 9 2 **Trumpet Lily**[17] 1685 3-9-3 74 RyanMoore 6 44
(J G Portman) *hld up: hdwy u.p over 2f out: wknd over 1f out* 15/2[3]

60-0 10 2 1/4 **Secret Gem (IRE)**[19] 1622 3-8-9 66 PhilipRobinson 17 31
(C G Cox) *prom over 5f* 12/1

51-2 11 nk **Bushy Dell (IRE)**[28] 1412 3-8-11 75 AmyBaker(7) 1 39
(Miss J Feilden) *sn outpcd* 25/1

5132 12 hd **Bookiebasher Babe (IRE)**[19] 1637 3-8-11 68 FrancisNorton 4 31
(M Quinn) *hld up: hdwy over 3f out: wknd over 2f out* 9/1

600- 13 hd **Maybe I Will (IRE)**[203] 6449 3-8-5 62 HayleyTurner 3 25
(S Dow) *sn outpcd* 33/1

030- 14 2 **Redeemed**[234] 5682 3-9-4 75 SebSanders 14 33
(B J Meehan) *chsd ldrs over 5f* 12/1

63-5 15 4 **Azure Mist**[21] 1575 3-8-10 67 JimmyQuinn 2 16
(M H Tompkins) *hld up: a in rr* 25/1

53-4 16 4 **Lullaby Lady**[16] 1709 3-8-7 64 MichaelHills 5 4
(B W Hills) *mid-div: wknd over 3f out* 20/1

30-0 17 2 3/4 **Farsighted**[30] 1381 3-8-12 69 DaleGibson 10 —
(J M P Eustace) *chsd ldrs over 4f* 50/1

1m 39.66s (1.06) **Going Correction** +0.20s/f (Good) **17 Ran SP% 126.3**

Speed ratings (Par 96): **102,100,99,93,90 86,86,84,82,80 79,79,79,77,73 69,66**

CSF £13.72 CT £120.61 TOTE £4.20: £1.10, £1.90, £3.10, £4.70; EX 16.00.

Owner Hamdan Al Maktoum **Bred** Shadwell Estate Company Limited **Trained** Newmarket, Suffolk

FOCUS

A modest fillies' handicap, run at an average pace. The form looks fair with the first three coming clear.

Bookiebasher Babe(IRE) Official explanation: jockey said filly was unsuited by the good to firm ground

Redeemed Official explanation: jockey said filly stopped very quickly

Azure Mist Official explanation: jockey said filly ran too free

2119 KING'S HEAD AT MOULTON MAIDEN STKS 1m 2f

6:55 (6:56) (Class 4) 3-Y-0 £5,180 (£1,541; £770; £384) Stalls Low

Form RPR

1 **Swinging Sixties (IRE)** 3-9-3 0 PhilipRobinson 3 92
(M A Jarvis) *hld up: racd keenly: hdwy over 2f out: chsd ldr over 1f out: rdn to ld towards fin* 11/2[3]

02- 2 nk **West With The Wind**[190] 6724 3-9-3 0 JohnEgan 1 91
(T P Tate) *chsd ldr tl led over 3f out: rdn over 1f out: hdd towards fin* 5/2[2]

0- 3 4 1/2 **Ucetek (IRE)**[186] 6777 3-8-12 0 RyanMoore 6 77
(Sir Michael Stoute) *hld up: outpcd over 3f out: hdwy over 1f out: styd on: nt trble ldrs* 20/1

04 4 3 1/4 **Closertobelieving**[14] 1748 3-9-3 0 TQuinn 2 76
(D R C Elsworth) *hdwy over 7f out: rdn and hung rt over 1f out: wknd fnl f* 16/1

0-6 5 11 **Piano Sonata**[20] 1599 3-8-12 0 MichaelHills 4 49
(B W Hills) *chsd ldrs: rdn 1/2-way: wknd over 2f out* 16/1

6 1/2 **Censored** 3-8-12 0 TPQueally 5 48
(Sir Michael Stoute) *s.i.s: a in rr* 33/1

7 3 3/4 **Catholic Hill (USA)** 3-9-3 0 RichardHughes 7 45
(B J Meehan) *sn chsng ldrs: rdn over 2f out: sn wknd* 33/1

6- 8 12 **Gainsborough's Art (IRE)**[196] 6602 3-9-3 0 SebSanders 9 21
(D R C Elsworth) *led over 6f: wknd 2f out* 25/1

4 P **King's Charm (FR)**[28] 1417 3-9-3 0 EddieAhern 8 —
(J Noseda) *hld up: hdwy 1/2-way: p.u 4f out* 10/11[1]

2m 6.24s (0.44) **Going Correction** +0.20s/f (Good) **9 Ran SP% 122.6**

Speed ratings (Par 101): **106,105,102,99,90 90,87,77,—**

CSF £20.19 TOTE £6.40: £2.10, £1.40, £2.50; EX 27.10.

Owner Sheikh Ahmed Al Maktoum **Bred** Darley **Trained** Newmarket, Suffolk

FOCUS

This should work out to be a fair three-year-old maiden. The first pair came nicely clear and the form has been rated positively.

2120 JACK & JILL CHILDREN'S FOUNDATION H'CAP 1m 2f

7:25 (7:25) (Class 3) (0-90,88) 4-Y-0+ £7,771 (£2,312; £1,155; £577) Stalls Low

Form RPR

-542 1 **Jeer (IRE)**[12] 1793 4-9-1 85 SebSanders 5 94
(E A L Dunlop) *a.p: chsd ldr over 1f out: sn rdn and hung lft: styd on to ld and edgd lft nr fin* 7/2[3]

121- 2 1/2 **Kaateb (IRE)**[204] 6439 5-9-1 85 RHills 7 96+
(W J Haggas) *hld up: swtchd lft 2f out: hdwy sn after: hmpd over 1f out: rdn to ld ins fnl f: hdd whn bmpd nr fin* 15/8[1]

-400 3 1 **Invasian (IRE)**[12] 1812 7-9-2 86 ShaneKelly 3 92
(P W D'Arcy) *led: rdn over 1f out: hdd and no ex ins fnl f* 16/1

565 4 1 1/2 **Lisathedaddy**[58] 927 6-8-12 82 RichardKingscote 1 85
(B G Powell) *s.i.s: hld up: hdwy over 3f out: rdn over 1f out: no ex fnl f* 8/1

-320 5 6 **Putra Square**[26] 1473 4-8-7 77 ow1 TQuinn 2 68
(P F I Cole) *chsd ldr: rdn over 2f out: wknd over 1f out* 12/1

3-05 6 1 3/4 **Sahrati**[22] 1568 4-9-4 88 RyanMoore 6 76
(C E Brittain) *chsd ldrs: lost pl 1/2-way: sn rdn: wknd over 1f out* 3/1[2]

300 7 19 **Quince (IRE)**[17] 1682 5-8-7 77 (v) JimmyQuinn 4 27
(J Pearce) *s.i.s: sn prom: wknd 2f out* 10/1

2m 5.87s (0.07) **Going Correction** +0.20s/f (Good) **7 Ran SP% 115.8**

Speed ratings (Par 107): **107,106,105,104,99 98,83**

CSF £10.80 TOTE £4.70: £2.20, £1.50; EX 11.00.

Owner Mohammed Jaber **Bred** Floors Farming And Side Hill Stud **Trained** Newmarket, Suffolk

FOCUS

A good little handicap, run at a fair pace. The form is a bit muddling but is best rated through the fourth.

NOTEBOOK

Jeer(IRE), a runner-up at Doncaster 12 days previously, proved game in going one better and winning his first handicap. He is versatile as regards underfoot conditions and this was his best effort to date, plus the Handicapper can hardly put him up too much for this. (op 9-2 tchd 5-1)

Kaateb(IRE), a dual winner last year, came through from off the pace to have every chance on this first run for 204 days. He was not done too many favours by the winner late on, but was losing that argument at the time and left the impression he may benefit for a step back up to 1m4f now. (op 2-1 tchd 9-4)

Invasian(IRE), with the eyeshield left off, had the run of things out in front yet this represented a much better effort in defeat from him. This is his grade and a return to 1m4f could see him get a little closer still.

Lisathedaddy ran her race on this return from a 58 days break and first outing on turf since October last year. She ought to come on a bit for the run and helps to set the standard of this form. (op 13-2)

Sahrati2lb lower, seems to need a strong pace to shine and he was not at his best on this drop back in trip. (op 10-3 tchd 4-1)

2121 WAGGON AND HORSES CONDITIONS STKS 1m

8:00 (8:01) (Class 3) 3-Y-0 £6,799 (£2,023; £1,011; £505) Stalls Low

Form RPR

13-0 1 **Without A Prayer (IRE)**[26] 1471 3-8-12 95 SebSanders 6 105
(R M Beckett) *mde all: rdn over 1f out: r.o gamely* 18/1

4-1 2 1/2 **Moyenne Corniche**[26] 1467 3-8-12 93 RyanMoore 7 104
(G Wragg) *chsd wnr: rdn and ev ch fr over 1f out: edgd lft: r.o* 5/2[2]

12- 3 nse **Fateh Field (USA)**[201] 6488 3-8-12 104 LDettori 8 104
(Saeed Bin Suroor) *hld up: hdwy over 2f out: rdn: edgd lft and ev ch ins fnl f: r.o* 9/4[1]

6-22 4 5 **Gaspar Van Wittel (USA)**[12] 1797 3-8-12 100 StephenDonohoe 3 93
(S A Callaghan) *hld up: swtchd rt over 1f out: nvr trbld ldrs* 13/2

1 5 2 1/4 **Fanjura (IRE)**[28] 1418 3-8-12 0 ShaneKelly 5 103+
(J Noseda) *trckd ldrs: rdn over 1f out: styng on whn hmpd and lost all ch ins fnl f: eased* 7/1

1- 6 1/2 **Cat Junior (USA)**[284] 4201 3-8-12 98 RichardHughes 4 86
(B J Meehan) *hld up: hdwy over 3f out: rdn over 2f out: wknd over 1f out* 4/1[3]

1 7 4 1/2 **Tri Nations (UAE)**[28] 1417 3-8-12 0 EddieAhern 2 76
(J W Hills) *hld up in tch: wknd over 1f out* 20/1

1m 40.19s (1.59) **Going Correction** +0.20s/f (Good) **7 Ran SP% 115.2**

Speed ratings (Par 103): **100,99,99,94,92 91,87**

CSF £63.88 TOTE £19.80: £3.50, £2.30; EX 81.60.

Owner McDonagh Murphy And Nixon **Bred** Brownstown Stud **Trained** Whitsbury, Hants

FOCUS
A decent three-year-old conditions event, but the early pace was only modest, however, and the first three were closely covered at the finish. The form can be rated around the third to his juvenile form.

NOTEBOOK
Without A Prayer(IRE), out the back in the Greenham on his seasonal debut 26 days previously, showed that effort to be all wrong and made all in brave fashion. He had the advantage of the stands' rail throughout, but the extra furlong enabled him to show his true colours and he is clearly smart - as his third in last year's Acomb backs up. (op 14-1)
Moyenne Corniche, a clear-cut winner of a Newbury maiden on his comeback 26 days previously, went down fighting and lost nothing in defeat. Whether he was as suited by the quicker ground has to be in some doubt and he would have really also preferred a stronger pace, so it is still unlikely we have seen the best of him. Official explanation: jockey said colt hung both ways in latter stages (op 3-1)
Fateh Field(USA), who showed smart form in two outings last year, was stepping back up from 6f for this three-year-old debut. Ridden patiently early on, he emerged with every chance when the race became really serious and was eventually not beaten at all far. Considering the early pace was only modest it is hard to know whether he really stayed this distance, but he has clearly trained on this season and does looks set for further successes. (op 2-1 tchd 5-2)
Gaspar Van Wittel(USA), a runner-up on both his previous outings this year, was unable to go with the principles nearing the final furlong and was put in his place. He did little wrong, however, and does help to set the level of this form. (op 10-1 tchd 6-1)
Fanjura(IRE), a narrow winner of the second division of the Wood Ditton over course and distance 28 days previously, must rate a good deal better than the bare form as he was hampered when coming with his challenge nearing the final furlong. Official explanation: jockey said colt suffered interference 1f out and lost its action (tchd 8-1)
Cat Junior(USA), a ready winner on his sole outing as a juvenile, was one of the first to be beaten on this return to the track. It may be that this step up in trip was beyond him at present, and he is entitled to improve for the run, but he does now have a little to prove all the same. (tchd 9-2)
Tri Nations(UAE), the winner of the first division of the Wood Ditton, travelled kindly on the rail until the race started to hot up. He is probably capable of better, but he is another who now has it to prove. (tchd 16-1 and 25-1)

2122 BETTER ON NEWMARKET HIGH STREET H'CAP — 5f
8:30 (8:30) (Class 5) (0-75,77) 3-Y-O — £3,885 (£1,156; £577; £288) Stalls Low

Form — RPR
5321 **1** **Espy**[10] 1852 3-9-4 77 6ex WilliamBuick(3) 13 — 82+
(S Kirk) *hld up in tch: led and edgd lft 1f out: rdn out* 2/1[1]
1600 **2** ¾ **Helping Hand (IRE)**[23] 1548 3-8-11 67 HayleyTurner 12 — 69
(R Hollinshead) *chsd ldrs: rdn and ev ch fr over 1f out: styd on* 40/1
21-4 **3** ½ **Another Socket**[16] 1707 3-9-4 74 GrahamGibbons 4 — 74
(E S McMahon) *chsd ldrs: rdn over 1f out: styd on* 16/1
445- **4** ½ **Mandelieu (IRE)**[166] 7000 3-9-0 70 LiamJones 10 — 68
(W J Haggas) *hld up: hdwy over 1f out: r.o: nt rch ldrs* 16/1
2400 **5** hd **Extreme North (USA)**[19] 1635 3-8-5 61 (v) EdwardCreighton 5 — 59
(Miss V Haigh) *hld up in tch: plld hrd: rdn over 1f out: styd on* 40/1
15-4 **6** hd **Wavertree Princess (IRE)**[35] 1284 3-9-0 70 TPQueally 14 — 67
(N P Littmoden) *hld up: hdwy over 1f out: nt rch ldrs* 12/1
-342 **7** nk **Monsieur Reynard**[43] 1155 3-9-2 72 RyanMoore 9 — 77+
(B J Meehan) *hld up: racd keenly: nt clr run over 1f out: r.o ins fnl f: nt rch ldrs* 4/1[2]
5-43 **8** 1¾ **Cracking Nick (IRE)**[23] 1548 3-9-0 70 AdamKirby 1 — 60
(W R Swinburn) *mid-div: sn drvn along: styd on ins fnl f: nvr trbld ldrs* 9/1
2324 **9** ¾ **Jalons Bridewell**[64] 855 3-8-13 69 (v[1]) FrancisNorton 11 — 56
(M Quinn) *chsd ldr: led wl over 1f out: rdn and hdd 1f out: wknd towards fin* 20/1
32-4 **10** ½ **Doric Lady**[14] 1737 3-9-0 70 AlanMunro 7 — 55
(J A R Toller) *hld up: rdn and edgd lft over 1f out: wknd fnl f* 8/1[3]
4250 **11** 1 **Shatter Resistant (IRE)**[6] 1958 3-8-4 60 oh6 (e) JimmyQuinn 3 — 41
(M D Squance) *s.s: hld up: hmpd over 1f out: nvr nr to chal* 14/1
600- **12** 1½ **Rough Rock (IRE)**[210] 6282 3-9-2 72 DarryllHolland 2 — 48
(Miss Gay Kelleway) *chsd ldrs: lost pl 3f out: sn bhd* 20/1
0-53 **13** 1¼ **Second Opinion (IRE)**[26] 1475 3-8-11 67 RichardHughes 6 — 39
(J M P Eustace) *led: rdn and hdd wl over 1f out: sn wknd* 9/1

60.80 secs (1.70) **Going Correction** +0.20s/f (Good) 13 Ran SP% **125.0**
Speed ratings (Par 99): **94,92,92,91,90 90,90,87,86,85 83,81,79**
CSF £117.42 CT £1109.72 TOTE £2.90: £1.40, £10.90, £5.20; EX 140.60 Place 6 £64.26, Place 5 £47.07.
Owner P D Merritt J Davies T Sharman **Bred** Miss Brooke Sanders **Trained** Upper Lambourn, Berks

FOCUS
A modest three-year-old sprint handicap which saw the first seven closely covered at the finish. There are doubts over the runner-up and fifth and the form looks ordinary.
Monsieur Reynard Official explanation: jockey said gelding was denied a clear run
Shatter Resistant(IRE) Official explanation: jockey said gelding missed the break and was denied a clear run
Rough Rock(IRE) Official explanation: jockey said gelding was intimidated in running by the closely packed field
Second Opinion(IRE) Official explanation: jockey said filly stopped very quickly
T/Plt: £130.30 to a £1 stake. Pool: £65,753.80. 368.30 winning tickets. T/Qpdt: £96.20 to a £1 stake. Pool: £3,901.37. 30.00 winning tickets. CR

1835 SALISBURY (R-H)
Thursday, May 15

OFFICIAL GOING: Good
Wind: Nil Weather: Overcast

2123 DIXON SCAFFOLDING TRANSMISSION MAIDEN FILLIES' STKS — 1m 1f 198y
1:50 (1:52) (Class 5) 3-Y-O+ — £3,885 (£1,156; £577; £288) Stalls Low

Form — RPR
5-3 **1** **Arthur's Girl**[27] 1444 3-8-12 0 JimCrowley 11 — 89+
(G Wragg) *trckd ldrs: drvn and swtchd lft ins fnl 2f: led 1f out: styd on strly* 9/2[2]
2 ½ **Ghaidaa (IRE)** 3-8-12 0 RichardKingscote 8 — 87+
(M A Jarvis) *t.k.h: trckd ldrs: drvn to chal over 1f out: stl ev ch ins fnl f: no ex cl home* 9/1
24- **3** 3 **Quotation**[205] 6411 3-8-9 0 WilliamBuick(3) 4 — 81
(Sir Michael Stoute) *trckd ldrs: slt advantage over 2f out: sn rdn: hdd 1f out: wknd ins fnl f* 2/1[1]
03- **4** 4½ **Gingham**[222] 6015 3-8-12 0 DaneO'Neill 13 — 72+
(L M Cumani) *plld hrd: chsd ldrs: stl keen over 3f out: rdn over 2f out: kpt on same pce* 8/1
0- **5** 1¼ **Dedicate**[202] 6470 3-8-12 0 SteveDrowne 9 — 70+
(R Charlton) *in tch: rdn and one pce over 2f out: styd on again ins fnl f* 6/1[3]
0- **6** ½ **Siyasa (USA)**[285] 4169 3-8-12 0 TQuinn 5 — 69
(Saeed Bin Suroor) *sn slt ld: rdn and hdd over 2f out: wknd over 1f out* 8/1
40- **7** 2½ **King's Kazeem**[201] 6493 3-8-12 0 MartinDwyer 6 — 64
(B W Hills) *sn chsng ldrs: rdn 3f out: wknd ins fnl 2f* 14/1
0- **8** 1¼ **Turfani (IRE)**[205] 6411 3-8-12 0 PaulDoe 7 — 61?
(W J Knight) *in rr: pushed along over 3f: sme prog fr over 1f out: nvr in contention* 100/1
9 ½ **Yonder**[41] 4-9-10 0 TravisBlock(3) 10 — 61
(H Morrison) *drvn along 4f out: mod prog fnl f* 16/1
0- **10** nk **Selsey**[194] 6648 3-8-12 0 J-PGuillambert 12 — 59
(Sir Michael Stoute) *w ldr: rdn 3f out: wknd ins fnl 2f* 14/1
0 **11** 5 **Poppy Gregg**[16] 1695 3-8-9 0 KevinGhunowa(3) 1 — 49?
(Dr J R J Naylor) *carried lft s: a in rr* 100/1
0- **12** 2¼ **Lambda (USA)**[219] 6093 3-8-12 0 TPO'Shea 3 — 45+
(Sir Michael Stoute) *wnt lft s: sn rcvrd: chsd ldrs 5f out: wknd fr 3f out* 20/1
13 1¼ **Lovespell (USA)** 3-8-12 0 EdwardCreighton 2 — 42
(H Morrison) *carried lft s: a towards rr* 100/1
0 **14** ¾ **Burry Green**[16] 1695 3-8-12 0 RichardHughes 14 — 41
(R Hannon) *in rr: mod prog over 4f out: sn in rr again* 33/1

2m 10.47s (0.57) **Going Correction** +0.15s/f (Good)
WFA 3 from 4yo 15lb 14 Ran SP% **127.9**
Speed ratings (Par 100): **103,102,100,96,95 95,93,92,91,91 87,85,84,84**
CSF £46.81 TOTE £6.10: £2.30, £2.80, £1.70; EX 38.40.
Owner A E Oppenheimer **Bred** Hascombe And Valiant Studs **Trained** Newmarket, Suffolk
■ Stewards' Enquiry : Jim Crowley one-day ban: careless riding (May 29)

FOCUS
An interesting maiden featuring some well-bred and lightly raced fillies and the form has been rated fairly positively.
Poppy Gregg Official explanation: jockey said filly suffered interference at the start

2124 AVONBRIDGE AT WHITSBURY STUD MAIDEN STKS — 5f
2:20 (2:21) (Class 3) 2-Y-O — £6,476 (£1,927; £963; £481) Stalls High

Form — RPR
33 **1** **Sun Ship (IRE)**[15] 1714 2-9-3 0 RichardHughes 6 — 85
(R Hannon) *mde all: shkn up over 1f out: in command thrght fnl f: readily* 2/1[1]
0 **2** 1¾ **Shiva Adiva**[17] 1680 2-8-12 0 RichardKingscote 3 — 74
(Tom Dascombe) *chsd ldrs: rdn and styd on to go 2nd 1f out: kpt on but a readily hld by wnr* 20/1
3 2½ **Penny's Gift** 2-8-12 0 DaneO'Neill 7 — 65+
(R Hannon) *s.i.s: green in rr: pushed along 3f out: hdwy fr 2f out: styd on ins fnl f but no ch w ldng duo* 9/1
4 nk **Macdillon** 2-9-3 0 LPKeniry 4 — 69
(W S Kittow) *chsd ldrs: rdn over 2f out: edgd lft u.p over 1f out: one pce* 16/1
3 **5** ½ **Desire To Excel (IRE)**[11] 1832 2-9-3 0 TQuinn 1 — 67
(P F I Cole) *chsd wnr: rdn over 2f out: wknd fnl f* 11/4[2]
6 1½ **Belle Des Airs (IRE)** 2-8-12 0 JamesDoyle 8 — 56
(R M Beckett) *in rr: drvn and hdwy over 2f out: crossed and swtchd rt over 1f out: kpt on but nvr in contention* 28/1
2 **7** nk **The Desert Saint**[10] 1851 2-9-0 0 WilliamBuick(3) 2 — 60
(A M Balding) *chsd ldrs: rdn 1/2-way and no imp on ldrs: wknd appr fnl f* 4/1[3]
8 2¼ **Russian Art** 2-9-3 0 GeorgeBaker 9 — 52
(R M Beckett) *green early: a towards rr* 8/1
9 ½ **Mattamia (IRE)** 2-8-12 0 JamesMillman(5) 5 — 50
(B R Millman) *s.i.s: green: a in rr* 20/1

62.05 secs (1.25) **Going Correction** +0.15s/f (Good) 9 Ran SP% **120.0**
Speed ratings (Par 97): **96,93,89,88,87 85,85,81,80**
CSF £49.12 TOTE £3.20: £1.50, £4.70, £2.00; EX 62.70 Trifecta £119.80 Part won. Pool: £168.74. 0.10 winning units..
Owner Michael Pescod **Bred** Captain T Bulwer-Long & Myriad Bldstck & Communic **Trained** East Everleigh, Wilts

FOCUS
A fair maiden in which only three had previous racecourse experience and that proved important. The winner is one to respect in a better grade.

NOTEBOOK
Sun Ship(IRE) ran out a comfortable winner. He had come up against the useful Baycat on both his starts and had reportedly not handled the soft ground on the second occasion. His trainer thinks something of him and he could take his chance in the Windsor Castle at Royal Ascot, especially if the ground is fast. (op 11-4 tchd 15-8)
Shiva Adiva is bred to be speedy and showed the benefit of her debut to chase home the winner. She was cheaply bought and could pick up an auction maiden at least. (tchd 16-1 and 22-1)
Penny's Gift ◆ was arguably the eyecatcher in that she missed the break quite badly on this debut before keeping on well in the closing stages. She is another that did not cost a great deal and can pick up an ordinary maiden with normal improvement. (op 16-1)
Macdillon, who was backed in the morning, was quite coltish in the paddock but his mind was fully on the job in the race and he kept on well in the closing stages. (op 14-1 tchd 20-1)
Desire To Excel(IRE) showed plenty of early pace but faded out of contention in the latter stages. (op 5-2 tchd 9-4)
Belle Des Airs(IRE), out of an unraced half-sister to Smart Enough, put up a fair effort and may have been closer had she not been stopped in her run below the distance. (op 25-1)
The Desert Saint had his chance but hung left into the centre of the track when put under pressure. (op 7-2 tchd 9-2)

2125 EUROPEAN BREEDERS FUND FILLIES' H'CAP — 1m 4f
2:50 (2:50) (Class 4) (0-85,73) 4-Y-O+ — £7,123 (£2,119; £1,059; £529) Stalls High

Form — RPR
1135 **1** **Naughty Thoughts (IRE)**[16] 1697 4-8-6 61 RichardKingscote 3 — 64
(Tom Dascombe) *trckd ldrs in cl 3rd: led over 3f out: rdn and edgd lft 1f out: kpt on wl* 4/7[1]
-261 **2** 2¼ **Uig**[6] 1959 7-8-13 73 6ex HaddenFrost(5) 2 — 72
(H S Howe) *t.k.h: led first f: styd chsng ldr: rdn and outpcd over 3f out: styd on fr 2f out to chse wnr fnl f but no imp* 3/1[2]
2-00 **3** 1¼ **Star Of Pompey**[18] 1643 4-8-3 61 oh6 ow2 KirstyMilczarek(3) 4 — 58
(A B Haynes) *led after 1f: rdn and hdd over 3f out: styd chsng wnr tl wknd 1f out* 12/1
00-0 **4** 2¾ **Fascinatin Rhythm**[26] 1472 4-9-4 73 EdwardCreighton 1 — 66
(M R Channon) *cl 4th: rdn to press ldrs 3f out: wknd ins fnl 2f* 13/2[3]

2m 38.77s (0.77) **Going Correction** +0.15s/f (Good) 4 Ran SP% **109.7**
Speed ratings (Par 102): **103,101,100,98**
CSF £2.63 TOTE £1.60; EX 2.40.

Owner 123 Racing Partnership **Bred** Dr John Hollowood And Aiden Murphy **Trained** Lambourn, Berks

FOCUS

A disappointing turnout for the feature race with a small field and the top weights running off marks 12lb below the race ceiling and the form is weak for the grade.

2126 TURFTV CLAIMING STKS — 6f 212y

3:25 (3:31) (Class 5) 3-Y-O — **£3,238** (£963; £481; £240) **Stalls** High

Form — RPR

-524 **1** **Party In The Park**[9] [1897] 3-9-0 67 .... PatrickHills(5) 4 — 68
(R Hannon) *chsd ldrs: rdn over 2f out: chal fnl f and styd on fnl to ld fnl 50yds: all out* **11/4**[2]

2406 **2** *nk* **Admirals Way**[14] [1743] 3-8-6 52 .... MatthewDavies(7) 10 — 61
(C N Kellett) *in rr: hdwy over 2f out: styng on to chal whn hung bdly rt thrght fnl f: nt run on cl home* **10/1**

0-00 **3** *½* **Bahamian Blue (IRE)**[16] [1696] 3-8-5 56 .... (b[1]) JamesDoyle 9 — 52
(H J L Dunlop) *led: hrd rdn fr over 2f out: styd on to hold narrow advantage tl hdd and no ex fnl 50yds* **15/2**

1561 **4** *2 ¼* **Secret Meaning**[20] [1603] 3-8-5 61 .... (v) JackDean(5) 8 — 51
(W G M Turner) *in rr: hdwy u.p fr 2f out: chsd ldng trio ins fnl f but sn fnd no ex* **9/2**[3]

223 **5** *3 ¼* **Caprio (IRE)**[13] [1777] 3-9-5 70 .... (p) JimCrowley 11 — 51
(J R Boyle) *chsd ldrs: rdn 3f out: wknd over 1f out* **9/4**[1]

000- **6** *4 ½* **Starfinch**[271] [4593] 3-7-13 48 .... RossAtkinson(7) 15 — 26
(J J Bridger) *chsd ldrs: rdn: hung lft and wknd ins fnl 2f* **80/1**

-236 **7** *7* **Mama Leo**[97] [486] 3-8-2 59 ow1 .... (v) KirstyMilczarek(3) 6 — 6
(J G M O'Shea) *rdn and hung bdly lft over 2f out: nvr in contention* **12/1**

0 **8** *4* **Owain James**[11] [1836] 3-9-1 0 .... NeilChalmers 14 — 5
(M Salaman) *sn rdn: a in rr* **50/1**

00 **9** *9* **La Zarza**[44] [1125] 3-8-0 0 .... NickyMackay 1 — —
(S C Williams) *chsd ldrs over 4f* **33/1**

0 **10** *7* **True And Fair (IRE)**[27] [1445] 3-8-10 0 .... (t) RichardKingscote 13 — —
(Tom Dascombe) *early spd: wknd rapidly over 3f out* **14/1**

11 *6* **Lady Silca** 3-8-2 59 ow2 .... RichardThomas 12 — —
(A D Smith) *slowly away: a in rr* **50/1**

1m 30.04s (1.04) **Going Correction** +0.15s/f (Good) — **11 Ran SP% 118.9**

Speed ratings (Par 99): **100,99,99,96,92 87,79,75,64,56 49**

CSF £29.14 TOTE £3.80: £1.60, £3.60, £2.20; EX 36.50.Party In The Park was claimed by Miss J Camacho for £12,000. Bahamian Blue was claimed by Ms P M Marks for £5,000.

Owner Sarah Whent Ron Gander & Betty Burchett **Bred** Lady Whent, Mrs B Burchett & R Hannon **Trained** East Everleigh, Wilts

FOCUS

An ordinary and uncompetitive claimer made less so by the scratching of Bridge Of Fermoy earlier in the day and the withdrawal of the well-backed Emir Bagatelle at the start by the vet. The form is rated around the first two but this is not a race to be with.

2127 WILKINS KENNEDY CHARTERED ACCOUNTANTS H'CAP — 6f

4:00 (4:02) (Class 5) (0-75,75) 3-Y-O — **£3,238** (£963; £481; £240) **Stalls** High

Form — RPR

5421 **1** **Nice Wee Girl (IRE)**[34] [1315] 3-9-1 72 .... LPKeniry 3 — 82
(S Kirk) *hld up in rr: str run fr 2f out: qcknd to ld ins fnl f: c clr nr fin: easily* **8/1**

4-66 **2** *2 ¼* **Farthermost (IRE)**[17] [1685] 3-8-13 70 .... DaneO'Neill 2 — 73
(R Hannon) *chsd ldrs: rdn to ld wl over 1f out: hdd ins fnl f and sn no ch w wnr but styd on wl for 2nd* **10/3**[1]

00-0 **3** *1 ½* **Infinite Patience**[43] [1161] 3-7-13 61 oh1 .... NataliaGemelova(5) 7 — 59
(J S Moore) *in rr: sn pushed along: plenty to do fr 2f out: rapid hdwy jst ins fnl f: gng on cl home but nt trble ldng duo* **8/1**

000- **4** *2 ½* **Belle Bellino (FR)**[273] [4540] 3-8-9 66 .... JamesDoyle 6 — 56
(B R Millman) *chsd ldrs: rdn over 2f out: styd on same pce fnl f* **20/1**

-036 **5** *¾* **Our Acquaintance**[16] [1707] 3-8-13 70 .... MartinDwyer 5 — 58
(W R Muir) *t.k.h: chsd ldrs tl led wl over 2f out: hdd wl over 1f out: wknd ins fnl f* **8/1**

51-5 **6** *2 ¼* **Outside Edge (IRE)**[19] [1611] 3-9-2 73 .... AdamKirby 1 — 53
(W R Swinburn) *in rr but in tch: rdn 3f out: effrt 2f out and no imp on ldrs* **13/2**[3]

6300 **7** *1 ¼* **Nawaaff**[12] [1819] 3-8-6 70 .... MatthewDavies(7) 11 — 46
(M R Channon) *sn rdn to chse ldrs: edgd rt u.p over 2f out: wknd wl over 1f out* **9/2**[2]

43-1 **8** *nse* **The Magic Blanket (IRE)**[57] [928] 3-8-11 68 .... MickyFenton 4 — 44
(Stef Liddiard) *t.k.h: chsd ldrs: rdn over 2f out: sn btn* **10/1**

055- **9** *5* **River N' Blues (IRE)**[176] [6897] 3-8-8 68 .... KevinGhunowa(3) 9 — 28
(Dr J R J Naylor) *led tl hdd wl over 2f out: sn btn* **28/1**

1044 **10** *½* **Bertbrand**[10] [1852] 3-8-13 73 .... KirstyMilczarek(3) 10 — 32
(M Botti) *chsd ldrs: rdn whn hmpd over 2f out: wknd sn after* **8/1**

241- **11** *1 ¼* **Replicator**[227] [5863] 3-9-4 75 .... PatDobbs 8 — 30
(Pat Eddery) *in tch: rdn 3f out: sn wknd* **12/1**

1m 15.73s (0.93) **Going Correction** +0.15s/f (Good) — **11 Ran SP% 124.0**

Speed ratings (Par 99): **99,96,94,90,89 86,85,84,78,77 75**

CSF £36.82 CT £234.64 TOTE £6.70: £2.20, £1.80, £3.40; EX 41.60.

Owner Family Amusements Ltd **Bred** John McLoughlin **Trained** Upper Lambourn, Berks

FOCUS

A fair handicap in which there was quite a lot of bunching in the first half of the race when the pace was modest. This was another personal best from the winner.

2128 AXMINSTER CARPETS APPRENTICE H'CAP (WHIPS SHALL BE CARRIED BUT NOT USED) — 6f 212y

4:35 (4:36) (Class 5) (0-70,73) 4-Y-O+ — **£3,238** (£963; £481; £240) **Stalls** High

Form — RPR

60-3 **1** **Vanadium**[11] [1842] 6-8-9 63 .... JemmaMarshall(3) 2 — 71
(G L Moore) *in tch: stdy hdwy fr 2f out: str run fnl f: led fnl strides* **6/1**[3]

00-4 **2** *hd* **Isphahan**[9] [1900] 5-8-3 59 .... DavidProbert(5) 15 — 66
(A M Balding) *led: drvn along over 2f out and kpt slt advantage tl ct fnl strides* **6/1**[3]

-321 **3** *nse* **Support Fund (IRE)**[10] [1867] 4-9-1 73 6ex .... DanielBlackett(7) 1 — 80+
(Eve Johnson Houghton) *towards rr but in tch: stdy hdwy fr 2f out: kpt on strly fnl f: clsng on line but nt quite get up* **11/2**[2]

600- **4** *2* **Charlie Delta**[223] [5981] 5-8-9 60 .... WilliamCarson 12 — 61
(J G M O'Shea) *in rr: rdn and hdwy fr 3f out: drvn to chal over 1f out: wknd ins fnl f* **16/1**

6252 **5** *¾* **Obe Royal**[28] [1431] 4-9-5 70 .... (b) RichardEvans 7 — 69
(P D Evans) *chsd ldrs: rdn to chal over 1f out: wknd ins fnl f* **7/1**

3436 **6** *1 ¼* **Imperium**[5] [1996] 7-7-13 57 .... (p) LindseyWhite(7) 5 — 53
(Jean-Rene Auvray) *slowly away: bhd: stl plenty to do fr 2f out: rapid hdwy appr fnl f: fin wl* **20/1**

00-0 **7** *2* **Ken's Girl**[24] [1522] 4-8-12 68 .... TimothyMeadows(5) 11 — 59
(W S Kittow) *in tch: rdn 3f out: no ch w ldrs fnl 2f* **20/1**

0-03 **8** *¾* **Tiger Trail (GER)**[11] [1835] 4-8-0 56 oh6 .... AmyScott(5) 4 — 45
(Mrs N Smith) *chsd ldrs: rdn and ev ch ins fnl 2f: wknd fnl f* **9/2**[1]

-030 **9** *¾* **Quantum Leap**[22] [1565] 11-8-5 61 .... (v) ThomasBubb(5) 9 — 48+
(S Dow) *in rr: kpt on fnl 2f: nvr in contention* **16/1**

3200 **10** *3 ¼* **Strut The Stage (IRE)**[23] [1533] 4-8-0 56 oh4 .... (bt) RosieJessop(5) 13 — 34
(B W Duke) *chsd ldrs over 4f* **25/1**

20-0 **11** *1* **Caustic Wit (IRE)**[10] [1872] 10-8-4 62 .... JakePayne(7) 14 — 37
(M S Saunders) *pressed ldr: ev ch and rdn fr 2f out: wknd over 1f out* **20/1**

30-5 **12** *nse* **Goose Green (IRE)**[18] [1645] 4-8-12 63 .... MatthewDavies 8 — 38
(R J Hodges) *a towards rr* **12/1**

1013 **13** *2* **Jessica Wigmo**[22] [1565] 5-8-3 57 .... SimonPearce(3) 10 — 27
(A W Carroll) *a towards rr* **10/1**

000- **14** *7* **Muffett's Dream**[156] [2628] 4-8-0 56 oh7 .... AshleyMorgan(5) 6 — 7
(J J Bridger) *early spd: sn bhd* **66/1**

3300 **15** *1* **Zazous**[18] [1641] 7-8-2 56 oh2 .... RossAtkinson(3) 3 — 4
(J J Bridger) *sn bhd* **20/1**

1m 29.36s (0.36) **Going Correction** +0.15s/f (Good) — **15 Ran SP% 127.6**

Speed ratings (Par 103): **103,102,102,100,99 98,95,95,94,90 89,89,86,78,77**

CSF £39.75 CT £223.45 TOTE £8.00: £2.50, £3.10, £2.70; EX 59.10 Place 6: £55.61, Place 5: £37.19..

Owner A V Racing **Bred** Bolton Grange **Trained** Woodingdean, E Sussex

FOCUS

This modest hands-and-heels apprentice race was run 0.68secs faster than the earlier claimer. However, the form looks sound enough rated around the principals.

Imperium Official explanation: jockey said gelding missed the break

T/Plt: £86.30 to a £1 stake. Pool: £47,361.07. 400.30 winning tickets. T/Qpdt: £30.60 to a £1 stake. Pool: £2,309.24. 55.70 winning tickets. ST

2103 YORK (L-H)

Thursday, May 15

OFFICIAL GOING: Good to firm (9.2)

The running rail was again in place one metre wide from the 9f pole to the home turn. 5mm water applied but the ground was 'quicker than Wednesday'.

Wind: Moderate half against Weather: Fine and dry

2129 ENTER THE FLAT TOTETENTOFOLLOW STKS (H'CAP) — 5f

1:40 (1:40) (Class 2) (0-100,100) 4-Y-O+ **£16,513** (£4,913; £2,455; £1,226) **Stalls** High

Form — RPR

20-0 **1** **Tournedos (IRE)**[8] [1917] 6-9-3 96 .... SilvestreDeSousa 1 — 107
(D Nicholls) *hld up in rr: hdwy on outer over 1f out: str run ins fnl f to ld fnl 50yds* **33/1**

0-03 **2** *½* **River Falcon**[33] [1325] 8-9-1 94 .... DanielTudhope 3 — 103
(J S Goldie) *hld up in rr: hdwy over 1f out: rdn ins fnl f and fin wl* **15/2**

6-01 **3** *hd* **Bertoliver**[8] [1917] 4-9-1 94 6ex .... KerrinMcEvoy 10 — 102
(D K Ivory) *prom: rdn to ld wl over 1f out: drvn ent fnl f: hdd and nt qckn fnl 50yds* **9/2**[1]

1522 **4** *hd* **Northern Empire (IRE)**[63] [866] 5-9-1 94 .... NCallan 7 — 102
(K A Ryan) *lw: trckd ldrs: effrt wl over 1f out: sn rdn and kpt on u.p ins fnl f* **9/1**

0-00 **5** *hd* **Special Day**[12] [1809] 4-8-9 88 .... MichaelHills 6 — 95
(B W Hills) *hld up: hdwy over 2f out: rdn over 1f out: kpt on ins fnl f* **11/2**[2]

05-0 **6** *½* **Tabaret**[29] [1393] 5-8-9 88 .... DeanMcKeown 15 — 93
(R M Whitaker) *cl up: effrt 2f out and sn ev ch tl drvn and no ex wl ins fnl f* **14/1**

-100 **7** *shd* **Conquest (IRE)**[11] [1831] 4-9-7 100 .... JimmyFortune 9 — 105
(W J Haggas) *hld up on rr: hdwy 2f out: rdn over 1f out: styd on ins fnl f: nrst fin* **14/1**

-040 **8** *½* **Strike Up The Band**[8] [1917] 5-9-2 95 .... AdrianTNicholls 4 — 98
(D Nicholls) *led: rdn along over 2f out: hdd wl over 1f out and grad wknd* **14/1**

5003 **9** *nk* **Fyodor (IRE)**[17] [1689] 7-8-13 92 .... JMurtagh 12 — 94
(W J Haggas) *chsd ldrs: rdn along 2f out and grad wknd* **15/2**

01-4 **10** *¾* **Aegean Dancer**[135] [5] 6-9-4 97 .... TomEaves 5 — 96
(B Smart) *chsd ldrs: effrt 2f out and ev ch tl rdn and wknd over 1f out* **6/1**[3]

-042 **11** *¾* **Green Park (IRE)**[8] [1917] 5-8-9 88 .... PaulHanagan 14 — 85
(R A Fahey) *lw: rrd s: a towards rr* **7/1**

58.46 secs (-0.84) **Going Correction** +0.075s/f (Good) — **11 Ran SP% 116.8**

Speed ratings (Par 109): **109,108,107,107,107 106,106,105,105,103 102**

CSF £262.52 CT £1370.27 TOTE £47.60: £9.00, £2.60, £2.10; EX 283.00 Trifecta £327.20 Pool: £1,425.03. 3.20 winning units..

Owner Mike Browne **Bred** Pat Grogan **Trained** Sessay, N Yorks

■ Stewards' Enquiry : N Callan caution: careless riding

FOCUS

A typically good competitive York sprint handicap in which early pace was strong and the first two came from the rear. The winner is rated back to his best with the runner-up to previous course form.

NOTEBOOK

Tournedos(IRE) who seems to have rediscovered his form since joining his current yard, had conditions to suit and everything fell right for him. The early pace was strong and he was able to cut through the pack in the centre of the track as the leaders tired and strike the front close home. He has been rated 9lb higher in the past but this appears about his level now although it would not be the first time his trainer has extracted more improvement from a seemingly exposed handicapper.

River Falcon, three times a previous course and distance winner, was 2lb higher than for that last success but like the winner things fell right and he came from virtually last over a furlong out and was closing down that rival at the line. He does not win very often but will always be a threat in these big sprint handicaps on flat tracks. (tchd 7-1)

Bertoliver is a really useful front-running sprinter and he did his best to follow up the previous week's Chester victory with another brave effort. At the head of the stands'-side group from the start, he got to the overall lead inside the last quarter-mile and only failed to resist the firast two, who finished fast and late. He deserves plenty of credit for this effort. (op 11-2)

Northern Empire(IRE), back from a short break following a decent campaign on the All-Weather during the winter, put up a fine effort. He has not had that much racing for one of his age and could be capable of further improvement judged on his recent efforts. (op 16-1)

Special Day, another lightly-raced performer, has found things more difficult following a good spell last spring and summer but looked to be on the way back here. She has dropped to a mark that she looks capable of winning off. (op 13-2)

Tabaret has not scored since winning here as a juvenile in 2005, but showed plenty of enthusiasm on this occasion and is down to his lowest-ever mark. (op 12-1)

Conquest(IRE) had the headgear left off this time and was keeping on in the closing stages but is not one to trust to put it all in.

Strike Up The Band showed plenty of pace up the middle of the track before fading.
Fyodor(IRE) Official explanation: jockey said gelding was denied a clear run closing stages
Aegean Dancer, well backed on this return from a break, has gone well fresh in the past and showed plenty of pace before tiring. (op 9-2)

2130 TOTESCOOP6 SPECIAL MIDDLETON STKS (GROUP 3) (F&M) 1m 2f 88y

2:10 (2:10) (Class 1) 4-Y-O+ **£28,385** (£10,760; £5,385; £2,685; £1,345) **Stalls** Low

Form				RPR
412-	1		**Promising Lead**[221] 6042 4-8-12 115 RyanMoore 3	115+
			(Sir Michael Stoute) *lw: hld up in tch: hdwy over 3f out: led wl over 1f out: sn pushed clr* **2/5**[1]	
35-0	2	3 ¾	**Under The Rainbow**[11] 1829 5-8-12 104 (p) NCallan 4	107
			(B W Hills) *trckd ldng pair: hdwy to ld wl over 2f out and sn rdn: hdd wl over 1f out: sn drvn and nt match pce of wnr* **8/1**[3]	
0-14	3	7	**Flying Clarets (IRE)**[41] 1199 5-8-12 100 (p) PaulHanagan 5	93
			(R A Fahey) *led: rdn along over 3f out: hdd wl over 2f out: sn drvn and one pce* **6/1**[2]	
12-5	4	1 ¾	**Ronaldsay**[28] 1427 4-8-12 101 JimmyFortune 7	90
			(R Hannon) *swtg: hld up in rr: hdwy over 3f out: sn rdn along and no imp fnl 2f* **16/1**	
244-	5	28	**Sell Out**[209] 6299 4-8-12 100 TedDurcan 6	34
			(G Wragg) *chsd ldr: rdn along 4f out: wknd 3f out* **16/1**	

2m 8.20s (-4.30) **Going Correction** -0.025s/f (Good) **5 Ran SP% 108.6**
Speed ratings (Par 113): **116,113,107,106,83**
CSF £4.08 TOTE £1.40: £1.10, £3.10; EX 4.00.
Owner K Abdulla **Bred** Juddmonte Farms Ltd **Trained** Newmarket, Suffolk

FOCUS
An uncompetitive renewal of this Group 3 but the time was 1.30secs faster than the following Classic trial. The winner did not need to improve to score but is open to more improvement.

NOTEBOOK
Promising Lead ◆, who beat Sell Out in a Salisbury Listed race last season, progressed from that to finish second in the Prix de L'Opera, and on that form had plenty in hand. She scored in comfortable fashion and this should tee her up for a campaign in the top fillies' races, with the Pretty Polly at the Curragh the first on the agenda. (tchd 4-9 in places)
Under The Rainbow, dropped to the shortest trip she has run over since 2006, had the cheekpieces re-applied. She ran as well as she was entitled to on official ratings and earned some decent prizemoney but has not scored since her juvenile days. (op 11-1)
Flying Clarets(IRE) is an admirable and progressive mare whose rating has necessitated a step up into this grade. She set the pace as usual and kept on once headed to earn black type, which will increase her paddock value. (op 13-2 tchd 7-1 in a place)
Ronaldsay, another whose progression last season resulted in her having to take her chance in Pattern company, never really got involved and she appears best in the second half of the season, especially when there is cut in the ground. (op 14-1)
Sell Out ran the winner to two and a half lengths at Salisbury last season, but that filly has improve a good deal since and she is another who looks much more effective on soft going. Official explanation: jockey said filly was unsuited by the good to firm ground (op 12-1)

2131 TOTESPORT.COM DANTE STKS (GROUP 2) 1m 2f 88y

2:40 (2:41) (Class 1) 3-Y-O

£85,155 (£32,280; £16,155; £8,055; £4,035; £2,025) **Stalls** Low

Form				RPR
2-1	1		**Tartan Bearer (IRE)**[19] 1621 3-9-0 0 RyanMoore 6	119+
			(Sir Michael Stoute) *lw: hld up in rr: hdwy 3f out: rdn to chal over 1f out: led jst ins fnl f: sn drvn and kpt on wl towards fin* **10/1**	
0-	2	hd	**Frozen Fire (GER)**[201] 6489 3-9-0 0 JMurtagh 2	118
			(A P O'Brien, Ire) *swtg: lengthy: w'like: hld up in tch: hdwy 3f out: led 2f out and sn rdn: drvn and hdd jst ins fnl f: rallied u.p and ev ch tl no ex nr fin* **14/1**	
11-1	3	2 ½	**Twice Over**[28] 1421 3-9-0 120 TedDurcan 5	114
			(H R A Cecil) *lw: hld up in tch: hdwy on outer 3f out: effrt 2f out: sn rdn and ev ch tl drvn and one pce wl ins fnl f* **4/6**[1]	
12-1	4	5	**Centennial (IRE)**[19] 1632 3-9-0 105 JimmyFortune 3	104
			(J H M Gosden) *chsd ldr: effrt and cl up 3f out: sn rdn and wknd wl over 1f out* **5/1**[2]	
115-	5	3	**Young Pretender (FR)**[221] 6041 3-9-0 116 LDettori 4	98
			(Saeed Bin Suroor) *bit bkwd: chsd ldng pair: hdwy and cl up 3f out: rdn over 2f out and grad wknd* **12/1**	
110-	6	3	**McCartney (GER)**[208] 6333 3-9-0 115 KerrinMcEvoy 1	92
			(Saeed Bin Suroor) *bit bkwd: led: pushed along 4f out: rdn over 3f out: hdd 2f out and sn wknd* **8/1**[3]	

2m 9.50s (-3.00) **Going Correction** -0.025s/f (Good) **6 Ran SP% 111.2**
Speed ratings (Par 111): **111,110,108,104,102 100**
CSF £119.32 TOTE £7.90: £3.40, £4.30; EX 140.90.
Owner Ballymacoll Stud **Bred** Ballymacoll Stud Farm Ltd **Trained** Newmarket, Suffolk

FOCUS
A fair renewal of this Derby trial but the time was 1.3secs slower than the preceding Group 3 (although still respectable) and all six were in line at the quarter-mile pole. The form is not easy to pin down but it looks up to scratch.

NOTEBOOK
Tartan Bearer(IRE) ◆, a brother to Golan, had not impressed everyone when winning his maiden at Leicester on his seasonal debut, but the run had clearly brought him on and he came through from the rear to win this in tenacious fashion. He was made to work quite hard by the runner-up and, although he is now favourite for the Derby in some quarters, looks a galloper more than a speed horse. That may not stop him winning at Epsom as he is clearly on the upgrade, but he looks well suited by tracks such as this and may be the horse to give his trainer a first St Leger winner. (op 7-1 tchd 13-2)
Frozen Fire(GER) ◆, a Montjeu colt who cost a quarter of a million euros as a yearling, is from a high-class German family. He had shown promise in the Racing Post Trophy last season after winning a maiden on his debut and this was a test of his progression. He travelled well behind the pace and came through to hit the front inside the final 2f, and when the winner went past he drifted across to join that colt and responded well to pressure to push him all the way to the line. Murtagh did not appear to be unduly hard on him, especially as the colt still appeared to be green, and he could be capable of repaying that kindness if re-opposing the winner at Epsom. He is now the shortest priced of the Ballydoyle contenders at around 10/1. (tchd 16-1)
Twice Over, came into this unbeaten, having won the Craven and missed the 2000 Guineas in favour of coming here. He appeared to have every chance but had nothing more to give in the last furlong and, although his dam stayed the trip well enough, perhaps he resembles his sire and is more a miler. He did not look totally happy on the fast ground either but it was subsequently reported that his blood was not right. (tchd 4-5)
Centennial(IRE), who made all when winning the Sandown Classic Trial, was unable to lead with McCartney in the line-up but had every chance before weakening in the last furlong and a half. There were no excuses regarding trip and ground and his trainer is now looking towards the Irish Derby and St Leger for him. (op 11-2 tchd 9-2)
Young Pretender(FR), formerly trained by John Gosden, had appeared to have his limitations exposed behind Rio De La Plata in the Prix Jean-Luc Lagardere last season and that was confirmed here, as he had his chance but was not good enough. (op 14-1)
McCartney(GER), who was the shorter priced of the Godolphin pair despite being passed over by Dettori, cut out the running but had nothing in reserve once headed entering the final quarter-mile. It may be that he takes after his dam and that he will be dropped back in trip in future. (op 11-1 tchd 12-1 in a place)

2132 BANK OF SCOTLAND CORPORATE HAMBLETON STKS (H'CAP) (LISTED RACE) 1m

3:10 (3:11) (Class 1) (0-110,110) 4-Y-O+ **£20,741** (£7,843; £3,920; £1,960) **Stalls** Low

Form				RPR
1113	1		**Mia's Boy**[15] 1723 4-8-7 96 oh2 JimmyQuinn 3	111+
			(C A Dwyer) *hld up: hdwy on inner 3f out: nt clr run over 2f out and again over 1f out: swtchd rt and hdwy ent fnl f: rdn and styd on to ld nr fin* **15/2**	
26-1	2	¾	**Lang Shining (IRE)**[26] 1469 4-8-7 96 RyanMoore 4	104
			(Sir Michael Stoute) *lw: hld up in rr: niggled along and hdwy over 3f out: nt clr run and swtchd rt over 2f out: rdn to ld wl over 1f out: drvn ins fnl f: hdd and no ex nr fin* **8/11**[1]	
-245	3	2 ¾	**Blythe Knight (IRE)**[19] 1631 8-9-7 110 GrahamGibbons 2	112
			(J J Quinn) *prom: hdwy 3f out: rdn to ld briefly 2f out: sn hdd and drvn over 1f out: wknd ins fnl f* **11/2**[2]	
40-0	4	6	**Annemasse**[54] 960 4-8-7 96 oh1 PaulHanagan 5	84
			(R A Fahey) *prom: effrt 3f out and cl up tl rdn 2f out and grad wknd* **7/1**[3]	
005-	5	½	**New Seeker**[236] 5634 8-9-0 103 (b) TedDurcan 7	90
			(P F I Cole) *bit bkwd: led: rdn along 3f out: drvn and hdd 2f out: sn wknd* **8/1**	
0/05	6	10	**Clipperdown (IRE)**[25] 1503 7-8-7 96 oh4 SamHitchcott 6	60
			(E J Creighton) *chsd ldrs: rdn along over 3f out: sn wknd* **50/1**	

1m 37.41s (-1.39) **Going Correction** -0.025s/f (Good) **6 Ran SP% 110.6**
Speed ratings (Par 111): **105,104,101,95,95 85**
CSF £13.16 TOTE £6.60: £2.50, £1.10; EX 15.50.
Owner Iraj Parvizi **Bred** Sir Eric Parker **Trained** Burrough Green, Cambs

FOCUS
A high-class Listed handicap run at a sound gallop with the first two still progressing.

NOTEBOOK
Mia's Boy ◆, who has been in fine form since joining his current trainer earlier in the year, was racing from 2lb out of the handicap. He was effectively 9lb higher than his previous winning mark and was stepping up in grade, and despite the small field on this wide track was denied a run at what appeared to be a crucial stage. However, when he did get out he picked up really well to collar the odds-on favourite and score a shade cosily. He is likely to go for the Royal Hunt Cup but may have to campaign in Pattern events after that and there appears no reason to believe the progression has come to an end.
Lang Shining(IRE), a lightly-raced colt who had been raised 7lb for winning the Newbury Spring Cup on his reappearance, was held up at the back before sweeping past his rivals down the outside and looking sure to score. However, although he kept on, he could not respond to the winner's late challenge. Moore may have been guilty of a rare error of judgement in that he appeared to be just pushing the winner out and only asked for extra when it was too late, but in truth the winner would have got there anyway. This is another progressive colt and, like the winner, he could pay to follow at this sort of level this season. (op 4-5 tchd 5-6 in places)
Blythe Knight(IRE), last year's winner of this contest, got warm at the start and was quite keen early on. He got to the front inside the last but was brushed aside by the runner-up. However, he is a good guide to the level of this form (op 5-1)
Annemasse raced up with the leaders but was unable to pick up when the race began in earnest. (op 8-1)
New Seeker made the running as usual but faded out of things once headed. He is not as good as he once was but as a result has slipped down the ratings and should drop another few pounds after this, so could still be capable of picking up one of the big handicaps if things fall right. (op 9-1)

2133 RALPH RAPER MEMORIAL STKS (CONDITIONS RACE) 1m 208y

3:45 (3:45) (Class 3) 4-Y-O+ **£10,361** (£3,083; £1,540; £769) **Stalls** Low

Form				RPR
2/2-	1		**Charlie Farnsbarns (IRE)**[352] 2124 4-9-4 113 LDettori 3	103
			(B J Meehan) *sn cl up: effrt 3f out: led 2f out and sn rdn: drvn ins fnl f and hld on gamely* **3/1**[3]	
-212	2	shd	**Benandonner (USA)**[26] 1469 5-9-4 98 PaulHanagan 1	103
			(R A Fahey) *lw: t.k.h: trckd ldng pair: hdwy 3f out: swtchd rt and rdn to chal 2f out: ev ch tl drvn ins fnl f and no nex nr line* **7/4**[1]	
000-	3	1 ¼	**Royal Power (IRE)**[209] 6301 5-9-4 92 AdrianTNicholls 2	100
			(D Nicholls) *hld up in rr: hdwy over 2f out: rdn over 1f out: styd on and ch ins fnl f: drvn and no ex fnl 75yds* **12/1**	
326-	4	½	**Docofthebay (IRE)**[209] 6298 4-9-4 103 ShaneKelly 4	99+
			(J A Osborne) *hld up: hdwy over 2f out: rdn over 1f out: n.m.r and kpt on same pce ins fnl f* **5/2**[2]	
000-	5	1 ½	**Striving Storm (USA)**[194] 6655 4-9-4 100 AlanMunro 5	96
			(P W Chapple-Hyam) *led: qcknd over 3f out: sn rdn along and hdd 2f out: cl up tl drvn and wknd ins fnl f* **6/1**	

1m 51.65s (-0.35) **Going Correction** -0.025s/f (Good) **5 Ran SP% 111.9**
Speed ratings (Par 107): **100,99,98,98,97**
CSF £8.86 TOTE £3.00: £1.70, £1.50; EX 5.80.
Owner The English Girls **Bred** Tinnakill Partnership I **Trained** Manton, Wilts
■ Stewards' Enquiry : Paul Hanagan caution: careless riding

FOCUS
The winner, on the comeback trail, looked to have been found a first-class opportunity but he ran some way short of his official 113 rating. The third is rated to last year's form.

NOTEBOOK
Charlie Farnsbarns(IRE), runner-up to Authorised in the 2006 Racing Post Trophy, was only able to have one outing at three. Taken to post early, he kicked for home but in the end hung on by the skin of his teeth. He showed battling qualities and hopefully can build on this return. (op 5-2)
Benandonner(USA), whose Newbury defeat has worked out well, had a stone to find with the winner on official ratings but that is based on his two-year-old form. Switched to throw down the gauntlet, he gave his all but in the end was just denied. He would not want the ground any quicker but opportunities will be thin on the ground. (op 15-8 tchd 2-1)
Royal Power(IRE), winner of the German 2000 Guineas in 2006, has largely struggled since. Bought for 45,000gns, he had the least chance of these on official ratings yet was only found lacking inside the last. (op 22-1)
Docofthebay(IRE), who improved two stone at three, needs to be waited with and at times has looked less than straightforward but here he seemed to be given a very negative ride. His jockey never looked like switching him to the outside and he seemed to finish full of running. (op 3-1)
Striving Storm(USA), who rather lost his way after finishing runner-up in the Classic Trial at Sandown last spring, has been gelded. He stepped up the pace from the front but in the end was firmly put in his place. (tchd 13-2 in a place)

2134 CONSTANT SECURITY E B F MAIDEN STKS 6f

4:20 (4:20) (Class 3) 2-Y-O **£7,835** (£2,331; £1,165; £582) **Stalls** High

Form				RPR
3	1		**Lord Shanakill (USA)**[27] 1447 2-9-3 0 FergusSweeney 3	91+
			(K R Burke) *athletic: lw: mde virtually all: qcknd clr over 1f out: comf* **13/2**	

2 2 ¾ **Awinnersgame (IRE)** 2-9-3 0 LDettori 7 83
(J Noseda) *athletic: b.hind: lw: sltly hmpd s: trckd ldrs: rdn and hdwy 2f out: sn chsng wnr: edgd lft ent fnl f and kpt on same pce* 6/4[1]
3 2 **Shaweel** 2-9-3 0 JoeFanning 5 77
(M Johnston) *w'like: a.p: rdn along 2f out: kpt on same pce appr fnl f* 14/1
4 2 **Reve De Soleil (FR)** 2-9-3 0 JamieSpencer 6 71
(E J O'Neill) *cmpt: dwlt and towards rr: hdwy over 2f out: rdn and edgd lft over 1f out: kpt on ins fnl f: nrst fin* 14/1
5 2 ¾ **Whatyouwoodwishfor (USA)** 2-9-3 0 PaulHanagan 10 63
(R A Fahey) *prom: rdn along over 2f out: grad wknd* 20/1
6 ½ **Ay Tay Tate (IRE)** 2-9-3 0 FergalLynch 4 61
(I W McInnes) *w'like: bit bkwd: in tch: rdn along 2f out: sn one pce* 100/1
7 nse **Four Star General (IRE)**[25] 1506 2-9-3 0 JMurtagh 2 61
(A P O'Brien, Ire) *w'like: hld up in rr: hdwy 1/2-way: rdn along to chse ldrs 2f out: wknd over 1f out* 3/1[2]
8 3 ½ **Cook's Endeavour (USA)** 2-9-3 0 NCallan 9 50+
(K A Ryan) *dwlt and wnt lft s: sn prom: rdn 2f out and sn wknd* 9/2[3]
55 9 5 **Tagula Sunset (IRE)**[12] 1794 2-8-9 0 JamieMoriarty(3) 1 30
(P T Midgley) *lw: a towards rr* 100/1
10 2 **Luckette** 2-8-12 0 TWilliams 8 24
(M Brittain) *leggy: bit bkwd: wnt rt and sltly hmpd s: t.k.h and chsd ldrs to 1/2-way: sn wknd* 40/1

1m 12.05s (0.15) **Going Correction** +0.075s/f (Good) **10 Ran SP% 119.0**
Speed ratings (Par 97): **102,98,95,93,89 88,88,83,77,74**
CSF £16.78 TOTE £8.10: £2.10, £1.20, £2.90; EX 19.70.
Owner Mark T Gittins **Bred** Vimal Khosla, Gillian Khosla Et Al **Trained** Middleham Moor, N Yorks

FOCUS
Traditionally a strong maiden with the winner rated 90+ and only slightly below that level this time. The winner had clearly learnt plenty first time and the runner-up came with a big reputation.

NOTEBOOK
Lord Shanakill(USA), a lengthy, well-made colt, looked really well. He knew his job this time and stayed on much too well for the highly thought-of runner-up. He deserves a trip to Royal Ascot now. (op 7-1)
Awinnersgame(IRE), closely related to the Irish 1000 Guinees winner Saoire, is a quality-looking colt. Knocked sideways at the start, he worked hard to get on to the winner's tail a furlong out but in the end was very much second best. (op 7-4 tchd 5-4)
Shaweel ♦, a rangy, rather immature newcomer, looked fit enough beforehand but was not quite right in his coat. He proved very inexperienced yet deserves high marks for the way he stuck to his task in the closing stages. He looks a ready-made winner in ordinary maiden company. (op 12-1 tchd 11-1, 16-1 in a place)
Reve De Soleil(FR), a lengthy, narrow gelding, missed the break but made up a fair amount of ground in the second half of the contest despite a marked tendency to hang left. Hopefully the experience will have taught him plenty.
Whatyouwoodwishfor(USA), a lengthy, narrow type, showed plenty of toe and hopefully will have learnt a fair bit from this introductory run. (op 25-1)
Ay Tay Tate(IRE), a breeze-up purchase, looked on the big side and was noisy beforehand. He belied his greenness and long odds with a sound first run.
Four Star General(IRE), a May foal, is bred to be something special yet had finished only eighth on his debut at Leopardstown three weeks earlier. Put to sleep at the back, he threatened to enter the argument at one stage but in the end finished well beaten. (op 11-4 tchd 4-1)
Cook's Endeavour(USA), a good-bodied, big, powerful newcomer, took a bump at the start. He showed ability before tiring and can be expected to do a lot better in due course. (op 5-1 tchd 11-2)

2135 THERIPLEYCOLLECTION.COM STKS (H'CAP) 2m 2f
4:55 (4:55) (Class 4) (0-80,80) 4-Y-O+ **£7,123** (£2,119; £1,059; £529) **Stalls** Low

Form RPR
02-2 1 **Mighty Moon**[21] 1580 5-9-3 **70** PaulHanagan 1 82+
(R A Fahey) *hld up towards rr: stdy hdwy on inner over 3f out: effrt 2f out: rdn to ld jst over 1f out: styd on strly ins fnl f* 15/2
-502 2 3 ¾ **Mister Arjay (USA)**[6] 1972 8-8-13 **69** PJMcDonald(3) 9 76
(B Ellison) *led: rdn along 3f out: jnd and drvn 2f out: hdd appr fnl f: kpt on u.p* 8/1
20-1 3 nk **Noddies Way**[41] 1179 5-8-8 **61** KerrinMcEvoy 5 68
(J F Panvert) *trckd ldng pair: hdwy over 4f out: rdn to chal 3f out: drvn over 2f out: wknd appr fnl f* 11/2[2]
420- 4 1 **Kayf Aramis**[45] 6622 6-9-0 **70** MarcHalford(3) 8 76
(Miss Venetia Williams) *trckd ldrs: hdwy 4f out: rdn wl over 2f out: drvn and kpt on same pce fr over 1f out* 9/1
-034 5 ½ **Rose Bien**[10] 1856 6-8-9 **62** ow1 (p) NCallan 2 67
(P J McBride) *trckd ldrs: hdwy over 4f out: rdn along wl over 2f out: sn drvn and kpt on same pce* 11/1
1/65 6 nk **Numero Due**[19] 1625 6-9-13 **80** JamieSpencer 7 85
(G M Moore) *hld up and bhd: stdy hdwy on wd outside 3f out: rdn 2f out: drvn: edgd lft and no imp appr fnl f* 6/1[3]
5-60 7 3 ¼ **Thewhirlingdervish (IRE)**[19] 1625 10-9-7 **74** DavidAllan 13 76
(T D Easterby) *hld up towards rr: hdwy over 3f out: rdn along over 2f out: sn drvn and no imp* 22/1
511- 8 2 ½ **Inchpast**[164] 7008 7-9-13 **80** (b) PaulMulrennan 12 79
(M H Tompkins) *b.nr fore: hld up towards rr: hdwy on inner 3f out: rdn along over 2f out: sn btn* 10/1
/0-2 9 shd **Accordello (IRE)**[52] 988 7-8-8 **61** JoeFanning 15 60
(K G Reveley) *hld up and bhd: sme hdwy 3f out: sn rdn and nvr a factor* 13/2
0-50 10 14 **Great As Gold (IRE)**[24] 1518 9-9-6 **73** (p) TomEaves 6 56
(B Ellison) *hld up: a towards rr* 25/1
5515 11 1 **Flame Creek (IRE)**[12] 1798 12-8-4 **64** MCGeran(7) 16 46
(E J Creighton) *hld up: a in rr* 33/1
0112 12 5 **Bugsy's Boy**[36] 1267 4-8-12 **72** (p) TolleyDean(3) 11 49
(George Baker) *lw: trckd ldrs: effrt 4f out and sn cl up: rdn over 3f out and sn wknd* 5/1[1]
110- 13 41 **Strobe**[139] 5911 4-9-5 **76** JMurtagh 10 8
(Mrs L B Normile) *lw: chsd ldr: rdn along 4f out and sn wknd* 16/1

3m 57.39s (-1.01) **Going Correction** -0.025s/f (Good)
WFA 4 from 5yo+ 4lb **13 Ran SP% 127.0**
Speed ratings (Par 105): **101,99,99,98,98 98,96,95,95,89 89,86,68**
CSF £69.29 CT £369.30 TOTE £9.20: £3.00, £3.30, £2.60; EX 95.80 Place 6: £181.13, Place 5: £59.68..
Owner Enda Hunston **Bred** Angmering Park Stud **Trained** Musley Bank, N Yorks
■ Stewards' Enquiry : Tolley Dean one-day ban: careless riding (May 29)

FOCUS
A modest stayers' handicap and the pace was just steady but the form looks solid rated around the fourth and fifth. The winner did it well in the end and now heads for Galway.
T/Jkpt: Not won. T/Plt: £87.80 to a £1 stake. Pool: £119,405.71. 991.85 winning tickets. T/Qpdt: £22.90 to a £1 stake. Pool: £4,601.68. 148.50 winning tickets. JR

2136 - 2139a (Foreign Racing) - See Raceform Interactive

[1948] HAMILTON (R-H)
Friday, May 16

OFFICIAL GOING: Good to firm (9.6)
Wind: Almost nil Weather: Cloudy

2140 EUROPEAN BREEDERS' FUND MAIDEN STKS 5f 4y
6:20 (6:20) (Class 5) 2-Y-O **£3,885** (£1,156; £577; £288) **Stalls** Low

Form RPR
5 1 **Spin Cycle (IRE)**[13] 1813 2-9-3 0 RichardMullen 8 89+
(B Smart) *in tch: hdwy to ld appr fnl f: pushed out: comf* 6/5[1]
3 2 2 ½ **Peninsular War**[14] 1770 2-9-3 0 DarrenWilliams 7 80
(K R Burke) *cl up: led 1/2-way to appr fnl f: kpt on fnl f: nrst fin* 11/4[2]
3 6 **Gassal** 2-8-9 0 DarryllHolland 4 53+
(W J Haggas) *sn outpcd: shkn up and hdwy fnl f: no ch w first two* 6/1[3]
6 4 1 ¾ **Lady Fantasie**[35] 1303 2-8-9 0 AndrewMullen(3) 6 47
(Mrs A Duffield) *led to 1/2-way: no ex over 1f out* 40/1
3 5 3 ½ **Metroland**[12] 1821 2-8-12 0 JoeFanning 3 35
(M Johnston) *cl up tl outpcd fr 2f out* 7/1
4 6 1 ¼ **Tito Gobbi**[16] 1727 2-9-3 0 LeeEnstone 1 35
(P C Haslam) *chsd ldrs tl edgd rt and no ex fr 1/2-way* 8/1
7 5 **Pedregal** 2-9-0 0 TonyHamilton 2 14
(R A Fahey) *s.i.s: sn wl bhd: nvr on terms* 33/1

58.03 secs (-1.97) **Going Correction** -0.25s/f (Firm) **7 Ran SP% 115.4**
Speed ratings (Par 93): **105,101,91,88,83 81,73**
CSF £4.76 TOTE £2.20: £1.60, £1.90; EX 4.20.
Owner H E Sheikh Rashid Bin Mohammed **Bred** Mrs Lisa Kelly **Trained** Hambleton, N Yorks
■ Stewards' Enquiry : Tony Hamilton two-day ban: used whip with excessive frequency without giving colt time to respond (May 30-31)

FOCUS
This looked a fair event for the course and the decent gallop resulted in a quick time. The first two pulled clear and remain fair prospects.

NOTEBOOK
Spin Cycle(IRE) ♦, who shaped well in a race containing several previous winners on his debut, took the eye in the paddock as a strong, sturdy sort who looked in tremendous condition and he fully confirmed that promise, travelling strongly before needing only to be pushed out to assert. He is the type to hold his own in stronger company. (op 11-8)
Peninsular War, who ran creditably behind a Brian Smart newcomer on his debut, looked in good condition and probably ran to a similar level in defeat against a potentially fair sort. He should stay 6f and is sure to win races. (op 9-2)
Gassal, a leggy sort who cost 62,000gns, was on her toes but looked fit enough to do herself justice on this racecourse debut and she was not disgraced against a couple of more experienced rivals. She will be suited by the step up to 6f and is likely to be placed to best advantage. (op 5-1)
Lady Fantasie, who showed only modest form on her debut, was not disgraced in the face of a stiff task. She is vulnerable to the more progressive sorts in this grade and modest nurseries will see her in a better light. (tchd 33-1)
Metroland failed to build on her fair debut run but she is going to be seen to much better effect when upped to 6f and beyond in due course. She is well worth another chance. (op 4-1)
Tito Gobbi, who showed ability at a modest level on his debut at Pontefract in soft ground, failed to build on that effort on this much quicker ground. He is likely to continue to look vulnerable in this type of event. (op 12-1)
Pedregal Official explanation: jockey said colt hung right-handed throughout

2141 BRANDON HOMES WILLIAM WALLACE H'CAP 6f 5y
6:50 (6:51) (Class 4) (0-80,78) 3-Y-O **£7,123** (£2,119; £1,059; £529) **Stalls** Low

Form RPR
2105 1 **Opus Maximus (IRE)**[14] 1764 3-9-3 **72** JoeFanning 7 80
(M Johnston) *pressed ldr: rdn 2f out: kpt on wl fnl f: led nr fin* 9/2[3]
0225 2 nk **Leading Edge (IRE)**[6] 2014 3-9-3 **72** DarryllHolland 9 79
(M R Channon) *led: rdn over 1f out: kpt on fnl f: hdd nr fin* 4/1[2]
-011 3 nk **Great Charm (IRE)**[14] 1781 3-9-7 **76** RichardMullen 5 82
(M L W Bell) *prom: effrt whn blkd over 1f out: kpt on wl u.p fnl f* 5/2[1]
-010 4 1 **Legendary Guest**[6] 1988 3-9-1 **70** ChrisCatlin 3 73
(D W Barker) *hld up: hdwy over 1f out: edgd rt ins fnl f: r.o* 7/1
40-0 5 3 ¾ **Lady Benjamin**[13] 1819 3-9-4 **73** LeeEnstone 4 64
(P C Haslam) *hld up: hdwy 1/2-way: rdn and no ex over 1f out* 9/1
1-15 6 nk **Yankee Storm**[122] 170 3-9-3 **72** GregFairley 2 62
(M Johnston) *prom: effrt over 2f out: no ex over 1f out* 12/1
3430 7 shd **Andrasta**[20] 1611 3-7-13 **59** oh3 DanielleMcCreery(5) 8 49
(A Berry) *chsd ldrs tl rdn and wknd over 1f out* 33/1
0-00 8 4 ½ **Flight Plan**[20] 1623 3-9-9 **78** TonyHamilton 6 53
(R A Fahey) *t.k.h: chsd ldrs: hung rt and wknd over 1f out* 7/1
005- 9 8 **Swift Acclaim (IRE)**[220] 6073 3-8-4 **59** oh4 PaulFessey 1 9
(K R Burke) *wnt rt s: bhd: drvn and wknd fr over 2f out* 40/1

1m 10.45s (-1.75) **Going Correction** -0.25s/f (Firm) **9 Ran SP% 114.8**
Speed ratings (Par 101): **101,100,100,98,93 93,93,87,76**
CSF £22.72 CT £54.48 TOTE £5.50: £2.20, £1.30, £1.30; EX 19.50.
Owner Jim McGrath And Reg Griffin **Bred** Mrs Anne Marie Burns **Trained** Middleham Moor, N Yorks

FOCUS
A run-of-the-mill handicap but one run at a fair gallop and the form looks sound but ordinary, rated around the placed horses.

2142 GLASGOW STKS (LISTED RACE) (C&G) 1m 3f 16y
7:25 (7:25) (Class 1) 3-Y-O
£19,869 (£7,532; £3,769; £1,879; £941; £472) **Stalls** High

Form RPR
-115 1 **Captain Webb**[21] 1600 3-9-0 94 GregFairley 6 103+
(M Johnston) *cl up: led after 4f: mde rest: rdn and styd on strly fr 2f out* 11/8[1]
41- 2 3 **Love Galore (IRE)**[236] 5663 3-9-0 88 JoeFanning 4 98
(M Johnston) *t.k.h early: chsd ldrs: effrt and chsd wnr over 2f out: r.o same pce fnl f* 6/1
4-13 3 2 ¼ **Bold Choice (IRE)**[23] 1570 3-9-0 93 PhilipRobinson 3 94
(M A Jarvis) *t.k.h: hld up in tch: stdy hdwy over 3f out: effrt 2f out: sn one pce* 5/2[2]
50-6 4 3 **Ellmau**[62] 902 3-9-0 95 ChrisCatlin 1 89
(E J O'Neill) *plld hrd: prom tl rdn and outpcd fr 2f out* 18/1
16-2 5 ¾ **Meeriss (IRE)**[13] 1810 3-9-4 100 DarryllHolland 7 92
(M R Channon) *led 4f: cl up tl rdn and no ex 2f out* 3/1[3]
01-0 6 1 ½ **Doon Haymer (IRE)**[35] 1297 3-9-0 78 (v) PaulFessey 5 85?
(Miss L A Perratt) *hld up in tch: drvn 3f out: sn btn* 33/1
60-6 7 41 **Northwest**[12] 1823 3-9-0 52 DanielleMcCreery 2 16
(A Berry) *bhd: struggling 1/2-way: t.o* 200/1

000- **8** *nk* **Premier Class (IRE)**[210] 6305 3-9-0 46......................(p) TonyHamilton 8 15
(J S Wainwright) *bhd: outpcd over 5f out: sn lost tch* **200/1**
2m 19.32s (-6.28) **Going Correction** -0.25s/f (Firm) course record **8** Ran SP% **119.2**
Speed ratings (Par 107): **112,109,108,106,105 104,74,74**
CSF £11.33 TOTE £2.60: £1.60, £2.20, £1.10; EX 13.40.
Owner Sheikh Hamdan Bin Mohammed Al Maktoum **Bred** Gainsborough Stud Management Ltd **Trained** Middleham Moor, N Yorks

FOCUS
A useful event but one run at just a fair pace in the first mile, although the overall time was decent for the grade. The winner is a progressive sort who turned in a career-best and remains one to keep on the right side while the third sets the standard.

NOTEBOOK
Captain Webb ◆, a shade disappointing - though far from disgraced in terms of form - after racing keenly and hanging at Sandown last time, had the run of the race and turned in his best effort on this first run on quick ground. He will stay 1m4f and he is the type to hold his own in stronger company. (op 2-1)
Love Galore(IRE), who bettered his debut effort when winning at this course on his final start of last year, ran creditably in the face of a stiff task behind his stablemate. He should come on for this run and is sure to win races this term. (op 4-1)
Bold Choice(IRE), far from disgraced behind Derby hopeful Curtain Call at Nottingham on his previous start, was not disgraced in after failing to settle in this muddling event back on quicker ground. A stronger gallop will see him in a better light and he is not one to write off yet. (op 9-4)
Ellmau looked to have something to find in this company but he ran creditably over this longer trip considering he failed to settle. He is likely to remain vulnerable in this type of event and is on a stiff mark for handicaps, though. (op 20-1 tchd 16-1)
Meeriss(IRE), conceding weight all round, had a decent chance at the weights and the run of the race but proved a disappointment. He may not be the easiest to place successfully this year. (op 4-1)
Doon Haymer(IRE) faced a very stiff task on these terms on this first start in Listed company and he will be seen to better effect in ordinary handicaps.

2143 LUDDON CONSTRUCTION MAIDEN STKS — 1m 1f 36y
8:00 (8:00) (Class 5) 3-Y-0+ **£2,590** (£770; £385; £192) **Stalls** High

Form RPR
44 **1** **Stock Market (USA)**[13] 1814 3-8-13 0................................ JimCrowley 5 76+
(E A L Dunlop) *hld up in tch: hdwy to ld over 2f out: clr whn edgd rt ins fnl f: eased nr fin* **6/5**[1]
65-3 **2** *3 ½* **Society Venue**[28] 1448 3-8-13 74.. TonyHamilton 6 66
(Jedd O'Keeffe) *prom: drvn and outpcd over 2f out: rallied to chse wnr wl ins fnl f: no imp* **9/2**[3]
0- **3** *¾* **Shady Gloom (IRE)**[191] 6724 3-8-13 0.................................... NCallan 9 64
(K A Ryan) *cl up: led over 3f out to over 2f out: no ex and lost 2nd wl ins fnl f* **25/1**
4 *1 ¼* **Hunting Country** 3-8-13 0.. JoeFanning 7 62+
(M Johnston) *s.i.s: t.k.h in rr: kpt on wl fr 2f out: nrst fin* **10/1**
03- **5** *1 ¼* **Mardood**[199] 6571 3-8-13 0.. DarryllHolland 2 59
(W J Haggas) *hld up: effrt over 3f out: no imp fnl 2f* **5/2**[2]
0/6 **6** *3 ¼* **Nelson Vettori**[35] 1307 4-9-5 0.. BMcHugh[(7)] 4 52
(Miss L A Perratt) *hld up in tch: drvn over 3f out: outpcd over 2f out* **100/1**
0 **7** *1* **Mytexie (FR)**[31] 1382 3-8-13 0.. GregFairley 10 50
(M Johnston) *led to over 3f out: sn no ex* **33/1**
0 **8** *½* **Notnowrosie (IRE)**[35] 1307 3-8-5 0................................ AndrewMullen[(3)] 8 44
(A G Foster) *prom tl wknd over 2f out* **200/1**
43 **9** *9* **Prince Rhyddarch**[12] 1825 3-8-13 0.................................... PaulFessey 1 30
(Miss L A Perratt) *hld up in tch: drvn 4f out: wknd over 2f out* **16/1**
1m 58.13s (-1.57) **Going Correction** -0.25s/f (Firm)
WFA 3 from 4yo 13lb **9** Ran SP% **115.5**
Speed ratings (Par 103): **96,92,92,91,90 87,86,85,77**
CSF £6.96 TOTE £2.00: £1.20, £1.40, £4.20; EX 8.40.
Owner Gainsborough **Bred** Gainsborough Farm Llc **Trained** Newmarket, Suffolk

FOCUS
Not the strongest of maidens and a muddling gallop but the winner is a fair sort who may well progress again. The runner-up is the best guide to the level.

2144 MCGRATTAN PILING BRAVEHEART STALES (H'CAP) (LISTED RACE) — 1m 4f 17y
8:35 (8:35) (Class 1) (0-110,109) 4-Y-0+ **£17,031** (£6,456; £3,231; £1,611; £807) **Stalls** High

Form RPR
4-22 **1** **Eradicate (IRE)**[23] 1569 4-8-9 **100**.................................... JoeFanning 6 103
(M Johnston) *set stdy pce: rdn over 2f out: hld on gamely fnl f* **5/2**[2]
110- **2** *hd* **Turbo Linn**[246] 5352 5-9-4 **109**.. NCallan 2 112
(G A Swinbank) *t.k.h: prom: stdy hdwy over 3f out: effrt over 2f out: kpt on fnl f: jst hld* **9/4**[1]
030- **3** *1 ¼* **Acropolis (IRE)**[269] 4690 7-8-4 **95** oh4......................(v) PaulFessey 3 96
(Miss L A Perratt) *hld up in tch: hdwy over 1f out: rdn and kpt on same pce fnl f* **12/1**
63-4 **4** *nk* **Night Crescendo (USA)**[23] 1569 5-8-7 **98**.......................... JimCrowley 5 99
(Mrs A J Perrett) *trckd ldrs: rdn and outpcd over 2f out: r.o fnl f* **9/4**[1]
45-1 **5** *½* **Gull Wing (IRE)**[44] 1158 4-8-5 **96**.................................... RichardMullen 1 96
(M L W Bell) *pressed wnr: ev ch and rdn over 2f out: outpcd wl over 1f out: sn n.d* **6/1**[3]
2m 35.09s (-3.51) **Going Correction** -0.25s/f (Firm) **5** Ran SP% **112.1**
Speed ratings (Par 111): **101,100,100,99,99**
CSF £8.71 TOTE £3.80: £1.70, £1.90; EX 10.00.
Owner A D Spence **Bred** Sir Eric Parker **Trained** Middleham Moor, N Yorks

FOCUS
A useful field but a slow gallop means this bare form is not reliable with the third to last year's mark despite being 4lb out of the handicap.

NOTEBOOK
Eradicate(IRE), who showed himself to be better than ever on his previous start, looked in tremendous shape and was allowed to do his own thing in front. He showed a fine attitude for pressure to notch his third win and, as he should not be going up too much for this, will remain of interest back in a more competitive handicap after reassessment. (op 11-4 tchd 3-1)
Turbo Linn ◆ really did look a picture in the preliminaries and showed she retains all her ability in a race that was not run to suit. A much stronger gallop would have been in her favour and she is sure to win races over middle distances this summer. (tchd 2-1 and 11-4 in places)
Acropolis(IRE), a one-time smart sort for Aidan O'Brien, was another that would have preferred a stronger gallop but, although he ran well in terms of form from 4lb out of the handicap he did not exactly impress with the way he went about his business. He would not be one to take too short a price about next time. (tchd 9-1)
Night Crescendo(USA), a useful performer up to middle distances, got closer to the winner than on his reappearance at Nottingham. However, he left the strong impression that a much stronger overall gallop would have suited and he will be of interest when it looks as though the pace will be a generous one. (op 11-4)
Gull Wing(IRE), whose two turf wins have been in testing ground, found a muddling event over this trip on a quick surface an insufficient test of stamina. She will be one to keep an eye on when the rains arrive. (op 5-1)

2145 CHARD CONSTRUCTION H'CAP — 5f 4y
9:05 (9:07) (Class 5) (0-75,75) 4-Y-0+ **£3,238** (£963; £481; £240) **Stalls** Low

Form RPR
-006 **1** **Steelcut**[20] 1624 4-9-8 **74**.. TonyHamilton 3 82
(R A Fahey) *prom: effrt over 2f out: kpt on wl fnl f to ld nr fin* **5/1**[3]
0361 **2** *shd* **Rothesay Dancer**[12] 1827 5-8-8 **65** 6ex........................ KellyHarrison[(5)] 4 73
(J S Goldie) *hld up in tch: effrt over 1f out: kpt on wl fnl f: jst hld* **9/2**[2]
0002 **3** *nk* **Hawaii Prince**[6] 1997 4-8-7 **59**.. SilvestreDeSousa 6 66
(S T Mason) *cl up: led appr fnl f: ct nr fin* **7/1**
30-3 **4** *nk* **Raccoon (IRE)**[6] 1997 8-8-11 **63**.. NCallan 12 69+
(Mrs R A Carr) *racd w one other far side: overall ldr tl wl ins fnl f: no ex* **4/1**[1]
05-0 **5** *¾* **Prince Namid**[29] 1430 6-9-6 **75**.................................... AndrewMullen[(3)] 9 78
(Mrs A Duffield) *towards rr: drvn and outpcd after 2f: hdwy over 1f out: nrst fin* **14/1**
00-5 **6** *½* **Nusoor (IRE)**[20] 1634 5-7-13 **58** ow2..................(v[1]) PatrickDonaghy[(7)] 1 59
(Peter Grayson) *led main stands' side gp to appr fnl f: kpt on same pce ins fnl f* **14/1**
-100 **7** *shd* **Howards Tipple**[12] 1826 4-8-13 **65**...............................(p) PaulFessey 8 66
(Miss L A Perratt) *prom: effrt over 2f out: no ex ins fnl f* **16/1**
0060 **8** *½* **Kings College Boy**[20] 1624 8-8-6 **58**.........................(b) RichardMullen 10 57
(R A Fahey) *bhd and outpcd: hdwy over 1f out: n.d* **8/1**
45-1 **9** *1 ¾* **Sandwith**[20] 1624 5-9-1 **70**....................................(p) PJMcDonald[(3)] 7 63
(J S Wainwright) *midfield: drvn over 2f out: btn fnl f* **9/2**[2]
5100 **10** *5* **Geordie Dancer (IRE)**[12] 1827 6-7-13 **56** oh11(b) DanielleMcCreery[(5)] 2 31
(A Berry) *s.i.s: nvr on terms* **50/1**
0-00 **11** *2 ¾* **Alfie Lee (IRE)**[12] 1827 11-8-2 **61** oh11 ow5................(t) PaulPickard[(7)] 5 26
(D A Nolan) *chsd far side ldr to 1/2-way: sn outpcd* **150/1**
00-0 **12** *4* **Howards Prince**[12] 1826 5-8-5 **57** oh11 ow1..................(t) GregFairley 11 8
(D A Nolan) *chsd ldrs tl wknd over 2f out* **150/1**
58.71 secs (-1.29) **Going Correction** -0.25s/f (Firm) **12** Ran SP% **119.1**
Speed ratings (Par 103): **100,99,99,98,97 96,96,95,93,85 80,74**
CSF £27.97 CT £160.04 TOTE £6.50: £2.20, £2.10, £3.10; EX 27.30 Place 6 £8.76, Place 5 £6.91.
Owner A Rhodes Haulage And P Timmins **Bred** Mrs B Skinner **Trained** Musley Bank, N Yorks

FOCUS
A run-of-the-mill handicap in which the pace was sound throughout. All bar two raced on or towards the stands' side and the form looks solid with those in the frame behind the winner close to their recent marks.
T/Plt: £8.70 to a £1 stake. Pool: £50,932.95. 4,256.55 winning tickets. T/Qpdt: £5.70 to a £1 stake. Pool: £3,597.35. 459.30 winning tickets. RY

1467 NEWBURY (L-H)
Friday, May 16

OFFICIAL GOING: Good
Wind: Moderate behind Weather: Dull & overcast

2146 SANDERSON WEATHERALL MAIDEN STKS (DIV I) — 6f 8y
1:20 (1:23) (Class 4) 2-Y-0 **£5,342** (£1,589; £794; £396) **Stalls** Centre

Form RPR
1 **Instalment** 2-9-3 0.. RichardHughes 8 83+
(R Hannon) *unf: scope: hld up in tch: shkn up: swtchd lft and hdwy over 1f out: str run ins fnl f: led fnl strides: readily* **11/4**[1]
2 *hd* **Great Art (IRE)** 2-9-3 0.. JamieSpencer 2 83+
(P W Chapple-Hyam) *unf: trckd ldrs: qcknd to ld over 1f out: rdn: length clr and styd on ins fnl f: ct fnl strides* **7/2**[2]
5 **3** *3 ½* **Duke Of Aquitaine (USA)**[25] 1523 2-9-3 0............................ JosedeSouza 5 72
(P F I Cole) *str: led: rdn over 2f out: hdd over 1f out: outpcd ins fnl f* **12/1**
4 *½* **Tudor Key (IRE)** 2-9-3 0.. JimCrowley 13 71+
(Mrs A J Perrett) *str: trckd ldrs: rdn and styd on over 1f out but nvr quite gng pce to chal: outpcd ins fnl f* **20/1**
5 *2 ¼* **Head Down** 2-9-3 0.. SteveDrowne 4 64
(R Hannon) *w'like: chsd ldrs: rdn and ev ch 2f out: sn hung lft u.p: wknd fnl f* **16/1**
6 *2* **Innactualfact** 2-8-12 0.. PaulDoe 14 53
(L A Dace) *leggy: s.i.s: sn drvn to rcvr: chsd ldrs over 2f out: wknd fnl f* **150/1**
7 *1 ½* **Talking Hands** 2-9-3 0.. GeorgeBaker 7 53
(S Kirk) *w'like: leggy: in rr: pushed along 1/2-way: styd on ins fnl f: gng on cl home* **12/1**
0 **8** *½* **Flawless Diamond (IRE)**[12] 1838 2-8-12 0.............................. LPKeniry 1 47
(J S Moore) *leggy: sn rdn along towards rr: kpt on ins fnl f but nvr in contention* **66/1**
9 *½* **Survivor's Song** 2-9-3 0.. RobertHavlin 3 50
(D K Ivory) *w'like: leggy: sn bhd: mod prog fnl f* **50/1**
10 *2 ¼* **Marsool** 2-9-3 0.. RHills 11 44+
(M P Tregoning) *w'like: athletic: trckd ldrs: ev ch 2f out: bmpd and wknd sn after* **7/2**[2]
11 *5* **Courageous Nature (IRE)** 2-8-10 0.................................... KMay[(7)] 10 29
(B J Meehan) *w'like: bit bkwd: chsd ldr: rdn over 2f out: wknd sn after* **18/1**
12 *19* **Daily Planet (IRE)** 2-9-3 0.. WandersonD'Avila 12 —
(B W Duke) *w'like: slowly away: outpcd* **50/1**
13 *2 ¼* **Oasis Knight (IRE)** 2-9-3 0.. WilliamBuick 6 —
(M P Tregoning) *w'like: sn rdn and outpcd* **8/1**[3]
1m 14.85s (1.85) **Going Correction** +0.175s/f (Good) **13** Ran SP% **119.6**
Speed ratings (Par 95): **94,93,89,88,85 82,80,80,79,76 69,44,41**
CSF £11.75 TOTE £3.90: £1.60, £1.70, £3.10; EX 16.70.
Owner The Queen **Bred** The Queen **Trained** East Everleigh, Wilts

FOCUS
A fair juvenile contest but run 1.46secs slower than the second division. The front pair came clear and can go on from this.

NOTEBOOK
Instalment ◆, representing a stable that has won this race twice in recent seasons, including with Major Cadeaux, is related to several winners at up to 1m2f. Sent off favourite, he was quite keen early but then lost his place mid-race. However, he picked up well when his rider got after him and ran down the runner-up near the line. The first two were clear and he looks to have a fair amount of ability, so he could be in line for a race like the Coventry Stakes after this. (op 3-1)

Great Art(IRE) ◆, an easy to back second favourite, is out of a middle-distance performer who has produced a 5f juvenile winner. He showed plenty of pace and looked the most likely winner going into the last furlong, only to be run down near the line. He should have no problem winning a similar contest with this under his belt and looks to have the scope to go on to better things. (op 3-1 tchd 4-1)

Duke Of Aquitaine(USA) had clearly improved from his Windsor debut and made the early running, but he could not respond when the principals went for home. However, they look a useful pair so it was no disgrace and he held off the rest well enough. (op 11-1)

Tudor Key(IRE) ◆, whose trainer won this race last season, is out of a half-sister to Annus Mirabilis as well as several other useful winners. He looked as if the outing was needed but he was getting the hang of things in the latter stages and, with plenty of scope, he should come on a good deal for the experience.

Head Down, a stable companion of the winner, he raced up with the early pace but tended to hang left when put under pressure. He did keep going however, and looks likely to appreciate another furlong before too long.

Innactualfact, a speedily-bred half-sister to seven winners, showed plenty of promise on this debut. She missed a beat at the start but worked her way into contention at about the quarter-mile pole before her effort flattened out. She can be placed to pick up a small contest.

Marsool, out of a half-sister to the top-class Dylan Thomas and Queen's Logic, was easy in the market and missed the break, but soon took up a position on the heels of the leaders. However, he lost his place just over a quarter of a mile from home and was beaten in the end. (op 11-4)

2147 BERRY BROS & RUDD FILLIES' CONDITIONS STKS 5f 34y
1:50 (1:53) (Class 3) 2-Y-O **£6,542** (£1,959; £979; £490; £244) **Stalls** Centre

Form RPR

31 **1** **Moss Likely (IRE)**[14] 1762 2-8-13 0 EdwardCreighton 2 87
(M R Channon) *trckd ldr: led appr fnl 2f: drvn over 1f out: hld on wl cl home* **4/1**[3]

12 **2** *nk* **April Pride**[12] 1838 2-8-13 0 RichardHughes 6 86
(R Hannon) *unf: scope: lw: sn pressing ldr: chsd wnr fr 2f out: rdn and styd on ins fnl f: fin wl but a jst hld* **7/2**[2]

1 **3** *1* **Glamorous Spirit (IRE)**[6] 1983 2-8-13 0 JamieSpencer 3 82
(J Noseda) *lw: stdd s: trckd ldrs: swtchd rt over 2f out: rdn over 1f out: styd on same pce ins fnl f* **8/13**[1]

125 **4** *12* **Sally's Dilemma**[12] 1838 2-8-10 0 TolleyDean(3) 1 39
(W G M Turner) *slt ld tl hdd appr fnl 2f: sn btn* **25/1**

5 *2 ¾* **Madison Belle** 2-8-7 0 RobertHavlin 5 23
(Mrs H Sweeting) *leggy: a in rr: no ch whn hung bdly lft ins fnl 2f* **100/1**

62.53 secs (1.13) **Going Correction** +0.175s/f (Good) **5** Ran SP% **109.0**
Speed ratings (Par 94): **97,96,94,75,71**
CSF £17.44 TOTE £4.70: £1.80, £1.80; EX 16.50.
Owner Ridgeway Downs Racing **Bred** Island Syndicate **Trained** West Ilsley, Berks

FOCUS
A decent conditions stakes despite the small field and the form looks reasonably sound.

NOTEBOOK
Moss Likely(IRE), whose previous form is working out pretty well, was a market drifter but she proved the strongest in the race. Going on from the early leader soon after halfway, she found plenty for pressure and was always holding her market rivals. She could go for the Queen Mary, which the stable won with Queen's Logic and Flashy Wings after they were successful here, but she will also be put in the Albany Stakes over an extra furlong. (op 9-4)

April Pride was deliberately kept towards the stands' side away from the leaders early on and travelled well but could never quite get to the winner in the last furlong and a half. She is probably a fair guide to the level. (op 6-1)

Glamorous Spirit(IRE), the most expensive of these at the sales, had won a four-runner maiden at Ascot. She was sent off favourite and was held up at the rear early but, when pulled out for her effort, kept changing her legs and did not really pick up as expected. She may be better back on truly fast ground. (op 8-11)

Sally's Dilemma, who has not been able to build on her Brocklesby win, finished 13 lengths behind the runner-up at Salisbury last time and finished a similar distance behind her here. (op 33-1 tchd 22-1)

Madison Belle, a sister to Lucayos, found this a bit too hot a race on her debut. (op 80-1)

2148 ULTIMATE TRAVEL STKS (REGISTERED AS THE CARNARVON STAKES) (LISTED RACE) 6f 8y
2:20 (2:23) (Class 1) 3-Y-O **£17,031** (£6,456; £3,231; £1,611) **Stalls** Centre

Form RPR

21-2 **1** **Fat Boy (IRE)**[30] 1400 3-9-3 112 RichardHughes 4 114
(P W Chapple-Hyam) *lw: mde all: rdn and edgd lft fnl f: r.o strly* **8/11**[1]

43-2 **2** *1 ¾* **Tajdeef (USA)**[16] 1718 3-9-0 111 RHills 2 105
(B W Hills) *hld up in cl 4th: qcknd to trck wnr over 1f out: styd on same pce u.p and edgd lft ins fnl f* **2/1**[2]

2-2 **3** *3 ½* **Skadrak (USA)**[21] 1601 3-9-0 0 JamieSpencer 5 94
(B J Meehan) *disp cl 2nd tl rdn and effrt to press wnr over 2f out: nvr quite upsides: wknd fnl f* **6/1**[3]

06-3 **4** *6* **Irish Pearl (IRE)**[43] 1170 3-8-9 88 JimCrowley 1 70
(K R Burke) *disp cl 2nd tl rdn over 2f out: sn btn* **20/1**

1m 12.86s (-0.14) **Going Correction** +0.175s/f (Good) **4** Ran SP% **110.3**
Speed ratings (Par 107): **107,104,100,92**
CSF £2.52 TOTE £1.80; EX 2.50.
Owner M Sines **Bred** Peter Mooney **Trained** Newmarket, Suffolk

FOCUS
Not the most competitive race for this Listed event and the time was only 0.53secs faster than the quicker of the two juvenile maidens. A straightforward race to rate, with the winner to form and the runner-up again a bit below his juvenile best.

NOTEBOOK
Fat Boy(IRE) had the highest official rating following his good second in the Free Handicap but had to give 3lb to the runner-up on this drop back in trip. However, he is a battle-hardened sprinter and, despite the ground not being as fast as he likes, he made all the running and stuck to his task determinedly. He deserves to win a Group race and, although he is entered in Group 1s at Royal Ascot, connections are now aiming for the Chipchase Stakes at Newcastle. (op 4-6 tchd 5-6)

Tajdeef(USA) finished third in the Middle Park last season and had made a decent return against Sir Gerry at Ascot. He had a good chance against the winner judged on official ratings and got a good lead into the race, but he could never get to grips with that rival and has yet to reproduce his juvenile form. (op 5-2 tchd 11-4)

Skadrak(USA) had finished runner-up in both his starts in maidens and this was a tough ask on this step up in grade. However, he performed with credit despite taking a keen hold, although no match for the first two. This effort will not have helped his chances of getting a decent handicap mark but he should be able to pick up a maiden before long. (op 9-2 tchd 4-1)

Irish Pearl(IRE) had a great deal to find judged on official ratings and it was unsurprising that she found the colts too tough. However, she did pick up some decent prizemoney. (op 33-1)

2149 SWETTENHAM STUD FILLIES' TRIAL STKS (LISTED RACE) 1m 2f 6y
2:50 (2:50) (Class 1) 3-Y-O
£17,031 (£6,456; £3,231; £1,611; £807; £405) **Stalls** Centre

Form RPR

4-1 **1** **Clowance**[28] 1440 3-8-12 87 SteveDrowne 7 104+
(R Charlton) *lw: trckd ldrs: drvn to ld over 1f out: pushed out fnl f* **11/8**[1]

124- **2** *1 ¾* **Kotsi (IRE)**[230] 5796 3-8-12 107 JamieSpencer 5 99
(E F Vaughan) *trckd ldrs: drvn and hdwy ins fnl 2f: kpt on u.p ins fnl f to take 2nd nr fin but no imp on wnr* **9/4**[2]

320- **3** *½* **Hobby**[202] 6498 3-8-12 92 JamesDoyle 1 98
(R M Beckett) *swtg: disp ld but a jst had narrow advantage: rdn ins fnl 3f: hdd over 1f out: sn no ch w wnr: lost 2nd nr fin* **20/1**

6-1 **4** *1* **Ada River**[37] 1270 3-8-12 85 WilliamBuick 8 96
(A M Balding) *lw: disp ld: rdn ins fnl 3f: outpcd over 1f out but stl kpt on ins fnl f* **7/1**[3]

24-1 **5** *4 ½* **Katimont (IRE)**[25] 1525 3-8-12 77 RHills 6 87
(B W Hills) *sltly hmpd s and sn in rr: stl bhd 3f out: rdn and effrt ins fnl 2f but nvr really travelling and nt rch ldrs: wknd fnl f* **7/1**[3]

20-5 **6** *12* **Shaker (IRE)**[12] 1833 3-8-12 86 RobertHavlin 2 63
(M L W Bell) *chsd ldrs: rdn 3f out: sn wknd* **12/1**

2-11 **7** *1 ½* **Longoria (IRE)**[20] 1637 3-8-12 77 NeilChalmers 4 60
(Lucinda Featherstone) *w'like: towards rr but in tch: rdn 3f out and sn wknd* **33/1**

2m 9.76s (0.96) **Going Correction** +0.175s/f (Good) **7** Ran SP% **113.3**
Speed ratings (Par 104): **103,101,101,100,96 87,86**
CSF £4.51 TOTE £2.20: £1.40, £1.80; EX 5.10 Trifecta £156.90 Part won. Pool: £221.01. 0.90 winning units..
Owner Seasons Holidays **Bred** B Hurley **Trained** Beckhampton, Wilts
■ Stewards' Enquiry : William Buick three-day ban: careless riding (May 30-Jun 1)

FOCUS
Just a fair renewal of this Listed contest, but a clear-cut winner. The form is not the most solid, but the winner appeared to improve, as did the third, fourth and fifth, but the runner-up was around 8lb off her May Hill form.

NOTEBOOK
Clowance, despite appearing to have a stiff task on official ratings, was well backed to follow up her course and distance maiden win, (in which she defeated subsequent Lingfield Oaks Trial winner Miracle Seeker) and did so in straightforward fashion. Always travelling well just behind the leaders, once she was asked to go to the front she found plenty and never looked likely to be reeled in. She is on course for the Oaks next and, as she is related to a number of winners in Germany, several of whom stayed well, she looks sure to get the trip. She needs to improve again but looks capable of doing so, as her rider reported she was not doing much in front. (op 6-4 tchd 5-4)

Kotsi(IRE), who set the standard on her second in the May Hill and fourth in the Fillies' Mile, was making her seasonal debut but looked fit enough beforehand. She did not respond that quickly when asked to go in pursuit of the winner but was keeping on at the end. She looks likely to come on for the outing but on breeding there is a question about her ability to stay any further and she may now not take up entires in the Ribblesdale and Irish Oaks. (op 2-1 tchd 5-2)

Hobby, who was well beaten in her only previous try in this grade on soft ground, had previously looked a decent performer on a sound surface. She made the running on this seasonal debut and kept on after being headed, and having earned more black type looks likely to aim to win at this level. Faster ground will be in her favour. (op 16-1)

Ada River, who adopted different tactics when scoring at Kempton last time, appeared to run her race but was outclassed. She may be better off in handicaps. (op 9-1)

Katimont(IRE), who beat a subsequent winner when taking her maiden at Windsor, was by the same sire as the winner and was stepping up in trip but never got into a challenging position. She looked uncomfortable in the closing stages so may have had some sort of problem. Official explanation: jockey said filly suffered interference on leaving stalls (op 11-1)

Longoria(IRE) was edgy in the paddock beforehand.

2150 SANDERSON WEATHERALL MAIDEN STKS DIV (II) 6f 8y
3:20 (3:24) (Class 4) 2-Y-O **£5,342** (£1,589; £794; £396) **Stalls** Centre

Form RPR

1 **Orizaba (IRE)** 2-9-3 0 EdwardCreighton 6 95+
(M R Channon) *w'like: scope: tall: trckd ldr: led ins fnl 2f: drvn clr fnl f: easily* **11/4**[2]

2 *9* **Johnny Rook (GER)** 2-9-3 0 SteveDrowne 12 68
(E A L Dunlop) *towards rr: hdwy fr 3f out: styd on wl to chse wnr 1f out: nvr any ch but hld on gamely for 2nd* **10/1**

6 **3** *shd* **Jazacosta (USA)**[12] 1832 2-9-3 0 JimCrowley 9 68
(Mrs A J Perrett) *athletic: lw: chsd ldrs: rdn and kpt on fnl 2f: disp wl hld 2nd fnl f* **10/1**

4 *2* **Donativum** 2-9-3 0 RobertHavlin 11 62
(J H M Gosden) *w'like: bit bkwd: chsd ldrs: c to stands' side and racd along fnl 2f: kpt on but nvr in contention* **14/1**

5 *½* **Sohcahtoa (IRE)** 2-8-12 0 HaddenFrost(5) 10 60+
(R Hannon) *w'like: tall: in tch: rdn and outpcd 1/2-way: styd on again ins fnl f* **20/1**

6 *¾* **Gallagher** 2-9-3 0 JamieSpencer 13 58+
(B J Meehan) *str: in tch: stdy hdwy to trck ldrs over 2f out: shkn up wl over 1f out and no imp: wknd ins fnl f* **5/2**[1]

6 **7** *5* **Robin The Till**[11] 1873 2-9-3 0 RichardHughes 2 43
(R Hannon) *w'like: str: wnt lft s and sn led: hdd and hung lft ins fnl 2f: wknd over 1f out* **14/1**

8 *3* **Motor Home** 2-9-3 0 WilliamBuick 5 34
(A M Balding) *w'like: s.i.s: outpcd: mod late prog* **20/1**

9 *¾* **Diamond Heist** 2-9-3 0 NelsonDeSouza 8 32
(M P Tregoning) *w'like: lw: sn pushed along towards rr: mod prog ins fnl f* **33/1**

10 *shd* **Taste The Wine (IRE)** 2-9-3 0 AdamKirby 3 31
(C G Cox) *w'like: leggy: chsd ldrs: rdn over 2f out and sn wknd* **18/1**

11 *3 ¾* **Strikemaster (IRE)** 2-8-10 0 GabrielHannon(7) 4 20
(J W Hills) *w'like: s.i.s: a in rr* **66/1**

12 *1* **Konka (USA)** 2-8-12 0 LPKeniry 7 12
(E F Vaughan) *tall: in tch to 1/2-way* **33/1**

13 *3 ½* **Ghaayer** 2-9-3 0 RHills 1 7
(M P Tregoning) *str: bit bkwd: hmpd s: green and a in rr* **6/1**[3]

1m 13.39s (0.39) **Going Correction** +0.175s/f (Good) **13** Ran SP% **123.2**
Speed ratings (Par 95): **104,92,91,89,88 87,80,76,75,75 70,69,64**
CSF £29.69 TOTE £4.50: £2.00, £2.50, £3.20; EX 41.30.
Owner Box 41 **Bred** W Powell-Harris **Trained** West Ilsley, Berks

FOCUS
The second division of this maiden produced a runaway winner in a time 1.46 secs faster than the first leg.

NOTEBOOK

Orizaba(IRE) ◆, well regarded at home, made a highly impressive debut, clearly knowing his job and coming right away from the rest when asked. The time was very good for a juvenile and much faster than the first division, so he looks to have real future. The stable seems to have several useful juveniles again this season but the Coventry seems a logical target and on this evidence he will take some beating there. (op 9-4 tchd 3-1)

Johnny Rook(GER), another with plenty of speed in his pedigree, ran on through the pack to do best of the rest but the winner had already put the race to bed. This was a decent effort though and the time puts him close to the principals in the first division, so he looks capable of winning his maiden at least. (op 7-1)

Jazacosta(USA), one of the few to have had an outing and from the stable who sent out last year's winner of this race, showed considerable improvement but was left trailing when the winner went for home. (op 12-1)

Donativum, a 120,000gns half-brother to several winners at around a mile, offered encouragement on this debut and looks sure to benefit from the experience. (tchd 16-1)

Sohcahtoa(IRE), a 65,000gns half-brother to a 7f juvenile winner and another who looks likely to benefit from a little further in time, was coltish in the paddock, but he showed some promise and should come on for the run. (op 16-1)

Gallagher, a 115,000gns son of the useful sprinter Roo, who has already produced a couple of winners, was clearly well fancied despite being from a yard whose juveniles normally need an outing. He showed up well enough for a long way before fading in the closing stages and better can be expected in time. (op 3-1)

Robin The Till Official explanation: jockey said colt hung left-handed

Motor Home was edgy in the preliminaries. (op 28-1)

Diamond Heist is a close-coupled colt.

Taste The Wine(IRE) got edgy in the paddock. (op 33-1)

Strikemaster(IRE) was another who was on edge beforehand.

Konka(USA) was also edgy in the paddock. (op 40-1)

Ghaayer, a 220,000gns half-brother to four winners, had clearly been showing something at home as he was well supported, but after getting hampered at the start was always out the back. He can be given another chance to show what he is capable of. (op 17-2 tchd 9-1)

2151 POWERSOLVE ELECTRONICS H'CAP — 1m 3f 5y

3:55 (3:56) (Class 4) (0-80,82) 3-Y-O — **£5,504** (£1,637; £818; £408) **Stalls Centre**

Form — RPR

6311 **1** **Allied Powers (IRE)**[9] 1919 3-9-3 **82** 6ex.................... TravisBlock(3) 16 — 97+
(M L W Bell) *lw: hld up in rr: stdy hdwy 4f out: led 2f out: styd on wl fnl f and a in command* **13/8**[1]

641- **2** *1 ¾* **Maxwil**[204] 6448 3-9-4 **80**.................... GeorgeBaker 4 — 89
(G L Moore) *swtg: hld up in rr: stdy hdwy fr 3f out: chsd wnr appr fnl f but a readily hld* **33/1**

515- **3** *2 ¼* **Black Jacari (IRE)**[215] 6194 3-9-2 **78**.................... SimonWhitworth 12 — 83
(A King) *in rr: hdwy on rails fr 3f out: n.m.r and swtchd rt ins fnl 2f: kpt on wl cl home but nt rch ldng duo* **33/1**

06-4 **4** *½* **Celt**[18] 1684 3-9-0 **76**.................... JamieSpencer 5 — 80+
(L M Cumani) *hld up in rr: hdwy on outside over 3f out: rdn over 2f out: styd on same pce appr fnl f* **7/2**[2]

55-6 **5** *1 ½* **Prairie Storm**[25] 1526 3-9-0 **76**.................... LPKeniry 7 — 78
(A M Balding) *chsd ldrs: rdn 3f out: wknd over 1f out* **16/1**

321- **6** *4 ½* **La Columbina**[226] 5914 3-9-2 **78**.................... RichardHughes 10 — 72
(R Hannon) *in rr: hdwy fr 3f out: nvr quite gng pce to rch ldrs: wknd ins fnl f* **16/1**

5-33 **7** *2 ¼* **Colorado Blue (IRE)**[18] 1684 3-9-1 **77**.................... SteveDrowne 9 — 67
(R Charlton) *mid-div: rdn along 3f out and styd on same pce* **12/1**

31-4 **8** *3 ¾* **Ragamuffin Man (IRE)**[29] 1424 3-9-3 **79**.................... PaulDoe 15 — 63
(W J Knight) *chsd ldrs: rdn 3f out: wknd over 2f out* **8/1**[3]

231- **9** *¾* **Fair Gale**[149] 7181 3-8-11 **78**.................... HaddenFrost(5) 8 — 61
(S Kirk) *lw: in rr: mod prog fnl 2f* **33/1**

03-3 **10** *nk* **Nino Cochise (IRE)**[23] 1572 3-8-9 **71**.................... WilliamBuick 14 — 53
(C R Egerton) *in rr: rdn over 4f out: mod prog fnl f* **14/1**

3-14 **11** *½* **Title Role**[25] 1527 3-8-11 **76**.................... TolleyDean(3) 3 — 57
(P F I Cole) *in tch: rdn 3f out: sn wknd* **28/1**

00-5 **12** *2* **Yathreb (USA)**[20] 1614 3-8-9 **71**....................(b[1]) RHills 13 — 49
(J L Dunlop) *chsd ldrs: led 4f out: hdd 2f out and wknd qckly* **16/1**

2411 **13** *12* **Forsyte Saga**[18] 1678 3-9-3 **79**.................... JimCrowley 2 — 36
(M Johnston) *slt ld tl hdd 4f out: wknd ins fnl 3f* **16/1**

41-0 **14** *¾* **Cossack Prince**[21] 1600 3-9-0 **76**.................... RobertHavlin 6 — 32
(B J Meehan) *w ldr to 4f out: wknd sn after* **28/1**

6-30 **15** *21* **Agente Romano (USA)**[15] 1746 3-8-11 **73**....................(t) AdamKirby 1 — —
(G A Butler) *chsd ldrs 7f* **50/1**

2m 22.46s (1.26) **Going Correction** +0.175s/f (Good) — 15 Ran SP% **127.0**

Speed ratings (Par 101): **102,100,99,98,97 94,92,90,89,89 88,87,78,78,62**

CSF £81.02 CT £1429.32 TOTE £2.70: £1.50, £6.30, £8.20; EX 52.30.

Owner David Fish And Edward Ware **Bred** Saad Bin Mishrif **Trained** Newmarket, Suffolk

FOCUS

This handicap was full of relatively unexposed performers and looks a race that could produce several future winners. The progressive winner was close to his Chester form and again won with a bit more in hand than the bare facts suggest. The placed horses were both lightly raced maiden winners who were entitled to improve, and the fourth was even less exposed.

2152 JOHN SMITH'S H'CAP — 1m 2f 6y

4:30 (4:30) (Class 4) (0-85,83) 4-Y-0+ — **£4,209** (£1,252; £625; £312) **Stalls Centre**

Form — RPR

1-01 **1** **Kavachi (IRE)**[15] 1742 5-9-1 **80**.................... GeorgeBaker 6 — 92+
(G L Moore) *hld up in rr: stl plenty to do 3f out: sn swtchd rt to outside and str run to ld appr fnl f: readily* **14/1**

00-0 **2** *2 ½* **Ascalon**[27] 1473 4-9-1 **80**.................... PaulEddery 9 — 87
(Pat Eddery) *lw: pressed ldr: rdn along 5f out: chal tl slt advantage 2f out: hdd over 1f out: styd on wl for 2nd but no ch w wnr* **13/2**[3]

0-14 **3** *¾* **Haarth Sovereign (IRE)**[26] 1502 4-8-13 **78**.................... AdamKirby 11 — 84
(W R Swinburn) *chsd ldrs: rdn over 2f out: kpt on fnl f but nvr gng pce to rch ldng duo* **9/1**

-563 **4** *½* **Red Somerset (USA)**[16] 1719 5-8-12 **82**.................... HaddenFrost(5) 14 — 87
(R J Hodges) *in tch: rdn to chse ledrs fr ins fnl 3f: kpt on same pce appr fnl f* **7/1**

2 **5** *1 ¾* **Indicible (FR)**[8] 1935 4-9-3 **82**.................... RichardHughes 1 — 83
(A King) *narrow ldr: rdn over 3f out: hdd 2f out: wknd fnl f* **11/2**[2]

16-0 **6** *½* **Nur Tau (IRE)**[27] 1473 4-9-4 **83**.................... SteveDrowne 12 — 83+
(H Morrison) *in rr: hdwy to chse ldrs 3f out: rdn: n.m.r and lost position over 2f out: kpt on again ins fnl f* **14/1**

130- **7** *½* **Encircled**[302] 3691 4-9-2 **81**.................... RobertHavlin 10 — 80+
(D Haydn Jones) *bit bkwd: in rr: stdy hdwy to chse ldrs over 2f out: shkn up over 1f out: wknd ins fnl f* **20/1**

4-32 **8** *shd* **Nutkin**[15] 1742 4-8-11 **76**.................... JamieSpencer 3 — 75
(J R Fanshawe) *lw: trckd ldrs on rails 4f out: rdn and n.m.r over 2f out: edgd rt over 1f out: sn btn* **10/3**[1]

114- **9** *3* **Good Effect (USA)**[18] 4847 4-8-7 **72**.................... CatherineGannon 4 — 65
(C P Morlock) *drvn into mid-div after 1f: rdn 3f out: wknd over 2f out* **33/1**

0156 **10** *2* **Golden Prospect**[20] 1630 4-8-7 **72**.................... RHills 5 — 61
(J W Hills) *t.k.h towards rr: nvr gng pce to get into contention* **10/1**

1210 **11** *4 ½* **Safari Sundowner (IRE)**[37] 1273 4-8-13 **78**.................... SaleemGolam 7 — 58
(P Winkworth) *chsd ldrs: rdn 3f out: wknd 2f out* **25/1**

0-45 **12** *hd* **Danski**[24] 1532 5-8-9 **77**.................... TravisBlock(3) 13 — 56
(P J Makin) *chsd ldrs: rdn 3f out: wkng whn hmpd over 1f out* **14/1**

50-0 **13** *7* **Press The Button (GER)**[20] 1633 5-9-4 **83**.................... WilliamBuick 8 — 48
(J R Boyle) *a towards rr* **14/1**

2m 11.38s (2.58) **Going Correction** +0.175s/f (Good) — 13 Ran SP% **121.6**

Speed ratings (Par 105): **96,94,93,93,91 91,90,90,88,86 83,82,77**

CSF £101.89 CT £884.84 TOTE £14.10: £3.70, £2.50, £3.10; EX 121.60.

Owner Bryan Pennick & Roy Martin **Bred** Gainsborough Stud Management Ltd **Trained** Woodingdean, E Sussex

FOCUS

A decent competitive handicap but the pace was ordinary early on. In the circumstances the winner did well to come from the back of the field, and he is clearly improving. The form looks sound enough, rated around the placed horses.

2153 M AND C CARPETS STKS (H'CAP) — 1m 4f 5y

5:05 (5:05) (Class 5) (0-75,78) 4-Y-0+ — **£2,590** (£770; £385; £192) **Stalls Centre**

Form — RPR

6-33 **1** **Mae Cigan (FR)**[20] 1613 5-8-8 **65** ow1.................... SteveDrowne 9 — 73
(M Blanshard) *mid-div: rdn over 2f out: squeezed through and styd on strly fnl f to ld fnl strides* **10/1**

31/0 **2** *shd* **Show Winner**[18] 1682 5-9-2 **73**.................... LPKeniry 13 — 81
(A M Balding) *lw: chsd ldrs: drvn to ld appr fnl 2f: edgd rt over 1f out: kpt on u.p ins fnl f: ct fnl strides* **16/1**

32-4 **3** *¾* **Coyote Creek**[28] 1458 4-9-4 **75**.................... GeorgeBaker 6 — 82
(E F Vaughan) *chsd ldrs: rdn to chal fr 3f out: kpt on u.p fnl f: no ex nr fin* **9/1**

00-2 **4** *1* **Natural Action**[18] 1691 4-9-1 **72**.................... JamieSpencer 3 — 77
(W Jarvis) *s.i.s: in rr: stl plenty to do whn swtchd rt to outside fr 3f out: rdn and styng on whn edgd lft ins fnl 2f: pushed rt over 1f out whn styng on: no ex ins fnl f* **8/1**

-314 **5** *1 ½* **Rising Force (IRE)**[33] 586 5-8-8 **68**....................(b) TolleyDean(3) 14 — 71
(J L Spearing) *t.k.h in rr: wd bnd 7f out: hdwy on outside room 3f out: chal 2f out: styng on whn pushed rt over 1f out: wknd ins fnl f* **18/1**

0-02 **6** *¾* **Aegean Prince**[11] 1874 4-9-2 **73**.................... RichardHughes 15 — 77+
(R Hannon) *hld up in rr: drvn and sme hdwy 3f out: kpt on but nvr gng pce to be competitive* **5/1**[2]

4-43 **7** *nk* **Pocketwood**[23] 198 6-8-8 **65**.................... StephenCarson 16 — 66
(Jean-Rene Auvray) *pressed ldr: chal over 3f out tl 3f out: wknd fnl f* **15/2**

51-1 **8** *½* **Aypeeyes (IRE)**[7] 1963 4-9-4 **78** 6ex.................... TravisBlock(3) 2 — 79
(A King) *lw: chsd ldrs: rdn over 2f out: wknd fnl f* **4/1**[1]

230/ **9** *nk* **Emile Zola**[31] 4868 6-8-8 **65**.................... JamesDoyle 7 — 65
(Miss Venetia Williams) *in tch: rdn and outpcd over 3f out: styd on again u.p fr over 1f out* **33/1**

034- **10** *½* **Kasban**[336] 2628 4-9-3 **74**.................... FrankieMcDonald 11 — 73
(Jane Chapple-Hyam) *mid-div: pushed along towards outside 3f out: mod prog fnl f* **16/1**

16-0 **11** *½* **Etain (IRE)**[18] 1682 4-8-12 **69**.................... AdamKirby 1 — 67
(W R Swinburn) *led tl hdd & wknd appr fnl 2f* **16/1**

0-00 **12** *nk* **Invention (USA)**[13] 1799 5-9-1 **72**.................... WilliamBuick 4 — 70
(Miss E C Lavelle) *chsd ldrs: rdn 3f out: wknd fr 2f out* **33/1**

-042 **13** *2 ¼* **Cruise Director**[7] 1947 8-8-13 **75**.................... HaddenFrost(5) 12 — 69
(Ian Williams) *chsd ldrs: rdn to chal 3f out: wknd over 2f out* **6/1**[3]

0-54 **14** *2 ¼* **Damascus Gold**[24] 1539 4-8-6 **63** oh4 ow2....................(b) SamHitchcott 8 — 54
(Miss Z C Davison) *s.i.s: in rr tl styd on fr over 1f out* **50/1**

0 **15** *shd* **L'Homme De Nuit (GER)**[18] 1682 4-8-6 **63**.................... RobertHavlin 5 — 54
(G L Moore) *mid-div: hdwy 3f out: sn wknd: eased whn no ch fnl f* **33/1**

334- **16** *1* **Snark (IRE)**[226] 5916 5-9-0 **71**.................... PaulEddery 10 — 60
(Simon Earle) *a in rr* **28/1**

2m 39.12s (3.62) **Going Correction** +0.175s/f (Good) — 16 Ran SP% **130.1**

Speed ratings (Par 103): **94,93,93,92,91 91,91,90,90,90 89,89,88,86,86 85**

CSF £164.02 CT £1526.71 TOTE £16.50: £2.80, £4.70, £2.90, £1.70; EX 278.90 Place 6 £59.51, Place 5 £33.82..

Owner A D Jones **Bred** Jonathan Jay **Trained** Upper Lambourn, Berks

FOCUS

An ordinary handicap for the track, with moderate prizemoney. A steady pace contributed to a close finish, and the form does not look the most solid, although the first three all ran close to their marks.

Coyote Creek Official explanation: jockey said gelding hung right-handed

Cruise Director Official explanation: jockey said gelding ran flat

T/Plt: £62.80 to a £1 stake. Pool: £47,968.90. 557.55 winning tickets. T/Qpdt: £32.30 to a £1 stake. Pool: £2,737.78. 62.60 winning tickets. ST

1217 NEWCASTLE (L-H)

Friday, May 16

OFFICIAL GOING: Good to firm (good in places; 8.3)

The riders were full of praise for the ground, 'near perfect going' was their verdict.

Wind: Light, half-against Weather: overcast and very cool

2154 PLATE TICKETS NOW ON SALE NOVICE STKS — 6f

6:10 (6:12) (Class 4) 2-Y-O — **£4,047** (£1,204; £601; £300) **Stalls High**

Form — RPR

1 **Prime Spirit (IRE)** 2-8-12 0.................... TomEaves 6 — 73+
(B Smart) *dwlt: sn trcking ldrs: effrt 2f out: r.o to ld nr fin* **3/1**[1]

016 **2** *hd* **Saxford**[28] 1447 2-9-5 0.................... ShaneKelly 5 — 79
(Mrs L Stubbs) *stmbld s: led tl hdd wl ins fnl f: no ex* **9/1**

1 **3** *2 ¼* **Toby Tyler**[16] 1727 2-9-2 0.................... JamieMoriarty(3) 4 — 71
(P T Midgley) *trckd ldrs: effrt 2f out: styd on appr fnl f* **3/1**[1]

0 **4** *nk* **Orphaned Annie**[25] 1515 2-8-0 0.................... LanceBetts(7) 7 — 58
(B Ellison) *s.i.s: in rr tl styd on wl appr fnl f* **40/1**

612 **5** *3 ¾* **Gone Hunting**[28] 1447 2-8-9 0.................... JackDean(5) 1 — 54
(W G M Turner) *lw: ldrs: edgd lft and fdd fnl f* **7/2**[2]

21 **6** *2 ¼* **Veronicas Boy**[12] 1821 2-9-2 0.................... AndrewElliott 3 — 49
(G M Moore) *w ldr: wknd over 1f out* **9/2**[3]

1m 14.77s (-0.43) **Going Correction** -0.175s/f (Firm) — 6 Ran SP% **102.8**

Speed ratings (Par 95): **95,94,91,90,85 82**

CSF £23.19 TOTE £4.10: £1.60, £5.70; EX 49.30.

Owner Prime Equestrian **Bred** Frank Gleeson **Trained** Hambleton, N Yorks

FOCUS
Four previous winners in the line-up and the winner will improve for the outing and the experience. The form is rated as positively as it can be at this stage.

NOTEBOOK
Prime Spirit(IRE), first foal of a mare that won over 2m, has size and scope but was very noisy and on his toes in the paddock. After missing a beat at the start he travelled easily best and came with a sustained run to lead near the line. This will have taught him plenty and he looks a fair prospect. (tchd 7-2)
Saxford, who had two handlers in the paddock, stumbled leaving the stalls. Nailed near the line, he lost nothing in defeat. (op 10-1 tchd 17-2)
Toby Tyler, very keen to post, was racing on much quicker ground. After being caught rather flat-footed he stayed on in willing fashion thoroughly appreciating the step up to six. (op 9-2 tchd 5-1)
Orphaned Annie, nothing at all to look at and stoutly-bred on her dam's side, made a tardy start but was putting in some solid work in the sixth and final furlong. (op 20-1)
Gone Hunting, over seven lengths ahead of the runner-up when narrowly beaten by a subsequent York winner at Thirsk, was inclined to be coltish in the paddock and did not seem to appreciate the extra furlong. (op 10-3 tchd 11-4)
Veronicas Boy, encountering much quicker ground, was the first beaten. (op 5-1 tchd 4-1)

2155 CHAMPAGNE & SWING NIGHT 29TH MAY H'CAP — 1m 2f 32y
6:40 (6:42) (Class 4) (0-80,75) 4-Y-0+ **£4,533** (£1,348; £674; £336) **Stalls** Centre

Form RPR
1 **Summer Gold (IRE)**[327] 2922 4-9-1 **72** ShaneKelly 3 81
(E J Alston) *trckd ldrs: led over 2f out: clr over 1f out: rdn out* **10/1**
2454 2 1 3/4 **Sudden Impulse**[9] 1909 7-9-2 **73** AndrewElliott 7 78
(A D Brown) *trckd ldrs: wnt 2nd appr fnl f: kpt on: nt rch wnr* **5/1**[2]
11-6 3 1 3/4 **Cheshire Prince**[31] 1388 4-9-0 **71** LiamJones 8 73
(W M Brisbourne) *hld up in rr: hdwy on outer over 2f out: styd on fnl f* **12/1**
56-5 4 2 1/4 **Demolition**[25] 1520 4-9-1 **72** GrahamGibbons 4 69
(N Wilson) *sn trcking ldrs: effrt over 2f out: kpt on same pce* **4/1**[1]
042- 5 hd **Titinius (IRE)**[140] 6727 8-8-7 **64** DO'Donohoe 5 61
(Micky Hammond) *chsd ldrs: drvn 3f out: one pce* **20/1**
40-0 6 1 **Shy Glance (USA)**[12] 1822 6-8-9 **66** TomEaves 13 61+
(P Monteith) *t.k.h in midfield: kpt on fnl 2f: nvr nr ldrs* **20/1**
01-0 7 shd **Snow Dancer (IRE)**[20] 1613 4-8-10 **67** PatrickMathers 1 61
(H A McWilliams) *s.i.s: hld up in midfield: effrt over 2f out: one pce* **40/1**
2/50 8 hd **Polish Corridor**[20] 1613 9-9-1 **72** DaleGibson 11 66
(M Dods) *hld up in rr: styd on fnl 2f: nvr nr ldrs* **8/1**[3]
0460 9 1/2 **Wovoka (IRE)**[13] 1815 5-9-2 **73** FergalLynch 12 68
(D W Barker) *t.k.h in rr: nt clr run over 2f out: kpt on* **12/1**
01-0 10 1/2 **Painted Sky**[19] 962 5-9-3 **74** PaulHanagan 10 66
(R A Fahey) *hld up in rr: hdwy on outside over 4f out: hung rt and nvr nr ldrs* **4/1**[1]
5/40 11 3/4 **Rehearsal**[54] 981 7-9-4 **75** RobertWinston 6 66
(L Lungo) *led: shkn up and qcknd pce over 3f out: hdd over 2f out: wknd fnl f: eased towards fin* **10/1**
-065 12 1/2 **Ahlawy (IRE)**[13] 1793 5-8-9 **73** NSLawes(7) 14 63
(M W Easterby) *s.s: a in rr* **11/1**
100/ 13 nk **Seyaadi**[718] 2079 6-8-13 **70** DeanMcKeown 2 59
(Miss Tracy Waggott) *trckd ldrs: t.k.h: effrt over 2f out: one pce whn n.m.r 1f out: sn wknd* **66/1**
602- 14 3 3/4 **Hawkit (USA)**[195] 6636 7-8-12 **72** JamieMoriarty(3) 9 53
(P Monteith) *in rr: bhd fnl 2f* **22/1**

2m 11.89s (-0.01) **Going Correction** -0.025s/f (Good) **14 Ran SP% 127.5**
Speed ratings (Par 105): **105,103,102,100,100 99,99,99,98,98 97,97,97,94**
CSF £59.38 CT £633.92 TOTE £13.50: £3.60, £1.30, £3.80; EX 118.00.
Owner J Stephenson **Bred** Rathbarry Stud **Trained** Longton, Lancs

FOCUS
A fair handicap but no real gallop until turning for home and it was hard to make significant ground from off the pace. The placed horses set the standard.
Wovoka(IRE) Official explanation: jockey said gelding ran too keen early and was then denied a clear run
Painted Sky Official explanation: jockey said gelding hung right-handed throughout

2156 BENFIELD RENAULT MEDIAN AUCTION MAIDEN STKS — 1m 2f 32y
7:15 (7:15) (Class 5) 3-Y-0 **£3,885** (£1,156; £577; £288) **Stalls** Centre

Form RPR
5-23 1 **Woolfall Treasure**[13] 1811 3-9-3 85 SebSanders 4 76+
(G G Margarson) *mde all: clr over 1f out: eased towards fin* **1/10**[1]
46 2 8 **Miss Mactango**[9] 1918 3-8-12 0 LiamJones 5 52
(W M Brisbourne) *trckd wnr: drvn 5f out: kpt on: no ch w wnr* **12/1**[3]
0- 3 2 1/4 **Fortunella**[263] 4875 3-8-12 0 ShaneKelly 3 48
(P Howling) *trckd ldrs: pushed along over 4f out: one pce fnl 2f* **20/1**
00- 4 3 **Northgate Maisie**[210] 6303 3-8-12 0 AndrewElliott 2 42
(Jedd O'Keeffe) *chsd ldrs: one pce fnl 3f* **66/1**
0 5 1 1/4 **Red Rouge**[15] 1751 3-8-12 0 KimTinkler 1 39
(N Tinkler) *hld up in last: pushed along 7f out: sme hdwy over 2f out: one pce* **20/1**
6 9 **Lady Fire (USA)** 3-8-12 0 PhillipMakin 6 21
(M Dods) *dwlt: t.k.h: hdwy 5f out: wknd over 2f out* **11/1**[2]

2m 12.73s (0.83) **Going Correction** -0.025s/f (Good) **6 Ran SP% 118.0**
Speed ratings (Par 99): **102,95,93,91,90 83**
CSF £2.92 TOTE £1.10: £1.02, £3.90; EX 2.40.
Owner J F Bower **Bred** Serpentine Bloodstock Et Al **Trained** Newmarket, Suffolk

FOCUS
A non-event with the winner not needing to run to his previous form to score.

2157 CHRISTMAS PARTIES AT BRANDLING HOUSE H'CAP — 2m 19y
7:50 (7:50) (Class 5) (0-70,68) 4-Y-0+ **£3,885** (£1,156; £577; £288) **Stalls** High

Form RPR
633- 1 **Mr Crystal (FR)**[27] 4821 4-9-2 **59** PaulHanagan 4 72+
(Micky Hammond) *trckd ldng pair: led over 2f out: clr over 1f out: eased towards fin* **3/1**[3]
554- 2 2 1/2 **Daylami Dreams**[149] 4758 4-9-11 **68** MickyFenton 7 75+
(T P Tate) *hld up in rr: hdwy whn stmbld bdly over 3f out: styd on to take 2nd ins fnl f* **11/4**[2]
5-05 3 1/2 **Rocknest Island (IRE)**[25] 1518 5-9-0 **55** (p) RobertWinston 6 58
(P D Niven) *hld up: hdwy to trck ldrs 9f out: pushed along over 5f out: wnt 2nd 1f out: kpt on same pce* **11/2**
03-4 4 8 **Forrest Flyer (IRE)**[14] 1773 4-8-8 **51** TomEaves 2 45
(Miss L A Perratt) *led tl over 2f out: wknd 1f out* **9/4**[1]
65/0 5 27 **Nounou**[45] 320 7-9-10 **65** FergalLynch 3 26
(Miss J E Foster) *hld up in rr: effrt over 3f out: wknd 2f out: sn bhd* **20/1**
050- 6 11 **Roll Em Over**[303] 3638 5-8-6 **47** oh2 LiamJones 5 —
(A Crook) *chsd ldr: pushed along 6f out: wknd over 3f out: sn bhd* **50/1**
232- R **Kristiansand**[175] 5586 8-9-1 **56** PaulMulrennan 8 —
(P Monteith) *ref to r: tk no part* **8/1**

3m 34.4s (-1.80) **Going Correction** -0.025s/f (Good)
WFA 4 from 5yo+ 2lb **7 Ran SP% 115.7**
Speed ratings (Par 103): **103,101,101,97,84 78,—**
CSF £12.02 CT £42.28 TOTE £3.40: £1.80, £2.10; EX 14.20.
Owner S Henderson **Bred** Gerard Schence **Trained** Middleham Moor, N Yorks

FOCUS
A moderate contest in which the winner stole first run and the runner-up was unlucky not to give him something to do. The form looks relatively weak.

2158 BENFIELD RENAULT H'CAP — 7f
8:25 (8:25) (Class 3) (0-90,85) 4-Y-0 **£6,938** (£2,076; £1,038; £519; £258) **Stalls** High

Form RPR
4-06 1 **Southandwest (IRE)**[6] 1985 4-9-4 **85** RobertWinston 11 93
(J S Moore) *trckd ldrs on inner: nt clr run over 2f out: edgd lft 1f out: sn led: edgd rt: hld on towards fin* **5/1**[3]
00-2 2 hd **Il Castagno (IRE)**[14] 1774 5-8-13 **80** TomEaves 9 87
(B Smart) *led: qcknd 2f out: hdd ins fnl f: r.o* **3/1**[1]
0-00 3 1 1/2 **Countdown**[13] 1815 6-8-10 **77** DavidAllan 8 87+
(T D Easterby) *rrd s: hld up in mid-div: gd hdwy over 1f out: styng on same pce whn nt clr run towards fin* **14/1**
0601 4 3/4 **Daaweitza**[10] 1891 5-9-1 **82** 6ex PaulHanagan 1 83
(B Ellison) *prom: outpcd over 3f out: hdwy to chse ldrs 2f out: kpt on same pce fnl f* **7/1**
0046 5 3/4 **Jamieson Gold (IRE)**[41] 1218 5-8-13 **80** (p) PhillipMakin 4 79
(Miss L A Perratt) *hld up in rr: hdwy 2f out: nvr trbld ldrs* **11/1**
0-40 6 2 1/4 **Middlemarch (IRE)**[6] 1982 8-8-8 **80** (v) GaryBartley(5) 3 73
(J S Goldie) *hld up in rr: kpt on fnl 2f: nvr nr ldrs* **7/1**
354- 7 2 1/2 **Chicken Soup**[146] 7223 6-9-4 **85** SebSanders 5 71
(S Parr) *dwlt: sn trcking ldrs: n.m.r over 2f out: wknd appr fnl f* **7/1**
000- 8 2 1/4 **Baltimore Jack (IRE)**[195] 6639 4-8-7 **74** PaulMulrennan 7 54
(M W Easterby) *sn trcking ldr: wkng whn hmpd 1f out* **12/1**
460- 9 1 3/4 **Macedon**[188] 6753 5-8-12 **79** MickyFenton 6 54
(T P Tate) *chsd ldrs: outpcd over 3f out: hdwy 2f out: n.m.r and sn wknd* **4/1**[2]
0-00 10 1 1/2 **Jalamid (IRE)**[15] 1747 6-8-5 **72** oh26 ow1 (t) DeanMcKeown 2 43
(M A Barnes) *in rr: effrt on wd outside over 2f out: sn chsng ldrs: lost pl over 1f out* **28/1**

1m 26.45s (-0.95) **Going Correction** -0.175s/f (Firm) **10 Ran SP% 125.3**
Speed ratings (Par 107): **107,106,105,104,103 100,97,95,93,91**
CSF £22.09 CT £186.31 TOTE £8.00: £2.60, £1.80, £5.80; EX 26.60.
Owner Wall To Wall Partnership **Bred** Paul Hardy **Trained** Upper Lambourn, Berks
■ Stewards' Enquiry : Robert Winston one-day ban: careless riding (May 30)

FOCUS
A competitive handicap even though top-weight was 5lb below the race ceiling. The runner-up sets the standard with the third rate a half-length winner.

NOTEBOOK
Southandwest(IRE), a dual winner at two, was due to race from a 3lb lower mark next day. Tucked away on the inner he met traffic problems then caused trouble when edging out for a run. In the end he had to give his all. (op 11-2 tchd 9-2)
Il Castagno(IRE), 5lb higher than his last win almost a year ago, is a natural front-runner. He wound it up from the front and to his credit battled back all the way to the line. (op 4-1)
Countdown, who has never won before July, exited the stalls on his hind legs. He was on the heels of the first two when running out of racing room near the line. He is now 6lb lower than his last success and his time is not that far away now. (op 12-1)
Daaweitza, raised 4lb after his Catterick success, had a 6lb penalty. He could have done with a more flat out gallop and in the circumstances ran with plenty of credit. (op 11-2)
Jamieson Gold(IRE), running from his lowest ever mark, wore sidewhisker for the first time. His new stable will have had their hopes raised by this improved effort. (tchd 10-1)
Middlemarch(IRE), 5lb higher than his last success here in August, was well backed but he was set an impossible task and did well to finish as close as he did. (op 12-1)

2159 PARKLANDS MINIGOLF FAMILY TICKETS ONLY £10 FILLIES' H'CAP — 5f
8:55 (8:55) (Class 5) (0-70,68) 3-Y-0+ **£3,885** (£1,156; £577; £288) **Stalls** High

Form RPR
1-00 1 **Revue Princess (IRE)**[20] 1611 3-9-1 **65** DavidAllan 13 71
(T D Easterby) *trckd ldrs on inner: led 2f out: hld on wl towards fin* **10/1**
4060 2 3/4 **Lambency (IRE)**[6] 2009 5-8-7 **54** oh2 GaryBartley(5) 1 60+
(J S Goldie) *hld up towards rr on wl outside: gd hdwy over 1f out: edgd lft and no ex wl ins fnl f* **7/2**[1]
0-00 3 3/4 **Toy Top (USA)**[10] 1893 5-9-0 **56** (b) PhillipMakin 5 60
(M Dods) *led 1f: chsd ldrs: kpt on same pce ins fnl f* **8/1**[3]
060- 4 shd **Hansomis (IRE)**[305] 3583 4-8-12 **54** oh2 DaleGibson 12 57
(B Mactaggart) *towards rr: hdwy over 1f out: styd on ins fnl f* **22/1**
0-06 5 3/4 **Darcy's Pride (IRE)**[6] 1997 4-9-10 **66** FergalLynch 3 67
(D W Barker) *chsd ldrs: kpt on same pce fnl f* **7/2**[1]
00-0 6 1 **Miacarla**[35] 1309 5-8-12 **54** oh1 PatrickMathers 4 51
(H A McWilliams) *mid-div: effrt over 2f out: kpt on: nvr trbld ldrs* **16/1**
30-0 7 1 3/4 **Violet's Pride**[3] 2088 4-8-12 **54** oh9 KimTinkler 2 45
(N Tinkler) *mid-div: effrt over 2f out: kpt on same pce: nvr rchd ldrs* **16/1**
52-0 8 1/2 **Best Suited**[13] 1819 3-8-10 **60** GrahamGibbons 9 46
(J J Quinn) *s.i.s: in rr: kpt on fnl 2f: nvr on terms* **8/1**[3]
0035 9 1 **Princess Charlmane (IRE)**[28] 1454 5-8-5 **54** oh9.(t) DeclanCannon(7) 7 39
(C J Teague) *led after 1f tl 2f out: wknd appr fnl f* **25/1**
0032 10 6 **Baileys Outshine**[32] 1373 4-9-12 **68** RobertWinston 10 32
(J G Given) *mid-div: t.k.h: lost pl over 2f out: eased fnl f* **4/1**[2]
0-00 11 13 **Just Joey**[13] 1818 4-9-6 **62** DO'Donohoe 6 —
(J R Weymes) *in rr: reminders after 1f: sn bhd: eased over 1f out* **16/1**
2-55 12 8 **Firewalker**[105] 397 3-9-3 **67** TomEaves 11 —
(B Smart) *mid-div: lost pl over 2f out: bhd whn eased over 1f out* **16/1**

60.41 secs (-0.29) **Going Correction** -0.175s/f (Firm)
WFA 3 from 4yo+ 8lb **12 Ran SP% 127.5**
Speed ratings (Par 100): **95,93,92,92,91 89,86,86,84,74 54,41**
CSF £48.40 CT £315.07 TOTE £11.20: £2.60, £2.10, £3.50; EX 57.50 Place 6 £69.75, Place 5 £27.72.
Owner S A Heley **Bred** Raymond Shanahan **Trained** Great Habton, N Yorks

FOCUS
A low-grade distaff sprint handicap but the form seems sound.
Firewalker Official explanation: jockey said filly lost its action
T/Plt: £233.70 to a £1 stake. Pool: £49,926.87. 155.90 winning tickets. T/Qpdt: £15.60 to a £1 stake. Pool: £3,812.39. 180.15 winning tickets. WG

2117

NEWMARKET (ROWLEY) (R-H)

Friday, May 16

OFFICIAL GOING: Good to soft

Wind: Light across Weather: Overcast

2160 BETINTERNET.COM E B F MAIDEN FILLIES' STKS 6f

2:00 (2:02) (Class 4) 2-Y-O £4,533 (£1,348; £674; £336) Stalls High

Form RPR

1 **Full Of Nature** 2-9-0 0.. TPO'Shea 5 78+
(K A Ryan) *s.i.s: sn prom: rdn to chse ldr 2f out: styd on to ld wl ins fnl f* **18/1**

3 2 ½ **Mambo Light (USA)**[29] 1419 2-9-0 0.. TQuinn 9 77
(P F I Cole) *led: rdn over 1f out: edgd lft and hdd wl ins fnl f* **13/8**[1]

3 ½ **Honest Quality (USA)** 2-9-0 0.. TedDurcan 6 75+
(H R A Cecil) *chsd ldrs: lost pl over 4f out: hdwy over 1f out: nt clr run ins fnl f: r.o* **5/2**[2]

4 1 ¼ **Gal Aloud (USA)** 2-9-0 0.. PatDobbs 2 71+
(R Hannon) *chsd ldrs: rdn over 2f out: edgd lft and outpcd over 1f out: styd on ins fnl f* **15/2**[3]

5 ¾ **Cornish Rose (IRE)** 2-9-0 0.. JimmyQuinn 7 69+
(M H Tompkins) *sn outpcd: hdwy over 1f out: nt rch ldrs* **25/1**

6 5 **Africa's Star (IRE)** 2-9-0 0.. MichaelHills 3 54+
(M A Jarvis) *s.i.s: sn pushed along in rr: bmpd wl over 1f out: n.d* **10/1**

7 8 **Dubai Tsunami** 2-9-0 0.. StephenDonohoe 4 30
(E A L Dunlop) *chsd ldr 4f: sn rdn: hung rt and wknd* **14/1**

8 ¾ **Hosanna** 2-9-0.. JimmyFortune 1 28
(B J Meehan) *prom: rdn over 2f out: hung lft and wknd wl over 1f out* **9/1**

1m 15.42s (3.22) **Going Correction** +0.375s/f (Good) **8 Ran SP% 113.3**
Speed ratings (Par 92): **93,92,91,90,89 82,71,70**
CSF £46.99 TOTE £28.30: £5.50, £1.10, £1.20; EX 85.60.Betws Y Coed was withdrawn. Price at time of withdrawal 33/1. Rule 4 does not apply.
Owner M G White **Bred** Whitsbury Manor Stud **Trained** Hambleton, N Yorks
■ Stewards' Enquiry : T Quinn two-day ban: careless riding (May 30-31).

FOCUS
A decent-looking maiden featuring some well-bred newcomers and a solid-looking favourite. The form is not easy to rate at this stage but should stand up.

NOTEBOOK
Full Of Nature, a half-sister to four winners, including Secret Place and Ektimaal, wore down the favourite in the closing stages to record a win that the market had not expected. Using the runner-up as a guide, she could be good enough to go for something like the Albany Stakes. (op 16-1)
Mambo Light(USA), who ran a race full of promise behind Danehill Destiny at the Craven meeting in a race that has worked out well, looked to hold solid claims, and she tried to put that previous experience to good use by making the running. She was worn down close home by the Ryan newcomer, but the chances are this was a good race and she should soon make amends, especially on faster ground, as she is by Kingmambo. (tchd 15-8 and 6-4)
Honest Quality(USA), a half-sister to First Defence, a high-class colt who was placed at Group One level over 7f on dirt in the US, and to Phantom Rose, a dual 1m winner in France, was a bit unlucky as the gap she went for between the winner and runner-up closed on her half a furlong out. She might not have won with a clear run but she would have gone close, and she should not be long in putting the record straight. (op 4-1)
Gal Aloud(USA), whose dam was a triple sprint winner, including on turf, in the US, showed her greenness by wandering about under pressure, but she was keeping on again at the finish and should have learnt plenty from this. (op 8-1)
Cornish Rose(IRE), a half-sister to Simpsons Gamble, a dual 6f winner on Polytrack, struggled in the early stages but began to get the hang of what was required later on. She should improve for this debut and quicker ground will probably help her. (tchd 20-1)
Africa's Star(IRE), who cost 230,000euros, is the first foal of a mare from an excellent family. Her trainer's first juvenile runner of the year, she was green and got unbalanced running into the Dip. She will do better with this outing under her belt. (op 11-2)
Dubai Tsunami, whose dam is well related and won over 1m at three, tried to keep the favourite honest at the head of affairs and paid the price in the latter stages. She is bred to want quite a bit further in time.
Hosanna, whose dam was placed in the Park Hill Stakes, is an April foal and was the youngest filly in the field. She showed up well to 2f out but then hung left and weakened. She can do better in time. (op 11-1)

2161 WA HILLS H'CAP 1m

2:30 (2:32) (Class 5) (0-75,75) 3-Y-O £3,885 (£1,156; £577; £288) Stalls High

Form RPR

0-33 1 **Mexican Venture**[26] 1504 3-9-3 **74**.. LDettori 13 82
(W Jarvis) *s.i.s: hld up: racd centre: hdwy over 2f out: led over 1f out: drvn out* **6/1**[1]

61-4 2 ½ **Astrodonna**[24] 1540 3-8-13 **70**.. JimmyQuinn 12 77
(M H Tompkins) *hld up: racd centre: hdwy over 2f out: rdn to chse wnr fnl f: r.o* **11/1**

55-4 3 ½ **Game Park (USA)**[14] 1781 3-9-1 **72**.. JimmyFortune 4 78+
(J R Fanshawe) *hld up: racd centre: swtchd rt over 2f out: hdwy and hmpd wl over 1f out: sn rdn: r.o* **10/1**

2101 4 3 ¼ **Desiderio**[7] 1958 3-8-7 **71** 6ex..............................(b) CharlesEddery(7) 19 69
(R Hannon) *led far side trio: overall ldr over 4f out: hdd over 3f out: sn rdn: edgd rt over 1f out: styd on same pce fnl f* **8/1**[3]

0-60 5 hd **Mr Fantozzi (IRE)**[42] 1186 3-7-11 **61** oh1..............................(b[1]) AmyBaker(7) 8 59
(Miss J Feilden) *overall ldr in centre over 3f: rdn over 2f out: styd on same pce fnl f* **50/1**

-000 6 ½ **Averoo**[23] 1572 3-8-5 **62**.. RichardKingscote 6 59
(M D Squance) *hld up: racd centre: swtchd rt over 2f out: hdwy and hmpd over 1f out: nt rch ldrs* **33/1**

02-4 7 1 ¼ **Hyde Lea Flyer**[15] 1750 3-9-2 **73**.. StephenDonohoe 15 67
(E S McMahon) *s.i.s: hld up: racd far side: hdwy to chse ldr 5f out: led that gp and overall ldr over 3f out: rdn: edgd lft and hdd over 1f out: wknd ins fnl f* **17/2**

316 8 ¾ **Sir Billy Nick**[18] 1686 3-9-4 **75**.. TPQueally 14 67
(J Noseda) *racd centre: chsd ldrs: rdn over 2f out: wknd fnl f* **6/1**[1]

5-22 9 4 ½ **Totally Focussed (IRE)**[24] 1546 3-9-2 **73**.. IanMongan 2 55
(S Dow) *hmpd s: racd centre: hld up: hdwy u.p over 2f out: wknd fnl f* **7/1**[2]

0-23 10 1 ¼ **Maximus Aurelius (IRE)**[24] 1540 3-8-11 **71**.. LukeMorris(3) 1 50
(J Jay) *racd centre: chsd ldrs: rdn and wknd over 1f out* **14/1**

10-0 11 nk **Writingonthewall (IRE)**[28] 1448 3-9-2 **73**.. DaneO'Neill 5 51
(M L W Bell) *racd centre: mid-div: rdn over 3f out: wknd over 2f out* **16/1**

060- 12 1 ¾ **Wabbraan (USA)**[205] 6436 3-8-6 **68**.. AhmedAjtebi(5) 18 42
(D M Simcock) *chsd ldr far side 3f: rdn and wknd over 1f out* **33/1**

5-06 13 4 **Redsensor**[60] 918 3-8-11 **68**.. FrancisNorton 17 33
(M Quinn) *racd centre: chsd ldrs: rdn over 3f out: wknd 2f out* **20/1**

0-60 14 2 **King's Alchemist**[17] 1695 3-8-3 **63**.. KirstyMilczarek(3) 3 24
(M D I Usher) *hmpd s: racd centre: a in rr* **16/1**

00-0 15 3 ¼ **Rescue Me**[18] 1671 3-8-12 **69**.. PatDobbs 10 22
(R Hannon) *s.i.s: racd centre: hld up: hdwy over 3f out: rdn and wknd 2f out* **28/1**

030- 16 4 ½ **Art Value**[161] 7051 3-9-2 **73**.. AdrianMcCarthy 7 16
(P W Chapple-Hyam) *racd centre: mid-div: rdn over 4f out: wknd 3f out* **14/1**

435- 17 23 **Southern Mistral**[228] 5871 3-8-9 **66**.. TGMcLaughlin 16 —
(M Wigham) *racd centre: hld up: wknd over 3f out* **16/1**

1m 41.2s (2.60) **Going Correction** +0.375s/f (Good) **17 Ran SP% 127.2**
Speed ratings (Par 99): **102,101,101,97,97 97,95,95,90,89 89,87,83,81,78 73,50**
CSF £69.59 CT £692.98 TOTE £5.70: £1.60, £3.70, £2.00, £2.30; EX 100.10.
Owner The Mexican Venture Partnership **Bred** Leydens Farm Stud **Trained** Newmarket, Suffolk
■ Stewards' Enquiry : Luke Morris one-day ban: failed to ride to draw (Jun 8)
Charles Eddery caution: careless riding

FOCUS
A competitive three-year-old handicap in which the first three came clear. The fourth is probably the best guide to the level having come here on the back of a personal best, but the proximity of the fifth and sixth does not do a lot for the value of the form.
King's Alchemist Official explanation: jockey said colt suffered interference immediately after start

2162 PLAY LIVE DEALER CASINO AT BETINTERNET.COM H'CAP 6f

3:00 (3:01) (Class 3) (0-95,95) 3-Y-O £9,066 (£2,697; £1,348; £673) Stalls High

Form RPR

1- 1 **Wingbeat (USA)**[206] 6409 3-8-9 **86**.. LDettori 5 100+
(Saeed Bin Suroor) *trckd ldrs in centre: racd keenly: led over 1f out: shkn up and r.o* **1/1**[1]

00-0 2 1 ¼ **Spanish Bounty**[30] 1404 3-8-10 **87**.. TPQueally 1 93
(J G Portman) *chsd ldr in centre: rdn and ev ch over 1f out: styd on same pce fnl f* **33/1**

12-6 3 1 ½ **Striking Spirit**[30] 1404 3-8-13 **90**.. MichaelHills 2 91
(B W Hills) *led cntre over 4f, no ex fnl f* **2/1**[2]

60-3 4 ¾ **Shifting Star (IRE)**[14] 1764 3-8-4 **81**.. JimmyQuinn 6 80
(W R Swinburn) *rcd alone fr side to1/2 way: overall ldr over 4f, no ex fnl f* **5/1**[3]

0-10 5 3 ¾ **Vhujon (IRE)**[30] 1404 3-9-4 **95**.. TGMcLaughlin 7 82
(P D Evans) *s.i.s: hld up plld hrd: racd centre tl swtchd to far side 1/2-way: rdn and wknd over 1f out* **14/1**

1m 14.76s (2.56) **Going Correction** +0.375s/f (Good) **5 Ran SP% 109.6**
Speed ratings (Par 103): **97,95,93,92,87**
CSF £28.00 TOTE £1.90: £1.40, £4.70; EX 30.90.
Owner Godolphin **Bred** Darley **Trained** Newmarket, Suffolk

FOCUS
An interesting little sprint but they only went an ordinary gallop and the form could be rated higher. The winner looks one to keep on-side, though.

NOTEBOOK
Wingbeat(USA) ◆, easy winner of a backend Yarmouth maiden on his only start at two, raced a bit keenly off the ordinary pace, but he picked up well when Dettori pressed the button and came home for a clear win under just a hand ride. He has Group 1 entries in the St James's Palace Stakes and Golden Jubilee Stakes, but is likely to go for a conditions or Listed race next. (tchd 6-5)
Spanish Bounty looked to bounce back to the best of his two-year-old form in chasing home the easy winner, but whether this was a flash in the pan or a sign that he is returning to form remains to be seen.
Striking Spirit, who led the main group, could not confirm recent course form with Spanish Bounty in this smaller field, and this must go down as a disappointing effort. In fairness, though, the ground was softer than he had encountered before. (op 7-4 tchd 13-8)
Shifting Star(IRE), who made a pleasing return on the Polytrack earlier in the month, raced apart from the rest for a fair way. He too was racing on ground that was softer than he had encountered before, and was below his best. (op 8-1)
Vhujon(IRE) was taken over the far-side rail in search of better ground, but the ploy failed. (op 11-1 tchd 10-1)

2163 GET BEST ODDS GUARANTEED AT BETINTERNET.COM H'CAP 7f

3:35 (3:36) (Class 3) (0-95,94) 4-Y-O+ £9,066 (£2,697; £1,348; £673) Stalls High

Form RPR

3-53 1 **Froissee**[9] 1910 4-8-4 **80** oh4.. TPO'Shea 2 88
(S A Callaghan) *hld up: hdwy over 2f out: chsd ldr over 1f out: rdn to ld ins fnl f: jst hld on* **12/1**

-504 2 hd **Compton's Eleven**[6] 2013 7-8-6 **82**.. TedDurcan 4 89
(M R Channon) *hld up: swtchd lft 1/2-way: hdwy u.p over 1f out: r.o wl* **15/2**

1-14 3 ½ **Transcend**[14] 1765 4-9-4 **94**.. JimmyFortune 3 100
(J H M Gosden) *hld up: hdwy over 1f out: sn rdn: styd on* **13/8**[1]

206- 4 1 ¾ **King's Caprice**[161] 7053 7-9-1 **91**..............................(t) DaneO'Neill 7 92
(J A Geake) *led and sn clr: rdn over 1f out: edgd lft: hdd and no ex ins fnl f* **16/1**

51-2 5 2 ½ **King's Bastion (IRE)**[34] 1327 4-8-1 **80** oh2.. LukeMorris(3) 1 74
(M L W Bell) *trckd ldrs: racd keenly: rdn over 1f out: wknd ins fnl f* **7/2**[2]

-300 6 1 ½ **Trafalgar Square**[6] 1982 6-8-7 **86**.. KirstyMilczarek(3) 6 76
(M J Attwater) *chsd ldrs: rdn whn hmpd over 2f out: wknd fnl f* **9/2**[3]

6-45 7 1 **The Kiddykid (IRE)**[7] 1942 8-8-9 **85**.. TGMcLaughlin 5 72
(P D Evans) *chsd clr ldr: hung rt and reminder over 4f out: wknd fnl f* **9/1**

1m 27.04s (1.64) **Going Correction** +0.375s/f (Good) **7 Ran SP% 113.8**
Speed ratings (Par 107): **105,104,104,102,99 97,96**
CSF £94.57 TOTE £14.20: £4.00, £3.30; EX 102.30.
Owner Mrs T A Foreman **Bred** Rosyground Stud **Trained** Newmarket, Suffolk
■ Stewards' Enquiry : T G McLaughlin two-day ban: careless riding (May 30-31)

FOCUS
A fair handicap run at a good gallop. The winner is progressive and the form looks solid rated through the third.

NOTEBOOK
Froissee was 4lb out of the handicap but the ground had changed in her favour and they went a decent pace, which suits her. Dropping back in distance, she travelled up well two furlongs out and, once shaken up, picked up to take the leader's measure. She does not seem to like being in front too soon and the runner-up was closing fast at the finish, but she probably won with a bit more in hand than the margin suggests. Her style of running means she might be able to keep one step ahead of the Handicapper, but her trainer plans to turn her out quickly under a penalty. (op 8-1)
Compton's Eleven has a poor strike-rate but he likes a good pace to run off and that is what he got here. Closing down the winner at the line, he might well have got up in a few more yards, but there is no guarantee that he will repeat this effort next time. (op 9-1 tchd 10-1)
Transcend, who did not have things fall right on the Polytrack last time, still looked fairly treated on a mark of 94, and the easing of the ground played to his strengths. In the circumstances this was a disappointing effort. (op 6-4 tchd 7-4)

King's Caprice, the only confirmed front-runner in the field, looked sure to gain an uncontested lead, and so it proved, as he had a clear lead at halfway. However, he had not run since December, and setting a good gallop eventually told on him. He should come on for the outing and is well handicapped on his best form. (op 14-1)
King's Bastion(IRE), 2lb wrong at the weights, was too keen for his own good and taking on a grade of opposition he is not used to. He is better than this. (op 4-1 tchd 10-3)
Trafalgar Square, who won this race last year on his seasonal reappearance off a 2lb lower mark, is an in-and-out performer, and this was not one of his better efforts. Official explanation: jockey said gelding ran flat (op 8-1)
The Kiddykid(IRE) is probably more effective around a sharp track over this sort of distance. (op 15-2 tchd 13-2)

2164 FA CUP FINAL AT BETINTERNET.COM MAIDEN FILLIES' STKS 1m 4f
4:10 (4:13) (Class 4) 3-Y-O £5,180 (£1,541; £770; £384) Stalls Centre

Form RPR
55- **1** **Inchwood (IRE)**[206] 6414 3-9-0 0 JimmyQuinn 8 75
(M A Jarvis) *s.i.s: hld up: hdwy over 3f out: led over 2f out: rdn out* **8/1**[3]
5 **2** *1/2* **Maria Di Scozia**[83] 674 3-9-0 0 AdrianMcCarthy 1 75
(P W Chapple-Hyam) *hld up: hdwy over 2f out: sn rdn: r.o* **66/1**
23 **3** *hd* **Victoria Montoya**[24] 1542 3-9-0 0 FrancisNorton 4 74
(A M Balding) *chsd ldr: rdn over 2f out: r.o* **5/1**[2]
5 **4** *hd* **Gravitation**[28] 1444 3-9-0 0 TQuinn 5 74
(W Jarvis) *hld up: nt clr run over 2f out: swtchd rt and hdwy over 1f out: r.o* **4/1**[1]
320- **5** *1 3/4* **Saleima (IRE)**[195] 6652 3-9-0 78 LDettori 9 71
(P W Chapple-Hyam) *hld up in tch: nt clr run over 2f out: swtchd lft and outpcd over 1f out: r.o ins fnl f* **4/1**[1]
06-5 **6** *1/2* **Hamsat Elqamar**[12] 1840 3-9-0 0 JimmyFortune 13 70
(J H M Gosden) *chsd ldr: rdn and ev ch over 2f out: no ex fnl f* **12/1**
7 *11* **Single Vote** 3-9-0 0 TedDurcan 12 53
(H R A Cecil) *s.i.s: sn prom: rdn and ev ch over 2f out: hung lft and wknd over 1f out* **4/1**[1]
0- **8** *4* **Montreal (GER)**[203] 6470 3-9-0 0 TPQueally 2 46
(H R A Cecil) *s.i.s: hld up: rdn over 3f out: a in rr: bhd whn hung rt over 1f out* **20/1**
0- **9** *8* **Zia Zabel (IRE)**[203] 6470 3-9-0 0 TPO'Shea 6 34
(J L Dunlop) *prom: rdn over 4f out: wknd over 3f out* **14/1**
0-0 **10** *2* **Marie Tempest**[28] 1440 3-9-0 0 MichaelHills 11 30
(B W Hills) *led: rdn and hdd over 2f out: wkng whn hmpd wl over 1f out* **33/1**
0 **11** *23* **Pure Song**[28] 1444 3-9-0 0 DaneO'Neill 7 —
(J L Dunlop) *chsd ldrs over 8f* **12/1**
2m 37.38s (3.88) **Going Correction** +0.375s/f (Good) **11** Ran SP% **119.0**
Speed ratings (Par 98): **102,101,101,101,100 99,92,89,84,83 67**
CSF £457.79 TOTE £8.70: £2.20, £9.10, £2.00; EX 586.00.
Owner Sheikh Ahmed Al Maktoum **Bred** Woodcote Stud Ltd **Trained** Newmarket, Suffolk
■ Stewards' Enquiry : L Dettori caution: careless riding.
FOCUS
A fairly steady early pace led to a bunch finish. The form might not be totally reliable, although the fifth set a fair standard beforehand.
Pure Song Official explanation: jockey said filly stopped quickly

2165 BETINTERNET.COM H'CAP 1m 2f
4:45 (4:47) (Class 5) (0-75,72) 4-Y-O+ £3,885 (£1,156; £577; £288) Stalls High

Form RPR
1-13 **1** **Sir Duke (IRE)**[23] 1564 4-8-12 66 FrancisNorton 5 75
(P W D'Arcy) *a.p: rdn and hung rt fr over 2f out: led over 1f out: styd on u.p* **13/2**[3]
0-52 **2** *3/4* **King Of Rhythm (IRE)**[7] 1963 5-9-2 70 TedDurcan 4 77
(D Carroll) *hld up: hdwy over 2f out: rdn to chse wnr and hung rt fnl f: styd on* **7/2**[2]
4-00 **3** *2* **Sintenis Mac (GER)**[14] 1780 5-8-1 58 oh5 LukeMorris(3) 1 61
(P J O'Gorman) *hld up: hdwy over 4f out: led over 2f out: rdn: hung lft and hdd over 1f out: styng on same pce whn hung rt towards fin* **12/1**
2-12 **4** *1/2* **Granary**[25] 1520 4-9-2 70 DaneO'Neill 3 72
(H Candy) *hld up: hdwy and hung rt over 1f out: nt rch ldrs* **7/2**[2]
0-26 **5** *1 1/4* **Billy One Punch**[48] 1085 6-8-12 66 TPQueally 8 66
(D Shaw) *s.i.s: hld up: hdwy over 2f out: rdn over 1f out: no ex fnl f* **14/1**
0231 **6** *7* **Resplendent Ace (IRE)**[23] 1564 4-8-10 64 JimmyQuinn 6 50
(P Howling) *hld up in tch: rdn over 2f out: wknd over 1f out* **8/1**
23-1 **7** *10* **Smirfy's Silver**[20] 1620 4-8-13 67 StephenDonohoe 9 33
(E S McMahon) *chsd ldr 8f out: rdn and wknd over 2f out* **11/4**[1]
-000 **8** *1* **Old Romney**[16] 1732 4-8-7 64 KirstyMilczarek(3) 2 28
(M Wigham) *led: clr 1/2-way: hdd & wknd over 2f out* **33/1**
/03- **9** *39* **Montrose Man**[177] 6901 4-9-4 72 JimmyFortune 7 —
(B J Meehan) *trckd ldrs: racd keenly: wknd and eased over 2f out* **20/1**
2m 7.51s (1.71) **Going Correction** +0.375s/f (Good) **9** Ran SP% **117.6**
Speed ratings (Par 103): **108,107,105,105,104 98,90,90,58**
CSF £30.11 CT £271.14 TOTE £6.90: £1.90, £1.70, £3.40; EX 29.40.
Owner Mrs Jan Harris **Bred** Southern Bloodstock **Trained** Newmarket, Suffolk
FOCUS
A modest contest but straightforward form to rate, with the first four all running close to their pre-race marks.
Montrose Man Official explanation: jockey said gelding moved badly and hung left

2166 CHAMPIONS LEAGUE FINAL AT BETINTERNET.COM H'CAP 5f
5:20 (5:20) (Class 4) (0-80,79) 4-Y-O+ £4,857 (£1,445; £722; £360) Stalls High

Form RPR
5031 **1** **What Do You Know**[19] 1646 5-9-2 77 (v) DavidKinsella 7 87
(A M Hales) *mde all: rdn over 1f out: edgd lft fnl f: r.o* **4/1**[2]
30-0 **2** *3/4* **Millfields Dreams**[27] 1488 9-8-1 65 oh6 (p) LukeMorris(3) 10 72
(P Leech) *a.p: rdn to chse wnr fnl f: hung lft: r.o* **12/1**
00-1 **3** *3/4* **Dragon Flame (IRE)**[28] 1454 5-8-5 66 (v) FrancisNorton 2 70
(M Quinn) *stmbld s: sn chsng ldr: rdn 1/2-way: outpcd over 1f out: r.o ins fnl f* **11/1**[3]
1113 **4** *1 3/4* **After The Show**[15] 1739 7-8-13 74 JimmyFortune 9 72
(Rae Guest) *hld up: rdn over 1f out: nt trble ldrs* **15/8**[1]
26-3 **5** *1* **Pretty Miss**[24] 1537 4-8-11 72 FergusSweeney 4 66
(H Candy) *hld up: hdwy 2f out: sn rdn: wknd ins fnl f* **15/8**[1]
000- **6** *4* **Bold Minstrel (IRE)**[161] 7059 6-8-9 70 TPQueally 1 50
(M Quinn) *hld up: rdn 1/2-way: wknd fnl f* **20/1**
60.23 secs (1.13) **Going Correction** +0.375s/f (Good) **6** Ran SP% **110.4**
Speed ratings (Par 105): **105,103,102,99,98 91**
CSF £44.44 CT £456.80 TOTE £4.60: £2.00, £5.40; EX 69.20 Place 6 £776.38, Place 5 £564.46..
Owner Brick Farm Racing **Bred** C G Reid **Trained** Preston Capes, Northants

FOCUS
A fairly average handicap and there are doubts over the form with the runner-up 6lb wrong at the weights.
T/Plt: £426.00 to a £1 stake. Pool: £54,311.20. 93.05 winning tickets. T/Qpdt: £168.00 to a £1 stake. Pool: £2,316.89. 10.20 winning tickets. CR

2129 YORK (L-H)
Friday, May 16

OFFICIAL GOING: Good to firm (9.0)
Wind: Virtually nil Weather: Overcast

2167 LANGLEYS SOLICITORS EBF MARYGATE STKS (LISTED RACE) (FILLIES) 5f
1:40 (1:40) (Class 1) 2-Y-O £14,815 (£5,602; £2,800; £1,400) Stalls High

Form RPR
11 **1** **Bahamian Babe**[28] 1447 2-8-12 0 HayleyTurner 9 93
(M L W Bell) *cl up: led after 1 1/2f: hdd wl over 1f out: rdn to ld ins fnl f: edgd lft and kpt on wl* **6/1**[3]
1 **2** *1/2* **Langs Lash (IRE)**[15] 1736 2-8-12 0 AlanMunro 10 91
(M G Quinlan) *in tch: hdwy to chse ldrs 2f out and sn rdn: drvn and styd on to chal ins fnl f: no ex towards fin* **8/1**
12 **3** *1/2* **Aspen Darlin (IRE)**[9] 1914 2-8-12 0 PaulHanagan 7 89
(A Bailey) *hmpd s and bhd: swtchd outside and hdwy over 1f out: sn rdn and styd on strly ins fnl f: nrst fin* **6/1**[3]
13 **4** *1/2* **Doughnut**[8] 1927 2-8-12 0 RyanMoore 4 88
(R Hannon) *led 1 1/2f: cl up: rdn along 2f out and ev ch tl drvn and one pce ins fnl f* **7/1**
2 **5** *3/4* **Fazbee (IRE)**[18] 1680 2-8-12 0 DarryllHolland 5 85
(P W D'Arcy) *chsd ldrs: rdn along 2f out: sn drvn and one pce appr fnl f* **4/1**[2]
331 **6** *1* **Knavesmire (IRE)**[15] 1749 2-8-12 0 PhilipRobinson 11 81
(M Brittain) *towards rr: hdwy 2f out: sn rdn and kpt on ins fnl f: nt rch ldrs* **20/1**
1 **7** *1/2* **To The Point**[11] 1866 2-8-12 0 RichardMullen 3 80
(E S McMahon) *wnt lft s: trckd ldrs: smooth hdwy on outer 2f out: qcknd to ld wl over 1f out: sn rdn: hdd ins fnl f and sn wknd* **7/2**[1]
13 **8** *3 1/2* **Lisburn (IRE)**[13] 1813 2-8-12 0 TWilliams 8 67
(M Brittain) *prom: rdn along 1/2-way: sn wknd* **25/1**
11 **9** *nse* **Dispol Kylie (IRE)**[13] 1813 2-8-12 0 JamieMoriarty 6 67
(P T Midgley) *wnt rt s: sn cl up tl rdn along 2f out and sn wknd* **15/2**
59.62 secs (0.32) **Going Correction** +0.125s/f (Good) **9** Ran SP% **114.8**
Speed ratings (Par 98): **102,101,100,99,98 96,96,90,90**
CSF £52.66 TOTE £6.70: £2.20, £2.60, £2.20; EX 72.00 Trifecta £122.00 Pool: £515.70. 3.00 winning units..
Owner Mrs P D Gray And H J P Farr **Bred** Mrs P D Gray And H Farr **Trained** Newmarket, Suffolk
FOCUS
The fourth running of this Listed event, which has quickly developed into a good trial for the Queen Mary and Albany Stakes at Royal Ascot. Eight of the nine fillies in this line-up had already notched a win and it looked a competitive heat; the form is not that solid although it can be given a chance.
NOTEBOOK
Bahamian Babe, a winner of her first two starts on Fibresand and good to soft ground, had to prove she could be as effective on this quicker surface. She answered in the affirmative, indeed her rider insisted it was an advantage afterwards, for she did not hang left as she had on her previous two starts. Having shown up prominently from the start, she kept on strongly to fend off the closers, but it is questionable whether this is Queen Mary winning form. She deserves to take her chance at the Royal meeting, though, and was given an 8-1 quote by Coral. (op 5-1)
Langs Lash(IRE), clear winner of an ordinary maiden at Folkestone on her debut, had a lot more on her plate here, but the quicker ground promised to suit this daughter of Noverre and, seeing her race out well, gave every indication that she will be suited by another furlong. (op 15-2)
Aspen Darlin(IRE), for whom this sharp 5f was a worry beforehand, was slowly away but predictably put in some good late work. She shapes as though she will be very much suited by a step up to 6f and the Albany Stakes will surely be her Royal Ascot target. (tchd 11-2)
Doughnut, in contrast, showed great early speed but did not quite get home. (op 8-1)
Fazbee(IRE) was the only maiden in the field but she had shown just as much in getting beaten by Beat Seven on her debut as a number of these had done in winning their maidens. She ran alright on this step up in grade and will have no trouble winning a little race. (op 6-1)
Knavesmire(IRE), the most experienced filly in the line-up, had done all her previous racing on softish ground and she struggled to go the early pace in this better company on this quicker surface.
To The Point was the disappointment of the race. She promised to be suited by conditions and showed good early speed and travelled well in the van to 2f out, but once she came under pressure she did not find as much as expected and was swamped inside the last. She must be better than this. (tchd 4-1 in places)
Lisburn(IRE) was well beaten, but she still managed to reverse recent Thirsk form with Dispol Kylie. It is possible that she needs softer ground to be seen at her best.
Dispol Kylie(IRE) was disappointing, dropping right out after travelling perhaps too strongly towards the front end to the quarter-mile pole. Official explanation: trainer said filly had scoped dirty after race (tchd 8-1)

2168 RELAND JORVIK STKS (HERITAGE H'CAP) 1m 4f
2:10 (2:10) (Class 2) (0-105,104) 4-Y-O+
£31,155 (£9,330; £4,665; £2,335; £1,165; £585) Stalls Centre

Form RPR
0-22 **1** **Luberon**[26] 1503 5-8-7 87 JoeFanning 9 97
(M Johnston) *led: qcknd 4f out: rdn and qcknd again over 2f out: styd on wl fnl f* **6/1**[2]
50-0 **2** *1/2* **Pevensey (IRE)**[23] 1569 6-8-11 91 GrahamGibbons 8 100+
(J J Quinn) *hld up in midfield: hdwy on inner 4f out: rdn over 1f out: styd on strly u.p ins fnl f* **20/1**
23-1 **3** *1 1/4* **Sugar Ray (IRE)**[24] 1531 4-8-13 93 RyanMoore 3 100
(Sir Michael Stoute) *a.p: effrt 3f out: rdn to chse wnr over 1f out: sn drvn and edgd lft ins fnl f: kpt on same pce* **3/1**[1]
01-2 **4** *1* **Furmigadelagiusta**[48] 1070 4-9-4 98 JMurtagh 15 103
(K R Burke) *hld up in midfield: hdwy on outer 3f out: rdn to chse ldrs 2f out: drvn and ev ch whn edgd lft ent fnl f: kpt on same pce* **18/1**
-011 **5** *nse* **Watamu (IRE)**[14] 1766 7-9-10 104 (v) SebSanders 1 109
(P J Makin) *trckd ldrs: hdwy 3f out: rdn wl over 1f out: drvn and hld whn n.m.r and wknd ins fnl f* **12/1**
110- **6** *5* **Pippa Greene**[188] 6759 4-9-3 97 NCallan 2 94
(P F I Cole) *plld hrd: chsd ldrs whn stmbld bdly after 1f: styd in tch: effrt over 3f out: sn rdn along and kpt on same pce fnl 2f* **7/1**[3]

1-00 **7** ¾ **Gordonsville**[35] 1299 5-7-12 78 oh2 NickyMackay 13 74
(J S Goldie) *chsd ldrs: rdn along over 3f out: drvn over 2f out and kpt on same pce* **25/1**

3410 **8** 2¼ **Sgt Schultz (IRE)**[48] 1076 5-8-12 92 DarryllHolland 11 85
(J S Moore) *s.i.s and bhd: hdwy on inner 3f out: rdn along and kpt on fnl 2f: nt rch ldrs* **33/1**

032- **9** hd **Bergonzi (IRE)**[233] 5724 4-8-7 87 RichardMullen 4 79
(J Howard Johnson) *hld up in rr: hdwy 3f out: sn rdn and kpt on: nt rch ldrs* **28/1**

-141 **10** 1½ **Birkside**[2] 2107 5-7-11 84 6ex JamieKyne(7) 7 74
(D Carroll) *hld up in rr: effrt whn n.m.r 3f out: sn rdn and nvr nr ldrs* **8/1**

1160 **11** ½ **Basalt (IRE)**[7] 1947 4-8-3 83 GregFairley 10 72
(T J Pitt) *chsd wnr: rdn along 4f out: wknd 3f out* **28/1**

153- **12** 7 **Dansili Dancer**[251] 5215 6-9-9 103 PhilipRobinson 12 81
(C G Cox) *in tch: effrt to chse ldrs 3f out: sn rdn along and wknd over 1f out* **8/1**

4-34 **13** 2 **Rayhani (USA)**[13] 1812 5-8-13 93 AlanMunro 5 68
(M P Tregoning) *dwlt: a towards rr* **8/1**

00-0 **14** 1 **Peruvian Prince (USA)**[23] 1569 6-8-6 86 PaulHanagan 16 59
(R A Fahey) *hld up in rr: effrt and sme hdwy on outer whn edgd lft 3f out: sn rdn and nvr a factor* **22/1**

6- **15** 3 **Lepido (ITY)**[377] 1475 4-8-13 93 PatCosgrave 14 61
(L M Cumani) *plld hrd in midfield: effrt and sme hdwy over 3f out: sn rdn and wknd* **33/1**

2m 32.08s (-1.12) **Going Correction** +0.025s/f (Good) **15** Ran SP% **123.8**
Speed ratings (Par 109): **104,103,102,102,102 98,98,96,96,95 95,90,89,88,86**
CSF £126.86 CT £436.06 TOTE £6.50: £2.20, £6.80, £1.80; EX 106.60 Trifecta £912.30 Part won. Pool: £1285.04. 0.40 winning units..
Owner Brian Yeardley Continental Ltd **Bred** Card Bloodstock **Trained** Middleham Moor, N Yorks

FOCUS
A decent middle-distance handicap, but it was very much a tactical affair with the early pace steady. The form appears sound enough despite the winner getting the run of the race.

NOTEBOOK
Luberon, who had rediscovered his form on Polytrack of late, got to race off a 12lb lower mark back on turf, and given that this time last year he was rated 105 it was not difficult to see why he was popular in the market having been available at 9-1 in the morning. Granted an easy lead on a track which often favours those who race handily, he took full advantage, setting a steady gallop, but he was travelling best approaching the 2f marker and, when kicked for home, was never going to be caught. Even after reassessment he will remain well handicapped on his best form, so he will not be one to dismiss when he tries to follow up, perhaps in the Duke of Edinburgh Stakes at Royal Ascot.
Pevensey(IRE), down to a mark 1lb higher than when successful at Royal Ascot last summer, came through from off the pace with a challenge up the inside rail. He shaped well considering that the early pace would not have seen him to best advantage, and presumably a return to Ascot and an attempt to notch another win in the Duke of Edinburgh Stakes is the plan. (tchd 16-1)
Sugar Ray(IRE) had few excuses as he was always well placed if good enough tracking the leader on the rail. It just seemed to be a case of him finding the 8lb higher mark too much to handle against better rivals. (op 4-1)
Furmigadelagiusta may need softer ground to be seen at his very best, but he had been put up 6lb for running second in a conditions event on his reappearance and that put paid to his chances here. (op 16-1)
Watamu(IRE), a progressive performer on Polytrack, was running on turf for the first time since August 2004. He looked to have a bit to do off a 5lb higher mark than when last successful, though, and probably ran as well as could be expected. (op 11-1 tchd 10-1)
Pippa Greene deserves plenty of credit as he stumbled or clipped heels and almost got rid of his rider early in the race. He recovered well but he was very keen to get on with things on his reappearance and simply did too much in the early stages. This was only his fifth-ever start and one can expect further improvement from him, especially in a stronger-run race, and perhaps with some cut in the ground. (op 15-2 tchd 8-1)
Gordonsville was 2lb wrong at the weights but the ground was back in his favour. Having shown stamina for 1m6f though, he would have preferred a stronger pace over this distance. (tchd 28-1)
Sgt Schultz(IRE) was running off a 12lb higher mark than when last seen on the turf, although he had won two races on Polytrack in the interim. In last place 3f out, he was another not suited by the way this race was run. Official explanation: jockey said gelding missed the break
Bergonzi(IRE), sold out of John Gosden's yard for 140,000gns in October, lacked a recent run and was racing off a career-high mark, so he had plenty on his plate. He finished well having not enjoyed the best of runs though, and should be all the better for the run. (op 33-1)
Birkside, a winner of 11 of his last 17 starts, was tackling much tougher opposition than he normally encounters - he had done all his previous racing in Class 4 company or lower on the Flat. Official explanation: jockey said he lost his stirrup 3f out
Dansili Dancer dropped out when the pace hotted up, as though in need of this seasonal reappearance. (op 10-1)
Rayhani(USA) was very disappointing, never getting involved from off the pace. (op 9-1)

2169 EMIRATES AIRLINE YORKSHIRE CUP (GROUP 2) 1m 6f
2:40 (2:42) (Class 1) 4-Y-0+

£79,478 (£30,128; £15,078; £7,518; £3,766; £1,890) **Stalls** Low

Form RPR

522- **1** **Geordieland (FR)**[221] 6054 7-8-12 114 ShaneKelly 2 119
(J A Osborne) *hld up and bhd: smooth hdwy 3f out: nt clr run and swtchd rt 2f out: n.m.r over 1f out: chsd wnr ins fnl f: styd on strly to chal whn edgd fnl strides: led on line* **13/2**[3]

31-1 **2** hd **Royal And Regal (IRE)**[27] 1468 4-8-12 116 NCallan 6 119
(M A Jarvis) *led: rdn clr over 2f out: drvn ins fnl f: edgd rt fnl strides: hdd on line* **3/1**[2]

320- **3** 5 **Samuel**[244] 5408 4-8-12 103 EddieAhern 4 112
(J L Dunlop) *chsd ldr: rdn along over 3f out: drvn 2f out: kpt on same pce u.p appr fnl f* **16/1**

330- **4** shd **Honolulu (IRE)**[208] 6374 4-8-12 0 JMurtagh 1 112
(A P O'Brien, Ire) *hld up in tch: effrt over 3f out and sn rdn along: drvn wl over 1f out: styd on same pce* **5/4**[1]

65-0 **5** 8 **Sergeant Cecil**[27] 1468 9-8-12 108 AlanMunro 5 101
(B R Millman) *hld up towards rr: hdwy and in tch over 5f out: rdn along 4f out: sn drvn and btn over 2f out* **11/1**

63-3 **6** 1¼ **Alfie Flits**[19] 1655 6-8-12 106 RobertWinston 7 99
(G A Swinbank) *t.k.h: chsd ldrs: rdn along 3f out: drvn 2f out and sn wknd* **12/1**

33-0 **7** 5 **Veenwouden**[44] 1158 4-8-9 105 KerrinMcEvoy 8 89
(E F Vaughan) *hld up: a in rr* **50/1**

25-0 **8** ½ **Young Mick**[6] 1980 6-8-12 108 (v) RyanMoore 3 91
(G G Margarson) *prom: hdwy 6f out: rdn along 3f out: drvn over 2f out and sn wknd* **14/1**

3m 2.47s (2.27) **Going Correction** +0.025s/f (Good) **8** Ran SP% **113.3**
Speed ratings (Par 115): **94,93,91,90,86 85,82,82**
CSF £25.84 TOTE £7.30: £1.60, £1.40, £3.70; EX 26.10 Trifecta £585.50 Part won. Pool: £824.70. 0.80 winning units..
Owner Mountgrange Stud **Bred** Mle Michele Bliard **Trained** Upper Lambourn, Berks

FOCUS
A fair renewal but lacking the stars of the division, and because nothing wanted to go on it was run at a fairly steady early gallop. The front pair were clear and are rated to form.

NOTEBOOK
Geordieland(FR) has been called a few names in the past, and rightly so as he does not like being in front for long, but no-one has ever doubted his class, for in recent seasons he has finished second to Yeats in both the Goodwood Cup and Gold Cup, and second to Septimus in the Doncaster Cup, not forgetting his second to Sergeant Cecil in this race last year. Kelly rode a brilliant race on him here, settling him out the back and timing his challenge just right so that he would lead just before the line. He got to the front with a few yards to run, and for a split second it looked like he might still have got there too soon, but the line came, denying the runner-up the chance to rally. He was cut to a top price of 16-1 for the Gold Cup, which looks fair, but this performance was a reminder that he is not short of speed - he was a Group 2 winner over 1m4f in France as a four-year-old - and it would be interesting to see how he would get on over slightly shorter. (op 7-1)
Royal And Regal(IRE) was down in the paper as only a runner in the event of suitable ground, and given that he took part connections must have been satisfied that the track had been watered sufficiently. Taken to the front when no-one else appeared keen to lead, he was able to dictate a steady pace and have the run of the race. Quickening things up early in the straight, he soon had a healthy advantage over the chasing pack and only Geordieland had the speed to pick him up close home. It was a great ride from Callan and a sound effort from the horse on ground that was quicker than ideal. (op 10-3 tchd 7-2)
Samuel, like the winner was making his seasonal reappearance, was keen in the early stages, he plugged on well, just holding off the staying-on Honolulu for third. He must be one of the highest rated horses in the land who has yet to win a race, and a confidence-boosting maiden win might do him some good. (op 20-1 tchd 22-1)
Honolulu(IRE) did not always look straightforward last season, but he was sent off a short price to build on promising efforts which included a second place in the Ebor and third place in the St Leger. The lack of early pace was against him, though, as he only really got motoring in the closing stages when the first two had already gone beyond recall. A step up to 2m and a stronger gallop looks sure to suit him and, as his stablemates have all been improving bundles for their reappearances, it is reasonable to expect the same from him too. (tchd 6-5)
Sergeant Cecil beat Geordieland in this race last year but he did not show a lot after that and his seasonal reappearance at Newbury gave little cause for optimism. He was returning to a track where his form figures read 121115 though, and if he was to show his old sparkle it would be here. The steady pace followed by a sprint to the line would not have suited him, but in all honesty it looks as though his best days are now behind him. (op 12-1 tchd 10-1)
Alfie Flits could have done with a stronger pace as he did not get cover and was always doing a bit too much in the early stages. (op 10-1)
Veenwouden picked up some valuable black type last backend, her best effort coming when third and only two and a quarter lengths behind Royal And Regal in the Group 3 Jockey Club Cup, but she was well beaten on her reappearance and once again failed to get involved here.
Young Mick may have found this coming a bit quick after his reappearance at Ascot six days earlier. Official explanation: jockey said gelding had no more to give (op 16-1)

2170 MICHAEL SEELY MEMORIAL FILLIES' STKS (LISTED RACE) 1m
3:10 (3:13) (Class 1) 3-Y-0

£17,031 (£6,456; £3,231; £1,611; £807; £405) **Stalls** Low

Form RPR

331- **1** **Raymi Coya (CAN)**[223] 6008 3-9-3 101 KerrinMcEvoy 7 99
(M Botti) *trckd ldr: cl up 3f out: rdn and ev ch 2f out: drvn ins fnl f: styd on gamely to ld nr line* **15/2**

1 **2** hd **Musical Bar (IRE)**[28] 1445 3-8-12 0 AlanMunro 3 94
(B W Hills) *set stdy pce: qcknd over 3f out: edgd rt 2f out: sn rdn and edgd lft over 1f out: drvn ins fnl f: hdd and no ex nr fin* **9/2**[2]

15-3 **3** 1 **Festivale (IRE)**[30] 1401 3-8-12 94 EddieAhern 1 91+
(J L Dunlop) *trckd ldrs: nt clr run 2f out: swtchd rt and hdwy to chal ent fnl f: sn rdn and ev ch tl nt qckn fnl 100yds* **5/1**[3]

10- **4** nk **Makaaseb (USA)**[209] 6336 3-8-12 97 SebSanders 4 93+
(M A Jarvis) *dwlt: sn trcking ldrs: hdwy on inner whn hmpd wl over 1f out: sn rdn and kpt on ins fnl f* **15/8**[1]

31-0 **5** 2 **Jeninsky (USA)**[34] 1332 3-8-12 84 NCallan 5 86
(P J McBride) *in rr: effrt and sme hdwy over 2f out: sn rdn and no imp* **25/1**

16- **6** nk **Mistress Greeley (USA)**[265] 4804 3-8-12 88 RyanMoore 6 85
(Sir Michael Stoute) *chsd ldrs: rdn along wl over 2f out: drvn and wknd appr fnl f* **8/1**

10-0 **7** ½ **Insaaf**[12] 1834 3-8-12 89 JMurtagh 2 84
(W J Haggas) *hld up towards rr: effrt 3f out: rdn 2f out and sn one pce* **11/2**

1m 39.83s (1.03) **Going Correction** +0.025s/f (Good) **7** Ran SP% **111.7**
Speed ratings (Par 104): **95,94,93,93,91 91,90**
CSF £38.87 TOTE £8.50: £3.20, £2.10; EX 29.60.
Owner C Pizarro **Bred** Anderson Farms Ont Inc & M Farrell **Trained** Newmarket, Suffolk

FOCUS
A fairly standard Listed contest which was run at a fairly steady early pace. The field finished quite well bunched and the form is somewhat muddling with the fifth tending to limit things.

NOTEBOOK
Raymi Coya(CAN) had to give 5lb to the rest of the field as a result of winning the Group 3 Oh So Sharp Stakes last backend. Stepping up to a mile for the first time, she was always well placed in a race not run at a strong gallop, and just got the better of Musical Bar in the final stages. She should pay her way at this sort of level, but may have to go to the continent for a shot at a bigger prize. (op 8-1)
Musical Bar(IRE), a winner on her debut at Newbury, was given a good front-running ride by Munro, who had her in the box seat throughout. Only run out it well inside the last, this well-bred filly looks the type to keep improving as the season goes on. (op 4-1 tchd 5-1)
Festivale(IRE), third in the Nell Gwyn on her reappearance, travelled well to 2f out but, once switched, did not pick up as well as she had promised. A mile looks to stretch her stamina but she can pick up a Listed race back over shorter. (op 11-2 tchd 6-1)
Makaaseb(USA), disappointing on her final start at two when sent off favourite for the Rockfel, was happier back on fast ground. She was not quick enough to take the gap that opened up on the inside a furlong and a half out, though, and once the door was shut she was unable to find a way past the front two. She looked unlucky not to finish closer, but whether she would have won with a clear run is open to debate. (op 2-1)
Jeninsky(USA), held up in last place in a race that was not run at a strong pace, found herself in the wrong position when the tap was turned. Following Makaaseb through on the rail, she failed to make much impression from a furlong out, but in fairness she did look to have plenty on her plate in this class. (op 20-1)
Mistress Greeley(USA) was not sure to be suited by the step up in trip and the way she finished suggests those fears were well founded. (op 6-1)

Insaaf, who wore the owner's second colours, was taking a big step up in class having been sent off 16-1 for a handicap off 89 on her reappearance. (op 7-1)

2171 AXIS INTERMODAL STKS (H'CAP) 5f
3:45 (3:47) (Class 3) (0-90,90) 3-Y-O £9,714 (£2,890; £1,444; £721) Stalls High

Form RPR

21-2 **1** **Hamish McGonagall**[27] 1484 3-9-3 **84** .... DavidAllan 2 94
(T D Easterby) *cl up: led 2f out: rdn over 1f out: drvn ins fnl f: edgd lft and hld on gamely* **4/1**[2]

44-5 **2** *hd* **Lesson In Humility (IRE)**[21] 1597 3-9-6 **87** .... AndrewElliott 5 97
(K R Burke) *cl up: rdn and ev ch 2f out: drvn and sltly outpcd over 1f out: styd on wl u.p ins fnl f: jst hld* **9/1**

11 **3** *3/4* **Marvellous Value (IRE)**[20] 1611 3-9-4 **85** .... PhillipMakin 10 92
(M Dods) *hld up: hdwy 2f out: swtchd lft and chsd ldrs ent fnl f: sn rdn and kpt on* **9/2**[3]

1604 **4** *1* **Style Award**[9] 1911 3-9-3 **84** .... NCallan 9 87
(W J H Ratcliffe) *chsd ldrs: rdn along 2f out: drvn and kpt on same pce appr fnl f* **16/1**

02-3 **5** *1/2* **Rash Judgement**[21] 1597 3-9-5 **86** .... RyanMoore 4 88
(W S Kittow) *trckd ldrs: effrt 2f out: sn rdn and kpt on same pce ins fnl f* **7/4**[1]

420- **6** *1 1/4* **Grudge**[230] 5802 3-8-4 **71** oh3 .... PaulHanagan 6 68
(D W Barker) *led: rdn along and hdd 2f out: grad wknd* **25/1**

60-0 **7** *nk* **Carleton**[30] 1404 3-9-9 **90** .... EddieAhern 11 86+
(W J Musson) *hld up towards rr: hdwy 2f out: sn rdn and no imp appr fnl f* **22/1**

1-0 **8** *3 1/2* **Mookhlesa**[30] 1404 3-9-1 **82** .... AlanMunro 12 65
(B W Hills) *chsd ldrs: rdn along 2f out: grad wknd* **22/1**

221- **9** *3/4* **Know No Fear**[242] 5480 3-8-7 **74** .... GrahamGibbons 7 55
(J J Quinn) *in tch: effrt whn hmpd wl over 1f out: nvr a factor* **14/1**

01-0 **10** *3 1/2* **Northern Bolt**[43] 1167 3-9-3 **84** .... AdrianTNicholls 8 52
(D Nicholls) *s.i.s: a in rr* **10/1**

150- **11** *2* **Whispering Desert**[240] 5529 3-8-1 **71** oh8 .... DuranFentiman(3) 1 32
(P T Midgley) *chsd ldrs: rdn along 1/2-way: sn wknd* **66/1**

58.62 secs (-0.68) **Going Correction** +0.125s/f (Good) **11** Ran SP% **120.2**
Speed ratings (Par 103): **110,109,108,106,106 104,103,98,96,91 88**
CSF £38.93 CT £174.39 TOTE £5.00: £1.80, £3.20, £1.80; EX 44.10.
Owner Reality Racing Syndicate No 1 **Bred** J P Coggan And Whitsbury Manor Stud **Trained** Great Habton, N Yorks

FOCUS
A competitive sprint handicap for three-year-olds that is rated positively around the third and sixth and should throw up future winners. As is the norm at this track, the pace held up well and those waited with struggled to land a blow.

NOTEBOOK
Hamish McGonagall, who won the race on his side at Thirsk on his reappearance, was just 3lb higher here, and he was the subject of good support beforehand. Prominent throughout, he led with 2f to run, which was probably early enough, as his advantage was diminishing quickly at the line. He held on to land the gamble and, as a result of this narrow victory, should not go up too much as a result. He looks progressive, though, and perhaps he will be held onto a bit longer in future. The William Hill Trophy here next month is the obvious target, although he seems more effective over 5f than 6f. (op 15-2)
Lesson In Humility(IRE), fifth in the handicap won by Corrybrough at Sandown on her reappearance, looked to have less to do in this company. Another who was never far off the pace at a track where that style of running often pays dividends, she finished her race off well and a few yards after the line she was in front. A similar race could well be hers granted her favoured fast ground. (op 15-2 tchd 10-1 in a place)
Marvellous Value(IRE), unbeaten in his previous two starts, had not run on ground this quick before and was running off a 12lb higher mark than when waltzing away with a handicap at Haydock last time. As a hold-up horse though, he did not have the ideal style of running for this track, and he probably ran as well as could be expected in third. He remains progressive and capable of better on a track where the leaders are more likely to come back to him. (op 5-1 tchd 11-2 in a place)
Style Award is on a mark which leaves her vulnerable to less-exposed rivals who are capable of improving past her. (op 20-1)
Rash Judgement, third in the Sandown handicap in which Lesson In Humility finished fifth, had the better draw of the two on that occasion, and could not confirm the form on a track that suits the handier horse. A stiffer track or a return to 6f will suit him better. (op 2-1 tchd 9-4)
Grudge, 3lb wrong at the weights, showed good speed for a long way but in the end lack of race-fitness told on his seasonal reappearance.
Carleton, a hold-up performer who would not be ideally suited by the demands of this track, remains on a stiff mark. (op 20-1)
Mookhlesa showed up well for a long way but dropped out tamely once push came to shove. Having also disappointed on her reappearance, she has something to prove now. (op 11-1)
Know No Fear travelled quite well to two furlongs out but he was hampered a furlong and a half out and then weakened. He should come on for this reappearance and easier ground will suit him in future. (tchd 11-1)

2172 SPORTING INDEX STKS (H'CAP) 6f
4:20 (4:20) (Class 2) (0-100,100) 4-Y-O+ £12,952 (£3,854; £1,926; £962) Stalls High

Form RPR

414- **1** **Tombi (USA)**[203] 6472 4-8-13 **92** .... RyanMoore 12 108
(J Howard Johnson) *cl up: rdn to ld wl over 1f out: drvn and kpt on wl fnl f* **7/1**[3]

4411 **2** *2 1/2* **Atlantic Story (USA)**[62] 904 6-8-9 **88** ....(bt) KerrinMcEvoy 10 96
(M W Easterby) *led: rdn 2f out: sn hdd and kpt on same pce fnl f* **10/1**

-040 **3** *2 1/4* **Hinton Admiral**[13] 1809 4-8-9 **95** .... FrederikTylicki(7) 9 96
(R A Fahey) *prom: rdn along 2f out: kpt on same pce u.p fnl f* **66/1**

0302 **4** *1/2* **Machinist (IRE)**[6] 1986 8-9-7 **100** .... SilvestreDeSousa 1 99
(D Nicholls) *dwlt: sn in tch: hdwy on wd outside over 1f out: sn rdn and kpt on ins fnl f: nrst fin* **8/1**

/30- **5** *1* **Dream Theme**[237] 5616 5-9-2 **95** .... MickyFenton 11 91
(D Nicholls) *dwlt: sn in tch: hdwy to chse ldrs 2f out: sn rdn and kpt on same pce ent fnl f* **40/1**

00-5 **6** *1 1/2* **Malcheek (IRE)**[27] 1481 6-8-10 **89** .... DavidAllan 3 80
(T D Easterby) *prom: rdn along 2f out: grad wknd* **12/1**

-422 **7** *shd* **Damika (IRE)**[13] 1809 5-9-4 **100** .... MichaelJStainton(3) 8 91+
(R M Whitaker) *towards rr and sn rdn along: hdwy 2f out: edgd lft and rdn over 1f out: no imp* **13/2**[2]

60-0 **8** *1 1/4* **Mutamared (USA)**[13] 1809 8-9-4 **97** .... NCallan 2 84
(K A Ryan) *hld up: hdwy to chse ldrs 2f out: rdn wl over 1f out and sn btn* **12/1**

000- **9** *1/2* **Mastership (IRE)**[205] 6437 4-9-0 **93** .... RobertWinston 13 78
(J J Quinn) *nvr bttr than midfield* **22/1**

0355 **10** *1 3/4* **Buachaill Dona (IRE)**[9] 1917 5-9-7 **100** .... AdrianTNicholls 6 80
(D Nicholls) *hld up in tch: hdwy to chse ldrs 2f out: sn rdn and wknd over 1f out* **7/1**[3]

30-6 **11** *1 1/4* **Wyatt Earp (IRE)**[30] 1393 7-8-7 **86** .... PaulHanagan 5 62
(R A Fahey) *hld up: effrt and hdwy 2f out: sn rdn: edgd lft and btn wl over 1f out* **7/2**[1]

020- **12** *2 3/4* **Sir Xaar (IRE)**[197] 6606 5-8-13 **92** ....(t) PaulMulrennan 4 59
(B Smart) *s.i.s: a towards rr* **20/1**

0-00 **13** *nk* **Barney McGrew (IRE)**[13] 1809 5-8-11 **90** .... PhillipMakin 16 81+
(M Dods) *hld up and bhd: swtchd lft and hdwy whn nt clr run and hmpd over 1f out: styng on whn hmpd and stmbld ins fnl f: eased* **18/1**

1-00 **14** *1 1/2* **Kostar**[29] 1420 7-9-7 **100** .... EddieAhern 7 61
(C G Cox) *chsd ldrs: rdn along and wkng whn hmpd appr fnl f and eased* **16/1**

0-00 **15** *1/2* **Zomerlust**[25] 1517 6-8-11 **90** ....(v) GrahamGibbons 14 50
(J J Quinn) *sn rdn along and a towards rr* **20/1**

1m 10.98s (-0.92) **Going Correction** +0.125s/f (Good) **15** Ran SP% **125.1**
Speed ratings (Par 109): **111,107,104,104,102 100,100,98,98,95 94,90,90,88,87**
CSF £72.91 CT £4294.68 TOTE £8.30: £2.80, £2.40, £13.70; EX 95.10.
Owner Transcend Bloodstock LLP **Bred** Sun Valley Farm **Trained** Billy Row, Co Durham

FOCUS
A competitive sprint handicap in which once again it proved a big advantage to race prominently. the first two are progressive suggesting the form is worth treating positively, but the proximity of the third and fifth tends to raise doubts.

NOTEBOOK
Tombi(USA), a progressive sprinter last season, had conditions to suit and came in for solid support on his reappearance. Showing up prominently throughout on his reappearance, he quickened up well with the runner-up inside the final two furlongs and drew clear of his only serious rival inside the last. He looks a serious sprinter and surely it will not be long before he is contesting Pattern company, although the Wokingham would look the logical first target. (op 9-1)
Atlantic Story(USA), a highly progressive horse on the All-Weather over the winter, winning five races over 7f and 1m, got to run on turf off a 15lb lower mark back on turf. The drop back to 6f was the worry, but he showed that to be completely unwarranted as he led this field of sprinters at a good clip to inside the final 2fs. He could not cope with the smart winner in the closing stages but beat the rest well enough, and on this evidence he will not be long in going one better. (op 12-1)
Hinton Admiral's performance does put a question mark on the value of the form, but he was a smart animal not so long ago and had been shown some leniency by the Handicapper, who had dropped him 10lb since the beginning of the season. This track also suits his prominent style of running. (tchd 100-1 in a place)
Machinist(IRE) raced on the wide outside when most of the pace was towards the stands' side. He kept on well for fourth, faring best of those held up, but he has nothing in hand of the Handicapper off his current mark and this track would not be ideal for him.
Dream Theme ◆, who has done all his winning over 7f, got outpaced approaching the 2f marker but then ran on again late. This was a decent reappearance and he looks the type who is trainer, who picked him up from the Barry Hills yard last summer, will be looking to win a decent pot with this year. The Buckingham Palace Stakes looks the race for him at Royal Ascot.
Malcheek(IRE), a winner of five of his 17 starts on ground officially described as good to firm or faster, showed good pace up the centre of the track. He is on a stiff mark now, though, 4lb higher than when last successful. (op 16-1)
Damika(IRE), who has gone up in the weights without winning this season, was apparently below par, but this track would not have suited his style of running ideally and it is probably unfair to crab him too much. (op 7-1)
Mutamared(USA) needs a stiffer course, where the leaders come back to him, to be seen at his best.
Buachaill Dona(IRE) ran well from a poor draw at Chester last time, but he was only running over 6f because his owner had Tournedos (who won) for the 5f race the previous day. He is arguably better over 5f in races in where he can pick off his rivals late from off the pace. (op 6-1)
Wyatt Earp(IRE), who won this race last year off a 2lb higher mark and has a great record in general at the track, had made a pleasing enough reappearance at Beverley and had clearly been prepared with this race in mind. He was desperately disappointing in the circumstances and patently failed to give his running for one reason or another. Official explanation: trainer had no explanation for the poor form shown (tchd 10-3, 4-1 in places)
Barney McGrew(IRE), who was attempting the impossible in trying to come from last to first, did not get the clearest of runs and actually stumbled badly inside the final furlong. He shaped better than the bare result suggests and, granted a little more leniency from the Handicapper, could pop up at some point this summer. Official explanation: jockey said gelding was denied a clear run (op 20-1)

2173 PHIL BENEST STKS (H'CAP) 1m 4f
4:55 (4:56) (Class 4) (0-80,79) 3-Y-O £7,123 (£2,119; £1,059; £529) Stalls Centre

Form RPR

5-32 **1** **Full Speed (GER)**[15] 1753 3-9-1 **76** .... PJMcDonald(3) 1 91+
(G A Swinbank) *trckd ldrs: hdwy on inner over 2f out: nt clr run and swtchd rt over 1f out: led jst ins fnl f: rdn out* **9/2**[2]

31-3 **2** *2 3/4* **Laterly (IRE)**[15] 1753 3-9-7 **79** .... MickyFenton 7 87
(T P Tate) *led: qcknd over 3f out: rdn 2f out: edgd lft over 1f out: drvn and hdd ins fnl f: kpt on same pce* **5/1**[3]

61-0 **3** *2* **Resplendent Light**[24] 1543 3-9-7 **79** .... AlanMunro 2 84
(W R Muir) *hld up in rr: hdwy over 2f out: swtchd outside and rdn over 1f out: chsd ldng pair and hung lft ent fnl f: kpt on same pce* **8/1**

-410 **4** *3 1/4* **Benedict Spirit (IRE)**[15] 1746 3-8-13 **71** .... PaulMulrennan 3 71
(M H Tompkins) *hld up in rr: hdwy on inner 3f out: rdn over 2f out: drvn and one pce fr over 1f out* **9/1**

0-64 **5** *hd* **Dramatic Solo**[20] 1614 3-8-7 **65** .... EddieAhern 4 64
(K R Burke) *prom: rdn along over 3f out: drvn over 2f out and grad wknd* **20/1**

-354 **6** *11* **King Kenny**[4] 2046 3-8-13 **74** .... DNolan(3) 6 56
(S Parr) *hld up: hdwy on outer 3f out: rdn 2f out: sn drvn and btn* **17/2**

50-3 **7** *3 1/4* **Pondapie (IRE)**[20] 1628 3-8-11 **72** .... MichaelJStainton(3) 8 49
(R M Whitaker) *trckd ldr: effrt 3f out: rdn along over 2f out: sn drvn and wknd* **10/1**

6011 **8** *3 1/2* **Cape Colony**[25] 1527 3-9-0 **72** .... RyanMoore 5 43
(R Hannon) *bmpd s: hdwy and in tch 1/2-way: effrt 3f out: rdn to chse ldrs over 2f out: sn drvn and btn* **6/4**[1]

2m 33.18s (-0.02) **Going Correction** +0.025s/f (Good) **8** Ran SP% **120.3**
Speed ratings (Par 101): **101,99,97,95,95 88,86,83**
CSF £28.80 CT £178.99 TOTE £5.70: £2.00, £2.00, £2.70; EX 18.20 Place 6 £398.44, Place 5 £157.66..
Owner P J Carr **Bred** Dr K Schulte **Trained** Melsonby, N Yorks

FOCUS
A fair handicap run at an ordinary gallop and there were plenty in with a chance three furlongs out. The form looks solid rated through the third.
Cape Colony Official explanation: jockey said colt was unsuited by the good to firm ground
T/Jkpt: Not won. T/Plt: £206.40 to a £1 stake. Pool: £155,513.98. 549.85 winning tickets. T/Qpdt: £33.50 to a £1 stake. Pool: £6,799.38. 149.90 winning tickets. JR

2174 - 2184a (Foreign Racing) - See Raceform Interactive

[1793]DONCASTER (L-H)

Saturday, May 17

OFFICIAL GOING: Good to firm (8.7)

55mm watering over the previous seven days. The running rail was again in place from the 10f start to the home turn 4m wide on 'slightly quick ground'.
Wind: light 1/2 behind Weather: fine but very cool

2185 DONCASTER FREE PRESS PROPERTY TODAY APPRENTICE H'CAP 1m 4f

6:10 (6:10) (Class 5) (0-70,67) 4-Y-0+ **£3,238** (£963; £481; £240) **Stalls** Low

Form RPR

06-0 **1** **Amanda Carter**[31] 1394 4-9-2 **64**........ JamieMoriarty 8 71
(R A Fahey) *t.k.h in midfield: swtchd rt and hdwy over 3f out: led 1f out: styd on wl* **11/2**[3]

0160 **2** 1 1/4 **Kames Park (IRE)**[45] 1137 6-9-0 **67**........ MarkCoumbe(5) 4 72
(R C Guest) *s.s: bhd: gd hdwy on wd outside over 1f out: styd on to take 2nd ins fnl f* **13/2**

006- **3** 1 **El Dececy (USA)**[204] 6475 4-9-5 **67**........ DNolan 1 70+
(S Parr) *prom: smooth hdwy to chal over 1f out: edgd rt and styd on same pce* **8/1**

4221 **4** 2 **Terminate (GER)**[3] 2100 6-8-13 **64** 6ex........ JamieJones(3) 9 64
(Ian Williams) *hld up in midfield: chal over 1f out: one pce* **3/1**[1]

0/0- **5** nk **Elite Land**[385] 1301 5-8-1 **54** oh8 ow1........ DeclanCannon(5) 10 54
(N Bycroft) *mid-div: hdwy over 5f out: led over 2f out: rdr dropped whip over 1f out: sn hdd: one pce* **50/1**

6160 **6** 1/2 **Sol Rojo**[8] 1963 6-8-6 **59**........ SimonPearce(5) 2 58
(J Pearce) *in rr: hdwy u.p 3f out: hrd rdn and kpt on fnl f* **9/1**

0-34 **7** nk **Sky Chart (IRE)**[99] 485 4-8-0 **53** oh5........ SophieDoyle(5) 5 51
(N J Vaughan) *s.s: in rr: hdwy over 5f out: edgd rt over 1f out: nvr trbld ldrs* **16/1**

-011 **8** 1 1/2 **Pegasus Prince (USA)**[19] 1679 4-8-5 **58**........ BMcHugh(5) 6 54
(Miss J A Camacho) *trckd ldrs: effrt over 3f out: wknd over 1f out* **7/2**[2]

005- **9** nk **Spume (IRE)**[199] 6598 4-8-9 **64**........ AJSmith(7) 11 59
(S Parr) *trckd ldrs: chal over 2f out: wknd 1f out* **16/1**

54 **10** 1 3/4 **Night Orbit**[47] 1119 4-8-12 **65**........ AmyBaker(5) 12 58
(Miss J Feilden) *trckd ldrs: chal over 2f out: kpt on same pce fnl f* **28/1**

200/ **11** 1 1/4 **Lodgician (IRE)**[599] 5080 6-8-6 **59**........ DanielleMcCreery(5) 7 50
(K G Reveley) *hld up towards rr: drvn over 3f out: nvr on terms* **14/1**

0-00 **12** 6 **Mujma**[15] 1779 4-8-6 **59**........ StacyRenwick(5) 3 40
(S Parr) *led: clr 7f out: hdd over 2f out: sn wknd* **50/1**

2m 36.3s (1.20) **Going Correction** +0.075s/f (Good) **12 Ran SP% 122.9**
Speed ratings (Par 103): **99,98,97,96,95 95,95,94,94,93 92,88**
CSF £42.37 CT £291.61 TOTE £7.30: £2.20, £2.20, £2.50; EX 41.30.
Owner Mrs Janis Macpherson **Bred** James G Thom **Trained** Musley Bank, N Yorks
■ Stewards' Enquiry : Jamie Moriarty one-day ban: used whip in incorrect place (May 31)

FOCUS
An ordinary handicap run at a steady early pace. The proximity of the fifth does not do a lot for the value of the form.

2186 DONCASTER FREE PRESS MOTORS TODAY MAIDEN AUCTION STKS 5f

6:40 (6:40) (Class 5) 2-Y-0 **£3,238** (£963; £481; £240) **Stalls** High

Form RPR

1 **Master Noverre (IRE)** 2-8-10 0........ PaulHanagan 3 83+
(R A Fahey) *mid-div: hdwy over 2f out: hung bdly rt over 1f out: led ins fnl f* **40/1**

44 **2** 1 1/4 **Russet Reward**[13] 1821 2-8-10 0 ow1........ DaneO'Neill 9 79
(Mrs L Stubbs) *led: hung lft thrght: hdd and no ex ins fnl f* **9/1**

3 1 **Bees River (IRE)** 2-8-8 0........ DavidAllan 6 73
(T D Easterby) *chsd ldrs: kpt on wl ins fnl f* **8/1**

366 **4** 2 1/4 **Smalljohn**[18] 1693 2-8-9 0........(v[1]) TGMcLaughlin 8 66
(P D Evans) *dwlt: hdwy over 1f out: nvr rchd ldrs* **17/2**

3 **5** 1 **Go Go Green (IRE)**[14] 1794 2-8-9 0........ BMcHugh(7) 7 69
(S Parr) *chsd ldrs: fdd appr fnl f* **7/2**[2]

6 1/2 **Jimwil (IRE)** 2-8-13 0........ PhillipMakin 1 64
(M Dods) *dwlt: hdwy over 1f out: nvr nr ldrs* **12/1**

5 **7** nk **Ritzy Wildcat (USA)**[12] 1851 2-8-13 0........ SebSanders 11 63
(S C Williams) *dwlt: in rr tl kpt on steadily fnl 2f* **10/3**[1]

2 **8** 2 1/2 **Where's Reiley (USA)**[13] 1821 2-8-9 0........ PaulFessey 12 50
(T D Barron) *mid-div: effrt over 2f out: wknd over 1f out* **4/1**[3]

9 2 1/2 **Excitable (IRE)** 2-8-4 0........ EdwardCreighton 4 36
(Miss V Haigh) *dwlt: in rr-div: sme hdwy over 2f out: sn wknd* **50/1**

0 **10** 2 1/4 **Pride Of Kings**[17] 1714 2-8-11 0........ JoeFanning 5 35
(M Johnston) *w ldrs: wknd over 1f out* **8/1**

11 3 1/2 **Port Ronan (USA)** 2-8-11 0........ GrahamGibbons 2 23
(J S Wainwright) *swvd rt s: sn chsng ldrs: lost pl 2f out* **40/1**

59.31 secs (-1.19) **Going Correction** -0.20s/f (Firm) **11 Ran SP% 122.6**
Speed ratings (Par 93): **101,99,97,93,92 91,90,86,82,79 73**
CSF £378.42 TOTE £48.20: £10.70, £3.70, £2.50; EX 443.80.
Owner Percy/Green Racing 1 **Bred** Barbara Prendergast **Trained** Musley Bank, N Yorks

FOCUS
A fair maiden in which the runner-up is probably the best guide to the level of the form and backed up by the time.

NOTEBOOK
Master Noverre(IRE), whose dam was unraced but is a half-sister to Ivy League, a smart, multiple winner at up to 1m3f in France, Heisse, a 1m4f winner, and Hunter's Glen, a dual 1m2f winner, is bred to get a good deal further than this in time, and that was reflected in his starting price, which suggested he had not been showing a great deal at home. He caused a surprise, though, racing wide and keeping on well to deny a more experienced and speedily bred rival in Russet Reward. He can only improve as he steps up to 6f and beyond. (op 28-1)
Russet Reward had the benefit of previous experience and the quicker ground promised to suit. Grabbing the rail, he tried to make every yard, but the winner, who raced furthest away from the rail, took his measure inside the last. This was a solid enough effort but he will remain vulnerable to similarly unexposed rivals. (op 13-2 tchd 11-1)
Bees River(IRE) is by Acclamation and is a half-sister to multiple winning sprinter Knot In Wood, multiple 5f winner Alugat, and 7f winner Mulan Princess, so she is bred to be fast. This was a pleasing performance for a stable whose juveniles usually improve plenty for their debuts. (op 13-2)
Smalljohn, the most experienced performer in the line-up, wore a visor for the first time but was still a bit slowly away. Staying on late, he shaped as though a sixth furlong will suit him. (op 14-1)
Go Go Green(IRE), who ran with some promise on his debut, was a bit disappointing as he failed to build on that effort and was outpaced from a furlong and a half out. He looks the type to do better in time once handicapped. (tchd 4-1)
Jimwil(IRE), whose dam was a 7f winner at three in France, is by One Cool Cat, who has made a good start with his first crop. He is entitled to come on for this. (op 16-1)
Ritzy Wildcat(USA) was well backed but failed to build on his debut effort. He will be more interesting back on the sand as he is bred for that surface. (op 7-1)
Where's Reiley(USA) finished almost three lengths in front of Russet Reward on his debut but completely failed to confirm that form on this quicker ground. (op 11-4)

2187 DONCASTER FREE PRESS JOBS TODAY MEDIAN AUCTION MAIDEN STKS 6f

7:15 (7:16) (Class 5) 3-4-Y-0 **£3,238** (£963; £481; £240) **Stalls** High

Form RPR

34-2 **1** **Harrison George (IRE)**[49] 1068 3-9-3 79........ PaulHanagan 7 81
(R A Fahey) *hld up in mid-div: stdy hdwy over 2f out: rdn to ld last 75yds* **10/3**[2]

3 **2** 3/4 **Mark Of Meydan**[26] 1519 3-9-3 0........ PhillipMakin 6 79
(M Dods) *w ldrs: led 3f out: hung lft: hdd wl ins fnl f* **5/1**

303- **3** 3 **Misplaced Fortune**[214] 6254 3-8-12 64........ KimTinkler 11 64
(N Tinkler) *dwlt: hdwy over 2f out: kpt on same pce appr fnl f* **28/1**

40 **4** 3/4 **Infinity Bond**[16] 1751 3-8-12 0........ SladeO'Hara(5) 10 67
(G R Oldroyd) *hld up in tch: hdwy over 2f out: hung lft: styd on fnl f* **50/1**

54- **5** nk **Pavershooz**[196] 6634 3-9-3 0........ GrahamGibbons 17 66
(N Wilson) *hld up in rr stands' side: hdwy over 2f out: hung bdly lft: styd on fnl f* **16/1**

4 **6** 1 **This Ones For Eddy**[8] 1960 3-9-0 0........ DNolan(3) 4 62
(S Parr) *w ldrs on outer: wknd ins fnl f* **8/1**

42 **7** 1 1/2 **Marchingontogether (IRE)**[14] 1795 3-8-12 0........ NCallan 3 53
(D Carroll) *trckd ldrs on outer: effrt over 2f out: wknd ins fnl f* **9/2**[3]

0-5 **8** hd **Upstairs**[23] 1581 4-9-9 0........ MarcHalford(3) 2 59
(D R C Elsworth) *sn chsng ldrs on wd outside: effrt over 2f out: edgd lft: one pce* **25/1**

0 **9** 1 **Jordi Roper (IRE)**[32] 1379 3-9-3 0........ MickyFenton 14 54
(S Parr) *chsd ldrs stands' side: outpcd over 2f out* **50/1**

300- **10** nk **Accused (IRE)**[225] 5971 3-9-3 74........ SebSanders 15 53
(J Noseda) *hld up toward rr: effrt over 2f out: nvr on terms* **3/1**[1]

11 1/2 **Flying Flute** 3-9-3 0........ DaneO'Neill 16 51
(H Candy) *dwlt: styd on fnl 2f: nvr a factor* **12/1**

6 **12** 1 3/4 **Charlie Allnut**[14] 1795 3-9-3 0........ DarrenWilliams 5 46
(K R Burke) *chsd ldrs: wknd over 1f out* **33/1**

040- **13** 8 **Call Me Rosy (IRE)**[220] 6100 4-9-7 52........ JamesDoyle 1 15
(J G Given) *w ldrs on outer: lost pl over 2f out* **40/1**

30 **14** 7 **Steel Mask (IRE)**[14] 1795 3-9-3 0........ TWilliams 9 —
(M Brittain) *mde most tl 3f out: sn wknd* **50/1**

00- **15** 1 1/2 **Banus Flyer (IRE)**[347] 2337 3-9-3 0........ TomEaves 8 —
(N Tinkler) *mid-div: lost pl 3f out* **100/1**

1m 12.48s (-1.12) **Going Correction** -0.20s/f (Firm)
WFA 3 from 4yo 9lb **15 Ran SP% 128.1**
Speed ratings (Par 103): **99,98,94,93,92 91,89,89,87,87 86,84,73,64,62**
CSF £20.41 TOTE £4.50: £1.70, £2.80, £8.10; EX 33.20.
Owner P D Smith Holdings Ltd **Bred** R P Ryan **Trained** Musley Bank, N Yorks

FOCUS
An ordinary maiden, and this time the stands' rail was largely shunned in favour of the centre of the track. The form looks pretty solid rated through the winner.

2188 DONCASTER RACECOURSE SPONSORSHIP CLUB H'CAP 6f

7:45 (7:46) (Class 4) (0-80,80) 4-Y-0+ **£4,857** (£1,445; £722; £360) **Stalls** High

Form RPR

00-0 **1** **Charles Darwin (IRE)**[36] 1300 5-9-2 **78**........(b[1]) JamesDoyle 5 86
(M Blanshard) *led centre: clr over 2f out: rdn out: unchal* **4/1**[2]

5-02 **2** 1 1/2 **Rainbow Fox**[8] 1952 4-8-5 **67**........ PaulHanagan 4 70
(R A Fahey) *dwlt: hld up stands' side: effrt over 2f out: wnt 2nd over 1f out: styd on: nvr able to chal* **7/2**[1]

0035 **3** nk **Cornus**[14] 1796 6-9-4 **80**........(be) SebSanders 7 82
(A J McCabe) *trckd ldrs stands' side: kpt on same pce fnl f* **5/1**[3]

33-4 **4** 1 **Charles Parnell (IRE)**[14] 1818 5-9-0 **76**........ FergalLynch 2 75
(M Dods) *racd towards stands' side: effrt over 2f out: kpt on: nvr nr to chal* **4/1**[2]

420- **5** 2 **Sir Nod**[183] 6836 6-9-4 **80**........ TomEaves 8 72
(Miss J A Camacho) *led stands' side gp: chsd wnr: edgd lft and wknd fnl f* **10/1**

1601 **6** 2 1/4 **Winthorpe (IRE)**[7] 2005 8-8-7 **69**........ GrahamGibbons 6 54
(J J Quinn) *chsd ldrs stands' side: wknd over 1f out* **5/1**[3]

0500 **7** 3 1/4 **Yungaburra (IRE)**[49] 1071 4-8-13 **75**........(b) DarrenWilliams 1 50
(S Parr) *hld up last of 3 centre: effrt over 2f out: wknd over 1f out* **25/1**

1260 **8** 7 **Financial Times (USA)**[21] 1617 6-9-4 **80**........(t) MickyFenton 3 32
(Stef Liddiard) *trckd ldr centre: lost pl over 1f out* **10/1**

1m 12.51s (-1.09) **Going Correction** -0.20s/f (Firm) **8 Ran SP% 117.6**
Speed ratings (Par 105): **99,97,96,95,92 89,85,75**
CSF £19.03 CT £71.79 TOTE £5.50: £1.50, £1.60, £1.60; EX 21.80.
Owner J M Beever **Bred** M And P Associates **Trained** Upper Lambourn, Berks

FOCUS
A fair handicap, dominated throughout by the gambled-on Charles Darwin. Once again the rail proved no advantage and the placed horses set the level.

2189 SOUTH YORKSHIRE TIMES H'CAP 7f

8:20 (8:21) (Class 4) (0-85,85) 3-Y-0 **£4,857** (£1,445; £722; £360) **Stalls** High

Form RPR

10 **1** **Throne Of Power (USA)**[13] 1834 3-9-4 **85**........ KerrinMcEvoy 6 99+
(M A Magnusson) *hld up in rr on stands' side: rdn 3f out: gd hdwy over 1f out: led ins fnl f: r.o* **5/2**[1]

560- **2** 1 1/2 **Firestreak**[245] 5410 3-9-4 **85**........ DaneO'Neill 8 95
(R Hannon) *trckd ldrs stands' side: styd on to ld 1f out: hdd and no ex ins fnl f* **9/1**

5-02 **3** 5 **Bere Davis (FR)**[11] 1899 3-9-0 **81**........ TGMcLaughlin 10 77
(P D Evans) *chsd ldrs stands' side: hrd rdn and kpt on same pce fnl 2f* **10/1**

2-1 **4** nk **Solar Spirit (IRE)**[26] 1519 3-8-12 **82**........ PJMcDonald(3) 5 77
(G A Swinbank) *trckd ldrs: led over 1f out: sn hdd: one pce* **7/2**[2]

3-61 **5** 2 **Jonny Lesters Hair (IRE)**[14] 1817 3-8-8 **75**........(e) DavidAllan 9 65
(T D Easterby) *racd stands' side: led 1f: chsd ldrs: one pce fnl 2f* **9/1**

01- **6** 4 1/2 **Parisian Gift (IRE)**[150] 7191 3-8-9 **76**........ RichardKingscote 7 54
(Tom Dascombe) *trckd ldrs: effrt 3f out: lost pl over 1f out* **11/2**[3]

3503 **7** nk **Atheer Dubai (IRE)**[47] 1113 3-8-10 **77**........(b) SebSanders 4 54
(C E Brittain) *prom: rdn 3f out: nvr a threat* **9/1**

-10R **8** 1 1/2 **Chrystal Venture (IRE)**[5] 2039 3-8-5 **72**........ NeilPollard 2 45
(A J McCabe) *s.i.s: racd alone v wd: led after 1f: edgd rt and hdd over 1f out: sn wknd* **50/1**

402 **9** *1 1/4* **Eastern Hills**[24] 1556 3-8-5 **72** .... JoeFanning 3 41
(M Johnston) *chsd ldrs: hung lft and lost pl over 1f out* **14/1**
40-0 **10** *5* **Azeer (USA)**[32] 1379 3-8-8 **80** .... AshleyHamblett(5) 11 36
(P W Chapple-Hyam) *in rr stands' side: bhd fnl 2f* **20/1**
5505 **11** *nk* **Afton View (IRE)**[55] 980 3-7-11 **71** oh12........ StacyRenwick(7) 12 26
(S Parr) *hld up in rr stands' side: edgd lft 3f out: sn bhd* **50/1**

1m 25.38s (-0.92) **Going Correction** -0.20s/f (Firm) **11** Ran SP% **120.6**
Speed ratings (Par 101): **97,95,89,89,86 81,81,79,78,72 72**
CSF £26.48 CT £197.14 TOTE £3.20: £1.60, £2.90, £3.50; EX 33.40.
Owner Eastwind Racing Ltd and Martha Trussell **Bred** Mineola Farm II Partnership Et Al **Trained** Upper Lambourn, Berks
■ Stewards' Enquiry : T G McLaughlin two-day ban; used whip with excessive frequency (Jun 1-2)

FOCUS
A decent little handicap run at a good pace and featuring one or two unexposed sorts. the third and fourth are rated 7lb off their latest marks.

2190 PROFILE FILLIES' H'CAP — 1m (R)
8:50 (8:53) (Class 4) (0-85,80) 3-Y-O+ **£4,857** (£1,445; £722; £360) **Stalls** High

Form RPR
0-1 **1** **Storyland (USA)**[16] 1751 3-8-9 **70** .... KerrinMcEvoy 6 75+
(W J Haggas) *hld up in rr: stdy hdwy on wd outside 3f out: styd on wl appr fnl f: led nr fin* **15/8**[1]
301- **2** *3/4* **Talk Of Saafend (IRE)**[224] 6012 3-9-5 **80** .... DaneO'Neill 3 80
(R Hannon) *trckd ldrs: t.k.h: effrt over 2f out: chal on ins 1f out: no ex nr fin* **9/2**[3]
26-4 **3** *hd* **Sam's Secret**[11] 1891 6-9-11 **77** .... PJMcDonald(3) 2 80
(G A Swinbank) *dwlt: hld up in rr: hdwy over 2f out: slt ld 1f out: hdd and no ex towards fin* **3/1**[2]
115- **4** *1 3/4* **Fly Kiss**[266] 4804 3-8-13 **79** .... AhmedAjtebi(5) 7 75
(C E Brittain) *trckd ldr: edgd rt 2f out: edgd lft and chal over 1f out: kpt on same pce* **14/1**
251- **5** *3* **Coachhouse Lady (USA)**[224] 6015 3-9-5 **80** .... NCallan 4 69
(K A Ryan) *led: t.k.h: qcknd over 2f out: hung rt over 1f out: sn hdd and fdd* **7/1**
1153 **6** *6* **Gallic Charm (IRE)**[17] 1730 3-9-1 **76** .... SebSanders 1 51
(D R C Elsworth) *tk fierce hold in rr: hdwy to chse ldrs 4f out: lost pl over 1f out: eased ins fnl f* **6/1**
0-30 **7** *11* **Mollyatti**[23] 1584 3-8-7 **68** .... EdwardCreighton 5 18
(Miss V Haigh) *trckd ldrs: drvn over 2f out: wknd and eased over 1f out* **22/1**

1m 41.19s (0.19) **Going Correction** +0.075s/f (Good)
WFA 3 from 6yo 12lb **7** Ran SP% **115.8**
Speed ratings (Par 102): **102,101,101,99,96 90,79**
CSF £11.03 TOTE £2.70: £1.70, £3.10; EX 10.00 Place 6 £ 368.55, Place 5 £ 127.64.
Owner Mr & Mrs R Scott **Bred** Arthur B Hancock III & James H Stone **Trained** Newmarket, Suffolk

FOCUS
They went a steady early pace in this fillies' handicap and it turned into something of a sprint. The third sets the level although the fourth is far from solid, so the form is a little messy.
Mollyatti Official explanation: jockey said filly had no more to give
T/Plt: £419.90 to a £1 stake. Pool: £78,840.08. 137.05 winning tickets. T/Qpdt: £15.60 to a £1 stake. Pool: £5,537.55. 261.20 winning tickets. WG

2146 NEWBURY (L-H)
Saturday, May 17

OFFICIAL GOING: Good
Wind: Moderate behind Weather: Overcast

2191 INSEAD MBA 1970 MAIDEN STKS (DIV I) — 1m 2f 6y
1:35 (1:35) (Class 4) 3-Y-O **£5,342** (£1,589; £794; £396) **Stalls** Centre

Form RPR
0- **1** **It's A Date**[281] 4362 3-9-3 0........ FergusSweeney 4 82
(A King) *chsd ldrs: rdn over 2f out: styd on gamely u.p fnl f to ld fnl stride* **16/1**
-322 **2** *shd* **Special Reserve (IRE)**[13] 1840 3-9-3 76........ RichardHughes 5 82
(R Hannon) *lw: trckd ldr: led gng wl appr fnl 2f: hrd rdn fnl f and kpt on: ct fnl stride* **7/2**[1]
3 *3 1/2* **Dancer In Demand (IRE)** 3-9-3 0........ RyanMoore 9 75+
(Sir Michael Stoute) *unf: scope: in rr: drvn along over 3f out: began to stay on fr 2f out: kpt on fnl f but nvr gng pce to get nr ldng duo* **6/1**
23 **4** *1 1/2* **Art Trend (IRE)**[29] 1446 3-9-3 0........ AlanMunro 2 72
(P W Chapple-Hyam) *swtg: led: rdn 3f out: hdd appr fnl 2f: wknd fnl f* **5/1**[3]
430- **5** *2 1/2* **Dubai Samurai**[236] 5680 3-9-3 82........ TQuinn 8 67
(J W Hills) *swtg: chsd ldrs: rdn fr 3f out: wknd over 1f out* **9/1**
0 **6** *nk* **Nisaal (IRE)**[31] 1398 3-9-3 0........ RHills 13 66
(J L Dunlop) *lw: in tch: rdn and effrt over 3f out: nt rch ldrs: wknd ins fnl 2f* **9/2**[2]
7 *3 1/4* **Filun** 3-9-3 0........ PatCosgrave 10 60
(L M Cumani) *w'like: s.i.s: sn rcvrd into mid-div: rdn 3f out: wknd 2f out* **16/1**
8 *nse* **Seven Stars** 3-9-3 0........ TedDurcan 6 60
(B J Meehan) *w'like: s.i.s: mid-div 1/2-way: rdn over 3f out: n.d* **33/1**
00 **9** *1/2* **Yellow Thunder (IRE)**[16] 1748 3-9-3 0........ JimCrowley 14 59
(Luke Comer, Ire) *lw: in rr: drvn along over 3f out: sme prog fnl f* **100/1**
00 **10** *hd* **Kijivu**[56] 974 3-8-5 0........ ThomasO'Brien(7) 1 53
(M R Channon) *chsd ldrs to 3f out: sn rdn: wknd over 2f out* **100/1**
11 *2 3/4* **Solar Max (IRE)** 3-9-3 0........ SebSanders 12 53
(C R Egerton) *w'like: scope: bit bkwd: a towards rr* **16/1**
12 *6* **One Oak (USA)** 3-8-12 0........ LDettori 15 36
(B J Meehan) *unf: scope: bit bkwd: a towards rr* **12/1**
13 *16* **Daarth** 3-9-0 0........ DJMoran(3) 3 9
(B W Duke) *w'like: s.i.s: a towards rr* **50/1**
14 *1* **Water Violet** 3-8-12 0........ JamieSpencer 11 2
(J R Fanshawe) *leggy: unf: stdd s: rdn 3f out: a in rr* **8/1**
15 *11* **Purlando (GER)** 3-9-0 0........ TravisBlock(3) 7 —
(H Morrison) *w'like: chsd ldrs to 3f out* **33/1**

2m 9.83s (1.03) **Going Correction** +0.125s/f (Good) **15** Ran SP% **127.6**
Speed ratings (Par 101): **100,99,97,95,93 93,91,91,90,90 88,83,70,69,61**
CSF £73.98 TOTE £20.10: £3.80, £1.70, £1.60; EX 77.90.
Owner Four Mile Racing **Bred** Mrs F M Gordon **Trained** Barbury Castle, Wilts

FOCUS
A good maiden with several future winners likely to have been in the line-up. The time was a shade slower than for division II and the form is rated around the runner-up.
Water Violet Official explanation: jockey said filly hung left-handed throughout

2192 ENTER THE FLAT TOTETENTOFOLLOW STKS (REGISTERED AS THE ASTON PARK STAKES) (LISTED RACE) — 1m 5f 61y
2:10 (2:11) (Class 1) 4-Y-O+ **£17,031** (£6,456; £3,231; £1,611; £807) **Stalls** Centre

Form RPR
4-04 **1** **Tranquil Tiger**[13] 1829 4-9-1 110........ TedDurcan 3 117
(H R A Cecil) *lw: mde all: drvn and qcknd fr 3f out: unchal* **5/1**[3]
114- **2** *10* **Regal Flush**[245] 5408 4-8-12 112........ LDettori 2 104+
(Saeed Bin Suroor) *lw: racd in 3rd: drvn and styd on to chse wnr ins fnl 3f but a wl hld* **11/10**[1]
10-3 **3** *4* **Spanish Hidalgo (IRE)**[45] 1158 4-9-1 106........ SebSanders 5 96
(J L Dunlop) *chsd wnr: rdn and dropped bk to 3rd ins fnl 3f: styd on same pce* **6/1**
42-0 **4** *4* **Balkan Knight**[13] 1829 8-9-1 110........ JimmyFortune 4 90
(D R C Elsworth) *b.hind: stdd in rr and a wl off pce: rdn over 3f out and styd on to take mod 4th sn after* **9/2**[2]
-106 **5** *23* **Malt Or Mash (USA)**[13] 1829 4-9-1 106........ RichardHughes 1 56
(R Hannon) *lw: racd in modest 4th tl rdn and lost tch fr 3f out* **7/1**

2m 52.31s (0.31) **Going Correction** +0.125s/f (Good) **5** Ran SP% **109.3**
Speed ratings (Par 111): **104,97,95,92,78**
CSF £10.91 TOTE £4.80: £2.10, £1.30; EX 8.80.
Owner K Abdulla **Bred** Juddmonte Farms Ltd **Trained** Newmarket, Suffolk

FOCUS
Smart performers, but a tactical-looking race with a potentially dubious outcome, though Tranquil Tiger should not be underestimated because of that. He has been rated as winning by 7l from the eased runner-up, and to his previous best.

NOTEBOOK
Tranquil Tiger was largely left alone in front, which undoubtedly made his task easier, but credit should still be given for the way he spreadeagled his rivals, showing much improved form, though rated value for seven lengths rather than ten. He may well stay 2m, and has the entries to back that up, but does not need a stamina test. (op 4-1)
Regal Flush is probably better than he looked in this tactical contest, and should be given another chance to show what he can do now he is with Godolphin. (op 5-4 tchd 11-8)
Spanish Hidalgo(IRE), the only one to make any attempt to chase the all-the-way winner, had been shaken off by the 2f pole. He is a generally reliable sort, but was not at his best here. (tchd 13-2)
Balkan Knight, given plenty to do in a tactical contest, never really became competitive and can do much better. A strong end-to-end gallop is ideal for his style of racing. (op 11-2)
Malt Or Mash(USA) was trying a longer trip, but the extra distance was not responsible for a poor effort. A largely progressive colt in the last year, he has plenty of scope and can be given another chance. (tchd 13-2 and 8-1)

2193 JUDDMONTE LOCKINGE STKS (GROUP 1) — 1m (S)
2:45 (2:50) (Class 1) 4-Y-O+
£113,540 (£43,040; £21,540; £10,740; £5,380; £2,700) **Stalls** Centre

Form RPR
42-0 **1** **Creachadoir (IRE)**[49] 1090 4-9-0 118........ LDettori 7 121
(Saeed Bin Suroor) *lw: led 1f: styd trcking ldrs: drvn to ld ins fnl 2f: kpt on wl fnl f and a in control* **3/1**[1]
11-1 **2** *3/4* **Phoenix Tower (USA)**[30] 1422 4-9-0 111........ TedDurcan 3 119
(H R A Cecil) *lw: t.k.h: trckd ldrs: rdn and styd on fr 2f out: chsd wnr and kpt on ins fnl f but a hld* **9/2**[3]
115- **3** *nk* **Tariq**[224] 6029 4-9-0 115........ JimmyFortune 10 119+
(P W Chapple-Hyam) *hld up in rr: nt clr run fr 2f out: hdwy and swtchd lft over 1f out: wnt lft again ins fnl f: styd on wl cl home but nvr quite gng pce to press ldng duo* **9/1**
40-1 **4** *hd* **Cesare**[17] 1716 7-9-0 120........ JamieSpencer 11 118
(J R Fanshawe) *lw: hld up in rr: hdwy on outside fr 2f out: styng on to chse ldrs whn pushed lft ins fnl f: edgd rt: kpt on cl home* **7/2**[2]
516- **5** *1/2* **Arabian Gleam**[210] 6332 4-9-0 114........ SebSanders 12 117
(J Noseda) *towards rr but in tch: rdn over 2f out: styd on to chse ldrs ins fnl f: kpt on but nvr gng pce to chal* **33/1**
6 *1 1/2* **Haradasun (AUS)**[196] 6663 5-9-0 0........ JMurtagh 9 118+
(A P O'Brien, Ire) *str: rangy: swtg: in tch: rdn 3f out: styd on ins fnl 2f and gng on whn hmpd ins fnl f: kpt on again cl home* **7/1**
06-3 **7** *hd* **Barshiba (IRE)**[14] 1807 4-8-11 106........ TQuinn 5 110
(D R C Elsworth) *t.k.h in rr: hdwy fr 3f out: chsd ldrs 2f out and sn hrd drvn: hung lft 1f out: wknd ins fnl f* **50/1**
20-2 **8** *3 1/4* **Al Qasi (IRE)**[21] 1619 5-9-0 114........ AlanMunro 8 106
(P W Chapple-Hyam) *s.i.s: t.k.h and sn mid-div: rdn over 2f out: nt pce to chal: wknd fnl f* **25/1**
25/2 **9** *nse* **Rob Roy (USA)**[21] 1631 6-9-0 111........ RyanMoore 2 105
(Sir Michael Stoute) *lw: bmpd s: led after 1f and tk field to stands' side: rdn over 2f out: hdd ins fnl 2f: wknd fnl f* **10/1**
41-0 **10** *4* **Majestic Roi (USA)**[49] 1090 4-8-11 116........ RichardHughes 1 93
(M R Channon) *lw: wnt rt s: sn trcking ldrs: rdn over 2f out: wknd over 1f out* **11/1**
340- **11** *1 1/2* **Astronomer Royal (USA)**[224] 4-9-0 0........ CO'Donoghue 4 93
(A P O'Brien, Ire) *t.k.h: pressed ldrs: rdn 3f out: wknd ins fnl 2f* **16/1**

1m 38.7s (-1.00) **Going Correction** +0.125s/f (Good) **11** Ran SP% **120.0**
Speed ratings (Par 117): **110,109,108,108,108 106,106,103,103,99 97**
CSF £16.65 TOTE £2.80: £1.20, £1.60, £2.70; EX 15.80 Trifecta £67.10 Pool: £9,302.21 - 98.40 winning units..
Owner Godolphin **Bred** Frank Dunne **Trained** Newmarket, Suffolk
■ Stewards' Enquiry : Jamie Spencer two-day ban; careless riding (May 31 - June 1)
Jimmy Fortune one-day ban; careless riding (May 31)

FOCUS
A decent line-up, but certainly not the best Lockinge of recent times, and the pace was not fast enough to be considered a testing Group 1. It was rather a muddling affair in which the winner benefited from a particularly astute ride, and if the first four meet again in the Queen Anne at Royal Ascot it is anybody's guess which order they will finish in.

NOTEBOOK
Creachadoir(IRE) deserved this Group 1 victory, having been runner-up in both the French and Irish 2000 Guineas last season. Though this was not a vintage Lockinge, he impressed with his willingness to battle in the face of several challenges, and must go to the Queen Anne at Royal Ascot with a sporting chance. (op 5-1)
Phoenix Tower(USA) was too keen early on, and would have been suited by a stronger gallop. His next race could be the Queen Anne, where a reversal of this result would be quite possible. However, he stays a bit farther than this, which also brings Group 1s over 1m2f into the equation. (op 5-1)
Tariq, unlike the first two, tried to come from the rear, and ran into traffic problems in the process, giving the impression that he may have been a shade unlucky. He could meet the first two again in the Queen Anne, and must have a chance of gaining revenge. Official explanation: jockey said colt ran too free (op 10-1 tchd 17-2)

Cesare was given plenty to do, but for a moment he looked like making his presence felt before flattening out a bit and edging right in the last 100 yards. Though not an unlucky loser, he will be at his best on his favourite track in the Queen Anne, so must be given serious consideration even if the three in front of him here also line up for that race. (tchd 4-1)

Arabian Gleam proved that he stays 1m, and did well to finish close behind better-fancied runners. (op 40-1)

Haradasun(AUS), a dual Group 1 winner in Australia, got warm in the preliminaries and was keen to post, which may account for his weakness in the betting. He made an encouraging British debut in a race that was not run to suit, and he should build on this as he acclimatises. A magnificent, powerful individual, he should make his mark in high-class races up to 1m2f before long. (op 7-2)

Barshiba(IRE) looked out of her depth, but ran a fine race especially as she was reluctant to settle out the back early on. (op 66-1)

Al Qasi(IRE) has yet to prove that 1m is his trip, but he used up too much energy by being over-headstrong.

Rob Roy(USA) had the run of the race, dictating no better than a medium tempo, but he was left standing when the race began to develop. (op 14-1 tchd 9-1)

Majestic Roi(USA) was one of only three Group 1 winners in the field, but she did not run much of a race. (op 14-1 tchd 10-1)

Astronomer Royal(USA) beat Creachadoir in last year's French 2000 Guineas, but he has only once run to that sort of level since. (op 20-1)

2194 TOTESCOOP6 LONDON GOLD CUP (HERITAGE H'CAP) 1m 2f 6y

3:20 (3:22) (Class 2) (0-105,98) 3-Y-O

£28,039 (£8,397; £4,198; £2,101; £1,048; £526) **Stalls** Centre

Form RPR

361- **1** **Strategic Mission (IRE)**[219] [6127] 3-8-10 **87**.......................... TQuinn 5 99
(P F I Cole) *lw: trckd ldrs: led ins fnl 2f: hrd rdn 1f out: styd on strly ins fnl f* **16/1**

03-2 **2** *1* **Midships (USA)**[22] [1600] 3-9-0 **91**.................................... JimCrowley 9 101
(Mrs A J Perrett) *lw: led: drvn along fr 3f out: narrowly hdd ins fnl 2f: nt pce of wnr ins fnl f but styd on wl for clr 2nd* **11/1**

01-1 **3** *1 3/4* **Colony (IRE)**[22] [1600] 3-8-8 **85**.. RyanMoore 12 91
(Sir Michael Stoute) *in tch: drvn along fr 3f out: styd on thrght fnl f but nvr gng pce to be competitive* **6/4**[1]

0-42 **4** *nse* **Ramona Chase**[14] [1811] 3-9-2 **93**.............................. DPMcDonogh 4 99
(S Kirk) *swtg: t.k.h and hld up in rr: hdwy fr 3f out: n.m.r 2f out: swtchd lft: hrd rdn and r.o u.p but nvr gng pce to be competitive* **8/1**[3]

1-20 **5** *1 1/4* **Whitcombe Minister (USA)**[21] [1632] 3-9-1 **92**............ GeorgeBaker 10 96
(Jamie Poulton) *swtg: towards rr: hdwy on outside fr 3f out: edgd lft 1f out but styd on ins fnl f: gng on cl home* **16/1**

3-10 **6** *nk* **Sundowner (IRE)**[26] [1524] 3-8-3 **80**.......................... HayleyTurner 14 83
(G A Butler) *lw: in rr: drvn along fr 5f out: n.m.r whn keeping on u.p over 1f out: styd on cl home but nvr gng pce to be competitive* **16/1**

21-0 **7** *3* **Trenchtown (IRE)**[22] [1600] 3-8-8 **85**............................ SteveDrowne 7 82+
(R Charlton) *swtg: in rr: rdn over 3f out: sme prog fnl 2f* **16/1**

1-21 **8** *nk* **Silver Rime (FR)**[26] [1524] 3-8-10 **87**......................... RichardHughes 8 85
(R Hannon) *lw: t.k.h: hld up in rr: rdn and effrt fr 3f out: nvr gng pce to rch ldrs: wknd fnl f* **10/1**

63-1 **9** *shd* **Jabal Tariq**[21] [1628] 3-8-7 **84** ow2................................... MichaelHills 1 80
(B W Hills) *chsd ldrs: rdn over 2f out: wknd over 1f out* **11/1**

6-41 **10** *2 1/4* **Master Spy**[18] [1701] 3-8-10 **87**..................................... JimmyFortune 2 79
(J H M Gosden) *lw: t.k.h in mid-div: rdn over 3f out: wknd 2f out* **16/1**

111 **11** *3/4* **William Blake**[31] [1395] 3-8-11 **88**.................................... GregFairley 11 78
(M Johnston) *chsd ldr: rdn 3f out: wknd 2f out* **13/2**[2]

42-0 **12** *1 1/4* **Palmerin**[49] [1074] 3-8-3 **80**.. FrancisNorton 15 68
(R Hannon) *chsd ldrs: rdn over 3f out: wknd over 2f out* **100/1**

0-63 **13** *nse* **Better Hand (IRE)**[14] [1810] 3-9-5 **96**............................... AlanMunro 6 84
(M R Channon) *t.k.h early: rdn over 3f out: a towards rr* **33/1**

4-00 **14** *hd* **Ruff Diamond (USA)**[21] [1632] 3-8-9 **86**............................ TedDurcan 3 73
(J R Best) *lw: rdn 6f out: a in rr* **33/1**

2m 7.97s (-0.83) **Going Correction** +0.125s/f (Good) **14** Ran SP% **126.5**
Speed ratings (Par 105): **108,107,105,105,104 104,102,101,101,100 99,98,98,98**
CSF £189.19 CT £430.96 TOTE £17.90: £4.80, £3.00, £1.50; EX 185.60 Trifecta £1329.70 Pool £9,738.94 - 5.20 winning units..

Owner H R H Sultan Ahmad Shah **Bred** Ruskerne Ltd **Trained** Whatcombe, Oxon

FOCUS

Just a good handicap in terms of ratings, but history suggests there will be some serious improvers in the field. The early tempo was a routine one, but it did increase around halfway. The fourth and fifth look the best guide to the form, but the first three are all expected to continue improving for a while yet.

NOTEBOOK

Strategic Mission(IRE) ◆, winner of a 1m maiden here last season, got the extra 2f really well on this handicap debut, and may now be ready for even longer trips. The 1m4f King George V Handicap at Royal Ascot is a possible target for this strapping sort, and he has the progressive profile that often works out well in that race. (op 20-1)

Midships(USA) looks well suited by 1m2f these days, though he may stay a bit farther as the season progresses. Already a winner of a maiden on his debut, he will be a force to be reckoned with in similarly competitive handicaps from now on. (op 12-1)

Colony(IRE), though unable to justify his short price, ran well enough considering the ground was probably plenty fast enough for him. Given a bit more juice, he looks a likely sort for a good prize this summer. (op 2-1)

Ramona Chase still needs to relax better, but if he finally gets the message he should develop into a smart 1m2f handicapper. (tchd 15-2 and 17-2)

Whitcombe Minister(USA) looks more at home in handicaps than among the Pattern company he tackled last time. However, he is racing off a challenging mark and could probably do with dropping a couple of pounds. (op 40-1)

Sundowner(IRE) looked a lazy customer, and blinkers may help him race with more enthusiasm. The ability is there if connections can encourage him to use it. (op 14-1)

Trenchtown(IRE) was going on pretty well at the finish, and should do better at 1m4f. (op 20-1 tchd 14-1)

William Blake, 8lb higher than when winning in lesser company last time, found it all too much. (op 8-1)

2195 TOTETENTOFOLLOW.CO.UK H'CAP 6f 8y

3:55 (3:57) (Class 2) (0-100,100) 4-Y-O+

£12,462 (£3,732; £1,866; £934; £466; £234) **Stalls** Centre

Form RPR

0264 **1** **Baby Strange**[14] [1809] 4-8-6 **88**...................................... JimCrowley 2 100
(D Shaw) *chsd ldr: rdn and stl 2 l down 1f out: styd on gamely u.p to ld fnl strides* **9/1**

5-11 **2** *nk* **Holbeck Ghyll (IRE)**[30] [1415] 6-8-4 **86** oh1.................. FrancisNorton 6 97
(A M Balding) *led: stl travelling ok and 2 l clr 1f out: hrd drvn ins fnl f: ct fnl strides* **12/1**

16-1 **3** *2 1/4* **Royal Rock**[19] [1689] 4-9-2 **98**.. GeorgeBaker 7 102
(C F Wall) *lw: trckd ldrs: drvn along over 1f out: kpt on same pce ins fnl f* **7/4**[1]

01-3 **4** *2 1/4* **Signor Peltro**[28] [1481] 5-8-7 **89**.............................(v[1]) FergusSweeney 1 86
(H Candy) *chsd ldrs: rdn 2f out: styd on same pce fnl f* **11/2**[3]

00-1 **5** *1/2* **Jimmy Styles**[7] [1985] 4-8-11 **93**.................................. PhilipRobinson 4 88
(C G Cox) *t.k.h early: hld up towards rr: hdwy and rdn 2f out: no imp on fnl f* **9/2**[2]

4550 **6** *4* **Ajigolo**[10] [1917] 5-8-6 **88**... SamHitchcott 9 70
(M R Channon) *towards rr: drvn and outpcd 1/2-way: styd on ins fnl f but nvr any threat* **40/1**

-044 **7** *3/4* **Dazed And Amazed**[7] [1985] 4-7-11 **86**.................... CharlesEddery(7) 10 66
(R Hannon) *in rr: hdwy over 2f out: nvr rchd ldrs and sn wknd* **25/1**

56-2 **8** *nk* **The Trader (IRE)**[29] [1442] 10-9-4 **100**......................(b) JamieSpencer 3 79
(M Blanshard) *lw: in rr: swtchd lft to outside and sme prog 2f out: nvr rchd ldrs and sn wknd* **14/1**

6010 **9** *1 3/4* **Bonnie Prince Blue**[21] [1617] 5-8-1 **86** oh3................(b) LukeMorris(3) 11 59
(B W Hills) *chsd ldrs: rdn over 2f out: sn btn* **40/1**

00-5 **10** *1* **Beauchamp Viceroy**[15] [1765] 4-8-8 **90**......................... RichardHughes 5 60
(G A Butler) *plld hrd and stdd rr: rdn over 2f out: no rspnse* **16/1**

210- **11** *3/4* **Tony The Tap**[169] [6972] 7-8-4 **86** oh1......................... RichardMullen 12 54
(W R Muir) *bit bkwd: stdd s: a in rr* **33/1**

113- **12** *3 3/4* **Sundae**[239] [5584] 4-8-11 **93**.. TedDurcan 8 49
(C F Wall) *a bhd: hung bdly rt ins fnl f* **7/1**

1m 12.53s (-0.47) **Going Correction** +0.125s/f (Good) **12** Ran SP% **124.3**
Speed ratings (Par 109): **108,107,104,101,100 95,94,94,91,90 89,84**
CSF £113.57 CT £284.89 TOTE £11.30: £2.90, £3.70, £1.40; EX 143.90 Trifecta £801.10 Part won. Pool: £1,128.33 - 0.70 winning units..

Owner Market Avenue Racing Club Ltd **Bred** Michael John Williamson **Trained** Danethorpe, Notts

FOCUS

A decent line-up, but the pace was not good for a 6f event, and the first two home were at the head throughout. In the circumstances, the hold-up performers had little chance. The bare form is not solid, but the winner is rated up 7lb on his recent efforts.

NOTEBOOK

Baby Strange was very well-in on his form of old, but he only just made it in the nick of time, so a trip back up the weights would make things tough for him at this trip. However, he is relatively unexposed at 7f and looked as if the extra furlong might suit these days. (op 15-2 tchd 10-1)

Holbeck Ghyll(IRE) has come from behind in recent races, but he was allowed to dictate a modest pace and nearly pulled it off. His current mark is a challenging one, but his opponents nearly played into his hands here. (tchd 10-1)

Royal Rock looked progressive before this, but the soft pace was not ideal for him, since he stays 7f. He can do better granted a decent gallop, and should win some nice prizes. (op 2-1 tchd 9-4)

Signor Peltro, visored instead of blinkered this time, alternates between 6f and 7f, so the modest tempo of this race was all against him. (op 9-2)

Jimmy Styles was one of several who needed a stronger pace to bring out the best in him. He is higher in the weights now, but should not be judged on this slightly disappointing effort. (op 5-1 tchd 11-2)

Ajigolo is back down to an interesting mark, but needs to show a bit more to encourage major support.

Beauchamp Viceroy Official explanation: jockey said gelding lost its action

Sundae made an awful seasonal debut, and must now show that he can continue the excellent work of 2007. Official explanation: jockey said gelding ran too free (op 12-1)

2196 CATRIDGE FARM STUD & MANOR FARM PACKERS FILLIES' H'CAP 7f (S)

4:30 (4:33) (Class 4) (0-85,85) 3-Y-O

£6,476 (£1,927; £963; £481) **Stalls** Centre

Form RPR

00-5 **1** **Clifton Dancer**[29] [1441] 3-8-6 **80**............................. RossAtkinson(7) 15 92
(Tom Dascombe) *led after 1f: rdn and edgd rt over 1f out: hld on wl fnl f* **8/1**[2]

21-0 **2** *1* **Shabiba (USA)**[31] [1401] 3-9-3 **84**.. RHills 9 93
(M P Tregoning) *lw: in tch: effrt 2f out: r.o to press wnr fnl 100yds: hld nr fin* **8/1**[2]

010- **3** *1 1/2* **Romany Princess (IRE)**[230] [5828] 3-8-10 **77**................. RyanMoore 4 82
(R Hannon) *mid-div: rdn to press ldrs 2f out: nt qckn fnl f* **11/1**

6-25 **4** *1 1/2* **Amylee (IRE)**[8] [1946] 3-8-13 **80**.............................(b[1]) PhilipRobinson 8 81
(C G Cox) *w ldrs: hrd rdn 2f out: one pce appr fnl f* **18/1**

4211 **5** *3/4* **Nice Wee Girl (IRE)**[2] [2127] 3-8-11 **78** 6ex.................. HayleyTurner 16 77+
(S Kirk) *dwlt: towards rr: drvn along 3f out: styd on wl fnl 2f: nrst fin* **15/2**[1]

10-5 **6** *2 1/2* **Edge Of Gold**[18] [1698] 3-8-13 **80**........................ CatherineGannon 18 72
(B Palling) *wnt lft s: t.k.h: sn trcking ldrs: hrd rdn 2f out: sn btn* **20/1**

3014 **7** *1 1/2* **Miss Mujanna**[35] [1336] 3-8-8 **75** ow1.............................. PatCosgrave 5 63
(J Akehurst) *broke wl: led 1f: w ldrs tl hrd rdn and wknd jst over 1f out* **40/1**

610- **8** *1/2* **Falcolnry (IRE)**[225] [5973] 3-9-1 **82**............................ JamieSpencer 19 69+
(J R Fanshawe) *lw: hld up in last pl: effrt and sme hdwy ins fnl 2f: nvr rchd ldrs* **15/2**[1]

1- **9** *1 1/4* **Hip**[285] [4232] 3-9-2 **83**.. JimmyFortune 1 66
(E A L Dunlop) *hld up in rr: hdwy and in tch 2f out: wknd over 1f out* **15/2**[1]

34-0 **10** *1* **Acquifer**[25] [1546] 3-8-5 **72**.. RichardMullen 2 53
(J L Dunlop) *bhd: drvn along over 2f out: n.d* **50/1**

221- **11** *nse* **Our Piccadilly (IRE)**[239] [5603] 3-8-13 **80**................. FergusSweeney 10 61
(W S Kittow) *bit bkwd: t.k.h in rr of midfield most of way: mod effrt 2f out: nt pce to chal* **20/1**

51-1 **12** *1 1/4* **Debonnaire**[19] [1688] 3-8-9 **76**... GregFairley 17 53
(M Johnston) *lw: dwlt: sn in midfield: drvn along 3f out: no imp* **9/1**[3]

10-4 **13** *2* **May Day Queen (IRE)**[13] [1837] 3-8-11 **78**................. RichardHughes 6 50
(R Hannon) *prom: rdn 2f out: sn wknd* **10/1**

613- **14** *1 3/4* **Princess India (IRE)**[242] [5516] 3-8-3 **73**...................... LukeMorris(3) 12 40
(P Winkworth) *bit bkwd: mid-div tl hrd rdn and wknd over 2f out* **40/1**

4-43 **15** *7* **Geestring (IRE)**[9] [1930] 3-8-6 **73**...................................... TPO'Shea 11 21
(R Hannon) *chsd ldrs 3f: sn rdn and lost pl: bhd fnl 2f* **14/1**

10-1 **16** *1 1/2* **Indian Diva (IRE)**[12] [1868] 3-9-3 **84**.....................(b) StephenDonohoe 14 28
(P A Blockley) *prom over 4f: drvn along and qckly lost pl* **22/1**

030- **17** *3 1/4* **Meridian Line (IRE)**[232] [5766] 3-9-2 **83**........................ JimCrowley 13 18
(J G Portman) *bit bkwd: mid-div tl rdn and wknd over 2f out* **66/1**

-310 **18** *17* **Centenerola (USA)**[29] [1448] 3-9-4 **85**............................ MichaelHills 3 —
(B W Hills) *lw: mid-div: hrd rdn over 2f out: sn bhd and eased* **16/1**

1m 25.13s (-0.57) **Going Correction** +0.125s/f (Good) **18** Ran SP% **132.6**
Speed ratings (Par 98): **108,106,105,103,102 99,98,97,96,94 94,93,91,89,81 79,75,56**
CSF £63.28 CT £648.08 TOTE £9.80: £3.10, £2.50, £4.10, £4.00; EX 117.70.

Owner Clifton Partners **Bred** Redmyre Bloodstock And Stuart McPhee **Trained** Lambourn, Berks

■ Stewards' Enquiry : Stephen Donohoe caution: allowed filly to coast home with no assistance

FOCUS
Probably a good handicap of its type, with the first two home having tackled Listed and Group 3 company respectively in earlier races. The pace was decent although little got into it from the rear. The first three were all improvers.

2197 INSEAD MBA 1970 MAIDEN STKS (DIV II) 1m 2f 6y
5:00 (5:03) (Class 4) 3-Y-O £5,342 (£1,589; £794; £396) Stalls Centre

Form RPR
1 **Secret Dancer (IRE)** 3-9-3 0 JamieSpencer 11 93+
(J R Fanshawe) *w/like: cl cpld: stdd s: hld up in rr: stl last whn swtchd rt 3f out: str run fr 2f out: qcknd ins fnl f to ld fnl 75yds: cosily* **9/1**
5 2 ¾ **Eqbaal**[28] 1467 3-9-3 0 RHills 4 86+
(J L Dunlop) *lw: chsd ldrs: drvn to ld ins fnl 2f: kpt on u.p: hdd and outpcd fnl 75yds* **5/2**[1]
4-6 3 2 ¾ **Belotto (IRE)**[29] 1444 3-8-12 0 SteveDrowne 9 75+
(R Charlton) *unf: towards rr but in tch: pushed along over 2f out: styd on wl fnl f but nt pce to rch ldng duo* **11/1**
5-2 4 2 ½ **Gaia Prince (USA)**[19] 1684 3-9-3 0 JimCrowley 14 75
(Mrs A J Perrett) *pressed ldr tl slt ld ins fnl 3f: hdd ins fnl 2f: wknd fnl f* **15/2**
5 4 **Amaakin (USA)** 3-9-3 0 AlanMunro 13 67
(P W Chapple-Hyam) *w/like: scope: trckd ldrs: pushed along and one pce 3f out: n.d after* **11/2**[3]
2 6 ½ **Ben Ami**[37] 1283 3-9-3 0 OscarUrbina 6 66
(Miss J R Gibney) *in tch 5f out: rdn over 3f out and sn one pce* **11/1**
0 7 1 ¾ **Dr Brass**[26] 1526 3-9-3 0 JimmyFortune 7 67+
(H J L Dunlop) *chsd ldrs: wknd fr 2f out: btn whn hmpd ins fnl f* **14/1**
8 nse **Tank Commander** 3-9-3 0 RichardMullen 10 62
(W R Muir) *w/like: lw: in rr: rdn 4f out: mod prog fnl f* **25/1**
9 2 **Purely By Chance** 3-8-12 0 FergusSweeney 12 53
(R M Beckett) *in rr tl sme progs fnl 2f* **33/1**
03 10 ½ **Byblos**[18] 1695 3-9-3 0 RichardHughes 2 57
(B J Meehan) *in tch: rdn over 3f out: wknd fr 2f out* **9/1**
60 11 ¾ **Hoar Frost**[61] 919 3-8-12 0 TPO'Shea 1 51
(M R Channon) *chsd ldrs: rdn 3f out: wknd over 2f out* **50/1**
0-0 12 1 ¾ **Teen Spirit (IRE)**[19] 1684 3-8-10 0 GabrielHannon(7) 5 52
(J W Hills) *prom early: bhd fnl 5f* **40/1**
0-3 13 1 ¼ **Crazy About You (IRE)**[33] 1367 3-8-12 0 MichaelHills 3 45
(B W Hills) *unf: led tl hdd ins fnl 3f: sn wknd* **9/2**[2]
14 37 **Shecher Para** 3-8-12 0 TedDurcan 8 —
(H R A Cecil) *slowly away: a bhd: t.o* **22/1**

2m 9.55s (0.75) **Going Correction** +0.125s/f (Good) **14 Ran SP% 132.8**
Speed ratings (Par 101): **102,101,99,97,94 93,92,92,90,90 89,88,87,57**
CSF £33.58 TOTE £9.50: £2.70, £1.70, £4.30; EX 54.40.
Owner Mr & Mrs Duncan Davidson **Bred** Airlie Stud **Trained** Newmarket, Suffolk

FOCUS
Slightly quicker than the first division, and probably the better race. The first three could turn out to be smart, particulary the winner who was value for extra, and some of the others should find races at a lower level.
Dr Brass Official explanation: jockey said colt suffered interference in running

2198 OLYMPIC COACH BUILDERS/HENDY VAN AND TRUCK MAIDEN STKS 7f (S)
5:35 (5:40) (Class 4) 3-Y-O £5,828 (£1,734; £866; £432) Stalls Centre

Form RPR
3- 1 **Aqlaam**[293] 3991 3-9-3 RHills 10 102+
(W J Haggas) *h.d.w: hld up wl in tch: smooth effrt to ld wl over 1f out: rdn clr: readily* **1/1**[1]
2 2 ¾ **Round The Cape** 3-8-12 RichardHughes 16 86
(R Hannon) *w/like: dwlt: t.k.h in tch: r.o to chse wnr fnl f: a hld* **33/1**
3 3 ¼ **Karoush (USA)** 3-9-3 AlanMunro 14 82
(P W Chapple-Hyam) *w/like: scope: str: in tch: effrt 2f out: one pce appr fnl f* **11/4**[2]
4 1 ¼ **Yahwudhee (FR)** 3-9-3 AdrianMcCarthy 11 79
(P W Chapple-Hyam) *athletic: w ldrs: led 3f out tl wl over 1f out: sn outpcd by wnr* **40/1**
05 5 1 **Capucci**[9] 1926 3-9-3 JimmyFortune 15 76+
(J H M Gosden) *lw: mid-div: rdn and r.o appr fnl f: gng on at fin* **25/1**
5- 6 hd **Film Maker (IRE)**[211] 6295 3-9-3 SteveDrowne 9 75
(B J Meehan) *lw: t.k.h: trckd ldrs: rdn 2f out: one pce* **9/2**[2]
7 nk **Fountains Abbey (USA)** 3-8-12 RyanMoore 19 70+
(Sir Michael Stoute) *w/like: attractive: lw: mid-div: rdn 2f out: kpt on fnl f: nvr able to chal* **12/1**
8 1 ¾ **Amber Queen (IRE)** 3-8-12 MichaelHills 18 65+
(B W Hills) *w/like: leggy: towards rr: rdn and styd on fnl 2f: nt rch ldrs* **20/1**
9 2 ½ **Diego Rivera** 3-9-3 RichardSmith 1 63
(P J Makin) *unf: scope: bit bkwd: swvd lft s: in tch tl wknd 2f out: btn whn hung lft over 1f out* **100/1**
0- 10 1 ¼ **Empire Seeker (USA)**[203] 6494 3-8-10 GabrielHannon(7) 13 60
(J W Hills) *prom 5f* **100/1**
60 11 ½ **Opening Hand**[25] 1529 3-9-3 FergusSweeney 12 58
(Evan Williams) *hld up in midfield: hrd rdn over 2f out: nt pce to chal* **100/1**
40 12 1 ½ **Mr Hichens**[8] 1957 3-9-3 JamieSpencer 17 54
(B J Meehan) *dwlt: bhd: rdn 2f out: mod late hdwy* **25/1**
04 13 hd **Style Icon**[15] 1763 3-9-3 TQuinn 2 54
(D R C Elsworth) *w ldrs tl wknd over 1f out* **28/1**
14 1 **Lightning Squall (USA)** 3-9-3 TedDurcan 8 51
(M Botti) *unf: dwlt: sn pushed along in rr of midfield: n.d* **33/1**
0 15 1 ¼ **First Tracks (IRE)**[15] 1763 3-8-12 PatrickHills(5) 5 48
(J W Hills) *led tl 3f out: wknd 2f out* **100/1**
16 hd **Triple Dream** 3-9-3 RichardMullen 7 47
(J L Dunlop) *w/like: bhd: rdn over 2f out: nvr nr ldrs* **50/1**
17 shd **Wivny (USA)** 3-8-12 StephenDonohoe 6 42
(P A Blockley) *unf: sn pshd along: a in rr* **100/1**
18 1 ¼ **Seven Royals (IRE)** 3-9-3 CatherineGannon 4 44
(Miss A M Newton-Smith) *str: bit bkwd: dwlt: t.k.h and sn in tch: rdn 3f out: sn wknd* **150/1**
19 3 ½ **Isle Of Capri** 3-8-12 JimCrowley 3 29
(R Hannon) *w/like: rdn over 2f out: a towards rr* **50/1**
0 20 3 ½ **Scary Movie (IRE)**[19] 1669 3-9-3 TPO'Shea 20 25
(D J Coakley) *s.s and swtchd lft to centre: a towards rr: rdn and no ch fnl 2f* **40/1**

1m 25.62s (-0.08) **Going Correction** +0.125s/f (Good) **20 Ran SP% 138.7**
Speed ratings (Par 101): **105,101,98,96,95 95,95,93,90,88 88,86,86,85,83 83,83,81,77,73**
CSF £59.33 TOTE £2.30: £1.40, £7.20, £1.80; EX 81.30 Place 6: £48.01, Place 5: £19.02..
Owner Hamdan Al Maktoum **Bred** Granham Farm **Trained** Newmarket, Suffolk

FOCUS
Probably a decent maiden with a number of likely improvers, and the winner looking potentially high-class. The form should work out.
Style Icon Official explanation: jockey said colt hung left-handed
T/Jkpt: Not won T/Plt: £96.20 to a £1 stake. Pool: £132,056.81. 1,001.94 winning tickets. T/Qpdt: £36.50 to a £1 stake. Pool: £7,329.80. 148.20 winning tickets. ST

2160

NEWMARKET (ROWLEY) (R-H)
Saturday, May 17

OFFICIAL GOING: Good to soft
Wind: Light across Weather: Overcast

2199 SIGN-UP BONUS@BETINTERNET.COM MAIDEN STKS 1m
1:50 (1:53) (Class 4) 3-Y-O £5,180 (£1,541; £770; £384) Stalls High

Form RPR
222- 1 **Rattan (USA)**[216] 6202 3-9-3 78 TPQueally 18 89+
(H R A Cecil) *chsd ldrs: led over 1f out: rdn clr* **5/2**[1]
4-2 2 5 **Hawk Island (IRE)**[24] 1573 3-9-3 0 RobertHavlin 9 77+
(G Wragg) *chsd ldrs: nt clr run and outpcd over 1f out: styd on ins fnl f* **10/3**[2]
03- 3 ½ **Deo Valente (IRE)**[225] 5971 3-8-10 0 KMay(7) 15 76
(B J Meehan) *led over 6f: no ex fnl f* **15/2**[3]
5 4 ½ **La Sarrazine (FR)**[16] 1748 3-8-12 0 RobertWinston 10 70
(J R Fanshawe) *hld up: hdwy over 3f out: swtchd lft and outpcd over 2f out: styd on fnl f* **14/1**
00-0 5 1 ¾ **Redarsene**[28] 1479 3-8-12 58 JamieJones(5) 12 71
(M G Quinlan) *hld up: racd keenly: hdwy over 2f out: rdn over 1f out: styd on same pce* **50/1**
0 6 3 **Sleeping**[26] 1519 3-8-12 0 JimmyQuinn 17 59
(M H Tompkins) *hld up in tch: rdn over 2f out: wknd fnl f* **100/1**
0- 7 ½ **Perez Prado (USA)**[197] 6618 3-9-3 0 J-PGuillambert 2 63+
(W Jarvis) *hld up: swtchd rt and hdwy over 3f out: rdn and ev ch over 1f out: wknd fnl f* **28/1**
0-5 8 nk **Trenchant**[32] 1380 3-9-3 0 AdamKirby 13 62+
(J R Fanshawe) *s.i.s: hld up: hdwy and hung rt over 1f out: n.d* **25/1**
05- 9 1 ¼ **Striving (IRE)**[228] 5881 3-8-12 0 KerrinMcEvoy 7 54
(Sir Michael Stoute) *chsd ldrs: rdn and ev ch over 2f out: wknd over 1f out* **8/1**
10 4 ½ **Spider Silk** 3-9-3 0 WilliamBuick 4 49
(W Jarvis) *sn pushed along: a in rr* **33/1**
0- 11 2 **Falcativ**[225] 5971 3-9-3 0 DaneO'Neill 3 44
(L M Cumani) *hld up: nvr nr to chal* **8/1**
12 1 ½ **Zuwaar** 3-9-3 0 (t) DavidKinsella 14 41
(J H M Gosden) *s.i.s: outpcd* **16/1**
6-0 13 2 **Brother Barry (USA)**[31] 1403 3-9-3 0 NeilPollard 8 36+
(W J Musson) *chsd ldrs 6f* **25/1**
0 14 6 **Zeeran**[36] 1298 3-8-12 0 AhmedAjtebi(5) 5 22
(C E Brittain) *chsd ldrs: rdn over 2f out: sn wknd* **50/1**
15 3 ½ **Vital Link (IRE)** 3-9-3 0 LiamJones 1 14
(W J Haggas) *s.i.s: a in rr* **16/1**
0 16 1 **Squire Boldwood (IRE)**[16] 1748 3-9-0 0 MarcHalford(3) 6 12
(D R C Elsworth) *mid-div: sn pushed along: hung lft 1/2-way: sn wknd* **40/1**

1m 41.01s (2.41) **Going Correction** +0.375s/f (Good) **16 Ran SP% 125.5**
Speed ratings (Par 101): **102,97,96,96,94 91,90,90,89,84 82,81,79,73,69 68**
CSF £9.80 TOTE £3.50: £1.80, £1.60, £2.80; EX 12.80.
Owner K Abdulla **Bred** Juddmonte Farms Inc **Trained** Newmarket, Suffolk
■ Stewards' Enquiry : Robert Winston two-day ban; careless riding (May 31-June 1)

FOCUS
A modest maiden apart from the winner, and the time was 1.38 secs slower than the following handicap. The form looks sound enough and has been rated at face value.
Trenchant Official explanation: jockey said gelding became unbalanced
Zuwaar Official explanation: jockey said, regarding running and riding, that his orders, on this the colt's debut, were to jump out, do his best, but not be unduly hard once it tired, adding that it showed signs of inexperience, being slowly away before struggling through greenness and possibly being unsuited by the good, good to soft places, ground; trainer's rep confirmed adding that the colt has had a wind operation necessitating the fitting of a tongue strap, appears moderate and is entered in the July sales.

2200 BEST ODDS GUARANTEED AT BETINTERNET.COM H'CAP 1m
2:25 (2:26) (Class 3) (0-95,92) 4-Y-O+ £9,066 (£2,697; £1,348; £673) Stalls High

Form RPR
231- 1 **Fondled**[241] 5545 4-8-9 83 KerrinMcEvoy 5 96+
(J R Fanshawe) *s.i.s: hld up: hdwy over 1f out: sn rdn: r.o to ld wl ins fnl f* **4/1**[3]
60-4 2 1 ¼ **Ace Of Hearts**[21] 1633 9-8-13 92 JackMitchell(5) 6 99
(C F Wall) *chsd ldrs: led over 2f out: rdn: edgd lft and hdd wl ins fnl f* **11/1**
00-0 3 1 ¼ **Billy Dane (IRE)**[15] 1774 4-8-6 80 TonyHamilton 10 84
(R A Fahey) *hld up: hdwy over 2f out: rdn and hung rt fr over 1f out: styd on* **28/1**
/406 4 1 ¼ **Royal Island (IRE)**[28] 1497 6-8-10 84 VinceSlattery 9 85
(M G Quinlan) *hld up in tch: chsd ldr 2f out: sn ev ch: wknd ins fnl f* **9/1**
42-2 5 17 **Oceana Gold**[13] 1828 4-9-0 88 WilliamBuick 3 50
(A M Balding) *sn chsng ldr: rdn over 2f out: wknd over 1f out* **2/1**[1]
51-1 6 ¾ **Viva Vettori**[12] 1857 4-8-11 88 MarcHalford(3) 7 48
(D R C Elsworth) *led: racd keenly: hdd over 2f out: wknd over 1f out* **9/4**[2]
1260 7 5 **Sri Kuantan (IRE)**[11] 1904 4-8-4 78 oh1 JimmyQuinn 4 27
(P F I Cole) *hld up: plld hrd: rdn and wknd over 2f out* **33/1**
0000 8 ¾ **Very Wise**[14] 1816 6-9-4 92 LiamJones 2 39
(W J Haggas) *s.i.s: sn chsng ldrs: hung rt and wknd over 2f out* **16/1**
2500 9 14 **Moonlight Man**[10] 1910 7-8-8 82 RobertWinston 1 —
(C R Dore) *hld up: rdn and wknd over 2f out* **50/1**

1m 39.63s (1.03) **Going Correction** +0.375s/f (Good) **9 Ran SP% 116.7**
Speed ratings (Par 107): **109,107,106,105,88 87,82,81,67**
CSF £46.31 CT £1091.65 TOTE £4.70: £1.60, £2.10, £5.10; EX 37.30 Trifecta £593.40 Pool: £919.50 - 1.10 winning units..
Owner Cheveley Park Stud **Bred** Cheveley Park Stud Ltd **Trained** Newmarket, Suffolk
■

FOCUS
A decent handicap run at a sound pace in the conditions, being 1.38secs faster than the opening maiden. The market leaders set the pace but where left behind in the last quarter-mile and the proximity of those in the frame behind the winner suggests the form is only ordinary.

NOTEBOOK

Fondled ◆, who progressed with racing last season, was 3lb higher than for a narrow win on her final start. She missed the break and looked to be struggling to get involved running down into the Dip, but she picked up really well once hitting the rising ground and in the end won with a little in hand. She was well suited by the ground, as her pedigree suggests she was likely to be, but in any case she looks a progressive sort and no doubt connections will be hoping she improves enough to earn black type at some stage. (tchd 9-2 in a place)

Ace Of Hearts ◆, from a yard that is going well at present, travelled well throughout and looked all over the winner running down into the Dip, but he could not hold off the winner up the hill. However, this was a decent effort from the veteran, especially as he is at is best on a fast surface and has not looked at his most effective at this track in the past. He often goes well on a turning right-handed track and on fast ground, so is one to bear in mind for when he gets those conditions. (op 10-1 tchd 8-1)

Billy Dane(IRE) has not shown much since finishing third in the Totesport Silver Bowl at around this time last year, and has dropped 10lb in the handicap as a result. This was a better performance and he may be able to build on this back on fast ground. (op 33-1)

Royal Island(IRE), having his first run for his current trainer having raced in Ireland from 2007 up until last month, was backed beforehand and travelled smoothly into the race, but he has not actually won since August 2005 and did not see it out. He was rated 19lb higher at around this time two years ago, so could prove well handicapped if able to build on this effort. (op 16-1)

Oceana Gold, who likes to race up with the pace, had every chance but faded pretty quickly in the closing stages. Official explanation: jockey said gelding was unsuited by the good to soft ground (op 5-2 tchd 11-4 in a place)

Viva Vettori, whose two recent wins have both been on Polytrack, made the running but stopped pretty quickly once headed and may have set too strong a gallop. Official explanation: jockey said colt was unsuited by the good to soft ground (tchd 5-2 and 11-4 in a place)

2201 BETINTERNET.COM H'CAP — 1m 4f

3:00 (3:01) (Class 3) (0-95,85) 3-Y-O — **£9,066** (£2,697; £1,348; £673) **Stalls** Centre

Form				RPR
4-12	**1**		**Enroller (IRE)**[21] 1618 3-9-9 **85** ... DO'Donohoe 5 (W R Muir) *a.p: rdn to ld over 2f out: edgd lft over 1f out: styd on wl* **13/8**[1]	96
2-21	**2**	*nk*	**Fiulin**[35] 1330 3-9-9 **85** ... KerrinMcEvoy 4 (M Botti) *hld up: swtchd lft and hdwy over 2f out: sn ev ch: styd on u.p* **15/8**[2]	96
2313	**3**	*6*	**Silver Waters**[17] 1731 3-8-10 **75** ... MarcHalford(3) 3 (D R C Elsworth) *chsd ldrs: rdn over 2f out: hung rt over 1f out: no ex fnl f* **13/2**	76
64-1	**4**	*5*	**Mazaaya (USA)**[16] 1746 3-9-9 **85** ... RobertWinston 2 (M Johnston) *chsd ldr tl rdn over 2f out: wknd over 1f out* **5/1**[3]	78
33-1	**5**	*2*	**Judgethemoment (USA)**[37] 1283 3-9-9 **85** ... TGMcLaughlin 6 (Jane Chapple-Hyam) *led: rdn and hdd over 2f out: wknd over 1f out* **14/1**	75

2m 39.24s (5.74) **Going Correction** +0.375s/f (Good) — **5** Ran SP% **109.5**

Speed ratings (Par 103): **95,94,90,87,86**

CSF £4.92 TOTE £2.60: £1.60, £1.70; EX 5.70.

Owner D G Clarke & C L A Edginton **Bred** Mrs Denise Brophy **Trained** Lambourn, Berks

■

FOCUS

A decent handicap despite the small field but there was no early pace and the time was ordinary. The winner is rated to his previous form with the winner raised 6lb compared with his previous mark.

NOTEBOOK

Enroller(IRE), whose close second at Leicester was boosted when the winner went on to be narrowly beaten in the Chester Vase, continued his progress with a battling success from his market rival. He could now be in line for a crack at the King George V Handicap, but will need some cut in the ground. (op 7-4 tchd 15-8)

Fiulin, who is progressing with experience, was held up before coming to have every chance running into the Dip. He pressed the winner all the way to the line but still looks a little green and, well clear of the rest, he has the potential to win a decent middle-distance/staying handicap before the season is out. Something like the Melrose Handicap at York appeals as a suitable long-term target. (op 5-2)

Silver Waters, probably found the ground too testing behind an improver last time and came up against a couple of similar sorts on this occasion. He will be helped by a drop in grade and it will be interesting to see how he performs on a sound surface, as it suited his sire well. (op 11-2 tchd 5-1)

Mazaaya(USA), who scored at great leighs on her previous outing, was 7lb higher and had to race off level weights with the market leaders. She had also not encountered easy ground before and was unable to run up to her previous mark on this step up in distance. (op 9-2)

2202 BETINTERNET.COM STKS (HERITAGE H'CAP) — 1m 6f

3:35 (3:38) (Class 2) (0-105,103) 4-Y-O+

£24,924 (£7,464; £3,732; £1,868; £932; £468) **Stalls** Centre

Form				RPR
14-1	**1**		**Ajaan**[14] 1812 4-9-2 **95** ... (b) TPQueally 11 (H R A Cecil) *hld up: hdwy over 4f out: led over 2f out: styd on wl* **15/8**[1]	108+
00-0	**2**	*3 ¼*	**Halla San**[10] 1916 6-8-13 **92** ... TonyHamilton 3 (R A Fahey) *chsd ldrs: ev ch over 2f out: sn rdn: styd on same pce fnl f* **16/1**	98
222-	**3**	*1*	**Sanbuch**[189] 6759 4-9-10 **103** ... DaneO'Neill 5 (L M Cumani) *hld up: rdn over 5f out: nt clr run 2f out: swtchd lft and hdwy over 1f out: styd on* **17/2**	107+
0-05	**4**	*1*	**Heron Bay**[21] 1629 4-9-5 **98** ... RobertHavlin 6 (G Wragg) *hld up: hdwy over 1f out: nt trble ldrs* **14/1**	101
333-	**5**	*4*	**Hot Diamond**[31] 6473 4-8-4 **83** ... WilliamBuick 4 (P J Hobbs) *s.i.s: hld up: hdwy over 2f out: rdn and hung rt over 1f out: wkng whn hung lft ins fnl f* **10/3**[2]	80
323	**6**	*1 ¾*	**Grande Caiman (IRE)**[25] 1544 4-9-1 **94** ... PatDobbs 10 (R Hannon) *hld up in tch: rdn over 2f out: wknd over 1f out* **20/1**	89
31/-	**7**	*shd*	**Backbord (GER)**[21] 6191 6-9-3 **96** ... IanMongan 8 (Mrs L Wadham) *led: rdn and hdd over 2f out: wknd over 1f out* **12/1**	91
35-3	**8**	*9*	**Sphinx (FR)**[21] 1625 10-8-9 **88** ... RobertWinston 7 (E W Tuer) *chsd ldr tl rdn over 2f out: wknd over 1f out* **8/1**[3]	70
32-2	**9**	*2*	**Four Miracles**[7] 1998 4-7-12 **77** oh1 ... JimmyQuinn 1 (M H Tompkins) *prom: rdn over 2f out: hung rt and wknd wl over 1f out* **8/1**[3]	56
45-1	**10**	*28*	**Chocolate Caramel (USA)**[23] 1583 6-8-9 **88** ... ShaneKelly 2 (Mrs A J Perrett) *s.i.s: hld up: rdn and wknd over 2f out* **18/1**	28

3m 5.13s (6.63) **Going Correction** +0.375s/f (Good) — **10** Ran SP% **120.9**

Speed ratings (Par 109): **96,94,93,93,90 89,89,84,83,67**

CSF £37.25 CT £219.28 TOTE £2.70: £1.30, £5.20, £3.10; EX 43.10 Trifecta £234.60 Pool: £1,024.70 - 3.10 winning units..

Owner Niarchos Family **Bred** Miss K Rausing & Course Investment Corporation **Trained** Newmarket, Suffolk

FOCUS

A good handicap with a decent prizemoney but the pace was again modest early on and ultimately an easy winner. The field raced up the centre of the track in the straight, whereas in the previous contests they stuck towards the far rail and those that came from off the pace dominated as the leaders dropped away. The winner is an improver but the third is rated to his best at this trip.

NOTEBOOK

Ajaan ◆, who has looked quirky on several occasions, is nevertheless improving with racing and on this occasion kept pretty straight once in front. Always travelling sweetly under restraint, he cruised into contention and won without turning a hair. He looks set to develop into a Pattern-race performer if the progress continues, but at this stage he looks a likely contender for the Ebor Handicap over this trip later in the summer. (op 9-4)

Halla San, who was hammered by the Handicapper for a wide-margin success at Catterick last spring, was subsequently campaigned over hurdles. Although dropped a couple of pounds, he is still a stone higher than his last winning mark on the Flat and so this was another creditable effort. He will not find things easy until the assessor gives him a bit more leeway. (tchd 20-1)

Sanbuch ◆, another who is well above his last winning mark, developed into a consistent performer at the end of last season. He put up an encouraging effort on this return to action and is the sort his patient trainer does so well with. He is another who could develop into an Ebor contender and a return to fast ground will be in his favour. (op 13-2 tchd 9-1)

Heron Bay, who broke his maiden when winning the King George V Handicap at Royal Ascot last season, but has struggled since off higher marks. The Handicapper has eased him 7lb since last backend but he never really got involved here, although this was the first time he had raced on such easy ground. (tchd 16-1)

Hot Diamond, who was backed against the winner, was returning to the Flat after running well over hurdles in the winter. He missed the break but moved up to have a chance at the quarter-mile pole, only to hang under pressure and fade up the hill. He does not totally convince with his attitude and connections may have to resort to some form of headgear to make him apply himself. (op 11-2)

Grande Caiman(IRE), a consistent performer on Polytrack, was having just his third start on turf and looks much less effective on it. (op 12-1)

Chocolate Caramel(USA) Official explanation: jockey said gelding stopped very quickly

2203 BETINTERNET.COM SPORTS BETTING H'CAP — 7f

4:10 (4:12) (Class 4) (0-80,79) 4-Y-O+ — **£4,857** (£1,445; £722; £360) **Stalls** High

Form				RPR
1-25	**1**		**King's Bastion (IRE)**[1] 2163 4-9-3 **78** ... DaneO'Neill 11 (M L W Bell) *hld up: hdwy 1/2-way: rdn to ld wl ins fnl f: jst hld on* **4/1**[2]	88
0/16	**2**	*shd*	**Jake The Snake (IRE)**[12] 1857 7-9-0 **75** ... RobertWinston 12 (A W Carroll) *hld up: hdwy wl over 2f out: led over 1f out: rdn and hdd wl ins fnl f: r.o* **7/2**[1]	85
63-0	**3**	*1*	**Aggravation**[17] 1729 6-8-6 **70** ... MarcHalford(3) 14 (D R C Elsworth) *hld up: hdwy over 1f out: r.o* **14/1**	77
0464	**4**	*2 ½*	**Resplendent Alpha**[9] 1928 4-8-11 **72** ... ShaneKelly 4 (P Howling) *hld up: hmpd 2f out: sn swtchd rt: r.o ins fnl f: nt trble ldrs* **12/1**	77+
333	**5**	*½*	**Resplendent Nova**[24] 1566 6-9-0 **75** ... JimmyQuinn 1 (P Howling) *chsd ldrs: led over 2f out: rdn and hdd over 1f out: no ex ins fnl f* **9/1**	74
1043	**6**	*2 ½*	**Desert Dreamer (IRE)**[7] 1996 7-9-0 **75** ... RichardKingscote 3 (Tom Dascombe) *s.s: hdwy 1/2-way: rdn and hung rt over 1f out: wknd fnl f* **13/2**[3]	67
3-06	**7**	*hd*	**Blue Charm**[22] 1604 4-8-12 **73** ... (t) SebSanders 7 (S Kirk) *prom: rdn and hung lft over 1f out: wknd fnl f* **8/1**	65
000-	**8**	*2 ½*	**Grizedale (IRE)**[196] 6651 9-8-6 **67** ... (t) PaulDoe 10 (M J Attwater) *chsd ldrs: led 3f out: rdn and hdd over 2f out: wknd fnl f* **12/1**	52
010-	**9**	*½*	**The Fifth Member (IRE)**[196] 6651 4-9-4 **79** ... KerrinMcEvoy 5 (J R Boyle) *prom: rdn over 2f out: wknd over 1f out* **8/1**	63
20-0	**10**	*nk*	**Orchestrator (IRE)**[12] 1876 4-8-4 **65** ... NeilPollard 9 (T G Mills) *dwlt: hld up: plld hrd: hmpd 2f out: n.d* **25/1**	48
06-0	**11**	*3 ¾*	**Kaballero (GER)**[17] 1719 7-8-9 **70** ... TPQueally 6 (S Gollings) *chsd ldrs: rdn over 2f out: sn edgd lft: wkng whn hung rt over 1f out* **28/1**	43
1000	**12**	*1 ¼*	**Super Frank (IRE)**[7] 1996 5-8-6 **67** ... J-PGuillambert 13 (J Akehurst) *led 4f: rdn and wknd over 1f out* **11/1**	37
/06-	**13**	*2*	**Emulate**[332] 2767 4-9-2 **77** ... IanMongan 2 (C F Wall) *hld up: racd keenly: hmpd 2f out: n.d* **20/1**	41

1m 28.08s (2.68) **Going Correction** +0.375s/f (Good) — **13** Ran SP% **130.2**

Speed ratings (Par 105): **99,98,97,94,94 91,91,88,87,87 83,81,79**

CSF £19.79 CT £172.31 TOTE £4.50: £1.90, £2.00, £4.40; EX 19.70.

Owner Edward J Ware **Bred** Floors Farming And Dominic Burke **Trained** Newmarket, Suffolk

FOCUS

A fair and pretty competitive handicap on paper but the pace was not strong and the race was dominated by the market leaders. The placed horses are rated to their marks in an ordinary handicap for the track.

Resplendent Alpha Official explanation: jockey said gelding suffered interference in running

Emulate Official explanation: jockey said filly suffered interference in running

2204 JOIN BETINTERNET.COM FOR CHAMPIONS LEAGUE FINAL NOVICE STKS — 6f

4:45 (4:47) (Class 4) 2-Y-O — **£5,180** (£1,541; £770; £384) **Stalls** High

Form				RPR
61	**1**		**Northern Tour**[37] 1276 2-9-0 0 ... NelsonDeSouza 8 (P F I Cole) *chsd ldrs: outpcd over 3f out: rallied to ld 1f out: r.o* **11/1**[3]	81
	2	*hd*	**I Am The Best** 2-8-7 0 ... AhmedAjtebi(5) 5 (D M Simcock) *s.i.s: hld up: racd keenly: nt clr run over 2f out: hdwy over 1f out: rdn and ev ch ins fnl f: r.o* **16/1**	78
	3	*1 ¼*	**Verlegen (IRE)** 2-8-7 0 ... PatDobbs 6 (R Hannon) *led to 1/2-way: rdn and ev ch 1f out: styd on same pce ins fnl f* **18/1**	70
010	**4**	*2*	**Bad Beat**[31] 1399 2-8-11 0 ... JerryO'Dwyer(3) 1 (V Smith) *prom: racd keenly: rdn and edgd lft over 1f out: styd on same pce fnl f* **16/1**	71
1	**5**	*2*	**Missile Dodger (USA)**[18] 1693 2-9-0 0 ... SebSanders 4 (R M Beckett) *chsd ldr tl led 1/2-way: rdn and hung lft over 1f out: sn hdd: wknd ins fnl f* **4/5**[1]	65
14	**6**	*3 ¾*	**Fuaigh Mor (IRE)**[14] 1813 2-8-8 0 ow1 ... RobertWinston 3 (A Bailey) *hld up in tch: jnd ldrs over 2f out: rdn: hung lft and wknd over 1f out* **10/1**[2]	47

1m 15.48s (3.28) **Going Correction** +0.375s/f (Good) — **6** Ran SP% **90.0**

Speed ratings (Par 95): **93,92,91,88,85 80**

CSF £83.49 TOTE £9.00: £2.60, £3.10; EX 68.70.

Owner Hunter, Maynard, Ward **Bred** Arbib Bloodstock Partnership **Trained** Whatcombe, Oxon

■ Exceptional Art (5/2) was withdrawn (reared up in stalls); Rule 4 applies, deduction 25p in the £.

■ Stewards' Enquiry : Ahmed Ajtebi one-day ban: careless riding (May 31)

FOCUS
This looked an uncompetitive race on paper and was made more so by the withdrawal of the second favourite. However, there was a surprise result with the favourite failing to make the frame. The form is best rated around the winner and fourth in a messy contest.

NOTEBOOK
Northern Tour, who made all when taking a four-runner maiden on similar ground at Folkestone last time, was virtually disregarded in the market despite the runner-up from that race having won since and his trainer going particularly well with his juveniles. Adopting less forceful tactics, he found plenty when asked to quicken and battled on up the hill to hold off the runner-up. Although he is no star, he has the right attitude and that should help him win more races. (op 9-1)
I Am The Best ◆, a 37,000gns first foal from a precocious family, missed the break but ran a fine race on this debut. Challenging up te hill but being unable to get past the more experienced winner. He looks sure to pick up a maiden on this evidence. (op 28-1 tchd 22-1 in a place)
Verlegen(IRE), a 68,000gns half-sister to Rag Top, is from a stable whose two-year-olds are in fine form and she clearly knew her job. Smartly away from the stalls she made the early running and battled back when the favourite headed her. She looks capable of winning a maiden against her own sex and a faster surface should be in her favour. (op 14-1 tchd 20-1)
Bad Beat, who finished well behind today's winner in the Brocklesby, had since won on Fibresand but had been well held in a conditions stakes on this track. He showed up for a fair way but is not up to this class and he may be best given a break and brought back for nurseries. (op 33-1)
Missile Dodger(USA), who made all to score in rain-softened ground on his debut at Bath, looked to have a fairly straightforward task once the second favourite was withdrawn. However, that race has not really worked out and, after travelling well enough into the lead, he began to flounder and dropped away quite tamely. He did not look totally at home on the undulations, so 5f back on a flatter track and a sounder surface may suit him better. (op 10-11 tchd evens in places)

2205 BETINTERNET.COM APPRENTICE H'CAP 6f
5:20 (5:21) (Class 5) (0-75,74) 4-Y-0+ £3,885 (£1,156; £577; £288) Stalls High

Form RPR
0-01 **1** **Mango Music**[16] 1739 5-9-5 **74** WilliamBuick 4 87
(M Quinn) *mde all: rdn out* **4/1**[2]
0-02 **2** ½ **Millfields Dreams**[1] 2166 9-8-0 **60** oh1 (p) PatrickDonaghy(5) 2 71
(P Leech) *chsd ldrs: rdn over 1f out: r.o* **10/1**
4400 **3** 2½ **Thoughtsofstardom**[7] 1996 5-8-2 **60** KellyHarrison(3) 10 63
(M Wigham) *trckd wnr: plld hrd: rdn over 1f out: no ex ins fnl f* **6/1**
-000 **4** 1 **Jimmy The Guesser**[19] 1683 5-8-12 **70** JackMitchell(3) 9 70
(N P Littmoden) *trckd ldrs: rdn over 1f out: styd on same pce ins fnl f* **17/2**
40-0 **5** ½ **Bateleur**[12] 1872 4-8-12 **72** MCGeran(5) 7 71
(M R Channon) *hld up: rdn over 1f out: styd on ins fnl f: nvr nrr* **11/2**[3]
05-2 **6** nk **Ingleby Princess**[13] 1826 4-8-7 **65** NeilBrown(3) 5 63+
(T D Barron) *s.s: outpcd: styd on ins fnl f: nvr nrr* **3/1**[1]
020- **7** 7 **Brunelleschi**[200] 6575 5-9-0 **74** (b) WilliamCarson(5) 1 49
(J Ryan) *s.s: outpcd* **8/1**
-632 **8** 3¾ **Double Bill (USA)**[11] 1901 4-8-10 **70** (b) DTDaSilva(5) 11 33
(P F I Cole) *chsd ldrs: rdn 1/2-way: wknd over 1f out* **9/1**
2300 **9** 8 **Lindbergh**[25] 1541 6-8-2 **60** oh1 (v) NicolPolli(3) 8 —
(J Ryan) *prom over 4f: eased* **14/1**

1m 13.96s (1.76) **Going Correction** +0.375s/f (Good) 9 Ran SP% **122.1**
Speed ratings (Par 103): **103,102,99,97,97 96,87,82,71**
CSF £46.19 CT £246.45 TOTE £4.20: £1.70, £4.00, £2.40; EX 45.10 Place 6: £214.96, Place 5 £162.39..
Owner Brian Morton **Bred** A G Antoniades **Trained** Newmarket, Suffolk

FOCUS
A modest apprentice handicap run 1.52secs faster than the preceding juvenile event. The winner is rated to last year's best with the runner-up close to his form of the previous day.
Ingleby Princess Official explanation: jockey said filly reared on leaving stalls
T/Plt: £257.00 to a £1 stake. Pool: £101,078.09. 287.10 winning tickets. T/Qpdt: £55.80 to a £1 stake. Pool: £4,788.96. 63.50 winning tickets. CR

2004 THIRSK (L-H)
Saturday, May 17

OFFICIAL GOING: Good changing to good (good to soft patches on top bend) after race 3 (3.10)
The ground was reckoned 'almost soft in the back straight, easy on the straight course'.
Wind: Nil Weather: Overcast

2206 E B F MARION GIBSON BROWN MEMORIAL MAIDEN FILLIES' STKS 5f
2:00 (2:01) (Class 4) 2-Y-0 £5,180 (£1,541; £770; £384) Stalls High

Form RPR
1 **Haigh Hall** 2-9-0 0 DavidAllan 11 84+
(T D Easterby) *s.i.s: sn in tch: swtchd lft and smooth hdwy 2f out: led ent fnl f: shkn up and kpt on* **4/1**[2]
2 ¾ **Excellent Show** 2-9-0 0 TomEaves 8 81+
(B Smart) *sn led: rdn along 2f out: hdd ent fnl f: kpt on u.p* **5/2**[1]
3 3¼ **Sparta Rebel (IRE)** 2-9-0 0 NCallan 9 70
(M J Wallace) *cl up on stands' rail: ev ch 2f out: sn rdn and kpt on same pce appr fnl f* **14/1**
4 5 **Black Salix (USA)** 2-9-0 0 MickyFenton 10 52
(Mrs P Sly) *in tch: effrt and cl up 1/2-way: sn rdn and wknd wl over 1f out* **16/1**
5 2¼ **Harriet's Girl** 2-9-0 0 AndrewElliott 7 44
(K R Burke) *dwlt: sn rdn along in rr: sme late hdwy* **22/1**
60 **6** 1 **Neo's Mate (IRE)**[9] 1924 2-8-7 0 AndrewHeffernan(7) 3 40
(Paul Green) *in rr and pushed along 1/2-way: sme late hdwy* **25/1**
03 **7** 2¼ **Dispol Toba**[11] 1889 2-9-0 0 PaulFessey 1 32
(P T Midgley) *wnt lft s: sn rdn along and nvr nr ldrs* **33/1**
30 **8** nk **Marygate (IRE)**[29] 1447 2-8-11 0 MarkLawson(3) 2 31
(M Brittain) *t.k.h: prom on outer tl rdn along 2f out and sn wknd* **8/1**[3]
9 7 **Daanaat (IRE)** 2-9-0 0 DarryllHolland 6 6+
(M R Channon) *prom: pushed along 1/2-way: sn rdn and wknd* **5/2**[1]
0 **10** 4½ **Real Diamond**[16] 1749 2-8-11 0 MichaelJStainton(3) 4 —
(A Dickman) *chsd ldrs: rdn along 2f out and sn wknd* **16/1**
11 107 **Kannie Annie** 2-9-0 0 DanielTudhope 5 —
(T J Pitt) *s.i.s: a outpcd: t.o fr 1/2-way* **33/1**

62.24 secs (2.64) **Going Correction** +0.35s/f (Good) 11 Ran SP% **120.8**
Speed ratings (Par 92): **92,90,85,77,74 72,68,68,57,49** —
CSF £14.21 TOTE £5.00: £1.90, £1.30, £4.70; EX 14.10.
Owner David W Armstrong **Bred** G Russell **Trained** Great Habton, N Yorks

FOCUS
Almost certainly a smart maiden fillies' race. The winner very highly regarded and the first pair finished clear.

NOTEBOOK
Haigh Hall ◆, a half-sister to the smart Dont Dili Dali, came with a big reputation. She did it nicely in the end and a trip to Beverley for the Hilary Needler is the favoured route ahead of the Queen Mary at Royal Ascot. (op 5-1)
Excellent Show ◆, whose dam is a half-sister to top sprinter Mind Games, knew her job but almost certainly met a smart filly on their respective debuts. She looks nailed on to go one better soon. (op 11-4)
Sparta Rebel(IRE) made a satisfactory debut but in the end proved no match for two very promising fillies. (op 12-1)
Black Salix(USA), a fourth foal, is out of a mare useful in sprints in the USA who has already produced three winners. She will have learnt plenty from this introduction. (tchd 14-1)
Harriet's Girl showed ability on her debut after a sluggish start and she will be better suited by 6f. (op 16-1)
Neo's Mate(IRE), having her third run, will be better off in nurseries. (op 33-1)
Daanaat(IRE) has a speedy pedigree, being a half-sister to smart juvenile Alzerra, but she was soon struggling to keep up. (op 15-8 tchd 11-4)

2207 WHITBY MAIDEN STKS 1m 4f
2:35 (2:36) (Class 5) 3-Y-0+ £3,885 (£1,156; £577; £288) Stalls Low

Form RPR
25 **1** **Touchdown**[25] 1539 3-8-10 0 JoeFanning 1 85+
(M Johnston) *t.k.h: trckd ldrs: led after 5f: rdn along 2f out: styd on wl u.p fnl f* **11/4**[2]
43 **2** 2½ **Dolly Penrose**[13] 1840 3-8-5 0 EdwardCreighton 15 72
(M R Channon) *in tch: hdwy 4f out: chsd wnr 2f out: sn rdn and kpt on same pce ins fnl f* **15/2**[3]
3 ½ **Indian Groom (IRE)** 3-8-10 0 TomEaves 6 79+
(J Howard Johnson) *hld up towards rr: hdwy on outer wl over 2f out: styd on wl appr fnl f: nrst fin* **33/1**
6-2 **4** nk **Warringah**[21] 1621 3-8-10 0 NCallan 7 76
(Sir Michael Stoute) *trckd ldrs: effrt over 2f out and sn rdn: ev ch over 1f out: styd on same pce: n.m.r and lost 3rd nr line* **4/6**[1]
3 **5** 3¾ **Kimbolton**[21] 1638 3-8-5 0 SaleemGolam 8 65
(H R A Cecil) *hld up towards rr: stdy hdwy on inner over 3f out: swtchd rt and rdn 2f out: no imp appr fnl f* **20/1**
5 **6** 2½ **Danesman**[32] 1382 3-8-10 0 ChrisCatlin 9 66
(E J O'Neill) *a.p: effrt to chse wnr 4f out: rdn along over 2f out: drvn and wknd over 1f out* **14/1**
7 4 **Enderby Light (FR)** 3-8-10 0 DavidAllan 2 59
(D Carroll) *midfield: effrt and hdwy 4f out: rdn along and in tch 3f out: sn drvn and grad wknd* **50/1**
00 **8** 12 **Slivovic (IRE)**[31] 1391 4-9-1 0 JamesRogers(7) 12 35
(J S Wainwright) *n.d* **200/1**
0 **9** 3¼ **Osteopathic Care (IRE)**[14] 1814 4-9-13 0 PhillipMakin 14 35
(Miss Tracy Waggott) *midfield: hdwy and in tch over 3f out: sn rdn and wknd* **66/1**
05-4 **10** 6 **Finnegans Rainbow**[92] 188 6-9-10 42 LeeVickers(3) 11 25
(M C Chapman) *prom: rdn along 6f out: sn wknd* **200/1**
00 **11** ½ **Victorias**[21] 1628 3-7-12 0 CharlotteKerton(7) 4 20
(A Crook) *a towards rr* **200/1**
0506 **12** 1 **Art Of Being (IRE)**[18] 1700 4-9-6 40 (p) NBazeley(7) 10 23
(M C Chapman) *led 5f: prom tl rdn along 4f out and sn wknd* **200/1**
35 **13** 22 **Boy Racer (IRE)**[19] 1690 3-8-10 0 AndrewElliott 3 —
(M Johnston) *in tch: pushed along over 5f out: sn wknd* **20/1**
500- **P** **Bobansheil (IRE)**[115] 2552 4-9-5 52 (p) PJMcDonald(3) 13 —
(J S Wainwright) *in rr whn p.u lame after 2f* **100/1**

2m 42.27s (6.07) **Going Correction** +0.50s/f (Yiel)
WFA 3 from 4yo+ 17lb 14 Ran SP% **124.0**
Speed ratings (Par 103): **99,97,97,96,94 92,89,81,79,75 75,74,60,**—
CSF £23.51 TOTE £3.70: £1.20, £1.90, £6.00; EX 31.00.
Owner Sheikh Hamdan Bin Mohammed Al Maktoum **Bred** The Hill Stud **Trained** Middleham Moor, N Yorks
■ Stewards' Enquiry : Edward Creighton caution: careless riding

FOCUS
A decent maiden for the track, rated through the runner-up.
Bobansheil(IRE) Official explanation: jockey said filly lost its action

2208 SANDS END H'CAP 1m
3:10 (3:13) (Class 6) (0-65,65) 3-Y-0 £2,590 (£770; £385; £192) Stalls Low

Form RPR
550- **1** **Metal Madness (IRE)**[282] 4323 3-8-12 **59** NCallan 14 66+
(M G Quinlan) *hld up in midfield: smooth hdwy on outer over 2f out rdn to ld 1f out: edgd lft ins fnl f: styd on wl* **16/1**
0-22 **2** 2¾ **Just Sam (IRE)**[12] 1870 3-8-12 **59** DavidAllan 2 60
(D Carroll) *trckd ldrs: hdwy over 2f out: rdn to ld briefly over 1f out: hdd 1f out and kpt on same pce u.p ins fnl f* **4/1**[2]
50-0 **3** nk **Defies Logic**[24] 1573 3-8-5 **52** JamesDoyle 16 55+
(J G Given) *hld up in midfield: hdwy over 2f out: effrt and nt clr run over 1f out: styd on ins fnl f: nrst fin* **25/1**
3205 **4** ½ **Turtle Dove**[4] 2090 3-8-13 **63** KirstyMilczarek(3) 7 62
(M Botti) *in tch: hdwy on inner over 2f out: rdn and kpt on same pce ent fnl f* **18/1**
-006 **5** 3¼ **Zabougg**[7] 2002 3-8-11 **58** FergalLynch 17 50
(D W Barker) *hld up towards rr: hdwy 2f out: sn rdn and kpt on ins fnl f: nrst fin* **25/1**
600- **6** hd **Smarterthanuthink (USA)**[221] 6072 3-9-1 **62** PaulHanagan 5 53
(R A Fahey) *prom: hdwy 3f out: rdn and ch 2f out: sn rdn and grad wknd* **6/4**[1]
450- **7** 1 **Gulf Coast**[208] 6388 3-8-13 **60** TomEaves 12 49
(T D Walford) *midfield: hdwy on outer over 3f out: rdn and outpcd 2f out: styd on ins fnl f* **10/1**
402- **8** 1 **Thanxforthat (USA)**[243] 5477 3-9-2 **63** GrahamGibbons 11 50
(J J Quinn) *led: rdn along over 2f out: hdd over 1f out and sn wknd* **16/1**
1000 **9** 8 **So Sublime**[12] 1870 3-8-4 **58** ow1 MarkCoumbe(7) 18 26
(M C Chapman) *stdd s: a in rr* **33/1**
06-U **10** ½ **Miss Olivia**[21] 1637 3-8-5 **52** SaleemGolam 4 19
(H R A Cecil) *t.k.h: prom: effrt to chal 2f out and ev ch tl rdn and wknd over 1f out* **11/1**
530- **11** 3¼ **Strictly Elsie (IRE)**[224] 6015 3-9-2 **63** DarrenWilliams 3 23
(J R Norton) *chsd ldrs: rdn along over 3f out: sn wknd* **66/1**
00-6 **12** 3¼ **Flaxton (UAE)**[7] 2008 3-8-6 **53** TWilliams 1 5
(M Brittain) *plld hrd: prom tl rdn along 3f out and sn wknd* **40/1**
1-65 **13** 2 **Alfredtheordinary**[44] 1163 3-9-2 **63** DarryllHolland 6 11
(M R Channon) *nvr bttr than midfield* **8/1**[3]
-053 **14** 1¾ **Polychrome**[16] 1740 3-8-11 **58** PaulMulrennan 15 2
(John Berry) *a towards rr* **25/1**

050- **15** *1 ½* **Honeycott (IRE)**^{221} [6075] 3-8-5 **52**........................ ChrisCatlin 8 —
(J D Bethell) *midfield: pushed along 1/2-way and sn lost pl* **80/1**

54-6 **16** *17* **Chaenomeles (USA)**^{23} [1575] 3-9-4 **65**........................ JoeFanning 13 —
(M Johnston) *a bhd* **16/1**

1m 44.55s (4.45) **Going Correction** +0.50s/f (Yiel) **16 Ran SP% 137.0**
Speed ratings (Par 97): **97,94,93,93,90 90,89,88,80,79 76,73,71,69,67 50**
CSF £80.80 CT £1737.95 TOTE £16.50: £2.80, £1.50, £7.10, £4.00; EX 120.20.
Owner P Bohan **Bred** Patrick Bohan **Trained** Newmarket, Suffolk

FOCUS
Modest form and a much improved effort from the winner on his handicap bow, rated up 12lb. The race has been rated through the runner-up.
Metal Madness(IRE) Official explanation: trainer's rep said, regarding running, that the colt was weak as a 2yo and had matured over the winter.
Flaxton(UAE) Official explanation: trainer said colt was not suited by the rain-softened ground
Polychrome Official explanation: trainer said filly was found to have pulled muscles in her hindquarters
Honeycott(IRE) Official explanation: jockey said filly was unsuited by the good (good to soft places top bend) ground
Chaenomeles(USA) Official explanation: trainer said filly was unsuited by the good (good to soft places top bend) ground

2209 RUNSWICK BAY H'CAP 1m
3:45 (3:47) (Class 4) (0-85,83) 3-Y-O **£5,180** (£1,541; £770; £384) **Stalls** Low

Form RPR

6-61 **1** **Summon Up Theblood (IRE)**^{19} [1685] 3-9-0 **79**.......... DarryllHolland 2 89
(M R Channon) *cl up: led over 5f out: pushed along over 2f out: rdn and edgd lft ent fnl f: styd on* **5/1**^{2}

421- **2** *2* **Inspector Clouseau (IRE)**^{242} [5502] 3-8-11 **76**.............. MickyFenton 8 81
(T P Tate) *led for over 2f: chsd wnr: effrt 3f out: rdn 2f out: drvn over 1f out: kpt on* **9/2**^{3}

106- **3** *1 ¾* **Montaquila**^{238} [5613] 3-9-4 **83**........................ PaulMulrennan 6 84
(J Howard Johnson) *hld up: hdwy 3f out: rdn 2f out: edgd lft and kpt on u.p fnl f* **15/2**

31-0 **4** *4* **Prince Hamlet (IRE)**^{36} [1297] 3-8-12 **77**........................ TomEaves 9 69
(B Smart) *hld up in tch: hdwy 3f out: rdn 2f out: drvn and one pce appr fnl f* **6/1**

15 **5** *8* **Yamal (IRE)**^{25} [1546] 3-8-10 **75**........................ JoeFanning 1 48
(M Johnston) *dwlt: t.k.h and sn chsng ldng pair: rdn along 3f out and sn wknd* **11/4**^{2}

14-0 **6** *3* **Shannersburg (IRE)**^{44} [1171] 3-9-3 **82**........................ ChrisCatlin 5 48
(E J O'Neill) *in tch: effrt 3f out: sn rdn along and wknd over 2f out* **16/1**

00-6 **7** *6* **Welcome Return (IRE)**^{31} [1395] 3-8-2 **70**..........(b) DuranFentiman$^{(3)}$ 4 23
(T D Easterby) *chsd ldrs: rdn along over 3f out and sn wknd* **33/1**

1m 43.71s (3.61) **Going Correction** +0.50s/f (Yiel) **7 Ran SP% 118.8**
Speed ratings (Par 101): **101,99,97,93,85 82,76**
CSF £12.41 CT £53.54 TOTE £2.80: £1.70, £1.80; EX 8.10.
Owner Derek And Jean Clee **Bred** D D And Mrs Jean P Clee **Trained** West Ilsley, Berks
■ Avertis (17/2) was withdrawn after breaking out of the stalls.

FOCUS
A fair handicap run 0.84secs faster than the preceding Class 6 handicap. The placed horses are the best guide, with the fourth 5lb off, so it could rate higher.

2210 HYGICARE H'CAP 6f
4:20 (4:21) (Class 3) (0-90,86) 4-Y-O+ **£7,771** (£2,312; £1,155; £577) **Stalls** High

Form RPR

-021 **1** **Valery Borzov (IRE)**^{24} [1567] 4-9-0 **82**..................(v) AdrianTNicholls 14 98
(D Nicholls) *qckly away: mde all: rdn and qcknd clr over 1f out: easily* **7/2**^{1}

0-20 **2** *3 ¾* **High Curragh**^{26} [1517] 5-9-4 **86**........................ NCallan 7 90
(K A Ryan) *trckd ldrs: swtchd lft and hdwy 2f out: rdn to chse wnr over 1f out: sn drvn and no imp* **11/2**^{2}

/00- **3** *½* **Johannes (IRE)**^{216} [6205] 5-9-0 **82**........................ ChrisCatlin 10 84
(E J O'Neill) *chsd ldrs: rdn along wl over 1f out: kpt on ins fnl f* **14/1**

5-00 **4** *1 ½* **Inter Vision (USA)**^{14} [1796] 8-9-3 **85**........................ DanielTudhope 2 83+
(A Dickman) *hld up in tch: hdwy whn nt clr run and hmpd wl over 1f out: styd on ins fnl f: nrst fin* **25/1**

00-0 **5** *1 ¼* **Sadeek**^{30} [1430] 4-8-10 **78**........................ TomEaves 13 72
(B Smart) *dwlt and wnt lft s: towards rr: hdwy 2f out: sn rdn and kpt on ins fnl f: nrst fin* **14/1**

1423 **6** *½* **Swinbrook (USA)**^{14} [1796] 7-8-7 **75**..................(p) PaulHanagan 1 71+
(R A Fahey) *hld up in rr: hdwy 2f out: rdn: swtchd lft and hmpd ins fnl f: kpt on* **6/1**^{3}

00-0 **7** *2 ¾* **Elkhorn**^{14} [1818] 6-8-9 **77**........................ PaulMulrennan 5 60
(Miss J A Camacho) *midfield: rdn along and swtchd lft wl over 1f out: nvr dangerous* **40/1**

520- **8** *¾* **Trojan Flight**^{247} [5356] 7-8-5 **80**........................ FrederikTylicki$^{(7)}$ 11 61
(R A Fahey) *in tch: swtchd outside and gd hdwy over 2f out: sn rdn and wknd over 1f out* **14/1**

0-40 **9** *2 ¼* **Coconut Moon**^{29} [1451] 6-8-9 **77**........................ DavidAllan 12 51
(E J Alston) *cl up: rdn along over 2f out and sn wknd* **22/1**

1045 **10** *nk* **Blue Tomato**^{8} [1969] 7-9-2 **84**........................ DarryllHolland 3 57+
(D Nicholls) *hld up in rr: sme hdwy 1/2-way: sn rdn and btn* **14/1**

354- **11** *1 ¾* **Soccerjackpot (USA)**^{224} [6016] 4-8-11 **82**.................. PJMcDonald$^{(3)}$ 9 49
(G A Swinbank) *towards rr: effrt and sme hdwy 1/2-way: sn rdn and btn* **7/2**^{1}

1320 **12** *7* **Distant Sun (USA)**^{28} [1481] 4-9-1 **83**........................ PhillipMakin 4 28
(Miss L A Perratt) *a towards rr* **14/1**

000- **13** *2 ½* **My Gacho (IRE)**^{238} [5638] 6-8-8 **76**..................(v) PaulFessey 6 13
(T D Barron) *chsd ldrs: rdn along wl over 2f out: sn wknd* **10/1**

1m 13.69s (0.99) **Going Correction** +0.35s/f (Good) **13 Ran SP% 127.2**
Speed ratings (Par 107): **107,102,101,99,97 97,93,92,89,88 86,77,73**
CSF £23.18 CT £263.69 TOTE £4.00: £1.80, £2.20, £4.90; EX 34.70.
Owner D Kilburn/I Hewitson/D Nicholls **Bred** Vincent Harrington **Trained** Sessay, N Yorks

FOCUS
A decent, competitive handicap on paper but the winner made all and was never in danger. The form looks solid with the placed horses rated to their marks.

NOTEBOOK
Valery Borzov(IRE) ◆ has rediscovered his form since having the visor fitted and put up a performance reminiscent of his namesake in running his rivals ragged. Drawn right under the stands' rail, he was always comfortable in showing his rivals a clean pair of heels and was never going to be caught. He is developing into a decent performer and there could be more to come from him. (op 3-1 tchd 11-4)
High Curragh, not as well drawn as the winner, is well suited by a flat track and ran a solid race in defeat. He looks capable of picking up a decent handicap this summer. (op 15-2 tchd 8-1)
Johannes(IRE), lightly raced last season, made a promising return to action. If he can build on this comeback display, he can surely capitalise on his attractive handicap mark. (op 22-1 tchd 25-1)
Inter Vision(USA), having shown nothing in his two previous starts this season, ran a whole lot better here, despite his poor draw. He tends to be at his best in the summer so may be now coming to hand.
Sadeek, who missed a beat at the start, kept on nicely late in the day. Comparatively lightly raced, he is very well treated if he can recapture his juvenile form. (op 22-1 tchd 25-1)
Swinbrook(USA), drawn widest of all and without his usual visor, did not really fire early on and was dropped across to the rails. He responded to pressure inside the final two furlongs, but he was stopped in his tracks inside the last when staying on well. (op 9-2)
Blue Tomato Official explanation: jockey said gelding was denied a clear run
Soccerjackpot(USA) was very well backed beforehand but may have needed this comeback outing, and this trip is too short for him in any case. (op 9-1)

2211 SCARBOROUGH H'CAP 5f
4:55 (4:56) (Class 2) (0-100,96) 4-Y-O+ **£11,656** (£3,468; £1,733; £865) **Stalls** High

Form RPR

00-6 **1** **Manzila (FR)**^{7} [2000] 5-9-3 **95**........................ SilvestreDeSousa 5 109+
(D Nicholls) *trckd ldrs: hdwy 2f out: swtchd lft and rdn to ld over 1f out: styd on wl* **13/2**^{3}

133- **2** *2 ½* **Ishetoo**^{203} [6487] 4-8-11 **92**........................ MichaelJStainton$^{(3)}$ 6 97
(A Dickman) *stmbld bdly s: sn cl up: led after 1f: rdn 2f out: hdd over 1f out: kpt on same pce ins fnl f* **3/1**^{2}

000- **3** *2 ¼* **Masta Plasta (IRE)**^{209} [6363] 5-9-4 **96**..........(v^{1}) AdrianTNicholls 3 93
(D Nicholls) *chsd ldrs: swtchd outside 2f out: sn rdn and kpt on same pce fnl f* **9/1**

36-2 **4** *1 ½* **Orpenindeed (IRE)**^{19} [1689] 5-8-11 **92**..........(t) KirstyMilczarek$^{(3)}$ 9 84
(M Botti) *chsd ldrs: pushed along 1/2-way: hdwy wl over 1f out: sn rdn and no imp ent fnl f* **7/4**^{1}

1025 **5** *3 ¾* **Canadian Danehill (IRE)**^{15} [1772] 6-9-3 **95**..................(p) NCallan 4 73
(R M H Cowell) *cl up: rdn along 2f out: edgd rt and wknd over 1f out* **14/1**

30-0 **6** *¾* **Invincible Force (IRE)**^{10} [1917] 4-8-7 **92**.............. AndrewHeffernan$^{(7)}$ 7 67
(Paul Green) *towards rr: sme hdwy 2f out: sn rdn and nvr nr ldrs* **12/1**

0016 **7** *½* **Bo McGinty (IRE)**^{4} [2082] 7-8-4 **82**..................(b) PaulHanagan 1 56
(R A Fahey) *cl up on outer: rdn along over 2f out and sn wknd* **16/1**

4364 **8** *3 ¼* **First Order**^{8} [1969] 7-8-6 **84**..................(v) TomEaves 2 46
(Miss L A Perratt) *hmpd after s and in rr: hdwy whn hmpd wl over 1f out: nt rcvr* **16/1**

0-30 **9** *5* **Classic Encounter (IRE)**^{19} [1689] 5-8-12 **90**.................. JoeFanning 8 34
(D M Simcock) *led 1f: prom tl rdn along 2f out and sn wknd* **8/1**

60.20 secs (0.60) **Going Correction** +0.35s/f (Good) **9 Ran SP% 121.9**
Speed ratings (Par 109): **109,105,101,99,93 91,91,85,77**
CSF £27.93 CT £183.07 TOTE £7.40: £2.20, £1.50, £2.50; EX 37.80.
Owner Michel Guerriche **Bred** H H The Aga Khan's Studs Sc **Trained** Sessay, N Yorks

FOCUS
A good sprint handicap and not surprisingly the fastest of the three races over the trip on the day. The winner is not far off Pattern class but there are doubts over the form with the placed horses reappearing and the favourite disappointing.

NOTEBOOK
Manzila(FR) came from off the pace and put this race to bed in emphatic style inside the last. A Listed winner when previously trained in France, she joined David Nicholls during the winter and was having her second outing for him here. She looks an interesting mare who could make her mark back in Pattern company. (op 16-1 tchd 20-1)
Ishetoo ◆, who made great strides last season when he won five times, made a cracking seasonal debut. Showing all his familiar speed, he was only outpointed inside the last. He is entitled to come on for this run and, although there will be no easy options for him this season, he looks the sort of horse who could well bag a major handicap. (op 7-2)
Masta Plasta(IRE), a stablemate of the winner, shaped well on his return to action, equipped with a first-time visor. The Handicapper has been unable to drop him much after some consistent efforts last season. (op 11-2)
Orpenindeed(IRE), dropped back to the minimum trip, was comfortably held, and as his last win in Italy was over 1m, a return to further looks likely. (op 9-4 tchd 6-4)
Canadian Danehill(IRE) was never able to land a telling blow when the chips were down. His current turf mark reflects his All-Weather form and he is clearly not as effective on grass. (op 12-1 tchd 11-1)
Classic Encounter(IRE) ran fast up the stands' rail, but faded quickly in the closing stages. (op 17-2 tchd 7-1)

2212 FILEY H'CAP 5f
5:30 (5:30) (Class 4) (0-85,84) 4-Y-O+ **£5,180** (£1,541; £770; £384) **Stalls** High

Form RPR

0161 **1** **Jilly Why (IRE)**^{7} [1997] 7-8-2 **75**..................(b) AndrewHeffernan$^{(7)}$ 1 84
(Paul Green) *swtchd rt s and sn pushed along in rr: hdwy 2f out: rdn and squeezed through to ld jst ins fnl f: edgd lft and sn clr* **12/1**

00-6 **2** *3 ½* **King Of Swords (IRE)**^{14} [1796] 4-9-0 **80**........................ FergalLynch 7 76
(N Tinkler) *hld up towards rr: hdwy wl over 1f out: sn rdn and kpt on to chse wnr ins fnl f: no imp towards fin* **8/1**

66-3 **3** *2 ¼* **Deserted Dane (USA)**^{14} [1818] 4-8-10 **79**.............. PJMcDonald$^{(3)}$ 10 67
(G A Swinbank) *trckd ldrs: smooth hdwy 2f out and sn ev ch rdn over 1f out and kpt on same pce ins fnl f* **15/8**^{1}

0-00 **4** *½* **Princess Ellis**^{21} [1624] 4-8-5 **71**........................ AdrianTNicholls 6 57
(E J Alston) *led: rdn along 2f out: drvn ent fnl f: sn hdd: edgd lft and one pce* **18/1**

200- **5** *nk* **Avertuoso**^{161} [7078] 4-9-4 **84**........................ TomEaves 5 69
(B Smart) *dwlt and towards rr: hdwy over 2f out: rdn over 1f out: kpt on ins fnl f* **14/1**

54-5 **6** *1 ½* **The Nifty Fox**^{14} [1818] 4-8-12 **78**........................ PaulMulrennan 9 58
(T D Easterby) *cl up: effrt 2f out and sn ev ch tl rdn and wknd over 1f out* **13/2**^{3}

210 **7** *5* **Stolt (IRE)**^{14} [1802] 4-8-10 **81**........................ AshleyHamblett$^{(5)}$ 4 43
(N Wilson) *cl up: rdn along 2f out: sn wknd* **8/1**

6-25 **8** *1* **Malapropism**^{14} [1802] 8-9-2 **82**........................ DarryllHolland 2 40
(M R Channon) *chsd ldrs on outer: rdn along 2f out and sn wknd* **8/1**

00-0 **9** *¾* **Strensall**^{11} [1893] 11-8-1 **70** oh7........................ DuranFentiman$^{(3)}$ 3 25
(R E Barr) *in tch: rdn along over 2f out and sn wknd* **40/1**

0110 **10** *1 ¼* **Harry Up**^{8} [1956] 7-9-2 **82**..................(p) NCallan 8 33
(K A Ryan) *cl up: ev ch 2f out: sn rdn: edgd lft and wknd over 1f out* **5/1**^{2}

61.43 secs (1.83) **Going Correction** +0.35s/f (Good) **10 Ran SP% 120.2**
Speed ratings (Par 105): **99,93,89,89,88 86,78,76,75,73**
CSF £107.49 CT £270.20 TOTE £11.50: £3.30, £3.00, £1.30; EX 129.50 Place 6: £146.11, Place 5 £81.76..
Owner Oaklea Racing **Bred** K And Mrs Cullen **Trained** Lydiate, Merseyside
■ Stewards' Enquiry : Darryll Holland one-day ban: allowed gelding to coast home with no assistance (May 31)
Fergal Lynch caution: careless riding

FOCUS
A fairly competitive sprint but run 1.21secs slower than the preceding Class 2 handicap. The runners unusually tended to race down the middle and the principals came from the rear.

T/Plt: £139.10 to a £1 stake. Pool: £59,843.36. 313.90 winning tickets. T/Qpdt: £16.80 to a £1 stake. Pool: £3,122.65. 136.90 winning tickets. JR

2213 - (Foreign Racing) - See Raceform Interactive

BADEN-BADEN (L-H)

Saturday, May 17

OFFICIAL GOING: Good

2214a 37.VON WERT BENAZET-RENNEN (GROUP 3) 6f

4:00 (4:01) 3-Y-0+ **£17,145** (£9,191; £3,676; £1,838)

RPR

1 **Abbadjinn (GER)** 4-9-6 .... TMundry 3 113
(P Rau, Germany) *pressed ldr: 3rd st: led 1 1/2f out: drvn out* **17/2**

2 *nk* **Dark Islander (IRE)**[15] 1767 5-9-6 .... EddieAhern 9 112
(J W Hills) *a cl up: 5th st: ev ch fnl f: unable qck cl home* **5/1**[3]

3 *1/2* **Tiza (SAF)**[23] 1593 6-9-6 .... CSoumillon 8 111
(A De Royer-Dupre, France) *hld up in rr: hdwy and swtchd lft wl over 1f out: hrd rdn and ev ch ins fnl f: no ex clsng stages* **4/5**[1]

4 *3 1/2* **Matrix (GER)**[47] 7-9-6 .... YLerner 10 100
(W Baltromei, Germany) *a.p: 2nd st: ev ch 1 1/2f out: one pce* **41/1**

5 *1 1/2* **Gainsbury (GER)**[195] 4-9-6 .... JiriPalik 7 96
(P Vovcenko, Germany) *pressed ldrs: 4th st: one pce fr wl over 1f out* **33/1**

6 *1 1/2* **Lucky Strike**[265] 4869 10-9-6 .... ADeVries 6 91
(A Trybuhl, Germany) *led to 1 1/2f out* **48/10**[2]

7 *2* **Florado (GER)**[20] 1660 5-9-6 .... THellier 5 85
(T Potters, Australia) *cl up to 2f out* **20/1**

8 *6* **Shinko's Best (IRE)**[20] 1660 7-9-6 .... ASuborics 4 67
(A Kleinkorres, Germany) *a outpcd* **76/10**

9 *8* **Key To Pleasure (GER)**[174] 8-9-6 .... AHelfenbein 1 43
(Mario Hofer, Germany) *early spd: bhd fnl 2f* **23/1**

10 *15* **Adamantinos**[20] 1660 4-9-6 .... LennartHammer-Hansen 2 —
(Frau E Mader, Germany) *spd to 1/2-way* **16/1**

1m 10.03s (-0.26) **10** Ran SP% **131.8**
(including ten euro stakes): WIN 95; PL 20, 19, 13; SF 937.
Owner Stall Schuoler-Gonzalez **Bred** Nathalie & Bruno Schuoler **Trained** Germany

NOTEBOOK
Abbadjinn(GER) ◆ was the worst-rated horse in the field, but was well backed nonetheless. He was close up throughout and battled on gamely when challenged by fancied rivals in the final furlong. He can continue to improve.
Dark Islander(IRE) showed plenty of speed and looked the likely winner inside the final furlong. However the winner kept on just the better. He won over 1m1f in the 2006 Oak Tree Derby at Santa Anita and will probably return to a longer trip.
Tiza(SAF) was at the back to the straight and had to angle towards the middle of the course to make his challenge. He looked capable of landing the odds entering the final furlong, but then flattened out. His trainer thought he was unsuited by the course.

PIMLICO (L-H)

Saturday, May 17

OFFICIAL GOING: Turf course - good; dirt course - fast

2215a PREAKNESS STKS (GRADE 1) (DIRT) 1m 1f 110y(D)

11:15 (11:17) 3-Y-0 **£301,508** (£100,503; £55,276; £30,151; £15,075)

RPR

1 **Big Brown (USA)**[14] 1820 3-9-0 .... KDesormeaux 7 118+
(Richard Dutrow Jr, U.S.A) *broke well, tracked leader after 2f, then 3rd in back straight, headway on outside to lead 2f out, soon clear, easily* **1/5**[1]

2 *5 1/4* **Macho Again (USA)**[21] 3-9-0 ....(b) JRLeparoux 1 104
(Dallas Stewart, U.S.A) *raced in 6th, switched out & headway on outside over 2f out, stayed on final f, never near winner* **40/1**

3 *1/2* **Icabad Crane (USA)**[28] 3-9-0 .... JRose 3 103
(H Graham Motion, U.S.A) *behind til headway 3f out, not clear run & switched outside over 2f out, stayed on one pace* **22/1**

4 *3/4* **Racecar Rhapsody (USA)**[28] 3-9-0 ....(b) RAlbarado 6 102
(Kenneth McPeek, U.S.A) *behind til headway from 3f out, disputed 2nd & hung left under pressure over 1f out, one pace* **25/1**

5 *4 1/4* **Stevil (USA)**[35] 3-9-0 ....(b) JRVelazquez 9 94
(N Zito, U.S.A) *went 4th 4f out, reached 3rd briefly well over 1f out, slightly hampered over 1f out, one pace* **41/1**

6 *3 3/4* **Kentucky Bear (USA)**[35] 3-9-0 .... JTheriot 8 87
(Reade Baker, Canada) *started slowly, reached 4th briefly over 3f out, not clear run on inside well over 1f out, one pace* **14/1**[3]

7 *1/2* **Hey Byrn (USA)**[35] 3-9-0 .... CCLopez 13 86
(E Plesa Jr, U.S.A) *raced in 4th til weakening from over 2f out* **34/1**

8 *1 3/4* **Giant Moon (USA)**[42] 3-9-0 ....(b) RADominguez 11 83
(R Schosberg, U.S.A) *never nearer than mid-division* **39/1**

9 *3/4* **Tres Borrachos (USA)**[35] 3-9-0 .... TBaze 2 81
(C B Greely, U.S.A) *stumbled start & hampered in first furlong, always in rear* **43/1**

10 *1 1/4* **Yankee Bravo (USA)**[42] 3-9-0 ....(b) ASolis 4 79
(Patrick Gallagher, U.S.A) *always behind* **24/1**

11 *7 1/4* **Gayego (USA)**[14] 1820 3-9-0 ....(b) MESmith 12 65
(P Lobo, U.S.A) *led on outside after 1 1/2f, headed 3f out, 3rd straight, soon weakened* **92/10**[2]

12 *nk* **Riley Tucker (USA)**[28] 3-9-0 ....(b) EPrado 10 64
(William Mott, U.S.A) *led 1 1/2f, led 3f out to 2f out, weakened quickly* **36/1**

1m 54.8s (-0.79) **12** Ran SP% **127.2**
PARI-MUTUEL (including $2 stakes): WIN 2.40; PL 2.60, 17.20; SHOW (1-2-3) 2.40, 10.40, 5.60; SF 36.60.
Owner IEAH Stables & P Pompa Jr **Bred** Monticule **Trained** USA

NOTEBOOK
Big Brown(USA), impressive winner of the Kentucky Derby, was sent off at prohibitive odds to follow up in this second leg of the Triple Crown, and rightly so as the opposition did not look as strong as that which he faced at Churchill Downs. Breaking smartly, he took up a prominent early position and his rider always looked comfortable, even looking round for dangers turning into the straight. Once in line for home he was shaken up and the response was explosive, as he quickened clear in a style rarely seen from a dirt horse. Within a few seconds he had gone beyond recall and his rider's only concern was to give him as easy a time as possible, with the third and final leg at Belmont clearly very much in his mind. His trainer now has three weeks to prepare him for the greater stamina test of the 1m4f Belmont Stakes, and he fully deserves to go there as a hot favourite. He will attempt to become the first winner of the Triple Crown since Affirmed in 1978, a feat which proved beyond War Emblem, Funny Cide and Smarty Jones earlier this century. They too won the first two legs but fell at the final hurdle in the Belmont. Big Brown will certainly face stiff competition in the form of the Japanese trained Casino Drive, who is bred to win the race, being a half-brother to the last two winners in Jazil and Rags To Riches.

1967 RIPON (R-H)

Sunday, May 18

OFFICIAL GOING: Good to firm (9.3)

The well watered ground was described as 'just on the quick side of good'.
Wind: Moderate, half-against Weather: Fine

2216 SKYBET.COM WOODEN SPOON CHARITY (S) STKS 6f

2:10 (2:15) (Class 6) 2-Y-O **£2,590** (£770; £385; £192) **Stalls** Low

Form RPR

6 1 **Kneesy Earsy Nosey**[29] 1480 2-8-9 0 .... KimTinkler 2 52
(N Tinkler) *chsd ldrs: styd on to ld ins fnl f: hld on wl* **8/1**

6 2 *1* **Jethro Bodine (IRE)**[15] 1794 2-9-0 0 .... PatCosgrave 4 54
(T J Pitt) *w ldrs: led over 2f out: hdd ins fnl f: no ex* **9/4**[1]

00 3 *hd* **French Forest**[8] 2004 2-8-9 0 .... TWilliams 5 48
(M Brittain) *towards rr: hdwy and swtchd outside over 2f out: kpt on wl fnl f* **50/1**

32 4 *2 3/4* **Rose Of Coma (IRE)**[8] 2004 2-8-9 0 .... TonyHamilton 11 40
(R A Fahey) *trckd ldrs: n.m.r 2f out: sn hrd rdn: kpt on same pce* **9/4**[1]

5 *2 1/4* **Petite Denise** 2-8-9 0 .... DaleGibson 10 33
(M W Easterby) *s.i.s: hdwy on outer over 2f out: hung rt: wknd over 1f out* **11/1**

6 6 *2 1/2* **Queen Of Dalyan (IRE)**[32] 1390 2-8-9 0 ....(p) LeeEnstone 3 26
(P C Haslam) *led tl over 2f out: wknd over 1f out* **7/1**[3]

0 7 *nk* **Dispol Bertie**[11] 1907 2-8-11 0 .... JamieMoriarty[(3)] 12 30
(P T Midgley) *w ldrs on outer: wandered and wknd 1f out* **33/1**

352 8 *5* **Syrup (IRE)**[25] 1555 2-8-9 0 .... RobertWinston 7 10
(P D Evans) *w ldrs: wkng whn n.m.r 2f out* **6/1**[2]

9 *12* **Ernies Keep** 2-8-11 0 .... DominicFox[(3)] 9 —
(W Storey) *s.v.s: detached in last thrght* **40/1**

1m 17.31s (4.31) **Going Correction** +0.15s/f (Good) **9** Ran SP% **115.1**
Speed ratings (Par 91): **77,75,75,71,68 65,65,58,42**
CSF £26.07 TOTE £8.80: £2.10, £1.30, £6.10; EX 28.80 TRIFECTA Not won..The winner was bought in for 5,000gns. Jethro Bodine was claimed by J. Sheard for £6,000.
Owner Mrs Christine Cawley **Bred** Jeremy Gompertz **Trained** Langton, N Yorks

FOCUS
A poor race even by selling race standards confirmed by the very slow time and not a race to dwell on.

NOTEBOOK
Kneesy Earsy Nosey, poorly drawn when a length and a quarter behind Rose Of Coma on their respective debuts at Thirsk a month ago, made very hard work of it but she had her head in front where it really matters. (old market op 9-1 tchd 7-1, new market op 15-2)
Jethro Bodine(IRE), easily the pick of the paddock, showed ahead but had to concede defeat in the shadow of the post. It was sufficient to see him claimed. (old market op 11-4, new market op 5-2)
French Forest, who had shown little in two previous starts, seemed to improve for the step up to six. (old market tchd 66-1)
Rose Of Coma(IRE), beaten favourite when placed on her two previous starts, had an outside draw. She was left short of racing room soon after the halfway mark but in the end that was no excuse. (old market op 15-8)
Petite Denise, a narrow filly, is a moderate walker. She showed just a glimmer of ability first time. (old market op 12-1 tchd 14-1 and 10-1)
Queen Of Dalyan(IRE), tried in cheekpieces and dropped in grade on just her second start, took them along but did not improve one jot for the extra furlong. (old market op 12-1 tchd 14-1)
Syrup(IRE) seems to be going the wrong way and her chance had already slipped when she was tightened up. (old market op 8-1 tchd 17-2)

2217 LEYBURN MAIDEN STKS 6f

2:40 (2:43) (Class 5) 2-Y-O **£3,561** (£1,059; £529; £264) **Stalls** Low

Form RPR

22 1 **Harwalla (IRE)**[16] 1770 2-9-3 0 .... RHills 6 80+
(M Johnston) *mde all: styd on strly: v readily* **4/6**[1]

0 2 *3* **Happy Anniversary (IRE)**[20] 1680 2-8-7 0 .... SCreighton[(5)] 8 66
(Miss V Haigh) *chsd ldrs: styd on to take 2nd ins fnl f: no imp* **50/1**

3 *1 1/4* **Custard Cream Kid (IRE)** 2-9-3 0 .... TonyHamilton 5 67
(R A Fahey) *s.i.s: sn drvn along: hdwy over 2f out: kpt on wl fnl f* **10/1**

0 4 *7* **Richo**[57] 957 2-9-3 0 .... RobertWinston 1 49+
(D H Brown) *in rr: hdwy over 2f out: nt clr run: hmpd 1f out: nt rch ldrs* **25/1**

5 *1 1/4* **Desert Falls** 2-9-0 0 .... MichaelJStainton[(3)] 10 43
(R M Whitaker) *dwlt: hdwy on outer to chse ldrs over 2f out: wknd appr fnl f* **40/1**

0 6 *2 3/4* **Nchike**[57] 957 2-9-3 0 .... AdrianTNicholls 9 34
(D Nicholls) *w ldrs: wknd over 1f out* **16/1**

253 7 *2* **Dispol Mulofky (IRE)**[22] 1627 2-8-9 0 .... JamieMoriarty[(3)] 14 23
(P T Midgley) *chsd ldrs on outside: wknd over 1f out* **14/1**

2 8 *5* **Cool Sonata (IRE)**[12] 1889 2-8-9 0 .... MarkLawson[(3)] 7 8
(M Brittain) *chsd ldrs: wkng whn hung rt 1f out* **13/2**[2]

230 9 *1 1/2* **Eilean Eeve**[18] 1727 2-8-12 0 .... NeilPollard 4 4
(A J McCabe) *chsd ldrs: nt clr run over 1f out: bmpd: pushed wd and hung rt 1f out: wknd* **22/1**

10 *3 1/4* **Captain Bradz (USA)** 2-9-3 0 .... PaulFessey 3 —
(P T Midgley) *chsd ldrs: wknd 2f out* **40/1**

11 *2 1/4* **Angela Tee (IRE)** 2-8-9 0 .... DuranFentiman[(3)] 13 —
(T D Easterby) *s.i.s: sn chsng ldrs on outer: lost pl over 1f out* **50/1**

2 **12** *6* **Carmanjoe**[16] 1778 2-9-3 0 PaulMulrennan 12 —
(M W Easterby) *chsd ldrs: wknd over 1f out* **9/1**[3]

1m 15.07s (2.07) **Going Correction** +0.15s/f (Good) **12** Ran SP% **122.0**
Speed ratings (Par 93): **92,88,86,77,75 71,69,62,60,56 53,45**
CSF £70.13 TOTE £1.70: £1.10, £7.60, £2.40; EX 51.10 Trifecta £190.60 Part won. Pool: £268.53, 0.60 w/u..

Owner Hamdan Al Maktoum **Bred** Senebrova Partnership **Trained** Middleham Moor, N Yorks

FOCUS
The winner had much the best form and had little difficulty going one better, the first three clear of dead wood. Not that easy to rate but the winner is rated aslight improver with the possibility the race could go higher.

NOTEBOOK
Harwalla(IRE), outspeeded by a promising newcomer at Musselburgh, proved suited by the extra furlong and always looked in total command. (op 10-11 tchd evens in places)
Happy Anniversary(IRE), well beaten on her debut three weeks earlier, proved well suited by the step up to six. (tchd 66-1)
Custard Cream Kid(IRE), who has size and scope, missed the break and took ages to grasp the nettle. Keeping on stoutly at the finish, this will have taught him plenty. (tchd 12-1)
Richo, who made his debut in the Brockelsby, had a nightmare run and is a fair bit better than he was able to show here. Official explanation: jockey said gelding was denied a clear run
Desert Falls, with a double figure draw, showed ability on his debut and is the type to do better in time. (op 28-1)
Dispol Mulofky(IRE) Official explanation: trainer said filly had scoped dirty after the race
Eilean Eeve Official explanation: jockey said filly hung right-handed throughout

2218 RIPON, YORKSHIRE'S GARDEN RACECOURSE H'CAP 1m
3:10 (3:11) (Class 2) (0-100,97) 4-Y-**£10,092** (£3,020; £1,510; £755; £376) **Stalls** High

Form				RPR
3-6U	**1**		**Laa Rayb (USA)**[8] 1982 4-9-4 **97** JoeFanning 2 (M Johnston) *trckd ldrs: wnt 2nd over 3f out: led 1f out: hung rt: styd on* **5/2**[1]	108
01-2	**2**	*1 1/2*	**Jewelled Dagger (IRE)**[9] 1970 4-8-11 **90** (b) RobertWinston 8 (Miss L A Perratt) *led: hrd rdn and hung rt 2f out: hdd 1f out: kpt on same pce* **11/4**[2]	98
00-4	**3**	*3 3/4*	**My Paris**[15] 1816 7-8-8 **90** AndrewMullen(3) 5 (Ollie Pears) *chsd ldrs: n.m.r on ins and swtchd lft 2f out: styd on to take 3rd ins fnl f* **5/1**[3]	91
-150	**4**	*1*	**Collateral Damage (IRE)**[11] 1910 5-8-2 **84** DuranFentiman(3) 1 (T D Easterby) *hood removed v late: hdwy to chse ldrs over 5f out: kpt on same pce fnl 2f* **14/1**	81
0/00	**5**	*nse*	**Another Bottle (IRE)**[29] 1481 7-8-4 **83** JimmyQuinn 3 (J J Quinn) *hld up in rr: hdwy 3f out: kpt on ins fnl f* **14/1**	80
30-0	**6**	*2 1/4*	**Vicious Warrior**[15] 1816 9-8-5 **84** DeanMcKeown 9 (R M Whitaker) *chsd ldr: wknd over 1f out* **16/1**	75
0005	**7**	*1/2*	**Fremen (USA)**[29] 1497 8-8-13 **92** AdrianTNicholls 4 (D Nicholls) *hld up in rr: effrt 4f out: kpt on: nvr rchd ldrs* **7/1**	82
0-10	**8**	*9*	**Best Prospect (IRE)**[25] 1569 6-9-0 **93** (t) PhillipMakin 6 (M Dods) *hld up in last: drvn 3f out: nvr a factor: eased ins fnl f* **10/1**	62

1m 40.01s (-1.39) **Going Correction** +0.15s/f (Good) **8** Ran SP% **112.7**
Speed ratings (Par 109): **112,110,106,105,105 103,102,93**
CSF £9.25 CT £30.21 TOTE £3.00: £1.60, £1.30, £1.50; EX 10.40 Trifecta £26.00 Pool: £490.68, 13.38 w/u.

Owner Sheikh Ahmed Al Maktoum **Bred** Darley **Trained** Middleham Moor, N Yorks

FOCUS
A competitive handicap run at a strong pace. The form looks rock solid with the third and fourth the best guides.

NOTEBOOK
Laa Rayb(USA), gelded since last year, put his bizarre Ascot exit behind him. He had the leader covered but tended to hang and took an age to get the better of him. A mile is his trip and he should continue to pay his way. (tchd 11-4)
Jewelled Dagger(IRE), 3lb higher, took them along at a stong pace. He hung into the fence but went down fighting. (op 5-2)
My Paris, runner-up in this a year ago from a 4lb higher mark, was unable to dominate this time. He is clearly in very good form for his new yard. (tchd 9-2 and 11-2)
Collateral Damage(IRE), who had the blindfold removed at the very last minute, is 3lb higher than Pontefract and he does not want the ground this quick. (op 12-1)
Another Bottle(IRE), who cut no ice over hurdles, has slipped to a lenient mark and here he showed he is no back-number. (op 11-1)
Vicious Warrior ran as if still in need of this outing, only his second this time, and these days he prefers much softer ground. (op 25-1 tchd 28-1 and 14-1)

2219 C. B. HUTCHINSON MEMORIAL CHALLENGE CUP (FILLIES' H'CAP) 6f
3:40 (3:40) (Class 3) (0-95,89) 3-Y-0 **£7,885** (£2,360; £1,180; £590; £293) **Stalls** Low

Form				RPR
4-15	**1**		**Valley Of The Moon (IRE)**[17] 1755 4-8-10 **75** JamieMoriarty(3) 3 (R A Fahey) *trckd ldrs: effrt and n.m.r over 1f out: r.o to ld ins fnl f* **13/2**[3]	84
6010	**2**	*1 1/4*	**Carcinetto (IRE)**[8] 2013 6-9-0 **83** RichardEvans(7) 5 (P D Evans) *w ldr: led 1f out: sn hdd and no ex* **9/1**	88
3-32	**3**	*3/4*	**Angus Newz**[35] 1346 5-9-13 **89** (v) FrancisNorton 2 (M Quinn) *led tl 1f out: no ex* **5/4**[1]	92
4-25	**4**	*1 1/2*	**Gallery Girl (IRE)**[5] 2082 5-9-4 **80** DavidAllan 1 (T D Easterby) *chsd ldrs: effrt over 2f out: nvr able to chal* **9/4**[2]	78
000-	**5**	*1/2*	**Playful**[181] 6876 5-9-6 **82** JamesDoyle 4 (R M Beckett) *t.k.h: trckd ldrs: effrt 2f out: wknd fnl f* **8/1**	78

1m 13.2s (0.20) **Going Correction** +0.15s/f (Good) **5** Ran SP% **109.7**
Speed ratings (Par 104): **104,102,101,99,98**
CSF £53.47 TOTE £6.80: £2.20, £5.00; EX 67.80.

Owner T Elsey,S A Elsey,R Mustill,J Tunstall **Bred** Mrs P Grubb **Trained** Musley Bank, N Yorks

FOCUS
A decent fillies' handicap run at a strong pace which seemed to suit the winner, who also seemed happier with the sixth furlong. The third and fourth ran slightly below the level they achieved when first and second in this race in 2007.

NOTEBOOK
Valley Of The Moon(IRE), happy to take a lead, burst through between horses to win going away. The sixth furlong seemed to suit her. (op 6-1 tchd 11-2 and 7-1)
Carcinetto(IRE) took on last year's winner. She went on a furlong out but was almost immediately overtaken by the winner. (tchd 8-1)
Angus Newz took this a year ago from just a 1lb lower mark. She was taken in for the lead and in the end was simply not good enough. (tchd 6-5 and 11-8)
Gallery Girl(IRE), runner-up in this a year ago, is struggling to make much impact at present. (op 11-4)
Playful, absent all last year, has slipped 5lb so far this time but she will need to learn to settle better is she is to add to her record of two wins as a juvenile. (op 15-2 tchd 7-1)

2220 MIDDLEHAM TRAINERS ASSOCIATION H'CAP 1m 1f 170y
4:10 (4:10) (Class 4) (0-85,83) 4-Y-0+ **£4,857** (£1,445; £722; £360) **Stalls** High

Form				RPR
0-26	**1**		**Veiled Applause**[11] 1910 5-9-0 **79** GrahamGibbons 6 (J J Quinn) *trckd ldrs: led 1f out: r.o wl: readily* **9/2**[1]	89+
326-	**2**	*1*	**Just Lille (IRE)**[256] 5145 5-9-1 **83** (p) AndrewMullen(3) 9 (Mrs A Duffield) *trckd ldrs: drvn and outpcd over 3f out: styd on strly fnl f* **16/1**	89
1420	**3**	*1/2*	**Intersky Charm (USA)**[57] 962 4-8-10 **75** DeanMcKeown 10 (R M Whitaker) *hld up in rr: effrt and nt clr run over 2f out: styd on wl fnl f* **12/1**	80
50-0	**4**	*1 1/2*	**Goodbye Mr Bond**[11] 1910 8-9-2 **81** DavidAllan 1 (E J Alston) *hld up in mid-div: effrt over 2f out: kpt on same pce fnl f* **11/2**[3]	83
-345	**5**	*1 1/4*	**Charlie Tipple**[11] 1910 4-8-10 **75** (p) PaulMulrennan 8 (T D Easterby) *trckd ldrs: nt clr run over 2f out tl over 1f out: nt rcvr* **6/1**	77+
-560	**6**	*1 1/4*	**Bed Fellow (IRE)**[16] 1771 4-7-12 **70** oh4 ow1 DeclanCannon(7) 11 (Paul Murphy) *trckd ldrs: n.m.r over 3f out: one pce fnl 2f* **50/1**	67
6-40	**7**	*shd*	**Getrah**[8] 2007 4-8-4 **69** oh2 JimmyQuinn 3 (N Wilson) *dwlt: hld up in rr: effrt 4f out: kpt on fnl f: nvr a threat* **17/2**	65
5230	**8**	*1*	**Lucayan Dancer**[9] 1947 8-8-6 **71** AdrianTNicholls 5 (D Nicholls) *hld up in rr: stmbld bnd over 6f out: nt clr run and eased ins fnl f* **7/1**	76+
0-50	**9**	*nk*	**Bajan Pride**[11] 1910 4-8-6 **71** (p) TonyHamilton 4 (R A Fahey) *led tl hdd & wknd 1f out* **7/1**	65
00-0	**10**	*1/2*	**Instructor**[9] 1970 7-8-11 **76** RobertWinston 2 (C A Mulhall) *chsd ldr: chal over 3f out: wknd appr fnl f: eased towards fin* **28/1**	69
050-	**11**	*hd*	**Wind Star**[218] 6185 5-8-12 **80** PJMcDonald(3) 7 (G A Swinbank) *hld up towards rr: stdy hdwy 3f out: shkn up 2f out: wknd fnl f* **5/1**[2]	72

2m 5.41s (0.01) **Going Correction** +0.15s/f (Good) **11** Ran SP% **119.0**
Speed ratings (Par 105): **105,104,103,102,101 100,100,99,99,99 98**
CSF £78.36 CT £818.69 TOTE £5.80: £1.80, £3.50, £3.20; EX 80.90 TRIFECTA Not won..

Owner Far 2 Many Sues **Bred** P J McCalmont **Trained** Settrington, N Yorks

FOCUS
A fair handicap run at just a steady early gallop with the resulting traffic problems. The form does not look that solid and is best rated around the first two.

Charlie Tipple Official explanation: jockey said gelding was denied a clear run
Lucayan Dancer Official explanation: jockey said gelding was denied a clear run
Instructor Official explanation: jockey said gelding became unbalanced in closing stages and was eased

2221 RIPON-RACES.CO.UK MAIDEN STKS 1m 1f
4:40 (4:43) (Class 5) 3-Y-O **£3,561** (£1,059; £529; £264) **Stalls** High

Form				RPR
53-	**1**		**Mangham (IRE)**[226] 5965 3-9-3 73 PaulMulrennan 14 (D H Brown) *mde all: styd on fnl 3f: hld on towards fin* **9/2**[3]	79
43-	**2**	*1/2*	**Tatbeeq (IRE)**[337] 2658 3-8-12 0 RHills 3 (M A Jarvis) *chsd wnr: effrt over 2f out: kpt on fnl f: a looked jst hld* **15/8**[2]	73
0-	**3**	*2*	**Miss Rochester (IRE)**[268] 4774 3-8-12 0 RobertWinston 8 (Sir Michael Stoute) *s.s: in rr: hdwy over 3f out: wnt 3rd over 1f out: styd on* **13/8**[1]	69+
003	**4**	*7*	**Grey Command (USA)**[8] 2008 3-9-0 70 MarkLawson(3) 10 (M Brittain) *chsd ldrs: one pce fnl 3f* **8/1**	58
	5	*1 3/4*	**Whipma Whopma Gate (IRE)** 3-8-12 0 DavidAllan 11 (D Carroll) *mid-div: hdwy over 2f out: kpt on one pce* **25/1**	49
0-0	**6**	*2 1/4*	**Willkandoo (USA)**[15] 1817 3-9-0 0 AndrewMullen(3) 12 (K A Ryan) *mid-div: kpt on fnl 3f: nvr a factor* **50/1**	49
P-00	**7**	*3 1/2*	**Templetuohy Max (IRE)**[31] 1429 3-9-3 0 JimmyQuinn 4 (J D Bethell) *mid-div: one pce fnl 3f* **80/1**	42
0-	**8**	*shd*	**Marramed**[280] 4422 3-8-12 0 DanielTudhope 2 (J O'Reilly) *chsd ldrs: wknd over 1f out* **100/1**	36
6-	**9**	*2 1/4*	**Nayarna**[285] 4247 3-8-5 0 FrederikTylicki(7) 13 (R A Fahey) *s.i.s: sme hdwy over 3f out: nvr on terms* **25/1**	31
	10	*2 1/4*	**Herrera (IRE)** 3-8-5 0 BMcHugh(7) 15 (R A Fahey) *s.s: nvr on terms* **25/1**	26
	11	*nk*	**Linby (IRE)** 3-9-3 0 KimTinkler 9 (N Tinkler) *s.s: last and detached 4f out: nvr on terms* **50/1**	31
	12	*2 3/4*	**Doctor Delta** 3-9-3 0 TWilliams 6 (M Brittain) *s.s: in rr: hung rt over 2f out* **40/1**	25
0	**13**	*1 1/2*	**Rye Rocket**[25] 1573 3-9-3 0 LeeEnstone 7 (K R Burke) *mid-div: wkng whn sltly hmpd over 2f out* **66/1**	21
0-F	**14**	*18*	**Jontobel**[22] 1628 3-9-3 0 AndrewElliott 16 (Jedd O'Keeffe) *trckd ldrs: t.k.h: wkng whn sltly hmpd over 2f out* **100/1**	—
0-00	**15**	*9*	**Viscount Monty**[22] 1626 3-8-10 35 MarzenaJeziorek(7) 5 (N Tinkler) *hld up in rr: racd wd: bhd fnl 3f* **200/1**	—

1m 56.17s (1.47) **Going Correction** +0.15s/f (Good) **15** Ran SP% **125.3**
Speed ratings (Par 99): **99,98,96,90,89 87,83,83,81,79 79,77,75,59,51**
CSF £13.05 TOTE £4.80: £1.90, £1.40, £1.10; EX 15.60 Trifecta £26.30 Pool: £322.00 - 8.69 winning units. Place 6 £98.50, Place 5 £45.08.

Owner Ron Hull **Bred** Dr Dean Harron **Trained** Tickhill, S Yorks

■ A first Flat winner for trainer David Brown who has renewed his licence this year.

FOCUS
An average maiden but the well-beaten fourth has an official rating of 70. The winner was up 6lb on her two-year-old form with the second to her mark.

Linby(IRE) Official explanation: jockey said gelding hung left-handed in home straight

T/Jkpt: £23,777.30 to a £1 stake. Pool: £184,191.00. 5.50 winning tickets. T/Plt: £180.00 to a £1 stake. Pool: £81,430.00. 330.15 winning tickets. T/Qpdt: £34.60 to a £1 stake. Pool: £4,696.28. 100.30 winning tickets. WG

2027 CAPANNELLE (R-H)
Sunday, May 18

OFFICIAL GOING: Good

2230a PREMIO PRESIDENTE DELLA REPUBBLICA (GROUP 1) 1m 2f
4:00 (4:13) 4-Y-0+ **£132,353** (£58,235; £31,765; £15,882)

RPR

1 **Saddex**[21] 1665 5-9-2 .... KerrinMcEvoy 5 116
(P Rau, Germany) *settled in 7th: effrt on outside 3f out: r.o to go 2nd appr fnl f: rdn to chal 100 yds out: led fnl strides* **94/100**[1]

2 *hd* **Pressing (IRE)**[196] 6689 5-9-2 .... NCallan 9 116
(M A Jarvis) *racd in cl 3rd: hdwy to ld 2f out: rdn and 3 l clr 1 1/2f out: r.o u.p fnl f: hdd cl home* **37/10**[2]

3 *2 1/2* **Freemusic (IRE)**[14] 4-9-2 .... GMarcelli 7 111
(F Scherillo, Italy) *hld up in 8th: hdwy 1 1/2f out: wnt 3rd 150 yds out: styd on* **62/1**

4 *2* **Golden Titus (IRE)**[22] 1667 4-9-2 .... DVargiu 8 107
(A Renzoni, Italy) *disp 5th: 5th st: hdwy to go 4th 2f out: disputing 2nd appr fnl f: rdn and no ex fnl 150 yds* **53/10**

5 *nk* **Selmis**[22] 1667 4-9-2 .... MDemuro 2 106
(V Caruso, Italy) *hld up in last: styd on in centre fr 1 1/2f out: nrest at fin* **143/10**

6 *3/4* **Sopran Promo (IRE)**[35] 4-9-2 .... GArena 4 105
(B Grizzetti, Italy) *racd in 4th: pushed along 3 1/2f out: rdn and one pce fr over 2f out* **29/1**

7 *1/2* **Hattan (IRE)**[23] 1596 6-9-2 .... SebSanders 1 104
(C E Brittain) *disp 5th: 6th st: drvn 3f out: hrd rdn and disputing 3rd 2f out: no ex and eased ins fnl f* **99/10**

8 *1/2* **Axxos (GER)**[22] 1667 4-9-2 .... AStarke 6 103
(P Schiergen, Germany) *led to 2f out: wknd over 1f out* **47/10**[3]

9 *1/2* **Shrek (GER)**[21] 1662 4-9-2 .... EBotti 3 102
(A Wohler, Germany) *racd in 2nd til rdn and wknd 2f out* **134/10**

2m 2.60s (-0.70) **9** Ran SP% **133.8**
(Including 1 Euro stake): WIN 1.94; PL 1.29, 1.85, 6.16; DF 4.14.
Owner Stall Avena **Bred** The Niarchos Family **Trained** Germany

NOTEBOOK
Saddex came with a sustained run and stayed on to put his head in front close home. Although he ran really well in the Ganay and was good enough to land the odds here, he is now likely to return to a more suitable 1m4f - the distance of all his races last year. His objective is the Grand Prix de Saint-Cloud on June 29th.
Pressing(IRE) had to settle for runner-up spot in this contest for the second year. He moved smoothly into the lead and ran on gamely under a strong drive. He returned with a cut on his near hind, but his trainer was delighted with his performance and did not use that as an excuse. It was his first appearance since winning the Premio Roma over course and distance in November and it should not be long before he is winning again.
Freemusic(IRE) ran far above any previous form.
Golden Titus(IRE) failed to stay and is likely to revert to 1m at which distance he will prove a tough opponent..
Hattan(IRE) was slightly hampered when disputing fourth and trying to pull off the rails from behind the weakening leader inside the final 2f. He was again squeezed up with a furlong to run and would have finished closer with better luck.

2231a PREMIO REGINA ELENA EMIRATES AIRLINE (GROUP 3) (FILLIES) 1m
4:45 (4:54) 3-Y-0 **£70,313** (£30,938; £16,875; £8,438)

RPR

1 **Love Of Dubai (USA)**[29] 1470 3-8-11 .... (p) DarryllHolland 6 105
(C E Brittain) *hld up towards rr to st: swtchd outside over 3f out: hdwy over 2f out: hrd rdn wl over 1f out: led 1f out: drvn out* **6/1**

2 *2* **Vattene (IRE)**[17] 3-8-11 .... NMurru 17 101
(M Gasparini, Italy) *hdwy over 2f out: ev ch 1f out: r.o same pce* **58/10**[3]

3 *nk* **Fairy Efisio**[22] 3-8-11 .... DVargiu 11 100
(B Grizzetti, Italy) *bhd to traight: hdwy over 2f out: r.o to take 3rd last strides* **18/10**[1]

4 *1/2* **Sensazione World (IRE)**[22] 3-8-11 .... MDemuro 12 99
(B Grizzetti, Italy) *hdwy over 2f out: nt clr run appr fnl f: r.o* **18/10**[1]

5 *3/4* **L'Indiscreta**[21] 1659 3-8-11 .... PConvertino 7 98
(B Grizzetti, Italy) *a.p: 3rd st: led 2f out: sn rdn: hdd 1f out: one pce* **18/10**[1]

6 *2* **Yacht Woman (USA)**[49] 3-8-11 .... ASanna 2 93
(E Borromeo, Italy) *5th st: ev ch on rails appraoching fnl f: one pce* **13/1**

7 *2 1/2* **Ecoute Moi (IRE)**[17] 3-8-11 .... (b) MMonteriso 18 88
(A & G Botti, Italy) *mid-div: styd on at one pce fnl 2f* **22/1**

8 *hd* **Smorova (IRE)**[21] 1659 3-8-11 .... MEsposito 4 87
(F Saggiomo, Italy) *cl up til one pce fnl 2f* **28/1**

9 *1 1/2* **Short Affair**[22] 3-8-11 .... GMarcelli 15 84
(M Gasparini, Italy) *nvr a factor* **16/1**

10 *3* **Harlem Madness (IRE)**[203] 3-8-11 .... PBorrelli 5 77
(M Massimi Jr, Italy) *nvr nrr than mid-div* **47/1**

11 *2* **Miss Galileo (IRE)** 3-8-11 .... URispoli 14 73
(L Camici, Italy) *nvr in contention* **57/10**[2]

12 *3* **Defaillance (IRE)**[17] 3-8-11 .... MSanna 16 66
(M Gasparini, Italy) *a bhd* **58/10**[3]

13 *3/4* **Sea Sex Sun**[17] 3-8-11 .... SUrru 13 65
(B Grizzetti, Italy) *nvr nrr than mid-div* **9/1**

14 *3 1/2* **Veddasca (IRE)** 3-8-11 .... NCallan 19 57
(L Brogi, Italy) *mid-div: eased whn btn wl over 1f out* **29/1**

15 *1/2* **Melody Break (USA)**[22] 3-8-11 .... EBotti 9 56
(A & G Botti, Italy) *disp 2nd over 3f: 4th st: waekened 2f out* **62/10**

16 *3* **Dalkey Girl (IRE)**[15] 1811 3-8-11 .... AStarke 10 49
(V Smith) *a bhd* **64/1**

17 *4* **Ventana (IRE)**[56] 3-8-11 .... DPorcu 1 41
(D Gambarota, Italy) *trckd ldr: 2nd st: wknd over 2f out* **15/1**

18 *1/2* **Lia Rumma (ITY)**[17] 3-8-11 .... FBranca 8 39
(F Folco, Italy) *led to 2f out* **18/1**

19 *1/2* **Golden Liberty (IRE)**[154] 3-8-11 .... PAragoni 3 38
(A Peraino, Italy) *bhd fnl 4f* **39/1**

1m 37.1s (-2.70) **19** Ran SP% **231.4**
WIN 7.02; PL 2.61, 2.82, 1.95; DF 61.94.
Owner Mohammed Al Shafar **Bred** M G G Holdings **Trained** Newmarket, Suffolk

NOTEBOOK
Love Of Dubai(USA), who wore cheekpieces, stood out in the preliminaries. Her jockey had been riding work on her and advised that she should be held up longer. She was almost last on the rails entering the straight, but was soon moved out to make her run on the outside. She had quite a hard race, but stuck it out gamely and her trainer thinks he could have another Crimplene who won the German 1000 and then a hat-trick of Group 1 races after finishing third here in 2000. She will follow Crimplene's path to Dusseldorf on June 1st and then the Coronation Stakes at Royal Ascot.
Vattene(IRE) was a smart two-year-old, but flopped on her reappearance. She clearly has recovered her form.
Fairy Efisio stayed on too late and will be much better suited by the extra 3f of the Oaks d'Italia on June 15th.
Dalkey Girl(IRE) was never in the race.

JAGERSRO (R-H)
Sunday, May 18

OFFICIAL GOING: Standard

2232a SKANSKAN JAGERSRO SPRINT (LISTED RACE) (DIRT) 6f (D)
2:50 (2:52) 3-Y-0+ **£18,648** (£6,216; £3,108; £1,943; £1,166)

RPR

1 **Completo (IRE)**[252] 5262 5-9-6 .... (b) MRodriguez 4 92
(F Castro, Sweden)

2 *3 1/2* **Miyasaki (CHI)**[17] 6-9-6 .... (b) JJohansen 3 81
(Rune Haugen, Norway) **133/10**[2]

3 *shd* **Ticmosic (FR)**[17] 5-9-6 .... CLopez 2 81
(Eva Sundbye, Sweden)

4 *2* **Pipoldchap (CHI)**[280] 8-9-6 .... (b) MMartinez 10 75
(F Castro, Sweden)

5 *2 1/2* **Aahayson**[31] 1420 4-9-6 .... FergusSweeney 7 68
(K R Burke) *mid-div: 7th st: rdn and late hdwy fr 1f out: n.d* **33/10**[1]

6 *nk* **Media Hora (CHI)**[266] 8-9-6 .... YvonneDurant 1 67
(F Castro, Sweden)

7 *nk* **Not Secret**[192] 4-9-6 .... (b) LSantos 6 66
(Eva Sundbye, Sweden)

8 *nk* **Maxim's (ARG)**[280] 7-9-6 .... (b) MSantos 5 65
(L Reuterskiold, Sweden)

9 *2 1/2* **September Sunrise (IRE)** 4-9-2 .... MLarsen 9 53
(B McGann, Sweden)

10 *7* **Cavorting**[616] 5225 6-9-6 .... P-AGraberg 8 36
(B Bo, Sweden)

1m 13.5s (73.50) **10** Ran SP% **30.2**
(Including Skr1 stake): WIN 7.88; PL 2.19, 4.55, 4.64; DF 138.14.
Owner Metalimo I Malmo AB & F Castro **Bred** Sean Finnegan **Trained** Sweden

NOTEBOOK
Aahayson is best when able to dominate, but did not come out of the stalls as quick as the battle-hardened locals and, although not disgraced, never got competitive.

2233a PRAMMS MEMORIAL (LISTED RACE) (DIRT) 1m 143y(D)
3:20 (3:20) 4-Y-0+ **£46,620** (£23,310; £11,655; £3,885; £3,885)

RPR

1 **Peas And Carrots (DEN)**[217] 5-9-4 .... MSantos 2 99
(L Reuterskiold, Sweden)

2 *shd* **Maybach**[217] 7-9-4 .... P-AGraberg 12 99
(B Bo, Sweden)

3 *2* **Salt Track (ARG)**[94] 564 8-9-4 .... ESki 9 95
(Niels Petersen, Norway)

4 *hd* **Highway (IRE)**[217] 5-9-4 .... (b) NCordrey 1 94
(F Castro, Sweden)

4 *dht* **Eldfote (SWE)** 5-9-4 .... JJohansen 7 94
(E Van Doorn, Sweden)

6 *5* **Quilboquet (BRZ)**[16] 5-9-4 .... CLopez 11 84
(L Kelp, Denmark)

7 *3* **Ancient Egypt**[299] 6-9-4 .... MRodriguez 3 78
(Annelie Larsson, Sweden)

8 *3* **Electric Warrior (IRE)**[13] 1857 5-9-4 .... FergusSweeney 6 71
(K R Burke) *broke wl: racd in 2nd: led briefly 2f out: grad wknd* **24/1**[1]

9 *1/2* **Volo Cat (FR)**[16] 4-9-4 .... WilliamBuick 4 70
(B Olsen, Norway)

10 *2* **Pecoiquen (CHI)**[217] 7-9-4 .... (b) YvonneDurant 10 66
(F Castro, Sweden)

11 **Wazir (USA)**[252] 6-9-4 .... (b) LSantos 8 66
(L Reuterskiold, Sweden)

1m 47.9s (107.90) **11** Ran SP% **4.0**
WIN 3.97; PL 1.53, 1.96, 1.49; DF 22.08.
Owner O Zawawi **Bred** Havreholms Stutteri **Trained** Sweden

NOTEBOOK
Electric Warrior(IRE) was taking a big step up in class here and ran as well as could have been expected. Always prominent, he had a brief moment in front passing the quarter mile pole but was soon found wanting.

KRANJI (L-H)
Sunday, May 18

OFFICIAL GOING: Good

2234a SINGAPORE AIRLINES INTERNATIONAL CUP (GROUP 1) 1m 2f
12:50 (12:52) 3-Y-0+
£595,819 (£211,672; £107,143; £52,265; £20,906; £10,453)

RPR

1 **Jay Peg (SAF)**[50] 1090 5-9-0 .... (b) AMarcus 7 121
(H J Brown, South Africa) *drvn to ld after 1 1/2f then 2nd: led again over 1 1/2f out: rdn and r.o wl fnl f: rdn out*

2 *1 3/4* **Recast (AUS)**[450] 542 8-9-0 .... NCallow 2 118
(L Laxon, Singapore) *a in tch: 5th and drvn st: hdwy and hrd rdn fnl f: wnt 2nd 100yds out: r.o*

3 *3/4* **Balius (IRE)**[21] 1666 5-9-0 .... (b) BPrebble 10 116
(C Laffon-Parias, France) *hld up towards rr: 14th and rdn st: gd hdwy fnl f: tk 3rd fnl strides*

4 *hd* **World Delight (NZ)** 6-9-0 .... JPowell 1 116
(S Burridge, Singapore) *hld up: 7th on ins st: hdwy 1 1/2f out: hrd rdn fnl f: jst missed 3rd*

5 *nk* **Sir Slick (NZ)**[21] 1666 7-9-0 .... BHerd 4 115
(Graeme Nicholson, New Zealand) *prom in 3rd: shkn up 1 1/2f out: styd on steadily: lost 3rd fnl strides*

6 *nk* **Cosmo Bulk (JPN)**[50] 7-9-0 .... MMatsuoka 9 114
(K Tabe, Japan) *towards rr: styd on fnl f but nvr in chalng position*

7 *1* **Spin Around (AUS)**[36] 8-9-0 .... GMcKeon 13 112
(S Cooper, Australia) *mid-div: drvn along st: styd on at one pce tl no ex last 100yds*

8 *nk* **Mourilyan (IRE)**[50] 1091 4-9-0 .... WCMarwing 3 112
(H J Brown, South Africa) *mid-div: styd on fnl f: nrest at fin*

9 *1* **Onceuponatime (NZ)** 4-8-9 .... DBeasley 14 105
(D Hill, Hong Kong) *hld up: rdn on outside 2f out: hdwy 1 1/2f out: sltly bmpd 1f out but looked hld at the time*

10 *3* **Traffic Guard (USA)**[31] 1422 4-9-0 .... JohnEgan 12 104
(Jane Chapple-Hyam) *mid-div: 6th and rdn in centre st: one pce fnl 1 1/2f*

11 *½* **Trigger Express (AUS)** 7-9-0 ....(b) ELegrix 8 103
(S Burridge, Singapore) *mid-div: hdwy 3 1/2f out: 4th and drvn st: rdn and one pce fnl 1 1/2f*

12 *½* **King And King (AUS)**[364] 1877 8-9-0 .... KBSoo 11 102
(D Koh, Singapore) *in rr: last and rdn st: nvr a factor*

13 *6* **Mr Line (ARG)**[553] 6-9-0 .... RFradd 16 90
(P Shaw, Singapore) *mid-div: n.d*

14 *9* **Musical Way (FR)**[21] 1666 6-8-11 .... RonanThomas 15 69
(P Van De Poele, France) *bhd: 15th st: nvr a factor*

15 *1 ½* **Chevron (IRE)** 5-9-0 .... JSaimee 6 69
(C Leck, Singapore) *prom: drvn to ld after 1 1/2f: hdd 1 1/2f out: wknd*

16 *18* **Itmaybeyou (NZ)** 6-9-0 .... DMOliver 5 33
(B Dean, New Zealand) *a towards rr*

2m 0.90s (120.90) **16** Ran
(including SIN$5 stakes): WIN 17; PL 6, 27, 9; DF 125.
Owner M Shirtliff,E Braun, P Loomes, S Marcus **Bred** High Season Stud **Trained** South Africa

NOTEBOOK
Jay Peg(SAF), who won the Dubai Duty Free when last seen, was given a good ride. His rider always had him prominent and he found plenty for pressure. In contrast to the third, he enjoyed the run of the race. The Cox Plate is apparently his next big target, although Ascot are keen to persuade his connections to bring him over for the Prince of Wales's Stakes.
Balius(IRE), whose regular rider Olivier Doleuze was stood down earlier in the day for failing a random urine test, had to make do with Brett Pebble aboard, and he was not given the best of rides. Given a lot to do, he was brought very wide into the straight and, although he ran on strongly at the finish, the line was always going to come too soon.
Traffic Guard(USA), who was not well drawn, travelled well enough to the turn but failed to pick up in the straight.

2235a KRISFLYER INTERNATIONAL SPRINT 6f
1:40 (1:42) 3-Y-0+
£201,742 (£70,557; £35,714; £17,423; £6,969; £3,484)

RPR

1 **Takeover Target (AUS)**[22] 9-9-0 .... JayFord 2 122
(J Janiak, Australia) *a cl up on rails: led ent st (jst over 2f out): drvn out*
8/5[1]

2 *½* **Magnus (AUS)**[22] 6-9-0 ....(p) DMOliver 11 120
(Peter G Moody, Australia) *chsd ldrs: 4th on outside st: wnt 2nd 1f out: kpt on same pce* **9/1**

3 *nse* **Sanziro (AUS)**[17] 7-9-0 ....(b) DBeasley 3 120
(C Fownes, Hong Kong) *last to st but saved grnd on ins: str run fnl f: jst missed 2nd* **18/1**

4 *1 ¼* **Waikato (NZ)** 5-9-0 ....(b) JPowell 8 116
(L Laxon, Singapore) *towards rr early: 7th st: stdy run on outside to take 4th wl ins fnl f* **16/1**

5 *½* **Star Crowned (USA)**[50] 1089 5-9-0 .... WCMarwing 1 115
(R Bouresly, Kuwait) *mid-div on ins: 6th st: 4th 1f out: one pce* **74/10**[3]

6 *2* **Capablanca (AUS)**[261] 7-9-0 .... NCallow 5 109
(D Baertschiger, Singapore) *broke wl: disp 2nd: 3rd st: rdn and ev ch over 1f out: grad wknd* **8/1**

7 *1 ¾* **Lovelace**[57] 959 4-9-0 .... RoystonFfrench 7 103
(M Johnston) *towards rr: 8th st: rdn wl over 1f out: carried rt by 2nd 1 1/2f out: kpt on same pce* **53/1**

8 *nk* **Universal Ruler (AUS)**[57] 4-8-11 .... JWhiting 13 99
(D McAuliffe, Australia) *10th st and c wdst: nvr a factor* **78/10**

9 *3 ¼* **Salaam Dubai (AUS)**[73] 814 7-9-0 ....(b) AMarcus 12 93
(A Sevratnam, UAE) *9th st: a outpcd* **53/1**

10 *nk* **Ace And Aces (NZ)**[138] 5-9-0 ....(b) RFradd 4 92
(L Laxon, Singapore) *pressed ldrs: 6th st: sn one pce* **53/1**

11 *1* **Why Be (AUS)**[161] 7089 6-9-0 ....(b) JSaimee 6 89
(L Laxon, Singapore) *led to jst over 2f out: sn wknd* **14/1**

P **Absolute Champion (AUS)**[91] 7-9-0 .... BPrebble 9 —
(D Hall, Hong Kong) *w ldrs whn broke down after 1f: p.u* **42/10**[2]

68.80 secs (68.80) 12 Ran SP% **125.4**
WIN 13; PL 5, 15, 22; DF 43.
Owner J & B Janiak **Bred** Meringo Stud Farm **Trained** Australia

NOTEBOOK
Takeover Target(AUS) soon grabbed the rail. He was always in the first three or four and took over as they hit the straight. He was driven out to maintain much the same margin over the second throughout the final furlong. He shaved one fifth of a second off the course record and can now continue his journey to Royal Ascot having proved that he is as good as ever at the age of nine, a birthday he will not actually celebrate until September 29th.
Magnus(AUS), not as well drawn as the winner, was well there on the outside throughout. He reached second at the furlong marker but, though he tried hard, could not haul in the winner and would have been caught by Sanziro in another stride. He beat Takeover Target half a length when they were third and fourth in last year's King's Stand, but disappointed in two later attempts in England.
Lovelace was one of three extreme outsiders, all of whom started at about 53-1. He ran at least as well as predicted and was keeping on under pressure when carried right by the third more than one furlong from home. It was a creditable effort over a distance which may be short of his best, but it remains to be seen how long he requires to recover from the long journey.

2031 LONGCHAMP (R-H)
Sunday, May 18
OFFICIAL GOING: Good to soft

2236a PRIX VICOMTESSE VIGIER (GROUP 2) 1m 7f 110y
1:10 (1:10) 4-Y-0+ **£54,485** (£21,029; £10,037; £6,691)

RPR

1 **Coastal Path**[21] 1663 4-9-0 .... SPasquier 3 119
(A Fabre, France) *trckd ldr 3f: wnt 2nd again over 7f out: led over 2f out: sn clr: pushed out and r.o wl* **1/5**[1]

2 *5* **Orion Star (FR)**[21] 1663 6-8-12 .... JVictoire 2 109
(H-A Pantall, France) *led over 6f: 3rd st: rdn to go 2nd 1 1/2f out: no imp on wnr* **56/10**[2]

3 *4* **Ponte Tresa (FR)**[21] 1663 5-8-8 .... CSoumillon 4 101
(Y De Nicolay, France) *wnt 2nd after 3f: led 9f out to over 2f out: sn one pce* **76/10**[3]

4 *10* **Le Miracle (GER)**[21] 1663 7-9-2 .... DBoeuf 1 98
(W Baltromei, Germany) *s.s: last thrght: wl bhd fnl 2f* **10/1**

3m 18.6s (-2.90) **Going Correction** +0.20s/f (Good)
WFA 4 from 5yo+ 1lb 4 Ran SP% **119.2**
Speed ratings: **115,112,110,105**
PARI-MUTUEL (including one euro stakes): WIN 1.20; PL 1.10, 1.10; SF2.20.
Owner K Abdulla **Bred** Juddmonte Farms Ltd **Trained** Chantilly, France

NOTEBOOK
Coastal Path put up another outstanding performance. He was cruising throughout the contest which he took by the scruff of the neck at the 2f marker. He then built up an unassailable lead and was pushed out to the line. He has yet to be asked a really serious question in six outings to date and now goes for the Gold Cup at Ascot where his jockey feels sure the extra half-mile will not be a problem.
Orion Star(FR) tried to make all the running, but is not in the same class as the winner and just stayed on at one pace throughout the final 2f.
Ponte Tresa(FR), always handy during the early part of the race, had little left in the straight and just stayed on to take third place.
Le Miracle(GER) ran well below his best and was always in last position. He was beaten before the entrance to the straight and apparently just had an off-day. He will have to put this performance behind him if he is to perform well again at Ascot in the Gold Cup.

2237a MONTJEU COOLMORE PRIX SAINT-ALARY (GROUP 1) (FILLIES) 1m 2f
2:50 (2:50) 3-Y-0 **£105,037** (£42,022; £21,011; £10,496; £5,257)

RPR

1 **Belle Et Celebre (FR)**[26] 3-9-0 .... C-PLemaire 6 110
(A De Royer-Dupre, France) *sn led: rdn and r.o 1f out: r.o wl to line*
132/10

2 *¾* **Gagnoa (IRE)**[37] 1323 3-9-0 .... JVictoire 3 108
(A Fabre, France) *in tch: 4th 1/2-way: sn pushed along st: rdn and wnt 3rd 1 1/2f out: wnt 2nd 1f out: nt rch wnr* **3/1**[3]

3 *nse* **Proviso**[21] 1664 3-9-0 .... SPasquier 5 108
(A Fabre, France) *hld up in last: pushed along 2f out: rdn in centre over 1f out: styd on to take 3rd post* **19/10**[2]

4 *½* **Madaway**[19] 3-9-0 .... OPeslier 1 107
(C Laffon-Parias, France) *first to show and prom: 3rd 1/2-way: rdn and 4th 1 1/2f out: wnt 3rd again 100yds out: lost pl post* **12/1**

5 *nse* **Albisola (IRE)**[42] 1238 3-9-0 .... CSoumillon 7 107
(Robert Collet, France) *hld up: 6th 1/2-way: pushed along on outside 2f out: stdy hdwy fr over 1f out: kpt on* **13/10**[1]

6 *2* **Place De L'Etoile (IRE)**[206] 3-9-0 .... TGillet 2 103
(J E Hammond, France) *in tch: 5th 1/2-way: outpcd fr over 1 1/2f out* **3/1**[3]

7 *nse* **Wait And See (FR)**[21] 1664 3-9-0 .... DBoeuf 4 103
(Robert Collet, France) *prom: 2nd 1/2-way: pushed along to chal 2f out: wknd appr fnl f* **13/10**[1]

2m 10.0s (3.10) **Going Correction** +0.20s/f (Good) 7 Ran SP% **186.2**
Speed ratings: **95,94,94,93,93 92,92**
PARI-MUTUEL: WIN 14.20; PL 5.00, 2.60, SF 64.40.
Owner Mme G Forien **Bred** Mme Aliette & Gilles Forien **Trained** Chantilly, France

NOTEBOOK
Belle Et Celebre(FR) came out best in a tactical race and much of the credit for this Group 1 success must be put down to her jockey who rode an inspired race. After a furlong, he realised the race was going along at a crawl so decided to take the initiative and for the rest of the trip he dominated the situation at the head of affairs. Setting a steady pace, he gradually increased the momentum in the straight. The filly responded bravely and proceeded to fend off all her rivals. This was a big step up as she was winning for the first time and this race was only chosen at the last moment. She appears to have further room for improvement and all being well the Prix de Diane is the next target.
Gagnoa(IRE), totally unsuited by the lack of early pace, took a hold but did eventually settle in third position. She was asked for a forward move from the 2f marker and ran on at one pace to the line. She may have been the winner if the race had not been run at a false pace and she will definitely stay further. Connections are now looking at the Juddmonte Oaks and the Darley Irish Oaks, whilst she is also in the Prix de Diane.
Proviso put up a much-improved performance and she looked to have done well physically since her seasonal debut. Ridden from behind on this occasion, she also pulled early on. Making her effort over a furlong put, she was putting in her best work at the finish and she will be a force to be reckoned with in the Diane if she continues to go the right way.
Madaway did not put up a bad effort for an inexperienced filly. She was settled in behind the leaders and kept up the good work throughout the final furlong and a half. She battled on well to take fourth place by inches and was only beaten a length and a half by the winner. A Group event will surely come her way later in the season.

2238a PRIX D'ISPAHAN (GROUP 1) 1m 1f 55y
3:20 (3:21) 4-Y-0+ **£105,037** (£42,022; £21,011; £10,496; £5,257)

RPR

1 **Sageburg (IRE)**[21] 1665 4-9-2 .... OPeslier 1 123
(A De Royer-Dupre, France) *sn racing in 3rd: pushed along 2f out: r.o appr fnl f: rdn to ld 150yds out: r.o wl* **109/10**

2 *2 ½* **Darjina (FR)**[50] 1090 4-8-13 .... CSoumillon 3 115
(A De Royer-Dupre, France) *racd in 2nd: drvn to chse ldr 2f out: rdn and led briefly 150yds out: sn hdd: no ex* **4/5**[1]

3 *½* **Loup Breton (IRE)**[42] 1240 4-9-2 .... C-PLemaire 5 117
(E Lellouche, France) *last: 5th 1/2-way: styd on fr 1 1/2f out: tk 3rd 50yds out: nrest at fin* **9/1**[3]

The Form Book, Raceform Ltd, Compton, RG20 6NL

4 1 1/2 **Turfrose (GER)**[17] 1761 4-8-13 SPasquier 2 111
(A Fabre, France) *led: pushed along and r.o st: hdd 150yds out: one pce cl home* **9/1**[3]
5 3 **Boris De Deauville (IRE)**[42] 1240 5-9-2 TThulliez 6 108
(S Wattel, France) *racd in 5th: last 1/2-way: rdn over 1 1/2f out: n.d* **15/1**
6 2 1/2 **Literato (FR)**[50] 1090 4-9-2 LDettori 4 102
(Saeed Bin Suroor) *racd in 4th: drvn 2f out: no rspnse* **28/10**[2]
1m 53.7s (-2.60) **Going Correction** +0.20s/f (Good) **6** Ran SP% **116.5**
Speed ratings: **119,116,116,115,112 110**
PARI-MUTUEL: WIN 11.90; PL 2.90, 1.30; SF 32.30.
Owner H H Aga Khan **Bred** Snc Lagardere Elevage **Trained** Chantilly, France

NOTEBOOK
Sageburg(IRE) finally showed the class which his is known to have possessed for some considerable time. Since changing stables, he has really settled down and he looked a picture in the paddock. Settled in third place, he was extricated to challenge from halfway up the straight and took the lead inside the final furlong. He then quickened and built up a lead which was getting longer with every stride. He was perfectly suited to this distance, but may well be allowed to take his chance in the Prince of Wales Stakes at Royal Ascot. If he can keep his act together, another Group 1 is sure to come his way.
Darjina(FR), who went off at odds-on, probably needed this outing as she was prepared early in the season and ran with great credit when second in the Dubai Duty Free. Given every possible chance, she settled behind the leader and then took things up at the furlong pole. She was then a little one-paced and had nothing in reserve to repel her stable companion. Connections have now decided to take her back to 1m and the Queen Anne Stakes at Royal Ascot is now the target. Hopefully the ground at the Berkshire track will be good as her previous efforts there were ruined by a testing surface.
Loup Breton(IRE) put up a pretty sound performance after being given a waiting ride. He started his challenge over a furlong out, quickened really well and would have caught the runner up in another 50 yards. Connections were pleased by this first effort at this level and he has not been ruled out of a trip to Royal Ascot for the Prince of Wales Stakes.
Turfrose(GER) was asked to go from pillar to post. She kept up the good work until the furlong marker, but was then one-paced to the line. She may be difficult to place this season as she carries a Group 1 penalty after her victory in Rome last November and she needs cut to show her best. Races like the Pretty Polly and the Nassau might be taken into account as well as the Prix d'Astarte at Deauville. She has been entered in the Arc and will also be entered in the Grand Prix de Saint-Cloud, but as a soft-ground specialist she will start her main campaign at the backend of the season.
Literato(FR) put up another disappointing effort and finished behind several old rivals. He appeared to be going well during the descent to the straight, but was a spent force by the 2f marker and was then not given a hard race. His jockey reported he ran flat and would have preferred softer ground, but he is only a shadow of the horse he was during 2007.

2097 BATH (L-H)
Monday, May 19

OFFICIAL GOING: Good to firm
Wind: Virtually nil. Weather: Dull

2239 E.B.F./LINDLEY CATERING NOVICE STKS 5f 11y
2:00 (2:00) (Class 5) 2-Y-O **£3,302** (£982; £491; £245) **Stalls** Centre

Form RPR
6 1 **Zezao**[7] 2042 2-8-12 0 NCallan 3 73+
(B J Meehan) *trckd ldr: led 2f out: c clr in own time: eased ins fnl f: canter* **8/15**[1]
1254 2 6 **Sally's Dilemma**[3] 2147 2-8-9 0 (t) JackDean(5) 8 42
(W G M Turner) *led tl hdd 2f out: no ch w eased down wnr sn after* **5/2**[2]
3 25 **Loched Up** 2-8-12 0 TPO'Shea 7 —
(P A Blockley) *s.i.s: no ch after 100yds and a in wl btn 3rd* **12/1**[3]
4 8 **Red Myth** 2-8-7 0 ChrisCatlin 2 —
(Karen George) *slowly away: wl bhd after 100yds and a last* **14/1**
62.33 secs (-0.17) **Going Correction** -0.225s/f (Firm) **4** Ran SP% **108.2**
Speed ratings (Par 93): **92,82,42,29**
CSF £2.10 TOTE £1.60; EX 2.10.
Owner Mrs Sheila Tucker **Bred** P A Mason **Trained** Manton, Wilts

FOCUS
Four key withdrawals left Zezao with little to beat. A weak race and the form is worth little.

NOTEBOOK
Zezao, very green when sixth on his recent Windsor debut, had his task simplified enormously by the withdrawals and he was left with only the regressive Sally's Dilemma to beat. Sent on two out, he gradually came clear and was eased right down close home. He should stay further in time and holds several sales race entries for later in the season. (op 5-6)
Sally's Dilemma has gone the wrong way from her Brocklesby win, slowly regressing with each run, the latest of which came at Newbury just three days previously. She looked Zezao's only credible threat, but aftersetting the pace was beaten with ease. The first-time tongue tie evidently failed to have an impact. (tchd 2-1)
Loched Up, whose dam was a middle-distance winner in France, was soon behind following a slow start and showed little promise. (op 9-2)
Red Myth, another who is bred to need further, being out of a 1m2f winner, was soon toiling at the back of the field and showed nothing. (op 16-1)

2240 PREMIER CONSERVATORY ROOFS MEDIAN AUCTION MAIDEN STKS 5f 11y
2:30 (2:32) (Class 6) 3-4-Y-O **£1,942** (£578; £288; £144) **Stalls** Centre

Form RPR
/2-5 1 **Whiskey Junction**[27] 1529 4-9-8 72 LPKeniry 2 73
(A M Balding) *led: narrowly hdd ins fnl 2f: styd w ldr tl led again jst ins fnl f: pushed out: readily* **7/4**[1]
223- 2 1 1/2 **Wotashirtfull (IRE)**[264] 4937 3-9-0 77 NCallan 7 65
(K A Ryan) *trckd ldr: drvn to take narrow ld jst ins fnl 2f: hdd jst ins fnl f: kpt on but a hld by wnr* **9/4**[2]
2665 3 nk **Spic 'n Span**[5] 2099 3-9-0 64 TGMcLaughlin 1 64
(R A Harris) *chsd ldrs: rdn and kpt on u.p ins fnl f: no ex nr fin* **8/1**
5522 4 4 1/2 **Walragnek**[41] 1259 4-9-8 62 SebSanders 5 51
(J G M O'Shea) *chsd ldrs: wd bnd 3f out: rdn and effrt over 2f out: nvr gng pce to be competitive and wknd fnl f* **5/1**[3]
5 2 3/4 **Admiral Bond (IRE)** 3-9-0 0 ChrisCatlin 6 38
(G R Oldroyd) *s.i.s: in rr: hdwy and rdn 2f out: nvr rchd ldrs: wknd fnl f* **17/2**
0 6 1 **Cherries On Top (IRE)**[44] 1215 3-8-11 0 KirstyMilczarek(3) 4 34
(I A Wood) *s.i.s: wnt lft s: drvn and in tch 1/2-way: wknd over 1f out* **20/1**
040- 7 11 **Mr Funshine**[210] 6386 3-8-9 60 JackMitchell(5) 3 —
(Mrs P N Dutfield) *sn outpcd* **25/1**
61.19 secs (-1.31) **Going Correction** -0.225s/f (Firm)
WFA 3 from 4yo 8lb **7** Ran SP% **114.0**
Speed ratings (Par 101): **101,98,98,90,86 84,67**
CSF £5.85 TOTE £2.70: £1.50, £1.50; EX 6.10.
Owner Kingsclere Racing CLub **Bred** Mrs I A Balding **Trained** Kingsclere, Hants

FOCUS
A typically weak three-year-old plus sprint maiden with the third struggling recently and the runner-up in line with much of his two-year-old form.

2241 MATTHEW CLARK FILLIES' H'CAP 1m 5f 22y
3:00 (3:00) (Class 5) (0-70,69) 4-Y-O+ **£2,590** (£770; £385; £192) **Stalls** High

Form RPR
40-2 1 **Spring Dream (IRE)**[20] 1697 5-9-2 67 RichardHughes 4 74+
(A King) *hld up in rr but in tch: n.m.r ins fnl 2f tl swtchd rt and qckned 1f out: led ins fnl f: pushed out* **6/4**[1]
5333 2 1/2 **Bassinet (USA)**[26] 1563 4-9-1 69 KirstyMilczarek(3) 6 75+
(J A R Toller) *in rr but in tch: hdwy on ins 2f out: sn n.m.r and again 1f out: swtchd rt ins fnl f and fin strly: nt rchd wnr* **9/2**[3]
3251 3 1/2 **Rose Row**[20] 1697 4-9-0 65 HayleyTurner 1 67
(Mrs Mary Hambro) *chsd ldrs in 3rd: drvn along 3f out: styd on to ld appr fnl f: hdd ins fnl f: styd on same pce* **5/2**[2]
6-64 4 3 1/2 **Adage**[7] 2051 5-8-9 60 (t) FergusSweeney 7 57
(David Pinder) *chsd ldr: drvn to chal 2f out and stl upsides 1f out: wknd ins fnl f* **13/2**
51-4 5 4 **Gamesters Lady**[20] 1697 5-9-0 65 LiamJones 3 55
(W M Brisbourne) *led: rdn and hung lft fr 2f out: hdd appr fnl f and sn wknd* **8/1**
5/0- 6 nk **Queen Excalibur**[84] 2946 9-7-11 55 oh10 (p) DavidProbert(7) 2 45
(C Roberts) *chsd ldrs: rdn 3f out: wknd 2f out* **66/1**
2m 54.2s (2.20) **Going Correction** -0.15s/f (Firm) **6** Ran SP% **112.7**
Speed ratings (Par 100): **87,86,86,84,81 81**
CSF £8.82 TOTE £2.30: £1.50, £2.50; EX 7.40.
Owner W H Ponsonby **Bred** R N Auld **Trained** Barbury Castle, Wilts

FOCUS
This modest handicap was run in a moderate time with first two rated a bit better than the bare form in a weak contest.
Gamesters Lady Official explanation: jockey said mare hung left

2242 MATTHEW CLARK H'CAP 5f 161y
3:30 (3:31) (Class 5) (0-70,70) 4-Y-O+ **£2,590** (£770; £385; £192) **Stalls** Centre

Form RPR
40-6 1 **Buy On The Red**[114] 313 7-9-4 70 RichardMullen 4 78
(W R Muir) *hld up in rr: stl plenty to do fr 2f out: qcknd on rails ins fnl f: str run to ld cl home* **14/1**
3024 2 1/2 **Misaro (GER)**[10] 1956 7-8-13 70 (b) HaddenFrost(5) 10 77
(R A Harris) *disp ld tl def advantage after 2f: rdn 2f out: styd on u.p fnl f: ct cl home* **5/1**[2]
2133 3 1/2 **High Reach**[40] 1275 8-8-4 56 oh4 HayleyTurner 5 61
(J G M O'Shea) *chsd ldrs: rdn and styd on strly ins fnl f: no ex cl home* **9/1**
2-22 4 shd **Prince Of Delphi**[30] 1488 5-9-3 69 (p) SebSanders 1 74
(R M Beckett) *chsd ldrs: rdn to go 2nd over 1f out: sn hrd drvn and kpt on same pce* **4/1**[1]
45-1 5 nk **Bold Argument (IRE)**[10] 1966 5-8-2 59 ow1 JackMitchell(5) 6 63
(Mrs P N Dutfield) *s.i.s: in rr: stl plenty to do whn swtchd sharply rt to outside 2f out: rapid hdwy ins fnl f: fin strly: nt rch ldrs* **9/1**
0-00 6 1 3/4 **Caustic Wit (IRE)**[4] 2128 10-8-8 60 FergusSweeney 2 58+
(M S Saunders) *in tch: rdn 2f out: styd on on fnl f but nvr gng pce to rch ldrs* **11/1**
40-0 7 2 1/2 **Pic Up Sticks**[11] 1928 9-9-4 70 TQuinn 9 59
(B G Powell) *hld up in tch: stdy hdwy to trck ldrs 2f out: rdn over 1f out: wknd fnl f* **14/1**
-005 8 2 1/2 **Harrison's Flyer (IRE)**[9] 1997 7-8-11 63 (p) DaneO'Neill 17 44
(J M Bradley) *s.i.s: rr tl styd on fr over 1f out* **7/1**[3]
5564 9 2 1/4 **Game Lady**[30] 1488 4-8-3 58 ow1 (p) KirstyMilczarek(3) 8 31
(I A Wood) *pressed ldrs 3f: wknd ins fnl 2f* **11/1**
0-00 10 2 1/4 **Makabul**[16] 1800 5-9-4 70 DarryllHolland 12 35
(B R Millman) *chsd ldrs: rdn 1/2-way: sn wknd* **12/1**
20-0 11 1 3/4 **Willhewiz**[127] 149 8-8-7 59 (v) ChrisCatlin 3 18
(M S Saunders) *led 2f: wknd 2f out* **12/1**
00-0 12 nk **Edge End**[10] 1966 4-8-4 56 oh3 DavidKinsella 7 14
(R A Farrant) *early spd: sn bhd* **40/1**
00-0 13 6 **Iguacu**[13] 1900 4-8-5 57 ow1 PaulFitzsimons 15 —
(J L Spearing) *a outpcd* **40/1**
4-00 14 1 1/4 **Nordic Light (USA)**[21] 1683 4-9-1 70 TolleyDean(3) 11 —
(J M Bradley) *a outpcd* **40/1**
1m 10.38s (-0.82) **Going Correction** -0.225s/f (Firm) **14** Ran SP% **121.9**
Speed ratings (Par 103): **96,95,94,94,94 91,88,85,82,79 76,76,68,66**
CSF £82.76 CT £693.45 TOTE £14.60: £3.90, £2.00, £2.80; EX 94.30 TRIFECTA Not won..
Owner R Haim **Bred** J Gittins And Capt J H Wilson **Trained** Lambourn, Berks

FOCUS
A modest but highly competitive sprint handicap with the winner to last year's turf mark and the third to form.
Edge End Official explanation: jockey said gelding hung right throughout

2243 GREGORY THAIN H'CAP 1m 5y
4:00 (4:00) (Class 5) (0-70,67) 4-Y-O+ **£2,590** (£770; £385; £192) **Stalls** Low

Form RPR
33-0 1 **Bold Cross (IRE)**[15] 1842 5-8-13 62 PaulFitzsimons 8 71
(E G Bevan) *s.i.s: in rr: stl plenty to do over 2f out: rapid hdwy on ins sn after to ld jst ins fnl f: hld on wl u.p* **16/1**
20-0 2 hd **Magroom**[22] 1641 4-9-2 65 WilliamBuick 2 73
(R J Hodges) *trckd ldrs: rdn and outpcd over 2f out: rdn and styd on again to press ldrs 1f out: styd on u.p but nt quite get up* **7/1**[3]
-000 3 3/4 **Strike Force**[15] 1842 4-8-7 56 ChrisCatlin 13 62
(K F Clutterbuck) *in rr: stl plenty to do whn plld to outside 2f out: rapid hdwy 1f out: fin strly but nt rch ldng duo* **40/1**
0512 4 1 **Unlimited**[5] 2101 6-8-11 63 KirstyMilczarek(3) 6 67
(A W Carroll) *sn led: rdn over 2f out: kpt slt advantage tl hdd jst ins fnl f: wknd cl home* **5/2**[1]
0-22 5 2 3/4 **Winning Show**[18] 1747 4-8-13 62 LPKeniry 4 60
(A M Balding) *mid-div: rdn 3f out: hdwy over 1f out: kpt on ins fnl f but nvr gng pce to get into contention* **7/1**[3]

50-4 **6** *nse* **Semi Detached (IRE)**^{47} [1160] 5-8-8 **57**.................. SimonWhitworth 12 55+
(J W Unett) *towards the rr tl hdwy over 3f out: rdn over 2f out: styd on ins fnl f but nvr gng pce to be competitive* **16/1**

00-2 **7** *hd* **Moves Goodenough**^{15} [1842] 5-8-13 **62**........................ HayleyTurner 15 59
(Andrew Turnell) *in rr: wd bnd over 4f out: continued on outer and rdn 3f out: styd on fnl f but nvr gng pce to be competitive* **6/1**^{2}

5200 **8** *3/4* **Prince Charlemagne (IRE)**^{11} [1932] 5-8-8 **62**..........(p) JackMitchell$^{(5)}$ 3 57
(R M Stronge) *chsd ldrs: rdn to chal over 2f out: wknd 1f out* **25/1**

1-00 **9** *hd* **Golden Brown (IRE)**^{14} [1853] 4-8-8 **57** ow1...........(b^{1}) FergusSweeney 1 52
(David Pinder) *mid-div: rdn over 3f out: wknd 2f out* **25/1**

013- **10** *3 1/2* **Parthenope**^{250} [5336] 5-8-4 **53** oh3.................................. DavidKinsella 9 40
(J A Geake) *chsd ldrs over 5f* **16/1**

56-6 **11** *3/4* **Kansas Gold**^{129} [128] 5-8-12 **61**.. NCallan 10 46
(J Mackie) *chsd ldrs over 5f* **8/1**

000- **12** *2* **Laish Ya Hajar (IRE)**^{170} [6997] 4-9-1 **64**................................ DaneO'Neill 5 45
(P R Webber) *chsd ldrs: rdn over 2f out: wknd over 1f out: eased whn no ch ins fnl f* **10/1**

63-0 **13** *3 1/2* **Thomas Lawrence (USA)**^{27} [1534] 7-8-4 **53** oh3.............. TPO'Shea 11 26
(P A Blockley) *slowly away: a bhd* **33/1**

3006 **14** *6* **Cavalry Guard (USA)**^{66} [888] 4-9-2 **65**.......................... PatCosgrave 7 24
(J R Boyle) *a in rr* **33/1**

1m 39.51s (-1.29) **Going Correction** -0.15s/f (Firm) **14** Ran SP% **121.7**
Speed ratings (Par 103): **100,99,99,98,95 95,95,94,94,90 89,87,84,78**
CSF £119.13 CT £4524.27 TOTE £26.30: £5.40, £2.50, £16.00; EX 185.90 Trifecta £237.50 Part won. Pool: £334.54 - 0.10 winning units..
Owner E G Bevan **Bred** M Hosokawa **Trained** Ullingswick, H'fords

FOCUS
A moderate handicap but the form looks pretty solid for the grade rated around the winner and the third.
Unlimited Official explanation: jockey said gelding ran too free
Semi Detached(IRE) Official explanation: jockey said gelding was denied a clear run

2244 BET365 BEST ODDS GUARANTEED ON EVERY H'CAP 1m 2f 46y
4:30 (4:32) (Class 5) (0-75,73) 3-Y-O £2,719 (£809; £404; £202) **Stalls** Low

Form RPR

43-3 **1** **Stow**^{28} [1516] 3-8-10 **68**.. TravisBlock$^{(3)}$ 6 80
(H Morrison) *sn pushed along in rr: gd hdwy over 2f out to take slt ld appr fnl f: hrd drvn and hld on wl* **7/2**^{2}

3-52 **2** *1/2* **Mezzanisi (IRE)**^{7} [2043] 3-8-13 **68**.. HayleyTurner 8 79+
(M L W Bell) *hld up in rr: stdy hdwy over 2f out: drvn and qcknd to press wnr ins fnl f: kpt on but a jst hld by wnr* **2/1**^{1}

-123 **3** *3 1/4* **Kyrie Eleison (IRE)**^{16} [1805] 3-8-9 **67**.............................. PatrickHills$^{(3)}$ 2 71
(R Hannon) *chsd ldrs: wnt 2nd over 2f out: drvn to chal over 1f out: wknd ins fnl f* **15/2**

0-01 **4** *1* **Challow Hills (USA)**^{14} [1870] 3-8-10 **65**.............................. MichaelHills 3 67
(B W Hills) *trck ldr: led 6f out: rdn over 2f out: hdd appr fnl f and sn wknd* **16/1**

40-0 **5** *1 1/2* **Silk Hall (UAE)**^{15} [1839] 3-9-2 **71**.................................. FergusSweeney 10 70
(D W P Arbuthnot) *in tch: rdn over 2f out: styd on same pce* **33/1**

3-00 **6** *2* **Bid Art (IRE)**^{10} [1958] 3-8-7 **62**... WilliamBuick 13 57
(A M Balding) *in rr: hdwy on outside fr 3f out: rdn over 2f out: nvr gng pce to rch ldrs and wknd over 1f out* **18/1**

050- **7** *2 1/4* **Red Merlin (IRE)**^{227} [5971] 3-9-4 **73**.................................. RichardMullen 4 64
(C G Cox) *in tch: rdn 3f out: nvr gng pce to rch ldrs and no ch fnl 2f* **16/1**

0000 **8** *1 3/4* **Asmodea**^{32} [1412] 3-8-4 **59** oh2... TPO'Shea 12 46
(D J Coakley) *t.k.h: led tl hdd 6f out: wknd 2f out* **66/1**

4-33 **9** *1* **Flying Time**^{10} [1959] 3-8-13 **68**.. EdwardCreighton 11 53
(M R Channon) *in tch: rdn to chse ldrs 3f out: wknd sn after* **14/1**

5-32 **10** *1* **King Bathwick (IRE)**^{20} [1696] 3-8-13 **68**.............................(t) DaneO'Neill 7 51
(B R Millman) *chsd ldrs: rdn over 3f out: wknd appr fnl 2f* **7/1**^{3}

00-0 **11** *1/2* **Lady Petrus**^{23} [1621] 3-8-4 **59** oh2.. FrancisNorton 5 41
(H J L Dunlop) *t.k.h: chsd ldrs tl wknd fr 3f out* **18/1**

-000 **12** *shd* **Ruby Delta**^{10} [1958] 3-8-5 **60**.. SimonWhitworth 9 42
(P D Cundell) *t.k.h early: a in rr* **50/1**

4-34 **13** *15* **Al Azy (IRE)**^{28} [1516] 3-8-13 **68**...(b^{1}) SebSanders 1 20
(J L Dunlop) *chsd ldrs: rdn and wknd over 2f out: eased whn no ch fnl f* **9/1**

2m 9.58s (-1.42) **Going Correction** -0.15s/f (Firm) **13** Ran SP% **125.2**
Speed ratings (Par 99): **99,98,96,95,94 92,90,89,88,87 87,87,75**
CSF £11.34 CT £52.48 TOTE £4.90: £1.80, £1.50, £2.60; EX 16.30 Trifecta £200.60 Pool: £367.40 - 1.30 winning units..
Owner Gillian, Lady Howard De Walden **Bred** Plantation Stud **Trained** East Ilsley, Berks

FOCUS
Two progressive types came away in what was a modest handicap. The form looks sound with the next three home close to recent handicap form.
Al Azy(IRE) Official explanation: jockey said colt stopped quickly

2245 PREMIER CONSERVATORY ROOFS H'CAP (FOR AMATEUR RIDERS) 2m 1f 34y
5:00 (5:00) (Class 6) (0-65,62) 4-Y-O+ £1,846 (£567; £283) **Stalls** Low

Form RPR

4430 **1** **Brave Bugsy (IRE)**^{14} [1856] 5-10-13 **54**.......... MissGDGracey-Davison 3 67+
(A M Balding) *hld up in rr: gd hdwy fr 4f out: drvn to ld ins fnl 2f: styd on u.p: all out* **11/1**

54-0 **2** *nk* **Directa's Digger (IRE)**^{17} [67] 4-10-10 **58**..................(v) MrJMahot$^{(5)}$ 4 71
(M J Scudamore) *in tch: hdwy on outside over 3f out: stl wd and styd on to chse wnr fnl f: kpt on wl but a jst hld* **25/1**

0/30 **3** *6* **Zeloso**^{19} [1726] 10-10-4 **45**..(v) MissSBrotherton 7 51
(M F Harris) *in rr: styd on fr 3f out: kpt on to chse ldrs ins fnl f but nvr any ch of troubling ldng duo* **10/1**

3044 **4** *2* **Sand Repeal (IRE)**^{27} [1551] 6-11-0 **60**..........................(v) MrRBirkett$^{(5)}$ 8 63
(Miss J Feilden) *chsd ldrs: rdn 3f out: wknd over 1f out* **17/2**^{3}

600/ **5** *1* **Dancing Bear**^{725} [1958] 7-9-13 **45**................................ MrBMMorris$^{(5)}$ 11 47
(C Roberts) *in tch: hdwy over 4f out: slt ld over 2f out: hdd ins fnl 2f: wknd fnl f* **40/1**

35-3 **6** *1/2* **Jenny Soba**^{18} [238] 5-9-13 **45**...............................(v) JPFeatherstone$^{(5)}$ 1 46
(Lucinda Featherstone) *in rr: rdn and sme hdwy 3f out: nvr rchd ldrs and sn btn* **20/1**

00-4 **7** *3 1/2* **Miss Porcia**^{13} [1898] 7-9-11 **45**.. MissCBoxall$^{(7)}$ 2 42
(P A Blockley) *mid-div: rdn and effrt over 3f out: nvr gng pce to chal and wknd ins fnl 2f: fin 7th, plcd 6th* **12/1**

/00- **8** *1 1/2* **Maximix**^{21} [5500] 5-11-2 **62**... MrSPHanson$^{(5)}$ 13 58
(G L Moore) *chsd ldr: slt advantage 5f out to 3f out: sn wknd* **16/1**

55-0 **9** *1 1/2* **Grasp**^{17} [14] 6-10-7 **55**...(b) MrJoshuaMoore$^{(7)}$ 15 49
(G L Moore) *led tl narrowly hdd 5f out: slt ld again 3f out: hdd & wknd over 2f out* **9/1**

0635 **10** *1/2* **Bobsleigh**^{7} [2051] 9-10-2 **50**...................................... MrGavinHall$^{(7)}$ 9 43
(H S Howe) *chsd ldrs tl wknd 3f out* **14/1**

2400 **11** *13* **Dreams Jewel**^{8} [1824] 8-10-10 **56**....................... MissIsabelTompsett$^{(5)}$ 14 34
(C Roberts) *chsd ldrs: racd wd: wknd fr 3f out* **12/1**

2540 **12** *3 1/2* **Ronsard (IRE)**^{14} 6-10-4 **45**.. MissEFolkes 10 18
(P D Evans) *a towards rr* **5/1**^{2}

240- **13** *1 1/4* **Linlithgow (IRE)**^{16} [2628] 4-10-6 **54**......................(b^{1}) MrDFDevereux$^{(5)}$ 16 26
(P Bowen) *chsd ldrs: rdn 4f out: sn wknd* **12/1**

5-00 **14** *31* **Finished Article (IRE)**^{7} [2051] 11-9-13 **45**.......................(t) MrRPFlint$^{(5)}$ 5 —
(Mrs D Thomas) *chsd ldrs to 1/2-way: sn wknd: t.o* **50/1**

5-16 **D** *hd* **Dansilver**^{9} [2012] 4-11-3 **60**... MrSWalker 6 62
(D J Wintle) *in tch: drvn and hdwy to chse ldrs fr 3f out: no imp 2f out: wknd over 1f out: fin 6th, nk, 6l, 2l, 1l, hd: disq(prohibited substance)* **4/1**^{1}

3m 52.65s (0.75) **Going Correction** -0.15s/f (Firm)
WFA 4 from 5yo+ 2lb **15** Ran SP% **123.3**
Speed ratings (Par 101): **92,91,89,88,87 87,85,85,84,84 78,76,75,61,87**
CSF £272.31 CT £2841.95 TOTE £12.90: £4.60, £10.20, £2.20; EX 326.40 TRIFECTA Not won. Place 6 £66.66, Place 5 £47.75..
Owner West Mercia Fork Trucks Ltd **Bred** James F Hanly **Trained** Kingsclere, Hants
■ Stewards' Enquiry : Mr D F Devereux four-day ban: used whip when out of contention (Jun 11,16,23, Jul 6)

FOCUS
A weak, slowly-run staying handicap in which the first two were clear but the form is not solid.
T/Jkpt: Not won. T/Plt: £102.30 to a £1 stake. T/Qpdt: £55.40 to a £1 stake. Pool: £2,704.27. 36.10 winning tickets. ST

1769 MUSSELBURGH (R-H)
Monday, May 19

OFFICIAL GOING: Good to firm (good in places; 8.1)
Wind: Light, half behind Weather: Dry and fine

2246 TURFTV MEDIAN AUCTION MAIDEN STKS 1m
2:10 (2:10) (Class 5) 3-5-Y-O £2,590 (£770; £385; £192) **Stalls** High

Form RPR

5-23 **1** **Marning Star**^{13} [1894] 3-9-0 76.. AdrianTNicholls 6 71
(D Nicholls) *mde all: rdn along 2f out: drvn ent fnl f: styd on gamely* **6/4**^{1}

-042 **2** *hd* **Randama Bay (IRE)**^{26} [1572] 3-9-0 73................................ FergalLynch 8 70
(I A Wood) *trckd wnr: effrt 3f out: rdn to chal wl over 1f out: drvn and ev ch ins fnl f tl no ex nr fin* **3/1**^{3}

50-0 **3** *6* **Wilmington**^{17} [1771] 4-9-9 60.. AndrewMullen$^{(3)}$ 3 59
(Mrs J C McGregor) *wnt rt s: trckd ldrs: hdwy 3f out: rdn to chse ldng pair wl over 1f out: sn drvn and no imp* **20/1**

00- **4** *10* **Mandalay King (IRE)**^{217} [6242] 3-9-0 0.......................... PaulMulrennan 7 33
(Mrs Marjorie Fife) *chsd ldrs: rdn along 3f out: drvn 2f out and sn wknd* **40/1**

066- **5** *1 1/2* **Oriental Gift (FR)**^{245} [5488] 4-9-12 39.................................. DavidAllan 5 33
(H A McWilliams) *chsd ldrs: rdn along 3f out: drvn over 2f out and sn wknd* **100/1**

6 *shd* **Ayrpassionata** 3-8-9 0.. PaulHanagan 1 25
(Miss L A Perratt) *a in rr* **22/1**

000- **7** *12* **Warm Tribute (USA)**^{264} [4935] 4-9-12 45.......................... RobertHavlin 2 —
(A G Foster) *a towards rr* **80/1**

5 **8** *18* **Sir John Lilley (USA)**^{29} [1504] 3-9-0 0.......................... RobertWinston 4 —
(M Johnston) *hmpd s: sn pushed along in tch: rdn along 3f out: sn wknd and eased* **7/4**^{2}

1m 41.7s (0.50) **Going Correction** -0.05s/f (Good)
WFA 3 from 4yo 12lb **8** Ran SP% **115.1**
Speed ratings (Par 103): **95,94,88,78,77 77,65,47**
CSF £6.16 TOTE £2.60: £1.10, £1.40, £4.60; EX 5.20.
Owner N Martin **Bred** P And Mrs A G Venner **Trained** Sessay, N Yorks

FOCUS
An ordinary maiden especially with the second favourite running no sort of race, though the pace was a fair one. The front pair occupied those positions throughout and nothing else ever got into it. The third sets the level but the field finished spread out all over East Lothian and there is nothing to get excited about amongst the also-rans.
Ayrpassionata Official explanation: jockey said filly hung left-handed throughout
Sir John Lilley(USA) Official explanation: trainer had no explanation for the poor form shown

2247 TURFTV BETTING SHOP SERVICE H'CAP 1m
2:40 (2:40) (Class 6) (0-60,60) 3-Y-O £2,266 (£674; £337; £168) **Stalls** High

Form RPR

-640 **1** **Bourse (IRE)**^{26} [1558] 3-9-1 **60**.. PJMcDonald$^{(3)}$ 8 65
(J S Wainwright) *hld up towards rr: hdwy over 2f out: rdn to ld ent fnl f: sn drvn and kpt on wl* **7/1**

06-0 **2** *nk* **Addwaitya**^{20} [1696] 3-9-4 **60**.. IanMongan 7 64+
(C F Wall) *hld up in rr: rdn along and outpcd 1/2-way: hdwy on outer wl over 2f out: str run to chal ent fnl f: sn drvn and ev ch tl no ex nr fin* **3/1**^{2}

0-65 **3** *nk* **Talon (IRE)**^{26} [1558] 3-8-8 **50** ow1.. RobertWinston 9 53
(G A Swinbank) *trckd ldrs on inner: pushed along over 3f out: rdn and ev ch 2f out: drvn ent fnl f: kpt on u.p towards fin* **5/1**^{3}

52-4 **4** *2 1/4* **Flashy Max**^{12} [1912] 3-8-8 **50**.. AndrewElliott 1 48
(Jedd O'Keeffe) *led: rdn along 2f out: drvn over 1f out: hdd ent fnl f: kpt on same pce* **14/1**

000- **5** *1 1/2* **Aleatricis**^{192} [6748] 3-8-4 **46** oh1.. DO'Donohoe 3 41
(Sir Mark Prescott) *dwlt: rdn along and sn in tch: hdwy to trck ldrs over 2f out: rdn and ev ch over 1f out: sn drvn and one pce* **5/2**^{1}

-034 **6** *nse* **Jevington Star (IRE)**^{10} [1968] 3-8-4 **46** oh1.............. RoystonFfrench 10 40
(B Ellison) *in tch: rdn along 3f out: drvn and one pce fnl 2f* **11/1**

00-1 **7** *1 1/2* **Wogan's Sister**^{67} [873] 3-9-1 **57**.. PaulHanagan 2 48
(I A Wood) *t.k.h: chsd ldrs: rdn along 3f out: drvn over 2f out and sn wknd* **9/1**

060 **8** *1 3/4* **Miss Understanding**^{9} [2008] 3-8-8 **50**.............................. GrahamGibbons 6 37
(J R Weymes) *a towards rr* **50/1**

0000 **9** *15* **Dawn Wind**^{27} [1553] 3-8-6 **48**..(p) FergalLynch 4 —
(I A Wood) *chsd ldrs: rdn along 3f out: sn wknd* **28/1**

000- **P** **Scarlet Royal**^{277} [4522] 3-8-7 **49**.. PaulMulrennan 5 —
(Mrs Marjorie Fife) *sn outpcd and bhd: t.o 1/2-way: p.u fnl 2f* **50/1**

1m 42.27s (1.07) **Going Correction** -0.05s/f (Good) **10** Ran SP% **115.1**
Speed ratings (Par 97): **92,91,91,89,87 87,86,84,69,—**
CSF £27.62 CT £108.15 TOTE £10.40: £2.20, £1.40, £2.20; EX 33.50.
Owner M Sawers **Bred** Darley **Trained** Kennythorpe, N Yorks

FOCUS
A modest handicap and they went no pace early. As a result the winning time was over half a second slower than the opening maiden and the race is best judged through the third and fourth. Unlike the preceding contest, the first two home both came from well back.

Bourse(IRE) Official explanation: trainer said, regarding apparent improvement in form, that the gelding was suited by the better ground and the step up in trip.
Scarlet Royal Official explanation: jockey said filly had a breathing problem

2248 EDINBURGH HOLIDAY CLAIMING STKS 5f
3:10 (3:10) (Class 6) 4-Y-O+ **£2,266** (£674; £337; £168) **Stalls** Low

Form RPR
0-00 **1** **Angelofthenorth**[7] 2040 6-8-13 43 .... PaulHanagan 3 53
(C J Teague) *towards rr and pushed along 1/2-way: swtchd rt and hdwy 2f out: rdn ent fnl f: styd on to ld on line* **14/1**[2]
1402 **2** *shd* **Blackheath (IRE)**[7] 2036 12-8-1 60 .... KellyHarrison(5) 4 46
(S T Mason) *trckd ldrs: effrt 2f out: rdn to ld ins fnl f: sn drvn: hdd and nt qckn on line* **9/4**[1]
005- **3** *1/2* **Distant Vision (IRE)**[336] 2709 5-8-7 35 .... DavidAllan 1 45
(H A McWilliams) *cl up: pushed along and sltly outpcd over 1f out: swtchd rt and rdn ent fnl f: styd on wl towards fin* **50/1**
00-6 **4** *1 1/4* **Best Lead**[7] 2036 9-8-11 50 ....(b) DeclanCannon(7) 5 52
(Ian Emmerson) *cl up: rdn to ld wl over 1f out: drvn and hdd ins fnl f: wknd* **25/1**[3]
5-20 **5** *1 1/2* **Funfair Wane**[13] 1893 9-8-10 64 .... AdrianTNicholls 2 38
(D Nicholls) *sn led: rdn along 2f out: sn hdd & wknd* **9/4**[1]
4-03 **6** *1/2* **Whinhill House**[13] 1893 8-9-4 62 ....(v) RobertWinston 8 44+
(D W Barker) *sltly hmpd s: in rr tl effrt and n.m.r 2f out: nvr a factor* **9/4**[1]
-000 **7** *3 3/4* **Alfie Lee (IRE)**[3] 2145 11-8-1 41 ....(tp) PatrickDonaghy(7) 6 21
(D A Nolan) *chsd ldrs: rdn along over 2f out and sn wknd* **100/1**
59.80 secs (-0.60) **Going Correction** -0.25s/f (Firm) 7 Ran SP% **105.8**
Speed ratings (Par 101): **94,93,93,91,88 87,81**
CSF £39.11 TOTE £12.70: £3.80, £2.10; EX 39.50.
Owner Collins Chauffeur Driven Executive Cars **Bred** Jephanil **Trained** Station Town, Co Durham

FOCUS
A modest claimer full of moderate performers or horses that have seen better days. The winner is rated 43 and the third 35, with the fourth the best guide to the level.
Angelofthenorth Official explanation: tariner said, regarding apparent improvement in form, that the mare settled better and was suited by the return to a 5f trip
Whinhill House Official explanation: jockey said gelding was denied a clear run

2249 SCOTTISH RACING YOUR BETTER BET H'CAP 1m 4f
3:40 (3:40) (Class 4) (0-80,77) 4-Y-O+ **£5,504** (£1,637; £818; £408) **Stalls** High

Form RPR
2131 **1** **Royal Amnesty**[10] 1953 5-8-10 66 ....(b) RobertWinston 3 75+
(Miss L A Perratt) *hld up in rr: stdy hdwy on inner 3f out: swtchd lft and nt clr run over 1f out: swtchd rt and nt clr run ins fnl f: swtchd lft and qcknd to ld fnl 50yds* **4/1**[3]
33-1 **2** *3/4* **Lochiel**[15] 1825 4-8-10 66 .... PaulMulrennan 8 74
(Mrs S C Bradburne) *a.p: effrt over 2f out: rdn to ld over 1f out: drvn and wandered ent fnl f: hung lft and hdd fnl 50yds* **7/1**
160- **3** *4* **Grand Art (IRE)**[55] 6422 4-9-3 73 .... TonyHamilton 5 75
(J Howard Johnson) *hld up in tch: hdwy 3f out: rdn to chse ldrs 2f out: sn drvn and kpt on same pce* **12/1**
1602 **4** *1* **Kames Park (IRE)**[2] 2185 6-8-4 67 .... MarkCoumbe(7) 1 67
(R C Guest) *dwlt and in rr: hdwy over 2f out: rdn over 1f out: kpt on same pce* **7/2**[2]
-000 **5** *3/4* **Wild Fell Hall (IRE)**[25] 1585 5-9-7 77 .... AndrewElliott 6 76
(A D Brown) *chsd ldr: rdn to chal over 2f out: drvn over 1f out: wknd ent fnl f* **14/1**
0-00 **6** *2 3/4* **Moonwalking**[13] 1904 4-8-7 63 .... PaulHanagan 2 57
(Jedd O'Keeffe) *hld up in tch: hdwy on outer 3f out: rdn along 2f out: sn drvn and wknd wl over 1f out* **8/1**
04-0 **7** *6* **Marieschi (USA)**[31] 1449 4-7-12 61 ow1 .... PatrickDonaghy(7) 7 46
(R F Fisher) *chsd ldrs: rdn along 3f out: sn wknd* **10/1**
502 **8** *nk* **Key Decision (IRE)**[16] 1814 4-9-2 75 .... PJMcDonald(3) 4 59
(G A Swinbank) *led: rdn along 3f out: drvn 2f out: sn hdd & wknd* **10/3**[1]
2m 37.43s (-2.27) **Going Correction** -0.05s/f (Good) 8 Ran SP% **112.4**
Speed ratings (Par 105): **105,104,101,101,100 98,94,94**
CSF £30.70 CT £303.47 TOTE £4.20: £1.60, £1.40, £3.20; EX 19.90.
Owner Mrs Francesca Mitchell **Bred** Brick Kiln Stud, Mrs L Hicks & Partners **Trained** Carluke, S Lanarks

FOCUS
A reasonable handicap and with the favourite going off at a rate of knots the pace was sound. There was a bit of trouble in the home straight, but no real hard-luck stories. The winner is value for more with the runner-up rated to his best maiden form, but there was little solid behind.
Key Decision(IRE) Official explanation: trainer had no explanation for the poor form shown

2250 LADIES OF LINKS (S) STKS 1m
4:10 (4:11) (Class 6) 4-Y-O+ **£1,942** (£578; £288; £144) **Stalls** High

Form RPR
-021 **1** **Royal Dignitary (USA)**[13] 1902 8-9-3 85 .... AdrianTNicholls 2 64
(D Nicholls) *mde all: qcknd over 3f out: rdn 2f out: drvn and styd on wl fnl f* **4/5**[1]
50-0 **2** *1 1/4* **Papa's Princess**[33] 1406 4-8-7 47 .... FergalLynch 3 51
(J S Goldie) *towards rr: hdwy on outer wl over 2f out: sn rdn and styd on strly fnl f: nrst fin* **22/1**
0000 **3** *nk* **Buzzin'Boyzee (IRE)**[7] 2040 5-8-9 48 .... MarkLawson(3) 10 55
(D W Barker) *midfield: hdwy on outer wl over 2f out: rdn wl over 1f out: drvn and hung rt ent fnl f: kpt on* **50/1**
0151 **4** *2* **Boundless Prospect (USA)**[38] 1301 9-9-3 77 .... RoystonFfrench 8 56
(Ollie Pears) *s.i.s and bhd: hdwy wl over 2f out: sn rdn and styd on wl fnl f* **5/1**[2]
0-00 **5** *1 1/4* **Malguru**[38] 1305 4-8-12 45 ....(p) RobertHavlin 11 48
(A G Foster) *chsd ldrs: rdn along 3f out: drvn 2f out and grad wknd* **100/1**
00-0 **6** *1/2* **College Land Boy**[22] 1221 4-8-12 48 .... PaulMulrennan 5 47
(A Kirtley) *chsd ldrs: rdn along 3f out: sn drvn and kpt on same pce* **100/1**
4-36 **7** *3/4* **Defi (IRE)**[57] 978 6-8-12 60 ....(b) RobertWinston 9 45
(Miss L A Perratt) *cl up: rdn along and sltly outpcd 3f out: chal 2f out and ev ch tl drvn and wknd ent fnl f* **6/1**[3]
00-0 **8** *1 3/4* **Roman History (IRE)**[38] 1305 5-8-9 45 ....(p) JamieMoriarty(3) 4 41
(Miss Tracy Waggott) *in tch: rdn along 3f out: sn wknd* **66/1**
06/0 **9** *11* **Katie's Biscuit**[7] 2038 6-8-2 49 ....(v) KellyHarrison(5) 6 11
(Ian Emmerson) *a in rr* **80/1**
-300 **10** *2 1/4* **Tizzy May (FR)**[19] 1729 8-8-12 58 ....(p) PaulHanagan 12 10
(B Ellison) *a in rr* **6/1**[3]
4200 **11** *36* **Local Poet**[20] 1705 7-8-12 50 ....(p) TonyHamilton 7 —
(Ollie Pears) *a towards rr* **28/1**
1m 41.12s (-0.08) **Going Correction** -0.05s/f (Good) 11 Ran SP% **115.3**
Speed ratings (Par 101): **98,96,96,94,93 92,91,90,79,76 40**
CSF £26.05 TOTE £1.70: £1.10, £4.80, £10.90; EX 24.60.The winner was bought in for 12,000 guineas.
Owner Middleham Park Racing XXXVI **Bred** Bentley Smith, J Michael O'Farrell Jr , Joan Thor **Trained** Sessay, N Yorks
■ Stewards' Enquiry : Robert Winston caution: allowed gelding to coast home with no assistance

FOCUS
A very uncompetitive seller containing a wide variety of abilities and it is hard to be positive over the form with poor performers close up. The pace was fair thanks to the favourite and the winning time was the fastest of the three races over the trip at the meeting, but that is not saying very much.
Tizzy May(FR) Official explanation: jockey said gelding was unsuited by the good to firm (good in places) ground

2251 MUSSELBURGH-RACECOURSE.CO.UK NORTH H'CAP 7f 30y
4:40 (4:40) (Class 5) (0-70,70) 4-Y-O+ **£2,914** (£867; £433; £216) **Stalls** High

Form RPR
00-1 **1** **Stellite**[17] 1775 8-8-10 62 .... DanielTudhope 10 73+
(J S Goldie) *trckd ldrs: hdwy over 2f out: rdn to ld ent fnl f: kpt on* **5/1**[1]
3500 **2** *1* **Sands Of Barra (IRE)**[9] 2007 5-9-0 66 .... AndrewElliott 3 73
(I W McInnes) *chsd ldr: rdn along 2f out: ch whn n.m.r and swtchd ent fnl f: sn drvn and kpt on* **14/1**
4033 **3** *shd* **Poppy's Rose**[7] 2039 4-8-9 61 .... RoystonFfrench 11 68
(I W McInnes) *led: rdn along over 2f out: drvn: hdd and hung bdly lft ent fnl f: kpt on same pce* **11/2**[2]
-214 **4** *shd* **The Salwick Flyer (IRE)**[95] 560 5-8-4 56 .... PaulFessey 4 62
(Miss L A Perratt) *prom: rdn along to chal 2f out and ev ch whn carried lft and swtchd ent fnl f: sn drvn and kpt on towards fin* **8/1**[3]
000- **5** *2 1/4* **Heureux (USA)**[254] 5228 5-8-13 65 ....(b) RobertWinston 6 65+
(J Howard Johnson) *hld up in rr: hdwy wl over 2f out: rdn over 1f out: kpt on: nrst fin* **10/1**
0/00 **6** *1/2* **Woodsley House (IRE)**[17] 1775 6-8-8 60 .... RobertHavlin 2 59
(A G Foster) *chsd ldrs: rdn along over 2f out: kpt on same pce* **28/1**
-024 **7** *3/4* **Stoic Leader (IRE)**[17] 1774 8-9-4 70 .... PaulHanagan 1 67
(R F Fisher) *chsd ldrs: rdn along over 2f out: sn drvn and no imp* **5/1**[1]
0-00 **8** *1 1/2* **Kirkby's Treasure**[31] 1449 10-8-7 62 .... PJMcDonald(3) 8 55
(G A Swinbank) *hld up and bhd: hdwy over 2f out: kpt on appr fnl f: nvr a factor* **9/1**
-050 **9** *2* **Yorkshire Blue**[10] 1952 9-8-10 67 .... GaryBartley(5) 7 55
(J S Goldie) *a towards rr* **9/1**
5500 **10** *1* **Inca Soldier (FR)**[17] 1775 5-8-8 60 .... DeanMcKeown 9 45
(R C Guest) *s.i.s: a in rr* **10/1**
0015 **11** *2 3/4* **Newgate (UAE)**[24] 1602 4-7-13 56 ....(b) DanielleMcCreery(5) 5 33
(Mrs R A Carr) *hld up in tch: hdwy on outer and wd st: rdn over 2f out and sn wknd* **16/1**
1m 29.86s (-0.44) **Going Correction** -0.05s/f (Good) 11 Ran SP% **114.0**
Speed ratings (Par 103): **100,98,98,98,96 95,94,92,90,89 86**
CSF £72.43 CT £403.19 TOTE £6.70: £1.90, £6.10, £2.50; EX 120.80.
Owner S Bruce **Bred** Cheveley Park Stud Ltd **Trained** Uplawmoor, E Renfrews
■ Stewards' Enquiry : Royston Ffrench caution: careless riding

FOCUS
An ordinary handicap, but a rather messy contest and the winner certainly got the run of the race. However, the form seems sound enough rated around those in the frame.
Newgate(UAE) Official explanation: jockey said gelding failed to handle the bend

2252 TURFTV A MATTER OF COURSE APPRENTICE H'CAP 2m
5:10 (5:11) (Class 6) (0-65,65) 4-Y-O+ **£2,590** (£770; £385; £192) **Stalls** Low

Form RPR
200/ **1** **Silver Seeker (USA)**[43] 5568 8-8-7 46 .... PJMcDonald 4 69+
(Miss P Robson) *hld up: smooth hdwy to trck ldrs 5f out: led over 2f out and sn clr: easily* **5/2**[1]
5634 **2** *10* **Easibet Dot Net**[38] 1304 8-8-10 52 ....(p) KellyHarrison(3) 3 58
(Miss L A Perratt) *hld up in rr: hdwy 3f out: rdn to chse wnr wl over 1f out: no imp* **13/2**
126- **3** *2 1/2* **Spanish Conquest**[196] 6697 4-8-11 59 .... RosieJessop(7) 2 62
(Sir Mark Prescott) *trckd ldrs: chsd ldr after 5f: rdn along over 3f out: kpt on same pce* **7/2**[2]
-100 **4** *2 1/2* **Rare Coincidence**[15] 1824 7-9-10 63 ....(p) DNolan 5 63
(R F Fisher) *cl up: led after 3f: rdn along 3f out: hdd over 2f out: sn drvn and btn* **5/1**[3]
2662 **5** *10* **Coronado's Gold (USA)**[13] 1892 7-9-2 60 .... LanceBetts(5) 7 48
(B Ellison) *chsd ldng pair: rdn along over 3f out and sn wknd* **7/2**[2]
300- **6** *30* **King's Envoy (USA)**[200] 2825 9-8-7 46 oh1 .... AndrewMullen 8 —
(Mrs J C McGregor) *led 3f: prom tl rdn along 4f out and sn wknd* **33/1**
00-0 **7** *18* **Erte**[10] 1972 7-8-2 46 oh1 ....(b) DeclanCannon(5) 6 —
(V Thompson) *trckd ldrs on inner: rdn along 6f out: lost pl qckly and sn bhd* **28/1**
3m 30.56s (-5.54) **Going Correction** -0.05s/f (Good)
WFA 4 from 7yo+ 2lb 7 Ran SP% **109.4**
Speed ratings (Par 101): **111,106,104,103,98 83,74**
CSF £17.52 CT £50.19 TOTE £3.70: £1.80, £3.60; EX 18.40 Place 6: £70.61, Place 5: £45.11..
Owner Hale Racing Limited **Bred** Darley Stud Management, L L C **Trained** Kirkharle, Northumberland
■ Pauline Robson's first runner, and winner, on the Flat.

FOCUS
A modest staying handicap, but they went a very decent pace in this and it became a proper test of stamina, hence the very healthy margins separating the seven runners. The winning time was very decent for a race of its class and the winner hacked up, with the runner-up setting the level.

T/Plt: £84.20 to a £1 stake. Pool: £47,236.29. 409.09 winning tickets. T/Qpdt: £20.60 to a £1 stake. Pool: £2,989.17. 107.30 winning tickets. JR

2042 WINDSOR (R-H)

Monday, May 19

OFFICIAL GOING: Good to firm changing to good to firm (good in places) after race 2 (6.40)

Wind: Light, against Weather: Fine but cloudy

2253 EUROPEAN BREEDERS' FUND MAIDEN FILLIES' STKS 5f 10y

6:10 (6:12) (Class 5) 2-Y-O £3,626 (£1,079; £539; £269) Stalls High

Form RPR

1 **Baileys Cacao (IRE)** 2-9-0 0 RichardHughes 2 84+
(R Hannon) *pressed ldr: hung lft after 2f: shkn up to ld over 1f out: sn clr* 11/4[1]

2 2 ¾ **Stan's Cool Cat (IRE)** 2-9-0 0 NelsonDeSouza 8 74+
(P F I Cole) *sn pushed along: bdly outpcd and rn green: sme prog fr 1/2-way: r.o strly fnl f to take 2nd last 75yds* 7/1

0402 3 2 ¼ **Amosite**[10] [1961] 2-9-0 0 (v) ShaneKelly 9 66
(J R Jenkins) *cl up: led against nr side rail over 2f out: hdd over 1f out: sn outpcd: lost 2nd wl ins fnl f* 9/2[3]

4 4 nse **Bahamian Ceilidh**[23] [1610] 2-9-0 0 TPQueally 7 66
(B R Millman) *t.k.h: cl up: shkn up and outpcd over 1f out: one pce after* 8/1

2 5 1 ½ **Forward Feline (IRE)**[14] [1866] 2-9-0 0 CatherineGannon 10 60
(B Palling) *led to over 2f out: nt qckn over 1f out: fdd fnl f* 4/1[2]

6 2 ½ **Deal Clincher** 2-9-0 0 JimmyFortune 3 51
(P Winkworth) *nt on terms w ldrs in midfield: outpcd fr 2f out* 12/1

7 ½ **Hameildaeme** 2-9-0 0 SaleemGolam 6 50
(S C Williams) *dwlt: bdly outpcd and wl bhd: styd on fr over 1f out: nrst fin* 66/1

8 2 **Hollow Green (IRE)** 2-9-0 0 StephenDonohoe 11 42
(P D Evans) *s.s: bdly outpcd and rn green: wl bhd tl styd on fnl f* 25/1

9 nk **Luxuria (IRE)** 2-9-0 0 RichardSmith 5 41
(R Hannon) *nt on terms in midfield: no prog 2f out: fdd* 11/1

10 3 ½ **Abby Belle (IRE)** 2-9-0 0 JamesDoyle 1 29
(J G Portman) *chsd ldrs: wknd sn after 1/2-way* 40/1

11 17 **Piste** 2-9-0 0 JamieSpencer 4 —
(B J Meehan) *s.s: rcvrd and in tch after 1f: wknd rapidly 1/2-way: t.o* 10/1

61.95 secs (1.65) **Going Correction** +0.20s/f (Good) 11 Ran SP% **121.4**

Speed ratings (Par 90): **94,89,86,85,83 79,78,75,75,69 42**

CSF £23.10 TOTE £3.20: £1.50, £2.20, £2.10; EX 20.80.

Owner William Durkan **Bred** Miss Mary Davison **Trained** East Everleigh, Wilts

FOCUS

There was not a great deal of strength in depth to this maiden but Baileys Cacao won well and the race could rate higher.

NOTEBOOK

Baileys Cacao(IRE), whose sales price increased to 160,000euros as a yearling, is out of a 7f scorer who is a half-sister to Chesham Stakes winner Fair Cop. She won comfortably on this debut despite showing her inexperience and will probably head to Ascot for either the Queen Mary or the Albany Stakes now, but she will need to improve to take a hand there. (tchd 2-1 and 3-1)

Stan's Cool Cat(IRE) ◆ could not go the pace and still had only two behind her entering the final quarter-mile, but she clicked into gear in the final furlong and passed several rivals for second without her rider being hard on her. There is a good deal of stamina on her dam's side and an extra furlong should soon see her off the mark. (op 8-1)

Amosite, who showed a fair level of form in four previous starts, was visored again. She came through against the rail to have her chance, but was outpaced by the winner before being run out of second place inside the final furlong. (op 4-1 tchd 5-1)

Bahamian Ceilidh, fourth on easy ground on her debut at Haydock, ran another fair race. She looks a nursery type, perhaps over 6f. (op 9-1 tchd 12-1)

Forward Feline(IRE), runner-up on her debut at Warwick, showed pace to lead until halfway before steadily dropping out of contention. (op 13-2)

Deal Clincher has an attractive sprinting pedigree, being a half-sister to sprint winner Tipsy Prince out of a dual 5f winner. She was never a factor on this debut but should come on for the run. (tchd 14-1)

Abby Belle(IRE) Official explanation: jockey said filly hung right

2254 WEATHERBYS BANK CONDITIONS STKS 5f 10y

6:40 (6:40) (Class 2) 2-Y-O £11,354 (£3,398; £1,699; £849) Stalls High

Form RPR

13 1 **White Shift (IRE)**[12] [1914] 2-8-9 0 StephenDonohoe 2 87
(P D Evans) *mde virtually all: drvn and hrd pressed fnl f: jst hld on* 5/2[2]

2 shd **Sayif (IRE)** 2-8-10 0 ow2 JimmyFortune 3 88+
(P W Chapple-Hyam) *dwlt: last tl effrt on outer 2f out: vigorously rdn to press wnr fnl f: upsides nr fin: jst pipped* 8/11[1]

3 1 **Square Eddie (CAN)** 2-8-8 0 LPKeniry 4 82+
(J R Best) *cl up: effrt 2f out: nt qckn and n.m.r over 1f out: green but renewed effrt fnl f: kpt on wl* 22/1

1 4 11 **Fault**[14] [1873] 2-9-0 0 RichardHughes 1 48
(R Charlton) *mostly chsd wnr to wl over 1f out: wknd rapidly and eased* 4/1[3]

61.68 secs (1.38) **Going Correction** +0.20s/f (Good) 4 Ran SP% **110.8**

Speed ratings (Par 99): **96,95,94,76**

CSF £4.92 TOTE £3.10; EX 6.30.

Owner Premier Cru Racing **Bred** Grange Stud **Trained** Pandy, Monmouths

FOCUS

A decent conditions event with the winner putting her experience to good use and rated to her Chester form.

NOTEBOOK

White Shift(IRE) was third in Chester's Lily Agnes Stakes last time, a place behind subsequent Listed third Aspen Darlin. Once again showing bags of pace, she showed a likeable attitude to hold off the runner-up after a good tussle. The Hilary Needler at Beverley looks the obvious immediate target for her. (op 3-1)

Sayif(IRE), at 200,000gns the most expensive yearling in Kheleyf's first crop, is a half-brother to Hunter Street who won the Cornwallis Stakes for this yard when it was run at Salisbury. He ran a fine race on this debut, just missing out to a filly who had the benefit of previous experience, and arguably would have won had he not carried 2lb overweight. He should not be long in losing his maiden tag although he did have a fairly hard race. (op 5-6 tchd 10-11)

Square Eddie(CAN) ◆, a $200,000 yearling by the sire of Curlin, made a promising debut despite running noticeably green. He travelled well on the rail, just behind the leader, but when he tried to make his effort between horses he did not have quite enough speed and then found the door closing on him. To his credit he came back for more and chased the two principals hard through the final furlong. A maiden should come his way. (tchd 20-1 and 25-1)

Fault was successful here on his debut on easy ground, but disappointed under the penalty. After going with the winner he was the first under pressure and was eased when beaten. This was not his running. Official explanation: jockey said colt ran too free (op 3-1 tchd 9-2 in places)

2255 GET A BONUS AT WILLIAMHILLCASINO.COM CLAIMING STKS 6f

7:10 (7:11) (Class 5) 3-Y-O+ £2,593 (£765; £383) Stalls High

Form RPR

0001 1 **Dressed To Dance (IRE)**[7] [2040] 4-8-13 55 (v) JimmyFortune 11 63
(N Tinkler) *rrd s: t.k.h and hld up in midfield: prog over 1f out: hrd rdn and styd on to ld last strides* 7/1[3]

0-04 2 hd **Guest Connections**[7] [2040] 5-9-8 72 (v) JamieSpencer 5 72
(D Nicholls) *hld up in rr: hanging to outer fr 1/2-way: coaxed along and clsd on ldrs fr 2f out: rdn to ld last 75yds: hdd last strides* 9/2[2]

1223 3 ¾ **Savile's Delight (IRE)**[11] [1928] 9-9-6 75 RichardKingscote 10 67
(Tom Dascombe) *restless stalls: pressed ldng pair: narrow ld 2f out: hrd pressed 1f out: hdd last 75yds* 6/4[1]

6560 4 ¾ **Teen Ager (FR)**[10] [1954] 4-9-6 57 TQuinn 12 65
(P Burgoyne) *trckd ldrs: effrt nr side 2f out: chal 1f out: one pce last 100yds* 25/1

240 5 ¾ **Doubtful Sound (USA)**[9] [1997] 4-9-8 65 RichardHughes 6 65
(John A Harris) *dwlt: hld up in rr: plld out wd and effrt 2f out: drvn to cl on ldrs 1f out: nt qckn ins fnl f: eased nr fin* 12/1

20-0 6 ½ **Rainbow Bay**[9] [1997] 5-9-0 60 (v) StephenDonohoe 15 55
(P D Evans) *settled in midfield: prog fr 2f out: pressed ldrs 1f out: nvr quite able to chal* 10/1

-030 7 hd **Scarlett Heart (IRE)**[22] [1642] 4-8-9 53 PaulDoe 16 49
(S Curran) *hld up against nr side rail: nt clr run over 2f out: prog and nt clr run over 1f out: kpt on but unable to chal* 16/1

6010 8 5 **Majestical (IRE)**[21] [1670] 6-9-0 58 (p) SaleemGolam 9 38
(V Smith) *trckd ldrs: waiting to chal 2f out: sn rdn and wknd tamely* 33/1

531 9 1 ½ **Jal Music**[17] [1777] 3-8-13 69 ShaneKelly 13 42
(R A Harris) *mde most to 2f out: wknd sn after* 12/1

2000 10 1 **Kempsey**[22] [1646] 6-9-6 54 (b) TPQueally 4 36
(J J Bridger) *towards rr: rdn and effrt 2f out: no prog over 1f out: wknd fnl f* 100/1

-401 11 hd **Kenmore**[7] [2036] 6-9-0 70 PatrickMathers 1 30
(I W McInnes) *racd alone out wd and nt on terms: carried further wd over 2f out: sme prog 2f out: wknd over 1f out* 14/1

06-6 12 ½ **Currency**[9] [2010] 11-9-4 56 LPKeniry 3 32
(J M Bradley) *sn pushed along in rr: drvn and effrt 2f out: sn no prog* 40/1

4053 13 3 **Monashee Prince (IRE)**[9] [2010] 6-9-0 57 (v) DaneO'Neill 2 19
(J R Best) *nvr on terms w ldrs: no ch fr over 1f out* 16/1

40-0 14 2 ¾ **Peer Pressure**[18] [1743] 3-9-3 59 SamHitchcott 7 22
(B R Johnson) *dwlt: nvr beyond midfield: wknd wl over 1f out* 100/1

5 15 19 **Quws Vision (IRE)**[39] [1283] 5-8-9 0 (p) FrankieMcDonald 14 —
(Mrs L C Jewell) *w ldr to over 2f out: wknd rapidly: t.o* 200/1

0436 16 7 **Mileaminutemurphy**[51] [1081] 3-8-5 55 RichardSmith 8 —
(R Hannon) *a in rr: t.o over 1f out* 66/1

1m 14.4s (1.40) **Going Correction** +0.20s/f (Good)

WFA 3 from 4yo+ 9lb 16 Ran SP% **126.8**

Speed ratings (Par 103): **98,97,96,95,94 94,93,87,85,83 83,82,78,75,49 40**

CSF £39.13 TOTE £8.60: £1.90, £2.30, £1.50; EX 37.30.The winner was claimed by P D Evans for £8,000.

Owner W K Syndicate **Bred** John Doyle **Trained** Langton, N Yorks

FOCUS

The first seven finished in a heap, clear of the rest, in this reasonable claimer. The second and third are good types for the grade but the next two have little or no turf form.

Guest Connections Official explanation: jockey said gelding hung right throughout

Jal Music Official explanation: jockey said gelding was unsuited by the ground

2256 GET ON WITH WILLIAM HILL 0800 44 40 40 H'CAP 1m 3f 135y

7:40 (7:40) (Class 4) (0-85,83) 3-Y-O £4,857 (£1,445; £722; £360) Stalls Centre

Form RPR

031- 1 **Inventor (IRE)**[231] [5858] 3-9-2 81 JimmyFortune 5 89
(B J Meehan) *mostly trckd ldr: rdn and effrt over 2f out: clsd and edgd rt 1f out: led last 150yds: drvn out* 9/2[3]

43-0 2 1 ¼ **The Betchworth Kid**[32] [1424] 3-9-4 83 JamieSpencer 2 89
(M L W Bell) *hld up in last: effrt on wd outside over 2f out: hrd rdn and styd on fnl f: tk 2nd nr fin: unable to chal* 9/2[3]

61- 3 shd **First Avenue**[202] [6574] 3-9-3 82 PhilipRobinson 6 87
(M A Jarvis) *swvd rt s: hld up in 5th: effrt on outer over 2f out: rdn and nt qckn over 1f out: styd on ins fnl f* 11/4[1]

0-1 4 nk **Killcara Boy**[15] [1840] 3-8-13 78 DaneO'Neill 7 83
(H Candy) *mde most: drvn over 2f out: bmpd rival ent fnl f: sn hdd and btn* 4/1[2]

40-3 5 2 ¼ **Winter Bloom (USA)**[18] [1746] 3-9-3 82 TPQueally 4 87+
(H R A Cecil) *trckd ldng pair: waiting for gap to appear fr over 2f out: effrt against rail over 1f out: squeezed out ent fnl f: nt rcvr* 8/1

-422 6 2 ¾ **Higgy's Boy (IRE)**[15] [1839] 3-8-13 78 RichardHughes 1 75
(R Hannon) *hld up in 4th: rdn over 2f out: nt qckn and btn over 1f out* 13/2

64-0 7 ½ **Sainglend**[14] [1854] 3-8-10 75 PaulDoe 3 71
(S Curran) *hld up in 6th: rdn and no prog 2f out: btn over 1f out* 20/1

2m 29.77s (0.27) **Going Correction** +0.05s/f (Good) 7 Ran SP% **112.2**

Speed ratings (Par 101): **101,100,100,99,98 96,96**

CSF £23.90 CT £64.25 TOTE £5.90: £2.70, £3.70; EX 42.20.

Owner Highclere Thoroughbred Racing (Lake Con) **Bred** Brendan Holland And P Connell **Trained** Manton, Wilts

FOCUS

This fairly good handicap was run at an ordinary pace. Decent form, rated around the fourth and the unfortunate Winter Bloom has been rated the length winner.

Winter Bloom(USA) Official explanation: jockey said filly suffered interference in running

2257 MICHA CLEMENTS BIRTHDAY MAIDEN FILLIES' STKS 1m 67y

8:10 (8:13) (Class 5) 3-Y-O+ £2,729 (£806; £403) Stalls High

Form RPR

3 1 **Illusion**[19] [1721] 3-8-12 0 JimmyFortune 9 85
(J H M Gosden) *led after 1f: mde rest: drvn and hrd pressed over 1f out: edgd lft fnl f: styd on wl* 9/2[2]

4- 2 1 **Red Dune (IRE)**[206] [6470] 3-8-12 0 PhilipRobinson 7 82
(M A Jarvis) *t.k.h early: led 1f: restrained bhd wnr: effrt to chal again wl over 1f out: nt qckn and hld fnl f* 4/7[1]

3 1 ½ **Lee Miller (IRE)** 3-8-12 0 DaneO'Neill 11 79+
(L M Cumani) *hld up in midfield: effrt over 2f out: prog to go 3rd over 1f out: styd on but nvr able to chal* 40/1

0- **4** 2 **Filigree Lace (USA)**[198] 6649 3-8-12 0 J-PGuillambert 14 74
(Sir Michael Stoute) *cl up: pushed along to chse ldng pair over 2f out but sn outpcd: one pce* **25/1**

46 **5** 1 ¾ **Eureka Moment**[9] 2015 3-8-5 0 WilliamCarson(7) 12 70
(E A L Dunlop) *trckd ldrs: pushed along and outpcd fr 2f out: nt on terms after* **28/1**

0- **6** nk **Sterope (FR)**[223] 6087 3-8-12 0 TPQueally 1 70
(H R A Cecil) *hld up in midfield: prog on outer over 2f out: no imp over 1f out: fdd ins fnl f* **20/1**

4- **7** nk **Debdene Bank (IRE)**[296] 3968 5-9-10 0 GeorgeBaker 4 72+
(Mrs Mary Hambro) *s.s: mostly in last pair: shkn up and styd on fnl 2f: nvr nrr* **66/1**

8 2 **Mischief Lady** 3-8-12 0 StephenDonohoe 13 64+
(E A L Dunlop) *s.s: wl in rr: shkn up on outer over 2f out: kpt on: n.d but nrst fin* **33/1**

9 hd **Russian Empress (USA)** 3-8-12 0 RichardHughes 5 64+
(Sir Michael Stoute) *wl in rr: pushed along and modest late prog: nvr nr ldrs* **8/1**[3]

03- **10** ½ **Broken Moon**[230] 5881 3-8-12 0 JamieSpencer 2 63
(J R Fanshawe) *hld up in midfield on inner: pushed along and grad lost pl fnl 2f* **10/1**

11 4 **Bountiful Bay** 3-8-5 0 GabrielHannon(7) 10 54
(B J Meehan) *dwlt: a in rr: urged along and no real prog fnl 2f* **100/1**

0- **12** 6 **Plumage**[164] 7051 3-8-12 0 JamesDoyle 6 40
(M Blanshard) *plld hrd: mostly chsd ldng pair to over 2f out: wknd* **66/1**

13 10 **Young Ollie** 3-8-12 0 LPKeniry 8 17
(E A Wheeler) *dwlt: a in rr:* **150/1**

14 shd **Thirtyfourthstreet (IRE)** 3-8-12 0 RichardMullen 3 17
(W R Muir) *a wl in rr: t.o* **100/1**

1m 43.67s (-1.03) **Going Correction** +0.05s/f (Good)
WFA 3 from 5yo 12lb **14** Ran SP% **125.1**
Speed ratings (Par 100): **107,106,104,102,100 100,100,98,97,97 93,87,77,77**
CSF £7.24 TOTE £5.00: £1.60, £1.10, £9.40; EX 10.30.
Owner Cheveley Park Stud **Bred** Cheveley Park Stud Ltd **Trained** Newmarket, Suffolk

FOCUS
An above average fillies' maiden, the winner setting a fair standard, and a decent winning time for a race like this. The winner sets a fair standard and there should be a few future winners down the field.
Debdene Bank(IRE) Official explanation: jockey said mare missed the break
Broken Moon Official explanation: jockey said filly hung right from the start

2258 GET YOUR BALLS AT WILLIAMHILLBINGO.COM H'CAP 5f 10y
8:40 (8:40) (Class 4) (0-85,85) 3-Y-O **£4,857** (£1,445; £722; £360) **Stalls** High

Form RPR

3-03 **1** **Good Gorsoon (USA)**[11] 1925 3-9-3 **84** MichaelHills 11 92
(B W Hills) *hld up bhd ldrs: prog against nr side rail to ld gp jst over 1f out: edgd lft u.p but r.o fnl f to ld last strides* **2/1**[1]

2-06 **2** hd **Bosun Breese**[14] 1852 3-9-1 **82** RichardHughes 2 89
(P W D'Arcy) *racd alone towards far side: wl on terms: def advntage fr 2f out: collared last strides* **16/1**

205- **3** 1 **Little Pete (IRE)**[324] 3077 3-9-1 **82** LPKeniry 9 86
(A M Balding) *trckd ldng pair: rdn and effrt over 1f out: edgd lft but styd on fnl f: a hld* **25/1**

-441 **4** ¾ **Blue Jack**[12] 1911 3-8-9 **76** RichardMullen 6 77
(W R Muir) *hld up in tch of main gp: rdn and effrt 2f out: styd on: nvr able to chal* **6/1**

3420 **5** nk **Monsieur Reynard**[4] 2122 3-8-6 **73** ow1 JamieSpencer 5 73
(B J Meehan) *t.k.h: hld up in last pair: prog on outer fr 2f out: clsd on ldrs ins fnl f: nt qckn last 100yds* **4/1**[3]

-310 **6** 3 ¾ **Barraland**[30] 1484 3-8-4 **78** MCGeran(7) 12 64
(M R Channon) *led main gp: hdd jst over 1f out: hung lft and wknd* **16/1**

02-6 **7** ¾ **Perfect Flight**[24] 1597 3-8-13 **80** JamesDoyle 3 64
(M Blanshard) *trckd ldrs tl wknd over 1f out* **16/1**

1316 **8** ¾ **Orpen's Art (IRE)**[52] 1066 3-7-13 **73** CharlesEddery(7) 10 54
(S A Callaghan) *t.k.h: hld up in last pair: rdn and wknd over 1f out* **28/1**

-305 **9** 4 ½ **Enodoc**[14] 1852 3-8-9 **76** ShaneKelly 4 41
(W R Muir) *in tch at rr of main gp: wknd over 1f out* **40/1**

13-0 **10** 1 ¾ **Just A Dancer (IRE)**[15] 1834 3-8-13 **80** TQuinn 8 39
(B W Hills) *w ldr to 2f out: wknd* **20/1**

105- **11** 4 ½ **Regal Step**[318] 3269 3-9-4 **85** JimmyFortune 7 27
(R M H Cowell) *pressed ldrs tl wknd qckly 2f out* **7/2**[2]

61.10 secs (0.80) **Going Correction** +0.20s/f (Good) **11** Ran SP% **122.0**
Speed ratings (Par 101): **101,100,99,97,97 91,90,89,81,79 71**
CSF £38.05 CT £664.17 TOTE £3.40: £1.50, £4.60, £3.30; EX 84.70 Place 6 £58.10, Place 5 £39.73..
Owner Triermore Stud & Partner **Bred** Jayeff 'B' Stables **Trained** Lambourn, Berks

FOCUS
A decent handicap with an improved run from Good Gorsoon. The form is rated through the fourth to his mark.
Just A Dancer(IRE) Official explanation: jockey said filly hung left final 2f
Regal Step Official explanation: jockey said filly ran too free
T/Plt: £113.30 to a £1 stake. Pool: £78,441.99. 505.10 winning tickets. T/Qpdt: £24.70 to a £1 stake. Pool: £5,689.86. 170.30 winning tickets. JN

2048 WOLVERHAMPTON (A.W) (L-H)
Monday, May 19

OFFICIAL GOING: Standard
Wind: Light half-against Weather: Overcast

2259 RINGSIDE CONFERENCE SUITE CLASSIFIED STKS 1m 141y(P)
6:50 (6:51) (Class 6) 3-Y-O+ **£2,047** (£604; £302) **Stalls** Low

Form RPR

1250 **1** **Wisdom's Kiss**[25] 1578 4-9-0 55 (b) JimmyQuinn 6 73
(J D Bethell) *trckd ldrs: led over 2f out: rdn clr fr over 1f out* **3/1**[2]

6-66 **2** 9 **Holden Caulfield (IRE)**[27] 1533 3-7-8 45 DavidProbert(7) 1 51
(Mouse Hamilton-Fairley) *s.i.s: hld up: hdwy u.p over 1f out: nt clr run and swtchd lft ins fnl f: no ch w wnr* **18/1**

0300 **3** nk **Natural Rhythm (IRE)**[7] 2041 3-8-1 55 LiamJones 2 50
(Mrs R A Carr) *hld up: hdwy over 1f out: rdn and edgd lft whn bmpd ins fnl f: tried to bite rival nr fin: nvr nrr* **7/1**

4232 **4** shd **One Called Alice**[24] 1603 3-7-12 55 LukeMorris(3) 9 50
(A W Carroll) *s.i.s and hmpd s: hdwy over 3f out: rdn over 2f out: sn edgd lft: wknd over 1f out* **6/1**[3]

5360 **5** 1 ¾ **Moorside Diamond**[23] 1626 4-9-0 39 SilvestreDeSousa 7 48
(A D Brown) *chsd ldr: rdn over 2f out: wknd over 1f out* **33/1**

000- **6** 1 **Bid To The Beat**[194] 6723 3-8-3 53 ow5 KirstyMilczarek(3) 10 48
(H J Collingridge) *sn led: rdn and hdd over 2f out: wknd over 1f out* **9/1**

0-04 **7** nk **Colleoni (IRE)**[108] 396 3-8-1 54 WilliamBuick 8 43
(G A Butler) *hld up: rdn and hung lft over 1f out: nvr nrr* **11/4**[1]

000 **8** nk **Cape Tycoon (IRE)**[17] 1763 3-8-1 52 DaleGibson 4 42
(S A Callaghan) *mid-div: hmpd over 7f out: rdn over 3f out: n.d* **20/1**

00-0 **9** 6 **Shoot Pontoon (IRE)**[35] 1367 3-8-2 55 ow1 ChrisCatlin 12 29
(S A Callaghan) *prom: rdn over 3f out: wkng whn nt clr run over 2f out* **22/1**

542- **10** ¾ **Foreland Sands (IRE)**[209] 6402 4-8-11 55 TolleyDean(3) 13 28
(Mrs L Williamson) *s.i.s: hld up: racd keenly: rdn over 2f out: sn wknd* **16/1**

0645 **11** 4 ½ **Takeanoteofthat (IRE)**[41] 1259 6-9-0 32 VinceSlattery 11 18
(D Burchell) *chsd ldr over 6f out: rdn and wknd over 1f out* **100/1**

60-0 **12** 12 **Jimmy Dean**[7] 2055 3-7-10 49 (p) NicolPolli(5) 5 —
(M Wellings) *hld up: rdn 1/2-way: wknd over 3f out* **66/1**

0-50 **13** 13 **Cobbold Point**[18] 1741 3-7-12 45 (b[1]) DominicFox(3) 3 —
(S W Hall) *led early: chsd ldrs tl wknd wl over 3f out: hmpd sn after* **66/1**

1m 49.56s (-0.94) **Going Correction** -0.025s/f (Stan)
WFA 3 from 4yo+ 13lb **13** Ran SP% **115.6**
Speed ratings (Par 101): **103,95,94,94,93 92,91,91,86,85 81,71,59**
CSF £49.44 TOTE £4.50: £1.80, £3.60, £2.30; EX 67.60.
Owner Ms Linda J Hipkiss **Bred** Snowdrop Stud Co Ltd **Trained** Middleham Moor, N Yorks

FOCUS
A weak race and little solid, with nothing to take into the future behind the winner.

2260 WOLVERHAMPTON-RACECOURSE.CO.UK H'CAP 7f 32y(P)
7:20 (7:20) (Class 6) (0-60,59) 3-Y-O **£2,047** (£604; £302) **Stalls** High

Form RPR

000- **1** **Master Of Arts (USA)**[257] 5126 3-9-3 **58** SebSanders 1 85
(Sir Mark Prescott) *s.i.s: drvn to ld over 6f out: rdn and hung rt over 2f out: r.o wl: eased nr fin* **7/2**[2]

-302 **2** 6 **Dancing Maite**[7] 2041 3-9-2 **57** PhillipMakin 12 68
(S R Bowring) *trckd ldrs: wnt 2nd over 2f out: rdn and edgd rt over 1f out: no ex fnl f* **15/8**[1]

0-66 **3** 5 **Solo River**[21] 1672 3-8-13 **57** TravisBlock(3) 2 54
(P J Makin) *chsd ldrs: rdn over 3f out: wknd over 1f out* **12/1**

560- **4** 1 ½ **Janet's Delight**[190] 6775 3-9-0 **58** KirstyMilczarek(3) 5 51
(S Curran) *s.i.s: hld up: plld hrd: hdwy over 1f out: nvr trbld ldrs* **12/1**

-051 **5** 1 ¼ **Just Jimmy (IRE)**[13] 1897 3-8-10 **58** RichardEvans(7) 9 48
(P D Evans) *s.s: hld up: racd keenly: hdwy over 1f out: n.d* **11/2**[3]

446 **6** nse **Night Premiere (IRE)**[21] 1672 3-9-3 **58** PatDobbs 8 47
(R Hannon) *led: hdd over 6f out: chsd wnr: rdn 1/2-way: wknd over 1f out* **14/1**

0-60 **7** 2 **Expediter**[21] 1672 3-8-9 **57** AmyScott(7) 10 41
(H Candy) *hld up in tch: rdn and nt clr run over 2f out: wknd over 1f out* **16/1**

040- **8** 4 ½ **Purple Ransom (IRE)**[288] 4198 3-9-4 **59** (t) VinceSlattery 11 31
(D J Wintle) *mid-div: rdn 1/2-way: sn wknd* **50/1**

00-0 **9** 5 **Keeparryappy (IRE)**[38] 1315 3-9-4 **59** DarrenWilliams 3 17
(K R Burke) *hld up in tch: plld hrd: rdn and wkng whn hung lft over 1f out* **14/1**

300 **10** 2 ¾ **Queen Macha (IRE)**[45] 1176 3-8-10 **56** JamieJones(5) 4 7
(A M Hales) *hld up: rdn 1/2-way: sn wknd* **40/1**

1350 **11** 4 ½ **Talamahana**[66] 876 3-9-4 **59** (b) NCallan 6 —
(A B Haynes) *hld up: rdn 3f out: sn wknd* **20/1**

1m 29.21s (-0.39) **Going Correction** -0.025s/f (Stan) **11** Ran SP% **116.2**
Speed ratings (Par 97): **101,94,88,86,85 85,82,77,72,68 63**
CSF £10.06 CT £70.26 TOTE £2.80: £1.50, £1.20, £4.90; EX 12.80.
Owner Eclipse Thoroughbreds-Osborne House III **Bred** Cyril Humphris **Trained** Newmarket, Suffolk

FOCUS
A mostly exposed field of three-year-olds were taken apart by the one potential blot on the handicap, who is one to follow until he is beaten. The form appears solid.
Master Of Arts(USA) ◆ Official explanation: trainer said, regarding running, that the gelding had benefited from the extra furlong, being gelded and having time off over the winter.

2261 HORIZONS RESTAURANT RATING RELATED MAIDEN STKS 7f 32y(P)
7:50 (7:51) (Class 5) 3-Y-O+ **£2,456** (£725; £362) **Stalls** High

Form RPR

00-4 **1** **Dream Express (IRE)**[26] 1556 3-8-13 70 PhillipMakin 6 76
(M Dods) *dwlt: hld up: hdwy 2f out: sn rdn and hung lft: led 1f out: edgd rt ins fnl f: styd on wl* **5/1**[3]

040- **2** 3 ¼ **The Wily Woodcock**[289] 4172 4-9-10 64 ChrisCatlin 3 71
(G Wragg) *hld up: nt clr run over 2f out: hdwy over 1f out: r.o: no ch w wnr* **25/1**

300- **3** 2 ¼ **Bishopbriggs (USA)**[191] 6756 3-8-13 69 DarrenWilliams 10 61
(S Parr) *led: rdn over 2f out: hdd 1f: edgd rt and wknd wl ins fnl f* **50/1**

024 **4** 1 ½ **Cheveton**[21] 1674 4-9-3 69 RichardEvans(7) 11 61
(R J Price) *trckd ldrs: racd keenly: rdn over 2f out: nt clr run and swtchd rt 1f out: wknd ins fnl f* **33/1**

06-4 **5** ½ **Totem Flower (IRE)**[19] 1721 3-8-11 70 ow1 SebSanders 12 54
(R Charlton) *trckd ldrs: racd keenly: rdn over 2f out: wknd fnl f* **5/2**[2]

036- **6** ¾ **Vineyard**[217] 6234 3-8-13 70 LiamJones 5 54
(W J Haggas) *mid-div: sn pushed along: rdn 1/2-way: styng on whn nt clr run 1f out: n.d* **15/8**[1]

0-63 **7** 1 ¼ **Pennygee**[20] 1709 4-9-7 60 JimmyQuinn 4 51
(S R Bowring) *hld up: nvr nr* **40/1**

0-04 **8** 1 ¼ **Yes Eighteen (IRE)**[45] 1194 3-8-10 67 PatrickHills(3) 9 47
(J W Hills) *s.s: a in rr* **25/1**

-240 **9** ¾ **Always Certain (USA)**[38] 1306 3-8-13 67 GregFairley 1 45
(M Johnston) *chsd ldr to 1/2-way: rdn and wknd 2f out* **12/1**

03-0 **10** shd **Zhebe**[33] 1398 3-8-13 69 (t) NCallan 2 49
(P J McBride) *hld up in tch: rdn 1/2-way: wknd over 1f out* **10/1**

5-64 **11** ¾ **High Plains (FR)**[26] 1572 3-8-13 69 PatDobbs 8 42
(R Hannon) *hld up: rdn and wknd over 2f out* **20/1**

-620 **12** 20 **Twiglet (IRE)**[14] 1867 3-8-7 70 TolleyDean(3) 7 —
(George Baker) *hld up in tch: rdn 1/2-way: wknd over 2f out* **40/1**

1m 29.42s (-0.18) **Going Correction** -0.025s/f (Stan)
WFA 3 from 4yo 11lb **12** Ran SP% **119.0**
Speed ratings (Par 103): **100,96,93,92,91 90,89,87,86,86 85,63**
CSF £125.78 TOTE £6.30: £1.70, £7.80, £13.10; EX 308.50.
Owner J A Wynn-Williams Les Waugh **Bred** Quay Bloodstock **Trained** Denton, Co Durham
■ Stewards' Enquiry : Richard Evans one-day ban: careless riding (Jun 2)

FOCUS
A maiden for horses rated 70 and below, run at a good lick throughout. The winner did it well, and the horses in the frame should all find races before too long.

2262 HOTEL & CONFERENCING AT WOLVERHAMPTON H'CAP 1m 141y(P)
8:20 (8:21) (Class 4) (0-80,80) 4-Y-0+ **£5,046** (£1,510; £755; £282; £282) **Stalls** Low

Form RPR
5103 **1** **Justcallmehandsome**[11] 1936 6-8-6 **75**........................(v) BillyCray(7) 5 84
(D J S Ffrench Davis) *hld up: hdwy over 3f out: styd on to ld wl ins fnl f* **9/1**
/00- **2** ½ **Kafuu (IRE)**[213] 6301 4-9-4 **80**........................ SebSanders 1 88
(S A Callaghan) *led: rdn over 1f out: hdd wl ins fnl f* **11/2**[2]
1013 **3** 1 ¼ **King's Ransom**[41] 1256 5-8-8 **75**........................ JamieJones(5) 4 80
(S Gollings) *chsd ldr: rdn over 2f out: styd on same pce fnl f* **8/1**[3]
2130 **4** ¾ **Supercast (IRE)**[31] 1449 5-8-3 **68** ow1................ KirstyMilczarek(3) 12 71
(N J Vaughan) *hld up: hdwy over 1f out: edgd lft and styd on same pce ins fnl f* **8/1**[3]
4120 **4** *dht* **Kildare Sun (IRE)**[28] 1520 6-8-12 **74**........................ PhillipMakin 7 77
(J Mackie) *hld up: hdwy u.p over 1f out: edgd lft: nt rch ldrs* **14/1**
6 *hd* **Lend A Grand (IRE)**[227] 5991 4-8-13 **78**................ TravisBlock(3) 11 81
(Miss Jo Crowley) *hld up: hdwy over 1f out: nt rch ldrs* **40/1**
1120 **7** ¾ **Dushstorm (IRE)**[11] 1935 7-8-5 **67**........................ LiamJones 8 68
(C R Dore) *hld up: hdwy over 1f out: nt rch ldrs* **25/1**
121 **8** 6 **Arthur's Edge**[24] 1604 4-8-9 **74**........................ TolleyDean(3) 10 61+
(B Palling) *chsd ldrs: rdn over 2f out: sn outpcd* **4/1**[1]
3300 **9** 1 ¼ **Harare**[9] 2013 7-8-7 **69**........................ WilliamBuick 2 53+
(R J Price) *hld up: rdn over 2f out: bhd whn hmpd ins fnl f* **8/1**[3]
0/65 **10** ½ **Fly Free**[11] 1935 4-8-13 **75**........................(v) HayleyTurner 9 58
(M L W Bell) *chsd ldrs: rdn over 2f out: wknd over 1f out* **25/1**
00-0 **11** ¾ **Mountain Cat (IRE)**[19] 1729 4-9-1 **77**........................ TPO'Shea 6 59
(W J Musson) *chsd ldrs: rdn 2f out: sn wknd: edgd lft ins fnl f* **14/1**

1m 49.56s (-0.94) **Going Correction** -0.025s/f (Stan) **11** Ran SP% **102.2**
Speed ratings (Par 105): **103,102,101,100,100 100,99,94,93,93 92**
CSF £40.16 CT £189.85 TOTE £9.40: £3.00, £1.70, £3.10; EX 82.30.
Owner Mrs J E Taylor **Bred** Mrs J E Taylor **Trained** Lambourn, Berks
■ Axiom was withdrawn (4/1, unruly in stalls). R4 applies, deduct 20p in the £.
■ Stewards' Enquiry : Hayley Turner one-day ban: careless riding (Jun 2)

FOCUS
A fair handicap featuring mostly exposed sorts, and the strong pace set by the eventual runner-up certainly sorted them out, with only the winner able to get into the race from off the pace. The form is somewhat messy for the grade.
Arthur's Edge Official explanation: trainer had no explanation for the poor form shown

2263 STAY AT THE WOLVERHAMPTON HOLIDAY INN H'CAP 5f 216y(P)
8:50 (8:51) (Class 6) (0-65,64) 4-Y-0+ **£2,047** (£604; £302) **Stalls** Low

Form RPR
2131 **1** **Kingsmaite**[6] 2081 7-9-0 **60** 6ex........................(b) PhillipMakin 8 66
(S R Bowring) *a.p: rdn 1f out: styd on same pce: fin 2nd, 3½l: awrdd r* **11/2**[3]
3062 **2** 4¼ **Mambazo**[23] 1634 6-8-8 **59**........................(e) AshleyHamblett(5) 6 63
(S C Williams) *s.i.s: hdwy over 3f out: rdn over 1f out: styd on same pce fin 3rd, 3½l and 3/4l; plcd 2nd* **8/1**
36-2 **3** 2 ¼ **Scuba (IRE)**[20] 1705 6-8-9 **58**........................(b) TravisBlock(3) 2 54
(H Morrison) *chsd ldrs: rdn over 2f out: wknd over 1f out: fin 4th, plcd 3rd* **9/2**[2]
6020 **4** *hd* **Gilded Cove**[55] 1015 8-9-3 **63**........................ HayleyTurner 7 59
(R Hollinshead) *sn outpcd: hdwy u.p over 1f out: nrst fin: fin 5th, plcd 4th* **8/1**
5005 **5** ½ **Music Box Express**[20] 1703 4-8-9 **62**................(t) MatthewDavies(7) 13 56
(G Baker) *s.i.s: sn chsng ldrs: rdn over 1f out: wknd ins fnl f: fin 6th, plcd 5th* **16/1**
30-0 **6** *shd* **All You Need (IRE)**[9] 2005 4-9-4 **64**........................ DaleGibson 11 58
(R Hollinshead) *chsd ldrs: rdn 2f out: wknd over 1f out: fin 7th, plcd 6th* **20/1**
3160 **7** ¾ **Green Pirate**[31] 1455 6-9-0 **63**................(b) KirstyMilczarek(3) 10 54
(C R Dore) *rrd s: outpcd: nvr nrr: fin 8th, plcd 7th* **22/1**
0-00 **8** ½ **Ryedane (IRE)**[9] 2005 6-8-13 **62**................(b) DuranFentiman(3) 1 52
(T D Easterby) *led over 4f: wknd ins fnl f: fin 9th, plcd 8th* **11/1**
0350 **9** 1 **Mind Alert**[20] 1703 7-8-10 **59**........................(v) TolleyDean(3) 4 46
(D Shaw) *hld up: hdwy u.p over 1f out: wknd ins fnl f: fin 10th, plcd 9th* **28/1**
3320 **10** *hd* **Dasheena**[9] 2005 5-9-4 **64**........................(be) SebSanders 5 50
(A J McCabe) *sn outpcd: fin 11th, plcd 10th* **8/1**
42-1 **11** *shd* **Strabinios King**[74] 806 4-9-4 **64**........................ FrancisNorton 12 50+
(M Wigham) *broke wl: stdd and lost pl after 1f: plld hrd: rdn whn nt clr run over 2f out: hung lft and wknd over 1f out: fin 12th, plcd 11th* **7/2**[1]
00-0 **12** 5 **Law Maker**[37] 1338 8-8-12 **58**........................(v) MickyFenton 9 28
(A Bailey) *chsd ldrs: rdn 1/2-way: wkng whn n.m.r sn after: fin13th, plcd 12th* **66/1**
1543 **D** **Mafaheem**[72] 839 6-9-2 **62**........................(b[1]) NCallan 3 79
(A B Haynes) *chsd ldrs: rdn 1/2-way: led over 1f out: styd on wl: fin 1st: disq* **12/1**

1m 14.5s (-0.50) **Going Correction** -0.025s/f (Stan) **13** Ran SP% **125.1**
Speed ratings (Par 101): **97,96,93,93,92 92,91,90,89,89 88,82,102**
CSF £77.39 CT £580.51 TOTE £22.90: £5.00, £2.80, £4.00; EX 139.80.
Owner S R Bowring **Bred** S R Bowring **Trained** Edwinstowe, Notts

FOCUS
The usual suspects for this modest sprint handicap, which they tend to win in their turn. The placed horses were close to recent form but any pounds-for-lengths reading of the form is fraught with danger. Mafaheem subs disq (prohibited substance in sample).
Green Pirate Official explanation: jockey said gelding reared leaving stalls
Strabinios King Official explanation: trainer had no explanation for the poor form shown

2264 SPONSOR A RACE BY CALLING 01902 390009 H'CAP 1m 4f 50y(P)
9:20 (9:20) (Class 4) (0-85,85) 4-Y-0+ **£5,046** (£1,510; £755; £377; £188) **Stalls** Low

Form RPR
-131 **1** **Sir Duke (IRE)**[3] 2165 4-8-5 **72** 6ex........................ FrancisNorton 7 79
(P W D'Arcy) *mde all: rdn and edgd rt over 1f out: hung lft ins fnl f: styd on* **9/4**[2]
15-3 **2** 1 ½ **Dawn Sky**[14] 1874 4-9-3 **84**........................ NCallan 1 89
(M A Jarvis) *a.p: chsd wnr over 2f out: rdn over 1f out: styd on* **11/4**[3]
13-3 **3** ¾ **Tifernati**[16] 1793 4-9-1 **82**........................ LiamJones 6 86
(W J Haggas) *hld up: hdwy over 2f out: rdn over 1f out: styd on u.p* **2/1**[1]
20-0 **4** 4 **Penang Cinta**[58] 963 5-8-4 **71** oh2................ CatherineGannon 5 68
(P D Evans) *hld up: hdwy over 5f out: rdn 2f out: styd on same pce* **16/1**
63-4 **5** 2 ½ **Wild Pitch**[7] 2059 7-8-10 **77**........................(b) MickyFenton 2 70
(Stef Liddiard) *s.i.s: hld up: hdwy wl over 1f out: sn rdn: hung rt and wknd fnl f* **12/1**
6-60 **6** *nk* **Corum (IRE)**[9] 1998 5-9-1 **82**........................ VinceSlattery 4 75
(Mrs K Waldron) *prom: lost pl over 3f out: sn rdn: wknd fnl f* **25/1**
060/ **7** ½ **Rathkenny (IRE)**[14] 2514 10-8-4 **71** oh26................ WilliamBuick 3 63?
(William Coleman O'Brien, Ire) *hld up: rdn and wknd over 1f out* **33/1**
002- **8** 1 ¼ **Baizically (IRE)**[240] 5640 5-9-1 **85**........................ TolleyDean(3) 8 75
(George Baker) *trckd wnr: plld hrd: rdn over 2f out: wknd over 1f out* **14/1**

2m 42.7s (1.60) **Going Correction** -0.025s/f (Stan) **8** Ran SP% **117.8**
Speed ratings (Par 105): **93,92,91,88,87 86,86,85**
CSF £9.27 CT £13.84 TOTE £3.40: £1.70, £1.40, £1.10; EX 11.70 Place 6 £140.50, Place 5 £57.49..
Owner Mrs Jan Harris **Bred** Southern Bloodstock **Trained** Newmarket, Suffolk

FOCUS
A warm little handicap, the three four-year-olds at the head of the market, all well-bred sorts from Newmarket yards, fighting out the finish and pulling well clear of the exposed remainder. The form is rated around the placed horses but with the pace moderate the form is dubious.
T/Plt: £272.90 to a £1 stake. Pool: £68,632.39. 183.55 winning tickets. T/Qpdt: £46.40 to a £1 stake. Pool: £4,743.66. 75.50 winning tickets. CR

2265 - 2267a (Foreign Racing) - See Raceform Interactive

1907 BEVERLEY (R-H)
Tuesday, May 20

OFFICIAL GOING: Good to firm
The well watered ground was reckoned 'quick but very safe and a good covering of grass'.
Wind: Moderate 1/2 behind Weather: Fine and sunny but cool

2268 TURFTV (S) STKS 5f
2:20 (2:20) (Class 5) 3-Y-0 **£2,428** (£722; £361; £180) **Stalls** High

Form RPR
3506 **1** **Hot Bertie**[22] 1674 3-8-11 56........................ PaulMulrennan 8 55
(Jedd O'Keeffe) *chsd ldrs: styd on wl fnl f: led nr fin* **14/1**
-605 **2** ½ **My Mate Pete (IRE)**[18] 1777 3-8-11 68........................ PaulHanagan 3 53
(Mrs L Stubbs) *w ldrs: led 1f out: hdd nr fin* **9/1**
50 **3** ½ **Foxy Jane**[48] 1139 3-8-6 0........................ JimmyQuinn 7 46+
(M Brittain) *wnt lft s: mid-div: hdwy: nt clr run and swtchd lft over 1f out: fin wl* **66/1**
64-0 **4** *shd* **Bahama Baileys**[11] 1952 3-8-11 67........................ JoeFanning 14 51
(M Johnston) *mde most tl 1f out: kpt on same pce* **7/2**[1]
60-0 **5** ¾ **Foreign Rhythm (IRE)**[17] 1795 3-8-6 63........................ KimTinkler 9 43
(N Tinkler) *chsd ldrs: edgd rt ins fnl f: one pce* **5/1**[2]
-040 **6** 3 **Wave Hill (IRE)**[19] 1740 3-8-4 58........................(v[1]) KMay(7) 13 37
(B J Meehan) *stmbld s: hdwy to chse ldrs over 3f out: fdd appr fnl f* **11/2**[3]
3356 **7** ½ **Planet Paradise (IRE)**[7] 2074 3-8-6 46........................ DeanMcKeown 12 31
(D Shaw) *s.i.s: in rr: kpt on fnl f* **14/1**
434- **8** ½ **Mill Creek**[244] 5520 3-8-6 42........................(b) RoystonFfrench 6 29
(Jedd O'Keeffe) *hmpd s: sn mid-div: wknd over 1f out* **50/1**
0-00 **9** 1 ½ **Caught In Paradise (IRE)**[8] 2041 3-8-11 58................(t) DO'Donohoe 15 28
(D W Thompson) *in tch 2f: sn lost pl: kpt on fnl f* **16/1**
5-00 **10** *nk* **Watch This Place**[14] 1894 3-8-11 35................(v[1]) FergusSweeney 17 27
(K R Burke) *wnt lft s: in rr: sme late hdwy* **20/1**
000- **11** 2 **Sandies Choice**[245] 5501 3-7-13 42........................ MatthewLawson(7) 16 15
(M Brittain) *sn outpcd and wl bhd: edgd lft: sme late hdwy* **40/1**
3321 **12** *hd* **Our Sunnie**[19] 1754 3-8-11 58........................(v) AdrianTNicholls 10 19
(D Nicholls) *w ldrs: carried hd high: wknd 1f out* **7/2**[1]
5640 **13** 16 **Rightcar Hull (IRE)**[27] 1560 3-8-6 43........................ LPKeniry 11 —
(Peter Grayson) *in rr: bhd fnl 2f: virtually p.u* **40/1**

63.36 secs (-0.14) **Going Correction** -0.35s/f (Firm) **13** Ran SP% **118.8**
Speed ratings (Par 99): **87,86,85,85,84 79,78,77,75,74 71,71,45**
CSF £128.37 TOTE £21.20: £3.80, £2.20, £11.20; EX 163.60.The winner was sold to Peter Grayson for £10,200.
Owner A Walker **Bred** Iain Wilson **Trained** Middleham Moor, N Yorks

FOCUS
A moderate time, even for a race like this. The proximity of the seventh, eighth and tenth limits the form of this weak seller.
Planet Paradise(IRE) Official explanation: jockey said filly missed the break
Mill Creek Official explanation: jockey said filly was hampered at start

2269 JOCKEYS LOFT FOR GREAT FOOD MAIDEN STKS 7f 100y
2:50 (2:50) (Class 5) 3-Y-0 **£2,428** (£722; £361; £180) **Stalls** High

Form RPR
626- **1** **Art Currency (USA)**[248] 5399 3-9-3 75........................ DO'Donohoe 6 81
(M J Wallace) *trckd ldrs: wnt 2nd over 1f out: styd on to ld last strides* **10/3**[2]
003 **2** *hd* **Tartan Gigha (IRE)**[19] 1748 3-9-3 80........................ JoeFanning 8 80
(M Johnston) *led: hung lft fnl f: jst ct* **5/1**[3]
2 **3** 9 **Hippolytus**[19] 1751 3-9-3 0........................ GrahamGibbons 7 57
(J J Quinn) *chsd ldrs: rdn over 2f out: kpt on same pce* **11/8**[1]
4 1 ½ **Urban Farmer** 3-9-3 0........................ PaulHanagan 2 53
(R A Fahey) *dwlt: in rr: kpt on fnl 2f* **9/1**
4-4 **5** ¾ **Salerosa (IRE)**[33] 1429 3-8-12 0........................ RoystonFfrench 11 46
(Mrs A Duffield) *mid-div: drvn 3f out: kpt on: nvr rchd ldrs* **12/1**
00 **6** ¾ **Royal Avenue (IRE)**[10] 2008 3-9-0 0........................ MickyFenton(3) 3 49
(T D Easterby) *w ldr: wknd over 1f out* **66/1**
0-0 **7** 1 **Marramed**[2] 2221 3-8-9 0........................ DNolan(3) 1 41
(J O'Reilly) *chsd ldrs: lost pl over 1f out* **80/1**
8 3 **King Of Sparta (USA)** 3-9-0 0........................ PJMcDonald(3) 10 38
(T J Fitzgerald) *dwlt: sme hdwy on outer over 2f out: nvr a factor* **20/1**
6- **9** 1 ¾ **Our Dolly**[197] 6694 3-8-12 0........................ PaulEddery 12 29
(Garry Moss) *in tch: wknd over 2f out* **80/1**
550- **10** 2 ¼ **Starlight Girl**[328] 2984 3-8-12 67........................ LeeEnstone 5 23
(T D Easterby) *in tch: lost pl 2f out* **11/1**
0 **11** 12 **White Rose George**[29] 1519 3-9-3 0........................(t) TGMcLaughlin 9 —
(J O'Reilly) *dwlt: t.k.h in rr: hung bdly lft bnd 4f out: sn bhd* **200/1**

1m 32.65s (-1.15) **Going Correction** -0.25s/f (Firm) **11** Ran SP% **117.1**
Speed ratings (Par 99): **96,95,85,83,82 82,80,77,75,72 59**
CSF £19.92 TOTE £4.90: £1.60, £1.50, £1.10; EX 26.00.
Owner Matthew Green **Bred** Liberation Farm And Brandywine Farm Llc **Trained** Newmarket, Suffolk

FOCUS
The first two finished clear of the favourite, who was well off his debut form. The winner stepped up markedly on his juvenile form, the runner-up sets the standard.

2270 KEVIN DONKIN MEMORIAL H'CAP 5f
3:20 (3:20) (Class 5) (0-70,69) 4-Y-0+ **£2,590** (£770; £385; £192) **Stalls** High

Form RPR
6-13 **1** **Baybshambles (IRE)**[16] 1827 4-8-8 **59**........................ RoystonFfrench 14 75
(R E Barr) *chsd ldrs: wnt 2nd 1f out: kpt on gamely to ld last 75yds* **11/2**[3]

-044 **2** 2 3/4 **Mr Rooney (IRE)**[14] 1893 5-8-5 **56** AdrianTNicholls 17 62
(D Nicholls) *led: hdd and no ex ins fnl f* **7/2**[1]

-530 **3** 1 **Colorus (IRE)**[14] 1893 5-9-2 **67** JoeFanning 16 69
(W J H Ratcliffe) *chsd ldrs: kpt on same pce fnl f* **4/1**[2]

123- **4** 1/2 **Royal Composer (IRE)**[203] 6562 5-8-8 **59** (b) PaulEddery 15 59
(T D Easterby) *awkward s: sn chsng ldrs: kpt on same pce appr fnl f* **8/1**

35-0 **5** 2 1/4 **Niteowl Lad (IRE)**[31] 1476 6-8-7 **58** (p) PaulMulrennan 7 50
(J Balding) *in tch: kpt on wl fnl f* **16/1**

5006 **6** 1/2 **No Time (IRE)**[11] 1966 8-8-6 **57** DO'Donohoe 4 47+
(A J McCabe) *in rr: hdwy over 1f out: styd on wl towards fin* **33/1**

0404 **7** nse **Spirit Of Coniston**[14] 1901 5-8-9 **60** PaulQuinn 11 50
(D Nicholls) *mid-div: rdn over 2f out: styd on fnl f* **14/1**

211- **8** 2 1/4 **Nomoreblondes**[267] 4896 4-9-4 **69** (p) MickyFenton 10 51
(P T Midgley) *chsd ldrs: wknd over 1f out* **14/1**

3006 **9** nk **Royal Challenge**[13] 1908 7-9-2 **67** PatrickMathers 2 48
(I W McInnes) *rr-div: sme hdwy 2f out: nvr on terms* **33/1**

50-0 **10** nse **Welcome Approach**[13] 1908 5-9-1 **66** GrahamGibbons 6 47
(J R Weymes) *swtchd rt s: in tch: outpcd over 3f out: hdwy over 1f out: no threat* **16/1**

30F- **11** nk **Uace Mac**[357] 2120 4-8-9 **60** JimmyQuinn 3 40
(N Bycroft) *rr-div: sme hdwy over 1f out: nvr on terms* **100/1**

6-40 **12** 1/2 **Woqoodd**[24] 1624 4-8-11 **62** PaulHanagan 13 40
(R A Fahey) *sn towards rr* **12/1**

4400 **13** nk **Paddywack (IRE)**[33] 1431 11-7-13 **55** (b) DanielleMcCreery(5) 8 32
(Mrs R A Carr) *s.s: sme hdwy over 1f out: nvr on terms* **28/1**

202 **14** nk **Regal Royale**[41] 1275 5-8-6 **57** oh2 ow2 (v) LPKeniry 9 33
(Peter Grayson) *sn outpcd in rr: sme hdwy over 1f out: nvr on terms* **12/1**

-056 **15** 2 3/4 **Signor Panettiere**[14] 1893 7-7-11 **55** oh5 KMay(7) 12 21
(A D Brown) *tubed: chsd ldrs: lost pl 2f out* **22/1**

6-00 **16** 9 **Mormeatmic**[14] 1893 5-8-3 **61** ow1 BradleyRoper(7) 1 —
(M W Easterby) *dwlt: swtchd lft after s: a bhd: eased ins fnl f* **66/1**

61.35 secs (-2.15) **Going Correction** -0.35s/f (Firm) **16** Ran SP% **125.4**
Speed ratings (Par 103): **103,98,97,96,92 91,91,88,87,87 87,86,85,85,80 66**
CSF £24.27 CT £87.59 TOTE £6.30: £1.90, £1.80, £1.30, £1.90; EX 33.40.
Owner Miss S Haykin **Bred** Mrs H F Mahr **Trained** Seamer, N Yorks

FOCUS
High-drawn horses filled the first four places and their form looks solid at this level. The late developing winner is clearly on the up.
Paddywack(IRE) Official explanation: jockey said gelding missed the break

2271 SIEMENS IN PROCESS H'CAP — 1m 100y
3:50 (3:50) (Class 3) (0-90,81) 4-Y-0+ **£6,799** (£2,023; £1,011; £505) **Stalls** High

Form RPR

23-6 **1** **Crocodile Bay (IRE)**[52] 1067 5-9-2 **79** AdrianTNicholls 1 93
(D Nicholls) *led after 1f: qcknd 3f out: rdn clr appr fnl f: styd on strly* **5/1**

-005 **2** 6 **Nevada Desert (IRE)**[24] 1612 8-9-1 **78** DeanMcKeown 4 78
(R M Whitaker) *hld up: hdwy to chse wnr over 6f out: kpt on to regain 2nd last strides* **9/4**[2]

1423 **3** nk **Princess Cocoa (IRE)**[21] 1711 5-8-13 **76** PaulHanagan 3 76
(R A Fahey) *led 1f: trckd ldrs: effrt 3f out: wnt 2nd over 1f out: kpt on same pce* **3/1**[3]

3221 **4** 2 3/4 **Yes One (IRE)**[17] 1815 4-9-4 **81** DO'Donohoe 2 74
(K A Ryan) *trckd ldrs: t.k.h: effrt 3f out: edgd rt over 1f out: sn wknd* **7/4**[1]

1m 44.89s (-2.71) **Going Correction** -0.25s/f (Firm) **4** Ran SP% **108.8**
Speed ratings (Par 107): **103,97,96,93**
CSF £16.03 TOTE £4.90; EX 19.20.
Owner Ian Bishop **Bred** James And Joe Brannigan **Trained** Sessay, N Yorks

FOCUS
The winner dominated and in the end came right away, his rider deserving full marks. He has been rated to his best but it is not hard to have doubts over the form.

NOTEBOOK
Crocodile Bay(IRE) wound it up once in line for home and in the end won going right away under a well-judged, tactical ride. If anything the extended trip was in his favour. (op 6-1 tchd 9-2)
Nevada Desert(IRE), whose last win was here from a 6lb higher mark, never gave up trying and was rewarded with second spot near the line. (op 100-30 tchd 4-1)
Princess Cocoa(IRE), in good form on the sand, is 11lb higher than her last turf success. This trip is her bare minimum. (op 11-4 tchd 5-2)
Yes One(IRE), 7lb higher, has never won going right-handed. (op 11-8 tchd 15-8)

2272 BEST UK RACECOURSES ON TURFTV H'CAP — 1m 1f 207y
4:20 (4:21) (Class 5) (0-75,73) 3-Y-0 **£3,238** (£963; £481; £240) **Stalls** High

Form RPR

0-01 **1** **Excape (IRE)**[8] 2043 3-8-13 **71** 6ex (b) MarcHalford(3) 8 81+
(D R C Elsworth) *trckd ldr: led 1f out: hld on wl* **11/4**[1]

2-45 **2** 3/4 **Just Rob**[14] 1899 3-9-3 **72** GrahamGibbons 9 78
(R Hollinshead) *trckd ldrs: chal jst ins fnl f: no ex towards fin* **7/1**

34-4 **3** 2 1/4 **Shaloo Diamond**[8] 2037 3-9-4 **73** DeanMcKeown 2 75
(R M Whitaker) *hld up in rr: hdwy over 4f out: kpt on fnl 2f: nvr able to chal* **14/1**

4-42 **4** 2 3/4 **Highland Love**[26] 1575 3-8-10 **65** PaulMulrennan 6 61
(Jedd O'Keeffe) *led: qcknd 3f out: hdd 1f out: sn wknd* **10/3**[2]

2556 **5** nk **Roundthetwist (IRE)**[48] 1140 3-8-13 **68** FergusSweeney 4 63
(K R Burke) *chsd ldrs: drvn over 3f out: hung rt and wknd over 1f out* **25/1**

50-4 **6** 2 1/4 **Top Vision**[14] 1899 3-9-3 **72** EdwardCreighton 1 63
(M R Channon) *swvd bdly lft s: in rr: kpt on fnl 3f: nvr nr ldrs* **11/1**

50-4 **7** 3 3/4 **Medici Time**[27] 1558 3-8-4 **59** oh2 PaulHanagan 5 42
(T D Easterby) *hld up in rr: hdwy over 5f out: effrt on inner 2f out: sn rdn and wknd* **15/2**

410- **8** 3 1/2 **Lanterns Of Gold**[230] 5914 3-9-0 **72** PJMcDonald(3) 7 48
(G A Swinbank) *hld up in rr: stdy hdwy 3f out: sn rdn: nvr a threat* **7/2**[3]

00-6 **9** 5 **Prince's Decree**[29] 1516 3-8-5 **60** RoystonFfrench 3 26
(G M Moore) *in rr: drvn over 5f out: sn bhd* **33/1**

2m 4.60s (-2.40) **Going Correction** -0.25s/f (Firm) **9** Ran SP% **118.0**
Speed ratings (Par 99): **99,98,96,94,94 92,89,86,82**
CSF £23.30 CT £232.53 TOTE £3.70: £1.50, £2.20, £2.90; EX 28.80.
Owner Raymond Tooth **Bred** Kildaragh Stud **Trained** Newmarket, Suffolk

FOCUS
A tactical affair and the winner was always in the right place. Ordinary form but sound at this level.
Top Vision Official explanation: jockey said filly missed the break

2273 RACING AGAIN HERE THIS SATURDAY H'CAP — 1m 4f 16y
4:50 (4:51) (Class 6) (0-60,60) 3-Y-0 **£2,428** (£722; £361; £180) **Stalls** High

Form RPR

06-4 **1** **Caffari (GER)**[57] 991 3-8-11 **53** FergusSweeney 4 65+
(K R Burke) *in rr: gd hdwy on outside over 2f out: styd on wl to ld post* **11/1**

0-05 **2** nse **River Kent**[24] 1628 3-8-10 **52** RoystonFfrench 10 57
(Mrs A Duffield) *led early: trckd ldrs: wnt 2nd over 2f out: edgd lft and led ins fnl f: jst ct* **20/1**

0-05 **3** 1 1/2 **Intersky Melody (USA)**[29] 1516 3-8-12 **54** (b[1]) DeanMcKeown 3 57
(R M Whitaker) *t.k.h: jnd ldr 7f out: led 3f out: hrd rdn and hung rt over 1f out: hdd ins fnl f* **8/1**

4-60 **4** 3 **Saturday Boy**[24] 1614 3-8-10 **52** PaulMulrennan 6 50
(Paul Green) *in rr: hdwy over 2f out: styd on same pce* **10/1**

6104 **5** 1 **Chanteuse De Rue (IRE)**[11] 1950 3-8-8 **50** JoeFanning 12 47
(M Johnston) *mid-div: shkn up 7f out: one pce fnl 3f* **4/1**[2]

00-0 **6** 4 1/2 **Dream Bee**[11] 1959 3-9-4 **60** TGMcLaughlin 11 49
(E A L Dunlop) *hld up in rr: drvn over 4f out: kpt on: nvr nr to chal* **8/1**

0-00 **7** 1 **Kuriyama (IRE)**[34] 1403 3-9-3 **59** JimmyQuinn 1 47+
(M H Tompkins) *hld up in rr: effrt over 3f out: nvr nr ldrs* **12/1**

00-0 **8** 13 **Blazing Mask (IRE)**[34] 1391 3-8-5 **47** SaleemGolam 9 14
(Mrs A Duffield) *in rr: sme hdwy 3f out: lost pl over 1f out* **25/1**

060- **9** 1/2 **Astrodome**[188] 6805 3-9-1 **57** DO'Donohoe 8 23+
(Sir Mark Prescott) *sn led: hdd 3f out: lost pl and eased over 1f out* **7/2**[1]

00-0 **10** 2 1/4 **Generous Boy**[29] 1516 3-8-11 **53** MickyFenton 2 16
(T D Easterby) *mid-div: drvn over 4f out: wkng whn n.m.r 2f out* **14/1**

6560 **11** 36 **Royal Soverin**[12] 1938 3-8-11 **53** PaulHanagan 5 —
(M J Wallace) *in rr: lost pl and t.o 3f out* **11/2**[3]

00-0 **12** 4 **Bollin Guil**[27] 1558 3-8-10 **52** GrahamGibbons 7 —
(T D Easterby) *sn trcking ldrs: pushed along 6f out: hung lft and lost pl over 3f out: sn bhd: t.o* **28/1**

2m 37.39s (-3.51) **Going Correction** -0.25s/f (Firm) **12** Ran SP% **123.7**
Speed ratings (Par 97): **101,100,99,97,97 94,93,84,84,83 59,56**
CSF £220.57 CT £1873.57 TOTE £17.90: £3.20, £3.70, £3.50; EX 264.20.
Owner Richards, Gittins, Burke **Bred** Gestut Gorlsdorf **Trained** Middleham Moor, N Yorks

FOCUS
A low-grade handicap run at just a steady pace and the winner did well to come from behind in the home straight. The form is rated through the third and fourth.

2274 TURFTV BETTING SHOP SERVICE H'CAP — 1m 100y
5:20 (5:21) (Class 6) (0-60,60) 4-Y-0+ **£2,558** (£755; £378) **Stalls** High

Form RPR

00-5 **1** **Paraguay (USA)**[82] 731 5-8-13 **55** EdwardCreighton 6 67
(Miss V Haigh) *hld up in rr: hdwy on outer 3f out: carried lft ins fnl f: styd on to ld nr fin* **28/1**

23-5 **2** 1/2 **Ours (IRE)**[133] 80 5-9-0 **56** DO'Donohoe 14 67
(John A Harris) *mid-div: effrt over 2f out: edgd rt and led 1f out: edgd lft and hdd wl ins fnl f* **7/1**[2]

55-0 **3** 2 **Alberts Story (USA)**[11] 1953 4-8-6 **55** BMcHugh(7) 3 61
(R A Fahey) *in tch: hdwy 3f out: styd on wl fnl f* **12/1**

0-64 **4** 1 1/2 **It's A Dream (FR)**[31] 1491 5-9-3 **59** (t) JimmyQuinn 4 62
(M W Easterby) *trckd ldrs: styd on same pce appr fnl f* **10/1**

-313 **5** 1 **Moonstreaker**[11] 1953 5-9-4 **60** DeanMcKeown 11 61
(R M Whitaker) *chsd ldrs: kpt on same pce appr fnl f* **5/1**[1]

3430 **6** nk **Latif (USA)**[10] 2003 7-9-0 **56** (b) PaulMulrennan 15 56
(Paul Green) *s.s: hld up detached in last: hdwy over 2f out: styd on fnl f* **14/1**

122- **7** 1 1/2 **Myfrenchconnection (IRE)**[208] 6447 4-9-4 **60** MickyFenton 9 57
(P T Midgley) *racd freely: w ldr: led over 3f out: hdd 1f out: sn wknd* **17/2**

156- **8** shd **Contemplation**[76] 6304 5-9-0 **59** PJMcDonald(3) 17 55
(G A Swinbank) *trckd ldrs: effrt over 2f out: kpt on same pce* **8/1**

1143 **9** 1 1/2 **Playtotheaudience**[25] 1604 5-9-4 **60** (v) PaulHanagan 2 53
(R A Fahey) *rr-div: effrt on outside over 3f out: edgd rt over 1f out: nvr nr ldrs* **9/1**

14-0 **10** 2 1/2 **Mister Fizzbomb (IRE)**[123] 207 5-9-0 **59** (p) DNolan(3) 5 46
(J S Wainwright) *in tch: effrt 3f out: wknd over 1f out* **22/1**

3260 **11** 1 1/2 **Only A Grand**[26] 1578 4-8-9 **51** SaleemGolam 7 35
(R Bastiman) *mid-div: effrt 3f out: nvr a factor* **33/1**

0-60 **12** nk **Scutch Mill (IRE)**[26] 1578 6-9-2 **58** (t) LeeEnstone 10 41
(P C Haslam) *a towards rr* **33/1**

1600 **13** 1/2 **General Feeling (IRE)**[10] 2003 7-8-7 **56** (p) DeclanCannon(7) 12 38
(S T Mason) *reminders after s: mid-div: hdwy on ins 3f out: wknd over 1f out* **40/1**

2/43 **14** 3 1/2 **Basinet**[34] 1391 10-8-11 **53** (p) GrahamGibbons 13 27
(J J Quinn) *in rr: rdn 3f out: kpt on: nvr a factor* **15/2**[3]

620- **15** nk **Kimono My House**[249] 5388 4-8-11 **53** JoeFanning 16 26
(J G Given) *led tl over 3f out: wknd qckly 1f out* **8/1**

-006 **16** 3 1/4 **Empire Dancer (IRE)**[7] 2087 5-9-0 **56** PatrickMathers 8 22
(I W McInnes) *trckd ldrs: lost pl over 2f out* **40/1**

1m 44.7s (-2.90) **Going Correction** -0.25s/f (Firm) **16** Ran SP% **125.7**
Speed ratings (Par 101): **104,103,101,100,99 98,97,97,95,93 91,91,90,87,87 83**
CSF £209.87 CT £2617.05 TOTE £38.50: £3.90, £2.90, £3.80, £2.30; EX 455.00 Place 6 £1,695.53, Place 5 £174.93..
Owner R J Budge **Bred** Nutbush Farm **Trained** Wiseton, Notts

FOCUS
A low-grade handicap run at a sound pace. The form looks sound at this level.
Latif(USA) Official explanation: jockey said gelding missed the break
Myfrenchconnection(IRE) Official explanation: jockey said gelding ran too free
T/Jkpt: Not won. T/Plt: £3,466.50 to a £1 stake. Pool: £55,084.63. 11.60 winning tickets. T/Qpdt: £117.60 to a £1 stake. Pool: £4,068.99. 25.60 winning tickets. WG

1616 LEICESTER (R-H)
Tuesday, May 20

OFFICIAL GOING: Good to firm (firm in places)
Wind: Light, across Weather: Cloudy with sunny spells

2275 E B F/EMIL ADAM MAIDEN STKS — 5f 2y
6:20 (6:20) (Class 4) 2-Y-0 **£4,533** (£1,348; £674; £336) **Stalls** Low

Form RPR

5 **1** **Light The Fire (IRE)**[20] 1714 2-9-3 0 LDettori 7 88+
(B J Meehan) *mde all: shkn up over 1f out: sn clr* **8/13**[1]

2 3 3/4 **Lucky Redback (IRE)** 2-9-3 0 PatDobbs 3 69
(R Hannon) *chsd ldrs: outpcd 1/2-way: rallied over 1f out: chsd wnr ins fnl f: no imp* **40/1**

3 1/2 **Eagles Call (USA)** 2-9-3 0 AlanMunro 2 67
(P W Chapple-Hyam) *dwlt: hdwy over 3f out: rdn and swtchd rt over 1f out: styd on same pce* **9/2**[2]

00 **4** 2 **Rich Red (IRE)**[19] 1736 2-9-3 0 DaneO'Neill 1 60
(R Hannon) *chsd ldrs: rdn 1/2-way: wknd fnl f* **33/1**

5 1 1/4 **Titus Andronicus (IRE)** 2-9-3 0 NCallan 4 55+
(K A Ryan) *chsd wnr: rdn 1/2-way: wknd fnl f* 10/1
6 6 **Cherry Belle (IRE)** 2-8-12 0 StephenDonohoe 6 28
(P D Evans) *sn outpcd* 40/1
7 3 3/4 **Silent Hero** 2-9-3 0 PhilipRobinson 5 20
(M A Jarvis) *s.s: outpcd* 7/1[3]

60.62 secs (0.62) **Going Correction** -0.175s/f (Firm) **7** Ran SP% **109.5**
Speed ratings (Par 95): **88,82,81,78,76 66,60**
CSF £32.59 TOTE £1.50: £1.10, £12.40; EX 26.00.
Owner Joe L Allbritton **Bred** A Panetta **Trained** Manton, Wilts

FOCUS
Not easy to rate but probably a modest juvenile maiden. The winner rates value for a little further.

NOTEBOOK
Light The Fire(IRE) ◆, whose debut fifth behind Baycat at Ascot last month is working out nicely, showed he has improved markedly for that experience and made all for a comfortable success. He showed much greater early speed on this quicker ground, which no doubt suited better, and looks a colt worth following. (op 5-6)
Lucky Redback(IRE), a 21,000gns April foal, hails from a stable known for their power in the juvenile division and was allowed to go off at very big odds for this racecourse bow. He ran as though the race was needed, but still showed fair ability and shaped as if another furlong will be right up his street. It should be noted that he played up in the preliminaries, however, and could have temperament issues. (op 33-1)
Eagles Call(USA), a 100,000gns purchase whose pedigree suggests a mix of speed and stamina, proved easy to back and ran distinctly green through the first half of the contest. He can be expected to come on a deal for this debut experience. (op 4-1 tchd 10-3)
Rich Red(IRE) showed early speed and posted his best effort to date in defeat on this quicker ground, but he still looks only moderate at this stage. (tchd 40-1)
Titus Andronicus(IRE), a 50,000euros first foal of a 6f juvenile winner, showed up well enough early on yet failed to sustain his effort when it counted most. It may prove that another furlong is required before he shines, but he could also prefer easier ground than this. (op 7-1)
Silent Hero is a half-brother to several winners and his dam was a triple 1m2f winner at 3 and 4. Sent off seemingly unfancied in the betting ring, he was never in the hunt after missing the break and clearly needed the experience, but it would be very surprising were he not to prove a deal wiser next time out. Official explanation: jockey said colt missed the break (op 13-2 tchd 15-2)

2276 36 BEDFORD ROW H'CAP 7f 9y
6:50 (6:50) (Class 4) (0-80,80) 3-Y-O **£4,209** (£1,252; £625; £312) **Stalls** High

Form RPR
511- 1 **High Standing (USA)**[211] [6388] 3-9-0 76 JamieSpencer 10 88+
(S A Callaghan) *hld up: swtchd lft and hdwy over 1f out: led ins fnl f: hung rt: drvn out* 2/1[1]
10-0 2 1 1/2 **The Jostler**[15] [1868] 3-8-13 75 MichaelHills 5 80
(B W Hills) *hld up: hdwy over 2f out: led over 1f out: sn rdn: edgd rt and hdd ins fnl f: styd on same pce* 5/1[2]
04-0 3 2 3/4 **Rowaad**[31] [1467] 3-8-12 74 RHills 11 72
(M P Tregoning) *chsd ldrs: led over 2f out: rdn and hdd over 1f out: no ex ins fnl f* 20/1
41-6 4 1 **Sahaadi**[14] [1899] 3-8-12 74 PatDobbs 2 69
(R Hannon) *led: hdd over 4f out: rdn over 1f out: styd on same pce* 16/1
-0U3 5 1/2 **Ten Pole Tudor**[15] [1868] 3-9-3 79 ChrisCatlin 3 73
(R A Harris) *s.i.s: hld up: rdn over 2f out: edgd rt and styd on ins fnl f: nvr nrr* 20/1
0-10 6 1/2 **Bombardier Wells**[28] [1546] 3-9-0 76 EddieAhern 12 69
(Eve Johnson Houghton) *hld up: hdwy over 2f out: rdn over 1f out: wknd fnl f* 16/1
05-0 7 1/2 **Sweet Kiss (USA)**[12] [1925] 3-9-4 80 PaulEddery 6 71
(B J Meehan) *s.i.s: hld up: hdwy and hmpd wl over 1f out: no ex ins fnl f* 50/1
000- 8 3/4 **Just Sort It**[225] [6052] 3-8-13 75 AlanMunro 7 64
(W Jarvis) *chsd ldrs: rdn over 2f out: wknd fnl f* 16/1
33-6 9 1 3/4 **Afram Blue**[15] [1868] 3-8-13 75 RichardKingscote 4 60
(W J Knight) *chsd ldrs: rdn over 2f out: wknd over 1f out* 9/1
0-40 10 1 1/2 **May Day Queen (IRE)**[3] [2196] 3-9-2 78 DaneO'Neill 1 58
(R Hannon) *prom: racd keenly: rdn over 2f out: wknd over 1f out* 8/1
0000 11 1 **Gross Prophet**[15] [1868] 3-8-5 74 RossAtkinson(7) 8 52
(Tom Dascombe) *w ldr tl led over 4f out: rdn and hdd over 2f out: wknd over 1f out* 20/1
32-2 12 5 **Connor's Choice**[18] [1763] 3-9-1 77 AlanDaly 9 41
(Andrew Turnell) *prom: racd keenly: rdn over 2f out: wknd wl over 1f out* 6/1[3]

1m 24.68s (-1.52) **Going Correction** -0.175s/f (Firm) **12** Ran SP% **119.3**
Speed ratings (Par 101): **101,99,96,95,94 93,93,92,90,88 87,81**
CSF £10.61 CT £159.99 TOTE £3.30: £1.30, £2.30, £5.90; EX 20.70.
Owner SP Racing Investments S A **Bred** Dr Melinda Blue **Trained** Newmarket, Suffolk
■ Stewards' Enquiry : Jamie Spencer two-day ban: careless riding (Jun 3-4)

FOCUS
A decent three-year-old handicap for the class, and solid form. The first three are all potential improvers.

2277 JAMES WARD (S) STKS 7f 9y
7:20 (7:20) (Class 6) 3-Y-O+ **£1,748** (£520; £260; £129) **Stalls** High

Form RPR
-206 1 **Cap St Jean (IRE)**[28] [1550] 4-9-7 59 (p) HayleyTurner 8 66
(R Hollinshead) *s.i.s: hld up: hdwy 1/2-way: rdn to ld ins fnl f: r.o: eased last strides* 5/1[3]
-565 2 2 3/4 **Fly In Johnny (IRE)**[63] [924] 3-8-10 69 PatDobbs 3 55
(R Hannon) *a.p: rdn over 2f out: styd on* 12/1
234- 3 2 **Million Percent**[255] [5233] 9-9-7 70 LiamJones 12 53
(C R Dore) *trckd ldr: plld hrd: led over 2f out: rdn over 1f out: hdd and no ex ins fnl f* 7/1
-615 4 hd **Mountain Pass (USA)**[36] [1369] 6-9-12 65 (p) ChrisCatlin 1 58
(B J Llewellyn) *s.i.s: hld up: rdn over 2f out: hung rt and styd on ins fnl f: nvr nrr* 14/1
6421 5 2 **Shot To Fame (USA)**[22] [1670] 9-9-12 65 AdrianTNicholls 11 52
(D Nicholls) *led over 4f: rdn and hung rt over 1f out: wknd ins fnl f* 11/4[2]
2-33 6 3 1/2 **One More Round (USA)**[8] [2040] 10-9-7 87 (b) RoystonFfrench 10 38
(Ollie Pears) *s.i.s: hld up: hdwy over 2f out: rdn over 1f out: sn wknd* 9/4[1]
2400 7 3 1/2 **Tiepie**[7] [2069] 3-8-10 60 (b) DaneO'Neill 2 24
(J Akehurst) *sn pushed along and prom: lost pl 5f out: rdn and wknd over 2f out* 25/1
6230 8 8 **Sweet World**[14] [1895] 4-9-7 62 (p) StephenDonohoe 4 7
(B J Llewellyn) *chsd ldrs over 4f* 12/1

1m 26.31s (0.11) **Going Correction** -0.175s/f (Firm)
WFA 3 from 4yo+ 11lb **8** Ran SP% **112.5**
Speed ratings (Par 101): **92,88,86,86,84 80,76,66**
CSF £59.64 TOTE £7.00: £2.10, £2.50, £3.00; EX 51.10.The winner was bought in for 4,200gns.
Owner Edenbrook Partnership **Bred** Drumhass Stud **Trained** Upper Longdon, Staffs

FOCUS
A very moderate winning time, even for a seller, mainly due to the lack of early pace. The form is not solid and worth treating with some caution, but the winner still rates value for further.
Shot To Fame(USA) Official explanation: jockey said gelding was unsuited by the good to firm (firm in places) ground
One More Round(USA) Official explanation: jockey said gelding had no more to give

2278 SPORTSGURU.CO.UK 40TH BIRTHDAY H'CAP 1m 1f 218y
7:50 (7:50) (Class 4) (0-80,80) 4-Y-O+ **£4,209** (£1,252; £625; £312) **Stalls** High

Form RPR
0260 1 **Speedy Sam**[15] [1874] 5-9-4 80 FergusSweeney 3 89
(K R Burke) *mde all: rdn and hung lft ins fnl f: styd on* 11/4[2]
253- 2 1/2 **Candy Mountain**[187] [6822] 4-9-0 76 JimmyFortune 5 84
(L M Cumani) *hld up in tch: rdn over 1f out: chsd wnr fnl f: styd on* 7/4[1]
0-41 3 2 3/4 **Snowed Under**[13] [1909] 7-9-1 77 PhilipRobinson 2 81+
(J D Bethell) *a.p: chsd wnr over 2f out tl rdn and no ex ins fnl f* 11/4[2]
6-44 4 1 3/4 **Ross Moor**[26] [1585] 6-8-4 66 oh2 WilliamBuick 4 65
(Mike Murphy) *in rr: swtchd rt over 2f out: hmpd sn after: swtchd lft over 1f out: styd on ins fnl f: nvr trbld ldrs* 5/1[3]
1120 5 7 **Contra Mundum (USA)**[97] [540] 5-8-11 73 HayleyTurner 1 58
(B G Powell) *trckd wnr over 6f out: rdn over 2f out: wknd over 1f out* 14/1

2m 5.49s (-2.41) **Going Correction** -0.10s/f (Good) **5** Ran SP% **113.0**
Speed ratings (Par 105): **105,104,102,101,95**
CSF £8.26 TOTE £3.40: £1.60, £2.00; EX 9.20.
Owner Mrs Maura Gittins **Bred** Cheveley Park Stud Ltd **Trained** Middleham Moor, N Yorks

FOCUS
A steadily run handicap and as a result the form is not totally reliable. The winner took advantage of a good mark and the race is rated around the runner-up.

2279 SARTORIUS MAIDEN STKS 5f 218y
8:20 (8:22) (Class 5) 3-Y-O **£2,590** (£770; £385; £192) **Stalls** High

Form RPR
0 1 **Onceaponatime (IRE)**[52] [1073] 3-9-3 0 AlanMunro 5 84+
(P W Chapple-Hyam) *chsd ldr tl led over 1f out: rdn out* 7/2[3]
3- 2 nk **Carniolan**[341] [2600] 3-9-3 0 AdamKirby 9 83+
(W R Swinburn) *trckd ldrs: rdn to chse wnr and hung rt 1f out: r.o: hung rt nr fin* 11/8[1]
0-3 3 3 **Chelsea Girl**[16] [1836] 3-8-12 0 PhilipRobinson 2 69
(C G Cox) *sn led: rdn and hdd over 1f out: no ex ins fnl f* 2/1[2]
6-0 4 12 **Croeso Cusan**[11] [1960] 3-8-12 0 SteveDrowne 1 30
(J L Spearing) *prom to 1/2-way* 40/1
5 hd **High Coincidence** 3-9-3 0 AlanDaly 6 35
(Andrew Turnell) *dwlt: outpcd* 16/1
6 8 **Azzaamm** 3-9-3 0 JimmyQuinn 10 9
(C A Dwyer) *s.i.s: hdwy 1/2-way: wknd over 1f out* 12/1

1m 11.32s (-1.68) **Going Correction** -0.175s/f (Firm) **6** Ran SP% **113.7**
Speed ratings (Par 99): **104,103,99,83,83 72**
CSF £8.96 TOTE £3.80: £1.60, £1.30; EX 11.20.
Owner Mrs Susan Roy **Bred** Dermot O'Rourke **Trained** Newmarket, Suffolk

FOCUS
The time was decent and this looks better form than might have been expected, the runner-up setting the standard and the first two big improvers.
Croeso Cusan Official explanation: jockey said filly was unsuited by the good to firm (firm in places) ground

2280 HENRY ALKEN H'CAP 1m 3f 183y
8:50 (8:50) (Class 5) (0-70,70) 3-Y-O **£2,590** (£770; £385; £192) **Stalls** High

Form RPR
40-1 1 **Ovthenight (IRE)**[28] [1553] 3-9-0 66 MickyFenton 4 71
(Mrs P Sly) *led: hdd over 7f out: chsd ldr tl led over 2f out: rdn over 1f out: styd on gamely* 5/1[2]
0-00 2 1/2 **Paddy Rielly (IRE)**[21] [1696] 3-8-4 56 oh1 JimmyQuinn 2 60
(P D Evans) *hld up: hdwy 1/2-way: rdn and hung rt fr over 1f out: ev ch ins fnl f: nt qckn nr fin* 10/1
0-10 3 1 **Mista Rossa**[21] [1696] 3-9-4 70 SteveDrowne 3 73
(H Morrison) *hld up: hdwy u.p over 1f out: edgd rt ins fnl f: styd on* 11/2[3]
2513 4 2 **Black Dahlia**[8] [2037] 3-8-12 64 JamesDoyle 5 63
(A J McCabe) *hld up: hdwy over 1f out: nt clr run ins fnl f: edgd rt and styd on same pce towards fin* 11/2[3]
0-05 5 2 3/4 **Eddie Dowling**[17] [1814] 3-9-4 70 AlanMunro 6 65
(M R Channon) *chsd ldrs: rdn over 1f out: edgd rt and wknd ins fnl f* 16/1
46-0 6 3/4 **Fearless Warrior**[16] [1839] 3-8-13 65 EddieAhern 1 58
(J L Dunlop) *chsd ldrs: rdn over 1f out: wknd ins fnl f* 15/2
000- 7 3 1/4 **Potemkin (USA)**[204] [6536] 3-8-6 58 FergusSweeney 9 46
(A King) *hld up: hdwy over 3f out: sn rdn: wknd over 1f out* 20/1
000- 8 1 **All Lit Up**[225] [6058] 3-8-4 56 ChrisCatlin 10 42
(A King) *prom: lost pl over 6f out: hdwy over 3f out: sn rdn: wknd over 1f out* 16/1
2310 9 1/2 **Oberlin (USA)**[29] [1516] 3-8-13 65 JimmyFortune 7 51
(T Keddy) *chsd ldr tl led over 7f out: rdn and hdd over 2f out: wknd fnl f* 16/1
-421 10 9 **Gunnadoit (USA)**[37] [1350] 3-8-10 62 JamieSpencer 8 49
(M L W Bell) *hld up: hdwy over 2f out: rdn and wknd over 1f out: eased* 5/2[1]

2m 34.06s (0.16) **Going Correction** -0.10s/f (Good) **10** Ran SP% **119.3**
Speed ratings (Par 99): **95,94,94,92,90 90,88,87,87,81**
CSF £55.48 CT £289.03 TOTE £7.60: £2.60, £2.80, £2.50; EX 133.70 Place 6 £47.84, Place 5 £32.95.
Owner D Bayliss, T Davies, G Libson & P Sly **Bred** Derek Veitch And Mark Tong **Trained** Thorney, Cambs

FOCUS
Modest handicap form, and a moderate pace. It is doubtful if the winner had to improve on his Southwell form.
Gunnadoit(USA) Official explanation: jockey said filly was unsuited by the good to firm (firm in places) ground

T/Plt: £54.80 to a £1 stake. Pool: £58,782.36. 782.45 winning tickets. T/Qpdt: £31.20 to a £1 stake. Pool: £4,940.84. 116.90 winning tickets. CR

[2246]MUSSELBURGH (R-H)

Tuesday, May 20

OFFICIAL GOING: Good to firm (8.6)

Wind: Light half across Weather: Overcast and dry

2281 EUROPEAN BREEDERS' FUND MEDIAN AUCTION MAIDEN STKS 5f

2:10 (2:11) (Class 5) 2-Y-O **£3,885** (£1,156; £577; £288) **Stalls** Low

Form RPR

52 **1** **Mullglen**[11] [1967] 2-9-3 0 DavidAllan 5 79
(T D Easterby) *cl up: rdn to ld over 1f out: drvn ins fnl f and kpt on wl* **11/10**[1]

2 1 1/4 **Taazur** 2-9-3 0 GregFairley 2 75+
(M Johnston) *s.i.s and bhd: hdwy 2f out: rtidden to chse wnr ent fnl f: ev ch tl no ex last 50yds* **7/2**[2]

55 **3** 1 3/4 **Amorachy**[18] [1770] 2-9-3 0 FergalLynch 4 68
(K A Ryan) *cl up: led after 2f: rdn and hdd over 1f out: kpt on same pce* **7/2**[2]

4 7 **Eldorado Days (IRE)** 2-9-3 0 DarrenWilliams 3 43
(K R Burke) *led 2f: rdn along 1/2-way: sn wknd* **4/1**[3]

60.44 secs (0.04) **Going Correction** -0.40s/f (Firm) **4** Ran SP% **112.1**

Speed ratings (Par 93): **83,81,78,67**

CSF £5.45 TOTE £1.80; EX 3.00.

Owner Richard Taylor & Philip Hebdon **Bred** Rosyground Stud **Trained** Great Habton, N Yorks

■ El Bobby was withdrawn (9/2, bolted bef s). R4 applies, deduct 15p in the £. New market formed.

FOCUS

A very slow winning time, even for a race like this. A modest little event in which the winner was much more the finished article than the runner-up.

NOTEBOOK

Mullglen tracked the pace before going on over a furlong out and asserting inside the last. A likely type for nurseries, he did not need to improve much on his Ripon second to take this. (old market op 6-4 tchd 13-8, new market op 5-4 tchd Evens)

Taazur, a half-brother to three winners at between 5f and 1m2f, made a promising debut and shaped as the best long-term prospect in the field. He found himself outpaced in last place before picking up with two furlongs to run and coming with what looked potentially a winning challenge before the effort flattened out. He will know much more next time. (old market op 100-30 tchd 4-1)

Amorachy stepped up slightly on the form of his previous run and looks the type for nurseries later in the year, perhaps over 6f. (old market op 7-1)

Eldorado Days(IRE) was green in the preliminaries and in the race too, but he did show early pace. He is sure to improve from this very moderate starting level. (old market op 5-1)

2282 ST JAMES SHOPPING "SOMETHING TO TALK ABOUT" H'CAP 7f 30y

2:40 (2:40) (Class 5) (0-70,69) 3-Y-O **£2,914** (£867; £433; £216) **Stalls** High

Form RPR

6-54 **1** **Novellen Lad (IRE)**[10] [2008] 3-9-7 69 WJSupple 3 77
(E J Alston) *trckd ldrs: carried wd home turn: led over 2f out: clr over 1f out: rdn ins fnl f and kpt on* **6/1**[3]

450- **2** 1 1/4 **Red Tarn**[199] [6634] 3-9-5 67 PhillipMakin 9 72+
(B Smart) *stmbld sltly s: t.k.h in rr: gd hdwy over 2f out: rdn to chse wnr and edgd rt ent fnl f: sn drvn and kpt on wl* **7/2**[1]

4-25 **3** 7 **Viscountess (IRE)**[39] [1302] 3-9-5 67 GregFairley 8 53
(M Johnston) *chsd ldrs: hdwy 3f out: rdn 2f out: drvn and one pce fr over 1f out* **4/1**[2]

160- **4** 3/4 **Princess Rhianna (IRE)**[195] [6722] 3-9-2 64 DavidAllan 5 48
(Mrs G S Rees) *hld up towards rr: effrt over 2f out: sn rdn and kpt on same pce* **16/1**

56-0 **5** 2 3/4 **Orpen Bid (IRE)**[17] [1817] 3-8-4 55 DominicFox(3) 2 31
(A M Crow) *in tch: hdwy on outer 3f out: sn rdn along and kpt on same pce fnl 2f* **28/1**

00-3 **6** 1 1/4 **Kingstyle (IRE)**[46] [1187] 3-8-4 52 (b) TWilliams 7 25
(M Brittain) *prom: rn wd home turn: rdn along 3f out: drvn 2f out and grad wknd* **16/1**

0250 **7** 1 1/2 **Thomas Malory (IRE)**[19] [1743] 3-8-6 59 ow1 SCreighton(5) 10 28
(Miss V Haigh) *a towards rr* **4/1**[2]

00-6 **8** 5 **Veronicas Way**[34] [1396] 3-8-7 55 PaulFessey 1 10
(G M Moore) *chsd ldrs: hdwy to ld 1/2-way: rdn along and hdd over 2f out: sn drvn and wknd* **10/1**

0-05 **9** 1 **Arcetri (IRE)**[26] [1592] 3-8-10 58 FergalLynch 4 11
(K A Ryan) *led to 1/2-way: sn rdn along and wknd over 2f out* **7/1**

00-3 **10** 3/4 **Sweet Mind**[49] [1132] 3-8-7 55 TonyHamilton 6 6
(R A Fahey) *a towards rr* **16/1**

1m 28.93s (-1.37) **Going Correction** -0.20s/f (Firm) **10** Ran SP% **119.2**

Speed ratings (Par 99): **99,97,89,88,85 84,82,76,75,74**

CSF £27.96 CT £97.87 TOTE £7.40: £2.50, £1.50, £1.70; EX 25.30.

Owner Con Harrington **Bred** Mrs Chris Harrington **Trained** Longton, Lancs

FOCUS

A modest handicap in which the first two finished clear, although they may not be as progressive as the gap to the rest suggests.

Kingstyle(IRE) Official explanation: jockey said colt failed to handle bend turning into straight

Veronicas Way Official explanation: jockey said filly hung left on final bend

2283 TURFTV MAIDEN STKS 5f

3:10 (3:11) (Class 5) 3-Y-O+ **£2,590** (£770; £385; £192) **Stalls** Low

Form RPR

-622 **1** **Rio Sands**[24] [1611] 3-8-11 69 MichaelJStainton(3) 7 72
(R M Whitaker) *trckd ldrs: hdwy 2f out: rdn to ld and hung rt ent fnl f: drvn out* **11/4**[2]

2 3/4 **He's Got Rhythm (IRE)**[39] [1316] 3-9-0 0 (b) FergalLynch 10 69
(David Marnane, Ire) *wnt lft s: sn chsng ldrs: hdwy 2f out: rdn to ld over 1f out: hdd and bmpd ent fnl f: kpt on* **5/1**[3]

0-0 **3** 3 1/4 **Embra (IRE)**[26] [1581] 3-9-0 0 GregFairley 6 58
(T J Etherington) *midfield: hdwy 2f out: sn rdn and kpt on ins fnl f* **33/1**

40- **4** 1/2 **Proud Linus (USA)**[228] [5975] 3-9-0 0 DavidAllan 3 56
(D Carroll) *wnt lft s: sn in tch: rdn along wl over 1f out: kpt on same pce* **1/1**[1]

0503 **5** 1 1/2 **Johnston's Glory (IRE)**[11] [1951] 4-9-3 58 (b) WJSupple 4 49+
(E J Alston) *hmpd s and in rr tl styd on appr fnl f: nrst fin* **17/2**

05-0 **6** nk **Tumbleweed Di**[8] [2038] 4-8-12 45 SladeO'Hara(5) 9 47
(G R Oldroyd) *hmpd s: swtchd wd and hdwy 1/2-way: rdn wl over 1f out: sn wknd* **25/1**

7 4 **Still Life (IRE)**[23] [1654] 4-9-8 0 TonyHamilton 1 38
(T F Lacy, Ire) *chsd ldrs: rdn along 2f out: sn wknd* **40/1**

000- **8** 3 **Compton Lad**[229] [5930] 5-9-3 41 (t) GaryBartley(5) 5 27
(D A Nolan) *prom: rdn along 2f out: wknd appr fnl f* **150/1**

00-0 **9** 1/2 **Sokoke**[39] [1309] 7-9-5 43 MarkLawson(3) 8 25
(D A Nolan) *led: rdn along 2f out: drvn and hdd over 1f out: sn wknd* **200/1**

10 4 1/2 **Irish Brooke (IRE)** 3-8-9 0 PhillipMakin 11 —
(B Smart) *s.i.s: a bhd* **22/1**

0 **11** 1 3/4 **Orangina Wood (GER)**[26] [1579] 5-9-3 40 DanielTudhope 12 —
(A Berry) *a towards rr* **150/1**

35-0 **12** hd **Next Best**[57] [993] 3-8-9 50 PaulFessey 13 —
(A Berry) *a towards rr* **40/1**

0 **13** 1 **White Elephant**[14] [1894] 4-9-5 0 DominicFox(3) 2 —
(W Storey) *hmpd s: a bhd* **100/1**

58.40 secs (-2.00) **Going Correction** -0.40s/f (Firm)

WFA 3 from 4yo+ 8lb **13** Ran SP% **122.7**

Speed ratings (Par 103): **100,98,93,92,90 89,83,78,77,70 67,67,66**

CSF £16.51 TOTE £3.70: £1.40, £1.50, £10.40; EX 17.40.

Owner Barry & The Barflys **Bred** Hellwood Farm And J B Pemberton **Trained** Scarcroft, W Yorks

■ Stewards' Enquiry : Slade O'Hara caution: allowed filly to coast home with no assistance

FOCUS

A weak maiden with the favourite and form horse running poorly. The winner is rated to his best.

Proud Linus(USA) Official explanation: jockey said colt was unbalanced throughout

Still Life(IRE) Official explanation: jockey said gelding was unsuited by the good to firm going

2284 THOROUGHBRED BREEDERS ASSOCIATION GOLF DAY FILLIES' H'CAP 1m

3:40 (3:41) (Class 4) (0-85,83) 4-Y-O+ **£6,476** (£1,927; £963; £481) **Stalls** High

Form RPR

34-2 **1** **Kasumi**[10] [1981] 5-9-4 83 TravisBlock(3) 2 91+
(H Morrison) *trckd ldrs: hdwy 3f out: rdn and edgd rt over 1f out: drvn and styd on ins fnl f to ld nr fin* **1/2**[1]

1333 **2** nk **Cha Cha Cha**[18] [1774] 4-9-6 82 CatherineGannon 3 88
(K A Ryan) *trckd ldng pair: hdwy 3f out: chal 2f out: sn rdn and ev ch: drvn and edgd lft ins fnl f: sn led: rdr lost whip fnl 100yds: hdd and no ex nr fin* **9/2**[2]

3 1 1/4 **Fancy Feathers (IRE)**[18] [1790] 4-8-8 70 FergalLynch 5 73
(David Marnane, Ire) *led: rdn along and jnd over 2f out: drvn over 1f out: edgd rt and hdd ins fnl f: no ex* **14/1**

0-61 **4** 6 **Keisha Kayleigh (IRE)**[16] [1822] 5-8-4 66 (v) GregFairley 6 55
(B Ellison) *hld up in rr: hdwy 3f out: rdn along 2f out: sn btn* **6/1**[3]

-060 **5** hd **Grethel (IRE)**[16] [1822] 4-7-13 66 oh14 ow2 KellyHarrison(5) 1 55?
(A Berry) *cl up: rdn along 3f out: sn wknd* **66/1**

1m 40.01s (-1.19) **Going Correction** -0.20s/f (Firm) **5** Ran SP% **107.3**

Speed ratings (Par 102): **97,96,95,89,89**

CSF £2.87 TOTE £1.50: £1.10, £1.60; EX 2.60.

Owner Viscountess Trenchard **Bred** Fonthill Stud **Trained** East Ilsley, Berks

■ Stewards' Enquiry : Catherine Gannon caution: used whip with excessive frequency

FOCUS

Only five runners, but this was a fair fillies' handicap. The form is straightforward at face value with the second and third running to their marks, but the fifth was close enough from a long way wrong.

2285 RECTANGLE GROUP H'CAP 7f 30y

4:10 (4:11) (Class 6) (0-60,60) 4-Y-O+ **£2,266** (£674; £337; £168) **Stalls** High

Form RPR

00-1 **1** **Zabeel Tower**[10] [2009] 5-8-13 55 (p) TonyHamilton 5 63
(R Allan) *sn led: hdd after 1 1/2f: trckd ldng pair tl swtchd lft and hdwy to ld over 1f out: rdn ins fnl f and kpt on wl* **12/1**

40-0 **2** 1 **Grand Diamond (IRE)**[16] [1822] 4-9-3 59 (p) DanielTudhope 1 65
(J S Goldie) *a.p: led over 2f out: sn rdn and hdd over 1f out: drvn and kpt on wl fnl f* **33/1**

0-03 **3** hd **Wind Shuffle (GER)**[18] [1775] 5-8-13 60 GaryBartley(5) 3 65
(J S Goldie) *chsd ldrs: rdn along on outer and outpcd over 2f out: sn drvn and styd on strly ins fnl f* **10/1**

3-34 **4** hd **Maison Dieu**[16] [1826] 5-8-12 54 WJSupple 7 58
(E J Alston) *hld up towards rr: hdwy 3f out: rdn wl over 1f out: chsd ldrs ent fnl f: sn drvn and one pce* **13/2**[2]

4562 **5** 1 **Zennerman (IRE)**[19] [1752] 5-8-13 60 KellyHarrison(5) 10 62
(G A Swinbank) *t.k.h: in tch: hdwy to trck ldrs 3f out: rdn wl over 1f out and sn one pce* **3/1**[1]

-552 **6** shd **Five Wishes**[10] [2009] 4-9-1 57 (be) PhillipMakin 8 58
(M Dods) *towards rr: hdwy over 2f out: sn rdn and kpt on ins fnl f: nrst fin* **7/1**[3]

00-0 **7** 1 1/4 **Mister Jingles**[18] [1780] 5-9-0 59 (v) MichaelJStainton(3) 6 57
(R M Whitaker) *t.k.h: chsd ldrs: hdwy over 2f out: sn rdn and ev ch tl drvn and wknd appr fnl f* **14/1**

-434 **8** 4 1/2 **Franksalot (IRE)**[23] [1641] 8-9-0 56 FergalLynch 11 42
(I W McInnes) *midfield: effrt on inner 3f out: rdn 2f out and sn no imp* **8/1**

5-60 **9** 2 **Wadnagin (IRE)**[45] [1209] 4-9-2 58 DarrenWilliams 9 39
(I A Wood) *a towards rr* **18/1**

-005 **10** hd **Valdan (IRE)**[36] [1371] 4-9-1 57 (t) CatherineGannon 2 37
(M A Barnes) *s.i.s: in tch on outer 1/2-way: rdn along wl over 2f out and sn wknd* **14/1**

06-0 **11** 2 **Give Her A Whirl**[15] [1867] 4-8-13 55 DavidAllan 4 30
(G A Swinbank) *cl up: led after 1 1/2f: rdn along 3f out: sn hdd & wknd* **14/1**

4114 **12** 5 **Shunkawakhan (IRE)**[18] [1775] 5-9-1 57 (p) PaulFessey 12 18
(Miss L A Perratt) *midfield: rdn along 3f out and sn wknd* **7/1**[3]

1m 28.61s (-1.69) **Going Correction** -0.20s/f (Firm) **12** Ran SP% **119.4**

Speed ratings (Par 101): **101,99,99,99,98 98,96,91,89,89 86,81**

CSF £350.86 CT £4059.97 TOTE £15.10: £3.50, £10.20, £3.10; EX 490.90.

Owner R. H. I. Ltd **Bred** Gainsborough Stud Management Ltd **Trained** Duns, Scottish Borders

■ Stewards' Enquiry : Michael J Stainton caution: careless riding

FOCUS

A moderate handicap. Straightforward to rate, with the second and third running to their marks and the winner up 4lb.

Franksalot(IRE) Official explanation: jockey said gelding ran flat

Shunkawakhan(IRE) Official explanation: jockey said gelding finished distressed

2286 RACING REPLAY TO SKY CHANNEL 432 H'CAP 1m 4f

4:40 (4:40) (Class 6) (0-60,60) 4-Y-O+ **£2,266** (£674; £337; £168) **Stalls** High

Form RPR

0-31 **1** **Annibale Caro**[14] [1890] 6-8-12 54 PhillipMakin 11 68+
(Grant Tuer) *hld up towards rr: hdwy 3f out: rdn to chal wl over 1f out: led ent fnl f and styd on wl* **5/2**[1]

10-4 **2** *1 ¾* **Living On A Prayer**[42] [1262] 5-8-8 **50** .... FergalLynch 6 58
(Thomas McLaughlin, Ire) *hld up towards rr: gd hdwy on outer over 2f out: rdn and ev ch ent fnl f: drvn: hung rt and one pce towards fin* **3/1**[2]

0062 **3** *nk* **Hugs Destiny (IRE)**[8] [2051] 7-8-4 **46** oh1..............(t) CatherineGannon 10 54
(M A Barnes) *led: hdd 4f out: led again 3f out: rdn over 2f out: drvn and hdd ent fnl f: kpt on same pce* **6/1**[3]

00-0 **4** *shd* **Barbirolli**[28] [1528] 6-8-10 **52**..................................... DarrenWilliams 3 59
(W M Brisbourne) *trckd ldrs: smooth hdwy 3f out: rdn wl over 1f out and ev ch tl drvn and one pce ins fnl f* **16/1**

003- **5** *4 ½* **Hits Only Vic (USA)**[268] [4845] 4-9-4 **60**............................ DavidAllan 9 60
(D Carroll) *chsd ldrs: effrt and n.m.r on inner over 2f out: sn rdn and no imp* **12/1**

450- **6** *8* **The Quantum Kid**[267] [4902] 4-8-13 **55**........................... GregFairley 7 42
(T J Etherington) *in tch on inner: rdn along whn n.m.r 3f out: sn rdn and wknd* **28/1**

2555 **7** *2 ½* **Qaasi (USA)**[55] [771] 6-8-12 **57**.............................. MarkLawson(3) 12 40
(M Brittain) *trckd ldng pair on inner: effrt 3f out: sn rdn along and edgd lft and rt: sn wknd* **10/1**

23-6 **8** *1* **Chip N Pin**[14] [1892] 4-8-6 **48**...(b¹) WJSupple 4 30
(T D Easterby) *in tch whn bdly hmpd bnd after 2f: bhd after* **6/1**[3]

000/ **9** *5* **Madge**[14] [3379] 6-8-1 **46** oh1..(v) DominicFox(3) 1 20
(W Storey) *chsd ldrs: hung in bnd after 2f: rdn along over 3f out and sn wknd* **50/1**

05-6 **10** *10* **Stravonian**[58] [982] 8-8-4 **46** oh1.................................... PaulFessey 8 4
(D A Nolan) *s.i.s: a in rr* **100/1**

00-0 **11** *3 ¾* **Fardi (IRE)**[39] [1305] 6-8-4 **46** oh1.............................. TWilliams 2 —
(K W Hogg) *trckd ldr: led 4f out: rdn and hdd 3f out: sn wknd* **100/1**

3-00 **12** *3 ½* **Falimar**[55] [1025] 4-7-13 **46** oh1.............................. KellyHarrison(5) 5 —
(C W Fairhurst) *in tch whn hmpered bnd after 2f: bhd after* **33/1**

2m 36.04s (-3.66) **Going Correction** -0.20s/f (Firm) 12 Ran SP% **115.1**
Speed ratings (Par 101): **104,102,102,102,99 94,92,91,88,81 79,77**
CSF £9.25 CT £38.99 TOTE £3.60: £1.40, £1.50, £2.90; EX 11.40.
Owner G Tuer **Bred** Cyril Humphris **Trained** Birkby, N Yorks
■ Stewards' Enquiry : Dominic Fox six-day ban: careless riding (Jun 3-8)
T Williams two-day ban: careless riding (June 2-4)

FOCUS
A moderate handicap but the form is sound enough. The winner looks a bit better than the bare form.

2287 TURFTV A MATTER OF COURSE H'CAP 5f
5:10 (5:10) (Class 6) (0-65,64) 3-Y-O **£2,266** (£674; £337; £168) **Stalls** Low

Form RPR

06-4 **1** **Discanti (IRE)**[28] [1548] 3-9-5 **62**.............................. DavidAllan 13 75+
(T D Easterby) *qckly away: mde all: rdn over 1f out and styd on strly* **11/2**[3]

-506 **2** *2 ¾* **Speedy Senorita (IRE)**[24] [1611] 3-9-3 **60**.................. DarrenWilliams 11 63
(K R Burke) *cl up: ev ch 2f out: sn rdn and kpt on ins fnl f: no ch w wnr* **5/1**[2]

0-04 **3** *1 ¾* **Handsinthemist (IRE)**[18] [1769] 3-8-10 **53**.....................(p) PhillipMakin 4 50
(P T Midgley) *towards rr: hdwy 2f out: nt clr run and swtchd lft over 1f out: n.m.r ent fnl f: sn rdn and kpt on: tk 3rd nr fin* **8/1**

3-00 **4** *nk* **Mr Lu**[27] [1560] 3-8-11 **54**... DanielTudhope 5 50
(G A Swinbank) *towards rr: hdwy 2f out: sn rdn and kpt on ins fnl f: nrst fin* **11/1**

4005 **5** *1 ¼* **Extreme North (USA)**[5] [2122] 3-8-13 **61**...................... SCreighton(5) 2 52+
(Miss V Haigh) *hmpd s and bhd: hdwy and nt clr run wl over 1f out: swtchd lft and nt clr run 1f out: swtchd rt and styd on ins fnl f: nrst fin* **8/1**

6-05 **6** *½* **Curio**[14] [1897] 3-8-6 **52**.. MichaelJStainton(3) 6 41
(R M Whitaker) *midfield: hdwy 2f out: sn rdn and no imp appr fnl f* **17/2**

1113 **7** *1 ½* **Killer Class**[27] [1560] 3-9-7 **64**.................................... FergalLynch 9 48
(J S Goldie) *hld up: hdwy 1/2-way: rdn to chse ldrs over 1f out: sn no imp* **4/1**[1]

00-0 **8** *hd* **Red River Boy**[17] [1795] 3-8-5 **53**............................. KellyHarrison(5) 10 36
(C W Fairhurst) *prom: rdn along over 2f out: sn drvn and wknd* **25/1**

0- **9** *nk* **Nimbelle (IRE)**[18] [1786] 3-8-13 **56**............................... TonyHamilton 3 38
(T F Lacy, Ire) *a towards rr* **14/1**

03-6 **10** *¾* **Lekin Sedona (IRE)**[42] [1257] 3-8-7 **50**............................(p) PaulFessey 8 29
(Joss Saville) *midfield: hdwy on inner to chse ldrs 1/2-way: sn rdn and wknd wl over 1f out* **20/1**

-030 **11** *1 ¾* **Dalarossie**[18] [1769] 3-9-4 **61**... WJSupple 1 34
(E J Alston) *chsd ldrs on inner: rdn along and lost pl over 2f out: sn in rr* **7/1**

00-0 **12** *1 ¼* **La Guancha**[18] [1769] 3-8-4 **47** ow2.................................(t) GregFairley 12 16
(D A Nolan) *chsd ldrs: rdn along 2f out: sn wknd* **80/1**

0-00 **13** *2 ¾* **Lady Aviator**[32] [1452] 3-8-2 **45**................................ CatherineGannon 7 4
(T D Easterby) *rrd s: a in rr* **28/1**

58.43 secs (-1.97) **Going Correction** -0.40s/f (Firm) **13** Ran SP% **125.6**
Speed ratings (Par 97): **99,94,91,91,89 88,86,85,85,84 81,79,74**
CSF £33.72 CT £235.46 TOTE £7.50: £2.20, £2.30, £2.30; EX 50.70 Place 6 £99.77, Place 5 £45.67..
Owner The Lapin Blanc Racing Partnership **Bred** Glending Bloodstock **Trained** Great Habton, N Yorks

FOCUS
A moderate sprint handicap.
Nimbelle(IRE) Official explanation: trainer said filly was found to be in season on returning home
Lekin Sedona(IRE) Official explanation: jockey said gelding was unsuited by the good to firm going
Lady Aviator Official explanation: jockey said filly reared as the stalls opened
T/Plt: £58.80 to a £1 stake. Pool: £48,243.86. 598.50 winning tickets. T/Qpdt: £19.00 to a £1 stake. Pool: £2,388.09. 92.80 winning tickets. JR

2080 SOUTHWELL (L-H)
Tuesday, May 20

OFFICIAL GOING: Standard
All races hand-timed except 4.00.
Wind: Light against Weather: Fine

2288 DINE IN THE QUEEN MOTHER RESTAURANT H'CAP 1m (F)
2:30 (2:31) (Class 5) (0-70,71) 3-Y-O **£3,275** (£967; £483) **Stalls** Low

Form RPR

5414 **1** **Montiboli (IRE)**[10] [2002] 3-8-12 **69**.............................. NeilBrown(5) 7 76
(K A Ryan) *mid-div: pushed along over 5f out: hdwy over 2f out: rdn and edgd rt to stands' rail over 1f out: led ins fnl f: r.o* **16/1**

-012 **2** *½* **Always Brave**[24] [1622] 3-9-4 **70**................................ AndrewElliott 10 76
(M Johnston) *a.p: rdn and ev ch 2f out: r.o ins fnl f* **15/2**

-154 **3** *½* **Golden Penny**[8] [2043] 3-9-4 **70**............................... SteveDrowne 4 75
(H Morrison) *a.p: wnt 2nd 3f out: rdn and ev ch over 1f out: kpt on ins fnl f* **3/1**[2]

1320 **4** *1 ¼* **Bookiebasher Babe (IRE)**[5] [2118] 3-9-2 **68**.................. FrancisNorton 6 70
(M Quinn) *led: rdn 2f out: hdd ins fnl f: no ex towards fin* **13/2**[3]

-402 **5** *9* **Queen's Speech (IRE)**[8] [2052] 3-9-4 **70**...................... JimmyFortune 3 51
(J H M Gosden) *hld up and bhd: hdwy on ins over 3f out: wknd over 2f out* **11/4**[1]

40-6 **6** *¾* **Morocchius (USA)**[32] [1448] 3-9-4 **70**............................ ShaneKelly 11 50
(Miss J A Camacho) *hld up in tch: wknd over 2f out* **11/1**

2604 **7** *1 ¾* **Coral Shores**[12] [1938] 3-8-4 **56** oh2.................................(v) ChrisCatlin 1 32
(P W Hiatt) *a bhd* **28/1**

05-0 **8** *12* **Lu's Woman**[13] [1912] 3-8-4 **56** oh2.............................. DaleGibson 8 4
(M W Easterby) *sn w ldr: wknd over 2f out* **50/1**

-200 **9** *9* **Ogmore Junction (IRE)**[10] [2002] 3-8-6 **65**..................... MCGeran(7) 12 —
(Mrs S Leech) *s.i.s: a in rr* **12/1**

50-2 **10** *½* **Xtravaganza (IRE)**[31] [1479] 3-8-10 **62**............................ JamesDoyle 9 —
(J W Hills) *reminders over 5f out: a bhd* **10/1**

1m 43.2s (-0.50) **Going Correction** +0.05s/f (Slow) **10** Ran SP% **113.2**
Speed ratings (Par 99): **104,103,103,101,92 92,90,78,69,68**
CSF £127.00 CT £470.54 TOTE £19.50: £4.90, £2.70, £1.30; EX 100.30 Trifecta £268.60 Part won. Pool £378.34 - 0.20 winning units..
Owner Dales Homes Ltd **Bred** Amanda Brudenell, James Boughey And Tric **Trained** Hambleton, N Yorks

FOCUS
A modest-looking handicap but solid form. The first four home were nicely clear of the remainder.
Queen's Speech(IRE) Official explanation: jockey said filly ran flat
Xtravaganza(IRE) Official explanation: jockey said filly was never travelling

2289 BOOK YOUR HOSPITALITY PACKAGES H'CAP 1m (F)
3:00 (3:00) (Class 5) (0-75,79) 4-Y-O+ **£3,238** (£963; £481; £240) **Stalls** Low

Form RPR

0200 **1** **Sun Catcher (IRE)**[6] [2101] 5-8-8 **65** ow1.......................(p) SteveDrowne 4 81
(P G Murphy) *a.p: led wl over 1f out: rdn clr and edgd lft fnl f* **9/2**[3]

-131 **2** *7* **Dado Mush**[7] [2083] 5-9-5 **79** 6ex.............................(p) KirstyMilczarek(3) 8 79
(T T Clement) *hld up in mid-div: hdwy on outside over 2f out: wnt 2nd ins fnl f: no ch w wnr* **2/1**[1]

-300 **3** *2* **Kabis Amigos**[32] [1450] 6-8-11 **68**.............................. SilvestreDeSousa 1 63
(D Nicholls) *led: rdn and hdd wl over 1f out: one pce* **8/1**

1026 **4** *hd* **Elusive Warrior (USA)**[7] [2081] 5-8-4 **61**...........................(p) NeilPollard 6 56
(A J McCabe) *chsd ldr: swtchd rt wl over 1f out: sn rdn: one pce* **12/1**

2632 **5** *5* **Jord (IRE)**[14] [1903] 4-9-4 **75**..................................... AndrewElliott 2 58+
(A J McCabe) *s.i.s: sn prom: pushed along over 4f out: rdn and wknd over 2f out* **7/2**[2]

6-06 **6** *2 ½* **Umpa Loompa (IRE)**[93] [596] 4-8-4 **61** oh9........................ HayleyTurner 7 39
(B J McMath) *pushed along 5f out: a bhd* **40/1**

0-06 **7** *3 ¼* **Nothingtodeclaire**[20] [1725] 4-8-4 **61** oh2............................ ChrisCatlin 3 31
(V Smith) *a bhd* **25/1**

1533 **8** *6* **Indian's Feather (IRE)**[14] [1903] 7-8-8 **70**.................... HaddenFrost(5) 5 26
(N Tinkler) *a bhd* **8/1**

1m 42.1s (-1.60) **Going Correction** +0.05s/f (Slow) **8** Ran SP% **112.8**
Speed ratings (Par 103): **110,103,101,100,95 93,90,84**
CSF £13.51 CT £68.18 TOTE £4.60: £1.20, £1.20, £2.30; EX 15.40 TRIFECTA Not won..
Owner Golden Anorak Partnership & Mike Conway **Bred** Johnston King **Trained** East Garston, Berks

FOCUS
A smart winning time but the form might be a bit unreliable, as Sun Catcher rarely wins, Dado Mush is probably high enough in the weights and Kabis Amigos and Elusive Warrior are better at 7f. The form has been rated at face value.
Kabis Amigos ◆ Official explanation: jockey said gelding hung right
Indian's Feather(IRE) Official explanation: jockey said mare was never travelling

2290 SOUTHWELL RACECOURSE FOR CONFERENCES H'CAP 1m 4f (F)
3:30 (3:31) (Class 6) (0-55,61) 4-Y-O+ **£2,047** (£604; £302) **Stalls** Low

Form RPR

0-00 **1** **Tykie Two**[14] [1890] 4-8-9 **50**.. LiamJones 5 60
(S Wynne) *w ldr: rdn to ld over 2f out: r.o wl* **100/1**

001 **2** *1 ¾* **Wizard Looking**[8] [2053] 7-9-6 **61** 6ex........................... ChrisCatlin 10 68+
(D E Cantillon) *hmpd after 1f: hdwy over 8f out: rdn over 2f out: kpt on ins fnl f* **9/2**[2]

3634 **3** *1* **Amwell Brave**[19] [1459] 7-8-9 **50**.................................... EddieAhern 12 55
(J R Jenkins) *hld up and bhd: hmpd after 1f: rdn and hdwy over 2f out: nt qckn ins fnl f* **9/2**[2]

1202 **4** *1 ½* **Mid Valley**[21] [1704] 5-9-0 **55**....................................... WilliamBuick 3 58+
(J R Jenkins) *hld up and bhd: rdn and hdwy on ins over 2f out: one pce fnl f* **4/1**[1]

366- **5** *nse* **Giddywell**[165] [7060] 4-8-12 **53**..................................... HayleyTurner 9 56
(R Hollinshead) *t.k.h towards rr: hdwy on ins over 4f out: one pce fnl f* **25/1**

120- **6** *3* **Red River Rebel**[294] [4040] 10-9-0 **55**............................... ShaneKelly 2 53
(J R Norton) *led: rdn and hdd over 2f out: swtchd rt over 1f out: wknd fnl f* **33/1**

3203 **7** *½* **Starcross Maid**[21] [1704] 6-8-12 **53**................................ TPQueally 11 50
(J F Coupland) *hld up and bhd: stdy hdwy on outside 6f out: rdn over 2f out: wknd over 1f out* **16/1**

5305 **8** *13* **Dream Forest (IRE)**[25] [1606] 5-8-9 **50**........................... SteveDrowne 1 27
(P W Hiatt) *prom tl wknd 2f out: eased whn btn fnl f* **33/1**

30-0 **9** *9* **Bolckow**[93] [602] 5-8-9 **50**... DaleGibson 8 12
(J T Stimpson) *bdly hmpd after 1f: a bhd* **33/1**

23-0 **10** *1 ¼* **Fire In Cairo (IRE)**[13] [1913] 4-8-1 **49**....................(t) PatrickDonaghy(7) 6 9
(P C Haslam) *hld up in mid-div: bhd fnl 4f* **28/1**

00/0 **11** *5* **Muskatsturm (GER)**[40] [1280] 9-8-2 **50**............................. MHarley(7) 14 2
(Shaun Harley, Ire) *prom: edgd lft after 1f: rdn and wknd over 4f out* **9/1**

/655 **12** *nse* **Wednesdays Boy (IRE)**[18] [1776] 5-8-10 **54**........(p) JamieMoriarty(3) 13 6
(P D Niven) *t.k.h: prom tl wknd over 4f out* **8/1**[3]

0026 **13** *13* **David's Cavalier**[13] [1913] 4-8-13 **54**............................(p) JimmyFortune 4 —
(R Hollinshead) *a bhd: eased whn no ch over 2f out* **4/1**[1]

300- **14** *1 ¼* **Jentris Girl (IRE)**[37] [3997] 4-8-8 **52**.......................... AndrewMullen(3) 7 —
(A C Whillans) *a bhd: rdn over 7f out: eased whn no ch over 2f out* **40/1**

2m 42.9s (1.90) **Going Correction** +0.05s/f (Slow) **14** Ran SP% **122.9**
Speed ratings (Par 101): **95,93,93,92,92 90,89,81,75,74 70,70,62,61**
CSF £507.39 CT £2530.20 TOTE £125.30: £16.90, £2.10, £2.40; EX 697.70 TRIFECTA Not won..

Owner L R Owen **Bred** L R Owen **Trained** Whitchurch, Shropshire
■ Steve Wynne's first winner on the Flat.
■ Stewards' Enquiry : M Harley eight-day ban: careless riding (Jun 3-10)

FOCUS
A modest winning time. The tempo increased rounding the home bend, which caught a lot of the field out. The form has been rated through the runner-up but may not prove too reliable.

2291 FIBRESAND MAIDEN STKS 1m 3f (F)
4:00 (4:00) (Class 5) 3-4-Y-O £3,238 (£963; £481; £240) Stalls Low

Form RPR
3 **1** **Deadly Silence (USA)**[24] 1621 3-8-11 0 SteveDrowne 5 86+
(Dr J D Scargill) *hld up in tch: led wl over 1f out: sn clr: eased wl ins fnl f* **9/4**[1]
2 *8* **Catching The Light (USA)** 3-8-6 0 TPQueally 11 62
(H R A Cecil) *a.p: rdn to ld over 2f out: hdd wl over 1f out: sn no ch w wnr* **16/1**
33 **3** *1 1/2* **Sea Chorus**[20] 1728 3-8-6 0 HayleyTurner 14 59
(M L W Bell) *hld up in mid-div: hdwy over 3f out: rdn over 2f out: one pce* **4/1**[3]
00 **4** *1 3/4* **Goldrenched (IRE)**[24] 1621 3-8-6 0 AndrewElliott 6 57
(M L W Bell) *chsd ldr: led over 4f out: rdn and hdd over 2f out: one pce* **66/1**
5 *nk* **Friendly King**[35] 4-9-9 0 (t) TolleyDean(3) 10 61
(George Baker) *s.i.s: hld up and bhd: hdwy on ins over 2f out: one pce fnl f* **20/1**
6 **6** *1 1/4* **Cyborg**[12] 1931 4-9-12 0 RobertHavlin 13 59
(D R C Elsworth) *s.i.s: hld up and bhd: hdwy over 3f out: one pce fnl 2f* **10/1**
06 **7** *1* **Force Tradition (IRE)**[10] 1994 3-8-6 0 NicolPolli(5) 2 57+
(M H Tompkins) *in rr: styd on fnl 2f: nvr nrr* **66/1**
40 **8** *hd* **World Time**[24] 1621 3-8-11 0 JimmyFortune 9 57+
(J H M Gosden) *s.i.s: hld up in mid-div: no hdwy fnl 3f* **11/4**[2]
9 *1 1/2* **Soomar** 3-8-11 0 ShaneKelly 8 54
(T G Mills) *s.i.s: sn mid-div: hdwy 6f out: rdn over 4f out: wknd over 2f out* **28/1**
-643 **10** *2* **Reprieved**[7] 2080 3-8-5 0 ow1 MarkCoumbe(7) 1 52
(M C Chapman) *prom: rdn over 2f out: sn wknd* **66/1**
5- **11** *3/4* **Al Cobra (IRE)**[193] 6742 3-8-6 0 WilliamBuick 7 45
(M A Jarvis) *prom tl wknd over 5f out* **9/1**
12 *9* **Lemonesse (USA)** 3-8-6 0 EddieAhern 3 29
(H R A Cecil) *a towards rr: eased whn no ch over 2f out* **14/1**
44 **13** *3/4* **Spanish Cruise (IRE)**[24] 1621 4-9-12 0 AlanDaly 12 33
(Andrew Turnell) *mid-div tl wknd 4f out* **20/1**
0- **14** *10* **Binyamina**[199] 6648 3-8-6 0 ChrisCatlin 4 11
(Miss J R Gibney) *led: hdd over 4f out: sn rdn: wknd 3f out* **100/1**

2m 28.12s (0.12) **Going Correction** +0.05s/f (Slow) 14 Ran SP% **127.5**
WFA 3 from 4yo 15lb
Speed ratings (Par 103): **101,95,94,92,92 91,90,90,89,88 87,81,80,73**
CSF £42.07 TOTE £3.70: £1.60, £4.90, £1.50; EX 66.00 Trifecta £157.80 Part won. Pool £222.27 - 0.40 winning units..
Owner Silent Partners **Bred** Oceanic Bloodstock Et Al **Trained** Newmarket, Suffolk
■ Stewards' Enquiry : Tolley Dean three-day ban: careless riding (Jun 3-6)
FOCUS
A modest early pace, but probably not a bad maiden with some big stables represented. The favourite eventually turned it into a procession.

2292 BOOK YOUR TICKETS ONLINE AT SOUTHWELL-RACECOURSE.CO.UK H'CAP 5f (F)
4:30 (4:30) (Class 4) (0-85,91) 4-Y-O+ £5,180 (£1,541; £770; £384) Stalls High

Form RPR
4113 **1** **Garlogs**[35] 1378 5-8-4 71 oh1 HayleyTurner 3 84
(R Hollinshead) *chsd ldr: led over 1f out: drvn out* **7/2**[2]
4651 **2** *1 3/4* **Figaro Flyer (IRE)**[14] 1901 5-8-4 71 oh3 FrancisNorton 4 78
(P Howling) *chsd ldrs: rdn over 2f out: wnt 2nd jst ins fnl f: kpt on same pce* **5/1**
1001 **3** *3 1/4* **Luscivious**[7] 2082 4-9-10 91 6ex (b) PatCosgrave 2 86
(A J McCabe) *s.i.s: sn prom: rdn over 1f out: wknd wl ins fnl f* **5/2**[1]
3024 **4** *1 1/2* **Pawan (IRE)**[13] 1908 8-8-9 81 (b) AnnStokell(5) 6 71
(Miss A Stokell) *sn outpcd: sme hdwy over 1f out: nvr trbld ldrs* **8/1**
3330 **5** *3/4* **Almaty Express**[13] 1908 6-9-0 81 (b) ChrisCatlin 5 68
(J R Weymes) *chsd ldrs tl wknd over 2f out* **20/1**
5450 **6** *1/2* **Diminuto**[6] 2102 4-7-11 71 oh5 RossAtkinson(7) 1 56
(M D I Usher) *sn outpcd: rdn and some hdwy over 1f out: n.d* **14/1**
-146 **7** *1 1/2* **Bookiesindex Boy**[26] 1582 4-8-9 76 (v) WilliamBuick 8 56
(J R Jenkins) *led over 3f: rdn and wknd ins fnl f* **11/1**
4-00 **8** *9* **Prospect Court**[17] 1818 6-8-4 74 AndrewMullen(3) 7 22
(A C Whillans) *s.i.s: a in rr* **4/1**[3]

59.30 secs (-0.40) **Going Correction** +0.05s/f (Slow) 8 Ran SP% **118.3**
Speed ratings (Par 105): **105,102,97,94,93 92,90,75**
CSF £22.25 CT £51.52 TOTE £4.10: £2.10, £1.70, £1.10; EX 22.20 Trifecta £40.20 Pool £276.67 - 4.88 winning units..
Owner Peter G Freeman **Bred** Peter Taplin **Trained** Upper Longdon, Staffs
FOCUS
Quite a decent handicap and the pace set by Bookiesindex Boy was furious - the first 2f was covered in 22.79 seconds - but he paid for that and several of the others could not cope with the tempo. Also the centre of the track was the place to be. Garlogs is rated up 7lb.
Pawan(IRE) Official explanation: jockey said gelding would not face the kick-back

2293 SOUTHWELL-RACECOURSE.CO.UK H'CAP 6f (F)
5:00 (5:00) (Class 4) (0-80,80) 4-Y-O+ £4,533 (£1,348; £674; £336) Stalls Low

Form RPR
1213 **1** **Diriculous**[22] 1683 4-9-1 76 JimmyFortune 8 85+
(T G Mills) *hld up in mid-div: smooth hdwy over 1f out: sn rdn: r.o to ld towards fin* **15/8**[1]
4010 **2** *1 1/4* **Varadouro (BRZ)**[11] 1952 6-9-4 79 SilvestreDeSousa 3 84+
(D Nicholls) *chsd ldrs: n.m.r on ins over 1f out: rdn and kpt on to take 2nd post* **3/1**[2]
3043 **3** *shd* **Steel City Boy (IRE)**[8] 2036 5-8-7 73 ow4 AnnStokell(5) 10 78
(Miss A Stokell) *a.p: led jst over 1f out: hdd towards fin* **20/1**
50-0 **4** *3/4* **Whitbarrow (IRE)**[33] 1415 9-8-11 77 (b) JamesMillman(5) 6 80
(B R Millman) *chsd ldrs: rdn and ev ch 2f out: nt qckn ins fnl f* **12/1**
5301 **5** *shd* **Cerebus**[7] 2077 6-9-5 80 6ex (b) PatCosgrave 11 82
(A J McCabe) *led: rdn and edgd lft over 1f out: sn hdd: no ex wl ins fnl f* **12/1**
20-0 **6** *2* **Minaash (USA)**[48] 1146 4-8-9 75 AhmedAjtebi(5) 7 71
(D M Simcock) *s.i.s: bhd: hdwy over 3f out: swtchd lft over 2f out: one pce fnl f* **16/1**
3666 **7** *1/2* **Dickie Le Davoir**[14] 1901 4-8-9 70 ChrisCatlin 2 64
(John A Harris) *outpcd and bhd: hdwy u.p fnl f: nrst fin* **8/1**
2605 **8** *3* **Tag Team (IRE)**[7] 2081 7-8-4 65 AndrewElliott 1 50
(John A Harris) *a bhd* **25/1**
4P12 **9** *1 3/4* **Bartercard (USA)**[7] 2085 7-9-0 75 TPQueally 5 54
(Stef Liddiard) *s.i.s: rdn over 3f out: a bhd* **11/2**[3]
-006 **10** *8* **Paris Bell**[11] 1969 6-8-11 75 JamieMoriarty(3) 9 28
(T D Easterby) *dwlt: outpcd* **20/1**
000- **11** *9* **Never Without Me**[202] 6594 8-7-11 65 oh2 AndrewHeffernan(7) 4 —
(J F Coupland) *mid-div: rdn over 3f out: sn bhd* **50/1**

1m 16.8s (0.30) **Going Correction** +0.05s/f (Slow) 11 Ran SP% **122.9**
Speed ratings (Par 105): **100,98,98,97,97 94,93,89,87,76 64**
CSF £7.30 CT £90.24 TOTE £2.60: £1.20, £1.60, £5.70; EX 10.10 Trifecta £101.70 Pool £385.61 - 2.69 winning units. Place 6 £32.63, Place 5 £9.20..
Owner Sherwoods Transport Ltd **Bred** Sherwoods Transport Ltd **Trained** Headley, Surrey
■ Stewards' Enquiry : Pat Cosgrave one-day ban: careless riding (Jun 3)
FOCUS
A modest race run at a fair pace. Those that raced prominently from the start dominated throughout and little else ever got into it. Pretty ordinary form at face value but the winner should continue to pay his way.
T/Plt: £27.30 to a £1 stake. Pool: £51,797.98. 1,383.85 winning tickets. T/Qpdt: £5.40 to a £1 stake. Pool: £3,351.89. 457.49 winning tickets. KH

2294 - (Foreign Racing) - See Raceform Interactive

AYR (L-H)
Wednesday, May 21
2295 Meeting Abandoned - Patch of false ground.
The meeting was called off 20 minutes after the scheduled start time of the first race.

1926 GOODWOOD (R-H)
Wednesday, May 21
OFFICIAL GOING: Good (good to firm in places; 8.8)
Wind: Moderate, behind. Weather: Sunny.

2302 ALAN BALL MEMORIAL STKS (H'CAP) 1m 1f
2:15 (2:18) (Class 4) (0-85,85) 3-Y-O
£4,361 (£1,306; £653; £326; £163; £81) Stalls High

Form RPR
-230 **1** **Mcconnell (USA)**[17] 1839 3-8-7 74 RyanMoore 10 82
(G L Moore) *chsd ldrs: swtchd lft over 2f out: sn rdn: led ins fnl f: kpt on wl: rdn out* **9/2**[2]
1-24 **2** *1/2* **Formation (USA)**[53] 1074 3-8-12 79 JamieSpencer 8 86
(E A L Dunlop) *hld up towards rr: swtchd lft and hdwy over 2f out: sn encouraged along: wnt 2nd jst ins fnl f: rdn and kpt on fnl 100yds but a hld* **6/1**[3]
52-0 **3** *2 1/4* **Border Owl (IRE)**[15] 1896 3-8-10 77 RichardHughes 11 79
(R Hannon) *chsd ldrs: rdn over 2f out: nt clr run briefly over 1f out: kpt on* **50/1**
11-0 **4** *1/2* **Goodwood Starlight (IRE)**[34] 1424 3-8-12 79 EddieAhern 12 86+
(J L Dunlop) *mid-div: rdn and hdwy 2f out: nt clr run over 1f out and ent fnl f: styd on* **10/1**
-045 **5** *1/2* **Legislation**[20] 1746 3-9-3 84 (b[1]) JimmyFortune 2 84
(J H M Gosden) *led after 1f: rdn 2f out: hdd ins fnl f: no ex* **9/1**
00-0 **6** *3/4* **Tamara Moon (IRE)**[53] 1074 3-8-6 73 ChrisCatlin 4 71
(M R Channon) *broke wl: led for 1f: trckd ldr: rdn 2f out: ev ch ent fnl f: kpt on same pce* **33/1**
1- **7** *1 3/4* **Mystery Sail (USA)**[242] 5633 3-9-0 81 JimCrowley 13 75
(Mrs A J Perrett) *trckd ldrs: rdn over 2f out: ev ch and edgd lft over 1f out: fdd ins fnl f* **12/1**
-115 **8** *1* **Air Chief**[22] 1696 3-8-10 77 JimmyQuinn 7 69
(H J L Dunlop) *slipped leaving stalls: towards rr: steadily rcvrd into midfield: rdn and edgd rt fr over 1f out: kpt on same pce fnl f* **12/1**
21-3 **9** *1 1/2* **The Which Doctor**[30] 1524 3-8-12 79 TPQueally 5 68
(J Noseda) *mid-div: rdn 3f out: no imp* **5/2**[1]
16-6 **10** *2 1/2* **Mujaadel (USA)**[53] 1074 3-9-4 85 RHills 6 68
(E A L Dunlop) *a towards rr* **8/1**
0-54 **11** *hd* **King's Icon (IRE)**[23] 1688 3-8-10 77 PatDobbs 1 60
(M P Tregoning) *a towards rr* **16/1**
4-40 **12** *nse* **Talayeb**[29] 1539 3-8-8 75 AlanMunro 9 58
(M P Tregoning) *hld up towards rr: hdwy into midfield over 3f out: rdn over 2f out: wknd over 1f out* **20/1**
05-4 **13** *6* **Royal Straight**[16] 1854 3-8-11 78 LPKeniry 3 48
(A M Balding) *mid-div: lost pl over 4f out: rdn 3f out: wknd 2f out* **28/1**

1m 56.97s (0.67) **Going Correction** +0.10s/f (Good) 13 Ran SP% **125.6**
Speed ratings (Par 101): **101,100,98,98,97 97,95,94,93,91 90,90,85**
CSF £32.32 CT £1238.25 TOTE £5.80: £2.50, £2.30, £10.10; EX 49.80.
Owner Joe McCarthy **Bred** Hall Et Al Farm **Trained** Woodingdean, E Sussex
FOCUS
A good three-year-old handicap, run at a sound pace, which saw those drawn high at an advantage. The runner-up is rated to his mark with the winner 5lb off.
Goodwood Starlight(IRE) Official explanation: jockey said colt was denied a clear run
Air Chief Official explanation: jockey said gelding slipped on leaving stalls

2303 DAVID WILSON HOMES STKS (REGISTERED AS THE COCKED HAT STAKES) (LISTED RACE) (C&G) 1m 3f
2:50 (2:51) (Class 1) 3-Y-O
£17,031 (£6,456; £3,231; £1,611; £807; £405) Stalls High

Form RPR
12-6 **1** **City Leader (IRE)**[34] 1421 3-9-5 111 JamieSpencer 2 109+
(B J Meehan) *trckd ldrs: tk narrow advantage wl over 1f out: r.o wl: rdn out* **3/1**[2]
1-00 **2** *3/4* **Scintillo**[18] 1808 3-9-5 109 RichardHughes 7 108
(R Hannon) *hld up in last pair: clsd on ldrs 2f out: sn rdn: swtchd lft over 1f out: r.o: wnt 2nd fnl 100yds* **14/1**
14 **3** *1 1/4* **Top Lock**[25] 1632 3-9-0 100 KerrinMcEvoy 4 101
(A M Balding) *led for 1f: trckd ldr: nudged along 4f out: rdn to chal 3f out: ev ch ent fnl f: no ex* **7/1**
01-2 **4** *1 1/2* **Whistledownwind**[25] 1632 3-9-0 104 LDettori 6 98
(P W Chapple-Hyam) *s.i.s: rcvrd to ld after 1f: rdn and hrd pressed fr 3f out: narrowly hdd wl over 1f out: rallied: no ex ins fnl f* **5/4**[1]

-044	5	½	**Siberian Tiger (IRE)**[18] 1811 3-9-3 98 ... RyanMoore 5		101
			(M R Channon) *trckd ldrs: rdn over 2f out: one pce fnl f*	12/1	
4-61	6	nk	**Savarain**[13] 1931 3-9-0 96 ... DaneO'Neill 1		97
			(L M Cumani) *hld up in last pair: rdn over 2f out: nt pce to chal*	11/2[3]	

2m 26.48s (-1.82) **Going Correction** +0.10s/f (Good) 6 Ran SP% **111.7**
Speed ratings (Par 107): **110,109,108,107,107 106**
CSF £39.21 TOTE £3.80: £2.10, £6.00; EX 39.20.
Owner Sangster Family **Bred** Swettenham Stud **Trained** Manton, Wilts

FOCUS
A good line-up for this Listed race. It was run at a sound pace and the form looks solid with the first pair, both penalised, coming clear late on, although the winner did not need to run to his best to score.

NOTEBOOK
City Leader(IRE), a well-beaten sixth under a penalty in the Craven on his seasonal return in April, showed his true colours on this step up in trip and did the job in determined fashion. He showed a decent attitude when asked to hit the front after passing the 2f pole and, relishing the longer distance, was always holding the runner-up at the business end. His stable are in much better form now and there is no doubt he is open to a good deal of improvement over this sort of trip, but he is unlikely to be heading for the Derby next month as connections favour a trip to Royal Ascot for the Group 2 King Edward VII Stakes. (op 10-3 tchd 7-2)
Scintillo, out the back in the 2000 Guineas last time, was another to relish the step up to this distance and managed to get closer to the winner than had been the case on his seasonal debut in the Craven last month. He deserves to be ridden more prominently over this trip now and this Group 1 winner looks to be coming back to himself again now. Official explanation: vet said colt finished sore (op 10-1)
Top Lock ◆ is developing into a relentless galloper and did nothing wrong in defeat, keeping on gamely inside the final furlong. Another furlong looks in order now, indeed he may enjoy even further as the season develops, and he can strike in this class before all that long. (op 15-2)
Whistledownwind, just held by Centennial in the Classic Trial at Sandown on his comeback 25 days previously, failed to confirm that form with the third over this extra furlong and may well not have been suited by this quicker surface. The best of him has probably still to be seen. Official explanation: jockey said colt did not handle the track (op 11-8 tchd 6-4 in places)
Siberian Tiger(IRE), whose stable took this event last year with Halicarnassus, was stepping up in trip and grade so was not disgraced in defeat. He ran very close to his official rating, but a drop back in trip now looks on the cards. (op 16-1)
Savarain, a maiden winner at the track 13 days previously, looked to have been fairly harsly assessed by the Handicapper on a mark of 96, despite still holding an entry in the Derby, and was taking a forced step up in class. A more positive ride would have likely seen him in a better light over this slightly shorter trip, but it is hard to really crab him and he still ran right up to his official rating in defeat. He is in the right hands and still one to keep a close eye on. (tchd 5-1)

2304 BAKER TILLY STKS (H'CAP) 1m 4f
3:25 (3:25) (Class 4) (0-80,80) 4-Y-0+ £5,180 (£1,541; £770; £384) Stalls Low

Form					RPR
1-41	1		**Hatton Flight**[25] 1639 4-8-7 69 ... (b) WilliamBuick 7		79+
			(A M Balding) *mid-div: nudged along and stdy prog fr 3f out: rdn to ld ent fnl f: styd on strly: won gng away*	5/1[2]	
12-5	2	1¾	**Potentiale (IRE)**[12] 1963 4-8-9 71 ... EddieAhern 10		78
			(J W Hills) *mid-div: smooth hdwy over 3f out: rdn to ld jst ins 2f out: hdd ent fnl f: no ex*	6/1[3]	
56-5	3	2¼	**Zaif (IRE)**[7] 2107 5-9-3 79 ... GeorgeBaker 11		82
			(Simon Earle) *hld up towards rr: hdwy 3f out: rdn 2f out: sn swtchd lft: styd on*	8/1	
212	4	1½	**Alonso De Guzman (IRE)**[19] 1768 4-8-6 68 ... JamieSpencer 3		69
			(J R Boyle) *led: rdn and narrowly hdd 2f out: rallied: fdd fnl 100yds*	12/1	
15-0	5	nk	**Optimus (USA)**[29] 1532 6-9-4 80 ... TQuinn 6		81
			(B G Powell) *slowly away: sn shoved along and detached: styd on ent fnl f: fin wl: nvr nrr*	33/1	
-101	6	nk	**Apache Fort**[19] 1768 5-8-7 69 ... ShaneKelly 4		69
			(T Keddy) *mid-div: hdwy 3f out: rdn to chse ldrs over 1f out: one pce fnl f*	14/1	
4-21	7	1	**Dove Cottage (IRE)**[13] 1929 6-9-0 76 ... FergusSweeney 2		74
			(W S Kittow) *trckd ldr: chal 3f out: led briefly 2f out: slipped on bnd after 2f out: wknd fnl f*	11/4[1]	
052-	8	1	**Venir Rouge**[197] 6709 4-9-0 76 ... TGMcLaughlin 1		73
			(M Salaman) *trckd ldrs: struggling whn nt clr run and snatched up over 1f out: wknd*	20/1	
3513	9	¾	**Wait For The Will (USA)**[13] 1929 12-8-4 66 oh1 ... (b) JoeFanning 8		62
			(G L Moore) *hld up towards rr: rdn and sme prog over 2f out: nvr trbld ldrs*	11/1	
2/0-	10	102	**South O'The Border**[19] 1621 6-9-1 77 ... LDettori 9		—
			(Miss Venetia Williams) *trckd ldrs: rdn over 3f out: sn wknd: virtually p.u wl over 1f out*	10/1	
21-6	11	dist	**Royal Jasra**[13] 1935 4-8-13 75 ... RyanMoore 5		—
			(E A L Dunlop) *hld up towards rr: lost action and virtually p.u 3f out*	13/2	

2m 41.41s (3.01) **Going Correction** +0.10s/f (Good) 11 Ran SP% **121.5**
Speed ratings (Par 105): **93,91,90,89,89 88,88,87,87,—,—**
CSF £36.47 CT £242.88 TOTE £6.90: £2.10, £2.80, £3.10; EX 48.80 Trifecta £635.50 Pool £984.70 - 1.10 winning units..
Owner David Brownlow **Bred** Fittocks Stud Ltd **Trained** Kingsclere, Hants

FOCUS
A modest handicap, run at a sound pace. The winner is progressive and the form can be rated through the placed horses.
Optimus(USA) Official explanation: jockey said gelding was slowly away
Dove Cottage(IRE) Official explanation: jockey said gelding slipped on first bend
South O'The Border Official explanation: jockey said gelding was unsuited by the track and moved poorly
Royal Jasra Official explanation: jockey said colt slipped and felt wrong after

2305 HEIGHT OF FASHION STKS (LISTED RACE) (FILLIES) 1m 1f 192y
4:00 (4:01) (Class 1) 3-Y-O £17,778 (£6,723; £3,360; £1,680) Stalls High

Form					RPR
1-0	1		**Michita (USA)**[32] 1470 3-9-0 92 ... JimmyFortune 9		107+
			(J H M Gosden) *travelled wl in mid-div: smooth hdwy fr 3f out: led wl over 1f out: rdn and forged clr fnl 150yds: quite impressive*	5/1[2]	
32-0	2	4½	**Annie Skates (USA)**[32] 1470 3-9-0 102 ... KerrinMcEvoy 1		98
			(Jane Chapple-Hyam) *hld up in rr: smooth hdwy on rails 3f out to trck ldrs: waited for clr run tl over 1f out: styd on to go 2nd ins fnl f: no ch w wnr*	10/1	
154-	3	1	**Rosa Grace**[214] 6336 3-9-0 99 ... ChrisCatlin 5		96
			(Rae Guest) *hld up towards rr: hdwy and nt clr run over 2f out: swtchd lft over 1f out: rdn and styd on wl fnl f: wnt 3rd towards fin*	12/1	
5-63	4	½	**Don't Forget Faith (USA)**[17] 1833 3-9-0 97 ... PhilipRobinson 4		95
			(C G Cox) *stmbld s: sn led: rdn and hdd wl over 1f out: kpt on same pce*	6/1[3]	
12-1	5	hd	**Jazz Jam**[39] 1332 3-9-3 92 ... TQuinn 2		98
			(P F I Cole) *chsd ldrs: rdn 3f out: ev ch 2f out: kpt on same pce*	9/1	
3-14	6	3	**Queen Of Naples**[14] 1915 3-9-0 98 ... (b[1]) RobertHavlin 8		89
			(J H M Gosden) *trckd ldr: chal jst ins 3f out: rdn whn drifted lft and bmpd 2f out: sn wknd*	17/2	
315-	7	½	**Celtic Slipper (IRE)**[220] 6222 3-9-5 108 ... RyanMoore 7		93
			(R M Beckett) *mid-div: rdn and hdwy over 2f out: wknd fnl f*	7/2[1]	
0-41	8	17	**Rosaleen (IRE)**[21] 1715 3-9-0 97 ... LDettori 6		54
			(B J Meehan) *hld up towards rr: rdn and hdwy over 2f out but nvr able to mount a chal: wknd over 1f out*	7/2[1]	
	9	30	**Really Ransom**[229] 5997 3-9-0 0 ... JoeFanning 3		—
			(P C Haslam) *settled in mid-div: rdn over 3f out: sn wknd: virtually p.u*	33/1	

2m 7.45s (-0.55) **Going Correction** +0.10s/f (Good) 9 Ran SP% **115.6**
Speed ratings (Par 104): **106,102,101,101,101 98,98,84,60**
CSF £53.79 TOTE £7.20: £2.50, £2.90, £2.50; EX 61.40.
Owner Stonerside Stable Llc **Bred** Stonerside Stable **Trained** Newmarket, Suffolk

FOCUS
A decent field for a Listed event and the winning time was not too bad. The winner was by far the best horse in the race and should progress through the season. Don't Forget Faith looks the benchmark to the form.

NOTEBOOK
Michita(USA), disappointing behind Muthabara in the Dubai Duty Free (Fred Darling) Stakes, burst clear of her rivals over a furlong from home and came home a very comfortable winner. Her trainer has every intention of running this powerfully-built sort in the Oaks next, for which she is generally a 12/1 shot, and feels that she will stay the extra 2f (the sire has produced horses that stay, but there must be a slight doubt on the dam's side of the pedigree). She has lots of scope for improvement and should continue to improve. (op 13-2)
Annie Skates(USA), who finished in front of today's winner last time, had to wait for an opening up the inside rail and lost some valuable ground on Michita. However, her acceleration was nothing like that of her rival and she shaped like a horse who could be better over further. (op 14-1 tchd 9-1)
Rosa Grace ◆, having her first start since her fine effort in the Rockfel Stakes last year, shaped really nicely and looks sure to win races this season. A step up in trip will probably suit her and her trainer stated that she must have quick ground. (op 8-1)
Don't Forget Faith(USA) did all the hard work in front but failed to raise her game once joined. The winner comprehensively reversed form with her on their meeting at Newbury and a slight drop in trip might make her task easier. (op 11-2 tchd 7-1)
Jazz Jam, stepping up in trip and back on turf, was not disgraced but looked a bit one-paced in the final couple of furlongs. She did not seem to have any obvious excuses. (op 12-1)
Queen Of Naples, in first-time blinkers, took a nice tow off Don't Forget Faith in the early stages and looked a big threat about 3f from home. However, she never picked up when asked to quicken and momentarily lost her footing, which saw her drop back through the field. (op 10-1 tchd 8-1)
Celtic Slipper(IRE), who was proven over the course, ran a lifeless race on her seasonal debut and has plenty to prove. (tchd 4-1)
Rosaleen(IRE) had performed well this season but this was a dreadful effort. The step up in trip was not the reason for the poor showing, as she was going backwards at the top of the home straight. Official explanation: trainer said filly was unsuited by the track and the good ground (tchd 3-1)

2306 E B F ALAN BALL SUPPORTERS' MAIDEN FILLIES' STKS 6f
4:35 (4:37) (Class 5) 2-Y-O £3,561 (£1,059; £529; £264) Stalls Low

Form					RPR
	1		**Elusive Wave (IRE)** 2-9-0 0 ... RichardHughes 5		83+
			(R Hannon) *trckd ldrs: led ent fnl f: r.o wl: readily*	4/1[2]	
	2	3¾	**Straitjacket** 2-9-0 0 ... RyanMoore 10		72
			(R Hannon) *s.i.s and wnt rt s: in tch: hdwy 3f out: rdn and ev ch ent fnl f: kpt on but nt pce of wnr*	2/1[1]	
4	3	nse	**Kerrys Requiem (IRE)**[16] 1866 2-9-0 0 ... ChrisCatlin 6		72
			(M R Channon) *plld hrd: led: rdn whn edgd rt and hdd ent fnl f: kpt on but nt pce of wnr*	4/1[2]	
	4	2	**Amber Sunset** 2-9-0 0 ... JimmyFortune 9		66
			(J Jay) *trckd ldrs: rdn and ev ch ent fnl f: one pce*	25/1	
	5	8	**Azwa** 2-9-0 0 ... RHills 8		42+
			(E A L Dunlop) *s.i.s: towards rr: effrt to cl on ldrs over 3f out: wknd 1f out*	4/1[2]	
0	6	1¾	**Miss Mojito (IRE)**[16] 1851 2-9-0 0 ... EddieAhern 7		37
			(J W Hills) *wnt rt s: sn prom: hung rt fr over 3f out: bit slipped through mouth over 2f out: sn btn*	10/1[3]	
00	7	½	**Percys Corismatic**[42] 1263 2-9-0 0 ... FergusSweeney 3		35
			(J Gallagher) *struggling to go pce fr over 4f out: a towards rr*	100/1	
	8	4	**Song Of Praise** 2-9-0 0 ... JamesDoyle 1		23
			(M Blanshard) *chsd ldrs: rdn over 2f out: wknd over 1f out*	40/1	
0	P		**Misty Glade**[12] 1961 2-9-0 0 ... JamieSpencer 4		—
			(B J Meehan) *trcking ldrs whn lost action and p.u after 2f*	12/1	

1m 12.2s **Going Correction** +0.025s/f (Good) 9 Ran SP% **117.4**
Speed ratings (Par 90): **101,96,95,93,82 80,79,74,—**
CSF £12.53 TOTE £5.70: £1.60, £1.40, £1.70; EX 14.00.
Owner Andrew Russell **Bred** Pier House Stud **Trained** East Everleigh, Wilts

FOCUS
A decent-looking fillies maiden but hard to quantify the form. The winner did it well.

NOTEBOOK
Elusive Wave(IRE), the lesser-fancied of the Hannon pair, quickened nicely clear of her rivals at around the furlong pole to win with plenty in hand. Both of the dam's previous offspring went on to be very useful performers, and there is no reason to think she will be any different. The Albany Stakes at Royal Ascot is on the agenda. (op 5-1)
Straitjacket, whose price doubled from a foal to a yearling, showed a professional attitude on her debut but lacked the acceleration of her stablemate. She should be good enough to win at this trip but should be better over further. (op 3-1 tchd 10-3 and 7-2 in a place)
Kerrys Requiem(IRE), who finished fourth in a race that has not worked out on her debut, showed some good pace but did not look suited by the course. She ought to be good enough to land at least an ordinary maiden. Official explanation: jockey said filly hung badly right (op 10-3 tchd 3-1)
Amber Sunset ◆, whose dam won as a 2yo, showed a good deal of promise on her debut and should be a lot wiser for the run. She looks sure to win a maiden at one of the lesser tracks. (tchd 20-1)
Azwa, a filly with plenty of substance, did not appear as clued up as some of her rivals and was a bit disappointing. However, she is definitely worth another chance, especially on a more conventional track. (op 9-2 tchd 7-2)
Miss Mojito(IRE) Official explanation: jockey said bit slipped through filly's mouth

The Form Book, Raceform Ltd, Compton, RG20 6NL

Misty Glade Official explanation: jockey said filly lost its action

2307 EVERTONIANS REMEMBER ALAN BALL MAIDEN FILLIES' STKS 7f
5:10 (5:11) (Class 5) 3-Y-O

£3,115 (£933; £466; £233; £116; £58) **Stalls** High

Form				RPR
	1		**Baby Houseman** 3-9-0 0 ... JimmyFortune 7 (J H M Gosden) *mid-div: nt clr run on rails 3f out: sn swtchd lft: rdn and qckd up wl over 1f out: led jst ins fnl f: r.o strly: readily* **11/2**[3]	88+
0-	2	3 3/4	**Victoria Reel**[200] 6649 3-9-0 0 ... PatDobbs 1 (R Hannon) *sn prom: led 3f out: rdn over 1f out: hdd jst ins fnl f: nt pce of wnr* **10/1**	74
6	3	1 1/2	**Theory**[12] 1957 3-9-0 0 ... SteveDrowne 2 (J H M Gosden) *mid-div: hdwy jst over 2f out: effrt over 1f out: kpt on same pce ins fnl f* **9/4**[2]	70
0-	4	1 1/2	**Jennie Jerome (IRE)**[230] 5949 3-9-0 0 ... DaneO'Neill 3 (L M Cumani) *trckd ldrs: rdn over 2f out: kpt on same pce fnl f* **5/4**[1]	66
0	5	7	**New Havens**[12] 1957 3-9-0 0 ... WilliamBuick 8 (C R Egerton) *trckd ldrs: rdn 3f out: wknd 2f out* **22/1**	47
	6	1/2	**Rockfield Rose** 3-9-0 0 ... TPQueally 6 (J A Osborne) *a towards rr* **14/1**	46
0	7	3 1/2	**Giadiniera**[16] 1869 3-9-0 0 ... IanMongan 4 (C F Wall) *led tl 3f out: wknd 2f out* **40/1**	36
56-	8	1/2	**Bluebell Ridge (IRE)**[217] 6262 3-9-0 0 ... FergusSweeney 5 (D W P Arbuthnot) *hld up: rdn 3f out: wknd 2f out* **16/1**	35

1m 28.24s (0.84) **Going Correction** +0.10s/f (Good) **8 Ran SP% 119.0**
Speed ratings (Par 96): **99,94,93,91,83 82,78,78**
CSF £60.55 TOTE £5.50: £1.80, £2.00, £1.20; EX 44.10.
Owner Normandie Stud Ltd **Bred** Normandie Stud Ltd **Trained** Newmarket, Suffolk

FOCUS
A fair-looking event and a very impressive winner. The first four were a long way superior to the rest of the field and the form is rated around the favourite.
Bluebell Ridge(IRE) Official explanation: jockey said filly was in season

2308 CONGRATULATIONS TO PORTSMOUTH FC STKS (H'CAP) 1m
5:45 (5:45) (Class 4) (0-85,85) 4-Y-0+ **£4,533** (£1,348; £674; £336) **Stalls** High

Form				RPR
6000	1		**Orchard Supreme**[11] 1982 5-9-2 **83** ... JimmyFortune 7 (R Hannon) *trckd ldrs: w.w tl qcknd up wl to ld fnl 100yds: drifted rt: rdn clr* **10/1**	97+
2106	2	1 3/4	**Count Ceprano (IRE)**[11] 1982 4-8-13 **80** ... RichardSmith 6 (M D I Usher) *mid-div: rdn and hdwy 2f out: ev ch ins fnl f: nt pce of wnr* **9/1**	87
16-4	3	shd	**Young Bertie**[30] 1520 5-8-4 **71** ...(v) ChrisCatlin 4 (H Morrison) *chsd ldrs: led over 2f out: sn rdn: hdd fnl 100yds: nt pce of wnr and lost 2nd nr fin* **9/2**[2]	78
4-60	4	1 3/4	**Rambling Light**[25] 1630 4-8-8 **75** ... LPKeniry 5 (A M Balding) *trckd ldr: jnd ldrs 3f out: rdn 2f out: ev ch ent fnl f: kpt on same pce* **16/1**	78
0-02	5	1	**Formax (FR)**[18] 1799 6-9-4 **85** ... PatDobbs 2 (M P Tregoning) *hld up bhd: rdn and sme prog over 1f out: kpt on fnl f: nvr trbld ldrs* **7/1**	85
2121	6	1	**Emperor Court (IRE)**[23] 1682 4-9-0 **81** ... SteveDrowne 9 (P J Makin) *set decent pce: rdn and hdd over 2f out: hung lft and wknd fnl f* **5/1**[3]	79
6002	7	nse	**Northern Spy (USA)**[16] 1857 4-8-11 **78** ... DaneO'Neill 1 (S Dow) *mid-div: rdn over 2f out: no imp* **11/2**	76
0000	8	1	**Alfresco**[11] 2013 4-8-12 **79** ...(b) WilliamBuick 8 (I A Wood) *rdn over 3f out: a towards rr* **16/1**	75
0-26	9	4	**Murrin (IRE)**[21] 1719 4-8-8 **75** ... JamieSpencer 3 (T G Mills) *a towards rr* **3/1**[1]	62

1m 39.81s (-0.09) **Going Correction** +0.10s/f (Good) **9 Ran SP% 118.6**
Speed ratings (Par 105): **104,102,102,100,99 98,98,97,93**
CSF £98.35 CT £467.80 TOTE £14.90: £3.10, £3.20, £1.90; EX 166.40 Place 6 £179.35, Place 5 £63.88..
Owner Brian C Oakley **Bred** Mrs M H Goodrich **Trained** East Everleigh, Wilts

FOCUS
A sound-looking handicap. The pace looked fair and the form, rated around the placed horses, should work out.
Emperor Court(IRE) Official explanation: jockey said colt hung left
T/Jkpt: Not won. T/Plt: £465.40 to a £1 stake. Pool: £87,071.00. 136.55 winning tickets. T/Qpdt: £39.50 to a £1 stake. Pool: £6,759.28. 126.60 winning tickets. TM

1630 SANDOWN (R-H)
Wednesday, May 21

OFFICIAL GOING: Good to firm (firm in places) abandoned after race 3 (7.05) due to unsafe ground.
Last three races abandoned due to unsafe ground.
Wind: Light, behind Weather: Sunny

2309 PANMURE GORDON SMALL COMPANIES E B F MAIDEN FILLIES' STKS 5f 6y
6:00 (6:02) (Class 4) 2-Y-O **£4,533** (£1,348; £674; £336) **Stalls** High

Form				RPR
	1		**Crystal Moments** 2-9-0 0 ... RyanMoore 7 (E A L Dunlop) *pressed ldng pair: rdn to ld 1f out: styd on wl* **9/2**[2]	79+
	2	1 1/2	**Our Wee Girl (IRE)** 2-8-9 0 ... HaddenFrost[(5)] 1 (S Kirk) *dwlt and wnt lft s: off the pce in 6th: prog on outer 1/2-way: cl enough 1f out: kpt on same pce* **9/2**[2]	73+
	3	nk	**Tropical Paradise (IRE)** 2-9-0 0 ... JimCrowley 8 (P Winkworth) *pressed ldr: led ins fnl 2f to 1f out: one pce* **11/2**[3]	72
5	4	2 1/4	**Nativity**[16] 1866 2-8-11 0 ... TolleyDean[(3)] 3 (J L Spearing) *led to wl over 1f out: grad fdd* **22/1**	64
4	5	1 3/4	**Street Of Hope (USA)**[19] 1762 2-9-0 0 ... EddieAhern 4 (J W Hills) *chsd ldng trio: rdn and nt qckn 2f out: sn btn* **9/2**[2]	58
	6	3 3/4	**Miss Fritton (IRE)** 2-9-0 0 ... RichardHughes 2 (R Hannon) *nvr bttr than 5th and pushed along over 3f out: struggling fnl 2f* **15/8**[1]	45
0	7	6	**Baby Special**[11] 2011 2-9-0 0 ... PhilipRobinson 5 (C G Cox) *outpcd and a bhd in last* **33/1**	23

60.45 secs (-1.15) **Going Correction** -0.35s/f (Firm) **7 Ran SP% 112.0**
Speed ratings (Par 92): **95,92,92,88,85 79,70**
CSF £23.79 TOTE £5.10: £2.30, £2.70; EX 25.80.
Owner Mohammed Jaber **Bred** Lady Jennifer Green And John Eyre **Trained** Newmarket, Suffolk

FOCUS
A modest event, but the front pair put up promising performances and should be capable of better. The race is rated around the balance of those with previous experience.

NOTEBOOK
Crystal Moments, an early foal whose yard won with its first juvenile runner of the season at York last week, is bred to want a bit further in time, but she knew her job and was soon in the stalking position. Driven to the front over a furlong out, she found plenty under pressure and was always doing enough, providing her sire Haafhd with his first winner as a stallion. She will improve for a little further in time, but has plenty of speed and it would not surprise to see her given her chance in the Albany Stakes at Royal Ascot. (op 17-2)
Our Wee Girl(IRE) ◆, a 24,000euros daughter of Choisir, had a tricky draw to overcome and she was done no favours by going left out of the gates. However, she showed good mid-race speed to reach a challenging position although that move took its toll on the rise to the line. This was a highly promising debut and winning an ordinary maiden should prove a formality. (op 4-1)
Tropical Paradise(IRE), a 42,000euros daughter of Verglas, comes from a yard that can ready the odd newcomer and she knew her job. The winner had too much for her though and, although losing out on second, she too can find an ordinary maiden. (op 7-1 tchd 8-1)
Nativity, ultimately well beaten on her debut at Warwick, again showed good early speed and she saw it out a little better this time. An easier 5f at one of the lesser tracks should present an opportunity for her. (op 25-1 tchd 33-1)
Street Of Hope(USA), who shaped with plenty of promise following a slow start on her debut at Lingfield, knew more this time, but she could not pick up under pressure and was disappointing. She may be more of a nursery type now. (op 11-4)
Miss Fritton(IRE), a 76,000gns daughter of Refuse To Bend, is bred to need further than this in time, but her yard has been doing well with their juvenile fillies and she was understandably made favourite. The experience looked needed though as she was never quite going the pace. Not given a hard time, she should learn from this and much better can be expected next time, possibly over 6f. (op 7-4 tchd 2-1 in places)
Baby Special, always outpaced over 6f on debut, was not helped by this drop back to 5f and she is clearly going to be more of a nursery type. (op 20-1)

2310 PANMURE GORDON CORPORATE FINANCE H'CAP 1m 6f
6:30 (6:32) (Class 4) (0-85,84) 3-Y-O **£5,828** (£1,734; £866; £432) **Stalls** High

Form				RPR
0-1	1		**Amerigo (IRE)**[23] 1690 3-9-9 **84** ... PhilipRobinson 9 (M A Jarvis) *t.k.h: hld up in 6th: plenty to do whn prog wl over 2f out: sustained effrt to ld ent fnl f: urged along and styd on wl* **13/2**[3]	91+
4-21	2	1 1/2	**Criterion**[18] 1814 3-9-2 **77** ... RyanMoore 6 (Sir Michael Stoute) *trckd ldng trio: clsd fr 3f out: rdn to ld over 1f out: hdd ent fnl f: kpt on* **7/2**[1]	81
0041	3	1 1/2	**Fairfield Flame (GER)**[12] 1962 3-8-2 **66** ...(b) MarcHalford[(3)] 3 (D R C Elsworth) *hld up in 7th: outpcd 3f out: effrt and hung bdly lft 2f out: prog then hung rt ins fnl f: r.o to take 3rd nr fin* **8/1**	68
2-13	4	1 1/4	**Downhiller (IRE)**[25] 1618 3-9-9 **84** ... EddieAhern 10 (J L Dunlop) *t.k.h: trckd ldr 3f: 3rd after: stmbld sltly bnd over 3f out: sn rdn: rallied to press ldr over 1f out: one pce fnl f* **7/2**[1]	84
15	5	2 1/4	**Tourism (IRE)**[25] 1618 3-9-5 **80** ... J-PGuillambert 4 (M Johnston) *mostly in 5th: rdn over 3f out and no imp: kpt on fnl 2f: n.d* **8/1**	77
-540	6	1 1/4	**Hadron Collider (FR)**[9] 2045 3-8-8 **69** ... RichardHughes 5 (R Hannon) *dwlt: hld up in 9th: already wl outpcd whn rdn 3f out: kpt on fnl 2f: nrst fin* **16/1**	64
-214	7	2 3/4	**Kiribati King (IRE)**[12] 1962 3-8-9 **70** ... DarryllHolland 7 (M R Channon) *dwlt: settled in 8th: rdn and wl outpcd 3f out: no real imp after* **9/2**[2]	62
3210	8	nk	**Always Bold (IRE)**[25] 1618 3-9-7 **82** ... JoeFanning 2 (M Johnston) *t.k.h: trckd ldr after 3f: clr of rest 4f out: led over 2f out: hdd & wknd over 1f out* **9/1**	73
2032	9	3 3/4	**Lord's Bidding**[16] 1871 3-8-4 **65** oh3 ...(v) DavidKinsella 8 (R Ingram) *led: kicked on over 4f out: hdd over 2f out: losing pl whn hmpd wl over 1f out: wknd* **20/1**	51
4410	10	41	**Boy On A Swing (USA)**[29] 1543 3-9-3 **78** ...(t) ShaneKelly 1 (J A Osborne) *stdd s and rrd bdly: hld up: a last: wknd wl over 2f out: eased: t.o* **40/1**	6

3m 3.87s (-2.73) **Going Correction** -0.15s/f (Firm) **10 Ran SP% 121.3**
Speed ratings (Par 101): **101,100,99,98,97 96,95,94,92,69**
CSF £30.80 CT £190.95 TOTE £6.00: £1.70, £1.60, £2.80; EX 13.50.
Owner B E Nielsen **Bred** Bjorn Nielsen **Trained** Newmarket, Suffolk

FOCUS
A good handicap that looks sound enough on paper rated through the sixth, despite the steady early pace.

2311 PANMURE GORDON INSTITUTIONAL EQUITIES H'CAP 1m 14y
7:05 (7:08) (Class 4) (0-85,84) 3-Y-O **£5,828** (£1,734; £866; £432) **Stalls** High

Form				RPR
1-44	1		**Mukhber**[23] 1686 3-9-8 **83** ... RHills 7 (J H M Gosden) *hld up in 6th: stdy prog on outer fr 3f out: rdn to ld over 1f out: jnd 100yds out: fnd ex and jst hld on* **11/4**[1]	92
01F-	2	nse	**Redesignation (IRE)**[244] 5551 3-9-9 **84** ... RyanMoore 13 (R Hannon) *hld up in last: plld out and gd prog u.p fr over 2f out: jnd wnr last 100yds: jst pipped* **10/1**	96+
4-03	3	1 1/2	**Ellemujie**[16] 1875 3-9-5 **80** ... JimCrowley 8 (D K Ivory) *hld up in 5th: effrt over 2f out: pressed wnr jst over 1f out: kpt on same pce fnl f* **8/1**	86
0222	4	3	**Brave Hawk**[53] 1082 3-8-13 **74** ...(p) PhilipRobinson 2 (M A Jarvis) *awkward s: wl in rr: drvn and sme prog fr over 2f out: nvr able to rch ldrs but kpt on* **8/1**	73
3-21	5	nk	**Mega Watt (IRE)**[15] 1899 3-9-3 **78** ... AlanMunro 11 (W Jarvis) *hld up wl in rr: last and rdn over 2f out: sme prog over 1f out: styd on steadily fnl f: nvr nrr* **6/1**[3]	76+
166-	6	3/4	**Spell Caster**[223] 6120 3-9-4 **79** ... GeorgeBaker 4 (R M Beckett) *hld up in rr: rdn and sme prog fr over 2f out: edgd rt fr over 1f out: nvr gng pce to rch ldrs* **5/1**[2]	76
501-	7	3 3/4	**Blues Minor (IRE)**[230] 5937 3-9-5 **80** ... RichardHughes 12 (R Hannon) *t.k.h: hld up in midfield: effrt on inner over 2f out: no imp over 1f out: pushed along and one pce fnl f* **14/1**	68
3-54	8	1/2	**Polmaily**[14] 1918 3-9-7 **82** ... EddieAhern 9 (B J Meehan) *trckd ldng trio: effrt to ld 2f out: hdd over 1f out: wknd and eased* **12/1**	69
1400	9	2	**Ike Quebec (FR)**[16] 1875 3-8-10 **76** ...(b[1]) HaddenFrost[(5)] 3 (J R Boyle) *trckd ldng pair: cl enough 2f out: wknd and eased fnl f* **40/1**	58
10	10	1/2	**Rehabilitation**[29] 1546 3-9-3 **78** ... AdamKirby 6 (W R Swinburn) *hld up in rr: u.p and struggling 3f out: sn btn* **22/1**	59
4-41	11	4	**Dr Livingstone (IRE)**[17] 1839 3-9-5 **80** ... ShaneKelly 5 (C R Egerton) *racd freely: led to 2f out: wkng whn n.m.r 1f out* **12/1**	52

0-40 12 19 **St Michael's Mount**[22] 1701 3-8-6 **67** .... JoeFanning 14 —
(M P Tregoning) *plld hrd: pressed ldr tl wknd wl over 2f out: t.o* **25/1**
1m 42.09s (-1.21) **Going Correction** -0.15s/f (Firm) 12 Ran SP% **121.6**
Speed ratings (Par 101): **100,99,98,95,95 94,90,90,88,87 83,64**
CSF £31.68 CT £207.50 TOTE £4.30: £1.30, £4.20, £2.90; EX 32.90 Place 6 £13.48, Place 5 £5.07..
Owner Hamdan Al Maktoum **Bred** Shadwell Estate Company Limited **Trained** Newmarket, Suffolk
FOCUS
A competitive event for three-year-olds and with the finish fought out by the two at the head of the handicap, both lightly-raced improvers, the form looks solid with the third setting a decent standard.
Brave Hawk Official explanation: jockey said colt slipped on leaving stalls
St Michael's Mount Official explanation: jockey said gelding ran too free

2312 HARRY PANMURE GORDON MEMORIAL H'CAP 1m 2f 7y
() (Class 3) (0-90,) 3-Y-O £

2313 PANMURE GORDON LIVERPOOL MAIDEN STKS 1m 2f 7y
() (Class 5) 3-4-Y-O £

2314 PANMURE GORDON STOCKBROKING FILLIES' H'CAP 1m 1f
() (Class 5) (0-75,) 3-Y-O+ £

T/Plt: £11.70 to a £1 stake. T/Qpdt: £1.90 to a £1 stake. JN

2302 GOODWOOD (R-H)
Thursday, May 22

OFFICIAL GOING: Good to firm (9.2)
Wind: Virtually Nil

2324 E B F GOODWOOD.CO.UK MEDIAN AUCTION MAIDEN STKS 6f
2:15 (2:16) (Class 5) 2-Y-O **£3,561** (£1,059; £529; £264) **Stalls** Low

Form RPR
4 1 **Indian Art (IRE)**[17] 1851 2-9-3 0 .... RichardHughes 1 80
(R Hannon) *trckd ldrs: drvn and qcknd over 1f out: styd on strly ins fnl f to ld fnl strides* **4/1**[1]
4 2 shd **In Transit (IRE)**[10] 2054 2-9-3 0 .... TPO'Shea 13 80
(M R Channon) *w'like: chsd ldrs: rdn 2f out: led ins fnl f: styd on u.p: ct fnl strides* **6/1**[2]
3 1 1/2 **Fareer** 2-9-3 0 .... JimmyFortune 9 75
(E A L Dunlop) *w'like: chsd ldrs: slt advantage fr 2f out: sn drvn: hdd ins fnl f: outpcd nr fin* **11/1**
3 4 1/2 **Burning Flute**[8] 2098 2-9-3 0 .... LDettori 16 74
(B J Meehan) *lw: strong: chsd ldrs towards centre of crse: drvn to chal fr 2f out: stl upsides 1f: outpcd ins fnl f* **4/1**[1]
2 5 2 **Rio Royale (IRE)**[19] 1804 2-9-3 0 .... JimCrowley 11 68
(Mrs A J Perrett) *chsd ldrs: rdn 2f out: hrd drvn and one pce appr fnl f* **8/1**[3]
6 hd **Advertise** 2-9-3 0 .... WilliamBuick 15 67
(A M Balding) *w'like: s.i.s: sn rcvrd: in tch towards centre 1/2-way: rdn 2f out: styd on same pce fr over 1f out* **25/1**
7 1 3/4 **Barwell Bridge** 2-9-3 0 .... JamieSpencer 14 62+
(S Kirk) *leggy: slowly away and detached early: gd hdwy towards far side 2f out: nvr quite gng pce to rch ldrs: fdd ins fnl f* **10/1**
8 1/2 **Super Fourteen** 2-9-3 0 .... RyanMoore 12 60
(R Hannon) *w'like: in tch: rdn and effrt 1/2-way: nvr quite gng pce to be competitive: wknd ins fnl f* **10/1**
0 9 1/2 **Josiah Bartlett (IRE)**[17] 1851 2-9-3 0 .... AlanMunro 8 59
(J W Hills) *chsd ldrs: rdn over 2f out: wknd fnl f* **66/1**
10 nk **Zebrano** 2-9-3 0 .... MickyFenton 3 58
(Miss E C Lavelle) *leggy: s.i.s: sn in tch: rdn over 2f out: wknd fnl f* **66/1**
44 11 1 **Lucky Punt**[8] 2098 2-9-3 0 .... TQuinn 2 55
(B G Powell) *lw: in tch: rdn 3f out: one pce fnl 2f* **28/1**
0 12 1/2 **Hatchet Man**[23] 1693 2-9-3 0 .... StephenCarson 4 53
(P Winkworth) *neat: s.i.s: in rr and sn drvn along: styd on fr over 1f out: running on cl home but nvr in contention* **66/1**
13 1 1/2 **Champagne Future** 2-8-12 0 .... AdamKirby 5 44+
(W R Swinburn) *w'like: scope: plld hrd early: a towards rr* **8/1**[3]
14 nk **Charlie Tiger (USA)** 2-9-3 0 .... EddieAhern 7 48+
(C G Cox) *w'like: in tch: rdn 1/2-way: wknd 2f out* **12/1**
0 15 1/2 **Speak The Truth (IRE)**[10] 2049 2-9-3 0 .... AmirQuinn 6 47
(J R Boyle) *plld hrd: chsd ldrs over 3f* **100/1**
0 16 5 **Herecomesbella**[12] 1987 2-8-12 0 .... NeilPollard 10 27
(A P Jarvis) *led tl hdd 2f out: sn wknd* **80/1**
1m 12.25s (0.05) **Going Correction** +0.025s/f (Good) 16 Ran SP% **124.7**
Speed ratings (Par 93): **100,99,97,97,94 94,91,91,90,90 88,88,86,85,85 78**
CSF £26.98 TOTE £4.30: £1.80, £2.70, £3.50; EX 31.80.
Owner Matthew Green **Bred** Michael Woodlock And Seamus Kennedy **Trained** East Everleigh, Wilts
FOCUS
The action took place down the middle of the track. Difficult to rate the form anything special, but a race which should produce a few winners nevertheless.
NOTEBOOK
Indian Art(IRE), fourth over 5f on Polytrack on his debut, took the step up in trip in his stride. Drawn alongside the rail, he steadily tacked across to race in the centre of the track but on the stands'-side flank of the pack. He disputed the lead with over a furlong to run and showed with a definite advantage close home. Epsom's Woodcote Stakes looks a suitable target. (op 6-1)
In Transit(IRE) duly improved from his debut effort over 5f and just missed out after showing prominently throughout. The Channon two-year-olds are in fine form at present and he should soon get off the mark. (op 11-2)
Fareer ◆, who was sold for 160,000gns as a yearling, is out of a multiple winner over 5f. An individual with a bit of scope, he got to the front with around two to run and only gave best inside the last. He was a little green and will be more the finished article next time. (op 9-1)
Burning Flute was expected to improve on his debut effort over 5f last week, with Dettori taking over from a 7lb claimer. He was rather isolated from his high draw and ran a respectable race in the circumstances, sticking on for fourth. (tchd 9-2)
Rio Royale(IRE), runner-up over 5f here on his debut earlier in the month, could not go with the leaders on the run to the final furlong but kept on for a respectable fifth. (op 15-2 tchd 13-2)
Advertise ◆, his sire's first runner, gave ground away when standing still as the stalls opened but soon recovered to chase the eventual fourth down the centre of the track, rather lacking cover. He kept on nicely in the latter stages without being given a hard time and considerable improvement should follow. (op 20-1)
Barwell Bridge ◆ is the first foal of a smart winner at 1m-1m1f and will stay further in time. He was slow to break and ran green in a detached last place until past halfway, before picking up well and making eyecatching headway. The effort flattened out late on but this was a taking introduction. (op 12-1)
Super Fourteen, out of a couple of useful winning sprinters and a stablemate of the winner, made a pleasing first racecourse appearance. (op 14-1)
Hatchet Man Official explanation: jockey said the colt hung left

2325 LETHEBY & CHRISTOPHER FESTIVAL STKS (LISTED RACE) 1m 1f 192y
2:50 (2:54) (Class 1) 4-Y-O+ **£17,031** (£6,456; £3,231; £1,611; £807) **Stalls** High

Form RPR
00-2 1 **Sixties Icon**[18] 1829 5-8-12 114 .... RyanMoore 5 118+
(J Noseda) *lw: trckd ldrs in 3rd: qcknd fr 3f out to ld 2f out: pushed clr fnl f: easily* **8/13**[1]
-403 2 5 **Sweet Lilly**[19] 1801 4-8-10 103 .... RichardHughes 4 106
(M R Channon) *trckd ldrs in cl 5th: hdwy on ins 2f out: shkn up and flashed tail whn qcknd to chse wnr jst ins fnl f: nvr any ch but kpt on for clr 2nd* **11/1**
-323 3 1 1/4 **Spice Route**[14] 1921 4-8-12 106 .... JamieSpencer 3 106
(M L W Bell) *swtg: led: rdn 3f out: hdd 2f out: sn no ch w wnr: outpcd and lost 2nd jst ins fnl f* **15/2**[3]
-261 4 9 **Ballinteni**[13] 1970 6-8-12 93 .... MickyFenton 2 88
(Miss Gay Kelleway) *b.hind: chsd ldr tl ins fnl 3f: sn rdn: wknd qckly 2f out* **33/1**
663- 5 36 **Blue Ksar (FR)**[216] 6298 5-9-1 112 .... (t) LDettori 1 19
(Saeed Bin Suroor) *trckd ldrs in cl 4th: rdn and effrt 3f out: nvr gng pce to be competitive: wknd 2f out: eased whn no ch sn after: t.o* **3/1**[2]
2m 8.31s (0.31) **Going Correction** +0.10s/f (Good) 5 Ran SP% **110.0**
Speed ratings (Par 111): **102,98,97,89,61**
CSF £8.45 TOTE £1.60: £1.10, £3.20; EX 7.70.
Owner Mrs Susan Roy **Bred** Lordship Stud **Trained** Newmarket, Suffolk
FOCUS
The pace was modest. Sixties Icon was entitled to beat the opposition in the fashion he did, with his only serious rival running poorly.
NOTEBOOK
Sixties Icon had not run over a trip this short since taking a Windsor maiden two years ago, but it was never likely to be a problem at this level and he ran out a pretty comfortable winner. This was not the most competitive race of its type, with his market rival failing to give his running, but the fluent victory will have boosted his confidence. He is set to revert to 1m4f in the Hardwicke Stakes at Ascot next, with the Arlington Million, back at this trip, a possible target later on. (op 5-6)
Sweet Lilly, back up in trip, stayed on from the rear in the straight to grab second in the final half-furlong, but never had a chance with the favourite. Not for the first time she showed signs of temperament. (tchd 14-1)
Spice Route, who became rather worked up before the race, was taken to the front in a race which lacked an obvious front runner. He set an ordinary pace but could do nothing about the winner easing past at the quarter-mile pole. (op 7-1 tchd 8-1)
Ballinteni, winner of a Ripon handicap off a mark of 87 last time, was very much up against it in this company. (tchd 40-1 tchd 50-1 in a place)
Blue Ksar(FR), making his seasonal reappearance, failed to pick up when brought under pressure and was eased right down with Dettori appearing concerned. The horse seemed fine afterwards, but this was obviously not his running and the fast ground seemed the likely reason. Official explanation: jockey said the horse was unsuited by the going (op 5-2)

2326 THOMAS EGGAR STKS (H'CAP) 5f
3:25 (3:25) (Class 2) (0-100,98) 4-Y-O+ **£10,361** (£3,083; £1,540; £769) **Stalls** Low

Form RPR
6-60 1 **Elhamri**[19] 1802 4-8-5 **85** .... RichardKingscote 2 95
(S Kirk) *b.hind: trckd ldrs: led appr fnl f: hrd drvn and hld on wl thrght fnl f* **5/1**[2]
34-1 2 nk **Safari Mischief**[19] 1802 5-8-3 **86** .... LukeMorris(3) 4 95
(P Winkworth) *chsd ldrs: rdn and effrt whn rdr dropped reins briefly appr fnl f: kpt on strly to press wnr ins fnl f: no ex cl home* **15/8**[1]
00-3 3 1 3/4 **Sweet Afton (IRE)**[23] 1698 5-8-6 **86** .... WilliamBuick 7 89
(M S Saunders) *outpcd towards rr: drvn along 1/2-way: styd on to cl on ldrs and edgd lft ins fnl f: nvr gng pce to trble ldng duo* **6/1**[3]
-300 4 3/4 **Woodcote (IRE)**[12] 1985 6-8-4 **84** oh2 .... (p) JimmyQuinn 6 84
(P R Chamings) *pressed ldrs: led ins fnl 2f: hdd appr fnl f: wknd cl home* **14/1**
04-0 5 3/4 **Golden Dixie (USA)**[12] 1985 9-8-12 **92** .... RyanMoore 5 89
(R A Harris) *lw: in rr and outpcd: rdn 1/2-way: r.o ins fnl f but nvr gng pce to be competitive* **5/1**[2]
200- 6 3/4 **The Jobber (IRE)**[231] 5953 7-9-4 **98** .... SteveDrowne 1 93
(M Blanshard) *lw: chsd ldrs: rdn over 2f out: wknd fnl f* **13/2**
-300 7 1 3/4 **Classic Encounter (IRE)**[5] 2211 5-8-10 **90** .... RichardMullen 3 78
(D M Simcock) *swtg: sn led: hdd ins fnl 2f: hung rt u.p and nt keen fnl f* **10/1**
57.34 secs (-1.06) **Going Correction** +0.025s/f (Good) 7 Ran SP% **111.5**
Speed ratings (Par 109): **109,108,105,104,103 102,99**
CSF £14.06 TOTE £7.30: £3.40, £1.30; EX 18.70.
Owner Norman Ormiston **Bred** Highfield Stud Ltd **Trained** Upper Lambourn, Berks
FOCUS
Not a great turnout for the money. The winner is rated to the pick of his 3yo form, and it was another slight step up from the second.
NOTEBOOK
Elhamri took a bump leaving the stalls before racing close up. He got to the front approaching the final furlong and held on well from the favourite. He reportedly failed to grow at three after winning the Windsor Castle Stakes and the Weatherbys Super Sprint as a juvenile, but he has been slipping down the handicap and looks to have found his level again.. (op 7-1)
Safari Mischief was raised 6lb for his win over course and distance at the beginning of the month. He clearly likes this track and ran well again, just failing to peg back the winner. His jockey momentarily dropped his reins but it did not affect the outcome. (op 2-1 tchd 9-4)
Sweet Afton(IRE), third in a Bath Listed race on soft ground last time, could never get close enough to land a blow on this different surface but was running on at the end. (op 5-1 tchd 9-2)
Woodcote(IRE) wore cheekpieces for the first time since this race last year, although he has tried other forms of headgear in the meantime. He is hard to win with. Official explanation: jockey said the gelding lost a shoe
Golden Dixie(USA) found himself outpaced at the back of the field and although he did pick up inside the last to pass a couple of rivals, it all came much too late. Bigger fields than this suit him. (op 11-2 tchd 13-2)
The Jobber(IRE) had not been seen since October. (op 6-1 tchd 11-2)
Classic Encounter(IRE) got into a state in the preliminaries and dropped away pretty tamely. He remains one to be wary of. (op 8-1)

2327 M-REAL STKS (H'CAP) 1m 3f
4:00 (4:01) (Class 4) (0-85,80) 3-Y-O **£4,533** (£1,348; £674; £336) **Stalls** Low

Form RPR
44-0 1 **Celtic Dragon**[23] 1695 3-8-12 **74** .... JimCrowley 6 78+
(Mrs A J Perrett) *hld up in rr: rdn and swtchd lft to outside over 2f out: styd on u.p to ld fnl 100yds: hld on all out* **10/1**

-123 **2** ¾ **Summer Winds**[18] 1839 3-9-2 **78**.............................. JamieSpencer 2 81+
(T G Mills) *led 1f: hld up in tch: trckd ldrs and gng smoothly whn n.m.r 2f out: rdn and kpt on fr over 1f out: styd on strly ins fnl f to take 2nd cl home but nt rch wnr* **7/2**[3]

3-21 **3** nk **Top Ticket (IRE)**[23] 1695 3-9-4 **80**.............................. RichardMullen 1 82
(D M Simcock) *swtg: chsd ldrs: led 3f out: rdn over 2f out: styd on u.p tl hdd fnl 100yds: lost 2nd cl home* **15/2**

01-4 **4** 1 ½ **Trianon**[18] 1839 3-9-2 **78**.............................. SteveDrowne 4 78
(R Charlton) *chsd ldr 7f out: drvn to chal fr 3f out tl wknd ins fnl f* **9/4**[2]

6-00 **5** 2 **Forget It**[24] 1684 3-8-6 **68**.............................. RichardHughes 7 65
(R Hannon) *lw: hld up in rr: hdwy fr 5f out: trcking ldrs but drvn whn n.m.r 2f out: swtchd rt and sn no imp u.p* **7/4**[1]

60-0 **6** 13 **Shaama Rose (FR)**[12] 2015 3-8-10 **72**.............................. EdwardCreighton 5 46
(M R Channon) *a towards rr: no ch fr 3f out* **50/1**

62-0 **7** 5 **Funseeker (UAE)**[109] 419 3-8-8 **70**.............................. IanMongan 3 36
(Jamie Poulton) *s.i.s: drvn to ld after 1f: hdd 3f out: wknd over 2f out* **50/1**

2m 28.68s (0.38) **Going Correction** +0.10s/f (Good) **7** Ran SP% **114.1**
Speed ratings (Par 101): **102,101,101,100,98 89,85**
CSF £44.56 TOTE £12.80: £4.20, £1.80; EX 61.20.
Owner M Dawson & Kevin Mercer **Bred** Usk Valley Stud **Trained** Pulborough, W Sussex

FOCUS
A fair handicap in which the winner appreciated the quicker ground and produced a big turnaround with the third on their Bath running. The second and fourth ran close to their previous Salisbury form.
Celtic Dragon Official explanation: trainer said, regarding the improved form shown, colt appeared to be better suited by the good to firm going

2328 ELECTROLUX CENTRE OF EXCELLENCE KITCHENS MAIDEN FILLIES' STKS 1m 1f
4:35 (4:37) (Class 5) 3-Y-O **£3,238** (£963; £481; £240) **Stalls** High

Form RPR
5 **1** **Casilda (IRE)**[31] 1525 3-9-0 0.............................. PaulDoe 5 76
(W J Knight) *w'like: trckd ldrs: drvn and kpt on to press wnr 1f out: styd on wl to ld fnl 50yds: kpt on* **16/1**

00 **2** ½ **Sunny Peace**[17] 1876 3-9-0 0.............................. TQuinn 7 75
(B G Powell) *led: drvn over 2f out: kpt advantage tl hdd fnl 50yds: no ex* **80/1**

3-4 **3** ½ **My Aunt Fanny**[22] 1715 3-9-0 0.............................. LPKeniry 6 74
(A M Balding) *in tch: hrd drvn and hdwy over 2f out: styd on u.p fnl f but nt pce to press ldng duo* **7/1**[3]

2-30 **4** hd **Madame Hoi (IRE)**[18] 1833 3-9-0 90.............................. RyanMoore 12 74+
(M R Channon) *mid-div: rdn over 2f out: swtchd lft to outside over 1f out: r.o strly ins fnl f: gng on cl home* **11/4**[2]

40- **5** 1 ½ **Shesha Bear**[188] 6827 3-9-0 0.............................. DO'Donohoe 4 70
(W R Muir) *chsd ldrs: rdn over 2f out: kpt on fnl f but nvr quite gng pce to chal* **66/1**

0-2 **6** nk **Finmore Queen (USA)**[138] 52 3-9-0 0.............................. JamieSpencer 11 70+
(J R Fanshawe) *t.k.h: in tch: n.m.r 2f out and edgd lft: swtchd rt and n.m.r 1f out and qcknd to chse ldrs: sn one pce* **7/1**[3]

4-4 **7** 1 **Quirina**[13] 1946 3-9-0 0.............................. JimmyFortune 14 67+
(J H M Gosden) *chsd ldrs: rdn 2f out: wknd ins fnl f and eased cl home* **7/4**[1]

04- **8** nse **Stormy View (USA)**[267] 4947 3-9-0 0.............................. RobertHavlin 10 67+
(J H M Gosden) *s.i.s: in rr: pushed along and hdwy over 2f out: styd on fnl f but nvr gng pce to be competitive* **16/1**

9 1 **Look To This Day** 3-9-0 0.............................. SteveDrowne 8 65+
(R Charlton) *w'like: in rr: edgd lft 4f out: styd on thrght fnl 2f but nvr in contention* **33/1**

5-44 **10** 1 ¼ **Lush (IRE)**[19] 1803 3-9-0 76.............................. RichardHughes 9 62
(R Hannon) *in tch: rdn and effrt 2f out: nvr quite gng pce to rch ldrs: wknd fnl f* **12/1**

11 nk **Romantic Retreat** 3-9-0 0.............................. NickyMackay 1 62+
(L M Cumani) *w'like: bit bkwd: in rr tl mod prog fnl f* **33/1**

12 1 ½ **Sevenna (FR)** 3-9-0 0.............................. TedDurcan 3 58+
(H R A Cecil) *in rr whn bmpd and pushed lft bnd 4f out: mod prog ins fnl f* **20/1**

0 **13** 10 **Thirtyfourthstreet (IRE)**[3] 2257 3-9-0 0.............................. RichardMullen 13 36
(W R Muir) *chsd ldrs: rdn 5f out: wknd 3f out* **100/1**

14 2 ¾ **Lady Special (IRE)** 3-9-0 0.............................. AdamKirby 2 30
(C G Cox) *w'like: sn rdn in rr: a bhd* **50/1**

1m 58.0s (1.70) **Going Correction** +0.10s/f (Good) **14** Ran SP% **123.8**
Speed ratings (Par 96): **96,95,95,94,93 93,92,92,91,90 90,88,79,77**
CSF £956.03 TOTE £19.70: £4.50, £11.50, £2.30; EX 2340.30.
Owner Mrs P G M Jamison **Bred** David Jamison Bloodstock And G Roddick **Trained** Patching, W Sussex

FOCUS
An ordinary maiden at best, and muddling form with it an advantage to race on the pace. The form is rated around the third and fourth.

2329 O'SULLEVANS CAFE STKS (H'CAP) 7f
5:10 (5:10) (Class 4) (0-80,78) 4-Y-O+ **£4,533** (£1,348; £674; £336) **Stalls** High

Form RPR
4053 **1** **Councellor (FR)**[9] 2083 6-8-10 **70**.............................. (t) MickyFenton 3 81
(Stef Liddiard) *led: drvn 2f out: styd on wl whn strly chal thrght fnl f* **9/2**[2]

1-05 **2** hd **Golden Desert (IRE)**[12] 2013 4-9-3 **77**.............................. JimmyFortune 9 87
(T G Mills) *chsd ldrs: wnt 2nd 3f out: drvn and str chal fr over 1f out but a jst hld by wnr thrght fnl f* **7/2**[1]

-060 **3** 5 **Blue Charm**[5] 2203 4-8-13 **73**.............................. RichardHughes 7 70
(S Kirk) *hld up towards rr: hdwy and swtchd rt ins fnl 2f: one pce over 1f out and nvr any ch w ldng duo* **8/1**

3-50 **4** shd **Titan Triumph**[19] 1809 4-9-4 **78**.............................. (t) PaulDoe 8 74
(W J Knight) *chsd ldrs: rdn over 2f out and no imp: one pce fr over 1f out* **9/2**[2]

0140 **5** 1 ¼ **Hessian (IRE)**[19] 1809 4-8-5 **65**.............................. RichardKingscote 2 58
(M D Squance) *in rr: rdn and sme hdwy over 2f out: nvr rchd ldrs and sn btn* **16/1**

1510 **6** 1 **Millfield (IRE)**[8] 2101 5-8-13 **73**.............................. JimCrowley 4 63
(P R Chamings) *in rr: rdn 3f out: styd on fr over 1f out and kpt on ins fnl f: gng on cl home* **10/1**

0-02 **7** nse **Rydal Mount (IRE)**[17] 1872 5-8-12 **72**.............................. TQuinn 10 62
(W S Kittow) *lw: stmbld bdly s: chsd ldrs 4f out: rdn 3f out: wknd 2f out* **7/1**[3]

40-0 **8** 8 **Coeur Courageux (FR)**[14] 1936 6-8-10 **70**.............................. WilliamBuick 1 38
(G L Moore) *chsd wnr to 3f out: sn wknd* **20/1**

0262 **9** 8 **Apache Dawn**[24] 1670 4-8-10 **70**.............................. (be) RyanMoore 5 17
(G L Moore) *a towards rr* **7/1**[3]

1m 28.25s (0.85) **Going Correction** +0.10s/f (Good) **9** Ran SP% **114.4**
Speed ratings (Par 105): **99,98,93,92,91 90,90,81,72**
CSF £20.43 CT £121.79 TOTE £5.50: £1.90, £1.40, £3.20; EX 25.30 Trifecta £353.10 Pool: £596.80. 1.20 winning units..
Owner ownaracehorse.co.uk **Bred** Janus Bloodstock & Pontchartrain Stud **Trained** Great Shefford, Berks

FOCUS
Pretty modest form, and not the most solid with many of these more at home on the sand. The first two came clear.
Rydal Mount(IRE) Official explanation: jockey reported that the mare stumbled soon after start.

2330 TURFTV.CO.UK APPRENTICE H'CAP 5f
5:45 (5:45) (Class 5) (0-70,65) 4-Y-O+ **£3,238** (£963; £481; £240) **Stalls** Low

Form RPR
1400 **1** **Crimson Fern (IRE)**[8] 2102 4-9-5 **65**.............................. PatrickHills 8 84
(M S Saunders) *hld up in tch: hdwy to ld jst ins fnl 2f: c clr ins fnl f: comf* **8/1**

2032 **2** 3 ¼ **Rocker**[25] 1646 4-8-13 **62**.............................. (b[1]) MCGeran[(3)] 7 69
(B R Johnson) *chsd ldrs: rdn and ev ch ins fnl 2f: kpt on u.p to hold narrow 2nd thrght fnl f but no ch w wnr* **3/1**[2]

40-2 **3** shd **Matterofact (IRE)**[8] 2102 5-8-7 **53**.............................. HaddenFrost 2 60
(M S Saunders) *chsd ldrs: rdn and ev ch ins fnl 2f: styd on to dispute 2nd ins fnl f but nvr any ch w wnr* **5/2**[1]

-230 **4** 3 **Azygous**[12] 1997 5-9-2 **62**.............................. JamieJones 6 58
(J Akehurst) *chsd ldrs: rdn to chal 2f out: wknd ins fnl f* **8/1**

0050 **5** ½ **Harrison's Flyer (IRE)**[3] 2242 7-8-12 **63**.............................. (p) RossAtkinson[(5)] 1 57
(J M Bradley) *b. rdn and pushed along towards rr 1/2-way: nvr gng pce to be competitive* **16/1**

00-3 **6** nk **Puskas (IRE)**[17] 1865 5-8-0 **51** oh1.............................. (b) PietroRomeo[(5)] 5 44
(J M Bradley) *sn pushed along: outpcd most of way* **8/1**

0-00 **7** hd **Peopleton Brook**[12] 1997 6-8-7 **56**.............................. RichardEvans[(3)] 3 48
(J M Bradley) *s.i.s: rdn and sme prog on outside 2f out: sn wknd* **12/1**

2101 **8** 1 ¾ **Trinculo (IRE)**[12] 2010 11-9-0 **65**.............................. (b) DavidProbert[(5)] 4 51
(R A Harris) *b.hind: sn led: hdd & wknd ins fnl 2f* **5/1**[3]

58.03 secs (-0.37) **Going Correction** +0.025s/f (Good) **8** Ran SP% **117.1**
Speed ratings (Par 103): **103,97,97,92,92 91,91,88**
CSF £33.13 CT £79.40 TOTE £9.50: £2.80, £1.30, £1.30; EX 41.90 Place 6: £209.16, Place 5: £105.00..
Owner M S Saunders **Bred** David Brickley **Trained** Green Ore, Somerset

FOCUS
Only a modest handicap, but Crimson Fern produced a big step up and was quite impressive. The form is sound enough.
T/Jkpt: Not won. T/Plt: £154.70 to a £1 stake. Pool: £78,291.71. 369.30 winning tickets. T/Qpdt: £53.90 to a £1 stake. Pool: £3,227.50. 44.30 winning tickets. ST

1986 HAYDOCK (L-H)
Thursday, May 22

OFFICIAL GOING: Good to firm (firm in places)
Wind: Fresh, behind Weather: Overcast

2331 BLACKPOOL TOWER AND CIRCUS MAIDEN AUCTION STKS 5f
2:25 (2:27) (Class 5) 2-Y-O **£2,590** (£770; £385; £192) **Stalls** Centre

Form RPR
3 **1** **Fivefootnumberone (IRE)**[14] 1924 2-8-9 0.............................. GrahamGibbons 7 81+
(J J Quinn) *pressed ldr: rdn to ld jst over 1f out: r.o wl* **11/8**[1]

5 **2** 1 ¼ **Rievaulx World**[14] 1924 2-8-13 0.............................. NCallan 9 80+
(K A Ryan) *racd keenly: led: rdn and hdd jst over 1f out: nt qckn ins fnl f* **4/1**[3]

2 **3** 1 ¾ **Camelot Communion (IRE)**[31] 1515 2-8-11 0.............................. RoystonFfrench 8 72
(Mrs A Duffield) *dwlt: sn chsd ldrs: rdn over 1f out: kpt on same pce fnl f* **9/4**[2]

4 3 ¼ **Lookafternumberone (IRE)** 2-8-13 0.............................. PaulHanagan 4 62+
(J G Given) *chsd ldrs and rn green: rdn along 1/2-way: outpcd over 1f out* **12/1**

5 5 **Charismatic Charli (IRE)** 2-8-9 0.............................. FrancisNorton 2 40+
(P W D'Arcy) *rn green: sn outpcd: nvr on terms* **11/1**

6 15 **That Boy Ronaldo** 2-8-5 0 ow1.............................. GregFairley 3 —
(A Berry) *s.s: racd keenly towards rr: pushed along 3f out: lost tch wl over 1f out* **18/1**

59.80 secs (-0.70) **Going Correction** -0.30s/f (Firm) **6** Ran SP% **114.2**
Speed ratings (Par 93): **93,91,88,83,75 51**
CSF £7.56 TOTE £2.80: £1.50, £2.10; EX 5.90.
Owner Maxilead Limited **Bred** Arne Stang **Trained** Settrington, N Yorks

FOCUS
Probably a fair event of its type, the three with experience having it to themselves throughout and all rated as improvers. The winner managed to dip under the one-minute barrier, and is one to keep on-side.

NOTEBOOK
Fivefootnumberone(IRE) ◆ confirmed the promise of his debut run at Chester and clocked a fast time in the process. He is a strong sort with scope but nicely balanced to boot. He can go on to better things. (op 5-4 tchd 6-4)
Rievaulx World finished under a length behind the winner at Chester when both horses made their racecourse bow but could not get any closer here. He changed his legs a few times inside the last 2f in a manner which suggested he was feeling the ground. (tchd 10-3)
Camelot Communion(IRE) was well supported in the market but did not really improve much for her debut second at Pontefract. (op 7-2)
Lookafternumberone(IRE) was not at all knocked about and will do better.
Charismatic Charli(IRE) was always outpaced and never really balanced. He should come on for the experience. (op 9-1)

2332 MOONDARRA STKS (H'CAP) 1m 6f
3:00 (3:00) (Class 4) (0-80,78) 4-Y-O+ **£5,180** (£1,541; £770; £384) **Stalls** Low

Form RPR
34-2 **1** **Bukit Tinggi (IRE)**[19] 1798 4-9-5 **74**.............................. PhilipRobinson 6 87+
(M A Jarvis) *racd keenly in midfield: hdwy over 3f out: led over 2f out: rdn over 1f out: r.o wl and in command fnl f comf* **9/4**[1]

1214 **2** 2 ½ **Inspirina (IRE)**[13] 1947 4-9-5 **74**.............................. PaulHanagan 4 80
(R Ford) *s.i.s: hld up in rr: hdwy over 3f out: rdn to chse ldrs and hung lft over 1f out: styd on to take 2nd post: nt trble wnr* **8/1**

0-50 **3** shd **Hawridge King**[17] 1877 6-9-2 **76**.............................. JamesMillman[(5)] 7 82
(W S Kittow) *hld up: hdwy over 3f out: chsd ldrs over 2f out: wnt 2nd 1f out: no imp on wnr fnl f: lost 2nd post* **11/2**

1-04 **4** ½ **Plane Painter (IRE)**[12] 1984 4-9-4 **73**.................... GregFairley 9 78
(M Johnston) *prom: led 9f out: rdn and hdd over 2f out: styd on same pce after* **9/2**[3]

50/4 **5** 1¾ **Markington**[12] 1998 5-8-12 **67**....................(p) FergusSweeney 5 70
(P Bowen) *midfield: rdn 4f out: hdwy over 3f out: chalng over 2f out: kpt on u.p after 1f no ex towards fin* **12/1**

/40- **6** 4 **Mith Hill**[35] 2860 7-9-9 **78**.................... StephenDonohoe 2 75
(Ian Williams) *hld up: pushed along 4f out: kpt on fr 1f out: nvr on terms w ldrs* **33/1**

/551 **7** 4½ **Hill Billy Rock (IRE)**[20] 1773 5-8-12 **70**.................... PJMcDonald(3) 8 61
(G A Swinbank) *chsd ldrs: rdn to take 2nd briefly 4f out: sn hung lft: wknd 2f out* **7/2**[2]

00/4 **8** 17 **Mt Desert**[13] 1972 6-9-1 **70**.................... PaulMulrennan 3 37
(E W Tuer) *chsd ldrs: rdn 4f out: wknd over 3f out* **40/1**

3-32 **9** 27 **Command Marshal (FR)**[12] 2012 5-9-6 **75**.................... NCallan 1 4
(M J Scudamore) *led: hdd 9f out: remained prom tl wknd over 3f out* **16/1**

3m 1.56s (-2.74) **Going Correction** -0.05s/f (Good) **9** Ran SP% **116.6**
Speed ratings (Par 105): **105,103,103,103,102 99,97,87,72**
CSF £21.59 CT £89.68 TOTE £3.30: £1.30, £2.60, £2.60; EX 20.10.
Owner H R H Sultan Ahmad Shah **Bred** Hrh Sultan Ahmad Shah **Trained** Newmarket, Suffolk

FOCUS
Not a bad race by any means and, although not the most solid, with the three four-year-olds in the race finishing first, second and fourth, the form looks like it will carry well into the future.

2333 WOODWARD FOODSERVICE H'CAP 7f 30y
3:35 (3:36) (Class 4) (0-80,80) 3-Y-O £4,533 (£1,348; £674; £336) **Stalls** Low

Form RPR

1-00 **1** **Elysee Palace (IRE)**[37] 1381 3-9-0 **76**.................... PhilipRobinson 10 80
(M A Jarvis) *a.p: led narrowly jst over 2f out: rdn over 1f out: r.o whn pressed ins fnl f: a doing enough* **12/1**

2 **2** ½ **San Jose City (IRE)**[20] 1781 3-8-10 **72**.................... DavidAllan 8 75
(D Carroll) *midfield: hdwy over 2f out: str chal ins fnl f: r.o u.p* **20/1**

04-1 **3** 1½ **Blindspin**[29] 1556 3-9-2 **78**.................... PhillipMakin 13 80+
(M Dods) *hld up: hdwy whn nt clr run 2f out and again over 1f out: prog ins fnl f: styd on wl towards fin wout rching front pair* **16/1**

233- **4** ¾ **Green Diamond**[165] 7084 3-9-1 **77**.................... GregFairley 6 74
(M Johnston) *chsd ldrs: rdn over 2f out: styd on same pce fnl f* **9/1**

022- **5** shd **Majeen**[205] 6574 3-9-0 **76**.................... MichaelHills 3 73+
(W J Haggas) *racd keenly: trckd ldrs: hung lft fr 3f out: kpt on same pce fnl f* **10/3**[2]

16- **6** hd **Brasingaman Hifive**[215] 6328 3-9-1 **77**.................... GrahamGibbons 11 73
(Mrs G S Rees) *midfield: hdwy on outside 2f out: rdn 1f out: kpt on wl fnl f wout troubling ldrs* **50/1**

-1 **7** 1¾ **Mr Macattack**[115] 343 3-8-10 **72**.................... KerrinMcEvoy 5 63+
(N J Vaughan) *dwlt: in rr: rdn and hung lft fr over 1f out: kpt on: nvr able to chal* **7/1**[3]

505- **8** ¾ **Shanafarahan (IRE)**[209] 6469 3-8-7 **69**.................... PaulHanagan 4 58
(T P Tate) *racd keenly in midfield: lost pl over 2f out: no imp after* **18/1**

-440 **9** hd **Kool Katie**[12] 2002 3-8-4 **66** oh3.................... LiamJones 7 55
(Mrs G S Rees) *s.s: hld up: effrt over 2f out: one pce fr over 1f out:* **50/1**

42-1 **10** 3¼ **Thannaan (USA)**[30] 1535 3-9-4 **80**.................... RHills 2 60+
(B W Hills) *led: hdd jst over 2f out: sn rdn: losing pl whn n.m.r and hmpd jst ins fnl f: sn eased* **6/4**[1]

200- **11** 6 **La Chicaluna**[226] 6075 3-9-4 **80**.................... RoystonFfrench 1 44
(J G Given) *racd keenly: prom: rdn 2f out: sn wknd* **14/1**

03-3 **12** ½ **Topflightrebellion**[136] 74 3-8-4 **66**.................... DaleGibson 12 29
(Mrs G S Rees) *a bhd: pushed along over 3f out: nvr on terms* **100/1**

1m 28.99s (-1.21) **Going Correction** -0.05s/f (Good) **12** Ran SP% **120.8**
Speed ratings (Par 101): **104,103,101,100,100 100,98,97,97,93 86,86**
CSF £232.51 CT £3820.94 TOTE £16.00: £4.10, £5.20, £4.30; EX 322.10.
Owner Sheikh Ahmed Al Maktoum **Bred** Darley **Trained** Newmarket, Suffolk

FOCUS
A decent handicap for three-year-olds, and with the lack of early pace and the hot favourite not giving his true running, the form is slightly muddling and best rated around the fourth and fifth.
Thannaan(USA) Official explanation: trainer had no explanation for the poor form shown

2334 BANK OF SCOTLAND CORPORATE STKS (H'CAP) 1m 30y
4:10 (4:11) (Class 3) (0-90,89) 4-Y-O+ £8,095 (£2,408; £1,203; £601) **Stalls** Low

Form RPR

-210 **1** **Ansells Pride (IRE)**[15] 1910 5-8-12 **83**.................... TomEaves 3 90+
(B Smart) *sn led: rdn over 1f out: kpt on ins fnl f* **4/1**[3]

00-6 **2** ¾ **Danehillsundance (IRE)**[75] 834 4-9-4 **89**.................... KerrinMcEvoy 2 94+
(S Parr) *hld up: rdn and hdwy over 1f out: swtchd rt ins fnl f: r.o wl and gaining at fin* **3/1**[2]

6203 **3** ½ **Lord Theo**[10] 2057 4-8-8 **79**.................... NCallan 6 83
(N P Littmoden) *a.p: chalng 2f out: sn rdn: nt qckn ins fnl f* **13/2**

45-0 **4** ¾ **Russian Epic**[17] 1857 4-8-7 **78** ow1.................... PhilipRobinson 5 80
(M A Jarvis) *racd keenly: a.p: rdn 2f out: kpt on same pce ins fnl f* **8/1**

-056 **5** 1¼ **Hoh Wotanite**[14] 1920 5-8-12 **83**....................(v) GrahamGibbons 1 82
(R Hollinshead) *broke wl: trckd ldrs: rdn 2f out: styd on same pce tl no ex wl ins fnl f* **20/1**

0000 **6** 1¼ **Ella Woodcock (IRE)**[14] 1920 4-8-11 **82**.................... DavidAllan 4 79
(E J Alston) *midfield: lost pl over 3f out: rdn over 1f out: hung rt ent fnl f: kpt on but nvr able to chal* **14/1**

1-33 **7** 3¼ **Major Magpie (IRE)**[26] 1612 6-8-9 **80**.................... PhillipMakin 8 69
(M Dods) *hld up: effrt over 2f out: no imp fr wl over 1f out* **5/2**[1]

/320 **8** shd **Claret And Amber**[100] 531 6-8-6 **77**.................... PaulHanagan 7 66
(R A Fahey) *cl up: stdd after 2f: racd off pce tl hdwy over 3f out: rdn and wknd over 1f out* **16/1**

1m 41.83s (-1.97) **Going Correction** -0.05s/f (Good) **8** Ran SP% **115.3**
Speed ratings (Par 107): **107,106,105,105,103 102,99,99**
CSF £16.61 CT £75.96 TOTE £5.20: £1.60, £1.40, £2.30; EX 21.20.
Owner Ansells Of Watford **Bred** E Lonergan **Trained** Hambleton, N Yorks

FOCUS
A decent handicap but they only went a modest pace early, before things quickened up appreciably in the second half of the contest and the final time was not at all bad. The winner got the run of the race whilst the runner-up did not and, with the third setting the level, generally this was a contest which favoured those that raced handily.

NOTEBOOK
Ansells Pride(IRE) ◆ showed his Beverley running to be all wrong and successfully reverted to the tactics which had previously served him so well at Musselburgh. He dictated virtually from the start, quickened from the front when he wanted and was always holding his rivals. Obviously a versatile sort when it comes to ground conditions, this was a decent effort off an 8lb higher mark than for his last win and he still seems to be progressing. (op 9-2 tchd 5-1 in places)

Danehillsundance(IRE) ◆, back on his last winning mark and making his debut for the yard, was patiently ridden and can possibly be counted unlucky as he was held in for a crucial length of time by Russian Epic when he was trying to angle out for a run. By the time he did get out it was just too late and it should not be long before he gains compensation. (op 4-1)

Lord Theo, still 1lb higher than for his last win more than a year ago, soon took his usual handy position but although he tried his best he could never quite get to grips with the winner and was deined second place close to the line. He is yet to win beyond 7f, but he does stay this trip and more and what he needs most is a little help from the Handicapper. (op 7-1)

Russian Epic's trainer and jockey had landed the two previous contests so were hardly lacking in confidence, but he did not help his chances by taking a grip in the slowly run early part of the race and when eventually asked for his effort, there was not a lot there. He may well have found this ground plenty quick enough.

Hoh Wotanite was never far away against the inside rail and tried his best, but once off the bridle he could never really land much of a blow. The early pace here would not have suited him, but although he has run some creditable races on turf he is at his best in strongly run races around Wolverhampton. (op 16-1 tchd 14-1)

Major Magpie(IRE) is another who was done no favours by the modest early pace and he also saw far too much daylight down the wide outside in the home straight. (op 11-4 tchd 3-1)

2335 LOUIS TUSSAUDS BLACKPOOL H'CAP 1m 2f 120y
4:45 (4:45) (Class 5) (0-75,73) 4-Y-O+ £2,590 (£770; £385; £192) **Stalls** High

Form RPR

04-3 **1** **Tufton**[93] 309 5-9-4 **73**.................... StephenDonohoe 2 84
(Ian Williams) *hld up: hdwy 3f out: chsd ldr 1f out: r.o to ld towards fin* **14/1**

-101 **2** shd **Cherri Fosfate**[13] 1968 4-8-9 **64**.................... DavidAllan 7 75
(D Carroll) *in tch: rdn to ld over 1f out: r.o u.p: hdd towards fin* **7/1**[3]

4006 **3** 4½ **Sforzando**[13] 1963 7-8-11 **66**.................... TomEaves 8 69
(Mrs L Stubbs) *in tch: rdn over 3f out: hdwy on outside over 1f out: styd on to take 3rd wl ins fnl f: no imp on front pair* **9/2**[2]

6-62 **4** 2¼ **Pitbull**[12] 2001 5-8-9 **64**....................(p) LiamJones 4 63
(Mrs G S Rees) *s.i.s: hld up: hdwy over 3f out: rdn over 1f out: kpt on one pce fnl f* **8/1**

20-6 **5** shd **Nightspot**[17] 1874 7-9-1 **70**.................... NCallan 1 69
(Eve Johnson Houghton) *led: rdn over 2f out: hdd over 1f out: fdd wl ins fnl f* **4/1**[1]

20-0 **6** 1¾ **Mulaazem**[13] 1963 5-8-7 **62**....................(t) AdrianTNicholls 6 58
(J Mackie) *in tch: rdn to chal 2f out: nt qckn over 1f out: wknd ins fnl f* **9/1**

34-0 **7** 1 **Snark (IRE)**[6] 2153 5-9-2 **71**.................... PaulEddery 10 68
(Simon Earle) *bhd: rdn over 2f out: eased whn no real imp wl ins fnl f* **22/1**

5060 **8** 1¾ **Byron Bay**[12] 2007 6-9-0 **69**.................... DeanMcKeown 3 60
(R C Guest) *hld up: rdn over 2f out: sn hung lft: nvr on terms* **25/1**

00-2 **9** hd **Boo**[23] 1711 6-9-4 **73**.................... MichaelHills 9 63
(J W Unett) *racd keenly: trckd ldrs: rdn and hung lft 2f out: wknd over 1f out* **7/1**[3]

43-4 **10** 6 **Crystal Prince**[13] 1963 4-9-3 **72**.................... PaulHanagan 5 51
(T P Tate) *prom: rdn over 2f out: wknd over 1f out* **9/2**[2]

2m 14.82s (-1.88) **Going Correction** -0.05s/f (Good) **10** Ran SP% **117.3**
Speed ratings (Par 103): **104,103,100,99,98 97,96,95,95,91**
CSF £109.17 CT £519.73 TOTE £14.70: £3.60, £2.20, £2.50; EX 82.40.
Owner Dr Marwan Koukash **Bred** Gainsborough Stud Management Ltd **Trained** Portway, Worcs

FOCUS
An ordinary handicap and another race that was run at a modest pace early before turning into something of a sprint. The front pair pulled well clear of the others and set the level.

2336 JUNGLE JIM'S AT BLACKPOOL TOWER MAIDEN STKS 1m 3f 200y
5:20 (5:20) (Class 5) 3-Y-O+ £2,590 (£770; £385; £192) **Stalls** High

Form RPR

2 **1** **Icon Project (USA)**[27] 1599 3-8-7 0 ow1.................... NCallan 6 88+
(B J Meehan) *racd keenly: trckd ldrs: led 2f out: rdn over 1f out: jst under 1f up whn edgd lft and tightened up rival ins fnl f: kpt on wl* **8/13**[1]

-03 **2** 2 **Factotum**[24] 1690 4-10-0 0.................... JoeFanning 2 92+
(L M Cumani) *led: rdn and hdd 2f out: stl jst under 1l down whn n.m.r and snatched up ins fnl f: eased whn unable to fully rcvr towards fin* **11/1**

6-23 **3** 6 **Wells Lyrical (IRE)**[19] 1814 3-8-11 75.................... TomEaves 3 73
(B Smart) *trckd ldrs: rdn over 3f out: wknd over 2f out* **15/2**[3]

432 **4** ½ **Dolly Penrose**[5] 2207 3-8-6 0.................... PaulHanagan 4 67
(M R Channon) *prom: chalng 3f out: rdn and wknd over 1f out* **4/1**[2]

56-2 **5** 3¼ **Spiritonthemount (USA)**[49] 1173 3-8-11 70.................... MichaelHills 5 67
(B W Hills) *racd keenly: rdn over 4f out: sn lost pl: n.d after* **12/1**

6 7 **Lisbon Lion (IRE)** 3-8-11 0.................... SamHitchcott 8 56
(N J Vaughan) *hld up: rdn over 3f out: no imp* **50/1**

7 1¾ **Tamerlano (USA)** 3-8-11 0.................... RoystonFfrench 9 53
(M Johnston) *in rr: rdn over 4f out: nvr on terms* **18/1**

003 **8** 6 **Princess Flame (GER)**[16] 1896 6-9-2 0.................... KylieManser(7) 7 38
(B G Powell) *pushed along over 3f out: a bhd* **33/1**

2m 31.83s (-1.37) **Going Correction** -0.05s/f (Good)
WFA 3 from 4yo+ 17lb **8** Ran SP% **119.9**
Speed ratings (Par 103): **102,100,96,96,94 89,88,84**
CSF £9.96 TOTE £1.80: £1.10, £3.10, £1.80; EX 8.40 Place 6: £186.04, Place 5: £111.02..
Owner Andrew Rosen **Bred** Ronald Carter Family Trust **Trained** Manton, Wilts
■ Stewards' Enquiry : N Callan two-day ban: careless riding (Jun 5, 8)

FOCUS
Not the most competitive of maidens and the pace was ordinary. The first two pulled well clear and there is little to get excited about amongst the others, with the form rated around the third and fifth.
Princess Flame(GER) Official explanation: jockey said mare never travelled
T/Plt: £323.40 to a £1 stake. Pool: £54,054.54. 122.00 winning tickets. T/Qpdt: £34.60 to a £1 stake. Pool: £2,643.80. 56.40 winning tickets. DO

2123 SALISBURY (R-H)
Thursday, May 22

OFFICIAL GOING: Good to firm (firm in places; 9.4)
Wind: virtually nil Weather: overcast but dry

2337 BATHWICK TYRES LADY RIDERS' SERIES H'CAP 6f
6:10 (6:07) (Class 6) (0-65,64) 4-Y-O+ £2,810 (£871; £435; £217) **Stalls** High

Form RPR

00-4 **1** **Charlie Delta**[7] 2128 5-10-2 **60**....................(b) MissARyan(3) 8 72
(J G M O'Shea) *hld up towards rr: hdwy towards stands' side over 2f out: hung rt and led wl over 1f out: fin on far side rails but r.o wl: rdn out* **12/1**

3204 **2** 2 **Sovereignty (JPN)**[18] 1842 6-9-13 **61**.................... MissECrossman(7) 12 67
(D K Ivory) *mid-div: rdn over 2f out: hdwy over 1f out: styd on to go 2nd ins fnl f: nt rch wnr* **18/1**

214- **3** *nk* **Shaded Edge**[221] 6210 4-10-5 **60** MissGDGracey-Davison 3 65
(D W P Arbuthnot) *towards rr: hdwy and nt clr run briefly 2f out: sn rdn: styd on ins fnl f: wnt 3rd nr fin* **20/1**

4430 **4** *shd* **Binnion Bay (IRE)**[14] 1932 7-9-9 **50** (b) MissLEllison 15 54
(J J Bridger) *sn struggling and nudged along in rr: hdwy over 1f out: styd on fnl f: nrst fin* **14/1**

00-0 **5** *1 3/4* **Exit Strategy (IRE)**[44] 1254 4-10-0 **60** (b) MissAngharadFrieze(5) 11 59
(R A Harris) *s.i.s: sn rcvrd to chse ldrs: rdn and ev ch whn edgd lft wl over 1f out one pce fnl f* **33/1**

030- **6** *nk* **Spice Gardens (IRE)**[204] 6582 4-10-0 **55** MissSBrotherton 18 53
(W Jarvis) *hld up towards rr: gd hdwy over 2f out: rdn to chse ldrs over 1f out: one pce after* **5/1**[3]

20-0 **7** *nk* **Conjecture**[18] 1827 6-9-9 **55** MissRBastiman(5) 9 52
(R Bastiman) *prom: rdn and ev ch 2f out: sn one pce* **20/1**

0-31 **8** *4* **Vanadium**[7] 2128 6-10-3 **63** MissFCumani(5) 17 47
(G L Moore) *hld up towards rr: hdwy and nt clr run 3f out: sn swtchd lft: styd on but nvr able to get on terms* **5/2**[1]

000/ **9** *2 1/2* **Boldinor**[558] 6436 5-9-2 **50** MissRachelKing(7) 16 26
(M R Bosley) *chsd ldrs: rdn over 2f out: wknd over 1f out* **40/1**

0062 **10** *shd* **Elusive Dreams (USA)**[10] 2055 4-10-0 **55** (v) MrsMMorris 14 31
(D Shaw) *led: rdn whn edgd lft and hdd wl over 1f out: wknd* **9/2**[2]

6460 **11** *1 3/4* **Quality Street**[18] 1842 6-10-3 **63** (p) MissZoeLilly(5) 6 33
(P Butler) *a towards rr* **40/1**

422- **12** *3/4* **Choreography**[209] 6467 5-10-8 **63** MissEJJones 5 31
(Jim Best) *s.i.s: a towards rr* **17/2**

0060 **13** *1* **George The Second**[48] 1191 5-9-5 **53** MissNMCook(7) 4 17
(Mrs H Sweeting) *chsd ldrs for over 3f* **33/1**

0050 **14** *1* **Mulberry Lad (IRE)**[25] 1642 6-9-6 **50** oh5 MrsMarieKing(3) 13 11
(P W Hiatt) *mid-div: rdn over 2f out: sn btn* **66/1**

2432 **15** *1 1/2* **Over To You Bert**[17] 9-10-5 **60** MissCHannaford 10 16
(R J Hodges) *chsd ldrs for over 3f* **16/1**

000- **16** *1* **Blessed Place**[193] 6773 8-10-6 **61** (t) MissFayeBramley 7 14
(D J S Ffrench Davis) *chsd ldrs tl wknd over 2f out* **40/1**

1m 14.32s (-0.48) **Going Correction** +0.025s/f (Good) **16** Ran SP% **123.7**
Speed ratings (Par 101): **104,101,100,100,98 98,97,92,89,88 86,85,84,82,80 79**
CSF £195.42 CT £4407.44 TOTE £10.10: £1.80, £5.00, £3.60, £2.70; EX 172.50.
Owner The Lovely Jubbly's **Bred** P K Gardner **Trained** Elton, Gloucs

FOCUS
A moderate sprint handicap restricted to lady amateurs. They went a strong pace and the form rated around the first three looks sound for the type of race.

2338 BATHWICK TYRES E B F MAIDEN STKS 5f
6:40 (6:44) (Class 4) 2-Y-O **£4,371** (£1,300; £650; £324) **Stalls** High

Form RPR

3 **1** **Tishtar**[12] 1987 2-9-3 0 RichardHughes 2 82+
(R Hannon) *mde all: kpt on wl: comf* **8/11**[1]

64 **2** *2 3/4* **Klynch**[31] 1523 2-9-3 0 RobertHavlin 6 70
(B J Meehan) *chsd ldrs: rdn 2f out: kpt on to go 2nd ins fnl f but a hld* **15/2**

3 *1 3/4* **Mesyaal** 2-9-3 0 EdwardCreighton 7 64+
(M R Channon) *chsd ldrs: effrt 2f out: kpt on same pce fnl f* **6/1**[3]

3 **4** *1 1/2* **Finnegan McCool**[19] 1804 2-9-3 0 SebSanders 1 58
(R M Beckett) *chsd wnr: rdn to chal 2f out: fdd ins fnl f* **5/1**[2]

5 **5** *1 1/4* **Madison Belle**[6] 2147 2-8-5 0 GabrielHannon(7) 4 49
(Mrs H Sweeting) *s.i.s: towards rr: hdwy and hung bdly lft over 2f out: kpt on but no further imp* **66/1**

6 *5* **Captain Kallis (IRE)** 2-9-3 0 RichardThomas 3 36
(D J S Ffrench Davis) *uns rdr on way to s: chsd ldrs tl wknd 2f out* **66/1**

7 *1 1/2* **Magical Illusion** 2-8-12 0 TGMcLaughlin 8 26
(P D Evans) *sn outpcd and a towards rr* **28/1**

8 *4* **Applehays** 2-8-7 0 (t) JackDean(5) 5 11
(W G M Turner) *awkward leaving stalls: mid-div tl wknd 2f out* **66/1**

9 *14* **Short Cut** 2-9-3 0 SteveDrowne 9 —
(S Kirk) *s.i.s: a bhd: hung lft fr 2f out* **14/1**

61.55 secs (0.75) **Going Correction** +0.025s/f (Good) **9** Ran SP% **115.2**
Speed ratings (Par 95): **95,90,87,85,83 75,73,66,44**
CSF £6.84 TOTE £1.70: £1.10, £1.50, £1.90; EX 7.50.
Owner The Waney Racing Group Inc **Bred** Waney Racing Group Inc **Trained** East Everleigh, Wilts

FOCUS
They finished reasonably strung out considering the trip and the bare form looks just fair but should work out.

NOTEBOOK
Tishtar ◆ confirmed the promise he showed when third on his debut over 6f at Haydock. Quickly away on this drop in trip, he showed plenty of speed to lead and sustained his effort to the line. He had his rivals strung out and looks a useful sprinter. (op Evens tchd 11-10 tchd 5-4 in a place)
Klynch is improving with racing and this was his best effort yet. He was no match for the useful winner, but was a clear second and might be up to finding a maiden before the nursery season. (op 10-1 tchd 7-1)
Mesyaal ◆, by Alhaarth out of a smart 5f juvenile winner, was a big drifter on course and found a couple too good. He should learn plenty from this and can show improved form next time. (op 7-2)
Finnegan McCool showed plenty of early speed but he finished up well held and did not really improve on the form he showed when third on his debut at Goodwood. (op 15-2 tchd 9-2)
Madison Belle, last of five on her debut in a good race at Newbury, ran surprisingly well considering she hung badly left under pressure and ended up towards the stands' rail. Official explanation: jockey reported that the filly hung left-handed. (op 50-1)

2339 BATHWICK TYRES H'CAP 6f
7:10 (7:14) (Class 4) (0-85,83) 4-Y-O+ **£4,209** (£1,252; £625; £312) **Stalls** High

Form RPR

5-51 **1** **Seamus Shindig**[14] 1928 6-8-8 **80** AmyScott(7) 11 88
(H Candy) *trckd ldrs: shkn up over 1f out: swtchd rt ins fnl f: r.o wl to ld fnl 50yds* **9/2**[1]

-000 **2** *nk* **Stamford Blue**[24] 1683 7-8-9 **77** (b) KevinGhunowa(3) 10 84
(R A Harris) *sn pushed into ld: rdn 2f out: kpt on but no ex whn hdd fnl 50yds* **14/1**

0-06 **3** *1/2* **China Cherub**[14] 1928 5-8-10 **75** (b) SebSanders 9 80
(S Dow) *trckd ldr: rdn over 2f out: kpt on ins fnl f* **8/1**

0-00 **4** *nk* **Tony James (IRE)**[19] 1800 6-9-1 **80** PatDobbs 3 84
(K O Cunningham-Brown) *mid-div: rdn over 2f out: clsd on ldrs ent fnl f: kpt on* **33/1**

6-40 **5** *shd* **Fleuret**[12] 1993 4-9-1 **80** (t) StephenCarson 7 84
(Eve Johnson Houghton) *chsd ldrs: rdn over 3f out: kpt on ins fnl furlong* **10/1**

303- **6** *1/2* **Flying Goose (IRE)**[213] 6391 4-9-1 **80** TGMcLaughlin 5 83+
(R A Harris) *settled in rr: swtchd rt and rdn 2f out: kpt on ins fnl f: nt rch ldrs* **11/1**

-400 **7** *3/4* **Kyle (IRE)**[24] 1683 4-8-12 **77** EddieAhern 2 77
(R Hannon) *hld up towards rr: rdn and hdwy over 2f out: nt pce to chal* **5/1**[2]

4-26 **8** *shd* **Adantino**[17] 1872 9-8-10 **75** (b) AlanMunro 8 75
(B R Millman) *mid-div: rdn wl over 2f out: sn one pce* **8/1**

5042 **9** *3/4* **Compton's Eleven**[6] 2163 7-9-3 **82** TedDurcan 6 79
(M R Channon) *mid-div: rdn 3f out: one pce fnl 2f* **9/2**[1]

3000 **10** *3/4* **Gallantry**[13] 1942 6-9-1 **83** TolleyDean(3) 1 78
(D Shaw) *hld up in rr: rdn over 2f out: no imp* **16/1**

-232 **11** *3* **North South Divide (IRE)**[14] 1928 4-8-10 **75** (p) DaneO'Neill 4 60
(R A Teal) *plld hrd: hld up in rr: rdn 2f out: wknd fnl f* **11/2**[3]

1m 14.08s (-0.72) **Going Correction** +0.025s/f (Good) **11** Ran SP% **123.6**
Speed ratings (Par 105): **105,104,103,103,103 102,101,101,100,99 95**
CSF £72.11 CT £393.12 TOTE £5.30: £2.20, £5.60, £3.00; EX 81.80.
Owner Henry Candy **Bred** R S A Urquhart **Trained** Kingston Warren, Oxon

FOCUS
This looked a fair sprint handicap beforehand, but the first three home were pretty much in the first three throughout, and the form, rated around the winner, fifth and sixth, needs treating with caution.

2340 BATHWICK TYRES SALISBURY H'CAP 1m 4f
7:40 (7:41) (Class 6) (0-65,65) 3-Y-O **£2,914** (£867; £433; £216) **Stalls** High

Form RPR

1-03 **1** **Any Given Day (IRE)**[10] 2043 3-9-3 **64** RichardMullen 2 76
(D M Simcock) *s.i.s: sn pushed along to go prom: led 3f out: rdn clr over 1f out: styd on strly: readily* **7/2**[1]

6233 **2** *5* **King Supreme (IRE)**[10] 2045 3-9-4 **65** (b) RichardHughes 3 69
(R Hannon) *hld up towards rr: stdy prog u.p fr over 2f out: styd on: wnt 2nd ins fnl f: no ch w wnr* **5/1**[3]

0-63 **3** *1/2* **King Of Pentacles**[12] 1994 3-9-1 **62** EddieAhern 12 65
(H Morrison) *chsd ldrs: rdn over 3f out: wnt 2nd over 2f out: no ch w wnr fr over 1f out: lost 2nd ins fnl f* **4/1**[2]

00-0 **4** *2* **Mount Lavinia (IRE)**[49] 1172 3-8-13 **60** JamesDoyle 1 60
(R M Beckett) *mid-div: gd prog to join ldrs briefly after 3f: sn bk in mid-div: rdn and hdwy over 2f out: styd on* **16/1**

5023 **5** *1/2* **Si Belle (IRE)**[49] 1163 3-9-3 **64** AlanMunro 9 63
(Rae Guest) *mid-div: rdn 3f out: styd on fr over 1f out: nvr trbld ldrs* **14/1**

5-00 **6** *1 1/4* **No Rules**[10] 2045 3-9-1 **62** JimmyQuinn 14 59
(M H Tompkins) *mid-div: rdn and hdwy 2f out: one pce fnl f* **16/1**

0-00 **7** *5* **Daddy's Boy**[17] 1871 3-9-4 **65** (b[1]) JimCrowley 6 54
(Mrs A J Perrett) *chsd ldrs: rdn over 3f out: one pce fnl 2f* **28/1**

-266 **8** *2 3/4* **Zen Factor**[23] 1696 3-9-4 **65** VinceSlattery 8 50
(J G Portman) *led after 2f: rdn and hdd 3f out: wknd over 1f out* **14/1**

10-0 **9** *1/2* **Blandys Wood**[23] 1696 3-9-3 **64** EdwardCreighton 13 48
(M R Channon) *hld up towards rr: hdwy over 3f out: sn rdn: wknd over 1f out* **33/1**

5-50 **10** *1* **Tantris (IRE)**[21] 1737 3-9-4 **65** ShaneKelly 5 47
(J A Osborne) *hld up towards rr: rdn whn swtchd lft 3f out: no imp* **14/1**

-423 **11** *hd* **Okafranca (IRE)**[23] 1710 3-8-13 **60** DO'Donohoe 11 42
(W R Muir) *a towards rr* **10/1**

64-0 **12** *3 3/4* **Sparkling Montjeu (IRE)**[26] 1622 3-9-2 **63** TQuinn 4 39
(J W Hills) *chsd ldrs tl dropped to midfield over 6f out: rdn over 3 out: wknd 2f out* **14/1**

000- **13** *shd* **Iron Cross (IRE)**[210] 6451 3-8-13 **60** SebSanders 7 36
(Sir Mark Prescott) *s.i.s: bhd: rdn and hdwy over 4f out: wknd over 2f out* **9/1**

00-0 **14** *4* **Leitmotif (USA)**[18] 1839 3-9-3 **64** TedDurcan 10 34
(J L Dunlop) *led for 2f: chsd ldrs: rdn over 3f out: wknd over 2f out* **14/1**

2m 36.34s (-1.66) **Going Correction** -0.20s/f (Firm) **14** Ran SP% **129.5**
Speed ratings (Par 97): **97,93,93,92,91 90,87,85,85,84 84,82,81,79**
CSF £22.31 CT £78.22 TOTE £4.30: £1.60, £2.00, £1.80; EX 21.70.
Owner Malcolm Martin Partnership **Bred** Ralph And Helen O'Brien **Trained** Newmarket, Suffolk

FOCUS
A modest handicap but solid form rated around the placed horses.
Okafranca(IRE) Official explanation: trainer said that the gelding was unsuited by the ground.

2341 BATHWICK TYRES MAIDEN FILLIES' STKS 6f
8:10 (8:12) (Class 5) 3-Y-O+ **£3,885** (£1,156; £577; £288) **Stalls** High

Form RPR

3-23 **1** **Dubai Power**[24] 1688 3-8-7 83 AhmedAjtebi(5) 7 77
(C E Brittain) *prom: led 2f out: r.o wl: comf* **2/1**[1]

2-2 **2** *2 3/4* **Orange Pip**[18] 1836 3-8-12 0 RichardHughes 11 68
(R Hannon) *trckd ldrs: nt clr run over 2f out: rdn and edgd rt over 1f out: kpt on but no ch w wnr* **2/1**[1]

00 **3** *3/4* **Milldown Bay**[17] 1869 3-8-12 0 AlanMunro 3 66
(B R Millman) *prom: rdn and ev ch 2f out: 2nd and hld ent fnl f: lost 2nd towards fin* **50/1**

5-3 **4** *2 1/2* **Compton Rose**[21] 1737 3-8-12 0 TQuinn 4 58
(H Candy) *racd freely: prom: rdn whn travelling wl 2f out: nt qckn: fdd fnl 75yds* **9/2**[2]

-220 **5** *nk* **Erlydors (IRE)**[13] 1946 3-8-12 0 AdamKirby 2 57
(W R Swinburn) *hld up towards rr: hdwy 3f out: sn rdn: styd on but nvr trbld ldrs* **7/1**[3]

6 *3/4* **Holly Cleugh** 3-8-12 0 SebSanders 9 54+
(J R Fanshawe) *mid-div: rdn over 2f out: styd on fnl f: nvr trbld ldrs* **14/1**

50 **7** *1/2* **Little Cee (IRE)**[13] 1960 3-8-9 0 MarcHalford(3) 1 53
(D R C Elsworth) *swtchd rt sn after s: bhd: swtchd lft and rdn over 2f out: styd on fnl f: nvr a danger* **50/1**

- **8** *hd* **Siren Party** 3-8-12 0 NickyMackay 5 52+
(L M Cumani) *a mid-div* **20/1**

000- **9** *1 1/2* **Lady Maya**[211] 6418 3-8-9 48 KevinGhunowa(3) 12 47
(Dr J R J Naylor) *swtchd rt 2f out: mainly towards rr* **200/1**

0- **10** *3/4* **Apple Pie Order (IRE)**[259] 5162 3-8-12 0 SteveDrowne 14 45
(R J Hodges) *prom: rdn over 2f out: wknd fnl f* **200/1**

6 **11** *1* **Where's Dids**[18] 1835 3-8-12 0 EdwardCreighton 13 42
(M R Channon) *led tl 2f out: sn wknd* **25/1**

12 *3/4* **Yatir (FR)**[156] 3-8-12 77 JimCrowley 6 39
(E F Vaughan) *chsd ldrs: effrt 3f out: sn wknd* **20/1**

05 **13** *nk* **Acclimate**[18] 1835 3-8-12 0 DaneO'Neill 8 38
(W S Kittow) *plld hrd early: a towards rr* **16/1**

14 *3 1/4* **Frosty's Gift** 4-9-7 0 PatDobbs 15 28
(J C Fox) *s.i.s: a bhd* **100/1**

1m 14.73s (-0.07) **Going Correction** +0.025s/f (Good)
WFA 3 from 4yo 9lb **14** Ran SP% **129.2**
Speed ratings (Par 100): **101,97,96,93,92 91,90,90,88,87 86,85,84,80**
CSF £5.65 TOTE £3.60: £1.50, £1.50, £7.50; EX 9.80.
Owner Dr Ali Ridha **Bred** Malih L Al Basti **Trained** Newmarket, Suffolk

FOCUS
A reasonable sprint maiden for fillies but the winner did not need to run up to her best to score and the form looks limited.
Siren Party Official explanation: jockey reported that the filly ran green.
Acclimate Official explanation: jockey reported that the filly ran too free.

2342 BATHWICK TYRES SUPPORTS "HEROS" REHOMING EX-RACEHORSES H'CAP — 1m 1f 198y
8:40 (8:40) (Class 5) (0-75,75) 3-Y-O — £3,238 (£963; £481; £240) Stalls High

Form			Horse	Jockey	RPR
30-0	1		**Mon Plaisir (USA)**29 1572 3-8-13 70	TedDurcan 1	78
			(J L Dunlop) *hld up towards rr: gd hdwy fr 2f out: edgd rt ent fnl f: led fnl 100yds: r.o wl: rdn out* **18/1**		
0-44	2	1 1/2	**Mizooka**19 1805 3-8-11 68	SebSanders 4	73+
			(R M Beckett) *trckd ldrs: led wl over 2f out: sn rdn: hdd fnl 100yds: no ex* **12/1**		
05-6	3	1 1/2	**Dusk**37 1389 3-8-6 63	JimmyQuinn 6	65
			(J L Dunlop) *hld up towards rr: stdy prog fr over 2f out: rdn over 1f out: wnt 3rd ent fnl f: styd on* **14/1**		
00-0	4	1/2	**Krisnando**23 1696 3-8-4 61 oh1	WilliamBuick 10	62
			(G L Moore) *rrd bdly s: bhd: swtchd lft and hdwy over 1f out: styd on wl: nrst fin* **18/1**		
66-2	5	5	**Sheer Bluff (IRE)**21 1746 3-9-1 75	MarcHalford(3) 3	66
			(D R C Elsworth) *mid-div: hdwy over 3f out: rdn and ev ch 2f out: wknd ins fnl f* **8/1**3		
245-	6	3/4	**Doctor Robert**162 7114 3-9-4 75	RichardKingscote 8	64
			(Tom Dascombe) *plld hrd: trckd ldr: led over 3f out: rdn and hdd wl over 2f out: wknd ins fnl f* **14/1**		
30-0	7	1 3/4	**Havanavich**45 1243 3-8-11 68	RichardHughes 11	53
			(S Kirk) *mid-div: rdn 3f out: hdwy wl over 1f out: fdd ins fnl f* **33/1**		
00-2	8	3 3/4	**Dark Camellia**24 1669 3-9-1 72	EddieAhern 12	50
			(H J L Dunlop) *hld up towards rr: hdwy over 3f out: sn rdn: wknd 1f out* **12/1**		
404-	9	8	**Driven (IRE)**202 6616 3-9-4 75	JimCrowley 5	36
			(Mrs A J Perrett) *mid-div: rdn 3f out: wknd over 1f out* **7/1**2		
456-	10	12	**Spent**220 6233 3-8-11 68	TQuinn 7	5
			(Mouse Hamilton-Fairley) *racd freely: led tl 3f out: sn wknd* **20/1**		
002	11	19	**Persian Wish (IRE)**16 1896 3-8-9 66	DaneO'Neill 9	—
			(J W Mullins) *trckd ldrs: rdn over 3f out: wknd over 2f out* **40/1**		
01-1	12	8	**Sleepy Hollow**10 2045 3-9-3 74 6ex	SteveDrowne 2	—
			(H Morrison) *mid-div: struggling over 4f out: wknd qckly and eased* **10/11**1		

2m 9.65s (-0.25) **Going Correction** -0.20s/f (Firm) 12 Ran SP% **125.4**
Speed ratings (Par 99): **93,91,90,90,86 85,84,81,74,65 50,43**
CSF £225.71 CT £3130.02 TOTE £24.30: £5.10, £3.50, £3.70; EX 258.40 Place 6: £273.27, Place 5 £48.67..
Owner Robin F Scully **Bred** Clovelly Farms **Trained** Arundel, W Sussex

FOCUS
An ordinary handicap and the winning time was modest. The favourite ran too badly to be true and three of the first four came from off the pace with the runner-up rated to form the best guide.
Krisnando Official explanation: jockey reported the filly reared as the stalls opened.
Sleepy Hollow Official explanation: jockey said that the gelding stopped quickly; vet said gelding had an irregular heartbeat
T/Plt: £408.30 to a £1 stake. Pool: £50,397.27. 90.10 winning tickets. T/Qpdt: £116.30 to a £1 stake. Pool: £5,834.19. 37.10 winning tickets. TM

2343 - 2345a (Foreign Racing) - See Raceform Interactive

2214 BADEN-BADEN (L-H)
Thursday, May 22

OFFICIAL GOING: Good

2346a BETTY BARCLAY-RENNEN (GROUP 3) — 2m
4:00 (4:11) 4-Y-0+ — £22,059 (£9,191; £3,676; £1,838)

		Horse	Jockey	RPR
1		**Caudillo (GER)**21 5-8-12	J-PCarvalho 1	106
		(Dr A Bolte, Germany) *hld up on ins in 6th or 7th: swtchd outside and hdwy ent st: led ins fnl f: rdn out* **15/2**		
2	2	**Waldvogel (IRE)**21 4-8-12	EPedroza 9	106
		(A Wohler, Germany) *hld up in 6th or 7th: 4th st: led narrowly jst over 1f out tl ins fnl f: one pce* **37/10**2		
3	3/4	**Brisant (GER)**25 1662 6-8-12	WMongil 3	103
		(M Trybuhl, Germany) *hld up in last: hdwy 2f out: styd on down outside to take 3rd fnl 100yds: kpt on* **67/10**		
4	2 1/2	**Dragon Fly (GER)**21 6-8-12	ASuborics 8	100
		(Frau Jutta Mayer, Germany) *hld up in 8th: hdwy on wd outside and 5th st: styd on at one pce: tk 4th cl home* **141/10**		
5	1/2	**Sereth (IRE)**21 5-8-12	TPQueally 7	100
		(J Hirschberger, Germany) *led: set solid pce: hdd jst over 1f out: wknd and lost 4th cl home* **26/10**1		
6	10	**Emporio (GER)**21 4-8-12	(b) AStarke 4	91
		(P Schiergen, Germany) *racd in 4th: 3rd st: sn rdn and nt qckn: outpcd fnl f* **92/10**		
7	3	**Anton Chekhov**270 4872 4-9-2	ADeVries 6	92
		(W Hickst, Germany) *racd in 2nd on outside: wknd over 1 1/2f out* **54/10**3		
8	21	**Stephenson (FR)**21 7-8-9	DBoeuf 5	59
		(W Baltromei, Germany) *racd in 5th: outpcd fr over 2f out* **102/10**		
9	14	**Swan Queen**18 1841 5-8-5	JAuge 2	40
		(J L Dunlop) *trckd ldr in 3rd on ins: rdn over 5f out: btn wl over 2f out: eased: t.o* **56/10**		

3m 20.44s (-3.15)
WFA 4 from 5yo+ 2lb 9 Ran SP% **129.9**
(including 10 Euro stake): WIN 85; PL 21, 16, 23; SF 308.
Owner Frau B & H Kuhlmann **Bred** Frau B & H Kuhlmann **Trained** Germany

NOTEBOOK
Swan Queen, stepping up in both trip and grade, was close enough early on but was in trouble some way out and was allowed to come home in her own time when beaten. She was beaten too early for the distance to have been a factor and the drying ground was more of a problem.

1850 FRANKFURT (L-H)
Thursday, May 22

OFFICIAL GOING: Good

2347a GROSSER PREIS DER FRANKFURTER VOLKSBANK (LISTED RACE) (FILLIES) — 1m
4:15 (4:17) 4-Y-0+ — £19,853 (£8,088; £4,412; £2,941; £1,471)

		Horse	Jockey	RPR
1		**Nans Joy (IRE)**19 1801 4-8-13	THellier 7	103
		(E J O'Neill) *racd in 4th: pushed along over 2f out: hdwy to press ldr appr fnl f: styd on gamely u.p to ld cl home* **22/10**1		
2	nk	**Flashing Colour (GER)**319 4-8-11	MCadeddu 1	101
		(P Rau, Germany) **49/10**		
3	3/4	**Ledicea**32 4-8-11	NRichter 3	99
		(P Rau, Germany) **116/10**		
4	1/2	**Rovana Jowe (GER)**350 2408 5-8-11	JBojko 2	98
		(A Wohler, Germany) **148/10**		
5	1 1/2	**Hashbrown (GER)**32 4-9-2	WPanov 4	99
		(C Sprengel, Germany) **32/10**3		
6	nk	**Pinea (GER)**242 6-8-11	JiriPalik 5	94
		(Frau Nina Bach, Germany) **79/10**		
7	3/4	**Chantra (GER)**25 1660 4-9-4	TMundry 9	99
		(P Rau, Germany) **31/10**2		
8	1 3/4	**Banderella (IRE)**180 6940 4-8-11	FilipMinarik 8	88
		(W Hickst, Germany) **86/10**		

1m 34.34s (94.34) 8 Ran SP% **132.3**
(including 10 Euro stake): WIN 32; PL 15, 18, 20; SF 182.
Owner Frank Cosgrove **Bred** Mrs Brid Cosgrove **Trained** Averham Park, Notts

NOTEBOOK
Nans Joy(IRE), who has been making the running in similar races in Britain, was settled just off the pace this time and proved game under pressure in getting up close home to land her first Listed success. She will try to step up into Group company at Hamburg at the beginning of July.

2067 BRIGHTON (L-H)
Friday, May 23

OFFICIAL GOING: Good to firm (firm in places)
Wind: Light half behind Weather: Cloudy

2349 SKY BET SUPPORTING THE LILY FOUNDATION E B F MAIDEN STKS — 5f 213y
2:00 (2:00) (Class 5) 2-Y-O — £3,626 (£1,079; £539; £269) Stalls Low

Form			Horse	Jockey	RPR
34	1		**Mazzola**15 1927 2-9-3 0	EdwardCreighton 6	76+
			(M R Channon) *chsd ldr: led 3f out: drvn clr over 1f out: readily* **1/1**1		
50	2	6	**Ritzy Wildcat (USA)**6 2186 2-8-12 0	MACleere(5) 1	56
			(S C Williams) *plld v hrd: disp 3rd pl: effrt and hung bdly lft and rt away fr whip fnl 2f: kpt on to take 2nd fnl 100yds* **2/1**2		
	3	1 3/4	**Satwa Boy** 2-9-3 0	TGMcLaughlin 4	51
			(E A L Dunlop) *disp 3rd pl: rdn to chse wnr over 2f out: no imp and lost 2nd fnl 100yds* **7/1**3		
P	4	2 3/4	**Rigged**13 2011 2-9-3 0	ShaneKelly 5	43
			(J A Osborne) *led tl 3f out: wknd 2f out* **14/1**		
	5	9 3/4	**Graysland** 2-8-12 0	SaleemGolam 7	8
			(W G M Turner) *s.i.s: bhd: rdn after 2f: no ch fr 1/2-way: fin 6th, plcd 5th* **20/1**		
	D		**Teneo Vestri** 2-8-10 0	PNolan(7) 2	34
			(A B Haynes) *dwlt: sn pushed along: a bhd: fin 5th, 6l, 13/4l, 23/4l, 7l: plcd last* **20/1**		

69.96 secs (-0.24) **Going Correction** -0.20s/f (Firm) 6 Ran SP% **112.0**
Speed ratings (Par 93): **93,85,82,79,66 75**
CSF £3.16 TOTE £1.80: £1.10, £1.80; EX 3.30.
Owner M Channon **Bred** Mrs E C Dowling **Trained** West Ilsley, Berks

FOCUS
The winner is improving with racing and looks above average for this track and grade. He thrashed his opponents, who were admittedly a moderate bunch, and can do better again.

NOTEBOOK
Mazzola proved a cut above these rivals, and seemed to appreciate the extra furlong, though his rider reported him to have idled in front up the final climb. He is a likeable individual, and should continue to make an impression.. (tchd 10-11)
Ritzy Wildcat(USA) was heavily backed again, but he is - to put it mildly - something of a handful and connections will have to work on him to make the best use of his speed. Not helped by having a rival crossing in front of him, he pulled like crazy early on but then wandered all over the track away from the whip when Cleere went for the whip. His trainer will doubtless try to find a handicap for him, and it looks worth letting him do his own thing from the front on a flatter track. (op 10-3 tchd 7-2)
Satwa Boy, a Royal Applause newcomer out of a winning half-sister to Dr Fong, made a satisfactory if unspectacular debut. He has some ability but will have to improve dramatically to be anything out of the ordinary. (op 5-1)
Rigged, who changed hands for just £5000 this year, is a half-brother to Females Fun, a multiple winner in Sweden up to 1m. Pulled up on his debut after swerving at the start, he fared a bit better here but does not look one to get too interested in yet. (op 12-1 tchd 16-1)
Graysland, a Silver Patriarch debutante out of Celtic Island, who won at trips up to 1m2f, will need much farther than this in due course. Quickly left behind, she confirmed that sprinting is unlikely to be her game. (op 14-1)
Teneo Vestri, an 11,000gns foal who changed hands for just 5,000gns as a yearling, has plenty of speedy winners in the family. However, he was too slowly away to show whether he has inherited any of their pace. He was susequently disqualified due to morphine in his sample. (op 33-1)

2350 SKY BET PRESS RED TO BET H'CAP — 5f 213y
2:30 (2:30) (Class 5) (0-70,70) 4-Y-0+ — £2,396 (£712; £356; £177) Stalls Low

Form			Horse	Jockey	RPR
-006	1		**Caustic Wit (IRE)**4 2242 10-8-8 60	FergusSweeney 8	63
			(M S Saunders) *dwlt: towards rr: rdn and hdwy 2f out: led ins fnl f: drvn out* **7/2**3		
0-65	2	3/4	**Jayanjay**10 2075 9-8-6 58	RichardSmith 7	59
			(B R Johnson) *hld up in tch: effrt and hrd rdn 2f out: led 1f out tl ins fnl f: kpt on* **7/1**		
-000	3	3/4	**Nordic Light (USA)**4 2242 4-9-4 70	(b1) WilliamBuick 5	69
			(J M Bradley) *chsd ldrs: outpcd 2f out: hrd rdn over 1f out: rallied and r.o fnl f* **14/1**		

6060 **4** *nk* **Tamino (IRE)**[32] [1522] 5-9-2 **68**..(t) JimmyQuinn 1 66
(P Howling) *rdn to ld: hrd rdn and hdd 1f out: one pce: disputing 3rd and btn whn n.m.r nr fin* **11/4**[1]

3056 **5** *hd* **Star Strider**[42] [1312] 4-8-13 **65**.. JimCrowley 6 62
(Miss Gay Kelleway) *in tch: swtchd rt 2f out: effrt and hrd rdn over 1f out: nt qckn fnl f* **10/3**[2]

0530 **6** *nk* **Monashee Prince (IRE)**[4] [2255] 6-8-5 **57**....................(v) SaleemGolam 9 53
(J R Best) *settled in 6th pl on outside: hrd rdn 2f out: no imp* **11/2**

000- **7** *2 1/4* **Valeesha**[227] [6090] 4-8-5 **57** oh11 ow1.................. SimonWhitworth 2 46
(M S Saunders) *s.s: bhd: rdn over 2f out: nvr rchd ldrs* **50/1**

00-0 **8** *1/2* **Exponential (IRE)**[31] [1534] 6-8-4 **56** oh10.................. CatherineGannon 3 43
(J M Bradley) *chsd ldr tl hrd rdn and wknd over 1f out* **25/1**

69.43 secs (-0.77) **Going Correction** -0.20s/f (Firm) **8** Ran SP% **112.3**
Speed ratings (Par 103): **97,96,95,94,94 93,90,90**
CSF £27.00 CT £298.95 TOTE £4.60: £1.30, £1.90, £2.50; EX 18.60.
Owner Mrs Sandra Jones **Bred** Gainsborough Stud Management Ltd **Trained** Green Ore, Somerset

FOCUS
A typical Brighton sprint handicap. Muddling form.

2351 SKY BET FREEPHONE BETTING 08000 722 421 H'CAP 5f 59y
3:05 (3:05) (Class 5) (0-75,75) 4-Y-0+ **£2,525** (£751; £375; £187) **Stalls** Low

Form RPR

4431 **1** **Best One**[57] [1035] 4-8-10 **70**.. KevinGhunowa(3) 6 79
(R A Harris) *w ldrs: hung lft and led 1f out: drvn out* **5/1**[3]

-055 **2** *1 1/4* **One Way Ticket**[70] [883] 8-8-4 **61** oh2..........................(p) WilliamBuick 3 65
(J M Bradley) *pressed ldr: led 3f out: hrd rdn and hdd 1f out: one pce ins fnl f* **12/1**

-200 **3** *nk* **Cosmic Destiny (IRE)**[9] [2102] 6-8-10 **70**........................ TravisBlock(3) 5 73
(E F Vaughan) *stdd s: hld up towards rr: nt clr run 2f out: hdwy to press ldrs 1f out: one pce* **9/2**[2]

3134 **4** *3/4* **Desperate Dan**[11] [2050] 7-8-6 **70**..............................(b) GihanArnolda(7) 9 74+
(A B Haynes) *dwlt: sn rdn in rr: effrt and nt clr run over 1f out: swtchd sharply lft: disputing 2nd and running on whn hit rail fnl 50yds* **7/1**

-000 **5** *2* **Peopleton Brook**[1] [2330] 6-7-11 **61** oh5...................... RossAtkinson(7) 8 54
(J M Bradley) *chsd ldrs on outside: rdn and outpcd fnl 2f* **10/1**

000- **6** *shd* **Peter Island (FR)**[193] [6794] 5-8-13 **70**..............................(v) JimCrowley 7 63
(J Gallagher) *sn chsng ldrs: outpcd 2f out: btn whn hung lft fnl f* **4/1**[1]

031- **7** *2* **Our Fugitive (IRE)**[172] [7005] 6-8-8 **65**........................... SamHitchcott 2 51
(C Gordon) *led 2f: prom on ins rail tl hrd rdn and wknd over 1f out* **10/1**

4150 **8** *1* **Multahab**[13] [1997] 9-8-10 **67**..(t) JimmyQuinn 4 49
(M Wigham) *hld up in 6th pl: rdn to chse ldrs 2f out: wknd fnl f* **9/2**[2]

61.38 secs (-0.92) **Going Correction** -0.20s/f (Firm) **8** Ran SP% **111.4**
Speed ratings (Par 103): **99,97,96,95,92 91,88,87**
CSF £58.45 CT £280.26 TOTE £6.40: £2.00, £2.50, £1.90; EX 51.70.
Owner The Govin Partnership **Bred** Darley **Trained** Earlswood, Monmouths
■ Stewards' Enquiry : William Buick one-day ban: used whip with excessive frequency (Jun 8)

FOCUS
Ordinary form, but a slight personal best from the winner on his debut for a new stable.

2352 SKY BET EURO 2008 IN-PLAY BETTING (S) STKS 1m 1f 209y
3:40 (3:41) (Class 6) 3-5-Y-0 **£1,683** (£501; £250; £125) **Stalls** High

Form RPR

6343 **1** **Pab Special (IRE)**[10] [2070] 5-9-8 58.................................. RichardSmith 4 62
(B R Johnson) *t.k.h: prom: led over 2f out: sn 5 l clr: tired fnl f but a holding on: rdn out* **11/4**[1]

0 **2** *1 1/4* **Sceilin (IRE)**[35] [1455] 4-9-3 42..(t) SaleemGolam 3 54
(Miss D Mountain) *dwlt: sn in midfield: sltly hmpd over 5f out: hdwy and bmpd jst ins fnl 2f: chsd wnr over 1f out: clsng at fin: a hld* **12/1**

2R0- **3** *4* **Prince Des Neiges (FR)**[163] [7120] 5-9-3 53..................... NicolPolli(5) 8 51
(M R Hoad) *s.i.s: rapid hdwy to ld after 2f and slowed pce: hdd and edgd rt over 2f out: one pce* **25/1**

3452 **4** *3/4* **Not Now Lewis (IRE)**[14] [1968] 4-10-0 57.............................. JimCrowley 7 56
(Miss Gay Kelleway) *hld up towards rr: hdwy to chse ldrs 3f out: rdn whn bmpd jst ins fnl 2f: styd on same pce fnl 3f* **7/2**[2]

2551 **5** *4* **Ledgerwood**[10] [2089] 3-9-0 63...(p) JamesDoyle 2 48+
(J W Hills) *in tch: tk clsr order 4f out: chsng ldrs whn bdly hmpd over 2f out: nt rcvr* **9/2**[3]

0060 **6** *1 1/4* **Lay The Cash (USA)**[37] [1408] 4-9-8 37..........................(bt) WilliamBuick 1 39
(B G Powell) *t.k.h: led 2f: prom tl awkward on road crossing after 4f: sn lost pl and pushed along: styd on again fnl 2f* **12/1**

0-00 **7** *shd* **Art Gallery**[10] [2070] 4-9-8 43..(b) FergusSweeney 10 39
(G L Moore) *t.k.h in rr: hdwy into midfield 4f out: hrd rdn over 2f out: no imp* **22/1**

4004 **8** *shd* **Bollywood (IRE)**[40] [1350] 5-9-8 42............................ RichardKingscote 12 39
(J J Bridger) *t.k.h: in tch: rdn 4f out: sn outpcd* **20/1**

5303 **9** *hd* **Lancaster Lad (IRE)**[10] [2089] 3-8-8 47........................(p) SamHitchcott 13 38
(A B Haynes) *hld up towards rr: hdwy on outside 3f out: hrd rdn 2f out: sn hung lft and wknd* **25/1**

0004 **10** *13* **Fortunes Maid (IRE)**[10] [2089] 3-8-3 46...........................(b) JimmyQuinn 11 —
(M H Tompkins) *t.k.h: in tch to 1/2-way: sn rdn and lost pl: bhd fnl 3f* **20/1**

4500 **11** *7* **Lady Firecracker (IRE)**[11] [2056] 4-9-0 40........................(v) TravisBlock(3) 5 —
(J R Best) *prom: rdn whn bdly squeezed over 2f out: nt rcvr* **33/1**

0404 **12** *3 1/4* **The Dagger**[10] [2069] 4-9-8 58..(b) GeorgeBaker 14 —
(G L Moore) *s.s: bhd: hdwy into midfield 3f out: wknd and hung lft 2f out: eased fnl f* **11/2**

2m 2.73s (-0.87) **Going Correction** -0.20s/f (Firm)
WFA 3 from 4yo+ 14lb **12** Ran SP% **122.3**
Speed ratings (Par 101): **95,94,90,90,87 86,85,85,85,75 69,67**
CSF £34.09 TOTE £3.60: £1.20, £4.30, £5.90; EX 49.20.The winner was bought in for 9,000 guineas. Sceilin was claimed by W I Bloomfield for £5,000.
Owner T Dempsey **Bred** Ballyhane Stud **Trained** Ashtead, Surrey

FOCUS
A poor race, with some jostling in the straight that ended the chance of at least two runners.
Not Now Lewis(IRE) Official explanation: jockey said gelding did not handle the track
The Dagger Official explanation: jockey said gelding was unsuited by the track

2353 SKYBET.COM EURO 2008 SPECIALS H'CAP 1m 1f 209y
4:15 (4:17) (Class 6) (0-60,60) 4-Y-0+ **£1,942** (£578; £288; £144) **Stalls** High

Form RPR

0213 **1** **Silver Blue (IRE)**[9] [2097] 5-8-9 **51** 6ex................................ LiamJones 7 61+
(W K Goldsworthy) *towards rr: rdn and hdwy over 2f out: r.o to ld ins fnl f* **15/8**[1]

416/ **2** *1 1/4* **Kangrina**[97] 6-9-4 **60**.. GeorgeBaker 13 67
(George Baker) *hld up in midfield: rdn to chse ldrs over 2f out: n.m.r over 1f out: kpt on to take 2nd fnl 75yds* **9/1**[3]

40-2 **3** *1/2* **Astrolibra**[10] [2072] 4-8-8 **50**.. JimmyQuinn 14 56
(M H Tompkins) *hld up in tch: rdn to ld over 1f out: hdd and one pce ins fnl f* **9/1**[3]

1030 **4** *1 1/2* **Granary Girl**[25] [1692] 6-8-6 **48**.. JamesDoyle 4 51
(J Pearce) *towards rr: pushed along 4f out: hdwy to chse ldrs over 1f out: hrd rdn: one pce* **10/1**

3003 **5** *2* **Personify**[17] [1895] 6-8-5 **50**......................................(p) KevinGhunowa(3) 16 49
(R A Harris) *mid-div on outside: rdn to chse ldrs over 2f out: n.m.r over 1f out: kpt on again ins fnl f* **7/1**[2]

00-0 **6** *hd* **Muffett's Dream**[8] [2128] 4-8-7 **49**............................ RichardKingscote 10 48
(J J Bridger) *t.k.h in midfield: pushed along and sltly outpcd 4f out: kpt on fnl 2f* **100/1**

2321 **7** *nse* **Faraday (IRE)**[58] [1031] 5-8-10 **52**................................ TGMcLaughlin 12 51
(A P Stringer) *led: hrd rdn and hdd over 1f out: sn wknd* **7/1**[2]

-430 **8** *1* **Border Edge**[100] [537] 10-7-13 **48**................................ RossAtkinson(7) 11 45
(J J Bridger) *prom tl hrd rdn and wknd over 1f out* **20/1**

3243 **9** *1/2* **Looks The Business (IRE)**[10] [2072] 7-8-13 **55**...........(t) SaleemGolam 2 51
(W G M Turner) *mid-div: drvn along over 2f out: nt pce to chal* **16/1**

2350 **10** *nk* **Prince Valentine**[10] [2070] 7-8-11 **53**..........................(p) FergusSweeney 15 48
(G L Moore) *stdd s and swtchd to ins: plld hrd in last pl: hdwy and swtchd lft over 1f out: nt rch ldrs* **16/1**

004- **11** *4 1/2* **Trevian**[193] [6796] 7-8-10 **52**.. WilliamBuick 3 38
(J M Bradley) *towards rr: swtchd wd and rdn 2f out: nvr able to chal: eased whn no ch fnl f* **20/1**

6610 **12** *hd* **Oasis Sun (IRE)**[70] [881] 5-8-12 **54**..................................(v) JimCrowley 8 40
(J R Best) *chsd ldrs tl wknd 2f out* **16/1**

0044 **13** *3 1/2* **Bandits Pistol (NZ)**[24] [1694] 8-8-5 **47** oh1 ow1......(v) EdwardCreighton 1 26
(M Madgwick) *towards rr: hrd rdn over 3f out: no rspnse* **33/1**

0-30 **14** *shd* **Lord Laing (USA)**[100] [541] 5-8-4 **46**................................ DavidKinsella 5 24
(H J Collingridge) *chsd ldrs tl hrd rdn and wknd over 2f out: wkng in midfield whn hmpd over 1f out* **14/1**

2160 **15** *24* **Competitor**[24] [1694] 7-8-6 **48**..(v) SimonWhitworth 9 —
(J Akehurst) *chsd ldr tl wknd over 3f out: sn lost pl: bhd and eased fnl 2f* **33/1**

2m 0.86s (-2.74) **Going Correction** -0.20s/f (Firm) **15** Ran SP% **129.6**
Speed ratings (Par 101): **102,101,100,99,97 97,97,96,96,96 92,92,89,89,70**
CSF £19.38 CT £137.57 TOTE £3.20: £1.10, £5.90, £2.30; EX 31.70.
Owner Mrs L A Goldsworthy **Bred** Mrs T V Ryan **Trained** Yerbeston, Pembrokes
■ Stewards' Enquiry : Jimmy Quinn one-day ban: used whip with excessive frequency (June 8)

FOCUS
Potentially fair form for the grade. The winner has run at Listed level in the past, and is staging a good revival under his new trainer. The runner-up looked nicely treated on old form too.
Lord Laing(USA) Official explanation: jockey said gelding suffered interference at furlong mark

2354 PLAY DEAL OR NO DEAL AT SKYVEGAS.COM FILLIES' H'CAP 1m 3f 196y
4:50 (4:50) (Class 6) (0-65,66) 4-Y-0+ **£1,942** (£578; £288; £144) **Stalls** High

Form RPR

24-1 **1** **Susie May**[51] [1148] 4-9-4 **64**.. GeorgeBaker 1 77+
(G L Moore) *hld up in tch: drvn to chse ldrs over 2f out: styd on to ld ins fnl f: rdn out* **15/8**[1]

36-1 **2** *1 3/4* **Summer Of Love (IRE)**[10] [2071] 4-9-6 **66** 6ex.........(b) FergusSweeney 2 76
(A King) *t.k.h: trckd ldrs: wnt 2nd 1/2-way: led over 1f out tl ins fnl f: nt qckn* **2/1**[2]

1546 **3** *5* **Saraba (FR)**[14] [1959] 7-9-4 **64**.. IanMongan 5 66
(Mrs L J Mongan) *hld up in rr: hdwy to chse ldrs over 2f out: one pce* **8/1**

1202 **4** *1/2* **Snake Skin**[10] [2071] 5-9-2 **62**.. JimCrowley 7 63
(J Gallagher) *disp ld: led after 4f tl over 1f out: wknd fnl f* **9/2**[3]

06-0 **5** *10* **Theatre Royal**[119] [299] 5-8-4 **50** oh4............................ WilliamBuick 3 35
(Mouse Hamilton-Fairley) *in tch: mod effrt on outside over 2f out: hrd rdn and hung lft wl over 1f out: wknd* **8/1**

505 **6** *16* **Coco L'Escargot**[31] [1542] 4-8-4 **50**.................................... LiamJones 6 10
(J R Jenkins) *chsd ldrs 5f: rdn and bhd fr 1/2-way* **25/1**

60-0 **7** *3 3/4* **Silver Surprise**[15] [1929] 4-8-4 **50** oh5.............................. JimmyQuinn 4 4
(J J Bridger) *disp ld 4f: wknd 4f out: bhd fnl 3f* **40/1**

2m 29.21s (-3.49) **Going Correction** -0.20s/f (Firm) **7** Ran SP% **114.8**
Speed ratings (Par 98): **103,101,98,98,91 80,78**
CSF £5.99 TOTE £2.40: £1.30, £1.80; EX 5.40.
Owner Mrs Charles Cyzer **Bred** Bottisham Heath Stud **Trained** Woodingdean, E Sussex

FOCUS
The first two are improving for their new trainers and set a fair standard for the course, but the rest are moderate at best.

2355 PLAY POKER AT SKYPOKER.COM H'CAP 6f 209y
5:25 (5:25) (Class 6) (0-60,57) 4-Y-0+ **£1,942** (£578; £288; £144) **Stalls** Low

Form RPR

5550 **1** **Batchworth Blaise**[44] [1269] 5-8-6 **45**.................................... LiamJones 15 56
(E A Wheeler) *patiently rdn fr rr: gd hdwy fr 2f out: r.o to ld fnl 100yds* **20/1**

6530 **2** *3/4* **Patavium Prince (IRE)**[31] [1528] 5-8-9 **51**...................... TravisBlock(3) 7 60
(Miss Jo Crowley) *w ldr: led 3f out: hrd rdn over 1f out: hdd and one pce fnl 100yds* **8/1**[3]

4366 **3** *1/2* **Imperium**[8] [2128] 7-9-4 **57**..(b) GeorgeBaker 10 65
(Jean-Rene Auvray) *hld up in rr of midfield gng wl: hdwy 2f out: drvn to chal whn swvd lft over 1f out: one pce ins fnl f* **4/1**[1]

2025 **4** *2 3/4* **Tilsworth Charlie**[11] [2055] 5-9-2 **55**.................................(b) JimCrowley 6 55
(J R Jenkins) *in tch: rdn to chse ldrs over 2f out: one pce appr fnl f* **13/2**[2]

3506 **5** *3/4* **Fun In The Sun**[10] [2070] 4-8-9 **48**.................................... SamHitchcott 3 46
(A B Haynes) *chsd ldrs on rail: drvn to chal over 1f out: no ex ins fnl f* **16/1**

0-66 **6** *nk* **Border Artist**[28] [1602] 9-9-4 **57**.. JimmyQuinn 4 54
(J Pearce) *towards rr: hdwy and in tch 2f out: hrd rdn and no imp over 1f out* **12/1**

4064 **7** *4* **Metropolitan Chief**[10] [2075] 4-8-7 **53**............................ MCGeran(7) 11 40
(P Burgoyne) *rrd s: hld up towards rr: sme hdwy into midfield 3f out: nt pce to chal* **9/1**

-106 **8** *1 1/2* **Turkish Sultan (IRE)**[13] [2003] 5-8-6 **52**....................(b[1]) RossAtkinson(7) 9 35
(J M Bradley) *in tch: rdn and lost pl 1/2-way: hung bdly lft over 1f out: n.d* **9/1**

0004 **9** *3/4* **Djalalabad (FR)**[11] [2055] 4-8-11 **50**................................ TGMcLaughlin 1 30
(Mrs C A Dunnett) *led tl 3f out: wknd over 1f out* **25/1**

00-0 **10** *shd* **Brean Dot Com (IRE)**[17] [1906] 4-8-6 **45**............................ PaulEddery 13 25
(Mrs P N Dutfield) *sn bhd and rdn along: sme late hdwy* **66/1**

0-60 **11** *1/2* **Charming Ballet (IRE)**[35] [1455] 5-8-6 **45**................(b) SimonWhitworth 8 24
(G L Moore) *prom tl wknd over 2f out* **10/1**

00-0 **12** *2 1/4* **Inwaan (IRE)**[10] [2075] 5-9-0 **53**..(p) JamesDoyle 2 26
(P R Webber) *prom tl wknd over 2f out* **13/2**[2]

-000 **13** 2 ½ **Baba Ghanoush**[100] 535 6-8-6 **45** .... PaulDoe 12 11
(M J Attwater) *bolted to post: dwlt: sn wl bhd* **33/1**

0660 **14** 2 ½ **Tuning Fork**[46] 1248 8-8-6 **45** .... DavidKinsella 14 4
(M J Attwater) *chsd ldrs tl hrd rdn and wknd over 2f out* **16/1**

0606 **15** 1 ¼ **Smokin Joe**[45] 1256 7-8-11 **50** ....(b) FergusSweeney 5 6
(J R Best) *mid-div on rail: drvn along and lost pl 3f out: bhd and eased fnl f* **11/1**

1m 21.52s (-1.58) **Going Correction** -0.20s/f (Firm) **15** Ran SP% **127.7**
Speed ratings (Par 101): **101,100,99,96,95 95,90,88,88,87 87,84,81,79,77**
CSF £176.37 CT £812.53 TOTE £33.40: £11.10, £5.70, £1.20; EX 294.30 Place 6: £48.63 Place 5: £43.49 .
Owner Astrod TA Austin Stroud & Co **Bred** Mrs D Price **Trained** Whitchurch-on-Thames, Oxon

FOCUS
A modest race, featuring few reliable yardsticks, but it was run at a good pace.
Brean Dot Com(IRE) Official explanation: jockey said gelding was unsuited by the good to firm (firm in places) ground
Smokin Joe Official explanation: jockey said gelding lost its action
T/Plt: £29.70 to a £1 stake. Pool: £51,245.15. 1,257.00 winning tickets. T/Qpdt: £8.10 to a £1 stake. Pool: £3,047.90. 275.10 winning tickets. LM

2331 HAYDOCK (L-H)
Friday, May 23

OFFICIAL GOING: Good to firm (firm in places)
Wind: Light, behind Weather: Overcast

2356 GEORGE DUFFIELD APPRENTICE H'CAP 5f
6:20 (6:22) (Class 5) (0-75,73) 4-Y-0+ **£3,043** (£905; £452; £226) **Stalls** Centre

Form RPR

-000 **1** **Mandurah (IRE)**[20] 1818 4-8-10 **64** .... MarkCoumbe 6 74
(D Nicholls) *squeezed s: sn trckd ldrs: rdn to chal over 1f out: r.o to ld towards fin* **7/2**[1]

-544 **2** ½ **Comptonspirit**[13] 1997 4-8-6 **63** .... DeclanCannon(3) 5 71
(B P J Baugh) *w ldr: rdn to ld 1f out: hdd towards fin* **15/2**

0462 **3** ½ **Timber Treasure (USA)**[13] 2005 4-8-8 **67** ....(b) AndrewHeffernan(5) 3 73+
(Paul Green) *broke wl: sn dropped towards rr: rdn and hdwy over 1f out: r.o and gaining towards fin* **7/1**

-036 **4** *nk* **Whinhill House**[4] 2248 8-8-8 **62** ....(v) GaryBartley 8 67
(D W Barker) *led: rdn and hdd 1f out: nt qckn ins fnl f* **9/2**[2]

0-20 **5** ½ **Green Lagonda (AUS)**[13] 1997 6-8-9 **63** .... MatthewDavies 4 67
(J G Given) *in tch: effrt 2f out: chalng and ev ch over 1f out: no ex wl ins fnl f* **13/2**[3]

242- **6** 3 **Hotham**[195] 6762 5-9-0 **73** .... SamuelDrury(5) 2 66
(N Wilson) *bhd: rdn over 1f out: styd on fnl f: nt pce to rch ldrs* **7/1**

0-60 **7** 2 **The History Man (IRE)**[20] 1818 5-8-7 **68** ow3........(be) MJMurphy(7) 7 54
(M Mullineaux) *chsd ldrs: rdn 1/2-way: wknd over 1f out* **16/1**

11-3 **8** *hd* **Lady Bahia (IRE)**[11] 2050 7-8-12 **66** ....(b) ClGillies 10 51
(Peter Grayson) *missed break: sn in midfield: rdn and hung lft over 1f out: wknd ins fnl f* **12/1**

31/6 **9** ½ **Wicked Wilma (IRE)**[22] 1755 4-8-5 **59** oh1........ DanielleMcCreery 1 42
(A Berry) *racd keenly: handy for 1f: sn racd off the pce: rdn and hung lft over 1f out: wknd ins fnl f* **33/1**

00-0 **10** 2 ¼ **Spanish Ace**[31] 1537 7-9-1 **72** .... BillyCray(3) 9 47
(J M Bradley) *chsd ldrs: rdn 1/2-way: wknd 2f out* **8/1**

59.63 secs (-0.87) **Going Correction** -0.225s/f (Firm) **10** Ran SP% **118.1**
Speed ratings (Par 103): **97,96,95,94,94 89,86,85,85,81**
CSF £30.54 CT £176.85 TOTE £4.50: £2.00, £2.90, £2.30; EX 37.50.
Owner Martin Hignett **Bred** Michael Lyons **Trained** Sessay, N Yorks

FOCUS
A modest sprint, confined to apprentice riders. The first five were fairly closely covered at the finish and the form appears straightforward and solid for the grade.

2357 E B F LAMBRINI MAIDEN FILLIES' STKS 6f
6:50 (6:50) (Class 5) 2-Y-O **£3,853** (£1,146; £572; £286) **Stalls** Centre

Form RPR

3 **1** **Undaunted Affair (IRE)**[14] 1961 2-9-0 0........ NCallan 9 88+
(K A Ryan) *wnt rt s: in tch: led 1/2-way: drawing clr whn edgd lft over 1f out: rn wl: eased down towards fin* **6/4**[1]

2 2 ½ **Maid For Music (IRE)** 2-9-0 0........ AdrianTNicholls 8 77+
(E S McMahon) *handy: rdn 2f out: wnt 2nd over 1f out: nt pce of wnr fnl f* **2/1**[2]

3 ½ **Dubai's Gazal** 2-9-0 0........ TPO'Shea 2 75+
(M R Channon) *w ldrs: rdn 2f out: kpt on same pce fr over 1f out* **20/1**

4 7 **Desert Sunset** 2-9-0 0........ RobertWinston 6 54+
(M Johnston) *hmpd s: rn green and outpcd: kpt on fnl f: nvr on terms w ldrs* **14/1**

53 **5** 2 ¼ **Rosabee (IRE)**[22] 1749 2-9-0 0........ GregFairley 7 47
(Miss V Haigh) *hld up bhd ldrs: hdwy 1/2-way: rdn 2f out: hung lft fr over 1f out: sn wknd* **12/1**

6 2 ¼ **Haven't A Clue** 2-9-0 0........ SebSanders 3 41
(Sir Mark Prescott) *w ldr: lost pl 1/2-way: outpcd after* **11/2**[3]

0 **7** 6 **Wigan Pier**[27] 1610 2-9-0 0........ GrahamGibbons 4 23
(T D Easterby) *racd keenly: led to 1/2-way: wknd over 1f out* **16/1**

0 **8** 20 **Avonlini**[27] 1610 2-8-11 0........ TolleyDean(3) 1 —
(B P J Baugh) *sn bhd* **100/1**

1m 12.95s (-1.05) **Going Correction** -0.225s/f (Firm) **8** Ran SP% **114.7**
Speed ratings (Par 90): **98,94,94,84,81 78,70,44**
CSF £4.66 TOTE £2.50: £1.10, £1.50, £2.80; EX 6.40.
Owner K Lee & L M Rutherford **Bred** J Collins **Trained** Hambleton, N Yorks

FOCUS
A fair fillies' maiden which saw the first three come clear. The winner rates value for further and this could prove an above-average contest.

NOTEBOOK
Undaunted Affair(IRE) ◆, third on debut at Nottingham a fortnight previously, could have been expected to have learned a good deal for that initial experience and not surprisingly proved a warm order in the betting ring. She eventually got the job done with plenty left in the tank, rating value for at least double the winning margin, and is clearly a filly on the up. The extra furlong was ideal and a step up in class now beckons. (op 7-4 tchd 2-1)
Maid For Music(IRE), whose dam was a 6f juvenile debutante winner, knew her job and was soon racing on the early pace. She eventually got put in her place when the winner quickened late on, but this rates as a pleasing debut effort and she has one of these within her compass in the coming weeks. (op 7-2)
Dubai's Gazal, whose stable have now hit top gear with it's juveniles, is bred to enjoy another furlong or so in due course and was allowed to go off at big odds for this racecourse bow. She ran a respectable race in defeat, shaping as though another will suit before long, and is entitled to come on nicely for the experience. (op 8-1)
Desert Sunset, who has speed in her pedigree, was done no favours at the start and then proved too green to do herself full justice. She ought to come on a bundle for this debut effort. (op 10-1 tchd 9-1)
Rosabee(IRE) Official explanation: jockey said filly hung left
Haven't A Clue, who holds a Listed entry, was the first juvenile runner from her stable and she proved distinctly green from halfway. Another furlong should suit in due course and it would be a surprise were she not to prove a lot sharper next time out. (op 6-1 tchd 5-1)

2358 CHAMPAGNE LANSON STKS (H'CAP) 6f
7:20 (7:25) (Class 4) (0-85,84) 4-Y-0+ **£5,310** (£1,580; £789; £394) **Stalls** Centre

Form RPR

-063 **1** **Obe Gold**[14] 1969 6-9-3 **83**........(v) AdrianTNicholls 7 98
(D Nicholls) *trckd ldrs: led 2f out: rdn over 1f out: asserted fnl f* **3/1**[1]

-000 **2** 3 ¾ **Heywood**[14] 1942 4-9-2 **82**........ TPO'Shea 5 85
(D Nicholls) *trckd ldrs: rdn to chal 2f out: outpcd by wnr fnl f* **7/1**

0-20 **3** 1 ½ **Manchurian**[25] 1683 4-8-11 **77**........ DO'Donohoe 6 75
(M J Wallace) *hld up: rdn and hdwy over 1f out: edgd lft ins fnl f: kpt on: nt pce of ldrs* **10/3**[2]

10-0 **4** 3 ¼ **Ellens Academy (IRE)**[42] 1300 13-9-1 **81**........ SebSanders 1 69
(E J Alston) *stdd s: hld up in rr: hdwy 2f out: one pce fnl f* **16/1**

00-1 **5** 1 **Pacific Pride**[14] 1969 5-8-13 **79**........ GrahamGibbons 4 64
(J J Quinn) *w ldr: rdn 2f out: wknd ins fnl f* **5/1**

3356 **6** 1 ¼ **Distinctly Game**[32] 1517 6-9-4 **84**........ NCallan 8 65
(K A Ryan) *racd keenly: led: hdd 2f out: wknd over 1f out* **7/2**[3]

0016 **7** 5 **Imperial Echo (USA)**[17] 1891 7-8-6 **75** ow1........ TolleyDean(3) 3 40
(D Shaw) *hld up: rdn and hdwy 2f out: wknd fnl f* **11/1**

1m 11.86s (-2.14) **Going Correction** -0.225s/f (Firm) **7** Ran SP% **113.7**
Speed ratings (Par 105): **105,100,98,93,92 90,84**
CSF £23.91 CT £72.48 TOTE £3.70: £1.90, £3.50; EX 20.50.
Owner Middleham Park Racing XLIV **Bred** Mrs M Mason **Trained** Sessay, N Yorks

FOCUS
A good sprint for the class, but it was run at just a modest early pace. The winner is rated to last year's best and there could be more to come.

2359 HARVEY NICHOLS H'CAP 5f
7:50 (7:50) (Class 3) (0-90,85) 4-Y-0+ **£10,167** (£3,025; £1,511; £755) **Stalls** Centre

Form RPR

6 **1** **Mondovi**[14] 1956 4-9-0 **81**........ FergalLynch 7 95
(N J Vaughan) *hld up bhd ldrs on stands' side: swtchd lft and hdwy under 2f out: edgd rt and led over 1f out: r.o wl* **14/1**

60-0 **2** 2 ½ **Fantasy Explorer**[30] 1571 5-9-3 **84**........ GrahamGibbons 8 89
(J J Quinn) *racd bhd ldrs on stands' side: rdn and hdwy over 1f out: styd on ins fnl f: nt pce of wnr* **4/1**[2]

60-0 **3** ¾ **Mambo Spirit (IRE)**[20] 1796 4-8-13 **80**........ SebSanders 2 82
(J G Given) *chsd ldr on far side: rdn over 1f out: led sole rival on that side ins fnl f: kpt on but no ch w stands' side gp* **4/1**[2]

03-0 **4** *nk* **Bahamian Ballet**[16] 1908 6-8-12 **79**........ RichardMullen 5 80
(E S McMahon) *prom on stands' side: rdn whn n.m.r and hmpd over 1f out: kpt on same pce after* **6/1**

1431 **5** ¾ **Royal Envoy (IRE)**[20] 1818 5-8-11 **81**........ TolleyDean(3) 4 80
(D Shaw) *chsd ldrs on stands' side: rdn 2f out: one pce fr over 1f out* **5/1**[3]

0046 **6** 2 ¼ **Cape Royal**[20] 1802 8-9-4 **85**........(bt) NCallan 6 75
(J M Bradley) *racd on stands' rail: led: rdn and hdd over 1f out: hung lft whn wkng ins fnl f* **8/1**

-400 **7** *hd* **Coconut Moon**[6] 2210 6-8-10 **77**........ RobertWinston 1 67
(E J Alston) *led sole rival on far side: rdn over 1f out: hdd on that side ins fnl f: sn wknd* **20/1**

1611 **8** 1 ½ **Jilly Why (IRE)**[6] 2212 7-8-7 **81** 6ex........(b) AndrewHeffernan(7) 3 65
(Paul Green) *slipped s: racd stands' side: a bhd* **7/2**[1]

59.05 secs (-1.45) **Going Correction** -0.225s/f (Firm) **8** Ran SP% **115.7**
Speed ratings (Par 107): **102,98,96,96,95 91,91,88**
CSF £70.00 CT £273.76 TOTE £15.30: £3.40, £1.60, £1.80; EX 103.20.
Owner K Dyer & C Bellamy **Bred** Branston Stud Ltd **Trained** Hampton Heat, Cheshire
■ Stewards' Enquiry : N Callan one-day ban: failed to ride to draw (Jun 9)
Fergal Lynch one-day ban: careless riding (Jun 8)

FOCUS
A fair sprint handicap which all but two raced on the favoured stands' side. The level is somewhat fluid with the winner seemingly progressive.

NOTEBOOK
Mondovi ◆ showed the clear benefit of her comeback run a fortnight previously and, with the aid of the stands' rail, came home to score most readily. This ex-German filly looks progressive, clearly enjoys quick ground, and is versatile as regards her best trip. She is one to follow. (tchd 16-1 in places)
Fantasy Explorer, like the winner, was another to improve on the level of his seasonal debut and was keeping on with promise inside the final furlong. This proves he still has an engine, a quick surface is much more to his liking, and a return to another furlong can see him finish closer still. (op 9-2)
Mambo Spirit(IRE) ◆ was yet another to show the benefit of his return to action 20 days previously and emerged best of the pair who raced far side. He is attractively handicapped at present and looks ready to strike in the coming weeks. (op 9-2)
Bahamian Ballet would have finished a little closer with a clearer passage nearing the final furlong and this was a definite step in the right direction from him. (op 8-1)
Royal Envoy(IRE) had his chance, but simply looked to be found out by his 7lb higher mark. Official explanation: jockey said gelding was unsuited by the good to firm (firm in places) ground (tchd 9-2)
Jilly Why(IRE), bidding for a hat-trick under her penalty, lost her chance when slipping soon after the start and should really be given another chance. However, she is due to race from a 4lb higher future mark now. Official explanation: jockey said mare stumbled leaving stalls and never travelled after (op 10-3)

2360 BINGLEY TBS MAIDEN STKS 1m 30y
8:20 (8:21) (Class 5) 3-Y-O+ **£3,043** (£905; £452; £226) **Stalls** Low

Form RPR

33-2 **1** **Missioner (USA)**[11] 2056 3-8-13 0........ GregFairley 14 89+
(M Johnston) *chsd ldrs: cl 2nd over 3f out: rdn to ld narrowly 2f out: r.o gamely thrght fnl f: pushed out towards fin* **6/4**[1]

2 **2** *nk* **Liberation Spirit (USA)**[22] 1748 3-8-13 0........ ShaneKelly 10 88+
(J Noseda) *stmbld sltly s: racd keenly: chsd ldr: led over 3f out: hdd narrowly 2f out: continued to chal strly: r.o u.p thrght fnl f* **5/2**[2]

3 4 **Presvis** 4-9-4 0........ MJMurphy(7) 3 82+
(L M Cumani) *stdd s: hld up bhd: hdwy whn n.m.r over 2f out: rn green: styd on ins fnl f: nt rch front pair: can improve* **50/1**

0- **4** ½ **Ebn Malk (IRE)**[206] 6571 3-8-13 0........ PhilipRobinson 12 78
(M A Jarvis) *racd keenly: chsd ldrs: rdn over 2f out: kpt on same pce and no imp on ldrs fnl 2f* **5/1**[3]

3-0 **5** *2* **Ezdeyaad (USA)**[13] 2008 4-9-11 0........................ TPO'Shea 2 76+
(G A Swinbank) *led: clr 5f out: hdd over 3f out: kpt on same pce fr 2f out tl no ex ins fnl f* **33/1**

4-0 **6** *shd* **Dear Maurice**[15] 1926 4-9-11 0........................ SebSanders 4 76
(E A L Dunlop) *midfield: rdn over 2f out: kpt on same pce fnl f* **8/1**

0- **7** *5* **Theonebox (USA)**[284] 4454 3-8-13 0........................ FergalLynch 1 62
(N J Vaughan) *bhd: pushed along and sme hdwy over 2f out: nvr trbld ldrs* **125/1**

64- **8** *1 1/4* **La Fortalesa (IRE)**[223] 6184 3-8-13 0........................ NCallan 11 59
(K A Ryan) *in tch: rdn and wknd 3f out* **16/1**

6-3 **9** *7* **Media Stars**[18] 1855 3-8-13 0........................ GrahamGibbons 5 43
(J A Osborne) *racd keenly: in tch: wknd 4f out* **33/1**

40 **10** *3 1/4* **Daralym (IRE)**[16] 1918 3-8-6 0........................ AndrewHeffernan(7) 6 35
(Paul Green) *midfield: rdn over 4f out: wknd over 2f out* **100/1**

11 *1/2* **Border Fox**[65] 5-9-11 0........................ PaddyAspell 9 37
(L Lungo) *s.v.s: a bhd* **33/1**

12 *nk* **Soviet (IRE)** 3-8-13 0........................ RobertWinston 8 33
(M Johnston) *s.s: pushed along 4f out: a bhd* **20/1**

0- **13** *29* **Diplomatic Dan (IRE)**[393] 1259 5-9-11 0........................ AdrianTNicholls 7 —
(E J Alston) *rdn over 3f out: a bhd* **100/1**

1m 42.04s (-1.76) **Going Correction** -0.125s/f (Firm)
WFA 3 from 4yo+ 12lb **13** Ran SP% **120.6**
Speed ratings (Par 103): **103,102,98,98,96 96,91,89,82,79 79,78,49**
CSF £4.88 TOTE £2.60: £1.20, £1.50, £10.80; EX 7.20.
Owner Sheikh Hamdan Bin Mohammed Al Maktoum **Bred** Gainsborough Farm Inc **Trained** Middleham Moor, N Yorks

FOCUS
This was just a modest maiden, but the pace was strong, the form makes sense and the first pair came clear and can both rate higher.
Presvis Official explanation: jockey said gelding was slowly into stride on leaving stalls and ran green

2361 JASPER STKS (H'CAP) 1m 3f 200y
8:50 (8:50) (Class 5) (0-75,74) 4-Y-O+ **£5,310** (£1,580; £789; £394) **Stalls** High

Form RPR

-100 **1** **Bull Market (IRE)**[20] 1793 5-8-13 **69**........................ StephenDonohoe 1 79
(Ian Williams) *hld up: hdwy over 3f out: led wl over 2f out: clr over 1f out: styd on wl: dismntd after line* **7/1**[3]

000/ **2** *3 1/4* **Bad Boy Al (IRE)**[629] 5025 4-8-4 **60** oh15........................ FergalLynch 4 65
(N J Vaughan) *w ldr: rdn over 2f out: kpt on same pce: n.d to wnr fnl f* **20/1**

2155 **3** *1/2* **Punta Galera (IRE)**[13] 2006 5-8-6 **62**........................ FrancisNorton 6 66
(Paul Green) *trckd ldrs: rdn over 2f out: kpt on same pce* **9/2**[2]

40-4 **4** *3* **Pretty Demanding (IRE)**[34] 1482 4-9-3 **73**........................ TPO'Shea 7 73
(M G Quinlan) *hld up: rdn and hung lft over 2f out: fnd nil* **2/1**[1]

00-2 **5** *2 1/4* **Wyeth**[25] 1692 4-8-8 **64** ow1........................ RobertWinston 3 60
(J R Fanshawe) *led: rdn and hdd wl over 2f out: wknd 1f out* **2/1**[1]

225/ **6** *dist* **Burnbank (IRE)**[30] 2224 5-8-11 **67**........................ NCallan 5 —
(P Bowen) *trckd ldrs: rdn and wknd qckly over 3f out: t.o fr 2f out: virtually p.u fnl f* **8/1**

2m 33.97s (0.77) **Going Correction** -0.125s/f (Firm) **6** Ran SP% **113.2**
Speed ratings (Par 103): **92,89,89,87,86** —
CSF £112.24 TOTE £9.50: £4.10, £2.40; EX 143.20 Place 6 £ 295.23, Place 5 £ 139.77.
Owner Dr Marwan Koukash **Bred** King Bloodstock **Trained** Portway, Worcs

FOCUS
A modest handicap which produced a very moderate winning time for the class, due to the lack of early pace and there are some doubts over the form.
Burnbank(IRE) Official explanation: jockey said gelding hung left
T/Plt: £640.00 to a £1 stake. Pool: £56,158.53. 64.05 winning tickets. T/Qpdt: £1,096.90 to a £1 stake. Pool: £4,002.30. 2.70 winning tickets. DO

2154 NEWCASTLE (L-H)
Friday, May 23

OFFICIAL GOING: Good to firm (firm in places)
Wind: Breezy, half behind Weather: Dry, sunny

2362 MITIE MEDIAN AUCTION MAIDEN STKS 6f
2:10 (2:10) (Class 6) 2-Y-O **£2,428** (£722; £361; £180) **Stalls** High

Form RPR

1 **Folsomprisonblues (IRE)** 2-9-3 0........................ ChrisCatlin 7 78+
(E J O'Neill) *s.i.s: bhd and outpcd: gd hdwy 2f out: led and drifted lft ins fnl f: hld on wl* **9/2**[2]

3 **2** *hd* **Faraway Sound (IRE)**[36] 1425 2-9-3 0........................ LeeEnstone 10 74
(P C Haslam) *led: rdn and edgd lft 2f out: hdd ins fnl f: rallied: jst hld* **6/1**

02 **3** *nse* **Happy Anniversary (IRE)**[5] 2217 2-8-12 0........................ MickyFenton 11 69
(Miss V Haigh) *trckd ldrs: drvn and outpcd over 2f out: kpt on strly fnl f: jst hld* **7/2**[1]

0 **4** *1 1/4* **Tagula Breeze (IRE)**[11] 2035 2-9-3 0........................ RoystonFfrench 4 70
(I W McInnes) *hld up: effrt over 2f out: kpt on ins fnl f* **50/1**

4 **5** *4 1/2* **Blow Your Mind**[17] 1889 2-9-3 0........................ PaulHanagan 2 57
(Karen McLintock) *w ldrs tl wknd over 1f out* **20/1**

6 *4 1/2* **Rapid Release (CAN)** 2-9-3 0........................ SebSanders 6 43
(Sir Mark Prescott) *trckd ldrs: outpcd over 2f out: sn btn* **11/2**[3]

7 *1 1/4* **Great Charter (USA)** 2-9-3 0........................ JoeFanning 8 43+
(M Johnston) *w ldrs: rn green and outpcd 2f out: sn btn* **9/2**[2]

8 *3 1/4* **Ten Cents A Dance** 2-9-3 0........................ DavidAllan 12 30
(T D Easterby) *bhd and sn outpcd: nvr on terms* **10/1**

3 **9** *hd* **Sorrel Ridge (IRE)**[43] 1276 2-9-0 0........................ JerryO'Dwyer(3) 5 29
(M G Quinlan) *chsd ldrs tl wknd over 1f out* **14/1**

10 *16* **Cotton N Silk** 2-8-9 0........................ DuranFentiman(3) 9 —
(T D Easterby) *s.i.s: sn wl bhd* **40/1**

11 *nk* **Ed's Pride (IRE)** 2-9-3 0........................ PaulMulrennan 1 —
(K A Ryan) *s.i.s: a struggling* **20/1**

1m 13.42s (-1.78) **Going Correction** -0.50s/f (Hard) **11** Ran SP% **117.9**
Speed ratings (Par 91): **91,90,90,89,83 77,75,71,70,49 49**
CSF £30.35 TOTE £5.60: £2.10, £2.00, £1.40; EX 26.20 Trifecta £90.00 Part won: Pool: £126.79, 0.40 winning units..
Owner Phil Cunningham **Bred** G W Robinson **Trained** Averham Park, Notts

FOCUS
An ordinary event in which the gallop was sound throughout. The form is fairly solid and the winner is the type to progress again.

NOTEBOOK
Folsomprisonblues(IRE) ◆, a half-brother to several useful sprinters, is a medium-sized, lengthy sort who created a favourable impression on this racecourse debut. He did well given his apparent inexperience, looks better than the bare form and is the type to progress again and win more races. (op 3-1)
Faraway Sound(IRE), who shaped well over 5f on easy ground on his debut, had the run of the race and bettered that effort over this longer trip on quicker ground. While showing a tendency to edge off the rail, he looks more than capable of winning a similar event. (op 5-1 tchd 4-1)
Happy Anniversary(IRE) has improved with every outing and turned in her best effort yet. She will be well suited by the step up to 7f and, although vulnerable to the more progressive sorts in this grade, is capable of picking up a similar event. (op 4-1 tchd 3-1)
Tagula Breeze(IRE), easy to back and well beaten on his debut, left that form well behind over this longer trip. He should be suited by 7f in due course and is capable of picking up an ordinary event this summer.
Blow Your Mind, who hinted at ability at a modest level on his debut, probably ran to a similar level over this longer trip. Modest nursery company will provide him with his best chance of success. (op 28-1)
Rapid Release(CAN), out of a US turf winner, holds a Derby entry but that looks optimistic on the evidence of this debut run. He is sure to be better for the experience, though, and may well fare better once qualified for a nursery mark. (op 8-1)
Great Charter(USA), took the eye in the paddock, despite his greenness, showed his inexperience in the race as well and was ultimately well beaten. However, he is sure to come on for this run and is not one to write off. (op 7-2 tchd 5-1 tchd 11-2 in a place)

2363 HALL & PARTNERS MEDIAN AUCTION MAIDEN STKS 1m 4f 93y
2:45 (2:45) (Class 6) 3-4-Y-O **£2,428** (£722; £361; £180) **Stalls** Centre

Form RPR

0-02 **1** **Blimey O'Riley (IRE)**[23] 1731 3-8-10 72........................ PaulMulrennan 4 67+
(M H Tompkins) *set stdy pce: rdn over 2f out: kpt on wl fnl f* **10/11**[1]

2 *2 1/2* **Hollins**[34] 4-9-13 0........................ PaulHanagan 2 63
(Micky Hammond) *prom: effrt over 2f out: kpt on fnl f to take 2nd post: nt rch wnr* **8/1**

0 **3** *nse* **Yonder**[8] 2123 4-9-8 0........................ SteveDrowne 5 58
(H Morrison) *presed wnr: rdn 3f out: sn ev ch: one pce fnl f: ct for 2nd post* **11/4**[2]

4 *1 1/2* **Bocciani (GER)** 3-8-10 0........................(b[1]) JoeFanning 1 60
(M Johnston) *trckd ldrs: n.m.r and swtchd rt over 2f out: effrt over 1f out: no imp fnl f* **6/1**[3]

6 **5** *3 1/2* **Fleurs De Censier**[22] 1741 3-8-5 0........................ ChrisCatlin 3 49
(D M Simcock) *last but in tch: sn niggled along: drvn 3f out: no imp fr 2f out* **22/1**

2m 45.84s (0.24) **Going Correction** -0.225s/f (Firm)
WFA 3 from 4yo 17lb **5** Ran SP% **108.8**
Speed ratings (Par 101): **90,88,88,87,84**
CSF £8.61 TOTE £1.70: £1.10, £3.00; EX 7.60.
Owner Trevor Benton **Bred** Mrs Ann Kennedy **Trained** Newmarket, Suffolk

FOCUS
An uncompetitive event and a muddling gallop resulted in a very moderate winning time, over 4 secs slower than the following handicap. The form looks weak with the third the best guide.

2364 EVERSHEDS H'CAP 1m 4f 93y
3:20 (3:20) (Class 6) (0-60,60) 4-Y-O+ **£2,590** (£770; £385; £192) **Stalls** Centre

Form RPR

-311 **1** **Annibale Caro**[3] 2286 6-9-1 **60** 6ex........................ PJMcDonald(3) 11 74+
(Grant Tuer) *midfield: smooth hdwy to ld over 1f out: drvn out fnl f* **11/4**[1]

03-5 **2** *2 1/4* **Hits Only Vic (USA)**[3] 2286 4-9-4 **60**........................ DavidAllan 3 70
(D Carroll) *prom: effrt and ev ch wl over 1f out: kpt on ins fnl f: nt pce of wnr* **10/1**

0/04 **3** *1 1/2* **Smoothly Does It**[24] 277 7-8-8 **50**........................ PaulHanagan 12 58
(R A Fahey) *t.k.h in midfield: effrt and rdn over 2f out: kpt on u.p ins fnl f* **6/1**[3]

33-6 **4** *1* **Hi Dancer**[21] 1776 5-8-5 **54**........................ PatrickDonaghy(7) 8 60
(P C Haslam) *midfield: drvn over 3f out: kpt on fnl f: nrst fin* **14/1**

2506 **5** *hd* **Fenners (USA)**[81] 778 5-8-11 **60**........................ BradleyRoper(7) 1 66
(M W Easterby) *midfield: effrt over 2f out: kpt on u.p fnl f* **16/1**

-652 **6** *nk* **Thorny Mandate**[11] 2053 6-8-11 **53**........................ FergalLynch 16 59+
(W M Brisbourne) *stdd in last pl: stdy hdwy over 2f out: n.m.r over 1f out: kpt on: nvr nr ldrs* **9/1**

5555 **7** *2* **Tour D'Amour (IRE)**[25] 1679 5-8-1 **48**........................(b) KellyHarrison(5) 9 50
(R Craggs) *cl up: led over 2f out to over 1f out: sn no ex* **14/1**

/4-6 **8** *nk* **San Deng**[30] 1559 6-9-1 **57**........................ PaulMulrennan 15 59
(Micky Hammond) *bhd: drvn over 3f out: sme late hdwy: nvr on terms* **50/1**

0-60 **9** *1 1/2* **Welcome Cat (USA)**[32] 1518 4-8-11 **53**........................ SilvestreDeSousa 10 53
(A D Brown) *hld up: drvn over 3f out: n.d* **80/1**

066- **10** *shd* **Bollin Freddie**[268] 4943 4-8-6 **48**........................ RoystonFfrench 17 47
(A J Lockwood) *dwlt: hld up: drvn 3f out: n.d* **28/1**

0-32 **11** *3/4* **Bijou Dan**[17] 1890 7-9-1 **57**........................ SebSanders 6 55+
(G M Moore) *hld up: rdn 3f out: hdwy on ins whn nt clr run over 1f out: sn n.d* **4/1**[2]

0-40 **12** *1 1/2* **Miss Havisham (IRE)**[21] 1773 4-8-1 **46**........................(b[1]) AndrewMullen(3) 4 42
(J R Weymes) *in tch: drvn 4f out: wknd 2f out* **40/1**

30-0 **13** *9* **Bond Casino**[14] 1972 4-8-13 **55**........................ ChrisCatlin 13 36
(G R Oldroyd) *prom: drvn over 4f out: wknd fnl 2f* **25/1**

0-63 **14** *3/4* **Ja Myford**[14] 1968 4-8-10 **52**........................(p) MickyFenton 7 32
(P T Midgley) *led to over 2f out: wknd over 1f out* **12/1**

060- **15** *5* **Sendali (FR)**[272] 4821 4-8-6 **48**........................ JoeFanning 14 20
(J D Bethell) *t.k.h: hld up: drvn over 3f out: sn wknd* **12/1**

2m 41.79s (-3.81) **Going Correction** -0.225s/f (Firm) **15** Ran SP% **127.6**
Speed ratings (Par 101): **103,101,100,99,99 99,98,97,96,96 96,95,89,88,85**
CSF £31.92 CT £164.27 TOTE £3.90: £1.90, £3.40, £2.90; EX 39.50 Trifecta £212.20 Pool: £301.93, 1.01 winning units.
Owner G Tuer **Bred** Cyril Humphris **Trained** Birkby, N Yorks

FOCUS
A run-of-the-mill handicap but one run at a decent gallop throughout and this bare form looks solid and should prove reliable. The winner showed improved form while the running of the sixth caught the eye.
Thorny Mandate Official explanation: jockey said gelding was denied a clear run

2365 CROFT TECHNOLOGY H'CAP 1m 2f 32y
3:55 (3:57) (Class 6) (0-65,65) 4-Y-O+ **£2,752** (£818; £409; £204) **Stalls** Centre

Form RPR

6-03 **1** **Dechiper (IRE)**[19] 1822 6-8-9 **63**........................ PatrickDonaghy(7) 17 71
(R Johnson) *hld up: smooth hdwy on outside over 3f out: rdn to ld ins fnl f: drvn out* **8/1**

2-06 **2** ½ **Dan Tucker**[13] 2006 4-9-4 **65** PhillipMakin 13 72
(N Tinkler) *hld up: hdwy over 2f out: kpt on fnl f: wnt 2nd cl home* **5/1**[3]

000- **3** shd **Nesno (USA)**[300] 3955 5-8-12 **59** JoeFanning 2 66
(J D Bethell) *t.k.h: pressed ldr: led appr fnl f to ins fnl f: no ex and lost 2nd cl home* **10/1**

2316 **4** nk **Resplendent Ace (IRE)**[7] 2165 4-9-3 **64** PaulHanagan 8 70
(P Howling) *in tch: drvn and outpcd over 2f out: rallied over 1f out: kpt on wl* **9/2**[2]

60-5 **5** 1 **African Pursuits (USA)**[15] 1932 4-9-3 **64** SteveDrowne 1 68
(H Morrison) *led to appr fnl f: kpt on same pce* **4/1**[1]

03-0 **6** ¾ **Foreign Edition (IRE)**[48] 1207 6-8-1 **51** oh1 AndrewMullen(3) 7 54
(Miss J A Camacho) *trckd ldrs: drvn over 2f out: no ex fnl f* **25/1**

0-00 **7** 2¾ **Joshua's Gold (IRE)**[38] 1383 7-8-10 **64** PaulPickard(7) 15 61
(D Carroll) *hld up: hdwy 2f out: no imp fnl f* **25/1**

260- **8** 1¼ **Crosby Jemma**[246] 5563 4-8-4 **51** oh1 ChrisCatlin 6 46
(J R Weymes) *t.k.h: in tch: drvn over 2f out: btn fnl f* **20/1**

26-0 **9** hd **Farne Island**[14] 1953 5-8-12 **59** PaulMulrennan 16 53
(Micky Hammond) *hld up: rdn 3f out: kpt on fnl f: nvr rchd ldrs* **25/1**

155- **10** ½ **Awaken**[256] 5286 7-8-7 **54** DeanMcKeown 12 47
(Miss Tracy Waggott) *hld up: rdn 3f out: n.d* **16/1**

03-0 **11** 1 **Campli (IRE)**[13] 2006 6-8-13 **60** TonyHamilton 3 51
(Micky Hammond) *s.i.s: bhd: hdwy over 2f out: sn no imp* **14/1**

4-00 **12** 1 **Naledi**[129] 168 4-8-4 **51** oh4 (b) RoystonFfrench 4 40
(J R Norton) *prom tl rdn and wknd fr 2f out* **18/1**

35-0 **13** 1¾ **March Mate**[13] 2009 4-8-3 **57** oh1 ow6 AnthonyBetts(7) 5 43
(B Ellison) *chsd ldrs to 2f out: sn wknd* **25/1**

0-00 **14** 5 **Roman History (IRE)**[4] 2250 5-8-4 **51** oh6 (p) SilvestreDeSousa 9 27
(Miss Tracy Waggott) *in tch tl drvn and wknd over 3f out* **25/1**

00-0 **15** 2 **Bright Sun (IRE)**[14] 1963 7-9-1 **62** KimTinkler 10 34
(N Tinkler) *in tch tl wknd over 2f out* **14/1**

40-0 **16** 35 **Grafty Green (IRE)**[13] 2001 5-8-6 **53** FergalLynch 11 —
(W M Brisbourne) *hld up: rdn 3f out: sn btn: t.o* **50/1**

0-00 **17** 5 **Ellies Faith**[17] 1890 4-8-5 **52** oh6 ow1 (b) AndrewElliott 14 —
(L R James) *in tch: effrt on outside 1/2-way: wknd 4f out: t.o* **100/1**

2m 10.82s (-1.08) **Going Correction** -0.225s/f (Firm) **17** Ran SP% **126.5**
Speed ratings (Par 101): **101,100,100,100,99 98,96,95,95,95 94,93,92,88,86 58,54**
CSF £44.38 CT £422.01 TOTE £6.40: £1.40, £2.10, £2.30, £2.00; EX 33.50 TRIFECTA Not won..
Owner L Armstrong **Bred** Tommy Burns **Trained** Newburn, Tyne & Wear

FOCUS
Another modest handicap butd one in which the gallop was fair and the form looks sound but ordinary rated through the runner-up.
Farne Island Official explanation: jockey said gelding hung right-handed throughout
Bright Sun(IRE) Official explanation: jockey said gelding slipped turning into home straight
Grafty Green(IRE) Official explanation: jockey said gelding lost its action

2366 PRICEWATERHOUSECOOPERS H'CAP 7f
4:30 (4:30) (Class 5) (0-75,74) 3-Y-O **£3,238** (£963; £481; £240) **Stalls High**

Form RPR

503- **1** **We'Re Delighted**[235] 5863 3-8-12 **68** PaulMulrennan 6 72
(T D Walford) *prom: effrt 2f out: led and edgd lft wl ins fnl f: r.o* **11/2**

2-03 **2** ½ **Dolly No Hair**[22] 1751 3-8-6 **62** FergalLynch 9 65
(D W Barker) *led: rdn and edgd lft fr over 1f out: hdd wl ins fnl f: r.o* **14/1**

3643 **3** 2 **Splash The Cash**[42] 1306 3-8-1 **60** AndrewMullen(3) 8 58
(K A Ryan) *hld up: hdwy over 1f out: kpt on fnl f: nt rch first two* **4/1**[2]

4-22 **4** 2¼ **Prince Kalamoun (IRE)**[42] 1307 3-8-13 **72** PJMcDonald(3) 7 64+
(G A Swinbank) *hld up in tch: drvn and outpcd 1/2-way: kpt on fnl f: no imp* **10/3**[1]

40-2 **5** 5 **Sylvias Grove**[13] 2014 3-8-12 **71** DNolan(3) 5 49
(D Carroll) *hld up in tch: drvn over 2f out: sn wknd* **9/2**[3]

300- **6** ½ **Bohobe (IRE)**[218] 6282 3-9-0 **70** SilvestreDeSousa 4 47
(J G Given) *plld hrd: cl up tl wknd over 2f out* **10/1**

7 3¾ **Princess Rose Anne (IRE)**[207] 6551 3-9-4 **74** ChrisCatlin 2 41
(E F Vaughan) *t.k.h: cl up tl wknd wl over 1f out* **12/1**

5020 **8** 17 **Dnata Flyer (USA)**[14] 1952 3-8-9 **65** JoeFanning 3 —
(M Johnston) *racd wd in tch: hung lft and wknd fr over 2f out* **5/1**

1m 25.62s (-1.78) **Going Correction** -0.50s/f (Hard) **8** Ran SP% **116.8**
Speed ratings (Par 99): **99,98,96,93,87 87,83,63**
CSF £78.33 CT £342.89 TOTE £9.50: £2.40, £3.70, £1.90; EX 125.80 Trifecta £212.10 Part won: Pool: £298.75, 0.10 winning units..
Owner B Selective Partnership **Bred** W T Whittle **Trained** Sheriff Hutton, N Yorks

FOCUS
An ordinary but open handicap on paper but one in which those racing up with the pace held the edge and being against the nearside rail proved an advantage.

2367 EAGLE BAR DINER HAS LANDED H'CAP 1m 3y(S)
5:05 (5:05) (Class 6) (0-65,65) 3-Y-O **£2,752** (£818; £409; £204) **Stalls Centre**

Form RPR

33-0 **1** **Hasty Retreat**[39] 1367 3-9-4 **65** JoeFanning 10 76+
(E A L Dunlop) *cl up: led gng wl over 2f out: pushed clr fr over 1f out: readily* **8/1**

-043 **2** 3 **Castlebury (IRE)**[13] 2014 3-9-0 **64** PJMcDonald(3) 11 71+
(G A Swinbank) *midfield: effrt and hdwy 2f out: sn chsng wnr: kpt on fnl f: no imp* **5/1**[3]

-015 **3** 3¾ **Casino Night**[11] 2041 3-8-13 **65** NeilBrown(5) 13 60
(J R Weymes) *in tch: effrt over 2f out: kpt on same pce fnl f* **8/1**

3-06 **4** 3½ **Portrush Storm**[22] 1737 3-8-13 **63** DNolan(3) 8 50
(D Carroll) *hld up: hdwy over 2f out: nvr rchd ldrs* **14/1**

3003 **5** nse **Natural Rhythm (IRE)**[4] 2259 3-8-8 **55** (v) TonyHamilton 6 42
(Mrs R A Carr) *hld up in tch: effrt over 2f out: no imp fnl f* **18/1**

5-04 **6** 2¾ **Mrs Summersby (IRE)**[14] 1958 3-9-2 **63** SteveDrowne 12 44
(H Morrison) *prom: effrt over 2f out: edgd lft: wknd over 1f out* **3/1**[2]

2066 **7** ½ **Caltire (GER)**[18] 1871 3-8-10 **60** (b) JerryO'Dwyer(3) 1 39
(M G Quinlan) *bhd and sn pushed along: nvr rchd ldrs* **14/1**

2260 **8** 7 **Whaston (IRE)**[29] 1592 3-8-10 **57** ChrisCatlin 14 20
(J D Bethell) *bhd: drvn 1/2-way: nvr on terms* **18/1**

56-0 **9** 3¼ **Sand Maiden (IRE)**[31] 1553 3-8-6 **56** (b) DuranFentiman(3) 9 12
(T D Easterby) *led to over 2f out: sn btn* **33/1**

-462 **10** 12 **Rossini's Dancer**[37] 1396 3-8-10 **60** JamieMoriarty(3) 4 —
(R A Fahey) *chsd ldrs: drvn 3f out: wknd wl over 1f out: eased* **2/1**[1]

0-00 **11** hd **Ursus**[35] 1453 3-8-1 **51** oh2 AndrewMullen(3) 7 —
(C R Wilson) *bhd: drvn 1/2-way: nvr on terms* **100/1**

3304 **12** 26 **Persistent (IRE)**[29] 1592 3-8-8 **55** (p) MickyFenton 2 —
(P T Midgley) *in tch on outside: hung lft and wknd over 2f out: eased whn no ch* **28/1**

1m 39.59s (-3.81) **Going Correction** -0.50s/f (Hard) **12** Ran SP% **128.5**
Speed ratings (Par 97): **100,97,93,89,89 86,86,79,76,64 64,38**
CSF £51.50 CT £347.42 TOTE £6.20: £3.00, £2.10, £3.10; EX 61.90 Trifecta £221.10 Part won: Pool: £311.47, 0.20 winning units. Place 6: £ 74.70 Place 5: £ 49.48 .
Owner Mrs Susan Roy **Bred** Mrs S M Roy **Trained** Newmarket, Suffolk

FOCUS
A run-of-the-mill handicap in which the two market leaders disappointed. The pace was sound and the winner showed improved form.
Caltire(GER) Official explanation: jockey said gelding never travelled
Rossini's Dancer Official explanation: jockey said colt lost its action 2f out
Persistent(IRE) Official explanation: jockey said gelding lost its action
T/Jkpt: £33,190.20 to a £1 stake. Pool: £46,746.85. 0.50 winning tickets. T/Plt: £155.60 to a £1 stake. Pool: £56,469.55. 264.90 winning tickets. T/Qpdt: £85.80 to a £1 stake. Pool: £3,445.80. 29.70 winning tickets. RY

2199 NEWMARKET (ROWLEY) (R-H)
Friday, May 23

OFFICIAL GOING: Good to firm
Wind: Light across Weather: Overcast with the sun breaking through late on

2368 NGK SPARK PLUGS E B F MAIDEN FILLIES' STKS 6f
2:20 (2:20) (Class 4) 2-Y-O **£4,857** (£1,445; £722; £360) **Stalls Low**

Form RPR

1 **Kissing The Camera** 2-9-0 0 RyanMoore 5 79+
(J Noseda) *w'like: w ldr: rdn to ld ins fnl f: r.o* **3/1**[2]

0 **2** nk **Misdaqeya**[36] 1419 2-9-0 0 RHills 1 78
(B W Hills) *lw: led: rdn and hdd ins fnl f: r.o* **11/4**[1]

3 2¼ **Daheeya** 2-9-0 0 DarryllHolland 9 71
(M R Channon) *cmpt: s.i.s: racd keenly and sn prom: rdn and edgd lft over 1f out: no ex ins fnl f* **7/1**

4 ½ **Moonburst** 2-9-0 0 StephenDonohoe 3 70+
(E A L Dunlop) *neat: b.hind: s.i.s: hdwy over 3f out: outpcd 2f out: r.o ins fnl f* **8/1**

5 1½ **Redhead (IRE)** 2-9-0 0 RichardHughes 2 65
(R Hannon) *leggy: scope: trckd ldrs: racd keenly: rdn over 1f out: styd on same pce* **7/2**[3]

6 5 **Refuse To Decline** 2-9-0 0 RichardMullen 6 50
(D M Simcock) *w'like: s.i.s: outpcd* **8/1**

7 ½ **Tamarah** 2-9-0 0 (t) EddieAhern 7 49
(Miss D Mountain) *wl grwn: s.i.s: hld up: hdwy over 2f out: rdn over 1f out: sn wknd* **40/1**

8 2¾ **Mistress Mary** 2-9-0 0 AdrianMcCarthy 8 41
(G G Margarson) *leggy: scope: prom: lost pl over 3f out: wknd 2f out* **33/1**

1m 15.38s (3.18) **Going Correction** +0.325s/f (Good) **8** Ran SP% **114.0**
Speed ratings (Par 92): **91,90,87,86,84 78,77,73**
CSF £11.63 TOTE £3.40: £1.60, £1.30, £1.80; EX 12.10.
Owner P Makin **Bred** Paulyn Limited **Trained** Newmarket, Suffolk

FOCUS
Little previous form to go on in this maiden fillies' event, and the steady pace means the form should not be taken too literally, but some of these are likely to improve a good deal and winners should emerge from it.

NOTEBOOK
Kissing The Camera ◆, an 88,000gns yearling, is a half-sister to three winners as two-year-olds out of a high-class miler in North America who also scored at two, so there was every chance that she would click at the first time of asking. She certainly knew her job and, having raced prominently from the start, battled on well to get the better of a rival with previous experience. She should get further and can go on from here. (tchd 7-2 in places)
Misdaqeya, the only filly with a run under her belt, having finished seventh in a maiden here last month that has already produced four winners, tried to make her experience count over this extra furlong and attempted to make every yard against the stands' rail. She did not do much wrong and just came up against a better filly on the day. Like the winner, she will appreciate further in time. (tchd 5-2 and 3-1)
Daheeya ◆, who cost just 5,000gns as a yearling, is a half-sister to a winner in Serbia out of a winner at up to 1m4f. Never far away, she looked a big danger to the front pair when ranging alongside a furlong out but then appeared to blow up. She should come on for this and her pedigree suggests she will appreciate much further. (op 6-1 tchd 15-2)
Moonburst ◆, out of a winning half-sister to Medicean, attracted market support but did not help her cause with a tardy start. The way she stayed on late rather backs up what her breeding would have suggested, that she will improve a fair amount once stepped up in trip. She is one to take a close interest in next time. (op 11-1)
Redhead(IRE), an 80,000gns filly out of a half-sister to Umniya and Lady Links, was rather weak in the market. A little disorganised soon after leaving the stalls, she could not go with the leaders over the last furlong or so. She should have learnt from this and ought to be up to winning a race when the market speaks more in her favour. (op 11-4)
Refuse To Decline, a 45,000gns filly out of a winner over 1m4f, was a springer in the market but she missed the break and it was a struggle thereafter. She is obviously thought capable of better. (op 16-1)
Tamarah Official explanation: jockey said filly was unsuited by the good to firm ground

2369 FRONTRUNNER FOR WINDOWS H'CAP 1m 2f
2:55 (2:55) (Class 4) (0-85,91) 4-Y-O+ **£4,857** (£1,445; £722; £360) **Stalls Low**

Form RPR

420- **1** **Ask The Butler**[336] 2816 4-9-0 **81** DaneO'Neill 1 92+
(L M Cumani) *hld up: hdwy: nt clr run and hmpd 1f out: r.o to ld nr fin: comf* **11/2**[3]

5421 **2** ½ **Jeer (IRE)**[8] 2120 4-9-10 **91** 6ex RyanMoore 6 96
(E A L Dunlop) *chsd ldr: rdn to ld over 1f out: hdd nr fin* **2/1**[1]

113- **3** hd **Spirit Of Adjisa (IRE)**[186] 6878 4-8-7 **74** PatDobbs 7 79
(Pat Eddery) *lw: led: rdn and hdd over 1f out: edgd rt ins fnl f: r.o* **17/2**

10-0 **4** 2 **Mount Hermon (IRE)**[41] 1335 4-8-10 **77** RobertHavlin 3 78
(H Morrison) *chsd ldrs: rdn over 3f out: outpcd 2f out: r.o ins fnl f* **6/1**

05-2 **5** 2 **Shake On It**[25] 1682 4-9-2 **83** (t) StephenCarson 5 80
(Eve Johnson Houghton) *hld up: hdwy 3f out: rdn over 1f out: wknd ins fnl f* **7/2**[2]

0-30 **6** nse **Northern Jem**[30] 1569 4-9-0 **81** EddieAhern 4 78
(G G Margarson) *prom: rdn and n.m.r over 1f out: wknd ins fnl f* **13/2**

116- **7** 24 **Robert The Brave**[149] 7236 4-8-10 **77** RichardHughes 2 26
(P R Webber) *s.i.s: hld up: racd keenly: hdwy over 6f out: rdn and wknd 2f out: eased fnl f* **16/1**

2m 8.25s (2.45) **Going Correction** +0.325s/f (Good) **7** Ran SP% **115.0**
Speed ratings (Par 105): **103,102,102,100,99 99,80**
CSF £17.16 TOTE £6.60: £2.80, £1.80; EX 19.40.

Owner R J Baines **Bred** Skymarc Farm Inc **Trained** Newmarket, Suffolk

FOCUS

A smallish field, but an eventful race and much of that was due to the modest pace which caused a few to take a grip and one or two traffic problems, especially for the eventual winner, who did well to get out of jail and has been rated value for three lengths.

2370 SIAS BUILDING SERVICES ANNIVERSARY MAIDEN STKS 1m 2f

3:30 (3:34) (Class 4) 3-Y-O £5,180 (£1,541; £770; £384) Stalls Low

Form RPR

1 **Ancient Lights** 3-9-3 0 EddieAhern 4 89+
(H R A Cecil) *gd sort: chsd ldr: led 2f out: styd on wl* 2/1[1]

2 1 1/4 **Meethaaq (USA)** 3-9-3 0 RHills 6 87+
(Sir Michael Stoute) *w'like: a.p: chsd wnr over 1f out: styd on wl* 3/1[2]

3 6 **Seventh Cavalry (IRE)** 3-9-3 0 RyanMoore 1 75
(H R A Cecil) *wl grwn: bit bkwd: chsd ldrs: rdn over 1f out: wknd ins fnl f* 10/3[3]

4 3/4 **Kossack** 3-9-3 0 DaneO'Neill 7 73
(L M Cumani) *gd sort: bit bkwd: s.i.s: hld up: rdn over 1f out: wknd fnl f* 5/1

5 1 3/4 **Crusoe's Return** 3-9-3 0 PatCosgrave 2 70
(L M Cumani) *cmpt: s.i.s: hld up: rdn over 1f out: sn wknd* 18/1

00- 6 2 1/4 **Hellzapoppin**[217] 6294 3-9-3 0 AlanMunro 3 65
(D R Lanigan) *led: rdn and hdd 2f out: wknd fnl f* 17/2

2m 8.57s (2.77) **Going Correction** +0.325s/f (Good) 6 Ran SP% **113.9**

Speed ratings (Par 101): **101,100,95,94,93 91**

CSF £8.47 TOTE £2.70: £1.40, £1.90; EX 10.50.

Owner Ennismore Racing II **Bred** C R Mason **Trained** Newmarket, Suffolk

FOCUS

Not the most competitive of maidens and the pace was ordinary. The front pair pulled a long way clear and should both go on to better things, but there was limited promise amongst the others.

2371 RE-OFFER.COM 1ST JUNE BREEZE UP H'CAP 7f

4:05 (4:05) (Class 3) (0-90,90) 4-Y-0+ £7,771 (£2,312; £1,155; £577) Stalls Low

Form RPR

0030 1 **Plum Pudding (IRE)**[14] 1942 5-9-4 90 (p) RyanMoore 6 104
(R Hannon) *lw: mde all: rdn clr fr over 1f out* 7/2[2]

4-40 2 5 **Dingaan (IRE)**[15] 1928 5-8-8 80 LPKeniry 7 81
(A M Balding) *trckd ldrs: racd keenly: wnt 2nd over 1f out: styd on same pce* 9/1

112- 3 1 1/4 **Big Noise**[244] 5635 4-9-2 88 RichardHughes 3 85
(Dr J D Scargill) *lw: hld up: hdwy 1/2-way: chsd wnr over 2f out tl rdn over 1f out: no ex* 6/4[1]

-500 4 1 **Purus (IRE)**[13] 1982 6-8-11 86 LukeMorris(3) 8 80
(R A Teal) *chsd ldrs: outpcd over 2f out: hung lft over 1f out: styd on ins fnl f* 6/1[3]

00-0 5 3/4 **Jedburgh**[18] 1857 7-9-2 88 (b) JimmyFortune 4 80
(J L Dunlop) *lw: s.i.s: hld up: hdwy over 1f out: sn rdn: wknd ins fnl f* 17/2

000- 6 2 3/4 **Ivory Lace**[159] 7165 7-9-3 89 EddieAhern 5 74
(S Woodman) *bit bkwd: hld up: rdn over 2f out: wknd over 1f out* 40/1

0-61 7 3/4 **Phluke**[13] 2013 7-8-12 84 StephenCarson 2 67
(Eve Johnson Houghton) *chsd ldr tl rdn over 2f out: wknd over 1f out* 8/1

-000 8 3 1/4 **Forest Dane**[15] 1928 8-8-4 76 NickyMackay 1 50
(Mrs N Smith) *hld up: hdwy 1/2-way: rdn over 2f out: sn wknd* 25/1

1m 26.29s (0.89) **Going Correction** +0.325s/f (Good) 8 Ran SP% **114.4**

Speed ratings (Par 107): **107,101,99,98,97 94,93,90**

CSF £34.63 CT £65.38 TOTE £4.70: £1.50, £3.00, £1.10; EX 50.80.

Owner Hyde Sporting Promotions Limited **Bred** Tom Deane **Trained** East Everleigh, Wilts

FOCUS

A decent handicap, but the winner is a dangerous horse to grant an easy lead and he held all the aces from the start. Very few others got into it and the form is far from solid.

NOTEBOOK

Plum Pudding(IRE), whose three previous wins have all been gained over 1m here, was given a well-judged ride from the front. Racing more towards the centre of the track, he was always travelling very smoothly and when asked to quicken he left his rivals for dead. If back to his best he had an obvious chance off a 3lb lower mark than for his last win, but he will be hit hard for this and will not get another chance to race on the Rowley Mile until September. (op 5-1)

Dingaan(IRE), without a win in almost a year and now 4lb lower than when last successful, was another to race more towards the centre of the track. He tried hard to get to the winner over the last couple of furlongs, but was firmly put in his place and it is debatable what he achieved as there was only one horse in it from some way out. (op 10-1 tchd 8-1)

Big Noise was returning from an eight-month absence and 5lb higher than at the end of a highly progressive 2007 campaign in which he was never been out of the first two in five starts. He was backed to make a winning return, but he came off the bridle some way out and although slipstreaming the winner entering the last couple of furlongs, was then completely left behind. There is the chance that he needed it, though he was successful on his racecourse debut a year ago. (op 7-4 tchd 15-8 in places)

Purus(IRE), not disgraced in the Victoria Cup last time, started off widest off all but, after getting his second wind, drifted left and ended up right against the stands' rail. He is still 3lb above his last winning mark and probably needs to come down a bit more. (op 5-1)

Jedburgh, patiently ridden early, made an effort racing into the Dip but could not maintain it up the final climb. Rated 106 at his best, he is a long way from the horse that won a Curragh Group 3 in the middle of 2006 and his lengthy losing run continues despite a slipping handicap mark. (op 7-1 tchd 9-1)

Phluke, raised 4lb for his Warwick victory, was kept tight against the stands' rail throughout and that may not have been ideal considering the action all took place down the centre, but it is probably more significant that all 11 of his victories have come around a bend. (op 7-1)

2372 BUY HORSES AT RE-OFFER.COM H'CAP 1m 4f

4:40 (4:40) (Class 3) (0-90,90) 4-Y-0+ £7,771 (£2,312; £1,155; £577) Stalls Centre

Form RPR

003/ 1 **Punjabi**[28] 5908 5-8-5 77 oh1 ow1 EddieAhern 4 98
(N J Henderson) *hld up: hdwy over 3f out: hung rt and led over 2f out: rdn over 1f out: jst hld on* 2/1[2]

122- 2 nk **Mad Rush (USA)**[331] 2999 4-9-2 88 RyanMoore 10 108+
(L M Cumani) *lw: hld up: hdwy over 2f out: swtchd lft over 1f out: sn rdn to chse wnr: r.o wl* 13/8[1]

3-53 3 7 **Shela House**[18] 1877 4-8-13 85 KerrinMcEvoy 7 94
(J R Fanshawe) *hld up: hdwy over 1f out: sn rdn: no ex ins fnl f* 12/1

25-3 4 3 1/4 **Ollie George (IRE)**[31] 1531 5-8-13 85 LPKeniry 6 89
(A M Balding) *chsd ldr tl led 8f out: rdn and hdd over 2f out: wknd fnl f* 16/1

4062 5 4 1/2 **Prince Sabaah (IRE)**[9] 2107 4-8-10 82 (p) RichardHughes 3 79
(R Hannon) *lw: led 4f: chsd ldrs: rdn over 2f out: wknd over 1f out* 11/2[3]

3-6 6 1/2 **Rajeh (IRE)**[9] 2107 5-8-12 84 AdamKirby 1 80
(J L Spearing) *lw: mid-div: effrt over 3f out: hmpd over 2f out: sn wknd* 25/1

331- 7 8 **Candle**[232] 5940 5-9-4 90 DaneO'Neill 5 73
(H Candy) *mid-div: hdwy over 7f out: rdn whn nt clr run over 2f out: sn wknd* 16/1

400- 8 10 **Know The Law**[168] 7055 4-8-4 79 (b) MarcHalford(3) 2 46
(D R C Elsworth) *s.i.s: hld up: rdn: hung lft and wknd over 2f out* 40/1

000- 9 nse **Mikao (IRE)**[217] 6302 7-9-1 87 DarryllHolland 8 54
(M H Tompkins) *chsd ldrs over 11f* 33/1

1101 10 55 **Maslak (IRE)**[14] 1947 4-9-3 89 DarrenWilliams 9 —
(P W Hiatt) *prom: rdn over 3f out: wknd over 2f out: eased* 25/1

2m 30.9s (-2.60) **Going Correction** 0.0s/f (Good) 10 Ran SP% **119.3**

Speed ratings (Par 107): **108,107,103,100,97 97,92,85,85,48**

CSF £5.53 CT £29.62 TOTE £3.30: £1.50, £1.20, £2.50; EX 8.20.

Owner Raymond Tooth **Bred** Capt J H Wilson **Trained** Upper Lambourn, Berks

FOCUS

A decent race, but there were a couple of potential blots on the handicap and they dominated the finish. Both still look capable of better.

NOTEBOOK

Punjabi ◆, a fair handicapper for Geraldine Rees when last seen on the Flat, was effectively 2lb wrong with his rider's 1lb overweight, but was still thrown in if he could transfer his recent top-class hurdling form back on to the level. Buried away early, his rider's decision to commit him when he did was probably crucial as he took a couple of lengths out of the favourite and soon built enough of an advantage for him to eventually just hold on all-out. The margin of victory would suggest that perhaps he does not have that much in hand of the Handicapper, but the runner-up is probably a decent sort and this performance is best measured by how far the pair pulled clear of the others. (tchd 9-4 and 5-2 in places)

Mad Rush(USA) ◆ was returning from 11 months off, but the market did not suggest that fitness would be a problem. Held up further back than the eventual winner, he did not exactly meet interference when eventually asked for his effort, but he did have to change course a few times and whilst he was doing that the winner was making the best of his way home. He finished very strongly, but had been left with just too much ground to make up and his rival was not stopping. It is only a matter of time before he goes one better and he looks to have a very decent handicap in him, perhaps even a race like the Ebor. (op 7-4 tchd 2-1 in places and 15-8 in places)

Shela House plugged on late to win the separate race for third and was almost certainly well beaten by a couple of decent sorts. He does not look well handicapped himself, however, now being 9lb higher than for his only win. (tchd 14-1)

Ollie George(IRE) had conditions to suit and the main question was whether he would come on or bounce from his promising return from a lengthy absence last month. Ridden up with the pace until finding it all too much over the last furlong or so, he probably still progressed from that reappearance and just found himself in a stronger race than would usually be the case for this level. He should be cherry-ripe now. (tchd 20-1 in a place)

Prince Sabaah(IRE), 1lb lower than when beaten a whisker at York, was the only one to start at less than 12-1 outside the big two, but having raced up with the pace from the start in the first-time cheekpieces, he failed to get home. His only win came on Polytrack and he is yet to win on grass after 15 attempts. (op 6-1)

Rajeh(IRE), well behind Prince Sabaah at York, had only a 1lb pull and did not improve from that reappearance effort as might have been hoped. (op 28-1)

Candle, returning from a seven-month absence off an 8lb higher mark, but from a stable in form and not unbacked, already looked to be feeling the strain when getting involved in some argy-bargy inside the last 3f. (op 25-1)

Mikao(IRE) Official explanation: jockey said gelding was unsuited by the good to firm ground

2373 SELL HORSES AT RE-OFFER.COM H'CAP 1m

5:15 (5:17) (Class 5) (0-75,75) 4-Y-0+ £3,885 (£1,156; £577; £288) Stalls Low

Form RPR

-320 1 **Oat Cuisine**[18] 1867 4-8-8 65 ow1 RichardHughes 9 80+
(M L W Bell) *racd centre: broke wl: lost pl over 6f out: hdwy over 2f out: rdn over 1f out: nt clr run and swtchd lft ins fnl f: r.o to ld nr fin* 14/1

130- 2 nk **Princess Taylor**[171] 7017 4-9-4 75 (t) DarryllHolland 2 86
(M Botti) *racd stands' side: chsd ldr tl led that gp and overall ldr over 2f out: rdn over 1f out: hdd nr fin* 16/1

300- 3 1 1/4 **Hannicean**[212] 6423 4-8-13 70 KerrinMcEvoy 16 78+
(M A Jarvis) *racd centre: hld up: swtchd lft and hdwy over 1f out: r.o: nrst fin* 12/1

-061 4 1/2 **Dream Of Fortune (IRE)**[23] 1725 4-8-9 71 (t) JamieJones(5) 3 78+
(M G Quinlan) *racd stands' side: s.i.s: hdwy 1/2-way: rdn and ev ch fr over 1f out tl no ex wl ins fnl f* 20/1

0-00 5 1/2 **Obezyana (USA)**[15] 1936 6-8-10 70 DominicFox(3) 18 76
(A Bailey) *overall ldr in centre over 4f: rdn: edgd lft and ev ch over 1f out: no ex ins fnl f* 33/1

00-5 6 1 3/4 **Sonny Parkin**[40] 1349 6-8-8 72 (v) SimonPearce(7) 19 74
(J Pearce) *racd centre: hld up: hdwy over 1f out: sn rdn and hung lft: nt run on* 20/1

0-10 7 hd **Hazytoo**[17] 1900 4-8-11 68 EddieAhern 10 69
(S A Callaghan) *lw: racd centre: hld up: hdwy over 2f out: rdn over 1f out: no ex ins fnl f* 20/1

440- 8 2 **Networker**[289] 4268 5-8-13 70 RyanMoore 13 67
(P J McBride) *racd centre: hld up: hdwy 2f out: rdn over 1f out: hmpd sn after: wknd wl ins fnl f* 6/1[2]

3-03 9 1 1/2 **Aggravation**[6] 2203 6-8-10 70 MarcHalford(3) 6 63+
(D R C Elsworth) *b.hind: racd centre: s.i.s: hld up: nt clr run over 2f out: styd on appr fnl f: nvr nrr* 7/2[1]

3000 10 4 **Harare**[4] 2262 7-8-5 69 (v) WilliamCarson(7) 17 53
(R J Price) *racd centre: hld up: hdwy over 2f out: wknd fnl f* 16/1

2053 11 2 1/4 **Tanforan**[24] 1708 6-8-5 62 NeilPollard 11 41
(B P J Baugh) *racd centre: chsd ldrs: rdn over 2f out: wknd over 1f out* 50/1

4-56 12 3 1/4 **Rain Stops Play (IRE)**[23] 1729 6-8-11 68 PatCosgrave 1 39
(M Quinn) *led stands' side: overall ldr over 3f out: rdn and hdd over 2f out: hung rt and wknd over 1f out* 9/1

051- 13 2 1/2 **Sister Act**[226] 6097 4-9-4 75 OscarUrbina 7 41
(J R Fanshawe) *lw: racd stands' side: hld up: hdwy over 2f out: wknd over 1f out* 10/1

340- 14 nk **Silent Applause**[246] 5559 5-8-6 66 LukeMorris(3) 5 31
(Dr J D Scargill) *lw: racd stands' side: chsd ldrs: rdn and lost pl over 3f out: bhd whn hung lft over 1f out* 7/1[3]

-134 15 10 **Garden Party**[84] 752 4-9-2 73 JimmyFortune 15 15
(Jane Chapple-Hyam) *racd centre: chsd ldrs: rdn over 2f out: wknd over 1f out: hung lft fnl f* 12/1

060 16 5 **Obrigado (USA)**[29] 1585 8-8-10 67 AdamKirby 14 —
(G L Moore) *racd centre: chsd ldrs over 5f* 16/1

40-3 17 1/2 **Bedizen**[22] 1742 5-9-4 75 AlanMunro 8 —
(Mrs P Sly) *swtg: racd centre: chsd ldrs over 5f* 16/1

00-0 **18** *24* **Leptis Magna**[25] 1682 4-8-11 **68**........................ LPKeniry 4 —
(D R C Elsworth) *lw: swtg: s.i.s: racd stands' side: hld up: rdn over 3f out: sn wknd* **33/1**

1m 39.53s (0.93) **Going Correction** +0.325s/f (Good) **18** Ran SP% **135.8**
Speed ratings (Par 103): **108,107,106,105,105 103,103,101,100,96 93,90,88,87,77 72,72,48**
CSF £224.27 CT £2885.58 TOTE £12.00: £2.30, £4.90, £3.80, £3.10; EX 301.30.
Owner Mrs G Rowland-Clark **Bred** Glebe Stud & J F Dean **Trained** Newmarket, Suffolk
■ Stewards' Enquiry : Simon Pearce three-day ban: careless riding (Jun 8-10)

FOCUS
A modest handicap for Newmarket, but fiercely competitive and both the pace and the winning time were decent. The field split into two early with the larger group of 12 coming down the middle, whilst six stayed against the stands' rail. The groups had merged by the time the field reached the 3f pole and there seemed no great advantage as two of the stands'-side group finished in the first four. The first four all showed improved form.
Rain Stops Play(IRE) Official explanation: jockey said gelding hung right
Garden Party Official explanation: jockey said gelding hung left and may have been unsuited by the good to firm ground
Leptis Magna Official explanation: jockey said gelding had no more to give

2374 BOLLINGER CHAMPAGNE CHALLENGE SERIES H'CAP (FOR GENTLEMAN AMATEUR RIDERS) 1m 2f
5:50 (5:52) (Class 5) (0-70,69) 4-Y-0+ **£3,123** (£968; £484; £242) **Stalls** Low

Form RPR
640 **1** **Artreju (GER)**[15] 1932 5-10-10 **65**........................ MrJoshuaMoore(7) 3 76+
(G L Moore) *lw: hld up: hdwy over 3f out: led over 1f out: rdn out* **9/2**[2]
6-06 **2** *2 1/2* **Iceman George**[17] 1904 4-10-4 **57**........................(b) MrBMMorris(5) 8 63
(D Morris) *s.i.s: sn prom: rdn and ev ch over 1f out: styd on same pce* **10/1**
51-0 **3** *3 1/4* **Moonlight Fantasy (IRE)**[118] 316 5-10-7 **60**......... JPFeatherstone(5) 2 59
(Lucinda Featherstone) *hld up: racd keenly: hdwy over 3f out: rdn and ev ch over 1f out: wknd ins fnl f* **8/1**
-003 **4** *9* **Sintenis Mac (GER)**[7] 2165 5-10-7 **55** oh2........................ MrSWalker 4 36
(P J O'Gorman) *lw: hld up: rdn over 3f out: n.d* **9/4**[1]
000- **5** *1 1/4* **Rasmani**[148] 7247 4-10-2 **55** oh10........................ MrPCollington(5) 11 34
(Miss Gay Kelleway) *chsd ldrs: led 3f out: rdn and hdd over 1f out: sn hung lft and wknd* **50/1**
00-0 **6** *1 1/4* **Psycho Cat**[53] 1116 5-10-4 **55** oh7........................ MrBenBrisbourne(3) 9 31
(W M Brisbourne) *hld up in tch: rdn and wknd over 2f out* **33/1**
06-4 **7** *3 1/4* **Sky Quest (IRE)**[15] 1932 10-10-12 **67**........................ MrBAdams(7) 10 37
(J R Boyle) *hld up: hdwy 1/2-way: rdn and wknd wl over 1f out* **5/1**[3]
000- **8** *nse* **Bournonville**[330] 3036 5-10-2 **55** oh10........................ MrSRees(5) 5 24
(M Wigham) *b. led 5f: sn rdn: wknd wl over 1f out* **66/1**
6260 **9** *1/2* **Flight Dream (FR)**[13] 2001 5-10-3 **58**........................ MrJMQuinlan(7) 1 26
(M G Quinlan) *hld up: rdn over 2f out: sn wknd* **8/1**
0-34 **10** *1/2* **Bavarica**[10] 2078 6-11-2 **69**........................ MrRBirkett(5) 6 36
(Miss J Feilden) *prom: racd keenly: lost pl over 4f out: rallied 3f out: hung rt and wknd over 2f out* **6/1**
0-00 **11** *18* **Canary Girl**[44] 1269 5-10-0 **55** oh10........................(p) MrJPearce(7) 7 —
(Miss Diana Weeden) *trckd ldr: plld hrd: wknd over 3f out* **80/1**

2m 11.54s (5.74) **Going Correction** +0.325s/f (Good) **11** Ran SP% **118.8**
Speed ratings (Par 103): **90,88,85,78,77 76,73,73,73,72 58**
CSF £48.56 CT £354.86 TOTE £6.60: £1.90, £2.70, £2.60; EX 73.40 Place 6: 23.47 Place 5: £ 14.65 .
Owner The Winning Hand **Bred** Mrs P Suerland **Trained** Woodingdean, E Sussex
■ A first winner under Rules for Joshua Moore, younger brother of Ryan and Jamie.

FOCUS
A modest race and they only went steadily early, which resulted in something of a sprint. The front three pulled a very long way clear of the others.
Sky Quest(IRE) Official explanation: jockey said gelding lost its action in the dip
T/Plt: £43.90 to a £1 stake. Pool: £69,135.88. 1,147.38 winning tickets. T/Qpdt: £15.80 to a £1 stake. Pool: £3,400.80. 159.10 winning tickets. CR

1727 PONTEFRACT (L-H)
Friday, May 23

OFFICIAL GOING: Good to firm (9.1)
Wind: Virtually nil Weather: Overcast

2375 ST. JOHN AMBULANCE H'CAP 1m 4y
6:30 (6:35) (Class 5) (0-70,70) 4-Y-0+ **£3,238** (£963; £481; £240) **Stalls** Low

Form RPR
260- **1** **Motafarred (IRE)**[230] 6016 6-9-3 **69**........................ TQuinn 2 82
(Micky Hammond) *cl up on inner: led 1/2-way: rdn clr over 1f out: kpt on strly* **6/1**[3]
2-00 **2** *4* **Aussie Blue (IRE)**[32] 1520 4-8-6 **61**........................ MichaelJStainton(3) 12 65
(R M Whitaker) *hld up in rr: hdwy on outer 2f out: rdn and styd on to chse wnr ins fnl f: sn drvn and no imp* **13/2**
441- **3** *1/2* **Drawn Gold**[203] 6623 4-8-12 **67**........................ RussellKennemore(3) 5 70+
(R Hollinshead) *towards rr: hdwy whn n.m.r over 2f out: swtchd to outside and rdn over 1f out: styd on wl fnl f: nrst fin* **15/2**
-000 **4** *2 1/4* **Society Music (IRE)**[20] 1815 6-9-4 **70**........................ PhillipMakin 11 67
(M Dods) *hld up towards rr: effrt and nt clr run wl over 2f out: hdwy over 1f out: sn rdn and kpt on same pce ins fnl f* **7/1**
-005 **5** *1 1/4* **Malinsa Blue (IRE)**[13] 2007 6-8-10 **62**........................(p) RoystonFfrench 7 57
(B Ellison) *in tch: effrt 3f out: sn rdn along and outpcd over 2f out: kpt on u.p appr fnl f: n.d* **11/2**[2]
000- **6** *1 3/4* **Medici Pearl**[195] 6753 4-9-3 **69**........................ DavidAllan 13 60
(T D Easterby) *plld hrd: chsd ldrs on outer: effrt to chal 2f out: sn rdn and wknd appr fnl f* **16/1**
6-50 **7** *hd* **The Graig**[28] 1602 4-7-11 **56** oh7........................ StacyRenwick(7) 6 46
(J R Holt) *chsd ldrs: rdn along 3f out: grad wknd* **66/1**
0-03 **8** *hd* **Holiday Cocktail**[23] 1729 6-8-7 **59**........................ PaulHanagan 3 49
(J J Quinn) *dwlt: sn in tch on inner: pushed along and outpcd 3f out: rdn and hdwy 2f out: sn btn* **5/2**[1]
1025 **9** *4* **Ming Vase**[24] 1702 6-7-11 **56** oh8........................ AndreaAtzeni(7) 10 36
(P T Midgley) *led to 1/2-way: sn rdn along and wknd wl over 2f out* **40/1**
0-00 **10** *3 1/2* **Deadline (UAE)**[13] 2007 4-8-10 **62**........................(p) PaulFessey 4 34
(P T Midgley) *chsd ldrs: rdn along over 3f out and sn wknd* **16/1**
/040 **11** *2 1/2* **Apres Ski (IRE)**[10] 2087 5-8-8 **60**........................ FrancisNorton 8 27
(J F Coupland) *s.i.s: plld hrd and rapid prog on outer to join ldrs after 3f: rdn along over 2f out and sn wknd* **25/1**
0150 **12** *3 1/2* **Newgate (UAE)**[4] 2251 4-8-4 **56**........................(b) DaleGibson 1 15
(Mrs R A Carr) *a in rr* **25/1**

1m 44.05s (-1.85) **Going Correction** -0.15s/f (Firm) **12** Ran SP% **119.2**
Speed ratings (Par 103): **103,99,98,96,95 93,93,92,88,85 82,79**
CSF £43.62 CT £305.14 TOTE £6.50: £2.70, £2.60, £2.20; EX 51.30.
Owner R D Bickenson **Bred** Shadwell Estate Company Limited **Trained** Middleham Moor, N Yorks
■ Stewards' Enquiry : Andrea Atzeni one-day ban: used whip when out of contention (Jun 8)

FOCUS
They went no early gallop and Motafarred was always well positioned meanign the form is a bit messy. The second and third ran close to their marks and are the ones to take from the race.
Apres Ski(IRE) Official explanation: jockey said gelding ran too freely early and later had no more to give

2376 MSK FILLIES' H'CAP 1m 2f 6y
7:00 (7:01) (Class 5) (0-70,70) 3-Y-0+ **£3,238** (£963; £481; £240) **Stalls** Low

Form RPR
31-2 **1** **Suzi's Decision**[8] 2118 3-9-5 **69**........................ FrancisNorton 6 85+
(P W D'Arcy) *hld up in tch: hdwy over 3f out: pushed along to chse ldr over 1f out: rdn and styd on to chal ent fnl f: sn led and styd on strly* **4/5**[1]
6-01 **2** *3 3/4* **Amanda Carter**[6] 2185 4-10-0 **64**........................ PaulHanagan 4 73
(R A Fahey) *led: rdn and qcknd over 2f out: drvn over 1f out: hdd jst ins fnl f and kpt on same pce* **3/1**[2]
0-00 **3** *2 1/2* **Sabancaya**[23] 1721 3-8-12 **62**........................ PhillipMakin 3 65
(W J Haggas) *hld up towards rr: hdwy over 3f out: rdn to chse ldrs wl over 1f out: kpt on u.p ins fnl f* **14/1**
006- **4** *2 1/2* **Red Lily (IRE)**[226] 6107 3-9-3 **67**........................ PaulMulrennan 2 65
(J R Fanshawe) *chsd ldrs: rdn along and outpcd 4f out: drvn and plugged on one pce fnl 2f* **12/1**[3]
0535 **5** *4 1/2* **Double On Red**[11] 2052 3-9-0 **64**........................ RoystonFfrench 5 53
(J M P Eustace) *trckd ldrs: hdwy to chse ldr 1/2-way: rdn along wl over 2f out: drvn over 1f out and grad wknd* **12/1**[3]
2-36 **6** *5* **Pharaohs Queen (IRE)**[11] 2052 3-9-6 **70**........................ StephenDonohoe 7 49
(E A L Dunlop) *dwlt: hld up in rr: sme hdwy 4f out: rdn along 3f out and nvr a factor* **14/1**
2-50 **7** *nk* **Molly Ann (IRE)**[21] 1781 3-8-12 **62**........................ DavidAllan 9 40
(T D Easterby) *wnt rt s: hld up and a in rr* **33/1**
004- **8** *shd* **Sendefaa (IRE)**[205] 6585 3-8-6 **63**........................ AndreaAtzeni(7) 8 41
(M Botti) *a in rr* **25/1**
60-5 **9** *16* **Ma Al Salamah (IRE)**[21] 1763 3-8-10 **65**........................ AhmedAjtebi(5) 1 11
(C E Brittain) *chsd ldr: rdn along over 3f out and sn wknd* **14/1**

2m 10.6s (-3.10) **Going Correction** -0.15s/f (Firm)
WFA 3 from 4yo 14lb **9** Ran SP% **122.7**
Speed ratings (Par 100): **106,103,101,99,95 91,91,91,78**
CSF £3.58 CT £20.31 TOTE £1.80: £1.20, £1.40, £3.90; EX 5.20.
Owner Greenstead Hall Racing **Bred** David And Mrs Vicki Fleet **Trained** Newmarket, Suffolk

FOCUS
A decent contest for the grade run at a sound pace and a race that should produce winners.

2377 DRURY PSM YOUNGSTERS CONDITIONS STKS 6f
7:30 (7:31) (Class 2) 2-Y-0 **£9,346** (£2,799; £1,399; £700) **Stalls** Low

Form RPR
21 **1** **Shampagne**[18] 1851 2-9-0 0........................ TQuinn 1 90
(P F I Cole) *led over 2f: cl up tl led again 2f out: sn rdn and styd on strly fnl f* **9/2**[3]
2 *3 3/4* **Salsa Star (USA)** 2-8-3 0........................ PaulHanagan 3 68
(R A Fahey) *t.k.h early: trckd ldrs: hdwy 2f out: chsd wnr wl over 1f out: rdn and edgd lft ent fnl f: kpt on same pce* **11/2**
51 **3** *4* **River Rye (IRE)**[11] 2042 2-8-9 0........................ PatDobbs 2 62
(R Hannon) *trckd ldrs: effrt 2f out: rdn over 1f out and sn no imp* **7/2**[2]
1 **4** *9* **Go Nani Go**[21] 1770 2-8-11 0........................ PaulMulrennan 4 37+
(B Smart) *plld hrd: cl up tl led over 3f out: rdn and hdd 2f out: sn btn and eased fnl f* **10/11**[1]

1m 16.85s (-0.05) **Going Correction** -0.15s/f (Firm) **4** Ran SP% **108.2**
Speed ratings (Par 99): **94,89,83,71**
CSF £24.26 TOTE £4.00; EX 24.20.
Owner Sisters Syndicate **Bred** Stringston Farm **Trained** Whatcombe, Oxon

FOCUS
A decent litte contest that has thrown up the likes of Coventry fourth and first Sir Xaar and Hellvelyn in recent years. Brian Smart was out of luck this time though as his Go Nani Go pulled his chance away, leaving the gritty Shampagne to win well. The winner could go to Royal Ascot and could be better than rated as the third and fourth appeared to run below their previous marks.

NOTEBOOK
Shampagne, readily off the mark in a 5f event at Kempton last time, again adopted his prominent role, but seemed happy enough to take a lead off Go Nani Go when that one pulled its way to the front. Despite giving weight all round, he raced away from them in the straight and, for the second time in three races, Quinn excelled. He lacks star quality, but has a good way of racing and is entitled to take his chance in something at Royal Ascot. (op 7-2)
Salsa Star(USA), a daughter of Giant's Causeway who is related to sprint winners, was not allowed to go off too big a price despite it being her racecourse debut and she showed any amount of promise in second. Keen early on, she travelled up like the winner rounding for home, but ran green under pressure and was unable to match the winner. She had River Rye well beaten off in third though and winning a maiden should prove a formality. (op 6-1 tchd 9-2)
River Rye(IRE), who looked as though this trip would improve when winning at Windsor last time, was happy to track the early speed, but she was outpaced before the turn in and could not pick up under pressure. This was disappointing and it is probable she will need to go down the nursery route now. (tchd 4-1)
Go Nani Go, whose trainer took this in 2005 and 2006 with Sir Xaar and Hellvelyn (latter went on to win Coventry) had earmarked the Royal Ascot event for the son of Kyllachy following a smart winning debut at Musselburgh and he was made a hot favourite. However, he failed to settle and tanked his way to the front just before halfway. It was always going to be tough to win from then on and, having been headed, he was eased off inside the final furlong. This was evidently not his form and perhaps a return to 5f is the answer for the time being. Official explanation: jockey said colt ran too freely early (op 11-10 tchd 5-6)

2378 CONSTANT SECURITY SERVICES H'CAP 1m 4y
8:00 (8:00) (Class 4) (0-85,82) 3-Y-O **£5,180** (£1,541; £770; £384) **Stalls** Low

Form RPR
-026 **1** **Premier Danseur (IRE)**[13] 1988 3-9-1 **79**........................ JoeFanning 6 84+
(M Johnston) *trckd ldrs: pushed along and sltly outpcd 1/2-way: hdwy wl over 2f out: rdn to chse ldr over 1f out: drvn ins fnl f and styd on wl to ld last 75yds* **7/4**[1]
2-40 **2** *nk* **Ninefineirishmen (IRE)**[18] 1868 3-8-9 **73** ow1........................ DarrenWilliams 2 78
(K R Burke) *led: rdn and qcknd 2f out: drvn 1f out: hdd and no ex last 75yds* **8/1**
10-0 **3** *2 1/2* **Bonny Rose**[32] 1524 3-8-8 **72**........................ RoystonFfrench 4 71
(M Johnston) *chsd ldr: rdn along over 2f out: drvn over 1f out and kpt on same pce* **20/1**
6310 **4** *3/4* **Canary Islands**[48] 1208 3-9-4 **82**........................ SteveDrowne 1 79
(E A L Dunlop) *trckd ldrs: hdwy on inner 2f out and sn rdn: drvn ent fnl f and kpt on same pce* **6/1**[3]

4-40 **5** *hd* **Joinedupwriting**[17] 1899 3-8-9 73 ..... DeanMcKeown 3 70
(R M Whitaker) *chsd ldrs: pushed along and sltly outpcd over 3f out: hdwy 2f out: sn rdn and one pce appr fnl f* **7/1**

53-1 **6** *2* **Rankayo Hitam (USA)**[132] 135 3-9-1 79 ..... TQuinn 5 71
(P F I Cole) *hld up towards rr: hdwy 3f out: rdn along 2f out and sn no imp* **10/3**[2]

105 **7** *½* **Khazina (USA)**[11] 2039 3-8-1 70 ..... AhmedAjtebi(5) 7 61
(C E Brittain) *hld up: a towards rr* **16/1**

1-55 **8** *20* **Thunderstruck**[29] 1576 3-8-13 77 ..... PaulMulrennan 8 22
(K A Ryan) *a in rr* **12/1**

1m 44.46s (-1.44) **Going Correction** -0.15s/f (Firm) 8 Ran SP% **115.7**
Speed ratings (Par 101): **101,100,98,97,97 95,94,74**
CSF £17.00 CT £211.41 TOTE £2.90: £1.30, £2.90, £2.30; EX 22.70.

Owner Sheikh Hamdan Bin Mohammed Al Maktoum **Bred** Darley **Trained** Middleham Moor, N Yorks

FOCUS
A fair handicap run in a simialr time to the opening race and the form looks reasonable rated around the third and fourth..

Thunderstruck Official explanation: jockey said gelding was unsuited by the good to firm ground

2379 CONSTANT SECURITY SERVING YORKSHIRE RACECOURSES H'CAP 1m 4f 8y
8:30 (8:30) (Class 4) (0-85,83) 4-Y-0+ **£5,180** (£1,541; £770; £384) **Stalls** Low

Form RPR

6-35 **1** **Charlotte Vale**[42] 1299 7-8-8 73 ..... PaulHanagan 1 82
(Micky Hammond) *led tl hdd over 6f out: cl up tl led again 3f out: rdn clr over 1f out: easily* **15/8**[1]

1040 **2** *6* **Tartan Tie**[20] 1812 4-9-4 83 ..... JoeFanning 4 82
(M Johnston) *cl up: effrt over 2f out: rdn to chse wnr wl over 1f out: sn drvn and one pce* **15/8**[1]

242/ **3** *1 ½* **Sculastic**[149] 6052 5-9-4 83 ..... PaulMulrennan 3 80
(J Howard Johnson) *t.k.h: trckd ldng pair: hdwy over 2f out: sn rdn and one pce appr fnl f* **3/1**[2]

203- **4** *11* **Dium Mac**[195] 6760 7-8-12 77 ..... PhillipMakin 2 56
(N Bycroft) *plld hrd: trckd ldng pair tl rapid hdwy on outer to ld over 6f out: rdn along and hdd 3f out: sn wknd* **11/2**[3]

2m 39.16s (-1.64) **Going Correction** -0.15s/f (Firm) 4 Ran SP% **109.9**
Speed ratings (Par 105): **99,95,94,86**
CSF £5.75 TOTE £2.40; EX 5.50.

Owner Peter J Davies **Bred** Snailwell Stud Co Ltd **Trained** Middleham Moor, N Yorks

FOCUS
A small field for this fair handicap and a moderate winning time. The winner did not appear to have to improve to score but is in-foal and could be underestimated.

2380 SHORTY'S 50TH BIRTHDAY MAIDEN STKS 6f
9:00 (9:03) (Class 5) 3-Y-0 **£3,238** (£963; £481; £240) **Stalls** Low

Form RPR

40-0 **1** **Another Decree**[20] 1817 3-9-3 74 ..... PhillipMakin 2 69
(M Dods) *in tch: rdn along over 2f out: hdwy over 1f out: sn rdn and styd on ins fnl f to ld nr line* **16/1**

50 **2** *shd* **Bahamian Kid**[20] 1808 3-9-0 0 ..... RussellKennemore(3) 5 68
(R Hollinshead) *in tch: hdwy to trck ldrs over 2f out: rdn to ld over 1f out and sn hung bdly lft: drvn ins fnl f: hdd nr line* **8/1**[1]

3 *1 ¼* **Hardanger (IRE)** 3-9-0 0 ..... JamieMoriarty(3) 12 64
(T J Fitzgerald) *dwlt: sn in tch: hdwy to chse ldrs 2f out: sn rdn and kpt on u.p fnl f* **40/1**

0-02 **4** *2* **Tanley**[25] 1674 3-9-3 57 ..... (p) RoystonFfrench 8 58
(J F Coupland) *t.k.h: cl up: led 2f out: sn rdn and hdd over 1f out: wknd ent fnl f* **40/1**

46 **5** *hd* **This Ones For Eddy**[6] 2187 3-9-3 0 ..... DarrenWilliams 1 57
(S Parr) *hld up: hdwy over 2f out: rdn to chse ldrs over 1f out: kpt on ins fnl f: nrst fin* **16/1**

6 **6** *nse* **Carpe Diem**[55] 1068 3-9-3 0 ..... PaulMulrennan 4 57+
(W J Haggas) *dwlt: sn in tch: hdwy on outer wl over 1f out: sn rdn and kpt on ins fnl f: nrst fin* **11/1**[3]

40 **7** *2 ¾* **Deep Winter**[11] 2038 3-8-12 0 ..... PaulHanagan 10 43+
(R A Fahey) *hld up in rr: hdwy wl over 1f out: sn rdn and no imp* **14/1**

50 **8** *nk* **Merrion Tiger (IRE)**[20] 1817 3-9-3 0 ..... AndrewElliott 14 47
(K R Burke) *midfield on outer: rdn along over 2f out and no hdwy* **50/1**

9 *½* **Into The Light** 3-9-3 0 ..... TQuinn 3 46
(E S McMahon) *prom: rdn along over 2f out and sn wknd* **20/1**

00 **10** *shd* **Jordi Roper (IRE)**[6] 2187 3-9-3 0 ..... LeeEnstone 13 46
(S Parr) *a towards rr* **80/1**

11 *hd* **Important News** 3-9-3 0 ..... JoeFanning 9 45
(M Johnston) *hld up: hdwy to chse ldrs on inner 3f out: rdn along 2f out and sn wknd* **10/1**[2]

12 *2* **Royal Grace** 3-8-12 0 ..... DavidAllan 11 33
(T D Easterby) *s.i.s: a in rr* **25/1**

34 **13** *6* **Imperial Djay (IRE)**[17] 1894 3-9-0 0 ..... DNolan(3) 6 19
(D Carroll) *led: rdn along and hdd 2f out: sn wknd* **11/1**[3]

1m 17.59s (0.69) **Going Correction** -0.15s/f (Firm) 13 Ran SP% **72.0**
Speed ratings (Par 99): **89,88,87,84,84 84,80,80,79,79 79,76,68**
CSF £32.51 TOTE £12.90: £3.30, £1.90, £8.80; EX 59.20 Place 6 £ 375.54, Place 5 £ 88.59.

Owner Mrs Karen S Pratt **Bred** D A Yardy **Trained** Denton, Co Durham
■ Palace Moon (8/13F) withdrawn (refused to enter stalls); Rule 4 applies, deduction 60p in the £.

FOCUS
A very moderate winning time, 0.74 seconds slower than the two-year-old race. The race lost much of its interest when hot favourite Palace Moon failed to enter the stalls and although the form makes sense at face value there are doubts about it.

Carpe Diem Official explanation: jockey said gelding hung right-handed in straight

Royal Grace Official explanation: jockey said filly missed the break

T/Plt: £111.50 to a £1 stake. Pool: £49,170.10. 321.83 winning tickets. T/Qpdt: £36.90 to a £1 stake. Pool: £2,635.30. 52.80 winning tickets. JR

2381 - 2387a (Foreign Racing) - See Raceform Interactive

2268

BEVERLEY (R-H)
Saturday, May 24

OFFICIAL GOING: Good to firm (firm in places)
Wind: Strong, half behind Weather: Sunny and dry

2388 TURFTV MEDIAN AUCTION MAIDEN STKS 5f
1:55 (1:57) (Class 4) 2-Y-O **£3,561** (£1,059; £529; £264) **Stalls** High

Form RPR

2 **1** **Officer Mor (USA)**[15] 1948 2-9-3 0 ..... AndrewElliott 1 71+
(K R Burke) *wnt bdly lft s: sn prom and led after 1f: rdn clr over 1f out: kpt on* **3/1**[2]

2 *3* **Secret Venue** 2-9-3 0 ..... TonyHamilton 10 60
(Jedd O'Keeffe) *led 1f: cl up: rdn along 2f out: drvn and kpt on same pce ent fnl f* **8/1**

3 *hd* **Captain Scooby** 2-9-0 0 ..... MichaelJStainton(3) 8 59
(R M Whitaker) *towards rr and pushed along on inner 1/2-way: hdwy over 1f out: swtchd lft and rdn ent fnl f: kpt on wl* **9/2**[3]

4 *nk* **Calley Ho** 2-9-3 0 ..... CatherineGannon 4 58
(Mrs L Stubbs) *chsd ldrs: rdn wl over 1f out: kpt on same pce fnl f* **22/1**

0 **5** *1 ¼* **Drachenfels**[12] 2035 2-9-3 0 ..... TPO'Shea 5 54+
(K A Ryan) *dwlt and in rr tl hdwy on outer over 1f out: rdn and edgd rt ins fnl f: nrst fin* **12/1**

6 *¾* **Northumberland** 2-9-3 0 ..... JohnEgan 3 51
(M Johnston) *cl up: rdn along 2f out: wknd appr last* **11/4**[1]

7 *1 ¼* **Nimmy's Special** 2-8-12 0 ..... RichardMullen 2 42
(B Smart) *chsd ldrs on outer: rdn along 2f out: sn wknd* **13/2**

0 **8** *11* **Rios Boy (IRE)**[24] 1727 2-9-0 0 ..... DuranFentiman(3) 6 7
(T D Easterby) *a outpcd in rr* **33/1**

63.47 secs (-0.03) **Going Correction** -0.20s/f (Firm) 8 Ran SP% **109.3**
Speed ratings (Par 95): **92,87,86,86,84 83,81,63**
CSF £23.59 TOTE £3.70: £1.40, £2.40, £1.60; EX 26.20.

Owner Cyril Wall **Bred** Carolyn McDonald **Trained** Middleham Moor, N Yorks
■ Darknstormy was withdrawn (9/1, unruly in stalls). Deduct 10p in the £ under Rule 4.

FOCUS
A modest juvenile maiden. The winner rated a slight improver from his debut, is full value for the winning margin and can do better.

NOTEBOOK
Officer Mor(USA) shot left coming out of the gates, but soon recovered to adopt a handy position and it was clear nearing the final furlong he was the one to beat. He kept on willingly at the business end, despite still looking green, and rates full value for the winning margin. A step into novice company should now tell us some more about this colt. (op 10-3)

Secret Venue, a 32,00gns half-brother to numerous winning sprinters, failed to trouble the winner yet still shaped with fair ability on this racecourse bow. He should really come on a bundle for this and evidently has a future. (op 7-1 tchd 9-1 and 12-1 in aplace)

Captain Scooby, who has speed in his pedigree, proved too green through the early parts to do himself full justice. He was noted keeping on when the penny dropped, however, and looks sure to learn a good deal for this debut experience. (op 10-1)

Calley Ho, bred to be suited by sprinting this year, posted a pleasing debut effort and was only found wanting nearing the final furlong. He should strip fitter next time out. (op 16-1 tchd 25-1)

Northumberland, a 100,00gns foal, has plenty of speed in his pedigree and proved popular in the betting for this racecourse debut. He eventually faded after showing some early dash and ran as though the race was needed. It will be no surprise to see this scopey colt rate a deal higher as he gains further experience and it must also be noted his powerful yard has yet to hit top gear with its juveniles this term. (tchd 3-1)

Rios Boy(IRE) Official explanation: jockey said colt hung left-handed throughout

2389 RACING AGAIN ON WEDNESDAY EVENING STKS (H'CAP) 7f 100y
2:25 (2:25) (Class 4) (0-85,88) 4-Y-0+ **£4,209** (£1,252; £625; £312) **Stalls** High

Form RPR

3511 **1** **Mujood**[12] 2057 5-9-7 88 ..... RichardMullen 3 96
(Eve Johnson Houghton) *trckd ldr: effrt 2f out: rdn over 1f out: drvn to chal ent fnl f: edgd rt and styd on to ld last 100yds* **11/8**[1]

260- **2** *½* **Stonehaugh (IRE)**[245] 5617 5-8-9 76 ..... (t) RoystonFfrench 1 83
(J Howard Johnson) *led: pushed along over 2f out: rdn over 1f out: drvn ins fnl f: edgd lft and hdd last 100yds* **5/1**

1-23 **3** *1 ¼* **Flying Bantam (IRE)**[11] 2085 7-8-4 71 oh2 ..... DaleGibson 4 75
(R A Fahey) *trckd ldng pair: hdwy 3f out: rdn to chal and ev ch ent fnl f: sn drvn and n.m.r: no ex last 100yds* **7/2**[3]

-531 **4** *1 ½* **Froissee**[8] 2163 4-9-1 82 ..... TPO'Shea 2 82
(S A Callaghan) *dwlt and hld up in rr: tk clsr order 3f out: effrt 2f out: rdn appr fnl f and sn btn* **11/4**[2]

1m 33.1s (-0.70) **Going Correction** -0.10s/f (Good) 4 Ran SP% **107.7**
Speed ratings (Par 105): **100,99,98,96**
CSF £8.08 TOTE £2.00; EX 8.50.

Owner Eden Racing **Bred** Bloomsbury Stud & The Hon Sir David Sieff **Trained** Blewbury, Oxon

FOCUS
Not a bad little handicap but it was run at a modest early pace. The first three basically ran to form.

2390 JOYCE AND KEITH SAUNDERS CONDITIONS STKS 5f
2:55 (2:55) (Class 2) 3-Y-0+
£12,462 (£3,732; £1,866; £934; £466; £234) **Stalls** High

Form RPR

5-41 **1** **Look Busy (IRE)**[15] 1945 3-7-13 100 ..... FrankieMcDonald 3 104
(A Berry) *prom: hdwy to chal wl over 1f out: rdn to ld appr fnl f: kpt on wl* **10/3**[3]

1-40 **2** *2 ¾* **Aegean Dancer**[9] 2129 6-8-12 97 ..... RoystonFfrench 2 102
(B Smart) *chsd ldrs: hdwy wl over 1f out: sn rdn and styd on ins fnl f: tk 2nd nr fin* **6/1**

03-0 **3** *½* **Something (IRE)**[121] 291 6-8-12 0 ..... SilvestreDeSousa 6 100
(D Nicholls) *led: rdn along wl over 1f out: drvn and hdd appr fnl f: kpt on same pce* **11/4**[2]

0-10 **4** *shd* **Utmost Respect**[10] 2106 4-9-5 107 ..... TonyHamilton 5 107
(R A Fahey) *cl up: rdn along and outpcd 1/2-way: hdwy over 1f out: kpt on u.p ins fnl f* **9/4**[1]

-105 **5** *2* **Vhujon (IRE)**[8] 2162 3-8-4 95 ..... CatherineGannon 4 90
(P D Evans) *prom: rdn along whn n.m.r 2f out: sn drvn and wknd over 1f out* **14/1**

6-01 **6** *hd* **Not My Choice (IRE)**[16] 1925 3-8-4 83 ..... JohnEgan 7 89
(S Parr) *stmbld s: a in rr* **9/1**

050/ **7** *8* **Blue Maeve**[557] 6478 8-8-12 0 AndrewElliott 1 63
(A D Brown) *wnt lft s: a bhd* **100/1**

60.97 secs (-2.53) **Going Correction** -0.20s/f (Firm)
WFA 3 from 4yo+ 8lb 7 Ran SP% 112.5
Speed ratings (Par 109): **112,107,106,106,103 103,90**
CSF £22.55 TOTE £3.40: £1.30, £2.40; EX 28.70.
Owner A Underwood **Bred** Tom And Hazel Russell **Trained** Cockerham, Lancs

FOCUS
A decent conditions sprint, run at a solid pace. The form looks solid with the runner-up to form and the fifth and sixth close to their marks.

NOTEBOOK
Look Busy(IRE), who showed her best form to date when winning off 93 in a Chester handicap last time, followed up with another career-best display in this higher grade. She had looked useful last term, but is clearly now really coming into her own and further step up into Listed company now looks a must while she is in such form. (op 9-4)
Aegean Dancer had not been beaten that far on his last two outings since scoring on the All-Weather and, officially rated 3lb inferior to the winner, ran right up to form in defeat. (tchd 5-1)
Something(IRE), having his first-ever run over the minimum trip, posted a brave effort in defeat and showed a lot of early speed. This was just his second outing for current connections and, entitled to strip fitter for the outing, he can certainly build on it. (op 7-2)
Utmost Respect was not at all disgraced on this drop back in trip under his big weight. He just lacks the speed for this trip on such ground, however, as he really wants it easier. (op 5-2 tchd 10-3)
Vhujon(IRE) ran more encouragingly in defeat, but is likely to continue to prove hard to place from his current official rating. (op 16-1 tchd 10-1)
Not My Choice(IRE), behind the winner at Chester last time, really lost his chance when falling out of the stalls. However, he was still beaten around the same margin by Look Busy as had been the case previously. Official explanation: jockey said colt stumbled leaving stalls (op 12-1 tchd 8-1)

2391 BEVERLEY ELECTRIC STKS (H'CAP) 1m 100y
3:25 (3:25) (Class 5) (0-70,69) 4-Y-0+ **£2,752** (£818; £409; £204) **Stalls** High

Form RPR
-265 **1** **Billy One Punch**[8] 2165 6-9-0 **65** RichardMullen 8 75
(D Shaw) *chsd ldrs: rdn along 2f out: n.m.r and swtchd lft over 1f out: drvn ins fnl f and styd on to ld last 100yds* **10/3**[2]
422- **2** *1* **Shotley Mac**[218] 6310 4-8-11 **62** ChrisCatlin 7 70
(N Bycroft) *led 2f: prom: rdn along 2f out: drvn over 1f out: ev ch ins fnl f tl no ex last 100yds* **11/2**
22-0 **3** *2 1/4* **Myfrenchconnection (IRE)**[4] 2274 4-8-9 **60** FrankieMcDonald 1 63
(P T Midgley) *in tch: hdwy and cl up after 3f: led 3f out: rdn over 1f out: drvn ins fnl f: hdd & wknd last 100yds* **3/1**[1]
-600 **4** *3/4* **Kingsholm**[14] 2007 6-8-13 **64** AndrewElliott 6 65
(I W McInnes) *dwlt: plld hrd and hld up in rr: hdwy on outer wl over 1f out: styd on strly ins fnl f: nrst fin* **8/1**
000- **5** *nk* **Riley Boys (IRE)**[199] 6727 7-9-1 **66** RoystonFfrench 2 66
(J G Given) *hld up in rr: hdwy on inner 2f out: rdn whn n.m.r over 1f out: swtchd lft and kpt on u.p ins fnl f* **5/1**[3]
622- **6** *8* **Motu (IRE)**[384] 1488 7-8-8 **66** (v) DonnaCaldwell[(7)] 4 48
(I W McInnes) *cl up: led after 2f: pushed along and hdd 3f out: sn rdn and wknd wl over 1f out* **11/1**
421/ **7** *7* **Dance In Style**[1020] 4230 7-8-4 **55** oh6 SilvestreDeSousa 3 21
(A Crook) *chsd ldrs: rdn along over 3f out: sn wknd* **18/1**
0-00 **8** *59* **Bolton Hall (IRE)**[14] 2007 6-8-9 **60** (p) TonyHamilton 9 —
(R A Fahey) *v.s.a: virtually ref to r* **11/2**

1m 46.18s (-1.42) **Going Correction** -0.10s/f (Good) 8 Ran SP% 120.2
Speed ratings (Par 103): **103,102,99,99,98 90,83,24**
CSF £23.36 CT £62.16 TOTE £4.00: £1.90, £2.00, £1.50; EX 24.50.
Owner Norcroft Park Stud **Bred** Norcroft Park Stud, And A J Hollis **Trained** Danethorpe, Notts

FOCUS
A moderate handicap in which the form is rated through the runner-up and looks sound but ordinary.

2392 BRIAN YEARDLEY CONTINENTAL TWO YEAR OLD TROPHY (CONDITIONS STKS) (C&G) 5f
3:55 (3:58) (Class 2) 2-Y-0
£9,346 (£2,799; £1,399; £700; £349; £175) **Stalls** High

Form RPR
1 **1** **Able Master (IRE)**[15] 1967 2-9-0 0 RoystonFfrench 5 81
(B Smart) *chsd ldrs: rdn along 1/2-way: hdwy to ld ent fnl f: drvn and hld on wl towards fin* **11/10**[1]
344 **2** *hd* **Kingswinford (IRE)**[12] 2042 2-8-12 0 CatherineGannon 6 78?
(P D Evans) *hld up in tch: hdwy over 1f out: rdn ent fnl f and sn ev ch tl drvn and no ex nr fin* **17/2**[3]
5 **3** *3* **Desert Falls**[6] 2217 2-8-12 0 DeanMcKeown 2 67
(R M Whitaker) *led: rdn along 2f out: hdd ent fnl f and kpt on same pce* **22/1**
13 **4** *1/2* **Toby Tyler**[8] 2154 2-9-2 0 JamieMoriarty 4 70+
(P T Midgley) *sn rdn along and outpcd towards rr: hdwy wl over 1f out: styd on ins fnl f: nrst fin* **10/1**
21 **5** *2* **Red Cell (IRE)**[18] 1889 2-8-12 0 ChrisCatlin 3 58
(E J O'Neill) *chsd ldr: rdn and ch over 1f out: drvn and wknd ent fnl f* **7/2**[2]
0 **6** *29* **Moon Warrior**[42] 1324 2-8-12 0 AndrewHeffernan 1 —
(C Smith) *a in rr: outpcd fnl 2f* **125/1**

62.59 secs (-0.91) **Going Correction** -0.20s/f (Firm) 6 Ran SP% 94.6
Speed ratings (Par 99): **99,98,93,93,89 43**
CSF £7.28 TOTE £1.70: £1.10, £3.70; EX 7.20.
Owner Ron Hull **Bred** Scuderia Miami Di Sandro Guerra And Co **Trained** Hambleton, N Yorks
■ Fathey was withdrawn (4/1, ref to enter stalls). Deduct 20p in the £ unde Rule 4).

FOCUS
Just an average renewal of this juvenile contest. The form looks sound enough with the first pair pulling clear.

NOTEBOOK
Able Master(IRE), bred to be effective at up to 1m, made it two wins from as many starts with a dogged display. He responded gamely to pressure nearing the final furlong and, while hard at work, he always looked like holding off the runner-up where it mattered. This quicker ground proved no problem and further improvement should be forthcoming when he tries another furlong in due course. It will be interesting to see where he goes next for the hat-trick bid. (op 5-4 tchd 11-8)
Kingswinford(IRE) ◆ had posted fair form in defeat on his previous three outings, but he stepped up a gear in this higher grade and only just lost out in a driving finish. Clear of the remainder in second, compensation should await him in the coming weeks. (tchd 10-1)
Desert Falls showed benefit of his debut experience at Ripon and clearly has some speed. He should really find a race when dropping back down in class. (op 28-1 tchd 33-1)
Toby Tyler struggled for early pace on this drop back a furlong and was always staying on too late. He is capable of better over a stiffer test and goes some way to putting this form into perspective. (tchd 17-2 and 11-1)
Red Cell(IRE), comfortably of the mark at Catterick last time, was found wanting inside the final furlong and can have no real excuses. (op 4-1 tchd 3-1)

2393 BRANTINGHAM STAYERS H'CAP 2m 35y
4:25 (4:25) (Class 5) (0-75,74) 4-Y-0+ **£2,752** (£818; £409; £204) **Stalls** High

Form RPR
5022 **1** **Mister Arjay (USA)**[9] 2135 8-9-11 **72** TonyHamilton 4 78
(B Ellison) *mde all: set stdy pce: qcknd 3f out: rdn wl over 1f out: drvn ins fnl f and styd on wl* **3/1**[2]
33-1 **2** *1 3/4* **Mr Crystal (FR)**[8] 2157 4-9-2 **68** MichaelJStainton[(3)] 5 72
(Micky Hammond) *trckd ldrs: hdwy on outer over 2f out: rdn to chal over 1f out: drvn and ev ch ins fnl f: no ex last 100yds* **13/8**[1]
06-3 **3** *1 3/4* **El Dececy (USA)**[7] 2185 4-9-1 **67** DNolan[(3)] 3 69
(S Parr) *hld up in tch: smooth hdwy over 2f out: n.m.r wl over 1f out: chal and ev ch ent fnl f: sn rdn and one pce* **8/1**
5/05 **4** *1 3/4* **Nounou**[8] 2157 7-8-13 **60** ChrisCatlin 1 60
(Miss J E Foster) *trckd ldr: effrt 3f out: rdn along 2f out: drvn and wknd appr fnl f* **33/1**
-053 **5** *3* **Rocknest Island (IRE)**[8] 2157 5-8-8 **55** (p) RoystonFfrench 2 51
(P D Niven) *trckd ldng pair: rdn along on inner over 2f out: sn wknd* **11/2**
3101 **6** *10* **Synonymy**[14] 2012 5-8-13 **60** (b) JamesDoyle 7 44
(M Blanshard) *hld up in rr: effrt over 3f out: sn rdn and btn* **4/1**[3]

3m 41.92s (2.12) **Going Correction** -0.10s/f (Good)
WFA 4 from 5yo+ 2lb 6 Ran SP% 112.5
Speed ratings (Par 103): **90,89,88,87,85 80**
CSF £8.36 CT £32.29 TOTE £3.10: £1.70, £1.70; EX 4.90.
Owner Keith Middleton **Bred** Barbara Hunter **Trained** Norton, N Yorks

FOCUS
A modest staying handicap, run at an uneven pace and the winner dictated. The winning time was slow and the form is muddling.
Synonymy Official explanation: trainer had no explanation for the poor form shown

2394 BEVERLEY LADY AMATEUR RIDERS' H'CAP 1m 1f 207y
5:00 (5:04) (Class 5) (0-70,67) 4-Y-0+ **£2,654** (£823; £411; £205) **Stalls** High

Form RPR
-605 **1** **Active Asset (IRE)**[24] 1725 6-10-3 **63** MissARyan[(3)] 5 75
(A J McCabe) *hld up towards rr: hdwy over 2f out: rdn to ld over 1f out: sn clr* **5/2**[1]
3000 **2** *7* **Tizzy May (FR)**[5] 2250 8-10-1 **58** (v[1]) MissLEllison 10 56
(B Ellison) *trckd ldrs: hdwy 2f out: rdn to chse wnr ent fnl f: sn drvn and no imp* **4/1**[2]
-022 **3** *3* **Penel (IRE)**[38] 1391 7-10-0 **62** (p) MissWGibson[(5)] 9 54
(P T Midgley) *in tch: hdwy over 2f out: sn rdn: kpt on same pce fr over 1f out* **6/1**[3]
5-00 **4** *hd* **Scotty's Future (IRE)**[38] 1391 10-9-5 **53** oh8 MissLAllan[(5)] 7 45
(A Berry) *chsd ldrs: rdn along over 2f out: drvn and one pce appr fnl f* **25/1**
3145 **5** *1 1/4* **Rising Force (IRE)**[8] 2153 5-10-10 **67** (b) MissEJJones 2 56
(J L Spearing) *s.i.s: hld up in rr: hdwy on inner 2f out: rdn over 1f out: kpt on same pce* **5/2**[1]
050/ **6** *2 3/4* **The Plainsman**[802] 634 6-9-7 **53** oh8 MrsMarieKing[(3)] 3 37
(P W Hiatt) *led: rdn along and hdd 3f out: grad wknd* **40/1**
-000 **7** *2 1/2* **Mujma**[7] 2185 4-9-11 **54** MissSBrotherton 6 33
(S Parr) *prom: led 3f out: rdn 2f out: hdd over 1f out and sn wknd* **9/1**
000/ **8** *9* **Parisian Playboy**[374] 6552 8-9-5 **53** oh8 MissBeverleyKendall[(5)] 8 14
(A D Brown) *s.i.s and wnt lft s: a bhd* **40/1**
0-35 **9** *3/4* **Dark Charm (FR)**[25] 1704 9-10-1 **65** (p) MissNVorster[(7)] 4 24
(R A Fahey) *chsd ldrs: pushed along over 3f out: sn wknd* **9/1**

2m 7.83s (0.83) **Going Correction** -0.10s/f (Good) 9 Ran SP% 120.2
Speed ratings (Par 103): **92,86,84,83,82 80,78,71,70**
CSF £13.15 CT £54.48 TOTE £3.60: £1.40, £1.60, £1.80; EX 15.60 Place 6 £41.60, Place 5 £15.96.
Owner Brian Morton **Bred** Rathasker Stud **Trained** Babworth, Notts
■ Stewards' Enquiry : Miss S Brotherton two-day ban: careless riding (Jun 11-12)

FOCUS
A moderate handicap for the grade, run at a strong early pace. The form is basically weak with the winner a stone off his old form.
Rising Force(IRE) Official explanation: jockey said gelding was upset in stalls
T/Plt: £16.00 to a £1 stake. Pool: £46,024.25. 2,089.55 winning tickets. T/Qpdt: £4.90 to a £1 stake. Pool: £2,368.70. 357.70 winning tickets. JR

1889 CATTERICK (L-H)
Saturday, May 24

OFFICIAL GOING: Good to firm (firm in places)
Wind: Fresh, half against Weather: Cloudy, bright

2395 TOTEPLACEPOT (S) STKS 1m 3f 214y
2:15 (2:15) (Class 6) 4-Y-0+ **£2,047** (£604; £302) **Stalls** Low

Form RPR
55-3 **1** **Eijaaz (IRE)**[18] 1890 7-8-11 52 DO'Donohoe 4 56+
(G A Harker) *hld up: plenty to do ent st: gd hdwy over 1f out: led wl ins fnl f: pushed out* **5/2**[1]
0-04 **2** *3/4* **Caraman (IRE)**[17] 1913 10-8-11 53 GrahamGibbons 9 55
(J J Quinn) *cl up: led and edgd lft over 1f out: hdd wl ins fnl f: r.o* **7/2**[3]
-315 **3** *1/2* **Court Of Appeal**[18] 1890 11-9-0 66 (tp) PJMcDonald[(3)] 3 61+
(B Ellison) *prom: effrt and ev ch whn n.m.r and swtchd rt appr fnl f: r.o* **11/4**[2]
00-0 **4** *3/4* **Parchment (IRE)**[139] 69 6-8-6 50 (b) GaryBartley[(5)] 10 53
(A J Lockwood) *hld up: hdwy over 3f out: kpt on u.p ins fnl f* **10/1**
00-0 **5** *6* **Resaass (USA)**[43] 1296 5-8-12 55 ow1 (b[1]) DanielTudhope 6 44
(J O'Reilly) *led to over 1f out: sn btn* **33/1**
6 *hd* **Funky Town (IRE)**[353] 6-8-7 0 ow1 NeilBrown[(5)] 5 44
(Grant Tuer) *missed break: hld up: hdwy and prom 1/2-way: rdn and wknd fr 2f out* **9/2**
00-5 **7** *13* **Airedale Lad (IRE)**[18] 1895 7-8-6 39 NataliaGemelova[(5)] 2 22
(R M Whitaker) *prom: lost pl 1/2-way: n.d after* **28/1**
50 **8** *1 3/4* **Jayne Dean**[28] 1626 4-8-6 0 LiamJones 8 14
(A Crook) *towards rr: drvn 1/2-way: sn wknd* **125/1**
0-00 **9** *8* **Fardi (IRE)**[4] 2286 6-8-11 20 TWilliams 7 6
(K W Hogg) *in tch: hdwy outside 1/2-way: wknd over 3f out* **200/1**

0/00 **10** *10* **Time Dancer (IRE)**[43] 1305 4-8-11 23........................(b) PatrickMathers 1 —
(H A McWilliams) *trckd ldrs tl wknd fr 4f out* **300/1**

2m 39.32s (0.42) **Going Correction** +0.05s/f (Good) **10** Ran SP% **112.7**
Speed ratings (Par 101): **100,99,99,98,94 94,85,84,79,72**
CSF £11.01 TOTE £4.10: £1.20, £1.50, £1.40; EX 12.80.There was no bid for the winner. Caraman was claimed by Mrs G. B. Walford for £6,000.
Owner A S Ward **Bred** Shadwell Estate Company Limited **Trained** Thirkleby, N Yorks
■ Stewards' Enquiry : Graham Gibbons two-day ban: careless riding (Jun 8-9)
FOCUS
A modest event in which the pace was just fair and the form is rated around the placed horses.

2396 BET TOTEPOOL ON ALL UK RACING MEDIAN AUCTION MAIDEN STKS 5f

2:45 (2:45) (Class 6) 3-Y-O **£2,047** (£604; £302) **Stalls** Low

Form RPR

1 **Mayoman (IRE)** 3-9-3 0... LiamJones 7 70+
(Paul Green) *s.i.s: bhd: hdwy 1/2-way: led and edgd lft ins fnl f: r.o* **10/1**

0-52 **2** *1* **Kyzer Chief**[31] 1560 3-8-12 47.. NeilBrown(5) 4 66
(R E Barr) *in tch: effrt 2f out: ev ch ins fnl f: r.o* **9/1**

20-6 **3** *1 3/4* **Grudge**[8] 2171 3-9-3 68.. HayleyTurner 8 60
(D W Barker) *cl up: outpcd and edgd lft over 1f out: kpt on fnl f* **11/4**[1]

44-0 **4** *1/2* **Le Toreador**[28] 1611 3-9-3 72.......................................(t) FergalLynch 10 58
(K A Ryan) *cl up: led over 1f out to ins fnl f: kpt on same pce* **11/2**[3]

20-0 **5** *1/2* **Actabou**[15] 1960 3-9-0 70.. PJMcDonald(3) 9 56+
(M Dods) *bhd and outpcd: styd on fr over 1f out: nrst fin* **6/1**

00-3 **6** *1/2* **Bishopbriggs (USA)**[5] 2261 3-9-3 69........................... DarrenWilliams 3 54
(S Parr) *led to over 1f out: kpt on same pce* **10/3**[2]

2- **7** *3/4* **Marias Buddy**[22] 1786 3-8-12 0.................................. GrahamGibbons 2 47
(Eamon Tyrrell, Ire) *chsd ldrs tl rdn and no ex over 1f out* **12/1**

0-0 **8** *5* **Abitofafath (IRE)**[21] 1795 3-9-3 0.............................. OscarUrbina 6 34
(J G Given) *in tch tl edgd lft and wknd wl over 1f out* **66/1**

2-60 **9** *5* **Paddy Jack**[31] 1556 3-9-3 65.......................................(b[1]) DO'Donohoe 5 16
(J R Weymes) *s.i.s: a outpcd* **14/1**

61.11 secs (1.31) **Going Correction** +0.20s/f (Good) **9** Ran SP% **114.4**
Speed ratings (Par 97): **97,95,92,91,91 90,89,81,73**
CSF £94.86 TOTE £12.00: £3.00, £2.60, £1.40; EX 84.30.
Owner Tom Tuohy **Bred** James Cosgrove **Trained** Lydiate, Merseyside
■ Stewards' Enquiry : Darren Williams caution: prematurely eased gelding app line
FOCUS
A modest maiden, as indicated by the proximity of the runner-up, who came into this race on a 47 mark. The pace was sound but the form is tricky to pin down and so needs treating with caution.
Paddy Jack Official explanation: trainer's rep said gelding did not face the first time blinkers

2397 TOTEPOOL A BETTER WAY TO BET H'CAP 7f

3:15 (3:15) (Class 3) (0-90,86) 4-Y-O+ **£7,771** (£2,312; £1,155; £577) **Stalls** Low

Form RPR

6014 **1** **Daaweitza**[8] 2158 5-8-12 **80**.. DO'Donohoe 7 88
(B Ellison) *hld up: hdwy 2f out: edgd lft: ev ch fnl f: kpt on wl to ld nr fin* **7/2**[3]

1-00 **2** *nk* **Captain Jacksparra (IRE)**[14] 1982 4-9-4 **86**.................. FergalLynch 1 93
(K A Ryan) *led: rdn 2f out: kpt on fnl f: hdd nr fin* **11/4**[2]

-610 **3** *1/2* **Phluke**[1] 2371 7-9-2 **84**.. HayleyTurner 3 90
(Eve Johnson Houghton) *prom: outpcd 1/2-way: rallied over 1f out: kpt on fin* **5/2**[1]

0604 **4** *1 1/4* **H Harrison (IRE)**[25] 1708 8-8-10 **78**.......................... PatrickMathers 6 80
(I W McInnes) *in tch: effrt over 2f out: kpt on u.p fnl f* **18/1**

00-0 **5** *2 3/4* **Hartshead**[17] 1910 9-8-12 **83**.. PJMcDonald(3) 5 85+
(G A Swinbank) *hld up: effrt on ins whn n.m.r and swtchd rt over 1f out: no imp fnl f* **9/2**

54-0 **6** *8* **Chicken Soup**[8] 2158 6-9-0 **82**.................................(v) DarrenWilliams 4 55
(S Parr) *chsd ldrs: effrt over 2f out: wknd over 1f out* **12/1**

0050 **7** *4 1/2* **Nuit Sombre (IRE)**[18] 1891 8-8-4 **77**..........................(p) KellyHarrison(5) 8 38
(G A Harker) *cl up tl rdn and wknd fr over 2f out* **25/1**

1m 26.57s (-0.43) **Going Correction** +0.05s/f (Good) **7** Ran SP% **112.4**
Speed ratings (Par 107): **104,103,103,101,98 89,84**
CSF £13.08 CT £26.78 TOTE £6.20: £2.80, £3.50; EX 16.10.
Owner Mrs Andrea M Mallinson **Bred** C Mallinson **Trained** Norton, N Yorks
FOCUS
A fair handicap in which the gallop was a sound one and the winner is rated to his best.
NOTEBOOK
Daaweitza, in good form of late, appreciated the strong gallop and notched his second course and distance win of the month. He should prove equally effective returned to 1m and should continue to give a good account. (tchd 4-1)
Captain Jacksparra(IRE) ◆ had been soundly beaten on his two previous starts but returned to form down in the weights and in grade. He may be a bit better than the bare form as he was up with the strong pace throughout and is one to keep an eye on in similar company, especially when it looks as though he may be able to dominate. (op 4-1)
Phluke, who was allowed an easy lead when winning this race the previous year, ran creditably turned out after his exertions at Newmarket the previous day. He seems best around sharp left-handed courses. (tchd 11-4 and 9-4)
H Harrison(IRE), well beaten on Polytrack this year, is on a fair mark and was not disgraced. He can make the running or sit handy and is not one to write off just yet. (op 12-1)
Hartshead ◆ has slipped to a handy mark and shaped as though better than this bare form after meeting trouble when starting his run. A strongly run race around this trip on quick ground are his requirements and he is one to keep an eye on. Official explanation: jockey said gelding was denied a clear run (op 5-1 tchd 11-2)
Chicken Soup, soundly beaten on his reappearance run, got a good tow from the leaders but was again well below his best. He will have to show a fair bit more before he is worth a bet. (op 9-1 tchd 17-2)

2398 BET TOTEPOOL ON ALL IRISH RACING H'CAP 5f 212y

3:50 (3:52) (Class 4) (0-85,85) 4-Y-O+ **£4,209** (£1,252; £625; £312) **Stalls** Low

Form RPR

-004 **1** **Inter Vision (USA)**[7] 2210 8-9-4 **85**............................ DanielTudhope 3 99
(A Dickman) *hld up: gd hdwy over 1f out: led ins fnl f: sn clr* **3/1**[1]

5-05 **2** *3* **Prince Namid**[8] 2145 6-8-1 **75**...................................... PatrickDonaghy(7) 6 79
(Mrs A Duffield) *hld up in tch: drvn and outpcd 1/2-way: rallied over 1f out: kpt on: no ch w wnr* **17/2**

6605 **3** *3/4* **Red Cape (FR)**[12] 2058 5-8-4 **71** oh1.................................(b) LiamJones 5 73
(Mrs R A Carr) *pressed ldr: led over 1f out: hung lft and hdd ins fnl f: no ex* **16/1**

3640 **4** *hd* **First Order**[7] 2211 7-9-0 **81**...(v) FergalLynch 4 82
(Miss L A Perratt) *prom: effrt 2f out: kpt on same pce fnl f* **15/2**

0050 **5** *shd* **Mr Wolf**[14] 2005 7-8-4 **71** oh2...(p) HayleyTurner 8 72
(D W Barker) *led to over 1f out: no ex ins fnl f* **8/1**

001- **6** *1 1/2* **Dig Deep (IRE)**[215] 6381 6-9-4 **85**................................. GrahamGibbons 2 81+
(J J Quinn) *hld up: effrt and hdwy on ins whn nt clr run over 1f out: no imp fnl f* **12/1**

20-5 **7** *1* **Sir Nod**[7] 2188 6-8-8 **78**.. PJMcDonald(3) 7 71
(Miss J A Camacho) *hld up in tch: pckd 1/2-way: sn outpcd: no imp over 1f out* **9/2**[3]

2121 **8** *2 1/4* **Expensive Art (IRE)**[12] 2058 4-8-13 **80**........................ OscarUrbina 1 66
(S A Callaghan) *hld up in tch: drvn wl over 1f out: sn btn* **10/3**[2]

1m 13.15s (-0.45) **Going Correction** +0.05s/f (Good) **8** Ran SP% **113.2**
Speed ratings (Par 105): **105,101,100,99,99 97,96,93**
CSF £28.25 CT £345.02 TOTE £3.30: £2.60, £1.90, £5.80; EX 37.90.
Owner Mrs D Hodgkinson **Bred** William A Carl **Trained** Sandhutton, N Yorks
FOCUS
Another fair handicap and a strongly run one to boot. This form should prove reliable rated around the first two.
Expensive Art(IRE) Official explanation: trainer's rep said filly became upset in stalls and ran flat

2399 TOTEEXACTA MEDIAN AUCTION MAIDEN FILLIES' STKS 5f 212y

4:20 (4:21) (Class 6) 3-4-Y-O **£2,047** (£604; £302) **Stalls** Low

Form RPR

30-4 **1** **Cassie's Choice (IRE)**[12] 2039 4-9-0 65.......................... NeilBrown(5) 7 68
(B Smart) *prom: rdn to ld over 1f out: hld on wl towards fin* **5/2**[1]

554 **2** *nk* **Leonid Glow**[12] 2038 3-8-7 64...................................... PJMcDonald(3) 3 65
(M Dods) *prom: effrt and ev ch over 1f out: kpt on: jst hld* **5/2**[1]

26-0 **3** *3 1/4* **Recent Times**[12] 2038 3-8-10 67................................... GrahamGibbons 1 55
(T D Easterby) *cl up: led 1/2-way to over 1f out: kpt on same pce* **5/2**[1]

4 *1 1/4* **Optional Dream (IRE)**[10] 2116 3-8-10 0........................ LiamJones 6 51
(Eamon Tyrrell, Ire) *in tch: drvn over 2f out: one pce over 1f out* **28/1**

30-5 **5** *1* **Bahamian Ballad**[21] 1795 3-8-10 65............................... HayleyTurner 11 47+
(J D Bethell) *hld up: hdwy and edgd lft over 1f out: kpt on: nvr able to chal* **15/2**[2]

4-04 **6** *2* **Little Bones**[11] 2088 3-8-10 53.......................................(t) FergalLynch 8 41
(J F Coupland) *s.i.s: bhd tl hdwy 2f out: no imp fnl f* **16/1**[3]

5-40 **7** *3/4* **Carnival Dream**[43] 1306 3-8-10 57................................. PatrickMathers 4 39
(H A McWilliams) *cl up tl outpcd over 2f out: n.d after* **20/1**

3600 **8** *2* **Nabra**[12] 2038 4-8-12 45.. AdamCarter(7) 9 34
(M Brittain) *midfield on outside: outpcd 1/2-way: n.d after* **50/1**

000/ **9** *12* **Frill A Minute**[570] 6296 4-9-0 0...................................... SladeO'Hara(5) 5 —
(Miss L C Siddall) *bhd: outpcd over 3f out: n.d after* **200/1**

050- **10** *13* **Champagne Sue**[257] 5282 4-9-0 35.................................. GaryBartley(5) 10 —
(D W Barker) *led to 1/2-way: sn struggling* **50/1**

1m 14.11s (0.51) **Going Correction** +0.05s/f (Good)
WFA 3 from 4yo 9lb **10** Ran SP% **116.0**
Speed ratings (Par 98): **98,97,93,91,90 87,86,83,67,50**
CSF £8.19 TOTE £2.70: £1.40, £1.60, £1.60; EX 9.70.
Owner EKOS Pinnacle Partnership **Bred** And Mrs James J Lenehan **Trained** Hambleton, N Yorks
FOCUS
An uncompetitive maiden but a race in which the pace was sound. The runner-up is rated 5lb higher than his Redcar effort through the third.
Little Bones Official explanation: jockey said filly missed the break

2400 TOTETRIFECTA H'CAP 7f

4:55 (4:56) (Class 5) (0-75,75) 4-Y-O+ **£2,729** (£806; £403) **Stalls** Low

Form RPR

246- **1** **Turn Me On (IRE)**[179] 6956 5-7-13 **61** oh2.................... KellyHarrison(5) 9 73
(T D Walford) *hld up: hdwy and swtchd rt 2f out: kpt on to ld wl ins fnl f* **11/1**

0322 **2** *1/2* **Violent Velocity (IRE)**[11] 2087 5-8-12 **69**.................. GrahamGibbons 12 79
(J J Quinn) *hld up in tch: effrt 2f out: ev ch wl ins fnl f: kpt on* **11/4**[1]

0240 **3** *3/4* **Stoic Leader (IRE)**[5] 2251 8-8-6 **70**.............................. PatrickDonaghy(7) 1 78
(R F Fisher) *w ldr: led over 1f out: hdd wl ins fnl f: no ex* **9/1**

-552 **4** *1 3/4* **Mandarin Spirit (IRE)**[14] 2010 8-8-1 **61**.......................(b) LukeMorris(3) 5 65
(G C H Chung) *chsd ldrs: ev ch 2f out: one pce fnl f* **11/2**[2]

00-0 **5** *3/4* **Onatopp (IRE)**[14] 2007 4-8-3 **63**.................................. DuranFentiman(3) 6 65
(T D Easterby) *hmpd s: bhd tl styd on fnl f: nrst fin* **33/1**

1010 **6** *hd* **Dudley Docker (IRE)**[21] 1815 6-9-2 **73**...........................(b) LiamJones 11 74
(C R Dore) *missed break: bhd tl kpt on fnl f: n.d* **12/1**

6-01 **7** *1* **Cheery Cat (USA)**[15] 1952 4-8-6 **63**..............................(p) FergalLynch 4 61
(D W Barker) *slt ld to over 1f out: sn no ex* **8/1**[3]

-460 **8** *shd* **King Harson**[18] 1891 9-8-8 **65**.. HayleyTurner 7 63
(J D Bethell) *hld up: hdwy 2f out: one pce fnl f* **10/1**

00-0 **9** *1 1/4* **Pay Time**[18] 1891 9-8-5 **62**... PatrickMathers 2 57
(R E Barr) *chsd ldrs: drvn 1/2-way: no ex over 1f out* **66/1**

50-6 **10** *1 1/2* **Flying Valentino**[20] 1826 4-8-8 **68**................................. PJMcDonald(3) 3 59
(G A Swinbank) *prom tl rdn and wknd over 1f out* **8/1**[3]

34-3 **11** *12* **Angaric (IRE)**[14] 2007 5-8-11 **73**................................(t) NeilBrown(5) 10 31
(B Smart) *chsd ldrs on outside: drvn 3f out: wknd 2f out* **11/2**[2]

1m 26.15s (-0.85) **Going Correction** +0.05s/f (Good) **11** Ran SP% **119.2**
Speed ratings (Par 103): **106,105,104,102,101 101,100,100,98,97 83**
CSF £41.91 CT £300.00 TOTE £19.80: £5.10, £1.50, £2.60; EX 97.70 TRIFECTA Not won. Place 6 £25.92, Place 5 £21.29.
Owner Ms M Austerfield **Bred** Brendan Lavery **Trained** Sheriff Hutton, N Yorks
FOCUS
An ordinary handicap in which the pace was sound throughout. This form, rated around the placed horses, should stand up at a similar level.
Angaric(IRE) Official explanation: jockey said gelding ran too free
T/Plt: £26.80 to a £1 stake. Pool: £48,366.20. 1,312.60 winning tickets. T/Qpdt: £15.20 to a £1 stake. Pool: £2,381.70. 115.50 winning tickets. RY

2356 HAYDOCK (L-H)

Saturday, May 24

OFFICIAL GOING: Good to firm (firm in places)
Wind: Strong, behind Weather: Sunny

2401 BETFREDCASINO H'CAP 5f

2:05 (2:05) (Class 2) (0-105,104) 4-Y-O+ **£14,571** (£4,335; £2,166; £1,082) **Stalls** Centre

Form RPR

0030 **1** **Fyodor (IRE)**[9] 2129 7-8-11 **92**.......................................(v[1]) MichaelHills 7 101
(W J Haggas) *lw: racd keenly in midfield: hdwy whn n.m.r jst over 1f out: r.o to burst through gap and ld wl ins fnl f: jst hld on fnl strides* **8/1**

200- **2** *nse* **Intrepid Jack**[294] 4150 6-9-7 **102**.................................. RyanMoore 6 111+
(H Morrison) *hld up: shkn up whn swtchd rt and hdwy ent fnl f: str run towards fin: jst failed* **9/2**[1]

0-06 **3** 1 **Invincible Force (IRE)**^{7} 2211 4-8-9 **90**....................(b^{1}) FrancisNorton 4 95
(Paul Green) *racd keenly: led: rdn over 1f out: hdd wl ins fnl f: nt qckn fnl strides* **10/1**

10-1 **4** 2 **Northern Fling**^{42} 1325 4-9-8 **103**.................................. AdrianTNicholls 2 101
(D Nicholls) *a.p: pushed along 1/2-way: rdn to chal fr over 1f out: no ex wl ins fnl f* **7/1**

0200 **5** nk **Knot In Wood (IRE)**^{21} 1809 6-9-4 **99**............................ PaulHanagan 3 96
(R A Fahey) *hld up: rdn over 1f out: styd on wl fnl f: nt rch ldrs* **9/2**^{1}

465- **6** nk **Green Manalishi**^{233} 5953 7-9-9 **104**.................................. NCallan 9 100
(K A Ryan) *lw: midfield: effrt over 1f out: one pce ins fnl f* **9/2**^{1}

0-53 **7** ½ **Bond City (IRE)**^{31} 1571 6-8-11 **92**.................................. JamieSpencer 8 86
(G R Oldroyd) *prom: rdn 1f out: sn btn* **13/2**^{3}

4004 **8** nk **Indian Trail**^{14} 1986 8-9-9 **104**......................................(v) LDettori 1 97
(D Nicholls) *hld up: hdwy 1/2-way: rdn to chal over 1f out: fdd wl ins fnl f* **5/1**^{2}

58.87 secs (-1.63) **Going Correction** -0.275s/f (Firm) **8** Ran SP% **117.2**
Speed ratings (Par 109): **102,101,100,97,96 96,95,94**
CSF £44.92 CT £369.22 TOTE £11.70: £3.20, £1.70, £2.70; EX 62.80 TRIFECTA Not won..
Owner The Fyodor Partnership **Bred** E J Banks And D I Scott **Trained** Newmarket, Suffolk

FOCUS
Perhaps not the strongest form for the grade, with several of them having questions to answer over trip or ground. The winner was back to form in the visor, and the second ran a good Wokingham trial.

NOTEBOOK
Fyodor(IRE), down to a mark 6lb lower than when last winning, was not beaten too far at York the previous week and the application of a first-time visor enabled him to improve enough to get his head in front. Meeting a bit of trouble in running seemed to suit and he got up in the nick of time, but it remains to be seen whether the headgear has the same effect next time. He now heads to the 'Dash' at Epsom on Derby Day. (op 10-1)
Intrepid Jack, off due to injury since finishing 10th behind Zidane in the Stewards Cup, is ideally suited by an extra furlong, but he is fully effective at this trip and he showed plenty of zip. He finished strongly and would have won in another couple of strides. This should set him up nicely for a repeat bid at the Wokingham, a race he was second in off a mark of 100 last year. (op 6-1)
Invincible Force(IRE) has been below his best in a couple of starts this year, but the first-time blinkers saw him in a better light and he showed plenty of zip up front. He was unable to repel the front pair, but this was certainly a step back in the right direction. (op 11-1)
Northern Fling, raised 7lb for last month's soft-ground Doncaster victory, seemed to find 5f on fast ground too much of a speed test. A return to 6f may now be in order. (op 11-2)
Knot In Wood(IRE) , who did best of those drawn low in a really competitive Newmarket handicap last time, looked a player off the same mark here, but he never really looked like getting into it and evidently found the drop in trip against him. He can be given another chance and is another Wokingham possible. (op 13-2)
Green Manalishi needed to have improved to make a winning reappearance off a mark of 104 and he never looked like doing it. (op 4-1 tchd 5-1 in places)
Bond City(IRE) ran well to a point, but needs soft ground ideally. Official explanation: jockey said gelding was unsuited by the good to firm (firm in places) ground (op 8-1)
Indian Trail, 2lb higher than when winning over course and distance in September, has yet to hit top form and this was a slightly disappointing effort. (op 9-2 tchd 6-1)

2402 BETFRED E B F JOAN WESTBROOK PINNACLE STKS (LISTED RACE) (F&M) 1m 3f 200y
2:35 (2:36) (Class 1) 4-Y-O+

£19,869 (£7,532; £3,769; £1,879; £941; £472) **Stalls** High

Form RPR

13-1 **1** **Folk Opera (IRE)**^{10} 2103 4-8-12 94.. LDettori 8 107
(Saeed Bin Suroor) *lw: chsd clr ldr: clsd under 2f out: led ent fnl f: pushed out fnl 100yds* **2/1**^{1}

5-02 **2** 1 ¾ **Under The Rainbow**^{9} 2130 5-8-12 104..................................(p) NCallan 5 104
(B W Hills) *handy in chsng gp: clsd under 2f out: styd on to chal ent fnl f: nt qckn fnl 100yds* **11/4**^{2}

4-2 **3** 1 ½ **Miramare (GER)**^{63} 968 4-8-12 0................................... JamieSpencer 6 102
(A P Stringer) *racd keenly: led: sn clr: rdn 2f out: hdd ent fnl f: kpt on same pce after* **7/1**

15-6 **4** 1 ¾ **Pentatonic**^{21} 1812 5-8-12 91... RyanMoore 4 99
(L M Cumani) *hld up: hdwy 3f out: styd on fnl f: nvr able to chal ldrs* **8/1**

2-54 **5** 1 ¾ **Ronaldsay**^{9} 2130 4-8-12 101.. FrancisNorton 1 96
(R Hannon) *racd keenly: handy in chsng gp: rdn over 3f out: plugged on u.p fnl 2f* **16/1**

1-06 **6** shd **Pelican Waters (IRE)**^{42} 1331 4-8-12 85.................................. LPKeniry 7 96
(E F Vaughan) *hld up: rdn and sme hdwy 3f out: plugged on u.p: nvr rchd ldrs* **66/1**

/1-1 **7** 26 **Abandon (USA)**^{26} 1691 5-8-12 86................................. MichaelHills 10 54
(W J Haggas) *lw: handy in chsng gp: rdn 3f out: wknd over 2f out: eased whn wl btn fnl f* **6/1**^{3}

14-0 **8** 4 **Maid To Believe**^{21} 1812 4-8-12 95...................................... EddieAhern 2 48
(J L Dunlop) *hld up: struggling 3f out: nvr on terms: eased whn wl btn fnl f* **16/1**

12-0 **9** 2 ¼ **Hanella (IRE)**^{14} 1980 5-8-12 80....................................... DavidAllan 9 44
(S C Williams) *hld up: rdn and wknd 3f out: eased whn wl btn fnl f* **80/1**

2m 30.42s (-2.78) **Going Correction** -0.125s/f (Firm) **9** Ran SP% **112.4**
Speed ratings (Par 111): **104,102,101,100,99 99,82,79,77**
CSF £7.19 TOTE £2.60: £1.20, £1.50, £1.90; EX 9.40 Trifecta £44.40 Pool: £551.00 - 8.80 winning units..
Owner Godolphin **Bred** Abbeville And Meadow Court Partners **Trained** Newmarket, Suffolk

FOCUS
Not the strongest of contests for the grade and the trail-blazing Miramare ensured few got into it. The form looks sound enough though.

NOTEBOOK
Folk Opera(IRE), ready winner of a 1m2f handicap at York on her seasonal reappearance, had disappointed in last year's Lingfield Oaks trial, but she proved herself up to Listed level with a gallant victory under a fine ride from Dettori. She has a good attitude and is clearly progressing well, so looks to have earned herself a step up in grade. (op 15-8)
Under The Rainbow is without a win since October 2005, but she is always on the premises in these events and has accumulated plenty of black-type in her time. Second to Promising Lead at York the previous week, the reapplication of cheekpieces seem to have helped and she stuck on willingly under pressure, but is always going to remain vulnerable to less-exposed animals. (op 3-1)
Miramare(GER), a free-going sort who had finished a good second to Malt Or Mash at Kempton in March, failed to settle and was soon in a clear lead. She briefly looked to have them all in trouble, but it became clear from two out she was going to be caught. This was a good effort from the lightly-raced filly, but she will not fulfil her potential until she learns to settle. (op 8-1 tchd 17-2)
Pentatonic came up short on her one previous try at Listed level and she again missed out on gaining some black-type, getting going too late. This represented a big step up on her recent Newmarket effort though and she seems to be coming to hand. (tchd 15-2)
Ronaldsay, another behind Promising Lead at York, was unable to reverse form with Under The Rainbow and she has yet to recapture the best of her form from last season. (op 20-1)
Pelican Waters(IRE), up half a mile in distance, had finished well behind Heaven Scent at Kempton last time and she performed better than entitled to. That said, she was ridden to try and snatch a place and is going to continue to struggle at this level.
Abandon(USA), a ready winner off 80 on her reappearance at Yarmouth, has not been the easiest to train and this was just the sixth start of her career. She struggled and ultimately proved disappointing, but judging by the way she dropped out it is probable something went amiss. Official explanation: jockey said mare had no more to give (op 11-2)
Maid To Believe Official explanation: jockey said filly was unsuited by the good to firm (firm in places) ground

2403 BETFRED SILVER BOWL (HERITAGE H'CAP) 1m 30y
3:05 (3:07) (Class 2) 3-Y-O

£62,310 (£18,660; £9,330; £4,670; £2,330; £1,170) **Stalls** Low

Form RPR

1-41 **1** **Staying On (IRE)**^{19} 1875 3-9-1 93.................................... AdamKirby 4 105
(W R Swinburn) *led: rdn over 2f out: hdd narrowly over 1f out: battled to regain ld fnl 100yds: gamely* **6/1**^{3}

111 **2** hd **Commander Cave (USA)**^{29} 1595 3-9-1 93............................ EddieAhern 5 105
(R Hannon) *in tch: rdn over 2f out: led narrowly over 1f out: hdd fnl 100yds: r.o u.p* **12/1**

1-11 **3** 1 ¼ **Jaser**^{39} 1381 3-8-12 90.. LDettori 1 99
(P W Chapple-Hyam) *midfield: rdn and hdwy over 2f out: chalng and ev ch wl ins fnl f: nt qckn towards fin* **13/2**

40-2 **4** ½ **Flawed Genius**^{21} 1806 3-9-2 94.. RyanMoore 13 104+
(Sir Michael Stoute) *lw: hld up: hdwy over 2f out: nt clr run over 1f out and again whn chsng ldrs ins fnl f: kpt on but unable to chal ldrs towards fin* **7/2**^{1}

21-0 **5** 1 **Endless Luck (USA)**^{28} 1632 3-8-12 90.............................. GregFairley 3 95
(M Johnston) *chsd ldrs: rdn over 1f out: sltly outpcd over 1f out: styd on again towards fin* **14/1**

0-21 **6** ½ **Duntulm**^{21} 1806 3-9-1 93.. DaneO'Neill 11 97
(H Candy) *b. lw: swtg: hld up: hdwy whn nt clr run over 2f out: nt clr run again wl over 1f out: sn rdn and hung lft: one pce wl ins fnl f* **4/1**^{2}

22-1 **7** 1 ½ **Tiger Dream**^{14} 2008 3-8-11 89.. NCallan 8 90
(K A Ryan) *in tch: rdn and outpcd over 2f out: kpt on again ins fnl f wout threatening ldrs* **16/1**

55-6 **8** ¾ **Jedediah**^{29} 1595 3-9-4 96....................................... FrancisNorton 14 98+
(A M Balding) *in rr: rdn and hdwy whn nt clr run and tried to switch rt over 1f out: styng on whn nt clr run again ins fnl f: no imp fnl 100yds* **40/1**

12-4 **9** 3 ¾ **Zakhaaref**^{29} 1598 3-8-12 90..................................... AdrianTNicholls 7 80
(M Johnston) *prom: rdn whn chalng 2f out: wknd wl over 1f out* **25/1**

4-11 **10** 2 ¾ **Huzzah (IRE)**^{16} 1923 3-9-7 99.. MichaelHills 10 83
(B W Hills) *racd keenly in midfield: effrt over 2f out: no imp: wknd fnl f* **9/1**

2-1 **11** 3 ¼ **Austintatious (USA)**^{19} 1854 3-8-11 89................................ IanMongan 6 65
(B J Meehan) *s.i.s: racd keenly and sn prom: rdn and wknd over 2f out* **12/1**

30-2 **12** ½ **Burnwynd Boy**^{15} 1949 3-9-6 98.. PhillipMakin 12 73
(Miss L A Perratt) *midfield: pushed along 3f out: sn wknd* **40/1**

11-2 **13** 2 ¾ **Unbreak My Heart (IRE)**^{29} 1595 3-9-1 93.......................... PaulHanagan 9 62
(R Charlton) *lw: hld up: rdn over 2f out: btn over 1f out* **10/1**

1m 40.91s (-2.89) **Going Correction** -0.125s/f (Firm) **13** Ran SP% **125.6**
Speed ratings (Par 105): **109,108,107,107,106 105,104,103,99,96 93,93,90**
CSF £79.09 CT £377.36 TOTE £7.40: £2.40, £4.30, £2.60; EX 94.70 Trifecta £709.00 Pool: £14,180.21 - 14.20 winning units..
Owner M H Dixon **Bred** M H Dixon **Trained** Aldbury, Herts

FOCUS
A high quality handicap contested by any number of progressive and unexposed three-year-olds. Solid form up front, with the first five all improvers, and several in behind with claims of being unlucky. Top three-year-old handicap form.

NOTEBOOK
Staying On(IRE) appreciated the return to 1m when winning grittily at Windsor last time and he looked open to further improvement, despite a 7lb rise. Soon in front, he kept finding for pressure and, having been headed by Commander Cave over a furlong out, he battled back against the rail under a strong ride from Kirby. His excellent attitude will continue to stand him in good stead and the Brittania at Royal Ascot looks the next logical step. He will have a lot more on his plate there though. (op 15-2 tchd 8-1 in places)
Commander Cave(USA), on a four-timer following back-to-back handicap wins at Kempton and Sandown, was up another 5lb and he looked like defying it when edging ahead over a furlong out. The winner did not give in though and he was unable to hold the lead for long. This was another improved effort and he could progress again back on a slightly slower surface. (tchd 14-1)
Jaser, another in search of a four-timer, has won two 1m soft-ground Nottingham handicaps and he performed really well faced with these contrasting conditions. He had been raised 12lb for his latest victory and the son of Alhaarth is clearly still on the up, with better to be expected again back on a slightly easier surface. (tchd 6-1 and 7-1)
Flawed Genius ◆, who did not really have things fall his way when second to Duntulm at Newmarket, had been raised 7lb and he was made favourite to reverse the form. He managed to do so, but twice got blocked at a vital time and was unable to find any extra inside the final furlong. This was another step forward and he must have gone close with a clear run. (op 11-2)
Endless Luck(USA), who faded out of things late on in what looks to be a fairly weak renewal of the Sandown Classic Trial, has clearly come on a good deal from that run and he ran a nice race back in fifth, keeping on well under pressure. A son of Giant's Causeway, he looks well worth another try at 1m2f, but needs to progress further to win off his current rating.
Duntulm, who put up a remarkable performance to win after losing around nine lengths at the start at Newmarket on his reappearance, was 2lb worse off with Flawed Genius, but still expected by many to confirm the form. Held up early, he too suffered interference at a crucial stage and then failed to pick up once in the clear. He had reportedly worked flat earlier in the week, so it is possible he was not quite at his best. He seems to have plenty of speed and it would be interesting to see him dropped back to 7f. (tchd 9-2 and 5-1 in places)
Tiger Dream made hard work of winning a weak Thirsk maiden on his reappearance, but he had shown some useful placed form at two and this was a lot more promising. His dam stayed 1m2f and he looks well worth a try at that distance. (op 20-1)
Jedediah ◆ was highly tried towards the end of his two-year-old career and could make no impression off a mark of 98 behind Commander Cave on his reappearance. This was better, the 40/1 shot looking rather unlucky not to finish a lot closer having been denied a clear run on more than one occasion, and he could soon become of interest. (op 33-1)
Zakhaaref still seems to be struggling for a suitable trip. There are mixed messages from his pedigree, but he looks well worth a try over 1m2f. It is possible that he is just too high in the handicap.
Huzzah(IRE) has returned with two battling wins in highly competitive handicaps at Newbury and Chester, but he was up another 6lb and seemed unsuited by not racing as prominently as he usually does. (tchd 10-1)

Austintatious(USA) won his maiden well at Kempton last time, but dropped away tamely on this handicap debut and has a bit to prove now.

2404 BETFRED.COM TEMPLE STKS (GROUP 2) 5f
3:35 (3:37) (Class 1) 3-Y-O+
£56,770 (£21,520; £10,770; £5,370; £2,690; £1,350) **Stalls** Centre

Form RPR

312- **1** **Fleeting Spirit (IRE)**[232] 5973 3-8-11 117 .... RyanMoore 3 124
(J Noseda) *awkward leaving stalls: towards rr: hdwy over 1f out: str run to ld wl ins fnl f: won gng away: impressive* **7/2**[2]

22-1 **2** *2* **Borderlescott**[22] 1772 6-9-4 111 .... PatCosgrave 1 119
(R Bastiman) *pressed ldrs: rdn to ld 1f out: hdd wl ins fnl f: nt pce of wnr towards fin* **10/1**

30-2 **3** *1 1/2* **Desert Lord**[22] 1772 8-9-4 108 ....(b) NCallan 10 113
(K A Ryan) *pressed ldr: rdn and hung lft whn led briefly over 1f out: styd on same pce wl ins fnl f* **11/2**[3]

-522 **4** *3/4* **Tax Free (IRE)**[22] 1783 6-9-4 110 .... AdrianTNicholls 4 111
(D Nicholls) *chsd ldrs: rdn 2f out: styd on ins fnl f: nt pce to chal* **17/2**

22-3 **5** *3/4* **Enticing (IRE)**[20] 1831 4-9-1 107 .... MichaelHills 7 105
(W J Haggas) *led: rdn and hdd over 1f out: fdd wl ins fnl f* **8/1**

0-01 **6** *1 1/4* **Off The Record**[21] 1809 4-9-4 99 .... PaulHanagan 13 104
(J G Given) *hld up: rdn and hdwy whn hung bdly lft over 1f out: styd on ins fnl f: nt rch ldrs* **25/1**

31-0 **7** *hd* **Judd Street**[20] 1831 6-9-4 107 .... PhillipMakin 12 103
(Eve Johnson Houghton) *midfield: rdn over 1f out: one pce* **16/1**

0-33 **8** *2* **Fullandby (IRE)**[21] 1809 6-9-4 103 .... GregFairley 9 96
(T J Etherington) *bhd: sn pushed along: kpt on fnl f: nt pce to trble ldrs* **33/1**

03-0 **9** *nse* **Cake (IRE)**[38] 1400 3-8-7 102 .... FrancisNorton 2 92
(R Hannon) *w ldrs to 1/2-way: sn lost pl and outpcd* **66/1**

320- **10** *1 1/2* **Dandy Man (IRE)**[230] 6039 5-9-4 116 .... LDettori 8 90
(Saeed Bin Suroor) *chsd ldrs: rdn whn bmpd over 1f out: wknd fnl f* **2/1**[1]

20-0 **11** *5* **Spirit Of Sharjah (IRE)**[38] 1400 3-8-10 110 .... KShea 6 72
(P W Chapple-Hyam) *s.i.s: alwys bhd* **40/1**

-240 **12** *2* **Matsunosuke**[17] 1917 6-9-4 96 .... DavidAllan 11 65
(A B Coogan) *in tch: pushed along 3f out: wknd 2f out* **66/1**

57.15 secs (-3.35) **Going Correction** -0.275s/f (Firm) course record
WFA 3 from 4yo+ 8lb **12** Ran SP% **119.8**
Speed ratings (Par 115): **115,111,109,108,107 105,104,101,101,99 91,87**
CSF £37.29 TOTE £4.30: £1.80, £3.10, £2.10; EX 41.60 Trifecta £90.90 Pool: £1,792.70 - 14.00 winning units..
Owner The Searchers **Bred** Mrs Bernadette Hayden **Trained** Newmarket, Suffolk
■ The first running of this race at its new venue, having been moved from Sandown.

FOCUS
A really good sprint. Dandy Man set the standard, but he failed to run his race and it was Fleeting Spirit who emerged as the new sprinting star. The winner shattered the 5f course record by over a second, though this race was a few grades higher than anything previously run over the trip here. Reliable form.

NOTEBOOK
Fleeting Spirit(IRE), second to only Kingsgate Native in the 5f juvenile pecking order last term (did beat him at Goodwood though) met with her two defeats behind Nahoodh and Natagora over 6f and she made an impressive three-year-old debut. Usually a prominent racer, she had no choice but to sit off the pace on this occasion having been awkward coming away from the stalls, but it seemed to suit her and she quickened nicely inside the final furlong to win going away. Unlike many in the past, she seems to have made the successful transition from top-class two-year-old sprinter and it will be interesting to see if connections opt to drop her in off the pace next time. With her sex allowance she now sets the standard in the King's Stand Stakes at Royal Ascot, for which she heads the market. (op 3-1 tchd 4-1)
Borderlescott, a really admirable sprinter who hardly ever runs a bad race, gained a deserved win in a conditions stakes at Musselburgh on his seasonal debut and it was no surprise to see him put up a bold show on this return to Group level, running right up to form with Desert Lord. The winner proved a different league in the end, but he looks sure to continue to give a good account and connections now plan on finding him a Listed race somewhere. (op 9-1)
Desert Lord is a top-class sprinter on his day, as shown by winning the Abbaye and finishing second to Kingsgate Native in last year's Nunthorpe. Second to Borderlescott at Musselburgh on his reappearance, this faster ground was expected to bring an improved effort and it was a little disappointing he failed to reverse the form. He did himself no favours by hanging, but still had every chance and will now bid to improve on last season's King's Stand sixth. Official explanation: trainer said gelding hung left and lost its front shoe (op 7-1)
Tax Free(IRE) has been running well in defeat in Ireland and he posted an improved effort on this return to fast ground. He has often fallen short at Group 2 level, but is just as effective at 5f and 6f and looks sure to continue to pay his way. (op 10-1 tchd 8-1)
Enticing(IRE) lost her unbeaten first-time-up record when third to another high-class three-year-old sprinter in Captain Gerrard in the Palace House Stakes at Newmarket last time and, having shown tons of early pace to lead here, she gradually backed out of it. Yet to prove she is as good as last year, the daughter of Pivotal may need her sights lowering slightly. (op 15-2)
Off The Record, an all-the-way winner of a hugely competitive 6f handicap at Newmarket's Guineas Meeting, was up markedly in grade this time and he lacked the early speed to take up his usual prominent role. He made a little late headway, but hung left under pressure and was never getting near the principals. He should still be competitive in handicaps off a mark in the high 90s.
Judd Street, whose stable are in cracking form at present, had finished well down the field behind Enticing in the Palace House and was again unable to make an impression, for all he got a lot closer to the filly. (op 20-1 tchd 25-1)
Dandy Man(IRE) has never hit the big time, twice looking a shade unlucky in the King's Stand, but he is usually on the premises in the top sprints and he looked to set a decent standard on this first start for Godolphin. However, having held an ideal early sit, he found nothing for pressure and it was later reported he had lost a shoe leaving the stalls. He probably deserves another chance. Official explanation: vet said horse lost its front shoe (op 5-2 tchd 15-8)
Spirit Of Sharjah(IRE) Official explanation: jockey said colt was unbalanced

2405 BETFREDPOKER H'CAP 7f 30y
4:10 (4:11) (Class 3) (0-95,89) 3-Y-O **£9,714** (£2,890; £1,444; £721) **Stalls** Low

Form RPR

0-12 **1** **Fervent Prince**[16] 1923 3-8-10 84 .... TravisBlock(3) 6 93
(H Morrison) *chsd ldr: led 2f out: edgd lft ins fnl f: given easy time by rdr towards fin: jst hld on* **11/2**[3]

31-6 **2** *hd* **Kal Barg**[36] 1441 3-9-4 89 .... NCallan 5 98+
(M A Jarvis) *lw: chsd ldrs: rdn over 1f out: r.o to take 2nd wl ins fnl f: gaining towards fin: nt quite get up: flattered sltly* **11/4**[1]

421- **3** *2 1/2* **Nezami (IRE)**[244] 5665 3-9-2 87 .... LDettori 1 89
(B J Meehan) *midfield: hdwy over 3f out: rdn whn chsd ldrs over 1f out: nt qckn ins fnl f* **8/1**

1-60 **4** *3/4* **Ramatni**[16] 1923 3-8-13 84 .... IanMongan 3 84
(M Johnston) *led: rdn and hdd 2f out: kpt on same pce fnl f* **25/1**

1-42 **5** *nk* **Cape Vale (IRE)**[14] 1988 3-9-2 87 .... AdrianTNicholls 7 86
(D Nicholls) *midfield: rdn and hdwy 2f out: styd on ins fnl f: nvr able to chal ldrs* **4/1**[2]

10-0 **6** *nse* **Bellomi (IRE)**[20] 1834 3-9-2 87 .... EddieAhern 9 86
(W J Haggas) *midfield: rdn and hdwy 2f out: styd on ins fnl f* **16/1**

202- **7** *1 1/2* **Flowing Cape (IRE)**[210] 6486 3-9-1 86 .... RyanMoore 11 85+
(R Hollinshead) *bmpd s: hld up: hdwy whn hung lft over 1f out: continually denied a run after: eased fnl 100yds* **9/1**

-305 **8** *1/2* **Silver Wind**[16] 1925 3-9-0 85 ....(v) TGMcLaughlin 2 81
(P D Evans) *chsd ldrs: rdn over 1f out: one pce fnl f* **16/1**

103- **9** *1 1/2* **Blue Sky Basin**[223] 6201 3-8-6 77 .... FrancisNorton 10 69+
(A M Balding) *wnt rt s: racd keenly: hld up: rdn 2f out: hdwy over 1f out: one pce fnl f* **8/1**

10-0 **10** *2 1/4* **Feisty Royale**[42] 1336 3-8-11 82 .... GregFairley 12 66
(M Johnston) *lw: hld up: rdn 2f out: no imp* **50/1**

510- **11** *2 1/2* **Cat Whistle**[232] 5974 3-8-11 82 .... PaulHanagan 8 59
(R A Fahey) *racd keenly: chsd ldrs: lost pl whn pce lifted over 2f out: n.d after* **16/1**

3-10 **12** *12* **American Art (IRE)**[21] 1806 3-9-0 85 ....(t) MichaelHills 13 29
(B W Hills) *hld up: eased whn hung lft and no imp over 1f out* **14/1**

1m 30.17s (-0.03) **Going Correction** -0.125s/f (Firm) **12** Ran SP% **124.4**
Speed ratings (Par 103): **95,94,91,91,90 90,88,88,86,84 81,67**
CSF £22.04 CT £127.20 TOTE £5.50: £2.10, £1.50, £3.20; EX 20.50.
Owner Thurloe Finsbury II **Bred** Fonthill Stud **Trained** East Ilsley, Berks

FOCUS
This wasn't as strongly run as the other races on the round course, but it was still a decent handicap. It has been rated positively and look sure to produce winners.

NOTEBOOK
Fervent Prince ◆, an unlucky loser behind Huzzah at Chester last time, had been raised 5lb and was back slightly in trip, but he was sent to the front plenty soon enough and was always doing enough, even if his rider did take it a little too easy. This looked a fair contest and the son of Averti seems to be progressing well, so it was no surprise to hear talk of the Brittania Stakes afterwards. He should get 1m and could run a big race there. (op 9-2)
Kal Barg ◆, sixth in a competitive handicap won by Huzzah at Newbury on his reappearance, looked to hold strong claims with that race having worked out so well and he ran a fine race, but was never quite getting to the winner. He was a couple of lengths clear of the remainder though and will appreciate a stronger pace or a little further. (op 7-2 tchd 4-1 in places)
Nezami(IRE), 6lb higher than when winning a 6f Hamilton handicap on his final start at two, had earlier shown himself to be as effective at this distance and he made a highly satisfactory return. The run may have been needed and he should be capable of winning off this mark, whether it be 6f or 7f. (op 10-1)
Ramatni, a tough and progressive juvenile who looked as though she may not have trained on in two previous starts this term, will no doubt have delighted connections with this effort in fourth. Soon in front, she was brushed aside readily enough, but kept finding for pressure and held fourth. This was certainly a step back in the right direction. (op 20-1)
Cape Vale(IRE) looked in need of this trip when just failing to get there over 6f at the course last time and he again seemed to hit top stride too late in the day. He looks worth persevering with at this distance though and perhaps a more positive ride or softer going would help in future. (op 7-2)
Bellomi(IRE), who ran well for a long way at Newmarket on his reappearance, had been dropped 2lb and he gave an improved performance under a more restrained ride. He should stay 1m and may yet have more to offer. (op 25-1)
Flowing Cape(IRE) ◆, second off a mark of 82 at Doncaster last backend, failed to get a prominent position having been bumped early and he received little luck in the final furlong, continually getting blocked. He would have been closer and will be of obvious interest next time. Official explanation: jockey said colt was bumped leaving stalls and later denied a clear run (op 8-1)
Blue Sky Basin never really threatened to get into this, but it was his seasonal debut and better can be expected next time. (op 11-1)
American Art(IRE) Official explanation: jockey said gelding was unsuited by the good to firm (firm in places) ground

2406 TEXT BETFRED TO 83080 FOR MOBILE BETTING H'CAP 1m 30y
4:45 (4:45) (Class 4) (0-80,82) 4-Y-O+ **£5,180** (£1,541; £770; £384) **Stalls** Low

Form RPR

-005 **1** **Obezyana (USA)**[1] 2373 6-8-5 70 .... DominicFox(3) 11 85+
(A Bailey) *a.p: led 2f out: rdn clr over 1f out: styd on wl: eased down towards fin* **10/1**

62-0 **2** *2* **Just Bond (IRE)**[15] 1970 6-8-9 71 .... RichardKingscote 8 78
(G R Oldroyd) *hld up: hdwy on outside 2f out: sn rdn: wnt 2nd 1f out: no real imp on wnr* **5/1**[3]

1112 **3** *2 1/4* **Xpres Maite**[11] 2082 5-9-6 82 ....(v) PhillipMakin 4 84
(S R Bowring) *trckd ldrs: rdn 2f out: kpt on same pce fnl f* **4/1**[2]

42-0 **4** *1 3/4* **Jawaab (IRE)**[24] 1719 4-8-10 72 .... RyanMoore 6 70
(M A Buckley) *lw: midfield: rdn and hdwy 2f out: kpt on one pce fnl f* **11/4**[1]

2044 **5** *hd* **Memphis Man**[14] 1996 5-8-10 72 .... TGMcLaughlin 10 69
(P D Evans) *dwlt: racd keenly: hld up: rdn over 2f out: styd on fnl f: nvr nrr* **12/1**

500- **6** *3 1/4* **Sotik Star (IRE)**[203] 6651 5-8-9 71 ow1 .... NCallan 13 61
(P J Makin) *in tch: rdn over 1f out: wknd fnl f* **10/1**

4-05 **7** *1/2* **Chicken George (IRE)**[22] 1771 4-8-9 71 .... AdrianTNicholls 5 60
(D Nicholls) *midfield: rdn over 3f out: wknd 2f out* **4/1**[2]

00-2 **8** *1 3/4* **Fantasy Parkes**[12] 2039 4-9-1 77 .... DavidAllan 2 62
(E J Alston) *led: rdn and hdd 2f out: wknd over 1f out* **12/1**

-000 **9** *85* **Lap Of Honour (IRE)**[28] 1612 4-9-2 78 .... GregFairley 12 —
(Jennie Candlish) *trckd ldrs: wnt wrong and lost pl qckly 4f out: virtually p.u fnl f* **20/1**

1m 41.79s (-2.01) **Going Correction** -0.125s/f (Firm) **9** Ran SP% **121.7**
Speed ratings (Par 105): **105,103,100,99,98 95,95,93,8**
CSF £62.55 CT £242.08 TOTE £16.60: £3.80, £2.20, £1.80; EX 118.60.
Owner Phil Buchanan **Bred** Stone Canyon Thoroughbreds **Trained** Newmarket, Suffolk

FOCUS
A fair handicap. Solid form which could go higher.
Lap Of Honour(IRE) Official explanation: jockey said gelding lost its action on the bend

2407 BETFREDBINGO H'CAP 6f
5:15 (5:18) (Class 4) (0-80,80) 3-Y-O **£4,533** (£1,348; £674; £336) **Stalls** Centre

Form RPR

42-0 **1** **Castles In The Air**[43] 1297 3-8-8 70 .... PaulEddery 6 79
(Pat Eddery) *lw: a prom: rdn to ld over 1f out: r.o wl fnl f* **9/2**[2]

531- **2** *2* **Maryolini**[148] 7260 3-9-0 76 .... LDettori 10 78
(N J Vaughan) *led: rdn and hdd over 1f out: nt qckn ins fnl f* **11/2**[3]

641 **3** *3/4* **Atlantic Beach**[15] 1971 3-8-10 72 .... PaulHanagan 9 72
(R A Fahey) *lw: in tch: rdn and outpcd 2f out: styd on towards fin: nt rch front pair* **9/2**[2]

010- **4** *1 ¼* **Tyfos**[182] 6936 3-9-3 **79** .... EddieAhern 11 75
(W M Brisbourne) *hld up: hdwy 1/2-way: sn rdn: intimidated over 1f out: kpt on ins fnl f* **33/1**

0-00 **5** *nse* **Hunt The Bottle (IRE)**[14] 1988 3-8-11 **73** .... MichaelHills 3 69
(B W Hills) *hld up: rdn and hdwy over 1f out: kpt on ins fnl f: nvr able to chal* **11/2**[3]

0-00 **6** *1* **Reel Gift**[14] 2000 3-9-4 **80** ....(b[1]) DaneO'Neill 12 73
(R Hannon) *chsd ldrs: rdn and chalng whn edgd rt over 1f out: no ex ins fnl f* **8/1**

5-32 **7** *3 ¾* **Supermassive Muse (IRE)**[17] 1911 3-8-11 **73** .... RyanMoore 2 54
(E S McMahon) *in tch: rdn over 1f out: wknd ins fnl f* **4/1**[1]

-231 **8** *23* **Pha Mai Blue**[22] 1764 3-9-4 **80** .... RichardKingscote 1 —
(W J Knight) *sn bhd: eased whn wl btn over 1f out* **11/2**[3]

1m 12.18s (-1.82) **Going Correction** -0.275s/f (Firm) **8** Ran SP% **116.6**
Speed ratings (Par 101): **101,98,97,95,95 94,89,58**
CSF £29.99 CT £118.12 TOTE £5.80: £1.70, £2.20, £1.60; EX 36.50 Place 6 £133.18, Place 5 £42.18.
Owner Reg Griffin And Jim McGrath **Bred** Newgate Stud Company **Trained** Nether Winchendon, Bucks

FOCUS
None of the principals here were fully exposed. The winner was improving to the tune of around 6lb, but the second and third were a shade off their best.
Pha Mai Blue Official explanation: jockey said colt knocked itself leaving stalls and never travelled
T/Jkpt: Not won. T/Plt: £212.50 to a £1 stake. Pool: £141,034.02. 484.30 winning tickets. T/Qpdt: £24.90 to a £1 stake. Pool: £7,144.85. 211.90 winning tickets. DO

2368
NEWMARKET (ROWLEY) (R-H)
Saturday, May 24

OFFICIAL GOING: Firm
Wind: Fresh, across Weather: Fine

2408 NATIONAL EXPRESS FAIRWAY STKS (LISTED RACE) 1m 2f
2:20 (2:20) (Class 1) 3-Y-O
£17,031 (£6,456; £3,231; £1,611; £807) **Stalls** High

Form RPR

2-12 **1** **Unnefer (FR)**[15] 1943 3-9-0 **109** .... TedDurcan 5 107
(H R A Cecil) *hld up: hdwy over 2f out: led over 1f out: rdn out* **10/11**[1]

13 **2** *1* **Pampas Cat (USA)**[16] 1922 3-9-0 **103** .... JimmyFortune 4 105
(J H M Gosden) *s.i.s: sn prom: led 2f out: rdn: hung lft and hdd over 1f out: styd on same pce ins fnl f: eased last strides* **15/8**[2]

1-1 **3** *1* **Age Of Reason (UAE)**[127] 217 3-9-0 **93** .... RHills 3 103
(M Johnston) *led: rdn and hdd 2f out: hung lft and outpcd over 1f out: styd on wl towards fin* **9/1**[3]

-125 **4** *4 ½* **Drill Sergeant**[21] 1811 3-9-0 **93** .... JoeFanning 2 94
(M Johnston) *chsd ldr 6f: rdn and wknd over 1f out* **25/1**

-224 **5** *1 ¼* **Gaspar Van Wittel (USA)**[9] 2121 3-9-0 **100** .... KerrinMcEvoy 1 92
(S A Callaghan) *hld up: hdwy over 3f out: rdn over 2f out: wknd over 1f out* **12/1**

2m 10.37s (4.57) **Going Correction** +0.275s/f (Good) **5** Ran SP% **108.7**
Speed ratings (Par 107): **92,91,90,86,85**
CSF £2.73 TOTE £1.80: £1.10, £1.30; EX 2.80.
Owner Niarchos Family **Bred** S Niarchos **Trained** Newmarket, Suffolk

FOCUS
This was anything but truly run and the pace did not pick up until entering the last 2f, hence the moderate time. The five runners, who raced down the centre of the track, were in a line soon after but despite the way the race was run, the better horses still dominated the finish. It is more likely that the winner was below his best than that the second and third were big improvers.

NOTEBOOK
Unnefer(FR) only needed reproduce the form of his narrow defeat in the Dee Stakes in order to take this. Produced with his effort towards the far side of the group, apart from one crack with the whip he only needed to be pushed out under hands and heels to see off his main market rival. He is very consistent and is still capable of winning a Group race. (op 5-6 tchd Evens)
Pampas Cat(USA), from the stable that took this last year with the subsequent St Leger winner Lucarno, was beaten rather further in the Chester Vase than the winner was in the Dee Stakes. Back to the scene of his debut victory, this drop back in trip may not have been totally ideal, especially in such a moderately run race. He had every chance, but lacked the pace to get the better of the favourite and may need a return to further. He remains open to a bit more improvement. (op 2-1 tchd 13-8 and 9-4 in places)
Age Of Reason(UAE), returning from four months off and previously unbeaten in two starts on Polytrack, was allowed a soft lead on this grass debut over a longer trip. He could not go with the big two when the tempo increased entering the last couple of furlongs, but despite edging to the stands' rail he got his second wind up the final climb and finished right on the heels of the front pair. He gives the impression that he would appreciate a more strongly run race over the trip and may even get further. (op 8-1 tchd 15-2)
Drill Sergeant, well beaten off 95 in a handicap here last time, was content to track his stable companion for much of the way, but he did race a little keenly and did not look totally happy on the ground on this undulating track in the latter stages. Fading right out of it late on, he was up against it at this level anyway but may still be capable of finding something back on easier ground. (op 16-1)
Gaspar Van Wittel(USA), trying his longest trip to date, was switched off out the back but after moving closer on the nearside approaching the last 2f, his effort soon petered out. He appeared not to stay, but he does have an exposed look to him now and he will continue to be a hard horse to place. (op 14-1 tchd 20-1)

2409 CORAL.CO.UK KING CHARLES II STKS (LISTED RACE) 7f
2:50 (2:51) (Class 1) 3-Y-O
£17,031 (£6,456; £3,231; £1,611; £807; £405) **Stalls** High

Form RPR

1- **1** **Calming Influence (IRE)**[225] 6156 3-9-0 **99** ....(t) KerrinMcEvoy 10 109+
(Saeed Bin Suroor) *hld up: hdwy over 2f out: chsd ldr over 1f out: edgd lft ins fnl f: r.o to ld nr fin* **9/2**[3]

2-10 **2** *hd* **Stimulation (IRE)**[21] 1808 3-9-4 **110** .... SteveDrowne 1 112
(H Morrison) *s.i.s: hdwy to chse ldr 6f out: led 2f out: rdn: hung lft and hdd nr fin* **3/1**[2]

24-3 **3** *nk* **Red Alert Day**[35] 1471 3-9-0 **107** .... ShaneKelly 6 107
(S A Callaghan) *hld up: hdwy over 1f out: r.o wl* **11/1**

13-4 **4** *9* **Exhibition (IRE)**[15] 1949 3-9-0 **103** .... TedDurcan 4 83
(S A Callaghan) *s.i.s: hld up: rdn over 1f out: nvr nr to chal* **33/1**

50-2 **5** *½* **Bobs Surprise**[35] 1471 3-9-0 **107** .... WilliamBuick 3 82
(B W Hills) *chsd ldrs: rdn over 2f out: wknd over 1f out* **7/1**

0-21 **6** *nk* **Tasdeer (USA)**[42] 1328 3-9-0 **93** .... RHills 8 81
(M A Jarvis) *chsd ldrs: rdn over 1f out: sn wknd* **8/1**

20-5 **7** *4* **Maze (IRE)**[38] 1400 3-9-4 **102** .... PaulMulrennan 7 74
(B Smart) *hld up: effrt over 2f out: wknd over 1f out* **22/1**

21- **8** *7* **Western Art (USA)**[323] 3269 3-9-4 **100** .... AlanMunro 2 55
(P W Chapple-Hyam) *s.i.s: hld up: rdn over 2f out: sn wknd* **25/1**

315- **9** *1 ½* **Luck Money (IRE)**[217] 6333 3-9-0 **113** .... TQuinn 5 47
(P F I Cole) *led 5f: sn rdn and wknd* **11/4**[1]

1m 26.01s (0.61) **Going Correction** +0.275s/f (Good) **9** Ran SP% **112.9**
Speed ratings (Par 107): **107,106,106,96,95 95,90,82,80**
CSF £17.51 TOTE £5.50: £1.60, £1.50, £2.40; EX 20.40 Trifecta £141.20 Pool: £537.30 - 2.70 winning units..
Owner Godolphin **Bred** Mrs Helen Lyons **Trained** Newmarket, Suffolk

FOCUS
The runners all raced towards the far side of the track this time. A race that was well up to its Listed status and the pace was solid, if far from breakneck. The way the front three pulled miles clear of the others suggest they are the ones to focus on and it is also worth noting that for the past two years the winner of this has gone on to win the Jersey Stakes at Royal Ascot. The winner improved around 14lb on his maiden form and would be fancied to confirm the placings with the runner-up at level weights if they met again.

NOTEBOOK
Calming Influence(IRE) ◆ was the least exposed in the field, having won a York maiden on his only previous start last October, a race that has since produced its share of winners. Sporting a tongue-tie for this reapperance, he belied his inexperience with a thoroughly professional performance and despite having plenty of ground to make up on the runner-up a furlong from home, he put in quite a finish to get up near the line. This was a good effort - only one of his eight rivals had a lower official rating than him - and further improvement is on the cards. He must not be underestimated if connections attempt to carry on the recent trend of winners of this race and head for the Jersey at Royal Ascot. (op 4-1 tchd 11-2)
Stimulation(IRE), back over the distance of his Free Handicap victory, having only put up an ordinary performance in the 2000 Guineas in the meantime, sat on the shoulder of the favourite for much of the way and when he was sent for home and quickly established a clear lead entering the final furlong, the race looked his. On the face of it, the fact that he had the race snatched from him close to the line would suggest he did not quite get up the hill, but the distance the front three put between themselves and the rest might suggest otherwise. Therefore the likelihood is that he ran right up to his best under his penalty. (op 4-1)
Red Alert Day, back on a more suitable surface, was given plenty to do but stayed on very strongly up the final climb and was putting in a strong finish between the front pair. He does look a little exposed now, but this was a good effort and he can find a Listed race over this trip at some stage. (op 12-1)
Exhibition(IRE), disappointing on his return to action, was switched off right out the back before staying on to win the separate race for fourth. Given how far he was beaten it is hard to be sure what he achieved, but he probably needs this trip now and it may be significant that his only win came on much softer ground. Official explanation: jockey said colt was slowly into its stride
Bobs Surprise, who finished four lengths in front of Red Alert Day in the Greenham, failed to confirm that form by some margin and looks as though he will be a hard horse to place. (tchd 13-2 and 8-1 in places)
Tasdeer(USA), runner-up to Paco Boy in a Listed race on Polytrack last time, form that meant he was closely matched with a couple of these on a line through the winner's subsequent victory in the Greenham, nonetheless had plenty to find on offcial ratings. After racing keenly just behind the leaders against the far rail, he was eventually put firmly in his place. Official explanation: jockey said colt lost its action (op 9-1)
Luck Money(IRE), not seen since finishing fifth in the Dewhurst, had plenty in hand of his rivals on official ratings and was soon in front. The way he capitulated tamely once headed suggests he may not have trained on, though more evidence is needed. Official explanation: jockey said colt lost its action (op 5-2 tchd 9-4 and 3-1 in places)

2410 CORAL.CO.UK SPRINT (HERITAGE H'CAP) 6f
3:20 (3:22) (Class 2) (0-105,99) 3-Y-O
£24,924 (£7,464; £3,732; £1,868; £932; £468) **Stalls** High

Form RPR

42-6 **1** **Ancien Regime (IRE)**[20] 1834 3-9-3 **95** .... PhilipRobinson 8 106+
(M A Jarvis) *chsd ldrs: led over 2f out: rdn and hung lft fr over 1f out: r.o* **9/2**[2]

0-00 **2** *¾* **Carleton**[8] 2171 3-8-9 **87** .... StephenDonohoe 11 96
(W J Musson) *hld up: hdwy over 1f out: rdn and ev ch ins fnl f: r.o* **16/1**

1-13 **3** *1 ¼* **Prohibit**[24] 1718 3-9-3 **95** .... JimmyFortune 13 100
(J H M Gosden) *hld up: racd keenly: hdwy over 2f out: rdn over 1f out: hung lft ins fnl f: styd on same pce* **5/2**[1]

4-00 **4** *1 ½* **Brave Prospector**[38] 1400 3-9-6 **98** ....(t) KerrinMcEvoy 14 98
(P W Chapple-Hyam) *prom: rdn over 1f out: hung lft and no ex ins fnl f* **10/1**

6540 **5** *nk* **Mister Hardy**[14] 1999 3-8-9 **87** .... PaulMulrennan 6 86
(R A Fahey) *mid-div: hdwy 1/2-way: outpcd over 1f out: r.o towards fin* **25/1**

-401 **6** *1 ¼* **Victorian Bounty**[20] 1837 3-8-13 **91** .... MickyFenton 7 86
(Stef Liddiard) *led over 3f: no ex fnl f* **9/1**

3-50 **7** *2 ½* **Oasis Wind**[20] 1837 3-9-3 **95** ....(b[1]) TQuinn 10 82
(P F I Cole) *chsd ldr: rdn over 2f out: wknd fnl f* **14/1**

34-6 **8** *3* **Sophie's Girl**[24] 1718 3-8-7 **92** .... KMay[(7)] 9 69
(B J Meehan) *mid-div: hdwy 1/2-way: sn rdn: wknd over 1f out* **20/1**

-541 **9** *2 ¾* **Brassini**[14] 1995 3-8-8 **86** .... AlanMunro 3 55
(B R Millman) *prom: lost pl over 4f out: n.d after* **11/1**

01-3 **10** *3* **Quest For Success (IRE)**[14] 1999 3-8-9 **87** .... SteveDrowne 12 46
(D J G Murray Smith) *hld up: rdn and wknd over 2f out* **25/1**

1051 **11** *½* **Opus Maximus (IRE)**[8] 2141 3-7-12 **76** oh1 .... JimmyQuinn 2 33
(M Johnston) *hld up: rdn over 1f out: a in rr* **8/1**[3]

10-3 **12** *1* **C'Mon You Irons (IRE)**[20] 1837 3-8-4 **82** .... AdrianMcCarthy 5 36
(M R Hoad) *chsd ldrs over 3f* **16/1**

010- **13** *¾* **Westwood**[210] 6488 3-8-12 **90** .... TedDurcan 4 42
(D Haydn Jones) *s.i.s: hld up: a in rr* **66/1**

1-30 **14** *2 ¾* **Fol Hollow (IRE)**[29] 1597 3-9-7 **99** .... JoeFanning 1 42
(D Nicholls) *unruly in stalls: s.i.s: hdwy over 3f out: hung rt and wknd over 2f out* **12/1**

1m 12.67s (0.47) **Going Correction** +0.275s/f (Good) **14** Ran SP% **125.4**
Speed ratings (Par 105): **107,106,104,102,101 100,96,92,89,85 84,83,82,78**
CSF £74.77 CT £225.89 TOTE £5.40: £2.20, £6.50, £1.20; EX 136.10 TRIFECTA Not won..
Owner Sheikh Ahmed Al Maktoum **Bred** Deer Forest Stud **Trained** Newmarket, Suffolk

FOCUS
Perhaps not quite the strength in depth we are used to in this race, but it was won by a progressive sort again. Several of the beaten horses are still open to improvement and the form has been rated fairly positively. The field tended to group towards the centre in the early stages, but with a few hanging late on they eventually used the whole width of the track.

NOTEBOOK

Ancien Regime(IRE) ◆, who seemed to find 7f just too far for him at the Guineas meeting, was nonetheless all the better for that reappearance effort. Never far way and always going well, he was sent for home entering the Dip, but he then threatened to throw it away by hanging badly away to his left. However, with the rail to straighten him and with Robinson at his strongest, he was lifted over the line in front and can be considered to have had a bit more in hand than the official margin. He still does not look the finished article, but the stable's three-year-old sprinters are always worth respecting and he now reportedly heads for a valuable 6f handicap at York. (op 7-2 tchd 5-1 in places)

Carleton, who finished behind three of these here on his reappearance, reversed the form with all of them. Switched off out the back, he was produced with his effort towards the far side and looked at one stage as though he might take advantage of the winner hanging, but once his rival was straightened he proved too good for him. The Handicapper is now giving him a chance, but it is worth noting that both of his wins have come on easier ground. (op 14-1)

Prohibit, third in an Ascot Listed race last time, was 9lb higher than when winning a handicap over course and distance on his reappearance when he had a few of these rivals behind him. He was brought through to hold every chance and did not go down without a fight, but he did carry his head rather high up the hill and he may not have appreciated this ground even though he has won on it. He will still need to find further improvement in order to defy this sort of mark. (op 7-2)

Brave Prospector, last of the 11 runners in the Free Handicap last time, has paid dearly in the weights for finishing fourth in last season's Horris Hill but he did not go off unbacked here and ran well back over this shorter trip in the first-time tongue-tie. This would have been the quickest ground he has encountered and this effort suggests this stiff-looking mark may not be totally beyond him. (op 14-1)

Mister Hardy has rather struggled since winning his first two starts as a juvenile but did not run at all badly here on ground that would have been plenty fast enough. He was doing some solid late work, and shaped as though worth another try over 7f. He lacks the scope of a few of these, but he is far from a lost cause. (op 33-1)

Victorian Bounty, raised 5lb for his victory over a subsequent winner at Salisbury last time, tried to make every yard once again but a combination of the higher mark and stiffer track seemed to find him out. (op 10-1)

Oasis Wind failed to improve for the application of blinkers and still looks too high in the weights. (op 18-1 tchd 20-1)

Brassini had been raised a whopping 9lb for his easy Lingfield victory and that was enough to anchor him in this much better contest. (op 8-1)

Opus Maximus(IRE) Official explanation: jockey said gelding lost its action closing stages

C'Mon You Irons(IRE) Official explanation: jockey said gelding was unsuited by the firm ground

Westwood Official explanation: jockey said gelding was unsuited by the firm ground

Fol Hollow(IRE) misbehaved beforehand and though back in touch at halfway following a tardy start, was soon on the retreat again. This was disappointing, but he lacks scope and also looks handicapped right up to the hilt. Official explanation: jockey said gelding never travelled (tchd 14-1)

2411 STANSTED EXPRESS E B F MAIDEN STKS 6f

4:00 (4:01) (Class 4) 2-Y-O **£4,533** (£1,348; £674; £336) **Stalls** High

Form RPR

1 **Alkhafif** 2-9-3 0 .... RHills 7 78+
(E A L Dunlop) *trckd ldrs: rdn to ld ins fnl f: r.o* **5/2**[2]

2 ½ **Weald Park (USA)** 2-9-3 0 .... TedDurcan 2 76+
(R Hannon) *wnt lft s: sn chsng ldr: rdn over 1f out: edgd lft: r.o* **5/2**[2]

3 ½ **Kingship Spirit (IRE)** 2-9-3 0 .... ShaneKelly 4 74+
(J Noseda) *led: rdn over 1f out: put hd in air and hdd ins fnl f: styd on same pce* **6/5**[1]

4 5 **Calaloo (IRE)** 2-9-3 0 .... SteveDrowne 3 56+
(C R Egerton) *hld up in tch: rdn over 1f out: hung rt and wknd ins fnl f* **12/1**[3]

1m 19.11s (6.91) **Going Correction** +0.275s/f (Good) 4 Ran SP% **110.3**
Speed ratings (Par 95): **64,63,62,56**
CSF £9.02 TOTE £3.50; EX 11.40.
Owner Hamdan Al Maktoum **Bred** Bearstone Stud **Trained** Newmarket, Suffolk

FOCUS

A race badly affected by three non-runners and the remaining four newcomers went only a very moderate pace. The winning time was therefore pedestrian - 6.44 seconds slower than the preceding handicap - and it is very hard to be sure what the form amounts to. Difficult to rate the form that highly, but all four runners had good pedigrees and represented decent yards, so it may have been underestimated.

NOTEBOOK

Alkhafif, a 180,000gns half-brother to four winners including Queen Mary Stakes winners Romantic Myth and Romantic Liaison, was given a well-judged debut ride here as his jockey found him cover despite the small field. That proved a major help to him when he was asked for his effort up the final climb and he showed a good attitude to score. The very slow time makes it difficult to establish the merit of the form, but he is bred to be a sprinter and obviously has the ability. (op 11-4 tchd 10-3)

Weald Park(USA), a 90,000gns half-brother to five winners at up to 1m including Fantastic View, went badly away to his left exiting the stalls but was soon back on an even keel. He had every chance and was still going forward at the line. He should know more next time and his breeding suggests he will get further. (tchd 11-4)

Kingship Spirit(IRE), a 100,000gns half-brother to a winner over 7f here and to three other winners in Italy, set the modest pace but as soon as he hit the rising ground he put his head up and was run down by the front pair. It may be worth giving him the benefit of the doubt, as he was entitled to be green on this debut and he may also not have handled this quick ground on an undulating track. Although by a sprinter, the dam's side of his pedigree suggests he will get further. (op 5-4 tchd Evens and 6-4 in a place)

Calaloo(IRE), a 115,000gns colt out of a half-sister to the high-class Latino Magic, was completely left behind when the pace quickened exiting the Dip. He probably needs more time and is more likely to come into his own over further. (op 9-1)

2412 NATIONAL EXPRESS LET'S GO H'CAP 1m

4:35 (4:37) (Class 3) (0-90,90) 3-Y-O **£7,771** (£2,312; £1,155; £577) **Stalls** High

Form RPR

21-2 1 **Yaddree**[26] 1686 3-9-0 **86** .... PhilipRobinson 13 102
(M A Jarvis) *chsd ldrs: led over 2f out: rdn out* **7/2**[1]

2-31 2 1¾ **Masaalek**[22] 1763 3-9-3 **89** .... RHills 4 104+
(M P Tregoning) *s.i.s: hld up: hdwy over 1f out: sn rdn: r.o* **7/2**[1]

2-21 3 3¾ **Glorious Gift (IRE)**[39] 1380 3-8-13 **85** .... AlanMunro 9 88
(P W Chapple-Hyam) *a.p: rdn over 1f out: styd on same pce* **11/2**[2]

15 4 ½ **House Of Lords (USA)**[32] 1543 3-8-7 **79** .... TQuinn 2 81
(M L W Bell) *s.i.s: hld up: hdwy u.p over 1f out: nt rch ldrs* **33/1**

15-6 5 shd **Noble Citizen (USA)**[21] 1811 3-8-10 **82** .... WilliamBuick 6 84
(D M Simcock) *chsd ldr tl led 1/2-way: rdn and hdd over 2f out: wknd ins fnl f* **14/1**

12 6 nk **Born Tobouggie (GER)**[24] 1730 3-8-12 **84** .... TedDurcan 8 85
(H R A Cecil) *s.i.s: hld up: hdwy over 2f out: rdn over 1f out: wknd ins fnl f* **10/1**

2-61 7 nk **Irish Mayhem (USA)**[26] 1686 3-8-13 **85** .... RobertHavlin 11 86
(B J Meehan) *hld up: rdn over 2f out: hdwy over 1f out: styd on* **12/1**

2-5 8 7 **Meydan Dubai (IRE)**[21] 1806 3-9-3 **89** .... JimCrowley 12 73
(J R Best) *chsd ldrs 6f* **9/1**[3]

01-2 9 nk **Talk Of Saafend (IRE)**[7] 2190 3-8-8 **80** .... DarryllHolland 3 64
(R Hannon) *dwlt: hld up: rdn and hung rt over 3f out: n.d* **14/1**

13-0 10 11 **Harlech Castle**[21] 1806 3-8-11 **90** .... DTDaSilva(7) 5 49
(P F I Cole) *chsd ldrs over 5f* **40/1**

11-4 11 22 **Billion Dollar Kid**[20] 1834 3-9-3 **89** .... JimmyFortune 10 —
(S A Callaghan) *led to 1/2-way: rdn and wknd 2f out: eased fnl f* **11/2**[2]

1m 39.9s (1.30) **Going Correction** +0.275s/f (Good) 11 Ran SP% **120.7**
Speed ratings (Par 103): **104,102,98,98,97 97,97,90,90,79 57**
CSF £15.30 CT £68.95 TOTE £5.10: £2.20, £1.60, £2.60; EX 24.50.
Owner Sheikh Ahmed Al Maktoum **Bred** Darley **Trained** Newmarket, Suffolk

FOCUS

Quite a decent little handicap run at a fair pace and the front pair, who stood out as potential improvers, pulled clear. The field came down the centre and the form ought to stand up.

NOTEBOOK

Yaddree ◆, edged out by Irish Mayhem on his Yarmouth reappearance, was only 1lb better off here but his rival had the benefit of a previous outing then and the form was comprehensively turned around. Always close to the pace, once committed he kept on finding more than enough in front and was always holding his rivals. He is still improving and could yet develop into a Britannia contender. (op 9-2 tchd 5-1)

Masaalek ◆, making his handicap debut after winning his maiden on the Lingfield Polytrack, was held up out the back over this longer trip. He managed to find traffic problems when asked to take closer order and needed to change direction a couple of times in order to get a run, but although he stayed on well up the hill and would have finished closer it would be pushing things to say that he would have beaten the winner. He remains open to further improvement, however, and there will be another day. (op 9-2)

Glorious Gift(IRE), raised 5lb for his victory in soft ground at Nottingham on his handicap debut, was brought through to hold every chance but could not match the finishing pace of the front pair up the hill. He has run well on fast ground before, but is probably better with some cut. (op 9-2)

House Of Lords(USA) ◆, making his turf debut after two runs on Polytrack and dropping back from 1m3f, was doing his best work late and it would be no surprise to see him stepped back up in trip. He still has some scope.

Noble Citizen(USA), back over a more suitable trip, was a springer in the market but, after travelling up with the pace for a long way, he did not get home. He may need a less demanding track and may also need to be ridden with a bit more restraint. (op 25-1)

Born Tobouggie(GER) ◆, whose two previous outings had been on much softer ground, gradually made progress entering the last couple of furlongs and had every chance passing the furlong pole, but she looked most unhappy on the ground and was not beaten up from then on. She is still unexposed and will be of much more interest back on an easier surface. (op 8-1)

Irish Mayhem(USA), 1lb worse off with Yaddree after edging him out at Yarmouth last time despite losing a shoe, had his chance but failed to confirm the form with his old rival, who had obviously come on from that seasonal reappearance. He may be worth another try over a longer trip. (op 16-1)

Talk Of Saafend(IRE) got herself into a state in the stalls, fluffed the start and never looked happy at any stage. She is better than this. (tchd 16-1)

Billion Dollar Kid, trying this trip for the first time, made much of the running but eventually stopped as if shot. Even allowing for the extra furlong, this was too bad to be true. Official explanation: vet said colt was found to have a breathing problem (op 5-1 tchd 9-2 and 7-1 in a place)

2413 NATIONAL EXPRESS MAKING TRAVEL SIMPLER MAIDEN STKS 1m

5:10 (5:11) (Class 4) 3-Y-O **£5,180** (£1,541; £770; £384) **Stalls** High

Form RPR

0-2 1 **Resurge (IRE)**[16] 1926 3-9-3 0 .... ShaneKelly 11 85+
(J Noseda) *hld up in tch: shkn up to ld over 1f out: rdn out* **5/2**[2]

2- 2 ½ **Timetable**[281] 4584 3-9-3 0 .... TedDurcan 8 84+
(H R A Cecil) *hld up in tch: rdn over 1f out: carried hd high and wandered ins fnl f: r.o* **9/4**[1]

0 3 hd **Schopenhauer (USA)**[16] 1926 3-9-3 0 .... GeorgeBaker 7 83
(L M Cumani) *s.i.s: hld up: hdwy over 1f out: r.o* **25/1**

2 4 nse **Expresso Star (USA)**[15] 1957 3-9-3 0 .... JimmyFortune 1 83
(J H M Gosden) *chsd ldr tl led over 4f out: rdn and hdd over 1f out: styd on* **5/2**[2]

5 3¼ **Myanmar (IRE)** 3-9-3 0 .... WilliamBuick 12 76
(J Noseda) *s.s: hld up: hdwy and hung rt over 1f out: nt trble ldrs* **33/1**

30 6 1¼ **Miss Brown To You (IRE)**[15] 1946 3-8-12 0 .... JimCrowley 4 68
(M L W Bell) *led: hdd over 4f out: rdn over 1f out: wknd ins fnl f* **25/1**

7 ½ **Spouk** 3-8-5 0 .... HeatherMcGee(7) 3 67+
(L M Cumani) *s.s: hld up: hung rt over 1f out: nt trble ldrs* **40/1**

05 8 1¾ **De Facto**[19] 1854 3-9-3 0 .... RobertHavlin 9 67
(J H M Gosden) *hld up: rdn over 3f out: hung rt over 1f out: nvr trbld ldrs* **50/1**

0-5 9 ¾ **Ministerofinterior**[14] 1994 3-8-12 0 .... JackMitchell(5) 6 66
(C F Wall) *chsd ldrs: rdn over 2f out: wknd over 1f out* **100/1**

0- 10 nk **Almoutezah (USA)**[203] 6648 3-8-12 0 .... RHills 2 60+
(M A Jarvis) *chsd ldrs tl rdn and wknd over 1f out* **8/1**[3]

1m 41.62s (3.02) **Going Correction** +0.275s/f (Good) 10 Ran SP% **115.0**
Speed ratings (Par 101): **95,94,94,94,91 89,89,87,86,86**
CSF £7.90 TOTE £3.50: £1.30, £1.50, £5.50; EX 10.30.
Owner Cheveley Park Stud **Bred** Sweetmans Bloodstock **Trained** Newmarket, Suffolk
■ Stewards' Enquiry : Heather McGee caution: careless riding

FOCUS

Quite an interesting maiden despite the time being 1.72 seconds slower than the preceding handicap. The front four, three of whom had finished runner-up in their most recent starts, finished in a bit of a heap but they pulled well clear of the others and they are all probably capable of more. Some of the others, especially amongst the longer-priced ones, are likely to show more once handicapped. Again the field came down the centre.

2414 NATIONAL EXPRESS WHITTLESFORD PARKWAY H'CAP 1m 6f

5:45 (5:47) (Class 4) (0-85,82) 4-Y-O+ **£5,180** (£1,541; £770; £384) **Stalls** Centre

Form RPR

6212 1 **Trachonitis (IRE)**[79] 810 4-9-4 **77** .... DarryllHolland 1 86+
(J R Jenkins) *hld up: hdwy and swtchd lft over 1f out: shkn up to ld ins fnl f: r.o wl* **6/1**

06-1 2 2¼ **Brief Goodbye**[19] 1877 8-9-1 **74** .... MickyFenton 7 80
(John Berry) *a.p: chsd ldr 1/2-way: rdn to ld wl over 1f out: hdd and unable qck ins fnl f* **7/1**

4141 3 ¾ **Pass The Port**[14] 1998 7-9-9 **82** .... TedDurcan 3 87
(D Haydn Jones) *hld up: hdwy over 2f out: rdn over 1f out: styd on* **7/2**[2]

0/06 4 4 **Alfie Noakes**[19] 1877 6-9-4 **77** .... JimCrowley 4 76
(Mrs A J Perrett) *s.s: hld up: hdwy over 4f out: rdn over 1f out: wknd ins fnl f* **5/1**[3]

4131 5 10 **Wind Flow**[16] 1933 4-9-0 **73** .... JimmyQuinn 2 58
(C A Dwyer) *chsd ldrs: rdn over 4f out: wknd over 1f out* **6/1**

20-0 **6** *32* **Irish Quest (IRE)**42 1337 4-9-7 **80** PhilipRobinson 6 21
(M A Jarvis) *led: rdn and hdd wl over 1f out: hmpd and wknd sn after: eased* **2/1**1

23-5 **7** *3/4* **Power Player**31 1563 4-8-11 **70** (v1) JoeFanning 5 10
(D J Coakley) *chsd ldr to 1/2-way: wknd wl over 2f out* **20/1**

3m 5.81s (7.31) **Going Correction** +0.275s/f (Good) **7** Ran SP% **118.1**
Speed ratings (Par 105): **90,88,88,86,80 62,61**
CSF £48.48 TOTE £5.40: £2.50, £3.10; EX 47.50 Place 6 £30.07, Place 5 £27.53.
Owner Jim McCarthy **Bred** D H W Dobson **Trained** Royston, Herts
■ Stewards' Enquiry : Darryll Holland caution: careless riding

FOCUS
A fair staying handicap on paper, but they went a dawdle early and it developed into a sprint over the last 2f. The runners were keen to come centre to stands' side once into the home straight. The winner did it nicely in the end, but with the favourite running such a wretched race the form may not amount to much.
Irish Quest(IRE) Official explanation: jockey said colt stopped very quickly
Power Player Official explanation: jockey said gelding was unsuited by the firm ground
T/Plt: £42.50 to a £1 stake. Pool: £110,860.20. 1,901.15 winning tickets. T/Qpdt: £17.90 to a £1 stake. Pool: £4,245.90. 174.80 winning tickets. CR

2415 - 2416a (Foreign Racing) - See Raceform Interactive

1878

CURRAGH (R-H)

Saturday, May 24

OFFICIAL GOING: Firm

2417a WEATHERBYS IRELAND GREENLANDS STKS (GROUP 3) 6f
3:10 (3:10) 3-Y-O+ **£38,235** (£11,176; £5,294; £1,764)

RPR

1 **Astronomer Royal (USA)**7 2193 4-10-0 114 CO'Donoghue 2 116
(A P O'Brien, Ire) *settled bhd ldrs: 7th 1/2-way: swtchd and hdwy to 5th over 1f out: r.o strly fnl f to ld cl home* **8/1**

2 *1/2* **Abraham Lincoln (IRE)**37 1420 4-9-9 102 JAHeffernan 5 109
(A P O'Brien, Ire) *hld up: hdwy to 4th 2f out: impr to ld under 1f out: kpt on wl: hdd cl home* **7/1**

3 *1 3/4* **Snaefell (IRE)**35 1495 4-9-9 110 PJSmullen 6 104
(M Halford, Ire) *chsd ldrs: 3rd 1/2-way: impr to ld 1 1/2f out: hdd under 1f out: no ex: kpt on same pce* **6/1**3

4 *1/2* **Galeota (IRE)**10 2106 6-9-9 RichardHughes 1 102
(R Hannon) *sn chsd ldr: 2nd 1/2-way: rdn in 3rd 1f out: no ex fnl f* **5/1**2

5 *3/4* **Myboycharlie (IRE)**251 5458 3-9-5 122 JMurtagh 7 105
(T Stack, Ire) *sn led: rdn and hdd 1 1/2f out: no ex in 4th 1f out: kpt on same pce* **11/8**1

6 *3 1/2* **An Tadh (IRE)**22 1783 5-9-9 105 KLatham 4 90
(G M Lyons, Ire) *chsd ldrs: 5th 1/2-way: rdn 2f out: no ex in 6th over 1f out: kpt on one pce* **16/1**

7 *1/2* **Great Rumpuscat (USA)**37 1421 3-9-0 98 DavidMcCabe 3 88
(A P O'Brien, Ire) *a towards rr* **25/1**

8 *3 1/2* **Finicius (USA)**22 1783 4-9-9 109 DPMcDonogh 8 78
(Eoin Griffin, Ire) *chsd ldrs on outer: 4th 1/2-way: rdn and wknd over 2f out: eased fnl f* **9/1**

1m 12.49s (-2.01) **Going Correction** -0.05s/f (Good)
WFA 3 from 4yo+ 9lb **8** Ran SP% **116.4**
Speed ratings: **113,112,110,109,108 103,103,98**
CSF £63.32 TOTE £9.60: £2.30, £3.90, £2.40; DF 96.10.
Owner Derrick Smith **Bred** ClassicStar **Trained** Ballydoyle, Co Tipperary

NOTEBOOK
Astronomer Royal(USA), who finished last of 11 in the Lockinge on his seasonal return a week previously, bounced right back to form on this first run over the shorter trip since his juvenile campaign. He had clearly come on for his comeback effort, settled a lot better, and showed a neat turn of foot when asked to win his race. This now increases his options with the Golden Jubilee next month a likely target. (op 8/1 tchd 9/1)
Abraham Lincoln(IRE), who shaped as though the race was needed in the Abernant Stakes on his return 37 days previously, turned in a career-best effort on ground he would have found plenty quick enough. He was nicely clear of the rest and, relatively lightly raced, it could well prove he is now ready to shine as a four-year-old. (op 12/1)
Snaefell(IRE), unbeaten in his two previous runs this term, was racing on vastly quicker ground and was not at all disgraced against this better company. There will still be other days for him. (op 7/1)
Galeota(IRE) recorded his best run of the current campaign and did nothing wrong in defeat. (op 13/2)
Myboycharlie(IRE) proved very easy to back for this anticipated three-year-old debut, probably due to doubts about this quick surface. He showed early speed before tiring late on and, while this could be deemed as disappointing, his next run really ought to reveal a lot more. (op 4/5)

2418a BOYLESPORTS IRISH 2,000 GUINEAS (GROUP 1) (ENTIRE COLTS & FILLIES) 1m
3:45 (3:49) 3-Y-O **£182,720** (£56,250; £26,838; £9,191; £6,250)

RPR

1 **Henrythenavigator (USA)**21 1808 3-9-0 121 JMurtagh 7 126+
(A P O'Brien, Ire) *trckd ldrs in 3rd: cl up travelling wl 2f out: rdn over 1f out: qckn wl ins fnl f to ld last 100yds: comf* **5/4**2

2 *1 3/4* **New Approach (IRE)**21 1808 3-9-0 126 KJManning 4 121
(J S Bolger, Ire) *sn led: rdn over 2f out: kpt on u.p: hdd last 100yds and no ex* **11/10**1

3 *3 1/2* **Stubbs Art (IRE)**21 1808 3-9-0 SebSanders 8 113
(D R C Elsworth) *prom early: sn chsd ldr: rdn in cl 2nd 2f out: no ex fnl f* **20/1**

4 *4 1/2* **Jupiter Pluvius (USA)**208 6549 3-9-0 109 JAHeffernan 5 103
(A P O'Brien, Ire) *hld up: mainly 5th: 4th under 3f out: rdn 1 1/2f out: no ex: kpt on same pce* **7/1**3

5 *5 1/2* **Nownownow (USA)**211 6484 3-9-0 (t) OPeslier 1 90
(David Wachman, Ire) *hld up: mainly 4th: rdn in 5th under 3f out: no imp fr over 2f out* **25/1**

1m 39.63s (-2.27) **Going Correction** +0.125s/f (Good) **8** Ran SP% **113.2**
Speed ratings: **116,114,110,106,100**
CSF £3.08 TOTE £3.10: £1.90, £1.10; DF 3.70.
Owner Mrs John Magnier **Bred** Westrn Bloodstock **Trained** Ballydoyle, Co Tipperary
■ Henrythenavigator was emulating Rock Of Gibraltar (2002) and Cockney Rebel (2007), the most recent dual Guineas winners.

FOCUS
A repeat of the Newmarket 1-2-3, although with extended margins. The smallest ever field for this race (three NRs) so quality rather than quantity was the watchword here, and it was an impressive performance by Henrythenavigator, who has been rated value for a shade further and up 3lb on his Newmarket form. The form has been assessed through third-placed Stubbs Art, with New Approach a touch below his best on ground that was plenty quick enough.

NOTEBOOK
Henrythenavigator(USA) confirmed himself the season's leading three-year-old colt with a most taking display to follow up his Newmarket victory. He moved smoothly up to the leaders passing the 2f pole and once asked to pick up New Approach he did so with ease, beating that rival with far more authority than had been the case last time. As a former Coventry winner one can see why he was given big entries at the start of the season from 5f to 1m4f, as his pedigree does give hope to him staying further than 1m. He would be a fascinating contender if lining up in the Epsom Derby, for which he was immediately placed near the top of most ante-post lists, and should he last home his value as a stallion would be astronomical. However, it would be surprising if a colt with as much speed as he has were able to see out 1m4f well enough to win a Derby, and there is a danger the experience might compromise his prospects of winning good races back at shorter distances later on. (op 5/4 tchd 11/10)
New Approach(IRE), beaten just a nose by the winner at Newmarket on his comeback 21 days previously, was given his customary front-running ride yet it was clear approaching the final furlong that he was a sitting duck. He may have been better off going off harder in the lead, but it was more likely that this quicker ground was really against him. It is not clear where he will now head next, as the ground will have to be in his favour for the Irish Derby, but it is certainly far too soon to be writing him off. He also promises to find more improvement as he steps up in trip. (op 5/4 tchd 11/8)
Stubbs Art(IRE), supplemented for this after his excellent third to the first pair in the 2,000 Guineas at Newmarket last time, posted another solid effort in defeat and has been rated as running right up to his previous level. He rates the benchmark for this form and this proves his previous effort to be no fluke. His connections indicated he is likely to head for the St James's Palace at Royal Ascot next and he ought to hold every chance, assuming he avoids the two principals there. (op 16/1)
Jupiter Pluvius(USA), unbeaten in two outings last season, had been forced to miss out Newmarket due to being held up in his work. He was unable to land a serious blow here, but was not disgraced and left the impression he will benefit a great deal for the run. (op 7/1 tchd 6/1)
Nownownow(USA), last seen beating Achill Island in the Breeders' Cup Juvenile Turf last October, was equipped with a first-time tongue tie for this debut for his new stable. He was never a factor from off the pace, but he probably needs easier ground to really shine and is another who should come on a deal for the run. (op 20/1)

2420a RIDGEWOOD PEARL STKS (GROUP 3) (F&M) 1m
4:50 (4:51) 4-Y-O+ **£45,404** (£13,272; £6,286; £2,095)

RPR

1 **Grecian Dancer**19 1880 5-8-12 99 FMBerry 4 106
(Charles O'Brien, Ire) *towards rr: hdwy 1 1/2f out: led 1f out: clr fnl f: easily* **14/1**

2 *5* **Mooretown Lady (IRE)**19 1880 5-8-12 97 (p) PShanahan 6 94
(H Rogers, Ire) *hld up: hdwy in 7th 2f out: 5th 1f out: kpt on to mod 3rd fnl f: wnt 2nd cl home* **20/1**

3 *shd* **Cheyenne Star (IRE)**19 1880 5-9-1 108 PJSmullen 10 97
(Ms F M Crowley, Ire) *chsd ldrs: 5th 2f out: rdn in 3rd 1f out: mod 2nd ins fnl f: lost 2nd cl home* **7/2**2

4 *2 1/2* **Arch Swing (USA)**259 5241 4-8-12 113 MJKinane 8 88
(John M Oxx, Ire) *led: hdd after 3f: chal 2f out: led again 1 1/2f out: hdd 1f out: no ex* **3/1**1

5 *1* **She's Our Mark**19 1880 4-9-1 106 DMGrant 9 89
(Patrick J Flynn, Ire) *chsd ldrs: 4th 2f out: rdn and no ex in 6th 1f out: kpt on same pce* **5/1**3

6 *1/2* **Navajo Moon (IRE)**20 1847 4-8-12 103 JMurtagh 3 85
(David Wachman, Ire) *chsd ldrs: 5th 3f out: rdn in 6th 2f out: kpt on same pce* **7/1**

7 *shd* **Jalmira (IRE)**55 1104 7-8-12 105 WJLee 7 84
(C F Swan, Ire) *towards rr: 8th 2f out: sn no imp* **8/1**

8 *1 1/2* **Dimenticata (IRE)**19 1880 4-8-12 102 CDHayes 1 81
(Kevin Prendergast, Ire) *mid-div: dropped to rr 1/2-way: no imp fr 2f out* **8/1**

9 *1 1/4* **Dani's Girl (IRE)**9 2138 5-8-12 93 WJSupple 5 78
(P A Fahy, Ire) *chsd ldrs: 3rd 2f out: rdn 1 1/2f out: sn no ex and wknd* **14/1**

10 *3 1/2* **Akua'Ba (IRE)**55 1105 4-8-12 92 (tp) KJManning 2 70
(J S Bolger, Ire) *chsd ldrs: led after 3f: rdn and hdd 1 1/2f out: wknd over 1f out* **16/1**

1m 39.69s (-2.21) **Going Correction** +0.125s/f (Good) **10** Ran SP% **122.6**
Speed ratings: **116,111,110,108,107 106,106,105,104,100**
CSF £271.30 TOTE £17.80: £2.70, £8.90, £2.30; DF 556.70.
Owner Dr M V O'Brien **Bred** John Ellis **Trained** Straffan, Co Kildare

FOCUS
They went a good pace and the first two came from the rear. A career best from Grecian Dancer.

NOTEBOOK
Grecian Dancer came home to score easily, showing by far her best form to date, and register her first success in Group company. The quick ground was much to her liking and she looks well up to adding to her tally now in this sort of company, but her trainer later indicated she is in foal to Galileo so has likely run her last race. (op 16/1)
Mooretown Lady(IRE) had finished two places behind the winner in the Athasi Stakes last time and, coming from a similar position as that rival from off the pace, ran right up to her previous level. She helps to put the form into perspective.
Cheyenne Star(IRE), who won this last year, showed the benefit of her comeback in the Athasi Stakes and enjoyed the quicker ground. This was a much-improved effort, but still some way below her previous best. (op 7/2 tchd 3/1)
Arch Swing(USA), who showed high-class form at three last season, was given an aggressive ride on this seasonal bow. She eventually tired out of contention before the final furlong, however, and performed well below her best. She can be expected to come on a lot for the run, but does have a little to prove now. (op 3/1 tchd 7/2)

2419 - 2422a (Foreign Racing) - See Raceform Interactive

2408

NEWMARKET (ROWLEY) (R-H)

Sunday, May 25

OFFICIAL GOING: Good
Wind: Fresh, across Weather: Showers

2423 COUNTRYSIDE DAY LADIES' H'CAP (FOR LADY AMATEUR RIDERS) (IN MEMORY OF LUCINDA STOPFORD-SACKVILLE) 1m 4f
2:20 (2:22) (Class 5) (0-70,72) 4-Y-0+ **£3,123** (£968; £484; £242) **Stalls** Centre

Form RPR

6414 **1** **Bienheureux**12 2071 7-9-8 **57** (t) MissEJJones 8 66
(Miss Gay Kelleway) *chsd ldrs: lost pl 10f out: hmpd over 7f out: sn drvn along: hdwy over 4f out: chsd ldr 3f out: styd on u.p to ld towards fin* **7/1**

The Form Book, Raceform Ltd, Compton, RG20 6NL

1332 **2** *1* **Friends Hope**[11] 2097 7-10-9 **72**.............................. MissFayeBramley 1 79
(P A Blockley) *hld up: hdwy 1/2-way: led over 3f out: rdn over 1f out: hdd towards fin* **3/1**[1]

34-4 **3** *6* **Its Moon (IRE)**[15] 2006 4-10-0 **70**.............................. MissERamstrom(7) 7 68
(T D Walford) *chsd ldr 4f: sn lost pl: hdwy 3f out: styd on same pce appr fnl f* **3/1**[1]

5312 **4** *3/4* **Our Kes (IRE)**[12] 2078 6-9-8 **62**.............................. MissAWallace(5) 6 59
(P Howling) *dwlt: bhd: hdwy over 3f out: rdn and hung rt fnl 2f: styd on same pce* **5/1**[3]

-004 **5** *3* **Great View (IRE)**[15] 2012 9-10-5 **68**..............................(p) MissLEllison 4 60
(Mrs A L M King) *hld up: hdwy to chse clr ldr 8f out: rdn over 4f out: sn lost pl* **7/2**[2]

430/ **6** *13* **Greenwich Village**[692] 3156 5-9-7 **63** ow1.............................. MrsEJJKnight(7) 5 34
(W J Knight) *hld up: plld hrd: hdwy 1/2-way: wknd 3f out* **12/1**

/05- **7** *35* **Traditionalist (IRE)**[361] 2132 4-9-8 **64**.............................. MissKMSalisbury(7) 3 —
(T T Clement) *led and sn clr: hdd over 3f out: wknd over 2f out* **40/1**

2m 41.33s (7.83) **Going Correction** +0.425s/f (Yiel) **7** Ran SP% **111.5**
Speed ratings (Par 103): **90,89,85,84,82 74,50**
CSF £26.82 CT £74.46 TOTE £7.70: £3.60, £2.00; EX 30.20.

Owner Mr & Mrs I Henderson **Bred** N R Shields **Trained** Exning, Suffolk

FOCUS
They went a solid pace in this lady riders' handicap but the form is only modest, rated through the placed horses.

2424 BUILDBASE MAIDEN STKS 5f
2:55 (2:56) (Class 4) 2-Y-O **£4,533** (£1,348; £674; £336) **Stalls** High

Form RPR

1 **Saucy Brown (IRE)** 2-9-3 0.............................. JimmyFortune 3 79+
(R Hannon) *s.i.s: sn prom: rdn to ld ins fnl f: r.o wl* **11/2**[3]

2 *1* **Aakef (IRE)** 2-9-3 0.............................. RHills 6 76+
(M A Jarvis) *chsd ldr: led 3f out: rdn over 1f out: edgd lft and hdd insde fnl f: styd on same pce* **15/8**[2]

3 *nse* **Thunderous Mood (USA)** 2-9-3 0.............................. JohnEgan 9 76+
(P F I Cole) *led: hdd 3f out: rdn and ev ch ins fnl f: styd on* **6/4**[1]

4 *1 3/4* **Party Cat (IRE)** 2-9-3 0.............................. PatDobbs 2 69+
(R Hannon) *hld up: rdn over 1f out: hung lft and r.o ins fnl f: nt rch ldrs* **16/1**

5 *1/2* **Grand Stitch (USA)** 2-9-3 0.............................. DeanMcKeown 5 68
(P A Blockley) *a.p: shkn up over 1f out: styd on* **20/1**

3 **6** *1 1/4* **Love You Louis**[20] 1873 2-9-3 0.............................. LDettori 8 63
(J R Jenkins) *wnt lft s: chsd ldrs: rdn over 1f out: wknd ins fnl f* **7/1**

7 *1 3/4* **Rocket Ruby** 2-8-9 0.............................. TolleyDean(3) 4 52
(D Shaw) *sn pushed along in rr: hdwy 1/2-way: wknd over 1f out* **66/1**

8 *6* **Clerical (USA)** 2-9-3 0.............................. StephenDonohoe 7 35
(M J Gingell) *s.i.s: outpcd* **100/1**

63.30 secs (4.20) **Going Correction** +0.425s/f (Yiel) **8** Ran SP% **115.8**
Speed ratings (Par 95): **83,81,81,78,77 75,72,63**
CSF £16.38 TOTE £6.90: £2.30, £1.10, £1.40; EX 16.30.

Owner The Heffer Syndicate **Bred** Churchtown House Stud **Trained** East Everleigh, Wilts

FOCUS
This looked a fair maiden on paper, but they did not go a great early gallop and as a result the winning time was very moderate. The form is rated through the sixth, the only one to have had a run, and there should be more to come from the winner.

NOTEBOOK
Saucy Brown(IRE), a half-brother to Sahend, a winner over 1m at three in Italy, saw his sales price drop from 56,000euros as a foal to 25,000gns as a yearling. He looked the better of the Hannon pair according to the market, though, and picked up well in the race itself as he hit the rising ground. He will get another furlong in time and looks to have a future. (op 5-1 tchd 9-2)
Aakef(IRE), who cost 210,000gns, the highest priced of his sire's yearlings to sell at auction last year, is out of a mare who is a half-sister to high-class middle-distance filly Gull Nook, later the dam of King George winner Pentire. Showing up well from the outset, he ran a promising race on his debut, and a maiden win should be a formality on this evidence. (tchd 7-4 and 2-1)
Thunderous Mood(USA) ◆, whose sales price rose from $400,000 as a yearling to $575,000 as a two-year-old, is a brother to 7f Listed winner Royal Tigress, and half-brother to Norfolk Stakes winner Warm Heart and juvenile Listed sprint winner Miguel Cervantes. He led early before being headed by the first two home, and then rallying in the closing stages. He would have regained second in another stride and looks sure to have benefited from this debut. (op 13-8 tchd 15-8 and 2-1 in a place)
Party Cat(IRE), a half-brother to five winners at various distances up to 1m2f, was not expected to do much according to the market, especially in relation to his stablemate. He showed definite signs of greenness, hanging left in the closing stages, but he was running on late and looks the type to improve for the experience. (op 14-1)
Grand Stitch(USA), whose sales price rose from $32,000 as a yearling to £34,000 as a two-year-old, is out of a smart dam who was a prolific winner on turf in the US and is herself a half-sister to seven winners over there, including six over sprint distances on dirt. Although bred to go a bit, he is a May foal and was the youngest in this field. He will do better with time. (op 25-1)
Love You Louis was the only one in the field with the benefit of a previous run, but he was up against better opposition here than he met at Windsor on his debut, and he could not make that edge in experience tell. He is one for ordinary handicap company in time. (op 10-1)

2425 CAPITAL SPREADS H'CAP 1m 2f
3:30 (3:31) (Class 2) (0-100,95) 3-Y-O **£11,656** (£3,468; £1,733; £865) **Stalls** High

Form RPR

11-1 **1** **Bronze Cannon (USA)**[38] 1424 3-9-3 **94**.............................. JimmyFortune 2 112+
(J H M Gosden) *s.i.s: hld up: hdwy over 3f out: led 2f out: clr fnl f: easily* **4/9**[1]

-231 **2** *2 1/4* **Woolfall Treasure**[9] 2156 3-8-8 **85**.............................. JohnEgan 4 94
(G G Margarson) *chsd ldrs: rdn over 3f out: wnt 2nd 1f out: no ch w wnr* **9/1**[3]

41-2 **3** *1 1/2* **Love Galore (IRE)**[9] 2142 3-8-13 **90**.............................. JoeFanning 3 96
(M Johnston) *a.p: chsd wnr 2 out: sn rdn: no ex fnl f* **4/1**[2]

-630 **4** *4 1/2* **Better Hand (IRE)**[8] 2194 3-9-4 **95**.............................. DarryllHolland 6 92
(M R Channon) *chsd ldr tl rdn 3f out: wknd over 2f out* **33/1**

0-55 **5** *3/4* **Bencoolen (IRE)**[20] 1875 3-8-5 **82**.............................. ChrisCatlin 1 78
(R Charlton) *hld up: rdn over 3f out: wknd over 2f out* **14/1**

51-0 **6** *2 1/4* **Almoutaz (USA)**[37] 1441 3-8-6 **83** ow1.............................. RHills 5 74
(B W Hills) *led 8f: sn rdn and wknd* **16/1**

2m 8.58s (2.78) **Going Correction** +0.425s/f (Yiel) **6** Ran SP% **114.7**
Speed ratings (Par 105): **105,103,102,98,97 96**
CSF £5.85 TOTE £1.50: £1.10, £2.60; EX 3.90.

Owner A E Oppenheimer **Bred** Hascombe And Valiant Studs **Trained** Newmarket, Suffolk

FOCUS
A lop-sided handicap with the favourite looking well in despite a 10lb hike for his win last time out. It has been rated through the fourth with Bronze Cannon value for four and a half lengths.

NOTEBOOK
Bronze Cannon(USA), who beat Doctor Fremantle in a hot handicap over this course and distance at the Craven meeting, still looked well ahead of the Handicapper off a 10lb higher mark and was rightly sent off at prohibitive odds. He quickened up well to put his seal on the race and only had to be pushed out to win easily. He is clearly a Pattern horse in the making and the Derby, for which he is a top-priced 25-1, is understandably under consideration. He already holds an entry at Epsom so there will be no need to supplement, and considering the exploits of Doctor Fremantle since and his likely addition to the race, this fellow probably deserves to take his chance. The extra two furlongs should be within his compass, but as yet he is unproven on fast ground. (op 8-11 tchd 4-5 in places)
Woolfall Treasure, who was found a soft race to finally get off the mark at Newcastle last time, was under pressure from some way out here but kept responding and ran on well to take second behind the well-handicapped winner. The assessor knows where he stands with him. (op 8-1 tchd 15-2)
Love Galore(IRE), runner-up in the Glasgow Stakes last time, looked the main danger to the favourite back in handicap company, but he was a bit disappointing. He will appreciate a step up to 1m4f, though, and remains open to further improvement. (op 3-1)
Better Hand(IRE) looks too high in the handicap for what he has achieved. Official explanation: jockey said colt hung left throughout
Bencoolen(IRE) has not built on the promise he showed in his reappearance at Windsor, but if it is the case that he simply needs fast ground then he can be excused this effort. (op 12-1)
Almoutaz(USA), who got very warm beforehand, took them along to 2f out but then hit the wall. He looks like a miler on this evidence, and faster ground will surely not go amiss. Official explanation: jockey said colt had a breathing problem (tchd 20-1)

2426 GOLDSTAR TRANSPORT H'CAP 6f
4:05 (4:06) (Class 2) (0-100,100) 4-Y-O+ **£11,656** (£3,468; £1,733; £865) **Stalls** High

Form RPR

5506 **1** **Ajigolo**[8] 2195 5-8-4 **86** oh1.............................. TPO'Shea 11 99+
(M R Channon) *hld up: hdwy over 2f out: led on bit over 1f out: shkn up and r.o wl* **25/1**

100- **2** *1 3/4* **Express Wish**[255] 5356 4-8-7 **89**.............................. ShaneKelly 7 97
(J Noseda) *chsd ldr tl led over 3f out: rdn and hdd over 1f out: styd on* **5/1**[2]

143- **3** *1/2* **Everymanforhimself (IRE)**[224] 6205 4-8-5 **87**..............(b) ChrisCatlin 12 93
(K A Ryan) *chsd ldrs: rdn and ev ch over 1f out: styd on same pce* **14/1**

2641 **4** *3/4* **Baby Strange**[8] 2195 4-8-11 **93**.............................. JimCrowley 9 97
(D Shaw) *s.i.s: hld up: hdwy over 2f out: rdn over 1f out: styd on* **5/1**[2]

0-00 **5** *shd* **Prior Warning**[22] 1809 4-9-3 **99**..............................(t) EddieAhern 4 102
(Miss D Mountain) *hld up: swtchd rt over 1f out: r.o ins fnl f: nrst fin* **33/1**

4-1 **6** *shd* **Cape**[44] 1300 5-8-10 **92**.............................. JamieSpencer 5 95
(P Howling) *s.i.s: hld up: swtchd rt and hdwy over 1f out: hrd rdn ins fnl f: styd on same pce* **7/2**[1]

00-3 **7** *1* **Phantom Whisper**[15] 1985 5-8-10 **92**.............................. AlanMunro 3 92
(B R Millman) *prom: outpcd over 1f out: styd on ins fnl f* **7/1**[3]

-103 **8** *hd* **Pusey Street Lady**[15] 1986 4-8-10 **92**.............................. JoeFanning 13 91
(J Gallagher) *chsd ldrs: rdn and ev ch over 1f out: wknd ins fnl f* **14/1**

101- **9** *nk* **Premio Loco (USA)**[246] 5635 4-8-10 **92**.............................. IanMongan 8 90
(C F Wall) *hld up: nt clr run over 2f out: nvr nr to chal* **10/1**

3400 **10** *1 1/2* **Beaver Patrol (IRE)**[11] 2106 6-9-4 **100**..............................(v) JimmyFortune 10 93
(Eve Johnson Houghton) *prom: rdn over 2f out: wknd fnl f: eased nr fin* **9/1**

06-0 **11** *4 1/2* **Daniella**[15] 1993 6-8-4 **86** oh1.............................. WilliamBuick 6 65
(Rae Guest) *hld up: rdn over 2f out: wknd over 1f out* **28/1**

-323 **12** *5* **Angus Newz**[7] 2219 5-8-7 **89**..............................(v) FrancisNorton 1 52
(M Quinn) *led: hdd over 3f out: rdn and wknd over 1f out* **11/1**

30-5 **13** *3* **Dream Theme**[9] 2172 5-8-11 **93**.............................. AdrianTNicholls 2 46
(D Nicholls) *s.i.s: hld up: sme hdwy over 2f out: sn rdn: hung rt and wknd* **16/1**

1m 13.14s (0.94) **Going Correction** +0.425s/f (Yiel) **13** Ran SP% **124.9**
Speed ratings (Par 109): **110,107,107,106,105 105,104,104,103,101 95,89,85**
CSF £150.20 CT £1878.18 TOTE £37.10: £8.80, £2.70, £4.20; EX 294.40 TRIFECTA Not won..

Owner Timberhill Racing Partnership **Bred** Timber Hill Racing Partnership **Trained** West Ilsley, Berks

FOCUS
A decent, competitive sprint handicap, and solid form rated through the third. The winner was close to his best.

NOTEBOOK
Ajigolo, as had been previously noted, was down to a mark off which he could win. Nothing travelled better into the final furlong and he quickened up on the climb to the line to score with a bit to spare. While in this form it would be dangerous to assume he could not follow up off a higher mark. (tchd 22-1)
Express Wish, a lightly-raced four-year-old making his seasonal reappearance off a fair mark, looked interesting. Showing pace throughout, he could not cope with the winner's turn of foot in the closing stages, but he showed plenty of guts to hold off the rest. He did by far the best of those who raced prominently throughout, and would not have to find any improvement to pick up a similar race in the coming weeks. (op 9-2 tchd 11-2)
Everymanforhimself(IRE) was debuting for a new stable and it was not hard to imagine Kevin Ryan extracting some improvement from this four-year-old. This was a promising reappearance especially as a sharper 6f might suit him ideally. (op 16-1)
Baby Strange gives the form a solid look as he has been in fine form during the first part of this turf campaign. (tchd 6-1)
Prior Warning, held up at the back of the field, was switched to the far-side rail for his finishing effort. He ran on well late, but the good pace did mean that the race was run to suit the likes of him. This was the first piece of form shown by this ex-French Listed winner in this country. (op 25-1)
Cape, running off a career-high mark, had conditions as she would like them and, being held up in a contest run at a good clip, seemingly had the race run to suit as well. However, she could never quite get to there this time (op 4-1 tchd 9-2)
Phantom Whisper, who ran a promising race on his reappearance, again shaped well, but the fact remains that he is still on a mark higher than when last successful. (op 13-2 tchd 6-1)
Pusey Street Lady has looked held by the Handicapper since being hiked up a substantial amount for bolting up at Doncaster on her reappearance. (op 16-1)
Premio Loco(USA) ◆, reappearing off a 9lb higher mark than when successful at Newbury last September, had never raced over a trip this short before. He looked to find it an inadequate test, but will be a different proposition back over 7f with this run under his belt. (op 8-1)
Beaver Patrol(IRE), who prefers fast ground, is difficult to place off his current mark. (op 14-1)
Dream Theme Official explanation: jockey said gelding hung right

2427 BOYTON HALL EQUINE CENTRE, MONKS ELEIGH MAIDEN STKS 7f
4:40 (4:43) (Class 4) 3-Y-O **£5,180** (£1,541; £770; £384) **Stalls** High

Form RPR

431- **1** **Classic Descent**[205] 6616 3-9-3 82.............................. SebSanders 8 90+
(P J Makin) *hld up in tch: led over 1f out: shkn up and r.o wl* **3/1**[2]

3-6 **2** *5* **E Major**[31] 1579 3-8-10 0 .... JPHamblett(7) 10 73+
(Sir Michael Stoute) *s.i.s: hld up: hdwy over 1f out: hung lft ins fnl f: nvr nr to chal* **11/1**

3 *2* **Without Prejudice (USA)** 3-9-3 0 .... ShaneKelly 7 67
(J Noseda) *chsd ldrs tl led over 2f out: rdn: hung lft and hdd over 1f out: wknd ins fnl f* **6/4**[1]

44-2 **4** *4 1/2* **Strategic Mover (USA)**[22] 1803 3-9-3 92 .... (t) TQuinn 6 55
(P F I Cole) *chsd ldr: rdn and ev ch over 2f out: wknd over 1f out* **3/1**[2]

-323 **5** *4* **Bowder Stone (IRE)**[15] 2002 3-9-3 74 .... JimmyQuinn 2 44
(M H Tompkins) *prom: rdn over 2f out: hung rt and wknd over 1f out* **13/2**[3]

4-0 **6** *shd* **Hurricane Harriet**[37] 1454 3-8-12 0 .... ChrisCatlin 9 38
(R M H Cowell) *led over 4f: rdn and wknd over 1f out* **66/1**

7 *hd* **Hundonette** 3-8-12 0 .... EddieAhern 1 38
(R M H Cowell) *s.s: effrt over 2f out: wknd over 1f out* **80/1**

8 *6* **Confident Warrior (IRE)** 3-8-10 0 .... (t) SimonPearce(7) 3 26
(J Pearce) *hld up in tch: wknd over 2f out* **66/1**

9 *14* **David Lloyd George** 3-9-0 0 .... LukeMorris(3) 4 —
(S W James) *s.i.s: sn pushed along in rr: hung lft and wknd over 2f out* **100/1**

1m 27.88s (2.48) **Going Correction** +0.425s/f (Yiel) **9** Ran SP% **116.9**
Speed ratings (Par 101): **102,96,94,88,84 84,83,77,61**
CSF £35.12 TOTE £4.70: £1.60, £2.40, £1.50; EX 41.30.
Owner Joseph Joyce **Bred** Mrs M L Parry **Trained** Ogbourne Maisey, Wilts

FOCUS
A fair maiden but it is questionable what the winner needed to run to to win this. He is rated value for 6l.

2428 EUROPEAN BREEDERS' FUND FILLIES' H'CAP — 6f
5:15 (5:15) (Class 4) (0-85,85) 3-Y-O — **£5,828** (£1,734; £866; £432) **Stalls** High

Form — RPR

32-1 **1** **Temple Of Thebes (IRE)**[35] 1499 3-8-13 **80** .... StephenDonohoe 9 93+
(E A L Dunlop) *chsd ldrs: led over 2f out: rdn and hung lft fr over 1f out: r.o* **6/1**[3]

2115 **2** *1 3/4* **Nice Wee Girl (IRE)**[8] 2196 3-8-12 **79** .... LPKeniry 6 86+
(S Kirk) *hld up: hdwy over 1f out: r.o u.p: nt rch wnr* **7/1**

2-11 **3** *2* **Requisite**[116] 364 3-8-5 **75** .... KirstyMilczarek(3) 1 76
(I A Wood) *always prom: rdn and ev ch over 1f out: hun glft and no ex ins fnl f* **16/1**

41-0 **4** *1/2* **Wise Melody**[15] 1999 3-8-13 **80** .... LiamJones 13 79
(W J Haggas) *led over 3f: rdn over 1f out: styd on same pce* **16/1**

10 **5** *shd* **Savannah Poppy (IRE)**[36] 1470 3-8-9 **76** .... JamieSpencer 12 75+
(M L W Bell) *s.s: hld up: hdwy over 1f out: styd on* **5/1**[2]

2252 **6** *2 3/4* **Leading Edge (IRE)**[9] 2141 3-8-7 **74** .... ChrisCatlin 10 64
(M R Channon) *chsd ldr to 1/2-way: rdn and wknd over 1f out* **10/1**

10-0 **7** *hd* **Masada (IRE)**[26] 1698 3-9-4 **85** .... LDettori 7 78
(B J Meehan) *trckd ldrs: plld hrd: rdn over 1f out: wknd ins fnl f: eased towards fin* **11/1**

04-1 **8** *1* **Fifty (IRE)**[21] 1835 3-8-10 **77** .... PatDobbs 4 63
(R Hannon) *prom over 4f* **14/1**

212 **9** *6* **Maslaha**[55] 1113 3-9-2 **83** .... PhilipRobinson 5 50
(M A Jarvis) *chsd ldrs: rdn over 2f out: wkng whn hung lft fnl f* **5/2**[1]

63 **10** *1 1/4* **Applesnap (IRE)**[12] 2077 3-8-8 **75** .... HayleyTurner 2 38
(Mrs C A Dunnett) *broke wl: trckd ldrs: wknd over 2f out* **50/1**

01-5 **11** *7* **Swanky Lady**[24] 1745 3-8-11 **78** .... JimmyFortune 3 19
(R Hannon) *trckd ldrs 4f* **15/2**

1m 14.34s (2.14) **Going Correction** +0.425s/f (Yiel) **11** Ran SP% **121.6**
Speed ratings (Par 98): **102,99,97,96,96 92,92,90,82,81 71**
CSF £49.46 CT £666.50 TOTE £6.60: £2.10, £2.50, £3.60; EX 35.50.
Owner Cliveden Stud **Bred** Cliveden Stud Ltd **Trained** Newmarket, Suffolk
■ Stewards' Enquiry : Liam Jones one-day ban: failed to ride to draw (Jun 8)

FOCUS
A fair sprint handicap for fillies, in which the first four all showed improvement. The form is rated through the fifth.
Requisite Official explanation: jockey said filly hung left in latter stages
Masada(IRE) Official explanation: jockey said filly had a breathing problem
Maslaha Official explanation: jockey said filly hung left
Swanky Lady Official explanation: jockey said filly moved badly throughout

2429 NCRD.CO.UK H'CAP — 7f
5:50 (5:52) (Class 5) (0-70,72) 3-Y-O — **£3,885** (£1,156; £577; £288) **Stalls** High

Form — RPR

45-0 **1** **Burnbrake**[24] 1748 3-9-1 **67** .... RobertHavlin 19 76
(J A R Toller) *a.p: rdn over 1f out: styd on to ld nr fin* **25/1**

005- **2** *hd* **El Fuser**[295] 4181 3-8-10 **65** .... TravisBlock(3) 5 74
(P J Makin) *hld up in tch: rdn to ld over 1f out: hdd nr fin* **12/1**

-230 **3** *1 1/4* **Christophers Quest**[36] 1467 3-8-13 **65** .... AlanMunro 15 70+
(A W Carroll) *hld up: swtchd lft over 1f out: sn rdn: r.o ins fnl f: nt rch ldrs* **25/1**

-621 **4** *nk* **All In The Red (IRE)**[31] 1581 3-9-4 **70** .... JimmyFortune 2 74
(Miss Gay Kelleway) *hld up: hdwy over 2f out: rdn over 1f out: styd on* **13/2**[2]

-446 **5** *1/2* **Tamasou (IRE)**[22] 1819 3-8-12 **64** .... ChrisCatlin 3 67
(Garry Moss) *chsd ldrs: rdn over 1f out: styd on same pce ins fnl f* **20/1**

50-1 **6** *1 1/4* **Metal Madness (IRE)**[8] 2208 3-9-0 **66** .... NCallan 7 65
(M G Quinlan) *prom: rdn over 1f out: styd on same pce fnl f* **13/2**[2]

-333 **7** *hd* **Koraleva Tectona (IRE)**[10] 2118 3-8-13 **65** .... PaulEddery 10 66+
(Pat Eddery) *led: edgd rt and hdd over 1f out: wknd towards fin* **3/1**[1]

33-0 **8** *1/2* **Creative (IRE)**[13] 2047 3-8-13 **65** .... JimmyQuinn 9 62
(M H Tompkins) *hld up in tch: rdn over 1f out: no ex fnl f* **40/1**

0-60 **9** *nk* **Loveinaelevator**[16] 1964 3-9-0 **66** .... JamieSpencer 17 70+
(M L W Bell) *hld up: swtchd rt over 2f out: nt clr run over 1f out: styd on: nvr trbld ldrs* **14/1**

5-32 **10** *3/4* **Tina's Best (IRE)**[13] 2047 3-9-1 **72** .... HaddenFrost(5) 14 74+
(R Hannon) *dwlt: hld up: nt clr run over 1f out: r.o ins fnl f: nvr nrr* **9/1**

44-3 **11** *1 1/4* **Candle Sahara (IRE)**[72] 885 3-9-4 **70** .... DarryllHolland 11 61
(M R Channon) *prom: rdn over 2f out: wknd fnl f* **11/1**

052- **12** *1/2* **Broughtons Flight (IRE)**[150] 7245 3-9-1 **67** .... StephenDonohoe 18 56
(W J Musson) *mid-div: effrt over 1f out: n.d* **25/1**

2 **13** *hd* **Kargan (IRE)**[57] 1073 3-8-10 **65** .... PJMcDonald(3) 8 54
(J S Wainwright) *s.s: hld up: n.d* **8/1**[3]

5-60 **14** *1 1/2* **Balata**[23] 1781 3-8-13 **70** .... JamesMillman(5) 20 55
(B R Millman) *chsd ldrs: rdn over 2f out: wknd fnl f* **16/1**

00-3 **15** *1 1/2* **Karky Schultz (GER)**[24] 1743 3-8-12 **64** .... ShaneKelly 12 45
(J M P Eustace) *hld up: stmbld: n.m.r and lost pl over 5f out: hdwy 1/2-way: rdn and hung rt over 1f out: sn wknd* **16/1**

1000 **16** *2* **Young Ivanhoe**[45] 1277 3-8-9 **68** .... JPHamblett(7) 16 43
(C A Dwyer) *chsd ldrs: rdn over 2f out: wknd over 1f out* **66/1**

40-6 **17** *17* **Imperial Decree**[24] 1738 3-9-1 **67** .... LiamJones 4 —
(John Berry) *a in rr: wknd over 2f out* **33/1**

40-0 **18** *1 1/4* **Langham House**[13] 2047 3-8-12 **64** .... PaulDoe 1 —
(J R Jenkins) *hld up: a in rr: wknd over 2f out* **66/1**

1m 28.4s (3.00) **Going Correction** +0.425s/f (Yiel) **18** Ran SP% **131.9**
Speed ratings (Par 99): **99,98,97,97,96 95,94,94,93,93 91,91,90,89,87 85,65,64**
CSF £301.02 CT £7660.26 TOTE £52.90: £8.90, £3.70, £5.20, £2.10; EX 837.40 Place 6 £76.10, Place 5 £30.28.
Owner M E Wates **Bred** M E Wates **Trained** Newmarket, Suffolk

FOCUS
A competitive but ordinary handicap for the track. It was dominated by unexposed types and has been rated through the third, fifth, sixth and ninth.
Loveinaelevator ◆ Official explanation: jockey said filly hung right throughout
Tina's Best(IRE) Official explanation: jockey said filly missed the break
Imperial Decree Official explanation: trainer said filly was found to have pulled muscles in its hind quarters
T/Jkpt: Not won. T/Plt: £142.80 to a £1 stake. Pool: £64,652.60. 330.35 winning tickets. T/Qpdt: £74.90 to a £1 stake. Pool: £3,880.10. 38.30 winning tickets. CR

2430 - 2431a (Foreign Racing) - See Raceform Interactive

2415 CURRAGH (R-H)
Sunday, May 25

OFFICIAL GOING: Firm

2432a TATTERSALLS GOLD CUP (GROUP 1) — 1m 2f 110y
3:00 (3:01) 4-Y-0+ — **£136,764** (£41,911; £19,852; £6,617; £2,205)

RPR

1 **Duke Of Marmalade (IRE)**[28] 1665 4-9-0 120 .... JMurtagh 6 126+
(A P O'Brien, Ire) *trckd ldr in 2nd: clsr ent st: led over 1 1/2f out: sn strly pressed: rdn and kpt on wl fnl f* **1/3**[1]

2 *1 1/4* **Finsceal Beo (IRE)**[57] 1090 4-8-11 119 .... KJManning 3 120
(J S Bolger, Ire) *trckd ldrs: mainly 4th: 3rd 4f out: clsr 2f out: chal 1 1/2f out: rdn over 1f out: no ex fnl f: kpt on* **7/2**[2]

3 *6* **Red Rock Canyon (IRE)**[260] 5243 4-9-0 115 .... JAHeffernan 1 112
(A P O'Brien, Ire) *led: clr after 2f: reduced advantage ent st: rdn and hdd over 1 1/2f out: kpt on one pce* **14/1**[3]

4 *2* **Halicarnassus (IRE)**[38] 1422 4-9-0 .... RichardHughes 4 108
(M R Channon) *settled 5th: rdn and no imp 2f out: kpt on into mod 4th over 1f out: n.d* **16/1**

5 *2 1/2* **Arch Rebel (USA)**[168] 7090 7-9-0 113 .... (p) FMBerry 5 103
(Noel Meade, Ire) *chsd ldrs: mainly 3rd: 4th 4f out: rdn and no imp 2f out: kpt on one pce* **20/1**

6 *3 1/2* **Mooretown Lady (IRE)**[1] 2420 5-8-11 97 .... PShanahan 2 94
(H Rogers, Ire) *a bhd* **66/1**

2m 15.77s (0.77) **Going Correction** +0.25s/f (Good) **6** Ran SP% **116.0**
Speed ratings: **107,106,101,100,98 95**
CSF £2.03 TOTE £1.50: £1.02, £1.80; DF 3.20.
Owner Mrs John Magnier **Bred** Southern Bloodstock **Trained** Ballydoyle, Co Tipperary

FOCUS
A clear step up from Duke Of Marmalade, the form rated through the second and sixth.

NOTEBOOK
Duke Of Marmalade(IRE) ◆ had no trouble with this much quicker surface and followed up his win in the Prix Ganay in fine style. The race was run just to suit him and he again showed a determined attitude when asked to put the race to bed. This rates his best effort to date and he is no doubt coming into his own now as a four-year-old. The step up to 1m4f also promises to see him in an even better light and his trainer later nominated the Prince Of Wales's Stakes at Royal Ascot as a likely next target in which he will bid for the hat-trick. (op 4/9)
Finsceal Beo(IRE), a respectable fifth on her first outing of the year in Dubai 57 days previously, returned to something like her previous best without seriously threatening the winner. She was well clear of the remainder at the finish and, while this is certainly as far as she wants to go, this performance gives more than hope that she will add to her tally of Group 1 wins this season. (op 7/2 tchd 100/30)
Red Rock Canyon(IRE), amazingly still a maiden, set the race up perfectly for his winning stable companion and performed right up to his very best in the process. He is entitled to improve nicely for the run and richly deserves to find an opening.
Halicarnassus(IRE) ran close enough to the level of his Newmarket run 38 days previously and was never in the hunt from off the pace. He needs to drop back down in class.

2433a BOYLESPORTS IRISH 1,000 GUINEAS (GROUP 1) (FILLIES) — 1m
3:35 (3:39) 3-Y-O

£165,073 (£56,250; £26,838; £9,191; £6,250; £3,308)

RPR

1 **Halfway To Heaven (IRE)**[14] 2033 3-9-0 112 .... JAHeffernan 5 109
(A P O'Brien, Ire) *trckd ldrs: led 2 1/2f out: chal 1 1/2f out: kpt on wl fnl f: all out cl home* **13/2**

2 *hd* **Mad About You (IRE)**[231] 6040 3-9-0 110 .... PJSmullen 12 108
(D K Weld, Ire) *trckd ldrs: 6th 1/2-way: impr into 2nd 2f out: chal 1 1/2f out: kpt on wl fnl f: no ex cl home: fin 3rd, hd & hd: plcd 2nd* **7/1**

3 *hd* **Carribean Sunset (IRE)**[14] 2024 3-9-0 105 .... RyanMoore 8 107
(D K Weld, Ire) *hld up towards rr: hdwy in 7th 2f out: rdn in 3rd 1 1/2f out: 4th 1f out: carried lft fnl f: kpt on wl: fin 4th, hd, hd & nk: plcd 3rd* **7/1**

4 *nk* **Tuscan Evening (IRE)**[11] 2116 3-9-0 100 .... DMGrant 13 109
(John Joseph Murphy, Ire) *prom early: sn mid-div: 8th 2f out: hdwy into 4th 1 1/2f out: rdn in 3rd 1f out: drifted lft and kpt on wl fnl f: jst failed: fin 2nd, hd: disq: plcd 4th* **66/1**

5 *8* **Saoirse Abu (USA)**[21] 1830 3-9-0 111 .... (b) KJManning 11 89
(J S Bolger, Ire) *hld up towards rr: hdwy into 5th 2f out: rdn in 7th 1 1/2f out: no ex: kpt on one pce* **7/2**[2]

6 *2 1/2* **Savethisdanceforme (IRE)**[21] 1830 3-9-0 112 .... CO'Donoghue 3 83
(A P O'Brien, Ire) *hld up towards rr: hdwy into 6th 2f out: rdn in 8th 1 1/2f out and no ex: kpt on one pce* **14/1**

7 *1* **Nahoodh (IRE)**[21] 1830 3-9-0 .... RichardHughes 4 81
(M R Channon) *hld up towards rr: hdwy into 4th 2f out: rdn in 5th and no ex 1 1/2f out: wknd over 1f out* **3/1**[1]

8 *2* **Eva's Request (IRE)**[14] 2024 3-9-0 .... MJKinane 2 76
(M R Channon) *mid-div: 8th 1/2-way: hdwy into 4th 3f out: rdn in 3rd 2f out: sn no ex and wknd* **25/1**

9 *nk* **Queen Jock (USA)**[49] 1230 3-9-0 93 .... PShanahan 10 76
(Tracey Collins, Ire) *mid-div: rdn and no imp 2 1/2f out* **100/1**

10 *1 1/2* **Kitty Matcham (IRE)**[21] 1830 3-9-0 105 .... JMurtagh 9 72
(A P O'Brien, Ire) *chsd ldrs: 5th 1/2-way: rdn 3f out: sn no ex and wknd* **5/1**[3]

11 1 1/2 **Milton Of Campsie**[13] 2038 3-9-0 .... DNolan 6 69
(S Parr) *chsd ldrs: 4th 1/2-way: rdn into 2nd over 3f out: sn no ex and wknd* **100/1**

12 13 **Mystical Lady (IRE)**[4] 2318 3-9-0 90.. SMLevey 7 39
(A P O'Brien, Ire) *led after 1f: rdn and hdd 2 1/2f out: sn wknd: trailing fnl f* **100/1**

13 22 **Soinlovewithyou (USA)**[21] 1847 3-9-0 88.................... DavidMcCabe 1 —
(A P O'Brien, Ire) *rdn to sn dispute ld: 2nd 1/2-way: sn rdn and wknd: t.o* **100/1**

1m 40.82s (-1.08) **Going Correction** +0.125s/f (Good) **13** Ran SP% **118.2**
Speed ratings: **110,109,109,109,101 98,97,95,95,94 92,79,57**
CSF £50.09 TOTE £7.20: £2.10, £3.40, £1.80; DF 51.50.
Owner Michael Tabor **Bred** T Stewart **Trained** Ballydoyle, Co Tipperary

■ The third time Aidan O'Brien has won both the Irish 2000 Guineas and 1000 Guineas, following similar feats in 1997 and 2001.

■ Stewards' Enquiry : D M Grant four-day ban: two days for 2 sepate incidents of careless riding (Jun 8-9, 11-13)

FOCUS
A blanket finish and unexceptional form by Classic standards. The race has been rated through the winner running to her French Guineas mark, with the second, third and fourth all improvers.

NOTEBOOK
Halfway To Heaven(IRE), third in the French 1,000 Guineas a fortnight previously, paid a compliment to her conquerer there, the high-class Zarkava, and gamely got her head in front where it mattered. She had been just held by Carribean Sunset over 7f on her seasonal bow, but she is obviously an improving filly who loves this sort of ground. A trip to the Coronation Stakes at Royal Ascot now looks on the cards and she will be entitled to considerable respect there. (op 9/1)
Mad About You(IRE) ◆, last seen finishing third to Zarkava in the Prix Marcel Boussac on Arc weekend, ran a blinder in defeat on this seasonal return and only just lost out in the driving finish. She has bundles of scope, should really enjoy a step up in trip this year, and looks a genuine Group 1 filly in the making. While still entered in the Epsom Oaks, it is most likely that will come too soon and the Group 2 Ribblesdale at Royal Ascot would appeal as a more logical next step. She ought to get the 1m4f there, especially considering her stable won that particular event with her dam in 2002.
Carribean Sunset(IRE) came into this having won both the domestic trials for this event at Leopardstown, including when just holding off Halfway To Heaven over 7f in April. Ridden more patiently this time, she was done no favours when Tuscan Evening carried her left inside the final furlong and she has to be rated a little better than the bare form. Whether it cost her a winning chance is uncertain, but the stewards' decision to later promote her to third was indeed the correct move. This daughter of Danehill Dancer looks well worth another chance and could well renew rivalry with the winner at Royal Ascot next month. (op 7/1 tchd 8/1)
Tuscan Evening(IRE), still a maiden, produced a vastly-improved effort and for a brief moment actually looked like pulling off a massive shock. She had some fair form at two but she is a quirky customer as well. This was advertised as she hung left late in the day, carrying Carribean Sunset with her, and not that surprisingly the stewards later demoted her to fourth spot.
Saoirse Abu(USA), third in the 1,000 Guineas at Newmarket last time, was well held back in fifth yet still confirmed her previous form with Nahoodh. This ground may well have been too quick for her. (op 4/1)
Nahoodh(IRE), unluckly at Newmarket behind Natagora last time, travelled well enough until passing the 2f pole where she appeared not to let herself down on this quicker ground. She now has something to prove, but it would be surprising were she not to leave this behind again in due course. (op 3/1 tchd 100/30)
Eva's Request(IRE) was unable to land a serious blow and finished further behind Carribean Sunset than had been the case at Leopardstown on her comeback a fortnight previously. She is probably happier when ridden more positively, yet a drop back down in class now looks a must.
Kitty Matcham(IRE) had run below expectations at Newmarket on her seasonal bow and again disappointed here. She may need further, and also softer ground, but she can only really be watched at present. (op 9/2)
Milton Of Campsie was predictably outclassed and found this a totally different league than when winning her maiden over 6f at Redcar 13 days previously.

2435a AIRLIE STUD GALLINULE STKS (GROUP 3) 1m 2f
4:40 (4:42) 3-Y-O **£38,294** (£11,235; £5,352; £1,823)

RPR

1 **Hebridean (IRE)**[21] 1846 3-9-1 106.. JMurtagh 1 115+
(A P O'Brien, Ire) *hld up: mod 7th 1/2-way: clsr in 6th 2f out: 4th 1 1/2f out: rdn to ld under 1f out: kpt on strly fnl f* **6/4**[1]

2 2 **Lisvale (IRE)**[238] 5845 3-9-1 104.. WMLordan 5 108
(David Wachman, Ire) *trckd ldrs: mod 5th 1/2-way: 4th 3f out: impr to cl 3rd 2f out: rdn to ld briefly over 1f out: kpt on same pce in 2nd fnl f* **12/1**

3 2 **Central Station (IRE)**[11] 2114 3-9-1 .... PJSmullen 7 104
(D K Weld, Ire) *trckd ldrs: mod 4th 1/2-way: rdn in 5th 2f out: 4th over 1f out: kpt on same pce to 3rd fnl f* **4/1**[2]

4 1 1/2 **Mr Medici (IRE)**[20] 1879 3-9-1 102.. DPMcDonogh 4 101
(Kevin Prendergast, Ire) *towards rr: hdwy into 6th 1f out: kpt on same pce fnl f* **10/1**

5 1/2 **Raydiya (IRE)**[24] 1758 3-8-12 .... MJKinane 9 97
(John M Oxx, Ire) *hld up in rr: stl bhd over 1f out: kpt on wl fnl f* **13/2**

6 3/4 **Toirneach (USA)**[14] 2024 3-8-12 100.. KJManning 2 96
(J S Bolger, Ire) *trckd ldrs: mod 3rd 1/2-way: clsr 2 1/2f out: rdn in 4th 2f out: sn no ex* **9/2**[3]

7 4 1/2 **Minneapolis**[21] 1846 3-9-1 103.. JAHeffernan 3 90
(A P O'Brien, Ire) *led after 1f: reduced advantage 2 1/2f out: rdn and hdd over 1f out: no ex and wknd* **20/1**

8 1 3/4 **The Fist Of God (IRE)**[9] 2184 3-9-1 98..(b) FMBerry 8 86
(Noel Meade, Ire) *mid-div: mod 6th 1/2-way: rdn in 7th 3f out: no imp* **8/1**

9 5 1/2 **Pyrenees (IRE)**[233] 5997 3-9-1 91.. DMGrant 6 75
(David Wachman, Ire) *led: hdd after 1f and chsd ldr: rdn 2f out: no ex in 3rd 1 1/2f out: sn wknd* **40/1**

2m 12.05s (2.55) **Going Correction** +0.25s/f (Good) **9** Ran SP% **126.6**
Speed ratings: **99,97,95,94,94 93,90,88,84**
CSF £25.46 TOTE £2.20: £1.50, £3.70, £1.50; DF 31.50.
Owner Mrs A M O'Brien **Bred** Whisperview Trading Ltd **Trained** Ballydoyle, Co Tipperary

FOCUS
Hebridean continues to improve and won easily. The fourth looks the best yardstick.

NOTEBOOK
Hebridean(IRE) showed himself to be a progressive three-year-old and followed up his win at Gowran three weeks previously under a confident ride. He was entitled to win this on his previous form this season, but he still had to prove himself on the much quicker ground and was taking a drop back in trip. While he cannot run in the Derby as he has been gelded, he looks well worthy of a chance at a bigger prize now and would have to be given respect if lining up for the King Edward VII Stakes at Royal Ascot next month. (op 5/4 tchd 7/4)
Lisvale(IRE), a dual winner at two, recorded a very pleasing return from his seasonal break. He got the longer trip well and is entitled to improve for the run, so has every chance of bettering this career-best effort next time out.
Central Station(IRE), a maiden winner on his debut at Naas 11 days previously, was facing a totally different test on this second career start and stepped up with a respectable effort in defeat. He left the impression he would relish 1m4f and is obviously open to further improvement. (op 4/1 tchd 9/2)

2434 - 2437a (Foreign Racing) - See Raceform Interactive

1667 SAN SIRO (R-H)
Sunday, May 25

OFFICIAL GOING: Soft

2438a PREMIO PAOLO MEZZANOTTE (GROUP 3) (F&M) 1m 2f
3:15 (3:18) 4-Y-O+ **£26,801** (£11,793; £6,432; £3,216)

RPR

1 **Mimetico (IRE)**[15] 4-8-9 .... DVargiu 4 104
(B Grizzetti, Italy) *mde all: rdn 1f out: r.o wl* **17/10**[1]

2 2 1/2 **Cottonmouth (IRE)**[15] 4-8-9 .... NPinna 9 99
(A & G Botti, Italy) *a.p: 3rd st: chsd wnr fnl 2f: hrd rdn and one pce fr over 1f out* **134/10**

3 1 1/2 **My Central (ITY)**[21] 4-8-9 .... URispoli 5 96
(A & G Botti, Italy) *5th st: hdwy 3f out on outside: rchd 3rd 1 1/2f out: one pce* **54/10**

4 4 **Lamentation**[15] 4-8-9 .... NMurru 8 89
(M Gasparini, Italy) *trckd wnr: 2nd s: one pce fnl 2f* **61/10**

5 1/2 **Go East (GER)**[14] 2027 4-8-9 .... EBotti 6 88
(V Valiani, Italy) *8th st: last 3f out: no real hdwy* **32/10**[2]

6 1 1/2 **Mia Kross (IRE)**[15] 5-8-9 .... MDemuro 2 85
(B Grizzetti, Italy) *7th st: hdwy on ins to go 3rd over 3f out: sn btn* **11/1**

7 3 1/2 **Penthouse Serenade (IRE)**[15] 4-8-9 .... ACarboni 3 78
(M Gonnelli, Italy) *4th st: bhd fr over 2f out* **80/1**

8 1 **Vinea Federspiel (IRE)**[203] 6688 4-8-9 .... GBocskai 7 76
(C Bocksai, Germany) *a towards rr* **23/1**

9 3 1/2 **Connessa (IRE)**[21] 4-8-9 .... CColombi 1 70
(V Valiani, Italy) *6th st: bhd fr over 2f out* **36/10**[3]

2m 6.30s (-0.40) **9** Ran SP% **133.0**
(including one euro stakes): WIN 2.69; PL 1.51, 1.79, 1.95; DF 21.90.
Owner Scuderia Francesco Aletti Montano **Bred** Azienda Agricola Razza Emiliana Srl **Trained** Italy

2439a PREMIO MARIO INCISA DELLA ROCHETTA (GROUP 3) (FILLIES) 1m 2f
4:25 (4:32) 3-Y-O **£26,801** (£11,793; £6,432; £3,216)

RPR

1 **Rosa Del Dubai (IRE)**[15] 3-8-11 .... DVargiu 1 103
(B Grizzetti, Italy) *hld up in rr: 8th st: hdwy to ld over 1 1/2f out: r.o strly* **19/10**[1]

2 2 1/4 **Radhakunda**[231] 6047 3-8-11 .... GForte 4 99
(S Billeri, Italy) *hld up: 5th st: hrd rdn 2f out: styd on u.str.p fnl f to take 2nd cl home* **82/10**

3 nk **Ragiam (ITY)**[15] 3-8-11 .... URispoli 8 98
(A & G Botti, Italy) *racd in 2nd tl led over 4f out: hdd over 1 1/2f out: one pce: lost 2nd cl home* **29/10**[2]

4 1 3/4 **Tremoto**[231] 6047 3-8-11 .... OFancera 3 95
(F & L Camici, Italy) *hld up: 6th st: in rr and looked wl btn 2f out: styd on u.p to take 4th cl home* **78/10**

5 3/4 **West Act** 3-8-11 .... EBotti 7 93
(A & G Botti, Italy) *hld up in rr: last st: hdwy to dispute 4th over 1f out: one pce: lost 4th cl home* **51/10**[3]

6 2 **River Best (IRE)** 3-8-11 .... MDemuro 5 90
(V Caruso, Italy) *led to over 4f out: one pce fnl 2f: stl disputing 4th tl wl ins fnl f: wknd cl home* **77/10**

7 4 **Kokkola (IRE)**[15] 3-8-11 .... CColombi 2 82
(V Valiani, Italy) *6th st: outpcd fnl 2f* **15/2**

8 6 **Fuente Apache (IRE)**[15] 3-8-11 .... DPorcu 9 71
(R Feligioni, Italy) *cl up: 3rd st: wknd over 2f out* **25/1**

9 8 **Mystic Lipstick (IRE)**[231] 6047 3-8-11 .... PConvertino 6 55
(J Heloury, Italy) *cl up: 4th st: wknd 3f out* **111/10**

2m 9.70s (3.00) **9** Ran SP% **134.1**
WIN 2.96; PL 1.38, 1.99, 1.43; DF 16.96.
Owner Allevamento Dei Sette **Bred** Azienda Agricola Del Vigna **Trained** Italy

2346 BADEN-BADEN (L-H)
Sunday, May 25

OFFICIAL GOING: Good

2440a GROSSER PREIS DER BADISCHEN UNTERNEHMEN (GROUP 2) 1m 3f
4:00 (4:08) 4-Y-O+ **£40,441** (£14,706; £7,353; £3,676)

RPR

1 **It's Gino (GER)**[42] 1359 5-8-11 .... KerrinMcEvoy 4 115
(P Vovcenko, Germany) *racd in 4th to st: brought to stands' side: led 1f out: rdn out* **19/10**[2]

2 1 1/2 **Egerton (GER)**[49] 1237 7-8-11 .... TMundry 3 112
(P Rau, Germany) *first to show: then disp 2nd bhd clr ldr: 2nd st: led on stands' rail 1 1/2f out to 1f out: r.o one pce* **3/1**[3]

3 2 **Poseidon Adventure (IRE)**[28] 1662 5-8-11 ....(b) ADeVries 1 109
(W Figge, Germany) *hld up: 5th st and mde grnd in middle: ev ch 1f out: one pce* **12/1**

4 1/2 **Lord Hill (GER)**[56] 4-8-11 .... J-PCarvalho 9 108
(C Zeitz) *carried rt s: sn in 2nd: led over 2f out to 1 1/2f out: one pce* **19/1**

5 10 **Oriental Tiger (GER)**[28] 1662 5-9-0 ....(b) THellier 8 94
(U Ostmann, Germany) *wnt rt s: plld his way to the front after 1f: 8 l clr after 3f: hdd over 2f out: 3rd st: eased* **11/10**[1]

6 4 **Dwilano (GER)**[20] 1888 5-8-11 .... AStarke 2 84
(P Remmert, Germany) *broke wl: sn racing in 4th: 6th and btn st* **11/1**

7 6 **Blushing King (FR)**[49] 1237 6-8-11 .... LHammerHansen 7 74
(Frau E Mader, Germany) *a in rr: last and btn st* **25/1**

2m 17.42s (-1.85) **7** Ran SP% **132.0**
PARI-MUTUEL: WIN 29.00; PL 16.00, 16.00, 21.00; SF 157.00.
Owner Stall 5-Stars **Bred** Frau B Nuttelmann **Trained** Germany

CARLISLE (R-H)

Monday, May 26

OFFICIAL GOING: Good to firm (firm in places; 9.8)

Wind: Strong, half against Weather: Cloudy, bright

2443 EUROPEAN BREEDERS' FUND MAIDEN STKS 5f

2:15 (2:17) (Class 5) 2-Y-O £3,626 (£1,079; £539; £269) Stalls High

Form				RPR
	1		**Effort** 2-9-3 0 DeanMcKeown 7 *(M Johnston) cl up: led and rn green over 2f out: pushed out fnl f* 2/1[1]	80+
	2	1 1/4	**Hysterical Lady** 2-8-12 0 AdrianTNicholls 5 *(D Nicholls) chsd ldrs: effrt and wnt 2nd over 2f out: kpt on ins fnl f* 85/40[2]	71+
	3	4 1/2	**Uramazin (IRE)** 2-9-0 0 PJMcDonald(3) 3 *(G A Swinbank) s.i.s: bhd tl hdwy over 1f out: kpt on: nt rch first 2* 8/1	59+
	4	2	**Visterre (IRE)** 2-8-12 0 PhillipMakin 1 *(B Smart) dwlt: outpcd unttil hdwy and edgd rt 2f out: no imp fnl f* 9/2[3]	47+
0	5	6	**Scarlet Blade**[40] 1390 2-9-3 0 (p) RoystonFfrench 6 *(Mrs A Duffield) in tch tl rdn and wknd fr 2f out* 25/1	31
20	6	3 3/4	**Cool Sonata (IRE)**[8] 2217 2-8-9 0 MarkLawson(3) 2 *(M Brittain) wnt lft s: bhd: rdn and edgd rt over 2f out: sn btn* 12/1	12
	7	nk	**Chipolini (IRE)** 2-9-3 0 FergalLynch 8 *(D Carroll) led to over 2f out: rdn and wknd over 1f out* 11/1	16
	8	19	**Royal Premium** 2-9-3 0 TonyHamilton 4 *(H A McWilliams) dwlt: rdn and wknd fr 1/2-way: t.o* 50/1	—

61.38 secs (0.58) **Going Correction** -0.05s/f (Good) 8 Ran SP% **116.5**

Speed ratings (Par 93): **93,91,83,80,71 65,64,34**

CSF £6.68 TOTE £2.60: £1.10, £1.20, £2.50; EX 6.80.

Owner Sheikh Hamdan Bin Mohammed Al Maktoum **Bred** Watership Down Stud **Trained** Middleham Moor, N Yorks

■ Stewards' Enquiry : Dean McKeown one-day ban: careless riding (Jun 9)

FOCUS

Little strength in depth but a race in which the first two pulled clear in the closing stages. The winner did it well.

NOTEBOOK

Effort ◆, a 140,000gns half-brother to high-class sprinter Titus Livius and smart German 7f winner Briseida, was green in the paddock and in the race but nevertheless created a favourable impression. He will be suited by the step up to 6f and is the type to win more races. (op 5-4)

Hysterical Lady ◆, an 85,000euro first foal of a fairly useful juvenile winner, shaped well on this racecourse debut. She pulled clear of the remainder and appeals as the sort to win races over sprint distances for this yard. (op 5-1)

Uramazin(IRE), a 45,000euro second foal of a multiple middle-distance winner abroad, was far from disgraced on this racecourse debut. He will be suited by a much stiffer test of stamina and is likely to fare better. (tchd 7-1)

Visterre(IRE), who cost 47,000euros and is out of a multiple 7f winner, showed ability on this racecourse debut. The step up to 6f+ will be in her favour and she is likely to fare better with this experience behind her. (op 5-1)

Scarlet Blade, well beaten on his debut at Beverley on easy ground, again had his limitations exposed on this quicker ground in the first-time cheekpieces. He is likely to remain vulnerable in this type of event. (op 20-1)

Cool Sonata(IRE), was again a long way below the form she showed on her debut and she remains one to field against in this type of event. Official explanation: jockey said filly was unsuited by the good to firm (firm in places) ground (op 11-1 tchd 10-1)

2444 RACING UK FREE TO AIR 31ST MAY H'CAP 5f 193y

2:50 (2:50) (Class 5) (0-70,70) 4-Y-O+ £2,590 (£770; £385; £192) Stalls High

Form				RPR
0-06	1		**Gap Princess (IRE)**[17] 1952 4-8-9 61 TonyHamilton 1 *(R A Fahey) towards rr nr side gp: effrt 2f out: styd on to ld nr fin* 8/1[3]	70
510-	2	1/2	**Quicks The Word**[235] 5935 8-8-5 57 DeanMcKeown 7 *(T A K Cuthbert) led nr side gp: overall ldr over 1f out: kpt on: hdd nr fin: 2nd of 10 in gp* 50/1	64
6534	3	1/2	**Avontuur (FR)**[16] 2009 6-8-4 56 oh5 (p) DaleGibson 4 *(Mrs R A Carr) in tch nr side gp: effrt over 1f out: edgd rt ins fnl f: r.o: 3rd of 10 in gp* 25/1	61
-001	4	1/2	**The Bear**[22] 1826 5-8-11 66 PJMcDonald(3) 16 *(R Johnson) led far side: rdn over 1f out: kpt on fnl f: nt rch stands' side ldrs: 1st of 5 in gp* 4/1[1]	70+
6000	5	3/4	**Circuit Dancer (IRE)**[16] 2005 8-9-2 68 AdrianTNicholls 6 *(D Nicholls) chsd nr side ldrs: effrt 2f out: one pce fnl f: 4th of 10 in gp* 20/1	69
5-26	6	3/4	**Ingleby Princess**[9] 2205 4-8-8 65 NeilBrown(5) 5 *(T D Barron) midfield nr side gp: effrt over 2f out: kpt on fnl f: no imp: 5th of 10 in gp* 10/1	64
24-2	7	3/4	**Miss Daawe**[63] 987 4-8-1 60 oh3 ow4 LanceBetts(7) 14 *(B Ellison) chsd far side ldr: effrt over 2f out: kpt on same pce fnl f: 2nd of 5 in gp* 8/1[3]	57+
06-4	8	nk	**Opal Noir**[17] 1952 4-8-10 62 PhillipMakin 11 *(Miss L A Perratt) sn swtchd to nr side gp: effrt over 1f out: kpt on: no imp: 6th of 10 in gp* 7/1[2]	58
6016	9	nk	**Winthorpe (IRE)**[9] 2188 8-9-3 69 GrahamGibbons 2 *(J J Quinn) towards rr nr side: drvn 1/2-way: sme late hdwy: 7th of 10 in gp* 22/1	64
0-50	10	shd	**Chin Wag (IRE)**[38] 1450 4-8-5 57 (p) FergalLynch 3 *(J S Goldie) bhd nr side tl sme late hdwy: n.d: 8th of 10 in gp* 8/1[3]	51
0-44	11	1/2	**Dark Champion**[16] 2005 8-8-9 61 RoystonFfrench 8 *(R E Barr) cl up nr side tl wknd over 1f out: 9th of 10 in gp* 11/1	54
-000	12	1/2	**Sea Land (FR)**[30] 1624 4-8-5 57 GregFairley 15 *(B Ellison) s.i.s: hdwy far side 1/2-way: one pce over 1f out: 3rd of 5 in gp* 22/1	48+
60-0	13	4 1/2	**Mundo's Magic**[16] 2005 4-8-7 62 MarkLawson(3) 10 *(G M Moore) chsd far side ldrs tl wknd over 1f out: 4th of 5 in gp* 20/1	39+
6-50	14	6	**Argentine (IRE)**[17] 1952 4-8-10 65 JamieMoriarty(3) 12 *(L Lungo) swtchd to nr side gp after 1f: bhd: effrt on outside over 2f out: sn wknd: last of 10 in gp* 16/1	23
4326	15	1	**Guto**[23] 1818 5-8-13 70 KellyHarrison(5) 13 *(W J H Ratcliffe) prom far side tl wknd wl over 1f out: last of 5 in gp* 14/1	24+

1m 12.9s (-0.80) **Going Correction** -0.05s/f (Good) 15 Ran SP% **119.8**

Speed ratings (Par 103): **103,102,101,101,100 99,98,97,97,97 96,95,89,81,80**

CSF £377.15 CT £9369.95 TOTE £10.20: £2.90, £8.70, £7.30; EX 360.50.

Owner Dr W D Ashworth **Bred** D Veitch And Musagd Abo Salim **Trained** Musley Bank, N Yorks

FOCUS

The field split into two groups but those racing against the near-side rail held the edge in the closing stages. The pace was sound throughout. Sound form, the winner rated back to his best.

2445 CLEANEVENT CARLISLE BELL TRIAL H'CAP 7f 200y

3:25 (3:25) (Class 4) (0-80,76) 4-Y-O+ £4,533 (£1,348; £674; £336) Stalls High

Form				RPR
2403	1		**Stoic Leader (IRE)**[2] 2400 8-8-12 70 RoystonFfrench 4 *(R F Fisher) midfield: hdwy on outside to ld over 1f out: drvn out fnl f* 10/1	79
23-0	2	1 1/4	**Champain Sands (IRE)**[20] 1891 9-8-10 68 GrahamGibbons 5 *(E J Alston) hld up: smooth hdwy over 1f out: chsd wnr ent fnl f: kpt on* 20/1	74
0-32	3	1/2	**Hula Ballew**[26] 1729 8-8-12 70 PhillipMakin 3 *(M Dods) chsd ldrs: drvn over 2f out: kpt on u.p fnl f* 9/4[1]	75
020-	4	nk	**Sunnyside Tom (IRE)**[217] 6380 4-8-9 67 DaleGibson 8 *(R A Fahey) hld up: effrt and hdwy over 1f out: kpt on fnl f: nrst fin* 16/1	71
60-3	5	3 1/4	**Musca (IRE)**[23] 1815 4-9-4 76 TonyHamilton 2 *(C Grant) in tch: effrt over 2f out: no ex over 1f out* 9/1	72
60-1	6	1/2	**Motafarred (IRE)**[3] 2375 6-9-3 75 6ex DeanMcKeown 1 *(Micky Hammond) t.k.h: cl up: led over 2f out to over 1f out: sn no ex* 11/4[2]	70
5-66	7	1/2	**Regent's Secret (USA)**[17] 1953 8-8-10 68 (p) FergalLynch 7 *(J S Goldie) bhd: drvn 3f out: nvr rchd ldrs* 12/1	62
3-26	8	3/4	**Grand Opera (IRE)**[54] 1138 5-8-10 71 PJMcDonald(3) 9 *(J Howard Johnson) midfield: drvn and outpcd 3f out: n.d after* 8/1[3]	63
-060	9	3 1/2	**Dakota Rain (IRE)**[23] 1818 6-9-4 76 GregFairley 6 *(Jennie Candlish) t.k.h: early ldr: cl up: chal over 2f to wl over 1f out: sn btn* 20/1	60
3003	10	27	**Kabis Amigos**[6] 2289 6-8-10 68 AdrianTNicholls 10 *(D Nicholls) dwlt: sn led: hdd over 2f out: wknd over 1f out* 12/1	—

1m 39.8s (-0.20) **Going Correction** +0.10s/f (Good) 10 Ran SP% **118.4**

Speed ratings (Par 105): **105,103,103,102,99 99,98,97,94,67**

CSF £192.08 CT £605.26 TOTE £8.70: £2.70, £4.70, £1.50; EX 165.10.

Owner Alan Willoughby **Bred** P J Higgins **Trained** Ulverston, Cumbria

FOCUS

An ordinary handicap run at just a modest gallop. It is doubtful if the winner had to improve on recent efforts to take this.

Motafarred(IRE) Official explanation: jockey said gelding ran too free early

Kabis Amigos Official explanation: jockey said gelding was unsuited by the good to firm (firm in places) ground

2446 CBS OUTDOOR ADVERTISING H'CAP 1m 1f 61y

4:00 (4:00) (Class 6) (0-65,65) 4-Y-O+ £1,942 (£578; £288; £144) Stalls High

Form				RPR
35/6	1		**Rainbow Zest**[25] 1752 5-8-13 60 PhillipMakin 11 *(W Storey) hld up: hdwy and swtchd lft appr fnl f: led ins fnl f: styd on wl* 14/1	67+
42-5	2	1/2	**Titinius (IRE)**[10] 2155 8-9-2 63 TonyHamilton 10 *(Micky Hammond) trckd ldrs: effrt and led over 1f out: hdd ins fnl f: r.o* 9/2[2]	68
0050	3	2 1/2	**Valdan (IRE)**[6] 2285 4-8-3 57 (t) SophieDoyle(7) 4 *(M A Barnes) hld up: hdwy and hung rt 2f out: sn ev ch: one pce fnl f* 9/1	57
/60-	4	2	**Still Calm**[231] 6057 4-8-13 60 (e[1]) FergalLynch 6 *(N J Vaughan) led to over 2f out: sn lost pl: rallied fnl f: no imp* 9/1	56
5004	5	1/2	**Muncaster Castle (IRE)**[17] 1953 4-8-6 53 RoystonFfrench 9 *(R F Fisher) cl up: ev ch over 2f out: no ex over 1f out* 7/1[3]	48
3242	6	1	**Pianoforte (USA)**[17] 1953 6-9-4 65 (b) GrahamGibbons 2 *(E J Alston) plld hrd: trckd ldrs: led over 2f out: hung rt and hdd over 1f out: sn no ex* 11/4[1]	58
1-00	7	nse	**Snow Dancer (IRE)**[10] 2155 4-8-11 65 BMcHugh(7) 5 *(H A McWilliams) hld up in tch on outside: rdn whn n.m.r 2f out: sn btn* 7/1[3]	58
3435	8	1 1/4	**Sparky Vixen**[16] 2003 4-7-13 51 oh1 KellyHarrison(5) 7 *(C J Teague) hld up in tch: drvn over 2f out: sn outpcd* 9/2[2]	41

1m 57.65s (0.05) **Going Correction** +0.10s/f (Good) 8 Ran SP% **114.7**

Speed ratings (Par 101): **103,102,100,98,98 97,97,96**

CSF £75.89 CT £607.23 TOTE £12.50: £3.00, £1.60, £2.90; EX 71.20.

Owner Raymond Tooth **Bred** Fittocks Stud **Trained** Muggleswick, Co Durham

FOCUS

Not a strong race by any means and run at just an ordinary gallop. Muddling and weak form but the winner won with a bit in hand and may be capable of better.

Pianoforte(USA) Official explanation: jockey said gelding ran too free

2447 CBS OUTDOOR CUMBERLAND PLATE TRIAL H'CAP 1m 3f 107y

4:35 (4:35) (Class 4) (0-80,78) 4-Y-O+ £4,533 (£1,348; £674; £336) Stalls Low

Form				RPR
05-0	1		**Bajan Parkes**[17] 1947 5-9-4 78 GrahamGibbons 4 *(E J Alston) mde all at decent gallop: clr 3f out: kpt on wl fnl f: unchal* 9/1	85
5020	2	1 3/4	**Key Decision (IRE)**[7] 2249 4-8-12 75 PJMcDonald(3) 6 *(G A Swinbank) hld up: hdwy 2f out: chsd wnr ent fnl f: r.o fin* 10/1	80
250-	3	2 3/4	**La Vecchia Scuola (IRE)**[16] 5805 4-8-6 66 FergalLynch 5 *(J S Goldie) hld up: effrt on outside 2f out: edgd rt: kpt on u.p fnl f* 11/10[1]	66
0005	4	shd	**Wild Fell Hall (IRE)**[7] 2249 5-9-3 77 (p) PhillipMakin 7 *(A D Brown) prom: effrt and drvn over 2f out: one pce over 1f out* 16/1	77
0623	5	3/4	**Hugs Destiny (IRE)**[6] 2286 7-7-12 65 oh17 ow1 (t) SophieDoyle(7) 8 *(M A Barnes) chsd ldr: drvn over 2f out: no ex over 1f out* 16/1	64?
3010	6	5	**Calzaghe (IRE)**[21] 1877 4-8-4 71 (v) DeclanCannon(7) 2 *(K R Burke) in tch: rdn and edgd rt 2f out: wknd over 1f out* 8/1[3]	62
-030	7	1 3/4	**Nelsons Column (IRE)**[19] 1909 5-8-9 69 RoystonFfrench 1 *(G M Moore) hld up: drvn over 3f out: wknd 2f out* 8/1[3]	57
03-3	8	hd	**Tsaroxy (IRE)**[63] 992 6-9-1 75 TonyHamilton 3 *(J Howard Johnson) hld up: struggling 3f out: sn btn* 5/1[2]	63

2m 23.18s (0.08) **Going Correction** +0.10s/f (Good) 8 Ran SP% **117.4**

Speed ratings (Par 105): **103,101,99,99,99 95,94,94**

CSF £95.55 CT £176.86 TOTE £10.00: £2.00, £2.80, £1.10; EX 65.20.

Owner Joseph Heler **Bred** Joseph Heler **Trained** Longton, Lancs

■ Stewards' Enquiry : Sophie Doyle caution: used whip with excessive frequency

FOCUS

Mainly exposed performers. The winner was given an enterprising ride and allowed a fairly easy lead, and it is doubtful he had to improve. The fifth holds down the form.

Bajan Parkes Official explanation: trainer said, regarding the apparent improvement in form, that the gelding got the run of the race today

2448 CBS OUTDOOR H'CAP 5f
5:10 (5:10) (Class 6) (0-60,59) 4-Y-0+ £2,047 (£604; £302) Stalls High

Form RPR
-000 1 **Just Joey**[10] 2159 4-9-1 56....(b) PhillipMakin 5 70
(J R Weymes) *pressed ldr: led over 1f out: drvn out* 25/1
0-10 2 2 **Jun Fan (USA)**[30] 1634 6-8-6 54.... LanceBetts(7) 17 61
(B Ellison) *trckd ldrs: effrt and wnt 2nd ins fnl f: kpt on same pce nr fin* 18/1
0442 3 shd **Mr Rooney (IRE)**[6] 2270 5-9-1 56.... AdrianTNicholls 11 63+
(D Nicholls) *dwlt: sn midfield: effrt whn nt clr run and swtchd over 1f out: r.o fnl f* 7/2[1]
402- 4 ½ **Smirfys Gold (IRE)**[254] 5420 4-8-12 53.... GrahamGibbons 6 58
(E S McMahon) *prom: effrt over 2f out: one pce fnl f* 11/1
0600 5 1 **Kings College Boy**[10] 2145 8-8-12 56....(b) JamieMoriarty(3) 13 57
(R A Fahey) *hld up: effrt over 1f out: kpt on ins fnl f: no imp* 15/2
0126 6 ¾ **A Big Sky Brewing (USA)**[24] 1775 4-8-13 59....(b) NeilBrown(5) 12 58
(T D Barron) *towards rr: drvn 1/2-way: styd on fnl f: nrst fin* 6/1[3]
5035 7 1 **Johnston's Glory (IRE)**[6] 2283 4-9-3 58....(b) DeanMcKeown 16 53
(E J Alston) *led to over 1f out: sn no ex* 10/1
0602 8 nk **Lambency (IRE)**[10] 2159 5-8-9 55.... GaryBartley(5) 2 49+
(J S Goldie) *bhd centre: swtchd to r alone stands' side over 2f out: kpt on fnl f: no imp* 4/1[2]
50-0 9 ½ **Greek Secret**[33] 1561 5-8-10 54.... DNolan(3) 7 46
(J O'Reilly) *hld up: short lived effrt 2f out: sn wknd* 25/1
630- 10 nse **Brigadore**[213] 6467 9-9-2 57.... TonyHamilton 8 49
(J G Given) *bhd and sn rdn along: nvr rchd ldrs* 20/1
000- 11 1¾ **Alugat (IRE)**[293] 4251 5-9-0 55....(p) RoystonFfrench 14 41
(Mrs A Duffield) *chsd ldrs tl rdn and wknd over 1f out* 33/1
0206 12 hd **Overstayed (IRE)**[22] 1827 5-9-1 56....(be) GregFairley 10 41
(M Mullineaux) *towards rr: drvn 1/2-way: sn btn* 10/1
0565 13 14 **Sharp Indian**[33] 1561 4-9-0 55.... FergalLynch 4 —
(W J H Ratcliffe) *racd centre thrght: a bhd* 25/1
0-06 14 1¾ **Miacarla**[10] 2159 5-8-4 52.... BMcHugh(5) 15 —
(H A McWilliams) *virtually ref to r: t.o thrght* 16/1

60.61 secs (-0.19) **Going Correction** -0.05s/f (Good) 14 Ran SP% 125.2
Speed ratings (Par 101): **99,95,95,94,93 92,90,89,89,89 86,85,63,60**
CSF £410.23 CT £2034.53 TOTE £32.30: £6.30, £6.60, £1.90; EX 755.10 Place 6: £372.58, Place 5: £277.07..
Owner High Moor Racing 4 **Bred** Mrs D O Joly **Trained** Middleham Moor, N Yorks

FOCUS
A modest sprint run at a good gallop in which all bar one raced centre to far side. The winner returned to form from out of the blue and is rated to his latter 3yo form.
Just Joey Official explanation: trainer said, regarding the apparent improvement of form, that the filly benefited from the reapplication of blinkers and the faster ground.
Kings College Boy Official explanation: jockey said gelding was denied a clear run
Miacarla Official explanation: jockey said mare missed the break
T/Plt: £421.90 to a £1 stake. Pool: £59,270.90. 102.55 winning tickets. T/Qpdt: £64.20 to a £1 stake. Pool: £2,970.50. 34.20 winning tickets. RY

[1895] CHEPSTOW (L-H)
Monday, May 26

OFFICIAL GOING: Soft (6.5)
A dramatic change in the going after 8mm of rain in the morning following 9mm the previous day.
Wind: Strong across Weather: Cloudy

2449 FREE SPORTS BETS@FREEBETS.CO.UK MAIDEN STKS 1m 14y
2:20 (2:23) (Class 5) 3-Y-0+ £2,460 (£732; £365; £182) Stalls High

Form RPR
00 1 **Blue Spartan (IRE)**[21] 1876 3-9-1 0.... EddieAhern 16 82+
(B J Meehan) *a.p: led over 2f out: rdn over 1f out: clr ins fnl f: r.o wl* 3/1[2]
2 4 **Akarshan (IRE)** 3-9-1 0.... FergusSweeney 14 73
(Evan Williams) *s.s: hdwy over 2f out: edgd lft over 1f out: wnt 2nd ins fnl f: no ch w wnr* 28/1
3 3 3 **Light From Mars**[33] 1573 3-9-1 0.... AlanMunro 1 66
(B R Millman) *a.p: rdn and one pce fnl 2f* 5/2[1]
4 2 **Addiena** 4-9-8 0.... CatherineGannon 10 56
(B Palling) *s.i.s: t.k.h: stmbld after 1f: sn mid-div: rdn over 2f out: styd on fnl f* 50/1
6-0 5 1 **Earlsmedic**[34] 1535 3-9-1 0.... SaleemGolam 11 59
(S C Williams) *led: hdd over 2f out: rdn over 1f out: wknd ins fnl f* 33/1
6 1 **I Confess**[39] 1434 3-9-1 86.... StephenDonohoe 9 57
(P D Evans) *prom: rdn over 2f out: wknd over 1f out* 3/1[2]
0-6 7 ¾ **Cinerama (IRE)**[38] 1440 3-8-10 0.... RichardMullen 7 50
(M P Tregoning) *hld up in tch: pushed along over 2f out: wknd over 1f out* 8/1[3]
-500 8 10 **The Graig**[3] 2375 4-9-13 49.... FrancisNorton 3 32
(J R Holt) *s.i.s: sn in tch: wknd over 2f out* 25/1
0-0 9 nk **Empire Seeker (USA)**[9] 2198 3-8-8 0.... GabrielHannon(7) 5 31
(J W Hills) *s.i.s: bhd: pushed along 3f out: sn no ch* 33/1
00- 10 2 **Askar Tau (FR)**[212] 6493 3-9-1 0.... DarryllHolland 12 27
(M P Tregoning) *hld up and bhd: no ch fnl 2f* 14/1
0 11 5 **Ci Vediamo (IRE)**[35] 1525 3-8-10 0.... SebSanders 6 10
(R M Beckett) *w ldr tl rdn over 2f out: sn wknd: eased fnl f* 16/1
00 12 14 **Heartsanddiamonds**[20] 1896 4-9-5 0.... JerryO'Dwyer(3) 2 —
(A W Carroll) *in tch 4f* 80/1
0 13 4½ **Young Ollie**[7] 2257 3-8-3 0.... DavidProbert(7) 13 —
(E A Wheeler) *s.i.s: rdn over 4f out: a bhd* 150/1
0 14 20 **Smart Artist**[33] 1563 3-9-1 0.... LPKeniry 4 —
(S Kirk) *bhd: rdn over 5f out: sn struggling: t.o* 80/1

1m 39.88s (3.68) **Going Correction** +0.45s/f (Yiel)
WFA 3 from 4yo+ 12lb 14 Ran SP% 120.5
Speed ratings (Par 103): **99,95,92,90,89 88,87,77,76,74 69,55,51,31**
CSF £93.75 TOTE £3.40: £1.80, £5.50, £1.80; EX 120.10.
Owner W A Harrison-Allan **Bred** Fortbarrington Stud **Trained** Manton, Wilts

FOCUS
The stalls on the straight course were moved from their intended position on the stands' side over to the far side, due to the 17mm of rain that fell in the preceding 24 hours, changing the going to soft.\n\x\x This was no more than a fair maiden and there was little soft-ground form to go on. A step up from the winner but the form may not prove too solid.

2450 FREE BET@FREEBETS.CO.UK (S) STKS 6f 16y
2:55 (2:56) (Class 6) 2-Y-0 £1,910 (£564; £282) Stalls High

Form RPR
44 1 **Come On Buckers (IRE)**[44] 1324 2-8-11 0.... TGMcLaughlin 10 60
(P D Evans) *a.p: rdn over 1f out: led ins fnl f: r.o* 9/4[1]
130 2 ¾ **Heaven Or Hell (IRE)**[37] 1480 2-9-2 0.... StephenDonohoe 4 63
(P D Evans) *led: rdn over 2f out: hdd ins fnl f: no ex towards fin* 4/1[3]
3 ¾ **Comghaire (IRE)** 2-8-7 0 ow1.... EddieAhern 2 52
(John R Upson) *s.i.s: sn in tch: ev ch wl over 1f out: sn rdn: nt qckn wl ins fnl f* 18/1
654 4 10 **Talulah Bells**[32] 1574 2-8-3 0.... LukeMorris(3) 9 21
(A W Carroll) *hld up in tch: rdn over 2f out: wknd wl over 1f out* 9/2
400 5 nse **Forzando Bloom**[14] 2049 2-8-8 0.... KevinGhunowa(3) 3 26
(R A Harris) *w ldr 3f: sn rdn: wknd over 1f out* 40/1
5 6 19 **Kuwinda**[44] 1341 2-8-6 0.... SamHitchcott 6 —
(M R Channon) *half-rrd s: bhd: pushed along 3f out: sn lost tch: t.o* 11/1
6423 7 nk **Dazzling Dust (IRE)**[16] 2004 2-8-4 0....(p) AshleyMorgan(7) 8 —
(W G M Turner) *bhd: rdn over 3f out: sn lost tch: t.o* 11/4[2]
55 8 1½ **Sweet Mujahid**[14] 2049 2-8-11 0....(b[1]) LPKeniry 1 —
(R A Harris) *wnt rt s: prom tl wknd qckly over 3f out: t.o* 40/1

1m 15.9s (3.00) **Going Correction** +0.45s/f (Yiel) 8 Ran SP% 114.1
Speed ratings (Par 91): **98,97,96,82,82 57,56,54**
CSF £11.56 TOTE £3.30: £1.40, £1.70, £3.20; EX 15.00.There was no bid for the winner. Comghaire was claimed by P D Evans for £5,400.
Owner Derek Buckley **Bred** D Houlihan **Trained** Pandy, Monmouths

FOCUS
Hand-timed. Probably an above-average seller with the winner having been sent off as favourite for a maiden at Doncaster last time. The first three finished a long way clear and their form might be underestimated.

NOTEBOOK
Come On Buckers(IRE) is nothing special but is another good advertisement for his trainer's ability to place his juveniles to good effect. Entitled to win this on the basis of two promising runs in maidens, he needed the extra furlong he was faced with here to get on top of his stablemate. (op 5-2 tchd 3-1, 10-3 and 7-2 in a place)
Heaven Or Hell(IRE) started off his career with three races in 10 days last month, and he has obviously been freshened up by a short break since then as he bounced right back to the form of his debut success at Bath, making his stablemate pull out all the stops. He can continue to go close in this grade despite his penalty. (op 3-1 tchd 9-2)
Comghaire(IRE) ◆ was an almost unheard of juvenile representative of a yard more associated with staying chasers. However she belied her bargain-basement purchase price by making a very promising racecourse bow, travelling as well as any throughout the race and just getting run out of it close home by a pair with more experience. She was claimed by David Evans afterwards. (op 22-1 tchd 25-1 and 14-1)
Dazzling Dust(IRE) has had five races in seven weeks and is not at all progressing with his racing. (op 10-3 tchd 7-2)
Sweet Mujahid Official explanation: jockey said gelding hung right-handed

2451 BET@FREEBETS.CO.UK H'CAP 1m 14y
3:30 (3:35) (Class 5) (0-70,70) 3-Y-0 £2,719 (£809; £404; £202) Stalls High

Form RPR
00-1 1 **Master Of Arts (USA)**[7] 2260 3-8-12 64 6ex.... SebSanders 2 76+
(Sir Mark Prescott) *hld up in tch: led over 3f out: sn grad drifted rt: shkn up over 1f out: readily* 4/5[1]
-014 2 1¼ **Challow Hills (USA)**[7] 2244 3-8-13 65.... AlanMunro 16 72
(B W Hills) *hld up in mid-div: hdwy over 3f out: rdn over 2f out: wnt 2nd wl over 1f out: kpt on ins fnl f: nt trble wnr* 5/1[2]
00-0 3 4 **Latin Scholar (IRE)**[14] 2047 3-8-10 65.... TravisBlock(3) 5 63
(A King) *hld up in tch: rdn and one pce fnl 2f* 16/1
00-2 4 1¼ **Tara's Garden**[21] 1869 3-8-13 65.... FrancisNorton 14 60
(M Blanshard) *t.k.h in tch: lost pl over 3f out: styd on fnl f* 14/1
4 5 ½ **Simarian (IRE)**[34] 1535 3-9-3 69.... FergusSweeney 7 63
(Evan Williams) *hld up and bhd: rdn over 2f out: hdwy over 1f out: styd on fnl f* 20/1
10-0 6 ½ **Sawpit Sunshine (IRE)**[16] 2014 3-9-0 66.... LiamJones 15 59
(J L Spearing) *t.k.h in tch: ev ch 3f out: rdn and wknd over 1f out* 16/1
5441 7 1 **Coole Dodger (IRE)**[30] 1622 3-8-11 70.... GabrielHannon(7) 4 60
(M D I Usher) *s.s: swtchd rt to stands' side and hdwy over 3f out: wknd over 1f out* 12/1[3]
0-55 8 1¼ **Follow Your Spirit**[21] 1870 3-8-4 56.... CatherineGannon 1 44
(B Palling) *prom: ev ch 3f out: rdn and wknd 2f out* 28/1
000- 9 13 **Reve Vert (FR)**[223] 6246 3-8-1 56 oh2.... LukeMorris(3) 6 14
(A W Carroll) *s.i.s: t.k.h towards rr: pushed along over 3f out: sn struggling* 80/1
3000 10 1 **Boss Hog**[20] 1897 3-8-9 61 oh1 ow1.... StephenDonohoe 17 16
(P A Blockley) *hld up towards rr: hdwy 3f out: sn rdn: wknd over 1f out: eased ins fnl f* 20/1
-440 11 3¼ **Lawton**[28] 1685 3-9-2 68.... PaulFitzsimons 11 16
(Miss J R Tooth) *chsd ldr: led briefly over 3f out: sn rdn: wknd qckly over 2f out* 40/1
3-00 12 4½ **Black Or Red (IRE)**[16] 2014 3-9-0 66.... RichardThomas 12 4
(I A Wood) *bhd fnl 5f* 66/1
06-0 13 nk **Robbmaa (FR)**[22] 1836 3-8-10 62.... EddieAhern 13 —
(A W Carroll) *hld up and bhd: rdn over 3f out: sn toiling* 40/1
-650 14 ¾ **Alfredtheordinary**[9] 2208 3-8-8 60.... SamHitchcott 9 —
(M R Channon) *hld up and bhd: rdn over 3f out: sn struggling* 33/1
0000 15 4½ **New Minerton (IRE)**[20] 1897 3-8-4 56 oh11....(b) TPO'Shea 10 —
(B R Millman) *t.k.h: led: rdn and hdd over 3f out: wknd 2f out* 100/1
-352 16 10 **Jemiliah**[18] 1938 3-8-4 56.... RichardKingscote 8 —
(B G Powell) *wnt lft s: rdn over 3f out: a in rr* 20/1

1m 40.09s (3.89) **Going Correction** +0.45s/f (Yiel) 16 Ran SP% 127.6
Speed ratings (Par 99): **98,96,92,91,91 90,89,88,75,74 71,66,66,65,60 50**
CSF £4.19 CT £46.51 TOTE £2.00: £1.10, £1.30, £2.80, £3.20; EX 6.70.
Owner Eclipse Thoroughbreds-Osborne House III **Bred** Cyril Humphris **Trained** Newmarket, Suffolk

FOCUS
Just a run-of-the-mill handicap won by a typical improver from the Sir Mark Prescott yard. He was value for a bit extra but still did not need to match his Wolverhampton form. The runner-up was up 5lb in beating the rest.
Coole Dodger(IRE) Official explanation: jockey said colt hung badly right-handed
Boss Hog Official explanation: jockey said gelding lost its action
Black Or Red(IRE) Official explanation: jockey said colt was unsuited by the soft ground
Robbmaa(FR) Official explanation: jockey said gelding was unsuited by the soft ground

Jemiliah Official explanation: jockey said filly was unsuited by the soft ground

2452 FREEBETS@FREEBETS.CO.UK FILLIES' H'CAP — 6f 16y
4:05 (4:07) (Class 5) (0-70,69) 3-Y-O — £2,719 (£809; £404; £202) Stalls High

Form				RPR
0133	1		**Oceana Blue**[28] 1671 3-8-9 **67**.....(t) DavidProbert(7) 12 — (A M Balding) *hld up: hdwy 3f out: led jst over 1f out: rdn out* **10/1**	75+
40-1	2	1 1/4	**Rosie Says No**[25] 1743 3-8-12 **63**..... SebSanders 10 — (R M H Cowell) *hld up: rdn 2f out: hdwy over 1f out: r.o to take 2nd wl ins fnl f: nt trble wnr* **5/1**[3]	67
6-65	3	1 1/4	**Whiteoak Lady (IRE)**[24] 1781 3-9-4 **69**..... FrancisNorton 13 — (J L Spearing) *t.k.h: w ldr: led 3f out: hdd jst over 1f out: sn rdn: no ex ins fnl f* **4/1**[2]	69
0054	4	1 1/4	**Easy Wonder (GER)**[12] 2102 3-8-6 **60**..... KirstyMilczarek(3) 16 — (I A Wood) *hld up: hdwy 2f out: sn rdn: one pce fnl f* **6/1**	56
6-32	5	1 1/4	**Filligree (IRE)**[20] 1897 3-8-10 **61**..... SaleemGolam 1 — (Rae Guest) *hld up: rdn and hdwy over 1f out: no further prog fnl f* **3/1**[1]	53
-504	6	2 3/4	**Our Kally**[25] 1740 3-8-1 **55** oh7..... LukeMorris(3) 2 — (M D I Usher) *w ldrs tl rdn over 2f out: wknd wl over 1f out* **25/1**	38
0-03	7	1/2	**Infinite Patience**[11] 2127 3-8-9 **60**..... LPKeniry 6 — (J S Moore) *trckd ldrs tl rdn and wknd over 1f out* **7/1**	42
36-0	8	4	**Edie Superstar (USA)**[12] 2102 3-9-3 **68**..... EddieAhern 15 — (M A Magnusson) *led 3f: wknd over 1f out* **14/1**	37
40-0	9	hd	**Elizabeth's Quest**[56] 1115 3-8-6 **57**..... CatherineGannon 14 — (A W Carroll) *hld up: hdwy 3f out: rdn and wknd wl over 1f out* **14/1**	25
-300	10	30	**Mollyatti**[9] 2190 3-8-13 **64**..... EdwardCreighton 4 — (Miss V Haigh) *w ldrs tl rdn 3f out: wknd qckly: t.o* **33/1**	—

1m 15.12s (2.22) **Going Correction** +0.45s/f (Yiel) **10 Ran SP% 117.7**
Speed ratings (Par 96): **103,101,99,98,96 92,92,86,86,46**
CSF £59.97 CT £237.64 TOTE £11.20: £2.20, £2.10, £1.90; EX 35.80.
Owner J Spence **Bred** The C H F Partnership **Trained** Kingsclere, Hants

FOCUS
A contest hit hard by six non-runners, five of them due to the ground. This was just a fair race of its type and although the stalls were against the far rail, the field came down the centre. Those drawn low never really got a look in. Pretty sound form considering the ground, the winner cofirming her impressive Kempton win.
Infinite Patience Official explanation: jockey said filly was unsuited by the soft ground

2453 E.B.F./FREEBETS.CO.UK FILLIES' H'CAP — 1m 4f 23y
4:40 (4:40) (Class 5) (0-75,74) 4-Y-O+ — £3,885 (£1,156; £577; £288) Stalls Low

Form				RPR
-021	1		**Stringsofmyheart**[13] 2078 4-8-12 **65**..... DarryllHolland 6 — (Miss Gay Kelleway) *led: hdd over 3f out: rdn over 2f out: rallied to ld last strides* **3/1**[2]	72
/0-6	2	hd	**Queen Excalibur**[7] 2241 9-7-9 **55** oh10.....(p) DavidProbert(7) 9 — (C Roberts) *a.p: wnt 2nd over 5f out: led over 3f out: rdn over 1f out: hdd last strides* **50/1**	61
3322	3	2	**Friends Hope**[1] 2423 7-9-5 **72**..... TPO'Shea 2 — (P A Blockley) *dropped out s: hld up in rr: hmpd bnd 6f out: hdwy on ins over 3f out: rdn 2f out: nt qckn ins fnl f* **3/1**[2]	75
56-0	4	1	**Looktheotherway (IRE)**[12] 2100 4-8-0 **56**..... LukeMorris(3) 7 — (J G M O'Shea) *towards rr: hdwy over 4f out: rdn over 3f out: styd on same pce fnl f* **10/1**	57
54-0	5	12	**Prelude**[32] 1577 7-9-1 **68**..... LiamJones 5 — (W M Brisbourne) *prom: chsd ldr over 9f out tl over 5f out: rdn 4f out: wknd wl over 2f out* **5/1**[3]	50
6641	6	18	**Karmest**[32] 1577 4-9-0 **67**.....(b) SilvestreDeSousa 3 — (A D Brown) *hld up: stdy hdwy over 6f out: wknd 4f out* **5/2**[1]	20
0-10	7	21	**Harvest Joy (IRE)**[30] 1620 4-9-7 **74**..... FergusSweeney 10 — (J Gallagher) *a bhd: lost tch 4f out: t.o* **12/1**	—
560-	8	19	**Sea Cookie**[57] 6060 4-8-2 **55** oh10.....(p) CatherineGannon 4 — (W De Best-Turner) *chsd ldr over 2f: n.m.r and checked on ins bnd 6f out: sn wknd: t.o* **33/1**	—

2m 47.95s (8.95) **Going Correction** +0.825s/f (Soft) **8 Ran SP% 116.9**
Speed ratings (Par 100): **103,102,101,100,92 80,66,54**
CSF £121.86 CT £492.81 TOTE £4.40: £1.50, £9.90, £1.70; EX 269.60.
Owner bettingjobs.com **Bred** Wretham Stud **Trained** Exning, Suffolk
■ Stewards' Enquiry : David Probert three-day ban: careless riding (Jun 9-11)

FOCUS
An ordinary fillies' handicap, but they went a very decent pace thanks to the eventual winner and the winning time was over two seconds quicker than the following maiden. The form looks weak with the runner-up 17lb wrong and this does not look a race to be with.
Harvest Joy(IRE) Official explanation: jockey said filly never travelled

2454 FREEBETS.CO.UK MAIDEN STKS — 1m 4f 23y
5:15 (5:19) (Class 5) 3-Y-O — £2,590 (£770; £385; £192) Stalls Low

Form				RPR
2-25	1		**Nemo Spirit (IRE)**[18] 1931 3-9-3 85..... RichardMullen 7 — (W R Muir) *s.i.s: hdwy over 7f out: rdn to ld over 1f out: edgd rt wl ins fnl f: r.o* **5/1**[3]	81+
5-24	2	1 1/4	**Manyriverstocross (IRE)**[18] 1931 3-9-3 90..... EddieAhern 10 — (A King) *t.k.h: a.p: rdn wl over 1f out: chsd wnr jst ins fnl f: nt qckn* **10/11**[1]	80+
04	3	6	**Swingkeel (IRE)**[22] 1840 3-9-3 0..... PatDobbs 11 — (J L Dunlop) *hld up: hdwy after 3f: rdn over 3f out: outpcd 2f out: styd on to take 3rd wl ins fnl f* **14/1**	69
6	4	1 1/2	**Karashar (IRE)**[34] 1539 3-9-3 0..... FergusSweeney 2 — (Evan Williams) *s.s: hdwy 5f out: led wl over 1f out: sn rdn and hdd: wknd ins fnl f* **66/1**	67
04	5	1 1/4	**Abstract Colours (IRE)**[20] 1896 3-9-3 0..... LPKeniry 9 — (A M Balding) *w ldr: led over 2f out: rdn and hdd wl over 1f out: wknd fnl f* **40/1**	65
06-	6	6	**Bosamcliff (IRE)**[208] 6585 3-8-9 0..... KevinGhunowa(3) 15 — (A B Haynes) *t.k.h: prom: lost pl after 3f: no real prog fnl 2f* **50/1**	50
3	7	4	**Albarouche**[31] 1599 3-8-12 0..... DarryllHolland 6 — (M A Jarvis) *led: rdn and hdd over 2f out: wknd over 1f out* **9/4**[2]	44
0	8	4 1/2	**Seedless**[31] 1599 3-8-12 0..... FrancisNorton 8 — (A M Balding) *t.k.h: sn stdd into mid-div: rdn over 5f out: bhd fnl 3f* **14/1**	37
-0	9	10	**Kennyboy**[30] 1621 3-8-10 0..... KylieManser(7) 1 — (Mrs H Sweeting) *prom: lost pl over 6f out: bhd fnl 5f* **150/1**	26
0	10	2 1/4	**Lovespell (USA)**[11] 2123 3-8-9 0..... TravisBlock(3) 14 — (H Morrison) *sn in rr* **66/1**	17
0	11	8	**Fielder (IRE)**[34] 1549 3-9-3 0..... TPO'Shea 4 — (J G Portman) *s.i.s: a bhd* **100/1**	9
6	12	45	**Heroic Lad**[34] 1549 3-8-10 0..... GihanArnolda(7) 13 — (A B Haynes) *plld hrd: mid-div: wknd over 4f out: t.o* **100/1**	—

2m 50.08s (11.08) **Going Correction** +0.825s/f (Soft) **12 Ran SP% 124.2**
Speed ratings (Par 99): **96,95,91,90,89 85,82,79,73,71 66,36**
CSF £10.31 TOTE £5.80: £1.60, £1.10, £2.90; EX 12.20 Place 6: £19.40, Place 5: £11.31..
Owner Mrs Monique V Bruce Copp **Bred** Gainsborough Stud Management Ltd **Trained** Lambourn, Berks

FOCUS
An uncompetitive maiden with only three of the 12 runners starting at less than 14-1 and the front pair, rated 85 and 90 respectively, proved far too good for the rest. Neither had to run to their best and some of those behind could be flattered to a degree. The pace was only ordinary and the time was over two seconds slower than the fillies' handicap.
Karashar(IRE) Official explanation: jockey said gelding lost its action 1f out
Lovespell(USA) Official explanation: jockey said filly hung left-handed
T/Plt: £21.70 to a £1 stake. Pool: £62,232.90. 2,084.80 winning tickets. T/Qpdt: £7.20 to a £1 stake. Pool: £3,344.30. 341.70 winning tickets. KH

2275 LEICESTER (R-H)
Monday, May 26

OFFICIAL GOING: Good to firm (firm in places; 9.8) (last race abandoned due to unsafe ground)
Last race abandoned due to unsafe ground on home turn.
Wind: half against Weather: Overcast

2455 KIBWORTH HARCOURT MEDIAN AUCTION MAIDEN STKS — 7f 9y
2:00 (2:02) (Class 5) 3-Y-O — £2,590 (£770; £385; £192) Stalls High

Form				RPR
4	1		**Yahwudhee (FR)**[9] 2198 3-9-3 0..... AdrianMcCarthy 8 — (P W Chapple-Hyam) *trckd ldrs: wnt 2nd 1/2-way: rdn over 1f out: styd on to ld wl ins fnl f* **8/11**[1]	79
4	2	1 1/4	**Caro George (USA)**[28] 1669 3-8-12 0..... SteveDrowne 12 — (R Charlton) *led: rdn and hdd wl ins fnl f* **11/4**[2]	71
	3	3 1/4	**Saintly Gaze** 3-9-3 0..... AdamKirby 10 — (W R Swinburn) *chsd ldr to 1/2-way: rdn over 1f out: styd on same pce* **16/1**	67
40	4	3/4	**Zaarmit (IRE)**[21] 1876 3-9-0 0..... MarcHalford(3) 9 — (D M Simcock) *prom: rdn over 2f out: styd on same pce appr fnl f* **10/1**[3]	65
	5	1 3/4	**Da Bomber (IRE)** 3-9-3 0..... PatrickMathers 6 — (J W Unett) *sn pushed along in rr: hdwy over 2f out: styd on same pce appr fnl f* **50/1**	60
50	6	2 1/2	**Plum Asset (USA)**[27] 1709 3-8-12 0..... JamesDoyle 5 — (R M Beckett) *hld up: hdwy 1/2-way: rdn over 1f out: sn wknd* **16/1**	48
06	7	2 3/4	**Poulaine Bleue**[21] 1869 3-8-12 0..... HayleyTurner 3 — (M L W Bell) *hld up: nvr nr to chal* **40/1**	41
50	8	7	**Benhego**[25] 1748 3-8-10 0..... WilliamCarson(7) 7 — (S C Williams) *hld up: a in rr: wknd over 2f out* **20/1**	27
	9	1 1/2	**Mensadil** 3-9-3 0..... DaneO'Neill 1 — (Mrs L Stubbs) *wnt lft s: sn prom: rdn 1/2-way: wknd over 2f out* **50/1**	23

1m 27.95s (1.75) **Going Correction** +0.20s/f (Good) **9 Ran SP% 119.5**
Speed ratings (Par 99): **98,96,92,92,90 87,84,76,74**
CSF £2.71 TOTE £1.80: £1.10, £1.10, £2.80; EX 2.70 Trifecta £17.40 Pool: £244.91 - 9.97 winning units..
Owner Jaber Abdullah **Bred** Gainsborough Stud Management Ltd **Trained** Newmarket, Suffolk

FOCUS
An ordinary maiden in which the front two finished clear. Sound form.
Plum Asset(USA) Official explanation: jockey said filly hung left-handed
Benhego Official explanation: jockey said gelding hung right-handed

2456 GILMORTON (S) STKS — 1m 1f 218y
2:35 (2:35) (Class 6) 3-5-Y-O — £1,942 (£578; £288; £144) Stalls High

Form				RPR
2511	1		**One Night In Paris (IRE)**[30] 1636 5-9-0 70..... RichardEvans(7) 8 — (P D Evans) *hld up in tch: chsd ldr 3f out: led 2f out: sn hung rt: styd on* **11/4**[1]	61
-040	2	1 1/2	**Hester Brook (IRE)**[47] 1269 4-9-2 42..... HayleyTurner 9 — (J G M O'Shea) *hld up: hdwy over 3f out: rdn to chse wnr over 1f out: styd on* **16/1**	53
0346	3	5	**Just Intersky (USA)**[10] 1853 5-9-7 60.....(e) DaneO'Neill 1 — (V Smith) *s.s: hld up: hmpd 1/2-way: styd on ins fnl f: nvr nrr* **3/1**[2]	48
5650	4	3/4	**Bothar Brugha (IRE)**[20] 1895 4-9-4 43..... RussellKennemore(3) 4 — (J G M O'Shea) *chsd ldrs: slipped on bnd 1/2-way and rn wd: led over 3f out: rdn and hdd 2f out: wknd over 1f out* **50/1**	46
40-0	5	3 1/4	**Miss Percy**[31] 1602 4-9-2 50.....(p) LeeEnstone 5 — (I W McInnes) *chsd ldrs: rdn over 2f out: wknd over 1f out* **14/1**	35
5040	6	2 1/2	**Skye But N Ben**[20] 1890 4-9-7 48.....(p) JamesDoyle 10 — (G A Harker) *s.i.s: hld up: hmpd 1/2-way: hdwy u.p over 1f out: wknd fnl f* **6/1**	35
05	7	4	**Brutus Maximus**[40] 1391 5-9-7 0.....(b) PatrickMathers 12 — (I W McInnes) *hld up: rdn over 3f out: wknd over 1f out* **25/1**	27
3000	8	3/4	**Queen Macha (IRE)**[7] 2260 3-8-2 56..... DavidKinsella 13 — (A M Hales) *chsd ldrs: rdn over 3f out: wknd over 1f out* **14/1**	20
/0-5	9	8	**Bond Cruz**[30] 1636 5-9-7 37..... SteveDrowne 7 — (D Burchell) *sn led: rdn and hdd over 3f out: wknd over 2f out* **28/1**	9
4033	10	64	**Mick Is Back**[13] 2069 4-9-7 53.....(vt) GeorgeBaker 2 — (G G Margarson) *hld up: hmpd 1/2-way: eased* **5/1**[3]	—
00-0	11	30	**Mellifluous (IRE)**[21] 1855 3-8-2 45..... ChrisCatlin 6 — (J W Hills) *hld up: hmpd 1/2-way: eased* **22/1**	—
600-	F		**Flamestone**[11] 6108 4-9-0 40.....(p) BillyCray(7) 3 — (A E Price) *hld up: slipped and fell 1/2-way* **66/1**	—

2m 10.7s (2.80) **Going Correction** +0.325s/f (Good)
WFA 3 from 4yo+ 14lb **12 Ran SP% 116.9**
Speed ratings (Par 101): **101,99,95,95,92 90,87,86,80,29 5,—**
CSF £44.28 TOTE £3.30: £1.50, £5.00, £1.40; EX 61.10 Trifecta £34.50 Pool: £224.62 - 4.61 winning units..There was no bid for the winner.
Owner Diamond Racing Ltd **Bred** Ken Carroll **Trained** Pandy, Monmouths

FOCUS
A weak seller in which the winner was the clear pick on her best form. Flamestone came down after slipping at around halfway, hampering several of his rivals.

Bothar Brugha(IRE) Official explanation: jockey said gelding hung badly left

2457 LEICESTER MERCURY FAMILY FUN DAY FILLIES' H'CAP 7f 9y

3:10 (3:11) (Class 4) (0-80,80) 4-Y-0+

£6,231 (£1,866; £933; £467; £233; £117) **Stalls** High

Form				RPR
5-30	1		**Farley Star**[34] 1545 4-9-4 **80** SteveDrowne 6	88
			(R Charlton) *chsd ldrs: rdn to ld ins fnl f: r.o* **9/4**[2]	
1405	2	*nk*	**Hessian (IRE)**[4] 2329 4-8-4 **66** oh1 ChrisCatlin 8	73
			(M D Squance) *hld up: nt clr run: swtchd lft and hdwy over 1f out: rdn and hung rt ins fnl f: r.o* **4/1**[3]	
-015	3	*2 1/4*	**Secret Night**[51] 1211 5-8-11 **73** AdamKirby 5	74
			(C G Cox) *led: rdn over 1f out: hdd and unable qck ins fnl f* **2/1**[1]	
1023	4	*1 1/2*	**High 'n Dry (IRE)**[17] 1954 4-8-7 **69** (p) PaulDoe 2	66
			(M A Allen) *chsd ldrs: rdn over 1f out: styd on same pce fnl f* **15/2**	
3200	5	*3 1/4*	**Dasheena**[7] 2263 5-7-11 **66** oh2 (v[1]) MCGeran(7) 9	54
			(A J McCabe) *chsd ldr: rdn and ev ch over 1f out: wknd ins fnl f* **25/1**	
-104	6	*1 1/4*	**Cinnamon Hill**[21] 1858 4-8-9 **71** HayleyTurner 1	56
			(Eve Johnson Houghton) *wnt lft s: hld up: plld hrd: rdn over 2f out: hmpd wl over 1f out: wknd fnl f* **14/1**	
06-0	7	*2 1/4*	**Emulate**[9] 2203 4-8-11 **73** IanMongan 10	52
			(C F Wall) *hld up: hdwy over 1f out: rdn and wknd over 1f out* **12/1**	

1m 27.1s (0.90) **Going Correction** +0.20s/f (Good) 7 Ran SP% **114.1**
Speed ratings (Par 102): **102,101,99,97,93 92,89**
CSF £11.69 CT £19.76 TOTE £3.30: £1.70, £2.20; EX 14.60 Trifecta £38.90 Pool: £540.65 - 9.86 winning units..
Owner A Parker (London) **Bred** Alan Parker **Trained** Beckhampton, Wilts
■ Stewards' Enquiry : Chris Catlin two-day ban: careless riding (Jun 9-10)

FOCUS
Just a fair fillies' handicap run at a good pace. The winner ran to her best sand form, with the second up 9lb on old turf form.

2458 ENDERBY MEDIAN AUCTION MAIDEN STKS 5f 2y

3:45 (3:46) (Class 5) 2-Y-0 **£2,590** (£770; £385; £192) **Stalls** Low

Form				RPR
2	1		**Brae Hill (IRE)**[11] 2117 2-9-3 0 HayleyTurner 9	94+
			(M L W Bell) *mde all: shkn up over 1f out: r.o strly* **11/10**[1]	
6	2	*7*	**Liturgical (USA)**[12] 2098 2-9-3 0 KerrinMcEvoy 7	69
			(M A Magnusson) *s.i.s: hld up: hdwy 1/2-way: rdn to chse wnr and hung lft 1f out: no ex* **5/1**[3]	
2	3	*2 1/2*	**Lucky Redback (IRE)**[6] 2275 2-9-3 0 DaneO'Neill 4	60
			(R Hannon) *prom: racd keenly: rdn over 1f out: wkng whn hung rt ins fnl f* **6/1**	
35	4	*shd*	**Desire To Excel (IRE)**[11] 2124 2-9-3 0 TQuinn 8	60
			(P F I Cole) *chsd ldrs: rdn 1/2-way: wkng whn hmpd 1f out* **9/4**[2]	
	5	*6*	**Time Loup** 2-9-3 0 SteveDrowne 2	38
			(Miss E C Lavelle) *hld up in tch: shkn up and hung lft fr 1/2-way: sn wknd* **33/1**	
04	6	*3/4*	**Taurus Twins**[17] 1955 2-8-12 0 JackDean(5) 6	35
			(W G M Turner) *chsd wnr: rdn 1/2-way: wknd over 1f out* **33/1**	
6	7	*6*	**August Days (IRE)**[22] 1838 2-8-12 0 JamesDoyle 3	9
			(R M Beckett) *chsd ldrs to 1/2-way* **20/1**	
	8	*10*	**Blushing Bertie** 2-9-3 0 PatrickMathers 5	—
			(J W Unett) *sn outpcd* **50/1**	
	9	*30*	**Colin Staite** 2-9-3 0 IanMongan 1	—
			(R Brotherton) *s.s: outpcd* **66/1**	

62.20 secs (2.20) **Going Correction** +0.20s/f (Good) 9 Ran SP% **123.4**
Speed ratings (Par 93): **90,78,74,74,65 63,54,38,—**
CSF £7.66 TOTE £2.30: £1.10, £1.70, £1.70; EX 4.00 Trifecta £22.00 Pool: £501.47 - 16.18 winning units..
Owner Thurloe Partners **Bred** James Doyle **Trained** Newmarket, Suffolk

FOCUS
An ordinary maiden, but an impressive winner in the form of Brae Hill who thrashed the opposition, although it is hard to tell exactly what he achieved.

NOTEBOOK
Brae Hill(IRE) built on the form he showed when second on his debut at Newmarket with an impressive performance, drawing well clear in the closing stages having shown good pace throughout. He may now be aimed at the Windsor Castle at Royal Ascot. (op 6-5 tchd evens and 5-4)
Liturgical(USA) was well held on his debut at Bath, but this was a little better. He was still beaten a long way, and it remains to be seen exactly what he achieved, but he seems to be going the right way. (op 8-1)
Lucky Redback(IRE) did not really build on the promise he showed when second at 40/1 on his debut over course and distance six days earlier. (tchd 5-1)
Desire To Excel(IRE) failed to build on his debut third at Newmarket when only fifth at Salisbury last time, and this was another ordinary effort. He does not seem to be progressing. (op 5-2 tchd 7-2 in places)
Time Loup, a 2,000gns son of Loup Sauvage, half-brother to a multiple winner in US, out of a triple 7f-1m winner at three, was beaten a long way and probably needs more time. (op 50-1)
Colin Staite Official explanation: jockey said colt missed the break

2459 SKEFFINGTON CLAIMING STKS 5f 218y

4:20 (4:20) (Class 6) 2-Y-0 **£2,331** (£693; £346; £173) **Stalls** High

Form				RPR
30	1		**Asian Tale (IRE)**[14] 2035 2-8-10 0 LeeEnstone 4	73+
			(P C Haslam) *hld up in tch: led over 1f out: shkn up and sn clr* **9/4**[2]	
550	2	*10*	**Crewezando**[18] 1924 2-8-5 0 SimonWhitworth 3	37
			(P D Evans) *chsd ldrs: led over 2f out: rdn and hdd over 1f out: wknd ins fnl f* **4/1**[3]	
	3	*hd*	**Inca Slew (IRE)** 2-8-8 0 DeanHeslop(7) 1	46+
			(P C Haslam) *dwlt and wnt lft s: outpcd: styd on ins fnl f: nvr trbld ldrs* **11/1**	
242	4	*2 1/4*	**Sub Prime (IRE)**[14] 2049 2-8-13 0 SteveDrowne 2	37
			(J A Osborne) *chsd ldrs: rdn and wknd over 1f out* **15/8**[1]	
3520	5	*8*	**Syrup (IRE)**[8] 2216 2-8-1 0 ow1 ChrisCatlin 6	1
			(P D Evans) *led: rdn and hdd over 2f out: wknd wl over 1f out* **10/1**	
	6	*4 1/2*	**Inn Swinger (IRE)** 2-8-3 0 JackDean(5) 5	—
			(W G M Turner) *chsd ldrs: rdn and ev ch over 2f out: hung rt and wknd wl over 1f out* **9/1**	

1m 15.42s (2.42) **Going Correction** +0.20s/f (Good) 6 Ran SP% **113.0**
Speed ratings (Par 91): **91,77,77,74,63 57**
CSF £11.80 TOTE £3.00: £2.10, £2.50; EX 13.10.The winner was claimed by A B Haynes for £11,000.
Owner Middleham Park Racing XXXIX **Bred** Hong Kong Breeders Club **Trained** Middleham Moor, N Yorks

FOCUS
A weak juvenile claimer in which the easy winner could be a fair bit better than rated.

NOTEBOOK
Asian Tale(IRE) had shown just moderate form in a couple of 5f maidens, but she absolutely bolted up over this extra furlong on this drop in grade. She looks a little better than this level and was claimed for £11,000 by Andy Haynes. (op 5-2 tchd 2-1 and 11-4 in places)
Crewezando, without the visor on this drop in grade and step up in trip, was no match for the winner and ran to a very moderate level. (op 11-4 tchd 9-2)
Inca Slew(IRE), a 6,500gns gelded son of City On A Hill, brother to triple 5f-6f two-year-old winner Hucking Hill, was soon detached after starting slowly, but he eventually got the hang of things and finished well. He can improve significantly for this experience. (op 14-1 tchd 10-1)
Sub Prime(IRE) was a major disappointment on his first start on turf and has now been a beaten favourite on his last three starts. (op 9-4)

2460 LEICESTERSHIRE AND RUTLAND LIFE H'CAP 5f 218y

4:55 (4:56) (Class 4) (0-80,80) 3-Y-0 **£4,209** (£1,252; £625; £312) **Stalls** High

Form				RPR
6125	1		**We Have A Dream**[22] 1837 3-9-2 **78** KerrinMcEvoy 8	84
			(W R Muir) *mde all: rdn over 1f out: jst hld on* **3/1**[1]	
14-1	2	*nse*	**Mission Impossible**[54] 1155 3-8-13 **75** LeeEnstone 10	81
			(P C Haslam) *a.p: chsd wnr over 3f out: rdn over 1f out: ev ch ins fnl f: r.o* **7/1**	
0-21	3	*3/4*	**Opera Prince**[16] 2014 3-9-1 **77** SteveDrowne 2	85+
			(S Kirk) *slipped leaving stalls: outpcd: hung rt and r.o wl ins fnl f: nt rch ldrs* **4/1**[2]	
01-0	4	*nk*	**Flashy Photon**[39] 1426 3-9-1 **77** DaneO'Neill 5	79
			(H Candy) *hld up: hdwy over 2f out: rdn over 1f out: styd on* **9/2**[3]	
33-0	5	*4*	**Lake Sabina**[16] 1988 3-8-11 **73** TQuinn 4	63
			(E S McMahon) *prom: rdn over 1f out: wknd fnl f* **12/1**	
3-61	6	*hd*	**Capone (IRE)**[23] 1819 3-8-13 **75** ChrisCatlin 7	64
			(Garry Moss) *chsd ldrs: rdn over 1f out: hung rt and wknd ins fnl f* **7/1**	
5-50	7	*4 1/2*	**Tadalavil**[53] 1167 3-8-11 **80** MCGeran(7) 1	55
			(M R Channon) *chsd ldrs over 4f* **13/2**	
-261	8	*4*	**Magical Speedfit (IRE)**[13] 2068 3-9-1 **77** AdamKirby 3	39
			(G G Margarson) *chsd ldrs: rdn over 2f out: wkng whn n.m.r wl over 1f out* **14/1**	

1m 13.83s (0.83) **Going Correction** +0.20s/f (Good) 8 Ran SP% **115.9**
Speed ratings (Par 101): **102,101,100,100,95 94,88,83**
CSF £24.86 CT £85.40 TOTE £4.00: £1.30, £2.70, £2.00; EX 23.50 Trifecta £73.90 Pool: £437.52 - 4.20 winning units. Place 6: £15.87, Place 5: £13.62..
Owner The Dreaming Squires **Bred** Whitsbury Manor Stud **Trained** Lambourn, Berks

FOCUS
A fair sprint handicap. The winner recorded a slight career best and the third looked unlucky.
Opera Prince ◆ Official explanation: jockey said gelding stumbled on leaving stalls

2461 TIGERS APPRENTICE H'CAP 1m 3f 183y

() (Class 6) (0-60,) 4-Y-0+ £

T/Plt: £13.00 to a £1 stake. Pool: £55,502.90. 3097.20 winning tickets. T/Qpdt: £11.00 to a £1 stake. Pool: £2,864.20. 191.10 winning tickets. CR

2035 REDCAR (L-H)

Monday, May 26

OFFICIAL GOING: Good to firm (firm in places)
Wind: Moderate against Weather: Sunny and windy

2462 WINNING SYNDICATES WITH MIDDLEHAM PARK RACING MAIDEN AUCTION STKS 5f

2:05 (2:07) (Class 5) 2-Y-0 **£2,456** (£725; £362) **Stalls** Centre

Form				RPR
	1		**Rowayton** 2-8-8 0 PhilipRobinson 3	76+
			(J D Bethell) *trckd ldrs: smooth hdwy to ld over 1f out: sn rdn clr* **6/1**	
26	2	*2 3/4*	**Musical Bridge**[18] 1924 2-8-13 0 TolleyDean(3) 6	74
			(Mrs L Williamson) *prom: effrt 2f out and sn ev ch rdn over 1f out and kpt on same pce ins fnl f* **7/2**[3]	
53	3	*1/2*	**The Magic Of Rio**[14] 2048 2-8-9 0 RHills 8	65
			(W J Haggas) *cl up: led 2f out: rdn and hdd over 1f out: one pce ins fnl f* **10/3**[2]	
3	4	*nk*	**Favourite Girl (IRE)**[40] 1390 2-8-9 0 DavidAllan 12	64
			(T D Easterby) *in tch: hdwy 2f out and sn ev ch: rdn over 1f out and kpt on same pce ins fnl f* **3/1**[1]	
00	5	*3*	**Lucky Buddha**[17] 1967 2-8-11 0 PaulHanagan 4	55
			(Jedd O'Keeffe) *chsd ldrs: rdn along 2f out and grad wknd* **20/1**	
0	6	*1 1/2*	**Compton Ford**[51] 1220 2-9-3 0 PaulMulrennan 1	56
			(M Dods) *led: rdn along 1/2-way: hdd 2f out: sn rdn and grad wknd* **20/1**	
300	7	*3 1/4*	**Marygate (IRE)**[9] 2206 2-8-4 0 TWilliams 11	31
			(M Brittain) *towards rr: rdn along 1/2-way: nvr a factor* **25/1**	
	8	*shd*	**Miss Gibboa (IRE)** 2-8-7 0 TedDurcan 7	34
			(G A Swinbank) *a in rr* **12/1**	
02	9	*4 1/2*	**El Bobby (IRE)**[14] 2035 2-8-9 0 DO'Donohoe 9	19
			(J R Weymes) *chsd ldrs: rdn along 1/2-way: sn wknd* **7/1**	
0	10	*3*	**Excitable (IRE)**[9] 2186 2-8-4 0 JimmyQuinn 10	—
			(Miss V Haigh) *in tch: rdn along 1/2-way: sn wknd* **40/1**	
6	11	*5*	**Sally Bond (IRE)**[19] 1907 2-8-2 0 (b[1]) DuranFentiman(3) 2	—
			(T D Easterby) *a in rr* **50/1**	

60.16 secs (1.56) **Going Correction** +0.15s/f (Good) 11 Ran SP% **122.5**
Speed ratings (Par 93): **93,88,87,87,82 80,74,74,67,62 54**
CSF £26.81 TOTE £8.50: £2.50, £1.70, £1.70; EX 45.10.
Owner Mrs J E Vickers **Bred** Miss R J Dobson **Trained** Middleham Moor, N Yorks

FOCUS
An average juvenile maiden in which the placed horses set the standard.

NOTEBOOK
Rowayton, who is bred to be all about speed, has been working with older horses at home and she knew her job. Always going nicely, she quickly settled the issue over a furlong out and ran out a stylish winner. A trip to Royal Ascot beckons for the daughter of Lujain, but she will obviously find things a lot tougher there. (op 8-1)
Musical Bridge, who lost all chance when hampered mid-race at Chester last time, had been beaten just a nose on his debut at Bath and this was more like his true form. He will benefit from an extra furlong before long and looks capable of winning an ordinary maiden. (tchd 10-3)
The Magic Of Rio, who improved on her debut effort to finish third at Wolverhampton last time, was made more use of on this occasion and again ran well, but the winner proved too classy. She is another for whom a sixth furlong will suit. (op 3-1 tchd 7-2)
Favourite Girl(IRE), who came home well for third on her debut at Beverley, was made favourite, but she had looked to be crying out for 6f that day and again gave that impression. She is only ordinary, but may yet be capable of improvement at further and in nurseries. (op 7-2)

Lucky Buddha has improved a little with each start and he will be of definite interest once nurseries roll around. (op 40-1 tchd 18-1)

2463 SUBSCRIBE TO RACING UK (S) STKS 7f
2:40 (2:41) (Class 6) 3-5-Y-O £1,774 (£523; £262) **Stalls Centre**

Form RPR

250- **1** **Lewis Lloyd (IRE)**[198] 4920 5-9-2 44 SladeO'Hara(5) 4 57
(R E Barr) *in tch: hdwy over 2f out: rdn to ld ent fnl f: drvn out* **33/1**

3200 **2** *2 1/2* **Desert Hunter (IRE)**[68] 933 5-9-7 46 JimmyQuinn 11 50
(Micky Hammond) *hld up towards rr: swtchd lft and hdwy over 2f out: rdn to chse wnr ent fnl f: kpt on* **10/1**

0346 **3** *3 3/4* **Jevington Star (IRE)**[7] 2247 3-8-10 44 (b[1]) J-PGuillambert 10 36
(B Ellison) *prom: led 3f out: rdn 2f out: drvn and hdd ent fnl f: kpt on same pce* **12/1**

0003 **4** *nk* **Buzzin'Boyzee (IRE)**[7] 2250 5-9-8 48 JimCrowley 12 40
(D W Barker) *midfield: hdwy over 2f out: sn rdn and kpt on ins fnl f: nrst fin* **7/1[3]**

-000 **5** *3/4* **First Valentini**[14] 2036 4-9-2 38 PaulFessey 7 32
(N Bycroft) *prom: rdn along over 2f and ev ch tl wknd ent fnl f* **80/1**

0-06 **6** *1/2* **College Land Boy**[7] 2250 4-9-7 48 PaulMulrennan 1 36
(A Kirtley) *chsd ldrs far side: rdn along and outpcd 3f out: styd on u.p fnl f* **28/1**

-604 **7** *1* **Kadia**[25] 1752 5-9-2 45 MickyFenton 6 28
(P T Midgley) *prom tl rdn along 2f out and grad wknd* **12/1**

4530 **8** *1/2* **Jaassey**[14] 2040 5-9-7 45 (t) DO'Donohoe 14 32
(J S Wainwright) *s.i.s and bhd tl styd on wl fnl 2f* **14/1**

0056 **9** *1/2* **Scruffy Skip (IRE)**[14] 2041 3-8-10 53 (p) PaulHanagan 17 26
(C R Dore) *in tch stands' side: rdn along over 2f out: sn no imp* **8/1**

6035 **10** *nse* **Hero Heart**[37] 1487 3-8-10 45 FrankieMcDonald 2 26
(Jane Chapple-Hyam) *chsd ldrs on outer: rdn along over 2f out: sn drvn and wknd* **25/1**

00-0 **11** *1/2* **Harlequinn Danseur (IRE)**[17] 1968 3-8-10 51 KimTinkler 9 25
(N Tinkler) *chsd ldrs: rdn along over 2f out: sn no imp* **40/1**

0006 **12** *2 3/4* **River Gleam (IRE)**[17] 1968 3-8-5 44 (v) WilliamBuick 15 12
(A P Jarvis) *led: pushed along and hdd 3f out: sn rdn and grad wknd* **16/1**

-200 **13** *3 1/2* **Piccolo Pete**[19] 1912 3-8-10 57 (p) JohnEgan 20 8
(T P Tate) *towards rr stands' side: hdwy 1/2-way: rdn along and in tch 3f out: sn wknd* **13/2[2]**

3210 **14** *hd* **Our Sunnie**[6] 2268 3-8-3 58 (v) AdeleRothery(7) 19 7
(D Nicholls) *in tch stands' side: rdn along over 2f out and sn wknd* **7/1[3]**

-650 **15** *nk* **Grey Vision**[40] 1391 5-8-9 37 (b) AdamCarter(7) 8 6
(M Brittain) *chsd ldrs 3f: sn wknd* **33/1**

00-0 **16** *4 1/2* **Crafty Fox**[56] 1116 5-9-7 47 (b) DanielTudhope 13 —
(John A Harris) *a towards rr* **20/1**

4-04 **17** *2 3/4* **Bahama Baileys**[6] 2268 3-8-10 67 JoeFanning 5 —
(M Johnston) *prom: rdn along 2f out and sn wknd* **5/1[1]**

000- **18** *9* **Diamond Hurricane (IRE)**[171] 7057 4-9-0 36 (t) SamuelDrury(7) 18 —
(M Wellings) *s.i.s: a bhd* **66/1**

00-0 **19** *7* **Kiowa Princess**[33] 1560 3-8-2 44 AndrewMullen(3) 3 —
(M Dods) *s.i.s: a bhd* **50/1**

-000 **20** *2 1/4* **Watch This Place**[6] 2268 3-8-10 35 (v) AndrewElliott 16 —
(K R Burke) *in tch stands' side to 1/2-way: sn lost pl and bhd* **50/1**

1m 27.93s (3.43) **Going Correction** +0.15s/f (Good)
WFA 3 from 4yo+ 11lb **20** Ran SP% **130.2**
Speed ratings (Par 101): **86,83,78,78,77 77,75,75,74,74 74,71,67,66,66 61,58,47,39,37**
CSF £330.88 TOTE £45.70: £10.00, £3.40, £4.50; EX 501.20.There was no bid for the winner.
Owner Brian Morton **Bred** Brian Delahunt **Trained** Seamer, N Yorks

FOCUS
A weak contest for the grade and the time was slow. The winner returned to his best form.
Jevington Star(IRE) Official explanation: jockey said gelding stumbled on leaving stalls

2464 TOTESPORT BETXTRA WIN ONLY H'CAP 1m 2f
3:15 (3:15) (Class 4) (0-85,84) 3-Y-O £6,476 (£1,927; £963; £481) **Stalls Low**

Form RPR

0-22 **1** **Indian Days**[12] 2109 3-9-2 79 J-PGuillambert 8 92+
(J G Given) *trckd ldrs: smooth hdwy 3f out: led 2f out and sn clr: comf* **5/2[1]**

-231 **2** *3 1/2* **St Jean Cap Ferrat**[37] 1477 3-9-0 77 TedDurcan 7 85+
(G Wragg) *hld up in rr: hdwy on inner 3f out: nt clr run 2f out: rdn to chse wnr appr fnl f: sn no imp* **7/1**

1-03 **3** *3/4* **Mystery Star (IRE)**[12] 2109 3-9-7 84 PaulMulrennan 3 88
(M H Tompkins) *in tch: hdwy over 3f out: rdn 2f out: kpt on same pce* **7/2[3]**

22-0 **4** *4 1/2* **Bavarian Nordic (USA)**[32] 1579 3-8-8 74 AndrewMullen(3) 5 69
(Mrs A Duffield) *hld up towards rr: hdwy over 3f out: rdn along 2f out and kpt on same pce* **20/1**

436- **5** *nk* **Reel Buddy Blaze**[244] 5702 3-8-7 70 MickyFenton 2 64
(T P Tate) *led 2f: cl up tl led again 3f out: sn rdn and hdd 2f out: grad wknd* **20/1**

-006 **6** *2* **Lady Sorcerer**[18] 1930 3-8-6 69 WilliamBuick 6 59
(A P Jarvis) *hld up: rdn along and reminders 1/2-way: sme hdwy 3f out: nvr a factor* **18/1**

-314 **7** *3/4* **Fujin Dancer (FR)**[12] 2109 3-8-8 71 PaulHanagan 4 60
(R A Fahey) *trckd ldng pair: hdwy on inner 3f out and ev ch tl rdn 2f out and sn btn* **11/4[2]**

16 **8** *5* **Al Samha (USA)**[21] 1875 3-9-7 84 JoeFanning 1 63
(M Johnston) *cl up: led after 2f: rdn along and hdd 3f out: sn wknd* **8/1**

2m 6.86s (-0.24) **Going Correction** +0.15s/f (Good) **8** Ran SP% **115.9**
Speed ratings (Par 101): **106,103,102,99,98 97,96,92**
CSF £20.96 CT £59.43 TOTE £3.00: £1.80, £2.10, £1.80; EX 23.40.
Owner D J Fish **Bred** Mrs C C Regalado-Gonzalez **Trained** Willoughton, Lincs
■ Stewards' Enquiry : Paul Mulrennan one-day ban: careless ring (Jun 9)

FOCUS
A decent handicap in which Indian Days extended his York superiority over today's third and seventh. The form looks sound.
Fujin Dancer(FR) Official explanation: trainer had no explanation for the poor form shown

2465 TOTESPORT BETXTRA ZETLAND GOLD CUP (HERITAGE H'CAP) 1m 2f
3:50 (3:52) (Class 2) (0-105,103) 3-Y-O+£32,380 (£9,635; £4,815; £2,405) **Stalls Low**

Form RPR

2030 **1** **Capable Guest (IRE)**[12] 2103 6-8-12 91 (v) JoeFanning 10 100
(M R Channon) *hld up towards rr: stdy hdwy on outer 3f out: chal wl over 1f out: rdn to ld ent fnl f: kpt on wl* **25/1**

21-3 **2** *1/2* **Fragrancy (IRE)**[16] 1981 4-8-12 91 PhilipRobinson 2 99
(M A Jarvis) *a.p: hdwy 3f out: led 2f out and sn rdn: hdd ent fnl f: drvn and kpt on wl towards fin* **7/2[1]**

216- **3** *1/2* **Monte Alto (IRE)**[233] 6011 4-9-6 99 NickyMackay 7 106+
(L M Cumani) *in tch: hdwy on outer 3f out: rdn and ev ch over 1f out: drvn and kpt on wl fnl f* **4/1[2]**

26-4 **4** *hd* **Docofthebay (IRE)**[11] 2133 4-9-10 103 ShaneKelly 9 110
(J A Osborne) *hld up: hdwy over 2f out: rdn and styd on ins fnl f: nrst fin* **7/1**

06-4 **5** *1* **Smart Instinct (USA)**[12] 2103 4-9-1 94 (p) PaulHanagan 5 101+
(R A Fahey) *in tch: pushed along and outpcd 3f out: rdn and hdwy wl over 1f out: styng on whn nt clr run and hmpd ins fnl f: swtchd rt and kpt on* **11/2[3]**

5064 **6** *3/4* **Snoqualmie Boy**[36] 1503 5-9-4 97 JohnEgan 4 100
(Jane Chapple-Hyam) *chsd ldrs: rdn along over 3f out: drvn 2f out and grad wknd* **14/1**

4101 **7** *1* **Re Barolo (IRE)**[26] 1724 5-9-7 100 (t) JimmyQuinn 1 101
(M Botti) *chsd ldrs: rdn along wl over 2f out: drvn and wknd wl over 1f out* **10/1**

5525 **8** *nk* **Yarqus**[34] 1545 5-8-6 90 (tp) AhmedAjtebi(5) 13 91
(C E Brittain) *hld up towards rr: hdwy on inner 3f out: rdn to chse ldrs 2f out: sn drvn and one pce appr fnl f* **16/1**

-211 **9** *3* **First Buddy**[24] 1771 4-9-4 97 TedDurcan 8 92
(G A Swinbank) *prom: rdn along 3f out: sn drvn and wknd fnl 2f* **8/1**

1-22 **10** *nk* **Jewelled Dagger (IRE)**[8] 2218 4-8-11 90 (b) DanielTudhope 15 84
(Miss L A Perratt) *led: rdn along 3f out: hdd 2f out and sn wknd* **14/1**

-056 **11** *3* **Grand Passion (IRE)**[58] 1077 8-9-9 102 JimCrowley 14 90
(G Wragg) *hld up: a towards rr* **16/1**

6-66 **12** *8* **Smart Enough**[24] 1767 5-9-10 103 MickyFenton 3 75+
(M A Magnusson) *dwlt: in rr whn stmbld bnd over 5f out: a bhd* **25/1**

040- **13** *10* **Fort Churchill (IRE)**[233] 6011 7-8-8 87 (bt) J-PGuillambert 12 39
(B Ellison) *v s.i.s: a bhd* **50/1**

2m 6.75s (-0.35) **Going Correction** +0.15s/f (Good) **13** Ran SP% **125.1**
Speed ratings (Par 109): **107,106,106,106,105 104,103,103,101,100 98,92,84**
CSF £114.37 CT £448.02 TOTE £31.30: £6.20, £2.00, £2.10; EX 96.80 Trifecta £640.20 Pool: £901.80 - 1 winning unit.
Owner John Guest **Bred** Mountarmstrong Stud **Trained** West Ilsley, Berks

FOCUS
A high-quality and very competitive handicap, but it was a bit messy and was run in a relatively modest time. Capable Guest was a surprise winner, rated to his best form of the last two years.

NOTEBOOK
Capable Guest(IRE), who has not won as many races as his ability has entitled him to over the years, finished last of 12 behind Folk Opera at York last time and looked to hold little chance. Somebody knew better was expected though, the outsider being nibbled at in the market beforehand, and, having moved strongly into contention, he found plenty under pressure to hold on well. This was the highest mark he has ever won off and there must be some doubt as to whether he can go in again off a mark in the mid-to-high 90s. Official explanation: trainer's rep said, regarding the apparent improvement in form, gelding had benefited from a change of tactics in that he had been kept wide of the field on this oocasion and possibly improved for a reaaplication of a visor (op 33-1)
Fragrancy(IRE), third off this mark at Ascot on her reappearance, was trying this trip for the first time and she saw it out well under a positive ride, but was unable to match the gritty winner. She seems to be improving still. (op 5-1)
Monte Alto(IRE), a most progressive three-year-old who finished sixth off this mark in the Cambridgeshire on his final start last term, responded well to pressure and came with what looked a winning challenge inside the final furlong, but he was unable to go past and may just have needed it. This was a bright start to his campaign. (tchd 7-2 and 9-2)
Docofthebay(IRE), who would not have been suited by the small field on his reappearance at York, took his racing well last season and this effort again suggested he will pay his way in competitive handicaps. He was a shade unfortunate not to finish closer, being a bit pressed for room, and can be rated a little better than the bare form. (op 15-2 tchd 13-2)
Smart Instinct(USA), well ahead of Capable Guest at York last time, had the cheekpieces back on and he looked unlucky not to finish closer, being impeded inside the final furlong. He too can be rated better than the bare form. (op 6-1 tchd 7-1)
Snoqualmie Boy has always struggled in handicaps and he ran about as well as could have been expected. He is not an easy horse to win with. (op 16-1)
Re Barolo(IRE), a dual All-Weather winner this season, struggled in this more competitive handicap and seemed to find a mark of 100 beyond him. Official explanation: jockey said horse lost its action (op 11-1 tchd 12-1)
First Buddy has been most progressive in soft ground, but the faster conditions and 12lb higher mark seemed to find him out on this hat-trick bid. (op 7-1)
Smart Enough lost his footing on the bend and never threatened thereafter. Official explanation: jockey said gelding slipped on the bend (op 28-1)
Fort Churchill(IRE) Official explanation: jockey said gelding missed the break

2466 MARKET CROSS JEWELLERS MEDIAN AUCTION MAIDEN STKS 6f
4:25 (4:26) (Class 5) 3-Y-O £2,331 (£693; £346; £173) **Stalls Centre**

Form RPR

5-6 **1** **Film Maker (IRE)**[9] 2198 3-9-3 0 RobertHavlin 3 82+
(B J Meehan) *hld up in tch: hdwy on outer 2f out: shkn up to ld over 1f out and sn clr: easily* **4/5[1]**

2 *6* **Monaadema (IRE)** 3-8-12 0 RHills 11 58
(W J Haggas) *prom: effrt and ev ch 2f out: sn rdn and kpt on same pce appr fnl f* **13/2[2]**

-043 **3** *nk* **Bertie Vista**[17] 1971 3-9-3 65 (b) DavidAllan 1 62
(T D Easterby) *led: rdn along and hdd 2f out: sn drvn and kpt on same pce* **16/1**

000- **4** *4 1/2* **Peltre**[291] 4328 3-8-12 30 TWilliams 6 43
(M Brittain) *chsd ldrs: rdn along over 2f out: sn drvn and wknd* **200/1**

20- **5** *nk* **Habbie Heights**[289] 4378 3-8-12 0 DarrenWilliams 8 42
(R Bastiman) *dwlt: hdwy over 2f out: sn rdn and styd on appr fnl f: nvr nr ldrs* **50/1**

02 **6** *1 1/4* **Tangerine Trees**[17] 1971 3-9-3 0 (v) PaulMulrennan 10 43
(B Smart) *t.k.h: cl up: led briefly 2f out: sn rdn and wknd qckly over 1f out* **7/1[3]**

4-5 **7** *2* **Howards Way**[17] 1951 3-9-3 0 PaulFessey 7 36
(Miss L A Perratt) *chsd ldrs: rdn along 1/2-way: sn drvn and wknd* **9/1**

0-05 **8** *nk* **Actabou**[2] 2396 3-9-3 70 PaulHanagan 2 42+
(M Dods) *midfield: rdn along 1/2-way and nvr a factor* **14/1**

00-0 **9** *10* **Accused (IRE)**[9] 2187 3-9-3 70 TedDurcan 9 3
(J Noseda) *a in rr* **9/1**

00-0 **10** *1 1/4* **Lay Down Darling**[25] 1754 3-8-5 26 MarzenaJeziorek(7) 4 —
(N Tinkler) *a in rr* **100/1**

1m 12.84s (1.04) **Going Correction** +0.15s/f (Good) **10** Ran SP% **117.4**
Speed ratings (Par 99): **99,91,90,84,84 82,79,79,66,64**
CSF £6.56 TOTE £1.60: £1.20, £2.10, £2.60; EX 7.60.
Owner Bayardo **Bred** Mountarmstrong Stud **Trained** Manton, Wilts

FOCUS
A typically weak three-year-old plus sprint maiden. The winner did not need to match his debut figure, with the fourth casting doubt on the solidity of this form.
Tangerine Trees Official explanation: jockey said gelding ran too free early stages
Actabou Official explanation: jockey said gelding hung right-handed throughout

2467 TOTESPORT BETXTRA SHOW ONLY H'CAP 1m 6f 19y
5:00 (5:00) (Class 6) (0-65,65) 4-Y-0+ **£1,942** (£578; £288; £144) **Stalls** Low

Form				RPR
00/1	**1**		**Silver Seeker (USA)**[7] 2252 8-8-2 **46** PaulFessey 14 (Miss P Robson) *hld up towards rr: stdy hdwy 3f out: chal 2f out and sn led: rdn clr appr fnl f: comf* **5/6**[1]	57+
3-64	**2**	3½	**Hi Dancer**[3] 2364 5-8-3 **54** PatrickDonaghy(7) 13 (P C Haslam) *midfield: hdwy 4f out: rdn to chse ldrs over 2f out: kpt on appr fnl f: no ch w wnr* **8/1**[2]	60
2200	**3**	¾	**On Every Street**[20] 1890 7-8-2 **46** oh1 (vt) DO'Donohoe 5 (R Bastiman) *chsd ldrs: hdwy 4f out: led 3f out: rdn and hung lft 2f out: sn hdd and kpt on same pce* **50/1**	51
36-0	**4**	1½	**Abstract Folly (IRE)**[23] 1798 6-9-7 **65** PhilipRobinson 2 (J D Bethell) *hld up in rr: stdy hdwy over 3f out: rdn to chse ldrs 2f out: drvn and no imp appr fnl f* **12/1**	68
6003	**5**	1¼	**Just Waz (USA)**[20] 1892 6-8-3 **47** PaulQuinn 1 (R M Whitaker) *midfield: hdwy over 4f out: rdn along to chse ldrs wl over 2f out: sn drvn and kpt on same pce* **11/1**	48
0/00	**6**	*nk*	**Toss The Caber (IRE)**[20] 1892 6-8-2 **46** oh1 PaulHanagan 4 (K G Reveley) *hld up in tch: hdwy over 3f out: rdn to chse ldrs over 2f out: hld whn hmpd over 1f out* **20/1**	47
6500	**7**	¾	**Able Dara**[32] 1579 5-8-2 **46** oh1 AndrewElliott 6 (N Bycroft) *prom: effrt and cl up over 3f out: rdn along over 2f out and sn wknd* **100/1**	46
/000	**8**	2½	**Mozayada (USA)**[16] 2001 4-8-8 **52** TWilliams 7 (M Brittain) *nvr bttr than midfield* **100/1**	48
00-5	**9**	2½	**Foxxy**[20] 1892 4-8-2 **46** oh1 JimmyQuinn 8 (J R Norton) *a midfield* **28/1**	39
20-0	**10**	4	**Let It Be**[20] 1890 7-9-3 **61** PaulMulrennan 11 (K G Reveley) *chsd ldrs: rdn along 3f out: sn drvn and grad wknd* **9/1**[3]	48
650-	**11**	11	**Apsara**[181] 5738 7-8-8 **52** JoeFanning 15 (G M Moore) *cl up: rdn along over 3f out: grad wknd* **28/1**	24
6625	**12**	1	**Coronado's Gold (USA)**[7] 2252 7-9-2 **60** J-PGuillambert 12 (B Ellison) *hld up and bhd: hmpd bnd over 5f out and no ch after* **14/1**	30+
-463	**13**	12	**Title Deed (USA)**[17] 1972 4-9-1 **59** DarrenWilliams 9 (A P Jarvis) *led: rdn along and hdd 3f out: sn wknd* **22/1**	12
/405	**14**	13	**Meohmy**[46] 1281 5-7-12 **49** oh1 ow3 MatthewDavies(7) 10 (M R Channon) *s.i.s and towards rr whn slipped bnd over 5f out and again over 4f out: bhd after* **25/1**	—+
46-5	**F**		**Dance Sauvage**[45] 1304 5-8-1 **48** AndrewMullen(3) 3 (C W Thornton) *hld up towards rr whn slipped and fell bnd over 5f out* **16/1**	—

3m 6.34s (1.64) **Going Correction** +0.15s/f (Good) **15** Ran SP% **128.0**
Speed ratings (Par 101): **101,99,98,97,97 96,96,94,93,91 84,84,77,70,—**
CSF £7.46 CT £231.84 TOTE £1.70: £1.50, £2.10, £15.10; EX 10.30 Place 6: £60.57, Place 5: £23.25..
Owner Hale Racing Limited **Bred** Darley Stud Management, L L C **Trained** Kirkharle, Northumberland
■ Stewards' Enquiry : D O'Donohoe two-day ban: careless riding (Jun 9-10)

FOCUS
A weak handicap in which Silver Seeker was a stone well in. There was an enquiry following the race as to the safety of the final bend, which Dance Sauvage slipped up on.
Coronado's Gold(USA) Official explanation: jockey said gelding was hampered by Meohmy which slipped on the bend
Meohmy Official explanation: jockey said mare slipped on the bend

2468 RACING HERE TOMORROW MAIDEN H'CAP 1m 6f 19y
5:30 (5:53) (Class 6) (0-65,65) 3-Y-O **£2,047** (£604; £302) **Stalls** Low

Form				RPR
-054	**1**		**Trip The Light**[27] 1710 3-8-2 **46** (v[1]) PaulHanagan 15 (R A Fahey) *in tch: hdwy over 4f out: led 3f out: rdn clr and edgd lft wl over 1f out: styd on* **8/1**[3]	56
065	**2**	2½	**Capal Dubh Alainn (IRE)**[44] 1330 3-9-0 **58** (t) WilliamBuick 16 (T J Pitt) *hld up towards rr: gd hdwy on outer over 2f out: rdn to chse wnr and edgd lft over 1f out: no imp ins fnl f* **7/1**[2]	65
00-0	**3**	1½	**Sonny Sam (IRE)**[59] 1059 3-8-12 **56** PaulMulrennan 5 (M H Tompkins) *hld up and bhd: hdwy 3f out: swtchd rt and rdn wl over 1f out: styd on ins fnl f: nrst fin* **11/1**	64+
00-5	**4**	4	**Jemima's Art**[95] 644 3-8-3 **47** oh1 ow1 FrankieMcDonald 10 (M W Easterby) *midfield: hdwy 4f out: rdn along to chse ldrs 2f out: sn drvn and kpt on same pce* **33/1**	46
050-	**5**	1½	**Warsaw Waltz**[240] 5812 3-9-5 **63** J-PGuillambert 6 (J G Given) *hld up in midfield: gd hdwy on outer over 3f out: rdn to chal 2f out: sn drvn and kpt on same pce* **33/1**	60
0-00	**6**	1¾	**Teen Spirit (IRE)**[9] 2197 3-9-3 **61** TedDurcan 2 (J W Hills) *chsd ldrs: hdwy over 3f out: rdn along over 2f out: sn one pce* **18/1**	55
00-0	**7**	1¼	**Dance Easily**[52] 1186 3-8-2 **46** oh1 JimmyQuinn 14 (J L Dunlop) *trckd ldrs on inner: hdwy 4f out: rdn along wl over 2f out and grad wknd* **12/1**	39
0-43	**8**	2¼	**Kalokairi (IRE)**[21] 1871 3-9-3 **61** PhilipRobinson 4 (J L Dunlop) *hld up in midfield: hdwy 4f out: rdn to chse ldrs over 2f out: drvn and wkng whn n.m.r wl over 1f out* **15/8**[1]	53+
6-44	**9**	1¾	**Dancing Dik**[14] 2045 3-9-7 **65** JimCrowley 12 (Mrs A J Perrett) *prom: effrt to ld 4f out: sn rdn along and hdd 3f out: sn wknd* **7/2**[2]	52
00-0	**10**	2	**Mathool (IRE)**[17] 1965 3-8-2 **46** oh1 TWilliams 3 (C W Thornton) *a midfield* **66/1**	30
000-	**11**	2¼	**Jetta Joy (IRE)**[242] 5749 3-8-1 **48** PaulQuinn(3) 13 (Mrs A Duffield) *a in rr* **40/1**	29
000	**12**	½	**Kijivu**[9] 2191 3-8-11 **55** JoeFanning 11 (M R Channon) *in tch: hdwy to trck ldrs 4f out: effrt and ev ch tl rdn and n.m.r wl over 1f out: sn wknd* **16/1**	35+
000	**13**	7	**Victorias**[9] 2207 3-7-9 **46** oh1 CharlotteKerton(7) 1 (A Crook) *a bhd* **100/1**	17
000-	**14**	2½	**Casual Garcia**[197] 6776 3-8-2 **46** oh1 (b[1]) DO'Donohoe 8 (Sir Mark Prescott) *led 1f: prom tl rdn along 4f out and sn wknd* **14/1**	13
00-0	**15**	21	**Premier Class (IRE)**[10] 2142 3-8-2 **46** (b[1]) PaulFessey 9 (J S Wainwright) *t.k.h: led after 1f: rdn along and hdd 4f out: sn wknd* **40/1**	—

3m 7.54s (2.84) **Going Correction** +0.15s/f (Good) **15** Ran SP% **126.3**
Speed ratings (Par 97): **97,95,94,92,91 90,89,88,87,86 85,84,80,79,67**
CSF £71.21 CT £727.98 TOTE £12.10: £3.00, £2.00, £3.20; EX 118.30.
Owner The Matthewman One Partnership **Bred** Darley **Trained** Musley Bank, N Yorks

FOCUS
The final bend which had caused so much trouble in the previous race was deemed safe enough for this last race to take place, following a lengthy enquiry. This was a moderate handicap run at a steady gallop, but the form looks reasonable for the grade.
Kalokairi(IRE) Official explanation: jockey said filly tired in the closing stages
Premier Class(IRE) Official explanation: jockey said gelding hung right-handed throughout
T/Jkpt: Not won. T/Plt: £140.20 to a £1 stake. Pool: £87,765.55. 456.80 winning tickets. T/Qpdt: £3.30 to a £1 stake. Pool: £4,344.40. 948.25 winning tickets. JR

2469 - 2471a (Foreign Racing) - See Raceform Interactive

WOODBINE (L-H)
Sunday, May 25

OFFICIAL GOING: Good to firm

2472a CONNAUGHT CUP (GRADE 3) 1m 110y
9:36 (9:36) 4-Y-0+
£50,510 (£16,836; £9,260; £4,591; £2,295; £204)

			RPR
1		**Rahy's Attorney (CAN)**[210] 4-8-9 (b) SCallaghan 9 (Ian Black, Canada) **16/1**	113
2	½	**Society's Chairman (CAN)** 5-8-6 ow1 JCJones 6 (Roger L Attfield, Canada) **38/10**[2]	109
3	1¾	**French Beret (CAN)**[78] 5-8-5 (b) RLandry 5 (Mark Frostad, Canada) **42/10**[3]	104
4	1¼	**Artie Hot (USA)**[29] 4-8-7 ERosaDaSilva 7 (Nicholas Gonzalez, U.S.A) **295/10**	103
5	*hd*	**Royal Oath (USA)**[80] 818 5-8-7 (b) PHusbands 8 (J H M Gosden) *started slowly, towards rear, 7th 3f out, headway around outside to go 4th approaching final f, one pace* **49/20**[1]	103
6	2½	**Shillelagh Slew (CAN)**[329] 5-8-5 JBaird 4 (M DePaulo, U.S.A) **403/10**	95
7	½	**Skipped Bail (CAN)**[184] 5-8-5 TPizarro 10 (E Coatrieux, Canada) **72/10**	94
8	*nk*	**Moonshine Hall (USA)**[1715] 4932 8-8-5 EmmaJayneWilson 2 (Mark Casse, Canada) **125/10**	94
9	*nse*	**Jiggs Coz (CAN)**[315] 4-8-7 DavidClark 3 (Sid Attard, Canada) **77/10**	95
10	4½	**Touched By Madness (USA)**[135] 6-8-5 JMcAleney 11 (Lorne Richards, Canada) **178/10**	84
11	19	**Good And Lucky (USA)**[36] 5-8-5 ERamsammy 1 (Josie Carroll, Canada) **249/10**	42

1m 39.53s (99.53) **11** Ran SP% **120.9**
PARI-MUTUEL (including $2 stake): WIN 34.10; PL (1-2) 12.20, 7.20;SHOW (1-2-3) 6.80, 4.90, 3.30; SF 245.20.
Owner Ellie-Boje Farm, Read Peters & McClennan **Bred** Ellie-Boje Farm **Trained** Canada

2449 CHEPSTOW (L-H)
Tuesday, May 27

OFFICIAL GOING: Soft (5.9)
The planned inspection was cancelled after only 4mm of rain overnight.
Wind: Almost nil Weather: Fine

2473 DIGIBET.CO.UK MAIDEN AUCTION STKS 5f 16y
2:20 (2:21) (Class 5) 2-Y-O **£2,914** (£867; £433; £216) **Stalls** High

Form				RPR
3	**1**		**Penny's Gift**[12] 2124 2-8-8 0 ow1 DaneO'Neill 7 (R Hannon) *w ldr: rdn to ld over 1f out: rdn out* **11/4**[1]	77+
25	**2**	1½	**Forward Feline (IRE)**[8] 2253 2-8-8 0 CatherineGannon 8 (B Palling) *hld up and bhd: hdwy over 2f out: rdn over 1f out: kpt on ins fnl f: nt trble wnr* **8/1**	72
2	**3**	3¼	**Lesley's Choice**[17] 2011 2-8-9 0 FrankieMcDonald 1 (P A Blockley) *led: rdn and hdd over 1f out: sn edgd lft: wknd wl ins fnl f* **6/1**	61
3442	**4**	1	**Kingswinford (IRE)**[3] 2392 2-8-13 0 StephenDonohoe 5 (P D Evans) *in tch: outpcd 3f out: r.o fnl f* **3/1**[2]	61+
326	**5**	1½	**Meg Jicaro**[20] 1914 2-7-12 0 SophieDoyle(7) 6 (Mrs L Williamson) *bhd: hung lft over 3f out: rdn 2f out: kpt on ins fnl f* **16/1**	48
523	**6**	1¾	**Riflessione**[43] 1363 2-8-13 0 LPKeniry 2 (J S Moore) *prom tl rdn and wknd wl over 1f out* **7/2**[3]	50
	7	3¼	**Campbeltown Trader (IRE)** 2-8-11 0 RichardKingscote 4 (Tom Dascombe) *n.m.r s: outpcd* **25/1**	36
	8	8	**Haulit** 2-8-11 0 JohnEgan 9 (R A Harris) *dwlt: outpcd* **66/1**	7
	9	2½	**Silent Treatment (IRE)** 2-8-7 0 JamesDoyle 3 (R M Beckett) *prom over 2f* **33/1**	—

62.60 secs (3.30) **Going Correction** +0.375s/f (Good) **9** Ran SP% **113.4**
Speed ratings (Par 93): **88,85,80,78,76 73,68,55,51**
CSF £24.41 TOTE £4.30: £1.50, £2.30, £2.00; EX 36.10.
Owner Malcolm Brown & Mrs Penny Brown **Bred** Capt A L Smith-Maxwell **Trained** East Everleigh, Wilts
■ Stewards' Enquiry : James Doyle three-day ban: careless riding (Jun 10-12)

FOCUS
This could have been an above-average event for its type and the form seems solid, rated through the second. The fourth was well off his best.

NOTEBOOK
Penny's Gift put the experience of her third behind a better-fancied stablemate to good use and coped well with the soft ground. She should get further in due course. (op 5-2)
Forward Feline(IRE) ◆ was a bit disappointing on faster ground last time after showing promise on her debut in similar conditions. A step up to 6f with some give underfoot should see her off the mark. (op 14-1)
Lesley's Choice ◆ showed no tendency to hang right this time but did not get home after making the running in these more demanding conditions. He is worth another chance on a sounder surface. (op 9-1 tchd 10-1)

Kingswinford(IRE), making a quick reappearance, had already run well on this type of ground and shaped as though he wants another furlong now. Official explanation: jockey said gelding was unsuited by the soft ground (op 11-4 tchd 9-4 and 10-3)
Meg Jicaro, highly tried at Chester last time, did not appear likely to finish so close when she started to hang left. She is another who appears to want further. (op 20-1 tchd 25-1)
Riflessione folded up disappointingly given that he was already proven in these conditions. (op 10-3 tchd 3-1)

2474 JENKINSONS CATERERS 1ST CHOICE FOR HOSPITALITY CLAIMING STKS 5f 16y
2:50 (2:52) (Class 6) 3-Y-O+ **£1,813** (£539; £269; £134) **Stalls High**

Form RPR
0-40 **1** **Luloah**[112] [440] 5-8-5 42 LukeMorris(3) 3 49
(J G M O'Shea) *a.p: rdn to ld ent fnl f: edgd rt ins fnl f: r.o* **20/1**
0-05 **2** 1 1/4 **Exit Strategy (IRE)**[5] [2337] 4-9-3 60 (b) LPKeniry 10 54
(R A Harris) *s.i.s: hdwy 2f out: rdn over 1f out: r.o to take 2nd nr fin* **9/2**[2]
1344 **3** hd **Desperate Dan**[4] [2351] 7-9-7 70 DaneO'Neill 1 57
(A B Haynes) *hld up and bhd: rdn and hdwy over 2f out: r.o ins fnl f* **7/2**[1]
40/0 **4** 1 1/2 **Danzili Bay**[15] [2036] 6-8-10 70 MarkCoumbe(7) 4 47
(A W Carroll) *a.p: led wl over 1f out: hdd ent fnl f: no ex towards fin* **14/1**
0-00 **5** 1 3/4 **Exponential (IRE)**[4] [2350] 6-9-5 46 WilliamBuick 9 43
(J M Bradley) *a.p: ev ch 2f out: rdn and wandered over 1f out: wknd ins fnl f* **22/1**
532 **6** 1 1/4 **Night Prospector**[15] [2050] 8-8-13 56 (p) AlanMunro 7 33
(R A Harris) *chsd ldrs: no hdwy fnl 2f* **7/2**[1]
5640 **7** 3/4 **Game Lady**[8] [2242] 4-8-12 57 PaulDoe 14 29
(I A Wood) *prom tl rdn and wknd wl over 1f out* **15/2**[3]
000- **8** nk **Seven No Trumps**[270] [4996] 11-8-4 48 PietroRomeo(7) 5 27
(J M Bradley) *hld up and bhd: hdwy 2f out: rdn over 1f out: swtchd lft ins fnl f: n.d* **16/1**
4-50 **9** 4 1/2 **Casla Beag (IRE)**[116] [397] 3-8-0 59 CatherineGannon 2 8
(B Palling) *led: rdn and hdd wl over 1f out: sn wknd* **20/1**
0064 **10** 1/2 **Pajada**[28] [1705] 4-8-6 43 (b) HayleyTurner 8 4
(M D I Usher) *reminder over 3f out: a bhd* **12/1**
250 **11** 1/2 **Maraagel (USA)**[22] 5-8-13 45 FrankieMcDonald 13 9
(G A Ham) *s.i.s: a in rr* **14/1**
6000 **12** 9 **Marysedge**[14] [2084] 3-7-13 42 ow2 MCGeran(7) 6 —
(R Brotherton) *s.i.s: a bhd* **100/1**
0-00 **13** 3/4 **Indian Lady (IRE)**[22] [1865] 5-8-1 45 (p) KMay(7) 16 —
(Mrs A L M King) *prom on stands' rail: wknd wl over 1f out* **33/1**

61.99 secs (2.69) **Going Correction** +0.375s/f (Good)
WFA 3 from 4yo+ 8lb **13 Ran SP% 119.1**
Speed ratings (Par 101): **93,91,90,88,85 83,82,81,74,73 73,58,57**
CSF £102.59 TOTE £28.70: £6.20, £2.50, £1.60; EX 152.10.
Owner W R Baddiley **Bred** Mrs S M Lee **Trained** Elton, Gloucs

FOCUS
A competitive if distinctly modest sprint claimer. Messy form, and none too solid.

2475 JENKINSONS CATERERS 1ST CHOICE FOR CONFERENCING H'CAP 1m 4f 23y
3:20 (3:20) (Class 6) (0-60,60) 3-Y-O **£2,331** (£693; £346; £173) **Stalls Low**

Form RPR
4-64 **1** **Captain Mainwaring**[35] [1553] 3-8-8 55 JackMitchell(5) 17 65
(N P Littmoden) *led over 1f: led over 2f out: clr whn edgd lft ins fnl f: rdn out* **12/1**
-500 **2** 7 **Io (IRE)**[18] [1962] 3-9-0 56 DaneO'Neill 14 55
(J L Dunlop) *hld up: hdwy over 3f out: rdn over 2f out: chsd wnr and edgd lft jst over 1f out: no imp* **11/2**[3]
5-46 **3** shd **Loveofmylife**[21] [1896] 3-8-13 55 JamesDoyle 8 54
(R M Beckett) *hld up in mid-div: rdn and hdwy over 3f out: styd on ins fnl f* **16/1**
00-5 **4** 1/2 **Smetana**[22] [1871] 3-8-11 56 TravisBlock(3) 15 54
(H Morrison) *hld up in tch: rdn and one pce fnl 2f* **9/2**[1]
00-6 **5** 2 1/2 **Flash Of Fire (USA)**[27] [1731] 3-9-0 56 JohnEgan 11 50
(J M P Eustace) *hld up and bhd: hdwy 4f out: rdn 2f out: one pce: eased whn btn towards fin* **20/1**
-030 **6** 3 1/4 **Balais Folly (FR)**[22] [1871] 3-8-7 49 CatherineGannon 4 38
(B Palling) *s.i.s: hdwy on ins 5f out: lost pl over 3f out: btn whn nt clr run and swtchd rt wl over 1f out* **25/1**
0-6 **7** shd **Titfer (IRE)**[38] [1478] 3-8-9 54 LukeMorris(3) 1 43
(A W Carroll) *led over 10f out: rdn and hdd over 3f out: wknd over 1f out* **12/1**
004- **8** shd **Special Feature (IRE)**[200] [6748] 3-8-13 55 ShaneKelly 13 44
(C R Egerton) *hld up in mid-div: hdwy over 3f out: sn rdn: wknd over 2f out* **13/2**
6-05 **9** 1 1/2 **Sarah's First**[33] [1586] 3-9-0 56 StephenDonohoe 12 42
(E A L Dunlop) *a bhd* **9/1**
4230 **10** 1/2 **Okafranca (IRE)**[5] [2340] 3-9-4 60 HayleyTurner 7 45
(W R Muir) *t.k.h in mid-div: wknd over 2f out* **5/1**[2]
0-00 **11** 1/2 **Shoot Pontoon (IRE)**[8] [2259] 3-8-13 55 WilliamBuick 9 40
(S A Callaghan) *wknd over 3f out: a bhd* **33/1**
04-0 **12** 18 **Yes Meg**[55] [1147] 3-9-0 56 TQuinn 3 12
(P F I Cole) *prom: rdn 3f out: sn wknd: eased whn no ch fnl f* **16/1**
3600 **13** 10 **Duneen Dream (USA)**[22] [1871] 3-8-12 54 (t) AlanMunro 2 —
(W J Musson) *a towards rr: eased whn no ch fnl f* **16/1**

2m 49.61s (10.61) **Going Correction** +0.75s/f (Yiel) **13 Ran SP% 118.1**
Speed ratings (Par 97): **94,89,89,88,87 85,85,84,83,83 83,71,64**
CSF £74.07 CT £1075.48 TOTE £16.20: £4.90, £1.80, £5.40; EX 115.00.
Owner John B Waterfall **Bred** N P Littmoden **Trained** Newmarket, Suffolk

FOCUS
A moderate handicap. The form seems sound enough, rated through the placed horses.
Yes Meg Official explanation: jockey said filly was unsuited by the soft ground

2476 JENKINSONS CATERERS WELCOME TO CHEPSTOW RACECOURSE H'CAP 1m 2f 36y
3:50 (3:55) (Class 5) (0-75,75) 4-Y-O+ **£3,561** (£1,059; £529; £264) **Stalls Low**

Form RPR
0/4- **1** **Celticello (IRE)**[73] [1559] 6-8-6 70 ow1 RichardEvans(7) 9 79+
(P D Evans) *reluctant to go to post: dropped out s: hld up in rr: stdy hdwy over 2f out: led wl ins fnl f: cleverly* **5/1**[2]
1-10 **2** 1/2 **Ryedale Ovation (IRE)**[29] [1682] 5-8-6 63 FergusSweeney 10 71
(M Hill) *hld up and bhd: hdwy over 3f out: led 2f out: sn rdn: hdd wl ins fnl f* **10/1**
0/60 **3** 4 **Master Mahogany**[13] [2101] 7-8-12 69 WilliamBuick 4 69
(R J Hodges) *led 1f: prom: rdn to ld briefly over 2f out: wknd ins fnl f* **10/1**
0-50 **4** 1 3/4 **New Star (UAE)**[18] [1947] 4-8-12 69 JamesDoyle 8 66
(W M Brisbourne) *hld up and bhd: rdn and hdwy over 2f out: one pce fnl f* **11/2**[3]
-041 **5** 2 3/4 **Davenport (IRE)**[19] [1932] 6-9-4 75 AlanMunro 2 66
(B R Millman) *hld up in tch: rdn over 2f out: wknd over 1f out* **13/8**[1]
6-00 **6** 3 3/4 **Shabahar (IRE)**[59] [1072] 4-8-13 70 ShaneKelly 5 54
(M J McGrath) *led after 1f: rdn and hdd over 2f out: wknd wl over 1f out* **10/1**
06-4 **7** 6 **Red Current**[144] [40] 4-8-10 67 LPKeniry 1 39
(R A Harris) *prom: n.m.r on ins bnd 6f out: wknd 3f out* **28/1**
8 8 **Amir El Jabal (FR)**[15] 5-8-8 65 (tp) DaneO'Neill 7 21
(D E Pipe) *s.i.s: sn pushed along: reminder after 1f: hdwy to chse ldr over 6f out: wknd 3f out* **20/1**
224- **9** 22 **Dr McFab**[189] [1059] 4-8-11 71 TravisBlock(3) 6 —
(Miss Tor Sturgis) *hld up in tch: wknd over 4f out: t.o fnl 3f* **7/1**

2m 17.22s (6.62) **Going Correction** +0.75s/f (Yiel) **9 Ran SP% 118.1**
Speed ratings (Par 103): **103,102,99,98,95 92,88,81,64**
CSF £55.03 CT £486.62 TOTE £7.00: £2.10, £2.60, £3.50; EX 72.10.
Owner R Edwards & Steve Hughes **Bred** P D Savill **Trained** Pandy, Monmouths

FOCUS
There were question marks hanging over most of these in this modest affair with the first three all potentially well-treated on their old form. The runner-up is perhaps the best guide.
Dr McFab Official explanation: jockey said filly was unsuited by the soft ground

2477 JENKINSONS CATERERS 1ST CHOICE FOR HOSPITALITY H'CAP 1m 14y
4:20 (4:24) (Class 5) (0-70,76) 4-Y-O+ **£3,238** (£963; £481; £240) **Stalls High**

Form RPR
44-2 **1** **Dancing Storm**[21] [1898] 5-8-6 58 FergusSweeney 3 71
(W S Kittow) *hld up in tch: led 2f out: rdn ins fnl f: r.o wl* **7/2**[1]
2451 **2** 3 1/2 **Ermine Grey**[21] [1898] 7-8-3 58 LukeMorris(3) 7 63
(A W Carroll) *hld up and bhd: hdwy over 3f out: rdn and ev ch 2f out: one pce* **7/2**[1]
0-02 **3** 4 1/2 **Magroom**[8] [2243] 4-8-13 65 WilliamBuick 9 60
(R J Hodges) *bhd: pushed along and hdwy over 3f out: ev ch whn rdn and hung lft over 2f out: wknd ins fnl f* **9/2**[3]
-000 **4** nk **The Gaikwar (IRE)**[13] [2101] 9-8-4 56 oh1 (b) RichardKingscote 12 50
(R A Harris) *prom: n.m.r briefly over 2f out: wknd over 1f out* **12/1**
-000 **5** shd **Outer Hebrides**[23] [1842] 7-8-1 60 (v) PietroRomeo(7) 11 54
(J M Bradley) *plld hrd: sn w ldr: led 3f out to 2f out: wknd over 1f out* **25/1**
0-45 **6** 3/4 **Indian Edge**[21] [1900] 7-9-2 68 CatherineGannon 5 60
(B Palling) *led 5f: wknd wl over 1f out* **4/1**[2]
0-00 **7** 5 **Coup D'Etat**[13] [2101] 6-8-13 65 (b) JohnEgan 2 46
(R A Harris) *a bhd* **16/1**
0-00 **8** 3 **Iguacu**[8] [2242] 4-8-5 57 ow1 PaulFitzsimons 1 31
(J L Spearing) *hld up: rdn over 3f out: sn struggling* **50/1**
11 **9** 2 1/4 **Climate (IRE)**[43] [1369] 9-8-9 68 RichardEvans(7) 6 36
(P D Evans) *hld up towards rr: rdn over 2f out: sn struggling* **8/1**
00-0 **10** 7 **Surprise Act**[21] [1898] 4-8-10 62 JimCrowley 13 14
(P R Chamings) *prom: rdn over 3f out: n.m.r and wknd over 2f out* **16/1**

1m 38.48s (2.28) **Going Correction** +0.375s/f (Good) **10 Ran SP% 119.0**
Speed ratings (Par 103): **103,99,95,94,94 93,88,85,83,76**
CSF £16.08 CT £56.74 TOTE £4.70: £1.70, £2.20, £1.30; EX 16.70.
Owner The Quintet Partnership **Bred** D R Tucker **Trained** Blackborough, Devon

FOCUS
This ordinary contest was decimated by seven withdrawals because of the soft ground. The winner was up 8lb on her latest form but there was little solid in behind.

2478 JENKINSONS CATERERS 1ST CHOICE FOR CONFERENCING APPRENTICE H'CAP 6f 16y
4:50 (4:53) (Class 6) (0-65,68) 4-Y-O+ **£2,331** (£693; £346; £173) **Stalls High**

Form RPR
65-0 **1** **Witchry**[22] [1872] 6-9-2 62 JemmaMarshall 1 69
(A G Newcombe) *hld up in rr: plenty to do whn gd hdwy fr over 1f out: str run to ld post* **25/1**
0-22 **2** nse **Kyllachy Storm**[22] [1865] 4-8-7 53 PatrickDonaghy 11 60
(R J Hodges) *hld up in mid-div: rdn and hdwy over 1f out: led last strides: hdd post* **9/2**[1]
1010 **3** hd **Trinculo (IRE)**[5] [2330] 11-9-5 65 (b) MatthewDavies 7 71
(R A Harris) *led: clr over 1f out: rdn and ct last strides* **17/2**
60-0 **4** 1 **Lordship (IRE)**[17] [2010] 4-9-1 61 MarkCoumbe 2 64
(A W Carroll) *stdd s: hld up in rr: hdwy over 2f out: rdn over 1f out: kpt on ins fnl f* **12/1**
0505 **5** 1/2 **Harrison's Flyer (IRE)**[5] [2330] 7-9-0 63 (p) RossAtkinson(3) 6 65
(J M Bradley) *a.p: rdn and kpt on same pce fnl f* **14/1**
00-0 **6** 2 1/4 **Morse (IRE)**[22] [1872] 7-8-11 64 MarieLequarre(7) 9 58
(J A Osborne) *chsd ldrs: no hdwy fnl 2f* **33/1**
1333 **7** 1 1/2 **High Reach**[8] [2242] 8-8-6 52 MCGeran 4 42
(J G M O'Shea) *hld up in tch: rdn wl over 1f out: wknd wl ins fnl f* **7/1**[3]
5431 **8** 1 1/4 **Mafaheem**[8] [2263] 6-9-3 68 6ex (b) PNolan(5) 8 54
(A B Haynes) *wnt lft s: towards rr: swtchd lft jst ins fnl f: nvr nr ldrs* **11/2**[2]
5466 **9** hd **Linda Green**[13] [2102] 7-9-2 62 ThomasO'Brien 12 47
(M R Channon) *hld up: swtchd to stands' rail: a bhd* **9/1**
0-00 **10** 1 1/2 **Barbar**[17] [2010] 5-7-13 52 DanielBlackett(7) 17 32
(Eve Johnson Houghton) *s.i.s: a bhd* **9/1**
0600 **11** 1 1/4 **George The Second**[5] [2337] 5-8-7 53 KylieManser 3 29
(Mrs H Sweeting) *chsd ldr 4f: sn wknd* **12/1**
/000 **12** 1 3/4 **Man Of Letters (UAE)**[25] [1780] 7-8-6 52 AmyBaker 15 23
(M Hill) *chsd ldrs over 3f* **10/1**
3-00 **13** 4 1/2 **Thomas Lawrence (USA)**[8] [2243] 7-8-5 51 oh1 (v) SophieDoyle 13 7
(P A Blockley) *dwlt: a bhd* **14/1**
5500 **14** 11 **Decider (USA)**[17] [1997] 5-8-9 60 DavidProbert(5) 16 —
(R A Harris) *hld up in tch: wknd 2f out* **20/1**

1m 14.6s (1.70) **Going Correction** +0.375s/f (Good) **14 Ran SP% 126.0**
Speed ratings (Par 101): **103,102,102,101,100 97,95,94,93,91 90,87,81,67**
CSF £137.83 CT £1110.35 TOTE £37.70: £9.50, £2.30, £4.40; EX 150.40 Place 6: £219.49, Place 5: £111.26.
Owner M K F Seymour **Bred** Darley **Trained** Yarnscombe, Devon

FOCUS
They were soon well spread out in this low-key sprint handicap which was run at a good pace especially considering the ground. Straightforward form.
T/Jkpt: Not won. T/Plt: £616.70 to a £1 stake. Pool: £84,400.77. 99.90 winning tickets. T/Qpdt: £122.50 to a £1 stake. Pool: £4,288.20. 25.90 winning tickets. KH

2455 LEICESTER (R-H)

Tuesday, May 27

OFFICIAL GOING: Round course - good (good to firm in places); straight course - good to firm (good in places)

Wind: Light across Weather: Light rain

2479 E B F LADBROKES.COM MAIDEN FILLIES' STKS — 5f 2y

2:00 (2:02) (Class 4) 2-Y-O — **£4,533** (£1,348; £674; £336) **Stalls** Low

Form — RPR

1 **Please Sing** 2-9-0 0 ... DarryllHolland 12 — 82
(M R Channon) *chsd ldrs: led wl over 1f out: sn edgd lft and hdd: rallied to ld ins fnl f: r.o wl* **11/4**2

2 2 1 1/4 **Our Wee Girl (IRE)**6 2309 2-9-0 0 ... JamieSpencer 6 — 77
(S Kirk) *hld up in tch: rdn to ld and hung rt fr over 1f out: hdd and unable qck ins fnl f* **15/8**1

3 hd **Prowl** 2-9-0 0 ... JimmyFortune 1 — 76+
(E A L Dunlop) *hld up: pushed along 1/2-way: hdwy over 1f out: edgd rt ins fnl f: r.o wl* **13/2**

3 4 3 **Verlegen (IRE)**10 2204 2-9-0 0 ... RichardHughes 4 — 65
(R Hannon) *led: hung rt thrght: rdn and hdd wl over 1f out: wknd ins fnl f* **6/1**3

5 shd **Golden Rosie (IRE)** 2-9-0 0 ... MichaelHills 2 — 68+
(B W Hills) *hld up: pushed along 1/2-way: r.o ins fnl f: nvr nrr* **17/2**

6 2 1/4 **Dance Club (IRE)** 2-9-0 0 ... KerrinMcEvoy 3 — 57
(W Jarvis) *mid-div: outpcd 1/2-way: hdwy over 1f out: wknd ins fnl f* **20/1**

7 nse **Cecily** 2-9-0 0 ... SebSanders 10 — 57+
(Sir Mark Prescott) *w ldrs tl rdn over 1f out: wkng whn hmpd ins fnl f* **25/1**

8 7 **Bitza Baileys (IRE)** 2-9-0 0 ... JoeFanning 9 — 32
(J G Given) *sn outpcd* **50/1**

9 3/4 **Lady Norlela** 2-9-0 0 ... PatDobbs 8 — 29
(R Hannon) *sn outpcd* **80/1**

10 nk **Rock On Ciara (IRE)** 2-9-0 0 ... VinceSlattery 7 — 28
(D J Wintle) *s.s: hld up: racd keenly: wknd 1/2-way* **150/1**

11 1 1/2 **Sonett** 2-9-0 0 ... NeilPollard 14 — 22
(A J McCabe) *s.s: a in rr* **100/1**

00 12 2 1/4 **Agnes Love**18 1955 2-9-0 0 ... RobertHavlin 13 — 14
(Mrs H Sweeting) *chsd ldrs: lost pl 3f out: sn bhd* **100/1**

61.51 secs (1.51) **Going Correction** +0.05s/f (Good) — **12** Ran SP% **114.0**

Speed ratings (Par 92): **89,87,86,81,81 78,78,66,65,65 62,59**

CSF £7.58 TOTE £3.60: £2.00, £1.10, £2.20; EX 13.80 Trifecta £144.30 Pool: £770.41 - 3.79 winning units.

Owner Mrs Ann C Black **Bred** Mrs R D Peacock **Trained** West Ilsley, Berks

FOCUS

A much above-average maiden confined to fillies, featuring a number of promising debuts, most notably from the winner. The second and fourth help with the early level.

NOTEBOOK

Please Sing ◆ seemed to know her job very well and, always well placed throughout, just had to be pushed out to account for a promising field of fillies. Out of a full-sister to Clive Brittain's trans-continental trailblazer Bold Arrangement (runner-up to Ferdinand in the 1986 Kentucky Derby), she is bred to appreciate at least an extra furlong, giving her connections a pleasant choice of Royal Ascot engagements. (op 5-2)

Our Wee Girl(IRE), the subject of strong support in the market beforehand, could not ultimately improve on the runner-up position she filled on her promising debut at Sandown last week after leading inside the final furlong. Time might tell that she caught a bit of a tartar in the winner however, and she remains likely to pick up a similar event soon. (op 10-3)

Prowl ◆, out of a half-sister to Oaks winner Lady Carla, is very well thought of and was not at all knocked about on her racecourse bow. She is sure to do better in due course. (op 4-1)

Verlegen(IRE) seemed slightly ill-at-ease on the fast surface after such a promising debut with cut in the ground at Newmarket. (op 5-1 tchd 13-2)

Golden Rosie(IRE) ◆ was never nearer than at the finish and looks like benefiting from the extra furlong next time. (op 9-1)

Dance Club(IRE) ◆ is a speedily-bred filly, being a half-sister to Group 1 Haydock Park Sprint Cup winner Red Clubs, out of a listed-winning sprinter who herself was a half-sister to 1990 Windsor Castle Stakes winner Gipsy Fiddler. Further back, her maternal grand-dam is a full-sister to Vernons Sprint Cup winner and renowned sire of sprinters Petong. Given time to find her stride, she made good progress before getting tired in the final furlong. She is sure to do better next time. (op 14-1)

Cecily ◆'s pedigree is all speed, with her being a half-sister to Group 3 winners Violette (Firth of Clyde Stakes) and Silca's Gift (Nell Gwyn), her maternal grand-dam being Jim Leigh's 1990 Queen Mary Stakes heroine On Tiptoes. She showed up well for a long way on this debut, and can only improve. (op 22-1)

2480 LADBROKES.COM CLAIMING STKS — 7f 9y

2:30 (2:32) (Class 6) 3-Y-O — **£2,331** (£693; £346; £173) **Stalls** High

Form — RPR

-360 1 **Nikolaievich (IRE)**15 2043 3-9-0 60 ...(b1) NelsonDeSouza 10 — 65
(P F I Cole) *chsd ldrs: led 2f out: rdn and edgd lft ins fnl f: styd on* **14/1**

5652 2 3/4 **Fly In Johnny (IRE)**7 2277 3-8-6 69 ow1 ... PatrickHills(3) 2 — 58
(R Hannon) *led 1f: chsd ldr tl led 4f out: hdd 2f out: sn rdn: edgd rt ins fnl f: styd on* **3/1**2

-000 3 nk **Flight Plan**11 2141 3-8-11 73 ... JamieMoriarty(3) 7 — 62
(R A Fahey) *stdd s: plld hrd and sn prom: rdn over 1f out: nt clr run ins fnl f: styd on* **5/2**1

-6 4 1/2 **Betonart**28 1709 3-8-7 0 ...(p) KerrinMcEvoy 6 — 54
(R M Beckett) *s.i.s: hld up: hdwy over 1f out: nt rch ldrs* **28/1**

2-40 5 2 1/4 **James Dean (IRE)**22 1854 3-9-10 75 ...(b1) JimmyFortune 3 — 65
(P F I Cole) *trckd ldrs: racd keenly: rdn and edgd rt over 1f out: styd on same pce* **10/1**

-124 6 2 **Lord Deevert**120 339 3-8-5 65 ...(p) JackDean(5) 8 — 45
(W G M Turner) *hld up: rdn over 1f out: n.d* **10/1**

0-31 7 1/2 **Sistos Fascination**120 335 3-9-1 65 ... KirstyMilczarek(3) 5 — 52
(M Botti) *hld up: rdn and nt clr run over 1f out: n.d* **13/2**3

-350 8 1 1/4 **Saafend Geezer**18 1958 3-8-8 59 ...(b1) RobertHavlin 12 — 39
(B J Meehan) *hld up in tch: rdn over 1f out: wknd ins fnl f* **7/1**

3 9 6 **Gioacchino (IRE)**55 1135 3-8-9 0 ... KevinGhunowa(3) 1 — 26
(R A Harris) *wnt lft s: rcvrd to ld 6f out: hdd 4f out: rdn over 2f out: wknd over 1f out* **40/1**

00-0 10 7 **Bozeman Trail**15 2043 3-9-0 61 ...(b1) JamieSpencer 11 — 10
(P F I Cole) *hld up: rdn: wkng over 2f out* **17/2**

1m 28.39s (2.19) **Going Correction** +0.05s/f (Good) — **10** Ran SP% **120.7**

Speed ratings (Par 97): **89,88,87,87,84 82,81,80,73,65**

CSF £57.92 TOTE £12.80: £4.00, £1.20, £1.40; EX 84.10 Trifecta £269.20 Pool: £4388.37 - 11.57 winning units.

Owner The Fairy Story Partnership **Bred** Deepwood Farm Stud **Trained** Whatcombe, Oxon

FOCUS

A claimer mostly filled with disappointing types although the form could rate higher at face value. Little of note to take into the future.

2481 LADBROKES.COM ABBEY PARK H'CAP — 7f 9y

3:00 (3:01) (Class 4) (0-80,80) 3-Y-O — **£4,209** (£1,252; £625; £312) **Stalls** High

Form — RPR

-220 1 **Ink Spot**17 1988 3-9-1 77 ... JamieSpencer 4 — 87
(M L W Bell) *hld up: rdn and hung rt fr over 2f out: hdwy over 1f out: r.o u.p to ld wl ins fnl f* **5/1**3

43-5 2 nk **Arabian Spirit**19 1934 3-8-13 75 ... JimmyFortune 5 — 84
(E A L Dunlop) *chsd ldr tl led 2f out: rdn and hdd over 1f out: ev ch ins fnl f: r.o* **9/1**

6-05 3 1 1/2 **Kiwi Bay**17 1988 3-8-13 75 ... PhillipMakin 12 — 80
(M Dods) *hld up: hdwy 1/2-way: led over 1f out: rdn and hdd wl ins fnl f* **9/2**2

10-3 4 1 1/2 **Romany Princess (IRE)**10 2196 3-9-4 80 ... RichardHughes 6 — 81
(R Hannon) *hld up: hdwy over 1f out: sn rdn: nt clr run ins fnl f: styd on same pce* **7/2**1

206- 5 1 1/4 **Thunder Gorge (USA)**206 6644 3-8-11 73 ... RobertHavlin 1 — 71
(Mouse Hamilton-Fairley) *s.i.s: hld up: hdwy and hung rt fr over 1f out: hmpd sn after: styd on* **66/1**

100- 6 3 **Night Skier (IRE)**229 6120 3-9-1 77 ... KerrinMcEvoy 3 — 67
(J L Dunlop) *chsd ldrs: rdn over 2f out: sn outpcd* **16/1**

-231 7 1 1/4 **Tawzeea (IRE)**18 1951 3-9-4 80 ... RHills 9 — 66
(M Johnston) *chsd ldrs: rdn and ev ch over 1f out: wknd ins fnl f* **7/2**1

0U35 8 1 **Ten Pole Tudor**7 2276 3-9-0 79 ... KevinGhunowa(3) 2 — 62
(R A Harris) *chsd ldrs: rdn over 2f out: n.m.r and wknd over 1f out* **28/1**

3-12 9 5 **Liberty Valance (IRE)**104 538 3-9-1 77 ... PatDobbs 8 — 47
(S Kirk) *s.i.s: sn prom: rdn and wknd over 1f out* **28/1**

2224 10 2 **Salt Of The Earth (IRE)**89 737 3-8-11 73 ...(b1) JoeFanning 7 — 38
(T G Mills) *led 5f: wknd over 1f out* **14/1**

42-1 11 21 **Divine Power**23 1836 3-9-2 78 ... SebSanders 10 — —
(R M Beckett) *s.i.s: hld up: effrt over 2f out: wknd over 1f out* **16/1**

1m 26.7s (0.50) **Going Correction** +0.05s/f (Good) — **11** Ran SP% **116.1**

Speed ratings (Par 101): **99,98,96,95,93 90,88,87,82,79 55**

CSF £48.00 CT £221.73 TOTE £7.30: £1.90, £3.20, £1.80; EX 54.50 Trifecta £130.30 Pool: £2014.76 - 10.97 winning units..

Owner Mrs Lucille Bone **Bred** L A Garfield **Trained** Newmarket, Suffolk

■ Stewards' Enquiry : Jamie Spencer two -day ban: careless riding (Jun 10-11); one-day ban: excessive use of the whip (Jun 12)

FOCUS

A fair handicap and the form looks solid. The winner is rated up 5lb.

2482 LADBROKESCASINO.COM H'CAP — 1m 3f 183y

3:30 (3:31) (Class 5) (0-70,70) 4-Y-O+ — **£2,590** (£770; £385; £192) **Stalls** High

Form — RPR

-016 1 **Royal Premier (IRE)**19 1929 5-9-0 66 ...(v) SebSanders 8 — 73+
(H J Collingridge) *a.p: led over 2f out: rdn and hung rt over 1f out: styd on* **11/4**1

0020 2 1 1/2 **One To Follow**19 1929 4-8-13 65 ... AdamKirby 7 — 70
(C G Cox) *chsd ldr: hmpd over 6f out: led over 3f out: rdn and hdd over 2f out: nt clr run over 1f out: styd on same pce fnl f* **7/1**

61-6 3 3 1/2 **Ommadawn (IRE)**25 1779 4-8-13 65 ...(t) JamieSpencer 9 — 68+
(J R Fanshawe) *s.s: hld up: rdn over 3f out: hdwy over 2f out: edgd rt fnl f: eased whn btn towards fin* **5/1**

0-00 4 9 **Wester Ross (IRE)**18 1963 4-9-4 70 ...(b1) DarryllHolland 4 — 55
(J M P Eustace) *chsd ldrs: led wl over 3f out: sn hdd: wknd 2f out* **10/1**

6-30 5 5 **Is It Me (USA)**125 268 5-9-3 69 ... TedDurcan 2 — 46
(A W Carroll) *led: hdd wl over 3f out: wknd over 2f out* **3/1**2

0-04 6 1 **King Of The Beers (USA)**13 2100 4-8-4 56 oh7 ...(p) LiamJones 1 — 31
(W K Goldsworthy) *hld up in tch: rdn over 4f out: wknd over 2f out* **9/2**3

2m 34.81s (0.91) **Going Correction** +0.175s/f (Good) — **6** Ran SP% **108.1**

Speed ratings (Par 103): **103,102,99,93,90 89**

CSF £20.02 CT £77.75 TOTE £3.50: £2.20, £1.50; EX 21.30 Trifecta £22.20 Pool: £800.02 - 25.52 winning units..

Owner Maynard Durrant Partnership I **Bred** Mrs Anne Hughes **Trained** Exning, Suffolk

FOCUS

Just a modest handicap, the first three home pulling well clear of the others. Indeed, those in fourth, fifth and sixth spots appear well out of form at the moment and are best watched for now. It is doubtful if the winner had to improve.

2483 LADBROKES.COM FOREST H'CAP — 1m 1f 218y

4:00 (4:00) (Class 5) (0-70,69) 4-Y-O+ — **£2,590** (£770; £385; £192) **Stalls** High

Form — RPR

3121 1 **Princelywallywogan**17 2001 6-8-10 61 ... PatCosgrave 10 — 72
(John A Harris) *trckd ldr: racd keenly: rdn over 1f out: styd on u.p to ld wl ins fnl f* **5/1**3

0566 2 3/4 **Zach's Harmoney (USA)**17 2001 4-8-9 60 ... JoeFanning 7 — 69
(P W Hiatt) *led: rdn over 1f out: hdd wl ins fnl f* **12/1**

/-03 3 2 1/2 **Bold Bobby Be (IRE)**18 1963 4-9-1 66 ... KerrinMcEvoy 8 — 70
(J L Dunlop) *trckd ldrs: racd keenly: rdn over 1f out: styd on same pce* **3/1**1

6012 4 1 **Aphrodisia**19 1932 4-9-4 69 ... JamieSpencer 12 — 71
(S C Williams) *hld up: hdwy over 2f out: rdn over 1f out: styd on same pce ins fnl f* **7/2**2

0-23 5 7 **Urban Warrior**12 1065 4-9-4 69 ... SebSanders 6 — 57
(Ian Williams) *prom: rdn over 2f out: hung rt and wknd over 1f out* **13/2**

2646 6 1 3/4 **Amical Risks (FR)**47 1280 4-8-5 56 ... NeilPollard 11 — 41
(W J Musson) *s.s: hld up: n.d* **7/1**

2-65 7 1 3/4 **He's Mine Too**32 1605 4-8-12 63 ... AdrianTNicholls 13 — 44
(D G Bridgwater) *hld up in tch: plld hrd: rdn and wknd over 2f out* **33/1**

00/0 8 1 **Seyaadi**11 2155 6-9-0 65 ... DeanMcKeown 4 — 44
(Miss Tracy Waggott) *s.i.s: hld up: rdn and wknd over 2f out* **40/1**

0-40 9 1 1/2 **The Flying Cowboy (IRE)**27 1725 4-8-12 63 ... TGMcLaughlin 2 — 39
(Jane Chapple-Hyam) *hld up: rdn and wknd over 3f out* **20/1**

210 10 28 **Miss Marauder**14 2078 4-8-13 67 ... KirstyMilczarek(3) 1 — —
(M Botti) *s.s: hld up: bhd fr 1/2-way* **10/1**

2m 10.48s (2.58) **Going Correction** +0.175s/f (Good) — **10** Ran SP% **116.6**

Speed ratings (Par 103): **96,95,93,92,87 85,84,83,82,59**

CSF £61.53 CT £211.43 TOTE £5.70: £1.90, £3.90, £1.10; EX 66.80 TRIFECTA Not won..

Owner Mrs A E Harris **Bred** Mrs J A Gawthorpe **Trained** Eastwell, Leics

FOCUS

A moderate handicap won by the in-form Princewallywogan who is gradually creeping back to his old mark. The first four were in much the same order throughout.

The Flying Cowboy(IRE) Official explanation: jockey said gelding ran flat

Miss Marauder Official explanation: jockey said filly never travelled

2484 LADBROKES.COM H'CAP — 5f 218y
4:30 (4:30) (Class 5) (0-75,73) 4-Y-0+ £3,238 (£963; £481; £240) Stalls High

Form | | | | RPR
1115 1 **Toms Laughter**[49] [1261] 4-9-0 72 (p) KevinGhunowa(3) 10 86
(R A Harris) *mde all: shkn up and r.o* 7/1
-224 2 1 3/4 **Prince Of Delphi**[8] [2242] 5-9-0 69 (p) SebSanders 8 77
(R M Beckett) *hld up: racd keenly: hdwy over 1f out: rdn to chse wnr ins fnl f: styd on* 10/3[1]
5524 3 2 **Mandarin Spirit (IRE)**[3] [2400] 8-8-6 61 (b) OscarUrbina 6 63
(G C H Chung) *hld up in tch: plld hrd: rdn over 1f out: no ex ins fnl f* 4/1[3]
0-05 4 3 3/4 **Bateleur**[10] [2205] 4-9-1 70 (v[1]) DarryllHolland 2 60
(M R Channon) *prom: rdn over 2f out: wknd fnl f* 9/2
0-20 5 2 **Bertie Swift**[35] [1541] 4-8-5 60 TPO'Shea 1 44
(J Gallagher) *chsd wnr over 3f: wknd over 1f out* 20/1
0-00 6 3/4 **Balakiref**[24] [1818] 9-9-4 73 PhillipMakin 9 54
(M Dods) *trckd ldrs: rdn over 2f out: wknd over 1f out* 8/1
4644 7 2 3/4 **Resplendent Alpha**[10] [2203] 4-9-3 72 JamieSpencer 3 50
(P Howling) *hld up: plld hrd: edgd rt over 1f out: eased* 7/2[2]

1m 14.12s (1.12) **Going Correction** +0.05s/f (Good) 7 Ran SP% 111.9
Speed ratings (Par 103): **94,91,89,84,81 80,76**
CSF £29.12 CT £104.55 TOTE £9.00: £4.20, £2.30; EX 23.10 Trifecta £161.90 Pool: £1092.73 - 4.79 winning units. Place 6: £42.55, Place 5: £32.76.
Owner Five To Follow **Bred** Mrs D J Hughes **Trained** Earlswood, Monmouths

FOCUS
A modest handicap with little strength in depth. Toms Laughter improved again back on turf.
Bateleur Official explanation: jockey said gelding ran around a lot
T/Plt: £72.20 to a £1 stake. Pool: £62086.97. 626.90 winning tickets. T/Qpdt: £35.70 to a £1 stake. Pool: £3125.10. 64.60 winning tickets. CR

2462 REDCAR (L-H)
Tuesday, May 27

OFFICIAL GOING: Good to firm (firm in places; 10.0)
Wind: Moderate across Weather: Overcast

2485 EUROPEAN BREEDERS' FUND MEDIAN AUCTION MAIDEN FILLIES' STKS — 6f
2:10 (2:14) (Class 5) 2-Y-0 £3,399 (£1,011; £505; £252) Stalls Centre

Form | | | | RPR
6 1 **Ares Choix**[18] [1961] 2-9-0 0 EddieAhern 6 80+
(P C Haslam) *mde most: rdn wl over 1f out: kpt on wl and clr ins fnl f* 9/4[1]
5 2 3 **Harriet's Girl**[10] [2206] 2-9-0 0 AndrewElliott 4 69
(K R Burke) *in tch: hdwy to chal 2f out: sn rdn and ev ch tl hung lft and one pce ent fnl f* 4/1[3]
3 1 3/4 **On Offer (IRE)** 2-9-0 0 DavidAllan 13 64+
(T D Easterby) *dwlt: hdwy and in tch 1/2-way: rdn 2f out: kpt on ins fnl f: nrst fin* 9/1
4 1 1/4 **Pacific Bay (IRE)** 2-9-0 0 RoystonFfrench 10 60
(Mrs A Duffield) *trckd ldrs: hdwy over 2f out: sn rdn and kpt on same pce* 9/1
5 4 **Royal Muwasim** 2-9-0 0 EdwardCreighton 7 48
(M R Channon) *cl up: rdn along over 2f out and grad wknd* 10/3[2]
0 6 3 3/4 **Madame Jourdain (IRE)**[41] [1390] 2-8-11 0 (b[1]) DuranFentiman(3) 2 37
(T D Easterby) *outpcd and in rr tl sme late hdwy* 100/1
05 7 2 1/2 **Sandies Sister**[20] [1907] 2-8-11 0 MarkLawson(3) 11 29
(M Brittain) *chsd ldrs: rdn along 1/2-way: wknd 2f out* 40/1
6 8 1 **Transformation (IRE)**[21] [1889] 2-9-0 0 ChrisCatlin 12 26
(J R Weymes) *a towards rr* 40/1
9 6 **Ga Ga** 2-9-0 0 PaulMulrennan 1 —
(M W Easterby) *cl up: rdn along 1/2-way and sn wknd* 50/1
10 14 **One Cool Pet (IRE)** 2-9-0 0 LeeEnstone 9 —
(P C Haslam) *dwlt: a in rr* 11/1

1m 13.84s (2.04) **Going Correction** +0.20s/f (Good) 10 Ran SP% 110.0
Speed ratings (Par 90): **94,90,87,86,80 75,72,71,63,44**
CSF £10.24 TOTE £2.40: £1.10, £1.90, £3.20; EX 9.10.
Owner Mrs R J Jacobs **Bred** Newsells Park Stud Limited **Trained** Middleham Moor, N Yorks
■ Outsiders Bella Fighetta and Coniston Wood were both withdrawn after proving unruly in the stalls. No Rule 4 deductions.

FOCUS
Ordinary maiden form. The winner was value for a shade more but there was not much strength in depth.

NOTEBOOK
Ares Choix, whose dam won a Listed race over 1m2f in France, shaped well on her debut at Nottingham and put that experience to good use, showing speed from the off and coming clear in the closing stages. This was only a modest race but she should pay her way in nursery company in time. (op 5-2)
Harriet's Girl, who shaped on her debut as though she would be suited by this extra furlong, was keeping on at the finish and made it a one-two for her sire Choisir. (op 5-1 tchd 3-1)
On Offer(IRE), a half-sister to a number of winners over various distances up to 1m2f, ran a promising race on her debut and looks the type to do better over further in time. (op 8-1)
Pacific Bay(IRE), whose dam won over a mile at two in France, is by Diktat and may well appreciate more dig in the ground. (op 6-1)
Royal Muwasim, whose dam was placed over 7f at two and is a half-sister to Royal Millennium, was popular in the market on her debut. She showed good early pace but did not get home. (tchd 9-2)
Madame Jourdain(IRE), a half-sister to Ask Don't Tell, a dual winner at 5f and 7f at two, was keeping on at the finish and looks the type to do better in ordinary handicap company later in the year.

2486 REDCAR A COURSE FOR ALL REASONS CLAIMING STKS — 1m 2f
2:40 (2:41) (Class 6) 3-Y-O £2,047 (£604; £302) Stalls Low

Form | | | | RPR
-000 1 **Sabre Light**[36] [1516] 3-8-0 58 (p) DuranFentiman(3) 4 56
(P T Midgley) *hld up towards rr: stdy hdwy 3f out: trckd ldrs over 1f out: swtchd rt to chal ent fnl f: sn rdn and styd on to ld last 100yds* 16/1
6-02 2 1 **Hurstpierpoint (IRE)**[20] [1912] 3-8-2 55 ChrisCatlin 3 53
(R A Fahey) *trckd ldrs: hdwy over 2f out: swtchd rt and rdn to ld over 1f out: drvn ent fnl f: edgd lft and hdd last 100yds* 15/8[2]
05 3 1 3/4 **Red Rouge**[11] [2156] 3-8-8 0 TomEaves 5 56
(N Tinkler) *a.p: effrt over 2f out: sn rdn and ev ch: drvn and kpt on u.p ins fnl f: tk 3rd on line* 25/1
21-3 4 shd **Ogre (USA)**[15] [2052] 3-9-4 68 EddieAhern 9 65
(J R Boyle) *trckd ldrs: smooth hdwy to ld over 2f out: rdn and hdd over 1f out: eased and lost 3rd on line* 6/5[1]
150 5 7 **Silver Spruce**[14] [2080] 3-8-11 59 (b[1]) PatrickMathers 2 44
(I W McInnes) *dwlt and sn chsd along to be in tch: effrt 4f out: rdn along over 3f out and sn wknd* 8/1[3]
0-60 6 10 **Northwest**[11] [2142] 3-8-0 46 DanielleMcCreery(5) 7 18
(A Berry) *a bhd* 33/1
0-00 7 12 **Marlena (IRE)**[26] [1754] 3-8-4 48 RoystonFfrench 8 —
(T D Easterby) *t.k.h: sn cl up: rdn along 3f out: wknd 2f out* 16/1
0-00 8 7 **Sun In Splendour (USA)**[22] [1855] 3-9-3 48 DarrenWilliams 1 —
(A P Jarvis) *led: rdn along 4f out: hdd over 2f out and sn wknd* 33/1
00-0 9 16 **Eighty Twenty**[38] [1478] 3-7-13 42 ow1 DaleGibson 6 —
(M W Easterby) *a bhd* 50/1

2m 9.96s (2.86) **Going Correction** +0.20s/f (Good) 9 Ran SP% 114.8
Speed ratings (Par 97): **96,95,93,93,88 80,70,64,52**
CSF £45.16 TOTE £20.50: £3.40, £1.10, £2.40; EX 61.20.Sabre Light was claimed by Alan Bailey for £5000.
Owner P T Midgley **Bred** D J And Mrs Deer **Trained** Westow, N Yorks

FOCUS
A moderate claimer run in a slow time. Weak form.

2487 WEATHERBYS PRINTING H'CAP — 1m 1f
3:10 (3:10) (Class 5) (0-70,70) 4-Y-0+ £2,331 (£693; £346; £173) Stalls Low

Form | | | | RPR
-261 1 **Daniel Thomas (IRE)**[18] [1954] 6-9-2 68 EddieAhern 1 75+
(Mrs A L M King) *trckd ldng pair: smooth hdwy 3f out: led over 2f out: pushed clr wl over 1f out: easily* 11/8[1]
-000 2 3 **Bailieborough (IRE)**[13] [2107] 9-9-1 67 (v) TomEaves 9 62
(B Ellison) *hld up: hdwy and n.m.r over 2f out: effrt and n.m.r whn swtchd rt over 1f out: sn rdn and styd on ins fnl f: nrst fin* 4/1[2]
2420 3 nk **Inside Story (IRE)**[64] [992] 6-9-2 68 (b) PaulMulrennan 6 63
(M W Easterby) *t.k.h: trckd ldrs: hdwy over 2f out: rdn to chse wnr wl over 1f out: sn drvn and one pce* 5/1[3]
-000 4 nk **Roman History (IRE)**[4] [2365] 5-8-4 56 oh11 (p) SilvestreDeSousa 8 50
(Miss Tracy Waggott) *chsd ldrs: hdwy on outer 3f out: rdn 2f out: drvn and hung lft appr fnl f: one pce* 20/1
000- 5 nk **Betteras Bertie**[244] [5739] 5-8-4 56 oh11 JimmyQuinn 4 49
(M Brittain) *dwlt and in rr: hdwy on outer wl over 2f out: sn rdn and styd on wl fnl f: nrst fin* 33/1
0-00 6 1 1/2 **Bright Sun (IRE)**[4] [2365] 7-8-10 62 KimTinkler 5 52
(N Tinkler) *chsd ldrs: rdn along over 2f out: drvn over 1f out and sn one pce* 10/1
50/5 7 2 1/4 **Emirate Isle**[18] [1951] 4-9-3 69 FergalLynch 7 54+
(C Grant) *hld up: hdwy on inner over 2f out: rdn and n.m.r over 1f out: sn wknd* 14/1
0000 8 1 1/4 **Provost**[24] [1815] 4-9-4 70 DaleGibson 3 52
(M W Easterby) *cl up: rdn along 4f out: drvn 3f out and sn wknd* 12/1
000- 9 6 **Take To The Skies (IRE)**[229] [6123] 4-8-5 57 AndrewElliott 2 26
(A P Jarvis) *led: rdn along 3f out: hdd over 2f out and sn wknd* 25/1

1m 55.0s (2.00) **Going Correction** +0.20s/f (Good) 9 Ran SP% 113.8
Speed ratings (Par 103): **99,96,96,95,95 94,92,91,85**
CSF £6.39 CT £20.48 TOTE £2.20: £1.30, £1.30, £1.40; EX 7.50.
Owner George Martin **Bred** Lawn Stud **Trained** Wilmcote, Warwicks

FOCUS
The winner did it well but there has to be a question mark about what he beat in this modest contest as both the fourth and fifth, who finished fairly close up, were a long way wrong at the weights. Dubious form.

2488 WEATHERBYS BLOODSTOCK INSURANCE MAIDEN STKS — 1m 2f
3:40 (3:41) (Class 5) 3-Y-O+ £2,331 (£693; £346; £173) Stalls Low

Form | | | | RPR
5-23 1 **Military Power**[19] [1926] 3-8-12 83 EddieAhern 7 88
(J W Hills) *trckd ldrs: smooth hdwy 3f out: led over 2f out: rdn clr over 1f out: comf* 15/8[1]
4 2 3 **Hunting Country**[11] [2143] 3-8-12 0 GregFairley 12 82
(M Johnston) *cl up: led 4f out: rdn along and hdd over 2f out: kpt on u.p appr last: nt pce of wnr* 9/1
3-40 3 2 1/4 **Green Wadi**[19] [1923] 3-8-12 77 EdwardCreighton 15 78
(M R Channon) *hld up towards rr: hdwy 3f out: rdn along 2f out: styd on fnl f: nrst fin* 5/2[2]
02 4 nk **King Fingal (IRE)**[17] [2008] 3-8-12 0 GrahamGibbons 5 78
(J J Quinn) *trckd ldrs: hdwy 4f out: rdn along 2f out: drvn over 1f out: sn one pce* 11/2[3]
430 5 7 **Plenilune (IRE)**[31] [1628] 3-8-12 70 TWilliams 14 63
(M Brittain) *towards rr: hdwy 3f out: sn rdn and kpt on same pce fnl 2f* 50/1
60- 6 5 **Brandane (IRE)**[277] [4782] 3-8-12 0 RoystonFfrench 6 53
(Mrs A Duffield) *chsd ldrs: hdwy on outer 3f out: rdn over 2f out: sn hung lft and btn* 40/1
220- 7 2 1/4 **Madison Heights (IRE)**[274] [4892] 3-8-12 68 TomEaves 1 48
(J Howard Johnson) *hld up towards rr: sme hdwy 3f out: sn rdn along and nvr a factor* 16/1
8 hd **Bonny Bright Eyes** 3-8-7 0 PaulMulrennan 13 43
(P C Haslam) *a in rr* 25/1
053- 9 6 **Fly With The Stars (USA)**[202] [6725] 3-8-12 80 (t) ChrisCatlin 10 36
(E J O'Neill) *chsd ldng pair: rdn along 3f out and sn wknd* 8/1
10 24 **Mill Beattie** 3-8-7 0 AndrewElliott 8 —
(G M Moore) *sn outpcd and bhd fr 1/2-way* 66/1
11 1 1/4 **Stellando (IRE)** 3-8-12 0 (t) DavidAllan 2 —
(T D Easterby) *s.i.s: a bhd* 50/1
0 12 15 **Monte Pattino (USA)**[64] [991] 4-9-9 0 (t) LeeVickers(3) 9 —
(C J Teague) *s.i.s: a bhd* 250/1
00-0 13 15 **Banus Flyer (IRE)**[10] [2187] 3-8-12 45 (v[1]) KimTinkler 3 —
(N Tinkler) *t.k.h: sn led: rdn along and hdd 4f out and sn wknd* 250/1

2m 6.75s (-0.35) **Going Correction** +0.20s/f (Good)
WFA 3 from 4yo 14lb 13 Ran SP% 118.2
Speed ratings (Par 103): **109,106,104,104,98 94,93,93,88,69 68,56,44**
CSF £19.41 TOTE £2.40: £1.20, £3.50, £1.30; EX 23.30.
Owner H R H Princess Haya Of Jordan **Bred** Paul Hearson Bloodstock **Trained** Upper Lambourn, Berks

FOCUS
Solid maiden form rated through the winner and third. The pace was good.
Fly With The Stars(USA) Official explanation: trainer said gelding had a breathing problem

Banus Flyer(IRE) Official explanation: jockey said gelding lost its action

2489 WEATHERBYS BANK H'CAP 5f
4:10 (4:12) (Class 4) (0-85,91) 4-Y-0+ **£4,209** (£1,252; £625; £312) **Stalls Centre**

Form RPR

0041 **1** **Inter Vision (USA)**[3] 2398 8-9-10 **91** 6ex........................ DanielTudhope 3 100
(A Dickman) *in rr: hdwy on outer 2f out: rdn ent fnl f: styd on wl to ld fnl stride* **7/2**[1]

4-56 **2** *nse* **The Nifty Fox**[10] 2212 4-8-8 **75**........................ DavidAllan 5 84
(T D Easterby) *hld up: hdwy 2f out: effrt and n.m.r over 1f out: rdn to ld last 100yds: drvn and hdd on line* **9/1**

1-52 **3** *hd* **Ocean Blaze**[18] 1956 4-8-13 **80**........................ ChrisCatlin 1 88
(B R Millman) *led: rdn wl over 1f out: drvn ins fnl f: hdd and nt qckn last 100yds* **7/2**[1]

-250 **4** *1* **Malapropism**[10] 2212 8-9-0 **81**........................ EdwardCreighton 4 86
(M R Channon) *chsd ldr: rdn along 2f out: chal and ev ch ent fnl f: sn drvn and nt qckn* **12/1**

-204 **5** *shd* **Caribbean Coral**[20] 1917 9-9-0 **81**........................ GrahamGibbons 7 87+
(J J Quinn) *trckd ldrs: effrt over 1f out: rdn and nt clr run ent fnl f: kpt on* **11/2**[2]

00-5 **6** *nk* **Avertuoso**[10] 2212 4-9-1 **82**........................ TomEaves 10 85
(B Smart) *cl up: effrt 2f out: sn rdn and ev ch tl drvn and wknd ins fnl f* **10/1**

1330 **7** *1* **Feelin Foxy**[17] 2000 4-8-9 **76**........................ J-PGuillambert 9 75
(J G Given) *in tch: hdwy over 1f out: sn rdn and kpt on same pce ins fnl f* **14/1**

0-00 **8** *½* **Rasaman (IRE)**[39] 1451 4-8-8 **75**........................ PaulMulrennan 2 73
(K A Ryan) *chsd ldrs: rdn along and edgd lft wl over 1f out: grad wknd* **16/1**

03-4 **9** *1 ¼* **Hypnosis**[26] 1755 5-8-9 **76**........................ TonyHamilton 6 69
(D W Barker) *dwlt and wnt rt s: in rr tl hdwy over 1f out: rdn and hanging whn n.m.r ent fnl f: no imp* **8/1**[3]

0-62 **10** *3 ¾* **King Of Swords (IRE)**[10] 2212 4-9-0 **81**........................ KimTinkler 8 61
(N Tinkler) *chsd ldrs: rdn 2f out: sn drvn and wknd* **12/1**

58.67 secs (0.07) **Going Correction** +0.20s/f (Good) **10 Ran SP% 118.0**
Speed ratings (Par 105): **107,106,106,105,104 104,102,101,99,93**
CSF £36.43 CT £119.41 TOTE £4.50: £1.50, £3.40, £1.60; EX 48.10.
Owner Mrs D Hodgkinson **Bred** William A Carl **Trained** Sandhutton, N Yorks

FOCUS
A competitive sprint handicap run at a good pace. The form looks solid and should prove reliable.
Caribbean Coral Official explanation: jockey said gelding was denied a clear run and was unable to ride out fully closing stages
Hypnosis Official explanation: jockey said mare missed the break

2490 GO RACING IN YORKSHIRE SUMMER FESTIVAL H'CAP 6f
4:40 (4:41) (Class 5) (0-70,70) 3-Y-0 **£2,331** (£693; £346; £173) **Stalls Centre**

Form RPR

6200 **1** **Moonage Daydream (IRE)**[34] 1572 3-8-8 **60**..............(b[1]) DavidAllan 4 66
(T D Easterby) *trckd ldrs: hdwy over 2f out: rdn to ld over 1f out: hung rt ent fnl f: drvn out* **20/1**

03-3 **2** *1* **Misplaced Fortune**[10] 2187 3-8-12 **64**........................ KimTinkler 15 67
(N Tinkler) *in tch: hdwy 2f out: sn edgd rt and rdn: ev ch tl drvn and one pce ins fnl f* **11/1**

560- **3** *shd* **Planet Queen**[319] 3492 3-8-4 **56** oh1........................ AndrewElliott 14 59
(K R Burke) *prom: effrt 2f out and sn ev ch: rdn over 1f out and kpt on same pce ins fnl f* **16/1**

1563 **4** *1* **Fulford**[24] 1819 3-8-8 **63**........................ MarkLawson(3) 7 62
(M Brittain) *towards rr: hdwy over 2f out and sn rdn: drvn over 1f out: kpt on ins fnl f: nrst fin* **8/1**[3]

003 **5** *1 ½* **Take It Easee (IRE)**[15] 2038 3-8-9 **64**........................ PJMcDonald(3) 11 59+
(G A Swinbank) *chsd ldrs: pushed along and outpcd over 2f out: rdn and hdwy over 1f out: swtchd lft and styd on wl fnl f: nrst fin* **8/1**[3]

0055 **6** *½* **Extreme North (USA)**[7] 2287 3-8-9 **61**..............(v) EdwardCreighton 8 54
(Miss V Haigh) *towards rr: hdwy 2f out: sn rdn and styd on ins fnl f: nrst fin* **8/1**[3]

50-4 **7** *hd* **Jaconet (USA)**[39] 1454 3-8-8 **60**........................ PaulFessey 6 52
(T D Barron) *hld up towards rr: hdwy 2f out: sn rdn and styd on ins fnl f: nrst fin* **16/1**

0104 **8** *2* **Legendary Guest**[11] 2141 3-9-4 **70**........................ TonyHamilton 3 56
(D W Barker) *cl up: led 1/2-way: rdn 2f out: hdd over 1f out and sn wknd* **11/2**[2]

3235 **9** *2* **Irish Music (IRE)**[26] 1737 3-9-3 **69**........................ DarrenWilliams 9 49
(A P Jarvis) *in tch: hdwy and cl up 1/2-way: rdn wl over 1f out and sn wknd* **10/1**

0-40 **10** *¾* **Select Committee**[31] 1611 3-8-10 **62**........................ GrahamGibbons 12 39
(J J Quinn) *towards rr: hdwy 2f out and sn rdn: edgd lft and no imp ins fnl f* **5/1**[1]

4-21 **11** *½* **Flying Indian**[13] 2099 3-8-13 **65**........................ PaulMulrennan 10 41
(J Balding) *prom: rdn along over 2f out: sn wknd* **9/1**

30-6 **12** *shd* **Kiwi Princess**[106] 527 3-8-4 **56** oh2........................ TWilliams 2 31
(M Brittain) *led: hdd 1/2-way: sn rdn along and wknd 2f out* **40/1**

0-00 **13** *nk* **Musical Charm (IRE)**[41] 1396 3-8-8 **60**..............(b[1]) FergalLynch 13 34
(T D Easterby) *hld up: a towards rr* **28/1**

60-0 **14** *1* **Danzig Fox**[19] 1925 3-9-4 **70**........................ ChrisCatlin 1 41
(M Mullineaux) *in tch on outer: hdwy over 2f out: sn rdn and btn* **16/1**

000- **15** *2 ¼* **Resolute Defender (IRE)**[277] 4775 3-8-8 **60**........................ TomEaves 16 24
(J Howard Johnson) *hld up towards rr: hdwy on wd outside 2f out: rdn whn hmpd and lost action povre 1f out: eased* **16/1**

1m 12.72s (0.92) **Going Correction** +0.20s/f (Good) **15 Ran SP% 127.0**
Speed ratings (Par 99): **101,99,99,98,96 95,95,92,89,88 88,88,87,86,83**
CSF £232.12 CT £3704.83 TOTE £31.30: £7.20, £2.80, £7.00; EX 247.80.
Owner Rio Grande Partnership **Bred** Miss Nicola Kent **Trained** Great Habton, N Yorks

FOCUS
Ordinary sprint handicap form, but solid enough rated through the runner-up and fourth.
Resolute Defender(IRE) Official explanation: jockey said gelding lost its action

2491 THE COMMITMENTS ARE HERE IN AUGUST AMATEUR RIDERS' MAIDEN H'CAP 6f
5:10 (5:10) (Class 6) (0-60,57) 4-Y-0+ **£1,977** (£608; £304) **Stalls Centre**

Form RPR

46-4 **1** **Staked A Claim (IRE)**[23] 1827 4-10-12 **53**........................ MrPCollington(5) 13 62
(T D Barron) *towards rr: hdwy over 2f out: rdn over 1f out: styd on strly ins fnl f to ld last 75yds* **2/1**[1]

6-42 **2** *1* **Willie Ever**[32] 1602 4-11-0 **50**........................ MissLEllison 2 56
(B Ellison) *installed early: a.p: effrt over 2f out: rdn to ld over 1f out: drvn ins fnl f: hdd and nt qckn last 75yds* **11/4**[2]

-256 **3** *¾* **High Window (IRE)**[117] 371 8-10-4 **45**........................ MrCCollins(5) 11 49
(G P Kelly) *prom: led 1/2-way: rdn 2f out: hdd over 1f out: kpt on ins fnl f* **9/1**

-000 **4** *½* **Cryptic Clue (USA)**[29] 1674 4-10-9 **45**........................ MissADeniel 6 47
(Mrs R A Carr) *midfield: hdwy 2f out: rdn over 1f out: styd on to chse ldrs ent fnl f: one pce* **40/1**

0-00 **5** *3* **Violet's Pride**[11] 2159 4-10-9 **45**........................ MissSBrotherton 14 37
(N Tinkler) *prom: rdn along 2f out: drvn and wknd ent fnl f* **10/1**

0056 **6** *1 ½* **Jabraan (USA)**[28] 1705 6-10-6 **45**........................ MissARyan(3) 16 33
(Mrs R A Carr) *in tch on wd outside: hdwy and ch 2f out: sn rdn and wknd appr fnl f* **16/1**

000/ **7** *nk* **She Who Dares Wins**[742] 1763 8-10-4 **45**........................ MrKJames(5) 12 32
(L R James) *in tch: rdn along over 2f out: kpt on same pce* **50/1**

-060 **8** *1* **Wee Ellie Coburn**[15] 2053 4-10-4 **45**..............(be[1]) MissMMullineaux(5) 5 28
(M Mullineaux) *chsd ldrs: rdn along over 2f out: drvn over 1f out and grad wknd* **25/1**

5-56 **9** *nk* **Swallow Senora (IRE)**[109] 479 6-10-2 **45**........................ MrHSensoy(7) 8 27
(M C Chapman) *bhd tl styd on fnl 2f* **40/1**

6-00 **10** *1* **Give Her A Whirl**[7] 2285 4-11-5 **55**........................ MrSDobson 9 34
(G A Swinbank) *prom: rdn along over 2f out: wknd over 1f out* **10/1**

6050 **11** *½* **Only A Splash**[15] 2036 4-10-4 **45**........................ MrBMMorris(5) 1 23
(Mrs R A Carr) *dwlt: sn led: hdd 1/2-way: sn rdn along and wknd: btn whn hmpd over 1f out* **25/1**

530- **12** *hd* **Vogarth**[232] 6062 4-11-0 **57**........................ MrPMillman(7) 4 34
(B R Millman) *hld up towards rr: hdwy 2f out: swtchd lft and rdn over 1f out: sn wknd* **8/1**[3]

0-60 **13** *½* **Bovered (IRE)**[124] 289 4-10-2 **45**..............(p) MrJMQuinlan(7) 10 20
(A Berry) *a in rr* **80/1**

50-0 **14** *2 ¼* **Summer Gift**[34] 1561 5-10-3 **46**..............(v[1]) MissACOlley(7) 15 14
(J O'Reilly) *in tch: rdn along over 2f out and sn wknd* **28/1**

00 **15** *3* **Orangina Wood (GER)**[7] 2283 5-10-4 **45**........................ MissWGibson(5) 7 4
(A Berry) *a in rr* **66/1**

/000 **16** *5* **Fiona Fox**[15] 2036 4-10-9 **45**..............(tp) MrsMMorris 3 —
(J Balding) *prom: rdn along 1/2-way and sn wknd* **40/1**

1m 14.45s (2.65) **Going Correction** +0.20s/f (Good) **16 Ran SP% 128.3**
Speed ratings (Par 101): **90,88,87,87,83 81,80,79,78,77 76,76,75,72,68 62**
CSF £6.99 CT £45.79 TOTE £3.50: £1.50, £1.20, £2.00, £7.40; EX 8.80 Place 6: £109.97, Place 5: £70.02.
Owner Chris McHale **Bred** J Callanan **Trained** Maunby, N Yorks
■ Stewards' Enquiry : Mr P Millman two-day ban: careless riding (Jun 11, 16)

FOCUS
A poor contest with more than half of the field wrong at the weights even in this low grade, but the right horses came to the fore.
T/Plt: £127.40 to a £1 stake. Pool: £46,804.95. 268.15 winning tickets. T/Qpdt: £52.20 to a £1 stake. Pool: £2,866.80. 40.60 winning tickets. JR

2492 - 2494a (Foreign Racing) - See Raceform Interactive

2388 BEVERLEY (R-H)
Wednesday, May 28

OFFICIAL GOING: Good to firm (good in places)
Wind: Light across Weather: Overcast and showers

2495 SUPABED QUALITY PAPER BEDDING H'CAP 1m 4f 16y
6:35 (6:36) (Class 5) (0-70,68) 3-Y-0 **£2,914** (£867; £433; £216) **Stalls High**

Form RPR

-322 **1** **Princess Lomi (IRE)**[19] 1950 3-9-4 **68**........................ DeanMcKeown 3 75
(E J O'Neill) *hld up in tch: smooth hdwy 3f out: led wl over 1f out: rdn clr ent fnl f: styd on* **9/2**[3]

1051 **2** *2 ¼* **An Scaribh**[15] 2080 3-8-11 **68**........................ RichardEvans(7) 5 71
(P D Evans) *hld up in rr: swtchd outside and hdwy 3f out: rdn over 1f out: styd on wl fnl f: nrst fin* **14/1**

66-2 **3** *nk* **Bouggler**[42] 1397 3-8-8 **58**........................ TomEaves 4 61
(Miss J A Camacho) *cl up: led 3f out: rdn 2f out: drvn and hdd wl over 1f out: kpt on same pce* **9/1**

3650 **4** *8* **Tripod Molly (IRE)**[19] 1959 3-8-8 **58**..............(t) FrancisNorton 8 48
(P J McBride) *hld up in rr: swtchd outside and hdwy over 2f out: sn rdn and styd on fnl f: nrst fin* **25/1**

-324 **5** *shd* **Graylyn Ruby (FR)**[28] 1731 3-9-3 **67**........................ RyanMoore 10 57
(J Jay) *hld up in rr: hdwy over 2f out: styd on ins fnl f: nrst fin* **10/3**[2]

0-46 **6** *2* **Sea Admiral**[19] 1962 3-9-2 **66**........................ PaulHanagan 11 52
(R Charlton) *chsd ldrs: hdwy 3f out: rdn over 2f out and sn one pce* **3/1**[1]

00-0 **7** *3 ½* **Rivington Pike (IRE)**[65] 991 3-8-13 **63**........................ GrahamGibbons 1 44
(J J Quinn) *s.i.s: a in rr* **18/1**

0-24 **8** *1* **Milanollo**[55] 1163 3-9-1 **65**........................ HayleyTurner 7 44
(M L W Bell) *t.k.h: prom on inner tl rdn along over 2f out and sn wknd* **10/1**

0-00 **9** *5* **Premier Class (IRE)**[2] 2468 3-8-4 **54** oh8..............(b) RoystonFfrench 9 25
(J S Wainwright) *t.k.h: sn led: rdn along and hdd 3f out: sn wknd* **66/1**

000- **10** *17* **Two Imposters (USA)**[293] 4323 3-8-9 **59**........................ JoeFanning 6 —
(J R Best) *prom: effrt over 3f out: rdn along over 2f out and sn wknd* **20/1**

6-41 **P** **Caffari (GER)**[8] 2273 3-8-9 **59** 6ex........................ FergusSweeney 12 —
(K R Burke) *t.k.h: trckd ldrs: sddle slipped after 4f: in rr and p.u 3f out* **7/1**

2m 43.29s (2.39) **Going Correction** +0.15s/f (Good) **11 Ran SP% 119.9**
Speed ratings (Par 99): **98,96,96,90,90 89,87,86,83,71** —
CSF £65.58 CT £553.50 TOTE £5.80: £1.60, £5.90, £3.00; EX 98.20.
Owner Miss A H Marshall **Bred** Frank Dunne **Trained** Averham Park, Notts

FOCUS
A modest handicap run at a modest early gallop. The first three came clear and this is ordinary form.
Caffari(GER) Official explanation: jockey said saddle slipped

2496 GUEST AND PHILIPS H'CAP 1m 100y
7:05 (7:05) (Class 5) (0-70,70) 3-Y-0 **£2,914** (£867; £433; £216) **Stalls High**

Form RPR

435 **1** **Shadowtime**[16] 2037 3-9-2 **68**........................ DeanMcKeown 6 73
(Miss Tracy Waggott) *hld up in tch: hdwy over 2f out: rdn to ld appr fnl f: kpt on wl u.p towards fin* **9/1**

05-5 **2** *nk* **Smooth As Silk (IRE)**[24] 1836 3-9-0 **66**........................ ShaneKelly 10 70+
(C R Egerton) *dwlt: in rr tl hdwy on outer 3f out: rdn wl over 1f out: drvn ins fnl f and styd on wl* **7/2**[2]

6401 **3** *1 ½* **Bourse (IRE)**[9] 2247 3-8-11 **66** 6ex........................ PJMcDonald(3) 3 67
(J S Wainwright) *hmpd s and bhd: hdwy over 2f out: sn rdn and styd on wl fnl f: nrst fin* **9/1**

50-0 **4** *hd* **Gulf Coast**[11] 2208 3-8-6 **58** ... GrahamGibbons 11 58
(T D Walford) *chsd ldrs: hdwy on inner over 2f out: rdn and ch over 1f out: sn drvn and kpt on same pce ins fnl f* **6/1**[3]
60-0 **5** *3 1/4* **Darley Star**[58] 1115 3-8-10 **62** ... RobertWinston 8 55
(C E Brittain) *chsd ldrs: rdn along and sltly outpcd 3f out: styd on u.p appr fnl f* **33/1**
15 **6** *3/4* **Lizzie Wiggins**[19] 1959 3-9-3 **69** ... HayleyTurner 2 60
(M L W Bell) *wnt lft s: in rr tl hdwy over 2f out: sn rdn and kpt on ins fnl f: nrst fin* **10/1**
4340 **7** *2 1/4* **Ace Of Spies (IRE)**[16] 2037 3-8-6 **65** ... MarieLussiana(7) 9 51
(M Johnston) *led: rdn along over 2f out: drvn and edgd rt over 1f out: hdd appr fnl f and sn wknd* **18/1**
600- **8** *3* **Jackday (IRE)**[221] 6328 3-8-10 **62** ... DavidAllan 4 41
(T D Easterby) *sltly hmpd and stdd s: a in rr* **33/1**
0122 **9** *nk* **Always Brave**[8] 2288 3-9-4 **70** ... JoeFanning 1 48
(M Johnston) *carried lft s: sn cl up: effrt 3f out: rdn over 2f out: wknd wl over 1f out* **11/4**[1]
4-65 **10** *3 3/4* **Diamond Royal (IRE)**[19] 1965 3-9-2 **68** ... RyanMoore 5 38
(E A L Dunlop) *prom: rdn along 3f out: drvn over 2f out and sn wknd* **7/1**
0-66 **11** *12* **Morocchius (USA)**[8] 2288 3-9-4 **70** ... TomEaves 7 12
(Miss J A Camacho) *a in rr* **14/1**

1m 48.97s (1.37) **Going Correction** +0.15s/f (Good) **11** Ran SP% **122.6**
Speed ratings (Par 99): **99,98,97,97,93 93,90,87,87,83 71**
CSF £42.33 CT £305.61 TOTE £11.00: £3.30, £2.20, £2.00; EX 86.00.
Owner H Conlon **Bred** Darley **Trained** Spennymoor, Co Durham

FOCUS
Just a modest handicap but run at a decent gallop so the form, while ordinary, should stand up well enough. The winner returned to his debut level.

2497 HILARY NEEDLER TROPHY (LISTED RACE) (FILLIES) 5f
7:35 (7:36) (Class 1) 2-Y-O

£12,205 (£4,626; £2,315; £1,154; £578; £290) **Stalls High**

Form RPR
3316 **1** **Knavesmire (IRE)**[12] 2167 2-8-12 0 ... JoeFanning 8 90
(M Brittain) *chsd ldrs: hdwy over 2f out: rdn to chal ent fnl f: drvn and kpt on gamely to ld last 100yds* **40/1**
212 **2** *nk* **Carانbola**[14] 2108 2-8-12 0 ... TWilliams 11 89
(M Brittain) *prom: rdn to ld over 1f out: drvn ins fnl f: hdd and no ex last 100yds* **12/1**
123 **3** *3 1/4* **Aspen Darlin (IRE)**[12] 2167 2-8-12 0 ... PaulHanagan 5 77
(A Bailey) *in tch: hdwy 2f out: sn rdn and kpt on u.p fnl f* **9/2**[2]
2 **4** *shd* **Aahaygirl (IRE)**[32] 1610 2-8-12 0 ... FergusSweeney 3 77
(K R Burke) *in tch on outer: rdn along 2f out: drvn over 1f out: kpt on same pce u.p ins fnl f* **28/1**
1 **5** *shd* **Haigh Hall**[11] 2206 2-8-12 0 ... DavidAllan 2 77
(T D Easterby) *in tch: hdwy to chse ldrs 2f out: rdn over 1f out and kpt on same pce* **10/3**[1]
6 *6* **Alectrona (FR)** 2-8-9 0 ... RyanMoore 1 52
(J R Best) *in tch on outer: effrt 2f out: sn rdn and btn* **20/1**
7 *3 1/2* **Ohiyesa (IRE)**[14] 2112 2-8-12 0 ... ShaneKelly 12 42
(G M Lyons, Ire) *cl up: effrt 2f out and ev ch tl rdn over 1f out and sn wknd* **9/1**[3]
8 *nk* **Minotaurious (IRE)** 2-8-9 0 ... AndrewElliott 13 38
(K R Burke) *led: rdn along 2f out: drvn and hdd over 1f out: wknd qckly* **16/1**
131 **9** *3* **White Shift (IRE)**[9] 2254 2-9-3 0 ... StephenDonohoe 10 36
(P D Evans) *outpcd and bhd fr 1/2-way* **9/1**[3]
1 **10** *3 3/4* **Glorious Dreams (USA)**[16] 2048 2-8-12 0 ... FrancisNorton 4 17
(T J Pitt) *dwlt: a in rr* **16/1**

63.58 secs (0.08) **Going Correction** -0.025s/f (Good) **10** Ran SP% **91.4**
Speed ratings (Par 98): **98,97,92,92,92 82,76,76,71,65**
CSF £271.08 TOTE £29.40: £4.60, £3.40, £1.10; EX 149.90.
Owner Mel Brittain **Bred** Michael O'Mahony **Trained** Warthill, N Yorks
■ Percolator was withdrawn (11/4, unruly in stalls.) R4 applies, deduct 25p in the £.
■ Stewards' Enquiry : T Williams caution: used whip with excessive frequency

FOCUS
A shock result to this Listed contest and weak form for the grade in all probability. Mel Brittain saddled the first two, the pair clear and both showing improved form.

NOTEBOOK
Knavesmire(IRE) was not beaten far despite finishing sixth in a Listed race at York last time, and this stiffer track and watered/rain-softened ground suited her better. Prominent from the outset, she saw the trip out strongly and got on top inside the last. She and her stable-companion finished clear of the rest but neither is likely to go to Royal Ascot and the form is open to question. (op 33-1)
Caranbola, the better fancied of the Mel Brittain pair, was also up with the pace throughout and only narrowly seen off by her stablemate. She only cost 2,000gns so has proved a bit of a bargain. (op 20-1)
Aspen Darlin(IRE), third in the York Listed race in which Knavesmire was sixth, promised to be suited by this stiffer track and ran a sound race in third. Another furlong is likely to be to her benefit in future. (tchd 5-1)
Aahaygirl(IRE), whose stable won this race in 2005, gave the form of her maiden run at Haydock behind Maggie Lou a boost with a solid run in fourth. Winning a maiden should be a formality on this evidence.
Haigh Hall made an impressive debut at Thirsk and her stable had won four of the last ten renewals of this race, so she was understandably sent off favourite. She had a poor draw in stall two, though, and this watered ground was perhaps not in her favour. (op 3-1 tchd 7-2)
Alectrona(FR), whose price rose from 85,000euros as a foal to 195,000euros as a yearling, is a half-sister to Darjeeling, a smart, prolific winner over 1m in France, Danielli, a multiple winner between 6f and 1m2f, Reina de Mexico, a triple 1m winner in Italy, and Dominicana, a 1m winner at two. She did not run too badly on her debut and there will be easier opportunities for her.
Ohiyesa(IRE) Official explanation: trainer later said filly was found to have pulled a muscle high up and was very lame post race

2498 BEVERLEY RACECOURSE CONDITIONS STKS 5f
8:05 (8:06) (Class 3) 3-Y-O

£6,542 (£1,959; £979; £490; £244; £122) **Stalls High**

Form RPR
21-1 **1** **Corrybrough**[33] 1597 3-9-1 100 ... RyanMoore 7 111
(H Candy) *hld up in rr: hdwy on outer 2f out: shkn up over 1f out: str run ins fnl f: led last 100yds and sn clr* **1/2**[1]
0-30 **2** *2 1/2* **Hammadi (IRE)**[17] 2034 3-9-1 102 ... DO'Donohoe 4 102
(K A Ryan) *cl up: led 1/2-way: rdn over 1f out: drvn ins fnl f: hdd and one pce last 100yds* **20/1**
1-23 **3** *1 1/2* **Inxile (IRE)**[29] 1712 3-9-1 100 ... AdrianTNicholls 5 97
(D Nicholls) *trckd ldrs: hdwy 2f out: rdn over 1f out: kpt on ins fnl f* **5/1**[2]
0-14 **4** *5* **Mey Blossom**[19] 1945 3-8-7 90 ... MichaelJStainton(3) 2 74
(R M Whitaker) *chsd ldrs: rdn along 2f out: drvn and one pce appr fnl f* **20/1**
13-6 **5** *nk* **Secret Asset (IRE)**[19] 1945 3-9-1 93 ... DavidAllan 6 78
(W M Brisbourne) *led: hdd 1/2-way: sn rdn and wknd wl over 1f out* **20/1**
62-4 **6** *11* **Dubai Princess (IRE)**[18] 2000 3-8-10 98 ... ShaneKelly 3 33
(J A Osborne) *a in rr* **13/2**[3]
0-60 **7** *4 1/2* **Prigsnov Dancer (IRE)**[41] 1426 3-8-12 72 ... (v1) LeeEnstone 1 19
(J O'Reilly) *wnt lft s: a in rr* **200/1**

62.00 secs (-1.50) **Going Correction** -0.025s/f (Good) **7** Ran SP% **111.4**
Speed ratings (Par 103): **111,107,104,96,96 78,71**
CSF £15.56 TOTE £1.50: £1.10, £4.30; EX 11.00.
Owner Thurloe Thoroughbreds XXI **Bred** Mrs Sheila Oakes **Trained** Kingston Warren, Oxon

FOCUS
An excellent conditions event which revolved to a large degree around the favourite, who had been touted as a future star of the sprinting division. He did not disappoint and has been rated up 9lb. The form is rated through the runner-up.

NOTEBOOK
Corrybrough ◆ confirmed himself on course for a tilt at Listed company in a fortnight's time with a convincing win. His rider seemed intent on bringing him up the middle of the track, and his trainer confirmed afterwards that he thought that was where the better ground was. In order to execute this manoeuvre Moore had to miss the kick, in effect giving those at the head of affairs a five-length start. This proved no problem to the son of Kyllachy as he came with a strong run inside the final furlong to mow down obviously inferior rivals. The Scurry Stakes at Sandown is his next port of call. (op 8-15 tchd 4-7)
Hammadi(IRE) probably put up his best effort for a while in taking up the running around halfway and keeping on to the line. The position of the second and third horses implies that he ran right up to his handicap mark. Clearly possessing bags of speed, he won't always run into horses of the calibre of the winner. (op 14-1)
Inxile(IRE), on only his fourth start, ran a solid race without ever looking like winning. As a young, inexperienced sprinter he is certainly in the right hands to exploit his ability to the full. (op 7-2)
Mey Blossom was far from disgraced at the weights. She keeps finishing off her races well to imply that another crack at 6f would not go amiss. (op 25-1)
Secret Asset(IRE) showed plenty of dash through the first half of the race and would be of some interest back in handicaps. Official explanation: jockey said gelding was unsuited by the good to firm ground (tchd 18-1)
Dubai Princess(IRE) Official explanation: jockey said filly was unsuited by the good to firm ground

2499 WEATHERBYS BLOODSTOCK INSURANCE H'CAP 1m 1f 207y
8:35 (8:35) (Class 4) (0-85,86) 4-Y-0+ **£4,209** (£1,252; £625; £312) **Stalls High**

Form RPR
26-2 **1** **Just Lille (IRE)**[10] 2220 5-9-4 **83** ... (p) RoystonFfrench 8 91
(Mrs A Duffield) *trckd ldng pair: hdwy over 2f out: rdn to chse ldr over 1f out: drvn ins fnl f: styd on wl to ld last 75yds* **11/4**[1]
2601 **2** *1 1/4* **Speedy Sam**[8] 2278 5-9-7 **86** 6ex ... FergusSweeney 6 91
(K R Burke) *led 2f: cl up tl led again over 2f out: rdn over 1f out: drvn ins fnl f: hdd and no ex fnl 75yds* **5/1**[3]
2-24 **3** *2* **Little Jimbob**[15] 2073 7-8-7 **72** ... PaulHanagan 3 73
(R A Fahey) *cl up: led after 2f: rdn along and hdd over 2f out: drvn over 1f out: kpt on same pce* **15/2**
2-01 **4** *hd* **Roodolph**[16] 2060 4-8-10 **75** ... StephenCarson 9 76
(Eve Johnson Houghton) *hld up in tch: hdwy 3f out: rdn to chse ldrs over 2f out: drvn over 1f out and no imp* **5/1**[3]
3455 **5** *2 1/4* **Charlie Tipple**[10] 2220 4-8-10 **75** ... (p) PaulMulrennan 2 71
(T D Easterby) *t.k.h: chsd ldrs: hdwy over 2f out: rdn wl over 1f out and no imp* **13/2**
4542 **6** *4 1/2* **Sudden Impulse**[12] 2155 7-8-10 **75** ... SilvestreDeSousa 5 62
(A D Brown) *hld up in rr: hdwy over 2f out: rdn over 1f out and n.d* **9/2**[2]
/11- **7** *7* **Tendalay (USA)**[454] 589 4-9-1 **80** ... DavidAllan 1 53
(D Carroll) *hld up in rr: hdwy on outer 3f out: rdn 2f out and sn btn* **16/1**

2m 8.11s (1.11) **Going Correction** +0.15s/f (Good) **7** Ran SP% **113.9**
Speed ratings (Par 105): **101,100,98,98,96 92,87**
CSF £15.00 CT £80.68 TOTE £3.10: £2.20, £2.70; EX 13.90.
Owner Miss Helen Wynne **Bred** Sweetmans Bloodstock **Trained** Constable Burton, N Yorks
■ Stewards' Enquiry : Fergus Sweeney caution: careless riding

FOCUS
A fair handicap and probably sound enough with the front pair coming here bang in form. A career best so far from the winner.

2500 RACING AGAIN ON 13TH JUNE MAIDEN FILLIES' STKS 7f 100y
9:05 (9:07) (Class 5) 3-Y-0+ **£2,428** (£722; £270; £270) **Stalls High**

Form RPR
42-2 **1** **Lindelaan (USA)**[19] 1946 3-8-10 78 ... RyanMoore 5 70+
(Sir Michael Stoute) *in tch: pushed along 3f out: swtchd outside and shkn up over 1f out: rdn and styd on strly to ld ins fnl f* **4/9**[1]
00-5 **2** *1 1/2* **Romantic Destiny**[16] 2038 3-8-10 75 ... FergalLynch 4 66
(K A Ryan) *prom: hdwy to ld over 2f out: rdn wl over 1f out: drvn and hdd ins fnl f: kpt on* **12/1**[3]
6-0 **3** *2 1/2* **Nayarna**[10] 2221 3-8-3 0 ... FrederikTylicki(7) 3 60
(R A Fahey) *in tch: hdwy on outer 3f out: rdn to chal wl over 1f out and ev ch tl wknd ent fnl f* **66/1**
5- **3** *dht* **Signora (IRE)**[200] 6754 3-8-10 0 ... JoeFanning 12 60
(M Johnston) *a.p: effrt and pushed along over 2f out: rdn and ch appr fnl f: kpt on same pce* **11/2**[2]
6 **5** *3* **Cheeky Chilli**[15] 2084 3-8-10 0 ... DanielTudhope 8 53
(A J McCabe) *towards rr: hdwy 2f out: sn rdn and kpt on: nt rch ldrs* **40/1**
04 **6** *2* **Dhahab (USA)**[19] 1971 3-8-5 0 ... AhmedAjtebi(5) 10 51
(C E Brittain) *led: rdn along and hdd over 2f out: sn wknd* **12/1**[3]
0-05 **7** *2 3/4* **Miss Taboo (IRE)**[37] 1519 4-9-4 46 ... JamieMoriarty(3) 11 45
(P T Midgley) *dwlt: sn chsng ldrs: rdn along over 3f out and sn wknd* **20/1**
0-0 **8** *3* **Aura**[19] 1965 3-8-10 0 ... HayleyTurner 1 33
(M L W Bell) *uns rdr and bolted bef s: a in rr* **28/1**
9 *3* **Micallef** 3-8-10 0 ... PaulHanagan 7 26
(R A Fahey) *s.i.s: a in rr* **20/1**
-0 **10** *29* **Annawanna**[42] 1410 4-9-7 0 ... LeeEnstone 9 —
(S Wynne) *chsd ldrs: rdn along 1/2-way: sn wknd* **200/1**

1m 35.7s (1.90) **Going Correction** +0.15s/f (Good)
WFA 3 from 4yo 11lb **10** Ran SP% **117.4**
Speed ratings (Par 100): **95,93,90,90,87 84,81,78,74,41**
CSF £6.26 TOTE £1.40: £1.02, £3.10; EX 6.00 TRIFECTA 3rd Place Tote Nayarna 8.40, Signora 0.80. Place 6 £ 68.00, Place 5 £ 20.75.
Owner Mrs R J Jacobs **Bred** Kinsman Farm **Trained** Newmarket, Suffolk

FOCUS
A very ordinary and slowly run fillies' maiden, the Newmarket raider having to work hard to land the odds. It is doubtful if the first two had to run to their best.
T/Plt: £111.20 to a £1 stake. Pool: £72,773.30. 477.50 winning tickets. T/Qpdt: £7.00 to a £1 stake. Pool: £4,190.50. 439.50 winning tickets. JR

2073 GREAT LEIGHS (A.W) (L-H)

Wednesday, May 28

OFFICIAL GOING: Standard

The first meeting at this new track when the general public was admitted, but it needed a late BHA inspection before being given the go-ahead.

Wind: fresh behind Weather: overcast

2501 LOOKERS LAND ROVER H'CAP — 5f (P)

2:30 (2:30) (Class 4) (0-85,85) 4-Y-O+ **£4,533** (£1,348; £674; £336) **Stalls** Low

Form RPR

3305 **1** **Almaty Express**[8] 2292 6-9-0 **81**.....(b) DarryllHolland 2 93
(J R Weymes) *mde all: clr wl over 1f out: unchal* **9/1**

4-00 **2** *1 ½* **Russian Symphony (USA)**[131] 210 7-8-6 **73**.....(b) WilliamBuick 5 80
(C R Egerton) *bhd: rdn over 2f out: styd on front over 1f out: wnt 2nd towards fin: no ch w wnr* **9/1**

0112 **3** *½* **Lord Of The Reins (IRE)**[25] 1802 4-8-12 **79**..... J-PGuillambert 1 84
(J G Given) *in tch: rdn and effrt over 2f out: chsd wnr 1f out: no imp: lost 2nd towards fin* **7/2[1]**

-136 **4** *2* **Hammer Of The Gods (IRE)**[23] 1865 8-8-8 **75**.....(bt) EddieAhern 7 73
(G C Bravery) *chsd ldrs: rdn wl over 1f out: kpt on same pce* **6/1[3]**

-000 **5** *hd* **Ice Planet**[25] 1796 7-9-3 **84**..... AdrianTNicholls 3 81
(D Nicholls) *bhd: pushed along and hdwy over 2f out: nt clr run briefly wl over 1f out: nvr trbld ldrs* **9/2[2]**

0660 **6** *3 ¾* **Silver Prelude**[19] 1956 7-9-4 **85**..... TedDurcan 4 68
(D K Ivory) *chsd wnr: rdn wl over 1f out: wknd qckly fnl f* **10/1**

-055 **7** *2 ¾* **New York Oscar (IRE)**[34] 1582 4-8-7 **74**.....(p) JamesDoyle 8 47
(A J McCabe) *sn bustled along in rr: n.d* **9/2[2]**

0-60 **8** *¾* **Diane's Choice**[116] 411 5-9-1 **82**..... MickyFenton 6 53
(Miss Gay Kelleway) *chsd ldrs: rdn 3f out: wknd qckly wl over 1f out* **9/1**

59.34 secs (-0.86) **Going Correction** -0.05s/f (Stan) **8** Ran SP% **112.0**

Speed ratings (Par 105): **104,101,100,97,97 91,86,85**

CSF £81.95 CT £337.83 TOTE £14.60: £2.10, £4.50, £1.50; EX 94.90.

Owner Sporting Occasions Racing No 5 **Bred** P G Airey **Trained** Middleham Moor, N Yorks

FOCUS

A fair sprint handicap, run at a sound pace. The winner produced a career best, up 6lb.

2502 GREATLEIGHS.COM MAIDEN AUCTION STKS — 6f (P)

3:00 (3:03) (Class 5) 2-Y-O **£3,238** (£963; £481; £240) **Stalls** Low

Form RPR

1 **Mister Green (FR)** 2-9-0 0..... FergalLynch 10 81+
(M J Wallace) *in tch: hdwy over 3f out: rdn to ld jst over 1f out: in command fnl f* **11/4[1]**

2 *1 ¾* **Solo Attempt** 2-8-10 0..... JohnEgan 4 72+
(M Botti) *chsd ldr tl 2f out: sn switch lft: chsd wnr fnl f: kpt on same pce* **10/1**

3 *nk* **Sir Geoffrey (IRE)** 2-8-11 0..... NeilPollard 3 72
(A J McCabe) *s.i.s: bhd: rdn and hung rt wl over 1f out: hdwy and edgd lft over 1f out: r.o wl fnl f:* **25/1**

00 **4** *3 ½* **Speak The Truth (IRE)**[6] 2324 2-8-12 0..... AmirQuinn 1 62
(J R Boyle) *sn pushed up to ld: rdn 2f out: hdd jst over 1f out: wknd fnl f* **50/1**

2 **5** *4* **Yokozuna**[15] 2086 2-8-13 0..... StephenDonohoe 8 51
(E A L Dunlop) *rrd in stalls and v.s.a: stl last but in tch 4f out: rdn and struggling wl over 2f out: no ch after* **3/1[2]**

6 *hd* **Tasman Gold** 2-9-4 0..... WilliamBuick 5 56
(A M Balding) *dwlt: sn chsng ldrs: rdn over 2f out: sn struggling* **5/1**

7 *2 ¾* **Victorian Tycoon (IRE)** 2-8-11 0..... ChrisCatlin 6 41
(E J O'Neill) *chsd ldrs: lost pl and rdn over 3f out: no ch fnl 2f* **10/3[3]**

1m 14.45s (0.75) **Going Correction** -0.05s/f (Stan) **7** Ran SP% **106.3**

Speed ratings (Par 93): **93,90,90,85,80 80,76**

CSF £25.69 TOTE £3.60: £1.40, £5.10; EX 21.90.

Owner A D Dale **Bred** Gainsborough Stud Management Ltd **Trained** Newmarket, Suffolk

■ Canadian Rockie was withdrawn (14/1, rdr uns and inj bef s). R4 applies, deduct 5p in the £.

FOCUS

An unsatisfactory race in some aspects with the forecast favourite Yokozuna drifting badly in the betting in favour of the eventual winner and then running no sort of race after rearing as the stalls opened. The winner scored in emphatic style and could prove useful. The time was 2.36secs slower than the later handicap.

NOTEBOOK

Mister Green(FR) ◆, a 16,000gns Green Desert colt out of a dual 1m juvenile winner, including at Group 3 level, looks well bought at that price given his pedigree and the ability he showed on this debut. Backed into favourite beforehand, he was always close up, took the lead early in the straight and from then on the result was never in doubt. He should be as effective on turf and can be expected to go on from this. (op 15-2)

Solo Attempt, a 19,000gns daughter of a high-class 1m2f performer in the USA, was another who knew her job on this debut and, although no match for the winner, showed enough promise to suggest she can win a similar contest before long. (op 9-1 tchd 8-1)

Sir Geoffrey(IRE), a cheaply-bought brother to dual 6f winner Caprio from the family of the same owner's No Time, missed the break and took a while to get the hang of things. Despite running green, he finished well and looks capable of emulating his relatives if making normal progress. (tchd 20-1)

Speak The Truth(IRE), who has been well beaten in two outings, including a claimer on Polytrack, appeared to run better this time but sets the standard and holds the form down at the same time. (tchd 66-1)

Yokozuna, who showed plenty of promise when unfancied in a fast-ground maiden on his debut, drifted badly in the pre-race betting and lost his race when rearing badly as the stalls opened. He never got into contention and can be given another chance, but on a note of caution he is clearly not straightforward as he wore a blanket for stalls entry. Official explanation: jockey said, regarding running and riding, that his orders were to be positive, jump out and hopefully make the running, adding that the colt reared prior to stalls opening, was always outpaced and resented the kickback, adding further that the rug fitted to aid colt in stalld had slpped off and colt became unsettled. (op 11-10)

Tasman Gold, a 30,000gns half-brother to Oceana Gold and Snake Skin amongst others, was another to miss the break and was never in the race, but was not given a hard time and can benefit from the experience. (op 7-1)

Victorian Tycoon(IRE), a speedily-bred half-brother to five winners but out of a mile winner in the USA, is from a yard whose juveniles are often ready to do themselves justice first time out. However, he was quite disappointing, losing his place soon after halfway. (op 4-1 tchd 3-1)

2503 NEW HOLLAND CONDITIONS STKS — 1m 2f (P)

3:35 (3:36) (Class 3) 4-Y-O+ **£6,938** (£2,076; £1,038; £519; £258) **Stalls** Low

Form RPR

42-2 **1** **Mutajarred**[40] 1457 4-8-12 100..... RHills 4 113
(W J Haggas) *pressed ldr: rdn over 2f out: led 1f out: a holding runner up after* **2/1[2]**

2-02 **2** *nk* **Many Volumes (USA)**[18] 1990 4-9-2 108..... TedDurcan 3 116
(H R A Cecil) *rearing in stalls: led: qcknd 4f out rdn over 2f out: hdd 1f out: kpt on battling but a jst hld* **5/4[1]**

0006 **3** *6* **Impeller (IRE)**[14] 2103 9-8-12 102..... JohnEgan 5 100
(Jane Chapple-Hyam) *t.k.h: trckd ldrs: rdn over 2f out: sn outpcd by ldng pair: lost action fnl strides: dead* **12/1**

03-4 **4** *2* **Pinpoint (IRE)**[18] 1990 6-8-12 109..... AdamKirby 2 96
(W R Swinburn) *t.k.h: hld up in tch: rdn and hanging bnd over 3f out: no ch w ldrs fnl 2f* **4/1[3]**

460- **5** *¾* **Secret World (IRE)**[286] 4543 5-8-12 107..... EddieAhern 1 95
(J Noseda) *stdd s: hld up in last pair: rdn over 3f out: outpcd wl over 2f out: no ch after* **9/1**

0/46 **6** *7* **Frank Sonata**[28] 1717 7-8-12 97..... PatDobbs 6 81
(M G Quinlan) *hld up in last pl: rdn 4f out: sn outpcd* **20/1**

2m 5.02s (-3.58) **Going Correction** -0.05s/f (Stan) **6** Ran SP% **120.2**

Speed ratings (Par 107): **112,111,106,105,104 99**

CSF £5.38 TOTE £3.10: £1.20, £1.90; EX 5.60.

Owner Hamdan Al Maktoum **Bred** Floors Farming & Beckhampton Stables Ltd **Trained** Newmarket, Suffolk

FOCUS

A decent conditions race that was close to Listed level. The first two in the betting dominated in the straight and the time was 2.05 secs faster than the later handicap. Mutajarred is rated up 5lb.

NOTEBOOK

Mutajarred, one of the lowest rated judged on official marks, was nevertheless one of only a couple who had no question marks over him regarding form and fitness. He was close to the pace from the start and, after getting to the front halfway up the straight, was always going to hold on. He has now won half of his eight starts and looks progressive enough to believe he can make up into a Listed performer, but he has yet to encounter fast turf and so his ability to handle it is an unknown. (op 3-1 tchd 10-3)

Many Volumes(USA), whose best form on turf has all been on fast ground, was quite restive in the stalls but jumped well enough and made the running on this Polytrack debut. The winner got past him halfway up the straight but he rallied and did not go down without a fight. He has been runner-up in four of his last five races now but does not appear to do much wrong. (tchd 15-8)

Impeller(IRE) tracked the leaders from the start but was left behind by the principals in the straight. Sadly he lost his action near the line and suffered an injury to his pastern that proved fatal. He was the winner of nine of his 96 races. (tchd 10-1)

Pinpoint(IRE) had not run on Polytrack since his debut back in June 2005. He looked in need of the outing but has got to come on a good deal to be effective off his current mark, which is 9lb higher than for his last win over a year ago. (op 11-2 tchd 7-2)

Secret World(IRE) has had his problems and has never fulfilled the promise of his debut. He is another who looks as if he needs to drop in the ratings before he can be expected to win again. (op 8-1 tchd 10-1)

2504 ESSEX RACING CLUB H'CAP — 6f (P)

4:10 (4:10) (Class 3) (0-90,90) 4-Y-O-**£6,938** (£2,076; £1,038; £519; £258) **Stalls** Low

Form RPR

1110 **1** **Came Back (IRE)**[46] 1325 5-9-4 **90**..... FergalLynch 7 100+
(K A Ryan) *trckd ldrs: effrt wl over 1f out: led and edgd lft over 1f out: r.o wl* **7/1**

0631 **2** *¾* **Obe Gold**[5] 2358 6-9-3 **89** 6ex.....(v) AdrianTNicholls 9 97
(D Nicholls) *sn bustled in rr: swtchd rt wl over 1f out: r.o wl fnl f: wnt 2nd towards fin: nt trble wnr* **2/1[1]**

2405 **3** *¾* **Tilly's Dream**[22] 1901 5-8-1 **76** oh6..... LukeMorris[(3)] 5 82
(G C Bravery) *in tch in midfield: rdn and hdwy 2f out: edgd lft jst over 1f out: chsd wnr jst ins fnl f: kpt on same pce: lost 2nd towards fin* **33/1**

-122 **4** *1 ¾* **Sweet Pickle**[134] 173 7-8-8 **80**.....(e) EddieAhern 2 80
(J R Boyle) *hld up in tch: effrt and n.m.r jst over 1f out: kpt on same pce fnl f* **15/2**

4064 **5** *2 ¾* **Royal Island (IRE)**[11] 2200 6-8-11 **83**..... VinceSlattery 6 74
(M G Quinlan) *s.i.s: bhd: hdwy on outer 3f out: kpt on fnl f but nvr pce to trble ldrs* **15/2**

-011 **6** *1 ½* **Mango Music**[11] 2205 5-8-4 **76** oh2..... ChrisCatlin 3 62
(M Quinn) *led: rdn 2f out: hdd over 1f out: wknd fnl f* **11/2[3]**

2-05 **7** *½* **Rainbow Mirage (IRE)**[18] 1985 4-8-10 **82**..... DarryllHolland 4 67
(E S McMahon) *stdd s: bhd: effrt and rdn 2f out: nvr threatened ldrs* **9/2[2]**

1245 **8** *¾* **Fromsong (IRE)**[19] 1956 10-9-1 **87**..... TedDurcan 1 69
(D K Ivory) *chsd ldrs on inner: rdn and short of room jst over 1f out: sn wknd* **12/1**

3015 **9** *¾* **Cerebus**[8] 2293 6-8-7 **79**.....(b) JamesDoyle 8 59
(A J McCabe) *chsd ldr: rdn over 2f out: wkng whn short of room over 1f out: no ch after* **9/1**

1m 12.09s (-1.61) **Going Correction** -0.05s/f (Stan) **9** Ran SP% **123.6**

Speed ratings (Par 107): **108,107,106,103,100 98,97,96,95**

CSF £23.01 CT £462.42 TOTE £10.40: £2.90, £1.60, £5.00; EX 21.50.

Owner Mrs Ger O'Driscoll **Bred** Yeomanstown Stud **Trained** Hambleton, N Yorks

FOCUS

A fair sprint, run at a solid pace. The winner continues to progress and, while the third was 6lb out of the handicap, the form still looks sound enough rated through the second and fourth.

NOTEBOOK

Came Back(IRE), below par on the turf 46 days previously, showed he is still an improving sprinter on the All-Weather and bagged his fifth consectutive success on sand. He has been a revelation since joining current connections and the way in which he quickened, despite carrying top weight, to seal this race nearing the final furlong would suggest he still has more to offer despite going up again for this. (op 13-2 tchd 8-1)

Obe Gold, penalised for his ready win at Haydock five days previously, was officially 3lb well in for this as he has now been raised to a mark of 92. He never really travelled through the first half of the race, however, and by the time he really hit top gear in the home straight the winner had gone beyond recall. The manner in which he stayed on late in the day would suggest he remains in top form and a return to turf could well see him defy his new mark in the coming weeks. (op 9-4 tchd 5-2)

Tilly's Dream posted by far her best form for some time considering she raced from 6lb out of the handicap. She will go up for this, but a quick turnout in a lower grade could see her back to winning ways. (op 25-1 tchd 40-1)

Sweet Pickle, who is in foal, was returning from a 134-day break and, after travelling nicely for most of the way, eventually left the impression she would come on for the run. She helps to put this form into perspective. (op 12-1 tchd 7-1)

Royal Island(IRE) was unable to go the early pace on this further drop back in distance, but a slow start hardly helped his cause on that front. He is no doubt weighted to win at present, but he has developed the losing habit and just what his best trip is nowadays is uncertain. (op 7-1 tchd 8-1)

Rainbow Mirage(IRE) Official explanation: jockey said gelding would not face the kickback

2505 IKANDI INTERIORS FILLIES' H'CAP — 1m 2f (P)

4:45 (4:46) (Class 3) (0-95,87) 3-Y-O+ **£6,938** (£2,076; £1,038; £519; £258) **Stalls** Low

Form				RPR
161-	**1**		**Zaskar**218 6410 3-7-12 **71** ... AdrianMcCarthy 1 (Tom Dascombe) *in tch: hdwy on inner over 2f out: led jst over 2f out: clr over 1f out: v easily* **11/4**1	87+
3-10	**2**	3 ½	**Dancing Abbie (USA)**21 1915 3-8-12 **85** ... MickyFenton 6 (M L W Bell) *t.k.h: hld up in tch: rdn and effrt 2f out: kpt on to go 2nd fnl 100yds: no ch w wnr* **4/1**2	91
4-03	**3**	¾	**Fongs Gazelle**16 2059 4-9-9 **82** ... GregFairley 3 (M Johnston) *led: rdn over 2f out: hdd jst over 2f out: no ch w wnr fnl f: lost 2nd fnl 100yds* **7/1**	86
0-46	**4**	¾	**Folly Lodge**25 1801 4-10-0 **87** ... SteveDrowne 10 (G Wragg) *t.k.h: hld up in rr: rdn and effrt over 2f out: kpt on fnl f but no ch w wnr* **11/2**3	90
654	**5**	hd	**Lisathedaddy**13 2120 6-9-12 **85** ... RichardKingscote 4 (B G Powell) *s.i.s: bhd: rdn 3f out: swtchd rt over 1f out: kpt on same pce u.p* **6/1**	87
0-00	**6**	1 ½	**Dusty Moon**20 1930 3-8-3 **79** ... LukeMorris(3) 8 (W J Knight) *bhd: rdn over 3f out: n.d* **14/1**	78+
1133	**7**	5	**Cape Velvet (IRE)**31 1645 4-8-12 **71** oh2 ... JamesDoyle 2 (J W Hills) *t.k.h: chsd ldrs: rdn over 2f out: wknd qckly wl over 1f out* **9/1**	60
1351	**8**	5	**Naughty Thoughts (IRE)**13 2125 4-8-5 **71** oh9 ... RossAtkinson(7) 7 (Tom Dascombe) *chsd ldr tl over 2f out: sn wknd: wl bhd fnl f* **8/1**	50

2m 7.07s (-1.53) **Going Correction** -0.05s/f (Stan)
WFA 3 from 4yo+ 14lb — **8** Ran SP% **116.6**
Speed ratings (Par 104): **104,101,100,100,99 98,94,90**
CSF £14.07 CT £69.38 TOTE £3.80: £2.70, £1.60, £2.00; EX 14.60.

Owner P A Deal & M J Silver **Bred** Darley **Trained** Lambourn, Berks

FOCUS
A decent fillies' handicap that was run 2.05 secs slower than the earlier conditions race. The first two came here unexposed and this is solid form.

NOTEBOOK
Zaskar ◆, who won two of her three starts as a juvenile and suffered her only defeat in a hot nursery that has since produced nine individual winners, was well backed on this return to action. Locked away on the inside, she made her ground turning in and, getting the split nearest the rail, she swept through to score with plenty in hand. Clearly better than her current rating, she is likely to go up a good deal for this and connections are likely to attempt to earn black type in the Listed Prix Urban Sea at Le Lion D'Angers next. (op 7-2 tchd 4-1 in places)

Dancing Abbie(USA), whose win came in an ordinary fillies' maiden on this surface at Wolverhampton, was quite keen early but ran on in the closing stages, although she was no match for the winner. Time may tell she had a tough task in trying to concede a stone. (tchd 5-1)

Fongs Gazelle, who was in good form at this time last year, was 5lb above her last winning mark but appeared to run her race and sets the standard. (op 6-1 tchd 9-2)

Folly Lodge was one of several that were keen under restraint early and she never really got involved despite staying on. This was her first attempt at the trip and she seemed to get it. (op 13-2)

Lisathedaddy, all of whose wins have been over 1m2f on Lingfield's Polytrack, has not scored for over a year but is still 2lb above her last winning mark as she has been running consistently. She missed the break before staying on in the closing stages but has more to find to get back to winning ways. (op 13-2)

Dusty Moon, whose debut win came on this surface, has been well beaten on turf since and the return to Polytrack failed to bring about a revival. (op 16-1)

2506 W20.NET H'CAP — 5f (P)

5:15 (5:17) (Class 5) (0-75,74) 3-Y-O **£2,590** (£770; £385; £192) **Stalls** Low

Form				RPR
-156	**1**		**Yankee Storm**12 2141 3-9-0 **70** ... GregFairley 5 (M Johnston) *s.i.s: bhd: rdn and hdwy 2f out: swtchd rt 1f out: hrd drvn to ld towards fin* **13/2**	77
3160	**2**	¾	**Orpen's Art (IRE)**9 2258 3-8-10 **73** ... HollyHall(7) 6 (S A Callaghan) *prom: ev ch 2f out: rdn to ld 1f out: hdd and no ex towards fin* **16/1**	77
41-0	**3**	¾	**Replicator**13 2127 3-9-2 **72** ... PatDobbs 10 (Pat Eddery) *chsd ldrs: lost pl over 3f out: drvn wl over 2f out: styd on u.p fnl f: wnt 3rd towards fin: nt rch ldng pair* **10/1**	76+
4241	**4**	nk	**Maggie Kate**15 2074 3-8-9 **65** ... RobertHavlin 8 (R Ingram) *in tch: rdn over 2f out: no hdwy tl styd on u.p ins fnl f: wnt 4th nr fin* **9/2**3	65
31-	**5**	1 ½	**Quaroma**203 6721 3-9-4 **74** ... JohnEgan 4 (Jane Chapple-Hyam) *pressed ldr: rdn to ld over 1f out: hdd 1f out: wknd and lost 2 pls fnl 100yds* **4/1**2	69
00-0	**6**	½	**L'Art Du Silence (IRE)**30 1674 3-8-7 **63** ... (p) EddieAhern 1 (J R Boyle) *bhd: detached last and lost tch wl over 3f out: c v wd wl over 1f out: r.o fnl f: nvr threatened ldrs* **20/1**	56
5-46	**7**	1	**Wavertree Princess (IRE)**13 2122 3-9-0 **70** ... JamesDoyle 3 (N P Littmoden) *in tch: rdn over 2f out: no imp u.p fr over 1f out* **10/3**1	59
3-10	**8**	½	**The Magic Blanket (IRE)**13 2127 3-8-10 **66** ... MickyFenton 2 (Stef Liddiard) *led: rdn 2f out: hdd over 1f out: wkng whn short of room ins fnl f: eased after* **9/1**	54
006-	**R**		**Fitolini**237 5932 3-8-10 **66** ... TedDurcan 9 (Mrs G S Rees) *ref to r* **9/1**	—

60.31 secs (0.11) **Going Correction** -0.05s/f (Stan) — **9** Ran SP% **114.3**
Speed ratings (Par 99): **97,95,94,94,91 90,89,88,—**
CSF £101.64 CT £1032.39 TOTE £7.30: £2.80, £4.50, £2.10; EX 110.30 Place 6: £106.50, Place 5: £47.54..

Owner Greenstead Hall Racing **Bred** Mark Johnston Racing Ltd **Trained** Middleham Moor, N Yorks

FOCUS
A modest three-year-old handicap. Fair form for the grade with the fourth a decent guide.

Wavertree Princess(IRE) Official explanation: jockey said filly lost its action

T/Plt: £377.20 to a £1 stake. Pool: £55,013.80. 106.45 winning tickets. T/Qpdt: £58.40 to a £1 stake. Pool: £3,152.70. 39.90 winning tickets. SP

2086 YARMOUTH (L-H)

Wednesday, May 28

OFFICIAL GOING: Good (good to firm in places)
Wind: fresh against Weather: fine

2507 EUROPEAN BREEDERS' FUND/TOTEPLACEPOT NOVICE STKS — 6f 3y

2:10 (2:11) (Class 5) 2-Y-O **£3,885** (£1,156; £577; £288) **Stalls** High

Form				RPR
4	**1**		**Imperial Guest**23 1873 2-8-12 0 ... RyanMoore 6 (G G Margarson) *sn pushed along in rr: hdwy over 2f out: led over 1f out: rdn clr* **22/1**	84+
341	**2**	3 ¾	**Mazzola**5 2349 2-8-12 0 ... MCGeran(7) 4 (M R Channon) *led 2f: led again over 2f out: rdn and hdd over 1f out: hung lft ins fnl f: no ex* **3/1**2	80
16	**3**	1 ½	**Kate The Great**25 1813 2-9-0 0 ... PatCosgrave 5 (M J Wallace) *s.i.s: sn prom: rdn over 1f out: no ex fnl f* **25/1**	71
21	**4**	1	**Soul Sista (IRE)**42 1392 2-8-11 0 ... LiamJones 2 (J L Spearing) *chsd ldrs: edgd lft thrght: rdn and ev ch over 2f out: wknd fnl f* **9/1**3	65
	5	2	**Suruor (IRE)** 2-8-12 0 ... JimmyFortune 1 (M Johnston) *s.s: outpcd: rdn over 2f out: nt trble ldrs* **12/1**	60
	6	8	**Secret Society** 2-8-12 0 ... JamieSpencer 7 (M L W Bell) *s.s: hdwy over 2f out: wknd over 1f out* **8/11**1	36+
130	**7**	1 ¾	**Lisburn (IRE)**12 2167 2-8-11 0 ... MarkLawson(3) 3 (M Brittain) *w ldr tl led 4f out: rdn and hdd over 2f out: wknd over 1f out* **12/1**	32

1m 15.92s (1.52) **Going Correction** +0.15s/f (Good) — **7** Ran SP% **116.5**
Speed ratings (Par 93): **95,90,88,86,84 73,71**
CSF £89.65 TOTE £22.40: £5.30, £2.20; EX 96.00.

Owner John Guest **Bred** John Guest Racing Ltd **Trained** Newmarket, Suffolk

FOCUS
A fair contest rated around the placed horses and the form look solid.

NOTEBOOK
Imperial Guest, soon outpaced when fourth on his debut at Windsor, was always likely to be suited by this extra furlong and the booking of Moore looked significant. Again struggling to go the early pace, he started to pick up from just past halfway and had it in the bag from over a furlong out. The form looks only fair, even with hot favourite Secret Society disappointing, and there should be more improvement to come. He will stay further in time and may take his chance in the Chesham Stakes at Royal Ascot. (op 18-1)

Mazzola, readily off the mark at Brighton the other day, appreciating the step up to 6f, had 7lb offset by his rider's claim and was made plenty of use of. He ran well without being able to match the unexposed winner and should pay his way in nurseries later in the campaign. (tchd 11-4 and 10-3)

Kate The Great, a disappointment at Thirsk last time, having previously won on debut, took a marked step forward here and seemed suited by the extra furlong. This was a really good effort considering she was giving weight all round and, although no match for the winner, she is another likely type for nurseries. (op 20-1 tchd 28-1)

Soul Sista(IRE), a good winner at Beverley last time, was up a furlong in trip here and she was unable to take a further step forward. She remains capable of better back at 5f. (op 11-1 tchd 12-1 in a place)

Suruor(IRE), who is going to need further than this in time, comes from a yard whose juveniles are needing a run this season and he was soon in trouble following a slow start. He can be expected to improve on this next time. Official explanation: jockey said colt ran very green (tchd 14-1)

Secret Society, a Group 1 Pheonix Stakes entry who is evidently well thought-of by connections, was strongly supported in the market and clearly expected to make a winning start. He was very slow out of the gates though and, despite making a promising forward move, the early running he had to do took its toll. This was clearly below expectations and he deserves another chance. Official explanation: jockey said colt moved poorly (op 10-11 tchd Evens)

Lisburn(IRE) Official explanation: jockey said filly hung right

2508 TOTEEXACTA (S) STKS — 6f 3y

2:40 (2:42) (Class 6) 2-Y-O **£1,683** (£501; £250; £125) **Stalls** High

Form				RPR
400	**1**		**Missy Que (IRE)**19 1961 2-8-6 0 ... RichardMullen 2 (W R Muir) *chsd ldrs: led over 1f out: drvn out* **11/4**3	53
	2	nk	**Coconut Shy** 2-8-6 0 ... TPO'Shea 6 (M G Quinlan) *unruly in stalls: s.s: hdwy over 1f out: rdn and ev ch ins fnl f: r.o* **9/4**2	52+
636	**3**	½	**Kheley (IRE)**18 2004 2-8-6 0 ... LiamJones 1 (W M Brisbourne) *hld up in tch: led wl over 1f out: sn rdn: hung lft and hdd: nt qckn ins fnl f* **9/1**	51
4540	**4**	3 ¾	**Lagan Handout**14 2098 2-8-8 0 ... KevinGhunowa(3) 4 (Dr J R J Naylor) *disp ld tl hdd wl over 1f out: hmpd sn after: wknd ins fnl f* **15/8**1	44
6	**5**	4 ½	**The Wonkey Donkey**16 2049 2-7-13 0 ... PatrickDonaghy(7) 5 (K J Burke) *disp ld tl rdn and wknd over 1f out* **16/1**	26

1m 17.56s (3.16) **Going Correction** +0.15s/f (Good) — **5** Ran SP% **108.1**
Speed ratings (Par 91): **84,83,82,77,71**
CSF £8.96 TOTE £3.40: £1.80, £1.70; EX 10.20.There was no bid for the winner. Coconut Shy was claimed by G Prodromou for £5,000.

Owner Quaintance Partnership & Partners **Bred** James Waldron **Trained** Lambourn, Berks

FOCUS
A fair seller by course standards with the winner dropping in grade, but not a race to be with.

NOTEBOOK
Missy Que(IRE), down the field behind fair sorts in two of her three maidens, looked of obvious interest on this drop in grade and she battled on well once hitting the front to deny newcomer Coconut Shy. She may prove a little better than this grade and should make her mark at a modest level in nurseries. (op 10-3)

Coconut Shy, a 4,500gns daughter of Bahamian Bounty, is bred for speed and her yard does quite well here. Introduced at a lowly level, she was unruly in the stalls and lost her race there, coming out very slowly. She did well to finish as close as she did, just losing out, and should have little trouble winning a race at this level. (op 2-1)

Kheley(IRE) is exposed at this level, but she again ran well and this represented a slight improvement. (op 12-1)

Lagan Handout had shown enough to suggest a race at this level would come his way and he was expected to prove suited by the extra furlong. However, having shown good early speed, he did not find much for pressure and already looked beaten when getting slightly hampered. Perhaps a drop back to 5f is needed. Official explanation: jockey said colt ran flat (op 13-8 tchd 2-1)

The Wonkey Donkey improved on her debut effort, but was still well beaten and winning a race is not going to be easy. (op 20-1)

2509 TOTESPORT 0800 221 221 MAIDEN STKS 1m 3y

3:15 (3:17) (Class 5) 3-Y-O+ £2,914 (£867; £433; £216) Stalls High

Form RPR

22- **1** **Tazeez (USA)**[210] 6597 4-9-12 0 JimmyFortune 12 97+
(J H M Gosden) *racd centre: chsd ldrs: led overall over 2f out: rdn out* 4/1[2]

3 **2** 3 1/4 **Decameron (USA)**[16] 2056 3-9-0 0 RyanMoore 14 87+
(Sir Michael Stoute) *racd centre: hld up in tch: chsd wnr 2f out: edgd lft over 1f out: styd on same pce* 4/7[1]

-20 **3** 6 **French Art**[20] 1926 3-9-0 83 SebSanders 2 73
(D R C Elsworth) *led far side duo and overall ldr tl jnd centre and hdd over 2f out: wknd fnl f* 5/1[3]

4 3/4 **Kidlat** 3-9-0 0 DaneO'Neill 7 71+
(L M Cumani) *racd centre: s.s: bhd tl styd on appr fnl f: nvr nrr* 50/1

5 **5** 3/4 **Dolcetto (IRE)**[28] 1721 3-8-9 0 JamieSpencer 16 64+
(J R Fanshawe) *s.i.s: racd centre: hld up: hdwy over 2f out: shkn up over 1f out: nt trble ldrs* 16/1

6 **6** 1/2 **Mont Cervin**[16] 2056 3-9-0 0 AlanMunro 9 68
(W J Haggas) *racd centre: chsd ldrs: rdn over 2f out: wknd over 1f out* 33/1

0- **7** 2 **Lilburn (IRE)**[299] 4130 3-9-0 0 TPO'Shea 13 64
(J R Fanshawe) *racd centre: s.s: hld up: hdwy over 1f out: nvr trbld ldrs* 100/1

8 2 **Ghufa (IRE)** 4-9-5 0 WilliamCarson(7) 8 62
(E A L Dunlop) *racd centre: chsd ldrs: hung lft and wknd over 2f out* 50/1

0 **9** nk **Battling Lil (IRE)**[23] 1869 4-9-4 0 TolleyDean(3) 15 56
(J L Spearing) *racd centre: hld up: rdn over 2f out: wknd over 1f out* 100/1

00 **10** nk **Golden Bishop**[27] 1748 3-9-0 0 RichardMullen 5 58
(M L W Bell) *racd centre: mid-div: rdn 1/2-way: wknd over 2f out* 100/1

11 3/4 **Selfish Option (IRE)** 3-8-11 0 PatCosgrave(3) 4 56
(H Morrison) *racd centre: hld up: n.d* 100/1

06 **12** 7 **Sleeping**[11] 2199 3-8-9 0 JimmyQuinn 1 35
(M H Tompkins) *trckd ldr far side tl jnd centre gp 1/2-way: wknd 3f out* 100/1

6-0 **13** 1 **Gainsborough's Art (IRE)**[13] 2119 3-8-11 0 MarcHalford(3) 11 37
(D R C Elsworth) *led centre gp over 5f: sn edgd lft and wknd* 100/1

0 **14** shd **Nefaf (IRE)**[41] 1418 3-9-0 0 LiamJones 10 37
(C E Brittain) *racd centre: chsd ldrs: rdn 1/2-way: wknd over 2f out* 100/1

0- **15** 3/4 **Siena**[211] 6574 3-8-9 0 TGMcLaughlin 6 30
(Mrs C A Dunnett) *racd centre: s.s: a in rr* 100/1

0 **16** 1 3/4 **Lightning Squall (USA)**[11] 2198 3-9-0 0 OscarUrbina 3 31
(M Botti) *racd centre: hld up: hung lft 1/2-way: sn wknd* 80/1

1m 41.02s (0.42) **Going Correction** +0.15s/f (Good)
WFA 3 from 4yo 12lb 16 Ran SP% 122.2
Speed ratings (Par 103): **103,99,93,93,92 91,89,87,87,87 86,79,78,78,77 75**
CSF £6.51 TOTE £5.20: £1.40, £1.02, £1.70; EX 8.50 Trifecta £21.80 Pool: £484.85. 15.73 winning units..
Owner Hamdan Al Maktoum **Bred** Clovelly Farms **Trained** Newmarket, Suffolk

FOCUS
A good maiden, although there was not much strength in depth - as the fact they bet 16/1 bar three testifies - but two very useful prospects came clear.
Dolcetto(IRE) Official explanation: trainer later said filly found the going (good, good to firm in places) too lively

2510 TOTESPORT.COM H'CAP 1m 3y

3:50 (3:51) (Class 6) (0-65,65) 4-Y-O+ £1,942 (£578; £288; £144) Stalls High

Form RPR

02-5 **1** **Navene (IRE)**[26] 1780 4-8-9 56 AlanMunro 2 67
(C F Wall) *trckd ldrs: plld hrd: led 2f out: drvn out* 6/1[2]

00-2 **2** 1 1/4 **Haasem (USA)**[31] 1645 5-9-4 65 RyanMoore 12 73
(J R Jenkins) *hld up: hdwy over 1f out: edgd rt and chsd wnr ins fnl f: r.o* 7/1[3]

5020 **3** 1 1/2 **Hits Only Cash**[15] 2087 6-9-4 65 JamieSpencer 15 70
(J Pearce) *hld up: racd keenly: swtchd lft over 2f out: hdwy over 1f out: sn edgd rt and chsng wnr: rdn and no ex ins fnl f* 7/2[1]

5003 **4** 3/4 **Libre**[22] 1898 8-8-11 58 TGMcLaughlin 7 61+
(F Jordan) *hld up: nt clr run fr over 2f out tl r.o ins fnl f: edgd lft: nt rch ldrs* 12/1

0-50 **5** 1 3/4 **Upstairs**[11] 2187 4-8-10 60 MarcHalford(3) 10 59+
(D R C Elsworth) *s.s: hld up: hdwy 2f out: rdn over 1f out: styd on same pce* 20/1

1143 **6** 1 1/2 **Wodhill Schnaps**[15] 2087 7-9-0 61 (b) JimmyFortune 3 56
(D Morris) *prom: rdn over 1f out: no ex fnl f* 5/1[1]

6004 **7** 2 1/2 **Kingsholm**[4] 2391 6-9-3 64 SebSanders 9 54
(I W McInnes) *hld up: nt clr run fr over 2f out: nvr trbld ldrs* 5/1[1]

-004 **8** 2 **Split The Wind (USA)**[18] 2003 4-8-5 52 RichardMullen 1 37
(Eve Johnson Houghton) *prom: rdn over 3f out: wknd fnl f* 9/1

05-0 **9** 3/4 **Spume (IRE)**[11] 2185 4-9-0 61 LiamJones 4 44
(S Parr) *w ldr tl led 1/2-way: rdn and hdd 2f out: wknd over 1f out* 10/1

0200 **10** 2 3/4 **Grey Gurkha**[18] 2009 7-8-6 53 PatrickMathers 13 30
(I W McInnes) *hld up: rdn 1/2-way: hdwy over 2f out: wknd over 1f out* 33/1

66-5 **11** 3/4 **Life's A Whirl**[16] 2057 6-8-5 52 (p) DMylonas 8 27
(Mrs C A Dunnett) *chsd ldrs over 5f* 20/1

0-65 **12** 6 **Carefree**[131] 214 4-8-7 54 PaulEddery 6 15
(Mrs R A Carr) *hld up in tch: rdn 1/2-way: sn lost pl* 66/1

5-03 **13** 1 **Dubai Shadow (IRE)**[20] 1938 4-8-9 56 KShea 5 15
(C E Brittain) *mid-div: rdn over 2f out: sn wknd* 16/1

-200 **14** 1 1/4 **Fairy Festival (IRE)**[27] 1747 4-8-8 55 (b[1]) LPKeniry 16 11
(J S Moore) *led to 1/2-way: edgd lft and wknd over 2f out* 17/2

1m 41.9s (1.30) **Going Correction** +0.15s/f (Good) 14 Ran SP% 120.2
Speed ratings (Par 101): **99,97,96,95,93 92,89,87,87,84 83,77,76,75**
CSF £44.64 CT £372.72 TOTE £7.60: £2.00, £3.30, £3.60; EX 53.80 Trifecta £230.10 Part won. Pool: £324.17. 0.30 winning units..
Owner Dr Philip Brown **Bred** Louis A Walshe **Trained** Newmarket, Suffolk
■ Stewards' Enquiry : D Mylonas caution: used whip when out of contention

FOCUS
A modest but competitive handicap. Pretty sound form, the winner up 3lb.

2511 TOTESPORTCASINO.COM H'CAP 6f 3y

4:25 (4:25) (Class 5) (0-70,70) 4-Y-O+ £2,590 (£770; £385; £192) Stalls High

Form RPR

4000 **1** **Avoncreek**[40] 1453 4-7-11 56 oh11 SoniaEaton(7) 2 58
(B P J Baugh) *racd centre: hld up: plld hrd: hdwy over 1f out: r.o to ld post* 100/1

4240 **2** hd **Commander Wish**[18] 1997 5-8-5 57 (p) LiamJones 1 58
(Lucinda Featherstone) *racd centre: prom: rdn over 2f out: edgd rt and led 1f out: hdd post* 12/1

-100 **3** 2 1/2 **Russian Rocket (IRE)**[19] 1966 6-8-5 57 DMylonas 9 50
(Mrs C A Dunnett) *racd centre: chsd ldrs: rdn and ev ch over 1f out: styd on same pce* 8/1

-106 **4** 3/4 **Fast Freddie**[61] 1047 4-9-2 68 JamieSpencer 7 59
(S Parr) *racd centre: mde most over 3f: rdn and ev ch over 1f out: no ex* 15/2

5051 **5** 1/2 **Gone'N'Dunnett (IRE)**[15] 2075 9-7-11 56 oh4 (v) AmyBaker(7) 3 45
(Mrs C A Dunnett) *racd centre: chsd ldrs: rdn over 1f out: styd on same pce* 20/1

31-6 **6** 3/4 **Cape Cobra**[29] 1703 4-8-13 65 (b) JimmyFortune 4 52
(J H M Gosden) *rdr slow removing hood: racd centre: sn prom: rdn over 1f out: nt run on* 5/2[1]

0-13 **7** 3/4 **Dragon Flame (IRE)**[12] 2166 5-9-0 66 (v) SebSanders 10 51
(M Quinn) *racd alone stands' side: w ldrs tl led over 2f out: rdn and edgd lft over 1f out: sn hdd: wknd towards fin* 4/1[2]

0604 **8** 2 3/4 **Tamino (IRE)**[5] 2350 5-9-2 68 (t) JimmyQuinn 11 44
(P Howling) *swtchd to r centre 5f out: hld up: rdn and wknd over 1f out* 6/1[3]

012- **9** hd **Efisio Princess**[211] 6575 5-8-11 63 RichardThomas 8 38
(J E Long) *racd centre: chsd ldrs: rdn over 1f out: wknd and eased fnl f* 13/2

1m 16.04s (1.64) **Going Correction** +0.15s/f (Good) 9 Ran SP% 112.5
Speed ratings (Par 103): **95,94,91,90,89 88,87,84,83**
CSF £994.25 CT £10378.56 TOTE £188.50: £23.80, £3.30, £2.50; EX 402.20 TRIFECTA Not won..
Owner Messrs Chrimes, Winn & Wilson **Bred** J H Chrimes **Trained** Audley, Staffs

FOCUS
The winner was 17lb wrong, so the form makes little sense and is probably not worth much.
Avoncreek Official explanation: trainer said, regarding the apparent improvement in form, that gelding is inconsistent but performed well on this occasion.
Efisio Princess Official explanation: trainer said mare was unsuited by the good (good to firm in places) ground

2512 TOTESPORTGAMES.COM H'CAP 1m 3f 101y

4:55 (4:55) (Class 6) (0-65,64) 4-Y-O+ £1,780 (£529; £264; £132) Stalls Low

Form RPR

5000 **1** **Inch Lodge**[30] 1692 6-8-10 56 (t) PaulEddery 3 63
(Miss D Mountain) *mde all: rdn over 1f out: styd on: eased nr fin* 9/2[3]

00-0 **2** 1 3/4 **Dawn Mystery**[31] 1643 4-8-4 50 oh5 (b[1]) NickyMackay 4 54
(Rae Guest) *chsd wnr: rdn over 2f out: styd on* 14/1

0400 **3** 2 **Summer Bounty**[30] 1692 12-7-12 51 oh1 ow1 PatrickDonaghy(7) 2 52
(F Jordan) *s.s: hld up: hdwy over 2f out: rdn over 1f out: no ex ins fnl f* 15/2

0-04 **4** 2 3/4 **Barbirolli**[8] 2286 6-8-6 52 (b[1]) LiamJones 6 49
(W M Brisbourne) *hld up: rdn over 2f out: nt trble ldrs* 15/8[1]

1441 **5** 7 **Lough Beg (IRE)**[53] 1206 5-9-4 64 (t) DaneO'Neill 7 49
(Miss Tor Sturgis) *hld up: prom: rdn over 3f out: wknd over 1f out* 5/2[2]

000/ **6** 3/4 **Plain Champagne (IRE)**[583] 6132 6-8-3 52 oh5 ow2 KevinGhunowa(3) 5 36
(Dr J R J Naylor) *trckd ldrs: racd keenly: rdn over 3f out: wknd 2f out: eased fnl f* 10/1

2m 32.18s (3.48) **Going Correction** +0.15s/f (Good) 6 Ran SP% 109.1
Speed ratings (Par 101): **93,91,90,88,83 82**
CSF £54.33 CT £415.94 TOTE £5.70: £2.80, £3.90; EX 56.20 Trifecta £274.00 Part won. Pool: £386.04 - 0.40 winning units..
Owner David Fremel **Bred** Gainsborough Stud Management Ltd **Trained** Newmarket, Suffolk

FOCUS
A moderate handicap in which the winner was given an easy lead and the runner-up was out of the handicap. Poor form which might not work out.
Lough Beg(IRE) Official explanation: jockey said gelding lost its action

2513 TOTESPORTBINGO.COM H'CAP 1m 2f 21y

5:25 (5:30) (Class 6) (0-55,55) 4-Y-O+ £1,780 (£529; £264; £132) Stalls Low

Form RPR

1510 **1** **Jarvo**[30] 1692 7-8-13 54 (v) PatrickMathers 8 58
(I W McInnes) *mid-div: rdn over 3f out: hdwy over 2f out: styd on to ld nr fin* 16/1

0330 **2** nk **Mick Is Back**[2] 2456 4-8-12 53 (vt) DaneO'Neill 13 56
(G G Margarson) *hld up in tch: rdn and ev ch fr over 2f out: led wl ins fnl f: hdd nr fin* 14/1

2-51 **3** nse **Nassar (IRE)**[27] 1747 5-8-9 53 KirstyMilczarek(3) 3 56
(G Prodromou) *chsd ldrs: rdn to ld over 2f out: hdd wl ins fnl f: styd on* 7/1

6064 **4** 1 **Barry Island**[16] 2060 9-8-9 53 MarcHalford(3) 6 54
(D R C Elsworth) *dwlt: hld up: hdwy over 1f out: styd on* 10/1

566- **5** 3/4 **Samahir (USA)**[180] 6975 4-8-11 52 SebSanders 4 54+
(T T Clement) *hld up: hdwy over 2f out: rdn over 1f out: styd on* 16/1

-324 **6** 1 1/2 **Beech Games**[86] 239 4-8-13 54 TGMcLaughlin 15 51
(F Jordan) *hld up: rdn over 2f out: hdwy and hung lft fr over 1f out: nt rch ldrs* 40/1

-004 **7** 3/4 **Desert Hawk**[26] 1776 7-8-10 51 LiamJones 1 46
(W M Brisbourne) *prom: rdn over 3f out: styd on same pce appr fnl f* 6/1[2]

2665 **8** 4 **Don Pasquale**[88] 769 6-8-3 47 ow1 (v) KevinGhunowa(3) 12 34
(J T Stimpson) *hld up: nt clr run over 2f out: hdwy over 1f out: no ex ins fnl f* 25/1

4430 **9** nse **Putra Laju (IRE)**[20] 1932 4-8-13 54 (p) AlanMunro 2 41
(J W Hills) *hld up: sme hdwy over 1f out: n.d* 7/1

2-03 **10** 4 **Bold Phoenix (IRE)**[53] 1207 7-8-5 46 oh1 (v[1]) TPO'Shea 16 25
(A P Stringer) *hld up: nt clr run over 2f out: n.d* 12/1

-331 **11** 1 3/4 **Formidable Guest**[30] 1673 4-8-8 49 JamieSpencer 10 25
(J Pearce) *hld up: nt clr run over 2f out: n.d* 5/1[1]

-300 **12** 6 **General Flumpa**[20] 1929 7-8-9 55 HaddenFrost(5) 11 19
(Miss Tor Sturgis) *s.i.s: hdwy over 7f out: rdn over 4f out: wknd over 2f out* 25/1

0-00 **13** *27* **Royal Choir**[19] 1966 4-8-1 **49** DebraEngland(7) 14 —
(C E Brittain) *chsd ldr: rdn and wknd over 2f out* **50/1**
2063 **14** *20* **Club Captain (USA)**[49] 1269 5-8-5 **46** oh1 JimmyQuinn 9 —
(T D McCarthy) *chsd ldrs: rdn over 4f out: n.m.r and wknd over 2f out* **20/1**
225/ **15** *3 ¾* **Valverde (IRE)**[238] 5927 5-8-8 **52** (t) TolleyDean(3) 7 —
(George Baker) *led: rdn and hdd over 2f out: sn wknd* **13/2**[3]

2m 11.68s (1.18) **Going Correction** +0.15s/f (Good) **15 Ran SP% 121.4**
Speed ratings (Par 101): **101,100,100,99,99 98,97,94,94,91 89,84,63,47,44**
CSF £211.11 CT £1725.92 TOTE £21.00: £7.00, £3.10, £2.90; EX 312.80 TRIFECTA Not won. Place 6: £1618.40, Place 5: £437.85..
Owner F S W Partnership **Bred** Lloyd Farm Stud **Trained** Catwick, E Yorks

FOCUS
A very moderate handicap contested by fully exposed horses.
Formidable Guest Official explanation: trainer said filly was unsuited by the good (good to firm in places) ground
General Flumpa Official explanation: jockey said gelding had no more to give
T/Jkpt: Not won. T/Plt: £8,067.30 to a £1 stake. Pool: £72,937.95. 6.60 winning tickets. T/Qpdt: £1,317.70 to a £1 stake. Pool: £3,917.60. 2.20 winning tickets. CR

2514 - 2520a (Foreign Racing) - See Raceform Interactive

AYR (L-H)
Thursday, May 29

OFFICIAL GOING: Good to firm (9.2)
Wind: breezy, half against Weather: sunny, dry

2521 EUROPEAN BREEDERS' FUND MAIDEN STKS 6f
2:20 (2:21) (Class 4) 2-Y-O **£4,857** (£1,445; £722; £360) **Stalls High**

Form RPR
3 **1** **Shaweel**[14] 2134 2-9-3 0 GregFairley 1 85+
(M Johnston) *mde all: qcknd clr over 1f out: easily* **1/2**[1]
4 **2** *6* **Verinco**[17] 2035 2-9-3 0 TomEaves 3 67+
(B Smart) *chsd wnr: rdn over 2f out: sn one pce* **3/1**[2]
3 *3 ¾* **Night Of Fortune** 2-9-3 0 SebSanders 2 53+
(Sir Mark Prescott) *t.k.h: in tch: pushed along and rn green over 2f out: sn outpcd* **10/1**[3]
4 *7* **An Carrig** 2-9-3 0 AndrewElliott 4 32+
(K R Burke) *t.k.h: prom: pushed along over 2f out: sn btn* **16/1**

1m 11.4s (-2.20) **Going Correction** -0.40s/f (Firm) **4 Ran SP% 106.6**
Speed ratings (Par 95): **98,90,85,75**
CSF £2.17 TOTE £1.50; EX 1.50.
Owner Sheikh Ahmed Al Maktoum **Bred** P C Hunt **Trained** Middleham Moor, N Yorks

FOCUS
Not a competitive race and just an ordinary gallop but plenty to like about the performance of the winner. The form is hard to quantify but should be at least this good and could be better.

NOTEBOOK
Shaweel ◆, who showed promise on his debut at York, had the rub of this uncompetitive race and showed improved form to win with plenty in hand. There is plenty of room for improvement, he should have no problems with 7f and he appeals as the sort to hold his own in stronger company this summer. (op 8-13 tchd 4-6)
Verinco, who showed promise at an ordinary level on his debut, was not disgraced over this longer trip but had his limitations exposed against a potentially useful sort. He is not the biggest around but is capable of picking up an ordinary event. (op 11-4 tchd 9-4)
Night Of Fortune, related to several winners, notably smart middle-distance performer Tam Lin, is a fair sort on looks but showed his inexperience and was well beaten on this racecourse debut. His Derby entry is optimistic on this evidence but he can be expected to leave this bare form a long way behind over further in due course. (op 7-1)
An Carrig, out of a dam who finished fourth in the Oaks, was easy to back and well beaten on this racecourse debut. A stiffer test of stamina is going to suit in due course. (op 14-1)

2522 DAWN DEVELOPMENTS MAIDEN AUCTION STKS 5f
2:50 (2:50) (Class 5) 2-Y-O **£3,070** (£906; £453) **Stalls High**

Form RPR
442 **1** **Russet Reward**[12] 2186 2-8-11 0 TomEaves 1 76
(Mrs L Stubbs) *mde all: rdn over 1f out: edgd lft ins fnl f: hld on wl* **4/1**[2]
35 **2** *nk* **Metroland**[14] 2140 2-8-10 0 GregFairley 3 74
(M Johnston) *pressed wnr: rdn and ev ch fr over 1f out: kpt on fnl f* **16/1**[3]
32 **3** *1 ¼* **Peninsular War**[13] 2140 2-9-1 0 DarrenWilliams 2 74
(K R Burke) *stdd bhd ldrs: effrt and rdn over 1f out: edgd lft: kpt on same pce fnl f* **1/4**[1]

59.55 secs (-0.55) **Going Correction** -0.40s/f (Firm) **3 Ran SP% 105.9**
Speed ratings (Par 93): **88,87,85**
CSF £21.59 TOTE £3.60; EX 19.00.
Owner P G Shorrock **Bred** Beech Park Bloodstock Ltd **Trained** Norton, N Yorks

FOCUS
Another uncompetitive maiden and one that did not take as much winning as seemed likely beforehand. The pace was moderate and the winner is rated to form in a muddling race.

NOTEBOOK
Russet Reward, the most experienced of the trio, took advantage of the below-par run of the market leader and probably did not have to improve to get off the mark. He left the impression this ground was plenty quick enough but would be no good thing to follow up under a penalty. (op 3-1)
Metroland, who failed to build on her debut effort at Hamilton back at the same course next time, showed that to be all wrong and returned to her best. She will be suited by 6f and is capable of picking up a modest event. (op 11-1)
Peninsular War looked the one to beat on his form behind a couple of useful Brian Smart juveniles on his first two starts but he proved a disappointment. The quick ground may have been the cause for this defeat but he is well worth another chance to confirm previous promise. Official explanation: trainer had no explanation for the poor form shown (op 4-11)

2523 NEILSON BINNIE-MCKENZIE H'CAP 1m 1f 20y
3:20 (3:21) (Class 6) (0-60,61) 4-Y-0+ **£2,914** (£867; £433; £216) **Stalls Low**

Form RPR
-005 **1** **Malguru**[10] 2250 4-8-6 **45** (p) GregFairley 1 53
(A G Foster) *chsd ldrs: rdn 3f out: led wl over 1f out: hrd pressed fnl f: hld on wl* **10/1**
22-3 **2** *nse* **Lady Valentino**[35] 1577 4-8-11 **50** PhillipMakin 6 58
(M Dods) *in tch: effrt 2f out: ev ch fnl f: jst failed* **3/1**[1]
62-6 **3** *1 ¾* **Oeuf A La Neige**[25] 1822 8-9-4 **57** TomEaves 7 61
(Miss L A Perratt) *hld up: hdwy over 1f out: r.o fnl f: nrst fin* **15/2**
40-6 **4** *hd* **Grandad Bill (IRE)**[43] 1406 5-8-11 **50** DanielTudhope 5 54
(J S Goldie) *midfield: rdn and hdwy wl over 1f out: r.o fnl f* **6/1**[3]
0-11 **5** *nse* **Zabeel Tower**[9] 2285 5-9-8 **61** 6ex (p) TonyHamilton 10 65
(R Allan) *prom: effrt wl over 1f out: kpt on same pce fnl f* **7/2**[2]
60-0 **6** *3 ¼* **Crosby Jemma**[6] 2365 4-8-11 **50** RobertWinston 3 47
(J R Weymes) *t.k.h early: midfield: effrt wl over 1f out: wknd ins fnl f* **12/1**
25-6 **7** *¾* **Botham (USA)**[126] 283 4-8-12 **51** FergalLynch 12 46
(J S Goldie) *hld up: hdwy on ins 2f out: no imp fnl f* **9/1**
05-6 **8** *1* **Rock Haven (IRE)**[46] 1350 6-8-10 **49** SebSanders 4 42
(W M Brisbourne) *hld up: drvn over 2f out: btn fnl f* **16/1**
045- **9** *2 ¼* **Anthemion (IRE)**[216] 6479 11-8-5 **47** AndrewMullen(3) 2 36
(Mrs J C McGregor) *led to wl over 1f out: sn btn* **28/1**
5/6- **10** *1 ¼* **Templet (USA)**[461] 533 8-8-3 **45** DuranFentiman(3) 11 31
(W G Harrison) *bhd: drvn over 2f out: nvr rchd ldrs* **40/1**
300- **11** *nk* **Jane Of Arc (FR)**[216] 6464 4-8-10 **54** (p) GaryBartley(5) 9 39
(J S Goldie) *chsd ldrs tl hung lft and wknd over 2f out* **20/1**
0-00 **12** *1* **Fan Club**[27] 1776 4-8-9 **48** (b) DaleGibson 13 31
(Mrs R A Carr) *hld up in tch: drvn over 2f out: sn btn* **40/1**
21/0 **13** *18* **Dance In Style**[5] 2391 7-8-10 **49** AndrewElliott 8 —
(A Crook) *dwlt: hld up outside: rdn 3f out: edgd lft and sn wknd* **33/1**

1m 55.08s (-3.32) **Going Correction** -0.40s/f (Firm) **13 Ran SP% 122.0**
Speed ratings (Par 101): **98,97,96,96,96 93,92,91,89,88 88,87,71**
CSF £38.87 CT £246.77 TOTE £14.50: £3.50, £1.50, £2.30; EX 72.10.
Owner Lothian Recycling Limited **Bred** Mrs M Walsh **Trained** Cousland, Midlothian

FOCUS
A low-grade handicap in which the pace was fair. The third, fourth and sixth were close to their marks.
Malguru Official explanation: trainer said, regarding the apparent improvement in form, that gelding appreciated the drop back in trip to 1m 1f.

2524 BURNS MALL KILMARNOCK H'CAP 1m
3:50 (3:52) (Class 5) (0-75,72) 4-Y-0+ **£3,885** (£1,156; £577; £288) **Stalls Low**

Form RPR
0001 **1** **Osteopathic Remedy (IRE)**[19] 2007 4-9-4 **72** PhillipMakin 4 88+
(M Dods) *t.k.h: trckd ldr: led over 1f out: edgd lft: kpt on strly: eased nr fin* **6/4**[1]
2-00 **2** *2 ¼* **Esoterica (IRE)**[19] 2007 5-8-8 **67** (b) GaryBartley(5) 2 77
(J S Goldie) *led to over 1f out: kpt on u.p fnl f: no ch w wnr* **13/2**[3]
0-06 **3** *4* **Shy Glance (USA)**[13] 2155 6-8-8 **62** DaleGibson 5 63
(P Monteith) *trckd ldrs: effrt over 2f out: edgd lft: one pce over 1f out* **10/3**[2]
2426 **4** *3 ½* **Pianoforte (USA)**[3] 2446 6-8-11 **65** (b) WJSupple 6 58
(E J Alston) *hld up in tch: effrt over 2f out: no ex over 1f out* **7/1**
000- **5** *1 ¼* **Darfour**[236] 6016 4-9-1 **69** FergalLynch 7 59
(J S Goldie) *hld up: pushed along over 2f out: kpt on fnl f: n.d* **10/1**
02-0 **6** *¾* **Hawkit (USA)**[13] 2155 7-9-4 **72** RobertWinston 9 60
(P Monteith) *stdd last: rdn over 2f out: nvr rchd ldrs* **16/1**
0-03 **7** *1 ¾* **Wilmington**[10] 2246 4-8-3 **60** AndrewMullen(3) 3 44
(Mrs J C McGregor) *prom tl rdn and wknd 2f out* **16/1**
404- **8** *2 ¾* **Jordan's Light (USA)**[394] 1378 5-8-10 **64** TonyHamilton 8 42
(P Monteith) *bhd: drvn over 3f out: sn btn* **14/1**
05-0 **9** *½* **Ulysees (IRE)**[20] 1952 9-8-5 **59** oh10 ow1 GregFairley 1 36
(J Barclay) *in tch: slipped bnd over 3f out: rdn and wknd over 2f out* **40/1**

1m 39.33s (-4.47) **Going Correction** -0.40s/f (Firm) **9 Ran SP% 118.9**
Speed ratings (Par 103): **106,103,99,96,95 94,92,89,89**
CSF £12.36 CT £29.72 TOTE £2.20: £1.30, £2.30, £1.30; EX 11.70.
Owner Kevin Kirkup **Bred** Airlie Stud **Trained** Denton, Co Durham

FOCUS
Only a fair handicap and those racing prominently held the edge. The runner-up is rated to his mark with the winner back to his best.
Hawkit(USA) Official explanation: jockey said gelding was unsuited by the good to firm ground
Wilmington Official explanation: jockey said gelding ran flat
Ulysees(IRE) Official explanation: jockey said gelding slipped on bend turning into home straight

2525 MACDONALD SOLICITORS H'CAP 1m 7f
4:20 (4:21) (Class 4) (0-85,80) 4-Y-0+ **£5,828** (£1,734; £866) **Stalls Low**

Form RPR
13-1 **1** **Alleviate (IRE)**[16] 2076 4-9-10 **80** SebSanders 1 91+
(Sir Mark Prescott) *t.k.h: trckd ldr: led and rdn 2f out: styd on wl fnl f* **1/3**[1]
-044 **2** *¾* **Plane Painter (IRE)**[7] 2332 4-9-3 **73** GregFairley 3 83
(M Johnston) *set stdy pce to 2f out: rallied: kpt on fnl f* **11/4**[2]
02/0 **3** *93* **Stolen Light (IRE)**[26] 1798 7-8-12 **67** (b) TonyHamilton 2 —
(A Crook) *chsd ldrs: rdn and lost tch fr 1/2-way* **20/1**[3]

3m 18.81s (-1.59) **Going Correction** -0.40s/f (Firm)
WFA 4 from 7yo 1lb **3 Ran SP% 106.4**
Speed ratings (Par 105): **88,87,38**
CSF £1.51 TOTE £1.40; EX 1.30.
Owner Mrs Sonia Rogers **Bred** Miss K Rausing And Airlie Stud **Trained** Newmarket, Suffolk

FOCUS
A moderate gallop to this uncompetitive handicap. The runner-up is rated to his best and the winner remains capable of better.

2526 WESTERN HOUSE HOTEL FOR WEDDINGS H'CAP 6f
4:50 (4:51) (Class 4) (0-85,82) 3-Y-O **£5,828** (£1,734; £866; £432) **Stalls High**

Form RPR
0-05 **1** **Rubirosa (IRE)**[19] 1999 3-9-2 **80** PhillipMakin 3 87
(M Dods) *trckd ldrs: shkn up over 1f out: kpt on wl to ld nr fin* **11/4**[2]
54-5 **2** *¾* **Pavershooz**[12] 2187 3-8-6 **70** WJSupple 4 75
(N Wilson) *led: rdn and hung lft over 1f out: kpt on: hdd nr fin* **8/1**
4-1 **3** *1 ½* **Fabreze**[20] 1960 3-9-4 **82** SebSanders 1 82
(P J Makin) *racd wd: cl up: ev ch and rdn wl over 1f out: one pce fnl f* **8/11**[1]
1040 **4** *1 ¾* **Legendary Guest**[2] 2490 3-8-6 **70** TonyHamilton 2 65
(D W Barker) *chsd ldrs: effrt 2f out: no ex fnl f* **7/1**[3]

1m 11.26s (-2.34) **Going Correction** -0.40s/f (Firm) **4 Ran SP% 108.2**
Speed ratings (Par 101): **99,98,96,93**
CSF £19.35 TOTE £3.40; EX 13.50.
Owner Pedro Rosas **Bred** Bendis Partnership **Trained** Denton, Co Durham

FOCUS
Not the strongest of handicaps and one that took less winning than seemed likely with the favourite proving a shade disappointing. The winner is rated to his juvenile form.

2527 GILES GLASGOW FAIR MEETING 21ST JULY H'CAP 5f
5:20 (5:20) (Class 5) (0-70,68) 3-Y-O **£2,914** (£867; £433; £216) **Stalls High**

Form RPR
5062 **1** **Speedy Senorita (IRE)**[9] 2287 3-8-13 **60** AndrewElliott 3 73
(K R Burke) *mde all: rdn 2f out: styd on wl fnl f* **9/4**[1]
250- **2** *hd* **Ridge Wood Dani (IRE)**[201] 6756 3-9-5 **66** WJSupple 6 78
(E J Alston) *pressed wnr: effrt and ev ch over 1f out: kpt on ins fnl f: jst hld* **5/2**[2]
1130 **3** *3* **Killer Class**[9] 2287 3-8-12 **64** GaryBartley(5) 9 65
(J S Goldie) *prom: effrt wl over 1f out: kpt on fnl f: nt rch first two* **15/2**

The Form Book, Raceform Ltd, Compton, RG20 6NL

-600 **4** *3 1/2* **Paddy Jack**[5] 2396 3-9-4 **65** RobertWinston 1 54
(J R Weymes) *in tch tl rdn and no ex over 1f out* **20/1**
2-64 **5** *1 1/4* **Richardthesecond (IRE)**[33] 1635 3-9-3 **64** SebSanders 2 48
(W M Brisbourne) *rrd s: bhd and pushed along: nvr rchd ldrs* **9/2**[3]
013 **6** *1 1/4* **Stoneacre Sarah**[76] 882 3-8-10 **64** PatrickDonaghy(7) 4 44
(Peter Grayson) *bhd: rdn 1/2-way: nvr on terms* **14/1**
0-53 **7** *2 1/2* **Miss Sunshine**[27] 1769 3-8-0 **50** ow1 (p) AndrewMullen(3) 5 21
(J S Goldie) *in tch 2f: sn rdn and outpcd* **8/1**
6052 **8** *hd* **My Mate Pete (IRE)**[9] 2268 3-9-7 **68** TonyHamilton 7 38
(Mrs L Stubbs) *towards rr: drvn and outpcd after 2f: nvr on terms* **12/1**

58.21 secs (-1.89) **Going Correction** -0.40s/f (Firm) **8** Ran SP% **119.5**
Speed ratings (Par 99): **99,98,93,88,86 84,80,79**
CSF £8.57 CT £36.29 TOTE £3.20: £1.10, £2.00, £2.00; EX 10.60.
Owner Market Avenue Racing Club Ltd **Bred** R McEnery And Vincent Millett **Trained** Middleham Moor, N Yorks

FOCUS
A modest sprint in which the two market leaders had the race to themselves from a long way out. The pace seemed fair but the form does not look solid.
Richardthesecond(IRE) Official explanation: jockey said gelding reared as stalls opened
My Mate Pete(IRE) Official explanation: jockey said gelding was unsuited by the good to firm ground
T/Plt: £142.30 to a £1 stake. Pool: £37,184.30. 190.70 winning tickets. T/Qpdt: £38.60 to a £1 stake. Pool: £2,206.20. 42.20 winning tickets. RY

2501 GREAT LEIGHS (A.W) (L-H)
Thursday, May 29

OFFICIAL GOING: Standard
Wind: virtually nil Weather: raining

2528 UMA LOUNGE MEDIAN AUCTION MAIDEN STKS 1m 2f (P)
2:30 (2:33) (Class 6) 3-5-Y-O £1,942 (£578; £288; £144) Stalls Low

Form RPR
5- **1** **Unleashed (IRE)**[226] 6248 3-8-12 0 TedDurcan 13 73+
(H R A Cecil) *in tch: rdn and effrt over 2f out: rdr dropped reins and wnt lft over 1f out: ev ch 1f out: led wl ins fnl f* **11/10**[1]
62-3 **2** *3/4* **Pediment**[31] 1685 3-8-8 75 ow1 JamieSpencer 12 67+
(J R Fanshawe) *hld up towards rr: stdy hdwy fr 7f out: chsd ldrs and rdn wl over 1f out: edgd lft u.p: wnt 2nd nr fin* **13/8**[2]
3-2 **3** *1/2* **Shy**[28] 1741 3-8-7 0 StephenCarson 1 65
(P Winkworth) *led: rdn 2f out: hdd and no ex wl ins fnl f* **12/1**[3]
00- **4** *1* **Princess Gee**[201] 6763 3-8-7 0 ShaneKelly 7 63
(B J McMath) *t.k.h: chsd ldrs: wnt 2nd jst over 2f out: ev ch over 1f out: no ex wl ins fnl f* **200/1**
05 **5** *2 1/2* **Tewin Green**[21] 1937 3-8-4 0 KirstyMilczarek(3) 14 58
(M Botti) *t.k.h: chsd ldrs: rdn over 2f out: kpt on same pce fr over 1f out* **66/1**
50-0 **6** *nk* **Heart Of Dubai (USA)**[20] 1957 3-8-12 58 (p) HayleyTurner 9 62
(C E Brittain) *hld up in midfield: hdwy over 4f out: chsd ldrs and rdn over 2f out: kpt on same pce fr over 1f out* **50/1**
7 *2* **Dream Esteem** 3-8-7 0 KerrinMcEvoy 15 53
(E J O'Neill) *s.i.s: t.k.h: hld up in rr: hdwy over 4f out: rdn and no imp fr wl over 1f out* **16/1**
5322 **8** *3* **Director's Chair**[16] 2090 3-8-9 64 (b) JerryO'Dwyer(3) 11 52
(Miss J Feilden) *s.i.s: bhd: rdn and hdwy 3f out: kpt on but nvr threatened ldrs* **16/1**
0- **9** *shd* **Three Gold Leaves**[223] 6307 3-8-12 0 J-PGuillambert 16 52
(J G Given) *t.k.h: hld up in midfield: rdn over 2f out: no prog after* **40/1**
00 **10** *1* **Don't Stop Me Now (IRE)**[17] 2046 3-8-7 0 RHills 10 45
(J W Hills) *bhd: sme hdwy fr over 1f out: n.d* **33/1**
0 **11** *hd* **Beau Fighter**[17] 2046 3-8-12 0 LiamJones 2 50
(C F Wall) *t.k.h: hld up in midfield: rdn and lost pl wl over 3f out: no ch fnl 2f* **25/1**
00 **12** *1* **Janshe Gold**[24] 1869 3-8-7 0 JamesDoyle 4 43
(J G Portman) *chsd ldrs: rdn over 3f out: wknd 2f out* **100/1**
13 *11* **Bordes Lane** 3-8-12 0 LPKeniry 5 26
(A M Balding) *racd in midfield tl lost pl and pushed along over 6f out: wl bhd last 3f* **33/1**
-000 **14** *12* **Tagula Sands (IRE)**[25] 1836 4-9-7 37 HaddenFrost(5) 3 2
(J C Fox) *t.k.h: w ldr tl 2f out: sn wknd: eased ins fnl f: t.o* **200/1**
000 **P** **Too Much To Do**[31] 1669 3-8-12 37 AdamKirby 8 —
(T D McCarthy) *a bhd: rdn and lost tch over 4f out: t.o whn p.u 1f out* **200/1**
P **Hungry For More**[108] 4-9-12 0 JimmyQuinn 6 —
(M R Hoad) *s.i.s: hung rt thrght: hdwy over 4f out: hung bdly rt bnd over 3f out: p.u 2f out* **200/1**

2m 8.85s (0.25) **Going Correction** -0.075s/f (Stan)
WFA 3 from 4yo 14lb **16** Ran SP% **123.8**
Speed ratings (Par 101): **96,95,95,94,92 91,90,87,87,87 86,86,77,67,— —**
CSF £2.83 TOTE £3.00: £1.10, £1.40, £1.90; EX 4.10.
Owner Ennismore Racing II **Bred** Davin Investments Ltd **Trained** Newmarket, Suffolk

FOCUS
A big field for this maiden, but it was only a two-horse race according to the market and the winning time was over 3 secs slower than the later handicap. The market principals ultimately filled the first two places, but things were far from straightforward for either of them and the form looks shaky.
Don't Stop Me Now(IRE) Official explanation: jockey said, regarding running and riding, that his orders were to jump out and sit mid-division, adding that on leaving stalls he took a pull on the filly, it threw its head in the air and he found himself further back than he wanted and stayed on one pace in straight; vet said filly was found to be coughing
Too Much To Do Official explanation: jockey said gelding was distressed
Hungry For More Official explanation: jockey said gelding hung badly right and was unsteerable

2529 BARCLAY WEST H'CAP 5f (P)
3:00 (3:03) (Class 3) (0-95,95) 3-Y-0 £6,623 (£1,982; £991; £371; £371) Stalls Low

Form RPR
20-1 **1** **Befortyfour**[51] 1255 3-9-2 **90** PhilipRobinson 4 102+
(M A Jarvis) *chsd ldr tl led over 1f out: in command ins fnl f: r.o wl* **7/4**[1]
14-6 **2** *1 1/4* **Royal Intruder**[25] 1837 3-8-13 **87** RyanMoore 8 89
(R Hannon) *outpcd in last pair: hanging rt bnd over 3f out: swtchd rt wl over 1f out: r.o wl to go 2nd nr fin: no ch w wnr* **5/1**[3]
414 **3** *1* **Prime Factor**[90] 756 3-8-2 **76** oh2 WilliamBuick 2 74
(B W Hills) *outpcd in last: rdn over 2f out: hdwy on inner wl over 1f out: chsd wnr fnl 100yds: no imp after: lost 2nd nr fin* **28/1**
60-0 **4** *1 1/4* **Lady Avenger (IRE)**[34] 1597 3-9-6 **94** KerrinMcEvoy 6 88
(J M P Eustace) *outpcd in rr: hdwy over 2f out: rdn over 1f out: kpt on but nt pce to threaten wnr* **12/1**
22-1 **4** *dht* **Maimoona (IRE)**[28] 1737 3-8-9 **83** RHills 3 77
(W J Haggas) *off the pce in midfield: pushed along 4f out: hdwy over 2f out: rdn 2f out: kpt on to chse wnr briefly jst ins fnl f: sn no imp and lost 3 pls after* **3/1**[2]
2103 **6** *2 3/4* **Kinout (IRE)**[24] 1852 3-8-2 **76** JimmyQuinn 7 60
(K A Ryan) *chsd ldng pair: rdn 2f out: wkng whn swtchd rt jst ins fnl f* **16/1**
2110 **7** *1/2* **Ten Down**[20] 1945 3-8-9 **82** ow1 (b) DarryllHolland 5 65
(Miss Gay Kelleway) *led at fast pce: rdn and hdd over 1f out: sn edgd lft and rt: wknd fnl f* **14/1**
105- **U** **Lytton**[229] 6182 3-9-7 **95** AdamKirby 1 —
(W R Swinburn) *rrd as stalls opened: veered rt and uns rdr* **5/1**[3]

60.14 secs (-0.06) **Going Correction** -0.075s/f (Stan) **8** Ran SP% **118.4**
Speed ratings (Par 103): **97,95,93,91,91 87,86,—**
CSF £11.49 CT £184.67 TOTE £3.50: £1.60, £1.80, £3.90; EX 7.80.
Owner M F Bailey **Bred** Slatch Farm Stud **Trained** Newmarket, Suffolk

FOCUS
Quite a decent sprint handicap run at a strong pace and the form looks solid enough, although unexceptional, the winner apart.

NOTEBOOK
Befortyfour ◆, easy winner of a moderate Lingfield maiden on his return to action when long odds-on, did at least show there that he could handle this surface. Getting a nice tow from Ten Down on this handicap debut, he picked him off comfortably enough and never looked like getting caught despite still showing some signs of greenness. There is probably still plenty more improvement in him. (op 9-4 tchd 11-8)

Royal Intruder, making his sand debut, was racing around a bend for the first time and it showed as he did not take the turn at all well and seemed to have no chance on straightening up. Brought widest which is no bad thing here, he finished in great style but the favourite had gone beyond recall. A return to 6f will not bother him and he should be able to go one better back on a straight track. (op 6-1 tchd 9-2)

Prime Factor, 2lb wrong, was completely taken off his feet early but, sticking closest to the inside rail, he stayed on as the front-runners started to come back to finish a highly-commendable third. He should be up to winning more races and could be very interesting if running off his proper mark in the near future. (op 16-1)

Lady Avenger(IRE), making her sand debut, was another unable to go the early gallop but, although she stayed on, she never looked like troubling the favourite. She still looks in need of more respite from the Handicapper. (op 16-1 tchd 20-1 and 11-1)

Maimoona(IRE), in good form on soft ground on turf, found this surface a totally different kettle of fish on this handicap debut and she could never land a blow despite having every chance. She looks in need of a slightly stiffer test. (op 16-1 tchd 20-1 and 11-1)

Ten Down, winner of five of his last six starts on Polytrack, was off a 4lb higher mark than for his last win and had the blinkers back on. He attempted his usual trailblazing tactics, but he was up against some progressive sorts here and was comfortably picked off. (op 10-1 tchd 16-1)

Lytton disgraced himself by jumping in the air as the stalls opened and he then quickly dislodged his rider. Judging by his reaction, Kirby was far from impressed. (op 8-1)

2530 LOOKERS LAND ROVER CONDITIONS STKS 6f (P)
3:30 (3:31) (Class 3) 3-Y-O+ £6,799 (£2,023; £1,011; £505) Stalls Low

Form RPR
/00- **1** **Nota Bene**[341] 2858 6-9-1 100 MarcHalford(3) 5 111
(D R C Elsworth) *chsd ldr: clr of remainder: led over 1f out: styd on wl* **8/1**
211- **2** *1 1/4* **Tamagin (USA)**[207] 6668 5-9-4 101 NCallan 1 107
(K A Ryan) *led at fast gallop: rdn and hdd over 1f out: no ex ins fnl f* **2/1**[1]
32-0 **3** *4 1/2* **Berbice (IRE)**[43] 1400 3-8-9 106 RyanMoore 6 93
(R Hannon) *outpcd in midfield: rdn wl over 3f out: wnt modest 3rd ins fnl f: no ch w ldrs* **9/4**[2]
2300 **4** *3* **Capricorn Run (USA)**[82] 832 5-9-7 105 (v) SteveDrowne 3 86
(A J McCabe) *sn wl outpcd in last: sme late hdwy: nvr on terms* **8/1**
-550 **5** *1* **Woodnook**[19] 2000 5-8-13 89 TPQueally 2 75
(J A R Toller) *chsd ldng pair: outpcd 3f out: no ch w ldrs after* **16/1**
1400 **6** *1* **Fajr (IRE)**[68] 960 6-9-4 110 (b) DarryllHolland 7 77
(Miss Gay Kelleway) *sn outpcd in last pair: n.d* **4/1**[3]
060- **7** *4 1/2* **Jebel Tara**[237] 5974 3-8-9 93 (t) HayleyTurner 4 62
(C E Brittain) *outpcd in midfield: rdn 4f out: wl bhd fnl 2f out: t.o* **33/1**

1m 11.52s (-2.18) **Going Correction** -0.075s/f (Stan)
WFA 3 from 5yo+ 9lb **7** Ran SP% **115.1**
Speed ratings (Par 107): **111,109,103,99,98 96,90**
CSF £24.82 TOTE £10.90: £3.90, £2.10; EX 38.30.
Owner D R C Elsworth **Bred** Usk Valley Stud **Trained** Newmarket, Suffolk

FOCUS
A decent little conditions sprint and they went a furious pace which proved far too much for the majority of the field. The front pair held those positions throughout and the winner is rated back to his three-year-old form.

NOTEBOOK
Nota Bene, who looked a possible star sprinter at the beginning of his three-year-old career, became very dispointing after bursting in the 2005 Temple Stakes and has been very lightly raced since. His trainer, who now also owns him, has obviously not lost faith in him though and he attracted market support for this belated sand debut. The confidence proved spot-on too, as he slipstreamed the favourite travelling well throughout and, once sent past him, showed a decent attitude to keep on going and keep his rallying rival at bay. He has won after a break before, so may not necessarily come on that much for this first run in 11 months, but this was still a decent effort and he can win a few more unless his old problems reoccur. (op 12-1)

Tamagin(USA) only knows how to run one way and again attempted his normal tactics from the rails draw. He ran most of his rivals into the ground, but the winner was always stalking him and, though he battled on once headed, as befits a horse that stays further, he was always being held. He has won after a similar break in the past, so like the winner may not come on that much for it but he will surely win more races under these tactics this term. (op 7-4 tchd 13-8 and 9-4)

Berbice(IRE), well beaten in the Free Handicap on his return to action, found everything happening too quickly for him and, though he plugged on to finish a clear third, he was never anywhere near the front pair. Another try over further looks in order, but off a mark of 106 he also strikes as the type that will remain hard to place. (op 3-1)

Capricorn Run(USA), who has done his recent racing over further, completely fluffed the start and in a race run at a scorching pace that sealed his fate. (op 10-1 tchd 11-1)

Woodnook had little chance at these weights and dropped away after trying to hang to the coat-tails of the front pair. She has struggled ever since winning a handicap off 84 nearly 15 months ago. (op 14-1)

Fajr(IRE), racing over a trip this short for the first time in his 33rd start, found everything happening far too quickly for him. (op 7-2 tchd 9-2)

2531 STANJAMESUK.COM H'CAP 1m 2f (P)
4:00 (4:01) (Class 3) (0-90,90) 4-Y-0+ **£6,623** (£1,982; £991; £495; £246) **Stalls** Low

Form RPR
2511 **1** **Art Man**[21] 1935 5-9-0 **86** RyanMoore 10 93+
(G L Moore) *s.i.s: hld up in rr: pushed along and hdwy over 3f out: rdn over 1f out: r.o wl to ld nr fin* **3/1**[1]

403 **2** *nk* **Vainglory (USA)**[21] 1920 4-9-3 **89** RichardMullen 4 95
(D M Simcock) *chsd ldrs: rdn 4f out: hdwy u.p over 2f out: led ins fnl f: hdd and no ex* **7/1**[3]

24-5 **3** *½* **Sign Of The Cross**[24] 1874 4-8-8 **80** ow1 JamieSpencer 1 85
(J R Fanshawe) *t.k.h: chsd ldrs: jnd ldr gng wl jst over 2f out: led wl over 1f out: sn rdn: fnd little u.p: hdd ins fnl f: nt qckn* **7/1**[3]

-231 **4** *hd* **Curzon Prince (IRE)**[30] 1711 4-8-13 **85** AlanMunro 6 90
(C F Wall) *hld up in midfield: hdwy 3f out: rdn and ev ch jst over 1f out: keeping on same pce whn rdr dropped whip wl ins fnl f* **7/2**[2]

0410 **5** *shd* **Folio (IRE)**[25] 1828 8-8-3 **82** DebraEngland(7) 8 86
(W J Musson) *hld up in rr: rdn and hdwy over 1f out: r.o wl fnl f: nt quite rch ldrs* **20/1**

1133 **6** *3 ¼* **Scamperdale**[55] 1180 6-9-1 **87** TPQueally 7 85
(B P J Baugh) *awkward leaving stalls and v.s.a: bhd: hdwy 4f out: chsd ldrs u.p wl over 1f out: sn edgd rt: wknd 1f out* **8/1**

-014 **7** *2 ½* **Gold Prospect**[30] 1711 4-8-9 **81** TedDurcan 2 74
(M L W Bell) *s.i.s: sn in midfield: rdn and effrt over 2f out: wknd fnl f* **10/1**

4003 **8** *8* **Invasian (IRE)**[14] 2120 7-9-4 **90** ShaneKelly 3 67
(P W D'Arcy) *chsd ldr: clsd 5f out: led 4f out: jnd and rdn jst over 2f out: hdd wl over 1f out: sn wknd: eased fnl f* **9/1**

1312 **9** *½* **Dado Mush**[9] 2289 5-8-3 **78** oh1 ow2 (p) KirstyMilczarek(3) 11 54
(T T Clement) *a bhd: rdn over 4f out: n.d* **14/1**

6325 **10** *2 ½* **Jord (IRE)**[9] 2289 4-8-4 **76** oh1 WilliamBuick 5 47
(A J McCabe) *led and sn clr: hdd 4f out: wknd over 2f out: wl bhd and eased ins fnl f* **33/1**

2m 5.84s (-2.76) **Going Correction** -0.075s/f (Stan) 10 Ran SP% **116.8**
Speed ratings (Par 107): **108,107,107,107,107 104,102,96,95,93**
CSF £24.45 CT £136.54 TOTE £4.20: £2.00, £2.80, £2.20; EX 30.10.
Owner Matthew Green **Bred** Lady Lonsdale **Trained** Woodingdean, E Sussex

FOCUS
A decent handicap and they went a serious pace thanks to Jord which makes it all the more surprising that the front five finished in a heap. The form looks rock solid with the four immediately behind the winner close to their marks.

NOTEBOOK
Art Man ◆, already proven here and 5lb higher in his bid for a hat-trick, was given a superb ride. His jockey was in no hurry with him and allowed the pace-setters to get on with it whilst he dropped out last. He still had plenty to do although much closer starting up the home straight as he had a wall of horses in front of him, but a gap appeared just in time and he whipped through it to snatch the race near the line. He only just does enough and has really taken to this track, so the four-timer cannot be ruled out provided the race is again run to suit him. (op 11-4 tchd 7-2 and 4-1 in a place)
Vainglory(USA) ◆ deserves plenty of credit as he raced prominently in a race run at a scorching pace and he kept battling all the way to the line. He is 7lb higher than for his last win, but this effort suggests he is perfectly capable of winning off it. (op 13-2 tchd 6-1)
Sign Of The Cross, all the better for his return to action, was another that raced handily throughout and he kept on going, but he was rather inclined to look around him rather than put his head down and battle. As in the opener, Spencer's 1lb overweight could be considered significant, but the gelding's attitude was probably a bigger issue. (op 13-2)
Curzon Prince(IRE), raised 2lb for his Wolverhampton victory, moved into contention turning for home and, racing closest to the inside rail, battled on to the line. Whether his rider losing his whip inside the last half-furlong made any difference is hard to say, but one thing this proves beyond doubt is that he gets every yard of this trip. (op 5-1)
Folio(IRE), 6lb higher than when winning over course and distance two starts ago, proved well suited by the strong pace and was dropped right out alongside the eventual winner. He finished strongly down the outside in the home straight and would probably have finished third in another stride. (op 16-1)
Scamperdale can be rated a length or two closer than his final position as he fluffed the start and was then forced very wide into the home straight as he tried to get closer. He remains 5lb above his last winning mark though, so will still need to find improvement from somewhere in order to defy it. (op 9-1)
Invasian(IRE), back on a winning mark and a springer in the market, was denied his preferred pacemaking role by Jord and although he managed to get past him on the home bend, it was not long before the cavalry arrived. (op 14-1)
Dado Mush, a Fibresand specialist and effectively 3lb wrong, never looked happy here. (op 12-1)
Jord(IRE), third behind Folio here last month on her only previous try over this trip, did far too much early this time and fell in a hole rounding the home bend.

2532 SODEXO PRESTIGE H'CAP 1m (P)
4:30 (4:33) (Class 4) (0-85,85) 3-Y-0 **£4,209** (£1,252; £625; £312) **Stalls** Low

Form RPR
34-1 **1** **Aromatherapy**[29] 1721 3-9-1 **82** TedDurcan 9 93
(H R A Cecil) *hld up in midfield: hdwy 4f out: rdn to chal over 1f out: led ins fnl f: r.o wl* **9/4**[1]

203 **2** *¾* **August Gale (USA)**[34] 1601 3-8-12 **79** J-PGuillambert 8 88
(M Johnston) *chsd ldrs: rdn 3f out: chsd ldr jst over 2f out: drvn to ld over 1f out: edgd rt 1f out: hdd and no ex ins fnl f* **14/1**

1-02 **3** *½* **Sky Dive**[28] 1745 3-9-1 **82** JamieSpencer 7 90
(L M Cumani) *hld up in tch: hdwy jst over 2f out: rdn and hung lft fr over 1f out: r.o: nt quite rch ldng pair* **9/4**[1]

4-10 **4** *2 ¼* **Hustle (IRE)**[41] 1441 3-9-4 **85** RyanMoore 1 88
(R Hannon) *in tch in midfield: rdn and effrt over 2f out: kpt on same pce u.p fnl f* **8/1**[3]

0-51 **5** *4 ½* **Dancer's Legacy**[19] 2002 3-8-12 **79** (t) SteveDrowne 2 72
(E A L Dunlop) *led: rdn 3f out: hdd over 1f out: wknd over 1f out* **11/1**

61 **6** *4* **Snowdrop Princess**[113] 447 3-8-6 **73** LiamJones 5 56
(W J Haggas) *s.i.s: sn bustled along in rr: hdwy over 4f out: rdn and outpcd over 2f out: no ch after* **20/1**

6-25 **7** *4 ½* **Sheer Bluff (IRE)**[7] 2342 3-8-5 **75** MarcHalford(3) 4 48
(D R C Elsworth) *s.i.s: hld up bhd: rdn 3f out: no prog: wl btn fnl f 2f* **6/1**[2]

15-4 **8** *¾* **Fly Kiss**[12] 2190 3-8-7 **79** AhmedAjtebi(5) 3 50
(C E Brittain) *w ldr tl over 2f out: sn wknd* **25/1**

21-0 **9** *7* **Honky Tonk Sally**[47] 1332 3-9-3 **84** TPQueally 6 39
(M L W Bell) *stdd after s: hld up in last trio: rdn and outpcd wl over 2f out: no ch after: eased ins fnl f* **16/1**

1m 38.85s (-1.05) **Going Correction** -0.075s/f (Stan) 9 Ran SP% **116.4**
Speed ratings (Par 101): **102,101,100,98,94 90,85,84,77**
CSF £38.95 CT £79.07 TOTE £2.90: £1.20, £2.80, £1.40; EX 43.60.
Owner K Abdulla **Bred** Juddmonte Farms Ltd **Trained** Newmarket, Suffolk

■ Stewards' Enquiry : J-P Guillambert two-day ban: careless riding (Jun 12-13)

FOCUS
A fair little handicap run at a decent pace thanks to a contested early lead. The form looks pretty solid rated through the third.

2533 WESTMINSTER TEAK H'CAP 1m (P)
5:00 (5:04) (Class 6) (0-65,69) 4-Y-0+ **£1,942** (£578; £288; £144) **Stalls** Low

Form RPR
2501 **1** **Wisdom's Kiss**[10] 2259 4-9-0 **61** 6ex (b) JimmyQuinn 5 77+
(J D Bethell) *t.k.h: hld up in midfield: hdwy wl over 1f out: rdn to ld over 1f out: in command fnl f: comf* **5/1**[1]

32-0 **2** *2* **Luck Will Come (IRE)**[24] 1867 4-8-9 **59** KirstyMilczarek(3) 7 68
(H J Collingridge) *t.k.h: chsd ldrs: rdn 2f out: chsd wnr ins fnl f: kpt on but nt pce to trble wnr* **12/1**

1510 **3** *¾* **Dinner Date**[24] 1853 6-8-11 **65** AshleyMorgan(7) 10 72
(T Keddy) *s.i.s: bhd: rdn over 2f out: swtchd lft over 1f out: styd on fnl f: nvr pce to chal* **16/1**

40-2 **4** *hd* **The Wily Woodcock**[10] 2261 4-9-3 **64** StephenCarson 16 71
(G Wragg) *hld up in midfield: hdwy on outer over 3f out: rdn and edging lft over 1f out: kpt on but nvr pce to chal* **6/1**[2]

4303 **5** *½* **Magic Warrior**[28] 1747 8-8-9 **61** ow1 HaddenFrost(5) 9 67
(J C Fox) *hld up in midfield: hdwy over 3f out: rdn over 2f out: kpt on steadily u.p but nvr pce to trble wnr* **16/1**

4-25 **6** *1 ½* **Surwaki (USA)**[29] 1729 6-9-4 **65** ShaneKelly 6 67
(R M H Cowell) *t.k.h: led: rdn 2f out: hdd over 1f out: wknd ins fnl f* **8/1**

60-0 **7** *1* **Lindy Lou**[20] 1959 4-9-0 **61** (t) IanMongan 15 61
(C F Wall) *t.k.h: hld up wl in tch: hrd rdn and unable qckn 2f out: one pce* **15/2**[3]

-225 **8** *nse* **Winning Show**[10] 2243 4-9-1 **62** LPKeniry 4 62
(A M Balding) *chsd ldrs on inner: rdn wl over 2f out: no imp fr jst over 1f out* **8/1**

6-00 **9** *1 ¾* **Kaballero (GER)**[12] 2203 7-9-4 **65** J-PGuillambert 1 61
(S Gollings) *s.i.s: hld up towards rr on inner: hdwy and swtchd lft wl over 1f out: sn no imp* **33/1**

606- **10** *½* **Bluebelle Dancer (IRE)**[224] 6277 4-8-11 **58** RichardMullen 14 53
(W R Muir) *s.i.s: bhd: rdn and effrt over 2f out: no real prog* **16/1**

-245 **11** *nk* **Anthill**[36] 1565 4-9-0 **61** TPQueally 12 55
(I A Wood) *t.k.h: prom: rdn jst over 2f out: wknd fnl f* **16/1**

2001 **12** *½* **Sun Catcher (IRE)**[9] 2289 5-9-8 **69** 6ex (p) SteveDrowne 13 62
(P G Murphy) *a towards rr: rdn jst over 2f out: sn no imp: eased whn wl btn ins fnl f* **5/1**[1]

0060 **13** *6* **Cavalry Guard (USA)**[10] 2243 4-9-4 **65** AmirQuinn 2 44
(J R Boyle) *a bhd: rdn over 2f out: sn struggling* **50/1**

000- **14** *3 ½* **Hypnotic**[246] 5737 6-9-1 **62** SimonWhitworth 11 33
(D Nicholls) *t.k.h: w ldr: rdn jst over 2f out: wknd qckly over 1f out* **25/1**

6-60 **15** *¾* **To The Max (IRE)**[29] 1725 4-8-13 **60** AdamKirby 3 29
(Mrs C A Dunnett) *flyj. leaving stalls: a bhd* **40/1**

1m 38.92s (-0.98) **Going Correction** -0.075s/f (Stan) 15 Ran SP% **124.0**
Speed ratings (Par 101): **101,99,98,98,97 96,95,95,93,92 92,91,85,82,81**
CSF £65.18 CT £918.37 TOTE £6.80: £2.50, £2.80, £4.80; EX 81.30.
Owner Hornblower Racing **Bred** Snowdrop Stud Co Ltd **Trained** Middleham Moor, N Yorks

FOCUS
A big field and several had a chance in a line across the track a furlong from home, but the form is probably modest as the winning time was fractionally slower than the preceding three-year-old handicap.
Sun Catcher(IRE) Official explanation: jockey said gelding never travelled
T/Plt: £23.20 to a £1 stake. Pool: £48,512.80. 1,520.70 winning tickets. T/Qpdt: £13.40 to a £1 stake. Pool: £2449.60. 134.60 winning tickets. SP

2362 NEWCASTLE (L-H)
Thursday, May 29
OFFICIAL GOING: Good to firm (firm in places)
Wind: Virtually nil Weather: Fine and dry

2534 FORTRESS ARCHITECTURAL SYSTEMS LLP MAIDEN FILLIES' STKS 6f
6:30 (6:31) (Class 4) 2-Y-O **£4,857** (£1,445; £722; £360) **Stalls** High

Form RPR
33 **1** **Barbee (IRE)**[14] 2117 2-9-0 0 JoeFanning 9 78
(E A L Dunlop) *dwlt: t.k.h and sn trcking ldrs on inner: swtchd outside 1/2-way and hdwy to chal 2f out: rdn to take marginal ld ent fnl f: kpt on wl* **7/2**[1]

4 **2** *hd* **Spring Tale (USA)**[42] 1413 2-9-0 0 PaulHanagan 4 77
(M J Wallace) *a cl up: led over 2f out: sn jnd and rdn: hdd ent fnl f: drvn and kpt on wl u.p* **13/2**[3]

0 **3** *1 ¾* **Common Diva**[17] 2035 2-9-0 0 PatCosgrave 6 72+
(A J McCabe) *a.p: rdn 2f out: kpt on u.p ins fnl f* **40/1**

4 **4** *½* **Honimiere (IRE)**[27] 1770 2-8-11 0 PJMcDonald(3) 7 71
(G A Swinbank) *trckd ldrs: hdwy over 2f out: rdn over 1f out: kpt on same pce ins fnl f* **5/1**[2]

5 *nk* **Mutually Mine (USA)** 2-9-0 0 MickyFenton 8 70
(Mrs P Sly) *midfield: effrt and swtchd lft 2f out: sn rdn and kpt on ins fnl f: nrst fin* **11/1**

54 **6** *2* **Voulez Vous**[20] 1961 2-9-0 0 ChrisCatlin 5 64
(E J O'Neill) *t.k.h: sn led: rdn along and hdd over 2f out: grad wknd* **7/2**[1]

23 **7** *1* **Camelot Communion (IRE)**[7] 2331 2-9-0 0 RoystonFfrench 3 61+
(Mrs A Duffield) *t.k.h: hld up towards rr: sltly hmpd after 1f: effrt and sme hdwy over 2f out: sn rdn and btn* **7/2**[1]

26 **8** *hd* **Woteva**[33] 1627 2-9-0 0 GrahamGibbons 1 62+
(J J Quinn) *hld up in rr: pushed along 1/2-way: rdn and hld whn hmpd 2f out* **11/1**

9 *4 ½* **Jaslyn (IRE)** 2-9-0 0 PaulMulrennan 2 47+
(J R Weymes) *s.i.s: a in rr* **50/1**

1m 12.93s (-2.27) **Going Correction** -0.50s/f (Hard) 9 Ran SP% **117.7**
Speed ratings (Par 92): **95,94,92,91,91 88,87,87,81**
CSF £27.54 TOTE £4.10: £1.10, £1.60, £15.30; EX 29.10.
Owner Ballygallon Stud Limited **Bred** Ballygallon Stud Limited **Trained** Newmarket, Suffolk
■ Stewards' Enquiry : Graham Gibbons two-day ban: careless riding (Jun 12-13)
Micky Fenton two-day ban: careless riding (Jun 12-13)

FOCUS
A modest fillies' maiden with the bare form no better than average for the grade and track.

The Form Book, Raceform Ltd, Compton, RG20 6NL

NOTEBOOK

Barbee(IRE), who was stepping up in trip, had shaped on her debut as if 6f would suit her and came up against a couple of Royal Ascot-bound colts next time. After being switched off the rail at around halfway, she picked up well to challenge and edged ahead close home, her jockey noticeably less hard on his mount than the rider of the second. (tchd 10-3 and 9-2)

Spring Tale(USA) knew more on this second run and saw out the extra furlong well, but after taking a slender lead going to the final furlong she was just denied. A race should come her way. (op 9-2)

Common Diva, whose dam is a half-sister to Ebor winner Mudawin, had hinted on her Redcar debut that this longer trip would suit and she was keeping on at the end. (op 33-1)

Honimiere(IRE) saw out the extra furlong but may prove better suited by an easier surface, having been withdrawn from a recent engagement at Haydock because the ground, officially good to firm like here, was thought unsuitable. (op 15-2 tchd 9-2)

Mutually Mine(USA) is a half-sister to the useful filly America America who was a multiple winner in the USA at up to 9f. She was staying on at the and is sure to be sharper for this debut experience. (op 8-1)

Voulez Vous, whose unraced dam is a half-sister to Lincoln winner Babodana, was having her first run on fast ground. She showed pace but raced keenly and did not get home, and is perhaps best kept at 5f for now. She is now qualified for nurseries. (op 4-1 tchd 3-1)

Camelot Communion(IRE) was a bit disappointing on this third run, and it did not seem a case of the extra furlong being to blame. (op 4-1 tchd 9-2)

Woteva Official explanation: jockey said filly never travelled

2535 DECKE NEWCASTLE LTD H'CAP 7f

7:05 (7:05) (Class 4) (0-80,85) 4-Y-O+ £4,857 (£1,445; £722; £360) Stalls High

Form RPR

-500 **1** **Handsome Falcon**[22] 1908 4-8-5 **67**.............................. PaulHanagan 9 77
(R A Fahey) *trckd ldrs: effrt 2f out and sn rdn: nt clr run over 1f out and appr fnl f: styd on u.p to ld last 50yds* **7/1**[3]

3-61 **2** ½ **Crocodile Bay (IRE)**[9] 2271 5-9-9 **85** 6ex................ AdrianTNicholls 11 94
(D Nicholls) *cl up: rdn to ld over 1f out: drvn and edgd lft ins fnl f: hdd and no ex last 50yds* **5/2**[1]

0-05 **3** 1 ¾ **Sadeek**[12] 2210 4-9-0 **76**.. TomEaves 12 80
(B Smart) *midfield: hdwy over 2f out: sn rdn and styd on u.p ins fnl f: nrst fin* **5/1**[2]

-254 **4** 1 **Ancient Cross**[26] 1815 4-8-6 **68**.................................. JoeFanning 7 70+
(M W Easterby) *towards rr: gd hdwy 1/2-way: chal over 2f out and ev ch tl drvn ent fnl f and wknd* **12/1**

40-0 **5** 2 ½ **Viva Volta**[42] 1430 5-8-12 **74**.............................(b) DavidAllan 3 69
(T D Easterby) *sn led: rdn along over 2f out: drvn and hdd over 1f out: wknd ins fnl f* **9/1**

0500 **6** ½ **Yorkshire Blue**[10] 2251 9-8-5 **67**.............................. RoystonFfrench 10 60
(J S Goldie) *sn rdn along in rr: hdwy 2f out: styd on ins fnl f: nt rch ldrs* **10/1**

0353 **7** hd **Cornus**[12] 2188 6-9-4 **80**...(be) PaulMulrennan 4 73
(A J McCabe) *midfield: effrt over 2f out: sn rdn along and no imp* **14/1**

-006 **8** nk **Balakiref**[2] 2484 9-8-8 **73**.............................. PJMcDonald[(3)] 1 65
(M Dods) *stdd and swtchd lft s: a in rr* **22/1**

0-00 **9** 1 ½ **Neon Blue**[23] 1900 7-8-5 **67** ow1.............................. DeanMcKeown 8 55
(R M Whitaker) *prom: rdn along wl over 2f out and sn wknd* **16/1**

-406 **10** 2 **Middlemarch (IRE)**[13] 2158 8-9-2 **78**.....................(v) DanielTudhope 5 61
(J S Goldie) *sn outpcd and a bhd* **8/1**

210- **11** 14 **Piper's Song (IRE)**[228] 6209 5-9-1 **77**.....................(v) PatCosgrave 2 22
(D J G Murray Smith) *chsd ldrs on outer: rdn along over 3f out and sn wknd* **22/1**

-000 **12** 2 ¾ **Jalamid (IRE)**[13] 2158 6-7-11 **66** oh21........................(t) SophieDoyle[(7)] 6 3
(M A Barnes) *sn outpcd: a in rr* **66/1**

1m 24.57s (-2.83) **Going Correction** -0.50s/f (Hard) **12** Ran SP% **118.4**
Speed ratings (Par 105): **105,104,102,101,98 97,97,97,95,93 77,74**
CSF £24.20 CT £96.01 TOTE £8.50: £2.40, £1.40, £2.40; EX 36.70.
Owner B Shaw **Bred** Miss D Fleming **Trained** Musley Bank, N Yorks

FOCUS

A fair handicap. Those drawn high held the call with the winner back to his best backed up by the third and fourth.

Yorkshire Blue Official explanation: jockey said gelding never travelled

Middlemarch(IRE) Official explanation: jockey said gelding never travelled

2536 J & G ARCHIBALD BUILDERS MERCHANTS MAIDEN FILLIES' STKS 1m 2f 32y

7:35 (7:37) (Class 5) 3-Y-O+ £3,561 (£1,059; £529; £264) Stalls Centre

Form RPR

2-2 **1** **Crystal Capella**[20] 1964 3-8-10 0.................................. TomEaves 3 79+
(Sir Michael Stoute) *dwlt and pushed along to trck ldrs: hdwy to ld over 4f out: shkn up over 2f out: rdn clr appr fnl f* **4/7**[1]

0 **2** 3 ½ **Herrera (IRE)**[11] 2221 3-8-7 0.............................. JamieMoriarty[(3)] 6 68+
(R A Fahey) *bhd: rdn along over 4f out: gd hdwy on outer over 3f out: rdn and hung lft 2f out: styd on wl u.p ins fnl f: tk 2nd nr fin* **66/1**

4 **3** 1 ½ **Maha Dubai (USA)**[33] 1628 3-8-10 0.............................. JoeFanning 2 65
(M Johnston) *trckd ldrs: hdwy over 2f out: rdn and ch whn edgd lft wl over 1f out: sn drvn and kpt on same pce* **7/1**[3]

3 **4** ½ **Gulch's Rose (USA)**[62] 1054 3-8-10 0.............................. PaulHanagan 8 64
(J Noseda) *cl up: effrt 3f out: rdn over 2f out and ev ch tl drvn over 1f out and sn one pce* **4/1**[2]

600- **5** 10 **Josephine Malines**[258] 5385 4-9-10 73.............................. RoystonFfrench 5 44
(Mrs A Duffield) *trckd ldrs: hdwy 4f out: rdn along 3f out: sn drvn and outpcd* **11/1**

5- **6** 3 ¼ **Volvoretas Rainbow**[253] 5524 3-8-10 0.............................. PaulMulrennan 7 38
(P C Haslam) *chsd ldrs: pushed along 1/2-way: sn rdn and wknd 4f out* **16/1**

00- **7** nk **Stones Of Venice (IRE)**[219] 6414 3-8-10 0.............................. DeanMcKeown 4 37
(R M Whitaker) *a in rr* **66/1**

000 **8** 43 **Fluoree (FR)**[23] 1894 4-9-10 35.............................. AdrianTNicholls 1 —
(D W Thompson) *led: rdn along and hdd over 4f out: sn wknd* **250/1**

2m 10.29s (-1.61) **Going Correction** -0.30s/f (Firm)
WFA 3 from 4yo 14lb **8** Ran SP% **113.8**
Speed ratings (Par 100): **100,97,96,95,87 85,84,50**
CSF £54.19 TOTE £1.60: £1.02, £14.50, £1.70; EX 54.00.
Owner Sir Evelyn De Rothschild **Bred** Southcourt Stud **Trained** Newmarket, Suffolk

■ Stewards' Enquiry : Paul Mulrennan one-day ban: careless riding (Jun 12)

FOCUS

An ordinary maiden run at a modest pace with little solid form behind the winner and the fourth the best guide.

2537 ESH CHARITABLE TRUST (S) STKS 1m (R)

8:10 (8:10) (Class 6) 3-5-Y-O £1,942 (£578; £288; £144) Stalls Centre

Form RPR

360- **1** **Practicallyperfect (IRE)**[225] 6269 4-9-0 75.............. RoystonFfrench 2 54
(Ollie Pears) *trckd ldng pair: hdwy 3f out: chal 2f out and sn rdn: drvn ins fnl f: kpt on gamely to ld nr fin* **11/10**[1]

-010 **2** hd **Ghafeer (USA)**[41] 1449 4-9-10 58..............................(p) TomEaves 4 63
(B Ellison) *led 2f: cl up tl led again 2f out: sn rdn: drvn ent fnl f: hdd and no ex nr fin* **11/4**[2]

0034 **3** 2 ¾ **Buzzin'Boyzee (IRE)**[3] 2463 5-9-5 48.............................. FergalLynch 6 52
(D W Barker) *trckd ldng pair tl led after 2f: rdn along 3f out: hdd 2f out: sn drvn and kpt on same pce ins fnl f* **4/1**[3]

4-40 **4** ¾ **Soldier Field**[132] 209 4-9-2 52..............................(p) PJMcDonald[(3)] 3 50
(J S Wainwright) *chsd ldrs: rdn along wl over 2f out: drvn wl over 1f out: one pce* **9/1**

/00- **5** 17 **Princess Of Aeneas (IRE)**[5] 6835 5-9-0 49................(p) PaulHanagan 1 6
(R Johnson) *a in rr: outpcd and bhd fr 1/2-way* **16/1**

1m 43.58s (-0.12) **Going Correction** -0.30s/f (Firm) **5** Ran SP% **110.2**
Speed ratings (Par 101): **88,87,85,84,67**
CSF £4.37 TOTE £1.80: £1.10, £1.90; EX 4.10.The winner was sold to B E Holland for £16,000.
Owner Diamond Racing Ltd **Bred** Epona Bloodstock Ltd **Trained** Norton, N Yorks

FOCUS

The favourite made hard work of landing this moderate seller with the third and fourth the best guides.

2538 TARMAC H'CAP 6f

8:40 (8:40) (Class 3) (0-90,97) 4-Y-O £6,938 (£2,076; £1,038; £519; £258) Stalls High

Form RPR

-000 **1** **Barney McGrew (IRE)**[13] 2172 5-9-4 **90**.............................. PhillipMakin 10 102+
(M Dods) *hld up in tch: hdwy 2f out: effrt and nt clr run ent fnl f: squeezed through to ld last 100yds* **13/2**[3]

0135 **2** ¾ **Stevie Gee (IRE)**[27] 1774 4-8-13 **88**.............................. PJMcDonald[(3)] 13 95
(G A Swinbank) *trckd ldrs: hdwy 2f out: rdn and ev ch ins fnl f: sn drvn and nt qckn last 100yds* **5/1**[1]

14-0 **3** shd **Gunfighter (IRE)**[61] 1069 5-8-12 **84**.............................. GrahamGibbons 11 91+
(J S Wainwright) *dwlt and towards rr: pushed along and hdwy over 2f out: swtchd lft and rdn over 1f out: styd on wl fnl f* **10/1**

2-30 **4** hd **Northern Dare (IRE)**[26] 1809 4-9-1 **87**.............................. AdrianTNicholls 4 93
(D Nicholls) *cl up: rdn to ld over 1f out: drvn ins fnl f: hdd & wknd last 100yds* **11/2**[2]

0411 **5** ½ **Inter Vision (USA)**[2] 2489 8-9-11 **97** 12ex.............................. DanielTudhope 14 105+
(A Dickman) *hld up towards rr: gd hdwy 2f out: swtchd lft and qcknd 1f out: nt clr run ins fnl f: kpt on* **11/2**[2]

1656 **6** ½ **Ingleby Arch (USA)**[31] 1689 5-9-2 **88**.............................. PaulFessey 12 91
(T D Barron) *led: rdn along 2f out: drvn and hdd over 1f out: wknd ins fnl f* **8/1**

4-51 **7** 3 **Geojimali**[26] 1796 6-8-10 **82**.............................. SaleemGolam 6 75+
(J S Goldie) *dwlt and bhd: rdn along 1/2-way: styd on appr fnl f: n.d* **7/1**

3200 **8** ½ **Distant Sun (USA)**[12] 2210 4-8-8 **80**.............................. RoystonFfrench 8 72
(Miss L A Perratt) *chsd ldrs: rdn along wl over 2f out: sn drvn and wknd wl over 1f out* **33/1**

20-0 **9** ½ **Trojan Flight**[12] 2210 7-8-6 **78**.............................. PaulHanagan 2 68
(R A Fahey) *hld up in midfield: hdwy on outer 1/2-way: rdn 2f out and sn btn* **25/1**

00-3 **10** 1 ¼ **Johannes (IRE)**[12] 2210 5-8-10 **82**.............................. ChrisCatlin 5 68
(E J O'Neill) *chsd ldrs: rdn along over 2f out: sn drvn and wknd wl over 1f out* **10/1**

5-06 **11** shd **Tabaret**[14] 2129 5-9-1 **87**.............................. DeanMcKeown 3 79+
(R M Whitaker) *chsd ldrs: effrt and nt clr run 2f out: no ch after* **16/1**

01-4 **12** 4 **Curtail (IRE)**[82] 836 5-9-2 **88**.............................. TomEaves 1 61
(Miss L A Perratt) *chsd ldrs on outer: rdn along wl over 2f out and sn wknd* **20/1**

1m 12.23s (-2.97) **Going Correction** -0.50s/f (Hard) **12** Ran SP% **120.0**
Speed ratings (Par 107): **99,98,97,97,96 96,92,91,90,89 89,83**
CSF £38.56 CT £329.55 TOTE £6.00: £3.10, £1.70, £4.70; EX 40.70.
Owner Andrew Tinkler **Bred** Mrs H B Raw **Trained** Denton, Co Durham

FOCUS

A decent handicap and high numbers again held the call, in a somewhat messy race. Despite that, the horses in the frame behind the winner were close to their marks.

NOTEBOOK

Barney McGrew(IRE) confirmed the promise of his recent run at York, where he did not get the breaks. He had to wait for a run here too, but picked up well when in the clear and won a shade readily. The Wokingham at Ascot is reportedly his target. (op 15-2 tchd 6-1, 8-1 in a place)

Stevie Gee(IRE), like the winner, had to bide his time before the gap appeared, but he did not pick up as well as his rival and seemed to hang to his left a little. This was still a respectable effort on this drop back in trip. (op 9-2)

Gunfighter(IRE) came from the rear to stay on strongly down the outside in the latter stages. He needs a return to 7f or 1m. (tchd 9-1)

Northern Dare(IRE), always up with the pace, showed ahead going to the last but was swallowed up in the last half-furlong. This was a commendable effort from his low draw. (op 8-1 tchd 5-1)

Inter Vision(USA), back up in trip, was saddled with a double penalty on this bid for a third win in six days. He was well drawn against the stands' rail but, after beginning to run on strongly from the rear from about 2f out, he ran right out of room inside the last and his rider had to give up. He would probably have been second and remains in top form. (tchd 13-2)

Ingleby Arch(USA) ran well, albeit from a favourable high draw, and was only knocked out of the frame inside the last. He is perhaps a shade high in the weights on turf. (tchd 17-2)

Geojimali, raised 5lb for his win at Doncaster earlier in the month, made late progress from the rear. (tchd 6-1)

Tabaret can be rated as better than his final placing as he was hampered quite badly when attempting to improve his position. Official explanation: jockey said gelding was denied a clear run

2539 GILWOOD MAST MECHANICAL ELECTRICAL & PLUMBING CONTRACTORS H'CAP 1m 3y(S)

9:10 (9:10) (Class 4) (0-85,78) 3-Y-O £4,857 (£1,445; £722; £360) Stalls High

Form RPR

0-01 **1** **Gala Casino Star (IRE)**[17] 2037 3-8-9 69.............................. PaulHanagan 4 76+
(R A Fahey) *chsd ldng pair: rdn along and sltly outpcd over 2f out: drvn and hdwy to ld ins fnl f: edgd rt and kpt on* **5/2**[3]

215- **2** 1 ½ **Celtic Strand (IRE)**[184] 6960 3-9-2 76.............................. MickyFenton 3 80
(T P Tate) *led: rdn along 2f out: drvn over 1f out: hdd and no ex ins fnl f* **12/1**

-402 **3** 4 1/2 **Ninefineirishmen (IRE)**[6] 2378 3-8-12 **72**.................. DarrenWilliams 2 66
(K R Burke) *cl up: effrt 2f out: sn rdn and ev ch tl drvn and edgd lft ent fnl f: one pce* **7/4**[2]

00-0 **4** 7 **Giant Love (USA)**[42] 1424 3-9-4 **78**.................................... JoeFanning 5 56
(M Johnston) *stdd s: t.k.h in rr: effrt 3f out: sn rdn along and btn* **13/8**[1]

1m 39.29s (-4.11) **Going Correction** -0.50s/f (Hard) **4** Ran SP% **110.7**
Speed ratings (Par 101): **102,100,96,89**
CSF £22.66 TOTE £3.00; EX 23.80 Place 6 £47.12, Place 5 £16.45.
Owner The Friar Tuck Racing Club **Bred** Glashare House Stud **Trained** Mulsey Bank, N Yorks

FOCUS
The pace was decent for a four-runner race but probably only the front pair showed their form.
T/Plt: £72.20 to a £1 stake. Pool: £57,371.70. 579.50 winning tickets. T/Qpdt: £18.70 to a £1 stake. Pool: £3,613.20. 142.45 winning tickets. JR

2309 SANDOWN (R-H)
Thursday, May 29

OFFICIAL GOING: Sprint course - soft; round course - good to soft changing to soft after race 2 (6.40)
Wind: Almost nil

2540 BETFAIR SP H'CAP — 1m 2f 7y
6:10 (6:11) (Class 4) (0-85,84) 4-Y-0+ **£4,533** (£1,348; £674; £336) **Stalls** High

Form RPR

03/1 **1** **Punjabi**[6] 2372 5-9-1 **81** 6ex.................................... EddieAhern 10 97+
(N J Henderson) *hld up in tch: hdwy fr 3f out: led appr fnl f: styd on* **10/11**[1]

0224 **2** 1 3/4 **Dakiyah (IRE)**[24] 1877 4-8-11 **77**.................................(p) PaulDoe 6 89
(Mrs L J Mongan) *led tl rdn and hdd appr fnl f: kpt on but no imp after* **16/1**

0-60 **3** 5 **Mustajed**[40] 1473 7-8-13 **84**................................ JamesMillman(5) 3 86
(B R Millman) *a in tch: rdn 2f out: kpt on one pce* **16/1**

221 **4** hd **Trans Siberian**[24] 1874 4-9-2 **82**.......................... FrancisNorton 7 84
(P F I Cole) *lw: chsd ldrs: rdn and kpt on one pce ins fnl 2f* **6/1**[2]

-026 **5** 2 1/4 **Aegean Prince**[13] 2153 4-8-8 **77**........................ PatrickHills(3) 11 74
(R Hannon) *stdd s: hdwy over 2f out: nt qckn fr over 1f out* **12/1**

-005 **6** 10 **Krugerrand (USA)**[31] 1682 9-8-5 **71**.......................... NeilPollard 9 48
(W J Musson) *a in rr and lost tch 2f out* **12/1**

5-00 **7** 14 **Novikov**[29] 1719 4-9-2 **82**...(bt[1]) JimmyFortune 1 31
(J H M Gosden) *racd wd: trckd ldr tl rdn over 2f out: sn wknd* **10/1**

5634 **8** 13 **Red Somerset (USA)**[13] 2152 5-9-2 **82**...................... RichardHughes 5 5
(R J Hodges) *a in rr: wl bhd 2f out: eased fnl f* **15/2**[3]

2m 11.97s (1.47) **Going Correction** +0.275s/f (Good) **8** Ran SP% **114.7**
Speed ratings (Par 105): **105,103,99,99,97 89,78,68**
CSF £18.16 CT £147.37 TOTE £1.90: £1.30, £2.80, £4.70; EX 20.40.
Owner Raymond Tooth **Bred** Capt J H Wilson **Trained** Upper Lambourn, Berks

FOCUS
Some useful sorts on show here, but ultimately the race revolved around the odds-on favourite Punjabi, who, before his recent winning return at Newmarket had made up into a top-class hurdler since he was last seen on the level. Even with the penalty he still looked very leniently treated, and he probably did not need to improve on the Newmarket form to win well. The runners tended to race some distance away from the rail down the far side, and came right over to the stands' rail in the straight.
Red Somerset(USA) Official explanation: jockey said gelding was unsuited by the soft ground

2541 BETFAIR BETTING AS IT SHOULD BE NATIONAL STKS (LISTED RACE) — 5f 6y
6:40 (6:44) (Class 1) 2-Y-0
£12,205 (£4,626; £2,315; £1,154; £578; £290) **Stalls** High

Form RPR

011 **1** **Icesolator (IRE)**[21] 1927 2-9-5 0.................................. RichardHughes 6 101
(R Hannon) *trckd ldr: led wl over 1f out: drvn out fnl f* **11/2**[3]

1 **2** 1 1/2 **Finjaan**[25] 1832 2-9-0 0.. RHills 4 91+
(M P Tregoning) *lw: t.k.h: hld up: r.o to chse wnr ins fnl f* **2/1**[1]

1 **3** 3/4 **Foundation Room (IRE)**[25] 1838 2-8-12 0.................. FrancisNorton 8 86
(A M Balding) *in tch tl rdn 1/2-way: kpt on ins fnl f* **9/4**[2]

25 **4** nk **Fazbee (IRE)**[13] 2167 2-8-9 0.. DarryllHolland 1 82
(P W D'Arcy) *a.p: kpt on but nt qckn ins fnl f* **7/1**

013 **5** 3 1/4 **Calypso Girl (IRE)**[25] 1838 2-8-9 0.......................... StephenDonohoe 3 70
(P D Evans) *led tl rdn and hdd wl over 1f out: wknd ins fnl f* **12/1**

2 **6** 1 1/2 **Agente Parmigiano (IRE)**[19] 1983 2-9-0 0................... HayleyTurner 5 70
(G A Butler) *prom tl rdn and wknd 2f out* **15/2**

7 20 **Pocket's Pick (IRE)** 2-9-0 0.. GeorgeBaker 9 —
(G L Moore) *str: v.s.a: a bhd: t.o* **20/1**

64.89 secs (3.29) **Going Correction** +0.70s/f (Yiel) **7** Ran SP% **116.2**
Speed ratings (Par 101): **101,98,97,96,91 89,57**
CSF £17.50 TOTE £5.60: £3.00, £1.80; EX 14.10.
Owner B Bull **Bred** Pier House Stud **Trained** East Everleigh, Wilts
■ Another National Stakes win for Richard Hannon, who has dominated the event for many years.

FOCUS
Although the ground would not have been to every runner's liking, the form of this Listed race looks well up to standard. The winner, who raced up the far rail, continues to progress, and the runner-up improved a couple of pounds despite racing too keen. It was the only race run on the straight course.

NOTEBOOK
Icesolator(IRE), unlucky not to finish closer on his debut at Newmarket before winning a couple of small-field events at Goodwood, including a conditions race on his latest start, continued his progression with a ready success, despite conceding upwards of 5lb all round. He was there to be shot at once leading inside the final 2f, and there was plenty to like about the way he stuck to his task, but it has to be noted he raced against the far rail, which is often the place to be on the straight course, and he might be a touch flattered. Whatever the case, he is very tough and is clearly improving. He is held in high regard by the Hannon camp and will now head to Royal Ascot, with the Norfolk Stakes the most likely target. (op 9-2)
Finjaan, the owner's second string when winning on his debut at Newmarket, was far too keen under restraint early on, but he dropped his head once switched into the clear. However, that meant he had to make his move widest of all under Richard Hills and, after briefly looking dangerous passing the furlong pole, his run flattened out, with the combination of his earlier exertions and the possibly slower ground taking its toll. He seemed to handle the going, which was much softer than on his debut, but he will need to settle better in future. (op 3-1 tchd 4-1)
Foundation Room(IRE), the surprise winner of a conditions race on her debut at Salisbury, followed the winner through against the rail, but could not muster the pace to get in a serious blow. She should be suited by 6f. (tchd 15-8 tchd 5-2 in places)
Fazbee(IRE), racing on the softest ground she has encountered to date, ran well in the face of a stiff task. She should win a maiden before stepping back up in class. Official explanation: jockey said filly was unsuited by the soft ground (op 5-1)
Calypso Girl(IRE) had the ground to suit, but she was not good enough. (op 14-1 tchd 11-1)
Agente Parmigiano(IRE) could not confirm the promise of his debut second at Newmarket and, even though he is a son of Captain Rio, who loved the mud, this ground was probably softer than he wants. (op 12-1 tchd 7-1)
Pocket's Pick(IRE), a £55,000 son of Exceed And Excel, hails from a stable that seldom overfaces their horses, so he was an interesting contender, and was clipped into 20/1 form 25/1 on course. However, he was always struggling after losing five lengths at the start and was too green to do himself justice. (op 25-1)

2542 BETFAIR HENRY II STKS (GROUP 2) — 2m 78y
7:15 (7:17) (Class 1) 4-Y-0+
£47,970 (£18,184; £9,100; £4,537; £2,273; £1,140) **Stalls** Centre

Form RPR

335- **1** **Finalmente**[258] 5376 6-9-2 110.......................................(p) LDettori 7 109
(S A Callaghan) *led: rdn and hrd pressed fr 2f out: hdd briefly ins fnl f: rallied to hold on cl home* **16/1**

2-04 **2** hd **Balkan Knight**[12] 2192 8-9-2 110................................ JamieSpencer 6 109
(D R C Elsworth) *hld up: rdn and hdwy 2f out: led briefly ins fnl f: foiled cl home* **10/1**

1-12 **3** nse **Royal And Regal (IRE)**[13] 2169 4-9-0 116...................... NCallan 5 109+
(M A Jarvis) *lw: t.k.h early: chsd ldrs: outpcd wl over 1f out: rallied and styd on again ins fnl f* **1/1**[1]

65-2 **4** 1 1/2 **Peppertree Lane (IRE)**[29] 1717 5-9-2 110................ JimmyFortune 9 107
(M Johnston) *trckd wnr tl rdn over 1f out: nt qckn ins fnl f* **5/1**[3]

5-05 **5** 1 1/2 **Sergeant Cecil**[13] 2169 9-9-2 108.................................. AlanMunro 1 105
(B R Millman) *t.k.h: hld up in tch: effrt 2f out: one pce fnl f* **33/1**

040- **6** nse **Enjoy The Moment**[222] 6335 5-9-2 99............................ ShaneKelly 8 105
(J A Osborne) *hld up in rr: effrt 2f out: nvr nr to chal* **33/1**

0 **7** 2 1/4 **Thundering Star (SAF)**[32] 1663 5-9-7 0.............................. KShea 11 107
(M F De Kock, South Africa) *w'like: str: mid-div: hdwy 1/2-way: wknd wl over 1f out* **33/1**

231- **8** 1 **Allegretto (IRE)**[214] 6526 5-9-4 113........................... RyanMoore 4 103
(Sir Michael Stoute) *mid-div: hdwy on rails over 2f out: wknd appr fnl f* **3/1**[2]

3m 54.3s (14.80) **Going Correction** +0.475s/f (Yiel)
WFA 4 from 5yo+ 2lb **8** Ran SP% **115.5**
Speed ratings (Par 115): **82,81,81,81,80 80,79,78**
CSF £157.36 TOTE £24.10: £3.30, £1.90, £1.10; EX 147.40.
Owner Edward M Kirtland **Bred** Helshaw Grange Stud Ltd **Trained** Newmarket, Suffolk

FOCUS
They went a very steady pace for much of the way and the form looks far from reliable, with several of the principals not at their best. The winner was allowed to dictate under a great front-running ride, and he would struggle to confirm the form with several he beat here in a proper race.

NOTEBOOK
Finalmente, returning from over eight months off the track, but fit enough, was absolutely gifted the lead and set a very steady pace for most of the contest. He could never get away from his rivals once coming under strong pressure in the straight, and was narrowly headed by Balkan Knight inside the final furlong, but he forced his head back in front close home to record a game success. The form is not worth much, however, and at least one or two of these would be expected to reverse the placings in a stronger-run race. He now goes for the Ascot Gold Cup, in which he was fourth last year. (op 20-1 tchd 22-1)
Balkan Knight, second to Allegretto in this race last year, was again just denied, but this was a fine effort in defeat considering he did not have the race run to suit. A confirmed hold-up horse, the steady pace was totally against him, but he still produced a big effort in the straight, coming from well back to briefly hit the front inside the final furlong, before just being run out of it near the line. (op 8-1)
Royal And Regal(IRE) was getting weight from all of his rivals, but he did not have things go his way and probably should have won. He made the running when a close second in the Yorkshire Cup on his latest start, so it was a real surprise he was restrained off a very modest early gallop this time, and he raced a little freely as a result. He was then short of room when trying to mount a challenge in the straight, lacking the pace to take a gap and being kept in by the same owner's Peppertree Lane. He ran on well once switched to the stands' rail, but the line came too soon. While Callan has to take much of the blame, it would be interesting to know what instructions both he and Jimmy Fortune (rider of Peter Savill's other runner, Peppertree Lane) were given, as neither horse was ridden to his strengths. He may now be rested until the autumn. (op 5-4)
Peppertree Lane(IRE) had conditions to suit but, like the same owner's Royal And Regal, the steady pace was totally against him - he raced keenly - and it is surprising he did not put more pressure on the lead considering he has made all in the past. (op 9-2)
Sergeant Cecil, who was not right in his coat, was a little keen down the far side. He briefly looked dangerous inside the final two furlongs, but his run flattened out late on. He needs better ground and a stronger-run race.
Enjoy The Moment, returning from over seven months off, would not have minded the ground, but he was never involved having been held up well off the steady gallop. He had a stiff task and did well to finish so close the way the race was run, so he will be well worth a close look if bidding to repeat last year's success in the Queen Alexandra Stakes at Royal Ascot.
Thundering Star(SAF) was a Grade 1 winner over this trip in South Africa last year, but he was well beaten on his European debut at Longchamp last time and was again well held, albeit he was conceding weight all round. He might be capable of better on a quicker surface off a stronger pace, but he still has something to prove. (op 20-1)
Allegretto(IRE), who looked fit enough for her reappearance, won this race last year (second time out), as well as the Goodwood Cup and a Group 1 in France, but the steady pace was against her this time and she was soundly beaten after seven months off. (op 7-2)

2543 BETFAIR BRIGADIER GERARD STKS (GROUP 3) — 1m 2f 7y
7:45 (7:52) (Class 1) 4-Y-0+
£26,681 (£10,114; £5,061; £2,523; £1,264; £634) **Stalls** High

Form RPR

1-16 **1** **Smokey Oakey (IRE)**[42] 1422 4-9-0 101........................... JimmyQuinn 13 113
(M H Tompkins) *s.i.s: towards rr tl hdwy over 2f out: strly rdn to ld wl ins fnl f* **20/1**

50-2 **2** nk **Maraahel (IRE)**[21] 1921 7-9-5 117...(v) RHills 1 117
(Sir Michael Stoute) *s.i.s: hdwy over 2f out: led 1f out: rdn and hdd wl ins fnl f* **12/1**

11-3 **3** 1/2 **Pipedreamer**[42] 1422 4-9-0 110.................................... RyanMoore 11 111+
(J H M Gosden) *wl in rr: rdn and hdwy over 2f out: styd on fnl f: nvr nrr* **9/4**[1]

3-01 **4** nk **Regime (IRE)**[24] 1882 4-9-3 112.................................. RichardHughes 15 114
(M L W Bell) *a in tch: rdn and ev ch 1f out: kpt on but no ex towards fin* **8/1**

/2-1 **5** 1 3/4 **Charlie Farnsbarns (IRE)**[14] 2133 4-9-0 110..................... NCallan 12 107
(B J Meehan) *trckd ldr: led briefly over 1f out: no ex ins fnl f* **16/1**

0-03 **6** 2 **Petara Bay (IRE)**[19] 1980 4-9-0 105............................... ShaneKelly 8 103
(T G Mills) *towards rr: rdn and styd on fr 2f out: nvr nrr* **50/1**

345/ **7** 3/4 **Fight Club (GER)**[642] 4828 7-9-0 105 .... KerrinMcEvoy 9 102
(R Brotherton) *led tl rdn and hdd appr fnl f: one pce after* **100/1**

111- **8** 1 1/2 **Buccellati**[229] 6169 4-9-0 101 .... WilliamBuick 6 99
(A M Balding) *mid-div: rdn over 2f out: one pce after* **25/1**

1 **9** 7 **Happy Boy (BRZ)**[133] 204 5-9-3 0 .... LDettori 14 88
(Saeed Bin Suroor) *w'like: b: b.hind: in tch: tl rdn 2f out: sn btn* **6/1**[3]

1-10 **10** 3 **Dansant**[61] 1091 4-9-0 112 .... EddieAhern 7 79
(G A Butler) *swtg: mid-div: in rr fnl 2f* **20/1**

411- **11** 1 1/4 **Lucarno (USA)**[257] 5408 4-9-7 115 .... JimmyFortune 4 83+
(J H M Gosden) *lw: in tch on outside tl wknd wl over 2f out* **4/1**[2]

-120 **12** 9 **Hattan (IRE)**[11] 2230 6-9-3 113 ....(p) DarryllHolland 2 61
(C E Brittain) *lw: racd wd: a bhd* **22/1**

00-0 **13** 1/2 **Classic Punch (IRE)**[19] 1980 5-9-0 110 .... TQuinn 5 57
(D R C Elsworth) *prom tl wknd over 2f out* **40/1**

33-4 **14** 23 **Passage Of Time**[26] 1807 4-8-11 115 .... TedDurcan 3 8
(H R A Cecil) *in tch to 1/2-way: sn rdn and wknd: eased over 1f out: t.o* **6/1**[3]

2m 11.57s (1.07) **Going Correction** +0.475s/f (Yiel) **14** Ran SP% **127.1**
Speed ratings (Par 113): **114,113,113,113,111 110,109,108,102,100 99,92,91,73**
CSF £240.09 TOTE £29.50: £4.50, £3.80, £1.70; EX 333.80.

Owner Judi Dench and Bryan Agar **Bred** Hyde Park Stud **Trained** Newmarket, Suffolk

FOCUS

A terrific renewal of this Group 3 contest. Twelve of the runners were entire horses, an extraordinary figure given their ages, and a statistic which probably accounts for the number of magnificent-looking thoroughbreds now on show in the paddock beforehand. Once again they tended to keep off the rail down the back and came across towards the stands' side in the straight. The winner, a soft-ground specialist, appeared to improve by around 8lb. The runner-up has been rated to his recent Chester level.

NOTEBOOK

Smokey Oakey(IRE) proved once again the merit of top-quality handicap form even against proven Group performers like those he defeated here. The Lincoln winner did boast previous winning form over this trip, albeit off a handicap mark of only 82, but the key to him appears to be soft going, and he revelled in the prevailing conditions. Settling much better off the decent pace set by Fight Club than he did when they dawdled in the Earl Of Sefton last time, he came through with a strong run from the rear and still had enough in the tank to outbattle the runner-up. (op 22-1 tchd 25-1)

Maraahel(IRE) was slowly away as is often his wont, and came with a sweeping run from the rear to lead near the stands' rail in the final furlong. Carrying the 5lb Group 2 winner's penalty, this was not far off last season's best, and he remains a credit to his yard. (op 14-1)

Pipedreamer ◆ has made up into the finished article from three to four and looked well beforehand. He was given a lot to do as the race panned out, having to make up an awful lot of ground just to get into the race, and not surprisingly, his effort flattened out late on. His jockey reported that he was never comfortable on the soft ground, and on a better surface he certainly looks up to making his mark in this company. (op 11-4 tchd 3-1)

Regime(IRE) looked wonderful beforehand and, having become something of a frustrating sort last year, it was good that he followed up his win at the Curragh with another creditable effort here. (op 10-1)

Charlie Farnsbarns(IRE) was always handy and briefly took the lead approaching the furlong marker, only to be run out of it by those finishing from the rear. This was only his third start since chasing up Authorized in the Racing Post Trophy on heavy ground at Newbury as a juvenile, and it will be interesting to see if he can build on it. (op 22-1)

Petara Bay(IRE) has made up into a good sort and came from well off the pace to finish a never-nearer sixth. He has obviously had his problems, hence his infrequent visits to the racecourse but, if he can be kept sound, the ability is certainly still there. (op 66-1)

Fight Club(GER) was a proven Pattern-race performer in his native Germany but had not seen the racecourse for nearly two years and was picked up by current connections for just £3,000 at Tattersalls December Sales. For all that he was probably advantaged in having his own way up front, he had plenty of these off the bit turning in, and did not come under pressure himself until around the 2f pole. On the other hand, the Hunt Cup, for which he is entered, will be run at a very different beat to this race, and his handicap mark of 105 still looks high.

Happy Boy(BRZ) looked awesome when blitzing a field of admittedly unknown quantities in Dubai last time. Transferred to Godolphin soon after, he must have had a problem not to have reappeared during the Carnival and, after this effort, the jury is well and truly out on him. Official explanation: jockey said horse was unsuited by the soft ground (op 5-1 tchd 7-1)

Lucarno(USA) has done really well from three to four and last year's St Leger winner is now a quite magnificent specimen. Having raced widest of all down the back, he travelled well into the straight before finding little when let down. Not at all knocked about on going he would not have encountered before, he should leave this form behind when next seen. (op 11-2)

Passage Of Time is a big filly and it was hoped she might have improved plenty on her comeback effort at Newmarket. Indeed, she looked better in her coat than at the Guineas meeting. Alas, she did not look at all happy during the race, racing with her head held high on going she was proven on, and it is beginning to look as though she hasn't trained on. Official explanation: jockey said filly ran flat (op 11-2 tchd 5-1)

2544 BETFAIR POKER HERON STKS (LISTED RACE) 1m 14y

8:20 (8:24) (Class 1) 3-Y-O

£14,760 (£5,595; £2,800; £1,396; £699; £351) **Stalls** High

Form RPR

-441 **1** **Redolent (IRE)**[26] 1797 3-8-12 100 ....(p) RyanMoore 8 107
(R Hannon) *mde all: shkn up over 1f out: r.o wl* **11/2**[3]

23-3 **2** 2 1/2 **Iguazu Falls (USA)**[26] 1797 3-8-12 105 .... LDettori 4 101
(Saeed Bin Suroor) *lw: t.k.h: trckd wnr thrght: rdn over 1f out: no imp ins fnl f* **2/1**[1]

22-1 **3** 1 1/2 **Virtual**[43] 1403 3-8-12 94 .... JimmyFortune 6 99+
(J H M Gosden) *lw: awkward leaving stalls: effrt 2f out: no imp on ldng pair fnl f* **2/1**[1]

21 **4** 2 1/2 **Khateeb (IRE)**[24] 1855 3-8-12 98 ....(t) RHills 1 92
(M A Jarvis) *lw: in tch: rdn 2f out: one pce after* **5/1**[2]

2245 **5** 4 1/2 **Gaspar Van Wittel (USA)**[5] 2408 3-8-12 100 .... JamieSpencer 5 82
(S A Callaghan) *in rr: rdn 2f out: no hdwy after* **10/1**

1- **6** 4 1/2 **Fr Dominic (USA)**[251] 5598 3-8-12 87 .... KerrinMcEvoy 3 72
(R M Beckett) *hld up: a bhd* **14/1**

1m 46.93s (3.63) **Going Correction** +0.675s/f (Yiel) **6** Ran SP% **114.5**
Speed ratings (Par 107): **108,105,104,101,97 92**
CSF £17.45 TOTE £5.80: £2.50, £2.20; EX 18.70.

Owner De La Warr Racing **Bred** R O'Callaghan And D Veitch **Trained** East Everleigh, Wilts

FOCUS

This was a decent renewal of a race that often featured colts stopping off en route to better things when run on the erstwhile turf course at nearby Kempton, but the soft ground looked against a couple of the principals. They kept a good six or seven horse widths off the rail down the far side, but gradually came across towards the stands' rail up the home straight, instead of angling straight for it as in previous events. The runners practically occupied the same positions throughout, suggesting that in this race at least, it was nigh on impossible to quicken in the prevailing conditions.

NOTEBOOK

Redolent(IRE) had the run of the race from the front but is a difficult horse to pass, particularly on his favoured soft ground. Left alone to do what he wanted in the lead, Moore was able to come across to the stands' rail in the straight in his own time, and never looked like being caught, clocking a time almost half a second faster than a smart type in the following handicap. This is as good as he is. (op 8-1)

Iguazu Falls(USA) had by far the best two-year-old form of these and his reappearance flop at Doncaster had come at a time when Godolphin's representatives were still re-adjusting to the British climate. Proven on the going, he ran much better here without ever really looking like getting to the winner. (op 10-3)

Virtual came into the race with a very progressive profile and while the going might have stopped him showing what he is capable of, his St James's Palace entry looks a little fanciful now. (tchd 9-4)

Khateeb(IRE) was something of a joker in the pack, having only run in maiden company so far, and it is a pity that the ground went as soft as it did as we didn't really find out that much more about him. He matched his Kempton form nevertheless, and could still be anything. (op 10-3 tchd 11-2 in a place)

Gaspar Van Wittel(USA) was a useful juvenile but he is found wanting in this company and with an uncompetitive handicap mark he is going to be hard to place. (op 9-1 tchd 11-1)

Fr Dominic(USA) had been off the course for eight months since a fast-ground maiden win on his debut at Newmarket and could never get into the race. (op 10-1)

2545 BETFAIR RADIO WHITSUN CUP H'CAP 1m 14y

8:50 (8:54) (Class 3) (0-95,94) 4-Y-O+

£9,346 (£2,799; £1,399; £700; £349; £175) **Stalls** High

Form RPR

31 **1** **Bushman**[38] 1526 4-9-2 92 .... RichardMullen 4 110+
(D M Simcock) *lw: in tch and a gng wl: shkn up to ld 2f out: sn clr: eased towards fin* **7/4**[1]

-600 **2** 4 1/2 **Little White Lie (IRE)**[60] 1105 4-9-4 94 .... DarryllHolland 7 97
(J R Jenkins) *hld up: hdwy over 1f out: r.o to go 2nd wl ins fnl f* **12/1**

-604 **3** 3/4 **Zero Cool (USA)**[26] 1799 4-8-5 81 .... AlanMunro 9 82
(G L Moore) *trckd ldrs: rdn and ev ch 2f out: kpt on but lost 2nd wl ins fnl f* **14/1**

2614 **4** 1/2 **Ballinteni**[7] 2325 6-9-3 93 .... NCallan 2 93
(Miss Gay Kelleway) *trckd ldr to 2f out: one pce fnl f* **9/2**[2]

0000 **5** 3/4 **Very Wise**[12] 2200 6-8-11 87 ....(p) RHills 1 85
(W J Haggas) *hld up in rr: mde sme hdwy ins fnl 2f* **9/1**[3]

-504 **6** hd **Twilight Star (IRE)**[21] 1936 4-8-1 80 oh2 ....(t) LukeMorris(3) 8 78
(R A Teal) *slowly away: effrt over 2f out: no ex ins fnl f* **20/1**

5434 **7** 2 **Bahar Shumaal (IRE)**[21] 1920 6-8-9 85 .... RyanMoore 6 78
(C E Brittain) *led tl rdn and hdd 2f out: wknd appr fnl f* **9/2**[2]

0001 **8** 1 1/2 **Orchard Supreme**[8] 2308 5-8-13 89 6ex .... RichardHughes 11 79
(R Hannon) *a in rr* **11/1**

-541 **9** 10 **Masai Moon**[16] 2085 4-8-11 92 .... JamesMillman(5) 5 59
(B R Millman) *chsd ldrs tl rdn 3f out: sn wknd* **10/1**

1m 47.37s (4.07) **Going Correction** +0.675s/f (Yiel) **9** Ran SP% **119.3**
Speed ratings (Par 107): **106,101,100,100,99 97,95,85**
CSF £26.41 CT £236.16 TOTE £2.50: £1.60, £4.10, £2.90; EX 33.00 Place 6 £29.26, Place 5 £17.70.

Owner Khalifa Dasmal **Bred** Darley **Trained** Newmarket, Suffolk

FOCUS

Just an ordinary handicap for the grade, but a very impressive winner. The winning time was 0.44 seconds slower than the previous three-year-old Listed contest, but the ground was deteriorating. They raced towards the stands' side in the straight, but not tight against the rail. Few solid yardsticks in the line-up, but Bushman impressed and looked value for nearer 7 lengths.

NOTEBOOK

Bushman ◆ has had his problems but looked a smart prospect when bolting up from the useful Woolfall Treasure in a Windsor maiden and a mark of 92 for his handicap debut was not that harsh. The testing going was much more of a concern, as his sire was a fast-ground horse, but he coped well. Having travelled nicely enough, he drew well clear when asked for his effort and was eased close home, looking value for at least a couple more lengths. He may well improve again when stepped back up in distance, and he looks capable of making his mark in Group company. In the short term he will be aimed at the Listed Wolferton Handicap at Royal Ascot, provided the ground is not too quick. (op 9-4 tchd 5-2)

Little White Lie(IRE) was formerly trained by Ger Lyons in Ireland, where he was a dual winner on heavy ground, so he had conditions to suit on his debut for new connections and ran well behind the smart winner. (op 10-1 tchd 8-1)

Zero Cool(USA), dropped back in trip, seemed to have his chance and can have few excuses. (op 12-1)

Ballinteni should not have minded the ground and he attracted good market support, but he finished up well held, suggesting he is plenty high enough in the weights. (op 13-2)

Very Wise has not been in much form this year, despite a declining handicap mark, but he had his ground and showed a bit more here in first-time cheekpieces. Official explanation: jockey said gelding got upset in stalls (op 12-1)

Bahar Shumaal(IRE) would appear to need better ground. (tchd 5-1)

T/Plt: £22.90 to a £1 stake. Pool: £96,575.02. 3,068.81 winning tickets. T/Qpdt: £7.90 to a £1 stake. Pool: £4,997.70. 468.10 winning tickets. JS

2507 YARMOUTH (L-H)

Thursday, May 29

OFFICIAL GOING: Good to firm (good in places)(8.2) changing to good after race 3 (3.10) changing to good to soft after race 5 (4.10)

Wind: Light behind Weather: Overcast turning to rain after race 2

2546 WATERAID MEDIAN AUCTION MAIDEN STKS 6f 3y

2:10 (2:14) (Class 6) 3-5-Y-O **£2,266** (£674; £337; £168) **Stalls** High

Form RPR

0- **1** **Valatrix (IRE)**[219] 6409 3-8-7 0 .... JackMitchell(5) 4 76
(C F Wall) *mde all: shkn up over 1f out: r.o* **5/1**[3]

2 1 1/4 **Buddhist Monk** 3-9-3 0 .... DO'Donohoe 6 77
(Sir Mark Prescott) *chsd wnr: shkn up over 1f out: edgd lft ins fnl f: r.o* **10/1**

0 **3** 3 1/2 **Thumbs Up**[27] 1763 3-9-3 0 .... NickyMackay 3 66
(L M Cumani) *trckd ldrs: outpcd 2f out: styd on ins fnl f* **5/1**[3]

24-5 **4** 1 1/4 **Sunny Sprite**[55] 1194 3-9-0 74 .... LukeMorris(3) 1 62
(J M P Eustace) *s.i.s: sn chsng ldrs: rdn over 2f out: wknd ins fnl f* **8/1**

00 **5** 3 3/4 **Isabella's Fancy**[26] 1795 3-8-12 0 .... OscarUrbina 9 45
(J R Fanshawe) *hld up: rdn over 2f out: wknd over 1f out* **10/1**

50-3 **6** 3/4 **Sister Moonshine**[20] 1960 3-8-12 66 .... DaneO'Neill 2 42
(W R Muir) *chsd ldrs: rdn over 2f out: wknd over 1f out* **11/4**[1]

0 **7** 3 3/4 **Dalla Finestra**[26] 1795 3-8-12 0 .... IanMongan 8 30
(C F Wall) *hld up: plld hrd: wknd 2f out* **4/1**[2]

8 1¾ **Dubai To Barnsley** 3-8-10 0 MarkCoumbe(7) 7 30
(Garry Moss) *s.i.s: hld up: rdn over 2f out: sn wknd* **50/1**

9 9 **Savanna's Gold** 4-9-7 0 DMylonas 5 —
(G Prodromou) *dwlt: plld hrd: bhd fnl 4f* **33/1**

1m 12.29s (-2.11) **Going Correction** -0.325s/f (Firm)
WFA 3 from 4yo 9lb 9 Ran SP% **114.2**
Speed ratings (Par 101): **101,99,94,93,88 87,82,79,67**
CSF £53.05 TOTE £6.50: £2.30, £3.00, £2.10; EX 58.30 Trifecta £339.60 Part won. Pool: £478.34. 0.49 winning units..
Owner Mrs Valerie Gordon **Bred** Michael Boland **Trained** Newmarket, Suffolk

FOCUS
A modest maiden and, although the level is quite fluid, the form should work out.
Dubai To Barnsley Official explanation: jockey said gelding lost its action 2f out

2547 AQUAZONE CLAIMING STKS 6f 3y
2:40 (2:42) (Class 6) 3-Y-O+ £1,683 (£501; £250; £125) **Stalls** High

Form RPR

405 **1** **Doubtful Sound (USA)**[10] 2255 4-9-2 65 (b[1]) MarkCoumbe(7) 5 68
(John A Harris) *dwlt: hld up: racd keenly: hdwy over 3f out: chsd ldr 2f out: sn rdn: hung rt ins fnl f: r.o to ld towards fin* **7/1[3]**

-042 **2** 1¾ **Guest Connections**[10] 2255 5-9-6 72 (b[1]) JamieJones(5) 8 64
(D Nicholls) *hld up: rdn over 2f out: swtchd lft and r.o ins fnl f: nt rch wnr* **13/8[1]**

4310 **3** *shd* **Mafaheem**[2] 2478 6-9-8 62 (b) TGMcLaughlin 7 61
(A B Haynes) *trckd ldrs: racd keenly: led 2f out: sn rdn and hung lft: hdd towards fin* **5/2[2]**

0100 **4** 1 **Majestical (IRE)**[10] 2255 6-9-2 58 (p) DaneO'Neill 3 52
(V Smith) *hld up: rdn over 1f out: r.o ins fnl f: nt trble ldrs* **8/1**

4235 **5** 2 **Time Share (IRE)**[16] 2088 4-8-9 47 KellyHarrison(5) 6 43
(M Wigham) *plld hrd and prom: rdn over 1f out: no ex fnl f* **14/1**

4206 **6** ¾ **Blackmalkin (USA)**[16] 2088 4-9-9 63 RobertHavlin 4 50
(M Quinn) *led 4f: wknd ins fnl f* **7/1[3]**

5540 **7** 8 **Ela Aleka Mou**[55] 1189 4-9-0 55 (t) PaulEddery 1 15
(Miss D Mountain) *chsd ldr to 1/2-way: wknd over 1f out* **33/1**

1m 12.88s (-1.52) **Going Correction** -0.325s/f (Firm)
WFA 3 from 4yo+ 9lb 7 Ran SP% **112.4**
Speed ratings (Par 101): **97,94,94,93,90 89,78**
CSF £18.21 TOTE £8.30: £2.80, £1.20; EX 22.90 Trifecta £70.70 Pool: £326.89. 3.28 winning units..
Owner Shaun Taylor **Bred** Millsec, Ltd **Trained** Eastwell, Leics

FOCUS
A moderate claimer and not a race to be too positive about, and the form is best rated through the winner to his turf best.

2548 BLP WATERAID (S) STKS 5f 43y
3:10 (3:11) (Class 6) 2-Y-O £1,683 (£501; £250; £125) **Stalls** High

Form RPR

6 **1** **Simple Rhythm**[33] 1616 2-8-4 0 DominicFox(3) 6 68+
(M G Quinlan) *mde all: qcknd clr fr over 1f out: easily* **3/1[1]**

00 **2** 4 **Elusive Ronnie (IRE)**[14] 2117 2-8-12 0 TPO'Shea 2 53+
(S A Callaghan) *hld up: hdwy over 2f out: rdn to chse wnr over 1f out: sn outpcd* **7/2[2]**

03 **3** 5 **Makaluna**[17] 2049 2-8-5 0 WilliamCarson(7) 3 35
(W G M Turner) *chsd wnr tl rdn over 1f out: wknd fnl f* **8/1**

53 **4** 2¾ **In The Moment**[36] 1555 2-8-2 0 JackDean(5) 4 20
(W G M Turner) *s.i.s: hld up: rdn over 2f out: n.d* **13/2**

0 **5** *hd* **Champagne Leader**[44] 1384 2-8-7 0 SamHitchcott 5 19
(A B Haynes) *chsd ldrs: rdn and hung lft over 2f out: sn wknd* **16/1**

6544 **6** 6 **Talulah Bells**[3] 2450 2-8-4 0 LukeMorris(3) 8 —
(A W Carroll) *prom: rdn over 2f out: sn hung lft and wknd* **11/2**

7 3¼ **Hunch** 2-8-8 0 ow3 MarkCoumbe(7) 7 —
(Garry Moss) *s.i.s: outpcd* **20/1**

8 7 **Maj William Martin** 2-8-12 0 FergusSweeney 1 —
(M Quinn) *swvd lft s: outpcd* **9/2[3]**

63.35 secs (1.15) **Going Correction** -0.15s/f (Firm) 8 Ran SP% **115.9**
Speed ratings (Par 91): **84,77,69,65,64 55,50,38**
CSF £13.87 TOTE £4.30: £1.50, £1.70, £2.90; EX 15.30 Trifecta £191.30 Pool: £406.96. 1.51 winning units..The winner was bought in for 12,500gns. Elusive Ronnie was claimed by Trina Cornwell for £5,000.
Owner P T Quinlan **Bred** P Quinlan **Trained** Newmarket, Suffolk

FOCUS
A dire juvenile affair but the easy winner should be rated value for a good deal further.

NOTEBOOK
Simple Rhythm, who produced a horror show on her debut a month ago, was very well supported for this drop into the lowest grade and she showed her true colours with an effortless success. She is evidently now going the right way, is doubtless better than a plater, and should be high on confidence after this. Her connections later went to 12,500gns to buy her back in. (op 5-2 tchd 7-2)
Elusive Ronnie(IRE) showed his best form to date for the drop in class, but must rate flattered by his proximity to the easy winner. He has now found his level and looks ready to try another furlong now. (tchd 3-1 and 4-1)
Makaluna ran a little better on this return to turf, but still dropped out tamely before the final furlong and looks very moderate indeed. He still helps to put this form into perspective, however. (tchd 10-1)
In The Moment missed the kick and was always playing catch-up thereafter. This was the quickest ground she has encountered to date and she is still learning her trade. (op 8-1 tchd 9-1)
Hunch Official explanation: jockey said colt hung left throughout
Maj William Martin Official explanation: jockey said colt swerved left at start

2549 HOLLERAN H'CAP 7f 3y
3:40 (3:41) (Class 6) (0-60,60) 3-Y-O £1,942 (£578; £288; £144) **Stalls** High

Form RPR

4062 **1** **Admirals Way**[14] 2126 3-8-7 56 MarkCoumbe(7) 7 65
(C N Kellett) *chsd ldrs: led and hung rt fr over 2f out: rdn out* **12/1**

0-43 **2** ¾ **Peas In A Pod**[17] 2055 3-8-8 50 OscarUrbina 8 57
(J R Fanshawe) *hld up: hmpd 1/2-way: hdwy over 1f out: chsd wnr ins fnl f: r.o* **9/2[1]**

04-4 **3** 1¾ **Flower**[17] 2052 3-9-4 60 MichaelHills 15 62
(W J Haggas) *s.i.s: hld up: hdwy 1/2-way: rdn and nt clr run over 1f out: styd on same pce ins fnl f* **5/1[2]**

00-2 **4** *shd* **My Flame**[28] 1740 3-8-13 55 DO'Donohoe 9 57
(J R Jenkins) *chsd ldrs: rdn over 1f out: styd on* **10/1**

0006 **5** 1¼ **Averoo**[13] 2161 3-9-4 60 TGMcLaughlin 13 59
(M D Squance) *s.i.s: hld up: rdn 1/2-way: hdwy and hung lft over 2f out: rdn and hung rt over 1f out: no ex wl ins fnl f* **6/1[3]**

0-00 **6** 2 **Carmela Maria**[20] 1957 3-8-13 60 JackMitchell(5) 16 53
(C F Wall) *s.i.s: hld up: rdn over 2f out: styd on ins fnl f: nvr nrr* **11/1**

00-1 **7** 4½ **King Of Cadeaux (IRE)**[31] 1672 3-8-12 54 FergusSweeney 6 35
(M A Magnusson) *hld up: hdwy over 2f out: rdn and edgd lft over 1f out: wknd fnl f* **13/2**

560- **8** 2¾ **Cryptonite Diamond (USA)**[230] 6150 3-9-1 57 DaneO'Neill 1 36+
(W R Swinburn) *s.i.s: hld up: hdwy over 2f out: rdn over 1f out: wknd fnl f: eased* **14/1**

6-U0 **9** 3½ **Miss Olivia**[12] 2208 3-8-8 50 CatherineGannon 2 14
(H R A Cecil) *chsd ldrs: rdn over 2f out: wknd over 1f out* **16/1**

206- **10** 2¼ **Bettys Touch**[290] 4453 3-8-8 55 ow1 JamieJones(5) 12 13
(W J Musson) *s.i.s: hld up: hmpd over 2f out: n.d* **25/1**

4-00 **11** ¾ **Amber Ridge**[48] 1315 3-8-13 55 (p) JohnEgan 3 11
(B P J Baugh) *prom: rdn and wknd over 2f out* **33/1**

040- **12** 3¾ **Demure Princess**[279] 4762 3-8-9 56 JackDean(5) 4 2
(W G M Turner) *chsd ldrs over 4f* **33/1**

-050 **13** ½ **Minwir (IRE)**[40] 1479 3-9-4 60 RobertHavlin 14 5
(M Quinn) *hld up: hdwy 1/2-way: wknd over 2f out* **12/1**

00-0 **14** ½ **Nisbah**[29] 1721 3-8-10 52 SilvestreDeSousa 5 —
(C E Brittain) *mid-div: sn drvn along: wknd wl over 1f out* **33/1**

-606 **15** *nse* **Galley Slave (IRE)**[114] 444 3-8-4 53 ow1 NBazeley(7) 11 —
(M C Chapman) *prom: sn drvn along: lost pl 1/2-way: sn bhd* **50/1**

05 **16** ½ **Cheeky Try (USA)**[16] 2089 3-8-8 50 (b) DMylonas 10 —
(G Prodromou) *sn led: rdn and hdd over 2f out: sn wknd* **20/1**

1m 26.0s (-0.60) **Going Correction** -0.15s/f (Firm) 16 Ran SP% **127.2**
Speed ratings (Par 97): **97,96,94,94,92 90,85,82,78,75 74,70,69,69,69 68**
CSF £63.47 CT £333.44 TOTE £15.70: £2.80, £1.80, £1.90, £2.50; EX 68.80 Trifecta £179.40 Pool: £356.45. 1.41 winning units..
Owner J E Titley **Bred** Juddmonte Farms Ltd **Trained** Woodlane, Staffs
■ Stewards' Enquiry : Silvestre De Sousa caution: allowed filly to coast home with no assistance

FOCUS
The ground was officially changed to "good" prior to this moderate handicap for three-year-olds. The form looks fair and pretty sound rated through the fifth.
Peas In A Pod Official explanation: jockey said gelding lost a front shoe
King Of Cadeaux(IRE) Official explanation: jockey said gelding was unsuited by the good ground

2550 ESSEX & SUFFOLK WATER H'CAP 7f 3y
4:10 (4:14) (Class 5) (0-70,68) 4-Y-O+ £2,590 (£770; £385; £192) **Stalls** High

Form RPR

16-1 **1** **Grand Vizier (IRE)**[21] 1936 4-8-12 67 JackMitchell(5) 7 78+
(C F Wall) *s.i.s: hld up: hdwy over 2f out: rdn to ld 1f out: r.o* **4/1[1]**

0-00 **2** ¾ **Kunte Kinteh**[19] 2005 4-8-10 60 SilvestreDeSousa 11 69
(D Nicholls) *a.p: rdn over 1f out: hung lft ins fnl f: r.o* **7/1[3]**

-053 **3** 1¼ **Farefield Lodge (IRE)**[23] 1900 4-9-2 66 (v[1]) DaneO'Neill 1 72
(C G Cox) *chsd ldrs: led 3f out: rdn and hdd 2f out: styd on same pce ins fnl f* **9/2[2]**

3142 **4** 1¼ **Marmooq**[20] 1966 5-8-5 55 (e) AdrianMcCarthy 6 57
(M J Attwater) *mid-div: sn drvn along: hdwy u.p over 1f out: styd on* **15/2**

-030 **5** ¾ **Grey Boy (GER)**[16] 2087 7-8-6 63 MarkCoumbe(7) 8 63
(A W Carroll) *chsd ldrs: led 2f out: rdn and hdd 1f out: no ex* **15/2**

0-04 **6** 1¾ **Billy Red**[28] 1739 4-8-11 61 (b) JohnEgan 4 57
(J R Jenkins) *trckd ldrs: plld hrd: n.m.r and lost pl over 2f out: styd on ins fnl f* **14/1**

-100 **7** *hd* **Hazytoo**[6] 2373 4-9-4 68 TPO'Shea 13 63+
(S A Callaghan) *stdd s: bhd tl styd on ins fnl f: nvr nr to chal* **8/1**

0040 **8** 2¾ **Djalalabad (FR)**[6] 2355 4-8-4 54 oh6 CatherineGannon 10 42
(Mrs C A Dunnett) *chsd ldrs: rdn 2f out: wknd fnl f* **25/1**

060 **9** ½ **Louisiade (IRE)**[41] 1449 7-8-5 62 ow2 (p) NBazeley(7) 9 57+
(M C Chapman) *led 4f: wknd over 1f out: eased* **25/1**

645- **10** ¾ **Massams Lane**[205] 6704 4-8-0 57 MCGeran(7) 14 41
(G C Bravery) *hld up: rdn over 2f out: sn wknd* **20/1**

310- **11** 4 **Whistleupthewind**[253] 5546 5-8-1 54 LukeMorris(3) 3 27
(J M P Eustace) *trckd ldrs: plld hrd: rdn over 1f out: sn hung lft and wknd* **9/1**

42-0 **12** 16 **Foreland Sands (IRE)**[10] 2259 4-8-4 54 oh9 (p) DO'Donohoe 5 —
(Mrs L Williamson) *hld up: rdn and wknd over 2f out* **40/1**

1m 26.56s (-0.04) **Going Correction** +0.05s/f (Good) 12 Ran SP% **116.9**
Speed ratings (Par 103): **102,101,99,98,97 95,95,92,91,90 86,67**
CSF £29.80 CT £133.59 TOTE £4.20: £1.80, £2.70, £1.90; EX 30.50 Trifecta £398.30 Part won. Pool: £561.05. 0.20 winning units..
Owner Hintlesham SP Partners **Bred** Yeomanstown Stud **Trained** Newmarket, Suffolk
■ Stewards' Enquiry : Jack Mitchell caution: used whip with excessive frequency

FOCUS
Another moderate handicap. The form is rated through the second and third.
Hazytoo Official explanation: jockey said gelding dwelt out of the stalls
Louisiade(IRE) Official explanation: jockey said saddle slipped

2551 MOUCHEL H'CAP 5f 43y
4:40 (4:46) (Class 5) (0-75,73) 3-Y-O+ £2,590 (£770; £385; £192) **Stalls** High

Form RPR

-065 **1** **Equuleus Pictor**[24] 1872 4-8-11 63 JackDean(5) 9 75
(J L Spearing) *trckd ldrs: rdn to ld over 1f out: r.o* **4/1[1]**

3443 **2** 1¼ **Desperate Dan**[2] 2474 7-9-9 70 (b) TGMcLaughlin 5 77
(A B Haynes) *s.i.s: swtchd lft and hdwy over 1f out: r.o* **15/2**

4003 **3** 3¼ **Thoughtsofstardom**[12] 2205 5-8-8 60 KellyHarrison(5) 3 55
(M Wigham) *hld up: hdwy over 1f out: nt rch ldrs* **15/2**

-022 **4** 1 **Millfields Dreams**[12] 2205 9-9-4 65 (p) DavidKinsella 11 57
(P Leech) *chsd ldrs: rdn 1/2-way: styd on same pce appr fnl f* **13/2**

0-34 **5** *shd* **Raccoon (IRE)**[13] 2145 8-9-4 65 DaneO'Neill 2 56
(Mrs R A Carr) *chsd ldrs: rdn over 1f out: no ex ins fnl f* **5/1[2]**

2500 **6** 7 **Shatter Resistant (IRE)**[14] 2122 3-8-7 62 oh5 ow3 (e) JohnEgan 4 28
(M D Squance) *s.i.s: sn pushed along in rr: n.d* **6/1[3]**

00-3 **7** 2 **Only In Jest**[16] 2068 3-8-11 66 RichardThomas 1 25
(J Gallagher) *got loose on the way to post: unruly in stalls: mde most over 3f: wknd fnl f* **16/1**

1460 **8** 2¾ **Bookiesindex Boy**[9] 2292 4-9-7 68 DO'Donohoe 6 17
(J R Jenkins) *trckd ldrs: rdn over 1f out: wknd fnl f* **10/1**

1064 **9** 3½ **Fast Freddie**[1] 2511 4-9-0 68 MCGeran(7) 8 4
(S Parr) *chsd ldrs over 3f* **15/2**

00-6 **10** 10 **Bold Minstrel (IRE)**[13] 2166 6-9-6 67 FergusSweeney 12 —
(M Quinn) *prom: rdn 1/2-way: wknd wl over 1f out* **16/1**

62.04 secs (-0.16) **Going Correction** +0.05s/f (Good)
WFA 3 from 4yo+ 8lb 10 Ran SP% **120.4**
Speed ratings (Par 103): **103,101,95,94,94 82,79,75,69,53**
CSF £35.47 CT £226.13 TOTE £5.30: £1.80, £3.20, £3.00; EX 44.70 Trifecta £257.50 Pool: £464.37. 1.28 winning units..
Owner Masonaires **Bred** A J And Mrs L Brazier **Trained** Kinnersley, Worcs

The Form Book, Raceform Ltd, Compton, RG20 6NL

FOCUS
A modest sprint handicap. The form looks ordinary but straightforward rated through the second, third and fourth.

2552 CARILLION H'CAP 1m 2f 21y
5:10 (5:12) (Class 6) (0-55,56) 3-Y-O £1,813 (£539; £269; £134) Stalls Low

Form RPR
-430 1 **Millie's Rock (IRE)**[17] 2041 3-9-0 55 DaneO'Neill 14 64+
(M J Wallace) *hld up: swtchd rt over 3f out: hdwy and swtchd rt over 1f out: r.o to ld nr fin* 4/1[2]
-000 2 ½ **South Wales**[93] 705 3-8-6 47 NickyMackay 10 52+
(S C Williams) *hld up in tch: led 2f out: sn rdn: hdd nr fin* 16/1
6455 3 1½ **Scientific**[55] 1193 3-8-11 52 (b) CatherineGannon 13 54
(G Prodromou) *hld up: hmpd over 3f out: hdwy and hung lft fr over 1f out: styd on* 16/1
-046 4 ¾ **Ba Dreamflight**[37] 1553 3-8-6 47 RichardSmith 7 47
(H Morrison) *chsd ldrs: rdn over 2f out: unable qckn towards fin* 7/1[3]
400 5 nk **Mganga**[17] 2045 3-8-7 55 MCGeran(7) 16 54+
(M R Channon) *hld up: hdwy over 2f out: sn rdn no ex ins fnl f* 10/1
0005 6 2¾ **Lady Florence**[21] 1938 3-8-11 52 MichaelHills 2 46
(A B Coogan) *led: rdn and hdd 2f out: wknd wl ins fnl f* 12/1
-343 7 1 **Yakama (IRE)**[40] 1478 3-8-7 48 (p) RichardThomas 3 40
(D J S Ffrench Davis) *prom: rdn over 2f out: wknd ins fnl f* 5/2[1]
000- 8 1 **Latimer House (IRE)**[261] 5308 3-8-5 46 DavidKinsella 5 36
(Dr J D Scargill) *hld up: hdwy over 3f out: rdn over 1f out: wknd fnl f* 33/1
005- 9 3¾ **Police Officer**[199] 6791 3-8-7 48 FergusSweeney 8 30
(W J Musson) *hld up: nvr nrr* 10/1
-400 10 14 **Dear Will**[24] 1870 3-9-0 55 OscarUrbina 11 9
(J R Fanshawe) *hld up: hdwy over 3f out: wknd over 1f out* 16/1
0000 11 14 **Dawn Wind**[10] 2247 3-8-7 48 (v[1]) TPO'Shea 12 —
(I A Wood) *s.i.s: hdwy over 6f out: rdn and wknd over 2f out* 33/1
00-0 12 14 **Bunty Malenoir**[29] 1721 3-8-9 50 ow1 (v[1]) TGMcLaughlin 15 —
(Mrs C A Dunnett) *chsd ldrs: wkng whn hmpd over 3f out: eased over 1f out* 50/1
-555 13 6 **Pie O My (IRE)**[30] 1710 3-9-0 55 (b[1]) RobertHavlin 1 —
(J Jay) *chsd ldrs 9f: eased over 1f out* 12/1
0000 14 ½ **So Sublime**[12] 2208 3-8-8 56 ow1 NBazeley(7) 6 —
(M C Chapman) *hld up: plld hrd: rdn and wknd over 3f out: eased over 1f out* 40/1
600 15 10 **Threecheersforanby (IRE)**[20] 1960 3-8-12 53 (t) JohnEgan 9 —
(S Parr) *s.i.s: sn pushed along in rr: wknd 4f out: eased over 1f out* 22/1

2m 11.15s (0.65) **Going Correction** +0.05s/f (Good) 15 Ran SP% 126.9
Speed ratings (Par 97): **99,98,97,96,96 94,93,92,89,78 67,56,51,50,42**
CSF £66.88 CT £964.59 TOTE £5.10: £2.30, £6.10, £3.40; EX 119.80 TRIFECTA Not won..
Owner Mike & Denise Dawes **Bred** Mrs U Schwarzenbach **Trained** Newmarket, Suffolk
■ Stewards' Enquiry : Dane O'Neill three-day ban: careless riding (June 12-14)

FOCUS
A weak handicap, run at an average pace, and moderate form overall.
Pie O My(IRE) Official explanation: jockey said colt stumbled 2f out
T/Jkpt: £207,817.80 to a £1 stake. Pool: £1,024,454.19. 3.50 winning tickets. T/Plt: £111.30 to a £1 stake. Pool: £107,557.18. 705.20 winning tickets. T/Qpdt: £12.30 to a £1 stake. Pool: £4,926.80. 295.80 winning tickets. CR

2064 SAINT-CLOUD (L-H)
Thursday, May 29

OFFICIAL GOING: Soft

2553a PRIX CORRIDA (GROUP 2) (F&M) 1m 2f 110y
2:20 (2:21) 4-Y-O+ £54,485 (£21,029; £10,037; £6,691; £3,346)

RPR
1 **Fair Breeze (GER)**[30] 1713 5-8-11 J-PCarvalho 4 107
(Mario Hofer, Germany) *a in tch: clsd up to go 3rd st: led over 1f out: rdn out* 21/10[2]
2 ¾ **La Boum (GER)**[30] 1713 5-8-11 CSoumillon 6 106
(Robert Collet, France) *5th st: pressed wnr over 1f out: kpt on u.p fnl f* 8/1
3 nse **Believe Me (IRE)**[30] 1713 4-8-9 (p) OPeslier 8 104
(J-M Beguigne, France) *hld up in rr: hdwy on outside over 1f out: disp 2nd fnl f: no ex cl home* 47/10[3]
4 ½ **Hapsburg (FR)**[30] 1713 4-8-9 TThulliez 3 103
(E Libaud, France) *wnt 3rd at 1/2-way: cl 4th on ins st: styd on same pce fnl f* 66/1
5 1 **Avanti Polonia (GER)**[30] 1713 4-8-11 DBonilla 5 103
(F Head, France) *6th st: hdwy on outside 2f out: kpt on one pce fr over 1f out* 24/1
6 3 **Mrs Lindsay (USA)**[32] 1665 4-9-2 C-PLemaire 2 102
(F Rohaut, France) *trckd ldr: led wl over 2f out to over 1f out: wknd qckly* 8/5[1]
7 5 **Guardia (GER)**[249] 5669 4-8-9 SPasquier 7 86
(A Fabre, France) *a in rr* 14/1
8 4 **Claire Et Bleu (FR)**[30] 1713 4-8-9 AlexisBadel 1 78
(Mme M Bollack-Badel, France) *led to wl over 2f out: 2nd st: sn btn* 16/1

2m 15.9s (-3.70) 8 Ran SP% 117.4
PARI-MUTUEL: WIN 3.10; PL 1.30, 2.10, 1.50; DF 16.80.
Owner Stall Margarethe **Bred** *unknown **Trained** Germany

NOTEBOOK
Fair Breeze(GER) had conditions to suit and she was able to follow up her recent Chantilly success. Fourth through the early stages, she went to the head of affairs early in the straight and stayed on bravely to the line. Her big target now is the Prix de l'Opera at Longchamp in October and she will probably have an outing before then in the Prix Jean Romanet at Deauville in August. She is certainly improving with age and is a high-class performer on a testing surface.
La Boum(GER) followed the winner for much of the way and looked dangerous a furlong out, but she could not quite get there. She battled on well for second and reversed the form with many of her recent rivals on this occasion.
Believe Me(IRE) was given a waiting ride and ran pretty free early on. She was brought with a run up the centre of the track and only just failed to get second.
Hapsburg(FR) ran on in the closing stages but was rather one-paced.
Mrs Lindsay(USA) was well below her best, even allowing for the fact she was conceding weight all round, and this ground was probably softer than she wants.

2349 BRIGHTON (L-H)
Friday, May 30

OFFICIAL GOING: Good to soft (7.4)
Running rail moved out 2 metres from 6f to 2.5f mark adding 15yds to advertised distances.
Wind: slight, half behind

2554 TOTESPORTCASINO.COM MEDIAN AUCTION MAIDEN STKS 5f 213y
2:35 (2:35) (Class 5) 2-Y-O £2,590 (£770; £385; £192) Stalls Low

Form RPR
42 1 **In Transit (IRE)**[8] 2324 2-9-3 0 TPO'Shea 5 77+
(M R Channon) *a in tch: rdn over 2f out: kpt on u.p fnl f to ld nr fin* 8/13[1]
02 2 nk **Hay Fever (IRE)**[29] 1736 2-9-3 0 StephenCarson 4 76
(Eve Johnson Houghton) *trckd ldr: ev ch ins fnl f: kpt on nr fin* 3/1[2]
6 3 ½ **Rapid Release (CAN)**[7] 2362 2-8-10 0 RosieJessop(7) 1 75
(Sir Mark Prescott) *led: rdn over 2f out: hdd and lost 2nd wl ins fnl f* 25/1
25 4 1¾ **Rio Royale (IRE)**[8] 2324 2-9-3 0 TPQueally 3 69
(Mrs A J Perrett) *chsd ldrs: rdn 1/2-way: n.m.r wl over 1f out: one pce fnl f* 9/2[3]
0 5 59 **Dubai Tsunami**[14] 2160 2-8-12 0 StephenDonohoe 2 —
(E A L Dunlop) *t.k.h: hld up: wl bhd fr 2f out: eased and t.o* 25/1

1m 12.54s (2.34) **Going Correction** +0.30s/f (Good) 5 Ran SP% 112.8
Speed ratings (Par 93): **96,95,94,92,13**
CSF £2.90 TOTE £1.80: £1.20, £1.40; EX 3.20.
Owner Tim Corby I **Bred** Tally-Ho Stud **Trained** West Ilsley, Berks
■ Stewards' Enquiry : Rosie Jessop caution: careless riding

FOCUS
An ordinary juvenile maiden. They raced stands' side in the straight. Straightforward form and the winner can do better on this evidence.

NOTEBOOK
In Transit(IRE) had shown plenty of ability on his first two starts, including when beaten just a short-head at Goodwood last time, but he made hard work of landing the odds. Racing on easy ground for the first time, he found himself stuck out wide once the field switched over to the stands' side, which was not the place to be, and he was forced to battle to deny Hay Fever, who had the benefit of the rail. He is probably a little better than the bare form implies. (op 4-5 tchd 10-11, Evens in places)
Hay Fever(IRE), an improved second over 5f at Folkestone on his previous start, grabbed the often favoured stands' rail in the straight and had every chance, but he was just denied by a better rival on the day. He is going the right way. (op 9-2)
Rapid Release(CAN)'s debut sixth on quick ground at Newcastle represented just moderate form, and with a 7lb claimer taking over he looked the type who would be best watched until sent handicapping, but he ran surprisingly well, producing a much-improved performance. He showed bags of speed and, to her credit, Rosie Jessop looked quite a capable apprentice, but the horse raced one off the possibly favoured rail in the straight and was just run out of it. He could improve again. (op 16-1)
Rio Royale(IRE) had a little bit to find with In Transit and Hay Fever on RPRs and that was how it worked out. (op 7-2 tchd 10-3)
Dubai Tsunami did not show much on her debut at Newmarket and she was beaten a mile this time. Official explanation: jockey said saddle slipped (op 20-1)

2555 OVER 100 GAMES AT TOTESPORTCASINO.COM H'CAP 5f 213y
3:10 (3:10) (Class 5) (0-75,75) 3-Y-O £2,525 (£751; £375; £187) Stalls Low

Form RPR
3442 1 **Valhillen**[16] 2099 3-9-0 71 (p) HayleyTurner 9 70
(M D I Usher) *trckd ldr: rdn over 2f out and briefly lost pl: kpt on u.str.p to ld nr fin* 10/3[2]
-110 2 hd **Lieutenant Pigeon**[43] 1426 3-9-4 75 PaulEddery 3 73
(G D Blake) *led: hdd briefly appr fnl f: rdn and hdd nr fin* 4/1[3]
00-0 3 hd **Rough Rock (IRE)**[15] 2122 3-8-7 69 (b) NicolPolli(5) 4 67
(Miss Gay Kelleway) *in tch: nt clr run and swtchd rt over 1f out: r.o strly ins fnl f: nvr nrr* 16/1
05-3 4 ½ **Lodi (IRE)**[20] 1995 3-9-2 73 PatCosgrave 2 69
(J Akehurst) *t.k.h: rdn 2f out to ld briefly appr fnl f: no ex towards fin* 9/4[1]
3000 5 nse **Nawaaff**[15] 2127 3-8-11 68 TPO'Shea 8 64
(M R Channon) *trckd ldrs: rdn 1/2-way: hung lft over 1f out but kpt on ins fnl f* 7/1
640- 6 1¾ **Oxbridge**[220] 6410 3-8-3 63 ow2 KirstyMilczarek(3) 1 53
(J M Bradley) *in tch: one pce fr over 1f out* 10/1
2240 7 nk **Salt Of The Earth (IRE)**[3] 2481 3-9-2 73 StephenDonohoe 5 62
(T G Mills) *s.i.s: rdn over 2f out: kpt on but n.d after* 8/1

1m 12.35s (2.15) **Going Correction** +0.30s/f (Good) 7 Ran SP% 112.4
Speed ratings (Par 99): **97,96,96,95,95 93,93**
CSF £16.43 CT £180.47 TOTE £3.80: £1.50, £3.20; EX 18.00 Trifecta £103.00 Pool: £399.13. 2.75 winning units..
Owner Saxon House Racing **Bred** Lady Hardy **Trained** Upper Lambourn, Berks
■ Stewards' Enquiry : Paul Eddery one-day ban: used whip with excessive frequency (Jun 13)

FOCUS
A modest but very competitive sprint handicap in which they finished in a heap. They raced stands' side in the straight.

2556 TOTESPORTGAMES.COM H'CAP 6f 209y
3:45 (3:45) (Class 6) (0-65,65) 4-Y-O+ £2,396 (£712; £356; £177) Stalls Low

Form RPR
50-0 1 **Pragmatist**[25] 1867 4-8-12 59 StephenCarson 10 68
(P Winkworth) *trckd ldr: rdn over 1f out: led wl ins fnl f* 7/1[3]
4331 2 ¾ **The Jailer**[17] 2069 5-8-6 60 MCGeran(7) 3 67
(J G M O'Shea) *sn led: rdn over 1f out: edgd lft and hdd wl ins fnl f* 7/2[2]
0-04 3 ½ **Lordship (IRE)**[3] 2478 4-8-11 61 LukeMorris(3) 2 67
(A W Carroll) *mid-div: hdwy over 2f out: ev ch whn sltly hmpd and swtchd lft ent fnl f: r.o* 2/1[1]
06-0 4 2½ **Finsbury**[33] 1645 5-9-1 65 KirstyMilczarek(3) 6 64
(J M Bradley) *mid-div: rdn 3f out: running on whn edgd lft fr over 1f out: styd on ins fnl f* 12/1
5604 5 ½ **Teen Ager (FR)**[11] 2255 4-8-10 57 TPQueally 11 55
(P Burgoyne) *trckd ldrs: rdn over 2f out: kpt on one pce fnl f* 8/1
60-0 6 1¾ **Tipsy Prince**[7] 2081 4-9-2 63 FergusSweeney 5 56
(David Pinder) *in rr: rdn and hdwy 2f out: fdd ins fnl f* 16/1
00-0 7 ¾ **Valeesha**[7] 2350 4-8-5 52 oh6 ow1 SimonWhitworth 8 43
(M S Saunders) *s.i.s: rdn 1/2-way: nvr on terms* 40/1
00-0 8 nse **Lady Lorins**[25] 1865 4-8-5 52 oh6 ow1 AlanDaly 1 43
(Andrew Turnell) *in tch tl rdn and wknd over 1f out* 33/1

0000 **9** *5* **Super Frank (IRE)**[13] 2203 5-9-3 **64**.............................. PatCosgrave 12 41
(J Akehurst) *in tch: rdn and no hdwy whn nt clr run fr over 1f out* **12/1**
0-00 **10** *3/4* **Orchestrator (IRE)**[13] 2203 4-9-2 **63**.............................. StephenDonohoe 9 38
(T G Mills) *trckd ldrs: rdn and wknd wl over 1f out* **15/2**

1m 24.59s (1.49) **Going Correction** +0.30s/f (Good) **10** Ran SP% **117.6**
Speed ratings (Par 101): **103,102,101,98,98 96,95,95,89,88**
CSF £32.01 CT £69.22 TOTE £9.60: £2.40, £1.90, £1.30; EX 38.70 Trifecta £127.80 Pool: 394.24. 2.19 winning units..
Owner Mrs Jenny Willment **Bred** Mrs Jenny Willment **Trained** Chiddingfold, Surrey
■ Stewards' Enquiry : M C Geran one-day ban: careless riding (Jun 13)

FOCUS
A very moderate handicap and, with the pace just ordinary, the first two home were in the first two throughout. They again raced stands' side in the straight, although the principals drifted back towards the centre of the course late on. Straightforward form.
Finsbury ◆ Official explanation: jockey said gelding was denied a clear run
Super Frank(IRE) Official explanation: jockey said gelding was denied a clear run

2557 PLAY ROULETTE AT TOTESPORTCASINO.COM CLAIMING STKS 7f 214y
4:20 (4:20) (Class 6) 4-Y-0+ **£1,683** (£501; £250; £125) **Stalls** Low

Form RPR
3302 **1** **Mick Is Back**[2] 2513 4-8-11 53...(vt) TPQueally 4 58
(G G Margarson) *trckd ldrs: led over 1f out: drvn clr* **15/8**[2]
2315 **2** *3 1/4* **Red Rudy**[18] 2040 6-8-5 69 ow1.............................. MarkCoumbe(7) 6 52
(A W Carroll) *t.k.h: led over 2f out: rdn and hdd over 1f out: edgd lft: kpt on one pce* **11/8**[1]
0040 **3** *1/2* **Corlough Mountain**[21] 1954 4-8-13 67.....................(p) SimonWhitworth 5 51
(M J McGrath) *led tl hdd over 2f out: rdn over 1f out and lost 2nd ins fnl f* **6/1**[3]
0606 **4** *2* **Lay The Cash (USA)**[7] 2352 4-8-5 35..................................(bt) TPO'Shea 3 39
(B G Powell) *trckd ldrs: rdn 1/2-way: one pce fr over 1f out* **16/1**
00-0 **5** *1/2* **Knickyknackienoo**[134] 193 7-8-3 36 ow1.............. KirstyMilczarek(3) 2 39
(T T Clement) *s.i.s: a bhd* **25/1**
0-54 **6** *1 3/4* **Measured Response**[24] 1895 6-8-2 47.................(b) ThomasO'Brien(7) 1 38
(J G M O'Shea) *t.k.h: in rr: wknd over 1f out* **15/2**

1m 38.18s (2.18) **Going Correction** +0.30s/f (Good) **6** Ran SP% **112.7**
Speed ratings (Par 101): **101,97,97,95,94 93**
CSF £4.87 TOTE £2.60: £1.40, £1.50; EX 4.50.
Owner M Jenner & G Margarson **Bred** J E Abbey **Trained** Newmarket, Suffolk

FOCUS
A pretty weak claimer in which both the second and third home were clearly below their official marks. The winner is the best guide to the form. They headed towards the stands' side in the straight, but edged back towards the middle of the track in the closing stages.

2558 PLAY BLACKJACK AT TOTESPORTCASINO.COM H'CAP 1m 3f 196y
4:55 (4:55) (Class 5) (0-75,72) 4-Y-0+ **£2,525** (£751; £375; £187) **Stalls** High

Form RPR
00-6 **1** **Transvestite (IRE)**[24] 97 6-9-1 **72**.............................. PatrickHills(3) 6 78
(J W Hills) *t.k.h: led: rdn over 2f out: hdd 1f out: rallied u.p to ld again towards fin* **9/1**
3332 **2** *1/2* **Bassinet (USA)**[11] 2241 4-8-11 **68**.......................... KirstyMilczarek(3) 4 73
(J A R Toller) *hld up: rdn and hdwy to ld 1f out: hdd towards fin* **13/8**[1]
114 **3** *1/2* **Bridgewater Boys**[49] 1296 7-9-0 **68**.............................. FergusSweeney 5 72
(G L Moore) *chsd ldrs: outpcd over 2f out: r.o wl and clsng ins fnl f* **4/1**[3]
4141 **4** *1* **Bienheureux**[5] 2423 7-8-9 **63** 6ex.....................(t) HayleyTurner 1 66
(Miss Gay Kelleway) *trckd wnr: rdn and ev ch 1f out: one pce after* **7/2**[2]
2131 **5** *1/2* **Silver Blue (IRE)**[7] 2353 5-8-5 **59** 6ex.............................. LiamJones 3 62+
(W K Goldsworthy) *hld up: hdwy whn n.m.r and swtchd lft over 1f out: edgd lft and no imp after* **7/2**[2]

2m 38.31s (5.61) **Going Correction** +0.30s/f (Good) **5** Ran SP% **112.5**
Speed ratings (Par 103): **93,92,92,91,91**
CSF £24.73 TOTE £11.40: £3.20, £1.60; EX 25.30.
Owner Tony Waspe Partnership **Bred** Rathasker Stud **Trained** Upper Lambourn, Berks

FOCUS
The eventual winner, Transvestite, set a muddling gallop, resulting in a very moderate winning time for the grade, and the form, which is pretty ordinary, needs treating with caution. They raced middle to stands' side in the straight.
Silver Blue(IRE) ◆ Official explanation: jockey said gelding was denied a clear run and finished distressed

2559 PLAY VIDEO POKER AT TOTESPORTCASINO.COM H'CAP 1m 1f 209y
5:25 (5:27) (Class 6) (0-65,65) 3-Y-0 **£2,525** (£751; £375; £187) **Stalls** High

Form RPR
0660 **1** **Caltire (GER)**[7] 2367 3-8-8 **60**...(b) JamieJones(5) 8 66
(M G Quinlan) *hld up: rdn and hdwy over 2f out: r.o to ld wl ins fnl f* **8/1**
0-50 **2** *1 3/4* **Italian Goddess**[18] 2052 3-9-3 **64**.............................. HayleyTurner 3 66
(M L W Bell) *t.k.h: trckd ldr: led after 2f: clr 3f out: rdn and hdd wl ins fnl f* **5/1**[3]
45-0 **3** *nk* **Nordic Commander (IRE)**[34] 1622 3-9-4 **65**.......... StephenDonohoe 4 66
(E A L Dunlop) *in rr: rdn over 4f out: hdwy and ev ch 1f out: kpt on* **7/2**[1]
0-00 **4** *1* **Blandys Wood**[8] 2340 3-9-3 **64**.............................. TPO'Shea 10 63
(M R Channon) *hld up: swtchd lft over 3f out: hdwy and kpt on one pce fr over 1f out* **12/1**
5402 **5** *1 1/4* **What's For Tea**[22] 1937 3-8-8 **55**.............................. RichardKingscote 1 52
(P Butler) *led for 2f: styd prom: rdn 2f out: no imp fr over 1f out* **4/1**[2]
0-06 **6** *3/4* **Threestoneburn (USA)**[132] 225 3-8-13 **60**.............. FergusSweeney 5 55
(J R Boyle) *trckd ldrs: rdn 2f out: no imp fr over 1f out* **12/1**
050- **7** *2 1/2* **Crimsonwing (IRE)**[212] 6585 3-8-10 **62**.............................. NicolPolli(5) 9 52
(A M Hales) *s.i.s: sn swtchd lft: in tch: rdn to hold ev ch over 1f out: wknd ins fnl f* **9/1**
20-0 **8** *6* **Townkab (IRE)**[58] 1161 3-9-3 **64**...(t) LiamJones 2 42
(N P Littmoden) *mid-div: hdwy 3f out: rdn and wknd over 1f out* **11/2**
000- **9** *1/2* **Jay Gee Wigmo**[225] 6274 3-8-1 **51** oh6.............................. LukeMorris(3) 12 28
(A W Carroll) *mid-div: rdn 4f out: bhd fnl 2f* **33/1**
2304 **10** *3/4* **Rhode Island Red (USA)**[25] 1870 3-8-6 **53**.................. SaleemGolam 7 29
(H J L Dunlop) *in rr: effrt over 2f out: sn btn* **6/1**
6-00 **11** *14* **Nathan Dee**[38] 1533 3-8-3 **53** oh3 ow2...................(p) KirstyMilczarek(3) 6 1
(Mrs H Sweeting) *prom tl rdn and wknd over 1f out* **20/1**

2m 8.26s (4.66) **Going Correction** +0.30s/f (Good) **11** Ran SP% **132.8**
Speed ratings (Par 97): **93,91,91,90,89 88,86,82,81,81 69**
CSF £54.27 CT £175.94 TOTE £11.60: £3.30, £2.80, £1.80; EX 100.90 Trifecta £215.70 Pool: £303.88. 1.00 winning units..
Owner N J Jones **Bred** L & K Zimmermann **Trained** Newmarket, Suffolk

FOCUS
A modest handicap run at a reasonable pace. The winner ran to his sand form. They raced middle to stands' side in the straight.
Italian Goddess Official explanation: jockey said filly ran too free
Nathan Dee Official explanation: jockey said gelding ran too free

T/Plt: £37.30 to a £1 stake. Pool: £50,743.90. 992.35 winning tickets. T/Qpdt: £7.00 to a £1 stake. Pool: £3,149.90. 330.80 winning tickets. JS

2324 GOODWOOD (R-H)
Friday, May 30

OFFICIAL GOING: Soft (6.8)
First 2f of 1m course out 5 metres, top bend out 3 metres.
Wind: Almost nil Weather: Fine but cloudy

2560 GOODWOOD FLYING SCHOOL MAIDEN FILLIES' STKS (DIV I) 1m
1:55 (1:58) (Class 5) 3-Y-0 **£2,752** (£818; £409; £204) **Stalls** High

Form RPR
2 **1** **Round The Cape**[13] 2198 3-9-0 0.............................. RichardHughes 10 85
(R Hannon) *trckd ldrs: effrt 2f out: led 1f out and immediately pressed: shkn up and r.o wl* **1/1**[1]
5 **2** *nk* **Soft Shoe Shuffle (IRE)**[21] 1964 3-9-0 0.......................... AdamKirby 4 85
(W R Swinburn) *t.k.h: hld up wl in rr: prog wl over 2f out: swtchd lft sn after: effrt to chal fnl f: r.o but a hld* **16/1**
0 **3** *3 3/4* **Fountains Abbey (USA)**[13] 2198 3-9-0 0.............................. PatDobbs 8 76
(Sir Michael Stoute) *led 2f: led again 1/2-way: rdn and hdd 1f out: sn outpcd* **10/1**
5 **4** *1 1/4* **Ainia**[17] 2079 3-9-0 0.. SaleemGolam 7 73
(D M Simcock) *hld up in rr: shkn up over 2f out: sn outpcd: drvn and styd on wl fr over 1f out: nrst fin* **50/1**
0-3 **5** *1 3/4* **Moon Sister (IRE)**[21] 1946 3-9-0 0.............................. SebSanders 5 69
(W Jarvis) *trckd ldrs: brought alone towards nr side in st: nt on terms w ldrs fnl 2f* **4/1**[2]
4- **6** *1/2* **La Troupe (IRE)**[209] 6649 3-9-0 0.............................. JimmyFortune 1 68
(J H M Gosden) *racd wd: trckd ldrs: wnt 2nd over 2f out to over 1f out: wknd* **6/1**[3]
0 **7** *2* **Fancy Footsteps (IRE)**[25] 1869 3-9-0 0.............................. DaneO'Neill 11 63
(C G Cox) *in tch: shkn up and cl enough over 2f out: sn lft bhd by ldrs* **40/1**
-304 **8** *2 1/4* **Madame Hoi (IRE)**[8] 2328 3-9-0 90.............................. DarryllHolland 9 58
(M R Channon) *trckd ldrs on outer: rdn over 2f out: no prog and btn sn after* **15/2**
00 **9** *3* **Quinzey's Best (IRE)**[22] 1926 3-9-0 0.............................. PaulDoe 6 51
(W J Knight) *hld up wl in rr: nudged along and no prog over 2f out* **100/1**
10 *6* **Telephonist** 3-9-0 0.. JimCrowley 3 37
(Norma Twomey) *s.s: in tch in rr to 3f out* **100/1**
0 **11** *1/2* **Bountiful Bay**[11] 2257 3-9-0 0.. RobertHavlin 2 36
(B J Meehan) *w ldr: led after 2f to 1/2-way: wknd rapidly over 2f out* **100/1**

1m 42.38s (2.48) **Going Correction** +0.40s/f (Good) **11** Ran SP% **118.4**
Speed ratings (Par 96): **103,102,98,97,95 95,93,91,88,82 81**
CSF £21.08 TOTE £2.00: £1.30, £3.90, £2.80; EX 21.20.
Owner P T Tellwright **Bred** P T Tellwright **Trained** East Everleigh, Wilts

FOCUS
A decent winning time for a race like this and over half a second quicker than the second division, so the first two in particular could turn out to be useful. The form looks sound enough.
La Troupe(IRE) Official explanation: jockey said filly hung left

2561 GOODWOOD AERODROME STKS (H'CAP) 1m 1f
2:25 (2:28) (Class 5) (0-70,70) 4-Y-0+ **£3,238** (£963; £481; £240) **Stalls** High

Form RPR
0-51 **1** **Paraguay (USA)**[10] 2274 5-8-9 **61** 6ex.............................. JamieSpencer 8 75
(Miss V Haigh) *s.i.s: hld up in last trio: stdy prog gng wl fr over 3f out: rdn to chal 1f out: led fnl 150yds: jst hld on* **6/1**[3]
2354 **2** *shd* **Merrymadcap (IRE)**[16] 2101 6-8-8 **60**.............................. SteveDrowne 4 74
(M Blanshard) *hld up towards rr: stdy prog gng wl fr over 3f out: led over 1f out: drvn and hdd fnl 150yds: kpt on wl: jst failed* **9/1**
3526 **3** *8* **Megalala (IRE)**[22] 1932 7-8-2 **57**.............................. MarcHalford(3) 10 54
(J J Bridger) *led to 3f out: sn hrd rdn: kpt on to ld again briefly wl over 1f out: no ch w ldng pair fnl f: fdd* **9/1**
0-45 **4** *2* **Lunar River (FR)**[36] 1577 5-8-5 **57**.........................(t) SaleemGolam 9 50
(David Pinder) *trckd ldrs: led on inner 3f out: drvn and hdd wl over 1f out: wknd* **9/1**
20-0 **5** *1 3/4* **Cormorant Wharf (IRE)**[22] 1932 8-9-2 **68**.............................. JimCrowley 11 57
(T E Powell) *reluctant to go in stalls: dwlt: mostly in last pair: rdn over 3f out: sme prog over 2f out: nvr on terms w ldrs* **12/1**
143- **6** *1/2* **Palmetto Point**[229] 6199 4-9-1 **70**.........................(p) TravisBlock(3) 6 58
(H Morrison) *trckd ldng pair: rdn wl over 2f out: wknd wl over 1f out: fin tired* **5/1**[2]
00-0 **7** *11* **Brave Quest (IRE)**[22] 1932 4-8-10 **62**.............................. IanMongan 14 27
(Mrs L J Mongan) *chsd ldrs: hrd rdn and lost pl 1/2-way: no ch fnl 3f* **9/1**
8 *4 1/2* **Dispatch Box**[255] 4-9-0 **66**.. PaulDoe 7 22
(W Jarvis) *racd wd: trckd ldrs: rdn over 3f out: lft bhd fr over 2f out* **9/2**[1]
405- **9** *5* **Montjeu's Melody (IRE)**[273] 5007 4-8-9 **66**......... NataliaGemelova(5) 13 11
(J E Long) *sn pushed along in midfield: struggling bef 1/2-way: brief rally over 3f out: sn wknd* **8/1**
4-00 **10** *2 1/4* **Snark (IRE)**[8] 2335 5-9-2 **68**.............................. SebSanders 12 9
(Simon Earle) *hld up bhd ldrs: lost pl 4f out: sn rdn: struggling fnl 3f* **8/1**
0556 **11** *10* **Mtoto Girl**[32] 1673 4-7-11 **56** oh11.............................. BillyCray(7) 1 —
(J J Bridger) *a in rr: wd and detached in last 4f out: bhd after* **100/1**
0600 **12** *25* **Cavalry Guard (USA)**[1] 2533 4-8-13 **65**.............................. AmirQuinn 15 —
(J R Boyle) *w ldr to 1/2-way: wknd rapidly: t.o and eased over 1f out* **33/1**

1m 59.81s (3.51) **Going Correction** +0.40s/f (Good) **12** Ran SP% **123.0**
Speed ratings (Par 103): **100,99,92,91,89 89,79,75,70,68 59,37**
CSF £61.59 CT £501.99 TOTE £4.30: £1.70, £2.50, £3.60; EX 20.10.
Owner R J Budge **Bred** Nutbush Farm **Trained** Wiseton, Notts

FOCUS
A modest race for the course. The first two finished clear but the overall form is not that solid.
Cavalry Guard(USA) Official explanation: jockey said gelding had no more to give

2562 CASCO MAIDEN AUCTION STKS 6f
3:00 (3:00) (Class 5) 2-Y-0 **£3,238** (£963; £481; £240) **Stalls** Low

Form RPR
1 **Creshendo** 2-8-9 0.. SebSanders 7 75
(R M Beckett) *prom: rdn over 2f out: effrt to ld narrowly over 1f out: hrd pressed fnl f: hld on wl* **11/2**[3]
2 *shd* **Woolston Ferry (IRE)** 2-8-11 0.............................. DarryllHolland 10 77
(M R Channon) *pressed ldr: rdn 2f out: chal wnr fnl f: styd on u.p: jst hld* **3/1**[2]

3 3 **Measurement (IRE)** 2-8-13 0 .... JimmyFortune 9 70
(R Hannon) *dwlt: sn in tch: shkn up and effrt 2f out: styd on to take 3rd ins fnl f: no ch w ldng pair* **17/2**

4 1 1/2 **Minder** 2-9-1 0 .... JamesDoyle 3 67
(J G Portman) *s.s: last tl stdy prog fr 1/2-way: rdn wl over 1f out: kpt on same pce* **16/1**

6 **5** hd **Black N Brew (USA)**[20] 2011 2-8-11 0 .... DaneO'Neill 11 63
(J R Best) *hld up in last pair: prog over 2f out: shkn up and kpt on same pce fr over 1f out* **14/1**

4 **6** 2 1/4 **Mr Clearview**[58] 1156 2-8-11 0 .... JimCrowley 13 56
(B R Millman) *led: hanging rt fr 1/2-way: hdd over 1f out: wkng whn edgd lft and rt fnl f* **25/1**

05 **7** 1/2 **Noworneva**[34] 1616 2-8-9 0 .... LPKeniry 8 54+
(S Kirk) *hld up towards rr: effrt over 2f out: keeping on one pce whn hmpd ins fnl f* **25/1**

5 **8** 2 3/4 **Head Down**[14] 2146 2-9-2 0 .... RichardHughes 1 57+
(R Hannon) *racd against nr side rail: pressed ldrs: rdn 2f out: sn btn: eased fnl f* **13/8**[1]

0 **9** 3 3/4 **Diamond Heist**[14] 2150 2-8-11 0 .... PatDobbs 6 35
(M P Tregoning) *racd against nr side rail: in tch: rdn over 3f out: rn green and btn over 2f out: wknd* **10/1**

10 4 **Ain't Talkin'** 2-8-9 0 .... PaulDoe 12 21
(M J Attwater) *trckd ldrs on outer to 1/2-way: sn wknd and bhd* **40/1**

1m 15.3s (3.10) **Going Correction** +0.40s/f (Good) **10** Ran SP% **120.8**
Speed ratings (Par 93): **95,94,90,88,88 85,84,81,76,70**
CSF £22.83 TOTE £6.90: £2.20, £1.60, £2.40; EX 25.90.

Owner Mrs David Aykroyd **Bred** Mrs David Aykroyd **Trained** Whitsbury, Hants

FOCUS
Debutants filled the first four places, and the form of the others was not solid, so difficult to assess with any confidence.

NOTEBOOK
Creshendo is a Kyllachy colt who was retained for just £1,500 as a yearling. There is a bit more stamina on his dam's side, but he showed plenty of speed throughout, and battled well to hold on. (op 6-1)

Woolston Ferry(IRE), an 18,000euro Fath half-brother to a couple of speedy sorts in Nights Cross and Cantgetyourbreath, showed plenty of promise on this debut. He nearly nicked it from the winner, and looks an obvious sort to get off the mark before long. (op 4-1 tchd 9-2 in a place)

Measurement(IRE), a 17,000gns yearling son of Viking Ruler, high-class in Australia at 1m and just beyond, is out of an Unfuwain mare who was useful up to 1m2f. Though never loking likely to trouble the first pair, he made an encouraging debut and appeals as a maiden winner in the near future, with longer trips certain to suit as the season progresses. (op 9-1 tchd 8-1)

Minder, a brother to decent juvenile sprinter Mesmerize Me and half-brother to four winners including Blue Charm and Threezeddzz, is bred to be speedy. By the top-class sprinter Mind Games and out of a winning miler, he can do much better with a level break, and should win his share of races. (op 14-1)

Black N Brew(USA) has shown ability in two races to date, and should find his in niche in nurseries after his final qualifying run. However, a minor maiden is not out of reach. (tchd 12-1)

Mr Clearview ran better than on his debut, this time - in stark contrast - getting away much better and making the running. However, he was all over the place in the home straight, and in any case looks a nursery type in the making. (op 20-1)

Noworneva looked better suited by the extra furlong, and will be more interesting in nurseries from now on, with 7f likely to suit before long. (op 33-1)

Head Down disappointed his connections, for no obvious reason, and deserves another a chance to recapture the promise he had shown on his debut. Official explanation: trainer had no explanation for the poor form shown (op 7-4 tchd 15-8)

2563 INTERNATIONAL BUREAU OF AVIATION STKS (H'CAP) 1m
3:35 (3:37) (Class 5) (0-70,70) 3-Y-O **£3,238** (£963; £481; £240) **Stalls** High

Form RPR

0-11 **1** **Master Of Arts (USA)**[4] 2451 3-9-4 **70** 12ex .... SebSanders 5 87+
(Sir Mark Prescott) *dwlt: wl in rr: pushed along and prog over 3f out: chsd ldr over 2f out: clsd to ld 1f out: punched clr: readily* **8/13**[1]

030- **2** 3 **Stand In Flames**[241] 5882 3-8-8 **60** .... ShaneKelly 10 70
(Pat Eddery) *led to over 4f out and again over 3f out: clr over 2f out: hdd 1f out: styd on but no ch w wnr* **50/1**

-135 **3** 3 3/4 **Benedetto**[34] 1622 3-9-1 **67** ....(p) JimCrowley 11 68
(Mrs A J Perrett) *t.k.h: bmpd after 1f: hld up in tch: gng wl enough over 2f out: chsd ldng pair over 1f out but no ch: drvn and jst hld on for 3rd* **12/1**[3]

00-5 **4** nk **Oriental Girl**[51] 1271 3-8-7 **59** ow1 ....(p) SteveDrowne 7 60
(J A Geake) *hld up in midfield and racd wd: lost pl 3f out: effrt 2f out: rdn and kpt on to press for 3rd nr fin* **33/1**

-255 **5** 1 1/2 **Kashmina**[20] 2002 3-8-13 **65** .... DarryllHolland 15 62
(M R Channon) *prom on inner: drvn to dispute 3rd 2f out: one pce* **12/1**[3]

0-41 **6** 1 1/2 **Longevity**[17] 2084 3-9-4 **70** .... RichardHughes 3 64
(W Jarvis) *prom: chsd ldr 3f out to over 2f out: sn btn: grad eased fnl f* **5/1**[2]

400- **7** 3 1/2 **Cosmea**[218] 6449 3-8-11 **63** .... DaneO'Neill 13 49
(A King) *hld up in midfield: lost pl and wl in rr over 3f out: no ch after: racd awkwardly but kpt on fnl 2f* **25/1**

64-0 **8** 1 **Bainisteoir**[18] 2047 3-8-12 **64** .... LPKeniry 4 47
(S Kirk) *hld up fr wd draw and swtchd to inner: in tch: wl outpcd fr over 2f out: nt clr run briefly over 1f out: styd on* **50/1**

00-0 **9** 1 3/4 **Presto Levanter**[18] 2047 3-8-11 **63** .... PatDobbs 16 42
(R Hannon) *hld up in midfield on inner: outpcd fr over 2f out: fdd* **16/1**

6252 **10** 3 1/2 **Too Grand**[63] 1051 3-8-2 **57** oh5 ow1 .... MarcHalford(3) 2 28
(J J Bridger) *racd wd in tch: rdn 3f out: wkng whn edgd rt fr 2f out* **25/1**

0-00 **11** 1 1/2 **Rettorical Lad**[32] 1669 3-8-11 **63** .... RobertHavlin 6 31
(Jamie Poulton) *hld up: dropped to last over 3f out: struggling after* **33/1**

266- **12** 6 **Celtic Charlie (FR)**[154] 7252 3-8-13 **65** .... IanMongan 9 19
(P M Phelan) *w ldr: narrow ld over 4f out tl taken wd bnd over 3f out: lost pl rapidly fr over 2f out: eased fnl f* **16/1**

0060 **13** 3 **Estella Mai**[32] 1671 3-7-11 **56** oh9 .... BillyCray(7) 14 —
(J J Bridger) *t.k.h: bmpd after 1f: midfield tl wknd over 3f out: sn bhd* **100/1**

1m 43.15s (3.25) **Going Correction** +0.40s/f (Good) **13** Ran SP% **124.2**
Speed ratings (Par 99): **99,96,92,91,90 88,85,84,82,79 77,71,68**
CSF £65.34 CT £260.81 TOTE £1.60: £1.10, £14.50, £3.40; EX 60.70.

Owner Eclipse Thoroughbreds-Osborne House III **Bred** Cyril Humphris **Trained** Newmarket, Suffolk

■ Stewards' Enquiry : Shane Kelly four-day ban: careless riding (Jun 13-16)

FOCUS
A modest race on the whole, but the winner, who was still officially 5lb well-in under the double penalty, looks a typical Prescott improver.

2564 GOODWOOD VINTAGE FLY IN STKS (H'CAP) 1m 1f 192y
4:10 (4:11) (Class 4) (0-80,79) 3-Y-O **£5,180** (£1,541; £770; £384) **Stalls** High

Form RPR

15-3 **1** **Black Jacari (IRE)**[14] 2151 3-9-3 **78** .... JimmyFortune 8 89
(A King) *hld up towards rr: prog over 3f out: n.m.r over 2f out and swtchd rt to r against rail: gng best and got through to ld 1f out: drvn clr* **4/1**[2]

-011 **2** 1 1/2 **Buddy Holly**[31] 1696 3-8-10 **71** .... PatDobbs 3 79
(Pat Eddery) *pressed ldr: led 3f out: drvn and hdd 1f out: styd on same pce* **11/2**[3]

5-65 **3** 1 3/4 **Prairie Storm**[14] 2151 3-8-13 **74** .... LPKeniry 1 78
(A M Balding) *wl plcd bhd ldrs: effrt to press ldr 2f out: kpt on same pce fr over 1f out* **10/1**

-521 **4** hd **Dubai Petal (IRE)**[32] 1681 3-8-12 **73** .... EddieAhern 15 77
(J S Moore) *hld up towards rr: shkn up over 2f out: taken to outer and r.o fnl f: nrst fin* **8/1**

-031 **5** 2 **Seattle Storm (IRE)**[18] 2046 3-9-4 **79** .... RobertHavlin 7 79
(D R C Elsworth) *hld up in rr: prog into midfield 4f out: rdn to chse ldrs 2f out: no imp over 1f out: fdd* **14/1**

4-45 **6** 1 1/4 **Rock Peak (IRE)**[46] 1367 3-8-10 **74** .... TravisBlock(3) 14 72
(H Morrison) *hld up on inner towards rr: cl up 3f out: nt qckn over 2f out: styd on fnl f* **11/1**

2-00 **7** 1 3/4 **Palmerin**[13] 2194 3-9-0 **75** .... RichardHughes 13 69
(R Hannon) *trckd ldrs: lost pl over 2f out: drvn and hanging over 1f out: nt keen* **16/1**

-522 **8** 3/4 **Mezzanisi (IRE)**[11] 2244 3-8-12 **73** .... JamieSpencer 2 66
(M L W Bell) *dwlt: hld up in last pair: sme prog on outer over 2f out: rdn and no rspnse over 1f out: no ch after* **11/4**[1]

66-3 **9** 3 1/2 **Hawk House**[102] 610 3-7-11 **65** oh1 .... KMay(7) 11 51
(B W Hills) *prom: lost pl wl over 2f out: struggling after* **25/1**

-430 **10** 1 **Geestring (IRE)**[13] 2196 3-8-11 **72** ....(p) DaneO'Neill 9 56
(R Hannon) *dwlt: hld up in last pair: shkn up wl over 1f out: nvr a factor* **20/1**

00-0 **11** 3 1/4 **Dancing Marabout (IRE)**[25] 1868 3-8-10 **71** .... ShaneKelly 6 48
(C R Egerton) *led to 3f out: sn lost pl and btn* **50/1**

30-5 **12** 2 3/4 **Dubai Samurai**[13] 2191 3-9-4 **79** .... DarryllHolland 4 51
(J W Hills) *chsd ldrs: wd in st: sn lost pl: wknd over 2f out* **25/1**

24-6 **13** nk **Red Icon**[22] 1926 3-9-0 **75** .... SebSanders 5 46
(R M Beckett) *a towards rr: rdn over 3f out: no real prog: wknd 2f out* **11/1**

2m 12.92s (4.92) **Going Correction** +0.40s/f (Good) **13** Ran SP% **125.9**
Speed ratings (Par 101): **96,94,93,93,91 90,89,88,85,85 82,80,80**
CSF £26.75 CT £215.99 TOTE £5.50: £2.00, £2.00, £4.00; EX 24.90.

Owner David Bellamy & Alan King **Bred** Allevamento Gialloblu S R L **Trained** Barbury Castle, Wilts

FOCUS
A decent race of its type and the form should work out. The progressive winner did well considering he is a hurdler in the making.

Palmerin Official explanation: jockey said colt hung left

Mezzanisi(IRE) Official explanation: jockey said gelding boiled over

2565 GOODWOOD AERO CLUB STKS (H'CAP) 7f
4:45 (4:45) (Class 4) (0-85,85) 4-Y-O+ **£4,533** (£1,348; £674; £336) **Stalls** High

Form RPR

3-43 **1** **Idle Power (IRE)**[27] 1800 10-8-13 **80** .... AmirQuinn 7 89
(J R Boyle) *fast away: mde all: gng best 2f out: drvn fnl f: hld on* **9/2**[2]

3-15 **2** 1/2 **The Snatcher (IRE)**[30] 1719 5-9-3 **84** .... JimmyFortune 5 92
(R Hannon) *chsd wnr 2f and again 3f out: hrd rdn wl over 1f out: tried to chal fnl f: a hld* **15/8**[1]

0-05 **3** 2 **Mason Ette**[22] 1928 4-8-9 **76** ....(b) EddieAhern 4 79
(C G Cox) *hld up in last: prog on inner over 2f out: drvn and kpt on one pce over 1f out* **12/1**

606- **4** 2 **Jo'Burg (USA)**[292] 4420 4-9-4 **85** ....(b[1]) JimCrowley 1 82
(Mrs A J Perrett) *t.k.h: hld up in midfield: effrt on outer 2f out: one pce u.p over 1f out* **9/1**

6463 **5** 1 **Lunces Lad (IRE)**[18] 2058 4-8-10 **77** ....(v[1]) DarryllHolland 6 72
(M R Channon) *t.k.h: hld up in rr: rdn and no rspnse over 2f out: plugged on* **5/1**[3]

60-0 **6** 2 3/4 **Starlight Gazer**[62] 1069 5-8-8 **78** .... TravisBlock(3) 2 65
(J A Geake) *hld up in rr: rdn over 2f out: no prog fnl 2f* **13/2**

000- **7** 1 3/4 **Out After Dark**[217] 6472 7-9-4 **85** ....(p) AdamKirby 3 67
(C G Cox) *chsd wnr after 2f to 3f out: wknd 2f out* **18/1**

0-35 **8** 6 **Crystal Gazer (FR)**[73] 925 4-8-11 **78** .... RichardHughes 8 44
(R Hannon) *cl up: hmpd on inner after 2f: midfield after: wknd 2f out: virtually p.u nr fin* **7/1**

1m 29.35s (1.95) **Going Correction** +0.40s/f (Good) **8** Ran SP% **118.4**
Speed ratings (Par 105): **104,103,101,98,97 94,92,85**
CSF £13.92 CT £96.15 TOTE £6.20: £1.90, £1.10, £4.30; EX 16.20.

Owner The Idle B's **Bred** Mountarmstrong Stud **Trained** Epsom, Surrey

FOCUS
A reasonable sprint for the track, with Idle Power landing his 13th win on his 100th outing. He is rated to his recent best.

2566 GOODWOOD FLYING SCHOOL MAIDEN FILLIES' STKS (DIV II) 1m
5:15 (5:18) (Class 5) 3-Y-O **£2,752** (£818; £409; £204) **Stalls** High

Form RPR

1D **Cosmopolitan** 3-9-0 0 .... JimmyFortune 10 83+
(J H M Gosden) *trckd ldrs: wnt 2nd over 2f out: urged along to ld over 1f out: fnd enough to hold on fnl f: fin 1st, nk: subs disq* **10/1**

54 **1** **La Sarrazine (FR)**[13] 2199 3-9-0 0 .... JamieSpencer 2 82
(J R Fanshawe) *hld up in midfield: prog to chse ldng pair 2f out: rdn over 1f out: styd on ins fnl f to snatch 2nd on line: fin 2nd, nk: subs awrdd r* **5/2**[2]

0-2 **2** nk **Victoria Reel**[9] 2307 3-9-0 0 .... RichardHughes 4 82
(R Hannon) *trckd ldr: led wl over 2f out and gng strly: rdn and hdd over 1f out: jst hld by wnr after: lost 2nd fnl stride: fin 3rd, nk & shd; plcd 2nd* **5/1**

020- **3** 6 **Thought Is Free**[238] 5974 3-9-0 95 .... SebSanders 9 68
(P F I Cole) *hld up in midfield on inner: effrt 3f out: nt on terms w ldng trio over 1f out: lost more grnd after: fin 4th, plcd 3rd* **9/4**[1]

0-5 **4** 2 3/4 **Driven Snow**[117] 416 3-9-0 0 .... JimCrowley 1 62
(E F Vaughan) *s.s: swtchd fr wd draw and hld up in last: sme prog on outer over 2f out: reminders over 1f out: kpt on but no ch: fin 5th, plcd 4th* **25/1**

-3 **5** 1 1/2 **Siren Sound**[27] 1803 3-9-0 0 .... SteveDrowne 7 58
(H Morrison) *trckd ldrs: cl enough over 2f out: sn rdn: wknd tamely over 1f out: eased fnl f: fin 6th, plcd 5th* **4/1**[3]

0-0 **6** 1 3/4 **Turfani (IRE)**[15] 2123 3-9-0 0 .... PaulDoe 3 54
(W J Knight) *a in rr: lost tch 3f out: plugged on: fin 7th, plcd 6th* **50/1**

00- **7** 4 1/2 **Lady Selkirk**[251] 5633 3-9-0 0 .... DaneO'Neill 11 44
(R Charlton) *dwlt: a wl in rr: lost tch fr 3f out: fin 8th, plcd 7th* **33/1**

50 **8** 1 3/4 **Sir Kyffin's Folly**[2] 1965 3-9-0 0 .... RichardThomas 5 40
(J A Geake) *pressed ldng pair to 3f out: sn wknd: fin 9th, plcd 8th* **33/1**

0-0 **9** 4 1/2 **Charming Tale (USA)**[39] 1525 3-9-0 0 .... RobertHavlin 8 30
(B J Meehan) *rdn in midfield over 4f out: bhd fnl 2f: fin 10th, plcd 9th* **33/1**

10 1 1/2 **Ma Vie En Rose (IRE)**[245] 5786 3-9-0 0 .... LPKeniry 6 26
(A M Balding) *led to wl over 2f out: wknd rapidly: fin11 th, plcd 10th* **40/1**

1m 42.91s (3.01) **Going Correction** +0.40s/f (Good) **11** Ran SP% **122.2**
Speed ratings (Par 96): **100,99,99,93,90 89,87,83,81,76 75**
CSF £34.94 TOTE £9.70: £2.40, £1.40, £1.50; EX 38.20.
Owner H R H Princess Haya Of Jordan **Bred** G S Shropshire **Trained** Newmarket, Suffolk

FOCUS
This was run in a time only half a second slower than division one, and it was a shade quicker than the handicap, which is not bad considering it was the seventh race run on the soft ground. The first three finished clear and a slightly positive view has been taken of their form.
Sir Kyffin's Folly Official explanation: jockey said filly lost its action

2567 GOODWOOD AIRCRAFT ENGINEERING STKS (H'CAP) 2m
5:50 (5:50) (Class 5) (0-70,67) 4-Y-0+ £3,238 (£963; £481; £240) Stalls High

Form RPR

5230 **1** **At The Money**[17] 2076 5-9-7 63 .... RichardHughes 9 74
(J M P Eustace) *mde all: kicked 2 l clr wl over 2f out: drvn and kpt on wl fnl f* **15/2**[3]

04-1 **2** 1 1/2 **Lady Dedlock**[53] 1246 4-9-8 66 .... PaulDoe 16 75
(Jamie Poulton) *pushed up to chse ldrs: effrt 3f out: drvn to go 2nd 2f out: kpt on but no real imp on wnr* **9/1**

0531 **3** 1 **Whaxaar (IRE)**[30] 1726 4-9-2 60 .... RobertHavlin 14 68
(R Ingram) *prom: disp 2nd fr 12f out to 6f out: chsd wnr again over 4f out to 2f out: one pce* **11/1**

30-2 **4** 1 3/4 **Go Amwell**[20] 1518 5-9-0 56 .... SebSanders 11 62+
(J R Jenkins) *wl in rr: rdn over 3f out: no prog tl styd on u.p fnl 2f: nrst fin* **3/1**[1]

-302 **5** 2 3/4 **Bob's Your Uncle**[16] 2100 5-9-2 58 .... JamieSpencer 15 60
(J G Portman) *hld up in last pair: prog fr 4f out: wnt 4th 2f out: no imp on ldng trio: wknd fnl f* **11/1**

3151 **6** 4 1/2 **Coda Agency**[25] 1856 5-9-2 58 .... JimCrowley 6 55
(D W P Arbuthnot) *wl in tch: rdn over 3f out: no imp on ldrs over 2f out: wl btn over 1f out* **11/2**[2]

3645 **7** 2 3/4 **Mister Completely (IRE)**[38] 1547 7-9-0 56 ....(v) JamesDoyle 4 50
(Ms J S Doyle) *hld up in last pair: nt clr run 4f out to 3f out: modest prog whn in the clr fr over 2f out* **12/1**

/00- **8** 3 **Papeete (GER)**[19] 5120 7-8-13 55 .... SteveDrowne 10 45
(Mrs N Smith) *chsd ldrs: rdn and lost pl over 3f out: n.d after: wknd* **20/1**

/455 **9** 1 **Songmaster (USA)**[22] 1929 5-9-6 62 .... JimmyFortune 1 51
(A King) *nvr beyond midfield: no imp on ldrs 3f out: fdd* **8/1**

0-24 **10** 22 **Jafaru**[26] 1824 4-9-7 65 ....(b) EddieAhern 7 28
(G A Butler) *a towards rr: u.p and struggling over 4f out: t.o and virtually p.u nr fin* **9/1**

5463 **11** 52 **Saraba (FR)**[7] 2354 7-9-8 64 .... IanMongan 13 —
(Mrs L J Mongan) *wl in tch: prog to chse wnr 6f out to over 4f out: wknd over 2f out: 8th 1f out: virtually p.u and walked in* **25/1**

/50- **12** 81 **Twill (IRE)**[14] 354 5-9-11 67 .... GeorgeBaker 12 —
(G L Moore) *mostly chsd wnr to 6f out: wknd rapidly over 4f out: wl t.o and walked in* **20/1**

3m 39.94s (6.74) **Going Correction** +0.40s/f (Good)
WFA 4 from 5yo+ 2lb **12** Ran SP% **121.0**
Speed ratings (Par 103): **99,98,97,96,95 93,91,90,89,78 52,12**
CSF £72.74 CT £752.59 TOTE £7.70: £2.80, £3.00, £3.40; EX 81.20.
Owner Harold Nass **Bred** Rockville Pike Partnership **Trained** Newmarket, Suffolk

FOCUS
This moderate event was the first race staged around the recambered Oak Tree bend, which is used only for races of 1m6f and upwards. Ordinary form, rated through the third.
Twill(IRE) Official explanation: jockey said he felt there was something amiss with the gelding
T/Plt: £58.60 to a £1 stake. Pool: £63,671.60. 792.00 winning tickets. T/Qpdt: £18.60 to a £1 stake. Pool: £2,829.40. 112.35 winning tickets. JN

2401 HAYDOCK (L-H)
Friday, May 30

OFFICIAL GOING: Good (7.8)
Rail realignment added 10yds to the advertised distances of races of 1m and over.
Wind: Almost nil Weather: Overcast

2568 LAMBRINI H'CAP (FOR LADY AMATEUR RIDERS) 1m 2f 120y
6:40 (6:40) (Class 5) (0-70,70) 4-Y-0+ £2,637 (£811; £405) Stalls High

Form RPR

4510 **1** **Hucking Heat (IRE)**[16] 2097 4-9-0 56 oh3 ....(p) MissRKneller[(7)] 4 67
(R Hollinshead) *trckd ldrs: wnt 2nd over 4f out: r.o to ld ins fnl f: pushed out towards fin* **10/1**

0503 **2** 1 1/2 **Valdan (IRE)**[4] 2446 4-9-3 57 ....(t) MissAngelaBarnes[(5)] 5 65
(M A Barnes) *s.s: rcvrd to ld after 2f: hdd ins fnl f: no ex towards fin* **11/2**[3]

-062 **3** 3 **Dan Tucker**[7] 2365 4-10-2 65 .... MissRDavidson 12 67
(N Tinkler) *midfield: rdn over 2f out: hdwy over 1f out: styd on ins fnl f: nvr threatened front pair* **3/1**[1]

0-04 **4** nk **Penang Cinta**[11] 2264 5-10-6 69 .... MissEFolkes 14 71
(P D Evans) *bhd: hdwy on outside over 2f out: chsd ldrs over 1f out: kpt on fnl f but unable to chal* **9/1**

56-0 **5** 3 1/4 **Contemplation**[10] 2274 5-9-10 59 .... MrsCBartley 6 55
(G A Swinbank) *hld up: rdn and hdwy over 1f out: plugged on at one pce fnl f: no imp on ldrs* **7/1**

0605 **6** 4 1/2 **Grethel (IRE)**[10] 2284 4-9-2 56 oh6 .... MissWGibson[(5)] 15 43
(A Berry) *prom: rdn over 2f out: wknd fnl f* **20/1**

2214 **7** nse **Terminate (GER)**[13] 2185 6-10-0 63 .... MissSBrotherton 2 50
(Ian Williams) *stdd s: hld up: sme hdwy over 3f out: no imp fnl 2f* **4/1**[2]

640 **8** 2 **Moment Of Clarity**[62] 1085 6-10-0 63 ....(p) MissCharmaineO'Neill 3 46
(R C Guest) *hld up: effrt over 1f out: nvr able to trble ldrs* **14/1**

4530 **9** shd **Bobering**[35] 1606 8-9-2 56 oh11 .... MissMMullineaux[(5)] 11 39
(B P J Baugh) *s.i.s: hld up: rdn and sme hdwy over 2f out: no imp on ldrs: wknd over 1f out* **33/1**

2056 **10** 7 **Candy Anchor (FR)**[65] 1031 9-9-0 56 oh11 .... MissSPeacock[(7)] 9 26
(R E Peacock) *led for 2f: remained prom: wknd 4f out* **50/1**

24/0 **11** 2 **Woody Valentine (USA)**[24] 1891 7-10-0 70 .... MissECSayer[(7)] 7 36
(Mrs Dianne Sayer) *dwlt: midfield: hdwy 4f out: rdn and hung rt fr over 2f out: wknd over 1f out* **25/1**

-350 **12** 12 **Dark Charm (FR)**[6] 2394 9-9-9 65 ....(p) MissNVorster[(7)] 10 8
(R A Fahey) *trckd ldrs tl wknd over 2f out* **20/1**

2m 19.44s (2.74) **Going Correction** +0.125s/f (Good) **12** Ran SP% **116.9**
Speed ratings (Par 103): **95,93,91,91,89 85,85,84,84,79 77,69**
CSF £58.96 CT £208.40 TOTE £13.40: £3.20, £2.50, £1.60; EX 90.30.
Owner Ed Weetman (haulage & Storage) Ltd **Bred** Thomas J Reid **Trained** Upper Longdon, Staffs
■ A first winner for 21-year-old jockey Rachel Kneller.

FOCUS
Not a great race though the pace was sound and very few ever got into it. Moderate form, the winner rated to his turf mark.

2569 E B F MAIDEN STKS 6f
7:10 (7:11) (Class 5) 2-Y-0 £3,399 (£1,011; £505; £252) Stalls Centre

Form RPR

2 **1** **Awinnersgame (IRE)**[15] 2134 2-9-3 0 .... LDettori 13 85+
(J Noseda) *a.p: rdn to ld over 1f out: r.o ins fnl f: pushed out towards fin* **4/7**[1]

2 **2** 2 **Servoca (CAN)**[44] 1399 2-9-3 0 .... MichaelHills 3 80+
(B W Hills) *racd keenly: in tch: upsides over 1f out: sn rdn: nt qckn ins fnl f* **11/4**[2]

3 1/2 **Canwinn (IRE)** 2-9-3 0 .... EdwardCreighton 12 78+
(M R Channon) *a.p: rdn and nt qckn over 1f out: styd on ins fnl f* **10/1**[3]

4 2 **Watergate (IRE)** 2-9-3 0 .... J-PGuillambert 2 72+
(Sir Mark Prescott) *in tch: pushed along over 1f out: kpt on fnl f: nt pce to chal: can improve* **25/1**

5 4 1/2 **Jobekani (IRE)** 2-9-0 0 .... TolleyDean[(3)] 4 58
(Mrs L Williamson) *led: rdn and hdd over 1f out: wknd fnl f* **100/1**

3664 **6** 1/2 **Smalljohn**[13] 2186 2-9-3 0 ....(v) NCallan 10 57
(P D Evans) *prom: rdn over 1f out: sn wknd* **16/1**

7 1 3/4 **Buckers Beauty (IRE)** 2-8-12 0 .... CatherineGannon 9 46
(P D Evans) *handy for 1f: sn pushed along and lost pl: edgd lft fr over 1f out: no real imp after* **66/1**

8 5 **Tee Gee Cee** 2-9-0 0 .... DuranFentiman[(3)] 7 36
(T D Easterby) *hld up: rdn 2f out: no imp on ldrs* **66/1**

9 3/4 **Miss Xu Xia** 2-8-7 0 .... SladeO'Hara[(5)] 11 29
(G R Oldroyd) *bhd: pushed along after 2f: nvr on terms* **100/1**

10 4 1/2 **Talsarnau (IRE)** 2-9-3 0 .... DanielTudhope 14 21
(W M Brisbourne) *hld up: rdn over 2f out: sn btn* **100/1**

11 shd **Strevelyn** 2-9-3 0 .... RoystonFfrench 1 20
(Mrs A Duffield) *racd keenly in tch: rdn over 2f out: sn wknd* **66/1**

12 16 **Redolini** 2-9-3 0 .... GrahamGibbons 6 —
(W M Brisbourne) *cl up early: pushed along and wknd bef 1/2-way* **66/1**

1m 15.28s (1.28) **Going Correction** +0.125s/f (Good) **12** Ran SP% **118.1**
Speed ratings (Par 93): **96,93,92,90,84 83,81,74,73,67 67,45**
CSF £2.15 TOTE £1.50: £1.02, £1.30, £2.50; EX 2.20.
Owner Saeed Suhail **Bred** J Joyce **Trained** Newmarket, Suffolk

FOCUS
A strong maiden ultimately dominated by the form horses, although there was plenty of dead wood with seven of the 12 runners starting at 66-1 or longer. The field came down the middle and the front four pulled well clear, which makes them the ones to focus on. The form has been rated positively.

NOTEBOOK
Awinnersgame(IRE) probably only had to reproduce his York effort to win this and though he had to be nudged out to make sure of it after being produced on the stands' side, he always seemed to have matters under control. He should continue to progress. (op 8-13 tchd 1-2 and 4-6 in places)
Servoca(CAN), like the winner a runner-up on his debut, had no problem with the extra furlong and had every chance, but the favourite had the legs of him where it mattered. A routine maiden is waiting for him. (tchd 10-3)
Canwinn(IRE) ◆, a 40,000gns foal but a 90,000gns yearling, is a half-brother to five winners, the majority of them as juveniles. He was never far away and kept on very well to finish close to a couple of rivals that had already posted decent efforts on their debuts. It should not be long before he gets off the mark. (op 8-1)
Watergate(IRE) ◆, a 60,000euros half-brother to four winners, was noted staying on very nicely towards the far side of the track and he pulled a long way clear of the others. He should get a bit further and looks to be a winner waiting to happen. (op 33-1)
Jobekani(IRE), who fetched £13,000 as a two-year-old, is out of a winning half-sister to three other winners. He showed a fair amount of speed towards the far side of the track and although he was eventually beaten far enough for it to be a mistake to get too carried away by this, he could be interesting in a modest event in the near future especially if dropped to the minimum.

2570 ZANUSSI H'CAP 5f
7:40 (7:41) (Class 4) (0-85,85) 3-Y-0 £6,476 (£1,927; £963; £481) Stalls Centre

Form RPR

05-3 **1** **Little Pete (IRE)**[11] 2258 3-9-6 82 .... FrancisNorton 10 95+
(A M Balding) *in tch: led over 1f out: r.o ins fnl f: pushed out towards fin* **9/2**[3]

4205 **2** 1 1/2 **Monsieur Reynard**[11] 2258 3-8-10 72 .... LDettori 5 80
(B J Meehan) *hld up: rdn and hdwy over 1f out: sn chsd wnr and upsides: nt qckn and hld fnl 75yds* **4/1**[2]

6-41 **3** 1 **Discanti (IRE)**[10] 2287 3-8-6 68 6ex .... DavidAllan 12 72+
(T D Easterby) *slipped s: bhd: hdwy 1f out: sn rdn to chse ldrs: drifted lft ins fnl f: one pce and no imp towards fin* **11/4**[1]

3211 **4** 1 **Espy**[15] 2122 3-9-5 81 .... RyanMoore 9 82
(S Kirk) *hld up: hdwy over 1f out: sn rdn to press ldrs: hung lft ins fnl f: one pce fnl 100yds* **11/4**[1]

21-0 **5** 1/2 **Know No Fear**[14] 2171 3-8-11 73 .... GrahamGibbons 4 72
(J J Quinn) *chsd ldrs: chalng whn hung lft 1f out: no ex fnl 100yds* **17/2**

1-0 **6** 7 **Firenza Bond**[41] 1484 3-8-13 80 .... SladeO'Hara[(5)] 7 54
(G R Oldroyd) *chsd ldrs: rdn over 1f out: sn wknd* **28/1**

3106 **7** 1/2 **Barraland**[11] 2258 3-9-2 78 .... EdwardCreighton 8 50
(M R Channon) *led: rdn and hdd over 1f out: wknd ins fnl f* **33/1**

0-05 **8** 1/2 **Bazguy**[20] 1995 3-8-6 68 ....(b) CatherineGannon 3 38
(P D Evans) *w ldr: rdn and wnt lft over 1f out: sn wknd* **33/1**

10-0 **9** 2 **Pearl Dealer (IRE)**[22] 1925 3-9-1 77 .... SamHitchcott 1 40
(N J Vaughan) *sluggish s: a outpcd and bhd* **40/1**

6002 **10** 1/2 **Helping Hand (IRE)**[15] 2122 3-7-13 68 .... DavidProbert[(7)] 2 29
(R Hollinshead) *w ldrs: rdn and wkng whn sltly hmpd over 1f out* **16/1**

60.79 secs (0.29) **Going Correction** +0.125s/f (Good) **10** Ran SP% **119.7**
Speed ratings (Par 101): **102,99,98,96,95 84,83,82,79,78**
CSF £22.81 CT £60.91 TOTE £5.50: £1.90, £1.90, £1.70; EX 23.50.
Owner Friends of Saunton Sands **Bred** Larry Ryan **Trained** Kingsclere, Hants

FOCUS
Quite a competitive three-year-old sprint handicap and the front five pulled miles clear of the others. The form looks solid enough and Little Pete is on the upgrade.

Know No Fear ◆ Official explanation: jockey said gelding hung left
Firenza Bond Official explanation: jockey said gelding was slowly into stride

2571 OCS GROUP UK LTD MAIDEN STKS — 1m 30y
8:10 (8:12) (Class 5) 3-Y-O+ — **£2,590** (£770; £385; £192) **Stalls** Low

Form — RPR

22 **1** **Bramaputra (IRE)**[30] 1715 3-8-9 0 .... AlanMunro 4 83+
(B R Millman) *chsd ldrs: rdn over 3f out: hung rt over 1f out: r.o ins fnl f to ld towards fin* **13/8**[1]

0- **2** *1* **Navajo Joe (IRE)**[210] 6616 3-9-0 0 .... LDettori 11 86+
(B J Meehan) *midfield: hdwy 3f out: chsd ldr over 2f out: led over 1f: hdd and no ex towards fin* **4/1**[3]

3 **3** *4* **Persian Sea (UAE)**[21] 1964 3-8-9 0 .... PhilipRobinson 14 72
(M A Jarvis) *racd keenly: led: edgd rt 2f out: rdn and hdd over 1f out: no ex wl ins fnl f* **9/4**[2]

03- **4** *2 1/4* **Tourist**[217] 6469 3-9-0 0 .... MichaelHills 9 72
(B W Hills) *midfield: rdn over 1f out: kpt on fnl f wout troubling ldrs* **14/1**

0 **5** *7* **Border Fox**[7] 2360 5-9-12 0 .... PaddyAspell 2 59
(L Lungo) *hld up and bhd: sme hdwy over 2f out: nvr able to chal* **100/1**

6 *2 1/2* **Trireme (IRE)**[19] 4-9-12 0 .... GrahamGibbons 1 53
(K A Morgan) *s.s: bhd: rdn over 2f out: nvr on terms* **100/1**

0/0- **7** *1* **Sweet Seville (FR)**[155] 7239 4-9-7 0 .... DaleGibson 3 45
(Mrs G S Rees) *hld up: rdn over 3f out: nvr on terms* **150/1**

2 **8** *6* **Al Wasef (USA)**[43] 1429 3-9-0 0 .... JoeFanning 6 34
(M Johnston) *prom tl rdn and wknd over 2f out* **8/1**

9 *3* **Deer Lake (IRE)** 3-9-0 0 .... RyanMoore 13 27
(J Noseda) *rdn over 4f out: a bhd* **16/1**

000- **10** *7* **Bagenalstown (IRE)**[195] 6855 3-9-0 30 .... DanielTudhope 8 11
(M Wellings) *s.i.s: hld up: pushed along over 3f out: nvr on terms* **200/1**

-00 **11** *52* **Annawanna**[2] 2500 4-9-7 0 .... LeeEnstone 5 —
(S Wynne) *chsd ldrs: rdn over 4f out: wknd over 3f out: t.o* **200/1**

1m 44.19s (0.39) **Going Correction** +0.125s/f (Good)
WFA 3 from 4yo+ 12lb — 11 Ran SP% **116.2**
Speed ratings (Par 103): **103,102,98,95,88 86,85,79,76,69 17**
CSF £8.59 TOTE £3.00: £1.20, £1.70, £1.40; EX 11.10.
Owner Mrs Mette Campbell-Andenaes **Bred** John Costello **Trained** Kentisbeare, Devon

FOCUS
Not as competitive a maiden as the numbers would suggest with only six of the 11 runners starting at less than 100-1. The pace was a sound one though and the fact that they finished very well spread out suggests the form is solid enough, among the first four at any rate. The winner did not match her Ascot form.
Tourist Official explanation: jockey said colt hung left

2572 SHOWERS & EYEBATHS H'CAP — 1m 6f
8:40 (8:41) (Class 5) (0-70,70) 4-Y-O+ — **£2,590** (£770; £385; £192) **Stalls** Low

Form — RPR

4-02 **1** **Directa's Digger (IRE)**[11] 2245 4-8-6 **58** .... (v) JoeFanning 7 71+
(M J Scudamore) *in tch: impr over 3f out: led 2f out: edgd rt over 1f out: styd on wl to draw clr fnl f: eased towards fin* **8/1**

244- **2** *6* **Rudry World (IRE)**[217] 6481 5-9-3 **69** .... RyanMoore 12 73+
(M Mullineaux) *hld up: rdn 2f out: hdwy over 1f out: styd on to take 2nd wl ins fnl f: nt trble wnr* **11/2**[3]

-025 **3** *1/2* **Blue Jet (USA)**[21] 1972 4-8-4 **56** oh2 .... PaulQuinn 5 59
(R M Whitaker) *midfield: rdn over 2f out: hdwy over 1f out: kpt on u.p ins fnl f to chal for pls: n.d to wnr* **16/1**

3205 **4** *shd* **Opera Writer (IRE)**[22] 1933 5-7-11 **56** .... DavidProbert[(7)] 8 59
(R Hollinshead) *racd keenly in midfield: hdwy on outside over 3f out: wnt 2nd wl over 1f out: no imp on wnr: lost 2nd wl ins fnl f: kpt on same pce* **16/1**

4-43 **5** *3 3/4* **Its Moon (IRE)**[5] 2423 4-9-4 **70** .... GrahamGibbons 2 68
(T D Walford) *trckd ldrs: rdn over 2f out: one pce fnl f: eased whn hld fnl 100yds* **5/1**[2]

1-24 **6** *1 1/2* **Toboggan Lady**[39] 1518 4-8-12 **64** .... RoystonFfrench 3 60
(Mrs A Duffield) *trckd ldrs: rdn over 4f out: outpcd over 3f out: styd on again wout being a danger towards fin* **11/4**[1]

-340 **7** *3/4* **Sky Chart (IRE)**[13] 2185 4-7-11 **56** oh8 .... SophieDoyle[(7)] 13 50
(N J Vaughan) *stdd s: plld hrd: hld up: hdwy to trck ldrs 8f out: hung lft 2f out: one pce after* **20/1**

0-55 **8** *1 3/4* **Merrymaker**[20] 2012 8-9-1 **67** .... NCallan 14 59
(W M Brisbourne) *hld up: rdn over 3f out: sn outpcd* **8/1**

4232 **9** *1/2* **Leyte Gulf (USA)**[22] 1933 5-8-8 **60** .... ChrisCatlin 6 51
(C C Bealby) *hld up: rdn whn nt clr run 3f out: kpt on 1f out: nvr trbld ldrs* **9/1**

30-0 **10** *2 1/4* **Icansingarainbow**[20] 2012 4-8-4 **56** oh1 .... DaleGibson 1 44
(R Hollinshead) *racd keenly in midfield: rdn 3f out: wknd and eased fnl f* **50/1**

610- **11** *shd* **Mcqueen (IRE)**[184] 6558 8-8-5 **60** ow1 .... RussellKennemore[(3)] 11 48
(J T Stimpson) *led: rdn and hdd 2f out: wknd fnl f* **33/1**

4306 **12** *1* **Latif (USA)**[10] 2274 7-8-4 **56** .... FrancisNorton 15 43
(Paul Green) *dwlt: racd keenly: hld up: rdn 3f out: wl btn over 1f out* **16/1**

00-0 **13** *2 1/2* **Don Jose (USA)**[120] 374 5-8-1 **56** oh11 .... (e[1]) DominicFox[(3)] 10 39
(N J Vaughan) *prom: rdn over 4f out: wknd 2f out* **28/1**

3m 4.91s (0.61) **Going Correction** +0.125s/f (Good) — 13 Ran SP% **121.7**
Speed ratings (Par 103): **103,99,99,99,97 96,95,94,94,93 93,92,91**
CSF £50.69 CT £704.73 TOTE £6.60: £2.20, £2.60, £5.80; EX 51.20.
Owner I J Anderson **Bred** J Dorrian **Trained** Bromsash, Herefordshire
■ A first winner for trainer Michael Scudamore, brother of Tom, son of Peter and grandson of Michael senior.

FOCUS
An ordinary staying handicap run at a rather uneven pace, but eventually turned into a procession by the winner. The form is rated through the third.

2573 HARVEY NICHOLS MAIDEN STKS — 1m 3f 200y
9:10 (9:13) (Class 5) 3-Y-O+ — **£2,590** (£770; £385; £192) **Stalls** High

Form — RPR

62-5 **1** **North Parade**[21] 1943 3-8-9 **88** .... (t) NCallan 4 70+
(B J Meehan) *racd keenly: trckd ldrs: led under 3f out: rdn ins fnl f and kpt on* **10/11**[1]

0- **2** *1 1/2* **Cherokee Star**[252] 5605 3-8-9 0 .... SamHitchcott 12 67
(C C Bealby) *trckd ldrs: rdn 4f out: sn outpcd: rallied over 2f out: wnt 2nd 1f out: styd on u.p to cl on wnr towards fin* **66/1**

3 *1 1/4* **Erdeli (IRE)**[167] 6151 4-9-12 0 .... ChrisCatlin 11 66
(P R Webber) *hld up in rr: stdy hdwy fr over 3f out: styd on to chse ldrs ins fnl f: no imp towards fin* **14/1**

4 *1 1/2* **Motarid (USA)** 3-8-9 0 .... GrahamGibbons 7 63
(T D Walford) *hld up: hdwy over 2f out: rdn over 1f out whn chsd ldrs: kpt on ins fnl f but unable to chal* **20/1**

0-34 **5** *1/2* **Dubai's Wonder (IRE)**[63] 1059 3-8-9 **70** .... MichaelHills 13 62+
(B W Hills) *midfield: outpcd 3f out: styd on ins fnl f: nt pce to chal ldrs* **9/2**[2]

4 **6** *1 3/4* **Bocciani (GER)**[7] 2363 3-8-9 0 .... (b) JoeFanning 8 59
(M Johnston) *racd keenly: prom: upsides 3f out: one pce fnl 2f* **14/1**

0- **7** *1 3/4* **Syriana**[209] 6648 3-8-1 0 .... DominicFox[(3)] 1 51
(A Bailey) *midfield: rdn over 3f out: kpt on one pce fnl f* **28/1**

0 **8** *2 1/4* **River Danube**[27] 1814 5-9-12 0 .... DavidAllan 5 53
(T J Fitzgerald) *trckd ldrs: rdn over 2f out: sn edgd lft: wknd over 1f out* **14/1**

24 **9** *4 1/2* **Evelith Regent (IRE)**[26] 1825 5-9-12 0 .... DanielTudhope 6 46
(G A Swinbank) *led: hdd under 3f out: rdn and wknd over 1f out* **15/2**[3]

10 *8* **Sherbet Lemon** 3-8-4 0 .... RoystonFfrench 10 28
(Miss J A Camacho) *pushed along after 4f: a bhd* **16/1**

00 **11** *26* **Monte Pattino (USA)**[3] 2488 4-9-9 0 .... (t) LeeVickers[(3)] 9 —
(C J Teague) *s.i.s: midfield: rdn and lost pl over 4f out: bhd after* **250/1**

2m 37.64s (4.44) **Going Correction** +0.125s/f (Good)
WFA 3 from 4yo+ 17lb — 11 Ran SP% **118.3**
Speed ratings (Par 103): **90,89,88,87,86 85,84,83,80,74 57**
CSF £110.63 TOTE £1.90: £1.20, £10.70, £3.80; EX 110.00 Place 6 £12.08, Place 5 £6.67.
Owner E H Jones (paints) Ltd **Bred** Le Thenney S A **Trained** Manton, Wilts

FOCUS
A modest middle-distance maiden in which the pace was ordinary and the time was slow. The proximity of a 66-1 shot in second does little for the form and North Parade was well below his level in success.
T/Plt: £19.00 to a £1 stake. Pool: £65,789.05. 2,523.40 winning tickets. T/Qpdt: £10.50 to a £1 stake. Pool: £3,470.10. 244.30 winning tickets. DO

2281 MUSSELBURGH (R-H)
Friday, May 30

OFFICIAL GOING: Good (7.6)
Wind: Virtually nil Weather: Overcast

2574 E B F/MICHAEL PAGE FINANCE WORLD ERVICE MAIDEN STKS — 5f
6:50 (6:50) (Class 5) 2-Y-O — **£3,885** (£1,156; £577) **Stalls** Low

Form — RPR

2 **1** **Excellent Show**[13] 2206 2-8-12 0 .... TomEaves 4 85+
(B Smart) *dwlt and wnt rt s: sn cl up: shkn up over 1f out: led ent fnl f: pushed out* **1/3**[1]

52 **2** *2* **Rievaulx World**[8] 2331 2-9-3 0 .... FergalLynch 1 81
(K A Ryan) *led: rdn along 2f out: drvn and ehaded ent fnl f: one pce* **5/2**[2]

64 **3** *7* **Lady Fantasie**[14] 2140 2-8-9 0 .... AndrewMullen[(3)] 2 51
(Mrs A Duffield) *chsd ldng pair: rdn along 2f out and sn outpcd* **25/1**[3]

60.84 secs (0.44) **Going Correction** -0.05s/f (Good) — 3 Ran SP% **107.4**
Speed ratings (Par 93): **94,90,79**
CSF £1.47 TOTE £1.20; EX 1.20.
Owner H E Sheikh Rashid Bin Mohammed **Bred** Bearstone Stud And T Herbert Jackson **Trained** Hambleton, N Yorks

FOCUS
A small field but a pleasing performance from the very useful-looking winner. The form should prove reliable.

NOTEBOOK
Excellent Show, who found only the promising Haigh Hall too good for her on her debut at Thirsk, was always travelling strongly and only had to be pushed out to score comfortably. Her trainer now plans to send her to Royal Ascot for the Queen Mary, and she could well put up a bold show there. (op 1-2)
Rievaulx World had shown enough in his previous two starts to suggest he can win a maiden, and this sharp 5f was right up his street, but he came up against a potentially smart rival in Excellent Show and was never going to be anything but second to her. (op 7-4)
Lady Fantasie finished up well held but she still picked up £577.80 for turning up. (tchd 20-1)

2575 BIBBY FINANCIAL SERVICES BICENTENNIAL H'CAP — 7f 30y
7:20 (7:21) (Class 4) (0-85,80) 3-Y-O — **£5,180** (£1,541; £770; £384) **Stalls** High

Form — RPR

321 **1** **Always A Rock (IRE)**[44] 1410 3-9-5 **78** .... GregFairley 1 92
(M Johnston) *led: rdn 3f out: hdd briefly 2f out: sn drvn to ld again wl over 1f out: styd on gamely u.p ins fnl f* **6/4**[1]

1-04 **2** *1 3/4* **Prince Hamlet (IRE)**[13] 2209 3-9-1 **74** .... TomEaves 3 83
(B Smart) *trckd ldrs: hdwy 1/2-way: chal 3f out and sn rdn: drvn to ld briefly 2f out: sn hdd and kpt on same pce ins fnl f* **7/2**[3]

0153 **3** *6* **Casino Night**[7] 2367 3-7-13 **65** .... PatrickDonaghy[(7)] 4 58
(J R Weymes) *trckd wnr to 1/2-way: rdn along and outpcd wl over 2f out: drvn and kpt on u.p appr fnl f* **7/1**

-132 **4** *3/4* **Sparton Duke (IRE)**[22] 1934 3-9-7 **80** .... (p) DO'Donohoe 5 71
(K A Ryan) *dwlt: sn trcking ldrs: rdn along 3f out: sn drvn and one pce* **10/3**[2]

33-1 **5** *2 1/4* **Island Music (IRE)**[18] 2039 3-8-12 **74** .... JamieMoriarty[(3)] 2 59
(J J Quinn) *hld up in tch: effrt 3f out: sn rdn along and btn 2f out* **5/1**

1m 31.01s (0.71) **Going Correction** -0.05s/f (Good) — 5 Ran SP% **114.5**
Speed ratings (Par 101): **93,91,84,83,80**
CSF £7.42 TOTE £2.40: £1.60, £1.90; EX 9.60.
Owner Always Trying Partnership IV **Bred** Ascagnano S P A **Trained** Middleham Moor, N Yorks

FOCUS
An ordinary handicap run at a steady early gallop, so there has to be a question mark on the value of the form. That said, the winner looks nicely progressive.

2576 NAIRN'S OATCAKES LTD (S) STKS — 5f
7:50 (7:50) (Class 6) 3-Y-O+ — **£1,942** (£578; £288; £144) **Stalls** Low

Form — RPR

-205 **1** **Funfair Wane**[11] 2248 9-9-3 64 .... AdrianTNicholls 6 65
(D Nicholls) *sn led: rdn over 1f out: clr whn edgd rt ins fnl f* **11/8**[1]

0350 **2** *3 1/4* **Princess Charlmane (IRE)**[14] 2159 5-8-9 43 .... (t) PJMcDonald[(3)] 3 48
(C J Teague) *chsd wnr: rdn along wl over 1f out: drvn ent fnl f and kpt on same pce* **8/1**

-001 **3** *3/4* **Angelofthenorth**[11] 2248 6-9-4 50 .... TomEaves 9 51
(C J Teague) *in tch: hdwy on outer 2f out: sn rdn and kpt on same pce* **11/4**[2]

0000 **4** *hd* **Alfie Lee (IRE)**[11] 2248 11-8-10 41 .... (tp) PatrickDonaghy[(7)] 5 50
(D A Nolan) *chsd ldrs: rdn wl over 1f out: kpt on same pce appr fnl f* **40/1**

0-00 **5** 1 1/4 **La Guancha**[10] 2287 3-8-1 42 ow4....(bt[1]) PaulPickard(7) 4 44
(D A Nolan) *in tch: hdwy to chse ldrs whn n.m.r appr fnl f: swtchd lft: rdn and no imp* **33/1**
0-00 **6** 6 **Howards Prince**[14] 2145 5-8-12 40.... GaryBartley(5) 7 23
(D A Nolan) *chsd ldrs: rdn 2f out and sn wknd* **50/1**
000 **7** 1 1/4 **Notforloveormoney**[39] 1519 3-8-5 0 ow1.... GregFairley 2 15
(A G Foster) *a towards rr* **40/1**
616- **8** 1 3/4 **Glenluji**[302] 4098 3-8-9 66.... FergalLynch 8 13
(J S Goldie) *s.i.s: a in rr* **10/3**[3]
000- **9** 13 **Mister Marmaduke**[238] 5969 7-9-0 38.... JamieMoriarty(3) 1 —
(D A Nolan) *s.i.s: a bhd* **100/1**

60.51 secs (0.11) **Going Correction** -0.05s/f (Good)
WFA 3 from 5yo+ 8lb **9** Ran SP% **113.7**
Speed ratings (Par 101): **97,91,90,90,88 78,76,73,53**
CSF £12.88 TOTE £2.40: £1.10, £1.70, £1.60; EX 15.00.There was no bid for the winner.
Owner The Wayward Lads **Bred** J K Keegan **Trained** Sessay, N Yorks
FOCUS
Moderate form, but it seems to make sense with the winner and third close to their marks.
Glenluji Official explanation: jockey said gelding missed the break
Mister Marmaduke Official explanation: jockey said gelding missed the break

2577 LANDSBANKI SECURITIES (UK) LTD H'CAP 2m
8:20 (8:20) (Class 4) (0-80,79) 4-Y-0+ **£6,476** (£1,927; £963; £481) **Stalls** Low

Form RPR
/656 **1** **Numero Due**[15] 2135 6-9-6 79.... PJMcDonald(3) 5 88+
(G M Moore) *trckd ldr: hdwy 3f out: rdn to ld over 1f out: drvn ins fnl f and styd on gamely* **11/4**[2]
-221 **2** 2 1/4 **Danzatrice**[21] 1972 6-8-9 65.... TomEaves 2 71
(C W Thornton) *hld up in rr: gd hdwy on outer 3f out: rdn to chse ldrs wl over 1f out: drvn to chse wnr and edgd rt ins fnl f: one pce* **9/4**[1]
3-12 **3** 1 3/4 **Mr Crystal (FR)**[6] 2393 4-8-10 68.... DO'Donohoe 1 72
(Micky Hammond) *trckd ldng pair: hdwy to ld 1/2-way: hdd over 4f out: rdn along 3f out: drvn over 1f out: kpt on same pce* **4/1**[3]
2212 **4** 3/4 **Fregate Island (IRE)**[25] 1877 5-9-8 78.... FergalLynch 4 81
(A G Newcombe) *led to 1/2-way: cl up tl led again 4f out: rdn along over 2f out: drvn and hdd over 1f out: wknd ins fnl f* **11/4**[2]
60-3 **5** 4 1/2 **Grand Art (IRE)**[11] 2249 4-8-12 73.... JamieMoriarty(3) 3 71
(J Howard Johnson) *hld up: effrt and hdwy 3f out: sn rdn and btn 2f out* **14/1**

3m 33.3s (-2.80) **Going Correction** -0.05s/f (Good)
WFA 4 from 5yo+ 2lb **5** Ran SP% **110.8**
Speed ratings (Par 105): **105,103,103,102,100**
CSF £9.40 TOTE £4.00: £2.00, £1.50; EX 8.70.
Owner J W Andrews **Bred** London Thoroughbred Services Ltd **Trained** Middleham Moor, N Yorks
FOCUS
They went an average pace in this fair staying handicap. The form seems sound enough.

2578 BERNARD HUNTER CRANE HIRE CLAIMING STKS 1m
8:50 (8:51) (Class 4) 4-Y-0+ **£5,180** (£1,541; £770; £384) **Stalls** High

Form RPR
0-26 **1** **Abbondanza (IRE)**[133] 218 5-9-11 83....(p) TomEaves 5 82
(Miss L A Perratt) *trckd ldrs: hdwy on inner to ld over 3f out: rdn 2f out: drvn ins fnl f and styd on wl* **6/1**[3]
0211 **2** 1 1/4 **Royal Dignitary (USA)**[11] 2250 8-9-2 85.... AdrianTNicholls 2 70
(D Nicholls) *cl up: effrt 3f out: rdn 2f out and ev ch tl drvn and kpt on same pce ins fnl f* **7/4**[2]
3200 **3** hd **Claret And Amber**[8] 2334 6-8-12 77.... JamieMoriarty(3) 8 69
(R A Fahey) *in tch: hdwy over 3f out: swtchd lft and rdn to chse ldng pair over 1f out: drvn and styd on wl fnl f* **8/1**
0-02 **4** 5 **Papa's Princess**[11] 2250 4-8-7 47.... FergalLynch 3 49
(J S Goldie) *chsd ldrs: rdn along 3f out: drvn 2f out and sn no imp* **14/1**
6-43 **5** 1/2 **Sam's Secret**[13] 2190 6-8-10 77.... PJMcDonald(3) 4 54
(G A Swinbank) *hld up in tch: hdwy 3f out: rdn along 2f out: sn drvn and no imp* **6/4**[1]
30-0 **6** 1 3/4 **Mis Chicaf (IRE)**[32] 1675 7-8-1 45 ow7.... PaulPickard(7) 6 45
(D Carroll) *in tch: hdwy to chse ldrs 3f out: rdn over 2f out: sn drvn and wknd* **50/1**
0/00 **7** 1 1/4 **Donna's Double**[49] 1305 13-8-1 37 ow1....(p) AndrewMullen(3) 7 38
(Karen McLintock) *a in rr* **50/1**
0-00 **8** 5 **Noble Edge**[32] 1679 5-8-6 42....(v[1]) PaulFessey 9 29
(Karen McLintock) *dwlt: a in rr* **50/1**
0/00 **9** 30 **Maylea Gold (IRE)**[21] 1951 5-8-10 36.... GaryBartley(5) 1 —
(Mrs S C Bradburne) *t.k.h: racd wd and sn ld: rn wd and hdd bnd over 3f out: sn wknd* **100/1**

1m 42.24s (1.04) **Going Correction** -0.05s/f (Good) **9** Ran SP% **115.3**
Speed ratings (Par 105): **92,90,90,85,85 83,82,77,47**
CSF £16.87 TOTE £8.50: £1.50, £1.20, £2.30; EX 21.30.
Owner Joseph Leckie & Sons Ltd **Bred** M Nolan **Trained** Carluke, S Lanarks
FOCUS
Not the worst claimer ever seen, but it was run in a moderate time, even for a race of this type. The first three and the favourite are fair for the grade, but the fourth limits the form.

2579 MARSHALL-TUFFLEX ODYSSEY CUP H'CAP 1m 4f
9:20 (9:20) (Class 5) (0-70,70) 4-Y-0+ **£3,238** (£963; £481; £240) **Stalls** High

Form RPR
3-12 **1** **Lochiel**[11] 2249 4-9-3 66.... PaulMulrennan 7 78
(Mrs S C Bradburne) *trckd ldng pair: hdwy over 3f out: led over 2f out and sn rdn: drvn ent fnl f and styd on strly* **5/2**[2]
6235 **2** 3 **Hugs Destiny (IRE)**[4] 2447 7-8-4 53 oh4 ow2....(t) AdrianTNicholls 6 60
(M A Barnes) *led 4f: chsd ldr: rdn along 3f out and sn ev ch tl drvn and kpt on same pce fnl f* **11/2**[3]
3111 **3** 1/2 **Annibale Caro**[7] 2364 6-9-0 66 12ex.... PJMcDonald(3) 5 72
(Grant Tuer) *hld up in tch: smooth hdwy 3f out: chsd ldrs 2f out: swtchd lft and rdn over 1f out: sn drvn and one pce ins fnl f* **5/4**[1]
06-0 **4** 1 **Kyber**[67] 988 7-8-6 55.... FergalLynch 3 60
(J S Goldie) *hld up and bhd: gd hdwy on outer over 2f out: rdn wl over 1f out: kpt on ins fnl f* **15/2**
4-60 **5** 11 **San Deng**[7] 2364 6-8-8 57.... DO'Donohoe 1 44
(Micky Hammond) *trckd ldr tl led after 4f and sn clr: rdn along over 3f out: hdd over 2f out and sn wknd* **25/1**
6342 **6** 2 1/4 **Easibet Dot Net**[11] 2252 8-8-3 52....(v) PaulFessey 4 35
(Miss L A Perratt) *hld up: a in rr* **9/1**
7 34 **Kwitara (GER)**[229] 4-9-7 70.... TomEaves 2 —
(P Monteith) *a towards rr: bhd fr 1/2-way* **33/1**

2m 38.18s (-1.52) **Going Correction** -0.05s/f (Good) **7** Ran SP% **117.0**
Speed ratings (Par 103): **103,101,100,100,92 91,68**
CSF £17.34 TOTE £3.30: £2.00, £3.10; EX 8.90 Place 6 £17.17, Place 5 £12.27.
Owner A Campbell **Bred** D W Barker **Trained** Cunnoquhie, Fife
FOCUS
A modest handicap and pretty ordinary form, with an improved effort from Lochiel. The pace was fair.
T/Plt: £28.60 to a £1 stake. Pool: £43,627.15. 1,110.85 winning tickets. T/Qpdt: £11.30 to a £1 stake. Pool: £2,815.00. 183.00 winning tickets. JR

[2167]YORK (L-H)
Friday, May 30

OFFICIAL GOING: Good (8.0)
4mm overnight rain resulted in 'good ground, just a shade loose on top'. Home bend moved out 3 metres adding 7yds to race distances.
Wind: light 1/2 against Weather: overcast

2580 PD PORTS STKS (CONDITIONS RACE) 7f
2:10 (2:10) (Class 3) 3-Y-0+ **£9,714** (£2,890; £1,444; £721) **Stalls** Low

Form RPR
113 **1** **King Of Dixie (USA)**[20] 1982 4-9-2 98.... RyanMoore 8 115+
(W J Knight) *lw: stdd s: in rr: pushed along over 3f out: nt clr run 2f out: styd on to ld ins fnl f: drvn out* **9/4**[1]
12-3 **2** 2 1/2 **Fateh Field (USA)**[15] 2121 3-8-5 104.... KerrinMcEvoy 4 104
(Saeed Bin Suroor) *lw: trckd ldrs: led 1f out: hdd and no ex ins fnl f* **3/1**[2]
054- **3** 2 **Easy Target (FR)**[237] 6017 3-8-7 100.... TomEaves 10 100
(B Smart) *sn drvn along: hdwy on wd outside to join ldrs over 2f out: kpt on same pce fnl f* **33/1**
-055 **4** 1 1/4 **Advanced**[20] 1986 5-9-2 107.... NCallan 7 99
(K A Ryan) *w ldrs: led 2f out: hdd 1f out: no ex* **12/1**
14-1 **5** 2 3/4 **Celtic Sultan (IRE)**[21] 1942 4-9-2 103.... MickyFenton 3 92
(T P Tate) *w ldr: led over 3f out: hdd 2f out: faltered and fdd fnl f* **15/2**
0-10 **6** nse **Dabbers Ridge (IRE)**[20] 1982 6-9-4 102.... MichaelHills 6 93
(B W Hills) *hld up: hdwy to trck ldrs over 2f out: rdn and wknd 1f out* **14/1**
0-02 **7** 3 3/4 **Diamond Tycoon (USA)**[20] 1989 4-9-2 105.... AlanMunro 1 81
(B J Meehan) *trckd ldrs: lost pl over 1f out* **6/1**[3]
00-0 **8** 8 **Levera**[18] 2044 5-9-2 100.... TedDurcan 9 60
(A King) *w ldrs: sn pushed along: lost pl over 2f out* **16/1**
3-03 **9** 6 **Something (IRE)**[6] 2390 6-9-2 0.... AdrianTNicholls 11 44+
(D Nicholls) *swtg: t.k.h in midfield: effrt over 2f out: lost pl over 1f out* **12/1**
05-5 **10** 15 **New Seeker**[15] 2132 8-9-2 99....(b) JoeFanning 2 3
(P F I Cole) *led tl over 3f out: sn lost pl: bhd and eased over 1f out* **25/1**

1m 24.63s (-0.67) **Going Correction** +0.15s/f (Good)
WFA 3 from 4yo+ 11lb **10** Ran SP% **116.5**
Speed ratings (Par 107): **109,106,103,102,99 99,94,85,78,61**
CSF £8.83 TOTE £3.00: £1.40, £1.40, £7.80; EX 9.20.
Owner Hesmonds Stud **Bred** Bee Zee LLC **Trained** Patching, W Sussex
FOCUS
Decent form bordering on Listed class. The winner continues to progress and the race has been rated around the placed horses.
NOTEBOOK
King Of Dixie(USA), an edgy sort, wore a Monty Roberts-type rope halter. Dropped in, he made hard work of it but scored in convincing fashion in the end. He is clearly going the right way and should make his mark in Listed company. (op 5-2 tchd 11-4)
Fateh Field(USA), who looked bright and well, was dropping back in trip. He travelled smoothly, but after taking the lead was very much second best at the line. (op 7-2)
Easy Target(FR), who is not that big, was taken to post early and became very warm behind the stalls. Soon making hard work of it, he moved up on the wide outside and kept going all the way to the line. (op 40-1)
Advanced, best in on official figures, is hard to predict at present and he has yet to win beyond 6f. (tchd 10-1)
Celtic Sultan(IRE), stepping up in grade, helped take them along but he seemed to falter as if something had gone amiss. He was reported to have returned sound afterwards. Official explanation: jockey said colt lost its action but returned sound (op 8-1 tchd 7-1)
Dabbers Ridge(IRE), conceding weight all round, is perhaps better these days with a lot more give underfoot. (op 12-1)
Diamond Tycoon(USA), loaded with a Monty Roberts rug, seemed to fold rather tamely. He has plenty to prove now. (tchd 13-2)
Levera Official explanation: jockey said gelding had no more to give

2581 E B F YORKSHIRE REGIMENT MAIDEN STKS 5f
2:45 (2:45) (Class 3) 2-Y-0 **£7,123** (£2,119; £1,059; £529) **Stalls** High

Form RPR
3 **1** **Thunderous Mood (USA)**[5] 2424 2-9-3 0.... JohnEgan 5 82+
(P F I Cole) *w ldr: led 2f out: hld on wl* **6/4**[1]
2 **2** 3/4 **Viva Ronaldo (IRE)**[22] 1924 2-9-3 0.... PaulHanagan 4 79+
(R A Fahey) *wnt rt s: hdwy to chse ldrs over 2f out: chal and hung lft 1f out: no ex ins fnl f* **6/4**[1]
3 6 **Secret City (IRE)** 2-9-3 0.... DarrenWilliams 1 57
(R Bastiman) *w'like: swvd lft s: hdwy to chse ldrs over 2f out: edgd rt and wknd 1f out* **20/1**
45 **4** 2 1/4 **Steel Stockholder**[16] 2108 2-9-3 0.... TWilliams 6 49
(M Brittain) *w ldrs: wknd over 1f out* **14/1**[3]
355 **5** 4 **Kings House**[20] 2004 2-9-3 0.... PaulMulrennan 3 35
(M W Easterby) *led tl 2f out: sn wknd* **50/1**
3 **U** **Bees River (IRE)**[13] 2186 2-8-12 0.... DavidAllan 2 —
(T D Easterby) *stmbld bdly and uns rdr leaving stalls* **5/1**[2]

61.31 secs (2.01) **Going Correction** +0.25s/f (Good) **6** Ran SP% **110.1**
Speed ratings (Par 97): **93,91,82,78,72** —
CSF £3.62 TOTE £2.20: £1.40, £1.20; EX 3.50.
Owner Mrs Fitri Hay **Bred** Barnett Enterprises **Trained** Whatcombe, Oxon
FOCUS
A modest event overall for a race carrying £11,000 prize money, but the first two finished clear and are decent juveniles. The form could have been rated higher.
NOTEBOOK
Thunderous Mood(USA), who is not a good mover, knew his job this time and fought off his market rival, the pair clear. (op 7-4 tchd 15-8 and 2-1)
Viva Ronaldo(IRE), edgy beforehand, went right exiting the stalls and seemed to bang the sides. He threw down his challenge but looked slightly awkward and was second best at the line. He is still learning and should find a race or two. (tchd 11-8 and 13-8)
Secret City(IRE), a close-coupled, good-walking newcomer, had nothing on his outside and went left leaving the stalls. He rolled off a straight line and tired in the final furlong but this should have taught him something. (op 25-1 tchd 16-1)
Steel Stockholder, having his third race in quick succession, was warm and edgy in the preliminaries. He is at least now qualified for a nursery mark. (op 16-1)
Kings House had finished well beaten in selling company on his previous start. (tchd 40-1)

Bees River(IRE), who is not that big, being more of an atheltic, chunky sort, stumbled and gave her rider no chance leaving the stalls. (op 7-2)

2582 SKF STKS (H'CAP) 1m 2f 88y

3:20 (3:21) (Class 3) (0-90,90) 4-Y-0+ £11,009 (£3,275; £1,637; £817) Stalls Low

Form RPR

0/25 1 **Humble Opinion**[26] 1828 6-9-3 **86** AlanMunro 13 95
(B J Meehan) *lw: hld up in midfield: effrt over 2f out: led jst ins fnl f: all out* 13/2[2]

0-00 2 *hd* **Peruvian Prince (USA)**[14] 2168 6-8-12 **81** PaulHanagan 6 90
(R A Fahey) *broke smartly and led early: hld up in midfield: effrt 3f out: chal jst ins fnl f: no ex nr line* 13/2[2]

0-30 3 *hd* **Celtic Change (IRE)**[41] 1473 4-8-9 **78** PhillipMakin 8 86
(M Dods) *trckd ldrs: chal 3f out: no ex wl ins fnl f* 14/1

-011 4 *1/2* **Kavachi (IRE)**[14] 2152 5-9-4 **87** RyanMoore 1 94
(G L Moore) *stdd s: hld up in last: hdwy on wd outside 3f out: kpt on wl fnl f* 7/2[1]

-261 5 *3/4* **Veiled Applause**[12] 2220 5-9-2 **85** 6ex GrahamGibbons 3 91
(J J Quinn) *hld up in midfield: hdwy on inner over 3f out: upsides jst ins fnl f: no ex* 8/1[3]

6163 6 *shd* **Granston (IRE)**[21] 1970 7-9-0 **83** KerrinMcEvoy 5 92+
(J D Bethell) *hld up in midfield: nt clr run over 2f out: styd on wl ins fnl f* 9/1

0-00 7 *1* **Philanthropy**[22] 1920 4-9-2 **85** NCallan 17 89
(K A Ryan) *swtg: prom: hdwy to ld 3f out: hdd jst ins fnl f: fdd* 33/1

50-0 8 *1 3/4* **Wind Star**[12] 2220 5-8-11 **80** TedDurcan 7 80
(G A Swinbank) *mid-div: hdwy on ins 3f out: chalng over 1f out: wknd ins fnl f* 20/1

00-4 9 *hd* **Film Festival (USA)**[21] 1970 5-9-0 **83** J-PGuillambert 4 83
(B Ellison) *lw: trckd ldrs: outpcd over 2f out: kpt on fnl f* 25/1

-432 10 *1 1/2* **Rosbay (IRE)**[23] 1909 4-9-1 **84** DavidAllan 15 81
(T D Easterby) *in rr: styd on u.p fnl 3f: nvr nr ldrs* 14/1

4203 11 *hd* **Intersky Charm (USA)**[12] 2220 4-8-7 **76** oh1 DeanMcKeown 10 72
(R M Whitaker) *prom: drvn over 2f out: one pce whn sltly hmpd over 1f out* 20/1

1210 12 *hd* **Blue Spinnaker (IRE)**[16] 2103 9-8-6 **82** NSLawes(7) 14 78
(M W Easterby) *rr-div: kpt on fnl 3f: nvr a factor* 16/1

1206 13 *5* **Man Of Gwent (UAE)**[21] 1947 4-8-9 **78** JohnEgan 16 64
(P D Evans) *b.hind: in rr: reminders 4f out: sn lost pl* 25/1

20-0 14 *1/2* **Hurlingham**[23] 1910 4-8-7 **76** PaulMulrennan 11 61
(M W Easterby) *swtg: chsd ldrs: wkng whn n.m.r over 2f out* 28/1

52-0 15 *1 1/2* **New Beginning (IRE)**[91] 757 4-8-11 **85** NeilBrown(5) 2 67
(Mrs S Lamyman) *in rr: sme hdwy 4f out: lost pl over 2f out* 22/1

U0-0 16 *1 1/2* **Fort Amhurst (IRE)**[16] 2103 4-8-10 **79** DaleGibson 18 58
(M W Easterby) *hld up in rr: hdwy on outside 3f out: wknd over 1f out* 66/1

-600 17 *1 1/2* **Mesbaah (IRE)**[16] 2103 4-8-12 **88** BMcHugh(7) 12 64
(R A Fahey) *swtg: trckd ldrs: chal 3f out: sn wknd* 33/1

0-43 18 *7* **My Paris**[12] 2218 7-9-7 **90** ChrisCatlin 9 52
(Ollie Pears) *t.k.h: sn led: hdd 3f out: sn lost pl* 14/1

2m 11.7s (-0.80) **Going Correction** +0.10s/f (Good) **18** Ran SP% **128.3**
Speed ratings (Par 107): **107,106,106,106,105 105,104,103,103,102 101,101,97,97,96 94,93,88**
CSF £43.68 CT £597.17 TOTE £7.80: £2.50, £2.00, £4.70, £1.70; EX 64.50 Trifecta £436.60 Pool: £922.56. 1.50 winning units..
Owner Paul & Jenny Green **Bred** P C Green **Trained** Manton, Wilts

FOCUS
A competitive handicap and the form should prove rock solid.

NOTEBOOK
Humble Opinion, who missed 2007, really took the eye in the paddock. Skilfully settled, after taking charge he had to dig deep and it was a scramble at the line. (op 6-1 tchd 7-1)
Peruvian Prince(USA), not the best of movers, became very warm at the start. He seemed to charge the gates and emerged in front but was soon settled in mid-field. In the end he only just missed out and is clearly right back to his best. (op 7-1)
Celtic Change(IRE), who looked in great shape beforehand but was on his toes, as usual travelled well only to just miss out in the end. This looks his trip now. (op 16-1)
Kavachi(IRE), 7lb higher, was put to sleep in last place. He made his effort widest of all and was cutting back the first three at the line. As it transpired he was almost certainly racing on the slower part of the track. (op 5-1)
Veiled Applause, who accounted for a subsequent winner at Ripon, was undone by his 6lb penalty. (op 15-2 tchd 7-1)
Granston(IRE), just 1lb higher than Doncaster, travelled strongly but met severe traffic problems. He stayed on really well inside the last and an eighth career success is surely just around the corner. Official explanation: jockey said gelding was denied a clear run (op 11-1)
Philanthropy, with the cheekpieces left off, ran much better but he is not easy to predict.
New Beginning(IRE) Official explanation: trainer said gelding had suffered interference early on and had been unable to regain its momentum thereafter

2583 GWP ARCHITECTS STKS (H'CAP) 5f

3:55 (3:56) (Class 4) (0-80,81) 4-Y-0+ £7,123 (£2,119; £1,059; £529) Stalls High

Form RPR

2100 1 **Stolt (IRE)**[13] 2212 4-9-2 **80** AshleyHamblett(5) 1 93
(N Wilson) *racd towards far side: mde all: edgd lft ins fnl f: hld on towards fin* 22/1

4001 2 *nk* **Crimson Fern (IRE)**[8] 2330 4-8-7 **66** oh1 FrancisNorton 2 78
(M S Saunders) *lw: rrd s: sn trcking ldrs far side: chal over 1f out: edgd rt ins fnl f: no ex nr fin* 5/2[1]

0-00 3 *2* **He's A Humbug (IRE)**[27] 1818 4-9-4 **77** (p) NCallan 12 82
(K A Ryan) *chsd ldrs: kpt on same pce appr fnl f* 20/1

3-44 4 *nk* **Charles Parnell (IRE)**[13] 2188 5-9-2 **75** RichardMullen 11 79+
(M Dods) *lw: s.s: hdwy 2f out: kpt on same pce ins fnl f* 7/1[2]

3612 5 *1 1/2* **Rothesay Dancer**[14] 2145 5-8-4 **68** KellyHarrison(5) 15 66
(J S Goldie) *hld up: hdwy and nt clr run 2f out: r.o fnl f* 14/1

6-33 6 *nse* **Deserted Dane (USA)**[13] 2212 4-9-5 **78** KerrinMcEvoy 13 76
(G A Swinbank) *hld up in mid-div: effrt 2f out: kpt on ins fnl f* 9/1

5303 7 *hd* **Colorus (IRE)**[10] 2270 5-8-8 **67** JoeFanning 10 64
(W J H Ratcliffe) *chsd ldrs: kpt on same pce fnl 2f* 12/1

0311 8 *1 1/4* **What Do You Know**[14] 2166 5-9-7 **80** (v) DavidKinsella 3 73
(A M Hales) *chsd ldrs far side: wknd jst ins fnl f* 9/1

450 9 *nse* **Supreme Speedster**[90] 766 4-8-0 **66** oh11 RossAtkinson(7) 5 59
(M Brittain) *prom: one pce fnl 2f* 50/1

0005 10 *3/4* **Circuit Dancer (IRE)**[4] 2444 8-8-9 **68** SilvestreDeSousa 18 58+
(D Nicholls) *towards rr stands' side: hung lft and kpt on fnl 2f: nvr a factor* 8/1[3]

0433 11 *3/4* **Steel City Boy (IRE)**[10] 2293 5-8-5 **69** oh6 ow3 AnnStokell(5) 6 56
(Miss A Stokell) *swtg: chsd ldrs: wknd over 1f out* 25/1

5330 12 *1/2* **Highland Warrior**[34] 1624 9-8-11 **70** MickyFenton 9 55
(P T Midgley) *chsd ldrs: wknd over 1f out* 16/1

3010 13 *1 3/4* **Brut**[20] 1997 6-8-11 **70** (p) PaulHanagan 16 49
(D W Barker) *racd towards stands' side: chsd ldrs: lost pl over 1f out* 33/1

-151 14 *1 1/2* **Valley Of The Moon (IRE)**[12] 2219 4-9-1 **81** 6ex FrederikTylicki(7) 17 55
(R A Fahey) *racd towards stands' side: a in rr* 16/1

-254 15 *2 1/2* **Gallery Girl (IRE)**[12] 2219 5-9-7 **80** DavidAllan 14 45
(T D Easterby) *racd towards stands' side: a towards rr* 12/1

59.89 secs (0.59) **Going Correction** +0.25s/f (Good) **15** Ran SP% **123.9**
Speed ratings (Par 105): **105,104,101,100,98 98,98,96,95,94 93,92,89,87,83**
CSF £74.48 CT £1215.71 TOTE £37.40: £7.90, £1.80, £7.30; EX 124.50.
Owner Dixon, McIntyre, Tobin **Bred** Seamus Phelan **Trained** Flaxton, N Yorks
■ Stewards' Enquiry : Ashley Hamblett two-day ban: careless riding (Jun 13-14)

FOCUS
Those racing towards the far side seemed to enjoy a big advantage. An ordinary sprint handicap but the form looks reliable.
Stolt(IRE) Official explanation: trainer said, regarding the apparent improvement in form, gelding seemed to benefit from getting the run of the race today
What Do You Know Official explanation: jockey said gelding had no more to give
Circuit Dancer(IRE) Official explanation: jockey said gelding hung left-handed

2584 GARBUTT & ELLIOTT MAIDEN AUCTION STKS 6f

4:35 (4:36) (Class 4) 2-Y-0 £6,152 (£1,830; £914; £456) Stalls High

Form RPR

1 **Chicago Cop (IRE)** 2-9-0 0 SilvestreDeSousa 7 83
(D Nicholls) *w'like: dwlt: hdwy to chse ldrs over 2f out: led jst ins fnl f: styd on wl* 20/1

4 2 *2 3/4* **Reve De Soleil (FR)**[15] 2134 2-8-10 0 ChrisCatlin 3 71
(E J O'Neill) *lw: w ldr: led over 1f out: hdd and no ex ins fnl f* 7/4[1]

560 3 *2* **Premier Krug (IRE)**[18] 2048 2-8-7 0 JohnEgan 2 62
(P D Evans) *led tl over 1f out: kpt on same pce* 25/1

0 4 *1 1/4* **The Kilkenny Kat (IRE)**[27] 1794 2-8-11 0 TedDurcan 5 62+
(T D Easterby) *w'like: str: in rr: hdwy over 2f out: kpt on fnl f* 25/1

04 5 *nse* **Richo**[12] 2217 2-8-11 0 PaulMulrennan 13 62
(D H Brown) *lw: chsd ldrs towards stands' side: outpcd over 2f out: kpt on wl fnl f* 20/1

2 6 *2* **Cutting Comments**[30] 1727 2-9-3 0 PhillipMakin 4 62
(M Dods) *lengthy: leggy: w ldrs: wknd over 1f out* 5/2[2]

6 7 *2 1/2* **Herring Senior (IRE)**[15] 2117 2-9-2 0 NelsonDeSouza 8 53
(P F I Cole) *chsd ldrs: outpcd fnl 2f* 16/1

5 8 *2 1/4* **Whatyouwoodwishfor (USA)**[15] 2134 2-9-2 0 PaulHanagan 11 47+
(R A Fahey) *dwlt: in rr: sme hdwy 2f out: nvr nr ldrs* 9/2[3]

9 *3* **Nassau Beach (IRE)** 2-9-3 0 DavidAllan 1 39
(T D Easterby) *lengthy: scope: bit bkwd: sn w ldrs: drvn over 3f out: lost pl 2f out* 20/1

10 *1* **Mill Pond** 2-8-7 0 JoeFanning 6 26
(M Johnston) *w'like: neat: bit bkwd: mid-div: outpcd over 2f out: sn lost pl* 11/1

11 *2 1/2* **Keeptheboatafloat (USA)** 2-9-0 0 AndrewElliott 12 25
(K R Burke) *cmpt: dwlt: in rr: swtchd to r far side sn after s: hdwy over 3f out: lost pl 2f out* 50/1

0 12 *1 1/4* **Luckette**[15] 2134 2-8-4 0 TWilliams 9 11
(M Brittain) *chsd ldrs: wknd 2f out* 66/1

0 13 *1/2* **Look For Value**[21] 1967 2-8-5 0 KimTinkler 10 11
(N Tinkler) *leggy: sn outpcd and in rr* 66/1

1m 14.4s (2.50) **Going Correction** +0.25s/f (Good) **13** Ran SP% **125.2**
Speed ratings (Par 95): **93,89,86,85,84 82,78,75,71,70 67,65,64**
CSF £53.92 TOTE £29.60: £6.70, £1.10, £4.50; EX 90.00.
Owner The Untouchable Partnership **Bred** Roundhill Stud & Gleadhill House Stud Ltd **Trained** Sessay, N Yorks

FOCUS
This looks pretty strong form for a maiden auction, albeit at a top track. The runner-up ran to his debut form and there is more to come from the winner.

NOTEBOOK
Chicago Cop(IRE), a medium-sized newcomer, is a good walker. He missed a beat at the start but won going right away in the end and can go on to better things. (op 16-1)
Reve De Soleil(FR), who looked really well, came home in a straight line this time but in the end the winner proved much too good. (tchd 11-8 and 2-1)
Premier Krug(IRE), having her fourth start and back on turf, seemed to show vastly improved form.
The Kilkenny Kat(IRE), who blew his chance at the start when gambled on first time, shaped a lot better and will improve again. (op 16-1)
Richo, having his third start, found himself rather marooned towards the stands' side. He stuck on in good style at the finish and will be interesting in nursery company. (tchd 25-1)
Cutting Comments, very keen, was taken quietly to post. Encountering totally different ground and up a furlong, he dropped out in disappointing fashion. (op 5-1)
Luckette did not look great in her coat. (op 50-1)
Look For Value was another who did not look great in her coat.

2585 BOLLINGER CHAMPAGNE CHALLENGE SERIES FOR GENTLEMAN AMATEUR RIDERS (H'CAP) 1m 4f

5:05 (5:06) (Class 4) (0-80,80) 4-Y-0+ £6,246 (£1,937; £968; £484) Stalls Centre

Form RPR

5603 1 **Crossbow Creek**[20] 1799 10-11-10 **80** MrMRimell 6 88
(M G Rimell) *trckd ldrs: effrt over 2f out: styd on u.p on ins to ld fnl 75yds* 10/1

6032 2 *1 1/2* **Bazart**[20] 2006 6-11-2 **77** MrPCollington(5) 3 83
(K R Burke) *trckd ldr: led after 2f: hdd ins fnl 75yds: no ex* 13/2[2]

1-13 3 *1/2* **Harry The Hawk**[34] 1620 4-11-0 **70** MrSWalker 2 75
(T D Walford) *t.k.h: stdd and hld up after 2f: hdwy over 6f out: wnt 2nd over 3f out: chal over 1f out: no ex wl ins fnl f* 7/4[1]

0-24 4 *shd* **Natural Action**[14] 2153 4-10-11 **72** (p) MrJoshuaMoore(5) 10 77+
(W Jarvis) *hld up in rr: hdwy on ins and nt clr run over 2f out: swtchd rt: hdwy and nt clr run over 1f out: plld wd: styd on wl ins fnl f* 7/1[3]

-233 5 *1/2* **Collette's Choice**[16] 2107 5-10-3 **66** oh1 (p) MrBenHamilton(7) 7 70
(R A Fahey) *lw: jnd ldrs after 3f: outpcd over 2f out: styd on fnl f* 8/1

3-34 6 *2* **Sporting Gesture**[16] 2107 11-10-9 **70** MrOGreenall(5) 9 71
(M W Easterby) *trckd ldrs: one pce fnl 2f* 9/1

00-0 7 *hd* **Tcherina (IRE)**[16] 2107 6-10-8 **69** MrCCollins(5) 11 70
(T D Easterby) *hld up in rr: hdwy on wd outside 4f out: one pce fnl 2f* 9/1

6024 8 *1/2* **Kames Park (IRE)**[11] 2249 6-10-6 **69** MrCAHarris(7) 8 69
(R C Guest) *s.v.s: hdwy to chse ldrs over 2f out: fdd fnl f* 28/1

204/ 9 *14* **Restart (IRE)**[948] 3283 7-10-5 **66** oh16 JPFeatherstone(5) 5 44
(Lucinda Featherstone) *chsd ldrs: lost pl over 4f out: sn bhd* 33/1

1-63 10 *1 1/2* **Cheshire Prince**[14] 2155 4-10-12 **71** MrBenBrisbourne(3) 4 46
(W M Brisbourne) *hld up towards rr: hdwy 4f out: wknd over 1f out* 12/1

2-00 **11** 2 **Kalasam**30 1732 4-10-7 70 .... MrJakeGreenall(7) 1 42
(M W Easterby) *t.k.h: led 2f: rdn and wknd over 2f out* **14/1**

2m 36.95s (3.75) **Going Correction** +0.10s/f (Good) **11** Ran SP% **123.1**
Speed ratings (Par 105): **91,90,89,89,89 87,87,87,78,77 75**
CSF £77.21 CT £171.77 TOTE £16.50: £4.20, £2.10, £1.60; EX 85.70.
Owner Mark Rimell **Bred** Mrs M R T Rimell **Trained** Leafield, Oxon

FOCUS
A strong pace yet half-a-dozen almost upsides inside the final furlong. The form looks rock solid at this level with the first five close to their pre-race marks.
T/Jkpt: Not won. T/Plt: £16.20 to a £1 stake. Pool: £93,829.25. 4,208.57 winning tickets. T/Qpdt: £9.60 to a £1 stake. Pool: £4,164.00. 319.40 winning tickets. WG

2586 - 2590a (Foreign Racing) - See Raceform Interactive

2185

DONCASTER (L-H)

Saturday, May 31

OFFICIAL GOING: Good (good to firm in places on straight course; 8.3)
Wind: Virtually nil Weather: Cloudy and warm, suny periods

2591 SAN ROSSORE H'CAP 1m 4f
2:00 (2:02) (Class 4) (0-85,85) 4-Y-0+ **£4,857** (£1,445; £722; £360) **Stalls** Low

Form RPR

2-43 **1** **Coyote Creek**15 2153 4-8-9 76 .... (v1) KShea 8 92
(E F Vaughan) *trckd ldng pair: hdwy to ld over 2f out: rdn clr appr fnl f: r.o wl* **15/2**

6-54 **2** 6 **Demolition**15 2155 4-8-5 72 .... KerrinMcEvoy 7 78
(N Wilson) *hld up towards rr: swtchd outside and hdwy 3f out: rdn to chse wnr and edgd lft appr fnl f: sn no imp* **7/1**3

6410 **3** nk **Red Wine**17 2107 9-8-2 76 .... StacyRenwick(7) 6 82
(A J McCabe) *hld up in rr: stdy hdwy on wd outside over 3f out: rdn to chse ldrs over 1f out: kpt on ins fnl f* **11/1**

036- **4** 1 1/4 **Bollin Felix**241 5911 4-8-6 76 .... (b) DuranFentiman(3) 1 80+
(T D Easterby) *hld up towards rr: hdwy over 3f out: rdn 2f out: styd on ins fnl f: nrst fin* **20/1**

0-02 **5** hd **Ascalon**15 2152 4-9-1 82 .... PaulEddery 10 85
(Pat Eddery) *chsd ldr: rdn along 5f out: led over 3f out: hdd over 2f out: sn drvn and grad wknd* **7/2**1

6-06 **6** 1/2 **Nur Tau (IRE)**15 2152 4-8-13 80 .... MartinDwyer 4 82
(H Morrison) *hld up and bhd: hdwy 3f out: sn rdn along and kpt on same pce fnl 2f* **9/2**2

252- **7** 1/2 **Duty Free (IRE)**240 5955 4-9-4 85 .... PaulMulrennan 3 87
(C R Egerton) *hld up in tch: stdy hdwy 4f out: swtchd ins and effrt over 2f out: sn rdn and ch tl drvn and wknd ent fnl f* **7/2**1

-310 **8** 3 **Boz**18 2076 4-9-2 83 .... SebSanders 5 80
(L M Cumani) *in tch: hdwy 4f out: rdn along 3f out: wknd over 1f out* **8/1**

0-00 **9** 12 **Instructor**13 2220 7-8-5 72 .... RoystonFfrench 9 50
(C A Mulhall) *prom: rdn along over 3f out: wknd over 2f out* **50/1**

15-5 **10** 34 **Princely Ted (IRE)**87 802 7-8-4 71 oh15 .... TWilliams 2 —
(W Clay) *led: rdn along over 4f out: hdd over 3f out and wknd qckly: sn bhd* **66/1**

2m 34.05s (-1.05) **Going Correction** -0.075s/f (Good) **10** Ran SP% **114.6**
Speed ratings (Par 105): **100,96,95,94,94 94,94,92,84,61**
CSF £57.03 CT £575.74 TOTE £8.70: £3.00, £1.80, £2.60; EX 33.50 Trifecta £321.30 Pool: £719.71, 1.59 winning units.
Owner Gibson, Goddard, Hamer & Hawkes **Bred** Lord Halifax **Trained** Newmarket, Suffolk
■ A first win in Britain for South African champion Kevin Shea.
■ Stewards' Enquiry : Paul Eddery one-day ban: careless riding (Jun 14)

FOCUS
A reasonable handicap, but they went a modest pace and there was only one horse in it throughout the last furlong. The form has been taken at face value and looks sound.

2592 EUROPEAN BREEDERS' FUND MAIDEN STKS 6f
2:35 (2:36) (Class 5) 2-Y-0 **£3,561** (£1,059; £529; £264) **Stalls** High

Form RPR

1 **Himalya (IRE)** 2-9-3 0 .... SebSanders 2 89+
(J Noseda) *sn prom: hdwy to ld over 2f out: rdn and edgd rt over 1f out: rn green ins fnl f: styd on* **4/6**1

2 **2** 3/4 **Seaway**21 1987 2-9-3 0 .... KerrinMcEvoy 7 84+
(J H M Gosden) *prom: effrt to chse wnr 2f out: sn rdn and kpt on ins fnl f* **15/8**2

6 **3** 5 **Ay Tay Tate (IRE)**16 2134 2-9-3 0 .... PatrickMathers 5 69
(I W McInnes) *midfield: hdwy 2f out: sn rdn and styd on wl fnl f: nrst fin* **100/1**

4 nse **Dr Smart (IRE)** 2-9-3 0 .... RoystonFfrench 8 69+
(B Smart) *in tch: hdwy to chse ldrs 2f out: sn rdn and kpt on ins fnl f* **16/1**

5 3/4 **Auld Arty (FR)** 2-9-3 0 .... JohnEgan 4 67+
(T G Mills) *chsd ldrs: rdn along and sltly outpcd 2f out: kpt on wl u.p ins fnl f* **50/1**

6 2 1/2 **Mohanad (IRE)** 2-9-0 0 .... LukeMorris(3) 11 62+
(M R Channon) *midfield: hdwy over 2f out: rdn to chse ldrs whn nt clr run and swtchd rt over 1f out: kpt on ins fnl f* **14/1**3

7 nk **Fastnet Storm (IRE)** 2-9-0 0 .... DNolan(3) 15 60+
(T P Tate) *s.i.s and bhd: hdwy over 2f out: swtchd lft over 1f out and styd on wl fnl f: nrst fin* **100/1**

8 hd **Thunderball** 2-9-3 0 .... AndrewElliott 10 58
(A J McCabe) *in tch: rdn along 2f out: kpt on same pce* **100/1**

0 **9** nk **Port Ronan (USA)**14 2186 2-9-0 0 .... MarkLawson(3) 14 57
(J S Wainwright) *chsd ldrs: rdn along 2f out: grad wknd* **200/1**

2300 **10** 3 **Eilean Eeve**13 2217 2-8-12 0 .... TWilliams 16 43
(A J McCabe) *in tch: rdn along over 2f out: sn wknd* **80/1**

11 nse **Threestepstoheaven** 2-9-3 0 .... PaulEddery 6 48
(B W Hills) *midfield: hdwy to chse ldrs 2f out: sn rdn and wknd over 1f out* **40/1**

12 nse **Dark Oasis** 2-8-12 0 .... NeilBrown(5) 12 47
(K A Ryan) *a towards rr* **100/1**

13 3/4 **Takaatuf (IRE)** 2-9-3 0 .... MartinDwyer 1 45+
(M Johnston) *chsd ldrs on wd outside: rdn along over 2f out and sn wknd* **33/1**

14 1 **Indian Fiesta (IRE)** 2-9-3 0 .... LeeEnstone 9 42
(B G Powell) *s.i.s: a in rr* **150/1**

15 2 1/2 **Tartan Turban (IRE)** 2-9-3 0 .... CRajendra 3 35
(R Hannon) *led: rdn along and hdd over 2f out: sn drvn and wknd* **50/1**

16 1 1/2 **Rawaaj** 2-9-3 0 .... KShea 13 30+
(Sir Michael Stoute) *a towards rr* **20/1**

1m 13.61s (0.01) **Going Correction** -0.075s/f (Good) **16** Ran SP% **127.7**
Speed ratings (Par 93): **96,95,88,88,87 83,83,83,82,78 78,78,77,76,73 71**
CSF £2.02 TOTE £1.90: £1.10, £1.10, £10.90; EX 2.90 Trifecta £66.00 Pool: £599.88, 6.45 winning units.
Owner Ms Gillian Khosla **Bred** Lodge Park Stud **Trained** Newmarket, Suffolk

FOCUS
Not many could be seriously considered in this and the pair who dominated the market also dominated the race, but they do look above-average types whilst there were also some eye-catching performances in behind. The runner-up sets the standard and the form looks sensible with the first two clear.

NOTEBOOK
Himalya(IRE) ◆, a 210,000gns colt out of the useful miler Lady Miletrian, was backed as though defeat was out of the question on this debut. He duly scored, but he did see plenty of daylight down the wide outside and also proved as green as grass inside the last furlong, so this performance was probably even better than it looked. He is likely to progress a good deal from this and may now head for the Coventry Stakes, but he should eventually stay further. (op 5-6 tchd evens in a place)
Seaway ◆, who already has form on the board, had every chance and pulled miles clear of the main body of the field but came up against a very nice prospect. That will not always be the case and he should soon go one better. (op 9-4 tchd 5-2)
Ay Tay Tate(IRE) ◆, who did offer some encouragement when 100-1 for a York maiden on his debut in a contest that has already produced a couple of winners, started that price again here despite the promise and he again caught the eye with the way he stayed on to snatch third, albeit adrift of a couple of useful propects. Bred to stay much further, he should have no problem winning a maiden.
Dr Smart(IRE) ◆, a 34,000gns half-brother to a winning juvenile, did not go unbacked and the way he stayed on late on this racecourse debut suggests he has a future. (op 25-1)
Auld Arty(FR) ◆, a £52,000 two-year-old and a half-brother to a couple of winners at up to 1m4f, was doing some good late work up the stands' rail and is likely to make his mark over further in due course. (tchd 40-1)
Mohanad(IRE), a 70,000gns colt out of a half-sister to the high-class Idris, would never have got close to the front pair but he would not have been beaten so far had he not run into traffic problems passing the furlong pole. He can be expected to come on for this. (op 8-1)
Port Ronan(USA), last on his debut here a fortnight earlier, ended up well beaten once again but he again showed speed for a long way and he could well eventually find a small race in the north once his sights are lowered. (op 125-1)

2593 MOSS PROPERTIES H'CAP 1m 2f 60y
3:10 (3:10) (Class 3) (0-95,92) 4-Y-0+ **£9,714** (£2,890; £1,444; £721) **Stalls** Low

Form RPR

13-1 **1** **Ezdiyaad (IRE)**42 1473 4-9-3 91 .... MartinDwyer 7 105+
(M P Tregoning) *prom: hdwy and cl up over 3f out: led wl over 2f out: rdn and wandered bdly over 1f out and ins fnl f: drvn out* **1/1**1

066- **2** 2 1/2 **Nanton (USA)**173 6359 6-8-8 82 .... RoystonFfrench 6 91
(J S Goldie) *trckd ldrs: hdwy 4f out: rdn along over 2f out: drvn to chse wnr over 1f out: kpt on ins fnl f* **25/1**

30-0 **3** 3 1/2 **Encircled**15 2152 4-8-6 80 .... KerrinMcEvoy 3 82
(D Haydn Jones) *hld up in rr: gd hdwy on inner over 3f out: rdn and ev ch over 2f out: drvn and one pce appr fnl f* **7/1**3

6-0 **4** 4 1/2 **Lepido (ITY)**15 2168 4-9-2 90 .... SebSanders 5 83
(L M Cumani) *hld up: hdwy 4f out: rdn along 3f out: no imp fnl 2f* **14/1**

4-35 **5** 1 3/4 **Bid For Glory**28 1812 4-9-4 92 .... KShea 1 82
(H J Collingridge) *chsd ldr: hdwy and cl up over 4f out: rdn along 3f out: drvn over 2f out and sn wknd* **3/1**2

4100 **6** 3 1/2 **Sgt Schultz (IRE)**15 2168 5-8-9 86 .... LukeMorris(3) 4 69
(J S Moore) *hld up in rr: sme hdwy on outer 3f out: sn rdn and n.d* **11/1**

1123 **7** nk **Xpres Maite**7 2406 5-8-6 80 .... (v) PaulEddery 2 62
(S R Bowring) *led and clr: jnd 4f out and sn rdn along: hdd wl over 2f out and sn wknd* **14/1**

2m 8.90s (-2.30) **Going Correction** -0.075s/f (Good) **7** Ran SP% **113.0**
Speed ratings (Par 107): **106,104,101,97,96 93,93**
CSF £29.58 CT £121.40 TOTE £1.90: £1.30, £4.80; EX 27.80 Trifecta £276.60 Pool: £689.75, 1.77 winning units.
Owner Hamdan Al Maktoum **Bred** Shadwell Estate Co Ltd **Trained** Lambourn, Berks
■ Suits Me (9/1) w/d after rider John Egan could not do the weight (8-6). Deduct 10p in the £ under rule 4. New market formed.

FOCUS
A fair handicap and although the early pace was not strong, things eventually quickened up and they finished well spread out. The form looks solid enough rated through the runner-up.

NOTEBOOK
Ezdiyaad(IRE) ◆, raised a whopping 9lb for his Newbury win and on quicker ground here, moved to the front smoothly enough halfway up the home straight, but once there he started to hang about though he was stretching away again at the line. He gives the impression there is still more to come from him and he also looks well worth another try over further. A trip to Royal Ascot for the Duke Of Edinburgh Handicap appears to be on the cards. (old market op 7-4 tchd 15-8 in places, new market op 6-4 tchd 10-11)
Nanton(USA) ◆, not seen since finishing unplaced on his hurdling debut in December, was making his debut for the yard and he looked a brief threat to the winner a furlong out, but only because his rival was idling. This was still a decent enough return though and the stable can be expected to find an opportunity for him especially as he is now back on his last winning mark. (old market op 16-1 new market op 12-1)
Encircled, all the better for her Newbury return, put in a strong effort on the inside rail halfway up the home straight but was making no impression on the front pair throughout the last furlong. Still 9lb higher than for her last win, she needs to drop a little bit more. (old market op 15-2 new market op 13-2 tchd 9-1)
Lepido(ITY) was returning just 15 days after reappearing from a year off at York last month so this may have come soon enough. He was not disgraced, but is still to reproduce the sort of form he was showing in Italy. (old market op 9-1 new market op 8-1)
Bid For Glory, back over a more suitable trip, was down 5lb and he had every chance having been up there all the way, but he again did not get home. (old market op 9-2 new market op 7-2)
Sgt Schultz(IRE) saw plenty of daylight on the outside and a brief effort in the home straight came to little. He is still to win on turf. (old market op 17-2 new market op 7-1)
Xpres Maite, better known as a sand performer though he has won on grass, was off a 15lb higher mark than when last on turf. He had questions marks against his stamina over this trip though, and after making much of the running he eventually dropped right out. (old market op 9-1 new market op 8-1)

2594 "ROVERS ARE UP!" CLASSIFIED STKS 6f
3:40 (3:42) (Class 2) 3-Y-0 **£11,656** (£3,468; £1,733; £865) **Stalls** High

Form RPR

4-52 **1** **Lesson In Humility (IRE)**15 2171 3-8-7 92 .... AndrewElliott 4 97
(K R Burke) *prom: hdwy to ld over 2f out: rdn and hdd briefly ins fnl f: sn led again and drvn out* **8/1**

1055 **2** *1 3/4* **Vhujon (IRE)**[7] 2390 3-8-10 91.......................... KShea 3 94
(P D Evans) *hld up in rr: swtchd lft and gd hdwy over 2f out: rdn to ld briefly ins fnl f: sn hdd and kpt on* **16/1**

1-1 **3** *1 3/4* **Wingbeat (USA)**[15] 2162 3-8-10 94.......................... KerrinMcEvoy 1 88+
(Saeed Bin Suroor) *stdd s and sn swtchd rt: hld up in rr: pushed along and swtchd lft 2f out: rdn and styng on whn nt clr run over 1f out: kpt on ins fnl f* **5/4**[1]

01 **4** *hd* **Light Hearted**[18] 2067 3-8-7 89.......................... MartinDwyer 8 85
(J Noseda) *trckd ldrs: effrt over 2f out: sn rdn and kpt on same pce ent fnl f* **10/3**[2]

6044 **5** *2 1/4* **Style Award**[15] 2171 3-8-7 84.......................... PatrickMathers 2 78
(W J H Ratcliffe) *chsd ldrs: rdn along over 2f out: grad wknd* **66/1**

3-05 **6** *1* **Highland Daughter (IRE)**[31] 1718 3-8-8 94 ow1.......... SebSanders 5 75
(C G Cox) *chsd ldrs: rdn along over 2f out: sn btn* **14/1**

6-50 **7** *6* **Dubai Dynamo**[17] 2104 3-8-10 95..........................(b[1]) JohnEgan 7 58
(P F I Cole) *led: rdn along and hdd over 2f out: sn drvn and wknd* **7/2**[3]

00-0 **8** *3/4* **Loch Jipp (USA)**[32] 1698 3-8-7 95.......................... RoystonFfrench 6 53
(J S Wainwright) *cl up: rdn along over 2f out and sn wknd* **25/1**

1m 12.0s (-1.60) **Going Correction** -0.075s/f (Good) **8** Ran SP% **118.7**
Speed ratings (Par 105): **107,104,102,102,99 97,89,88**
CSF £126.32 TOTE £10.20: £2.00, £4.30, £1.10; EX 123.80 TRIFECTA Not won..
Owner M Nelmes-Crocker **Bred** Kevin Quinn **Trained** Middleham Moor, N Yorks

FOCUS
A decent three-year-old sprint handicap and although the favourite got into a bit of trouble the form looks solid rated around the first two.

NOTEBOOK
Lesson In Humility(IRE) ◆ proved well suited by this return to 6f as she needed every yard of it in order to regain the advantage from Vhujon after being headed. She looks a progressive young sprinter and a race like the William Hill Trophy at York in a couple of weeks could be a realistic target.
Vhujon(IRE), over seven lengths behind Wingbeat at Newbury last month, had a 9lb pull even though he was 3lb badly with him on these terms. Probably helped by this better ground, he looked the winner when taking it up a furlong from home, but he could never stamp his authority on the contest and that gave the filly another bite at the cherry. He lacks scope, but does look capable of winning off this lower mark provided he is not shoved up again for this. (op 25-1 tchd 14-1)
Wingbeat(USA) was unbeaten in two starts coming into this, but this would have been the quickest ground he has raced on. Switched off out the back against the stands' rail, he did have to be manoeuvred left in order to find daylight and did not get the best of runs, but he did not exactly take off once in the clear and it is hard to argue that he would have won with a clear passage. (op Evens tchd 6-4)
Light Hearted, taking a big step up in class after bolting up at odds-on in a Brighton maiden, had every chance but she probably found this too demanding at this stage of her career. (op 3-1 tchd 5-2 and 7-2)
Style Award, worst in at the weights and with plenty to find with Lesson In Humility on York running, ran as well as could be expected under the circumstances but is yet to win beyond the minimum. (op 50-1)
Highland Daughter(IRE), who has been plying her trade in Pattern company since making a winning racecourse debut, probably needs easier ground but even so she is looking a hard filly to place. (tchd 16-1)
Dubai Dynamo, who has been racing over 7f since beating Vhujon in the Redcar Two-Year-Old Trophy last October, almost certainly did too much too soon in the first-time blinkers. Official explanation: jockey said colt was unsuited by the good to firm ground (op 17-2 tchd 9-1)

2595 DONCASTER FREE PRESS BUSINESS MONTHLY H'CAP 7f
4:15 (4:18) (Class 2) (0-100,100) 4-Y-O+
£15,577 (£4,665; £2,332; £1,167; £582; £292) **Stalls** High

Form RPR
-050 **1** **Dhaular Dhar (IRE)**[22] 1942 6-8-1 90.......................... DeanHeslop[(7)] 4 101
(J S Goldie) *t.k.h: in tch: hdwy over 2f out and sn rdn along: styd on u.p to ld ins fnl f* **16/1**

0403 **2** *3/4* **Hinton Admiral**[15] 2172 4-8-5 94.......................... FrederikTylicki[(7)] 10 103
(R A Fahey) *trckd ldr: led over 2f out: rdn over 1f out: drvn and hdd ins fnl f: kpt on* **10/1**

240- **3** *nse* **Artimino**[225] 6301 4-9-1 97.......................... MartinDwyer 2 106+
(J R Fanshawe) *wnt lft s: trckd ldrs: effrt to chse ldr over 1f out: sn rdn and ev ch ins fnl f tl no ex fnl 100yds* **11/2**[2]

00-0 **4** *1 1/2* **Flipando (IRE)**[28] 1816 7-8-7 94.......................... NeilBrown[(5)] 14 99+
(T D Barron) *hld up towards rr: gd hdwy over 2f out: rdn over 1f out: fin wl* **20/1**

00-0 **5** *3* **Giganticus (USA)**[21] 1982 5-9-4 100.......................... KShea 3 97
(B W Hills) *hmpd s and towards rr: gd hdwy on outer over 2f out: sn rdn and kpt on ins fnl f: nrst fin* **9/1**

20-0 **6** *1/2* **Sir Xaar (IRE)**[15] 2172 5-8-8 90..........................(b) RoystonFfrench 7 85
(B Smart) *hld up: hdwy over 2f out: styd on ins fnl f: nrst fin* **20/1**

0-62 **7** *nk* **Danehillsundance (IRE)**[9] 2334 4-8-8 90.......................... KerrinMcEvoy 8 85
(S Parr) *chsd ldrs: rdn 2f out: sn drvn and one pce* **9/2**[1]

54-4 **8** *2 1/4* **Burning Incense (IRE)**[63] 1071 5-8-8 90.......................... PhillipMakin 16 78+
(M Dods) *in rr tl sme late hdwy* **6/1**[3]

-200 **9** *3/4* **Fishforcompliments**[21] 1982 4-8-8 97..........................(v[1]) BMcHugh[(7)] 9 83
(R A Fahey) *chsd ldrs: rdn over 2f out: sn wknd* **6/1**[3]

6040 **10** *nk* **Vortex**[77] 904 9-9-4 100..........................(t) JohnEgan 17 86
(Miss Gay Kelleway) *a in midfield* **25/1**

150- **11** *3 1/4* **Game Lad**[308] 3941 6-8-2 87.......................... DuranFentiman[(3)] 11 64
(T D Easterby) *a towards rr* **33/1**

1060 **12** *3/4* **Bazroy (IRE)**[77] 904 4-8-7 96..........................(b) RichardEvans[(3)] 15 71
(P D Evans) *a towards rr* **33/1**

0301 **13** *28* **Plum Pudding (IRE)**[8] 2371 5-8-11 98..........................(p) HaddenFrost[(5)] 1 —
(R Hannon) *led: rdn along and hdd over 2f out: sn wknd* **6/1**[3]

0565 **14** *11* **Hoh Wotanite**[9] 2334 5-7-11 86 oh4..........................(v) PatrickDonaghy[(7)] 12 —
(R Hollinshead) *stmbld and almost uns rdr stalls: a bhd* **33/1**

1m 24.09s (-2.21) **Going Correction** -0.075s/f (Good) **14** Ran SP% **123.6**
Speed ratings (Par 109): **109,108,108,106,102 102,102,99,98,98 94,93,61,49**
CSF £156.83 CT £1030.47 TOTE £16.40: £3.10, £3.40, £2.40; EX 191.40 TRIFECTA Not won..
Owner Middleham Park Racing LVIII **Bred** Gainsborough Stud Management Ltd **Trained** Uplawmoor, E Renfrews

FOCUS
A competitive handicap and unlike in the earlier races the field came down the centre of the track. It paid to race handily and the front four pulled clear, so the form looks solid and should work out.

NOTEBOOK
Dhaular Dhar(IRE) had not been in much form for some time now, but he was 4lb lower than for his last win just over a year ago. Never far away, he was produced with precision timing to foil the gamble and gain his first victory on a straight track. Now that he has hit form, he may be able to win again. (op 14-1)
Hinton Admiral, much more feasibly handicapped now, was back up to the trip over which he gained his last win. The substantial support for him on the market suggested he was expected to run a big race under his young rider and he duly did so having been up with the pace throughout. He looked like winning a furlong out and it must have been heartbreaking for his supporters to see him get nailed. Obviously he is capable of winning off this sort of mark, but the cat is rather out of the bag now. (op 25-1)
Artimino ◆, returning from seven months off and without his usual tongue-tie, was tucked in behind the leaders for most of the journey and seemed to be travelling best of all a furlong out, but once switched right he did not find quite as much as had looked likely. Sure to be all the better for this, he won second time out in his first two seasons so is obviously worth watching out for next time. (op 6-1 tchd 7-1)
Flipando(IRE) ◆, racing over a shorter trip than usual, stepped up from his reappearance effort and was doing all his best work late. Now 2lb lower than when winning last season's Zetland Gold Cup, he is well worth looking out for back up in trip.
Giganticus(USA) ◆ looked dangerous when produced with his effort towards the far side of the track and was close enough a furlong out before fading. He may well have still just needed this and he should be cherry-ripe now. (op 17-2 tchd 8-1 and 10-1)
Danehillsundance(IRE), whose last win came over course and distance last September off a 1lb lower mark, was close enough for a long way but found nothing at all off the bridle and this was disappointing. (op 4-1 tchd 7-2)
Vortex Official explanation: jockey said gelding lost its action
Plum Pudding(IRE), raised 8lb for his Newmarket win, managed to get the lead but folded tamely once the runner-up headed him and showed again that he is just not the same horse away from the Rowley Mile. Official explanation: vet said gelding finished distressed (op 7-1 tchd 15-2)
Hoh Wotanite Official explanation: jockey said horse stumbled badly leaving stalls

2596 BLUEBELL WOOD GOLDEN MILE CHALLENGE H'CAP 5f
4:50 (4:52) (Class 5) (0-75,75) 4-Y-O+ **£3,238** (£963; £481; £240) **Stalls** High

Form RPR
00-4 **1** **Total Impact**[66] 1023 5-9-4 75.......................... KerrinMcEvoy 13 87+
(R A Fahey) *hld up towards rr: gd hdwy on stands' rail 2f out: rdn to ld ent fnl f: kpt on* **5/1**[2]

5442 **2** *3/4* **Comptonspirit**[8] 2356 4-8-7 64.......................... JohnEgan 7 73
(B P J Baugh) *a cl up: rdn and ev ch over 1f out: drvn and kpt on ins fnl f* **12/1**

5-05 **3** *1 3/4* **Niteowl Lad (IRE)**[11] 2270 6-8-1 61 oh4..........................(p) AndrewMullen[(3)] 9 64
(J Balding) *hld up: hdwy 2f out: sn rdn and styd on wl fnl f: nrst fin* **12/1**

0001 **4** *hd* **Mandurah (IRE)**[8] 2356 4-8-4 68.......................... MarkCoumbe[(7)] 4 70+
(D Nicholls) *cl up: led 1/2-way: rdn and hdd ent fnl f: edgd lft and one pce: eased and lost 3rd cl home* **15/2**

6125 **5** *3/4* **Rothesay Dancer**[1] 2583 5-8-6 68.......................... KellyHarrison[(5)] 8 68
(J S Goldie) *in tch: rdn 2f out: kpt on ins fnl f* **8/1**

-131 **6** *1 1/4* **Baybshambles (IRE)**[11] 2270 4-8-9 66.......................... RoystonFfrench 2 61+
(R E Barr) *in tch: hdwy on outer 2f out: sn rdn and styng on whn carried sltly lft and no imp ins fnl f* **4/1**[1]

-006 **7** *nk* **Windjammer**[21] 2005 4-8-2 62.......................... DuranFentiman[(3)] 10 56
(T D Easterby) *dwlt: sn in tch: effrt and hdwy 2f out: sn rdn and no imp appr fnl f* **6/1**[3]

0023 **8** *3/4* **Hawaii Prince**[15] 2145 4-8-4 61.......................... AndrewElliott 12 52
(S T Mason) *chsd ldrs: rdn along over 2f out and grad wknd appr fnl f* **14/1**

0-00 **9** *1* **Welcome Approach**[11] 2270 5-8-6 63.......................... MartinDwyer 11 51
(J R Weymes) *in tch: rdn along over 2f out and sn wknd* **16/1**

0066 **10** *1* **No Time (IRE)**[11] 2270 8-7-11 61 oh5.......................... MCGeran[(3)] 3 45
(A J McCabe) *dwlt and sltly hmpd s: a in rr* **20/1**

500 **11** *2 1/4* **Supreme Speedster**[1] 2583 4-8-0 64 oh6 ow3.......... RossAtkinson[(7)] 6 40
(M Brittain) *chsd ldrs: rdn along 1/2-way: sn wknd* **50/1**

3260 **12** *1 1/4* **Guto**[5] 2444 5-8-6 70.......................... PatrickDonaghy[(7)] 5 42
(W J H Ratcliffe) *led: rdn along and hdd 1/2-way: sn drvn and wknd wl over 1f out* **33/1**

5114 **13** *3/4* **Sands Crooner (IRE)**[57] 1195 5-8-5 67..........................(v) SCreighton[(5)] 1 36
(J G Given) *a in rr* **14/1**

59.13 secs (-1.37) **Going Correction** -0.075s/f (Good) **13** Ran SP% **118.1**
Speed ratings (Par 103): **107,105,103,102,101 99,99,97,96,94 91,89,87**
CSF £61.85 CT £710.00 TOTE £5.70: £2.70, £3.20, £3.60; EX 68.20 TRIFECTA Not won..
Owner R A Fahey **Bred** C A Cyzer **Trained** Musley Bank, N Yorks
■ Stewards' Enquiry : Mark Coumbe 10-day ban: failed to ride out for third place (June 14-23)

FOCUS
A decent sprint for the grade and no hanging about with a contested lead. The field raced centre to stands' side early, but with a few hanging late on they covered almost the width of the track at the line. The form looks solid rated around the placed horses.

2597 NORTHERN RACING COLLEGE APPRENTICE H'CAP 1m (S)
5:25 (5:27) (Class 6) (0-60,60) 4-Y-O+ **£2,914** (£867; £433; £216) **Stalls** High

Form RPR
425 **1** **Shosolosa (IRE)**[30] 1747 6-8-4 50.......................... StacyRenwick[(5)] 12 60
(R C Guest) *towards rr: hdwy over 2f out: sn rdn and styd on strly to ld ins fnl f: kpt on wl* **22/1**

3-52 **2** *1* **Ours (IRE)**[11] 2274 5-9-5 60.......................... KellyHarrison 2 68
(John A Harris) *dwlt and bhd: stdy hdwy on wd outside 3f out: swtchd rt and rdn over 1f out: ev ch ent fnl f: sn drvn and no ex fnl 100yds* **11/2**[1]

2-02 **3** *1 1/4* **Brouhaha**[21] 2003 4-8-9 55.......................... SimonPearce[(5)] 4 60+
(B J McMath) *chsd ldrs: hdwy on outer over 2f out: rdn to ld wl over 1f out: drvn and hdd ins fnl f: one pce* **13/2**[2]

4512 **4** *1* **Ermine Grey**[4] 2477 7-9-0 58.......................... MarkCoumbe[(3)] 15 61
(A W Carroll) *bhd and rdn along towards stands' rail: hdwy over 2f out: styd on wl u.p appr fnl f: nrst fin* **13/2**[2]

6000 **5** *shd* **General Feeling (IRE)**[11] 2274 7-7-7 53.......................... DeclanCannon[(5)] 9 55
(S T Mason) *s.i.s and bhd: gd hdwy over 2f out: rdn wl over 1f out: styd on ins fnl f: nrst fin* **50/1**

-000 **6** *3 1/4* **Hollywood George**[22] 1966 4-9-0 55.......................... NicolPolli 1 50
(Miss M E Rowland) *chsd ldrs: hdwy to ld over 2f out: sn rdn and hdd wl over 1f out: one pce appr fnl f* **50/1**

00-6 **7** *1/2* **Distant Pleasure**[40] 1520 4-8-13 59.......................... JohnCavanagh[(5)] 19 53
(M Dods) *in tch towards stands' rail: hdwy over 2f out: sn rdn and styd on same pce appr fnl f* **16/1**

3413 **8** *1 1/4* **King Of Legend (IRE)**[96] 703 4-9-1 56..........................(p) NeilBrown 13 47
(A G Foster) *midfield: hdwy over 2f out: sn rdn and kpt on same pce appr fnl f* **11/1**

-660 **9** *1/2* **Thermidor (USA)**[48] 1345 5-8-13 59..........................(b[1]) BMcHugh[(5)] 7 49
(Lady Herries) *in tch: rdn along and lost pl over 2f out: styd on u.p appr fnl f: nvr a factor* **20/1**

0-01 **10** *2 1/2* **Wahoo Sam (USA)**[21] 2003 8-9-2 60.......................... RichardEvans[(3)] 3 44
(P D Evans) *led: rdn 3f out: hdd over 2f out and sn wknd* **8/1**[3]

5540 **11** *1* **Film Queen (IRE)**[23] 1938 4-8-8 52.......................... KylieManser[(3)] 6 34
(B G Powell) *s.i.s: a in rr* **33/1**

0-02 **12** ¾ **Grand Diamond (IRE)**^{11} [2285] 4-9-2 **60**..................(p) GaryBartley$^{(3)}$ 20 40
(J S Goldie) *cl up towards stands' rail: rdn along over 2f out and sn wknd* **12/1**

0F-0 **13** 1 ¼ **Uace Mac**^{11} [2270] 4-9-2 **57**.................................... SladeO'Hara 16 34
(N Bycroft) *chsd ldrs towards stands' side: rdn 2f out: sn edgd lft and wknd* **50/1**

0555 **14** *nk* **Parkview Love (USA)**^{32} [1708] 7-9-2 **60**................ MatthewDavies$^{(3)}$ 18 36
(J G Given) *chsd ldrs towards stands' rail: rdn along over 2f out and sn wknd* **16/1**

5242 **15** 1 ½ **Guildenstern (IRE)**^{29} [1780] 6-8-13 **57**.................... JPHamblett$^{(3)}$ 10 30
(P Howling) *chsd ldrs: rdn along 3f out: sn wknd* **8/1**^{3}

00-0 **16** *hd* **Borodinsky**^{27} [1826] 7-8-13 **57**................................ PatrickDonaghy$^{(3)}$ 14 30
(R E Barr) *bhd fr 1/2-way* **40/1**

0245 **17** 3 ½ **Silidan**^{21} [2009] 5-8-6 **52**.. AdamCarter$^{(5)}$ 17 17
(M Brittain) *prom towards stands' rail: rdn along over 2f out and sn wknd* **16/1**

20-0 **18** ½ **Kimono My House**^{11} [2274] 4-8-8 **52**............................ SCreighton$^{(3)}$ 8 15
(J G Given) *cl up: rdn along 1/2-way: sn wknd* **25/1**

040- **19** 1 **Triple Shadow**^{180} [7005] 4-8-12 **58**............................ DeanHeslop$^{(5)}$ 11 19
(M A Peill) *cl up: rdn along over 3f out: sn wknd* **20/1**

-066 **20** 3 ¼ **Umpa Loompa (IRE)**^{11} [2289] 4-9-2 **60**............................(b^{1}) AmyBaker$^{(3)}$ 5 14
(B J McMath) *cl up tl rdn along and wknd 1/2-way* **20/1**

1m 39.22s (-0.08) **Going Correction** -0.075s/f (Good) **20** Ran SP% **131.7**
Speed ratings (Par 101): **97,96,94,93,93 90,89,88,88,85 84,83,82,82,80 80,77,76,75,72**
CSF £134.07 CT £927.79 TOTE £31.50: £5.90, £2.00, £2.50, £2.00; EX 86.10 TRIFECTA Not won. Place 6: £209.88, Place 5: £43.95.
Owner Pinewood Racing Limited **Bred** David John Brown **Trained** Carburton, Notts

FOCUS
A moderate apprentice handicap, though given the size of the field it was extremely competitive and the form is rated around the runner-up and fourth, who are both solid markers. The field split into two early with the main group coming down the middle whilst six stayed towards the stands' side, but the two groups had converged by halfway.
T/Plt: £175.50 to a £1 stake. Pool: £71,092.18. 295.65 winning tickets. T/Qpdt: £59.40 to a £1 stake. Pool: £3,706.09. 46.10 winning tickets. JR

2560 GOODWOOD (R-H)
Saturday, May 31

OFFICIAL GOING: Soft
First 2f of 1m course out 5 metres, top bend out 3 metres.
Wind: Almost nil

2598 GOODWOOD.CO.UK STKS (H'CAP) 6f
2:30 (2:30) (Class 2) (0-100,99) 3-Y-0+
£12,462 (£3,732; £1,866; £934; £466; £234) **Stalls** Low

Form RPR

00-0 **1** **Viking Spirit**^{28} [1809] 6-9-10 **98**.. AdamKirby 7 105
(W R Swinburn) *trckd ldr: led wl over 1f out: pushed out* **5/2**^{1}

0244 **2** 2 **Pawan (IRE)**^{11} [2292] 8-8-6 **85** oh7....................(b) AnnStokell$^{(5)}$ 1 86
(Miss A Stokell) *chsd ldrs: rdn and kpt on to go 2nd ins fnl f* **20/1**

0600 **3** ½ **Hurricane Spirit (IRE)**^{35} [1619] 4-9-6 **94**.................... GeorgeBaker 4 93
(J R Best) *hld up: nt clr run over 1f out: r.o to go 3rd ins fnl f* **16/1**

3633 **4** *hd* **Ebraam (USA)**^{24} [1917] 5-9-4 **95**............................ TolleyDean$^{(3)}$ 6 94
(D Shaw) *t.k.h: trckd ldrs: rdn 2f out: kpt on one pce fnl f* **5/1**^{3}

1000 **5** *hd* **Conquest (IRE)**^{16} [2129] 4-9-11 **99**............................ RichardHughes 5 97+
(W J Haggas) *stdd s and hmpd sn after: held up twrds rr: nt clr rn and outpcd over 1f out: r.o ins fnl f* **4/1**^{2}

0-30 **6** *nse* **C'Mon You Irons (IRE)**^{7} [2410] 3-8-2 **85** oh3............ AdrianMcCarthy 2 81
(M R Hoad) *led tl rdn and hdd wl over 1f out: one pce after* **8/1**

40-0 **7** 7 **The Lord**^{85} [824] 8-8-11 **85**.. AlanDaly 8 61
(W G M Turner) *in tch tl rdn and wknd qckly ins fnl f* **33/1**

2-01 **8** 7 **Swift Princess (IRE)**^{30} [1755] 4-8-11 **85** oh1..........(v) FergusSweeney 3 38
(K R Burke) *stmbld and wnt rt sn after s: wknd over 1f out: eased: lame* **5/2**^{1}

1m 14.05s (1.85) **Going Correction** +0.375s/f (Good)
WFA 3 from 4yo+ 9lb **8** Ran SP% **118.5**
Speed ratings (Par 109): **102,99,98,98,98 98,88,79**
CSF £58.11 CT £683.69 TOTE £3.40: £1.30, £3.80, £3.90; EX 57.00 Trifecta £319.10 Part won. Pool: £449.50, 0.10 winning units..
Owner The Masterminds **Bred** Bearstone Stud **Trained** Aldbury, Herts

FOCUS
Three of these - including the winner - are entered for the Wokingham, and three in Epsom's Dash, but it was a modest turnout for the money. The early pace was not good for a 6f sprint at this level and the form is nothing special. The winner did not need to be at his best.

NOTEBOOK
Viking Spirit had gained two of his three previous victories with some cut in the ground, and is clearly well at home in the soft since he runs on it more often than most. He now heads for the Wokingham, for which he just missed the cut last year, and he is a 25-1 chance with Coral and William Hill. The 5lb penalty guarantees him a run, and faster ground would not be a worry to connections. (op 3-1)
Pawan(IRE) has not won since August 2006, but his mark is significantly higher these days and he usually runs a good race - as he did here from out of the handicap. Though he has been campaigned over 5f of late, this was a reminder that he is also effective over an extra furlong or two. (op 25-1)
Hurricane Spirit(IRE) put in a more positive effort this time, and may yet recapture some of his earlier promise. Soft ground looks to suit him well now following his injury problem after last year's 2,000 Guineas.
Ebraam(USA) showed he does act on soft ground with a solid effort from a testing mark. However, he was far too keen early on, and would be suited by a stronger pace. (tchd 13-2)
Conquest(IRE) handled the soft ground well enough, and ran as if 6f ought to suit him better than 5f this season. He would have finished closer with a clear run, and on this evidence he may even stay 7f, but he is not one to totally rely on. Official explanation: jockey said gelding suffered interference 1f after start (op 5-1)
C'Mon You Irons(IRE) was nicely backed and ran a decent race from out of the handicap. This lightly-raced sort is capable of finding a race. (op 14-1)
Swift Princess(IRE) lost her footing early in the race and finished lame, which explains her lack-lustre effort. Official explanation: vet said filly was lame (op 2-1)

2599 GOODWOOD HOSPITALITY STKS (H'CAP) 1m 4f
3:00 (3:00) (Class 3) (0-90,90) 4-Y-0+ **£7,771** (£2,312; £1,155; £577) **Stalls** Low

Form RPR

-025 **1** **Formax (FR)**^{10} [2308] 6-8-13 **85**.. RichardMullen 7 94
(M P Tregoning) *hld up in rr: stdy hdwy fr over 2f out: squeezed through gap and r.o wl to ld wl ins fnl f* **15/2**

304- **2** ¾ **Akarem**^{108} [6994] 7-9-0 **86**.. FergusSweeney 12 94
(K R Burke) *trckd ldrs: hdwy to ld 3f out: rdn and r.o: hdd wl ins fnl f* **15/2**

5533 **3** *nk* **Rudry Dragon (IRE)**^{24} [1909] 4-8-7 **79**........................ SimonWhitworth 9 86
(P A Blockley) *hld up in rr: hdwy 3f out: rdn over 1f out: kpt on fnl f* **12/1**

31-0 **4** ½ **Candle**^{8} [2372] 5-9-2 **88**.. DaneO'Neill 3 94
(H Candy) *trckd ldrs: rdn over 2f out: ev ch 1f out: kpt on ins fnl f* **6/1**^{3}

1/02 **5** 1 ½ **Show Winner**^{15} [2153] 5-8-4 **76** oh1.............................. FrancisNorton 10 81+
(A M Balding) *a.p: ev ch ent fnl f: wknd ins fnl f* **4/1**^{2}

03-5 **6** 1 ½ **Tears Of A Clown (IRE)**^{38} [1569] 5-9-2 **88**.................... RichardHughes 4 90
(J A Osborne) *hld up towards rr: hdwy over 2f out: wknd fnl f* **3/1**^{1}

0-00 **7** 1 ½ **Birkspiel (GER)**^{23} [1935] 7-8-7 **79**........................(t) DeanMcKeown 6 78
(S Dow) *sn led: hdd 3f out: wknd ent fnl f* **66/1**

120/ **8** *nse* **Climate Change (USA)**^{54} [5690] 6-8-7 **82**................ TravisBlock$^{(3)}$ 11 81
(Miss Venetia Williams) *in tch: rdn 1/2-way: wknd 2f out* **16/1**

00-0 **9** *nk* **Mikao (IRE)**^{8} [2372] 7-8-12 **84**.. SaleemGolam 1 83
(M H Tompkins) *mid-div: effrt over 2f out: sn btn* **14/1**

-030 **10** 1 ¼ **Ainama (IRE)**^{17} [2107] 4-8-7 **79**.. OscarUrbina 2 76
(M Wigham) *mid-div: wkng whn hung rt over 1f out* **8/1**

11 1 **Daltaban (FR)**^{37} 4-9-4 **90**.. JimmyQuinn 8 85
(Miss E C Lavelle) *mid-div: bhd fnl 5f* **25/1**

2m 43.66s (5.26) **Going Correction** +0.375s/f (Good) **11** Ran SP% **119.5**
Speed ratings (Par 107): **97,96,96,95,94 93,92,92,92,91 91**
CSF £63.84 CT £678.03 TOTE £8.90: £2.40, £2.40, £2.90; EX 68.90 Trifecta £437.50 Part won. Pool: £616.27, 0.10 winning units..
Owner Mr And Mrs A E Pakenham **Bred** Mathieu Daguzan-Garros & Mme P Menard **Trained** Lambourn, Berks

FOCUS
A competitive handicap of a reasonable standard for the course. Solid form.

NOTEBOOK
Formax(FR) took an age to find a gap, but when it appeared he rattled through it to score in style. He looks effective from 1m to 1m4f, with this trip looking ideal, but connections say he is best when covered up like this, so there will always be an element of risk. (op 10-1)
Akarem, who had suffrered a cut leg over hurdles in February, showed he is none the worse for that with a sterling effort. He is on a tempting mark at present, and this run may bring him on, so he must have a good chance in similar company next time. (op 10-1 tchd 7-1)
Rudry Dragon(IRE), who continues to run with admirable consistency, got the trip really well and looks worth another try at 1m4f. (tchd 14-1)
Candle improved on her seasonal debut, and looks very effective on soft ground, having won in similar conditions at this track last season. She is higher in the weights this season, but has trained on well. (op 9-2)
Show Winner does not need soft ground, but won his maiden on it and clearly acts well with cut. However, though going close over this trip at Newbury last time, this was a greater test of stamina and he did not quite make it home from a 3lb higher mark. (op 9-2)
Tears Of A Clown(IRE) is very effective at 1m2f, but has yet to completely convince that he fully stays 1m4f, and the testing conditions made certain of it here. (op 7-2)
Ainama(IRE) Official explanation: jockey said gelding moved poorly throughout

2600 ON THE HOUSE STKS (LISTED RACE) 1m
3:35 (3:40) (Class 1) 3-Y-0+
£17,031 (£6,456; £3,231; £1,611; £807; £405) **Stalls** High

Form RPR

11-1 **1** **Bankable (IRE)**^{31} [1719] 4-9-5 94.. DaneO'Neill 7 117+
(L M Cumani) *a in tch and gng wl: shkn up to ld over 1f out: sn clr: readily* **7/4**^{1}

21-2 **2** 3 ¾ **Lady Gloria**^{28} [1801] 4-9-3 104.. AdamKirby 8 103
(J G Given) *in rr: swtchd lft over 2f out: hdwy on outside and r.o to go 2nd ins fnl f* **13/2**^{3}

-336 **3** ¾ **Babodana**^{35} [1631] 8-9-5 100.. SaleemGolam 6 103
(M H Tompkins) *a.p: rdn over 1f out: kpt on one pce fnl f* **9/1**

-205 **4** *nse* **Whitcombe Minister (USA)**^{14} [2194] 3-8-7 92................ RobertHavlin 9 100
(Jamie Poulton) *in tch on ins: rdn over 1f out: styd on ins fnl f* **25/1**

5-51 **5** *hd* **Ordnance Row**^{19} [2044] 5-9-8 106.................................... RichardHughes 1 106
(R Hannon) *led to 1/2-way: styd prom tl lost pl over 2f out: rallied wl over 1f out: fdd ins fnl f* **5/1**^{2}

-6U1 **6** ¾ **Laa Rayb (USA)**^{13} [2218] 4-9-5 97.................................... DeanMcKeown 5 101
(M Johnston) *trckd ldr: led 1/2-way: rdn and hdd over 1f out: wknd ins fnl f* **5/1**^{2}

03-4 **7** 4 ½ **Caldra (IRE)**^{31} [1716] 4-9-5 108.. GeorgeBaker 3 91
(S Kirk) *t.k.h: a in rr* **15/2**

0-33 **8** 2 ¾ **Vanderlin**^{29} [1767] 9-9-5 102.. FrancisNorton 4 84
(A M Balding) *in tch: effrt over 2f out: wknd 1f out: lame* **16/1**

0065 **9** 2 ¾ **Final Verse**^{19} [2044] 5-9-5 100.. FrankieMcDonald 2 78
(Jane Chapple-Hyam) *trckd ldrs tl wknd over 1f out* **33/1**

1m 40.52s (0.62) **Going Correction** +0.375s/f (Good)
WFA 3 from 4yo+ 12lb **9** Ran SP% **117.5**
Speed ratings (Par 111): **111,107,106,106,106 105,101,98,95**
CSF £13.91 TOTE £2.40: £1.40, £1.60, £2.40; EX 13.80 Trifecta £147.40 Pool: £789.22, 3.80 winning units..
Owner Ronchalon Racing (UK) Ltd **Bred** Barronstown Stud And Cobra **Trained** Newmarket, Suffolk

FOCUS
A fascinating Listed race featuring six Hunt Cup entries, among them the ante-post favourite Bankable, who looked a future Group winner and will go to Royal Ascot with outstanding prospects under a penalty. Sound form overall, despite a couple of disappointments.

NOTEBOOK
Bankable(IRE) ◆ had plenty to find on official ratings, but he had looked a highly progressive sort and took another leap in the right direction here, travelling well throughout and looking better and better throughout the final furlong. He heads for the Royal Hunt Cup as a short-priced favourite and this big strong individual will be very hard to beat there with just a 5lb penalty, unless the draw wrecks his chance, for he looks more than capable of making his mark in Group company in due course. (tchd 13-8 and 9-4 tchd 5-2 in places)
Lady Gloria, with hindsight, did not have the slightest chance against the rapidly improving Bankable, so it is probably best to assess her performance by ignoring the winner. In the circumstances, she ran an excellent race against the boys and ought to have a good season at this sort of level. (op 8-1)
Babodana planted himself at the 5f pole going to post and only consented to move after every strategy had been used, which included the peculiar sight of his jockey placing a towel over the horse's head like a blindfold, and then waving it at his rear end. More amenable going into and out of the stalls, he lacked tactical speed in the straight but plodded on as if he might stay a bit farther these days. (tchd 17-2 and 10-1)
Whitcombe Minister(USA), who had the lowest adjusted rating in the line-up, ran really well against his elders in this classy event. He stays at least 1m2f, and has plenty of options, so this lightly-raced sort looks a potential winner if his trainer can find the right one. (op 20-1)
Ordnance Row was one of the leading contenders on official ratings despite having to concede weight all round. Though fading out of the frame late on, he was not beaten far by the placed horses, and can be deemed to have run his race. (tchd 4-1)
Laa Rayb(USA) seemed to handle the ground alright, but it left him with nothing to give as he reached the limit of his stamina. (op 7-1)

Caldra(IRE) Official explanation: jockey said gelding hung left throughout
Vanderlin Official explanation: vet said gelding finished lame and was struck into on left hind

2601 NICK BROOKS E B F MAIDEN STKS 6f
4:05 (4:08) (Class 4) 2-Y-O **£4,371** (£1,300; £650; £324) **Stalls** Low

Form				RPR
	1		**Versaki (IRE)** 2-9-3 0 DaneO'Neill 5 (R Hannon) *trckd ldrs: led over 2f out: r.o wl fnl f* **13/2**[3]	85+
	2	2 1/2	**Noble Jack (IRE)** 2-9-3 0 RichardHughes 7 (R Hannon) *slowly away: in rr tl rdn and hdwy over 1f out: wnt 2nd ins fnl f: no ch w wnr* **15/8**[1]	77+
0	3	hd	**Motor Home**[15] 2150 2-9-3 0 FrancisNorton 8 (A M Balding) *led tl hdd over 2f out: kpt on but nt qckn fnl f* **12/1**	76
4	4	2 1/4	**Party Cat (IRE)**[6] 2424 2-9-3 0 RichardMullen 4 (R Hannon) *trckd ldrs: rdn over 2f out: kpt on one pce after* **9/4**[2]	69
	5	3/4	**Managua** 2-9-3 0 TPO'Shea 1 (M R Channon) *towards rr: rdn over 1f out: one pce* **8/1**	72+
	6	1/2	**Penton Hook** 2-9-3 0 StephenCarson 3 (P Winkworth) *trckd ldr to over 2f out: sn btn* **33/1**	65
	7	9	**Hellbender (IRE)** 2-9-3 0 GeorgeBaker 6 (S Kirk) *racd on outside: in tch tl wknd over 1f out: eased* **15/2**	38
0	8	1 1/2	**Courageous Nature (IRE)**[15] 2146 2-9-3 0 RobertHavlin 2 (B J Meehan) *s.i.s: hdwy over 2f out: wknd qckly appr fnl f* **10/1**	34

1m 15.14s (2.94) **Going Correction** +0.375s/f (Good) **8 Ran SP% 121.5**
Speed ratings (Par 95): **95,91,91,88,87 86,74,72**
CSF £20.44 TOTE £10.10: £2.50, £1.40, £3.40; EX 30.80.
Owner J A Lazzari **Bred** Peter Kelly And Ms Wendy Daly **Trained** East Everleigh, Wilts

FOCUS
A race with a mixed history, but won by the top-class miler Dubawi back in 2004. Only three of these had run before, but the time and the fourth suggest it is worth taking a positive view of the form. The winner looks useful, and the runner-up is a sure-fire maiden winner.

NOTEBOOK
Versaki(IRE) ◆ was the most expensive in the field at 100,000euros, and he was nicely backed even though he was the longest-priced of the Hannon trio. He is by the smart sprinter-miler Verglas and out of a mare who won over 1m2f in France, but there are winners at shorter trips in the family, and he clearly possesses his share of speed, so the future looks good following this decisive debut success. (op 14-1)
Noble Jack(IRE) ◆ came from behind to chase his less-fancied stablemate without every looking likely to get to him. A 55,000gns yearling Elusive City half-brother to winners up to 1m3f, he should win a maiden and shaped as if he will stay farther as he matures. (op 13-8 tchd 5-2)
Motor Home had missed the break on his debut, but this time he got out much better and made the running. A half-brother to eight winners up to 1m4f, his sire Toubougg stayed middle distances but his dam was very speedy, so it is not easy to predict his optimum trip. However, it is clear that he has more pace than he showed on his first appearance and his family history suggests he should win races. (op 14-1)
Party Cat(IRE) was a bit disappointing considering he started much shorter than his winning stablemate. Well-rated, he had looked promising on his debut and may just have found the ground too soft or this second appearance coming too soon, so deserves another chance. (op 11-4 tchd 15-8)
Managua is a 50,000gns son of high-class French miler Kaldounevees, whose progeny often improve as they mature. His dam won between 1m and 1m2f, and it is likely that he will settle round at 1m or just beyond, so this was a fair debut and gives him a sound base to build on. (op 13-2 tchd 11-2)
Penton Hook, a son of the top-class Hong Kong miler Lucky Owners, cost just £3,400 as a yearling, and was gelded for this debut. However, his dam won over 7f and 1m2f on the Flat, and was also placed over hurdles, so he would not be a hopeless cause by any means following this low-key but satisfactory debut which suggested that he would already be suited by 7f. (tchd 50-1 in a place)
Hellbender(IRE), a 48,000euros yearling, later re-sold for 65,000gns, would have finished closer but for being eased when beaten. He is a son of the top-class Australian sprinter Exceed and Excel, and should do better on faster ground. (op 8-1 tchd 7-1)

2602 RACING UK FREE TO AIR TODAY STKS (H'CAP) 5f
4:40 (4:40) (Class 5) (0-70,70) 3-Y-O **£3,238** (£963; £481; £240) **Stalls** Low

Form				RPR
44-0	1		**Brazilian Brush (IRE)**[21] 1995 3-9-1 70 (t) TravisBlock(3) 7 (H Morrison) *a.p: led over 1f out: hrd rdn ins fnl f: jst hld on* **5/1**[2]	76
000-	2	nse	**Cheshire Rose**[218] 6462 3-8-13 65 JimmyQuinn 5 (T D Barron) *trckd ldrs: swtchd rt over 1f out: chal wnr thrght fnl f: jst failed* **5/1**[3]	70
331	3	2 3/4	**Jane's Payoff (IRE)**[35] 1635 3-9-2 68 RichardThomas 1 (Mrs L C Jewell) *a.p: rdn over 1f out: kpt on fnl f but no ch w first 2* **7/2**[2]	63
55-0	4	2 1/4	**River N' Blues (IRE)**[16] 2127 3-8-10 65 KevinGhunowa(3) 3 (Dr J R J Naylor) *led tl rdn and hdd over 1f out: wknd fnl f* **12/1**	52
3102	5	1 3/4	**Ben**[18] 2068 3-8-12 64 (v) DaneO'Neill 8 (P G Murphy) *slowly away: effrt and swtchd rt over 1f out: wknd ins fnl f* **5/2**[1]	45
-640	6	8	**Penrice Castle**[32] 1699 3-8-10 62 RichardHughes 6 (R Hannon) *a in rr: eased whn no ch ins fnl f* **10/1**	14

61.12 secs (2.72) **Going Correction** +0.375s/f (Good) **6 Ran SP% 112.8**
Speed ratings (Par 99): **93,92,88,84,82 69**
CSF £15.49 CT £42.27 TOTE £3.30: £2.20, £2.60; EX 19.00.
Owner Betfair Club ROA **Bred** Mrs T Mahon **Trained** East Ilsley, Berks
■ Our Acquaintance was withdrawn on vet's advice (100/30, deduct 20p in the £ under rule 4).
■ Stewards' Enquiry : Jimmy Quinn caution: used whip with excessive frequency

FOCUS
A modest race for the course, with little progressive in the line-up.

2603 MICHAEL (GERRY) GERMON "LIFETIME IN RACING" STKS (H'CAP) 1m 3f
5:15 (5:15) (Class 5) (0-70,70) 3-Y-O **£3,238** (£963; £481; £240) **Stalls** Low

Form				RPR
-055	1		**Moment's Notice**[19] 2043 3-9-0 66 GeorgeBaker 8 (S Kirk) *in rr: making hdwy whn short of room and swtchd lft over 2f out: squeezed through to ld appr fnl f: forged clr: easily* **7/1**	81+
06-4	2	5	**Red Lily (IRE)**[8] 2376 3-8-13 65 OscarUrbina 16 (J R Fanshawe) *mid-div: swtchd lft over 2f out: styd on to go 2nd nr fin: no ch w wnr* **9/2**[2]	69
0-00	3	1/2	**Fiume**[19] 2043 3-9-4 70 RichardHughes 2 (R Hannon) *led tl rdn and hdd over 1f out: no ex and lost 2nd cl home* **16/1**	73
-600	4	4	**King's Alchemist**[15] 2161 3-8-5 60 EmmettStack(3) 1 (M D I Usher) *slowly away: hdwy to go into mid-div after 2f: effrt over 3f out: kpt on: nvr nr to chal* **14/1**	56
6-30	5	2 1/2	**Tamrai Dancer**[39] 1530 3-8-8 63 KirstyMilczarek(3) 4 (R M Beckett) *mid-div: effrt over 3f out: one pce after* **15/2**	55
05-0	6	2 1/4	**Striving (IRE)**[14] 2199 3-8-10 62 DaneO'Neill 7 (Sir Michael Stoute) *towards rr: kpt on fnl 2f but nvr nrr than fin* **4/1**[1]	50
605-	7	3/4	**Red Twist**[196] 6855 3-9-1 70 TravisBlock(3) 9 (H Morrison) *trckd ldr: rdn over 3f out: wknd wl over 1f out* **10/1**	57
004-	8	1/2	**Appointment**[227] 6262 3-9-0 66 StephenCarson 14 (Mrs A J Perrett) *trckd ldrs: bdly hmpd on ins over 2f out and nvr a danger after* **12/1**	52
03-5	9	hd	**Mardood**[15] 2143 3-9-2 68 SaleemGolam 12 (W J Haggas) *hld up in rr: a bhd* **7/1**	54
000-	10	2 1/2	**Flower Song**[212] 6601 3-8-5 60 RussellKennemore(3) 13 (J Gallagher) *a in rr* **50/1**	42
400	11	12	**World Time**[11] 2291 3-9-0 66 (b[1]) RobertHavlin 3 (J H M Gosden) *slowly away: chsd ldrs after 2f: rdn and hung rt fr over 2f out: sn btn* **11/2**[3]	27
100	12	10	**Mrs Jefferson (IRE)**[44] 1412 3-8-9 66 JackDean(5) 6 (J G Portman) *mid-div: effrt 4f out: wknd 2f out: eased* **33/1**	10
5565	13	19	**Roundthetwist (IRE)**[11] 2272 3-8-13 65 FergusSweeney 5 (K R Burke) *trckd ldrs tl wknd rapidly 2f out* **16/1**	—

2m 32.12s (3.82) **Going Correction** +0.375s/f (Good) **13 Ran SP% 130.4**
Speed ratings (Par 99): **101,97,97,94,92 90,90,89,89,87 79,71,57**
CSF £42.24 CT £516.00 TOTE £8.30: £2.80, £2.40, £6.80; EX 42.50.
Owner C Wright & The Hon Mrs J M Corbett **Bred** Stratford Place Stud **Trained** Upper Lambourn, Berks

FOCUS
This looked an ordinary race for the course, and the pace was nothing special either, so the winner did well to come from so far back. He has been rated back to last year's best AW level, with the second and third both showing improved form and the rest well held.
Flower Song Official explanation: jockey said filly hung left

2604 RACING UK 4TH BIRTHDAY CELEBRATION STKS (H'CAP) 1m
5:50 (5:51) (Class 2) (0-100,92) 4-Y-O£9,969 (£2,985; £1,492; £747; £372) **Stalls** High

Form				RPR
3-30	1		**Salient**[21] 1982 4-8-9 86 KirstyMilczarek(3) 3 (M J Attwater) *mde all: r.o wl fnl f* **4/1**	92
5111	2	1/2	**Mujood**[7] 2389 5-9-3 91 StephenCarson 2 (Eve Johnson Houghton) *chsd wnr thrght: rdn over 1f out: no imp fnl f* **10/3**[3]	96
0005	3	1 1/2	**Very Wise**[2] 2545 6-8-13 87 (p) RichardMullen 6 (W J Haggas) *hld up in rr: hdwy and kpt on to go 3rd ins fnl f* **3/1**[2]	89
4-15	4	1 1/2	**Cape Hawk (IRE)**[35] 1633 4-9-4 92 RichardHughes 4 (R Hannon) *prom: rdn over 1f out and no hdwy appr fnl f* **15/8**[1]	90
03/	5	14	**Frederick Ozanam (IRE)**[579] 6262 4-9-4 92 RobertHavlin 1 (B J Meehan) *t.k.h: in tch: rdn 3f out: wknd 2f out* **14/1**	58

1m 41.82s (1.92) **Going Correction** +0.375s/f (Good) **5 Ran SP% 109.5**
Speed ratings (Par 109): **105,104,103,101,87**
CSF £17.06 TOTE £4.90: £2.30, £1.80; EX 20.00 Place 6: £278.92, Place 5: £99.83..
Owner Canisbay Bloodstock **Bred** Hesmonds Stud Ltd **Trained** Epsom, Surrey

FOCUS
A disappointing turnout for the prize money, and slight doubts about the form.

NOTEBOOK
Salient's three previous wins were all at 7f, but he had some previous form at 1m and Milczarek judged the front-running tactics to perfection. He goes well at Goodwood, and these tactics continue to suit. (op 6-1)
Mujood has been creeping up the weights, but he is in flying form at present and put in another good effort, just failing to make it a four-timer. Admirably effective from 6f to 1m, and on any ground, he is better than ever this season. (op 9-4 tchd 7-2)
Very Wise is on a generous mark at present, and would be very dangerous if returning to top form. There were signs here that some progress is being made, and he is probably worth trying back over a slightly longer trip. (op 4-1 tchd 11-4)
Cape Hawk(IRE) has been disappointing in two recent races on turf - the other on good going - and may just be best on Polytrack, although fast ground on turf is also a possiblity. He travelled really well here, and looked a potential problem for the winner 2f out, but found little when shaken up. (op 2-1 tchd 7-4)
Frederick Ozanam(IRE), a smart ex-Irish winner on soft ground, showed little on this first race since October 2006. While few conclusions can be drawn at this stage, his previous form had been up to 7f though admittedly that was as a juvenile. (op 8-1)
T/Plt: £615.30 to a £1 stake. Pool: £92,296.97. 109.50 winning tickets. T/Qpdt: £34.20 to a £1 stake. Pool: £4,102.04. 88.60 winning tickets. JS

2568 HAYDOCK (L-H)
Saturday, May 31

OFFICIAL GOING: Good changing to good to firm (good in places) after race 2 (3.15)
Rail realignment added 21yds to advertised distances of races of a mile and above.
Wind: Almost nil Weather: Warm and Sunny

2605 RECTANGLE GROUP SANDY LANE STKS (LISTED RACE) 6f
2:10 (2:11) (Class 1) 3-Y-O
£17,031 (£6,456; £3,231; £1,611; £807; £405) **Stalls** Centre

Form				RPR
1-21	1		**Fat Boy (IRE)**[15] 2148 3-9-3 112 TPQueally 9 (P W Chapple-Hyam) *mde all: rdn and hung lft over 1f out: r.o and a doing enough ins fnl f* **10/11**[1]	116
3-22	2	3/4	**Tajdeef (USA)**[15] 2148 3-9-0 109 MichaelHills 6 (B W Hills) *in tch: impr to chse wnr over 1f out: rdn to chal and hung lft ins fnl f: nt qckn towards fin* **11/2**[3]	111
233-	3	2 1/2	**Swiss Franc**[283] 4721 3-9-0 108 RyanMoore 1 (D R C Elsworth) *hld up: pushed along 2f out: hdwy over 1f out: styd on to take 3rd ins fnl f: no imp on front pair* **9/2**[2]	103
11-6	4	2 3/4	**Beacon Lodge (IRE)**[42] 1471 3-9-5 107 PhilipRobinson 10 (C G Cox) *dwlt: racd keenly and chsd ldrs: rdn and hung lft fr over 1f out: one pce ins fnl f* **11/1**	99
-133	5	1 3/4	**Prohibit**[7] 2410 3-9-0 95 (b[1]) SteveDrowne 11 (J H M Gosden) *hld up: rdn and hdwy over 1f out: keeping on whn nt clr run ins fnl f: no imp after* **13/2**	93
1-05	6	1/2	**Jeninsky (USA)**[15] 2170 3-8-9 88 GregFairley 8 (P J McBride) *chsd ldrs: rdn over 1f out: wknd ins fnl f* **50/1**	82
410-	7	6	**Unilateral (IRE)**[239] 5973 3-9-0 106 TomEaves 3 (B Smart) *towards rr: rdn over 1f out: nvr a threat* **20/1**	68

600- **8** *6* **Sudden Impact (IRE)**[211] 6619 3-8-9 89.......................... HayleyTurner 4 44
(Paul Green) *racd keenly: prom tl wknd qckly 1/2-way* **66/1**

1m 13.15s (-0.85) **Going Correction** +0.125s/f (Good) **8** Ran SP% **115.8**
Speed ratings (Par 107): **110,109,105,102,99 99,91,83**
CSF £6.41 TOTE £1.80: £1.10, £1.40, £1.50; EX 4.50 Trifecta £11.40 Pool: £429.34, 26.60 winning units.
Owner M Sines **Bred** Peter Mooney **Trained** Newmarket, Suffolk

FOCUS
A decent Listed contest run at a reasonable gallop and sound form for the grade.

NOTEBOOK
Fat Boy(IRE) confirmed Newbury form with Tajdeef on the same terms, and he won in similar style to Newbury, making every yard of the running. He deserves a crack at a Group race now, but the top Group 1 sprints at Royal Ascot might be flying a bit high, at least at this stage of the season. (op 6-5 tchd 5-4 in places)
Tajdeef(USA), runner-up to Sir Gerry at Ascot and now to Fat Boy on two occasions, all in Listed company, certainly has the ability to win a race of this nature. He finished nicely clear of the rest and the form looks solid for this grade of race. (op 9-2)
Swiss Franc, absent since being sent off favourite and finishing third in the Gimcrack last August, made a pleasing reappearance. He should be all the better for the run and will always be seen to best effect when able to settle off a decent pace. (tchd 5-1)
Beacon Lodge(IRE), disappointing in the Greenham on his reappearance, was dropping back in trip, but the drying ground was not in his favour, and he confirmed it by hanging. Official explanation: jockey said colt found the good ground too fast (op 10-1 tchd 9-1)
Prohibit, third in a handicap off 95 last time, had blinkers on for the first time. He was comfortably held and is not quite up to this class. (op 8-1 tchd 9-1)
Jeninsky(USA), chasing some black type, was back over a more suitable trip, but she was the lowest-rated runner in the field and lacked the class to get involved. (tchd 66-1)
Unilateral(IRE), a Group 3 winner at two, probably needs more cut in the ground and was entitled to need her reappearance.

2606 TIMEFORM SILVER SALVER (REGISTERED AS THE CECIL FRAIL STKS) (LISTED RACE) (F&M) 6f
2:45 (2:47) (Class 1) 3-Y-0+

£17,031 (£6,456; £3,231; £1,611; £807; £405) **Stalls** Centre

Form RPR
40-1 **1** **Perfect Polly**[22] 1949 3-8-7 104.......................... ShaneKelly 9 103
(J Noseda) *racd keenly in midfield: hdwy over 2f out: led wl over 1f out: sn rdn: r.o: a doing enough towards fin* **9/2**[3]
2 *1* **Aine (IRE)**[34] 1652 3-8-7 0.......................... WMLordan 8 100
(T Stack, Ire) *hld up: rdn and hdwy whn swtchd rt over 1f out: chsd wnr wl ins fnl f: r.o towards fin but nvr gng to get there* **11/2**
2-42 **3** *2* **Crystany (IRE)**[21] 2000 3-8-7 95.......................... TPQueally 4 93
(H R A Cecil) *in tch: rdn and swtchd lft over 1f out: sn tried to chal: nt qckn wl ins fnl f* **4/1**[2]
0102 **4** *2 1/4* **Carcinetto (IRE)**[13] 2219 6-9-2 83.......................... StephenDonohoe 5 88
(P D Evans) *led to 1/2-way: sn pushed along: kpt on same pce fr over 1f out* **66/1**
0-32 **5** *hd* **Dark Missile**[32] 1698 5-9-2 103.......................... HayleyTurner 6 87
(A M Balding) *racd keenly w ldr: led 1/2-way: hdd wl over 1f out: fdd ins fnl f* **7/4**[1]
120- **6** *3/4* **Vive Les Rouges**[238] 6017 3-8-7 99.......................... IanMongan 10 83
(C F Wall) *racd keenly: prom: rdn over 1f out: wknd ins fnl f* **16/1**
-231 **7** *nk* **Dubai Power**[9] 2341 3-8-7 83.......................... LiamJones 7 82
(C E Brittain) *hmpd s: bhd: pushed along 2f out: prog ent fnl f: nt pce to chal* **20/1**
6640 **8** *nse* **Ripples Maid**[21] 2000 5-9-6 93.......................... ChrisCatlin 1 88
(J A Geake) *w ldr: rdn over 1f out: wknd ins fnl f* **25/1**
222- **9** *nse* **Sakhee's Song (IRE)**[41] 4-9-2 103.......................... RyanMoore 3 84
(D R C Elsworth) *hld up: pushed along over 1f out: nvr trbld ldrs* **12/1**
1-10 **10** *3/4* **Quiet Elegance**[45] 1401 3-8-7 94.......................... WJSupple 12 79
(E J Alston) *hld up: rdn over 1f out: hung lft whn no imp ent fnl f* **16/1**

1m 13.44s (-0.56) **Going Correction** +0.125s/f (Good)
WFA 3 from 4yo+ 9lb **10** Ran SP% **119.5**
Speed ratings (Par 111): **108,106,104,101,100 99,99,99,99,98**
CSF £29.71 TOTE £5.50: £1.90, £1.90, £1.90; EX 33.50 Trifecta £171.30 Pool: £555.18, 2.30 winning units.
Owner Red Man Bloodstock **Bred** Old Peartree Stud **Trained** Newmarket, Suffolk

FOCUS
Average Listed form, with the 83-rated Carcinetto finishing fourth and limiting things. The time was 0.29sec slower than that recorded by Fat Boy in the previous race.

NOTEBOOK
Perfect Polly, who made a winning reappearance in a little race at Hamilton, stepped up on that effort up in grade. Her fourth in the Cheveley Park last season gave her every chance in this company and she looks the type to gain further success in Listed and Group 3 contests this season. (op 13-2 tchd 7-1)
Aine(IRE), unbeaten in two previous starts, is a daughter of Danehill Dancer and had done her racing to date on easier ground. These quicker conditions were perhaps not entirely suitable but she showed that she is up to winning in this grade when things are more in her favour. (op 9-2 tchd 4-1)
Crystany(IRE), runner-up in a similar event at Nottingham last time out, is a fairly reliable sort, and the ground was drying out in her favour. She ran a sound race. (tchd 9-2)
Carcinetto(IRE), thoroughly exposed and beaten in a handicap off 83 last time out, holds the form down as it is difficult to believe that she has suddenly improved 10lb. (op 80-1)
Dark Missile was back over her ideal distance, but she raced keenly towards the front end and did not get home. (op 15-8 tchd 13-8)
Vive Les Rouges was another who did not help her chances of seeing out her race by racing keenly in the early stages. In fairness, though, this was her seasonal reappearance, and she is entitled to come on for it. (tchd 20-1)
Dubai Power had a stiff task in this company. Official explanation: jockey said filly was hampered leaving stalls (op 22-1)

2607 J.W.LEES STKS (REGISTERED AS THE JOHN OF GAUNT STAKES) (GROUP 3) 7f 30y
3:15 (3:17) (Class 1) 4-Y-0+

£28,385 (£10,760; £5,385; £2,685; £1,345; £675) **Stalls** Low

Form RPR
5-21 **1** **Major Cadeaux**[35] 1631 4-9-5 113.......................... RyanMoore 2 119+
(R Hannon) *sddle slipped early: hld up: hdwy 2f out: nt clr run over 1f out: qcknd up to chal ent fnl f: sn led: kpt on wl* **10/11**[1]
0220 **2** *1/2* **Big Timer (USA)**[17] 2106 4-9-0 100.......................... TomEaves 3 113
(Miss L A Perratt) *racd keenly: hld up: nt clr run over 2f out: rdn and hdwy over 1f out: pressed ldrs ins fnl f: styd on wl but a looked hld* **33/1**
5051 **3** *hd* **Appalachian Trail (IRE)**[21] 1989 7-9-0 112..................(b) FergalLynch 7 112
(Miss L A Perratt) *hld up: rdn and hdwy over 1f out: running on whn swtchd lft ins fnl f: hld fnl strides* **5/1**[2]
50-0 **4** *3/4* **Silver Touch (IRE)**[26] 1880 5-9-0 108.......................... EdwardCreighton 9 110
(M R Channon) *midfield: hdwy over 2f out: rdn to ld jst over 1f out: hdd ins fnl f: nt qckn towards fin* **7/1**[3]
2-54 **5** *5* **Tell**[35] 1631 5-9-0 108..........................(b) SteveDrowne 6 97
(J L Dunlop) *prom: led over 2f out: rdn and hdd jst over 1f out: wknd ins fnl f* **12/1**
0453 **6** *nk* **Beckermet (IRE)**[17] 2106 6-9-0 110.......................... ChrisCatlin 4 96
(R F Fisher) *racd keenly: led: rdn and hdd over 2f out: wknd over 1f out* **9/1**
-300 **7** *1 1/2* **Lovelace**[13] 2235 4-9-3 108.......................... WJSupple 5 95
(M Johnston) *trckd ldrs: rdn and upsides fr over 2f out: n.m.r whn hld ent fnl f: n.d after* **9/1**
-140 **8** *6* **Excusez Moi (USA)**[44] 1420 6-9-0 103.......................... PhilipRobinson 1 75
(C E Brittain) *trckd ldrs: niggled along whn n.m.r and hmpd 2f out: sn dropped away* **20/1**

1m 29.98s (-0.22) **Going Correction** +0.125s/f (Good) **8** Ran SP% **116.9**
Speed ratings (Par 113): **106,105,105,104,98 98,96,89**
CSF £39.49 TOTE £1.90: £1.10, £5.90, £1.60; EX 36.20 Trifecta £139.90 Pool: £648.32, 3.29 winning units.
Owner N A Woodcock, A C Pickford & David Mort **Bred** Earl Richard Evain **Trained** East Everleigh, Wilts

FOCUS
They went only a fair gallop and those who were held up dominated at the finish. The time was modest for a Group 3 race and there are slight doubts over the form.

NOTEBOOK
Major Cadeaux defied his Group 2 penalty in good style, quickening up well between horses to put the race to bed, and he deserves extra credit because his saddle slipped early on in the race, making things a good deal more difficult for his rider. He is better than the bare form suggests and, while he could run in the Golden Jubilee at Royal Ascot, the Sussex Stakes was mentioned as his main summer target. He would not want extremes of going. (op 5-4 tchd 11-8)
Big Timer(USA) defied his long odds and led home the Linda Perratt-trained pair. His stable is in form at the moment but he was probably flattered here as he benefited from the leaders going off too quick and stayed on from the back when they had run their races.
Appalachian Trail(IRE), comprehensive winner of a Listed contest over this course and distance last time out, had the good pace he needs to deliver a late challenge, and so he can have few excuses. (op 7-2 tchd 100-30)
Silver Touch(IRE) made her move earlier than the eventual winner and placed horses and did not see it out as well. She ran a bit better than her finishing position suggests and this was far more encouraging than her effort in Ireland on her reappearance. (tchd 8-1)
Tell travelled up well 3f out but it turned out he had done too much too soon and he emptied from a furlong out. (tchd 10-1)
Beckermet(IRE) set a strong gallop which he was unable to sustain, and merely set it up for the hold-up merchants. (op 14-1 tchd 8-1)
Lovelace also had too much use made of him. (op 8-1)

2608 EBF MRS LESLIE BUCKLEY BIRTHDAY MAIDEN STKS 5f
3:50 (3:53) (Class 5) 2-Y-O

£3,399 (£1,011; £505; £252) **Stalls** Centre

Form RPR
5 **1** **Dabbers Chief (USA)**[43] 1439 2-9-3 0.......................... MichaelHills 5 86+
(B W Hills) *s.i.s: sn trckd ldrs: led 2f out: qcknd clr ent fnl f: r.o wl and wl in commnd after* **2/1**[1]
2 *5* **Carnaby Haggerston (IRE)** 2-9-3 0.......................... DO'Donohoe 7 68+
(K A Ryan) *s.i.s: rn green: towards rr: pushed along over 3f out: hdwy over 1f out: sn edgd lft: wnt 2nd ins fnl f: no ch w wnr: can improve* **7/2**[2]
3 *1* **Khor Dubai (IRE)** 2-9-3 0.......................... SteveDrowne 3 63
(Saeed Bin Suroor) *trckd ldrs: rn green: shkn up and edgd lft over 1f out: one pce ins fnl f* **4/1**[3]
4 *2* **Rio Cobolo (IRE)** 2-8-10 0.......................... AndrewHeffernan(7) 2 56
(Paul Green) *w ldr: rdn 2f out: fdd ins fnl f* **33/1**
5 *3/4* **Night Seed (IRE)** 2-8-12 0.......................... RyanMoore 9 49
(R Hannon) *hld up: effrt over 1f out: nvr able to chal* **7/2**[2]
6 *hd* **Tropical Blue** 2-9-3 0.......................... HayleyTurner 1 53
(Jennie Candlish) *in tch: rdn 2f out and rn green: btn over 1f out* **16/1**
40 **7** *7* **Bethie**[26] 1866 2-8-12 0.......................... TomEaves 6 23
(R Brotherton) *upset in stalls: racd keenly: led: hdd 2f out: sn rdn and wknd* **25/1**

62.17 secs (1.67) **Going Correction** +0.125s/f (Good) **7** Ran SP% **110.4**
Speed ratings (Par 93): **91,83,81,78,77 76,65**
CSF £8.58 TOTE £3.10: £1.60, £2.40; EX 11.60.
Owner South Bank Thoroughbred Racing **Bred** Jerry Squyres & Liz Squyres **Trained** Lambourn, Berks
■ Mythical Blue was withdrawn after refusing to enter the stalls (12/1, deduct 5p in the £ under rule 4).

FOCUS
A fair maiden in which, not for the first time, previous experience counted for plenty. This form could be underestimated with newcomers filling the frame behind the winner.

NOTEBOOK
Dabbers Chief(USA), too green to do himself justice on his debut, was a well-backed favourite, and he justified the support with a commanding success, bounding clear of the newcomers to win with plenty in hand. Well regarded at home, he could go for the Norfolk Stakes or Windsor Castle Stakes next. (op 5-2)
Carnaby Haggerston(IRE), who cost 260,000euros, is a half-brother to Den's Gift, a dual 7f-1m winner at three, but Invincible Spirit should in theory give him more speed. He showed signs of inexperience for much of the race, but was running on at the finish as he began to get the hang of things, and on this evidence he will have learnt plenty from this debut. (op 13-2)
Khor Dubai(IRE), whose price rose from 30,000euros as a yearling to 130,000gns as a two-year-old, is out of a dual winner in France at 1m4f plus. Godolphin's first juvenile runner of the year, he ran green on his debut but showed ability, and another furlong is likely to suit him in time. (op 11-4)
Rio Cobolo(IRE), whose dam won over 7f at three, was a cheap purchase, but he showed good speed for a long way. Being by Captain Rio, he may appreciate softer ground in future. (op 25-1)
Night Seed(IRE), a half-sister to Fielding, a prolific winner between 6f and 1m4f in Italy, Burning Incense, a dual 6f winner, and Cartronageeraghlad, a dual 6f-7f winner at two, is bred to go a bit. She was a bit disappointing on her debut considering she was quite well fancied, but the run should bring her on experience-wise. (op 3-1 tchd 4-1)
Bethie Official explanation: jockey said filly lost its action

2609 OPTION HYGIENE STKS (H'CAP) 2m 45y
4:20 (4:20) (Class 2) (0-100,97) 4-Y-0+

£12,462 (£3,732; £1,866; £934; £466; £234) **Stalls** Low

Form RPR
01-5 **1** **Gee Dee Nen**[21] 1984 5-9-1 87.......................... TPQueally 6 95
(M H Tompkins) *stdd off the pce: hdwy over 2f out: rdn to chse ldr over 1f out: r.o to ld fnl f to nose ahd post* **9/2**[2]
32-0 **2** *nse* **Colloquial**[27] 1841 7-9-7 93..........................(v) HayleyTurner 8 101
(H Candy) *a.p: led over 2f out: rdn over 1f out: ct post* **4/1**[1]

The Form Book, Raceform Ltd, Compton, RG20 6NL

30-3 **3** 3 **Acropolis (IRE)**[15] 2144 7-9-8 **94**..........................(v) TomEaves 16 98
(Miss L A Perratt) *hld up: hdwy 5f out: rdn to chse ldrs over 1f out: one pce and no imp ins fnl f* **7/1**

41-0 **4** *nk* **Missoula (IRE)**[24] 1916 5-8-13 **85**.................................. SamHitchcott 4 89
(Miss Suzy Smith) *trckd ldrs: pushed along over 4f out: outpcd over 1f out: styd on towards fin* **16/1**

03-0 **5** 2 1/4 **Greenwich Meantime**[24] 1916 8-9-7 **93**.................... DaleGibson 5 94
(R A Fahey) *midfield: hdwy 5f out: rdn 3f out: one pce fnl f* **11/2**[3]

26-4 **6** *hd* **Dr Sharp (IRE)**[35] 1625 8-8-7 **79**.............................. MickyFenton 2 80
(T P Tate) *s.i.s: bustled along and rcvrd to sn ld: rdn and hdd over 2f out: wknd fnl f* **13/2**

30-5 **7** 1 **Baddam**[31] 1717 6-9-8 **94**.................................... StephenDonohoe 3 94
(Ian Williams) *led early: remained prom: lost pl 1/2-way: struggling towards rr over 4f out: plugged on again fnl f wout troubling ldrs* **16/1**

1/-0 **8** 3/4 **Backbord (GER)**[14] 2202 6-9-6 **92**.......................... PaddyAspell 17 91
(Mrs L Wadham) *prom: rdn over 4f out: sn wknd* **13/2**

5-36 **9** 2 **Wing Collar**[24] 1916 7-9-11 **97**................................(p) DavidAllan 9 94
(T D Easterby) *hld up: effrt over 3f out: no imp* **13/2**

5-30 **10** 7 **Sphinx (FR)**[14] 2202 10-8-13 **85**..........................(p) DO'Donohoe 15 73
(E W Tuer) *hld up: rdn 2f out: no hdwy* **16/1**

3m 35.02s (-1.98) **Going Correction** +0.125s/f (Good)
WFA 4 from 5yo+ 2lb **10** Ran SP% **123.7**
Speed ratings (Par 109): **109,108,107,107,106 106,105,105,104,100**
CSF £24.48 CT £129.69 TOTE £5.40: £2.10, £2.20, £3.10; EX 29.20.
Owner David P Noblett **Bred** Kingwood Bloodstock **Trained** Newmarket, Suffolk

FOCUS
A fair staying handicap run at a good gallop. The form looks sound rated around the principals. There were seven non-runners in this event, five on account of the ground.

NOTEBOOK
Gee Dee Nen, all the better for his reappearance at Ascot, appreciated the decent pace and quick ground and stayed on strongly to get up by the shortest of short margins. Another crack at the Northumberland Plate is up next, and he should acquit himself well - he was seventh in it last year from a poor draw on unsuitably soft ground. (op 6-1)
Colloquial ◆, who won this race last year, ran very well considering he was never too far off the decent gallop. He was travelling as well as anything going to 3f out and, while he did not go on to win as he had threatened to do, he was only narrowly denied and, considering the way the race was run, can take great credit. He undoubtedly has a race in him off this sort of mark. (op 13-2)
Acropolis(IRE) has not convinced over staying trips when tried over them in the past, but he was having a second outing for his new and in-form stable and he shaped quite well, without quite suggesting he wants to go as far as this. Perhaps he can find a race back over 1m6f. (op 8-1)
Missoula(IRE), who was staying on at the finish, gets even further than this and easier ground would have put an even greater premium on stamina. (op 14-1)
Greenwich Meantime, back on the mark he won the Chester Cup off last year, was a bit disappointing and has not quite hit form yet. (op 13-2)
Dr Sharp(IRE) needs softer ground to be seen at his best and he did too much in the early stages this time. (op 7-1)

2610 TOMBOY CAVANAGH H'CAP 1m 3f 200y
4:55 (5:02) (Class 2) (0-100,100) 3-Y-O
£12,462 (£3,732; £1,866; £934; £466; £234) **Stalls High**

Form RPR

1-32 **1** **Patkai (IRE)**[24] 1919 3-9-4 **95**.................................. RyanMoore 5 109+
(Sir Michael Stoute) *s.i.s: hld up: hdwy over 2f out: led wl over 1f out: wanted to lug lft whn r.o wl and in command ins fnl f: pushed out towards fin* **6/5**[1]

1-00 **2** 2 3/4 **Trenchtown (IRE)**[14] 2194 3-8-6 **83**.......................... SteveDrowne 4 90
(R Charlton) *hld up: nt clr run whn hdwy over 2f out: rdn and hung lft over 1f out: styd on to take 2nd towards fin: nt trble wnr* **15/2**[3]

3-02 **3** 1/2 **The Betchworth Kid**[12] 2256 3-8-6 **83**.................... MickyFenton 2 89
(M L W Bell) *midfield: hdwy over 3f out: rdn whn bmpd over 1f out: sn chsd wnr but no imp: kpt on same pce ins fnl f: lost 2nd towards fin* **14/1**

0-64 **4** 3 **Ellmau**[15] 2142 3-8-11 **88**.. ChrisCatlin 3 89
(E J O'Neill) *prom: led over 3f out: rdn and hdd jst over 2f out: one pce fnl f* **33/1**

311- **5** 3 **Tomintoul Flyer**[235] 6092 3-8-8 **85**.............................. TPQueally 6 81
(H R A Cecil) *in tch: rdn to ld jst over 2f out: hdd wl over 1f out: sn hung lft and btn* **3/1**[2]

31-1 **6** *shd* **Inventor (IRE)**[12] 2256 3-8-8 **85**.............................. WJSupple 8 81
(B J Meehan) *midfield: rdn and hdwy to chse ldrs over 2f out: wknd fnl f* **8/1**

10-6 **7** 15 **Safari Sunup (IRE)**[36] 1600 3-8-13 **90**.......................... TomEaves 10 62
(P Winkworth) *midfield: lost pl over 4f out: n.d after* **20/1**

0135 **8** 2 **No To Trident**[24] 1919 3-8-7 **84** ow1.................... StephenDonohoe 13 53
(P D Evans) *hld up: brief effrt over 3f out: hung lft whn btn over 1f out* **50/1**

6-25 **9** 1 1/4 **Meeriss (IRE)**[15] 2142 3-9-9 **100**.......................... EdwardCreighton 7 67
(M R Channon) *led: rdn and hdd over 3f out: wknd over 2f out* **33/1**

1110 **10** 4 1/2 **William Blake**[14] 2194 3-8-11 **88**.......................... GregFairley 11 48
(M Johnston) *trckd ldrs tl rdn and wknd over 3f out* **12/1**

2m 31.19s (-2.01) **Going Correction** +0.125s/f (Good) **10** Ran SP% **120.3**
Speed ratings (Par 105): **111,109,108,106,104 104,94,93,92,89**
CSF £11.18 CT £91.48 TOTE £2.00: £1.20, £2.60, £2.60; EX 13.20 Place 6: £10.14, Place 5: £8.70..
Owner Ballymacoll Stud **Bred** Ballymacoll Stud Farm Ltd **Trained** Newmarket, Suffolk

FOCUS
A good-quality handicap run in a decent winning time for the type of race. The first three all came from well off the pace with the third and fourth setting the level.

NOTEBOOK
Patkai(IRE), runner-up to a well-treated rival in a well-contested handicap at Chester last time, looked sure to be more at home on this more galloping track, and the way the race was run suited him down to the ground. They went a good gallop and set it up for him, having been held up out the back early. He is a progressive sort and will get further than this in time, but in the short term the King George V Handicap at Royal Ascot looks his type of race. He would probably be ideally suited by ground that does not ride as quick as it was here. (op 5-4 tchd 6-4)
Trenchtown(IRE), like the winner, held up out the back in the early stages, came through late as those who raced more prominently fell in a hole. He was only beaten by a rival who could well prove himself Pattern class in time, so there was no disgrace in this, and he certainly seems to be finding his ideal trip now. (op 10-1)
The Betchworth Kid proved his stamina for this sort of trip when chasing home Inventor at Windsor last time and he again stayed on well for a place. He will not always have a rival of the quality of Patkai to beat at this sort of level. (op 16-1)
Ellmau ◆ has been given a chance by the Handicapper, who dropped him 7lb following his fourth in a Listed race last time. Running in a handicap for the first time, he ran a blinder considering he chased the leader for much of the race - his fellow prominent racers finished last and second-last - and he could well pop up at a price in a similar heat.
Tomintoul Flyer, who holds a King Edward VII entry, was making his seasonal reappearance. He travelled well chasing the pace but then hung under pressure and perhaps the ground was too quick for him. He looks capable of better. (op 100-30 tchd 4-1)
Inventor(IRE) was disappointing considering he was only 4lb worse off with The Betchworth Kid compared with when he beat him at Windsor last time. There looked no obvious excuse. (op 7-1)
T/Jkpt: £11,257.50 to a £1 stake. Pool: £15,855.64. 1.00 winning ticket. T/Plt: £10.20 to a £1 stake. Pool: £129,582.90. 9,194.50 winning tickets. T/Qpdt: £4.00 to a £1 stake. Pool: £3,939.24. 712.80 winning tickets. DO

1990 LINGFIELD (L-H)
Saturday, May 31

OFFICIAL GOING: Turf course - good to soft (6.4); all-weather - standard
Wind: Almost nil Weather: Overcast, warm

2611 DORMANSLAND PRIMARY SCHOOL (S) STKS 1m 4f (P)
6:05 (6:05) (Class 6) 3-Y-O
£1,774 (£523; £262) **Stalls Low**

Form RPR

0 **1** **Ericarrow (IRE)**[27] 1840 3-8-0 0.......................... DavidProbert(7) 11 59
(A M Balding) *dwlt: t.k.h: hld up in midfield: smooth prog to trck ldr 3f out: led over 1f out: rdn wl clr* **3/1**[1]

0000 **2** 7 **Kijivu**[5] 2468 3-8-7 55.. CatherineGannon 4 48
(M R Channon) *cl up: rdn 3f out: nt qckn over 2f out: kpt on fr over 1f out to take 2nd fnl 100yds* **6/1**

0-0 **3** 1/2 **Soundbyte**[21] 1994 3-8-10 0 ow1.............................. JerryO'Dwyer(3) 3 53
(J Gallagher) *pushed along in rr 1/2-way: u.p and no prog over 4f out: hrd rdn and styd on fr over 2f out: tk 3rd nr fin* **50/1**

50-6 **4** 3/4 **Has To Be Abacus (IRE)**[95] 704 3-8-12 53.............. DavidKinsella 5 51
(A B Haynes) *plld hrd: cl up: prog to ld over 3f out: hdd over 1f out: wknd and lost 2 pls fnl 100yds* **5/1**[3]

0-60 **5** 1 1/2 **Lady Jinks**[18] 2080 3-8-0 46.................................... BillyCray(7) 10 44
(M D I Usher) *cl up: gng wl on outer over 3f out: rdn over 2f out: no imp: fdd over 1f out* **20/1**

00 **6** 9 **Toon Army**[26] 1869 3-8-4 0................................(t) DominicFox(3) 6 29
(Miss D Mountain) *in tch: rdn over 4f out: wknd over 2f out* **25/1**

0000 **7** *hd* **Cape Tycoon (IRE)**[12] 2259 3-8-12 49.......................... VinceSlattery 9 34
(S A Callaghan) *settled midfield: rdn and effrt 3f out: no prog: wknd rapidly over 1f out* **4/1**[2]

00-0 **8** 10 **Pay Pay Pay**[32] 1694 3-8-7 45.................................. SimonWhitworth 12 13
(P D Evans) *in tch: rdn over 3f out: at rr of main gp over 2f out: sn wknd rapidly* **22/1**

02P0 **9** 11 **Herrbee (IRE)**[37] 1586 3-8-12 46.............................. AdamKirby 13 —
(P Butler) *hld up in last: reminder 7f out: lost tch 5f out: t.o* **8/1**

0-00 **10** 5 **Charlie Be (IRE)**[32] 1694 3-8-7 47.......................... JackMitchell(5) 1 —
(Mrs P N Dutfield) *t.k.h: mde most to 4f out: wknd rapidly: t.o* **12/1**

2600 **11** 5 **Poppy Red**[23] 1938 3-8-7 49.................................. PaulFitzsimons 7 —
(Miss J R Tooth) *t.k.h: w ldr: led 4f out to over 3f out: wknd rapidly: t.o* **10/1**

-660 **12** 8 **Hiss And Boo**[23] 1937 3-8-12 50........................(b) FrancisNorton 2 —
(P Howling) *a towards rr: lost tch over 5f out: t.o* **14/1**

2m 33.31s (0.31) **Going Correction** -0.05s/f (Stan) **12** Ran SP% **125.4**
Speed ratings (Par 97): **96,91,91,90,89 83,83,76,69,66 62,57**
CSF £21.50 TOTE £4.10: £1.60, £2.00, £8.80; EX 9.80.The winner was sold to M Harris for 10,200gns. Kijivu was claimed by A Lidderdale for £6,000
Owner Kingsclere Racing CLub **Bred** Kingsclere Stud **Trained** Kingsclere, Hants

FOCUS
A weak and uncompetitive seller. The form is sound, rated through the second and fourth.
Herrbee(IRE) Official explanation: jockey said gelding was never travelling

2612 ALAN MCCONNOCHIE MEMORIAL MAIDEN STKS 1m 2f (P)
6:35 (6:37) (Class 5) 3-Y-O
£2,331 (£693; £346; £173) **Stalls Low**

Form RPR

5 **1** **Never Ending Tale**[44] 1417 3-9-3 0.......................... AdrianMcCarthy 12 76
(W Jarvis) *hld up in tch: prog 3f out: chal 2f out: narrow ld over 1f out: drvn out* **7/1**

45 **2** *nk* **Classic Remark (IRE)**[21] 1991 3-8-12 0.......................... EddieAhern 11 70
(H J L Dunlop) *prom: wnt 2nd 1/2-way: jnd ldr 2f out: w wnr over 1f out: nt qckn fnl 100yds* **5/4**[1]

26 **3** 4 **Ben Ami**[14] 2197 3-9-0 0.. JerryO'Dwyer(3) 8 67
(Miss J R Gibney) *s.s: towards rr: rdn 3f out: styd on u.p over 1f out: tk 3rd nr fin* **10/1**

0 **4** 3/4 **Drum Major (IRE)**[33] 1684 3-9-3 0.............................. PaulDoe 3 66
(Sir Michael Stoute) *led: stdd pce 1/2-way: kicked on 3f out: jnd 2f out: hdd over 1f out: wknd and lost 3rd nr fin* **11/2**[3]

5 1 **Hendersyde (USA)** 3-9-3 0.. AdamKirby 9 64+
(W R Swinburn) *towards rr: bustled along 1/2-way: no prog tl styd on fnl f: nrst fin* **7/2**[2]

0 **6** 1 **Zuwaar**[14] 2199 3-9-3 0..(t) DavidKinsella 14 62
(J H M Gosden) *racd wd: hld up in midfield: rdn 3f out: no prog and hung lft over 1f out* **25/1**

7 *nk* **Bramalea** 3-8-12 0.. DeanMcKeown 10 56
(B W Duke) *s.s: sn trckd ldng trio: outpcd over 2f out: wknd over 1f out* **50/1**

8 1 **One Oi** 3-9-3 0.. SimonWhitworth 1 59
(D W P Arbuthnot) *restrained s: hld up in last pair: shkn up over 1f out: nvr in the hunt* **33/1**

9 1 3/4 **Day Trip (IRE)** 3-9-3 0.. PaulFitzsimons 6 55
(B J Meehan) *s.s: hld up in last pair: stl there whn rn into bk of wkng rival over 1f out: nvr in the hunt* **16/1**

60 **10** 8 **Heroic Lad**[5] 2454 3-9-0 0.................................... KevinGhunowa(3) 2 39
(A B Haynes) *plld hrd: chsd ldr to 1/2-way: wknd u.p 3f out: eased fnl f* **100/1**

2m 7.62s (1.02) **Going Correction** -0.05s/f (Stan) **10** Ran SP% **119.3**
Speed ratings (Par 99): **93,92,89,88,88 87,87,86,84,78**
CSF £16.28 TOTE £8.20: £1.70, £1.30, £2.10; EX 13.70.
Owner Ali Saeed **Bred** Gainsborough Stud Management Ltd **Trained** Newmarket, Suffolk

FOCUS
An ordinary maiden run in a time 0.81 seconds slower than the following 46-60 handicap. The form does not look too solid with the runner-up rated a stone off her previous best.
Hendersyde(USA) Official explanation: jockey said colt was never travelling

Heroic Lad Official explanation: vet said gelding lost a shoe

2613 GLEEDS H'CAP — 1m 2f (P)

7:10 (7:10) (Class 6) (0-60,63) 3-Y-O — £2,047 (£604; £302) Stalls Low

Form					RPR
040	1		**Ramprakash**68 997 3-9-4 60	AdamKirby 7	65
			(M L W Bell) *trckd ldrs: rdn and prog on outer fr 3f out: hrd drvn to ld over 1f out: hld on*	15/2	
550-	2	1	**Highly Regal (IRE)**219 6451 3-9-2 58	GeorgeBaker 1	61
			(R A Teal) *hld up wl in rr: stdy prog over 2f out: drvn and hanging bdly over 1f out: forced along and tk 2nd ins fnl f: nt rch wnr*	10/1	
56-0	3	2	**Looter (FR)**59 1161 3-9-4 60	EddieAhern 6	59
			(J L Dunlop) *trckd ldrs: rdn and effrt 2f out: no real prog tl styd on to take 3rd fnl f: unable to chal*	11/4[1]	
3106	4	1	**Novestar (IRE)**37 1592 3-9-3 59	SimonWhitworth 11	56
			(G J Smith) *led: drvn and hdd over 1f out: fdd fnl f*	12/1	
02-0	5	¾	**Bobal Girl**33 1671 3-8-13 60	JackMitchell(5) 4	56
			(E F Vaughan) *trckd ldng pair: cl up and rdn 2f out: nt qckn over 1f out: fdd fnl f*	33/1	
000	6	1 ¾	**Tallest Peak (USA)**26 1854 3-9-2 58	VinceSlattery 3	50
			(M G Quinlan) *trckd ldrs: effrt on inner 2f out: rdn in cl 4th over 1f out but nowhere to go: lost pl fnl f*	5/1[3]	
6-02	7	1 ½	**Addwaitya**12 2247 3-9-7 63	IanMongan 10	52
			(C F Wall) *racd wd in midfield: rdn 3f out: no imp on ldrs fnl 2f*	4/1[2]	
531	8	1 ¼	**Tapas Lad (IRE)**23 1938 3-8-13 58	(v) KevinGhunowa(3) 8	45
			(G J Smith) *trckd ldrs: cl up 3f out: steadily wknd fnl 2f*	7/1	
503	9	1	**Elzeeza (USA)**26 1869 3-9-4 60	JimmyQuinn 12	45
			(E A L Dunlop) *stdd s: hld up in rr: rdn wl over 1f out: one pce and no real prog*	14/1	
-400	10	4 ½	**Treasure Islands (IRE)**26 1870 3-8-13 58	JerryO'Dwyer(3) 14	34
			(S W Hall) *stdd s: hld up in rr: rdn and no prog over 3f out*	50/1	
0-00	11	hd	**Moluccella**26 1870 3-8-12 57	TravisBlock(3) 13	32
			(H Morrison) *mostly chsd ldr to 3f out: losing pl whn hmpd 2f out*	33/1	
3540	12	6	**Thankuforthemusic (IRE)**42 1478 3-9-2 58	FrancisNorton 2	21
			(C Tinkler) *settled in rr: lost tch w main gp over 2f out: bhd after*	16/1	
42-0	13	17	**Mairead's Boy (IRE)**143 98 3-8-10 59	(v) ThomasO'Brien(7) 5	—
			(P Butler) *dwlt and drvn in last pair: wknd 4f out: t.o*	33/1	

2m 6.81s (0.21) **Going Correction** -0.05s/f (Stan) 13 Ran SP% **127.7**
Speed ratings (Par 97): **97,96,94,93,93 91,90,89,88,85 85,80,66**
CSF £83.98 CT £266.06 TOTE £10.50: £2.60, £3.70, £1.40; EX 157.30.
Owner Scotney,Asplin,Symonds & Chellingworth **Bred** Ashbrittle Stud **Trained** Newmarket, Suffolk

FOCUS
A modest if competitive handicap run at just an ordinary pace. The winning time was 0.81 seconds quicker than the previous maiden. The bare form is probably not up to much, but seems sound. The first three should be capable of a bit better.

2614 BENGAL VILLAGE MAIDEN FILLIES' STKS — 6f

7:40 (7:40) (Class 5) 2-Y-O — £2,331 (£693; £346; £173) Stalls High

Form					RPR
4	1		**Skruton (IRE)**30 1749 2-8-11 0	JerryO'Dwyer(3) 10	73
			(M G Quinlan) *racd against nr side rail: mde all: rdn fnl f: kpt on wl*	8/1[3]	
	2	1	**Predict** 2-9-0 0	SebSanders 7	70+
			(Sir Mark Prescott) *racd against nr side rail: trckd ldrs: wnt 2nd 2f out: tried to cl fnl f but a hld*	5/2[2]	
6	3	4	**Innactualfact**15 2146 2-9-0 0	PaulDoe 4	58
			(L A Dace) *dwlt: sn in tch: effrt to dispute 2nd 2f out: nt qckn over 1f out: fdd u.p fnl f*	14/1	
	4	¾	**Samara Valley (IRE)** 2-9-0 0	EddieAhern 1	56
			(H R A Cecil) *dwlt: pushed along towards rr 1/2-way: effrt over 1f out: kpt on but nvr pce to threaten*	10/11[1]	
	5	shd	**Isabella Romee (IRE)** 2-9-0 0	IanMongan 8	55
			(Jane Chapple-Hyam) *dwlt: towards rr: shkn up and styd on fr over 1f out: nrst fin*	20/1	
	6	9	**Bella Rowena** 2-9-0 0	FrancisNorton 3	28
			(A M Balding) *chsd ldrs: hanging and wknd rapidly fnl 2f*	12/1	
	7	6	**Redsetgo** 2-8-11 0	DominicFox(3) 2	10
			(S W Hall) *dwlt and awkward s: nvr on terms: wknd 2f out: t.o*	33/1	
	8	nse	**Winterbourne** 2-9-0 0	JimmyQuinn 6	10
			(M Blanshard) *mostly chsd wnr to 2f out: wknd rapidly: t.o*	25/1	
0	9	½	**Four Green Fields (IRE)**33 1680 2-9-0 0	WandersonD'Avila 5	9
			(B W Duke) *racd v wd: prom tl wknd bdly 2f out: t.o*	66/1	

1m 12.45s (1.25) **Going Correction** +0.125s/f (Good) 9 Ran SP% **119.5**
Speed ratings (Par 90): **96,94,89,88,88 76,68,68,67**
CSF £28.48 TOTE £10.20: £1.80, £1.20, £2.80; EX 37.20.
Owner A Pettinari **Bred** Rathasker Stud **Trained** Newmarket, Suffolk

FOCUS
An ordinary juvenile maiden for fillies and few got involved. The winner stepped up on her debut form and the first two came clear.

NOTEBOOK
Skruton(IRE) improved significantly on the form she showed when fourth on her debut over 5f at Redcar. Soon in front against the often-favoured stands' rail, she stuck on well to the line and never looked in much danger. She clearly has a fair amount of ability, and is open to further improvement, but it is worth remembering everything went right for her this time. (tchd 7-1)
Predict, a daughter of Oasis Dream, half-sister to 1m winner Ricci De Mare, tracked the pace against the stands' rail and ran on to the line. She is open to improvement. (tchd 11-4)
Innactualfact, who showed some ability on her debut at Newbury, ran a respectable race in third and should find her level in nurseries. (op 16-1)
Samara Valley(IRE), a 150,000gns daughter of Dalakhani, first foal of a champion two-year-old filly in Italy, who was also second in the Prix de l'Abbaye at three, was a warm order to make a winning debut, but she was never involved and looked in need of the experience. She should improve for the run, but may require a little further in time. (op 11-10 tchd 6-5 and 5-6)
Isabella Romee(IRE), a daughter of Bahri, was never seen with a chance after starting slowly and she will be a lot better for the experience. (op 16-1 tchd 12-1)

2615 M & M MORTGAGE MANAGEMENT H'CAP — 7f

8:15 (8:17) (Class 5) (0-75,75) 4-Y-O+ — £2,331 (£693; £346; £173) Stalls High

Form					RPR
05-0	1		**My Learned Friend (IRE)**27 1842 4-8-6 63	FrancisNorton 10	72+
			(A M Balding) *trckd ldrs: prog to ld over 2f out: rdn and pressed 1f out: styd on wl*	9/2[3]	
2-06	2	1 ½	**Valentino Swing (IRE)**25 1900 5-8-11 68 ow1	AdamKirby 2	73
			(Miss T Spearing) *hld up in midfield: prog over 2f out: swtchd to nr side and cshd wnr wl over 1f out: chal ent fnl f: no imp fnl 100yds*	12/1	
0140	3	½	**Kensington (IRE)**33 1683 7-9-4 75	(p) EddieAhern 9	79
			(P D Evans) *trckd ldrs: gng strly over 2f out: drvn and nt qckn wl over 1f out: kpt on fnl f*	8/1	
3123	4	3	**Follow The Flag (IRE)**64 1058 4-8-8 70	JackMitchell(5) 11	66
			(C F Wall) *wl in rr against nr side rail: effrt over 2f out: kpt on but nvr able to rch ldrs*	7/2[2]	
005-	5	½	**Dr Synn**221 6413 7-8-4 61 oh1	DavidKinsella 7	55
			(M J Attwater) *stdd s: pushed along in last over 4f out: drvn and styd on fnl 2f: nrst fin*	16/1	
200-	6	3 ½	**Torquemada (IRE)**173 7099 7-8-9 69	TolleyDean(3) 8	54
			(M J Attwater) *dwlt: nvr on terms w ldrs: rdn and plugged on reluctantly fr over 2f out*	16/1	
335	7	¾	**Resplendent Nova**14 2203 6-9-3 74	JimmyQuinn 5	57
			(P Howling) *pressed ldr: upsides over 2f out: wknd wl over 1f out: b.b.v*	11/4[1]	
00-0	8	3 ½	**Grizedale (IRE)**14 2203 9-8-8 65	(t) PaulDoe 1	38
			(M J Attwater) *nvr beyond midfield: wknd on outer wl over 1f out*	20/1	
1340	9	13	**Garden Party**8 2373 4-8-11 71	KirstyMilczarek(3) 4	9
			(Jane Chapple-Hyam) *prom on wd outside 3f: sn wknd: t.o*	12/1	
5-10	10	hd	**Vintage (IRE)**23 1928 4-8-11 68	IanMongan 12	6
			(J Akehurst) *led against nr side rail to over 2f out: wknd and heavily eased: t.o*	15/2	

1m 24.75s (1.45) **Going Correction** +0.125s/f (Good) 10 Ran SP% **121.9**
Speed ratings (Par 103): **96,94,93,90,89 85,84,80,66,65**
CSF £60.14 CT £437.70 TOTE £5.80: £2.00, £3.60, £2.40; EX 84.50.
Owner DR E Harris **Bred** B Kennedy **Trained** Kingsclere, Hants

FOCUS
A modest handicap, run at a fair pace and rated through the runner-up. The winner is potentially well treated on his 2yo form.
Torquemada(IRE) Official explanation: jockey said gelding lost its action
Resplendent Nova Official explanation: jockey said gelding bled from the nose
Garden Party Official explanation: jockey said gelding lost its action
Vintage(IRE) Official explanation: jockey said gelding was unsuited by the track

2616 NATIONAL CENTRE FOR YOUNG PEOPLE WITH EPILEPSY FILLIES' H'CAP — 5f

8:45 (8:45) (Class 5) (0-70,68) 3-Y-O+ — £2,331 (£693; £346; £173) Stalls High

Form					RPR
1521	1		**Wibbadune (IRE)**18 2088 4-9-1 56	AdamKirby 9	70
			(D Shaw) *t.k.h: hld up bhd ldrs: plld out and effrt 2f out: rdn to ld 1f out: styd on wl*	3/1[3]	
-012	2	2 ½	**Black Moma (IRE)**18 2088 4-9-7 62	DavidKinsella 2	67
			(A B Haynes) *trckd ldr: led 2f out: rdn and hdd 1f out: one pce*	9/4[1]	
-530	3	1 ½	**Second Opinion (IRE)**16 2122 3-8-13 65	KirstyMilczarek(3) 3	62
			(J M P Eustace) *racd against nr side rail: led to 2f out: rdn and grad fdd fr over 1f out*	7/1	
-451	4	½	**Dualagi**17 2102 4-9-12 67	GeorgeBaker 7	65
			(M R Bosley) *taken to post early and steadily: s.s: hld up in last pair: shkn up and no prog over 2f out: kpt on fnl f*	11/4[2]	
0-44	5	1 ½	**Red Amaryllis**26 1867 3-9-5 68	EddieAhern 8	57
			(H J L Dunlop) *chsd ldrs: rdn 1/2-way: wknd over 1f out*	9/1	
4506	6	7	**Diminuto**11 2292 4-9-3 65	BillyCray(7) 4	32
			(M D I Usher) *led to s and mounted at post: a in last pair: struggling on outer fr 1/2-way*	20/1	

58.81 secs (0.61) **Going Correction** +0.125s/f (Good)
WFA 3 from 4yo+ 8lb 6 Ran SP% **116.4**
Speed ratings (Par 100): **100,96,93,92,90 79**
CSF £9.64 CT £35.17 TOTE £4.40: £2.00, £1.70; EX 8.60 Place 6: £105.91, Place 5: £44.95..
Owner Simon Mapletoft Racing I **Bred** Ballyhane Stud **Trained** Danethorpe, Notts

FOCUS
A moderate sprint, run at a solid pace. The progressive winner is rated up a further 9lb.
T/Plt: £110.90 to a £1 stake. Pool: £53,963.07. 355.20 winning tickets. T/Qpdt: £78.60 to a £1 stake. Pool: £3,901.18. 36.70 winning tickets. JN

2191 NEWBURY (L-H)

Saturday, May 31

OFFICIAL GOING: Soft (good to soft in places; 5.7)
Wind: Moderate, behind

2617 BATHWICK TYRES LADY RIDERS' H'CAP — 1m 2f 6y

6:20 (6:21) (Class 5) (0-70,69) 4-Y-O+ — £3,123 (£968; £363; £363) Stalls High

Form					RPR
-504	1		**New Star (UAE)**4 2476 4-10-7 69	MissEJJones 3	75
			(W M Brisbourne) *chsd ldrs: rdn to ld jst ins fnl f: hrd rdn and hung lft nr fin: all out*	4/1[2]	
0000	2	nk	**Gala Sunday (USA)**21 2001 8-9-8 56	(bt) MissSBrotherton 1	61
			(M W Easterby) *in rr: stdy hdwy over 2f out: styd on wl fnl f: edgd rt cl home and fin wl: nt quite get up*	25/1	
0002	3	1 ¼	**Tizzy May (FR)**7 2394 8-9-9 57	(v) MissLEllison 9	60
			(B Ellison) *chsd ldrs: slt ld 1f out: hdd sn after: wkng whn hmpd and snatched up cl home*	4/1[2]	
0/0-	3	dht	**Bay Hawk**83 6848 6-10-1 68	MissCLWills(5) 2	71
			(B G Powell) *in rr: hdwy over 2f out: styd on wl thrght fnl f to join 3rd but nt rch ldng duo*	11/1	
-065	5	3 ¼	**Love Angel (USA)**18 2072 6-9-7 55 oh10	(v) MissGDGracey-Davison 5	51
			(J J Bridger) *slowly away: sn rcvrd to tack on to main gp: rdn over 2f out: styd on wl fnl f but nt rch ldrs*	33/1	
505-	6	2 ¼	**Golden Alchemist**98 2006 5-9-7 55 oh2	MissFayeBramley 4	47
			(M D I Usher) *chsd ldrs: rdn over 2f out: sn btn*	11/2[3]	
2445	7	½	**Kylkenny**37 1589 13-9-3 56 oh1 ow1	MissVCartmel(5) 6	47
			(H Morrison) *in tch: rdn and one pce fr over 2f out*	10/3[1]	
000-	8	nk	**Barathea Dreams (IRE)**357 2467 7-10-1 63	MrsSMoore 10	53
			(J S Moore) *t.k.h: sn led and 8l clr 7f out: rdn 3f out: wknd 2f out: hdd 1f out and sn btn*	13/2	
650-	9	2 ¼	**Piano Man**310 3868 6-9-2 55 oh5	MissSarah-JaneDurman(5) 8	40
			(J C Fox) *bhd most of way*	18/1	
60-0	10	hd	**Scottish River (USA)**26 1853 9-9-5 60	MissCNosworthy(7) 7	45
			(M D I Usher) *t.k.h: a in rr*	20/1	

2m 15.11s (6.31) **Going Correction** +0.70s/f (Yiel) 10 Ran SP% **116.9**
Speed ratings (Par 103): **102,101,100,100,98 96,95,95,93,93**
Tote Places: Bay Hawk £1.60, Tizzy May £0.90. Tri-cast: New Star/Gala Sunday/Bay Hawk £512.51; New Star/Gala Sunday/Tizzy May £214.14. CSF £101.93 TOTE £4.10: £1.90, £3.90; EX 62.00.
Owner Shropshire Wolves **Bred** Darley **Trained** Great Ness, Shropshire
■ Stewards' Enquiry : Miss S Brotherton three-day ban: careless riding (Jun 14,16,23)
Miss E J Jones three-day ban: used whip with excessive frequency (Jun 14,16,23)

FOCUS
Many of these lady riders looked far from convincing, and the leader, Barathea Dreams, seemed to go off a little too fast, so this is form to treat with real caution. The main action took place up the centre of the track in the straight.

2618 BATHWICK TYRES MAIDEN AUCTION FILLIES' STKS — 6f 8y
6:50 (6:53) (Class 5) 2-Y-O — **£3,885** (£1,156; £577; £288) **Stalls** High

Form — RPR
3 **1** **Accede**[26] 1866 2-8-8 0 ... PatCosgrave 12 — 78
(J G Portman) *w'like: tall: chsd ldrs: outpcd over 2f out: drvn and rallied over 1f out: swtchd rt ins fnl f and fin strly fnl 75yds: led last stride* **22/1**
23 **2** *shd* **Raggle Taggle (IRE)**[42] 1474 2-8-6 0 ... JamesDoyle 4 — 76
(R M Beckett) *lw: pressed ldrs tl slt ld over 1f out: styd on wl whn chal thrght fnl f: ct fnl stride* **5/2**[1]
02 **3** *hd* **Souter's Sister (IRE)**[22] 1955 2-8-3 0 ... PatrickHills(3) 8 — 75
(R Hannon) *lw: chsd ldrs: drvn to chal fr ins fnl f: no ex fnl strides* **6/1**[3]
4 *½* **Deyas Dream** 2-8-8 0 ... SteveDrowne 5 — 76
(A M Balding) *athletic: b.hind: in tch: rdn over 2f out: styd on to chse ldrs ins fnl f: styd on wl cl home but nvr quite gng pce to chal* **18/1**
5 *1* **Bouggie Daize** 2-8-4 0 ... NeilPollard 11 — 69+
(C G Cox) *w'like: str: lw: s.i.s: sn drvn along: styd on appr fnl f and gng on cl home* **33/1**
6 *1¼* **Infamous Angel** 2-8-6 0 ... RichardSmith 16 — 67
(R Hannon) *w'like: scope: s.i.s: sn rcvrd to chse ldrs: led 2f out: hdd over 1f out: wknd ins fnl f* **22/1**
02 **7** *½* **Shiva Adiva**[16] 2124 2-8-4 0 ... RichardKingscote 14 — 63
(Tom Dascombe) *sn led: rdn and hdd 2f out: wknd fnl f* **7/2**[2]
8 *3½* **Milly Rose** 2-8-8 0 ... FrankieMcDonald 1 — 57
(M Blanshard) *lengthy: sn pushed along in rr: mod prog ins fnl f* **33/1**
9 *¾* **Very Distinguished** 2-8-11 0 ... TPQueally 10 — 58+
(M G Quinlan) *w'like: bit bkwd: pressed ldrs: rdn 2f out: wknd over 1f out* **16/1**
10 *1¼* **Nun Today (USA)** 2-8-3 0 ... LukeMorris(3) 2 — 49
(J S Moore) *w'like: leggy: bit bkwd: in tch: rdn and bhd fr 1/2-way* **50/1**
3 **11** *13* **Daheeya**[8] 2368 2-8-4 0 ... TPO'Shea 3 — 20+
(M R Channon) *trckd ldrs: rdn over 2f out: sn wknd* **7/2**[2]
12 *1* **Fong's Alibi** 2-7-13 0 ... NataliaGemelova(5) 6 — 5
(J S Moore) *w'like: slowly away: a in rr* **20/1**
13 *13* **Duchess Of Doom (IRE)** 2-7-13 0 ... KMay(7) 13 — —
(B W Hills) *w'like: scope: lengthy: swtg: pressed ldrs to 1/2-way* **20/1**

1m 15.97s (2.97) **Going Correction** +0.50s/f (Yiel) — **13** Ran SP% **124.5**
Speed ratings (Par 90): **100,99,99,98,97 95,95,90,89,87 70,69,51**
CSF £74.82 TOTE £29.70: £6.00, £1.40, £1.90; EX 89.20.
Owner Mrs D Joly **Bred** Mrs D Joly And D F Powell **Trained** Compton, Berks

FOCUS
A big field for this fillies' maiden, and the race should produce some winners, but the bare form is just ordinary. The winning time was decent, 0.11 seconds quicker than the later three-year-old maiden, although the ground would have been more chewed up by the time that race was run. They raced middle to stands' side early on, but the main action took place towards the near rail late on.

NOTEBOOK
Accede improved on the form she showed when third on her debut over 5f at Warwick, but she needed every yard of this extra furlong. Having shown some early speed down the centre of the track, she lost her place when coming under pressure, still looking green, and she appeared set to finish down the field, but she gradually responded to pressure and picked up well when getting a gap towards the stands' rail inside the final furlong. She should progress a fair bit again. (op 28-1)
Raggle Taggle(IRE), just beaten on her debut on Lingfield's Polytrack before looking a little unlucky at Nottingham, did nothing wrong on this step up to 6f, but was just caught near the line. She showed good pace up the centre of the track early and kept on well after edging towards the stands' rail in the closing stages. (op 7-2 tchd 4-1)
Souter's Sister(IRE), a beaten favourite when well held in second on the turf over 5f at Lingfield on her previous start, ran a solid race and deserves extra credit as she made her challenge on the outside of runners. (tchd 11-2 and 15-2)
Deyas Dream, a 25,000gns foal, daughter of Clodovil, half-sister to among others, quite useful Norisan, a multiple 7f winner at two to three, is an attractive filly and knew her job more than some of these, faring best of the newcomers and showing a fair level of ability. (op 25-1)
Bouggie Daize ◆, a daughter of Tobougg, half-sister to Fox's Den, placed over 5f at two, out of a dual 5f juvenile winner, showed plenty of ability and gave the impression she will improve a fair bit for the run.
Infamous Angel ◆, a 9,000gns daughter of Exceed And Excel, half-sister to Aviva, who was placed over 6f at two, showed lots of natural speed against the stands' rail before getting tired. She should be better for the run and will not mind a drop back to 5f. (op 18-1 tchd 16-1)
Shiva Adiva, who was on her toes beforehand, took them along towards the stands' side early, but she weakened out of contention, proving unable to build on her recent second at Salisbury, and this ground was probably softer than she wants. (op 4-1)
Very Distinguished ◆, a 26,000gns daughter of Diktat, half-sister to Personify, a triple 6f-1m winner at two and four, out of a very useful dual 7f-1m juvenile winner in France, was conceding weight all round. She travelled well down the centre of the track early on, showing good speed, but offered little once coming under pressure and might need a little more time. She is not without ability. (op 14-1)
Daheeya, edgy beforehand, could not confirm the promise she showed when third on her debut over this trip on quick ground at Newmarket. She was caught out wide down the centre of the track and was never really going, not looking happy on the easy surface. Official explanation: jockey said filly never travelled (tchd 4-1)

2619 WEDGEWOOD ESTATES H'CAP — 1m (S)
7:25 (7:26) (Class 4) (0-80,83) 4-Y-0+ — **£5,504** (£1,637; £818; £408) **Stalls** High

Form — RPR
/0-1 **1** **Ben Chorley**[40] 1520 4-9-4 80 ... TPQueally 12 — 90
(D R Lanigan) *disp ld tl def advantage after 2f: drvn over 2f out and kpt slt ld tl asserted fnl 100yds and sn in command* **7/2**[1]
60-0 **2** *1¾* **Prince Golan (IRE)**[40] 1520 4-8-6 68 ... RichardKingscote 8 — 74
(J W Unett) *chsd ldrs tl wnt 2nd 2f out: kpt on u.p thrght fnl f: outpcd fnl 100yds* **66/1**
56-2 **3** *1* **Last Sovereign**[131] 246 4-8-13 75 ... FrankieMcDonald 9 — 79
(Jane Chapple-Hyam) *lw: in tch: chsd ldrs over 2f out: styd on ins fnl f but nvr gng pce to chal* **12/1**
-240 **4** *nk* **Montrachet**[28] 1801 4-8-13 75 ... SteveDrowne 6 — 78
(M L W Bell) *in tch: rdn over 2f out: kpt on thrght fnl f but nvr gng pce to be competitive* **14/1**
00-2 **5** *¾* **Kafuu (IRE)**[12] 2262 4-9-7 83 ... RichardHughes 13 — 84
(S A Callaghan) *lw: in tch: rdn and effrt over 2f out: nvr gng pce to be competitive and no imp ins fnl f* **11/2**
4214 **6** *nse* **Full Victory (IRE)**[18] 2083 6-9-3 79 ... DaneO'Neill 2 — 80
(R A Farrant) *towards rr: rdn and hdwy over 2f out: kpt on fnl f but nvr gng pce to get into contention* **9/2**[3]
0006 **7** *1¼* **Moody Tunes**[43] 1456 5-9-2 78 ... PatCosgrave 5 — 76
(K R Burke) *mid-div: rdn over 2f out: styd on fnl f but nvr a danger* **16/1**
0000 **8** *2* **Alfresco**[10] 2308 4-8-13 75 ... (b) JamesDoyle 14 — 69
(I A Wood) *s.i.s: t.k.h: rdn over 2f out: sme prog fnl f* **16/1**
5/5- **9** *2* **Balnagore**[287] 4608 4-8-10 72 ... RichardMullen 1 — 61
(J L Dunlop) *in rr: mod prog fnl 2f* **14/1**
0-00 **10** *7* **Mountain Cat (IRE)**[12] 2262 4-8-4 66 ... TPO'Shea 7 — 39
(W J Musson) *w wnr 2f and styd chalng to 3f out: wknd over 2f out* **33/1**
006- **11** *6* **Namid Reprobate (IRE)**[213] 6596 5-9-2 78 ... JosedeSouza 10 — 37
(P F I Cole) *bhd most of way* **33/1**
/162 **12** *11* **Jake The Snake (IRE)**[14] 2203 7-9-0 79 ... LukeMorris(3) 11 — 13
(A W Carroll) *chsd ldrs tl wknd over 2f out: eased whn no ch ins fnl f* **4/1**[2]
0063 **13** *26* **Bomber Command (USA)**[26] 1857 5-8-9 74 ... (v) PatrickHills(3) 3 — —
(J W Hills) *sn rdn in rr: dropped away fr 1/2-way* **9/1**

1m 41.99s (2.29) **Going Correction** +0.50s/f (Yiel) — **13** Ran SP% **126.0**
Speed ratings (Par 105): **108,106,105,104,104 104,102,100,98,91 85,74,48**
CSF £267.85 CT £2588.15 TOTE £5.10: £1.80, £13.80, £4.00; EX 486.40.
Owner Diamond Racing Ltd **Bred** Mrs A Yearley **Trained** Newmarket, Suffolk

FOCUS
A fair handicap with the winner rated 5lb higher than her Pontefract form. Nothing could make much impression from off the pace.
Montrachet Official explanation: jockey said filly hung right-handed
Jake The Snake(IRE) Official explanation: jockey said gelding lost its action

2620 BATHWICK TYRES MAIDEN STKS — 6f 8y
7:55 (7:59) (Class 5) 3-Y-O — **£3,885** (£1,156; £577; £288) **Stalls** High

Form — RPR
44 **1** **Badweia (USA)**[22] 1964 3-8-12 0 ... RichardMullen 14 — 75
(J L Dunlop) *lw: trckd ldrs: drvn to ld jst ins fnl f: asserted fnl 100yds: readily* **9/2**[2]
3- **2** *1¼* **Muhajaar (IRE)**[358] 2432 3-9-3 0 ... PatCosgrave 1 — 76
(L M Cumani) *str: bit bkwd: racd towards centre: trckd ldrs: rdn to ld ins fnl 2f: hdd jst ins fnl f: kpt on but nt pce to wnr* **7/2**[1]
3 *1¼* **Vienna Affair** 3-8-12 0 ... OscarUrbina 6 — 67
(J R Fanshawe) *w'like: str: chsd ldrs: rdn over 1f out: kpt in ins fnl f but nvr gng pce of ldng duo* **14/1**
0-0 **4** *1¼* **Apple Pie Order (IRE)**[9] 2341 3-8-12 0 ... SteveDrowne 15 — 63
(R J Hodges) *in tch: rdn 2f out: styd on ins fnl f but nvr gng pce to be competitive* **66/1**
55- **5** *½* **Dan Chillingworth (IRE)**[215] 6530 3-9-3 0 ... TPQueally 3 — 66
(J R Fanshawe) *racd towards centre of crse: styd on to press ldr over 1f out: wknd ins fnl f* **12/1**
5- **6** *1* **Lekita**[220] 6434 3-8-12 0 ... SaleemGolam 4 — 58
(W R Swinburn) *bit bkwd: racd towards centre: chsd ldrs: rdn 2f out: wknd ins fnl f* **5/1**[3]
04 **7** *½* **Priti Fabulous (IRE)**[27] 1836 3-8-12 0 ... LiamJones 7 — 57
(W J Haggas) *in tch: rdn over 2f out: kpt on ins fnl f but nvr gng pce to be competitive* **10/1**
0 **8** *nk* **Seven Royals (IRE)**[14] 2198 3-9-3 0 ... ChrisCatlin 13 — 61
(Miss A M Newton-Smith) *bhd: pushed along 3f out: styd on ins fnl f but nvr in contention* **100/1**
6 **9** *¾* **Mr Rio (IRE)**[22] 1971 3-9-3 0 ... NeilPollard 10 — 58
(A P Jarvis) *w'like: bit bkwd: led: hdd ins fnl 2f: sn btn* **50/1**
10 *nk* **Celtic Spring (IRE)** 3-8-12 0 ... FergusSweeney 8 — 52
(J R Boyle) *leggy: s.i.s: bhd tl kpt on fr over 1f out* **22/1**
0 **11** *hd* **Flying Flute**[14] 2187 3-9-3 0 ... DaneO'Neill 12 — 57
(H Candy) *rangy: in tch: rdn and kpt on same pce fnl 2f* **20/1**
20- **12** *¾* **Storm Sir (USA)**[232] 6138 3-9-3 0 ... (t) RichardHughes 11 — 54
(B J Meehan) *lw: trckd ldr: rdn over 2f out: wknd over 1f out* **7/2**[1]
00 **13** *3* **First Tracks (IRE)**[14] 2198 3-8-10 0 ... GabrielHannon(7) 2 — 45
(J W Hills) *lw: racd towards centre: chsd ldrs tl rdn and wknd fr 2f out* **33/1**
60 **14** *4½* **Where's Dids**[9] 2341 3-8-12 0 ... TPO'Shea 5 — 25
(M R Channon) *a in rr* **50/1**
15 *13* **Red Century** 3-8-12 0 ... PaulEddery 9 — —
(G D Blake) *leggy: scope: s.i.s: a in rr* **33/1**

1m 16.08s (3.08) **Going Correction** +0.50s/f (Yiel) — **15** Ran SP% **124.1**
Speed ratings (Par 99): **99,97,95,94,93 92,91,90,89,89 89,88,84,78,60**
CSF £19.65 TOTE £5.90: £2.30, £2.30, £4.00; EX 22.90.
Owner Hamdan Al Maktoum **Bred** Shadwell Farm LLC **Trained** Arundel, W Sussex

FOCUS
Quite a good sprint maiden that should produce some winners, although the form is muddling. The winning time was 0.11 seconds slower than the earlier juvenile fillies' maiden, although that race was run on fresher ground. They raced in two groups early on, with four racing up the middle and the majority racing towards the stands' side, but they merged as one late on.

2621 RACING UK 4TH BIRTHDAY H'CAP — 1m 5f 61y
8:30 (8:30) (Class 5) (0-75,75) 4-Y-0+ — **£2,590** (£770; £385; £192) **Stalls** High

Form — RPR
0-53 **1** **Cleaver**[18] 2076 7-9-9 75 ... RichardHughes 5 — 85+
(Lady Herries) *hld up in tch: hdwy 2f out: hrd rdn over 1f out and styd on ins fnl f to ld fnl 100yds: drvn out* **10/3**[1]
-430 **2** *1¼* **Pocketwood**[15] 2153 6-8-11 63 ... StephenCarson 4 — 71
(Jean-Rene Auvray) *led: rdn 3f out: hdd ins fnl 2f: rallied u.p to chse wnr fnl 75yds but a hld* **8/1**
4515 **3** *1* **The King And I (IRE)**[25] 1904 4-9-0 73 ... (b) DavidProbert(7) 7 — 80
(Miss E C Lavelle) *t.k.h towards rr: gd hdwy over 3f out to ld ins fnl 2f: hrd rdn over 1f out: hdd fnl 100yds: wknd and lost 2nd fnl 75yds* **20/1**
34-0 **4** *¾* **Kasban**[15] 2153 4-9-6 72 ... FrankieMcDonald 1 — 77
(Jane Chapple-Hyam) *chsd ldrs: rdn fr 3f out: styd on fnl 2f but nvr quite gng pce to chal* **8/1**
2635 **5** *¾* **Salute (IRE)**[41] 1501 9-9-9 75 ... RobertHavlin 10 — 79
(P G Murphy) *lw: chsd ldrs: rdn over 3f out: styd on same pce fnl 2f* **20/1**
-331 **5** *dht* **Mae Cigan (FR)**[15] 2153 5-9-2 68 ... SteveDrowne 16 — 72+
(M Blanshard) *in rr: rdn and hdwy over 2f out: kpt on u.p fr over 1f out but nvr gng pce to trble ldrs* **7/2**[2]
0-51 **7** *¾* **Rock 'N' Roller (FR)**[39] 1538 4-9-8 74 ... RichardMullen 9 — 77
(W R Muir) *chsd ldrs: hrd drvn fr over 2f out: styd on same pce fr over 1f out* **6/1**[3]
0-02 **8** *¾* **Bold Adventure**[18] 2076 4-9-1 67 ... NeilPollard 11 — 69+
(W J Musson) *swtg: hld up in rr: kpt on fnl 2f: nvr in contention* **10/1**
5150 **9** *6* **Flame Creek (IRE)**[16] 2135 12-8-2 61 ... MCGeran(7) 12 — 54
(E J Creighton) *in rr: rdn and effrt over 2f out: nvr in contention* **20/1**
6035 **10** *2½* **They All Laughed**[21] 1998 5-9-6 72 ... ChrisCatlin 6 — 61
(P W Hiatt) *in rr: hdwy 5f out: rdn and wknd 3f out* **16/1**

1402 **11** 3/4 **Mandalay Prince**[31] 1732 4-8-13 65 TPO'Shea 13 53
(W J Musson) *a in rr* **9/1**
2000 **12** 40 **Prince Charlemagne (IRE)**[12] 2243 5-8-7 59 (p) JamesDoyle 14 —
(R M Stronge) *chsd ldr: rdn over 4f out: wknd 3f out: t.o* **33/1**
0000 **13** 29 **Old Romney**[15] 2165 4-8-10 62 SaleemGolam 15 —
(M Wigham) *chsd ldrs tl wknd qckly over 3f out: t.o* **33/1**

2m 59.88s (7.88) **Going Correction** +0.70s/f (Yiel) **13** Ran SP% **127.0**
Speed ratings (Par 103): **103,102,101,101,100 100,100,99,96,94 94,69,51**
CSF £30.02 CT £481.83 TOTE £4.50: £1.70, £3.20, £5.20; EX 46.00.
Owner Lady Herries and Friends **Bred** J M Greetham **Trained** Patching, W Sussex

FOCUS
Just a modest handicap run at a fair pace and rated around the placed horses. They raced up the centre of the track in the straight.
Prince Charlemagne(IRE) Official explanation: jockey said gelding was unsuited by the soft (good to soft places) ground

2622 RELYON CLEANING NEWBURY FILLIES' H'CAP 7f (S)
9:00 (9:04) (Class 5) (0-75,74) 3-Y-O+ **£2,590** (£770; £385; £192) **Stalls** High

Form RPR
-020 **1** **Rydal Mount (IRE)**[9] 2329 5-10-0 72 FergusSweeney 1 92
(W S Kittow) *chsd ldrs: led over 2f out: drvn clr fnl f* **13/2**[2]
40-3 **2** 5 **Superduper**[18] 2067 3-9-0 69 RichardHughes 15 72
(R Hannon) *swtg: racd stands' side and narrow overall ldr tl hdd over 2f out: kpt on but no ch w wnr fnl f* **8/1**
4-30 **3** 2 1/4 **Poppets Sweetlove**[17] 2097 4-9-6 64 SteveDrowne 8 65
(A B Haynes) *t.k.h: chsd ldrs: rdn and kpt on same pce fnl 2f* **7/1**[3]
0-15 **4** 1 1/4 **Binfield (IRE)**[23] 1930 3-9-4 73 DaneO'Neill 2 67
(B G Powell) *in tch: rdn over 2f out: kpt on fr over 1f out but nvr gng pce to rch ldrs* **12/1**
0140 **5** 1 3/4 **Miss Mujanna**[14] 2196 3-9-5 74 PatCosgrave 11 63
(J Akehurst) *s.i.s: towards rr: rdn and hdwy over 2f out: swtchd rt over 1f out and kpt on but nvr gng pce to trble ldrs* **10/1**
00-0 **6** hd **Scarlet Oak**[26] 1872 4-9-5 63 RichardThomas 14 56
(D J S Ffrench Davis) *racd stands' side: chsd ldrs 3f out: rdn sn after: wknd fnl f* **14/1**
10-2 **7** 1 3/4 **Danseuse Volante (IRE)**[22] 1958 3-9-4 73 TPQueally 6 57
(J W Hills) *chsd ldrs: rdn over 2f out: wknd fnl f* **5/2**[1]
0-60 **8** 1 3/4 **Kannon**[23] 1926 3-8-4 59 (v[1]) RichardKingscote 4 39
(W J Knight) *chsd ldrs: rdn over 2f out: wknd over 1f out* **25/1**
0-06 **9** nk **Tamara Moon (IRE)**[10] 2302 3-9-2 71 ChrisCatlin 5 50
(M R Channon) *pressed ldrs and upsides after 2f: wknd ins fnl 2f* **12/1**
-113 **10** 1 **Silca Destination**[87] 797 3-8-11 66 TPO'Shea 9 42
(M R Channon) *in tch: rdn and effrt over 2f out: sn wknd* **11/1**
-145 **11** 1 1/4 **Bookish**[70] 975 3-9-4 73 RobertHavlin 7 46
(Jamie Poulton) *in tch: rdn 3f out: wknd 2f out* **33/1**
32-0 **12** 3 1/2 **Monashee Rock (IRE)**[89] 772 3-9-1 70 RichardMullen 12 34
(M Salaman) *chsd ldrs stands' side over 4f* **12/1**
56-0 **13** 3 1/4 **Istria (USA)**[22] 1957 3-8-10 65 JamesDoyle 10 21
(R M Beckett) *chsd ldrs stands' side over 4f* **50/1**
-500 **14** 1 3/4 **Ishibee (IRE)**[125] 327 4-8-9 53 oh2 (p) LiamJones 3 8
(J J Bridger) *a outpcd* **66/1**
/0-4 **15** 15 **Night Rainbow (IRE)**[22] 1966 5-8-2 53 oh4 MCGeran(7) 13 —
(Mrs S Leech) *s.i.s: t.k.h on stands' side but a towards rr* **40/1**

1m 29.03s (3.33) **Going Correction** +0.50s/f (Yiel) **15** Ran SP% **125.4**
WFA 3 from 4yo+ 11lb
Speed ratings (Par 100): **100,94,91,90,88 88,86,84,83,82 81,77,73,71,54**
CSF £57.76 CT £396.50 TOTE £7.70: £2.70, £2.20, £2.90; EX 77.50 Place 6: £179.56, Place 5: £58.27..
Owner Reg Gifford **Bred** D R Tucker **Trained** Blackborough, Devon

FOCUS
A fair fillies' handicap but the form makes sense rated around the fourth that finished immediately behind the winner. They raced middle to stands' side early, with the larger group up the centre, but they were spread all over the track at the line.
Monashee Rock(IRE) Official explanation: jockey said filly was unsuited by the soft (good to soft places) ground
Night Rainbow(IRE) Official explanation: jockey said mare lost its action
T/Plt: £177.00 to a £1 stake. Pool: £74,024.65. 305.20 winning tickets. T/Qpdt: £68.70 to a £1 stake. Pool: £4,617.45. 49.70 winning tickets. ST

2580 YORK (L-H)
Saturday, May 31

OFFICIAL GOING: Good (good to firm in places)
Meeting switched from Musselburgh. The ground was described as 'good to firm, quicker in places'. Home bend moved out 3m adding 7y to race distances.
Wind: Light 1/2 against Weather: Fine, sunny and warm

2623 CSL SCAFFOLDING STKS (CLAIMING RACE) 1m 4f
2:20 (2:20) (Class 4) 4-Y-O+ **£7,123** (£2,119; £1,059; £529) **Stalls** Centre

Form RPR
5-10 **1** **Chocolate Caramel (USA)**[14] 2202 6-8-13 85 JimCrowley 7 78
(Mrs A J Perrett) *mid-div: stdy hdwy 4f out: chal 2f out: rdn to ld ins fnl f: hld on wl* **11/2**
-540 **2** 1/2 **Inchloch**[21] 1998 6-9-0 75 LDettori 11 78
(B G Powell) *hld up in rr: effrt over 3f out: sn chsng ldrs: styd on wl ins fnl f* **5/1**[3]
1410 **3** 1 1/4 **Birkside**[15] 2168 5-9-7 82 NCallan 1 83
(D Carroll) *hld up in midfield: hdwy over 3f out: led over 2f out: hdd and no ex ins fnl f* **2/1**[1]
4233 **4** 1/2 **Princess Cocoa (IRE)**[11] 2271 5-8-11 74 PaulHanagan 4 72
(R A Fahey) *wnt rt s: chsd ldr: chal over 2f out: kpt on same pce ins fnl f* **9/2**[2]
-060 **5** 2 **Longspur**[17] 2107 4-9-0 75 NSLawes(7) 5 79
(M W Easterby) *hld up in rr: effrt 4f out: styd on fnl f* **25/1**
3153 **6** 1 1/4 **Court Of Appeal**[7] 2395 11-8-9 65 (tp) J-PGuillambert 6 65
(B Ellison) *chsd ldrs: hung rt and one pce fnl 2f* **8/1**
2-40 **7** 3 1/4 **Wraith**[21] 1998 4-9-4 66 TedDurcan 9 69
(H R A Cecil) *chsd ldrs: effrt over 3f out: wknd over 1f out* **12/1**
150- **8** 8 **Muraco**[256] 5500 4-8-11 69 AndrewMullen(3) 2 52
(Mrs A Duffield) *chsd ldrs: drvn 4f out: wknd 2f out* **40/1**
000- **9** 8 **Peak Seasons (IRE)**[5] 1750 5-8-4 40 (b) NBazeley(7) 12 36
(M C Chapman) *t.k.h: sn long way clr: edgd rt and hdd over 2f out: sn lost pl* **200/1**
314/ **10** 8 **High Command**[610] 5660 5-8-9 92 BradleyRoper(7) 8 28
(M W Easterby) *swtchd lft after star: t.k.h in rr: drvn 4f out: sn wknd* **12/1**
000- **11** dist **Water Pistol**[13] 1406 6-8-5 44 ow3 MarkCoumbe(7) 10 —
(M C Chapman) *chsd ldrs: lost pl after 3f: sn wl bhd: hopelessly t.o fnl 5f* **200/1**

2m 34.36s (1.16) **Going Correction** -0.075s/f (Good) **11** Ran SP% **117.3**
Speed ratings (Par 105): **93,92,91,91,90 89,87,81,76,71** —
CSF £32.71 TOTE £6.70: £2.30, £2.20, £1.10; EX 32.00.The winner was claimed by R Fahey for £14,000. Inchloch was claimed by Miss C Dyson for £16,000
Owner Mrs Priscilla Graham **Bred** Sierra Thoroughbreds **Trained** Pulborough, W Sussex

FOCUS
A decent claimer but not easy to rate. The sixth and seventh look the best guide for the time being.

2624 ORGANS FOR LIFE STKS (H'CAP) 7f
2:50 (2:51) (Class 3) (0-90,90) 3-Y-O **£9,714** (£2,890; £1,444; £721) **Stalls** Low

Form RPR
2-1 **1** **Tawaash (USA)**[22] 1957 3-9-7 90 RHills 6 98
(M A Jarvis) *mde all: styd on wl fnl 2f: gamely* **4/1**[1]
1-34 **2** 1 **Swift Gift**[17] 2104 3-9-3 86 LDettori 5 92
(B J Meehan) *hld up: nt clr run over 2f out: rdn to chal over 1f out: no ex wl ins fnl f* **11/2**[3]
4-21 **3** 1 **Harrison George (IRE)**[14] 2187 3-8-10 79 PaulHanagan 2 82
(R A Fahey) *w ldrs: styd on same pce ins fnl f* **15/2**
0510 **4** hd **Opus Maximus (IRE)**[7] 2410 3-8-7 76 oh1 JoeFanning 10 78
(M Johnston) *w ldrs: hung lft over 2f out: kpt on same pce appr fnl f* **16/1**
2-20 **5** 1 **Elna Bright**[23] 1923 3-9-2 85 EddieAhern 3 85
(B J Meehan) *w ldrs: fdd fnl f* **16/1**
02-0 **6** shd **Flowing Cape (IRE)**[7] 2405 3-9-3 86 NCallan 8 85
(R Hollinshead) *hld up: effrt over 2f out: kpt on: nvr rchd ldrs* **6/1**
1- **7** nk **Naval Review (USA)**[218] 6469 3-8-7 76 oh1 AlanMunro 9 75
(Sir Michael Stoute) *hld up in rr: effrt and swtchd rt over 2f out: rdn and hung lft appr fnl f: nvr rchd ldrs* **7/1**
4-13 **8** 3 1/2 **Blindspin**[9] 2333 3-8-8 80 PJMcDonald(3) 7 69
(M Dods) *chsd ldrs: effrt over 2f out: wknd over 1f out* **12/1**
0-02 **9** 2 **The Jostler**[11] 2276 3-8-9 78 TedDurcan 4 62
(B W Hills) *trckd ldrs: drvn 3f out: lost pl over 1f out* **12/1**
2-1 **10** 1 1/2 **The Oil Magnate**[50] 1298 3-9-3 86 PhillipMakin 1 66
(M Dods) *trckd ldrs: effrt over 2f out: sn wknd* **9/2**[2]

1m 24.86s (-0.44) **Going Correction** 0.0s/f (Good) **10** Ran SP% **119.3**
Speed ratings (Par 103): **102,100,99,99,98 98,97,93,91,89**
CSF £26.65 CT £161.62 TOTE £4.90: £1.90, £2.20, £2.30; EX 31.90.
Owner Hamdan Al Maktoum **Bred** G Watts Humphrey Jr & Louise I Humphrey **Trained** Newmarket, Suffolk

FOCUS
A very competitive three-year-old handicap rated through the third. Improved efforts from the first two and the form looks very solid.

NOTEBOOK
Tawaash(USA), making his handicap debut, looked very fit. He made every hard and, really buckling down, was going away at the line. He will take his chance in the Jersey Stakes at Royal Ascot. (op 9-2)
Swift Gift travelled strongly but had to wait for an opening. After throwing down the gauntlet, he was very definitely second best at the line. He is clearly progressing very nicely. (op 7-1)
Harrison George(IRE), stepping up in trip, ran out of his skin on his handicap debut. He looks to be thriving. (op 16-1)
Opus Maximus(IRE), on his toes beforehand, tended to hang but to his credit kept going all the way to the line.
Elna Bright keeps running well but looks rated to the very limit. (op 18-1 tchd 20-1)
Flowing Cape(IRE), happy to sit at the back, stayed on when it was all over. He can surely win any average maiden race. (op 9-2)
Naval Review(USA), winner of a backend maiden on his only start, was lethargic beforehand and looked to be carrying condition. Eventually making his way to the wide outside, he was keeping on nicely at the finish. He is open to plenty of improvement. (op 5-1 tchd 9-2)
The Oil Magnate, still on the weak side, was making his handicap debut on just his third career start. He didn't run up to expectations and may not want the ground as quick as this. (tchd 5-1)

2625 STOWE FAMILY LAW LLP GRAND CUP (LISTED RACE) 1m 6f
3:25 (3:27) (Class 1) 4-Y-O+
£17,031 (£6,456; £3,231; £1,611; £807; £405) **Stalls** Low

Form RPR
20-3 **1** **Samuel**[15] 2169 4-9-0 111 EddieAhern 8 116
(J L Dunlop) *hld up in mid-div: effrt on inner over 3f out: styd on wl to ld fnl 75yds* **12/1**
-041 **2** 1 3/4 **Tranquil Tiger**[14] 2192 4-9-3 117 TedDurcan 1 117
(H R A Cecil) *reluctant to go to post: trckd ldrs: led on inner over 3f out: shkn up 2f out: rdn and hdd wl ins fnl f* **4/1**[2]
14-2 **3** 2 **Regal Flush**[14] 2192 4-9-0 112 LDettori 2 111
(Saeed Bin Suroor) *hld up towards rr: effrt on inner over 3f out: styd on same pce appr fnl f* **2/1**[1]
31-5 **4** 1 3/4 **Lion Sands**[21] 1980 4-9-3 110 NCallan 10 112
(L M Cumani) *hld up in rr: stdy hdwy on inner over 3f out: kpt on same pce fnl f* **9/2**[3]
5-54 **5** nk **Red Gala**[22] 1944 5-9-0 105 AlanMunro 11 108
(Sir Michael Stoute) *hld up in mid-div: hdwy on outer 4f out: kpt on fnl f* **17/2**
0-14 **6** hd **Soapy Danger**[31] 1717 5-9-0 106 JoeFanning 5 108
(M Johnston) *chsd ldrs: outpcd on outer over 2f out: kpt on fnl f* **10/1**
-054 **7** 5 **Heron Bay**[14] 2202 4-9-0 97 PaulHanagan 12 101
(G Wragg) *hld up in mid-div: effrt on outside 4f out: wknd ins fnl f* **25/1**
40-2 **8** 11 **Supersonic Dave (USA)**[22] 1944 4-9-0 106 RHills 9 86
(B J Meehan) *hld up in rr: effrt over 3f out: sn btn* **14/1**
10-4 **9** 4 1/2 **Tungsten Strike (USA)**[21] 1980 7-9-3 111 JimCrowley 6 82
(Mrs A J Perrett) *led 2f: chsd ldrs: rdn and hung lft over 2f out: sn lost pl* **14/1**
00-2 **10** 1 1/4 **Dunaskin (IRE)**[35] 1629 8-9-0 107 J-PGuillambert 7 78
(B Ellison) *led after 2f: hdd over 3f out: sn wknd* **33/1**
2-00 **11** 1 **Hanella (IRE)**[7] 2402 5-8-9 80 NickyMackay 3 71
(S C Williams) *chsd ldrs: drvn 6f out: outpcd over 3f out: sn lost pl* **100/1**
063- **12** hd **Lost Soldier Three (IRE)**[457] 598 7-9-0 108 AdrianTNicholls 4 76
(D Nicholls) *hld up in rr: drvn over 3f out: nvr a factor* **40/1**

2m 55.03s (-5.17) **Going Correction** -0.075s/f (Good) **12** Ran SP% **122.4**
Speed ratings (Par 111): **111,110,108,107,107 107,104,98,95,95** **94,94**
CSF £60.28 TOTE £14.50: £3.40, £1.70, £1.40; EX 72.30 Trifecta £174.10 Pool: £1,054.55, 4.30 winning units.
Owner Normandie Stud Ltd **Bred** Normandie Stud Ltd **Trained** Arundel, W Sussex

FOCUS
A strong Listed race, well worth Group 3 status. The form looks very solid with the maiden Samuel showing further improvememnt.

NOTEBOOK
Samuel, who looked a picture of health, enjoyed a dream run on the inner and really stuck to his guns to put his head in front near the line, finally breaking his duck on his eighth start. (op 16-1)
Tranquil Tiger proved reluctant to go to the post and had to be dismounted and led down. He took it up full of running and looked in total command, matched at 1.03 on the exchanges. His rider picked his whip up after checking on the big screen that Samuel was closing on his inside and they were picked off near the line. (op 7-2)
Regal Flush, beaten ten lengths by today's runner-up on easier ground at Newbury, closed the gap but was still not good enough. He improved with racing at three and the same pattern looks likely under Godolphin. (op 3-1)
Lion Sands, suited by the return to 1m6f, improved on his Ascot return effort and will be suited by 2m. (tchd 5-1)
Red Gala, stepping up in trip, made his effort on the slower ground towards the centre. Staying on at the finish, there is even better to come. (op 8-1)
Soapy Danger, another to find himself rather marooned towards the centre of the track, stuck to his guns and is close to his best now after serious injury curtailed his three-year-old career. (tchd 9-1)
Dunaskin(IRE) Official explanation: jockey said gelding was unsuited by the good (good to firm in places) ground

2626 NATIONAL EXPRESS SCOTTISH SPRINT CUP (HERITAGE H'CAP) 5f
3:55 (3:58) (Class 2) (0-105,102) 3-Y-O+

£31,155 (£9,330; £4,665; £2,335; £1,165; £585) **Stalls** High

Form				RPR
00-3	**1**		**Masta Plasta (IRE)**[14] 2211 5-8-11 **96** .... AdeleRothery(7) 11 (D Nicholls) *led stands' side and overall ldr: edgd lft over 1f out: kpt on wl* **16/1**	111
43-3	**2**	*1*	**Everymanforhimself (IRE)**[6] 2426 4-8-9 **87** .... (b) NCallan 16 (K A Ryan) *chsd wnr: kpt on wl fnl f* **11/1**	98
33-2	**3**	*1 1/4*	**Ishetoo**[14] 2211 4-8-12 **93** .... MichaelJStainton(3) 17 (A Dickman) *mid-div: effrt 2f out: edgd lft and styd on wl fnl f* **8/1**[2]	100+
-060	**4**	*nse*	**Tabaret**[2] 2538 5-8-9 **87** .... JimCrowley 19 (R M Whitaker) *chsd ldrs: edgd lft and kpt on wl fnl f* **16/1**	94
164-	**5**	*1*	**Siren's Gift**[238] 6003 4-9-3 **95** .... LPKeniry 4 (A M Balding) *racd far side: trckd ldr: led that side over 1f out: kpt on same pce* **12/1**	98
0040	**6**	*hd*	**Indian Trail**[7] 2401 8-9-10 **102** .... (v) JoeFanning 18 (D Nicholls) *dwlt: hld up in rr: styd on appr fnl f: nt rch ldrs* **33/1**	104+
3024	**7**	*nk*	**Machinist (IRE)**[15] 2172 8-9-7 **99** .... SilvestreDeSousa 3 (D Nicholls) *racd far side: chsd ldrs: drvn over 3f out: one pce fnl 2f* **8/1**[2]	100
0-02	**8**	*nk*	**Fantasy Explorer**[8] 2359 5-8-7 **85** .... GrahamGibbons 14 (J J Quinn) *chsd ldrs: one pce fnl 2f* **20/1**	85
-005	**9**	*1 1/4*	**Special Day**[16] 2129 4-8-10 **88** .... AlanMunro 12 (B W Hills) *chsd ldrs: one pce fnl 2f* **14/1**	84
30-5	**10**	*hd*	**How's She Cuttin' (IRE)**[38] 1571 5-8-7 **85** .... PaulFessey 20 (T D Barron) *in rr: hdwy over 1f out: nvr nr ldrs* **25/1**	80
0301	**11**	*1*	**Fyodor (IRE)**[7] 2401 7-9-4 **96** .... (v) PaulMulrennan 5 (W J Haggas) *dwlt: racd far side: sn trcking ldrs: effrt over 2f out: fdd over 1f out* **14/1**	87
-601	**12**	*nk*	**Elhamri**[9] 2326 4-8-12 **90** .... LDettori 15 (S Kirk) *chsd ldrs: wknd 1f out* **10/1**	80
0-14	**13**	*3/4*	**Northern Fling**[7] 2401 4-9-10 **102** .... AdrianTNicholls 7 (D Nicholls) *in rr: effrt over 2f out: nvr a factor* **11/1**	90
-032	**14**	*hd*	**River Falcon**[16] 2129 8-9-3 **95** .... DanielTudhope 10 (J S Goldie) *hld up in rr: effrt 2f out: nvr a factor* **13/2**[1]	82
2400	**15**	*3/4*	**Matsunosuke**[7] 2404 6-9-8 **100** .... EddieAhern 2 (A B Coogan) *racd far side: hld up: nvr a factor* **20/1**	84+
10-0	**16**	*1 1/2*	**Blazing Heights**[69] 983 5-8-5 **83** .... NelsonDeSouza 8 (J S Goldie) *hld up in rr: nvr on terms* **33/1**	62
-013	**17**	*3/4*	**Bertoliver**[16] 2129 4-9-4 **96** .... TedDurcan 1 (D K Ivory) *led far side gp of 6: wknd over 1f out* **9/1**[3]	72
0420	**18**	*3*	**Green Park (IRE)**[16] 2129 5-8-10 **88** .... PaulHanagan 6 (R A Fahey) *racd far side: trckd ldrs: lost pl over 1f out* **12/1**	53

58.13 secs (-1.17) **Going Correction** 0.0s/f (Good) **18** Ran SP% **131.0**
Speed ratings (Par 109): **109,107,105,105,103 103,102,102,100,100 98,98,96,96,95 92,91,86**
CSF £180.75 CT £1544.95 TOTE £23.20: £4.80, £3.30, £2.10, £4.80; EX 380.60 Trifecta £3191.60 Pool: £1,2586.93, 2.80 winning units.
Owner Lady O'Reilly **Bred** Shane Doyle **Trained** Sessay, N Yorks

FOCUS
Unlike the previous day the draw was insignificant. The back-to-his-best winner made all with only Indian Trail able to make significant ground from off the pace.

NOTEBOOK
Masta Plasta(IRE), without a win since his Norfolk Stakes success here in 2005, had the visor left off. He blitzed from the off and, despite drifting towards the far side, he always looked like holding on. He is all speed and now heads forEpsom's 'Dash'. (op 20-1)
Everymanforhimself(IRE), trying the minimum trip for the first time since his juvenile days, was in pursuit of the winner throughout and never gave up the fight. There is surely a good handicap to be won with him by his new connections. (op 14-1)
Ishetoo, running from a career-high mark, made tremendous improvement at three and he looks likely to make further progress this time.
Tabaret, having his second outing in three days, is a 5f fast-ground specialist but he is on a long losing run and the handicapper is reluctant to slacken his grip.
Siren's Gift, out of a dam-line that tends to improve with age, made a highly satisfactory return.
Indian Trail, back on his last winning mark, showed a return to form after a trip to Dubai in the winter. Last away, he was the only one to make significant ground from off the pace and is sure to be a big player in the major sprint handicaps again this year.
How's She Cuttin'(IRE) was putting in some pleasing work in the closing stages and looks on the verge of regaining her very best form. (op 20-1)
Elhamri Official explanation: jockey said gelding lost his action
River Falcon, making his 16th appearance at this track and seeking his third course-and-distance win, never looked like making ground from off the pace. There will be another day. (op 8-1)
Bertoliver Official explanation: trainer had no explanation for the poor form shown

2627 PARSONAGE COUNTRY HOUSE HOTEL E B F MAIDEN FILLIES' STKS 6f
4:30 (4:30) (Class 3) 2-Y-O

£6,605 (£1,965; £982; £490) **Stalls** High

Form				RPR
3	**1**		**Honest Quality (USA)**[15] 2160 2-9-0 0 .... TedDurcan 8 (H R A Cecil) *hld up: hdwy to ld over 2f out: edgd rt ins fnl f: hld on wl* **15/8**[1]	88+
	2	*1 1/4*	**African Skies** 2-9-0 0 .... NCallan 7 (K A Ryan) *dwlt: effrt over 2f out: upsides 1f out: edgd lft: no ex wl ins fnl f* **11/1**	84+
	3	*1 3/4*	**Sanvean (IRE)** 2-9-0 0 .... AlanMunro 9 (M R Channon) *hld up: effrt over 2f out: hung lft and kpt on same pce fnl f* **9/1**	79+
2	**4**	*nk*	**Stan's Cool Cat (IRE)**[12] 2253 2-9-0 0 .... NelsonDeSouza 6 (P F I Cole) *w ldrs: chal over 1f out: kpt on same pce* **11/4**[2]	78
	5	*2*	**My Sweet Georgia (IRE)** 2-9-0 0 .... RHills 3 (B W Hills) *trckd ldrs: effrt and swtchd lft over 1f out: kpt on same pce* **8/1**	72
	6	*7*	**Damselfly** 2-9-0 0 .... JoeFanning 4 (M Johnston) *w ldrs: wkng whn hmpd over 1f out* **14/1**	51
	7	*hd*	**Lady Salama** 2-9-0 0 .... DarrenWilliams 2 (K R Burke) *t.k.h: trckd ldrs: effrt over 2f out: wkng whn sltly hmpd over 1f out* **22/1**	54+
	8	*2 3/4*	**Fleeting Star (USA)** 2-9-0 0 .... LDettori 1 (J Noseda) *dwlt: t.k.h: sn trcking ldrs: rdn and edgd lft 1f out: sn wknd and eased* **4/1**[3]	60+
	9	*6*	**Ennovy** 2-9-0 0 .... KimTinkler 5 (N Tinkler) *led tl hdd & wknd over 2f out: sn bhd* **66/1**	24

1m 12.79s (0.89) **Going Correction** 0.0s/f (Good) **9** Ran SP% **123.4**
Speed ratings (Par 94): **94,92,90,89,86 77,77,73,65**
CSF £26.71 TOTE £2.80: £1.30, £3.40, £3.20; EX 24.60.
Owner K Abdulla **Bred** Juddmonte Farms Inc **Trained** Newmarket, Suffolk
■ Stewards' Enquiry : R Hills three-day ban: careless riding (Jun 14-16)

FOCUS
A decent fillies' maiden race sure to throw up some future winners, notably the runner-up.

NOTEBOOK
Honest Quality(USA), who is not that big, knew what was required this time and she stuck on in game fashion despite a tendency to edge right. (op 9-4 tchd 5-2)
African Skies ◆, out of an unraced daughter of an Irish 1,000 Guineas winner, was much the biggest in the field. Noisy beforehand, she missed the break but came there looking a big threat only to edge to her left in the final furlong. This will bring her on a ton and, sure to be wiser next time, she looks a fine prospect. (op 20-1)
Sanvean(IRE), a lengthy, well-made newcomer, showed her inexperience but kept going all the way to the line. This will have taught her plenty. (op 7-1 tchd 10-1)
Stan's Cool Cat(IRE), stepping up a furlong, gave a good account of herself and can surely find a lesser maiden race. (op 7-2)
My Sweet Georgia(IRE), a lengthy newcomer, had to switch to find racing room. She stuck on in her own time and the experience will not be lost on her. (op 9-1)
Damselfly, bought relatively cheaply, was on the retreat when completely knocked out of her stride by My Sweet Georgia. (op 18-1 tchd 12-1)
Fleeting Star(USA), who cost $490,000 at a breeze-up sale in Florida, looks very weak. She was keen to get on with it but stopped in a matter of strides and was heavily eased. Official explanation: jockey said filly lost its action (op 11-4)

2628 COLDSTREAM GUARDS ASSOCIATION STKS (H'CAP) 2m 88y
5:05 (5:05) (Class 4) (0-80,79) 4-Y-O+ **£7,123** (£2,119; £1,059; £529) **Stalls** Low

Form				RPR
4-21	**1**		**Bukit Tinggi (IRE)**[9] 2332 4-9-10 **79** .... PhilipRobinson 1 (M A Jarvis) *hld up in tch: hdwy on outside to ld over 2f and edge lft: rdn over 2 l clr ent fnl f: eased nr fin: shkn up last stride and hld on* **4/6**[1]	94+
1600	**2**	*nk*	**Basalt (IRE)**[15] 2168 4-9-7 **76** .... PaulHanagan 2 (T J Pitt) *chsd ldrs: kpt on to take 2nd 1f out: styd on wl ins fnl f: jst denied* **20/1**	86
210-	**3**	*3 1/2*	**Indonesia**[165] 6335 6-9-9 **76** .... GrahamGibbons 6 (T D Walford) *mid-div: effrt over 3f out: rallied over 1f out: styd on same pce* **20/1**	82
20-4	**4**	*hd*	**Kayf Aramis**[16] 2135 6-9-0 **70** .... MarcHalford(3) 10 (Miss Venetia Williams) *chsd ldrs: keeping on same pce whn sltly hmpd over 1f out* **9/1**[2]	76
54-2	**5**	*2 1/2*	**Daylami Dreams**[15] 2157 4-9-3 **72** .... JoeFanning 9 (T P Tate) *trckd ldrs: led over 3f out: hdd over 2f out: wknd ins fnl f* **10/1**[3]	75
4-2	**6**	*6*	**Winged D'Argent (IRE)**[42] 1472 7-9-9 **76** .... (b) LPKeniry 3 (B J Llewellyn) *prom: drvn 9f out: wknd over 1f out* **16/1**	71
-600	**7**	*1*	**Thewhirlingdervish (IRE)**[16] 2135 10-9-5 **72** .... TedDurcan 8 (T D Easterby) *in rr: hdwy on ins 4f out: nvr nr ldrs* **14/1**	66
1241	**8**	*3/4*	**Capitalise (IRE)**[18] 2091 5-8-8 **61** .... AlanMunro 12 (V Smith) *hld up in rr: hdwy over 3f out: hung lft: nvr nr ldrs* **14/1**	54
0221	**9**	*1 1/2*	**Mister Arjay (USA)**[7] 2393 8-9-5 **75** .... PJMcDonald(3) 11 (B Ellison) *led tl over 3f out: wknd 2f out* **10/1**[3]	66
6030	**10**	*4*	**Trance (IRE)**[21] 1998 8-8-12 **65** .... (p) PaulFessey 5 (T D Barron) *in rr: drvn 8f out: nvr on terms* **18/1**	52
11-0	**11**	*6*	**Inchpast**[16] 2135 7-9-11 **78** .... (b) PaulMulrennan 7 (M H Tompkins) *mid-div: drvn over 4f out: sn wknd* **14/1**	57

3m 33.46s (-3.34) **Going Correction** -0.075s/f (Good)
WFA 4 from 5yo+ 2lb **11** Ran SP% **128.8**
Speed ratings (Par 105): **105,104,103,103,101 98,98,97,97,95 92**
CSF £21.35 CT £195.23 TOTE £1.80: £1.60, £8.10, £5.60; EX 40.70 Place 6: £41.82, Place 5: £27.53..
Owner H R H Sultan Ahmad Shah **Bred** Hrh Sultan Ahmad Shah **Trained** Newmarket, Suffolk

FOCUS
The progressive winner was value for at least three lengths. The form looks solid rated through the third, fourth and fifth.
Thewhirlingdervish(IRE) Official explanation: jockey said gelding was unsuited by the good (good to firm in places) ground
Capitalise(IRE) Official explanation: jockey said gelding hung left
T/Plt: £70.00 to a £1 stake. Pool: £120,765.27. 1,258.72 winning tickets. T/Qpdt: £13.40 to a £1 stake. Pool: £5,252.78. 288.30 winning tickets. WG

2629 - 2636a (Foreign Racing) - See Raceform Interactive

[2348] LONGCHAMP (R-H)
Saturday, May 31

OFFICIAL GOING: Soft

2637a PRIX DU PALAIS ROYAL (GROUP 3) 7f
3:15 (3:16) 3-Y-O+ **£29,412** (£11,765; £8,824; £5,882; £2,941)

			RPR
1		**Garnica (FR)**[17] 2106 5-9-6 .... SPasquier 3 (D Nicholls) *trckd ldr tl led 2f out: drvn wl over 1f out: r.o wl fnl f* **58/10**	110
2	*1/2*	**Bellifiore (FR)**[16] 4-9-1 .... TJarnet 8 (Mlle S-V Tarrou, France) *hld up: last st: str run on outside fr over 1f out: drvn to take 2nd cl home* **10/1**	104
3	*hd*	**Tiza (SAF)**[14] 2214 6-9-8 .... CSoumillon 7 (A De Royer-Dupre, France) *hld up: 6th st: hdwy 2f out: drvn to go 2nd 100yds out: no ex clsng stages* **27/10**[1]	110

4 *1* **Welsh Emperor (IRE)**[21] [1989] 9-9-4 .... IMendizabal 4 104
(T P Tate) *racd in 3rd to 1f out: rdn and one pce* **29/10[2]**
5 *1* **Wilki (FR)**[20] [2034] 3-8-4 .... C-PLemaire 1 98
(A De Royer-Dupre, France) *set gd pce tl hdd 2f out: stl 2nd ins fnl f: one pce* **82/10**
6 *1* **Skagerrak (USA)**[37] [1593] 4-9-4 .... OPeslier 5 98
(D Smaga, France) *racd in 4th to st: one pce fnl 2f* **15/1**
7 *2* **Captain Marvelous (IRE)**[35] [1619] 4-9-4 .... TThulliez 6 93
(B W Hills) *restrained to r in 5th: rdn over 2f out: nvr able to chal* **41/10[3]**
8 *nk* **Prince Fasliyev**[8] 4-9-4 .... JVictoire 9 92
(H-A Pantall, France) *7th st: a in rr* **27/1**

1m 21.0s (0.10) **Going Correction** +0.35s/f (Good)
WFA 3 from 4yo+ 11lb 8 Ran SP% **116.8**
Speed ratings: **113,112,112,111,109 108,106,106**
PARI-MUTUEL: WIN 6.80; PL 2.00, 2.20, 1.60; DF 31.40.
Owner Lady O'Reilly, Eamon Maher **Bred** Jean Pierre Dubois **Trained** Sessay, N Yorks

NOTEBOOK
Garnica(FR) certainly saves his best efforts for his native country. Back at Longchamp after changing hands last October, he put up a fine performance by winning this event for the second year running. Settled in second position early on, he quickened to take control of the race at the furlong marker and stayed on well to fend off all challengers as the race came to a close. He was very well suited by the soft ground which did not prevail when he made his seasonal debut at York over 6f. One of his main future targets will be the Prix Maurice de Gheest at Deauville and then it will be back to Longchamp for the Group 1 Prix de la Foret in October.
Belliflore(FR) raced in last place for the early part of this race and was brought wide to make his challenge early in the straight. He quickened from one out and finished best of all.
Tiza(SAF) was another to be given a waiting race. He made a forward move a furlong and a half out and was only just touched off for second place.
Welsh Emperor(IRE) was never going really well. He was being pushed along before the straight and just stayed on one-paced.
Captain Marvelous(IRE) tried to make his final run up the rail but was never really seen with a chance.

2239 BATH (L-H)
Sunday, June 1

OFFICIAL GOING: Good (good to soft in places; 7.8) changing to soft after race 5 (4.10)
The going was changed considerably after the 4.10.
Wind: Nil Weather: Heavy rain just before and for a while after the 4.10 race

2638 TOTEPLACEPOT MEDIAN AUCTION MAIDEN FILLIES' STKS 5f 161y
2:10 (2:14) (Class 6) 2-Y-O £2,072 (£616; £308; £153) Stalls Centre

Form RPR
3 **1** **Dubai's Gazal**[9] [2357] 2-9-0 0.................................. TPO'Shea 5 78
(M R Channon) *a.p: rdn wl over 1f out: edgd lft ent fnl f: r.o to ld last strides* **10/3[1]**
2 *hd* **Qalahari (IRE)** 2-9-0 0.................................. AdamKirby 12 77
(D J Coakley) *w ldr: led over 3f out: rdn wl over 1f out: ct last strides* **10/1**
3 *1 3/4* **Like For Like (IRE)** 2-9-0 0.................................. RichardHughes 9 72+
(R Hannon) *s.s: hld up and bhd: hdwy 2f out: rdn over 1f out: kpt on ins fnl f* **9/1**
3 **4** *1/2* **Sparta Rebel (IRE)**[15] [2206] 2-9-0 0.................................. PatCosgrave 13 70
(M J Wallace) *a.p: chsd ldr over 2f out: rdn over 1f out: no ex wl ins fnl f* **10/3[1]**
40 **5** *5* **Readily**[23] [1961] 2-9-0 0.................................. RichardKingscote 16 54
(J G Portman) *hld up in mid-div: rdn and hdwy 2f out: wknd over 1f out* **22/1**
6 **6** *nk* **Deal Clincher**[13] [2253] 2-9-0 0.................................. JimCrowley 7 53
(P Winkworth) *led: hdd over 3f out: pushed along over 2f out: wknd wl over 1f out* **40/1**
5 **7** *1* **You've Been Mowed**[34] [1680] 2-9-0 0.................................. SaleemGolam 10 50
(D K Ivory) *w ldrs: rdn and wknd over 1f out* **8/1[3]**
6 **8** *2 1/2* **Dream City (IRE)**[30] [1762] 2-9-0 0.................................. PatDobbs 11 41
(M P Tregoning) *hld up in tch: pushed along and wknd over 1f out* **5/1[2]**
9 *3/4* **Monte Mayor Eagle** 2-9-0 0.................................. TQuinn 1 39
(D Haydn Jones) *s.s: nvr nr ldrs* **66/1**
55 **10** *1/2* **Madison Belle**[10] [2338] 2-9-0 0.................................. RobertHavlin 14 37
(Mrs H Sweeting) *s.i.s: sn hld up in mid-div: wknd over 2f out* **66/1**
11 *1/2* **Jhinga Palak (IRE)** 2-8-7 0.................................. RichardEvans(7) 8 36
(P D Evans) *s.s: rdn and sme hdwy over 1f out: no further prog* **16/1**
12 *3/4* **Heartsease** 2-9-0 0.................................. JamesDoyle 2 33
(J G Portman) *chsd ldrs tl wknd over 2f out* **18/1**
13 *1 3/4* **Samba Queen (IRE)** 2-8-11 0.................................. TravisBlock(3) 3 28
(J L Spearing) *s.s: a in rr* **50/1**
04 **14** *3/4* **Blushing Maid**[28] [1838] 2-9-0 0.................................. MickyFenton 15 25+
(H S Howe) *s.i.s: sme hdwy on outside over 2f out: wknd and eased over 1f out* **16/1**
15 *2* **Goodenough Magic** 2-9-0 0.................................. HayleyTurner 6 19
(Andrew Turnell) *a bhd* **28/1**
16 *29* **Zaftil (IRE)** 2-8-9 0.................................. HaddenFrost(5) 4 —
(H S Howe) *s.s: a in rr: eased whn no ch over 1f out: fin lame* **100/1**

1m 12.39s (1.19) **Going Correction** +0.05s/f (Good) 16 Ran SP% **126.2**
Speed ratings (Par 88): **94,93,91,90,84 83,82,79,78,77 76,75,73,72,69 31**
CSF £37.99 TOTE £3.70: £1.30, £3.70, £2.90; EX 39.90 Trifecta £94.10 Part won..
Owner Jaber Abdullah **Bred** Gainsborough Stud Management Ltd **Trained** West Ilsley, Berks

FOCUS
The first four finished clear in a race where there was little previous form to go on but the level looked strong and reliable.

NOTEBOOK
Dubai's Gazal, a half-sister to a dual winning miler in Germany, built on the promise of her fast-ground debut third over 6f at Haydock. She needed every yard of this slightly shorter trip despite the slower going and a return to a longer distance would appear to be on the cards. (op 3-1 tchd 11-4)
Qalahari(IRE) ◆, a half-sister to a 7f winner in Ireland, was the most expensive in the field costing 20,000 guineas at public auction. She could not have gone much closer to making a winning debut and can soon go one better. (op 9-1 tchd 8-1 and 11-1)
Like For Like(IRE) ◆ is a half-sister to Bella Chica who won the valuable 6f Irish Tattersalls sales race. She showed plenty of promise after a tardy start and improvement can be expected. (op 15-2 tchd 7-1)
Sparta Rebel(IRE), a half-sister to two multiple winners in Italy and another in Spain, came up against a couple of promising sorts at Thirsk. This was another pretty solid performance by one who is bred to need further in due course. (tchd 3-1 and 7-2 tchd 4-1 in a place)
Readily could only manage a short-lived effort. (op 20-1)
Deal Clincher showed far more than on her debut at Windsor although the end result was much the same.
Heartsease Official explanation: jockey said filly suffered interference in running
Zaftil(IRE) Official explanation: vet said filly finished lame in front

2639 TOTEEXACTA H'CAP 1m 5y
2:40 (2:45) (Class 6) (0-60,60) 3-Y-O £2,072 (£616; £308; £153) Stalls Low

Form RPR
00-0 **1** **Maybe I Will (IRE)**[17] [2118] 3-9-4 **60**.................................. HayleyTurner 4 66
(S Dow) *hld up in tch: rdn to ld ins fnl f: drvn out* **33/1**
043- **2** *hd* **The Willowy Wigeon**[244] [5869] 3-9-0 **56**.................................. JimCrowley 10 62
(P Winkworth) *a.p: rdn to ld over 1f out: hdd ins fnl f: r.o* **7/1[3]**
4-60 **3** *2 3/4* **Karmei**[76] [918] 3-9-4 **60**.................................. JamesDoyle 2 59
(J W Hills) *hld up in mid-div: hdwy over 2f out: hrd rdn over 1f out: kpt on same pce ins fnl f* **14/1**
-662 **4** *nk* **Holden Caulfield (IRE)**[13] [2259] 3-8-3 **52**.................................. DavidProbert(7) 1 51
(Mouse Hamilton-Fairley) *s.i.s: sn prom: led over 3f out: rdn and hdd over 1f out: no ex ins fnl f: edgd lft nr fin* **10/1**
5600 **5** *3/4* **Bon Ton Roulet**[48] [1364] 3-8-11 **53**.................................. RichardHughes 5 50
(R Hannon) *s.i.s: hld up and bhd: rdn over 2f out: hdwy over 1f out: styng on same pce whn n.m.r on ins nr fin* **14/1**
060- **6** *1* **Daisy Nook**[213] [6611] 3-8-10 **52**.................................. LPKeniry 14 47+
(S Kirk) *hld up in mid-div: rdn and sltly outpcd over 2f out: hdwy 1f out: kpt on ins fnl f* **10/1**
-250 **7** *2 1/2* **Supporting Role (IRE)**[33] [1696] 3-9-1 **57**..................(p) RichardMullen 15 46
(E S McMahon) *hld up and bhd: rdn and sme hdwy on ins over 1f out: no imp fnl f* **10/1**
-003 **8** *1/2* **Hla Tun (USA)**[38] [1592] 3-9-3 **59**.................................. AdamKirby 6 47
(W R Swinburn) *led: hdd over 3f out: w ldr whn hrd rdn 2f out: wknd over 1f out* **11/2[1]**
0000 **9** *1 1/4* **Asmodea**[13] [2244] 3-8-13 **55**.................................. TPO'Shea 8 40
(D J Coakley) *bhd: rdn 4f out: nvr nrr* **14/1**
00-0 **10** *nk* **Madame Bountiful**[24] [1938] 3-8-13 **55**.................................. FergusSweeney 7 39
(A King) *hld up in tch: rdn over 1f out: wknd fnl f* **14/1**
000 **11** *1 1/4* **Grit (IRE)**[20] [2056] 3-8-7 **56**.................................. MCGeran(7) 13 37+
(M R Channon) *hld up and bhd: pushed along and sme hdwy whn nt clr run jst ins fnl f: n.d* **18/1**
00-0 **12** *3/4* **Rockjumper**[34] [1684] 3-8-7 **52**.................................. TravisBlock(3) 3 31+
(H Morrison) *hld up in tch: wkng whn nt clr run jst ins fnl f* **6/1[2]**
5550 **13** *3/4* **Landikhaya (IRE)**[20] [2045] 3-9-4 **60**..................(b[1]) SaleemGolam 9 38
(D K Ivory) *hld up in mid-div: hdwy on wd outside over 2f out: rdn and wknd over 1f out* **6/1[2]**
2-40 **14** *3 1/2* **Sunshine Lady (IRE)**[20] [2052] 3-9-2 **58**.................................. TQuinn 12 28
(D Haydn Jones) *hld up in mid-div: rdn over 2f out: sn bhd* **20/1**
000 **15** *34* **Minerton Mountain**[28] [1835] 3-8-11 **58** ow1............ JamesMillman(5) 11 —
(B R Millman) *a in rr: eased whn no ch over 1f out* **33/1**

1m 43.29s (2.49) **Going Correction** +0.05s/f (Good) 15 Ran SP% **126.3**
Speed ratings (Par 97): **89,88,86,85,85 84,81,81,79,79 78,77,76,73,39**
CSF £256.95 CT £3500.74 TOTE £30.80: £5.80, £3.20, £5.90; EX 448.50 TRIFECTA Not won..
Owner Mrs Alicia Aldis **Bred** Cheval Court Stud **Trained** Epsom, Surrey
■ Stewards' Enquiry : David Probert one-day ban: careless riding (June 15)

FOCUS
A tightly-knit modest affair with the winning time 1.29 seconds slower than the later older-horse handicap which was run in heavy rain. The winner is rated to her juvenile form.

2640 TOTEQUADPOT H'CAP 1m 2f 46y
3:10 (3:11) (Class 6) (0-65,65) 4-Y-O+ £2,072 (£616; £308; £153) Stalls Low

Form RPR
04-0 **1** **Acapulco Bay**[32] [843] 4-7-9 **46** oh1.................................. DavidProbert(7) 5 56
(D Burchell) *t.k.h in tch: led gng wl over 1f out: rdn ins fnl f: drvn out* **14/1**
6-00 **2** *1 3/4* **Double Spectre (IRE)**[135] [207] 6-9-4 **62**.................................. RobertHavlin 7 68+
(Jean-Rene Auvray) *hld up towards rr: stdy hdwy over 2f out: rdn over 1f out: r.o ins fnl f: wnt 2nd nr fin* **20/1**
-250 **3** *1/2* **Gracechurch (IRE)**[24] [1932] 5-8-12 **56**.................................. RichardHughes 8 61
(R J Hodges) *hld up in tch: rdn and ev ch over 1f out: nt qckn ins fnl f: lost 2nd nr fin* **6/1[3]**
03-6 **4** *2 1/2* **April Fool**[23] [1954] 4-8-9 **56**..................(v) TravisBlock(3) 17 56
(J A Geake) *a.p: rdn over 1f out: one pce* **14/1**
4215 **5** *nk* **Ryan's Future (IRE)**[18] [2097] 8-9-6 **64**.................................. LPKeniry 15 63+
(J S Moore) *hld up in rr: swtchd rt and hdwy 2f out: sn rdn: styd on ins fnl f: nvr nrr* **4/1[2]**
-454 **6** *1* **Lunar River (FR)**[2] [2561] 5-8-13 **57**..................(t) FergusSweeney 4 54
(David Pinder) *hld up and bhd: stdy hdwy over 2f out: rdn and one pce fnl f* **17/2**
16-6 **7** *1* **Jacaranda (IRE)**[18] [2097] 8-9-2 **65**.................................. JamesMillman(5) 12 60
(B R Millman) *s.i.s: hld up in rr: rdn and hdwy over 1f out: one pce fnl f* **9/1**
50/0 **8** *3 3/4* **Achilles Wings (USA)**[24] [776] 12-8-8 **52** ow2.................................. MickyFenton 2 40
(Karen George) *hld up in mid-div: rdn over 2f out: no hdwy* **50/1**
0004 **9** *1/2* **The Gaikwar (IRE)**[5] [2477] 9-8-11 **55**..................(b) RichardKingscote 16 42
(R A Harris) *t.k.h: led: hdd over 4f out: rdn and lost 2nd 2f out: sn wknd: eased wl ins fnl f* **16/1**
00-4 **10** *1/2* **Follow The Colours (IRE)**[27] [1853] 5-9-1 **62**.................................. PatrickHills(3) 14 48
(J W Hills) *plld hrd: w ldr: hung rt and rn sltly wd whn led over 4f out: rdn over 2f out: hdd over 1f out: wknd and eased ins fnl f* **14/1**
6610 **11** *3* **Cumae (USA)**[30] [1776] 4-8-4 **48**.................................. JimmyQuinn 6 28
(J Pearce) *t.k.h in mid-div: rdn over 2f out: sn struggling* **16/1**
0003 **12** *3/4* **Strike Force**[13] [2243] 4-9-0 **58**.................................. ChrisCatlin 11 36
(K F Clutterbuck) *a bhd* **16/1**
/005 **13** *1 1/2* **Old Time Dancing**[33] [1694] 5-7-13 **46** oh1.................................. LukeMorris(3) 1 21
(J F Panvert) *rdn over 3f out: a towards rr* **50/1**
4-00 **14** *9* **Blockley (USA)**[24] [1938] 4-8-7 **51** ow1.................................. StephenDonohoe 10 8
(Ian Williams) *a bhd: fin lame* **7/2[1]**
0220 **15** *10* **Mighty Mover (IRE)**[80] [872] 6-8-13 **57**.................................. CatherineGannon 9 —
(B Palling) *s.i.s: a bhd* **16/1**
00P- **16** *13* **Captain Marryat**[290] [4535] 7-8-2 **46** oh1.................................. DavidKinsella 13 —
(M J Attwater) *a towards rr: eased whn no ch fnl f* **50/1**

2m 12.38s (1.38) **Going Correction** +0.05s/f (Good) 16 Ran SP% **131.2**
Speed ratings (Par 101): **96,94,94,92,91 91,90,87,86,86 84,83,82,75,67 56**
CSF £287.51 CT £1883.71 TOTE £16.20: £4.70, £6.10, £1.60, £4.00; EX 880.50 TRIFECTA Not won..
Owner J Parfitt **Bred** Mrs S Camacho **Trained** Briery Hill, Blaenau Gwent

FOCUS
Not many came into this low-grade contest in decent form and although it could rate higher, there is little solid form to go on and it is probably not a race to take too literally.
Jacaranda(IRE) Official explanation: jockey said gelding missed the break
Follow The Colours(IRE) Official explanation: jockey said gelding hung right-handed

Blockley(USA) Official explanation: vet said gelding was lame behind
Mighty Mover(IRE) Official explanation: jockey said gelding missed the break
Captain Marryat Official explanation: jockey said gelding had no more to give

2641 TOTETRIFECTA FILLIES' H'CAP — 1m 3f 144y
3:40 (3:40) (Class 6) (0-65,63) 4-Y-0+ **£2,072** (£616; £308; £153) **Stalls** Low

Form — RPR
0355 **1** **Shandelight (IRE)**[40] 1551 4-8-4 **46** ow1 (p) RoystonFfrench 7 — 63
(Mrs A Duffield) *chsd ldr: led wl over 2f out: pushed clr fnl f: easily* **3/1**[2]
0-40 **2** *9* **Miss Porcia**[13] 2245 7-8-3 **45** TPO'Shea 4 — 48
(P A Blockley) *hld up in tch: chsd wnr over 2f out: sn rdn: no imp* **9/1**[3]
2430 **3** *3/4* **Still Dreaming**[18] 1408 4-8-2 **51** RossAtkinson[(7)] 6 — 52
(R J Price) *hld up and bhd: pushed along and hdwy 2f out: styd on to take 3rd towards fin: n.d* **12/1**
244- **4** *1 1/2* **Adorabella (IRE)**[234] 6132 5-9-7 **63** FergusSweeney 1 — 62
(A King) *t.k.h in tch: rdn 2f out: one pce* **5/4**[1]
2-60 **5** *1* **Party Palace**[19] 1181 4-8-3 **45** CatherineGannon 9 — 42
(H S Howe) *led: clr over 7f out: hdd wl over 2f out: sn rdn: wknd wl over 1f out* **16/1**
021- **6** *5* **Ful Of Grace (IRE)**[12] 6570 4-8-11 **53** (b) JimmyQuinn 3 — 42
(D E Pipe) *s.i.s: in rr: rdn and struggling over 2f out: nvr nr ldrs* **12/1**
6-05 **7** *9* **Theatre Royal**[9] 2354 5-8-4 **46** (p) ChrisCatlin 8 — 21
(Mouse Hamilton-Fairley) *hld up: rdn and struggling over 2f out* **14/1**
325- **8** *2* **Sweet Request**[205] 6751 4-9-3 **62** KevinGhunowa[(3)] 2 — 34
(Dr J R J Naylor) *hld up: rdn over 2f out: sn struggling* **16/1**
6100 **9** *26* **Oasis Sun (IRE)**[9] 2353 5-8-9 **51** (v) LPKeniry 5 — —
(J R Best) *in rr: rdn 3f out: sn toiling: t.o* **33/1**

2m 31.77s (1.17) **Going Correction** +0.05s/f (Good) **9** Ran SP% **116.2**
Speed ratings (Par 98): **98,92,91,90,89 86,80,79,61**
CSF £30.44 CT £284.90 TOTE £4.10: £1.50, £2.90, £3.70; EX 43.40 Trifecta £185.50 Pool £261.33 - 1 winning unit..
Owner Lee Bolingbroke David Andrew Rod Jordan **Bred** Limestone And Tara Studs **Trained** Constable Burton, N Yorks
■ This was Ann Duffield's first winner at Bath.

FOCUS
A weak fillies' handicap with the first three having all tried their luck at around 2m on their previous outings. The form is not solid with the runner-up the best guide.
Oasis Sun(IRE) Official explanation: jockey said mare ran flat

2642 BET TOTEPOOL ON ALL UK RACING H'CAP — 1m 5y
4:10 (4:10) (Class 5) (0-70,69) 4-Y-0+ **£2,914** (£867; £433; £216) **Stalls** Low

Form — RPR
0-03 **1** **Willow Dancer (IRE)**[24] 1932 4-9-4 **66** (p) AdamKirby 3 — 76
(W R Swinburn) *hld up in mid-div: swtchd rt and hdwy over 1f out: rdn to ld jst ins fnl f: drvn out* **15/2**[3]
0-40 **2** *1 1/2* **Moyoko (IRE)**[18] 2097 5-8-2 **50** oh2 JimmyQuinn 1 — 57
(M Blanshard) *s.i.s: hld up and bhd: nt clr run on ins over 2f out: rdn and hdwy over 1f out: r.o u.p to take 2nd towards fin* **20/1**
3-01 **3** *1 1/4* **Bold Cross (IRE)**[13] 2243 5-9-4 **66** PaulFitzsimons 4 — 70
(E G Bevan) *hld up towards rr: swtchd rt and hdwy over 1f out: rdn and ev ch jst ins fnl f: no ex towards fin* **12/1**
-000 **4** *3/4* **Coup D'Etat**[5] 2477 6-9-3 **65** (b) RichardKingscote 6 — 67
(R A Harris) *hld up in mid-div: stdy hdwy over 2f out: nt clr run over 1f out: swtchd lft ent fnl f: nt qckn towards fin* **33/1**
0-50 **5** *4* **Goose Green (IRE)**[17] 2128 4-8-12 **60** RichardHughes 5 — 53
(R J Hodges) *hld up towards rr: hdwy whn nt clr run and swtchd rt over 1f out: sn rdn: eased whn btn towards fin* **14/1**
/603 **6** *1 3/4* **Master Mahogany**[5] 2476 7-7-9 **69** TQuinn 7 — 58
(R J Hodges) *hld up in mid-div: rdn over 2f out: hdwy wl over 1f out: wknd fnl f* **6/1**[1]
-532 **7** *1 1/2* **Recalcitrant**[19] 2070 5-8-7 **55** JamesDoyle 14 — 40
(S Dow) *chsd ldrs: rdn to ld wl over 1f out: hdd jst ins fnl f: sn wknd* **13/2**[2]
-010 **8** *1 1/2* **Wahoo Sam (USA)**[1] 2597 8-8-6 **61** ow1 RichardEvans[(7)] 9 — 43
(P D Evans) *a.p: led over 4f out: hdd wl over 1f out: sn rdn: wknd fnl f* **16/1**
604 **9** *5* **Under Fire (IRE)**[18] 2097 5-8-6 **61** MarkCoumbe[(7)] 8 — 31
(A W Carroll) *s.i.s: bhd: rdn 2f out: no rspnse* **18/1**
-015 **10** *1 1/2* **Don Pietro**[18] 2101 5-9-6 **68** TPO'Shea 11 — 35
(P A Blockley) *hld up in mid-div: hdwy over 2f out: sn rdn: wknd fnl f* **6/1**[1]
-560 **11** *2* **Rain Stops Play (IRE)**[9] 2373 6-9-3 **65** (p) ChrisCatlin 2 — 27
(M Quinn) *t.k.h in tch: pushed along and wknd 2f out* **11/1**
-456 **12** *shd* **Indian Edge**[5] 2477 7-8-13 **68** MatthewDavies[(7)] 13 — 30
(B Palling) *led: hdd over 4f out: rdn over 2f out: wknd over 1f out* **12/1**
000- **13** *4 1/2* **Vehari**[94] 6056 5-8-7 **55** ow5 StephenDonohoe 10 — 7
(Ian Williams) *s.s: a wl in rr* **14/1**
00-3 **14** *8* **Monda**[40] 1528 6-8-0 **51** DominicFox[(3)] 12 — —
(M Hill) *hld up in tch: rdn over 2f out: wkng whn n.m.r wl over 1f out* **6/1**[1]

1m 42.0s (1.20) **Going Correction** +0.05s/f (Good) **14** Ran SP% **123.9**
Speed ratings (Par 103): **96,94,93,92,88 86,85,83,78,77 75,75,70,62**
CSF £153.07 CT £1171.10 TOTE £9.40: £2.30, £7.40, £4.30; EX 372.50 TRIFECTA Not won..
Owner Mrs G Godfrey & Mrs A Horner **Bred** Exors Of The Late R E Sangster **Trained** Aldbury, Herts

FOCUS
The heavens opened just in time for this ordinary handicap. The form is pretty solid rated around the placed horses with the winner up 6lb.
Wahoo Sam(USA) Official explanation: jockey said gelding ran too free

2643 BET TOTEPOOL ON ALL IRISH RACING H'CAP — 2m 1f 34y
4:40 (4:42) (Class 6) (0-60,68) 4-Y-0+ **£2,072** (£616; £308; £153) **Stalls** Low

Form — RPR
0403 **1** **Arabian Sun**[32] 1726 4-8-9 **51** (v) MickyFenton 8 — 61
(M J Attwater) *mde all: rdn wl over 1f out: styd on wl to go clr ins fnl f* **11/2**[3]
0-6 **2** *5* **Pochard**[14] 461 5-8-13 **54** RichardHughes 13 — 58
(J M P Eustace) *a.p: rdn over 4f out: sltly outpcd over 2f out: styd on to take 2nd wl ins fnl f* **13/2**
0V-0 **3** *1/2* **L'Oiseau De Feu (USA)**[22] 2001 4-8-13 **55** VinceSlattery 6 — 58
(Mrs K Waldron) *hld up in mid-div: hdwy on ins over 4f out: chsd wnr jst over 2f out: sn rdn: lost 2nd wl ins fnl f* **50/1**
5400 **4** *1 1/4* **Ronsard (IRE)**[13] 2245 6-8-5 **46** oh1 SaleemGolam 11 — 48
(P D Evans) *hld up in rr: hdwy over 3f out: rdn over 2f out: one pce fnl f* **14/1**
1016 **5** *nk* **Synonymy**[8] 2393 5-9-5 **60** (b) JamesDoyle 4 — 62
(M Blanshard) *hld up in tch: rdn 2f out: one pce* **11/1**
/60- **6** *3 1/4* **Rajam**[42] 5000 10-8-5 **46** oh1 ChrisCatlin 2 — 44
(W K Goldsworthy) *prom: wnt 2nd over 9f out: ev ch 3f out: rdn over 1f out: wknd wl ins fnl f* **10/3**[1]
6/00 **7** *1* **Sir Night (IRE)**[13] 1779 8-7-12 **46** oh1 AmyBaker[(7)] 5 — 43
(M Hill) *hld up in mid-div: hdwy 3f out: sn rdn: wknd 2f out* **40/1**
3413 **8** *1 1/4* **Sovietta (IRE)**[20] 2051 7-8-9 **50** (t) StephenDonohoe 1 — 46
(Ian Williams) *hld up and bhd: stdy hdwy over 4f out: rdn over 2f out: sn wknd* **4/1**[2]
4-06 **9** *6* **Marquee (IRE)**[26] 1895 4-9-0 **56** TPO'Shea 7 — 45
(P A Blockley) *stdd s: hld up in rr: rdn over 2f out: sn struggling* **16/1**
6350 **10** *1* **Bobsleigh**[13] 2245 9-8-5 **46** CatherineGannon 14 — 34
(H S Howe) *hld up in tch: lost pl 5f out: n.d after* **18/1**
035- **11** *1 1/4* **Teorban (POL)**[241] 5948 9-8-0 **48** ow1 RossAtkinson[(7)] 10 — 35
(Mrs N S Evans) *hld up in mid-div: bhd fnl 4f* **14/1**
35P5 **12** *34* **Kofi**[19] 1405 6-8-5 **46** oh1 JimmyQuinn 15 — —
(Karen George) *swtchd lft sn after s: a in rr: rdn over 2f out: sn struggling: eased whn no ch over 1f out* **20/1**
00/0 **13** *26* **Dance Hall Diva**[36] 1621 6-8-6 **47** HayleyTurner 12 — —
(M D I Usher) *t.k.h in tch: lost pl 5f out: t.o and eased over 2f out* **14/1**

(8.10) **Going Correction** +0.475s/f (Yiel)
WFA 4 from 5yo+ 1lb **13** Ran SP% **120.4**
Speed ratings (Par 101): **99,96,96,95,95 94,93,93,90,89 89,73,60**
CSF £40.84 CT £1639.38 TOTE £6.70: £2.20, £2.50, £11.20; EX 47.50 TRIFECTA Not won..
Owner The Attwater Partnership **Bred** Usk Valley Stud **Trained** Epsom, Surrey

FOCUS
A slowly-run minor staying handicap with the runners coming up the stands' side in the home straight, the rain having got into the ground. The form is not that solid despite the placed horses being close to their marks.

2644 BET TOTEPOOL AT TOTESPORT.COM H'CAP — 5f 161y
5:10 (5:13) (Class 4) (0-85,84) 3-Y-0+ **£4,209** (£1,252; £625; £312) **Stalls** Centre

Form — RPR
000- **1** **Barons Spy (IRE)**[171] 6651 7-9-3 **77** RussellKennemore[(3)] 1 — 88
(R J Price) *hld up: hdwy 3f out: chsd ldr 2f out: rdn to ld ins fnl f: drvn out* **12/1**
0002 **2** *3/4* **Stamford Blue**[10] 2339 7-9-4 **78** (b) KevinGhunowa[(3)] 2 — 86
(R A Harris) *led: rdn and hdd ins fnl f: kpt on* **9/1**
0244 **3** *1 1/4* **Cheveton**[13] 2261 4-8-9 **66** SaleemGolam 7 — 70
(R J Price) *chsd ldrs: rdn over 2f out: kpt on towards fin* **14/1**
1033 **4** *1/2* **Digital**[25] 1908 11-9-8 **79** ChrisCatlin 9 — 81
(M R Channon) *in rr: rdn and hdwy over 1f out: kpt on same pce ins fnl f* **7/2**[1]
0-01 **5** *3 3/4* **Charles Darwin (IRE)**[15] 2188 5-9-13 **84** (b) JamesDoyle 6 — 74
(M Blanshard) *prom: chsd wnr 3f out to 2f out: rdn and wknd over 1f out* **9/1**
0224 **6** *3/4* **Millfields Dreams**[3] 2551 9-8-5 **65** (p) LukeMorris[(3)] 8 — 52
(P Leech) *chsd ldrs: rdn over 2f out: wknd over 1f out* **5/1**[3]
1134 **7** *1 1/4* **After The Show**[16] 2166 7-9-2 **73** TQuinn 5 — 56
(Rae Guest) *hld up: sn bhd: sme hdwy over 2f out: wknd fnl f* **13/2**
516- **8** *2* **Damhsoir (IRE)**[216] 6528 4-8-8 **65** oh20 JimmyQuinn 3 — 41
(H S Howe) *s.i.s: hld up towards rr: outpcd over 2f out: n.d after* **40/1**
4214 **9** *12* **Hereford Boy**[19] 2082 4-9-9 **80** RobertHavlin 10 — 15
(D K Ivory) *a bhd* **6/1**
0-56 **10** *1 1/4* **Edge Of Gold**[15] 2196 3-9-0 **79** CatherineGannon 4 — 10
(B Palling) *prom: rdn 3f out: sn wknd* **9/2**[2]

1m 13.2s (2.00) **Going Correction** +0.475s/f (Yiel)
WFA 3 from 4yo+ 8lb **10** Ran SP% **121.5**
Speed ratings (Par 105): **105,104,102,101,96 95,94,91,75,73**
CSF £119.85 CT £1581.12 TOTE £15.30: £4.90, £2.60, £4.20; EX 237.90 TRIFECTA Not won..
Owner Barry Veasey **Bred** Tally-Ho Stud **Trained** Ullingswick, H'fords

FOCUS
They raced middle to stands' side in the rain-softened ground. The form is given a chance with the runner-up and third setting the level.
T/Jkpt: Not won. T/Plt: £2,359.20 to a £1 stake. Pool: £93,563.48. 28.95 winning tickets. T/Qpdt: £126.80 to a £1 stake. Pool: £6,713.00. 39.15 winning tickets. KH

2649 - (Foreign Racing) - See Raceform Interactive

2294 CHANTILLY (R-H)
Sunday, June 1

OFFICIAL GOING: Soft

2650a PRIX DE ROYAUMONT (GROUP 3) (FILLIES) — 1m 4f
2:10 (2:16) 3-Y-0 **£29,412** (£11,765; £8,824; £5,882; £2,941)

RPR
1 **Sub Rose (IRE)**[35] 3-9-0 CSoumillon 7 — 110
(A De Royer-Dupre, France) *racd in 4th: 5th st: wnt 2nd under 2f out: rdn 1 1/2f out: led 1f out: r.o wl: comf* **4/1**[2]
2 *3* **Treat Gently**[17] 3-9-0 SPasquier 9 — 105
(A Fabre, France) *racd in 3rd: led 2f out: rdn appr fnl f: sn hdd and one pce* **11/4**[1]
3 *5* **Balladeuse (FR)**[21] 2031 3-9-0 OPeslier 4 — 97
(A Fabre, France) *hld up in 7th or 8th: 6th st on ins: swtchd lft and hdwy 2f out: wnt 3rd 1 1/2f out: kpt on at one pce* **16/1**
4 *1 1/2* **Folle Allure (FR)**[41] 3-9-0 C-PLemaire 2 — 95
(J-C Rouget, France) *s.i.s: racd in 9th: last st: hdwy down outside fr under 2f out: tk 4th 100yds out* **4/1**[2]
5 *1* **Myakoda (FR)**[26] 3-9-0 LDettori 8 — 93
(Y De Nicolay, France) *bhd tl hdwy 3f out: 8th st: wnt 4th 1 1/2f out: lost 4th 100yds out* **14/1**
6 *6* **Prudenzia (IRE)**[21] 2031 3-9-0 TThulliez 5 — 83
(P Bary, France) *hld up in 7th or 8th: 9th st: swtchd lft and hdwy 2f out: disp 4th briefly over 1f out: sn btn* **4/1**[2]
7 *4* **Mischief Making (USA)**[28] 1833 3-9-0 RyanMoore 10 — 77
(E A L Dunlop) *racd in 2nd: pushed along ent st: wknd 2f out* **20/1**
8 *1* **Seal Bay (IRE)**[21] 2031 3-9-0 DBoeuf 1 — 75
(D Smaga, France) *racd in 6th: 4th st: wknd 2f out* **10/1**[3]
9 *15* **Tangaspeed (FR)**[26] 3-9-0 J-BEyquem 3 — 51
(Y Fouin, France) *led to 2f out: wknd qckly* **18/1**
10 *3/4* **Party Lover (FR)**[19] 3-9-0 (b) AlexisBadel 6 — 50
(Mme M Bollack-Badel, France) *in midfield: 7th st: sn wknd* **33/1**

2m 31.5s (0.90) **Going Correction** +0.30s/f (Good) **10** Ran SP% **121.3**
Speed ratings: **109,107,103,102,102 98,95,94,84,84**
PARI-MUTUEL: WIN 3.70; PL 1.60, 1.70, 3.70; DF 5.50.
Owner 6c Racing Ltd **Bred** Azienda Agricola Rosati Colarieti **Trained** Chantilly, France

NOTEBOOK
Sub Rose(IRE) is a high-class middle-distance filly in the making. Racing for just the second time, she looked a different class to the others in this Group 3 race. Held up early on in fifth place, she cruised into the lead one out and drew clear to pass the post on her own. Further improvement can be expected and she now heads for the Prix de Malleret at Saint-Cloud at the end of the month. No doubt connections will be looking at the Prix Vermeille later in the season, but the filly has not been entered in the Prix de L'Arc de Triomphe.
Treat Gently ran a fair race after settling down in third place early on. She went to the head affairs two out, but failed to quicken like the winner. Another filly with scope for improvement, she should make it at Group level later in the season.
Balladeuse(FR) was putting in her best work at the finish. Virtually last early on, she had slight traffic problems early in the straight before quickening over a furlong out. She was running on at the finish and can be rated better than the bare form.
Folle Allure(FR) did herself no favours with a sluggish start and she was brought up the centre of the track in the straight. She was staying on at the end and is another who can be rated a bit better than the bare form.
Mischief Making(USA), who soon found herself in a prominent position, was a spent force early in the straight. She gradually dropped out of contention and was beaten over 20 lengths at the finish.

2651a PRIX DE SANDRINGHAM (GROUP 2) (FILLIES) 1m
2:40 (2:47) 3-Y-O £54,485 (£21,029; £10,037; £6,691; £3,346)

RPR
1 **Modern Look**[21] 2033 3-8-11 .... SPasquier 5 114+
(D Smaga, France) *mde all: rdn appr fnl f: drew clr ins fnl f: comf* **8/13**[1]
2 3 **Mousse Au Chocolat (USA)**[49] 1360 3-8-11 .... C-PLemaire 3 107
(J-C Rouget, France) *trckd ldr in 3rd: rdn ins fnl f: styd on to take 2nd on line* **7/1**[3]
3 nse **Albisola (IRE)**[14] 2237 3-8-11 .... CSoumillon 4 107
(Robert Collet, France) *racd in 2nd: rdn over 1f out: one pce: lost 2nd on line* **7/2**[2]
4 snk **Lady Deauville (FR)**[28] 1830 3-8-11 .... DBoeuf 1 107
(P A Blockley) *racd in 4th: rdn 2f out: styd on down outside to press for 2nd cl home* **20/1**
5 2 ½ **Nijoom Dubai**[21] 2033 3-8-11 .... RyanMoore 2 101
(M R Channon) *last thrght: pushed along and detached over 3f out: kpt on at same pce fnl 2f* **9/1**

1m 38.5s (0.70) **Going Correction** +0.30s/f (Good) 5 Ran SP% **111.4**
Speed ratings: **108,105,104,104,102**
PARI-MUTUEL: WIN 1.70; PL 1.30, 1.80; SF 5.20.
Owner K Abdulla **Bred** Juddmonte Farms Ltd **Trained** Lamorlaye, France

NOTEBOOK
Modern Look won this as she was entitled to. Soon at the head of affairs, she was asked to quicken one and a half out and then drew clear of her four rivals. A lazy filly at home, she might not have been quite fit enough when fourth in the Pouliches but is certainly spot-on now and may have earned a tilt at the Coronation Stakes at Royal Ascot.
Mousse Au Chocolat(USA) took time before quickening in the straight, after being in third position early on. She did quicken on the rail from a furlong out and snatched second place literally on the line.
Albisola(IRE) was found wanting for pace in the straight. Settled behind the winner for much of the race, she tried to get on terms from one and a half out but was then one paced to the line. Beaten by inches for second place, connections are now looking at the longer Prix de Pysche at Deauville.
Lady Deauville(FR), fourth rounding the final turn, she was outpaced in the straight before running on inside the final furlong and only narrowly failed to take second place. This soft-ground specialist is likely to be back in France later in the season.
Nijoom Dubai was never at the races and always in last position. It was a disappointing effort by this filly who ran way below her best form.

2652a PRIX DU GROS-CHENE (GROUP 2) 5f
3:15 (3:19) 3-Y-O+ £54,485 (£21,029; £10,037; £6,691; £3,346)

RPR
1 **Marchand D'Or (FR)**[175] 7089 5-9-9 .... DBonilla 3 126
(F Head, France) *missed break and sltly hmpd s: sn rcvrd: 7th 3f out: hdwy to ld 100yds out: r.o strly* **8/1**
2 nk **Equiano (FR)**[12] 3-8-10 .... CSoumillon 5 116
(M Delcher Sanchez, Spain) *cl up trcking ldr: hdwy against ins rail to ld over 1f out: hdd 100yds out: no ex* **18/1**
3 3 **Sir Gerry (USA)**[32] 1718 3-9-0 .... KerrinMcEvoy 1 109+
(J R Fanshawe) *hld up in rr: 10th 3f out: styd on wl fnl f: nrst fin* **4/1**[2]
4 ¾ **Captain Gerrard (IRE)**[28] 1831 3-8-12 .... TomEaves 4 104
(B Smart) *led to over 1f out: one pce* **5/2**[1]
5 ¾ **Benbaun (IRE)**[175] 7089 7-9-9 ....(v) PJSmullen 2 109
(M J Wallace) *wnt rt s: in midfield on ins: kpt on at same pce fnl 2f* **13/2**[3]
6 nk **Only Answer**[21] 2034 4-8-13 .... OPeslier 7 98+
(A Fabre, France) *in midfield: 5th 3f out: kpt on at one pce fnl 2f* **15/2**
7 1 ½ **Calbuco (FR)**[21] 2034 4-9-2 .... WMongil 6 95
(B Dutruel, France) *racd in 2nd to 1 1/2f out: wknd* **28/1**
8 1 ½ **Mariol (FR)**[94] 741 5-9-2 .... C-PLemaire 8 90+
(Robert Collet, France) *a bhd* **33/1**
9 ½ **Reverence**[22] 1986 7-9-2 .... WJSupple 11 88+
(E J Alston) *cl up: 6th 3f out: rdn 2f out: wknd* **11/1**
10 ¾ **The Trader (IRE)**[15] 2195 10-9-2 ....(b) RyanMoore 9 85+
(M Blanshard) *a bhd* **25/1**
11 **Mood Music**[21] 2034 4-9-2 ....(b) DBoeuf 12 —
(Mario Hofer, Germany) *hld up towards centre: 9th 3f out: nvr a factor* **25/1**
12 **Desert Lord**[8] 2404 8-9-2 ....(b) NCallan 10 —
(K A Ryan) *prom in centre: 4th 3f out: rdn under 2f out: wknd* **11/1**

57.20 secs (-0.90) **Going Correction** +0.20s/f (Good)
WFA 3 from 4yo+ 7lb 12 Ran SP% **120.8**
Speed ratings: **115,114,109,108,107 106,104,102,101,100 100,100**
PARI-MUTUEL: WIN 6.20; PL 2.80, 5.30, 5.70; DF 56.30.
Owner Mme J-L Giral **Bred** Mme C Giral **Trained** France

NOTEBOOK
Marchand D'Or(FR), running for the first time this season and carrying joint top weight, was dropped out as usual in the early stages of this sprint. He came with a progressive run from one and a half out and took the lead 50 yards from the line. This was the first time the gelding has run over the minimum distance and this effort bodes well for the rest of the season. He is now to be aimed at the Golden Jubilee Stakes at Royal Ascot and no doubt he will then go to Deauville to try and land a hat-trick in the Maurice de Gheest.
Equiano(FR), a Spanish raider, put up an excellent performance by finishing so close to a top-class performer. He was tucked in behind the leaders early on before taking the lead one and a half out. He did his best but just could not hold the winner inside the final 50 yards. This improving three-year-old is another bound for Ascot and he will run in the King's Stand Stakes.
Sir Gerry(USA), having his first run at the distance, produced a fine effort without suggesting this is his trip. He still had plenty to do at the halfway stage and really did not get motoring until the final furlong. He ran on well but the race for the first two places was already over. He now goes for the Golden Jubilee and the distance will be much more in his favour.
Captain Gerrard(IRE), who put up a smart effort to win the Palace House Stakes at Newmarket on his three-year-old debut, was smartly away but he was already beaten a furlong out. He stayed on bravely to the line and only lost third place inside the final furlong. He will also probably line up for the King's Stand at Royal Ascot next time out.
Benbaun(IRE), smartly away from his inside draw, settled just behind the leading group. When things quickened up one and a half out, he looked a bit one paced but did stay on until the line. This was not a bad effort from the seven-year-old as he had not been out since December so he should strip much better next time out and he also goes for the Golden Jubilee.
Reverence was mid-division for much of this race but could not quicken when pace was injected one and a half furlongs from the post. His best days are behind him.
The Trader(IRE) was never really seen with a chance and was always towards the tail of the field.
Desert Lord was unable to get the lead and failed to run his race.

2653a GRAND PRIX DE CHANTILLY (GROUP 2) 1m 4f
3:50 (3:51) 4-Y-O+ £54,485 (£21,029; £10,037; £6,691; £3,346)

RPR
1 **Doctor Dino (FR)**[64] 1091 6-9-4 .... OPeslier 4 121
(R Gibson, France) *hld up in 6th: 5th st: sn pushed along: hdwy to ld narrowly ins fnl f: drvn out* **15/8**[1]
2 ½ **Zambezi Sun**[35] 1665 4-9-4 .... SPasquier 5 121
(P Bary, France) *racd in 4th: led 1 1/2f out to ins fnl f: kpt on: jst hld on for 2nd* **5/2**[2]
3 shd **Not Just Swing (IRE)**[27] 1888 4-8-11 .... LDettori 8 113
(A Fabre, France) *hld up in rr: last st: swtchd lft and hdwy over 1 1/2f out: styd on wl down the outside fnl f: jst missed 2nd* **7/1**
4 1 ½ **Noble Prince (GER)**[27] 1888 4-8-11 .... JMurtagh 1 111
(A Fabre, France) *trckd ldr in 3rd: n.m.r on ins over 1 1/2f out: swtchd lft: styd on u.p fr over 1f out* **9/1**
5 ¾ **First Stream (GER)**[35] 1662 4-8-11 .... C-PLemaire 3 110
(Mario Hofer, Germany) *racd in 5th: 6th st: rdn over 1f out: kpt on* **33/1**
6 ¾ **Varevees**[217] 6526 5-8-9 .... CSoumillon 7 107
(R Gibson, France) *led 1f: pressed ldr in 2nd: pushed along 3f out: jnd ldr 2f out to 1 1/2f out: one pce* **20/1**
7 1 **Bucintoro (IRE)**[26] 4-8-11 .... TGillet 6 107
(J E Hammond, France) *hld up in rr: 7th st: nvr a factor* **33/1**
8 ½ **Galactic Star**[28] 1829 5-8-11 .... RyanMoore 2 106
(Sir Michael Stoute) *led after 1f: set slow pce: jnd 2f out: hdd 1 1/2f out: one pce: eased cl home* **4/1**[3]

2m 35.4s (4.80) **Going Correction** +0.30s/f (Good) 8 Ran SP% **116.5**
Speed ratings: **96,95,95,94,94 93,92,92**
PARI-MUTUEL: WIN 2.20; PL 1.10, 1.50, 1.30; DF 4.90.
Owner J Martinez Salmean **Bred** Ecurie Pelder **Trained** Lamorlaye, France

NOTEBOOK
Doctor Dino(FR), who was supplemented into this Group 2 event, put up a fine effort. Towards the tail of the field in the early stages, he began to make a forward move halfway up the straight and then quickened impressively to take the lead well inside the final furlong. He went well on the soft ground and is now to be aimed at the Grand Prix de Saint-Cloud. If all goes well there, connections will be looking at the King George at Ascot. This much travelled horse still seems to enjoy his racing and is getting better with age, and is a great credit to his trainer.
Zambezi Sun looked the likely winner at the furlong marker. He had always been well up from the start and went to the front a furlong and a half from the line. He was just outpaced as the mile and a half event came to an end but will have a chance to take his revenge on the winner as he is also going for the Grand Prix de Saint-Cloud. He has taken a little time to find his form since a training setback after winning last year's Juddmonte Grand Prix de Paris, but he certainly looks on course now for another successful season.
Not Just Swing(IRE) was not suited by a lack of early pace and pulled a little early on. He made a forward move up the centre of the track from a furlong and a half out and finished really well, but he is not quite up to this standard, although he is improving.
Noble Prince(GER) was certainly unsuited by the slow early pace, being a horse known to stay a longer distance. His jockey had to wait a little before being able to make his final effort, and the pair just ran on one paced to the line.
Galactic Star was allowed to dictate a steady pace out in front. He tried to quicken things up early in the straight but was soon under pressure and gradually dropped out of contention to finish last, but he was only beaten a total of five lengths.

2654a PRIX DU JOCKEY CLUB (GROUP 1) (C&F) 1m 2f 110y
4:35 (4:41) 3-Y-O £630,221 (£252,132; £126,066; £62,912; £31,544)

RPR
1 **Vision D'Etat (FR)**[38] 1594 3-9-2 .... IMendizabal 4 122
(E Libaud, France) *cl up: 5th st: rdn to ld 1f out: hld on gamely whn strly pressed clsng stages: drvn out* **14/1**
2 hd **Famous Name**[56] 1232 3-9-2 .... PJSmullen 17 122
(D K Weld, Ire) *towards rr: 14th st: angled out over 2f out: str run down outside to press for 2nd 1f out: wnt 2nd 100yds out: r.o* **12/1**
3 1 ½ **Natagora (FR)**[28] 1830 3-8-13 .... LDettori 11 116
(P Bary, France) *2nd early: 3rd st: led jst over 1 1/2f out to 1f out: lost 2nd last 100yds* **7/2**[2]
4 1 ½ **High Rock (IRE)**[49] 1362 3-9-2 .... C-PLemaire 5 116
(J-C Rouget, France) *in tch: 6th st: wnt 2nd 1 1/2f out to appr fnl f: one pce* **11/4**[1]
5 1 ½ **Chinchon (IRE)**[41] 3-9-2 .... MBlancpain 2 114
(C Laffon-Parias, France) *in tch on ins: 7th st: swtchd lft 1 1/2f out: kpt on* **33/1**
6 2 ½ **Hello Morning (FR)**[21] 2032 3-9-2 .... AlexisBadel 1 109
(Mme C Head-Maarek, France) *in midfield: 9th st: n.m.r and swtchd lft 1 1/2f out: kpt on fnl f* **22/1**
7 1 ½ **Trincot (FR)**[19] 2096 3-9-2 .... TThulliez 13 106
(P Demercastel, France) *in rr: hdwy and 15th st: n.m.r 1 1/2f out: kpt on at one pce fnl f* **33/1**
8 1 **Prospect Wells (FR)**[20] 2064 3-9-2 .... OPeslier 7 105
(A Fabre, France) *in rr: 19th st: hmpd over 2f out: styd on wl fr over 1f out: nrst fin* **10/1**
9 1 ½ **Zack Dream (FR)**[19] 3-9-2 .... DBoeuf 6 102
(M Delzangles, France) *in midfield: 10th st: rdn and one pce fnl 2f* **150/1**
10 nse **Thewayyouare (USA)**[21] 2032 3-9-2 .... SPasquier 8 102
(A Fabre, France) *in midfield: 8th st: rdn and disputing 6th 1f out: one pce: eased clsng stages* **5/1**[3]
11 ½ **Magadan (IRE)**[38] 1594 3-9-2 .... ACrastus 14 101
(E Lellouche, France) *in rr: 18th st: nvr a factor* **25/1**
12 ¾ **Salsalavie (FR)**[20] 2064 3-9-2 .... FBlondel 18 100
(P Demercastel, France) *in rr: detached last ent st: modest late prog* **66/1**

13 5 **Blue Bresil (FR)**[27] 1887 3-9-2 .... WMongil 20 91
(Mlle B Halley des Fontaines, France) *wnt 2nd after 4f: stl 2nd tl wknd 1 1/2f out* **50/1**

14 1/2 **Starlish (IRE)**[27] 1887 3-9-2 .... TJarnet 15 90
(E Lellouche, France) *cl up: 4th st: wknd over 1 1/2f out* **20/1**

15 6 **Montmartre (FR)**[35] 3-9-2 .... CSoumillon 12 79
(A De Royer-Dupre, France) *hld up: 12th st: nvr a factor* **14/1**

16 2 **Trois Rois (FR)**[20] 2064 3-9-2 .... DBonilla 16 75
(F Head, France) *16th st: a towards rr* **25/1**

17 2 1/2 **Mayweather**[19] 2096 3-9-2 .... GBenoist 10 71
(J-C Rouget, France) *led to jst over 1 1/2f out: wknd* **150/1**

18 1/2 **Democrate**[27] 1887 3-9-2 .... KerrinMcEvoy 3 70
(A Fabre, France) *17th st: a in rr* **16/1**

19 3 **Achill Island (IRE)**[23] 1943 3-9-2 .... JMurtagh 9 64
(A P O'Brien, Ire) *in midfield: 11th st: btn over 1 1/2f out* **22/1**

20 8 **Full Of Gold (FR)**[27] 1887 3-9-2 .... TGillet 19 50
(Mme C Head-Maarek, France) *in tch on outside: 13th and already wkng ent st* **33/1**

2m 8.60s (1.60) **Going Correction** +0.30s/f (Good) **20** Ran SP% **136.3**
Speed ratings: **106,105,104,103,102 100,99,98,97,97 97,96,93,92,88 87,85,84,82,76**
PARI-MUTUEL: WIN 8.20; PL 2.90, 11.60, 3.10; DF 183.80.
Owner J Detre **Bred** Gaetan Gilles **Trained** France

FOCUS
A big field and a good renewal of the Prix du Jockey Club, with Vision D'Etat provisionally given the highest RPR for a winner of this race since Dalakhani in 2003.

NOTEBOOK
Vision D'Etat(FR), an unfashionably bred colt who cost only 39,000euros when picked up at the sales in December 2006, put 19 others in their place in good style. He was given a great ride and was never far from the leading group. Things opened up nicely in the straight and he took the lead at the furlong marker, then ran on gamely to fend off the runner-up. He is now unbeaten in five races and is still considered a little immature, so further improvement can be expected. He is now being given a holiday and no plans have been made for the moment, but he could be trained for the Arc de Triomphe, with a run before in the Prix Niel. A half-brother to the David Pipe-trained chaser Milan Deux Mille, he certainly has plenty of stamina on his dam's side. He became just the second provincially-trained horse to win a Classic at Chantilly.
Famous Name, a late withdrawal from the Irish 2,000 Guineas because of the fast ground, put in a fine performance considering his wide outside draw. Still towards the rear entering the straight, he was brought with a run up the centre of the track but could never quite peg back the winner. With a better draw who knows what might have happened, but it was certainly a creditable effort. Connections may now be looking at races like the Prix Eugene Adam and the Prix Guillaume d'Ornano at Deauville, but he is certainly a colt who prefers some cut in the ground.
Natagora(FR), rideden by Dettori as Lemaire was claimed to partner High Rock, put in another fine performance. Smartly out of the stalls, she settled in second place early on and, asked to go on early in the straight, took the lead two out and held it for a furlong. It was only sheer courage that kept her going to keep third place as her stamina had certainly run out. She is a truly marvellous filly and will be given a well-deserved rest now. Not surprisingly, she will now drop back to a mile and will be aimed at the Prix Rothschild (formerly Prix d'Astarte) at Deauville in early August. The Moulin de Longchamp is also being talked about later in the season, as is the Queen Elizabeth II Stakes at Ascot.
High Rock(IRE) was on his toes during the parade and was once again rather free during the race. He was given every possible chance and was well there when things quickened up in the straight. He tried to lengthen his stride but just stayed on at the same pace. Connections felt deeper ground would have been an advantage but his main problem is settling during a race. He looks likely to take on the runner-up in the Eugene Adam and/or the Guillaume d'Ornano next, but perhaps 1m will prove his best distance.
Prospect Wells(FR) was unlucky not to finish closer. A brother to high-class middle-distance performer Prospect Park, he found himself well behind early and then got interfered with at a vital stage. He can be rated much better than the bare form and may now head for the Grand Prix De Paris.
Thewayyouare(USA) is a fine-looking beast and he made a pleasing reappearance in the French Guineas. However, he did not improve as expected for the extra distance and was eased off close home. He may be worth another chance, but it is possible he has been over-rated.
Montmartre(FR) looked one of the more interesting ones, but he was too inexperienced and never got into it. He still rates a bright long-term prospect.
Achill Island(IRE), whose powerful yard have yet to win this contest, did not look up to Group 1 level and he never threatened.

DUSSELDORF (R-H)
Sunday, June 1

OFFICIAL GOING: Good

2655a GERMAN 1000 GUINEAS (GROUP 2) (FILLIES) 1m
4:00 (4:16) 3-Y-O **£55,882** (£20,588; £10,294; £5,147)

RPR

1 **Briseida**[224] 6371 3-9-2 .... MartinDwyer 1 109
(P Schiergen, Germany) *mid-div: 7th st: gd hdwy to ld appr fnl f: drvn out* **202/10**

2 2 1/2 **Rosenreihe (IRE)**[20] 2065 3-9-2 .... FilipMinarik 5 103
(P Schiergen, Germany) *a in tch: 3rd on ins st: ev ch 1f out: r.o one pce* **66/10**[3]

3 2 **Love Of Dubai (USA)**[14] 2231 3-9-2 ....(p) DarryllHolland 7 99
(C E Brittain) *hld up: hdwy wl over 1f out: r.o one pce fnl f* **29/10**[2]

4 1 1/2 **Love Academy (GER)**[20] 2065 3-9-2 .... THellier 6 96
(P Schiergen, Germany) *a in tch: 5th st: styd on same pce on outside fr over 1f out: nvr able to chal* **21/10**[1]

5 1 **Manipura (GER)**[20] 2065 3-9-2 .... TMundry 13 94
(A Wohler, Germany) *sn in mid-div: 4th st: ev ch wl over 1f out: one pce fnl f* **22/1**

6 1 1/2 **Themelie Island (IRE)**[20] 2065 3-9-2 .... ADeVries 8 90
(A Trybuhl, Germany) *last st: sme prog on ins over 1f out: nvr a factor* **103/10**

7 3/4 **Sutra (GER)**[326] 3-9-2 .... J-PCarvalho 9 89
(H Blume, Germany) *nvr nrr than mid-div* **135/10**

8 shd **Global Rose (GER)**[43] 3-9-2 .... RPiechulek 12 88
(Frau K Haustein, Germany) *led to appr fnl f* **81/10**

9 2 **Giocita (GER)** 3-9-2 .... HGrewe 11 84
(Andreas Lowe, Germany) *a towards rr* **134/10**

10 3 1/2 **Every Day (GER)**[43] 3-9-2 .... LennartHammer-Hansen 2 76
(Mario Hofer, Germany) *pressed ldr: 2nd st: sn wknd* **16/1**

11 11 **Picobella (GER)**[43] 3-9-2 .... EPedroza 4 52
(A Wohler, Germany) *prom: trckd ldr 1/2-way: 6th st: sn wknd* **107/10**

S **Tathkaar**[22] 1993 3-9-2 .... KShea 3 —
(C E Brittain) *last whn slipped up on bnd appr st* **26/1**

1m 36.29s (-4.87) **12** Ran SP% **131.9**
PARI-MUTUEL: WIN 212; PL 61, 28, 23; SF 840.
Owner Stall Litex **Bred** Watership Down Stud **Trained** Germany

NOTEBOOK
Briseida was the least fancied of Peter Schiergen's three runners and reportedly needed the race. After struggling to go the early clip, she came with a strong run to lead at the furlong pole and saw the trip out well. She could renew rivalry with the runner-up in a Group 3 at Hamburg on July 2.
Love Of Dubai(USA) stood stock still behind the stalls for several minutes while the others circled around her, even though Holland tried to stir her into action a couple of times. Held up, she kept on well up the straight without threatening the front two and may need a stiffer test.
Tathkaar was in last place when slipping up on the final turn. Both horse and rider were unscathed.

2438 SAN SIRO (R-H)
Sunday, June 1

OFFICIAL GOING: Good to soft

2656a PREMIO CARLO VITTADINI (EX PREMIO TURATI) (GROUP 2) 1m
4:25 (4:32) 3-Y-O+ **£42,188** (£18,563; £10,125; £5,063)

RPR

1 **King Jock (USA)**[31] 1761 7-9-6 .... RBurke 2 112
(R J Osborne, Ire) *with leaders early, restrained to race in 5th after 2f, headway 3f out, led over 1f out, ran on well* **212/10**

2 3/4 **Eustachione (IRE)**[14] 3-8-9 .... NMurru 4 110
(M Gasparini, Italy) *close up when snatched up early & lost place, 6th straight, last 2f out, ran on under pressure on stands side of group to take 2nd well ins final f* **106/10**

3 1/2 **Gris De Gris (IRE)**[31] 1761 4-9-6 .... MMonteriso 6 109
(J-M Capitte, France) *led after 1f, brought field into middle of course entering straight, headed over 1f out, one pace & lost 2nd well inside final f* **19/20**[1]

4 1 1/4 **Selmis**[14] 2230 4-9-6 .... MDemuro 8 106
(V Caruso, Italy) *held up, last straight, headway on far side of group 3f out, disputed 2nd 2f out, kept on same pace* **62/10**[3]

5 1/2 **Sunday's Brunch (IRE)**[15] 5-9-6 .... DVargiu 3 105
(B Grizzetti, Italy) *held up, 7th straight, kept on one pace final 2f, never near to challenge* **67/10**

6 1/2 **Sopran Promo (IRE)**[14] 2230 4-9-6 .... PConvertino 5 104
(B Grizzetti, Italy) *first to show, 2nd straight, ridden 3f out, beaten well over 1f out, stayed on same pace* **22/1**

7 1/2 **Golden Titus (IRE)**[14] 2230 4-9-6 .... MEsposito 7 103
(A Renzoni, Italy) *always in touch, 4th straight, tracked leader 3f out, one pace final 2f* **19/10**[2]

8 hd **Miles Gloriosus (USA)**[28] 5-9-6 .... LManiezzi 9 103
(R Menichetti, Italy) *3rd straight, ridden over 2f out, soon last but kept on* **25/1**

1m 40.9s (-1.20)
WFA 3 from 4yo+ 11lb **8** Ran SP% **134.0**
(including one euro stakes): WIN 22.25; PL 4.01, 2.24, 1.35; DF 109.74.
Owner Thistle Bloodstock Limited **Bred** Kenneth L Ramsey & Sarah K Ramsey **Trained** Naas, Co Kildare

2443 CARLISLE (R-H)
Monday, June 2

OFFICIAL GOING: Good (good to soft in places)
Wind: Light, half against Weather: Overcast

2657 RACING UK MEDIAN AUCTION MAIDEN STKS 5f
2:15 (2:18) (Class 6) 2-Y-O **£2,590** (£770; £385; £192) **Stalls** High

Form RPR

1 **South Central (USA)** 2-9-3 0 .... RobertWinston 9 99+
(J Howard Johnson) *mde all: shkn up and qcknd clr over 1f out: eased wl ins fnl f: impressive* **11/1**

2 13 **What A Fella** 2-9-3 0 .... RoystonFfrench 13 52
(Mrs A Duffield) *s.i.s: bhd tl hdwy over 1f out: wnt 2nd ins fnl f: no ch w wnr* **14/1**

3 1/2 **Hel's Angel (IRE)** 2-8-9 0 .... AndrewMullen(3) 10 45
(Mrs A Duffield) *towards rr: drvn and hdwy on outside over 1f out: kpt on fnl f: nrst fin* **33/1**

4 3 **Abu Derby (IRE)** 2-9-3 0 .... J-PGuillambert 6 40
(J G Given) *unruly in preliminaries: in tch: effrt 2f out: one pce fnl f* **25/1**

32 5 1/2 **Faraway Sound (IRE)**[10] 2362 2-9-3 0 ....(p) LeeEnstone 8 38
(P C Haslam) *prom: effrt 2f out: kpt on same pce fnl f* **5/4**[1]

3 6 hd **Bragging Rights (IRE)**[24] 1948 2-9-3 0 .... PaulMulrennan 11 37
(K A Ryan) *trckd ldrs: effrt and wnt 2nd over 1f out: wknd ins fnl f* **5/2**[2]

0 7 3 1/4 **Chipolini (IRE)**[7] 2443 2-9-0 0 .... DNolan(3) 4 25
(D Carroll) *trckd ldrs tl rdn and wknd over 1f out* **40/1**

6 8 2 3/4 **Northumberland**[9] 2388 2-9-3 0 .... GregFairley 2 15
(M Johnston) *cl up tl rdn and wknd over 1f out* **13/2**[3]

9 1/2 **Kheylide (IRE)** 2-9-3 0 .... EdwardCreighton 7 14
(Miss V Haigh) *unruly in paddock: dwlt: a bhd* **50/1**

10 2 1/4 **Court Judgement (IRE)** 2-9-3 0 .... DavidAllan 5 —
(T D Easterby) *missed break: a outpcd* **28/1**

6 11 1 3/4 **Lonsdale Lad**[33] 1722 2-8-10 0 .... StacyRenwick(7) 1 —
(R C Guest) *bhd and outpcd: nvr on terms* **100/1**

62.08 secs (1.28) **Going Correction** +0.125s/f (Good) **11** Ran SP% **117.0**
Speed ratings (Par 91): **94,73,72,67,66 66,61,56,56,52 49**
CSF £136.72 TOTE £13.80: £2.60, £3.50, £7.30; EX 101.30.
Owner Transcend Bloodstock LLP **Bred** Tony Holmes & Walter Zent **Trained** Billy Row, Co Durham

FOCUS
The two market leaders disappointed but this was all about South Central, who created a hugely favourable impression and is the type to hold his own in stronger company.

NOTEBOOK
South Central(USA) ◆, a £60,000 half-brother to five winners in the US, took the eye in the paddock as a strong sort with scope and he created a striking impression on this racecourse debut. He was value for at least another four lengths and appeals strongly as the sort to hold his own in stronger company, perhaps the Norfolk Stakes at Ascot. (tchd 16-1)

What A Fella, out of a half-sister to a staying Flat/hurdle winner, showed ability at an ordinary level on this racecourse debut. He is entitled to improve for the experience and will be suited by a much stiffer test of stamina. (op 12-1 tchd 16-1)

Hel's Angel(IRE), a 5,500euro purchase and half-sister to a couple of winners from 7f to 1m1f, was not disgraced on this racecourse debut. She will be much better suited by a stiffer test of stamina in due course.

Abu Derby(IRE), a 20,000gns half-brother to a 6f winner, was not disgraced given he gave plenty of trouble in the preliminaries on this racecourse debut. He is entitled to be all the better for this experience, though, and has the scope to progress if his temperament holds up. (op 16-1)

Faraway Sound(IRE), who showed fair form on his first two starts, looked to have fair claims but he was disappointing in first-time cheekpieces. It is debatable whether he would have got anywhere near the winner even had he been at his best but he is worth another chance in ordinary company. (op 13-8 tchd Evens)

Bragging Rights(IRE), who ran creditably in a race that has been franked at Hamilton on his debut, failed to build on that form and was disappointing. It is too soon to be writing him off and he may be better on quicker ground. Official explanation: jockey said colt hung left throughout (op 3-1 tchd 7-2)

Northumberland, who took the eye in the paddock as a good, deep-bodied sort with plenty of physical scope, failed by some way to build on his debut run. However his stable does well with this type and he is not one to be writing off yet. (op 11-2)

2658 CARLISLE CONFERENCE GROUP AND WAVERLEY TBS CLAIMING STKS 7f 200y

2:45 (2:45) (Class 6) 3-Y-O+ £2,047 (£604; £302) Stalls High

Form RPR

2003 1 **Claret And Amber**[3] 2578 6-9-9 75 PaulHanagan 12 79
(R A Fahey) *prom: n.m.r and swtchd lft over 2f out: led over 1f out: drvn out* 11/4[1]

0-30 2 2 3/4 **Efidium**[23] 2007 10-8-12 62 NeilBrown(5) 10 66
(N Bycroft) *hld up: hdwy whn n.m.r over 2f out: kpt on to chse wnr ins fnl f: r.o* 12/1

0652 3 3 1/2 **Bobski (IRE)**[86] 833 6-9-9 76 (p) FergalLynch 11 63
(P J McBride) *hld up: stdy hdwy over 3f out: effrt over 1f out: one pce* 7/2[2]

5526 4 hd **Five Wishes**[13] 2285 4-9-0 57 (be) PhillipMakin 3 54
(M Dods) *bhd: pushed along and hdwy 2f out: r.o fnl f* 9/2[3]

-004 5 1/2 **Scotty's Future (IRE)**[9] 2394 10-9-3 45 PatrickMathers 13 56
(A Berry) *sn drvn in rr: hdwy on outside 2f out: nvr rchd ldrs* 40/1

0030 6 1 1/2 **Kabis Amigos**[7] 2445 6-9-7 67 (t) SilvestreDeSousa 8 56
(D Nicholls) *chsd ldrs: led and hung rt over 2f out: hdd over 1f out: sn no ex* 8/1

/00- 7 3 1/4 **Diktatorial**[25] 4690 6-9-9 78 RobertWinston 9 50
(J Howard Johnson) *midfield: effrt over 2f out: wknd over 1f out* 8/1

-000 8 12 **Kirkby's Treasure**[14] 2251 10-9-7 60 PaulMulrennan 7 18
(G A Swinbank) *hld up: rdn and hdwy over 2f out: wknd over 1f out* 11/1

-000 9 8 **On The Map**[21] 2055 4-9-0 47 (b) MickyFenton 4 —
(Joss Saville) *led to 1/2-way: wknd 3f out* 50/1

00-5 10 2 3/4 **Susiedil (IRE)**[153] 2 7-8-7 35 KellyHarrison(5) 2 —
(S T Mason) *bhd: drvn along 1/2-way: n.d* 100/1

0-06 11 3 3/4 **Mis Chicaf (IRE)**[3] 2578 7-8-9 45 (b[1]) DNolan(3) 5 —
(D Carroll) *dwlt: bhd and pushed along 1/2-way: nvr rchd ldrs* 28/1

66-5 12 15 **Oriental Gift (FR)**[14] 2246 4-9-4 39 DavidAllan 1 —
(H A McWilliams) *prom tl rdn and wknd wl over 1f out* 100/1

0000 13 5 **Stir Crazy (IRE)**[21] 2040 4-9-2 43 (p) PaulQuinn 6 —
(D W Barker) *cl up: led 1/2-way to over 2f out: sn wknd* 50/1

1m 41.94s (1.94) **Going Correction** +0.40s/f (Good) 13 Ran SP% 117.1
Speed ratings (Par 101): **106,103,99,99,99 97,94,82,74,71 67,52,47**
CSF £35.50 TOTE £3.20: £1.60, £4.00, £1.40; EX 41.60.Bobski was claimed by Miss Gay Kelleway for £12000.
Owner The Matthewman Partnership **Bred** D R Tucker **Trained** Musley Bank, N Yorks
■ Stewards' Enquiry : Silvestre De Sousa one-day ban: careless riding (Jun 16)
Paul Hanagan one-day ban: careless riding (Jun 16)

FOCUS
An ordinary claimer but one in which the pace was sound. This form should stand up at a similar level although it is limited a bit by the fifth.

2659 AZURE FILLIES' H'CAP 1m 1f 61y

3:15 (3:15) (Class 5) (0-70,69) 3-Y-O £4,533 (£1,348; £674; £336) Stalls High

Form RPR

-064 1 **Portrush Storm**[10] 2367 3-8-10 61 DNolan(3) 8 64
(D Carroll) *prom: effrt over 2f out: rallied to ld ins fnl f: styd on wl* 10/3[1]

4-60 2 4 **Chaenomeles (USA)**[16] 2208 3-9-0 62 GregFairley 10 57
(M Johnston) *led: clr over 2f out: hdd ins fnl f: no ex* 16/1

2-50 3 1 **Salsa Time**[24] 1964 3-9-3 65 RobertWinston 5 58
(Miss J A Camacho) *hld up: hdwy 2f out: kpt on fnl f: nrst fin* 8/1[3]

00-0 4 1/2 **Princess Maria (USA)**[26] 1912 3-8-2 50 oh5 PaulHanagan 9 42
(R A Fahey) *chsd ldr: effrt over 2f out: one pce fnl f* 9/2[2]

00-0 5 3/4 **Pentandra (IRE)**[30] 1817 3-8-12 60 J-PGuillambert 6 50
(J G Given) *in tch: effrt whn n.m.r briefly over 3f out: one pce fr 2f out* 9/1

000- 6 3 1/2 **Marie Camargo**[216] 6572 3-8-2 50 oh4 RoystonFfrench 4 33
(R A Fahey) *s.i.s: bhd: effrt 3f out: no ex over 1f out* 16/1

3-30 7 3/4 **Topflightrebellion**[11] 2333 3-9-0 62 AndrewElliott 1 43
(Mrs G S Rees) *hld up: drvn 3f out: sn btn* 25/1

00-2 8 3 3/4 **Midnight Mystique (IRE)**[58] 1222 3-9-2 69 NeilBrown(5) 7 42
(T D Barron) *chsd ldrs tl edgd rt and wknd fr 2f out* 10/3[1]

605 9 9 **Cheers For Thea (IRE)**[23] 2008 3-8-7 55 DavidAllan 2 10
(T D Easterby) *hld up: drvn over 3f out: nvr on terms* 12/1

6-05 10 12 **Orpen Bid (IRE)**[13] 2282 3-8-4 52 PatrickMathers 3 —
(A M Crow) *hld up: effrt outside 3f out: sn wknd* 16/1

2m 2.51s (4.91) **Going Correction** +0.40s/f (Good) 10 Ran SP% 114.6
Speed ratings (Par 96): **94,90,89,89,88 85,84,81,73,62**
CSF £58.34 CT £395.17 TOTE £4.40: £1.50, £4.90, £2.70; EX 83.00.
Owner M Symes G H & G J Briers S & A Franks **Bred** Northmore Stud **Trained** Sledmere, E Yorks

FOCUS
A modest fillies' handicap in which the pace was fair. The form seems to make sense.
Midnight Mystique(IRE) Official explanation: trainer's rep had no explanation for the poor form shown

2660 CUMBRIA COMMUNITY FOUNDATION H'CAP 5f 193y

3:45 (3:46) (Class 6) (0-65,66) 3-Y-O £2,729 (£806; £403) Stalls High

Form RPR

-003 1 **Turn And River (IRE)**[32] 1754 3-8-8 55 MarkLawson(3) 1 64
(M Brittain) *cl up: led over 2f out: hung rt over 1f out: drvn out* 25/1

54-3 2 2 1/4 **Shakespeare's Son**[27] 1897 3-8-9 56 DuranFentiman(3) 6 58
(H J Evans) *prom: effrt over 2f out: chsd wnr over 1f out: kpt on: nt rch wnr* 12/1

60-0 3 1 3/4 **Klarity**[44] 1475 3-8-11 55 PhillipMakin 5 51
(J Pearce) *in tch: drvn 1/2-way: kpt on fnl f: nrst fin* 18/1

013- 4 1 **Lujano**[164] 7210 3-9-2 60 PaulMulrennan 10 53
(Ollie Pears) *cl up: led briefly 1/2-way: one pce over 1f out* 14/1

3004 5 1 1/4 **Complete Frontline (GER)**[30] 1819 3-9-0 58 AndrewElliott 11 47+
(K R Burke) *prom: effrt over 2f out: one pce over 1f out* 13/2[3]

2001 6 1/2 **Moonage Daydream (IRE)**[6] 2490 3-9-8 66 6ex (b) DavidAllan 16 53+
(T D Easterby) *midfield: drvn and effrt over 2f out: no ex over 1f out* 11/2[2]

7 1 **Distant Rock**[222] 6440 3-9-4 65 DNolan(3) 3 49
(D Carroll) *bhd until styd on fnl f: nvr rchd ldrs* 16/1

05-0 8 1 1/4 **Swift Acclaim (IRE)**[17] 2141 3-8-3 54 (v[1]) DeclanCannon(7) 2 34
(K R Burke) *w ldrs tl hung rt and wknd over 1f out* 40/1

2500 9 hd **Thomas Malory (IRE)**[13] 2282 3-8-12 56 (v) EdwardCreighton 14 35
(Miss V Haigh) *sn rdn along in rr: effrt 1/2-way: no imp fr 2f out* 14/1

0-00 10 nse **Piverina (IRE)**[26] 1912 3-8-11 55 RobertWinston 7 34
(Miss J A Camacho) *hld up: drvn 1/2-way: no imp fnl 2f* 12/1

5-05 11 1 3/4 **Scanno (IRE)**[35] 1674 3-9-0 58 GregFairley 8 31
(M Mullineaux) *led to 1/2-way: sn lost pl* 28/1

0-40 12 3 1/2 **Jaconet (USA)**[6] 2490 3-9-2 60 PaulFessey 9 22
(T D Barron) *in tch to 1/2-way: sn lost pl* 10/1

004- 13 6 **Rio Sabotini**[220] 6462 3-9-0 61 PJMcDonald(3) 12 3
(G A Swinbank) *midfield: drvn over 3f out: wknd fr 2f out* 12/1

50-0 14 3 1/2 **Whispering Desert**[17] 2171 3-9-5 63 MickyFenton 15 —
(P T Midgley) *bhd: drvn 1/2-way: sn btn* 16/1

5634 15 nk **Fulford**[6] 2490 3-9-5 63 TWilliams 17 —
(M Brittain) *dwlt: sn midfield on outside: rdn and wknd over 2f out* 5/1[1]

06-R 16 33 **Fitolini**[5] 2506 3-9-5 63 J-PGuillambert 13 —
(Mrs G S Rees) *dwlt: bhd: wknd over 2f out: t.o* 16/1

1m 14.88s (1.18) **Going Correction** +0.125s/f (Good) 16 Ran SP% 123.5
Speed ratings (Par 97): **97,94,91,90,88 88,86,85,84,84 82,77,69,65,64 20**
CSF £300.24 CT £3063.16 TOTE £28.70: £5.30, £2.30, £4.80, £3.30; EX 208.70.
Owner Northgate Poker **Bred** Miss Jane Hogan **Trained** Warthill, N Yorks

FOCUS
A truly run handicap in which the action unfolded against the near-side rail. Very modest form, the winner running her best race since her debut in the Brocklesby.
Distant Rock Official explanation: jockey said, regarding running and riding, that his orders were to educate the filly as it had been green in its home work, and do his best, adding that it was outpaced around half way before staying on under a hands and heels ride.
Fulford Official explanation: jockey said gelding missed the break

2661 TURFTV H'CAP 5f

4:15 (4:16) (Class 6) (0-60,60) 3-Y-O £2,729 (£806; £403) Stalls High

Form RPR

0-00 1 **Red River Boy**[13] 2287 3-8-3 50 KellyHarrison(5) 6 53
(C W Fairhurst) *cl up nr side: led that gp ins fnl f: pushed out* 20/1

243 2 1 **Regal Veil**[41] 1536 3-8-4 46 PaulFessey 1 46
(S C Williams) *prom nr side: drvn over 2f out: kpt on fnl f: nt rch wnr: 2nd of 10 in gp* 15/2

44-0 3 nk **Socceroo**[21] 2036 3-8-13 58 DNolan(3) 4 57
(S Parr) *led nr side to ins fnl f: kpt on same pce: 3rd of 10 in gp* 12/1

0545 4 1 **Gelert (IRE)**[40] 1560 3-8-10 52 PatrickMathers 2 47
(Peter Grayson) *prom nr side: drvn over 2f out: one pce fnl f: 4th of 10 in gp* 16/1

0-11 5 shd **Big Slick (IRE)**[31] 1769 3-9-4 60 TWilliams 7 55+
(M Brittain) *prom stands' side: outpcd 2f out: rallied fnl f: r.o: 5th of 10 in gp* 5/1[1]

34-0 6 shd **Mill Creek**[13] 2268 3-8-4 46 oh1 AndrewElliott 13 40+
(Jedd O'Keeffe) *in tch nr side: drvn over 2f out: kpt on fnl f: 6th of 10 in gp* 25/1

00-5 7 nk **Cool Fashion (IRE)**[115] 487 3-8-8 50 (v) PaulMulrennan 9 43
(Ollie Pears) *bhd nr side tl styd on fnl f: n.d: 7th of 10 in gp* 50/1

0300 8 2 1/4 **Captain Turbot (IRE)**[31] 1769 3-8-1 46 oh1 AndrewMullen(3) 3 31
(D W Barker) *prom nr side tl rdn and no ex over 1f out: 8th of 10 in gp* 14/1

00-0 9 1 1/2 **Stormy Journey**[40] 1560 3-8-12 57 PJMcDonald(3) 10 37
(Mrs K Walton) *bhd nr side: drvn 1/2-way: nvr rchd ldrs: 9th of 10 in gp* 20/1

-043 10 1/2 **Handsinthemist (IRE)**[13] 2287 3-8-11 53 (p) MickyFenton 15 31
(P T Midgley) *cl up far side: led that gp appr fnl f: nt pce of nr side: 1st of 5 in gp* 11/2[2]

4300 11 1 **Andrasta**[17] 2141 3-8-13 55 DanielTudhope 12 29
(A Berry) *cl up far side: effrt over 2f out: no imp over 1f out: 2nd of 5 in gp* 12/1

0-05 12 nk **Foreign Rhythm (IRE)**[13] 2268 3-9-1 57 FergalLynch 16 30
(N Tinkler) *led far side to appr fnl f: no ex: 3rd of 5 in gp* 7/1[3]

-000 13 hd **Lady Aviator**[13] 2287 3-8-1 46 oh1 DuranFentiman(3) 5 19
(T D Easterby) *missed break: a bhd nr side: last of 10 in gp* 40/1

0-20 14 hd **Maahe (IRE)**[20] 2074 3-8-6 48 PaulHanagan 17 20
(R A Fahey) *racd far side: towards rr: hung rt 1/2-way: n.d: 4th of 5 in gp* 9/1

2-00 15 nk **Best Suited**[17] 2159 3-9-1 57 GrahamGibbons 11 28
(J J Quinn) *in tch far side: outpcd 1/2-way: n.d after: last of 5 in gp* 9/1

63.33 secs (2.53) **Going Correction** +0.125s/f (Good) 15 Ran SP% 122.0
Speed ratings (Par 97): **84,82,81,80,80 80,79,75,73,72 71,70,70,70,69**
CSF £156.79 CT £1909.91 TOTE £26.80: £7.30, £2.30, £5.00; EX 248.50.
Owner John Gibb **Bred** Southill Stud **Trained** Middleham Moor, N Yorks

FOCUS
A very slow winning time for a race like this, 1.25 seconds slower than the earlier two-year-old median auction maiden. The main near-side group held a big edge over the quintet that raced far side. Weak form which has been rated negatively.
Red River Boy Official explanation: trainer's rep said, regarding running, that the gelding had been very immature and had benefited from being covered up and racing amongst others.

2662 CARLISLE-RACES.CO.UK APPRENTICE H'CAP 7f 200y

4:45 (4:45) (Class 6) (0-65,66) 4-Y-O+ £2,047 (£604; £302) Stalls High

Form RPR

600 1 **Boy Dancer (IRE)**[23] 2009 5-9-2 52 JamieMoriarty 15 60
(J J Quinn) *hld up: effrt over 2f out: styd on wl fnl f to ld post* 14/1

600- 2 shd **Reddy Ronnie (IRE)**[256] 5567 4-8-4 47 PaulPickard(7) 17 54
(D Carroll) *trckd ldrs: led 2f out: kpt on wl: hdd post* 66/1

-050 3 1 **Apache Nation (IRE)**[24] 1966 5-9-6 56 NeilBrown 16 61+
(M Dods) *hld up: styd on wl fnl 2f: nrst fin* 9/1

-033 4 3/4 **Wind Shuffle (GER)**[13] 2285 5-9-7 60 GaryBartley(3) 13 63
(J S Goldie) *t.k.h early: cl up: chal 2f out: sn rdn and wandered: one pce ins fnl f* 8/1[3]

-511 **5** *1 3/4* **Paraguay (USA)**[3] 2561 5-9-13 **66** 6ex .... SCreighton(3) 8 69+
(Miss V Haigh) *hld up: stdy hdwy over 2f out: rdn and one pce fnl f* **4/1**[1]
6-00 **6** *3/4* **Farne Island**[10] 2365 5-9-7 **57** .... AndrewMullen 1 54
(Micky Hammond) *bhd: hdwy on ins over 1f out: no imp fnl f* **20/1**
005 **7** *1 3/4* **Gee Ceffyl Bach**[35] 1687 4-8-4 **45** .... StacyRenwick(5) 7 37
(R C Guest) *prom: shkn up over 1f out: sn no ex* **25/1**
0-03 **8** *nk* **Emperor's Well**[39] 1578 9-9-1 **56** .... BradleyRoper(5) 14 48
(M W Easterby) *prom tl rdn and no ex over 1f out* **10/1**
5625 **9** *6* **Zennerman (IRE)**[13] 2285 5-9-9 **59** .... PJMcDonald 4 36
(G A Swinbank) *prom: outpcd 3f out: n.d after* **7/1**[2]
0100 **10** *nk* **Shava**[35] 1687 8-8-9 **50** .... DeclanCannon(5) 9 26
(H J Evans) *hld up: pushed along 2f out: nvr on terms* **33/1**
6056 **11** *1 3/4* **Grethel (IRE)**[3] 2568 4-9-0 **50** .... DuranFentiman 12 22
(A Berry) *t.k.h: in tch tl wknd fr 2f out* **22/1**
-066 **12** *hd* **College Land Boy**[7] 2463 4-8-5 **46** ow1 .... SamuelDrury(5) 5 17
(A Kirtley) *cl up tl wknd over 2f out* **33/1**
6404 **13** *shd* **Cool Sands (IRE)**[34] 1703 6-8-6 **45** .... MatthewDavies(3) 6 16
(J G Given) *hld up: outpcd 3f out: sn btn* **11/1**
5-03 **14** *1 1/2* **Alberts Story (USA)**[13] 2274 4-9-0 **55** .... BMcHugh(5) 11 22
(R A Fahey) *midfield: struggling 3f out: sn btn* **4/1**[1]
0040 **15** *1/2* **Cadogen Square**[34] 1705 6-8-6 **45** .... DanielleMcCreery(3) 3 11
(Mrs R A Carr) *sn led: hdd 2f out: wknd* **80/1**

1m 42.94s (2.94) **Going Correction** +0.40s/f (Good) **15** Ran SP% **119.3**
Speed ratings (Par 101): **101,100,99,99,97 96,94,94,88,88 86,86,86,84,84**
CSF £741.95 CT £4920.88 TOTE £14.10: £5.90, £12.50, £4.70; EX 646.00 Place 6: £11571.67, Place 5 £1079.82.
Owner A Turton & S Brown **Bred** Azienda Agricola Razza Emiliana **Trained** Settrington, N Yorks
■ Stewards' Enquiry : Gary Bartley two-day ban: careless riding (Jun 16, 22)

FOCUS
Another low-grade handicap and one in which the pace was sound. Those drawn near the far rail enjoyed a sizeable advantage. The winner is rated to last year's form.
T/Jkpt: Not won. T/Plt: Part won. £42,191.80 to a £1 stake. Pool: £57,797.03. 0.65 winning tickets. T/Qpdt: Part won. £3,758.00 to a £1 stake. Pool: £5,078.48. 0.90 winning tickets. RY

2479 LEICESTER (R-H)

Monday, June 2

OFFICIAL GOING: Good (good to soft in places; 7.5)
Wind: Almost nil Weather: Overcast turning showery after race 6

2663 PYTCHLEY MAIDEN STKS 5f 218y
2:00 (2:01) (Class 4) 2-Y-O **£3,885** (£1,156; £577; £288) **Stalls** High

Form RPR
1 **Free Agent** 2-9-3 0 .... RichardHughes 9 86+
(R Hannon) *trckd ldrs: rdn to ld 1f out: hmpd wl ins fnl f: r.o* **12/1**[3]
4 **2** *5* **Donativum**[17] 2150 2-9-3 0 .... JimmyFortune 8 83+
(J H M Gosden) *w ldr: rdn to ld over 1f out: sn hung lft and hdd: running on whn swvd rt and bmpd wnr wl ins fnl f: lost action and eased* **2/1**[2]
54 **3** *1* **Senatorial**[25] 1924 2-9-3 0 .... MichaelHills 5 68
(B W Hills) *led: racd keenly: rdn and hdd over 1f out: no ex ins fnl f* **6/4**[1]
4 *2 3/4* **Battle Of Hastings** 2-9-3 0 .... JamieSpencer 7 60+
(M L W Bell) *hld up: pushed along 1/2-way: hdwy over 1f out: nt trble ldrs* **12/1**[3]
5 *1 1/4* **Special Cuvee** 2-9-3 0 .... SebSanders 1 56
(Sir Mark Prescott) *s.i.s: sn prom: rdn and wkng whn edgd rt over 1f out* **25/1**
53 **6** *nk* **Duke Of Aquitaine (USA)**[17] 2146 2-9-3 0 .... JosedeSouza 3 55
(P F I Cole) *chsd ldrs over 4f* **12/1**[3]
7 *hd* **Superstitious Me (IRE)** 2-8-12 0 .... CatherineGannon 10 50
(B Palling) *prom: rdn over 2f out: wknd wl over 1f out* **100/1**
8 *6* **Billy Beetroot (USA)** 2-8-10 0 .... WilliamCarson(7) 2 37
(S C Williams) *hld up: hdwy over 3f out: wknd wl over 1f out* **66/1**

1m 14.07s (1.07) **Going Correction** +0.10s/f (Good) **8** Ran SP% **102.7**
Speed ratings (Par 95): **96,89,88,84,82 82,82,74**
CSF £28.80 TOTE £12.00: £1.80, £1.20, £1.10; EX 36.20 Trifecta £91.20 Part won: Pool: £128.49 - 0.49 winning units..
Owner The Queen **Bred** The Queen **Trained** East Everleigh, Wilts
■ Zaffaan (7/1) & Distinctive Spirit (40/1) were withdrawn after proving unruly at the start. Rule 4 applies, deduct 10p in the £.

FOCUS
A fair juvenile maiden, run at an average pace. The winner impressed although is slightly flattered by his winning margin.

NOTEBOOK
Free Agent, from a successful middle-distance family, ran out a somewhat surprisingly ready debutant winner over this sprint distance. He knew his job and displayed a turn of foot when asked to win the race, but he is a little flattered by the winning margin as the runner-up lost ground when barging into him late on. This is another advertisement of his trainer's excellent skills with juveniles and he no doubt has a future, with improvement assured from this experience. His connections later indicated a trip to Royal Ascot for the Chesham Stakes is now likely for him and the extra furlong should really prove right up his street, so a bold bid should be expected there. (op 11-1 tchd 8-1)
Donativum, well backed, looked held as Free Agent went past entering the final furlong but after getting a smack from his rider he found an extra gear and was closing again before hanging badly left and eventually coming across to bump into that rival. That ended his chance and his jockey was not hard on him thereafter, so while he is clearly very much still learning his trade, he has to be rated better than the bare form. This experience should again not be lost on him and he certainly has a maiden over this trip within his compass. (op 10-3 tchd 7-2)
Senatorial, who did not have things go his way at Chester last time in a maiden his stable often win, proved a little free through the early parts and was made to look one-paced when the first two made their moves for home. He rates the benchmark for this form and, while it is too soon to be writing him off just yet, he is now starting to look exposed. (op 2-1)
Battle Of Hastings, an already gelded tenth foal of a dam who was a smart 5f-1m2f winner, struggled to really got the early pace and was never seriously involved. He comes from a yard that knows the time of day with its juveniles, however, and this 62,000gns purchase can be expected to come on nicely for this debut experience. (op 14-1 tchd 16-1 and 9-1)
Special Cuvee is a half-brother to three winners at up to 1m, most notably Joseph Henry, and out of a dam who was herself a winner at 5f. Having made a sluggish start he was allowed to find his feet without being put under any real pressure and left the impression he would come on a good deal for this run. (op 20-1)

2664 HICKLING (S) STKS 5f 218y
2:30 (2:30) (Class 6) 3-5-Y-O **£1,942** (£578; £288; £144) **Stalls** High

Form RPR
00/0 **1** **Boldinor**[11] 2337 5-9-5 47 .... GeorgeBaker 3 62
(M R Bosley) *hld up: hdwy 1/2-way: rdn over 1f out: led and edgd rt ins fnl f: jst hld on* **12/1**
051 **2** *nse* **Doubtful Sound (USA)**[4] 2547 4-9-3 65 ....(b) MarkCoumbe(7) 6 67+
(John A Harris) *s.i.s: hld up: stmbld over 2f out: hdwy over 1f out: hung rt and r.o ins fnl f: jst failed* **10/3**[2]
45-0 **3** *1 1/4* **Avertitop**[27] 1899 3-8-11 70 .... RichardHughes 5 56
(R Hannon) *sn pushed along in rr: hdwy over 2f out: rdn over 1f out: nt qckn nr fin* **15/8**[1]
0-06 **4** *nk* **Rainbow Bay**[14] 2255 5-9-5 58 ....(v) StephenDonohoe 9 57
(P D Evans) *s.i.s: hdwy 4f out: led 1/2-way: sn rdn: hdd ins fnl f: no ex towards fin* **7/2**[3]
0506 **5** *1 3/4* **Swift Cut (IRE)**[27] 1898 4-8-12 49 ....(p) DavidProbert(7) 4 51
(D Burchell) *prom: rdn over 1f out: sn hung rt: styd on same pce* **11/1**
46-5 **6** *1 3/4* **Accolation**[143] 121 4-9-5 45 .... DaneO'Neill 10 46
(Pat Eddery) *chsd ldrs: rdn over 2f out: wknd ins fnl f* **14/1**
550- **7** *5* **Mannello**[166] 7188 5-9-0 50 .... RichardThomas 2 25
(Jim Best) *chsd ldrs: lost pl 1/2-way: sn hung rt: n.d after* **16/1**
0-00 **8** *7* **Summer Gift**[6] 2491 5-9-0 46 ....(v) ChrisCatlin 8 2
(J O'Reilly) *chsd ldrs: rdn over 2f out: sn wknd* **33/1**
5500 **9** *4* **Her Name Is Rio (IRE)**[26] 1912 3-8-11 50 ....(b) TomEaves 7 —
(Mrs S Lamyman) *led to 1/2-way: wknd 2f out* **50/1**
10 *18* **Bubbles Darling** 3-8-6 0 .... RichardKingscote 1 —
(M R Bosley) *dwlt: outpcd: hung lft fr 1/2-way* **80/1**

1m 13.4s (0.40) **Going Correction** +0.10s/f (Good)
WFA 3 from 4yo+ 8lb **10** Ran SP% **114.8**
Speed ratings (Par 101): **101,100,99,98,96 94,87,78,72,48**
CSF £50.81 TOTE £23.20: £4.40, £1.40, £1.40; EX 117.80 Trifecta £116.10 Pool: £227.31 - 1.39 winning units.The winner was bought in for 4,000 guineas. Doubtful Sound was claimed by Mr R A Harris for £7,000. Avertitop was claimed by Mr J Gallagher for £7,000.
Owner Ron Collins **Bred** Ron Collins **Trained** Lockeridge, Wilts

FOCUS
A typically moderate seller, run at a sound pace. The first pair came clear late on and the winner is rated 7lb off his old turf form.
Bubbles Darling Official explanation: jockey said filly hung left

2665 RICHARD BURLEY HALF CENTURY BIRTHDAY H'CAP 1m 1f 218y
3:00 (3:02) (Class 4) (0-85,85) 3-Y-O **£4,209** (£1,252; £625; £312) **Stalls** High

Form RPR
12-0 **1** **Dona Alba (IRE)**[38] 1600 3-9-5 **83** .... EddieAhern 4 94+
(J L Dunlop) *chsd ldrs: led over 3f out: rdn over 1f out: styd on* **11/1**
01-1 **2** *3/4* **Cool Judgement (IRE)**[30] 1805 3-9-7 **85** .... PhilipRobinson 9 94+
(M A Jarvis) *hld up: hdwy over 2f out: sn rdn and hung rt: styd on ins fnl f: nt rch wnr* **11/4**[1]
-011 **3** *2 1/4* **Excape (IRE)**[13] 2272 3-8-9 **76** ....(b) MarcHalford(3) 12 81
(D R C Elsworth) *led: hdd over 3f out: sn rdn: styd on same pce fnl f* **9/1**
210 **4** *nse* **Sweet Lightning**[19] 2109 3-9-3 **81** .... MartinDwyer 10 85+
(W R Muir) *hld up in tch: rdn over 2f out: nt clr run ins fnl f: styd on* **14/1**
-330 **5** *1* **Colorado Blue (IRE)**[17] 2151 3-8-11 **75** .... SebSanders 1 77
(R Charlton) *chsd ldrs: rdn over 3f out: no ex fnl f* **9/1**
0-31 **6** *3/4* **Hepburn Bell (IRE)**[39] 1579 3-8-13 **77** .... JamieSpencer 2 78+
(J R Fanshawe) *hld up: rdn and hung rt fr over 2f out: styd on ins fnl f: nt rch ldrs* **14/1**
0-1 **7** *3* **It's A Date**[16] 2191 3-9-6 **84** .... FergusSweeney 14 79
(A King) *dwlt: hld up: rdn over 2f out: nvr trbld ldrs* **6/1**[3]
0-21 **8** *3/4* **Conquisto**[37] 1614 3-9-5 **83** .... AdamKirby 8 76+
(C G Cox) *hld up: plld hrd: rdn over 2f out: n.d* **11/2**[2]
310- **9** *1/2* **Suzi Spends (IRE)**[206] 6750 3-8-9 **73** .... ChrisCatlin 13 65
(H J Collingridge) *prom: rdn 3f out: wknd over 1f out* **66/1**
31-0 **10** *3 1/4* **Fair Gale**[17] 2151 3-9-0 **78** .... RichardHughes 7 64
(S Kirk) *chsd ldrs: rdn over 2f out: wknd over 1f out* **33/1**
051- **11** *9* **Wing Play (IRE)**[198] 6855 3-8-13 **77** .... SteveDrowne 5 45
(H Morrison) *s.s: hld up: rdn over 3f out: a in rr* **12/1**
1150 **12** *2 1/4* **Air Chief**[12] 2302 3-8-12 **76** .... JimmyQuinn 6 39
(H J L Dunlop) *plld hrd and prom: rdn and wknd over 2f out* **20/1**
50-5 **13** *2 1/2* **Transmission (IRE)**[40] 1572 3-8-8 **72** .... TomEaves 11 30
(B Smart) *hld up: rdn over 4f out: sn wknd* **25/1**
3-16 **14** *15* **Rankayo Hitam (USA)**[10] 2378 3-9-1 **79** .... JohnEgan 3 7
(P F I Cole) *hld up: bhd fnl 3f* **50/1**

2m 7.61s (-0.29) **Going Correction** +0.10s/f (Good) **14** Ran SP% **120.7**
Speed ratings (Par 101): **105,104,102,102,101 101,98,98,97,95 87,86,84,72**
CSF £39.45 CT £297.12 TOTE £13.00: £3.70, £1.30, £2.60; EX 47.40 Trifecta £308.60 Part won: Pool: £434.73 - 0.59 winning units..
Owner Windflower Overseas Holdings Inc **Bred** Windflower Overseas Holdings Inc **Trained** Arundel, W Sussex
■ Stewards' Enquiry : Philip Robinson two-day ban: used whip with excessive frequency without giving colt time to respond (Jun 16, 22)

FOCUS
A good handicap for the grade. The early pace was only modest, however and it looked an advantage to race prominently. The form looks sound.
Rankayo Hitam(USA) Official explanation: jockey said colt hung badly left

2666 CHARNWOOD FOREST FILLIES' CONDITIONS STKS 7f 9y
3:30 (3:32) (Class 2) 3-Y-O+
£12,462 (£3,732; £1,866; £934; £466; £234) **Stalls** High

Form RPR
52-0 **1** **Dixey**[30] 1806 3-8-7 88 ow1 .... PhilipRobinson 7 92
(M A Jarvis) *mde all: rdn over 1f out: styd on gamely* **12/1**
5-1 **2** *nk* **Danae**[46] 1423 3-8-6 92 .... FergusSweeney 5 90
(H Candy) *trckd ldrs: rdn and ev ch fr over 1f out: edgd lft: styd on* **9/4**[1]
5-03 **3** *1/2* **Kay Es Jay (FR)**[33] 1715 3-8-7 95 ow1 .... MichaelHills 6 90
(B W Hills) *hld up: hdwy over 1f out: sn rdn: styd on* **10/1**
/50- **4** *shd* **Silca Chiave**[348] 2752 4-8-12 104 .... DarryllHolland 3 89
(M R Channon) *hld up: rdn and hung rt over 1f out: r.o ins fnl f: nt rch ldrs* **11/2**[3]
31-6 **5** *1* **Steam Cuisine**[23] 1993 4-8-12 94 .... TPO'Shea 2 86
(M G Quinlan) *chsd ldrs: rdn over 1f out: no ex ins fnl f* **3/1**[2]

00-0 **6** 6 **Gone Fast (USA)**[47] 1401 3-8-6 93 RichardMullen 9 70
(D M Simcock) *hld up in tch: rdn over 2f out: wknd fnl f* **16/1**

20-0 **7** nk **Broken Applause (IRE)**[23] 2000 3-8-4 100 DaleGibson 10 67
(D J G Murray Smith) *chsd wnr: rdn over 2f out: wknd fnl f* **16/1**

6110 **8** 10 **Jilly Why (IRE)**[10] 2359 7-8-12 84 (b) TPQueally 8 42
(Paul Green) *hld up: rdn over 2f out: sn wknd* **20/1**

1m 25.68s (-0.52) **Going Correction** +0.10s/f (Good)
WFA 3 from 4yo+ 10lb **8** Ran SP% **104.5**
Speed ratings (Par 96): **106,105,105,104,103 96,96,85**
CSF £32.71 TOTE £16.60: £3.40, £1.40, £2.20; EX 33.30 Trifecta £192.80 Pool: 374.75. - 1.38 winning units..
Owner T G Warner **Bred** Red House Stud **Trained** Newmarket, Suffolk
■ Edge Of Light (12/1) was withdrawn after proving unruly at the start. Deduct 5p in the £ under rule 4.

FOCUS
A decent fillies' conditions event, run at a reasonable pace. The first five came nicely clear. There are doubts over the form, however, and it has not been rated too positively.

NOTEBOOK
Dixey bounced right back to form on this return to 7f and ran out a dogged winner from the front. She had finished last of 13 on her comeback at Newmarket in early May, but this was much more like it and her performance is made more meritorious by the fact her rider put up 1lb overweight. (op 14-1)
Danae was produced with every chance, but was always being held by the winner at the business end. This rates a solid effort in defeat and the way this lightly-raced filly kept on here would suggest the move up to 1m may just bring about some more improvement now. There will certainly still be other days for her. (op 5-2 tchd 2-1)
Kay Es Jay(FR) looks to be coming good again now and posted another improved effort in defeat. She looks best kept to this trip at present, was another whose rider carried 1lb overweight, and her turn does not look at all far off again now. (op 12-1)
Silca Chiave caught the eye staying on with some purpose on this return from a 348-day break. She had some smart form as a juvenile and, granted the normal improvement, looks sure to get closer next time now she has this encouraging return effort under her belt. (op 4-1 tchd 6-1)
Steam Cuisine failed to really improve as may have been expected from her seasonal debut 23 days previously, but still had her chance and did nothing wrong in defeat. (op 5-2)
Gone Fast(USA) proved too free for her own good early on and still has to prove she has really trained on from two to three. (tchd 18-1)

2667 LEICESTER RACECOURSE CONFERENCE CENTRE CLAIMING STKS 1m 1f 218y
4:00 (4:01) (Class 5) 4-Y-0+ **£2,331** (£693; £346; £173) **Stalls** High

Form RPR
1514 **1** **Boundless Prospect (USA)**[14] 2250 9-8-9 75 JamieSpencer 9 67
(Ollie Pears) *hld up: hdwy and hung rt over 1f out: sn rdn: styd on to ld at post* **9/4**[1]

00/0 **2** nse **Channel Crossing**[27] 1890 6-8-11 45 LiamJones 5 69
(S Wynne) *chsd ldrs: rdn to ld wl ins fnl f: hdd post* **66/1**

-010 **3** 1/2 **Rowan Lodge (IRE)**[18] 1752 6-8-9 64 (b) TomEaves 10 66
(Ollie Pears) *hld up in tch: rdn to ld ins fnl f: sn hdd: styd on* **7/1**

0/12 **4** 1 1/2 **Penny Island (IRE)**[27] 1895 6-9-1 68 DaneO'Neill 2 69
(John A Harris) *chsd ldrs: led 7f out: rdn over 1f out: hdd and unable qck ins fnl f* **11/4**[2]

3-45 **5** 6 **Wild Pitch**[14] 2264 7-9-5 72 (v[1]) EddieAhern 8 61
(Stef Liddiard) *hld up in tch: lost pl 7f out: hdwy over 2f out: sn rdn: wknd ins fnl f* **8/1**

5060 **6** 1 1/2 **Good Cause (IRE)**[52] 1296 7-8-9 50 DO'Donohoe 7 48
(Mrs S Lamyman) *s.s: hdwy 7f out: rdn over 2f out: wknd over 1f out* **33/1**

3152 **7** 1 1/4 **Red Rudy**[3] 2557 6-8-11 69 SebSanders 6 48
(A W Carroll) *s.i.s: hld up: hdwy over 2f out: wknd over 1f out* **10/3**[3]

50/6 **8** 1 1/2 **The Plainsman**[9] 2394 6-8-11 39 ChrisCatlin 4 45
(P W Hiatt) *plld hrd and prom: rdn and wknd over 1f out* **66/1**

3050 **9** 6 **Dream Forest (IRE)**[13] 2290 5-8-11 43 JimCrowley 1 33
(P W Hiatt) *racd wd: led 3f: chsd ldrs: rdn over 2f out: sn wknd* **20/1**

00/ **10** 30 **Follow The Buzz**[593] 6050 4-8-9 0 JoeFanning 3 —
(M Wellings) *s.i.s: hld up: bhd fr 1/2-way* **100/1**

2m 8.74s (0.84) **Going Correction** +0.10s/f (Good) **10** Ran SP% **115.8**
Speed ratings (Par 103): **100,99,99,98,93 92,91,90,85,61**
CSF £171.19 TOTE £3.50: £1.20, £14.20, £2.30; EX 143.60 Trifecta £198.80 Pool: £677.77 - 2.42 winning units..The winner was subject to a friendly claim.
Owner Diamond Racing Ltd **Bred** Mrs Edgar Scott Jr & Mrs Lawrence Macelree **Trained** Norton, N Yorks

FOCUS
A weak claimer all in all. The first three came clear and the proximity of the runner-up raises serious doubts over the form.

2668 COPLOW MAIDEN STKS (DIV I) 1m 3f 183y
4:30 (4:31) (Class 5) 3-Y-0 **£2,104** (£626; £312; £156) **Stalls** High

Form RPR
2 **1** **Meethaaq (USA)**[10] 2370 3-9-3 0 RHills 4 90+
(Sir Michael Stoute) *hld up: hdwy and nt clr run 2f out: swtchd rt over 1f out: r.o to ld last strides* **8/15**[1]

2 nk **Inquisitive Look** 3-8-12 0 AdrianMcCarthy 7 77
(P W Chapple-Hyam) *hld up: hdwy over 4f out: led over 2f out: rdn clr over 1f out: shkn up and hdd last strides* **33/1**

24 **3** 6 **Coin Of The Realm (IRE)**[33] 1728 3-9-3 0 JimmyFortune 8 73
(E A L Dunlop) *chsd ldr: rdn and ev ch over 2f out: wknd ins fnl f* **9/1**[3]

4 1 1/2 **London Times (IRE)**[69] 3-9-3 0 JoeFanning 13 70
(M Johnston) *led: rdn and hdd over 2f out: wknd fnl f* **16/1**

342- **5** 1/2 **Mushtaaq (USA)**[238] 6051 3-9-3 85 MartinDwyer 3 70
(M A Jarvis) *prom: rdn over 2f out: wknd over 1f out* **3/1**[2]

0 **6** 1 1/2 **Requia**[38] 1599 3-8-12 0 DaneO'Neill 5 62
(H Candy) *chsd ldrs: rdn over 2f out: hung rt and wknd over 1f out* **66/1**

55 **7** 1 **Solas Alainn (IRE)**[21] 2046 3-9-3 0 AdamKirby 10 66+
(J R Fanshawe) *hld up: hdwy over 3f out: wknd over 1f out* **50/1**

0-0 **8** 1 **Zia Zabel (IRE)**[17] 2164 3-8-12 0 TPO'Shea 6 59
(J L Dunlop) *hld up: hdwy and nt clr run over 1f out: swtchd lft: nt trble ldrs* **50/1**

9 nk **Miss Serena** 3-8-12 0 JimmyQuinn 9 59
(Mrs P Sly) *s.s: a in rr* **50/1**

0 **10** 2 1/4 **Enderby Light (FR)**[16] 2207 3-9-3 0 DO'Donohoe 12 60
(D Carroll) *hld up: hdwy over 7f out: rdn over 2f out: sn hung rt and wknd* **80/1**

00 **11** 6 **Squire Boldwood (IRE)**[16] 2199 3-9-3 0 (b[1]) SebSanders 1 50
(D R C Elsworth) *hld up: plld hrd: hdwy 8f out: rdn and wknd over 2f out* **80/1**

0- **12** 4 1/2 **Lake Nayasa**[208] 6723 3-8-9 0 TravisBlock(3) 11 38
(H Morrison) *prom: shkn up 1/2-way: rdn and wknd over 2f out* **100/1**

00 **13** 10 **Silver Willow**[21] 2046 3-8-7 0 NicolPolli(5) 2 22
(Miss Gay Kelleway) *hld up: pushed along over 7f out: wknd over 3f out* **200/1**

0 **14** 13 **Daarth**[16] 2191 3-9-3 0 ChrisCatlin 14 6
(B W Duke) *a in rr* **250/1**

2m 36.38s (2.48) **Going Correction** +0.10s/f (Good) **14** Ran SP% **120.8**
Speed ratings (Par 99): **95,94,90,89,89 88,87,87,86,85 81,78,71,63**
CSF £34.42 TOTE £1.50: £1.02, £6.80, £2.20; EX 28.90 Trifecta £80.40 Pool: £495.43. - 4.37 winning units.
Owner Hamdan Al Maktoum **Bred** W S Farish & E J Hudson Jr Ir **Tr Trained** Newmarket, Suffolk
■ Stewards' Enquiry : Adrian McCarthy ten-day ban: failed to ride out on a horse that could have won (Jun 16-25)

FOCUS
This controversial maiden was run at just an average pace, resulting in a slower winning time than the second division, but still looks the stronger of the pair. The first two came clear and the form makes sense.
Miss Serena Official explanation: jockey said filly missed the break and ran freely

2669 COPLOW MAIDEN STKS (DIV II) 1m 3f 183y
5:00 (5:02) (Class 5) 3-Y-0 **£2,104** (£626; £312; £156) **Stalls** High

Form RPR
54 **1** **Gravitation**[17] 2164 3-8-12 0 TPQueally 11 76
(W Jarvis) *hld up: hdwy 7f out: swtchd lft over 1f out: rdn to ld wl ins fnl f* **5/1**[2]

52 **2** 1 1/4 **Maria Di Scozia**[17] 2164 3-8-12 0 AdrianMcCarthy 7 74
(P W Chapple-Hyam) *a.p: led 2f out: rdn: hung lft and hdd wl ins fnl f* **15/2**

634- **3** 2 1/4 **Blue Citadel (USA)**[223] 6410 3-9-3 78 JimCrowley 6 75
(Mrs A J Perrett) *led: hdd over 8f out: lft in ld 5f out: rdn and hdd 2f out: styd on same pce fnl f* **6/1**[3]

0-5 **4** 2 3/4 **Dedicate**[18] 2123 3-8-12 0 SteveDrowne 5 65
(R Charlton) *hld up in tch: rdn over 3f out: styd on same pce fnl 2f* **10/1**

0-52 **5** 1 **Dalhaan (USA)**[25] 1931 3-9-3 93 RHills 13 69
(J L Dunlop) *chsd ldrs: rdn over 3f out: wknd fnl f* **13/8**[1]

0 **6** 1 3/4 **Waarid**[37] 1628 3-9-3 0 (b[1]) MartinDwyer 4 66
(W J Haggas) *chsd ldr: led over 8f out: hung lft and hdd 5f out: rdn over 2f out: styd on same pce* **80/1**

7 2 **Lough Diver (IRE)** 3-9-3 0 JimmyQuinn 14 63+
(M H Tompkins) *s.s: styd on fr over 2f out: n.d* **50/1**

0 **8** 10 **Filun**[16] 2191 3-9-3 0 DaneO'Neill 8 46+
(L M Cumani) *s.s: hld up: rdn over 3f out: n.d* **11/1**

9 10 **Beautiful Dreamer** 3-8-12 0 RyanMoore 9 25
(Sir Michael Stoute) *prom: rdn over 5f out: wknd over 2f out* **12/1**

0 **10** 1 1/4 **Tank Commander**[16] 2197 3-9-3 0 GeorgeBaker 10 28
(W R Muir) *hld up: sme hdwy over 3f out: sn wknd* **28/1**

11 7 **Nastjir** 3-9-3 0 DarryllHolland 3 16
(M A Jarvis) *hld up: bhd fnl 4f* **50/1**

3 **12** 8 **Dance The Star (USA)**[54] 1272 3-9-3 0 SebSanders 1 3
(D M Simcock) *a in rr: bhd whn hung rt fr over 3f out* **28/1**

00- **P** **Tagula King (IRE)**[283] 4783 3-9-3 0 DO'Donohoe 2 —
(D Carroll) *in rr whn p.u after 2f* **300/1**

2m 34.47s (0.57) **Going Correction** +0.10s/f (Good) **53** Ran SP% **118.3**
Speed ratings (Par 99): **102,101,99,97,97 96,94,88,81,80 75,70,—**
CSF £40.31 TOTE £6.70: £2.00, £2.50, £2.60; EX 36.60 Trifecta £140.90 Pool: £395.01. - 1.99 winning units.
Owner Gillian, Lady Howard De Walden **Bred** Plantation Stud **Trained** Newmarket, Suffolk

FOCUS
A fair maiden likely to produce winners. The time was quicker than the first division and this is sound maiden form, the third setting the standard.
Waarid Official explanation: jockey said gelding hung left
Tank Commander Official explanation: jockey said gelding had no more to give
Tagula King(IRE) Official explanation: jockey said colt lost its action after 2f

2670 SIS FILLIES' H'CAP 7f 9y
5:30 (5:32) (Class 5) (0-70,70) 3-Y-0+ **£3,238** (£963; £481; £240) **Stalls** High

Form RPR
04-1 **1** **Oh So Saucy**[21] 2055 4-9-7 **60** GeorgeBaker 1 75
(C F Wall) *hld up: hdwy wl over 1f out: led 1f out: shkn up and sn clr* **4/1**[2]

5-10 **2** 6 **Bert's Memory**[39] 1578 4-8-11 **50** (b[1]) SebSanders 3 49
(J Mackie) *led: rdn and hdd 1f out: no ex* **10/1**

6002 **3** nk **Stormburst (IRE)**[44] 1489 4-8-11 **50** CatherineGannon 6 48
(A J Chamberlain) *hld up: hdwy u.p over 1f out: no ex whn rdr dropped whip ins fnl f* **33/1**

0130 **4** 4 1/2 **Jessica Wigmo**[18] 2128 5-8-8 **54** MarkCoumbe(7) 2 40
(A W Carroll) *s.i.s: in rr tl mod late prog* **16/1**

0-25 **5** 3 1/4 **Sylvias Grove**[10] 2366 3-9-7 **70** DO'Donohoe 4 47
(D Carroll) *chsd ldrs: rdn over 2f out: wknd fnl f* **14/1**

61- **6** 1 **Romantic Verse**[210] 6694 3-9-0 **63** LiamJones 7 37
(W J Haggas) *prom: rdn over 2f out: wknd fnl f* **8/1**[3]

6145 **7** 3 3/4 **Alucica**[52] 1313 5-9-0 **53** (v) JimCrowley 10 17
(D Shaw) *mid-div: hdwy 1/2-way: rdn and wknd over 1f out* **10/1**

0 **8** 2 1/4 **Ornella**[33] 1729 4-9-11 **67** TravisBlock(3) 12 25
(H Morrison) *chsd ldrs 5f* **16/1**

4052 **9** 1/2 **Hessian (IRE)**[7] 2457 4-9-9 **62** ChrisCatlin 8 19+
(M D Squance) *hld up: rdn over 2f out: wknd over 1f out* **13/8**[1]

06-0 **10** 3 1/2 **Bewdley**[44] 1478 3-7-11 **53** ow1 SophieDoyle(7) 5 —
(Mrs K Waldron) *hld up: a in rr* **100/1**

00-0 **11** 13 **Geordie Girl**[23] 2002 3-9-2 **65** JimmyQuinn 9 —
(R C Guest) *prom over 4f* **33/1**

11-3 **12** 1 3/4 **Shepherds Warning (IRE)**[122] 393 3-9-6 **69** RichardKingscote 11 —
(N J Vaughan) *chsd ldr tl rdn 1/2-way: wknd over 2f out* **16/1**

1m 26.23s (0.03) **Going Correction** +0.10s/f (Good)
WFA 3 from 4yo+ 10lb **12** Ran SP% **118.6**
Speed ratings (Par 100): **103,96,95,90,86 85,81,78,78,74 59,57**
CSF £43.43 CT £1185.79 TOTE £5.50: £2.30, £3.30, £6.00; EX 59.80 Trifecta £373.10 Part won: Pool: £525.54. - 0.10 winning units. Place 6: £11.88, Place 5: £ 9.87.
Owner The Eight Of Diamonds **Bred** Mrs C J Walker **Trained** Newmarket, Suffolk

FOCUS
A modest fillies' handicap, but they went a decent pace and it ultimately became a one-horse race. The field came right down the centre of the track. The winner is on the upgrade but this form is none too solid.
T/Plt: £7.50 to a £1 stake. Pool: £57,548.42. 5,558.77 winning tickets. T/Qpdt: £4.90 to a £1 stake. Pool: £3,695.68. 550.80 winning tickets. CR

2206 THIRSK (L-H)
Monday, June 2

OFFICIAL GOING: Good to soft
Wind: Virtually nil Weather: Overcast and warm

2671 SCARBOROUGH FAIR (S) STKS 6f
6:15 (6:16) (Class 5) 2-Y-O £3,885 (£1,156; £577; £288) Stalls High

Form RPR
06 1 **Madame Jourdain (IRE)**[6] 2485 2-8-7 0 ....(b) DavidAllan 12 62+
(T D Easterby) *in tch: hdwy over 2f out: rdn to ld 1 1/2f out: clr ent fnl f: styd on wl* **22/1**
324 2 3 3/4 **Rose Of Coma (IRE)**[15] 2216 2-8-7 0 .... TonyHamilton 5 49
(R A Fahey) *in tch: hdwy to chse ldrs 2f out: sn rdn and kpt on ins fnl f* **5/1**[2]
1302 3 hd **Heaven Or Hell (IRE)**[7] 2450 2-9-3 0 .... RobertWinston 13 58
(P D Evans) *led: rdn and hdd over 2f out: drvn over 1f out: edgd lft and one pce ins fnl f* **9/4**[1]
34 4 4 **Rioja Ruby (IRE)**[23] 2004 2-8-0 0 .... PatrickDonaghy(7) 8 36
(P C Haslam) *cl up: led over 2f out: sn rdn and hdd 1 1/2f out: wknd appr fnl f* **7/1**[3]
61 5 1/2 **Kneesy Earsy Nosey**[15] 2216 2-8-12 0 .... KimTinkler 2 40+
(N Tinkler) *dwlt and bhd tl styd on fnl 2f: nvr nr ldrs* **9/1**
0 6 4 1/2 **Approved**[21] 2035 2-8-7 0 .... J-PGuillambert 6 21
(M W Easterby) *towards rr and sn rdn along: hdwy over 2f out: styd on u.p appr fnl f: nrst fin* **12/1**
003 7 1 1/2 **French Forest**[15] 2216 2-8-7 0 .... AlanMunro 1 17
(M Brittain) *nvr nr ldrs* **8/1**
5 8 shd **Petite Denise**[15] 2216 2-8-7 0 .... DaleGibson 9 16
(M W Easterby) *a towards rr* **16/1**
9 13 **Willin Dillon (IRE)** 2-8-9 0 .... DominicFox(3) 11 —
(W Storey) *cmpt: bit bkwd: s.i.s: a bhd* **66/1**
5 10 3 1/4 **Ron's Princess (IRE)**[39] 1574 2-8-0 0 ....(p) DeanHeslop(7) 10 —
(P C Haslam) *leggy: prom: rdn along bef 1/2-way and sn wknd* **25/1**
11 4 1/2 **Fathtastic (IRE)** 2-8-12 0 .... EdwardCreighton 7 —
(Miss V Haigh) *str: chsd ldrs: rdn along 1/2-way: sn wknd* **40/1**
5502 12 1 **Crewezando**[7] 2459 2-8-12 0 .... PhillipMakin 3 —
(P D Evans) *chsd ldrs on wd outside: rdn along 1/2-way: sn wknd* **7/1**[3]

1m 15.5s (2.80) **Going Correction** +0.30s/f (Good) 12 Ran SP% **119.2**
Speed ratings (Par 93): **93,88,87,82,81 75,73,73,56,51 45,44**
CSF £126.45 TOTE £21.10: £6.00, £2.20, £1.30; EX 179.30.The winner was bought by Nigel Sennett for £7,200.
Owner Habton Farms **Bred** Tally-Ho Stud **Trained** Great Habton, N Yorks
■ Stewards' Enquiry : Kim Tinkler two-day ban: careless riding (Jun 16, 22)

FOCUS
A very moderate bunch of juveniles, most of whom have been campaigning solely at this level, the winner being one of the few exceptions. The form is rated through the placed horses.

NOTEBOOK
Madame Jourdain(IRE), dropping out of maiden company for the first time, always travelled best and quickly put the race to bed when given the office two furlongs out. She looks a touch above this grade. (op 20-1)
Rose Of Coma(IRE) is consistent but not really improving with racing. She will need to be found a weak seller to break her duck. (op 11-2 tchd 6-1)
Heaven Or Hell(IRE) is becoming a standing dish in sellers all over the country and while he again ran his race, his winner's penalty is making it hard for him to add to his debut success. (op 5-2 tchd 11-4)
Rioja Ruby(IRE) showed good speed before getting tired in the last furlong. A return to the minimum trip is on the cards for her. (op 17-2)
Kneesy Earsy Nosey missed the break and was switched from her centre-field draw across to the stands' rail before making good late progress. She can win again in this grade. (op 7-1)
Fathtastic(IRE) Official explanation: jockey said colt had no more to give
Crewezando Official explanation: jockey said gelding hung left-handed throughout

2672 STUBBS IN YORK EXHIBITION H'CAP 1m
6:45 (6:45) (Class 5) (0-75,72) 4-Y-O+ £3,885 (£1,156; £577; £288) Stalls Low

Form RPR
-323 1 **Hula Ballew**[7] 2445 8-9-5 70 .... PhillipMakin 5 84
(M Dods) *trckd ldrs: effrt 3f out: rdn to chal 2f out: drvn ent fnl f: styd on wl to ld nr fin* **85/40**[1]
-302 2 nk **Celtic Step**[23] 2007 4-9-5 70 .... PaulHanagan 2 83
(P D Niven) *lw: led: rdn along over 2f out: drvn over 1f out: hdd and no ex towards fin* **6/1**[2]
-500 3 4 **Chin Wag (IRE)**[7] 2444 4-8-6 57 .... FergalLynch 1 61
(J S Goldie) *dwlt and towards rr: hdwy over 3f out: rdn to chse ldrs 2f out: sn drvn and no imp appr fnl f* **15/2**[3]
2-02 4 3 1/4 **Just Bond (IRE)**[9] 2406 6-9-1 71 .... SladeO'Hara(5) 14 67
(G R Oldroyd) *lw: midfield: hdwy 3f out: rdn to chse ldrs whn hung rt over 1f out: no imp ins fnl f* **8/1**
0-16 5 2 1/2 **Dispol Isle (IRE)**[23] 2007 6-9-7 72 .... PaulFessey 13 65
(T D Barron) *dwlt: midfield: hdwy over 2f out: rdn and n.m.r wl over 1f out: sn swtchd rt and kpt on same pce* **11/1**
4203 6 3 3/4 **Inside Story (IRE)**[6] 2487 6-9-3 68 ....(b) PaulMulrennan 8 50
(M W Easterby) *hld up and bhd: hdwy over 2f out: kpt on appr fnl f: nrst fin* **14/1**
0600 7 2 1/2 **Byron Bay**[11] 2335 6-9-0 65 ....(p) TonyHamilton 15 41
(R C Guest) *hld up: a towards rr* **12/1**
1000 8 2 1/2 **Guadaloup**[59] 1188 6-8-2 53 .... TWilliams 9 23
(M Brittain) *in tch: hdwy 3f out: rdn along over 2f out and sn wknd* **25/1**
/060 9 6 **Gramm**[30] 1815 5-9-2 67 .... DaleGibson 11 24
(M W Easterby) *chsd ldrs: rdn along over 3f out: sn wknd* **28/1**
000- 10 1/2 **Kaymich Perfecto**[250] 5737 8-8-6 60 .... MichaelJStainton(3) 7 16
(R M Whitaker) *stmbld s: sn prom: rdn along over 2f out and sn wknd* **50/1**
112- 11 1 **Prince Noel**[195] 6885 4-9-0 70 .... AshleyHamblett(5) 6 23
(N Wilson) *cl up: rdn along wl over 2f out and sn wknd* **12/1**
5330 12 4 1/2 **Indian's Feather (IRE)**[13] 2289 7-9-2 67 .... TomEaves 12 10
(N Tinkler) *chsd ldrs on outer: rdn along 3f out and sn wknd* **12/1**

1m 40.1s **Going Correction** +0.15s/f (Good) 12 Ran SP% **116.5**
Speed ratings (Par 103): **106,105,101,98,95 92,89,87,81,80 79,75**
CSF £13.43 CT £79.77 TOTE £3.00: £1.20, £1.60, £3.20; EX 13.20.
Owner Mrs J W Hutchinson & Mrs P A Knox **Bred** T K & Mrs P A Knox **Trained** Denton, Co Durham

FOCUS
Just a fair handicap, where it paid to race close to the pace. Pretty solid form. The winner is something of a course specialist and was winning this race for the third year in a row.
Just Bond(IRE) Official explanation: jockey said gelding hung right
Inside Story(IRE) Official explanation: jockey said gelding lost its action

2673 BUCK INN THORNTON WATLASS MAIDEN STKS 7f
7:15 (7:18) (Class 5) 3-Y-O+ £3,885 (£1,156; £577; £288) Stalls Low

Form RPR
22 1 **San Jose City (IRE)**[11] 2333 3-9-2 75 .... DavidAllan 7 81
(D Carroll) *t.k.h: trckd ldrs: hdwy over 2f out: rdn and squeezed through to ld over 1f out: drvn ins fnl f and hld on wl* **10/1**
3 2 nk **Karoush (USA)**[16] 2198 3-9-2 0 .... AlanMunro 5 80
(P W Chapple-Hyam) *prom: effrt 2f out: sn rdn and ev ch: drvn ins fnl f and kpt on* **4/11**[1]
22 3 4 **Strawberry Moon (IRE)**[24] 1951 3-8-11 0 .... TomEaves 6 64
(B Smart) *chsd ldrs: hdwy 3f out: rdn and ev ch 2f out: drvn and kpt on same pce appr fnl f* **15/2**[3]
52-0 4 nse **Penchesco (IRE)**[24] 1957 3-9-2 76 .... PaulEddery 10 69
(Pat Eddery) *lw: cl up: led after 1f: rdn along wl over 2f out: drvn and hdd over 1f out: kpt on same pce* **40/1**
3 5 1 1/2 **Presvis**[10] 2360 4-9-5 0 .... MJMurphy(7) 4 78+
(L M Cumani) *lw: towards rr: hdwy over 2f out: n.m.r over 1f out: kpt on* **6/1**[2]
64-0 6 5 **La Fortalesa (IRE)**[10] 2360 3-9-2 73 .... NCallan 3 52
(K A Ryan) *led 1f: cl up tl rdn over 2f out and grad wknd* **28/1**
6 7 1 3/4 **Sosostris Pitch (FR)**[42] 1519 3-9-2 0 .... PaulMulrennan 8 47
(P C Haslam) *str: midfield: effrt 3f out: sn rdn along and no imp* **100/1**
4 8 6 **Phantom Serenade (IRE)**[32] 1751 3-9-2 0 .... PhillipMakin 9 31
(M Dods) *tall: lengthy: s.i.s: a in rr* **50/1**
0 9 nk **Important News**[10] 2380 3-9-2 0 .... GregFairley 1 30
(M Johnston) *chsd ldrs: rdn along 3f out: sn wknd* **50/1**
00- 10 6 **Trojan Hero (IRE)**[283] 4781 3-9-2 0 .... DanielTudhope 2 14
(A Dickman) *a in rr* **150/1**
0- 11 2 1/2 **Mighty Alfred (IRE)**[360] 2424 3-9-2 0 .... JoeFanning 12 7
(E A L Dunlop) *a towards rr* **50/1**

1m 27.9s (0.70) **Going Correction** +0.15s/f (Good)
WFA 3 from 4yo 10lb 11 Ran SP% **121.9**
Speed ratings (Par 103): **102,101,97,97,95 89,87,80,80,73 70**
CSF £14.50 TOTE £11.40: £2.30, £1.02, £1.80; EX 26.10.
Owner Declan Gardiner **Bred** Bryan Ryan **Trained** Sledmere, E Yorks

FOCUS
Only a fair maiden which looked like a penalty kick for Karoush beforehand, but in the end the 75-rated winner had too many guns for him. The form is pretty sound with the first six close to their pre-race marks.
Phantom Serenade(IRE) Official explanation: jockey said gelding missed the break

2674 WEATHERBYS BLOODSTOCK INSURANCE H'CAP 7f
7:45 (7:46) (Class 4) (0-85,83) 3-Y-O £5,180 (£1,541; £770; £384) Stalls Low

Form RPR
0-03 1 **Lindoro**[23] 1988 3-9-7 83 .... AdamKirby 4 91+
(W R Swinburn) *lw: hld up in midfield: n.m.r on inner and swtchd rt over 2f out: rdn to chse ldrs over 1f out: drvn and styd on ins fnl f to ld fnl 100yds* **3/1**[1]
00-0 2 3/4 **La Chicaluna**[11] 2333 3-9-1 77 .... J-PGuillambert 10 83
(J G Given) *led: rdn along over 2f out: drvn over 1f out: hdd and no ex fnl 100yds* **25/1**
0-41 3 3/4 **Dream Express (IRE)**[14] 2261 3-8-10 72 .... PhillipMakin 3 76
(M Dods) *lw: plld hrd: chsd ldrs: effrt to chse ldr and hung lft over 2f out: drvn and carried hd high over 1f out: swtchd rt and kpt on ins fnl f* **9/2**[2]
2-10 4 2 1/2 **Minus Fifteen (IRE)**[23] 1988 3-9-2 78 .... NCallan 5 75
(K A Ryan) *t.k.h: chsd ldrs: rdn along over 2f out: drvn and hung bdly rt ent fnl f: one pce* **12/1**
421 5 1 3/4 **Baunagain (IRE)**[25] 1934 3-9-6 82 .... PatCosgrave 13 75
(M J Wallace) *hld up: hdwy on outer over 2f out: rdn to chse ldrs whn carried rt ent fnl f: kpt on same pce* **11/2**[3]
0-05 6 2 **Lady Benjamin**[17] 2141 3-8-1 70 .... PatrickDonaghy(7) 6 57
(P C Haslam) *in rr: hdwy over 2f out: sn rdn and kpt on appr fnl f: nrst fin* **25/1**
-615 7 1/2 **Jonny Lesters Hair (IRE)**[16] 2189 3-8-13 75 ....(e) DavidAllan 11 61
(T D Easterby) *cl up: rdn along over 2f out and grad wknd* **8/1**
03-1 8 3/4 **We'Re Delighted**[10] 2366 3-8-11 73 .... GrahamGibbons 14 57
(T D Walford) *midfield: hdwy 3f out: rdn along 2f out and sn no imp* **11/1**
340 9 1/2 **Imperial Djay (IRE)**[10] 2380 3-8-7 69 .... TonyHamilton 2 51
(D Carroll) *t.k.h: chsd ldrs on inner: rdn along over 2f out and sn wknd* **25/1**
0-00 10 3/4 **Feisty Royale**[9] 2405 3-9-4 80 .... GregFairley 9 60+
(M Johnston) *a towards rr* **16/1**
06-0 11 3 1/4 **Semah Harold**[28] 1868 3-8-8 70 .... JoeFanning 12 42
(E S McMahon) *a in rr* **40/1**
24-0 12 1 1/2 **Beetuna (IRE)**[88] 812 3-9-1 77 .... TomEaves 7 45
(B Smart) *a in rr* **33/1**
06-3 13 11 **Montaquila**[16] 2209 3-9-7 83 .... RobertWinston 8 21
(J Howard Johnson) *chsd ldrs: rdn along 3f out: sn wknd* **13/2**
10-0 14 30 **Fyodorovich (USA)**[37] 1623 3-8-12 74 ....(v) MickyFenton 1 —
(J S Wainwright) *wnt bdly rt s: sn bhd* **50/1**

1m 27.74s (0.54) **Going Correction** +0.15s/f (Good) 14 Ran SP% **123.8**
Speed ratings (Par 101): **102,101,100,97,95 93,92,91,91,90 86,84,72,38**
CSF £92.82 CT £357.61 TOTE £4.00: £1.80, £6.20, £2.40; EX 95.10.
Owner Exors Of The Late Mrs P W Harris **Bred** Pigeon House Stud **Trained** Aldbury, Herts

FOCUS
A very decent handicap for three-year-olds run at a good lick to imply that the form will stand up well in the coming weeks. The winner shaped a bit better than the bare form.
Montaquila Official explanation: jockey said gelding lost its action
Fyodorovich(USA) Official explanation: jockey said colt hung right throughout; trainer said blinkers became dislodged

2675 CARLETON FURNITURE H'CAP 1m 4f
8:15 (8:16) (Class 4) (0-85,81) 3-Y-O £5,180 (£1,541; £770; £384) Stalls Low

Form RPR
1-32 1 **Laterly (IRE)**[17] 2173 3-9-6 80 .... MickyFenton 2 91
(T P Tate) *lw: mde all: rdn clr over 2f out: drvn ent fnl f: jst hld on* **7/2**[3]
0-1 2 shd **Ephorus (USA)**[33] 1728 3-9-4 78 .... J-PGuillambert 14 89
(Sir Michael Stoute) *trckd ldrs: hdwy over 2f out: rdn over 1f out: drvn ins fnl f and fin strly: jst failed* **11/4**[1]
-233 3 2 **Wells Lyrical (IRE)**[11] 2336 3-9-1 75 .... TomEaves 9 83
(B Smart) *prom: hdwy 3f out: rdn along 2f out: drvn and kpt on ins fnl f* **14/1**

-256 **4** *3* **My Mate Max**19 2109 3-8-12 **72**........ GrahamGibbons 6 75
(R Hollinshead) *hld up towards rr: hdwy over 2f out: rdn to chse ldrs over 1f out: drvn and same pce ins fnl f* **16/1**

20-5 **5** *2* **Saleima (IRE)**17 2164 3-9-1 **75**........ AlanMunro 1 75
(P W Chapple-Hyam) *lw: trckd ldrs: hdwy to chse wnr 3f out: rdn over 2f out: sn drvn and wknd appr fnl f* **10/3**2

32-0 **6** *1 ½* **Black Rain**46 1424 3-9-7 **81**........(t) FergalLynch 10 79
(P J McBride) *hld up towards rr: hdwy over 2f out: rdn and kpt on appr fnl f: nrst fin* **25/1**

1-44 **7** *½* **Trianon**11 2327 3-9-4 **78**........ PaulHanagan 5 75
(R Charlton) *lw: t.k.h: trckd ldrs: hdwy over 2f out: rdn wl over 1f out and sn wknd* **9/2**

155 **8** *6* **Tourism (IRE)**12 2310 3-9-4 **78**........ GregFairley 7 65
(M Johnston) *in tch: rdn along 3f out: drvn over 2f out and no hdwy* **14/1**

2-04 **9** *4 ½* **Bavarian Nordic (USA)**7 2464 3-9-0 **74**........ RoystonFfrench 13 54
(Mrs A Duffield) *a towards rr* **33/1**

3-15 **10** *7* **Judgethemoment (USA)**16 2201 3-9-7 **81**........ PaulMulrennan 8 50
(Jane Chapple-Hyam) *chsd wnr: rdn along over 3f out: sn wknd* **33/1**

304- **11** *53* **Manuka Bee**230 6255 3-8-8 **68** ow1........ RobertWinston 11 —
(J Howard Johnson) *sn outpcd and bhd fr 1/2-way* **40/1**

060 **P** **St Johns Wood**23 2008 3-8-8 **68**........ DaleGibson 3 —
(M W Easterby) *unruly stalls and dwlt: sn in midfield tl lost pl and p.u over 7f out* **40/1**

2m 38.04s (1.84) **Going Correction** +0.15s/f (Good) **12** Ran SP% **124.0**
Speed ratings (Par 101): **99,98,97,95,94 93,92,88,85,81 45,—**
CSF £13.60 CT £123.58 TOTE £5.50: £1.40, £1.60, £3.40; EX 13.60.
Owner Mrs Sylvia Clegg **Bred** Gestut Fahrhof Stiftung **Trained** Tadcaster, N Yorks

FOCUS
Runners from some big yards made the journey north to contest this handicap for three-year-olds, but the prize stayed in Yorkshire thanks to Tom Tate's progressive winner. He and the second are on the up and the form looks sound.
Bavarian Nordic(USA) Official explanation: jockey said colt never travelled

2676 YORKSHIRE MOORS & COAST TOURISM FILLIES' H'CAP 5f
8:45 (8:46) (Class 5) (0-75,75) 3-Y-0+ **£3,885** (£1,156; £577; £288) **Stalls** High

Form RPR

4-20 **1** **Miss Daawe**7 2444 4-8-3 **53**........ LanceBetts(7) 14 61
(B Ellison) *lw: cl up stands' side: rdn to ld and overall ldr over 1f out: kpt on wl* **7/2**2

1303 **2** *1 ½* **Killer Class**4 2527 3-8-13 **63**........ FergalLynch 16 63+
(J S Goldie) *lw: trckd ldrs stands' side: effrt and nt clr run over 1f out: swtchd rt and rdn ent fnl f: styd on* **3/1**1

303 **3** *nse* **Nigella**49 1373 5-10-0 **71**........ GrahamGibbons 15 73
(E S McMahon) *cl up stands' side: rdn over 1f out: kpt on ins fnl f* **15/2**3

0-00 **4** *nk* **Rue Soleil**29 1827 4-8-9 **52**........ RobertWinston 13 53
(J R Weymes) *chsd ldrs stands' side: rdn wl over 1f out: drvn: edgd lft and and kpt on ins fnl f* **20/1**

-003 **5** *1* **Toy Top (USA)**17 2159 5-8-12 **55**........(b) PhillipMakin 10 53
(M Dods) *lw: chsd ldrs stands' side: rdn wl over 1f out: kpt on ins fnl f* **15/2**3

040- **6** *nk* **Yorke's Folly (USA)**245 5861 7-8-4 **52** oh7........(v) KellyHarrison(5) 8 49
(C W Fairhurst) *hld up stands' side: hdwy over 1f out: rdn and kpt on ins fnl f: nrst fin* **50/1**

00-0 **7** *¾* **Safranine (IRE)**23 2010 11-8-5 **53** oh4 ow1........ AnnStokell(5) 12 47
(Miss A Stokell) *dwlt and towards rr stands' side: rdn and hdwy over 1f out: kpt on u.p ins fnl f: nrst fin* **50/1**

214- **8** *1 ¼* **Choisette**206 6741 3-9-4 **68**........ TomEaves 7 54+
(B Smart) *overall ldr stands' side: rdn 2f out: hdd over 1f out: wknd ins fnl f* **10/1**

60-0 **9** *1 ¾* **Metal Guru**134 241 4-8-13 **59**........ RussellKennemore(3) 11 42
(R Hollinshead) *chsd ldrs stands' side: rdn 2f out: drvn ent fnl f and wknd* **20/1**

-065 **10** *1 ¾* **Darcy's Pride (IRE)**17 2159 4-9-7 **64**........ TonyHamilton 4 41
(D W Barker) *led far side gp: rdn over 1f out: kpt on: no ch w stands' side gp* **12/1**

0320 **11** *2 ¼* **Baileys Outshine**17 2159 4-9-4 **68**........ MatthewDavies(7) 9 37
(J G Given) *chsd ldrs stands' side: rdn along 2f out: sn wknd* **20/1**

-001 **12** *¾* **Revue Princess (IRE)**17 2159 3-9-5 **69**........ DavidAllan 6 32
(T D Easterby) *lw: chsd ldrs stands' side: rdn over 2f out and sn wknd* **14/1**

1-00 **13** *1 ½* **Morristown Music (IRE)**44 1476 4-9-1 **61**........ PJMcDonald(3) 3 22
(J S Wainwright) *dwlt: racd far side: a towards rr* **20/1**

5465 **14** *1* **Alabama Spirit (USA)**32 1738 3-8-7 **60**........ MichaelJStainton(3) 2 14
(J Balding) *dwlt: racd far side: a towards rr* **25/1**

1-0 **15** *3 ¾* **Well Informed**31 1764 3-9-11 **75**........ NCallan 1 16
(K A Ryan) *chsd ldr far side: rdn along over 2f out: nvr a factor* **12/1**

100- **16** *6* **Splendidio**195 6887 4-8-9 **52** oh4........(p) RoystonFfrench 5 —
(A Crook) *a in rr stands' side* **40/1**

61.02 secs (1.42) **Going Correction** +0.30s/f (Good)
WFA 3 from 4yo+ 7lb **16** Ran SP% **131.1**
Speed ratings (Par 100): **100,97,97,97,95 94,93,91,88,86 82,81,78,77,71 61**
CSF £13.83 CT £79.52 TOTE £5.50: £1.70, £1.60, £2.70, £4.40; EX 16.90 Place 6: £8.60, Place 5: £4.71..
Owner Mrs Andrea M Mallinson **Bred** N R C Trading Ltd **Trained** Norton, N Yorks

FOCUS
The old Thirsk draw bias returned with a vengeance in this handicap for fillies with the four drawn closest to the stands' rail filling the first four placings. Those drawn 1-4 went far side and had no chance. Weak form.
Safranine(IRE) Official explanation: jockey said mare reared and missed the break
Well Informed Official explanation: jockey said filly had no more to give
T/Plt: £9.30 to a £1 stake. Pool: £64,687.89. 5,042.25 winning tickets. T/Qpdt: £6.30 to a £1 stake. Pool: £4,485.18. 523.90 winning tickets. JR

2253 WINDSOR (R-H)
Monday, June 2

OFFICIAL GOING: Good to soft
Wind: Almost nil Weather: Overcast becoming murky and wet from race 5

2677 EBF TRAILFINDERS AWARD-WINNING TRAVEL NOVICE STKS 5f 10y
6:30 (6:30) (Class 5) 2-Y-0 **£3,626** (£1,079; £539; £269) **Stalls** High

Form RPR

1 **1** **Danehill Destiny**46 1419 2-9-0 0........ RyanMoore 4 90+
(W J Haggas) *racd against nr side rail: w ldr: led after 2f: shkn up fnl f: rdn out nr fin* **6/4**2

1 **2** *½* **Prolific (IRE)**18 2117 2-9-2 0........ RichardHughes 1 90+
(R Hannon) *cl up on outer: chsd wnr 2f out: sn rdn: styd on but a hld* **4/6**1

3 *¾* **Shyrl** 2-8-7 0........ TedDurcan 3 80+
(S A Callaghan) *cl up: tried for gap between 1st pair over 1f out and nudged by runner-up: shkn up and styd on: encouraging debut* **25/1**3

6 **4** *25* **Captain Kallis (IRE)**11 2338 2-8-12 0........ RichardThomas 2 —
(D J S Ffrench Davis) *t.k.h and hanging: led 2f: wknd rapidly 2f out: t.o* **100/1**

61.44 secs (1.14) **Going Correction** +0.15s/f (Good) **4** Ran SP% **104.8**
Speed ratings (Par 93): **96,95,94,54**
CSF £2.65 TOTE £2.30; EX 2.50.
Owner Cheveley Park Stud **Bred** T G Mills And Mr J Humphreys **Trained** Newmarket, Suffolk
■ Stewards' Enquiry : Ted Durcan two-day ban: careless riding (Jun 16,22)

FOCUS
A strong and informative race that is likely to have a bearing on one, if not, two of the juvenile races at Royal Ascot. The winner will need to improve again at Ascot but looks capable of doing so and the second was not disgraced trying to concede weight.

NOTEBOOK
Danehill Destiny, who created a strong impression when quickening smartly to win at Newmarket on debut (race could hardly have worked out better with the second, fourth, fifth and ninth already winning) faced a good test here with smart-looking colt Prolific in opposition and she proved up to it. In front after a couple of furlongs, she always looked to be finding under pressure and the favourite was unable to get past. There should be more improvement to come from the daughter of Danehill Dancer and the only question which remains is how will she handle quick ground in future. This win confirms her to be the best sprinting juvenile filly around though and she looks set to take the beating in the Queen Mary at Royal Ascot, a race for which she is currently 4/1 favourite. (op 11-8 tchd 13-8)
Prolific(IRE), another to have shown a nice change of gear when making a winning debut at Newmarket (second bolted up since and third also won), was conceding just 2lb to Danehill Destiny and he was rightly made favourite, with his stable continuing to churn out the two-year-old winners. One doubt about him though was his ability to act with cut in the ground, as his win came on good to firm and his pedigree is very much that of a fast-ground performer. He loomed up on the outside over two out, but could not quicken under pressure and was always being held. This still represented a step forward and he remains open to further improvement on genuine quick ground. He will head to Royal Ascot for either the Norfolk or Windsor Castle. (op 4-5 tchd 4-7 and 5-6 in a place)
Shyrl, whose price rose considerably to 70,000gns as a two-year-old, is related to numerous winners and bred for plenty of speed being by Acclamation. This was a stiff introduction against two smart sorts, but she ran a blinder and may well have gone close had she not bumped into the runner-up when creating a gap over a furlong out. Her rider was not hard on her once she flattened out and the experience should not be lost on her. She is well worth a shot at the Queen Mary on this evidence and should benefit from faster ground in future. (op 16-1)
Captain Kallis(IRE) gave trouble before the start on his recent Salisbury debut and he was always going to struggle to make an impact against these. He showed early speed, but quickly backed out of it. Nurseries are more likely to be his thing. (tchd 80-1)

2678 TRAILFINDERS TAILORMADE TRAVEL H'CAP 1m 67y
7:00 (7:01) (Class 5) (0-70,70) 3-Y-0 **£2,729** (£806; £403) **Stalls** High

Form RPR

36-6 **1** **Vineyard**14 2261 3-9-3 **68**........ RyanMoore 8 74
(W J Haggas) *fast away: mde virtually all: hrd rdn and strly pressed fr over 1f out: jst hld on* **6/1**3

000- **2** *nse* **Politeia (USA)**270 5162 3-9-2 **67**........ RichardHughes 1 73
(R Hannon) *trckd wnr after 3f: rdn to chal 2f out: upsides fnl f: jst pipped* **10/1**

60-5 **3** *1* **Dark Prospect**21 2056 3-9-5 **70**........ PhilipRobinson 7 74
(M A Jarvis) *trckd ldrs: tried to chal fr 2f out: hrd rdn and styd on: a hld ins fnl f* **7/2**1

534- **4** *shd* **Addikt (IRE)**185 6973 3-9-3 **68**........ LPKeniry 10 72+
(S Kirk) *mostly in midfield: u.p and n.m.r 2f out: styd on fr over 1f out: nrst fin* **8/1**

400 **5** *¾* **Mr Hichens**16 2198 3-9-5 **70**........ WilliamBuick 2 72
(B J Meehan) *trckd ldrs and racd on outer: rdn and effrt 2f out: kpt on wl enough but nvr quite able to chal* **20/1**

-603 **6** *½* **Feasible**21 2047 3-9-2 **67**........ EddieAhern 14 68
(J G Portman) *trckd wnr 3f: styd v cl up against nr side rail: poised to chal 2f out: reminder over 1f out: nt qckn and hld fnl f* **13/2**

0-04 **7** *hd* **Seventh Hill**23 2014 3-9-5 **70**........ JamesDoyle 11 70
(M Blanshard) *cl up bhd ldrs: rdn 2f out: kpt on fr over 1f out: nvr able to chal* **20/1**

044 **8** *½* **Closertobelieving**18 2119 3-9-5 **70**........ TedDurcan 13 69+
(D R C Elsworth) *s.i.s: sn rcvrd: hld up in midfield on inner: gng wl fr over 2f out but nowhere to go and nvr asked a question* **11/2**2

5240 **9** *hd* **Themwerethedays**27 1896 3-9-5 **70**........ JamieSpencer 9 69+
(S Kirk) *hld up in last pair: gng wl but stl last 2f out: swtchd lft to wd outside over 1f out: styd on: no ch* **25/1**

4410 **10** *½* **Coole Dodger (IRE)**7 2451 3-8-12 **70**........ GabrielHannon(7) 5 68
(M D I Usher) *taken down early and free to post: t.k.h: hld up in midfield: lost pl over 2f out: kpt on but no real imp fr over 1f out* **12/1**

06-5 **11** *½* **Hawk Flight (IRE)**54 1265 3-9-3 **68**........ RichardMullen 12 64
(W R Muir) *s.i.s: wl in rr: rdn over 2f out: hanging lft but kpt on fr over 1f out: n.d* **16/1**

6-44 **12** *hd* **Where's Susie**28 1876 3-9-3 **68**........ RobertHavlin 4 64
(D K Ivory) *hld up in midfield: effrt on outer 3f out: chsng ldrs 2f out: fdd fnl f* **18/1**

3205 **13** *1 ¼* **Calistos Quest**21 2047 3-8-13 **67**........(t) KirstyMilczarek(3) 3 60
(M Botti) *t.k.h: hld up in rr: prog on outer over 2f out: pressed ldrs over 1f out: wknd fnl f* **12/1**

650- **14** *1* **Stage Acclaim (IRE)**228 6282 3-8-12 **68**........ JamesMillman(5) 6 59
(B R Millman) *hld up in last pair: effrt on outer over 2f out: cl enough wl over 1f out: fdd* **40/1**

1m 45.93s (1.23) **Going Correction** +0.15s/f (Good) **14** Ran SP% **127.8**
Speed ratings (Par 99): **99,98,97,97,97 96,96,95,95,95 94,94,93,92**
CSF £65.88 CT £257.62 TOTE £6.80: £2.40, £3.60, £2.00; EX 64.50.
Owner Highclere Thoroughbred Racing (VCI) **Bred** Petra Bloodstock Agency **Trained** Newmarket, Suffolk

FOCUS
A modest but interesting handicap that should produce winners at the right level. The winner set only an ordinary pace and he and the second were always to the fore. The form looks pretty sound.
Closertobelieving Official explanation: jockey said colt was denied a clear run
Themwerethedays Official explanation: jockey said colt moved poorly throughout and was denied a clear run

Coole Dodger(IRE) Official explanation: jockey said colt hung right-handed

2679 TRAILFINDERS TRAVEL EXPERTS H'CAP 6f
7:30 (7:30) (Class 4) (0-80,80) 4-Y-O+ **£4,857** (£1,445; £722; £360) **Stalls** High

Form RPR

4000 **1** **Kyle (IRE)**11 2339 4-9-2 **75** EddieAhern 10 86
(R Hannon) *hld up in tch in chsng gp: prog 1/2-way: rdn and hung lft over 1f out: kpt on to ld ins fnl f: all out* **13/2**3

2320 **2** *nk* **North South Divide (IRE)**11 2339 4-9-2 **75** (p) DaneO'Neill 14 85
(R A Teal) *taken down early: sn hld up in chsng gp: prog over 2f out: str chal ins fnl f: jst hld* **12/1**

0011 **3** *1 1/2* **Dressed To Dance (IRE)**14 2255 4-8-6 **65** (v) StephenDonohoe 1 70
(P D Evans) *wl in rr: rdn and effrt 2f out: gd prog over 1f out: r.o to take 3rd nr fin* **10/1**

00-0 **4** *1 1/4* **Blessed Place**11 2337 8-7-9 **61** oh4 BillyCray(7) 8 62
(D J S Ffrench Davis) *taken down early: led and sn clr: maintained advantage tl wknd and hdd ins fnl f* **50/1**

0-30 **5** *1 1/4* **Cheap Street**35 1683 4-8-13 **72** RyanMoore 6 73+
(J G Portman) *hld up wl in rr: effrt whn hmpd 2f out: swtchd rt to nr side rail: styd on but no ch* **5/1**1

-350 **6** *nk* **Crystal Gazer (FR)**3 2565 4-9-5 **78** (p) RichardHughes 2 74
(R Hannon) *racd towards far side: wl on terms w main gp: looked upsides 1f out: wknd ins fnl f* **16/1**

1354 **7** *1* **Kelamon**20 2085 4-8-11 **70** WilliamBuick 11 63
(M D I Usher) *rrd s: outpcd in last and bhd: taken towards far side after 2f: clsd on ldr fr 2f out: nvr on terms* **11/2**2

0061 **8** *3/4* **Caustic Wit (IRE)**10 2350 10-8-4 **63** FrancisNorton 5 53
(M S Saunders) *taken down early: towards rr: prog on outer in chsng gp 2f out: no imp fnl f* **10/1**

-260 **9** *1 1/4* **Adantino**11 2339 9-8-10 **74** (b) JamesMillman(5) 4 60
(B R Millman) *wl in rr: no prog whn n.m.r 2f out: plugged on fnl f* **8/1**

345 **10** *2 1/4* **Hits Only Jude (IRE)**27 1891 5-9-5 **78** DeanMcKeown 12 57
(P A Blockley) *n.m.r and lost pl after 2f: a towards rr rest of r* **9/1**

5542 **11** *1/2* **Cativo Cavallino**21 2058 5-8-12 **76** NataliaGemelova(5) 13 54
(J E Long) *prom in chsng gp tl wknd 2f out* **10/1**

0020 **12** *1 1/4* **Lucayos**25 1928 5-8-11 **77** KylieManser(7) 9 51
(Mrs H Sweeting) *dwlt: rcvrd and prom in chsng gp 1/2-way: wknd 2f out* **20/1**

0-06 **13** *9* **Minaash (USA)**13 2293 4-8-9 **73** AhmedAjtebi(5) 15 18
(D M Simcock) *prom in chsng gp but sn pushed along: wknd 2f out: eased* **28/1**

000- **14** *18* **Yerevan**205 6753 4-8-11 **70** JohnEgan 7 —
(R T Phillips) *mostly chsd clr ldr to over 2f out: wknd rapidly: eased: t.o* **20/1**

1m 14.67s (1.67) **Going Correction** +0.425s/f (Yiel) **14 Ran SP% 122.3**
Speed ratings (Par 105): **105,104,102,100,99 98,97,96,94,91 91,89,77,53**
CSF £79.73 CT £806.37 TOTE £8.30: £3.20, £4.60, £2.70; EX 116.40.
Owner Noodles Racing **Bred** John Cullinan **Trained** East Everleigh, Wilts

FOCUS
A competitive handicap. The winner is rated back to his 3yo level but the fourth lends doubts to the form.
Dressed To Dance(IRE) Official explanation: jockey said filly got upset in the stalls
Cheap Street Official explanation: jockey said gelding suffered interference in running

2680 TRAILFINDERS WORLDWIDE TRAVEL LEISURE STKS (LISTED RACE) 6f
8:00 (8:03) (Class 1) 3-Y-O+
£14,760 (£5,595; £2,800; £1,396; £699; £351) **Stalls** High

Form RPR

4-00 **1** **Balthazaar's Gift (IRE)**19 2106 5-9-0 112 JimmyFortune 5 115
(L M Cumani) *dwlt: hld up in last pair: prog and hrd rdn fr 2f out: styd on to ld fnl 75yds* **10/3**1

220- **2** *nk* **Lipocco**261 5407 4-9-0 102 JamesDoyle 9 114
(R M Beckett) *led: tk field down centre crse: rdn over 1f out: hdd fnl 75yds: kpt on but a hld* **25/1**

-400 **3** *1/2* **Prime Defender**19 2106 4-9-0 106 MichaelHills 3 112
(B W Hills) *stdd s: t.k.h and hld up in tch: prog 1/2-way: rdn to chal over 1f out: nt qckn ins fnl f* **13/2**3

50-6 **4** *hd* **Confuchias (IRE)**37 1619 4-9-0 107 TedDurcan 6 112
(K R Burke) *t.k.h: hld up wl in rr: effrt over 1f out: eased to outer and r.o fnl f: fin wl* **14/1**

60-5 **5** *1 1/2* **Hoh Mike (IRE)**19 2106 4-9-0 109 JamieSpencer 1 107
(M L W Bell) *hld up in last pair: prog on outer 2f out: pressed ldrs 1f out: wknd fnl 100yds* **4/1**2

0-12 **6** *1 1/4* **Edge Closer**31 1765 4-9-0 104 RichardHughes 10 103
(R Hannon) *t.k.h: mostly chsd ldr to over 1f out: fdd ins fnl f* **13/2**3

0/0- **7** *nk* **Pivotal Flame**429 847 6-9-0 107 DarryllHolland 4 102
(E S McMahon) *t.k.h: pressed ldrs: cl enough 1f out: fdd* **33/1**

2140 **8** *1* **Sonny Red (IRE)**19 2106 4-9-0 107 (p) RyanMoore 8 99
(R Hannon) *t.k.h: hld up rt bhd ldrs: rdn over 1f out: fdd* **4/1**2

10-3 **9** *1 1/2* **Eisteddfod**37 1619 7-9-4 106 NelsonDeSouza 2 98
(P F I Cole) *chsd ldrs: rdn and no imp 2f out: fdd fnl f* **16/1**

-16 **10** *nk* **Cape**8 2426 5-8-9 92 ShaneKelly 7 88
(P Howling) *dwlt: wl in rr: effrt towards nr side 2f out: no prog 1f out: fdd* **33/1**

405- **11** *3* **Pivotal Point**261 5416 8-9-0 105 EddieAhern 11 83
(P J Makin) *dwlt: in tch towards rr: rdn and no prog 2f out: wknd fnl f* **40/1**

1m 13.91s (0.91) **Going Correction** +0.425s/f (Yiel) **11 Ran SP% 114.5**
Speed ratings (Par 111): **110,109,108,108,106 105,104,103,101,100 96**
CSF £91.95 TOTE £4.40: £1.60, £6.70, £2.70; EX 120.50.
Owner Ms Nicola Mahoney & De La Warr Racing **Bred** Pat Beirne **Trained** Newmarket, Suffolk

FOCUS
A competitive Listed sprint and this time the whole field came down the centre of the track. The winning time was about what you would expect for a race like this in the conditions. The form looks generally solid although the runner-up was showing improvement.

NOTEBOOK
Balthazaar's Gift(IRE) has not had things go his way in his two previous starts this season, but he is at least up to this class on his day and everything was in his favour here, not least that he was best in at the weights plus the softening ground. Brought with his effort towards the stands' side of the group, he had to be given the full Fortune treatment but always looked like getting there. He now heads for the Golden Jubilee in which he narrowly missed out to Les Arcs two years ago and his chances would be that much stronger if the ground came up like this. (op 11-4 tchd 7-2)
Lipocco, having his first outing in more than eight months and in Listed company for the first time, was up against it as only one of his rivals was worse in than him on adjusted official ratings, so under the circumstances he ran a blinder from the front and only the favourite was able to run him down. Were he able to reproduce this form in the Wokingham, in which he carries 9st 3lb, he would have to have a serious chance especially as he would not mind if the ground was quicker, but the dreaded 'bounce' may also become a factor.
Prime Defender, in front of Balthazaar's Gift in both the Abernant and the Duke Of York, was produced with his effort towards the far side in plenty of time and tried hard, but was never quite getting there under pressure. He ran his race, but does look better on quicker ground. (op 8-1)
Confuchias(IRE) ◆, having his first start for Karl Burke following a solitary appearance for Walter Swinburn after arriving from Ireland, loves to get his toe in so conditions had come in his favour. Switched towards the far side to make his final effort, he finished in good style to finish right alongside the front three and a stiffer track or even a step back up to 7f will not inconvenience him. (op 16-1)
Hoh Mike(IRE), switched off out the back in order to conserve his stamina, looked like getting involved when switched towards the far side to make his challenge, but his effort eventually petered out and 6f on an easy surface is just too much for him. (op 3-1)
Edge Closer raced freely behind the leaders, but did not get home. The ground should not have been a problem so the likelihood is that he is not quite up to this class. (op 8-1)
Sonny Red(IRE) was well supported in the ring despite having finished behind three of these in the Duke Of York, presumably because he loves soft ground. However, after showing prominently for a long way he dropped out and there seemed no obvious excuse. (op 11-2)

2681 TRAILFINDERS FLY-DRIVE EXPERTS MAIDEN STKS 1m 2f 7y
8:30 (8:31) (Class 5) 3-Y-O **£2,729** (£806; £403) **Stalls** Low

Form RPR

3- **1** **Porthole (USA)**241 5977 3-9-3 0 MichaelHills 9 87+
(B W Hills) *mde all: drew clr wl over 2f out: at least 5 l clr fnl f: heavily eased nr fin* **6/4**1

2 *2 1/2* **Torphichen** 3-9-3 0 PhilipRobinson 3 71
(M A Jarvis) *a chsng wnr: shkn up over 3f out: lft bhd fr over 2f out: kpt on* **8/1**

2- **3** *1 1/4* **Cuban Rhythm (USA)**228 6285 3-8-12 0 SteveDrowne 7 63
(R Charlton) *prom: pushed along fr 3f out: tried to chal for 2nd fr 2f out: one pce* **11/4**2

4 *nk* **Mvuto** 3-8-12 0 RichardThomas 4 62
(C G Cox) *hld up in midfield: shuffled along fr 3f out: styd on steadily: nrst fin* **66/1**

6 **4** *dht* **April's Daughter**24 1965 3-8-12 0 JimCrowley 15 62
(B R Millman) *mostly trckd ldng pair: appeared short of room on inner fr 2f out: nudged along and kpt on steadily* **40/1**

6 *1/2* **Voice Coach (IRE)** 3-9-3 0 PatDobbs 5 66
(Sir Michael Stoute) *hld up in midfield: prog over 2f out: jnd chsers over 1f out: kpt on steadily* **16/1**

7 *1 3/4* **Civitas Filius (USA)** 3-9-3 0 RichardMullen 11 63+
(D M Simcock) *settled in midfield: pushed along 3f out: kpt on steadily at one pce* **66/1**

8 *nse* **Ask Nicely** 3-8-12 0 DO'Donohoe 8 58
(W R Muir) *s.s: plld hrd and hld up in last trio: sme prog on inner fnl 2f: nvr nrr* **66/1**

9 *3 1/4* **Pimento (IRE)** 3-9-3 0 PaulDoe 12 56
(J L Dunlop) *s.s: hld up in last quartet: sme prog 2f out: reminder over 1f out: styd on steadily* **33/1**

10 *nk* **Capstan** 3-9-3 0 DaneO'Neill 1 56
(L M Cumani) *s.s: hld up in last trio: pushed along on outer over 2f out: rn green and awkwardly: kpt on* **20/1**

6-3 **11** *1/2* **Opening Act**27 1905 3-9-3 0 NelsonDeSouza 16 55
(P F I Cole) *chsd ldrs: rdn and nt keen over 2f out: sn lost pl and btn* **33/1**

03- **12** *2* **Valvigneres (IRE)**189 6948 3-9-3 0 TedDurcan 2 51
(E A L Dunlop) *wl enough plcd bhd ldrs: pushed along over 3f out: steadily lost pl* **28/1**

13 *2* **Dixie Dean (USA)** 3-9-3 0 RyanMoore 6 47
(Sir Michael Stoute) *hld up towards rr: pushed along and no prog 3f out* **7/1**3

14 *2 1/2* **Amir Pasha (UAE)** 3-9-3 0 TQuinn 10 42
(W R Swinburn) *s.s: rn v green in last: a bhd* **16/1**

15 *3/4* **One Night In May (IRE)** 3-8-12 0 MartinDwyer 14 35
(W R Muir) *hld up towards rr: brief effrt on wd outside over 2f out: sn wknd* **40/1**

2m 13.0s (4.30) **Going Correction** +0.425s/f (Yiel) **15 Ran SP% 125.5**
Speed ratings (Par 99): **99,97,96,95,95 95,93,93,91,91 90,89,87,85,84**
CSF £13.81 TOTE £2.90: £1.10, £3.00, £1.70; EX 18.80.
Owner K Abdulla **Bred** Juddmonte Farms Inc **Trained** Lambourn, Berks

FOCUS
A routine maiden for Windsor, run at an ordinary pace, and not as competitive as the numbers might suggest though a few did catch the eye and look capable of better. Not many ever got into it and the runners stuck close to the stands' rail this time. The winner, the clear form choice coming into the race, was value for more than the bare margin.

2682 TRAILFINDERS NO HIDDEN EXTRAS H'CAP 1m 3f 135y
9:00 (9:00) (Class 5) (0-75,75) 4-Y-O+ **£3,070** (£906; £453) **Stalls** Low

Form RPR

2513 **1** **Rose Row**14 2241 4-8-11 **65** RyanMoore 4 72
(Mrs Mary Hambro) *mde all: gng strly over 2f out: drvn whn pressed fnl f: hld on wl* **5/2**1

0-21 **2** *3/4* **Spring Dream (IRE)**14 2241 5-9-3 **71** RichardHughes 11 77
(A King) *cl up: wnt 2nd over 2f out: drvn to chal 1f out: styd on but a hld* **4/1**2

14-0 **3** *1 1/2* **Good Effect (USA)**17 2152 4-9-2 **70** GeorgeBaker 6 73
(C P Morlock) *prom: disp 2nd 2f out: rdn and kpt on same pce fr over 1f out* **12/1**

0124 **4** *3 1/2* **Street Life (IRE)**42 1521 10-8-6 **60** StephenDonohoe 9 58
(W J Musson) *hld up in last pair: rdn wl over 2f out: kpt on fr over 1f out: n.d* **4/1**2

-100 **5** *nk* **Harvest Joy (IRE)**7 2453 4-9-6 **74** (b1) JimCrowley 10 71
(J Gallagher) *hld up in last trio: styd alone towards nr side fnl 3f: sme prog but nvr on terms w ldrs* **25/1**

03-0 **6** *8* **Jebel Ali (IRE)**25 1932 5-9-0 **68** JamesDoyle 7 53
(B Gubby) *cl up: rdn wl over 2f out: wknd over 1f out* **33/1**

0-00 **7** *5* **Polish Red**28 1877 4-9-7 **75** JohnEgan 8 52
(G G Margarson) *wl in tch: effrt to dispute 2nd over 3f out: wknd 2f out: heavily eased* **4/1**2

1-50 **8** *6* **Garafena**23 2012 5-9-0 **68** TQuinn 12 35
(B G Powell) *mostly chsd wnr to 3f out: wknd u.p over 2f out* **9/1**3

014/ 9 2 1/2 **Precious Dancer**[260] 1740 5-8-4 58 ....(p) WilliamBuick 5 21
(P Bowen) *dwlt: a in last pair: rdn and no prog 3f out: sn bhd* **16/1**

2m 33.32s (3.82) **Going Correction** +0.425s/f (Yiel) **9 Ran SP% 118.9**
Speed ratings (Par 103): **104,103,102,100,99 94,91,87,85**
CSF £12.99 CT £102.23 TOTE £3.50: £1.20, £1.90, £3.20; EX 11.20 Place 6: £110.31, Place 5: £29.87..
Owner Richard Hambro **Bred** Cotswold Stud **Trained** Bourton-on-the-Hill, Gloucs

FOCUS
Just an ordinary handicap and another race where the winner made all, but they went quite a decent pace and this time the runners went to the far side of the track up the home straight. This was the third recent meeting between the first two and there is little between them.
Jebel Ali(IRE) Official explanation: jockey said gelding was unsuited by the good to soft ground
Precious Dancer Official explanation: jockey said gelding lost its action
T/Plt: £89.40 to a £1 stake. Pool: £83,509.09. 681.85 winning tickets. T/Qpdt: £23.20 to a £1 stake. Pool: £6,899.28. 219.86 winning tickets. JN

2110 NAAS (L-H)
Monday, June 2

OFFICIAL GOING: Good to firm

2685a COOLMORE CHOISIR NAAS SPRINT STKS (LISTED RACE) 5f
3:40 (3:41) 3-Y-0+ £28,720 (£8,426; £4,014; £1,367)

RPR

1 **Tax Free (IRE)**[9] 2404 6-9-12 .... AdrianTNicholls 5 117
(D Nicholls) *trckd ldrs: 3rd 1/2-way: impr to 2nd 2f out: rdn to ld 1f out: kpt on wl fnl f* **5/4**[1]

2 1 3/4 **Day By Day**[23] 2000 4-9-4 ....(b) NCallan 9 102
(B J Meehan) *chsd ldr: led 1/2-way: rdn and hdd 1f out: no ex: kpt on fnl f* **10/1**

3 3 **Snaefell (IRE)**[9] 2417 4-9-10 110.... PJSmullen 2 98+
(M Halford, Ire) *chsd ldrs: 6th 1/2-way: rdn into 5th 1f out: kpt on same pce fnl f* **5/1**[3]

4 1 1/4 **An Tadh (IRE)**[9] 2417 5-9-7 103....(p) KLatham 8 90
(G M Lyons, Ire) *towards rr early: 8th 1/2-way: rdn in 6th 2f out: styd on to 4th 1f out: kpt on same pce fnl f* **16/1**

5 1/2 **Osterhase (IRE)**[274] 5075 9-9-7 95....(b) FMBerry 6 88
(J E Mulhern, Ire) *led: hdd 1/2-way: rdn in 2nd over 2f out: no ex in 3rd over 1f out: kpt on same pce* **25/1**

6 hd **The Loan Express (IRE)**[12] 2316 3-8-11 100.... WMLordan 7 81
(T Stack, Ire) *chsd ldrs early: sn towards rr: rdn in 8th over 1f out: kpt on same pce fnl f* **10/1**

7 hd **Peak District (IRE)**[17] 2175 4-9-7 95.... JAHeffernan 10 87
(David Wachman, Ire) *chsd ldrs: 7th 1/2-way: rdn in 5th 2f out: no ex in 6th 1f out: kpt on one pce* **8/1**

8 2 1/2 **Littlemisssunshine (IRE)**[3] 2587 3-8-11 95....(p) PShanahan 11 72
(Tracey Collins, Ire) *stmbld leaving stalls: chsd ldrs: 4th 1/2-way: rdn and no ex 2f out: wknd over 1f out* **20/1**

9 3 **Contest (IRE)**[31] 1783 4-9-10 106.... JMurtagh 4 70
(David Wachman, Ire) *hmpd and stmbld shortly after s: a bhd* **4/1**[2]

10 shd **Fly By Magic (IRE)**[17] 2175 4-9-4 82.... CO'Donoghue 1 64
(Patrick Carey, Ire) *a towards rr on far rail* **66/1**

11 3 **Inourthoughts (IRE)**[17] 2175 4-9-4 95.... DJMoran 3 53
(Francis Ennis, Ire) *towards rr early: 5th 1/2-way: rdn and wknd over 2f out* **20/1**

58.70 secs (-3.30)
WFA 3 from 4yo+ 7lb **11 Ran SP% 131.1**
CSF £17.43 TOTE £2.30: £1.20, £3.70, £2.40; DF 14.50.
Owner Ian Hewitson **Bred** Denis & Mrs Teresa Bergin **Trained** Sessay, N Yorks

NOTEBOOK
Tax Free(IRE), fourth in the Temple Stakes last time, ran out a deserved winner and followed up his win in this last year with a typically resolute effort. He is a solid Group 3 sprinter, is versatile as regards underfoot conditions, and has developed into a very likeable performer. He looks set to miss out Royal Ascot, a track where he has failed to perform in the past, and is more likely to continue to search for opportunties abroad. (op 7/4)
Day By Day was given a very positive ride on this drop back to the minimum and was the only one to give the winner a serious time of things at the business end. This was her best effort to date and she is evidently up to finding a race of this class on similar ground. (op 12/1)
Snaefell(IRE) had his chance on this drop back in trip/class. He again left the impression that he wants it softer, however, and it is a little surprising that he is being kept on the go at present while the ground is riding fast. (op 4/1)

2686a CATHAL RYAN MEMORIAL SWORDLESTOWN STUD SPRINT STKS (GROUP 3) (FILLIES) 6f
4:10 (4:11) 2-Y-0 £47,867 (£14,044; £6,691; £2,279)

RPR

1 **Cuis Ghaire (IRE)**[19] 2110 2-8-12 .... KJManning 2 105+
(J S Bolger, Ire) *mde all: rdn and kpt on strly fnl f: easily* **1/1**[1]

2 3 1/2 **Marquesa (USA)**[17] 2178 2-8-12 .... WMLordan 1 94+
(David Wachman, Ire) *chsd ldrs: 5th 1/2-way: hdwy to 3rd 2f out: rdn into 2nd over 1f out: no imp wnr fnl f* **8/1**

3 2 **Undaunted Affair (IRE)**[10] 2357 2-8-12 .... NCallan 9 88
(K A Ryan) *sn chsd ldrs: 4th 1/2-way: hdwy to 2nd over 2f out: rdn in 3rd and no ex over 1f out: kpt on same pce* **3/1**[2]

4 2 1/2 **Empress of France (USA)**[19] 2110 2-8-12 .... JMurtagh 6 80+
(A P O'Brien, Ire) *chsd ldrs: 3rd 1/2-way: rdn in 5th under 2f out: no ex over 1f out: kpt on same pce* **6/1**[3]

5 4 1/2 **Cool Tarifa (IRE)**[64] 1101 2-8-12 .... FMBerry 8 67
(J G Burns, Ire) *dwlt: towards rr: hdwy to 5th 2f out: sn 4th: rdn and wknd over 1f out* **8/1**

6 2 **Sky Mystic (IRE)** 2-8-12 .... DJMoran 7 61
(J S Bolger, Ire) *bhd: rdn 1/2-way: sn no imp: kpt on one pce* **25/1**

7 1 1/2 **Daffodil Walk (IRE)**[9] 2416 2-8-12 .... WJSupple 5 56
(P D Deegan, Ire) *chsd ldr: 2nd 1/2-way: rdn and wknd 2 1/2f out* **25/1**

8 3 1/2 **Carygali (IRE)** 2-8-12 .... DMGrant 4 46
(John Joseph Murphy, Ire) *chsd ldrs early: 6th 1/2-way: sn rdn and wknd* **50/1**

69.30 secs (-3.90) **9 Ran SP% 121.2**
CSF £10.99 TOTE £1.80: £1.10, £2.60, £1.20; DF 12.10.
Owner Mrs J S Bolger **Bred** J S Bolger **Trained** Coolcullen, Co Carlow

NOTEBOOK
Cuis Ghaire(IRE) ◆ confirmed the promise of her debut win over course and distance in May and followed up with a taking success from the front. She could have been called the winner a fair way out here and has to be rated value for a deal further than the winning margin, so is clearly one of the best juvenile fillies to have been seen so far this year in either Ireland or Britain. Her leading trainer was true to form after the race and was uncertain as to where she will turn up next, leaning more towards domestic prizes in preference to a trip to Royal Ascot. Wherever she is pitched in next she will no doubt take all the beating.
Marquesa(USA) ◆, from an in-form yard, had finished runner-up at Dundalk on her debut and this represented a big step up on that effort. She was a clear second-best and winning her maiden should be a formality on this evidence. (op 9/1)
Undaunted Affair(IRE), an easy maiden winner at Haydock last time, ran her race without ever seriously threatening and has been rated as performing right up to her previous level. (op 3/1 tchd 7/2)
Empress of France(USA), well behind the winner on her debut last month, showed a lot more on this big step up in class yet never looked like getting involved all the same. This half-sister to the top-class sprinter Fasliyev is clearly well regarded and should come on again for this experience, so is definitely one to keep tabs on. (op 13/2)
Daffodil Walk(IRE) Official explanation: jockey said filly ran short of room approx 2 1/2f out

2687 - 2689a (Foreign Racing) - See Raceform Interactive

1736 FOLKESTONE (R-H)
Tuesday, June 3

OFFICIAL GOING: Good to soft (good in places)
Wind: Almost nil Weather: Overcast

2690 SCIZZOR SISTERZ LIVE HERE JULY 24TH H'CAP 5f
6:20 (6:21) (Class 5) (0-75,75) 3-Y-0 £3,238 (£963; £481; £240) Stalls Low

Form RPR

00-0 1 **Liberty Belle (IRE)**[24] 1995 3-8-13 67.... LPKeniry 2 73
(J R Best) *racd against nr side rail: led 2f: led again over 1f out: sn rdn clr: in command after* **12/1**

114 2 2 1/4 **Wynberg (IRE)**[21] 2068 3-9-2 70.... JimCrowley 7 68+
(S A Callaghan) *dropped in last fr wd draw and hanging: swtchd to outer and effrt 2f out: styd on to take 2nd ins fnl f and edgd lft: no ch w wnr* **11/1**

45-4 3 nk **Mandelieu (IRE)**[19] 2122 3-9-2 70.... LiamJones 1 67
(W J Haggas) *trckd ldrs: nt qckn over 1f out and lost pl sltly: kpt on ins fnl f: nvr able to chal* **15/8**[1]

3050 4 1 **Enodoc**[15] 2258 3-9-3 71.... RichardMullen 5 64
(W R Muir) *hld up in 5th: effrt towards outer over 1f out: one pce and no real imp* **11/1**

-200 5 shd **Hobson**[24] 1995 3-9-5 73.... StephenCarson 4 66
(Eve Johnson Houghton) *restless bef s: pushed up to chse ldrs: rdn and did nt qckn over 1f out: fdd ins fnl f* **7/2**[2]

-015 6 3/4 **Swindon Town Flyer (IRE)**[21] 2068 3-9-5 73....(b) DavidKinsella 6 63
(A B Haynes) *pressed ldr: led after 2f to over 1f out: wknd ins fnl f* **8/1**

3-00 7 1 **Just A Dancer (IRE)**[15] 2258 3-9-7 75.... WilliamBuick 3 62
(B W Hills) *a in last trio: rdn and no rspnse wl over 1f out* **9/2**[3]

60.24 secs (0.24) **Going Correction** +0.05s/f (Good) **7 Ran SP% 110.7**
Speed ratings (Par 99): **100,96,95,94,94 92,91**
CSF £120.73 TOTE £19.30: £6.50, £3.30; EX 293.30.
Owner Heading For The Rocks Partnership **Bred** Dr Dean Harron **Trained** Hucking, Kent

FOCUS
A modest sprint handicap for three-year-olds. The form is rated through the third and the winner rates value for a little further than the winning margin.

2691 HOBBS PARKER TELECOM MAIDEN FILLIES' STKS 6f
6:50 (6:52) (Class 5) 2-Y-0 £3,238 (£963; £481; £240) Stalls Low

Form RPR

6 1 **Haven't A Clue**[11] 2357 2-9-0 0.... DO'Donohoe 1 78+
(Sir Mark Prescott) *racd against nr side rail: mde all: pressed fr 2f out: styd on wl* **33/1**

3 2 1 1/2 **Tropical Paradise (IRE)**[13] 2309 2-9-0 0.... JimCrowley 9 74
(P Winkworth) *trckd ldrs: prog on outer to chse wnr wl over 1f out: tried to chal fnl f: readily hld last 150yds* **5/2**[2]

3 3 1 **Gassal**[18] 2140 2-9-0 0.... MartinDwyer 6 71
(W J Haggas) *dwlt: rcvrd into midfield bef 1/2-way: rdn to chse ldng pair over 1f out: one pce after* **8/1**

0 4 3/4 **Balladiene (IRE)**[19] 2117 2-9-0 0.... TPQueally 8 68
(M H Tompkins) *chsd ldrs: rdn and sltly outpcd 1/2-way: effrt again on outer 2f out: kpt on same pce* **50/1**

5 3/4 **Wohaida (IRE)** 2-9-0 0.... DarryllHolland 2 66+
(M R Channon) *trckd ldrs: n.m.r and lost pl 2f out: tried to rally over 1f out: one pce and no prog fnl f* **2/1**[1]

6 2 3/4 **Eliza Griffith (IRE)** 2-9-0 0.... RyanMoore 4 58
(R Hannon) *sn lost chsng position: off the pce in 8th and rdn 1/2-way: plugged on fnl f but no imp on ldrs* **6/1**[3]

5603 7 3/4 **Premier Krug (IRE)**[4] 2584 2-8-7 0.... RichardEvans(7) 12 56
(P D Evans) *cl up towards outer: steadily wknd fr wl over 1f out* **16/1**

8 1 1/4 **Tobizzy** 2-9-0 0.... SimonWhitworth 11 55+
(J R Jenkins) *dwlt: outpcd and sn wl bhd: styd on fr over 1f out* **80/1**

9 2 **Today's The Day** 2-9-0 0.... WilliamBuick 7 46
(M A Jarvis) *dwlt: outpcd and sn wl bhd: kpt on fr over 1f out* **16/1**

4 10 shd **Amber Sunset**[13] 2306 2-9-0 0.... J-PGuillambert 10 45
(J Jay) *chsd wnr to wl over 1f out: sn wknd and lost pl qckly* **9/1**

11 9 **Sister Clement (IRE)** 2-9-0 0.... ShaneKelly 3 18
(C R Egerton) *dwlt: outpcd and sn wl bhd: t.o* **20/1**

1m 13.74s (1.04) **Going Correction** +0.05s/f (Good) **11 Ran SP% 120.0**
Speed ratings (Par 90): **95,93,91,90,89 86,85,83,80,80 68**
CSF £115.05 TOTE £21.10: £5.50, £1.10, £2.60; EX 201.70.
Owner Lady Fairhaven **Bred** Lady Fairhaven **Trained** Newmarket, Suffolk

FOCUS
A modest juvenile maiden for fillies. The winner made all against the stands' rail and the form can be rated through the placed horses.

NOTEBOOK
Haven't A Clue, sixth on debut at Haydock 11 days previously when sent off at just 11/2, showed the clear benefit of her initial experience and made all against the stands' rail for a ready success. She enjoyed this easier ground, clearly stays this trip very well, and should really improve again now her confidence will have been boosted. This was the first juvenile winner for her yard. (op 28-1)
Tropical Paradise(IRE), third on debut at Sandown 13 days previously, was given a positive ride and had her chance. She finished nicely enough clear in second, got the extra furlong well enough, and also acted on this softer ground. (op 11-4 tchd 7-2)

Gassal posted improved form for the step up to this extra furlong, yet never looked like getting to the front at any stage. She still looks to be learning her trade and is one for nurseries in due course. (tchd 13-2 and 17-2)
Balladiene(IRE) had finished out the back on her debut, but that was in a hotter contest at Newmarket and she kept on to post an improved effort in defeat. She still looks green and ought to do better still as she gains further experience. (tchd 66-1)
Wohaida(IRE), whose dam was a triple 1m winner at three, lacked the tactical pace when it was required on this racecourse bow and left the impression the run would certainly not be lost on her. Another furlong should also see her in a better light in due course. (op 15-8 tchd 13-8)

2692 INVICTA MOTORS H'CAP 6f
7:20 (7:20) (Class 5) (0-75,78) 4-Y-0+ **£3,238** (£963; £481; £240) **Stalls** Low

Form RPR
1151 **1** **Toms Laughter**[7] [2484] 4-9-7 **78** 6ex..........(p) KevinGhunowa[(3)] 2 93+
(R A Harris) *trckd ldng pair: pushed into ld over 1f out: drvn out fnl f* **11/4**[1]
6410 **2** *1 1/2* **Love On Sight**[62] [1146] 4-9-0 **68**.......... JimCrowley 1 75
(J R Boyle) *dwlt: hld up wl in rr: prog 1/2-way: swtchd to outer over 1f out: r.o to take 2nd last 75yds: unable to chal* **12/1**
31-0 **3** *1/2* **Our Fugitive (IRE)**[11] [2351] 6-8-10 **64**.......... SamHitchcott 6 69
(C Gordon) *hld up bhd ldrs: effrt 2f out: chsd wnr ent fnl f: hd high and nt qckn: lost 2nd last 75yds* **20/1**
-030 **4** *3* **Tiger Trail (GER)**[19] [2128] 4-9-1 **69**.......... GeorgeBaker 7 65
(Mrs N Smith) *stdd s: hld up towards rr: prog 1/2-way: rdn and kpt on one pce fnl 2f* **16/1**
4600 **5** *shd* **Bertie Southstreet**[21] [2087] 5-8-13 **67**..........(b[1]) LPKeniry 3 62
(J R Best) *racd against nr side rail: led to over 1f out: hanging rt and sn btn* **12/1**
0-04 **6** *1* **Whitbarrow (IRE)**[14] [2293] 9-9-2 **75**..........(b) JamesMillman[(5)] 4 67
(B R Millman) *w ldr at decent pce: steadily lost pl fr over 1f out* **15/2**
5306 **7** *1 1/4* **Monashee Prince (IRE)**[11] [2350] 6-8-2 **56** oh1.......(v) AdrianMcCarthy 5 44
(J R Best) *chsd ldng trio to 2f out: sn struggling* **18/1**
2525 **8** *nk* **Obe Royal**[19] [2128] 4-8-9 **70**..........(b) RichardEvans[(7)] 9 57
(P D Evans) *sn pushed along in rr and wl off the pce: nvr rchd ldrs* **15/2**
6620 **9** *1 1/4* **Reigning Monarch (USA)**[24] [1996] 5-7-12 **59** ow2.. RossAtkinson[(7)] 10 42
(Miss Z C Davison) *rrd s: hld up: pushed along and no real prog 2f out* **6/1**[3]
4265 **10** *6* **Proud Killer**[45] [1476] 5-8-8 **62**.......... DarryllHolland 8 26
(J R Jenkins) *a towards rr: rdn bef 1/2-way and struggling after* **5/1**[2]
60-0 **11** *3 1/4* **Looks Could Kill (USA)**[30] [1842] 6-8-6 **60**.......... DavidKinsella 12 14
(A B Haynes) *a struggling in last pair: nvr a factor* **16/1**

1m 12.45s (-0.25) **Going Correction** +0.05s/f (Good) **11 Ran SP% 118.3**
Speed ratings (Par 103): **103,101,100,96,96 94,93,92,91,83 78**
CSF £38.12 CT £568.99 TOTE £3.80: £1.60, £3.80, £5.90; EX 43.10.
Owner Five To Follow **Bred** Mrs D J Hughes **Trained** Earlswood, Monmouths

FOCUS
A modest handicap, run at a solid early pace. The winner continues to progress and this form is worth taking at face value.
Obe Royal Official explanation: jockey said gelding was unsuited by the track
Looks Could Kill(USA) Official explanation: jockey said gelding had no more to give

2693 SMITH AND WILLIAMSON H'CAP 7f (S)
7:50 (7:51) (Class 4) (0-80,80) 4-Y-0+
£6,854 (£2,052; £1,026; £513; £256; £128) **Stalls** Low

Form RPR
00-3 **1** **Royal Storm (IRE)**[20] [2101] 9-8-9 **73** ow3.......... JamesMillman[(5)] 1 84
(B R Millman) *racd against nr side rail: mde all and sn clr: rdn over 2f out: pressed over 1f out: styd on stoutly* **8/1**
-402 **2** *1 3/4* **Dingaan (IRE)**[11] [2371] 5-9-7 **80**.......... LPKeniry 8 86
(A M Balding) *trckd wnr: clsd fr over 2f out: produced to chal over 1f out: n.g.t w effrt and hld fnl f* **6/1**
-043 **3** *shd* **Lordship (IRE)**[4] [2556] 4-7-13 **61**.......... LukeMorris[(3)] 7 67
(A W Carroll) *chsd ldrs: hrd rdn and effrt 2f out: tried to chal on outer jst over 1f out: nt qckn* **10/3**[1]
10-0 **4** *1 1/2* **The Fifth Member (IRE)**[17] [2203] 4-9-5 **78**.......... IanMongan 3 80
(J R Boyle) *trckd ldng pair: rdn and lost pl 2f out: nt qckn and no imp after* **9/2**[3]
0436 **5** *1 1/2* **Desert Dreamer (IRE)**[17] [2203] 7-8-8 **74**..........(t) RossAtkinson[(7)] 5 72
(Tom Dascombe) *taken down early: v awkward s: wl bhd in last pair: tried to cl fr over 2f out: hanging bdly but kpt on* **20/1**
1403 **6** *1 3/4* **Kensington (IRE)**[3] [2615] 7-8-9 **75**..........(p) RichardEvans[(7)] 2 68
(P D Evans) *dwlt: sn in tch: effrt towards outer over 2f out: nt qckn wl over 1f out: sn lost pl* **4/1**[2]
03-6 **7** *12* **Flying Goose (IRE)**[12] [2339] 4-9-7 **80**.......... ShaneKelly 6 41
(R A Harris) *racd on outer: hld up bhd ldrs: floundering and wknd 2f out* **16/1**
40-0 **8** *8* **Networker**[11] [2373] 5-8-10 **69**.......... RyanMoore 9 8
(P J McBride) *hld up in last pair and wl off the pce: no prog over 2f out: eased over 1f out* **6/1**

1m 27.2s (-0.10) **Going Correction** +0.05s/f (Good) **8 Ran SP% 111.6**
Speed ratings (Par 105): **102,100,99,98,96 94,80,71**
CSF £52.23 CT £188.43 TOTE £11.20: £2.90, £1.80, £1.40; EX 63.00.
Owner Mrs H Brain **Bred** E Campion **Trained** Kentisbeare, Devon
■ Stewards' Enquiry : Luke Morris 13-day ban (takes into account previous offences; two days deferred): careless riding (Jun 20-30)

FOCUS
Hand-timed. A fair handicap for the class. Royal Storm became the third winner to make all up the stands' rail, cashing on a decent mark. The form is rated through the third.
Flying Goose(IRE) Official explanation: trainer said gelding was unsuited by the good to soft (good in places) going
Networker Official explanation: jockey said gelding was never travelling

2694 ARENALEISUREPLC.COM CLASSIFIED STKS 1m 4f
8:20 (8:20) (Class 6) 3-Y-0+ **£2,047** (£604; £302) **Stalls** Low

Form RPR
1003 **1** **Shenandoah Girl**[27] [1913] 5-9-7 51..........(p) DarryllHolland 5 56+
(Miss Gay Kelleway) *hld up in last trio: prog on wd outside 3f out: sn drvn: sustained effrt u.p to ld ins fnl f: kpt on* **5/1**[3]
2-15 **2** *3/4* **Compton Charlie**[27] [1913] 4-9-7 54.......... RyanMoore 11 55
(J G Portman) *led 1f: restrained behnd ldng pair: effrt on inner to ld over 1f out: hdd and no ex ins fnl f* **11/4**[1]
000 **3** *shd* **Glitz (IRE)**[43] [1525] 3-8-6 55.......... RichardMullen 3 55
(M L W Bell) *hld up in midfield: effrt 2f out: rdn to chal 1f out: fnd little and hld ins fnl f* **16/1**
00-5 **4** *2 1/4* **Capistrano**[42] [1550] 5-9-7 55.......... PaulEddery 6 54+
(G D Blake) *hld up in last: effrt whn nt clr run over 2f out: prog over 1f out: kpt on one pce fnl f* **20/1**
00-0 **5** *1 3/4* **Hawkstar Express (IRE)**[24] [1994] 3-8-6 55.......... MartinDwyer 9 48
(J R Boyle) *led after 1f to over 1f out: wknd ins fnl f* **15/2**
04-0 **6** *1* **Special Feature (IRE)**[7] [2475] 3-8-7 55 ow1.......... ShaneKelly 13 48
(C R Egerton) *hld up in midfield: effrt on inner over 2f out: sn rdn and no prog* **4/1**[2]
0-02 **7** *1/2* **Dawn Mystery**[6] [2512] 4-9-7 44..........(b) NickyMackay 10 46
(Rae Guest) *t.k.h: trckd ldrs: rdn to chal 2f out: fnd nil and btn over 1f out* **4/1**[2]
050 **8** *2 1/4* **Eddystone (IRE)**[71] [545] 4-9-7 50..........(v[1]) LPKeniry 7 42
(Mrs L C Jewell) *t.k.h: trckd ldr over 9f out: rdn over 3f out: wknd tamely 2f out* **40/1**
0/ **9** *2* **Drombeg Pride (IRE)**[285] [4750] 4-9-0 42.......... JemmaMarshall[(7)] 14 39
(G P Enright) *hld up in rr: pushed along and no prog over 2f out* **25/1**
00-5 **10** *8* **Pay The Grey**[59] [1205] 3-8-6 45.......... RichardSmith 8 26
(R Hannon) *a in rr: last and losing tch u.p over 3f out* **18/1**

2m 46.5s (5.60) **Going Correction** +0.275s/f (Good)
WFA 3 from 4yo+ 15lb **10 Ran SP% 117.3**
Speed ratings (Par 101): **92,91,91,89,88 88,87,86,84,79**
CSF £18.83 TOTE £6.50: £1.70, £1.40, £5.30; EX 15.40.
Owner Miss Gay Kelleway **Bred** Julian Czerpak And Robert Cole **Trained** Exning, Suffolk

FOCUS
Hand-timed. A weak affair, run at a strong pace. The form is rated around the runner-up with the winner rated to her best.

2695 BOOK ON-LINE FOR DISCOUNTED TICKETS H'CAP 1m 1f 149y
8:50 (8:52) (Class 5) (0-70,70) 3-Y-O **£3,238** (£963; £481; £240) **Stalls** Centre

Form RPR
6-20 **1** **Everybody Knows**[26] [1931] 3-9-7 **70**.......... TPQueally 4 74
(M L W Bell) *t.k.h early: sn trckd ldr: led 2f out: drvn and styd on wl fnl f* **16/1**
50-0 **2** *3/4* **Red Merlin (IRE)**[15] [2244] 3-9-7 **70**.......... RichardMullen 10 73
(C G Cox) *taken steadily to post: trckd ldrs: rdn and nt qckn 2f out: styd on wl again fnl f to take 2nd nr fin: nt rch wnr* **10/1**
0-10 **3** *3/4* **Classical Rhythm (IRE)**[22] [2043] 3-9-2 **65**.......... AmirQuinn 7 66
(J R Boyle) *reluctant to go to s: hld up in midfield: prog on outer 3f out: chsd wnr over 1f out: hld fnl f: lost 2nd nr fin* **7/1**[3]
6-53 **4** *1 1/2* **El Duende (USA)**[33] [1745] 3-9-7 **70**.......... J-PGuillambert 2 68+
(W Jarvis) *hld up wl in rr: gng wl enough 3f out: rdn and prog jst over 2f out: styd on wl to take 4th nr fin: no ch of rching ldrs* **17/2**
-230 **5** *nse* **Dream Sea**[22] [2052] 3-9-5 **68**.......... DarryllHolland 14 66
(M R Channon) *t.k.h early: trckd ldng pair: rdn and cl enough 2f out: nt qckn and hld over 1f out* **6/1**[2]
0-50 **6** *hd* **Trenchant**[17] [2199] 3-9-6 **69**.......... WilliamBuick 1 66+
(J R Fanshawe) *dwlt: hld up in last trio: rdn over 2f out: no prog tl styd on fr over 1f out: nrst fin* **14/1**
0-04 **7** *shd* **Krisnando**[12] [2342] 3-8-11 **60**.......... RyanMoore 8 57+
(G L Moore) *s.v.s: hld up in last trio: prog over 2f out: kpt on one pce and nvr rchd ldrs* **7/4**[1]
3-00 **8** *1 1/2* **It's Josr**[67] [1057] 3-9-0 **63**.......... RichardThomas 3 57
(I A Wood) *prom: rdn wl over 2f out: steadily lost pl over 1f out* **66/1**
1014 **9** *1 1/2* **Desiderio**[18] [2161] 3-9-0 **70**..........(b) CharlesEddery[(7)] 5 61
(R Hannon) *racd freely: led to 2f out: sn wknd* **8/1**
3-00 **10** *nse* **Zhebe**[15] [2261] 3-9-4 **67**.......... JimCrowley 12 60
(P J McBride) *dwlt: sn in midfield: outpcd 2f out: one pce and no ch whn hmpd last 100yds* **28/1**
-066 **11** *10* **Threestoneburn (USA)**[4] [2559] 3-8-11 **60**.......... MartinDwyer 6 30
(J R Boyle) *a in rr: last and struggling over 3f out: no ch after* **18/1**
500 **12** *1 1/4* **Sunny Spells**[25] [1960] 3-8-4 **60**.......... WilliamCarson[(7)] 11 27
(S C Williams) *heavily restrained s and sn in last pair: rdn and brought wd bnd over 2f out: no ch* **22/1**
6-30 **13** *16* **Media Stars**[11] [2360] 3-9-7 **70**.......... ShaneKelly 13 3
(J A Osborne) *trckd ldrs: rdn and lost pl wl over 2f out: heavily eased whn no ch fnl f* **33/1**

2m 7.83s (2.93) **Going Correction** +0.275s/f (Good) **13 Ran SP% 123.9**
Speed ratings (Par 99): **99,98,97,96,96 96,96,95,93,93 85,84,72**
CSF £167.95 CT £1245.28 TOTE £14.80: £3.90, £3.50, £2.70; EX 232.20 Place 6: £4714.81 Place 5: £138.67.
Owner W J Gredley **Bred** Middle Park Stud Ltd **Trained** Newmarket, Suffolk
■ Stewards' Enquiry : J-P Guillambert one-day ban: careless riding (Jun 22)

FOCUS
A modest handicap for three-year-olds, run at a steady pace. The form looks fair with the winner up 5lb and the third the best guide.
Krisnando Official explanation: jockey said filly reared leaving stalls
Desiderio Official explanation: jockey said colt ran too free
Threestoneburn(USA) Official explanation: jockey said saddle slipped
Sunny Spells Official explanation: trainer said gelding had reared on exiting the stalls and had been unable into contention thereafter
T/Plt: £451.20 to a £1 stake. Pool: £69,481.95. 112.40 winning tickets. T/Qpdt: £68.60 to a £1 stake. Pool: £6,433.49. 69.30 winning tickets. JN

2216 RIPON (R-H)
Tuesday, June 3

OFFICIAL GOING: Soft changing to heavy after race 2 (3.00)
Wind: Virtually nil Weather: Overcast and raining

2696 E B F BISHOPTON MAIDEN STKS 5f
2:30 (2:30) (Class 5) 2-Y-O **£4,209** (£1,252; £625; £312) **Stalls** Low

Form RPR
1 **Charging Indian (IRE)** 2-9-3 0.......... EdwardCreighton 2 73
(M R Channon) *towards rr and green early: hdwy 1/2-way: swtchd rt and rdn over 1f out: styd on to chal ins fnl f: led nr line* **5/1**[2]
2 *nse* **Black Attack (IRE)** 2-8-10 0.......... AndrewHeffernan[(7)] 1 73
(Paul Green) *chsd ldng pair: hdwy 2f out: rdn to ld ins fnl f: sn drvn and hdd nr line* **18/1**
5 **3** *3 1/2* **Titus Andronicus (IRE)**[14] [2275] 2-9-3 0.......... NCallan 6 60+
(K A Ryan) *cl up: led 2f out: rdn over 1f out: edgd rt and hdd ins fnl f: wknd* **12/1**
4 *2 1/4* **Mo Mhuirnin (IRE)** 2-8-12 0.......... PaulHanagan 4 47
(R A Fahey) *led: rdn along and hdd 2f out: sn wknd* **7/1**[3]

2 **5** 4 ½ **Taazur**[14] 2281 2-9-3 0 RHills 3 36
(M Johnston) *s.i.s: rr tl pushed along and sme hdwy 1/2-way: rdn and btn over 2f out* **8/13**[1]

6 15 **Gems Star** 2-9-3 0 GrahamGibbons 5 —
(J J Quinn) *rrd s: chsd ldrs: rdn along and lost pl 1/2-way: sn bhd and eased* **40/1**

63.52 secs (2.82) **Going Correction** +0.40s/f (Good) **6** Ran SP% **106.5**
Speed ratings (Par 93): **93,92,87,83,76 52**
CSF £68.59 TOTE £5.50: £2.50, £5.60; EX 65.90.
Owner Saif Ali & Saeed H Altayer **Bred** Samac Ltd **Trained** West Ilsley, Berks

FOCUS
Probably just a modest contest, with newcomers dominating and the form choice failing to give his running.

NOTEBOOK
Charging Indian(IRE), a 50,000gns son of Chevalier, comes from a yard who can do little wrong with their juveniles at present and he overcame greenness to score. The below-par effort of the favourite obviously made his task easier, but he made his ground well and showed a good attitude. The step up to 6f is going to suit before long and he is open to further improvement. (op 4-1)
Black Attack(IRE), a half-brother to a 1m winner in Italy, is by Invincible Spirit and he ran a cracking race on this racecourse debut. He clearly knew his job and went down fighting, but Charging Indian just had a bit too much for him in the finish. He is entitled to improve for the experience. (op 16-1)
Titus Andronicus(IRE) did not show a great deal on his debut at Leicester, but he lasted longer this time and ran an improved race. He is clearly no star, but should make his mark at a modest level and may benefit from a faster surface next time.
Mo Mhuirnin(IRE), who cost £27,000 as a two-year-old, was soon in front and she clearly knew her job, but it proved too much in the end and she faded out of it. Better ground may be more to her liking in future. (op 8-1)
Taazur made a really pleasing debut when second at Musselburgh, overcoming a slow start and greenness, and he was rightly made a hot favourite. However, he was once again slow out of the gate and never travelled, possibly resenting the soft ground. His first season-sire Needwood Blade has yet to hit the target, but he probably deserves another chance back on better ground. Official explanation: jockey said colt missed the break and hung left (tchd 4-6 in places)
Gems Star, a half-brother to very useful sprinter Yorkies Boy, is a late foal and he was eased right down late on. Official explanation: jockey said colt hung right throughout (op 33-1)

2697 NFU MUTUAL CHALLENGE H'CAP 1m 1f 170y
3:00 (3:00) (Class 5) (0-70,70) 4-Y-0+ **£2,914** (£867; £433; £216) **Stalls** High

Form RPR

3135 **1** **Moonstreaker**[14] 2274 5-8-7 **59** MichaelJStainton(3) 4 70
(R M Whitaker) *trckd ldr: cl up 2f out: led 2f out: rdn appr fnl f and kpt on strly* **12/1**

-614 **2** 2 ¾ **Keisha Kayleigh (IRE)**[14] 2284 5-9-3 **66** (v) NCallan 9 71
(B Ellison) *hld up: gd hdwy 4f out: trckd ldrs 2f out: rdn to chse wnr ent fnl f: drvn and kpt on* **7/1**[3]

/043 **3** 1 ¾ **Smoothly Does It**[11] 2364 7-8-3 **52** PaulHanagan 5 57+
(R A Fahey) *trckd ldrs: pushed along 3f out: n.m.r and swtchd lft wl over 1f out: rdn and kpt on fnl f* **7/4**[1]

1012 **4** 2 **Cherri Fosfate**[12] 2335 4-9-5 **68** DavidAllan 3 65
(D Carroll) *hld up: hdwy 4f out: rdn to chse ldrs 2f out: one pce ent fnl f* **11/2**[2]

2300 **5** 2 ¾ **Lucayan Dancer**[16] 2220 8-9-7 **70** AdrianTNicholls 7 62
(D Nicholls) *hld up in tch: hdwy 3f out: rdn to chse ldrs 2f out: sn no imp* **9/1**

06-0 **6** 8 **San Antonio**[43] 1520 8-9-5 **68** (b) MickyFenton 11 43
(Mrs P Sly) *led: rdn along 3f out: hdd 2f out and sn wknd* **11/1**

00-5 **7** ½ **Betteras Bertie**[7] 2487 5-8-3 **52** oh6 ow1 RoystonFfrench 8 26
(M Brittain) *a in rr* **33/1**

-030 **8** nk **Holiday Cocktail**[11] 2375 6-8-9 **58** GrahamGibbons 1 31
(J J Quinn) *a towards rr* **8/1**

-624 **9** 2 ½ **Pitbull**[12] 2335 5-9-0 **63** (p) JimmyQuinn 6 31
(Mrs G S Rees) *s.i.s and rr: hdwy over 3f out: rdn over 2f out and sn wknd* **14/1**

0-00 **10** 54 **Rodeo**[43] 1520 5-9-2 **65** (b) LeeEnstone 2 —
(C W Thornton) *chsd ldrs: rdn along over 4f out and sn wknd* **40/1**

2m 10.43s (5.03) **Going Correction** +0.60s/f (Yiel) **10** Ran SP% **113.4**
Speed ratings (Par 103): **103,100,99,97,95 89,88,88,86,43**
CSF £90.83 CT £219.01 TOTE £11.90: £3.10, £2.90, £1.10; EX 97.70 Trifecta £75.30 Pool: £424.32 - 4.00 winning units.
Owner Ian B Ender **Bred** Hellwood Stud Farm **Trained** Scarcroft, W Yorks

FOCUS
A moderate handicap. The winner produced a career high but the form is not entirely solid.
Betteras Bertie Official explanation: jockey said gelding was never travelling
Holiday Cocktail Official explanation: jockey said gelding was unsuited by the heavy ground

2698 NICK WILMOT-SMITH MEMORIAL H'CAP 6f
3:30 (3:30) (Class 3) (0-95,95) 3-Y-0+ **£8,200** (£2,454; £1,227; £613; £305) **Stalls** Low

Form RPR

0000 **1** **Rising Shadow (IRE)**[20] 2106 7-9-12 **93** JimmyQuinn 1 101
(N Wilson) *hld up towards rr: hdwy over 2f out: swtchd rt and rdn over 1f out: styd on to ld last 100yds* **4/1**[3]

0211 **2** ¾ **Valery Borzov (IRE)**[17] 2210 4-9-11 **92** AdrianTNicholls 10 98
(D Nicholls) *cl up: rdn over 1f out: led ent fnl f and sn drvn: hdd and no ex last 100yds* **7/2**[2]

6530 **3** ¾ **Bel Cantor**[28] 1891 5-8-9 **79** (p) AndrewMullen(3) 6 83
(W J H Ratcliffe) *led: rdn along 2f out: drvn over 1f out: hdd ent fnl f: kpt on* **6/1**

4236 **4** 1 **Swinbrook (USA)**[17] 2210 7-8-9 **76** oh1 (v) PaulHanagan 2 76
(R A Fahey) *chsd ldrs: swtchd rt and rdn wl over 1f out: drvn ins fnl f and kpt on same pce* **9/4**[1]

00-0 **5** 3 **Grazeon Gold Blend**[27] 1908 5-8-12 **79** GrahamGibbons 8 70
(J J Quinn) *s.i.s and bhd tl styd on fnl 2f: n.d* **25/1**

-202 **6** 2 **High Curragh**[17] 2210 5-9-5 **86** NCallan 7 70
(K A Ryan) *cl up: rdn along 1/2-way: wknd 2f out* **4/1**[3]

000/ **7** 55 **Dazzling Bay**[598] 5957 8-8-12 **79** DavidAllan(3) 5 —
(T D Easterby) *chsd ldrs: rdn along 1/2-way: sn lost pl and bhd: eased* **40/1**

1m 16.01s (3.01) **Going Correction** +0.70s/f (Yiel) **7** Ran SP% **113.6**
Speed ratings (Par 107): **107,106,105,103,99 97,23**
CSF £18.10 CT £81.50 TOTE £5.30: £2.90, £2.10; EX 21.50 Trifecta £135.80 Pool: £455.55 - 2.38 winning units.
Owner G Morrill **Bred** 6c Stallions Ltd **Trained** Flaxton, N Yorks
■ Stewards' Enquiry : Adrian T Nicholls caution: used whip down shoulder in forehand position

FOCUS
A fair handicap sprint, rated through the runner-up. The winner ran his best race for this yard but was still 12lb off last year's best.

NOTEBOOK
Rising Shadow(IRE), a pound lower than when registering his last handicap win back in 2006, contested the Duke Of York Stakes on his reappearance and this obviously represented a drop in grade. A lover of soft ground, everything looked in his favour for a big run and, having been held up early on, he came with a strong run inside the final furlong to get well on top. This was his first win in 14 months and it will be interesting to see if he is out under a penalty. (op 13-2)
Valery Borzov(IRE) has finally got his act together and he came into this on a hat-trick, having registered wins at Kempton and Thirsk. Raised 10lb, and without the visor, he was soon up with the pace and driven to the front over a furlong out, but it soon became clear the winner had his move covered and he was worn down. He continues to progress, but things are not going to get any easier. (op 11-4)
Bel Cantor, still 2lb higher than when last winning on turf, enjoys some cut in the ground and it was no surprise to see him run well off the front end. He stays further than this and should continue to give a good account. (op 8-1 tchd 17-2)
Swinbrook(USA) has generally been running well and he managed to get a lot closer to Valery Borzov than he had done at Thirsk, but the weight turnaround was not enough for him to reverse form and he failed to pick up out of the ground. (tchd 11-4)
Grazeon Gold Blend, who finished last in a first-time eyeshield at Beverley on his reappearance, ran much more encouragingly without the headgear and remains handily weighted. (op 22-1)
High Curragh dropped out having shown early speed and the heavy ground may have been too taxing for him. (tchd 7-2 and 9-2)
Dazzling Bay, off the course since October 2006, was always likely to struggle in these conditions and he was not given a hard time from two out, being eased right off. Official explanation: jockey said gelding was unsuited by the heavy ground (op 25-1)

2699 WEATHERBYS BLOODSTOCK INSURANCE H'CAP 1m 1f 170y
4:00 (4:01) (Class 4) (0-80,80) 3-Y-0 **£4,533** (£1,348; £674; £336) **Stalls** High

Form RPR

4-43 **1** **Shaloo Diamond**[14] 2272 3-8-10 **72** MichaelJStainton(3) 4 81
(R M Whitaker) *trckd ldrs on outer: hdwy 3f out: rdn to chse ldng pair over 1f out: drvn and styd on ins fnl f to ld last 100yds* **7/1**

-452 **2** 1 **Just Rob**[14] 2272 3-9-2 **75** GrahamGibbons 12 82
(R Hollinshead) *trckd ldrs on inner: hdwy to chse ldr wl over 2f out: rdn over 1f out and ev ch tl drvn and nt qckn wl ins fnl f* **9/2**[2]

53-1 **3** shd **Mangham (IRE)**[16] 2221 3-9-5 **78** PaulMulrennan 7 85
(D H Brown) *led: rdn along over 2f out: drvn over 1f out: hdd and no ex last 100yds* **12/1**

5360 **4** 11 **Harry Gee**[39] 1600 3-9-5 **78** SteveDrowne 8 62
(G Wragg) *in tch: effrt 4f out: rdn to chse ldrs over 2f out: sn drvn and no imp* **3/1**[1]

0-24 **5** ¾ **Indy Driver**[31] 1817 3-9-1 **74** NCallan 1 56
(J R Fanshawe) *towards rr: hdwy over 3f out: rdn wl over 2f out: nvr rch ldrs* **8/1**

104- **6** 2 ¾ **Annaliesse (IRE)**[255] 5613 3-8-12 **71** PaulHanagan 2 47
(R A Fahey) *t.k.h: hld up towards rr: hdwy on outer over 3f out: sn rdn and btn* **11/1**

2-40 **7** 5 **Hasty Lady**[29] 1867 3-8-6 **68** AndrewMullen(3) 6 34
(K A Ryan) *dwlt: a towards rr* **50/1**

4305 **8** 19 **Plenilune (IRE)**[7] 2488 3-8-8 **70** MarkLawson(3) 5 —
(M Brittain) *prom: rdn along 4f out: sn drvn and wknd 3f out* **25/1**

33-4 **9** 10 **Green Diamond**[12] 2333 3-9-3 **76** JoeFanning 10 —
(M Johnston) *chsd ldrs: rdn along over 3f out: sn wknd* **9/1**

441 **10** 9 **Stock Market (USA)**[18] 2143 3-9-7 **80** TedDurcan 11 —
(E A L Dunlop) *in tch: effrt 4f out: sn rdn along: drvn and wknd wl over 2f out: bhd and eased wl over 1f out* **5/1**[3]

2m 11.5s (6.10) **Going Correction** +0.70s/f (Yiel) **10** Ran SP% **115.3**
Speed ratings (Par 101): **103,102,102,93,92 90,86,71,63,56**
CSF £38.09 CT £373.73 TOTE £8.50: £2.30, £1.90, £3.40; EX 42.80 Trifecta £277.20 Pool: £624.81 - 1.60 winning units.
Owner G B Bedford **Bred** Hellwood Stud Farm **Trained** Scarcroft, W Yorks
■ Stewards' Enquiry : Steve Drowne caution: careless riding

FOCUS
A fair handicap on paper, but most of these were below form, probably failing to handle the testing conditions, and the front three finished a long way clear. The first two were close to their previous Beverley form.
Plenilune(IRE) Official explanation: jockey said colt was unsuited by the heavy ground
Stock Market(USA) Official explanation: jockey said colt was unsuited by the heavy ground

2700 DAVENHAM PROPERTY FINANCE MAIDEN STKS 1m
4:30 (4:31) (Class 5) 3-Y-0 **£2,914** (£867; £433; £216) **Stalls** High

Form RPR

0-4 **1** **Ebn Malk (IRE)**[11] 2360 3-9-3 0 PhilipRobinson 1 82+
(M A Jarvis) *t.k.h: cl up: led 3f out: rdn wl over 1f out: drvn and hung lft ent fnl f: styd on* **6/5**[1]

4304 **2** 2 ¼ **Jollyhockeysticks**[19] 2118 3-8-12 71 EdwardCreighton 8 66
(M R Channon) *in tch: hdwy 3f out: rdn to chal over 1f out: swtchd rt and drvn ins fnl f: kpt on same pce* **3/1**[2]

05-0 **3** 2 **Eton Fable (IRE)**[73] 961 3-9-0 65 AndrewMullen(3) 6 66
(W J H Ratcliffe) *trckd ldrs: effrt over 2f out: sn rdn and kpt on same pce* **12/1**

4 **4** 2 ¾ **Sirvino**[40] 1579 3-9-3 0 PaulFessey 11 60
(T D Barron) *in tch: hdwy 3f out: rdn 2f out and sn no imp* **7/1**

5 11 **Liberty Key (IRE)** 3-9-3 0 MickyFenton 10 35
(T P Tate) *led: rdn along and hdd 3f out: sn wknd* **11/2**[3]

40- **6** ¾ **Hawk Mountain (UAE)**[225] 6384 3-9-3 0 GrahamGibbons 4 33
(J J Quinn) *a towards rr* **33/1**

6- **7** 41 **Rascasse**[255] 5621 3-9-3 0 RoystonFfrench 7 —
(Bruce Hellier) *s.i.s: a in rr* **66/1**

00 **8** 1 ½ **Mytexie (FR)**[18] 2143 3-9-3 0 JoeFanning 3 —
(M Johnston) *chsd ldrs on outer: rdn along 3f out: sn drvn and wknd* **28/1**

1m 47.14s (5.74) **Going Correction** +0.80s/f (Soft) **8** Ran SP% **113.9**
Speed ratings (Par 99): **103,100,98,96,85 84,43,41**
CSF £4.76 TOTE £2.20: £1.30, £1.10, £2.30; EX 5.30 Trifecta £62.60 Pool: £489.65 - 5.55 winning units.
Owner Sheikh Ahmed Al Maktoum **Bred** Tony Doyle **Trained** Newmarket, Suffolk
■ Stewards' Enquiry : Graham Gibbons one-day ban: careless riding (Jun 22)

FOCUS
A modest and uncompetitive maiden, but the winner did it well and the form looks sound.

2701 BAKER TILLY H'CAP 1m 4f 10y
5:00 (5:00) (Class 5) (0-70,70) 4-Y-0+ **£2,914** (£867; £433; £216) **Stalls** High

Form RPR

3-52 **1** **Hits Only Vic (USA)**[11] 2364 4-9-1 **64** DavidAllan 9 76
(D Carroll) *hld up in tch: smooth hdwy over 3f out: led wl over 1f out: rdn clr ent fnl f: drvn out* **5/1**

-320 **2** *2 1/4* **Bijou Dan**[11] 2364 7-8-8 **57** .... GregFairley 7 65
(G M Moore) *hld up in tch: hdwy 1/2-way: cl up 4f out: led 3f out and sn rdn: hdd wl over 1f out and sn drvn: kpt on u.p ins fnl f* **9/2**[3]

-312 **3** *3* **Pee Jay's Dream**[30] 1824 6-9-6 **69** .... DaleGibson 14 72
(M W Easterby) *a.p: effrt 3f out and ev ch tl rdn wl over 1f out and kpt on same pce* **9/4**[1]

0-35 **4** *1/2* **Aleron (IRE)**[10] 1779 10-9-0 **63** ....(p) GrahamGibbons 1 65
(J J Quinn) *trckd ldrs: hdwy over 4f out: rdn along 3f out: drvn over 2f out and kpt on same pce* **7/2**[2]

0-01 **5** *9* **Saluscraggie**[41] 1559 6-8-9 **63** .... DanielleMcCreery(5) 4 51
(R E Barr) *trckd ldrs: hdwy on outer over 4f out: rdn along wl over 2f out and sn btn* **7/1**

5550 **6** *8* **Qaasi (USA)**[14] 2286 6-8-5 **54** .... JoeFanning 6 29
(M Brittain) *led: rdn along 4f out: hdd 3f out and sn wknd* **16/1**

242/ **7** *18* **Prince Of Love (IRE)**[537] 6816 5-8-11 **60** .... LeeEnstone 10 6
(Jedd O'Keeffe) *in tch: rdn along over 3f out and sn wknd* **12/1**

2m 47.27s (10.57) **Going Correction** +0.90s/f (Soft) 7 Ran SP% **113.9**
Speed ratings (Par 103): **100,98,96,96,90 84,72**
CSF £27.29 CT £63.54 TOTE £5.90: £2.50, £2.80; EX 27.10 Trifecta £78.00 Pool: £460.54 - 4.19 winning units. Place 6: £210.31 Place 5: £45.28.
Owner Kell-Stone & Watson **Bred** Peter E Blum **Trained** Sledmere, E Yorks

FOCUS
A modest handicap run in what by now was pretty bad ground. There were seven non-runners, five of them due to the conditions. The winner is much improved and the form makes sense.
T/Jkpt: Not won. T/Plt: £482.60 to a £1 stake. Pool: £168,150.34. 254.30 winning tickets. T/Qpdt: £34.40 to a £1 stake. Pool: £10,295.76. 220.95 winning tickets. JR

2288 SOUTHWELL (L-H)
Tuesday, June 3

OFFICIAL GOING: Standard
First five races hand-timed.
Wind: Light behind Weather: Raining

2702 LADBROKES.COM LEADS THE WAY MEDIAN AUCTION MAIDEN STKS 5f (F)
2:15 (2:16) (Class 6) 2-Y-O £1,774 (£523; £262) **Stalls High**

Form RPR

30 **1** **La Brigitte**[25] 1961 2-8-12 0 .... SebSanders 3 75+
(A J McCabe) *mde all: rdn out* **15/8**[1]

2 *1* **Aunt Nicola** 2-8-12 0 .... HayleyTurner 5 71
(M L W Bell) *chsd ldrs: rdn and ev ch over 1f out: styd on same pce ins fnl f* **5/2**[2]

20 **3** *4* **Carmanjoe**[16] 2217 2-9-3 0 .... TomEaves 4 62
(M W Easterby) *chsd ldrs: rdn over 3f out: styd on same pce fnl 2f* **8/1**

0P **4** *nk* **Misty Glade**[13] 2306 2-8-12 0 .... StephenDonohoe 2 56
(B J Meehan) *chsd ldrs: rdn 1/2-way: wknd ins fnl f* **13/2**

5 *4 1/2* **Miss Moloney (IRE)** 2-8-12 0 .... RobertWinston 6 40
(Mrs S Lamyman) *chsd ldrs: rdn over 1f out: wknd fnl f* **50/1**

6 *11* **Smitain** 2-9-3 0 .... PhillipMakin 7 —
(Mrs S Lamyman) *dwlt: outpcd* **66/1**

7 *1 1/4* **Ba Globetrotter** 2-9-3 0 .... ChrisCatlin 1 —
(M R Channon) *s.s: outpcd* **4/1**[3]

59.60 secs (-0.10) **Going Correction** -0.225s/f (Stan) 7 Ran SP% **111.3**
Speed ratings (Par 91): **91,89,83,82,75 57,55**
CSF £6.36 TOTE £3.60: £1.50, £2.00; EX 7.60.
Owner Paul J Dixon **Bred** M And Mrs V L Ritchie **Trained** Babworth, Notts

FOCUS
Probably just a standard median auction maiden for the track, but the front two are speedy types and they can progress.

NOTEBOOK
La Brigitte put her racecourse experience to good use by pinging out and making all. Her future lies in the hands of the handicapper. (op 10-3)
Aunt Nicola, uneasy in the market beforehand, ran a fine race on this debut, on a surface she wouldn't have encountered before. Her trainer's two-year-olds normally come on for their first run. (op 11-10)
Carmanjoe had finished in front of the winner when both made their debut here two starts ago but had trailed in last at Ripon since. He ran respectably, but lacked the pace to go with the front two. (op 10-1 tchd 11-1)
Misty Glade was well backed in the market beforehand despite being pulled up at Goodwood last time. Her limitations were exposed here. (op 12-1)
Miss Moloney(IRE) Official explanation: jockey said filly had no more to give
Ba Globetrotter, whose stable's juveniles are hitting top gear at the moment, was slowly away and never seemed to be facing the kickback. He is worth another chance away from this surface. (op 9-2 tchd 7-2)

2703 LADBROKES 24/7 FREE PHONE BETTING 0800 777 888 CLAIMING STKS 7f (F)
2:45 (2:47) (Class 6) 3-Y-O+ £1,774 (£523; £262) **Stalls Low**

Form RPR

6-34 **1** **Dancing Deano (IRE)**[32] 1780 6-9-3 57 .... RussellKennemore(3) 7 75
(R Hollinshead) *a.p: led over 1f out: rdn clr* **11/1**

0264 **2** *5* **Elusive Warrior (USA)**[14] 2289 5-9-8 60 ....(p) JamesDoyle 10 64
(A J McCabe) *chsd ldrs: led 1/2-way: rdn and hdd over 1f out: styd on same pce* **7/1**

1000 **3** *3 3/4* **Ugenius**[55] 1266 4-9-2 50 .... StephenDonohoe 4 47
(P A Blockley) *sn outpcd: hdwy u.p over 2f out: nt trble ldrs* **33/1**

2040 **4** *1 1/2* **Strathmore (IRE)**[32] 1775 4-9-3 65 .... JamieMoriarty(3) 6 47
(R A Fahey) *hld up: hdwy u.p over 1f out: n.d* **10/1**

3210 **5** *shd* **West End Lad**[36] 1679 5-9-4 54 ....(b) PhillipMakin 3 45
(S R Bowring) *sn pushed along and prom: outpcd 3f out: rdn and hung lft 2f out: n.d after* **16/1**

6660 **6** *1/2* **Dickie Le Davoir**[14] 2293 4-9-7 68 .... MarkCoumbe(7) 2 54
(John A Harris) *sn pushed along in rr: hdwy 3f out: rdn and wknd over 1f out* **10/1**

513 **7** *4 1/2* **Blue Empire (IRE)**[28] 1902 7-8-9 57 ....(p) JackMitchell(5) 11 28
(John A Harris) *s.i.s: nvr nrr* **11/2**[3]

-600 **8** *2 1/4* **Gilded Youth**[28] 1900 4-9-6 68 .... DaneO'Neill 12 27
(H Candy) *s.i.s: sn chsng ldrs: rdn and wknd 2f out* **9/2**[2]

4000 **9** *7* **Government (IRE)**[28] 1906 7-9-1 41 .... NBazeley(7) 8 11
(M C Chapman) *mid-div: rdn 4f out: wknd 3f out* **100/1**

060- **10** *2 3/4* **Head To Head (IRE)**[333] 3281 4-9-2 49 .... SilvestreDeSousa 9 —
(A D Brown) *chsd ldr: rdn over 2f out: wknd over 1f out* **66/1**

0456 **11** *3 3/4* **Ninth House (USA)**[26] 1936 6-10-0 82 ....(bt) SebSanders 13 —
(N P Littmoden) *hld up: rdn 1/2-way: eased over 2f out* **11/4**[1]

4000 **12** *hd* **Orchestration (IRE)**[28] 1906 7-8-13 38 ....(v) AhmedAjtebi(5) 1 —
(Garry Moss) *chsd ldrs over 4f* **100/1**

5300 **13** *3 1/4* **Zorn**[21] 2075 9-9-4 46 .... RobertWinston 5 —
(P Howling) *sn rdn to ld: hdd 1/2-way: wknd over 2f out* **40/1**

00/ **14** *47* **Miss Tiddlypush**[9] 4226 7-8-9 0 ....(b[1]) TPO'Shea 14 —
(Miss Kariana Key) *dwlt: outpcd: t.o fr 1/2-way* **250/1**

1m 28.5s (-1.80) **Going Correction** -0.175s/f (Stan) 14 Ran SP% **114.4**
Speed ratings (Par 101): **103,97,93,91,91 90,85,82,74,71 67,67,63,9**
CSF £80.51 TOTE £12.30: £3.60, £2.40, £9.00; EX 76.00.Blue Empire was claimed by Mr Ollie Pears for £5000. Ninth House was claimed by Mrs R Carr for £12000.
Owner Ron Wood **Bred** Mrs Olivia Farrell **Trained** Upper Longdon, Staffs

FOCUS
Just a moderate claimer featuring mainly out-of-form sorts, the front two, although wrong at the weights, being in the minority as having run well recently. They pulled well clear of the remainder with some of the form horses not running their races on the wet track. The runner-up looks the best guide.
Ninth House(USA) Official explanation: jockey said horse was never travelling

2704 BET IN PLAY AT LADBROKES.COM H'CAP 7f (F)
3:15 (3:17) (Class 6) (0-55,55) 3-Y-O £1,774 (£523; £262) **Stalls Low**

Form RPR

2324 **1** **One Called Alice**[15] 2259 3-8-11 **52** .... HayleyTurner 7 56
(A W Carroll) *s.i.s: sn prom: rdn to chse ldr over 1f out: styd on to ld post* **4/1**[1]

0560 **2** *hd* **Scruffy Skip (IRE)**[8] 2463 3-8-9 **53** ....(b[1]) PJMcDonald(3) 13 56
(C R Dore) *chsd ldrs: led 2f out: sn rdn: hdd post* **12/1**

0-06 **3** *1 1/2* **Amicable Terms**[21] 2067 3-8-12 **53** .... ChrisCatlin 4 52
(Rae Guest) *w ldrs: rdn over 2f out: styd on same pce ins fnl f* **22/1**

6350 **4** *2 1/4* **Mujahope**[22] 2041 3-8-9 **55** ....(v[1]) KellyHarrison(5) 14 48
(C J Teague) *hld up: hdwy 1/2-way: rdn over 1f out: no ex* **16/1**

0200 **5** *2 3/4* **Magical Song**[29] 1870 3-8-12 **53** .... StephenDonohoe 10 38+
(P A Blockley) *sn outpcd: bhd and rdn 1/2-way: r.o ins fnl f: nt trble ldrs* **9/2**[2]

5-46 **6** *nk* **Aquarian Dancer**[27] 1912 3-8-10 **51** .... SebSanders 1 36
(Jedd O'Keeffe) *chsd ldrs: rdn over 2f out: wknd over 1f out* **6/1**[3]

1434 **7** *3/4* **Note Perfect**[60] 1187 3-8-4 **52** ....(b) BradleyRoper(7) 3 35
(M W Easterby) *s.i.s: hdwy 1/2-way: rdn over 2f out: sn outpcd* **12/1**

0035 **8** *2 1/4* **Natural Rhythm (IRE)**[11] 2367 3-8-11 **52** ....(b) DaneO'Neill 12 29
(Mrs R A Carr) *hld up: rdn 1/2-way: n.d* **7/1**

00-4 **9** *9* **Mandalay King (IRE)**[15] 2246 3-8-9 **50** ow2 .... TomEaves 6 2
(Mrs Marjorie Fife) *led 1f: chsd ldrs: rdn and ev ch 2f out: sn wknd* **18/1**

6000 **10** *1 3/4* **Threecheersforanby (IRE)**[5] 2552 3-8-5 **53** .....(b[1]) CharlotteKerton(7) 9 1
(S Parr) *s.s: effrt 1/2-way: wknd over 2f out* **66/1**

0-00 **11** *3 1/4* **Whenineedyou**[80] 903 3-8-8 **49** ....(t) FergalLynch 2 —
(I A Wood) *led 6f out: rdn and hdd over 2f out: wknd over 1f out* **50/1**

0-00 **12** *13* **Marramed**[14] 2269 3-8-9 **50** .... PhillipMakin 11 —
(J O'Reilly) *sn outpcd* **16/1**

0220 **13** *17* **Rich James (IRE)**[53] 1315 3-8-10 **51** ow1 .... RobertWinston 8 —
(J D Bethell) *prom: lost pl 4f out: bhd fnl 3f* **9/1**

1m 30.4s (0.10) **Going Correction** -0.175s/f (Stan) 13 Ran SP% **115.2**
Speed ratings (Par 97): **92,91,90,87,84 84,83,80,70,68 64,49,30**
CSF £49.75 CT £966.69 TOTE £4.20: £1.80, £4.20, £4.40; EX 51.90.
Owner J T Billson **Bred** Miss K Rausing **Trained** Cropthorne, Worcs

FOCUS
A truly forgettable heat contested by some exposed, moderate and not entirely straightforward animals. It was much the slowest of the three C/D races and this is weak form.
Marramed Official explanation: jockey said filly had no more to give

2705 LADBROKES.COM LEADS THE WAY H'CAP 7f (F)
3:45 (3:47) (Class 5) (0-75,75) 3-Y-O £2,456 (£725; £362) **Stalls Low**

Form RPR

3-42 **1** **Fools Gold**[61] 1166 3-8-8 **62** .... OscarUrbina 2 76
(G D Blake) *hld up in tch: led over 2f out: rdn clr over 1f out: eased ins fnl f* **14/1**

4141 **2** *6* **Montiboli (IRE)**[14] 2288 3-9-0 **73** .... NeilBrown(5) 6 71
(K A Ryan) *hld up: outpcd 1/2-way: hdwy u.p over 1f out: wnt 2nd ins fnl f: no ch w wnr* **7/2**[2]

6214 **3** *nk* **All In The Red (IRE)**[9] 2429 3-9-2 **70** ....(e[1]) FergalLynch 8 67
(Miss Gay Kelleway) *s.i.s: sn outpcd: hdwy u.p over 1f out: nvr nrr* **6/1**[3]

-142 **4** *2 1/2* **Top Draw (USA)**[59] 1216 3-9-4 **72** .... HayleyTurner 10 62
(M L W Bell) *w ldr: rdn and ev ch over 2f out: wknd fnl f* **8/1**

3-52 **5** *3 1/2* **Arabian Spirit**[7] 2481 3-9-7 **75** .... RobertWinston 5 56
(E A L Dunlop) *sn led: hdd 5f out: rdn 3f out: wknd fnl f* **2/1**[1]

6430 **6** *8* **Reprieved**[14] 2291 3-8-0 **61** .... SophieDoyle(7) 1 20
(M C Chapman) *s.i.s: sn pushed along and prom: wknd 1/2-way* **50/1**

1-36 **7** *1 1/2* **The Twelve Steps**[24] 1995 3-9-6 **74** ....(b[1]) TQuinn 7 29
(P F I Cole) *trckd ldrs: plld hrd: rdn and wknd over 2f out* **8/1**

10R0 **8** *4* **Chrystal Venture (IRE)**[17] 2189 3-9-4 **72** ....(p) JamesDoyle 3 17
(A J McCabe) *s.i.s: sn chsng ldrs: led 5f out: rdn and hdd over 2f out: wknd wl over 1f out* **20/1**

3-40 **9** *32* **Candida's Beau**[30] 1836 3-9-2 **70** ....(b[1]) SebSanders 9 —
(R M Beckett) *sn drvn along in rr: wknd 1/2-way* **16/1**

1m 28.9s (-1.40) **Going Correction** -0.175s/f (Stan) 9 Ran SP% **111.3**
Speed ratings (Par 99): **101,94,93,90,86 77,76,71,34**
CSF £57.63 CT £290.88 TOTE £12.50: £2.10, £1.60, £1.70; EX 74.40.
Owner Dale And Ann Wilsdon **Bred** Larksborough Stud Limited **Trained** Aylesbury, Bucks
■ Climaxtackledotcom was withdrawn (10/1, broke out of stalls). R4 applies, deduct 5p in the £.
■ Stewards' Enquiry : James Doyle two-day ban: careless riding (Jun 22-23)

FOCUS
A fair handicap for three-year-olds and while the second and third deserve extra credit for running on from unpromising positions, the winner is clearly better than this grade. That said, he could have been flattered as he raced up the supposedly favoured far rail which had been harrowed.
The Twelve Steps Official explanation: jockey said colt hung left-handed

2706 PAWN IN LIFE H'CAP 6f (F)
4:15 (4:16) (Class 6) (0-60,60) 3-Y-O+ £1,774 (£523; £262) **Stalls Low**

Form RPR

2454 **1** **Limonia (GER)**[36] 1675 6-8-9 **47** .... FergalLynch 8 60
(Mike Murphy) *hld up: all: drvn out* **6/1**[3]

30-0 **2** *3 1/4* **Whozart (IRE)**[30] 1827 5-8-12 **50** .... DanielTudhope 4 53
(A Dickman) *chsd wnr: rdn over 1f out: styd on same pce* **9/1**

-000 **3** *2* **Mormeatmic**[14] 2270 5-8-10 **55** .... NSLawes(7) 9 51
(M W Easterby) *prom: rdn and hung lft 2f out: styd on same pce appr fnl f* **66/1**

2130 **4** *1 ¾* **Rambling Socks**[32] 1780 5-8-13 **51**..............(p) PhillipMakin 2 42
(S R Bowring) *hld up: hdwy over 2f out: sn rdn: styd on same pce* **12/1**

3032 **5** *3* **Owed**[21] 2081 6-9-7 **59**..............(tp) RobertWinston 13 40
(R Bastiman) *chsd ldrs: rdn over 2f out: wknd fnl f* **5/2**[1]

0000 **6** *3* **Arfinnit (IRE)**[24] 2010 7-9-2 **54**..............(v) SebSanders 14 25
(Mrs A L M King) *chsd ldrs: rdn 1/2-way: wknd over 1f out* **14/1**

0103 **7** *½* **Polar Force**[21] 2075 8-9-0 **52**.............. ChrisCatlin 1 22
(Mrs C A Dunnett) *mid-div: rdn over 2f out: sn wknd* **12/1**

-000 **8** *nse* **Give Her A Whirl**[7] 2491 4-8-12 **50**.............. TPO'Shea 10 20
(G A Swinbank) *chsd ldrs: lost pl over 4f out: n.d after* **18/1**

0-00 **9** *1 ¾* **Megalo Maniac**[21] 2081 5-9-5 **60**.............. JamieMoriarty[(3)] 7 24
(R A Fahey) *s.s: outpcd* **17/2**

0-04 **10** *9* **Gracie's Gift (IRE)**[24] 2010 6-9-2 **54**.............. DaneO'Neill 6 —
(A G Newcombe) *dwlt: outpcd* **4/1**[2]

05-P **11** *4 ½* **Admiralcollingwood**[22] 2041 3-8-12 **58**.............. HayleyTurner 11 —
(T P Tate) *s.s: outpcd* **12/1**

1m 15.6s (-0.90) **Going Correction** -0.175s/f (Stan)
WFA 3 from 4yo+ 8lb 11 Ran SP% **119.9**
Speed ratings (Par 101): **99,94,92,89,85 81,81,80,78,66 60**
CSF £60.34 CT £3243.96 TOTE £7.00: £2.40, £3.70, £12.50; EX 98.40.
Owner M Murphy **Bred** D Furstin Zu Oettingen-Wallerstein **Trained** Westoning, Beds

FOCUS
Quite a few struggling for form in a typically modest handicap at this track and the in-foal winner gained reward for a string of consistent efforts this spring. Ordinary form for the grade. The first three all raced down the far side.
Arfinnit(IRE) Official explanation: trainer said gelding was unsuited by the going
Gracie's Gift(IRE) Official explanation: jockey said gelding didn't face the kick-back; jockey said, regarding the running and riding, his orders were to jump out and sit handy but he was unable to do so as the gelding was not striding out on the saturated track and would not face the kick-back.

2707 ARENALEISUREPLC.COM H'CAP 1m 4f (F)
4:45 (4:46) (Class 6) (0-60,60) 4-Y-0+ £1,774 (£523; £262) **Stalls** Low

Form RPR

0110 **1** **Pegasus Prince (USA)**[17] 2185 4-9-0 **56**.............. TomEaves 13 72+
(Miss J A Camacho) *a.p: chsd ldr over 2f out: led over 1f out: rdn out* **4/1**[2]

0-00 **2** *5* **Bolckow**[14] 2290 5-7-12 **47**.............. PatrickDonaghy[(7)] 2 55
(J T Stimpson) *a.p: chsd ldr over 4f out: led over 3f out: rdn and hdd over 1f out: styd on same pce fnl f* **40/1**

-001 **3** *3 ¼* **Tykie Two**[14] 2290 4-8-13 **55**.............. RobertWinston 9 58
(S Wynne) *chsd ldr tl led over 4f out: rdn and hdd over 3f out: wknd fnl f* **14/1**

66-5 **4** *1 ½* **Giddywell**[14] 2290 4-8-11 **53**.............. HayleyTurner 10 53
(R Hollinshead) *hld up: hdwy over 7f out: rdn and c stands' side over 2f out: wknd over 1f out* **11/1**

0/00 **5** *3* **Senor Set (GER)**[38] 1639 7-8-0 **49**.............. SophieDoyle[(7)] 8 45
(D Shaw) *hld up: hdwy over 6f out: lost pl 4f out: rdn and hung lft fr over 2f out: n.d after* **28/1**

2403 **6** *½* **Trysting Grove (IRE)**[38] 1639 7-9-0 **56**.............. SaleemGolam 6 51
(E G Bevan) *hld up: hdwy 5f out: rdn over 3f out: wknd 2f out* **7/1**[3]

0260 **7** *8* **David's Cavalier**[14] 2290 4-8-8 **53**..............(p) RussellKennemore[(3)] 11 35
(R Hollinshead) *mid-div: sn pushed along: wknd over 4f out* **12/1**

2021 **8** *2 ¼* **Nimello (USA)**[84] 843 12-8-13 **60**.............. KellyHarrison[(5)] 3 38
(A G Newcombe) *hld up: n.d* **11/1**

4210 **9** *8* **Key Partners (IRE)**[20] 2100 7-9-1 **57**.............. StephenDonohoe 12 23
(P A Blockley) *s.i.s: hld up: hdwy over 5f out: rdn over 3f out: wkng whn c stands' side over 2f out* **20/1**

3605 **10** *15* **Moorside Diamond**[15] 2259 4-8-5 **47**.............. SilvestreDeSousa 7 —
(A D Brown) *trckd ldrs: racd keenly: rdn over 4f out: wknd over 2f out* **66/1**

060 **11** *8* **Nothingtodeclaire**[14] 2289 4-9-2 **58**..............(p) ChrisCatlin 14 —
(V Smith) *hld up: bhd fr 1/2-way* **14/1**

26-3 **12** *32* **Spanish Conquest**[15] 2252 4-9-3 **59**.............. SebSanders 5 —
(Sir Mark Prescott) *sn pushed along to ld: rdn and hdd over 4f out: wknd and eased over 3f out* **2/1**[1]

2040 **13** *12* **George Henson (IRE)**[46] 1459 4-8-6 **48**.............. FergalLynch 1 —
(Garry Moss) *sn pushed along in rr: bhd fr 1/2-way* **10/1**

2m 39.19s (-1.81) **Going Correction** -0.175s/f (Stan) 13 Ran SP% **124.8**
Speed ratings (Par 101): **99,95,93,92,90 90,84,83,78,68 62,41,33**
CSF £171.89 CT £2096.41 TOTE £4.70: £1.40, £10.00, £4.80; EX 236.50 Place 6: £935.00 Place 5: £674.58.
Owner David W Armstrong **Bred** Liberty Road Stables **Trained** Norton, N Yorks

FOCUS
Little strength in depth in this moderate handicap and with the favourite flopping on his first attempt at Fibresand it was left to the course specialist son of Fusaichi Pegasus to come home a comfortable winner. Modest but sound form.
David's Cavalier Official explanation: jockey said gelding was never travelling
Nothingtodeclaire Official explanation: jockey said colt wouldn't face the kick-back
Spanish Conquest Official explanation: jockey had no explanation for the poor run
George Henson(IRE) Official explanation: jockey said gelding was never travelling
T/Plt: £1,904.20 to a £1 stake. Pool: £54,518.55. 20.90 winning tickets. T/Qpdt: £139.30 to a £1 stake. Pool: £4,951.12. 26.30 winning tickets. CR

TABY (R-H)
Tuesday, June 3

OFFICIAL GOING: Good to firm

2708a STOCKHOLMS STORA PRIS (GROUP 3) 1m 1f 165y
8:00 (8:09) 4-Y-0+ £42,735 (£19,425; £9,324; £6,216; £3,885)

RPR

1 **Peas And Carrots (DEN)**[16] 2233 5-9-2.............. EddieAhern 4 —
(L Reuterskiold, Sweden) *always in touch, 4th straight, quickened to lead over 1f out, driven clear (3.98/1)* **4/1**[2]

2 *2 ½* **Appel Au Maitre (FR)**[17] 4-9-2.............. FJohansson 13 —
(Wido Neuroth, Norway) *always prominent, close 3rd on outside straight, every chance approaching final f, ran on same pace* **1/1**[1]

3 *1 ½* **Fly Society (DEN)**[32] 7-9-2.............. KAndersen 6 —
(S Jensen, Denmark) *towards rear final 2f, ran on well final 2f, nearest at finish* **36/1**

4 *hd* **Sheriffen (IRE)** 5-9-2.............. MadeleineSmith 15 —
(Ann Michanek) *led after 2f til headed over 1f out, lost 3rd last strides* **23/1**

5 *1 ½* **The Pirate (DEN)**[17] 5-9-2.............. ESki 7 —
(Niels Petersen, Norway) *always in touch, 5th straight, one pace* **104/10**

6 *hd* **Tertullus (FR)**[345] 5-9-2.............. LDettori 12 —
(Rune Haugen, Norway) *pressed leader, 2nd straight, every chance over 1f out, soon weakened* **18/1**

7 *shd* **Illustrious Blue**[39] 1596 5-9-2.............. RichardKingscote 5 —
(W J Knight) *towards rear when hampered on turn after 2f, some progress final 2f, never nearer* **47/10**[3]

8 *1 ½* **Luca Brasi (FR)**[17] 4-9-2..............(b) MMartinez 10 —
(F Castro, Sweden) *towards rear to straight, never nearer* **31/1**

9 *½* **Alnitak (USA)**[32] 7-9-2..............(b) MRodriguez 1 —
(B Olsen, Norway) *last til half-way, some late progress* **69/1**

10 *1 ½* **Crimson And Gold**[32] 6-9-2.............. FDiaz 2 —
(L Reuterskiold, Sweden) *never nearer than mid-division* **56/1**

11 *1* **Highway (IRE)**[16] 2233 5-9-2..............(b) NCordrey 8 —
(F Castro, Sweden) *led 2f, close up to half-way, 6th & beaten straight* **47/1**

12 *1 ½* **Calistoga (DEN)**[255] 9-9-2.............. CCLopez 11 —
(L Reuterskiold, Sweden) *always in rear* **55/1**

13 *3 ½* **Shareholder (GER)**[17] 4-9-2.............. JMcLaughlin 14 —
(L Kelp, Denmark) *always in rear* **102/1**

14 *1 ½* **Alpacco (IRE)**[17] 6-9-2..............(b) DeanMcKeown 9 —
(L Kelp, Denmark) *mid-division, dropped to last 3f out* **13/1**

1m 57.7s (-1.60) 14 Ran SP% **126.7**
(including one krona stakes): WIN 4.98; PL 1.51, 1.29, 3.22; DF 18.45.
Owner O Zawawi **Bred** Havreholms Stutteri **Trained** Sweden

NOTEBOOK
Illustrious Blue never got into contention after being hampered on the bend in the early stages.

[1851]KEMPTON (A.W) (R-H)
Wednesday, June 4

OFFICIAL GOING: Standard
Wind: Light, behind Weather: Fine

2709 EURO 2008 LAUNCH PARTY TONIGHT MEDIAN AUCTION MAIDEN STKS 5f (P)
6:10 (6:11) (Class 6) 2-Y-0 £2,047 (£604; £302) **Stalls** High

Form RPR

642 **1** **Klynch**[13] 2338 2-9-3 0.............. RyanMoore 11 84
(B J Meehan) *mde all: rdn clr fr over 1f out: r.o wl* **1/1**[1]

2 *5* **Red Rossini (IRE)** 2-9-3 0.............. RichardHughes 9 66
(R Hannon) *pressed wnr to 2f out: lft bhd fr over 1f out: hld on for 2nd* **4/1**[2]

0 **3** *nk* **Scrapper Smith (IRE)**[25] 1987 2-9-3 0.............. LPKeniry 5 65
(E F Vaughan) *trckd ldrs: prog on inner 2f out: pressed for 2nd fnl f but no ch w wnr* **10/1**

4 *3 ¾* **Kitty Allen** 2-8-12 0.............. TedDurcan 1 52+
(M Botti) *at bk of main gp: pushed along and passed 6 rivals fnl f to snatch 4th on line* **33/1**

5 *hd* **Dalepak Flyer (IRE)** 2-9-3 0.............. PaulEddery 8 53
(G D Blake) *pressed ldng pair on outer: rdn and easily outpcd fr over 1f out* **20/1**

6 **6** *½* **The Saucy Snipe**[37] 1680 2-8-12 0.............. StephenCarson 6 46
(P Winkworth) *pressed ldng trio but racd on wd outside: lost grnd bnd 2f out: n.d after* **10/1**

7 *1* **Norfolk Broads (IRE)** 2-8-12 0.............. GregFairley 10 42
(M Johnston) *s.s: sn in tch in rr: sme prog on inner over 1f out: one pce and no ch after* **18/1**

5 **8** *¾* **Fyelehk (IRE)**[62] 1168 2-9-3 0.............. AlanMunro 2 44+
(B R Millman) *rrd s: at bk of main gp: shuffled along over 1f out: no real prog but kpt on* **20/1**

0 **9** *½* **Betoula**[30] 1866 2-8-12 0.............. EddieAhern 4 38
(Mrs A L M King) *in tch towards rr: no prog 2f out: fdd* **100/1**

10 *7* **Farriers Gate** 2-8-12 0.............. J-PGuillambert 7 12
(T Keddy) *chsd ldrs tl wknd 2f out* **50/1**

11 *9* **Kingsgate Storm (IRE)** 2-9-3 0.............. GeorgeBaker 3 —
(J R Best) *nrly uns rdr leaving stalls: a detached in last after: eased fnl f* **6/1**[3]

61.49 secs (0.99) **Going Correction** +0.125s/f (Slow) 11 Ran SP% **123.1**
Speed ratings (Par 91): **97,89,88,83,83 82,80,79,78,67 53**
CSF £4.99 TOTE £2.50: £1.40, £1.70, £3.00; EX 8.60.
Owner L P R Partnership **Bred** J C S Wilson Bloodstock **Trained** Manton, Wilts

FOCUS
A fairly interesting auction maiden on paper and the market got it right. The time was less that half a second slower than the following handicap.

NOTEBOOK
Klynch, the well-backed favourite and most experienced runner in the race, took advantage of his rail draw by making all and coming right away in the final furlong for an easy first success. He has progressed with racing, has scope and looks capable of getting an extra furlong, but in the meantime connections are considering something like the Windsor Castle at Royal Ascot. (op 6-4 tchd 7-4)
Red Rossini(IRE), a 65,000gns first foal of a mile winner, had clearly been showing a fair amount at home and ran well for his in-form yard, despite being no match for the winner. He looks more than capable of winning races on this evidence. (op 10-3 tchd 3-1)
Scrapper Smith(IRE) showed considerable improvement on his debut and the drop in trip seemed to suit. (op 15-2 tchd 6-1)
Kitty Allen did best of the remainder in running on from the rear, is from a speedy family and can be expected to do better as she had the worst of the draw. (tchd 28-1)
Dalepak Flyer(IRE) showed early speed before tiring. A half-brother to Little Wing, he cost less than half his yearling price when re-sold earlier this year but showed he has some ability. (op 14-1)
Fyelehk(IRE) Official explanation: jockey said colt missed the break and would not face kickback
Kingsgate Storm(IRE) lost his chance with a slow start, having apparently stumbled upon leaving the stalls. Official explanation: jockey said colt stumbled on leaving stalls (op 8-1)

2710 DONKEY HARNESS RACING HERE NEXT WEDNESDAY H'CAP 5f (P)
6:40 (6:40) (Class 5) (0-70,70) 3-Y-0+ £2,590 (£770; £385; £192) **Stalls** High

Form RPR

0-00 **1** **Fairfield Princess**[105] 620 4-9-1 **57**.............. DaneO'Neill 11 66
(M S Saunders) *trckd ldng trio: prog on inner and led ent fnl f: drvn and jst hld on* **10/1**

0623 **2** *hd* **Mambazo**[16] 2263 6-8-12 **59**........(p) AshleyHamblett(5) 5 67
(S C Williams) *hld up in rr: hanging but prog over 1f out: r.o to take 2nd last 50yds and clsng fast on wnr at fin* **7/1**[3]

2304 **3** *1/2* **Azygous**[13] 2330 5-9-4 **60**........(p) AlanMunro 2 66+
(J Akehurst) *chsd ldrs: effrt u.p 2f out: clsd fr over 1f out: nvr quite pce to chal* **12/1**

4566 **4** *3/4* **Desert Opal**[50] 1378 8-9-10 **66**........(b) LiamJones 4 70
(C R Dore) *pressed ldng pair: tried to chal over 1f out: kpt on same pce u.p* **20/1**

1-40 **5** *nse* **Smokin Beau**[41] 1582 11-9-10 **69**........ KirstyMilczarek(3) 9 72
(N P Littmoden) *pressed ldr: nt qckn and lost pl jst over 1f out: tried to rally ins fnl f: one pce* **9/2**[2]

223 **6** *1 1/4* **Spoof Master (IRE)**[29] 1901 4-10-0 **70**........ TPQueally 10 69
(C R Dore) *led: hdd ent fnl f: wknd last 100yds* **4/1**[1]

-205 **7** *4* **Green Lagonda (AUS)**[12] 2356 6-9-6 **62**........ GeorgeBaker 1 46
(J G Given) *nvr bttr than midfield: u.p and outpcd wl over 1f out* **7/1**[3]

1-30 **8** *1/2* **Lady Bahia (IRE)**[12] 2356 7-9-6 **62**........(b) LPKeniry 8 45
(Peter Grayson) *s.s: wl in rr: pushed along and outpcd fnl 2f: nvr nr ldrs* **12/1**

0-00 **9** *1/2* **Willhewiz**[16] 2242 8-9-1 **57**........ FergusSweeney 7 38
(M S Saunders) *chsd ldrs: rdn 1/2-way: sn struggling* **14/1**

0000 **10** *nse* **Gross Prophet**[15] 2276 3-9-7 **70**........ RichardKingscote 12 51
(Tom Dascombe) *outpcd and last after 2f: nvr a factor* **11/1**

5000 **11** *1* **Decider (USA)**[8] 2478 5-9-6 **65**........ KevinGhunowa(3) 6 42
(R A Harris) *rdn in midfield bef 1/2-way: no prog: wknd over 1f out* **14/1**

-100 **12** *13* **The Magic Blanket (IRE)**[7] 2506 3-9-3 **66**........ MickyFenton 3 —
(Stef Liddiard) *stalls opening as blindfold removed: plld hrd and hld up in rr: sme prog on wd outside 1/2-way: wknd over 1f out: t.o* **25/1**

61.00 secs (0.50) **Going Correction** +0.125s/f (Slow)
WFA 3 from 4yo+ 7lb **12** Ran SP% **117.9**
Speed ratings (Par 103): **101,100,99,98,98 96,90,89,88,88 86,66**
CSF £77.96 CT £870.13 TOTE £9.50: £2.30, £2.20, £3.40; EX 72.50.
Owner Lockstone Business Services Ltd **Bred** Lady Fairhaven **Trained** Green Ore, Somerset

FOCUS
A modest sprint handicap run 0.49 secs faster than the opening maiden despite the early pace appearing to be strong. Sound form, if ordinary for the grade.
Lady Bahia(IRE) Official explanation: jockey said mare missed the break
The Magic Blanket(IRE) Official explanation: jockey said gelding lost its action

2711 DIGIBET REDFERN H'CAP 1m 2f (P)
7:10 (7:11) (Class 3) (0-95,95) 4-Y-0+
£6,542 (£1,959; £979; £490; £244; £122) **Stalls** High

Form RPR

2100 **1** **Safari Sundowner (IRE)**[19] 2152 4-8-0 **77**........ LukeMorris(3) 11 89
(P Winkworth) *settled in midfield: pushed along and struggling 1/2-way: taken to outer and rapid prog u.p over 2f out to ld over 1f out: styd on* **16/1**

-023 **2** *2 1/4* **Pinch Of Salt (IRE)**[33] 1766 5-9-6 **94**........ FrancisNorton 5 101
(A M Balding) *hld up in rr: prog 1/2-way into midfield: hdwy on outer to ld wl over 1f out: sn hdd and drvn: one pce* **15/2**

064 **3** *nk* **Kayak (SAF)**[94] 6-9-2 **95**........ AhmedAjtebi(5) 9 101
(D M Simcock) *chsd ldr 4f: cl up 2f out: drvn to chse ldng pair over 1f out: kpt on* **20/1**

0-50 **4** *1 1/4* **Beauchamp Viceroy**[18] 2195 4-9-4 **92**........ EddieAhern 12 98+
(G A Butler) *hld up wl in rr: tk clsr order over 2f out: prog and shkn up jst over 1f out: running on and looked likely to take 3rd whn eased last 75yds* **16/1**

6613 **5** *1* **Basra (IRE)**[27] 1935 5-8-7 **84**........ TravisBlock(3) 7 86
(Miss Jo Crowley) *wl in rr: drvn over 2f out: styd on fr over 1f out: nt pce to trble ldrs* **12/1**

221- **6** *1/2* **Spring City (GER)**[317] 3794 4-9-1 **89**........ KerrinMcEvoy 6 90+
(Saeed Bin Suroor) *dwlt: mostly in last pair: shkn up over 1f out: styd on fnl f: no ch of rching ldrs* **7/2**[2]

14-2 **7** *hd* **Tropical Strait (IRE)**[31] 1841 5-9-1 **89**........ FergusSweeney 8 90
(D W P Arbuthnot) *chsd ldrs: rdn 3f out and losing pl: no real hdwy after* **9/2**[3]

0424 **8** *2 3/4* **Mataram (USA)**[27] 1935 5-8-8 **82**........ AlanMunro 2 77
(W Jarvis) *trckd ldng trio: lost pl 2f out: sn btn* **12/1**

1-16 **9** *1 1/4* **Viva Vettori**[18] 2200 4-9-0 **88**........ TQuinn 10 81
(D R C Elsworth) *led at generous pce: hdd wl over 1f out and immediately wknd rapidly* **10/3**[1]

-534 **10** *16* **Rapid City**[23] 2057 5-8-10 **84**........ ShaneKelly 4 45
(Miss J Feilden) *a in rr: rdn and struggling over 3f out: sn bhd: t.o* **14/1**

1004 **11** *20* **Samarinda (USA)**[33] 1766 5-9-7 **95**........ MickyFenton 3 16
(Mrs P Sly) *dwlt: rushed up to go prom after 2f: chsd ldr 6f out to over 2f out: wkng rapidly whn hmpd wl over 1f out: eased and t.o* **14/1**

2m 6.77s (-1.23) **Going Correction** +0.125s/f (Slow) **11** Ran SP% **120.5**
Speed ratings (Par 107): **109,107,106,105,105 104,104,102,101,88 72**
CSF £134.27 CT £2434.21 TOTE £25.60: £6.20, £2.60, £4.20; EX 136.30.
Owner P Winkworth **Bred** Michael Phelan **Trained** Chiddingfold, Surrey

FOCUS
A decent handicap featuring several unexposed performers and the time was decent for the grade. A good race for the grade, and solid form.

NOTEBOOK
Safari Sundowner(IRE), who was stepping up in grade, looked in trouble on the far side, but then swept around his field and ran on strongly to score. He loves this surface and, although this is the highest grade he has won in, his winning run does not look over quite yet.
Pinch Of Salt(IRE) ranged up alongside the leader turning for home looking all over the winner, but he could not find the extra gear when challenged. He has a good record on this track but both his wins here were over further and he may need to return to 1m4f. (op 9-1)
Kayak(SAF), a multiple winner in South Africa, was making his Polytrack debut and ran much better than on his first outing here. (op 16-1)
Beauchamp Viceroy, having his first try here, had gained all his wins on a similar surface at Wolverhampton and this was a welcome return to something like his old form, as he has not had much racing in the last two years.
Basra(IRE) is another who has gone well on other Polytrack venues and ran reasonably on his first try here. (tchd 11-1)
Spring City(GER) lost his chance with a slow start and, although running on, never got involved. He should be better for the outing, his first since last July. Official explanation: jockey said colt missed the break (op 3-1)
Tropical Strait(IRE) gained both his previous wins over further but was outpaced after trying to race prominently on this drop back in trip and is likely to step up in distance next time. (op 5-1 tchd 4-1)
Viva Vettori previously had an unbeaten record on this surface and made the running, but may have gone a shade too fast as he dropped right away. (op 9-2)
Samarinda(USA) Official explanation: jockey said gelding had no more to give

2712 DIGIBET ACHILLES STKS (LISTED RACE) 5f (P)
7:40 (7:43) (Class 1) 3-Y-0+
£14,760 (£5,595; £2,098; £2,098; £699; £351) **Stalls** High

Form RPR

0-30 **1** **Stoneacre Lad (IRE)**[47] 1442 5-9-3 92........(b) GeorgeBaker 10 106
(Peter Grayson) *cl up: effrt 2f out: drvn to ld jst over 1f out: edgd lft but drew clr fnl f* **10/1**

3-00 **2** *2 1/4* **Cake (IRE)**[11] 2404 3-8-5 100........ RichardSmith 5 90
(R Hannon) *led: rdn and hdd jst over 1f out: sn no ch w wnr but hld on for 2nd* **14/1**

65-6 **3** *hd* **Green Manalishi**[11] 2401 7-9-3 103........ DO'Donohoe 2 97
(K A Ryan) *prom: rdn to chal over 1f out: nt qckn and sn btn* **14/1**

01-0 **3** *dht* **Biniou (IRE)**[24] 2034 5-9-7 102........ EddieAhern 8 101
(R M H Cowell) *t.k.h: hld up: prog on inner 2f out: shkn up and styd on fnl f: nrst fin* **33/1**

4000 **5** *1* **Matsunosuke**[4] 2626 6-9-3 100........ KerrinMcEvoy 12 94+
(A B Coogan) *hld up in rr: effrt whn nt clr run over 1f out tl ent fnl f: pushed along and styd on* **7/2**[2]

1-00 **6** *hd* **Judd Street**[11] 2404 6-9-7 106........ StephenCarson 9 97
(Eve Johnson Houghton) *t.k.h: n.m.r over 3f out: trckd ldrs 2f out: plld out over 1f out but hanging and no prog* **4/1**[3]

0 **7** *1/2* **Mocha Java (SAF)**[25] 2000 6-8-12 97........(b) TPQueally 7 86+
(E F Vaughan) *t.k.h: n.m.r after 1f: sn dropped to last: nvr on terms after* **16/1**

12-0 **8** *nse* **Rowe Park**[31] 1831 5-9-10 111........ LPKeniry 1 98
(Mrs L C Jewell) *dwlt: hld up in rr on outer: effrt and nt clr run over 1f out: no ch* **10/1**

-004 **9** *4* **Galeota (IRE)**[11] 2417 6-9-7 104........ RyanMoore 4 80
(R Hannon) *chsd ldr to over 1f out: wknd rapidly* **3/1**[1]

112- **10** *1/2* **Group Therapy**[380] 1897 3-8-10 101........ ShaneKelly 6 72
(J A Osborne) *t.k.h: n.m.r after 1f: in tch on outer 1/2-way: wknd over 1f out* **12/1**

59.96 secs (-0.54) **Going Correction** +0.125s/f (Slow)
WFA 3 from 4yo+ 7lb **10** Ran SP% **115.3**
Speed ratings (Par 111): **109,105,105,105,103 103,102,102,95,95**
PL: Biniou £2.60, Green Manalishi £2.50 CSF £138.66 TOTE £14.90: £3.40, £3.50; EX 175.00.
Owner Richard Teatum **Bred** Mrs Annie Hughes **Trained** Formby, Lancs

FOCUS
An interesting Listed sprint and something of a surprise result. Pretty ordinary form for the grade, and the form may not stand up.

NOTEBOOK
Stoneacre Lad(IRE), who was well drawn and got a good lead in the early stages, squeezed through a narrow gap at the furlong marker, then ran on strongly to score his first success at this level. Having beaten a number of rivals with ratings in the low 100s his opportunities in handicaps may be somewhat limited from now on, but the intention is for him to try to repeat last year's success in the Hong Kong Jockey Club Sprint at Ascot at the end of next month. (op 14-1 tchd 16-1)
Cake(IRE) ◆ won her sole start on Polytrack on her racecourse debut last year and had not raced on the All-Weather since, but she broke really well from her middle draw, made the running and stayed on really well when headed. She has some good form to her name having won in this grade and been placed at Group level and she may be able to add to her score, especially against her own sex. (op 16-1)
Biniou(IRE) has looked something of a soft-ground performer and had been well beaten on his only previous try on this surface, but this was a step up. He is likely to be of most interest when returning to race in France. (op 20-1)
Green Manalishi has form on Polytrack in the past and ran well on his first try on the surface for almost two years. A flat track suits him well and he can score again at this level. (op 20-1)
Matsunosuke was well backed but could never land a blow, having been held up in the rear and then not getting a clear passage. (op 4-1 tchd 3-1)
Judd Street was quite keen early but his rider reported that he failed to handle the bend and he could make no impression in the straight. Official explanation: jockey said gelding failed to handle the bend (op 9-2 tchd 5-1)
Mocha Java(SAF), a multiple winning sprinter in South Africa, was the victim of some interference in the early stages before staying on. Official explanation: jockey said mare suffered interference in running
Galeota(IRE) raced up with the early pace set by his stable companion but dropped out tamely. (tchd 11-4 and 7-2)

2713 DIGIBET SPORTS BETTING E B F NOVICE STKS 6f (P)
8:10 (8:11) (Class 4) 2-Y-0 **£4,857** (£1,445; £722; £360) **Stalls** High

Form RPR

10 **1** **Asaint Needs Brass (USA)**[49] 1399 2-9-0 0........ JackMitchell(5) 4 84
(R M Beckett) *led to over 4f out: sn in 3rd: swtchd to inner and quick prog to ld wl over 1f out: hung lft ent fnl f: hld on* **10/1**

421 **2** *1/2* **In Transit (IRE)**[5] 2554 2-8-9 0........ MCGeran(7) 3 80
(M R Channon) *led over 4f out: hdd and nt qckn wl over 1f out: styd on ins fnl f: nt get bk to wnr* **9/2**[3]

2 **3** *nk* **I Am The Best**[18] 2204 2-8-12 0........ RichardMullen 2 75+
(D M Simcock) *hld up in 4th: outpcd and shkn up over 2f out: struggling tl styd on jst over 1f out: gaining steadily at fin* **11/10**[1]

5 **4** *1 3/4* **Redhead (IRE)**[12] 2368 2-8-7 0........ RichardHughes 1 65
(R Hannon) *trckd ldr after 2f to 2f out: nt qckn and hld after* **9/2**[3]

5 *1/2* **Syrinx (IRE)** 2-8-7 0........ ShaneKelly 5 63+
(J Noseda) *dwlt: rn green and a last: outpcd over 2f out: styd on ins fnl f* **4/1**[2]

1m 15.88s (2.78) **Going Correction** +0.125s/f (Slow) **5** Ran SP% **113.1**
Speed ratings (Par 95): **86,85,84,82,81**
CSF £52.24 TOTE £14.50: £4.10, £2.50; EX 41.20.
Owner Tony Perkins, J Cameron & Wendy Smith **Bred** Fred Seitz **Trained** Whitsbury, Hants

FOCUS
A fair juvenile novice contest that was dominated by the two most experienced runners, who set a steady pace between them which resulted in a slow winning time for a race of its class.

NOTEBOOK
Asaint Needs Brass(USA) made the early running but was headed on the turn and his rider gave him a breather before asking him for his effort halfway up the straight. He responded well and ran on strongly to get the better of the runner-up, who had led him into the straight. He looks a decent sort on this surface and the Sirenia Stakes at the end of the summer appeals as a likely target providing he continues to progress. (op 6-1 tchd 11-2)
In Transit(IRE) took the advantage off the winner on the bend and battled on well, but could not hold off his rival's renewed effort. He is also improving with racing and lost little in defeat. (op 4-1 tchd 7-2)
I Am The Best was somewhat unlucky on his debut at Newmarket but the third has been well beaten since and that race may not be as strong as it promised to be. However, he did not look entirely happy on the track and a return to a straight track on turf might suit him better. (op 11-8 tchd 13-8)

Redhead(IRE), an 80,000gns yearling from the family of the stable's good juvenile Lady Links, had looked in need of the experience on her debut but ran quite free and could not build on that effort, fading late on. (op 4-1 tchd 5-1 in places)

Syrinx(IRE) cost 230,000gns as a yearling but never got out of last place on this racecourse debut. (op 13-2 tchd 15-2)

2714 JIM ELLIS 50TH BIRTHDAY CELEBRATION H'CAP (LONDON MILE QUALIFIER) 1m (P)

8:40 (8:43) (Class 4) (0-80,80) 3-Y-O **£4,209** (£1,252; £625; £312) **Stalls** High

Form				RPR
403	1		**Naughty Frida (IRE)**[43] 1546 3-9-4 **77** .... JohnEgan 12	83
			(M Botti) *hld up in midfield: clsd on ldrs over 2f out: forced way through jst over 1f out to chse ldr: drvn to ld last 75yds* **16/1**	
515-	2	*hd*	**King Columbo (IRE)**[214] 6650 3-9-4 **80** .... JerryO'Dwyer(3) 13	86
			(Miss J Feilden) *trckd ldrs and racd on inner: effrt to ld over 1f out: drvn and worn down last 75yds* **9/1**	
-331	3	*hd*	**Mexican Venture**[19] 2161 3-9-7 **80** .... KerrinMcEvoy 5	89+
			(W Jarvis) *hld up in last pair: nt clr run over 2f out and again whn prog wl over 1f out: eased lft and r.o wl fnl f: unlucky* **9/2**[2]	
2-03	4	*1 1/2*	**Border Owl (IRE)**[14] 2302 3-9-4 **77** .... RichardHughes 14	79
			(R Hannon) *racd on inner in midfield and n.m.r: lost pl over 2f out: drvn and prog to press wnr over 1f out: hung lft and wknd last 100yds* **8/1**	
24-3	5	*3/4*	**Barliffey (IRE)**[22] 2079 3-9-2 **75** .... TPO'Shea 3	75+
			(D J Coakley) *hld up in last pair: brought wd in st: prog whn bmpd 1f out: r.o after: nrst fin* **20/1**	
5-43	6	*shd*	**Game Park (USA)**[19] 2161 3-9-2 **75** .... DaneO'Neill 4	75
			(J R Fanshawe) *racd wd towards rr: rdn over 2f out: styd on fr over 1f out: nt rch ldrs* **7/1**[3]	
0-60	7	*1 1/2*	**Prince Desire (IRE)**[25] 1988 3-9-2 **75** .... RichardKingscote 2	72
			(Tom Dascombe) *racd wd: trckd ldrs: tried to cl 2f out: nt qckn and no imp fnl f* **16/1**	
-200	8	*1/2*	**Last Of The Line**[29] 1899 3-9-2 **75** .... (b[1]) FrancisNorton 7	71
			(H J L Dunlop) *racd wd and cl up: prog to chal over 1f out: fnd nil and sn wknd* **33/1**	
6-15	9	*1*	**Rockfield Tiger (IRE)**[110] 573 3-9-6 **79** .... ShaneKelly 9	78+
			(J A Osborne) *sn hld up in rr: nt clr run 2f out: sme prog whn nt clr run again over 1f out: pushed along and kpt on* **16/1**	
1-30	10	*hd*	**The Which Doctor**[14] 2302 3-9-6 **79** .... TPQueally 11	72+
			(J Noseda) *n.m.r after 1f and hld up in rr: nt clr run fr over 2f out to over 1f out: bmpd sn after: kpt on one pce fnl f* **4/1**[1]	
04-0	11	*2 3/4*	**Emerald Crystal (IRE)**[51] 1367 3-9-2 **75** .... (b[1]) AlanMunro 6	61+
			(B J Meehan) *led to over 1f out: wkng whn hmpd sn after* **25/1**	
-504	12	*1 3/4*	**Artsu**[30] 1875 3-9-4 **77** .... RichardMullen 10	59
			(M L W Bell) *plld hrd: hld up bhd ldrs: effrt and cl up over 2f out: wknd rapidly over 1f out* **20/1**	
61	13	*3 3/4*	**Mooted (UAE)**[30] 1876 3-9-2 **75** .... SteveDrowne 8	49+
			(R Charlton) *nvr beyond midfield: struggling in rr whn bmpd 1f out* **7/1**[3]	
222-	14	*1*	**Regal Bird (USA)**[178] 7084 3-9-3 **76** .... EddieAhern 1	48+
			(M A Magnusson) *t.k.h: trckd ldr: upsides gng easily 2f out: nt qckn and losing pl whn bmpd jst over 1f out: eased* **14/1**	

1m 40.59s (0.79) **Going Correction** +0.125s/f (Slow) **14 Ran SP% 124.9**
Speed ratings (Par 101): **101,100,100,99,98 98,96,96,95,95 92,90,86,85**
CSF £151.47 CT £792.26 TOTE £17.60: £3.40, £3.80, £2.60; EX 235.40.
Owner Giuliano Manfredini **Bred** J Hanly **Trained** Newmarket, Suffolk

■ Stewards' Enquiry : John Egan two-day ban (reduced from three days on appeal): careless riding (Jun 22-23)

Kerrin McEvoy one-day ban: careless riding (Jun 22)

FOCUS
A fair contest with several unexposed performers that developed into a rough race but produced a good finish. Around half the field were hampered, of which the third home looked the most unlucky, and it is hard to be too positive about the bare form.
The Which Doctor Official explanation: jockey said gelding was denied a clear run

2715 WEATHERBYS BLOODSTOCK INSURANCE APPRENTICE H'CAP (ROUND 1) 1m 4f (P)

9:10 (9:10) (Class 6) (0-65,65) 4-Y-0+ **£2,047** (£604; £302) **Stalls** Centre

Form				RPR
005/	1		**Tomina**[102] 5559 8-9-3 **63** .... DavidProbert(5) 5	78+
			(Miss E C Lavelle) *sn trckd ldr: upsides fr 1/2-way: edgd lft 2f out but sn led: drew clr u.p* **16/1**	
5332	2	*5*	**Alexander Guru**[30] 1853 4-9-9 **64** .... JackMitchell 9	71
			(M Blanshard) *hld up in last trio: nt clr run briefly over 2f out: prog over 1f out: styd on to take 2nd last 100yds: no ch w wnr* **9/2**[3]	
0-24	3	*2*	**Critical Stage (IRE)**[16] 551 9-9-4 **59** .... HaddenFrost 3	63
			(J D Frost) *mde most: hit rail over 2f out: hdd wl over 1f out: fdd* **6/1**	
1330	4	*1*	**Floodlight Fantasy**[8] 2001 5-9-0 **58** .... (b) JPHamblett(3) 2	60
			(Dr R D P Newland) *trckd ldrs: rdn and no prog over 2f out: n.d after* **7/1**	
2302	5	*1*	**Mixing**[42] 1562 6-9-1 **56** .... AshleyHamblett 7	57
			(M J Attwater) *prom: rdn over 2f out: fdd over 1f out* **9/4**[1]	
-060	6	*1/2*	**Saloon (USA)**[23] 2051 4-9-0 **58** .... WilliamCarson(3) 6	58
			(S Curran) *hld up in last: rdn wl over 3f out: sme prog 2f out: kpt on but n.d* **14/1**	
0000	7	*9*	**Spellman**[47] 1459 4-8-2 **46** oh1 .... (b) JackDean(3) 4	31
			(N P Littmoden) *dwlt: pushed along most of way to stay in tch: rn v wd bnd 3f out and btn after* **20/1**	
20-1	8	*6*	**Ardmaddy (IRE)**[11] 485 4-9-1 **59** .... (b) JemmaMarshall(3) 1	35
			(G L Moore) *trckd ldrs: rdn 4f out: wd bnd 3f out and wknd* **4/1**[2]	
1606	9	*3 1/4*	**Sol Rojo**[18] 2185 6-9-5 **65** .... (v) SimonPearce(5) 8	71
			(J Pearce) *hld up in last trio: prog over 2f out: rdn to go 2nd jst over 1f out whn broke down bdly and virtually p.u: dead* **12/1**	

2m 35.9s (1.40) **Going Correction** +0.125s/f (Slow) **9 Ran SP% 120.7**
Speed ratings (Par 101): **100,96,95,94,94 93,87,83,81**
CSF £90.42 CT £497.50 TOTE £14.80: £4.70, £1.80, £2.30; EX 166.50 Place 6 £10,114.48, Place 5 £7,720.26.
Owner Paul G Jacobs **Bred** P G Jacobs **Trained** Wildhern, Hants

FOCUS
A very moderate apprentice handicap that resulted in a surprise success. The form looks sound, however.
T/Jkpt: Not won. T/Plt: £1,673.80 to a £1 stake. Pool: £71,767.29. 31.30 winning tickets. T/Qpdt: £706.20 to a £1 stake. Pool: £4,580.88. 4.80 winning tickets. JN

2611 LINGFIELD (L-H)

Wednesday, June 4

OFFICIAL GOING: Turf course - good (good to soft in places; 7.6) all-weather - standard
Wind: fairly modest against Weather: partly cloudy with brighter spells

2716 BET EURO 2008 - BETDAQ MAIDEN FILLIES' STKS (DIV I) 1m 2f

1:50 (1:53) (Class 5) 3-Y-0+ **£1,845** (£549; £274; £137) **Stalls** Low

Form				RPR
2-5	1		**Elmaleeha**[47] 1440 3-8-9 0 .... RHills 5	70
			(J L Dunlop) *lw: mde all: hrd pressed and rdn 3f out: battled on gamely: hld on wl fnl 100yds* **15/8**[1]	
0-6	2	*nk*	**Siyasa (USA)**[20] 2123 3-8-9 0 .... KerrinMcEvoy 11	69
			(Saeed Bin Suroor) *lw: chsd ldng pair: effrt and hanging lft fr 2f out: ev ch 1f out: wnt 2nd ins fnl f: hld towards fin* **10/1**[3]	
0-	3	*1 3/4*	**Basanti (USA)**[214] 6649 3-8-9 0 .... MichaelHills 6	66
			(B W Hills) *s.i.s: sn pushed up to press wnr: rdn and ev ch 3f out: no ex ins fnl f* **11/1**	
0-3	4	*2*	**Miss Rochester (IRE)**[17] 2221 3-8-9 0 .... RyanMoore 9	62+
			(Sir Michael Stoute) *hld up bhd: rdn over 3f out: plugged on steadily u.p: wnt 4th ins fnl f: nt pce to threaten ldrs* **15/8**[1]	
00-	5	*1 1/4*	**Corking (IRE)**[239] 6093 3-8-6 0 .... PatrickHills(3) 3	59
			(Eve Johnson Houghton) *in tch: rdn over 2f out: outpcd by ldrs wl over 1f out: kpt on same pce* **66/1**	
30	6	*2*	**Sphere (IRE)**[32] 1814 3-8-9 0 .... DaneO'Neill 7	55
			(J R Fanshawe) *leggy: in tch: rdn and unable qck 3f out: kpt on same pce u.p after* **14/1**	
	7	*1/2*	**Colourways (IRE)** 3-8-9 0 .... JimCrowley 1	54
			(Mrs A J Perrett) *unf: scope: hld up in tch: effrt and hung lft 3f out: no imp after* **6/1**[2]	
66	8	*2*	**Code Violation**[61] 1176 3-8-9 0 .... FrankieMcDonald 8	50
			(Jean-Rene Auvray) *hld up in midfield: hdwy on outer 4f out: rdn over 3f out: sn no imp* **100/1**	
	9	*2 1/4*	**Ginos Destination** 3-8-6 0 .... KirstyMilczarek(3) 10	46
			(M Botti) *str: stdd s: hld up in last: n.d* **40/1**	
0-0	10	*3/4*	**Rabeera**[47] 1440 3-8-9 0 .... FrancisNorton 4	44
			(A M Balding) *rn in snatches: racd in midfield: rdn 3f out: sn outpcd* **14/1**	
0	11	*nk*	**Bobster**[30] 1869 3-8-9 0 .... FergusSweeney 2	44
			(B R Millman) *leggy: t.k.h: chsd ldrs tl stdd and in rr after 1f: rdn 3f out: no prog* **66/1**	

2m 14.29s (3.79) **Going Correction** +0.40s/f (Good) **11 Ran SP% 121.0**
Speed ratings (Par 100): **100,99,98,96,95 94,93,92,90,89 89**
CSF £24.74 TOTE £2.70: £1.30, £2.90, £2.80; EX 28.30 Trifecta £117.30 Pool: £361.97. 2.19 winning units..
Owner Hamdan Al Maktoum **Bred** Shadwell Estate Company Limited **Trained** Arundel, W Sussex

FOCUS
An ordinary maiden run at a steady pace. The winning time was 0.88 seconds slower than the second division, and 0.36 seconds slower than 56-75 fillies' handicap. The form is not that solid and it is doubtful if the winner had to match her reappearance effort.
Bobster Official explanation: jockey said filly lost its action

2717 BET EURO 2008 - BETDAQ MAIDEN FILLIES' STKS (DIV II) 1m 2f

2:20 (2:24) (Class 5) 3-Y-0+ **£1,845** (£549; £274; £137) **Stalls** Low

Form				RPR
42	1		**Qui Moi (CAN)**[23] 2046 3-8-9 0 .... DaneO'Neill 10	80
			(J R Fanshawe) *chsd ldrs: wnt 2nd 3f out: led 2f out: sn rdn clr and in command: idled ins fnl f: rdn out* **4/1**[2]	
5-0	2	*1/2*	**Syvilla**[26] 1964 3-8-9 0 .... JimCrowley 6	79
			(Rae Guest) *in tch: rdn and unable qck over 2f out: styd on again ins fnl f: chsd wnr fnl 100yds: clsng on idling wnr towards fin* **66/1**	
32-2	3	*1 3/4*	**Desert Chill (USA)**[26] 1965 3-8-9 81 .... KerrinMcEvoy 7	75
			(Saeed Bin Suroor) *lw: t.k.h: led after 1f out: hdd 2f out: sn rdn: kpt on same pce fnl f* **6/4**[1]	
24-	4	*1/2*	**Full Marks**[219] 6543 3-8-9 0 .... (t) ShaneKelly 8	74
			(J Noseda) *led for 1f: chsd ldr after: rdn and unable qck jst over 2f out: edgd rt over 1f out: kpt on same pce* **6/1**[3]	
6-40	5	*7*	**Sayyedati Symphony (USA)**[21] 2105 3-8-9 94 .... DarryllHolland 9	60
			(C E Brittain) *lw: nvr travelling wl in midfield: rdn and no prog 3f out* **4/1**[2]	
0-5	6	*3 1/4*	**Rockellio (IRE)**[67] 1073 3-8-9 0 .... MichaelHills 3	54+
			(B W Hills) *a bhd: no ch fnl 3f* **14/1**	
	7	*1*	**Winners Chant (IRE)** 3-8-9 0 .... RyanMoore 1	52
			(Sir Michael Stoute) *w'like: a bhd: rdn and no hdwy 3f out* **14/1**	
0-	8	*3*	**Shraayef**[257] 5596 3-8-9 0 .... JohnEgan 2	46
			(M Botti) *unf: a bhd: no ch fnl 3f* **33/1**	
0-0	9	*3 3/4*	**Montreal (GER)**[19] 2164 3-8-9 0 .... TedDurcan 11	38
			(H R A Cecil) *chsd ldrs: rdn over 3f out: wknd qckly over 2f out* **25/1**	
	10	*34*	**Between Dreams**[21] 5-9-8 0 .... LPKeniry 5	—
			(Miss E C Lavelle) *s.i.s: a bhd: rdn and lost tch over 3f out: t.o and virtually p.u fnl f* **100/1**	

2m 13.41s (2.91) **Going Correction** +0.40s/f (Good)
WFA 3 from 5yo 13lb **10 Ran SP% 116.9**
Speed ratings (Par 100): **104,103,102,101,96 93,92,90,87,60**
CSF £245.83 TOTE £5.30: £1.60, £8.40, £1.20; EX 246.50 TRIFECTA Not won..
Owner Mrs C C Regalado-Gonzalez **Bred** Hedgestone Management **Trained** Newmarket, Suffolk

FOCUS
A reasonable maiden run at a good pace, and the better of the two divisions.The winning time was 0.88 seconds faster than the first division, and 0.52 seconds quicker than the 56-75 fillies' handicap, so the form should work out.
Sayyedati Symphony(USA) Official explanation: jockey said filly never travelled
Montreal(GER) Official explanation: jockey said filly had no more to give

2718 BACK OR LAY AT BETDAQ FILLIES' H'CAP 1m 2f

2:50 (2:52) (Class 5) (0-75,71) 4-Y-0+ **£2,331** (£693; £346; £173) **Stalls** Low

Form				RPR
0211	1		**Stringsofmyheart**[9] 2453 4-9-7 **71** 6ex .... DarryllHolland 2	82
			(Miss Gay Kelleway) *lw: mde all: pushed along at times: rdn 2f out: clr over 1f out: r.o strly* **9/2**[3]	
5-40	2	*6*	**Idesia (IRE)**[26] 1963 4-9-7 **71** .... AdamKirby 1	70
			(W R Swinburn) *lw: chsd wnr thrght: rdn wl over 2f out: hung rt u.p over 1f out: btn whn edgd lft 1f out: hld on for 2nd* **15/2**	
050-	3	*nk*	**Regal Curtsy**[230] 6278 4-8-9 **59** .... JimCrowley 6	57
			(P R Chamings) *stdd s: hld up in last: hdwy on outer 5f out: rdn wl over 2f out: kpt on but no ch w wnr fr over 1f out* **25/1**	

-124 **4** *shd* **Granary**[19] [2165] 4-9-6 **70**.............................. DaneO'Neill 3 68
(H Candy) *chsd ldrs: rdn 3f out: outpcd by wnr over 1f out: plugged on fnl f* **2/1**[1]

100 **5** *1 ¾* **Tinnarinka**[27] [1932] 4-9-2 **66**.............................. RyanMoore 4 61
(R Hannon) *hld up in last pair: rdn and effrt on inner 3f out: no ch w wnr fr over 1f out: eased towards finsh* **5/1**

34-2 **6** *14* **Jill Dawson (IRE)**[26] [1954] 5-8-11 **64**.............................. KirstyMilczarek(3) 7 53
(John Berry) *in tch in last trio: dropped to last and rdn over 3f out: no ch fnl 2f: virtually p.u ins fnl f* **5/2**[2]

2m 13.93s (3.43) **Going Correction** +0.40s/f (Good) 6 Ran SP% **112.4**
Speed ratings (Par 100): **102,97,96,96,95 84**
CSF £36.07 TOTE £4.40: £2.10, £4.20; EX 29.50.
Owner bettingjobs.com **Bred** Wretham Stud **Trained** Exning, Suffolk

FOCUS
An ordinary fillies' handicap for the grade, with the two top weights rated 4lb below the ceiling of 75. The winner produced a personal best but the form is not too solid. The winning time was 0.36 seconds quicker than the first division of the maiden, but 0.52 seconds slower than the second division.
Jill Dawson(IRE) Official explanation: jockey said mare was unsuited by the good (good to soft places) ground

2719 BET 3RD TEST - BETDAQ H'CAP 1m 3f 106y
3:20 (3:20) (Class 6) (0-60,61) 3-Y-O **£2,047** (£604; £302) **Stalls** High

Form RPR

0-66 **1** **Love And Glory (FR)**[23] [2045] 3-9-4 **59**.............................. RyanMoore 4 70
(G L Moore) *hld up in midfield: hdwy over 3f out: chsd ldr 2f out: led over 1f out: sn rdn clr: in command whn flashed tail ins fnl f* **3/1**[2]

-641 **2** *3 ½* **Captain Mainwaring**[8] [2475] 3-9-1 **61** 6ex.............................. JackMitchell(5) 10 66
(N P Littmoden) *lw: sn chsng ldr: led over 3f out: rdn 3f out: hdd over 1f out sn outpcd by wnr: kpt on* **5/2**[1]

00-0 **3** *½* **Potemkin (USA)**[15] [2280] 3-9-0 **55**.............................. DaneO'Neill 7 59
(A King) *stdd after s: t.k.h: hld up towards rr: hdwy over 4f out: styd on u.p fr over 2f out: wnt 3rd towards fin: no ch w wnr* **12/1**[3]

00-0 **4** *¾* **All Lit Up**[15] [2280] 3-8-12 **53**.............................. FergusSweeney 12 56
(A King) *lw: bhd: rdn and hanging lft fr over 3f out: styd on u.p: wnt 4th towards fin: nvr trbld ldrs* **12/1**[3]

00-5 **5** *1 ¾* **Aleatricis**[16] [2247] 3-8-4 **45**.............................. DO'Donohoe 11 45
(Sir Mark Prescott) *lw: s.i.s: rdn along to chse ldrs after 2f: reminders 7f out: chsd ldr u.p jst over 2f out tl 2f out: one pce after: lost 2 pls fnl 100yds* **5/2**[1]

0-00 **6** *1* **Abfabfong (IRE)**[27] [1938] 3-8-5 **46**.............................. (v[1]) FrankieMcDonald 6 44
(Mrs L C Jewell) *hld up in tch in midfield: rdn and effrt 3f out: one pce and hung lft u.p after: nvr threatened ldrs* **66/1**

0-00 **7** *6* **Lady Petrus**[16] [2244] 3-9-0 **55**.............................. JamesDoyle 8 43
(H J L Dunlop) *hld up towards rr: swtchd rt and effrt jst over 3f out: hung lft over 2f out: no imp* **16/1**

46-0 **8** *¾* **Poppy Dean (IRE)**[63] [1147] 3-9-2 **57**.............................. TPQueally 2 44
(J G Portman) *t.k.h: chsd ldrs: wnt 2nd 3f out: sn rdn: lost 2nd over 2f out: wknd qckly over 1f out* **33/1**

00-0 **9** *3 ¼* **Great Future**[46] [1477] 3-8-7 **48**.............................. SimonWhitworth 5 29
(J R Holt) *a bhd: rdn 3f out: and no hdwy 3f out: plugged on past btn horses fnl f* **80/1**

600 **10** *4 ½* **Hoar Frost**[18] [2197] 3-9-1 **56**.............................. SamHitchcott 14 30
(M R Channon) *s.i.s: a bhd: rdn 8f out: wl bhd fnl 3f* **25/1**

00-5 **11** *5* **Teadancer (IRE)**[43] [1553] 3-8-13 **54**.............................. JimCrowley 9 19
(J G Portman) *hld up in tch: rdn 3f out: wknd qckly over 2f out: wl bhd fnl f* **16/1**

-000 **12** *7* **Whatalotofbuts**[27] [1938] 3-8-7 **48**.............................. (p) LPKeniry 3 1
(B De Haan) *a towards rr: pushed along 7f out: t.o fnl 2f* **50/1**

0100 **13** *6* **Rosy Dawn**[37] [1681] 3-8-7 **55**.............................. (b) SophieDoyle(7) 1 —
(Ms J S Doyle) *led tl over 3f out: wknd qckly over 2f out: t.o* **33/1**

-U06 **14** *½* **Malt Empress (IRE)**[68] [1054] 3-8-11 **52**.............................. LiamJones 15 —
(B W Duke) *s.i.s: a bhd: t.o fnl 2f* **33/1**

2m 36.24s (4.74) **Going Correction** +0.40s/f (Good) 14 Ran SP% **126.6**
Speed ratings (Par 97): **98,95,95,94,93 92,88,87,85,82 78,73,68,68**
CSF £11.02 CT £84.26 TOTE £3.80: £1.80, £1.70, £3.30; EX 12.90 Trifecta £39.90 Pool: £317.06. 5.64 winning units..
Owner Paul Hancock **Bred** Petra Bloodstock Agency Ltd **Trained** Woodingdean, E Sussex

FOCUS
Modest quality, but a big field and a competitive handicap of its type especially with several being backed. Solid form from the first two.
Love And Glory(FR) Official explanation: jockey said, regarding running, that the colt appreciated the drop in class after its last run on good to firm ground
Lady Petrus Official explanation: jockey said filly hung left in straight
Teadancer(IRE) Official explanation: jockey said filly was unsuited by the good (good to soft places) ground

2720 LOOK FOR BETTER ODDS AT BETDAQ (S) STKS 5f (P)
3:50 (3:50) (Class 6) 2-Y-O **£1,774** (£523; £262) **Stalls** High

Form RPR

3355 **1** **Just The Lady**[28] [1914] 2-8-1 0.............................. JackDean(5) 4 64+
(W G M Turner) *lw: mde all: in command fr 1/2-way: eased ins fnl f: v easily* **30/100**[1]

6 **2** *4* **Inn Swinger (IRE)**[9] [2459] 2-8-3 0.............................. LukeMorris(3) 2 46+
(W G M Turner) *leggy: chsd wnr for 1f and again over 2f out: kpt on but no ch w wnr* **22/1**

3 *6* **Twinkle De Star** 2-8-6 0.............................. LPKeniry 6 24
(J S Moore) *leggy: s.i.s: outpcd in last: hdwy 2f out: wnt modest 3rd 1f out: nvr nr ldng pair* **8/1**[2]

5446 **4** *2* **Talulah Bells**[6] [2548] 2-8-7 0 ow1.............................. (b[1]) ShaneKelly 3 18
(A W Carroll) *s.i.s: racd off the pce in midfield: rdn 1/2-way: no ch fnl f* **12/1**[3]

65 **5** *1 ¼* **The Wonkey Donkey**[7] [2508] 2-8-6 0.............................. (p) GregFairley 5 12
(K J Burke) *leggy: bhd: rdn 1/2-way: wl bhd fnl 2f* **16/1**

05 **6** *2 ½* **Champagne Leader**[6] [2548] 2-8-6 0.............................. SamHitchcott 1 3
(A B Haynes) *leggy: lt-f: s.i.s: pushed up to chse wnr after 1f tl over 2f out: wknd* **14/1**

60.85 secs (2.05) **Going Correction** 0.0s/f (Stan) 6 Ran SP% **112.6**
Speed ratings (Par 91): **83,76,67,63,61 57**
CSF £9.67 TOTE £1.30: £1.10, £6.40; EX 9.90.The winner was sold to I Bishop for 7,800gns
Owner Mrs M S Teversham **Bred** Mrs Monica Teversham **Trained** Sigwells, Somerset

FOCUS
A very poor race and a slow time, even for a seller. This race will not live long in the memory and the form amounts to nothing, with the winner making light of a simple task. She did not have to match her previous form.

NOTEBOOK
Just The Lady, whose trainer has a fine record in this race, had finished fifth in the Lily Agnes at Chester last time and could hardly have been in more contrasting company here. All she had to do was go down to the start, ping the gates, and saunter back.and she would hardly have known that she had even been in a race. She was sold for 7,800gns at the subsequent auction and now joins Ollie Pears. (op 4-11 tchd 2-7, 2-5 in places)
Inn Swinger(IRE), a tailed-off last in a Leicester claimer on her debut, was always in about the same place and though finishing a clear second, was totally outclassed by her stable companion. This was an improvement, but she probably still did not achieve much. (op 20-1 tchd 25-1)
Twinkle De Star, out of a half-sister to a winner at up to 1m4f in France, plugged on from the back to finish a very remote third. She may improve for further, but will need to come on a huge amount from this to have any chance of ever winning a race. (op 9-1)
Talulah Bells, the most experienced of these, is already exposed as very poor and this switch to Polytrack and first-time blinkers failed to bring about any improvement. (tchd 10-1 and 14-1)
The Wonkey Donkey, well beaten in two previous outings at a similar level, even managed to regress from those efforts here.
Champagne Leader may have had only very moderate form to her name, but even so she seems to be going the wrong way. Official explanation: jockey said filly veered left at start (op 12-1 tchd 16-1)

2721 BET EPSOM DERBY - BETDAQ CLAIMING STKS 6f (P)
4:20 (4:20) (Class 6) 3-Y-O+ **£1,774** (£523; £262) **Stalls** Low

Form RPR

445 **1** **Marko Jadeo (IRE)**[37] [1670] 10-8-11 60.............................. KevinGhunowa(3) 1 57
(R A Harris) *taken down early: t.k.h: chsd ldr: rdn 3f out: styd on u.p fnl f to ld fnl 75yds* **11/2**

-336 **2** *nk* **One More Round (USA)**[15] [2277] 10-8-11 75.............................. (b) RichardEvans(7) 7 60
(Ollie Pears) *lw: hld up in rr: hdwy 2f out: swtchd rt jst over 1f out: rdn and r.o fnl f: wnt 2nd wl ins fnl f: nt quite rch wnr* **5/2**[1]

000- **3** *nk* **Half A Tsar (IRE)**[27] [5947] 4-8-9 45.............................. JackDean(5) 8 55
(Mark Gillard) *led: rdn 2f out: clr over 1f out: worn down and hdd wl ins fnl f: lost 2nd towards fin* **40/1**

4000 **4** *2 ¼* **Southwest Star (IRE)**[26] [1958] 3-8-12 70.............................. (b[1]) LPKeniry 2 52
(J S Moore) *chsd ldrs on outer: rdn over 2f out: wknd jst ins fnl f* **8/1**

-405 **5** *nk* **James Dean (IRE)**[8] [2480] 3-8-13 75.............................. DTDaSilva(7) 5 59
(P F I Cole) *lw: wnt lft s: sn pushed up into midfield: rdn and unable qck jst over 2f out: kpt on again ins fnl f* **9/1**

6522 **6** *nk* **Fly In Johnny (IRE)**[8] [2480] 3-8-5 62.............................. PatrickHills(3) 3 46
(R Hannon) *in tch: hdwy 3f out: drvn and nt qckn 2f out: kpt on again ins fnl f* **11/4**[2]

0300 **7** *nk* **Scarlett Heart (IRE)**[16] [2255] 4-8-11 53.............................. PaulDoe 4 42
(S Curran) *stdd s: hld up bhd: hdwy on outer over 2f out: hrd rdn and unable qck 2f out: kpt on again ins fnl f* **9/2**[3]

-400 **8** *1 ¼* **Ile Royale**[30] [1870] 3-8-7 55.............................. (v) RichardSmith 6 40
(B R Johnson) *t.k.h: hld up in tch: hdwy over 3f out: rdn jst over 2f out: sn outpcd: wknd fnl f* **20/1**

1m 13.14s (1.24) **Going Correction** 0.0s/f (Stan)
WFA 3 from 4yo+ 8lb 8 Ran SP% **117.1**
Speed ratings (Par 101): **91,90,90,87,86 86,86,84**
CSF £20.21 TOTE £7.10: £2.10, £1.40, £6.30; EX 23.80 Trifecta £480.40 Part won. Pool: £676.72. 0.30 winning units..
Owner Ron Harris & David Thornton **Bred** P Casey **Trained** Earlswood, Monmouths

FOCUS
A moderate claimer, contested by horses of very varied ability, and the finish was fought out between a pair of ten-year-olds. The pace was surprisingly moderate for a sprint and the winning time was slow. The close proximity of a 45-rated horse in third does nothing for the form either.

2722 CASH BONUS @ BETDAQPOKER.CO.UK H'CAP 1m (P)
4:50 (4:50) (Class 5) (0-75,75) 4-Y-O+ **£2,331** (£693; £346; £173) **Stalls** High

Form RPR

0-00 **1** **Glencalvie (IRE)**[25] [1996] 7-9-3 **71**.............................. (p) IanMongan 11 81
(J Akehurst) *mde all: rdn 2f out: styd on strly fnl f: eased nr fin* **33/1**

352- **2** *2* **Carmenero (GER)**[159] [7253] 5-9-5 **73**.............................. DO'Donohoe 5 78
(W R Muir) *trckd ldrs: disp 2nd 2f out: chsd wnr and rdn 1f out: unable qck and btn fnl 100yds* **5/1**[3]

5-15 **3** *1* **Mumbleswerve (IRE)**[27] [1936] 4-9-7 **75**.............................. KerrinMcEvoy 12 78
(W Jarvis) *t.k.h: chsd ldrs: disp 2nd 2f out: sn hanging lft: one pce fnl f* **3/1**[1]

3-26 **4** *½* **Effigy**[35] [1732] 4-8-9 **63**.............................. DaneO'Neill 4 65
(H Candy) *in tch in midfield: rdn and sltly outpcd jst over 2f out: styd on again u.p fnl f: nt pce to threaten ldrs* **11/2**

-260 **5** *hd* **Murrin (IRE)**[14] [2308] 4-9-5 **73**.............................. JimCrowley 8 74+
(T G Mills) *midfield whn clipped heels and stmbld after 1f: rn in snatches after: hdwy u.p 2f out: styd on fnl f: nt rch ldrs* **7/2**[2]

0-00 **6** *3* **Coeur Courageux (FR)**[13] [2329] 6-8-13 **67**.............................. FergusSweeney 6 62
(G L Moore) *hld up in last trio: hdwy over 2f out: rdn wl over 1f out: no imp fnl f* **14/1**

5106 **7** *2* **Millfield (IRE)**[13] [2329] 5-9-4 **72**.............................. FrancisNorton 1 62+
(P R Chamings) *taken down early: s.i.s: t.k.h: hld up in rr: hdwy on inner 2f out: nt clr run over 1f out: swtchd rt 1f out: n.d* **15/2**

1200 **8** *¾* **Dushstorm (IRE)**[16] [2262] 7-8-12 **66**.............................. LiamJones 2 54
(C R Dore) *s.i.s: hld up towards rr: effrt on inner 2f out: swtchd rt jst over 1f out: n.d* **14/1**

-000 **9** *2 ¼* **Golden Brown (IRE)**[16] [2243] 4-8-2 **56** oh1.............................. (b) AdrianMcCarthy 10 39
(David Pinder) *in tch: hdwy and rdn over 3f out: wknd wl over 1f out* **33/1**

0-66 **10** *shd* **Lopinot (IRE)**[135] [246] 5-8-11 **70**.............................. HaddenFrost(5) 9 53
(M R Bosley) *a towards rr: n.d* **12/1**

1230 **11** *2 ½* **Wrighty Almighty (IRE)**[97] [730] 6-9-0 **68**.............................. PaulDoe 7 45
(P R Chamings) *s.i.s: a bhd* **12/1**

1-60 **12** *1 ½* **Power Ballad**[38] [1645] 4-8-13 **67**.............................. AmirQuinn 3 41
(W J Knight) *chsd ldr tl 2f out: wknd rapidly over 1f out* **33/1**

1m 37.59s (-0.61) **Going Correction** 0.0s/f (Stan) 12 Ran SP% **128.6**
Speed ratings (Par 103): **103,101,100,99,99 96,94,93,91,91 88,87**
CSF £204.69 CT £676.90 TOTE £26.90: £5.70, £2.30, £1.90; EX 203.50 Trifecta £313.60 Place 6: £50.87, Place 5: £23.34. Part won. Pool: £441.79. 0.10 winning units..
Owner Tattenham Corner Racing **Bred** Top Of The Form Syndicate **Trained** Epsom, Surrey
■ Stewards' Enquiry : Adrian McCarthy four-day ban: careless riding (Jun 26-29)

FOCUS
An ordinary handicap, but they did go a solid pace thanks to the winner. The first three were always up with the pace. Sound form.
T/Plt: £48.40 to a £1 stake. Pool: £55,025.25. 829.70 winning tickets. T/Qpdt: £15.10 to a £1 stake. Pool: £3,713.08. 181.20 winning tickets. SP

1997 NOTTINGHAM (L-H)

Wednesday, June 4

2723 Meeting Abandoned - Waterlogged

2696 RIPON (R-H)

Wednesday, June 4

OFFICIAL GOING: Soft (7.6)

The ground, heavy the previous day, had dried out and was described as 'very sticky, tacky'.

Wind: almost nil Weather: fine and sunny

2730 EURA AUDIT UK YORKSHIRE'S SMALL BUSINESS ACCOUNTANTS MAIDEN STKS — 6f
6:50 (6:50) (Class 5) 2-Y-O £2,914 (£867; £433; £216) Stalls Low

Form RPR

4 1 **Sweet Smile (IRE)**[25] 1987 2-9-3 0 ... NCallan 1 70
(K A Ryan) *chsd ldr: swtchd rt after 1f: styd on to ld last 150yds: kpt on wl towards fin* 11/8[1]

2 *nk* **Becausewecan (USA)** 2-9-3 0 ... JoeFanning 2 69
(M Johnston) *s.i.s: sn chsng ldrs: chal ins fnl f: no ex nr fin* 9/2[3]

4 3 *1 1/4* **Lookafternumberone (IRE)**[13] 2331 2-9-3 0 ... PaulHanagan 4 65
(J G Given) *led: swtchd lft after 1f: rdr lost whip 1f out: hung rt and hdd jst ins fnl f: kpt on same pce* 2/1[2]

4 *4* **Scarth Hill (IRE)** 2-9-3 0 ... RoystonFfrench 6 53
(Mrs A Duffield) *swvd rt s: sn outpcd and drvn along: kpt on fnl 2f: nvr on terms* 8/1

5 *11* **Shifting Gold (IRE)** 2-9-3 0 ... PaulMulrennan 5 21
(K A Ryan) *s.i.s: reminders and swtchd lft after 1f: a wl outpcd* 20/1

1m 16.46s (3.46) **Going Correction** +0.275s/f (Good) **5 Ran SP% 109.5**
Speed ratings (Par 93): **87,86,84,79,64**
CSF £7.84 TOTE £2.50: £1.50, £2.30; EX 7.60.
Owner Brendan P Hayes **Bred** Kilfrush Stud **Trained** Hambleton, N Yorks

FOCUS
A modest maiden in all probability but the winner will improve again and the runner-up will come on a good deal for this first outing. The third sets the standard.

NOTEBOOK
Sweet Smile(IRE), still carrying plenty of condition, did enough in the end and will improve again. (op 13-8 tchd 6-5)
Becausewecan(USA) ◆, a May foal, has size and scope and was noisy in the paddock. Racing wide of the other two after a tardy start, in the end he was just held at bay. This will have taught him plenty and he looks a ready-made winner. (op 5-2 tchd 5-1)
Lookafternumberone(IRE), on his toes beforehand, cut out the pace but hung away from the fence and his rider's whip was knocked out of his hand. (op 11-4)
Scarth Hill(IRE), whose dam won over 1m4f, is not the best of movers. Ducking right leaving the stalls, he kept on in his own time and will do better over further in time. (op 12-1 tchd 15-2)
Shifting Gold(IRE), a March foal, looked to be carrying tons of condition. He made a tardy start and was soon being run off his feet. (op 12-1 tchd 25-1 in a place)

2731 TONY AND GERRY NOW (S) H'CAP — 1m 4f 10y
7:20 (7:20) (Class 6) (0-60,49) 4-5-Y-O £2,590 (£770; £385; £192) Stalls High

Form RPR

/0-5 1 **Elite Land**[18] 2185 5-9-2 47 ... JimmyQuinn 7 52
(N Bycroft) *prom: drvn over 1f out: led 1f out: jst hld on* 7/1[3]

0-06 2 *hd* **Psycho Cat**[12] 2374 5-8-12 46 ... DuranFentiman(3) 12 51
(W M Brisbourne) *s.s: in rr: hdwy over 3f out: hung bdly lft 2f out: ended up stands' side: fin strly: jst failed* 20/1

30-6 3 *3/4* **Leprechaun's Gold (IRE)**[20] 1694 4-9-0 45 ... NCallan 11 48
(B J Llewellyn) *mid-div: effrt and nt clr run 3f out: styd on wl fnl f* 15/2

640- 4 *1 1/2* **Cecina Marina**[229] 6308 5-8-9 45 ... KellyHarrison(5) 2 46
(Mrs K Walton) *w ldrs: led 3f out tl 1f out: kpt on same pce* 9/1

4425 5 *hd* **Cape Dancer (IRE)**[26] 1968 4-8-11 45 ... PJMcDonald(3) 9 46
(J S Wainwright) *mid-div: effrt over 3f out: nvr rchd ldrs* 8/1

0406 6 *1 1/4* **Skye But N Ben**[9] 2456 4-9-3 48 ... (p) PaulMulrennan 10 47
(G A Harker) *hld up in rr: hdwy on ins 4f out: nvr nr ldrs* 8/1

-002 7 *1 1/2* **Classic Hall (IRE)**[36] 1694 5-9-0 45 ... JoeFanning 5 41
(J Akehurst) *led after 1f: hdd 3f out: wknd fnl f* 7/1[3]

3-00 8 *4* **Fire In Cairo (IRE)**[11] 2290 4-8-8 46 ... (t) PatrickDonaghy(7) 3 36
(P C Haslam) *dwlt: sn prom: wknd over 2f out* 11/2[2]

-000 9 *nk* **Ellies Faith**[12] 2365 4-9-0 45 ... AndrewElliott 6 34
(L R James) *led 1f: chsd ldrs: drvn over 4f out: wknd 2f out* 40/1

0006 10 *9* **Prince Rossi (IRE)**[43] 1528 4-9-1 46 ... (p) HayleyTurner 4 21
(A E Price) *dwlt: hld up in rr: effrt over 4f out: nvr a factor: bhd fnl 2f* 9/2[1]

000 11 *6* **Slivovic (IRE)**[18] 2207 4-8-7 45 ... JamesRogers(7) 8 10
(J S Wainwright) *mid-div: drvn 7f out: lost pl over 2f out: sn bhd* 18/1

2m 43.91s (7.21) **Going Correction** +0.275s/f (Good) **11 Ran SP% 115.0**
Speed ratings: **86,85,85,84,84 83,82,79,79,73 69**
CSF £133.96 CT £1076.77 TOTE £8.20: £2.80, £3.20, £2.70; EX 162.40.There was no bid for the winner
Owner Mrs J Dickinson **Bred** T Umpleby **Trained** Brandsby, N Yorks

FOCUS
A very slow winning time, even for a seller. Rock-bottom stuff with the weight range just 3lb.
Prince Rossi(IRE) Official explanation: jockey said gelding missed the break

2732 SKY TELEVISION H'CAP — 6f
7:50 (7:50) (Class 4) (0-85,82) 3-Y-O £4,533 (£1,348; £674; £336) Stalls Low

Form RPR

0113 1 **Great Charm (IRE)**[19] 2141 3-9-2 77 ... NCallan 6 87
(M L W Bell) *chsd ldrs: led 1f out: styd on wl: readily* 3/1[3]

6221 2 *2* **Rio Sands**[15] 2283 3-8-8 72 ... MichaelJStainton(3) 8 75
(R M Whitaker) *w ldr: led over 2f out: hdd 1f out: no ex* 11/2

4-12 3 *1 1/2* **Mission Impossible**[9] 2460 3-8-7 75 ... PatrickDonaghy(7) 3 73
(P C Haslam) *chsd ldrs: styd on same pce fnl 2f* 9/4[1]

0010 4 *7* **Storey Hill (USA)**[36] 1707 3-9-2 77 ... DeanMcKeown 5 53
(D Shaw) *rrd s: hld up: hdwy and drvn along over 3f out: wknd 2f out* 18/1

0-4 5 *8* **Legal Eagle (IRE)**[27] 1925 3-9-7 82 ... RobertHavlin 1 32
(J H M Gosden) *led: hung rt and hdd over 2f out: sn wknd: eased ins fnl f* 5/2[2]

1-50 6 *17* **Incomparable**[46] 1484 3-9-3 78 ... (b[1]) PatCosgrave 2 —
(A J McCabe) *chsd ldrs: sn drvn along: lost pl over 2f out: sn bhd and eased* 14/1

1m 14.44s (1.44) **Going Correction** +0.275s/f (Good) **6 Ran SP% 111.7**
Speed ratings (Par 101): **101,98,96,87,76 53**
CSF £19.15 CT £41.47 TOTE £3.40: £2.00, £3.10; EX 24.70.
Owner Mr & Mrs G Middlebrook **Bred** G And Mrs Middlebrook **Trained** Newmarket, Suffolk

FOCUS
The winner is going the right way and the form looks sound at this level rated through the placed horses.
Legal Eagle(IRE) Official explanation: trainer had no explanation for the poor form shown
Incomparable Official explanation: jockey said gelding was unsuited by the soft ground

2733 DIRECTORS CUP (H'CAP) — 1m
8:20 (8:20) (Class 3) (0-95,87) 4-Y-O **£7,885** (£2,360; £1,180; £590; £293) Stalls High

Form RPR

1216 1 **Exit Smiling**[41] 1590 6-8-7 76 ... JamieMoriarty(3) 2 91
(P T Midgley) *hld up: smooth hdwy over 3f out: led over 1f out: shot clr: v readily* 20/1

225- 2 *5* **Observatory Star (IRE)**[219] 6539 5-8-12 78 ... (p) DavidAllan 6 81
(T D Easterby) *hld up in rr: nt clr run and swtchd outside over 1f out: tk 2nd jst ins fnl f: no ch w wnr* 6/1

4300 3 *3/4* **Wigwam Willie (IRE)**[28] 1910 6-9-0 80 ... (p) NCallan 5 81
(K A Ryan) *chsd ldrs: kpt on same pce appr fnl f* 4/1[1]

0240 4 *3* **Moheebb (IRE)**[26] 1970 4-8-9 75 ... (b) JoeFanning 10 69+
(Mrs R A Carr) *hld up: effrt in ins 4f out: nt clr run tl swtchd lft ins fnl f: kpt on* 8/1

0-03 5 *nk* **Billy Dane (IRE)**[18] 2200 4-9-0 80 ... PaulHanagan 9 74
(R A Fahey) *trckd ldrs: effrt over 2f out: fdd over 1f out* 4/1[1]

0-06 6 *1* **Vicious Warrior**[17] 2218 9-9-2 82 ... DeanMcKeown 4 73
(R M Whitaker) *led tl over 1f out: sn fdd* 11/2[3]

1023 7 *hd* **Tencendur (IRE)**[29] 1891 4-8-11 77 ... SilvestreDeSousa 1 68
(D Nicholls) *trckd ldrs: chal over 2f out: fdd fnl f* 8/1

-612 8 *10* **Crocodile Bay (IRE)**[6] 2535 5-9-7 87 ... TonyHamilton 3 55
(D W Barker) *w ldrs: wknd 2f out: eased ins fnl f* 9/2[2]

1m 42.2s (0.80) **Going Correction** +0.275s/f (Good) **8 Ran SP% 114.8**
Speed ratings (Par 107): **107,102,101,98,97 96,96,86**
CSF £134.53 CT £591.47 TOTE £21.60: £4.60, £2.50, £2.10; EX 127.00.
Owner Peter Mee **Bred** Mrs D O Joly **Trained** Westow, N Yorks

FOCUS
They went a strong gallop in the conditions and the first two came from way off the pace. The form looks very solid at this level rated through the placed horses.

NOTEBOOK
Exit Smiling, absent for six weeks after finishing distressed at Southwell, was ridden with bags of confidence. He came there travelling strongly and had this won in a matter of strides when popped the question. He is a credit to his trainer. (op 14-1 tchd 25-1 in a place)
Observatory Star(IRE), who ended last term in good form, resumed 10lb higher than his last success. Put to sleep at the back, he had to be pulled wide for a run but the winner had flown. (op 11-2 tchd 5-1)
Wigwam Willie(IRE), back on his last winning mark, had the ground in his favour but he had no excuse whatsoever. (op 9-2 tchd 5-1)
Moheebb(IRE), given a three-week break, was drawn against the rail and he found himself trapped there all the way up the home straight. Only able to pull wide inside the last, he looked to finish full of running. Official explanation: jockey said gelding was denied a clear run (tchd 9-1)
Billy Dane(IRE), who has slipped to a lenient mark, in the end did not see it out on this sticky ground. (op 6-1)
Vicious Warrior, 1lb lower than his last winning mark, won the battle for the lead but he did too much and was readily picked off in the end. (op 5-1 tchd 9-2 and 6-1)
Crocodile Bay(IRE), 8lb higher than Beverley, has changed stables in the last week since Newcastle. He lost the battle for the lead and, in the end dropping right out, was heavily eased. Official explanation: trainer had no explanation for the poor form shown (op 11-2 tchd 4-1)

2734 RIPON FARM SERVICES H'CAP — 2m
8:50 (8:50) (Class 5) (0-75,73) 4-Y-O+ £2,914 (£867; £433; £216) Stalls Low

Form RPR

303/ 1 **Ritsi**[649] 4777 5-8-10 62 ... PJMcDonald(3) 3 68
(Grant Tuer) *trckd ldrs: nt clr run over 2f out: barged through over 1f out: led ins fnl f: hld on wl* 15/2[3]

2212 2 *1/2* **Danzatrice**[5] 2577 6-9-2 65 ... RobertWinston 6 70
(C W Thornton) *dwlt: hld up: shkn up over 6f out: hdwy to trck ldrs 4f out: rdn and upsides whn bmpd over 1f out: upsides ins fnl f: no ex* 2/5[1]

254- 3 *2 1/2* **Industrial Star (IRE)**[269] 5256 7-9-6 69 ... (p) TonyHamilton 1 71
(Micky Hammond) *led tl over 2f out: upsides ins fnl f: one pce* 11/2[2]

00/0 4 *1 3/4* **Fair Spin**[51] 1017 8-8-5 54 oh9 ... (p) PaulHanagan 4 54
(Micky Hammond) *trckd ldr: chal 4f out: slt ld over 2f out: hdd ins fnl f: wknd towards fin* 16/1

0000 5 *36* **Mozayada (USA)**[9] 2467 4-8-4 54 oh2 ... JoeFanning 7 11
(M Brittain) *hld up in last: effrt over 3f out: wknd over 2f out: eased fnl f* 16/1

3m 44.39s (12.59) **Going Correction** +0.275s/f (Good)
WFA 4 from 5yo+ 1lb **5 Ran SP% 110.3**
Speed ratings (Par 103): **79,78,77,76,58**
CSF £11.29 TOTE £9.60: £2.80, £1.10; EX 13.80.
Owner G Tuer **Bred** Haras Du Bois Carrouges & Hammersfield Bloodstock **Trained** Birkby, N Yorks
■ Stewards' Enquiry : P J McDonald four-day ban: careless riding (Jun 22-25)

FOCUS
A pedestrian winning time for the class and four upsides inside the final furlong. The actual top-weight was 6lb below the race ceiling and the winner had to barge his way out. The out-of-the-handicap fourth limits the form.

2735 EURA AUDIT UK MAIDEN STKS — 1m 1f 170y
9:20 (9:21) (Class 5) 3-Y-O+ £2,914 (£867; £433; £216) Stalls High

Form RPR

3-22 1 **Wood Chorus**[29] 1905 3-8-6 78 ... HayleyTurner 15 76+
(M L W Bell) *trckd ldrs: t.k.h: led over 2f out: drvn clr ins fnl f* 8/15[1]

3/ 2 *3 3/4* **Alqaahir (USA)**[1358] 5570 6-9-10 0 ... RobertWinston 6 74
(J S Wainwright) *tracd ldrs: effrt 3f out: wnt 2nd over 1f out: hung rt and no imp* 8/1[3]

2 3 *8* **Hollins**[12] 2363 4-9-10 0 ... PaulHanagan 14 57
(Micky Hammond) *led: hdd over 2f out: one pce* 5/1[2]

0 4 *8* **Doctor Delta**[17] 2221 3-8-8 0 ... MarkLawson(3) 8 40
(M Brittain) *s.i.s: hdwy and in tch 4f out: hrd rdn: one pce* 50/1

0 5 *3* **Micallef**[7] 2500 3-8-7 0 ow1 ... TonyHamilton 5 29
(R A Fahey) *in rr: sn pushed along: nvr a factor* 33/1

000- 6 *2 1/4* **Firestorm (IRE)**[245] 5906 4-9-10 41 ... PaulMulrennan 12 30
(C W Fairhurst) *in tch: hdwy 4f out: wknd over 2f out* 33/1

5 7 1 1/2 **Arch**[31] 1825 5-9-10 0 PatrickMathers 16 26
(A M Crow) *s.s: sme hdwy on outer over 3f out: wknd 2f out* **50/1**
-0 8 6 **Missycomelightly**[50] 1382 5-9-5 0 TomEaves 7 9
(W J H Ratcliffe) *in rr: hdwy 6f out: lost pl over 2f out* **50/1**
50 9 107 **Sir John Lilley (USA)**[16] 2246 3-8-11 JoeFanning 11 —
(M Johnston) *chsd ldrs: lost pl and eased 3f out: sn wl bhd: hopelessly t.o* **10/1**
2m 10.03s (4.63) **Going Correction** +0.275s/f (Good)
WFA 3 from 4yo+ 13lb 9 Ran SP% **113.9**
Speed ratings (Par 103): **92,89,82,76,73 72,70,66,—**
CSF £5.07 TOTE £1.50: £1.02, £2.20, £1.80; EX 4.20 Place 6 £ 62.66, Place 5 £ 40.75.
Owner H J P Farr **Bred** Worksop Manor Stud **Trained** Newmarket, Suffolk

FOCUS
A modest winning time. No strength in depth to this maiden, in which there were seven non-runners, and the 78-rated winner was not winning out of turn.
Sir John Lilley(USA) Official explanation: trainer had no explanation for the poor form shown
T/Plt: £90.60 to a £1 stake. Pool: £75,862.15. 611.18 winning tickets. T/Qpdt: £9.30 to a £1 stake. Pool: £5,331.39. 421.00 winning tickets. WG

2736 - 2737a (Foreign Racing) - See Raceform Interactive

2514 LEOPARDSTOWN (L-H)
Wednesday, June 4

OFFICIAL GOING: Good to firm

2738a BALLYOGAN STKS (GROUP 3) (F&M) 6f
7:00 (7:06) 3-Y-O+ **£33,455** (£9,779; £4,632; £1,544)

RPR
1 **Age Of Chivalry (IRE)**[21] 2111 3-8-12 103 FMBerry 4 106
(John M Oxx, Ire) *hld up: 7th appr st: 5th over 1f out: kpt on wl u.p to ld last strides* **8/1**
2 hd **Eastern Romance**[38] 1659 3-8-12 FergalLynch 2 105
(K A Ryan) *trckd ldr in 2nd: impr to ld 1f out: strly pressed cl home: hdd last strides* **16/1**
3 1 1/4 **Cartimandua**[25] 2000 4-9-6 GrahamGibbons 9 103
(E S McMahon) *trckd ldrs: 3rd 3f out: 2nd 1f out: kpt on same pce ins fnl f* **9/4**[1]
4 1/2 **Campfire Glow (IRE)**[30] 1880 3-9-3 106 PJSmullen 5 105
(D K Weld, Ire) *chsd ldrs: 5th 3f out: 3rd 1f out: kpt on wl cl home* **8/1**
5 nk **Aleagueoftheirown (IRE)**[303] 4237 4-9-6 97 WMLordan 11 101
(David Wachman, Ire) *hld up: 7th 2f out: kpt on to go 5th cl home* **25/1**
6 1 1/4 **Forthefirstime**[263] 5435 3-8-12 99 MJKinane 10 95
(John M Oxx, Ire) *hld up: sme late prog on outer st: kpt on wout threatening fnl f* **9/1**
7 nk **That's Hot (IRE)**[264] 5392 5-9-6 102 JMurtagh 8 96
(G M Lyons, Ire) *mid-div: 6th 3f out: kpt on one pce fnl f* **10/1**
8 1 3/4 **Emily Blake (IRE)**[30] 1880 4-9-6 100 PTownend 3 91
(J C Hayden, Ire) *chsd ldrs: 4th 3f out: pushed along and no imp fr 2f out* **11/1**
9 5 1/2 **My Girl Sophie (USA)**[2] 2684 3-8-12 98 KJManning 1 72
(J S Bolger, Ire) *led: hdd over 1f out: no ex ins fnl f* **13/2**[3]
10 3 1/2 **Manzila (FR)**[18] 2211 5-9-6 AdrianTNicholls 6 64
(D Nicholls) *mid-div: 7th 3f out: rdn and no imp st* **9/2**[2]
1m 14.64s (0.54) **Going Correction** +0.10s/f (Good)
WFA 3 from 4yo+ 8lb 11 Ran SP% **121.7**
Speed ratings: **100,99,98,97,97 95,94,92,85,80**
CSF £132.44 TOTE £11.40: £2.60, £3.60, £1.10; DF 188.20.
Owner Plantation Stud **Bred** Perle O'Rourke **Trained** Currabeg, Co Kildare

NOTEBOOK
Age Of Chivalry(IRE), so narrowly denied under top weight in handicap company last month, this time got the better of a bobbing finish and registered a deserved success. She is developing into a consistent sprinter and this was undoubtedly her best effort to date, so she ought to still have a more to offer this season. (op 9/1)
Eastern Romance posted another improved effort, but yet again had to settle for the silver medal. She was nicely clear of the remainder at the finish, helps to set the standard of this form, and richly deserves a change of fortune now. (op 10/1)
Cartimandua, chasing a four-timer, had her chance yet probably would have found the recent easing of the ground against her. There will still be other days for her. (op 100/30)
Campfire Glow(IRE) did little wrong in defeat, but looked to find this sharper test against her. She is in danger of becoming a "tripless" filly at present, but still has the class for this sort of grade all the same and is worthy of another chance. (op 7/1)

2740a GLENCAIRN STKS (LISTED RACE) 1m
8:00 (8:00) 4-Y-O+ **£23,933** (£7,022; £3,345; £1,139)

RPR
1 **Mustameet (USA)**[374] 2064 7-9-1 111 CPGeoghegan 3 105+
(Kevin Prendergast, Ire) *settled 3rd: impr into 2nd 3f out: chal 1f out: disp ld under 1f out: kpt on wl to ld cl home* **3/1**[2]
2 1/2 **Akua'Ba (IRE)**[11] 2420 4-8-12 89 (tp) KJManning 2 101
(J S Bolger, Ire) *settled 4th: 3rd appr st: disp ld under 1f out: hdd cl home: kpt on* **8/1**
3 1/2 **Ferneley (IRE)**[24] 2026 4-9-6 111 WJSupple 4 108
(Francis Ennis, Ire) *led: strly pressed fnl f: jnd ins fnl f: hdd 150yds fr home: kpt on* **10/11**[1]
4 7 **Jalmira (IRE)**[11] 2420 7-9-1 102 WJLee 1 89
(C F Swan, Ire) *trckd ldr in 2nd: dropped to 3rd and pushed along appr st: no ex fr 2f out* **7/2**[3]
1m 42.3s (1.10) **Going Correction** +0.10s/f (Good) 5 Ran SP% **110.7**
Speed ratings: **98,97,97,90**
CSF £21.27 TOTE £2.80; DF 20.90.
Owner Hamdan Al Maktoum **Bred** Shadwell Farm LLC **Trained** Friarstown, Co Kildare

NOTEBOOK
Mustameet(USA) found the drop into this grade right up his street and got back to winning ways, despite the lack of early pace over this shorter trip being against him. He was still some way below his official rating here and he is not really the force of old, but no doubt this will serve his confidnce well. (op 5/2)
Akua'Ba(IRE) has been struggling for form previously this season and, while this was a greatly-improved effort in defeat, she does limit the form.
Ferneley(IRE), an easy winner over course and distance in Group 3 company last time, was just held under his penalty and would have likely been better off going faster on the early lead. (op Evs tchd 11/10)
Jalmira(IRE) was not given too hard a time when his chance became apparent, which accentuated the margin of his defeat. He has yet to look like recapturing last season's form.

2739 - 2742a (Foreign Racing) - See Raceform Interactive

FONTAINEBLEAU
Wednesday, June 4

OFFICIAL GOING: Soft

2743a PRIX MELISANDE (GRAND PRIX DE FONTAINEBLEAU) (LISTED RACE) (FILLIES) 1m 2f
2:35 (2:34) 3-Y-O **£20,221** (£8,088; £6,066; £4,044; £2,022)

RPR
1 **Yarastar**[26] 1979 3-8-12 JVictoire 2 100
(H-A Pantall, France)
2 3/4 **Antiquities**[34] 1760 3-9-2 MGuyon 3 102
(A Fabre, France)
3 1 **Madaway**[17] 2237 3-8-12 OPeslier 8 96
(C Laffon-Parias, France)
4 shd **Grenadia (USA)**[26] 1979 3-8-12 C-PLemaire 4 96
(J-C Rouget, France)
5 1/2 **Ballerina Blue (IRE)**[34] 1760 3-8-12 TThulliez 7 95
(Y De Nicolay, France)
6 4 **Perfect Hand**[26] 3-8-12 SPasquier 1 87
(P Bary, France)
7 1/2 **Courageuse (FR)**[34] 1760 3-8-12 ACrastus 6 86
(E Lellouche, France)
8 1 1/2 **Don't Forget Faith (USA)**[14] 2305 3-8-12 (v) CSoumillon 5 83
(C G Cox) *racd in 2nd on outside: niggled along 3 1/2f out: rdn over 2f out: sn wknd* **9/1**[1]
2m 1.20s (121.20) 8 Ran SP% **10.0**
PARI-MUTUEL (inlcuding 1 Euro stake): WIN 16.10; PL 2.20, 1.30, 1.30;DF 19.50.
Owner Ecurie Skymarc Farm **Bred** Castlemartin Stud & Ecurie Skymarc Farm **Trained** France

NOTEBOOK
Don't Forget Faith(USA), looking for some more black type, was fitted with a visor for the first time. However, she finished well beaten and the soft ground may not have suited, as her best efforts have been on a faster surface.

2656 SAN SIRO (R-H)
Wednesday, June 4

OFFICIAL GOING: Very soft

2744a PREMIO ARONA (UNRACED FILLIES) 7f
2:05 (12:00) 2-Y-O **£6,618** (£2,912; £1,588; £794)

RPR
1 **Queen Sensazione (IRE)** 2-9-0 DVargiu 1 —
(B Grizzetti, Italy)
2 3 1/4 **Desert Love (IRE)** 2-9-0 FBossa 9 —
(M Ciciarelli, Italy)
3 nse **Touchet Marie (IRE)** 2-9-0 PConvertino 4 —
(M Marcialis, Italy)
4 nse **Miss Devious (ITY)** 2-9-0 MColombi 3 —
(J Bindi, Italy)
5 1 1/4 **Valtraud (FR)** 2-9-0 SMereu 12 —
(M Simondi, Italy)
6 2 3/4 **Miesque Girl (FR)** 2-9-0 WGambarota 5 —
(J Heloury, Italy)
7 2 **Right Edge (USA)** 2-9-0 OFancera 6 —
(F & L Camici, Italy)
8 2 1/4 **Mac Waterloo** 2-9-0 SLandi 7 —
(M G Quinlan) *s.s: effrt on outside ent st: nvr a factor* **57/10**[1]
9 7 **Nina Morena (USA)** 2-9-0 LManiezzi 10 —
(R Menichetti, Italy)
10 3 1/4 **Desert Star (ITY)** 2-9-0 LSorrentino 2 —
(S Benedetti, Italy)
1m 32.9s (4.70) 10 Ran SP% **14.9**
(including 1 Euro stake): WIN 1.56; PL 1.18, 1.94, 2.52; DF 7.62.
Owner Scuderia Blueberry **Bred** Scuderia Blueberry **Trained** Italy

NOTEBOOK
Mac Waterloo, making her racecourse debut, missed the break and was never able to get involved.

2745a PREMIO LUINO (UNRACED COLTS & GELDINGS) 7f
2:40 (12:00) 2-Y-O **£6,618** (£2,912; £1,588; £794)

RPR
1 **Abaton** 2-9-0 MDemuro 2 —
(V Caruso, Italy)
2 4 1/2 **Autre Gemme (IRE)** 2-9-0 URispoli 5 —
(A & G Botti, Italy)
3 5 1/2 **Halling Machine (UAE)** 2-9-0 MEsposito 3 —
(A Feligioni, Italy)
4 nse **Doctor Kris** 2-9-0 FBossa 12 —
(M Ciciarelli, Italy)
5 3 1/4 **Lord Fasliyev (IRE)** 2-9-0 GArena 7 —
(L D'Auria, Italy)
6 3 **Mon Colonel (IRE)** 2-9-0 LManiezzi 14 —
(R Menichetti, Italy)
7 snk **Il Ranzani (ITY)** 2-9-0 DPorcu 8 —
(V Toccolini)
8 1 1/4 **Gold Plus (IRE)** 2-9-0 WGambarota 10 —
(M Bebbu, Italy)
9 1/2 **Ekrajeu (ITY)** 2-9-0 EBotti 9 —
(Gianfranco Verricelli, Italy)
10 1 1/2 **Zemlinsky (IRE)** 2-9-0 SUrru 1 —
(B Grizzetti, Italy)
11 8 **Rahymi (USA)** 2-9-0 OFrancera 13 —
(F & L Camici, Italy)
12 12 **Thunder Jodys (USA)** 2-9-0 DVargiu 4 —
(B Grizzetti, Italy)
13 15 **Mac Warren** 2-9-0 SLandi 6 —
(M G Quinlan) *in tch to 1/2-way: wknd qckly: eased* **8/1**[1]
1m 30.7s (2.50) 13 Ran SP% **11.1**
WIN 2.92; PL 1.67, 2.79, 2.92; DF 15.15.

Owner Scuderia Incolinx **Bred** Azienda Agricola Rosati Colarieti **Trained** Italy

NOTEBOOK
Mac Warren, a son of Falbrav and another making his debut, showed up for the first half of the race but dropped away badly and was eased down as though something was amiss.

[2140] HAMILTON (R-H)

Thursday, June 5

OFFICIAL GOING: Good to firm (good in places)
Wind: almost nil Weather: overcast

2746 SEXUAL HEALTH SPRINT MAIDEN AUCTION STKS — 6f 5y
2:10 (2:10) (Class 6) 2-Y-O — **£2,590** (£770; £385; £192) **Stalls** Low

Form — RPR

4 **1** **Calley Ho**[12] 2388 2-8-10 0 TonyHamilton 3 — 68
(Mrs L Stubbs) *hld up: hdwy wl over 1f out: 2l 3rd and styng on whn lft in ld cl home* **8/1**

5 **2** *1 1/4* **Going Time (USA)**[27] 1948 2-8-11 0 JoeFanning 10 — 65+
(M Johnston) *w ldrs: rdn 2f out: 3l 4th and one pce whn lft 2nd cl home* **9/2**[3]

3 **3** *1* **Custard Cream Kid (IRE)**[18] 2217 2-9-1 0 PaulHanagan 11 — 66+
(R A Fahey) *in tch: drvn and outpcd 1/2-way: rallied fnl f: lft 3rd cl home: no imp* **7/2**[1]

4 *1* **Little Tokyo (USA)** 2-9-1 0 RobertWinston 5 — 63
(J Howard Johnson) *cl up tl rdn and no ex over 1f out: hld whn lft 4th cl home* **6/1**

5 *6* **The Canny Dove (USA)** 2-8-10 0 GrahamGibbons 6 — 40
(T D Barron) *sn bhd and outpcd: no imp fr 2f out* **8/1**

6 *1* **Aegean Warning** 2-8-10 0 DO'Donohoe 12 — 39+
(K A Ryan) *hld up outside: drvn 1/2-way: n.d* **25/1**

06 **7** *nk* **Nchike**[18] 2217 2-8-9 0 AdrianTNicholls 8 — 35+
(D Nicholls) *in tch tl wknd over 2f out* **20/1**

8 *nk* **Another Echo** 2-8-3 0 TWilliams 2 — 28
(W Storey) *bhd and hung rt thrght: nvr on terms* **40/1**

0 **9** *5* **Ed's Pride (IRE)**[13] 2362 2-8-12 0 PaulMulrennan 7 — 22
(K A Ryan) *cl up to 1/2-way: sn lost pl* **66/1**

42 **U** **Verinco**[7] 2521 2-9-3 0 TomEaves 4 — 74+
(B Smart) *led: rdn over 2f out: edgd rt over 1f out: edgd lft ins fnl f: 1 1/2l in front and in command whn jinked rt and uns rdr cl home* **4/1**[2]

U **Lucky Dan (IRE)** 2-8-3 0 AndrewHeffernan(7) 9 — 71+
(Paul Green) *s.i.s: sn prom: effrt 2f out: 1 1/2l 2nd and keeping on whn bdly hmpd and uns rdr cl home* **12/1**

1m 12.66s (0.46) **Going Correction** -0.175s/f (Firm) — 11 Ran SP% **117.1**
Speed ratings (Par 91): **89,87,86,84,76 75,74,74,67,— —**
CSF £42.21 TOTE £9.00: £2.40, £1.40, £1.40; EX 58.10.
Owner Des Thurlby **Bred** Whitsbury Manor Stud & Pigeon House Stud **Trained** Norton, N Yorks

FOCUS
Ordinary form but a most eventful race in which the picture changed dramatically near the finish. The unseaters are rated as having finished first and second with the first three close to previous form, but the fourth home may be the best long-term proposition.

NOTEBOOK
Calley Ho, who shaped with credit on his debut, was in the process of running at least as well when left in front near the finish over this longer trip. He was a most fortuitous winner but shapes as though he will stay further and may be capable of better. (op 12-1)
Going Time(USA), who shaped as though a fair bit better than her debut effort, looked in good condition and ran well for a long way. She was held when left in second place close home and has the ability to pick up an uncompetitive event. (op 3-1)
Custard Cream Kid(IRE), who shaped with promise in an ordinary event on his debut, looked in good shape in the paddock and ran to a similar level. He left the impression that a stiffer test over this trip or the step up to 7f would suit and he remains the type to win a race. (op 11-4)
Little Tokyo(USA) ◆, a $37,000 first foal of a useful spriting dirt winner in the US, was arguably the nicest type in the paddock but he both looked and ran as though this debut outing was needed. He should come on a fair bit for this and is sure to win a race. (op 9-1)
The Canny Dove(USA), a workmanlike colt with scope who looked as though the race would do him good, showed only ordinary form on this racecourse debut but is entitled to improve and will be of more interest once qualified for a nursery mark. (op 22-1)
Aegean Warning, a 10,000gns purchaser who has several winners up to 7f in his pedigree, was very easy to back and offered little immediate promise on this racecourse debut. He is entitled to improve for the run.
Verinco, bandaged behind, was colty in the paddock and looked less than straightforward once pressure was applied but looked to have the race in safe keeping before jinking and unseating his rider close home. He does not look entirely straighforward but clearly has the ability to win races on this evidence. (tchd 14-1)
Lucky Dan(IRE), an 11,000euro half-brother to several winners from sprint distances to 1m, was in the process of running creditably but looked held when badly hampered and unseating his rider close home. He showed enough to suggest a similar race can be found. (tchd 14-1)

2747 RECTANGLE GROUP CLAIMING STKS — 6f 5y
2:40 (2:42) (Class 6) 3-4-Y-O — **£2,047** (£604; £302) **Stalls** Low

Form — RPR

6606 **1** **Dickie Le Davoir**[2] 2703 4-8-11 68 MarkCoumbe(7) 5 — 63
(John A Harris) *hld up: hdwy over 2f out: edgd lft and led over 1f out: drvn out* **4/1**[3]

061 **2** *1* **Gap Princess (IRE)**[10] 2444 4-9-1 61 PaulHanagan 6 — 62+
(R A Fahey) *t.k.h: prom: effrt whn hmpd over 1f out: styd on wl towards fin: nt rch wnr* **6/4**[1]

3000 **3** *nk* **Andrasta**[3] 2661 3-7-11 55 DanielleMcCreery(5) 11 — 49
(A Berry) *prom: effrt and ev ch over 1f out: kpt on fnl f: lost 2nd nr fin* **16/1**

50-0 **4** *1 3/4* **Beaumont Boy**[139] 214 4-8-13 46 (p) PJMcDonald(3) 8 — 51
(A G Foster) *towards rr: effrt over 2f out: prom over 1f out: one pce fnl f* **50/1**

150- **5** *1/2* **Jennifer's Dream (IRE)**[216] 6619 3-8-8 80 AndrewMullen(3) 2 — 50
(K A Ryan) *t.k.h in midfield: hdwy and chsng ldrs whn nt clr run and swtchd rt over 1f out: one pce fnl f* **7/1**

0R- **6** *2 1/4* **Polish Star**[10] 2759 4-8-12 54 GrahamGibbons 7 — 38
(R Johnson) *dwlt: hdwy and in tch over 2f out: wknd ins fnl f* **20/1**

14-6 **7** *2 1/2* **Jim Martin**[106] 632 3-8-8 80 TomEaves 1 — 32
(Miss L A Perratt) *bhd: drvn and outpcd 1/2-way: n.d after* **7/2**[2]

-040 **8** *5* **Binario Uno**[33] 1795 3-8-6 63 (v) AdrianTNicholls 12 — 14
(D Nicholls) *sn swtchd to stands' side fr wdst draw: led and clr: edgd rt and hdd over 1f out: btn and eased ins fnl f* **14/1**

00 **9** *5* **White Elephant**[16] 2283 4-9-10 0 PaddyAspell 3 — 10
(W Storey) *chsd ldrs tl wknd over 2f out* **80/1**

000- **10** *3 1/2* **Caribbean Cruiser**[229] 6329 3-8-5 47 (b) TWilliams 9 — —
(Bruce Hellier) *bhd: struggling 1/2-way: nvr on terms* **50/1**

00 **11** *18* **Deer Park Lord**[27] 1951 4-8-9 0 (t) PaulPickard(7) 4 — —
(D A Nolan) *towards rr: wkng whn lost action wl over 2f out: t.o* **150/1**

1m 11.21s (-0.99) **Going Correction** -0.175s/f (Firm)
WFA 3 from 4yo 8lb — 11 Ran SP% **117.9**
Speed ratings (Par 101): **99,97,97,94,94 91,87,81,74,69 45**
CSF £10.15 TOTE £4.90: £1.70, £1.50, £4.40; EX 12.70.
Owner Stan Wright Shaun Taylor **Bred** P And Mrs A G Venner **Trained** Eastwell, Leics
■ Stewards' Enquiry : Mark Coumbe one-day ban: careless riding (June 24)

FOCUS
The usual mixed bag but, although the pace was sound, this looks ordinary form at best. The runner-up looked arguably unlucky with the third rated to this year's best.
Binario Uno Official explanation: jockey said gelding hung right-handed throughout

2748 STRATHCLYDE PARK GOLF DRIVING RANGE H'CAP — 5f 4y
3:10 (3:11) (Class 6) (0-65,63) 3-Y-O+ — **£2,047** (£604; £302) **Stalls** Low

Form — RPR

-002 **1** **Ronnie Howe**[30] 1893 4-9-12 61 FergalLynch 4 — 72
(M Dods) *cl up: rdn to ld appr fnl f: kpt on fnl f* **4/1**[1]

4313 **2** *3/4* **Mineral Rights (USA)**[27] 1952 4-10-0 63 (v) TomEaves 15 — 71
(Miss L A Perratt) *racd alone centre: a cl up: chal over 1f out: kpt on to pull clr of remainder fnl f* **9/2**[2]

00-0 **3** *5* **Bungie**[109] 596 4-8-3 45 (b[1]) AndrewHeffernan(7) 7 — 35
(Paul Green) *chsd ldrs: effrt over 2f out: one pce over 1f out* **14/1**

0-65 **4** *nse* **Falmassim**[27] 1966 5-8-12 47 RobertWinston 8 — 37
(Miss J A Camacho) *in tch: drvn 1/2-way: kpt on same pce fnl f* **6/1**

1000 **5** *nse* **Howards Tipple**[20] 2145 4-10-0 63 TonyHamilton 6 — 53
(Miss L A Perratt) *hld up: hdwy 2f out: rdn and nt qckn fnl f* **10/1**

6020 **6** *nk* **Lambency (IRE)**[10] 2448 5-9-1 55 GaryBartley(5) 12 — 44
(J S Goldie) *bhd tl hdwy over 1f out: nvr rchd ldrs* **11/2**[3]

6005 **7** *shd* **Kings College Boy**[10] 2448 8-9-7 56 (b) PaulHanagan 14 — 44
(R A Fahey) *hld up bhd ldrs: drvn and outpcd 2f out: kpt on u.p fnl f* **6/1**

0560 **8** *2* **Signor Panettiere**[16] 2270 7-9-1 50 (p) SilvestreDeSousa 2 — 31
(A D Brown) *led to appr fnl f: sn btn* **14/1**

45-0 **9** *1/2* **City For Conquest (IRE)**[62] 1185 5-8-7 45 (b) PJMcDonald(3) 9 — 24
(John A Harris) *midfield: drvn whn swtchd lft over 1f out: sn btn* **20/1**

3-00 **10** *1 1/2* **Fern House (IRE)**[143] 153 6-8-10 45 RoystonFfrench 3 — 19
(Bruce Hellier) *bhd: drvn 1/2-way: nvr on terms* **18/1**

0060 **11** *1 3/4* **Spinning Game**[24] 2036 4-8-5 45 (b) DanielleMcCreery(5) 11 — 13
(Mrs R A Carr) *dwlt: a bhd* **33/1**

50-0 **12** *5* **She's Our Beauty (IRE)**[148] 100 5-8-5 45 (p) KellyHarrison(5) 10 — —
(S T Mason) *dwlt: t.k.h and sn prom: edgd rt and wknd over 1f out* **20/1**

000- **13** *1 3/4* **Seafield Towers**[249] 5836 8-8-10 45 (p) DavidAllan 1 — —
(D A Nolan) *towards rr: drvn and outpcd 1/2-way: nvr on terms* **50/1**

58.90 secs (-1.10) **Going Correction** -0.175s/f (Firm) — 13 Ran SP% **124.3**
Speed ratings (Par 101): **101,99,91,91,91 91,91,87,87,84 81,73,71**
CSF £21.57 CT £246.66 TOTE £5.50: £1.90, £2.00, £5.60; EX 28.00.
Owner Mrs C E Dods **Bred** R Howe **Trained** Denton, Co Durham

FOCUS
An ordinary handicap in which the pace was sound but very few figured. The form is rated fairly positively as the front two pulled clear and may be capable of better.
Spinning Game Official explanation: jockey said filly missed the break

2749 TOKIO MARINE H'CAP (QUALIFIER FOR THE RBS SCOTTISH TROPHY HANDICAP SERIES FINAL) — 1m 65y
3:40 (3:41) (Class 5) (0-70,69) 4-Y-O+ — **£3,238** (£963; £481; £240) **Stalls** High

Form — RPR

-644 **1** **It's A Dream (FR)**[16] 2274 5-8-10 58 (t) GrahamGibbons 9 — 69+
(M W Easterby) *hld up in midfield: n.m.r briefly over 2f out: hdwy to ld ins fnl f: r.o wl* **7/2**[1]

6-33 **2** *1 1/4* **El Dececy (USA)**[12] 2393 4-9-5 67 JoeFanning 5 — 75
(S Parr) *led: rdn and qcknd over 2f out: hdd ins fnl f: kpt on same pce* **8/1**

2-63 **3** *1/2* **Oeuf A La Neige**[7] 2523 8-8-9 57 DO'Donohoe 4 — 64
(Miss L A Perratt) *bhd tl hdwy 2f out: kpt on wl fnl f: nrst fin* **6/1**[3]

1304 **4** *2 1/2* **Supercast (IRE)**[17] 2262 5-9-6 68 SamHitchcott 2 — 74+
(N J Vaughan) *in tch: drvn and outpcd 3f out: rallied fnl f: nrst fin* **14/1**

45-0 **5** *nk* **Anthemion (IRE)**[7] 2523 11-8-1 52 oh3 ow2 AndrewMullen(3) 10 — 53
(Mrs J C McGregor) *chsd ldr: drvn 3f out: one pce over 1f out* **33/1**

0025 **6** *1 1/4* **King Of The Moors (USA)**[27] 1953 5-8-13 68 DeanHeslop(7) 1 — 66
(T D Barron) *prom: effrt over 2f out: no ex over 1f out* **16/1**

-063 **7** *1 1/4* **Shy Glance (USA)**[7] 2524 6-9-0 62 RobertWinston 13 — 57
(P Monteith) *prom: drvn over 2f out: wknd over 1f out* **5/1**[2]

/45- **8** *nk* **Until When (USA)**[210] 6731 4-9-6 68 TomEaves 7 — 62
(B Smart) *hld up: pushed along over 2f out: nvr rchd ldrs* **11/1**

5/61 **9** *1* **Rainbow Zest**[10] 2446 5-9-4 66 6ex PaulHanagan 6 — 58
(W Storey) *hld up: drvn and outpcd over 2f out: n.d after* **7/1**

-360 **10** *1 3/4* **Defi (IRE)**[17] 2250 6-8-10 58 (b) TonyHamilton 8 — 46
(Miss L A Perratt) *chsd ldrs tl rdn and wknd over 1f out* **12/1**

0-60 **11** *1/2* **Frank Crow**[42] 1308 5-9-2 69 GaryBartley(5) 3 — 56
(J S Goldie) *hld up and bhd: drvn over 3f out: nvr on terms* **12/1**

406- **12** *18* **Mangano**[245] 5936 4-7-13 52 DanielleMcCreery(5) 11 — —
(A Berry) *t.k.h: hld up: struggling 3f out: sn btn* **50/1**

1m 44.57s (-3.83) **Going Correction** -0.40s/f (Firm) — 12 Ran SP% **118.0**
Speed ratings (Par 103): **103,101,101,98,98 97,95,95,94,92 92,74**
CSF £31.31 CT £167.23 TOTE £4.40: £2.00, £2.80, £1.80; EX 43.20.
Owner Matthew Green **Bred** Serge Bernereau Sarl **Trained** Sheriff Hutton, N Yorks

FOCUS
An ordinary handicap in which the pace was decent throughout and this bare form is solid and should prove reliable.

2750 DM HALL H'CAP — 1m 3f 16y
4:10 (4:10) (Class 6) (0-65,65) 3-Y-O — **£2,047** (£604; £302) **Stalls** High

Form — RPR

00-6 **1** **Smarterthanuthink (USA)**[19] 2208 3-9-4 62 (p) PaulHanagan 10 — 71+
(R A Fahey) *mde all: set modest gallop: rdn clr fr 2f out: kpt on wl fnl f* **4/1**[1]

0-54 **2** *3 3/4* **Jemima's Art**[10] 2468 3-8-2 46 oh1 (b[1]) DaleGibson 13 — 49+
(M W Easterby) *hld up ins: hdwy to chse wnr over 1f out: kpt on fnl f: no imp* **12/1**

-604 **3** *2 1/4* **Saturday Boy**[16] 2273 3-8-9 53 ow3 PaulMulrennan 7 — 52
(Paul Green) *prom: rdn to chse wnr briefly over 1f out: kpt on same pce fnl f* **15/2**

-563 **4** *1* **Zaplamation (IRE)**[29] 1912 3-8-0 47 ow1 AndrewMullen(3) 6 44
(D W Barker) *hld up outside: hdwy 3f out: rdn 2f out: kpt on same pce fnl f* **17/2**

20 **5** *1 1/4* **Kargan (IRE)**[11] 2429 3-9-7 65 GrahamGibbons 9 60+
(J S Wainwright) *dwlt: hld up: nt clr run 3f out and over 2f out: styd on fnl f: n.d* **5/1**[2]

5-25 **6** *shd* **Livvy Inn (USA)**[27] 1950 3-8-12 56 RobertWinston 12 51
(Miss Lucinda V Russell) *hld up: stdy hdwy on outside over 3f out: rdn and no imp fr 2f out* **6/1**[3]

1045 **7** *3/4* **Chanteuse De Rue (IRE)**[16] 2273 3-8-3 47 (b[1]) RoystonFfrench 5 41
(M Johnston) *hld up: drvn and outpcd 4f out: no imp fr 2f out* **8/1**

-050 **8** *1 1/2* **Arcetri (IRE)**[16] 2282 3-8-10 54 DO'Donohoe 11 45
(K A Ryan) *t.k.h: cl up tl wknd wl over 1f out* **16/1**

462 **9** *4* **Miss Mactango**[20] 2156 3-8-12 56 DavidAllan 8 40
(W M Brisbourne) *hld up: drvn over 4f out: nvr on terms* **14/1**

5223 **10** *1/2* **Love Empire (USA)**[78] 940 3-9-6 64 (b) JoeFanning 1 47
(M Johnston) *cl up: effrt and ch 3f out: wknd wl over 1f out* **9/1**

430 **11** *1 1/4* **Prince Rhyddarch**[20] 2143 3-8-11 55 TomEaves 2 36
(Miss L A Perratt) *hld up in tch: hdwy over 3f out: wknd fr 2f out* **20/1**

00-4 **12** *1 1/4* **Northgate Maisie**[20] 2156 3-8-3 47 AndrewElliott 3 26
(Jedd O'Keeffe) *prom tl edgd rt and wknd fr 2f out* **50/1**

00 **13** *5* **Ceduna Roadhouse (IRE)**[27] 1951 3-8-4 48 AdrianTNicholls 4 19
(A M Crow) *in tch: drvn 1/2-way: wknd fr 3f out* **50/1**

2m 22.21s (-3.39) **Going Correction** -0.40s/f (Firm) 13 Ran SP% **123.3**
Speed ratings (Par 97): **96,93,91,90,90 89,89,88,85,85 84,83,79**
CSF £54.38 CT £355.58 TOTE £5.60: £2.00, £4.70, £3.30; EX 85.40.
Owner David And Jackie Knaggs **Bred** Chelsea Virginia Llc **Trained** Musley Bank, N Yorks

FOCUS
Just an ordinary gallop to this moderate handicap but a much-improved effort from Smarterthanuthink, who looks a fair way ahead of his current mark. The form behind though is a bit fluid.

Smarterthanuthink(USA) ◆ Official explanation: trainer said, regarding running, colt may have benefited from the fitting of cheek pieces and been suited by the step up in trip, although he may drop him back in the future

Kargan(IRE) Official explanation: jockey said gelding was denied a clear run

2751 SAM COLLINGWOOD-CAMERON H'CAP 6f 5y
4:40 (4:40) (Class 5) (0-70,69) 4-Y-0+ **£3,238** (£963; £481; £240) **Stalls** Low

Form RPR

6-40 **1** **Opal Noir**[10] 2444 4-9-0 62 DO'Donohoe 5 74
(Miss L A Perratt) *prom: effrt 2f out: led ins fnl f: drvn out* **18/1**

0014 **2** *1 1/4* **The Bear**[10] 2444 5-9-4 66 GrahamGibbons 2 74
(R Johnson) *led: rdn over 2f out: hdd ins fnl f: kpt on u.p* **9/2**[1]

5006 **3** *1* **Yorkshire Blue**[7] 2535 9-9-3 65 DanielTudhope 9 70+
(J S Goldie) *bhd: plenty to do 1/2-way: n.m.r and swtchd over 1f out: styd on strly fnl f: nt rch first two* **8/1**

0014 **4** *1/2* **Mandurah (IRE)**[5] 2596 4-9-6 68 AdrianTNicholls 1 71
(D Nicholls) *prom: effrt over 2f out: kpt on same pce fnl f* **13/2**[3]

-022 **5** *1/2* **Rainbow Fox**[19] 2188 4-9-6 68 PaulHanagan 6 70
(R A Fahey) *midfield: drvn 1/2-way: rallied over 1f out: kpt on fnl f* **11/2**[2]

4045 **6** *hd* **Coleorton Dancer**[27] 1952 6-9-4 69 AndrewMullen(3) 16 70
(K A Ryan) *hld up: hdwy 2f out: kpt on ins fnl f: no imp* **10/1**

0-41 **7** *shd* **Cassie's Choice (IRE)**[12] 2399 4-9-4 66 TomEaves 13 67
(B Smart) *hld up in midfield: drvn over 2f out: r.o ins fnl f* **16/1**

-010 **8** *hd* **Cheery Cat (USA)**[12] 2400 4-9-1 63 (p) TonyHamilton 11 63
(D W Barker) *prom tl rdn and no ex over 1f out* **16/1**

6231 **9** *1 1/4* **Imperial Sword**[31] 1865 5-8-0 55 (b) DeanHeslop(7) 14 51
(T D Barron) *bhd and outpcd: hdwy over 1f out: nvr rchd ldrs* **8/1**

60-4 **10** *3/4* **Hansomis (IRE)**[20] 2159 4-8-5 53 DaleGibson 15 47
(B Mactaggart) *midfield on outside: drvn and outpcd over 2f out: sn btn* **25/1**

0003 **11** *1/2* **Union Jack Jackson (IRE)**[30] 1906 6-8-3 51 oh5 ow1(b) RoystonFfrench 7 43
(John A Harris) *midfield: drvn and outpcd over 2f out: n.d after* **22/1**

25-3 **12** *nk* **Cross Of Lorraine (IRE)**[32] 1826 5-9-2 64 (b) RobertWinston 8 55
(C Grant) *bhd and outpcd: nvr rchd ldrs* **8/1**

5343 **13** *1 1/4* **Avontuur (FR)**[10] 2444 6-8-3 51 (p) AndrewElliott 10 38
(Mrs R A Carr) *dwlt: sn prom drvn and wknd wl over 1f out* **12/1**

1000 **14** *3 1/2* **Geordie Dancer (IRE)**[20] 2145 6-7-11 50 oh5..(b) DanielleMcCreery(5) 3 26
(A Berry) *chsd ldrs tl wknd fr 2f out* **100/1**

45-3 **15** *2* **Irish Conection (IRE)**[58] 1259 5-8-2 50 TWilliams 4 19
(Thomas McLaughlin, Ire) *bhd and outpcd: nvr on terms* **40/1**

000- **16** *2 1/2* **The Thrifty Bear**[245] 5930 5-7-13 52 oh5 ow2 KellyHarrison(5) 12 13
(C W Fairhurst) *prom tl wknd over 2f out* **50/1**

1m 10.64s (-1.56) **Going Correction** -0.175s/f (Firm) 16 Ran SP% **127.6**
Speed ratings (Par 103): **103,101,100,99,98 98,98,98,96,95 94,94,92,87,85 81**
CSF £98.10 CT £761.69 TOTE £21.10: £4.50, £2.00, £3.00, £1.90; EX 212.90.
Owner R Hyndman **Bred** J K And Mrs Keegan **Trained** Carluke, S Lanarks

FOCUS
A run-of-the-mill sprint in which the field raced centre to stands' side. The pace was sound but very few got competitive, although the form looks solid with several with sound recent form close up.

2752 CASH FOR KIDS NEXT WEEK H'CAP 1m 5f 9y
5:10 (5:10) (Class 5) (0-70,66) 4-Y-0+ **£3,238** (£963; £481; £240) **Stalls** High

Form RPR

50-3 **1** **La Vecchia Scuola (IRE)**[10] 2447 4-9-7 66 DanielTudhope 7 85
(J S Goldie) *hld up: rdn 3f out: led wl over 1f out: sn clr* **15/8**[1]

0-42 **2** *8* **Living On A Prayer**[16] 2286 5-8-6 51 AndrewElliott 3 58
(Thomas McLaughlin, Ire) *hld up: hdwy over 3f out: disp 2nd over 1f out: kpt on u.p* **11/4**[2]

00/2 **3** *shd* **Bad Boy Al (IRE)**[13] 2361 4-9-0 59 FergalLynch 6 66
(N J Vaughan) *in tch: hdwy to dispute 2nd over 1f out: kpt on ins fnl f* **5/1**[3]

00-0 **4** *3 1/4* **Jane Of Arc (FR)**[7] 2523 4-8-9 54 JoeFanning 2 56
(J S Goldie) *chsd ldr to 1/2-way: effrt and ev ch 2f out: sn no ex* **22/1**

-501 **5** *5* **Wulimaster (USA)**[29] 1913 5-8-7 55 MarkLawson(3) 8 50
(D W Barker) *hld up: effrt and prom 2f out: wknd appr fnl f* **5/1**[3]

3426 **6** *1 3/4* **Easibet Dot Net**[6] 2579 8-8-7 50 ow2 (b) TomEaves 10 44
(Miss L A Perratt) *led and clr: hdd wl over 1f out: wknd qckly* **16/1**

0-06 **7** *15* **Asrar**[15] 1304 6-8-2 47 oh2 (p) DO'Donohoe 11 16
(Miss Lucinda V Russell) *chsd ldrs: wnt 2nd 1/2-way tl wknd over 3f out* **66/1**

5-60 **8** *4 1/2* **Stravonian**[4] 2286 8-8-3 47 oh2 ow8 PaulPickard(7) 9 18
(D A Nolan) *prom tl wknd over 4f out* **40/1**

/00- **9** *28* **Knight Valliant**[45] 1966 5-7-13 51 RobbieEgan(7) 5 —
(J Howard Johnson) *t.k.h: hld up in tch: rdn and lost tch fnl 4f* **9/1**

2m 47.28s (-6.62) **Going Correction** -0.40s/f (Firm) 9 Ran SP% **118.9**
Speed ratings (Par 103): **104,99,99,97,93 92,83,80,63**
CSF £7.28 CT £22.12 TOTE £3.00: £1.10, £1.90, £2.00; EX 7.60 Place 6: £30.52, Place 5: £17.52..
Owner John Connor Graham Brown **Bred** Maurice Craig **Trained** Uplawmoor, E Renfrews
■ Stewards' Enquiry : Paul Pickard two-day ban: used whip when out of contention (Jun 22-23)

FOCUS
A modest handicap but one in which the pace was soon sound and the form looks solid with those in the frame behind the winner close to their marks. The winner appeals as the type to win more races on the Flat.
T/Jkpt: Not won. T/Plt: £37.00 to a £1 stake. Pool: £71,704.68. 1,411.07 winning tickets. T/Qpdt: £22.30 to a £1 stake. Pool: £2,802.69. 92.70 winning tickets. RY

2716 LINGFIELD (L-H)
Thursday, June 5

OFFICIAL GOING: Standard
Wind: virtually nil Weather: bright, partly cloudy

2753 FELBRIDGE (S) STKS 7f (P)
2:20 (2:20) (Class 6) 3-Y-0+ **£1,774** (£523; £262) **Stalls** Low

Form RPR

3362 **1** **One More Round (USA)**[1] 2721 10-9-7 75 (b) TPQueally 8 62
(Ollie Pears) *stdd s: hld up bhd: smooth hdwy on outer over 2f out: carried rt over 1f out: rdn to ld wl ins fnl f* **5/2**[1]

/00- **2** *1/2* **Miracle Baby**[503] 183 6-8-11 32 HaddenFrost(5) 5 56
(J A Geake) *t.k.h: in tch in midfield: hdwy and rdn 2f out: ev ch ins fnl f: unable qckn towards fin* **40/1**

5614 **3** *nk* **Secret Meaning**[21] 2126 3-8-7 61 (b[1]) JackDean(5) 3 57
(W G M Turner) *chsd ldrs: rdn and hanging rt fr 2f out: kpt on u.p fnl f* **16/1**

34-3 **4** *2* **Million Percent**[16] 2277 9-9-7 67 LiamJones 1 55
(C R Dore) *chsd ldr tl over 3f out: rdn jst over 2f out: led jst ins fnl f: hdd wl ins fnl f: fdd towards fin* **5/1**[3]

4423 **5** *hd* **Moayed**[23] 2073 9-9-7 65 (b) GeorgeBaker 12 54
(N P Littmoden) *stdd s: hld up wl bhd: hdwy wl over 1f out: r.o fnl f: nvr pce to rch ldrs* **7/2**[2]

5226 **6** *1* **Fly In Johnny (IRE)**[1] 2721 3-8-11 62 RichardHughes 6 47
(R Hannon) *chsd ldrs: wnt 2nd over 3f out: rdn to ld wl over 1f out: hdd jst ins fnl f: sn btn* **11/2**

3500 **7** *3/4* **Saafend Geezer**[9] 2480 3-8-11 59 (v[1]) RobertHavlin 9 45
(B J Meehan) *stdd after s: hld up bhd: hdwy on inner 2f out: rdn 1f out: sn no imp* **16/1**

6000 **8** *1* **Sir Douglas**[30] 1900 5-9-13 62 (p) TGMcLaughlin 7 53
(R A Harris) *taken down early: stdd s: hld up bhd: hdwy on outer over 2f out: hung rt over 1f out: nvr nr ldrs* **12/1**

00-0 **9** *2 1/2* **Agon Eyes (USA)**[62] 1186 3-8-6 44 TPO'Shea 11 31
(D J Coakley) *in tch in midfield: lost pl and rdn jst over 2f out: no ch after* **50/1**

033- **10** *2 1/2* **Ballad Maker (IRE)**[198] 6457 4-9-4 69 JerryO'Dwyer(3) 4 33
(Mrs S J Humphrey) *in tch in midfield: rdn 3f out: lost pl jst over 2f out: no ch after* **8/1**

0000 **11** *1 1/2* **Orchestration (IRE)**[2] 2703 7-9-7 38 (v) ChrisCatlin 13 29
(Garry Moss) *sn led: rdn jst over 2f out: hdd wl over 1f out: wknd qckly* **66/1**

-006 **12** *5* **Wilford Maverick (IRE)**[40] 1636 6-9-4 35 (v) KevinGhunowa(3) 10 16
(Garry Moss) *racd in midfield on outer: lost pl and rdn over 2f out: sn wl btn* **66/1**

0-00 **13** *8* **Valeesha**[6] 2556 4-9-2 45 SimonWhitworth 2 —
(M S Saunders) *v.s.a: bhd: lost tch over 2f out: t.o* **33/1**

1m 25.94s (1.14) **Going Correction** +0.10s/f (Slow)
WFA 3 from 4yo+ 10lb 13 Ran SP% **123.7**
Speed ratings (Par 101): **97,96,96,93,93 92,91,90,87,84 83,77,68**
CSF £126.31 TOTE £3.60: £1.40, £18.30, £3.90; EX 175.00 TRIFECTA Not won..The winner was bought in for 5,600gns
Owner Diamond Racing Ltd **Bred** Kenneth L Ramsey And Sarah K Ramsey **Trained** Norton, N Yorks

FOCUS
An ordinary seller containing a mixed bag of abilities and several were still within a length or so of each other passing the furlong pole. Despite being won by a 75-rated horse, the form of this race looks very modest with the runner-up rated just 32 and the third is the best guide for now.

2754 COPTHORNE MEDIAN AUCTION MAIDEN STKS 6f (P)
2:50 (2:53) (Class 6) 2-Y-0 **£2,266** (£674; £337; £168) **Stalls** Low

Form RPR

33 **1** **Daddy's Gift (IRE)**[24] 2042 2-8-12 0 RichardHughes 2 74
(R Hannon) *chsd ldr: rdn 2f out: styd on u.p to ld fnl 50yds* **11/4**[1]

63 **2** *1/2* **Rapid Release (CAN)**[6] 2554 2-9-3 0 SebSanders 1 78+
(Sir Mark Prescott) *s.i.s: sn rcvrd and in tch on inner: hdwy to chse ldng pair 2f out: kpt on u.p to go 2nd nr fin* **3/1**[2]

0 **3** *3/4* **Zebrano**[14] 2324 2-9-3 0 ShaneKelly 7 75
(Miss E C Lavelle) *chsd ldrs tl led after 1f: stdd pce over 3f out: rdn and qcknd 2f out: hdd fnl 50yds: no ex* **16/1**

4 *3 1/2* **Temperence Hall (USA)** 2-9-3 0 GeorgeBaker 4 65+
(J R Best) *t.k.h: hld up wl in tch: rdn and unable qck 2f out: kpt on but no ch w ldng trio after* **12/1**

5 *6* **Sapphire Prince (USA)** 2-9-3 0 LPKeniry 12 47
(J R Best) *s.i.s: dropped in and pushed along early: clsd whn pce slowed over 3f out: rdn and outpcd jst over 2f out: no ch after* **33/1**

5 **6** *nk* **Inside Knowledge (USA)**[31] 1873 2-9-3 0 JimCrowley 6 46
(Mrs A J Perrett) *chsd ldrs: rdn over 4f out: lost pl qckly jst over 2f out: plugged on again fnl f* **5/1**[3]

0 **7** *3/4* **Mr Melodious**[75] 957 2-9-3 0 MichaelHills 11 44
(B W Hills) *sn outpcd and rdn in rr: rn wd bnd over 2f out: nvr on terms* **13/2**

8 *nk* **Catenaccio (IRE)** 2-9-3 0 StephenCarson 8 43
(P Winkworth) *t.k.h: hld up towards rr: hdwy on outer over 3f out: chsd ldrs jst over 2f out: sn outpcd* **20/1**

9 *shd* **Satwa Street (IRE)** 2-9-3 0 RichardMullen 9 42
(D M Simcock) *a towards rr: rdn and effrt over 2f out: sn outpcd and wl bhd* **20/1**

5 **10** 2 **Time Loup**[10] 2458 2-9-3 0 ChrisCatlin 3 36
(Miss E C Lavelle) *led for 1f: chsd ldrs tl 2f out: wknd qckly* **50/1**

1m 13.51s (1.61) **Going Correction** +0.10s/f (Slow) **10** Ran SP% **109.7**
Speed ratings (Par 91): **93,92,91,86,78 78,77,76,76,74**
CSF £8.45 TOTE £2.90: £1.70, £1.10, £3.50; EX 6.50 Trifecta £32.00 Pool: £201.49. 4.47 winning units..
Owner Charlee & Hollie Allan **Bred** Vincent Dunne **Trained** East Everleigh, Wilts

FOCUS
Not a particularly competitive maiden, made less so by the late withdrawal of the third-favourite Marsool (4/1, refused to enter stalls, deduct 20p in the £ under Rule 4). The pace was a fair one and the front three pulled clear of the others, with the form rated around the first two.

NOTEBOOK
Daddy's Gift(IRE), third in a maiden and a novice event at Windsor, had no problem with the extra furlong and produced a nice turn of foot to cut down the leader. This was a nice effort against the colts and she should continue to progress. (tchd 2-1)
Rapid Release(CAN), with the stable jockey back on following his improved effort at Brighton, put in a strong late effort up the inside rail but the winner was finishing just as fast out wider. Nurseries may be his thing in a few weeks' time and an extra furlong would not come amiss. (tchd 7-2)
Zebrano ◆, well beaten on his Goodwood debut, did not go off unbacked. Given a positive ride, he looked the possible winner starting up the home straight but, although he did not do much wrong, he was swamped on both sides near the line. He is going the right way. (op 25-1)
Temperence Hall(USA) ◆, a $72,000 half-brother to winners in the US and Japan, took a bit of time to realise what was required. Although unable to get anywhere near the front three, he stayed on steadily in the closing stages and pulled well clear of the rest. He is bred to be suited by this surface and he should have learned something from this. (tchd 10-1 and 14-1)
Sapphire Prince(USA), out of a dual winner over 1m in the US, was not expected to show much on this debut according to the market. Starting from the outside stall, he looked very much in need of the experience.
Inside Knowledge(USA), fifth of six on his Windsor debut when backed, attracted market support again but appeared to find even this trip too sharp despite the extra furlong. (op 8-1)
Mr Melodious, not seen since ruining his chance in the Brocklesby with a tardy start having been very well supported in the market, repeated the feat having been well backed again here and still looked horribly green. He needs more time and probably a longer trip in due course. (op 12-1 tchd 14-1)

2755 NUTFIELD H'CAP — 1m 4f (P)
3:20 (3:20) (Class 6) (0-55,55) 4-Y-0+ **£2,047** (£604; £302) **Stalls** Low

Form RPR
000 **1** **Camera Shy (IRE)**[68] 1082 4-8-8 **49** ow1 PatCosgrave 4 57
(K A Morgan) *t.k.h: chsd ldr for 3f: styd prom: rdn over 2f out: styd on wl u.p to ld towards fin* **7/1**[3]
00-5 **2** ½ **Moonshine Creek**[22] 2100 6-8-5 **46** oh1 ChrisCatlin 6 53
(P W Hiatt) *t.k.h: chsd ldrs: wnt 2nd 9f out: led over 3f out: rdn over 2f out: hdd and no ex towards fin* **11/2**[1]
2430 **3** nk **Looks The Business (IRE)**[13] 2353 7-8-9 **55** (t) JackDean(5) 12 62
(W G M Turner) *t.k.h: chsd ldrs: wnt 2nd 3f out: ev ch and rdn fr over 2f out: unable qckn fnl f* **8/1**
30-0 **4** 1 **Swords**[24] 2051 6-8-9 **50** EddieAhern 9 55
(R E Peacock) *stdd s: hld up in midfield: hdwy 4f out: chsd ldng trio and rdn jst over 2f out: kpt on but nt pce to chal ldrs* **9/1**
00-4 **5** ½ **Makai**[25] 1643 5-7-13 **47** oh1 ow1 RossAtkinson(7) 14 51
(M R Hoad) *t.k.h: hld up in midfield: hdwy over 3f out: chsd ldrs and rdn over 2f out: kpt on but nvr quite pce to rch ldrs* **16/1**
4-20 **6** 1 **Andorran (GER)**[12] 345 5-8-7 **48** (b) FrancisNorton 10 51+
(A Bailey) *t.k.h: hld up in rr: stl bhd and swtchd rt 3f out: pushed along and styd on fr over 1f out: nt rch ldrs* **15/2**
0403 **7** 5 **Artzola (IRE)**[43] 1562 8-8-11 **52** TQuinn 11 47
(C A Horgan) *taken down early: stdd s: t.k.h: hld up bhd: hdwy over 4f out: rdn 3f out: hung lft and no imp fr 2f out* **6/1**[2]
006- **8** 2¼ **Laughing Game**[324] 3624 4-8-9 **50** HayleyTurner 1 41
(A M Hales) *t.k.h: hld up in tch: bmpd 5f out: rdn over 2f out: sn wknd* **16/1**
-500 **9** 4½ **Ruwain**[35] 1747 4-8-5 **46** oh1 TPO'Shea 7 30
(W J Musson) *hmpd s: t.k.h: hld up in rr: n.d* **10/1**
3650 **10** 4½ **Lordswood (IRE)**[24] 2053 4-8-11 **52** LPKeniry 8 29
(J R Best) *t.k.h: hld up bhd: hdwy over 4f out: rdn over 2f out: sn struggling* **12/1**
0-45 **11** hd **Ground Patrol**[38] 1673 7-8-9 **50** JohnEgan 3 26
(N R Mitchell) *a towards rr: rdn over 4f out: sme hdwy u.p 3f out: sn struggling* **7/1**[3]
/00- **12** 6 **Our Glenard**[501] 203 9-8-0 **46** oh1 NataliaGemelova(5) 13 13
(J E Long) *stdd s: a bhd: wl bhd last 3f: t.o* **33/1**
560- **13** hd **Ireland Dancer (IRE)**[359] 2545 4-9-0 **55** IanMongan 5 21
(P M Phelan) *t.k.h: hld up in midfield: hmpd and lost pl wl over 4f out: bhd after: t.o* **25/1**
0P-0 **14** nse **Captain Marryat**[4] 2640 7-8-6 **47** oh1 ow1 PaulDoe 2 13
(M J Attwater) *dwlt: sn bustled up to ld: rdn and hdd over 3f out: sn wknd: t.o* **33/1**

2m 35.27s (2.27) **Going Correction** +0.10s/f (Slow) **14** Ran SP% **125.8**
Speed ratings (Par 101): **96,95,95,94,94 93,90,88,85,82 82,78,78,78**
CSF £46.62 CT £324.55 TOTE £10.00: £2.40, £2.00, £3.70; EX 72.40 TRIFECTA Not won..
Owner Michael Ogburn **Bred** Haras D'Etreham And Madame Lily Ades **Trained** Little Marcle, H'fords

FOCUS
A moderate middle-distance handicap in which the early pace was steady and it developed into a sprint. It paid to be handy and the front six pulled a long way clear of the others. The form is not solid despite the placed horses being close to their recent form.
Camera Shy(IRE) Official explanation: trainer's rep said, regarding running, that the gelding was better suited by the longer trip allowing it to settle.
Artzola(IRE) Official explanation: jockey said mare lost a near-fore shoe and hung left in straight
Ireland Dancer(IRE) Official explanation: jockey said gelding hung badly left throughout
Captain Marryat Official explanation: trainer's rep said gelding had made a noise

2756 OUTWOOD MEDIAN AUCTION MAIDEN STKS — 7f (P)
3:50 (3:51) (Class 6) 3-4-Y-0 **£2,388** (£705; £352) **Stalls** Low

Form RPR
34- **1** **Transfer**[215] 6644 3-9-0 0 WilliamBuick 7 92+
(A M Balding) *chsd ldr tl led 3f out: rdn clr wl over 1f out: rdn out: readily* **11/4**[2]
-220 **2** 3¼ **Totally Focussed (IRE)**[20] 2161 3-9-0 73 IanMongan 10 80
(S Dow) *t.k.h: hld up in midfield: rdn and hdwy over 2f out: chsd wnr 1f out: no imp* **3/1**[3]
0-20 **3** 6 **Dark Camellia**[14] 2342 3-8-9 72 EddieAhern 8 59
(H J L Dunlop) *trckd ldrs: rdn to chse wnr 2f out: sn outpcd by wnr: lost modest 2nd 1f out* **7/1**
-662 **4** 3¼ **Farthermost (IRE)**[21] 2127 3-9-0 70 RichardHughes 2 55
(R Hannon) *trckd ldrs on inner: swtchd rt and rdn jst over 2f out: sn outpcd and btn: wnt poor 4th ins fnl f* **9/4**[1]
0406 **5** 1¼ **Ma Ridge**[24] 2055 4-9-10 47 RichardThomas 6 55
(T D McCarthy) *led tl 3f out: sn rdn: wknd qckly wl over 1f out* **66/1**
500- **6** ¾ **Rondeau (GR)**[202] 6827 3-9-0 68 JimCrowley 5 49
(P R Chamings) *t.k.h: hld up wl in tch: rdn and sltly hmpd jst over 2f out: sn outpcd and wl btn* **16/1**
5 **7** 2¼ **Al Gillani (IRE)**[79] 923 3-9-0 0 PatCosgrave 13 43
(J R Boyle) *s.i.s: hld up bhd: sme hdwy over 3f out: rdn over 2f out: sn outpcd and wl btn* **33/1**
0- **8** ½ **Silver Diamond**[247] 5881 3-8-9 0 AdrianMcCarthy 14 37
(W Jarvis) *in tch in midfield on outer: rdn 3f out: wl bhd fnl 2f* **100/1**
0 **9** 1 **Hundonette**[11] 2427 3-8-9 0 ShaneKelly 1 34
(R M H Cowell) *s.i.s: nvr on terms* **33/1**
5- **10** ½ **World View (IRE)**[241] 6065 3-8-9 0 PatDobbs 4 33
(M P Tregoning) *in tch in midfield: rdn 3f out: sn struggling: wl bhd fnl 2f* **20/1**
11 1¼ **Shadayid Khanum (IRE)** 3-8-9 0 MartinDwyer 3 30
(M P Tregoning) *s.i.s: bhd: rdn 3f out: sn lost tch* **16/1**
0-00 **12** 23 **Eau Sauvage**[94] 772 4-9-5 37 (v[1]) HayleyTurner 12 —
(M J Attwater) *a bhd: rdn and lost tch over 4f out: t.o fnl 2f* **100/1**
-64 **13** 30 **Betonart**[9] 2480 3-8-9 0 SebSanders 9 —
(R M Beckett) *bhd: lost tch and eased fr over 2f out: t.o: sddle slipped* **14/1**
0600 **14** 2 **Sweet Refrain**[27] 1959 3-8-9 51 (v[1]) PaulDoe 11 —
(M J Attwater) *s.i.s: racd awkwardly in rr: wl t.o fnl 2f: virtually p.u ins fnl f* **66/1**

1m 24.97s (0.17) **Going Correction** +0.10s/f (Slow)
WFA 3 from 4yo 10lb **14** Ran SP% **129.0**
Speed ratings (Par 101): **103,99,92,88,87 86,83,83,82,81 80,53,19,17**
CSF £11.99 TOTE £3.90: £1.30, £1.60, £3.00; EX 14.80 Trifecta £66.40 Pool: £534.04. 5.71 winning units..
Owner D H Back **Bred** Kingsclere Stud **Trained** Kingsclere, Hants

FOCUS
A modest and uncompetitive maiden with plenty of dead wood and the race was dominated by those with form on the board who also dominated the market. The form looks sound with the runner-up rated to his best.
Totally Focussed(IRE) Official explanation: jockey said bit pulled through colt's mouth
Betonart Official explanation: jockey said saddle slipped

2757 BLINDLEY HEATH FILLIES' H'CAP — 6f (P)
4:20 (4:29) (Class 5) (0-75,75) 3-Y-0 **£2,331** (£693; £346; £173) **Stalls** Low

Form RPR
0 **1** **Princess Rose Anne (IRE)**[13] 2366 3-9-4 **72** LPKeniry 3 78
(E F Vaughan) *mde all: rdn jst over 2f out: clr ins fnl f: tiring fnl 50yds: hld on* **9/1**
2526 **2** hd **Leading Edge (IRE)**[11] 2428 3-9-6 **74** ChrisCatlin 7 79
(M R Channon) *bhd and rdn after 2f: gd hdwy u.p on inner over 1f out: chsd wnr fnl 100yds: clsng qckly but nt quite rch wnr* **8/1**
0-12 **3** ½ **Rosie Says No**[10] 2452 3-8-9 **63** ShaneKelly 1 66
(R M H Cowell) *chsd wnr tl 4f out: chsd ldng pair after: rdn and nt qckn jst over 2f out: styd on again fnl f: wnt 3rd wl ins fnl f* **3/1**[1]
-113 **4** 3¾ **Requisite**[11] 2428 3-9-7 **75** SebSanders 10 66
(I A Wood) *chsd ldrs on outer: wnt 2nd 4f out: clr w wnr over 2f out: ev ch tl wknd qckly jst ins fnl f: lost 2 pls fnl 100yds* **4/1**[2]
33-3 **5** ¾ **Midnight Fling**[42] 1587 3-9-2 **70** WilliamBuick 4 59
(R Charlton) *chsd ldrs: rdn and unable qckn jst over 2f out: no ch w ldrs after* **12/1**
3402 **6** ½ **Firespin (USA)**[23] 2074 3-8-3 **57** (t) JohnEgan 6 44
(M Botti) *t.k.h: rdn over 2f out: sn outpcd by ldrs and n.d after* **7/1**
0-36 **7** 1½ **Pantherii (USA)**[38] 1671 3-8-9 **61** ow3 NelsonDeSouza 8 46
(P F I Cole) *racd in midfield: lost pl and rdn over 2f out: n.d after* **6/1**
030- **8** 2½ **Hawk Eyed Lady (IRE)**[197] 6897 3-9-5 **73** TPQueally 9 48
(J A Osborne) *racd wd: a bhd* **16/1**
526- **9** ¾ **My Pin Up**[167] 7216 3-9-4 **72** PatDobbs 2 44
(Christian Wroe) *s.i.s: a towards rr: rdn 3f out: no prog* **33/1**
-400 **10** 2½ **May Day Queen (IRE)**[16] 2276 3-9-6 **74** (b[1]) RichardHughes 5 38
(R Hannon) *a towards rr: rdn over 2f out: nvr on terms* **9/2**[3]

1m 12.34s (0.44) **Going Correction** +0.10s/f (Slow) **10** Ran SP% **127.6**
Speed ratings (Par 96): **101,100,100,95,94 93,91,88,87,83**
CSF £86.49 CT £282.47 TOTE £12.40: £3.30, £2.80, £1.60; EX 123.30 Trifecta £399.60 Part won. Pool: £562.91. 0.60 winning units..
Owner Miss Rose-Anne Galligan **Bred** C McCarthy **Trained** Newmarket, Suffolk

FOCUS
An ordinary fillies' handicap, but they went a serious pace in this and the front three pulled well clear of the others with the third setting the level.

2758 ARDINGLY H'CAP — 7f (P)
4:50 (4:54) (Class 6) (0-65,65) 4-Y-0+ **£2,047** (£604; £302) **Stalls** Low

Form RPR
2-10 **1** **Strabinios King**[17] 2263 4-9-5 **63** FrancisNorton 7 73
(M Wigham) *t.k.h: chsd ldrs: swtchd ins and rdn over 1f out: r.o wl u.p to ld wl ins fnl f* **11/2**[1]
12-4 **2** ½ **The City Kid (IRE)**[142] 173 5-9-2 **60** PaulEddery 4 69
(G D Blake) *chsd ldng pair: chsd ldr u.p wl over 1f out: led jst over 1f out: hdd and no ex wl ins fnl f* **13/2**[2]
6101 **3** 1¾ **Napoletano (GER)**[39] 1641 7-9-4 **62** (p) SebSanders 13 66
(S Dow) *dropped in bhd after s: t.k.h: hld up in rr: hdwy and grad edgd out rt fr wl over 1f out: r.o strly to snatch 3rd last strides: nt threaten ldng pair* **10/1**
14-3 **4** hd **Shaded Edge**[14] 2337 4-9-2 **60** FergusSweeney 14 63
(D W P Arbuthnot) *chsd ldrs: rdn and unable qckn wl over 1f out: styd on again u.p fnl f* **13/2**[2]
20-0 **5** 1½ **Run For Ede'S**[32] 1842 4-9-5 **63** (p) IanMongan 8 62
(P M Phelan) *t.k.h: led: rdn over 2f out: hdd jst over 1f out: fdd fnl 100yds* **25/1**
6045 **6** shd **Teen Ager (FR)**[6] 2556 4-9-7 **65** LPKeniry 11 64
(P Burgoyne) *t.k.h: hld up in midfield: rdn and effrt 2f out: kpt on same pce* **9/1**
0045 **7** 1 **Norcroft**[31] 1865 6-9-7 **65** (p) JohnEgan 1 61
(Mrs C A Dunnett) *bhd: hdwy on inner 2f out: swtchd rt and sme hdwy u.p over 1f out: kpt on same pce ins fnl f* **14/1**

50-1 **8** 3/4 **High Class Problem (IRE)**[141] 176 5-8-12 **56**............. ChrisCatlin 12 50
(D C O'Brien) *t.k.h: chsd ldr tl wl over 1f out: sn drvn: wknd jst over 1f out* **20/1**

5565 **9** *hd* **Double Valentine**[58] 1253 5-8-11 **55**.............. ShaneKelly 6 49
(R Ingram) *s.i.s: sn in midfield: hdwy on outer over 3f out: rdn and outpcd bnd 2f out: n.d after* **16/1**

-620 **10** 1 1/4 **Rhapsilian**[31] 1872 4-9-3 **61**.............................. RobertHavlin 2 51
(J A Geake) *stdd s: t.k.h: hld up in rr: nvr trbld ldrs* **12/1**

2042 **11** *nk* **Sovereignty (JPN)**[14] 2337 6-8-12 **61**...................... JamesMillman(5) 10 51
(D K Ivory) *t.k.h: hld up in midfield: rdn and lost pl over 2f out: n.d after* **8/1**[3]

3663 **12** 1 1/4 **Imperium**[13] 2355 7-8-11 **58**....................................(v) TravisBlock(3) 9 44
(Jean-Rene Auvray) *t.k.h: hld up in midfield: hmpd and lost pl 5f out: bhd fnl 2f* **10/1**

040 **13** *nk* **Trivia (IRE)**[43] 1565 4-9-6 **64**............................... JamesDoyle 3 49
(Ms J S Doyle) *in tch in midfield on inner: rdn over 2f out: wknd 2f out: sn bhd* **14/1**

1m 25.77s (0.97) **Going Correction** +0.10s/f (Slow) **13** Ran SP% **128.0**
Speed ratings (Par 101): **98,97,95,95,93 93,92,91,91,89 89,87,87**
CSF £35.60 CT £275.32 TOTE £5.60: £1.90, £2.90, £2.40; EX 52.10 Trifecta £213.00 Place 6: £63.23, Place 5: £23.96. Part won. Pool: £300.06. 0.40 winning units..Anthill was withdrawn. Price at time of withdrawal 8/1. Rule 4 applies to all bets. Deduct 10p in the pound.
Owner Val Kelly **Bred** Newsells Park Stud Limited **Trained** Newmarket, Suffolk

FOCUS
Competitive if modest fare and the form is ordinary but sound, rated through the runner-up and sixth.
T/Plt: £90.50 to a £1 stake. Pool: £60,252.97. 485.85 winning tickets. T/Qpdt: £60.50 to a £1 stake. Pool: £2,743.20. 33.50 winning tickets. SP

2540 SANDOWN (R-H)
Thursday, June 5

OFFICIAL GOING: Sprint course - soft (good to soft in places); round course - good to soft (good in places)

2759 SODEXO PRESTIGE MAIDEN AUCTION STKS — 5f 6y
6:15 (6:18) (Class 5) 2-Y-O — **£3,885** (£1,156; £577; £288) **Stalls** High

Form RPR

36 **1** **Love You Louis**[11] 2424 2-8-9 0................................ JimCrowley 10 76
(J R Jenkins) *mde virtually all and slt ld tl asserted ins fnl 2f: hrd drvn fnl f: jst hld on* **14/1**

023 **2** 3/4 **Souter's Sister (IRE)**[5] 2618 2-8-4 0......................... RichardSmith 1 68+
(R Hannon) *chsd ldrs: wnt 2nd jst ins fnl f: styd on wl u.p cl home: jst failed* **9/4**[1]

3 *shd* **Bobs Dreamflight** 2-8-6 0.................................... DuranFentiman(3) 6 73+
(D K Ivory) *str: bit bkwd: towards rr and rdn 3f out: hdwy appr fnl f and edgd lft: styd on strly fnl 75yds: gng on cl home* **66/1**

4 *nk* **Hail Promenader (IRE)** 2-8-13 0.............................. MichaelHills 11 76+
(B W Hills) *w'like: s.i.s: bhd: pushed along 2f out: gd hdwy appr fnl f: swtchd lft: styd on strly fnl 75yds: fin wl* **11/4**[2]

0 **5** 2 1/4 **Sweet Applause (IRE)**[27] 1967 2-8-4 0...................... RichardThomas 5 58
(A P Jarvis) *w wnr: rdn 1/2-way: lost 2nd jst ins fnl f: fdd cl home* **33/1**

6 1 3/4 **Timeteam (IRE)** 2-8-9 0.. PaulDoe 4 57
(S Kirk) *w'like: leggy: t.k.h: in tch: rdn 2f out: fading whn nudged lft 1f out* **9/1**

7 *hd* **Amour Propre** 2-8-9 0... DaneO'Neill 8 56
(H Candy) *unf: chsd ldrs: rdn 2f out: wknd over 1f out* **14/1**

440 **8** 4 **Lucky Punt**[14] 2324 2-8-11 0...................................... PatDobbs 9 44
(B G Powell) *in tch: rdn 1/2-way: sn btn* **14/1**

9 1 1/4 **Arachnophobia (IRE)** 2-8-11 0................................. PaulEddery 2 40
(Pat Eddery) *w'like: leggy: s.i.s: drvn and outpcd most of way* **16/1**

10 2 **Vien (IRE)** 2-8-9 0.. RyanMoore 7 30
(R Hannon) *str: s.i.s: a outpcd* **5/1**[3]

64.19 secs (2.59) **Going Correction** +0.425s/f (Yiel) **10** Ran SP% **114.4**
Speed ratings (Par 93): **96,94,94,94,90 87,87,81,79,75**
CSF £44.83 TOTE £13.00: £3.60, £1.20, £8.00; EX 33.50.
Owner J Pepper **Bred** Mrs Wendy Jenkins **Trained** Royston, Herts
■ Stewards' Enquiry : Richard Smith one-day ban: used whip with excessive frequency (Jun 22)

FOCUS
An ordinary looking maiden and, as is often the case here, the rail proved a big advantage. The form looks messy and unsatisfactory.

NOTEBOOK
Love You Louis had less to do here than at Newmarket and, crucially, he bagged the far-side rail. He took full advantage, making almost all the running. He was tiring at the finish but he is a speedy type and a sharper track will probably suit him in handicap company. (tchd 12-1)
Souter's Sister(IRE), who ran over 6f at Newbury last time, was drawn worst of all. She stayed on well down the outside and was only beaten by a rival who had the advantage of racing on the rail. (op 5-2 tchd 11-4 in a place)
Bobs Dreamflight, whose dam won over 6f and was placed in three Listed races over that trip, did best of the newcomers, belying his long odds. He should have learnt plenty from this and better ground might suit this son of Royal Applause.
Hail Promenader(IRE), a half-brother to five winners, was fancied on his debut but he missed the break. Held up, but on the favoured far rail, he kept on well late and is another who should be all the better for this debut outing. (op 5-2 tchd 3-1)
Sweet Applause(IRE), a half-sister to Eternally, a 5f winner at two, showed good early speed to keep the eventual winner company to a furlong and a half out. (op 50-1)
Timeteam(IRE), a brother to Chauvinism, a 6f winner at two and later a useful performer at 6f to 1m in Hong Kong, was a bit too keen on this debut. (op 7-1)
Amour Propre cost only 1,500gns but his dam is a half-sister to Corrybrough, Artie and Kingscross, from the family of top-class sprinter Cape Of Good Hope, so he is bred to go a bit.

2760 WISECALL CLAIMS INSURANCE ASSISTANCE H'CAP — 5f 6y
6:45 (7:04) (Class 4) (0-85,85) 3-Y-O+ — **£5,180** (£1,541; £770; £384) **Stalls** High

Form RPR

0012 **1** **Crimson Fern (IRE)**[6] 2583 4-9-1 **75**......................... PatrickHills(3) 13 88+
(M S Saunders) *trckd ldr tl led after 2f: hrd drvn and qckly 2l clr 1f out: hld on wl cl home* **11/2**[2]

3300 **2** 3/4 **Highland Warrior**[6] 2583 9-8-13 **70**......................... MickyFenton 2 79+
(P T Midgley) *stdd s and swtchd rt to far rail: rdn 1/2-way: hdwy u.p over 1f out: styd on to take 2nd fnl 50yds but nvr quite gng pce to rch wnr* **20/1**

0-42 **3** 3/4 **Glasshoughton**[29] 1908 5-9-12 **83**........................... PhillipMakin 10 89
(M Dods) *slt ld 2f: styd chsng wnr tl no ex fnl 50yds* **4/1**[1]

6410 **4** 1/2 **Judge 'n Jury**[40] 1624 4-9-3 **74**..................................(t) JohnEgan 12 78
(R A Harris) *lw: chsd ldrs: rdn over 2f out: styd on same pce fnl f* **8/1**

2131 **5** 2 1/2 **Diriculous**[16] 2293 4-9-9 **80**...................................... JimCrowley 3 75+
(T G Mills) *lw: in tch: rdn over 2f out: kpt on ins fnl f but nvr gng pce to rch ldrs* **7/1**[3]

6-63 **6** *nk* **River Thames**[48] 1451 5-9-9 **80**.............................. JamieSpencer 6 74
(K A Ryan) *swtg: in rr: rdn 1/2-way: styd on u.p fnl f but nvr in contention* **11/2**[2]

2450 **7** 1 **Fromsong (IRE)**[8] 2504 10-9-9 **80**............................. DaneO'Neill 8 71
(D K Ivory) *mid-div: rdn over 2f out: a struggling to go pce* **25/1**

0-00 **8** 1/2 **The Lord**[5] 2598 8-10-0 **85**...................................... AlanDaly 9 74
(W G M Turner) *chsd ldrs: rdn 3f out: wknd ins fnl 2f* **25/1**

2601 **9** 3/4 **Namir (IRE)**[29] 1908 6-8-12 **72**...............................(vt) DuranFentiman(3) 4 58
(D Shaw) *lw: s.i.s: swtchd rt to far rail: t.k.h early: a outpcd* **16/1**

36-0 **10** *shd* **Don Pele (IRE)**[56] 1278 6-9-10 **84**..........................(p) KevinGhunowa(3) 1 70
(R A Harris) *sn drvn and outpcd: sme prog fnl f* **33/1**

0-61 **11** 2 **Zowington**[27] 1956 6-9-13 **84**................................. IanMongan 11 62+
(C F Wall) *slowly away: rdn 1/2-way and a outpcd* **8/1**

0440 **12** *nk* **Dazed And Amazed**[19] 2195 4-9-12 **83**.......................(b) RyanMoore 5 60
(R Hannon) *in tch: rdn 1/2-way: nvr in contention and wknd over 1f out* **8/1**

1-56 **13** 7 **Annes Rocket (IRE)**[127] 364 3-8-4 **68**....................... RichardSmith 7 20
(J C Fox) *slowly away: a bhd* **50/1**

63.00 secs (1.40) **Going Correction** +0.425s/f (Yiel)
WFA 3 from 4yo+ 7lb **13** Ran SP% **119.8**
Speed ratings (Par 105): **105,103,102,101,97 97,95,94,93,93 90,89,78**
CSF £117.58 CT £508.61 TOTE £5.90: £2.20, £5.80, £2.00; EX 125.30.
Owner M S Saunders **Bred** David Brickley **Trained** Green Ore, Somerset

FOCUS
A fair sprint handicap in which once again a high draw proved helpful. The runner-up rated to this year's form sets the level.
Fromsong(IRE) Official explanation: jockey said gelding had a breathing problem
Annes Rocket(IRE) Official explanation: jockey said colt missed the break and never travelled

2761 CHARLES RUSSELL H'CAP — 7f 16y
7:20 (7:22) (Class 4) (0-85,84) 3-Y-O — **£5,180** (£1,541; £770; £384) **Stalls** High

Form RPR

4020 **1** **Eastern Hills**[19] 2189 3-8-11 **72**.............................. GregFairley 8 80
(M Johnston) *in rr tl hdwy on ins 3f out: swtchd lft ins fnl 2f and sn led: drvn out fnl f* **11/1**

0111 **2** 2 **Topazes**[24] 2047 3-9-1 **76**...................................... JamieSpencer 10 79+
(M L W Bell) *lw: trckd ldrs: hdwy and rdn 2f out: sn n.m.r and hung rt u.p: rdn and wnt rt again ins fnl f: styd on to chse wnr sn after but a readily hld* **11/4**[1]

310- **3** 1 1/2 **Non Sucre (USA)**[243] 6017 3-9-2 **77**.......................... StephenDonohoe 11 76
(P A Blockley) *led: rdn and hdd ins fnl 2f: styd on same pce fnl f* **25/1**

120 **4** 1/2 **Magnitude**[28] 1923 3-9-9 **84**.................................. MichaelHills 4 82
(W J Haggas) *lw: in rr tl hdwy on outside over 3f out: chsd ldrs and rdn ins fnl 2f: one pce appr fnl f* **3/1**[2]

6550 **5** 3/4 **Desert Clover (USA)**[26] 1988 3-9-0 **75**...................... NelsonDeSouza 2 71
(P F I Cole) *chsd ldrs: rdn over 2f out: sn one pce: styd on again cl home* **16/1**

-254 **6** *nk* **Amylee (IRE)**[19] 2196 3-9-5 **80**.............................(b) PhilipRobinson 1 75
(C G Cox) *lw: s.i.s: sn rcvrd: chsd ldr over 2f out: wknd ins fnl f* **7/1**

1-20 **7** 1 3/4 **Talk Of Saafend (IRE)**[12] 2412 3-9-5 **80**.................... JimmyFortune 9 76+
(R Hannon) *towards rr but in tch: hdwy whn bdly hmpd ins fnl 2f: styd on again ins fnl f: nt rcvr* **10/1**

10-0 **8** 4 **Errigal Lad**[68] 1074 3-9-0 **80**................................... NeilBrown(5) 5 59
(K A Ryan) *in rr whn hmpd ins fnl 2f: nt rcvr* **14/1**

0-5 **9** 16 **Shamrock Lady (IRE)**[31] 1868 3-9-0 **75**..................... TPO'Shea 7 11
(J Gallagher) *rrd stalls: slowly away: a bhd* **20/1**

01-0 **10** 1 1/2 **Blues Minor (IRE)**[15] 2311 3-9-4 **79**.......................... RyanMoore 6 11+
(R Hannon) *lw: chsd ldr: rdn whn bdly hmpd ins fnl 2f: sn btn and eased* **6/1**[3]

1m 30.81s (1.31) **Going Correction** +0.225s/f (Good) **10** Ran SP% **117.0**
Speed ratings (Par 101): **101,98,97,96,95 95,93,88,70,68**
CSF £41.56 CT £614.86 TOTE £14.80: £4.40, £1.10, £7.00; EX 52.40.
Owner Sheikh Hamdan Bin Mohammed Al Maktoum **Bred** Azienda Agricola Patrizia **Trained** Middleham Moor, N Yorks
■ Stewards' Enquiry : Greg Fairley five-day ban: careless riding (June 19-23)

FOCUS
An average handicap run at a fair pace but a somewhat messy race with the runner-up to his bare Windsor form.
Eastern Hills Official explanation: trainer had no explanation for the apparent improvement in form
Talk Of Saafend(IRE) Official explanation: jockey said filly suffered interference in running
Blues Minor(IRE) Official explanation: jockey said colt suffered interference in running

2762 IGINDEX.CO.UK H'CAP — 1m 14y
7:50 (7:52) (Class 3) (0-90,87) 4-Y-O+ — **£6,799** (£2,023; £1,011; £505) **Stalls** High

Form RPR

5046 **1** **Twilight Star (IRE)**[7] 2545 4-9-0 **78**..........................(t) TedDurcan 8 89+
(R A Teal) *t.k.h towards rr but in tch: swtchd rt ins fnl 3f: drvn to ld ins fnl 2f: hld on whn pressed cl home* **16/1**

5211 **2** *hd* **Carlitos Spirit (IRE)**[26] 1996 4-8-12 **76**...................... AlanMunro 3 83
(B R Millman) *chsd ldrs: drvn along 2f out: styd on wl thrght fnl f: gng on cl home: nt quite get up* **6/1**

0-13 **3** *hd* **Cactus King**[40] 1630 5-9-2 **80**................................ IanMongan 1 87
(P M Phelan) *in rr: hdwy fr 3f out: swtchd rt over 1f out: styd on strly ins fnl f: gng on cl home* **16/1**

514/ **4** 1/2 **Overturn (IRE)**[607] 5805 4-9-9 **87**............................. AdamKirby 9 93+
(W R Swinburn) *slt advantage after 1f: narrowly hdd over 2f out: styd pressing ldrs u.p fr over 1f out: kpt on gamely: outpcd nr fin* **5/1**[3]

5-04 **5** 1 1/2 **Russian Epic**[14] 2334 4-8-13 **77**................................ PhilipRobinson 6 79
(M A Jarvis) *led 1f: styd trcking ldr tl led again over 2f out: hdd ins fnl quarter m: styd on same pce fnl f* **9/2**[2]

2146 **6** 1 1/4 **Full Victory (IRE)**[5] 2619 6-9-1 **79**........................... JimmyFortune 12 79
(R A Farrant) *chsd ldrs: hrd drvn fr over 2f out: kpt on same pce: wknd ins fnl f* **10/3**[1]

6043 **7** 1/2 **Zero Cool (USA)**[7] 2545 4-9-3 **81**.............................. RyanMoore 2 79
(G L Moore) *in rr: rdn and styd on fr 3f out: nvr gng pce to rch ldrs: wknd ins fnl f* **11/2**

510 **8** 1 **Rock Anthem (IRE)**[29] 1910 4-8-10 **74**........................ PatDobbs 10 70
(Mike Murphy) *in rr: sme hdwy on ins over 2f out: nvr rchd ldrs: wknd fnl f* **14/1**

00-6 **9** 1 3/4 **Ivory Lace**[13] 2371 7-9-9 **87**.................................... JimCrowley 5 79
(S Woodman) *s.i.s: bhd: sme prog fnl 2f* **40/1**

/40- **10** 5 **Kestrel Cross (IRE)**[438] 783 6-9-7 **85**........................ DaneO'Neill 4 66
(L M Cumani) *chsd ldrs: pushed lft ins fnl 3f: sn wknd* **10/1**

11 2 **Right Stuff (FR)**[162] 5-8-8 72 FergusSweeney 11 48
(G L Moore) *bit bkwd: a towards rr* **20/1**

1m 43.21s (-0.09) **Going Correction** +0.225s/f (Good) **11** Ran SP% **122.3**
Speed ratings (Par 107): **109,108,108,108,106 105,104,103,102,97 95**
CSF £113.46 CT £1619.60 TOTE £21.10: £4.40, £2.70, £3.50; EX 203.70.
Owner G M Harris **Bred** D G Hardisty Bloodstock **Trained** Ashtead, Surrey

FOCUS
A bunched finish to this competitive handicap, but the form looks sound enough rated around the placed horses.

NOTEBOOK
Twilight Star(IRE) gave progressive handicapper Bushman a bit of a boost as he was well held behind him over this course and distance a week earlier. He picked up in good style when asked to go on and, while the bunch were closing in on him in the final strides, the way he travelled into the race suggests he might be capable of better still. (op 20-1)
Carlitos Spirit(IRE), chasing a hat-trick, kept on well in the latter stages and was edging closer at the line. He remains progressive but, with another little rise likely following this effort, the Handicapper might just be in charge now. (op 11-2 tchd 7-1)
Cactus King, who appreciates time between his races, had had 40 days off since he last ran. He stays further than this and the stiff finish here suits him. (op 14-1)
Overturn(IRE) had not been seen since finishing fourth in the Group 3 Autumn Stakes back in October 2006, but a mark of 87 gave him a chance on his return. He was not without his supporters either, and he ran well, being prominent throughout. There should be a race in him off this sort of mark. (op 6-1 tchd 7-1)
Russian Epic, back on softish ground, tends to run well enough to ensure that the Handicapper does not drop him much, and he generally runs into one or two better weighted. Official explanation: jockey said gelding has a breathing problem (tchd 4-1)
Full Victory(IRE), a previous course and distance winner, had conditions to suit so was a little disappointing in the circumstances. (op 4-1 tchd 9-2)
Zero Cool(USA) could not confirm last week's course and distance form over Twilight Star. (op 13-2 tchd 7-1)
Kestrel Cross(IRE), returning from a 438-day absence, is potentially well handicapped if his new stable can get him back to his best. His winning form in Ireland was on good ground and faster. (op 7-1)

2763 IGINDEX.CO.UK MAIDEN STKS 1m 2f 7y
8:25 (8:31) (Class 5) 3-Y-O £3,885 (£1,156; £577; £288) Stalls High

Form RPR
- 1 **Kensington Oval** 3-9-3 0 RyanMoore 12 88+
(Sir Michael Stoute) *w'like: scope: in rr but in tch: hdwy over 2f out: str run over 1f out: led fnl 100yds: won gng away* **7/2**[2]
52 2 1 1/4 **Eqbaal**[19] [2197] 3-9-3 0 RHills 6 85
(J L Dunlop) *led 3f: styd trcking ldr: upsides 3f out: slt ld appr fnl 2f: styd on tl hdd and outpcd fnl 100yds* **4/5**[1]
3 1 1/4 **King Olav (UAE)** 3-9-3 0 PhilipRobinson 8 83+
(M A Jarvis) *athletic: in rr: shkn up and hdwy over 2f out: green and hung rt sn after and again over 1f out: green but styd on thrght fnl f and gaining on ldng duo cl home* **16/1**
3 4 1 3/4 **Seventh Cavalry (IRE)**[13] [2370] 3-9-3 0 TedDurcan 7 79
(H R A Cecil) *trckd ldr: led 7f out: hdd appr fnl 2f: wknd ins fnl f* **8/1**[3]
4 5 3 **Kossack**[13] [2370] 3-9-3 0 DaneO'Neill 4 73+
(L M Cumani) *in rr: hdwy over 2f out: styng on whn faltered ins fnl f and momentarily eased: styd on again cl home* **10/1**
6 1 **Intercom** 3-9-3 0 TPQueally 11 71
(H R A Cecil) *w'like: scope: in tch: rdn and hdwy over 2f out: nvr quite gng pce to rch ldrs: wknd ins fnl f* **16/1**
-320 7 3 **King Bathwick (IRE)**[17] [2244] 3-9-3 67 ChrisCatlin 3 65
(B R Millman) *chsd ldrs: rdn over 2f out: wknd over 1f out* **25/1**
8 9 **Alkyoni (IRE)** 3-8-12 0 (p) JohnEgan 2 42
(Jane Chapple-Hyam) *w'like: leggy: rdn along 6f out: a towards rr* **50/1**
0 9 5 **Catholic Hill (USA)**[21] [2119] 3-9-3 0 JamieSpencer 10 37
(B J Meehan) *t.k.h: chsd ldrs: rdn 3f out: sn wknd* **33/1**
10 1/2 **Unique (IRE)** 3-9-3 0 JimCrowley 9 36
(N P Littmoden) *str: s.i.s: a in rr* **66/1**

2m 13.27s (2.77) **Going Correction** +0.225s/f (Good) **10** Ran SP% **120.0**
Speed ratings (Par 99): **97,96,95,93,91 90,88,80,76,76**
CSF £6.68 TOTE £4.40: £1.40, £1.10, £3.40; EX 7.80.Colour Trooper (66/1) and Watercolours (66/1) were withdrawn. Rule 4 does not apply.
Owner The Duke Of Devonshire & Mrs J Magnier **Bred** The Duke Of Devonshire And Globe Bstock **Trained** Newmarket, Suffolk

FOCUS
A decent looking maiden, with the runner-up and seventh appearing to give a good guide to the level. They went steady early, though, so the form, rated around the second, fourth and fifth, may not be entirely reliable.
Catholic Hill(USA) Official explanation: jockey said colt lost its action

2764 IGSPORT.COM H'CAP 1m 2f 7y
8:55 (9:02) (Class 4) (0-80,80) 4-Y-O+ £4,533 (£1,348; £674; £336) Stalls High

Form RPR
-444 1 **Ross Moor**[16] [2278] 6-8-7 64 ow1 FergusSweeney 4 73
(Mike Murphy) *in rr: hdwy 4f out: styd on to ld ins fnl 2f: drvn out fnl f* **8/1**
00-3 2 3 3/4 **Hannicean**[13] [2373] 4-9-0 71 PhilipRobinson 9 73+
(M A Jarvis) *lw: chsd ldrs: rdn over 2f out: styd on to chse wnr ins fnl f but nvr any ch* **15/8**[1]
52-0 3 hd **Venir Rouge**[15] [2304] 4-9-4 75 TGMcLaughlin 5 76+
(M Salaman) *in rr: hdwy fr 2f out: styd on strly u.p fnl f: gng on cl home* **8/1**
6-53 4 1 1/4 **Zaif (IRE)**[15] [2304] 5-9-8 79 GeorgeBaker 3 78
(Simon Earle) *lw: chsd ldrs: rdn and kpt on fr 2f out: one pce ins fnl f* **13/2**
13-3 5 1 **Spirit Of Adjisa (IRE)**[13] [2369] 4-9-5 76 PatDobbs 2 73
(Pat Eddery) *led to 7f out: rdn and outpcd over 2f out: styd on again ins fnl f* **11/2**[3]
00-0 6 1/2 **Olimpo (FR)**[31] [1877] 7-9-2 78 JamesMillman[(5)] 1 74
(B R Millman) *t.k.h: chsd ldr: led 7f out: qcknd 4l clr over 3f out: hdd ins fnl 2f and sn wknd* **14/1**
3344 7 shd **Blacktoft (USA)**[40] [1630] 5-9-3 74 (e) RyanMoore 8 69
(S C Williams) *plld hrd in rr: styd on fnl 2f: nvr in contention* **5/1**[2]
221- 8 23 **Abydos**[231] [6286] 4-9-9 80 TPQueally 6 29
(A P Stringer) *t.k.h: in tch tl wknd over 3f out* **10/1**

2m 13.31s (2.81) **Going Correction** +0.225s/f (Good) **8** Ran SP% **118.1**
Speed ratings (Par 105): **97,94,93,92,92 91,91,73**
CSF £24.30 CT £128.97 TOTE £10.60: £2.40, £1.30, £2.50; EX 33.90 Place 6 £147.70, Place 5 £55.04.
Owner M Murphy **Bred** R T And Mrs Watson **Trained** Westoning, Beds

FOCUS
Again the early pace was steady and the race developed into something of a sprint. The form is rated at face value but looks less than solid.

T/Plt: £75.60 to a £1 stake. Pool: £81,221.02. 783.45 winning tickets. T/Qpdt: £20.20 to a £1 stake. Pool: £5,336.79. 195.00 winning tickets. ST

2765 - 2768a (Foreign Racing) - See Raceform Interactive

[2638] BATH (L-H)
Friday, June 6

OFFICIAL GOING: Good (7.7)
Wind: Moderate, against Weather: Fine

2769 E B F/WBX.COM DERBY DAY PROMOTIONS MAIDEN STKS 5f 161y
6:25 (6:26) (Class 5) 2-Y-O £3,626 (£1,079; £539; £269) Stalls Centre

Form RPR
34 1 **Burning Flute**[15] [2324] 2-9-3 0 TPO'Shea 7 74
(B J Meehan) *mde all: rdn 2f out: r.o* **7/4**[1]
2 3/4 **Sparkling Crystal (IRE)** 2-8-12 0 WilliamBuick 9 66
(B W Hills) *hld up: swtchd lft and hdwy wl over 1f out: swtchd rt ins fnl f: kpt on* **16/1**
0 3 2 1/2 **Magical Illusion**[15] [2338] 2-8-12 0 CatherineGannon 10 58
(P D Evans) *a.p: rdn over 2f out: ev ch over 1f out: nt qckn fnl f* **66/1**
4 hd **Casting Couch (IRE)** 2-8-12 0 RobertHavlin 12 57+
(B W Hills) *hld up: hdwy 2f out: reminder over 1f out: kpt on same pce fnl f* **16/1**
3 5 shd **Mesyaal**[15] [2338] 2-9-3 0 EdwardCreighton 3 62
(M R Channon) *a.p: rdn and ev ch over 1f out: nt qckn fnl f* **9/4**[2]
6 3/4 **Swift Chap** 2-8-12 0 JamesMillman[(5)] 1 59
(B R Millman) *t.k.h early: chsd ldrs on ins: rdn and no hdwy fnl 2f* **40/1**
7 hd **Saharan Royal** 2-8-5 0 SophieDoyle[(7)] 11 54
(M Salaman) *hld up: hdwy on outside 2f out: no imp fnl f* **40/1**
8 9 **Pyrus Time (IRE)** 2-9-3 0 LPKeniry 2 28
(J S Moore) *t.k.h early: bhd fnl 2f* **16/1**
9 1 1/2 **Gilbertian** 2-9-3 0 GeorgeBaker 8 23
(R M Beckett) *prom: n.m.r 2f out: sn wknd* **5/1**[3]
10 1 1/4 **Hawkspur (IRE)** 2-9-3 0 SteveDrowne 5 18
(R Hannon) *hld up in tch: n.m.r and lost pl over 3f out: bhd fnl 2f* **8/1**
11 9 **Into My Arms** 2-8-12 0 FergusSweeney 6 —
(M S Saunders) *s.s: outpcd* **40/1**

1m 14.08s (2.88) **Going Correction** +0.25s/f (Good) **11** Ran SP% **121.4**
Speed ratings (Par 93): **90,89,85,85,85 84,84,72,70,68 56**
CSF £33.37 TOTE £2.70: £1.10, £2.80, £14.10; EX 46.40.
Owner Clipper Logistics **Bred** Wood Hall Stud Limited **Trained** Manton, Wilts

FOCUS
Probably a fair race, but little previous form to go on in a race where only three had previous racecourse experience.

NOTEBOOK
Burning Flute put his previous experience to good use and produced what was required from the front. (op 13-8 tchd 11-8)
Sparkling Crystal(IRE) ◆ made a promising debut especially considering she is bred to need further. Normal improvement will see her off the mark. (tchd 20-1)
Magical Illusion left behind the form of her Salisbury debut last month where she had finished over nine lengths behind Mesyaal. (op 50-1)
Casting Couch(IRE) ◆ is the first foal of a sister to a Group 3 winner and half-sister to Champion Hurdle winner Alderbrook. Not knocked about, she should do better over a longer trip in due course and seems sure to come on for the outing. (op 12-1)
Mesyaal was a bit disappointing and failed to confirm her nine-length superiority over Magical Illusion at Salisbury on his debut.
Swift Chap is a half-brother to multiple winners Summer Charm and Spree Vision. Like a few of these, he should come into his own when tackling further. (tchd 33-1)

2770 WBX.COM EURO 2008 SHIRTS FOR NEW ACCOUNTS H'CAP 1m 2f 46y
6:55 (6:55) (Class 5) (0-70,68) 4-Y-O+ £2,590 (£770; £385; £192) Stalls Low

Form RPR
21-1 1 **Auntie Mame**[23] [2097] 4-8-12 59 TPO'Shea 5 63
(D J Coakley) *hld up in tch: outpcd over 4f out: hdwy over 2f out: led 1f out: rdn and r.o* **3/1**[2]
0-65 2 3/4 **Nightspot**[15] [2335] 7-9-7 68 StephenCarson 2 71
(Eve Johnson Houghton) *set stdy pce: qcknd over 4f out: rdn and hdd 1f out: r.o* **5/1**[3]
2503 3 hd **Gracechurch (IRE)**[5] [2640] 5-8-9 56 FrancisNorton 4 58
(R J Hodges) *chsd ldrs: wnt 2nd 3f out: rdn and ev ch 1f out: kpt on* **3/1**[2]
/050 4 3/4 **Viscount Rossini**[23] [2100] 6-7-9 49 oh4 StacyRenwick[(7)] 8 50
(A W Carroll) *chsd ldr to 3f out: nt clr run on ins and swtchd rt wl ins fnl f: kpt on* **25/1**
3542 5 1 1/4 **Merrymadcap (IRE)**[7] [2561] 6-8-13 60 SteveDrowne 6 58
(M Blanshard) *hld up and bhd: hdwy over 2f out: rdn and one pce fnl f* **9/4**[1]
6 6 12 **Sayago (GER)**[24] [2071] 6-8-9 56 WilliamBuick 1 30
(C J Mann) *hld up: bhd fnl 4f* **20/1**
000- 7 115 **Gallego**[212] [6727] 6-8-9 63 SophieDoyle[(7)] 3 —
(R J Price) *bolted to s: dwlt: t.k.h and gd hdwy over 7f out: wknd over 4f out: eased whn no ch fnl 2f* **12/1**

2m 13.76s (2.76) **Going Correction** +0.375s/f (Good) **7** Ran SP% **113.7**
Speed ratings (Par 103): **103,102,102,101,100 91,—**
CSF £18.10 CT £47.45 TOTE £3.50: £2.10, £3.10; EX 15.90.
Owner Finders Keepers Partnership **Bred** Eclipse-Rogers Partnership **Trained** West Ilsley, Berks

FOCUS
A modest, falsely-run race with the first five covered by less than three lengths. The form is rated through the winner with the proximity of the fourth a worry.
Gallego Official explanation: jockey said gelding had bolted to the start

2771 EVENT MOBILE CATERING CLAIMING STKS 5f 11y
7:30 (7:30) (Class 6) 3-Y-O £1,748 (£520; £260; £129) Stalls Centre

Form RPR
-340 1 **Midnite Blews (IRE)**[23] [2099] 3-8-4 61 PNolan[(7)] 7 61
(A B Haynes) *sn pushed along and wl outpcd: gd hdwy over 1f out: led jst ins fnl f: sn edgd lft: r.o wl* **5/1**[2]
46-3 2 5 **Fast Feet**[120] [470] 3-9-5 75 NCallan 2 51
(K A Ryan) *chsd ldr: led wl over 1f out: sn rdn: hdd jst ins fnl f: one pce* **4/7**[1]
000- 3 nk **Rose De Rita**[212] [6721] 3-8-5 0 ow1 SimonWhitworth 5 36
(L P Grassick) *chsd ldrs: rdn over 1f out: one pce fnl f* **50/1**
00 4 hd **Flying Seasons**[23] [2099] 3-9-0 0 JamesMillman[(5)] 3 49
(B R Millman) *hld up: rdn over 1f out: nt clr run and swtchd rt jst ins fnl f: kpt on* **14/1**

 The Form Book, Raceform Ltd, Compton, RG20 6NL

40-0 **5** 2 ¼ **Mr Funshine**[18] 2240 3-9-0 58 JackMitchell(5) 6 41
(Mrs P N Dutfield) *a.p: rdn and ev ch whn edgd rt over 1f out: wknd towards fin* **12/1**
00-0 **6** 3 ¾ **No Point (IRE)**[23] 2099 3-8-3 42 ow1 TPO'Shea 4 12
(P A Blockley) *bhd: rdn 3f out: short-lived effrt over 1f out* **12/1**
-500 **7** ¾ **Casla Beag (IRE)**[10] 2474 3-8-2 59 (v[1]) CatherineGannon 1 8
(B Palling) *led: hdd wl over 1f out: rdn and wknd qckly ins fnl f* **9/1**[3]

64.72 secs (2.22) **Going Correction** +0.25s/f (Good) **7 Ran SP% 114.3**
Speed ratings (Par 97): **92,84,83,83,79 73,72**
CSF £8.24 TOTE £6.20: £2.40, £1.20; EX 10.10.
Owner A Moore & P Brett **Bred** Lodge Park Stud **Trained** Limpley Stoke, Bath

FOCUS
A weak affair won in a slow time with the leaders appearing to go off too fast.

2772 PALADIN GROUP MEDIAN AUCTION MAIDEN STKS 1m 5y
8:00 (8:05) (Class 6) 3-Y-O £1,942 (£578; £288; £144) Stalls Low

Form RPR
5-2 **1** **Pippbrook Gold**[32] 1876 3-9-3 0 FergusSweeney 1 78
(J R Boyle) *hld up in tch: rdn over 2f out: wnt 2nd over 1f out: edgd lft ins fnl f: r.o to ld cl home* **11/4**[2]
002 **2** ½ **Sunny Peace**[15] 2328 3-8-12 76 NCallan 11 72
(B G Powell) *led 1f: chsd ldr: led over 2f out: rdn whn rdr dropped rein briefly jst over 1f out: hdd cl home* **11/2**[3]
0-6 **3** 4 **Papuan Prince (IRE)**[32] 1876 3-8-12 0 HaddenFrost(5) 9 67
(S Kirk) *a.p: rdn over 2f out: one pce fnl f* **8/1**
00 **4** 1 ¾ **Scary Movie (IRE)**[20] 2198 3-9-3 0 TPO'Shea 10 63
(D J Coakley) *in rr: rdn over 1f out: sn swtchd rt: styd on ins fnl f: nvr nrr* **20/1**
42 **5** 2 **Caro George (USA)**[11] 2455 3-8-12 0 SteveDrowne 5 54
(R Charlton) *hld up in tch: rdn over 1f out: wknd wl ins fnl f* **5/4**[1]
6 1 ¾ **Zantic** 3-9-3 0 FrancisNorton 12 55
(P R Chamings) *s.i.s: sme hdwy on ins over 1f out: n.d* **25/1**
060- **7** hd **Ochenvay**[219] 6591 3-8-9 50 TolleyDean(3) 2 49?
(C J Down) *hld up towards rr: hdwy on ins over 3f out: pushed along over 2f out: wknd over 1f out* **66/1**
8 3 **Age Of Miracles (IRE)** 3-9-3 0 RobertHavlin 4 47
(G A Ham) *hld up in mid-div: hdwy on ins over 3f out: rdn over 1f out: wknd fnl f* **66/1**
0 **9** 2 ¾ **Alutando (IRE)**[28] 1964 3-8-12 0 CatherineGannon 6 36
(B Palling) *s.i.s: sn rcvrd: led after 1f: rdn and hdd over 2f out: wknd jst over 1f out* **16/1**
0- **10** 10 **Shybutwilling (IRE)**[359] 2569 3-8-7 0 JackMitchell(5) 3 13
(Mrs P N Dutfield) *prom: hmpd and lost pl over 5f out: hung rt and rn wd bnd over 4f out: sn bhd* **66/1**
-0 **11** 100 **Danse De Sioux (IRE)**[28] 1965 3-8-5 0 SophieDoyle(7) 8 —
(P A Blockley) *hung bdly rt thrght: a in rr: t.o whn rn v wd bnd over 3f out* **66/1**

1m 43.94s (3.14) **Going Correction** +0.375s/f (Good) **11 Ran SP% 118.1**
Speed ratings (Par 97): **99,98,94,92,90 89,88,85,83,73** —
CSF £17.38 TOTE £3.80: £1.40, £1.90, £2.80; EX 16.00.
Owner Prosser Family Partnership **Bred** Mrs R M Prosser **Trained** Epsom, Surrey

FOCUS
A modest maiden in which the form seems to make sense.
Shybutwilling(IRE) Official explanation: jockey said filly hung right
Danse De Sioux(IRE) Official explanation: jockey said filly hung badly right-handed throughout

2773 GURKHA WELFARE TRUST H'CAP 5f 161y
8:35 (8:36) (Class 4) (0-85,85) 3-Y-O+ £4,209 (£1,252; £625; £312) Stalls Centre

Form RPR
2-51 **1** **Whiskey Junction**[18] 2240 4-9-1 72 LPKeniry 8 88
(A M Balding) *led: hdd wl over 1f out: rdn to ld ins fnl f: r.o* **11/2**[2]
2443 **2** ½ **Cheveton**[5] 2644 4-8-9 66 FrancisNorton 5 80
(R J Price) *a.p: led wl over 1f out: sn rdn: hdd ins fnl f: kpt on* **7/1**
0334 **3** 2 ¾ **Digital**[5] 2644 11-9-1 79 ThomasO'Brien(7) 6 84
(M R Channon) *stdd s: sn bhd: hdwy on outside over 1f out: edgd lft wl ins fnl f: nt trble ldrs* **13/2**[3]
-063 **4** 1 ½ **China Cherub**[15] 2339 5-9-4 75 (b) FergusSweeney 2 75
(S Dow) *a.p: rdn over 1f out: no ex ins fnl f* **8/1**
0-33 **5** 3 ¾ **Sweet Afton (IRE)**[15] 2326 5-9-11 85 PatrickHills(3) 4 72
(M S Saunders) *hld up: hdwy on outside over 2f out: rdn over 1f out: sn edgd rt: wknd ins fnl f* **15/2**
1223 **6** 1 ½ **Alexander Huricane (IRE)**[27] 2005 4-9-1 72 NCallan 7 54
(K A Ryan) *a.p: ev ch over 1f out: sn rdn: wknd fnl f* **9/4**[1]
30-0 **7** 1 **Meridian Line (IRE)**[20] 2196 3-9-2 81 JamesDoyle 3 59
(J G Portman) *hld up: hrd rdn and shortlived effrt over 1f out* **25/1**
-210 **8** 3 ¾ **Nobilissima (IRE)**[34] 1796 4-9-8 82 TolleyDean(3) 1 48
(J L Spearing) *w wnr tl rdn over 2f out: sn wknd: eased ins fnl f* **9/1**
3004 **9** 39 **Woodcote (IRE)**[15] 2326 6-9-11 82 (p) PaulDoe 9 —
(P R Chamings) *rrd s: a in rr: eased whn no ch fnl 2f* **9/1**

1m 11.86s (0.66) **Going Correction** +0.25s/f (Good)
WFA 3 from 4yo+ 8lb **9 Ran SP% 118.7**
Speed ratings (Par 105): **105,104,100,98,93 91,90,85,33**
CSF £44.93 CT £259.46 TOTE £5.70: £2.20, £2.40, £2.10; EX 45.10.
Owner Kingsclere Racing CLub **Bred** Mrs I A Balding **Trained** Kingsclere, Hants

FOCUS
The two least-exposed runners fought out the finish and the form has been rated fairly positively.
Sweet Afton(IRE) Official explanation: jockey said mare hung right-handed
Woodcote(IRE) Official explanation: jockey said gelding was never travelling.

2774 INVENTURES FILLIES' H'CAP 5f 11y
9:05 (9:06) (Class 5) (0-70,69) 3-Y-O £2,590 (£770; £385; £192) Stalls Centre

Form RPR
333- **1** **Lambrini Lace (IRE)**[172] 7170 3-8-10 61 TolleyDean(3) 12 65
(Mrs L Williamson) *a.p: led jst over 1f out: sn rdn: r.o* **7/1**[3]
31-3 **2** 1 **Heaven**[23] 2102 3-9-6 68 NCallan 5 68
(P J Makin) *hld up: sn in tch: nt clr run briefly over 1f out: rdn and kpt on ins fnl f* **9/4**[1]
5046 **3** ¾ **Our Kally**[11] 2452 3-7-9 50 oh2 DavidProbert(7) 8 47
(M D I Usher) *hld up: hdwy over 2f out: rdn and ev ch wl over 1f out: nt qckn ins fnl f* **11/1**
3560 **4** ½ **Planet Paradise (IRE)**[17] 2268 3-8-2 50 oh5 CatherineGannon 10 46
(D Shaw) *s.i.s: hld up and bhd: hdwy on outside over 2f out: rdn wl over 1f out: kpt on towards fin* **28/1**
0-20 **5** ¾ **Rathmolyon**[23] 2102 3-9-4 66 RobertHavlin 11 59
(D Haydn Jones) *led: rdn and hdd jst over 1f out: no ex wl ins fnl f* **6/1**[2]
360- **6** nse **Miss Poppy**[228] 6386 3-9-7 69 FrancisNorton 2 62
(P R Chamings) *prom: rdn whn n.m.r 2f out: one pce fnl f* **10/1**
050 **7** nk **Acclimate**[15] 2341 3-8-8 56 FergusSweeney 3 48
(W S Kittow) *hld up towards rr: hdwy on ins over 2f out: nt clr run and swtchd rt over 1f out: rdn and edgd lft wl ins fnl f: one pce* **7/1**[3]
334 **8** 2 **Allium (IRE)**[99] 734 3-8-2 50 WilliamBuick 6 34
(B W Hills) *hld up in rr: hdwy over 1f out: sn rdn: wknd ins fnl f* **6/1**[2]
065- **9** ¾ **Pretty Bonnie**[214] 6693 3-7-12 53 StacyRenwick(7) 1 35
(A E Price) *w ldr tl over 2f out: sn rdn: wknd over 1f out* **12/1**
6-04 **10** 1 **Croeso Cusan**[17] 2279 3-7-11 52 ow1 SophieDoyle(7) 7 30
(J L Spearing) *hld up towards rr: pushed along over 2f out: rdn over 1f out: no rspnse* **16/1**
0-30 **11** 22 **Only In Jest**[8] 2551 3-8-11 66 JWStevenson(7) 4 —
(J Gallagher) *half-rrd and s.s: c wd over 3f out: a in rr* **16/1**

64.13 secs (1.63) **Going Correction** +0.25s/f (Good) **11 Ran SP% 124.7**
Speed ratings (Par 96): **96,94,93,92,91 91,90,87,86,84 49**
CSF £24.52 CT £186.83 TOTE £11.00: £3.50, £1.50, £3.20; EX 34.90 Place 6 £63.16, Place 5 £28.03.
Owner Mrs Judy Halewood **Bred** Louis Creaven **Trained** Saighton, Cheshire

FOCUS
A weak fillies' handicap with the third and fourth both running from out of the handicap.
Only In Jest Official explanation: jockey said filly reared as the stalls opened
T/Plt: £56.00 to a £1 stake. Pool: £44,919.38. 585.35 winning tickets. T/Qpdt: £12.90 to a £1 stake. Pool: £3,373.38. 192.89 winning tickets. KH

2395 CATTERICK (L-H)
Friday, June 6

OFFICIAL GOING: Good to soft (good to soft in places; 8.5)
Wind: light 1/2 against Weather: overcast

2775 EUROPEAN BREEDERS' FUND NOVICE STKS 5f
1:50 (1:51) (Class 5) 2-Y-O £4,094 (£1,209; £604) Stalls Low

Form RPR
1 **1** **Senor Mirasol**[35] 1778 2-9-0 0 FergalLynch 4 88
(K A Ryan) *mde all: kpt on wl fnl f* **10/1**
1 **2** 2 **Effort**[11] 2443 2-9-5 0 DeanMcKeown 6 86+
(M Johnston) *dwlt: hld up: hdwy over 3f out: chal over 1f out: edgd lft and no ex* **13/8**[1]
14 **3** 1 ½ **Go Nani Go**[14] 2377 2-9-2 0 TomEaves 1 77
(B Smart) *trckd ldrs: effrt 2f out: kpt on same pce* **2/1**[2]
1 **4** ¾ **Ykikamoocow**[44] 1555 2-8-7 0 SilvestreDeSousa 3 66+
(G A Harker) *chsd ldrs: edgd rt over 1f out: styd on ins fnl f* **13/2**[3]
5 ¾ **Lucky Art (USA)** 2-8-12 0 RobertWinston 5 68+
(J Howard Johnson) *w ldrs: rdn and hung bdly lft 1f out: sn wknd* **18/1**
216 **6** 1 ¾ **Veronicas Boy**[21] 2154 2-9-2 0 AndrewElliott 2 66
(G M Moore) *trckd ldrs: outpcd over 2f out: kpt on fnl f* **22/1**
0 **7** 8 **Igoyougo**[76] 957 2-8-12 0 MickyFenton 8 33
(P T Midgley) *sn outpcd and in rr* **8/1**
8 4 **Sweet Virginia (USA)** 2-8-7 0 PaulMulrennan 7 14
(K R Burke) *chsd ldrs: outpcd and lost pl after 2f* **50/1**

60.52 secs (0.72) **Going Correction** +0.05s/f (Good) **8 Ran SP% 116.5**
Speed ratings (Par 93): **96,92,90,89,88 85,72,66**
CSF £27.30 TOTE £13.00: £2.50, £1.40, £1.20; EX 38.90.
Owner Mrs Margaret Forsyth **Bred** P C Hunt **Trained** Hambleton, N Yorks

FOCUS
Five previous winners in the line-up and this is fairly solid novice form. The winner turned in an improved effort and is a likely type for a nursery.

NOTEBOOK
Senor Mirasol, a close-coupled, well-made type, had made a successful debut on the All-Weather at Southwell. He made every yard and won going away, and looks a fair prospect. (tchd 14-1)
Effort, on his toes in the paddock, missed a beat at the start. He moved upsides looking a real threat but tended to edge in behind the winner. This was altogether a different track to Carlisle and it did not suit him as well. (op 15-8 tchd 11-8)
Go Nani Go, taken to post well ahead of the rest, did nothing wrong but this seems to be as good as he is. (tchd 11-4)
Ykikamoocow, wide-margin winner of a seller here, ran really well in this much stronger company. Tending to edge right, she was sticking on in good style at the finish and should certainly win a claimer. (op 5-1)
Lucky Art(USA), on edge beforehand, hung badly left under pressure and will be seen to better advantage on a more conventional track. (op 16-1 tchd 22-1)
Veronicas Boy, back over five and encountering much easier ground, stuck on after getting outpaced and is now set for nurseries. (op 25-1 tchd 20-1)

2776 BILL HAGUE 90TH BIRTHDAY CELEBRATION (S) STKS 1m 5f 175y
2:25 (2:25) (Class 6) 4-Y-O+ £2,047 (£604; £302) Stalls Low

Form RPR
3202 **1** **Bijou Dan**[3] 2701 7-8-12 57 GregFairley 12 54
(G M Moore) *trckd ldrs: effrt over 3f out: led 2f out: styd on wl fnl f* **15/8**[1]
4 **2** 2 ¾ **Pendragon (USA)**[31] 1890 5-8-9 0 AndrewMullen(3) 5 50
(Mrs L B Normile) *trckd ldrs: effrt over 3f out: kpt on to take 2nd nr fin* **10/1**
1536 **3** nk **Court Of Appeal**[6] 2623 11-8-11 65 (tp) LanceBetts(7) 6 56
(B Ellison) *trckd ldrs: effrt over 3f out: chal 2f out: styd on same pce* **9/4**[2]
0-40 **4** 3 ½ **York Cliff**[49] 1459 10-8-12 52 LiamJones 7 45
(W M Brisbourne) *trckd ldrs: effrt over 3f out: one pce* **11/1**
5 nk **Sonnengold (GER)**[20] 7-8-7 0 TWilliams 9 40
(B J Llewellyn) *led at mod pce: qcknd over 7f out: hdd 2f out: fdd fnl f* **8/1**[3]
060 **6** ½ **Besi**[9] 989 6-8-8 41 ow1 SladeO'Hara(5) 11 45
(A Berry) *hld up in midfield: outpcd over 4f out: kpt on fnl 2f* **80/1**
4004 **7** ½ **Ronsard (IRE)**[5] 2643 6-8-6 40 ow1 RichardEvans(7) 4 44
(P D Evans) *hld up: effrt 4f out: edgd lft and kpt on fnl f* **9/1**
6 **8** ½ **Funky Town (IRE)**[13] 2395 6-8-9 0 PJMcDonald(3) 3 43
(Grant Tuer) *t.k.h in last: kpt on fnl 2f: nvr on terms* **11/1**
-000 **9** 21 **Fardi (IRE)**[13] 2395 6-8-7 15 DanielleMcCreery(5) 8 13
(K W Hogg) *t.k.h in midfield: lost pl over 2f out: sn bhd* **250/1**
00-P **10** 2 **Bobansheil (IRE)**[20] 2207 4-8-8 52 ow1 (v) TomEaves 2 —
(J S Wainwright) *hld up in rr: t.o 3f out* **25/1**

3m 8.25s (4.65) **Going Correction** +0.05s/f (Good) **10 Ran SP% 116.0**
Speed ratings (Par 101): **88,86,86,84,84 83,83,83,71,70**
CSF £21.90 TOTE £2.70: £1.02, £3.20, £1.40; EX 13.50.There was no bid for the winner.
Owner Bert Markey **Bred** James Thom And Sons **Trained** Middleham Moor, N Yorks

FOCUS
A weak seller. No gallop at all until the final mile and in the end the sixth, seventh and eighth are probably flattered.

Funky Town(IRE) Official explanation: jockey said, regarding running and riding, instructions were to drop horse out last and not make a move until 2f marker because gelding had been extremely keen in previous races; he added race had been run at a slow pace and things had not worked out as it had turned into a sprint; trainer said gelding had been difficult to teach to settle
Bobansheil(IRE) Official explanation: jockey said filly moved poorly throughout

2777 LIONWELD KENNEDY SPRINT H'CAP — 5f

3:00 (3:00) (Class 5) (0-70,70) 3-Y-0+ — **£2,590** (£770; £385; £192) — **Stalls** Low

Form — RPR

0060 **1** — **Windjammer**[6] 2596 4-9-6 **62** ....(b[1]) DavidAllan 6 — 73
(T D Easterby) *mde all: clr over 2f out: unchal* — **5/1**[2]

0650 **2** 1 3/4 **Darcy's Pride (IRE)**[4] 2676 4-9-8 **64** .... FergalLynch 9 — 69
(D W Barker) *chsd ldrs: kpt on to take 2nd jst ins fnl f: nt rch wnr* — **8/1**

-440 **3** 1 1/2 **Dark Champion**[11] 2444 8-9-5 **61** ....(v) TomEaves 3 — 61
(R E Barr) *chsd ldrs: styd on same pce fnl 2f* — **5/1**[2]

1/60 **4** 1 1/4 **Wicked Wilma (IRE)**[14] 2356 4-8-7 **54** .... DanielleMcCreery(5) 2 — 51+
(A Berry) *mid-div: hdwy on ins 2f out: kpt on: nvr rchd ldrs* — **25/1**

0100 **5** 1/2 **Brut**[7] 2583 6-9-7 **70** ....(p) AdeleRothery(7) 13 — 63
(D W Barker) *hld up in rr: hdwy on wd outside 2f out: styd on ins fnl f* **10/1**

0-56 **6** nk **Nusoor (IRE)**[21] 2145 5-8-7 **56** ....(b) PatrickDonaghy(7) 11 — 48
(Peter Grayson) *chsd ldrs: one pce fnl 2f* — **16/1**

0035 **7** nk **Toy Top (USA)**[4] 2676 5-8-13 **55** ....(b) PhillipMakin 4 — 46
(M Dods) *sn chsng wnr: wknd jst ins fnl f* — **4/1**[1]

-102 **8** 1 1/2 **Jun Fan (USA)**[11] 2448 6-8-5 **54** .... LanceBetts(7) 10 — 40
(B Ellison) *mid-div: hdwy 2f out: styng on same pce whn nt clr run wl ins fnl f* — **9/1**

0-00 **9** 1 1/4 **Strensall**[20] 2212 11-9-7 **63** .... RoystonFfrench 12 — 44
(R E Barr) *towards rr on outer: nvr on terms* — **28/1**

-004 **10** 1 1/2 **Rue Soleil**[4] 2676 4-8-10 **52** .... RobertWinston 7 — 28
(J R Weymes) *mid-div: effrt over 2f out: wknd fnl f* — **10/1**

-020 **11** 1/2 **Jakeini (IRE)**[27] 1997 5-9-8 **64** ....(p) TPQueally 8 — 38
(E S McMahon) *a towards rr: nvr a factor* — **7/1**[3]

0660 **12** nk **Percy Douglas**[31] 1893 8-8-6 **53** oh6 ow2.... AnnStokell(5) 1 — 26
(Miss A Stokell) *dwlt: a in rr* — **80/1**

60.42 secs (0.62) **Going Correction** +0.05s/f (Good) — **12** Ran SP% **119.5**
Speed ratings (Par 103): **97,94,91,89,89 88,88,85,83,81 80,79**
CSF £44.53 CT £217.09 TOTE £6.50: £1.90, £3.30, £1.90; EX 69.20.
Owner April Fools **Bred** Peter E Clinton **Trained** Great Habton, N Yorks

FOCUS
The winner, set alight by first-time blinkers, soon had these at full stretch and never looked in any danger. Overall the form looks sound at this level.
Jakeini(IRE) Official explanation: jockey said gelding was never travelling

2778 BOOK TICKETS ONLINE @ CATTERICKBRIDGE.CO.UK H'CAP — 5f 212y

3:35 (3:35) (Class 4) (0-85,84) 4-Y-0+ — **£4,209** (£1,252; £625; £312) — **Stalls** Low

Form — RPR

0002 **1** — **Heywood**[14] 2358 4-9-5 82 .... SilvestreDeSousa 2 — 92
(D Nicholls) *trckd ldr: led jst ins fnl f: kpt on wl* — **11/2**[3]

6044 **2** 1 **H Harrison (IRE)**[13] 2397 8-8-13 76 .... AndrewElliott 1 — 83
(I W McInnes) *led tl hdd and no ex jst ins fnl f* — **10/1**

5250 **3** 1/2 **Obe Royal**[3] 2692 4-8-4 70 ....(b) LukeMorris(3) 8 — 75
(P D Evans) *chsd ldrs: kpt on same pce fnl f* — **13/2**

3222 **4** 1 1/2 **Violent Velocity (IRE)**[13] 2400 5-8-5 71 .... AndrewMullen(3) 6 — 71
(J J Quinn) *dwlt: hdwy over 2f out: n.m.r over 1f out: nvr rchd ldrs* — **11/4**[1]

6-54 **5** hd **Makshoof (IRE)**[50] 1430 4-9-0 77 .... FergalLynch 5 — 77
(K A Ryan) *chsd ldrs on outside: kpt on same pce appr fnl f* — **9/2**[2]

-052 **6** 1 3/4 **Prince Namid**[13] 2398 6-8-12 75 .... RoystonFfrench 4 — 69
(Mrs A Duffield) *w ldrs on outer: drvn over 2f out: fdd fnl f* — **6/1**

0060 **7** 1 3/4 **Paris Bell**[17] 2293 6-8-12 75 .... DavidAllan 9 — 63
(T D Easterby) *hood removed v late: s.s: t.k.h in rr: a in rr* — **11/1**

01-6 **8** nk **Dig Deep (IRE)**[13] 2398 6-9-7 84 .... RobertWinston 7 — 71
(J J Quinn) *chsd ldrs: nt clr run over 1f out: nt rcvr: eased* — **8/1**

1m 13.92s (0.32) **Going Correction** +0.05s/f (Good) — **8** Ran SP% **116.4**
Speed ratings (Par 105): **99,97,97,95,94 92,90,89**
CSF £59.16 CT £370.80 TOTE £6.30: £2.20, £2.30, £2.30; EX 42.80.
Owner Martin Hignett **Bred** R F And S D Knipe **Trained** Sessay, N Yorks

FOCUS
The winner and runner-up were always in the right place. John Quinn's pair seemed to get in each other's way and the form does not look altogether reliable.
Dig Deep(IRE) Official explanation: jockey said gelding lost its action

2779 BARTON MAIDEN STKS — 1m 3f 214y

4:15 (4:22) (Class 5) 3-Y-0+ — **£2,590** (£770; £385; £192) — **Stalls** Low

Form — RPR

234 **1** — **Art Trend (IRE)**[20] 2191 3-8-11 83 .... TPQueally 3 — 81
(P W Chapple-Hyam) *trckd ldrs: led over 1f out: sn rdn: kpt on* — **4/9**[1]

0-3 **2** 1 3/4 **Shady Gloom (IRE)**[21] 2143 3-8-11 0 .... FergalLynch 2 — 78
(K A Ryan) *led tl over 1f out: kpt on same pce* — **6/1**[2]

0 **3** 13 **Bonny Bright Eyes**[10] 2488 3-8-6 0 .... RoystonFfrench 9 — 52
(P C Haslam) *chsd ldrs drvn over 4f out: one pce* — **16/1**

00- **4** 10 **Starlight Prince**[212] 6724 3-8-11 0 .... MickyFenton 4 — 41
(R Hollinshead) *t.k.h in rr: bhd fnl 5f* — **16/1**

00 **5** hd **Rye Rocket**[9] 2221 3-8-11 0 .... AndrewElliott 5 — 41
(K R Burke) *in rr: rdn and outpcd over 5f out* — **50/1**

0- **6** 19 **Rio Novo**[296] 4495 3-8-11 0 .... TomEaves 7 — 10
(J Howard Johnson) *chsd ldrs: outpcd over 5f out: sn lost pl* — **25/1**

7 3 1/4 **Brathay (IRE)** 4-9-12 0 .... PaulMulrennan 1 — 5
(M H Tompkins) *dwlt: sn chsng ldrs: outpcd 7f out: lost pl over 4f out* — **7/1**[3]

2m 37.96s (-0.94) **Going Correction** +0.05s/f (Good)
WFA 3 from 4yo 15lb — **7** Ran SP% **113.6**
Speed ratings (Par 103): **105,103,95,88,88 75,73**
CSF £3.61 TOTE £1.40: £1.30, £1.60; EX 3.40.
Owner Matthew Green **Bred** Abbeville And Meadow Court Partners **Trained** Newmarket, Suffolk

FOCUS
A very weakly contested maiden with just two in it from halfway. The winner did not have things his own way.

2780 PEN HILL H'CAP — 5f 212y

4:45 (4:47) (Class 6) (0-65,65) 3-Y-0+ — **£2,047** (£604; £302) — **Stalls** Low

Form — RPR

0000 **1** — **Royal Acclamation (IRE)**[44] 1558 3-9-0 **60** .... SilvestreDeSousa 2 — 71
(G A Harker) *chsd ldrs: styd on to ld jst ins fnl f: r.o* — **4/1**[2]

-201 **2** 2 **Miss Daawe**[4] 2676 4-9-0 **59** 6ex.... LanceBetts(7) 8 — 66
(B Ellison) *w ldrs: led over 1f out: hdd jst ins fnl f: no ex* — **10/3**[1]

-020 **3** hd **Soto**[38] 1703 5-9-11 **63** .... PaulMulrennan 5 — 69
(M W Easterby) *sn chsng ldrs: drvn over 3f out: kpt on fnl f* — **11/1**

6-04 **4** 1 **Orotund**[24] 2081 4-8-12 **50** .... DavidAllan 3 — 53
(T D Easterby) *led tl over 1f out: kpt on one pce* — **5/1**[3]

4423 **5** 1 3/4 **Mr Rooney (IRE)**[11] 2448 5-9-1 **56** .... PJMcDonald(3) 11 — 54
(D Nicholls) *chsd ldrs on outer: kpt on same pce fnl 2f* — **5/1**[3]

-600 **6** hd **Nufoudh (IRE)**[25] 2040 4-9-0 **52** .... DeanMcKeown 6 — 49
(Miss Tracy Waggott) *chsd ldrs: one pce fnl 2f* — **14/1**

020 **7** 1 1/2 **Regal Royale**[17] 2270 5-9-1 **53** ....(v) TomEaves 1 — 45
(Peter Grayson) *dwlt: kpt on fnl 2f: nvr nr ldrs* — **11/1**

-020 **8** hd **Campo Bueno (FR)**[33] 1826 6-9-7 **59** .... TPQueally 7 — 50
(A Berry) *mid-div: kpt on fnl 2f: nvr a threat* — **14/1**

4022 **9** 1 **Blackheath (IRE)**[18] 2248 12-9-2 **59** .... KellyHarrison(5) 12 — 47
(S T Mason) *chsd ldrs on outer: lost pl over 4f out: no threat after* — **16/1**

0060 **10** 1 **Royal Challenge**[17] 2270 7-9-13 **65** .... DanielTudhope 9 — 50
(I W McInnes) *in tch on outer: drvn and outpcd over 4f out: sn lost pl* **16/1**

00-0 **11** nk **Resolute Defender (IRE)**[10] 2490 3-9-0 **60** .... RobertWinston 4 — 42
(J Howard Johnson) *s.s: a in rr* — **50/1**

1m 14.16s (0.56) **Going Correction** +0.05s/f (Good)
WFA 3 from 4yo+ 8lb — **11** Ran SP% **120.1**
Speed ratings (Par 101): **98,95,95,93,91 91,89,88,87,86 85**
CSF £18.18 CT £140.92 TOTE £5.80: £2.80, £1.40, £3.40; EX 32.10.
Owner Good Breed Limited **Bred** The Susie Syndicate **Trained** Thirkleby, N Yorks
■ Stewards' Enquiry : Robert Winston caution: used whip when out of contention.

FOCUS
A moderate handicap. The race has been rated through the third's form this year, with improved form from the first two.
Royal Acclamation(IRE) Official explanation: trainer said, regarding apparent improvement in form, that gelding appreciated the drop back in trip and had a better draw.

2781 TURFTV BETTING SHOP SERVICE FILLIES' H'CAP — 7f

5:15 (5:16) (Class 5) (0-75,75) 3-Y-0+ — **£2,590** (£770; £385; £192) — **Stalls** Low

Form — RPR

00-6 **1** — **Medici Pearl**[14] 2375 4-9-13 **67** .... DavidAllan 7 — 82
(T D Easterby) *mid-div: hdwy on ins over 2f out: styd on to ld fnl 75yds* — **7/1**[3]

14-2 **2** 3/4 **Orpen Fire (IRE)**[32] 1867 3-9-11 **75** .... TPQueally 8 — 84
(E S McMahon) *led: hdd and no ex wl ins fnl f* — **11/4**[1]

1412 **3** 1 **Montiboli (IRE)**[3] 2705 3-9-4 **73** .... NeilBrown(5) 11 — 79
(K A Ryan) *mid-div: hdwy on outside over 3f out: kpt on wl fnl 2f* — **9/1**

0-60 **4** 1 1/4 **Flying Valentino**[13] 2400 4-9-8 **65** .... PJMcDonald(3) 3 — 72
(G A Swinbank) *hld up in tch: effrt 2f out: kpt on same pce* — **12/1**

0113 **5** 1/2 **Dressed To Dance (IRE)**[4] 2679 4-9-4 **65** ....(v) RichardEvans(7) 9 — 71
(P D Evans) *rr-div: hdwy on outer over 2f out: styd on same pce* — **5/1**[2]

3325 **6** 1 1/2 **Dorn Dancer (IRE)**[27] 2005 6-10-0 **68** .... FergalLynch 15 — 70
(D W Barker) *towards rr: effrt 2f out: styd on fnl f: nvr nr ldrs* — **9/1**

-604 **7** 3/4 **Vanatina (IRE)**[32] 1869 4-8-2 **49** .... DeanHeslop(7) 1 — 48
(W M Brisbourne) *chsd ldrs: one pce fnl 2f* — **16/1**

4-45 **8** 1 3/4 **Salerosa (IRE)**[17] 2269 3-8-9 **59** .... RoystonFfrench 6 — 50
(Mrs A Duffield) *chsd ldrs on outside: sn drvn along: hung rt and one pce fnl 2f* — **10/1**

60-4 **9** 3/4 **Princess Rhianna (IRE)**[17] 2282 3-8-12 **62** .... AndrewElliott 5 — 51
(Mrs G S Rees) *prom: effrt on inner over 2f out: hung lft and wknd over 1f out* — **28/1**

0-00 **10** 1/2 **Pay Time**[13] 2400 9-9-2 **59** .... MichaelJStainton(3) 13 — 50
(R E Barr) *rrd s: swtchd rt after s: nvr a factor* — **33/1**

0-60 **11** 1/2 **Veronicas Way**[17] 2282 3-7-13 **54** ow2.... KellyHarrison(5) 4 — 40
(G M Moore) *chsd ldrs: hung lft 2f out: sn wknd* — **18/1**

4300 **12** 1/2 **Lady Amberlini**[27] 2002 3-8-3 **60** .... PatrickDonaghy(7) 12 — 45
(P D Evans) *s.s: in rr: sme late hdwy* — **50/1**

546 **13** 5 **Mugeba**[32] 1867 7-9-2 **56** ....(t) MickyFenton 14 — 31
(Miss Gay Kelleway) *in rr: bhd fnl 2f* — **14/1**

-403 **14** 3 1/2 **Ensign's Trick**[27] 2009 4-8-11 **54** .... LukeMorris(3) 2 — 20
(W M Brisbourne) *chsd ldrs: lost pl 2f out* — **16/1**

1m 27.33s (0.33) **Going Correction** +0.05s/f (Good)
WFA 3 from 4yo+ 10lb — **14** Ran SP% **124.7**
Speed ratings (Par 100): **100,99,98,96,96 94,93,91,90,90 89,88,83,79**
CSF £27.01 CT £184.99 TOTE £9.00: £3.20, £1.30, £3.00; EX 35.00 Place 6: £22.38, Place 5: £17.12..
Owner Ryedale Partners No 3 **Bred** Larkwood Stud **Trained** Great Habton, N Yorks

FOCUS
Pretty solid form with the winner back on song and the fifth to her mark.
Salerosa(IRE) Official explanation: jockey said filly hung right-handed in home straight
T/Plt: £53.90 to a £1 stake. Pool: £50,125.74. 677.95 winning tickets. T/Qpdt: £33.50 to a £1 stake. Pool: £2,024.13. 44.60 winning tickets. WG

2591 DONCASTER (L-H)

Friday, June 6

OFFICIAL GOING: Straight course - good to firm (good in places); round course - good (good to firm in places) changing to good to soft (both courses) after race 2 (7.10)
Wind: Virtually nil Weather: Overcast and raining

2782 AJA FEGENTRI LADIES INVITATION H'CAP (LADY AMATEUR RIDERS) — 1m (R)

6:35 (6:36) (Class 6) (0-60,60) 4-Y-0+ — **£2,810** (£871; £435; £217) — **Stalls** Low

Form — RPR

4320 **1** — **Bivouac (UAE)**[33] 1822 4-10-3 **56** .... MrsCBartley 1 — 70
(G A Swinbank) *trckd ldrs: smooth hdwy to ld 3f out: rdn clr wl over 1f out: easily* — **4/1**[2]

5-00 **2** 5 **March Mate**[14] 2365 4-9-8 **47** .... MissLEllison 2 — 49
(B Ellison) *chsd ldrs on inner: pushed along over 3f out: rdn to chse wnr 2f out: sn drvn and kpt on same pce appr fnl f* — **8/1**

00-0 **3** nse **Jiminor Mack**[43] 1579 5-9-7 **46** oh1.... (p) MmeRUnrath 12 — 48
(W J H Ratcliffe) *stdd and hld up wl in rr: swtchd wd 4f out: rdn and hdwy wl over 1f out: styd on strly ins fnl f* — **33/1**

0-02 **4** 2 1/4 **Vesuvio**[35] 1775 4-10-0 **53** .... MissGDGracey-Davison 5 — 50
(C W Thornton) *midfield: hdwy over 3f out: rdn to chse ldrs over 2f out: drvn and kpt on same pce fr over 1f out* — **12/1**

0023 **5** 3/4 **Tizzy May (FR)**[6] 2617 8-10-4 **57** ....(v) MlleMPlat 8 — 52
(B Ellison) *chsd ldrs: rdn along: sltly outpcd and n.m.r over 3f out: kpt on u.p fnl 2f* — **9/1**

5032 **6** *1* **Valdan (IRE)**[7] 2568 4-10-0 **53**.....................(t) MissARyan 3 46
(M A Barnes) *s.i.s and bhd: gd hdwy on inner 4f out: swtchd rt and rdn to chse ldrs wl over 2f out: sn drvn and wknd wl over 1f out* **10/3**[1]
-024 **7** *nk* **Papa's Princess**[7] 2578 4-9-10 **49**..................... MissVCartmel 7 41
(J S Goldie) *towards rr tl sme late hdwy* **15/2**
-002 **8** *5* **Kunte Kinteh**[8] 2550 4-10-7 **60**..................... MissADeniel 11 41
(D Nicholls) *hld up in tch: hdwy to chse ldrs over 3f out: rdn over 2f out and sn btn* **6/1**[3]
0-00 **9** *2 1/2* **Just Oscar (GER)**[39] 1687 4-9-9 **48**..................... MissJAKidd 10 23
(W M Brisbourne) *a towards rr* **12/1**
4040 **10** *7* **Cantique (IRE)**[76] 972 4-9-7 **46** oh1..................... MissNJefferson 6 5
(R J Price) *led: rdn along and hdd 3f out: sn wknd* **50/1**
0600 **11** *1 3/4* **Sagunt (GER)**[27] 2003 5-10-4 **57**..................... MissFayeBramley 4 12
(S Curran) *cl up: rdn along over 4f out and sn wknd* **28/1**
-630 **12** *22* **Gifted Flame**[131] 328 9-9-7 **46** oh1..................... MissJKelly 9 —
(Miss A Stokell) *chsd ldrs to 1/2-way: sn wknd* **50/1**

1m 42.43s (1.43) **Going Correction** +0.225s/f (Good) **12** Ran SP% **115.9**
Speed ratings (Par 101): **101,96,95,93,92 91,91,86,84,77 75,53**
CSF £34.16 CT £925.62 TOTE £5.20: £1.90, £3.10, £5.90; EX 48.50.
Owner P J Hughes Developments Ltd **Bred** Darley **Trained** Melsonby, N Yorks
■ Stewards' Enquiry : Miss L Ellison one-day ban: careless riding (Jun 23)

FOCUS
A moderate handicap, confined to lady amateur riders, run at a fair pace. Bivouac was less exposed than most and did it well but the third limits the form.

2783 WESTSIDE MAIDEN AUCTION STKS 6f
7:10 (7:10) (Class 5) 2-Y-O £3,238 (£963; £481; £240) Stalls High

Form RPR
4 **1** **Classic Blade (IRE)**[41] 1616 2-8-9 0..................... RichardKingscote 3 83+
(Tom Dascombe) *sltly hmpd s: sn cl up: led 1/2-way: rdn over 1f out: kpt on gamely ins fnl f* **12/1**
34 **2** *1 1/4* **Favourite Girl (IRE)**[11] 2462 2-8-1 0..................... DuranFentiman(3) 8 74+
(T D Easterby) *trckd ldrs: swtchd lft and hdwy 2f out: rdn and n.m.r wl over 1f out: chsd wnr appr fnl f: sn drvn and kpt on* **11/4**[2]
6 **3** *3* **Jimwil (IRE)**[20] 2186 2-8-12 0..................... PhillipMakin 6 72
(M Dods) *trckd ldrs: effrt over 2f out: sn rdn and bmpd wl over 1f out: drvn and kpt on same pce appr fnl f* **7/1**[3]
4 **4** *1* **Watergate (IRE)**[7] 2569 2-9-1 0..................... SebSanders 7 72
(Sir Mark Prescott) *bmpd sltly s: sn trcking ldrs: swtchd lft and ev ch over 2f out: sn rdn and wknd over 1f out* **1/1**[1]
5 *3/4* **Tiger Goddess (IRE)** 2-8-7 0..................... LiamJones 5 62
(W J Haggas) *hld up in rr: hdwy over 2f out: swtchd lft and rdn over 1f out: kpt on ins fnl f: nrst fin* **14/1**
00 **6** *10* **Fasalee (IRE)**[27] 1987 2-8-9 0..................... JohnEgan 9 34
(A P Jarvis) *led: rdn along and hdd 1/2-way: sn wknd* **33/1**
0 **7** *6* **Free To Choose (IRE)**[51] 1399 2-8-9 0..................... DarrenWilliams 4 16
(A P Jarvis) *hmpd s: a in rr* **66/1**
4 **8** *13* **Flog It**[51] 1392 2-8-10 0 ow1..................... RobertWinston 2 —
(T D Easterby) *wnt rt s: cl up: rdn along over 2f out and wkng whn bmpd wl over 1f out* **40/1**
05 **9** *34* **Drachenfels**[13] 2388 2-9-1 0..................... DO'Donohoe 1 —
(K A Ryan) *chsd ldrs: rdn along 1/2-way: wknd over 2f out* **33/1**

1m 15.65s (2.05) **Going Correction** +0.175s/f (Good) **9** Ran SP% **113.3**
Speed ratings (Par 93): **93,91,87,86,85 71,63,46,1**
CSF £43.51 TOTE £17.40: £2.80, £1.50, £2.00; EX 73.00.
Owner The Classic Strollers Partnership **Bred** Ballybrennan Stud Ltd **Trained** Lambourn, Berks

FOCUS
A modest juvenile maiden. The form is nothing special, rated around the runner-up and the time, but the first two look capable of better.

NOTEBOOK
Classic Blade(IRE), fourth on his debut at Leicester, showed a much more professional attitude over this extra furlong and came home to score in determined fashion. The quicker ground proved more in his favour and he is not the first juvenile from this stable to show significant improvement from their debut efforts. A step into novice company now looks on the cards. (op 10-1 tchd 14-1)
Favourite Girl(IRE) was very well backed on this first outing over the extra furlong and had her chance. She ran right up to her previous level, getting the trip without much fuss, so rates the benchmark for this form. (op 5-1)
Jimwil(IRE) knew his job this time and posted a slightly improved effort for the step up to this distance. He already looks a nursery type and should get appreciate another furlong before the year is out. (tchd 9-1)
Watergate(IRE) had shown promise when fourth on his debut in a hotter race at Haydock a week previously, but he proved disappointing and was beaten before the final furlong pole. It is still too soon to be writing him off, however, and his next outing should reveal more. (op 4-5 tchd 4-6)
Tiger Goddess(IRE), a £37,000 purchase bred to be suited by this trip at two, took time to find her full stride on this racecourse bow. She kept on with some promise late on, however, and should really be all the sharper next time out. (tchd 16-1)

2784 RECTANGLE GROUP H'CAP 1m 2f 60y
7:40 (7:40) (Class 4) (0-85,85) 4-Y-O+ £6,476 (£1,927; £963; £481) Stalls Low

Form RPR
-514 **1** **Magic Echo**[31] 1903 4-9-2 **80**..................... PhillipMakin 1 92
(M Dods) *t.k.h: led and sn clr: shkn up over 2f out: rdn over 1f out: unchal* **16/1**
-020 **2** *5* **Eglevski (IRE)**[28] 1970 4-9-7 **85**..................... DaneO'Neill 7 87
(J L Dunlop) *trckd ldrs: hdwy to chse wnr 3f out: rdn wl over 1f out: sn drvn and no imp* **7/2**[2]
3115 **3** *1 1/2* **Shogun Prince (IRE)**[32] 1877 5-8-13 **77**..................... SebSanders 6 76
(W Jarvis) *trckd ldrs: hdwy 3f out: rdn wl over 1f out and kpt on same pce* **9/2**[3]
-002 **4** *1 1/4* **Peruvian Prince (USA)**[7] 2582 6-9-3 **81**..................... PaulHanagan 4 78
(R A Fahey) *trckd ldrs: hdwy 3f out: rdn along over 2f out: sn drvn and one pce* **15/8**[1]
0650 **5** *1 3/4* **Ahlawy (IRE)**[21] 2155 5-8-8 **72**..................... PaulMulrennan 9 65
(M W Easterby) *s.i.s: in rr tl hdwy 2f out: sn rdn and kpt on fnl f: nrst fin* **25/1**
/4-1 **6** *shd* **Celticello (IRE)**[10] 2476 6-8-6 **77** 6ex ow2..................... RichardEvans(7) 2 70
(P D Evans) *hld up towards rr: sme hdwy fnl 2f: nvr a factor* **11/2**
-413 **7** *10* **Snowed Under**[17] 2278 7-8-13 **77**..................... PatCosgrave 8 50
(J D Bethell) *chsd wnr: rdn along 4f out: wknd wl over 2f out* **16/1**
00-0 **8** *15* **Golden Dagger (IRE)**[69] 1072 4-8-12 **76**..................... DO'Donohoe 5 19
(K A Ryan) *a in rr* **33/1**
-134 **9** *6* **Kindlelight Blue (IRE)**[111] 591 4-8-11 **75**..................... MickyFenton 3 6
(N P Littmoden) *in tch: pushed along 1/2-way: rdn 4f out and sn wknd* **20/1**

2m 13.47s (2.27) **Going Correction** +0.375s/f (Good) **9** Ran SP% **113.9**
Speed ratings (Par 105): **105,101,99,98,97 97,89,77,72**
CSF £68.91 CT £300.24 TOTE £14.60: £3.10, £1.50, £1.70; EX 84.60.
Owner D C Batey **Bred** D C Batey **Trained** Denton, Co Durham

FOCUS
A fair handicap which saw Magic Echo make all decisively. Hard form to assess, as the winner did have an easy time in front.
Peruvian Prince(USA) Official explanation: jockey said gelding was unsuited by the good to soft ground
Kindlelight Blue(IRE) Official explanation: jockey said gelding hung left

2785 EASTSIDE H'CAP 1m 4f
8:15 (8:16) (Class 5) (0-70,69) 3-Y-O £4,857 (£1,445; £722; £360) Stalls Low

Form RPR
5611 **1** **Precision Break (USA)**[32] 1871 3-9-3 **65**..................... JohnEgan 2 74
(P F I Cole) *chsd ldr: effrt and cl up 4f out: rdn to ld wl over 2f out: drvn over 1f out: kpt on gamely u.p* **11/2**[1]
5134 **2** *1 1/2* **Black Dahlia**[17] 2280 3-9-1 **63**..................... PatCosgrave 15 69+
(A J McCabe) *hld up in rr: stdy hdwy 3f out: rdn to chse ldrs over 1f out: drvn and kpt on ins fnl f* **11/1**
0-11 **3** *3/4* **Ovthenight (IRE)**[17] 2280 3-9-7 **69**..................... MickyFenton 16 74
(Mrs P Sly) *sn led: jnd and rdn 3f out: sn hdd: drvn wl over 1f out: kpt on gamely u.p tl no ex ins fnl f* **12/1**
0066 **4** *1 1/4* **Lady Sorcerer**[11] 2464 3-9-7 **69**..................... DarrenWilliams 11 72
(A P Jarvis) *hld up in rr: hdwy on outer over 3f out: rdn to chse ldrs over 1f out: sn drvn and kpt on: nrst fin* **50/1**
-002 **5** *1* **Paddy Rielly (IRE)**[17] 2280 3-8-10 **58**..................... RobertWinston 14 61+
(P D Evans) *hld up towards rr: stdy hdwy 4f out: rdn to chse ldrs and styng on whn bdly hmpd 2f out: kpt on same pce after* **9/1**
333 **6** *1* **Sea Chorus**[17] 2291 3-9-6 **68**..................... HayleyTurner 5 68+
(M L W Bell) *in tch on inner: effrt and rdn whn hmpd 2f out: kpt on same pce after* **17/2**[3]
-055 **7** *3 1/4* **Eddie Dowling**[17] 2280 3-9-6 **68**..................... ChrisCatlin 9 63+
(M R Channon) *bhd tl styd on fnl 2f: nvr rchd ldrs* **33/1**
440- **8** *2 1/2* **Bigalo's Magic (UAE)**[223] 6486 3-9-0 **67**..................... NataliaGemelova(5) 6 58
(E J O'Neill) *chsd ldrs: rdn along 3f out: hung bdly lft 2f out: sn wknd* **12/1**
0-00 **9** *7* **Leitmotif (USA)**[15] 2340 3-8-11 **59**..................... DaneO'Neill 10 38
(J L Dunlop) *chsd ldrs: rdn along over 3f out: grad wknd* **18/1**
-003 **10** *5* **Sabancaya**[14] 2376 3-9-0 **62**..................... PhillipMakin 8 33
(W J Haggas) *a towards rr* **9/1**
6-62 **11** *1* **It's My Day (IRE)**[25] 2045 3-9-6 **68**..................... FrankieMcDonald 1 38
(Jane Chapple-Hyam) *midfield: rdn along over 4f out: sn lost pl and bhd* **8/1**[2]
0-30 **12** *1 3/4* **When Yer Ready (IRE)**[25] 2041 3-8-10 **58**.....................(b[1]) DavidAllan 7 25
(T D Easterby) *in tch: hdwy 4f out: rdn along to chse ldrs whn hmpd 2f out: sn wknd* **18/1**
0-33 **13** *5* **Dancing Sword**[36] 1741 3-9-5 **67**..................... SebSanders 4 26
(H J L Dunlop) *a in rr* **9/1**
-424 **14** *23* **Highland Love**[17] 2272 3-9-2 **64**..................... PaulMulrennan 3 —
(Jedd O'Keeffe) *plld hrd: chsd ldng pair tl rdn along and wknd over 2f out* **12/1**

2m 40.19s (5.09) **Going Correction** +0.375s/f (Good) **14** Ran SP% **113.9**
Speed ratings (Par 99): **98,97,96,95,95 94,92,90,85,82 81,80,77,62**
CSF £55.85 CT £523.79 TOTE £6.10: £1.90, £2.70, £4.50; EX 77.80.
Owner JMH Lifestyle Ltd **Bred** Gainesway Thoroughbreds Ltd **Trained** Whatcombe, Oxon
■ Trip The Light was withdrawn (9/1, unruly in stalls). R4 applies, deduct 10p in the £.

FOCUS
A modest handicap for three-year-olds. It was run at just a modest early pace, and the winner was always well placed, but the form still looks sound enough.
It's My Day(IRE) Official explanation: jockey said colt was unsuited by the good to soft ground
When Yer Ready(IRE) Official explanation: jockey said gelding ran too freely
Highland Love Official explanation: jockey said gelding ran too freely and hung right

2786 RMC CHERYL MARTIN MAIDEN STKS 7f
8:45 (8:55) (Class 5) 3-Y-O £3,238 (£963; £481; £240) Stalls High

Form RPR
3 **1** **Grande Annee (USA)**[28] 1957 3-8-12 0..................... ShaneKelly 19 71
(J Noseda) *cl up: led 1/2-way: rdn along 2f out: drvn ent fnl f: edgd rt and hld on wl* **2/1**[1]
2 *1* **Applaude** 3-9-3 0..................... RobertWinston 16 73+
(G A Swinbank) *towards rr: pushed along 1/2-way: hdwy over 2f out: rdn and ev ch ent fnl f: no ex towards fin* **16/1**
3-0 **3** *3/4* **Street Devil (USA)**[66] 1125 3-9-3 0..................... GregFairley 4 71
(P A Blockley) *prom: effrt 2f out: sn rdn and ev ch tl drvn: edgd rt and no ex ins fnl f* **50/1**
60 **4** *hd* **Gulf Stream Lady (IRE)**[28] 1946 3-8-12 0..................... DaneO'Neill 3 65
(B W Hills) *trckd ldrs: hdwy over 2f out: rdn over 1f out: ev ch ins fnl f: drvn and no ex towards fin* **4/1**[2]
65 **5** *2 3/4* **Cheeky Chilli**[9] 2500 3-8-12 0..................... DanielTudhope 7 58
(A J McCabe) *prom: rdn along 2f out and ev ch tl drvn and wknd ent fnl f* **40/1**
6 *1* **Muftarres (IRE)** 3-9-3 0..................... SebSanders 17 60+
(Sir Michael Stoute) *midfield: pushed along and outpcd 1/2-way: styd on appr fnl f: nrst fin* **8/1**[3]
5- **7** *1 1/2* **Kingdom Of Fife**[217] 6616 3-9-3 0..................... TomEaves 14 56+
(Sir Michael Stoute) *s.i.s and bhd: hdwy over 2f out: styd on appr fnl f: nrst fin* **4/1**[2]
4- **8** *nk* **Coach And Four (USA)**[210] 6783 3-9-3 0..................... VinceSlattery 11 55
(M G Quinlan) *bhd: rdn along 1/2-way: hdwy over 2f out: kpt on appr fnl f: nrst fin* **20/1**
9 *nk* **Half A Crown (IRE)** 3-9-3 0..................... FergalLynch 6 55
(D W Barker) *in tch: swtchd outside and gd hdwy over 2f out: rdn and wknd over 1f out* **66/1**
10 *1* **First Swallow** 3-9-3 0..................... DavidAllan 15 52
(R A Fahey) *in tch: rdn along over 2f out and sn wknd* **22/1**
4- **11** *2 1/2* **Paradise Island (IRE)**[241] 6093 3-8-12 0..................... DO'Donohoe 2 40
(E A L Dunlop) *in tch: rdn along over 2f out and grad wknd* **10/1**
0- **12** *2* **Headache**[377] 2041 3-9-3 0..................... MickyFenton 20 40
(B W Duke) *cl up on stands' rail: rdn along over 2f out and sn wknd* **11/1**
0- **13** *2 1/2* **Ubenkor (IRE)**[170] 7191 3-9-3 0..................... PaulMulrennan 12 33
(B Smart) *cl up: ev ch over 2f out: sn rdn and grad wknd* **80/1**
14 *13* **Willaby Lad** 3-9-3 0..................... PatrickMathers 1 —
(D Shaw) *wnt bdly lft s: a in rr* **100/1**
15 *9* **Spabreaksdotcom (IRE)** 3-8-9 0..................... PJMcDonald(3) 5 —
(J S Wainwright) *s.i.s: a bhd* **40/1**
00 **16** *9* **Ma Mirage (IRE)**[28] 1957 3-8-12 0..................... HayleyTurner 18 —
(S C Williams) *led: hdd 1/2-way and sn wknd* **100/1**

1m 30.25s (3.95) **Going Correction** +0.55s/f (Yiel) **16** Ran SP% **128.4**
Speed ratings (Par 99): **99,97,97,96,93 92,90,90,90,88 86,83,80,66,55 45**
CSF £39.47 TOTE £3.30: £1.30, £5.10, £14.70; EX 51.70.

Owner Tom Ludt **Bred** Grapestock Llc **Trained** Newmarket, Suffolk

FOCUS

A modest maiden for three-year-olds. The fifth is the best guide to the strength of the form and it is doubtful if the winner had to match her debut effort.

2787 REGIONAL MAGAZINE COMPANY H'CAP 1m (S)

9:15 (9:22) (Class 4) (0-80,81) 4-Y-0+ £6,476 (£1,927; £963; £481) **Stalls** High

Form				RPR
221-	1		**Axiom**241 6094 4-9-7 **80** DaneO'Neill 11 (L M Cumani) *hld up in rr: swtchd lft and hdwy 2f out: rdn over 1f out: led ins fnl f: styd on wl* **7/2**1	91+
345-	2	2	**Summer Dancer (IRE)**170 7193 4-9-2 **81** MarcHalford(3) 1 (D R C Elsworth) *hld up in rr: swtchd outside and hdwy to ld 2f out: rdn over 1f out: hdd and one pce ins fnl f* **4/1**2	84
-002	3	2 1/4	**Esoterica (IRE)**8 2524 5-8-8 **67** (b) HayleyTurner 4 (J S Goldie) *trckd ldrs: led 3f out: rdn and hdd 2f out: n.m.r over 1f out: swtchd lft and styd on u.p ins fnl f* **4/1**2	71+
-002	4	1/2	**Aussie Blue (IRE)**14 2375 4-7-11 **61** NataliaGemelova(5) 2 (R M Whitaker) *hld up towards rr: hdwy 3f out: cl up 2f out: sn rdn and ev ch tl drvn and wknd ent fnl f* **11/2**	61
/500	5	1 3/4	**Polish Corridor**21 2155 9-8-9 **68** PhillipMakin 5 (M Dods) *chsd ldrs: rdn along and sltly outpcd 2f out: kpt on u.p ins fnl f* **9/2**3	64+
-060	6	nk	**Fever**30 1909 4-8-12 **78** NSLawes(7) 3 (M W Easterby) *chsd ldrs: rdn along over 2f out: wknd over 1f out* **25/1**	73
2112	7	10	**Glenridding**118 509 4-8-13 **72** J-PGuillambert 7 (J G Given) *led: rdn along and hdd 3f out: drvn over 2f out and sn wknd* **10/1**	44
-325	8	3 1/2	**Thunderousapplause**31 1903 4-9-2 **75** (b1) PatCosgrave 9 (A J McCabe) *chsd ldrs: rdn along 3f out: sn wknd* **14/1**	39

1m 42.93s (3.63) **Going Correction** +0.60s/f (Yiel) **8 Ran SP% 115.4**

Speed ratings (Par 105): **105,103,100,100,98 98,88,84**

CSF £17.86 CT £58.12 TOTE £3.90: £2.00, £2.00, £1.50; EX 15.90 Place 6 £145.97, Place 5 £48.31.

Owner DIC Racing Syndicate **Bred** Cheveley Park Stud Ltd **Trained** Newmarket, Suffolk

■ Bailieborough was withdrawn on vet's advice (7/1, deduct 10p in the £ under rule 4). New market formed.

■ Stewards' Enquiry : Natalia Gemelova two-day ban: careless riding (Jun 22-23)

FOCUS

A fair handicap, run at a solid pace. The form is rated through the second and the winner can rate higher.

T/Plt: £143.20 to a £1 stake. Pool: £60,640.46. 309.00 winning tickets. T/Qpdt: £11.10 to a £1 stake. Pool: £4,617.79. 307.20 winning tickets. JR

EPSOM (L-H)

Friday, June 6

OFFICIAL GOING: Good

Rail dolled out approximately 5yards from 1 mile point, adding circa 12yards to advertised race distances.

Wind: fairly modest against Weather: overcast

2788 JUDDMONTE DIOMED STKS (GROUP 3) 1m 114y

1:40 (1:42) (Class 1) 3-Y-0+

£28,385 (£10,760; £5,385; £2,685; £1,345; £675) **Stalls** Low

Form				RPR
2453	1		**Blythe Knight (IRE)**22 2132 8-9-4 109 GrahamGibbons 5 (J J Quinn) *lw: chsd ldng pair: swtchd rt over 1f out: sn chsng ldr: led 1f out: edgd lft u.p: r.o wl* **6/1**	116
13-4	2	1/2	**Alexandros**28 1943 3-8-6 116 KerrinMcEvoy 8 (Saeed Bin Suroor) *chsd ldr: led 2f out: sn rdn: hdd 1f out: kpt on but a hld* **10/3**1	113
15-5	3	1 3/4	**Young Pretender (FR)**22 2131 3-8-9 115 LDettori 4 (Saeed Bin Suroor) *s.i.s: hld up in midfield: hdwy and rdn 3f out: chsd ldrs 2f out: kpt on same pce fnl f* **7/1**	112
-122	4	hd	**Don't Panic (IRE)**37 1716 4-9-4 105 AlanMunro 2 (P W Chapple-Hyam) *hld up in midfield: shkn up and effrt 3f out: rdn and sltly out pce 2f out: edgd lft and kpt on again ins fnl f* **4/1**2	110
1-00	5	1/2	**Majestic Roi (USA)**20 2193 4-9-8 115 RichardHughes 1 (M R Channon) *stdd after s: t.k.h: hld up in last pair: hdwy 3f out: rdn and effrt on outer 2f out: one pce u.p in fnl f* **14/1**	113
1131	6	1 3/4	**Mia's Boy**22 2132 4-9-4 104 JimmyQuinn 7 (C A Dwyer) *hld up towards rr: rdn over 3f out: nvr pce to threaten ldrs: btn whn short of room ins fnl f* **5/1**3	105
20-2	7	6	**Dunelight (IRE)**25 2044 5-9-4 109 (v) PhilipRobinson 6 (C G Cox) *lw: led at gd pce: rdn and hdd 2f out: wknd over 1f out* **7/1**	91
5233	8	17	**Metropolitan Man**25 2044 5-9-4 110 RichardMullen 3 (D M Simcock) *hld up in last: rdn over 3f out: sn struggling: eased ins fnl f: t.o* **10/1**	52

1m 45.5s (-0.60) **Going Correction** +0.25s/f (Good)

WFA 3 from 4yo+ 12lb **8 Ran SP% 114.8**

Speed ratings (Par 113): **112,111,110,109,109 107,102,87**

CSF £26.44 TOTE £6.70: £2.30, £1.50, £1.90; EX 30.30 Trifecta £60.40 Pool: £1073.18 - 12.60 winning units..

Owner Maxilead Limited **Bred** Gainsborough Stud Management Ltd **Trained** Settrington, N Yorks

■ The Diomed was formerly run on Derby day.

■ Stewards' Enquiry : Graham Gibbons two-day ban: careless riding (Jun 23-24)

FOCUS

An ordinary Group 3 race, and while they seemed to go a decent enough pace, the time was not much different from that recorded by the winner of the following handicap. Sound form though, with the winner to a similar level as in the 2007 running.

NOTEBOOK

Blythe Knight(IRE) loves it around here and made it three wins from five starts at the track. He won this race last year and, although weak in the market in his follow-up bid, was always well positioned tracking the first two. Switched to challenge inside the final two furlongs, he picked up well and showed he is as good as he has ever, although in fairness this will not be the strongest Group 3 race run this season. His trainer hinted that he will go pot hunting abroad now, and that hurdling is now off the agenda. (op 5-1 tchd 13-2)

Alexandros, fourth to Tajaaweed in the Dee Stakes on his seasonal reappearance, did not do that form any harm on the eve of the Derby. Easier ground promised to suit him as he showed his best form in France with give, but having had every chance the winner just had a bit too much toe for him at the finish. (op 9-2 tchd 5-1 in places)

Young Pretender(FR) represented the Dante form so he gave supporters of Tartan Bearer and Frozen Fire a bit of a boost with this effort. The drop back in trip promised to suit this son of Oasis Dream and he duly improved on his York run, but on this evidence his current rating flatters him. (tchd 13-2)

Don't Panic(IRE), second in Listed company on his last two starts, probably sets the level of the form, although softer ground might have suited him better. He is threatening to become a twilight horse now. (op 9-2 tchd 5-1 in places)

Majestic Roi(USA) had a stiff task at the weights under her 7lb penalty for winning the Sun Chariot Stakes last autumn. She threatened to throw down a challenge on the outside inside the final two furlongs but on this ground, which was on the easy side, she just could not pick up. Back on genuinely fast ground in a strongly-run race, her turn of foot may well see her pop up again in a decent event. (op 12-1)

Mia's Boy, who has progressed through the handicapping ranks this year, found this step up in class beyond him. He was receiving a stone from Blythe Knight when finishing three and a half lengths in front of him at York last time, but was unable to confirm that form off levels. (op 9-2)

Dunelight(IRE), who is a difficult horse to place, needs quicker ground to be seen at his best. (op 8-1)

Metropolitan Man finds winning difficult at the best of times, but he was never going on this occasion. (op 12-1)

2789 JEEP MILE (H'CAP) 1m 114y

2:10 (2:13) (Class 2) (0-105,105) 4-Y-0+

£18,693 (£5,598; £2,799; £1,401; £699; £351) **Stalls** Low

Form				RPR
6002	1		**Little White Lie (IRE)**8 2545 4-8-13 **94** DarryllHolland 11 (J R Jenkins) *lw: chsd ldrs: rdn and effrt to ld over 2f out: r.o gamely u.p: all out* **12/1**	103
660-	2	nk	**Unshakable (IRE)**244 6011 9-8-8 **89** PaulEddery 14 (Bob Jones) *s.i.s: t.k.h: hld up in midfield: rdn and hdwy over 2f out: chsd wnr over 1f out: kpt on wl u.p* **11/1**	97
4032	3	1/2	**Vainglory (USA)**8 2531 4-8-8 **89** RichardMullen 10 (D M Simcock) *lw: racd in midfield: rdn and effrt on outer 3f out: disp 2nd jst over 1f out: kpt on u.p* **9/1**	96
-015	4	2	**Vitznau (IRE)**35 1767 4-9-7 **102** RichardHughes 6 (R Hannon) *hld up in midfield: hdwy over 2f out: chsd ldrs and edgd lft ins fnl f: kpt on same pce* **10/1**	105
03-1	5	1 1/2	**Emerald Wilderness (IRE)**37 1723 4-9-0 **95** EddieAhern 2 (A King) *chsd ldng pair: gng wl 3f out: rdn to chse wnr 2f out: hld hd high u.p: lost 2nd over 1f out: wknd fnl f* **6/1**1	94
00-3	6	3/4	**Royal Power (IRE)**22 2133 5-9-0 **95** AdrianTNicholls 7 (D Nicholls) *lw: stdd s: hld up in rr: hdwy and n.m.r jst over 2f out: keeping on whn short of room and snatched up ins fnl f* **14/1**	97+
0-60	7	2 3/4	**Kingsdale Orion (IRE)**33 1828 4-8-6 **87** KerrinMcEvoy 12 (B Ellison) *s.i.s: hld up towards rr: rdn and little rspnse wl over 2f out: kpt on past btn horses fnl f* **10/1**	78
1112	8	1/2	**Mujood**6 2604 5-8-10 **91** StephenCarson 5 (Eve Johnson Houghton) *bustled up into midfield after s: hdwy on inner over 2f out: getting outpcd whn short of room and swtchd rt wl over 1f out: no ch after* **9/1**	81
4-62	9	nk	**Prince Of Thebes (IRE)**27 2013 7-8-5 **86** PaulDoe 13 (M J Attwater) *hld up in midfield on outer: rdn and hdwy over 2f out: wknd ent fnl f* **16/1**	75
4006	10	1 1/4	**Fajr (IRE)**8 2530 6-9-10 **105** (b) NCallan 4 (Miss Gay Kelleway) *hld up in rr: short lived effrt on inner wl over 2f out: sn btn* **33/1**	91
0044	11	7	**Charlie Tokyo (IRE)**50 1427 5-9-1 **99** (b) JamieMoriarty(3) 8 (R A Fahey) *s.i.s: a bhd* **20/1**	69
000-	12	2 1/4	**Prince Of Light (IRE)**350 2815 5-9-3 **98** JoeFanning 9 (M Johnston) *chsd ldr: rdn and ev ch 3f out: wknd qckly 2f out* **20/1**	63
0-04	13	hd	**Annemasse**22 2132 4-8-12 **93** PaulHanagan 3 (R A Fahey) *led tl rdn and hdd over 2f out: wkng whn short of room 2f out: eased fnl f* **7/1**3	58
4003	14	2	**Dream Lodge (IRE)**28 1942 4-8-12 **93** RyanMoore 1 (J G Given) *lw: racd in midfield tl lost pl and bhd over 5f out: wl bhd last 3f* **13/2**2	53

1m 45.47s (-0.63) **Going Correction** +0.25s/f (Good) **14 Ran SP% 119.3**

Speed ratings (Par 109): **112,111,111,109,108 107,105,104,104,103 97,95,94,93**

CSF £133.09 CT £837.86 TOTE £11.60: £3.40, £3.30, £3.50; EX 248.30 TRIFECTA Not won..

Owner The Three Honest Men **Bred** J L Hassett **Trained** Royston, Herts

■ Stewards' Enquiry : Richard Hughes one-day ban: careless riding (Jun 22)

FOCUS

A decent handicap run at a good pace, and the time compared favourably with the previous Group 3 race. Solid form, with the winner back to his best and the second to last year's mark in this race. The third has been raised 3lb in line with his AW form.

NOTEBOOK

Little White Lie(IRE), second to Bushman at Sandown last time in a race that is beginning to work out well - the sixth won next time out as well - was well placed entering the straight and, once sent on, was always going to be tough to catch. While his cushion over the rest was whittled down near the line, he never looked like getting caught. He would probably not want the ground any quicker than this at Ascot, where connections intend running him in the Royal Hunt Cup under a penalty. (op 9-1)

Unshakable(IRE) won this race last year off a 3lb lower mark, but he had not had a pipe-opener this time around. Conditions were as he would like them, though, and he ran a solid race, staying on well to close the winner down at the line. He now heads for a very valuable handicap at Sandown. (op 10-1)

Vainglory(USA) stays further than this, so the decent gallop suited him. He kept on well down the outside and posted a solid effort, but whether he has much in hand of the Handicapper off his current mark is open to question. (op 10-1 tchd 11-1 in places)

Vitznau(IRE) is on a stiff mark for handicaps but he does appreciate a good gallop and he is more likely to get the race run to suit in a big-field handicap than in a small-field conditions race. He travelled well as usual and, while he did not get the clearest of runs, he was not unlucky. (op 15-2)

Emerald Wilderness(IRE) again carried his head high but there is no suggestion that he is a monkey. He was racing off a 3lb higher mark than when successful on the Polytrack last time and probably ran close to that form. (op 7-1)

Royal Power(IRE) ◆ shaped well on his debut for Dandy Nicholls at York last month and he again showed that there is a decent handicap in him here. Held up at the back of the field, he had less than a clear passage and was hampered by Vitznau inside the last. With a clear run he might have been fourth, and there will be worse outsiders than this former German Classic winner if he lines up for the Hunt Cup. (op 10-1)

Kingsdale Orion(IRE) has not built on the promise of his run in the Newbury Spring Cup on his debut for his current yard. (op 12-1)

Mujood may just be feeling the effects of a busy first half to the campaign. (op 17-2 tchd 10-1)

Prince Of Thebes(IRE) gave away plenty of ground racing on the wide outside. (op 20-1 tchd 25-1 in places)

Prince Of Light(IRE), who is dropping back to a potentially good mark, would have preferred his own way up front. Official explanation: jockey said gelding had no more to give

Annemasse probably set too strong a pace for his own good. (op 8-1 tchd 10-1 in places)

Dream Lodge(IRE) Official explanation: jockey said colt losts its left-fore shoe

2790 TOTESPORT BETXTRA ROSE BOWL (HERITAGE H'CAP) 1m 2f 18y
2:45 (2:48) (Class 2) 4-Y-0+

£31,155 (£9,330; £4,665; £2,335; £1,165; £585) Stalls Low

Form RPR

156- **1** **Emirates Skyline (USA)**[311] 4043 5-9-10 103 LDettori 5 113+
(Saeed Bin Suroor) *lw: chsd ldrs: plld out 3f out: shkn up and qcknd to ld 2f out: sn rdn: r.o wl and in command after* 7/2[1]

0-50 **2** 1 1/4 **Ladies Best**[23] 2103 4-9-4 97 JamieSpencer 2 104
(L M Cumani) *hld up in midfield: swtchd rt and effrt jst over 3f out: rdn and hanging lft fr 2f out: chsd wnr ent fnl f: a hld* 4/1[2]

0-13 **3** 1 **Rationale (IRE)**[111] 592 5-8-5 84 KerrinMcEvoy 1 89
(S C Williams) *lw: hld up towards rr: bhd 3f out: hdwy 2f out: r.o wl fnl f to go 3rd nr fin: nvr rchd ldrs* 17/2

6-45 **4** nk **Smart Instinct (USA)**[11] 2465 4-9-0 93 (p) PaulHanagan 4 97
(R A Fahey) *led: jnd and rdn 3f out: hdd 2f out: kpt on one pce u.p after* 5/1[3]

5-25 **5** 2 3/4 **Shake On It**[14] 2369 4-8-4 83 (t) WilliamBuick 6 82
(Eve Johnson Houghton) *stdd s and dropped in bhd: hdwy on outer 3f out: hanging lft and no imp last 2f* 16/1

0020 **6** nk **Northern Spy (USA)**[16] 2308 4-7-13 78 JimmyQuinn 9 76
(S Dow) *hld up in last pair: effrt on inner 3f out: rdn over 2f out: sn no imp* 20/1

-221 **7** 2 **Eradicate (IRE)**[21] 2144 4-9-11 104 4ex JoeFanning 8 98
(M Johnston) *chsd ldr: rdn to chal 3f out: struggling whn sltly short of room jst over 2f out: wknd wl over 1f out* 6/1

0512 **8** 2 3/4 **Escape Route (USA)**[29] 1920 4-9-7 100 (p) JimmyFortune 7 89
(J H M Gosden) *hld up in midfield: rdn and effrt 3f out: no prog* 6/1

2404 **9** 6 **Moheebb (IRE)**[2] 2733 4-7-12 77 oh2 (b) AdrianMcCarthy 10 54
(Mrs R A Carr) *chsd ldng pair tl over 4f out: wkng whn bmpd over 3f out: sn bhd* 40/1

1212 **10** 12 **Mr Aviator (USA)**[35] 1766 4-9-9 102 RichardHughes 3 55
(R Hannon) *hld up in midfield: hdwy to chse ldng pair over 4f out: rdn and bmpd 3f out: wknd qckly over 2f out: virtually p.u ins fnl f* 8/1

2m 9.56s (-0.14) **Going Correction** +0.25s/f (Good) 10 Ran SP% 122.2
Speed ratings (Par 109): **110,109,108,107,105 105,103,101,96,87**
CSF £18.45 CT £114.40 TOTE £4.30: £1.80, £2.00, £3.20; EX 25.10 Trifecta £393.70 Pool: £1441.79 - 2.60 winning units.
Owner Godolphin **Bred** Darley **Trained** Newmarket, Suffolk
■ Stewards' Enquiry : L Dettori four-day ban: careless riding (Jun 22-25)

FOCUS
A decent handicap but not too many open to significant improvement. It was a clear personal best from the winner, who has a good record fresh, while the runner-up was to form and the third close to his best over his minimum trip.

NOTEBOOK
Emirates Skyline(USA), off the track and gelded since his last run in July, was always handily placed tracking the leader on the rail, but he had to barge his way out somewhat to get a clear run at the line. He quickened up well, though, and was never going to be caught from then on. Having won this off 103 he will have to move into Listed company now, but he is lightly raced for his age and might just be able to make the jump. (op 4-1 tchd 9-2 in places)
Ladies Best tracked the eventual winner for much of the race and did not enjoy the best of passages when angling for a run. He ran on well once in the clear, although his challenge was hindered by the fact that he kept hanging left on the camber. His current mark leaves him vulnerable to improvers. (op 9-2 tchd 5-1 in places)
Rationale(IRE), returning from a 111-day break, has won over as far as 1m6f, so over this trip he needs the pace to be frenetic. Staying on strongly at the finish, he will be suited by a return to further. (op 14-1)
Smart Instinct(USA) was kept out of trouble this time by being sent out to make the running. He did not seem to have any obvious excuse. (tchd 11-2)
Shake On It, who cannot have the ground too fast, threatened to get involved down the outside in the final two furlongs but hung left and could not pick up on this slightly easy ground.
Northern Spy(USA) has recorded his three highest RPRs on Polytrack. (op 25-1)
Eradicate(IRE) may not have been at home on the track. (tchd 13-2 in places)
Escape Route(USA), another 3lb higher, is a son of Elusive Quality so this ground, which was on the easy side of good, probably did not suit him ideally. He will be happier back on proper fast ground. (op 13-2)
Mr Aviator(USA) Official explanation: jockey said colt was unsuited by the track

2791 JUDDMONTE CORONATION CUP (GROUP 1) 1m 4f 10y
3:25 (3:31) (Class 1) 4-Y-0+

£113,540 (£43,040; £21,540; £10,740; £5,380; £2,700) Stalls Centre

Form RPR

115- **1** **Soldier Of Fortune (IRE)**[243] 6043 4-9-0 0 JMurtagh 7 124+
(A P O'Brien, Ire) *hld up off the pce in midfield: hdwy 6f out: 5th st: wnt 3rd over 2f out: chsd wnr over 1f out: led ins fnl f: edgd lft: r.o wl* 9/4[2]

42-5 **2** 3/4 **Youmzain (IRE)**[69] 1091 5-9-0 125 RichardHughes 3 123
(M R Channon) *hld up in rr: 9th st: hdwy on inner wl over 2f out: swtchd rt 1f out: r.o wl to go 2nd nr fin: could nt rch wnr* 15/2[3]

6-01 **3** 1 1/2 **Macarthur**[28] 1944 4-9-0 0 JAHeffernan 10 122+
(A P O'Brien, Ire) *lw: chsd clr ldr wl ahd of remainder: clsd 5f out: led 4f out: 6 l clr over 2f out: hdd ins fnl f: hld whn short of room and lost 2nd nr fin* 12/1

130- **4** nk **Papal Bull**[194] 6943 5-9-0 116 RyanMoore 8 120
(Sir Michael Stoute) *swtg: stdd after s: hld up bhd: 10th st: rdn and hanging lft over 2f out: swtchd rt over 1f out: little hdwy tl r.o ins fnl f: fin wl* 16/1

24-1 **5** 1 1/2 **Getaway (GER)**[33] 1829 5-9-0 0 SPasquier 11 118+
(A Fabre, France) *t.k.h: prom in main gp: 3rd st: rdn to go 6 l 2nd over 2f out: hanging bdly lft after: hemmed in over 1f out: swtchd rt jst ins fnl f: no imp after* 5/4[1]

30-1 **6** 3 1/2 **Red Rocks (IRE)**[27] 1990 5-9-0 116 LDettori 1 112
(B J Meehan) *prom in main gp: 4th st: rdn 3f out: no prog whn bmpd over 1f out* 14/1

10-2 **7** 1/2 **Turbo Linn**[21] 2144 5-8-11 110 NCallan 4 108
(G A Swinbank) *racd off the pce in midfield: effrt and 6th st: sn rdn and kpt on same pce* 40/1

116- **8** 4 1/2 **Anna Pavlova**[222] 6526 5-8-11 112 PaulHanagan 2 101
(R A Fahey) *s.i.s: sn in midfield: rdn and 8th st: nvr trbld ldrs* 33/1

5-44 **9** 5 **Multidimensional (IRE)**[29] 1921 5-9-0 111 TedDurcan 9 96
(H R A Cecil) *lw: hld up wl off the pce in midfield: 7th st: sn rdn and btn* 33/1

6-06 **10** 9 **Big Robert**[27] 1980 4-9-0 103 MartinDwyer 5 82
(W R Muir) *s.i.s: a bhd: last st: t.o* 100/1

060- **11** 2 1/2 **Song Of Hiawatha**[243] 6043 4-9-0 0 CO'Donoghue 6 78
(A P O'Brien, Ire) *led and clr tl hdd 4f out: 2nd st tl over 2f out: sn wknd* 200/1

2m 36.83s (-2.07) **Going Correction** +0.25s/f (Good) 11 Ran SP% 117.0
Speed ratings (Par 117): **116,115,114,114,113 110,110,107,104,98 96**
CSF £19.00 TOTE £3.60: £1.80, £1.60, £3.80; EX 19.90 Trifecta £121.90 Pool: £9353.72 - 54.46 winning units..
Owner Mrs John Magnier, M Tabor & D Smith **Bred** J S Bolger **Trained** Ballydoyle, Co Tipperary
■ Stewards' Enquiry : J Murtagh three-day ban: careless riding (Jun 22-24)

FOCUS
A high-class renewal run at a strong pace, making it a thorough test at the distance. The third and fourth have been rated as running personal bests so the race cannot really be rated much higher, and the winner has probably run closer to his Arc mark than his Irish Derby figure.

NOTEBOOK
Soldier Of Fortune(IRE) had not been seen since finishing fifth, one place behind Getaway, in the Arc last autumn, but his odds suggested he was fit enough, albeit he did not look great in his coat. The strong pace set by his stablemates set the race up nicely for him and as both he and Getaway closed in on Macarthur, Murtagh made sure that Getaway, who was on his inside, was denied a chance to angle out past the weakening leader. Team tactics may well have helped win the day on this occasion, but it would be a mistake to suggest that the wrong horse won. Connections will presumably be keen to win a big 1m2f race with Soldier Of Fortune, but this is his best trip, and the King George looks the ideal target. However, with pacemakers aplenty setting a scorching gallop, it is not out of the question that he could take a Group 1 race over 1m2f, perhaps the Eclipse, where the stiff finish would be in his favour. (tchd 2-1 and 5-2 in places)
Youmzain(IRE) has always been seen at his best in a strongly run event over 1m4f, and he had the race very much run to suit this time. Held up out the back, the winner got first run on him and, while he cut back the deficit greatly inside the last, the line was always going to come too soon. He has now finished second in an Arc, King George and Coronation Cup, but his only success at the top level came in Germany back in 2006. Connections are keen to get his head in front and could drop him a grade for the Hardwicke Stakes at Royal Ascot. (op 7-1)
Macarthur was impressive in the Ormonde Stakes last time but the competition was much stiffer here. Isolated clear of the main pack chasing his stablemate and pacemaker Song Of Hiawatha in the early stages, he took over entering the straight and, for a moment, threatened to nick the race. While getting tired in the final stages, he denied Getaway a run through on the rail, which helped Soldier Of Fortune's cause towards the outer, but this performance proved he has a big prize in him as well when ridden more conservatively. The Hardwicke appeals in the short term. (tchd 14-1 in places)
Papal Bull, like Youmzain, finished well from off the pace without threatening the principals. He has never been straightforward but has plenty of ability, and he is one of a number of potential Hardwicke Stakes candidates his trainer has at his disposal. (tchd 18-1)
Getaway(GER), who finished one place in front of Soldier Of Fortune in the Arc and had impressed on his reappearance when taking the Jockey Club Stakes, led the chasing pack entering the straight but had been racing quite keenly and hung towards the rail. That was his undoing as Soldier Of Fortune was quickly rushed up on his outside and when the pair caught up with Macarthur, Getaway had nowhere to go, blocked as he was by the winner's stablemate in front of him. He would have been second at worst but whether he would have beaten the Soldier Of Fortune is questionable. Nevertheless, he may have a chance of revenge in the King George, or perhaps connections will opt for the Grand Prix de Saint-Cloud instead. (tchd 11-8 and 6-4 in places)
Red Rocks(IRE), who had a confidence-boosting win in a little race at Lingfield last time, was a bit disappointing, although quicker ground suits him ideally. His whole season is being geared towards returning to America for the Breeders' Cup. Official explanation: jockey said horse lost its action (op 16-1)
Turbo Linn is a useful performer in mares-only company, but against some top-class colts she was outclassed.
Anna Pavlova, who needs very testing ground to be seen at her best, was up against hotter competition than she normally meets.
Multidimensional(IRE), who had his stamina to prove over this longer trip, has been disappointing this season and this effort did not signal any imminent return to form. A sore right shin was later put up as a possible explanation for this below-par effort. Official explanation: jockey said horse was never travelling
Big Robert never threatened to get involved after a slow start. While out of his depth here, he is much better than this and a locking stifle reportedly could explain his poor run. Official explanation: jockey said colt did not move well (tchd 125-1)
Song Of Hiawatha did his job of setting a strong pace for the first mile. (op 150-1)

2792 JUDDMONTE OAKS (GROUP 1) (FILLIES) 1m 4f 10y
4:05 (4:18) (Class 1) 3-Y-0

£208,118 (£78,892; £39,482; £19,686; £9,861; £4,949) Stalls Centre

Form RPR

1-2 **1** **Look Here**[27] 1991 3-9-0 94 SebSanders 13 121
(R M Beckett) *swtg: hld up in midfield: hdwy and 7th st: travelling wl over 2f out: led 2f out: sn rdn clr: r.o strly* 33/1

4 **2** 3 3/4 **Moonstone**[23] 2105 3-9-0 0 RichardHughes 10 114
(A P O'Brien, Ire) *hld up towards rr: 12th st: rdn and gd hdwy on outer wl over 2f out: chsd wnr wl over 1f out: r.o but no imp* 25/1

2 **3** 2 3/4 **Katiyra (IRE)**[26] 2024 3-9-0 0 MJKinane 11 110+
(John M Oxx, Ire) *lw: lengthy: hld up in midfield: nt handle gradient and lost pl 6f out:10th st: hdwy and hanging lft 3f out: chsd ldng pair over 1f out: kpt on but nvr r to chal* 9/2[2]

4-11 **4** 2 3/4 **Clowance**[21] 2149 3-9-0 101 LDettori 3 106
(R Charlton) *hld up towards rr: hdwy and 9th st: styd on steadily last 2f: nvr trbld ldrs* 11/1

-061 **5** 1/2 **Lush Lashes**[23] 2105 3-9-0 0 KJManning 8 105+
(J S Bolger, Ire) *lw: hld up in midfield: hdwy 5f out: 4th and travelling wl st: ev ch 2f out: sn rdn and btn: hung lft over 1f out: plugged on* 5/2[1]

1-2 **6** 1 1/2 **Cape Amber (IRE)**[23] 2105 3-9-0 104 JamieSpencer 6 102+
(P W Chapple-Hyam) *t.k.h: hld up towards rr: 11th st: gd hdwy jst over 3f out: chsd ldrs and rdn over 2f out: wkng whn hmpd over 1f out* 16/1

1-01 **7** 3 1/2 **Michita (USA)**[16] 2305 3-9-0 92 JimmyFortune 9 100+
(J H M Gosden) *hld up in midfield: nt handle gradient and lost pl 6f out: 14th st: rdn and hdwy over 3f out: hanging lft fr 2f out: nt rch ldrs: eased towards fin* 8/1

-206 **8** 1 1/2 **Savethisdanceforme (IRE)**[12] 2433 3-9-0 0 CO'Donoghue 15 94
(A P O'Brien, Ire) *hld up wl bhd: 13th st: gd hdwy on inner 3f out: rdn and no prog 2f out* 33/1

1 **9** 2 1/4 **Chinese White (IRE)**[33] 1847 3-9-0 0 PJSmullen 14 91
(D K Weld, Ire) *w'like: chsd ldrs: 3rd st: sn chsng ldr: led over 2f out: sn rdn: hdd 2f out: sn no ch w wnr: wknd over 1f out* 5/1[3]

11 **10** 2 1/4 **Saphira's Fire (IRE)**[33] 1833 3-9-0 98 MartinDwyer 1 87
(W R Muir) *hld up towards rr: nt handle gradient 6f out: 15th st: n.d* 40/1

3-31 **11** nk **Miracle Seeker**[27] 1991 3-9-0 96 AdamKirby 2 87
(C G Cox) *chsd ldng pair: chsd ldr wl over 4f out: 2nd st: sn rdn to ld: hdd over 2f out: wknd qckly* 40/1

6-12 **12** *18* **Sugar Mint (IRE)**[30] 1915 3-9-0 104 ....(t) MichaelHills 12 58
(B W Hills) *hld up in midfield: hdwy 5f out: 6th st: sn rdn and wknd: eased fnl f: t.o* **33/1**

1 **13** *6* **Sail (IRE)**[30] 1915 3-9-0 0 .... RyanMoore 4 48
(A P O'Brien, Ire) *lw: s.i.s: a wl bhd: 16th st: virtually p.u fnl f: t.o* **9/1**

2 **14** *1* **Tiffany Diamond (IRE)**[12] 2437 3-9-0 0 .... JAHeffernan 7 47
(A P O'Brien, Ire) *lw: chsd ldrs: 5th st: sn rdn and wknd: virtually p.u fnl f: t.o* **25/1**

1 **15** *14* **Adored (IRE)**[23] 2113 3-9-0 0 .... JMurtagh 16 24
(A P O'Brien, Ire) *lengthy: chsd ldr tl led after 2f: rdn and hdd over 3f out: sn wknd: virtually p.u fnl f: t.o* **9/1**

64 **16** *1 1/4* **Ice Queen (IRE)**[27] 1991 3-9-0 0 .... DavidMcCabe 5 22
(A P O'Brien, Ire) *bustled up and sn led: hdd after 2f: chsd ldr after tl wl over 4f out: 8th and wkng st: virtually p.u fnl f: t.o* **100/1**

2m 36.89s (-2.01) **Going Correction** +0.25s/f (Good) **16** Ran SP% **131.1**
Speed ratings (Par 110): **116,113,111,109,109 108,106,105,103,102 101,89,85,85,75 75**
CSF £709.38 CT £4401.63 TOTE £56.80: £13.40, £11.20, £2.40; EX 926.90 Trifecta £3463.60.
Owner J H Richmond-Watson **Bred** Lawn Stud **Trained** Whitsbury, Hants

■ A first Classic winner for Ralph Beckett, and a first domestic Classic winner for Seb Sanders. New sponsors for the Oaks.

FOCUS

This looked a good renewal, full of trial winners and with plenty of depth. Adored went off at a furious pace, which ensured this was a proper stamina test. Plenty of the fillies did not appear to handle the course but that could not be said of Look Here, who bounded clear once sent to the front. The time was decent and not that far off Soldier Of Fortune's winning figure for the Coronation Cup, so there is no reason to believe that the race will not work out. The front four have all been rated improvers, and the winner slightly above the average for the race.

NOTEBOOK

Look Here, somewhat unfortunate in the Lingfield Oaks Trial last time, sat in a good position and lengthened away like a smart sort once asked to win the race. She settled matters within a matter of strides and came home a comfortable winner. Some may want to dismiss this as a fluke because of her starting price, but she saw the trip out well and looks an above average Oaks winner. The Irish Oaks was not ruled out, but she is not that robust and likes a bit of time between races, besides which she would need supplementing. Whether she runs there or not, connections have the St Leger very much in mind, and there is plenty of stamina in the family. The Yorkshire Oaks could be on the agenda in the meantime, and there is no reason to think any of those she beat here would be turning the tables on her.

Moonstone, who was one of the favourites for this race before running moderately in the Musidora, ran a massive race. Settled towards the rear and wide of her rivals, she was unable to get to the winner, who had gone beyond recall, but finished strongly to claim second place despite edging to the inside of the course under pressure. Unraced at two, she looks sure to win a decent race before the end of the season and looks an obvious Irish Oaks type. (tchd 33-1 in places)

Katiyra(IRE), who was stepping up in trip by 4f, was unlucky not to have got closer to the winner, as she did not appear to handle Epsom's undulations at all well. Also, she did not have the smoothest passage up the home straight until finding room inside the final two furlongs. As with her seasonal debut, her head carriage under extreme pressure was not completely convincing and she may have her quirks. However, she deserves another chance in this grade and over this trip on a flatter track and is another heading for The Curragh. (op 6-1)

Clowance, who was ridden by Frankie Dettori for the first time, was closing on the leaders throughout the final furlong after having quite a bit to do as they turned in. The step up in distance suited her well and she would have been challenging for third had she got going earlier. She looks the right type for the Ribblesdale at Royal Ascot, if recovering in time. (op 10-1)

Lush Lashes was quite handy throughout but ultimately shaped like a non-stayer at this trip, which is somewhat surprising after her success in the Musidora at York. She has had a reasonably hard time of it already this season and may benefit from a little break now. On her return 1m2f will probably be her preferred distance. (op 3-1 tchd 10-3 and 7-2 in places)

Cape Amber(IRE), who was fairly keen early, got much closer to Lush Lashes than she had done at York but never really threatened to take a hand despite keeping on nicely. She was one of many who did not appear to handle the track very well and also suffered some interference when Moonstone hung across her about a furlong from home. Her trainer has always had a high opinion of his filly and she may still have more to come this season. (tchd 14-1)

Michita(USA) did not handle the course at all once under pressure and is a lot better than she showed. She is entitled to be given another chance on a flatter track, but one cannot help thinking that she will be ideally suited by 1m2f. (tchd 9-1)

Savethisdanceforme(IRE), who had been disappointing in both the English and Irish Guineas, was not guaranteed to stay 1m4f on pedigree and did not show enough to suggest she will relish middle distances. (op 40-1)

Chinese White(IRE) did not appear to get home after chasing the pacesetters. She cruised into the home straight and briefly got to the front before being passed a few strides later. It is too soon to write her off and she should be given the chance to prove this effort all wrong. (op 11-2 tchd 4-1)

Saphira's Fire(IRE), supplemented for the race after winning the Pretty Polly at Newmarket, had a lot to find with the best of these and came up a long way short. It emerged after the race that she came back with four large insect bites on her, which may have caused her to be edgy before the race. (op 50-1 tchd 66-1)

Miracle Seeker held every chance turning into the straight and briefly led the field. However, she was quickly joined and never looked like upholding the Lingfield Oaks form, where she beat Look Here, and ended well beaten. She looked far from happy on this undulating course, especially in the final 2f. (op 50-1 tchd 33-1 in places)

Sail(IRE), the winner of the Cheshire Oaks, did not get away too smartly and barely got involved. Her rider reported that she never travelled at any stage. Official explanation: jockey said filly was never travelling (op 10-1)

Tiffany Diamond(IRE) came in for some support prior to the off but was struggling from an early stage. (op 33-1)

Adored(IRE), Johnny Murtagh's pick of the Aidan O'Brien entry, was given an ultra positive ride and it was no surprise when she failed to get home. She had looked very progressive coming into the race. Official explanation: jockey said filly had no move to give (op 11-1)

2793 HELP FOR HEROES SURREY STKS (LISTED RACE) 7f
4:50 (4:52) (Class 1) 3-Y-O

£14,760 (£5,595; £2,800; £1,396; £699; £351) **Stalls** Low

Form RPR

3-32 **1** **Iguazu Falls (USA)**[8] 2544 3-8-13 105 .... LDettori 3 109+
(Saeed Bin Suroor) *lw: t.k.h: chsd ldr after 2f: led over 2f out: shkn up and sn clr: r.o strly* **13/8**[1]

5221 **2** *4* **Fathsta (IRE)**[23] 2104 3-8-13 93 .... RichardHughes 9 98
(S Kirk) *swtchd lft s: plld hrd and hld up in midfield: rdn to chse wnr wl over 1f out: no imp on wnr* **4/1**[2]

20 **3** *2 3/4* **Croi Mo Ri (IRE)**[23] 2111 3-8-13 0 .... KJManning 6 91
(P D Deegan, Ire) *t.k.h: hld up in midfield: effrt and rdn 3f out: hung lft and no prog 2f out: wnt 3rd towards fin* **14/1**

6-20 **4** *nk* **Dream Day**[26] 2033 3-8-8 101 .... RyanMoore 1 85
(R Hannon) *led for 1f: chsd ldrs after: rdn and effrt on inner 3f out: wknd wl over 1f out* **5/1**

5-61 **5** *nse* **Film Maker (IRE)**[11] 2466 3-8-13 0 .... JamieSpencer 8 90
(B J Meehan) *lw: t.k.h: led after 1f: rdn and hdd over 2f out: sn outpcd by wnr: wknd fnl f* **12/1**

1152 **6** *1 1/2* **Nice Wee Girl (IRE)**[12] 2428 3-8-8 79 .... MartinDwyer 4 81
(S Kirk) *nvr gng wl in last pair: rdn and hanging lft 3f out: nvr on terms* **16/1**

03-4 **7** *3 1/2* **Nacho Libre**[51] 1400 3-8-13 101 .... MichaelHills 2 77
(B W Hills) *s.i.s: a bhd* **9/2**[3]

1m 24.11s (0.81) **Going Correction** +0.25s/f (Good) **7** Ran SP% **113.2**
Speed ratings (Par 107): **105,100,97,96,96 95,91**
CSF £8.08 TOTE £2.40: £1.80, £2.90; EX 8.60.
Owner Godolphin **Bred** Darley **Trained** Newmarket, Suffolk

FOCUS

Not the strongest of Listed races, and run at only an even pace. The winner was much the best of these and should be able to handle a slight rise in class. Fathsta pulled much too hard, while Dream Day has not progressed since a good reappearance effort.

NOTEBOOK

Iguazu Falls(USA) ◆, dropped back a furlong after proving slightly disappointing at a mile, was nicely placed behind leader Film Maker and the race was over almost as soon as Frankie Dettori asked him for his effort. He was in no danger through the last two furlongs and was value for a bit more than the winning margin. This 7f is his optimum trip (he had some very sound form at the distance at 2) and the Jersey Stakes at Royal Ascot looks the right target for him. (op 7-4 tchd 6-4 and 15-8 in places)

Fathsta(IRE), having his 25th race in little more than a year, was quickly moved to the inside from a wide draw but ran much too freely once in midfield. A faster pace would have helped him to settle but his form did not entitle him to do any better than second as he was rated 12lb behind the winner on official figures. (op 9-2)

Croi Mo Ri(IRE) made his effort on the outside and only nudged himself into third in the final half a furlong. He did not seem to handle the track when placed under pressure but that had little bearing on the final result. (op 20-1)

Dream Day, who never figured at any stage in the French 1,000 Guineas last time, has become regressive since a promising start to her 3yo campaign. There was no obvious reason for the modest effort. (op 4-1 tchd 11-2)

Film Maker(IRE) set only a modest pace and was easily overwhelmed when the winner made his challenge. However, he is probably still capable of a bit more improvement, as this was only his fourth run. (tchd 10-1)

Nice Wee Girl(IRE) never got into it and looked uncomfortable down the hill.

Nacho Libre, not seen since finishing fourth place in the Free Handicap at the Craven meeting, was always at the back of the field and never looked like taking a hand. He is much better than this and can be given another chance. (op 5-1 tchd 7-2)

2794 TATTENHAM STKS (H'CAP) 7f
5:25 (5:25) (Class 2) (0-100,90) 3-Y-O

£12,462 (£3,732; £1,866; £934; £466; £234) **Stalls** Low

Form RPR

0-06 **1** **Bellomi (IRE)**[13] 2405 3-9-4 85 .... EddieAhern 11 94
(W J Haggas) *taken down early: hld up in midfield: hdwy over 2f out: led wl over 1f out: r.o wl* **12/1**

0-41 **2** *1* **Dubai Meydan (IRE)**[31] 1894 3-8-12 79 .... RyanMoore 9 85+
(Miss Gay Kelleway) *hmpd s: bhd: hdwy and burst through over 1f out: r.o strly to chse wnr last 100yds: no imp after* **13/2**

-411 **3** *2 3/4* **Slugger O'Toole**[33] 1834 3-9-9 90 .... MichaelHills 10 89
(B W Hills) *chsd ldrs: effrt to chse ldr over 2f out: ev ch 2f out: nt pce of wnr fnl f: lost 2nd last 100yds* **11/2**[3]

-213 **4** *2* **Opera Prince**[11] 2460 3-8-10 77 .... RichardHughes 4 75+
(S Kirk) *trckd ldrs on inner: nt clr run 3f out tl swtchd over 1f out: plugged on but nvr pce to threaten ldrs* **11/4**[1]

01 **5** *1 1/4* **East Drive (IRE)**[34] 1803 3-9-6 87 .... PhilipRobinson 7 77
(M A Jarvis) *chsd ldr tl over 2f out: one pce fr ovr 1f out.* **8/1**

50 **6** *shd* **Meydan Dubai (IRE)**[13] 2412 3-9-5 86 .... JimmyQuinn 2 76
(J R Best) *sltly hmpd s: hld up in rr: rdn effrt 2f out: sltly hmpd over 1f: kpt on fnl f but nvr trbld ldrs* **12/1**

-013 **7** *1/2* **Cross Fell (USA)**[98] 756 3-9-3 84 ....(p) MartinDwyer 8 72
(J R Boyle) *wnt rt s: sn led: hdd wl over 1f out: wknd fnl f* **25/1**

3550 **8** *4 1/2* **Geezers Colours**[23] 2104 3-9-6 87 .... RichardMullen 5 63
(K R Burke) *chsd ldrs: rdn 3f out: sn struggling* **28/1**

21-3 **9** *1 3/4* **Nezami (IRE)**[13] 2405 3-9-6 87 .... LDettori 3 59
(B J Meehan) *hld up in last trio: nvr trbld ldrs* **7/2**[2]

3230 **10** *3* **The Game**[29] 1925 3-8-10 77 .... PJSmullen 1 40
(J R Boyle) *stdd s: t.k.h: hld up in midfield: nt clr run on inner 3f out tl over 2f out: no prog last 2f: eased ins fnl f* **20/1**

4310 **11** *2 3/4* **Keep Discovering (IRE)**[23] 2104 3-9-8 89 .... AdrianTNicholls 6 45
(M Johnston) *t.k.h: hld up in midfield: hanging bdly lft fr over 3f out: no ch last 2f: eased ins fnl f* **16/1**

1m 24.97s (1.67) **Going Correction** +0.25s/f (Good) **11** Ran SP% **122.0**
Speed ratings (Par 105): **100,98,95,93,92 91,91,86,84,80 77**
CSF £89.12 CT £384.03 TOTE £17.30: £3.90, £2.60, £2.00; EX 162.40 Place 6: £268.29, Place 5 £133.10..
Owner Hit The Beach Partnership **Bred** Barronstown Stud **Trained** Newmarket, Suffolk

FOCUS

This looked an open race, but two horses finished clear of the pack. The pace looked sound enough and the form should be reliable. Much improved form from the first two, and to a lesser extent from the third.

NOTEBOOK

Bellomi(IRE), who was taken down early, settled well despite his wide draw. He travelled strongly through the race, and when he went to the front he was soon in charge, although the second was closing at the finish. He can continue paying his way in decent handicap company. (tchd 14-1)

Dubai Meydan(IRE) was thought good enough to take his chance in the Dewhurst at two, so a mark of 79 was potentially lenient, even allowing for his subsequent gelding and a narrow success in a Catterick maiden. Hampered by Cross Fell as he left the stalls, he was at the back of the field and stayed there until well into the straight. He edged right when making his effort on the outside and appeared to give Meydan Dubai a nudge before running on well. One would imagine that his shrewd connections will find the right sort of opportunities for him. (op 15-2 tchd 8-1)

Slugger O'Toole, looking to complete a hat-trick, had every chance in this and could not pull out extra when needed. He was less exposed than most in this, so is not one to give up on quite yet. (op 9-2)

Opera Prince did not have a lot of room up the inside rail when the tempo really increased, and would have finished much closer to Slugger O'Toole with a clear passage. (op 7-2)

East Drive(IRE) ◆ was far from disgraced on only his third-ever start and appeals as one to keep on the ride side of. This was a big improvement on his winning effort last time (that race has not worked out at all) and, on a flatter track, he can continue his progressive profile. (tchd 15-2)

Meydan Dubai(IRE) had plenty to do with two furlongs to go and never got on terms despite staying on nicely. He is still maiden and probably could do with a confidence-boosting success. (op 11-1 tchd 10-1)

Cross Fell(USA), returning from a layoff and having his first start on turf since October last year, was given a positive ride and led for much of the race. Eventually well held, he should come on for the run but has to improve off his current mark.

Nezami(IRE) never looked happy on the track and reportedly lost his action. Official explanation: jockey said gelidng lost its action (op 5-1)

The Form Book, Raceform Ltd, Compton, RG20 6NL

The Game, trying the trip for the first time, was much too keen in the early stages and did not get the clearest of runs from his inside pitch. He is on a handy mark again now and can win in his grade again soon. (op 14-1)

Keep Discovering(IRE) was keen under restraint and finished last. However, he looked all at sea on the course and this effort can be forgotten.

T/Jkpt: Not won. T/Plt: £540.20 to a £1 stake. Pool: £230,177.34. 311.00 winning tickets. T/Qpdt: £64.00 to a £1 stake. Pool: £11,686.93. 135.10 winning tickets. SP

2598 GOODWOOD (R-H)

Friday, June 6

OFFICIAL GOING: Good (good to soft in places; 8.0)

First 2f of mile course dolled out approximately 5metres, top bend dolled out 3m but no significant change to advertised distances.

Wind: Moderate, across

2795 ELM FARM ORGANIC RESEARCH CENTRE STKS (H'CAP) (FOR AMATEUR RIDERS) 1m 1f

6:15 (6:17) (Class 5) (0-70,74) 4-Y-0+ £3,123 (£968; £484; £242) Stalls High

Form	Pos	Dist	Horse / Trainer	Jockey	SP	RPR
62-4	1		**Im Ova Ere Dad (IRE)**[24] 2087 5-11-7 **70** (D E Cantillon) *hld up towards rr: gd hdwy over 2f out: led over 1f out: sn clr: easily*	MrSWalker 8	7/2[2]	87+
00-0	2	4 1/2	**Barathea Dreams (IRE)**[6] 2617 7-11-0 **63** (J S Moore) *mid-div: hdwy to ld over 2f out: hdd over 1f out: kpt on one pce*	MrsSMoore 14	14/1	70
0040	3	4	**The Gaikwar (IRE)**[5] 2640 9-10-3 **55** (b) (R A Harris) *mid-div: rdn over 3f out: kpt on to go 3rd ins fnl f*	MrRPFlint(3) 1	12/1	53
2611	4	1 1/4	**Daniel Thomas (IRE)**[10] 2487 6-11-4 **74** 6ex (Mrs A L M King) *mid-div: hdwy whn nt clr run and swtchd lft over 2f out: kpt on one pce ins fnl 2f*	MrOJMurphy(7) 12	3/1[1]	69
50-0	5	3/4	**Piano Man**[6] 2617 6-9-11 **51** oh1 (J C Fox) *hld up: hdwy over 2f out: nvr nr to chal*	MissSarah-JaneDurman(5) 7	33/1	44
00-0	6	1 1/2	**Laish Ya Hajar (IRE)**[18] 2243 4-10-4 **60** (P R Webber) *w ldrs: prom tl rdn 3f out: one pce after*	MrBBrackenbury(7) 10	20/1	50
3021	7	2	**Mick Is Back**[7] 2557 4-10-3 **59** 6ex (vt) (G G Margarson) *hld up towards rr: hdwy 3f out: one pce after*	MissKMargarson(7) 11	10/1	44
500-	8	1 1/4	**Path To Glory**[237] 6178 4-9-9 **51** oh5 (Miss Z C Davison) *prom on outside: rdn over 2f out: no hdwy after*	MrHGMiller(7) 4	25/1	33
43-6	9	3/4	**Palmetto Point**[7] 2561 4-11-2 **70** (p) (H Morrison) *in tch: rdn 3f out: sn btn*	MrRyanBird(5) 15	17/2[3]	51
5-60	10	1	**Rock Haven (IRE)**[8] 2523 6-10-0 **52** oh2 ow1 (W M Brisbourne) *prom tl rdn over 2f out: hung lft and wknd*	MrBenBrisbourne(3) 13	20/1	30
5	11	1	**Guilt**[89] 710 8-9-10 **52** (tp) (K J Burke) *hld up: a towards rr*	MissJMHindle(7) 5	50/1	28
501/	12	1/2	**Danish Monarch**[561] 5259 7-9-10 **52** (David Pinder) *led for 2f: rdn and wknd over 2f out*	MissNMCook(7) 17	40/1	27
3-04	13	1 1/2	**Mythical Charm**[149] 89 9-10-2 **51** oh1 (t) (J J Bridger) *nvr bttr than mid-div*	MrSDobson 3	14/1	22
1550	14	4 1/2	**Ruffie (IRE)**[67] 1116 5-9-11 **51** oh3 (Miss J Feilden) *prom tl wknd 3f out*	MrRBirkett(5) 9	25/1	12
6-40	15	3 1/4	**Sky Quest (IRE)**[14] 2374 10-10-9 **65** (J R Boyle) *mid-div early: rdn and wknd 3f out*	MrBAdams(7) 2	20/1	19
-650	16	2 1/2	**He's Mine Too**[10] 2483 4-10-9 **63** (p) (D G Bridgwater) *led after 2f: hdd over 2f out: wknd rapidly*	MrDanielChinn(5) 18	25/1	11
5606	17	20	**Bed Fellow (IRE)**[19] 2220 4-10-9 **65** (Paul Murphy) *slowly away: a in rr: t.o*	MissJKWilson(7) 6	40/1	—
6360	18	50	**Hansomelle (IRE)**[9] 1996 6-10-2 **58** (p) (Miss Sheena West) *slowly away: a bhd: t.o*	MissTHall(7) 16	25/1	—

1m 58.66s (2.36) **Going Correction** +0.225s/f (Good) **18 Ran SP% 127.3**

Speed ratings (Par 103): **98,94,90,89,88 87,85,84,83,82 82,81,80,76,73 71,53,8**

CSF £44.60 CT £575.91 TOTE £5.70: £1.40, £3.60, £2.60, £1.50; EX 78.80.

Owner Allan Milton **Bred** Golden Vale Stud **Trained** Newmarket, Suffolk

FOCUS

This amateurs' event was run at a good pace. Solid enough form for the grade and the winner proved himself a well-handicapped animal.

Piano Man Official explanation: jockey said gelding dwelt in the stalls

2796 SOIL ASSOCIATION EUROPEAN BREEDERS' FUND MAIDEN STKS 6f

6:45 (6:46) (Class 5) 2-Y-O £3,561 (£1,059; £529; £264) Stalls Low

Form	Pos	Dist	Horse / Trainer	Jockey	SP	RPR
5	1		**Sohcahtoa (IRE)**[21] 2150 2-9-3 0 (R Hannon) *led after 1f: drvn out fnl f*	RichardHughes 7	3/1[2]	84+
	2	1/2	**Total Gallery (IRE)** 2-9-3 0 (J S Moore) *slowly away: sn in tch: r.o to go 2nd ins fnl f: hld nr fin*	TedDurcan 8	16/1	82+
2	3	1 3/4	**Woolston Ferry (IRE)**[7] 2562 2-9-3 0 (M R Channon) *a.p: ev ch ent fnl f: lost 2nd ins fnl f*	DarryllHolland 4	6/5[1]	77
	4	1	**Gyr (IRE)** 2-9-3 0 (J L Dunlop) *hld up: hdwy 2f out: kpt on ins fnl f: nvr nrr*	KerrinMcEvoy 3	13/2	74+
	5	6	**Killmarnock** 2-9-3 0 (R A Teal) *led for 1f: ev ch tl wknd fnl f*	EddieAhern 5	33/1	56
	6	4	**Custody (IRE)** 2-9-3 0 (Sir Michael Stoute) *hld up: rdn over 2f out: sn btn*	JimmyFortune 2	5/1[3]	44
	7	1 1/4	**Arushore (IRE)** 2-9-3 0 (R Hannon) *slowly away: sn in tch: wknd over 1f out*	PatDobbs 6		40
	8	3/4	**Cashed Up** 2-9-3 0 (P Winkworth) *slowly away: a bhd*	JimCrowley 1	40/1	38

1m 13.41s (1.21) **Going Correction** +0.15s/f (Good) **8 Ran SP% 115.6**

Speed ratings (Par 93): **97,96,94,92,84 79,77,76**

CSF £46.60 TOTE £4.40: £1.50, £4.00, £1.10; EX 55.90.

Owner Mrs Sue Brendish **Bred** Knockainey Stud **Trained** East Everleigh, Wilts

FOCUS

A fair maiden on paper and, as is often the case, previous experience counted for plenty. The third is the best guide to the level.

NOTEBOOK

Sohcahtoa(IRE), one of only two in the race with the benefit of previous experience, put that to good use and, up there from the start, always looked like holding off his challengers inside the final furlong. Quicker ground will not be a problem for him and he looks one to look out for in decent nursery company next month. (op 9-2)

Total Gallery(IRE), whose dam was a triple 7f winner at three in Greece, is bred to be fairly speedy, but being by Namid the drying ground would probably not have been in his favour. He split a couple of rivals who had the benefit of previous experience and should not be long in going one better. (op 12-1 tchd 11-1)

Woolston Ferry(IRE), only narrowly beaten over this course and distance on his debut a week earlier, had quicker ground to deal with and this also looked a stronger race on paper. He had every chance and probably ran to a similar level. (op 11-8)

Gyr(IRE), a 180,000gns half-brother to ten winners including top-class sprinter Invincible Spirit, was of obvious interest on his debut. His stable's first two-year-old runner of the season, he shaped with promise, running on at the finish, and he should have learnt plenty from this. (tchd 15-2)

Killmarnock, whose dam was a triple 1m4f winner in France, is bred to want further than this in time while a number of his rivals were more sprint bred. He showed good early speed in the circumstannces. (op 40-1)

Custody(IRE), a half-brother to Satine, a 7f winner at two, is out of Shahtoush, who was second in the 1,000 Guineas and won the Oaks. Not particularly strong in the market, he is obviously bred to improve over a good deal further than this in time. (op 7-2)

2797 HILDON STKS (REGISTERED AS THE TAPSTER STAKES) (LISTED RACE) 1m 4f

7:20 (7:22) (Class 1) 4-Y-O+ £17,778 (£6,723; £3,360; £1,680) Stalls Low

Form	Pos	Dist	Horse / Trainer	Jockey	SP	RPR
5-24	1		**Peppertree Lane (IRE)**[8] 2542 5-9-0 110 (M Johnston) *led: rdn and hdd briefly jst ins fnl f: all out*	JoeFanning 6	8/1	116
/32-	2	hd	**Eastern Anthem (IRE)**[379] 1957 4-9-0 101 (t) (Saeed Bin Suroor) *trckd wnr: chal over 2f out: led briefly jst ins fnl f: kpt on to line*	TedDurcan 5	14/1	116
151-	3	shd	**Speed Gifted**[288] 4749 4-9-0 102 (L M Cumani) *hld up wl in rr: gd hdwy fr 3f out: hung bdly rt fr over 1f out but r.o and jst failed for 2nd*	JamieSpencer 1	5/1[3]	116+
0-13	4	1	**Al Shemali**[27] 1990 4-9-0 109 (t) (Saeed Bin Suroor) *a.p: rdn and chal 2f out: no ex ins fnl f*	LDettori 4	4/1[2]	114
0-10	5	5	**Raincoat**[28] 1944 4-9-0 109 (J H M Gosden) *hld up in rr: sme hdwy 2f out: n.d*	JimmyFortune 3	5/1[3]	106
30-0	6	4 1/2	**Dragon Dancer**[33] 1829 5-9-0 108 (G Wragg) *mid-div: rdn over 2f out: sn btn*	RichardHughes 7	12/1	99
5-00	7	nk	**Young Mick**[21] 2169 6-9-0 105 (v) (G G Margarson) *trckd ldrs: chal 3f out: wknd over 1f out*	DarryllHolland 10	40/1	98
4-00	8	2 1/2	**Maid To Believe**[13] 2402 4-8-9 90 (J L Dunlop) *t.k.h in mid-div: wknd over 2f out*	EddieAhern 8	50/1	89
226-	9	1 1/2	**Shahin (USA)**[272] 5220 5-9-0 112 (v) (M P Tregoning) *hld up in tch: rdn over 3f out: sn btn*	MartinDwyer 9	15/2	92
523-	10	nk	**Sagara (USA)**[243] 6043 4-9-0 122 (Saeed Bin Suroor) *t.k.h: a towards rr*	KerrinMcEvoy 2	11/4[1]	91

2m 37.82s (-0.58) **Going Correction** +0.225s/f (Good) **10 Ran SP% 121.6**

Speed ratings (Par 111): **110,109,109,109,105 102,102,100,99,99**

CSF £118.21 TOTE £10.40: £2.40, £4.80, £2.00; EX 121.40.

Owner P D Savill **Bred** Gestut Wittekindshof **Trained** Middleham Moor, N Yorks

FOCUS

A decent Listed race featuring only one horse with a rating below 101, but it developed into something of a tactical affair. Significant improvement from both the second and third, both of whom are relatively unexposed.

NOTEBOOK

Peppertree Lane(IRE), who stays much further than this, likes to be out in front, but he did not go a mad gallop. Quickening things up from the front three furlongs out, he proved tough to pass, and although he was briefly headed inside the final furlong, he rallied bravely to get his head back in front. The Group 3 Curragh Cup on June 28, which he won last year, is next up, and softer ground will suit him there. (tchd 9-1)

Eastern Anthem(IRE), lightly raced and not seen since finishing second in similar company at this track in May last year, wore a tongue tie for the first time. Despite having plenty on with most of his rivals - he was the Godolphin third string on jockey bookings - he ran well, racing prominently throughout and taking advantage of the slightly tactical nature of the race to maintain his position in the straight. (op 10-1)

Speed Gifted ◆ is another who has not had much racing. He won the Melrose Handicap on his final start last year and looked then the sort destined for greater things this time around. This was a promising reappearance as he did by far the best of the hold-up horses in a race not run to suit, and if he had not hung so badly right he would surely have won. Connections were satisfied and pointed the way to a step up in class next in the Hardwicke Stakes. Official explanation: jockey said colt ran hung badly right (op 10-3)

Al Shemali, the stable's first string on jockey bookings, did not run badly behind Red Rocks on his return to this country, but he failed to build on that here. Never too far off the pace in what was a fairly tactical affair, he might have found this trip a bit further than he cares for. (op 5-1)

Raincoat, who endured a nightmare run at Chester last month, had no such excuse this time and could only plug on one-paced in the closing stages. (op 15-2 tchd 9-2)

Dragon Dancer, ridden more patiently this time, is difficult to catch right. (op 16-1)

Young Mick is difficult to place these days. Official explanation: jockey said gelding hung right

Shahin(USA), runner-up to Ivy Creek in this race last year on his seasonal reappearance, was unable to repeat that effort despite solid support in the market. (op 10-1)

Sagara(USA), bought by Godolphin after finishing third in the Arc, had 10lb in hand of his nearest rival on official ratings, but he carried the second colours and never looked a danger on this reappearance. His connections will be hoping he steps up massively on this next time out. Official explanation: trainer said gelding was never travelling (op 7-2 tchd 4-1 in a place)

2798 WHEB VENTURES STKS (H'CAP) 6f

7:50 (7:54) (Class 5) (0-70,69) 4-Y-O+ £3,238 (£963; £481; £240) Stalls Low

Form	Pos	Dist	Horse / Trainer	Jockey	SP	RPR
0254	1		**Tilsworth Charlie**[14] 2355 5-8-5 **53** (b) (J R Jenkins) *hld up: gd hdwy fr over 1f out: r.o to ld ins fnl f: won gng away*	AdrianMcCarthy 8	16/1	65
0610	2	2 1/2	**Caustic Wit (IRE)**[4] 2679 10-9-1 **63** (p) (M S Saunders) *led gp of 3 on far side and sn overall ldr: rdn and hdd wl ins fnl f*	RichardHughes 15	15/2	67+
-222	3	shd	**Kyllachy Storm**[10] 2478 4-8-5 **53** (R J Hodges) *hld up: hdwy 2f out: ev ch ent fnl f: kpt on ins fnl f*	DavidKinsella 9	9/2[1]	56
6200	4	4 1/2	**Reigning Monarch (USA)**[3] 2692 5-8-2 **57** (Miss Z C Davison) *slowly away: sn chsd ldrs: rdn and edgd rt over 1f out: sn btn*	RossAtkinson(7) 6	9/1	46
2510	5	1	**Contented (IRE)**[84] 879 6-8-11 **59** (p) (Mrs L C Jewell) *led stands' side: hung rt and wknd appr fnl f*	JimCrowley 7	14/1	45
4315	6	3/4	**Hart Of Gold**[33] 1842 4-8-13 **68** (R A Harris) *chsd ldr far side: wknd over 1f out*	MatthewDavies(7) 14	8/1	51
50-4	7	1 3/4	**Sheriff's Silk**[43] 1591 4-9-6 **68** (b) (G D Blake) *prom far side tl wknd fnl f*	PaulEddery 13	40/1	46
-052	8	1/2	**Exit Strategy (IRE)**[10] 2474 4-8-11 **59** (b) (R A Harris) *prom tl wknd over 1f out*	TedDurcan 5	10/1	35
500-	9	2	**Who's Winning (IRE)**[129] 7094 7-8-9 **64** (B G Powell) *a towards rr*	KylieManser(7) 1	33/1	34
1-03	10	hd	**Our Fugitive (IRE)**[3] 2692 6-9-2 **64** (b) (C Gordon) *prom tl wknd over 1f out*	SamHitchcott 12	6/1[3]	33

0-06 11 5 **Morse (IRE)**[10] 2478 7-9-2 64 .... LDettori 11 17
(J A Osborne) *s.i.s: swtchd towards stands' side: a towards rr* **11/2**[2]

0003 12 3 1/2 **Nordic Light (USA)**[14] 2350 4-9-7 69 .... (b) JoeFanning 10 11
(J M Bradley) *chsd stands' side ldr tl wknd qckly over 1f out* **25/1**

1/00 13 14 **Tadlil**[32] 1872 6-9-1 63 .... EddieAhern 4 —
(J M Bradley) *a struggling in rr: t.o* **20/1**

1m 12.61s (0.41) **Going Correction** +0.15s/f (Good) **13** Ran SP% **116.4**
Speed ratings (Par 103): **103,99,99,93,92 91,88,88,85,85 78,73,55**
CSF £116.92 CT £575.35 TOTE £18.80: £5.70, £2.50, £1.80; EX 167.40.
Owner M Ng **Bred** Michael Ng **Trained** Royston, Herts
■ Figaro Flyer was withdrawn on vet's advice (10/1, deduct 5p in the £ under rule 4).
■ Stewards' Enquiry : L Dettori one-day ban: failed to ride to draw (Jun 26)

FOCUS
A competitive, if moderate handicap run at a good clip. Modest form, the winner rated to her best.
Reigning Monarch(USA) Official explanation: jockey said saddle slipped
Who's Winning(IRE) Official explanation: jockey said gelding missed the break
Morse(IRE) Official explanation: jockey said gelding lost its action
Tadlil Official explanation: jockey said gelding lost its action

2799 ECOLOGIST STKS (H'CAP) 1m 1f 192y
8:25 (8:25) (Class 4) (0-80,79) 4-Y-0+ **£4,533** (£1,348; £674; £336) **Stalls** High

Form RPR

2242 1 **Dakiyah (IRE)**[8] 2540 4-9-5 77 .... (p) IanMongan 5 85
(Mrs L J Mongan) *hld up: hdwy 4f out: nt clr run 3f out: swtchd lft and led 2f out: styd on wl fnl f* **11/8**[1]

6-42 2 1 1/4 **Multicultural**[25] 2060 5-8-9 67 .... MartinDwyer 3 72
(D M Simcock) *in rr: pushed along 1/2-way: hdwy 3f out: squeezed out 2f out: kpt on fnl f* **4/1**[3]

5263 3 3 1/4 **Megalala (IRE)**[7] 2561 7-7-12 63 oh3 ow3 .... RossAtkinson(7) 1 62
(J J Bridger) *trckd ldrs: ev ch over 2f out: kpt on* **12/1**

0-00 4 2 1/4 **Press The Button (GER)**[21] 2152 5-9-7 79 .... EddieAhern 4 73
(J R Boyle) *hld up: effrt over 2f out: one pce after* **7/2**[2]

4-62 5 4 **Cupid's Glory**[110] 605 6-9-2 74 .... (p) RichardHughes 2 60
(Mrs L C Jewell) *led after 1f: rdn and hdd 2f out: sn btn* **16/1**

306 6 27 **Northern Jem**[14] 2369 4-9-7 79 .... AdrianMcCarthy 6 11
(G G Margarson) *led for 1f: wknd over 2f out: eased 1f out* **6/1**

2m 8.80s (0.80) **Going Correction** +0.225s/f (Good) **6** Ran SP% **112.2**
Speed ratings (Par 105): **105,104,101,99,96 74**
CSF £7.16 TOTE £2.60: £1.90, £2.10; EX 5.10.
Owner Mrs P J Sheen **Bred** His Highness The Aga Khan's Studs S C **Trained** Epsom, Surrey
■ Stewards' Enquiry : Adrian McCarthy three-day ban: weighed in 2lbs less than the weight at which he weighed out (Jun 30-Jul 2)

FOCUS
The winner looked well in on her form behind Punjabi and did not need to run to that level to win. The runner-up is the guide to the level.
Cupid's Glory Official explanation: jockey said gelding lost its action in the final furlong

2800 GOODWOOD FARM SHOP MAIDEN FILLIES' STKS 1m
8:55 (9:01) (Class 5) 3-Y-0+ **£3,238** (£963; £481; £240) **Stalls** High

Form RPR

4-2 1 **Red Dune (IRE)**[18] 2257 3-8-12 0 .... PhilipRobinson 8 88+
(M A Jarvis) *mde all: pushed clr over 1f out: comf* **11/10**[1]

3 2 1 1/2 **Lee Miller (IRE)**[18] 2257 3-8-12 0 .... NickyMackay 10 79+
(L M Cumani) *trckd ldrs: rdn to chse wnr over 1f out: r.o* **9/4**[2]

3 3 1/4 **Suede** 3-8-12 0 .... PaulEddery 2 72+
(Pat Eddery) *hld up in rr: styd on fr over 1f out: nvr nrr* **33/1**

0-0 4 1 1/4 **Selsey**[22] 2123 3-8-12 0 .... RichardHughes 3 69+
(Sir Michael Stoute) *hld up towards rr: hdwy over 2f out: sn rdn and no imp after* **10/1**

0 5 3 1/4 **Isle Of Capri**[20] 2198 3-8-12 0 .... PatDobbs 1 61
(R Hannon) *prom: rdn over 2f out: one pce after* **50/1**

0-6 6 2 **Sterope (FR)**[18] 2257 3-8-12 0 .... TedDurcan 11 57+
(H R A Cecil) *mid-div: rdn over 2f out and nvr on terms after* **14/1**

7 2 1/4 **Citron Presse (USA)** 3-8-12 0 .... JimmyFortune 5 51
(J H M Gosden) *in tch tl wknd appr fnl f* **20/1**

005 8 2 1/4 **Miss Clonyn (IRE)**[77] 3-8-12 0 ....[1] EddieAhern 4 46
(Christian Wroe) *trckd wnr: rdn over 2f out: wknd over 1f out* **33/1**

9 8 **Titillate (IRE)** 3-8-12 0 .... LDettori 9 28
(Saeed Bin Suroor) *mid-div: rdn over 3f out and nvr on terms after* **5/1**[3]

3 10 1 1/4 **Twelfth Night (IRE)**[107] 633 4-9-9 0 .... JimCrowley 7 25
(J R Best) *slowly away: a bhd* **33/1**

1m 40.81s (0.91) **Going Correction** +0.225s/f (Good)
WFA 3 from 4yo 11lb **10** Ran SP% **126.4**
Speed ratings (Par 100): **104,102,99,98,94 92,90,88,80,79**
CSF £3.88 TOTE £2.30: £1.30, £1.40, £6.00; EX 4.70 Place 6 £32.27, Place 5 £18.98.
Owner Sheikh Ahmed Al Maktoum **Bred** Ballymacoll Stud Farm Ltd **Trained** Newmarket, Suffolk

FOCUS
A fair maiden which has been rated around the first two to their Windsor form. The winner was value for further.
T/Plt: £18.10 to a £1 stake. Pool: £70,571.81. 2,843.85 winning tickets. T/Qpdt: £10.30 to a £1 stake. Pool: £3,244.78. 230.90 winning tickets. JS

2259 WOLVERHAMPTON (A.W) (L-H)
Friday, June 6

OFFICIAL GOING: Standard
All races except 4.25 hand-timed.
Wind: Light across Weather: Cloudy with sunny spells

2801 LADBROKESCASINO.COM CLAIMING STKS 1m 1f 103y(P)
2:00 (2:00) (Class 6) 3-Y-0 **£2,047** (£604; £302) **Stalls** Low

Form RPR

1-34 1 **Ogre (USA)**[10] 2486 3-8-8 68 .... PatCosgrave 6 67
(J R Boyle) *hld up in tch: rdn to chse ldr 2f out: r.o to ld nr fin* **2/1**[1]

2-30 2 nk **Locum**[25] 2043 3-8-13 66 .... SaleemGolam 3 71
(M H Tompkins) *trckd ldr over 7f out: led over 2f out: rdn and hung lft ins fnl f: hdd nr fin* **5/2**[2]

3241 3 7 **One Called Alice**[3] 2704 3-8-6 52 .... HayleyTurner 1 49
(A W Carroll) *trckd ldrs: racd keenly: rdn over 2f out: wknd fnl f* **9/2**[3]

-060 4 2 1/2 **Redsensor**[21] 2161 3-9-3 64 .... ShaneKelly 8 55
(M Quinn) *sn led: rdn and hdd over 2f out: wknd over 1f out* **10/1**

-022 5 5 **Hurstpierpoint (IRE)**[10] 2486 3-8-7 60 .... TonyHamilton 5 35
(R A Fahey) *hld up: rdn and wknd over 2f out* **13/2**

-065 6 3 **Bahia Palace**[42] 1603 3-8-2 38 .... (p) FrancisNorton 2 23
(M D I Usher) *chsd ldrs: lost pl 6f out: rdn and wknd over 2f out* **40/1**

1505 7 7 **Silver Spruce**[10] 2486 3-8-11 59 .... (b) PatrickMathers 4 18
(I W McInnes) *s.i.s: hld up: rdn over 3f out: wknd over 2f out* **20/1**

2m 2.20s (0.50) **Going Correction** +0.025s/f (Slow) **7** Ran SP% **109.7**
Speed ratings (Par 97): **98,97,91,89,84 82,75**
CSF £6.54 TOTE £4.00: £1.20, £1.40; EX 7.10 Trifecta £24.80 Pool: £ 172.86 - 4.94 winning units.Hurstpierpoint (IRE) was claimed by Mr Mark Rimell for £9000.
Owner M Khan X2 **Bred** Gulf Coast Farms LLC **Trained** Epsom, Surrey

FOCUS
A moderate claimer run at a steady early pace. The form is not that solid behind the first three and the winner did not need to be at his best.

2802 LADBROKESPOKER.COM H'CAP 5f 20y(P)
2:35 (2:36) (Class 6) (0-55,55) 3-Y-0+ **£2,388** (£705; £352) **Stalls** Low

Form RPR

0-04 1 **Blessed Place**[4] 2679 8-8-9 49 .... BillyCray(7) 7 65
(D J S Ffrench Davis) *mde all: shkn up ins fnl f: r.o wl* **9/2**[2]

02-4 2 2 3/4 **Smirfys Gold (IRE)**[11] 2448 4-9-6 53 .... J-PGuillambert 9 59
(E S McMahon) *a.p: chsd wnr over 3f out: rdn fnl f: styd on same pce* **4/1**[1]

-210 3 1 **Charlotte Grey**[120] 469 4-8-12 50 .... JackMitchell(5) 2 52
(P J McBride) *chsd ldrs: n.m.r and lost pl over 3f out: styd on u.p fnl f* **15/2**

3060 4 3 **Ducal Regancy Red**[49] 1455 4-8-8 48 .... DeclanCannon(7) 6 39
(C J Teague) *chsd ldrs: rdn 1/2-way: wknd over 1f out* **10/1**

40-0 5 nk **Calypso King**[38] 1706 5-9-3 50 .... PatCosgrave 3 40
(Peter Grayson) *n.m.r s: hdwy over 3f out: rdn over 1f out: hung lft and wknd fnl f* **6/1**

3000 6 1/2 **Scarlett Heart (IRE)**[2] 2721 4-9-3 53 .... KirstyMilczarek(3) 4 42
(S Curran) *s.s: outpcd: styd on ins fnl f: nvr nrr* **6/1**

0023 7 1 3/4 **Stormburst (IRE)**[4] 2670 4-9-3 50 .... VinceSlattery 1 32
(A J Chamberlain) *sn outpcd* **9/1**

0-00 8 1/2 **Law Maker**[18] 2263 8-8-13 53 .... (v) NatashaEaton(7) 5 34
(A Bailey) *sn outpcd* **33/1**

4236 9 1 1/4 **Twinned (IRE)**[38] 1706 5-9-5 52 .... ShaneKelly 11 28
(Mike Murphy) *wnt rt s: hdwy over 3f out: rdn: hung rt and wknd over 1f out* **5/1**[3]

61.30 secs (-1.00) **Going Correction** +0.025s/f (Slow)
WFA 3 from 4yo+ 7lb **9** Ran SP% **117.2**
Speed ratings (Par 101): **109,104,103,98,97 96,94,93,91**
CSF £23.27 CT £133.63 TOTE £4.20: £1.10, £2.10, £5.00; EX 24.90 Trifecta £91.80 Part won..
Owner S J Edwards **Bred** Mrs W H Gibson Fleming **Trained** Lambourn, Berks

FOCUS
Moderate sprint handicap form, but pretty solid.

2803 MIDLAND TECHNICAL TRANSLATIONS 25TH ANNIVERSARY (S) STKS 5f 216y(P)
3:10 (3:10) (Class 6) 3-Y-0 **£2,047** (£604; £302) **Stalls** Low

Form RPR

1120 1 **Copperbottomed (IRE)**[23] 2099 3-9-3 68 .... (e) PatCosgrave 2 65
(J R Boyle) *hld up: hdwy over 2f out: shkn up to ld over 1f out: sn clr* **11/2**[3]

550- 2 2 3/4 **Varinia (IRE)**[253] 5751 3-8-4 57 .... KirstyMilczarek(3) 3 46
(M Brittain) *chsd ldrs: outpcd over 2f out: r.o u.p ins fnl f* **8/1**

1366 3 1/2 **Bahamarama (IRE)**[41] 1635 3-8-9 53 .... (p) KevinGhunowa(3) 1 50
(R A Harris) *led 1f: chsd ldr: rdn over 2f out: ev ch over 1f out: edgd lft and no ex fnl f* **10/1**

1246 4 2 1/4 **Lord Deevert**[10] 2480 3-8-7 65 .... (v) JackDean(5) 6 43
(W G M Turner) *s.i.s: hld up: nt clr run over 2f out: hdwy over 1f out: nt trble ldrs* **4/1**[2]

000 5 1 1/4 **Hapi**[24] 2084 3-8-5 37 .... (t) WilliamCarson(7) 9 39
(S C Williams) *prom: edgd lft over 3f out: rdn over 1f out: hung lft and wknd fnl f* **33/1**

5 6 1/2 **Bertha**[24] 2084 3-8-7 0 .... ShaneKelly 5 32
(J A Osborne) *prom: n.m.r and lost pl over 3f out: n.d after* **8/1**

500- 7 3 3/4 **Fraamington**[179] 7096 3-8-5 45 .... MCGeran(7) 8 25
(M R Channon) *hld up: rdn over 2f out: no ch whn hmpd ins fnl f* **28/1**

00 8 nse **Paris Hall**[31] 1894 3-8-12 0 .... PatrickMathers 10 25
(I W McInnes) *s.s: outpcd* **50/1**

0406 9 3 1/2 **Wave Hill (IRE)**[17] 2268 3-8-12 57 .... (b[1]) RobertHavlin 7 14
(B J Meehan) *n.m.r sn after s: hdwy over 4f out: rdn: hung rt and wknd wl over 1f out* **8/1**

432- 10 2 **Mystickhill (IRE)**[228] 6388 3-8-7 65 .... (t) ChrisCatlin 4 2
(J Balding) *led 5f out: rdn and hdd over 1f out: sn hung lft and wknd* **6/4**[1]

1m 15.8s (0.80) **Going Correction** +0.025s/f (Slow) **10** Ran SP% **126.2**
Speed ratings (Par 97): **95,91,90,87,86 85,80,80,75,72**
CSF £52.43 TOTE £6.30: £2.10, £3.40, £1.50; EX 71.70 Trifecta £271.40 Part won.Winner bought in for 6,500 guineas.
Owner M Khan X2 **Bred** Paul McEnery **Trained** Epsom, Surrey
■ Stewards' Enquiry : Chris Catlin three-day ban: careless riding (Jun 22-24)

FOCUS
A weak seller and the form has been rated negatively, but the pace was good.

2804 BET NOW WITH LADBROKES ON 0800 777 888 H'CAP 1m 4f 50y(P)
3:45 (3:45) (Class 5) (0-70,68) 4-Y-0+ **£3,238** (£963; £481; £240) **Stalls** Low

Form RPR

5065 1 **Fenners (USA)**[14] 2364 5-8-13 60 .... DaleGibson 7 66
(M W Easterby) *hld up in tch: shkn up 1/2-way: outpcd over 2f out: rallied over 1f out: rdn to ld wl ins fnl f* **13/2**

6-00 2 3/4 **Etain (IRE)**[21] 2153 4-9-5 66 .... SaleemGolam 2 71
(W R Swinburn) *chsd ldrs: rdn 4f out: styd on u.p* **5/1**[3]

033 3 nk **King's Fable (USA)**[27] 2012 5-8-13 63 .... (p) JerryO'Dwyer(3) 3 68+
(Karen George) *s.i.s: hld up: hdwy on outside over 2f out: rdn to ld and edgd lft over 1f out: hung rt and hdd wl ins fnl f* **11/2**

124 4 3/4 **Alonso De Guzman (IRE)**[16] 2304 4-9-7 68 .... PatCosgrave 1 71
(J R Boyle) *led: rdn over 2f out: edgd lft and hdd over 1f out: no ex ins fnl f* **9/4**[1]

5506 5 2 **Qaasi (USA)**[3] 2701 6-8-7 54 .... ChrisCatlin 4 54
(M Brittain) *hld up: racd keenly: nt clr run over 2f out: hdwy over 1f out: no ex ins fnl f* **8/1**

1044 6 1 **My Mentor (IRE)**[29] 1933 4-9-4 65 .... J-PGuillambert 5 63
(Sir Mark Prescott) *chsd ldr: rdn over 3f out: wknd towards fin* **4/1**[2]

0-50 7 31 **Desert Leader (IRE)**[41] 1639 7-8-13 60 .... TGMcLaughlin 6 9
(W M Brisbourne) *chsd ldrs: rdn 4f out: wknd wl over 2f out* **16/1**

2m 40.6s (-0.50) **Going Correction** +0.025s/f (Slow) **7** Ran SP% **113.1**
Speed ratings (Par 103): **102,101,101,100,99 98,78**
CSF £37.62 TOTE £9.40: £2.20, £2.10; EX 41.40.
Owner K Wreglesworth **Bred** Darley **Trained** Sheriff Hutton, N Yorks

FOCUS
Just a modest 1m4f handicap and a bunch finish. The winning time was moderate, as they did not seem to go very quickly in the early stages.

2805 BETTER PRICES, BIGGER WINS AT LADBROKES.COM H'CAP 1m 141y(P)
4:25 (4:33) (Class 6) (0-65,65) 3-Y-O £2,388 (£705; £352) Stalls Low

Form RPR
0-05 1 **Redarsene**[20] 2199 3-9-2 65 JamieJones(5) 5 71+
(M G Quinlan) *hld up: racd keenly: hdwy u.p over 1f out: edgd lft and led wl ins fnl f* 9/2[2]
2-00 2 1 ¾ **The Last Bottle (IRE)**[27] 2014 3-9-6 64 TGMcLaughlin 9 66
(W M Brisbourne) *chsd ldr: rdn to ld ins fnl f: sn hdd and unable qck* 9/1
6500 3 2 **Alfredtheordinary**[11] 2451 3-8-10 61 MCGeran(7) 3 58
(M R Channon) *sn led: rdn over 1f out: hdd and no ex ins fnl f* 14/1
322 4 nk **Zeffirelli**[43] 1587 3-9-4 62 PatCosgrave 7 59
(M Quinn) *chsd ldrs: rdn over 2f out: styd on same pce fnl f* 4/1[1]
4400 5 ¾ **Kool Katie**[15] 2333 3-9-4 62 DaleGibson 4 57
(Mrs G S Rees) *hld up in tch: rdn over 1f out: no ex ins fnl f* 9/1
56-0 6 ¾ **Spent**[15] 2342 3-9-4 65 TravisBlock(3) 8 58+
(Mouse Hamilton-Fairley) *hld up: swtchd rt over 1f out: styng on whn nt clr run and swtchd lft ins fnl f: nvr rchd ldrs* 14/1
220- 7 ½ **Artistic Light**[177] 7117 3-9-5 63 ShaneKelly 1 55
(W R Muir) *trckd ldrs: rdn over 1f out: wknd ins fnl f* 15/2[3]
40-0 8 3 ¼ **Purple Ransom (IRE)**[18] 2260 3-8-11 55 (t) VinceSlattery 13 40
(D J Wintle) *prom: rdn over 2f out: wkng whn edgd lft fr over 1f out* 50/1
0-03 9 1 ½ **Reel Man**[24] 2084 3-9-2 60 SaleemGolam 11 41
(D K Ivory) *hld up: n.d* 25/1
600 10 2 ¼ **Opening Hand**[20] 2198 3-9-4 62 (p) ChrisCatlin 2 38
(Evan Williams) *chsd ldrs: rdn over 2f out: sn wknd: edgd rt fr over 1f out* 16/1
-604 11 2 **Mouse White**[24] 2084 3-8-1 52 AmyScott(7) 6 23
(H Candy) *s.i.s: a in rr* 16/1
0-6U 12 119 **Dynamo Dave (USA)**[39] 1685 3-9-7 65 (t) J-PGuillambert 12 —
(B J Meehan) *mid-div: rdn 1/2-way: wknd 3f out: eased* 8/1
60-0 F **Wabbraan (USA)**[21] 2161 3-9-2 65 (b[1]) AhmedAjtebi(5) 10 —
(D M Simcock) *hld up: rdn over 3f out: no ch whn clipped heels and fell ins fnl f* 9/1

1m 51.81s (1.31) **Going Correction** +0.025s/f (Slow) 13 Ran SP% 122.0
Speed ratings (Par 97): **95,93,91,91,90 90,89,86,85,83 81,—,—**
CSF £45.99 CT £556.03 TOTE £4.10: £1.80, £4.30, £5.50; EX 35.00 Trifecta £166.60 Part won..
Owner N J Jones **Bred** Rockwell Bloodstock **Trained** Newmarket, Suffolk

FOCUS
Run at a steady pace, this was a very moderate handicap (many of the runners looked very badly handicapped) and it is extremely unlikely that many winners will emerge from the race. The form seems fairly sound.
Redarsene Official explanation: trainer said, regarding the apparent improvement in form, that colt was now wearing a cross-noseband which enabled it to settle better, helping him to win.
Dynamo Dave(USA) Official explanation: jockey said colt was never travelling

2806 BET & WATCH ALL RACES AT LADBROKES.COM H'CAP 7f 32y(P)
5:00 (5:02) (Class 6) (0-60,60) 4-Y-O+ £2,388 (£705; £352) Stalls High

Form RPR
-200 1 **Forced Upon Us**[28] 1954 4-8-11 58 (b) JackMitchell(5) 10 68
(P J McBride) *led 1f: chsd ldr: led again over 2f out: all out* 12/1
2420 2 shd **Guildenstern (IRE)**[6] 2597 6-9-1 57 TGMcLaughlin 11 67
(P Howling) *hld up: hdwy and edgd lft fr over 1f out: r.o* 10/1
1140 3 ½ **Shunkawakhan (IRE)**[17] 2285 5-9-1 57 (p) J-PGuillambert 6 65
(Miss L A Perratt) *hld up: hdwy over 2f out: rdn over 1f out: n.m.r wl ins fnl f: r.o* 9/2[3]
0006 4 2 ¼ **Hollywood George**[6] 2597 4-8-13 55 PatrickMathers 12 57
(Miss M E Rowland) *hld up: hdwy over 1f out: sn rdn: edgd lft ins fnl f: styd on* 14/1
0-00 5 nk **All You Need (IRE)**[18] 2263 4-9-1 60 RussellKennemore(3) 5 61
(R Hollinshead) *trckd ldrs: rdn over 1f out: no ex ins fnl f* 7/2[1]
1430 6 ¾ **Playtotheaudience**[17] 2274 5-9-4 60 (v) TonyHamilton 8 59
(R A Fahey) *s.i.s: sn drvn along in rr: r.o ins fnl f: nvr nrr* 4/1[2]
-600 7 shd **Wadnagin (IRE)**[17] 2285 4-9-0 56 ChrisCatlin 9 55
(I A Wood) *hld up: r.o ins fnl f: nvr nrr* 16/1
1600 8 1 **Green Pirate**[18] 2263 6-9-1 60 (v) KirstyMilczarek(3) 3 57
(C R Dore) *s.s: hdwy over 5f out: nt clr run over 2f out: sn rdn: styd on same pce fnl f* 10/1
5160 9 2 ¼ **Kitto Katsu**[27] 2010 4-9-2 58 PatCosgrave 7 48
(D J Coakley) *hld up in tch: rdn over 1f out: wkng whn hmpd ins fnl f* 20/1
0230 10 ½ **Bens Georgie (IRE)**[98] 749 6-9-0 56 SaleemGolam 1 45
(D K Ivory) *chsd ldrs: rdn over 2f out: wknd fnl f* 15/2
56-0 11 ¾ **Baylaw Star**[98] 749 7-8-8 57 DonnaCaldwell(7) 4 44
(I W McInnes) *hld up: bhd fnl 3f* 33/1
460/ 12 6 **Bigalo's Banjo**[900] 6617 5-8-13 55 ShaneKelly 2 26
(L A Mullaney) *led 6f out: hdd over 2f out: wknd over 1f out* 16/1

1m 29.7s (0.10) **Going Correction** +0.025s/f (Slow) 12 Ran SP% 124.2
Speed ratings (Par 101): **100,99,99,96,96 95,95,94,91,91 90,83**
CSF £132.64 CT £647.04 TOTE £17.70: £4.00, £2.60, £1.90; EX 92.40 Trifecta £196.90 Pool: £234.71 - 1.02 winning units. Place 6: £403.92, Place 5: £292.22..
Owner Mrs Julie King **Bred** Lady Fairhaven **Trained** Newmarket, Suffolk
■ Stewards' Enquiry : T G McLaughlin caution: careless riding
J-P Guillambert caution: careless riding

FOCUS
A very modest handicap run at a steady pace. The form looks weak, rated through the placed horses.
Bigalo's Banjo Official explanation: jockey said gelding ran too free
T/Plt: £631.50 to a £1 stake. Pool: £41,264.51. 47.70 winning tickets. T/Qpdt: £196.50 to a £1 stake. Pool: £2,230.91. 8.40 winning tickets. CR

2807 - 2817a (Foreign Racing) - See Raceform Interactive

2782 DONCASTER (L-H)
Saturday, June 7

OFFICIAL GOING: Good to soft (good in places on straight course; soft in places on round course)
Wind: Light, across Weather: Overcast

2818 BETDIRECT.COM H'CAP 7f
2:05 (2:06) (Class 3) (0-90,89) 4-Y-O+ £9,714 (£2,890; £1,444; £721) Stalls High

Form RPR
0420 1 **Compton's Eleven**[16] 2339 7-8-8 83 MCGeran(7) 4 91
(M R Channon) *a.p: led wl over 1f out: sn rdn: jst hld on* 14/1
-251 2 nk **King's Bastion (IRE)**[21] 2203 4-9-1 83 HayleyTurner 10 90
(M L W Bell) *hld up: hdwy over 2f out: rdn over 1f out: r.o* 5/1[2]
365- 3 nk **Carnivore**[174] 7165 6-8-11 79 DaneO'Neill 7 85+
(T D Barron) *s.i.s: hld up: hdwy over 1f out: swtchd rt ins fnl f: r.o* 15/2
4-30 4 1 **Angaric (IRE)**[14] 2400 5-8-2 70 RoystonFfrench 1 74
(B Smart) *trckd ldrs: racd keenly: rdn and ev ch over 1f out: styd on* 10/1
30-0 5 hd **Misphire**[51] 1430 5-8-8 76 PhillipMakin 3 79
(M Dods) *s.i.s: hld up: hdwy over 1f out: r.o* 12/1
3530 6 ½ **Cornus**[9] 2535 6-8-12 80 (be) JamesDoyle 15 82
(A J McCabe) *hld up: plld hrd: r.o ins fnl f: nvr nrr* 12/1
5000 7 1 ¼ **Moonlight Man**[21] 2200 7-8-11 79 (t) LiamJones 8 77
(C R Dore) *trckd ldr: rdn over 1f out: no ex ins fnl f* 28/1
-003 8 hd **Countdown**[22] 2158 6-8-11 79 DavidAllan 11 77
(T D Easterby) *prom: rdn 1/2-way: no ex fnl f* 6/1[3]
010- 9 ¾ **Musical Beat**[273] 5230 4-8-12 80 EdwardCreighton 5 76
(Miss V Haigh) *dwlt: hld up: hdwy 1/2-way: rdn and ev ch over 1f out: wknd wl ins fnl f* 50/1
0000 10 ½ **Lap Of Honour (IRE)**[14] 2406 4-8-10 78 JimmyQuinn 6 73
(Jennie Candlish) *sn led: rdn and hdd wl over 1f out: btn whn hmpd ins fnl f* 33/1
5001 11 1 ¼ **Handsome Falcon**[9] 2535 4-8-4 72 DaleGibson 9 63
(R A Fahey) *prom: rdn over 2f out: sn edgd lft: wknd fnl f* 8/1
12-3 12 10 **Big Noise**[15] 2371 4-9-6 88 SteveDrowne 16 52
(Dr J D Scargill) *hld up: rdn over 2f out: sn edgd lft and wknd* 9/2[1]
0-15 13 8 **Pacific Pride**[15] 2358 5-8-11 79 GrahamGibbons 12 22
(J J Quinn) *mid-div: trckd ldr: rdn over 1f out: wknd wl over 1f out* 20/1
00-0 14 24 **Steenberg (IRE)**[47] 1517 9-9-7 89 SebSanders 13 —
(M H Tompkins) *sn pushed along in rr: rdn and wknd wl over 2f out* 14/1

1m 27.93s (1.63) **Going Correction** +0.20s/f (Good) 14 Ran SP% 122.9
Speed ratings (Par 107): **98,97,97,96,95 95,93,93,92,92 90,79,70,42**
CSF £81.50 CT £600.31 TOTE £16.30: £3.90, £2.50, £3.30; EX 94.60 TRIFECTA Not won..
Owner PCM Racing **Bred** Lady Cobham **Trained** West Ilsley, Berks
■ Stewards' Enquiry : M C Geran one-day ban: used whip with excessive force (Jun 22)

FOCUS
The two withdrawals notably weakened this handicap, particularly the absence of the unbeaten Musaalem, and left it far from competitive for the money, nor was it run at better than a steady pace. The form makes sense.

NOTEBOOK
Compton's Eleven, who had been taken off his feet over 6f on his previous start, proved suited by this step back up in trip, leading well over a furlong out, after coming under pressure at the 2f pole, and just holding on in a tight finish. He has a poor strike-rate but is in decent heart. (op 16-1)
King's Bastion(IRE) confirmed himself in good form with a fine effort, just failing to catch the winner. Raised 5lb for winning last time, he was behind the winner two runs ago and could not get past him again. (op 11-2 tchd 6-1)
Carnivore ◆ deserves credit for an encouraging first run of the year. He stayed on powerfully inside the final furlong to grab a close third late on and should be much straighter for the effort. (op 14-1)
Angaric(IRE) shaped well after racing prominently and gave the impression that he was ready to win again soon, although he is hardly a regular visitor to the winner's enclosure. (op 16-1 tchd 18-1)
Misphire did not run too badly without any headgear on (something she has not done for a long time) and is potentially fairly treated again. She has only ever won at 6f, so one would expect to see her eased in trip fairly soon. (op 16-1 tchd 20-1)
Cornus stayed on quite nicely inside the final furlong after being keen early. He has gone quite a few races since his last success, which came off a 5lb lower mark. (op 14-1 tchd 16-1)
Countdown had quite a few things in his favour but failed to show much sparkle. Four of his five successes have come in either July or August. (op 9-2)
Musical Beat, having her first run since last September, caught the eye to some extent before fading late on. It was a good reappearance but she is a shade high in the weights at the moment. (op 40-1 tchd 66-1)
Lap Of Honour(IRE) was not beaten too far after setting the pace. It was a vast improvement on his dismal effort last time.
Handsome Falcon was in trouble at the midway point and did not finish his race off. Class 4 races are very much his level, so this company was a bit too hot for him.
Big Noise ran dreadfully and has yet to justify any of the market confidence in him this season. Official explanation: jockey said colt never travelled (op 4-1)
Steenberg(IRE) Official explanation: jockey said gelding never travelled

2819 CALL BETDIRECT FREE ON 0800 211 222 H'CAP 1m (S)
2:35 (2:36) (Class 2) (0-100,93) 3-Y-O £12,952 (£3,854; £1,926; £962) Stalls High

Form RPR
041- 1 **Redford (IRE)**[248] 5904 3-9-1 87 HayleyTurner 4 101+
(M L W Bell) *hld up in tch: plld hrd: led ins fnl f: rdn out* 8/1
31-0 2 nk **Choose Your Moment**[50] 1441 3-9-7 93 MichaelHills 12 106
(P C Haslam) *chsd ldr tl led over 5f out: rdn and edgd lft fr over 1f out: hdd ins fnl f: r.o* 6/1[2]
151- 3 2 ¼ **Lady Rangali (IRE)**[253] 5766 3-8-10 82 RoystonFfrench 10 90
(Mrs A Duffield) *hld up in tch: rdn and hung rt ins fnl f: r.o* 12/1
-121 4 ¾ **Albaqaa**[44] 1576 3-8-12 84 TonyHamilton 3 90
(R A Fahey) *s.i.s: hld up: hdwy over 1f out: edgd rt: r.o* 8/1
5-1 5 1 ½ **Lazy Days**[26] 2056 3-8-13 88 MarcHalford(3) 11 91+
(D R C Elsworth) *hld up in tch: outpcd 2f out: r.o ins fnl f* 8/1
1F-2 6 ½ **Redesignation (IRE)**[17] 2311 3-9-1 87 PatDobbs 16 88
(R Hannon) *led: hdd over 5f out: rdn over 2f out: styd on same pce fnl f* 7/1[3]
31 7 ¾ **Illusion**[19] 2257 3-8-11 83 JimmyFortune 2 83
(J H M Gosden) *hld up in tch: chsd ldr over 2f out: rdn over 1f out: nt clr run sn after: wknd ins fnl f* 4/1[1]
31-1 8 nse **Classic Descent**[13] 2427 3-9-4 90 SebSanders 1 90
(P J Makin) *hld up: hdwy over 2f out: wknd fnl f* 10/1
30-1 9 1 ½ **Tarkheena Prince (USA)**[45] 1573 3-8-7 82 PJMcDonald(3) 8 78
(G A Swinbank) *chsd ldrs: rdn over 2f out: wknd over 1f out* 16/1
216- 10 nk **Shamayel**[224] 6498 3-8-13 85 MartinDwyer 7 80+
(B W Hills) *hld up: rdn over 2f out: sme hdwy over 1f out: n.d* 33/1
21-0 11 1 ½ **Cuban Missile**[35] 1811 3-9-1 87 SteveDrowne 5 79
(R Charlton) *hld up: rdn over 2f out: wknd over 1f out* 16/1
1-66 12 10 **Speedy Dollar (USA)**[35] 1806 3-9-3 89 PhilipRobinson 6 58
(M A Jarvis) *chsd ldrs: rdn over 2f out: wknd over 1f out* 12/1
1-5 13 14 **Bright Falcon**[65] 1171 3-9-2 88 DaneO'Neill 9 25
(S Parr) *s.i.s: hld up: rdn 1/2-way: wknd over 2f out* 25/1

1m 39.84s (0.54) **Going Correction** +0.20s/f (Good) 13 Ran SP% 123.1
Speed ratings (Par 105): **105,104,102,101,100 99,98,98,97,97 95,85,71**
CSF £57.20 CT £606.05 TOTE £10.20: £2.60, £2.20, £4.30; EX 73.80 TRIFECTA Not won..
Owner Highclere T'bred Racing (Housemaster) **Bred** T J Rooney **Trained** Newmarket, Suffolk

FOCUS
Potentially a strong three-year-old handicap, with each of the 13 runners already a winner and plenty of them open to improvement. They went a good gallop, too, and this is just the sort of race likely to throw up winners. Solid form.

NOTEBOOK
Redford(IRE) ◆, having his first race since bolting up at Newcastle last October, raced a shade keenly before taking up the lead inside the final furlong. After travelling sweetly, his response was not as good as it promised to be in the closing stages but this was the first time he had been involved in a battle and he found the necessary to hold on. Lightly raced, he has to be a leading contender for the Britannia Handicap at Royal Ascot (op 11-2)
Choose Your Moment, trying a mile for the first time, proved that he has trained on into a useful three-year-old (his last run can be largely ignored) by making the well-regarded winner, who was getting weight from him, battle hard for victory. He will not find things very easy off his handicap mark, but should make up into a tough sort. (op 11-2)
Lady Rangali(IRE), the winner of over £150,000 in prize-money as a two-year-old, showed that she has trained on with a decent effort, keeping on despite hanging right in the latter stages. She appeared to handle most ground conditions last season, which should help connections find races for her. (op 20-1)
Albaqaa kept on well for pressure, proving he is still making progress for his new stable this season. He does need to improve a little bit to keep that momentum going, but he could land a nice handicap before the end of the season. He shapes as though he will stay a little bit further. (op 10-1 tchd 15-2)
Lazy Days ◆ kept on nicely after getting outpaced. He was one of the least experienced in the line-up and, considering his size, has further improvement in him, so it is worth following his progress. (op 13-2)
Redesignation(IRE) led to halfway before he was gathered in. He ran much better last time when held up, so a return to those tactics may suit him better. (op 15-2 tchd 8-1)
Illusion could not confirm the promise of her Windsor maiden win in this much stronger company, as she weakened inside the final furlong after holding every chance over a furlong out. Official explanation: jockey said filly hung right (op 9-2 tchd 7-2)
Classic Descent ran a bit better than his finishing position suggests, as he was not given a hard time in the final furlong. Seven furlongs will probably be his best distance (op 11-1)
Shamayel ◆ went off a long price considering her efforts at two. She ran much better than the bare form would suggest, as she quickened nicely at halfway before not being punished late on. There should be more to come from her. Official explanation: jockey said filly was unsuited by the good to soft ground
Bright Falcon Official explanation: jockey said gelding hung right

2820 BETDIRECT 0800 211 222 FILLIES' H'CAP — 1m 2f 60y
3:05 (3:06) (Class 2) (0-100,95) 4-Y-O+ **£16,190** (£4,817; £2,407; £1,202) **Stalls** Low

Form — RPR

-545 **1** **Ronaldsay**[14] [2402] 4-9-7 **95** .... JimmyFortune 3 — 103
(R Hannon) *hld up in tch: swtchd lft over 1f out: sn rdn: r.o to ld post* **3/1**[2]

-233 **2** *nk* **Royal Fantasy (IRE)**[40] [1691] 5-8-3 **77** .... HayleyTurner 7 — 84
(J R Fanshawe) *hld up: hdwy over 3f out: led over 1f out: rdn and hung lft ins fnl f: hdd post* **7/1**

2404 **3** *2* **Montrachet**[7] [2619] 4-8-2 **76** oh1 .... RoystonFfrench 1 — 80
(M L W Bell) *chsd ldrs: rdn over 1f out: styd on same pce* **4/1**[3]

53-2 **4** *5* **Candy Mountain**[18] [2278] 4-8-5 **79** .... (v[1]) JimmyQuinn 6 — 73
(L M Cumani) *trckd ldr: led over 2f out: rdn and hdd over 1f out: wknd ins fnl f* **5/2**[1]

-033 **5** *4* **Fongs Gazelle**[10] [2505] 4-8-8 **82** .... MartinDwyer 2 — 69
(M Johnston) *led: rdn and hdd over 2f out: wknd fnl f* **5/1**

545 **6** *23* **Lisathedaddy**[10] [2505] 6-8-6 **80** .... DaleGibson 4 — 23
(B G Powell) *s.i.s: hdwy over 6f out: rdn and wknd over 2f out* **12/1**

2m 15.24s (4.04) **Going Correction** +0.375s/f (Good) **6** Ran SP% **110.4**
Speed ratings (Par 96): **98,97,96,92,88 70**
CSF £22.52 CT £78.34 TOTE £4.60: £2.50, £2.50; EX 28.20 Trifecta £148.30 Pool: £592.55 - 1.40 winning units.
Owner S P Tindall **Bred** Stowell Hill Ltd **Trained** East Everleigh, Wilts

FOCUS
Some fairly useful fillies and mares in the line-up, but the withdrawal of Group 2 entry Fragrancy left the field decidedly short on obviously progressive performers. The pace was steady and the form is only fair, rated through the placed horses.

NOTEBOOK
Ronaldsay was far from unexposed after 16 starts and she has had her limitations revealed in Listed company, but she is fairly useful at her very best and proved just too strong in the final strides for Royal Fantasy. She has only won a single race in each of the three seasons she has been racing, so she needs to find more improvement to buck that trend. (op 4-1)
Royal Fantasy(IRE) moved smoothly into the lead over a furlong out but was caught close home in a driving finish. She has plenty of ability but, despite edging left under pressure, was beaten by a classier type. (op 11-2)
Montrachet, who attracted some market support, ran creditably on this step up in trip and seemed to stay 1m2f. It should open up a few more options for connections. (op 7-1)
Candy Mountain, wearing a first-time visor, came through to lead over two furlongs out but faded quickly, and was ultimately comfortably held. (op 2-1 tchd 11-4 in places)
Fongs Gazelle did a lot of the donkey work in front but was readily left behind when the tempo increased. She is still rated well above her highest winning mark. (op 11-2)

2821 E B F CROWNHOTEL-BAWTRY.COM MAIDEN FILLIES' STKS — 6f
3:45 (3:47) (Class 4) 2-Y-O **£4,533** (£1,348; £674; £336) **Stalls** High

Form — RPR

5 **1** **Golden Rosie (IRE)**[11] [2479] 2-9-0 0 .... MichaelHills 9 — 74+
(B W Hills) *a.p: led over 2f out: shkn up fnl f: styd on* **10/3**[1]

4 **2** *¾* **Gal Aloud (USA)**[22] [2160] 2-9-0 0 .... PatDobbs 15 — 72
(R Hannon) *w ldr: led over 3f out: hdd over 2f out: rdn over 1f out: edgd lft: styd on* **10/3**[1]

3 *nse* **Peter's Gift (IRE)** 2-9-0 0 .... FergalLynch 4 — 72
(K A Ryan) *a.p: rdn and edgd lft over 1f out: styd on* **14/1**

4 *½* **Rose Diamond (IRE)** 2-9-0 0 .... SteveDrowne 11 — 70+
(R Charlton) *prom: lost pl over 3f out: hdwy over 1f out: shkn up and edgd lft ins fnl f: styd on* **9/2**[2]

5 *2 ¼* **Ahla Wasahl** 2-9-0 0 .... RichardMullen 6 — 63
(D M Simcock) *chsd ldrs: rdn over 1f out: styd on same pce fnl f* **25/1**

6 *hd* **Rose Cheval (USA)** 2-9-0 0 .... EdwardCreighton 14 — 63
(M R Channon) *mid-div: sn drvn along: lost pl 4f out: swtchd lft over 1f out: r.o ins fnl f* **12/1**

7 *2* **Claphands** 2-9-0 0 .... JamesDoyle 1 — 57
(A J McCabe) *s.i.s: hdwy over 1f out: nt trble ldrs* **40/1**

0 **8** *½* **Sonett**[11] [2479] 2-9-0 0 .... GrahamGibbons 10 — 55
(A J McCabe) *sn prom: rdn and hung lft over 1f out: wknd fnl f* **66/1**

9 *1 ¾* **Sicilian Pink** 2-9-0 0 .... PhilipRobinson 5 — 50
(J L Dunlop) *dwlt: sme hdwy over 2f out: wknd over 1f out* **12/1**

6 **10** *hd* **Well Of Echoes**[28] [1987] 2-9-0 0 .... DaneO'Neill 17 — 49
(A J McCabe) *led: hdd over 3f out: rdn and hung lft over 2f out: wknd over 1f out* **20/1**

11 *½* **Alayala (IRE)** 2-9-0 0 .... MartinDwyer 3 — 48
(M Johnston) *prom: hung lft thrght: wknd wl over 1f out* **13/2**[3]

12 *1 ¼* **Colangnik (USA)** 2-9-0 0 .... JimmyQuinn 2 — 44
(J R Best) *s.i.s: a in rr* **33/1**

13 *3 ¾* **Halaak (USA)** 2-9-0 0 .... HayleyTurner 12 — 33
(D M Simcock) *unruly in stalls: s.i.s: hdwy over 3f out: rdn and wknd over 2f out* **20/1**

14 *3 ½* **Bella Olympia** 2-8-7 0 .... StacyRenwick(7) 13 — 22
(A J McCabe) *s.s: outpcd* **66/1**

1m 15.9s (2.30) **Going Correction** +0.20s/f (Good) **14** Ran SP% **121.5**
Speed ratings (Par 92): **92,91,90,90,87 87,84,83,81,81 80,78,73,69**
CSF £12.79 TOTE £3.80: £1.70, £1.70, £2.60; EX 11.60 Trifecta £143.50 Part won: Pool: £202.21 - 0.70 winning units..
Owner John C Grant **Bred** Yeomanstown Stud **Trained** Lambourn, Berks

FOCUS
Probably no more than a fair fillies' maiden, although a couple of these had shown promise and several of the newcomers looked interesting. The way the first four came clear marks them down as having the makings of decent performers though. Sound form.

NOTEBOOK
Golden Rosie(IRE) showed the benefit of her debut experience over 5f. She travelled nicely in the early stages, took up the running 2f from home and then ran on well when asked to quicken. She is unlikely to go to Royal Ascot but is just the sort to make her mark in decent company. (op 5-2 tchd 4-1)
Gal Aloud(USA), whose debut race has been working out fairly well, arguably stepped up on her first effort at Newmarket and is well up to winning a maiden. (op 4-1)
Peter's Gift(IRE), who is related to winning sprinters, did best of the newcomers and showed more than enough to suggest she will win races after racing prominently throughout. (op 16-1 tchd 12-1)
Rose Diamond(IRE) ◆ kept on nicely without being knocked about. The first foal of top-class sprinter Tante Rose, she travelled really nicely for much of the race and should do a good deal better next time with this experience under her belt. (op 4-1)
Ahla Wasahl, a Dubai Destination half-sister to winners, travelled well for a long way and is sure to improve for the outing. (op 20-1 tchd 18-1)
Rose Cheval(USA) ◆, a Johannesburg half-sister to a fairly useful juvenile on the turf in the US, was outpaced early but finished strongly inside the final furlong. Her stable are doing well with their two-year-olds this season, so she can reasonably be expected to come on for the run. (op 14-1 tchd 11-1)
Claphands was not expected to go that close, judging by her starting price, but she did not run too badly after missing the break from a low draw. (tchd 33-1)
Sicilian Pink, a half-sister to Scarlet Runner, a smart filly for the same connections over the last two seasons, did not break too smartly but ran a lot better than her final position implies. It would be no surprise to see her go a lot closer next time.
Well Of Echoes Official explanation: jockey said filly hung left
Alayala(IRE), who cost 100,000gns as a yearling, was never far away before hanging to the inside rail in the final 2f. (op 10-1 tchd 6-1)

2822 SOCIETY LIFESTYLE AND LEISURE MAGAZINE H'CAP — 1m 4f
4:30 (4:30) (Class 4) (0-85,85) 4-Y-O+ **£4,857** (£1,445; £722; £360) **Stalls** Low

Form — RPR

413 **1** **Cotton Eyed Joe (IRE)**[34] [1824] 7-8-10 **74** .... DeanMcKeown 11 — 83
(G A Swinbank) *hld up in tch: rdn over 3f out: led and hung lft fr over 1f out: styd on u.p* **8/1**

4103 **2** *nk* **Red Wine**[7] [2591] 9-8-5 **76** .... StacyRenwick(7) 15 — 85
(A J McCabe) *stdd s: hld up and bhd: hdwy over 2f out: edgd lft and ev ch fr over 1f out: shkn up ins fnl f: nt run on* **7/1**[3]

0-00 **3** *1* **Tcherina (IRE)**[8] [2585] 6-8-1 **68** .... DuranFentiman(3) 5 — 75
(T D Easterby) *led: rdn and hdd over 1f out: unable qck towards fin* **10/1**

1-10 **4** *2* **Aypeeyes (IRE)**[22] [2153] 4-9-1 **79** .... DaneO'Neill 17 — 85+
(A King) *hld up in tch: racd keenly: rdn and nt clr run over 1f out: styd on same pce ins fnl f* **7/1**[3]

0240 **5** *hd* **Kames Park (IRE)**[8] [2585] 6-8-4 **68** .... CatherineGannon 12 — 72
(R C Guest) *hld up: hdwy over 2f out: rdn and carried hd high over 1f out: nt trble ldrs* **20/1**

2323 **6** *3 ½* **Casual Affair**[28] [1998] 5-8-9 **73** .... JimmyQuinn 2 — 71
(J D Bethell) *chsd ldrs: rdn over 2f out: wknd ins fnl f* **7/2**[1]

0-45 **7** *nk* **Ursis (FR)**[31] [1909] 7-8-7 **76** .... JamieJones(5) 6 — 74
(S Gollings) *hld up: swtchd rt 3f out: sn rdn and edgd lft: hdwy over 1f out: no imp fnl f* **33/1**

651- **8** *3* **Bollin Derek**[387] [1794] 5-9-7 **85** .... DavidAllan 16 — 78
(T D Easterby) *prom: rdn over 2f out: edgd lft and wknd over 1f out* **9/1**

0/0- **9** *2* **Day To Remember**[22] [6490] 7-9-2 **80** .... (vt) GrahamGibbons 7 — 70
(J J Quinn) *prom: rdn over 3f out: wknd over 1f out* **12/1**

045- **10** *½* **Yossi (IRE)**[221] [6576] 4-9-1 **79** .... SebSanders 4 — 68
(M H Tompkins) *chsd ldr: rdn and ev ch over 1f out: wknd fnl f* **11/2**[2]

441/ **11** *14* **Burnt Oak (UAE)**[659] [4549] 6-9-2 **80** .... FergalLynch 13 — 47
(C W Fairhurst) *hld up: wknd over 2f out* **18/1**

0605 **12** *9* **Longspur**[7] [2623] 4-8-4 **75** .... BradleyRoper(7) 14 — 27
(M W Easterby) *dwlt: sn pushed along in rr: wknd over 3f out* **14/1**

4-2 **13** *34* **Mister Right (IRE)**[46] [1531] 7-8-10 **74** .... JamesDoyle 3 — —
(D J S Ffrench Davis) *hld up: hdwy over 4f out: rdn and wknd over 2f out* **9/1**

2m 37.84s (2.74) **Going Correction** +0.375s/f (Good) **13** Ran SP% **130.1**
Speed ratings (Par 105): **105,104,104,102,102 100,100,98,96,96 87,81,58**
CSF £68.98 CT £591.24 TOTE £6.70: £2.30, £2.00, £3.70; EX 44.10 Trifecta £193.90 Part won: Pool: £273.17 - 0.30 winning units..
Owner Mrs S Sanbrook **Bred** Tally-Ho Stud **Trained** Melsonby, N Yorks

FOCUS
A fair handicap and sound enough form.
Longspur Official explanation: jockey said gelding had a breathing problem
Mister Right(IRE) Official explanation: jockey said gelding lost its action

2823 HAPPY BIRTHDAY DARRYL BARKER MAIDEN STKS (DIV I) — 5f
5:00 (5:01) (Class 4) 3-Y-O+ **£4,047** (£1,204; £601; £300) **Stalls** High

Form — RPR

0 **1** **Royal Grace**[15] [2380] 3-8-12 0 .... DavidAllan 11 — 61
(T D Easterby) *chsd ldrs: led over 1f out: hung lft towards fin: rdn out* **6/1**

2 *1* **Safaseef (IRE)** 3-8-12 0 .... JamesDoyle 12 — 58
(K A Morgan) *s.i.s: hld up: hdwy u.p over 1f out: r.o* **13/2**

60 **3** *shd* **Champagne Lawn (USA)**[25] [2084] 3-8-12 0 .... GrahamGibbons 9 — 57
(T D Barron) *w ldrs: rdn to chse wnr and hung lft fr over 1f out: styd on* **25/1**

55- **4** *1 ¾* **Hucking Harkness**[196] [6926] 3-9-3 0 .... JimmyQuinn 3 — 56
(J R Best) *hld up: hdwy 1/2-way: rdn over 1f out: styd on* **8/1**

0-25 **5** *hd* **Linnet Park**[36] [1769] 3-8-12 57 .... DeanMcKeown 5 — 57+
(J G Given) *chsd ldrs: hmpd and lost pl over 1f out: styd on ins fnl f* **9/2**[2]

6 ½ **Mrs Bun** 3-8-12 0 FergalLynch 1 48
(K A Ryan) *s.i.s: hdwy and edgd lft 2f out: one pce ins fnl f* 11/2[3]

6 7 1½ **Azzaamm**[18] 2279 3-8-10 0 JPHamblett(7) 10 48
(C A Dwyer) *hld up: hdwy over 1f out: wknd ins fnl f* 33/1

4 8 5 **In Toto**[44] 1581 3-9-3 0 TGMcLaughlin 4 30
(M Wigham) *s.i.s: nvr nrr* 12/1

9 1¾ **Groundhog Day** 4-9-5 0 EdwardCreighton 8 19
(J Balding) *s.s and swvd lft: outpcd* 20/1

465 10 nk **This Ones For Eddy**[15] 2380 3-9-3 67 DarrenWilliams 2 23
(S Parr) *led over 3f: wknd fnl f* 11/4[1]

11 1 **Portugal** 3-8-12 0 DaneO'Neill 6 14
(T J Etherington) *s.i.s: sn chsng ldrs: rdn and edgd lft wl over 1f out: sn wknd* 20/1

500 12 1¾ **Feeling Pretty**[36] 1777 3-8-12 30 (p) CatherineGannon 7 8
(C Smith) *prom: rdn 1/2-way: wknd over 1f out* 66/1

61.73 secs (1.23) **Going Correction** +0.20s/f (Good)
WFA 3 from 4yo 7lb 12 Ran SP% 124.5
Speed ratings (Par 105): **98,96,96,93,93 92,89,81,79,78 77,74**
CSF £44.15 TOTE £7.00: £2.50, £2.60, £6.90; EX 26.00 TRIFECTA Not won..
Owner David W Armstrong **Bred** The Aston House Stud **Trained** Great Habton, N Yorks

FOCUS
A modest maiden and the slower of the two divisions. Modest form rated around the exposed fifth, with the winner a big improver.
Linnet Park Official explanation: jockey said filly ran too freely
In Toto Official explanation: jockey said gelding hung left
Groundhog Day Official explanation: jockey said filly ran very green
This Ones For Eddy Official explanation: jockey said gelding reared leaving stalls

2824 HAPPY BIRTHDAY DARRYL BARKER MAIDEN STKS (DIV II) 5f
5:30 (5:30) (Class 4) 3-Y-O+ £4,047 (£1,204; £601; £300) Stalls High

Form RPR

5 1 **Sir Boss (IRE)**[29] 1960 3-8-10 0 RosieJessop(7) 3 72
(D E Cantillon) *chsd ldrs: led 3f out: edgd rt ins fnl f: pushed out* 6/1[3]

43-3 2 1¼ **Terry's Tip (IRE)**[35] 1795 3-9-3 80 DaneO'Neill 9 67
(Mrs L Stubbs) *s.i.s: outpcd: hdwy u.p over 1f out: edgd lft: nt rch wnr* 11/10[1]

5 3 ¾ **Admiral Bond (IRE)**[19] 2240 3-8-12 0 SladeO'Hara(5) 1 64
(G R Oldroyd) *s.i.s: hdwy 1/2-way: rdn to chse wnr over 1f out: hung lft ins fnl f: styd on same pce* 16/1

6 4 2¼ **Holly Cleugh**[16] 2341 3-8-12 0 JimmyQuinn 8 51
(J R Fanshawe) *s.i.s: hld up: hdwy over 1f out: sn rdn: styd on same pce ins fnl f* 5/1[2]

6-03 5 1¾ **Recent Times**[14] 2399 3-8-12 63 DavidAllan 11 45
(T D Easterby) *prom: rdn whn hmpd wl over 1f out: n.d after* 5/1[2]

0-00 6 ½ **Abitofafath (IRE)**[14] 2396 3-9-3 47 DeanMcKeown 10 48
(J G Given) *hung lft thrght: led 2f: sn rdn: wknd over 1f out* 33/1

00 7 ¾ **Colour Of Money**[29] 1951 3-9-3 0 PatDobbs 5 46
(S A Callaghan) *s.s: outpcd* 16/1

400- 8 3½ **Archilini**[171] 7191 3-9-3 67 JamesDoyle 7 33
(K A Morgan) *chsd ldrs: rdn 1/2-way: wknd over 1f out* 18/1

30-0 9 2 **The Cube**[40] 1675 4-9-10 46 EdwardCreighton 6 26
(J Balding) *chsd ldrs: rdn 1/2-way: hmpd and wknd wl over 1f out* 33/1

61.33 secs (0.83) **Going Correction** +0.20s/f (Good)
WFA 3 from 4yo 7lb 9 Ran SP% 118.1
Speed ratings (Par 105): **101,99,97,94,91 90,89,83,80**
CSF £13.28 TOTE £8.20: £2.10, £1.10, £3.20; EX 14.60 Trifecta £127.50 Part won: Pool: £179.60 - 0.40 winning units. Place 6: £807.98 Place 5: £260.55.
Owner Don Cantillon **Bred** Mrs E R Cantillon **Trained** Newmarket, Suffolk

FOCUS
The stronger of the two divisions on paper, and it was run in a time 0.4sec quicker, but the form still looks fairly modest, rated around the second.
Abitofafath(IRE) Official explanation: jockey said gelding hung left
T/Plt: £5,757.90 to a £1 stake. Pool: £104,510.33. 13.25 winning tickets. T/Qpdt: £368.70 to a £1 stake. Pool: £3,787.50. 7.60 winning tickets. CR

2788 EPSOM (L-H)
Saturday, June 7

OFFICIAL GOING: Good
Wind: Virtually nil Weather: bright, partly cloudy

2825 TOTESPORTCASINO.COM STKS (HERITAGE H'CAP) 1m 2f 18y
1:40 (1:40) (Class 2) (0-105,100) 3-Y-O £31,155 (£9,330; £4,665; £2,335; £1,165; £585) Stalls Low

Form RPR

31-3 1 **Conduit (IRE)**[43] 1600 3-8-6 85 ow1 RyanMoore 6 104
(Sir Michael Stoute) *lw: hld up in last: stl last and plenty to do over 3f out: hdwy 3f out: str run on outside fr over 2f out: edgd lft but led ins fnl f: stormed clr: impressive* 11/8[1]

-424 2 6 **Ramona Chase**[21] 2194 3-9-2 95 RichardHughes 1 102
(S Kirk) *hld up in midfield: rdn and effrt 3f out: hung lft u.p fr wl over 1f out: kpt on to go 2nd nr fin: no ch w wnr* 8/1[3]

61-3 3 nk **First Avenue**[19] 2256 3-8-3 82 WilliamBuick 5 88
(M A Jarvis) *in tch: rdn and hdwy over 3f out: chsd clr ldr briefly and edgd lft wl over 1f out: kpt on to go 3rd nr fin* 17/2

0445 4 nk **Siberian Tiger (IRE)**[17] 2303 3-9-5 98 DarrylHolland 12 103
(M R Channon) *s.i.s: sn pushed along and in tch: hdwy to ld over 5f out: shkn up and clr over 3f out: hdd ins fnl f: immediately btn: lost 2 pls nr fin* 33/1

331- 5 5 **Rochefort (IRE)**[243] 6058 3-8-7 86 KerrinMcEvoy 3 81
(J H M Gosden) *hld up towards rr: rdn and effrt over 2f out: hanging lft over 1f out: nvr trbld ldrs* 14/1

3-22 6 3 **Midships (USA)**[21] 2194 3-9-3 96 JimCrowley 11 85
(Mrs A J Perrett) *w ldr tl over 5f out: disp 2nd and rdn 3f out: hanging lft after: wknd over 1f out* 13/2[2]

3222 7 2¾ **Special Reserve (IRE)**[21] 2191 3-8-4 83 TPO'Shea 4 67
(R Hannon) *lw: trckd ldrs on inner: rdn and outpcd over 3f out: wl bhd last 2f* 20/1

1-13 8 ¾ **Cobo Bay**[43] 1595 3-9-7 100 NCallan 9 82
(K A Ryan) *led tl over 5f out: chsd clr ldr after: rdn 3f out: no imp: wknd over 1f out* 16/1

6-60 9 ½ **Solent Ridge (IRE)**[26] 2066 3-8-13 92 MJKinane 8 73
(J S Moore) *t.k.h: in tch early: stdd and hld up in rr after 1f: rdn and effrt over 3f out: nvr trbld ldrs* 66/1

05-0 10 2¾ **Miss Bootylishes**[35] 1801 3-8-4 86 ow1 KevinGhunowa(3) 2 62
(A B Haynes) *hld up in rr: n.d* 50/1

01-0 11 4½ **Fitzroy Crossing (USA)**[35] 1811 3-8-8 87 GregFairley 7 54
(M Johnston) *t.k.h: hld up in midfield: rdn over 3f out: sn struggling: t.o* 50/1

-211 12 2½ **Tajweed (IRE)**[37] 1753 3-8-5 84 RHills 10 46
(M Johnston) *lw: t.k.h: chsd ldrs early tl stdd and hld up in midfield after 2f: rdn and struggling over 3f out: no ch after: t.o* 13/2[2]

2m 6.37s (-3.33) **Going Correction** +0.15s/f (Good) 12 Ran SP% 116.1
Speed ratings (Par 105): **119,114,113,113,109 107,105,104,104,101 98,96**
CSF £11.73 CT £70.06 TOTE £2.30: £1.10, £3.20, £3.20; EX 15.00 Trifecta £121.50 Pool: £1779.80 - 10.40 winning units.
Owner Ballymacoll Stud **Bred** Ballymacoll Stud Farm Ltd **Trained** Newmarket, Suffolk

FOCUS
Invariably a decent handicap for three-year-olds, but the betting for what should have been an open race was dominated by Conduit. While he looked to be given plenty to do, he proved himself a very well-handicapped horse and won in a style which suggests he is Listed class at the very least. The consistent runner-up is a good guide to the level.

NOTEBOOK
Conduit(IRE), who shaped with plenty of promise on his reappearance at Sandown, was representing a stable that had won this race twice in the previous four years. Even off a 6lb higher mark he looked attractively weighted, and he was a strongly-backed favourite. Given a very confident ride by Moore, who had him out the back for much of the race, he picked up in great style once angled him to the outside for his run. The way he stayed on strongly inside the last, winning going away by a wide margin, suggested he is a Group horse in the making and, being closely related to Great Voltigeur winner Hard Top, another two furlongs will be in his favour. The King George V Handicap at Royal Ascot or the John Smith's Cup at York could be suitable targets if the Handicapper is lenient enough to let him take his chance, but otherwise he may have to step up to Pattern company next. (tchd 6-4 in places)
Ramona Chase kept on well to just grab second close home, but he simply did not have the winner's pace in the closing stages. He is a very consistent animal but the Handicapper knows all about him now. (op 12-1)
First Avenue was one of the more interesting runners as he is well bred and this was only his fourth start, so he was open to improvement. Not for the first time, he did not impress with his head carriage, but easier ground is likely to suit him better, and so will a step up in distance. (op 8-1)
Siberian Tiger(IRE), who had a stiff task on the face of it, was given an enterprising ride by Holland, who, sensing the pace had slackened off, tried to nick it running down the hill. He still looked likely to be difficult to catch with a furlong and a half to run, but he soon hit the wall and in the end could not quite hold on to a place. It was a valiant effort, though, and he is now likely to be aimed for Royal Ascot's Hampton Court Stakes. (op 28-1)
Rochefort(IRE) had not been seen since winning a Windsor maiden last autumn and was stepping up two furlongs in distance. Difficult to ride out inside the final two furlongs as he was hanging left, he will be happier back on a more conventional track. Official explanation: jockey said colt hung left
Midships(USA) had form with the first two home so really should have been involved in the finish, but having had every chance three furlongs out he made no further progress. (tchd 7-1)
Special Reserve(IRE), who is a brother to Derby runner-up The Great Gatsby, did not handle the track as well as him, but perhaps he needs easier ground to be at his best. His current mark does not make him look particularly well handicapped, though.
Cobo Bay, trying a distance beyond a mile for the first time, did not get home. (tchd 20-1)
Tajweed(IRE), a son of Pivotal, has done his winning on soft ground and probably found conditions on the quick side. Official explanation: jockey said gelding suffered interference (op 11-2)

2826 WOODCOTE STKS (LISTED RACE) 6f
2:10 (2:11) (Class 1) 2-Y-O £14,192 (£5,380; £2,692; £1,342; £672; £337) Stalls High

Form RPR

412 1 **Smokey Storm**[30] 1927 2-9-0 0 AlanMunro 3 92
(W Jarvis) *chsd ldrs: rdn and hdwy over 2f out: drvn to ld over 1f out: r.o strly* 4/1[1]

41 2 2¼ **Indian Art (IRE)**[16] 2324 2-9-0 0 RichardHughes 10 85
(R Hannon) *lw: outpcd in rr: pushed along over 4f out: hdwy on outer wl over 1f out: r.o wl to go 2nd on line: nvr nr wnr* 9/2[2]

11 3 nse **Able Master (IRE)**[14] 2392 2-9-5 0 PaulMulrennan 2 90
(B Smart) *strong: lw: led for 1f: chsd ldrs after: rdn 3f out: ev ch 2f out: outpcd by wnr fnl f: lost 2nd on line* 8/1

4 4 ½ **Roly Boy**[28] 1983 2-9-0 0 RyanMoore 11 84+
(R Hannon) *lw: outpcd in rr: hanging lft over 3f out: gd hdwy on outer over 1f out: r.o wl fnl f* 10/1

3412 5 ½ **Mazzola**[10] 2507 2-9-0 0 DarryllHolland 6 82
(M R Channon) *chsd ldrs: rdn to ld over 2f out: hdd over 1f out: sn outpcd by wnr: wknd wl ins fnl f* 14/1

1 6 nk **Full Of Nature**[22] 2160 2-8-9 0 NCallan 5 76
(K A Ryan) *s.i.s: sn in midfield: rdn and hdwy wl over 2f out: keeping on same pce whn swtchd rt ins fnl f* 5/1[3]

31 7 1 **Fivefootnumberone (IRE)**[16] 2331 2-9-0 0 TPO'Shea 4 78
(J J Quinn) *racd in midfield: rdn and hdwy 3f out: kpt on same pce fr over 1f out* 17/2

5144 8 1¾ **Grand Honour (IRE)**[24] 2108 2-9-0 0 TPQueally 8 73
(P Howling) *towards rr: swtchd rt and hdwy over 2f out: no imp and hanging lft fr over 1f out* 50/1

22 9 3¾ **Our Wee Girl (IRE)**[11] 2479 2-8-9 0 JamieSpencer 9 57+
(S Kirk) *s.i.s: a bhd* 9/2[2]

502 10 18 **Ritzy Wildcat (USA)**[15] 2349 2-9-0 0 (b[1]) EddieAhern 7 8+
(S C Williams) *chsd ldrs tl led after 1f: clr 4f out: hdd over 2f out: sn wknd: eased fnl f* 40/1

1m 11.06s (1.66) **Going Correction** +0.15s/f (Good) 10 Ran SP% 114.8
Speed ratings (Par 101): **94,91,90,90,89 89,87,85,80,56**
CSF £21.53 TOTE £4.20: £1.80, £1.70, £2.80; EX 15.80 Trifecta £124.30 Pool: £1348.20 - 7.70 winning units.
Owner The Bk Partnership **Bred** P V And Mrs J P Jackson **Trained** Newmarket, Suffolk

FOCUS
A race that often struggles to live up to its Listed status, being early in the calendar for two-year-olds and around this tricky track, including Tattenham Corner after a couple of furlongs. Experience of a similar track and a low draw has proven the formula in recent years and so it proved again. The winner had the best previous form and has been rated around the average for the race. The second, third and fourth all showed improved form.

NOTEBOOK
Smokey Storm, who handled both Brighton and Goodwood well in races that have worked out nicely for early-season contests, was a ready winner despite having to sit and suffer around the bend in a pocket just off the pace. He dived through the gap left against the inside rail to put the race to bed into the final furlong, and was full value for the clear winning margin. He maintains a progressive profile but connections do not see him as a Royal Ascot contender, and are eyeing a Group 2 at the Curragh instead. (op 11-4)

Indian Art(IRE), a tall, scopey colt, had a poor draw and became unbalanced rounding Tattenham Corner, but he stayed on steadily down the middle to not be beaten that far. He can improve on the bare form back on a conventional track. (op 5-1 tchd 11-2 in places)
Able Master(IRE), who was enthusiastic to post, was far from disgraced under his 5lb penalty and emerges with as much credit as the winner. He will, however, find things become much tougher as the season unfolds. (op 11-1)
Roly Boy, a taking individual but lacking the experience of the principals, found it all happening too quickly for him. He was also all at sea on the track, hanging badly left down the camber all the way up the straight. This was nevertheless much improved form and he should win his maiden before going on to better things. He is bred to get another furlong. (tchd 11-1)
Mazzola showed plenty of dash but did not get home. This company was just too hot for him but he appeared to run his race. Official explanation: jockey said colt hung both ways in closing stages (op 20-1)
Full Of Nature hampered her chances with a slow start and never really got into contention. She is probably a bit better than this. (tchd 9-2)
Fivefootnumberone(IRE) got into the race about 3f from home but became unbalanced under pressure. However, he was not beaten that far and is worth another chance on a flatter track. (op 12-1)
Grand Honour(IRE) was not disgraced at long odds but rolled around under pressure, which hampered his finishing kick. Official explanation: trainer said colt was unsuited by the track
Our Wee Girl(IRE) palpably failed to handle the track after breaking slowly and sitting last. Official explanation: trainer said filly was unsuited by the track (op 11-2 tchd 6-1 in places)
Ritzy Wildcat(USA) ran much too freely in the first-time blinkers and dropped right out once joined. Official explanation: trainer said colt ran too free

2827 PRINCESS ELIZABETH STKS (SPONSORED BY VODAFONE) (GROUP 3) (F&M) 1m 114y

2:40 (2:42) (Class 1) 3-Y-O+

£28,385 (£10,760; £5,385; £2,685; £1,345; £675) **Stalls** Low

Form				RPR
1-22	**1**		**Lady Gloria**[7] 2600 4-9-6 104 ... TPQueally 6 (J G Given) *mde all: rdn 2 l clr 2f out: styd on gamely fnl f* **7/1**[3]	106
/02-	**2**	½	**Cicerole (FR)**[33] 1885 4-9-6 0 ... C-PLemaire 8 (J-C Rouget, France) *lengthy: lw: hld up in last trio: plld out and hdwy 2f out: str run to press ldrs ins fnl f: wnt 2nd on line: nt quite rch wnr* **7/2**[1]	105
54-1	**3**	shd	**Enforce (USA)**[35] 1801 5-9-6 105 ... WilliamBuick 5 (Mrs L Wadham) *chsd ldrs: rdn to chse wnr 1f out: kpt on u.p: lost 2nd on line* **15/2**	104
446-	**4**	nk	**Selinka**[259] 5661 4-9-6 107 ... RichardHughes 9 (R Hannon) *w.w in midfield: rdn and hdwy jst over 2f out: kpt on u.p fnl f: nvr quite pce to rch wnr* **17/2**	104
1201	**5**	shd	**Baharah (USA)**[28] 1981 4-9-6 109 ... EddieAhern 3 (G A Butler) *lw: hld up in last pair: hdwy on outer 2f out: r.o u.p fnl f: nt quite rch ldrs* **7/2**[1]	103
1-50	**6**	1 ½	**Eva's Request (IRE)**[13] 2433 3-8-11 100 ... MJKinane 2 (M R Channon) *chsd ldrs: rdn and effrt on inner over 2f out: wknd jst ins fnl f* **20/1**	101
2-15	**7**	nk	**Jamboretta (IRE)**[28] 1981 4-9-6 93 ... RyanMoore 4 (Sir Michael Stoute) *lw: dwlt: racd in midfield: effrt over 2f out: sn rdn: wknd ent fnl f* **8/1**	99
50-0	**8**	2	**Bahia Breeze**[42] 1631 6-9-6 106 ... PJSmullen 7 (Rae Guest) *chsd wnr: rdn jst over 2f out: lost 2nd 1f out: wknd ins fnl f* **16/1**	95
6-30	**9**	2 ¾	**Barshiba (IRE)**[21] 2193 4-9-6 108 ... JamieSpencer 1 (D R C Elsworth) *stdd s: a last: no ch whn hung bdly lft fnl f: eased* **5/1**[2]	88

1m 44.69s (-1.41) **Going Correction** +0.15s/f (Good)
WFA 3 from 4yo+ 12lb **9** Ran SP% **117.7**
Speed ratings (Par 113): **112,111,111,111,111 109,109,107,105**
CSF £32.38 TOTE £8.70: £2.30, £1.50, £2.60; EX 39.70 Trifecta £209.30 Pool: £1739.60 - 5.90 winning units.
Owner M H Tourle **Bred** M H And Mrs G Tourle **Trained** Willoughton, Lincs

FOCUS

This Group 3 has a mixed history, and Echelon, who went on to land a Group 1 in Ireland after landing this in 2006 and 2007 was an exception among recent winners. Lady Gloria was given a good ride from the front, and in a bunch finish the form looks pretty ordinary for the grade.

NOTEBOOK

Lady Gloria may have been a shade flattered as she was left alone up front and Tom Queally was allowed to dictate a pace to suit himself. When she kicked on up the straight the hold-up horses were left with a bit to do, and although four of her rivals had got to within three-quarters of a length of her at the finish none of them quite got to her. She was thought to be ground dependant previously, but she handled this drying going perfectly well, which broadens her options. (op 12-1)
Cicerole(FR), a three-time Listed race winner in France over a mile, did not break too well and was then held up in rear. She came with a good run towards the outside but was never quite getting there. (op 9-2)
Enforce(USA), who was a touch keen throughout, only just failed to hold on for second place. In-foal and in-form, she was ridden close to the pace but could have done with a stronger gallop. She now heads for the Windsor Forest at Royal Ascot. (tchd 7-1)
Selinka ◆, making her reappearance after being slow coming to hand once again, was one of the first off the bridle, but she stuck on really well without ever looking likely to win. She will be all the better for this and will also presumably head to Royal Ascot now for the Windsor Forest. (op 9-1 tchd 8-1, 10-1 in places)
Baharah(USA) ◆, who put up an outstanding handicap performance when winning well off 105 at Ascot last time, was left with too much ground to make up after being given a really patient ride at the rear of the field. She made relentless progress down the centre of the track once in the clear, but it was never enough. A return to Ascot could show her in a different light, and the Windsor Forest looks the race for her. Official explanation: trainer said filly was unsuited by the track (op 3-1 tchd 11-4 in places)
Eva's Request(IRE), dropped in class after finishing down the field in the Irish Guineas and carrying a 3lb penalty for last year's Group 3 win, ran well in the face of a stiff task, only getting run out of the places late on. She looks capable of holding her own in good company this season. (op 25-1)
Jamboretta(IRE), representing the connections that won this with Echelon in 2006 vand 2007, was held up and never looked all that happy, although she still finished close up without having as hard a race as some. (op 13-2)
Bahia Breeze, second in this last year, dropped out tamely after chasing the winner.
Barshiba(IRE) can look a difficult ride on the most conventional of tracks, so it was no surprise that she never looked happy. (op 6-1)

2828 TOTESPORT.COM "DASH" (HERITAGE H'CAP) 5f

3:15 (3:15) (Class 2) 3-Y-O+

£31,155 (£9,330; £4,665; £2,335; £1,165; £585) **Stalls** High

Form				RPR
-112	**1**		**Holbeck Ghyll (IRE)**[21] 2195 6-8-7 **85** ... WilliamBuick 8 (A M Balding) *swtchd rt after s: chsd ldrs: rdn 1f out: led last 100yds: r.o wl* **15/2**[3]	99
3043	**2**	½	**Merlin's Dancer**[29] 1956 8-8-5 **83** ... JohnEgan 19 (S Dow) *swtg: led stands' side: ev ch ins fnl f: unable qck last 100yds* **12/1**	95
4-12	**3**	½	**Safari Mischief**[16] 2326 5-8-5 **86** ... LukeMorris(3) 12 (P Winkworth) *lw: racd in midfield: rdn 1/2-way: r.o to press ldrs ins fnl f: kpt on* **17/2**	97
0-56	**4**	½	**Hogmaneigh (IRE)**[35] 1809 5-9-8 **100** ... SaleemGolam 17 (S C Williams) *stdd s: bhd on stands' rail: hdwy 2f out: r.o fnl f: nt quite rch ldrs* **9/2**[1]	109
0-31	**5**	nk	**Masta Plasta (IRE)**[7] 2626 5-9-1 **100** 4ex ... AdeleRothery(7) 6 (D Nicholls) *swtg: led in centre and overall: rdn and hdd last 100yds: fdd towards fin* **7/1**[2]	108+
20-3	**6**	nk	**Fathom Five (IRE)**[36] 1772 4-9-5 **97** ... PaulMulrennan 20 (B Smart) *lw: taken down early: s.i.s: sn chsng ldrs: rdn over 1f out: kpt on same pce ins fnl f* **8/1**	104
0400	**7**	nk	**Strike Up The Band**[23] 2129 5-8-13 **91** ... SilvestreDeSousa 7 (D Nicholls) *chsd ldrs: chsd overall ldr over 1f out tl ins fnl f: fdd towards fin* **18/1**	97
530	**8**	½	**Bond City (IRE)**[14] 2401 6-9-0 **92** ... AlanMunro 9 (G R Oldroyd) *s.i.s: bhd: styd on u.p fr over 1f out: nvr rchd ldrs* **20/1**	96
5224	**9**	¾	**Northern Empire (IRE)**[23] 2129 5-9-2 **94** ... NCallan 10 (K A Ryan) *restless stalls: burst through gate and awkward s: sn swtchd rt: hdwy 1/2-way: rdn over 1f out: kpt on same pce fnl f* **20/1**	95
0-01	**10**	1 ½	**Tournedos (IRE)**[23] 2129 6-9-4 **96** 4ex ... AdrianTNicholls 4 (D Nicholls) *taken down early: racd in midfield: rdn and effrt 2f out: wknd ent fnl f* **12/1**	92
2140	**11**	nk	**Hereford Boy**[6] 2644 4-8-1 **82** ow1 ... KirstyMilczarek(3) 5 (D K Ivory) *s.i.s: a towards rr: styng on whn swtchd lft ins fnl f: n.d* **40/1**	77
0061	**12**	nk	**Steelcut**[22] 2145 4-7-7 **78** 4ex ... DavidProbert(7) 13 (R A Fahey) *lw: prom tl 1/2-way: sn struggling* **33/1**	72
-050	**13**	½	**Magic Glade**[126] 411 9-8-2 **80** ... PatrickMathers 16 (Peter Grayson) *taken down early: restless stalls: chsd ldrs tl 1/2-way: steadily wknd* **40/1**	72
0255	**14**	¾	**Canadian Danehill (IRE)**[21] 2211 6-9-3 **95** ...(p) LDettori 18 (R M H Cowell) *racd in midfield: struggling 1/2-way: no ch after* **16/1**	84
0-10	**15**	nk	**Morinqua (IRE)**[28] 2000 4-9-3 **95** ... TPQueally 1 (J G Given) *chsd overall ldr in centre pair tl over 1f out: sn wknd* **16/1**	83
1050	**16**	½	**Evens And Odds (IRE)**[51] 1420 4-9-5 **102** ...(b) NeilBrown(5) 15 (K A Ryan) *racd in midfield: struggling 1/2-way: sn bhd* **11/1**	88
-523	**17**	¾	**Ocean Blaze**[11] 2489 4-8-2 **80** ... AdrianMcCarthy 3 (B R Millman) *chsd ldrs tl over 2f out: sn rdn: wknd over 1f out* **25/1**	64
00-0	**18**	nk	**Bigalos Bandit**[56] 1325 6-8-4 **82** ... SimonWhitworth 11 (D Nicholls) *s.i.s: a bhd* **50/1**	65
-600	**19**	1 ¼	**Diane's Choice**[10] 2501 5-8-4 **82** ... TPO'Shea 14 (Miss Gay Kelleway) *a bhd* **50/1**	60

55.33 secs (-0.37) **Going Correction** +0.15s/f (Good) **19** Ran SP% **129.9**
Speed ratings (Par 109): **108,107,106,105,105 104,104,103,102,99 99,98,98,96,96 95,94,93,91**
CSF £90.49 CT £821.97 TOTE £9.30: £2.50, £3.00, £2.20, £2.00; EX 127.20 Trifecta £3253.40 Pool: £18787.61- 4.10 winning units.
Owner Halsall Nicholson Partnership **Bred** David Brickley **Trained** Kingsclere, Hants

FOCUS

A very strong renewal of the race, which should give valuable clues to all the big sprint handicaps during the summer. Masta Plasta aside, those involved in the finish all raced towards the stands' side rail. Holbeck Ghyll was ahead of the handicapper in this early-closing race but seems better than ever. Merlins Dancer has been rated to last year's best and Hogmaneigh to the level he showed when winning this in 2007.

NOTEBOOK

Holbeck Ghyll(IRE), an unlucky fourth last year off a lower mark, broke well and was given a cool ride, sitting just off the strong pace set by Morinqua and Masta Plasta down the middle of the course, and Merlin's Dancer hard against the stands' rail. He is already due to go up 5lb, and while that suggests he is going to be hard to place, he has proved most progressive this year and confirmed it again in reversing last year's form with plenty of these. The Stewards' Cup looks a natural target for him. (op 8-1)
Merlin's Dancer, eighth last year off a 12lb higher mark, had a good draw and showed he is ready to strike again off his falling mark. Much like the winner, he has form at Goodwood, so one of the many sprint races at the Glorious meeting is likely to be on the agenda for him.
Safari Mischief has been rising through the ratings for his good start to the year and remains firmly on the upgrade, as he kept on strongly to the line. He is yet another candidate for one of the sprints at the Glorious Goodwood meeting later in the year. (op 10-1)
Hogmaneigh(IRE), last year's winner off a pound lower mark, tracked the leaders against the stands' rail and finished off strongly without being able to land a blow. It was a fine effort giving so much weight away. (op 5-1)
Masta Plasta(IRE) deserves plenty of credit for his effort away from the main body of the field for much of the race (only Morinqua went with him down the centre of the track). It is not too difficult to argue that he would have won had he been able to come down the stands'-side rail. He is in great heart and remains one to be interested in. (tchd 13-2)
Fathom Five(IRE) could not find an extra kick in the final furlong, suggesting the handicapper has caught up with him after his good 2007. He will probably be most effective in conditions races until his mark eases.
Strike Up The Band showed quite a bit of pace, as he usually does, from his low draw before not quite getting home. He has not won since late 2006 but is extremely well handicapped as a result. (op 20-1)
Bond City(IRE), seventh last year off a 9lb lower mark and second the year before, started slowly and could never land a blow despite staying on well. He has not won since 2006 and could do with getting back to winning ways soon. (op 18-1)
Northern Empire(IRE) reared as the stalls' opened, so did well to beat quite a few home.
Morinqua(IRE) showed plenty of speed down the middle of the track from stall 1.

2829 VODAFONE DERBY (GROUP 1) (ENTIRE COLTS & FILLIES) 1m 4f 10y

4:00 (4:08) (Class 1) 3-Y-O

£802,443 (£304,185; £152,233; £75,904; £38,023; £19,082) **Stalls** Centre

Form				RPR
1-22	**1**		**New Approach (IRE)**[14] 2418 3-9-0 0 ... KJManning 3 (J S Bolger, Ire) *lw: plld hrd: hld up towards rr: 13th st: hdwy wl over 2f out: nt clr run and swtchd lft 2f out: rdn and qcknd to ld jst over 1f out: wandered but a holding runner up after* **5/1**[2]	126+
2-11	**2**	½	**Tartan Bearer (IRE)**[23] 2131 3-9-0 116 ... RyanMoore 14 (Sir Michael Stoute) *lw: s.i.s and bustled along early: bhd: 14th st: gd hdwy on outer 3f out: rdn to ld 2f out: hdd jst over 1f out: r.o wl but a hld by wnr* **6/1**	125+
1	**3**	4 ½	**Casual Conquest (IRE)**[27] 2023 3-9-0 0 ... PJSmullen 10 (D K Weld, Ire) *rangy: lw: hld up in midfield: hdwy 6f out: 4th st: chsd ldr over 1f out tl 1f out: nt pce of ldng pair fnl f* **7/2**[1]	118

1-21 **4** *1 1/2* **Doctor Fremantle**[30] 1922 3-9-0 112........................... KerrinMcEvoy 13 116
(Sir Michael Stoute) *lw: t.k.h: hld up in midfield: hdwy to chse ldrs 6f out: chsd ldr 4f out: led wl over 2f: hdd and rdn 2f out: wknd ent fnl f* **11/2**[3]

22 **5** *3/4* **Washington Irving (IRE)**[27] 2023 3-9-0 0.................. CO'Donoghue 16 114
(A P O'Brien, Ire) *rangy: chsd ldrs on inner: 3rd st: rdn over 2f out: wknd over 1f out* **33/1**

41 **6** *shd* **Alessandro Volta**[28] 1992 3-9-0 0.................................. JAHeffernan 1 114
(A P O'Brien, Ire) *lw: s.i.s: bhd: sme hdwy and 12th st: styd on past btn horses fr over 1f out: nvr nr ldrs* **33/1**

14-2 **7** *1* **Rio De La Plata (USA)**[27] 2032 3-9-0 120.......................... LDettori 17 113+
(Saeed Bin Suroor) *lw: t.k.h: hld up in midfield: 8th st: effrt 3f out: keeping on same pce whn carried lft and hmpd 2f out: no ch after* **20/1**

10-1 **8** *1/2* **Tajaaweed (USA)**[29] 1943 3-9-0 110.. RHills 5 112+
(Sir Michael Stoute) *lw: hld up towards rr: hdwy 6f out: 7th st: effrt to chse ldrs and rdn over 2f out: wknd wl over 1f out* **10/1**

-120 **9** *1/2* **Bouguereau**[27] 2028 3-9-0 108.. AlanMunro 2 111
(P W Chapple-Hyam) *hld up in midfield: 10th st: effrt on inner 3f out: nvr pce to trble ldrs* **100/1**

15-1 **10** *1 1/4* **Curtain Call (FR)**[45] 1570 3-9-0 115............................ JamieSpencer 6 111+
(L M Cumani) *swtg: hld up in midfield: 11th st: effrt and hanging lft wl over 2f out: eased whn wl btn fnl f* **7/1**

0-2 **11** *1 1/4* **Frozen Fire (GER)**[23] 2131 3-9-0 0.................................. MJKinane 15 107
(A P O'Brien, Ire) *hld up in rr: 15th st: sme late hdwy: nvr on terms* **16/1**

0-52 **12** *9* **King Of Rome (IRE)**[28] 1992 3-9-0 0................................ JMurtagh 11 93
(A P O'Brien, Ire) *swtg: s.i.s: bhd: hdwy 6f out: 9th st: sn rdn: wknd 2f out* **16/1**

23-4 **13** *4 1/2* **Alan Devonshire**[28] 1992 3-9-0 102......................... PaulMulrennan 12 85
(M H Tompkins) *plld hrd: chsd ldrs: 6th and rdn st: wknd 3f out* **100/1**

1-21 **14** *14* **Kandahar Run**[35] 1810 3-9-0 105.............................. TedDurcan 8 63+
(H R A Cecil) *swtg: t.k.h: chsd ldrs: wnt 2nd 6f out: led 4f out: rdn and hdd wl over 2f out: sn btn and eased* **11/1**

15 *11* **Bashkirov**[27] 2021 3-9-0 0.. DavidMcCabe 9 45
(A P O'Brien, Ire) *w'like: scope: sn rdn to chse ldr: led 7f out: reminders over 5f out: hdd 4f out: 5th and wkng qckly st: t.o and eased fnl f* **125/1**

16 *39* **Maidstone Mixture (FR)**[13] 3-9-0 0......................... MichaelO'Connell 7 —
(Paul Murphy) *led tl 7f out: sn dropped out: t.o last st* **250/1**

2m 36.5s (-2.40) **Going Correction** +0.15s/f (Good) **465** Ran SP% **124.1**
Speed ratings (Par 113): **114,113,110,109,109 109,108,108,107,106 106,100,97,87,80 54**
CSF £34.67 TOTE £5.80: £2.30, £3.20, £1.50; EX 42.80 Trifecta £167.10 Pool: £25007.15 - 106.20 winning units.

Owner H R H Princess Haya Of Jordan **Bred** Lodge Park Stud **Trained** Coolcullen, Co Carlow

■ A first Derby for both Jim Bolger, who won the 1991 Oaks with Jet Ski Lady, and Kevin Manning.

■ Stewards' Enquiry : K J Manning three-day ban: careless riding (June 22-24)

FOCUS

A Derby that looked well up to standard beforehand, with the Guineas form represented by New Approach and the winners of all the major trials lining up in opposition to him. The early pace was not that strong and as a result one or two, including the winner, did not settle. This resulted in a time that was nothing special, but the form looks really solid, for nothing obviously holds it back for once. New Approach has been rated slightly above the ten-year average, and Tartan Bearer ran to a figure that would have been good enough to win three of the last five runnings.

NOTEBOOK

New Approach(IRE) was a welcome addition to the field in terms of adding quality to the race, but his trainer had made few friends with his misleading comments regarding the colt's likely participation prior to the race and there was some definite ill-feeling post-race as a result of punters having taken ante-post positions in the understandable belief that New Approach would not be lining up. Of course this takes nothing away from the colt or his trainer's great achievement in getting him here in top form having had tough races in both the Dewhurst last backend and the 2,000 Guineas on his reappearance. Stepping up half a mile in distance following a slightly below-par effort on quick ground in the Irish Guineas just two weeks earlier, his pedigree suggested it would suit, and this very tough, if a little quirky (as usual he was ponied to the start) son of Galileo showed that he had been crying out for the longer trip. Despite not settling at all - he was still pulling for his head entering the straight - and having to weave a passage between horses, he quickened up from a furlong out and saw the trip out in good style, holding off the strong staying Tartan Bearer a shade cosily in the process. He was a very worthy winner and the form looks pretty solid with the right horses in behind, so it will be interesting to see how he gets on in the coming months, especially when taking on older horses, as the impression left was that he is even better than the bare result suggests. With regard to targets, the Irish Derby is currently next on his agenda, but his trainer also mentioned most of the other top middle distance Group 1s as possibilities. (op 13-2 tchd 9-2)

Tartan Bearer(IRE) has improved considerably with each outing this term and, following a narrow win in the Dante, he progressed again to finish a fine second here, repeating the achievement of his brother Golan, who chased home Galileo in the 2001 Derby. He is bred to stay well, so the less-than-frenetic early pace would not have been in his favour, but once angled out for his run in the straight he picked up really well and drew clear with the winner inside the last. He would not have as much pace as New Approach, but he looks a real battler, and he will have prospects of reversing the form on the more galloping track at The Curragh. Longer term, he looks an ideal candidate for the St Leger. (op 9-2 tchd 7-1 in a place)

Casual Conquest(IRE), supplemented at a cost of £75,000, was the most impressive trial winner in the race, having won the Derrinstown Derby Trial by six lengths. His lack of experience was his trainer's main worry, though, and while he ran well in third, perhaps that concern was borne out. He had every chance at the two-furlong pole but was always just getting the worst of the argument with Tartan Bearer, and in the end the first two pulled away from him. He looks the type to keep improving as the season goes on, and he is another who will probably head for the Irish Derby next. (op 9-2 tchd 5-1 in places)

Doctor Fremantle, surprisingly well backed considering Ryan Moore had chosen Tartan Bearer in front of him, was another who had been added to the field at a cost of £75,000 following his win in the Chester Vase. Keen in the early stages, he hit the front with over two furlongs to run but was soon overhauled and could only plug on one-paced. He just seemed to be beaten by better horses, but can make his mark at a slightly lower level. It is difficult to see him reverse form with the first three at The Curragh, so the King Edward VII would seem the logical short-term target, providing it does not come too soon for him. (op 8-1)

Washington Irving(IRE) was not done any favours by New Approach, who crossed in front of him inside the final two furlongs, but he kept on, and he was actually staying on again as the line approached. Casual Conquest beat him six lengths in the Derrinstown Derby Trial but over this two-furlong longer trip he cut that deficit back to just over two lengths, despite not having as strong a pace as he would have liked to run off. Closely related to Oaks winner Alexandrova, he looks the type to do better on a more galloping track, and over further, so the St Leger will surely come into the reckoning for him.

Alessandro Volta, the Lingfield Derby Trial winner, did not get the clearest of runs, having been held up towards the back of the field in the early stages. He stayed on but the principals had gone beyond recall and he probably just ran to a similar level as at Lingfield.

Rio De La Plata(USA), runner-up in the French 2,000 Guineas, is not bred to get 1m4f and, while he travelled well enough to two furlongs out, he blatantly did not get home. He was hampered by the winner as that one crossed in front of him, but it made no huge difference to the result. Not knocked about in a lost cause, he can regain the winning thread back over a mile or 1m2f.

Tajaaweed(USA), who won the Dee Stakes, looked a leading candidate on that piece of form, but he had drifted in the betting in the days leading up to the race as a result of a minor scare relating to losing a shoe, and doubts about his stamina. His dam is a half-sister to Mr Greeley and in the event stamina fears appeared to be realised. He did not look at home on the track either and will be worth another chance when dropped back in distance. (tchd 11-1, 12-1 in places)

Bouguereau disappointed in the Italian Derby last time, but it transpired he lost a shoe and suffered a hoof injury. His previous form with Unnefer had been well advertised, but the drying ground would not have been in his favour here and he was shooting a bit high. He could have done with a more positive ride in a race that what was not that strongly run, and he was not disgraced. Connections are now eyeing the St Leger as his long-term target, and he would have prospects of Group-race success abroad in the meantime.

Curtain Call(FR) held his market position quite well considering the doubts about him. At his best with give in the ground, conditions were drying against him, and his trial win at Nottingham from a couple of handicappers had told us little we did not already know. His best piece of form, which was his three-length second to New Approach in the Futurity Stakes last year, came on desperate ground, and while his stamina looked guaranteed on paper, he never looked happy in the race itself. He was hanging left in the straight and was eased down inside the final furlong, having seemingly failed to cope with the undulating track and ground on the fast side. He is better than this, but while he reportedly returned sound connections will give him a bit of time now. (op 6-1)

Frozen Fire(GER) was only narrowly beaten by Tartan Bearer in the Dante and, given that that was his seasonal reappearance and he was not given a hard race, there were some who gave him a chance of reversing the form. He was rejected by Murtagh though, and having been held up at the back, made little headway in the straight. He did not look at home on the track, but he carries his head high and looks far from straightforward.

King Of Rome(IRE), runner-up in the Lingfield Derby Trial when a 16-1 shot, was bizarrely Murtagh's choice of the O'Brien quintet. He was by no means the stable's best chance on paper, but had apparently impressed Murtagh the most in work leading up to the race. Although slowly away, he had a squeak three furlongs out but soon dropped out and simply does not look up to this class. (tchd 14-1 in places)

Alan Devonshire had a mountain to climb in this class of race and he did not help his chances of seeing out the trip by completely failing to settle in the early stages. Official explanation: jockey said colt ran too free

Kandahar Run had his supporters both in the lead up to the race and on the day, but his pedigree suggested 1m4f was going to stretch his stamina massively, despite having won a minor Listed race over 1m2f last time - he is closely related to that top-class miler Grey Lilas. Keen early on, he was running on empty before reaching the two-furlong pole. (op 14-1 tchd 16-1 in places)

Bashkirov, the Ballydoyle pacemaker, was embarrassingly unable to get to the front ahead of the hurdler Maidstone Mixture. He simply was not good enough to take a Classic field along, which was a shame because the result was that the pace was not as strong as one would expect in a Derby, and on the whole that did not suit his stablemates. (op 200-1 tchd 100-1)

Maidstone Mixture(FR), last seen winning over hurdles in France, had no business being in the race, but his rider ensured that he got a namecheck by taking the field along during the early stages.

2830 NORTHERN DANCER STKS (H'CAP) 1m 4f 10y

4:45 (4:51) (Class 2) (0-100,98) 4-Y-O+

£15,577 (£4,665; £2,332; £1,167; £582; £292) **Stalls** Centre

Form RPR

100/ **1** **Bureaucrat**[30] 5436 6-8-13 **88**...................................... JamieSpencer 3 98
(P J Hobbs) *hld up in midfield: hdwy 3f out: rdn and wanting to hang lft after: chsd ldr over 1f out: led last 100yds: jst lasted* **11/1**

320- **2** *hd* **Bandama (IRE)**[210] 6759 5-8-13 **88**................................ RyanMoore 15 98
(Mrs A J Perrett) *hld up in midfield: lost pl 6f out: bhd 3f out: hdwy and swtchd lft over 2f out: running on and swtchd rt jst ins fnl f: r.o wl: nt quite get up* **9/2**[1]

4205 **3** *1/2* **Aureate**[29] 1947 4-8-8 **83**.. EddieAhern 9 92
(B Ellison) *hld up bhd: plenty to do 3f out: hdwy on outer after: edgd lft wl over 1f out: r.o strly fnl f: snatched 3rd on line* **14/1**

/4-0 **4** *nse* **King's Head (IRE)**[22] 315 5-9-2 **91**............................... TedDurcan 16 100
(G L Moore) *bhd: stl last 3f out: hdwy on outer over 2f out: edgd lft but r.o strly fnl f: nt quite rch ldrs* **33/1**

006/ **5** *1/2* **Wingman (IRE)**[85] 5671 6-8-4 **79** oh3.............................. TPO'Shea 6 87+
(G L Moore) *chsd ldrs: clr in ldng quartet 4f out: swtchd rt and rdn over 3f out: led 3f out: hdd last 100yds: lost 3 pls nr fin* **11/2**[2]

-045 **6** *2* **Prince Forever (IRE)**[30] 1920 4-9-9 **98**............................... NCallan 8 103
(M A Jarvis) *t.k.h: hld up in midfield: hdwy 3f out: chsd ldrs u.p 2f out: wknd last 100yds* **20/1**

4103 **7** *1/2* **Birkside**[7] 2623 5-8-7 **82**.. AlanMunro 10 86+
(D Carroll) *hld up in midfield: hdwy and edgd lft over 2f out: sltly hmpd wl over 1f out: kpt on but nvr pce to trble ldrs* **10/1**

430- **8** *3* **Misty Dancer**[56] 5215 9-9-1 **90**..................................... WilliamBuick 7 89
(Miss Venetia Williams) *hld up in midfield: rdn and nt qckning whn hmpd over 2f out: plugged on fnl f: nvr trbld ldrs* **16/1**

0/40 **9** *2* **Come On Jonny (IRE)**[34] 1841 6-9-5 **94**.................. NelsonDeSouza 12 90+
(R M Beckett) *t.k.h: chsd ldr tl led over 9f out: rdn and hdd 3f out: wknd over 1f out* **20/1**

0301 **10** *1 1/4* **Capable Guest (IRE)**[12] 2465 6-9-6 **95**.................(v) RichardHughes 11 91
(M R Channon) *stdd s: hld up bhd: hmpd and swtchd rt over 2f out: n.d* **8/1**

0-50 **11** *hd* **Dzesmin (POL)**[24] 2107 6-8-6 **81** ow2.........................(p) KerrinMcEvoy 2 77
(R C Guest) *stdd s: hld up bhd: hmpd over 2f out: n.d* **9/1**

40-0 **12** *2* **Fort Churchill (IRE)**[12] 2465 7-8-9 **87**...................(p) JerryO'Dwyer[(3)] 13 80
(B Ellison) *chsd ldrs: 5th and outpcd 5f out: rdn over 3f out: sn struggling* **66/1**

1430 **13** *1/2* **John Terry (IRE)**[63] 1212 5-9-4 **93**..................................... JimCrowley 1 85+
(Mrs A J Perrett) *chsd ldrs: clr in ldng quartet over 4f out: rdn over 2f out: sn hanging lft and fnd nil* **12/1**

-601 **14** *4 1/2* **Mull Of Dubai**[30] 1920 5-9-3 **92**.. JohnEgan 5 77
(T P Tate) *bhd: rdn and effrt whn hung lft over 2f out: n.d* **7/1**[3]

03-0 **15** *5* **Players Please (USA)**[70] 1076 4-9-9 **98**............................ GregFairley 14 75+
(M Johnston) *led tl over 9f out: chsd ldr after: clr in ldng quartet over 4f out: wkng whn hmpd over 2f out* **14/1**

2m 37.85s (-1.05) **Going Correction** +0.15s/f (Good) **15** Ran SP% **125.5**
Speed ratings (Par 109): **109,108,108,108,108 106,106,104,103,102 102,100,100,97,94**
CSF £59.61 CT £726.48 TOTE £14.50: £4.50, £2.50, £5.00; EX 77.00 Trifecta £1278.80 Pool: £1801.20 - 1.00 winning units.

Owner Peter Luff **Bred** Newgate Stud Co **Trained** Withycombe, Somerset

■ Stewards' Enquiry : Eddie AhernM one-day ban: used whip with excessive frequency (Jun 22)
T P O'SheaM one-day ban: used whip with excessive frequency (Jun 22)

FOCUS

A strong contest run at a good pace, although the front four raced fully four lengths clear of the pack through the middle part of the race and still held a healthy advantage off the home bend before all weakened out of the finish. Bureaucrat has been rated to his old Flat mark, and plenty of those down the field ran close to their marks too.

NOTEBOOK

Bureaucrat, from a stable that does very well with the handful they race on the Flat, proved a game winner after hanging for much of the final two furlongs. A winner over hurdles last time, he was desperate for the line in the last 100 yards and only just held on.

Bandama(IRE), from a stable that was looking for its third successive win in the race, was closing on Bureaucrat all the way to the line but could not quite get up. This was a taking seasonal reappearance against racefit rivals but it has been two years since his last win. (op 6-1)

Aureate kept on well in the latter stages, after being a long way off the pace turning in, but could not force his way to the front. He is still a shade high in the weights on the best of his form but continues to run plenty of good races. (tchd 16-1)

King's Head(IRE), who ran well over this course back in 2006, had plenty to do at the bottom of Tattenham Corner yet nearly managed an unlikely success. A gambled on winner over hurdles in early May before a moderate effort at Aintree last time, he is fairly treated on the Flat and is probably still good enough to go close in a decent handicap or two. (op 25-1)

Wingman(IRE), having his first outing since a poor effort in the County Hurdle at Cheltenham, made a bold move up the home straight, which initially looked to have gained him a winning advantage. However, he was caught inside the final furlong and run out of the places close to the line. He has not won on the Flat since landing a two-year-old maiden in 2004. (tchd 9-2 and 6-1)

Prince Forever(IRE), who was stepping up in trip again, kept on well without suggesting that the distance completely suited him. He is lightly raced for his age but connections do seem to be struggling to find his optimum trip. (op 16-1)

Birkside, beaten in a decent claimer last time, has made plenty of progress over the last year but appears to have reached his level, despite running a respectable race after suffering some interference. (op 9-1 tchd 8-1)

Misty Dancer, second in this race last year off a 10lb lower mark, shaped with only a modicum of promise on his first start since April. At the age of nine, he is not going to find things easy until coming down the weights a lot.

Come On Jonny(IRE) has come down the weights and showed enough in this to suggest he is one to keep an eye on. (tchd 22-1)

Capable Guest(IRE), the winner of the Zetland Stakes last time, was given plenty to do and never looked like troubling the leaders. Consistency is not his strongest point. (op 10-1)

Dzesmin(POL) is steadily coming back down to a winning mark but showed very little in this. (op 8-1)

Mull Of Dubai failed to reproduce the form that saw him get home in front at Chester last time. He has often struggled off a mark in the 90s, so this effort cannot have come as a complete shock.
Official explanation: jockey said gelding had no more to give (op 8-1 tchd 6-1, 5-1 in a place and 10-1 in a place)

2831 PRINCE'S STAND STKS (H'CAP) 6f

5:20 (5:21) (Class 2) (0-100,99) 4-Y-0+

£15,577 (£4,665; £2,332; £1,167; £582; £292) Stalls High

Form				RPR
10-0	1		**Mac Gille Eoin**[28] 1985 4-9-5 **93** ... JimCrowley 2	107
		(J Gallagher) *chsd ldr: led over 1f out: sn rdn clr: r.o wl*	**11/1**
0-00	2	1 1/2	**Our Faye**[35] 1809 5-8-8 **82** ... RichardKingscote 12	91
		(S Kirk) *hld up in midfield: hdwy and rdn over 2f out: chsd wnr over 1f out: kpt on but nvr able to chal*	**20/1**
0-00	3	1 1/2	**Gift Horse**[35] 1809 8-8-11 **85** ...(v) JamieSpencer 6	89+
		(D Nicholls) *hld up bhd: plld out and rdn wl over 1f out: r.o fnl f: snatched 3rd on line: nvr nr ldrs*	**9/2**[2]
1224	4	hd	**Sweet Pickle**[10] 2504 7-8-6 **80** ...(e) KerrinMcEvoy 3	84
		(J R Boyle) *t.k.h: hld up in midfield: hdwy over 1f out: r.o but nvr threatened ldrs*	**12/1**
-431	5	1/2	**Idle Power (IRE)**[8] 2565 10-8-10 **84** ... AmirQuinn 15	86
		(J R Boyle) *led at gd pce: hdd and rdn over 1f out: wknd ins fnl f*	**14/1**
130-	6	1	**Pearly Wey**[259] 5616 5-9-7 **95** ... NCallan 17	94
		(C G Cox) *toward rr: rdn and effrt over 2f out: nvr gng pce to trble ldrs*	**9/1**
2442	7	1	**Pawan (IRE)**[7] 2598 8-8-5 **84** ...(b) AnnStokell(5) 1	80
		(Miss A Stokell) *racd in midfield: kpt on same pce last 3f*	**33/1**
0200	8	1/2	**Lucayos**[5] 2679 5-7-12 **79** oh2 ... DavidProbert(7) 14	73
		(Mrs H Sweeting) *chsd ldrs: rdn over 2f out: wknd wl over 1f out*	**33/1**
0-24	9	4 1/2	**Joseph Henry**[29] 1942 6-9-4 **92** ... AdrianTNicholls 4	72
		(D Nicholls) *t.k.h: hld up in midfield: rdn over 2f out: sn struggling*	**4/1**[1]
-161	10	1	**Halsion Chancer**[105] 676 4-8-8 **82** ... JohnEgan 8	58
		(J R Best) *plld hrd: chsd ldrs: rdn and wknd over 2f out: eased ins fnl f*	**10/1**
6312	11	1	**Obe Gold**[10] 2504 6-9-4 **92** ...(v) TPO'Shea 16	65
		(D Nicholls) *a bhd: no ch and hanging lft 2f out*	**7/1**
0240	12	2 1/4	**Machinist (IRE)**[7] 2626 8-9-10 **98** ... SilvestreDeSousa 9	64+
		(D Nicholls) *sat down in stalls and lost many lengths: a bhd*	**5/1**[3]

69.41 secs (0.01) **Going Correction** +0.15s/f (Good) **12** Ran SP% **119.8**
Speed ratings (Par 109): **105,103,101,100,100 98,97,96,90,89 88,85**
CSF £215.20 CT £1154.29 TOTE £14.90: £4.10, £6.10, £2.00; EX 205.60 TRIFECTA Not won. Place 6: £41.02 Place 5: £26.43.
Owner M C S D Racing Partnership **Bred** M C S D Racing Ltd **Trained** Moreton-in-Marsh, Gloucs

FOCUS
A competitive enough sprint despite the smaller than usual field, but the leader didn't go mad. A clear personal best from Mac Gille Eoin, and Our Faye was only a shade off her best from an outside draw.

NOTEBOOK

Mac Gille Eoin was well drawn and proven on a downhill track - he has two wins from four starts at Goodwood - so he had to be of interest having had a pipe-opener at Ascot. He was always well placed chasing the leader and, when asked to go and pick him up, did it in good style. He was a comfortable winner in the end and races like the Wokingham and Stewards' Cup will have to be on his agenda now. Whether he is up to defying an even higher mark remains to be seen, though.
Official explanation: trainer said, regarding apparent improvement in form, that the colt was suited by the faster ground. (op 14-1)

Our Faye has dropped back down to her last winning mark and she bounced back to form here. Although never looking like catching the winner, it was a good effort from her wide draw. (tchd 16-1)

Gift Horse, who won this three years ago, has not won for a long time but he is on a good mark and showed there is still a race of this nature in him when things fall right. He could probably have done with easier ground. (op 4-1 tchd 7-2 in places)

Sweet Pickle, who had a good draw, appears to have run to a similar level of form to that which she has been running to on the All-Weather this year, but she simply looks held off her current mark. (tchd 11-1)

Idle Power(IRE), another who is at his best on softer ground than he had here, is at least happy on a downhill track, and he showed great early speed to cross over from his wide draw and lead.

Pearly Wey, who had a wide draw to overcome, threatened to run on for third up the inside but it came to nothing. He was making his seasonal reappearance, so there could be some improvement to come, but he has run well fresh before so that is not guaranteed. (op 12-1)

Pawan(IRE) takes his racing well and is often placed, but he has a poor strike-rate.

Joseph Henry had not run well on his previous two starts at this track and it was a similar story again. Official explanation: jockey said gelding did not handle the track (op 7-2 tchd 9-2 in places and 5-1 in places)

Halsion Chancer Official explanation: jockey said gelding did not handle the track

Machinist(IRE) Official explanation: jockey said gelding was late out of stalls

T/Jkpt: Not won. T/Plt: £63.50 to a £1 stake. Pool: £293,821.30. 3,372.52 winning tickets. T/Qpdt: £27.70 to a £1 stake. Pool: £11,475.30. 306.05 winning tickets. SP

2753 LINGFIELD (L-H)

Saturday, June 7

OFFICIAL GOING: Turf course - good to firm (8.4); all-weather - standard
Wind: Slight, half against

2832 PREMIER PENSIONS MANAGEMENT ACTUARIAL (S) STKS 1m 4f (P)

5:40 (5:41) (Class 6) 3-Y-0+ £1,149 (£1,149; £262) Stalls Low

Form				RPR
5130	1		**Wait For The Will (USA)**[17] 2304 12-10-1 63 ...(b) GeorgeBaker 3	59
		(G L Moore) *hld up: hdwy over 4f out: chsd ldrs 2f out: led 1f out: jnd post*	**10/11**[1]
00-	1	dht	**Trigger's Friend**[283] 4948 4-9-5 0 ... RobertHavlin 5	49+
		(Jamie Poulton) *in tch: rdn wl over 2f out: drvn to join ldr post*	**66/1**
3-45	3	3/4	**Missie Baileys**[38] 1726 6-9-10 45 ...(p) IanMongan 6	53
		(Mrs L J Mongan) *a.p: led over 2f out: hdd 1f out: no ex ins fnl f*	**12/1**
00-0	4	nse	**Soldiers Quest**[54] 1369 4-10-1 66 ... AdamKirby 10	58
		(Peter Grayson) *in rr: hdwy to chse ldrs 2f out: styd on ins fnl f*	**20/1**
5	hd	**Go On Ahead (IRE)**[43] 8-9-7 0 ... TravisBlock(3) 8	53
		(W S Kittow) *slowly away but ld after 1f: hdd 7f out: rallied appr fnl f: no ex nr fin*	**14/1**
2656	6	6	**Tabulate**[25] 2078 5-9-10 44 ... ShaneKelly 7	43
		(P Howling) *mid-div: hdwy over 3f out: wknd appr fnl f*	**14/1**
2224	7	3/4	**Perfect Storm**[41] 631 9-9-10 50 ... JackDean(5) 1	47
		(W G M Turner) *led for 1f: rdn over 2f out: wknd over 1f out*	**14/1**
0000	8	1/2	**Three Thieves (UAE)**[26] 2051 5-10-1 45 ... FergusSweeney 12	46
		(M S Saunders) *bhd: hdwy over 2f out: rdn and sn no imp*	**14/1**
300/	9	1 3/4	**Cellarmaster (IRE)**[30] 1909 7-9-12 62 ... PatrickHills(3) 2	43
		(Mark Gillard) *in rr: rdn over 4f out: kpt on appr fnl f: nvr nr to chal*	**9/1**[3]
1600	10	11	**Competitor**[15] 2353 7-9-12 60 ...(v) KirstyMilczarek(3) 11	26
		(J Akehurst) *prom: led 7f out: hdd over 2f out: wknd over 1f out*	**9/2**[2]
0-00	11	3	**Splinter Group**[33] 1853 4-9-10 57 ...(p) PatCosgrave 9	16
		(S A Callaghan) *slowly away: sn in tch: lost tch 4f out*	**40/1**
12	4 1/2	**Necker (FR)**[75] 7-9-8 0 ... RossAtkinson(7) 4	14
		(M R Hoad) *hld up: a in rr*	**66/1**
13	7	**Walking In Memphis (IRE)**[117] 4-9-10 0 ... StephenCarson 13	—
		(C P Morlock) *rrd up leaving stalls but sn in tch: wknd over 4f out*	**66/1**

2m 34.69s (1.69) **Going Correction** +0.05s/f (Slow) **13** Ran SP% **126.6**
Speed ratings (Par 101): **96,96,95,95,95 91,90,90,89,82 80,77,72**
WIN: Wait For The Will £0.80, Trigger's Friend £52.90; PL: Wait For The Will £1.20, Trigger's Friend £20.00, Missie Baileys £2.10; EX: WFTW-TF £117.40, TF-WFTW £237.80; CSF: WFTW-TF £61.57, TF-WFTW £66.64.There were no bid for the winners. Three Thieves was claimed by J. J. Best for £6,000.
Owner R W Huggins **Bred** R W Huggins **Trained** Lewes, E Sussex
Owner Rdm Racing **Bred** Paul Mellon **Trained** Woodingdean, E Sussex

FOCUS
A weak seller that produced a blanket finish resulting in a dead-heat. The favourite is rated a stone off his recent best with the third the best guide.
Competitor Official explanation: trainer said horse had a breathing problem

2833 PREMIER BENEFIT SOLUTIONS H'CAP 1m 2f (P)

6:10 (6:12) (Class 6) (0-60,60) 3-Y-O £2,047 (£604; £302) Stalls Low

Form				RPR
0040	1		**Borrowdale**[33] 1870 3-9-1 **57** ... ShaneKelly 1	59
		(J A Osborne) *a in tch: chal ent fnl f: drvn to ld cl home*	**20/1**
4301	2	shd	**Millie's Rock (IRE)**[9] 2552 3-9-4 **60** ... PatCosgrave 3	62+
		(M J Wallace) *a in tch: chal on ins over 1f out: kpt on u.p: jst failed*	**6/1**[2]
-222	3	shd	**Just Sam (IRE)**[21] 2208 3-9-4 **60** ... DNolan 2	61
		(D Carroll) *a in tch: rdn to ld jst ins fnl f: hdd and lost 2nd fnl strides*	**6/1**[2]
-663	4	hd	**Solo River**[19] 2260 3-8-11 **56** ... TravisBlock(3) 10	57
		(P J Makin) *trckd ldr on outside: led 2f out: hdd jst ins fnl f: kpt on towards fin*	**14/1**
065-	5	3/4	**Berry Baby (IRE)**[194] 6944 3-9-4 **60** ... EddieAhern 11	60+
		(G A Butler) *hld up: hdwy 4f out: chsd ldrs over 1f out: nvr nr to chal*	**5/2**[1]
0-05	6	3/4	**Orbital Orchid**[28] 2015 3-9-0 **56** ...(v) FergusSweeney 12	56+
		(W S Kittow) *chsd ldrs: ev ch ent fnl f: squeezed out wl ins fnl f: nt rcvr*	**16/1**
6-30	7	3 1/4	**Star Grazer**[26] 2052 3-8-13 **60** ... JackMitchell(5) 13	52
		(C F Wall) *mid-div: rdn and effrt over 3f out: nvr nr to chal*	**20/1**
04-0	8	1 1/4	**Sendefaa (IRE)**[15] 2376 3-9-1 **60** ... KirstyMilczarek(3) 8	49
		(M Botti) *mid-div: rdn 2f out: one pce fr over 3f out*	**14/1**
0006	9	3/4	**Tallest Peak (USA)**[7] 2613 3-9-1 **57** ... VinceSlattery 6	45+
		(M G Quinlan) *mid-div: wknd over 1f out*	**16/1**
000-	10	6	**Fleur De Montjeu (IRE)**[225] 6470 3-9-2 **58** ... AdamKirby 5	34
		(W R Swinburn) *towards rr: rdn 4f out: sn btn*	**16/1**
5515	11	3/4	**Ledgerwood**[15] 2352 3-9-1 **60** ...(p) PatrickHills(3) 4	34
		(J W Hills) *led tl hdd 2f out: wknd wl over 1f out*	**12/1**
45-0	12	1 1/2	**Kristal Glory (IRE)**[49] 1479 3-9-1 **57** ... TedDurcan 7	41+
		(J L Dunlop) *a in rr*	**9/1**[3]
00-0	13	dist	**Two Imposters (USA)**[10] 2495 3-9-1 **57** ... GeorgeBaker 9	—
		(J R Best) *slowly away: a bhd: t.o*	**11/1**

2m 7.65s (1.05) **Going Correction** +0.05s/f (Slow) **13** Ran SP% **123.7**
Speed ratings (Par 97): **97,96,96,96,96 95,92,91,91,86 85,84,—**
CSF £140.51 CT £826.63 TOTE £28.90: £6.80, £3.00, £1.80; EX 452.90.
Owner Mr & Mrs G Middlebrook **Bred** G And Mrs Middlebrook **Trained** Upper Lambourn, Berks
■ Stewards' Enquiry : D Nolan two-day ban: careless riding (Jun 22-23)

FOCUS
A moderate handicap with another blanket finish but a few unexposed sorts lurking in here and although low-grade fare, the form, rated around the third and fourth, could work out.
Two Imposters(USA) Official explanation: trainer's rep said gelding had a breathing problem

2834 PREMIER PENSIONS MANAGEMENT CONSULTANCY MAIDEN STKS 1m (P)

6:40 (6:46) (Class 5) 3-Y-O £2,456 (£725; £362) Stalls High

Form				RPR
0-2	1		**Navajo Joe (IRE)**[8] 2571 3-9-3 0 ... RichardHughes 3	85
		(B J Meehan) *trckd ldrs: hdwy on ins to ld jst ins fnl f: r.o wl*	**8/13**[1]
2	2	1 1/4	**Visions Of Johanna (USA)**[33] 1854 3-9-3 0 ... RyanMoore 10	82
		(J Noseda) *led tl hdd over 5f out: led again over 3f out: hdd jst ins fnl f: nt pce of wnr*	**11/4**[2]
0-	3	1 1/2	**Wikaala (USA)**[301] 4393 3-9-3 0 ... DarryllHolland 8	79
		(M P Tregoning) *a.p: wnt 2nd 2f out tl fdd ins fnl f*	**25/1**

The Form Book, Raceform Ltd, Compton, RG20 6NL

4 1 3/4 **Cave Lion (USA)** 3-9-3 0 RobertHavlin 4 75+
(J H M Gosden) *mid-div: hdwy over 1f out: kpt on one pce* **11/1**[3]
0 5 1 1/4 **Mischief Lady**[19] 2257 3-8-12 0 AdamKirby 7 67
(E A L Dunlop) *chsd ldrs: rdn 2f out: wknd ins fnl f* **20/1**
6 shd **Quail Landing** 3-8-12 0 AlanMunro 5 67
(M P Tregoning) *mid-div: hdwy over 2f out: sn rdn and no imp after* **50/1**
0 7 nk **Selfish Option (IRE)**[10] 2509 3-9-3 0 FergusSweeney 2 71+
(H Morrison) *towards rr: sme hdwy over 1f out but nvr on terms* **66/1**
5 8 1 1/2 **Myanmar (IRE)**[14] 2413 3-9-3 0 ShaneKelly 6 68
(J Noseda) *hld up towards rr: nvr on terms* **12/1**
9 4 1/2 **Brakey Hill (USA)** 3-9-3 0 EddieAhern 12 57
(B J Meehan) *slowly away: a bhd* **50/1**
10 1 **Island Treasure** 3-9-0 0 TravisBlock(3) 1 55
(H Morrison) *v.s.a: rdn over 2f out and a bhd* **50/1**
11 14 **Lekezia (IRE)** 3-8-12 0 WilliamBuick 11 18
(J W Hills) *led over 5f out: hdd over 3f out: sn lost pl and wknd* **66/1**

1m 38.16s (-0.04) **Going Correction** +0.05s/f (Slow) **11** Ran SP% **122.1**
Speed ratings (Par 99): **102,100,99,97,96 96,95,94,89,88 74**
CSF £2.37 TOTE £1.60: £1.02, £1.20, £7.90; EX 2.20.
Owner Joe L Allbritton **Bred** Killeen Castle Stud **Trained** Manton, Wilts

FOCUS
Probably an above-average maiden for the track with some top yards represented and some smart maiden form already in the book. The winner did not need to run to previous form to score but the race should work out.
Mischief Lady Official explanation: jockey said filly hung right
Myanmar(IRE) Official explanation: jockey said colt hung right

2835 E B F PREMIER PENSIONS MANAGEMENT LTD MAIDEN FILLIES' STKS 6f
7:10 (7:15) (Class 5) 2-Y-O **£3,302** (£982; £491; £245) **Stalls** High

Form RPR
1 **Foxtrot Alpha (IRE)** 2-9-0 0 StephenCarson 10 72
(P Winkworth) *a.p: tk narrow ld 2f out: drvn out fnl f* **33/1**
2 nk **Sterling Sound (USA)** 2-9-0 0 DarryllHolland 11 71
(M P Tregoning) *a.p: rdn and ev ch ins fnl f: no ex cl home* **12/1**
3 1 1/4 **Mawjaat (IRE)** 2-9-0 0 IanMongan 3 67+
(J L Dunlop) *in rr: rdn and hdwy over 1f out: fin strly to snatch 3rd cl home* **16/1**
4 shd **Peper Harow (IRE)** 2-9-0 0 WilliamBuick 12 67
(M D I Usher) *chsd ldrs: rdn and ev ch 1f out: one pce and lost 3rd cl home* **33/1**
2 5 2 **Straitjacket**[17] 2306 2-9-0 0 RichardHughes 9 61
(R Hannon) *trckd ldr: ev ch 2f out but hung lft u.p and no ex after* **10/11**[1]
6 1/2 **Select (IRE)** 2-9-0 0 AlanMunro 8 60
(P W Chapple-Hyam) *chsd ldrs: effrt over 2f out: one pce after* **6/1**[2]
7 shd **Starlarks (IRE)** 2-9-0 0 ShaneKelly 5 59
(W J Knight) *trckd ldrs: effrt over 1f out: sn btn* **11/1**
8 1 1/2 **Bobbie Soxer (IRE)** 2-9-0 0 TedDurcan 1 61+
(J L Dunlop) *c over towards stands' side fr wd draw after wnt lft s: a bhd* **16/1**
9 3/4 **Extremely So** 2-8-11 0 KirstyMilczarek(3) 7 53
(P J McBride) *outpcd and a bhd* **20/1**
54 10 3 **Nativity**[17] 2309 2-8-11 0 TolleyDean(3) 2 44
(J L Spearing) *led tl rdn and hdd 2f out: wknd qckly* **16/1**
11 1 **Good Queen Best** 2-9-0 0 AdamKirby 6 41
(B De Haan) *mid-div: effrt on outside over 2f out: sn wknd* **33/1**
12 1/2 **Cat Patrol** 2-9-0 0 EddieAhern 4 39
(H J L Dunlop) *prom tl rdn and wknd qckly 2f out* **8/1**[3]

1m 12.15s (0.95) **Going Correction** -0.075s/f (Good) **12** Ran SP% **125.0**
Speed ratings (Par 90): **90,89,87,87,85 84,84,82,81,77 76,75**
CSF £393.18 TOTE £31.90: £7.70, £3.60, £5.00; EX 247.40.
Owner Foxtrot Racing Partnership **Bred** Irish National Stud **Trained** Chiddingfold, Surrey

FOCUS
Not easy at all to assess but probably no more than a fair maiden with the time not good, the favourite below par and three of the first four drawn near the rail. Newcomers dominated, filling the first four places.

NOTEBOOK
Foxtrot Alpha(IRE) ◆, a 37,000euros half-sister to three winners including Todlea, was seemingly unfancied in the betting but she looked very professional on her debut, travelling nicely in touch with the pace and seeing her race out in determined style to prompt connections to talk of the Goffs Fillies Million, as she was bought at the Goffs Sales. She is highly regarded by Peter Winkworth, indeed connections were intimating afterwards that they have only one 2yo better than her at home, and this was a smart effort first time up, so she shouldn't be underestimated wherever she goes next.
Sterling Sound(USA) ◆, a $120,000 sister to Art Currency and half-sister to four other winners, ran a cracker in second, coming from off the pace to finish strongly and go down all guns blazing. Her dam won the Prix de Diane, so she's bred to be smart and she looks a nice prospect. (tchd 10-1)
Mawjaat(IRE) ◆, a half-sister to a dual-winner at up to 1m2f in Italy, was very green and unable to go the pace at halfway, but the penny really dropped in the closing stages and she picked up nicely from the back. She looks a surefire improver next time, especially granted the stiffer test of stamina she's bred to appreciate. (op 25-1)
Peper Harow(IRE), an 8,500gns half-sister to Lunar Wind and Kelamon, is therefore quite precociously bred and ran a nice race on her debut, keeping on up the stands' rail.
Straitjacket had shaped well when runner-up on her debut, but dropped out tamely and was well below that form here. Official explanation: vet said filly was found to have been struck into (tchd 5-6 and Evens)
Bobbie Soxer(IRE), a half-sister to connections' high-class performer Big Bad Bob, shaped better than the bare form from her poor draw and will surely leave this behind in time. (tchd 14-1)
Cat Patrol Official explanation: jockey said filly had no more to give

2836 RACE FOR JUDE FILLIES' H'CAP 5f
7:40 (7:45) (Class 5) (0-70,67) 3-Y-0+ **£2,456** (£725; £362) **Stalls** High

Form RPR
5211 1 **Wibbadune (IRE)**[7] 2616 4-10-0 **63** AdamKirby 7 79+
(D Shaw) *hld up in tch: hdwy and swtchd lft wl over 1f out: rdn to ld ins fnl f: sprinted clr* **2/1**[1]
0122 2 3 1/4 **Black Moma (IRE)**[7] 2616 4-9-13 **62** DavidKinsella 1 66
(A B Haynes) *a.p: led over 1f out: hdd ins fnl f: nt pce of wnr* **6/1**[3]
0-23 3 hd **Matterofact (IRE)**[16] 2330 5-9-7 **56** FergusSweeney 6 60
(M S Saunders) *trckd ldr: ev ch ent fnl f: edgd lft u.p: no ex* **9/4**[2]
000- 4 shd **Overwing (IRE)**[193] 6962 5-9-11 **60** ShaneKelly 8 63
(R M H Cowell) *led tl hdd over 1f out: rdn and sn short of room: swtchd lft ins fnl f: r.o* **13/2**
2-40 5 1 3/4 **Doric Lady**[23] 2122 3-9-11 **67** EddieAhern 3 64
(J A R Toller) *hld up: rdn over 1f out: nvr nr to chal* **11/1**
-300 6 1/2 **Lady Bahia (IRE)**[3] 2710 7-9-13 **62** (b) GeorgeBaker 5 57
(Peter Grayson) *a towards rr* **12/1**
16-0 7 2 1/2 **Damhsoir (IRE)**[6] 2644 4-8-11 **46** ow1 DarryllHolland 2 32
(H S Howe) *sn rdn and a in rr* **10/1**

57.40 secs (-0.80) **Going Correction** -0.075s/f (Good)
WFA 3 from 4yo+ 7lb **7** Ran SP% **116.8**
Speed ratings (Par 100): **103,97,97,97,94 93,89**
CSF £15.18 CT £28.90 TOTE £3.20: £2.40, £2.40; EX 11.60.
Owner Simon Mapletoft Racing I **Bred** Ballyhane Stud **Trained** Danethorpe, Notts

FOCUS
A moderate handicap run at a fast pace. The progressive Wibbadune had Black Moma back in second once again and there could be more to come yet.
Lady Bahia(IRE) Official explanation: jockey said mare hung left

2837 PREMIER PENSIONS MANAGEMENT ADMINISTRATION H'CAP 7f
8:10 (8:11) (Class 5) (0-75,75) 4-Y-0+ **£2,331** (£693; £346; £173) **Stalls** High

Form RPR
5-01 1 **My Learned Friend (IRE)**[7] 2615 4-8-7 **68** DavidProbert(7) 7 83
(A M Balding) *mde all: drvn clr ent fnl f: comf* **3/1**[1]
0000 2 3 1/4 **Alfresco**[7] 2619 4-9-4 **72** (v[1]) WilliamBuick 15 78
(I A Wood) *chsd ldrs: rdn to go 2nd over 1f out: r.o but no ch w wnr* **5/1**[2]
-062 3 2 1/4 **Valentino Swing (IRE)**[7] 2615 5-9-1 **69** AdamKirby 6 69
(Miss T Spearing) *a.p: hung rt over 1f out: no ex ins fnl f* **15/2**[3]
4304 4 nk **Binnion Bay (IRE)**[16] 2337 7-7-11 **58** oh6 ow2 (b) RossAtkinson(7) 2 57+
(J J Bridger) *slowly away: hld up: hdwy over 1f out: nvr nr to chal* **16/1**
6600 5 hd **Cornerstone**[44] 1578 4-7-13 **56** oh7 (vt) LukeMorris(3) 13 55
(S C Williams) *t.k.h: trckd wnr to over 1f out: nt qckn after* **20/1**
2242 6 shd **Prince Of Delphi**[11] 2484 5-9-1 **69** (p) GeorgeBaker 9 68
(R M Beckett) *hld up in rr: swtchd lft and hdwy over 1f out: nvr nrr* **3/1**[1]
00-6 7 1 3/4 **Torquemada (IRE)**[7] 2615 7-8-13 **67** PaulDoe 14 61
(M J Attwater) *t.k.h: in rr and nvr on terms* **12/1**
6440 8 hd **Resplendent Alpha**[11] 2484 4-9-2 **70** ShaneKelly 5 63
(P Howling) *hld up in rr: rdn over 2f out and no imp after* **11/1**
1436 9 nk **Wodhill Schnaps**[10] 2510 7-8-7 **61** ow1 (b) TedDurcan 11 53
(D Morris) *s.i.s: a bhd* **10/1**
P120 10 2 1/4 **Bartercard (USA)**[18] 2293 7-9-7 **75** PatCosgrave 1 61
(Stef Liddiard) *mid-div: rdn over 2f out: sn btn* **20/1**
0000 11 8 **Kempsey**[19] 2255 6-7-11 **56** oh4 (b) NicolPolli(5) 10 21
(J J Bridger) *mid-div tl wknd 2f out* **33/1**

1m 22.61s (-0.69) **Going Correction** -0.075s/f (Good) **11** Ran SP% **121.9**
Speed ratings (Par 103): **100,96,93,93,93 93,91,90,90,87 78**
CSF £18.01 CT £108.94 TOTE £3.00: £1.60, £2.40, £2.00; EX 24.90 Place 6 £193.66, Place 5 £106.13.
Owner DR E Harris **Bred** B Kennedy **Trained** Kingsclere, Hants

FOCUS
A modest handicap won in good style by My Learned Friend, who is rated back to his 2yo best. He was able to dictate a modest pace and the form is not that solid.
T/Plt: £169.60 to a £1 stake. Pool: £42,936.80. 184.75 winning tickets. T/Qpdt: £59.40 to a £1 stake. Pool: £3,846.70. 47.90 winning tickets. JS

2574 MUSSELBURGH (R-H)
Saturday, June 7

OFFICIAL GOING: Good to firm (good in places; 7.8)
Wind: Light, half behind Weather: Fine and sunny

2838 TOTEPOOL EDINBURGH CASTLE CONDITIONS STKS 5f
2:20 (2:21) (Class 2) 2-Y-O
£12,462 (£3,732; £1,866; £934; £466; £234) **Stalls** Low

Form RPR
51 1 **Spin Cycle (IRE)**[22] 2140 2-9-0 0 TomEaves 5 86
(B Smart) *trckd ldrs: hdwy 2f out: rdn to chal over 1f out: drvn and styd on to ld last half f* **11/10**[1]
221 2 nk **Harwalla (IRE)**[20] 2217 2-9-0 0 JoeFanning 4 85
(M Johnston) *led: rdn wl over 1f out: drvn and edgd rt ent fnl f: hdd and no ex last half f* **8/1**[3]
43 3 3/4 **Kerrys Requiem (IRE)**[17] 2306 2-8-6 0 ChrisCatlin 3 74
(M R Channon) *dwlt: sn in tch on outer: hdwy to chal and ev ch whn edgd lft ent fnl f: drvn and kpt on* **16/1**
4 1 **Elegant Cad (CAN)** 2-8-8 0 LPKeniry 2 73
(J R Best) *dwlt: in tch: hdwy over 1f out: rdn and kpt on ins fnl f: nrst fin* **10/1**
1 5 3/4 **Deadly Encounter (IRE)**[31] 1907 2-8-11 0 PaulHanagan 6 73
(R A Fahey) *cl up: pushed along and ev ch 2f out: sn rdn and edgd lft: wknd ent fnl f* **15/8**[2]
110 6 4 1/2 **Dispol Kylie (IRE)**[22] 2167 2-8-12 0 J-PGuillambert 1 65+
(P T Midgley) *cl up: pushed along 2f out: sn rdn and wknd appr fnl f: eased* **20/1**

58.98 secs (-1.42) **Going Correction** -0.30s/f (Firm) **6** Ran SP% **113.2**
Speed ratings (Par 99): **99,98,97,95,94 87**
CSF £11.07 TOTE £2.00: £1.10, £4.10; EX 10.20.
Owner H E Sheikh Rashid Bin Mohammed **Bred** Mrs Lisa Kelly **Trained** Hambleton, N Yorks

FOCUS
A decent conditions event featuring four previous winners, but probably some way below Listed form. The form looks reasonable assessed around the placed horses.

NOTEBOOK
Spin Cycle(IRE) has been sent off a short-priced favourite for all three starts, and though he disappointed first time up he clocked a fast time when winning at Hamilton on his next start and followed up here in a workmanlike manner. Connections are keen to go to Royal Ascot but on this showing he is going to need to find a deal of improvement to figure. (op 5-4 tchd 11-8)
Harwalla(IRE), having proved himself over 6f last time, was keen to stretch this field from the start but, while he had the speed to do so, he had no answer once the winner came at him. He is going to have plenty of weight in nurseries and will find it tough in Listed/Pattern comany. (op 17-2 tchd 9-1)
Kerrys Requiem(IRE) ◆ was slowly away and forced to challenge wide as a result. She could well have finished closer but for that and this speedy sort won't remain a maiden for much longer. (op 22-1 tchd 14-1)
Elegant Cad(CAN) ◆, who possesses a speedy US pedigree, was thrown in at the deep end on this debut and was certainly not disgraced. He will know more about what is required of him next time and a normal maiden could be his for the taking. (op 15-2 tchd 7-1)
Deadly Encounter(IRE) drifted badly in the market and dropped away tamely after having the speed to hold every chance. This ground might have been fast enough for him. (tchd 6-4)

Dispol Kylie(IRE) is quick but she was precocious and others have caught up and passed her now. Official explanation: jockey said filly hung right-handed in final furlong (tchd 18-1)

2839 TOTESPORT BETXTRA H'CAP 1m 6f
2:50 (2:50) (Class 3) (0-95,88) 4-Y-0+

£9,346 (£2,799; £1,399; £700; £349; £175) **Stalls** High

Form RPR

100- **1** **Record Breaker (IRE)**[273] 5215 4-9-7 **88** JoeFanning 6 98
(M Johnston) *trckd ldr: hdwy to ld wl over 2f out: rdn wl over 1f out: drvn and hdd jst ins fnl f: rallied u.p to ld again last 75yds* **5/2**[1]

1311 **2** *nk* **Sir Duke (IRE)**[19] 2264 4-8-8 **75** FrancisNorton 4 85
(P W D'Arcy) *trckd ldng pair: hdwy 3f out: rdn to chal over 1f out: led and edgd rt ins fnl f: sn drvn: hdd and no ex last 75yds* **9/2**[3]

-132 **3** *4* **Hue**[28] 1984 7-8-10 **77** J-PGuillambert 2 81
(B Ellison) *hld up in rr: hdwy on outer 3f out: rdn to chse ldng pair over 1f out: kpt on same pce* **11/4**[2]

-351 **4** *1* **Charlotte Vale**[15] 2379 7-8-9 **76** PaulHanagan 5 79
(Micky Hammond) *led: rdn along over 3f out: hdd and drvn wl over 2f out: grad wknd* **7/1**

/50- **5** *¾* **Motive (FR)**[30] 2093 7-9-4 **85** RobertWinston 1 87
(J Howard Johnson) *in tch: hdwy over 3f out: rdn wl over 2f out: sn one pce* **10/1**

1311 **6** *8* **Royal Amnesty**[19] 2249 5-8-7 **74** ow1 (b) TomEaves 3 65
(Miss L A Perratt) *hld up in rr: hdwy 3f out: rdn along on inner 2f out: sn btn* **11/2**

3m 4.67s (-0.63) **Going Correction** -0.225s/f (Firm) **6** Ran SP% **110.4**
Speed ratings (Par 107): **92,91,89,88,88 83**
CSF £13.49 TOTE £4.00: £2.10, £2.90; EX 17.80.
Owner Leung Kai Fai & Vincent Leung **Bred** Sir E J Loder **Trained** Middleham Moor, N Yorks
■ Stewards' Enquiry : Joe FanningM one-day ban: careless riding (Jun 22)

FOCUS
A slightly disappointing turnout for the money, it terms of both quality and quantity. The first two, the only four-year-olds in the race, pulled well clear. the winner did not need to improve on his best to score while the runner-up is progressive and raised another 4lb.

NOTEBOOK
Record Breaker(IRE) ended last term with a couple of disappointing efforts but had been progressive before that and the son of In The Wings showed himself to be right back on track with a battling success on his seasonal bow. He can build further on this. (op 10-3)
Sir Duke(IRE) has been in great form of late and looked sure to make it five wins from his last six starts when coming through to lead a furlong out. Just outbattled on this occasion, he will continue to go close from this sort of mark. (op 7-2)
Hue could have done with a faster pace to come off considering he was dropping back two furlongs in trip and would also appreciate some ease in the ground. (op 3-1 tchd 5-2)
Charlotte Vale had her own way up front and was allowed to dictate just a fair gallop but couldn't go with the principals once challenged. (op 11-2)

2840 TOTESCOOP6 TRADESMAN'S DERBY H'CAP 1m 4f
3:20 (3:21) (Class 4) (0-85,84) 3-Y-0

£15,577 (£4,665; £2,332; £1,167; £582; £292) **Stalls** High

Form RPR

1-03 **1** **Resplendent Light**[22] 2173 3-9-1 **78** DO'Donohoe 10 87
(W R Muir) *trckd ldng pair on inner: hdwy over 2f out: rdn wl over 1f out: styd on to ld jst ins fnl f: jst hld on* **16/1**

-106 **2** *shd* **Sundowner (IRE)**[21] 2194 3-9-3 **80** RobertWinston 12 89
(G A Butler) *in tch on inner: hdwy 3f out: rdn along 2f out: swtchd lft and drvn ent fnl f: styd on strly: jst failed* **4/1**[2]

-023 **3** *½* **The Betchworth Kid**[7] 2610 3-9-7 **84** AndrewElliott 5 92+
(M L W Bell) *hld up towards rr: gd hdwy on outer 3f out: rdn to chal over 1f out and ev ch whn hmpd and swtchd rt ent fnl f: sn drvn and kpt on* **8/1**

-410 **4** *½* **Yes Mr President (IRE)**[31] 1919 3-9-1 **78** (b[1]) JoeFanning 11 85
(M Johnston) *trckd ldr: led over 2f out: rdn and hung bdly lft appr fnl f: drvn and kpt on wl u.p* **33/1**

02-2 **5** *½* **West With The Wind**[23] 2119 3-9-5 **82** MickyFenton 2 88
(T P Tate) *dwlt and in rr tl gd hdwy on outer to trck ldrs after 4f: effrt 3f out: rdn along 2f out: sn drvn and one pce ent fnl f* **5/1**[3]

12-0 **6** *hd* **Step This Way (USA)**[24] 2109 3-9-3 **80** J-PGuillambert 13 86
(M Johnston) *led: rdn along 3f out: hdd over 2f out: drvn and stl ev ch 1f out: no ex ins fnl f* **16/1**

6-44 **7** *¾* **Celt**[22] 2151 3-9-0 **77** NickyMackay 3 82+
(L M Cumani) *hld up: hdwy over 2f out: rdn and styng on whn hmpd jst ins fnl f: kpt on towards fin* **4/1**[2]

1-21 **8** *1 ¼* **Suzi's Decision**[15] 2376 3-9-2 **79** FrancisNorton 8 82
(P W D'Arcy) *midfield: hdwy 3f out: rdn over 2f out: sn drvn and kpt on same pce* **7/2**[1]

-000 **9** *4 ½* **Ruff Diamond (USA)**[21] 2194 3-9-7 **84** LPKeniry 6 80
(J R Best) *a towards rr* **40/1**

-011 **10** *hd* **Gala Casino Star (IRE)**[9] 2539 3-8-10 **73** PaulHanagan 4 68
(R A Fahey) *hld up: a towards rr* **9/1**

5-32 **11** *1 ¼* **Society Venue**[22] 2143 3-8-10 **73** TomEaves 7 66
(Jedd O'Keeffe) *midfield: hdwy and in tch 1/2-way: effrt to chse ldrs 4f out: rdn along over 2f out: sn drvn and wknd* **40/1**

4013 **12** *½* **Bourse (IRE)**[10] 2496 3-7-12 **66** KellyHarrison(5) 1 58
(J S Wainwright) *hld up: a in rr* **33/1**

4-41 **13** *½* **Stop On**[37] 1741 3-8-9 **72** ChrisCatlin 9 64
(M R Channon) *chsd ldrs: rdn along 3f out: sn wknd* **25/1**

2m 36.56s (-3.14) **Going Correction** -0.225s/f (Firm) **13** Ran SP% **126.4**
Speed ratings (Par 101): **101,100,100,100,99 99,99,98,95,95 94,94,93**
CSF £80.48 CT £575.07 TOTE £21.00: £4.50, £2.40, £3.10; EX 123.10.
Owner Middleham Park Racing XLIX **Bred** Usk Valley Stud **Trained** Lambourn, Berks
■ Stewards' Enquiry : Joe Fanning caution: careless riding

FOCUS
An informative handicap featuring quite a number of three-year-olds stepping up markedly in trip and who, on paper, were more than likely to improve considerably for doing so. The race looks sound enough through the placed horses and should throw up plenty of winners in the coming weeks.
Yes Mr President(IRE) Official explanation: jockey said colt hung badly left-handed final 2f

2841 BALFOUR KILPATRICK SUPPLY CHAIN H'CAP 1m
3:50 (3:53) (Class 4) (0-80,78) 4-Y-0+

£4,673 (£1,399; £699; £350; £174; £87) **Stalls** High

Form RPR

20-4 **1** **Sunnyside Tom (IRE)**[12] 2445 4-8-10 **67** PaulHanagan 4 78
(R A Fahey) *sn led: pushed along over 2f out: jnd and rdn wl over 1f out: drvn ins fnl f and styd on wl* **7/2**[2]

0-11 **2** *¾* **Stellite**[19] 2251 8-8-10 **67** DanielTudhope 2 76
(J S Goldie) *trckd wnr: effrt over 2f out: sn rdn to chal and ev ch tl drvn ins fnl f and no ex last 75yds* **3/1**[1]

3-02 **3** *3 ¼* **Champain Sands (IRE)**[12] 2445 9-8-12 **69** JoeFanning 1 71
(E J Alston) *hld up towards rr: hdwy 3f out: rdn to chse ldng pair wl over 1f out: sn drvn and no imp ins fnl f* **5/1**

0256 **4** *3* **King Of The Moors (USA)**[2] 2749 5-8-4 **68** DeanHeslop(7) 6 63
(T D Barron) *chsd ldrs: effrt over 2f out: sn rdn and one pce fr over 1f out* **9/2**[3]

0055 **5** *2* **Malinsa Blue (IRE)**[15] 2375 6-8-4 **61** ow1 (p) ChrisCatlin 7 51
(B Ellison) *chsd ldrs: rdn along over 3f out: wknd over 2f out* **5/1**

0465 **6** *3 ½* **Jamieson Gold (IRE)**[22] 2158 5-9-7 **78** (p) RobertWinston 5 60
(Miss L A Perratt) *in tch: hdwy to chse ldrs 1/2-way: rdn along 3f out and sn wknd* **6/1**

0/0- **7** *13* **Tender Moments**[385] 1837 4-9-6 **77** TomEaves 3 29
(B Smart) *a in rr: bhd fnl 2f* **25/1**

1m 40.45s (-0.75) **Going Correction** -0.225s/f (Firm) **7** Ran SP% **116.9**
Speed ratings (Par 105): **94,93,90,87,85 81,68**
CSF £15.02 TOTE £4.40: £1.90, £2.20; EX 12.90.
Owner The Sunnyside Racing Partnership **Bred** S W D McIlveen **Trained** Musley Bank, N Yorks

FOCUS
A modest handicap and not that much pace on so the front two had it to themselves pretty much throughout. The form, as a consequence, does not look too reliable.
Jamieson Gold(IRE) Official explanation: jockey said gelding was unsuited by the good to firm (good in places) ground

2842 BULLEIT BOURBON SPIRIT OF ENDEAVOUR H'CAP 7f 30y
4:35 (4:36) (Class 4) (0-80,80) 3-Y-0 **£4,673** (£1,399; £699; £350; £174) **Stalls** High

Form RPR

-042 **1** **Prince Hamlet (IRE)**[8] 2575 3-9-3 **76** (b[1]) TomEaves 1 87
(B Smart) *plld hrd: cl up: effrt over 2f out and sn led: rdn clr over 1f out: styd on wl* **5/2**[2]

44-1 **2** *7* **Baron's Court**[136] 265 3-9-4 **77** J-PGuillambert 3 69
(M Johnston) *stmbld s: hld up in rr: hdwy over 2f out and sn rdn: drvn over 1f out: kpt on ins fnl f: nvr nr wnr* **9/2**

1-33 **3** *1* **Atabaas Pride**[44] 1576 3-9-7 **80** (b[1]) JoeFanning 2 69
(M Johnston) *stdd s: hld up and in rr whn rn wd home turn and sn wl bhd: rdn and hdwy on wd outside over 2f out: sn drvn and styd on ins fnl f* **9/4**[1]

1533 **4** *¾* **Casino Night**[8] 2575 3-7-11 **63** PatrickDonaghy(7) 5 50
(J R Weymes) *sn led: rdn along and hdd over 2f out: sn drvn and wknd over 1f out* **9/1**

4620 **5** *1 ¼* **Rossini's Dancer**[15] 2367 3-8-2 **61** oh2 PaulHanagan 4 45
(R A Fahey) *hld up: effrt 3f out: sn rdn along and btn over 2f out* **3/1**[3]

1m 27.87s (-2.43) **Going Correction** -0.225s/f (Firm) **5** Ran SP% **112.5**
Speed ratings (Par 101): **104,96,94,94,92**
CSF £13.98 TOTE £3.50: £1.90, £2.70; EX 15.40.
Owner H E Sheikh Rashid Bin Mohammed **Bred** Darley **Trained** Hambleton, N Yorks

FOCUS
A good little race but the pace set by Casino Night found all except the winner out and the remainder couldn't get into it. The form is a bit shaky with the placed horses not the most solid.

2843 LOTHIAN DAF H'CAP 5f
5:05 (5:06) (Class 4) (0-85,85) 3-Y-0+ **£5,180** (£1,541; £770; £384) **Stalls** Low

Form RPR

-004 **1** **Princess Ellis**[21] 2212 4-9-0 **69** J-PGuillambert 9 84
(E J Alston) *mde all: rdn wl over 1f out: styd on strly ins fnl f* **8/1**

0050 **2** *1 ¾* **Circuit Dancer (IRE)**[8] 2583 8-8-11 **66** MickyFenton 5 75+
(D Nicholls) *towards rr: hdwy 2f out: rdn and squeezed through over 1f out: styd on ins fnl f* **8/1**

-562 **3** *nk* **The Nifty Fox**[11] 2489 4-9-8 **77** RobertWinston 6 85
(T D Easterby) *chsd ldrs: rdn along wl over 1f out: drvn and styd on ins fnl f: nrst fin* **4/1**[1]

2504 **4** *½* **Malapropism**[11] 2489 8-9-12 **81** ChrisCatlin 10 87
(M R Channon) *cl up: rdn over 1f out and ev ch tl drvn and wknd wl ins fnl f* **10/1**

0450 **5** *¾* **Blue Tomato**[21] 2210 7-9-7 **83** PatrickDonaghy(7) 7 87
(D Nicholls) *chsd ldrs on outer: hdwy 2f out: rdn and ch over 1f out: one pce ins fnl f* **10/1**

0160 **6** *1 ¼* **Bo McGinty (IRE)**[21] 2211 7-9-5 **81** (b) BMcHugh(7) 4 80
(R A Fahey) *chsd ldrs: rdn along wl over 1f out: kpt on same pce appr fnl f* **20/1**

6404 **7** *½* **First Order**[14] 2398 7-9-11 **80** (v) TomEaves 11 77
(Miss L A Perratt) *trckd ldrs: hdwy 2f out and sn ev ch tl rdn and wknd appr fnl f* **11/1**

1255 **8** *hd* **Rothesay Dancer**[7] 2596 5-8-7 **67** KellyHarrison(5) 8 63
(J S Goldie) *in tch: effrt wl over 1f out: sn rdn and hld whn n.m.r appr fnl f* **6/1**[3]

5-10 **9** *hd* **Sandwith**[22] 2145 5-9-1 **70** (p) DO'Donohoe 12 66
(J S Wainwright) *chsd ldrs: rdn along 2f out: sn drvn and wknd* **11/1**

200- **10** *¾* **Inspainagain (USA)**[211] 6743 4-8-8 **70** DeanHeslop(7) 14 63
(T D Barron) *prom: rdn along 2f out: grad wknd* **14/1**

0-00 **11** *nk* **Blazing Heights**[7] 2626 5-9-11 **80** DanielTudhope 3 72
(J S Goldie) *midfield: hdwy to chse ldrs wl over 1f out: sn rdn and wknd* **12/1**

0004 **12** *2 ¼* **Alfie Lee (IRE)**[8] 2576 11-8-2 **64** oh18 (tp) PaulPickard(7) 2 48
(D A Nolan) *a in rr* **100/1**

-062 **13** *2 ½* **Bosun Breese**[19] 2258 3-9-9 **85** FrancisNorton 1 60
(P W D'Arcy) *t.k.h: hld up: a in rr* **9/2**[2]

00-0 **14** *7* **Seafield Towers**[2] 2748 8-8-8 **68** oh19 ow4 (p) GaryBartley(5) 13 18
(D A Nolan) *chsd ldrs towards outer: rdn along 2f out and sn wknd* **150/1**

58.27 secs (-2.13) **Going Correction** -0.30s/f (Firm)
WFA 3 from 4yo+ 7lb **14** Ran SP% **130.3**
Speed ratings (Par 105): **105,102,101,100,99 97,96,96,96,95 94,91,87,75**
CSF £76.25 CT £306.88 TOTE £11.70: £3.60, £3.40, £1.50; EX 82.20.
Owner John Jackson **Bred** J E Jackson **Trained** Longton, Lancs

FOCUS
A fair sprint handicap featuring all fully exposed sorts but three or four in grand heart at present and the form, rated around the third and fourth, should bear close scrutiny in the weeks ahead.

2844 STEPHEN HAY AND ASSOCIATES LTD APPRENTICE H'CAP 2m
5:35 (5:35) (Class 5) (0-70,65) 4-Y-0+ **£3,885** (£1,156; £577; £288) **Stalls** Low

Form RPR

6-04 **1** **Kyber**[8] 2579 7-9-2 **55** GaryBartley 3 64
(J S Goldie) *led: rdn along and hdd 2f out: drvn and rallied to ld again ins fnl f: styd on gamely* **9/2**[3]

-422 **2** *1* **Living On A Prayer**[2] 2752 5-8-9 **51**........................ DeclanCannon(3) 2 59
(Thomas McLaughlin, Ire) *trckd ldng pair: hdwy 3f out: led wl over 1f out and sn rdn: hdd and drvn ins fnl f: sn no ex* **9/4**[2]

0/11 **3** *2* **Silver Seeker (USA)**[12] 2467 8-9-7 **60**........................ ClGillies 4 66
(Miss P Robson) *plld hrd: trckd ldr: effrt 3f out: rdn to ld 2f out: sn drvn and hdd over 1f out: wknd ins fnl f* **5/6**[1]

0300 **4** *17* **Trance (IRE)**[7] 2628 8-9-5 **61**........................(b) DeanHeslop(3) 5 46
(T D Barron) *in rr: pushed along over 5f out: rdn 3f out: sn drvn and bhd* **10/1**

0 **P** **Kwitara (GER)**[8] 2579 4-9-8 **65**........................ BMcHugh(3) 1 —
(P Monteith) *a towards rr: rdn along and bhd over 3f out: p.u and dismntd over 2f out: lame* **25/1**

3m 32.84s (-3.26) **Going Correction** -0.225s/f (Firm)
WFA 4 from 5yo+ 1lb 5 Ran SP% **116.4**
Speed ratings (Par 103): **99,98,97,89,—**
CSF £15.87 TOTE £7.00: £2.30, £1.50; EX 16.70 Place 6: £77.57 Place 5: £44.65.
Owner Great Northern Partnership **Bred** P B Holmes **Trained** Uplawmoor, E Renfrews

FOCUS
A modest staying handicap for apprentices being basically a three-horse race. The form makes sense but looks weak.
Kwitara(GER) Official explanation: jockey said filly felt wrong behind
T/Plt: £197.10 to a £1 stake. Pool: £63,193.70. 234.05 winning tickets. T/Qpdt: £36.50 to a £1 stake. Pool: £2,580.90. 52.30 winning tickets. JR

2534 NEWCASTLE (L-H)
Saturday, June 7

OFFICIAL GOING: Good to soft (good in places; 7.0)
20mm rain four days before but it had dried out and was described as 'nearly good, a bit tacky in places'.
Wind: Light, half behind Weather: fine, sunny and warm

2845 PAR PETROLEUM MAIDEN AUCTION STKS 6f
6:50 (6:52) (Class 5) 2-Y-O **£3,238** (£963; £481; £240) **Stalls** Low

Form RPR

42 **1** **Spring Tale (USA)**[9] 2534 2-8-9 0........................ PaulHanagan 10 80+
(M J Wallace) *w ldr: led 3f out: shkn up and wnt clr over 1f out: pushed out* **5/6**[1]

2 *3* **Sunset Crest** 2-8-3 0........................ AndrewMullen(3) 9 67+
(Mrs A Duffield) *dwlt: sn chsng ldrs: styd on to go 2nd jst ins fnl f: no ch w wnr* **14/1**

66 **3** *4* **El Portet**[29] 1967 2-8-11 0........................ AndrewElliott 4 60
(G M Moore) *led 3f: fdd fnl f* **16/1**

454 **4** *shd* **Steel Stockholder**[8] 2581 2-8-10 0........................ TWilliams 8 59
(M Brittain) *hld up in tch: effrt over 2f out: styd on fnl f* **14/1**

30 **5** *1 3/4* **Fitzolini**[26] 2035 2-8-9 0........................ PhillipMakin 3 52
(A D Brown) *chsd ldrs: one pce fnl 2f* **12/1**

6 *5* **Hill Cross (IRE)** 2-8-12 0........................ RoystonFfrench 7 40
(Mrs A Duffield) *chsd ldrs: wknd over 1f out* **7/1**[3]

7 *4 1/2* **Topolski (IRE)** 2-9-1 0........................ JoeFanning 1 30
(M Johnston) *dwlt: a outpcd and bhd* **5/1**[2]

8 *1/2* **Coniston Reload** 2-8-10 0........................ DaleGibson 5 23
(M W Easterby) *unruly s: s.i.s: a in rr* **40/1**

9 *2 3/4* **Cleard For Action** 2-8-10 0........................ JamieMoriarty(3) 2 18
(J R Weymes) *mid-div: rdn and lost pl over 2f out* **20/1**

10 *7* **Southern Scarlet** 2-8-7 0 ow1........................ TonyHamilton 6 —
(Miss J A Camacho) *sn outpcd and bhd* **20/1**

1m 15.46s (0.26) **Going Correction** -0.075s/f (Good) 10 Ran SP% **122.6**
Speed ratings (Par 93): **95,91,85,85,83 76,70,69,66,56**
CSF £15.70 TOTE £1.70: £1.30, £4.70, £3.20; EX 20.90.
Owner B Walsh A Viner & Dr J Wallace **Bred** Sadler's Profile Syndicate **Trained** Newmarket, Suffolk
■ Stewards' Enquiry : Paul Hanagan one-day ban: failed to keep straight from the stalls (Jun 22)

FOCUS
A weak maiden auction race and the winner was doing no more than she was entitled to. The race has been rated through the third.

NOTEBOOK
Spring Tale(USA) is nothing much to look at but proved different class. Drawn ten of ten, her rider wasted no time getting across to the far side and she had only to be shaken up to shoot clear and score with plenty in hand. She looks ideal nursery material. (op Evens tchd 8-11)
Sunset Crest, a lengthy March foal, stayed on in willing fashion after a sluggish start and this will have taught her plenty. (op 16-1)
El Portet, having his third start, took them along but in the end did not truly see out the sixth furlong on this uphill track. (op 14-1)
Steel Stockholder, already having his fourth start, was putting in all his best work at the finish and 7f in a nursery will be more his cup of tea. (tchd 16-1)
Fitzolini, suited by the bit of give, is now qualified for a nursery company. (op 14-1)
Hill Cross(IRE), not the best of walkers, looked to be carrying tons of condition and the outing will have done him a power of good. (op 8-1 tchd 9-1)
Topolski(IRE), a moderate walker, was very green beforehand and after a trady start he never figured. (tchd 6-1)

2846 NEW COUNTY ROADS H'CAP 7f
7:20 (7:22) (Class 5) (0-70,70) 4-Y-O+ **£3,238** (£963; £481; £240) **Stalls** Low

Form RPR

0050 **1** **Gee Ceffyl Bach**[5] 2662 4-8-2 **51** oh6........................ DaleGibson 15 62
(R C Guest) *trckd one other stands' side: led that side over 1f out: str run to ld overall nr fin* **28/1**

-115 **2** *2 1/4* **Zabeel Tower**[9] 2523 5-8-11 **60**........................(p) TonyHamilton 6 65+
(R Allan) *chsd ldr: chal 1f out: kpt on same pce ins fnl f* **9/1**

0000 **3** *hd* **Bid For Gold**[34] 1826 4-8-11 **60**........................ AndrewElliott 8 64+
(Jedd O'Keeffe) *led overall on far side tl ins fnl f: no ex* **16/1**

0-02 **4** *1 1/4* **Prince Golan (IRE)**[7] 2619 4-9-7 **70**........................ PaulHanagan 11 71+
(J W Unett) *chsd ldrs: kpt on same pce fnl f* **11/2**[2]

3-05 **5** *hd* **Ezdeyaad (USA)**[15] 2360 4-9-7 **70**........................ RobertWinston 9 70+
(G A Swinbank) *hld up in midfield: hdwy over 2f out: styd on same pce ins fnl f* **4/1**[1]

1-66 **6** *3 3/4* **Cape Cobra**[10] 2511 4-9-0 **63**........................ JimmyFortune 3 53
(J H M Gosden) *hld up in midfield: effrt over 3f out: kpt on fnl f: nvr a threat* **7/1**

0-00 **7** *3* **Mundo's Magic**[12] 2444 4-8-9 **58**........................ RoystonFfrench 4 40
(G M Moore) *mid-div: drvn 3f out: nvr nr to chal* **22/1**

4600 **8** *1 1/2* **King Harson**[14] 2400 9-8-13 **62**........................ JoeFanning 14 40
(J D Bethell) *led one other stands' side: hung lft and hdd over 1f out: sn wknd* **9/1**

-300 **9** *5* **Maia**[28] 2005 4-9-0 **63**........................ PhillipMakin 2 28
(D Nicholls) *s.i.s: nvr a factor* **14/1**

251 **10** *hd* **Shosolosa (IRE)**[7] 2597 6-7-12 **54**........................ StacyRenwick(7) 13 18
(R C Guest) *swtchd lft s: bhd tl sme late hdwy* **8/1**

2144 **11** *2* **The Salwick Flyer (IRE)**[19] 2251 5-8-9 **58**........................ TomEaves 12 17
(Miss L A Perratt) *prom: wknd over 1f out* **6/1**[3]

0660 **12** *3* **College Land Boy**[5] 2662 4-8-2 **51** oh6........................ TWilliams 7 2
(A Kirtley) *chsd ldrs: lost pl over 1f out* **40/1**

50-1 **13** *2 1/4* **Lewis Lloyd (IRE)**[12] 2463 5-8-0 **52**........................ DuranFentiman(3) 1 —
(R E Barr) *s.i.s: a in rr* **25/1**

1500 **14** *28* **Newgate (UAE)**[15] 2375 4-7-11 **51** oh1...........(b) DanielleMcCreery(5) 10 —
(Mrs R A Carr) *racd centre: in tch: lost pl over 3f out: sn bhd and eased: virtually p.u* **40/1**

1m 26.7s (-0.70) **Going Correction** -0.025s/f (Good) 14 Ran SP% **122.4**
Speed ratings (Par 103): **103,100,100,98,98 94,90,89,83,83 80,77,74,42**
CSF £256.08 CT £4262.74 TOTE £40.80: £10.30, £3.70, £6.00; EX 515.50.
Owner Adrian Swingler **Bred** Phil Jen Racing **Trained** Carburton, Notts

FOCUS
A moderate handicap in which the winner and the eighth elected to race up the stands' side. The form makes sense at face value and looks pretty sound with the runner-up to his recent best.
King Harson Official explanation: jockey said gelding lost its action

2847 NEW COUNTY ROADS MAIDEN STKS 1m 2f 32y
7:50 (7:52) (Class 5) 3-Y-O+ **£3,238** (£963; £481; £240) **Stalls** Centre

Form RPR

62 **1** **Moonquake (USA)**[31] 1918 3-8-12 0........................ JimmyFortune 6 78+
(J H M Gosden) *trckd ldrs: smooth hdwy to go 2nd over 2f out: led over 1f out: pushed clr: eased towards fin* **2/5**[1]

0 **2** *2 1/4* **Dream Esteem**[9] 2528 3-8-7 0........................ PaulHanagan 1 66
(E J O'Neill) *chsd ldrs: wnt 2nd over 1f out: no ch w wnr* **20/1**

66 **3** *3/4* **Cyborg**[18] 2291 4-9-8 0........................ MarcHalford(3) 11 71
(D R C Elsworth) *hld up towards rr: hdwy over 2f out: wnt 3rd over 1f out: kpt on same pce* **10/1**[3]

02 **4** *3 1/4* **Always Cruising (USA)**[68] 1114 3-8-12 0........................ JoeFanning 5 63
(M Johnston) *mid-div: hdwy over 2f out: kpt on: nvr nr ldrs* **15/2**[2]

0 **5** *3* **Linby (IRE)**[20] 2221 3-8-12 0........................ DaleGibson 3 57
(N Tinkler) *s.i.s: bhd tl kpt on fnl 2f: nrst fin* **100/1**

6 *1* **Circus Clown (IRE)** 3-8-12 0........................ PhillipMakin 14 55
(Miss L A Perratt) *s.i.s: drvn 5f out: styd on fnl 2f: nvr nr ldrs* **33/1**

00- **7** *5* **Banquet (IRE)**[224] 6494 3-8-12 0........................ GrahamGibbons 9 45
(T D Walford) *chsd ldrs: wknd over 1f out* **33/1**

6 **8** *nk* **Lisbon Lion (IRE)**[16] 2336 3-8-12 0........................ AndrewElliott 10 44
(N J Vaughan) *led: clr over 5f out: hdd & wknd over 1f out* **25/1**

05 **9** *2* **Border Fox**[8] 2571 5-9-11 0........................ PaddyAspell 8 42
(L Lungo) *stdd s: t.k.h in rr: sme hdwy over 2f out: nvr on terms* **40/1**

10 *9* **Bertie Boo** 3-8-12 0........................ TomEaves 12 22
(B Smart) *in rr-div: sn pushed along: reminders over 3f out: sn bhd* **20/1**

0-0 **11** *1 1/2* **Three Gold Leaves**[9] 2528 3-8-12 0........................ J-PGuillambert 2 19
(J G Given) *chsd ldrs: wknd 2f out* **80/1**

0- **12** *1/2* **Endeavor**[248] 5904 3-8-9 0........................ PJMcDonald(3) 7 18
(P Monteith) *s.s: sme hdwy over 2f out: sn wknd* **100/1**

00 **13** *3/4* **Osteopathic Care (IRE)**[21] 2207 4-9-8 0........................ JamieMoriarty(3) 13 16
(Miss Tracy Waggott) *in tch: drvn over 3f out: sn lost pl* **50/1**

2m 14.25s (2.35) **Going Correction** +0.15s/f (Good)
WFA 3 from 4yo+ 13lb 13 Ran SP% **119.2**
Speed ratings (Par 103): **103,101,100,98,95 94,90,90,88,81 80,80,79**
CSF £14.40 TOTE £1.30: £1.02, £4.20, £2.70; EX 12.50.
Owner H R H Princess Haya Of Jordan **Bred** Stonestreet Mares Llc **Trained** Newmarket, Suffolk

FOCUS
The winner looked head and shoulders above the opposition and so it proved. He is value for four lengths but still 7lb below his best with the third setting the level and the form looks sound enough amongst the principals.

2848 NEW COUNTY ROADS PLANING H'CAP 1m 2f 32y
8:20 (8:21) (Class 5) (0-70,70) 4-Y-O+ **£3,238** (£722; £722; £240) **Stalls** Centre

Form RPR

-460 **1** **Trouble Mountain (USA)**[29] 1963 11-8-13 **62**.............(t) DaleGibson 10 68
(M W Easterby) *chsd ldrs: hrd drvn 6f out: rallied appr fnl f: styd on wl to ld nr fin* **8/1**

00-3 **2** *1/2* **Nesno (USA)**[15] 2365 5-8-11 **60**........................ JoeFanning 7 65
(J D Bethell) *w ldr: led over 2f out: hdd jst ins fnl f: regained ld last 75yds: hdd last strides* **5/1**[3]

/025 **2** *dht* **Calcutta Cup (UAE)**[28] 2001 5-8-9 **58**........................ TonyHamilton 5 63
(Karen McLintock) *trckd ldrs: led jst ins fnl f: hdd and no ex wl ins fnl f* **9/2**[2]

0/00 **4** *1 1/2* **Seyaadi**[11] 2483 6-8-11 **60**........................(v) RobertWinston 11 62
(Miss Tracy Waggott) *slowly away: t.k.h in rr: drvn over 3f out: hrd rdn and styd on fnl 2f: nt rch ldrs* **22/1**

0063 **5** *3/4* **Sforzando**[16] 2335 7-9-2 **65**........................ TomEaves 1 66
(Mrs L Stubbs) *mid-div: effrt 3f out: hrd rdn and styd on over 1f out: nt rch ldrs* **7/1**

00-0 **6** *1 1/2* **Camerooney**[31] 1913 5-8-2 **51** oh6........................ AndrewElliott 6 49
(A D Brown) *led tl over 2f out: one pce* **66/1**

04-0 **7** *1/2* **Jordan's Light (USA)**[9] 2524 5-8-10 **62**........................ PJMcDonald(3) 3 59
(P Monteith) *chsd ldrs: edgd rt and one pce fnl 2f* **20/1**

-031 **8** *1 1/4* **Dechiper (IRE)**[15] 2365 6-8-10 **66**........................ PatrickDonaghy(7) 4 60
(R Johnson) *hld up in rr: sme hdwy 4f out: drvn over 2f out: nvr a factor* **5/2**[1]

/-15 **9** *nse* **Twilight Dawn**[38] 1732 4-9-7 **70**........................ PaddyAspell 9 64
(L Lungo) *hld up in rr: hdwy over 2f out: hrd rdn over 1f out: nvr nr ldrs* **20/1**

2-52 **10** *7* **Titinius (IRE)**[12] 2446 8-9-1 **64**........................ PaulHanagan 8 44
(Micky Hammond) *mid-div: drvn along over 5f out: nvr a threat: wknd and eased 1f out* **13/2**

2m 14.38s (2.48) **Going Correction** +0.15s/f (Good) 10 Ran SP% **115.7**
Speed ratings (Par 103): **102,101,101,100,99 98,98,97,97,91**
WIN: £12.50; PL: Trouble Mountain £2.90, Nesno £2.50, Calcutta Cup £1.80; EX: Nesno £36.80, Calcutta Cup £30.00; CSF: Nesno £22.48, Calcutta Cup £20.70; TRICAST: Nesno £101.95, Calcutta Cup £100.19.
Owner Mrs Jean Turpin **Bred** Robert B Berger **Trained** Sheriff Hutton, N Yorks

FOCUS
A modest handicap in which the form is a bit messy and somewhat limited on a line through the sixth.
Dechiper(IRE) Official explanation: trainer had no explanation for the poor form shown

Titinius(IRE) Official explanation: jockey said gelding hung left throughout

2849 NEW COUNTY ROADS TRAFFIC MANAGEMENT H'CAP 2m 19y
8:50 (8:50) (Class 6) (0-65,65) 4-Y-0+ **£2,590** (£770; £385; £192) **Stalls** Low

Form RPR
60-0 **1** **Sendali (FR)**[15] 2364 4-8-6 **47** ow1 .... GrahamGibbons 9 57
(J D Bethell) *hld up in rr: hdwy over 3f out: led 1f out: hld on towards fin* **16/1**
116 **2** ½ **Cavendish**[26] 2051 4-9-10 **65** ....(b) RobertWinston 12 74
(J M P Eustace) *hld up in rr: rapid hdwy to ld over 2f out: sn hrd rdn and hung lft: hdd 1f out: no ex wl ins fnl f* **7/1**[3]
3-44 **3** 2 **Forrest Flyer (IRE)**[22] 2157 4-8-7 **48** ow1 .... TomEaves 4 55
(Miss L A Perratt) *hld up wl in tch: hdwy to chse ldrs over 2f out: keeping on same pce whn crowded ins fnl f* **5/1**[2]
0-00 **4** 3½ **Let It Be**[12] 2467 7-9-4 **58** .... PhillipMakin 5 61
(K G Reveley) *hld up in rr: hdwy over 2f out: kpt on one pce* **9/1**
-605 **5** 2¾ **San Deng**[8] 2579 6-8-13 **53** .... PaulHanagan 1 53
(Micky Hammond) *hld up in midfield: effrt 3f out: one pce* **10/1**
32-R **6** 4½ **Kristiansand**[10] 2157 8-8-13 **56** .... PJMcDonald(3) 3 50
(P Monteith) *hld up in rr-div: hdwy 6f out: wknd 2f out* **10/1**
0-00 **7** 3½ **Don Jose (USA)**[8] 2572 5-8-5 **45** ....(e) DaleGibson 2 35
(N J Vaughan) *chsd ldrs: drvn 9f out: hrd rdn and chal over 2f out: sn wknd* **33/1**
-246 **8** 2¾ **Toboggan Lady**[8] 2572 4-9-6 **61** .... RoystonFfrench 7 48
(Mrs A Duffield) *prom: pushed along 7f out: lost pl 2f out* **15/8**[1]
50-0 **9** 8 **Apsara**[12] 2467 7-8-10 **50** .... JoeFanning 10 27
(G M Moore) *led: qcknd 10f out: hdd over 2f out: sn lost pl* **25/1**
00/0 **10** ½ **Lodgician (IRE)**[21] 2185 6-9-2 **56** .... TonyHamilton 6 32
(K G Reveley) *in rr: drvn over 5f out: bhd fnl 3f* **22/1**
01/6 **11** 18 **Skit**[46] 1551 5-8-2 **45** .... DuranFentiman(3) 8 —
(W M Brisbourne) *sn chsng ldrs: drvn over 4f out: wknd 3f out: sn bhd and eased* **14/1**
0-50 **12** 9 **Foxxy**[12] 2467 4-8-4 **45** .... AndrewElliott 11 —
(J R Norton) *sn chsng ldrs: drvn 8f out: chal 4f out: wknd over 2f out: sn bhd and eased* **20/1**

3m 39.35s (3.15) **Going Correction** +0.15s/f (Good)
WFA 4 from 5yo+ 1lb **12 Ran SP% 120.6**
Speed ratings (Par 101): **98,97,96,95,93 91,89,88,84,84 75,70**
CSF £120.03 CT £656.01 TOTE £27.70: £4.90, £3.40, £2.30; EX 189.00.
Owner Elliott Brothers **Bred** Sarl Haras Du Taillis Et Al **Trained** Middleham Moor, N Yorks

FOCUS
A low-grade handicap run at a sound pace and the form looks sound rated through the third.

2850 NEW-COUNTY.CO.UK H'CAP 5f
9:20 (9:21) (Class 5) (0-75,72) 3-Y-0 **£3,238** (£963; £481; £240) **Stalls** Low

Form RPR
23-2 **1** **Wotashirtfull (IRE)**[19] 2240 3-9-4 **72** ....(p) JamieMoriarty(3) 2 79
(K A Ryan) *mde all: 4l clr over 1f out: rdn rt out: unchal* **7/2**[1]
-522 **2** 1 **Kyzer Chief**[14] 2396 3-8-9 **60** .... RoystonFfrench 8 63
(R E Barr) *racd wd: chsd ldrs: wnt 2nd and hung lft over 3f out: kpt on fnl f: nvr able to chal* **5/1**[3]
-115 **3** nk **Big Slick (IRE)**[5] 2661 3-8-9 **60** .... TWilliams 7 62
(M Brittain) *chsd ldrs: styd on same pce fnl f* **9/2**[2]
0-63 **4** ½ **Grudge**[14] 2396 3-9-1 **66** .... TonyHamilton 1 66
(D W Barker) *dwlt: in rr and sn drvn along: hdwy over 1f out: kpt on wl* **8/1**
0-03 **5** 1¼ **Embra (IRE)**[18] 2283 3-8-7 **61** ow1 .... PJMcDonald(3) 6 57
(T J Etherington) *dwlt: outpcd and bhd tl kpt on fnl f* **6/1**
5303 **6** shd **Second Opinion (IRE)**[7] 2616 3-8-12 **63** .... TomEaves 5 58
(J M P Eustace) *sn outpcd: hdwy 2f out: kpt on: nvr trbld ldrs* **7/1**
-400 **7** 1¾ **Select Committee**[11] 2490 3-8-8 **59** .... GrahamGibbons 3 48
(J J Quinn) *chsd ldrs: rdn over 2f out: fdd fnl f* **6/1**
-210 **8** 2½ **Flying Indian**[11] 2490 3-9-0 **65** .... RobertWinston 4 45
(J Balding) *chsd ldrs: lost pl over 1f out* **9/1**

61.77 secs (1.07) **Going Correction** -0.075s/f (Good) **8 Ran SP% 119.3**
Speed ratings (Par 99): **88,86,85,85,83 82,80,76**
CSF £22.17 CT £81.81 TOTE £3.80: £2.10, £1.20, £1.90; EX 16.30 Place 6 £174.56, Place 5 £104.88.
Owner Sporting Gunners Syndicate Two **Bred** Luke O'Reilly **Trained** Hambleton, N Yorks

FOCUS
A modest handicap run in a slow time but the form makes sense rated around the next four home behind the winner.
T/Plt: £326.60 to a £1 stake. Pool: £56,931.50. 127.25 winning tickets. T/Qpdt: £10.90 to a £1 stake. Pool: £4,572.80. 309.80 winning tickets. WG

2851 - 2857a (Foreign Racing) - See Raceform Interactive

BELMONT PARK (L-H)
Saturday, June 7

OFFICIAL GOING: Turd course - firm; dirt course - fast

2858a BELMONT STKS (GRADE 1) (DIRT) 1m 4f (D)
11:25 (11:31) 3-Y-0
£301,508 (£100,503; £42,714; £42,714; £15,075; £3,350)

RPR
1 **Da' Tara (USA)**[21] 3-9-0 .... AGarcia 5 115
(N Zito, U.S.A) *made all, ridden clear well over 2f out, driven out* **77/2**
2 5¼ **Denis Of Cork (USA)**[35] 1820 3-9-0 .... RAlbarado 4 107
(David M Carroll, U.S.A) *held up in 6th, headway 3f out, 2nd straight, kept on same pace* **72/10**[2]
3 2¾ **Ready's Echo (USA)**[28] 3-9-0 .... JRVelazquez 8 103
(Todd Pletcher, U.S.A) *outpaced & in rear til making headway on outside over 2f out, 6th straight, kept on steadily* **29/1**
3 dht **Anak Nakal (USA)**[35] 1820 3-9-0 .... JRLeparoux 7 103
(N Zito, U.S.A) *disputing 3rd on outside when carried wide on first turn, settled in 4th, went 3rd 3f out, soon one pace* **34/1**
5 3 **Macho Again (USA)**[21] 2215 3-9-0 ....(b) GKGomez 3 99
(Dallas Stewart, U.S.A) *raced in 5th, some progress on final turn, soon one pace* **174/10**
6 7¼ **Tale Of Ekati (USA)**[35] 1820 3-9-0 .... ECoa 6 88
(B Tagg, U.S.A) *tracked winner til weakening over 2f out* **29/2**[3]
7 6½ **Guadalcanal (USA)**[15] 3-9-0 .... JCastellano 2 78
(Frederick J Seitz, U.S.A) *stumbled start, always in rear* **25/1**
8 ½ **Icabad Crane (USA)**[21] 2215 3-9-0 .... JRose 9 77
(H Graham Motion, U.S.A) *always in rear* **17/1**
9 dist **Big Brown (USA)**[21] 2215 3-9-0 .... KDesormeaux 1 —
(Richard Dutrow Jr, U.S.A) *went right start, racing in 3rd & pulling when moved outside & bumped Anak Nakal on first turn, still 3rd until weakening quickly 3f out, pulled up* **30/100**[1]

2m 29.65s (0.69) **9 Ran SP% 119.1**
PARI-MUTUEL: WIN 79.00; PL (1-2) 28.00, 5.40; SHOW (1-2-3) 14.80, 4.10, 7.60 (Anak Nakal), 6.20 (Ready's Echo); SF 659.00.
Owner Robert V LaPenta **Bred** WinStar Farm LLC **Trained** USA

NOTEBOOK
Da' Tara(USA), who had won just once in his seven previous starts, made all the running and never looked like being caught in the straight. A son of Tiznow, his trainer reported that he is a late-developing sort who is improving with racing and time may show that, although this was a surprise, it was no fluke.
Big Brown(USA), bidding to become the first Triple Crown winner since Affirmed thirty years before, had suffered a cracked hoof since the Preakness but did not appear inconvenienced by it and went off at prohibitive odds. However, he was never going that well despite racing prominently, and eventually dropped right away. His rider looked after him once he was beaten and there was no obvious physical reason for his disappointment apparent immediately after the race.

2554 BRIGHTON (L-H)
Sunday, June 8

OFFICIAL GOING: Good to firm (8.5)
Wind: Moderate, against Weather: Sunny and warm

2859 E B F BE IN THE GAME - BETLIVE@WILLIAMHILL.COM NOVICE MEDIAN AUCTION STKS 5f 213y
2:30 (2:31) (Class 5) 2-Y-0 **£3,302** (£982; £368; £368) **Stalls** Low

Form RPR
22 **1** **The Dial House**[39] 1722 2-8-12 .... ShaneKelly 6 77
(J A Osborne) *stdd s: hld up in rr: rdn 3f out: hdwy 2f out: drvn to take narrow ld fnl 100yds* **6/4**[1]
254 **2** nk **Rio Royale (IRE)**[9] 2554 2-8-12 .... JimCrowley 4 76
(Mrs A J Perrett) *led: rdn wl over 1f out: hld on wl tl fnl 100yds: kpt on gamely* **7/1**
301 **3** 1½ **Asian Tale (IRE)**[13] 2459 2-8-11 .... SteveDrowne 3 72+
(A B Haynes) *s.s: bhd: rdn to chse ldrs ins fnl 2f: one pce fnl f* **4/1**[3]
4212 **3** dht **In Transit (IRE)**[4] 2713 2-8-11 .... MCGeran(7) 5 80+
(M R Channon) *trckd ldng pair: drvn along and outpcd whn n.m.r fr 2f out tl over 1f out: kpt on fnl f* **7/4**[2]
00 **5** 3¼ **Hatchet Man**[17] 2324 2-8-12 .... StephenCarson 2 62
(P Winkworth) *rdn leaving stalls to chse ldr: hung bdly lft and faltered 2f out: sn lost pl* **33/1**

1m 10.81s (0.61) **Going Correction** -0.05s/f (Good) **5 Ran SP% 111.8**
Speed ratings (Par 93): **93,92,90,90,86**
CSF £12.33 TOTE £2.20: £1.40, £2.30; EX 15.40.
Owner Martyn and Elaine Booth **Bred** Mrs E L Hunter **Trained** Upper Lambourn, Berks

FOCUS
An ordinary race of its type, but they went a good gallop. The form is rated around the principals.

NOTEBOOK
The Dial House gained his reward for finishing second in his first two races, with the extra furlong working in his favour. However, he took his time to get past the runner-up and was never able to shake him off, so this is probably as good as he is. (op 2-1)
Rio Royale(IRE) ran a brave race in defeat, making the favourite work hard for his victory. He can win a maiden or nursery. (op 11-2)
Asian Tale(IRE) gets the 6f well enough, but she had won a claimer last time and was just a shade outclassed here. (tchd 13-8 and 15-8 in a place)
In Transit(IRE) was short of room as the race developed from the 2f pole, but that was largely his own doing as he did not have the pace to hold his position at the time. Though he kept on reasonably well when in the clear, he was not an unlucky loser. (tchd 13-8 and 15-8 in a place)
Hatchet Man did not look happy on the camber when coming under pressure, and looks more a low-grade nursery type. Official explanation: jockey said colt hung left (op 20-1)

2860 GET YOUR BALLS AT WILLIAMHILLBINGO.COM H'CAP 6f 209y
3:00 (3:02) (Class 5) (0-75,74) 4-Y-0+ **£2,590** (£770; £385; £192) **Stalls** Low

Form RPR
505- **1** **Perfect Treasure (IRE)**[209] 6795 5-9-6 **73** .... RyanMoore 4 85
(J A R Toller) *hld up in 6th: effrt and drvn along ins fnl 2f: styd on to ld ins fnl f: won gng away* **10/3**[2]
020- **2** 2½ **Ede's Dot Com (IRE)**[229] 6406 4-8-9 **62** .... IanMongan 3 67
(P M Phelan) *chsd ldng pair: drvn to ld 1f out: hdd and nt pce of wnr ins fnl f* **20/1**
0531 **3** nk **Councellor (FR)**[17] 2329 6-9-7 **74** ....(t) MickyFenton 8 78
(Stef Liddiard) *chsd ldr: rdn over 2f out: lost 2nd pl 1f out: one pce* **10/3**[2]
1013 **4** 1 **Napoletano (GER)**[3] 2758 7-8-9 **62** ....(p) SteveDrowne 1 63
(S Dow) *stdd s: bhd: rdn and styd on fnl 2f: nt pce to chal* **11/4**[1]
0-61 **5** 2½ **Buy On The Red**[20] 2242 7-9-6 **73** .... MartinDwyer 7 68
(W R Muir) *racd in 5th: effrt and in tch 2f out: hrd rdn and wknd over 1f out* **8/1**
3312 **6** nk **The Jailer**[9] 2556 5-8-1 **61** ....(p) MCGeran(7) 2 55
(J G M O'Shea) *led and set gd pce: hdd & wknd 1f out* **11/2**[3]
5124 **7** 1¾ **Unlimited**[20] 2243 6-9-0 **67** .... JimCrowley 6 56
(A W Carroll) *racd in 4th tl hrd rdn and wknd 2f out* **8/1**

1m 20.97s (-2.13) **Going Correction** -0.05s/f (Good) **7 Ran SP% 115.2**
Speed ratings (Par 103): **110,107,106,105,102 102,100**
CSF £62.20 CT £238.94 TOTE £4.40: £2.60, £6.00; EX 90.30 Trifecta £160.50 Pool £228.38 - 1.01 winning units..
Owner John Drew **Bred** Patrick F Kelly **Trained** Newmarket, Suffolk

FOCUS
A fair race for the track, run at a blistering pace. Solid form.

2861 MAKING SPORT MORE EXCITING - BETLIVE@WILLIAMHILL.COM (S) STKS 6f 209y
3:30 (3:31) (Class 6) 3-Y-0+ **£1,748** (£520; £260; £129) **Stalls** Low

Form RPR
50-0 **1** **Mannello**[6] 2664 5-9-2 **50** ....(b) RichardThomas 6 59
(Jim Best) *in tch: squeezed out over 2f out: swtchd outside and rallied over 1f out: styd on to ld fnl 50yds* **16/1**
0403 **2** nk **Corlough Mountain**[9] 2557 4-9-7 **66** ....(p) ShaneKelly 2 63
(M J McGrath) *prom: led over 2f out: hrd rdn and kpt on fnl f: hdd fnl 50yds* **5/2**[2]
0040 **3** 1¼ **Split The Wind (USA)**[11] 2510 4-9-2 **50** ....(b[1]) StephenCarson 1 55
(Eve Johnson Houghton) *led 2f: chsd ldrs after: drvn to chal fnl 2f: nt qckn fnl 100yds* **10/1**

4-34 **4** ¾ **Million Percent**[3] 2753 9-9-7 67 LPKeniry 3 58
(C R Dore) *in tch: hmpd over 2f out: drvn to chal over 1f out: one pce fnl 100yds* 9/4[1]
-666 **5** 3 **Border Artist**[16] 2355 9-9-7 55 MickyFenton 5 50
(J Pearce) *settled towards rr: nt clr run and swtchd lft over 2f out: rdn and styd on: nt rch ldrs* 13/2
5400 **6** 1 **Film Queen (IRE)**[8] 2597 4-9-2 50 IanMongan 10 42
(Mrs L J Mongan) *bhd: drvn along over 2f out: sme late hdwy* 6/1[3]
2600 **7** ½ **Inontime (IRE)**[27] 2052 3-8-6 60 AndrewElliott 7 41
(K R Burke) *chsd ldrs: chal over 2f out: wknd wl over 1f out* 14/1
6300 **8** 4 ½ **Gifted Flame**[2] 2782 9-9-2 45 AnnStokell(5) 4 34
(Miss A Stokell) *stdd s: hld up in rr: sme hdwy on rail 2f out: wknd over 1f out: eased whn btn* 33/1
2P00 **9** 14 **Herrbee (IRE)**[8] 2611 3-8-4 42 (p) ThomasO'Brien(7) 9 —
(P Butler) *towards rr: drvn along 3f out: nvr trbld ldrs* 33/1
5000 **10** 3 **Golden Spectrum (IRE)**[33] 1895 9-9-0 40 (b) DavidProbert(7) 8 —
(R A Harris) *chsd ldr: led after 2f tl wknd over 2f out* 20/1

1m 22.42s (-0.68) **Going Correction** -0.05s/f (Good)
WFA 3 from 4yo+ 10lb 10 Ran SP% 119.2
Speed ratings (Par 101): **101,100,99,98,94 93,93,88,72,68**
CSF £56.40 TOTE £22.60: £4.20, £1.60, £2.10; EX 88.20 Trifecta £138.40 Part won. Pool £195.04 - 0.50 winning units..There was no bid for the winner. Corlough Mountain was claimed by P. Butler for £5,000.
Owner The Ace Partnership **Bred** Richard Moses **Trained** Lewes, E Sussex
FOCUS
A routine seller, with the winner scoring at the 26th attempt. The form is unlikely to prove too reliable.

2862 GET YOUR CHIPS @ WILLIAMHILLCASINO.COM MAIDEN STKS 1m 3f 196y
4:00 (4:01) (Class 5) 3-Y-O+ £2,525 (£751; £375; £187) Stalls High

Form RPR
4 **1** **Bell Island**[46] 1563 4-9-13 73 RichardKingscote 7 83
(Lady Herries) *chsd ldr: led 3f out: maintained narrow ld mainly under hands and heels: edgd lft fnl f: hld on gamely* 16/1
3-23 **2** nk **Shy**[10] 2528 3-8-7 72 StephenCarson 2 78
(P Winkworth) *led tl 3f out: kpt on gamely u.p and continued to press wnr: a narrowly hld* 8/1
56- **3** 4 ½ **Flam**[226] 6470 3-8-7 JimCrowley 6 71
(J R Fanshawe) *hld up in rr: 5th and rdn 4f out: kpt on to go 3rd ins fnl f: nt trble first two* 11/4[2]
20-2 **4** 2 ¼ **Baraari (USA)**[29] 2015 3-8-7 75 MartinDwyer 5 67
(J L Dunlop) *hld up in 4th: rdn to go 3rd over 2f out: nt pce to stay in tch w first two* 6/1[3]
0-3 **5** 15 **Ucetek (IRE)**[24] 2119 3-8-7 RyanMoore 3 43+
(Sir Michael Stoute) *awkward s: sn trcking ldng pair: shkn up and unbalanced on trck ins fnl 3f: lost action and eased 2f out* 10/11[1]
00 **6** 2 **Black Cloud**[31] 1931 5-9-6 HarryPoulton(7) 4 45
(A Ennis) *dwlt: hld up in rr: lost tch 5f out: drvn and no ch fnl 3f* 100/1
7 15 **Prince Joshua** 3-8-12 ChrisCatlin 1 21
(J Jay) *dwlt and wnt lft s: mainly 5th tl dropped to last 1/2-way: sn wl bhd* 50/1

2m 32.34s (-0.36) **Going Correction** -0.05s/f (Good)
WFA 3 from 4yo+ 15lb 7 Ran SP% 113.3
Speed ratings (Par 103): **99,98,95,94,84 82,72**
CSF £130.03 TOTE £21.60: £6.20, £3.00; EX 137.70.
Owner L G Lazarus **Bred** Juddmonte Farms Ltd **Trained** Patching, W Sussex
FOCUS
Probably only an ordinary maiden, weakened by the favourite not runing his race, but there should be better to come from the winner. The pace was weak until halfway.
Ucetek(IRE) Official explanation: jockey said filly hung badly left throughout

2863 GET ON WITH HILLS - 0800 44 40 40 H'CAP 1m 1f 209y
4:30 (4:31) (Class 6) (0-65,63) 4-Y-O+ £1,942 (£578; £288; £144) Stalls High

Form RPR
0-23 **1** **Astrolibra**[16] 2353 4-8-2 51 AshleyMorgan(7) 4 57
(M H Tompkins) *towards rr: hrd rdn 2f out: hdwy over 1f out: r.o to ld fnl strides* 9/2[3]
5662 **2** hd **Zach's Harmoney (USA)**[12] 2483 4-9-7 63 ChrisCatlin 9 69
(P W Hiatt) *led: hrd rdn and hld on gamely fnl 2f tl ct fnl strides* 10/3[1]
3500 **3** 1 ¾ **Prince Valentine**[16] 2353 7-8-8 50 (p) RyanMoore 1 52
(G L Moore) *hld up and bhd: plld wd and r.o wl fnl 2f: nt rch first two* 9/2[3]
0030 **4** 2 **Princess Flame (GER)**[17] 2336 6-9-1 57 JimCrowley 3 55
(B G Powell) *in tch: lost pl over 4f out: drvn along over 2f out: rallied and r.o fr over 1f out* 12/1
0030 **5** 1 ¼ **Tuscan Treaty**[26] 2072 8-8-3 45 (t) NickyMackay 6 41
(R W Price) *stdd s: sn cl up: jnd ldrs 3f out: wknd over 1f out* 33/1
3431 **6** 1 ¼ **Pab Special (IRE)**[16] 2352 5-9-2 58 RichardSmith 5 51
(B R Johnson) *t.k.h in midfield: drvn and in tch 2f out: no ex* 4/1[2]
050- **7** ½ **Surdoue**[214] 6713 8-8-3 45 AdrianMcCarthy 8 37
(J G M O'Shea) *t.k.h: chsd ldr: chal 2f out: wknd 1f out* 33/1
0304 **8** 1 ½ **Granary Girl**[16] 2353 6-7-12 47 JosephineBruning(7) 7 36
(J Pearce) *prom tl hrd rdn and wknd over 2f out* 12/1
0035 **9** 1 ½ **Personify**[16] 2353 6-8-9 51 ow2 (p) TGMcLaughlin 2 37
(R A Harris) *towards rr: mod effrt on outside over 2f out: sn wknd* 5/1

2m 2.70s (-0.90) **Going Correction** -0.05s/f (Good) 9 Ran SP% 117.4
Speed ratings (Par 101): **101,100,99,97,96 95,95,94,93**
CSF £20.28 CT £70.49 TOTE £5.10: £1.60, £1.80, £2.10; EX 21.80 Trifecta £38.70 Pool £421.74 - 7.73 winning units..
Owner Mystic Meg Limited **Bred** Mystic Meg Limited **Trained** Newmarket, Suffolk
FOCUS
A weak handicap. The form is rated through the second and fourth.

2864 EVERY MINUTE, EVERY MATCH BETLIVE@WILLIAMHILL.COM H'CAP 5f 59y
5:00 (5:00) (Class 5) (0-70,72) 3-Y-O £2,590 (£770; £385; £192) Stalls Low

Form RPR
0621 **1** **Speedy Senorita (IRE)**[10] 2527 3-9-1 64 AndrewElliott 8 68
(K R Burke) *mde all: rdn and hld on wl fnl 2f* 15/8[1]
5006 **2** ¾ **Shatter Resistant (IRE)**[10] 2551 3-8-5 54 (e) ChrisCatlin 6 55
(M D Squance) *in tch: chal 2f out: kpt on fnl f* 8/1
4-01 **3** 1 **Brazilian Brush (IRE)**[8] 2602 3-9-9 72 (t) SteveDrowne 1 70
(H Morrison) *prom: hmpd on rail after 1f: swtchd outside and rallied 1f out: r.o* 11/4[2]
5310 **4** ¾ **Jal Music**[20] 2255 3-9-6 69 TGMcLaughlin 4 64
(R A Harris) *sn chsng wnr: hrd rdn 2f out: one pce appr fnl f* 14/1
3401 **5** 1 ¼ **Midnite Blews (IRE)**[2] 2771 3-8-11 67 6ex PNolan(7) 5 58
(A B Haynes) *s.s: bhd: hdwy and hung bdly lft over 1f out: nt rch ldrs* 12/1
0-00 **6** 3 ¼ **Elizabeth's Quest**[13] 2452 3-7-11 53 SophieDoyle(7) 2 32
(A W Carroll) *sn outpcd at hd of rr gp: n.d* 16/1
3240 **7** ¾ **Jalons Bridewell**[24] 2122 3-9-4 67 ShaneKelly 9 43
(M Quinn) *t.k.h: prom tl wknd 2f out* 14/1
000- **8** 3 ¾ **Defnikov**[251] 5856 3-8-2 51 oh6 DavidKinsella 7 14
(A B Haynes) *dwlt: a bhd: no ch fnl 2f* 50/1
1025 **9** 1 ½ **Ben**[8] 2602 3-9-0 63 (v) MartinDwyer 3 20
(P G Murphy) *s.s: bhd: drvn along and modest effrt 2f out: sn wknd* 4/1[3]

62.19 secs (-0.11) **Going Correction** -0.05s/f (Good) 9 Ran SP% 121.4
Speed ratings (Par 99): **98,96,95,94,92 86,85,79,77**
CSF £19.29 CT £43.20 TOTE £2.80: £1.10, £2.60, £1.70; EX 20.60 Trifecta £79.00 Pool £368.32 - 3.31 winning units..
Owner Market Avenue Racing Club Ltd **Bred** R McEnery And Vincent Millett **Trained** Middleham Moor, N Yorks
FOCUS
A moderate sprint handicap, but the pace was strong. The form is rated through the placed horses.
Jal Music Official explanation: jockey said gelding hung left from the gate
Defnikov Official explanation: jockey said gelding hung right-handed throughout
T/Plt: £1,180.30 to a £1 stake. Pool: £72,197.00. 44.65 winning tickets. T/Qpdt: £70.00 to a £1 stake. Pool: £4,601.00. 48.60 winning tickets. LM

2702 SOUTHWELL (L-H)
Sunday, June 8

OFFICIAL GOING: Standard
Wind: Light, across Weather: fine, sunny and very warm

2865 REDUCE GLARE WITH PINDERS OPTOMETRISTS MAIDEN AUCTION FILLIES' STKS 5f (F)
2:10 (2:10) (Class 5) 2-Y-O £2,456 (£725; £362) Stalls High

Form RPR
1 **Excellerator (IRE)** 2-8-10 0 TedDurcan 7 74+
(George Baker) *sn trcking ldrs: led over 2f out: edgd lft fnl f: drvn out* 5/4[1]
6 **2** 3 **Hip Hip Hooray**[27] 2048 2-8-6 0 RichardMullen 6 55+
(E S McMahon) *dwlt: sn drvn along: hdwy and swtchd rt over 1f out: kpt on to take 2nd nr fin* 9/2[2]
0 **3** ½ **Bold Rose**[30] 1961 2-8-4 0 (t) PaulHanagan 5 51
(M D I Usher) *led tl over 2f out: kpt on same pce* 40/1
3 **4** nk **Eden Park**[32] 1907 2-8-10 0 PhillipMakin 2 56
(M Dods) *w ldrs: kpt on same pce appr fnl f* 12/1
5 3 ¼ **First Choice (IRE)** 2-8-10 0 PaulMulrennan 9 42
(K A Ryan) *w ldrs: t.k.h: wknd over 1f out* 7/1[3]
2530 **6** 1 **Dispol Mulofky (IRE)**[21] 2217 2-8-4 0 FrankieMcDonald 4 33
(P T Midgley) *chsd ldrs: rdn: outpcd and lost pl over 2f out: kpt on fnl f* 8/1
0 **7** 1 ¾ **Rocket Ruby**[14] 2424 2-8-1 0 DuranFentiman(3) 1 27
(D Shaw) *chsd ldrs: wknd over 1f out* 9/1
3265 **8** 17 **Meg Jicaro**[12] 2473 2-8-5 0 ow4 TolleyDean(3) 8 —
(Mrs L Williamson) *chsd ldrs: lost pl over 1f out: heavily eased* 9/1
9 6 **Fantasies (IRE)** 2-8-4 0 RoystonFfrench 3 —
(Garry Moss) *s.s: sn bhd: eased fnl f* 66/1

60.81 secs (1.11) **Going Correction** +0.025s/f (Slow) 9 Ran SP% 117.9
Speed ratings (Par 90): **92,87,86,85,79 78,75,48,38**
CSF £7.12 TOTE £2.00: £1.10, £2.10, £3.90; EX 9.20.
Owner The Excellerators **Bred** E Landi **Trained** Moreton Morrell, Warwicks
FOCUS
A modest maiden auction fillies' race but a well backed winner in the newcomer Excellerator who should be capable of much better.
NOTEBOOK
Excellerator(IRE) has some size about her. She clearly knew her job and came clear despite drifting towards the far side. She was all the rage in the betting and had clearly been showing plenty at home ahead of this debut effort. (op 15-8)
Hip Hip Hooray, who gave problems being mounted, is an habitual tail-swisher. She stayed on under strong driving after a tardy start and is crying out for a sixth furlong. (op 4-1 tchd 5-1)
Bold Rose, fitted with a tongue tie this time, took them along to halfway but the winner was different class. (op 25-1)
Eden Park, a well beaten third in fair company on her debut, showed plenty of dash and should improve again. (op 10-1)
First Choice(IRE), a close-coupled January foal, was very keen on her debut and did not last home. (tchd 8-1)
Dispol Mulofky(IRE), dropping back to five on her fifth outing, was badly tapped for toe at the halfway mark. (tchd 10-1)

2866 SHANE W DARBY MEMORIAL (S) H'CAP 7f (F)
2:40 (2:41) (Class 6) (0-60,60) 4-Y-O+ £1,774 (£523; £262) Stalls Low

Form RPR
2642 **1** **Elusive Warrior (USA)**[5] 2703 5-9-4 60 (p) JamesDoyle 9 72
(A J McCabe) *mde all: qcknd 3f out: clr over 1f out: rdn out* 9/4[1]
0003 **2** 2 ¾ **Ugenius**[5] 2703 4-8-5 50 KevinGhunowa(3) 8 54
(P A Blockley) *sn chsng ldrs: wnt 2nd over 1f out: kpt on: no threat* 4/1[2]
400/ **3** 6 **Uncle Bulgaria (IRE)**[947] 6247 6-8-13 55 SebSanders 6 43
(G C Bravery) *chsd ldrs: one pce fnl 2f* 7/1[3]
0-00 **4** ¾ **Crafty Fox**[13] 2463 5-8-4 46 oh1 (v) FrankieMcDonald 5 32
(John A Harris) *chsd ldrs: one pce fnl 3f* 25/1
4056 **5** 2 **Hi Spec (IRE)**[33] 1906 5-8-4 46 oh1 (p) GregFairley 1 27
(Miss M E Rowland) *mid-div: swtchd rt over 1f out: kpt on* 20/1
0030 **6** 1 ¾ **Union Jack Jackson (IRE)**[3] 2751 6-8-4 46 oh1 (b) DaleGibson 4 22
(John A Harris) *trckd ldrs: effrt over 2f out: one pce* 9/1
1/00 **7** 2 **Dance In Style**[10] 2523 7-8-4 46 RoystonFfrench 12 16
(A Crook) *chsd ldrs: outpcd 3f out: wknd over 1f out* 20/1
000- **8** 2 ¼ **Jellytot (USA)**[309] 4180 5-8-7 49 CatherineGannon 14 13
(J O'Reilly) *t.k.h on outside: lost pl over 4f out* 33/1
3600 **9** ½ **Goodbye Cash (IRE)**[35] 1842 4-8-12 54 TomEaves 11 17
(P D Evans) *in rr: kpt on fnl 2f: nvr on terms* 16/1
0440 **10** nk **Cabourg (IRE)**[55] 1371 5-8-11 53 RobertWinston 2 15
(R Bastiman) *chsd ldrs on inner: n.m.r and lost pl after 1f: swvd rt over 2f out* 8/1
0-00 **11** 1 ¾ **Murdoch**[33] 1898 4-8-10 52 RichardMullen 10 9
(E S McMahon) *chsd ldrs on outer: lost pl 3f out* 25/1
0640 **12** nk **Pajada**[12] 2474 4-7-11 46 oh1 (be) JustinaKay(7) 7 3
(M D I Usher) *in tch: lost pl over 4f out: sn bhd* 33/1
3506 **13** 3 ¼ **Compulsion**[67] 1150 5-8-8 50 PaulHanagan 3 —
(Pat Eddery) *lost pl over 4f out: sn bhd* 11/1

40-0 **14** *21* **Domesday (UAE)**[37] 1775 7-8-1 **46**......................(p) DuranFentiman(3) 13 —
(W G Harrison) *chsd ldrs on outer: lost pl over 4f out: sn bhd: t.o* **16/1**

1m 29.97s (-0.33) **Going Correction** +0.025s/f (Slow) **14** Ran SP% **127.6**
Speed ratings (Par 101): **102,98,92,91,88 86,84,82,81,81 79,78,75,51**
CSF £10.07 CT £58.01 TOTE £2.80: £1.60, £2.80, £3.10; EX 13.60.The winner was bought in for 6,500gns. Ugenius was claimed by Mr George Prodromou for £5,500.
Owner Paul J Dixon & Brian Morton **Bred** Steve Peskoff **Trained** Babworth, Notts

FOCUS
A weak selling handicap and in effect only really concerning the first two.
Cabourg(IRE) Official explanation: trainer said gelding was struck into

2867 LOOK SMART WITH PINDERS OPTOMETRISTS CLAIMING STKS 1m 4f (F)
3:10 (3:10) (Class 5) 3-Y-O+ **£2,456** (£725; £362) **Stalls** Low

Form RPR
1064 **1** **Novestar (IRE)**[8] 2613 3-8-5 58.............................. KevinGhunowa(3) 12 73
(G J Smith) *chsd ldr: led over 5f out: kpt on wl fnl f* **16/1**
324 **2** *3 3/4* **Black Falcon (IRE)**[29] 2001 8-9-4 73.............................. SebSanders 4 62
(M A Peill) *hld up: hdwy 6f out: wnt 2nd over 2f out: sn rdn and no real imp* **5/2**[2]
1122 **3** *7* **Yakimov (USA)**[26] 2083 9-9-13 85.............................. TPQueally 6 60
(Ollie Pears) *hld up in rr: hdwy on outside 5f out: sn chsng ldrs: kpt on same pce fnl 2f* **6/4**[1]
2030 **4** *3/4* **Starcross Maid**[19] 2290 6-8-8 51.............................. MarkCoumbe(7) 8 47
(J F Coupland) *hld up in rr: hdwy 5f out: chsng ldrs over 3f out: one pce fnl 2f* **14/1**
0202 **5** *9* **Kanisorn (SWE)**[17] 1702 6-9-6 63..............................(vt) TolleyDean(3) 13 40
(Mike Hammond) *in rr: reminders 7f out: kpt on fnl 2f: nvr on terms* **16/1**
/400 **6** *1 1/4* **Rehearsal**[23] 2155 7-9-13 73.............................. PaulHanagan 10 42
(L Lungo) *chsd ldrs: wknd over 2f out* **8/1**[3]
14/0 **7** *3* **High Command**[8] 2623 5-10-0 80.............................. PaulMulrennan 2 38
(M W Easterby) *chsd ldrs: lost pl over 2f out* **8/1**[3]
5-50 **8** *5* **Princely Ted (IRE)**[8] 2591 7-9-6 55.............................. LeeVickers(3) 3 25
(W Clay) *led: hdd over 5f out: wknd 3f out* **50/1**
9 *5* **Ice Lad (NZ)**[501] 9-9-5 0.............................. VinceSlattery 7 13
(R Brotherton) *mid-div: drvn over 5f out: lost pl 3f out* **100/1**
0400 **10** *9* **George Henson (IRE)**[5] 2707 4-9-0 48.............................. GihanArnolda(7) 1 —
(Garry Moss) *in rr: bhd fnl 3f* **66/1**
/6-0 **11** *shd* **Templet (USA)**[10] 2523 8-9-1 55..............................(b) DuranFentiman(3) 11 —
(W G Harrison) *in rr: bhd fnl 4f* **66/1**
000/ **12** *52* **Keepers Knight (IRE)**[647] 4954 7-9-6 0..........(v[1]) RussellKennemore(3) 9 —
(W Clay) *chsd ldrs: drvn over 7f out: sn wknd and bhd: t.o 4f out: virtually p.u* **100/1**
P **Goldsmeadow**[19] 9-9-4 0.............................. RobertWinston 5 —
(O Brennan) *s.s: detached in rr tl p.u over 7f out* **100/1**

2m 42.45s (1.45) **Going Correction** +0.025s/f (Slow) **13** Ran SP% **117.1**
WFA 3 from 4yo+ 15lb
Speed ratings (Par 103): **96,93,88,88,82 81,79,76,72,66 66,32,—**
CSF £55.12 TOTE £15.70: £3.70, £1.20, £1.10; EX 86.90.Black Falcon was claimed by Mr Shaun Taylor for £5,000.
Owner Graham Smith **Bred** Mrs Eithne Thompson **Trained** Six Hills, Leics

FOCUS
The winner had a lot to find and the form should be treated with suspicion on a day when it was difficult to make ground from off the pace.
Goldsmeadow Official explanation: jockey said gelding had a breathing problem

2868 SAM BOLDY MEMORIAL H'CAP 1m 4f (F)
3:40 (3:41) (Class 6) (0-65,63) 3-Y-O **£1,774** (£523; £262) **Stalls** Low

Form RPR
0235 **1** **Si Belle (IRE)**[17] 2340 3-9-7 **63**.............................. TedDurcan 2 78
(Rae Guest) *trckd ldrs: led on bit over 2f out: edgd rt: clr 1f out: eased ins fnl f* **11/4**[1]
0-54 **2** *9* **Smetana**[12] 2475 3-8-11 **56**.............................. TravisBlock(3) 7 57
(H Morrison) *chsd ldrs: drvn over 5f out: wnt 2nd over 1f out: no ch w wnr* **7/2**[3]
0-00 **3** *7* **Marie Tempest**[23] 2164 3-8-11 **53**.............................. RobertWinston 9 43
(B W Hills) *led tl over 2f out: fdd over 1f out* **10/1**
4210 **4** *16* **Gunnadoit (USA)**[19] 2280 3-9-6 **62**.............................. TPQueally 6 26
(M L W Bell) *hld up towards rr: effrt 5f out: sn wl outpcd* **10/3**[2]
4-00 **5** *8* **Pequeno Dinero (IRE)**[30] 1950 3-8-10 **52**.............................. DeanMcKeown 3 —
(C W Fairhurst) *sn chsng ldrs: reminders over 6f out: sn lost pl* **18/1**
-000 **6** *9* **Kuriyama (IRE)**[19] 2273 3-9-0 **56**.............................. PaulMulrennan 4 —
(M H Tompkins) *sn chsng ldrs: hrd drvn 6f out: sn lost pl* **16/1**
0-00 **7** *13* **Romford Car Two**[31] 1938 3-7-11 **46**..............................(b) AmyBaker(7) 5 —
(Miss J Feilden) *chsd ldrs: lost pl over 5f out: sn bhd* **16/1**
0- **8** *4 1/2* **Stop The Power (GER)**[42] 1658 3-8-3 **45**..................(tp) PaulHanagan 10 —
(Ruaidhri Joseph Tierney, Ire) *in rr: lost pl 6f out: sn bhd* **10/1**

2m 41.18s (0.18) **Going Correction** +0.025s/f (Slow) **8** Ran SP% **107.2**
Speed ratings (Par 97): **100,94,89,78,73 67,58,55**
CSF £10.72 CT £59.40 TOTE £2.40: £1.10, £1.50, £2.40; EX 14.20.
Owner Miss K Rausing **Bred** Airlie Stud And R N Clay **Trained** Newmarket, Suffolk

FOCUS
A low-grade three-year-old handicap, run at a decent pace. A much improved effort from the well-bred winner who looks a real stayer.
Pequeno Dinero(IRE) Official explanation: jockey said filly would not face the kickback

2869 PINDERS OPTOMETRISTS H'CAP 6f (F)
4:10 (4:12) (Class 6) (0-60,59) 4-Y-O+ **£1,774** (£523; £262) **Stalls** Low

Form RPR
0325 **1** **Owed**[5] 2706 6-9-4 **59**..............................(tp) RobertWinston 9 68
(R Bastiman) *chsd ldrs: chal and hung lft over 1f out: hrd rdn and led nr fin: all out* **7/1**[3]
4331 **2** *shd* **Blakeshall Quest**[33] 1906 8-9-2 **57**..............................(b) PaulMulrennan 6 66
(R Brotherton) *led: kpt on gamely: hdd nr fin: jst failed* **10/1**
0-02 **3** *1 1/2* **Whozart (IRE)**[5] 2706 5-8-9 **50**.............................. DanielTudhope 3 54
(A Dickman) *chsd ldrs: styd on same pce fnl f* **7/2**[2]
1304 **4** *2 1/4* **Rambling Socks**[5] 2706 5-8-10 **51**..............................(p) PhillipMakin 5 48
(S R Bowring) *trckd ldrs: kpt on same pce fnl 2f* **12/1**
00-6 **5** *2 3/4* **Jojesse**[152] 82 4-8-4 **45**.............................. PaulHanagan 1 33
(G A Swinbank) *hdwy on ins to chse ldrs over 4f out: one pce fnl 2f* **12/1**
0515 **6** *3* **Gone'N'Dunnett (IRE)**[11] 2511 9-8-11 **52**..............................(v) DMylonas 8 31
(Mrs C A Dunnett) *mid-div: drvn over 3f out: nvr on terms* **16/1**
4541 **7** *nk* **Limonia (GER)**[5] 2706 6-8-12 **53** 6ex.............................. RichardMullen 14 31
(Mike Murphy) *dwlt: hdwy on wd outside over 4f out: lost pl over 2f out* **7/2**[2]
0004 **8** *shd* **Cryptic Clue (USA)**[12] 2491 4-7-13 **45**.................. DanielleMcCreery(5) 7 22
(Mrs R A Carr) *mid-div: hdwy on ins 3f out: wknd over 1f out* **16/1**
0566 **9** *1 1/4* **Jabraan (USA)**[12] 2491 6-8-4 **45**..............................(b) DaleGibson 2 18
(Mrs R A Carr) *s.v.s: detached in rr: kpt on fnl 2f* **40/1**
0205 **10** *2* **White Ledger (IRE)**[29] 2010 9-8-8 **49**..............................(v) TomEaves 13 16
(R E Peacock) *hld up in rr: nvr on terms* **33/1**
00-4 **11** *nse* **Miss Mujahid Times**[27] 2036 5-8-4 **45**..................(b) SilvestreDeSousa 10 12
(A D Brown) *sn drvn along: lost pl over 4f out: sn bhd* **18/1**
6-24 **12** *1 1/4* **Scuba (IRE)**[20] 2263 6-8-13 **57**..............................(b) TravisBlock(3) 11 20
(H Morrison) *in rr: drvn over 2f out: nvr on terms* **3/1**[1]

1m 16.52s (0.02) **Going Correction** +0.025s/f (Slow) **12** Ran SP% **128.8**
Speed ratings (Par 101): **100,99,97,94,91 87,86,86,85,82 82,80**
CSF £82.12 CT £300.49 TOTE £7.70: £2.10, £2.60, £2.00; EX 61.80.
Owner Robin Bastiman **Bred** Helshaw Grange Stud, N Kent & H Phillips **Trained** Cowthorpe, N Yorks

■ Triple Shadow was withdrawn (12/1, uns rdr and ran loose bef start). R4 applies, deduct 5p in the £. New market formed.
■ Stewards' Enquiry : Robert Winston six-day ban: used whip with excessive frequency and down shoulder in forehand position (June 22-27)

FOCUS
The first five were the first five almost throughout. Another low-grade handicap, rated through the winner and the third.
Jabraan(USA) Official explanation: jockey said gelding missed the break
Scuba(IRE) Official explanation: jockey said gelding never travelled

2870 SEE CLEARLY WITH PINDERS - NIKON LENSES H'CAP 1m (F)
4:40 (4:41) (Class 6) (0-60,60) 4-Y-O+ **£1,774** (£523; £262) **Stalls** Low

Form RPR
0-50 **1** **Sularno**[31] 1933 4-9-1 **60**.............................. TravisBlock(3) 12 78+
(H Morrison) *w ldrs: led over 6f out: clr over 4f out: rdn over 1f out: heavily eased ins fnl f* **12/1**
00-0 **2** *5* **Bessemer (JPN)**[29] 2003 7-8-13 **55**..............................(t) DanielTudhope 8 58+
(Miss M E Rowland) *in rr-div: hdwy over 3f out: swtchd rt 2f out: kpt on to take 2nd jst ins fnl f* **25/1**
0250 **3** *1 3/4* **Ming Vase**[16] 2375 6-8-6 **48**.............................. FrankieMcDonald 14 47
(P T Midgley) *mid-div: hdwy over 2f out: kpt on fnl f* **16/1**
-513 **4** *1* **Nassar (IRE)**[11] 2513 5-8-13 **55**.............................. CatherineGannon 1 52
(G Prodromou) *sn bhd: styd on fnl 2f: lame* **8/1**[3]
-650 **5** *1/2* **Carefree**[11] 2510 4-8-10 **52**.............................. PaulHanagan 3 48
(Mrs R A Carr) *led over 1f: chsd wnr: one pce fnl 2f* **25/1**
1316 **6** *nk* **Welcome Releaf**[37] 1780 5-8-10 **59**.............................. MarkCoumbe(7) 7 54+
(P Leech) *in rr: kpt on fnl 2f: nvr a factor* **5/1**[1]
-101 **7** *1 1/2* **Komreyev Star**[112] 601 6-9-2 **58**.............................. SebSanders 5 50
(R E Peacock) *chsd ldrs: wknd over 1f out* **5/1**[1]
-500 **8** *1/2* **Bear Bottom**[38] 1747 4-7-13 **48**.............................. DebraEngland(7) 2 39
(W J Musson) *chsd ldrs on ins: one pce fnl 3f* **12/1**
-564 **9** *2* **Bowl Of Cherries**[59] 1282 5-8-8 **50**..............................(be) TPQueally 11 36
(I A Wood) *sn bhd: sme hdwy 2f out: nvr on terms* **13/2**[2]
4350 **10** *2 1/4* **Sparky Vixen**[13] 2446 4-7-13 **48**.............................. DeclanCannon(7) 6 29
(C J Teague) *prom: lost pl over 3f out* **11/1**
3045 **11** *4* **Zabeel House**[94] 809 5-9-2 **58**..............................(p) DeanMcKeown 9 30
(John A Harris) *s.i.s: a in rr* **8/1**[3]
6550 **12** *6* **Wednesdays Boy (IRE)**[19] 2290 5-8-9 **51**..............(b[1]) RobertWinston 10 9
(P D Niven) *s.i.s: a in rr* **8/1**[3]
000- **13** *3* **Ardent Prince**[235] 6265 5-8-0 **49**.............................. StacyRenwick(7) 13 —
(A J McCabe) *sn trcking ldrs on outer: lost pl over 3f out* **20/1**
40-0 **14** *7* **Call Me Rosy (IRE)**[22] 2187 4-8-8 **50**.............................. J-PGuillambert 4 —
(J G Given) *chsd ldrs: lost pl over 3f out* **33/1**

1m 43.93s (0.23) **Going Correction** +0.025s/f (Slow) **14** Ran SP% **125.0**
Speed ratings (Par 101): **99,94,92,91,90 90,88,88,86,84 80,74,71,64**
CSF £295.72 CT £4891.17 TOTE £14.40: £6.30, £9.50, £6.20; EX 278.70 Place 6 £168.56, Place 5 £109.41..
Owner Miss B Swire **Bred** Miss B Swire **Trained** East Ilsley, Berks

FOCUS
Another low-grade handicap. The winner blasted his opponents and was value double the official margin. The race has been rated through the third.
Nassar(IRE) Official explanation: trainer said horse pulled up lame
T/Jkpt: Not won. T/Plt: £575.30 to a £1 stake. Pool: £72,712.88. 92.25 winning tickets. T/Qpdt: £239.70 to a £1 stake. Pool: £4,017.00. 12.40 winning tickets. WG

2871 - 2874a (Foreign Racing) - See Raceform Interactive

[2650] CHANTILLY (R-H)
Sunday, June 8

OFFICIAL GOING: Good

2875a PRIX PAUL DE MOUSSAC (GROUP 3) (C&G) 1m
2:00 (2:09) 3-Y-O **£29,412** (£11,765; £8,824; £5,882; £2,941)

RPR
1 **Arcadia's Angle (USA)**[22] 2213 3-8-10.............................. C-PLemaire 8 109
(P Bary, France) *mde all: rdn out and r.o wl* **5/2**[2]
2 *1/2* **Senlis (IRE)**[28] 2028 3-8-12.............................. ASanna 1 110
(E Borromeo, Italy) *hld up: 7th st: hdwy and nt clr run on rails 1 1/2f out: drvn and r.o to take 2nd last strides* **14/1**
3 *nse* **Yorktown (FR)**[28] 2032 3-8-10.............................. IMendizabal 6 108
(J-C Rouget, France) *3rd on ins st: n.m.r wl over 1f out: swtchd out and unbalanced at dist: r.o u.p but lost 2nd last strides* **9/4**[1]
4 *snk* **Murcielago (FR)**[56] 1361 3-8-10.............................. TCastanheira 4 108
(P Demercastel, France) *hld up: last st: stl last 1 1/2f out: effrt on outside: fin wl* **14/1**
5 *2* **Moyenne Corniche**[24] 2121 3-8-10.............................. RichardHughes 5 103
(G Wragg) *a cl up: 4th st: disp 3rd wl over 1f out: kpt on one pce* **12/1**
6 *3/4* **Royal God (USA)**[44] 1607 3-8-10.............................. OPeslier 3 101
(F Head, France) *6th st: nvr able to chal* **7/1**
7 *1* **Gris Tendre (FR)**[76] 1011 3-8-10.............................. SPasquier 7 99
(J-C Rouget, France) *rushed up to go 2nd after 3f: rdn and btn 1f out* **4/1**[3]
8 *3* **Balios (GER)**[27] 2066 3-8-10.............................. CSoumillon 2 92
(A Wohler, Germany) *5th st: rdn and btn appr fnl f* **25/1**

1m 39.0s (1.20) **Going Correction** +0.175s/f (Good) **8** Ran SP% **116.7**
Speed ratings: **101,100,100,100,98 97,96,93**
PARI-MUTUEL: WIN 3.90; PL 1.70, 3.20, 1.40; DF 41.40.
Owner Niarchos Family **Bred** J F Orseno & J Bailry **Trained** Chantilly, France

NOTEBOOK

Arcadia's Angle(USA), a rapidly improving colt, may well make it to the top by the end of the season as he is turning into a really professional racehorse. He was asked to make all the running and he quickened well half way up the straight before running on strongly to the line. He has now been marked down for the Prix Jean Prat back at this track in July and it will be no surprise if he went on to the Jacques Le Marois at Deauville in August.

Senlis(IRE) was last into the straight before making up a lot of late ground. He did not have the best of runs and took second place well inside the final furlong. He was giving a kilo to the winner and he has to be considered a little unlucky. His jockey dislocated his shoulder during the race which was another added but genuine excuse. He was back to a much better distance and will have a chance to take his revenge in the Jean Prat.

Yorktown(FR) lost little in defeat. He looked dangerous halfway up the straight but did not quite go through with his final effort. He lost second place on the line. It would be no surprise if he also lined up for the Jean Prat.

Murcielago(FR) was given a waiting race and still had plenty to do rounding the final turn. He was brought with a late run up the centre of the track and was putting in his best work at the finish.

Moyenne Corniche ran a reasonable race and was mid division virtually throughout. He stayed on one-paced at the end. Connections felt he now needs a longer trip and softer ground to show his best.

2876a PRIX EQUIDIA (PRIX DU CHEMIN DE FER DU NORD) (GROUP 3) 1m

2:30 (2:40) 4-Y-0+ **£29,412** (£11,765; £8,824; £5,882; £2,941)

RPR

1 **Spirito Del Vento (FR)**[38] 1761 5-9-2 .... OPeslier 10 115
(J-M Beguigne, France) *hld up: 10th st: str run on outside fr 2f out to ld 1f out: edgd rt: r.o wl* **9/4**[1]

2 1 1/2 **Athanor (FR)**[16] 6-8-12 .... DBonilla 11 108
(F Head, France) *hld up: last st: trckd wnr on outside fr 2f out: rchd 2nd 120yds out: r.o one pce* **13/2**

3 2 **Mount Nelson**[34] 1882 4-8-12 .... JMurtagh 3 103
(A P O'Brien, Ire) *7th st: nt clr run wl over 1f out and again jst ins fnl f: swtchd outside and fin wl to take 3rd last strides* **4/1**[2]

4 shd **Hujum (IRE)**[24] 4-8-12 .... TGillet 9 103
(J E Hammond, France) *trckd ldr: led 1 1/2f out to 1f out: lost 3rd last strides* **6/1**[3]

5 1 **Runaway**[31] 6-8-12 .... TJarnet 5 101
(R Pritchard-Gordon, France) *4th st: cl 3rd 2f out: one pce but stl cl up whn squeezed out ins fnl f: fin 6th: plcd 5th* **14/1**

6 3/4 **King Jock (USA)**[7] 2656 7-9-2 .... RMBurke 8 100
(R J Osborne, Ire) *hld up: 8th st: hdwy wl over 1f out: cl 4th 1f out: kpt on one pce: fin 5th: disqualified: plcd 6th* **14/1**

7 1 1/2 **Molly Max (GER)**[21] 4-8-12 .... DBoeuf 7 96
(Frau K Haustein, Germany) *led to 1 1/2f out: hrd rdn and ev ch 1f out: wkng whn n.m.r on rails jst ins fnl f: eased* **25/1**

8 snk **Snow Key (USA)**[15] 4-8-8 .... TThulliez 1 91
(J E Pease, France) *3rd st: stl cl up bhd ldrs at dist: n.m.r ins fnl f: nt rcvr* **16/1**

9 2 **Holocene (USA)**[38] 1761 4-8-12 .... C-PLemaire 4 91
(P Bary, France) *7th st: rdn 1 1/2f out: sn btn* **6/1**[3]

10 6 **Jodhpur**[41] 4-8-12 .... SPasquier 2 77
(A Fabre, France) *5th st: btn over 1f out: eased* **11/1**

11 **Slickly Royal (FR)**[21] 4-8-12 .... IMendizabal 6 77
(P Demercastel, France) *9th st: a in rr* **33/1**

1m 36.5s (-1.30) **Going Correction** +0.175s/f (Good) 11 Ran SP% **127.0**
Speed ratings: **113,111,109,109,107 108,106,106,104,98 98**
PARI-MUTUEL: WIN 2.90; PL 1.30, 1.80, 2.00; DF 7.10.
Owner L Ciampi **Bred** Haras Des Sablonnets **Trained** France

NOTEBOOK

Spirito Del Vento(FR), who is a high-class performer when on song, carried joint top weight and, brought with a late run, he showed his usual brilliant acceleration to take the lead at the furlong marker. He definitely runs better on a right-handed track and when the going is good. If he recovers quickly enough, he will be off to Ascot for the Queen Anne Stakes.

Athanor(FR) never runs a bad race. He was at the tail of the field together with the winner but could not quicken quite so well, although he stayed on throughout the final two furlongs. Connections will now be looking for a similar event.

Mount Nelson, lightly raced since winning the Criterium International in 2006, put up a much better performance on this drop in trip and was unlucky in the straight. He could not be extracted to challenge a furlong and a half out but, once in the clear, made up a lot of late ground. This performance augers well for the future.

Hujum(IRE), smartly into his stride and second early on, was still well there a furlong and a half out but could not find another gear.

2877a PRIX DE DIANE (GROUP 1) (FILLIES) 1m 2f 110y

3:15 (3:22) 3-Y-0 **£336,118** (£134,471; £67,235; £33,588; £16,824)

RPR

1 **Zarkava (IRE)**[28] 2033 3-9-0 .... CSoumillon 8 124+
(A De Royer-Dupre, France) *hld up towards rr early: 8th st: hdwy on outside over 2f out: led dist: r.o wl* **1/3**[1]

2 3 **Gagnoa (IRE)**[21] 2237 3-9-0 .... JMurtagh 5 115
(A Fabre, France) *hld up: 10th st: trckd wnr on outside fr over 2f out: drvn 2f out: kpt on to take 2nd 100yds out: no ch w wnr* **20/1**

3 1 1/2 **Goldikova (IRE)**[28] 2033 3-9-0 .... OPeslier 6 112
(F Head, France) *a cl up: 2nd st: led over 2f out: hrd rdn 1 1/2f out: hdd dist: one pce* **9/1**[2]

4 snk **Proviso**[21] 2237 3-9-0 .... SPasquier 9 112
(A Fabre, France) *hdwy and 5th st: rchd 2nd ins fnl 2f: sn rdn: kpt on same pce* **12/1**[3]

5 2 1/2 **Satan's Circus (USA)**[44] 1608 3-9-0 .... C-PLemaire 2 107
(J-C Rouget, France) *mid-div: 6th st on ins: clsd up over 2f out: rdn wl over 1f out: one pce* **50/1**

6 1 1/2 **Wait And See (FR)**[21] 2237 3-9-0 .... DBoeuf 7 105
(Robert Collet, France) *hld up: 11th st: styd on fr 2f out: nvr a factor* **100/1**

7 1/2 **Top Toss (IRE)**[58] 1323 3-9-0 .... TThulliez 11 104
(Y De Nicolay, France) *broke out of stall bef s: 9th st: one pce fnl 2f* **40/1**

8 nk **Belle Allure (IRE)**[42] 1664 3-9-0 .... DBonilla 12 103
(R Pritchard-Gordon, France) *hld up in rr: last to st: nvr in contention* **50/1**

9 1/2 **Leo's Starlet (IRE)**[38] 1760 3-9-0 .... LDettori 4 102
(A De Royer-Dupre, France) *prom: 4th st: rdn over 2f out: wknd over 1f out* **14/1**

10 8 **Prima Luce (IRE)**[34] 1880 3-9-0 .... KJManning 3 87
(J S Bolger, Ire) *led over 1f: led over 4f out to over 2f out: wknd over 1f out: eased* **66/1**

11 8 **Belle Et Celebre (FR)**[21] 2237 3-9-0 .... IMendizabal 1 72
(A De Royer-Dupre, France) *prom early: 8th st: btn wl over 1f out* **25/1**

12 5 **Kitty Matcham (IRE)**[14] 2433 3-9-0 .... JAHeffernan 10 62
(A P O'Brien, Ire) *mid-div to 1/2-way: 12th st: bhd fnl 2f* **40/1**

13 8 **Sanjida (IRE)**[19] 2294 3-9-0 .... FDiFede 13 47
(A De Royer-Dupre, France) *led 9f out to over 4f out: 3rd st: sn wknd* **100/1**

2m 7.10s (0.10) **Going Correction** +0.175s/f (Good) 13 Ran SP% **120.3**
Speed ratings: **106,103,102,102,100 99,99,99,98,92 87,83,77**
PARI-MUTUEL: WIN 1.40 (coupled with Sanjida); PL 1.10, 3.00, 1.60;DF 13.70.
Owner H H Aga Khan **Bred** His Highness The Aga Khan's Studs S C **Trained** Chantilly, France

NOTEBOOK

Zarkava(IRE), stepping up in trip following her Pouliches success, put up another outstanding performance and never looked liked being beaten. Her jockey just let her bowl along towards the tail of the field early on before beginning a forward move coming out of the final turn. She was brought with a run up the centre of the track and quickened impressively to take the lead one and a half out. She is now unbeaten in five races and she will be given a rest before connections decided on a plan for the future. The most likely target is the Arc de Triomphe with a run in a shorter event before.

Gagnoa(IRE), who has progressed well since finishing well behind today's winner in the Marcel Boussac last autumn, put up another very sound effort. She followed the winner throughout but could not quicken in the same manner once the race warmed up. She was staying on at the finish but could never get in a serious blow and is crying out for 1m4f. The plan now is to go for the Irish Oaks and then the Prix Vermeille. Softer ground would also have been an advantage and she is definitely one to follow.

Goldikova(IRE), who finished runner-up in the Pouliches, played up somewhat in the preliminaries but did nothing wrong in the race. Well up with the pace from the start, she went to the head of affairs at the 2f marker but had nothing in reserve when tackled by the winner. She kept going up the far rail but this distance might have tested her stamina to the limit and she will now have a well-earned rest.

Proviso was given every possible chance but did run a little free in the early part of the race. She could not quicken early in the straight but did run on in the final stages and only failed by a narrow distance to take third place. Possibly another at the limit of her stamina.

1514 KREFELD (R-H)

Sunday, June 8

OFFICIAL GOING: Good

2879a KREFELDER STUTENPREIS (LISTED RACE) (F&M) 1m 2f 55y

3:20 (3:31) 4-Y-0+ **£8,824** (£3,235; £1,765; £882)

RPR

1 **Another World (GER)**[15] 5-9-2 .... ADeVries 8 97
(W Hickst, Germany)

2 1/2 **Nolas Lolly (IRE)**[29] 1981 4-9-0 .... JohnEgan 1 94
(M Botti) *racd in 3rd to st: chal 2f out: drvn to ld briefly ins fnl f: r.o same pce* **41/10**[1]

3 1 1/2 **Red Diva**[217] 4-9-0 .... StefanieHofer 9 91
(Mario Hofer, Germany)

4 nk **Now Again (GER)**[201] 6889 4-9-0 .... J-PCarvalho 6 91
(W Hickst, Germany)

5 nse **Foreign Music (FR)**[15] 4-9-2 .... FilipMinarik 2 92
(H J Groschel, Germany)

6 2 1/2 **Lilia (GER)** 4-9-0 .... J-LSilverio 3 86
(Frau E Mader, Germany)

7 1 **Elora (GER)**[15] 4-9-0 .... TMundry 7 84
(P Rau, Germany)

8 3 1/2 **La Bamba (GER)**[221] 4-9-0 .... JBojko 5 77
(A Wohler, Germany)

9 1/2 **The Fairy (GER)**[252] 5850 4-9-0 .... MCadeddu 4 76
(J Hirschberger, Germany)

2m 5.68s (125.68) 9 Ran SP% **19.6**
TOTE: WIN 29; PL 13, 17, 18; SF 157.
Owner J Erhardt **Bred** Joachim Erhardt **Trained** Germany

NOTEBOOK

Nolas Lolly(IRE), a winner at Compiegne last year and a close second in an Italian Listed race while trained by Urs Suter in France, went close again. She looked the winner when taking over from Another World inside the final furlong but her rival rallied to outstay her. This was her first attempt beyond 1m and it proved a little too far for her.

MUNICH (L-H)

Sunday, June 8

OFFICIAL GOING: Good

2880a GERMAN TOTE BAVARIAN CLASSIC (GROUP 3) 1m 2f

3:35 (3:53) 3-Y-0 **£23,529** (£7,353; £3,676; £2,206)

RPR

1 **Walzertraum (USA)** 3-9-2 .... THellier 4 101
(J Hirschberger, Germany) *hld up in 4th to st: hdwy on outside fr over 2f out: drvn to ld dist: r.o wl* **71/10**

2 3/4 **Il Divo (GER)**[27] 3-9-2 .... EPedroza 1 100
(A Wohler, Germany) *led to dist: r.o same pce* **5/1**[3]

3 2 **Idolino (GER)** 3-9-2 .... FJohansson 3 96
(J Hirschberger, Germany) *6th st: hdwy on ins to rch 2nd over 2f out: one pce fnl f* **14/1**

4 3/4 **Kamsin (GER)**[35] 1850 3-9-2 .... AStarke 7 94
(P Schiergen, Germany) *a.p: wnt 2nd after 4f: 2nd st: btn wl over 1f out* **2/5**[1]

5 3 **Lone Star (GER)**[52] 3-9-2 .... PVanDeKeere 6 88
(M Trybuhl, Germany) *s.i.s: last to st: nvr a factor* **21/1**

6 1 **Lancetto (FR)**[35] 1850 3-9-2 .... AHelfenbein 2 86
(Mario Hofer, Germany) *trckd ldr 4f: 3rd st: sn btn* **43/10**[2]

7 23 **Diacaro**[238] 6219 3-9-2 .... GBietolini 5 40
(H Blume, Germany) *uns rdr and rn loose bef s: 5th st: sn btn: eased* **16/1**

2m 12.39s (3.42) 7 Ran SP% **136.4**
TOTE: WIN 81; PL 29, 19, 41; SF 338.
Owner Gestut Schlenderhan **Bred** Gestut Schlenderhan **Trained** Germany

[2690]FOLKESTONE (R-H)

Monday, June 9

OFFICIAL GOING: Good to firm (8.1)

Wind: very slight across Weather: sunny and warm

2881 EASTWELL MANOR H'CAP — 5f
2:15 (2:16) (Class 6) (0-60,60) 4-Y-O+ £2,047 (£604; £302) Stalls Low

Form RPR

0033 1 **Thoughtsofstardom**[11] 2551 5-8-11 58 KellyHarrison(5) 1 68
(M Wigham) *trckd ldrs on stands' rail: nt clr run and swtchd rt over 1f out: r.o wl to ld last strides* **5/2**[1]

0040 2 hd **Fastrac Boy**[87] 883 5-8-5 47 MartinDwyer 3 56
(J R Best) *led narrowly: rdn 2f out: hdd over 1f out: kpt on gamely fnl f* **12/1**

0200 3 nk **Regal Royale**[3] 2780 5-8-11 53 (v) AdamKirby 8 61
(Peter Grayson) *racd in midfield: rdn 3f out: hdwy 1/2-way: ev ch fr wl over 1f out: unable qck nr fin* **13/2**[3]

3043 4 hd **Azygous**[5] 2710 5-9-4 60 (p) AlanMunro 10 67
(J Akehurst) *chsd ldrs: rdn and ev ch 2f out: led narrowly over 1f out tl hdd and lost 3 pls last strides* **7/1**

6232 5 2 1/4 **Mambazo**[5] 2710 6-8-1 46 oh1 (e) LukeMorris(3) 5 48+
(S C Williams) *taken down to s early: pressed ldr: rdn and ev ch fr over 2f out tl wknd last 100yds: btn whn sltly short of room towards fin* **9/2**[2]

55-6 6 1/2 **Valiant Romeo**[38] 1772 8-8-6 48 SaleemGolam 2 45
(R Bastiman) *towards rr: rdn 1/2-way: kpt on but nvr pce to chal* **8/1**

5055 7 1 **Harrison's Flyer (IRE)**[13] 2478 7-9-4 60 (p) DaneO'Neill 6 54
(J M Bradley) *bhd: rdn 1/2-way: kpt on but nvr pce to chal* **10/1**

0460 8 1 1/4 **Briery Lane (IRE)**[35] 1865 7-8-9 51 SteveDrowne 4 40
(J M Bradley) *a in rr: no ch last 2f* **10/1**

-005 9 10 **Exponential (IRE)**[13] 2474 6-8-6 48 LiamJones 9 1
(J M Bradley) *in tch: rdn 1/2-way: wknd 2f out: eased ins fnl f* **25/1**

610- 10 12 **Pretty Selma**[432] 918 4-8-8 50 (b) EddieAhern 7 —
(Mark Gillard) *stdd s: wl bhd fr 1/2-way: t.o* **40/1**

59.21 secs (-0.79) **Going Correction** -0.15s/f (Firm) **10** Ran SP% **115.9**
Speed ratings (Par 101): **100,99,99,98,95 94,92,90,74,55**
CSF £34.44 CT £180.77 TOTE £2.70: £1.30, £3.00, £2.50; EX 48.70 TRIFECTA Not won..
Owner Eventmaker Racehorses **Bred** B Bargh **Trained** Newmarket, Suffolk

FOCUS
A moderate sprint in which those drawn low proved at an advantage. The first four were very closely covered at the finish and the form is straightforward, with the first three rated to their marks.

2882 BETDAQ.CO.UK (S) STKS — 5f
2:45 (2:45) (Class 6) 2-Y-O £2,047 (£604; £302) Stalls Low

Form RPR

2424 1 **Sub Prime (IRE)**[14] 2459 2-9-0 0 ShaneKelly 2 55+
(J A Osborne) *led after 1f: mde rest: shkn up and in command wl over 1f out: comf* **2/5**[1]

033 2 1 1/2 **Makaluna**[11] 2548 2-8-7 0 WilliamCarson(7) 1 50
(W G M Turner) *led for 1f out: sn outpcd in 3rd: chsd wnr over 1f out: styd on u.p but nvr threatened wnr* **7/2**[2]

534 3 4 **In The Moment**[11] 2548 2-8-4 0 JackDean(5) 4 30
(W G M Turner) *chsd wnr over 3f out: rdn 1/2-way: outpcd by wnr wl over 1f out: lost 2nd over 1f out* **12/1**[3]

4 6 **Incy Wincy** 2-8-7 0 PietroRomeo(7) 3 14
(J M Bradley) *s.i.s: sn outpcd in fnl f* **20/1**

60.86 secs (0.86) **Going Correction** -0.15s/f (Firm) **4** Ran SP% **106.1**
Speed ratings (Par 91): **87,84,78,68**
CSF £1.96 TOTE £1.40; EX 2.00.There was no bid for the winner.
Owner Mrs F Walwyn **Bred** Mrs Claire Doyle **Trained** Upper Lambourn, Berks

FOCUS
A dire juvenile affair. The winner did the job pretty much as he was entitled to but this looks a race to be against.

NOTEBOOK
Sub Prime(IRE), a beaten favourite in claiming company the last twice, took advantage of this further drop in grade and opened his account at the fifth attempt. He was fully entitled to win this on his previous form, however, and he has clearly now found his level. (tchd 4-11 and 4-9)
Makaluna turned in his best effort to date in defeat and is now becoming a standing dish at this level, rating the benchmark for the lowly form. (op 5-1)
In The Moment has shown very little in her career to date and was again well beaten off here, but did at least shape as though she may be worth sending over an extra furlong. (op 13-2)

2883 BET ROMANIA V FRANCE - BETDAQ H'CAP — 6f
3:15 (3:15) (Class 4) (0-85,82) 3-Y-O £4,533 (£1,348; £674; £336) Stalls Low

Form RPR

1251 1 **We Have A Dream**[14] 2460 3-9-6 81 MartinDwyer 7 81
(W R Muir) *led narrrowly tl over 1f out: edgd rt u.p 1f out: kpt on gamely to ld again nr fin* **5/2**[2]

10-4 2 hd **Tyfos**[16] 2407 3-9-2 77 EddieAhern 5 77
(W M Brisbourne) *stdd s: sn chsng ldrs rdn 2f out: ev ch ent fnl f: unable qck nr fin* **10/1**

215 3 nk **Baunagain (IRE)**[7] 2674 3-9-7 82 PatCosgrave 1 81
(M J Wallace) *taken down early: racd keenly: pressed wnr: rdn and edgd rt 2f out: led narrowly over 1f out: hdd and no ex towards fin* **2/1**[1]

-500 4 1/2 **Tadalavil**[11] 2460 3-9-1 76 DarryllHolland 6 73
(M R Channon) *in tch: effrt and rdn jst over 2f out: ev ch ent fnl f: unable qck last 50yds* **6/1**[3]

30-5 5 nk **Alsadeek (IRE)**[31] 1971 3-8-11 72 RHills 2 73+
(J L Dunlop) *s.i.s: bhd: edgd out rt 1/2-way: rdn wl over 1f out: keeping on whn nt clr run ins fnl f: swtchd rt nr fin: nvr able to chal* **8/1**

-120 6 1 1/2 **Liberty Valance (IRE)**[13] 2481 3-9-1 76 RichardHughes 3 67
(S Kirk) *hld up in tch: swtchd rt and effrt wl over 1f out: ev ch u.p 1f out: fdd last 100yds* **16/1**

2-60 7 1/2 **Perfect Flight**[21] 2258 3-9-4 79 SteveDrowne 4 69
(M Blanshard) *hld up in tch: rdn over 2f out: kpt on but nvr pce to chal* **7/1**

1m 11.67s (-1.03) **Going Correction** -0.15s/f (Firm) **7** Ran SP% **114.8**
Speed ratings (Par 101): **100,99,99,98,98 96,95**
CSF £27.23 TOTE £2.90: £1.90, £5.80; EX 30.70.
Owner The Dreaming Squires **Bred** Whitsbury Manor Stud **Trained** Lambourn, Berks

FOCUS
A fair handicap for three-year-olds. The form looks straightforward enough but pretty ordinary, with five in line inside the final furlong. The fifth looked unlucky.

Alsadeek(IRE) Official explanation: jockey said colt was denied a clear run

2884 BET HOLLAND V ITALY - BETDAQ H'CAP — 1m 4f
3:45 (3:46) (Class 6) (0-60,59) 4-Y-O+ £2,047 (£604; £151; £151) Stalls Low

Form RPR

0012 1 **Wizard Looking**[20] 2290 7-8-12 53 RichardHughes 13 61
(D E Cantillon) *t.k.h: hld up in midfield: hdwy over 2f out: chal over 1f out: rdn to ld 1f out: drvn out* **2/1**[1]

2024 2 3/4 **Mid Valley**[20] 2290 5-8-13 54 KerrinMcEvoy 14 60
(J R Jenkins) *hld up in midfield: hdwy 2f out: hld hd high over 1f out: swtchd rt jst ins fnl f: r.o to go 2nd wl ins fnl f: nt rch wnr* **5/1**[2]

-044 3 nse **Barbirolli**[12] 2512 6-8-12 53 EddieAhern 4 59
(W M Brisbourne) *hld up in rr: hdwy 3f out: swtchd lft over 1f out: r.o wl fnl f: nt rch wnr* **8/1**[3]

0-00 3 dht **Brave Quest (IRE)**[10] 2561 4-9-4 59 IanMongan 1 65
(Mrs L J Mongan) *in tch: hdwy over 2f out: drvn wl over 1f out: pressed wnr ent fnl f: nt qckn u.p* **11/1**

20-1 5 1 1/2 **Chapter (IRE)**[27] 2072 6-8-8 49 (p) AlanMunro 5 53+
(Mrs A L M King) *stdd s: hld up bhd: c wd and rdn 2f out: styd on wl fnl f: nt rch ldrs* **9/1**

2003 6 nk **On Every Street**[14] 2467 7-8-8 49 ow1 (vt) PatCosgrave 3 52
(R Bastiman) *hld up bhd: reminders 6f out: rdn 3f out: no imp tl styd on ins fnl f: nvr trbld ldrs* **14/1**

-300 7 1 1/2 **Lord Laing (USA)**[17] 2353 5-8-6 47 ow1 JamesDoyle 12 48
(H J Collingridge) *in tch: rdn and effrt over 2f out: one pce u.p fr over 1f out* **14/1**

0-05 8 hd **Icannshift (IRE)**[48] 1538 8-9-0 55 FrankieMcDonald 10 55
(T M Jones) *chsd ldr tl wnt 2nd 6f out: rdn to ld 2f out: hdd 1f out: wknd qckly ins fnl f* **8/1**[3]

000- 9 1 1/2 **Colton**[16] 5018 5-9-2 57 MickyFenton 7 55
(J M P Eustace) *taken down early: s.i.s: sn rdn up to ld: clr 8f out: rdn 3f out: hdd 2f out: hit on nose by rival's whip over 1f out: wknd fnl f* **18/1**

0010 10 1 1/4 **Royal Audition**[62] 1262 7-7-8 52 (p) MarcHalford(3) 8 48
(T T Clement) *restless stalls: s.i.s: t.k.h: hld up in rr: rdn and effrt on inner 2f out: n.d* **33/1**

5004 11 3 1/4 **Kadouchski (FR)**[33] 863 4-8-12 53 DarryllHolland 6 44
(A B Coogan) *hld up towards rr: hdwy on outer 5f out: lost pl 3f out: n.d after* **11/1**

235- 12 2 1/2 **Papradon**[203] 6871 4-9-3 58 (v) JimmyQuinn 9 45
(J R Best) *led for 1f: chsd ldr tl 6f out: rdn and wknd over 2f out* **12/1**

2m 37.4s (-3.50) **Going Correction** -0.15s/f (Firm) **12** Ran SP% **128.1**
Speed ratings (Par 101): **105,104,104,104,103 103,102,102,101,100 98,96**
TRIFECTA: WL/MV/BQ £67.70 - 1.70 winning units WL/MV/B £12.40 - 9.22 winning units. Pool: £324.58 CSF £12.37 TOTE £2.80: £1.20, £2.40; EX 14.10 TRIFECTA PL: Brave Quest £2.30, Barbirolli £1.30. TRICAST: WL/MV/BQ £48.70, WL/MV/B £36.53..
Owner T H Heckingbottom **Bred** J G Phillips **Trained** Newmarket, Suffolk

FOCUS
A weak handicap, run at a decent pace. The winner took advantage of a 10lb lower turf mark and the form looks pretty solid, rated through the third.
Lord Laing(USA) Official explanation: trainer said gelding was struck into
Colton Official explanation: jockey said gelding stumbled on final bend
Royal Audition Official explanation: trainer said mare missed the break

2885 MAKE IT PAY AT BETDAQ MEDIAN AUCTION MAIDEN STKS — 1m 1f 149y
4:15 (4:18) (Class 6) 3-4-Y-O £2,266 (£674; £337; £168) Stalls Centre

Form RPR

66 1 **Mont Cervin**[12] 2509 3-8-13 0 EddieAhern 6 74
(W J Haggas) *mde all: rdn 2f out: styd on wl fnl f* **12/1**

2-32 2 1 1/4 **Pediment**[11] 2528 3-8-8 75 KerrinMcEvoy 5 66
(J R Fanshawe) *chsd ldr: chal wl over 1f out: sn rdn and unable qck: btn 1f out* **8/13**[1]

30- 3 1 **Dea Caelestis (FR)**[351] 2904 3-8-8 0 TPQueally 8 64
(H R A Cecil) *chsd ldng pair: rdn over 1f out: sn hanging rt: kpt on same pce* **11/2**[2]

00 4 2 1/4 **Beau Fighter**[11] 2528 3-8-13 0 IanMongan 9 65
(C F Wall) *chsd ldrs: rdn over 2f out: outpcd by ldrs wl over 1f out: kpt on* **33/1**

40-5 5 nk **Shesha Bear**[18] 2328 3-8-8 72 MartinDwyer 4 59
(W R Muir) *racd in midfield: rdn and outpcd jst over 2f out: styd on u.p fnl f: nvr threatened ldrs* **14/1**

253- 6 3/4 **Soggy Dollar**[235] 6274 3-8-13 74 JimmyQuinn 1 62+
(M H Tompkins) *stdd after s and hld up in rr: effrt and rdn 2f out: nvr pce to trble ldrs* **15/2**[3]

0-65 7 1 3/4 **Piano Sonata**[25] 2119 3-8-8 75 MichaelHills 2 54
(B W Hills) *hld up towards rr: hdwy on outer 6f out: chsd ldrs 4f out: rdn and wknd 2f out: eased wl ins fnl f* **12/1**

0 8 2 3/4 **Ubiquitous**[28] 2046 3-8-8 0 JamesDoyle 11 48
(S Dow) *hld up in midfield: rdn and no imp 2f out* **100/1**

00- 9 1 **Rutba**[208] 6805 3-8-8 0 RHills 7 46
(M P Tregoning) *hld up in rr: rdn 3f out: n.d* **33/1**

P 10 9 **Hungry For More**[11] 2528 4-9-9 0 KevinGhunowa(3) 3 32
(M R Hoad) *s.i.s: a last* **100/1**

2m 3.93s (-0.97) **Going Correction** -0.15s/f (Firm)
WFA 3 from 4yo 13lb **10** Ran SP% **119.0**
Speed ratings (Par 101): **97,96,95,93,93 92,91,88,88,80**
CSF £20.18 TOTE £13.50: £3.30, £1.02, £2.00; EX 27.90 Trifecta £446.80 Part won. Pool: £629.37 - 0.50 winning units..
Owner Mrs Charles Cyzer **Bred** C A Cyzer **Trained** Newmarket, Suffolk

FOCUS
A fair maiden which was slowly run, and few got into the equation from off the pace with the first four pretty much in that order throughout. The form is rated around the runner-up, with the winner up 11lb.

2886 STONE OF FOLCA H'CAP — 1m 1f 149y
4:45 (4:48) (Class 5) (0-70,70) 4-Y-O+ £2,331 (£693; £346; £173) Stalls Centre

Form RPR

-006 1 **Shabahar (IRE)**[13] 2476 4-9-2 65 PatCosgrave 8 75
(M J McGrath) *t.k.h: hld up in midfield: hdwy and rdn 2f out: r.o strly to ld ins fnl f: sn in command* **10/1**

50-5 2 1 3/4 **Princess Lavinia**[44] 1620 5-9-0 63 SteveDrowne 9 69
(G Wragg) *led for 1f: chsd ldr after tl over 4f out: styd handy: rdn to ld jst over 1f out: hdd and nt pce of wnr ins fnl f* **9/2**[3]

240- 3 1 1/2 **Daring Racer (GER)**[231] 5204 5-8-12 61 IanMongan 1 64
(Mrs L J Mongan) *chsd ldrs: wnt 2nd over 4f out: rdn jst over 2f out: one pce u.p* **20/1**

0-40 **4** *shd* **Follow The Colours (IRE)**[8] 2640 5-8-10 **62**.......... PatrickHills(3) 3 65
(J W Hills) *v.s.a: bhd: hdwy over 3f out: rdn and effrt on inner 2f out: kpt on but nt pce to rch ldrs* **11/1**

40-0 **5** *3/4* **Silent Applause**[17] 2373 5-9-1 **64**.......... MickyFenton 11 65+
(Dr J D Scargill) *hld up bhd: rdn 3f out: styd on fnl f: nvr trbld ldrs* **9/2**[3]

03-0 **6** *1 1/4* **Montrose Man**[24] 2165 4-9-0 **70**.......... KMay(7) 6 68
(B J Meehan) *hld up towards rr: rdn and unable qck 2f out: plugged on* **25/1**

1 **7** *nk* **Vinces**[30] 1994 4-9-7 **70**.......... EddieAhern 12 68
(T D McCarthy) *led after 1f: rdn 2fout: hdd jst over 1f out: wknd fnl f* **4/1**[2]

520 **8** *1/2* **Scripted (USA)**[51] 1486 4-9-5 **68**.......... (t) GeorgeBaker 7 65
(C F Wall) *chsd ldrs: rdn 2f out: wknd over 1f out* **7/2**[1]

-600 **9** *4 1/2* **Rock Haven (IRE)**[3] 2795 6-8-2 **51** oh3.......... LiamJones 4 38
(W M Brisbourne) *hld up in rr: rdn and brief effrt 2f out: sn wl btn* **16/1**

000- **10** *39* **Camp Attack**[407] 1319 5-8-2 **51** oh6.......... NickyMackay 10 —
(S Dow) *chsd ldrs tl wknd qckly 3f out: virtually p.u fr over 1f out* **25/1**

2m 2.22s (-2.68) **Going Correction** -0.15s/f (Firm) **10** Ran SP% **114.3**
Speed ratings (Par 103): **104,102,101,101,100 99,99,99,95,64**
CSF £52.11 CT £880.00 TOTE £12.40: £3.70, £1.70, £4.00; EX 59.90 Trifecta £278.10 Part won. Pool: £391.74 - 0.80 winning units. Place 6: £42.88 Place 5: £22.36..
Owner Gallagher Equine Ltd **Bred** His Highness The Aga Khan's Studs S C **Trained** East Malling, Kent

FOCUS
A modest handicap, run at a strong early pace. The form looks sound but limited, rated around the fourth.
Vinces Official explanation: jockey said gelding was unsuited by the good to firm going
Rock Haven(IRE) Official explanation: jockey said gelding lost its action
T/Plt: £63.60 to a £1 stake. Pool: £67,067.10. 769.35 winning tickets. T/Qpdt: £13.20 to a £1 stake. Pool: £4,016.50. 223.50 winning tickets. SP

2375 PONTEFRACT (L-H)

Monday, June 9

OFFICIAL GOING: Good (good to firm in places; 7.5)
Wind: Virtually nil Weather: Dry and sunny

2887 BRIAN LEIGHTON RENAULT MAIDEN AUCTION FILLIES' STKS 6f
6:50 (6:51) (Class 5) 2-Y-O **£3,238** (£963; £481; £240) **Stalls** Low

Form RPR

03 **1** **Common Diva**[11] 2534 2-8-4 0.......... WilliamBuick 2 72
(A J McCabe) *mde all: rdn wl over 1f out: kpt on strly ins fnl f* **7/1**[3]

3 **2** *3/4* **On Offer (IRE)**[13] 2485 2-8-6 0.......... DavidAllan 8 73+
(T D Easterby) *dwlt: rn green and in rr tl hdwy wl over 1f out: swtchd lft and rdn ent fnl f: styd on wl towards fin* **8/1**

2 **3** *1/2* **Maid For Music (IRE)**[17] 2357 2-8-8 0.......... RichardMullen 9 72
(E S McMahon) *trckd ldng pair: effrt 2f out and sn rdn: ch ent fnl f: sn drvn and kpt on* **10/11**[1]

4 *3 1/4* **Flying Lady (IRE)** 2-8-6 0.......... EdwardCreighton 5 61
(M R Channon) *midfield: hdwy over 2f out: sn rdn and kpt on u.p ins fnl f: nrst fin* **11/4**[2]

0 **5** *3 1/4* **Abby Belle (IRE)**[21] 2253 2-8-13 0.......... TomEaves 6 58+
(J G Portman) *chsd ldrs on outer: rdn wl over 1f out: kpt on same pce fnl f* **80/1**

5 **6** *nk* **Betws Y Coed (IRE)**[44] 1610 2-8-1 0.......... DominicFox(3) 10 48
(A Bailey) *towards rr: rdn along 1/2-way: hdwy over 1f out: swtchd lft ins fnl f and styd on: nrst fin* **66/1**

7 *5* **Digit** 2-8-4 0.......... PaulHanagan 7 36+
(B Smart) *a towards rr: rdn along and hung bdly lft wl over 1f out: sn eased* **25/1**

8 *nk* **Smoke Me A Kipper (IRE)** 2-8-6 0.......... RoystonFfrench 11 34
(Mrs A Duffield) *a bhd* **40/1**

9 *3/4* **Ishe Mac** 2-8-4 0.......... SilvestreDeSousa 3 30
(N Bycroft) *cl up: rdn 2f out and ev ch tl drvn and wknd appr fnl f* **80/1**

0 **10** *1 1/2* **Angela Tee (IRE)**[22] 2217 2-8-1 0.......... DuranFentiman(3) 4 25
(T D Easterby) *chsd ldrs: rdn along over 2f out and sn wknd* **100/1**

11 *hd* **Accomplishment (IRE)** 2-8-6 0.......... AndrewElliott 1 30+
(A P Jarvis) *a in rr* **20/1**

1m 17.45s (0.55) **Going Correction** +0.025s/f (Good) **11** Ran SP% **118.7**
Speed ratings (Par 90): **97,96,95,91,86 86,79,79,78,76 75**
CSF £58.43 TOTE £8.90: £2.00, £2.30, £1.10; EX 48.50.
Owner Alotincommon Partnership **Bred** Llety Stud **Trained** Babworth, Notts

FOCUS
A modest maiden run at a fairly strong pace. The favourite was below her debut form.

NOTEBOOK
Common Diva, who improved on her debut effort when stepping up to 6f at Newcastle last time, bounced out of the stalls and was soon in front. Putting all her experience to good use, she had to really dig in late on, but was always just doing enough. There may be more to come from her in nurseries. (tchd 8-1)
On Offer(IRE), a promising third over 6f at Redcar on debut, again hindered her chance by being sluggish out of the gate and she took an age to get going. She finished strongly though and may well have won in another 50 yards. She should continue to go the right way. (op 12-1)
Maid For Music(IRE), whose yard do well with their juveniles, finished second in a fair contest at Haydock on debut and she looked the one to beat with that run under her belt. She had an ideal early pitch, but could not match the winner for speed and only plugged on at the one pace. This was disappointing, but a small race should still come her way. (tchd Evens)
Flying Lady(IRE), a 26,000euros daughter of Hawk Wing, comes from a yard who have been going well with their two-year-olds, but her inexperience found her out on this racecourse debut. She finished well though and should know a lot more next time. (op 5-2 tchd 9-4)
Abby Belle(IRE) improved markedly on her debut effort and travelled up promisingly on the outside, only to tire in the straight. She will be qualified for a handicap mark following one more run and should fare better in nurseries. (tchd 100-1)
Digit Official explanation: jockey said filly hung badly left in the straight

2888 TONY BETHELL MEMORIAL H'CAP 2m 1f 22y
7:20 (7:20) (Class 4) (0-80,80) 4-Y-O+ **£4,533** (£1,348; £674; £336) **Stalls** Low

Form RPR

510 **1** **Rock 'N' Roller (FR)**[9] 2621 4-9-3 **73**.......... RichardMullen 5 83
(W R Muir) *in tch on inner: pushed along over 3f out: swtchd rt and rdn 2f out: drvn and styd on strly ins fnl f to ld fnl 75yds* **6/1**[3]

13-0 **2** *1* **Aphorism**[51] 1472 5-9-4 **73**.......... JamieSpencer 1 82
(J R Fanshawe) *dwlt: hld up in rr: hdwy on outer 4f out cl up 2f out: rdn to ld and hung lft ins fnl f: hdd and no ex fnl 100yds* **7/1**

2301 **3** *3* **At The Money**[10] 2567 5-8-13 **68**.......... RyanMoore 8 74
(J M P Eustace) *led: rdn along over 3f out: drvn over 1f out: edgd lft ent fnl f: sn hdd and kpt on same pce* **4/1**[1]

6000 **4** *1 1/2* **Thewhirlingdervish (IRE)**[9] 2628 10-9-0 **69**.......... DavidAllan 4 74+
(T D Easterby) *trckd ldrs: effrt on inner 2f out: rdn and nt clr run jst ins fnl f: swtchd rt and kpt on same pce* **4/1**[1]

-550 **5** *3 1/2* **Merrymaker**[10] 2572 8-8-10 **65**.......... KShea 6 66
(W M Brisbourne) *chsd ldrs: rdn along over 3f out: drvn 2f out and plugged on same pce* **16/1**

4301 **6** *2* **Brave Bugsy (IRE)**[21] 2245 5-8-5 **60** oh1.......... WilliamBuick 11 58
(A M Balding) *hld up in tch: effrt 4f out: rdn along 3f out and sn no imp* **5/1**[2]

0-50 **7** *3* **Tribe**[30] 1984 6-8-13 **68**.......... JoeFanning 9 63
(P R Webber) *rrd s and slowly away: in rr tl rapid hdwy on outer over 4f out: cl up over 2f out: sn rdn and wknd* **14/1**

110- **8** *1 3/4* **Colwyn Bay (IRE)**[46] 5533 6-8-8 **63**.......... (tp) PaulHanagan 10 56
(R M Stronge) *in tch: hdwy over 6f out: rdn along over 3f out and sn wknd* **12/1**

-500 **9** *8* **Great As Gold (IRE)**[25] 2135 9-8-12 **67**.......... (p) TomEaves 12 51
(B Ellison) *hld up towards rr: hdwy over 6f out: rdn along over 3f out: sn drvn and wknd* **10/1**

0/40 **10** *45* **Mt Desert**[18] 2332 6-8-11 **66**.......... RobertWinston 7 1
(E W Tuer) *prom: rdn along 4f out: wknd 3f out* **16/1**

3m 49.6s (-2.00) **Going Correction** +0.025s/f (Good)
WFA 4 from 5yo+ 1lb **10** Ran SP% **118.7**
Speed ratings (Par 105): **105,104,103,102,100 99,98,97,93,72**
CSF £48.54 CT £190.57 TOTE £7.40: £2.50, £2.40, £1.70; EX 61.80.
Owner D G Clarke & C L A Edginton **Bred** Eric Puerari, Oceanic Bloodstock Et Al **Trained** Lambourn, Berks

FOCUS
An ordinary staying handicap, rated through the second and third.
Thewhirlingdervish(IRE) Official explanation: jockey said gelding was denied a clear run
Mt Desert Official explanation: jockey said gelding ran too free

2889 HARRATTS WAKEFIELD RENAULT H'CAP 1m 2f 6y
7:50 (7:52) (Class 4) (0-85,85) 3-Y-O **£5,180** (£1,541; £770; £384) **Stalls** Low

Form RPR

-242 **1** **Formation (USA)**[19] 2302 3-9-5 **83**.......... JamieSpencer 3 87
(E A L Dunlop) *trckd ldrs: hdwy 2f out: swtchd lft and effrt to chal over 1f out: rdn to ld and swished tail ins fnl f: drvn and hld on towards fin* **2/1**[2]

3-21 **2** *shd* **Missioner (USA)**[17] 2360 3-9-7 **85**.......... GregFairley 2 89+
(M Johnston) *cl up: led 3f out: rdn 2f out: drvn and hdd ins fnl f: rallied wl towards fin* **5/4**[1]

214- **3** *2 1/4* **Merchant Of Dubai**[306] 4278 3-8-12 **76**.......... RobertWinston 4 76
(G A Swinbank) *chsd ldng pair: rdn along 3f out: drvn wl over 1f out: kpt on same pce fnl f* **11/2**[3]

310- **4** *7* **Resounding Glory (USA)**[226] 6486 3-9-4 **82**.......... PaulHanagan 8 68
(R A Fahey) *hld up in rr: effrt over 2f out: sn rdn and nvr a factor* **17/2**

210- **5** *2 3/4* **Bonjour Allure (IRE)**[270] 5350 3-9-1 **79**.......... RoystonFfrench 5 59
(Mrs A Duffield) *hld up: effrt 3f out: sn rdn along and btn 2f out* **14/1**

13-0 **6** *10* **Burriscarra**[7] 2688 3-8-11 **75**.......... AdrianTNicholls 6 35
(Eamon Tyrrell, Ire) *led: rdn along and hdd 3f out: drvn 2f out and sn wknd* **28/1**

2m 17.15s (3.45) **Going Correction** +0.025s/f (Good) **6** Ran SP% **113.8**
Speed ratings (Par 101): **87,86,85,79,77 69**
CSF £4.99 CT £9.82 TOTE £2.70: £1.80, £1.50; EX 4.70.
Owner Highclere Thoroughbred Racing (Tamarisk) **Bred** Loch Lea Farm **Trained** Newmarket, Suffolk

FOCUS
A poor turnout and no strength in depth but the first three home are talented. They went no pace at all in the early stages resulting in a very slow winning time for a race of its type. Slight improvement from the first two.
Bonjour Allure(IRE) Official explanation: jockey said filly ran too free

2890 WEATHERBYS BANK PIPALONG STKS (LISTED RACE) (F&M) 1m 4y
8:20 (8:20) (Class 1) 4-Y-O+
£16,824 (£6,405; £3,207; £1,602; £801; £402) **Stalls** Low

Form RPR

4-21 **1** **Kasumi**[20] 2284 5-8-12 85.......... TravisBlock 2 104
(H Morrison) *trckd ldrs: hdwy 2f out: rdn to ld appr fnl f: drvn: edgd lft and kpt on wl towards fin* **17/2**

-143 **2** *3/4* **Flying Clarets (IRE)**[25] 2130 5-8-12 100.......... (p) PaulHanagan 6 103
(R A Fahey) *led: rdn along and jnd 2f out: sn hdd: rallied wl u.p ins fnl f: kpt on* **7/2**[3]

1-65 **3** *3* **Steam Cuisine**[7] 2666 4-8-12 94.......... TPO'Shea 10 96
(M G Quinlan) *hld up: hdwy on inner wl over 1f out: swtchd rt and rdn ent fnl f: sn drvn and kpt on: nrst fin* **12/1**

4-25 **4** *1 1/2* **Chantilly Tiffany**[37] 1801 4-8-12 94.......... JoeFanning 8 92
(E A L Dunlop) *trckd ldr: chal 2f out: rdn to ld wl over 1f out: drvn and hdd appr fnl f: wknd* **10/1**

-464 **5** *1/2* **Folly Lodge**[12] 2505 4-8-12 86.......... WilliamBuick 3 91
(G Wragg) *in tch: hdwy over 2f out: sn rdn and no imp appr fnl f* **16/1**

00-6 **6** *3/4* **Passion Fruit**[28] 2039 7-8-12 83.......... AndrewElliott 9 89
(C W Fairhurst) *hld up in rr: swtchd outside and hdwy wl over 1f out: sn rdn and no imp fnl f* **50/1**

31-1 **7** *3 3/4* **Fondled**[23] 2200 4-8-12 88.......... JamieSpencer 1 81
(J R Fanshawe) *trckd ldrs: hdwy over 2f out: rdn wl over 1f out: drvn and carried rt ent fnl f: sn wknd* **2/1**[1]

0005 **8** *10* **Impetious**[37] 1807 4-9-1 0.......... (b) AdrianTNicholls 12 61
(Eamon Tyrrell, Ire) *a in rr* **50/1**

430- **9** *6* **Treat**[318] 3897 4-8-12 100.......... RyanMoore 4 44
(E A L Dunlop) *trckd ldng pair: effrt over 2f out: sn rdn and wknd wl over 1f out: eased* **10/3**[2]

1m 43.16s (-2.74) **Going Correction** +0.025s/f (Good) **9** Ran SP% **115.7**
Speed ratings (Par 111): **114,113,110,108,108 107,103,93,87**
CSF £38.47 TOTE £9.20: £1.80, £1.50, £2.90; EX 48.70.
Owner Viscountess Trenchard **Bred** Fonthill Stud **Trained** East Ilsley, Berks
■ Stewards' Enquiry : Paul Hanagan two-day ban: used whip with excessive frequency (Jun 23-24)

FOCUS
A wide variety of ability for this Listed event judged on official figures but it was one of those who seemed to have a stiff task who proved successful, although it was no fluke. The second is a good guideline as to the quality of the form and the winning time was a decent one too.

NOTEBOOK
Kasumi had plenty to find with most of these on official figures but the daughter of Inchinor has done nothing but improve with age and she showed a willing attitude to get the better of the runner-up who sets a good standard in this company. Connections are eyeing a Group 3 event in Germany as her next target. (op 9-1 tchd 10-1)

Flying Clarets(IRE) bounced out of the stalls and took them along at a good lick, finding plenty for pressure when challenged, and would have gained that elusive first win in Listed company in convincing style if for some reason Kasumi hadn't turned up. This trip is a bare minimum for her and she will have chances to go one better in similar company over 1m2f throughout the summer. (op 11-2)
Steam Cuisine passed a couple of beaten horses close home and it remains to be seen whether she will see out a truly run mile if she is put in the race with a chance at a more realistic stage.
Chantilly Tiffany led briefly at the furlong pole and, whilst this made it three consecutive respectable efforts in Listed company, she needs to find some improvement from somewhere to win a race as she is punitively handicapped if connections choose to go down that route. (op 9-1)
Folly Lodge probably ran up to her best as she had a very difficult task on official ratings.
Passion Fruit was beaten less than a length into third in this event last year and again ran above herself on this occasion. If she could reproduce this form in a handicap she would be something of a good thing but she often hasn't been able to do so in the recent past. (op 40-1)
Fondled was slightly interfered with in the closing stages but was already looking well held, and judged on this evidence the step up to listed company from handicaps is too much for her at this stage in her career. Official explanation: jockey said gelding was unsuited by the going (op 15-8 tchd 9-4 in a place)
Treat, who became very disappointing for Mick Channon last year after running fourth in the 1000 Guineas, has switched yards but to no effect judged on this display. Official explanation: trainer had no explanation for the poor form shown (op 7-2 tchd 3-1)

2891 SMITHS OF PETERBOROUGH RENAULT H'CAP — 6f
8:50 (8:50) (Class 5) (0-70,74) 3-Y-0+ — **£3,238** (£963; £481; £240) **Stalls** Low

Form				RPR
0003	1		**Bid For Gold**[2] 2846 4-9-6 **60** ... PaulHanagan 17 (Jedd O'Keeffe) *chsd ldng pair: hdwy to ld wl over 1f out and sn rdn: drvn ins fnl f and kpt on wl* **9/2**[1]	72
6061	2	3/4	**Dickie Le Davoir**[4] 2747 4-10-1 **74** 6ex ... MarkCoumbe(5) 5 (John A Harris) *in rr: hdwy on outer wl over 1f out: rdn to chse wnr ins fnl f: kpt on* **16/1**	83
1266	3	3/4	**A Big Sky Brewing (USA)**[14] 2448 4-9-0 **59** ...(b) NeilBrown(5) 2 (T D Barron) *trckd ldrs: hdwy 2f out: sn rdn and kpt on u.p ins fnl f* **6/1**[2]	66
0600	4	2 1/4	**Royal Challenge**[3] 2780 7-9-11 **65** ... DanielTudhope 12 (I W McInnes) *chsd ldrs: hdwy 2f out and sn rdn: drvn ent fnl f and kpt on same pce* **16/1**	65
30-0	5	1/2	**Brigadore**[14] 2448 9-9-1 **55** ... J-PGuillambert 11 (J G Given) *in tch: hdwy 2f out: rdn and chsd ldrs over 1f out: drvn and kpt on ins fnl f: nrst fin* **11/1**	53
0600	6	1/2	**Steel Blue**[31] 1952 8-9-7 **61** ... KShea 8 (R M Whitaker) *in tch: hdwy 2f out: sn rdn and kpt on ins fnl f: nrst fin* **12/1**	58
3430	7	3/4	**Avontuur (FR)**[4] 2751 6-9-2 **56** ...(p) DaleGibson 10 (Mrs R A Carr) *s.i.s and bhd: hdwy 2f out: sn rdn and styd on strly ins fnl f: nrst fin* **20/1**	50
2650	8	1	**Messiah Garvey**[30] 2005 4-9-6 **60** ... AdrianTNicholls 9 (D Nicholls) *in rr: swtchd outside and hdwy wl over 1f out: sn rdn and kpt on fnl f: nrst fin* **13/2**[3]	51
5002	9	nse	**Sands Of Barra (IRE)**[21] 2251 5-10-0 **68** ... AndrewElliott 7 (I W McInnes) *chsd ldrs: rdn along over 2f out: drvn: edgd rt and wknd over 1f out* **12/1**	59
0-30	10	2 1/4	**Karky Schultz (GER)**[15] 2429 3-9-1 **63** ... RobertWinston 13 (J M P Eustace) *a in rr* **11/1**	47
4330	11	nse	**Steel City Boy (IRE)**[10] 2583 5-9-1 **60** ... AnnStokell(5) 14 (Miss A Stokell) *a in midfield* **16/1**	43
-032	12	3/4	**Dolly No Hair**[17] 2366 3-9-4 **66** ... FergalLynch 1 (D W Barker) *cl up on inner: led over 2f out: sn rdn and hdd wl over 1f out: grad wknd* **9/1**	47
0160	13	3 1/2	**Winthorpe (IRE)**[14] 2444 8-9-11 **68** ... JamieMoriarty(3) 3 (J J Quinn) *a in rr* **11/1**	38
5-00	14	2 1/2	**Sea Rover (IRE)**[30] 2005 4-9-11 **65** ... TWilliams 16 (M Brittain) *sn led: rdn along and hdd over 2f out: wknd* **20/1**	27

1m 16.74s (-0.16) **Going Correction** +0.025s/f (Good) — **14** Ran SP% **123.4**
WFA 3 from 4yo+ 8lb
Speed ratings (Par 103): **102,101,100,97,96 95,94,93,93,90 90,89,84,81**
CSF £80.90 CT £451.81 TOTE £5.90: £2.40, £6.00, £2.40; EX 71.40.
Owner Paul Chapman And Ba'Tat Investments **Bred** B Minty **Trained** Middleham Moor, N Yorks

FOCUS
A fair sprint handicap for older horses featuring a few in-form animals and a couple threatening to strike form imminently. Solid form.
Avontuur(FR) Official explanation: jockey said gelding missed the break
Sea Rover(IRE) Official explanation: trainer later said colt was found to have a viral infection

2892 TRENTON HULL RENAULT H'CAP — 5f
9:20 (9:21) (Class 5) (0-75,75) 4-Y-0+ — **£3,238** (£963; £481; £240) **Stalls** Low

Form				RPR
6010	1		**Namir (IRE)**[4] 2760 6-9-1 **72** ...(vt) DuranFentiman(3) 11 (D Shaw) *prom: hdwy to chse ldr 1/2-way: rdn to chal over 1f out: drvn ins fnl f: styd on to ld last stride* **10/1**	81
0505	2	shd	**Mr Wolf**[16] 2398 7-9-1 **69** ...(p) TomEaves 13 (D W Barker) *sn led: jnd and rdn wl over 1f out: drvn ins fnl f: hdd last stride* **7/1**[2]	78
206-	3	1 3/4	**Pickering**[275] 5232 4-9-2 **70** ... DavidAllan 12 (E J Alston) *hld up in rr: hdwy on outer wl over 1f out: sn rdn and styd on ins fnl f: nrst fin* **10/1**	72+
0660	4	1 1/2	**No Time (IRE)**[9] 2596 8-8-2 **56** ... WilliamBuick 4 (A J McCabe) *hld up towards rr: hdwy on outer wl over 1f out: rdn and kpt on ins fnl f: nrst fin* **11/1**	53
0050	5	1/2	**Kings College Boy**[4] 2748 8-8-2 **56** oh1 ...(b) PaulHanagan 7 (R A Fahey) *sn chsng ldrs: rdn along wl over 1f out: drvn appr fnl f and kpt on same pce* **15/2**[3]	51
00-0	6	1/2	**Never Without Me**[20] 2293 8-8-6 **60** ... RoystonFfrench 3 (J F Coupland) *chsd ldrs: rdn along 2f out: drvn over 1f out: kpt on same pce* **25/1**	53+
-000	7	1	**Welcome Approach**[9] 2596 5-8-6 **60** ... AndrewElliott 2 (J R Weymes) *in tch on inner: rdn along 2f out: drvn over 1f out and no imp* **14/1**	50
50/0	8	1/2	**Blue Maeve**[16] 2390 8-9-2 **70** ... SilvestreDeSousa 8 (A D Brown) *chsd ldr: rdn along 2f out: drvn and wknd ent fnl f* **25/1**	58
3300	9	1/2	**Feelin Foxy**[13] 2489 4-9-7 **75** ... J-PGuillambert 9 (J G Given) *chsd ldrs: effrt 2f out: sn rdn and wknd appr fnl f* **16/1**	61
0004	10	3/4	**Jimmy The Guesser**[23] 2205 5-8-9 **68** ...(b) MarkCoumbe(5) 10 (N P Littmoden) *s.i.s: a in rr* **11/1**	51
6053	11	3/4	**Red Cape (FR)**[16] 2398 5-9-2 **70** ...(b) JohnEgan 14 (Mrs R A Carr) *in tch on outer: rdn along 2f out: wknd over 1f out* **12/1**	51
-444	12	1/2	**Charles Parnell (IRE)**[10] 2583 5-9-7 **75** ... FergalLynch 6 (M Dods) *s.i.s and bhd: hdwy on inner whn nt clr run over 1f out: swtchd rt and eased* **11/4**[1]	54+
2051	13	11	**Funfair Wane**[10] 2576 9-8-6 **60** ... AdrianTNicholls 5 (D Nicholls) *chsd ldrs: rdn along 2f out: wkng whn lost action jst ins fnl f and sn eased* **7/1**[2]	—

63.25 secs (-0.05) **Going Correction** +0.025s/f (Good) — **13** Ran SP% **126.2**
Speed ratings (Par 103): **101,100,98,95,94 94,92,91,90,89 88,87,70**
CSF £82.93 CT £528.48 TOTE £15.20: £4.40, £3.20, £3.00; EX 61.80 Place 6: £68.97, Place 5: £49.15..
Owner ownaracehorse.co.uk (Shakespeare) **Bred** B Kennedy **Trained** Danethorpe, Notts

FOCUS
A competitive sprint handicap run at a good pace. The first pair were always prominent and the form is pretty solid.
Jimmy The Guesser Official explanation: jockey said gelding stumbled leaving the stalls
Charles Parnell(IRE) Official explanation: jockey said gelding missed the break and was denied a clear run
Funfair Wane Official explanation: jockey said gelding lost its action
T/Jkpt: Part won. £442,863.41 to a £1 stake. Pool: £623,751.38. 0.50 winning tickets. T/Plt: £97.20 to a £1 stake. Pool: £105,623.57. 793.25 winning tickets. T/Qpdt: £37.70 to a £1 stake. Pool: £4,391.50. 86.00 winning tickets. JR

2677 WINDSOR (R-H)
Monday, June 9

OFFICIAL GOING: Good to firm (good in places; 8.6)
Wind: Light, behind Weather: Fine, warm

2893 PSP ASSOCIATION E B F MEDIAN AUCTION MAIDEN STKS — 6f
6:30 (6:31) (Class 5) 2-Y-0 — **£3,302** (£982; £491; £245) **Stalls** High

Form				RPR
	1		**Dark Mischief** 2-9-3 0 ... DaneO'Neill 16 (H Candy) *mde all and racd against nr side rail: rdn 1f out: styd on* **3/1**[1]	80+
	2	2	**Green Beret (IRE)** 2-9-3 0 ... JimmyFortune 6 (J H M Gosden) *chsd ldrs: effrt 2f out: rdn and kpt on fnl f: nvr able to chal* **4/1**[2]	72
	3	nse	**Young Dottie** 2-8-12 0 ... AmirQuinn 11 (P M Phelan) *pressed wnr: wandered whn rdn fr 2f out: hld fnl f and jst pipped for 2nd* **66/1**	67
	4	2	**Soul City (IRE)** 2-9-3 0 ... RichardHughes 9 (R Hannon) *dwlt: sn in tch: hanging lft fr over 2f out: shkn up and styd on: nvr able to chal* **9/2**[3]	66+
0	5	nk	**Blusher**[31] 1961 2-8-12 0 ... SamHitchcott 3 (M R Channon) *t.k.h: hld up bhd ldrs: hanging fr 2f out: no imp but kpt on* **50/1**	60
	6	6	**Yeoman Blaze** 2-9-3 0 ... FrancisNorton 12 (A M Balding) *bmpd s: nvr beyond midfield: shkn up over 2f out: one pce* **15/2**	52+
	7	nk	**Alderbed** 2-9-0 0 ... TolleyDean(3) 14 (George Baker) *wnt lft s: cl up: rdn 2f out: wknd over 1f out* **16/1**	46
	8	1	**Mr Willis** 2-9-3 0 ... LPKeniry 10 (J R Best) *s.s: hld up wl in rr: sme prog 2f out: swtchd lft over 1f out: green but plugged on* **25/1**	43
	9	hd	**Elusive Intentions (IRE)** 2-8-12 0 ... TGMcLaughlin 15 (P D Evans) *s.s: nvr beyond midfield: struggling fr over 2f out* **22/1**	37
0	10	1	**Kheylide (IRE)**[7] 2657 2-8-12 0 ... SCreighton(5) 2 (Miss V Haigh) *hld up in midfield: rn green fr 1/2-way: sn outpcd and btn* **100/1**	39
0	11	4	**Super Fourteen**[18] 2324 2-9-3 0 ... RichardSmith 1 (R Hannon) *s.s: swtchd fr wd draw: a wl in rr* **8/1**	27+
	12	3/4	**Brazilian Art** 2-9-3 0 ... AlanMunro 7 (P W Chapple-Hyam) *dwlt: sn pushed along and wl in rr: a bhd* **8/1**	25
	13	nk	**Prima Fonteyn** 2-8-5 0 ... MatthewDavies(7) 4 (M R Channon) *dwlt: a wl in rr: struggling fr 1/2-way* **20/1**	19
	14	nk	**Spring Quartet** 2-9-3 0 ... ShaneKelly 8 (Pat Eddery) *dwlt: nvr beyond midfield: rdn over 2f out: sn wknd* **20/1**	23
	15	26	**Jasper Cliff** 2-8-12 0 ... JackDean(5) 5 (Mark Gillard) *dwlt: outpcd and a bhd: t.o* **66/1**	—

1m 13.17s (0.17) **Going Correction** -0.225s/f (Firm) — **15** Ran SP% **126.7**
Speed ratings (Par 93): **89,86,86,83,83 75,74,73,73,71 66,65,65,64,30**
CSF £14.01 TOTE £4.20: £2.00, £2.00, £15.20; EX 17.70.
Owner First Of Many Partnership **Bred** Jeremy Green And Sons And Mr P Bickmore **Trained** Kingston Warren, Oxon

FOCUS
Few got involved and they finished strung out, indeed the first five were well clear of the remainder. There was not much strength in depth and the bare form is probably just ordinary, but the race should produce some winners.

NOTEBOOK
Dark Mischief, a 34,000gns son of Namid, half-brother to 1m7f winner Sargon, who was also a multiple hurdles winner, out of a 1m1f winner, knew his job and justified significant market support. Soon in front showing good speed, he had the benefit of the favoured stands' rail and ran on strongly to the line. It remains to be seen what he beat, but he looks a useful prospect and holds a Super Sprint entry. (op 6-1 tchd 13-2 in places)
Green Beret(IRE), a 120,000gns gelded son of Fayruz, brother to quite useful 5f juvenile Inxile, half-brother to very useful sprinter Tax Free, emerges with plenty of credit. He made his move out wide, which was far from ideal, and proved no match for the comfortable winner, who had the benefit of the rail, but he kept on quite well. He should learn from this. (op 7-2 tchd 6-1)
Young Dottie, a daughter of Desert Sun, first foal of a 5f juvenile winner, showed plenty of ability on her racecourse debut and might have been second had her rider not dropped his reins around a furlong out. She showed a lot of speed and should be able to win a similar race, possibly over 5f.
Soul City(IRE), an 88,000euros son of Elusive City, half-brother to among others the smart Sentinelese, a multiple 7f-1m winner, out a smart German sprinter at two and three, shaped nicely back in fourth. He could make no impression in a race in which the pace held up, but was noted doing some good late work and he should be sharper next time. (op 7-2)
Blusher showed very little on her debut at Nottingham, but this was a lot better.
Brazilian Art Official explanation: vet said colt spread a plate
Jasper Cliff Official explanation: jockey said colt was lame

2894 CANNON KIRK CLAIMING STKS — 1m 3f 135y
7:00 (7:00) (Class 5) 3-Y-0 — **£2,593** (£765; £383) **Stalls** Low

Form				RPR
0512	1		**An Scaribh**[12] 2495 3-9-1 **70** ... RichardEvans(7) 7 (P D Evans) *t.k.h: hld up in tch: prog to press ldrs 2f out: led 1f out: sn clr* **5/4**[1]	65

5100 **2** 3½ **Kryptonite (IRE)**[31] 1962 3-9-8 64..............................(p) TQuinn 4 59
(J W Hills) *mde most: rdn and hanging bdly lft 3f out: hung lft and hdd 1f out: kpt on* **15/2**[3]

6-63 **3** 1¼ **Sergeant Sharpe**[32] 1937 3-9-0 68.............................. SebSanders 5 49
(M H Tompkins) *s.i.s: hld up: prog to trck ldr over 3f out: chal 2f out: nt qckn and n.m.r 1f out: btn after* **15/8**[2]

0-06 **4** 1¼ **Howe's Jack (IRE)**[27] 2080 3-8-6 40..............(t) RussellKennemore(3) 2 42
(M C Chapman) *t.k.h: hld up: trckd ldrs whn nt clr run 2f out: hung lft and fnd nil fnl f* **66/1**

00-0 **5** 12 **Golddigging (IRE)**[73] 1059 3-8-11 45..............................(b[1]) JamesDoyle 3 23
(J G Portman) *in tch tl wknd 3f out* **33/1**

00-0 **6** 2½ **Illusionary**[66] 1186 3-8-12 46.............................. RichardKingscote 9 20
(J G Portman) *t.k.h: mostly trckd ldr after 2f to over 3f out: wknd over 2f out* **16/1**

0-50 **7** ½ **Pay The Grey**[6] 2694 3-8-9 45 ow1.............................. RichardHughes 1 16
(R Hannon) *prom tl rdn and lost pl 4f out* **16/1**

06-0 **8** ½ **Magnol**[35] 1869 3-8-2 49..............................(p) LukeMorris(3) 6 11
(J G M O'Shea) *dwlt: t.k.h: hld up: rdn and struggling over 4f out* **14/1**

2m 30.47s (0.97) **Going Correction** -0.10s/f (Good) **8** Ran SP% **113.9**
Speed ratings (Par 99): **92,89,88,88,80 78,78,77**
CSF £11.62 TOTE £2.10: £1.10, £1.70, £1.20; EX 12.80.The winner was claimed by Ian Saunders for £18,000.
Owner John P Jones **Bred** P Young **Trained** Pandy, Monmouths

FOCUS
A weak claimer rated through the first two, with the fourth doing nothing for the form.

2895 SEI INVESTMENT H'CAP 1m 2f 7y
7:30 (7:32) (Class 4) (0-80,80) 4-Y-0+ **£4,857** (£1,445; £722; £360) **Stalls** Low

Form RPR

1-44 **1** **Valrhona (IRE)**[30] 1981 4-9-7 80.............................. LDettori 8 88+
(J Noseda) *mde all and secured easy ld: shkn up over 3f out: drvn and kpt on wl fnl 2f* **10/11**[1]

014 **2** 1 **Roodolph**[12] 2499 4-9-1 74.............................. StephenCarson 6 80
(Eve Johnson Houghton) *t.k.h: trckd wnr after 2f: rdn 3f out: tried to chal fnl 2f: a hld* **7/1**[3]

0265 **3** ¾ **Aegean Prince**[11] 2540 4-9-3 76.............................. RichardHughes 3 81
(R Hannon) *hld up in 5th: pushed along to cl over 2f out: swtchd wd and effrt jst over 1f out: rdn and nt qckn* **3/1**[2]

1-60 **4** *hd* **Royal Jasra**[19] 2304 4-9-2 75.............................. JimmyFortune 4 79
(E A L Dunlop) *trckd wnr 2f: rdn over 3f out: one pce and no imp fnl 2f* **16/1**

00-0 **5** 2 **Know The Law**[17] 2372 4-9-0 76..............................(b) MarcHalford(3) 1 76
(D R C Elsworth) *rn wout front shoe: hld up in last: rdn 3f out: hanging and nt qckn fnl 2f: kpt on* **16/1**

0056 **6** *shd* **Krugerrand (USA)**[11] 2540 9-8-11 70.............................. StephenDonohoe 7 70
(W J Musson) *hld up in last pair: rdn and no imp fnl 3f* **8/1**

21-0 **7** 14 **Fantastic Morning**[72] 1072 4-9-6 79.............................. TGMcLaughlin 2 51
(F Jordan) *trckd ldng trio: rdn over 3f out: wknd rapidly over 1f out: eased: t.o* **33/1**

2m 7.98s (-0.72) **Going Correction** -0.10s/f (Good) **7** Ran SP% **115.7**
Speed ratings (Par 105): **98,97,96,96,94 94,83**
CSF £8.47 CT £14.68 TOTE £1.70: £1.40, £2.60; EX 4.90.
Owner Ballygallon Stud Limited **Bred** Ballygallon Stud Limited **Trained** Newmarket, Suffolk
■ Stewards' Enquiry : Richard Hughes one-day ban: careless riding (Jun 23)

FOCUS
An ordinary race for the grade. The winner is on the upgrade, but she had an easy lead here and the bare form is muddling.

2896 SMITH & WILLIAMSON H'CAP 5f 10y
8:00 (8:01) (Class 4) (0-80,78) 3-Y-O **£4,857** (£1,445; £722; £360) **Stalls** High

Form RPR

2052 **1** **Monsieur Reynard**[10] 2570 3-9-2 73.............................. LDettori 5 83
(B J Meehan) *in tch in rr: swtchd lft jst over 2f out: and effrt: drvn to chal 1f out: led fnl 100yds: eased fnl strides: jst hld on* **11/4**[2]

1-04 **2** *shd* **Wise Melody**[15] 2428 3-9-7 78.............................. LiamJones 3 87
(W J Haggas) *cl up: effrt to ld over 1f out: urged along fnl f: hdd fnl 100yds: kpt on: jst failed* **15/2**

4-05 **3** 2¾ **Kalligal**[41] 1699 3-8-10 67.............................. SteveDrowne 2 67
(R Ingram) *led: hanging lft fr 1/2-way: hdd over 1f out: outpcd fnl f* **25/1**

1060 **4** 3 **Barraland**[10] 2570 3-8-11 75.............................. MatthewDavies(7) 4 64
(M R Channon) *trckd ldr to over 2f out: swtchd lft sn after: nt qckn over 1f out: fdd* **18/1**

31-5 **5** 2 **Quaroma**[12] 2506 3-9-2 73.............................. KerrinMcEvoy 7 55
(Jane Chapple-Hyam) *trckd ldrs: hemmed in against rail fr 2f out: wknd fnl f* **6/1**[3]

0-14 **6** *nk* **Mullein**[30] 1988 3-9-3 74.............................. SebSanders 6 55
(R M Beckett) *s.i.s: hld up in last: no prog whn nt clr run briefly over 1f out: wknd fnl f* **11/8**[1]

1-43 **7** 2¼ **Another Socket**[25] 2122 3-9-3 74.............................. StephenDonohoe 1 47
(E S McMahon) *wnt lft s: in tch in rr on outer: wknd wl over 1f out* **8/1**

59.35 secs (-0.95) **Going Correction** -0.225s/f (Firm) **7** Ran SP% **115.0**
Speed ratings (Par 101): **98,97,93,88,85 84,81**
CSF £23.65 TOTE £3.50: £2.40, £3.50; EX 23.70.
Owner Mrs Sandy Briddon **Bred** The Hon Mrs R Pease **Trained** Manton, Wilts
■ Stewards' Enquiry : L Dettori one-day ban: careless riding (Jun 27)

FOCUS
A fair sprint handicap and the early pace looked strong. The front pair put distance between themselves and the rest and the form looks solid enough despite the disappointing run of the favourite.
Quaroma Official explanation: jockey said filly moved poorly in final furlong
Another Socket Official explanation: jockey said filly missed the break

2897 SCOTT WILSON H'CAP 1m 67y
8:30 (8:31) (Class 5) (0-75,75) 4-Y-0+ **£3,070** (£906; £453) **Stalls** High

Form RPR

4-06 **1** **Dear Maurice**[17] 2360 4-9-4 72.............................. SebSanders 4 88+
(E A L Dunlop) *trckd ldrs: rdn over 2f out: styd on to ld 1f out: sn drew clr* **7/2**[1]

00-6 **2** 2¼ **Sotik Star (IRE)**[16] 2406 5-9-0 68.............................. JimmyFortune 5 76
(P J Makin) *trckd ldr to 1/2-way: wnt 2nd again wl over 2f out: drvn to ld 2f out: hdd and outpcd 1f out* **12/1**

0-0 **3** 1½ **Australia Day (IRE)**[131] 357 5-9-0 68.............................. DaneO'Neill 13 73
(P R Webber) *rrd s: plld hrd and hld up in midfield: effrt over 2f out: styd on fr over 1f out to take 3rd nr fin* **12/1**

031- **4** ¾ **Quaglino Way (GR)**[228] 6457 4-8-13 67.............................. JimCrowley 6 70
(P R Chamings) *led: drvn and hdd 2f out: wknd fnl f* **20/1**

-030 **5** *hd* **Aggravation**[17] 2373 6-8-13 70.............................. MarcHalford(3) 1 72+
(D R C Elsworth) *hld up in last pair: shkn up 3f out: tried to make prog fr 2f out: urged along and kpt on: nvr nrr* **8/1**

6-11 **6** *nk* **Grand Vizier (IRE)**[11] 2550 4-8-13 72.............................. JackMitchell(5) 2 74
(C F Wall) *hld up bhd ldrs: taken to outer and effrt over 2f out: hanging and no imp on ldrs over 1f out* **4/1**[2]

405- **7** ½ **Eastern Emperor**[297] 4587 4-9-2 70.............................. AdamKirby 12 71
(W R Swinburn) *t.k.h: trckd ldrs: stl cl up 2f out: reminder over 1f out and edgd lft: eased ins fnl f* **11/1**

0614 **8** ½ **Dream Of Fortune (IRE)**[17] 2373 4-8-12 71..............(t) JamieJones(5) 8 70
(M G Quinlan) *hld up in rr: reminders and looked awkward over 2f out: nvr on terms: kpt on* **5/1**[3]

1560 **9** 1¼ **Golden Prospect**[24] 2152 4-9-4 72.............................. EddieAhern 7 69
(J W Hills) *dwlt: hld up in last pair: nudged along fr 3f out: nvr nr ldrs* **14/1**

0-00 **10** *nk* **Leptis Magna**[17] 2373 4-8-7 61 ow1.............................. TQuinn 11 57
(D R C Elsworth) *stdd s: hld up wl in rr: taken to outer and effrt over 2f out: wknd over 1f out* **28/1**

0600 **11** *shd* **Louisiade (IRE)**[11] 2550 7-7-13 60..............(p) CharlotteKerton(7) 14 56
(M C Chapman) *plld hrd: cl up: trckd ldr 1/2-way to wl over 2f out: wknd u.p* **66/1**

0415 **12** 1¾ **Davenport (IRE)**[13] 2476 6-9-7 75.............................. AlanMunro 10 67
(B R Millman) *hld up in midfield: taken to wd outside over 2f out and brief effrt: pushed along and grad lost pl fr over 1f out* **8/1**

-000 **13** 1½ **Briannsta (IRE)**[43] 1641 6-8-1 60.............................. NataliaGemelova(5) 9 48
(J E Long) *plld hrd: prom tl wknd over 2f out* **40/1**

1m 43.13s (-1.57) **Going Correction** -0.10s/f (Good) **13** Ran SP% **123.6**
Speed ratings (Par 103): **103,100,99,98,98 98,97,97,95,95 95,93,92**
CSF £46.90 CT £486.08 TOTE £4.30: £1.70, £4.20, £4.50; EX 66.50.
Owner Abdul Rahman Al Khalifa **Bred** Sheikh Abdulla Bin Isa Al-Khalifa **Trained** Newmarket, Suffolk
■ Stewards' Enquiry : Jimmy Fortune two-day ban: used whip with excessive force without allowing time to respond (Jun 23-24)

FOCUS
Quite a competitive little handicap and a solid pace set by Quaglino Way. It paid to race handily too and not many were able to make much impression from off the pace. The winner is on the upgrade.
Sotik Star(IRE) ◆ Official explanation: jockey said gelding hung right in the straight
Quaglino Way(GR) ◆ Official explanation: jockey said gelding hung left
Grand Vizier(IRE) ◆ Official explanation: jockey said gelding was unsuited by the good to firm, good in places ground
Leptis Magna Official explanation: jockey said gelding ran too keen

2898 K & L GATES FILLIES' H'CAP 6f
9:00 (9:00) (Class 5) (0-70,70) 3-Y-O **£2,729** (£806; £403) **Stalls** High

Form RPR

2-22 **1** **Orange Pip**[18] 2341 3-9-7 70.............................. RichardHughes 2 86+
(R Hannon) *led after 1f and racd against nr side rail sn after: drew clr fr over 2f out: at least 4l clr fnl f: eased fnl 100yds* **3/1**[1]

-600 **2** 1¾ **Kannon**[9] 2622 3-8-6 55..............................(v) RichardKingscote 6 58
(W J Knight) *in tch: prog to chse wnr over 2f out: no ch fr over 1f out: kpt on* **12/1**

0-00 **3** ¾ **Presto Levanter**[10] 2563 3-8-9 58.............................. DaneO'Neill 1 59
(R Hannon) *in tch: prog on outer over 2f out: disp 2nd over 1f out: no ch w wnr* **9/1**

10- **4** 1½ **Candela Bay (IRE)**[242] 6128 3-9-4 67.............................. SebSanders 8 63+
(W J Haggas) *hld up in last pair: effrt over 2f out: styd on fr over 1f out: no ch of chalng* **3/1**[1]

0-33 **5** 6 **Chelsea Girl**[20] 2279 3-9-4 67.............................. PhilipRobinson 3 44
(C G Cox) *sn prom on outer: wknd fr 2f out* **9/2**[2]

0-36 **6** ½ **Sister Moonshine**[11] 2546 3-9-0 63.............................. KerrinMcEvoy 7 38
(W R Muir) *led 1f: chsd wnr to 1/2-way: sn btn* **10/1**

06-5 **7** 1 **Tea Cake (IRE)**[42] 1671 3-9-0 63.............................. EddieAhern 5 35+
(H J L Dunlop) *hld up: gng strly over 2f out: nt clr run wl over 1f out: nudged along and lost tch* **10/1**

0-00 **8** 2¾ **Miss Okaloosa**[44] 1637 3-8-4 53.............................. SaleemGolam 10 16
(D M Simcock) *struggling in last pair bef 1/2-way: nvr a factor* **33/1**

006- **9** 1 **Noplace For A Lady**[302] 4422 3-8-2 51 oh2.............................. KimTinkler 4 11
(N Tinkler) *prom: urged along 1/2-way: wknd over 2f out* **8/1**[3]

1m 12.12s (-0.88) **Going Correction** -0.225s/f (Firm) **9** Ran SP% **118.1**
Speed ratings (Par 96): **96,93,92,90,82 82,80,77,75**
CSF £42.20 CT £297.33 TOTE £3.10: £1.60, £4.10, £3.10; EX 50.40 Place 6: £39.42, Place 5: £20.87..
Owner Lady Whent And Friends **Bred** Raffin Bloodstock **Trained** East Everleigh, Wilts

FOCUS
An ordinary fillies' handicap run at just a fair pace and the front four pulled a very long way clear of the rest.
T/Plt: £56.20 to a £1 stake. Pool: £83,184.65. 1,080.45 winning tickets. T/Qpdt: £19.90 to a £1 stake. Pool: £4,355.10. 161.65 winning tickets. JN

2899 - 2901a (Foreign Racing) - See Raceform Interactive

2553 SAINT-CLOUD (L-H)
Monday, June 9

OFFICIAL GOING: Good to soft

2902a PRIX DES LILAS (LISTED RACE) (FILLIES) 1m
2:35 (2:37) 3-Y-O **£20,221** (£8,088; £6,066; £4,044; £2,022)

RPR

1 **Azabara**[29] 2033 3-8-11.............................. SPasquier 1 100
(A Fabre, France)

2 1 **Sefroua (USA)**[25] 3-8-11.............................. C-PLemaire 5 98
(J-C Rouget, France)

3 *snk* **Kayaba**[29] 2033 3-8-11.............................. OPeslier 2 98
(C Laffon-Parias, France)

4 3 **Silent Sunday (IRE)**[29] 2033 3-8-11.............................. DBoeuf 6 91
(H-A Pantall, France)

5 *nk* **Kelowna (IRE)**[32] 1926 3-8-11.............................. CSoumillon 4 90
(J L Dunlop) *racd in 2nd to 2f out: one pce: lost 4th cl home* **61/10**[1]

6 3 **Zania (FR)**[29] 2031 3-8-11.............................. JAuge 7 84
(M Delzangles, France)

7 2½ **Luna Royale (IRE)**[57] 1360 3-8-11.............................. JVictoire 3 78
(H-A Pantall, France)

1m 42.9s (-4.60) **7** Ran SP% **14.1**
PARI-MUTUEL: WIN 1.90; PL 1.20, 1.50; SF 4.00.
Owner Mayfair Stud **Bred** Sunny Days Ltd **Trained** Chantilly, France

NOTEBOOK
Kelowna(IRE), a maiden winner over this trip on fast ground, was stepping up in trip and ran reasonably, chasing the leader until fading in the closing stages.

[1942]CHESTER (L-H)
Tuesday, June 10

OFFICIAL GOING: Good to firm (9.6)
Wind: Moderate, against Weather: Fine

2903 HIGHSTREETVOUCHERS.COM E B F MAIDEN STKS 5f 16y
6:45 (6:49) (Class 4) 2-Y-0 £5,180 (£1,541; £770; £384) Stalls Low

Form RPR
1 **Madame Trop Vite (IRE)** 2-8-12 0 .... NCallan 10 75+
(K A Ryan) *s.i.s: sn in midfield: hdwy to trck ldrs 3f out: n.m.r jst over 1f out: swtchd rt ins fnl f: str run to ld towards fin* 10/1

523 2 1/2 **Dedante**[39] 1762 2-8-12 0 .... AdrianMcCarthy 9 66
(D K Ivory) *chsd ldrs: effrt on wd outside 1/2-way: led jst under 2f out: rdn over 1f out: hdd towards fin* 8/1

3 nk **Tillers Satisfied (IRE)** 2-8-12 0 .... GrahamGibbons 12 65
(R Hollinshead) *towards rr: hdwy 1/2-way: rdn ins fnl f: r.o but nt pce to chal wnr towards fin* 40/1

4 1 1/2 **Impressible** 2-8-12 0 .... J-PGuillambert 6 60
(E J Alston) *w ldrs: rdn over 1f out: no ex wl ins fnl f* 7/1[3]

60 5 1 **Robin The Till**[25] 2150 2-8-12 0 .... HaddenFrost(5) 4 61
(R Hannon) *sn led: hdd after 1f: regained ld 3f out: hdd jst under 2f out: rdn over 1f out: wknd wl ins fnl f* 6/4[1]

6 6 3 3/4 **That Boy Ronaldo**[19] 2331 2-8-12 0 .... FrancisNorton 8 42
(A Berry) *s.i.s: chsd ldrs: rdn and lost pl over 1f out: n.d after* 20/1

7 3/4 **Usual Suspects** 2-8-12 0 .... PatrickMathers 5 40
(Peter Grayson) *s.i.s: towards rr: sme hdwy 1/2-way: outpcd over 1f out* 16/1

8 3/4 **Lily Waters** 2-8-12 0 .... LiamJones 1 37
(W M Brisbourne) *uns rdr and broke loose on way to post: a outpcd* 12/1

9 nk **Cognac Boy (USA)** 2-9-3 0 .... PatCosgrave 2 41
(D J G Murray Smith) *s.i.s: a outpcd* 5/1[2]

10 2 3/4 **Jack Jicaro** 2-9-0 0 .... TolleyDean(3) 11 31
(Mrs L Williamson) *s.i.s: a outpcd and bhd* 66/1

606 11 1 1/2 **Neo's Mate (IRE)**[24] 2206 2-8-12 0 .... PaulMulrennan 7 21
(Paul Green) *prom: led after 1f: hdd 3f out: n.m.r 2f out: sn wknd* 12/1

61.49 secs (0.49) **Going Correction** -0.125s/f (Firm) 11 Ran SP% 119.3
Speed ratings (Par 95): **91,90,89,87,85 79,78,77,76,72 70**
CSF £87.48 TOTE £13.00: £2.90, £2.20, £11.90; EX 90.80.
Owner Mrs T Marnane **Bred** Mark & Pippa Hackett **Trained** Hambleton, N Yorks

FOCUS
A modest maiden run at a good pace, and the winner came from behind. She is rated better than the bare facts, but overall the form looks very ordinary with the time modest.

NOTEBOOK
Madame Trop Vite(IRE), a half-sister to six winners including Gardasee, a dual winner over middle distances, gets her speed from her sire Invincible Spirit. Despite a wide draw, she was able to secure a good position chasing the leaders and, although short of room early in the straight, once switched she stayed on strongly to get up close home. She may go for the Queen Mary next, although that might prove to be flying a bit high. (op 9-1 tchd 7-1)
Dedante, having her fourth start but her first on turf, ran well considering that she challenged three or four wide rounding the turn into the straight. Given the ground she gave away it was a fine effort. (op 6-1)
Tillers Satisfied(IRE), a half-sister to Steal My Fire, who won over 6f on his juvenile debut, could not quite repeat the trick, but she posted a decent effort from her outside draw, running on late from off the pace. (op 33-1)
Impressible, a half-sister to six winners including top-class sprinter Reverence, showed good speed to race alongside the leader, and just weakened in the closing stages when her early efforts began to tell. She should improve.
Robin The Till was a well-backed favourite and showed good speed to lead on the rail, but he was not left alone and had to work hard to maintain that position, and in the end that effort told. Official explanation: jockey said colt hung left-handed (op 2-1 tchd 9-4)
That Boy Ronaldo, like on her debut, compromised his chance with a slow start. (op 33-1)
Cognac Boy(USA), whose price rose from $67,000 as a yearling to 140,000gns as a two-year-old, is out of a mare who was quite a useful multiple sprint winner at three in the US. He was too green to do himself justice on his debut. (tchd 9-2 and 11-2)
Neo's Mate(IRE) Official explanation: jockey said filly did not handle the track

2904 HOOLE HALL H'CAP 1m 2f 75y
7:15 (7:15) (Class 4) (0-85,82) 4-Y-0+ £5,180 (£1,541; £770; £384) Stalls High

Form RPR
013- 1 **Muhannak (IRE)**[242] 6144 4-9-9 82 .... PaulMulrennan 3 96
(M W Easterby) *mde all: rdn clr over 1f out: r.o wl and in command fnl f* 5/1[3]

41-3 2 4 1/2 **Drawn Gold**[18] 2375 4-8-8 67 .... GrahamGibbons 8 72
(R Hollinshead) *rrd bef s: s.s: sn in midfield: hdwy over 6f out: wnt 2nd over 1f out: no imp on wnr* 7/2[1]

1001 3 2 1/4 **Bull Market (IRE)**[18] 2361 5-9-0 73 .... StephenDonohoe 9 74
(Ian Williams) *hld up: rdn and hdwy 3f out: outpcd by ldrs over 1f out: kpt on u.p after* 6/1

10-0 4 nse **Piper's Song (IRE)**[12] 2535 5-9-3 76 .... PatCosgrave 4 76+
(D J G Murray Smith) *s.s: hld up: nt clr run and pushed wd under 3f out: r.o and prog ins fnl f: nvr gng to rch ldrs* 20/1

3005 5 nk **Lucayan Dancer**[7] 2697 8-8-11 70 .... AdrianTNicholls 5 70+
(D Nicholls) *midfield: lost pl and nt clr run 3f out: kpt on u.p fnl f: no imp on ldrs* 7/2[1]

-630 6 1 **Cheshire Prince**[11] 2585 4-8-11 70 .... LiamJones 2 68
(W M Brisbourne) *racd keenly: chsd wnr: rdn over 2f out: lost 2nd over 1f out: wknd ins fnl f* 4/1[2]

1010 7 13 **Komreyev Star**[2] 2870 6-8-1 63 oh5 .... LukeMorris(3) 1 35
(R E Peacock) *trckd ldrs: rdn over 4f out: wknd over 2f out: eased fnl f* 16/1

0-20 8 5 **Boo**[19] 2335 6-8-9 68 .... PatrickMathers 7 30
(J W Unett) *racd keenly: prom: stdd 6f out: rdn over 4f out: wknd over 2f out* 9/1

2m 10.68s (-1.52) **Going Correction** -0.125s/f (Firm) 8 Ran SP% 116.0
Speed ratings (Par 105): **101,97,95,95,95 94,84,80**
CSF £23.24 CT £107.58 TOTE £7.20: £2.10, £1.90, £1.50; EX 32.40.
Owner Woodford Group Plc **Bred** Mount Coote Stud **Trained** Sheriff Hutton, N Yorks

FOCUS
They went a steady pace here and the winner enjoyed the run of things out in front. The form is rated through the runner-up and the winner could be flattered.

2905 GROWHOW H'CAP 7f 2y
7:45 (7:45) (Class 3) (0-95,92) 4-Y-0 **£8,200** (£2,454; £1,227; £613; £305) **Stalls** Low

Form RPR
0141 1 **Daaweitza**[17] 2397 5-9-0 83 .... J-PGuillambert 5 94
(B Ellison) *hld up: hdwy 2f out: swtchd rt over 1f out: str run and rdr dropped whip ins fnl f: led post* 8/1[3]

0000 2 shd **Gallantry**[19] 2339 6-8-8 80 .... TolleyDean(3) 4 91
(D Shaw) *a.p: rdn to ld jst over 1f out: hdd post* 8/1[3]

-225 3 2 1/2 **Guilded Warrior**[31] 1982 5-9-4 87 .... DarryllHolland 14 91
(W S Kittow) *led after 1f: rdn and hdd jst over 1f out: no ex wl ins fnl f* 8/1[3]

051- 4 3/4 **Kings Point (IRE)**[267] 5479 7-8-8 82 .... AhmedAjtebi(5) 3 84
(D Nicholls) *a.p: rdn over 1f out: styd on same pce ins fnl f* 11/1

-002 5 hd **Captain Jacksparra (IRE)**[17] 2397 4-9-5 88 .... NCallan 9 90
(K A Ryan) *s.i.s: midfield: effrt over 1f out: kpt on ins fnl f: nt pce of ldrs* 9/1

6103 6 hd **Phluke**[17] 2397 7-9-2 85 .... StephenCarson 8 86
(Eve Johnson Houghton) *a.p: rdn 2f out: kpt on same pce fnl f* 8/1[3]

0021 7 nse **Heywood**[4] 2778 4-9-5 88 6ex .... AdrianTNicholls 6 89
(D Nicholls) *racd keenly in midfield: hdwy over 2f out: rdn whn nt clr run wl over 1f out: bmpd jst ins fnl f: one pce after* 6/1[2]

0-52 8 1 1/2 **Hazzard County (USA)**[41] 1723 4-9-0 83 .... RichardMullen 1 80
(D M Simcock) *s.i.s: bhd: effrt whn nt clr run over 1f out: no imp ins fnl f* 7/2[1]

505- 9 1 **Majuro (IRE)**[230] 6437 4-9-9 92 .... PaulMulrennan 12 86
(M W Easterby) *dwlt: sn swtchd lft: hld up: effrt whn pushed wd over 1f out: no imp after* 22/1

-606 10 1/2 **Overrule (USA)**[38] 1815 4-8-11 80 .... TonyHamilton 2 73
(B Ellison) *s.i.s: pushed along 4f out: a bhd* 12/1

-450 11 6 **The Kiddykid (IRE)**[25] 2163 8-9-2 85 .... TGMcLaughlin 13 62
(P D Evans) *in tch: rdn and wknd over 2f out* 20/1

3110 12 3 **Silver Hotspur**[70] 1133 4-9-6 89 .... FrancisNorton 11 58
(M Wigham) *in tch: rdn over 2f out: sn wknd* 20/1

1m 23.91s (-2.59) **Going Correction** -0.125s/f (Firm) course record 12 Ran SP% 120.8
Speed ratings (Par 107): **109,108,106,105,104 104,104,102,101,101 94,90**
CSF £69.84 CT £546.72 TOTE £8.90: £3.10, £2.60, £3.80; EX 96.10.
Owner Mrs Andrea M Mallinson **Bred** C Mallinson **Trained** Norton, N Yorks
■ Stewards' Enquiry : J-P Guillambert one-day ban: careless riding (Jun 24)

FOCUS
They went a good gallop in this decent and competitive handicap. Solid form.

NOTEBOOK
Daaweitza enjoyed the good gallop and, getting the gap in the straight, ran on well to lead right on the line. Progressive this term, the fact that he never wins by far has helped him stay one step ahead of the Handicapper. (op 7-1 tchd 9-1 in a place)
Gallantry, narrowly beaten in this race last year off 82, again came up just a tad short off a 2lb lower mark. He was well placed in the chasing group and came with what looked like a winning challenge, only to be collared on the line. (op 10-1)
Guilded Warrior did well to get to the front from his wide draw but used up too much energy forcing a good pace. He did well in the circumstances to hold on for third, although softer ground probably suits him ideally. (tchd 9-1)
Kings Point(IRE), claimed out of Richard Fahey's yard on his final start last year, ran a satisfactory race on his seasonal reappearance. He has reportedly had a wind operation since he last ran and should come on for this. (op 9-1)
Captain Jacksparra(IRE) was only 1lb better off with Daaweitza compared with when they met at Catterick last time, and that proved an insufficient turnaround in the weights to reverse the form. He and Phluke, who was third in the Catterick race, did appear to run close to that form, though. (op 8-1)
Phluke ran close to his Catterick form with Captain Jacksparra but Daaweitza, who finished under a length in front of him there, looks to have improved since. (op 9-1 tchd 7-1)
Hazzard County(USA) had a good draw but failed to take advantage of it as he was slowly away and struggled to take a hand. (op 4-1)
Silver Hotspur Official explanation: jockey said gelding was unsuited by the good to firm ground

2906 RATHBONES H'CAP 5f 16y
8:15 (8:16) (Class 4) (0-85,85) 3-Y-0+ £5,180 (£1,541; £770; £384) Stalls Low

Form RPR
0242 1 **Misaro (GER)**[22] 2242 7-8-9 71 ....(b) HaddenFrost(5) 4 80+
(R A Harris) *midfield: rdn and hdwy over 1f out: r.o to ld cl home* 9/2[1]

4311 2 nk **Best One**[18] 2351 4-9-0 74 ....(p) KevinGhunowa(3) 2 82
(R A Harris) *chsd ldrs: rdn to ld 1f out: sn hung lft: hdd post* 5/1[2]

0-03 3 1/2 **Mambo Spirit (IRE)**[18] 2359 4-9-9 80 .... J-PGuillambert 7 86+
(J G Given) *rrd s: missed break: hld up: hdwy whn swtchd rt over 1f out: r.o ins fnl f: gaining at fin* 6/1

100- 4 1 1/4 **Foxy Music**[293] 4726 4-9-9 80 .... PaulMulrennan 3 82
(E J Alston) *pressed ldr: led 3f out: sn hung rt: hdd 1f out: eased whn no ex towards fin* 12/1

4000 5 hd **Coconut Moon**[18] 2359 6-9-0 71 .... TonyHamilton 6 72
(E J Alston) *chsd ldrs: rdn over 1f out: styd on same pce ins fnl f* 8/1

2045 6 3/4 **Caribbean Coral**[14] 2489 9-9-10 81 .... GrahamGibbons 9 79
(J J Quinn) *bhd: rdn and hdwy over 1f out: styd on ins fnl f: nt pce to chal ldrs* 11/2[3]

2131 7 2 **Dodaa (USA)**[29] 2050 5-8-8 70 .... AshleyHamblett(5) 11 61
(N Wilson) *chsd ldrs: rdn over 1f out: wknd ins fnl f* 14/1

6 8 1 1/4 **I Confess**[15] 2449 3-9-4 82 .... TGMcLaughlin 10 69
(P D Evans) *bhd: kpt on fnl f: nvr rchd chalng position* 33/1

6606 9 3/4 **Silver Prelude**[13] 2501 7-9-2 73 .... DarryllHolland 8 57
(D K Ivory) *led: hdd 3f out: continued to chal: rdn over 1f out: wknd ins fnl f* 25/1

1100 10 1 1/4 **Jilly Why (IRE)**[8] 2666 7-9-13 84 ....(b) FrancisNorton 5 63
(Paul Green) *s.i.s: a bhd* 14/1

404- 11 1 **Bluebok**[211] 6794 7-9-0 74 ....(t) TolleyDean(3) 12 50
(J M Bradley) *midfield: rdn over 1f out: sn wknd* 33/1

1530 12 7 **Fire Up The Band**[34] 1917 9-9-6 82 .... SladeO'Hara(5) 1 33
(A Berry) *chsd ldrs: n.m.r and hmpd after 1f: sn dropped away: bhd after* 7/1

0466 13 14 **Cape Royal**[18] 2359 8-9-12 83 ....(bt) NCallan 14 —
(J M Bradley) *missed break: sn rcvrd to chse ldrs: eased whn sddled slipped over 3f out: lost pl over 2f out: sn bhd* 33/1

59.70 secs (-1.30) **Going Correction** -0.125s/f (Firm)
WFA 3 from 4yo+ 7lb 13 Ran SP% 121.8
Speed ratings (Par 105): **105,104,103,101,101 100,97,95,93,91 90,79,56**
CSF £26.09 CT £136.17 TOTE £5.70: £2.10, £2.50, £2.00; EX 22.70.

The Form Book, Raceform Ltd, Compton, RG20 6NL

Owner Messrs Criddle Davies Dawson & Villa **Bred** Wilhelm Fasching **Trained** Earlswood, Monmouths

FOCUS
A contested early lead resulted in the pace horses hitting the wall in the straight and those held up coming through to contest the finish. Ordinary form, but sound.

Silver Prelude Official explanation: jockey said gelding had a breathing problem

Cape Royal Official explanation: jockey said saddle slipped

2907 DANIEL STEWART H'CAP — 1m 2f 75y
8:45 (8:45) (Class 5) (0-70,70) 3-Y-O — **£3,561** (£1,059; £529; £264) **Stalls** High

Form — RPR

2400 **1** — **Always Certain (USA)**[22] 2261 3-9-4 **65** .... DarryllHolland 3 — 70
(M Johnston) *broke wl: a.p: rdn 2f out: rdr dropped rein over 1f out: sn rcvrd: r.o to ld wl ins fnl f* — **8/1**

-230 **2** 1 — **Maximus Aurelius (IRE)**[25] 2161 3-9-6 **70** .... LukeMorris(3) 5 — 73
(J Jay) *sn led: hung rt over 4f out: rdn over 1f out: hdd and nt qckn wl ins fnl f* — **7/1**

50-2 **3** 1 1/4 — **Sinbad The Sailor**[31] 2002 3-9-9 **70** .... NCallan 8 — 71
(J W Hills) *midfield: hdwy 3f out: chsd ldng pair 2f out: rdn and lugged lft fr over 1f out: no imp ins fnl f* — **7/4**[1]

6-02 **4** 2 1/4 — **Kiho**[31] 1994 3-9-6 **67** .... StephenCarson 10 — 63+
(Eve Johnson Houghton) *hld up: nt clr run fr 2f out: swtchd rt and hdwy over 1f out: r.o ins fnl f: nt rch front trio* — **11/2**[3]

400- **5** 2 1/4 — **Elusive Deal (USA)**[190] 7007 3-8-9 **56** .... PatCosgrave 4 — 48
(D J G Murray Smith) *plld hrd in midfield: effrt 2f out: one pce fnl f* — **25/1**

0462 **6** 3 — **Una Auroraborealis**[28] 2089 3-8-4 **51** oh5........(p) DavidKinsella 1 — 37
(J Ryan) *prom: lost pl 2f out: n.d after* — **25/1**

0641 **7** 1 — **Portrush Storm**[8] 2659 3-9-6 **67** 6ex........ DNolan 6 — 51
(D Carroll) *awkward s: racd keenly: hld up: hdwy 3f out: pushed wd over 1f out: sn btn* — **4/1**[2]

400 **8** 3 1/4 — **Daraiym (IRE)**[18] 2360 3-9-1 **62** .... PaulMulrennan 2 — 39
(Paul Green) *hld up: struggling 2f out: nvr on terms* — **16/1**

06-5 **9** 21 — **Seeking The Star (CAN)**[66] 1216 3-9-1 **67** .... AhmedAjtebi(5) 9 — —
(D M Simcock) *broke wl: prom: rdn and lost pl 4f out: wknd 3f out* — **12/1**

2m 12.86s (0.66) **Going Correction** -0.125s/f (Firm) — **9** Ran SP% **116.6**
Speed ratings (Par 99): **92,91,90,88,86 84,83,80,64**
CSF £63.31 CT £141.07 TOTE £9.10: £2.50, £2.20, £1.40; EX 69.00.

Owner Always Trying Partnership VI **Bred** Robert Harmon & Ashford Stud **Trained** Middleham Moor, N Yorks

FOCUS
A modest handicap run at an ordinary gallop in a moderate time and dominated by the front two throughout. The form is rated through the second.

2908 MERCEDES BENZ OF CHESTER H'CAP (FOR LADY AMATEUR RIDERS) — 1m 4f 66y
9:15 (9:15) (Class 5) (0-70,70) 4-Y-O+ — **£3,435** (£1,065; £532; £266) **Stalls** Low

Form — RPR

6526 **1** — **Thorny Mandate**[18] 2364 6-9-7 **55** .... MissADeniel 13 — 63
(W M Brisbourne) *stdd s: hld up: hdwy over 1f out: prog whn swtchd lft ins fnl f: r.o to ld post* — **7/1**[3]

1-45 **2** nse — **Gamesters Lady**[22] 2241 5-9-11 **62**........(p) MissMSowerby(3) 14 — 70
(W M Brisbourne) *chsd front pair tl 7f out: clsd to ld over 1f out: hdd post* — **14/1**

5101 **3** 3/4 — **Hucking Heat (IRE)**[11] 2568 4-9-7 **60**........(p) MissRKneller(5) 7 — 67
(R Hollinshead) *missed break: midfield: swtchd rt and hdwy over 1f out: chsd ldrs ins fnl f: r.o* — **8/1**

0000 **4** 1 3/4 — **Old Romney**[10] 2621 4-9-5 **60** .... MissMHugo(7) 5 — 64
(M Wigham) *chsd ldrs: chsd clr front pair 7f out tl over 2f out: sn outpcd: plugged on at one pce fnl f* — **25/1**

-305 **5** 1/2 — **Is It Me (USA)**[14] 2482 5-10-4 **66**........ MissGDGracey-Davison 4 — 69
(A W Carroll) *led: pushed along and hdd over 5f out: remained w ldr: rdn 2f out: kpt on same pce fnl f* — **10/1**

4-05 **6** 1 1/4 — **Prelude**[15] 2453 7-10-4 **66** .... MissARyan 2 — 67
(W M Brisbourne) *chsd ldrs: rdn over 2f out: edgd lft over 1f out: one pce fnl f* — **5/1**[1]

2140 **7** 1 — **Terminate (GER)**[11] 2568 6-9-11 **62** .... MissJCoward(3) 10 — 62
(Ian Williams) *hld up: hdwy on wd outside over 2f out: one pce fnl f* — **16/1**

2352 **8** 1 1/2 — **Hugs Destiny (IRE)**[11] 2579 7-9-2 **55**........(t) MissAngelaBarnes(5) 12 — 52
(M A Barnes) *w ldr: led over 5f out: rdn and hdd over 1f out: wknd and eased ins fnl f* — **12/1**

000- **9** 1/2 — **Compton Dragon (USA)**[203] 6883 9-9-12 **60** .... MrsCBartley 3 — 56
(W M Brisbourne) *s.i.s: hld up: rdn over 1f out: nvr on terms* — **20/1**

1414 **10** hd — **Bienheureux**[11] 2558 7-10-0 **62**........(t) MissEJJones 8 — 58
(Miss Gay Kelleway) *missed break: midfield: hdwy 5f out: chsd ldrs over 2f out: wknd ins fnl f* — **8/1**

0560 **11** hd — **Candy Anchor (FR)**[11] 2568 9-8-10 **51** oh6........ MissSPeacock(7) 9 — 47
(R E Peacock) *a bhd* — **66/1**

44-2 **12** 1 1/2 — **Rudry World (IRE)**[11] 2572 5-10-3 **70** .... MissMMullineaux(5) 1 — 63
(M Mullineaux) *s.i.s: a bhd* — **11/2**[2]

012- **13** 1/2 — **Sir Sandicliffe (IRE)**[164] 7273 4-9-11 **59** .... MissNCarberry 11 — 52
(W M Brisbourne) *midfield: rdn over 2f out: wknd over 1f out* — **5/1**[1]

2m 39.92s (0.02) **Going Correction** -0.125s/f (Firm) — **13** Ran SP% **122.9**
Speed ratings (Par 103): **98,97,97,96,95 95,94,93,93,93 92,91,91**
CSF £102.04 CT £815.71 TOTE £9.30: £3.00, £4.30, £2.90; EX 153.70 Place 6: £530.17 Place 5: £72.16.

Owner R C Naylor **Bred** Major W R Hern And W H Carson **Trained** Great Ness, Shropshire

FOCUS
Is It Me and Hugs Destiny took each other on for the lead and ensured a good gallop in this moderate handicap. The bare form makes sense amongst the placed horses.

T/Jkpt: Not won. T/Plt: £302.60 to a £1 stake. Pool: £130,304.67. 314.35 winning tickets. T/Qpdt: £49.40 to a £1 stake. Pool: £7,131.10. 106.70 winning tickets. DO

2485 REDCAR (L-H)
Tuesday, June 10

OFFICIAL GOING: Good to firm changing to good to firm (firm in places) after race 5 (4.30)

2909 REDCAR A COURSE FOR ALL REASONS MEDIAN AUCTION MAIDEN STKS — 6f
2:30 (2:30) (Class 5) 2-Y-O — **£2,331** (£693; £346; £173) **Stalls** Centre

Form — RPR

04 **1** — **Tagula Breeze (IRE)**[18] 2362 2-9-3 0........ RoystonFfrench 5 — 76
(I W McInnes) *trckd ldrs: hdwy to chse ldr over 1f out: swtchd rt and rdn ins fnl f: styd on to ld last 100yds* — **7/2**[2]

4 **2** 1/2 — **Countrywide City (IRE)**[26] 2117 2-9-3 0........ AlanMunro 4 — 75
(P W Chapple-Hyam) *led to 1/2-way: cl up tl led again wl over 1f out: rdn and edgd lft ins fnl f: hdd and no ex last 100yds* — **15/8**[1]

3 1 1/4 — **Needwood Lad** 2-9-3 0........ PaulHanagan 16 — 71+
(R A Fahey) *towards rr: hdwy over 2f out: rdn over 1f out: styd on wl fnl f* — **14/1**

4 4 1/2 — **Doric Echo** 2-9-3 0........ TomEaves 8 — 58+
(B Smart) *t.k.h: hld up: hdwy 2f out: swtchd lft over 1f out: kpt on ins fnl f: nrst fin* — **7/1**[3]

0 **5** 1 1/2 — **Pedregal**[25] 2140 2-9-3 0........ TonyHamilton 7 — 53
(R A Fahey) *chsd ldrs: rdn along 2f out: kpt on same pce appr fnl f* — **66/1**

6 nse — **Scenic Pass** 2-8-5 0........ MCGeran(7) 1 — 48
(M R Channon) *prom: rdn along over 2f out: wkng whn bmpd over 1f out* — **12/1**

0 **7** 1 3/4 — **Dispol Grand (IRE)**[32] 1967 2-9-0 0........ JamieMoriarty(3) 2 — 47
(P T Midgley) *midfield: hdwy over 2f out: sn rdn and one pce* — **25/1**

62 **8** hd — **Jethro Bodine (IRE)**[23] 2216 2-9-0 0........ AndrewMullen(3) 15 — 47
(W J H Ratcliffe) *prom: led 1/2-wayt: rdn and hdd wl over 1f out: grad wknd* — **15/2**

04 **9** 2 1/4 — **Orphaned Annie**[25] 2154 2-8-5 0........ LanceBetts(7) 12 — 35
(B Ellison) *a towards rr* — **16/1**

10 10 — **Moroccan Party** 2-9-3 0........ PaulMulrennan 11 — 10
(M W Easterby) *dwlt: hdwy and in tch 1/2-way: wknd over 2f out* — **40/1**

11 4 — **Bubbly Baby** 2-8-12 0........ DavidAllan 17 — —
(T D Easterby) *a towards rr* — **25/1**

12 2 — **Davana** 2-8-7 0........ KellyHarrison(5) 13 — —
(W J H Ratcliffe) *a out pce in rr* — **20/1**

13 2 1/4 — **Northern Shore (IRE)** 2-9-3 0........(t) DNolan 10 — —
(J O'Reilly) *wnt rt s: sn in tch: rdn along 1/2-way and sn wknd* — **66/1**

0 **14** 6 — **Ten Cents A Dance**[18] 2362 2-9-0 0........ DuranFentiman(3) 3 — —
(T D Easterby) *sn out pce and bhd* — **33/1**

1m 12.47s (0.67) **Going Correction** -0.05s/f (Good) — **14** Ran SP% **122.3**
Speed ratings (Par 93): **93,92,90,84,82 82,80,80,77,63 58,55,52,44**
CSF £9.83 TOTE £4.40: £1.30, £1.50, £4.20; EX 15.20.

Owner Terence Elsey **Bred** Michael And John Fahy **Trained** Catwick, E Yorks

■ Stewards' Enquiry : Royston Ffrench caution: careless riding; caution: used whip with excessive force

FOCUS
Despite the numbers this was a modest maiden, rated around the time and the winner. The first three pulled nicely clear of the remainder.

NOTEBOOK
Tagula Breeze(IRE) improved considerably on his debut effort when running fourth at Newcastle last time and, well backed in the market beforehand, he stepped up again on that form to get off the mark in workmanlike fashion. His future lies in the hands of the Handicapper. (op 5-1)
Countrywide City(IRE) had made his debut in a heat at Newmarket which has already yielded up a couple of winners so it was no surprise to see him sent off as favourite. Always in the vanguard, he was probably a little unlucky to come up against the winner in this grade of race here. (op 6-4 tchd 2-1)
Needwood Lad ◆ picked up really strongly in the closing stages once the penny started to drop. A grandson of Eric Alston's flying racemare Stack Rock on the distaff side of his pedigree, he won't be long in breaking his maiden. (op 11-1)
Doric Echo was not given a hard race once it was clear he couldn't go with the principals. This was a pleasing introduction. (tchd 13-2 and 15-2)
Pedregal showed up well for much of the way. This was a big improvement on his debut effort.
Scenic Pass ◆ showed good speed on her debut and wasn't at all knocked about once the leaders had got away from her. She will improve for this. Official explanation: jockey said filly hung right-handed throughout (op 14-1 tchd 11-1)

2910 RACING UK CHANNEL 432 MAIDEN CLAIMING STKS — 6f
3:00 (3:01) (Class 6) 2-Y-O — **£2,047** (£604; £302) **Stalls** Centre

Form — RPR

5 **1** — **Elaine's Folly**[29] 2035 2-8-11 0........ JoeFanning 8 — 56+
(P C Haslam) *cl up: led 1/2-way: rdn over 1f out: kpt on* — **5/2**[2]

0 **2** 1 1/4 — **Mimicker**[31] 2004 2-8-7 0........ DaleGibson 10 — 48+
(M W Easterby) *dwlt and bhd: hdwy over 2f out: rdn to chse wnr over 1f out: kpt on u.p ins fnl f* — **66/1**

060 **3** 1 1/4 — **Nchike**[5] 2746 2-9-2 0........ SilvestreDeSousa 9 — 54
(D Nicholls) *in tch: hdwy 1/2-way: rdn to chse ldrs wl over 1f out: kpt on ins fnl f* — **9/1**

46 **4** 4 — **Tito Gobbi**[25] 2140 2-9-1 0........ LeeEnstone 7 — 41
(P C Haslam) *cl up: rdn along over 2f out: sn drvn and grad wknd* — **6/1**[3]

05 **5** nse — **Scarlet Blade**[15] 2443 2-8-7 0........(p) RoystonFfrench 6 — 32
(Mrs A Duffield) *in tch: rdn along 2f out: kpt on same pce u.p fnl f* — **20/1**

030 **6** 1 1/2 — **Dispol Toba**[24] 2206 2-8-2 0 ow1........ FrankieMcDonald 11 — 23
(P T Midgley) *in tch on wd outside: pushed along over 2f out: rdn and hung lft over 1f out: kpt on u.p ins fnl f* — **9/1**

3 **7** 1 1/2 — **Inca Slew (IRE)**[15] 2459 2-8-7 0........ PatrickDonaghy(7) 2 — 30
(P C Haslam) *in rr and rdn along 1/2-way: sme late hdwy* — **10/1**

3 **8** nk — **Comghaire (IRE)**[15] 2450 2-8-10 0........ TomEaves 5 — 25
(P D Evans) *led: rdn along and hdd 1/2-way: sn wknd* — **9/4**[1]

0 **9** 1 3/4 — **Ennovy**[10] 2627 2-8-4 0........ KimTinkler 12 — 14
(N Tinkler) *a in rr* — **33/1**

00 **10** 4 — **Rios Boy (IRE)**[17] 2388 2-8-11 0........(b[1]) DavidAllan 3 — 9
(T D Easterby) *cl up: rdn along 1/2-way: sn wknd* — **40/1**

06 **11** 1 — **Approved**[8] 2671 2-8-7 0........ PaulMulrennan 1 — 2
(M W Easterby) *cl up: rdn along 1/2-way: sn wknd* — **14/1**

1m 14.08s (2.28) **Going Correction** -0.05s/f (Good) — **11** Ran SP% **121.0**
Speed ratings (Par 91): **82,80,78,73,73 71,69,68,66,61 59**
CSF £179.03 TOTE £3.10: £1.50, £15.10, £3.20; EX 249.80.

Owner S A B Dinsmore **Bred** Whatton Manor Stud **Trained** Middleham Moor, N Yorks

FOCUS
Pretty modest fare as you would expect for the grade, the juveniles finishing in a time over 1.5secs slower than their counterparts in the preceding maiden. Elaine's Folly did it well enough and the second produced a big step up.

NOTEBOOK
Elaine's Folly ran with some promise in a maiden here last month on debut but her trainer quickly dropped her into claiming company nevertheless and she ran out a decisive winner having always raced prominently. It is doubtful whether she will find much improvement on this. (op 9-4 tchd 11-4 in a place)
Mimicker was tailed off on her debut in a Thirsk seller, but that came at a time when Mick Easterby's horses were mostly out of sorts and the daughter of Kyllachy duly left that run well behind her despite a slow start which left her with plenty to do. She should find a little race. (op 100-1)
Nchike started off in the Brocklesby where he was far from disgraced but having not progressed from that run in two subsequent starts in maiden company has probably found his level here.
Tito Gobbi was dropping out of maiden company for the first time but still couldn't get competitive. (tchd 11-2 and 13-2)
Scarlet Blade could only plug on at one pace and looks limited. (op 22-1 tchd 25-1)

2911 ANDERSON BARROWCLIFF H'CAP 7f
3:30 (3:31) (Class 5) (0-75,75) 3-Y-O £2,331 (£693; £346; £173) Stalls Centre

Form RPR
-053 1 **Kiwi Bay**^{14} 2481 3-9-7 **75** TonyHamilton 15 89
(M Dods) *trckd ldrs: rdn over 2f out: led over 1f out: r.o wl* **7/2**^{1}
5241 2 5 **Party In The Park**^{26} 2126 3-8-13 **67** PaulHanagan 18 67
(Miss J A Camacho) *mid-div: hdwy over 2f out: rdn over 1f out: edgd lft ins fnl f: no ch w wnr* **9/1**
0-40 3 hd **Medici Time**^{21} 2272 3-7-13 **56** oh2 DuranFentiman(3) 16 55
(T D Easterby) *hld up: hdwy and nt clr run over 1f out: hung lft and r.o ins fnl f: nrst fin* **14/1**
0035 4 ½ **Take It Easee (IRE)**^{14} 2490 3-8-10 **64** RobertWinston 2 62
(G A Swinbank) *hld up: rdn over 2f out: hdwy over 1f out: nt trble ldrs* **12/1**
0-40 5 ¾ **Low Flyer (USA)**^{29} 2041 3-8-3 **57** SilvestreDeSousa 17 53
(T D Barron) *sn pushed along in rr: bhd and rdn 1/2-way: r.o ins fnl f: nvr nrr* **16/1**
0065 6 shd **Zabougg**^{24} 2208 3-8-2 **56** RoystonFfrench 19 52
(D W Barker) *hld up: rdn over 2f out: hung lft and styd on ins fnl f: n.d* **16/1**
3-32 7 nse **Misplaced Fortune**^{14} 2490 3-8-11 **65** KimTinkler 6 61
(N Tinkler) *s.i.s: sn pushed along and prom: rdn over 2f out: no ex fnl f* **12/1**
-500 8 2 **Molly Ann (IRE)**^{18} 2376 3-8-6 **60** ow2 (b^{1}) DavidAllan 5 50
(T D Easterby) *w ldrs: led over 4f out: rdn: hdd and hung lft over 1f out: wknd ins fnl f* **25/1**
0045 9 nk **Complete Frontline (GER)**^{8} 2660 3-8-4 **58** AndrewElliott 13 47
(K R Burke) *s.i.s: sn pushed along in rr: n.d* **14/1**
033- 10 1½ **Borasco (USA)**^{295} 4669 3-9-1 **69** AlanMunro 1 54
(T D Barron) *chsd ldrs: rdn over 2f out: wknd over 1f out* **16/1**
00-6 11 ½ **Bohobe (IRE)**^{18} 2366 3-9-0 **68** TPQueally 12 52+
(J G Given) *led 1f: chsd ldrs: rdn over 2f out: n.m.r over 1f out: wkng whn hmpd sn after* **20/1**
50-2 12 2 **Red Tarn**^{21} 2282 3-9-2 **70** TomEaves 4 49
(B Smart) *s.i.s: bhd fnl 3f* **4/1**^{2}
404 13 ½ **Infinity Bond**^{24} 2187 3-8-8 **67** SladeO'Hara(5) 9 44
(G R Oldroyd) *prom: rdn 1/2-way: wknd over 1f out* **20/1**
1-0 14 ½ **Harlem Shuffle (UAE)**^{43} 1685 3-9-5 **73** JoeFanning 8 49
(M Johnston) *led 6f out: hdd over 4f out: wknd over 2f out* **15/2**^{3}
30-5 15 2¼ **The Lady Granuaile (USA)**^{28} 2067 3-9-0 **68** (b^{1}) FergalLynch 14 38
(K A Ryan) *w ldrs: rdn over 2f out: sn wknd* **33/1**
30-0 16 7 **Strictly Elsie (IRE)**^{24} 2208 3-8-4 **61** AndrewMullen(3) 11 12
(J R Norton) *s.i.s: bhd fnl 1/2-way* **40/1**

1m 24.05s (-0.45) **Going Correction** -0.05s/f (Good) **16** Ran SP% **129.1**
Speed ratings (Par 99): **100,94,94,93,92 92,92,90,89,88 87,85,84,84,81 73**
CSF £34.70 CT £328.42 TOTE £4.70: £1.50, £2.30, £3.30, £2.80; EX 51.40.
Owner Kiwi Racing **Bred** Templeton Stud **Trained** Denton, Co Durham

FOCUS
A modest handicap for three-year-olds run in a good time thanks to the pacesetting exploits of Molly Ann. The horses drawn nearest the stands' rail filled five of the first six placings. The winner continues to progress and the form is sound enough.
Red Tarn Official explanation: jockey said gelding was never travelling
Strictly Elsie(IRE) Official explanation: jockey said filly was never travelling

2912 REDCAR CONFERENCE CENTRE MEDIAN AUCTION MAIDEN STKS 1m
4:00 (4:02) (Class 6) 3-5-Y-O £2,047 (£604; £302) Stalls Centre

Form RPR
2-2 1 **Timetable**^{17} 2413 3-8-13 **0** TedDurcan 9 68+
(H R A Cecil) *trckd ldrs: hdwy over 2f out: led wl over 1f out: shkn up appr fnl f and kpt on* **2/9**^{1}
0- 2 1¾ **Bollin Greta**^{265} 5524 3-8-8 **0** DavidAllan 6 59
(T D Easterby) *dwlt and hld up in rr: hdwy over 2f out and sn rdn along: chsd wnr over 1f out: sn drvn and one pce* **20/1**
0 3 5 **Ducal Regancy Duke**^{43} 1674 4-9-5 **0** KellyHarrison(5) 7 56
(C J Teague) *led: rdn along 3f out: hdd wedll over 1f out and kpt on same pce* **100/1**
3 4 hd **Times Vital (IRE)**^{67} 1194 3-8-13 **0** DeanMcKeown 8 52
(E J O'Neill) *in tch: hdwy to chse ldrs 2f out: sn rdn and no imp* **6/1**^{2}
5 1½ **Tump Mac** 4-9-5 **0** NeilBrown(5) 1 52
(N Bycroft) *prom: rdn along over 2f out: drvn: edgd lft and wknd over 1f out* **50/1**
000- 6 3 **Halton Castle**^{272} 5328 3-8-13 **0** DanielTudhope 4 42
(G M Moore) *hld up in rr: hdwy over 2f out: sn rdn and no imp fr over 1f out* **80/1**
0- 7 4½ **Calza Di Seta**^{365} 2504 3-8-8 **0** RoystonFfrench 2 27
(G M Moore) *chsd ldrs: rdn along wl over 2f out and sn wknd* **33/1**
8 2 **Snake Catcher** 3-8-6 **0** NSLawes(7) 11 27
(M W Easterby) *cl up: rdn along over 3f out and grad wknd* **100/1**
40 9 ¾ **Phantom Serenade (IRE)**^{8} 2673 3-8-10 **0** PJMcDonald(3) 5 25
(M Dods) *chsd ldrs: pushed along 1/2-way: sn wknd* **14/1**^{3}
10 1 **Peedee** 3-8-8 **0** TomEaves 10 18
(G R Oldroyd) *dwlt: a towards rr* **50/1**
11 7 **Ring Bertie** 3-8-13 **0** PaulHanagan 3 7
(Micky Hammond) *a in rr* **20/1**

1m 39.86s (1.86) **Going Correction** -0.05s/f (Good)
WFA 3 from 4yo 11lb **11** Ran SP% **122.4**
Speed ratings (Par 101): **88,86,81,81,79 76,72,70,69,68 61**
CSF £12.04 TOTE £1.30: £1.02, £3.80, £27.20; EX 8.30.
Owner K Abdulla **Bred** Juddmonte Farms Ltd **Trained** Newmarket, Suffolk

FOCUS
The well-bred winner faced something of a penalty kick in beating mainly modest sorts, though the runner-up shaped with promise. The fourth was below his dbut form. The time was slow.
Ring Bertie Official explanation: jockey said gelding slipped and stumbled leaving stalls

2913 BODDINGTONS REDCAR STRAIGHT-MILE CHAMPIONSHIP H'CAP (QUALIFIER) 1m
4:30 (4:30) (Class 3) (0-95,90) 3-Y-O+
£6,542 (£1,959; £979; £490; £244; £122) Stalls Centre

Form RPR
13- 1 **Gold Sovereign (IRE)**^{249} 5978 4-10-0 **90** TedDurcan 9 107+
(Saeed Bin Suroor) *hld up: hdwy over 2f out: led and edgd rt fr over 1f out: clr ins fnl f: eased towards fin* **1/1**^{1}
2101 2 3¼ **Ansells Pride (IRE)**^{19} 2334 5-9-10 **86** TomEaves 6 93
(B Smart) *chsd ldr: rdn and ev ch over 1f out: styd on same pce fnl f* **11/4**^{2}
0-05 3 hd **Hartshead**^{17} 2397 9-9-5 **81** DeanMcKeown 1 88
(G A Swinbank) *trckd ldrs: rdn and edgd rt over 1f out: styd on* **17/2**^{3}
-231 4 ¾ **Marning Star**^{22} 2246 3-8-3 **76** SilvestreDeSousa 4 78
(D Nicholls) *led: rdn and hdd over 2f out: ev ch over 1f out: no ex ins fnl f* **9/1**
4031 5 3 **Stoic Leader (IRE)**^{15} 2445 8-8-12 **74** PaulHanagan 8 72
(R F Fisher) *hld up in tch: plld hrd: rdn and hung lft over 1f out: sn btn* **12/1**
0-35 6 4½ **Musca (IRE)**^{15} 2445 4-8-12 **74** RobertWinston 5 78
(C Grant) *s.i.s: hdwy over 6f out: led over 2f out: rdn and hdd over 1f out: eased ins fnl f* **12/1**

1m 38.37s (0.37) **Going Correction** -0.05s/f (Good)
WFA 3 from 4yo+ 11lb **6** Ran SP% **112.6**
Speed ratings (Par 107): **96,92,92,91,88 84**
CSF £3.92 CT £12.63 TOTE £1.70: £1.40, £1.90; EX 3.30.
Owner Godolphin **Bred** Sunderland Holdings **Trained** Newmarket, Suffolk

FOCUS
A decent handicap. Godolphin have a pretty good record when throwing maiden winners into handicap company and their son of King's Best proved well up to coping with a handicap mark of 90. There is much better to come from him.

NOTEBOOK
Gold Sovereign(IRE) must have had his problems as he didn't see the racecourse until the autumn of his three-year-old year, but he obviously has plenty of ability and made it two wins from three career starts in fairly effortless fashion. He faces a sizable hike in the weights but it would be no surprise to see him take in a conditions event next. (tchd 11-10 and 6-5 in a place)
Ansells Pride(IRE) didn't have the firepower to go with the winner, but time might tell he faced an impossible task in reciept of just 4lb and he probably ran at least as well as when successful at Haydock from a 3lb lower mark last time. (op 3-1)
Hartshead hasn't won for two years but is 12lb lower than his last winning mark and shaping like he is at last coming to hand. (op 8-1 tchd 9-1)
Marning Star won a weak Musselburgh maiden last time and was facing a tough task in taking on his elders at this time of year. Having cut out the running, he was far from disgraced. (tchd 10-1)
Musca(IRE) Official explanation: vet said gelding finished lame

2914 THE COMMITMENTS ARE HERE IN AUGUST (S) STKS 1m 6f 19y
5:00 (5:00) (Class 6) 4-6-Y-O £1,774 (£523; £262) Stalls Low

Form RPR
422/ 1 **Alasoun (IRE)**^{705} 3231 5-9-0 **0** (tp) VinceSlattery 4 56+
(Evan Williams) *trckd ldrs: hdwy to ld over 3f out: rdn wl over 1f out: styd on strly* **5/2**^{1}
604- 2 2¾ **Kerry's Blade (IRE)**^{17} 5561 6-9-0 **47** (p) PaulHanagan 3 49
(Micky Hammond) *hld up towards rr: hdwy over 4f out: rdn over 2f out: chsd wnr appr fnl f: sn drvn and no imp* **16/1**
0-04 3 1¾ **Parchment (IRE)**^{17} 2395 6-8-9 **50** (b) GaryBartley(5) 10 47
(A J Lockwood) *hld up and bhd: hdwy 3f out: rdn wl over 1f out: styd on ins fnl f: nrst fin* **6/1**^{3}
60 4 1 **Funky Town (IRE)**^{4} 2776 6-8-11 **0** PJMcDonald(3) 2 45
(Grant Tuer) *plld hrd: chsd ldrs: effrt 3f out: sn chsng wnr: rdn wl over 1f out and kpt on same pce* **10/1**
00-3 5 2¾ **Blushing Hilary (IRE)**^{15} 654 5-8-9 **53** (b) TomEaves 9 36
(Miss J A Camacho) *in tch: hdwy 4f out: rdn along wl over 2f out: sn drvn and no imp* **5/2**^{1}
50-0 6 ¾ **Muraco**^{10} 2623 4-9-0 **69** RoystonFfrench 1 40
(Mrs A Duffield) *trckd ldr tl hld over 7f out: rdn along and hdd over 3f out: sn wknd* **5/1**^{2}
50-4 7 ½ **Revolving World (IRE)**^{29} 2053 5-8-11 **49** (t) RussellKennemore(3) 7 40
(L R James) *hld up: hdwy 4f out: rdn along on outer to chse ldrs 3f out: sn drvn and wknd* **14/1**
0-P0 8 6 **Bobansheil (IRE)**^{4} 2776 4-8-2 **52** (v) PatrickDonaghy(7) 5 26
(J S Wainwright) *a towards rr* **50/1**
0-05 9 5 **Resaass (USA)**^{17} 2395 5-9-0 **48** (b) DNolan 6 24
(J O'Reilly) *chsd ldrs: rdn along 3f out: drvn over 2f out and sn wknd* **33/1**
50-6 10 14 **Roll Em Over**^{25} 2157 5-8-6 **28** MichaelJStainton(3) 8 —
(A Crook) *led: hdd over 7f out: rdn along over 4f out and sn wknd* **66/1**

3m 7.43s (2.73) **Going Correction** -0.05s/f (Good) **10** Ran SP% **116.1**
Speed ratings: **90,88,87,86,85 84,84,81,78,70**
CSF £47.69 TOTE £3.10: £1.50, £4.10, £2.10; EX 40.80.There was no bid for the winner.
Owner R E R Williams **Bred** His Highness The Aga Khan's Studs S C **Trained** Llancarfan, Vale Of Glamorgan

FOCUS
Pretty desperate stuff, the winner making the long journey from South Wales worthwhile but running well below his official mark. The form is rated around the runner-up.
Blushing Hilary(IRE) Official explanation: jockey said mare ran flat

2915 GO RACING IN YORKSHIRE SUMMER FESTIVAL H'CAP 1m 2f
5:30 (5:32) (Class 6) (0-55,55) 3-Y-O £2,047 (£604; £302) Stalls Low

Form RPR
-063 1 **Amicable Terms**^{7} 2704 3-8-12 **53** TedDurcan 15 60
(Rae Guest) *hld up: hdwy over 2f out: rdn over 1f out: r.o to ld nr fin* **14/1**
0002 2 nk **South Wales**^{12} 2552 3-8-9 **50** NickyMackay 2 56
(S C Williams) *trckd ldrs: racd keenly: led over 1f out: sn rdn: hdd nr fin* **8/1**^{3}
0-06 3 1½ **Willkandoo (USA)**^{23} 2221 3-9-0 **55** FergalLynch 5 58+
(K A Ryan) *s.i.s: hld up: racd keenly: hdwy over 1f out: r.o* **14/1**
005 4 1 **Mganga**^{12} 2552 3-8-7 **55** MCGeran(7) 12 56
(M R Channon) *hld up: rdn over 1f out: r.o ins fnl f: nt rch ldrs* **8/1**^{3}

-050 **5** *hd* **Sarah's First**[14] 2475 3-8-13 **54**........ PaulHanagan 1 55
(E A L Dunlop) *dwlt: hld up: rdn and hung lft fr over 1f out: r.o ins fnl f: nrst fin* **12/1**

-053 **6** *1 1/2* **Intersky Melody (USA)**[21] 2273 3-9-0 **55**........(b) DeanMcKeown 14 53
(R M Whitaker) *s.i.s: hdwy 8f out: led over 2f out: rdn and hdd over 1f out: hung lft and no ex ins fnl f* **9/1**

5-00 **7** *1 1/4* **Jakam (IRE)**[35] 1894 3-8-9 **50**........ JoeFanning 13 46
(E J O'Neill) *chsd ldr tl led over 3f out: rdn and hdd over 2f out: wknd ins fnl f* **10/1**

6624 **8** *1* **Holden Caulfield (IRE)**[9] 2639 3-8-11 **52**........ TomEaves 7 46
(Mouse Hamilton-Fairley) *hld up: hdwy over 3f out: rdn over 1f out: sn edgd lft: wknd ins fnl f* **13/2**[2]

50-0 **9** *3/4* **Honeycott (IRE)**[24] 2208 3-8-9 **50**........ AlanMunro 9 42
(J D Bethell) *prom: racd keenly: rdn over 2f out: wknd fnl f* **40/1**

0003 **10** *1/2* **Glitz (IRE)**[7] 2694 3-9-0 **55**........ HayleyTurner 10 46
(M L W Bell) *chsd ldrs: rdn over 2f out: wknd fnl f* **11/1**

-000 **11** *nk* **Marramed**[7] 2704 3-8-9 **50**........ DNolan 3 40
(J O'Reilly) *hld up: rdn over 2f out: nt trble ldrs* **66/1**

0-03 **12** *2 1/4* **Defies Logic**[24] 2208 3-9-0 **55**........ TPQueally 8 41+
(J G Given) *prom: nt clr run and lost pl over 2f out: n.d after* **9/4**[1]

0400 **13** *1 1/4* **Chevaliers Dream (IRE)**[34] 1912 3-9-0 **55**........ DavidAllan 4 38
(T D Easterby) *s.i.s: hld up: hrd rdn 2f out: wknd fnl f* **25/1**

060- **14** *20* **Bond Scissorsister (IRE)**[256] 5766 3-8-9 **50**........ RoystonFfrench 11 —
(G R Oldroyd) *led: rdn and hdd over 3f out: wknd over 2f out* **40/1**

2m 7.67s (0.57) **Going Correction** -0.05s/f (Good) **14 Ran SP% 125.0**
Speed ratings (Par 97): **95,94,93,92,92 91,90,89,89,88 88,86,85,69**
CSF £123.77 CT £1630.85 TOTE £15.00: £3.20, £2.70, £5.20; EX 104.20 Place 6: £19.31 Place 5: £13.43.
Owner Sentinel Bloodstock **Bred** Brook Stud Bloodstock Ltd **Trained** Newmarket, Suffolk
■ Stewards' Enquiry : Nicky Mackay one-day ban: excessive use of whip (Jun 24)

FOCUS
Some moderate three-year-olds on show. The winner, showing improved form, completed a hat-trick for Durcan and was the third successful Newmarket raider on the card. The first three probably have more to offer.
Sarah's First Official explanation: jockey said filly hung left-handed throughout
Defies Logic Official explanation: jockey said gelding was denied a clear run and was carried back by weakening horses
T/Plt: £18.00 to a £1 stake. Pool: £61,028.65. 2,472.20 winning tickets. T/Qpdt: £7.00 to a £1 stake. Pool: £3,505.40. 367.85 winning tickets. JR

2337 SALISBURY (R-H)
Tuesday, June 10

OFFICIAL GOING: Good to firm
Wind: Moderate, half against

2916 GEORGE SMITH HORSEBOXES MAIDEN AUCTION STKS 6f
2:15 (2:23) (Class 5) 2-Y-O **£3,238** (£963; £481; £240) **Stalls** High

Form RPR

3 **1** **Measurement (IRE)**[11] 2562 2-8-12........ RichardHughes 3 77+
(R Hannon) *lw: a in tch: led over 1f out: r.o wl* **10/3**[1]

2 *1 1/4* **Blown It (USA)** 2-9-2........ SteveDrowne 2 77+
(J A Osborne) *str: lw: s.i.s: sn pshd along twrds rr: hdwy over 1f out: r.o to go 2nd ins fnl f* **9/1**

3 *1* **Damassin** 2-8-7........ WilliamBuick 4 65
(Eve Johnson Houghton) *leggy: scope: bit bkwd: mid-div: hdwy 2f out: rdn and kpt on fr over 1f out* **50/1**

4 **4** *2 1/2* **Minder**[11] 2562 2-9-2........ SebSanders 13 67
(J G Portman) *swtg: w ldrs tl wknd 1f out* **7/1**[3]

5 *nk* **Cavendish Road (IRE)** 2-8-12........ MartinDwyer 15 62
(W R Muir) *str: a.p: led over 2f out: hdd over 1f out: sn wknd* **25/1**

6 *shd* **Give (IRE)** 2-8-11........ RyanMoore 8 63+
(R Hannon) *w'like: towards rr: swtchd lft over 1f out: r.o: nvr nrr* **15/2**

7 *1 1/2* **Trigger McCann** 2-8-9........ LPKeniry 10 54
(J S Moore) *str: in tch: rdn over 2f out: one pce* **33/1**

8 *2* **City Diamond** 2-8-9........ TravisBlock(3) 9 51
(P J Makin) *w'like: bit bkwd: slowly away and wnt rt s: bhd: short of room and swtchd lft wl over 1f out: going on wl at fin* **40/1**

0 **9** *1/2* **Ba Globetrotter**[7] 2702 2-9-2........ SamHitchcott 16 58+
(M R Channon) *leggy: rrd up s: nvr bttr than mid-div* **50/1**

10 *nk* **Hi Shinko** 2-8-12........ FergusSweeney 17 49
(B R Millman) *w'like: bit bkwd: chsd ldrs: hung lft over 2f out: wknd over 1f out* **25/1**

11 *3/4* **Royal Executioner (USA)** 2-8-12........ KerrinMcEvoy 1 46
(P W Chapple-Hyam) *w'like: bit bkwd: racd on outside: n.d* **12/1**

12 *1* **My Best Man** 2-8-12........ DaneO'Neill 6 43
(B R Millman) *w'like: a in rr* **40/1**

13 *nk* **Lady Mulligan** 2-8-4........ JimmyQuinn 11 35
(M Blanshard) *leggy: w'like: bit bkwd: mid-div: wknd over 1f out* **66/1**

14 *nk* **Co Dependent (USA)** 2-9-2........ ShaneKelly 7 46
(J A Osborne) *w'like: scope: a bhd* **15/2**

15 *1 3/4* **Kosama** 2-8-5 ow1........ EdwardCreighton 14 29
(M R Channon) *athletic: bolted bef s: mid-div tl wknd over 2f out* **20/1**

16 *1* **Rocksy** 2-8-7........ TPO'Shea 12 28
(D J Coakley) *w'like: scope: bit bkwd: w ldrs tl rdn and wknd qckly wl over 1f out* **4/1**[2]

17 *3 1/2* **Endofmytether** 2-8-7........ CatherineGannon 18 18
(P D Evans) *leggy: swtg: led tl hdd over 2f out: wknd rapidly* **25/1**

18 *1 1/2* **Lucky Bid** 2-8-2........ PietroRomeo(7) 5 15
(J M Bradley) *w'like: bit bkwd: slowly away: a bhd* **150/1**

1m 15.54s (0.74) **Going Correction** -0.10s/f (Good) **18 Ran SP% 127.0**
Speed ratings (Par 93): **91,89,88,84,84 84,82,79,78,78 77,76,75,75,72 71,66,64**
CSF £30.98 TOTE £3.90: £1.60, £4.40, £12.80; EX 39.00.
Owner B Bull **Bred** Donagh Killilea **Trained** East Everleigh, Wilts

FOCUS
An interesting maiden, but little form to go on with only three of the 18 runners having raced before. The early pace was set by those drawn high towards the inside rail, but the finish was dominated by the finishers down the middle and the first three home were drawn 3, 2 and 4. The winner and the fourth set the standard.

NOTEBOOK
Measurement(IRE), with the benefit of previous experience, picked up well when asked to go and win his race and was well on top at the line. He should continue to improve and will have no difficulty staying an extra furlong. (op 11-4)
Blown It(USA) ◆, a 25,000gns colt out of a useful sprinting juvenile in the US, like his stable-companion Co Dependent came in for market support and justified it with a fine staying-on second. He should not take long in going one better. (op 14-1 tchd 17-2)
Damassin ◆, a 10,000gns half-sister to Ellway Queen and a multiple sprint-winner in the US, was not expected to make a successful debut according to the market, but as it turned out she ran a blinder. She was doing some very nice work late on and can be expected to improve. (tchd 66-1)
Minder, a length and a half behind Measurement on his Goodwood debut and 2lb worse off, got himself into a real state beforehand and unshipped his rider before stalls entry. Once under way he had every chance, but he must have taken plenty out of himself and probably did not run quite up to his best. (op 9-2 tchd 4-1)
Cavendish Road(IRE), a 14,000gns colt out of a dual winning sprinter in Italy, showed good speed for a long way before lack of a run took its toll. This gives his connections something to build on.
Give(IRE) ◆, a 24,000gns filly, is out of a winning half-sister to Harvest Queen and Coconut Queen and from the family of Golan, Tartan Bearer and North Light. A stable-companion of the winner though well backed in her own right, she took time to realise what was required but was noted finishing strongly and she should soon leave this form behind. (op 12-1)
Trigger McCann ◆, out of the prolific winning sprinter Roses Of Spring, showed some ability on this debut and would have finished closer had he not ran into a few traffic problems inside the final furlong. He looks to have a future.
City Diamond ◆, a 10,000gns brother to Scarlet Knight and half-brother to Sun Of The Sea, was a real eye-catcher. Slowest to break from the stalls, he tried to make up ground as the race progressed but repeatedly ran into traffic and he can be rated quite a bit better than his finishing position. From a stable not really noted for winning juvenile debutants, much better can be expected from him in due course. Official explanation: jockey said colt ran very green
Royal Executioner(USA), a $30,000 half-brother to a winner in the US, did not show a great deal on this debut but he was rather marooned on the wide outside from the lowest stall and is probably capable of better. (op 10-1 tchd 17-2)
Co Dependent(USA), re-sold for 23,000gns as a yearling, is out of a triple-winner in the US. Very well supported in the betting, he never got into the race but the market confidence suggests he is thought capable of much better. (op 22-1)
Kosama, a 14,500gns foal but only 5,500gns as a yearling, is a half-sister to four winners around Europe. She did her chances no good by running loose before the start so therefore should not be judged too harshly on this. (op 18-1)
Rocksy, a 10,000gns half-sister to two winners, one of whom was successful at up to 1m6f and also over hurdles, attracted market support but after showing up for a long way, she then dropped right out. (op 5-1 tchd 11-2)

2917 GERRY MCCANN "LIFETIME IN RACING" CLAIMING STKS 6f 212y
2:45 (2:53) (Class 5) 3-Y-O+ **£3,238** (£963; £481; £240) **Stalls** High

Form RPR

1200 **1** **Bartercard (USA)**[3] 2837 7-9-12 75........ EddieAhern 5 63
(Stef Liddiard) *in rr: hdwy fr 3f out: rdn and styd on over 1f out: swtchd rt to far rail ins fnl f: led fnl 75yds: kpt on wl* **7/1**[2]

4365 **2** *1 1/2* **Desert Dreamer (IRE)**[7] 2693 7-9-10 74........(t) RichardKingscote 2 57
(Tom Dascombe) *lw: in tch rdn and hung rt fr over 2f out: styd on u.p over 1f out and chsd wnr nr fin but a readily hld* **15/8**[1]

0-00 **3** *nk* **Takitwo**[116] 576 5-9-2 56........ SimonWhitworth 7 48
(P D Cundell) *chsd ldrs: rdn 3f out: pressed ldrs over 1f out: styd on same pce ins fnl f* **15/2**[3]

0155 **4** *1/2* **Landucci**[69] 1143 7-9-9 73........(p) PatrickHills(3) 16 57
(J W Hills) *lw: chsd ldrs: chal fr 2f out: led appr fnl f: hdd fnl 75yds and sn wknd* **7/1**[2]

0005 **5** *hd* **Outer Hebrides**[14] 2477 7-9-5 57........(v) WilliamBuick 11 53+
(J M Bradley) *t.k.h and stdd into mid-div 4f out: hdwy on ins and n.m.r over 2f out: styng on wl whn hmpd jst ins fnl f: kpt on again but nt rcvr* **14/1**

6 *hd* **Sticky Tape** 4-9-7........ ShaneKelly 10 51+
(J A Osborne) *w'like: stdd s and in rr: bmpd over 3f out: swtchd to outside over 2f out: styd on wl thrght fnl f: gng on cl home* **25/1**

5065 **7** *1/2* **Fun In The Sun**[18] 2355 4-9-4 46........ SamHitchcott 8 47
(A B Haynes) *chsd ldr over 5f out: rdn to chal over 2f out: wknd ins fnl f* **25/1**

0-00 **8** *1* **Convince (USA)**[28] 2069 7-9-2 42........(v) SteveDrowne 4 42
(J M Bradley) *rdn and outpcd towards rr 5f out: styd on fnl 2f but nvr gng pce to be competitive* **80/1**

1060 **9** *1/2* **Turkish Sultan (IRE)**[18] 2355 5-9-6 50........(p) DaneO'Neill 13 45
(J M Bradley) *sn mid-div: rdn and hdwy to chse ldrs over 2f out: wknd over 1f out* **16/1**

0 **10** *2 1/2* **Frosty's Gift**[19] 2341 4-9-2........ RichardSmith 3 34
(J C Fox) *in rr tl r.o fr over 1f out: nvr in contention* **100/1**

0403 **11** *1 3/4* **Cyfrwys (IRE)**[49] 1550 7-8-12 48........(p) CatherineGannon 1 25
(B Palling) *chsd ldrs: rdn over 3f out: wknd ins fnl 2f* **28/1**

-000 **12** *1* **Orchestrator (IRE)**[11] 2556 4-9-3 60........(p) JimCrowley 12 27
(T G Mills) *led: rdn over 2f out: hdd over 1f out and wknd qckly* **14/1**

1400 **13** *5* **Solicitude**[63] 1260 5-8-12 47........(p) RobertHavlin 6 9
(D Haydn Jones) *a in rr* **25/1**

0-00 **14** *3 1/4* **Bozeman Trail**[14] 2480 3-8-9 56........(b) TQuinn 14 7
(P F I Cole) *chsd ldrs tl rdn and wknd fr 3f out* **33/1**

-640 **15** *5* **High Plains (FR)**[22] 2261 3-8-13 67........ RichardHughes 15 —
(R Hannon) *chsd ldrs: rdn over 3f out: wknd 2f out: eased whn no ch ins fnl f* **8/1**

1m 28.13s (-0.87) **Going Correction** -0.10s/f (Good)
WFA 3 from 4yo+ 10lb **15 Ran SP% 122.0**
Speed ratings (Par 103): **100,98,97,97,97 96,96,95,94,91 89,88,82,79,73**
CSF £19.22 TOTE £8.20: £2.50, £1.60, £3.10; EX 26.70.
Owner Mrs Stef Liddiard **Bred** Red Gate Venture Llc **Trained** Great Shefford, Berks

FOCUS
A modest claimer run at a fair pace. The form has a messy look to it and is far from solid.
Outer Hebrides Official explanation: jockey said gelding suffered interference in the closing stages
High Plains(FR) Official explanation: jockey said colt lost its action

2918 RACING UK MAIDEN STKS (DIV I) 6f 212y
3:15 (3:22) (Class 5) 3-Y-O **£3,399** (£1,011; £505; £252) **Stalls** High

Form RPR

1 **Main Aim** 3-9-3 0........ RyanMoore 6 84+
(Sir Michael Stoute) *w'like: hld up in rr: t.k.h: shkn up 2f out: rdn and r.o to ld nr fin* **4/5**[1]

3-2 **2** *nk* **Carniolan**[21] 2279 3-9-3 0........ AdamKirby 8 83
(W R Swinburn) *chsd ldrs: rdn to ld appr fnl f: hdd towards fin* **11/4**[2]

6 **3** *2 3/4* **Profitability (USA)**[53] 1445 3-8-12 0........ JimmyFortune 10 71
(J H M Gosden) *lw: trckd ldrs: rdn and one pce fr over 1f out* **9/1**[3]

-540 **4** *shd* **Polmaily**[20] 2311 3-9-3 78........ EddieAhern 7 75
(B J Meehan) *towards rr: hdwy on ins 2f out: kpt on one pce fnl f* **10/1**

0 **5** *3* **Ma Vie En Rose (IRE)**[11] 2566 3-8-12 0........(t) LPKeniry 1 62
(A M Balding) *led tl rdn and hdd appr fnl f: wknd* **100/1**

4-03 **6** *1* **Rowaad**[21] 2276 3-9-3 72........ RHills 3 65
(M P Tregoning) *lw: trckd ldr tl rdn 2f out: wknd fnl f* **16/1**

00 **7** *4* **Flying Flute**[10] 2620 3-9-3 0........ DaneO'Neill 4 54
(H Candy) *b.hind: stdd s: in tch tl hung lft 2f out: sn btn* **40/1**

	8	10	**Gun For Sale (USA)** 3-9-3 0 ... SebSanders 9	27
			(P J Makin) *str: slowly away: a towards rr* **33/1**	
06	9	6	**Cherries On Top (IRE)**[22] 2240 3-9-3 0 ... RichardThomas 2	11
			(I A Wood) *stdd s: plld hrd: a bhd* **100/1**	

1m 28.62s (-0.38) **Going Correction** -0.10s/f (Good) **9** Ran SP% **114.6**
Speed ratings (Par 99): **98,97,94,94,90 89,85,73,66**
CSF £2.97 TOTE £2.10: £1.10, £1.20, £1.60; EX 3.90.

Owner K Abdulla **Bred** Juddmonte Farms Ltd **Trained** Newmarket, Suffolk

FOCUS
Just an ordinary maiden and the pace was steady through the early stages. The winning time was 1.22 seconds slower than the second division. Main Aim did it well and the form makes a good deal of sense, rated through the runner-up.

Flying Flute Official explanation: jockey said gelding hung left

Cherries On Top(IRE) Official explanation: jockey said colt ran too free

2919 RACING UK MAIDEN STKS (DIV II) — 6f 212y

3:45 (3:51) (Class 5) 3-Y-O — £3,399 (£1,011; £505; £252) Stalls High

Form				RPR
	1		**Kalahari Gold (IRE)** 3-9-3 ... LPKeniry 9	86+
			(A M Balding) *w'like: trckd ldrs: drvn along 3f out: staying on whn carried lft and bmpd over 1f out: sn rcvrd and styd on wl to ld fnl 50yds: readily* **16/1**	
4-	2	¾	**Credit Swap**[231] 6409 3-9-3 ... DaneO'Neill 10	84+
			(L M Cumani) *lw: chsd ldrs: led 1f out whn ldr veered lft: sn rdn: hdd and outpcd fnl 50yds* **5/1**[3]	
63	3	3½	**Theory**[20] 2307 3-8-12 ... JimmyFortune 8	70
			(J H M Gosden) *led: rdn and veered bdly lft over 1f out: nt rcvr and sn btn* **11/4**[1]	
4-24	4	3	**Strategic Mover (USA)**[16] 2427 3-9-3 85 ... TQuinn 1	67
			(P F I Cole) *in tch: rdn and styng on whn pushed lft over 2f out: swtchd rt over 1f out and styd on same pce* **11/4**[1]	
230-	5	¾	**Papillio (IRE)**[290] 4832 3-9-3 83 ... KerrinMcEvoy 4	65
			(J R Fanshawe) *pressed ldr: rdn over 2f out: wknd appr fnl f* **10/3**[2]	
0-	6	1	**Holden Eagle**[228] 6468 3-9-3 ... SteveDrowne 7	62
			(A G Newcombe) *w'like: scope: str: in rr: shkn up over 2f out: sme prog fr over 1f out: nvr in contention* **33/1**	
0	7	2½	**Diego Rivera**[24] 2198 3-9-3 ... RichardSmith 2	55
			(P J Makin) *t.k.h: chsd ldrs: rdn and hung lft over 2f out: sn btn* **11/1**	
	8	shd	**Sydneysider** 3-9-3 ... WilliamBuick 5	55
			(Eve Johnson Houghton) *str: s.i.s: rcvrd into mid-div 3f out: sn rdn: wknd over 2f out* **40/1**	
60	9	13	**Persian Flyer (IRE)**[37] 1835 3-9-3 ... JimmyQuinn 6	20
			(J W Mullins) *bit bkwd: a bhd* **100/1**	
	10	18	**Cape Roberto (IRE)** 3-9-3 ... RobertHavlin 3	—
			(Jamie Poulton) *slowly away: rcvrd into mid-div 4f out: sn rdn and wknd* **40/1**	

1m 27.4s (-1.60) **Going Correction** -0.10s/f (Good) **10** Ran SP% **116.1**
Speed ratings (Par 99): **105,104,100,96,95 94,91,91,76,56**
CSF £91.97 TOTE £17.50: £3.40, £1.80, £1.50; EX 100.70.

Owner The Toucan Syndicate **Bred** Mick McGinn And James Waldron **Trained** Kingsclere, Hants

FOCUS
There was probably more strength in depth than in the first division and the winning time was 1.22 seconds quicker, although it was still only identical to the later 46-65 handicap won by the 56-rated Grit. The form is rated through th second and third but looks a bit guessy

Credit Swap Official explanation: jockey said colt hung left

Theory Official explanation: vet said filly was lame on her left-fore

Cape Roberto(IRE) Official explanation: trainer said gelding lost its action after jumping the road

2920 E B F MARGADALE FILLIES' H'CAP — 1m 1f 198y

4:15 (4:23) (Class 4) (0-85,81) 3-Y-O+ — £6,476 (£1,927; £963; £481) Stalls High

Form				RPR
51	1		**Casilda (IRE)**[19] 2328 3-9-4 77 ... PaulDoe 7	83
			(W J Knight) *mid-div: rdn and hdwy to go 2nd over 1f out: led cl home* **12/1**	
3-43	2	hd	**My Aunt Fanny**[19] 2328 3-9-3 76 ... LPKeniry 9	82
			(A M Balding) *trckd ldr: led 3f out: wnt lft ins fnl f: hdd cl home* **16/1**	
0-11	3	nk	**Storyland (USA)**[24] 2190 3-9-0 73 ... KerrinMcEvoy 5	78+
			(W J Haggas) *twrds rr: hdwy on ins over 2f out: r.o wl fnl f: nvr nrr* **3/1**[1]	
21-6	4	1½	**La Columbina**[25] 2151 3-9-5 78 ... RichardHughes 14	80
			(R Hannon) *lw: trckd ldrs: rdn over 2f out: kpt on one pce* **8/1**	
66-6	5	½	**Spell Caster**[20] 2311 3-9-5 78 ... SebSanders 2	79+
			(R M Beckett) *twrds rr: hdwy 2f out: r.o: nvr nrr* **6/1**[3]	
04-5	6	1½	**Star Of Gibraltar**[46] 1599 3-9-7 80 ... EddieAhern 13	78
			(J L Dunlop) *mid-div: rdn over 2f out: one pce fnl f* **14/1**	
03-3	7	½	**Amhooj**[36] 1854 3-8-11 70 ... RHills 8	67+
			(M P Tregoning) *mid-div on outside: rdn over 2f out: no hdwy after* **16/1**	
	8	hd	**Atomic Winner (IRE)**[34] 4-10-0 74 ... DaneO'Neill 10	71
			(A King) *lw: mid-div: no hdwy fr over 1f out* **16/1**	
0-35	9	nk	**Winter Bloom (USA)**[22] 2256 3-9-8 81 ... JimmyFortune 4	77
			(H R A Cecil) *lw: mid-div: rdn over 2f out: wknd over 1f out* **7/2**[2]	
31-0	10	4½	**Trinkila (USA)**[54] 1412 3-9-1 74 ... TQuinn 1	61
			(P F I Cole) *chsd ldrs: rdn 3f out: wknd 2f out* **50/1**	
16-	11	3¼	**Mistress Eva**[252] 5883 3-9-0 73 ... JimCrowley 11	54
			(P Winkworth) *b: led tl hdd 3f out: sn wknd* **25/1**	
1-64	12	3	**Sahaadi**[21] 2276 3-8-13 72 ... RyanMoore 3	47
			(R Hannon) *stdd s: a bhd* **12/1**	
666-	13	41	**Lady Zabeen (IRE)**[255] 5801 3-8-13 72 ... MartinDwyer 6	—
			(D M Simcock) *hld up in rr: a bhd: eased 1f out: t.o* **25/1**	

2m 8.13s (-1.77) **Going Correction** -0.10s/f (Good)
WFA 3 from 4yo+ 13lb **13** Ran SP% **122.0**
Speed ratings (Par 102): **103,102,102,101,101 99,99,99,99,95 92,90,57**
CSF £190.46 CT £733.82 TOTE £13.00: £4.70, £4.90, £1.50; EX 145.20 Trifecta £296.10 Part won. Pool: 417.16 - 0.40 winning units..

Owner Mrs P G M Jamison **Bred** David Jamison Bloodstock And G Roddick **Trained** Patching, W Sussex

FOCUS
Probably just a fair fillies' handicap for the grade, with most of the field finishing well bunched off an ordinary pace. The first two ran to their latest form in a Goodwood maiden.

Lady Zabeen(IRE) Official explanation: trainer's rep said filly was unsuited by the good to firm ground

2921 DUTTON GREGORY H'CAP — 1m 4f

4:45 (4:51) (Class 5) (0-70,70) 4-Y-O+ — £3,238 (£963; £481; £240) Stalls High

Form				RPR
-002	1		**Double Spectre (IRE)**[9] 2640 6-8-13 62 ... DaneO'Neill 7	71
			(Jean-Rene Auvray) *rr: hdwy over 2f out: rdn: edgd rt and led 1f out: drvn out* **14/1**	
5-16	2	1	**Colonel Flay**[31] 1998 4-9-1 69 ... JackMitchell(5) 8	76
			(Mrs P N Dutfield) *hld up in rr: swtchd lft to outside and hdwy over 2f out: styd on u.p to chse wnr ins fnl f but a hld* **6/1**[3]	
30/6	3	1¼	**Greenwich Village**[16] 2423 5-8-13 62 ... AmirQuinn 10	67
			(W J Knight) *sn chsng ldr: chal 3f out: led sn after: hdd u.p ins fnl 2f: kpt on same pce ins fnl f* **16/1**	
6-12	4	nk	**Summer Of Love (IRE)**[18] 2354 4-9-4 67 ...(b) FergusSweeney 4	72
			(Mrs S J Humphrey) *towards rr: hdwy fr 3f out: drvn to press ldrs whn edgd rt 1f out: styd on same pce* **8/1**	
5564	5	¾	**Savannah**[40] 1744 5-8-13 65 ...(b) JerryO'Dwyer(3) 9	69
			(Luke Comer, Ire) *mid-div whn rdn and outpcd 4f out: swtchd lft 2f out and r.o u.p fnl f but nvr gng pce to rch ldrs* **16/1**	
-033	6	1¾	**Bold Bobby Be (IRE)**[14] 2483 4-9-3 66 ... KerrinMcEvoy 14	67+
			(J L Dunlop) *lw: in tch: rdn and one pce 2f out: styng on but nt gng pce to trble ldrs whn hmpd 1f out* **7/2**[1]	
0-25	7	hd	**Wyeth**[18] 2361 4-8-12 61 ... SebSanders 6	62
			(J R Fanshawe) *in rr: rdn 3f out: styd on fr over 1f out but nvr in contention* **6/1**[3]	
3164	8	¾	**Resplendent Ace (IRE)**[18] 2365 4-9-1 64 ... JimmyQuinn 2	65+
			(P Howling) *chsd ldrs: rdn 3f out: led ins fnl 2f: hdd over 1f out and sn wknd* **14/1**	
4-03	9	2¾	**Good Effect (USA)**[8] 2682 4-9-7 70 ... GeorgeBaker 3	71+
			(C P Morlock) *lw: in tch: chsd ldrs over 2f out: led over 1f out: narrowly hdd whn hmpd 1f out and sn wknd* **14/1**	
4445	10	3¼	**Generous Lad (IRE)**[28] 2071 5-9-4 67 ...(p) RichardHughes 13	66+
			(A B Haynes) *chsd ldrs: rdn ins fnl 3f: wkng and no ch whn hmpd 1f out* **20/1**	
0202	11	6	**One To Follow**[14] 2482 4-9-2 65 ... AdamKirby 12	45
			(C G Cox) *chsd ldrs: rdn 3f out: wknd fr 2f out: out of contention whn sltly hmpd 1f out* **5/1**[2]	
45-0	12	2¼	**Ocean Avenue (IRE)**[159] 27 9-9-2 65 ... JimmyFortune 11	42
			(C A Horgan) *led tl ins fnl 3f: sn wknd* **16/1**	

2m 36.51s (-1.49) **Going Correction** -0.10s/f (Good) **12** Ran SP% **121.0**
Speed ratings (Par 103): **100,99,98,98,97 96,96,96,94,92 88,86**
CSF £97.77 CT £1385.44 TOTE £18.50: £4.70, £2.30, £6.60; EX 131.20.

Owner The Dragon Partnership **Bred** R Bailey **Trained** Upper Lambourn, Berks

■ Stewards' Enquiry : Amir Quinn two-day ban: careless riding (Jun 24-25)
Jimmy Quinn two-day ban: careless riding (Jun 24-25)

FOCUS
A modest handicap run at an ordinary pace. It was something of a rough race but the first two avoided the trouble and the winner looks the best guide.

Summer Of Love(IRE) Official explanation: jockey said filly lost a near-fore shoe

One To Follow Official explanation: jockey said gelding suffered interference in running

2922 TURFTV H'CAP — 6f 212y

5:15 (5:23) (Class 6) (0-65,68) 3-Y-O — £2,914 (£867; £433; £216) Stalls High

Form				RPR
0000	1		**Grit (IRE)**[9] 2639 3-8-12 56 ... TPO'Shea 15	64
			(M R Channon) *mid-div: hdwy over 1f out: nosed ahd wl ins fnl f: jst hld on* **40/1**	
4-43	2	nse	**Flower**[12] 2549 3-9-2 60 ...(v[1]) RyanMoore 3	68
			(W J Haggas) *lw: stdd s: hld up and t.k.h: chal ins fnl f: jst failed* **10/3**[2]	
-432	3	2¼	**Peas In A Pod**[12] 2549 3-8-10 54 ... KerrinMcEvoy 9	56
			(J R Fanshawe) *lw: in rr: hdwy 2f out: rdn and ev ch ins fnl f: no ex towards fin* **3/1**[1]	
00-0	4	1¾	**Reve Vert (FR)**[15] 2451 3-8-5 52 ... KirstyMilczarek(3) 11	49+
			(A W Carroll) *in tch: rdn 2f out: kpt on one pce fnl f* **40/1**	
00-4	5	nk	**Belle Bellino (FR)**[26] 2127 3-9-7 65 ... DaneO'Neill 14	61
			(B R Millman) *lw: chsd ldrs: led wl over 1f out tl hdd & wknd ins fnl f* **20/1**	
00-6	6	½	**The Hoofer (IRE)**[61] 1279 3-8-8 52 ... EddieAhern 17	47+
			(J L Dunlop) *in tch: hdwy and kpt on fr over 1f out* **20/1**	
30-0	7	1½	**Xaravella (IRE)**[36] 1870 3-8-9 53 ... RobertHavlin 16	44
			(J G M O'Shea) *a in tch on ins: wknd fnl f* **66/1**	
-550	8	nk	**Follow Your Spirit**[15] 2451 3-8-9 53 ... CatherineGannon 2	43
			(B Palling) *prom tl rdn and wknd appr fnl f* **20/1**	
3601	9	¾	**Nikolaievich (IRE)**[14] 2480 3-9-7 65 ...(b) NelsonDeSouza 10	53
			(P F I Cole) *s.i.s: a towards rr* **16/1**	
6-00	10	nk	**Wooden King (IRE)**[48] 1558 3-8-9 53 ... ShaneKelly 5	40
			(P D Evans) *mid-div: chsd ldrs: rdn 3f out: wknd 2f out* **33/1**	
-030	11	6	**Infinite Patience**[15] 2452 3-8-10 59 ... NataliaGemelova(5) 13	30
			(J S Moore) *mid-div: outpcd 2f out and nvr on terms after* **12/1**	
-421	12	½	**Fools Gold**[7] 2705 3-9-10 68 6ex ... PaulEddery 7	38
			(G D Blake) *led tl hdd wl over 1f out: sn wknd* **8/1**	
0-33	13	1¼	**Ray Diamond**[111] 623 3-8-10 54 ... JimmyQuinn 12	20
			(M Madgwick) *a in rr* **33/1**	
04-6	14	½	**Karate Queen**[45] 1637 3-8-13 57 ...(t) LPKeniry 1	22
			(A M Balding) *racd on outside: nvr on terms* **20/1**	
0-44	15	½	**Billy Hot Rocks (IRE)**[37] 1835 3-9-7 65 ... SebSanders 8	29
			(R M Beckett) *mid-div tl wknd over 2f out* **9/2**[3]	
060-	16	¾	**Iamagrey (IRE)**[239] 6242 3-8-13 60 ... TravisBlock(3) 4	22
			(C J Down) *chsd ldrs tl wknd 3f out* **33/1**	
0-00	17	2	**Madame Bountiful**[9] 2639 3-8-11 55 ... FergusSweeney 18	11
			(A King) *w ldr: wknd qckly 2f out* **28/1**	

1m 27.4s (-1.60) **Going Correction** -0.10s/f (Good) **17** Ran SP% **128.6**
Speed ratings (Par 97): **105,104,102,100,100 99,97,97,96,96 89,88,87,86,86 85,83**
CSF £159.66 CT £577.11 TOTE £47.60: £7.10, £1.40, £1.30, £9.00; EX 347.80.

Owner M Channon **Bred** M G Masterson **Trained** West Ilsley, Berks

FOCUS
A moderate handicap, but probably not bad form for the grade and the race has been rated positively. They went a good pace and the time was good.

Grit(IRE) ◆ Official explanation: trainer's rep said, regarding the apparent improvement in form, that gelding had been broken in March, gelded and dropped back in trip

Flower Official explanation: jockey said filly lost her action

2923 AXMINSTER CARPETS APPRENTICE H'CAP (WHIPS SHALL BE CARRIED BUT NOT USED) 6f

5:45 (5:53) (Class 5) (0-75,81) 4-Y-0+ **£3,238** (£963; £481; £240) **Stalls High**

Form RPR

0/04 **1** **Danzili Bay**[14] 2474 6-8-9 **60** StacyRenwick 7 71
(A W Carroll) *chsd ldrs: pushed along fr 2f out: pressed ldr ins fnl f: led last stride* **16/1**

0-41 **2** *nse* **Charlie Delta**[19] 2337 5-9-0 **65** (v) WilliamCarson 6 76
(J G M O'Shea) *chsd ldrs: led appr fnl f: pushed along ins fnl f: ct last stride* **11/4**[1]

4432 **3** *2 1/2* **Desperate Dan**[12] 2551 7-9-0 **70** (b) PNolan(5) 5 73
(A B Haynes) *led tl hdd appr fnl f: wknd ins fnl f* **12/1**

5-01 **4** *1/2* **Witchry**[14] 2478 6-8-13 **64** JemmaMarshall 8 65+
(A G Newcombe) *plld hrd: in tch: rdn 2f out: styd on fnl f but nvr gng pce to trble ldng trio* **7/1**

0445 **5** *3/4* **Memphis Man**[17] 2406 5-9-5 **70** RichardEvans 9 70+
(P D Evans) *in rr tl hdwy appr fnl f styng on whn nt clr run fnl 100yds: nt rcvr* **5/1**[3]

0001 **6** *shd* **Kyle (IRE)**[8] 2679 4-9-11 **81** 6ex CharlesEddery(5) 2 86+
(R Hannon) *lw: in rr tl swtchd to outside and stdy hdwy fr 2f out: clsng on ldrs and shkn up whn sddle slipped ins fnl f and could nt rcvr* **7/2**[2]

054 **7** *1/2* **Bateleur**[14] 2484 4-9-3 **68** (v) MatthewDavies 3 65
(M R Channon) *in tch: rdn 2f out: wknd fnl f* **17/2**

26-5 **8** *1/2* **Brandywell Boy (IRE)**[157] 55 5-9-0 **68** BillyCray(3) 4 63
(D J S Ffrench Davis) *chsd ldrs: rdn over 2f out: wknd over 1f out* **9/1**

2503 **9** *nk* **Obe Royal**[4] 2778 4-9-0 **70** (b) AshleyMorgan(5) 1 65
(P D Evans) *outpcd* **10/1**

1m 14.39s (-0.41) **Going Correction** -0.10s/f (Good) **9 Ran SP% 121.2**
Speed ratings (Par 103): **98,97,94,93,92 92,92,91,91**
CSF £63.02 CT £575.51 TOTE £19.50: £4.70, £1.20, £2.60; EX 84.00 Place 6: £ 73.93 Place 5: £28.61.
Owner Winding Wheel Partnership **Bred** T Lightbowne **Trained** Cropthorne, Worcs

FOCUS
A modest 'hands and heels' sprint handicap restricted to apprentices. The winner produced his best form since his 3yo season.
Kyle(IRE) Official explanation: jockey said saddle slipped
T/Plt: £116.70 to a £1 stake. Pool: £74,803.95. 467.55 winning tickets. T/Qpdt: £53.70 to a £1 stake. Pool: £3,509.00. 48.30 winning tickets. JS

2495 BEVERLEY (R-H)

Wednesday, June 11

OFFICIAL GOING: Good to firm (firm in places on home bend)
The ground had dried out over the previous two days and was reckoned 'on the quick side of good, no jar whatsoever'.
Wind: moderate, half against Weather: overcast and breezy

2924 YORKSHIRE SUMMER FESTIVAL CLAIMING STKS 5f

2:20 (2:22) (Class 6) 2-Y-0 **£1,942** (£578; £288; £144) **Stalls High**

Form RPR

3551 **1** **Just The Lady**[7] 2720 2-8-8 0 TonyHamilton 6 61
(Ollie Pears) *mde all: rdn fnl f: hld on towards fin* **2/5**[1]

061 **2** *nk* **Madame Jourdain (IRE)**[9] 2671 2-8-5 0 (b) AshleyHamblett(5) 2 62
(N Wilson) *chsd wnr: wandered and kpt on fnl f: jst hld* **4/1**[2]

00 **3** *3 1/4* **Chipolini (IRE)**[9] 2657 2-9-5 0 DNolan 8 59
(D Carroll) *chsd ldrs: hdwy 2f out: edgd lft: kpt on same pce* **16/1**

50 **4** *4* **Petite Denise**[9] 2671 2-8-4 0 DaleGibson 1 30
(M W Easterby) *dwlt: outpcd and bhd: styd on fnl 2f* **28/1**

5 *2 1/4* **Kapowee** 2-8-8 0 PaulHanagan 3 26
(W J Musson) *dwlt: outpcd and bhd: sme hdwy 2f out: nvr nrr* **12/1**[3]

60 **6** *1* **Transformation (IRE)**[15] 2485 2-8-6 0 GrahamGibbons 4 20
(J R Weymes) *chsd ldrs: sn drvn along: lost pl over 1f out* **22/1**

7 *24* **Under The Table** 2-8-3 0 DuranFentiman(3) 7 —
(Miss J E Foster) *s.s: sn wl bhd* **33/1**

64.64 secs (1.14) **Going Correction** -0.05s/f (Good) **7 Ran SP% 115.7**
Speed ratings (Par 91): **88,87,82,75,72 70,32**
CSF £2.34 TOTE £1.50: £1.10, £1.70; EX 1.60.The winner was the subject of a friendly claim
Owner Ian Bishop **Bred** Mrs Monica Teversham **Trained** Norton, N Yorks
■ Coup De Feu was withdrawn after proving unruly in the paddock (12/1, deduct 5p in the £ under rule 4, new market formed).

FOCUS
A modest claimer rated through the first two, who were both having their first outing for new yards. The third lends doubts to the form.

NOTEBOOK
Just The Lady gave her new connections a quick return. All speed, in the end she just lasted home. Nurseries are on the horizon now. (old market op 4-7 new market op 1-2)
Madame Jourdain(IRE), another who has changed stables, was encountering much quicker conditions. She ducked and dived but was cutting down the winner at the line. (new market op 7-2)
Chipolini(IRE), down in grade, could never get to grips with the leading pair. Even so this was an improvement on his first two efforts. (old market op 16-1 new market op 14-1)
Petite Denise, well beaten on her first two outings, failed completely to go the pace. Picking up ground in her own time in the second half of the contest, she is crying out for a sixth or even seventh furlong. (new market op 33-1)
Kapowee, a leggy newcomer, missed a beat at the start and was soon being run off her feet. (new market op 14-1)

2925 CHRISTMAS PARTIES AT BEVERLEY RACECOURSE H'CAP 7f 100y

2:50 (2:50) (Class 5) (0-70,76) 4-Y-0+ **£4,533** (£1,348; £674; £336) **Stalls High**

Form RPR

22-2 **1** **Shotley Mac**[18] 2391 4-8-11 **65** NeilBrown(5) 12 74
(N Bycroft) *prom: effrt over 2f out: led appr fnl f: hld on wl* **11/2**[2]

0005 **2** *1* **Fiefdom (IRE)**[29] 2087 6-9-7 **70** TomEaves 13 77
(I W McInnes) *prom: wnt 2nd 1f out: no real imp* **11/1**

46-1 **3** *1/2* **Turn Me On (IRE)**[18] 2400 5-8-11 **65** KellyHarrison(5) 8 70
(T D Walford) *hld up in rr: hdwy over 2f out: edgd wd over 1f out: styd on wl* **13/2**[3]

-233 **4** *1 1/4* **Flying Bantam (IRE)**[18] 2389 7-9-7 **70** PaulHanagan 2 72+
(R A Fahey) *in rr: hdwy over 2f out: styd on wl fnl f* **10/1**

-522 **5** *1/2* **Ours (IRE)**[11] 2597 5-8-13 **62** PatCosgrave 10 63
(John A Harris) *sn drvn along in rr: hdwy 3f out: hung lft: styd on: nt rch ldrs* **5/1**[1]

0-05 **6** *1 1/2* **Onatopp (IRE)**[18] 2400 4-8-12 **61** DavidAllan 4 58
(T D Easterby) *prom: outpcd over 2f out: styd on ins fnl f* **14/1**

2-03 **7** *3/4* **Myfrenchconnection (IRE)**[18] 2391 4-8-8 **60** JamieMoriarty(3) 1 55
(P T Midgley) *in rr: hdwy on outside over 2f out: kpt on: nvr nr ldrs* **7/1**

0530 **8** *nk* **Tanforan**[19] 2373 6-8-11 **60** RobertWinston 11 55
(B P J Baugh) *s.i.s: hld up in rr: hdwy over 2f out: kpt on: nvr nr ldrs* **18/1**

0020 **9** *hd* **Sands Of Barra (IRE)**[2] 2891 5-9-5 **68** AndrewElliott 3 62
(I W McInnes) *chsd ldrs: led briefly over 1f out: sn wknd* **20/1**

0000 **10** *1 3/4* **Provost**[15] 2487 4-9-2 **65** GrahamGibbons 9 55
(M W Easterby) *s.i.s: a in rr* **18/1**

0-31 **11** *1/2* **Royal Storm (IRE)**[8] 2693 9-9-8 **76** 6ex JamesMillman(5) 7 64
(B R Millman) *led: hdd over 1f out: wknd and eased ins fnl f* **11/2**[2]

22-6 **12** *2 1/2* **Motu (IRE)**[18] 2391 7-9-2 **65** (v) RoystonFfrench 5 47
(I W McInnes) *hld up in rr: nvr on terms* **18/1**

5-30 **13** *2 1/4* **Northern Boy (USA)**[135] 342 5-8-13 **62** PaulMulrennan 14 39
(M W Easterby) *chsd ldrs: lost pl over 1f out* **18/1**

1m 31.01s (-2.79) **Going Correction** -0.25s/f (Firm) **13 Ran SP% 123.2**
Speed ratings (Par 103): **105,103,103,101,101 99,98,98,98,96 95,92,90**
CSF £67.15 CT £412.62 TOTE £7.40: £2.20, £5.20, £3.00; EX 111.30.
Owner J A Swinburne **Bred** N Bycroft **Trained** Brandsby, N Yorks

FOCUS
A modest handicap run at a strong pace. Solid form for the grade, with a career best from the winner.

2926 "I DO" WEDDING FAIR HERE 10TH AUGUST H'CAP 1m 4f 16y

3:20 (3:20) (Class 6) (0-55,55) 3-Y-0 **£2,266** (£674; £337; £168) **Stalls High**

Form RPR

00-0 **1** **Patthepainter (GER)**[53] 1478 3-8-10 **51** (b[1]) AndrewElliott 12 56
(K R Burke) *set str pce: rdn over 2f out: stmbld and hit rail over 1f out: hld on wl* **5/1**[3]

-052 **2** *1* **River Kent**[22] 2273 3-9-0 **55** RoystonFfrench 10 58
(Mrs A Duffield) *chsd ldrs: wnt 2nd over 1f out: hung rt over 1f out: no ex ins fnl f* **6/4**[1]

05-0 **3** *1 1/4* **Police Officer**[13] 2552 3-8-6 **47** PaulHanagan 2 48+
(W J Musson) *t.k.h in rr: hdwy over 3f out: hdwy over 2f out: styd on: nt rch first 2* **9/2**[2]

06-0 **4** *3 1/4* **Harrison's Star**[55] 1429 3-8-9 **53** RussellKennemore(3) 8 49
(G M Moore) *chsd ldrs: drvn over 3f out: one pce fnl 3f* **12/1**

0-40 **5** *2 1/4* **Northgate Maisie**[6] 2750 3-8-7 **48** ow1 TonyHamilton 9 41
(Jedd O'Keeffe) *chsd wnr drvn over 4f out: one pce fnl 3f* **25/1**

0-50 **6** *2 1/2* **Lady In Chief**[50] 1553 3-8-11 **52** TomEaves 3 41
(Miss J A Camacho) *rrd star: hdwy on outside 7f out: one pce fnl 3f* **8/1**

-000 **7** *9* **Templetuohy Max (IRE)**[24] 2221 3-8-8 **49** GrahamGibbons 5 23
(J D Bethell) *hld up in rr: drvn 4f out: sn wknd* **14/1**

00-0 **8** *8* **Hotel Felix**[50] 1549 3-8-9 **50** RobertWinston 11 11
(Miss Gay Kelleway) *trckd ldrs: t.k.h: lost pl 3f out* **12/1**

00-0 **9** *3 1/2* **Stones Of Venice (IRE)**[13] 2536 3-8-8 **52** MichaelJStainton(3) 4 8
(R M Whitaker) *mid-div: effrt over 3f out: sn wknd* **16/1**

5000 **10** *31* **Her Name Is Rio (IRE)**[9] 2664 3-8-9 **50** PaulMulrennan 6 —
(Mrs S Lamyman) *in rr: lost pl 5f out: t.o 3f out* **40/1**

2m 39.52s (-1.38) **Going Correction** -0.25s/f (Firm) **10 Ran SP% 120.2**
Speed ratings (Par 97): **94,93,92,90,88 87,81,75,73,52**
CSF £13.28 CT £37.55 TOTE £6.60: £1.80, £1.20, £1.70; EX 16.60.
Owner Mrs Maura Gittins **Bred** Gestut Brummerhof **Trained** Middleham Moor, N Yorks

FOCUS
They set off very fast but the pace slowed appreciably down the back straight. It was a weak, low-grade handicap and the winner justified market confidence. He is rated up 6lb on his maiden form.
Patthepainter(GER) Official explanation: trainer's rep said, regarding the improved form shown, gelding was suited by the step up in trip and the first-time blinkers
Her Name Is Rio(IRE) Official explanation: trainer said filly was unsuited by the good to firm ground

2927 ALAN WOOD & PARTNERS 40TH ANNIVERSARY H'CAP 1m 1f 207y

3:50 (3:53) (Class 5) (0-70,68) 4-Y-0+ **£4,533** (£1,348; £674; £336) **Stalls High**

Form RPR

00-5 **1** **Riley Boys (IRE)**[18] 2391 7-9-4 **65** RobertWinston 5 76
(J G Given) *hld up in rr: hdwy 3f out: styd on wl to ld fnl 150yds* **15/2**[3]

4-00 **2** *1 1/4* **Mister Fizzbomb (IRE)**[22] 2274 5-8-12 **59** (v) GrahamGibbons 9 68
(J S Wainwright) *chsd ldr: led 1f out: sn hdd and no ex* **14/1**

1211 **3** *1* **Princelywallywogan**[15] 2483 6-9-5 **66** PatCosgrave 7 73
(John A Harris) *chsd ldrs: hung rt over 1f out: kpt on same pce* **5/1**[2]

0124 **4** *1/2* **Cherri Fosfate**[8] 2697 4-9-7 **68** DavidAllan 11 74
(D Carroll) *hld up in mid-div: effrt over 2f out: n.m.r over 1f out: styd on same pce* **4/1**[1]

-000 **5** *hd* **Snow Dancer (IRE)**[16] 2446 4-9-1 **62** TonyHamilton 4 67
(H A McWilliams) *s.i.s: hdwy on outside over 2f out: kpt on fnl f* **14/1**

5/30 **6** *1 3/4* **Three Strings (USA)**[32] 2001 5-8-12 **59** (p) PaulMulrennan 15 61
(P D Niven) *led: hung lft and hdd 1f out: sn wknd* **9/1**

400 **7** *1/2* **Moment Of Clarity**[12] 2568 6-9-0 **61** (p) DeanMcKeown 6 62
(R C Guest) *in rr: hdwy on outside over 2f out: nvr rchd ldrs* **25/1**

0-51 **8** *1 3/4* **Elite Land**[7] 2731 5-8-6 **53** 6ex PaulHanagan 16 50
(N Bycroft) *mid-div: hdwy on ins over 2f out: wknd over 1f out* **12/1**

1351 **9** *1/2* **Moonstreaker**[8] 2697 5-9-1 **65** 6ex MichaelJStainton(3) 13 61
(R M Whitaker) *s.i.s: t.k.h in rr: kpt on fnl 2f: nvr nr ldrs* **9/1**

0005 **10** *1/2* **Mozayada (USA)**[7] 2734 4-8-5 **52** TWilliams 10 47
(M Brittain) *chsd ldrs: wknd over 1f out* **66/1**

0045 **11** *hd* **Scotty's Future (IRE)**[9] 2658 10-7-11 **49** oh4 DanielleMcCreery(5) 12 44
(A Berry) *s.i.s: nvr on terms* **22/1**

0-45 **12** *4 1/2* **Trans Sonic**[49] 1559 5-8-10 **62** (b[1]) NeilBrown(5) 14 48
(A J Lockwood) *prom: t.k.h: lost pl over 2f out* **8/1**

0223 **13** *1* **Penel (IRE)**[18] 2394 7-8-10 **60** (p) JamieMoriarty(3) 3 44
(P T Midgley) *a in rr* **18/1**

4040 **14** *2 3/4* **Cool Sands (IRE)**[9] 2662 6-8-2 **49** oh4 (v) RoystonFfrench 1 27
(J G Given) *trckd ldrs: drvn over 3f out: sn lost pl* **28/1**

0002 **15** *8* **Bailieborough (IRE)**[15] 2487 9-9-6 **67** (v) TomEaves 2 29
(B Ellison) *in rr: effrt on wd outside over 2f out: sn lost pl: eased* **9/1**

2m 3.54s (-3.46) **Going Correction** -0.25s/f (Firm) **15 Ran SP% 129.0**
Speed ratings (Par 103): **103,102,101,100,100 99,98,97,97,96 96,92,92,89,83**
CSF £111.39 CT £594.19 TOTE £7.00: £3.00, £4.20, £2.20; EX 159.00.
Owner Paul Riley **Bred** P J Makin **Trained** Willoughton, Lincs

FOCUS
Another low-grade handicap run at a strong pace. The winner loves this place and is undeniably well-treated after taking time to regain his form after a year off through injury. Pretty sound form overall.

Three Strings(USA) Official explanation: jockey said gelding hung left-handed throughout

2928 BEVERLEY ANNUAL BADGEHOLDERS FILLIES' H'CAP 5f

4:20 (4:20) (Class 6) (0-65,64) 3-Y-0+ £2,266 (£674; £337; £168) Stalls High

Form RPR

0-00 **1** **Metal Guru**[9] 2676 4-9-6 **59**............................(p) RussellKennemore(3) 13 70
(R Hollinshead) *prom: styd on fnl 2f: led last stride* **12/1**

2012 **2** *nse* **Miss Daawe**[5] 2780 4-9-2 **59** 6ex.......................... LanceBetts(7) 2 70
(B Ellison) *w ldr: led over 1f out: hdd last stride* **7/1**

-266 **3** *3* **Ingleby Princess**[16] 2444 4-9-9 **64**............................(b[1]) NeilBrown(5) 5 64
(T D Barron) *mid-div: effrt 2f out: kpt on wl fnl f* **10/1**

0001 **4** *1 1/4* **Just Joey**[16] 2448 4-9-12 **62**..................................(b) TomEaves 8 58
(J R Weymes) *w ldrs: styd on same pce fnl f* **6/1**[2]

0013 **5** *nk* **Angelofthenorth**[12] 2576 6-8-12 **51**.......................... DuranFentiman(3) 4 46
(C J Teague) *s.i.s: rr-div: hdwy 2f out: kpt on ins fnl f* **22/1**

-056 **6** *hd* **Curio**[22] 2287 3-8-7 **50**..................................(p) DeanMcKeown 11 41
(R M Whitaker) *hmpd s: hld up towards rr: styd on fnl f: nt rch ldrs* **14/1**

-060 **7** *1/2* **Miacarla**[16] 2448 5-9-2 **52**.. DavidAllan 15 44
(H A McWilliams) *chsd ldrs on ins: kpt on same pce appr fnl f* **12/1**

5-06 **8** *1 1/2* **Tumbleweed Di**[22] 2283 4-8-8 **49**.......................... SladeO'Hara(5) 9 36
(G R Oldroyd) *mid-div: hdwy over 1f out: nvr nr ldrs* **16/1**

0000 **9** *hd* **Lady Aviator**[9] 2661 3-8-2 **45**.......................... AndrewElliott 14 28
(T D Easterby) *in rr: sme hdwy whn edgd rt over 1f out: nvr on terms* **40/1**

4-03 **10** *nk* **Socceroo**[9] 2661 3-9-1 **58**.......................... GrahamGibbons 16 40
(S Parr) *led tl hdd & wknd 1f out* **4/1**[1]

40-6 **11** *1 1/4* **Yorke's Folly (USA)**[9] 2676 7-8-4 **45**.......................(v) KellyHarrison(5) 17 25
(C W Fairhurst) *stmbld s: rr-div: kpt on fnl f: nvr a factor* **13/2**[3]

0-40 **12** *1 1/2* **Myriola**[40] 1769 3-8-9 **52**.......................... RobertWinston 10 24
(S Gollings) *rr-div: sme hdwy over 1f out: nvr on terms* **25/1**

/604 **13** *2 3/4* **Wicked Wilma (IRE)**[5] 2777 4-9-4 **54**.......................... FrancisNorton 7 19
(A Berry) *w ldrs: lost pl over 1f out* **10/1**

606- **14** *5* **Steph The Ref**[236] 6306 3-8-11 **54**.......................... PaulHanagan 12 —
(R A Fahey) *swvd lft s: rr-div: sme hdwy on inner 2f out: sn wknd* **8/1**

5650 **15** *1* **Sharp Indian**[16] 2448 4-9-1 **54**.......................... AndrewMullen(3) 6 —
(W J H Ratcliffe) *in rr: hmpd over 1f out* **66/1**

63.40 secs (-0.10) **Going Correction** -0.05s/f (Good)
WFA 3 from 4yo+ 7lb 15 Ran SP% **129.5**
Speed ratings (Par 98): **98,97,93,91,90 90,89,87,86,86 84,81,77,69,67**
CSF £97.24 CT £921.76 TOTE £13.00: £4.20, £2.70, £3.20; EX 117.40.
Owner Moores Metals Ltd **Bred** Reg Hollinshead **Trained** Upper Longdon, Staffs

FOCUS
A low-grade fillies' handicap and for once a high draw was not vital. The runner-up, in effect drawn one, deserves plenty of praise. Modest form, best rated through the winner.
Yorke's Folly(USA) Official explanation: jockey said mare stumbled leaving the stalls

2929 RACING HERE ON 24TH JUNE MAIDEN STKS 7f 100y

4:50 (4:57) (Class 5) 3-Y-0+ £2,914 (£867; £433; £216) Stalls High

Form RPR

2-2 **1** **Ramaad**[36] 1894 3-8-13 0.......................... GrahamGibbons 7 80
(W J Haggas) *chsd ldrs: hung rt and led over 1f out: drvn out* **10/3**[3]

32 **2** *1* **Tableau Vivant (IRE)**[42] 1721 3-8-8 0.......................... J-PGuillambert 8 72
(Sir Michael Stoute) *trckd ldrs: smooth hdwy over 2f out: nt clr run and swtchd outside over 1f out: styd on u.p: nt rch wnr* **8/11**[1]

2032 **3** *9* **August Gale (USA)**[13] 2532 3-8-13 82.......................... DeanMcKeown 12 55
(M Johnston) *chsd ldr: chal 3f out: one pce over 1f out* **3/1**[2]

4 *1/2* **Hydrophonic** 3-8-7 0 ow6.......................... FrederikTylicki(7) 2 54
(R A Fahey) *s.i.s: sn drvn along: hdwy over 2f out: styd on fnl f* **33/1**

00 **5** *3 3/4* **Springfield Lass**[53] 1490 3-8-5 0.......................... AndrewMullen(3) 1 39
(Mrs A Duffield) *t.k.h in midfield: reminders over 2f out: nvr nr ldrs* **100/1**

660- **6** *1 3/4* **Sheik'N'Knotsterd**[281] 5117 3-8-13 60.......................... DavidAllan 11 40
(J F Coupland) *chsd ldrs: one pce whn sltly hmpd over 1f out* **50/1**

00-5 **7** *hd* **Rasmani**[19] 2374 4-9-1 35.......................... RussellKennemore(3) 13 37
(Miss Gay Kelleway) *led tl over 1f out: fdd* **33/1**

8 *2 1/2* **Anna Lane** 3-8-3 0.......................... KellyHarrison(5) 9 28
(W J H Ratcliffe) *s.s: bhd tl sme hdwy fnl 2f* **66/1**

0 **9** *2 1/4* **King Of Sparta (USA)**[22] 2269 3-8-10 0.......................... JamieMoriarty(3) 5 27
(T J Fitzgerald) *s.s: bhd tl sme hdwy fnl 2f* **80/1**

05-0 **10** *8* **Crossing Bridges**[36] 1894 3-8-8 45.......................... FrancisNorton 10 2
(T D Barron) *s.i.s: a towards rr* **50/1**

0000 **11** *6* **Fluoree (FR)**[13] 2536 4-9-4 35.......................... AndrewElliott 14 —
(D W Thompson) *chsd ldrs: lost pl 3f out* **200/1**

12 *19* **Always Optimistic**[41] 5-9-9 0.......................(t) TonyHamilton 4 —
(M Mullineaux) *s.s: wl bhd whn hung lft over 3f out: t.o* **66/1**

1m 32.11s (-1.69) **Going Correction** -0.25s/f (Firm)
WFA 3 from 4yo+ 10lb 12 Ran SP% **121.5**
Speed ratings (Par 103): **99,97,87,87,82 80,80,77,75,65 59,37**
CSF £6.18 TOTE £4.00: £1.20, £1.10, £1.30; EX 8.40 Place 6: £55.14, Place 5: £45.30..Lighting Shadow and Mr Burton were withdrawn. Prices at time of withdrawal 66/1 and 200/1 respectively. Rule 4 does not apply.
Owner Hamdan Al Maktoum **Bred** St Clare Hall Stud **Trained** Newmarket, Suffolk
■ Stewards' Enquiry : Graham Gibbons caution: careless riding

FOCUS
They bet 33/1 bar three and the first two finished some way ahead. The suspicion was that the best horse on the day did not win. Weak form behind the front pair.
T/Plt: £36.40 to a £1 stake. Pool: £61,848.64. 1,237.45 winning tickets. T/Qpdt: £7.30 to a £1 stake. Pool: £2,891.49. 289.60 winning tickets. WG

2859 BRIGHTON (L-H)

Wednesday, June 11

OFFICIAL GOING: Firm
Wind: Fresh, across

2930 CONNOLLY'S RED MILLS HORSEFEEDS CLAIMING STKS 7f 214y

2:00 (2:01) (Class 6) 3-Y-0+ £2,266 (£674; £337; £168) Stalls Low

Form RPR

6154 **1** **Mountain Pass (USA)**[22] 2277 6-9-8 62.......................(p) NCallan 10 59
(B J Llewellyn) *hld up in tch: hdwy and swtchd rt to go 2nd 2f out: led over 1f out: rdn out fnl f* **9/2**[1]

0403 **2** *1/2* **Split The Wind (USA)**[3] 2861 4-9-3 50.......................(b) HayleyTurner 1 53
(Eve Johnson Houghton) *a.p: led over 2f out: hdd over 1f out: rallied ins fnl f* **9/2**[1]

-603 **3** *3* **Karmei**[10] 2639 3-9-3 60.......................... EddieAhern 3 54
(J W Hills) *towards rr: kpt on one pce to go 3rd ins fnl f* **9/2**[1]

1450 **4** *nk* **Bookish**[11] 2622 3-8-7 69.......................(b[1]) KirstyMilczarek(3) 2 46
(Jamie Poulton) *t.k.h: chsd ldrs: kpt on one pce to go 3rd over 1f out: fdd ins fnl f* **7/1**[3]

/25- **5** *2* **Shrewd Dude**[24] 267 4-9-7 53.......................(p) NelsonDeSouza 6 45
(Carl Llewellyn) *mid-div: rdn over 3f out: nvr on terms after* **14/1**

605- **6** *nse* **Mamichor**[262] 5310 5-9-11 49.......................... RichardSmith 9 49
(B R Johnson) *trckd ldr: led after 2f: hdd over 2f out: sn btn* **14/1**

3060 **7** *shd* **Casablanca Minx (IRE)**[28] 2097 5-8-12 55.......................(v) RichardEvans(7) 11 42
(P D Evans) *slowly away: a bhd* **8/1**

-006 **8** *14* **Coeur Courageux (FR)**[7] 2722 6-9-10 67.......................(t) GeorgeBaker 5 15
(G L Moore) *rrd up leaving stalls: a bhd and nvr gng wl* **5/1**[2]

0-05 **9** *4* **Knickyknackienoo**[12] 2557 7-9-4 35.......................... MarcHalford(3) 7 3
(T T Clement) *mid-div: rdn over 3f out: sn btn* **50/1**

0-00 **10** *4 1/2* **Edge End**[23] 2242 4-9-8 50.......................(v[1]) ChrisCatlin 8 —
(R A Farrant) *t.k.h: led for 2f: wknd qckly over 3f out* **33/1**

1m 36.18s (0.18) **Going Correction** -0.05s/f (Good)
WFA 3 from 4yo+ 11lb 10 Ran SP% **113.1**
Speed ratings (Par 101): **97,96,93,93,91 91,91,77,73,68**
CSF £23.73 TOTE £4.10: £2.30, £1.60, £1.40; EX 25.40 Trifecta £206.80 winning units.Split The Wind was claimed by Miss Sheena West for £6,000.
Owner B J Llewellyn **Bred** Marablue Farm **Trained** Fochriw, Caerphilly

FOCUS
An ordinary claimer in which the form is rated around the winner and second.
Coeur Courageux(FR) Official explanation: jockey said gelding was never travelling

2931 FOR A WINNING CAREER VISIT RPJOBS.CO.UK H'CAP (FOR THE OPERATIC SOCIETY CHALLENGE CUP) 1m 3f 196y

2:30 (2:31) (Class 5) (0-70,70) 3-Y-0 £2,655 (£790; £394; £197) Stalls High

Form RPR

-466 **1** **Sea Admiral**[14] 2495 3-9-0 **63**.......................(b[1]) ChrisCatlin 3 73
(R Charlton) *led: hdd 2f out: led again u.p 1f out: jst hld on: all out* **11/4**[2]

0-02 **2** *nse* **Miss Jolyon (USA)**[33] 1959 3-9-7 **70**.......................... NCallan 6 80
(M A Jarvis) *trckd ldr: led 2f out to 1f out: rallied u.p: jst failed* **13/8**[1]

0020 **3** *13* **Persian Wish (IRE)**[20] 2342 3-9-0 **63**.......................... LPKeniry 2 52
(J W Mullins) *trckd ldrs tl rdn and wknd 2f out* **25/1**

25-6 **4** *6* **Spectrana**[50] 1540 3-9-2 **65**.......................... JimCrowley 1 45
(Mrs A J Perrett) *hld up in tch: effrt on outside over 2f out: sn wknd* **12/1**[3]

4450 **5** *1* **I Certainly May**[70] 1147 3-8-6 **55**.......................... HayleyTurner 4 33
(S Dow) *in rr: pushed along sn after 1/2-way: lost tch 3f out* **12/1**[3]

5002 **6** *13* **Io (IRE)**[15] 2475 3-8-8 **57**.......................... EddieAhern 5 14
(J L Dunlop) *in tch: rdn 4f out: wknd qckly 2f out: sn eased* **11/4**[2]

2m 33.04s (0.34) **Going Correction** -0.05s/f (Good) 6 Ran SP% **110.7**
Speed ratings (Par 99): **96,95,87,83,82 73**
CSF £7.40 TOTE £4.40: £1.40, £1.50; EX 8.70.
Owner Axom (IV) **Bred** Stratford Place Stud **Trained** Beckhampton, Wilts

FOCUS
A pretty weak handicap in which the first two finished well clear. Improved form from the winner.
Io(IRE) Official explanation: jockey said filly was unsuited to the firm ground

2932 BEST JOBS IN BETTING AT BETRECRUIT.COM (S) STKS 1m 1f 209y

3:00 (3:02) (Class 6) 3-5-Y-0 £1,748 (£520; £260; £129) Stalls High

Form RPR

0-55 **1** **African Pursuits (USA)**[19] 2365 4-9-1 62.......................(v[1]) TravisBlock(3) 6 65+
(H Morrison) *sn trckd ldr: rdn 3f out: led wl over 1f out: drvn clr: eased ins fnl f* **4/5**[1]

0402 **2** *4 1/2* **Hester Brook (IRE)**[16] 2456 4-8-13 47.......................... HayleyTurner 4 48
(J G M O'Shea) *slowly away and wl in rr: rdn 2f out: r.o strly to go 2nd ins fnl f* **13/2**[3]

3050 **3** *1 1/4* **Persian Fox (IRE)**[43] 1694 4-9-4 45.......................... VinceSlattery 3 51
(A G Juckes) *t.k.h: in tch: disputing 2nd fr over 1f out tl lost that position ins fnl f* **20/1**

2300 **4** *hd* **Sweet World**[22] 2277 4-9-4 60.......................... NCallan 1 50
(B J Llewellyn) *trckd ldrs: rdn to dispute 2nd fr over 1f out: no ex ins fnl f* **10/1**

6000 **5** *3* **Poppy Red**[11] 2611 3-7-11 47 ow4.......................... RossAtkinson(7) 7 42
(Miss J R Tooth) *in tch: led wl over 2f out: sn swtchd lft to ins: hdd wl over 1f out: wknd qckly fnl f* **50/1**

5150 **6** *nk* **Ledgerwood**[4] 2833 3-8-11 60.......................... EddieAhern 2 49
(J W Hills) *in tch: rdn 3f out: sn in rr* **11/2**[2]

1000 **7** *3 3/4* **Rosy Dawn**[7] 2719 3-8-7 55 ow1.......................(be) EdwardCreighton 5 37
(Ms J S Doyle) *led: clr 4f out: hdd wl over 2f out: sn wknd* **40/1**

000- **8** *15* **Veras Joy**[240] 6234 3-8-2 20 ow2.......................... ChrisCatlin 9 2
(B R Johnson) *in rr: lost tch over 4f out* **50/1**

R0-3 **9** *27* **Prince Des Neiges (FR)**[7] 2352 5-8-13 53.......................(p) NicolPolli(5) 8 —
(M R Hoad) *slowly away: sn t.o* **10/1**

2m 3.08s (-0.52) **Going Correction** -0.05s/f (Good)
WFA 3 from 4yo+ 13lb 9 Ran SP% **113.6**
Speed ratings (Par 101): **100,96,95,95,92 92,89,77,56**
CSF £5.98 TOTE £1.70: £1.20, £1.30, £5.40; EX 6.50 Trifecta £109.70 Pool: £508.44. 3.29 winning units..The winner was bought by Ron Huggins for 6,800gns.
Owner The Pursuits Partnership **Bred** Airlie Stud **Trained** East Ilsley, Berks

FOCUS
A modest seller. The winner is a cut above his rivals and did not need to show his best.

2933 WEATHERBYS BLOODSTOCK SERVICES H'CAP 6f 209y

3:30 (3:30) (Class 6) (0-65,66) 4-Y-0+ £2,525 (£751; £375; £187) Stalls Low

Form RPR

22-0 **1** **Choreography**[20] 2337 5-9-5 **63**.......................(p) PaulDoe 5 79
(Jim Best) *mid-div: hdwy on ins 2f out: led over 1f out: rdn out fnl f* **8/1**[3]

5302 **2** *1/2* **Patavium Prince (IRE)**[19] 2355 5-8-7 **54** ow1.......................... TravisBlock(3) 7 69
(Miss Jo Crowley) *in tch: led 3f out: hdd over 1f out: kpt on but no imp ins fnl f* **7/2**[1]

0100 **3** *1 1/4* **Wahoo Sam (USA)**[10] 2642 8-8-9 **60**.......................... RichardEvans(7) 8 71
(P D Evans) *a in tch: hung lft fr over 1f out: no imp on first 2 fnl f* **14/1**

2061 **4** *6* **Cap St Jean (IRE)**[22] 2277 4-9-7 **65**.......................(p) HayleyTurner 12 60
(R Hollinshead) *t.k.h early: hld up: styd on fnl f: nvr nr to chal* **11/2**[2]

0-01 **5** *1 1/4* **Mannello**[3] 2861 5-8-12 **56** 6ex.......................(b) RichardThomas 2 48
(Jim Best) *mid-div: rdn 3f out: no hdwy fnl 2f* **11/2**[2]

-000 **6** *3/4* **Bollin Franny**[29] 2075 4-8-1 **50**.......................... NataliaGemelova(5) 9 40
(J E Long) *trckd ldr: wknd over 1f out and hmpd sn after* **14/1**

6065 **7** *3* **Sir Liam (USA)**[68] 1182 4-9-3 **61**.......................... EddieAhern 3 55+
(R A Teal) *in rr: keeping on one pce whn hmpd ins fnl f* **9/1**

311 **8** *1 1/2* **Sion Hill (IRE)**[40] 1780 7-9-1 **64**.......................(p) MarkCoumbe(5) 4 42
(John A Harris) *led tl hdd 3f out: wknd over 1f out* **11/2**[2]

0-05 **9** *1 1/2* **Goodwood Spirit**[27] 1642 6-7-11 **48** oh1 ow2.......................(v) PietroRomeo(7) 10 21
(J M Bradley) *t.k.h in mid-div: bhd fnl 2f* **20/1**

00-0 **10** *1* **Barley Moon**[44] 1687 4-8-2 **46** oh1 ChrisCatlin 6 17
(T Keddy) *a bhd* **50/1**

040- **11** *1 3/4* **Summer Recluse (USA)**[237] 6290 9-9-1 **59** (t) JimCrowley 13 25
(J M Bradley) *a in rr* **20/1**

46-0 **12** *3 3/4* **Doctor's Cave**[43] 1703 6-9-0 **58** (b) RichardSmith 11 14
(K O Cunningham-Brown) *in tch: rdn 1/2-way: sn struggling in rr* **25/1**

1m 21.48s (-1.62) **Going Correction** -0.05s/f (Good) **12** Ran SP% **118.2**
Speed ratings (Par 101): **107,106,105,98,96 95,92,90,89,87 85,81**
CSF £34.27 CT £394.49 TOTE £6.20: £3.00, £1.50, £4.30; EX 29.60 TRIFECTA Not won..
Owner Bill Wallace **Bred** Cheveley Park Stud Ltd **Trained** Lewes, E Sussex
■ Stewards' Enquiry : Hayley Turner two-day ban: careless riding (Jun 25-26)

FOCUS
The first three finished clear in this modest handicap. Sound form.
Mannello Official explanation: jockey said mare ran flat
Sion Hill(IRE) Official explanation: jockey said gelding was unsuited by the firm ground

2934 JOIN BETFAIRCLUB ROA H'CAP 5f 59y
4:00 (4:01) (Class 6) (0-60,64) 3-Y-0+ **£2,525** (£751; £375; £187) **Stalls** Low

Form RPR

220- **1** **Croeso Bach**[280] 5139 4-8-11 **53** SophieDoyle(7) 2 61
(J L Spearing) *mde all: edgd lft u.p fnl f: all out* **6/1**[3]

0331 **2** *nk* **Thoughtsofstardom**[2] 2881 5-9-8 **64** 6ex TobyAtkinson(7) 4 71
(M Wigham) *trckd ldrs: wnt 2nd 2f out: pressed wnr thrght fnl f: jst hld on for 2nd* **9/4**[1]

6500 **3** *shd* **Racing Stripes (IRE)**[44] 1675 4-8-11 **46** oh1 RichardSmith 1 57+
(K O Cunningham-Brown) *t.k.h: hld up: hdwy on ins fr over 1f out: chalng whn short of room ins fnl f and swtchd rt: edgd rt but r.o strly: jst failed to go 2nd: possibly unlucky* **14/1**

4600 **4** *4 1/2* **Briery Lane (IRE)**[2] 2881 7-9-2 **51** EddieAhern 7 41
(J M Bradley) *in rr and outpcd: nvr nr to chal:* **4/1**[2]

-650 **5** *2* **Dancing Mystery**[36] 1901 14-9-11 **60** (b) LPKeniry 3 43
(E A Wheeler) *w wnr to 2f out: sn wknd* **6/1**[3]

0005 **6** *1 1/2* **Peopleton Brook**[19] 2351 6-9-4 **53** JimCrowley 6 31
(J M Bradley) *chsd ldrs tl rdn and wknd 2f out* **4/1**[2]

/00- **7** *2 1/4* **Clewer**[313] 894 4-8-11 **53** GihanArnolda(7) 5 23
(A B Haynes) *slowly away: a bhd* **25/1**

61.81 secs (-0.49) **Going Correction** -0.05s/f (Good) **7** Ran SP% **109.9**
Speed ratings (Par 101): **101,100,100,93,89 87,83**
CSF £18.33 TOTE £7.40: £3.00, £1.50; EX 22.40.
Owner Mrs Richard Evans **Bred** Richard Evans Bloodstock **Trained** Kinnersley, Worcs
■ Stewards' Enquiry : Sophie Doyle three-day ban: careless riding (Jun 25-27)

FOCUS
Modest form, rated though the second with the winner up 7lb. The third was unlucky.

2935 BETFAIR APPRENTICE TRAINING SERIES H'CAP 5f 213y
4:30 (4:31) (Class 6) (0-65,61) 3-Y-0 **£2,525** (£751; £375; £187) **Stalls** Low

Form RPR

-325 **1** **Filligree (IRE)**[16] 2452 3-9-10 **61** JPHamblett 7 72
(Rae Guest) *a in tch: led appr fnl f: rdn clr: kpt up to work* **2/1**[1]

432 **2** *4* **Regal Veil**[9] 2661 3-8-9 **46** WilliamCarson 3 44
(S C Williams) *led tl rdn and hdd appr fnl f: kpt on to hold on for 2nd* **4/1**[2]

-50 **3** *nk* **Rossini Byline (IRE)**[95] 837 3-9-2 **53** JackDean 4 50
(J L Spearing) *trckd ldr to wl over 1f out: rallied ins fnl f* **4/1**[2]

0544 **4** *3/4* **Easy Wonder (GER)**[16] 2452 3-9-5 **59** BMcHugh(3) 6 57+
(I A Wood) *hld up: hdwy whn hung lft fr wl over 1f out: kpt on ins fnl f* **4/1**[2]

604- **5** *1* **New Balls Please (IRE)**[217] 6722 3-9-1 **52** (p) JemmaMarshall 5 43
(P M Phelan) *trckd ldrs tl rdn and wknd wl over 1f out* **8/1**

40-6 **6** *7* **Oxbridge**[12] 2555 3-9-4 **60** PietroRomeo(5) 2 29
(J M Bradley) *chsd ldrs: wkng whn n.m.r wl over 1f out* **16/1**

5560 **7** *4 1/2* **Hold That Call (USA)**[50] 1533 3-8-10 **47** MarkCoumbe 8 2
(A J Chamberlain) *slowly away: racd wd: bhd fr over 2f out* **33/1**

2360 **8** *3 1/2* **Mama Leo**[27] 2126 3-9-5 **56** (b) MCGeran 1 —
(J G M O'Shea) *a outpcd in rr* **33/1**

1m 10.13s (-0.07) **Going Correction** -0.05s/f (Good) **8** Ran SP% **116.2**
Speed ratings (Par 97): **98,92,92,91,89 80,74,69**
CSF £10.39 CT £28.22 TOTE £3.00: £1.40, £1.30, £1.90; EX 10.60 Trifecta £20.50 Place 6: £10.80, Place 5: £7.44. Pool: £595.82. 20.58 winning units..
Owner The Filligree Partnership **Bred** T Hirschfeld **Trained** Newmarket, Suffolk

FOCUS
A weak handicap which took little winning. The winner was up 5lb on her previous handicap form.
T/Plt: £8.30 to a £1 stake. Pool: £50,744.97. 4,443.45 winning tickets. T/Qpdt: £4.10 to a £1 stake. Pool: £2,973.45. 536.40 winning tickets. JS

2746 HAMILTON (R-H)
Wednesday, June 11
OFFICIAL GOING: Good to firm (good in places; 9.3)
Wind: Breezy, half against Weather: Cloudy, fine

2936 JOHN SMITH'S AMATEUR RIDERS' H'CAP 6f 5y
6:40 (6:41) (Class 6) (0-60,58) 4-Y-0+ **£2,966** (£912; £456) **Stalls** Centre

Form RPR

5-60 **1** **Botham (USA)**[13] 2523 4-10-5 **49** MrPNorton(7) 5 61
(J S Goldie) *hld up in last: gd hdwy 2f out: led ins fnl f: r.o wl* **20/1**

0206 **2** *1 3/4* **Lambency (IRE)**[6] 2748 5-11-4 **55** MrsCBartley 13 61
(J S Goldie) *hld up: hdwy and swtchd lft over 1f out: chsd wnr wl ins fnl f: r.o* **6/1**[2]

0413 **3** *1/2* **Duke Of Milan (IRE)**[64] 1254 5-10-9 **53** MissOMaylam(7) 15 58
(G C Bravery) *t.k.h: hld up: hdwy over 1f out: kpt on fnl f: nrst fin* **8/1**

0-00 **4** *1/2* **Conjecture**[20] 2337 6-10-11 **53** MissRBastiman(5) 8 56
(R Bastiman) *prom: effrt and ev ch 1f out: kpt on same pce* **8/1**

10-2 **5** *1* **Quicks The Word**[16] 2444 8-11-2 **58** MissHCuthbert(5) 11 58
(T A K Cuthbert) *led: edgd rt over 1f out: hdd ins fnl f: one pce* **7/1**[3]

050 **6** *3/4* **Obe One**[41] 1752 8-10-1 **45** MrBlakeStorrie(7) 9 43
(A Berry) *prom tl rdn and no ex over 1f out* **66/1**

2002 **7** *1 1/4* **Desert Hunter (IRE)**[16] 2463 5-10-4 **46** MrsGHogg(5) 7 40
(Micky Hammond) *bhd tl hdwy over 1f out: nvr rchd ldrs* **8/1**

4340 **8** *2* **Franksalot (IRE)**[22] 2285 8-11-3 **54** MrSDobson 4 41
(I W McInnes) *towards rr: effrt 2f out: no imp fnl f* **6/1**[2]

6-41 **9** *nk* **Staked A Claim (IRE)**[15] 2491 4-11-1 **57** MrPCollington(5) 14 43
(T D Barron) *midfield on outside: drvn 1/2-way: btn over 1f out* **9/2**[1]

/006 **10** *1 1/4* **Woodsley House (IRE)**[23] 2251 6-11-0 **58** ALVoy(7) 2 40
(A G Foster) *in tch: outpcd over 2f out: n.d after* **16/1**

0500 **11** *shd* **Only A Splash**[15] 2491 4-10-5 **45** MrBenBrisbourne(3) 12 27
(Mrs R A Carr) *towards rr on outside: drvn 1/2-way: sn outpcd* **50/1**

3604 **12** *3/4* **Silly Gilly (IRE)**[36] 1906 4-10-4 **48** MissVBarr(7) 16 28
(R E Barr) *racd alone far side: no imp fr 1/2-way* **18/1**

6600 **13** *3* **Telepathic (IRE)**[138] 305 8-10-3 **45** (b) MissWGibson(5) 6 15
(A Berry) *prom tl rdn and wknd over 1f out* **66/1**

5660 **14** *1/2* **Jabraan (USA)**[3] 2869 6-10-8 **45** (v) MissARyan 3 13
(Mrs R A Carr) *in tch tl rdn and wknd wl over 1f out* **28/1**

0040 **15** *shd* **Cryptic Clue (USA)**[3] 2869 4-10-8 **45** MissADeniel 1 13
(Mrs R A Carr) *chsd ldrs to 2f out: sn wknd* **28/1**

1m 13.06s (0.86) **Going Correction** -0.05s/f (Good) **15** Ran SP% **120.3**
Speed ratings (Par 101): **92,89,89,88,87 86,84,81,81,79 79,78,74,73,73**
CSF £129.71 CT £1083.09 TOTE £23.60: £5.60, £2.50, £2.80; EX 125.60.
Owner J S Morrison **Bred** France Weiner & Neal Hayias **Trained** Uplawmoor, E Renfrews
■ A winner on his first ride for Paul Norton.
■ Stewards' Enquiry : Mr Blake Storrie four-day ban:careless riding (Jun 26,30, Jul 6, 25)

FOCUS
A 1-2 for Jim Goldie in this moderate amateur riders' handicap full of hard-to-win-with types. The form seems pretty sound.
Cryptic Clue(USA) Official explanation: jockey said gelding was struck into behind

2937 IRN BRU MAIDEN STKS 6f 5y
7:10 (7:10) (Class 4) 2-Y-0 **£4,533** (£1,348; £674; £336) **Stalls** Low

Form RPR

1 **Deadly Secret (USA)** 2-9-3 0 PaulHanagan 5 85+
(R A Fahey) *sn cl up: led after 1f: mde rest: drvn out fnl f* **20/1**

2 *3/4* **Master Rooney (IRE)** 2-9-3 0 TomEaves 1 83+
(B Smart) *rn green bhd ldrs: hdwy and hung rt 2f out: kpt on wl fnl f: bttr for r* **6/5**[1]

3 *1 1/4* **Pegasus Lad (USA)** 2-9-3 0 GregFairley 4 79+
(M Johnston) *chsd ldrs: effrt 2f out: kpt on same pce fnl f: improve* **5/2**[2]

4 *1 1/2* **Markyg (USA)** 2-9-3 0 FergusSweeney 2 75+
(K R Burke) *prom: effrt 2f out: one pce appr fnl f* **6/1**[3]

5 *1 3/4* **Flyit (IRE)** 2-9-3 0 TPO'Shea 3 69+
(M R Channon) *s.i.s: bhd and outpcd tl sme late hdwy* **6/1**[3]

6 *7* **Red China Blues (USA)** 2-9-3 0 RobertWinston 6 48+
(J Howard Johnson) *t.k.h: led 1f: cl up tl wknd wl over 1f out: eased whn no ch fnl f* **25/1**

1m 12.51s (0.31) **Going Correction** -0.05s/f (Good) **6** Ran SP% **111.2**
Speed ratings (Par 95): **95,94,92,90,88 78**
CSF £44.27 TOTE £15.90: £4.10, £1.10; EX 65.30.
Owner J J Staunton **Bred** Brushwood Stable **Trained** Musley Bank, N Yorks
■ Stewards' Enquiry : Greg Fairley caution: careless riding

FOCUS
This event was confined to unraced juveniles, but all six came from decent two-year-old stables and the race should work out. The time was modest.

NOTEBOOK
Deadly Secret(USA), a $115,000 son of Johannesburg, half-brother to quite useful dual 1m-1m2f winner Pinkhair, out of a smart triple winner at up to 1m2f, was friendless in the market but proved good enough to make a winning debut. It is hard to know exactly what he achieved, but he looks the type to progress and could be useful. (tchd 25-1)
Master Rooney(IRE) ◆, a 300,000gns son of Cape Cross, out of a quite useful dual 5f-6f winner at two, was well backed to make a winning debut, but he was just found out by his inexperience. He got the hang of things late on, finishing his race quite nicely, and he should come on a fair bit for this. (op Evens tchd 11-8)
Pegasus Lad(USA), a $90,000 son of Fusaichi Pegasus, half-brother to 2m2f winner Tribe, and 1m2f winner Leo Boy, out of a smart dual 1m2f winner in France, made a satisfactory debut in third. Like many of these, he should be better for the run and can make his mark in similar company. (op 11-4 tchd 9-4)
Markyg(USA), a 100,000gns half-brother to among others smart 1m juvenile winner Kid Mambo, ran a respectable race and is entitled to come on for this. (op 12-1)
Flyit(IRE), a 42,000gns son King's Best, half-brother to among others quite useful triple 6f juvenile winner Yajbill, out of a 7f three-year-old winner, was soon detached and getting reminders after a furlong or so, but he gradually got the hang of things. He should come on significantly for this. (tchd 7-1)

2938 CLYDE 1 ONE THOUSAND POUND SONG H'CAP 6f 5y
7:40 (7:40) (Class 3) (0-90,87) 4-Y-0+ **£10,361** (£3,083; £1,540; £769) **Stalls** Centre

Form RPR

4505 **1** **Blue Tomato**[4] 2843 7-9-5 **83** AdrianTNicholls 12 94
(D Nicholls) *in tch: hdwy over 1f out: led ins fnl f: r.o wl* **15/2**

00-0 **2** *1/2* **My Gacho (IRE)**[25] 2210 6-8-9 **73** (b) GregFairley 11 82
(M Johnston) *w ldr: led briefly 1f out: kpt on towards fin* **16/1**

0225 **3** *2 1/2* **Rainbow Fox**[6] 2751 4-8-4 **68** PaulHanagan 1 69
(R A Fahey) *towards rr: drvn whn hmpd over 1f out: rallied fnl f: r.o* **5/1**[2]

0063 **4** *1* **Yorkshire Blue**[6] 2751 9-8-4 **68** oh3 LiamJones 7 66
(J S Goldie) *bhd tl hdwy over 1f out: nt pce to chal* **13/2**

0-56 **5** *nk* **Avertuoso**[15] 2489 4-9-3 **81** (v) TomEaves 6 78
(B Smart) *set decent gallop: hdd 1f out: sn no ex* **16/1**

1-40 **6** *1 1/4* **Curtail (IRE)**[13] 2538 5-9-7 **85** PaulMulrennan 4 78
(Miss L A Perratt) *bhd tl hdwy over 1f out: no imp* **22/1**

6566 **7** *1* **Ingleby Arch (USA)**[13] 2538 5-9-9 **87** FergalLynch 8 77
(T D Barron) *cl up: rdn and edgd lft over 1f out: no ex* **15/2**

600- **8** *1/2* **Katie Boo (IRE)**[214] 6753 6-9-2 **80** RoystonFfrench 5 68
(A Berry) *in tch: drvn and outpcd whn hmpd over 1f out: sn btn* **33/1**

2000 **9** *nk* **Distant Sun (USA)**[13] 2538 4-8-13 **77** TPO'Shea 3 64
(Miss L A Perratt) *bhd: drvn 1/2-way: n.d* **20/1**

-510 **10** *2 1/4* **Geojimali**[13] 2538 6-9-4 **82** DanielTudhope 9 62
(J S Goldie) *bhd: shortlived effrt on outside over 1f out: sn wknd* **6/1**[3]

60-2 **11** *6* **Stonehaugh (IRE)**[18] 2389 5-9-0 **78** (t) RobertWinston 2 39
(J Howard Johnson) *in tch tl rdn and wknd 2f out: eased whn no ch fnl f* **10/1**

4-03 **L** **Gunfighter (IRE)**[13] 2538 5-9-4 **85** PJMcDonald(3) 10 —
(J S Wainwright) *ref to r* **9/2**[1]

1m 10.56s (-1.64) **Going Correction** -0.05s/f (Good) **12** Ran SP% **118.9**
Speed ratings (Par 107): **108,107,104,102,102 100,99,98,98,95 87,—**
CSF £117.96 CT £671.76 TOTE £8.00: £2.80, £5.50, £2.30; EX 212.10.
Owner Dab Hand Racing **Bred** Bearstone Stud **Trained** Sessay, N Yorks
■ Stewards' Enquiry : Fergal Lynch two-day ban: careless riding (Jun 25 -26)

FOCUS
Despite the favourite refusing to take part, this was still a decent sprint handicap and the front two came clear. The form is rated through the winner.

NOTEBOOK
Blue Tomato, disappointing since winning on his return to action, picked up well when asked to nail the runner-up and did it nicely. He is talented, but does seem to have two ways of running. (op 8-1)

My Gacho(IRE) ◆, tailed off on his return to action last month, was down to a mark 10lb lower than for his last win just over a year ago. After taking his usual position up with the pace, he never stopped trying and only the winner was able to get the better of him. There should be a race in him before too long off this sort of mark. (tchd 18-1)

Rainbow Fox ◆ can be considered unlucky not to have finished closer as he suffered quite badly at the end of the chain reaction started off by Ingleby Arch changing course passing the 2f pole. He is knocking at the door. (op 9-2)

Yorkshire Blue, 3lb wrong, was therefore that much worse off with Rainbow Fox who was a length behind him over course and distance six days earlier. He stayed on late, but never looked like getting there. (op 8-1)

Avertuoso, with the visor back on, showed his usual decent early speed and was still right there a furlong out before fading out of it. He does look better over the minimum trip.

Curtail(IRE), who is not very consistent, ran better than last time and was staying on late but he never looked like winning. (op 16-1)

Ingleby Arch(USA), tucked in behind the leaders for much of the way, caused a few problems in behind when switched left entering the last couple of furlongs but could never land a blow. He has only ever won once in handicap company on turf. (op 17-2 tchd 10-1)

Katie Boo(IRE) was already beaten when hampered by Ingleby Arch entering the last 2f. She suffered badly at the hands of the Handicapper for not being beaten far in a Listed race here last September and it is taking time for her to come back down the weights. (op 40-1)

Distant Sun(USA) Official explanation: jockey said gelding was denied a clear run

Gunfighter(IRE), 7lb higher than for his last win, disgraced himself by planting himself in the stalls and refusing to take part. (op 4-1)

2939 CASH FOR KIDS LANARK SILVER BELL H'CAP — 1m 4f 17y
8:10 (8:10) (Class 2) (0-90,88) 4-Y-O+

£21,808 (£6,531; £3,265; £1,634; £815; £409) Stalls High

Form — RPR

3-33 **1** **Tifernati**[23] 2264 4-9-4 **82** .... LiamJones 6 — 94+
(W J Haggas) *hld up: hdwy on outside over 2f out: led and edgd rt over 1f out: drvn out* **9/2**[2]

-000 **2** 1 1/4 **Gordonsville**[26] 2168 5-8-10 **74** .... FergalLynch 9 — 83+
(J S Goldie) *hld up: hdwy on ins whn nt clr run over 1f out: styd on wl fnl f to take 2nd nr fin* **6/1**[3]

0-31 **3** hd **La Vecchia Scuola (IRE)**[6] 2752 4-8-8 **72** 6ex .... DanielTudhope 1 — 79
(J S Goldie) *hld up in midfield: rdn 3f out: hdwy over 1f out: r.o fnl f* **2/1**[1]

/22- **4** 1/2 **Sin City**[375] 2245 5-8-12 **76** .... PaulHanagan 3 — 82
(R A Fahey) *prom: drvn and effrt 3f out: one pce ins fnl f* **8/1**

263- **5** nk **Whispering Death**[64] 5375 6-9-10 **88** .... RobertWinston 2 — 93
(J Howard Johnson) *hld up: drvn and outpcd 3f out: rallied and hdwy on outside over 1f out: kpt on fnl f* **20/1**

0-21 **6** 2 1/4 **Nero West (FR)**[38] 1824 7-8-8 **72** ....(b) TomEaves 12 — 74
(Miss L A Perratt) *cl up: chal 3f to 2f out: no ex appr fnl f* **16/1**

04-2 **7** 1/2 **Akarem**[11] 2599 7-9-10 **88** .... FergusSweeney 13 — 89
(K R Burke) *chsd ldrs tl rdn and wknd over 1f out* **8/1**

0-21 **8** 1 **Maneki Neko (IRE)**[32] 2006 6-8-6 **70** .... RoystonFfrench 11 — 69
(E W Tuer) *hld up in tch: drvn 3f out: wknd over 1f out* **20/1**

-660 **9** 2 **Regent's Secret (USA)**[16] 2445 8-8-2 **66** .... SilvestreDeSousa 10 — 62
(J S Goldie) *hld up: shortlived effrt on outside 3f out: btn over 1f out* **28/1**

5-01 **10** 1/2 **Bajan Parkes**[16] 2447 5-9-7 **85** .... AdrianTNicholls 7 — 80
(E J Alston) *led to over 1f out: sn btn* **16/1**

-121 **11** 5 **Lochiel**[12] 2579 4-8-10 **74** .... PaulMulrennan 5 — 61
(Mrs S C Bradburne) *prom: drvn over 3f out: wknd wl over 1f out* **10/1**

2m 33.92s (-4.68) **Going Correction** -0.15s/f (Firm) 11 Ran SP% **121.9**

Speed ratings (Par 109): **109,108,108,107,107 106,105,105,103,103 100**

CSF £32.07 CT £72.07 TOTE £6.00: £2.20, £3.40, £1.30; EX 37.80.

Owner Johnny Townsend **Bred** Miss S N Ralphs **Trained** Newmarket, Suffolk

■ This was the first running of the historic 'Bell' since 1977, after which Lanark racecourse closed.

FOCUS

A very competitive renewal for the return of this famous old race, as it should have been for the money. Despite a decent pace, the bulk of the field were still within a length or two of each other passing the 2f pole. A good race for the grade and the winner is better than the bare form, which is solid overall.

NOTEBOOK

Tifernati ◆, a proven stayer, was ridden with plenty of confidence and would have been suited by the decent tempo. Pulled widest of all, he quickened up nicely to take the lead and despite hanging once in front he was always doing enough. This was a decent effort as he had looked held off this sort of mark recently, so he is probably still improving. (op 8-1)

Gordonsville ◆, down to a more realistic mark, got the strong pace he needs this time but one thing he did not get was the gaps. When he did see daylight he finished in good style to snatch second, but the winner had gone beyond recall. He should go one better before too long. (op 8-1)

La Vecchia Scuola(IRE), carrying a 6lb penalty for her easy win over a furlong further here six days earlier, had every chance in this much better contest and stayed on to the line but the winner was much too good for her. She may be better suited by a slightly stiffer test. (tchd 9-4 in places)

Sin City, returning from a year off, was one of several in a line across the track passing the 2f pole and kept on to the end. He was only just edged out on his return from a similar lay-off last season, so it remains to be seen how much he will come on for this. (tchd 7-1)

Whispering Death, having his first start on the Flat since last September, has had a couple of spins over hurdles in the meantime. All five of his wins have come over further than this at up to 2m2f, so it was no surprise that he got outpaced after the intersection and looked more likely to finish last, but his stamina then came into play and he was finishing well down the outside. He will appreciate a step back up in trip. (tchd 18-1)

Nero West(FR), 6lb higher than when winning over 1m5f here last month, had every chance up the home straight but lacked the finishing pace of the principals. This was a fair effort considering all his best form has come on soft ground. (op 12-1)

2940 PATERSONS OF GREENOAKHILL (S) STKS — 1m 65y
8:40 (8:40) (Class 6) 4-Y-O+

£2,914 (£867; £433; £216) Stalls High

Form — RPR

4264 **1** **Pianoforte (USA)**[13] 2524 6-9-3 64 ....(b) PaulMulrennan 15 — 66
(E J Alston) *hld up on ins: hdwy to ld ent fnl f: hld on wl* **4/1**[1]

-002 **2** 3/4 **March Mate**[5] 2782 4-8-9 47 .... PJMcDonald(3) 10 — 59
(B Ellison) *trckd ldrs gng wl: led briefly appr fnl f: sn rdn: kpt on fnl f* **6/1**[3]

2600 **3** 3 **Only A Grand**[22] 2274 4-8-12 49 ....(b) DarrenWilliams 14 — 52
(R Bastiman) *t.k.h: prom: drvn whn edgd lft over 1f out: one pce fnl f* **25/1**

44-6 **4** 1/2 **Riverhill (IRE)**[79] 989 5-8-5 47 .... RobbieEgan(7) 7 — 51
(J Howard Johnson) *prom: effrt over 2f out: one pce over 1f out* **14/1**

0-06 **5** 1 1/2 **Crosby Jemma**[13] 2523 4-8-7 47 .... TPO'Shea 5 — 43
(J R Weymes) *bhd tl hdwy over 1f out: nrst fin* **14/1**

6-05 **6** nse **Contemplation**[12] 2568 5-9-3 56 ....(t) RobertWinston 6 — 52
(G A Swinbank) *hld up: hdwy whn hmpd over 1f out and ins fnl f: nt rcvr* **4/1**[1]

0-64 **7** shd **Grandad Bill (IRE)**[13] 2523 5-9-3 49 .... DanielTudhope 4 — 52
(J S Goldie) *hld up: effrt outside 3f out: no imp fr 2f out* **11/2**[2]

30-5 **8** 1 3/4 **Sarraaf (IRE)**[142] 250 12-9-3 50 .... TomEaves 8 — 48
(Miss L A Perratt) *cl up: led over 3f out to appr fnl f: sn no ex* **12/1**

5-00 **9** shd **Ulysees (IRE)**[13] 2524 9-9-3 48 .... RoystonFfrench 11 — 48
(J Barclay) *hld up: drvn whn hmpd over 1f out: sn btn* **33/1**

4360 **10** 10 **Not Another Cat (USA)**[51] 1521 4-8-12 60 ....(t) FergusSweeney 9 — 20
(K R Burke) *towards rr: drvn 3f out: sn btn* **11/1**

3500 **11** 2 3/4 **Dark Charm (FR)**[12] 2568 9-9-3 62 ....(p) PaulHanagan 16 — 19
(R A Fahey) *trckd ldrs: drvn 3f out: wknd 2f out* **7/1**

0-05 **12** 2 1/4 **Miss Percy**[16] 2456 4-8-7 47 ....(p) AdrianTNicholls 1 — —
(I W McInnes) *led to over 3f out: wknd 2f out* **25/1**

1m 47.37s (-1.03) **Going Correction** -0.15s/f (Firm) **12** Ran SP% **122.2**

Speed ratings (Par 101): **99,98,95,94,93 93,93,91,91,81 78,76**

CSF £27.93 TOTE £5.30: £2.20, £2.80, £3.90; EX 40.00.There was no bid for the winner

Owner Nigel Leadbeater Mrs Val Leadbeater **Bred** Cashmark Farm **Trained** Longton, Lancs

■ Stewards' Enquiry : Robert Winston one-day ban: eased mount prematureley (Jun 28)

Darren Williams six-day ban: careless riding (Jun 25-30)

FOCUS

A moderate but competitive seller. The form seems pretty sound.

Miss Percy Official explanation: jockey said filly failed to come down the hill

2941 HAPPY BIRTHDAY HELEN CLAIMING STKS — 1m 3f 16y
9:10 (9:11) (Class 6) 3-Y-O

£2,914 (£867; £433; £216) Stalls High

Form — RPR

6000 **1** **Hoar Frost**[7] 2719 3-8-3 57 ow1 .... TPO'Shea 6 — 48
(M R Channon) *chsd ldrs: drvn over 3f out: rallied and led 1f out: styd on gamely* **3/1**[2]

0-00 **2** 1/2 **Blazing Mask (IRE)**[22] 2273 3-8-2 44 .... RoystonFfrench 5 — 46
(Mrs A Duffield) *prom: effrt 3f out: chsd wnr ins fnl f: r.o* **7/1**

5650 **3** 2 3/4 **Roundthetwist (IRE)**[11] 2603 3-9-5 62 .... DarrenWilliams 7 — 58
(K R Burke) *cl up: led 3f to 1f out: one pce* **11/4**[1]

60- **4** 1 3/4 **Terrasini (FR)**[334] 3510 3-9-5 0 .... RobertWinston 4 — 56
(J Howard Johnson) *t.k.h: in tch: lost pl after 4f: drvn over 3f out: rallied over 1f out: no imp* **4/1**

00 **5** 3/4 **Notnowrosie (IRE)**[26] 2143 3-8-9 0 .... PJMcDonald(3) 1 — 47
(A G Foster) *prom: effrt over 2f out: edgd rt over 1f out: no ex* **20/1**

5050 **6** 6 **Silver Spruce**[5] 2801 3-8-7 56 .... FergalLynch 2 — 32
(I W McInnes) *hld up: drvn 3f out: outpcd fr 2f out* **7/2**[3]

-606 **7** hd **Northwest**[15] 2486 3-8-4 46 .... AdrianTNicholls 9 — 29
(A Berry) *hld up: drvn over 3f out: btn fnl 2f* **20/1**

0000 **8** 3 1/4 **Victorias**[16] 2468 3-8-0 28 .... SilvestreDeSousa 8 — 19
(A Crook) *led to 3f out: wknd 2f out* **50/1**

2m 23.93s (-1.67) **Going Correction** -0.15s/f (Firm) **8** Ran SP% **117.9**

Speed ratings (Par 97): **100,99,97,96,95 91,91,88**

CSF £24.23 TOTE £4.10: £1.90, £2.70, £1.10; EX 39.50.

Owner Chris & Karen Hoar **Bred** Mike Channon Bloodstock Ltd **Trained** West Ilsley, Berks

■ Indecision was withdrawn on vet's advice (7/2, deduct 20p in the £ under Rule 4).

■ Stewards' Enquiry : T P O'Shea caution: excessive use of whip

FOCUS

A dreadful contest that is unlikely to produce any winners in the foreseeable future. The runner-up is perhaps the best guide to the form.

2942 29 PRIVATE MEMBERS CLUB CHALLENGE CUP H'CAP — 1m 65y
9:40 (9:40) (Class 4) (0-80,78) 4-Y-O+

£5,180 (£1,541; £770; £384) Stalls High

Form — RPR

0004 **1** **Society Music (IRE)**[19] 2375 6-8-13 **68** ....(p) FergalLynch 2 — 73
(M Dods) *cl up: led over 2f out: drvn and hld on wl fnl f* **11/4**[2]

350- **2** nk **Bold Indian (IRE)**[223] 6610 4-8-7 **62** .... TomEaves 7 — 66
(Miss L A Perratt) *plld hrd early: in tch: hdwy over 1f out: kpt on fnl f: hld cl home* **7/1**[3]

-512 **3** nk **Bustan (IRE)**[30] 2057 9-9-9 **78** .... RobertWinston 6 — 81
(G C Bravery) *trckd ldrs: effrt 2f out: edgd rt: kpt on fnl f: hld towards fin* **8/11**[1]

00-5 **4** 1 **Darfour**[13] 2524 4-8-7 **67** .... GaryBartley(5) 1 — 68
(J S Goldie) *hld up: shkn up and hdwy over 1f out: kpt on fnl f: nvr nr ldrs* **8/1**

100- **5** 2 3/4 **Packers Hill (IRE)**[330] 3607 4-9-5 **74** .... PaulMulrennan 3 — 69
(G A Swinbank) *t.k.h: led to over 2f out: wknd over 1f out* **20/1**

1m 47.44s (-0.96) **Going Correction** -0.15s/f (Firm) **5** Ran SP% **112.9**

Speed ratings (Par 105): **98,97,97,96,93**

CSF £20.95 TOTE £4.30: £1.80, £1.80; EX 18.90 Place 6 £ 113.01, Place 5 £ 23.33.

Owner Mrs C M Hewitson **Bred** John Weld **Trained** Denton, Co Durham

FOCUS

A trappy race that ended in a bit of a sprint. The form looks pretty weak.

T/Plt: £136.10 to a £1 stake. Pool: £75,562.45. 405.15 winning tickets. T/Qpdt: £30.50 to a £1 stake. Pool: £4,917.38. 119.00 winning tickets. RY

2709 KEMPTON (A.W) (R-H)

Wednesday, June 11

OFFICIAL GOING: Standard

Wind: Moderate, against Weather: Fine

2943 WEATHERBYS PRINTING APPRENTICE H'CAP (ROUND 2) — 1m (P)
6:25 (6:26) (Class 5) (0-70,65) 4-Y-O+

£2,590 (£770; £385; £192) Stalls High

Form — RPR

3255 **1** **Onenightinlisbon (IRE)**[33] 1954 4-9-5 **63** .... HarryPoulton(3) 2 — 73
(J R Boyle) *trckd ldr: pushed along over 3f out: drvn to ld wl over 2f out and dashed clr: kpt on u.p: unchal* **12/1**

640 **2** 2 **Eagle Nebula**[116] 590 4-9-10 **65** .... JamieJones 6 — 70
(B R Johnson) *trckd ldrs: pushed along and effrt over 3f out: wnt 3rd over 2f out: urged along to chse wnr jst over 1f out: fnd little* **12/1**

5320 **3** 1 1/2 **Recalcitrant**[10] 2642 5-8-11 **55** .... WilliamCarson(3) 4 — 57
(S Dow) *led: drvn and hdd wl over 2f out: one pce* **5/1**[1]

0-56 **4** 3 1/4 **Sonny Parkin**[19] 2373 6-9-5 **65** .... SimonPearce(5) 1 — 59
(J Pearce) *s.i.s: last and racing awkwardly: effrt over 2f out: plugged on but nvr on terms* **15/2**

-402 **5** 3/4 **Moyoko (IRE)**[10] 2642 5-8-2 **48** .... RossAtkinson(5) 3 — 41
(M Blanshard) *towards rr: rdn and effrt wl over 2f out: no imp on ldrs: b.b.v* **5/1**[1]

110 **6** 2 **Climate (IRE)**[15] 2477 9-9-7 **65** .... RichardEvans(3) 7 — 53
(P D Evans) *hld up towards rr: rdn over 2f out: no rspnse and btn after* **15/2**

0526 **7** nk **Postmaster**[41] 1747 6-8-5 **51** .... AshleyMorgan(5) 9 — 38
(R Ingram) *settled in rr: rdn over 3f out: no imp on ldrs* **13/2**[3]

3035 **8** 1/2 **Magic Warrior**[13] 2533 8-9-5 **60** .... HaddenFrost 8 — 46
(J C Fox) *trckd ldng pair: rdn 3f out: wknd over 2f out* **11/2**[2]

600- **9** *5* **Fantasy Crusader**[245] 6096 9-8-4 **50** .... BillyCray(5) 5 25
(R M H Cowell) *chsd ldrs: wd bnd 3f out and lost grnd: sn struggling in rr* **13/2**[3]

1m 40.8s (1.00) **Going Correction** +0.125s/f (Slow) **9** Ran SP% **114.3**
Speed ratings (Par 103): **100,98,96,93,92 90,90,89,84**
CSF £143.52 CT £820.50 TOTE £7.20: £2.50, £5.00, £1.70; EX 99.80.
Owner Inside Track Racing Club **Bred** Stephen Moloney **Trained** Epsom, Surrey

FOCUS
This was not a strong race and the winner is the best guide to the form.
Moyoko(IRE) Official explanation: vet said mare had bled from the nose
Magic Warrior Official explanation: jockey said gelding had no more to give

2944 SPILLERS MAIDEN AUCTION STKS 6f (P)
6:55 (6:57) (Class 5) 2-Y-O £2,590 (£770; £385; £192) **Stalls** High

Form RPR
2 **1** **Solo Attempt**[14] 2502 2-8-7 0 .... JohnEgan 10 73
(M Botti) *trckd ldrs: prog on inner to go 2nd 2f out: drvn to ld jst ins fnl f: styd on wl* **4/1**[3]
3 **2** *1 1/4* **Sir Geoffrey (IRE)**[14] 2502 2-8-10 0 .... PatCosgrave 5 72
(A J McCabe) *racd freely: led: hrd rdn 2f out: hdd jst ins fnl f: kpt on same pce* **7/1**
3 **3** *1 1/4* **Like For Like (IRE)**[10] 2638 2-8-7 0 ow1 .... TedDurcan 1 66+
(R Hannon) *dwlt: in tch in midfield: 7th 1/2-way: rdn jst over 2f out: prog over 1f out to take 3rd ent fnl f: no imp on ldng pair after* **2/1**[1]
40 **4** *2 1/4* **Amber Sunset**[8] 2691 2-8-1 0 .... LukeMorris(3) 6 56
(J Jay) *chsd ldr: drvn over 2f out: grad fdd* **14/1**
5 *1 1/2* **River Captain (IRE)** 2-8-10 0 .... LPKeniry 4 57+
(S Kirk) *dwlt: t.k.h: hld up in last and sn wl off the pce: sme prog on inner over 2f out: nt clr run briefly 1f out: one pce* **40/1**
2 **6** *1 1/4* **Calahonda**[30] 2048 2-8-4 0 .... ChrisCatlin 7 48
(P W D'Arcy) *t.k.h: trckd ldrs: 5th over 2f out: sn struggling u.p* **5/2**[2]
0 **7** *2 3/4* **Song Of Praise**[21] 2306 2-8-5 0 .... RichardKingscote 2 40
(M Blanshard) *t.k.h: trckd ldrs on outer: edgd lft u.p 2f out: wknd* **50/1**
0 **8** *1 1/4* **Calypso Prince**[43] 1693 2-8-10 0 .... RichardSmith 12 42
(M D I Usher) *reminder after 1f: a in last trio: rdn and no imp over 2f out* **66/1**
9 *hd* **Craft (FR)** 2-8-11 0 .... NCallan 8 42
(B J Meehan) *chsd ldrs: 6th and hrd rdn over 2f out: wknd over 1f out* **14/1**
0 **10** *shd* **Paymaster In Chief**[43] 1693 2-8-9 0 .... HayleyTurner 3 40
(M D I Usher) *a in last trio: hanging and struggling wl over 2f out: no ch after* **66/1**

1m 14.6s (1.50) **Going Correction** +0.125s/f (Slow) **10** Ran SP% **115.1**
Speed ratings (Par 93): **95,93,91,88,86 85,81,79,79,79**
CSF £31.09 TOTE £4.70: £1.80, £2.20, £1.10; EX 22.30.
Owner Mrs R J Jacobs **Bred** Newsells Park Stud Limited **Trained** Newmarket, Suffolk
■ Stewards' Enquiry : Pat Cosgrave one-day ban: careless riding (Jun 25)

FOCUS
An ordinary maiden but a mixed bag formwise which could be out either way. The first two came from the same Great Leighs race.

NOTEBOOK
Solo Attempt looked as though the experience was needed when second in a modest Great Leighs maiden on her debut, finishing one place ahead of Sir Geoffrey, and she showed herself to be heading the right way by confirming the form. Well drawn in ten, she held a nice position against the rail and picked up nicely when asked to go on inside the final furlong. The daughter of Anabaa will want 7f before long and she remains capable of better. It will be interesting to see what mark she is given for nurseries. (tchd 3-1, 9-2 in a place)
Sir Geoffrey(IRE), who got going late after a slow start to finish a neck behind Solo Attempt at Great Leighs on his debut, was quick to grab the lead and he again showed obvious promise, but was unable to repel his old rival. He clearly possesses plenty of pace and has shown enough to suggest he can land a small maiden. (op 13-2 tchd 6-1)
Like For Like(IRE) comes from a yard that continues to churn out the juvenile winners and she did little wrong when finishing third behind a decent sort on her recent debut at Bath. The draw had not been kind to her though, having drawn stall one, and she was forced to race in midfield early. She got going too late, running on inside the final furlong for third, and already looks as though she will benefit from 7f. (tchd 15-8 and 5-2)
Amber Sunset, who seemed to struggle on slow ground at Folkestone, had earlier shaped well at Goodwood and this was a more promising effort. She will now be qualified for nurseries and should fare better in that sphere. (op 20-1)
River Captain(IRE), a half-brother to multiple winner Proper, comes from a yard that is capable of readying one and he made a promising debut back in fifth, running on late having been slowly away. He should learn from this experience. (op 33-1 tchd 50-1)
Calahonda, second to a fair type on debut at Wolverhampton, went the wrong way from that and ran rather flat. Official explanation: trainer later said filly was found to be lame on returning home (op 3-1 tchd 10-3)
Craft(FR), a Super Sprint entrant, offered little encouragement on this racecourse debut. (op 12-1)

2945 DIGIBET H'CAP 6f (P)
7:25 (7:27) (Class 4) (0-80,80) 3-Y-O £4,209 (£1,252; £625; £312) **Stalls** High

Form RPR
01 **1** **Onceaponatime (IRE)**[22] 2279 3-9-7 **80** .... AlanMunro 9 87+
(P W Chapple-Hyam) *nt as wl away as sme: sn trckd ldrs: shkn up over 2f out: prog on outer over 1f out: styd on to ld last 100yds: drvn out* **5/2**[1]
4143 **2** *3/4* **Prime Factor**[13] 2529 3-9-2 **75** .... NCallan 7 80
(B W Hills) *trckd ldrs: effrt over 2f out: drvn to ld jst over 1f out: hdd last 100yds: kpt on* **11/2**[3]
6-21 **3** *nk* **Honey Monster (IRE)**[60] 1339 3-9-2 **75** .... PatCosgrave 11 79+
(A J McCabe) *in rr of main gp: rdn and sme prog 2f out: no imp over 1f out: picked up again and fin wl last 150yds to take 3rd nr fin* **6/1**
1-03 **4** *1/2* **Replicator**[14] 2506 3-8-13 **72** .... PatDobbs 8 74
(Pat Eddery) *trckd ldrs: effrt on inner and cl up 2f out: drvn and nt qckn over 1f out: one pce after* **16/1**
31-2 **5** *1 1/4* **Maryolini**[18] 2407 3-9-1 **77** .... KirstyMilczarek(3) 6 75
(N J Vaughan) *led: hrd pressed fr over 2f out: hdd and fdd jst over 1f out* **4/1**[2]
2235 **6** *1/2* **Caprio (IRE)**[27] 2126 3-8-11 **70** .... RichardKingscote 4 66+
(Tom Dascombe) *v awkward s and lost many ls: wl bhd: pushed along over 2f out: styd on wl fr over 1f out: nrst fin* **14/1**
-050 **7** *1/2* **Bazguy**[12] 2570 3-8-7 **73** ....(b) RichardEvans(7) 5 68
(P D Evans) *trckd ldr: poised to chal gng wl fr 1/2-way: rdn and fnd nil 2f out: stl nrly upsides jst over 1f out: wknd* **25/1**
54-1 **8** *3/4* **Vigano (IRE)**[131] 397 3-8-8 **72** .... HaddenFrost(5) 1 64
(S Kirk) *restless stalls: trckd ldrs and racd on outer: grad lost grnd bnd 3f out: one pce in rr fnl 2f* **20/1**
2310 **9** *1 1/4* **Pha Mai Blue**[18] 2407 3-9-7 **80** .... LPKeniry 3 68
(W J Knight) *in rr of main gp: pushed along 1/2-way: no prog over 2f out: btn after* **25/1**
1353 **10** *nk* **Benedetto**[12] 2563 3-8-10 **69** ....(p) JimCrowley 10 56
(Mrs A J Perrett) *in rr of main gp: no prog u.p over 2f out* **8/1**
00-0 **11** *44* **Just Sort It**[22] 2276 3-8-11 **70** .... TedDurcan 2 —
(W Jarvis) *nrly sat down as stalls opened and jockey unable to remove blindfold: a t.o and allowed to coast rnd* **25/1**

1m 14.21s (1.11) **Going Correction** +0.125s/f (Slow) **11** Ran SP% **118.2**
Speed ratings (Par 101): **97,96,95,94,93 92,91,90,89,88 30**
CSF £15.34 CT £72.05 TOTE £3.50: £1.80, £1.70, £2.90; EX 19.30.
Owner Mrs Susan Roy **Bred** Dermot O'Rourke **Trained** Newmarket, Suffolk

FOCUS
A fair handicap run at an ordinary pace. There should be more to come from the winner.
Maryolini Official explanation: jockey said filly had no more to give
Caprio(IRE) Official explanation: jockey said colt missed the break
Just Sort It Official explanation: jockey said gelding missed the break

2946 DIGIBET FILLIES' H'CAP 7f (P)
7:55 (8:01) (Class 5) (0-70,70) 3-Y-O £2,590 (£770; £385; £192) **Stalls** High

Form RPR
040 **1** **Priti Fabulous (IRE)**[11] 2620 3-9-3 **66** .... DarryllHolland 6 79+
(W J Haggas) *trckd ldng pair: forced wd over 2f out and lost pl briefly: hrd rdn and prog to ld 1f out: styd on strly* **7/2**[1]
3000 **2** *3 1/4* **Lady Amberlini**[5] 2781 3-8-11 **60** .... JohnEgan 14 62
(P D Evans) *chsd ldrs: drvn and prog on inner to ld over 1f out: hdd and outpcd 1f out* **16/1**
-600 **3** *1/2* **Loveinanelevator**[17] 2429 3-9-3 **66** .... HayleyTurner 5 67+
(M L W Bell) *t.k.h: hld up in rr: gng wl 3f out: prog over 2f out: chsd ldng pair ins fnl f: nt qckn and no imp* **9/2**[2]
633- **4** *1 1/4* **Tense (IRE)**[175] 7190 3-9-6 **69** .... ShaneKelly 8 67
(J A Osborne) *led 2f: pressed ldr: led over 2f out to over 1f out: fdd ins fnl f* **8/1**
-335 **5** *1/2* **Asian Lady**[28] 2102 3-9-4 **67** .... ChrisCatlin 9 63
(R Charlton) *cl up: nt qckn and lost pl over 2f out: struggling after: styd on again fnl f* **9/2**[2]
0-31 **6** *1* **Rio L'Oren (IRE)**[110] 662 3-9-2 **65** .... JimmyQuinn 1 59
(N J Vaughan) *a in same pl: shkn up 2f out: one pce and no prog* **18/1**
000 **7** *2* **Your Golf Travel**[33] 1971 3-7-13 **51** oh6 .... LukeMorris(3) 12 39
(J S Wainwright) *wl in rr: rdn wl over 2f out: no real prog: plugged on* **33/1**
-400 **8** *3/4* **Hasty Lady**[8] 2699 3-9-5 **68** .... NCallan 11 54
(K A Ryan) *s.s: a in rr: drvn and no prog on inner fnl 2f* **13/2**[3]
500 **9** *nse* **Little Cee (IRE)**[20] 2341 3-8-7 **59** .... MarcHalford(3) 13 45
(D R C Elsworth) *dwlt: plld hrd: hld up in midfield: effrt over 2f out: wknd over 1f out* **20/1**
6-00 **10** *1/2* **Edie Superstar (USA)**[16] 2452 3-9-2 **65** ....(vt[1]) EddieAhern 7 50
(M A Magnusson) *led after 2f to over 2f out: wknd over 1f out* **12/1**
0-00 **11** *10* **Cheviot Red**[30] 2043 3-8-12 **61** .... AlanMunro 10 19
(B J Meehan) *sn detached in last pair: a bhd: t.o* **18/1**
04-0 **12** *11* **In Decorum**[160] 23 3-8-2 **51** oh6 ....(v) DavidKinsella 4 —
(J A Geake) *dwlt and early reminders: nvr gng wl and a detached: t.o* **66/1**

1m 26.99s (0.99) **Going Correction** +0.125s/f (Slow) **12** Ran SP% **122.2**
Speed ratings (Par 96): **99,95,94,93,92 91,89,88,88,87 76,63**
CSF £63.78 CT £268.33 TOTE £4.80: £1.90, £5.50, £1.60; EX 49.50.
Owner Kevin Murphy **Bred** Deln Ltd **Trained** Newmarket, Suffolk

FOCUS
A competitive fillies' handicap. The fourth is the best guide, with the winner showing big improvement on her handicap debut.
Hasty Lady Official explanation: jockey said filly had no more to give

2947 DIGIBET.COM H'CAP 7f (P)
8:25 (8:27) (Class 4) (0-85,85) 4-Y-O+ £4,209 (£1,252; £625; £312) **Stalls** High

Form RPR
3332 **1** **Cha Cha Cha**[22] 2284 4-8-8 **72** .... NCallan 9 85
(K A Ryan) *prom on inner: chsd ldr jst over 2f out: drvn to ld 1f out: styd on wl* **3/1**[1]
05-0 **2** *1/2* **Medicea Sidera**[32] 1981 4-9-6 **84** .... LPKeniry 5 96
(E F Vaughan) *led: drvn and clr w wnr over 1f out: hdd 1f out: kpt on wl but a hld* **10/1**
350 **3** *3* **Resplendent Nova**[11] 2615 6-9-7 **85** .... JimmyQuinn 7 89
(P Howling) *trckd ldrs: outpcd wl over 1f out: drvn into 3rd 1f out: no ch w ldng pair* **7/1**
0630 **4** *3/4* **Bomber Command (USA)**[11] 2619 5-9-2 **83** ....(v) PatrickHills(3) 11 85+
(J W Hills) *dwlt and n.m.r on inner sn after s: last trio tl rdn and styd on fnl 2f: nrst fin* **13/2**[3]
-100 **5** *3/4* **Vintage (IRE)**[11] 2615 4-8-5 **69** ow1 .... AlanMunro 10 69
(J Akehurst) *t.k.h: hld up towards rr: sme prog on inner 2f out: sn outpcd: one pce after* **16/1**
0201 **6** *1/2* **Rydal Mount (IRE)**[11] 2622 5-9-4 **82** .... ChrisCatlin 3 80
(W S Kittow) *chsd ldr tl jst over 2f out: fdd u.p* **12/1**
1024 **7** *1 3/4* **Carcinetto (IRE)**[11] 2606 6-9-0 **85** .... RichardEvans(7) 1 78
(P D Evans) *trckd ldrs: rdn and nt qckn over 2f out: sn struggling and btn* **14/1**
0645 **8** *1 1/2* **Royal Island (IRE)**[14] 2504 6-9-3 **81** .... VinceSlattery 6 70
(M G Quinlan) *sn last: rdn and wd bnd 3f out: nvr a factor* **14/1**
1000 **9** *2 1/4* **Hazytoo**[13] 2550 4-8-4 **68** .... WilliamBuick 2 51
(S A Callaghan) *racd wd and rn in snatches: brief effrt fr rr over 2f out: sn rdn and wknd* **6/1**[2]
3202 **10** *1/2* **North South Divide (IRE)**[9] 2679 4-8-11 **75** ....(p) DaneO'Neill 4 57
(R A Teal) *t.k.h: hld up in midfield: rdn over 2f out: sn wknd* **13/2**[3]
3360 **11** *5* **Hollow Jo**[50] 1541 8-8-2 **66** .... AdrianMcCarthy 8 34
(J R Jenkins) *dwlt: a in last trio: rdn and no prog 3f out: eased over 1f out* **20/1**

1m 25.58s (-0.42) **Going Correction** +0.125s/f (Slow) **11** Ran SP% **119.2**
Speed ratings (Par 105): **107,106,103,102,101 100,98,97,94,93 88**
CSF £34.69 CT £198.49 TOTE £3.00: £1.30, £2.90, £2.80; EX 44.10.
Owner Guy Reed **Bred** G Reed **Trained** Hambleton, N Yorks

FOCUS
The time was well over a second quicker than the earlier fillies' handicap over the same trip. The winner took full advantage of her 10lb lower sand mark, which is based mainly on her efforts on Fibresand, and overall this form has been rated positively.

2948 ING EQUITY MARKETS H'CAP — 1m 4f (P)
8:55 (8:56) (Class 4) (0-85,82) 3-Y-O — **£4,209** (£1,252; £625; £312) **Stalls** Centre

Form — RPR

5-1 **1** **Unleashed (IRE)**[13] [2528] 3-9-7 **82**.......... TedDurcan 3 94+
(H R A Cecil) *cl up: drvn to ld over 1f out: hung lft after but stdy on wl* **7/4**[1]

4-01 **2** 2 **Celtic Dragon**[20] [2327] 3-8-13 **74**.......... JimCrowley 1 83
(Mrs A J Perrett) *hld up in last: effrt on outer whn carried lft over 2f out: drvn and kpt on to take 2nd fnl f: no imp wnr* **9/2**[3]

005- **3** 1 3/4 **General Ting (IRE)**[249] [6022] 3-8-4 **65**.......... DO'Donohoe 6 71+
(Sir Mark Prescott) *led: veered lft bnd after 4f: hung bdly lft over 2f out: hung lft again over 1f out and hdd: nt qckn* **8/1**

1-1 **4** 1 1/4 **Relative Strength (IRE)**[50] [1543] 3-9-3 **78**.......... LPKeniry 5 82
(A M Balding) *trckd ldr: hmpd over 2f out: grad fdd u.p* **15/8**[2]

2-23 **5** 2 1/4 **Brexca (IRE)**[30] [2046] 3-9-2 **77**.......... (v[1]) AdamKirby 2 78
(C G Cox) *hld up in 4th: effrt on outer 3f out: hmpd over 2f out: fdd over 1f out* **8/1**

2m 35.06s (0.56) **Going Correction** +0.125s/f (Slow) **5** Ran SP% **111.6**
Speed ratings (Par 101): **103,101,100,99,98**
CSF £10.03 TOTE £2.50: £1.80, £2.30; EX 7.30.
Owner Ennismore Racing II **Bred** Davin Investments Ltd **Trained** Newmarket, Suffolk

FOCUS
The most interesting race of the evening, despite the small field, and it proved the most eventful, with the front-running General Ting jinking left on the bend racing away from the stand and then hanging in the same direction in the straight, interfering with all bar the winner in the process. The winner is on the up and the form has been rated fairly positively.

2949 TFM NETWORKS H'CAP — 1m 3f (P)
9:25 (9:27) (Class 6) (0-60,60) 4-Y-O+ — **£2,047** (£604; £302) **Stalls** High

Form — RPR

013 **1** **Top Seed (IRE)**[44] [1692] 7-9-3 **59**.......... StephenDonohoe 7 68+
(Ian Williams) *hld up in last: stl there 2f out: rapid prog on outer after: r.o wl to ld last 75yds: won gng away* **5/1**[2]

2365 **2** 1 1/2 **Medieval Maiden**[44] [1692] 5-9-0 **56**.......... PaulDoe 5 62
(Mrs L J Mongan) *prom: drvn to ld over 1f out: hdd and outpcd last 75yds* **14/1**

3025 **3** 2 **Mixing**[7] [2715] 6-8-11 **56**.......... KirstyMilczarek(3) 10 59
(M J Attwater) *hld up in last trio: prog over 2f out: r.o to take 3rd ins fnl f but nt pce of wnr* **11/2**[3]

600 **4** 1 1/4 **Nothingtodeclaire**[8] [2707] 4-9-2 **58**.......... ChrisCatlin 3 58
(V Smith) *led 2f: pressed ldr: rdn to chal and upsides 2f out: outpcd fnl f* **6/1**

040- **5** nk **Bundle Up**[338] [3387] 5-9-1 **57**.......... IanMongan 4 57
(Mrs L J Mongan) *t.k.h: hld up in midfield: clsd on ldrs over 2f out: swtchd rt and nrly upsides wl over 1f out: sn outpcd* **20/1**

0160 **6** hd **Noah Jameel**[50] [1528] 6-8-11 **53**.......... DaneO'Neill 9 53
(A G Newcombe) *hld up in midfield: effrt over 2f out: styd on same pce fr over 1f out: nvr able to chal* **9/2**[1]

0034 **7** 2 1/2 **Sintenis Mac (GER)**[19] [2374] 5-8-13 **55**.......... DarryllHolland 11 50
(P J O'Gorman) *rousted along to go prom: effrt on inner and n.m.r over 2f out: cl up over 1f out: wknd* **5/1**[2]

0644 **8** 3/4 **Barry Island**[14] [2513] 9-8-11 **53**.......... AlanMunro 1 47
(D R C Elsworth) *hld up wl in rr: no prog over 2f out: kpt on fr over 1f out: no ch* **12/1**

-000 **9** nse **Autograph Hunter**[129] [420] 4-8-4 **46** oh1.......... AdrianMcCarthy 13 40
(Peter Grayson) *towards rr: rdn and prog over 2f out: nt rch ldrs over 1f out: wknd fnl f* **25/1**

60-4 **10** 2 **Still Calm**[16] [2446] 4-9-4 **60**.......... (e) AdamKirby 2 51
(N J Vaughan) *led to post and mounted at s: led after 2f: wandered 1/2-way: kicked on over 3f out: hanging over 2f out: hdd & wknd over 1f out* **8/1**

4036 **11** 1/2 **Trysting Grove (IRE)**[8] [2707] 7-9-0 **56**.......... SaleemGolam 14 46
(E G Bevan) *hld up in last trio: rdn and no prog over 2f out* **14/1**

1200 **12** 4 **Siena Star (IRE)**[28] [2097] 10-9-4 **60**.......... MickyFenton 6 43
(Stef Liddiard) *t.k.h: trckd ldrs: cl enough over 2f out: wknd rapidly wl over 1f out* **16/1**

0630 **13** 7 **Club Captain (USA)**[14] [2513] 5-8-4 **46** oh1.......... (p) RichardThomas 12 17
(T D McCarthy) *racd awkwardly on inner: in tch tl wknd over 2f out* **40/1**

2m 24.3s (2.40) **Going Correction** +0.125s/f (Slow) **13** Ran SP% **130.3**
Speed ratings (Par 101): **96,94,93,92,92 92,90,89,89,88 87,85,79**
CSF £78.77 CT £417.96 TOTE £6.10: £2.00, £2.90, £2.60; EX 65.70 Place 6 £ 35.69, Place 5 £ 10.01.
Owner J Tredwell **Bred** Hugo Merry And Jack Dorrian **Trained** Portway, Worcs

FOCUS
A weak handicap full of exposed sorts which was steadily run. Modest form, the runner-up the best guide.
Still Calm Official explanation: jockey said gelding hung both ways
T/Plt: £28.20 to a £1 stake. Pool: £63,336.55. 1,638.05 winning tickets. T/Qpdt: £9.10 to a £1 stake. Pool: £4,343.93. 352.00 winning tickets. JN

1997 NOTTINGHAM (L-H)
Wednesday, June 11

OFFICIAL GOING: Good to firm (good in places) changing to good to firm after race 2 (2.10)
Wind: light half against

2950 TURFTV H'CAP — 6f 15y
1:40 (1:40) (Class 6) (0-65,65) 3-Y-O+ — **£2,047** (£604; £302) **Stalls** High

Form — RPR

5-15 **1** **Bold Argument (IRE)**[23] [2242] 5-9-2 **58**.......... JackMitchell(5) 15 73+
(Mrs P N Dutfield) *rrd s and s.i.s: bhd: hdwy and swtchd rt 2f out: sn rdn and styd on strly ins fnl f to ld nr line* **4/1**[1]

6512 **2** shd **Figaro Flyer (IRE)**[22] [2292] 5-9-12 **63**.......... IanMongan 7 78
(P Howling) *trckd ldrs: hdwy to ld wl over 1f out: rdn ins fnl f: hdd and no ex nr line* **8/1**

0-00 **3** 2 3/4 **Greek Secret**[16] [2448] 5-9-1 **52**.......... TGMcLaughlin 4 58
(J O'Reilly) *dwlt: hld up towards rr: hdwy 2f out: sn rdn and styd on same pce fnl f* **33/1**

1312 **4** 1/2 **Kingsmaite**[23] [2263] 7-9-1 **52**.......... (b) JimmyFortune 12 57
(S R Bowring) *in tch: hdwy 2f out: sn rdn and styd on same pce ins fnl f* **6/1**[3]

1003 **5** 1 3/4 **Russian Rocket (IRE)**[14] [2511] 6-9-4 **55**.......... KerrinMcEvoy 5 54
(Mrs C A Dunnett) *chsd ldr: rdn along 2f out: drvn and wknd appr fnl f* **15/2**

6050 **6** 2 1/4 **Tag Team (IRE)**[22] [2293] 7-9-0 **51**.......... StephenDonohoe 16 43
(John A Harris) *hld up in tch towards stands rail: hmpd 2f out: swtchd lft and sn rdn: kpt on ins fnl f: nrst fin* **14/1**

0103 **7** 3/4 **Trinculo (IRE)**[15] [2478] 11-9-11 **65**.......... (b) KevinGhunowa(3) 8 54
(R A Harris) *led: rdn along wl over 2f out: hdd wl over 1f out and grad wknd* **8/1**

6604 **8** nk **No Time (IRE)**[2] [2892] 8-9-5 **56**.......... TPQueally 17 44+
(A J McCabe) *hld up in tch on stands rail: n.m.r 2f out: sn rdn and no imp* **5/1**[2]

6-60 **9** 1 1/2 **Currency**[23] [2255] 11-9-0 **54**.......... TolleyDean(3) 3 38
(J M Bradley) *chsd ldrs on outer: rdn along 2f out: sn wknd* **33/1**

000 **10** 2 **Supreme Speedster**[11] [2596] 4-9-0 **58**.......... AdamCarter(7) 6 35
(M Brittain) *t.k.h: in tch: hdwy to chse ldrs after 2f: rdn along 2f out and sn wknd* **50/1**

04-0 **11** 1 1/2 **Regal Dream (IRE)**[48] [1578] 6-9-4 **55**.......... (t) AdamKirby 13 27
(J W Unett) *hld up: a towards rr* **16/1**

4010 **12** nse **Kenmore**[23] [2255] 6-9-13 **64**.......... PatrickMathers 2 36
(I W McInnes) *chsd ldrs on outer: rdn along 2f out: sn drvn and wknd* **20/1**

000- **13** 2 1/2 **High Ridge**[232] [6406] 9-9-9 **60**.......... (p) DaneO'Neill 11 24
(J M Bradley) *hmpd s: a towards rr* **20/1**

1m 15.02s (-0.08) **Going Correction** +0.025s/f (Good) **13** Ran SP% **114.9**
Speed ratings (Par 101): **101,100,97,96,94 91,90,89,87,85 83,83,79**
CSF £31.81 CT £948.14 TOTE £5.50: £2.00, £2.10, £9.50; EX 30.50.
Owner Simon Dutfield **Bred** K S Lee **Trained** Axmouth, Devon
■ Stewards' Enquiry : Jack Mitchell two-day ban: excessive use of whip (Jun 25-26)

FOCUS
A moderate sprint which saw the first pair come clear. The winner is value for further and the form is pretty sound.
Tag Team(IRE) Official explanation: jockey said gelding hung left-handed

2951 EUROPEAN BREEDERS' FUND MAIDEN STKS — 6f 15y
2:10 (2:17) (Class 5) 2-Y-O — **£3,626** (£1,079; £539; £269) **Stalls** High

Form — RPR

3 **1** **Uramazin (IRE)**[16] [2443] 2-9-3 0.......... KerrinMcEvoy 1 81+
(G A Swinbank) *hld up: hdwy over 2f out: hmpd over 1f out: rdn to ld ins fnl f: r.o* **7/1**[2]

2 1 1/4 **Mrs Kipling (IRE)** 2-8-12 0.......... LDettori 11 72
(S A Callaghan) *hld up in tch: rdn and ev ch fr over 1f out: styd on* **11/4**[1]

3 3/4 **Crackdown (IRE)** 2-9-3 0.......... JoeFanning 7 75
(M Johnston) *chsd ldrs: led wl over 2f out: rdn and hung lft fr over 1f out: hdd and unable qck ins fnl f* **28/1**

4 nse **Izzi Mill (USA)** 2-8-12 0.......... TQuinn 13 70+
(D R C Elsworth) *s.s: hld up: hdwy over 1f out: r.o: nt rch ldrs* **40/1**

5 1 1/4 **Churchills Victory (IRE)** 2-9-3 0.......... WilliamBuick 14 71
(W Jarvis) *chsd ldrs: ev ch over 2f out: rdn and hung lft fr over 1f out: styd on same pce* **12/1**

5 **6** nk **Kings Troop**[29] [2086] 2-9-3 0.......... TPQueally 6 71+
(H R A Cecil) *chsd ldrs: rdn whn hmpd over 1f out: styd on same pce* **14/1**

2 **7** 1/2 **Black Attack (IRE)**[8] [2696] 2-9-3 0.......... RyanMoore 12 69+
(Paul Green) *chsd ldrs: rdn over 1f out: styd on same pce* **11/4**[1]

8 1 **Oratory (IRE)** 2-9-3 0.......... RichardHughes 9 69+
(R Hannon) *s.i.s: hld up: styd on ins fnl f: nvr nrr* **15/2**[3]

9 1 3/4 **Dubai Hills** 2-9-3 0.......... TedDurcan 3 60
(B Smart) *s.s: hld up: rdn and nt clr run over 1f out: n.d* **8/1**

10 1 1/4 **Bob Stock (IRE)** 2-9-3 0.......... StephenDonohoe 10 57
(W J Musson) *s.s: a in rr* **66/1**

11 1/2 **Join Up** 2-9-3 0.......... AdamKirby 5 55
(W R Swinburn) *hld up: shkn up 1/2-way: a in rr* **16/1**

3 **12** 1 1/2 **Satwa Boy**[19] [2349] 2-9-3 0.......... TGMcLaughlin 2 51
(E A L Dunlop) *prom: rdn over 2f out: wknd over 1f out* **25/1**

0 **13** 28 **Ruby's Song (IRE)**[45] [1640] 2-8-9 0.......... (b[1]) TolleyDean(3) 8 —
(J M Bradley) *sn led: rdn and hdd wl over 2f out: sn wknd* **125/1**

1m 15.23s (0.13) **Going Correction** +0.025s/f (Good) **13** Ran SP% **121.0**
Speed ratings (Par 93): **100,98,97,97,95 95,94,93,90,89 88,86,49**
CSF £26.03 TOTE £8.00: £2.40, £1.40, £6.80; EX 33.00.
Owner Mrs T Blackett **Bred** Davin Investments Ltd **Trained** Melsonby, N Yorks

FOCUS
A fair juvenile maiden which will produce future winners. The sixth helps to set the level, which is somewhat guessy.

NOTEBOOK
Uramazin(IRE), third on his debut at Carlisle, relished the extra furlong and ran out a tidy winner in the end. He should be rated better than the bare margin as he met trouble in between the final two furlongs, being carried towards the far side, and also deserves a little extra credit as he was drawn in the outside stall. This colt will get further still before the year is out and rates a useful prospect. (op 9-1)

Mrs Kipling(IRE) ◆, a 55,000gns half-sister to a juvenile mile winner, came to the track with somewhat of a reputation and, while easy in the on-course betting ring, she still went off as joint favourite with Dettori on board. She emerged from off the pace with every chance, confirming her ability, and just got beaten by a more experienced horse on the day. She will be the one to beat wherever turning up next. (op 7-4 tchd 13-8)

Crackdown(IRE), a 60,000gns May foal, knew his job early on and was soon up with the pace. He ran green having been in front for some time nearing the final furlong, however, and left the clear impression this debut experience would be of real benefit to him. Another furlong will suit before that long and he has a future. Official explanation: jockey said colt hung left (op 25-1)

Izzi Mill(USA), a $70,000 purchase whose dam was a quite useful turf winner in the US, posted an encouraging debut effort and was noted doing all of her best work late on after making a sluggish start. She was given an educational ride and really ought to be a deal shaper next time out.

Churchills Victory(IRE), whose dam won over 1m1f at three, showed promise on this racecourse bow and was another to run green when put under serious pressure. He will come on a deal for this. (op 16-1)

Kings Troop stepped up on the level of his debut effort at Yarmouth and goes some way to helping set the level of this form. (op 20-1 tchd 12-1)

Black Attack(IRE), well backed, was in trouble before the furlong pole and failed to build on the promise of his debut second at Ripon eight days previously. He got the extra furlong well enough, but it may be that this came just a little too soon and possibly he may have found the quicker surface against him. (op 7-2 tchd 4-1)

2952 SHOWSEC H'CAP 1m 6f 15y
2:40 (2:43) (Class 5) (0-75,75) 4-Y-0+ **£2,914** (£867; £433; £216) **Stalls** Low

Form RPR

3-54 **1** **Lapina (IRE)**[34] 1929 4-8-7 **61**........(b) ShaneKelly 10 69
(Pat Eddery) *hld up towards rr: stdy hdwy 4f out: cl up 2f out: rdn and ev ch ent fnl f: sn drvn and edgd lft: styd on to ld fnl 50yds* **7/1**[2]

-212 **2** ½ **Spring Dream (IRE)**[9] 2682 5-9-3 **71**........ RichardHughes 8 78
(A King) *hld up: smooth hdwy 4f out: trckd ldrs on bit over 2f out: shkn up to chal and ev ch ent fnl f: sn rdn: edgd lft and nt qckn towards fin* **15/8**[1]

0350 **3** nk **They All Laughed**[11] 2621 5-9-3 **71**........ TGMcLaughlin 3 78
(P W Hiatt) *hld up and bhd: stdy hdwy on outer 3f out: rdn to ld appr fnl f: drvn and edgd lft ins fnl f: hdd and no ex fnl 50yds* **16/1**

30/0 **4** 2 ½ **Emile Zola**[26] 2153 6-8-9 **63**........ WilliamBuick 2 66
(Miss Venetia Williams) *chsd ldrs on inner: rdn along and outpcd 3f out: styd on u.p appr fnl f: tk 4th nr line* **15/2**[3]

3-43 **5** shd **Fourth Dimension (IRE)**[29] 2091 9-9-1 **69**........ AdamKirby 9 72
(Miss T Spearing) *stdd s and hld up towards rr: hdwy on outer over 3f out: rdn to chse ldrs 2f out: drvn and one pce ent fnl f: lost 4th nr line* **8/1**

-065 **6** 1 ½ **Muntami (IRE)**[14] 1121 7-8-4 **58**........ JimmyQuinn 6 59
(John A Harris) *hld up: hdwy and in tch over 3f out: rdn over 2f out: no imp appr fnl f* **9/1**

0-06 **7** ¾ **Mulaazem**[20] 2335 5-8-5 **59**........(t) JoeFanning 11 59
(J Mackie) *trckd ldrs: hdwy over 4f out: led wl over 2f out and sn rdn: drvn and hdd appr fnl f: wknd* **14/1**

212- **8** 1 ½ **Up In Arms (IRE)**[191] 7008 4-9-0 **68**........ StephenCarson 5 66
(P Winkworth) *chsd ldrs: rdn along 4f out: drvn 3f out and sn wknd* **15/2**[3]

-644 **9** ½ **Adage**[23] 2241 5-8-3 **57**........(t) AdrianMcCarthy 7 54
(David Pinder) *chsd ldrs: hdwy over 4f out: led over 4f out: rdn and hdd wl over 2f out: grad wknd* **11/1**

-606 **10** nse **Corum (IRE)**[23] 2264 5-9-4 **75**........(p) LeeVickers(3) 1 72
(Mrs K Waldron) *t.k.h: led 2f: cl up tl led again after 4f: rdn along and hdd 4f out: sn wknd* **33/1**

11 12 **Liverpool Echo (FR)**[100] 8-8-7 **64**........(v) DominicFox(3) 4 44
(Mrs K Waldron) *cl up: led after 2f: hdd after 4f: chsd ldrs tl rdn along 4f out and sn wknd* **50/1**

3m 4.43s (-2.87) **Going Correction** -0.35s/f (Firm) **11** Ran SP% **117.7**
Speed ratings (Par 103): **94,93,93,92,92 91,90,89,89,89 82**
CSF £20.42 CT £208.95 TOTE £7.60: £2.20, £1.30, £4.00; EX 19.60.
Owner Aitken & Phillips **Bred** W Maxwell Ervine **Trained** Nether Winchendon, Bucks
■ Stewards' Enquiry : Adam Kirby four-day ban: dropped his hands and lost 4th place (Jun 25-28)

FOCUS
A modest staying handicap, run at a moderate early pace. The first three came clear and the form is sound, if ordinary.

2953 BETFAIR H'CAP 1m 75y
3:10 (3:10) (Class 3) (0-95,89) 3-Y-0 **£6,799** (£2,023; £1,011; £505) **Stalls** Centre

Form RPR

3-1 **1** **Scuffle**[33] 1964 3-9-1 **83**........ SteveDrowne 9 94+
(R Charlton) *trckd ldrs: racd keenly: led over 2f out: rdn and edgd lft ins fnl f: jst hld on* **7/4**[1]

2-21 **2** nse **Lindelaan (USA)**[14] 2500 3-8-11 **79**........(v[1]) RyanMoore 4 90+
(Sir Michael Stoute) *hld up: hdwy over 2f out: rdn ins fnl f: r.o* **6/1**[3]

-210 **3** 3 ½ **Silver Rime (FR)**[25] 2194 3-9-5 **87**........ RichardHughes 3 90
(R Hannon) *a.p: ev ch 2f out: sn rdn and edgd lft: no ex ins fnl f* **4/1**[2]

43-5 **4** nk **Upton Grey (IRE)**[55] 1428 3-9-5 **87**........ JimmyFortune 2 89
(J H M Gosden) *trckd ldrs: plld hrd: rdn over 2f out: styd on same pce fnl f* **10/1**

1-26 **5** 1 ½ **Toto Skyllachy**[34] 1923 3-9-4 **86**........ MickyFenton 6 85
(T P Tate) *led: hdd after 1f: led again 1/2-way: hdd over 2f out: sn rdn: wknd ins fnl f* **9/1**

2-50 **6** 1 ½ **King Hafhafah**[67] 1213 3-9-5 **87**........ AdamKirby 7 82
(I A Wood) *hld up in tch: rdn over 3f out: hung lft over 1f out: styd on same pce* **50/1**

2621 **7** ½ **Mekong Melody (IRE)**[34] 1930 3-8-10 **78**........ KerrinMcEvoy 10 72+
(C G Cox) *hld up: nt clr run over 2f out: hmpd over 1f out: n.d* **11/1**

4-40 **8** 4 **Arctic Cape**[39] 1806 3-9-3 **85**........ JoeFanning 1 70
(M Johnston) *led after 1f: hdd 1/2-way: wknd over 1f out* **10/1**

10-6 **9** 1 ¾ **Quam Celerrime**[69] 1171 3-9-7 **89**........ StephenDonohoe 5 70
(P A Blockley) *s.i.s: hld up: rdn 1/2-way: a in rr* **66/1**

2-06 **10** nk **Eternal Luck (IRE)**[48] 1584 3-9-0 **82**........(p) PhilipRobinson 8 62
(M A Jarvis) *chsd ldrs: n.m.r and lost pl over 6f out: rdn over 2f out: wknd over 1f out* **10/1**

1m 43.35s (-2.05) **Going Correction** -0.35s/f (Firm) **10** Ran SP% **119.7**
Speed ratings (Par 103): **103,102,99,99,97 96,95,91,89,89**
CSF £12.96 CT £39.33 TOTE £3.00: £1.50, £1.80, £1.80; EX 8.30.
Owner K Abdulla **Bred** Juddmonte Farms Ltd **Trained** Beckhampton, Wilts

FOCUS
A decent little handicap run at a good pace and the front pair pulled clear, suggesting they are both above average. Form to take fairly positively.

NOTEBOOK
Scuffle ◆, making her handicap debut after winning her maiden in good style over course and distance last month, saw plenty of daylight on the outside of the field. Nonetheless, she quickened up nicely and though she was hard pressed by the runner-up late and only just held on, this was a good effort and she should continue to improve. (op 5-4 tchd 15-8)
Lindelaan(USA) ◆, making her handicap debut in a first-time visor over the longest trip she has attempted, came from further back than the winner and her strong late effort down the wide outside only just failed. There should be a race like this waiting for her off this sort of mark. (op 9-2)
Silver Rime(FR) was always up with the pace, but lacked the pace to go with the front pair late on. He was disappointing when tried over 1m2f last time, but that may have been down to racing too keenly rather than lack of stamina and he may be worth another try over that trip. (op 11-2 tchd 6-1)
Upton Grey(IRE), a springer in the market, raced keenly up with the pace but lacked the speed to go with the front pair. He may not want the ground as fast as this. (op 20-1)
Toto Skyllachy, given a positive ride, was given no peace by Arctic Cape and that eventually found him out. He may be best over a shorter trip on easier ground. (op 10-1)
King Hafhafah, making his turf debut after four outings on Polytrack, did not look at all happy amongst horses down the home straight and may not have liked this quick ground. (op 66-1)
Mekong Melody(IRE) Official explanation: jcokey said filly hung left
Eternal Luck(IRE) Official explanation: jcokey said gelding was unsuited by the good to firm ground

2954 PADDOCKS CONFERENCE CENTRE AT NOTTINGHAM RACECOURSE MAIDEN STKS (DIV I) 1m 75y
3:40 (3:41) (Class 5) 3-Y-0+ **£2,428** (£722; £361; £180) **Stalls** Centre

Form RPR

03-4 **1** **Tourist**[12] 2571 3-9-0 75........ WilliamBuick 5 80
(B W Hills) *trckd ldrs: hdwy over 3f out: rdn to chal wl over 1f out: drvn ins fnl f: styd on to ld nr fin* **10/3**[2]

43-2 **2** hd **Tatbeeq (IRE)**[24] 2221 3-8-9 73........ RHills 6 75
(M A Jarvis) *led: rdn along 2f out: drvn ent fnl f: hdd and no ex nr fin* **7/4**[1]

6- **3** 4 **Robert Burns (IRE)**[225] 6571 3-9-0 0........ JimmyFortune 7 71+
(J H M Gosden) *trckd ldrs: hdwy on outer 3f out: rdn to chal wl over 1f out and ev ch tl hung lft and one pce ins fnl f* **8/1**

4 1 ¾ **Dawnhill (GER)** 4-9-11 0........ KerrinMcEvoy 2 70+
(J R Fanshawe) *s.i.s and bhd: hdwy 3f out: styd on wl appr fnl f: nrst fin* **11/1**

6-5 **5** ½ **Ascot Lime**[49] 1573 3-9-0 0........ RyanMoore 11 66+
(Sir Michael Stoute) *stdd s and hld up in rr tl styd on wl fnl 2f: nvr nr ldrs* **4/1**[3]

4 **6** ¾ **Addiena**[16] 2449 4-9-6 0........ CatherineGannon 3 62
(B Palling) *chsd ldrs: rdn along 3f out: drvn and grad wknd fnl 2f* **16/1**

0 **7** ½ **Into The Light**[19] 2380 3-9-0 0........ StephenDonohoe 9 63
(E S McMahon) *towards rr: hdwy on inner over 2f out: sn rdn and kpt on appr fnl f: nrst fin* **50/1**

0 **8** 1 ¾ **Bramalea**[11] 2612 3-8-9 0........ TPQueally 8 54
(B W Duke) *chsd ldr: rdn along over 3f out: drvn over 2f out and sn wknd* **40/1**

6 **9** 4 **Trireme (IRE)**[12] 2571 4-9-6 0........ JackMitchell(5) 14 53
(K A Morgan) *s.i.s: a in rr* **100/1**

6- **10** 5 **Toballa**[175] 7181 3-8-9 0........(t) MickyFenton 10 33
(H J Collingridge) *s.i.s: a in rr* **100/1**

00 **11** 1 ¾ **Travelling Light (USA)**[37] 1854 3-8-9 0........ SteveDrowne 1 29
(R Charlton) *a towards rr* **20/1**

0-00 **12** 16 **Charlie Green (IRE)**[98] 803 3-9-0 41........(t) StephenCarson 12 —
(Paul Green) *s.i.s: a in rr* **100/1**

1m 45.17s (-0.23) **Going Correction** -0.35s/f (Firm)
WFA 3 from 4yo 11lb **12** Ran SP% **116.9**
Speed ratings (Par 103): **94,93,89,88,87 86,86,84,80,75 73,57**
CSF £9.08 TOTE £4.20: £1.30, £1.10, £2.10; EX 9.20.
Owner K Abdulla **Bred** Juddmonte Farms Ltd **Trained** Lambourn, Berks

FOCUS
The form horses fought out the finish and were nicely clear of some promising, if modest, sorts. It was the faster of the two divisions and the form is pretty solid, if ordinary.
Ascot Lime Official explanation: jockey said colt was unsuited by the good to firm ground.

2955 PADDOCKS CONFERENCE CENTRE AT NOTTINGHAM RACECOURSE MAIDEN STKS (DIV II) 1m 75y
4:10 (4:11) (Class 5) 3-Y-0+ **£2,428** (£722; £361; £180) **Stalls** Centre

Form RPR

53 **1** **Acrostic**[37] 1876 3-9-0 0........ NickyMackay 8 83+
(L M Cumani) *trckd ldrs: led over 1f out: shkn up and edgd lft ins fnl f: r.o* **2/1**[2]

2 1 **Alsace Lorraine (IRE)** 3-8-9 0........ KerrinMcEvoy 3 75+
(J R Fanshawe) *chsd ldrs: rdn over 1f out: r.o* **13/2**

025- **3** 1 ½ **Moville (IRE)**[273] 5321 3-9-0 83........ WilliamBuick 11 77
(B W Hills) *trckd ldr: rdn and ev ch over 1f out: edgd lft and no ex ins fnl f* **15/8**[1]

4 1 ¼ **Gifted Leader (USA)** 3-9-0 0........ ShaneKelly 9 74+
(Pat Eddery) *s.s: hld up: hdwy over 2f out: rdn over 1f out: styd on* **6/1**[3]

0 **5** 3 **Soviet (IRE)**[19] 2360 3-9-0 0........ JoeFanning 12 67
(M Johnston) *sn led: rdn over 2f out: hung lft and hdd over 1f out: wknd ins fnl f* **16/1**

00 **6** 4 **Battling Lil (IRE)**[14] 2509 4-9-3 0........ TolleyDean(3) 5 56
(J L Spearing) *hld up in tch: rdn over 3f out: wknd over 1f out* **33/1**

7 5 **Liberally (IRE)** 3-8-9 0........ RichardHughes 13 42+
(B J Meehan) *dwlt and rdr lost irons s: a in rr: wknd over 2f out* **12/1**

0 **8** 1 **Wivny (USA)**[25] 2198 3-8-9 0........ StephenDonohoe 7 39
(P A Blockley) *s.s: a in rr: wknd over 2f out* **50/1**

1m 46.77s (1.37) **Going Correction** -0.35s/f (Firm)
WFA 3 from 4yo 11lb **8** Ran SP% **114.2**
Speed ratings (Par 103): **86,85,83,82,79 75,70,69**
CSF £15.55 TOTE £2.60: £1.30, £2.10, £1.10; EX 15.20.
Owner L Marinopoulos **Bred** Mrs B A Matthews **Trained** Newmarket, Suffolk
■ Stewards' Enquiry : Nicky Mackay two-day ban: careless riding (Jun 25-26)

FOCUS
A very moderate winning time and by far the slowest of the three races over the trip at the meeting. Ordinary form, with the third the best guide. There were five non-runners because of the fast ground.

2956 CARLTON ROAD FILLIES' H'CAP 1m 2f 50y
4:40 (4:48) (Class 5) (0-75,73) 3-Y-0 **£3,238** (£963; £481; £240) **Stalls** Low

Form RPR

0-06 **1** **Houri (IRE)**[30] 2043 3-9-2 **68**........(p) AdamKirby 3 76+
(R M Beckett) *chsd ldrs: rdn along 3f out: drvn wl over 1f out: squeezed through ent fnl f: styd on to ld fnl 75yds* **9/1**

04-0 **2** nk **Stormy View (USA)**[20] 2328 3-9-4 **70**........ JimmyFortune 10 76+
(J H M Gosden) *hld up towards rr: hdwy over 2f out: swtchd rt and rdn over 1f out: drvn to chal ins fnl f and ev ch tl no ex towards fin* **5/2**[1]

03-4 **3** ¾ **Gingham**[27] 2123 3-9-7 **73**........ DaneO'Neill 15 77+
(L M Cumani) *hld up: hdwy 3f out: rdn over 1f out: styd on to ld jst ins fnl f: drvn: hdd and no ex fnl 75yds* **3/1**[2]

-240 **4** 2 ¼ **Milanollo**[14] 2495 3-8-12 **64**........ TPQueally 13 64
(M L W Bell) *trckd ldrs: hdwy 3f out: led wl over 1f out: sn rdn and hdd jst ins fnl f: kpt on same pce* **11/1**

6-00 **5** hd **Alseraaj (USA)**[32] 2015 3-9-6 **72**........(t) RHills 2 71
(Sir Michael Stoute) *dwlt: sn prom: hdwy to ld wl over 2f out: rdn: hung lft and hdd wl over 1f out: wknd* **8/1**[3]

4300 **6** ½ **Geestring (IRE)**[12] 2564 3-9-5 **71**........(b[1]) IanMongan 8 69
(R Hannon) *led: rdn along 3f out: sn hdd: drvn and wkng whn sltly hmpd ent fnl f* **14/1**

10-0 **7** 3 ¾ **Suzi Spends (IRE)**[9] 2665 3-9-7 **73**........ MickyFenton 9 64
(H J Collingridge) *in rr: hdwy on outer 3f out: rdn and ch whn rdr dropped whip over 1f out: wknd* **12/1**

5-50 **8** 1 3/4 **Jelly Mo**[27] 2118 3-8-11 63 ... DO'Donohoe 4 50
(J W Hills) *s.i.s and bhd: hdwy over 2f out: styng on whn hmpd wl over 1f out: nvr a factor* **20/1**

554- **9** 1/2 **Astania**[252] 5912 3-9-7 73 ... DarryllHolland 6 59
(P W D'Arcy) *chsd ldr: rdn along over 3f out: hung rt and wknd wl over 1f out* **8/1**[3]

5160 **10** 2 1/4 **Princess Livius (IRE)**[32] 2014 3-8-13 65 ... StephenDonohoe 12 47
(P A Blockley) *a in rr* **33/1**

563- **11** 18 **Flop (IRE)**[321] 3884 3-8-11 63 ... JimmyQuinn 7 9
(M Brittain) *midfield: rdn along over 4f out and sn wknd* **16/1**

2m 10.75s (-1.75) **Going Correction** -0.35s/f (Firm) **11** Ran SP% **122.1**
Speed ratings (Par 96): **99,98,98,96,96 95,92,91,91,89 74**
CSF £32.97 CT £87.90 TOTE £11.00: £2.80, £1.90, £1.30; EX 45.30.
Owner Mrs David Aykroyd **Bred** C H Wacker Iii **Trained** Whitsbury, Hants
■ Stewards' Enquiry : Adam Kirby caution: careless riding

FOCUS
An ordinary fillies' handicap and the winning time was about what you would expect, despite being significantly faster than the following handicap for older horses. There is better to come from the first thee, all of whom are relatively unexposed.
Houri(IRE) ◆ Official explanation: trainer's rep said, regarding the apparent improvement in form, filly appeared to have benefitted from the sheepskin cheek-pieces
Suzi Spends(IRE) Official explanation: jockey said filly hung left-handed

2957 BEST RACECOURSES ON TURFTV H'CAP — 1m 2f 50y
5:10 (5:10) (Class 6) (0-60,62) 4-Y-0+ — **£2,047** (£604; £302) **Stalls** Low

Form — RPR

5-31 **1** **Eijaaz (IRE)**[18] 2395 7-8-13 55 ... DO'Donohoe 15 62+
(G A Harker) *hld up: hdwy over 1f out: r.o to ld wl ins fnl f* **10/1**

4546 **2** 1/2 **Lunar River (FR)**[10] 2640 5-8-13 55 ... (t) AdamKirby 14 61
(David Pinder) *hld up in tch: led over 2f out: rdn and hdd wl ins fnl f* **12/1**

3124 **3** 1 **Our Kes (IRE)**[17] 2423 6-9-4 60 ... IanMongan 8 64
(P Howling) *hld up in tch: rdn over 2f out: styd on* **7/1**[3]

00-0 **4** 1 **Dr Light (IRE)**[32] 2001 4-8-12 54 ... LeeEnstone 11 56
(M A Peill) *hld up: swtchd rt and hdwy over 1f out: r.o: nt rch ldrs* **40/1**

000- **5** hd **Faith And Reason (USA)**[177] 5514 5-8-13 55 ... TPQueally 13 57
(A P Stringer) *hld up in tch: rdn over 2f out: hung lft over 1f out: no ex ins fnl f* **10/1**

-040 **6** 1 **Fossgate**[81] 963 7-9-0 56 ... PhilipRobinson 7 56
(J D Bethell) *chsd ldrs: rdn and ev ch over 2f out: no ex fnl f* **11/2**[2]

0034 **7** 1 1/4 **Libre**[14] 2510 8-9-1 57 ... TGMcLaughlin 10 54
(F Jordan) *hld up: hdwy over 1f out: no imp fnl f* **17/2**

5550 **8** 1 **Parkview Love (USA)**[11] 2597 7-9-0 59 ow1 ... LeeVickers(3) 9 54
(J G Given) *s.i.s: hld up: hdwy 4f out: rdn and nt clr run over 1f out: styd on same pce* **20/1**

-006 **9** 1/2 **Bright Sun (IRE)**[15] 2487 7-9-2 58 ... KimTinkler 4 52
(N Tinkler) *plld hrd: led after 1f: rdn and hdd over 2f out: wknd ins fnl f* **25/1**

-600 **10** 1/2 **Scutch Mill (IRE)**[14] 2274 6-8-6 55 ... (t) PatrickDonaghy(7) 16 48
(P C Haslam) *hld up: hdwy over 2f out: wknd fnl f* **14/1**

5101 **11** 1 **Jarvo**[14] 2513 7-9-1 57 ... (v) PatrickMathers 2 48
(I W McInnes) *chsd ldrs: rdn over 2f out: wknd over 1f out* **12/1**

0441 **12** 1 1/4 **King Of Connacht**[40] 1776 5-8-7 56 ... (p) SamuelDrury(7) 3 45
(M Wellings) *prom: racd keenly: lost pl over 3f out: n.d after* **9/2**[1]

0-60 **13** 1 1/4 **Distant Pleasure**[11] 2597 4-9-0 56 ... StephenDonohoe 6 42
(M Dods) *hld up in tch: rdn over 2f out: wknd over 1f out* **8/1**

000 **14** 3 1/2 **Passato (GER)**[121] 526 4-8-12 57 ... KevinGhunowa(3) 5 36
(R A Harris) *led 1f: chsd ldr tl rdn over 2f out: wknd over 1f out* **22/1**

2m 12.97s (0.47) **Going Correction** -0.35s/f (Firm) **14** Ran SP% **123.3**
Speed ratings (Par 101): **90,89,88,88,87 87,86,85,84,84 83,82,81,78**
CSF £121.75 CT £911.55 TOTE £8.20: £2.30, £5.30, £2.30; EX 246.20 Place 6: £11.23, Place 5 £4.00..
Owner A S Ward **Bred** Shadwell Estate Company Limited **Trained** Thirkleby, N Yorks

FOCUS
A moderate handicap and they went no pace early whch resulted in a slow winning time, 2.22 seconds slower than the preceding three-year-old fillies' handicap. The winner is possibly worth a bit more than the bare form, which is very moderate.
T/Jkpt: £49,210.50 to a £1 stake. Pool: £1,178,279.88. 17.00 winning tickets. T/Plt: £16.40 to a £1 stake. Pool: £82,712.11. 3,671.55 winning tickets. T/Qpdt: £1.70 to a £1 stake. Pool: £3,876.50. 1,604.10 winning tickets. JR

2958 - 2960a (Foreign Racing) - See Raceform Interactive

2736 LEOPARDSTOWN (L-H)
Wednesday, June 11
OFFICIAL GOING: Good to firm

2961a BALLYCORUS STKS (GROUP 3) — 7f
7:30 (7:31) 3-Y-0+ — **£33,455** (£9,779; £4,632; £1,544)

RPR

1 **Summit Surge (IRE)**[18] 2419 4-9-9 109 ... (t) KLatham 6 110
(G M Lyons, Ire) *chsd ldrs: 4th 1/2-way: wd ent st: rdn into 3rd 1f out: kpt on wl to ld cl home* **6/1**

2 1 1/4 **Great War Eagle (USA)**[37] 1879 3-8-13 106 ... WMLordan 2 102
(David Wachman, Ire) *sn led: rdn over 1f out: kpt on wl: hdd cl home* **5/1**[3]

3 1 **Prince Shaun (IRE)**[21] 2316 3-8-13 104 ... FMBerry 8 99
(Patrick J Flynn, Ire) *sn settled bhd ldrs: 5th 1/2-way: rdn into 2nd 1 1/2f out: no ex under 1f out: kpt on same pce* **7/2**[1]

4 nk **Captain Marvelous (IRE)**[11] 2637 4-9-9 ... MichaelHills 4 102
(B W Hills) *chsd ldrs: 3rd 1/2-way: rdn into 2nd 2f out: no ex in 4th 1f out: kpt on same pce* **9/2**[2]

5 shd **Excelerate (IRE)**[31] 2026 5-9-9 107 ... CDHayes 5 102
(Edward Lynam, Ire) *hld up in rr: wd ent st: 7th over 1f out: kpt on fnl f* **6/1**

6 nk **Akua'Ba (IRE)**[7] 2740 4-9-6 99 ... (tp) KJManning 1 98
(J S Bolger, Ire) *mid-div: 6th 1/2-way: rdn 2f out: kpt on same pce* **10/1**

7 1 1/4 **Campfire Glow (IRE)**[7] 2738 3-9-1 106 ... (b[1]) PJSmullen 7 96
(D K Weld, Ire) *towards rr: rdn and no imp 2f out* **11/2**

8 3 **Rock Of Rochelle (USA)**[59] 1356 3-8-13 101 ... (t) RPCleary 3 85
(A Kinsella, Ire) *sn chsd ldr: 2nd 1/2-way: rdn in 3rd 2f out: sn no ex and wknd* **14/1**

1m 26.49s (-3.81) **Going Correction** -0.425s/f (Firm)
WFA 3 from 4yo+ 10lb **8** Ran SP% **116.8**
Speed ratings: **104,102,101,101,100 100,99,95**
CSF £36.75 TOTE £6.40: £2.10, £2.00, £1.70; DF 34.10.
Owner W Bellew **Bred** Norelands Bloodstock **Trained** Dunsany, Co. Meath

NOTEBOOK
Summit Surge(IRE), a winner in handicap company 18 days previously, found a ready turn of foot to settle the issue at the business end and follow up in this hotter company. He may not have had to really improve to take this, but is in top form at present and is versatile as regards his best trip. (op 11/2)
Great War Eagle(USA) had every chance from the front, but was a sitting duck for the winner inside the final furlong. He had the tongue tie left off for this this and ran close enough to his recent level in defeat. (op 4/1)
Prince Shaun(IRE) looked a big player nearing the final furlong pole, but his effort proved one paced when it really mattered. He was below his mark here, but still performed creditably and the best of this gelding has probably still to be seen. (op 4/1 tchd 100/30)
Captain Marvelous(IRE) was not disgraced under his penalty, but never seriously looked like doing the business. This was more like is true form. (op 5/1)

2962 - 2964a (Foreign Racing) - See Raceform Interactive

2605 HAYDOCK (L-H)
Thursday, June 12
OFFICIAL GOING: Good to firm (8.5)
Wind: almost nil Weather: fine

2965 SUPPLY UK HIRE SHOPS MAIDEN CLAIMING STKS — 5f
2:30 (2:34) (Class 5) 2-Y-0 — **£2,590** (£770; £385; £192) **Stalls** Centre

Form — RPR

1 **Missus Christie** 2-8-3 0 ... DO'Donohoe 1 60
(N Tinkler) *chsd ldrs: pushed along 3f out: led 2f out: pushed clr ins fnl f* **14/1**[3]

643 **2** 3 **Lady Fantasie**[13] 2574 2-8-5 0 ... RoystonFfrench 2 51
(Mrs A Duffield) *led: hdd 2f out: rdn over 1f out: edgd rt whn no ex wl ins fnl f* **2/1**[1]

0 **3** 1 1/4 **Just Five (IRE)**[34] 1967 2-9-0 0 ... TomEaves 6 56
(M Dods) *towards rr: sn outpcd: styd on fr 1f out: nt pce to trble ldrs* **25/1**

3555 **4** 1 1/4 **Kings House**[13] 2581 2-8-6 0 ... DaleGibson 8 43
(M W Easterby) *chsd ldrs: pushed along 2f out: outpcd over 1f out: edgd lft ins fnl f: plugged on at one pce after* **7/2**[2]

344 **5** 1/2 **Rioja Ruby (IRE)**[10] 2671 2-7-12 0 ow3 ... (b[1]) PatrickDonaghy(7) 3 40
(P C Haslam) *w ldr: rdn over 1f out: u.p whn hung lft ent fnl f: sn wknd* **2/1**[1]

6 5 **Keen Rabbit** 2-8-1 0 ow1 ... AndrewElliott 4 18
(Micky Hammond) *a towards rr: sn outpcd* **20/1**

00 **7** 1/2 **Naughty Natz**[33] 2004 2-8-0 0 ow2 ... (p) FrankieMcDonald 7 16
(P T Midgley) *awkward s: pushed along and a outpcd* **20/1**

62.12 secs (1.62) **Going Correction** +0.10s/f (Good) **7** Ran SP% **108.9**
Speed ratings (Par 93): **91,86,84,82,81 73,72**
CSF £38.42 TOTE £9.30: £4.00, £1.30; EX 29.30.The winner was claimed by Ian Williams for £8,000.
Owner Mrs Janis Macpherson **Bred** Llety Stud **Trained** Langton, N Yorks

FOCUS
A very modest event.

NOTEBOOK
Missus Christie, who is out of a 5f winner, is a sister to winning sprinters Apollo Five and Mister Christie. Making her debut at a lowly level, she came under pressure before halfway and ran a little green once in front, but still came clear for a fairly comfortable success. She was claimed. (op 10-1 tchd 9-1)
Lady Fantasie, having her fourth start, looks exposed now. After making the running, she proved no match when headed by the winner but stuck on for second. (op 15-8 tchd 85-40 in a place)
Just Five(IRE) is out of an unraced daughter of Coronation Stakes winner Gold Splash. He showed nothing on his debut a month previously but there was more to like about this effort, as he eventually grasped what was needed in the latter part of the contest and stayed on from the back of the field for third. (op 8-1)
Kings House is fully exposed as a low-level performer and has already been beaten in a seller. (op 5-1 tchd 3-1)
Rioja Ruby(IRE) was blinkered for the first time on this drop back in trip. She showed decent pace again, but once coming off the bridle she hung across the track and finished well held. (op 5-2 tchd 11-4 in a place)

2966 BALFOUR BEATTY UTILITY SOLUTIONS MAIDEN STKS — 6f
3:00 (3:07) (Class 5) 3-Y-0+ — **£2,590** (£770; £385; £192) **Stalls** Centre

Form — RPR

3-2 **1** **Muhajaar (IRE)**[12] 2620 3-9-2 0 ... PatCosgrave 16 85+
(L M Cumani) *a.p: led wl over 1f out: pushed out and r.o wl fnl f* **15/8**[1]

3 **2** 1 3/4 **Without Prejudice (USA)**[18] 2427 3-9-2 0 ... ShaneKelly 4 79+
(J Noseda) *midfield: tk t.k.h and stdd after 2f: towards rr: nt clr run over 2f out: swtchd rt and hdwy over 1f out: edgd lft and styd on to take 2nd wl ins fnl f: nt trble wnr* **5/2**[2]

32-6 **3** 1 1/4 **Provence**[34] 1960 3-8-11 82 ... MichaelHills 9 70
(B W Hills) *midfield: rdn and hdwy to chse ldrs over 1f out: styd on: nt pce to chal ldrs towards fin* **4/1**[3]

0 **4** 1 1/4 **Beat The Bell**[68] 1215 3-9-2 0 ... FrancisNorton 17 71
(A Bailey) *a.p: chal over 1f out: rdn ins fnl f: no ex* **40/1**

60 **5** 4 1/2 **Charlie Allnut**[26] 2187 3-9-2 0 ... DarrenWilliams 5 57
(K R Burke) *bhd: rdn and hdwy over 1f out: styd on fnl f: nvr gng pce to be competitive* **33/1**

2- **6** shd **Royal Degree**[118] 3-9-2 0 ... TomEaves 2 56
(B Smart) *led: rdn and hdd wl over 1f out: wknd fnl f* **8/1**

45-0 **7** 2 1/4 **Cranworth Blaze**[33] 2008 4-9-2 45 ... (b) PJMcDonald(3) 6 46
(T J Etherington) *bmpd s: bhd: styd on fnl f: nt pce to chal* **200/1**

8 nk **Billy Bowmore** 3-9-2 0 ... TonyHamilton 14 48
(M Dods) *s.i.s: midfield: rdn 2f out: no hdwy* **33/1**

3 **9** nk **Hardanger (IRE)**[20] 2380 3-8-13 0 ... JamieMoriarty(3) 7 47
(T J Fitzgerald) *racd keenly: chsd ldrs: outpcd 1/2-way: no imp after* **12/1**

0350 **10** 1 1/4 **Johnston's Glory (IRE)**[17] 2448 4-9-5 57 ... (b) WJSupple 12 40
(E J Alston) *midfield: hdwy to chse ldrs 1/2-way: rdn over 1f out: fdd fnl f* **33/1**

11 3/4 **Nizhoni (USA)** 3-8-11 0 ... RoystonFfrench 1 36
(B Smart) *missed break: sn in midfield: hdwy 2f out: rdn over 1f out: sn wknd* **33/1**

0600 **12** 4 1/2 **Wee Ellie Coburn**[16] 2491 4-9-5 37 ... (be) TWilliams 3 23
(M Mullineaux) *prom tl rdn and wknd over 2f out* **200/1**

13 1 3/4 **Lydia's Legacy** 3-8-11 0 ... GregFairley 11 16
(T J Etherington) *missed break: a towards rr* **100/1**

0-5 **14** 3/4 **Noche De Reyes**[37] 1894 3-9-2 0 ... DavidAllan 10 18
(E J Alston) *chsd ldrs to 1/2-way: outpcd after* **66/1**

15 3 3/4 **Braille** 3-9-2 0 ... RobertWinston 15 6
(T D Walford) *edgy in stalls: s.i.s: midfield: rdn and wknd over 1f out* **25/1**

005- **16** *24* **Joint Agency (IRE)**[250] 6023 3-8-11 45..................... DanielTudhope 13 —
(N Wilson) *edgy in stalls: handy tl wknd 1/2-way: eased fnl f* **100/1**

1m 14.68s (0.68) **Going Correction** +0.10s/f (Good)
WFA 3 from 4yo 8lb **16** Ran SP% **124.7**
Speed ratings (Par 103): **99,96,95,93,87 87,84,83,83,81 80,74,72,71,66 34**
CSF £6.22 TOTE £2.60: £1.40, £1.70, £2.00; EX 8.80.

Owner Jaber Abdullah **Bred** Gainsborough Stud Management Ltd **Trained** Newmarket, Suffolk

FOCUS
The form horses finished to the fore in this sprint maiden but the form looks only ordinary.
Without Prejudice(USA) Official explanation: jockey said colt ran too free in the early stages and was hampered in running
Provence Official explanation: vet said filly was struck into and required stitches
Braille Official explanation: jockey said gelding hit its head several times on the stalls

2967 EBF WATERAID H'CAP — 6f
3:35 (3:36) (Class 3) (0-95,90) 3-Y-O **£9,714** (£2,890; £1,444; £721) **Stalls** Centre

Form — RPR

-541 **1** **Novellen Lad (IRE)**[23] 2282 3-8-8 75..................... WJSupple 9 82
(E J Alston) *midfield: hdwy over 2f out: r.o to ld wl ins fnl f* **8/1**

-051 **2** *hd* **Rubirosa (IRE)**[14] 2526 3-9-2 83..................... FergalLynch 12 89
(M Dods) *midfield: rdn and hdwy over 1f out: edgd lft ent fnl f: str chal after: r.o* **10/1**

0-02 **3** *nk* **Spanish Bounty**[27] 2162 3-9-8 89..................... TomEaves 5 94
(J G Portman) *led: rdn over 1f out: hdd wl ins fnl f: hld fnl strides* **25/1**

1324 **4** *1* **Sparton Duke (IRE)**[13] 2575 3-8-11 78.....................(p) RobertWinston 8 82+
(K A Ryan) *rdr briefly lost iron s: rdn and hdwy over 1f out: running on and gaining on ldrs whn n.m.r and snatched up fnl strides* **14/1**

5-01 **5** *2 1/2* **Aye Aye Digby (IRE)**[33] 1999 3-9-9 90..................... IanMongan 7 84
(H Candy) *prom: rdn over 2f out: hung lft over 1f out: no ex ins fnl f* **4/1**[2]

2-35 **6** *1* **Rash Judgement**[27] 2171 3-9-7 88..................... FergusSweeney 10 79
(W S Kittow) *racd keenly in midfield: rdn over 1f out: one pce ins fnl f* **3/1**[1]

4-06 **7** *3* **Irving Place**[35] 1925 3-8-9 76..................... TonyHamilton 4 57
(R A Fahey) *hld up: pushed along 2f out: styd on fnl f: nvr trbld ldrs* **33/1**

-144 **8** *1 1/4* **Mey Blossom**[15] 2498 3-9-5 89..................... MichaelJStainton(3) 1 66
(R M Whitaker) *in tch: rdn and wknd over 2f out* **16/1**

130- **9** *3/4* **Sam's Cross (IRE)**[229] 6488 3-9-6 87..................... AndrewElliott 6 62
(K R Burke) *racd keenly: chsd ldrs: rdn and lost pl 2f out: wkng whn hung lft over 1f out* **8/1**

-604 **10** *1 1/4* **Ramatni**[19] 2405 3-9-2 83.....................(b[1]) GregFairley 2 54
(M Johnston) *prom tl rdn and wknd over 1f out* **18/1**

005- **11** *1/2* **Monaazalah (IRE)**[225] 6588 3-9-0 81..................... MichaelHills 3 50
(B W Hills) *racd keenly in midfield: effrt 2f out: no imp whn carried lft over 1f out: wl btn after* **25/1**

21- **12** *7* **Messias Da Silva (USA)**[227] 6544 3-9-3 84.....................(t) ShaneKelly 11 31
(J Noseda) *hld up: pushed along 2f out: eased whn n.d 1f out* **7/1**[3]

1m 14.03s (0.03) **Going Correction** +0.10s/f (Good) **12** Ran SP% **117.3**
Speed ratings (Par 103): **103,102,102,101,97 96,92,90,89,88 87,78**
CSF £82.66 CT £1938.54 TOTE £10.30: £3.10, £4.20, £6.80; EX 100.70.

Owner Con Harrington **Bred** Mrs Chris Harrington **Trained** Longton, Lancs

FOCUS
A decent sprint handicap in which they raced down the centre but the gallop was not that strong. The form is sound enough although not as strong as it might have been with the placed horses pretty exposed.

NOTEBOOK
Novellen Lad(IRE), put up 6lb for his win at Musselburgh, followed up over this furlong-shorter trip. He travelled well in touch and ran on strongly once finding his full stride, getting there close home. On the upgrade, he will be suited by a stiffer gallop at this trip. (op 11-1)
Rubirosa(IRE), whose win in an uncompetitive event at Ayr saw him raised 3lb, was held up in midfield. He made good progress to challenge inside the last, perhaps even putting his head in front before succumbing late on. (op 14-1)
Spanish Bounty made a bold attempt to lead throughout and only gave way well inside the final furlong. This confirms his good effort at Newmarket was no fluke. (op 22-1)
Sparton Duke(IRE), back down in trip, had plenty to do entering the latter stages but began to pick up inside the last and would have finished a bit closer to the first three had he not been tightened up near the finish. This was his best run so far on turf. (op 10-1)
Aye Aye Digby(IRE), put up 7lb for his win at Nottingham a month ago, could not confirm that form on the revised terms with today's runner-up. (op 9-2)
Rash Judgement, whos has been climbing the handicap this term without winning, failed to settle on this return to 6f and could never really make his presence felt. (op 4-1)
Messias Da Silva(USA) Official explanation: jockey said filly lost action

2968 GALLAGHER LTD H'CAP — 6f
4:10 (4:10) (Class 5) (0-75,75) 4-Y-O+ **£2,590** (£770; £385; £192) **Stalls** Centre

Form — RPR

4623 **1** **Timber Treasure (USA)**[20] 2356 4-9-1 67.....................(b) FrancisNorton 15 83
(Paul Green) *trckd ldrs: led over 1f out: r.o wl and in command ins fnl f* **10/3**[1]

6006 **2** *3 1/2* **Steel Blue**[3] 2891 8-8-9 61..................... KShea 3 66
(R M Whitaker) *in tch: rdn over 1f out: styd on to take 2nd wl ins fnl f: nt pce to trble wnr* **15/2**[2]

00-0 **3** *3/4* **John Keats**[33] 2005 5-9-2 68..................... DanielTudhope 2 71
(J S Goldie) *bhd: rdn and hdwy to chse ldrs over 1f out: styd on same pce ins fnl f* **12/1**

00-6 **4** *nk* **Peter Island (FR)**[20] 2351 5-9-3 69.....................(v) FergusSweeney 11 71
(J Gallagher) *led: rdn and hdd over 1f out: kpt on same pce ins fnl f* **8/1**[3]

0333 **5** *1* **Poppy's Rose**[24] 2251 4-9-0 66..................... FergalLynch 10 64
(I W McInnes) *prom: rdn and edgd lft over 1f out: no ex ins fnl f* **8/1**[3]

00-0 **6** *2* **Hypnotic**[14] 2533 6-9-1 67..................... AdrianTNicholls 8 59
(D Nicholls) *bhd: rdn and hdwy over 1f out: styd on wl fnl f: nt rch ldrs: one to nte* **25/1**

100 **7** *1 1/2* **Cheery Cat (USA)**[7] 2751 4-8-11 63.....................(p) TonyHamilton 13 50
(D W Barker) *midfield: pushed along 1/2-way: one pce fnl f* **15/2**[2]

-000 **8** *4 1/2* **Rasaman (IRE)**[16] 2489 4-9-6 72..................... DO'Donohoe 16 45
(K A Ryan) *in tch: effrt over 1f out: no imp fnl f* **10/1**

0030 **9** *nk* **Nordic Light (USA)**[6] 2798 4-9-3 69.....................(b) StephenDonohoe 14 41
(J M Bradley) *bhd: u.p over 1f out: nvr trbld ldrs* **33/1**

0-00 **10** *1 1/4* **Gwilym (GER)**[35] 1928 5-9-4 70..................... RobertWinston 4 38
(D Haydn Jones) *prom: rdn 2f out: wknd over 1f out* **12/1**

0-20 **11** *1* **Fantasy Parkes**[19] 2406 4-9-9 75..................... WJSupple 5 40
(E J Alston) *midfield: pushed along 1/2-way: wknd over 1f out* **14/1**

/000 **12** *nk* **Tadlil**[6] 2798 6-8-11 63.....................(b[1]) ShaneKelly 12 27
(J M Bradley) *midfield: pushed along 1/2-way: sn outpcd* **33/1**

016- **13** *28* **Zamalik (USA)**[269] 5489 5-8-13 65..................... RoystonFfrench 6 —
(Mrs A Duffield) *prom tl rdn and wknd 2f out* **9/1**

1m 13.8s (-0.20) **Going Correction** +0.10s/f (Good) **13** Ran SP% **119.7**
Speed ratings (Par 103): **105,100,99,98,97 94,92,86,86,84 83,83,45**
CSF £26.68 CT £277.69 TOTE £3.80: £1.90, £3.20, £3.70; EX 34.20.

Owner Gary Williams **Bred** London Thoroughbred Services & Derry Meeting Farm **Trained** Lydiate, Merseyside

FOCUS
A modest handicap in which the winner could be better but there is little solid recent form amongst the placed horses.
Tadlil Official explanation: jockey said gelding hung right
Zamalik(USA) Official explanation: jockey said gelding lost action

2969 DHL EXEL H'CAP — 1m 30y
4:45 (4:45) (Class 3) (0-90,88) 4-Y-O+ **£8,095** (£2,408; £1,203; £601) **Stalls** Low

Form — RPR

-301 **1** **Farley Star**[17] 2457 4-9-6 85..................... FergusSweeney 9 96+
(R Charlton) *hld up: hdwy over 3f out: led over 1f out: r.o ins fnl f and a in command* **6/1**[3]

0051 **2** *1/2* **Obezyana (USA)**[19] 2406 6-8-10 78..................... DominicFox(3) 4 88
(A Bailey) *a.p: rdn 2f out: led briefly over 1f out: r.o ins fnl f but a looked hld* **9/2**[1]

0000 **3** *2 1/2* **Minority Report**[40] 1816 8-9-4 83..................... AdrianTNicholls 8 91+
(D Nicholls) *dwlt: bhd: swtchd rt and hdwy 2f out: swtchd lft to chse ldrs over 1f out: hld in 3rd whn eased towards fin* **12/1**

0-00 **4** *3 3/4* **Hurlingham**[13] 2582 4-8-7 72..................... DaleGibson 5 68
(M W Easterby) *in tch: effrt over 2f out: carried hd high u.p: kpt on but no imp on ldrs ins fnl f* **8/1**

0315 **5** *2 1/2* **Stoic Leader (IRE)**[2] 2913 8-8-9 74..................... RoystonFfrench 1 64
(R F Fisher) *racd keenly: trckd ldrs: rdn 3f out: wknd over 1f out* **9/1**

6120 **6** *1/2* **Crocodile Bay (IRE)**[8] 2733 5-9-9 88..................... FergalLynch 2 77
(D W Barker) *racd keenly: led: rdn and hdd over 1f out: wknd ins fnl f* **5/1**[2]

0060 **7** *2 3/4* **White Deer (USA)**[40] 1816 4-9-4 83..................... SilvestreDeSousa 6 65+
(D Nicholls) *towards rr: pushed along whn n.m.r 3f out: struggled after: eased whn n.d ins fnl f* **9/2**[1]

0052 **8** *1* **Fiefdom (IRE)**[1] 2925 6-8-5 70..................... AndrewElliott 7 50
(I W McInnes) *prom tl rdn and wknd over 2f out* **6/1**[3]

1m 44.38s (0.58) **Going Correction** -0.025s/f (Good) **8** Ran SP% **110.4**
Speed ratings (Par 107): **96,95,93,89,86 86,83,82**
CSF £30.72 CT £296.80 TOTE £3.80: £1.70, £1.80, £2.90; EX 19.50.

Owner A Parker (London) **Bred** Alan Parker **Trained** Beckhampton, Wilts

FOCUS
A decent handicap run at an ordinary pace and the form looks reasonable rated through the runner-up.

NOTEBOOK
Farley Star defied a 5lb rise for her recent win over 7f at Leicester. After coming with a sustained run to show ahead, she was always holding her nearest pursuers and gave the impression she was idling near the finish. She should continue to give a good account. (op 5-1)
Obezyana(USA) remained well treated on his old form despite being hoisted 8lb for his recent win over course and distance. Always towards the fore, he had every chance but ran into a progressive filly. (op 11-2)
Minority Report, a very useful performer for Luca Cumani last season, had shown little in four previous starts for this yard, albeit on easier ground, and had dropped 11lb in the weights in total. Led to the start, he made eyecatching progress from the back of the field in the straight, going after the two leaders when switched back towards the inner but held in third when his rider eased him close home, but for which he would have finished closer. This was an encouraging performance but he might not be one to place too much faith in. (op 6-1)
Hurlingham has fallen in the weights and ran his best race for some time, although he was well held if truth be told and did look a little unenthusiastic under pressure. (tchd 9-1)
Crocodile Bay(IRE) made the running as he likes to and tried to wind up the pace in the straight, but could not offer much resistance when headed. (op 6-1 tchd 13-2)
White Deer(USA) has dropped to an attractive mark, now a pound lower than when scoring at Thirsk a year ago for Mark Johnston, but he was never able to get into the action. Official explanation: trainer said, regarding the poor form, that gelding spread a plate at the start, ran without it and appeared to be feeling the ground (op 6-1 tchd 4-1)

2970 E C HARRIS WATERAID H'CAP — 1m 2f 120y
5:15 (5:15) (Class 4) (0-85,85) 4-Y-O+ **£5,504** (£1,637; £818; £408) **Stalls** High

Form — RPR

0013 **1** **Bull Market (IRE)**[2] 2904 5-8-11 73..................... StephenDonohoe 8 84
(Ian Williams) *hld up: hdwy 3f out: rdn to ld 2f out: a hrd pressed: hdd 100yds out: rallied to regain ld fnl strides* **4/1**[2]

4065 **2** *nk* **Suits Me**[34] 1970 5-9-4 80..................... RoystonFfrench 7 91
(T P Tate) *a.p: led over 3f out: rdn and hdd 2f out: continued to press ldr: rallied u.p to regain ld 100yds out: hdd fnl strides* **11/2**[3]

500- **3** *8* **Dar Es Salaam**[73] 6622 4-8-13 75..................... DanielTudhope 2 71
(J S Goldie) *hld up: rdn 3f out: hdwy on outside over 2f out: chsd front pair over 1f out but no imp* **18/1**

421- **4** *1 3/4* **Vanquisher (IRE)**[78] 5637 4-8-10 72..................... RobertWinston 4 65
(Ian Williams) *midfield: rdn over 3f out: hdwy to chse ldrs over 2f out: wl btn over 1f out* **9/1**

0140 **5** *1 1/2* **Gold Prospect**[14] 2531 4-9-3 79..................... MichaelHills 3 69
(M L W Bell) *dwlt: sn chsd ldrs: rdn over 2f out: wknd 1f out* **7/2**[1]

5041 **6** *12* **New Star (UAE)**[12] 2617 4-8-7 72..................... DuranFentiman(3) 5 39
(W M Brisbourne) *handy early: sn racd off pce: rdn over 3f out: n.d after* **14/1**

1-30 **7** *10* **Oddsmaker (IRE)**[47] 1625 7-8-13 82.....................(t) SophieDoyle(7) 1 30
(M A Barnes) *chsd ldrs tl rdn and wknd over 3f out* **8/1**

-010 **8** *15* **Bajan Parkes**[1] 2939 5-9-9 85..................... WJSupple 6 5
(E J Alston) *led: rdn and hdd over 3f out: wknd over 2f out* **4/1**[2]

2m 14.88s (-1.82) **Going Correction** -0.025s/f (Good) **8** Ran SP% **110.6**
Speed ratings (Par 105): **105,104,98,97,96 87,80,69**
CSF £24.40 CT £331.41 TOTE £4.50: £1.50, £2.20, £4.50; EX 30.20 Place 6: £211.33, Place 5: £93.02..

Owner Dr Marwan Koukash **Bred** King Bloodstock **Trained** Portway, Worcs

FOCUS
A fair handicap in which the first two finished well clear after a fine duel. The pace was decent and the form looks solid rated around the first two.
T/Jkpt: Not won. T/Plt: £198.60 to a £1 stake. Pool: £74,470.77. 273.70 winning tickets. T/Qpdt: £94.00 to a £1 stake. Pool: £3,050.40. 24.00 winning tickets. DO

2617 NEWBURY (L-H)

Thursday, June 12

OFFICIAL GOING: Good (good to soft in places) changing to good to soft after race 6 (4.25)

Wind: virtually nil

2971 DOYLE CLAYTON MAIDEN FILLIES' STKS (DIV I) 1m 2f 6y
1:40 (1:41) (Class 5) 3-Y-O £3,723 (£1,108; £553; £276) Stalls Low

Form RPR

0 **1** **Sevenna (FR)**[21] 2328 3-9-0 0 TedDurcan 5 85
(H R A Cecil) *hld up in rr: stdy hdwy 3f out: chsd ldr over 1f out: drvn to ld fnl 110yds: readily* **18/1**

2 1 1/4 **Caprivi (IRE)** 3-9-0 0 JimmyFortune 10 83
(J H M Gosden) *w'like: scope: bit bkwd: str: in rr tl hdwy 3f out: drvn to ld ins fnl 2f: hdd and outpcd fnl 110yds* **12/1**

3 3 3/4 **Dazzling Light (UAE)** 3-9-0 0 SteveDrowne 4 75
(R Charlton) *leggy: scope: in rr: drvn along 3f out: styd on fr over 1f out: kpt on ins fnl f but nvr any ch w ldng duo* **10/1**

22- **4** 7 **Siyabona (USA)**[233] 6411 3-9-0 0 LDettori 9 61
(Saeed Bin Suroor) *lw: trckd ldrs: drvn to chal over 2f out: sn outpcd: wknd fnl f* **2/1[1]**

0 **5** 1 1/4 **One Oak (USA)**[26] 2191 3-9-0 0 RyanMoore 3 59
(B J Meehan) *lw: in rr: rdn over 3f out: mod prog ins fnl f* **33/1**

6 **6** 1/2 **Alzaroof (USA)**[34] 1964 3-9-0 0 RHills 11 58
(E A L Dunlop) *tall: athletic: in rr: drvn along over 3f out: little rspnse tl sme hdwy fnl f* **5/2[2]**

4-6 **7** hd **La Troupe (IRE)**[13] 2560 3-9-0 0 RobertHavlin 7 57
(J H M Gosden) *lw: b.hind: chsd ldrs: wnt 2nd 4f out: chal 3f out and sn slt ld: hdd ins fnl 2f and wknd qckly* **10/1**

5- **8** 2 1/2 **Double Duty (IRE)**[245] 6130 3-9-0 0 RichardHughes 8 52
(B J Meehan) *lw: s.i.s: sn chsng ldrs: rdn 3f out: wknd 2f out* **4/1[3]**

00 **9** 2 1/4 **Poppy Gregg**[28] 2123 3-8-7 0 MatthewCosham(7) 6 48
(Dr J R J Naylor) *slowly away: rdn 5f out: a bhd* **100/1**

0 **10** 11 **Let Me Pass (USA)**[43] 1721 3-9-0 0 AlanMunro 1 26
(Jane Chapple-Hyam) *str: chsd ldr tl over 4f out: sn wknd* **100/1**

5- **11** 27 **Qasayed (USA)**[275] 5309 3-9-0 0 KerrinMcEvoy 2 —
(C E Brittain) *led: 8l clr fr 7f out to 5f out: hdd & wknd qckly ins fnl 3f* **33/1**

2m 8.44s (-0.36) **Going Correction** -0.05s/f (Good) 11 Ran SP% **120.9**
Speed ratings (Par 96): **99,98,95,89,88 88,87,85,84,75 53**
CSF £187.46 TOTE £22.50: £4.80, £2.50, £3.10; EX 247.30.
Owner Gestut Ammerland **Bred** Gestut Ittlingen & Arial Bloodstock **Trained** Newmarket, Suffolk
■ Stewards' Enquiry : R Hills one-day ban: careless riding (Jun 26)

FOCUS
Probably an average event of its type, though with Qasayed racing freely out in front at least the early pace was sound and the winning time was 1.43 seconds faster than the second division. The front pair pulled clear of the third, who in turn came right away from the rest but the level is still a little fluid.
Qasayed(USA) Official explanation: jockey said filly ran too free

2972 NEWVOICEMEDIA MAIDEN STKS 6f 8y
2:10 (2:14) (Class 4) 2-Y-O £5,828 (£1,734; £866; £432) Stalls Centre

Form RPR

1 **Sri Putra** 2-9-0 0 PhilipRobinson 4 85+
(M A Jarvis) *w'like: scope: str: chsd ldrs: led ins fnl 2f: drvn out ins fnl f* **6/1[3]**

2 **2** 1 1/2 **Noble Jack (IRE)**[12] 2601 2-9-0 0 RyanMoore 8 80
(R Hannon) *lw: chal 2f out: chsd wnr wl over 1f out: kpt on but a comf hld* **15/8[1]**

3 **3** 1 1/4 **Canwinn (IRE)**[13] 2569 2-9-0 0 EdwardCreighton 12 76
(M R Channon) *lw: chsd ldrs: rdn 2f out: styd on fnl f but no imp on ldng duo* **3/1[2]**

62 **4** 3 **Liturgical (USA)**[17] 2458 2-9-0 0 (v1) KerrinMcEvoy 15 67
(M A Magnusson) *t.k.h: led tl hdd ins fnl 2f: wknd fnl f* **16/1**

5 2 1/4 **Waahej** 2-9-0 0 RHills 11 61+
(J L Dunlop) *w'like: leggy: chsd ldrs: rdn over 2f out: wknd appr fnl f* **20/1**

24 **6** 1 1/2 **Heliodor (USA)**[39] 1832 2-9-0 0 RichardHughes 1 56+
(R Hannon) *chsd ldrs: rdn over 2f out: wknd over 1f out* **12/1**

7 2 1/2 **Smart Endeavour (USA)** 2-9-0 0 AdamKirby 10 49+
(W R Swinburn) *unf: scope: towards rr: pushed along 1/2-way: sme prog fnl f* **25/1**

8 1 1/4 **Captain Walcot** 2-9-0 0 JimmyFortune 6 45
(R Hannon) *str: bit bkwd: chsd ldrs: drvn along and green 3f out: wknd fr 2f out* **33/1**

9 hd **Pagan Force (IRE)** 2-9-0 0 JimCrowley 7 44
(Mrs A J Perrett) *w'like: str: in tch: rdn 3f out: wknd 2f out* **20/1**

0 **10** 4 1/2 **Oasis Knight (IRE)**[27] 2146 2-9-0 0 PatDobbs 3 31+
(M P Tregoning) *rdn in mid-div 1/2-way: sn btn* **66/1**

11 1 **Mons Calpe (IRE)** 2-9-0 0 TQuinn 9 28
(P F I Cole) *w'like: scope: rangy: in tch: drvn along over 3f out: wknd over 2f out* **12/1**

12 1 **My Kingdom (IRE)** 2-9-0 0 (t) SteveDrowne 2 25
(H Morrison) *w'like: scope: s.i.s: a outpcd* **20/1**

13 1 1/4 **Kyle Of Bute** 2-9-0 0 ChrisCatlin 14 21
(J L Dunlop) *leggy: bit bkwd: a outpcd* **50/1**

14 hd **Who Art Thou (USA)** 2-9-0 0 TPO'Shea 16 20
(P A Blockley) *leggy: a outpcd* **100/1**

15 hd **Supernoverre (IRE)** 2-9-0 0 TedDurcan 13 20
(Mrs A J Perrett) *w'like: bit bkwd: slowly away: a in rr* **50/1**

16 3 1/4 **Highway Magic (IRE)** 2-9-0 0 NeilPollard 5 10
(A P Jarvis) *w'like: bit bkwd: sn rdn and bhd* **100/1**

1m 14.87s (1.87) **Going Correction** -0.05s/f (Good) 16 Ran SP% **123.8**
Speed ratings (Par 95): **85,83,81,77,74 72,69,67,67,61 59,58,56,56,56 51**
CSF £16.14 TOTE £7.90: £2.40, £1.40, £1.60; EX 20.60.
Owner H R H Sultan Ahmad Shah **Bred** Glebe Stud And Partners **Trained** Newmarket, Suffolk

FOCUS
A big field for this maiden, but the winning time was moderate which does put a question mark against the form, though plenty of these are entitled to improve. The runners were inclined to come over towards the stands' rail soon after the start.

NOTEBOOK
Sri Putra ◆, a 240,000gns half-brother to the useful middle-distance performer/hurdler Duty, attracted significant market support for this debut. Racing virtually alone furthest from the stands' rail, he hit the front just after halfway and, despite hanging away to his right through greenness late on, he was always doing enough. Despite the modest time, this was a decent effort considering the placed horses already had form on the board and he should come on for it. (op 9-1 tchd 10-1)

Noble Jack(IRE), backed to confirm the promise of his Goodwood debut, had every chance but he came up against an above-average newcomer and could never quite get to him. He should be able to find a race, but may appreciate an extra furlong now. (op 7-4 tchd 2-1, 9-4 in places)

Canwinn(IRE), another that had shown ability on his debut, had his chance entering the last furlong but lacked the speed to get in an effective blow. An ordinary race should come his way sooner rather than later. (op 10-3 tchd 7-2)

Liturgical(USA), up a furlong on this third outing, bounced out of the gate and raced freely out in front against the stands' rail in the first-time visor. In view of that, he probably did well to hang in there for as long as he did, but it is debatable whether he improved much on his previous form and he lacks the scope of many of these. (op 20-1)

Waahej, a 130,000gns colt out of a half-brother to nine winners including the high-class sprinter Bolshoi, ran well for a long way and should have learnt something from this. (op 16-1 tchd 14-1)

Heliodor(USA) showed up for a while, but ran as though not seeing out the extra furlong. The way he drifted in the market beforehand was an ominous sign, but even so he is not fulfilling early promise. (op 7-1)

Smart Endeavour(USA) ◆, a $135,000 colt out of a half-sister to three winners including Moonshine Girl and Mount Hadley, was noted staying on in the latter stages without being knocked about. From a stable that tends to give its horses plenty of time, better is likely to be seen from him in due course.

2973 DOYLE CLAYTON MAIDEN FILLIES' STKS (DIV II) 1m 2f 6y
2:40 (2:43) (Class 5) 3-Y-O £3,723 (£1,108; £553; £276) Stalls Low

Form RPR

2 **1** **Ghaidaa (IRE)**[28] 2123 3-9-0 0 RHills 6 91+
(M A Jarvis) *athletic: lw: t.k.h early: chsd ldrs: led wl over 1f out: sn clr: easily* **1/2[1]**

0-62 **2** 3 1/2 **Siyasa (USA)**[8] 2716 3-9-0 0 LDettori 8 79
(Saeed Bin Suroor) *sn led: rdn and hung lft fr over 2f out: hdd wl over 1f out and sn no ch w wnr: hld on for 2nd* **6/1[2]**

3 1 1/2 **Solar Dance (USA)** 3-9-0 0 RobertHavlin 10 76+
(J H M Gosden) *w'like: str: s.i.s: in rr but in tch: drvn along over 3f out: styd on fr 2f out to take 3rd ins fnl f but nvr any ch w ldng duo* **40/1**

55- **4** 3 1/4 **Sweet Sara**[223] 6626 3-8-9 0 AhmedAjtebi(5) 7 69
(C E Brittain) *chsd ldr: rdn over 2f out: wknd over 1f out* **66/1**

5 1 **Sacred Flame (USA)** 3-9-0 0 RichardHughes 9 67
(B J Meehan) *w'like: leggy: in rr: drvn along over 3f out: mod prog fr over 1f out* **40/1**

6 1/2 **Orange River (IRE)** 3-9-0 0 JimmyFortune 4 66+
(J H M Gosden) *lengthy: scope: bit bkwd: t.k.h: hld up in rr but in tch: rdn over 3f out: mod prog fnl f* **16/1**

0 **7** 6 **Testimonial**[48] 1599 3-9-0 0 RyanMoore 2 54
(E A L Dunlop) *lw: in rr: effrt on ins over 3f out: nvr in contention and sn wknd* **16/1**

2-3 **8** 13 **Cuban Rhythm (USA)**[10] 2681 3-9-0 0 SteveDrowne 1 28
(R Charlton) *sn drvn to chse ldrs: wknd fr 3f out* **9/1[3]**

2 **9** 7 **Catching The Light (USA)**[23] 2291 3-9-0 0 TedDurcan 3 14
(H R A Cecil) *unf: chsd ldrs: rdn and btn 3f out* **9/1[3]**

0 **10** 3 3/4 **One Night In May (IRE)**[10] 2681 3-9-0 0 KerrinMcEvoy 5 7
(W R Muir) *w'like: leggy: in tch: rdn and btn over 3f out* **100/1**

2m 9.87s (1.07) **Going Correction** -0.05s/f (Good) 46 Ran SP% **120.1**
Speed ratings (Par 96): **93,90,89,86,85 85,80,70,64,61**
CSF £4.13 TOTE £1.60: £1.02, £1.90, £9.10; EX 5.20.
Owner Hamdan Al Maktoum **Bred** Shadwell Estate Company Limited **Trained** Newmarket, Suffolk

FOCUS
Like the first division this looked an ordinary maiden and the early pace was modest. As a result the winning time was 1.43 seconds slower. The fourth looks the best guide to the level.
Sacred Flame(USA) Official explanation: jockey said filly hung left
Testimonial Official explanation: jockey said filly hung left

2974 PERTEMPS H'CAP 1m (S)
3:15 (3:19) (Class 5) (0-75,75) 3-Y-O £2,590 (£770; £385; £192) Stalls Centre

Form RPR

055 **1** **Capucci**[26] 2198 3-9-6 75 (t) JimmyFortune 5 90+
(J H M Gosden) *lw: sn in tch: hdwy fr 3f out: led ins fnl 2f: hld on wl thrght fnl f* **15/8[1]**

0-40 **2** 3/4 **Trumpet Lily**[28] 2118 3-9-3 72 JimCrowley 8 84+
(J G Portman) *hld up in rr: hdwy and n.m.r over 2f out: qcknd over 1f out to chse wnr ins fnl f: kpt on wl but a hld* **25/1**

-000 **3** 2 1/4 **Palmerin**[13] 2564 3-9-2 71 RichardHughes 2 76
(R Hannon) *chsd ldrs: rdn and ev ch 2f out: veered rt jst ins fnl f: rcvrd and r.o again cl home* **10/1[3]**

3-22 **4** 3/4 **Barricado (FR)**[38] 1855 3-9-6 75 SteveDrowne 3 78
(R Charlton) *chsd ldrs: drvn to chal 2f out: on pce ins fnl f* **8/1[2]**

2224 **5** 2 1/2 **Brave Hawk**[22] 2311 3-9-5 74 (p) PhilipRobinson 9 74+
(M A Jarvis) *chsd ldrs: rdn to chal over 1f out: one pce whn hmpd jst ins fnl f: nt rcvr* **8/1[2]**

-320 **6** hd **Tina's Best (IRE)**[18] 2429 3-9-3 72 RyanMoore 4 69
(R Hannon) *towards rr: hdwy 3f out: pressed ldrs 2f out: wknd ins fnl f* **10/1[3]**

-216 **7** 1 1/4 **Spin Again (IRE)**[33] 2014 3-9-3 72 GeorgeBaker 12 70+
(R M Beckett) *hld up in rr: hdwy over 2f out: chsng ldrs whn hmpd jst ins fnl f: nt rcvr* **8/1[2]**

2263 **8** nk **Rich Kid (IRE)**[37] 1899 3-9-1 73 KevinGhunowa(3) 11 66
(R A Harris) *chsd ldrs: slt ld 2f out: sn hdd: wknd appr fnl f* **16/1**

-106 **9** 1 3/4 **Bombardier Wells**[23] 2276 3-9-5 74 WilliamBuick 7 63
(Eve Johnson Houghton) *lw: in rr: rdn over 2f out: mod prog fnl f* **40/1**

100 **10** 2 **Rehabilitation**[22] 2311 3-9-5 74 (v1) AdamKirby 14 59
(W R Swinburn) *in rr tl sme prog fnl f* **25/1**

10-0 **11** 8 **The Name Is Frank**[39] 1839 3-9-2 71 LPKeniry 6 37
(J W Mullins) *pressed ldrs tl wknd over 2f out* **50/1**

45-6 **12** 2 1/2 **Doctor Robert**[21] 2342 3-9-4 73 RichardKingscote 10 33
(Tom Dascombe) *led tl hdd 2f out: wknd qckly* **11/1**

3-60 **13** 1 1/2 **Afram Blue**[23] 2276 3-9-3 72 AlanMunro 16 29
(W J Knight) *in tch: rdn 3f out: wknd over 2f out* **40/1**

4-00 **14** 1 **Sainglend**[24] 2256 3-9-3 72 PaulDoe 15 27
(S Curran) *bhd fr 1/2-way* **25/1**

2630 **15** 1 1/4 **Speyside (IRE)**[30] 2090 3-9-3 72 TQuinn 13 24
(J W Hills) *chsd ldrs 5f* **50/1**

005- **16** 1/2 **Mystic Art (IRE)**[268] 5498 3-9-3 72 LDettori 1 23
(C R Egerton) *a in rr* **14/1**

1m 39.5s (-0.20) **Going Correction** -0.05s/f (Good) 16 Ran SP% **127.5**
Speed ratings (Par 99): **93,92,89,86,85 79,76,75,74,73 72**
CSF £64.21 CT £410.92 TOTE £2.70: £1.70, £8.30, £2.60, £1.80; EX 132.20.
Owner H R H Princess Haya Of Jordan **Bred** Meon Valley Stud **Trained** Newmarket, Suffolk
■ Stewards' Enquiry : Steve Drowne caution: careless riding

FOCUS
This was a modest handicap for three-year-olds, but a competitive one in which just 4lb covered the entire field. It was run at an average early pace and saw the field split into two groups early on, before meeting again down the middle of the track nearing 2f out. The form looks good for the grade and the three immediately behind those in the frame give it a solid look.
Capucci Official explanation: trainer said, regarding the apparently improved form, that colt had been running in high class maiden and is improving
Barricado(FR) Official explanation: jockey said colt hung left

2975 LORD WEINSTOCK MEMORIAL STKS (REGISTERED AS THE BALLYMACOLL STUD STAKES) (LISTED RACE) (FILLIES) 1m 2f 6y
3:50 (3:50) (Class 1) 3-Y-O
£17,031 (£6,456; £3,231; £1,611; £807; £405) **Stalls** Low

Form RPR
54-3 **1** **Rosa Grace**^{22} [2305] 3-8-12 98 ChrisCatlin 1 107+
(Rae Guest) *t.k.h: hld up in rr but in tch: hdwy and n.m.r 2f out: swtchd rt and drvn over 1f out: styd on u.p to ld fnl 100yds* **11/2**^{2}
4-21 **2** *1* **Melodramatic (IRE)**^{34} [1965] 3-8-12 98 SteveDrowne 3 102
(R Charlton) *lw: in rr but in tch: hdwy 2f out: drvn to ld wl over 1f out: hdd and no ex fnl 100yds* **5/2**^{1}
2-02 **3** *2* **Annie Skates (USA)**^{22} [2305] 3-8-12 100 KerrinMcEvoy 6 98
(Jane Chapple-Hyam) *hld up in rr: hdwy fr 2f out: kpt on fnl f to take 3rd cl home but nt imp on ldng duo* **11/2**^{2}
3 **4** *1/2* **Flure De Leise (IRE)**^{17} [2469] 3-8-12 0 WilliamBuick 5 97
(Eamon Tyrrell, Ire) *chsd ldrs on ins: rdn and styd on to go 3rd fnl f: no imp on ldng duo and lost 3rd cl home* **50/1**
5-26 **5** *1 1/2* **Silk Affair (IRE)**^{36} [1915] 3-8-12 94 RyanMoore 8 94
(M G Quinlan) *in rr but in tch: rdn and hdwy to chse ldrs 2f out: wknd ins fnl f* **25/1**
221 **6** *3* **Bramaputra (IRE)**^{13} [2571] 3-8-12 90 AlanMunro 2 88
(B R Millman) *led: rdn over 2f out: hdd & wknd qckly wl over 1f out* **14/1**
3-13 **7** *2 3/4* **Burn The Breeze (IRE)**^{36} [1919] 3-8-12 84 TedDurcan 7 83
(H R A Cecil) *lw: t.k.h: chsd ldrs: rdn 3f out: wknd 2f out* **7/1**^{3}
24-2 **8** *8* **Kotsi (IRE)**^{27} [2149] 3-8-12 102 LDettori 4 67
(E F Vaughan) *lw: sn chsng ldr: chal fr 3f out to 2f out: weaking whn hmpd over 1f out* **5/2**^{1}

2m 7.49s (-1.31) **Going Correction** -0.05s/f (Good) **8** Ran SP% **112.9**
Speed ratings (Par 104): **103,102,100,100,99 96,94,88**
CSF £19.14 TOTE £5.70: £1.70, £1.60, £1.60; EX 24.20.
Owner E P Duggan **Bred** Worksop Manor Stud **Trained** Newmarket, Suffolk

FOCUS
A reasonable three-year-old fillies' Listed contest and the form looks sound. The winning time was significantly faster than both divisions of the earlier fillies' maiden, and much quicker than the later amateur riders' race over this trip.

NOTEBOOK
Rosa Grace built on the promise she showed when third on her reappearance in this grade at Goodwood, reversing form with Annie Skates and overcoming trouble in-running to record a decisive success. Having travelled strongly in behind horses for much of the way, she was very much last off the bridle, but was continually denied a clear run when looking to make her move inside the final two furlongs and had to switch out wide. She did not pick up immediately once in the clear, but eventually recovered her momentum in time. Her thinks she is best suited by quick ground, so that makes this effort all the more creditable, and the Irish Oaks is under consideration. There is a lot of speed on the dam's side of her pedigree, but she shapes as though she will stay 1m4f. (op 8-1 tchd 5-1)
Melodramatic(IRE), the easy winner of a 1m maiden at Nottingham on her previous start, proved suited by this step up in trip and ran well in the face of a much stiffer task. She finished clear of the remainder and should continue to go well in similar company. (tchd 11-4)
Annie Skates(USA) was given plenty to do - she was still last when the pace began to increase inside the final half mile - and, although she stayed on, she never looked likely to confirm recent Goodwood form with Rosa Grace. She will probably benefit from more positive tactics in future. (op 6-1)
Flure De Leise(IRE), an Irish challenger who won a fillies' maiden at Ballinrobe on her most recent start, ran well on this significant step up in class and just missed out on some black type, despite not looking entirely happy on the easing ground. Her action when under pressure suggests she may do even better on a quicker surface. (op 40-1)
Silk Affair(IRE) did not build on the form she showed when sixth in the Cheshire Oaks on her previous start. (op 20-1)
Bramaputra(IRE), a Coronation Stakes entry who won a 1m maiden at Nottingham on her previous start, did not appear to stay this longer trip. (op 12-1)
Burn The Breeze(IRE) had a bit to find with some of these at the weights, but she was still below the form she showed when third in a good 1m4f handicap at Chester on her previous start. (op 8-1)
Kotsi(IRE) ran nowhere near the form she showed when second over course and distance to subsequent Oaks fourth Clowance on her most recent outing. Official explanation: trainer was unable to explain the poor form (op 9-4 tchd 11-4)

2976 BATHWICK TYRES NEWBURY H'CAP 7f (S)
4:25 (4:28) (Class 5) (0-75,75) 3-Y-O **£2,590** (£770; £385; £192) **Stalls** Centre

Form RPR
03-0 **1** **Blue Sky Basin**^{19} [2405] 3-9-7 75 WilliamBuick 2 87+
(A M Balding) *trckd ldr: chal over 1f out: led jst ins fnl f: drvn and in command fnl 100yds: readily* **5/1**^{2}
1-56 **2** *1 1/2* **Just Like A Woman**^{51} [1546] 3-9-4 72 RichardHughes 7 80
(M L W Bell) *in tch: hdwy 2f out: rdn and styd on u.p to chse wnr ins fnl f but a readily hld* **8/1**^{3}
05-2 **3** *4 1/2* **El Fuser**^{18} [2429] 3-9-1 69 RyanMoore 9 65+
(P J Makin) *lw: towards rr: hrd drvn and hdwy fr 2f out: styd on to go 3rd fnl f but nvr in contention w ldng pair* **9/4**^{1}
2-20 **4** *3/4* **Connor's Choice**^{23} [2276] 3-9-7 75 AlanDaly 14 69
(Andrew Turnell) *led: rdn over 2f out: hdd jst ins fnl f and sn wknd* **25/1**
04-0 **5** *2 1/2* **Driven (IRE)**^{21} [2342] 3-9-4 72 JimCrowley 8 59
(Mrs A J Perrett) *chsd ldrs: rdn over 2f out: wknd fnl f* **12/1**
005- **6** *1 1/2* **Cape Rock**^{232} [6436] 3-9-1 69 TQuinn 13 52+
(C A Horgan) *in rr tl styd on in fnl 2f: nvr in contention* **33/1**
331- **7** *1/2* **Flying Applause**^{221} [6665] 3-9-2 73 TravisBlock$^{(3)}$ 11 55
(A King) *chsd ldrs: hrd drvn over 2f out: wknd wl over 1f out* **9/1**
-300 **8** *3 1/2* **Ivory Silk**^{41} [1763] 3-9-4 72 AlanMunro 10 44
(D K Ivory) *in rr tl drvn into mid-div over 2f out: sn one pce* **50/1**
06-5 **9** *1 1/2* **Thunder Gorge (USA)**^{16} [2481] 3-9-5 73 RobertHavlin 5 41
(Mouse Hamilton-Fairley) *s.i.s: a towards rr* **16/1**
-540 **10** *2* **King's Icon (IRE)**^{22} [2302] 3-9-6 74 (v^{1}) PatDobbs 15 37
(M P Tregoning) *chsd ldrs: rdn 3f out: wknd 2f out* **25/1**
5262 **11** *hd* **Leading Edge (IRE)**^{7} [2757] 3-9-5 73 ChrisCatlin 12 35
(M R Channon) *chsd ldrs: rdn 3f out: sn btn* **10/1**
30-0 **12** *2 1/4* **Redeemed**^{28} [2118] 3-9-4 72 RHills 1 28
(B J Meehan) *a towards rr* **33/1**
530- **13** *3* **Deal Flipper**^{287} [4964] 3-9-3 71 PaulDoe 16 19
(P Winkworth) *s.i.s: sn chsng ldrs: wknd 3f out* **33/1**
502 **14** *hd* **Bahamian Kid**^{20} [2380] 3-9-2 70 KerrinMcEvoy 4 18
(R Hollinshead) *in tch 1/2-way: rdn and btn whn hung bdly lft fr 2f out* **9/1**

1m 26.87s (1.17) **Going Correction** +0.15s/f (Good) **14** Ran SP% **119.7**
Speed ratings (Par 99): **99,97,92,91,88 86,86,82,80,78 77,75,71,71**
CSF £41.11 CT £115.96 TOTE £6.70: £2.50, £2.60, £1.60; EX 34.60.
Owner George Strawbridge **Bred** George Strawbridge **Trained** Kingsclere, Hants

FOCUS
Just an ordinary handicap and, with the pace sensible on easing ground, very few got involved and the form has been rated cautiously. They tended to race up the middle of the track, avoiding both rails. The ground was changed to good to soft immediately after this contest.
Bahamian Kid Official explanation: jockey said colt hung badly left

2977 BATHWICK TYRES SWINDON H'CAP 1m 4f 5y
4:55 (4:59) (Class 5) (0-75,75) 3-Y-O **£2,590** (£770; £385; £192) **Stalls** Low

Form RPR
6-24 **1** **Warringah**^{26} [2207] 3-9-7 75 RyanMoore 4 100
(Sir Michael Stoute) *lw: mde all: drvn and styd on strly fnl 2f: readily* **13/8**^{1}
55-1 **2** *1 1/4* **Inchwood (IRE)**^{27} [2164] 3-9-7 75 PhilipRobinson 9 98
(M A Jarvis) *lw: chsd ldrs: rdn to chse wnr appr fnl f but a readily hld* **6/1**^{2}
1-42 **3** *3 3/4* **Tasheba**^{34} [1962] 3-9-4 72 AlanMunro 8 89
(P W Chapple-Hyam) *chsd ldrs: wnt 2nd 7f out: rdn 3f out: no imp on wnr fnl 2f: wknd into 3rd over 1f out* **7/1**^{3}
0110 **4** *6* **Cape Colony**^{27} [2173] 3-9-3 71 RichardHughes 14 77
(R Hannon) *stdd s and swtchd lft to rail: trckd ldrs after 4th: rdn and effrt 3f out: nvr gng pce to chal and wknd fr 2f out* **16/1**
5214 **5** *3* **Dubai Petal (IRE)**^{13} [2564] 3-9-5 73 JimmyFortune 11 74+
(J S Moore) *t.k.h in rr: swtchd to outside and rdn 4f out: kpt on fnl 2f but nvr in contention* **15/2**
045 **6** *3 1/2* **Abstract Colours (IRE)**^{17} [2454] 3-8-12 66 LPKeniry 10 61
(A M Balding) *towards rr: rdn 3f out: late prog fnl f but nvr any danger* **33/1**
3-30 **7** *nk* **Nino Cochise (IRE)**^{27} [2151] 3-9-2 70 LDettori 2 65
(C R Egerton) *chsd ldrs: rdn 4f out: wknd over 2f out* **25/1**
3221 **8** *nk* **Princess Lomi (IRE)**^{15} [2495] 3-9-7 75 ChrisCatlin 15 69
(E J O'Neill) *chsd ldrs: rdn 4f out: wknd qckly 2f out* **16/1**
3133 **9** *2* **Silver Waters**^{26} [2201] 3-9-6 74 TQuinn 12 65
(D R C Elsworth) *chsd ldrs: rdn 3f out: wknd over 2f out* **8/1**
641 **10** *1 3/4* **Murcar**^{37} [1896] 3-9-2 70 AdamKirby 1 58
(C G Cox) *in rr: rdn 3f out and nvr in contention* **12/1**
0-60 **11** *10* **Contrada**^{51} [1535] 3-8-11 65 SteveDrowne 7 36
(R Charlton) *chsd ldrs 8f* **25/1**
2564 **12** *6* **My Mate Max**^{10} [2675] 3-9-4 72 KerrinMcEvoy 13 33
(R Hollinshead) *a in rr* **14/1**
040- **13** *32* **Jasoora**^{211} [6805] 3-8-7 61 RHills 5 —
(M P Tregoning) *a in rr: t.o* **50/1**

2m 37.66s (2.16) **Going Correction** +0.15s/f (Good) **13** Ran SP% **126.5**
Speed ratings (Par 99): **98,97,94,90,88 86,86,85,84,83 76,72,51**
CSF £11.39 CT £60.17 TOTE £2.90: £1.50, £2.30, £2.80; EX 11.10.
Owner Philip Newton **Bred** Philip Newton **Trained** Newmarket, Suffolk

FOCUS
This looked like a decent handicap for the grade, with quite a few unexposed types from big stables, and the race has been rated positively and should work out.
My Mate Max Official explanation: jockey said gelding was unsuited by the good to soft ground

2978 BOLLINGER CHAMPAGNE CHALLENGE SERIES H'CAP (FOR GENTLEMAN AMATEUR RIDERS) 1m 2f 6y
5:25 (5:25) (Class 5) (0-70,76) 4-Y-O+ **£3,123** (£968; £484; £242) **Stalls** Low

Form RPR
540 **1** **Night Orbit**^{26} [2185] 4-10-8 62 MrPCollington$^{(5)}$ 13 73
(Miss J Feilden) *trckd ldrs: drvn fr 2f out: styd on wl to ld last strides* **20/1**
6141 **2** *nk* **Western Roots**^{30} [2073] 7-9-12 52 MrJoshuaMoore$^{(5)}$ 9 63
(A M Balding) *led: hrd drvn fr 2f out: hung rt but kpt on wl: ct last strides* **7/2**^{2}
-062 **3** *1 3/4* **Iceman George**^{20} [2374] 4-10-6 60 (b) MrBMMorris$^{(5)}$ 4 67
(D Morris) *chsd ldrs: rdn and effrt over 2f out: nvr quite gng pce to chal and one pce ins fnl f* **9/2**^{3}
-340 **4** *2 1/2* **Bavarica**^{20} [2374] 6-10-11 65 MrRBirkett$^{(5)}$ 7 67
(Miss J Feilden) *chsd ldrs: rdn and kpt on fnl 2f but nvr gng pce to chal* **20/1**
2-41 **5** *3/4* **Im Ova Ere Dad (IRE)**^{6} [2795] 5-11-13 76 6ex MrSWalker 10 77+
(D E Cantillon) *stdd s: t.k.h and hld up in rr: rdn over 2f out and styd on sn after: kpt on fnl f but nt rch ldrs* **2/1**^{1}
0-00 **6** *1 3/4* **Scottish River (USA)**^{12} [2617] 9-10-8 57 MrLeeNewnes 12 54
(M D I Usher) *stdd s: t.k.h: in rr: hdwy on outside over 3f out: kpt on same pce fnl 2f* **20/1**
450- **7** *1* **Everyman**^{184} [7109] 4-9-13 51 MrBenBrisbourne$^{(3)}$ 2 46
(A W Carroll) *chsd ldrs: rdn 3f out: wknd over 1f out* **20/1**
0635 **8** *1 1/4* **Sforzando**^{5} [2848] 7-10-11 65 MrCCollins$^{(5)}$ 6 58
(Mrs L Stubbs) *in rr: sme prog fnl 2f* **7/1**
560- **9** *3* **Act Three**^{232} [6420] 4-10-10 64 JPFeatherstone$^{(5)}$ 1 51
(Mouse Hamilton-Fairley) *slowly away: a in rr: hung rt fr 3f out* **33/1**
6-40 **10** *2 1/4* **Red Current**^{16} [2476] 4-10-13 65 MrRPFlint$^{(3)}$ 5 47
(R A Harris) *chsd ldrs: rdn 3f out: sn wknd* **28/1**
0/50 **11** *11* **Banjo Patterson**^{30} [2087] 6-11-0 70 MrJMQuinlan$^{(7)}$ 11 30
(M G Quinlan) *bhd most of way* **33/1**
24-0 **12** *31* **Dr McFab**^{16} [2476] 4-11-1 69 MrAshleePrice$^{(5)}$ 3 —
(Miss Tor Sturgis) *chsd ldrs 5f: sn wknd: t.o* **25/1**

2m 12.68s (3.88) **Going Correction** +0.15s/f (Good) **12** Ran SP% **118.5**
Speed ratings (Par 103): **90,89,88,86,85 84,83,82,80,78 69,44**
CSF £80.94 CT £381.41 TOTE £23.90: £5.20, £1.80, £1.50; EX 154.50 Place 6: £34.30, Place 5: £2.70..
Owner Stowstowquickquickstow Partnership **Bred** Juddmonte Farms Ltd **Trained** Exning, Suffolk

FOCUS
A modest handicap for amateur riders and they went a steady pace through the early stages. The runner-up has been rated to his old form for now with the winner a big improver.
T/Plt: £129.50 to a £1 stake. Pool: £79,423.02. 447.60 winning tickets. T/Qpdt: £4.70 to a £1 stake. Pool: £5,391.56. 846.85 winning tickets. ST

2546 YARMOUTH (L-H)

Thursday, June 12

OFFICIAL GOING: Good to firm (7.8)

Wind: fresh behind Weather: cloudy with sunny spells

2979 NORFOLK NELSON MUSEUM MAIDEN AUCTION STKS 6f 3y

2:20 (2:25) (Class 6) 2-Y-O **£2,137** (£635; £317; £158) **Stalls** High

Form RPR

26 **1** **Agente Parmigiano (IRE)**[14] 2541 2-9-1 0 EddieAhern 10 87+
(G A Butler) *mde all: pushed clr fnl f* **5/6**[1]

2 *4* **Pyrrha** 2-8-5 0 MartinDwyer 4 67+
(C F Wall) *hld up in tch: shkn up over 1f out: wnt 2nd ins fnl f: no ch w wnr* **20/1**

3 *1 ½* **Blue Arctic** 2-8-5 0 RichardMullen 2 61
(J M P Eustace) *chsd ldrs: rdn over 2f out: styd on same pce appr fnl f* **33/1**

4 *1 ¼* **One Cool Kitty** 2-8-9 0 TPQueally 5 61
(M G Quinlan) *chsd wnr: rdn over 1f out: wknd ins fnl f* **9/1**[3]

25 **5** *¾* **Yokozuna**[15] 2502 2-8-12 0 TGMcLaughlin 8 62
(E A L Dunlop) *mid-div: rdn over 2f out: styd on same pce appr fnl f* **9/1**[3]

6 *2 ¼* **Why Nee Amy** 2-8-4 0 LiamJones 1 47
(V Smith) *mid-div: effrt and edgd lft over 2f out: wknd over 1f out* **66/1**

0 **7** *1 ¾* **Bitza Baileys (IRE)**[16] 2479 2-8-8 0 JimmyQuinn 11 46
(J G Given) *chsd ldrs over 3f* **40/1**

8 *shd* **Siciliando** 2-8-13 0 NCallan 9 50+
(M L W Bell) *sn pushed along in rr: n.d* **7/2**[2]

9 *½* **Clerk's Choice (IRE)** 2-8-13 0 PaulHanagan 7 49
(W Jarvis) *s.s: outpcd: hung lft over 2f out* **16/1**

10 *15* **Benetti (IRE)** 2-8-11 0 DarryllHolland 3 —
(M R Channon) *s.i.s: outpcd: bhd fr 1/2-way* **20/1**

1m 12.97s (-1.43) **Going Correction** -0.25s/f (Firm) **10** Ran SP% **119.1**

Speed ratings (Par 91): **99,93,91,90,89 86,83,83,82,62**

CSF £26.96 TOTE £1.70: £1.10, £4.90, £5.20; EX 23.80 Trifecta £217.50 Pool: £435.04. 1.42 winning units..

Owner Damiano Drago **Bred** J Cullinan **Trained** Newmarket, Suffolk

■ The first winner for Gerard Butler since his move from Blewbury to Newmarket.

FOCUS

An ordinary juvenile maiden. The winner was in a different league.

NOTEBOOK

Agente Parmigiano(IRE), sixth in the Listed National Stakes last time, duly got his head in front at the third attempt on this big drop in grade and could hardly have done the job more readily. He obviously proved well suited by this step up in trip and should be high on confidence after this, so it will be interesting to see where this good-looking colt turns up next. This also confirms he is happiest on a sound surface. (op 11-8 tchd 8-11)

Pyrrha, half-sister to a 12f winner, caught the the eye staying with effect inside the final furlong and eventually finished nicely clear of the remainder. She has a deal of scope, will get another furlong before too long, and should prove a lot sharper now she has this debut experience under her belt. This was a bright start for her stable with their juveniles. (tchd 18-1)

Blue Arctic, half-sister to a 7f juvenile scorer, did nothing really wrong on this racecourse bow and looked suited by the trip. She is entitled to come on a good bit for the run. (tchd 40-1)

One Cool Kitty, 24,000gns purchase, showed some early pace before finding it all too hot passing the final-furlong marker. She was easy to back here and the debut experience will not be lost on her. (op 7-1)

Yokozuna, who reared at the gates on his All-Weather bow last time, performed more encouragingly yet was never seriously in the hunt. (op 12-1 tchd 8-1)

Siciliando, whose dam was a 7f debutante winner at two, proved very easy to back and ultimately proved far too green to do himself full justice. (op 5-2)

2980 GREAT YARMOUTH TOURISM (S) STKS 7f 3y

2:50 (3:01) (Class 6) 2-Y-O **£1,683** (£501; £250; £125) **Stalls** High

Form RPR

3242 **1** **Rose Of Coma (IRE)**[10] 2671 2-8-6 0 PaulHanagan 6 54
(R A Fahey) *chsd ldrs: led 4f out: rdn and hung lft fr over 1f out: r.o* **7/4**[1]

05 **2** *1 ¾* **Debbys Boy**[31] 2054 2-8-11 0 (b[1]) NCallan 4 55
(Miss Gay Kelleway) *trckd ldrs: plld hrd: outpcd over 1f out: r.o ins fnl f* **7/1**[3]

441 **3** *nk* **Come On Buckers (IRE)**[17] 2450 2-9-3 0 (v[1]) TGMcLaughlin 5 60
(P D Evans) *led 1f: chsd ldr: rdn and ev ch: styd on same pce ins fnl f* **2/1**[2]

000 **4** *¾* **Percys Corismatic**[22] 2306 2-8-6 0 MartinDwyer 1 47
(J Gallagher) *led 6f out: hdd 4f out: rdn and ev ch 2f out: no ex ins fnl f* **20/1**

6 **5** *¾* **Cherry Belle (IRE)**[23] 2275 2-8-6 0 RichardMullen 8 45
(P D Evans) *sn pushed along in rr: hdwy and hung lft fr over 2f out: no ex fnl f* **16/1**

6 *8* **Charly's Rose** 2-8-6 0 (v[1]) EddieAhern 2 25
(P C Haslam) *prom over 4f* **8/1**

7 *30* **Silver Thatch** 2-8-1 0 JackDean(5) 3 —
(W G M Turner) *mid-div: sn pushed along: bhd fr 1/2-way* **14/1**

3 **8** *1 ½* **Twinkle De Star**[8] 2720 2-8-1 0 NataliaGemelova(5) 7 —
(J S Moore) *s.i.s: sme hdwy 4f out: sn rdn and wknd* **25/1**

1m 27.8s (1.20) **Going Correction** -0.25s/f (Firm) **8** Ran SP% **114.5**

Speed ratings (Par 91): **83,81,80,79,78 69,35,33**

CSF £14.82 TOTE £2.80: £1.10, £1.80, £1.10; EX 10.20 Trifecta £24.50 Pool: £499.50. 14.44 winning units..The winner was sold for 6,000gns to the Whispering Wind Syndicate. Debbys Boy was subject to a friendly claim of £5000.

Owner R A Fahey **Bred** Pier House Stud **Trained** Musley Bank, N Yorks

FOCUS

A slow time, even for a two-year-old seller. The form is set by the penalised third.

NOTEBOOK

Rose Of Coma(IRE) ran out a deserved winner under a positive ride, despite hanging to her left when put under maximum pressure. This is her sort of level, but she remains open to a little more improvement over this longer trip. (tchd 13-8 and 15-8)

Debbys Boy, up in trip and down in grade, ran freely despite the application of first-time blinkers yet still posted his best effort to date in defeat. He is tricky, but has a race of this class within his range. (op 10-1 tchd 13-2)

Come On Buckers(IRE), off the mark in this class at Chepstow last time, raced in a first-time visor and was given every chance under his penalty. He got the extra furlong well enough and rates as the benchmark for this form. (op 3-1)

Percys Corismatic was ridden positively on this step up in trip and, having evry chance, turned in her most encouraging effort to date. She has now found her sort of level. (op 14-1)

2981 CUSTOM KITCHENS MAIDEN STKS 6f 3y

3:25 (3:30) (Class 5) 3-Y-O+ **£2,590** (£770; £385; £192) **Stalls** High

Form RPR

02-2 **1** **Choiseau (IRE)**[34] 1960 3-9-0 76 PaulHanagan 13 84+
(Pat Eddery) *trckd ldrs: rdn to ld ins fnl f: r.o* **15/8**[1]

50- **2** *1 ¼* **Silvanus (IRE)**[279] 5192 3-9-0 0 EddieAhern 6 80
(W J Haggas) *chsd ldrs: led and hung rt over 1f out: sn rdn: hdd and unable qckn ins fnl f* **5/2**[2]

36- **3** *1 ¼* **Danish Art (IRE)**[237] 6295 3-8-9 0 JackMitchell(5) 7 76+
(J A R Toller) *s.i.s: hld up: swtchd lft over 2f out: hdwy over 1f out: sn rdn: styd on* **8/1**[3]

5-00 **4** *1* **Sweet Kiss (USA)**[23] 2276 3-8-9 76 NCallan 1 68
(B J Meehan) *prom: rdn over 2f out: styd on same pce ins fnl f* **11/1**

5 *4* **State Function (IRE)** 3-9-0 0 DMylonas 9 60
(G Prodromou) *chsd ldr: led over 3f out: rdn and hdd whn n.m.r over 1f out: wknd ins fnl f* **66/1**

0-6 **6** *2* **Laa Baas (IRE)**[31] 2038 3-8-9 0 MartinDwyer 12 49
(M A Jarvis) *trckd ldrs: rdn over 2f out: wknd over 1f out* **22/1**

0 **7** *1* **Confident Warrior (IRE)**[18] 2427 3-9-0 0 (t) JimmyQuinn 3 50
(J Pearce) *hld up in tch: plld hrd: rdn and wknd over 1f out* **100/1**

03 **8** *shd* **Thumbs Up**[14] 2546 3-9-0 0 NickyMackay 14 50+
(L M Cumani) *hld up: racd keenly: shkn up over 1f out: nvr nr to chal* **14/1**

66 **9** *nse* **Carpe Diem**[20] 2380 3-9-0 0 LiamJones 11 50
(W J Haggas) *s.i.s: sn pushed along in rr: styd on ins fnl f: nvr nrr* **16/1**

55- **10** *nk* **Stormbeam (USA)**[208] 6850 3-9-0 0 HayleyTurner 10 49+
(G A Butler) *s.i.s: sn pushed along in rr: nvr nrr* **40/1**

11 *hd* **Malta (USA)** 3-8-9 0 DarryllHolland 16 43+
(J H M Gosden) *mid-div: pushed along 1/2-way: wknd over 2f out* **14/1**

2 **12** *nk* **Filemot**[42] 1737 3-8-6 0 KirstyMilczarek(3) 5 42
(John Berry) *led: rdn over 3f out: edgd lft over 1f out: sn wknd* **12/1**

00 **13** *1* **Hundonette**[7] 2756 3-8-9 0 PaulEddery 8 39
(R M H Cowell) *prom over 4f* **100/1**

14 *3 ½* **Harryana To** 3-8-9 0 AdrianMcCarthy 4 28
(B J McMath) *s.i.s: a in rr* **100/1**

15 *14* **Carry On Ellie (IRE)**[410] 1328 3-8-9 0 TPQueally 15 —
(J G Given) *hld up: plld hrd: rdn and wknd over 2f out* **66/1**

16 *6* **Summer Rose** 3-8-9 0 RichardMullen 2 —
(R M H Cowell) *s.s: outpcd* **66/1**

1m 12.36s (-2.04) **Going Correction** -0.25s/f (Firm) **16** Ran SP% **123.9**

Speed ratings (Par 103): **103,101,99,98,93 90,89,88,88,88 88,87,86,81,63 55**

CSF £6.20 TOTE £3.20: £1.80, £1.50, £2.50; EX 7.50 Trifecta £79.70 Pool: £314.34. 2.80 winning units..

Owner Pat Eddery Racing (Danehill Dancer) **Bred** J G Burns And J Hennessy **Trained** Nether Winchendon, Bucks

FOCUS

A modest maiden for three-year-olds. The form looks fair and pretty sound rated around the principals.

Malta(USA) Official explanation: jockey said filly hung throughout

Carry On Ellie(IRE) Official explanation: jiockey said filly hung right

2982 NORFOLK CHAMBER OF COMMERCE H'CAP 1m 3y

4:00 (4:02) (Class 6) (0-65,65) 3-Y-O **£1,813** (£539; £269; £134) **Stalls** High

Form RPR

00-0 **1** **Serious Choice (IRE)**[42] 1743 3-8-13 **62** JackMitchell(5) 14 73
(J R Boyle) *s.i.s: hld up: hdwy over 3f out: led 2f out: sn hung rt: pushed clr fnl f* **25/1**

0-16 **2** *4 ½* **Metal Madness (IRE)**[18] 2429 3-9-7 **65** NCallan 13 66
(M G Quinlan) *hld up: hdwy 3f out: rdn to chse wnr over 1f out: edgd rt: styd on same pce* **11/4**[2]

-605 **3** *2 ¾* **Mr Fantozzi (IRE)**[27] 2161 3-8-13 **60** (b) JerryO'Dwyer(3) 8 55
(Miss J Feilden) *led: rdn and hdd 2f out: sn hung rt: wknd fnl f* **16/1**

00-6 **4** *1 ¼* **Augmentation**[30] 2079 3-9-0 **58** EddieAhern 4 50
(P W D'Arcy) *hld up: hdwy 1/2-way: outpcd 2f out: styd on ins fnl f* **20/1**

0-04 **5** *1* **Danamight (IRE)**[31] 2047 3-9-4 **62** RichardMullen 7 52
(J L Dunlop) *dwlt: sn pushed along in rr: styd on appr fnl f: nrst fin* **15/2**[3]

660- **6** *¾* **Siryena**[260] 5729 3-8-13 **57** HayleyTurner 3 45
(E A L Dunlop) *s.i.s: hld up: rdn 1/2-way: styd on appr fnl f: nvr trbld ldrs* **50/1**

0-00 **7** *nk* **Townkab (IRE)**[13] 2559 3-9-4 **62** (t) TGMcLaughlin 2 49
(N P Littmoden) *hld up: rdn over 4f out: hdwy over 2f out: wknd fnl f* **22/1**

0-05 **8** *1 ½* **Ejeed (USA)**[38] 1855 3-9-7 **65** MartinDwyer 1 49
(J H M Gosden) *hld up: hdwy 1/2-way: rdn and ev ch 2f out: wknd fnl f* **9/4**[1]

3-00 **9** *3* **Creative (IRE)**[18] 2429 3-9-6 **64** JimmyQuinn 16 41
(M H Tompkins) *hld up: rdn over 2f out: sn wknd* **14/1**

2054 **10** *8* **Turtle Dove**[26] 2208 3-9-2 **63** KirstyMilczarek(3) 10 21
(M Botti) *chsd ldrs 6f* **12/1**

4306 **11** *3 ¾* **Reprieved**[9] 2705 3-8-10 **61** NBazeley(7) 15 11
(M C Chapman) *chsd ldr tl rdn and wknd over 2f out* **66/1**

4-00 **12** *7* **Bainisteoir**[13] 2563 3-8-9 **58** HaddenFrost(5) 12 —
(S Kirk) *mid-div: rdn 1/2-way: wknd over 2f out* **33/1**

0-05 **13** *9* **Pentandra (IRE)**[10] 2659 3-9-2 **60** TPQueally 9 —
(J G Given) *chsd ldrs tl rdn and wknd over 2f out: eased over 1f out* **18/1**

-230 **14** *5* **Kayflaa (IRE)**[31] 2037 3-9-7 **65** DarryllHolland 5 —
(M R Channon) *prom over 5f: eased over 1f out* **25/1**

0500 **15** *24* **Minwir (IRE)**[14] 2549 3-8-13 **57** PaulHanagan 6 —
(M Quinn) *hld up: rdn 1/2-way: wknd 3f out* **33/1**

1m 39.19s (-1.41) **Going Correction** -0.25s/f (Firm) **15** Ran SP% **120.8**

Speed ratings (Par 97): **97,92,89,88,87 86,86,84,81,73 70,63,54,49,25**

CSF £86.81 CT £1193.50 TOTE £54.20: £6.40, £1.50, £5.50; EX 148.80 TRIFECTA Not won..

Owner The Serious Choice Partnership **Bred** Ray Cullen **Trained** Epsom, Surrey

FOCUS

A moderate handicap for three-year-olds, run at an average early pace. The placed horses are rated to their recent marks.

Serious Choice(IRE) Official explanation: trainer said, regarding the improved form, that gelding had been a big, backward 2yo, had strengthened up over the winter and appreciated stepping up to 1m having run over 6f last time

Bainisteoir Official explanation: jockey said gelding was never travelling

Pentandra(IRE) Official explanation: jockey said filly was never travelling; trainer later said filly was found to be lame on her right hind the next day and also had muscle pain in her back

The Form Book, Raceform Ltd, Compton, RG20 6NL

Minwir(IRE) Official explanation: jockey said gelding lost action

2983 EASTERN EVENING NEWS H'CAP — 6f 3y
4:35 (4:38) (Class 5) (0-70,70) 3-Y-0+ £2,428 (£722; £361; £180) Stalls High

Form / RPR

630 **1** **Applesnap (IRE)**[18] 2428 3-9-6 **70** .... TPQueally 9 76
(Mrs C A Dunnett) *chsd ldrs: led over 1f out: rdn out* **25/1**

5030 **2** ¾ **Obe Royal**[2] 2923 4-9-7 **70** .... (b) RichardEvans(7) 10 76
(P D Evans) *s.i.s: hld up: hdwy over 2f out: rdn over 1f out: styd on* **9/2**[2]

-101 **3** ¾ **Strabinios King**[7] 2758 4-9-13 **69** 6ex .... TGMcLaughlin 1 73
(M Wigham) *hld up: hdwy over 1f out: styd on u.p* **4/1**[1]

0450 **4** 2 **Norcroft**[7] 2758 6-8-10 **52** .... (p) HayleyTurner 6 49
(Mrs C A Dunnett) *chsd ldrs: rdn over 1f out: styd on same pce* **5/1**[3]

0440 **5** 1 **Bertbrand**[28] 2127 3-9-3 **70** .... KirstyMilczarek(3) 8 62
(M Botti) *chsd ldrs: rdn over 1f out: wknd wl ins fnl f* **16/1**

-654 **6** 1¾ **Falmassim**[7] 2748 5-8-9 **51** oh4 .... PaulHanagan 5 39
(Miss J A Camacho) *rrd s: bhd: hdwy u.p over 1f out: nt trble ldrs* **5/1**[3]

6040 **7** ¾ **Tamino (IRE)**[15] 2511 5-9-10 **66** .... (t) JimmyQuinn 7 52
(P Howling) *led: rdn and hdd over 1f out: wknd fnl f* **17/2**

0400 **8** 4½ **Djalalabad (FR)**[14] 2550 4-8-9 **51** oh3 .... (v[1]) CatherineGannon 3 23
(Mrs C A Dunnett) *s.s: hdwy 1/2-way: rdn and wknd over 1f out* **25/1**

0-03 **9** *hd* **Rough Rock (IRE)**[13] 2555 3-9-5 **69** .... (b) DarryllHolland 2 38
(Miss Gay Kelleway) *prom: stdd and lost pl 4f out: n.d after* **6/1**

00-0 **10** 1¾ **Peak Seasons (IRE)**[12] 2623 5-8-2 **51** oh6 .... (v) CharlotteKerton(7) 11 16
(M C Chapman) *sn pushed along in rr: bhd fr 1/2-way* **66/1**

3000 **11** 2 **Lindbergh**[26] 2205 6-8-12 **57** .... (p) JerryO'Dwyer(3) 4 16
(J Ryan) *trckd ldrs: rdn over 2f out: sn wknd* **16/1**

1m 12.98s (-1.42) **Going Correction** -0.25s/f (Firm)
WFA 3 from 4yo+ 8lb — 11 Ran SP% 117.3
Speed ratings (Par 103): **99,98,97,94,93 90,89,83,83,81 78**
CSF £132.40 CT £571.73 TOTE £30.10: £5.20, £1.90, £1.80; EX 75.30 TRIFECTA Not won..
Owner Michael Bringloe **Bred** Rathasker Stud **Trained** Hingham, Norfolk

FOCUS
A modest sprint handicap in which the first three came clear and the placed horses set the level.
Falmassim Official explanation: jockey said gelding missed the break
Djalalabad(FR) Official explanation: jockey said filly missed the break

2984 LOWESTOFT JOURNAL H'CAP — 1m 3f 101y
5:05 (5:06) (Class 6) (0-65,65) 3-Y-0 £1,942 (£578; £288; £144) Stalls Low

Form / RPR

4000 **1** **World Time**[12] 2603 3-9-7 **65** .... RichardMullen 8 76+
(J H M Gosden) *s.i.s: hld up: hdwy 4f out: rdn to ld ins fnl f: r.o* **12/1**

000 **2** 2 **Golden Bishop**[15] 2509 3-8-13 **57** .... HayleyTurner 6 64+
(M L W Bell) *trckd ldr: racd keenly: led 2f out: rdn and hdd ins fnl f: styd on same pce* **11/4**[1]

60-0 **3** 3½ **Astrodome**[23] 2273 3-8-12 **56** .... JimmyQuinn 9 57+
(Sir Mark Prescott) *chsd ldrs: hung lft over 4f out: led over 3f out: rdn and hdd 2f out: no ex fnl f* **7/1**[3]

0-65 **4** *shd* **Flash Of Fire (USA)**[16] 2475 3-8-8 **55** .... LukeMorris(3) 5 56
(J M P Eustace) *hld up: hdwy 1/2-way: rdn over 1f out: styd on same pce* **10/1**

0001 **5** 1 **Sabre Light**[16] 2486 3-8-9 **58** .... (p) JackMitchell(5) 2 57
(A Bailey) *s.i.s: hld up: hdwy over 2f out: rdn and swtchd rt over 1f out: nt rch ldrs* **16/1**

50-2 **6** 2½ **Highly Regal (IRE)**[12] 2613 3-9-4 **62** .... EddieAhern 1 57
(R A Teal) *hld up in tch: rdn over 3f out: wknd over 1f out* **6/1**[2]

000- **7** *nk* **Amwell House**[238] 6274 3-7-9 **46** oh1 .... DavidProbert(7) 10 41
(J R Jenkins) *hld up: hdwy 1/2-way: rdn and wknd over 1f out* **50/1**

-000 **8** 3½ **Daddy's Boy**[21] 2340 3-9-2 **60** .... (b) MartinDwyer 7 49
(Mrs A J Perrett) *sn led: rdn and hdd over 3f out: wknd over 1f out* **10/1**

20-3 **9** 2 **Colorado Springs**[30] 2090 3-9-5 **63** .... TPQueally 4 48
(W Jarvis) *hld up: rdn and hung lft over 2f out: n.d* **11/1**

3520 **10** 1¼ **Jemiliah**[17] 2451 3-8-11 **55** .... NCallan 16 38
(B G Powell) *hld up: rdn over 2f out: n.d* **20/1**

-004 **11** 3¼ **Blandys Wood**[13] 2559 3-9-5 **63** .... DarryllHolland 3 41
(M R Channon) *hld up: hmpd 1/2-way: rdn 4f out* **14/1**

00-0 **12** 3½ **Latimer House (IRE)**[14] 2552 3-8-2 **46** .... DavidKinsella 11 18
(Dr J D Scargill) *hld up: a in rr* **50/1**

0-05 **13** 3¾ **Hawkstar Express (IRE)**[9] 2694 3-8-11 **55** .... TGMcLaughlin 14 20
(J R Boyle) *s.i.s: hdwy 10f out: rdn over 2f out: sn wknd* **40/1**

0-04 **14** 10 **Princess Maria (USA)**[10] 2659 3-8-2 **46** oh1 .... PaulHanagan 12 —
(R A Fahey) *hld up: a in rr: wknd over 3f out* **12/1**

055 **15** 4½ **Tewin Green**[14] 2528 3-9-4 **65** .... KirstyMilczarek(3) 13 6
(M Botti) *hld up: hdwy 1/2-way: rdn and wknd over 3f out* **25/1**

2m 31.3s (2.60) **Going Correction** +0.05s/f (Good) — 15 Ran SP% 122.9
Speed ratings (Par 97): **92,90,88,87,87 85,85,82,81,80 77,75,72,65,62**
CSF £43.44 CT £261.16 TOTE £16.30: £6.10, £1.60, £3.70; EX 66.70 TRIFECTA Not won..
Owner H R H Princess Haya Of Jordan **Bred** Lady Bamford **Trained** Newmarket, Suffolk

FOCUS
A moderate handicap for three-year-olds in which the form looks sound and should work out.
World Time ◆ Official explanation: trainer said, regarding the improved form, that colt benefitted from leaving the blinkers off which he wore last time and having been a backward colt is now maturing
Blandys Wood Official explanation: trainer said filly was unsuited by the good to firm ground

2985 GREAT YARMOUTH MERCURY H'CAP — 1m 6f 17y
5:35 (5:37) (Class 5) (0-70,69) 3-Y-0 £2,428 (£722; £361; £180) Stalls High

Form / RPR

2351 **1** **Si Belle (IRE)**[4] 2868 3-9-7 **69** 6ex .... RichardMullen 7 76
(Rae Guest) *hld up: hdwy over 2f out: rdn over 1f out: styd on to ld post* **10/3**[2]

-645 **2** *hd* **Dramatic Solo**[27] 2173 3-9-1 **63** .... NCallan 8 70
(K R Burke) *chsd ldrs: rdn to ld 1f out: edgd rt: hdd post* **10/1**

2140 **3** 1¼ **Kiribati King (IRE)**[22] 2310 3-9-6 **68** .... DarryllHolland 6 73
(M R Channon) *hld up: hdwy to ld over 9f out: rdn and hdd 1f out: styd on same pce towards fin* **5/1**[3]

0413 **4** ¾ **Fairfield Flame (GER)**[22] 2310 3-9-4 **69** .... (b) MarcHalford(3) 9 73
(D R C Elsworth) *sn pushed along and prom: rdn and hung lft fr over 2f out: nt run on* **13/2**

6-56 **5** 1¼ **Hamsat Elqamar**[27] 2164 3-9-4 **66** .... MartinDwyer 3 68
(J H M Gosden) *led: hdd over 9f out: rdn over 4f out: hung lft over 3f out: styd on same pce fnl f* **12/1**

0-03 **6** ½ **Sonny Sam (IRE)**[17] 2468 3-8-11 **59** .... JimmyQuinn 2 61
(M H Tompkins) *hld up: hdwy 1/2-way: rdn over 4f out: hdwy and n.m.r fr over 3f out: tl styd on same pce fnl f* **3/1**[1]

6-23 **7** ½ **Bouggler**[15] 2495 3-8-12 **60** .... TPQueally 4 61
(Miss J A Camacho) *plld hrd: trckd ldr: rdn over 2f out: sn swtchd rt: styd on same pce fnl f* **6/1**

0-00 **8** 22 **Dance Easily**[17] 2468 3-8-2 **50** oh5 .... DavidKinsella 5 20
(J L Dunlop) *hld up: wknd over 3f out* **40/1**

0-00 **9** 33 **Farsighted**[28] 2118 3-9-0 **65** .... LukeMorris(3) 1 —
(J M P Eustace) *prom: lost pl 6f out: bhd fnl 4f* **33/1**

3m 8.42s (0.82) **Going Correction** +0.05s/f (Good) — 9 Ran SP% 114.5
Speed ratings (Par 99): **99,98,98,97,97 96,96,83,65**
CSF £36.16 CT £164.14 TOTE £4.50: £1.90, £3.60, £2.10; EX 53.90 Trifecta £245.40 Place 6: £18.67, Place 5: £10.27. Pool: £411.37. 1.19 winning units..
Owner Miss K Rausing **Bred** Airlie Stud And R N Clay **Trained** Newmarket, Suffolk

FOCUS
A modest staying handicap for three-year-olds. The form is set by the runner-up backed up by the third and fourth and looks pretty sound.
Farsighted Official explanation: trainer said filly was unsuited by the good to firm ground
T/Plt: £36.90 to a £1 stake. Pool: £60,832.20. 1,200.30 winning tickets. T/Qpdt: £25.20 to a £1 stake. Pool: £2,433.20. 71.45 winning tickets. CR

2473 CHEPSTOW (L-H)
Friday, June 13

OFFICIAL GOING: Good to firm (8.9)
Wind: Almost nil Weather: Fine

2987 TOTEPLACEPOT EBF NOVICE STKS — 6f 16y
6:30 (6:30) (Class 4) 2-Y-0 £4,630 (£1,377; £688; £343) Stalls High

Form / RPR

31 **1** **Penny's Gift**[17] 2473 2-8-11 0 .... RichardHughes 6 87+
(R Hannon) *plld hrd early: trckd ldrs: led wl over 1f out: pushed out* **5/4**[1]

022 **2** 2½ **Hay Fever (IRE)**[14] 2554 2-8-12 0 .... StephenCarson 5 76
(Eve Johnson Houghton) *led: hdd over 3f out: led over 2f out tl wl over 1f out: rdn and kpt on same pce fnl f* **7/1**

2123 **3** *nse* **In Transit (IRE)**[5] 2859 2-8-9 0 .... MatthewDavies(7) 2 80
(M R Channon) *hld up in tch: rdn over 1f out: kpt on same pce ins fnl f* **9/2**[2]

4424 **4** 2¼ **Kingswinford (IRE)**[17] 2473 2-8-12 0 .... CatherineGannon 1 69
(P D Evans) *swtchd rt sn after s: pushed along over 3f out: hdwy 2f out: rdn over 1f out: one pce fnl f* **5/1**[3]

46 **5** 2 **Ridgeway Silver**[42] 1778 2-8-7 0 .... RichardSmith 8 58
(M D I Usher) *t.k.h: sn prom on stands' rail: lost pl 4f out: n.d after* **66/1**

61 **6** ¾ **Haven't A Clue**[10] 2691 2-9-0 0 .... DO'Donohoe 3 63
(Sir Mark Prescott) *prom tl rdn and wknd over 1f out* **5/1**[3]

550 **7** *nk* **Madison Belle**[12] 2638 2-8-0 0 .... DavidProbert(7) 7 55
(Mrs H Sweeting) *bhd: pushed along over 3f out: rdn over 2f out: btn whn edgd lft over 1f out* **40/1**

0 **8** 1½ **Hault**[17] 2473 2-8-12 0 .... TGMcLaughlin 4 55
(R A Harris) *w ldr: led over 3f out tl over 2f out: wknd over 1f out* **66/1**

1m 11.03s (-1.87) **Going Correction** -0.425s/f (Firm) — 8 Ran SP% 113.9
Speed ratings (Par 95): **95,91,91,88,85 84,84,82**
CSF £10.81 TOTE £1.80: £1.20, £2.50, £1.60; EX 10.60.
Owner Malcolm Brown & Mrs Penny Brown **Bred** Capt A L Smith-Maxwell **Trained** East Everleigh, Wilts

FOCUS
A fair contest for its type.

NOTEBOOK
Penny's Gift had no problem with the extra furlong back on fast ground despite racing freely down the hill. She is continuing to progress along the right lines. (op 11-8 tchd 11-10)
Hay Fever(IRE) ◆ turned around a neck defeat by In Transit on 4lb better terms. He will not always meet one as good at the winner and deserves to end his frustrating run of seconds. (op 8-1 tchd 13-2)
In Transit(IRE) could not quite confirm his neck defeat of Hay Fever at Brighton last month on 4lb worse terms ignoring his rider's claim. (op 7-1)
Kingswinford(IRE) was meeting the winner on 4lb better terms than when beaten nearly six lengths on soft ground over the minimum trip here last time. (op 13-2 tchd 7-1)
Ridgeway Silver was out of his depth in this company after making his best exit from the stalls so far. (op 80-1)
Haven't A Clue was unsuited by the good to firm ground according to his rider. Official explanation: jockey said filly was unsuited by the good to firm ground (op 11-4)

2988 BET TOTEPOOL ON ALL UK RACING (S) STKS — 7f 16y
7:00 (7:01) (Class 6) 3-Y-0+ £1,748 (£520; £260; £129) Stalls High

Form / RPR

0-4 **1** **Rich Harvest (USA)**[49] 1603 3-8-10 0 ow1 .... RichardHughes 13 58
(A P Jarvis) *led after 1f: rdn over 1f out: edgd rt wl ins fnl f: r.o* **8/1**

5065 **2** ¾ **Swift Cut (IRE)**[11] 2664 4-8-12 49 .... (p) DavidProbert(7) 5 59+
(D Burchell) *chsd ldrs: rdn over 1f out: kpt on to take 2nd cl home* **15/2**

4030 **3** 1 **Cyfrwys (IRE)**[3] 2917 7-9-0 48 .... (p) CatherineGannon 15 51
(B Palling) *sn w wnr: ev ch 2f out: sn rdn: no ex towards fin* **9/1**

3430 **4** 2¼ **Yakama (IRE)**[15] 2552 3-8-2 48 .... (v[1]) BillyCray(7) 6 46
(D J S Ffrench Davis) *sn bhd: swtchd lft and rdn over 3f out: hdwy over 1f out: edgd rt wl ins fnl f: nt trble ldrs* **9/2**[2]

-6U0 **5** ½ **Dynamo Dave (USA)**[7] 2805 3-8-9 65 .... (b[1]) SteveDrowne 7 35
(B J Meehan) *led 1f: prom: rdn over 2f out: one pce* **16/1**

-102 **6** ¾ **Bert's Memory**[11] 2670 4-9-5 50 .... (b) DarryllHolland 11 47
(J Mackie) *chsd ldrs: pushed along 4f out: rdn over 2f out: no imp fnl f* **4/1**[1]

0500 **7** 1¾ **Moon Forest (IRE)**[31] 2069 6-9-2 42 .... (b) KevinGhunowa(3) 4 42
(J M Bradley) *hld up in mid-div: rdn over 3f out: no hdwy* **25/1**

8 2½ **Kosciusko**[31] 7-8-9 0 .... HaddenFrost(5) 2 30
(J D Frost) *dwlt: rdn over 3f out: nvr nr ldrs* **10/1**

0400 **9** *hd* **Cantique (IRE)**[7] 2782 4-8-11 45 .... RussellKennemore(3) 17 30
(R J Price) *hld up in mid-div: rdn and sme hdwy over 3f out: wknd over 2f out* **25/1**

6-00 **10** ½ **Bewdley**[11] 2670 3-8-1 52 .... DominicFox(3) 14 24
(Mrs K Waldron) *hld up in mid-div: rdn over 3f out: wknd over 2f out* **50/1**

0-06 **11** 1½ **Tipsy Prince**[14] 2556 4-9-5 60 .... SaleemGolam 9 29
(David Pinder) *wnt to post early: s.i.s: a bhd* **13/2**[3]

-050 **12** 2¾ **Goodwood Spirit**[2] 2933 6-8-12 45 .... (v) PietroRomeo(7) 1 22
(J M Bradley) *t.k.h towards rr: hdwy over 3f out: wknd 2f out* **33/1**

-545 **13** 2 **Spy Gun (USA)**[141] 284 8-9-5 45 .... (p) GregFairley 12 17
(T Wall) *prom: rdn over 3f out: sn lost pl* **40/1**

000 **14** ½ **Tell Me What (FR)**[57] 1416 3-8-4 49 .... (tp) RichardThomas 8 6
(D J S Ffrench Davis) *bhd fnl 5f* **50/1**

0000 **15** 1 1/4 **Sir Douglas**[8] 2753 5-9-10 55....................(p) TGMcLaughlin 10 17
(R A Harris) *wnt to post early: s.s: racd alone on stands' rail fr over 3f out: rdn over 2f out: a bhd* **14/1**

500 **16** 2 **Maraagel (USA)**[17] 2474 5-9-5 45.................... AlanMunro 16 6
(G A Ham) *hld up in mid-div: bhd fnl 3f* **16/1**

0/0- **P** **Straw Boy**[298] 4658 4-9-2 52....................(t) LukeMorris(3) 3 —
(R Brotherton) *s.i.s: a in rr: p.u 3f out* **33/1**

1m 22.11s (-1.09) **Going Correction** -0.425s/f (Firm)
WFA 3 from 4yo+ 10lb 17 Ran SP% **131.8**
Speed ratings (Par 101): **89,88,87,84,83 83,81,78,77,77 75,72,70,69,68 65,—**
CSF £68.07 TOTE £11.00: £2.70, £3.50, £4.50; EX 118.10.The winner was sold to P D Evans for 3,800gns.
Owner Eurostrait Ltd **Bred** Dream With Me Stables Inc **Trained** Twyford, Bucks

FOCUS
There were questions hanging over most of these in this big field of platers. Ordinary selling form, the third the best guide.
Bert's Memory Official explanation: jockey said filly was unsuited by the good to firm ground
Kosciusko Official explanation: jockey said mare missed the break
Cantique(IRE) Official explanation: jockey said filly hung left
Tipsy Prince Official explanation: trainer said gelding bled from the nose
Sir Douglas Official explanation: jockey said gelding missed the break
Straw Boy Official explanation: jockey said gelding lost action

2989 BET TOTEPOOL ON ALL IRISH RACING MAIDEN FILLIES' STKS 1m 4f 23y
7:35 (7:36) (Class 5) 3-Y-0+ £2,590 (£770; £385; £192) Stalls Low

Form RPR

0 **1** **Calakanga**[35] 1964 3-8-12 0.................... GregFairley 3 75
(C E Brittain) *hld up in tch: rdn 3f out: swtchd rt 2f out: led ins fnl f: r.o* **18/1**

00-3 **2** 1 **Ethereal Flame**[34] 2015 3-8-12 75.................... RichardHughes 5 73
(H R A Cecil) *led after 1f: rdn over 2f out: hdd and nt qckn ins fnl f* **9/4**[2]

2 **3** 3 3/4 **Inquisitive Look**[11] 2668 3-8-12 0.................... AlanMunro 2 67
(P W Chapple-Hyam) *a.p: ev ch over 2f out: sn rdn: wknd towards fin* **4/6**[1]

0 **4** 1 3/4 **Purely By Chance**[27] 2197 3-8-12 0.................... NelsonDeSouza 8 64
(R M Beckett) *led 1f: prom: lost pl and rdn over 5f out: styd on fnl f* **10/1**

0 **5** 3 **Romantic Retreat**[22] 2328 3-8-12 0.................... DarryllHolland 7 59
(L M Cumani) *hld up in tch: impr to chse ldr over 6f out: wknd wl over 1f out* **8/1**[3]

0-0 **6** 24 **Lake Nayasa**[11] 2668 3-8-12 0....................(v[1]) SteveDrowne 1 21
(H Morrison) *a bhd* **33/1**

0-00 **7** nk **Great Future**[9] 2719 3-8-10 48 ow1.................... RussellKennemore(3) 6 22
(J R Holt) *hld up and bhd: hdwy over 5f out: rdn and wknd over 3f out* **100/1**

00 **8** 15 **Bombay Dreams**[34] 2015 5-9-13 0....................(p) TGMcLaughlin 4 —
(Karen George) *dwlt: a bhd: t.o* **100/1**

2m 37.82s (-1.18) **Going Correction** -0.20s/f (Firm)
WFA 3 from 5yo 15lb 8 Ran SP% **121.1**
Speed ratings (Par 100): **95,94,91,90,88 72,72,62**
CSF £62.33 TOTE £33.10: £3.50, £1.20, £1.02; EX 103.20.
Owner Saeed Manana **Bred** Darley **Trained** Newmarket, Suffolk

FOCUS
Not a bad contest for the grade but the favourite was disappointing. The winner showed big improvement and the form is generally sound.
Romantic Retreat Official explanation: jockey said filly failed to handle the track

2990 TOTEEXACTA H'CAP 1m 2f 36y
8:10 (8:11) (Class 5) (0-75,75) 4-Y-0+ £2,719 (£809; £404; £202) Stalls Low

Form RPR

1315 **1** **Silver Blue (IRE)**[14] 2558 5-8-4 58.................... CatherineGannon 8 74
(W K Goldsworthy) *hld up: hdwy over 5f out: led over 2f out: clr whn rdn and edgd lft over 1f out: r.o wl* **8/1**

612 **2** 9 **Uig**[29] 2125 7-8-11 70.................... HaddenFrost(5) 9 68
(H S Howe) *hld up: hdwy 5f out: rdn over 2f out: wnt 2nd 1f out: no ch w wnr* **9/1**

-652 **3** 1/2 **Nightspot**[7] 2770 7-9-0 68.................... StephenCarson 3 65
(Eve Johnson Houghton) *led: hdd over 8f out: w ldr: led over 5f out: rdn and hdd over 2f out: one pce* **5/1**[3]

4-16 **4** 1/2 **Celticello (IRE)**[7] 2784 6-9-0 75.................... RichardEvans(7) 7 71
(P D Evans) *hld up and bhd: hdwy 3f out: rdn over 1f out: one pce fnl f* **11/2**

2-03 **5** 2 **Venir Rouge**[8] 2764 4-9-7 75.................... TGMcLaughlin 10 67
(M Salaman) *hld up and bhd: rdn 4f out: styd on fnl f: n.d* **10/3**[2]

2111 **6** 1/2 **Stringsofmyheart**[9] 2718 4-9-7 75 6ex.................... DarryllHolland 2 66
(Miss Gay Kelleway) *w ldr: led over 8f out tl over 5f out: rdn over 2f out: wknd over 1f out* **11/4**[1]

320/ **7** nk **Spence Appeal (IRE)**[555] 6735 6-8-2 56 oh4.................... RichardThomas 5 46
(C Roberts) *hld up and bhd: pushed along over 3f out: nvr nr ldrs* **50/1**

25-0 **8** 1 1/2 **Sweet Request**[12] 2641 4-8-5 62.................... KevinGhunowa(3) 4 49
(Dr J R J Naylor) *hld up: hdwy on ins over 4f out: rdn over 3f out: wknd over 1f out* **25/1**

0-62 **9** 1/2 **Queen Excalibur**[18] 2453 9-7-11 58....................(p) DavidProbert(7) 1 44
(C Roberts) *chsd ldng pair: rdn over 3f out: wknd over 2f out* **9/1**

2m 7.72s (-2.88) **Going Correction** -0.20s/f (Firm) 9 Ran SP% **118.7**
Speed ratings (Par 103): **103,95,95,95,93 93,92,91,91**
CSF £79.41 CT £401.76 TOTE £11.90: £2.20, £2.00, £1.90; EX 78.90.
Owner D Hughes M Edwards G Miller & Partners **Bred** Mrs T V Ryan **Trained** Yerbeston, Pembrokes

FOCUS
What looked a fairly competitive minor handicap was turned into a one-horse race by Silver Blue, who stepped up on his recent form and is rated back to something like his latter 3yo best.

2991 TOTETRIFECTA MAIDEN H'CAP 6f 16y
8:45 (8:48) (Class 5) (0-70,70) 3-Y-0+ £2,590 (£770; £385; £192) Stalls High

Form RPR

0-32 **1** **Superduper**[13] 2622 3-9-13 69.................... RichardHughes 13 82
(R Hannon) *w ldrs: led 3f out: rdn ins fnl f: r.o wl* **5/1**[2]

6624 **2** 2 1/4 **Farthermost (IRE)**[8] 2756 3-10-0 70.................... AlanMunro 9 76
(R Hannon) *hld up: hdwy over 3f out: rdn over 1f out: r.o one pce fnl f* **8/1**[3]

40-6 **3** 1 **Sir Ike (IRE)**[40] 1836 3-9-8 64.................... DarryllHolland 4 67
(W S Kittow) *w ldrs: rdn and one pce fnl f* **8/1**[3]

-600 **4** 1 1/4 **Balata**[19] 2429 3-9-5 68....................(b[1]) DavidProbert(7) 11 67
(B R Millman) *a.p: rdn over 2f out: one pce* **20/1**

2223 **5** 1 1/4 **Kyllachy Storm**[7] 2798 4-9-1 54.................... HaddenFrost(5) 14 51
(R J Hodges) *w ldrs: rdn over 1f out: one pce* **3/1**[1]

00-4 **6** 1/2 **Hits Only Time**[120] 556 3-8-12 57.................... KevinGhunowa(3) 3 50+
(P A Blockley) *s.i.s: rdn over 1f out: hdwy fnl f: nvr nrr* **50/1**

-000 **7** 1 **Wooden King (IRE)**[3] 2922 3-8-11 53.................... TGMcLaughlin 2 43
(P D Evans) *hld up: hdwy over 2f out: sn rdn: wknd over 1f out* **22/1**

252- **8** nk **Towy Girl (IRE)**[191] 7029 4-9-7 60.................... MarkCoumbe(5) 8 51
(A W Carroll) *t.k.h towards rr: rdn and hdwy over 1f out: no further prog fnl f* **16/1**

2500 **9** 2 **Mr Rev**[34] 2010 5-9-2 57.................... PietroRomeo(7) 15 42
(J M Bradley) *hld up: hdwy 3f out: sn rdn: wknd over 1f out* **50/1**

5224 **10** 2 1/4 **Walragnek**[25] 2240 4-9-11 62.................... RussellKennemore(3) 17 39
(J G M O'Shea) *led: hdd 3f out: rdn over 2f out: wknd wl over 1f out* **33/1**

-430 **11** nk **Cracking Nick (IRE)**[29] 2122 3-10-0 70.................... SaleemGolam 10 44
(W R Swinburn) *hld up in mid-div: rdn over 2f out: wknd over 1f out* **8/1**[3]

3-04 **12** hd **Solemn**[45] 1699 3-9-6 65.................... LukeMorris(3) 16 39
(J M Bradley) *t.k.h: prom: lost pl over 3f out: rdn over 1f out: no rspnse* **33/1**

0-03 **13** nk **Klarity**[11] 2660 3-8-10 55.................... JerryO'Dwyer(3) 5 28
(J Pearce) *t.k.h in mid-div: rdn 2f out: sn wknd* **14/1**

3355 **14** 3 **Bold Diva**[94] 849 3-9-4 60.................... CatherineGannon 12 23
(A W Carroll) *rdn over 2f out: a bhd* **25/1**

00-5 **15** 2 **Valento**[35] 1957 3-9-13 69.................... StephenCarson 7 26
(Eve Johnson Houghton) *prom 3f* **12/1**

0-30 **16** nk **Saranome (IRE)**[34] 1995 3-9-13 69.................... SteveDrowne 6 25
(R Charlton) *prom tl wknd over 2f out* **11/1**

046 **17** 2 **Dhahab (USA)**[16] 2500 3-9-4 60.................... GregFairley 1 10
(C E Brittain) *prom tl rdn and wknd 3f out* **33/1**

1m 10.17s (-2.73) **Going Correction** -0.425s/f (Firm)
WFA 3 from 4yo+ 8lb 17 Ran SP% **129.3**
Speed ratings (Par 103): **101,98,96,95,93 92,91,90,88,85 84,84,84,80,77 77,74**
CSF £43.02 CT £340.22 TOTE £3.90: £2.40, £3.00, £1.90, £4.30; EX 53.40 Trifecta £79.20 Pool £178.57 - 1.60 winning units..
Owner David & Jennifer Sieff & Bloomsbury Stud **Bred** Bloomsbury Stud & The Hon Sir David Sieff **Trained** East Everleigh, Wilts

FOCUS
This may have only been a maiden handicap but it was the only race won in a time below standard. The form seems pretty sound.
Saranome(IRE) Official explanation: jockey said gelding was unsuited by the track

2992 BET TOTEPOOL AT TOTESPORT.COM H'CAP 7f 16y
9:15 (9:17) (Class 5) (0-75,70) 4-Y-0+ £2,719 (£809; £404; £202) Stalls High

Form RPR

0-42 **1** **Isphahan**[29] 2128 5-8-5 61.................... DavidProbert(7) 3 70
(A M Balding) *a.p: led over 3f out: rdn over 1f out: hld on wl cl home* **3/1**[2]

4-11 **2** shd **Oh So Saucy**[11] 2670 4-9-3 66 6ex.................... GeorgeBaker 8 75
(C F Wall) *hld up: hdwy over 1f out: sn rdn: str chal ins fnl f: r.o* **5/6**[1]

4455 **3** 1 1/4 **Memphis Man**[3] 2923 5-9-0 70.................... RichardEvans(7) 5 76
(P D Evans) *hld up: rdn and hdwy 1f out: rdr dropped whip ins fnl f: nt qckn* **15/2**[3]

2-00 **4** 2 3/4 **Gazboolou**[30] 2101 4-9-7 70.................... SaleemGolam 6 68
(David Pinder) *hld up in tch: rdn over 1f out: one pce* **20/1**

6-04 **5** nk **Finsbury**[14] 2556 5-9-1 64.................... RichardHughes 1 61
(J M Bradley) *led over 3f: wknd ins fnl f* **16/1**

-505 **6** 1/2 **Goose Green (IRE)**[12] 2642 4-8-11 60.................... SteveDrowne 7 56
(R J Hodges) *hld up: rdn over 1f out: nvr able to chal* **22/1**

460- **7** 1 3/4 **The Cayterers**[158] 5064 6-8-12 68.................... AshleyMorgan(7) 2 59
(J M Bradley) *prom: rdn over 2f out: wknd jst over 1f out* **28/1**

0004 **8** 3/4 **Coup D'Etat**[12] 2642 6-8-13 62....................(b) TGMcLaughlin 4 51
(R A Harris) *t.k.h in tch: rdn 2f out: sn wknd* **16/1**

1m 22.69s (-0.51) **Going Correction** -0.425s/f (Firm) 8 Ran SP% **115.6**
Speed ratings (Par 103): **85,84,83,80,79 79,77,76**
CSF £5.74 CT £15.33 TOTE £4.40: £1.40, £1.30, £1.80; EX 7.20 Place 6 £54.55, Place 5 £36.88..
Owner Mohamad Rafique **Bred** J H Wall **Trained** Kingsclere, Hants
■ Stewards' Enquiry : George Baker caution: careless riding

FOCUS
A cracking finish to this minor little handicap, which was run at a very steady pace. The form makes sense.
T/Plt: £46.00 to a £1 stake. Pool: £56,173.26. 890.65 winning tickets. T/Qpdt: £5.90 to a £1 stake. Pool: £4,065.26. 507.80 winning tickets. KH

2795 GOODWOOD (R-H)
Friday, June 13

OFFICIAL GOING: Good (8.4)
Wind: Fairly modest against Weather: Mainly cloudy with brighter spells

2993 EBF SOUTHERN DAILY ECHO FILLIES' STKS (H'CAP) 6f
6:20 (6:21) (Class 3) (0-95,90) 3-Y-0+ £9,714 (£2,890; £1,444; £721) Stalls Low

Form RPR

-002 **1** **Our Faye**[6] 2831 5-9-9 82.................... GeorgeBaker 6 92
(S Kirk) *racd in centre gp: in tch travelling wl: chsd ldr over 1f out: rdr dropped whip 1f out: pushed into ld ins fnl f: pushed out* **11/4**[1]

4053 **2** 3/4 **Tilly's Dream**[16] 2504 5-9-2 75.................... AdamKirby 11 83
(G C Bravery) *racd in centre gp: chsng ldrs: rdn to ld wl over 1f out: hdd ins fnl f: kpt on but nt pce of wnr* **16/1**

345 **3** 3 1/4 **Tia Mia**[34] 2000 3-9-9 90.................... JohnEgan 10 86
(M Botti) *racd in centre gp: s.i.s: hld up in tch: rdn and hdwy 2f out: one pce fnl f* **9/2**[3]

5-40 **4** 3/4 **Fly Kiss**[15] 2532 3-8-3 75.................... AhmedAjtebi(5) 9 68
(C E Brittain) *uns rdr bef s: racd in centre gp: s.i.s: sn chsng ldrs: rdn over 2f out: outpcd over 1f out* **33/1**

4-24 **5** nk **Nice To Know (FR)**[39] 1857 4-9-7 80.................... RyanMoore 5 74
(G L Moore) *racd in centre gp: s.i.s: hld up in tch: rdn and effrt 2f out: sn edgd rt and no imp* **3/1**[2]

3230 **6** 1/2 **Angus Newz**[19] 2426 5-10-0 87....................(v) FrancisNorton 2 80
(M Quinn) *racd in stands' side pair: overall ldr tl 1/2-way: wknd wl over 1f out* **14/1**

0240 **7** 1 1/4 **Carcinetto (IRE)**[2] 2947 6-9-12 85.................... JimmyFortune 3 74
(P D Evans) *racd in centre gp: prom: rdn 2f out: wknd wl over 1f out* **9/1**

21-0 **8** 3 **Street Star (USA)**[34] 1999 3-9-6 87.................... JamieSpencer 7 64
(J R Fanshawe) *racd in centre gp: chsd overall ldr tl led 1/2-way: rdn and hdd wl over 1f out: sn wknd* **12/1**

0520 **9** 3 1/4 **Hessian (IRE)**[11] 2670 4-8-11 70.................... ChrisCatlin 4 39
(M D Squance) *racd in centre gp: a bhd* **25/1**

2244 **10** 2 3/4 **Sweet Pickle**[6] 2831 7-9-7 **80**..(e) PatCosgrave 1 40
(J R Boyle) *racd in stands' side pair: hld up towards rr: rdn and brief effrt over 2f out: sn btn* **9/1**

1m 12.53s (0.33) **Going Correction** +0.175s/f (Good)
WFA 3 from 4yo+ 8lb **10** Ran SP% **116.9**
Speed ratings (Par 104): **104,103,98,97,97 96,94,90,86,82**
CSF £48.21 CT £195.13 TOTE £3.70: £1.30, £3.70, £1.90; EX 57.60.
Owner J B J Richards **Bred** J B J Richards **Trained** Upper Lambourn, Berks

FOCUS
A fair fillies' handicap. The principals avoided the stands' rail for much of the way and the first two finished clear. The form looks sound enough.

NOTEBOOK
Our Faye was 3lb well-in following her recent second at Epsom and she proved good enough to take advantage. She had to work hard to get the better of Tilly's Dream, but was well on top at the line and should remain competitive off higher marks. (op 2-1)
Tilly's Dream returned to form when third at 33/1 at Great Leighs on her previous start and this was another decent effort, pulling well clear of the remainder in second.
Tia Mia, fifth at Nottingham on her previous outing, was beaten a fair way into third on her return to handicap company. (op 7-1)
Fly Kiss, who got rid of her rider before the start, was noted doing some good late work and is probably best suited by 7f.
Nice To Know(FR) is another who is probably better over another furlong. (op 4-1)
Hessian(IRE) Official explanation: trainer said filly was found to be in season

2994 FRANKIE'S 21ST ANNIVERSARY MAIDEN STKS 1m
6:50 (6:54) (Class 5) 3-Y-O **£3,238** (£963; £481; £240) **Stalls** High

Form RPR
4- **1** **Regal Best (IRE)**[241] 6252 3-9-3 0.. JimCrowley 8 86+
(Mrs A J Perrett) *hld up in midfield: rdn and unable qck 3f out: wnt modest 3rd wl over 1f out: styd on strly u.p fnl f to ld towards fin* **10/1**[3]
2-23 **2** 1/2 **Desert Chill (USA)**[9] 2717 3-8-12 81.. LDettori 4 80
(Saeed Bin Suroor) *led: rdn over 2f out: clr ent fnl f: wknd last 100yds: hdd and no ex towards fin* **7/2**[2]
3 1 **Hall Hee (IRE)** 3-8-12 0.. MartinDwyer 5 78+
(M P Tregoning) *s.i.s: hld up in tch: nt clr run and swtchd rt over 2f out: rallied over 1f out: r.o wl fnl f: nt rch ldng pair* **14/1**
22 **4** 3 **Liberation Spirit (USA)**[21] 2360 3-9-3 0.. RyanMoore 6 76
(J Noseda) *chsd ldrs tl wnt 2nd over 4f out: drvn over 2f out: one pce and btn over 1f out: lost two pls fnl f* **1/2**[1]
0-66 **5** 5 **Timber Creek**[32] 2046 3-9-3 68.. FergusSweeney 9 64
(H Candy) *wnt lft s: t.k.h: hld up in tch: rdn wl over 2f out: outpcd fnl 2f* **40/1**
6 nk **Hevelius** 3-9-3 0.. AdamKirby 2 64+
(W R Swinburn) *s.i.s: sn rdn along in rr: plugged on past btn horses fnl f: nvr on terms* **25/1**
7 1/2 **Wouldn'Titbenice** 3-8-12 0.. ChrisCatlin 11 57?
(V Smith) *t.k.h early: hld up bhd: nvr trble ldrs* **100/1**
8 hd **Futurity** 3-8-12 0.. HayleyTurner 7 57+
(Eve Johnson Houghton) *s.i.s: wl bhd: swtchd lft jst over 2f out: sme late hdwy: n.d* **50/1**
0-0 **9** 3 3/4 **Headache**[7] 2786 3-9-3 0.. PatCosgrave 1 53
(B W Duke) *hld up in tch: rdn and effrt on outer 3f out: no hdwy and wl btn last 2f* **40/1**
0- **10** 9 **Harting Hill**[294] 4764 3-9-3 0.. PatDobbs 3 33
(M P Tregoning) *chsd ldrs: rdn wl over 2f out: sn wknd* **66/1**
0- **11** 2 3/4 **Royal Tartan (USA)**[268] 5536 3-8-12 0.. JimmyFortune 10 21
(G L Moore) *chsd ldr tl over 4f out: wkng whn hmpd over 2f out: sn wl bhd* **66/1**

1m 40.75s (0.85) **Going Correction** +0.10s/f (Good) **11** Ran SP% **119.3**
Speed ratings (Par 99): **99,98,97,94,89 89,88,88,84,75 73**
CSF £44.40 TOTE £11.90: £2.10, £1.50, £2.70; EX 56.60.
Owner A D Spence **Bred** J F Tuthill **Trained** Pulborough, W Sussex
■ Stewards' Enquiry : Martin Dwyer two-day ban: careless riding (Jun 27-28)

FOCUS
An ordinary maiden run at a fair pace. The favourite disappointed but the form seems sound enough, rated around the second and fifth.
Hevelius Official explanation: jockey said colt ran green

2995 CHEVIOT ASSET MANAGEMENT STKS (H'CAP) 7f
7:25 (7:28) (Class 4) (0-80,80) 4-Y-O+ **£4,533** (£1,348; £674; £336) **Stalls** High

Form RPR
-203 **1** **Manchurian**[21] 2358 4-9-2 **75**..(p) JamieSpencer 4 85
(M J Wallace) *stdd s: hld up bhd: stl plenty to do 2f out: hdwy after: rdn ent fnl f: r.o to ld last 75yds* **10/1**
-052 **2** 1/2 **Golden Desert (IRE)**[22] 2329 4-9-7 **80**.. JimmyFortune 8 89
(T G Mills) *hld up in midfield: swtchd lft over 2f out: gd hdwy wl over 1f out: rdn to ld ins fnl f: hdd and no ex last 75yds* **5/1**[2]
-405 **3** 3/4 **Fleuret**[22] 2339 4-9-7 **80**.. HayleyTurner 3 87
(Eve Johnson Houghton) *taken down early: towards rr: rdn and effrt on outer over 2f out: kpt on wl u.p fr over 1f out: wnt 3rd wl ins fnl f* **14/1**
5313 **4** 1 **Councellor (FR)**[5] 2860 6-9-1 **74**..(t) TPQueally 14 78
(Stef Liddiard) *led: rdn over 2f out: kpt on wl tl hdd ins fnl f: no ex last 100yds* **4/1**[1]
1062 **5** 1 1/4 **Count Ceprano (IRE)**[23] 2308 4-9-0 **80**.. GabrielHannon[(7)] 7 81
(M D I Usher) *hld up in midfield: hdwy on rail 3f out: edgd out lft 2f out: kpt on same pce u.p fnl f* **6/1**[3]
1020 **6** 2 1/2 **Buxton**[69] 1211 4-9-5 **78**..(t) RobertHavlin 15 72
(R Ingram) *chsd ldrs on rail: rdn wl over 1f out: outpcd ent fnl f* **12/1**
05-0 **7** 1/2 **Blue Java**[44] 1719 7-8-10 **72**.. TravisBlock[(3)] 5 65
(H Morrison) *chsd ldrs: rdn over 2f out: chsd ldr briefly over 1f out: wknd jst ins fnl f* **7/1**
603- **8** 1 1/4 **Gentle Guru**[274] 5360 4-9-5 **78**.. LDettori 1 67
(R T Phillips) *stdd s and dropped in bhd: hdwy towards inner 3f out: nt clr run and edgd out lft 2f out: nvr trbld ldrs* **10/1**
500- **9** 1 1/2 **Cape Of Luck (IRE)**[168] 7253 5-9-5 **78**.. IanMongan 13 63
(P M Phelan) *chsd ldr: rdn and ev ch 2f out: lost 2nd over 1f out: sn wknd* **14/1**
0-00 **10** nk **Grizedale (IRE)**[13] 2615 9-8-3 **62**.. DavidKinsella 9 47
(M J Attwater) *stdd s: hld up bhd: effrt on outer wl over 2f out: nvr on terms* **50/1**
4-00 **11** 1/2 **Wavertree Warrior (IRE)**[139] 314 6-9-4 **77**.. JimCrowley 2 60
(N P Littmoden) *hld up in rr: plld out 3f out: sn rdn and no hdwy* **16/1**
05-5 **12** 1 **Dr Synn**[13] 2615 7-7-11 **61** oh1.. NataliaGemelova[(5)] 12 42
(M J Attwater) *hld up in rr: n.d* **20/1**
2561 **13** 1/2 **Steig (IRE)**[61] 1345 5-9-0 **73**.. JamesDoyle 10 52
(Carl Llewellyn) *chsd ldrs: rdn and hung rt over 2f out: sn btn* **18/1**
-004 **14** 3 1/2 **Tony James (IRE)**[22] 2339 6-9-7 **80**.. ChrisCatlin 11 50
(K O Cunningham-Brown) *hld up in tch: rdn and struggling whn hmpd over 2f out: sn wl btn: eased ins fnl f* **14/1**

1m 27.63s (0.23) **Going Correction** +0.10s/f (Good) **14** Ran SP% **127.2**
Speed ratings (Par 105): **102,101,100,99,98 95,94,93,91,91 90,89,88,84**
CSF £57.26 CT £552.54 TOTE £11.80: £2.60, £2.30, £6.90; EX 59.80.
Owner Mrs P Good **Bred** J R And Mrs P Good **Trained** Newmarket, Suffolk
■ Vanadium (17/2) was withdrawn after being kicked at the start. Rule 4 applies, deduct 10p in the £.

FOCUS
A fair handicap run at a strong pace. The winner took advantage of a good turf mark and the form is rated through the fourth.
Steig(IRE) Official explanation: jockey said gelding hung right

2996 CRIMBOURNE STUD STKS (H'CAP) 1m 1f 192y
8:00 (8:01) (Class 4) (0-80,80) 3-Y-O **£6,476** (£1,927; £963; £481) **Stalls** High

Form RPR
1-04 **1** **Goodwood Starlight (IRE)**[23] 2302 3-9-6 **79**.. EddieAhern 6 93
(J L Dunlop) *hld up in tch: hdwy 4f out: rdn to ld 2f out: sn edgd rt: clr 1f out: styd on strly* **9/4**[1]
-033 **2** 5 **Ellemujie**[23] 2311 3-9-7 **80**.. LDettori 8 85+
(D K Ivory) *hld up towards rr: hdwy over 3f out: rdn to chse wnr ent fnl f: no imp: eased nr fin* **9/2**[3]
-140 **3** nk **Title Role**[28] 2151 3-8-11 **73**.. TolleyDean[(3)] 2 75
(P F I Cole) *chsd ldr tl over 5f out: rdn and outpcd 3f out: styd on again u.p fr over 1f out: wnt 3rd wl ins fnl f: no ch w wnr* **18/1**
4226 **4** shd **Higgy's Boy (IRE)**[25] 2256 3-9-5 **78**.. PatDobbs 4 80
(R Hannon) *hld up in last pair: rdn 3f out: plugged on steadily past btn horses fnl f: nvr nr wnr* **11/1**
2301 **5** 1 1/4 **Mcconnell (USA)**[23] 2302 3-9-6 **79**.. RyanMoore 1 79
(G L Moore) *chsd ldrs: wnt 2nd over 5f out: rdn 3f out: unable qck u.p: wknd over 1f out* **11/4**[2]
65-6 **6** 3 1/2 **Timbalier (USA)**[58] 1403 3-8-10 **69**.. MartinDwyer 9 61
(D M Simcock) *chsd ldrs: pushed along 6f out: rdn over 4f out: wknd wl over 2f out* **33/1**
-143 **7** nk **Greylami (IRE)**[52] 1543 3-9-7 **80**.. JimmyFortune 7 72
(T G Mills) *sn led: rdn over 2f out: hdd 2f out: wknd over 1f out* **5/1**
334- **8** 5 **Red Cauldron**[305] 4448 3-8-12 **71**.. ChrisCatlin 5 52
(E J O'Neill) *hld up bhd: rdn and lost tch 3f out* **25/1**
5-24 **9** 2 1/2 **Gaia Prince (USA)**[27] 2197 3-9-4 **77**.. JimCrowley 3 53
(Mrs A J Perrett) *hld up towards rr: hdwy on outer 4f out: rdn 3f out: sn struggling and btn* **14/1**

2m 8.68s (0.68) **Going Correction** +0.10s/f (Good) **9** Ran SP% **119.3**
Speed ratings (Par 101): **101,97,96,96,95 92,92,88,86**
CSF £13.30 CT £148.59 TOTE £3.00: £1.30, £2.00, £4.90; EX 12.90.
Owner Goodwood Racehorse Owners Group Fourteen **Bred** Lynn Lodge Stud **Trained** Arundel, W Sussex

FOCUS
A fair handicap. Solid form, with improvement from the winner.

2997 BLACK TIE PICNIC MAIDEN H'CAP 1m 6f
8:35 (8:36) (Class 5) (0-75,75) 3-Y-O **£3,238** (£963; £481; £240) **Stalls** Low

Form RPR
233 **1** **Victoria Montoya**[28] 2164 3-9-4 **70**.. FrancisNorton 5 80
(A M Balding) *s.i.s: hld up bhd: hdwy and swtchd lft over 3f out: ev ch u.p wl over 1f out: carried lft 1f out and again ins fnl f: rallied to ld on post* **3/1**[1]
4324 **2** shd **Dolly Penrose**[22] 2336 3-9-4 **70**.. EdwardCreighton 12 80
(M R Channon) *hld up towards rr: hdwy over 1f out: rdn to ld wl over 1f out: hung lft 1f out and again ins fnl f: hdd on post* **15/2**
0-05 **3** 4 **Silk Hall (UAE)**[25] 2244 3-9-2 **68**.. FergusSweeney 4 72
(D W P Arbuthnot) *rrd s and slowly away: hld up bhd: hdwy on outer over 3f out: kpt on to chse ldng pair ins fnl f: nvr pce to chal* **18/1**
0320 **4** 1 1/2 **Lord's Bidding**[23] 2310 3-8-10 **62**..(v) RobertHavlin 13 64
(R Ingram) *t.k.h: sn chsng ldr: rdn and ev ch over 3f out: kpt on same pce u.p* **16/1**
-006 **5** shd **Teen Spirit (IRE)**[18] 2468 3-8-6 **58**.. LiamJones 1 60
(J W Hills) *hrd pressed and rdn over 3f out: hdd wl over 1f out: one pce fr over 1f out* **33/1**
-006 **6** 3/4 **No Rules**[22] 2340 3-8-6 **58**.. MartinDwyer 10 59
(M H Tompkins) *chsd ldrs: rdn and pressed ldrs 4f out: one pce u.p last 2f* **14/1**
5406 **7** 1/2 **Hadron Collider (FR)**[23] 2310 3-9-0 **66**.. PatDobbs 9 66
(R Hannon) *hld up in midfield: hdwy on outer 6f out: rdn 3f out: no imp last 2f* **10/1**
-440 **8** 2 1/4 **Dancing Dik**[18] 2468 3-8-11 **63**.. JimmyFortune 14 65+
(Mrs A J Perrett) *t.k.h: in tch: rdn 3f out: btn whn swtchd rt 1f out: no ch whn nt clr run ins fnl f* **9/1**
-040 **9** 2 1/2 **Krisnando**[10] 2695 3-8-8 **60**.. RyanMoore 8 56+
(G L Moore) *s.i.s: hld up wl bhd: hdwy 3f out: chsd ldrs and rdn over 2f out: wknd over 1f out: eased ins fnl f* **4/1**[2]
043 **10** 3/4 **Swingkeel (IRE)**[18] 2454 3-9-9 **75**.. EddieAhern 3 67
(J L Dunlop) *t.k.h: hld up in midfield early: grad dropped to rr: hdwy 3f out: sn rdn and no hdwy* **6/1**[3]
0046 **11** 5 **Brave Boogie**[58] 1397 3-8-6 **58**.. JamesDoyle 11 43
(H J L Dunlop) *in tch in midfield: rdn over 3f out: sn wknd: eased ins fnl f* **66/1**
04-0 **12** 1/2 **Appointment**[13] 2603 3-8-13 **65**.. JimCrowley 7 50
(Mrs A J Perrett) *in tch: rdn over 3f out: wknd qckly over 2f out: eased ins fnl f* **16/1**
50-5 **13** 26 **Warsaw Waltz**[18] 2468 3-8-9 **61**.. TPQueally 2 9
(J G Given) *chsd ldrs: rdn and wknd wl over 2f out: eased fnl f: t.o* **16/1**
-223 **14** 3 3/4 **Montfjord (IRE)**[48] 1615 3-9-9 **75**.. ChrisCatlin 6 18
(E J O'Neill) *hld up in midfield: rdn and lost pl over 4f out: struggling whn hmpd over 3f out: wl bhd after: t.o* **20/1**

3m 6.52s (2.92) **Going Correction** +0.10s/f (Good) **14** Ran SP% **128.9**
Speed ratings (Par 99): **95,94,92,91,91 91,91,89,88,87 85,84,69,67**
CSF £27.27 CT £371.62 TOTE £3.90: £2.10, £2.60, £7.00; EX 22.80.
Owner Kingsclere Racing CLub **Bred** Kingsclere Stud **Trained** Kingsclere, Hants
■ Stewards' Enquiry : Edward Creighton two-day ban: careless riding (Jun 27-28)

FOCUS
A weak maiden handicap but the form seems sound enough. The first two are progressive.

Warsaw Waltz Official explanation: trainer said filly was found to be lame on near-hind next day

2998 LIZZY HARE STKS (H'CAP) 6f
9:05 (9:07) (Class 4) (0-85,85) 3-Y-0 £4,533 (£1,348; £674; £336) Stalls Low

Form				RPR
0-34	1		**Shifting Star (IRE)**[28] 2162 3-9-3 81 AdamKirby 3	95
			(W R Swinburn) *in tch in midfield: nt clr run and swtchd lft 2f out: r.o wl u.p to ld last 100yds: edgd rt nr fin* **8/1**	
4-13	2	¾	**Fabreze**[15] 2526 3-9-1 79 EddieAhern 7	91
			(P J Makin) *sltly hmpd s: sn in tch: rdn 1/2-way: hdwy and ev ch 2f out: led ent fnl f: hdd and no ex last 100yds* **3/1**[2]	
5410	3	1 ½	**Brassini**[20] 2410 3-9-7 85 JohnEgan 1	92
			(B R Millman) *chsd ldrs tl led after 2f: rdn jst over 2f out: sn edging rt: hdd wl over 1f out: kpt on same pce* **13/2**[3]	
2134	4	1	**Opera Prince**[7] 2794 3-8-13 77 JimmyFortune 12	81+
			(S Kirk) *in tch on outer: hdwy over 2f out: led wl over 1f out: sn rdn: hdd ent fnl f: wknd last 100yds* **5/2**[1]	
0-00	5	2	**Masada (IRE)**[19] 2428 3-9-4 82 RyanMoore 5	79
			(B J Meehan) *t.k.h: hld up bhd: hdwy and nt clr run 2f out: grad edgd out rt: kpt on same pce fnl f* **14/1**	
5-34	6	1 ½	**Lodi (IRE)**[14] 2555 3-8-9 73 IanMongan 11	66
			(J Akehurst) *in tch: hdwy 1/2-way: ev ch u.p over 1f out: wknd fnl f* **17/2**	
1-05	7	nk	**Hadaf (IRE)**[35] 1945 3-9-6 84 MartinDwyer 2	76
			(M P Tregoning) *t.k.h: hld up bhd: effrt 2f out: nvr pce to chal* **14/1**	
-306	8	¾	**C'Mon You Irons (IRE)**[13] 2598 3-9-4 82 AdrianMcCarthy 10	71
			(M R Hoad) *led for 2f: styd prom: ev ch and rdn wl over 1f out: wknd ent fnl f* **16/1**	
4421	9	2 ¾	**Valhillen**[14] 2555 3-8-8 72 (p) HayleyTurner 9	52
			(M D I Usher) *chsd ldrs: rdn 1/2-way: wkng whn n.m.r 2f out: wl bhd fnl f* **14/1**	
2310	10	1 ½	**Dubai Power**[13] 2606 3-9-0 83 AhmedAjtebi(5) 4	59
			(C E Brittain) *rrd stalls: sn rcvrd: pressed ldr after 2f: ev ch wl over 1f out: wknd qckly ent fnl f* **12/1**	
2-16	11	¾	**What Katie Did (IRE)**[36] 1934 3-8-5 74 JackMitchell(5) 6	47
			(P F I Cole) *wnt rt s: sn chsng ldrs: rdn and wkng whn hmpd 2f out: no ch after* **16/1**	

1m 12.59s (0.39) **Going Correction** +0.175s/f (Good) 11 Ran SP% **128.0**
Speed ratings (Par 101): **104,103,101,99,97 95,94,93,89,87 86**
CSF £35.21 CT £179.73 TOTE £11.90: £3.10, £1.80, £3.80; EX 38.10 Place 6 £157.04, Place 5 £81.99..
Owner Night Shadow Syndicate **Bred** Hardys Of Kilkeel Ltd **Trained** Aldbury, Herts

FOCUS
A good three-year-old sprint handicap. There seemed no advantage with the draw and the form is sound, rated through the third.
T/Plt: £143.00 to a £1 stake. Pool: £75,682.79. 386.25 winning tickets. T/Qpdt: £27.00 to a £1 stake. Pool: £4,711.00. 128.85 winning tickets. SP

2759 SANDOWN (R-H)
Friday, June 13

OFFICIAL GOING: Good (good to soft in places on round course; 7.5)
Wind: almost nil

2999 FIREX EBF MAIDEN STKS 5f 6y
2:10 (2:11) (Class 4) 2-Y-0 £4,533 (£1,348; £674; £336) Stalls High

Form				RPR
4	1		**Macdillon**[29] 2124 2-9-3 0 FergusSweeney 11	81
			(W S Kittow) *t.k.h early: trckd ldrs: drvn to ld jst ins fnl f: hld on all out* **8/1**[3]	
3	2	nk	**Kingship Spirit (IRE)**[20] 2411 2-9-3 0 LDettori 7	80
			(J Noseda) *hld up in rr: stdy hdwy fr 2f out: drvn and styd on to go 2nd ins fnl f: clsng on wnr nr fin but a jst hld* **4/6**[1]	
0	3	1 ½	**Pocket's Pick (IRE)**[15] 2541 2-9-3 0 GeorgeBaker 5	75
			(G L Moore) *led: rdn over 1f out: hdd jst ins fnl f: sn on pce* **25/1**	
2	4	1 ¼	**Red Rossini (IRE)**[9] 2709 2-9-3 0 RichardHughes 4	70
			(R Hannon) *chsd ldr tl over 1f out: wknd ins fnl f* **10/1**	
0	5	½	**Mattamia (IRE)**[29] 2124 2-9-3 0 AlanMunro 9	68
			(B R Millman) *chsd ldrs: rdn 1/2-way: wknd over 1f out* **50/1**	
34	6	4 ½	**Verlegen (IRE)**[17] 2479 2-8-12 0 RyanMoore 3	47
			(R Hannon) *chsd ldrs: rdn 2f out: wknd fnl f* **6/1**[2]	
	7	½	**Goldvil (IRE)** 2-9-3 0 JamieSpencer 1	50
			(B J Meehan) *towards rr: hdwy 1/2-way: nvr gng pce to to rch ldrs and wknd over 1f out* **14/1**	
	8	1 ¼	**Rocket Rob (IRE)** 2-9-3 0 JimCrowley 2	46
			(S A Callaghan) *s.i.s: in rr: sme hdwy fr over 1f out: nvr in contention* **50/1**	
0	9	1 ¼	**Mean Mr Mustard (IRE)**[35] 1955 2-9-3 0 TPQueally 8	41+
			(J A Osborne) *s.i.s: t.k.h early: a outpcd* **40/1**	
0	10	2 ¾	**Russian Art**[29] 2124 2-9-3 0 JamesDoyle 10	31+
			(R M Beckett) *rdn 1/2-way: a outpcd* **14/1**	
	11	6	**Rapanui Belle** 2-8-12 0 AdamKirby 6	5
			(G L Moore) *a outpcd* **66/1**	

63.01 secs (1.41) **Going Correction** +0.20s/f (Good) 11 Ran SP% **119.5**
Speed ratings (Par 95): **96,95,93,91,90 83,82,80,78,73 64**
CSF £13.62 TOTE £8.10: £1.90, £1.10, £6.50; EX 17.30.
Owner The Macdillon Partnership **Bred** Mrs Hopkins, Mr Kittow And Mrs Perry **Trained** Blackborough, Devon
■ Stewards' Enquiry : L Dettori caution: careless riding

FOCUS
A fair juvenile maiden run 0.40secs slower than the following handicap. As usual the far rail proved the place to be.

NOTEBOOK
Macdillon, who was backed before showing ability on his debut, was well drawn. He tracked the leaders before getting a run that took him into the lead a furlong out and he did enough to hold off the favourite. He had clearly learnt from his debut and looks as if he will improve again on this, and could return here for the Listed Dragon Stakes next.
Kingship Spirit(IRE), dropped in trip after fading up the hill on his debut, was coltish in the paddock. He was held up before making headway from 3f out and had to be switched to get a run, but tended to hang before eventually running on well in the final furlong. He again displayed an awkward head carriage and, although he clearly has ability, does not look one to be totally confident about. Some form of headgear may help, but it could be that gelding will be necessary in time. (op 8-13 tchd 4-7 in places)
Pocket's Pick(IRE) had learnt from his debut run in the National Stakes over course and distance and showed plenty of pace on this drop in grade. He had nothing more to give once headed but does look capable of picking up a maiden, possibly on a sharper track. (tchd 40-1 in places)
Red Rossini(IRE), who showed pace on his debut on Polytrack, again displayed speed until tiring in the final furlong. He looks the sort who can make his mark in nurseries after another outing. (op 11-1)
Mattamia(IRE) built on his debut effort when finishing last of nine in the race in which today's winner was fourth, staying on in the closing stages, and is another who can make his mark in handicaps in time.
Verlegen(IRE), having her third run, was close up until weakening a furlong out and is another who is likely to be contesting nurseries before long. Her best effort was over 6f on easy ground and she may need some cut. (op 15-2)
Goldvil(IRE) ◆, who at 30,000gns cost 20,000gns less at the breeze-ups than he had as a yearling, is a half-brother to the speedy sorts Mr Rooney and Desert Tiger and comes from the family of Ma Biche. Drawn on the outside on this debut, he had to race wide but showed a bit of promise despite being done no favours by the runner-up at one point. He should come on a fair amount for the experience. (op 16-1 tchd 12-1)
Russian Art Official explanation: jockey said colt hung left

3000 FIRE INDUSTRY DAY H'CAP 5f 6y
2:40 (2:42) (Class 5) (0-75,75) 3-Y-0 £4,533 (£1,348; £674; £336) Stalls High

Form				RPR
1134	1		**Requisite**[8] 2757 3-9-9 75 RyanMoore 12	82
			(I A Wood) *trckd ldrs: drvn and qcknd fnl f to ld fnl 100yds: r.o strly* **4/1**[1]	
2414	2	¾	**Maggie Kate**[16] 2506 3-8-13 65 RobertHavlin 10	69
			(R Ingram) *led: rdn fr 2f out: hdd and no ex fnl 100yds* **14/1**	
00-0	3	1 ¼	**First Trim (IRE)**[34] 1995 3-9-9 75 RichardHughes 11	75
			(B J Meehan) *towards rr: hdwy over 1f out: styd on strly thrght fnl f: gng on cl home but nt rch ldng duo* **8/1**	
-320	4	nk	**Supermassive Muse (IRE)**[20] 2407 3-9-7 73 StephenDonohoe 9	71
			(E S McMahon) *chsd ldr: rdn 2f out: one pce fnl f* **7/1**	
142	5	¾	**Wynberg (IRE)**[10] 2690 3-9-4 70 JimCrowley 3	66+
			(S A Callaghan) *in rr: rdn 2f out: styd on fnl f but nt trble ldrs* **10/1**	
0-04	6	½	**Apple Pie Order (IRE)**[13] 2620 3-9-1 67 SteveDrowne 8	61
			(R J Hodges) *chsd ldrs: rdn 2f out: one pce fnl f* **14/1**	
4346	7	hd	**The Little Fizzer (IRE)**[42] 1769 3-8-8 60 FergusSweeney 2	53+
			(K R Burke) *chsd ldrs: rdn 1/2-way: one pce whn j. patch jst ins fnl f and sn btn* **14/1**	
-013	8	2	**Brazilian Brush (IRE)**[5] 2864 3-9-3 72 (t) TravisBlock(3) 5	58
			(H Morrison) *chsd ldrs: rdn 1/2-way: wknd fnl f* **9/2**[2]	
0-01	9	1	**Liberty Belle (IRE)**[10] 2690 3-9-7 73 6ex LPKeniry 4	55
			(J R Best) *in tch whn rdn and sme prog 3f out: nvr in contention and wknd fnl f* **16/1**	
264-	10	nse	**Wreningham**[167] 7270 3-9-0 69 JerryO'Dwyer(3) 1	51
			(T Keddy) *outpcd most of way* **66/1**	
0504	11	hd	**Enodoc**[10] 2690 3-9-5 71 MartinDwyer 7	53
			(W R Muir) *outpcd* **16/1**	
105	12	1 ½	**Savannah Poppy (IRE)**[19] 2428 3-9-9 75 JamieSpencer 6	51
			(M L W Bell) *t.k.h: in rr: swtchd lft to outside 2f out: sn rdn and no ch* **5/1**[3]	

62.61 secs (1.01) **Going Correction** +0.20s/f (Good) 12 Ran SP% **120.8**
Speed ratings (Par 99): **99,97,95,95,94 93,93,89,88,88 87,85**
CSF £62.53 CT £346.60 TOTE £4.80: £2.00, £5.30, £3.10; EX 66.10.
Owner Paddy Barrett **Bred** Darley **Trained** Upper Lambourn, Berks

FOCUS
A fair handicap run 0.40secs faster than the opening juvenile maiden after the initial pace had not looked that strong. The draw played a major part in the outcome and the form is obviously a bit shaky.
Savannah Poppy(IRE) Official explanation: jockey said filly boiled over

3001 EMS RADIO FIRE & SECURITY MAIDEN STKS 7f 16y
3:15 (3:17) (Class 4) 2-Y-0 £5,180 (£1,541; £770; £384) Stalls High

Form				RPR
5	1		**Managua**[13] 2601 2-9-3 0 DarryllHolland 3	80
			(M R Channon) *trckd ldrs: chal over 1f out: rdn to take slt advantage ins fnl f: styd on wl cl home* **6/1**	
63	2	½	**Jazacosta (USA)**[28] 2150 2-9-3 0 JimCrowley 6	79
			(Mrs A J Perrett) *sn pressing for ld: slt advantage over 3f out: rdn 2f out: hdd ins fnl f: kpt on but a jst hld by wnr* **4/1**[2]	
	3	2 ½	**Perfect Citizen (USA)** 2-9-3 0 AdamKirby 7	73
			(W R Swinburn) *chsd ldrs: rdn 3f out: styd on same pce fr over 1f out* **16/1**	
	4	2	**Pachattack (USA)** 2-8-12 0 HayleyTurner 5	63
			(G A Butler) *s.i.s: bhd: rdn over 3f out: hdwy over 1f out: styd on wl cl home but nvr gng pce to be competitive* **16/1**	
	5	nse	**Muraweg (IRE)** 2-9-3 0 RHills 1	68
			(J H M Gosden) *in rr: rdn and hdwy over 2f out: kpt on fnl f but nvr gng pce to be competitive* **9/2**[3]	
	6	shd	**Andhaar** 2-9-3 0 MartinDwyer 4	67
			(E A L Dunlop) *s.i.s: in rr: rdn and styd on fr 2f out: kpt on ins fnl f but nvr a threat* **12/1**	
	7	3 ¾	**Pure Poetry (IRE)** 2-9-3 0 RichardHughes 12	58
			(R Hannon) *slt advantage tl narrowly hdd over 3f out: styd chalng tl appr fnl 2f: wknd over 1f out* **11/4**[1]	
	8	hd	**Sam Sharp (USA)** 2-9-3 0 TedDurcan 9	58
			(H R A Cecil) *in rr tl effrt and n.m.r 3f out: and again over 2f out: sayed on fnl forlong but nvr in contention* **8/1**	
	9	1 ½	**Beaubrav** 2-9-3 0 JamieSpencer 10	54
			(P W D'Arcy) *slowly away: in rr: awkward bnd 4f out and wd: rdn and sme prog over 2f out: nvr in contention: hung rt and wknd over 1f out* **7/1**	
	10	7	**Shape Shifter (USA)** 2-9-3 0 LPKeniry 11	36
			(J R Best) *in tch: rdn over 3f out and sn wknd* **33/1**	
0	11	2 ½	**Ain't Talkin'**[14] 2562 2-9-3 0 PaulDoe 8	30
			(M J Attwater) *chsd ldrs over 4f* **100/1**	
0	12	18	**Tightrope (IRE)**[43] 1736 2-9-3 0 RobertHavlin 2	—
			(T D McCarthy) *chsd ldrs tl wknd qckly over 2f out* **100/1**	

1m 31.85s (2.35) **Going Correction** +0.075s/f (Good) 12 Ran SP% **127.1**
Speed ratings (Par 95): **89,88,85,83,83 83,78,78,76,68 66,45**
CSF £32.52 TOTE £7.40: £2.40, £1.70, £5.70; EX 37.50.
Owner Capital **Bred** Brook Stud Bloodstock Ltd **Trained** West Ilsley, Berks

FOCUS
Just an ordinary maiden in which two of the three with previous experience fought out the finish.

NOTEBOOK
Managua, who showed promise on his debut over 6f, appreciated the step up in trip and the experience enabled him to wear down the runner-up in the closing stages. He races as if he will get further in time. (op 7-1 tchd 15-2)
Jazacosta(USA), who had built on his debut when upped to 6f last time, appreciated the extra furlong and ran his race, just losing out to the winner in the closing stages. He possibly raced a little free up with the leaders otherwise the result may have been different. He now qualifies for a handicap mark and looks more than capable of winning a race. (op 11-2 tchd 6-1)

Perfect Citizen(USA) ◆, a $160,000 half-brother to two turf winners in the USA, put up a decent effort on this raccourse debut, putting his head down and showing a good attitude in the closing stages. His yard is going well at present and he looks capable of scoring before long.
Pachattack(USA) ◆, another American-bred and closely related to the smart US filly La Mina, caught the eye on this debut with a strong finishing effort after being slow from the gate. She was the only filly in the line-up and looks sure to win races, especially against her own sex.
Muraweg(IRE), a 90,000gns half-brother to nine winners at various trips, made good ground from the rear before his effort flattened out and was not given a hard time once beaten. He is another who will benefit from the experience. (op 6-1)
Andhaar, the first foal of a mare who scored over a mile, is related to several winners for his owner. He missed the break but stayed on steadily although not quite so eye-catchingly as the fourth. He will nevertheless come on for the outing. (op 14-1)
Pure Poetry(IRE), whose stable has a good record here with their juvenile newcomers and had won this race with debutants twice in the last ten years, was well drawn and was sent off favourite but seemed to do too much in front and faded once headed. He is likely to prove capable of better with this behind him. (op 10-3)
Beaubrav, a cheaply-bought half-brother to several winners including the useful Ti Adora, who did so well for this yard, was quite short in the market given his pedigree and ran as if he will benefit from the experience. He is likely to make his mark in handicaps but possibly not until next season. Official explanation: jockey said colt lost his off-fore and near-hind shoe (op 8-1)
Shape Shifter(USA) Official explanation: jockey said colt stumbled on bend into home straight
Tightrope(IRE) Official explanation: trainer said colt was found to have mucus in its trachea

3002 MOUSETRAP CHALLENGE CUP H'CAP — 1m 14y
3:50 (3:51) (Class 4) (0-85,85) 3-Y-O — **£6,476** (£1,927; £963; £481) **Stalls** High

Form — RPR
1-50 **1** **Mountain Pride (IRE)**[41] 1811 3-9-6 **82** ... SteveDrowne 9 — 90
(J L Dunlop) *mde virtually all: rdn over 1f out: styd on wl thrght fnl f* **20/1**
3-1 **2** 2 1/4 **Diamond Yas (IRE)**[39] 1869 3-9-4 **80** ... TedDurcan 7 — 83
(H R A Cecil) *chsd ldrs: wnt 2nd 3f out: kpt on u.p fnl 2f but no ch w wnr fnl f* **11/2**[3]
3313 **3** 1/2 **Mexican Venture**[9] 2714 3-9-4 **80** ... JamieSpencer 1 — 82
(W Jarvis) *in rr but in tch: rdn and hdwy over 2f out: kpt on fnl f but nvr gng pce to be competitive* **15/8**[1]
-410 **4** shd **Master Spy**[27] 2194 3-9-9 **85** ... JimmyFortune 5 — 86
(J H M Gosden) *in tch: pushed along 3f out: hrd drvn fr 2f out: styd on same pce ins fnl f* **11/2**[3]
1-42 **5** 1 1/4 **Astrodonna**[28] 2161 3-8-12 **74** ... TPQueally 3 — 73
(M H Tompkins) *hld up in rr: hdwy over 2f out: sn chsng ldrs: wknd fnl f* **17/2**
021- **6** 1 1/2 **Howdigo**[212] 6805 3-9-5 **81** ... LPKeniry 6 — 76
(J R Best) *in tch: rdn 3f out: wknd fr 2f out* **33/1**
1-0 **7** 1/2 **Naval Review (USA)**[13] 2624 3-8-13 **75** ... RyanMoore 4 — 69
(Sir Michael Stoute) *in rr: sme prog whn nt clr run over 2f out: swtchd lft and rdn sn after: no rspnse* **9/4**[2]
03-3 **8** 5 **Deo Valente (IRE)**[27] 2199 3-8-13 **82** ... KMay(7) 8 — 64
(B J Meehan) *pressed wnr 2f: styd 2nd to 3f out: wknd qckly 2f out* **14/1**
1m 45.93s (2.63) **Going Correction** +0.075s/f (Good) **8** Ran SP% **121.2**
Speed ratings (Par 101): **89,86,86,86,84 83,82,77**
CSF £132.33 CT £316.27 TOTE £24.10: £3.30, £1.80, £1.40; EX 149.20.
Owner Ian Cameron **Bred** Raymond P Doyle **Trained** Arundel, W Sussex

FOCUS
A decent handicap but the early pace was steady and it was not easy to make ground from the rear. The winner enjoyed the run of the race and is rated up 5lb.
Mountain Pride(IRE) Official explanation: trainer said, regarding the improved form, that colt appeared to benefit from today's drop in trip to 1m

3003 WAGNER UK H'CAP — 1m 2f 7y
4:25 (4:25) (Class 4) (0-85,82) 4-Y-O+ — **£7,123** (£2,119; £1,059; £529) **Stalls** High

Form — RPR
/13- **1** **Crete (IRE)**[209] 6853 6-9-3 **76** ... MichaelHills 11 — 95+
(W J Haggas) *hld up in tch: qcknd to ld on bit over 1f out: pushed clr ins fnl f* **6/1**[3]
2214 **2** 4 1/2 **Trans Siberian**[15] 2540 4-9-9 **82** ... TQuinn 7 — 89
(P F I Cole) *led after 2f: rdn over 2f out: hdd over 1f out: sn no ch w wnr but kpt on wl to hold 2nd* **9/2**[1]
46-0 **3** 3/4 **Just Two Numbers**[46] 1682 4-9-4 **77** ... MartinDwyer 6 — 83
(W Jarvis) *mid-div: rdn over 2f out: styd on u.p fnl f to take 3rd: nt rch ldng duo* **20/1**
210- **4** 2 **Dustoori**[230] 6490 4-9-7 **80** ... RHills 9 — 84+
(E A L Dunlop) *mid-div: rdn over 2f out: styd on fr over 1f out and kpt on ins fnl f but nvr gng pce to be competitive* **5/1**[2]
1216 **5** 1/2 **Emperor Court (IRE)**[23] 2308 4-9-8 **81** ... RyanMoore 10 — 82
(P J Makin) *slt ld 2f: styd disputing 2nd: hrd rdn over 2f out: wknd fnl f* **12/1**
/5-0 **6** 2 1/2 **Balnagore**[13] 2619 4-8-10 **69** ... TedDurcan 2 — 71+
(J L Dunlop) *in rr tl styd on fnl 2f: nvr in contention* **12/1**
0-04 **7** 1 1/4 **Mount Hermon (IRE)**[21] 2369 4-9-0 **76** ... TravisBlock(3) 3 — 69
(H Morrison) *chsd ldrs: drvn along 6f out: kpt on same pce fr over 2f out* **12/1**
1153 **8** shd **Shogun Prince (IRE)**[7] 2784 5-9-4 **77** ... TPQueally 15 — 70
(W Jarvis) *disp 2nd 7f out to 3f out: wknd fr 2f out* **8/1**
422- **9** 3/4 **Del Mar Sunset**[216] 6765 9-9-5 **78** ... LiamJones 4 — 69
(W J Haggas) *in rr: rdn 3f out: sme prog over 1f out* **25/1**
0-44 **10** 3 3/4 **Pretty Demanding (IRE)**[21] 2361 4-8-10 **72** ow1 ... JerryO'Dwyer(3) 12 — 56
(M G Quinlan) *t.k.h in rr: rdn 3f out and no prog* **16/1**
4441 **11** hd **Ross Moor**[8] 2764 6-8-10 **69** 6ex ... FergusSweeney 13 — 52
(Mike Murphy) *s.i.s: in rr: rdn 3f out and no prog* **7/1**
4105 **12** 3 **Folio (IRE)**[15] 2531 8-9-9 **82** ... StephenDonohoe 5 — 59
(W J Musson) *a towards rr* **20/1**
3-06 **13** 8 **Jebel Ali (IRE)**[11] 2682 5-8-9 **68** ... JamesDoyle 14 — 29
(B Gubby) *chsd ldrs 7f* **50/1**
-143 **14** 9 **Haarth Sovereign (IRE)**[28] 2152 4-9-6 **79** ... AdamKirby 1 — 22
(W R Swinburn) *chsd ldrs to 3f out* **8/1**
2m 9.22s (-1.28) **Going Correction** +0.075s/f (Good) **14** Ran SP% **128.1**
Speed ratings (Par 105): **108,104,103,102,101 99,98,98,98,95 94,92,86,78**
CSF £33.84 CT £535.06 TOTE £7.80: £2.90, £2.00, £6.50; EX 43.10.
Owner Highclere Thoroughbred Racing (Crete) **Bred** Scuderia Siba S P A **Trained** Newmarket, Suffolk

FOCUS
A decent handicap run at a good gallop, being 2.04secs faster than the following race for three-year-olds. The form looks solid and should prove reliable.
Balnagore ◆ Official explanation: jockey said colt was denied a clear run
Haarth Sovereign(IRE) Official explanation: jockey said gelding lost action

3004 ADVANCED ELECTRONICS H'CAP — 1m 2f 7y
4:55 (4:59) (Class 5) (0-75,75) 3-Y-O — **£4,533** (£1,348; £674; £336) **Stalls** High

Form — RPR
0112 **1** **Buddy Holly**[14] 2564 3-9-8 **74** ... PatDobbs 17 — 84
(Pat Eddery) *chsd ldrs: chal over 1f out: led jst ins fnl f: drvn out* **15/2**[3]
22-2 **2** 3/4 **Heritage Coast (USA)**[53] 1527 3-9-9 **75** ... RyanMoore 9 — 84+
(Sir Michael Stoute) *chsd ldrs: rdn over 2f out: styd on u.p to chse wnr ins fnl f: kpt on but no imp cl home* **10/3**[1]
3-31 **3** 1 **Stow**[25] 2244 3-9-6 **75** ... TravisBlock(3) 1 — 82+
(H Morrison) *chsd ldrs: led 6f out: rdn whn chal fr over 2f out: hdd jst ins fnl f: sn one pce* **7/1**[2]
0-02 **4** 3/4 **Red Merlin (IRE)**[10] 2695 3-9-4 **70** ... AdamKirby 14 — 75
(C G Cox) *in tch: rdn 3f out: kpt on u.p fnl f: kpt on cl home* **12/1**
6-30 **5** 1/2 **Hawk House**[14] 2564 3-8-9 **61** ... MichaelHills 12 — 66+
(B W Hills) *led 2f: styd w ldrs: upsides 2f out: hmpd over 1f out and sn one pce* **33/1**
-661 **6** 1/2 **Love And Glory (FR)**[9] 2719 3-8-13 **65** 6ex ... FergusSweeney 8 — 68
(G L Moore) *mid-div: rdn over 3f out: styd on fr 2f out to chse ldrs: one pce fnl f* **9/1**
455- **7** 3 1/4 **Tyrrells Wood (IRE)**[209] 6857 3-9-9 **75** ... TedDurcan 10 — 72
(T G Mills) *in tch: rdn and styd on fr over 2f out: gng on cl home* **25/1**
-403 **8** 1 **Green Wadi**[17] 2488 3-9-9 **75** ... EdwardCreighton 6 — 70
(M R Channon) *towards rr: rdn over 3f out: kpt on fnl 2f but nvr rchd ldrs* **12/1**
-534 **9** 2 **El Duende (USA)**[10] 2695 3-9-4 **70** ... TPQueally 5 — 61
(W Jarvis) *chsd ldrs: rdn over 3f out: wknd 2f out* **12/1**
6-50 **10** 1 1/4 **Hawk Flight (IRE)**[11] 2678 3-9-2 **68** ... MartinDwyer 13 — 56
(W R Muir) *slowly away: in rr: sme prog fnl 2f* **16/1**
-400 **11** 1 1/4 **Straight And Level (CAN)**[43] 1745 3-9-9 **75** ... JamesDoyle 3 — 61
(Miss Jo Crowley) *chsd ldrs: rdn 3f out: wknd over 2f out* **66/1**
1220 **12** hd **Always Brave**[16] 2496 3-9-7 **73** ... JoeFanning 2 — 58
(M Johnston) *in rr: sme prog on outside 4f out: sn wknd* **16/1**
-340 **13** 1 3/4 **Al Azy (IRE)**[25] 2244 3-8-13 **65** ... (b) RHills 11 — 47
(J L Dunlop) *in rr: sme prog and n.m.r 3f out: no further prog and sn bhd* **25/1**
30-0 **14** 1 1/4 **Bathwick Man**[38] 1899 3-8-13 **65** ... TQuinn 7 — 44
(B R Millman) *a towards rr* **66/1**
2-40 **15** 1 3/4 **Hyde Lea Flyer**[28] 2161 3-9-5 **71** ... StephenDonohoe 4 — 47
(E S McMahon) *slowly away: a towards rr* **12/1**
0401 **16** 12 **Ramprakash**[13] 2613 3-9-0 **66** ... JamieSpencer 16 — 18+
(M L W Bell) *in tch: rdn and chsd ldrs 3f out: sn wknd* **7/1**[2]
3400 **17** 3 1/2 **Ace Of Spies (IRE)**[16] 2496 3-8-4 **63** ... CraigPettigrew(7) 15 — 8
(M Johnston) *led after 2f to 6f out: wknd fr 3f out* **40/1**
2m 11.26s (0.76) **Going Correction** +0.075s/f (Good) **17** Ran SP% **128.4**
Speed ratings (Par 99): **99,98,97,97,96 96,93,92,91,90 89,89,87,86,85 75,72**
CSF £32.33 CT £193.83 TOTE £8.50: £1.80, £1.60, £2.80, £2.60; EX 42.80 Place 6: £66.76, Place 5: £48.47.
Owner Hayman, Pearson, Phillips & McGuinness **Bred** R J & S A Carter **Trained** Nether Winchendon, Bucks

FOCUS
A fair handicap run 2.04secs slower than the preceding older-horse contest. The form is pretty solid and a positive view has been taken of the form.
Ramprakash Official explanation: jockey said colt had no more to give
T/Plt: £91.30 to a £1 stake. Pool: £88,580.32. 708.05 winning tickets. T/Qpdt: £21.60 to a £1 stake. Pool: £4,000.19. 136.80 winning tickets. ST

[2623] YORK (L-H)
Friday, June 13

OFFICIAL GOING: Good to firm (good in places; 8.3)
Wind: Light, half against Weather: Overcast

3005 EBF HSS HIRE MEDIAN AUCTION MAIDEN STKS — 5f
2:20 (2:20) (Class 4) 2-Y-O — **£6,929** (£2,061; £1,030; £514) **Stalls** High

Form — RPR
22 **1** **Viva Ronaldo (IRE)**[14] 2581 2-9-3 0 ... PaulHanagan 4 — 84
(R A Fahey) *led: pushed along and hdd 2f out: rdn to ld and edgd lft over 1f out: styd on wl u.p ins fnl f* **7/4**[2]
22 **2** 1 1/2 **Every Second**[32] 2042 2-9-3 0 ... RichardMullen 1 — 79
(E S McMahon) *cl up on outer: effrt 2f out and ev ch: sn rdn and kpt on same pce ins fnl f* **6/4**[1]
2 **3** 1 1/4 **Carnaby Haggerston (IRE)**[13] 2608 2-9-3 0 ... NCallan 9 — 74
(K A Ryan) *cl up: led 2f out: sn rdn and hdd over 1f out: kpt on same pce ins fnl f* **9/2**[3]
4 **4** hd **Eldorado Days (IRE)**[24] 2281 2-9-3 0 ... DarrenWilliams 7 — 73
(K R Burke) *trckd ldrs: hdwy 2f out: sn rdn and kpt on same pce ins fnl f* **33/1**
5 1 3/4 **Sea Crest** 2-8-12 0 ... TWilliams 8 — 62
(M Brittain) *dwlt: sn chsng ldrs: rdn along 2f out and grad wknd* **16/1**
0 **6** 3/4 **Norfolk Broads (IRE)**[5] 2709 2-8-12 0 ... RoystonFfrench 10 — 59
(M Johnston) *cl up: rdn along 1/2-way: grad wknd* **22/1**
6 **7** nk **Adozen Dreams**[62] 1324 2-8-8 0 ow1 ... SladeO'Hara(5) 2 — 59
(G R Oldroyd) *dwlt: towards rr and pushed along 1/2-way: rdn and sme hdwy 2f out: sn rdn and no imp* **50/1**
8 3 1/2 **Bulella** 2-8-12 0 ... AndrewElliott 6 — 46
(Garry Moss) *a in rr* **28/1**
0 **9** 15 **Cotton N Silk**[21] 2362 2-8-9 0 ... DuranFentiman(3) 3 — —
(T D Easterby) *sn rdn along and a in rr* **66/1**
59.78 secs (0.48) **Going Correction** 0.0s/f (Good) **9** Ran SP% **114.6**
Speed ratings (Par 95): **96,93,91,91,88 87,86,81,57**
CSF £4.43 TOTE £2.70: £1.20, £1.20, £1.30; EX 4.10.
Owner Aykroyd And Sons Ltd **Bred** Thomas Foy **Trained** Musley Bank, N Yorks

FOCUS
A fair juvenile maiden, run at a solid pace. The form looks straightforward.

NOTEBOOK
Viva Ronaldo(IRE) had finished runner-up on both his previous outings, including over course and distance last time, so this rates a deserved success. As was the case last time, he got pretty worked up beforehand and raced freely into the early lead. He still had too many guns for this field, however, and should really be high on confidence after this. (tchd 2-1)
Every Second, who like the winner had finished second on both of his previous starts, raced on the outside of the pack and was always up with the pace. He held every chance, only lacking the pace of the winner, and again finished a clear second best. While he may be deemed frustrating to follow, he does have ability and can find his feet when the nurseries start. (op 2-1)

Carnaby Haggerston(IRE), a well-held second on his debut at Haydock, showed good early pace and ran his race. He still looked in need of this race and no doubt has prizes within his grasp this season, especially when faced with another furlong in due course. (op 4-1 tchd 5-1)

Eldorado Days(IRE) stepped up nicely on the level of his Musselburgh debut 24 days previously and had his chance. He lacked a change of gear so may appreciate another furlong now, but should come on again for the run. (op 25-1)

Sea Crest, related to winners at around 6f, raced freely through the early parts and eventually paid the price. This was still a fair introduction, however, and she does have a future. (op 25-1)

Norfolk Broads(IRE) had the benefit of the stands' rail and improved a bit on the level of her debut at Kempton nine days previously, but she was still well beaten off in the end. Her Group 1 entry looks to be shooting at stars. (op 20-1 tchd 25-1)

3006 FIRST TRANSPENNINE EXPRESS STKS (H'CAP) 1m 208y

2:50 (2:51) (Class 4) (0-80,80) 4-Y-0+ **£6,799** (£2,023; £1,011; £505) **Stalls** Low

Form RPR

0-04 **1** **Goodbye Mr Bond**[26] 2220 8-9-9 **80**.................................. JimmyQuinn 5 93
(E J Alston) *hld up in tch gng wl: smooth hdwy 3f out: cl up 2f out: rdn to ld ent fnl f: sn drvn and r.o wl* **6/1**[2]

-024 **2** *1 1/4* **Just Bond (IRE)**[11] 2672 6-8-9 **71**.................................. SladeO'Hara(5) 15 81
(G R Oldroyd) *stdd s and hld up in rr: swtchd ins and hdwy 3f out: rdn to chal over 1f out and ev ch: drvn and hung rt ins fnl f: no ex towards fin* **25/1**

0052 **3** *1* **Nevada Desert (IRE)**[24] 2271 8-9-2 **76**................ MichaelJStainton(3) 6 84
(R M Whitaker) *trckd ldrs on inner: hdwy 3f out: chal 2f out: rdn to ld over 1f out: drvn and hdd ent fnl f: sn edgd lft and one pce towards fin* **9/1**

-035 **4** *2* **Billy Dane (IRE)**[9] 2733 4-9-9 **80**..................................(p) PaulHanagan 3 84
(R A Fahey) *led: rdn along wl over 2f out: drvn wl over 1f out and sn hdd: edgd lft and wknd ins fnl f* **10/1**

6505 **5** *3 1/2* **Ahlawy (IRE)**[7] 2784 5-9-1 **72**.................................. PaulMulrennan 13 69
(M W Easterby) *hld up: stdy hdwy over 3f out: chsd ldrs over 1f out: sn rdn: edgd lft and one pce* **8/1**

2651 **6** *hd* **Billy One Punch**[20] 2391 6-8-13 **70**.................................. RichardMullen 18 66
(D Shaw) *stdd s and hld up in rr: hdwy over 2f out: swtchd lft and rdn over 1f out: kpt on wl fnl f: nt rch ldrs* **12/1**

-560 **7** *3/4* **Cross The Line (IRE)**[39] 1857 6-9-5 **76**.................................. DarrenWilliams 7 71
(A P Jarvis) *hld up: hdwy 3f out: rdn to chse ldrs over 2f out: sn drvn and no imp* **14/1**

0010 **8** *2* **Bold Marc (IRE)**[41] 1815 6-9-8 **79**.................................. AndrewElliott 14 70
(K R Burke) *midfield: hdwy on outer 3f out: rdn along 2f out and sn no imp* **18/1**

2100 **9** *hd* **Blue Spinnaker (IRE)**[14] 2582 9-9-1 **79**.................. BradleyRoper(7) 17 69
(M W Easterby) *stdd s: hld up and a towards rr* **18/1**

0-00 **10** *4 1/2* **Fort Amhurst (IRE)**[14] 2582 4-9-3 **74**.................................. DaleGibson 11 55
(M W Easterby) *a towards rr* **33/1**

3022 **11** *2* **Celtic Step**[11] 2672 4-8-13 **70**.................................. RobertWinston 8 69+
(P D Niven) *cl up: rdn along over 2f out: drvn and edgd rt whn lost action over 1f out and sn eased* **9/2**[1]

0230 **12** *6* **Tencendur (IRE)**[9] 2733 4-9-6 **77**.................................. AdrianTNicholls 16 41
(D Nicholls) *in tch: rdn along 3f out: sn wknd* **25/1**

-522 **13** *1 1/2* **King Of Rhythm (IRE)**[28] 2165 5-9-1 **72**..................(v[1]) DavidAllan 10 33
(D Carroll) *chsd ldrs: rdn along 3f out: drvn over 2f out and sn wknd* **7/1**[3]

11-0 **14** *8* **Tendalay (USA)**[16] 2499 4-9-7 **78**.................................. DNolan 2 22
(D Carroll) *a in rr* **33/1**

014/ **15** *1 3/4* **Penryn**[609] 5944 5-8-11 **71**.................................. JamieMoriarty(3) 1 11
(P T Midgley) *dwlt: a towards rr* **40/1**

2033 **16** *21* **Lord Theo**[22] 2334 4-9-8 **79**.................................. NCallan 12 —
(N P Littmoden) *chsd ldng pair: rdn along 4f out: sn wknd* **12/1**

1m 49.95s (-2.05) **Going Correction** -0.10s/f (Good) **16** Ran SP% **123.8**
Speed ratings (Par 105): **105,103,103,101,98 97,97,95,95,91 89,84,82,75,74 55**
CSF £160.32 CT £1421.33 TOTE £5.10: £1.80, £5.30, £1.90, £2.90; EX 51.60.

Owner Peter J Davies **Bred** Michael Ng **Trained** Longton, Lancs

FOCUS
A good handicap, run at a sound pace. The form is solid, rated through the placed horses.

Celtic Step Official explanation: jockey said gelding lost its action

Lord Theo Official explanation: jockey said gelding never travelled

3007 HSS HIRE STKS (H'CAP) 2m 88y

3:25 (3:25) (Class 3) (0-95,88) 4-Y-0+ **£11,009** (£3,275; £1,637; £817) **Stalls** Low

Form RPR

2-20 **1** **Four Miracles**[27] 2202 4-8-11 **76**.................................. JimmyQuinn 5 82+
(M H Tompkins) *hld up in rr: smooth hdwy 3f out: trckd ldrs on bit 2f out: shkn up to ld jst ins fnl f: sn rdn and hung lft: drvn out* **8/1**

-021 **2** *1/2* **Directa's Digger (IRE)**[14] 2572 4-8-0 **70** oh1 ow1........(v) JackDean(5) 7 75
(M J Scudamore) *hld up in tch: hdwy on outer over 3f out: rdn along 2f out: styd on to chal over 1f out and ev ch tl drvn and no ex fnl 100yds* **5/1**[3]

36-4 **3** *1 1/4* **Bollin Felix**[13] 2591 4-8-10 **75**..................................(b) DavidAllan 2 79
(T D Easterby) *prom: hdwy to chal 3f out: rdn and ev ch 2f out: drvn and sltly outpcd appr fnl f: styd on wl u.p towards fin* **3/1**[2]

6561 **4** *nk* **Numero Due**[14] 2577 6-9-2 **83**.................................. PJMcDonald(3) 8 87
(G M Moore) *led: rdn along over 3f out: drvn 2f out: hdd jst ins fnl f: kpt on same pce* **5/2**[1]

151/ **5** *9* **Toldo (IRE)**[713] 3078 6-9-10 **88**.................................. DanielTudhope 1 81
(G M Moore) *trckd ldrs: hdwy over 3f out: chal 2f out and ev ch tl rdn and wknd ent fnl f* **10/1**

2-00 **6** *2 1/4* **New Beginning (IRE)**[14] 2582 4-9-2 **81**.................................. TomEaves 6 71
(Mrs S Lamyman) *hld up and bhd tl sme hdwy fnl 2f: nvr a factor* **18/1**

2335 **7** *9* **Collette's Choice**[14] 2585 5-8-5 **69** oh4........................(p) PaulHanagan 3 48
(R A Fahey) *hld up: hdwy on outer over 3f out: chal over 2f out: sn rdn and wknd* **8/1**

-300 **8** *26* **Sphinx (FR)**[13] 2609 10-9-4 **82**..................................(p) RobertWinston 4 30
(E W Tuer) *prom: chsd ldr 1/2-way: rdn along over 4f out and sn wknd* **9/1**

3m 33.87s (-2.93) **Going Correction** -0.10s/f (Good)
WFA 4 from 5yo+ 1lb **8** Ran SP% **116.8**
Speed ratings (Par 107): **103,102,102,101,97 96,91,78**
CSF £48.58 CT £148.91 TOTE £9.60: £2.70, £1.80, £1.60; EX 58.70.

Owner Pat Swayne and Partners **Bred** A G Antoniades **Trained** Newmarket, Suffolk

FOCUS
A fair staying handicap, run at a good pace. The form looks sound enough, if ordinary.

NOTEBOOK

Four Miracles, having travelled sweetly into contention, found a ready turn of foot when put under maximum pressure and got back to winning ways. The move up to this stiffer test no doubt suited and so did the return to quicker ground. She should also not really be going up too much for this, so appeals as one to keep on side as she is certainly open to more improvement over this distance. Official explanation: trainer said, regarding the improved form shown, filly had been better suited by the ground on this occasion

Directa's Digger(IRE) had been officially raised 10lb for his clear-cut win at Haydock a fortnight previously, yet was still racing from 1lb out of the handicap in this much better company. He was a touch free early on, but that did not stop him from displaying another career-best effort in defeat and he got the longer trip without too much fuss. (op 6-1 tchd 9-2)

Bollin Felix, well backed, failed to really raise his game as could have been expected for the step back up in trip. He still did little wrong in defeat, however, and left the impression he would prefer a stiffer track over this distance. It may well also be that this ground was as fast as he wants it. (op 7-2 tchd 4-1 in places)

Numero Due posted a brave effort from the front, ensuring this was a proper test, and stayed on gamely when headed. This rates a sound effort from his 4lb higher mark. (op 11-4 tchd 3-1)

Toldo(IRE) ◆, on his first outing since winning the Northumberland Plate back in 2006, having injured a tendon, was resuming from a 2lb higher mark and posted a very pleasing return. He travelled sweetly into the home straight and briefly looked a big player, but he found just the same pace when push eventually came to shove. That cannot be considered too surprising as he has been off the track so long and no doubt another crack at the Newcastle showpiece later this month will be firmly on connections' minds now. This race should really tee him up nicely for that too and it will be very interesting to see if the Handicapper cuts him a little slack for this. (op 7-1)

Sphinx(FR) Official explanation: jockey said gelding was unsuited by the good to firm (good in places) ground

3008 SKF ROUS (S) STKS 6f

4:00 (4:02) (Class 4) 2-Y-0 **£6,476** (£1,927; £963; £481) **Stalls** High

Form RPR

6646 **1** **Smalljohn**[14] 2569 2-8-11 0..................................(v) TomEaves 7 73
(P D Evans) *chsd ldng pair: hdwy to ld over 2f out: rdn wl over 1f out: kpt on wl u.p ins fnl f* **4/1**[2]

6 **2** *2* **Scenic Pass**[3] 2909 2-8-6 0.................................. TPO'Shea 5 62
(M R Channon) *in tch: hdwy over 2f out: rdn to chse wnr wl over 1f out: drvn ins fnl f and no imp towards fin* **7/2**[1]

3 *6* **Musical Maze** 2-8-3 0.................................. DuranFentiman(3) 13 44+
(W M Brisbourne) *towards rr: swtchd lft after 1f: rdn and hdwy 2f out: sn drvn and kpt on ins fnl f: nrst fin* **33/1**

0 **4** *3* **Miss Xu Xia**[14] 2569 2-8-6 0.................................. RoystonFfrench 4 35
(G R Oldroyd) *midfield: rdn along over 2f out: kpt on u.p appr fnl f: nrst fin* **33/1**

0 **5** *1/2* **Bold Account (IRE)**[34] 2004 2-8-11 0.................................. AndrewElliott 8 39
(K R Burke) *chsd ldrs: rdn along over 2f out: sn one pce* **16/1**

00 **6** *1 3/4* **Ed's Pride (IRE)**[8] 2746 2-8-11 0..................................(p) NCallan 10 33
(K A Ryan) *reminders s and towards rr tl styd on fnl 2f* **33/1**

3023 **7** *2* **Heaven Or Hell (IRE)**[11] 2671 2-8-11 0..................(v[1]) RobertWinston 9 27
(P D Evans) *led: rdn along and hdd over 2f out: sn drvn and wknd* **7/2**[1]

8 *1/2* **Kingaroo (IRE)** 2-8-11 0.................................. DeanMcKeown 15 26
(Garry Moss) *s.i.s: a towards rr* **50/1**

615 **9** *1* **Kneesy Earsy Nosey**[11] 2671 2-8-6 0.................................. KimTinkler 14 18
(N Tinkler) *sn rdn along in rr: nvr a factor* **9/1**

206 **10** *1/2* **Cool Sonata (IRE)**[18] 2443 2-8-6 0.................................. TWilliams 16 16
(M Brittain) *nvr bttr than midfield* **33/1**

61 **11** *1* **Dispol Diva**[50] 1574 2-8-6 0.................................. FrankieMcDonald 11 13
(P T Midgley) *rdn along 1/2-way: a in rr* **9/1**

0030 **12** *4 1/2* **French Forest**[11] 2671 2-8-6 0.................................. DavidAllan 3 —
(M Brittain) *midfield: rdn along 1/2-way: sn lost pl and bhd* **20/1**

050 **13** *21* **Sandies Sister**[17] 2485 2-8-6 0.................................. JimmyQuinn 12 —
(M Brittain) *midfield: rdn along 1/2-way: sn wknd and eased fnl 2f* **50/1**

0603 **14** *18* **Nchike**[3] 2910 2-8-11 0.................................. AdrianTNicholls 2 —
(D Nicholls) *chsd ldrs on outer: rdn along 1/2-way: sn wknd and eased wl over 1f out* **13/2**[3]

1m 12.53s (0.63) **Going Correction** 0.0s/f (Good) **14** Ran SP% **124.1**
Speed ratings (Par 95): **95,92,84,80,79 77,74,74,72,72 70,64,36,12**
CSF £17.78 TOTE £5.30: £2.00, £1.80, £5.20; EX 18.80.The winner was sold to Declan Carroll for £13,000.

Owner Christy Leo **Bred** W H R John And Partners **Trained** Pandy, Monmouths

FOCUS
A weak juvenile affair, but still a competitive race for the grade. The first pair came clear.

NOTEBOOK

Smalljohn found the drop into this company right up his street and he ran out a gutsy winner, under a no-nonsense ride. His latest sixth in a good maiden at Haydock was enough to give him a serious chance in this and he should be high on confidence after this career-first success, but he has now found his sort of level all the same. (tchd 9-2 in places)

Scenic Pass, sixth on her debut in a Redcar maiden just three days previously, proved popular in the betting ring on this quick reappearance and drop in class. She came through to have her chance, but found the winner too resolute at the business end and probably just found it coming a bit too soon. She was still well clear of the remainder at the finish and should not be long in going one better in this sort of grade. (op 3-1 tchd 11-4)

Musical Maze, a half-sister to her stable's 6-7f winner Roman Maze among others, took time to find her full stride on this racecourse bow and was doing her best work towards the finish. She should learn plenty for this, but is clearly only moderate.

Miss Xu Xia showed more encouragment on this drop in class, but still ran close enough to her debut form with the winner. She should come on again a little for the run. (op 25-1)

Heaven Or Hell(IRE), very well backed in the first-time visor, was given an aggressive ride and folded tamely inside the final furlong. This was the quickest ground he had encountered to date (op 8-1)

Sandies Sister Official explanation: jockey said filly hung right-handed throughout

Nchike Official explanation: jockey said gelding lost its action

3009 HSS.COM STKS (H'CAP) 5f

4:35 (4:36) (Class 3) (0-95,91) 3-Y-0+ **£8,289** (£2,466; £1,232; £615) **Stalls** High

Form RPR

020- **1** **Sohraab**[238] 6301 4-9-11 **88**.................................. JimmyQuinn 12 101
(H Morrison) *in tch: hdwy 2f out: rdn and qcknd to ld jst ins fnl f: drvn out* **14/1**

0-41 **2** *1* **Total Impact**[13] 2596 5-9-3 **80**.................................. PaulHanagan 2 89
(R A Fahey) *in tch: hdwy 2f out: rdn and ev ch ent fnl f: sn drvn and one pce towards fin* **4/1**[1]

1123 **3** *1/2* **Lord Of The Reins (IRE)**[16] 2501 4-9-2 **79**.................. AndrewElliott 15 86
(J G Given) *towards rr: hdwy 2f out: rdn over 1f out: kpt on wl fnl f* **20/1**

3-32 **4** *nk* **Everymanforhimself (IRE)**[13] 2626 4-9-13 **90**..................(b) NCallan 1 96
(K A Ryan) *cl up: rdn to chal 2f out and ev ch tl drvn and nt qckn ins fnl f* **4/1**[1]

1001 **5** *nse* **Stolt (IRE)**[14] 2583 4-9-5 **87**.......................... KellyHarrison(5) 6 93
(N Wilson) *led: rdn along 2f out: drvn over 1f out: hdd and one pce ins fnl f* **18/1**

1606 **6** *1/2* **Bo McGinty (IRE)**[6] 2843 7-8-11 **81**.................(b) FrederikTylicki(7) 14 85
(R A Fahey) *chsd ldrs: rdn along 2f out: drvn and one pce ent fnl f* **50/1**

5623 **7** *1/2* **The Nifty Fox**[6] 2843 4-9-0 **77**.. DavidAllan 4 79
(T D Easterby) *towards rr: hdwy 2f out: swtchd rt and rdn over 1f out: kpt on u.p ins fnl f: nrst fin* **11/1**[3]

-020 **8** *1/2* **Fantasy Explorer**[13] 2626 5-9-4 **84**....................... JamieMoriarty(3) 16 85
(J J Quinn) *cl up: rdn along 2f out: grad wknd appr fnl f* **11/1**[3]

0445 **9** *3/4* **Style Award**[13] 2594 3-8-7 **84**............................ PatrickDonaghy(7) 11 79
(W J H Ratcliffe) *towards rr: rdn along and hdwy 2f out: drvn and no imp ent fnl f* **33/1**

250- **10** *1* **Efistorm**[231] 6472 7-9-8 **88**.. PJMcDonald(3) 5 82
(C R Dore) *chsd ldrs: rdn over 2f out: sn drvn and grad wknd* **33/1**

-336 **11** *3/4* **Deserted Dane (USA)**[14] 2583 4-9-0 **77**....................... RobertWinston 18 69
(G A Swinbank) *midfield: effrot and sme hdwy on wd outside 2f out: sn rdn and wknd* **18/1**

620 **12** *nk* **King Of Swords (IRE)**[17] 2489 4-9-3 **80**........................ FergalLynch 13 70
(N Tinkler) *nvr bttr than midfield* **40/1**

300 **13** *1/2* **Bond City (IRE)**[6] 2828 6-9-9 **91**................................ SladeO'Hara(5) 7 80
(G R Oldroyd) *nvr bttr than midfield* **14/1**

0604 **14** *nk* **Tabaret**[13] 2626 5-9-10 **87**... DeanMcKeown 19 75
(R M Whitaker) *in tch on wd outside: rdn along 2f out: wknd appr fnl f* **15/2**[2]

411- **15** *1 3/4* **Divine Spirit**[266] 5581 7-9-8 **86**.............................. RoystonFfrench 3 67
(M Dods) *a in rr* **25/1**

3-04 **16** *1* **Bahamian Ballet**[21] 2359 6-9-2 **79**............................... WilliamBuick 10 57
(E S McMahon) *rrd s: slowly away and a in rr* **14/1**

300- **17** *1/2* **Jack Rackham**[255] 5891 4-9-7 **84**..................................... TomEaves 17 60
(B Smart) *a in rr* **22/1**

10-0 **18** *nk* **Tony The Tap**[27] 2195 7-9-7 **84**................................. RichardMullen 9 59
(W R Muir) *a towards rr* **40/1**

650- **19** *1 3/4* **Continent**[258] 5809 11-9-10 **87**............................ SilvestreDeSousa 8 56
(D Nicholls) *s.i.s and a bhd* **33/1**

58.31 secs (-0.99) **Going Correction** 0.0s/f (Good)
WFA 3 from 4yo+ 7lb **19** Ran SP% **127.6**
Speed ratings (Par 107): **107,105,104,104,104 103,102,101,100,98 97,97,96,95,93 91,90,90,87**
CSF £63.67 CT £1197.65 TOTE £15.70: £3.90, £1.70, £5.40, £1.60; EX 97.70 TRIFECTA Not won..
Owner Pangfield Racing **Bred** T J Billington **Trained** East Ilsley, Berks

FOCUS
A really competitive sprint handicap for the class. The form is solid and should work out.

NOTEBOOK
Sohraab showed he has improved for his time off the track and made a successful return from his 238-day break. This was his first success on turf, and he has been somewhat of a nearly horse until now, but he could well just be the type to improve as a four-year-old sprinter. (op 12-1)
Total Impact, 5lb higher, posted another improved effort in defeat and is evidently still on an upwards curve. He looks ready to tackle another furlong again now and there will be other days for him. (op 5-1 tchd 11-2)
Lord Of The Reins(IRE) has developed into a very consistent performer and, given his usual patient ride, he ran right up to his best in defeat. He helps to set the level of this form and deserves to find another opening now. (op 22-1)
Everymanforhimself(IRE), placed on his last three outings, was always on the pace and kept on to post another solid effort in defeat. He remains in good heart and richly deserves to win another prize, but the Handicapper looks to have his measure all the same. (op 9-2 tchd 5-1)
Stolt(IRE), up 7lb for his course-and-distance success a fortnight previously, ran a solid race from the front and gave the form a decent look. He too remains in great heart, but is another who now looks in the Handicapper's grip. (tchd 20-1)
Bond City(IRE) Official explanation: jockey said gelding was unsuited by the good to firm (good in places) ground
Tabaret likes this course and distance and appeared to have a good shout in this contest, but he ultimately ran a tame race. He was beaten 2f out and now has a good deal to prove. (op 8-1)
Bahamian Ballet Official explanation: jockey said gelding missed the break

3010 COLLINGWOOD CLEANING SERVICES APPRENTICE STKS (H'CAP) — 1m 4f

5:05 (5:05) (Class 4) (0-80,75) 4-Y-0+ **£6,476** (£1,927; £963; £481) **Stalls** Centre

Form RPR

3510 **1** **Naughty Thoughts (IRE)**[16] 2505 4-8-6 **62**............... RossAtkinson(5) 6 70
(Tom Dascombe) *in tch: hdwy on outer over 2f out: rdn to chal and edgd lft ent fnl f: styd on to ld nr fin* **8/1**

-346 **2** *hd* **Sporting Gesture**[14] 2585 11-8-11 **69**.............................. NSLawes(7) 12 77
(M W Easterby) *chsd ldrs: hdwy to ld 3f out: rdn 2f out and sn hung persistently lft: drvn ins fnl f: hdd and no ex nr fin* **10/1**

2-52 **3** *1 1/2* **Potentiale (IRE)**[23] 2304 4-9-9 **74**.................................. PatrickHills 2 80
(J W Hills) *trckd ldng pair: hdwy 3f out: rdn along 2f out: drvn to chal whn edgd lft over 1f out: kpt on same pce ins fnl f* **11/4**[1]

2142 **4** *1* **Inspirina (IRE)**[22] 2332 4-9-9 **74**.............................. AndrewMullen 7 79+
(R Ford) *trckd ldrs: hdwy 3f out: rdn 2f out: styng on whn nt clr run over 1f out: swtchd rt and kpt on ins fnl f* **7/2**[2]

0623 **5** *nk* **Dan Tucker**[14] 2568 4-8-10 **66**................................. PatrickDonaghy(5) 11 70
(N Tinkler) *hld up: hdwy over 3f out: rdn to chse ldrs 2f out and ch whn n.m.r on inner over 1f out: drvn and one pce ins fnl f* **12/1**

66-0 **6** *2 3/4* **Stretton (IRE)**[35] 1947 10-9-4 **69**.................................. JamieMoriarty 8 68
(J D Bethell) *towards rr: hdwy 3f out: rdn 2f out: kpt on nt rch ldrs* **18/1**

-120 **7** *2 1/2* **Proper (IRE)**[31] 2076 4-9-10 **75**....................................... WilliamBuick 4 70
(C J Mann) *towards rr: sme hdwy over 2f out: nvr plcd to chal* **6/1**[3]

-000 **8** *2 1/4* **Polish Red**[11] 2682 4-9-7 **75**... NeilBrown(3) 9 67
(G G Margarson) *towards rr: effrt and sme hdwy over 2f out: nvr a factor* **12/1**

0054 **9** *shd* **Wild Fell Hall (IRE)**[3] 2447 5-9-10 **75**..................... MichaelJStainton 5 66
(A D Brown) *led: rdn along 4f out: hdd 3f out: drvn and n.m.r over 2f out: sn wknd* **20/1**

56-0 **10** *7* **Intavac Boy**[58] 1394 7-8-0 **56** oh9....................................... AmyBaker(5) 3 36
(S P Griffiths) *chsd ldr: effrt 4f out: rdn over 3f out and sn wknd* **50/1**

050- **11** *7* **Boxhall (IRE)**[220] 6703 6-8-3 **61** ow3............................ SamuelDrury(7) 1 30
(N Wilson) *a in rr* **11/1**

2m 34.59s (1.39) **Going Correction** -0.10s/f (Good) **11** Ran SP% **119.1**
Speed ratings (Par 105): **91,90,89,89,89 87,85,84,83,79 74**
CSF £86.52 CT £279.22 TOTE £6.10: £1.90, £2.50, £1.60; EX 112.00 Place 6: £49.73, Place 5: £46.65..
Owner 123 Racing Partnership **Bred** Dr John Hollowood And Aiden Murphy **Trained** Lambourn, Berks
■ Stewards' Enquiry : N S Lawes two-day ban: careless riding (Jun 27-28); one-day ban: used whip with excessive frequency and in the incorrect place (Jun 29)

FOCUS
A modest handicap, confined to apprentice riders, which was run at just a moderate early pace. The runner-up sets the level and the form is sound.
T/Jkpt: Not won. T/Plt: £36.60 to a £1 stake. Pool: £105,939.07. 2,109.31 winning tickets. T/Qpdt: £12.30 to a £1 stake. Pool: £3,921.59. 235.70 winning tickets. JR

3011 - 3017a (Foreign Racing) - See Raceform Interactive

LE LION-D'ANGERS (R-H)

Friday, June 13

OFFICIAL GOING: Good

3018a PRIX URBAN SEA (LISTED RACE) (FILLIES) — 1m 3f 110y

3:05 (3:07) 3-Y-O **£20,221** (£8,088; £6,066; £4,044; £2,022)

RPR

1 **Loutka (FR)**[46] 3-8-11 ....(b) OPeslier 4 99
(J-M Beguigne, France)

2 *2 1/2* **Zaskar**[16] 2505 3-8-11 .... DBonilla 5 95
(Tom Dascombe) *plld hrd on outside in 6th: wdst of all ent st: swtchd lft and hdwy 1 1/2f out: tk 2nd 100yds out: no ch w wnr* **13/1**[2]

3 *nk* **Lune Rose**[36] 3-8-11 .... C-PLemaire 3 95
(P Bary, France)

4 *3* **Without Precedent (FR)**[60] 3-8-11 .... AClement 8 90
(Y De Nicolay, France)

5 *1/2* **Barring Decree (IRE)**[34] 2015 3-8-11 .... J-BEyquem 9 89
(E J O'Neill) *racd in 2nd on outside: rdn 2f out: lost 2nd 1f out: one pce* **12/1**[1]

6 *shd* **Orient Celebrity**[269] 3-8-11 .... TJarnet 2 89
(Mlle S-V Tarrou, France)

7 *2 1/2* **Kong Moon (FR)**[42] 3-8-11 ....(b) GToupel 7 85
(H-A Pantall, France)

8 *1 1/2* **Vraona**[15] 3-8-11 .... DBoeuf 6 82
(D Sepulchre, France)

9 *5* **Orion Queen (FR)**[43] 1760 3-8-11 .... JVictoire 1 74
(H-A Pantall, France)

2m 20.69s (140.69) **9** Ran SP% **14.8**
(including 1 Euro stake): WIN 4.20; PL 1.60, 2.90, 1.50; DF 8.80.
Owner E Ciampi & M Parrish **Bred** Eric Puerari & Oceanic Bloodstock Inc **Trained** France

NOTEBOOK
Zaskar, a lightly-raced filly who bolted up in a handicap at Great Leighs on her previous outing, was quite keen early then came wide entering the straight. She stayed on well but the winner was already home and hosed. She at least earned black type and looks capable of winning in this grade when things go her way.
Barring Decree(IRE), a narrow winner of a maiden at Warwick over this sort of trip, was stepping up in grade but appeared to have every chance before fading.

2769 BATH (L-H)

Saturday, June 14

OFFICIAL GOING: Good to firm (firm in places; 9.2)
Wind: Light, against Weather: Fine

3019 BATHWICK TYRES BRIDGEND MAIDEN AUCTION STKS — 5f 11y

2:25 (2:27) (Class 6) 2-Y-O **£1,942** (£578; £288; £144) **Stalls** Centre

Form RPR

6 **1** **Infamous Angel**[14] 2618 2-8-7 0 ow1............................ RichardHughes 8 80+
(R Hannon) *a gng wl: shkn up to ld jst over 1f out: rdn out* **4/9**[1]

6 **2** *2* **Timeteam (IRE)**[9] 2759 2-8-11 0.. PatDobbs 3 74+
(S Kirk) *a.p: nt clr run and swtchd rt 1f out: r.o to take 2nd ins fnl f: nt trble wnr* **9/1**[3]

262 **3** *2 1/4* **Musical Bridge**[19] 2462 2-8-13 0................................... TolleyDean(3) 7 71
(Mrs L Williamson) *hld up: hdwy on outside 2f out: sn rdn: no ex ins fnl f* **3/1**[2]

66 **4** *3 1/2* **The Saucy Snipe**[10] 2709 2-8-1 0.................................. LukeMorris(3) 5 46
(P Winkworth) *hld up: pushed along over 2f out: rdn and sme hdwy over 1f out: wknd ins fnl f* **16/1**

0 **5** *1 1/4* **Silent Treatment (IRE)**[18] 2473 2-8-6 0.....................(t) JamesDoyle 6 44
(R M Beckett) *w ldr: rdn over 1f out: wknd ins fnl f* **33/1**

46 **6** *1 1/4* **Mr Clearview**[15] 2562 2-8-11 0.. ChrisCatlin 1 44
(B R Millman) *led: shkn up and hdd jst over 1f out: wknd ins fnl f* **25/1**

7 *3 1/4* **Emerald Lass** 2-8-11 0... TPO'Shea 4 32
(D J Coakley) *hld up: shkn up jst over 1f out: sn struggling* **25/1**

8 *4* **Miss Leona** 2-8-4 0.. RoystonFfrench 2 11
(J M Bradley) *hld up: rdn over 2f out: sn bhd* **66/1**

62.89 secs (0.39) **Going Correction** -0.05s/f (Good) **8** Ran SP% **122.3**
Speed ratings (Par 91): **94,90,87,81,79 77,72,66**
CSF £6.26 TOTE £1.60: £1.02, £2.40, £1.20; EX 5.90 Trifecta £26.70 Pool £557.03 - 14.78 winning units..
Owner Geoff Howard-Spink & Peter Marshall **Bred** Bricklow Stud **Trained** East Everleigh, Wilts

FOCUS
This minor maiden was only 0.15 second slower than the following novice event and the winner could be fairly useful. She produced a big step up on her debut form.

NOTEBOOK
Infamous Angel, well backed, duly proved well suited to a drop back to 5f and her trainer reckons she needs this faster ground. She is likely to have one more outing before a possible tilt at the Newbury Super Sprint next month. (op 10-11)
Timeteam(IRE) ◆, another who had made his debut on soft ground, settled much better this time. He will not always meet one so useful as the winner in this type of contest and will be suited by a step up to 6f. (op 8-1 tchd 15-2)
Musical Bridge may have had more to do than when second at Redcar last time. (op 9-4 tchd 7-2)
The Saucy Snipe has yet to live up to the support she attracted when making a satisfactory debut at Windsor. (tchd 12-1)
Silent Treatment(IRE), tried in a tongue tie, lasted a lot longer on this much faster ground. (op 40-1 tchd 25-1)
Mr Clearview, reverting to the minimum trip, was another encountering a totally different surface. (op 20-1 tchd 16-1)

3020 BATHWICK TYRES CARDIFF AND EUROPEAN BREEDERS' FUND NOVICE STKS — 5f 11y

3:00 (3:03) (Class 4) 2-Y-O **£4,630** (£1,377; £688; £343) **Stalls** Centre

Form RPR

4421 **1** **Russet Reward**[16] 2522 2-9-2 0.................................... DarryllHolland 2 87
(Mrs L Stubbs) *mde all: rdn fnl f: r.o* **6/1**[3]

134 **2** 1 1/4 **Doughnut**[29] 2167 2-9-0 0 RichardHughes 6 80
(R Hannon) *a chsng wnr: ev ch over 1f out: rdn and nt qckn ins fnl f* **5/4**[1]

433 **3** 1 1/2 **Kerrys Requiem (IRE)**[7] 2838 2-8-7 0 ChrisCatlin 5 68
(M R Channon) *s.i.s: outpcd: rdn and sme hdwy over 1f out: kpt on ins fnl f* **7/4**[2]

4 1/2 **Green Poppy** 2-8-3 0 HayleyTurner 4 62+
(Eve Johnson Houghton) *dwlt: hdwy 2f out: sn pushed along: one pce fnl f* **14/1**

03 **5** 2 1/4 **Magical Illusion**[8] 2769 2-8-7 0 CatherineGannon 1 58
(P D Evans) *sn outpcd: rdn over 2f out: a bhd* **20/1**

00 **6** 2 1/4 **Courageous Nature (IRE)**[14] 2601 2-8-5 0 KMay(7) 3 55
(B J Meehan) *chsd ldrs: rdn 2f out: wknd fnl f* **25/1**

62.74 secs (0.24) **Going Correction** -0.05s/f (Good) **6** Ran SP% **110.4**
Speed ratings (Par 95): **96,94,91,90,87 83**
CSF £13.56 TOTE £5.80: £2.40, £1.30; EX 14.90.
Owner P G Shorrock **Bred** Beech Park Bloodstock Ltd **Trained** Norton, N Yorks

FOCUS
This fair novice event was 0.15 seconds faster than the opening maiden. Improvement from the winner, the form rated through the next two.

NOTEBOOK
Russet Reward made the long journey from North Yorkshire in search of fast ground worthwhile. Always doing enough to keep the favourite at bay, a step up to Listed class at Sandown next month is on the cards. (op 5-1)
Doughnut was made a warm favourite on the strength of her close fourth in a decent-looking Listed race at York. She had no excuses and was beaten fair and square. Official explanation: jockey said filly was unsuited by the god to firm, firm in places ground (tchd 6-5, 11-8 in places)
Kerrys Requiem(IRE) either seems to do too much in the lead or lose ground at the start. A return to 6f might help on this evidence. (op 2-1 tchd 9-4)
Green Poppy ◆ is a 26,000gns daughter of an unraced half-sister to the top-class Prix de la Foret winner Septieme Ciel. She showed plenty of promise after a tardy start and improvement can be expected. (op 10-1 tchd 9-1)

3021 BATHWICK TYRES SUPPORTS HEROS (S) STKS 5f 161y
3:35 (3:39) (Class 6) 3-Y-O+ £1,683 (£501; £250; £125) Stalls Centre

Form RPR

-600 **1** **Currency**[3] 2950 11-9-1 54 TolleyDean(3) 7 61
(J M Bradley) *a.p: rdn over 2f out: led wl ins fnl f: r.o* **16/1**

3/ **2** nk **Tune Up The Band**[795] 961 4-9-4 0 SteveDrowne 1 60
(R J Hodges) *led: rdn and hdd wl ins fnl f: r.o* **11/2**[2]

5326 **3** shd **Night Prospector**[18] 2474 8-9-4 56 (p) ChrisCatlin 5 60
(R A Harris) *a.p: nt clr run 2f out tl swtchd rt 1f out: rdn and kpt on ins fnl f* **10/1**

4451 **4** nk **Marko Jadeo (IRE)**[10] 2721 10-9-5 62 HaddenFrost(5) 3 65+
(R A Harris) *hld up in mid-div: hdwy on ins over 2f out: nt clr run over 2f out: squeezed through ins fnl f: n.m.r towards fin* **3/1**[1]

00-3 **5** 1 1/4 **Half A Tsar (IRE)**[10] 2721 4-8-11 54 RichardEvans(7) 9 54
(Mark Gillard) *hld up and bhd: hdwy 2f out: rdn jst over 1f out: r.o towards fin* **12/1**

3330 **6** 1 1/4 **High Reach**[18] 2478 8-9-10 56 HayleyTurner 10 56
(J G M O'Shea) *hld up in tch: rdn and ev ch over 1f out: fdd wl ins fnl f* **6/1**[3]

000- **7** 1/2 **Peruvian Style (IRE)**[254] 5947 7-9-4 47 RoystonFfrench 8 48
(J M Bradley) *mid-div: hdwy 2f out: no ex ins fnl f* **25/1**

-000 **8** 1/2 **Willhewiz**[10] 2710 8-9-4 55 StephenCarson 11 47
(M S Saunders) *w ldr: ev ch over 1f out: sn rdn: wknd ins fnl f* **8/1**

2464 **9** 2 3/4 **Lord Deevert**[8] 2803 3-8-3 59 (v) AshleyMorgan(7) 14 35
(W G M Turner) *towards rr: rdn and short-lived effrt over 1f out* **12/1**

4015 **10** hd **Midnite Blews (IRE)**[6] 2864 3-8-9 61 GihanArnolda(7) 15 41
(A B Haynes) *s.i.s: a bhd* **11/1**

0424 **11** 1/2 **Diademas (USA)**[43] 1777 3-8-10 58 (v) RichardHughes 6 33
(V Smith) *hld up in mid-div: rdn over 1f out: eased whn btn ins fnl f* **15/2**

000- **12** 2 1/2 **Parkside Pursuit**[203] 6925 10-8-11 40 SophieDoyle(7) 4 26
(J M Bradley) *a bhd* **50/1**

1300 **13** 6 **Piccostar**[66] 1275 5-8-12 49 PNolan(7) 16 7
(A B Haynes) *a bhd* **25/1**

040- **14** 1/2 **Stagnite**[192] 7034 8-9-4 43 AlanDaly 12 —
(D L Williams) *a in rr* **33/1**

0005 **15** 15 **Ace Club**[47] 1675 7-8-11 40 (b) StacyRenwick(7) 17 —
(Garry Moss) *racd wd: spd over 2f: wknd qckly* **33/1**

1m 11.92s (0.72) **Going Correction** -0.05s/f (Good)
WFA 3 from 4yo+ 8lb **15** Ran SP% **131.8**
Speed ratings (Par 101): **93,92,92,92,90 88,88,87,83,83 82,79,71,70,50**
CSF £105.89 TOTE £20.90: £6.70, £3.10, £2.90; EX 291.90 TRIFECTA Not won..There was no bid for the winner.
Owner Robert Bailey **Bred** Limestone Stud **Trained** Sedbury, Gloucs
■ Stewards' Enquiry : Tolley Dean caution: careless riding
Steve Drowne one-day ban: careless riding (Jun 28)

FOCUS
A classic case of quantity rather than quality in this sprint seller which resulted in a blanket finish.

3022 BATHWICK TYRES TETBURY H'CAP 1m 3f 144y
4:10 (4:10) (Class 5) (0-70,68) 3-Y-O £2,719 (£809; £404; £202) Stalls Low

Form RPR

0-04 **1** **Mount Lavinia (IRE)**[23] 2340 3-8-12 59 JamesDoyle 5 66
(R M Beckett) *a.p: wnt 2nd 3f out: rdn wl over 1f out: led jst ins fnl f: r.o* **11/2**

2332 **2** 3/4 **King Supreme (IRE)**[23] 2340 3-9-5 66 (b) RichardHughes 4 72
(R Hannon) *hld up and bhd: hdwy 5f out: rdn wl over 1f out: styd on u.p to take 2nd last strides* **5/2**[1]

025 **3** shd **Paddy Rielly (IRE)**[8] 2785 3-8-11 58 DarryllHolland 2 64
(P D Evans) *w ldr: led over 3f out: rdn and edgd rt over 1f out: hdd jst ins fnl f: edgd lft: lost 2nd last strides* **3/1**[2]

3-04 **4** 2 **Parson's Punch**[40] 1855 3-9-7 68 SimonWhitworth 7 70
(P D Cundell) *hld up: hdwy 2f out: sn rdn: no ex ins fnl f* **5/1**[3]

6-03 **5** 11 **Looter (FR)**[14] 2613 3-9-0 61 ChrisCatlin 3 45
(J L Dunlop) *hld up in tch: rdn over 2f out: wknd over 1f out* **5/1**[3]

-600 **6** 1/2 **Asian Classic (IRE)**[39] 1896 3-8-13 60 (b[1]) SteveDrowne 8 43
(R Charlton) *prom: lost pl over 5f out: rdn wl over 1f out: sn bhd* **14/1**

005- **7** 7 **Festival Dreams**[219] 6737 3-8-8 55 HayleyTurner 1 26
(Miss J S Davis) *hld up: pushed along over 3f out: bhd fnl 2f* **33/1**

00-0 **8** 2 1/2 **Jay Gee Wigmo**[15] 2559 3-8-2 49 oh4 CatherineGannon 9 16
(A W Carroll) *plld hrd: sn stdd into mid-div: bhd fnl 4f* **66/1**

6-30 **9** 8 **Opening Act**[12] 2681 3-8-13 63 TolleyDean(3) 6 16
(P F I Cole) *led: rdn and hdd over 3f out: wknd over 2f out: eased whn no ch over 1f out* **25/1**

2m 31.96s (1.36) **Going Correction** -0.05s/f (Good) **9** Ran SP% **117.2**
Speed ratings (Par 99): **93,92,92,91,83 83,78,77,71**
CSF £19.74 CT £49.41 TOTE £7.50: £1.70, £1.50, £1.60; EX 23.80 Trifecta £115.40 Pool £452.01 - 2.78 winning units..
Owner Thurloe Thoroughbreds XX **Bred** Knocklong House Stud **Trained** Whitsbury, Hants

FOCUS
A steadily-run and modest handicap with the first four eventually coming clear. The first two came from the same Salisbury form and this form is pretty ordinary.
Paddy Rielly(IRE) Official explanation: jockey said gelding was unsuited by the good to firm, firm in places ground
Opening Act Official explanation: jockey said gelding was never travelling

3023 BATHWICK TYRES BRISTOL FILLIES' H'CAP 1m 5y
4:40 (4:43) (Class 5) (0-70,69) 3-Y-O+ £2,719 (£809; £404; £202) Stalls Low

Form RPR

0-01 **1** **Maybe I Will (IRE)**[13] 2639 3-9-0 65 HayleyTurner 10 71
(S Dow) *hld up in tch: led 1f out: drvn out* **16/1**

30-2 **2** 1 **Stand In Flames**[15] 2563 3-8-12 63 PatDobbs 13 67
(Pat Eddery) *chsd ldr: rdn and ev ch 1f out: nt qckn* **8/1**

0-00 **3** 3/4 **Garland**[30] 2118 3-9-0 65 (t) RichardHughes 7 67
(R Hannon) *led: rdn and hdd 1f out: no ex towards fin* **16/1**

4-21 **4** 3/4 **Dancing Storm**[18] 2477 5-9-9 63 ChrisCatlin 16 66
(W S Kittow) *t.k.h: a.p: rdn and one pce fnl f* **9/2**[1]

1330 **5** nse **Cape Velvet (IRE)**[17] 2505 4-10-0 68 JamesDoyle 11 71+
(J W Hills) *hld up towards rr: rdn over 1f out: late hdwy nrst fin* **14/1**

2555 **6** nk **Kashmina**[15] 2563 3-8-12 63 DarryllHolland 15 62
(M R Channon) *hld up towards rr: stdy hdwy over 4f out: rdn over 1f out: one pce* **10/1**

04-3 **7** 1/2 **Silky Steps (IRE)**[36] 1958 3-9-1 66 RichardSmith 9 64
(P J Makin) *t.k.h in mid-div: clipped heels and stmbld after 1f: pushed along and hdwy over 2f out: rdn over 1f out: one pce* **6/1**[2]

006- **8** hd **Medici Gold**[298] 4683 3-8-1 52 CatherineGannon 6 50
(B G Powell) *hld up in tch: rdn over 2f out: fdd ins fnl f* **66/1**

0600 **9** 1/2 **Casablanca Minx (IRE)**[3] 2930 5-8-8 55 (v) RichardEvans(7) 12 55
(P D Evans) *hld up and bhd: rdn over 1f out: nvr trbld ldrs* **25/1**

0-55 **10** nk **Driven Snow**[15] 2566 3-9-1 66 RoystonFfrench 4 62
(E F Vaughan) *s.i.s: hld up in rr: rdn 3f out: n.d* **9/1**

1304 **11** nk **Jessica Wigmo**[12] 2670 5-8-5 52 StacyRenwick(7) 14 50
(A W Carroll) *s.s: rdn and swtchd lft to ins rail 1f out: n.d* **18/1**

5-52 **12** 1 **Smooth As Silk (IRE)**[17] 2496 3-9-4 69 SteveDrowne 8 62
(C R Egerton) *hld up in mid-div: rdn over 2f out: eased whn btn wl ins fnl f* **13/2**[3]

06-0 **13** 7 **Bluebelle Dancer (IRE)**[16] 2533 4-8-13 56 TolleyDean(3) 2 36
(W R Muir) *s.v.s: a in rr* **20/1**

000- **14** 13 **Ava Gee**[254] 5939 3-8-8 62 PatrickHills(3) 5 9
(B De Haan) *a towards rr* **50/1**

1m 41.73s (0.93) **Going Correction** -0.05s/f (Good)
WFA 3 from 4yo+ 11lb **14** Ran SP% **111.8**
Speed ratings (Par 100): **93,92,91,90,90 90,89,89,88,88 88,87,80,67**
CSF £106.78 CT £1359.96 TOTE £16.20: £3.80, £3.50, £3.00; EX 129.60 TRIFECTA Not won..
Owner Mrs Alicia Aldis **Bred** Cheval Court Stud **Trained** Epsom, Surrey

FOCUS
A wide-open but ordinary fillies' handicap. Modest form, with few progressive sorts in the race.
Ava Gee Official explanation: jockey said filly was never travelling

3024 BATHWICK TYRES SWINDON H'CAP 5f 161y
5:10 (5:10) (Class 4) (0-80,80) 3-Y-O+ £4,209 (£1,252; £625; £312) Stalls Centre

Form RPR

4635 **1** **Lunces Lad (IRE)**[15] 2565 4-9-9 75 (v) DarryllHolland 7 81
(M R Channon) *hld up: hdwy over 2f out: rdn over 1f out: edgd lft and r.o to ld last strides* **7/2**[1]

2426 **2** shd **Prince Of Delphi**[7] 2837 5-9-2 68 JamesDoyle 6 74
(R M Beckett) *hld up: hdwy whn nt clr run and swtchd lft wl over 1f out: sn rdn: led nr fin: hdd last strides* **7/2**[1]

0022 **3** 1 **Stamford Blue**[13] 2644 7-9-9 80 (b) HaddenFrost(5) 5 83
(R A Harris) *led: rdn ins fnl f: hdd and n.m.r nr fin* **7/2**[1]

064 **4** 1 1/4 **Rainbow Bay**[12] 2664 5-8-2 61 oh6 (v) AshleyMorgan(7) 2 59
(P D Evans) *hld up and bhd: pushed along over 2f out: hdwy on ins whn swtchd rt 1f out: kpt on ins fnl f* **9/1**[2]

0-00 **5** 4 1/2 **Spanish Ace**[22] 2356 7-8-12 67 (p) TolleyDean(3) 4 50
(J M Bradley) *w ldrs tl rdn over 2f out: wkng whn n.m.r briefly over 1f out* **20/1**

6166 **6** 1/2 **Drifting Gold**[80] 1033 4-9-8 74 (b) SteveDrowne 1 55
(C G Cox) *w ldrs on ins: rdn and wknd over 1f out* **16/1**[3]

6102 **7** nk **Caustic Wit (IRE)**[8] 2798 10-8-12 64 (p) RichardHughes 9 44
(M S Saunders) *w ldrs on outside: rdn and wknd 1f out* **7/2**[1]

00-0 **8** 5 **Loyal Royal (IRE)**[80] 1033 5-9-4 70 RoystonFfrench 3 33
(J M Bradley) *t.k.h: sn w ldrs: rdn and wknd 2f out* **20/1**

1m 11.86s (0.66) **Going Correction** -0.05s/f (Good) **8** Ran SP% **114.3**
Speed ratings (Par 105): **93,92,91,89,83 83,82,76**
CSF £15.39 CT £44.05 TOTE £6.00: £1.90, £1.70, £1.50; EX 16.90 Trifecta £108.70 Part won. Pool £153.21 - 0.99 winning units..
Owner Jon and Julia Aisbitt **Bred** Fortbarrington Stud **Trained** West Ilsley, Berks
■ Stewards' Enquiry : James Doyle three-day ban: used whip with excessive frequency, with an element of force and without allowing sufficient time to respond (Jun 28-30)

FOCUS
There were four 7/2 co-favourites in this little sprint handicap. Straightforward form.

3025 BATHWICK TYRES CHIPPENHAM H'CAP 1m 2f 46y
5:40 (5:41) (Class 6) (0-55,55) 4-Y-O+ £2,047 (£604; £302) Stalls Low

Form RPR

U00/ **1** **Cordage (IRE)**[15] 6621 6-8-5 46 oh1 FrankieMcDonald 14 54
(M F Harris) *mde all: rdn wl over 1f out: drvn out* **11/1**

6-50 **2** 1 **Beckenham's Secret**[133] 401 4-7-12 46 oh1 StacyRenwick(7) 15 52
(A W Carroll) *t.k.h towards rr: stdy hdwy over 3f out: swtchd rt 2f out: r.o ins fnl f: nt rch wnr* **12/1**

04-0 **3** 1 1/2 **Trevian**[22] 2353 7-8-9 50 SteveDrowne 13 53
(J M Bradley) *hld up in tch: rdn over 1f out: kpt on same pce ins fnl f* **14/1**

050 **4** 1 1/2 **Meohmy**[19] 2467 5-7-12 46 oh1 MatthewDavies(7) 6 46
(M R Channon) *hld up in tch: rdn over 2f out: no ex wl ins fnl f* **16/1**

4030 **5** shd **Artzola (IRE)**[9] 2755 8-8-9 50 DarryllHolland 12 50
(C A Horgan) *s.s: hld up in rr: hdwy on ins 3f out: kpt on ins fnl f* **8/1**

44-0 **6** 1 1/2 **Fair Sailing (IRE)**[33] 2055 4-9-0 **55** .... JamesDoyle 9 52
(J W Hills) *chsd ldr tl over 6f out: wnt 2nd again 4f out: rdn wl over 1f out: wknd ins fnl f* **12/1**

3246 **7** hd **Beech Games**[17] 2513 4-8-12 **53** .... RichardHughes 5 50
(F Jordan) *s.i.s: hld up and bhd: hdwy 2f out: sn rdn: wknd ins fnl f* **7/1**[3]

0000 **8** nk **The Grey One (IRE)**[35] 2001 5-8-7 **48** ....(p) PaulFitzsimons 8 44
(J M Bradley) *plld hrd: sn mid-div: rdn and no hdwy fnl 2f* **12/1**

-402 **9** 1 **Miss Porcia**[13] 2641 7-7-12 **46** oh1 .... SophieDoyle(7) 4 41
(P A Blockley) *plld hrd: prom: chsd wnr over 6f out to 4f out: rdn and wknd over 1f out* **9/2**[1]

2215 **10** 1/2 **Classic Blue (IRE)**[52] 1562 4-8-8 **49** .... HayleyTurner 10 43
(Ian Williams) *hld up in rr: pushed along and sme hdwy wl over 1f out: n.d* **9/2**[1]

0403 **11** 7 **The Gaikwar (IRE)**[8] 2795 9-8-8 **54** ....(b) HaddenFrost(5) 11 34
(R A Harris) *hld up in mid-div: lost pl over 7f out: bhd fnl 4f* **6/1**[2]

6100 **12** 3 **Cumae (USA)**[13] 2640 4-8-5 **46** oh1 .... RoystonFfrench 16 21
(J Pearce) *prom: rdn 3f out: sn wknd* **16/1**

420/ **13** 4 1/2 **Goldstar Dancer (IRE)**[50] 1201 6-7-12 **46** oh1 ....(t) KMay(7) 17 12
(K M Prendergast) *hld up in mid-div: pushed along 4f out: rdn and bhd 3f out* **33/1**

0-00 **14** 7 **Grafty Green (IRE)**[22] 2365 5-8-8 **52** .... PatrickHills(3) 1 5
(W M Brisbourne) *a towards rr* **20/1**

2m 10.26s (-0.74) **Going Correction** -0.05s/f (Good) **14** Ran SP% **131.8**
Speed ratings (Par 101): **100,99,98,96,96 95,95,95,94,93 88,85,82,76**
CSF £149.63 CT £1905.51 TOTE £17.60: £4.10, £6.00, £3.50; EX 355.30 TRIFECTA Not won. Place 6 £84.88, Place 5 £81.05..
Owner M Harris **Bred** M H Dixon **Trained** Edgcote, Northants

FOCUS
Three of the first four were a pound out of the handicap in this weak affair. Fairly sound, low-grade form.
Artzola(IRE) Official explanation: jockey said mare missed the break and hung left
The Gaikwar(IRE) Official explanation: jockey said gelding was never travelling
Grafty Green(IRE) Official explanation: jockey said gelding lost action but returned sound
T/Plt: £104.90 to a £1 stake. Pool: £64,311.54. 447.24 winning tickets. T/Qpdt: £50.30 to a £1 stake. Pool: £2,919.70. 42.90 winning tickets. KH

2663

LEICESTER (R-H)

Saturday, June 14

OFFICIAL GOING: Good to firm (firm in places)
Wind: Light, behind Weather: Overcast

3026 WIMPEY HOMES FILLIES' H'CAP 5f 218y
6:45 (6:46) (Class 5) (0-70,68) 3-Y-0+ **£3,238** (£963; £481; £240) **Stalls Low**

Form RPR

00-4 **1** **Overwing (IRE)**[7] 2836 5-9-8 **60** .... EddieAhern 4 74
(R M H Cowell) *mde all: sn clr: rdn over 1f out: edgd rt: r.o gamely* **4/1**[2]

612 **2** 2 1/4 **Gap Princess (IRE)**[9] 2747 4-9-9 **64** .... JamieMoriarty(3) 7 71
(R A Fahey) *chsd ldrs: rdn over 2f out: styd on* **9/4**[1]

221- **3** 1 1/2 **Mistress Cooper**[269] 5534 3-9-8 **68** .... StephenDonohoe 6 68
(W J Musson) *chsd wnr: rdn over 1f out: no ex ins fnl f* **11/1**

4660 **4** nse **Linda Green**[18] 2478 7-9-3 **60** .... MCGeran(5) 1 62
(M R Channon) *hld up: hdwy u.p over 1f out: styd on: eased last strides* **9/1**

2541 **5** 3/4 **Tilsworth Charlie**[8] 2798 5-9-8 **60** ....(b) AdrianMcCarthy 3 59
(J R Jenkins) *prom: rdn over 1f out: styd on same pce* **9/2**[3]

4514 **6** 1 **Dualagi**[14] 2616 4-10-0 **66** .... LPKeniry 9 62
(M R Bosley) *hld up: plld hrd: hdwy over 2f out: rdn over 1f out: no ex* **7/1**

1450 **7** 1 **Alucica**[12] 2670 5-9-0 **52** ....(v) DeanMcKeown 8 45
(D Shaw) *slipped s: hld up: rdn over 2f out: edgd rt: n.d* **12/1**

6000 **8** 3 3/4 **Nabra**[21] 2399 4-8-2 **47** oh2 .... MatthewLawson(7) 2 28
(M Brittain) *s.i.s: hld up: outpcd 1/2-way: n.d after* **33/1**

-046 **9** 16 **Little Bones**[21] 2399 3-8-3 **52** ....(t) DuranFentiman(3) 5 —
(J F Coupland) *s.s: plld hrd early: bhd fr 1/2-way* **40/1**

1m 13.21s (0.21) **Going Correction** -0.10s/f (Good)
WFA 3 from 4yo+ 8lb **9** Ran SP% **112.9**
Speed ratings (Par 100): **94,91,89,88,87 86,85,80,58**
CSF £13.03 CT £88.25 TOTE £4.70: £1.80, £1.10, £2.50; EX 10.70.
Owner Keith Robinson & Ian Robinson **Bred** Noel Finegan And Noel Cogan **Trained** Six Mile Bottom, Cambs

FOCUS
Just a modest sprint handicap for fillies won in good style by Overwing, who is rated to last year's mark.
Alucica Official explanation: jockey said mare lost action leaving stalls

3027 SIMPLY BATHROOMS, LEICESTER, MAIDEN FILLIES' STKS 5f 218y
7:15 (7:18) (Class 4) 2-Y-O **£3,885** (£1,156; £577; £288) **Stalls Low**

Form RPR

1 **Oasis Breeze** 2-9-0 0 .... OscarUrbina 11 75+
(G D Blake) *hld up in tch: shkn up over 2f out: swtchd rt over 1f out: rdn to ld wl ins fnl f* **28/1**

2 **2** hd **Predict**[14] 2614 2-9-0 0 .... SebSanders 6 74
(Sir Mark Prescott) *led: rdn over 1f out: hdd wl ins fnl f* **15/8**[1]

3 2 1/2 **Sneak Preview** 2-9-0 0 .... RichardMullen 8 67
(E S McMahon) *s.i.s: sn pushed along in rr: hdwy over 2f out: sn rdn: styd on same pce fnl f* **16/1**

00 **4** 3 **Wigan Pier**[22] 2357 2-9-0 0 .... DavidAllan 7 58
(T D Easterby) *plld hrd and prom: rdn over 1f out: wknd ins fnl f* **66/1**

5 nk **Polly's Choice (IRE)** 2-9-0 0 .... LPKeniry 3 57
(R Hannon) *s.i.s: hld up: swtchd rt over 2f out: hdwy and hung rt over 1f out: styd on same pce fnl f* **18/1**

6 1 1/2 **Exceedingly Good (IRE)** 2-9-0 0 .... TomEaves 1 52
(B Smart) *hld up in tch: outpcd 2f out: n.d after* **4/1**[3]

7 shd **Romantic Queen** 2-9-0 0 .... StephenDonohoe 4 52
(E A L Dunlop) *hld up: swtchd rt over 2f out: rdn and hung rt over 1f out: wknd fnl f* **7/2**[2]

8 1 **Franchesca's Gold** 2-9-0 0 .... AlanMunro 2 49
(B R Millman) *chsd ldrs: rdn over 2f out: wknd over 1f out* **33/1**

9 3/4 **Anjuna (USA)** 2-9-0 0 .... JimmyFortune 12 47
(J H M Gosden) *wnt rt s: sn trcking ldrs: racd keenly: rdn and hung rt over 1f out: wknd fnl f* **9/1**

4 **10** 11 **Black Salix (USA)**[28] 2206 2-9-0 0 .... MickyFenton 5 14
(Mrs P Sly) *hld up in tch: racd keenly: hmpd and lost pl over 2f out* **7/1**

1m 13.54s (0.54) **Going Correction** -0.10s/f (Good) **10** Ran SP% **118.5**
Speed ratings (Par 92): **92,91,88,84,84 82,81,80,79,64**
CSF £81.36 TOTE £29.10: £5.10, £1.40, £3.70; EX 138.50.
Owner Dale And Ann Wilsdon **Bred** P And Mrs A G Venner **Trained** Aylesbury, Bucks

FOCUS
Not easy to rate but probably just a fair fillies' maiden, the favourite the best guide to the form. The first two home are daughters of Oasis Dream.

NOTEBOOK
Oasis Breeze ◆ is clearly a useful prospect, defying her lack of racecourse experience to come from behind and pick up a fair filly who had the advantage of a previous run. She is the sixth winner to come from the eight foals produced by her American dam, and looks well up to a shot at a conditions event now. (tchd 25-1 and 33-1)
Predict put her experience to good use in pinging out of the stalls and getting across to the favoured stands' rail. If it wasn't for the presence of a clearly above-average newcomer she would have been a decisive winner, so this has to go down as a positive effort. She is clearly going to win races. (op 7-4 tchd 9-4)
Sneak Preview's trainer does very well with the juveniles in his care and after a slow start the daughter of Monsieur Bond showed enough to suggest that she will be winning one of these very soon. (op 12-1 tchd 11-1)
Wigan Pier ◆ had shown nothing in two previous starts but clearly has plenty of pace judged on this display and can go close in a nursery back at the minimum trip.
Polly's Choice(IRE) ended up racing towards the middle of the course having been slowly away from a stands'-side draw. She kept on well enough to suggest she has a future. (op 14-1 tchd 20-1)
Exceedingly Good(IRE) ◆, a 110,000gns purchase as a yearling, appeared to get outpaced when the leaders quickened just after halfway but kept on well once the penny started to drop and should leave this form a long way behind her in due course. (op 6-1 tchd 7-2)
Black Salix(USA) Official explanation: jockey said filly suffered interference in running

3028 ARTHUR PRINCE VOLKSWAGEN, LOUGHBOROUGH, SPRINT H'CAP 5f 2y
7:45 (7:47) (Class 3) (0-95,95) 3-Y-O
£8,723 (£2,612; £1,306; £653; £326; £163) **Stalls Low**

Form RPR

0-11 **1** **Befortyfour**[16] 2529 3-9-7 **95** .... PhilipRobinson 6 109
(M A Jarvis) *w ldr tl led 3f out: shkn up over 1f out: r.o wl: eased nr fin* **10/11**[1]

5-31 **2** 2 1/4 **Little Pete (IRE)**[15] 2570 3-8-13 **87** .... FrancisNorton 8 93
(A M Balding) *s.i.s: hld up: hdwy over 1f out: sn rdn: r.o* **5/2**[2]

-003 **3** 1/2 **Captain Dunne (IRE)**[38] 1911 3-8-0 **77** .... DuranFentiman(3) 2 81
(T D Easterby) *chsd ldrs: rdn over 1f out: styd on same pce ins fnl f* **16/1**

4414 **4** 1 **Blue Jack**[26] 2258 3-8-2 **76** .... DO'Donohoe 3 76
(W R Muir) *s.i.s: outpcd: swtchd rt and hdwy over 1f out: nt trble ldrs* **12/1**[3]

3-65 **5** 2 1/2 **Secret Asset (IRE)**[17] 2498 3-9-5 **93** .... DavidAllan 1 84
(W M Brisbourne) *chsd ldrs: rdn and hung rt fr over 1f out: sn wknd* **16/1**

11-5 **6** 3/4 **Weet A Surprise**[128] 470 3-8-2 **76** .... WilliamBuick 4 65
(R Hollinshead) *hld up: rdn 1/2-way: wknd fnl f* **40/1**

0620 **7** 1 3/4 **Bosun Breese**[7] 2843 3-8-10 **84** .... AlanMunro 7 66
(P W D'Arcy) *led: hdd 3f out: wknd fnl f* **16/1**

21-0 **8** 3 1/2 **Kashoof**[35] 1999 3-8-11 **85** .... MartinDwyer 9 55
(J L Dunlop) *prom: rdn 1/2-way: wknd fnl f* **16/1**

0-04 **9** 1/2 **Lady Avenger (IRE)**[16] 2529 3-9-4 **92** .... RichardMullen 10 60
(J M P Eustace) *s.i.s: rdn and hung rt 1/2-way: wknd over 1f out* **25/1**

59.33 secs (-0.67) **Going Correction** -0.10s/f (Good) **9** Ran SP% **118.5**
Speed ratings (Par 103): **101,97,96,95,91 89,87,81,80**
CSF £3.29 CT £20.23 TOTE £1.90: £1.30, £1.40, £5.80; EX 3.50.
Owner M F Bailey **Bred** Slatch Farm Stud **Trained** Newmarket, Suffolk

FOCUS
A very useful sprint handicap for three-year-olds. The progressive winner appears to be on his way to much better things and the second brought solid form into this.

NOTEBOOK
Befortyfour made it three wins from three starts this term with a comfortable success. Backed into odds-on favouritism despite having to lump top weight, Robinson allowed him to drift over to the stands' rail before a few shakes of the reins sent him clear at the furlong pole. Eased down close home, the son of Kyllachy looks as though he will be holding his own in Listed/Pattern company before too long. (op 11-8 tchd 5-6)
Little Pete(IRE) was slowly away and had to weave through the field to get a run, by which time the winner had flown. He won't always run into such an improver as Befortyfour, and can go one better soon. Official explanation: jockey said gelding lost action (op 9-4 tchd 11-4)
Captain Dunne(IRE) ran a solid race in the vanguard throughout without ever looking like going with the winner once he had set sail for home. He is probably a couple of pounds too high in the handicap at the moment. (op 12-1 tchd 20-1)
Blue Jack was badly outpaced in the early stages but really found his stride and began cutting through the pack when it was all too late. He looks in need of a return to 6f now. (tchd 11-1)
Secret Asset(IRE) Official explanation: jockey said gelding hung right
Lady Avenger(IRE) Official explanation: jockey said filly was unsuited by the good to firm, firm in places ground

3029 TENPIN DERBY & NOTTINGHAM H'CAP 1m 1f 218y
8:15 (8:15) (Class 5) (0-75,75) 4-Y-0+ **£3,561** (£1,059; £529; £264) **Stalls High**

Form RPR

3000 **1** **Quince (IRE)**[30] 2120 5-9-7 **75** ....(v) JimmyQuinn 6 84
(J Pearce) *hld up in tch: rdn to ld ins fnl f: r.o* **14/1**

0131 **2** 1 1/4 **Top Seed (IRE)**[3] 2949 7-8-11 **65** 6ex .... StephenDonohoe 7 72
(Ian Williams) *hld up: rdn over 3f out: r.o u.p ins fnl f: nt rch wnr* **85/40**[1]

3-10 **3** 1 1/4 **Smirfy's Silver**[29] 2165 4-8-13 **67** .... GrahamGibbons 1 71
(E S McMahon) *chsd ldr tl led over 1f out: sn rdn: hdd and unable qck ins fnl f* **12/1**

64-0 **4** 1/2 **Vincenzio (IRE)**[52] 1559 4-9-0 **68** ....(b[1]) SebSanders 3 71
(C R Egerton) *hld up: hdwy over 3f out: rdn over 1f out: styd on* **11/2**[3]

6240 **5** hd **Pitbull**[11] 2697 5-8-8 **62** ....(p) AlanMunro 5 65
(Mrs G S Rees) *s.s: hld up: rdn over 3f out: hdwy over 1f out: r.o* **8/1**

142 **6** 5 **Roodolph**[5] 2895 4-9-6 **74** .... StephenCarson 4 67
(Eve Johnson Houghton) *trckd ldrs: hung rt 1/2-way: rdn 3f out: wknd over 1f out* **7/2**[2]

3652 **7** 4 1/2 **Bramcote Lorne**[27] 1776 5-8-2 **56** oh4 ....(p) WilliamBuick 9 40
(R C Guest) *prom: rdn over 3f out: wknd over 1f out* **11/1**

0-30 **8** 3/4 **Bedizen**[22] 2373 5-9-5 **73** ....(p) MickyFenton 2 55
(Mrs P Sly) *led: rdn and hdd over 1f out: sn wknd* **33/1**

5426 **9** 5 **Sudden Impulse**[17] 2499 7-9-6 **74** .... SilvestreDeSousa 10 46
(A D Brown) *hld up: rdn and wknd over 2f out* **8/1**

2m 6.10s (-1.80) **Going Correction** -0.10s/f (Good) **9** Ran SP% **117.5**
Speed ratings (Par 103): **103,102,101,100,100 96,92,92,88**
CSF £44.85 CT £385.05 TOTE £13.80: £4.70, £1.20, £2.40; EX 63.50.
Owner D Leech **Bred** David Ryan **Trained** Newmarket, Suffolk

FOCUS
No more than a fair handicap but the runner-up has been in good form of late and the form should prove reliable, if pretty ordinary.

3030 VICTORIA CENTRE, NOTTINGHAM, H'CAP — 5f 218y
8:45 (8:48) (Class 6) (0-60,62) 3-Y-O — £2,266 (£674; £337; £168) Stalls Low

Form — RPR

-003 **1** **Presto Levanter**[5] 2898 3-9-2 58 .... JimmyFortune 5 — 66
(R Hannon) *wnt rt s: hld up: hdwy 2f out: rdn to ld ins fnl f: r.o* — **13/2**

00-0 **2** ¾ **Bilboa**[77] 1068 3-8-12 54 .... AlanMunro 6 — 60
(B R Millman) *hmpd s: hld up: swtchd lft and hdwy over 1f out: sn rdn: r.o* — **16/1**

360 **3** hd **Pantherii (USA)**[9] 2757 3-9-3 59 .... NelsonDeSouza 16 — 64
(P F I Cole) *sn led: rdn and edgd lft over 1f out: hdd ins fnl f: styd on* — **12/1**

0065 **4** ¾ **Averoo**[16] 2549 3-9-2 58 .... StephenDonohoe 12 — 61
(M D Squance) *hood removed late: bhd: hdwy over 2f out: rdn over 1f out: styd on* — **9/2**[1]

4-32 **5** 2¼ **Shakespeare's Son**[12] 2660 3-8-12 57 .... DuranFentiman(3) 2 — 52
(H J Evans) *trckd ldrs: rdn over 1f out: styd on same pce* — **6/1**[3]

3504 **6** 1 **Mujahope**[11] 2704 3-8-6 53 ....(v) KellyHarrison(5) 15 — 45
(C J Teague) *s.i.s: racd keenly and sn prom: rdn and hung rt over 1f out: no ex fnl f* — **20/1**

060 **7** ¾ **Lucky Character**[59] 1410 3-8-5 47 ....(t) GregFairley 10 — 37
(N J Vaughan) *mid-div: sn pushed along: outpcd 1/2-way: styd on ins fnl f* — **40/1**

0-10 **8** 1¼ **King Of Cadeaux (IRE)**[16] 2549 3-8-12 54 ....(b[1]) EddieAhern 7 — 40
(M A Magnusson) *slowly in to stride: hld up: hmpd over 2f out: styd on ins fnl f: nvr nrr* — **10/1**

600 **9** 1 **Where's Dids**[14] 2620 3-8-9 51 .... EdwardCreighton 1 — 34
(M R Channon) *s.i.s: outpcd: styng on whn nt clr run ins fnl f: nvr nrr* — **33/1**

-024 **10** ½ **Tanley**[22] 2380 3-9-4 60 ....(p) MickyFenton 4 — 41
(J F Coupland) *chsd ldrs: rdn over 1f out: wknd fnl f* — **16/1**

0-00 **11** nk **Rockjumper**[13] 2639 3-8-8 50 .... RichardMullen 11 — 30
(H Morrison) *prom: rdn 1/2-way: wknd over 1f out* — **16/1**

0515 **12** 1¼ **Just Jimmy (IRE)**[26] 2260 3-9-2 58 .... CatherineGannon 17 — 34
(P D Evans) *s.i.s: sn pushed along in rr: hdwy u.p over 2f out: wknd over 1f out* — **5/1**[2]

5604 **13** nse **Planet Paradise (IRE)**[8] 2774 3-8-4 46 .... FrancisNorton 18 — 22
(D Shaw) *s.i.s: hld up: plld hrd: hung rt over 4f out: hdwy over 2f out: sn rdn and wknd* — **16/1**

0031 **14** 1½ **Turn And River (IRE)**[12] 2660 3-9-3 62 .... MarkLawson(3) 8 — 33
(M Brittain) *chsd ldrs: wkng whn nt clr run over 2f out* — **10/1**

00-0 **15** ¾ **Framington**[8] 2803 3-7-13 46 .... MCGeran(5) 13 — 15
(M R Channon) *chsd ldrs over 4f* — **66/1**

50-2 **16** shd **Varinia (IRE)**[8] 2803 3-8-10 55 .... JamieMoriarty(3) 14 — 23
(M Brittain) *chsd ldrs: rdn 1/2-way: wknd over 2f out* — **20/1**

1m 12.72s (-0.28) **Going Correction** -0.10s/f (Good) **16 Ran SP% 128.3**
Speed ratings (Par 97): **97,96,95,94,91 90,89,87,86,85 85,83,83,81,80 80**
CSF £105.87 CT £1303.02 TOTE £8.30: £1.70, £4.10, £4.30, £1.60; EX 177.60.
Owner B Bull **Bred** Poulton Stud **Trained** East Everleigh, Wilts

FOCUS
Very modest fare despite the numbers and the form could be turned upside down if they met in future as the winner benefited greatly from the second and fourth enjoying no luck in running. However the time was the pick of the three races over the trip so the form is rated a bit more positively than it might have been.
Turn And River(IRE) Official explanation: jockey said filly was unsuited by the good to firm (firm in places) ground

3031 FENWICK OF LEICESTER H'CAP — 7f 9y
9:15 (9:16) (Class 4) (0-80,80) 3-Y-O — £4,415 (£1,321; £660; £330; £164) Stalls Low

Form — RPR

243- **1** **House**[255] 5920 3-9-4 77 .... SebSanders 6 — 90
(L M Cumani) *s.i.s: hld up: hdwy 1/2-way: led over 1f out: rdn clr* — **5/1**[2]

0621 **2** 3¾ **Admirals Way**[16] 2549 3-8-3 62 .... JimmyQuinn 2 — 65
(C N Kellett) *trckd ldrs: rdn over 1f out: edgd rt: styd on same pce fnl f* — **9/1**

26-2 **3** nk **Elk Trail (IRE)**[33] 2037 3-9-4 77 .... MickyFenton 1 — 79
(T P Tate) *sn outpcd: hung rt fr 1/2-way: hdwy u.p fr over 1f out: nt rch ldrs* — **9/1**

160 **4** 1½ **Al Samha (USA)**[19] 2464 3-9-7 80 .... GregFairley 7 — 78
(M Johnston) *chsd ldrs: rdn over 2f out: styd on same pce appr fnl f* — **16/1**

22-5 **5** 1 **Majeen**[23] 2333 3-9-2 75 .... LiamJones 10 — 70
(W J Haggas) *led: plld hrd: hdd over 1f out: wknd ins fnl f* — **11/4**[1]

010- **6** 2¼ **Dresden Doll (USA)**[276] 5322 3-9-4 77 .... EddieAhern 12 — 66
(M L W Bell) *chsd ldr: rdn and ev ch over 1f out: wknd ins fnl f* — **9/1**

1-56 **7** ½ **Outside Edge (IRE)**[30] 2127 3-8-12 71 ....(p) AdamKirby 5 — 59
(W R Swinburn) *hld up: outpcd 1/2-way: hdwy u.p over 1f out: wknd fnl f* — **18/1**

0-00 **8** ½ **Hawaana (IRE)**[31] 2104 3-9-7 80 .... MartinDwyer 3 — 67
(B W Hills) *chsd ldrs: rdn whn hmpd over 2f out: sn wknd* — **6/1**[3]

-200 **9** 1½ **Talk Of Saafend (IRE)**[9] 2761 3-9-7 80 .... JimmyFortune 11 — 63
(R Hannon) *hld up: hdwy u.p and hung lft over 1f out: wknd and eased ins fnl f* — **6/1**[3]

6-00 **10** 3½ **Semah Harold**[12] 2674 3-8-8 67 .... RichardMullen 8 — 40
(E S McMahon) *prom: rdn whn hmpd over 2f out: sn wknd* — **40/1**

0-00 **11** 3¼ **Azeer (USA)**[28] 2189 3-9-3 76 .... AlanMunro 9 — 40
(P W Chapple-Hyam) *mid-div: rdn 1/2-way: wknd over 2f out* — **18/1**

546- **12** 5 **Pinewood Lulu**[183] 7139 3-8-7 66 .... DeanMcKeown 4 — 17
(R C Guest) *stdd s: hld up: rdn and wknd over 2f out* — **66/1**

1m 24.96s (-1.24) **Going Correction** -0.10s/f (Good) **12 Ran SP% 122.2**
Speed ratings (Par 101): **103,98,98,96,95 92,92,91,90,86 82,76**
CSF £51.39 CT £409.07 TOTE £7.50: £2.10, £3.10, £3.10; EX 70.10 Place 6 £61.93, Place 5 £37.93..
Owner Antoniades Family **Bred** A G Antoniades **Trained** Newmarket, Suffolk

FOCUS
A few in-form and a few unexposed horses combined to make this a useful handicap for three-year-olds. Run at a strong pace and with the runner-up coming off the back of a victory, the form looks solid.
Admirals Way Official explanation: jockey said gelding hung right
Talk Of Saafend(IRE) Official explanation: jockey said filly hung left
T/Plt: £37.90 to a £1 stake. Pool: £63,387.83. 1,220.75 winning tickets. T/Qpdt: £19.90 to a £1 stake. Pool: £3,648.80. 135.50 winning tickets. CR

2832 LINGFIELD (L-H)
Saturday, June 14

OFFICIAL GOING: Turf course - good to firm; all-weather - standard
Wind: Moderate, half-behind Weather: Fine but cloudy

3032 E B F SWEDEN V SPAIN IN PLAY AT BETDAQ MEDIAN AUCTION MAIDEN FILLIES' STKS — 5f
5:55 (5:55) (Class 5) 2-Y-O — £3,302 (£982; £491; £245) Stalls High

Form — RPR

44 **1** **Bahamian Ceilidh**[26] 2253 2-9-0 0 .... TGMcLaughlin 13 — 77+
(B R Millman) *racd against nr side rail: mde all: at least 2 l clr over 1f out: drvn out fnl f to hold on* — **4/1**[2]

0 **2** ½ **Starlarks (IRE)**[7] 2835 2-9-0 0 .... PaulDoe 11 — 76+
(W J Knight) *dwlt: hld up bhd ldrs and racd against nr side rail: n.m.r jst over 2f out: chsd wnr over 1f out: chal fnl f: jst hld* — **11/2**[3]

0 **3** 3¾ **Hameildaeme**[26] 2253 2-8-7 0 .... WilliamCarson(7) 5 — 62+
(S C Williams) *dwlt: swtchd to r against nr side rail: in tch in rr: effrt 2f out: styd on same pce fnl f to take 3rd nr fin* — **25/1**

34 **4** ½ **Sparta Rebel (IRE)**[13] 2638 2-9-0 0 .... PatCosgrave 10 — 60
(M J Wallace) *racd three wd: prom: mostly chsd wnr to over 1f out: wknd fnl f* — **10/11**[1]

405 **5** 1¼ **Readily**[13] 2638 2-8-9 0 .... JackMitchell(5) 12 — 55
(J G Portman) *pressed ldrs to wl over 1f out: sn outpcd and btn* — **17/2**

6 1¼ **Place The Duchess** 2-9-0 0 .... FergusSweeney 4 — 51
(D W P Arbuthnot) *racd on outer: wl on terms to 2f out: hanging lft and wknd fnl f* — **33/1**

7 3¼ **Costa Lotta** 2-9-0 0 .... TQuinn 1 — 37
(E A L Dunlop) *outpcd in last pair and wl bhd: kpt on fnl f* — **20/1**

3 **8** 1 **True Britannia**[36] 1955 2-9-0 0 .... RobertHavlin 7 — 34
(S Kirk) *racd towards outer: spd to 1/2-way: sn btn* — **16/1**

00 **9** 4 **Herecomesbella**[23] 2324 2-9-0 0 .... NeilPollard 8 — 19
(A P Jarvis) *racd v awkwardly: nvr on terms: bhd fnl 2f* — **50/1**

000 **10** hd **Agnes Love**[18] 2479 2-8-11 0 .... TravisBlock(3) 3 — 19
(Mrs H Sweeting) *prom on wd outside to 1/2-way: sn wknd and wl bhd* — **100/1**

11 20 **Bold Escape** 2-9-0 0 .... PatrickMathers 2 — —
(Peter Grayson) *outpcd and a wl bhd in last: t.o* — **50/1**

57.58 secs (-0.62) **Going Correction** -0.175s/f (Firm) **11 Ran SP% 120.6**
Speed ratings (Par 90): **97,96,90,89,87 85,79,77,71,71 39**
CSF £25.27 TOTE £6.90: £1.60, £2.00, £7.20; EX 35.50.
Owner Paul Murphy **Bred** Redmyre Bloodstock And Stuart McPhee **Trained** Kentisbeare, Devon

FOCUS
A low-key maiden for juvenile fillies. The first three home raced against the favoured stands'-side rail. The form is hard to pin down accurately but the first two showed improvement.

NOTEBOOK
Bahamian Ceilidh is bred for speed and made it third time lucky on the racecourse with a pillar-to-post success. Her draw against the favoured rail was obviously a big help on this occasion and her future lies in the hands of the Handicapper. (op 9-2)
Starlarks(IRE) was held up slightly in her run before producing a strong challenge close home. She made her debut here over 6f and her immediate future is probably going to lie back at that trip. (op 6-1 tchd 9-2, 13-2 in a place)
Hameildaeme was again slowly away but stayed on well to pass beaten horses in the last furlong, suggesting than an extra furlong will suit. (op 16-1 tchd 33-1)
Sparta Rebel(IRE), backed into odds-on favouritism, seemed ill-at-ease on the fast ground and is starting to look a little disappointing. Official explanation: trainer was unable to explain the poor form shown (op 11-10)
Place The Duchess raced up the centre of the course from her low draw and showed good speed despite obvious signs of greenness. (op 16-1)

3033 CASH BONUS @ BETDAQPOKER.CO.UK H'CAP — 6f
6:25 (6:25) (Class 6) (0-65,69) 3-Y-O+ — £2,047 (£604; £302) Stalls High

Form — RPR

4215 **1** **Shot To Fame (USA)**[25] 2277 9-9-13 65 .... GeorgeBaker 18 — 78
(S Kirk) *racd against nr side rail: trckd ldrs: squeezed through fr over 1f out to chal ins fnl f: r.o to ld last 75yds* — **7/2**[2]

0006 **2** ¾ **Arfinnit (IRE)**[11] 2706 7-8-9 50 ....(v) KirstyMilczarek(3) 13 — 61
(Mrs A L M King) *racd towards nr side rail: w ldrs: led wl over 1f out: hdd and outpcd last 75yds* — **20/1**

2-01 **3** ½ **Choreography**[3] 2933 5-10-3 69 6ex ....(p) PaulDoe 14 — 78
(Jim Best) *trckd ldrs and racd towards nr side rail: effrt over 1f out: jnd ldr ins fnl f: nt qckn last 75yds* — **3/1**[1]

0100 **4** 3¼ **Kenmore**[3] 2950 6-9-7 64 .... SCreighton(5) 4 — 63+
(I W McInnes) *taken down early and wnt to post awkwardly: hld up in last: taken to wd outside and stl wl in rr 2f out: styd on fnl f to snatch 4th last strides* — **25/1**

2346 **5** nk **Grezie**[88] 922 6-8-5 46 oh1 .... LukeMorris(3) 17 — 44
(L A Dace) *hld up in rr against nr side rail: outpcd fr 2f out: styd on fnl f* — **20/1**

1030 **6** shd **Polar Force**[11] 2706 8-8-13 51 .... DMylonas 7 — 48+
(Mrs C A Dunnett) *racd on wd outside: trckd ldrs: hrd rdn and effrt 2f out: disp 4th fnl f but no ch* — **16/1**

2103 **7** shd **Charlotte Grey**[8] 2802 4-8-6 49 .... JackMitchell(5) 10 — 46
(P J McBride) *w ldrs tl wknd jst over 1f out* — **12/1**

5243 **8** shd **Mandarin Spirit (IRE)**[18] 2484 8-9-7 59 ....(b) RobertHavlin 1 — 56
(G C H Chung) *racd towards outer: overall ldr to wl over 1f out: wknd tamely* — **16/1**

-600 **9** 1¼ **Charming Ballet (IRE)**[22] 2355 5-8-8 46 oh1 ....(b) FergusSweeney 15 — 39
(G L Moore) *racd against nr side rail: on terms w ldrs tl 2f out: losing pl whn hmpd over 1f out* — **10/1**

-652 **10** ½ **Jayanjay**[22] 2350 9-9-6 58 .... RichardThomas 12 — 49
(B R Johnson) *trckd ldrs: swtchd to outer and effrt 2f out: no imp 1f out: fdd* — **9/1**[3]

2004 **11** 1 **Reigning Monarch (USA)**[8] 2798 5-8-10 55 .... RossAtkinson(7) 6 — 43
(Miss Z C Davison) *dwlt: a towards rr and racd towards outer: no prog fnl 2f* — **12/1**

0230 **12** hd **Stormburst (IRE)**[8] 2802 4-8-12 50 .... VinceSlattery 16 — 37
(A J Chamberlain) *racd towards nr side: a wl in rr: u.p and btn 2f out* — **20/1**

0-00 **13** 1 **Registrar**[36] 1966 6-8-13 51 .... PatCosgrave 2 — 35
(Mrs C A Dunnett) *a in rr: u.p and struggling 2f out* — **33/1**

0456 **14** 1¼ **Teen Ager (FR)**[9] 2758 4-9-5 57 .... TQuinn 8 — 37
(P Burgoyne) *trckd ldrs and racd towards outer: wknd over 1f out* — **11/1**

00-0 **15** 2¾ **Diamond Hurricane (IRE)**[19] 2463 4-8-3 46 oh1 ....(bt) NicolPolli(5) 11 — 17
(M Wellings) *restless stalls and dwlt: sn trckd ldrs: wknd u.p 2f out* — **66/1**

0660 **16** *13* **Umpa Loompa (IRE)**[14] 2597 4-9-1 **56**....................(v) JerryO'Dwyer(3) 9 —
(B J McMath) *nvr gng wl: a in rr: wknd and eased 2f out: t.o* **33/1**
-000 **17** *3 ½* **Iguacu**[18] 2477 4-8-6 **47**..(b[1]) MarcHalford(3) 5 —
(J L Spearing) *racd on wd outside: in tch to 1/2-way: sn wknd u.str.p* **33/1**
69.95 secs (-1.25) **Going Correction** -0.175s/f (Firm) **17** Ran SP% **130.2**
Speed ratings (Par 101): **101,100,99,95,94 94,94,94,92,91 90,90,88,87,83 66,61**
CSF £82.12 CT £227.61 TOTE £6.40: £2.30, £4.10, £1.80, £9.90; EX 142.20.
Owner Timothy Pearson & Dianne Fraser **Bred** Eric Puerari **Trained** Upper Lambourn, Berks
■ Stewards' Enquiry : George Baker one-day ban: careless riding (Jun 28)

FOCUS
Most of these would be better off in selling company and the winner, a Group 3 winner in his pomp, was able to outclass his rivals. He did have the best draw but this was a good start for his new yard.
Umpa Loompa(IRE) Official explanation: jockey said gelding hung right throughout

3034 BET EURO 2008 - BETDAQ H'CAP 7f
6:55 (6:58) (Class 6) (0-55,56) 3-Y-O+ **£2,047** (£604; £302) **Stalls** High

Form RPR
046- **1** **Imperial Lucky (IRE)**[294] 4828 5-9-6 **54**........................ PatCosgrave 16 64
(M J Wallace) *hld up bhd ldrs and racd against nr side rail: effrt to ld wl over 1f out: drvn out to hold on* **7/1**[2]
2204 **2** *nk* **Bentley**[46] 1706 4-9-5 **53**.. J-PGuillambert 18 62
(J G Given) *racd against nr side rail: wl on terms: edgd lft off rail over 2f out: rallied u.p to press wnr ins fnl f: jst hld* **10/1**
-023 **3** *1 ¼* **Brouhaha**[14] 2597 4-9-7 **55**.. TedDurcan 17 61
(B J McMath) *wl in rr and nt gng wl but racd against nr side rail: prog fr 2f out: styd on wl to take 3rd nr fin* **5/2**[1]
6005 **4** *nk* **Cornerstone**[7] 2837 4-9-3 **51**..............................(vt) GeorgeBaker 13 56
(S C Williams) *wl in rr: kpt towards nr side: hanging lft but styd on fr over 1f out: nrst fin* **8/1**[3]
13-0 **5** *¾* **Parthenope**[26] 2243 5-9-2 **50**.. DavidKinsella 10 53
(J A Geake) *trckd ldrs and sn tacked across towards nr side: effrt 2f out: outpcd fr over 1f out* **20/1**
1424 **6** *2 ¼* **Marmooq**[16] 2550 5-9-0 **55**..(e) HarryPoulton(7) 7 52+
(M J Attwater) *racd on outer: prom: on terms 2f out: grad fdd fnl f* **17/2**
1004 **7** *1* **Majestical (IRE)**[16] 2547 6-9-6 **54**..............................(p) NCallan 15 48+
(V Smith) *dwlt and nudged sn after s: trckd ldrs: effrt and swtchd towards centre 2f out: no imp after* **12/1**
2410 **8** *nk* **Balerno**[35] 2003 9-9-5 **53**.. IanMongan 6 46+
(Mrs L J Mongan) *hld up wl in rr: rdn and no prog over 2f out: plugged on towards nr side fnl f* **16/1**
/020 **9** *1 ¼* **Moverra (IRE)**[35] 2009 4-9-4 **52**..................................(p) TGMcLaughlin 1 42+
(M Wigham) *racd on wd outside: prom tl lost pl fr wl over 1f out* **25/1**
3400 **10** *hd* **Franksalot (IRE)**[3] 2936 8-9-3 **54**................................ LukeMorris(3) 4 43+
(I W McInnes) *hld up in rr: tried to make prog fr over 2f out but forced to r wd: no ch* **20/1**
6665 **11** *½* **Border Artist**[6] 2861 9-9-0 **55**.................................... SimonPearce(7) 8 43
(J Pearce) *dwlt: wl in rr: rdn 3f out: plugged on fr over 1f out: no ch* **28/1**
30-0 **12** *hd* **Vogarth**[18] 2491 4-9-2 **55**.. JamesMillman(5) 14 42
(B R Millman) *mde most towards nr side to wl over 1f out: wknd* **20/1**
0060 **13** *7* **Empire Dancer (IRE)**[25] 2274 5-9-5 **53**........................ PatrickMathers 2 22
(I W McInnes) *racd on wd outside: in tch to 3f out: sn no ch* **33/1**
-015 **14** *1 ½* **Mannello**[3] 2933 5-9-8 **56** 6ex..............................(p) RichardThomas 3 20
(Jim Best) *racd on outer: nvr gng wl: hanging and wknd u.p over 2f out* **20/1**
-340 **15** *hd* **Grand Assault**[129] 453 5-9-6 **54**................................(be) FergusSweeney 12 18
(G C Bravery) *chsd ldrs: hrd rdn 1/2-way: wknd over 2f out* **20/1**
0640 **16** *nse* **Metropolitan Chief**[22] 2355 4-9-3 **51**..............................(b) TQuinn 11 15
(P Burgoyne) *plld hrd: hld up in tch: wknd rapidly over 2f out* **20/1**
-600 **17** *3 ¾* **To The Max (IRE)**[16] 2533 4-9-7 **55**................................ DMylonas 9 9
(Mrs C A Dunnett) *prom towards outer: hrd rdn 3f out: sn wknd* **33/1**
34-0 **18** *51* **Park Valley Prince**[161] 56 4-9-3 **51**................................ TPO'Shea 5 —
(W R Muir) *chsd ldrs to 1/2-way: bhd and virtually p.u fnl f* **16/1**
1m 22.38s (-0.92) **Going Correction** -0.175s/f (Firm) **18** Ran SP% **133.0**
Speed ratings (Par 101): **98,97,96,95,95 92,91,90,89,89 88,88,80,78,78 78,74,15**
CSF £68.83 CT £207.78 TOTE £8.90: £2.30, £2.60, £1.20, £2.40; EX 57.80.
Owner David Cohen **Bred** Holborn Trust Co **Trained** Newmarket, Suffolk
■ Stewards' Enquiry : Pat Cosgrave two-day ban: used whip in an incorrect place (Jun 28-29)

FOCUS
With the first three home being drawn in the three boxes nearest the stands' rail, the overall form deserves treating with the utmost uncertainty. The form amongst the principals does make sense, though.
Mannello Official explanation: jockey said mare hung left
Park Valley Prince Official explanation: trainer said gelding was severely struck into

3035 BET GREECE V RUSSIA - BETDAQ MEDIAN AUCTION MAIDEN STKS 1m 4f (P)
7:25 (7:26) (Class 6) 3-4-Y-O **£2,266** (£674; £337; £168) **Stalls** Low

Form RPR
1D **Eventide** 3-8-6 0.. PaulDoe 9 68
(W J Knight) *prom: trckd ldr 3f out: rdn to ld wl over 1f out: rn green but styd on wl: fin 1st, 2½l: subs disq (prohibited substance)* **25/1**
0-06 **1** **Heart Of Dubai (USA)**[16] 2528 3-8-11 68................................ NCallan 3 69
(C E Brittain) *cl up: effrt and hanging 2f out: chsd wnr 1f out: kpt on but no imp: fin 2nd, 2½l: sus awrdd r* **10/1**[3]
2 *4 ¾* **Beauchamp Wonder** 3-8-7 0 ow1.......................... PaulMulrennan 10 61
(G A Butler) *trckd ldrs on outer: effrt over 2f out: outpcd over 1f out: kpt on to take 3rd last strides: fin 3rd, 2½l & 2¼l; plcd 2nd* **16/1**
34 **3** *nk* **Seventh Cavalry (IRE)**[9] 2763 3-8-11 0.............................. TedDurcan 8 67+
(H R A Cecil) *led: rdn and hdd wl over 1f out: wknd fnl f: lost 3rd last strides: fin 5th, plced 4th* **1/2**[1]
00 **4** *3* **Seedless**[19] 2454 3-7-13 0.. DavidProbert(7) 7 55+
(A M Balding) *hld up in last trio: outpcd and pushed along over 3f out: styd on steadily fnl 2f: nvr nrr: fin 5th, plcd 4th* **14/1**
65 **5** *1 ¾* **Fleurs De Censier**[22] 2363 3-8-3 0.............................. MarcHalford(3) 5 52
(D M Simcock) *hld up towards rr: effrt and sme prog over 3f out: nt on terms over 2f out: n.d after: fin 6th, plcd 5th* **50/1**
6 *½* **Munlochy Bay** 4-9-7 0.. FergusSweeney 11 51
(W S Kittow) *s.s: t.k.h early: hld up in last trio: outpcd over 3f out: no ch after: fin 7th, plcd 6th* **50/1**
3-50 **7** *5* **Power Player**[21] 2414 4-9-12 69..................................(v) TPO'Shea 6 48
(D J Coakley) *trckd ldr to 3f out: hanging bdly and nt run on over 2f out fin 8th, plcd 7th* **8/1**[2]
6- **8** *4 ½* **Green Wonder (GER)**[225] 6626 3-8-3 0.................. KirstyMilczarek(3) 4 36
(D M Simcock) *a towards rr: struggling fr 3f out: fin 9th, plcd 8th* **40/1**
06 **9** *3* **Bonzo**[32] 2090 3-8-11 0.. PatCosgrave 1 36
(P Howling) *hld up in last trio: wknd over 3f out: fin 10th plcd 9th* **66/1**
2300 **10** *1 ¾* **Okafranca (IRE)**[18] 2475 3-8-11 57..............................(p) J-PGuillambert 2 33
(W R Muir) *cl up tl wknd u.p over 4f out: fin 11th, plcd 10th* **14/1**
2m 34.33s (1.33) **Going Correction** +0.05s/f (Slow)
WFA 3 from 4yo 15lb **11** Ran SP% **117.8**
Speed ratings (Par 101): **97,95,93,93,91 90,90,86,83,81 80**
CSF £248.05 TOTE £26.20: £7.10, £2.80, £4.70; EX 132.70.
Owner Mrs Alison Ruggles **Bred** Mrs A R Ruggles **Trained** Patching, W Sussex

FOCUS
A modest maiden and with the favourite losing his action on his first experience of an All-Weather surface, the form is questionable.
Seventh Cavalry(IRE) Official explanation: jockey said colt lost action and hung right

3036 GET MATCHED NOW AT BETDAQ H'CAP 1m 2f (P)
7:55 (7:57) (Class 5) (0-70,68) 4-Y-O+ **£2,331** (£693; £346; £173) **Stalls** Low

Form RPR
0600 **1** **Obrigado (USA)**[22] 2373 8-9-4 **65**..................................(t) GeorgeBaker 9 77
(G L Moore) *stdd s: hld up in last pair: gd prog on outer over 3f out to go 2nd over 2f out: clsd to ld jst over 1f out: cajoled along and fnd enough* **5/1**[3]
0446 **2** *½* **My Mentor (IRE)**[8] 2804 4-9-1 **62**..............................(b) J-PGuillambert 12 73
(Sir Mark Prescott) *sn led and clr: 8 l up 4f out: c bk and hdd jst over 1f out: kpt on wl but a hld* **9/2**[2]
0234 **3** *3 ½* **High 'n Dry (IRE)**[19] 2457 4-9-7 **68**................................(p) PaulDoe 3 72
(M A Allen) *hld up in midfield: effrt over 2f out: hanging over 1f out: styd on to take 3rd ins fnl f: no ch w ldng pair* **7/1**
400- **4** *hd* **Tenement (IRE)**[374] 2362 4-8-2 **49** oh1.......................... DavidKinsella 10 53
(Jamie Poulton) *hld up wl in rr: effrt over 2f out: styd on fr over 1f out to press for 3rd ins fnl f* **33/1**
-030 **5** *4* **Dubai Shadow (IRE)**[17] 2510 4-8-9 **56** ow1...................... NCallan 6 52
(C E Brittain) *prom: chsd clr ldr over 3f out to over 2f out: wknd fnl f* **14/1**
0-02 **6** *1 ¾* **Barathea Dreams (IRE)**[8] 2795 7-8-9 **59**...................... LukeMorris(3) 7 51
(J S Moore) *rrd s: mostly in last trio: rdn wl over 3f out: no real imp fnl 2f* **4/1**[1]
2000 **7** *shd* **Dushstorm (IRE)**[10] 2722 7-9-3 **64**................................ IanMongan 8 56
(C R Dore) *prom in chsng gp: effrt over 2f out: nt qckn wl over 1f out: btn after* **12/1**
3310 **8** *1* **Formidable Guest**[17] 2513 4-8-7 **54**........................ FergusSweeney 11 44
(J Pearce) *a in rr: rdn and struggling over 3f out* **6/1**
0-04 **9** *½* **Soldiers Quest**[7] 2832 4-8-13 **60**............................ PatrickMathers 4 49
(Peter Grayson) *cl up on inner: rdn 4f out: steadily wknd fnl 2f* **20/1**
4546 **10** *½* **Art Market (CAN)**[31] 2101 5-9-1 **65**................................ TravisBlock(3) 2 53
(Miss Jo Crowley) *mostly chsd clr ldr to over 3f out: wknd over 2f out* **6/1**
3000 **11** *4* **Fateful Attraction**[53] 1528 5-9-0 **66**..........................(b) JackMitchell(5) 5 46
(I A Wood) *hld up in rr: sme prog over 3f out: no hdwy over 2f out: wknd over 1f out* **25/1**
2m 6.13s (-0.47) **Going Correction** +0.05s/f (Slow) **11** Ran SP% **121.8**
Speed ratings (Par 103): **103,102,99,99,96 95,94,94,93,93 90**
CSF £28.22 CT £162.60 TOTE £6.20: £2.00, £2.40, £2.90; EX 42.20.
Owner B R Phillips **Bred** Bradyleigh Farms Inc **Trained** Woodingdean, E Sussex
■ Stewards' Enquiry : Paul Doe caution: used whip down the shoulder in forehand position

FOCUS
Just a modest handicap and the pace set by runner-up found everything out bar the winner. The form looks reliable enough, assessed through the third.
Obrigado(USA) Official explanation: trainer said, regarding the improved form, that there had been a change of tactics today having made the running last time, and that gelding is better suited by the AW surface

3037 BETDAQ GOLF DAY AT CAMBERLEY HEATH H'CAP 1m (P)
8:25 (8:27) (Class 6) (0-60,59) 4-Y-O+ **£2,047** (£604; £302) **Stalls** High

Form RPR
3-64 **1** **April Fool**[13] 2640 4-8-11 **55**..................................(v) TravisBlock(3) 4 69+
(J A Geake) *mde all: rdn 2 l clr over 2f out: drvn over 1f out: kpt on and unchal* **7/2**[1]
3000 **2** *3 ½* **Zorn**[11] 2703 9-8-1 **45**.. LukeMorris(3) 6 51
(P Howling) *a chsng wnr: rdn and no imp fr over 2f out: jst hld on for 2nd* **25/1**
60-0 **3** *hd* **Reveur**[164] 10 5-8-3 **47** ow2.................................. KirstyMilczarek(3) 11 53+
(M Mullineaux) *hld up in last trio: pushed along over 2f out: rdn and styd on fr over 1f out to take 3rd nr fin* **11/1**
-505 **4** *½* **Upstairs**[17] 2510 4-9-1 **59**.. MarcHalford(3) 8 63
(D R C Elsworth) *dwlt: hld up towards rr: prog to chse ldng trio 2f out: tried to chal for 2nd on ins over 1f out: one pce fnl f* **9/2**[2]
6000 **5** *1* **Green Pirate**[8] 2806 6-9-3 **58**......................................(v) GeorgeBaker 5 60
(C R Dore) *stdd s: hld up in last trio: rdn 3f out: modest prog fr over 1f out: n.d* **8/1**
000- **6** *¾* **Dilwin (IRE)**[339] 3411 4-9-3 **58**.. TedDurcan 10 58
(P R Webber) *dwlt: hld up in last trio: rdn 3f out: no real imp and nvr on terms* **5/1**[3]
0005 **7** *1 ¾* **Copper King**[46] 1705 4-8-11 **52**.................................... FergusSweeney 12 48
(Miss Tor Sturgis) *chsd ldng trio: wnt 3rd over 3f out and chal for 2nd 2f out: wknd over 1f out* **7/1**
5506 **8** *22* **King After**[129] 453 6-9-0 **55**..(v) NCallan 2 —
(J R Best) *t.k.h: trckd ldng pair to over 3f out: wknd rapidly over 2f out: eased: t.o* **11/2**
00-0 **9** *12* **Take To The Skies (IRE)**[18] 2487 4-9-0 **55**...................... NeilPollard 1 —
(A P Jarvis) *dwlt: plld hrd and sn in midfield: wknd over 3f out: virtually p.u fnl 2f* **20/1**
1m 37.99s (-0.21) **Going Correction** +0.05s/f (Slow) **9** Ran SP% **113.0**
Speed ratings (Par 101): **103,99,99,98,97 97,95,73,61**
CSF £89.53 CT £869.48 TOTE £4.60: £2.00, £5.00, £3.40; EX 96.20 Place 6 £544.49, Place 5 £177.11..
Owner Miss B Swire **Bred** Miss B Swire **Trained** Kimpton, Hants

FOCUS
A poor handicap, with very few able to get into the race, but the time was not bad. The form is rated through the placed horses.
King After Official explanation: jockey said gelding hung left
T/Plt: £1,525.70 to a £1 stake. Pool: £55,280.90. 26.45 winning tickets. T/Qpdt: £269.30 to a £1 stake. Pool: £4,513.60. 12.40 winning tickets. JN

2999 SANDOWN (R-H)

Saturday, June 14

OFFICIAL GOING: Good (8.0)

Rail realignment added 6 yards to races on round course.

Wind: Nil.

3038 BETTERBET.COM H'CAP 1m 1f

1:55 (1:55) (Class 3) (0-90,85) 3-Y-O £7,771 (£2,312; £1,155; £577) Stalls High

Form				RPR
6-12	1		**Steele Tango (USA)**[50] 1598 3-9-9 **85** TedDurcan 2 (R A Teal) *in tch: hdwy over 3f out: drvn to ld ins fnl 2f: pushed out: readily* **16/1**	93
-104	2	1	**Hustle (IRE)**[16] 2532 3-9-9 **85** RyanMoore 7 (R Hannon) *chsd ldrs: rdn and kpt on fr 2f out: chsd wnr fnl f but a readily hld* **11/1**	91
41-2	3	½	**Maxwil**[29] 2151 3-9-9 **85** GeorgeBaker 4 (G L Moore) *hld up towards rr but in tch: hdwy on outside 3f out: rdn to chse ldrs ins fnl 2f: chal u.p for 2nd ins fnl f: no ex* **9/4**[1]	90
0455	4	¾	**Legislation**[24] 2302 3-9-6 **82** (b) RobertHavlin 3 (J H M Gosden) *sn led: rdn fr 3f out and kpt narrow advantage tl hdd ins fnl 2f: one pce ins fnl f* **15/2**[3]	85
0315	5	1	**Seattle Storm (IRE)**[15] 2564 3-9-2 **78** TQuinn 6 (D R C Elsworth) *in rr: puhed along 3f out: hdwy over 1f out: styd on wl fnl f and gng on cl home* **10/1**	79
001	6	shd	**Blue Spartan (IRE)**[19] 2449 3-9-4 **80** LDettori 1 (B J Meehan) *chsd ldrs: drvn to chal fr ins fnl 3f tl wknd fnl f* **4/1**[2]	81
0261	7	1	**Premier Danseur (IRE)**[22] 2378 3-9-8 **84** GregFairley 5 (M Johnston) *chsd ldrs: rdn over 3f out and nvr gng pce to chal: wknd fnl f* **4/1**[2]	82
4410	8	hd	**Stock Market (USA)**[11] 2699 3-9-4 **80** JimCrowley 8 (E A L Dunlop) *towards rr: styd on fr over 1f out but nvr gng pce to get into contention* **14/1**	78

1m 57.55s (1.25) **Going Correction** +0.075s/f (Good) **8** Ran SP% **112.5**

Speed ratings (Par 103): **97,96,95,95,94 94,93,92**

CSF £169.36 CT £554.79 TOTE £16.70: £3.30, £1.90, £1.30; EX 101.10.

Owner The Thirty Acre Racing Partnership **Bred** Tom Zwiesler **Trained** Ashtead, Surrey

FOCUS

A good handicap for three-year-olds. The field were fairly closely covered at the finish but the form is solid.

NOTEBOOK

Steele Tango(USA), officially raised 12lb for finishing second in a conditions event at this venue 50 days previously, confirmed himself a progressive three-year-old with a ready success under joint top weight. The extra furlong was to his liking and, lightly-raced, there should really still be more to come from him in handicap company. (op 14-1 tchd 12-1)

Hustle(IRE) got a positive ride and, while eventually put in his place by the winner, this rates an improved effort under joint top weight. His predigree suggests this trip may stretch him, but he got the distance without fuss. (op 14-1)

Maxwil, 5lb higher, looked to be travelling best of all shortly after turning for home yet in the end he failed to quicken like the winner and proved a bit one paced. He probably needs a stiffer test and is still capable of success from this new mark. (tchd 5-2)

Legislation had his chance from the front again and, while proving one paced, ran very close to his recent level in defeat. He helps to set the level of this form as he looks firmly in the Handicapper's grip now. (op 16-1)

Seattle Storm(IRE) really shaped as though he is crying out for a more positive ride over this distance or indeed the step up to a longer trip. It is still unlikely we have yet to quite see the best of him. (op 12-1 tchd 14-1)

Blue Spartan(IRE), comfortably off the mark at Chepstow 19 days previously, failed to raise his game on this switch to handicap company and was held in the end. Perhaps this ground was too quick. (op 7-2 tchd 3-1)

3039 BETTER NOW HAVE 40 SHOPS H'CAP 7f 16y

2:30 (2:30) (Class 3) (0-90,90) 3-Y-O £7,771 (£2,312; £1,155; £577) Stalls High

Form				RPR
2124	1		**Stevie Thunder**[40] 1868 3-8-12 **79** PaulMulrennan 4 (G A Swinbank) *trckd ldrs: rdn to ld ins fnl 2f: hrd drvn and styd on wl fnl f* **12/1**	86
-031	2	1	**Lindoro**[12] 2674 3-9-8 **89** AdamKirby 2 (W R Swinburn) *stdd s: slowly away: in rr tl gd hdwy on outside fr over 2f out: styd on wl u.p fnl f and sn chsng wnr but a hld* **8/1**[3]	93
10-0	3	¾	**Falcolnry (IRE)**[28] 2196 3-9-1 **82** JamieSpencer 1 (J R Fanshawe) *hld up in tch: hdwy over 2f out: hrd drvn and styd on to chse wnr over 1f out: no imp and outpcd into 3rd ins fnl f* **12/1**	84
5-01	4	1	**Burnbrake**[20] 2429 3-8-5 **72** MartinDwyer 3 (J A R Toller) *in rr tl swtchd lft and gd hdwy over 1f out: kpt on wl fnl f and gng on cl home* **16/1**	71
-342	5	nse	**Swift Gift**[14] 2624 3-9-7 **88** LDettori 10 (B J Meehan) *in tch whn n.m.r 2f out: swtchd lft and hdwy over 1f out: kpt on fnl f but nt trble ldrs* **6/1**[2]	90+
2-10	6	1 ¾	**Tiger Dream**[21] 2403 3-9-6 **87** NCallan 8 (K A Ryan) *chsd ldrs: hrd drvn fr 2f out: styd on same pce* **10/1**	81
60-0	7	½	**Jebel Tara**[16] 2530 3-9-4 **90** (t) AhmedAjtebi[(5)] 6 (C E Brittain) *chsd ldr: led over 2f out: hdd ins fnl 2f: wknd fnl f* **50/1**	83
1-25	8	nk	**Adversity**[37] 1923 3-9-2 **83** RyanMoore 11 (Sir Michael Stoute) *t.k.h: trckd ldrs: shkn up whn n.m.r over 1f out and lost position: nvr in contention after* **10/11**[1]	75+
4100	9	1	**Coole Dodger (IRE)**[12] 2678 3-7-11 **71** oh3 DavidProbert[(7)] 5 (M D I Usher) *towards rr: rdn and effrt on rails into mid-div over 2f out: nvr in contention and wknd fnl f* **40/1**	61
4-12	10	1	**Baron's Court**[7] 2842 3-8-9 **76** GregFairley 9 (M Johnston) *led tl hdd over 2f out: sn wknd* **20/1**	63

1m 30.0s (0.50) **Going Correction** +0.075s/f (Good) **10** Ran SP% **117.3**

Speed ratings (Par 103): **100,98,98,96,96 94,94,93,92,91**

CSF £102.84 CT £829.07 TOTE £15.50: £3.30, £2.20, £3.10; EX 127.30 TRIFECTA Not won..

Owner Steve Gray **Bred** Sir Eric Parker **Trained** Melsonby, N Yorks

FOCUS

Another good handicap for three-year-olds, run at an average pace. The hot favourite got no run, so the form should be treated with some caution, although overall it seems sound.

NOTEBOOK

Stevie Thunder, returning from a 40-day break, got a no-nonsense ride from Mulrennan and resumed winning ways in determined fashion. He got first run on a few of his rivals, but there was still no fluke about this effort and he remains progressive. On this evidence, he now looks ready to tackle a 1m again. (op 16-1)

Lindoro, raised 6lb for his Thirsk win 12 days previously, deserves extra credit as he lost ground with a slow start and had to come from behind. He is evidently back in decent form again now.

Falcolnry(IRE) ◆ came through from off the pace to have her chance and did nothing wrong in defeat. This was a much more encouraging effort and she looks one to be with when stepping up another furlong. (op 8-1 tchd 15-2)

Burnbrake showed himself to be an improving three-year-old with a solid effort in defeat from his 5lb higher mark. A more positive ride again over this trip in the future may well see him go in again. (op 14-1)

Swift Gift, another 2lb higher, did not get the best of runs in the home straight and can be rated a little better than the bare form indicates. That said, he hardly looks well handicapped now (op 13-2 tchd 7-1 in places)

Adversity, very well backed, proved free early on yet still looked to be travelling like the winner passing the 2f pole. However, he found himself behind horses with nowhere to go when the eventual winner kicked for home and quickly lost his position, with his rider soon accepting the situation. He ran on again inside the final furlong and has to rate very unlucky, so compensation should really be forthcoming. Official explanation: jockey said colt was denied a clear run (op 11-10 tchd 4-5)

3040 RBS H'CAP 7f 16y

3:05 (3:06) (Class 2) (0-100,99) 3-Y-O+

£12,462 (£3,732; £1,866; £934; £466; £234) Stalls High

Form				RPR
1-06	1		**Lady Grace (IRE)**[62] 1355 4-9-13 **98** (t) RyanMoore 8 (W J Haggas) *hld up in rr: str run on outside fr 2f out: drvn to ld fnl 75yds: kpt on wl* **4/1**[1]	108
00-0	2	1	**Binanti**[35] 1982 8-9-5 **90** GeorgeBaker 6 (P R Chamings) *hld up in rr: stdy hdwy fr 2f out: styd on u.p to chal fnl 75yds: kpt on but nt pce of wnr nr fin* **9/1**[3]	97
1352	3	shd	**Stevie Gee (IRE)**[16] 2538 4-9-4 **89** NCallan 4 (G A Swinbank) *chsd ldrs: drvn to chal ins fnl f: sn slt advantage tl hdd and one pce fnl 75yds* **4/1**[1]	96
00-1	4	½	**Barons Spy (IRE)**[13] 2644 7-8-8 **82** RussellKennemore[(3)] 1 (R J Price) *in tch: chsd ldrs fr 3f: str chal ins fnl f and sn upsides: one pce cl home* **16/1**	88
-011	5	1 ¼	**My Learned Friend (IRE)**[7] 2837 4-8-2 **80** oh4 DavidProbert[(7)] 9 (A M Balding) *trckd ldr after 2f: led ins fnl 2f: hrd drvn over 1f out: narrowly hdd ins fnl f: wknd nr fin* **4/1**[1]	82
4201	6	hd	**Compton's Eleven**[7] 2818 7-8-11 **87** MCGeran[(5)] 12 (M R Channon) *mid-div: hdwy over 2f out: styd on wl fnl f but nvr gng pce to trble ldrs* **12/1**	89
300-	7	1 ¼	**Lone Wolfe**[239] 6301 4-9-9 **94** JohnEgan 5 (Jane Chapple-Hyam) *in tch: drvn over 2f out: chal 1f out tl wknd fnl 100yds* **33/1**	92
00-0	8	1 ¾	**Out After Dark**[15] 2565 7-8-12 **83** ow1 (p) AdamKirby 10 (C G Cox) *in rr: rdn ins fnl 3f: styd on fnl f but nvr in contention* **20/1**	77
-301	9	1	**Salient**[14] 2604 4-9-0 **88** KirstyMilczarek[(3)] 7 (M J Attwater) *led after 1f: narrowly hdd ins fnl 3f: wknd ins fnl f* **7/1**[2]	79
460-	10	1	**Woodcote Place**[303] 4548 5-8-11 **82** JimCrowley 2 (P R Chamings) *in tch: rdn over 3f out: nvr in contention* **14/1**	70
406	11	4 ½	**Classic Port (FR)**[33] 2044 4-10-0 **99** TGMcLaughlin 11 (M Wigham) *led 1f: chsd ldrs tl wknd 2f out* **14/1**	75
03/5	12	½	**Frederick Ozanam (IRE)**[14] 2604 4-9-3 **88** JamieSpencer 3 (B J Meehan) *chsd ldrs: rdn: n.m.r and wknd qckly over 2f out* **20/1**	63

1m 29.16s (-0.34) **Going Correction** +0.075s/f (Good) **12** Ran SP% **121.9**

Speed ratings (Par 109): **104,102,102,102,100 100,99,97,95,94 89,89**

CSF £41.27 CT £157.44 TOTE £5.20: £1.70, £3.00, £2.00; EX 46.60 Trifecta £377.00 Pool £743.54 - 1.40 winning units,.

Owner F C T Wilson **Bred** Frank Barry **Trained** Newmarket, Suffolk

■ Stewards' Enquiry : Russell Kennemore two-day ban: used whip from above shoulder height (Jun 28-29)

N Callan caution: used whip down the shoulder in forehand position

FOCUS

A decent handicap, run at a solid pace. There were plenty still in with a chance passing the final furlong pole and the form looks solid, with a personal best from the winner.

NOTEBOOK

Lady Grace(IRE), well backed, showed the benefit of this drop down from Group 3 company and got back to winning ways. She relished the decent early pace and showed a willing attitude when asked to win her race on the outside of the pack from the 2f pole. Her stable remains in top form and she is currently in-foal to Nayef, so no doubt will now head in search of some black type again before retiring to the paddocks. (op 9-2 tchd 5-1 in places)

Binanti stepped up markedly on the level of his seasonal debut at Ascot, for which he had been dropped 3lb, and now looks to be coming right back to form. It is very interesting that he was second in this event last year before going on to land the Buckingham Palace Handicap at Royal Ascot and he will surely now head back there to defend his title from a 3lb higher mark. (op 11-1 tchd 8-1)

Stevie Gee(IRE) posted another solid effort in defeat on this return to the extra furlong and fared best of those to race up with the early pace. The stiff finish here probably just found him out. (tchd 7-2 and 9-2 in places)

Barons Spy(IRE), up 5lb for his Bath success, held every chance and posted another improved display on this step up in distance. He is probably just at his very best on easier ground. (op 20-1)

My Learned Friend(IRE) ran the race of his life on this quest for the hat-trick and kept on gamely once headed. He was effectively racing from a 12lb higher mark as he was 4lb out of the handicap here. (tchd 7-2 and 9-2 in places)

Compton's Eleven, 4lb higher, really needs to be ridden more prominently over this distance nowadays and, having been ridden more patiently this time, was motoring home inside the final furlong. There will be other days for him.

Lone Wolfe, who won on his seasonal bow last year, was still in with a chance passing the final furlong pole before eventually tiring out of contention. He is entitled to come on nicely for this first run in 239 days.

3041 BETTERCASINO.COM SCURRY STKS (LISTED RACE) 5f 6y

3:40 (3:40) (Class 1) 3-Y-O

£14,760 (£5,595; £2,800; £1,396; £699; £351) Stalls High

Form				RPR
1-11	1		**Corrybrough**[17] 2498 3-8-13 110 RyanMoore 3 (H Candy) *in rr tl pushed along and str run ins fnl 2f: chsd ldr 1f out: qcknd to ld fnl 100yds: won gng away* **4/7**[1]	114+
-233	2	1 ½	**Inxile (IRE)**[17] 2498 3-8-13 100 SilvestreDeSousa 8 (D Nicholls) *led after 1f: rdn over 2f out: kpt on fnl f tl hdd and outpcd fnl 100yds* **14/1**	109
14-0	3	2 ¼	**Philario (IRE)**[59] 1400 3-9-4 106 FergusSweeney 1 (K R Burke) *chsd ldrs: rdn fr 1/2-way: kpt on fnl f but nvr gng pce of ldng duo* **20/1**	106
-423	4	1 ¼	**Crystany (IRE)**[14] 2606 3-8-8 95 TedDurcan 7 (H R A Cecil) *towards rr: rdn 2f out: hdwy over 1f out: kpt on same pce ins fnl f* **12/1**[3]	91

-002 **5** 1 3/4 **Cake (IRE)**[10] 2712 3-8-11 100 .... JamieSpencer 2 88
(R Hannon) *led 1f: styd chsng ldrs: rdn 2f out: wknd ins fnl f* **14/1**

-222 **6** 1/2 **Tajdeef (USA)**[14] 2605 3-8-13 109 .... MartinDwyer 5 88
(B W Hills) *in rr: rdn 1/2-way: sme prog fnl f but nvr in contention* **3/1**[2]

0-00 **7** 3/4 **Loch Jipp (USA)**[14] 2594 3-8-11 90 .... (v[1]) PJMcDonald 10 84
(J S Wainwright) *chsd ldrs: rdn 1/2-way: wkng whn bmpd ins fnl f* **50/1**

-302 **8** 6 **Hammadi (IRE)**[17] 2498 3-8-13 102 .... NCallan 6 64
(K A Ryan) *chsd ldrs: rdn 2f out: wkng whn bmpd ins fnl f* **25/1**

10-0 **9** 1 1/4 **Westwood**[21] 2410 3-8-13 88 .... TQuinn 4 60
(D Haydn Jones) *sn bhd* **66/1**

60.48 secs (-1.12) **Going Correction** +0.20s/f (Good) 9 Ran SP% **121.7**
Speed ratings (Par 107): **116,113,110,108,105 104,103,93,91**
CSF £11.65 TOTE £1.60: £1.10, £3.80, £5.80; EX 16.90 Trifecta £140.20 Pool £790.36 - 4.00 winning units..
Owner Thurloe Thoroughbreds XXI **Bred** Mrs Sheila Oakes **Trained** Kingston Warren, Oxon

FOCUS
This Listed three-year-old sprint revolved around Corrbrough and he duly extended his winning sequence, being value for better than the bare margin. Decent form for the grade, with the winner up another 5lb.

NOTEBOOK
Corrybrough ◆ landed the four-timer with another taking display on this first crack in Listed company. He was more edgy at the start this time and was certainly not helped by having to race down the middle of the track, so should really be rated better than the bare margin. Always held in the highest regard by connections, he certainly looks a Group winner in waiting and promises to really come into his own when faced with another furlong. He also is probably happiest with more cut in the ground, so it is not too hard to see why his connections are considering a possible tilt at the Pix de l'Abbaye on Longchamp's Arc weekend in October. That test would be sharp enough for him at this stage and he would be taking on a different calibre of opponent, but on soft ground he would rate a fascinating contender in that. He is now due a deserved break so it will be facinating to see where he turns up next in preparation for a possible trip to France. (op 8-13 tchd 8-15, 8-11 in places and 4-6 in places)
Inxile(IRE) ◆, behind the winner at Beverley 17 days previously, got closer to that rival this time and posted a career-best effort. He too looks sure to enjoy another furlong again now and, nicely clear of the remainder, he can be placed to find success in this company.
Philario(IRE), seventh in the Free Handicap on his seasonal comeback in April, turned in a commendable effort under his 5lb penalty. He found this drop back in trip too sharp and, on this evidence, should really now relish a return to 6f.
Crystany(IRE) came through to run her race and was not disgraced, but simply found this too hot. She is a likeable filly, but her handicap mark would not want to go up for this as she will then be tricky to place successfully. (op 14-1 tchd 20-1 in a place)
Cake(IRE) showed decent early dash, but was a sitting duck for the principals in the final furlong. She is back in decent heart, but is another who is not simple to place now. (op 16-1)
Tajdeef(USA), a runner-up on each of his three previous starts this term, was ridden patiently on this first-ever run over the minimum distance and ultimately performed well below his previous best. He now has something to prove. (op 11-4 tchd 10-3 and 7-2 in places)
Hammadi(IRE) Official explanation: jockey said colt hung left in the early stages

3042 BETTERPOKER.COM H'CAP — 5f 6y
4:15 (4:16) (Class 4) (0-80,83) 4-Y-0+ **£5,180** (£1,541; £770; £384) **Stalls** High

Form RPR

4432 **1** **Cheveton**[8] 2773 4-8-11 68 .... JimCrowley 3 78
(R J Price) *trckd ldrs: led over 1f out: drvn out cl home* **7/1**

2111 **2** 1 1/2 **Wibbadune (IRE)**[7] 2836 4-9-2 73 .... AdamKirby 6 78
(D Shaw) *anticipated s: broke stalls and led 100yds: stdd into mid-div: hdwy: edgd rt and nt clr run over 1f out: styd on to chse wnr wl ins fnl f but no imp nr fin* **4/1**[1]

0502 **3** shd **Circuit Dancer (IRE)**[7] 2843 8-8-10 67 .... SilvestreDeSousa 2 72
(D Nicholls) *in tch: drvn along 2f out: kpt on wl fnl f but nvr gng pce to chal* **6/1**[3]

0651 **4** 1/2 **Equuleus Pictor**[16] 2551 4-8-4 66 .... JackDean(5) 9 71+
(J L Spearing) *in tch: hdwy on ins whn swtchd lft and hmpd over 1f out: kpt on again but nt rcvr* **9/2**[2]

-000 **5** hd **Gwilym (GER)**[2] 2968 5-8-13 70 .... TedDurcan 7 72
(D Haydn Jones) *bhd: stl plenty to do 2f out: str run fnl f fin wl* **8/1**

1511 **6** 1/2 **Toms Laughter**[11] 2692 4-9-9 83 .... (p) KevinGhunowa(3) 1 83
(R A Harris) *chsd ldrs: rdn 2f out: wknd fnl 100yds* **6/1**[3]

-041 **7** 1/2 **Blessed Place**[8] 2802 8-7-11 61 oh3 .... BillyCray(7) 4 60
(D J S Ffrench Davis) *led after 100yds: hdd over 1f out: styd on tl wknd fnl 100yds* **14/1**

3343 **8** 2 **Digital**[8] 2773 11-9-0 78 .... (v) ThomasO'Brien(7) 11 69+
(M R Channon) *sn detached in rr: rapid hdwy appr fnl f: fin wl but nvr in contention* **10/1**

6000 **9** 1 1/2 **Diane's Choice**[7] 2828 5-9-6 77 .... NCallan 8 63
(Miss Gay Kelleway) *chsd ldrs tl wknd 1f out* **12/1**

12-0 **10** 5 **Efisio Princess**[17] 2511 5-8-5 62 .... RichardThomas 5 30
(J E Long) *spd 3f* **22/1**

61.95 secs (0.35) **Going Correction** +0.20s/f (Good) 10 Ran SP% **118.2**
Speed ratings (Par 105): **105,102,102,101,101 100,99,96,94,86**
CSF £35.66 CT £181.40 TOTE £8.60: £2.60, £1.70, £2.40; EX 36.10.
Owner Mrs K Oseman **Bred** Miss K Rausing **Trained** Ullingswick, H'fords

FOCUS
A fair sprint in which the draw played little part. The form looks sound enough with the first two continuing to progress.

3043 RBS MAIDEN STKS — 1m 2f 7y
4:50 (4:51) (Class 5) 3-Y-0 **£3,885** (£1,156; £577; £288) **Stalls** High

Form RPR

6 **1** **Voice Coach (IRE)**[12] 2681 3-9-3 0 .... RyanMoore 3 87+
(Sir Michael Stoute) *chsd ldr 7f out: shkn up 3f out: led over 2f out: sn in command and forged clr fnl f* **7/4**[2]

540- **2** 4 1/2 **Craigstown**[234] 6418 3-9-3 77 .... LDettori 2 78
(Saeed Bin Suroor) *led: drvn and hdd over 2f out: no ch w wnr fnl f but comf 2nd best* **6/4**[1]

0 **3** 3 1/2 **Capstan**[12] 2681 3-9-3 0 .... PatCosgrave 8 71
(L M Cumani) *t.k.h: chsd ldrs: rdn 3f out: one pce fnl 2f* **14/1**

0 **4** 2 1/2 **Day Trip (IRE)**[14] 2612 3-9-3 0 .... NCallan 1 66
(B J Meehan) *chsd ldrs: rdn over 3f out: wknd fr 2f out* **14/1**

5 3 1/4 **Canyon Colours (USA)** 3-9-3 0 .... PaulMulrennan 5 60
(G A Butler) *a towards rr: rdn and no prog 3f out* **16/1**

0 **6** 7 **Amir Pasha (UAE)**[12] 2681 3-9-3 0 .... AdamKirby 6 46
(W R Swinburn) *s.i.s: a towards rr* **33/1**

0 **7** 8 **Shecher Para**[28] 2197 3-8-12 0 .... TedDurcan 4 25
(H R A Cecil) *in rr: shkn up: rn green and lost tch 3f out: eased whn no ch fnl f* **25/1**

0 **8** 7 **Seven Stars**[28] 2191 3-9-3 0 .... JamieSpencer 7 16
(B J Meehan) *in rr: effrt into mid-div over 3f out: sn wknd: eased whn no ch fnl f* **5/1**[3]

2m 12.01s (1.51) **Going Correction** +0.075s/f (Good) 8 Ran SP% **119.0**
Speed ratings (Par 99): **96,92,89,87,85 79,73,67**
CSF £5.00 TOTE £2.70: £1.20, £1.30, £2.90; EX 4.10.
Owner Ballymacoll Stud **Bred** Ballymacoll Stud Farm Ltd **Trained** Newmarket, Suffolk

FOCUS
This could prove to be a fair maiden in time. The form is rated around the runner-up and the winner should rate higher.

3044 RBS PRIVATE BANKING H'CAP — 1m 6f
5:20 (5:20) (Class 4) (0-85,85) 4-Y-0+ **£5,180** (£1,541; £770; £384) **Stalls** Centre

Form RPR

010- **1** **Desert Sea (IRE)**[238] 6335 5-9-9 85 .... RyanMoore 6 99
(D W P Arbuthnot) *hld up in rr tl str run fr 3f out to ld jst ins fnl 2f: clr over 1f out: easily* **7/1**[3]

311- **2** 4 1/2 **Whenever**[232] 6473 4-9-5 81 .... JohnEgan 10 89+
(R T Phillips) *in rr: rdn and hdwy over 2f out: chsd wnr fnl f but nvr any ch* **4/1**[1]

3-66 **3** shd **Rajeh (IRE)**[22] 2372 5-9-4 80 .... LiamJones 1 85
(J L Spearing) *towards rr: hrd rdn over 3f out: styd on fr over 1f out and kpt on cl home but nvr a threat: fin 4th: plcd 3rd* **16/1**

6-12 **4** 1 3/4 **Brief Goodbye**[21] 2414 8-8-13 75 .... TedDurcan 3 77+
(John Berry) *chsd ldrs: rdn over 3f out: one pce fnl 2f: fin 5th: plcd 4th* **17/2**

0-06 **5** 1 **Irish Quest (IRE)**[21] 2414 4-9-3 79 .... (p) NCallan 13 81+
(M A Jarvis) *chsd ldrs: rdn and no ch w ldrs whn hmpd wl ins fnl f: fin 6th: plcd 5th* **15/2**

65-4 **6** 3/4 **Velvet Heights (IRE)**[55] 1501 6-9-7 83 .... IanMongan 5 83
(J L Dunlop) *in tch: rdn 3f out: wknd ins fnl 2f: fin 7th: plcd 6th* **6/1**[2]

0-36 **7** shd **Ned Ludd (IRE)**[35] 1984 5-9-1 77 .... JimCrowley 12 77
(J G Portman) *in rr: rdn over 3f out: mod prog fr over 1f out: fin 8th: plcd 7th* **12/1**

20/0 **8** 2 1/4 **Climate Change (USA)**[14] 2599 6-9-0 76 .... AdamKirby 8 72
(Miss Venetia Williams) *chsd ldr tl over 3f out: sn wknd: fin 9th: plcd 8th* **16/1**

0300 **9** 2 1/2 **Ainama (IRE)**[14] 2599 4-9-2 78 .... JamieSpencer 4 71
(M Wigham) *chsd ldrs: led over 3f out: sn rdn: hdd jst ins fnl 2f and sn wknd: fin 10th: plcd 9th* **8/1**

1525 **10** 1 **Clear Reef**[83] 981 4-9-4 80 .... PaulMulrennan 7 71
(Jane Chapple-Hyam) *sn led: hdd over 3f out: sn wknd: fin 11th: plcd 10th* **12/1**

1130 **11** 1 1/2 **Calculating (IRE)**[35] 1984 4-9-0 83 .... GabrielHannon(7) 11 72
(M D I Usher) *in tch tl wknd fr 4f out: fin 12th: plcd 11th* **25/1**

1413 **D** 1 3/4 **Pass The Port**[21] 2414 7-9-6 82 .... LDettori 2 87
(D Haydn Jones) *in rr and pushed along over 3f out: kpt on fr 2f out and styd on into 3rd fnl f but no ch w ldng duo: fin 3rd: 4½l & 1 3/4l disq & plcd last: jockey drew incorrect weight* **6/1**[2]

3m 3.52s (-3.08) **Going Correction** +0.075s/f (Good) 12 Ran SP% **125.5**
Speed ratings (Par 105): **111,108,107,106,105 105,105,104,102,102 101,107**
CSF £37.27 CT £452.77 TOTE £8.30: £2.80, £2.10, £5.50; EX 50.00 Place 6 £53.84, Place 5 £21.24..
Owner Bonusprint **Bred** Peter McGlynn **Trained** Compton, Berks
■ Stewards' Enquiry : L Dettori three-day ban: weighed in light (Jun 28-30)

FOCUS
A good staying handicap, run at a strong pace. The winner is value for a deal further and the form is solid.
Clear Reef Official explanation: jockey said colt ran too free
T/Plt: £70.70 to a £1 stake. Pool: £116,200.95. 1,198.60 winning tickets. T/Qpdt: £4.00 to a £1 stake. Pool: £7,460.14. 1,370.10 winning tickets. ST

3005 YORK (L-H)
Saturday, June 14

OFFICIAL GOING: Good (good to firm in places; 8.3)
Heavy showers before racing resulted in 'ground quick underneath but dead on the surface'.
Wind: Fresh, half-against Weather: changeable, very breezy

3045 QUEEN MOTHER'S CUP STKS (LADY AMATEUR RIDERS) (H'CAP) — 1m 4f
2:15 (2:16) (Class 3) (0-95,95) 3-Y-0+ **£12,492** (£3,874; £1,936; £968) **Stalls** Centre

Form RPR

2-06 **1** **Step This Way (USA)**[7] 2840 3-8-10 80 .... MissADeniel 4 92
(M Johnston) *chsd clr ldr: hdwy to ld wl over 2f out: clr and rdn over 1f out: styd on strly* **14/1**

-000 **2** 4 1/2 **Philanthropy**[15] 2582 4-10-2 85 .... MissARyan 5 89
(K A Ryan) *in tch: hdwy 3f out: rdn to chse ldrs whn rdr dropped whip over 1f out: kpt on ins fnl f* **14/1**

0322 **3** nse **Bazart**[15] 2585 6-9-7 79 .... MissKellyBurke(3) 16 83
(K R Burke) *led and sn clr: pushed along 3f out: hdd wl over 2f out: kpt on same pce* **20/1**

20-1 **4** 2 1/4 **Ask The Butler**[22] 2369 4-10-3 89 .... MissFCumani(3) 6 90+
(L M Cumani) *hld up in midfield: effrt over 2f out: sn rdn: swtchd rt and styd on ins fnl f: nrst fin* **15/8**[1]

4212 **5** 1/2 **Jeer (IRE)**[22] 2369 4-10-10 93 .... MrsCBartley 3 93
(E A L Dunlop) *chsd ldrs: effrt 3f out: rdn 2f out: and kpt on same pce* **10/1**[3]

6440 **6** 3 **Resonate (IRE)**[40] 1874 10-9-7 76 oh1 .... MissCHannaford 13 71+
(A G Newcombe) *hld up towards rr: hdwy on outer 3f out: rdn along 2f out: styd on u.p appr fnl f: nvr rchd ldrs* **50/1**

-101 **7** 2 3/4 **Chocolate Caramel (USA)**[14] 2623 6-9-10 82 .... MrsVFahey(3) 9 73
(R A Fahey) *rrd s and slowly away: bhd tl hdwy over 2f out: sn rdn and styd on ins fnl f: nrst fin* **14/1**

1010 **8** 1/2 **Maslak (IRE)**[22] 2372 4-10-5 88 .... MrsMarieKing 14 78
(P W Hiatt) *chsd ldrs: rdn along over 2f out: drvn wl over 1f out and grad wknd* **40/1**

-211 **9** 2 **Nawamees (IRE)**[47] 1668 10-9-9 81 ow2 .... (p) MissHayleyMoore(3) 10 68
(G L Moore) *chsd ldng pair: hdwy over 3f out: rdn over 2f out: sn drvn and wknd* **22/1**

2053 **10** 2 **Aureate**[7] 2830 4-10-2 85 .... MissLEllison 17 69
(B Ellison) *hld up in tch: hdwy 4f out: rdn along wl over 2f out: drvn and wknd wl over 1f out* **10/1**[3]

0420 **11** ½ **Cruise Director**29 2153 8-9-7 76 MissGDGracey-Davison 12 59
(Ian Williams) *nvr nr to chal* **20/1**

1 **12** *shd* **Secret Dancer (IRE)**28 2197 3-9-9 93 MissRDavidson 1 76
(J R Fanshawe) *hld up: effrt 3f out: rdn and hung lft 2f out: nvr a factor* **11/4**2

0355 **13** *11* **Murfreesboro**35 1990 5-10-4 87 (be) MissFayeBramley 15 52
(K J Burke) *dwlt: t.k.h and hld up: a in rr* **66/1**

0106 **14** *2* **Calzaghe (IRE)**19 2447 4-9-4 76 oh5 (v) MissLEBurke(3) 2 38
(K R Burke) *a towards rr* **66/1**

6- **15** *19* **Risk (IRE)**247 6137 5-10-8 91 MissMSowerby 8 22
(C R Egerton) *a in rr* **33/1**

2m 33.88s (0.68) **Going Correction** +0.125s/f (Good)
WFA 3 from 4yo+ 15lb **15** Ran SP% **123.8**
Speed ratings (Par 107): **102,99,98,97,97 95,93,92,91,90 89,89,82,81,68**
CSF £183.29 CT £3899.69 TOTE £19.90: £5.50, £3.90, £6.40; EX 356.70 Trifecta £624.50 Part won. Pool £879.66 - 0.50 winning units..
Owner S R Counsell **Bred** Crescent Hill Farm And Dr W A Rood **Trained** Middleham Moor, N Yorks

FOCUS
One of the top lady amateur races of the season and a good early gallop, although the overall time was unexceptional and few got into contention from off the pace. The field tended to race nearer the far rail in the straight. The unexposed winner is rated up 9lb.

NOTEBOOK
Step This Way(USA), one of just two three-year-olds in the line-up, was off the same mark as when being beaten in a slightly lower-grade race on her previous attempt at this trip. However, she got a good lead from the eventual third and, sticking to the rail in the straight, ran on strongly to hold off the challengers. She is likely to go up a fair amount for this, so will not find things easy next time. (tchd 16-1)
Philanthropy seems to like this track, having won here last season and shown a return to form on his previous outing at the May meeting. He was always in the group chasing the leaders and kept going well to get the better of the long-time leader for the runner-up spot, but in truth he never looked like catching the winner.
Bazart, who ran well in an amateurs' race over course and distance at the end of last month, appeared to go off at a rate of knots but, despite being headed by the winner at the quarter-mile pole, stuck to his task and was only run out of second place late on. He is clearly in good heart at present and deserves to pick up a race. (op 18-1 tchd 25-1)
Ask The Butler, who won in such taking style on his first outing for Luca Cumani, was bidding to give the trainer and his daughter their third successive winner of this race. He seemed to travel well enough but the jockey began to show signs of anxiety halfway up the straight and from that point he was always being held, although he did run on again in the closing stages. (op 2-1)
Jeer(IRE), who had been narrowly but decisively beaten by the favourite at Newmarket, was 6lb better off this time but the margin was the same. He appeared to run his race, being given every chance by his capable rider, but looked to be found out by the longer trip, and a drop back to 1m2f will be in his favour. (op 9-1 tchd 8-1)
Resonate(IRE), who is getting on in age and has been struggling for form of late, has looked at his best from midsummer onwards in previous seasons and this running-on effort suggests he is on the way back.
Chocolate Caramel(USA), claimed after winning over course and distance at the end of last month, ran a remarkable race on his debut for new connections. He reared as the stalls opened and missed the break, and was still at the back until passing a number of horses in the final furlong. He has been dropped 3lb since taking that claimer, and stronger handling may see him score again as he appears to be holding his form this season. (tchd 11-1)
Secret Dancer(IRE), who had won in such promising fashion on his debut, was well backed against the favourite but missed the break, came wide into the straight and then hung under pressure, not looking an easy ride. He is surely better than this effort suggests. (op 10-3)

3046 CADOGAN SILVER SALVER STKS (H'CAP) 1m 208y
2:50 (2:50) (Class 2) (0-105,97) 3-Y-0+ **£17,485** (£5,202; £2,600; £1,298) **Stalls** Low

Form RPR

1010 **1** **Re Barolo (IRE)**19 2465 5-10-0 97 (t) JimmyQuinn 8 106
(M Botti) *hld up in rr: stdy hdwy over 2f out: led 1f out: hld on wl* **7/1**

6000 **2** ½ **Mesbaah (IRE)**15 2582 4-9-0 83 (b1) TonyHamilton 13 91
(R A Fahey) *chsd ldrs: effrt on wd outside over 2f out: hung lft and styd on wl ins fnl f: jst hld* **33/1**

1636 **3** *nk* **Granston (IRE)**15 2582 7-9-1 84 RobertWinston 1 91
(J D Bethell) *chsd ldrs: upsides over 1f out: no ex wl ins fnl f* **7/2**1

2000 **4** *nse* **Fishforcompliments**14 2595 4-9-12 95 PaulHanagan 2 102
(R A Fahey) *trckd ldrs: led over 1f out: sn hdd: no ex ins fnl f* **7/1**

32-0 **5** *1* **Free Offer**41 1828 4-9-3 86 EddieAhern 10 91
(J L Dunlop) *mid-div: hdwy over 2f out: upsides over 1f out: kpt on same pce ins fnl f* **11/2**2

306- **6** ¾ **Nine Stories (IRE)**267 5582 3-8-3 84 PaulFessey 3 85
(J Howard Johnson) *chsd ldrs: chal on ins over 1f out: fdd last 75yds* **33/1**

2615 **7** 2¾ **Veiled Applause**15 2582 5-9-3 86 GrahamGibbons 6 83
(J J Quinn) *mid-div: sn pushed along: hdwy over 2f out: chsng ldrs over 1f out: wknd ins fnl f* **9/1**

6012 **8** 2¼ **Speedy Sam**17 2499 5-9-4 87 AndrewElliott 9 80
(K R Burke) *mid-div: sn pushed along: hdwy 3f out: wknd fnl f* **8/1**

-220 **9** *9* **Jewelled Dagger (IRE)**19 2465 4-9-10 93 (b) TomEaves 11 67
(Miss L A Perratt) *set str pce and sn clr: hdd over 1f out: sn lost pl* **12/1**

024/ **10** *9* **Mister Genepi**1050 3932 6-10-0 97 RichardMullen 5 52
(W R Muir) *in rr: bhd fnl 4f* **33/1**

0440 **11** 2½ **Charlie Tokyo (IRE)**8 2789 5-9-11 97 (b) JamieMoriarty(3) 12 47
(R A Fahey) *s.i.s: in rr: bhd fnl 4f* **20/1**

15-6 **12** *57* **Tanweer (USA)**31 2104 3-8-11 92 KerrinMcEvoy 4 —
(Sir Michael Stoute) *in rr: bhd 4f out: virtually p.u over 1f out: t.o* **6/1**3

1m 50.99s (-1.01) **Going Correction** +0.125s/f (Good)
WFA 3 from 4yo+ 12lb **12** Ran SP% **119.3**
Speed ratings (Par 109): **109,108,108,108,107 106,104,102,94,86 84,33**
CSF £226.53 CT £949.60 TOTE £9.20: £3.10, £9.70, £1.60; EX 340.10 Trifecta £519.00 Part won. Pool £731.10 - 0.10 winning units..
Owner Effevi Snc Di Villa Felice & C **Bred** Luciano Bosio **Trained** Newmarket, Suffolk

FOCUS
A good handicap run at a sound gallop and producing a close finish. Solid, reliable form.

NOTEBOOK
Re Barolo(IRE), who reportedly lost his action when not beaten far in the Zetland Gold Cup, had been dropped 3lb for that and gained his first win on turf in this country in ultra-game fashion. He is a likeable sort and should continue to pay his way in good races this season. (op 8-1)
Mesbaah(IRE), who has been out of sorts this spring, having finished last-but-one in each of his three previous outings, was revived by the application of blinkers for the first time and stayed on well in the closing stages to just get up for second place. If the headgear works as well next time he could prove well handicapped, having begun the year racing off a 13lb higher mark. (op 25-1)
Granston(IRE), who has been racing over slightly further of late, appeared to have every chance but, carrying his head to one side, had nothing more to give in the last furlong. He is probably the best guide to the level of the form. (tchd 4-1)
Fishforcompliments, who has not won since his juvenile days, had the visor he wore last time left off on this step back up in trip but seemed to run his race back off the mark from which he ran so well on his seasonal debut. (op 8-1)
Free Offer, who appeared to benefit from her outing at Newmarket last month, is from a yard that is running into form and looked a big threat until flattening out in the last furlong. She is high enough in the weights at present but could be one to bear in mind as the season progresses. (op 6-1)
Nine Stories(IRE) ◆, a useful juvenile in the north last season, ran well on his seasonal debut over the longest trip he has tried to date. He tired in the final furlong after appearing to have every chance and looks the sort who can win a similar contest, possibly back at a mile, with this behind him. (tchd 40-1)
Jewelled Dagger(IRE) made the running but appeared to go too quickly for his own good and was in trouble halfway up the straight. (op 11-1)
Mister Genepi Official explanation: jockey said gelding lost its action
Tanweer(USA) was well supported but has not built on his promising and successful debut and, always in the rear, dropped out as if he had a problem. Official explanation: jockey said gelding oost its action (op 11-2 tchd 13-2)

3047 BETFAIR SPRINT (HERITAGE H'CAP) 6f
3:25 (3:26) (Class 2) (0-105,104) 3-Y-0 **£64,760** (£19,270; £9,630; £4,810) **Stalls** High

Form RPR

-004 **1** **Brave Prospector**21 2410 3-9-0 97 (t) AlanMunro 8 108
(P W Chapple-Hyam) *trckd ldrs: smooth hdwy 2f out: led over 1f out: rdn and qcknd ent fnl f: kpt on* **12/1**

4016 **2** 1½ **Victorian Bounty**21 2410 3-8-8 91 MickyFenton 4 97
(Stef Liddiard) *led: rdn along 2f out: drvn and hdd over 1f out: kpt on gamely u.p ins fnl f* **20/1**

2-61 **3** *nk* **Ancien Regime (IRE)**21 2410 3-9-6 103 PhilipRobinson 17 108
(M A Jarvis) *hld up: hdwy 2f out: rdn to chse ldrs over 1f out: drvn and kpt on same pce ins fnl f* **5/1**1

-031 **4** *nk* **Good Gorsoon (USA)**26 2258 3-8-7 90 ow1 MichaelHills 18 94
(B W Hills) *hld up in rr: hdwy over 2f out: rdn over 1f out: styd on u.p ins fnl f: nrst fin* **16/1**

4-20 **5** 1½ **Spitfire**41 1834 3-8-13 96 KerrinMcEvoy 16 95
(J R Jenkins) *hld up towards rr: hdwy 2f out: rdn to chse ldrs appr fnl f: sn drvn and kpt on same pce* **18/1**

6- **6** ¾ **Dohasa (IRE)**24 2316 3-9-0 104 EJMcNamara(7) 1 101
(G M Lyons, Ire) *hld up: hdwy on outer wl over 1f out: rdn and styd on ins fnl f: nrst fin* **28/1**

-002 **7** ½ **Carleton**21 2410 3-8-9 92 StephenDonohoe 15 87
(W J Musson) *hld up in rr: hdwy 2f out: sn rdn and styd on ins fnl f: nrst fin* **22/1**

0-00 **8** *hd* **Seeking Star (IRE)**57 1441 3-8-7 90 SamHitchcott 19 84
(M R Channon) *hld up in tch: hdwy 1/2-way: rdn along 2f out: drvn and edgd lft appr fnl f: sn no imp* **66/1**

1335 **9** *shd* **Prohibit**14 2605 3-9-0 97 (b) JimmyFortune 13 91
(J H M Gosden) *hld up: hdwy 2f out: rdn and n.m.r ent fnl f: sn no imp* **12/1**

05-U **10** *1* **Lytton**16 2529 3-8-12 95 SaleemGolam 7 86
(W R Swinburn) *chsd ldrs: swtchd lft and rdn along wl over 1f out: grad wknd* **40/1**

2-46 **11** *hd* **Dubai Princess (IRE)**17 2498 3-8-12 95 TPQueally 12 85
(J A Osborne) *in tch: effrt whn n.m.r wl over 1f out: sn rdn and no imp* **40/1**

1-21 **12** ¾ **Hamish McGonagall**29 2171 3-8-7 90 DavidAllan 9 78
(T D Easterby) *prom: rdn along 2f out: sn wknd* **8/1**

-123 **13** *nk* **Meydan Princess (IRE)**31 2104 3-8-7 90 EddieAhern 6 77
(J Noseda) *dwlt: a towards rr* **7/1**2

2212 **14** ½ **Fathsta (IRE)**8 2793 3-8-10 93 LPKeniry 5 78
(S Kirk) *towards rr: effrt 2f out: swtchd lft and rdn wl over 1f out: n.d* **8/1**

3-22 **15** *nk* **Baldemar**35 1999 3-8-7 90 AndrewElliott 14 74
(K R Burke) *prom: rdn along over 2f out: sn drvn and wknd* **16/1**

2-63 **16** *5* **Striking Spirit**29 2162 3-8-6 89 WilliamBuick 10 57
(B W Hills) *in midfield: rdn along after 2f: sn lost pl and bhd* **15/2**3

0552 **17** *6* **Vhujon (IRE)**14 2594 3-8-12 95 KShea 20 44
(P D Evans) *s.i.s: a in rr* **33/1**

0-50 **18** ½ **Maze (IRE)**21 2409 3-9-3 100 TomEaves 11 47
(B Smart) *a in rr* **25/1**

2113 **19** *hd* **Van Bossed (CAN)**36 1949 3-9-0 97 AdrianTNicholls 2 44
(D Nicholls) *chsd ldrs: rdn along over 2f out: sn wknd* **14/1**

1m 11.05s (-0.85) **Going Correction** +0.125s/f (Good) **19** Ran SP% **127.9**
Speed ratings (Par 105): **110,108,107,107,105 104,103,103,103,101 101,100,100,99,99 92,84,83,83**
CSF £244.67 CT £1411.72 TOTE £17.90: £4.20, £7.90, £2.10, £3.90; EX 792.40 Trifecta £7634.20 Pool £17,204.04 - 1.60 winning units..
Owner Saleh Al Homaizi & Imad Al Sagar **Bred** Times Of Wigan Ltd **Trained** Newmarket, Suffolk
■ New sponsors for this event, run previously as the William Hill Trophy.

FOCUS
Another competitive renewal of this good sprint handicap and the time was good for the grade, being 1.08secs faster than the later all-aged handicap. The form looks pretty sound despite the runner-up's apparent improvement.

NOTEBOOK
Brave Prospector ◆, a maiden coming into this, had shown a return to something like his useful juvenile form behind the favourite last time when fitted with a tongue tie. With the same equipment on again and appearing to have made the difference, he travelled well throughout and found plenty to run out a decisive winner in this competitive race. He was meeting the winner on 9lb better terms and ran close to form with his old rival, but this will have given him confidence and he can make up into a decent sprinter on this evidence. (tchd 11-1)
Victorian Bounty is an admirably consistent performer who has continued to progress since switching to his current trainer and ran close to previous form with the winner and third. He made the running but the winner cruised up to him and, although he stuck on gamely, he had no chance with that rival. His attitude is a big advantage in these tight-knit handicaps and he should win his share. (op 28-1)
Ancien Regime(IRE), who had the winner behind when scoring in a similar race at Newmarket, was 8lb higher but looked progressive that day and was made favourite to follow up. He ran his race and was pretty close to previous form with the first two, but gave the impression that he needs a stiffer track than this now. (tchd 11-2)
Good Gorsoon(USA), both of whose wins have been over 5f, nevertheless has form over this trip and came into this in good heart. He finished well from off the pace and looks capable of picking up a decent handicap this season on this evidence. (tchd 18-1)
Spitfire, dropped 3lb, seems well suited by a flat track and, dropping in trip, ran his race if not quite having the extra gear to get him into the frame. A return to 7f looks on the cards for him. (op 20-1)
Dohasa(IRE) has developed into a very useful sprinter on a sound surface in Ireland and ran well from his outside stall under his inexperienced rider. He gave the impression he could have finished closer if he had been drawn better. (op 33-1)

Carleton, who had finished runner-up to the favourite at Newmarket with the first two today behind, was 5lb higher but his usual waiting tactics were not suited to this speed-favouring track and, despite running on well, he never got in a blow. He will do better back on a stiffer course. (op 20-1)
Seeking Star(IRE), dropped 3lb, has been struggling for form this season but this was a better effort. (op 80-1)
Prohibit, who finished third in the Newmarket race that was key to this event, ran reasonably well but was another for whom waiting tactics did not work on this track. (op 14-1)
Hamish McGonagall, whose wins have been over 5f, including on this track last time, was 6lb higher and up in grade, but ran well enough until fading in the latter stages. (tchd 15-2)
Meydan Princess(IRE), dropping in trip, did not help herself by missing the break but had a chance of sorts at halfway before failing to pick up. (tchd 8-1)
Fathsta(IRE), another dropping in trip, did not appear to have the pace to lie up in this strongly-run contest.
Striking Spirit is relatively inexperienced and was always struggling, but he may prefer genuinely fast ground. Official explanation: jockey said colt was unsuited by the good (good to firm places) ground (op 8-1)
Van Bossed(CAN) Official explanation: jockey said gelding ran flat

3048 DANIEL PRENN ROYAL YORKSHIRE STKS (H'CAP) 1m 2f 88y
4:00 (4:01) (Class 2) (0-100,86) 3-Y-0 **£14,247** (£4,239; £2,118; £1,058) **Stalls** Low

Form RPR
-231 1 **Military Power**[18] 2488 3-9-6 **83** EddieAhern 2 88+
(J W Hills) *hld up bhd ldrs: stdy hdwy over 2f out: shkn up and qcknd to ld ins fnl f: readily* **7/1**
21-2 2 ¾ **Inspector Clouseau (IRE)**[28] 2209 3-9-1 **78** MickyFenton 4 82
(T P Tate) *led tl hdd and no ex ins fnl f* **11/1**
10-0 3 1 **Casa Catalina (IRE)**[31] 2109 3-9-4 **81** JoeFanning 1 83
(M Johnston) *chsd ldrs: chal over 2f out: styd on same pce ins fnl f* **33/1**
1 4 1 **Swinging Sixties (IRE)**[30] 2119 3-9-9 **86** PhilipRobinson 5 86+
(M A Jarvis) *t.k.h in rr: hdwy over 2f out: hung bdly lft ins fnl f: kpt on same pce* **15/8**[1]
31 5 ½ **Deadly Silence (USA)**[25] 2291 3-9-9 **86** JimmyQuinn 8 85
(Dr J D Scargill) *hld up in tch: hdwy over 3f out: chsng ldrs over 1f out: kpt on same pce* **5/2**[2]
5-31 6 6 **Black Jacari (IRE)**[15] 2564 3-9-8 **85** JimmyFortune 7 73
(A King) *hld up in rr: hdwy on outer over 5f out: hung rt and wknd over 1f out* **4/1**[3]
1-06 7 11 **Doon Haymer (IRE)**[29] 2142 3-9-1 **78** TomEaves 3 45
(Miss L A Perratt) *t.k.h in rr: effrt 3f out: sn lost pl* **25/1**
110- 8 ½ **Apollo Shark (IRE)**[296] 4743 3-9-6 **83** RobertWinston 6 49
(J Howard Johnson) *chsd ldrs: effrt over 3f out: wknd 2f out* **12/1**

2m 12.39s (-0.11) **Going Correction** +0.125s/f (Good) **8** Ran SP% **118.7**
Speed ratings (Par 105): **105,104,103,102,102 97,88,88**
CSF £82.11 CT £2380.32 TOTE £7.70: £2.00, £2.10, £4.40; EX 52.20 Trifecta £698.90 Part won. Pool £984.44 - 0.40 winning units..
Owner H R H Princess Haya Of Jordan **Bred** Paul Hearson Bloodstock **Trained** Upper Lambourn, Berks

FOCUS
A decent handicap, although not that strong for the grade with the top weight a stone below the race ceiling, and the early pace was not that strong. A fairly positive view has been taken of the form nevertheless.

NOTEBOOK
Military Power ◆ had proved well suited by the step up to 1m2f when winning his maiden last time, and he looked an improved performer on this handicap debut. Always travelling well in the slipstream of the leading group, he was ready to pounce from 2f out but had to wait for a gap. When it came he quickened up nicely to win in good style and he looks the sort who can improve again. He is likely to be aimed at Newmarket's July festival next. (tchd 13-2 and 15-2)
Inspector Clouseau(IRE), a consistent front-runner, was stepping up from a mile but was able to dictate a steady early gallop. He found plenty for pressure, fighting off several challenges before the winner swept by late on. He clearly stays and deserves plenty of credit for this. (op 12-1 tchd 10-1)
Casa Catalina(IRE), well beaten here on her return, ran much better this time, pestering the leader most of the way up the straight and only fading in the last furlong. She looks well capable of winning at this trip, possibly against her own sex. (op 20-1)
Swinging Sixties(IRE), who narrowly beat a stable companion of the runner-up on his debut, was favourite to build on that success but would not settle under restraint in the early stages and then hung left when delivering his challenge. He will need to settle better but clearly has plenty of ability and can be forgiven his antics on account of inexperience, and is certainly in the right hands to enable him to do so. (op 13-8 tchd 9-4)
Deadly Silence(USA), who made his debut behind subsequent Derby runner-up Tartan Bearer at Leicester, is a strapping sort who had since got off the mark at Southwell. He was backed against the favourite and appeared to have his chance before failing to find an extra gear late on. He is still relatively inexperienced and this should have brought him on again. (op 3-1 tchd 10-3)
Black Jacari(IRE), who came into this with some solid handicap form behind him, was 7lb higher than for his last win but should have run better. He was held up but, when asked for his effort, did not look totally happy on the ground, although he has handled fast going in the past. (op 9-2)

3049 LEONARD SAINER E B F MAIDEN STKS 6f
4:30 (4:32) (Class 3) 2-Y-0 **£6,929** (£2,061; £1,030; £514) **Stalls** High

Form RPR
1 **Wildcat Wizard (USA)** 2-9-3 0 JimmyFortune 5 79+
(P F I Cole) *trckd ldrs: hdwy to ld 2f out: rdn ins fnl f and styd on wl* **7/1**[3]
6 2 1 **Mohanad (IRE)**[14] 2592 2-9-3 0 EdwardCreighton 10 76+
(M R Channon) *trckd ldrs: hdwy 2f out: rdn to chse wnr over 1f out: drvn and kpt on same pce ins fnl f* **7/2**[2]
232 3 3 ¼ **Firth Of Fifth (IRE)**[45] 1714 2-9-3 0 RichardKingscote 13 66
(Tom Dascombe) *racd alone stands' rail: cl up: rdn and ev ch 2f out tl edgd lft and wknd ent fnl f* **6/4**[1]
4 ½ **Tepmokea (IRE)** 2-9-3 0 AndrewElliott 9 65
(K R Burke) *s.i.s and bhd: hdwy 2f out: styd on wl fnl f* **33/1**
5 ½ **Mintoe** 2-9-3 0 RichardMullen 6 63
(K A Ryan) *led: rdn along and hdd 2f out: grad wknd* **7/1**[3]
6 1 ¾ **Red Max (IRE)** 2-9-3 0 FergalLynch 8 58+
(T D Easterby) *towards rr: hdwy 2f out: styd on ins fnl f: nrst fin* **20/1**
50 7 3 ¾ **Whatyouwoodwishfor (USA)**[15] 2584 2-9-3 0 PaulHanagan 2 47
(R A Fahey) *cl up: rdn along over 2f out: sn wknd* **12/1**
8 ½ **Acclaben (IRE)** 2-9-3 0 RobertWinston 11 45
(G A Swinbank) *dwlt: sn rdn along and a in rr* **11/1**
9 hd **Waltzing Buddy** 2-8-12 0 MickyFenton 3 40+
(P T Midgley) *s.i.s: a in rr: lame* **66/1**
10 ¾ **All Spin (IRE)** 2-9-3 0 DarrenWilliams 1 42
(A P Jarvis) *chsd ldrs: rdn along over 2f out: grad wknd* **50/1**
0 11 ½ **Nassau Beach (IRE)**[15] 2584 2-9-3 0 DavidAllan 4 41
(T D Easterby) *a towards rr: rdn along and bhd fr 1/2-way* **33/1**
12 7 **Rossett Rose (IRE)** 2-8-5 0 AdamCarter(7) 7 15
(M Brittain) *chsd ldrs: rdn along over 2f out: sn wknd* **28/1**

1m 13.82s (1.92) **Going Correction** +0.125s/f (Good) **12** Ran SP% **120.8**
Speed ratings (Par 97): **92,90,86,85,85 82,77,77,76,75 75,65**
CSF £30.42 TOTE £6.10: £2.20, £1.80, £1.30; EX 36.70.
Owner A D Spence **Bred** Gulf Coast Farms LLC **Trained** Whatcombe, Oxon

FOCUS
An ordinary maiden run considerably slower than the two handicaps run over the trip. Tricky to rate, with most of the field previously unraced and the favouritte clearly below form. The runner-up showed big improvement.

NOTEBOOK
Wildcat Wizard(USA), an American-bred who cost 90,000gns at the breeze-ups, is from a yard whose juveniles have been going well and he clearly knew his job. He came through to score in decent fashion from two more experienced rivals and should be capable of winning again. (op 7-2)
Mohanad(IRE), who is also from a yard with some good two-year-olds, improved on his debut when he had traffic problems and was the only one to really trouble the winner. He should be up to winning his maiden before long. (tchd 3-1)
Firth Of Fifth(IRE), who was the most experienced runner and set the standard on his Ascot form with Baycat, came up the stands' rail by himself on a day when the majority of runners had raced towards the centre of the track. He appeared to have every chance before fading and will not find things easy as the better juveniles appear. His talented trainer may well try to find a small race as a confidence-booster now as he was cheap enough to qualify for maiden auctions. (op 9-4 tchd 11-4)
Tepmokea(IRE) ◆, a 70,000gns first foal of a dual 1m winner from a decent German family, missed the break on this debut but was noted staying on in good fashion in the closing stages. He will appreciate a longer trip and should improve for the experience.
Mintoe, a 38,000gns half-brother to two winners at up to 1m1f including Hoh Wotanite, showed plenty of pace on this debut before tiring in the closing stages. He is another who looks sure to be better for the run. (op 12-1)
Red Max(IRE), a 20,000gns son of a 7f juvenile winner and half-brother to three winners, was noted staying on quite nicely under a sympathetic ride and looks the sort his shrewd trainer will be able to place to win his share of races. (op 16-1 tchd 14-1)
Waltzing Buddy Official explanation: vet said filly returned lame

3050 CHARLES HENRY MEMORIAL STKS (H'CAP) 6f
5:05 (5:08) (Class 4) (0-80,79) 3-Y-0+ **£7,123** (£2,119; £1,059; £529) **Stalls** High

Form RPR
-213 1 **Harrison George (IRE)**[14] 2624 3-9-6 **79** PaulHanagan 18 88
(R A Fahey) *hld up in tch: hdwy 2f out: edgd lft ins fnl f: led nr fin: all out* **11/2**[1]
0-00 2 shd **Trojan Flight**[16] 2538 7-9-3 **75** BMcHugh(7) 13 86
(R A Fahey) *in rr and sn pushed along: gd hdwy over 1f out: upsides whn hmpd cl home: jst hld* **25/1**
42-6 3 hd **Hotham**[22] 2356 5-9-7 **72** JimmyQuinn 9 82+
(N Wilson) *chsd ldrs: led and edgd rt ins fnl f: hrd rdn and hdd cl home* **12/1**
2544 4 2 ¼ **Ancient Cross**[16] 2535 4-9-2 **67** TPQueally 1 70+
(M W Easterby) *hld up in midfield far side: hdwy over 2f out: styd on same pce fnl f* **8/1**[2]
5303 5 ½ **Bel Cantor**[11] 2698 5-9-11 **79** (p) AndrewMullen(3) 7 81
(W J H Ratcliffe) *led tl ins fnl f: wkng whn hmpd nr fin* **10/1**[3]
0422 6 1 ¼ **Guest Connections**[16] 2547 5-9-5 **70** (v) AdrianTNicholls 16 68
(D Nicholls) *chsd ldrs stands' side: kpt on same pce appr fnl f* **14/1**
0530 7 ½ **Red Cape (FR)**[5] 2892 5-9-2 **70** (b) MichaelJStainton(3) 6 66
(Mrs R A Carr) *mid-div: hdwy over 2f out: kpt on same pce: nvr rchd ldrs* **25/1**
-003 8 nk **He's A Humbug (IRE)**[15] 2583 4-9-13 **78** (p) RichardMullen 11 73
(K A Ryan) *chsd ldrs: kpt on same pce appr fnl f: sltly hmpd nr fin* **8/1**[2]
0060 9 4 ½ **Our Blessing (IRE)**[37] 1928 4-9-2 **67** DarrenWilliams 10 48
(A P Jarvis) *chsd ldrs: wknd appr fnl f* **28/1**
2-01 10 ½ **Castles In The Air**[21] 2407 3-9-4 **77** JimmyFortune 15 54
(Pat Eddery) *chsd ldrs stands' side: wknd 2f out* **11/2**[1]
3250 11 2 **Lujiana**[42] 1819 3-8-1 **60** TWilliams 12 31
(M Brittain) *in rr: nvr a factor* **66/1**
0-50 12 nk **Sir Nod**[21] 2398 6-9-10 **75** (v[1]) TonyHamilton 17 47
(Miss J A Camacho) *chsd ldrs: wknd over 1f out* **16/1**
1600 13 3 ½ **Winthorpe (IRE)**[5] 2891 8-9-3 **68** GrahamGibbons 5 28
(J J Quinn) *chsd ldrs: wknd over 1f out* **25/1**
5104 14 2 **Opus Maximus (IRE)**[14] 2624 3-9-3 **76** JoeFanning 19 28
(M Johnston) *hld up in midfield: lost pl over 3f out* **8/1**[2]
2663 15 ½ **Ingleby Princess**[3] 2928 4-8-8 **64** (b) NeilBrown(5) 3 16
(T D Barron) *chsd ldrs: lost pl over 2f out* **11/1**
6120 16 2 ½ **My Kaiser Chief**[35] 1988 3-8-8 **72** KellyHarrison(5) 4 14
(W J H Ratcliffe) *hld up in midfield: hung rt and lost pl over 2f out:* **25/1**
00-0 17 ¾ **Baltimore Jack (IRE)**[29] 2158 4-9-7 **72** KerrinMcEvoy 2 14
(M W Easterby) *mid-div on outer: lost pl over 2f out* **16/1**
4646 18 shd **Kalhan Sands (IRE)**[38] 1911 3-9-5 **78** RobertWinston 8 71
(G A Swinbank) *chsd ldrs: wknd and eased over 1f out* **33/1**
000- 19 17 **Top Bid**[238] 6331 4-9-5 **70** (b) FergalLynch 14 —
(T D Easterby) *in rr: bhd fnl 2f: t.o* **33/1**

1m 12.13s (0.23) **Going Correction** +0.125s/f (Good)
WFA 3 from 4yo+ 8lb **19** Ran SP% **133.9**
Speed ratings (Par 105): **103,102,102,99,98 97,96,96,90,89 86,86,81,79,78 75,74,74,51**
CSF £158.07 CT £1684.26 TOTE £5.30: £1.60, £5.50, £2.80, £3.20; EX 165.80.
Owner P D Smith Holdings Ltd **Bred** R P Ryan **Trained** Musley Bank, N Yorks
■ Stewards' Enquiry : Jimmy Quinn two-day ban: used whip without giving gelding time to respond (Jul 2-3)

FOCUS
A fair sprint handicap but run 1.08secs slower than the earlier Class 2 event over the trip and producing a close finish in which Hotham did no favours to several rivals. Solid form, with a personal best from the winner.
My Kaiser Chief Official explanation: jockey said gelding hung right-handed throughout
Kalhan Sands(IRE) Official explanation: jockey said gelding lost its action
Top Bid Official explanation: jockey said gelding lost its action

3051 MICHAEL SOBELL MAIDEN STKS 1m
5:35 (5:39) (Class 4) 3-Y-0 **£6,540** (£1,946; £972; £485) **Stalls** Low

Form RPR
32 1 **Decameron (USA)**[17] 2509 3-9-3 0 KerrinMcEvoy 2 89+
(Sir Michael Stoute) *mde all: styd on strly fnl 2f: unchal* **8/15**[1]
2 3 **Tanto Faz (IRE)** 3-9-3 0 MichaelHills 5 82+
(W J Haggas) *hld up: hdwy over 6f out: styd on to go 2nd 1f out: no imp* **4/1**[2]
3360 3 2 ¾ **Internationaldebut (IRE)**[31] 2109 3-8-10 **80** EJMcNamara(7) 7 76
(S Parr) *trckd wnr: styd on same pce fnl 2f* **6/1**[3]

20 **4** *1 1/4* **Al Wasef (USA)**[15] 2571 3-9-3 0........................ JoeFanning 6 73
(M Johnston) *trckd ldrs: wnt 2nd 2f out: wknd towards fin* **16/1**

\- **5** *10* **Eton Rifles (IRE)** 3-9-3 0........................ RobertWinston 1 50
(J Howard Johnson) *dwlt: outpcd over 5f out: hdwy over 3f out: lost pl over 1f out* **12/1**

6 *12* **Ateesh** 3-9-3 0........................ NickyMackay 4 22
(L M Cumani) *s.s: detached in last: rdn 4f out: sn bhd* **25/1**

1m 38.41s (-0.39) **Going Correction** +0.125s/f (Good) **6** Ran SP% **116.9**
Speed ratings (Par 101): **106,103,100,99,89 77**
CSF £3.33 TOTE £1.70: £1.40, £2.40; EX 3.80 Place 6 £2,386.35, Place 5 £136.83..
Owner Gainsborough **Bred** Gainsborough Farm Llc **Trained** Newmarket, Suffolk

FOCUS
An uncompetitive maiden run at a sound gallop and the winner made all. There is more to come from him.
T/Jkpt: Not won. T/Plt: £1,120.90 to a £1 stake. Pool: £186,719.27. 121.60 winning tickets.
T/Qpdt: £81.10 to a £1 stake. Pool: £10,050.65. 91.60 winning tickets. JR

2636 LONGCHAMP (R-H)
Saturday, June 14

OFFICIAL GOING: Good

3052a PRIX LA FLECHE (LISTED RACE) 5f (S)
3:00 (3:00) 2-Y-O **£20,221** (£8,088; £6,066; £4,044; £2,022)

RPR

1 **Percolator**[40] 1886 2-8-11........................ CSoumillon 3 103+
(P F I Cole) *fast away: mde all: pushed out fnl f: r.o strly* **7/10**[1]

2 *2 1/2* **Bargouzine (USA)**[32] 2-8-11........................ JVictoire 1 94
(A Fabre, France) **86/10**

3 *1 1/2* **Bluster (FR)**[28] 2-9-0........................ OPeslier 6 92
(C Baillet, France) **3/1**[2]

4 *2 1/2* **Pink Candie (FR)**[22] 2-8-11........................ YLerner 5 80
(Y De Nicolay, France) **14/1**

5 *2* **Smooth Operator (GER)**[32] 2-9-0........................ DBoeuf 4 75
(Mario Hofer, Germany) **64/10**[3]

6 *6* **Miguelight (FR)**[22] 2-9-0........................ C-PLemaire 2 54
(Mme P Alexanian, France) **31/1**

56.60 secs (-0.10) **Going Correction** -0.15s/f (Firm) **6** Ran SP% **117.5**
Speed ratings: **94,90,87,83,80 70**
PARI-MUTUEL: WIN 1.70; PL 1.30, 2.30; SF 7.80.
Owner A H Robinson **Bred** A H And C E Robinson Partnership **Trained** Whatcombe, Oxon

NOTEBOOK
Percolator, quickly out of the stalls, soon built up a two-length lead over the field, who never got a look in, and she covered the 5f in a very fast time for a two-year-old at this point in the season. Her trainer could aim her for the Group 2 Prix Robert Papin at Maison-Laffitte on July 27th.

3053a LA COUPE (GROUP 3) 1m 2f
3:30 (3:30) 4-Y-O+ **£29,412** (£11,765; £8,824; £5,882; £2,941)

RPR

1 **Crossharbour**[39] 4-8-12........................ JVictoire 3 108
(A Fabre, France) *hld up: wnt 4th 1/2-way: hdwy 2f out: rdn to ld ins fnl f: pushed out* **36/10**[3]

2 *3/4* **Spirit One (FR)**[48] 1665 4-9-2........................ CSoumillon 1 110
(P Demercastel, France) *led to ins fnl f: r.o same pce* **6/4**[1]

3 *4* **Boris De Deauville (IRE)**[27] 2238 5-8-12........................ TThulliez 4 98
(S Wattel, France) *a cl up: wnt 2nd appr st: ev ch wl over 1f out: one pce fnl f* **27/10**[2]

4 *2* **Fastmambo (USA)**[34] 5-8-12........................ DBonilla 6 94
(F Head, France) *hld up: last to st: wnt 4th wl over 1f out: nvr nr to chal* **10/1**

5 *2 1/2* **Freemusic (IRE)**[27] 2230 4-8-12........................ GMarcelli 5 89
(L Riccardi, Italy) *disp 3rd to 1/2-way: 5th st: rdn 2f out: sn btn* **13/1**

6 *3/4* **Axxos (GER)**[27] 2230 4-9-2........................ AStarke 2 92
(P Schiergen, Germany) *trckd ldr: cl 3rd st: btn 2f out* **69/10**

2m 2.00s (-4.90) **Going Correction** -0.15s/f (Firm) **6** Ran SP% **117.7**
Speed ratings: **113,112,109,107,105 105**
PARI-MUTUEL: WIN 4.60; PL 2.20, 1.50; SF 14.40.
Owner K Abdulla **Bred** Juddmonte Farms Ltd **Trained** Chantilly, France
■ Stewards' Enquiry : G Marcelli €200 fine: whip abuse

NOTEBOOK
Crossharbour sat in fifth position for much of the race and travelled sweetly off a good pace set by the leader. When the tempo increased turning into the straight he took a while to engage top gear but joined the eventual second one and a half out and these two battled to the line and he broke the race record. This was his first race in Group company and connections will be looking at something like the Group 2 Prix Gontaut-Biron with the long-term aim the Prix Dollar back at this track in October.
Spirit One(FR) was quickly at the head of affairs and set a strong pace. He battled up the far rail all the way to the line but could not hold off the persistent challenge of the winner. A race like the Prix Eugene Adam could be next on this colt's agenda.
Boris De Deauville(IRE), held up in third, pulled hard early on but turning into the straight he looked all over the winner. He got his nose in front one and a half out but could not sustain his challenge and his jockey reported that the going was too quick for him.
Fastmambo(USA), held up off the pace, he finally started to pick up halfway up the straight but it was too late to threaten the first three.

2818 DONCASTER (L-H)
Sunday, June 15

OFFICIAL GOING: Good to firm (9.8)
The ground had dried out and was described as 'on the fast side of good'. The running rail was extended to 6m from 9f out to the home turn.
Wind: Light 1/2 behind Weather: Fine

3054 HOWARD HUGHES MEMORIAL HEARTBEAT H'CAP 1m (S)
2:20 (2:26) (Class 4) (0-85,85) 4-Y-O+ **£4,533** (£1,348; £674; £336) **Stalls** High

Form RPR

1-2 **1** **Swop (IRE)**[38] 1936 5-9-7 **85**........................ JoeFanning 5 96+
(L M Cumani) *led 2f: hung lft and led over 2f out: kpt on wl ins fnl f* **9/4**[1]

-435 **2** *nk* **Sam's Secret**[16] 2578 6-8-13 **77**........................ KerrinMcEvoy 4 87
(G A Swinbank) *hld up: smooth hdwy 3f out: chal over 1f out: no ex wl ins fnl f* **7/1**

0000 **3** *4* **Harare**[23] 2373 7-8-2 **66**........................(v) JimmyQuinn 6 67
(R J Price) *t.k.h in rr: effrt over 3f out: kpt on same pce fnl 2f* **16/1**

4-46 **4** *2* **Habshan (USA)**[34] 2057 8-9-7 **85**........................ GeorgeBaker 2 82
(C F Wall) *hdwy to ld after 2f: hdd over 2f out: fdd appr fnl f* **7/2**[3]

0020 **5** *3/4* **Bailieborough (IRE)**[4] 2927 9-8-3 **67**........................(p) RoystonFfrench 3 62
(B Ellison) *dwlt: sn chsng ldrs: one pce fnl 2f* **11/1**

5306 **6** *2* **Cornus**[8] 2818 6-9-1 **79**........................(be) PatCosgrave 8 69
(A J McCabe) *t.k.h in rr: effrt over 2f out: wknd over 1f out* **20/1**

0512 **7** *9* **Obezyana (USA)**[3] 2969 6-8-11 **78**........................ DominicFox[(3)] 7 47
(A Bailey) *chsd ldrs: drvn over 3f out: lost pl 2f out* **11/4**[2]

-000 **8** *1* **Kalasam**[16] 2585 4-8-4 **68**........................ DaleGibson 1 35
(M W Easterby) *chsd ldrs: hrd drvn over 3f out: lost pl over 2f out* **22/1**

1m 38.39s (-0.91) **Going Correction** -0.225s/f (Firm) **8** Ran SP% **115.5**
Speed ratings (Par 105): **95,94,90,88,87 85,76,75**
CSF £18.99 CT £202.61 TOTE £2.70: £1.10, £2.20, £4.10; EX 11.50 Trifecta £84.10 Pool £302.40 - 2.66 winning units..
Owner Mrs Angie Silver **Bred** Rathbarry Stud **Trained** Newmarket, Suffolk

FOCUS
In the end the first two dominated with the lightly-raced winner likely to prove even better in due course.

3055 SOVEREIGN HEALTHCARE HEARTBEAT E B F MEDIAN AUCTION MAIDEN STKS 6f
2:50 (2:53) (Class 4) 2-Y-O **£4,857** (£1,445; £722; £360) **Stalls** High

Form RPR

3 **1** **Fareer**[24] 2324 2-9-3 0........................ MartinDwyer 9 73+
(E A L Dunlop) *racd wd: chsd ldr: rdn over 1f out: led jst ins fnl f: styd on* **1/3**[1]

2 **2** *1 1/4* **Secret Venue**[22] 2388 2-9-3 0........................ TonyHamilton 12 69
(Jedd O'Keeffe) *trckd ldrs on ins: hdwy to ld 2f out: hdd jst ins fnl f: no ex* **10/1**[2]

6 **3** *2 1/4* **Aegean Warning**[10] 2746 2-9-3 0........................ NCallan 5 63
(K A Ryan) *mid-div: hdwy over 2f out: styd on to take 3rd ins fnl f* **33/1**

00 **4** *1 1/2* **Port Ronan (USA)**[15] 2592 2-9-0 0........................ MarkLawson[(3)] 10 58
(J S Wainwright) *led tl 2f out: wknd ins fnl f* **33/1**

0 **5** *1 1/2* **Tee Gee Cee**[16] 2569 2-9-3 0........................ DavidAllan 6 54+
(T D Easterby) *rr-div: hdwy over 2f out: styd on ins fnl f* **50/1**

6 *1/2* **Shaker Style (USA)** 2-9-3 0........................ JimmyQuinn 3 52+
(J D Bethell) *mid-div: hdwy over 2f out: hung lft and kpt on* **33/1**

0 **7** *7* **Clerical (USA)**[21] 2424 2-9-3 0........................ PatCosgrave 4 31
(M J Gingell) *chsd ldrs: outpcd over 2f out: sn wknd* **66/1**

8 *2* **Ivor Novello (IRE)** 2-9-3 0........................ KerrinMcEvoy 2 25
(G A Swinbank) *mid-div: nvr on terms* **14/1**

0 **9** *2* **Great Charter (USA)**[23] 2362 2-9-3 0........................ JoeFanning 1 19
(M Johnston) *racd wd: w ldrs: sn drvn along: wknd 2f out* **14/1**

10 *3 1/4* **Huxaar** 2-9-3 0........................ TomEaves 7 9
(Mrs L Stubbs) *s.i.s: a outpcd and bhd* **33/1**

11 *11* **Gemini Jive (IRE)** 2-8-12 0........................ JamieSpencer 8 —
(M G Quinlan) *rrd s: a wl detached* **12/1**[3]

12 *1 1/2* **Always Gunner** 2-9-3 0........................ PaulMulrennan 11 —
(J O'Reilly) *dwlt: rn green and sn bhd* **66/1**

1m 13.9s (0.30) **Going Correction** -0.225s/f (Firm) **12** Ran SP% **121.8**
Speed ratings (Par 95): **89,87,84,82,80 79,70,67,65,60 46,44**
CSF £4.36 TOTE £1.30: £1.10, £1.50, £5.20; EX 4.60 Trifecta £71.50 Pool £205.03 - 2.12 winning units..
Owner Hamdan Al Maktoum **Bred** Bishopswood Bloodstock & Trickledown Stud **Trained** Newmarket, Suffolk

FOCUS
An ordinary maiden, no strength in depth and 33/1 bar five. The winner is rated to his debut mark and is the best guide for now.

NOTEBOOK
Fareer, whose Goodwood debut race has worked out well, raced wide. He made very hard work of it but was in command at the line. (op 1-2 tchd 4-7)
Secret Venue, who has plenty of size and scope, travelled strongly hard against the stands'-side rail stepping up in trip. He really threw down the gauntlet but in the end came off second best. He can surely go one better. (op 8-1 tchd 15-2)
Aegean Warning stepped up a good deal on his debut effort and will be suited by 7fs.
Port Ronan(USA), having his third start, showed bags of toe and a drop back to five in nursery company might suit. (op 25-1)
Tee Gee Cee took the eye running on steadily from the rear and looks a likely type for a 7f nursery with another outing under his belt. (tchd 40-1)
Shaker Style(USA), a close-coupled newcomer, showed ability staying on nicely despite a tendency to hang.
Gemini Jive(IRE) Official explanation: jockey said filly reared at start

3056 BRIAN GAYNOR MEMORIAL H'CAP 6f
3:25 (3:26) (Class 3) (0-95,95) 3-Y-O+ **£6,799** (£2,023; £1,011; £505) **Stalls** High

Form RPR

1-1 **1** **Musaalem (USA)**[33] 2087 4-9-3 **84**........................ MartinDwyer 7 101+
(W J Haggas) *trckd ldr stands' side: t.k.h: led over 2f out: pushed out* **13/8**[1]

00-0 **2** *1 3/4* **Mastership (IRE)**[30] 2172 4-9-10 **91**........................ GrahamGibbons 12 102
(J J Quinn) *trckd ldrs stands' side: t.k.h: wnt 2nd appr fnl f: kpt on: no real imp* **7/1**

6-24 **3** *2* **Orpenindeed (IRE)**[29] 2211 5-9-11 **92**........................(t) TedDurcan 13 97
(M Botti) *hld up stands' side: hdwy over 2f out: kpt on same pce fnl f* **6/1**[2]

13-0 **4** *nk* **Sundae**[29] 2195 4-9-11 **92**........................ GeorgeBaker 10 96+
(C F Wall) *hld up stands' side: hdwy over 2f out: kpt on fnl f* **10/1**

3-23 **5** *3/4* **Ishetoo**[15] 2626 4-9-9 **93**........................ MichaelJStainton[(3)] 4 95
(A Dickman) *trckd ldrs centre: effrt over 2f out: kpt on same pce fnl f* **13/2**[3]

0-56 **6** *1 1/2* **Malcheek (IRE)**[30] 2172 6-9-6 **87**........................ DavidAllan 8 84
(T D Easterby) *led on stands' side tl over 2f out: kpt on one pce* **18/1**

0-00 **7** *1 3/4* **Obe Brave**[114] 668 5-9-7 **95**........................ BMcHugh[(7)] 5 86
(R A Fahey) *w ldrs centre: hung rt and wknd over 1f out* **40/1**

0-05 **8** *hd* **Grazeon Gold Blend**[12] 2698 5-8-9 **76** oh1........................ PaulMulrennan 11 67
(J J Quinn) *hld up stands' side: kpt on fnl 2f: nvr a factor* **40/1**

5100 **9** *1 1/4* **Geojimali**[4] 2938 6-8-10 **82**........................ GaryBartley[(5)] 9 69
(J S Goldie) *s.i.s: in rr stands' side: sme hdwy over 1f out: nvr a factor* **12/1**

1510 **10** *3/4* **Valley Of The Moon (IRE)**[16] 2583 4-8-12 **79**........................ PaulHanagan 3 63
(R A Fahey) *racd centre: nvr trbld ldrs* **25/1**

0-60 **11** ½ **Wyatt Earp (IRE)**^{30} 2172 7-9-0 **84** JamieMoriarty(3) 1 67
(R A Fahey) *racd centre: effrt over 2f out: sn outpcd* **18/1**
1-0 **12** ¾ **Kashimin (IRE)**^{60} 1404 3-8-8 **83** KerrinMcEvoy 2 63
(G A Swinbank) *racd centre: w ldrs: wknd over 1f out* **16/1**
00-6 **13** *15* **The Jobber (IRE)**^{24} 2326 7-10-0 **95** JimmyQuinn 6 27
(M Blanshard) *chsd ldrs stands' side: wknd 2f out: eased ins fnl f* **33/1**
1m 11.09s (-2.51) **Going Correction** -0.225s/f (Firm)
WFA 3 from 4yo+ 8lb **13** Ran SP% **123.1**
Speed ratings (Par 107): **107,104,102,101,100 98,96,96,94,93 92,91,71**
CSF £12.90 CT £60.50 TOTE £2.80: £1.30, £3.20, £2.50; EX 17.40 Trifecta £305.70 Pool £495.85 - 1.20 winning units.
Owner Hamdan Al Maktoum **Bred** Shadwell Farm LLC **Trained** Newmarket, Suffolk

FOCUS
A competitive sprint handicap proved plain sailing for Musaalem who is now unbeaten in three starts. He should make further progress and overall the form looks rock solid.

NOTEBOOK
Musaalem(USA), who injured a pelvis at two, is making up for lost time. Raised 9lb and dropping back in trip, he was keen to get on with it. He scored with something in hand and should continue to climb the ladder, but he is still unfurnished and on the weak side. (op 2-1)
Mastership(IRE), who scored over an extended mile for his previous yard, was another to take a tug. He went in pursuit of the leader but was always going to have to settle for second spot. (op 15-2 tchd 6-1)
Orpenindeed(IRE), back over his best trip, ran with plenty of credit on ground plenty fast enough for him. (op 7-1 tchd 15-2)
Sundae, too keen last time, settled much better. He took three handicaps last year rising over a stone in the ratings and he should be spot on next time. (tchd 9-1 and 12-1)
Ishetoo, 8lb higher than his last winning mark seems better over the minimum trip. (op 11-2)
Malcheek(IRE) fitted with a crupper to prevent him getting his head under the stalls, has slipped to a mark just 2lb higher than his last success. (op 25-1)
Kashimin(IRE) Official explanation: jockey said colt hung left-handed
The Jobber(IRE) Official explanation: Jockey said gelding moved poorly in latter stages

3057 SIR RODNEY WALKER HEARTBEAT FILLIES' H'CAP 1m 2f 60y
4:00 (4:00) (Class 5) (0-75,75) 3-Y-O £3,238 (£963; £481; £240) Stalls Low

Form RPR
1342 **1** **Black Dahlia**^{9} 2785 3-8-11 **65** PatCosgrave 8 75+
(A J McCabe) *t.k.h in midfield: smooth hdwy over 2f out: led over 1f out: 5l ahd whn eased ins fnl f: v comf* **4/1**^{1}
4-60 **2** ¾ **Red Icon**^{16} 2564 3-9-3 **71** GeorgeBaker 12 79+
(R M Beckett) *hld up in rr: stdy hdwy whn n.m.r and hmpd 2f out: swtchd outside: fin fast to take 2nd ins fnl f: nt quite rch eased down wnr* **8/1**
0-46 **3** *3* **Top Vision**^{26} 2272 3-9-4 **72** TPO'Shea 13 71
(M R Channon) *hld up in rr: hdwy on outer over 2f out: tk 2nd 1f out: kpt on same pce* **20/1**
03-0 **4** *hd* **Broken Moon**^{27} 2257 3-9-2 **70** JamieSpencer 5 69
(J R Fanshawe) *hld up: hdwy over 2f out: hung rt and sn bmpd: kpt on* **6/1**^{3}
304- **5** *2* **Neve Lieve (IRE)**^{273} 5443 3-8-11 **65** TedDurcan 15 60
(M Botti) *prom: chal 2f out: kpt on same pce* **25/1**
616 **6** *3* **Snowdrop Princess**^{17} 2532 3-9-4 **72** NCallan 3 61
(W J Haggas) *mid-div: hdwy over 2f out: n.m.r over 1f out: kpt on one pce* **7/1**
-213 **7** 1¼ **Fantastic Lass**^{48} 1678 3-8-7 **61** PaulHanagan 9 48
(R A Fahey) *sn chsng ldrs: led over 2f out: hdd over 1f out: sn wknd* **8/1**
465 **8** 1¼ **Eureka Moment**^{27} 2257 3-9-3 **71** JoeFanning 11 56
(E A L Dunlop) *mid-div: effrt 3f out: wknd fnl f* **8/1**
4025 **9** *7* **Queen's Speech (IRE)**^{26} 2288 3-9-7 **75** KShea 2 46
(J H M Gosden) *trckd ldrs: nt clr run over 2f out: sn lost pl* **9/1**
16- **10** *5* **Fits Of Giggles (IRE)**^{293} 4899 3-9-7 **75** J-PGuillambert 7 37
(J G Given) *trckd ldrs: t.k.h: nt clr run 3f out: sn wknd* **20/1**
040- **11** *8* **Madam Carwell**^{261} 5766 3-8-4 **58** JimmyQuinn 10 5
(J G Given) *t.k.h: trckd ldrs: lost pl over 2f out* **40/1**
363- **12** *11* **Snowy Indian**^{227} 6611 3-9-7 **75** KerrinMcEvoy 6 1
(Sir Michael Stoute) *led: hdd over 2f out: wknd* **5/1**^{2}
0-06 **13** *8* **Lavender And Lace**^{31} 2118 3-8-4 **58** ow1 MartinDwyer 14 —
(T Keddy) *s.i.s: a last* **50/1**
2m 10.2s (-1.00) **Going Correction** +0.025s/f (Good) **13** Ran SP% **124.6**
Speed ratings (Par 96): **105,104,102,101,100 97,96,95,90,86 79,71,64**
CSF £35.47 CT £593.56 TOTE £3.90: £1.90, £2.80, £4.10; EX 32.60 TRIFECTA Not won..
Owner Paul J Dixon and D Sharp **Bred** Worksop Manor Stud **Trained** Babworth, Notts

FOCUS
A modest fillies-only handicap but the first two look of real interest.
Madam Carwell Official explanation: jockey said filly ran too free in the early stages

3058 ANN HUGHES HEARTBEAT MAIDEN STKS 1m 4f
4:35 (4:36) (Class 5) 3-Y-O+ £3,238 (£963; £481; £240) Stalls Low

Form RPR
1 **Maori**^{66} 3-8-12 0 JoeFanning 3 82+
(M Johnston) *mid-div: effrt on outside over 3f out: led 2f out: styd on strly* **11/1**
02 **2** *4* **Herrera (IRE)**^{17} 2536 3-8-7 0 PaulHanagan 15 66+
(R A Fahey) *trckd ldrs: effrt 4f out: sn wl outpcd: styd on wl appr fnl f: tk 2nd nr line* **8/1**
3 **3** *hd* **Erdeli (IRE)**^{16} 2573 4-9-13 0 JamieSpencer 12 70
(P R Webber) *hld up: smooth hdwy on outside 7f out: led and edgd lft over 2f out: sn hdd: kpt on same pce* **11/2**^{2}
-032 **4** *1* **Factotum**^{24} 2336 4-9-13 85 PatCosgrave 14 69
(L M Cumani) *trckd ldr: n.m.r and swtchd rt over 2f out: one pce* **4/5**^{1}
00-6 **5** *2* **Hellzapoppin**^{23} 2370 3-8-12 72 NCallan 7 65
(D R Lanigan) *trckd ldrs: t.k.h: effrt over 2f out: kpt on one pce* **28/1**
00 **6** *nk* **Enderby Light (FR)**^{13} 2668 3-8-12 0 DNolan 5 65
(D Carroll) *chsd ldrs: edgd rt over 1f out: kpt on* **66/1**
0 **7** *2* **Miss Serena**^{13} 2668 3-8-8 0 ow1 MickyFenton 13 58
(Mrs P Sly) *mid-div: drvn over 3f out: kpt on: nvr a factor* **50/1**
0-0 **8** *3* **Syriana**^{16} 2573 3-8-4 0 DominicFox(3) 9 52
(A Bailey) *chsd ldrs: lost pl over 2f out* **50/1**
6 **9** 1¼ **Enderby Princess (IRE)**^{57} 1477 3-8-7 0 DavidAllan 1 50
(D Carroll) *s.i.s: hdwy 5f out: one pce whn pushed wd over 1f out* **66/1**
04 **10** 1¼ **Drum Major (IRE)**^{15} 2612 3-8-12 0 KerrinMcEvoy 10 53
(Sir Michael Stoute) *led: hdd over 2f out: sn lost pl* **6/1**^{3}
11 *3* **Faraway Bay** 3-8-7 0 MartinDwyer 11 43
(E J O'Neill) *s.s: pushed along in rr* **25/1**
12 3½ **Thankfully (IRE)** 3-8-7 0 TPO'Shea 8 38
(W M Brisbourne) *s.s: a bhd* **66/1**
2m 35.6s (0.50) **Going Correction** +0.025s/f (Good)
WFA 3 from 4yo+ 15lb **12** Ran SP% **120.4**
Speed ratings (Par 103): **99,96,96,95,94 94,92,90,89,89 87,84**
CSF £92.90 TOTE £13.20: £2.70, £2.30, £1.70; EX 91.80 TRIFECTA Not won..
Owner Sheikh Hamdan Bin Mohammed Al Maktoum **Bred** Gainsborough Stud Management Ltd **Trained** Middleham Moor, N Yorks

FOCUS
A fair maiden with the fifth rated 72.

3059 LADY WALKER HEARTBEAT APPRENTICE H'CAP 1m 6f 132y
5:05 (5:06) (Class 5) (0-70,70) 4-Y-O+ £3,238 (£963; £481; £240) Stalls Low

Form RPR
-521 **1** **Hits Only Vic (USA)**^{12} 2701 4-9-2 **69** PaulPickard(7) 12 78+
(D Carroll) *trckd ldrs: led over 1f out: styd on wl* **6/1**^{3}
0345 **2** 2¼ **Rose Bien**^{31} 2135 6-8-11 **60** (p) JackMitchell(3) 4 66
(P J McBride) *trckd ldrs: wnt 2nd over 1f out: no imp* **7/2**^{1}
4303 **3** 2¾ **Still Dreaming**^{14} 2641 4-8-5 **51** oh1 KirstyMilczarek 11 54
(R J Price) *trckd ldrs: kpt on same pce fnl 2f* **10/1**
-000 **4** *1* **Don Jose (USA)**^{8} 2849 5-8-0 **51** oh6 (e) StacyRenwick(5) 6 52
(N J Vaughan) *hld up in rr: hdwy over 2f out: kpt on wl fnl f* **40/1**
0444 **5** *hd* **Sand Repeal (IRE)**^{27} 2245 6-8-6 **57** (v) AmyBaker(5) 8 58
(Miss J Feilden) *led after 1f: hrd rdn and hdd over 1f out: one pce* **9/1**
00/5 **6** *4* **Dancing Bear**^{27} 2245 7-8-1 **52** oh6 ow1 PatrickDonaghy(5) 10 48
(C Roberts) *dwlt: hdwy to trck ldrs after 3f: wknd over 2f out* **22/1**
0253 **7** ¾ **Blue Jet (USA)**^{16} 2572 4-8-10 **56** MichaelJStainton 3 51
(R M Whitaker) *led 1f: trckd ldrs: wknd over 1f out* **5/1**^{2}
5-20 **8** *shd* **Strong Survivor (USA)**^{38} 1933 5-9-6 **69** JamieJones(3) 9 64
(P R Webber) *in rr: kpt on fnl 3f: nvr a factor* **16/1**
3400 **9** 1¾ **Sky Chart (IRE)**^{16} 2572 4-8-5 **51** oh2 AndrewMullen 5 43
(N J Vaughan) *dwlt: t.k.h on outer in rr: sme hdwy over 3f out: sn wknd* **8/1**
-012 **10** 2½ **Amanda Carter**^{23} 2376 4-9-10 **70** JamieMoriarty 1 59
(R A Fahey) *had problems in stalls: hld up in rr: effrt over 3f out: nvr a factor* **7/2**^{1}
6-04 **11** 3¾ **Looktheotherway (IRE)**^{20} 2453 4-8-8 **54** LukeMorris 2 38
(J G M O'Shea) *mid-div: shkn up 7f out: lost pl over 3f out* **20/1**
50-6 **12** *14* **The Quantum Kid**^{26} 2286 4-8-3 **52** NicolPolli(3) 7 18
(T J Etherington) *hld up in mid-div: hdwy on outside over 3f out: rdn and hung bdly rt 2f out: sn bhd* **28/1**
3m 10.29s (3.59) **Going Correction** +0.025s/f (Good) **12** Ran SP% **126.5**
Speed ratings (Par 103): **91,89,88,87,87 85,85,85,84,82 80,73**
CSF £28.01 CT £218.45 TOTE £6.50: £2.80, £2.00, £2.20; EX 37.20 Trifecta £154.70 Pool £524.81 - 2.51 winning units. Place 6 £56.56, Place 5 £27.71..
Owner Kell-Stone & Watson **Bred** Peter E Blum **Trained** Sledmere, E Yorks
■ A first career success on his 87th ride for 21-year-old Paul Pickard.
■ Stewards' Enquiry : Amy Baker four-day ban: used whip with excessive frequency (Jun 29-Jul 2)

FOCUS
A low-grade apprentice handicap run at a steady pace.
Amanda Carter Official explanation: trainer said filly had jammed its nose in the bars of the stalls
The Quantum Kid Official explanation: jockey said colt hung right
T/Plt: £57.20 to a £1 stake. Pool: £76,606.52. 976.35 winning tickets. T/Qpdt: £20.10 to a £1 stake. Pool: £3,849.00. 141.10 winning tickets. WG

2916 SALISBURY (R-H)
Sunday, June 15

OFFICIAL GOING: Good to firm changing to good after race 3 (3.00)
Wind: Virtually nil Weather: Bright spells; showers earlier

3060 ALBERT SAMUEL "CITY BOWL" H'CAP 1m 4f
2:00 (2:00) (Class 4) (0-85,85) 4-Y-O+ £4,371 (£1,300; £650; £324) Stalls High

Form RPR
0-25 **1** **Paktolos (FR)**^{28} 1841 5-9-2 **80** (b^{1}) DaneO'Neill 13 91
(A King) *stmbld s: hld up in midfield: hdwy 3f out: rdn to ld over 1f out: clr ins fnl f: r.o wl* **10/1**
160- **2** *2* **Horseford Hill**^{255} 5955 4-9-4 **82** RyanMoore 2 90
(D R C Elsworth) *wnt rt s: hld up in rr: rdn over 3f out: plld out and hdwy 3f out: chsd wnr ent fnl f: kpt on* **13/2**^{3}
5-34 **3** ½ **Ollie George (IRE)**^{23} 2372 5-9-6 **84** LPKeniry 6 91
(A M Balding) *t.k.h: chsd ldrs: rdn and effrt over 2f out: chsd ldrs ent fnl f: kpt on* **3/1**^{1}
/064 **4** *3* **Alfie Noakes**^{22} 2414 6-8-10 **74** JimCrowley 3 76
(Mrs A J Perrett) *stdd s: hld up bhd: plld out and rdn 3f out: styd on fnl f but nvr pce to threaten ldrs* **15/2**
-603 **5** *1* **Mustajed**^{17} 2540 7-9-0 **83** JamesMillman(5) 1 84
(B R Millman) *t.k.h: chsd ldrs: wnt 2nd over 5f out: led over 2f out: sn rdn: hdd over 1f out: wknd fnl f* **5/1**^{2}
-235 **6** 1¼ **Urban Warrior**^{19} 2483 4-8-4 **68** ChrisCatlin 10 67
(Ian Williams) *chsd ldrs: rdn 3f out: struggling whn swtchd lft 2f out: no ch w ldrs fnl f* **25/1**
0-61 **7** *hd* **Transvestite (IRE)**^{16} 2558 6-8-8 **75** PatrickHills(3) 11 73
(J W Hills) *led tl rdn and hdd over 2f out: wknd over 1f out* **22/1**
315 **8** *nk* **Mae Cigan (FR)**^{15} 2621 5-7-13 **70** ow2 SophieDoyle(7) 8 68
(M Blanshard) *hld up in midfield: rdn and unable qckn whn short of room briefly wl over 2f out: n.d after* **9/1**
6031 **9** *hd* **Crossbow Creek**^{16} 2585 10-9-7 **85** RichardHughes 9 83
(M G Rimell) *stdd s: hld up in last pl: effrt on rail over 2f out: nvr trbld ldrs* **7/1**
-20 **10** *1* **Mister Right (IRE)**^{8} 2822 7-8-10 **74** RobertWinston 12 70
(D J S Ffrench Davis) *t.k.h: hld up towards rr: rdn and effrt 3f out: nvr trbld ldrs* **16/1**
3/0- **11** *13* **Scotland Yard (UAE)**^{29} 2736 5-9-5 **83** (p) JimmyFortune 4 58
(D E Pipe) *chsd ldr tl over 5f out: drvn 4f out: wknd and bhd last 3f* **16/1**
2m 36.42s (-1.58) **Going Correction** 0.0s/f (Good) **11** Ran SP% **118.3**
Speed ratings (Par 105): **105,103,103,101,100 99,99,99,99,98 90**
CSF £74.11 CT £246.69 TOTE £10.30: £2.70, £2.70, £1.60; EX 103.00.
Owner P Finnegan **Bred** Stilvi Compania **Trained** Barbury Castle, Wilts
■ Stewards' Enquiry : Patrick Hills one-day ban: careless riding (Jun 29)

FOCUS
A competitive handicap run at a fairly steady early gallop.

3061 BETFAIR MAIDEN FILLIES' STKS 1m
2:30 (2:36) (Class 5) 3-Y-O **£3,885** (£1,156; £577; £288) **Stalls** High

Form RPR

52 **1** **Soft Shoe Shuffle (IRE)**[16] 2560 3-9-0 0 AdamKirby 13 82+
(W R Swinburn) *t.k.h: hld up towards rr: swtchd lft and hdwy 3f out: chsd ldr ent fnl f: led ins fnl f: pushed out* **4/5**[1]

0-0 **2** *1 1/4* **Lambda (USA)**[31] 2123 3-9-0 0 RyanMoore 12 79
(Sir Michael Stoute) *t.k.h: hld up in midfield: hdwy over 3f out: rdn to chse ldr over 2f out: led over 1f out: hdd and nt pce of wnr ins fnl f* **11/1**

00 **3** *6* **Ci Vediamo (IRE)**[20] 2449 3-8-7 0 RichardFelton(7) 7 65
(R M Beckett) *led: rdn and hdd over 1f out: outpcd by ldng pair fnl f but plugged on to hold 3rd pl* **50/1**

05 **4** *nk* **Isle Of Capri**[9] 2800 3-9-0 0 RichardHughes 2 65
(R Hannon) *hld up in midfield: hdwy and edgd rt over 2f out: outpcd over 1f out: kpt on steadily* **12/1**

-36 **5** *1 3/4* **Siren Sound**[16] 2566 3-9-0 0 SteveDrowne 8 60
(H Morrison) *chsd ldrs: rdn 3f out: wknd over 1f out* **7/1**[3]

0-0 **6** *3/4* **Plumage**[27] 2257 3-9-0 0 LPKeniry 6 59
(M Blanshard) *s.i.s: sn in midfield: plld out and rdn 3f out: edgd rt and no imp last 2f* **50/1**

3- **7** *1/2* **La Famiglia**[272] 5470 3-9-0 0 DaneO'Neill 5 58
(H Candy) *chsd ldrs tl wnt 2nd 1/2-way: rdn and lost 2nd pl over 2f out: wknd 2f out* **9/2**[2]

8 *1 3/4* **Miss Pelling (IRE)** 3-9-0 0 StephenDonohoe 16 54
(B J Meehan) *s.i.s: towards rr: rdn 3f out: hung rt fr over 2f out: nvr trbld ldrs* **25/1**

6 **9** *7* **Rockfield Rose**[25] 2307 3-9-0 0 ChrisCatlin 10 37
(J A Osborne) *bhd: rdn 3f out: nvr on terms* **33/1**

00 **10** *shd* **Bobster**[11] 2716 3-9-0 0 FergusSweeney 15 37
(B R Millman) *s.i.s: t.k.h: hld up in rr: n.d* **100/1**

11 *hd* **Romiosini Way (GR)** 3-9-0 0 JimCrowley 1 37
(P R Chamings) *s.i.s: sn swtchd rt: bhd: plld out 3f out: sn edging rt: nvr trbld ldrs* **66/1**

05 **12** *1/2* **New Havens**[25] 2307 3-9-0 0 RobertWinston 4 36
(C R Egerton) *chsd ldrs: rdn over 2f out: wknd qckly over 1f out* **80/1**

0- **13** *2 3/4* **Redchete**[250] 6082 3-8-9 0 AhmedAjtebi(5) 3 29
(C E Brittain) *chsd ldr tl 1/2-way: wknd qckly wl over 2f out* **66/1**

14 *10* **Flipacoin** 3-9-0 0 IanMongan 9 —
(S Dow) *t.k.h: in tch: rdn 3f out: sn wknd: t.o* **50/1**

15 *30* **Miss Riviera Chic** 3-9-0 0 EddieAhern 14 —
(G Wragg) *a bhd: t.o last 2f* **16/1**

1m 41.99s (-1.51) **Going Correction** -0.275s/f (Firm) **15** Ran SP% **126.0**
Speed ratings (Par 96): **96,94,88,88,86 85,85,83,76,76 76,75,73,63,33**
CSF £11.32 TOTE £1.80: £1.20, £2.50, £14.30; EX 15.20.
Owner Exors Of The Late Mrs P W Harris **Bred** Pendley Farm **Trained** Aldbury, Herts

FOCUS
An ordinary maiden.
New Havens Official explanation: jockey said filly was unsuited by the good to firm going

3062 MANOR FARM MEATS H'CAP 5f
3:00 (3:06) (Class 4) (0-85,83) 3-Y-O+ **£4,371** (£1,300; £650; £324) **Stalls** High

Form RPR

230- **1** **Osiris Way**[198] 6970 6-9-13 **82** JimCrowley 4 92+
(P R Chamings) *chsd ldrs tl wnt 2nd 4f out: rdn 2f out: led jst ins fnl f: styd on wl* **10/1**

00-5 **2** *1/2* **Playful**[28] 2219 5-9-10 **79** JamesDoyle 7 87
(R M Beckett) *stdd s: hld up bhd: hdwy 1/2-way: rdn 2f out: chsd ldrs and hung lft ins fnl f: r.o to go 2nd toward fin: nt rch wnr* **7/1**

0121 **3** *1/2* **Crimson Fern (IRE)**[10] 2760 4-9-8 **80** PatrickHills(3) 12 86+
(M S Saunders) *uns rdr bef s and galloped loose to s: hld up in midfield: hdwy on inner 2f out: chsd wnr ins fnl f: kpt on same pce and lost 2nd towards fin* **11/4**[1]

6-35 **4** *1/2* **Pretty Miss**[30] 2166 4-9-2 **71** FergusSweeney 5 76
(H Candy) *sn led: rdn 2f out: hdd jst ins fnl f: fdd last 100yds* **6/1**[3]

0-00 **5** *3/4* **Pic Up Sticks**[27] 2242 9-8-13 **68** RyanMoore 3 70
(B G Powell) *s.i.s: bhd and sn rdn along: hdwy u.p 2f out: kpt on same pce fnl f* **11/2**[2]

222- **6** *3/4* **Even Bolder**[273] 5447 5-9-3 **72** StephenCarson 9 71
(E A Wheeler) *stdd after s: hld up in midfield: rdn and effrt 2f out: kpt on but nvr pce to threaten ldrs* **9/1**

4660 **7** *3/4* **Cape Royal**[5] 2906 8-9-11 **83** (bt) KevinGhunowa(3) 2 80
(J M Bradley) *prom: ev ch wl over 1f out: wkng whn sltly hmpd ins fnl f* **25/1**

04-0 **8** *1* **Bluebok**[5] 2906 7-9-5 **74** (t) StephenDonohoe 6 67
(J M Bradley) *racd in midfield: rdn and struggling 3f out* **11/1**

0040 **9** *2 1/4* **Woodcote (IRE)**[9] 2773 6-9-11 **80** (p) LPKeniry 11 65
(P R Chamings) *awkward s: sn chsng ldr tl 4f out: rdn 2f out: sn wknd* **10/1**

-005 **10** *hd* **Spanish Ace**[1] 3024 7-8-12 **67** (p) DaneO'Neill 8 51
(J M Bradley) *a towards rr: rdn 3f out: nvr trbld ldrs* **33/1**

5044 **11** *1* **Malapropism**[8] 2843 8-9-11 **80** SamHitchcott 1 60
(M R Channon) *sn bustled along in rr: n.d* **7/1**

60.34 secs (-0.46) **Going Correction** +0.05s/f (Good) **11** Ran SP% **124.6**
Speed ratings (Par 105): **105,104,103,102,101 100,99,97,93,93 91**
CSF £83.13 CT £256.82 TOTE £12.30: £3.60, £2.90, £1.30; EX 99.20.
Owner Mrs Alexandra J Chandris **Bred** Whitsbury Manor Stud **Trained** Baughurst, Hants

FOCUS
Run in a rainstorm, this was a competitive sprint handicap and the form looks solid enough for the grade.
Cape Royal Official explanation: jockey said gelding hung right

3063 AXMINSTER CARPETS CATHEDRAL STKS (LISTED RACE) 6f
3:35 (3:39) (Class 1) 3-Y-O+
£17,031 (£6,456; £3,231; £1,611; £807; £405) **Stalls** High

Form RPR

-126 **1** **Edge Closer**[13] 2680 4-9-4 104 RichardHughes 4 117
(R Hannon) *led for 1f: chsd ldr after tl led again 1/2-way: rdn wl over 1f out: r.o strly* **9/1**

2-12 **2** *2* **Borderlescott**[22] 2404 6-9-4 111 RobertWinston 1 111
(R Bastiman) *trckd ldrs: chsd ldr over 2f out: rdn 2f out: r.o but nt pce to chal wnr* **7/4**[1]

500- **3** *4 1/2* **Ashdown Express (IRE)**[324] 3894 9-9-4 100 JimmyFortune 8 96
(W J Knight) *stdd s: t.k.h: hld up in rr: hdwy 2f out: styd on past btn horses to go 3rd last 100yds: no ch w ldng pair* **25/1**

6400 **4** *1/2* **Ripples Maid**[15] 2606 5-8-13 92 DaneO'Neill 3 90
(J A Geake) *chsd ldrs: rdn wl over 2f out: chsd ldng pair 2f out: wknd ent fnl f: lost 3rd last 100yds* **33/1**

0-04 **5** *1/2* **Silver Touch (IRE)**[15] 2607 5-8-13 106 EdwardCreighton 6 88
(M R Channon) *stdd after s: hld up in tch: swtchd rt and effrt over 2f out: sn rdn: wknd over 1f out* **5/1**[3]

33-3 **6** *1 1/4* **Swiss Franc**[15] 2605 3-8-10 108 RyanMoore 7 89
(D R C Elsworth) *in tch in midfield: rdn 1/2-way: wknd over 1f out* **5/2**[2]

05-0 **7** *2 1/4* **Pivotal Point**[13] 2680 8-9-4 105 EddieAhern 5 82
(P J Makin) *hld up in rr: hdwy 1/2-way: rdn jst over 2f out: wknd wl over 1f out: eased wl ins fnl f* **18/1**

4536 **8** *1 1/2* **Beckermet (IRE)**[15] 2607 6-9-8 110 ChrisCatlin 2 81
(R F Fisher) *swtchd lft after s: led after 1f: hdd and rdn 1/2-way: wknd and bhd last 2f* **11/1**

-200 **9** *1 1/4* **The Trader (IRE)**[14] 2652 10-9-4 100 (b) SteveDrowne 9 73
(M Blanshard) *a bhd* **40/1**

1m 13.45s (-1.35) **Going Correction** +0.05s/f (Good)
WFA 3 from 4yo+ 8lb **9** Ran SP% **114.4**
Speed ratings (Par 111): **111,108,102,101,101 99,96,94,92**
CSF £24.59 TOTE £8.30: £2.20, £1.10, £5.60; EX 31.40.
Owner Lady Whent And Friends **Bred** Caroline Wilson **Trained** East Everleigh, Wilts

FOCUS
A solid race for the grade and, following the rain, they came towards the stands' side this time.

NOTEBOOK
Edge Closer does not mind a bit of ease so the change in ground conditions was no inconvenience to him. Up there throughout, he pulled clear for a comfortable win in the end and clearly retains a progressive profile. A quick reappearance in the Wokingham under a penalty is now on the cards. (op 10-1 tchd 8-1)
Borderlescott, a reliable performer who finished second to Fleeting Spirit in the Group 2 Temple Stakes last time, could not take advantage of the drop in grade, but he did finish well clear of the rest. Since he won the Stewards' Cup he has only won once but has finished second ten times. (op 6-4)
Ashdown Express(IRE), notoriously difficult to win with, would not have been suited by the rain easing the ground from his favoured fast, but he shaped well enough on his seasonal reappearance and first run for his new yard. (tchd 28-1)
Ripples Maid, who had the lowest official rating of those taking part, ran as well as could be expected. She will be more effective back in mares-only company. (op 40-1)
Silver Touch(IRE) has done all her winning over 7f but was not expected to have any trouble with the drop back in trip, especially with the ground easing in the run up to the race. She was a little disappointing in the circumstances. (op 11-2)
Swiss Franc, taking on older horses for the first time, was representing a generation that have acquitted themselves well in sprints so far this term, so this has to go down as a disappointing effort. Perhaps he has not trained on. (op 3-1)

3064 MARTIN PEARCE 50TH ANNIVERSARY FILLIES' H'CAP 6f 212y
4:10 (4:11) (Class 5) (0-75,75) 3-Y-O+ **£3,238** (£963; £481; £240) **Stalls** High

Form RPR

2-00 **1** **Monashee Rock (IRE)**[15] 2622 3-8-11 **68** TGMcLaughlin 6 75
(M Salaman) *hld up bhd: c stands' side 1/2-way: rdn 3f out: hdwy over 1f out: edgd rt but r.o strly to ld wl ins fnl f* **22/1**

0-20 **2** *1 1/4* **Danseuse Volante (IRE)**[15] 2622 3-9-2 **73** EddieAhern 12 77
(J W Hills) *led: styd on far rail 1/2-way: rdn over 2f out: hdd and no ex wl ins fnl f* **7/1**

4-10 **3** *nk* **Fifty (IRE)**[21] 2428 3-9-4 **75** RichardHughes 4 78
(R Hannon) *chsd ldrs: c stands' side and led that gp 1/2-way: ev ch u.p ent fnl f: kpt on same pce* **6/1**

0-15 **4** *1* **Glencal**[36] 1996 4-9-0 **64** TravisBlock(3) 7 68
(H Morrison) *chsd ldr: styd far side 1/2-way: ev ch u.p fr over 2f out: one pce fnl f* **3/1**[1]

-50 **5** *3* **Shamrock Lady (IRE)**[10] 2761 3-9-4 **75** LPKeniry 3 67
(J Gallagher) *in tch in midfield: c stands' side 1/2-way: rdn wl over 2f out: wknd over 1f out* **20/1**

4-00 **6** *1* **Acquifer**[29] 2196 3-8-13 **70** JimmyFortune 8 59
(J L Dunlop) *hld up in tch: styd far side 1/2-way: swtchd lft and effrt 3f out: chsd ldrs 2f out: hung lft and wknd ent fnl f* **10/1**

053 **7** *1 1/2* **Mason Ette**[16] 2565 4-10-0 **75** (b) AdamKirby 1 64
(C G Cox) *t.k.h: in tch: c stands' side 1/2-way: hdwy to press ldrs and rdn over 2f out: wknd over 1f out* **4/1**[3]

26-0 **8** *11* **My Pin Up**[10] 2757 3-8-13 **70** PatDobbs 10 26
(Christian Wroe) *stdd s: hld up bhd: c stands' side 1/2-way: rdn 3f out: sn lost tch* **33/1**

600- **9** *1* **Oronsay**[260] 5818 3-8-0 **57** AdrianMcCarthy 2 10
(B R Millman) *t.k.h: hld up in tch: c stands' side 1/2-way: rdn 3f out: sn bhd* **66/1**

400 **10** *9* **Trivia (IRE)**[10] 2758 4-9-1 **62** JamesDoyle 5 —
(Ms J S Doyle) *t.k.h: in tch: c stands' side 1/2-way: rdn and wknd qckly over 2f out: t.o* **14/1**

045- **11** *dist* **Calypso Charms**[233] 6470 3-9-4 **75** RyanMoore 11 —
(M L W Bell) *taken down early: t.k.h: in tch: c stands' side 1/2-way: wknd qckly 3f out: virtually p.u wl over 1f out: t.o* **7/2**[2]

1m 28.77s (-0.23) **Going Correction** +0.05s/f (Good)
WFA 3 from 4yo 10lb **11** Ran SP% **123.3**
Speed ratings (Par 100): **103,101,101,100,96 95,93,81,80,69 —**
CSF £171.06 CT £1085.53 TOTE £34.50: £6.70, £2.40, £1.90; EX 246.20.
Owner Mrs P G Lewin & D Grieve **Bred** M J Lewin And D Grieve **Trained** Baydon, Wilts

FOCUS
A modest fillies' handicap. They came both sides as they straightened up and there seemed no advantage.
Trivia(IRE) Official explanation: jockey said filly lost action

3065 PERTEMPS PEOPLE DEVELOPMENT "HANDS AND HEELS" APPRENTICE SERIES H'CAP 1m
4:45 (4:50) (Class 6) (0-65,65) 3-Y-O **£2,914** (£867; £433; £216) **Stalls** High

Form RPR

004- **1** **Slip**[256] 5918 3-9-1 **65** KatiaScallan(8) 1 78+
(M P Tregoning) *hld up bhd: hdwy over 4f out: led over 2f out: sn pushed along and in command: eased wl ins fnl f* **11/2**[2]

-600 **2** *2 3/4* **Miss Phoebe (IRE)**[38] 1930 3-9-1 **65** MatthewBirch(8) 11 69
(S Kirk) *led tl over 6f out: pushed along and lost pl 1/2-way: plugged on again fr jst over 1f out: wnt 2nd nr fin: no ch w wnr* **12/1**

1130 **3** *nk* **Silca Destination**[15] 2622 3-9-7 **63** AshleyMorgan 10 66
(M R Channon) *in tch in midfield: hdwy 1/2-way: led wl over 2f out: sn hdd and rdn: no ch w wnr fnl f: lost 2nd nr fin* **6/1**[3]

-605 **4** 2 1/4 **Lady Jinks**[15] 2611 3-7-10 **46** oh1 .... JustinaKay(8) 5 44
(M D I Usher) *hld up wl bhd: edgd rt over 4f out: styd on steadily past btn horses on far side last 2f: nvr trbld ldrs* **14/1**

0-20 **5** 1 1/2 **Xtravaganza (IRE)**[26] 2288 3-9-6 **62** .... AdeleRothery 7 57
(J W Hills) *bhd: hmpd over 4f out: styd on fr over 1f out: nvr trbld ldrs* **7/1**

000- **6** 2 **Pretty Officer (USA)**[230] 6535 3-8-7 **49** .... RichardEvans 3 39
(Rae Guest) *in tch: rdn and lost pl over 3f out: keeping on whn swtchd rt 1f out: nvr pce to trble ldrs* **9/1**

0000 **7** 2 **Ruby Delta**[27] 2244 3-8-13 **55** .... (b[1]) TobyAtkinson 13 40
(P D Cundell) *s.i.s: hld up in midfield: hdwy 3f out: shkn up over 2f out: fnd nil and sn btn* **8/1**

56-0 **8** 3/4 **Bluebell Ridge (IRE)**[25] 2307 3-9-4 **60** .... SimonPearce 6 44
(D W P Arbuthnot) *hld up towards rr: hmpd and stmbld over 3f out: nvr trbld ldrs* **14/1**

4-00 **9** 3/4 **In Decorum**[4] 2946 3-8-4 **46** oh1 .... BillyCray 4 28
(J A Geake) *racd in midfield: rdn and edgd rt over 3f out: no ch fr over 2f out* **40/1**

0000 **10** 3/4 **Dawn Wind**[17] 2552 3-8-4 **46** oh1 .... (v) RosieJessop 14 26
(I A Wood) *s.i.s: hld up in rr: n.d* **25/1**

00-0 **11** 2 1/2 **Bagenalstown (IRE)**[16] 2571 3-8-6 **48** oh1 ow2 .... SamuelDrury 12 23
(M Wellings) *uns rdr bef s: prom: led over 6f out tl 1/2-way: sn hanging lft: wknd over 1f out* **66/1**

00-0 **12** 3 3/4 **Lady Maya**[24] 2341 3-7-12 **48** .... (v[1]) MatthewCosham(8) 9 14
(Dr J R J Naylor) *pressed ldrs tl led 1/2-way: hdd over 2f out: sn wknd* **20/1**

-560 **13** 3 **Spiritofthestorm (USA)**[46] 1721 3-9-7 **63** .... RossAtkinson 2 22
(R A Teal) *prom: rdn 3f out: wknd qckly over 2f out* **7/1**

5003 **14** 3 **Alfredtheordinary**[9] 2805 3-9-1 **60** .... MatthewDavies(3) 8 12
(M R Channon) *prom tl 1/2-way: sn struggling: wl bhd whn eased ins fnl f* **9/2**[1]

1m 45.24s (1.74) **Going Correction** +0.05s/f (Good) **14** Ran SP% **127.5**
Speed ratings (Par 97): **93,90,89,87,86 84,82,81,80,79 77,73,70,67**
CSF £72.03 CT £436.06 TOTE £5.20: £2.50, £4.30, £2.30; EX 79.40 Place 6 £154.29, Place 5 £77.97..
Owner Mrs H Thomson Jones **Bred** Mrs H T Jones **Trained** Lambourn, Berks
■ A first winner for Katia Scallan.

FOCUS
A moderate race but it was won by an unexposed sort who is clearly well ahead of the Handicapper.
T/Jkpt: Not won. T/Plt: £108.10 to a £1 stake. Pool: £84,013.81. 567.09 winning tickets. T/Qpdt: £23.20 to a £1 stake. Pool: £4,031.90. 128.10 winning tickets. SP

3066 - 3069a (Foreign Racing) - See Raceform Interactive

2174 CORK (R-H)
Sunday, June 15

OFFICIAL GOING: Good to firm

3070a KERRY GROUP NOBLESSE STKS (F&M) (GROUP 3) 1m 4f
4:40 (4:41) 3-Y-0+ **£47,794** (£10,294; £10,294; £2,205)

RPR

1 **Ice Queen (IRE)**[9] 2792 3-8-9 88 .... CO'Donoghue 10 105+
(A P O'Brien, Ire) *trckd ldrs: prog to ld 1 1/2f out: rdn and swished tail continually fnl f: styd on wl: comf* **14/1**

2 1 3/4 **Profound Beauty (IRE)**[32] 2113 4-9-9 104 .... PJSmullen 3 101
(D K Weld, Ire) *towards rr: prog fr 3 out: rdn in 3rd over 1f out: wnt 2nd wout troubling wnr on line* **5/1**[1]

2 dht **Beach Bunny (IRE)**[28] 2225 3-8-9 99 .... CDHayes 4 102
(Kevin Prendergast, Ire) *towards rr: prog into 5th on outer 2 1/2f out: 2nd over 1f out: kpt on wout threatening wnr and jnd for 2nd on line* **5/1**[1]

4 2 1/2 **Nick's Nikita (IRE)**[49] 1655 5-9-12 106 .... RPCleary 7 100
(M Halford, Ire) *trckd ldrs in 3rd: rdn to dispute ld 2 1/2f out: hdd and no ex fr 1 1/2f out* **5/1**[1]

5 3/4 **Always Beautiful (USA)**[30] 2177 3-8-9 .... WMLordan 9 97
(David Wachman, Ire) *mid-div: prog into 4th 2 1/2f out: sn rdn: kpt on same pce* **6/1**[2]

6 1 1/4 **Galistic (IRE)**[220] 6367 5-9-9 100 .... DMGrant 5 94
(Patrick J Flynn, Ire) *trckd ldrs: rdn in 5th 4f out: kpt on same pce fr 2f out* **20/1**

7 1/2 **Love To Dance (IRE)**[4] 2964 3-8-9 56 .... JAHeffernan 6 94?
(A P O'Brien, Ire) *sn led: rdn and jnd 2 1/2f out: hdd 1 1/2f out: sn no ex* **16/1**

8 2 **Teacht An Earraig (USA)**[8] 2854 3-8-9 105 .... KJManning 2 91
(J S Bolger, Ire) *trckd ldrs: rdn and no imp fr 2 1/2f out: eased fnl f* **5/1**[1]

9 1 3/4 **Simawa (IRE)**[72] 1199 3-8-10 95 ow1 .... FMBerry 8 89
(John M Oxx, Ire) *settled in rr: effrt on inner early st whn nt clr run: bdly hmpd over 1f out: sn eased* **13/2**[3]

10 3 1/2 **Glowing (IRE)**[9] 2813 3-8-9 91 .... (t) DPMcDonogh 1 83
(Charles O'Brien, Ire) *trckd ldr in 2nd: rdn and wknd fr 2 1/2f out* **25/1**

2m 35.29s (-12.61)
WFA 3 from 4yo+ 15lb **10** Ran SP% **115.4**
PL: 4.40, Profound Beauty 2.00, Beach Bunny 1.90; Ex IQ/PB 27.40, IQ/BB 156.40; CSF IQ/PB 40.89, IQ/BB 40.89 TOTE £22.00.
Owner M Tabor, D Smith & Mrs John Magnier **Bred** March Thoroughbreds **Trained** Ballydoyle, Co Tipperary

NOTEBOOK
Ice Queen(IRE), who finished last after being deplyed as a pacemaker in the Oaks nine days previously, rather surprisingly came home to score in ready fashion on this drop in grade. This was by far her best effort to date and, while not one of her connections' better fillies, she could well have more to offer now her confidence should have been nicely boosted. This will have also significantly enhanced her paddock potential.
Profound Beauty(IRE) showed the benefit of the return to this extra distance and posted her best effort since finishing third to Peeping Fwan in last year's Irish Oaks. She ideally wants easier ground and her turn should not be far off when getting her favoured underfoot conditions once more. (op 5/1 tchd 11/2)
Beach Bunny(IRE), up in trip, has been progressive this season and this rates a career-best effort in defeat. She can go one better in this class, especially when ridden a little more positively again. (op 5/1 tchd 11/2)

3071 - 3072a (Foreign Racing) - See Raceform Interactive

2065 COLOGNE (R-H)
Sunday, June 15

OFFICIAL GOING: Good

3073a DIANA-TRIAL (EX SCHWARZGOLD-RENNEN) (GROUP 2) (FILLIES) 1m 3f
3:05 (3:16) 3-Y-0 **£29,412** (£11,029; £4,412; £2,941)

RPR

1 **Baila Me (GER)**[23] 3-9-0 .... DBoeuf 1 104
(W Baltromei, Germany) *racd in 2nd early: 3rd st: r.o fr over 1f out to ld fnl 100yds* **44/10**[3]

2 3/4 **Splash Mountain (IRE)**[24] 3-9-0 .... WMongil 5 103
(A Trybuhl, Germany) *set slow pce: jnd 1 1/2f out: rallied to ld again 1f out: hdd and no ex 100yds out* **40/1**

3 1 **Goathemala (GER)**[43] 3-9-0 .... MJKinane 4 101
(W Hickst, Germany) *racd in 5th: 4th st: kpt on steadily fnl 2f* **11/10**[1]

4 1/2 **Auentime (GER)**[42] 3-9-0 .... THellier 6 100
(Uwe Ostmann, Germany) *racd in 7th: 6th st: kpt on against ins rail fnl 2f* **5/1**

5 1 3/4 **Lady Siro (GER)**[35] 2030 3-9-0 .... EPedroza 2 97
(W Hickst, Germany) *racd in 3rd: wnt 2nd over 4f out: rdn to dispute ld 1 1/2f out: hdd 1f out: wknd* **153/10**

6 2 1/2 **Larella (GER)**[57] 3-9-0 .... MSuerland 8 93
(P Rau, Germany) *unruly bef s: led arnd rdrless bhd and into stalls: dropped out in last: 7th st: nvr a factor* **28/1**

7 7 **Servenya (GER)**[35] 2030 3-9-0 .... OPeslier 7 81
(J Hirschberger, Germany) *racd in 4th: dropped bk to last ent st: sn rdn: no rspnse* **28/10**[2]

8 1/2 **La Peinture (GER)**[35] 2030 3-9-0 .... ADeVries 3 80
(W Hickst, Germany) *racd in 6th: 5th st: sn wknd* **94/10**

2m 20.71s (-0.09) **8** Ran SP% **130.8**
TOTE: WIN 54; PL 17, 54, 14; SF 1607.
Owner Gestut Karlshof **Bred** Gestut Karlshof **Trained** Germany

3074a 173RD OPPENHEIM-UNION-RENNEN (GROUP 2) 1m 3f
4:15 (4:38) 3-Y-0 **£44,118** (£16,912; £8,824; £3,676)

RPR

1 **Liang Kay (GER)**[34] 2066 3-9-2 .... THellier 4 101
(U Ostmann, Germany) *disp last: 7th st: str run down outside to ld 150yds out: r.o wl* **36/10**[2]

2 1 3/4 **Little Fighter (GER)**[42] 3-9-2 .... J-PCarvalho 9 98
(H Blume, Germany) *racd in 2nd: ev ch 150yds out: kpt on* **177/10**

3 1 **Akiem (IRE)**[25] 3-9-2 .... WMongil 3 96
(Andreas Lowe, Germany) *racd in 5th: styd on wl fnl f to take 3rd on line* **83/10**

4 shd **Daressalam (GER)**[34] 3-9-2 .... ADeVries 6 96
(W Hickst, Germany) *reluctant ldr: set slow pce: hdd 150yds out: one pce: lost 3rd on line* **21/10**[1]

5 1/2 **Albahri (FR)**[21] 2441 3-9-2 .... DBoeuf 7 95
(M Delzangles, France) *racd in 4th: rdn over 1f out: one pce* **67/10**

6 2 **Duellant (IRE)**[42] 3-9-2 .... MJKinane 5 92
(P Schiergen, Germany) *cl up: 3rd st: one pce fnl 2f* **11/2**

7 2 **Santero (GER)**[34] 3-9-2 .... JLermyte 1 88
(N Sauer, Germany) *last st: nvr a factor* **42/1**

8 hd **Agapanthus (GER)**[24] 3-9-2 .... OPeslier 2 88
(J Hirschberger, Germany) *nvr a factor* **53/10**[3]

9 4 **All The Winds (GER)**[24] 3-9-2 .... EPedroza 8 81
(A Wohler, Germany) *a towards rr* **61/10**

2m 19.97s (-0.83) **9** Ran SP% **130.8**
TOTE: WIN 46; PL 19, 28, 24; SF 763.
Owner Stall Emina **Bred** Frau I Zimmermann **Trained** Germany

2744 SAN SIRO (R-H)
Sunday, June 15

OFFICIAL GOING: Heavy

3075a GRAN PREMIO DI MILANO (GROUP 1) 1m 4f
3:15 (3:22) 3-Y-0+ **£105,882** (£46,588; £25,412; £12,706)

RPR

1 **Quijano (GER)**[49] 1666 6-9-7 .... AStarke 4 113
(P Schiergen, Germany) *hld up in 4th: wnt 2nd 5f out: drvn over 1f out: led 150yds out: r.o wl* **4/6**[1]

2 1 1/4 **Voila Ici (IRE)**[35] 2028 3-8-6 .... MDemuro 1 111
(V Caruso, Italy) *trckd clr ldr to 5f out: cl 4th st: styd on fnl 2f to take 2nd cl home*

3 snk **Gimmy (IRE)**[35] 2027 4-9-7 .... DVargiu 3 111
(B Grizzetti, Italy) *led: 6l clr to st: stl 3l up 2f out: ct 150yds out: lost 2nd cl home*

4 3 **Dickens (GER)**[49] 1662 5-9-7 .... JVictoire 2 107
(H Blume, Germany) *racd in 6th to 1/2-way: 5th st: nvr nr to chal*

5 3 **Permesso**[35] 2028 3-8-6 .... LDettori 7 102
(F & L Camici, Italy) *racd in 5th: 6th st: rdn and btn 2f out*

6 1 1/4 **Rockmaster (IRE)**[35] 2027 5-9-7 .... URispoli 5 100
(G Pucciatti, Italy) *last to st: nvr a factor*

7 15 **Sopran Promo (IRE)**[14] 2656 4-9-7 .... PConvertino 6 78
(B Grizzetti, Italy) *3rd st: wknd over 2f out*

2m 34.7s (3.20)
WFA 3 from 4yo+ 15lb **7** Ran SP% **60.0**
TOTE: WIN 1.67; PL 1.35, 2.31; SF 12.79.
Owner Stiftung Gestut Fahrhof **Bred** Stiftung Gestt Fahrhof **Trained** Germany

NOTEBOOK
Quijano(GER) gained a deserved reward for some excellent performances around the world. This was his first important appearance on a testing surface and he responded well when driven to catch the front-running Gimmy. It was his first win since the Grosser Preis von Baden last September and that race will be his next objective. He will continue to follow last year's programme through the Canadian International and the Hong Kong Vase.

Voila Ici(IRE), a staying-on fifth in the Derby Italiano last time, appreciated the extra furlong of this race. He will not run again until the autumn but should find a decent prize then.
Permesso, who had finished in front of Voila Ici when second in the Derby, was never going well. However Dettori reported that he thought something was wrong before the straight and the colt might have tweaked a muscle in his back.

3076a OAKS D'ITALIA (GROUP 2) (FILLIES) 1m 3f
4:35 (5:02) 3-Y-O £132,353 (£58,235; £31,765; £15,882)

RPR
1 **Goose Bay (GER)**^{35} [2030] 3-8-11 .... AStarke 2 104
(P Schiergen, Germany) *a.p: 6th st: led over 2f out: rdn clr over 1f out: drvn out*
2 5 1/2 **Counterclaim**^{51} [1608] 3-8-11 .... JVictoire 14 95
(H-A Pantall, France) *a.p: 3rd st: jnd ldrs on outside 3f out: hrd rdn 2f out: kpt on same pce*
3 nse **Dancing Abbie (USA)**^{18} [2505] 3-8-11 .... HayleyTurner 5 95
(M L W Bell) *dwlt: settled towards rr: 16th st: hdwy fr over 2f out: styd on to jst miss 2nd*
4 1 1/4 **Presbyterian Nun (IRE)**^{36} [1991] 3-8-11 .... LDettori 13 93
(J L Dunlop) *hld up: 13th st: hdwy 3f out: styd on u.p to take 4th on line*
5 nse **Gerika (FR)**^{36} 3-8-11 .... NPinna 12 93
(A & G Botti, Italy) *trckd ldr: 2nd st: wknd jst over 2f out but kpt on to the end*
6 1 1/4 **Ragiam (ITY)**^{21} [2439] 3-8-11 ....(b) URispoli 8 91
(A & G Botti, Italy) *a.p: 4th st: hrd rdn and disp 2nd on rails 2f out: sn btn*
7 1 1/4 **Miss Galileo (IRE)**^{28} [2231] 3-8-11 .... MMonteriso 1 89
(L Camici, Italy) *in rr to st: last wl over 2f out: styd on fnl 1 1/2f: nvr a factor*
8 1/2 **Radhakunda**^{21} [2439] 3-8-11 .... GForte 15 88
(S Billeri, Italy) *mid-div: brought wd st: rdn and btn over 2f out*
9 3 **Belle Isnarde (IRE)**^{36} 3-8-11 .... MDemuro 3 83
(V Caruso, Italy) *mid-div: hdwy on ins over 2f out: btn over 1f out*
10 4 **Maiepoimai (IRE)** 3-8-11 .... NMurru 4 77
(M Gasparini, Italy) *replated in paddock: mid-div: 7th st: btn over 2f out*
11 2 **Sensazione World (IRE)**^{14} 3-8-11 .... SUrru 7 74
(B Grizzetti, Italy) *cl up to st: wknd over 2f out*
12 1 3/4 **Try Me (UAE)**^{39} [1915] 3-8-11 .... DarryllHolland 17 71
(C E Brittain) *a in rr*
13 3/4 **Cutter**^{36} 3-8-11 .... SebSanders 6 70
(M Gasparini, Italy) *5th st: wknd over 2f out*
14 hd **Short Affair**^{28} [2231] 3-8-11 .... FBranca 18 69
(M Gasparini, Italy) *a bhd*
15 5 **Melody Break (USA)**^{28} [2231] 3-8-11 .... SLandi 11 61
(A & G Botti, Italy) *led to over 2f out: eased*
16 2 **Polenta (ITY)**^{45} 3-8-11 .... MEsposito 9 58
(F & L Camici, Italy) *bhd fnl 2f*
17 2 1/2 **Tremoto**^{21} [2439] 3-8-11 .... OFancera 10 54
(F & L Camici, Italy) *7th st: btn over 2f out*
18 nse **Defaillance (IRE)**^{28} [2231] 3-8-11 .... MSanna 16 54
(M Gasparini, Italy) *a bhd*
19 8 **Fairy Efisio**^{28} [2231] 3-8-11 .... DVargiu 19 41
(B Grizzetti, Italy) *nvr nrr than mid-div: bhd fr over 2f out*

2m 20.3s (1.70) 19 Ran
WIN 4.41; PL 1.94, 3.01, 6.00; DF 30.52.
Owner Gestut Ebbesloh **Bred** Gestut Ebbesloh **Trained** Germany

FOCUS
There was plenty of rain between the Gran Premio and the Oaks. The official description of heavy had been questioned after Quijano's success but it was nearer that mark by the time of the classic.

NOTEBOOK
Goose Bay(GER) completed a Schiergen-Starke Group 1 double with a commanding performance. She will be hard to beat in the Preis der Diana (German Oaks) on August 3, particularly if the ground is soft again.
Counterclaim, whose form included two seconds on the Polytrack at Wolverhampton last autumn when in the care of Saeed Bin Suroor, was hurried along on the outside to go up to third at the end of the back straight. She was no match for the winner in the last 2f and was fortunate to hang on to second prize.
Dancing Abbie(USA) missed a beat at the start - perhaps intentionally - and was allowed to settle with only two or three behind her. Her prospects seemed minimal until she picked up well in the final quarter-mile and she would have been second in another stride.
Presbyterian Nun(IRE), the best supported of the three English runners, was well back until in the straight but responded to pressure to claim fourth on the line.
Try Me(UAE), encountering testing ground for the first time, never improved on her position at the back of the field.

^{2657}CARLISLE (R-H)
Monday, June 16

OFFICIAL GOING: Good to firm (good in places)
Wind: Cloudy, bright Weather: Fresh, half against

3077 ANDIDRAIN CLAIMING STKS 1m 1f 61y
2:15 (2:15) (Class 6) 3-Y-O+ £2,047 (£604; £302) Stalls High

Form RPR
-243 1 **Little Jimbob**^{19} [2499] 7-9-8 71 .... JamieMoriarty$^{(3)}$ 13 79
(R A Fahey) *mde all: rdn over 2f out: hld on wl fnl f* 7/2^{1}
-504 2 nk **Lauro**^{53} [1577] 8-8-4 55 .... DawnRankin$^{(7)}$ 5 64
(Miss J A Camacho) *in tch: hdwy over 1f out: chsd wnr ins fnl f: kpt on fin* 12/1
2036 3 2 1/2 **Inside Story (IRE)**^{14} [2672] 6-9-9 68 ....(b) PaulMulrennan 12 71
(M W Easterby) *cl up: effrt and ch over 1f out: sn rdn: no ex ins fnl f* 9/2^{2}
0103 4 3 **Rowan Lodge (IRE)**^{14} [2667] 6-9-4 64 ....(b) TomEaves 2 59
(Ollie Pears) *in tch: effrt and edgd rt over 1f out: no imp fnl f* 9/1
3242 5 3/4 **Black Falcon (IRE)**^{8} [2867] 8-9-2 59 .... PJMcDonald$^{(3)}$ 10 59
(John A Harris) *bhd tl hdwy over 1f out: nvr rchd ldrs* 7/2^{1}
-056 6 3 3/4 **Contemplation**^{5} [2940] 5-9-7 56 .... RobertWinston 8 53
(G A Swinbank) *dwlt: hld up: rdn and sme hdwy over 1f out: n.d* 5/1^{3}
0004 7 1/2 **Roman History (IRE)**^{20} [2487] 5-9-4 55 ....(p) TonyHamilton 3 49
(Miss Tracy Waggott) *chsd ldrs tl rdn and wknd wl over 1f out* 40/1
00-5 8 1 1/2 **Josephine Malines**^{18} [2536] 4-9-0 70 .... RoystonFfrench 9 42
(Mrs A Duffield) *t.k.h: towards rr: rdn and drifted rt over 1f out: nvr on terms* 8/1
55-0 9 12 **Awaken**^{24} [2365] 7-9-4 52 .... DeanMcKeown 1 21
(Miss Tracy Waggott) *hld up: rdn 3f out: sn btn* 20/1
100- 10 31 **Fadansil**^{266} [5676] 5-9-4 48 .... PaulFessey 4 —
(J Wade) *cl up: rdn 3f out: sn btn* 33/1

1m 57.06s (-0.54) **Going Correction** +0.10s/f (Good)
WFA 3 from 4yo+ 11lb 10 Ran SP% **118.2**
Speed ratings (Par 101): **106,105,103,100,100 96,96,95,84,56**
CSF £46.88 TOTE £3.90: £1.40, £5.10, £1.50; EX 34.20.
Owner Dale Scaffolding Co Ltd **Bred** D R Tucker **Trained** Musley Bank, N Yorks

FOCUS
A moderate contest. The form looks sound with the winner putting in a fair effort for the grade, rated to his form when winning this race last year.
Josephine Malines Official explanation: jockey said filly ran too free early on

3078 DONLEYS MAIDEN AUCTION STKS 5f 193y
2:45 (2:46) (Class 5) 2-Y-O £2,729 (£806; £403) Stalls High

Form RPR
342 1 **Favourite Girl (IRE)**^{10} [2783] 2-8-7 0 .... DavidAllan 12 77
(T D Easterby) *chsd ldrs: shkn up to ld over 1f out: kpt on wl fnl f* 11/8^{1}
2 1/2 **Kyllachy Star** 2-8-12 0 .... TonyHamilton 2 80+
(R A Fahey) *prom: shkn up and rn green over 2f out: hdwy over 1f out: kpt on wl fnl f: jst hld* 10/1
352 3 3 **Metroland**^{18} [2522] 2-8-7 0 .... GregFairley 6 66
(M Johnston) *led to over 1f out: kpt on same pce u.p* 11/4^{2}
4 hd **Inheritor (IRE)** 2-9-2 0 .... TomEaves 9 75+
(B Smart) *bhd: hdwy over 2f out: kpt on fnl f: nrst fin* 8/1^{3}
5 1/2 **The Kyllachy Kid** 2-8-12 0 .... MickyFenton 10 70+
(T P Tate) *s.i.s: bhd tl hdwy over 1f out: nrst fin* 16/1
305 6 6 **Fitzolini**^{9} [2845] 2-8-9 0 .... PaulMulrennan 5 47
(A D Brown) *cl up tl rdn and wknd fr 2f out* 20/1
7 nk **Classic Contours (USA)** 2-9-2 0 .... RobertWinston 8 53
(G A Swinbank) *hld up: drvn 1/2-way: nvr rchd ldrs* 9/1
8 1/2 **Inventing Paradise** 2-8-6 0 .... GrahamGibbons 11 42
(J D Bethell) *loose bef s: bhd and sn outpcd: no ch fr 1/2-way* 33/1
0 9 22 **Captain Bradz (USA)**^{29} [2217] 2-8-11 0 .... PaulFessey 7 —
(P T Midgley) *prom tl rdn and wknd over 2f out: eased whn no ch fnl f* 100/1

1m 14.17s (0.47) **Going Correction** +0.10s/f (Good) 9 Ran SP% **113.5**
Speed ratings (Par 93): **100,99,95,95,94 86,86,85,56**
CSF £15.99 TOTE £2.00: £1.10, £2.50, £1.40; EX 17.10.
Owner Peter C Bourke **Bred** Limestone And Tara Studs **Trained** Great Habton, N Yorks

FOCUS
A modest juvenile contest but a fair race of its type which could have been rated a bit higher. The winner built on her steadily progressive form.

NOTEBOOK
Favourite Girl(IRE), who showed improved form for the step up to 6f when second at Doncaster last time, was always likely to be suited by the stiff, uphill finish and she eventually got on top. Very much a nursery type, she will appreciate an extra furlong in time and it will be interesting to see what mark she is given by the Handicapper. (op 2-1 tchd 5-4)
Kyllachy Star, related to numerous winners, is bred to be effective at this distance and he made a highly satisfactory debut, closing right in on the winner as they passed the line. He will require an extra furlong before too long and looks to have a future. (op 7-1)
Metroland comes from a yard who have an excellent record with their juveniles at this course and she has looked to be crying out for this extra furlong. She ran well, possibly finding the stiff finish a bit too much having made the running, but is beginning to look exposed. (op 9-4 tchd 7-2)
Inheritor(IRE), whose dam won at up to 2m, has more speed on his sire's side and he made a pleasing start back in fourth, keeping on well close home. An extra furlong will benefit in time. (tchd 13-2)
The Kyllachy Kid, by a sprinter out of a mare who won over 1m4f, comes from a yard whose juveniles often need a run and as a result this has to go down as a pleasing first effort. He was clear of anything else and should learn from the experience/appreciate an extra furlong. (tchd 14-1)

3079 TELFORD HART ASSOCIATES - CONSTRUCTION COST CONSULTANTS H'CAP 5f 193y
3:15 (3:18) (Class 6) (0-60,60) 3-Y-O+ £2,047 (£604; £302) Stalls High

Form RPR
4300 1 **Avontuur (FR)**^{7} [2891] 6-9-7 56 ....(b) DaleGibson 8 67
(Mrs R A Carr) *hld up: gd hdwy fr 2f out: led ins fnl f: kpt on wl* 14/1
3036 2 1 3/4 **Wiltshire (IRE)**^{35} [2040] 6-9-7 56 ....(v) MickyFenton 15 61
(P T Midgley) *hld up ins: gd hdwy to press wnr ins fnl f: kpt on same pce towards fin* 14/1
-601 3 hd **Botham (USA)**^{5} [2936] 4-9-6 55 6ex .... DanielTudhope 5 59+
(J S Goldie) *racd wd in midfield: effrt and hdwy over 1f out: edgd rt ins fnl f: nrst fin* 4/1^{1}
0-05 4 nk **Brigadore**^{7} [2891] 9-9-6 55 .... J-PGuillambert 12 58
(J G Given) *midfield: hdwy and chsng ldrs whn carried rt and swtchd over 1f out: kpt on ins fnl f* 17/2^{3}
-044 5 2 1/4 **Orotund**^{10} [2780] 4-8-11 49 .... DuranFentiman$^{(3)}$ 2 45
(T D Easterby) *chsd ldr: effrt and rdn over 2f out: one pce fnl f* 10/1
0-00 6 1 1/2 **Roman Quintet (IRE)**^{38} [1966] 8-9-6 55 .... DeanMcKeown 13 46
(A J McCabe) *led: rdn and edgd rt over 1f out: hdd ins fnl f: no ex* 10/1
20-0 7 hd **Slip Star**^{35} [2038] 5-9-1 50 .... GregFairley 16 41
(T J Etherington) *in tch: drvn whn hmpd over 1f out: no ex* 20/1
00S- 8 1/2 **Orphan (IRE)**^{343} [3381] 6-9-8 60 .... PJMcDonald$^{(3)}$ 6 49
(G M Moore) *midfield: drvn over 2f out: no imp over 1f out* 20/1
-344 9 1 **Maison Dieu**^{27} [2285] 5-9-5 54 ....(b) DavidAllan 14 40
(E J Alston) *s.i.s: hdwy 1/2-way: nvr rchd ldrs* 11/2^{2}
0020 10 3/4 **Desert Hunter (IRE)**^{5} [2936] 5-8-11 46 .... RobertWinston 10 30
(Micky Hammond) *bhd and sn pushed along: n.d* 9/1
-300 11 1 3/4 **Attacca**^{45} [1775] 7-8-13 48 .... DO'Donohoe 4 26
(J R Weymes) *midfield: drvn fr 1/2-way: outpcd fnl 2f* 25/1
00 12 2 **Phinerine**^{146} [256] 5-8-9 47 ....(e) MichaelJStainton$^{(3)}$ 11 19
(Miss J E Foster) *bhd and sn rdn along: nvr rchd ldrs* 40/1
6500 13 5 **Social Rhythm**^{83} [1015] 4-9-6 60 .... NeilBrown$^{(5)}$ 7 16
(A C Whillans) *bhd and sn outpcd: nvr on terms* 14/1
0-00 14 1/2 **Stormy Journey**^{14} [2661] 3-8-10 52 ....(p) TomEaves 9 6
(Mrs K Walton) *in tch tl rdn and wknd 2f out* 33/1
06-0 15 3/4 **Steph The Ref**^{5} [2928] 3-8-5 54 .... FrederikTylicki$^{(7)}$ 17 6
(R A Fahey) *chsd ldrs tl wknd fr 2f out* 33/1
00-0 16 6 **Jellytot (USA)**^{8} [2866] 5-9-0 49 .... TonyHamilton 1 —
(J O'Reilly) *prom tl rdn and wknd 2f out* 33/1
00-0 17 15 **Monte Cassino (IRE)**^{60} [1429] 3-8-11 53 ....(b^{1}) PaulMulrennan 3 —
(J O'Reilly) *racd wd in midfield: drvn and lost tch fr over 2f out* 50/1

1m 14.06s (0.36) **Going Correction** +0.10s/f (Good)
WFA 3 from 4yo+ 7lb 17 Ran SP% **120.7**
Speed ratings (Par 101): **101,98,98,98,95 93,92,92,90,89 87,84,78,77,76 68,48**
CSF £174.97 CT £970.83 TOTE £16.30: £3.10, £3.70, £1.50, £2.30; EX 216.40.
Owner David W Chapman **Bred** Haras D'Etreham **Trained** Stillington, N Yorks
■ Stewards' Enquiry : Dean McKeown three-day ban: careless riding (Jun 30-Jul 2)

FOCUS
A most competitive handicap sprint, although the form is only moderate. A clear personal best from Avontuur.

3080 LAKELAND WILLOW WATER H'CAP 5f
3:45 (3:45) (Class 5) (0-70,69) 3-Y-0+ **£4,533** (£1,348; £674; £336) **Stalls** High

Form RPR
0505 **1** **Kings College Boy**[7] 2892 8-8-10 **55**....................(b) JamieMoriarty(3) 14 68
(R A Fahey) *midfield: drvn 1/2-way: hdwy over 1f out: kpt on wl to ld towards fin* **9/1**
0364 **2** ½ **Whinhill House**[24] 2356 8-9-5 **61**...............................(v) TonyHamilton 17 72
(D W Barker) *set str gallop: rdn over 1f out: kpt on: hdd and no ex towards fin* **12/1**
0014 **3** 1 ½ **Just Joey**[5] 2928 4-9-6 **62**...(b) DO'Donohoe 15 68
(J R Weymes) *towards rr and sn pushed along: gd hdwy over 1f out: r.o fnl f: nrst fin* **12/1**
11-0 **4** ½ **Nomoreblondes**[27] 2270 4-9-12 **68**...........................(p) MickyFenton 2 72+
(P T Midgley) *racd wd: cl up: effrt and edgd rt over 1f out: kpt on same pce ins fnl f* **25/1**
-160 **5** 1 ¾ **Invincible Lad (IRE)**[37] 2009 4-8-11 **53**.................. AdrianTNicholls 6 51+
(E J Alston) *midfield: nt clr run briefly 2f out: swtchd lft and effrt over 1f out: one pce fnl f* **8/1**
6502 **6** ¾ **Darcy's Pride (IRE)**[10] 2777 4-9-8 **64**.......................... RobertWinston 7 59
(D W Barker) *chsd ldrs: drvn over 2f out: no ex over 1f out* **15/2[3]**
-000 **7** 1 ½ **Fern House (IRE)**[11] 2748 6-8-8 **50** oh5.......................... TWilliams 11 39
(Bruce Hellier) *bhd tl kpt on fnl f: nvr rchd ldrs* **66/1**
3032 **8** hd **Killer Class**[14] 2676 3-9-2 **64**.. DanielTudhope 12 51
(J S Goldie) *bhd and pushed along: hdwy over 1f out: nvr nrr* **10/1**
14-0 **9** 1 **Choisette**[14] 2676 3-9-5 **67**... TomEaves 9 50
(B Smart) *sn drvn towards rr: no imp fr 1/2-way* **14/1**
0601 **10** ½ **Windjammer**[10] 2777 4-9-12 **68**...(b) DavidAllan 5 51
(T D Easterby) *disp ld tl wknd appr fnl f* **6/1[2]**
00-0 **11** 1 ½ **Inspainagain (USA)**[9] 2843 4-9-7 **68**............................. NeilBrown(5) 3 46
(T D Barron) *midfield: drvn over 2f out: sn no ex* **11/1**
3132 **12** 2 **Mineral Rights (USA)**[11] 2748 4-9-9 **65**............................(v) PaulFessey 4 36
(Miss L A Perratt) *cl up tl rdn and wknd over 1f out* **7/2[1]**
0600 **13** ½ **Miacarla**[5] 2928 5-8-10 **52**....................................... PatrickMathers 1 21
(H A McWilliams) *midfield: rdn over 2f out: wknd over 1f out* **50/1**
-500 **14** 1 ½ **Argentine (IRE)**[21] 2444 4-9-4 **60**...........................(tp) PaulMulrennan 13 23
(L Lungo) *sn outpcd and drvn along: nvr on terms* **20/1**
00-0 **15** 2 ½ **The Thrifty Bear**[11] 2751 5-8-3 **50** oh5......................(b) KellyHarrison(5) 16 —
(C W Fairhurst) *prom tl rdn and wknd fr 2f out* **50/1**

60.87 secs (0.07) **Going Correction** +0.10s/f (Good)
WFA 3 from 4yo+ 6lb **15 Ran SP% 122.9**
Speed ratings (Par 103): **103,102,99,99,96 95,92,92,90,89 87,84,83,81,77**
CSF £109.18 CT £863.33 TOTE £13.60: £3.30, £2.90, £4.40; EX 80.90 Trifecta £221.10 Part won. Pool: £298.81. 0.60 winning units..
Owner The Cosmic Cases **Bred** Lady Jennifer Green **Trained** Musley Bank, N Yorks

FOCUS
Any number looked in with a chance and Kings College Boy got well on top close home. Straightforward form.

3081 EDINBURGH WOOLLEN MILL FILLIES' H'CAP 6f 192y
4:15 (4:19) (Class 5) (0-70,66) 3-Y-0 **£2,590** (£770; £385; £192) **Stalls** High

Form RPR
05-0 **1** **Umverti**[35] 2041 3-8-9 **54**.. GrahamGibbons 3 59
(N Bycroft) *hld up: hdwy wl over 1f out: led ins fnl f: styd on strly* **16/1**
0-60 **2** 1 ¾ **Welcome Return (IRE)**[30] 2209 3-9-5 **64**..........................(b) DavidAllan 2 64
(T D Easterby) *prom: led and edgd lft 2f out: hdd ins fnl f: kpt on same pce* **9/1**
-342 **3** ½ **Wiseman's Diamond (USA)**[43] 1823 3-9-7 **66**............ MickyFenton 12 65
(P T Midgley) *prom: drvn and outpcd over 3f out: rallied over 1f out: kpt on fnl f* **6/1[2]**
0600 **4** 1 ¾ **Miss Understanding**[28] 2247 3-8-2 **47**.......................... DO'Donohoe 13 41
(J R Weymes) *bhd tl hdwy over 1f out: kpt on fnl f: no imp* **25/1**
-000 **5** hd **Piverina (IRE)**[14] 2660 3-8-4 **52**..................................... AndrewMullen(3) 10 46
(Miss J A Camacho) *bhd: drvn 1/2-way: hdwy fnl f: nrst fin* **7/1[3]**
20-5 **6** 2 ¼ **Habbie Heights**[21] 2466 3-8-13 **58**.............................. DarrenWilliams 11 46+
(R Bastiman) *dwlt: drvn in rr over 3f out: effrt and edgd rt 2f out: sn no imp: nt rch ldrs and eased ins fnl f* **16/1**
-430 **7** 1 **Kyllis**[38] 1952 3-9-2 **61**.. TomEaves 9 46
(B Smart) *led 2f: cl up tl rdn and wknd over 1f out* **11/1**
4005 **8** 1 ¾ **Kool Katie**[10] 2805 3-9-0 **59**.. DaleGibson 4 39
(Mrs G S Rees) *t.k.h: trckd ldrs: effrt whn n.m.r briefly 2f out: sn no ex* **7/1[3]**
-602 **9** 3 ¾ **Chaenomeles (USA)**[14] 2659 3-9-3 **62**............................. GregFairley 6 32
(M Johnston) *cl up: led after 2f to 2f out: sn wknd* **7/2[1]**
-650 **10** 5 **Diamond Royal (IRE)**[19] 2496 3-9-6 **65**.........................(b[1]) JoeFanning 8 22
(E A L Dunlop) *plld hrd in rr: short-lived effrt 2f out: sn btn* **8/1**
0-00 **11** 11 **Strictly Elsie (IRE)**[6] 2911 3-9-2 **61**............................. PaulMulrennan 7 —
(J R Norton) *missed break: a wl bhd* **33/1**
10-0 **12** 7 **Coffee Cup (IRE)**[59] 1448 3-9-2 **61**............................. RobertWinston 5 —
(G A Swinbank) *unruly bef s: a bhd* **8/1**

1m 28.09s (0.99) **Going Correction** +0.10s/f (Good) **12 Ran SP% 120.6**
Speed ratings (Par 96): **98,96,95,93,93 90,89,87,83,77 64,56**
CSF £155.59 CT £992.36 TOTE £22.60: £5.60, £3.40, £2.10; EX 207.40.
Owner Mrs C M Whatley **Bred** N Bycroft **Trained** Brandsby, N Yorks

FOCUS
A very moderate fillies' handicap, and the form looks somewhat dubious. The winner is rated up 10lb on her poor 2yo form.
Umverti Official explanation: trainer said, regarding the improved form, that filly had benefited from its first run in seven months having blown up last time out at Redcar on 12th May
Habbie Heights Official explanation: jockey said bit slipped through filly's mouth
Strictly Elsie(IRE) Official explanation: jockey said filly missed break

3082 BAINES WILSON LLP H'CAP 7f 200y
4:45 (4:46) (Class 5) (0-70,67) 4-Y-0+ **£2,590** (£770; £385; £192) **Stalls** High

Form RPR
-604 **1** **Flying Valentino**[10] 2781 4-9-1 **64**................................ PJMcDonald(3) 9 72
(G A Swinbank) *midfield: hdwy 2f out: disp ld and edgd rt u.p ins fnl f: styd on to ld nr fin* **8/1**
5-05 **2** hd **Anthemion (IRE)**[11] 2749 11-8-2 **48** oh1............................. PaulFessey 1 55
(Mrs J C McGregor) *led: rdn over 2f out: hrd pressed fnl f: hdd nr fin* **20/1**
0334 **3** nse **Wind Shuffle (GER)**[14] 2662 5-9-0 **60**.......................... DanielTudhope 13 67
(J S Goldie) *in tch: effrt ins over 2f out: kpt on fnl f: hld cl home* **9/2[1]**
6001 **4** nk **Boy Dancer (IRE)**[14] 2662 5-8-10 **56**.......................... GrahamGibbons 12 62
(J J Quinn) *hld up ins: effrt and hdwy over 1f out: kpt on wl fnl f* **5/1[2]**
0/50 **5** 1 ¾ **Emirate Isle**[20] 2487 4-9-7 **67**.. RobertWinston 6 69+
(C Grant) *trckd ldrs: effrt and rdn 2f out: keeping on whn n.m.r ins fnl f: no ex* **16/1**
-030 **6** 2 **Emperor's Well**[14] 2662 9-8-9 **55**.. DaleGibson 7 52
(M W Easterby) *cl up tl rdn and no ex over 1f out* **12/1**
-633 **7** 1 ¼ **Oeuf A La Neige**[11] 2749 8-8-11 **57**.............................. DO'Donohoe 11 51
(Miss L A Perratt) *hld up: drvn over 2f out: kpt on fnl f: n.d* **11/2[3]**
-302 **8** 1 ¼ **Efidium**[14] 2658 10-8-11 **62**... NeilBrown(5) 8 53
(N Bycroft) *hld up: pushed along over 2f out: nvr rchd ldrs* **15/2**
-006 **9** ¾ **Farne Island**[14] 2662 5-8-6 **55**....................................... AndrewMullen(3) 5 44
(Micky Hammond) *sn pushed along in rr: nvr on terms* **11/1**
0102 **10** 1 ½ **Ghafeer (USA)**[18] 2537 4-8-12 **58**..(p) TomEaves 3 43
(B Ellison) *cl up: rdn and edgd lft 2f out: sn wknd* **11/1**
000- **11** ¾ **Multitude (IRE)**[241] 6310 4-8-12 **58**.................................... DavidAllan 10 41
(T D Easterby) *bhd: drvn over 3f out: sn btn* **20/1**
0343 **12** ½ **Buzzin'Boyzee (IRE)**[18] 2537 5-8-6 **52**.......................... TonyHamilton 4 34
(D W Barker) *prom tl wknd fr 2f out* **20/1**
06-0 **13** 5 **Mangano**[11] 2749 4-8-6 **52**... JoeFanning 2 21
(A Berry) *racd wd in midfield: edgd rt and wknd fr 2f out* **50/1**

1m 40.11s (0.11) **Going Correction** +0.10s/f (Good) **13 Ran SP% 119.6**
Speed ratings (Par 103): **103,102,102,102,100 98,97,96,95,93 93,92,87**
CSF £163.17 CT £840.25 TOTE £10.50: £3.20, £10.40, £1.90; EX 321.40.
Owner Adrian Butler **Bred** Helshaw Grange Stud Ltd **Trained** Melsonby, N Yorks
■ Stewards' Enquiry : Paul Fessey three-day ban: used whip with excessive frequency (Jun 30-Jul 2)

FOCUS
A modest but very competitive handicap. Sound form.

3083 DOBIES CUMBRIA, WORKINGTON, CARLISLE & PENRITH H'CAP 1m 6f 32y
5:15 (5:15) (Class 5) (0-70,69) 4-Y-0+ **£2,590** (£770; £385; £192) **Stalls** High

Form RPR
0212 **1** **Directa's Digger (IRE)**[3] 3007 4-9-1 **68**..........................(v) JackDean(5) 8 76+
(M J Scudamore) *hld up: stdy hdwy over 6f out: rdn to ld over 1f out: edgd rt: styd on wl* **11/8[1]**
1101 **2** 1 ¾ **Pegasus Prince (USA)**[13] 2707 4-8-13 **61**........................ TomEaves 2 65
(Miss J A Camacho) *prom: effrt 3f out: edgd rt u.p 2f out: chsd wnr ins fnl f: r.o* **9/2[2]**
3520 **3** 3 **Hugs Destiny (IRE)**[6] 2908 7-8-7 **55**..........................(t) AdrianTNicholls 4 55
(M A Barnes) *led to 1/2-way: drvn and ev ch over 1f out: no ex ins fnl f* **5/1[3]**
0535 **4** 1 ½ **Rocknest Island (IRE)**[23] 2393 5-8-7 **55**...............(v[1]) GrahamGibbons 1 53
(P D Niven) *t.k.h: cl up: led 1/2-way: sn clr: hdd over 1f out: no ex* **7/1**
00-6 **5** 10 **Firestorm (IRE)**[12] 2735 4-8-2 **50** oh5.............................. PaulFessey 7 34
(C W Fairhurst) *in tch: drvn and outpcd 6f out: n.d after* **28/1**
606 **6** 6 **Besi**[10] 2776 6-7-11 **50** oh4.. DanielleMcCreery(5) 6 26
(A Berry) *hld up: rdn over 4f out: sn btn* **25/1**
240 **7** 3 ½ **Evelith Regent (IRE)**[17] 2573 5-9-7 **69**.......................... RobertWinston 3 40
(G A Swinbank) *t.k.h: hld up: rdn over 4f out: sn wknd* **7/1**

3m 8.33s (0.83) **Going Correction** +0.10s/f (Good) **7 Ran SP% 109.2**
Speed ratings (Par 103): **101,100,98,97,91 88,86**
CSF £6.94 CT £20.03 TOTE £2.00: £1.10, £3.10; EX 8.20 Place 6: £364.98, Place 5: £177.94..
Owner I J Anderson **Bred** J Dorrian **Trained** Bromsash, Herefordshire

FOCUS
This was not a strong race and Directa's Digger was always doing enough. The form makes sense at face value.
Evelith Regent(IRE) Official explanation: jockey said gelding ran too free in the early stages
T/Jkpt: Not won. T/Plt: £264.50 to a £1 stake. Pool: £82,998.35. 229.00 winning tickets. T/Qpdt: £156.60 to a £1 stake. Pool: £3,619.83. 17.10 winning tickets. RY

2010 WARWICK (L-H)
Monday, June 16

OFFICIAL GOING: Good to firm (8.6)
Wind: Almost nil Weather: Fine

3084 RACING UK AMATEUR RIDERS' H'CAP 1m 4f 134y
6:40 (6:40) (Class 6) (0-60,60) 4-Y-0+ **£1,977** (£608; £304) **Stalls** Low

Form RPR
6-02 **1** **Kokkokila**[39] 1929 4-11-6 **59**... MrSWalker 13 66
(Lady Herries) *hld up in tch: rdn to ld jst over 1f out: r.o* **4/1[1]**
32-5 **2** nk **Twist Bookie (IRE)**[40] 31 8-10-12 **56**........................... MrBJToomey(5) 8 63
(S Lycett) *w ldr: rdn over 1f out: ev ch fnl f: r.o* **6/1[3]**
0443 **3** ¾ **Barbirolli**[7] 2884 6-10-11 **53**.................................... MrBenBrisbourne(3) 1 58
(W M Brisbourne) *hld up in mid-div: rdn and hdwy over 1f out: kpt on ins fnl f* **9/2[2]**
4550 **4** nk **Songmaster (USA)**[17] 2567 5-10-12 **58**.............................. MrKYates(7) 9 63
(A King) *hld up in mid-div: hdwy over 5f out: rdn over 2f out: kpt on ins fnl f* **8/1**
4003 **5** 1 **Summer Bounty**[19] 2512 12-10-5 **49**......................... MrJoshuaMoore(5) 4 52
(F Jordan) *stdd s: hld up in ins 2f out: rdn and styd on fnl f* **14/1**
2054 **6** ½ **Opera Writer (IRE)**[17] 2572 5-10-12 **56**..........(p) MrStephenHarrison(5) 6 59
(R Hollinshead) *s.i.s: sn hld up in mid-div: rdn and hdwy on ins wl over 1f out: swtchd rt wl ins fnl f: nt rch ldrs* **6/1[3]**
0-15 **7** 1 ¼ **Chapter (IRE)**[7] 2884 6-10-3 **49**...............................(p) MrOJMurphy(7) 10 50
(Mrs A L M King) *hld up and bhd: rdn and hdwy on outside whn hung lft 2f out: no imp fnl f* **17/2**
-500 **8** nk **Princely Ted (IRE)**[8] 2867 7-11-2 **55**................................ MrSDobson 2 55
(W Clay) *hld up in tch: rdn over 1f out: wknd ins fnl f* **16/1**
3000 **9** shd **General Flumpa**[19] 2513 7-10-10 **54**.............................. MissFCumani(5) 3 54
(Miss Tor Sturgis) *led: rdn and hdd jst over 1f out: wknd ins fnl f* **20/1**
510- **10** 13 **Converti**[27] 4015 4-10-7 **53**... MrECookson(7) 11 34
(H J Manners) *hld up towards rr: sme hdwy over 5f out: rdn and wknd wl over 3f out* **50/1**
000 **11** 8 **Heartsanddiamonds**[21] 2449 4-10-12 **54** ow4.............. MrMJJSmith(3) 7 23
(A W Carroll) *plld hrd: prom tl wknd over 3f out* **50/1**
0103 **12** 1 **Take A Mile (IRE)**[11] 1643 6-10-9 **55**...........................(p) MrEElliott(7) 12 22
(C Gordon) *s.i.s: hld up: hdwy on outside over 5f out: wknd 4f out* **22/1**
0/0- **13** 6 **Monash Lad (IRE)**[12] 4246 6-11-0 **60**........................(p) MissMBryant(7) 5 18
(P Butler) *t.k.h early: a towards rr* **40/1**

2m 46.51s (1.91) **Going Correction** -0.30s/f (Firm) **13 Ran SP% 116.4**
Speed ratings (Par 101): **82,81,81,81,80 80,79,79,79,71 66,65,62**
CSF £25.36 CT £111.23 TOTE £3.80: £1.80, £2.10, £2.00; EX 26.00.

Owner Lady Mary Mumford J Woodcock & J Cowdrey **Bred** Lady Mary & Group Captain A Mumford **Trained** Patching, W Sussex
■ Stewards' Enquiry : Mr B J Toomey two-day ban: used whip with excessive force (Jul 6,25)

FOCUS
This moderate handicap, confined to amateur riders, was run at just a steady early pace. It resulted in a very moderate winning time, even for a race like this, and the first pair came clear. Limited form.

3085 EUROPEAN BREEDERS' FUND MAIDEN FILLIES' STKS 5f
7:10 (7:12) (Class 5) 2-Y-O **£3,626** (£1,079; £539; £269) **Stalls** Centre

Form RPR
0 **1** **Cecily**[20] 2479 2-9-0 0 SebSanders 1 74
(Sir Mark Prescott) *chsd ldrs: rdn to ld 1f out: drvn out* **5/2**[2]
24 **2** *shd* **Stan's Cool Cat (IRE)**[16] 2627 2-9-0 0 NelsonDeSouza 7 74
(P F I Cole) *led: rdn and hdd 1f out: r.o* **6/4**[1]
3 *1 1/4* **Jargelle (IRE)** 2-9-0 0 LiamJones 8 69
(W J Haggas) *w ldr: rdn and ev ch 1f out: nt qckn towards fin* **8/1**[3]
4 *4 1/2* **Boho Chic** 2-9-0 0 JamesDoyle 10 53
(R M Beckett) *hld up in mid-div: hdwy 2f out: nt clr run and swtchd rt jst over 1f out: sn rdn: one pce* **14/1**
5 **5** *shd* **First Choice (IRE)**[8] 2865 2-9-0 0 NCallan 6 53
(K A Ryan) *s.i.s: sn w ldrs: rdn and ev ch over 1f out: wknd ins fnl f* **8/1**[3]
6 *3/4* **Caledonia Princess** 2-9-0 0 TPO'Shea 4 50
(P A Blockley) *s.i.s: carried rt sn after s: sme hdwy on outside whn hung lft fr over 1f out: no further prog* **50/1**
0 **7** *6* **Monte Mayor Eagle**[15] 2638 2-9-0 0 EdwardCreighton 5 28+
(D Haydn Jones) *uns rdr and galloped loose to s: outpcd* **50/1**
8 *1* **Varsa (IRE)** 2-9-0 0 AndrewElliott 9 25
(K R Burke) *chsd ldrs tl wknd 2f out* **20/1**
9 *4 1/2* **Sparkling Suzie** 2-9-0 0 RichardHughes 3 8
(R Hannon) *s.i.s: wnt rt sn after s: sn outpcd* **8/1**[3]
10 *18* **Lady Aoy (IRE)** 2-9-0 0 VinceSlattery 2 —
(D J Wintle) *s.s: fly-jmpd and wnt rt: a t.o* **66/1**

59.42 secs (-0.18) **Going Correction** -0.20s/f (Firm) **10 Ran SP% 118.7**
Speed ratings (Par 90): **93,92,90,83,83 82,72,71,63,35**
CSF £6.59 TOTE £4.20: £1.50, £1.10, £2.60; EX 8.10.
Owner C G Rowles Nicholson **Bred** Limestone And Tara Studs **Trained** Newmarket, Suffolk
■ Stewards' Enquiry : Nelson De Souza three-day ban: used whip with excessive frequency and without allowing time to respond (Jun 30-Jul 2)

FOCUS
An ordinary juvenile fillies' maiden. The form is just fair for the grade but should work out. The winner stepped forward from her debut but the winner has not progressed from hers.

NOTEBOOK
Cecily, seventh on debut at Leicester 20 days previously, proved all the rage in the betting ring and opened her account in dogged fashion. She is clearly improving, enjoyed the sound surface, and it would be a surprise were she not to improve again for this experience. (op 7-1)
Stan's Cool Cat(IRE) set the standard on the level of her previous two outings and she was produced with every chance on this drop back from 6f. She only just lost out and deserves to find an opening now, but will most likely have to stick to one of the smaller tracks if she is to go one better in this company. (op 10-11 tchd 13-8)
Jargelle(IRE), related to winners at up to 7f, knew her job and posted a pleasing debut display. Her stable continue in fine form and she should come on for this experience, with the likelihood of another furlong going to suit before that long. (op 14-1)
Boho Chic, whose dam was a multiple 5-6f winner at two, found some trouble in the home straight, but still showed enough to suggest she has a future and really should come on a bundle for this debut experience. (tchd 10-1)
Monte Mayor Eagle Official explanation: jockey said filly ran green
Sparkling Suzie Official explanation: jockey said filly was unsuited by the good to firm ground

3086 LETHEBY & CHRISTOPHER FILLIES' H'CAP 6f
7:40 (7:40) (Class 6) (0-65,65) 3-Y-O **£2,729** (£806; £403) **Stalls** Centre

Form RPR
5542 **1** **Leonid Glow**[23] 2399 3-9-6 64 FergalLynch 3 76+
(M Dods) *sltly hmpd s: hld up and bhd: hdwy on ins 2f out: sn rdn: led ins fnl f: drvn out* **11/4**[1]
65-0 **2** *nk* **Pretty Bonnie**[10] 2774 3-8-1 50 NataliaGemelova[(5)] 10 61
(A E Price) *racd keenly w ldrs: rdn to ld jst over 1f out: hdd ins fnl f: r.o* **25/1**
61-6 **3** *3 1/4* **Romantic Verse**[14] 2670 3-9-4 62 LiamJones 1 62
(W J Haggas) *wnt rt s: sn chsng ldrs: rdn wl over 1f out: no ex wl ins fnl f* **7/2**[2]
4322 **4** *3/4* **Regal Veil**[5] 2935 3-7-13 46 LukeMorris[(3)] 14 44
(S C Williams) *chsd ldrs on outside: c wd bnd over 2f out: rdn wl over 1f out: one pce fnl f* **7/1**[3]
5444 **5** *3/4* **Easy Wonder (GER)**[5] 2935 3-9-1 59 SebSanders 13 55+
(I A Wood) *hld up and bhd: rdn and hdwy over 1f out: no further prog fnl f* **8/1**
-503 **6** *1 1/4* **Miss Firefly**[33] 2099 3-9-0 63 MCGeran[(5)] 12 55
(R J Hodges) *w ldr: led 3f out: rdn and hdd jst over 1f out: wknd ins fnl f* **14/1**
5-00 **7** *3/4* **Swift Acclaim (IRE)**[14] 2660 3-8-7 51 AndrewElliott 7 40
(K R Burke) *led 3f: rdn and wknd wl over 1f out* **33/1**
-460 **8** *shd* **Arrabiata**[95] 873 3-8-2 46 JimmyQuinn 11 35
(C N Kellett) *s.i.s: bhd: rdn wl over 1f out: nvr nr ldrs* **50/1**
445 **9** *1/2* **Red Amaryllis**[16] 2616 3-9-7 65 RichardKingscote 6 52
(H J L Dunlop) *chsd ldrs: rdn over 2f out: sn wknd* **17/2**
-006 **10** *2 1/2* **Elizabeth's Quest**[8] 2864 3-8-9 53 CatherineGannon 9 32
(A W Carroll) *stmbld sltly s: sn mid-div: rdn over 2f out: wknd 1f out* **33/1**
5-04 **11** *5* **River N' Blues (IRE)**[16] 2602 3-9-5 63 AlanDaly 5 26
(Dr J R J Naylor) *mid-div: rdn over 1f out: sn edgd lft and struggling* **16/1**
0000 **12** *3 1/4* **Marysedge**[20] 2474 3-8-0 51 oh1 ow5 PatrickDonaghy[(7)] 8 —
(R Brotherton) *prom: pushed along over 2f out: wknd wl over 1f out* **80/1**
4650 **13** *12* **Alabama Spirit (USA)**[14] 2676 3-8-8 55 (b[1]) TolleyDean[(3)] 2 —
(J Balding) *hmpd s: nvr gng wl: a in rr* **14/1**

1m 11.47s (-0.33) **Going Correction** -0.20s/f (Firm) course record **13 Ran SP% 115.2**
Speed ratings (Par 94): **94,93,89,88,87 85,84,84,83,80 73,69,53**
CSF £80.60 CT £254.33 TOTE £2.90: £1.20, £5.60, £1.70; EX 98.10.
Owner M J K Dods **Bred** Mrs G C Stanley **Trained** Denton, Co Durham
■ Stewards' Enquiry : Natalia Gemelova four-day ban: used whip with excessive frequency down shoulder in forehand position (Jun 30-Jul 3)
Fergal Lynch two-day ban: used whip with excessive frequency down shoulder in forehand position (Jun 30, Jul 1)

FOCUS
A moderate fillies' handicap. The form looks fair with the first pair coming clear and the progressive winner up 9lb.
River N' Blues(IRE) Official explanation: jockey said filly was unsuited by the good to firm ground
Alabama Spirit(USA) Official explanation: jockey said filly lost action

3087 PRICEWATERHOUSECOOPERS H'CAP 7f 26y
8:10 (8:12) (Class 4) (0-80,80) 4-Y-O+ **£4,857** (£1,445; £722; £360) **Stalls** Low

Form RPR
0002 **1** **Gallantry**[6] 2905 6-9-4 80 TolleyDean[(3)] 1 88
(P Howling) *a.p: rdn to ld over 1f out: drvn out* **10/3**[2]
-023 **2** *1/2* **Magroom**[20] 2477 4-8-2 68 PatrickDonaghy[(7)] 7 75
(R J Hodges) *chsd ldr: ev ch over 1f out: sn rdn: kpt on* **20/1**
0522 **3** *hd* **Golden Desert (IRE)**[3] 2995 4-9-7 80 RichardHughes 3 86
(T G Mills) *stdd s: plld hrd towards rr: hdwy over 1f out: rdn and kpt on same pce fnl f* **2/1**[1]
52-2 **4** *nk* **Carmenero (GER)**[12] 2722 5-9-1 74 NCallan 4 80
(W R Muir) *hld up in tch: rdn over 1f out: kpt on same pce ins fnl f* **8/1**
0153 **5** *1 1/2* **Secret Night**[21] 2457 5-9-0 73 SebSanders 8 75
(C G Cox) *s.i.s: hld up in rr: rdn and hdwy over 1f out: no ex wl ins fnl f* **9/1**
0442 **6** *1* **H Harrison (IRE)**[10] 2778 8-9-4 77 AndrewElliott 2 76
(I W McInnes) *set stdy pce: pushed along over 2f out: carried hd high and hdd over 1f out: wknd ins fnl f* **8/1**
-023 **7** *1/2* **Champain Sands (IRE)**[9] 2841 9-8-9 68 JimmyQuinn 5 66
(E J Alston) *s.i.s: t.k.h towards rr: pushed along wl over 1f out: no rspnse* **16/1**
-542 **8** *2 1/2* **Hiccups**[41] 1891 8-9-2 75 FergalLynch 9 66
(M Dods) *t.k.h in mid-div: lost pl 3f out: bhd fnl 2f* **13/2**[3]

1m 23.29s (-1.31) **Going Correction** -0.30s/f (Firm) **8 Ran SP% 112.6**
Speed ratings (Par 105): **95,94,94,93,92 91,90,87**
CSF £62.37 CT £164.45 TOTE £3.50: £1.80, £6.60, £1.10; EX 95.60.
Owner The Circle Bloodstock I Limited **Bred** Cheveley Park Stud Ltd **Trained** Newmarket, Suffolk

FOCUS
A fair handicap, run at a modest early pace. It was a very moderate winning time for a race of its class.

3088 TWEENHILLS FARM AND STUD WARWICKSHIRE OAKS STKS (LISTED RACE) (F&M) 1m 2f 188y
8:40 (8:40) (Class 1) 4-Y-O+
£14,760 (£5,595; £2,800; £1,396; £699; £351) **Stalls** Low

Form RPR
5451 **1** **Ronaldsay**[9] 2820 4-8-12 99 RichardHughes 7 103
(R Hannon) *chsd ldr: led wl over 1f out: rdn and edgd lft 1f out: drvn out* **8/1**
0-56 **2** *nse* **Cosmodrome (USA)**[44] 1807 4-8-12 101 SebSanders 3 103
(L M Cumani) *chsd ldrs: rdn over 1f out: str chal ins fnl f: r.o* **9/2**[3]
4-23 **3** *6* **Miramare (GER)**[23] 2402 4-8-12 100 TPQueally 2 94
(A P Stringer) *racd keenly in ld: rdn and hdd wl over 1f out: hld whn hmpd 1f out: wknd* **15/8**[1]
2332 **4** *4* **Royal Fantasy (IRE)**[9] 2820 5-8-12 80 HayleyTurner 6 85
(J R Fanshawe) *hld up and bhd: rdn and short-lived effrt on ins over 1f out* **16/1**
4032 **5** *2 1/2* **Sweet Lilly**[25] 2325 4-8-12 103 TPO'Shea 4 81
(M R Channon) *hld up and bhd: rdn wl over 1f out: no rspnse* **11/4**[2]
4230 **6** *19* **Baylini**[93] 906 4-8-12 94 JamesDoyle 5 48
(Ms J S Doyle) *chsd ldrs tl rdn and wknd over 2f out* **8/1**
1- **7** *12* **Velma Kelly**[287] 5102 4-8-12 64 SaleemGolam 8 27
(W R Swinburn) *stdd s: hld up in rr: rdn and lost tch 3f out* **40/1**

2m 14.98s (-6.12) **Going Correction** -0.30s/f (Firm) course record **7 Ran SP% 110.2**
Speed ratings (Par 111): **110,109,105,102,100 87,78**
CSF £40.23 TOTE £6.80: £3.50, £2.20; EX 46.70.
Owner S P Tindall **Bred** Stowell Hill Ltd **Trained** East Everleigh, Wilts

FOCUS
A fair renewal of this fillies' Listed prize but the form is only ordinary for the grade. It was run at a solid pace and the first two pulled clear.

NOTEBOOK
Ronaldsay, whose previous best effort was when second over this trip in Listed company last season, showed real battling qualities to repel the runner-up at the business end and follow up her Doncaster handicap success nine days previously, significantly enhancing her potential paddock value. It is possible she could find some further improvement when sent over 1m4f in due course and her connections are now keen to look abroad for further black-type opportunities. (op 4-1)
Cosmodrome(USA) bounced right back to form with a gallant effort and only lost out by the smallest of margins. She looks to be approaching something like her best again now and, well clear of the remainder at the finish, can be placed by her canny trainer to gain compensation in this grade again before that long. (op 5-1)
Miramare(GER), well backed, had been placed in this grade on both her previous outings this term and came into this in great form. She ultimately paid for running too freely on the early lead, however, and was a sitting duck for the first pair at the business end. (op 5-2 tchd 7-4)
Royal Fantasy(IRE) was just beaten by today's winner in a handicap last time and was 18lb worse off here, so faced a stiff task. She is a consistent sort and she ran her race again. (op 20-1)
Sweet Lilly was a big disappointment as she had been running well in this sort of company, but her response when asked to make up her ground from off the pace was very limited and she can only be watched at present. This longer trip was not solely to blame. (op 9-4)
Baylini Official explanation: jockey said filly stopped very quickly

3089 INCHCAPE TOYOTA H'CAP 1m 2f 188y
9:10 (9:11) (Class 6) (0-65,64) 4-Y-O+ **£2,388** (£705; £352) **Stalls** Low

Form RPR
44-5 **1** **Constant Cheers (IRE)**[42] 1853 5-8-13 63 DavidProbert[(7)] 1 78
(W R Swinburn) *a.p: rdn to ld 1f out: r.o wl* **7/2**[2]
02 **2** *2 3/4* **Sceilin (IRE)**[24] 2352 4-8-7 50 (t) TPO'Shea 7 60
(J Mackie) *led: rdn and hdd 1f out: no ex: jst hld on for 2nd* **15/2**[3]
00 **3** *nse* **Ornella**[14] 2670 4-9-4 64 TravisBlock[(3)] 5 74+
(H Morrison) *t.k.h towards rr: hdwy 2f out: sn rdn: r.o ins fnl f: jst failed to take 2nd* **28/1**
0340 **4** *2 1/4* **Libre**[5] 2957 8-9-0 57 RichardHughes 4 63
(F Jordan) *hld up in mid-div: rdn and hdwy whn edgd lft jst over 1f out: one pce fnl f* **17/2**
5300 **5** *1/2* **Chia (IRE)**[33] 2097 5-9-4 61 (p) NCallan 16 66
(D Haydn Jones) *plld hrd towards rr: stdy hdwy over 5f out: rdn and one pce fnl f* **20/1**
00-0 **6** *hd* **Gallego**[10] 2770 6-9-2 62 KirstyMilczarek[(3)] 3 67+
(R J Price) *dwlt: hld up in rr: styd on fnl f: nrst fin* **16/1**
0001 **7** *1/2* **Inch Lodge**[19] 2512 6-9-5 62 (t) PaulEddery 11 66
(Miss D Mountain) *t.k.h: chsd ldr tl rdn over 1f out: wknd ins fnl f* **17/2**
16/2 **8** *shd* **Kangrina**[24] 2353 6-9-5 62 SebSanders 2 66+
(George Baker) *hld up towards rr: rdn and hdwy 2f out: one pce fnl f* **9/4**[1]
/0-0 **9** *4* **Sweet Seville (FR)**[17] 2571 4-8-7 50 AndrewElliott 9 46
(Mrs G S Rees) *hld up in mid-div: rdn 2f out: sn struggling* **66/1**

000- **10** 3½ **Woodygo**[369] 2552 4-8-6 **49**.. JimmyQuinn 12 39
(J R Best) *t.k.h in tch: pushed along over 3f out: rdn and wknd wl over 1f out* **25/1**

1-03 **11** ¾ **Moonlight Fantasy (IRE)**[24] 2374 5-9-1 **58**...................... TPQueally 14 47
(Lucinda Featherstone) *s.i.s: plld hrd towards rr: sme hdwy 6f out: lost pl over 3f out* **11/1**

-400 **12** ½ **The Flying Cowboy (IRE)**[20] 2483 4-9-4 **61**........... FrankieMcDonald 8 49
(Jane Chapple-Hyam) *a in rr* **33/1**

2000 **13** 4½ **Siena Star (IRE)**[5] 2949 10-9-3 **60**................................ MickyFenton 15 40
(Stef Liddiard) *hld up in mid-div: pushed along over 3f out: sn bhd* **16/1**

-006 **14** 3½ **Winter Cruise (IRE)**[110] 722 4-8-4 **47**........................ HayleyTurner 17 20
(Ian Williams) *a in rr* **33/1**

2m 17.3s (-3.80) **Going Correction** -0.30s/f (Firm) **14** Ran SP% **125.3**
Speed ratings (Par 101): **101,99,98,97,96 96,96,96,93,90 90,90,86,84**
CSF £29.01 CT £663.19 TOTE £4.30: £2.00, £2.60, £11.80; EX 35.90 Place 6: £70.46, Place 5: £47.90..
Owner Mr & Mrs W R Swinburn **Bred** Pendley Farm **Trained** Aldbury, Herts

FOCUS
A moderate handicap run 2.32 secs slower than the preceding Listed race and it proved difficult to get involved from off the pace. The form looks pretty sound for the grade and the winner is generally progressive.
Gallego Official explanation: jockey said gelding hung right
The Flying Cowboy(IRE) Official explanation: jockey said gelding was unsuited by the good to firm ground
T/Plt: £88.60 to a £1 stake. Pool: £63,274.54. 520.79 winning tickets. T/Qpdt: £106.10 to a £1 stake. Pool: £3,227.90. 22.50 winning tickets. KH

[2893] WINDSOR (R-H)
Monday, June 16
OFFICIAL GOING: Good to firm (good in places; 8.6)
Wind: Almost nil Weather: Fine but cloudy

3090 CITY INDEX H'CAP 1m 67y
6:30 (6:30) (Class 5) (0-75,78) 4-Y-0+ **£3,070** (£906; £453) **Stalls** High

Form RPR

-061 **1** **Dear Maurice**[7] 2897 4-9-10 **78** 6ex.. RyanMoore 9 91+
(E A L Dunlop) *hld up in midfield: n.m.r 1/2-way and swtchd to wd outside over 3f out: prog over 2f out: rdn to ld over 1f out: in command fnl f* **8/11**[1]

-031 **2** 1¾ **Willow Dancer (IRE)**[15] 2642 4-9-3 **71**............................(p) AdamKirby 6 80
(W R Swinburn) *hld up wl in rr: prog on outer fr 3f out: rdn to chse wnr jst over 1f out: kpt on but no imp* **14/1**

0305 **3** ½ **Aggravation**[7] 2897 6-8-13 **70**.. MarcHalford(3) 3 78
(D R C Elsworth) *hld up wl in rr: prog on outer over 2f out: styd on to take 3rd fnl f: nvr able to chal* **16/1**

0-03 **4** nk **Australia Day (IRE)**[7] 2897 5-9-0 **68**.......................... JimmyFortune 13 75
(P R Webber) *free to post: racd freely: mde most to over 1f out: sn outpcd: hanging lft but kpt on* **16/1**

-604 **5** ¾ **Rambling Light**[26] 2308 4-9-5 **73**.. LPKeniry 14 79
(A M Balding) *trckd ldng pair: eased off rail to try to chal wl over 1f out: nt qckn and btn fnl f* **14/1**

-264 **6** 3¼ **Effigy**[12] 2722 4-8-12 **66**.. DaneO'Neill 11 64
(H Candy) *dwlt: rousted up to midfield sn after s: rdn 3f out: outpcd over 1f out* **20/1**

6-23 **7** 1¾ **Last Sovereign**[16] 2619 4-9-7 **75**...................................... JohnEgan 1 69
(Jane Chapple-Hyam) *hld up in midfield: nt qckn whn short of room jst over 2f out: no prog after* **12/1**[3]

3201 **8** 1 **Bivouac (UAE)**[10] 2782 4-8-11 **65**.................................. KerrinMcEvoy 4 57
(G A Swinbank) *free to post: t.k.h: hld up in midfield: no prog whn bmpd 2f out* **10/1**[2]

6036 **9** 3½ **Master Mahogany**[15] 2642 7-8-13 **67**............................ SteveDrowne 12 51
(R J Hodges) *a in midfield: rdn and no prog 2f out: eased whn no ch ins fnl f* **25/1**

16-0 **10** 1¼ **Robert The Brave**[24] 2369 4-9-7 **75**................................ ChrisCatlin 10 56
(P R Webber) *sn detached in last: no prog tl passed wkng rivals fnl f* **50/1**

260- **11** nk **Le Chiffre (IRE)**[200] 6293 6-9-2 **70**...................................(p) PaulDoe 8 50
(S Curran) *trckd ldng pair: losing pl and btn whn bmpd 2f out* **50/1**

450 **12** nk **Danski**[31] 2152 5-9-7 **75**..(p) EddieAhern 2 54
(P J Makin) *w ldr to jst over 2f out: wkng qckly whn bmpd arnd sn after* **22/1**

4300 **13** 3½ **Border Edge**[24] 2353 10-7-13 **60** oh9 ow4.................. RossAtkinson(7) 7 31
(J J Bridger) *a wl in rr: rdn and no prog 3f out* **50/1**

06-0 **14** 2¼ **Namid Reprobate (IRE)**[16] 2619 5-9-7 **75**............................ TQuinn 5 41
(P F I Cole) *free to post: s.s: hld up in last pair: nvr a factor: eased whn no ch fnl f* **25/1**

1m 42.12s (-2.58) **Going Correction** -0.20s/f (Firm) **14** Ran SP% **122.5**
Speed ratings (Par 103): **104,102,101,101,100 97,95,94,91,89 89,89,85,83**
CSF £11.08 CT £105.92 TOTE £1.50: £1.10, £3.40, £3.50; EX 13.60.
Owner Abdul Rahman Al Khalifa **Bred** Sheikh Abdulla Bin Isa Al-Khalifa **Trained** Newmarket, Suffolk

FOCUS
A fair handicap and solid form, with Dear Maurice confirming his recent course superiority over a couple of rivals.
Namid Reprobate(IRE) Official explanation: jockey said gelding missed the break

3091 BMS SOLUTIONS (S) STKS 6f
7:00 (7:03) (Class 6) 2-Y-0 **£2,047** (£604; £302) **Stalls** High

Form RPR

0 **1** **Anacaona (IRE)**[60] 1413 2-8-6 0.. RyanMoore 2 58+
(R Hannon) *towards rr and off the pce: rdn and prog over 2f out: sustained effrt to ld fnl 150yds: drvn clr* **9/2**[2]

4413 **2** 2¼ **Come On Buckers (IRE)**[4] 2980 2-9-2 0........................ PatCosgrave 10 61
(P D Evans) *sn chsd ldr: rdn to cl fr 2f out: tried to chal 1f out: kpt on but sn outpcd by wnr* **2/1**[1]

6363 **3** nk **Kheley (IRE)**[19] 2508 2-8-7 0 ow1...................................... JohnEgan 4 51
(W M Brisbourne) *led and sn at least 2 l clr: grabbed nr side rail after 2f: hdd and outpcd fnl 150yds* **11/2**[3]

4 4 **Time For Old Time** 2-7-13 0.. SophieDoyle(7) 11 38
(I A Wood) *dwlt: wl in rr and off the pce: prog fr 2f out: rn green but styd on: nrst fin* **16/1**

00 **5** 1 **Tyler**[37] 2011 2-8-11 0.. TGMcLaughlin 6 40
(W M Brisbourne) *trckd ldrs: gng wl 1/2-way: rdn 2f out: wandered over 1f out: fdd* **50/1**

0332 **6** 1¾ **Makaluna**[7] 2882 2-8-4 0.. WilliamCarson(7) 13 35
(W G M Turner) *cl up on inner: rdn over 2f out: wknd over 1f out* **7/1**

4005 **7** 6 **Forzando Bloom**[21] 2450 2-8-8 0.................................. KevinGhunowa(3) 5 17
(R A Harris) *chsd ldrs: rdn bef 1/2-way: wknd rapidly over 1f out* **66/1**

8 1¼ **Hold The Bucks (USA)** 2-8-11 0................................ SimonWhitworth 9 13
(J S Moore) *s.s: nvr on terms: no ch fnl 2f* **25/1**

5020 **9** 4½ **Crewezando**[14] 2671 2-8-11 0................................(v) StephenDonohoe 12 —
(P D Evans) *chsd ldrs to 1/2-way: wknd rapidly* **12/1**

0 **10** 6 **Kosama**[6] 2916 2-8-6 0.. SamHitchcott 7 —
(M R Channon) *dwlt: reluctant and sn drvn: a bhd* **10/1**

6 **11** 4 **Rhydian**[74] 1168 2-8-6 0..(b[1]) JackMitchell(5) 3 —
(R M Beckett) *nvr beyond midfield: wknd 1/2-way: wl bhd 2f out* **17/2**

1m 14.0s (1.00) **Going Correction** -0.025s/f (Good) **11** Ran SP% **119.9**
Speed ratings (Par 91): **92,89,88,83,81 79,71,69,63,55 50**
CSF £14.01 TOTE £3.70: £1.60, £1.40, £2.30; EX 11.10.The winner was bought in for £6,000.
Owner J A Lazzari **Bred** Yeomanstown Stud **Trained** East Everleigh, Wilts
■ Stewards' Enquiry : William Carson caution: used whip with excessive frequency

FOCUS
A reasonable juvenile seller, with the runner-up setting the standard. The winner proved her debut all wrong.

NOTEBOOK
Anacaona(IRE) failed to beat a rival when sent off favourite on her debut over 5f at Kempton back in April, but she was a different proposition on this drop in grade over an extra furlong, making light of a two-month break. She won going away and might be a little bit better than this level. (op 5-1 tchd 4-1)
Come On Buckers(IRE), with the visor left off on this drop in trip, was conceding weight all round, so this was a solid effort in defeat. (op 9-4 tchd 5-2)
Kheley(IRE), carrying 1lb overweight, had every chance if good enough and this was a respectable effort. (op 6-1 tchd 13-2)
Time For Old Time ◆, by Olden Times, out of a mare who was placed in a 5f Windsor maiden on her only start at two, caught the eye on her racecourse debut, keeping on well after running green. With the benefit of this experience, she should prove very hard to beat if kept to this grade next time. (tchd 20-1)
Tyler, a stablemate of the third, appreciated the drop in grade but still found a few too good.

3092 SUNSEEKER EBF MAIDEN STKS 5f 10y
7:30 (7:31) (Class 4) 2-Y-0 **£4,403** (£1,310; £654; £327) **Stalls** High

Form RPR

34 **1** **Finnegan McCool**[25] 2338 2-9-3 0................................ GeorgeBaker 6 81
(R M Beckett) *chsd clr ldrs: clsd fr 1/2-way: rdn to ld jst over 1f out: styd on wl: readily* **7/1**

5 **2** 1 **My Sweet Georgia (IRE)**[16] 2627 2-8-12 0...................... MichaelHills 8 72
(B W Hills) *dwlt: hld up in midfield: prog whn nt clr run briefly jst over 2f out: chsd wnr fnl f: clsd but nvr able to chal* **1/1**[1]

33 **3** ¾ **Like For Like (IRE)**[5] 2944 2-8-12 0.................................... PatDobbs 4 69
(R Hannon) *racd freely: mde most to jst over 1f out: one pce* **7/2**[2]

4 2¾ **Snoqualmie Girl (IRE)** 2-8-12 0.. TQuinn 5 59
(D R C Elsworth) *s.s: pushed along in last and wl off the pce: styd on encouragingly fnl 2f: nrst fin* **22/1**

5 3 **Barnezet (GR)** 2-8-12 0.. RyanMoore 3 49
(R Hannon) *towards rr: effrt on outer 1/2-way: sme prog but hung lft fr 2f out: wknd fnl f* **5/1**[3]

6 ½ **Louie's Lad** 2-9-3 0.. DaneO'Neill 2 52
(J A Geake) *chsd clr ldng pair to 1/2-way: edgd lft sn after: fdd over 1f out* **50/1**

0 **7** shd **Mr Willis**[7] 2893 2-9-3 0.. LPKeniry 1 51
(J R Best) *dwlt: nvr beyond midfield or on terms w ldrs: fdd over 1f out* **25/1**

8 6 **One Cool Quest (IRE)** 2-8-10 0................................ SophieDoyle(7) 9 30
(P A Blockley) *dwlt: a outpcd in last pair* **40/1**

0 **9** 10 **Applehays**[25] 2338 2-8-5 0.. WilliamCarson(7) 7 —
(W G M Turner) *w ldr to 1/2-way: wknd rapidly: t.o* **100/1**

60.76 secs (0.46) **Going Correction** -0.025s/f (Good) **9** Ran SP% **115.0**
Speed ratings (Par 95): **95,93,92,87,83 82,82,72,56**
CSF £14.02 TOTE £8.20: £2.10, £1.10, £1.50; EX 17.00.
Owner Lawrence & Wilkinson **Bred** D J And Mrs Deer **Trained** Whitsbury, Hants

FOCUS
An ordinary juvenile maiden which has been rated through the winner and third.

NOTEBOOK
Finnegan McCool failed to confirm the promise he showed on his debut at Goodwood when only fourth at Salisbury on his previous start, but this was a lot better. His trainer thinks he'll get 6f, but might let him take his chance in the Super Sprint. (op 9-1)
My Sweet Georgia(IRE) was well backed to improve on the form she showed when fifth on her debut at York, but she found one too good. (op 11-10 tchd 5-4)
Like For Like(IRE) raced a little freely on this return to the minimum trip but this was still a fair effort. (op 10-3)
Snoqualmie Girl(IRE) ◆ is a daughter of Montjeu, sister to smart 1m2f winner Snoqualmie Boy, so it was a real surprise to see her started off over this trip, and she ran very encouragingly considering. She can improve with both time and distance. (op 16-1 tchd 14-1)
Barnezet(GR), a 30,000gns daughter of Invincible Spirit, first foal of a multiple sprint winner, did not help her chance by hanging left towards the centre of the track and she looked in need of the experience. (tchd 9-2)

3093 VIRGIN H'CAP 6f
8:00 (8:01) (Class 4) (0-80,80) 4-Y-0+ **£5,051** (£1,503; £751; £375) **Stalls** High

Form RPR

1135 **1** **Dressed To Dance (IRE)**[10] 2781 4-8-7 **66** ow1..........(v) PatCosgrave 2 78
(P D Evans) *hld up in last trio: prog 2f out: shuffled along and r.o to ld fnl 100yds: sn clr: readily* **9/1**

0634 **2** 1¾ **China Cherub**[10] 2773 5-9-2 **75**..(b) RyanMoore 10 81
(S Dow) *racd against nr side rail: mde most: drvn 2f out: hdd and readily outpcd fnl 100yds* **10/3**[1]

-000 **3** 2¼ **Makabul**[28] 2242 5-8-8 **67**.. KerrinMcEvoy 3 66
(B R Millman) *chsd ldng pair: disp 2nd 1f out: sn outpcd* **14/1**

0002 **4** ½ **Alfresco**[9] 2837 4-8-13 **72**..(v) WilliamBuick 5 70
(I A Wood) *hld up in last trio: sme prog 2f out: n.m.r over 1f out: hanging sn after and kpt on one pce* **7/1**[3]

0-06 **5** 1½ **Scarlet Oak**[16] 2622 4-8-3 **62** oh1 ow1.................................. ChrisCatlin 7 55
(D J S Ffrench Davis) *nvr beyond midfield: u.p on over over 2f out: no real prog* **12/1**

6-00 **6** 1½ **Don Pele (IRE)**[11] 2760 6-9-3 **79**..............................(p) KevinGhunowa(3) 11 67
(R A Harris) *s.i.s: sn chsd ldrs: edgd lft under presusre fr 2f out and fdd* **12/1**

0223 **7** ¾ **Stamford Blue**[2] 3024 7-9-2 **80**................................(b) HaddenFrost(5) 6 66
(R A Harris) *w ldr to over 2f out: wknd over 1f out* **13/2**[2]

4036 **8** *3* **Kensington (IRE)**[13] 2693 7-9-2 75 (p) StephenDonohoe 4 51
(P D Evans) *a wl in rr: u.p and struggling sn after 1/2-way* **20/1**

-615 **9** *5* **Buy On The Red**[8] 2860 7-9-0 73 RichardMullen 8 33
(W R Muir) *a in last trio and sn struggling* **10/1**

1610 **10** *3 1/4* **Halsion Chancer**[9] 2831 4-9-7 80 JohnEgan 1 30
(J R Best) *chsd ldrs: rdn wl over 2f out: wknd rapidly wl over 1f out* **8/1**

1m 11.84s (-1.16) **Going Correction** -0.025s/f (Good) **10** Ran SP% **105.9**
Speed ratings (Par 105): **106,103,100,100,98 96,95,91,84,80**
CSF £32.46 CT £316.36 TOTE £10.30: £2.60, £1.70, £4.80; EX 44.00.
Owner Premier Cru Racing **Bred** John Doyle **Trained** Pandy, Monmouths
■ Eau Good was withdrawn on vet's advice (8/1, deduct 10p in the £ under Rule 4).

FOCUS
A fair little sprint handicap contested by a field of experienced handicappers and a few characters - six of the ten runners were sporting some sort of headgear. Ordinary form, with an improved run from the winner.
Stamford Blue Official explanation: jockey said gelding had no more to give
Buy On The Red Official explanation: jockey said gelding was never travelling
Halsion Chancer Official explanation: jockey said gelding lost action

3094 CLARENDON MAIDEN STKS — 1m 2f 7y
8:30 (8:32) (Class 5) 3-Y-0+ — **£2,729** (£806; £403) **Stalls** Centre

Form / RPR

3- **1** **Speed Ticket**[254] 6005 4-9-12 0 DaneO'Neill 12 82+
(L M Cumani) *trckd ldrs: effrt over 2f out: drvn to ld 1f out: hld on wl nr fin* **4/1**[3]

5 **2** *1/2* **Crusoe's Return**[24] 2370 3-8-9 0 AshleyHamblett(5) 13 81+
(L M Cumani) *dwlt: rchd midfield bef 1/2-way: prog on outer over 2f out: rdn to chal fnl f: pressed wnr but jst hld* **40/1**

0- **3** *1/2* **Woodcutter (IRE)**[311] 4362 3-9-0 0 JimmyFortune 14 80
(J H M Gosden) *led after 3f: drvn 2f out: hdd and nt qckn 1f out: kpt on u.p* **11/2**

42 **4** *2 1/4* **Hunting Country**[20] 2488 3-9-0 0 DarryllHolland 8 75
(M Johnston) *led 3f: pressed ldr: rdn over 2f out: nt qckn over 1f out: fdd ins fnl f* **9/4**[1]

5 **5** *1/2* **Hendersyde (USA)**[16] 2612 3-9-0 0 AdamKirby 16 74
(W R Swinburn) *wl in tch bhd ldrs: effrt 3f out: carried lft over 1f out: one pce* **16/1**

6 *hd* **Optimus Maximus (IRE)** 3-9-0 0 TQuinn 9 74
(P F I Cole) *trckd ldrs: pushed along over 3f out: effrt over 2f out: hung lft over 1f out: fdd* **14/1**

7 *1 1/2* **Ibn Qutaiba (USA)** 3-9-0 0 LDettori 5 71+
(Saeed Bin Suroor) *settled midfield: shkn up and struggling 4f out and sn in rr: sme prog 2f out: no imp over 1f out* **7/2**[2]

0 **8** *7* **Dixie Dean (USA)**[14] 2681 3-9-0 0 RyanMoore 7 57
(Sir Michael Stoute) *wl in rr: shkn up and adrift 3f out: modest late prog* **16/1**

00 **9** *3 1/2* **Tank Commander**[14] 2669 3-9-0 0 RichardMullen 11 50
(W R Muir) *wl in tch in midfield tl wknd 3f out* **100/1**

0 **10** *1* **Alkyoni (IRE)**[11] 2763 3-8-9 0 JohnEgan 2 43
(Jane Chapple-Hyam) *a wl in rr: pushed along and struggling 4f out* **100/1**

00 **11** *nk* **Catholic Hill (USA)**[11] 2763 3-9-0 0 EddieAhern 3 47+
(B J Meehan) *prom: pushed along over 3f out: wknd rapidly over 2f out: eased* **100/1**

12 *3 3/4* **Tuxedo** 3-9-0 0 ChrisCatlin 1 40
(P W Hiatt) *s.s: a in last trio: wl bhd 3f out* **100/1**

13 *5* **High Lady** 3-8-9 0 WilliamBuick 6 25
(C R Egerton) *restless stalls and dwlt: a in last pair: wl bhd fnl 3f* **66/1**

R **Red Rock Prince (IRE)** 3-9-0 0 KerrinMcEvoy 4 —
(P F I Cole) *hld up in midfield: 8th whn rn off the crse bnd over 5f out* **11/1**

2m 7.15s (-1.55) **Going Correction** -0.20s/f (Firm)
WFA 3 from 4yo+ 12lb **14** Ran SP% **123.0**
Speed ratings (Par 103): **98,97,97,95,95 94,93,88,85,84 84,81,77,—**
CSF £170.25 TOTE £5.70: £2.00, £11.20, £2.00; EX 139.50.
Owner Ronchalon Racing (UK) Ltd **Bred** Fittocks Stud **Trained** Newmarket, Suffolk

FOCUS
A one-two for Luca Cumani in what is potentially a decent maiden, run in a time 0.26 seconds slower than the following three-year-old handicap. A few of these have improvement in them and the form should work out.

3095 MCGEE GROUP H'CAP — 1m 2f 7y
9:00 (9:00) (Class 5) (0-70,70) 3-Y-0 — **£2,729** (£806; £403) **Stalls** Centre

Form / RPR

0440 **1** **Closertobelieving**[14] 2678 3-9-7 70 TQuinn 15 81
(D R C Elsworth) *dwlt: hld up wl in rr: swtchd to outer and prog 3f out: rdn 2f out: r.o to ld fnl 150yds: won gng away* **7/2**[1]

0-03 **2** *2* **Latin Scholar (IRE)**[21] 2451 3-9-2 65 FergusSweeney 1 72
(A King) *trckd ldng pair: effrt to go 2nd over 2f out: drvn to ld briefly 1f out: outpcd by wnr* **16/1**

5-06 **3** *3/4* **Striving (IRE)**[16] 2603 3-8-11 60 (v[1]) RyanMoore 11 66
(Sir Michael Stoute) *racd keenly: led after 3f out: drvn and hdd 1f out: outpcd* **7/1**[2]

1233 **4** *1 1/4* **Kyrie Eleison (IRE)**[28] 2244 3-9-4 67 DaneO'Neill 16 70
(R Hannon) *trckd ldrs: rdn and effrt over 2f out: kpt on same pce fr over 1f out* **7/2**[1]

0-50 **5** *1 1/2* **Ministerofinterior**[23] 2413 3-8-11 65 JackMitchell(5) 9 65
(C F Wall) *in tch in midfield: rdn and no imp over 2f out: kpt on fr over 1f out: nvr able to chal* **25/1**

5-63 **6** *1/2* **Dusk**[25] 2342 3-9-0 63 EddieAhern 12 62
(J L Dunlop) *in tch: prog on inner over 3f out: chsd ldrs 2f out: no ex over 1f out* **8/1**[3]

6-06 **7** *2* **Spent**[10] 2805 3-9-0 63 ChrisCatlin 2 58
(Mouse Hamilton-Fairley) *hld up wl in rr: prog over 4f out: chsd ldrs 2f out: wknd over 1f out* **50/1**

1-00 **8** *hd* **Cossack Prince**[31] 2151 3-9-7 70 RobertHavlin 3 65
(B J Meehan) *plld hrd: trckd ldrs: rdn over 2f out: hung lft and wknd over 1f out* **16/1**

5-03 **9** *nse* **Nordic Commander (IRE)**[17] 2559 3-9-2 65 StephenDonohoe 14 60
(E A L Dunlop) *dwlt: wl in rr: no prog 3f out: modest late hdwy* **16/1**

0-00 **10** *hd* **Havanavich**[25] 2342 3-9-2 65 GeorgeBaker 10 59
(S Kirk) *wl in tch in midfield: rdn and lost pl over 2f out: n.d after* **25/1**

0-24 **11** *1 3/4* **Tara's Garden**[21] 2451 3-9-2 65 SteveDrowne 6 56
(M Blanshard) *wl in rr: wd bnd 5f out: sme prog on wd outside 3f out: nvr on terms: wknd fnl f* **20/1**

050 **12** *shd* **De Facto**[23] 2413 3-9-4 67 JimmyFortune 7 57
(J H M Gosden) *dwlt: wl in rr: rdn and taken towards outer over 2f out: no real prog* **8/1**[3]

52-0 **13** *8* **Broughtons Flight (IRE)**[22] 2429 3-9-3 66 JohnEgan 5 40
(W J Musson) *a in rr: wd bnd 5f out: wknd 3f out: bhd after* **12/1**

0-00 **14** *11* **Dancing Marabout (IRE)**[17] 2564 3-9-3 66 (b[1]) WilliamBuick 8 18
(C R Egerton) *t.k.h: led 3f: w ldr to 3f out: wknd rapidly: t.o* **33/1**

423 **F** **Nags To Riches (IRE)**[112] 698 3-9-1 67 JerryO'Dwyer(3) 13 —
(J A Osborne) *wl in rr tl broke leg and fell 2f out: dead* **12/1**

2m 6.89s (-1.81) **Going Correction** -0.20s/f (Firm) **15** Ran SP% **129.6**
Speed ratings (Par 99): **99,97,96,95,94 94,92,92,92,92 90,90,84,75,—**
CSF £67.29 CT £396.33 TOTE £4.50: £2.50, £4.00, £3.10; EX 93.30 Place 6: £23.34, Place 5: £16.37..
Owner Gordon Li **Bred** Cheveley Park Stud Ltd **Trained** Newmarket, Suffolk
■ Castlebury was withdrawn (100/30, no suitable jockey available.) New market formed. Rule 4 does not apply.

FOCUS
A typically competitive Windsor three-year-old handicap and the winning time was 0.26 seconds faster than the preceding maiden. The form is pretty solid but with the exception of the winner the race lacked progressive types.
Dusk Official explanation: jockey said gelding lost action
Tara's Garden Official explanation: jockey said filly hung left
T/Plt: £45.00 to a £1 stake. Pool: £84,492.28. 1,369.60 winning tickets. T/Qpdt: £27.70 to a £1 stake. Pool: £4,842.90. 129.20 winning tickets. JN

3096 - 3099a (Foreign Racing) - See Raceform Interactive

1980 ASCOT (R-H)
Tuesday, June 17

OFFICIAL GOING: Good to firm (straight course 10.8; round course 8.9; overall 9.7)
Dolling out added 12yards to race distances on the round course.
Wind: Moderate, half against

3100 QUEEN ANNE STKS (GROUP 1) — 1m (S)
2:30 (2:37) (Class 1) 4-Y-0+
£154,698 (£58,642; £29,348; £14,633; £7,330; £3,678) **Stalls** Centre

Form / RPR

6 **1** **Haradasun (AUS)**[31] 2193 5-9-0 JMurtagh 10 123
(A P O'Brien, Ire) *swtg: prom on rail: rdn over 2f out: disp ld over 1f out: slt ld thrght fnl f: all out* **5/1**[2]

3-22 **2** *hd* **Darjina (FR)**[30] 2238 4-8-11 CSoumillon 5 120
(A De Royer-Dupre, France) *lw: hld up in midfield: rdn and hdwy 2f out: str chal and almost level w wnr fnl 200yds: r.o wl: jst hld* **5/1**[2]

5-52 **3** *3/4* **Finsceal Beo (IRE)**[23] 2432 4-8-11 KJManning 6 118
(J S Bolger, Ire) *hld up in tch: rdn over 2f out: disp ld and hung lft over 1f out: kpt on: hld by first 2 fnl 100yds* **9/2**[1]

0-14 **4** *nk* **Cesare**[31] 2193 7-9-0 118 JamieSpencer 3 121+
(J R Fanshawe) *dwlt: hld up towards rr: effrt whn nt clr run and bmpd ins fnl 2f: running on whn blocked ins fnl f: swtchd lft and nowhere to go: swtchd rt and r.o wl nr fin* **15/2**[3]

0-63 **5** *nk* **Mount Nelson**[9] 2876 4-9-0 JAHeffernan 2 120+
(A P O'Brien, Ire) *lw: prom: rdn over 2f out: squeezed out over 1f out: rallied and kpt on fnl f* **33/1**

5-31 **6** *nk* **Sageburg (IRE)**[30] 2238 4-9-0 (t) OPeslier 11 119
(A De Royer-Dupre, France) *lw: t.k.h: hld up towards rr: effrt over 2f out: drvn to press ldrs over 1f out: one pce* **15/2**[3]

-331 **7** *1/2* **Spirito Del Vento (FR)**[9] 2876 5-9-0 C-PLemaire 7 118
(J-M Beguigne, France) *swtg: hld up towards rr: effrt over 2f out: nt pce to chal* **20/1**

16-5 **8** *1* **Arabian Gleam**[31] 2193 4-9-0 114 SebSanders 4 116+
(J Noseda) *swtg: in tch: outpcd whn tempo qcknd and dropped to rr 3f out: trying to rally whn bmpd over 1f out: unable to rcvr position* **16/1**

15-3 **9** *nk* **Tariq**[31] 2193 4-9-0 115 JimmyFortune 1 115
(P W Chapple-Hyam) *dwlt: bhd: mod effrt over 2f out: n.d* **5/1**[2]

-140 **10** *shd* **Linngari (IRE)**[80] 1090 6-9-0 RyanMoore 8 115+
(Sir Michael Stoute) *swtg: t.k.h: trckd ldrs: rdn over 2f out: sing to lose pl whn bdly squeezed over 1f out: nt rcvr* **12/1**

3-00 **11** *2 3/4* **Honoured Guest (IRE)**[34] 2106 4-9-0 DavidMcCabe 9 109+
(A P O'Brien, Ire) *lw: led and set modest pce: crossed to stands' rail after 1f: rdn and increased tempo 3f out: hdd and btn whn squeezed over 1f out: eased whn wl hld fnl f* **100/1**

1m 38.98s (-1.62) **Going Correction** +0.125s/f (Good) **11** Ran SP% **114.0**
Speed ratings (Par 117): **113,112,112,111,111 111,110,109,109,109 106**
toteswinger: 1&2 £5.30, 1&3 £6.60, 2&3 £4.60. CSF £28.70 CT £121.94 TOTE £6.60: £2.70, £1.10, £2.40; EX 32.90 Trifecta £165.40 Pool: £13,453.65. 60.17 winning units..
Owner F Tagg/Mrs Magnier/F Meduri/G Moffitt **Bred** Arch Of Gold Syndicate Et Al **Trained** Ballydoyle, Co Tipperary
■ Stewards' Enquiry : K J Manning two-day ban: careless riding (Jul 1-2); 2nd incident three-day ban: careless riding (Jul 3,4,6)
J Murtagh three-day ban: used whip with excessive frequency down shoulder in forehand position (Jul 1-3)

FOCUS
A competitive renewal in which there looked no one outstanding candidate, and the tight finish seemed to confirm that impression. It was something of a tactical affair, not run at a strong gallop throughout, and the form may not be the most reliable with several looking unlucky. Haradasun got a better run than most, and the second and third ran close to their form in last year's French Guineas.

NOTEBOOK
Haradasun(AUS) was solid in the market beforehand, in contrast to before the Lockinge, when he clearly needed the run. He got a nice lead from his stablemate Honoured Guest, but if anything could probably have done with a stronger pace as he hit a flat spot three furlongs out, just as he did at Newbury, before picking up again and taking advantage of the gap left by his stablemate next to the rail. He stayed on strongly in the closing stages, always looking to be just holding Darjina close home, and one got the impression that in a stronger-run race he would have won even more easily. Connections had suggested beforehand that he would be retired to stud back in Australia after this race, and that was confirmed soon afterwards. (tchd 9-2 and 11-2 in places)
Darjina(FR), who had seen her chance compromised by softish ground on her two previous visits here, had conditions to suit this time and ran right up to her best. A stronger pace would probably have suited her, but she stuck her neck out in willing fashion and was only narrowly denied. Apparently the plan is now to go for the Falmouth Stakes. (tchd 11-2 and 6-1 in a place)
Finsceal Beo(IRE), backed into favouritism on this drop back in trip, is a tough sort who has only run one bad race in her life when the ground has been good to firm or faster. She too could have done with a stronger pace and connections are now planning to step her back up to 1m2f, despite the fact that she has yet to really impress over that sort of distance. (op 13-2 tchd 8-1 in a place and 7-1 in places)

Cesare, successful in four of his previous six visits to Ascot, is the type who needs plenty of luck in running as he has to be brought with a late challenge from off the pace. With the field coming up the stands'-side rail there was always the danger that he would not get a clear run, and with the tactical pace also not suiting those held up, that is what happened. He could be seen swinging away from two furlongs out, but he had to wait for a gap and it was not until well inside the last that he got into the clear. While he looked unlucky he is now 0-4 in Group 1 company, and has still to be placed at the top level. It is unlikely that he is improving at the age of seven, and he is likely to continue to find one or two too good in this grade. (op 7-1)

Mount Nelson, who did not run badly in France last time, was sent off an unconsidered 33-1 shot here, but he shaped with considerable promise. Caught in a sandwich between his stablemates as Haradasun made his move on the rail and Honoured Guest weakened, he never really got a chance to throw down a challenge, but this former Group 1 winner looks as though he is returning to his best.

Sageburg(IRE), supplemented into this race, had not run on ground this quick before. He could not get cover from his wide draw and raced keenly in the early stages so was probably not seen at his best in this rather tactical event. (op 13-2 tchd 8-1 in a place)

Spirito Del Vento(FR), another who was stuck out wide, could not confirm form with Mount Nelson from a Group 3 race in France nine days earlier. He might need softer ground to be seen at his best. (op 25-1)

Arabian Gleam shaped a bit better than his finishing position suggests, as he got bumped about towards the back of the field when staying on under pressure inside the final two furlongs. He is probably not up to this class, though. (op 20-1)

Tariq, third in the Lockinge, was unable to confirm Newbury form with any of the three who finished behind him that day. He was held up in a tactical affair and made his challenge widest of all, but he did not convince as a miler and hopefully he will now be dropped back to 7f or perhaps 6f. (tchd 11-2 in places)

Linngari(IRE) was well placed in what was quite a tactical affair but he was unable to take advantage. This was his first outing since returning to his original trainer Sir Michael Stoute and he should come on for the run. (op 10-1 tchd 9-1)

Honoured Guest(IRE) did his job for his stablemate and set the pace for him on the stands' rail before edging off it and letting him through.

3101 KING'S STAND STKS (BRITISH LEG OF THE GLOBAL SPRINT CHALLENGE) (GROUP 1) 5f

3:05 (3:10) (Class 1) 3-Y-O+

£141,925 (£53,800; £26,925; £13,425; £6,725; £3,375) **Stalls** Centre

Form RPR

3-2 **1** **Equiano (FR)**[16] 2652 3-8-12 0 OPeslier 5 119
(M Delcher Sanchez, Spain) *w/like: str: racd stands' side: overall ldr and mde all: rdn and edgd rt over 1f out: r.o whn pressed ins fnl f: a looked on top* **22/1**

42-1 **2** ½ **Takeover Target (AUS)**[30] 2235 9-9-4 0 JayFord 7 120
(J Janiak, Australia) *lw: racd stands' side: a.p: rdn over 1f out: str chal ins fnl f: r.o u.p but a looked hld: 2nd of 9 in gp* **6/1**[2]

12-1 **3** nk **Fleeting Spirit (IRE)**[24] 2404 3-8-9 118 RyanMoore 4 113
(J Noseda) *lw: wnt rt s: racd on stands' side: hld up in midfield: effrt and hdwy 2f out: pressed ldrs ins fnl f: r.o u.p: nt quite pce of front pair: 3rd of 9 in gp* **15/8**[1]

20-0 **4** hd **Dandy Man (IRE)**[24] 2404 5-9-4 114 (t) LDettori 15 118
(Saeed Bin Suroor) *lw: racd on far side: chsd ldr: effrt over 1f out: r.o to ld gp fnl 100yds: a hld by ldrs on other side: 1st of 4 in gp* **8/1**

0-55 **5** ¾ **Hoh Mike (IRE)**[15] 2680 4-9-4 109 JamieSpencer 8 115
(M L W Bell) *racd stands' side: in rr: hdwy and swtchd rt over 1f out: edgd rt whn running on ins fnl f: clsng towards fin: nt pce to rch ldrs: 4th of 9 in gp* **22/1**

10- **6** ½ **National Colour (SAF)**[444] 860 6-9-1 0 KShea 14 110
(S Tarry, South Africa) *racd on far side: led gp: rdn over 1f out: hdd fnl 100yds: nt qckn towards fin: 2nd of 4 in gp* **20/1**

10-5 **7** ½ **Benbaun (IRE)**[16] 2652 7-9-4 119 (v) PJSmullen 1 111
(M J Wallace) *stmbld s: racd stands' side: in tch: sn niggled along: kpt on u.p ins fnl f: nt pce to chal: 5th of 9 in gp* **12/1**

00-2 **8** nk **Magnus (AUS)**[30] 2235 6-9-4 0 (p) DMOliver 6 110
(Peter G Moody, Australia) *racd stands' side: prom: rdn over 1f out: no ex ins fnl f: 6th of 9 in gp* **13/2**[3]

0-02 **9** 1¼ **Abraham Lincoln (IRE)**[24] 2417 4-9-4 107 JMurtagh 9 106
(A P O'Brien, Ire) *racd stands' side: in rr: rdn over 1f out: no real imp whn n.m.r and hmpd ins fnl f: 7th of 9 in gp* **33/1**

212- **10** ½ **Kingsgate Native (IRE)**[254] 6039 3-8-12 118 JimmyQuinn 10 102
(J R Best) *swtchd to r stands' side: racd keenly: hld up in midfield on outside of gp: effrt 2f out: wknd ins fnl f: 8th of 9 in gp* **8/1**

110- **11** 2 **Moorhouse Lad**[299] 4746 5-9-4 110 TomEaves 13 97
(B Smart) *racd on far side: chsd ldrs: rdn over 1f out: sn outpcd: 3rd of 4 in gp* **33/1**

2-35 **12** hd **Enticing (IRE)**[24] 2404 4-9-1 105 (b[1]) EddieAhern 3 93
(W J Haggas) *wnt rt s: racd keenly on stands' side: in tch: rdn 2f out: wknd ins fnl f: 9th of 9 in gp* **28/1**

0005 **13** 5 **Matsunosuke**[13] 2712 6-9-4 100 KerrinMcEvoy 12 78
(A B Coogan) *racd on far side: a bhd: outpcd over 1f out: 4th of 4 in gp* **100/1**

59.35 secs (-1.15) **Going Correction** +0.125s/f (Good)
WFA 3 from 4yo+ 6lb **13** Ran SP% **116.1**
Speed ratings (Par 117): **114,113,112,112,111 110,109,109,107,106 103,102,94**
toteswinger: 1&2: £18.70, 1&3 £9.80, 2&3 £2.60. CSF £136.72 CT £373.59 TOTE £14.50: £2.90, £2.60, £1.30; EX 142.50 Trifecta £385.60 Pool: £10,522.65. 20.19 winning units..
Owner J Acheson **Bred** Ecurie Skymarc Farm **Trained** Spain

■ Spain's first Royal Ascot winner, and the first winner in Britain for Mauricio Delcher Sanchez.

FOCUS

The King's Stand has been restored to Group 1 status. With a field of just 13 this was also the smallest line-up since Piccolo beat nine rivals back in 1995, but the field were still responsible for 11 Grade 1 wins between them and there is little reason to think that this was not a very worthy renewal. The field split into two distinct groups with four electing to go far side and the remainder heading towards the stands' rail, and it was the near-side posse that emerged on top. It was a bit of a messy race, with the winner, rated up 6lb, setting an ordinary pace. Takeover Target is rated to last year's form in this race.

NOTEBOOK

Equiano(FR), a challenger from Spain, made just about all to score in ready fashion. He pinged out to grab the rail early on and was given an easy time in the lead through the first few furlongs, which ultimately proved decisive. It was clear entering the final furlong that he was the one to beat and he ran on strongly when asked for maximum effort. He relished this return to a quicker surface and confirmed last-time-out form with Benbaun, who was around the same margin behind him in France 16 days previously. Equiano will stay in Britain and joins Barry Hills, who will no doubt be leaning towards the likes of the July Cup, the Nunthorpe and Haydock Sprint Cup as likely future targets. Further improvement looks firmly on the cards and he fully deserves a chance to prove he is not flattered by this first Group 1 success. (op 20-1)

Takeover Target(AUS) ran another blinder in defeat and has to emerge with a lot of credit. He was always handy, but it was clear passing the furlong pole that he had it to do to catch the eventual winner. He was eating into that rival's advantage nearing the finish and probably ran right up to his form when successful in this race two years ago. He will now turn out quickly again for the Golden Jubilee and, with the likelihood that he will come on a touch for this run, he should be expected to be bang there in that race again this time around. The extra furlong there also suits him best these days. (op 11-2 tchd 13-2 in places)

Fleeting Spirit(IRE), the Temple Stakes winner, was produced with every chance. She posted a useful effort in defeat and is clearly a high-class filly, so there will doubtless still be other days for her in this grade. She will likely re-oppose the winner in the Nunthorpe. Her trainer felt that she may not have been totally at the top of her game on this occasion. (op 85-40 tchd 9-4 in places)

Dandy Man(IRE), not for the first time in his career, found himself on the wrong side. Electing to go with three others on the far side, he ran out a clear winner of that group, only just missing out on third. This proves his disappointment in the Temple Stakes (lost a shoe) to be all wrong, and he is a genuine Group 1 sprinter when things go his way. (op 9-1 tchd 11-1 in a place and 10 in places)

Hoh Mike(IRE), behind Fleeting Spirit last time, was doing all of his best work towards the finish and the stiffer track proved much more to his liking. He had his ideal conditions and ran the race of his life in defeat. (op 25-1 tchd 20-1)

National Colour(SAF), a raider from South Africa, is blessed with serious early pace and she again advertised that by leading the far-side group. She may have been leading overall at one stage, but not that surprisingly tired out of things on this first outing since running in Dubai in March last year. She is due to stay in Britain now, with the Nunthorpe at York in August looking an ideal target for her. (op 16-1)

Benbaun(IRE), just touched off in this by Takeover Target in 2006, did little wrong in defeat. He may just need an extra furlong to shine now. (op 11-1)

Magnus(AUS) ran below his best on this occasion and proved one-paced when asked to make up his ground. (op 7-1)

Abraham Lincoln(IRE) was quickly brought over to the stands' side and got a very patient ride. He was making up his ground inside the final furlong, albeit without ever threatening, and would have been a little closer had he not been slightly hampered.

Kingsgate Native(IRE), whose rider seemed unsure as to which group to tag on to from the gates, was the last runner to tack over to the stands' side. He failed to pick up when asked for maximum effort and, having proved keen through the early parts with no cover, he was below his previous best. It is too soon to write him off and it may well also prove that the step up to 6f is now what he really wants. (op 7-1)

Moorhouse Lad never looked a player on the far side. He should be a deal sharper next time, but is not going to prove easy to place this year. (op 40-1 tchd 50-1)

Enticing(IRE) raced freely through the early stages in the first-time blinkers and her effort petered out shortly after passing the furlong marker. She still ran close enough to her Haydock form with Fleeting Spirit and is another who is now tricky to place successfully. (op 33-1)

Matsunosuke was always playing catch-up on the far side and was predictably outclassed in the end.

3102 ST JAMES'S PALACE STKS (GROUP 1) (ENTIRE COLTS) 1m (R)

3:45 (3:49) (Class 1) 3-Y-O

£141,925 (£53,800; £26,925; £13,425; £6,725; £3,375) **Stalls** High

Form RPR

3-11 **1** **Henrythenavigator (USA)**[24] 2418 3-9-0 JMurtagh 6 128+
(A P O'Brien, Ire) *hld up towards rr: hdwy and swtchd lft ins fnl 2f: led jst over 1f out: drvn and a holding runner-up ins fnl f* **4/7**[1]

3-24 **2** ¾ **Raven's Pass (USA)**[45] 1808 3-9-0 116 JimmyFortune 8 125
(J H M Gosden) *lw: patiently rdn fr last pl: gd hdwy 2f out: chsd wnr fnl f: r.o wl and clsd grad: a hld* **7/1**[3]

1-13 **3** 2½ **Twice Over**[33] 2131 3-9-0 116 TedDurcan 5 118
(H R A Cecil) *lw: hld up in 6th pl: hdwy to go 2nd 2f out: led briefly over 1f out: one pce* **8/1**

1-6 **4** ½ **Cat Junior (USA)**[33] 2121 3-9-0 98 RichardHughes 7 117
(B J Meehan) *lw: led over 1f: prom: outpcd ent st: kpt on gamely fr over 1f out* **66/1**

1 **5** 2¾ **Falco (USA)**[37] 2032 3-9-0 OPeslier 2 112
(C Laffon-Parias, France) *lw: chsd ldrs: led 3f out tl wknd over 1f out* **13/2**[2]

-533 **6** 6 **Stubbs Art (IRE)**[24] 2418 3-9-0 112 SebSanders 9 98
(D R C Elsworth) *lw: in tch on rail tl rdn and wknd over 2f out* **25/1**

3-42 **7** 1½ **Alexandros**[11] 2788 3-9-0 116 LDettori 1 95
(Saeed Bin Suroor) *lw: wd and in tch: hdwy to chse ldrs ent st: wknd wl over 1f out* **28/1**

04-0 **8** 33 **Minneapolis**[23] 2435 3-9-0 JAHeffernan 4 19
(A P O'Brien, Ire) *swtg: hdwy to ld over 6f out and set gd gallop: hdd 3f out: wknd qckly over 2f out* **150/1**

1m 38.7s (-2.10) **Going Correction** +0.075s/f (Good) **8** Ran SP% **110.0**
Speed ratings (Par 113): **113,112,109,109,106 100,99,66**
toteswinger: 1&2 £1.50, 1&3 £1.40, 2&3 £4.20. CSF £4.44 CT £13.93 TOTE £1.60: £1.02, £2.80, £1.90; EX 5.30 Trifecta £20.00 Pool: 17,727.95. 655.42 winning units..
Owner Mrs John Magnier **Bred** Westrn Bloodstock **Trained** Ballydoyle, Co Tipperary

FOCUS

A quality contest that was run at a good gallop and produced a worthy winner in Henrythenavigator who showed his best form yet. He rates alongside Rock Of Gibraltar as the best winner of the race for the past ten years. The form should not be downgraded because of the performance of the 66-1 fourth as he is lightly raced and has always been well regarded.

NOTEBOOK

Henrythenavigator(USA) completed a famous treble by following up his two Guineas successes with victory here, repeating the feat achieved by Rock Of Gibraltar back in 2002. Once again his electric turn of pace was in evidence as he took Twice Over's measure a furlong out. He was always holding Raven's Pass thereafter and cemented his reputation as the leading three-year-old miler in Europe. With no outstanding older horse around in the miling division, he will surely be made a short price to take prizes such as the Sussex Stakes or Moulin if lining up, although connections will no doubt be keen to step him up to 1m2f at some point, too, which will bring in a host of other possible targets. (tchd 8-13 in places)

Raven's Pass(USA), fourth in the 2,000 Guineas, had quite a bit of ground to make up on Henrythenavigator on that piece of form, but that race came plenty soon enough after his big run in the Craven and, having had a nice break since Newmarket, he came here fresh. Tracking the favourite through in the straight, he was given every chance but simply could not get by his brilliant rival. Nevertheless, he pulled clear of the rest, proving without doubt that he stays a mile, and as long as the ground remains on the quick side he should take some beating in the top races over this trip, providing Henry does not show up of course. The Breeders' Cup Mile is his long-term target.

Twice Over, disappointing when sent off at odds-on for the Dante last month, had an excuse for that as his blood was found to be wrong afterwards. This was a return to form but on this track and on this ground he lacked the pace of the first two in the closing stages, prompting his trainer to suggest that he is probably more of a 1m2f horse than a miler. He remains unexposed and races like the Eclipse and Juddmonte International could well be on his agenda now. (tchd 15-2)

Cat Junior(USA) was disappointing at Newmarket on his reappearance but he had looked a Group horse in the making when winning impressively on his only start at two and this run confirmed that first impression. His performance should not cause the form to be devalued. (op 100-1)

Falco(USA), although flattered by the bare result of his clear-margin French Guineas win, was still disappointing. He took up the running early in the straight but was soon one-paced, and simply failed to advertise the Longchamp form. River Proud, who finished third in the French Guineas, had earlier been a well-held fourth in the Craven, so the form ties in quite well, suggesting the English/Irish milers are some way superior this year. (op 6-1 tchd 7-1 in a place)
Stubbs Art(IRE), third in the English and Irish 2,000 Guineas, could not match that level of performance. His run only gives further credit to the winner, who has maintained his form so well throughout the six and a half-week period since the first colts' Classic. (op 33-1)
Alexandros, runner-up in the Group 3 Diomed Stakes at Epsom 11 days earlier, looked out of his depth here, but all his form at two was on easier ground and he may do better when he can get his toe in. Official explanation: jockey said colt had no more to give (op 40-1)
Minneapolis did a fine job of pacemaking for his stable-companion. (op 125-1)

3103 COVENTRY STKS (GROUP 2) 6f
4:20 (4:25) (Class 1) 2-Y-O

£56,770 (£21,520; £10,770; £5,370; £2,690; £1,350) **Stalls** Centre

Form				RPR
11	**1**		**Art Connoisseur (IRE)**[62] 1399 2-9-1 0 JamieSpencer 2 (M L W Bell) *lw: hld up in rr: swtchd lft over 2f out: qcknd and rapid prog whn edgd rt over 1f out: led ins fnl f: r.o wl and sn in full control* **8/1**[3]	113+
	2	2 ¼	**Intense Focus (USA)**[23] 2431 2-9-1 0 KJManning 10 (J S Bolger, Ire) *w'like: athletic: a.p: rdn whn pressed ldr over 1f out: styd on u.p ins fnl f but nt pce of wnr* **12/1**	106
31	**3**	nse	**Lord Shanakill (USA)**[33] 2134 2-9-1 0 FergusSweeney 12 (K R Burke) *lw: a.p: led over 2f out: rdn over 1f out: hdd ins fnl f: kpt on u.p after but a hld* **12/1**	106
1	**4**	hd	**Himalya (IRE)**[17] 2592 2-9-1 0 SebSanders 18 (J Noseda) *midfield: hdwy 2f out: rdn whn chsd ldrs over 1f out: styd on u.p whn chalng for pls ins fnl f* **13/2**[2]	106+
1	**5**	2 ¾	**Orizaba (IRE)**[32] 2150 2-9-1 0 LDettori 1 (M R Channon) *lw: rrd s and missed break: hld up rdn and hdwy over 1f out: edgd rt and styd on ins fnl f: nt pce to get competitive w ldrs* **11/4**[1]	98+
21	**6**	2	**Awinnersgame (IRE)**[18] 2569 2-9-1 0 MJKinane 8 (J Noseda) *in tch: pushed along over 2f out: rdn whn chsd ldrs over 1f out: sn edgd rt: kpt on u.p fnl f* **25/1**	91
23	**7**	2	**I Am The Best**[13] 2713 2-9-1 0 TedDurcan 9 (D M Simcock) *midfield: rdn 2f out: rdn whn nt clr run over 1f out: kpt on w troubling ldrs fnl f* **66/1**	85
31	**8**	nk	**Shaweel**[19] 2521 2-9-1 0 KerrinMcEvoy 7 (M Johnston) *led: hdd over 2f out: sn rdn: wknd appr fnl f* **20/1**	84
	9	½	**Peter Tchaikovsky**[59] 1494 2-9-1 0 JMurtagh 14 (A P O'Brien, Ire) *str: missed break: racd keenly: hld up: rdn and hdwy over 1f out: plugged on fnl f: nt pce to chal* **11/1**	83+
2	**10**	1	**Blown It (USA)**[7] 2916 2-9-1 0 ShaneKelly 15 (J A Osborne) *lw: midfield: pushed along and outpcd over 2f out: sme hdwy over 1f out: nvr on terms w ldrs* **50/1**	80
3	**11**	¾	**Square Eddie (CAN)**[29] 2254 2-9-1 0 LPKeniry 4 (J R Best) *plld hrd: stdd into midfield after 1f: rdn over 1f out: btn ent fnl f* **40/1**	78
211	**12**	nk	**Shampagne**[25] 2377 2-9-1 0 TQuinn 13 (P F I Cole) *prom: rdn over 2f out: wknd over 1f out* **20/1**	77
0111	**13**	1	**Icesolator (IRE)**[19] 2541 2-9-1 0 RyanMoore 6 (R Hannon) *edgy in stalls: hld up: effrt 2f out: no real imp whn n.m.r over 1f out: n.d after* **12/1**	76+
1	**14**	3 ½	**Instalment**[32] 2146 2-9-1 0 RichardHughes 11 (R Hannon) *racd keenly: prom tl rdn and wknd 2f out* **25/1**	65+
4121	**15**	hd	**Smokey Storm**[10] 2826 2-9-1 0 AlanMunro 3 (W Jarvis) *midfield: hdwy 1/2-way: rdn and chsd ldrs 2f out: hung rt whn wkng over 1f out* **20/1**	63+
2212	**16**	nk	**Harwalla (IRE)**[10] 2838 2-9-1 0 RHills 5 (M Johnston) *chsd ldrs: rdn over 2f out: wknd over 1f out* **40/1**	62+
1	**17**	2	**Versaki (IRE)**[17] 2601 2-9-1 0 DaneO'Neill 17 (R Hannon) *handy: rdn over 2f out: wknd over 1f out* **25/1**	56+
31	**18**	5	**Thunderous Mood (USA)**[18] 2581 2-9-1 0 JohnEgan 16 (P F I Cole) *prom: pushed along 1/2-way: wknd over 1f out* **25/1**	41+

1m 13.59s (-0.81) **Going Correction** +0.125s/f (Good) 2y crse rec **18** Ran **SP% 123.3**
Speed ratings (Par 105): **110,107,106,106,103 100,97,97,96,95 94,93,92,87,87 87,84,77**
toteswinger: 1&2 £28.50, 1&3 £23.30, 2&3 £40.00. CSF £87.62 CT £1196.24 TOTE £8.70: £2.90, £4.40, £4.80; EX 134.20 Trifecta £4557.10 Part won. Pool: 6,158.33. 0.10 winning units..
Owner R A Green **Bred** D McDonnell **Trained** Newmarket, Suffolk

FOCUS
A typically competitive Coventry with only three of the 18 runners maidens, but despite the evidence of the earlier races the jockeys spurned the opportunity to come up the nearside of the track and instead raced down the centre as one big group. Even so, it may have been significant that the winner made his effort closest to the stands' rail. Despite being 1.13 seconds slower than Henrythenavigator took to win this race last year, the winning time was still smart when compared to the other races on the day and plenty of winners will come out of this. The impressive Art Connoisseur is rated the best Coventry winner since Three Valleys in 2003.

NOTEBOOK
Art Connoisseur(IRE) ◆ was originally to be aimed at the Norfolk after winning at Newmarket, but his rider was of the opinion that he would be suited by an extra furlong so he came here instead and the move paid off handsomely. What was particularly impressive about this win was that he came from last in order to achieve it and also had to circle the field in order to make his move closest to the stands' rail, though that may have meant he ended up on the most favoured part of the track. The burst of speed he showed to go past his rivals and win going away was spectacular though, and it is that speed which might place a doubt against his ability to stay 1m, but his pedigree does give some cause for optimism in that regard. He is likely to attempt 7f in the Dewhurst later in the season which will tell us more, though he will take in another high-class juvenile event or two along the way. (op 15-2)
Intense Focus(USA) ◆, whose Curragh maiden victory on his second start has not really worked out that well, was nonetheless a springer in the market and duly ran a cracker. He was always up with the pace and kept on battling all the way to the line, but like all the others he was completely swept away by the winner's turn of foot. He looks well up to winning a Pattern race at some stage this season on this evidence. (op 20-1)
Lord Shanakill(USA) ◆ could not dominate this field in quite the same way as he did last time, but he still put up a cracking effort having been prominent from the start and he extended the margin over the pair he had beaten at York, which suggests he is still improving. There will be other days. (op 14-1)
Himalya(IRE) ◆, very green despite winning on his Doncaster debut, was weak in the market this time and it also looked as though the highest stall might be a big disadvantage judged on earlier events, so the fact that the runners came down the centre rather than move over to the stands' rail was probably in his favour. His lack of experience was a bigger problem though and there were still signs of greenness here, but the way he kept on trying and very nearly got up for second does him great credit. He can be considered the second-best horse in the race and it will be a surprise if he cannot win a very decent contest in the coming weeks. (op 9-2)
Orizaba(IRE) ◆, in different ownership to when he made such a spectacular winning debut at Newbury, was very well backed to maintain his unbeaten record but he severely dented his chances by lurching out of the stalls as the gate opened and thereby giving himself plenty of ground to make up. He did stay on under pressure in the latter stages, but never looked like getting to the leaders and is well worth another chance to prove himself to be better than he was able to show here. (op 3-1 tchd 10-3 and 7-2 in places)
Awinnersgame(IRE), very much the stable's second string according to the market, was never far off the pace and kept on pretty well without being able to go with the leaders. Despite finishing further behind Lord Shanakill than he had on his York debut, this was still a very creditable effort.
I Am The Best ◆, one of three maidens in the field, ran with plenty of credit especially as he got caught up in a bit of crowding over a furlong from home. He can win a race before long provided his sights are lowered a bit.
Shaweel tried to do it the hard way, but found this much harder than the egg-and-spoon race he won at Ayr and also ended up further behind Lord Shanakill than he did on his York debut.
Peter Tchaikovsky, whose victory at Naas on his debut has worked out well, absolutely walked out of the stalls this time and even with his connections there was no way he was ever going to overcome that handicap at this level. He probably did as well as could be expected under the circumstances and will show himself to be much better than this. (op 12-1 tchd 14-1 in places)

3104 ASCOT STKS (H'CAP) 2m 4f
4:55 (4:59) (Class 2) (0-95,95) 4-Y-O+

£37,386 (£11,196; £5,598; £2,802; £1,398; £702) **Stalls** High

Form				RPR
1-04	**1**		**Missoula (IRE)**[17] 2609 5-9-0 **85** SamHitchcott 9 (Miss Suzy Smith) *mid-div: rdn 5f out: hdwy 2f out: styd on strly to ld fnl strides in blanket fin* **20/1**	92
0-	**2**	hd	**Mamlook (IRE)**[38] 3143 4-8-10 **83** RyanMoore 1 (D E Pipe) *lw: stdd s: hld up towards rr: rdn and hdwy 2f out: str run on outside to draw level nr fin: jst pipped* **8/1**	90
113/	**3**	shd	**Liberate**[38] 3877 5-9-1 **86** JamieSpencer 3 (P J Hobbs) *lw: sn chsng ldr: led over 2f out tl narrowly hdd 1f out: kpt on wl to press ldrs fnl f: nt qckn fnl strides* **9/2**[1]	93
-211	**4**	shd	**Bukit Tinggi (IRE)**[17] 2628 4-9-0 **87** PhilipRobinson 8 (M A Jarvis) *lw: mid-div: hdwy and edgd rt 2f out: slt ld 1f out and thrght fnl f tl hdd fnl strides* **5/1**[2]	94
0-32	**5**	½	**Som Tala**[41] 1916 5-9-10 **95** LDettori 17 (M R Channon) *in tch on rail: drvn along 3f out: styd on wl fnl 2f* **7/1**[3]	101
6002	**6**	½	**Basalt (IRE)**[17] 2628 4-8-7 **80** KerrinMcEvoy 5 (T J Pitt) *chsd ldrs: rdn and n.m.r over 1f out: styd on same pce* **12/1**	86
3-	**7**	¾	**Jawad (IRE)**[13] 2741 7-9-0 **85** MJKinane 19 (Ms Joanna Morgan, Ire) *in rr of mid-div: drvn and hdwy to chse ldrs over 1f out: kept on: no imp fnl f* **12/1**	90
52-0	**8**	2 ¼	**Duty Free (IRE)**[17] 2591 4-8-11 **84** RichardHughes 18 (C R Egerton) *mid-div: effrt over 2f out: no ex appr fnl f* **20/1**	87
0-50	**9**	½	**Baddam**[17] 2609 6-9-6 **91** JMurtagh 2 (Ian Williams) *in rr of mid-div: rdn 4f out: hdwy and in tch 2f out: no ex fnl f* **12/1**	93
/2-5	**10**	¾	**Tritonville Lodge (IRE)**[25] 1744 6-8-6 **77** HayleyTurner 12 (Miss E C Lavelle) *t.k.h in midfield: drvn along and no hdwy fnl 3f* **50/1**	79
100-	**11**	hd	**Power Of Future (GER)**[13] 2741 5-8-11 **82** JAHeffernan 20 (Andrew Oliver, Ire) *t.k.h: hld up in rr: shkn up over 2f out: sme hdwy over 1f out: nt rch ldrs* **20/1**	83
040-	**12**	1	**Galient (IRE)**[55] 5030 5-9-2 **87** EddieAhern 16 (N J Henderson) *chsd ldrs: nt clr run and snatched up over 2f out: btn whn n.m.r over 1f out* **8/1**	90+
500-	**13**	nk	**Vinando**[311] 4375 7-9-10 **95** (bt) SebSanders 15 (C R Egerton) *in tch tl hrd rdn and wknd fnl 2f* **66/1**	95
5250	**14**	6	**Clear Reef**[3] 3044 4-8-7 **80** TGMcLaughlin 13 (Jane Chapple-Hyam) *dwlt: t.k.h: settled in rr: rdn 3f out: nvr nr ldrs* **50/1**	74
1525	**15**	2 ½	**Legend Erry (IRE)**[59] 1472 4-8-7 **80** JohnEgan 10 (Jane Chapple-Hyam) *led tl over 2f out: sn wknd* **33/1**	72
6-64	**16**	4	**Hawridge Prince**[44] 1841 8-9-9 **94** JimCrowley 6 (B R Millman) *rdn 3f out: a bhd* **33/1**	82
0	**17**	7	**Daltaban (FR)**[17] 2599 4-8-12 **85** (b) AlanMunro 11 (Miss E C Lavelle) *prom: outpcd and btn whn squeezed over 2f out: sn lost pl* **50/1**	66
3-56	**P**		**Tears Of A Clown (IRE)**[17] 2599 5-9-2 **87** ShaneKelly 7 (J A Osborne) *hld up towards rr: lost action and p.u over 3f out: dead* **20/1**	—

4m 28.61s (7.81) **Going Correction** +0.075s/f (Good)
WFA 4 from 5yo+ 2lb **18** Ran **SP% 125.0**
Speed ratings (Par 109): **87,86,86,86,86 86,86,85,85,84 84,84,84,81,80 79,76,—**
toteswinger: 1&2 £51.30, 1&3 £26.40, 2&3 £7.40. CSF £160.77 CT £869.42 TOTE £30.90: £5.00, £2.20, £1.60, £1.90; EX 321.60 Trifecta £1642.40 Pool: £6,481.05. 2.92 winning units..
Owner M J Weaver & Pollards Bloodstock **Bred** Pollards Stables **Trained** Lewes, E Sussex
■ A first Flat winner for trainer Suzy Smith and a first Royal Ascot winner for jockey Sam Hitchcott.
■ Stewards' Enquiry : L Dettori caution: careless riding
Philip Robinson two-day ban: careless riding (Jul 1-2)

FOCUS
This race is not quite the lottery that it used to be with the safety limit reduced to 20 these days and this year's renewal was reduced further by two non-runners. Many of these had questions to answer over this marathon trip, but although the early pace looked generous enough, it appeared to slow down at around halfway and several were still in with a shout starting up the home straight. The fact that only a thick cigarette paper would have covered the first four at the line was a triumph for the handicapper but seemed to confirm that the pace was steady. The winning time was extremely slow for a race like this, over ten seconds slower than last year's event, and the form looks pretty ordinary for a handcap at this meeting.

NOTEBOOK
Missoula(IRE) had finished a long way behind Som Tala in the Chester Cup when she was apparently in season, but she had run much better at Haydock on her previous start. There was a question over her ability to show her best going right-handed and she must also have given her rider a bit of a fright at the start as she fly-jumped leaving the stalls, but despite that she was soon able to take a handy position just behind the leaders. Her chances did not look that bright when she came off the bridle running towards the home bend and several were travelling better than her at that point, but she answered her rider's every call and poked her head between Bukit Tinggi and Mamlook to steal the prize near the line. She still looks to be improving and is now likely to be aimed at the Cesarewitch in the autumn. (tchd 22-1 in a place)
Mamlook(IRE), from a stable with a fine record in this contest, had won over 1m5f when with Kevin Prendergast, but his three wins over hurdles for David Pipe last jumps season were all at around 2m so there was a slight question over the trip. Stamina was not an issue as things turned out, but he was forced to make his effort widest of all and had to cover plenty of ground to get into a challenging position. Despite that he did look like scoring at one point, but the mare snatched the prize from him near the line.

Liberate, a winner at up to 2m for Sir Mark Prescott, was making his Flat debut for his current yard, but having scored over 3m over hurdles last time he was unlikely to have much problem with this trip. Well backed beforehand, he was always handy and tried to steal the race soon after straightening up for home. To his great credit he battled back very gamely after being headed by Bukit Tinggi a furlong out and only went down narrowly, but his rider was of the opinion that they had not gone fast enough in order to truly bring his stamina into play. (op 5-1 tchd 11-2 in places)
Bukit Tinggi(IRE), bidding for a hat-trick off an 8lb higher mark, was always in a good position and looked likely to win when collaring Liberate a furlong out, but he could never quite stamp his authority on the contest and the last half-furlong may have just found him out. (op 9-2 tchd 11-2 and 6-1 in places)
Som Tala, third in this last year, had been hiked up 6lb after finishing runner-up in the Chester Cup and he ran another solid race after holding every chance, but he has not scored since September 2006. (op 8-1)
Basalt(IRE), a neck behind an eased-down Bukit Tinggi at York last time, also ran with plenty of credit and though he is yet to win on turf, he should put that right when dropped back to 2m. (op 14-1)
Jawad(IRE) stayed on without ever quite managing to land a blow and is another that would probably have benefited from a stronger pace. (op 14-1)
Duty Free(IRE) ran an improved race on this second start for Charles Egerton over this longer trip. (op 16-1)
Baddam, winner of this race off a 4lb lower mark in 2006 for Mick Channon before following up in the Queen Alexandra, was not disgraced on this return to handicap company having been mostly plying his trade at Pattern level since then, but he is probably still a bit too high in the weights. (op 14-1)
Galient(IRE), who has been running well over hurdles for Nicky Henderson this year, was still in with some sort of a chance when squeezed out between Som Tala and the weakening Daltaban approaching the last two furlongs, but for which he would have been closer. (tchd 9-1 and 10-1 in a place)

3105 WINDSOR CASTLE STKS (LISTED RACE) 5f

5:30 (5:42) (Class 1) 2-Y-O

£34,062 (£12,912; £6,462; £3,222; £1,614; £810) **Stalls** Centre

Form RPR

33 **1** **Flashmans Papers**43 [1851] 2-9-3 0 .... SteveDrowne 13 104
(J R Best) *in rr: swtchd lft and hdwy over 1f out: edgd rt and str run ins fnl f: led fnl 50yds: r.o* **100/1**

2 ½ **Bushranger (IRE)**12 [2767] 2-9-3 0 .... JMurtagh 11 102
(David Wachman, Ire) *w'like: str: in tch: carried rt 1/2-way: rdn to ld 2f out: hdd and no answer to wnr fnl 50yds* **4/1**1

1 **3** 1¼ **Mullionmileanhour (IRE)**61 [1413] 2-9-3 0 .... LPKeniry 25 98
(J R Best) *racd keenly: hld up: rdn and hdwy to press ldrs over 1f out: styd on u.p ins fnl f* **16/1**

12 **4** hd **Effort**11 [2775] 2-9-3 0 .... KerrinMcEvoy 20 97+
(M Johnston) *w'like: lengthy: lw: dwlt: hld up: swtchd rt and hdwy 2f out: pressed ldr over 1f out: nt qckn towards fin* **28/1**

1 **5** 2½ **Saucy Brown (IRE)**23 [2424] 2-9-3 0 .... RichardHughes 6 89+
(R Hannon) *lw: s.i.s: racd keenly: hld up: rdn and hdwy under 2f out: swtchd rt over 1f out: r.o ins fnl f: gaining at fin* **11/2**2

2 **6** ¾ **Total Gallery (IRE)**11 [2796] 2-9-3 0 .... TedDurcan 1 85
(J S Moore) *lw: hld up: rdn and hdwy over 1f out: sn chsd ldrs and edgd rt: styd on same pce ins fnl f* **66/1**

42 **7** 1 **Donativum**15 [2663] 2-9-3 0 .... (b1) JimmyFortune 22 82
(J H M Gosden) *lw: racd keenly: hld up: hdwy 2f out: rdn over 1f out: kpt on fnl f: nt pce to chal ldrs* **33/1**

0 **8** ½ **Kingsgate Storm (IRE)**13 [2709] 2-9-3 0 .... JimmyQuinn 8 80
(J R Best) *racd keenly: midfield: hdwy and edgd rt 1/2-way: one pce ins fnl f* **66/1**

3 **9** ½ **Khor Dubai (IRE)**17 [2608] 2-9-3 0 .... LDettori 4 78
(Saeed Bin Suroor) *lw: missed break: hld up bhd ldrs: nt clr run 1/2-way: nt clr run and swtchd rt over 1f out: nt pce to get competitive* **25/1**

51 **10** ¾ **Light The Fire (IRE)**28 [2275] 2-9-3 0 .... JamieSpencer 23 75
(B J Meehan) *lw: prom: rdn over 1f out: no ex ins fnl f* **16/1**

242 **11** ½ **Miss Hollybell**36 [2054] 2-8-12 0 .... JimCrowley 7 69
(J Gallagher) *pressed ldrs: led 1/2-way: sn rdn and hdd: wknd ent fnl f* **100/1**

21 **12** nk **Brae Hill (IRE)**22 [2458] 2-9-3 0 .... HayleyTurner 5 73
(M L W Bell) *lw: wnt rt s: prom: rdn 2f out: wknd over 1f out* **15/2**

13 1½ **Silver Shoon (IRE)**24 [2416] 2-8-12 0 .... PJSmullen 10 72+
(D K Weld, Ire) *w'like: lengthy: midfield: nt clr run 1/2-way: sn rdn: hmpd over 1f out: sn n.d* **7/1**3

15 **14** 1½ **Missile Dodger (USA)**31 [2204] 2-9-3 0 .... GeorgeBaker 21 62
(R M Beckett) *racd keenly in tch: rdn 2f out: outpcd over 1f out* **16/1**

4244 **15** nk **Kingswinford (IRE)**4 [2987] 2-9-3 0 .... CatherineGannon 26 61
(P D Evans) *in tch: rdn 1/2-way: wknd over 1f out* **100/1**

311 **16** ½ **Moss Likely (IRE)**32 [2147] 2-9-0 0 .... EdwardCreighton 18 56
(M R Channon) *midfield: rdn 2f out: wknd fnl f* **16/1**

2 **17** hd **Aakef (IRE)**23 [2424] 2-9-3 0 .... RHills 17 58
(M A Jarvis) *lw: hung rt thrght fnl f: in tch: rdn to chse ldrs 2f out: wknd fnl f* **7/1**3

3 **18** 1½ **Court Approval (IRE)**38 [1983] 2-9-3 0 .... ShaneKelly 24 56+
(T G Mills) *hld up bhd ldrs: rdn 2f out: btn over 1f out* **100/1**

341 **19** 1 **Burning Flute**11 [2769] 2-9-3 0 .... MJKinane 12 49
(B J Meehan) *in tch: n.m.r and hmpd 1/2-way: sn rdn and hung rt: wknd over 1f out* **66/1**

51 **20** nse **Dabbers Chief (USA)**17 [2608] 2-9-3 0 .... MichaelHills 15 49
(B W Hills) *lw: in tch: rdn over 1f out: wknd fnl f* **14/1**

21 **21** ½ **Officer Mor (USA)**24 [2388] 2-9-3 0 .... AndrewElliott 3 47
(K R Burke) *led to 1/2-way: sn wknd* **50/1**

163 **22** 1½ **Kate The Great**20 [2507] 2-8-12 0 .... PatCosgrave 16 37
(M J Wallace) *prom tl rdn and wknd over 1f out* **100/1**

10 **23** 7 **Glorious Dreams (USA)**20 [2497] 2-8-12 0 .... EddieAhern 19 12
(T J Pitt) *prom tl pushed along and lost pl 1/2-way* **100/1**

114 **24** 1¾ **She's A Shaw Thing**41 [1914] 2-8-12 0 .... TGMcLaughlin 9 5
(P D Evans) *chsd ldrs: rdn and wnt rt 1/2-way: sn wknd* **28/1**

101 **25** 9 **Asaint Needs Brass (USA)**13 [2713] 2-9-3 0 .... SebSanders 14 —+
(R M Beckett) *rrd bef s: sn in rr: pushed along 1/2-way: eased whn btn* **40/1**

60.60 secs (0.10) **Going Correction** +0.125s/f (Good) **25** Ran SP% **130.8**
Speed ratings (Par 101): **104,103,101,100,96 95,94,93,92,91 90,90,87,85,84 83,83,81,79,79 78,76,65,62,47**
toteswinger: 1&2 £236.50, 1&3 £378.40, 2&3 £11.20. CSF £471.37 CT £6922.76 TOTE £148.80: £27.90, £2.50, £4.50; EX 1309.30 Trifecta £3889.60 Place 6: £45.61, Place 5: £26.95. Part won. Pool: £5,256.25. 0.10 winning units..
Owner D Gorton **Bred** Cliveden Stud Ltd **Trained** Hucking, Kent
■ A shock result, and John Best's first Royal Ascot winner.

FOCUS
Perhaps not the classiest race at the meeting, but very competitive and the biggest field in recent years. Although the runners were spread right across the track, they stayed away from either rail and, as with the earlier Coventry Stakes, the winner made his effort closest to the stands' side. The form may not be totally reliable as a result but overall it reads sound enough, despite Flashmans Papers' huge price.

NOTEBOOK
Flashmans Papers, from the stable that provided the 66-1 runner-up in this race last year, had finished third in his two previous starts and winners have emerged from both contests, but it still required something of a leap of faith to see him winning this. Given plenty to do, he followed a similar route to the winner of the Coventry Stakes earlier in the afternoon in that he was switched right over to the stands' side in order to make his effort and he fairly flew home. Whether he can repeat the exploits of Kingsgate Native remains to be seen, but even though he may have benefited from a track bias this was still a big step in the right direction.
Bushranger(IRE) ◆, narrow winner of his only previous start, at Tipperary, went off the well-backed favourite and things looked good for his supporters entering the last couple of furlongs when he swept to the front, so it must have been galling for all concerned to have the prize snatched from him by a 100-1 rag. There should be a race at this level in him. (op 9-2 tchd 5-1 in a place)
Mullionmileanhour(IRE) ◆, easy winner of a Kempton Polytrack maiden on his debut that has produced winners, was weak in the market here but belied that with a decent effort behind his stable companion. Always racing with plenty of enthusiasm behind the leaders over on the far side of the group, he was produced with his effort in plenty of time and went down with all guns blazing. He should enjoy plenty more success this season. (op 11-1)
Effort, back on a stiffer track, was produced to hold every chance entering the last furlong and was only seen off inside the last 50 yards. His style of running and his breeding suggests he will appreciate another furlong. (op 33-1)
Saucy Brown(IRE), who beat another of today's runners Aakef when successful on his Windsor debut, was very popular in the market beforehand and his price halved. Unfortunately he appeared to take a bump from Brae Hill leaving the stalls and that may have meant he was further back than ideal. In any case his strong finishing effort was always falling short and he is almost certainly better than here showed here. (op 11-1)
Total Gallery(IRE) ◆ showed that his promising Goodwood debut was no fluke and although he was probably helped by making his effort on the favoured side of the track, it should not be long before he gets off the mark. (op 50-1)
Donativum, not surprisingly fitted with first-time blinkers following his wayward antics at Leicester, stayed on over the last furlong or so and this was a very creditable effort considering he was probably drawn on the wrong side.
Kingsgate Storm(IRE) ◆, who finished last of 11 on his Kempton Polytrack debut when nearly unseating his rider at the start, was from the same stable as the winner and third and did not let the side down. He showed more than enough to suggest that he can win a race.
Khor Dubai(IRE) did his chances little good with a tardy start before plugging on late, but although he reversed Haydock form with Dabbers Chief that is all he achieved. (tchd 28-1)
Light The Fire(IRE) showed good speed as he did when winning at Leicester, but he could not dominate in the same way and did not get home. (tchd 18-1)
Silver Shoon(IRE), still a maiden but narrowly beaten in Listed company last time, was just starting to stay on when badly squeezed out between Saucy Brown and Kingsgate Storm a furlong and a half out and there was no way back from there. She is better than this. (op 11-2 tchd 8-1 in a place)
Missile Dodger(USA), who failed to see out the extra furlong on soft ground at Newmarket last time, was a springer in the market on this return to the minimum but never looked like figuring. (op 33-1)
T/Jkpt: Not won. T/Plt: £89.50 to a £1 stake. Pool: £467,313.31. 3,808.28 winning tickets. T/Qpdt: £30.40 to a £1 stake. Pool: £16,008.87. 389.10 winning tickets.

2671 THIRSK (L-H)

Tuesday, June 17

OFFICIAL GOING: Firm
Wind: Virtually nil Weather: Cloudy

3106 FAIRFAX ARMS (S) STKS 6f

2:15 (2:17) (Class 5) 2-Y-O **£3,885** (£1,156; £577; £288) **Stalls** High

Form RPR

62 **1** **Scenic Pass**4 [3008] 2-8-9 0 .... DarryllHolland 13 62
(M R Channon) *led: rdn along and hdd over 1f out: drvn and rallied ins fnl f to ld nr line* **4/9**1

2 hd **Red Baron Dancer** 2-9-0 0 .... SilvestreDeSousa 1 67
(D Nicholls) *t.k.h: cl up on outer: hdwy to ld over 1f out: sn rdn and rn green: hdd nr fin* **14/1**3

0 **3** 8 **Maria Milena**64 [1363] 2-8-9 0 .... (v1) RobertWinston 8 40+
(M J Wallace) *wnt rt s: in rr tl hdwy 2f out: sn rdn and kpt on ins fnl f: nrst fin* **4/1**2

055 **4** nk **Scarlet Blade**7 [2910] 2-9-0 0 .... (v1) RoystonFfrench 5 40
(Mrs A Duffield) *prom: rdn along over 2f out: drvn and one pce fr wl over 1f out* **20/1**

6 **5** 2¾ **Sale Or Return (IRE)**57 [1515] 2-8-9 0 .... DavidAllan 2 26
(T D Easterby) *chsd ldrs: rdn along over 2f out: drvn and one pce fr over 1f out* **25/1**

0306 **6** 1½ **Dispol Toba**7 [2910] 2-8-7 0 ow1 .... JamieMoriarty(3) 12 22
(P T Midgley) *cl up: rdn along over 2f out and grad wknd* **20/1**

6 **7** 2¾ **Keen Rabbit**5 [2965] 2-8-9 0 .... TonyHamilton 11 13
(Micky Hammond) *chsd ldrs: rdn along over 2f out: grad wknd* **33/1**

0 **8** 1½ **Hunch**19 [2548] 2-8-11 0 .... MarkLawson(5) 9 13
(Garry Moss) *dwlt and bmpd s: a in rr* **80/1**

0 **9** hd **One Cool Pet (IRE)**21 [2485] 2-8-9 0 .... LeeEnstone 7 7
(P C Haslam) *a towards rr* **33/1**

0 **10** 4½ **Ga Ga**21 [2485] 2-8-9 0 .... PaulMulrennan 10 —
(M W Easterby) *prom: rdn along 1/2-way: sn wknd* **40/1**

0 **11** 2¾ **Ernies Keep**30 [2216] 2-8-9 0 .... KellyHarrison(5) 6 —
(W Storey) *dwlt: a in rr* **66/1**

0 **12** 4 **Canclodacancan (IRE)**46 [1770] 2-8-9 0 .... MickyFenton 14 —
(P T Midgley) *a bhd* **40/1**

1m 12.39s (-0.31) **Going Correction** -0.30s/f (Firm) **12** Ran SP% **122.8**
Speed ratings (Par 93): **90,89,79,78,75 73,69,67,67,61 57,52**
toteswinger: 1&2 £3.10, 1&3 £1.60, 2&3 £4.00. CSF £7.54 TOTE £1.50: £1.02, £3.30, £1.60; EX 10.70.There was no bid for the winner. Red Baron Dancer was claimed for £10,000 by Mustafa Khan.
Owner M Channon **Bred** Norman Court Stud **Trained** West Ilsley, Berks

FOCUS
The first two, who came well clear of the rest, are good types for the grade although the winner was a bit below her York form.

NOTEBOOK

Scenic Pass was sent off at cramped odds after her decent effort in a valuable seller at York last week, but she only got home by the skin of her teeth from her good draw and, indeed, she might well have been beaten had the runner-up had the benefit of a previous outing and been better drawn. She is not that good and this ground was probably lively enough for her; there was no bid at the subsequent auction. (op 4-6)

Red Baron Dancer, who was making his debut, ran a blinder. Drawn widest of all, he was produced to win his race from over a furlong out and he actually got in front, but looked inexperienced under pressure and was beaten on the nod. He changed hands after the race. (op 12-1 tchd 16-1)

Maria Milena, who was visored for the first time, hampered her chances with a slow start. She stayed on well inside the final furlong but was no match for the first two. Official explanation: jockey said filly was unsuited by the firm ground (op 11-4 tchd 9-2)

Scarlet Blade, equipped with a first-time visor, was comfortably held in fourth after racing prominently throughout. (tchd 25-1)

Sale Or Return(IRE), quickly dropped to selling grade after a moderate effort on her debut, was not disgraced from her poor draw. (op 20-1)

3107 HELEN SYKES FASHIONS MEDIAN AUCTION MAIDEN STKS — 7f

2:50 (2:54) (Class 5) 2-Y-O — **£3,885** (£1,156; £577; £288) — **Stalls** Low

Form — RPR

03 **1** — **Motor Home**[17] 2601 2-9-3 0 .... WilliamBuick 1 — 76+
(A M Balding) *mde all: rdn wl over 1f out: styd on wl fnl f* — **7/2**[1]

5 **2** 1 ¼ **Suruor (IRE)**[20] 2507 2-9-3 0 .... MartinDwyer 5 — 73
(M Johnston) *prom: chsd wnr 1/2-way: rdn to chal 2f out: sn hung lft: drvn ins fnl f and no ex fnl 100yds* — **7/2**[1]

3 5 **Kudu Country (IRE)** 2-9-3 0 .... MickyFenton 7 — 60+
(T P Tate) *chsd ldrs on outer: rdn along and outpcd wl over 2f out: styd on appr fnl f* — **16/1**

05 **4** nse **Blusher**[8] 2893 2-8-12 0 .... DarryllHolland 2 — 55
(M R Channon) *trckd ldrs: effrt 3f out: sn rdn and chsd ldng pair 2f out: drvn and one pce appr fnl f: lost 3rd nr line* — **7/1**[2]

04 **5** 5 **The Kilkenny Kat (IRE)**[18] 2584 2-9-3 0 .... GrahamGibbons 13 — 47
(T D Easterby) *chsd wnr to 1/2-way: prom and rdn along wl over 2f out: grad wknd* — **8/1**[3]

6 ½ **Carter** 2-9-0 0 .... DuranFentiman(3) 6 — 45
(W M Brisbourne) *bhd tl sme late hdwy* — **40/1**

7 nse **Dark Moment** 2-9-3 0 .... DaleGibson 3 — 45
(A Dickman) *chsd ldrs: rdn along wl over 2f out and sn one pce* — **50/1**

8 4 **Kladester (USA)** 2-9-3 0 .... RoystonFfrench 8 — 35
(B Smart) *a in rr* — **9/1**

0 **9** 1 ¾ **Holst (IRE)**[62] 1392 2-9-3 0 .... DavidAllan 10 — 30
(T D Easterby) *a in rr* — **50/1**

10 5 **El Guevara (IRE)** 2-9-3 0 .... NCallan 11 — 17
(K A Ryan) *in tch: rdn along 3f out and sn wknd* — **14/1**

0 **11** 8 **Talsarnau (IRE)**[18] 2569 2-9-3 0 .... DanielTudhope 12 — —
(W M Brisbourne) *a in rr* — **66/1**

63 **12** 95 **Ay Tay Tate (IRE)**[17] 2592 2-9-3 0 .... FergalLynch 4 — —
(I W McInnes) *s.i.s: a bhd: t.o fr 1/2-way* — **7/2**[1]

1m 26.11s (-1.09) **Going Correction** -0.30s/f (Firm) — **12** Ran SP% **120.7**

Speed ratings (Par 93): **94,92,86,86,81 80,80,75,73,68 59,—**

toteswinger: 1&2 £2.70, 1&3 £28.50, 2&3 £20.70. CSF £14.76 TOTE £3.90: £1.70, £1.70, £6.00; EX 12.30.Hunting Magic was withdrawn. Price at time of withdrawal 66/1. Rule 4 does not apply.

Owner Philip Eaton **Bred** Iain Wilson **Trained** Kingsclere, Hants

FOCUS

A fair race of its type with the first two finishing clear. The winner did it well.

NOTEBOOK

Motor Home got off the mark on his third attempt. Seemingly appreciating this extra furlong, he stuck to his task in grand style. He should hold his own in nursery company. (op 5-2)

Suruor(IRE), stepping up in trip, came out comfortably best of the remainder, but he was always just second-best to the winner and seemed to be hanging to his left, into the rails. He should improve with experience. (tchd 3-1 and 4-1)

Kudu Country(IRE) shaped nicely, taking time to grasp what was required on his debut, but doing some solid work in the closing stages. (op 20-1)

Blusher confirmed the hint of promise she showed last time and only got mugged for third on the line. (op 12-1)

The Kilkenny Kat(IRE), who shaped reasonably well last time, chased the leaders before fading in the final two furlongs. (op 12-1)

Kladester(USA) Official explanation: jockey said colt was unsuited by the firm ground

Ay Tay Tate(IRE) lost his action and trailed the field throughout. Official explanation: jockey said colt lost its action; vet said colt returned lame (tchd 10-3 and 4-1)

3108 CC H'CAP — 7f

3:25 (3:25) (Class 5) (0-75,74) 3-Y-O+ — **£3,885** (£1,156; £577; £288) — **Stalls** Low

Form — RPR

155 **1** — **Yamal (IRE)**[31] 2209 3-9-3 72 .... JoeFanning 8 — 85
(M Johnston) *prom: hdwy to ld over 2f out: rdn over 1f out: styd on wl fnl f* — **9/2**[2]

0023 **2** 1 ½ **Esoterica (IRE)**[11] 2787 5-9-7 67 .... (b) DanielTudhope 7 — 82+
(J S Goldie) *hld up towards rr: effrt and nt clr run 2f out: sn swtchd rt and rdn: styd on strly ins fnl f: nrst fin* — **7/2**[1]

00-5 **3** 1 ¼ **Heureux (USA)**[29] 2251 5-9-5 65 .... (b) RobertWinston 10 — 74
(J Howard Johnson) *trckd ldrs: hdwy over 2f out: rdn to chse wnr over 1f out: drvn and one pce ins fnl f* — **14/1**

2224 **4** 1 **Violent Velocity (IRE)**[11] 2778 5-9-8 71 .... JamieMoriarty(3) 4 — 77
(J J Quinn) *trckd ldrs: effrt over 2f out: sn rdn and kpt on same pce appr fnl f* — **7/2**[1]

1120 **5** 1 **Glenridding**[11] 2787 4-9-8 68 .... TPQueally 9 — 71
(J G Given) *led: rdn along 3f out: hdd over 2f out: sn drvn and wknd appr fnl f* — **16/1**

0-00 **6** 1 **Mister Jingles**[28] 2285 5-8-11 57 .... (b) DeanMcKeown 5 — 57
(R M Whitaker) *chsd ldrs: rdn along over 2f out: kpt on same pce* — **16/1**

0003 **7** 2 ¼ **Flight Plan**[21] 2480 3-8-10 65 .... (e[1]) DaleGibson 13 — 56
(R A Fahey) *towards rr: effrt and sme hdwy over 2f out: sn rdn and no imp* — **7/1**[3]

4560 **8** nk **Ninth House (USA)**[14] 2703 6-9-7 70 .... (b) PJMcDonald(3) 3 — 64
(Mrs R A Carr) *s.i.s: a in rr* — **20/1**

-000 **9** 2 **Pay Time**[11] 2781 9-8-10 56 .... RoystonFfrench 6 — 44
(R E Barr) *chsd ldr: rdn along 3f out: wknd 2f out* — **28/1**

4555 **10** 2 ¼ **Charlie Tipple**[20] 2499 4-10-0 74 .... (p) GrahamGibbons 14 — 56
(T D Easterby) *stdd s: hld up: a in rr* — **8/1**

1315 **11** 9 **Haroldini (IRE)**[121] 601 6-8-6 55 .... (p) TolleyDean(3) 11 — 13
(J Balding) *chsd ldrs: rdn along over 3f out: sn wknd* — **20/1**

1m 24.49s (-2.71) **Going Correction** -0.30s/f (Firm)

WFA 3 from 4yo+ 9lb — **11** Ran SP% **117.6**

Speed ratings (Par 103): **103,101,99,98,97 96,93,93,91,88 78**

toteswinger: 1&2 £3.90, 1&3 £11.90, 2&3 £12.00. CSF £20.00 CT £205.92 TOTE £5.90: £2.00, £1.90, £4.00; EX 23.00.

Owner Sheikh Hamdan Bin Mohammed Al Maktoum **Bred** Gainsborough Stud Management Ltd **Trained** Middleham Moor, N Yorks

FOCUS

Not the most competitive of Class 5 handicaps but the form is solid enough.

3109 EBF FIRST TRANSPENNINE EXPRESS FILLIES' H'CAP — 1m

4:00 (4:00) (Class 3) (0-90,85) 3-Y-O+ — **£9,714** (£2,890; £1,444; £721) — **Stalls** Low

Form — RPR

30-2 **1** — **Princess Taylor**[25] 2373 4-9-8 79 .... (t) DarryllHolland 6 — 90
(M Botti) *trckd ldrs: hdwy over 2f out: rdn to ld wl over 1f out: edgd lft ins fnl f: drvn out* — **7/2**[2]

211 **2** 1 **Maghya (IRE)**[33] 2118 3-9-0 81 .... MartinDwyer 7 — 87
(W J Haggas) *hld up in rr: hdwy on outer 3f out: rdn to chse ldrs and edgd lft over 1f out: drvn and kpt on ins fnl f* — **6/4**[1]

3231 **3** nk **Hula Ballew**[15] 2672 8-9-0 76 .... NeilBrown(5) 1 — 84
(M Dods) *trckd ldrs on inner: hdwy over 2f out: rdn and ev ch wl over 1f out: drvn and nt qckn ins fnl f* — **7/2**[2]

21-2 **4** 2 ½ **Badalona**[40] 1930 3-9-3 84 .... RichardMullen 9 — 84
(M L W Bell) *prom: effrt 3f out: rdn to ld briefly 2f out: sn drvn and hdd: wknd appr fnl f* — **15/2**[3]

000 **5** 1 ¾ **Feisty Royale**[15] 2674 3-8-10 77 .... GregFairley 4 — 73
(M Johnston) *prom: rdn along 3f out: drvn over 2f out and sn wknd* — **28/1**

3-15 **6** 5 **Island Music (IRE)**[18] 2575 3-8-5 72 .... GrahamGibbons 5 — 56
(J J Quinn) *hld up: a towards rr* — **33/1**

0-03 **7** nse **Bonny Rose**[25] 2378 3-8-5 72 .... JoeFanning 3 — 56
(M Johnston) *led: rdn along 3f out: hdd 2f out and sn wknd* — **16/1**

10-0 **8** 12 **Musical Beat**[10] 2818 4-9-8 79 .... PaulMulrennan 2 — 38
(Miss V Haigh) *t.k.h: chsd ldrs tl rdn and wknd over 2f out* — **16/1**

1m 37.9s (-2.20) **Going Correction** -0.30s/f (Firm)

WFA 3 from 4yo+ 10lb — **8** Ran SP% **114.4**

Speed ratings (Par 104): **99,98,97,95,93 88,88,76**

toteswinger: 1&2 £2.00, 1&3 £2.80, 2&3 £2.40. CSF £9.14 CT £18.70 TOTE £4.40: £1.30, £1.10, £1.70; EX 10.40.

Owner Rothmere Racing Limited **Bred** Blenheim Bloodstock **Trained** Newmarket, Suffolk

FOCUS

A messy gallop to this fillies' handicap, but the form reads pretty sound.

NOTEBOOK

Princess Taylor lead well over a furlong out and was always holding Maghya, who came from off the pace. This was only her second outing of the season and there should be more to come from her yet. (op 4-1 tchd 3-1)

Maghya(IRE), raised 7lb for her Newmarket win, was held up in a rather muddling race. Pulled to the outer in the straight, she gradually made ground as the tempo increased, but the winner was always ahead of her and she was unable to wear her down. (op 11-10)

Hula Ballew, who goes so well at Thirsk, ran a creditable race in third but could not follow her win up over the course and distance last time off this 6lb higher mark. (op 5-1)

Badalona, running off a 4lb higher mark than last time, shaped well until not quite getting home. (op 8-1 tchd 7-1)

Feisty Royale is unproven over this sort of distance and appeared not to stay again. However, she is down to a handy mark and will be of interest if dropped back down to a more suitable trip.

Bonny Rose Official explanation: jockey said filly hung right-handed in home straight

Musical Beat Official explanation: jockey said filly ran too free early stages; trainer said filly on being scoped had bled internally

3110 BIBENDUM WINE H'CAP — 1m 4f

4:35 (4:35) (Class 4) (0-80,76) 4-Y-O+ — **£5,180** (£1,541; £770; £384) — **Stalls** Low

Form — RPR

-411 **1** — **Hatton Flight**[27] 2304 4-9-7 76 .... (b) WilliamBuick 3 — 89+
(A M Balding) *trckd ldng pair: smooth hdwy 3f out: cl up 2f out: shkn up to ld over 1f out: pushed out* — **10/11**[1]

3514 **2** 1 ¾ **Charlotte Vale**[10] 2839 7-9-6 75 .... RobertWinston 1 — 82
(Micky Hammond) *cl up: led over 3f out and sn rdn: jnd 2f out: drvn and hdd over 1f out: kpt on same pce u.p fnl f* — **4/1**[3]

-422 **3** 2 **Multicultural**[11] 2799 5-8-12 67 .... RichardMullen 5 — 71
(D M Simcock) *hld up: hdwy 3f out: rdn and n.m.r 2f out: swtchd lft and drvn over 1f out: kpt on same pce* — **5/2**[2]

00-6 **4** 3 ¾ **Danish Rebel (IRE)**[39] 1970 4-9-5 74 .... (t) PaulMulrennan 4 — 72
(G A Charlton) *sn led: rdn along and hdd over 3f out: sn wknd* — **11/1**

2m 35.52s (-0.68) **Going Correction** -0.30s/f (Firm) — **4** Ran SP% **109.3**

Speed ratings (Par 105): **90,88,87,85**

CSF £4.92 TOTE £1.80; EX 3.20.

Owner David Brownlow **Bred** Fittocks Stud Ltd **Trained** Kingsclere, Hants

FOCUS

A moderate winning time for the grade. The form is sound enough and Hatton Flight continues on the upgrade.

3111 LADIES DAY H'CAP — 6f

5:10 (5:14) (Class 4) (0-85,82) 3-Y-O+ — **£5,180** (£1,541; £770; £384) — **Stalls** High

Form — RPR

0-03 **1** — **John Keats**[5] 2968 5-9-0 68 .... DanielTudhope 4 — 76
(J S Goldie) *towards rr: hdwy on outer wl over 2f out: sn rdn and edgd lft: led 1f out: drvn ins fnl f and kpt on wl* — **6/1**[3]

-636 **2** ¾ **River Thames**[12] 2760 5-9-11 79 .... NCallan 2 — 85
(K A Ryan) *hld up in rr: hdwy wl over 1f out: rdn and styd on strly ins fnl f* — **7/1**

3035 **3** ½ **Bel Cantor**[3] 3050 5-9-6 79 .... (p) KellyHarrison(5) 3 — 83+
(W J H Ratcliffe) *prom: hdwy to ld wl over 1f out: rdn and hdd 1f out: drvn and edgd lft ins fnl f: no ex towards fin* — **7/1**

3-05 **4** 1 **Lake Sabina**[22] 2460 3-8-9 70 .... RichardMullen 9 — 69
(E S McMahon) *dwlt and bhd: swtchd lft and hdwy 2f out: rdn over 1f out: styd on wl fnl f: nrst fin* — **16/1**

0526 **5** ½ **Prince Namid**[11] 2778 6-9-6 74 .... (p) RoystonFfrench 6 — 74
(Mrs A Duffield) *hld up: hdwy 2f out: sn rdn and kpt on ins fnl f: nrst fin* — **14/1**

5052 **6** 1 **Mr Wolf**[8] 2892 7-9-1 69 .... (p) FergalLynch 11 — 65
(D W Barker) *cl up: led over 2f out: sn rdn and hdd wl over 1f out: drvn: edgd lft and wknd appr fnl f* — **10/3**[2]

0-02 **7** nk **My Gacho (IRE)**[6] 2938 6-9-5 73 .... (b) GregFairley 10 — 68
(M Johnston) *chsd ldrs: rdn along over 2f out: sn drvn and wknd over 1f out* — **2/1**[1]

4403 **8** 2 3/4 **Dark Champion**[11] 2777 8-8-9 **63** oh3........................(v) PaulMulrennan 5 50
(R E Barr) *chsd ldrs: rdn along wl over 2f out and sn wknd* **16/1**

00/0 **9** 1 3/4 **Dazzling Bay**[14] 2698 8-9-7 **75**..................................(b) DavidAllan 7 56
(T D Easterby) *in tch: rdn along over 2f out and sn wknd* **25/1**

-600 **10** 10 **Prigsnov Dancer (IRE)**[20] 2498 3-8-11 **72**........................(v) TPQueally 1 19
(J O'Reilly) *led: rdn along 1/2-way: sn hdd & wknd* **50/1**

1m 10.82s (-1.88) **Going Correction** -0.30s/f (Firm)
WFA 3 from 5yo+ 7lb **10** Ran SP% **119.9**
Speed ratings (Par 105): **100,99,98,97,96 95,94,90,88,75**
toteswinger: 1&2 £7.60, 1&3 £6.90, 2&3 £7.40. CSF £49.10 CT £249.05 TOTE £8.10: £2.10, £2.00, £2.20; EX 61.50.
Owner Tough Construction Ltd **Bred** R Preece **Trained** Uplawmoor, E Renfrews

FOCUS
A fairly competitive handicap and straightforward form with the front four all rated to their best.

3112 ADORN HATS H'CAP 5f
5:40 (5:41) (Class 6) (0-65,65) 3-Y-0+ **£2,729** (£806; £403) **Stalls** High

Form RPR

0350 **1** **Toy Top (USA)**[11] 2777 5-8-12 **54**..............................(b) NeilBrown(5) 20 69
(M Dods) *led stands' side gp: shkn up and overall ldr 1f out: qcknd clr ins fnl f* **5/1**[2]

3030 **2** 3 1/4 **Colorus (IRE)**[18] 2583 5-10-0 **65**........................ RobertWinston 10 68
(W J H Ratcliffe) *cl up stands' side: rdn 2f out and ev ch tl one pce ins fnl f* **8/1**[3]

-345 **3** 1/2 **Raccoon (IRE)**[19] 2551 8-9-10 **64**............................ PJMcDonald(3) 4 66
(Mrs R A Carr) *led far side gp: rdn and ev ch over 1f out: kpt on same pce ins fnl f* **8/1**[3]

6000 **4** 1/2 **Miacarla**[1] 3080 5-9-1 **52**.. PatrickMathers 15 52
(H A McWilliams) *towards rr stands' side: rdn 2f out: styd on strly ent fnl f: nrst fin* **33/1**

05-3 **5** hd **Distant Vision (IRE)**[29] 2248 5-8-9 **46** oh1..................... DavidAllan 19 45
(H A McWilliams) *in rr on stands' side: rdn along 2f out: styd on strly ins fnl f: nrst fin* **16/1**

-053 **6** 3/4 **Niteowl Lad (IRE)**[17] 2596 6-9-7 **58**..............................(p) PaulMulrennan 12 54
(J Balding) *t.k.h: trckd ldrs stands' side: swtchd lft and hdwy 2f out: sn rdn and kpt on same pce ent fnl f* **8/1**[3]

1140 **7** 1/2 **Sands Crooner (IRE)**[17] 2596 5-9-13 **64**..............................(v) TPQueally 8 58
(J G Given) *chsd ldrs stands' side: rdn 2f out and ev ch tl drvn and wknd appr fnl f* **16/1**

-000 **8** hd **Strensall**[11] 2777 11-9-3 **57**...................................... DuranFentiman(3) 3 51
(R E Barr) *chsd ldrs far side: rdn along 2f out: sn one pce* **20/1**

4235 **9** 1/2 **Mr Rooney (IRE)**[11] 2780 5-9-5 **56**...................(t) SilvestreDeSousa 17 48
(D Nicholls) *chsd ldrs stands' side: rdn along over 2f out and sn wknd* **4/1**[1]

4040 **10** 3/4 **Spirit Of Coniston**[28] 2270 5-9-7 **58**............................. MickyFenton 2 47
(P T Midgley) *chsd ldr far side gp: rdn along 2f out: sn one pce* **25/1**

040- **11** 1 1/4 **Northern Chorus (IRE)**[273] 5507 5-8-13 **57**...........(b) AdeleRothery(7) 6 42
(J O'Reilly) *racd far side: rdn along over 2f out and grad wknd* **20/1**

40-0 **12** 1 1/2 **Triple Shadow**[17] 2597 4-9-1 **55**................................... LeeVickers(3) 13 34
(M A Peill) *chsd ldrs stands' side: rdn 2f out and grad wknd* **33/1**

-243 **13** hd **Bond Becks (IRE)**[123] 581 8-9-1 **57**................................ SladeO'Hara(5) 1 36
(G R Oldroyd) *prom far side: rdn along 1/2-way: sn wknd* **20/1**

-023 **14** 1 1/2 **Whozart (IRE)**[9] 2869 5-8-13 **50**..................................... DanielTudhope 7 23
(A Dickman) *racd alone centre: prom: rdn along and edgd lft 2f out: sn wknd* **17/2**

0200 **15** 1/2 **Jakeini (IRE)**[11] 2777 5-9-12 **63**..............................(p) RichardMullen 9 34
(E S McMahon) *a towards rr stands' side* **20/1**

00-0 **16** 2 1/2 **Alugat (IRE)**[22] 2448 5-9-1 **52**..................................(p) RoystonFfrench 16 14
(Mrs A Duffield) *racd stands' side: in rr fr 1/2-way* **28/1**

-000 **17** 1/2 **Mutayam**[44] 1827 8-8-8 **50** oh1 ow4.................................(t) GaryBartley(5) 5 11
(D A Nolan) *a towards rr far side* **80/1**

0230 **18** 2 1/2 **Hawaii Prince**[17] 2596 4-9-4 **60**.. KellyHarrison(5) 11 12
(S T Mason) *cl up stands' side: rdn along 1/2-way: sn wknd* **16/1**

57.79 secs (-1.81) **Going Correction** -0.30s/f (Firm) **18** Ran SP% **131.6**
Speed ratings (Par 101): **102,96,96,95,94 93,92,92,91,90 88,86,85,83,82 78,77,73**
toteswinger: 1&2 £12.50, 1&3 £15.40, 2&3 £20.70. CSF £41.39 CT £343.44 TOTE £5.40: £1.50, £2.60, £3.00, £6.70; EX 45.70 Place 6: £16.87, Place 5: £15.86..
Owner D Vic Roper **Bred** Lajos Kengye **Trained** Denton, Co Durham

FOCUS
A big field of run-of-the-mill handicappers, and a race of two halves, with six of the runners racing on the far side and and the remainder towards the stands' side, which fielded the winner Toy Top. She is rated back to form.
Mr Rooney(IRE) Official explanation: jockey said gelding never travelled
Hawaii Prince Official explanation: gelding hung left-handed throughout
T/Plt: £31.90 to a £1 stake. Pool: £49,617.69. 1,135.05 winning tickets. T/Qpdt: £20.10 to a £1 stake. Pool: £2,438.09. 89.50 winning tickets. JR

2979 YARMOUTH (L-H)
Tuesday, June 17

OFFICIAL GOING: Good to firm
Wind: Light against Weather: Overcast

3113 4HEAD APPRENTICE H'CAP 1m 2f 21y
6:30 (6:30) (Class 6) (0-60,57) 4-Y-0+ **£2,137** (£635; £317; £158) **Stalls** Low

Form RPR

2220 **1** **Wee Charlie Castle (IRE)**[52] 1639 5-8-8 **51**............ WilliamCarson(5) 8 67
(G C H Chung) *hld up: hdwy 4f out: led over 2f out: edgd lft: rdn clr fnl f* **13/2**[3]

-231 **2** 7 **Astrolibra**[9] 2863 4-9-0 **57** 6ex.................................. AshleyMorgan(5) 14 59
(M H Tompkins) *hld up: hdwy over 3f out: rdn to chse wnr over 1f out: styd on same pce fnl f* **3/1**[1]

0040 **3** 2 **Desert Hawk**[20] 2513 7-8-11 **49**... PatrickHills 6 47
(W M Brisbourne) *hld up: hdwy over 3f out: rdn over 1f out: edgd lft: styd on same pce* **11/2**[2]

4410 **4** 1/2 **King Of Connacht**[6] 2957 5-8-11 **56**..........................(p) SamuelDrury(7) 4 53
(M Wellings) *prom: chsd ldr over 3f out: rdn over 1f out: no ex* **7/1**

0000 **5** nse **Spellman**[13] 2715 4-8-7 **45**.....................................(b) KirstyMilczarek 10 42
(N P Littmoden) *s.i.s: hld up: rdn over 2f out: hung rt fr over 1f out: r.o ins fnl f* **16/1**

3040 **6** hd **Granary Girl**[9] 2863 6-8-4 **47**................................... SimonPearce(5) 9 44
(J Pearce) *hld up in tch: nt clr run over 2f out: rdn over 1f out: styd on same pce* **10/1**

4255 **7** 5 **Cape Dancer (IRE)**[13] 2731 4-8-0 **45**........................... JamesRogers(7) 3 32
(J S Wainwright) *chsd ldrs: rdn over 3f out: wknd over 2f out* **16/1**

00-0 **8** nk **King's Account (USA)**[42] 1898 6-8-2 **45**..............................(t) KMay(5) 12 31
(S Gollings) *prom: lost pl over 6f out: hdwy 4f out: rdn and wknd over 1f out* **25/1**

0000 **9** 1 1/2 **Prince Charlemagne (IRE)**[17] 2621 5-9-2 **57**..........(p) JackMitchell(3) 1 40
(R M Stronge) *hld up: hdwy 1/2-way: rdn and wknd over 1f out* **8/1**

5000 **10** 1/2 **Ruwain**[12] 2755 4-8-0 **45**.. DebraEngland(7) 7 27
(W J Musson) *chsd ldrs 8f* **20/1**

3-06 **11** 5 **Foreign Edition (IRE)**[25] 2365 6-8-11 **49**.................... AndrewMullen 11 21
(Miss J A Camacho) *led: rdn and hdd over 2f out: wknd over 1f out* **8/1**

0-05 **12** 3 3/4 **Wickedish**[72] 851 4-8-2 **47**..(t) TobyAtkinson(7) 2 11
(M J Gingell) *hld up: rdn over 2f out: a in rr* **50/1**

0-00 **13** 3 **Sibo Baggins (IRE)**[36] 2055 4-8-4 **47**................................ AmyBaker(5) 13 5
(Mrs C A Dunnett) *hld up: racd keenly: hdwy 7f out: rdn and wknd over 2f out* **40/1**

2m 9.18s (-1.32) **Going Correction** -0.10s/f (Good) **13** Ran SP% **122.3**
Speed ratings (Par 101): **101,95,93,93,93 93,89,88,87,87 83,80,77**
toteswinger: 1&2 £2.70, 1&3 £3.90, 2&3 £1.10. CSF £25.92 CT £119.24 TOTE £6.00: £1.70, £1.70, £2.30; EX 23.90.
Owner The Maybe This Time Partnership **Bred** Bryan Ryan **Trained** Newmarket, Suffolk

FOCUS
A moderate handicap for apprentices taken in good style by Wee Charlie Castle, who was not winning out of turn. The form is not strong.
Spellman Official explanation: jockey said gelding hung right
Cape Dancer(IRE) Official explanation: jockey said filly hung right
Foreign Edition(IRE) Official explanation: jockey said gelding hung right

3114 AEROPAK MAIDEN AUCTION STKS 5f 43y
7:00 (7:05) (Class 6) 2-Y-O **£2,266** (£674; £337; £168) **Stalls** High

Form RPR

232 **1** **Raggle Taggle (IRE)**[17] 2618 2-8-8 0.............................. JamesDoyle 4 82+
(R M Beckett) *mde all: shkn up and r.o wl ins fnl f: eased nr fin* **5/6**[1]

533 **2** 3 1/4 **The Magic Of Rio**[22] 2462 2-8-9 0.................................. LiamJones 9 69
(W J Haggas) *trckd ldrs: racd keenly: rdn and ev ch over 1f out: no ex ins fnl f* **7/1**[3]

3 1/2 **Sills Vincero** 2-8-7 0.. ChrisCatlin 3 66
(P W Chapple-Hyam) *dwlt: hdwy 2f out: styd on* **25/1**

60 **4** 3/4 **Dream City (IRE)**[16] 2638 2-8-8 0..................................... DO'Donohoe 5 64
(M P Tregoning) *racd keenly: w wnr tl rdn 2f out: styd on same pce appr fnl f* **9/1**

0 **5** 1 3/4 **Billy Beetroot (USA)**[15] 2663 2-8-9 0............................. SaleemGolam 7 59
(S C Williams) *s.i.s: hld up: hdwy over 1f out: edgd lft and no ex ins fnl f* **12/1**

0 **6** 2 1/4 **Samba Queen (IRE)**[16] 2638 2-8-6 0........................... AdrianTNicholls 10 50+
(J L Spearing) *hld up: rdn over 1f out: nt trble ldrs* **50/1**

4 **7** 3/4 **Kitty Allen**[13] 2709 2-8-6 0... OscarUrbina 1 45
(M Botti) *chsd ldrs: rdn over 1f out: wknd ins fnl f* **9/2**[2]

8 3 1/2 **Tillagirl** 2-8-5 0.. TPO'Shea 2 31
(G G Margarson) *dwlt: outpcd* **50/1**

3 **9** nk **Secret City (IRE)**[18] 2581 2-8-11 0............................. DarrenWilliams 6 36
(R Bastiman) *prom: rdn and n.m.r 1/2-way: sn wknd: eased ins fnl f* **17/2**

0 **10** 1/2 **Farriers Gate**[13] 2709 2-8-4 0.. NickyMackay 8 27
(T Keddy) *prom to 1/2-way* **80/1**

65.37 secs (3.17) **Going Correction** +0.225s/f (Good) **10** Ran SP% **122.5**
Speed ratings (Par 91): **83,77,77,75,73 69,68,62,62,61**
toteswinger: 1&2 £1.10, 1&3 £4.80, 2&3 £56.90. CSF £7.86 TOTE £1.90: £1.10, £2.10, £6.10; EX 7.20.
Owner Lady Marchwood **Bred** Keith Wills **Trained** Whitsbury, Hants

FOCUS
A modest maiden run in a slow time considering the Good to firm going. The winner basically outclassed her rivals and the form looks pretty solid.

NOTEBOOK
Raggle Taggle(IRE) was entitled to win this on the form of her three previous runs in better maidens and duly did so with the minimum of fuss. Whilst handicapping looks a realistic level for her, her trainer was keen to point out that she is entered in the Super Sprint at Newbury in the middle of next month. (op 11-10 tchd 4-5)
The Magic Of Rio is starting to look exposed and while she shouldn't be too harshly handicapped once the nurseries start, she is not improving with her racing. (op 11-2 tchd 5-1)
Sills Vincero, weak in the market, was slowly away before making some useful late gains. She will have learnt from this considerate introduction. (op 16-1)
Dream City(IRE) is pacey enough but her overall level of form means that she will start life in nurseries on not much more than a plater's mark. (op 6-1 tchd 10-1)
Billy Beetroot(USA), whose dam was an excellent sprinter, was the subject of good support in the market beforehand and ran much better than on his debut, making headway into the race after a slow start before getting tired close home. Keep an eye on him. (op 50-1)
Kitty Allen, by this year's leading first-season sire, was disappointing on her first crack at turf. Her pedigree implies that she could be better on an artificial surface. (op 13-2 tchd 15-2)
Farriers Gate Official explanation: jockey said filly lost its action

3115 DIOMED DEVELOPMENTS (S) STKS 1m 1f
7:30 (7:31) (Class 6) 3-Y-O **£1,813** (£539; £269; £134) **Stalls** Low

Form RPR

0015 **1** **Sabre Light**[5] 2984 3-8-13 58...(p) JackMitchell(5) 7 68
(A Bailey) *chsd ldrs: led over 2f out: rdn clr fr over 1f out* **11/4**[2]

053 **2** 10 **Red Rouge**[21] 2486 3-8-7 58.. DO'Donohoe 6 35
(N Tinkler) *led 2f: chsd ldr tl led over 3f out: rdn and hdd over 2f out: sn edgd lft: styd on same pce appr fnl f* **4/1**

6143 **3** 3/4 **Secret Meaning**[12] 2753 3-8-8 61.................................(v) JackDean(5) 2 39
(W G M Turner) *hld up: bmpd 7f out: hdwy over 2f out: sn rdn: styng on same pce whn edgd lft fnl f* **10/3**[3]

-633 **4** hd **Sergeant Sharpe**[8] 2894 3-8-5 68..............................(b[1]) AshleyMorgan(7) 4 38
(M H Tompkins) *s.i.s: hld up: racd keenly: bmpd 7f out: hdwy and n.m.r on ins fr over 4f out: stmbld over 2f out: styd on same pce* **5/2**[1]

66 **5** 3/4 **Pure Inspiration**[35] 2089 3-8-4 0...................................... LukeMorris(3) 3 31
(P Howling) *prom: racd keenly: hmpd and lost pl 4f out: hdwy 3f out: rdn and hung lft fr over 2f out: sn outpcd* **16/1**

0-00 **6** 5 **Whodouthinkur (IRE)**[74] 1193 3-8-12 45...........................(v[1]) ChrisCatlin 1 25
(Mrs C A Dunnett) *hld up: rdn over 3f out: wknd 2f out* **20/1**

6600 **7** 13 **Hiss And Boo**[17] 2611 3-8-12 44.. LiamJones 9 —
(P Howling) *hld up: rdn over 2f out: sn wknd* **28/1**

00-0 **8** 19 **Call Of Ktulu (IRE)**[39] 1968 3-8-12 16....................(b[1]) StephenDonohoe 5 —
(J S Wainwright) *s.i.s: sn drvn along: hdwy to ld 7f out: rdn and hdd over 3f out: sn wknd* **66/1**

1m 58.96s (3.16) **Going Correction** -0.10s/f (Good) **8** Ran SP% **113.9**
Speed ratings (Par 97): **81,72,71,71,70 66,54,37**
toteswinger: 1&2 £3.70, 1&3 £1.70, 2&3 £3.40. CSF £13.84 TOTE £3.80: £1.80, £1.10, £1.70; EX 16.70.The winner was bought in for 9,000gns. Red Rouge was claimed by Graham Smith for £4,500. Secret Meaning was subject to a friendly claim.

Owner Phil Buchanan **Bred** D J And Mrs Deer **Trained** Newmarket, Suffolk
FOCUS
A poor seller for three-year-olds run in a very slow winning time, even for allowing for the grade. The easy winner may not have needed to improve on his recent form.
Sergeant Sharpe Official explanation: jockey said gelding stumbled

3116 FREEDERM H'CAP — 1m 3y
8:00 (8:01) (Class 5) (0-75,75) 3-Y-0+ — **£2,914** (£867; £433; £216) **Stalls** High

Form — RPR
1- **1** **Avertis**[258] 5895 3-9-10 **74** ...... OscarUrbina 1 — 80
(M Botti) *a.p: shkn up over 3f out: rdn to ld ins fnl f: r.o* — **10/1**[3]
0-22 **2** *3/4* **Haasem (USA)**[20] 2510 5-10-0 **68** ...... StephenDonohoe 8 — 74+
(J R Jenkins) *hld up: hdwy over 1f out: nt clr run and hmpd ins fnl f: swtchd rt: r.o wl* — **10/1**[3]
-332 **3** *nk* **El Dececy (USA)**[12] 2749 4-10-0 **68** ......(p) FrancisNorton 2 — 73
(S Parr) *led: rdn and hung rt over 3f out: hdd over 2f out: rallied to ld and hung lft 1f out: hdd and unable qck ins fnl f* — **11/2**[2]
6-50 **4** *2 1/4* **Life's A Whirl**[20] 2510 6-8-9 **49** ......(p) ChrisCatlin 3 — 49
(Mrs C A Dunnett) *chsd ldrs: rdn over 2f out: styd on same pce fnl f* **33/1**
3-01 **5** *hd* **Hasty Retreat**[25] 2367 3-9-8 **72** ...... JamieSpencer 5 — 72
(E A L Dunlop) *trckd ldr: led over 2f out: rdn and hdd 1f out: no ex wl ins fnl f* — **8/15**[1]
6022 **6** *nse* **Rockfield Lodge (IRE)**[73] 1203 3-9-11 **75** ...... NeilPollard 6 — 72
(M E Rimmer) *s.i.s: hld up: racd keenly: hdwy over 1f out: no ex ins fnl f* — **33/1**
10-3 **7** *1/2* **Affrettando (IRE)**[59] 1491 4-9-11 **65** ...... RobertHavlin 4 — 63
(J A R Toller) *hld up: rdn over 2f out: nt trble ldrs* — **20/1**
-000 **8** *2 1/2* **Zhebe**[14] 2695 3-8-9 **64** ...... JackMitchell(5) 7 — 55
(P J McBride) *chsd ldrs: rdn over 2f out: wknd over 1f out* — **50/1**

1m 43.6s (3.00) **Going Correction** +0.225s/f (Good)
WFA 3 from 4yo+ 10lb — **8** Ran SP% **111.4**
Speed ratings (Par 103): **94,93,92,90,90 90,89,87**
toteswinger: 1&2 £5.30, 1&3 £3.30, 2&3 £3.50. CSF £91.09 CT £603.22 TOTE £12.80: £2.60, £2.50, £1.40; EX 52.80.
Owner Dr Ornella Carlini Cozzi **Bred** Mrs Sally Doyle **Trained** Newmarket, Suffolk
■ Stewards' Enquiry : Francis Norton two-day ban: careless riding (Jul 1-2); caution: used whip down shoulder in forehand position.
FOCUS
A fair handicap featuring some in-form older horses and a couple of unexposed three-year-olds. The favourite was below par.
El Dececy(USA) Official explanation: jockey said gelding anticipated the start
Hasty Retreat Official explanation: jockey said gelding finished distressed

3117 ADIOS RATING RELATED MAIDEN STKS — 7f 3y
8:30 (8:33) (Class 5) 3-Y-0 — **£2,914** (£867; £433; £216) **Stalls** High

Form — RPR
4-30 **1** **Candle Sahara (IRE)**[23] 2429 3-9-0 **68** ...... TPO'Shea 2 — 74
(M R Channon) *led 1f: led again 1/2-way: hrd rdn over 1f out: all out* — **8/1**
55-4 **2** *1/2* **Wise Hawk**[39] 1957 3-9-3 **70** ...... LiamJones 4 — 76
(W J Haggas) *trckd ldr: plld hrd: rdn and ev ch fr over 1f out: hung rt ins fnl f: nt run on* — **7/2**[2]
6-50 **3** *6* **Seeking The Star (CAN)**[7] 2907 3-8-12 **67** ......(p) AhmedAjtebi(5) 7 — 60
(D M Simcock) *edgd rt s: racd keenly: led 6f out: hdd 1/2-way: rdn over 1f out: styd on same pce* — **66/1**
040 **4** *1* **Style Icon**[31] 2198 3-9-0 **67** ...... MarcHalford(3) 12 — 57
(D R C Elsworth) *hld up: hdwy over 1f out: nvr nrr* — **16/1**
4-0 **5** *hd* **Coach And Four (USA)**[11] 2786 3-9-3 **67** ...... JamieSpencer 14 — 57
(M G Quinlan) *racd alone: hld up in tch: rdn over 2f out: hung lft over 1f out: one pce* — **9/4**[1]
3-50 **6** *4 1/2* **Azure Mist**[33] 2118 3-8-7 **63** ...... AshleyMorgan(7) 11 — 41
(M H Tompkins) *s.i.s: hld up: rdn 1/2-way: nvr nrr* — **33/1**
0-05 **7** *3/4* **Darley Star**[20] 2496 3-9-0 **60** ...... ChrisCatlin 3 — 39
(C E Brittain) *prom: rdn over 3f out: wknd 2f out* — **40/1**
4-54 **8** *1* **Sunny Sprite**[19] 2546 3-9-0 **70** ...... LukeMorris(3) 5 — 40
(J M P Eustace) *hld up in tch: rdn over 2f out: sn wknd* — **25/1**
62-4 **9** *shd* **Marraasi (USA)**[40] 1930 3-9-0 **69** ...... DO'Donohoe 8 — 36
(M P Tregoning) *hmpd s: trckd ldrs: rdn over 2f out: sn wknd* — **7/1**[3]
2-30 **10** *nk* **Adab (IRE)**[57] 1519 3-9-3 **70** ...... RobertHavlin 6 — 39
(J H M Gosden) *hld up: hdwy 1/2-way: rdn and wknd over 1f out* — **12/1**
425 **11** *22* **Kirkie (USA)**[96] 867 3-9-3 **69** ...... FrancisNorton 1 — —
(S Parr) *prom 5f* — **7/1**[3]
400 **12** *1 1/4* **Candida's Beau**[14] 2705 3-9-3 **68** ......(b) JamesDoyle 9 — —
(R M Beckett) *chsd ldrs over 4f* — **50/1**
24-0 **13** *18* **Jerry Hamilton (USA)**[38] 2014 3-9-3 **70** ...... AdrianTNicholls 13 — —
(M Johnston) *s.i.s: a in rr: rdn and wknd 1/2-way* — **20/1**

1m 28.28s (1.68) **Going Correction** +0.225s/f (Good) — **13** Ran SP% **120.1**
Speed ratings (Par 99): **99,98,91,90,90 85,84,83,82,82 57,56,35**
toteswinger: 1&2 £14.30, 1&3 not won, 2&3 not won. CSF £34.14 TOTE £10.60: £2.60, £1.40, £17.20; EX 49.90.
Owner Jaber Abdullah **Bred** John Cullinan **Trained** West Ilsley, Berks
FOCUS
This maiden was restricted to horses rated 70 and below. They finished well strung out behind the front two and the form probably isn't all that strong, with the winner still below her best.
Kirkie(USA) Official explanation: jockey said gelding moved poorly
Jerry Hamilton(USA) Official explanation: jockey said gelding never travelled

3118 BAZUKA H'CAP — 6f 3y
9:00 (9:03) (Class 6) (0-65,65) 3-Y-0 — **£2,201** (£655; £327; £163) **Stalls** High

Form — RPR
3251 **1** **Filligree (IRE)**[6] 2935 3-8-10 **61** ...... JPHamblett(7) 8 — 78+
(Rae Guest) *hld up in tch: led over 2f out: rdn clr fr over 1f out* — **10/11**[1]
000 **2** *6* **Ma Mirage (IRE)**[11] 2786 3-7-13 **46** oh1 ...... LukeMorris(3) 2 — 41
(S C Williams) *hld up: hdwy over 2f out: rdn over 1f out: no imp* — **50/1**
3321 **3** *hd* **Young Gladiator (IRE)**[50] 1674 3-9-4 **65** ...... AndrewMullen(3) 5 — 59
(Miss J A Camacho) *bmpd s: led: hdd over 4f out: rdn over 2f out: styd on same pce appr fnl f* — **7/1**[3]
0-00 **4** *6* **Framington**[3] 3030 3-8-3 **47** ow1 ...... TPO'Shea 3 — 22
(M R Channon) *sn outpcd: styd on ins fnl f: nvr nrr* — **33/1**
-123 **5** *1* **Rosie Says No**[12] 2757 3-9-7 **65** ...... JamieSpencer 9 — 37
(R M H Cowell) *hld up in tch: shkn up 1/2-way: wknd fnl f* — **7/2**[2]
-323 **6** *1/2* **Nice Dream**[54] 1581 3-9-0 **63** ...... AhmedAjtebi(5) 4 — 33
(C E Brittain) *chsd ldrs: rdn over 2f out: wkng whn hung rt fnl f* — **9/1**
503 **7** *nk* **Rossini Byline (IRE)**[6] 2935 3-8-4 **53** ...... JackDean(5) 6 — 22
(J L Spearing) *prom 4f* — **14/1**
005 **8** *3 3/4* **Wicksy Creek**[35] 2074 3-8-2 **46** ...... NickyMackay 7 — 3
(G C H Chung) *led over 4f out: hdd over 2f out: wknd over 1f out* — **20/1**
0-60 **9** *9* **Southwark Newsboy (IRE)**[60] 1454 3-8-2 **46** oh1 ......(v[1]) ChrisCatlin 1 — —
(Mrs C A Dunnett) *chsd ldrs over 3f* — **66/1**

1m 15.01s (0.61) **Going Correction** +0.225s/f (Good) — **9** Ran SP% **114.9**
Speed ratings (Par 97): **104,96,95,87,86 85,85,80,68**
toteswinger: 1&2 £86.80, 1&3 £1.20, 2&3 not won. CSF £73.54 CT £224.96 TOTE £1.90: £1.30, £13.60, £1.80; EX 82.00 Place 6: £49.74, Place 5 £30.59..
Owner The Filligree Partnership **Bred** T Hirschfeld **Trained** Newmarket, Suffolk
■ Stewards' Enquiry : Chris Catlin one-day ban: used whip when out of contention (Jul 1)
FOCUS
No strength in depth to this handicap and they came home at intervals behind the well-handicapped winner. She probably stepped up a bit further.
Rosie Says No Official explanation: jockey said filly moved poorly
T/Plt: £22.70 to a £1 stake. Pool: £60,238.15. 1,933.36 winning tickets. T/Qpdt: £10.70 to a £1 stake. Pool: £3,721.98. 256.60 winning tickets. CR

3100 ASCOT (R-H)
Wednesday, June 18

OFFICIAL GOING: Good to firm (firm in places; overall 10.0, straight course 11.0; round course 9.4)
Dolling out added 12yards to race distances on the round course.
Wind: Fresh, half against Weather: Mainly cloudy

3119 JERSEY STKS (GROUP 3) — 7f
2:30 (2:32) (Class 1) 3-Y-0
£39,739 (£15,064; £7,539; £3,759; £1,883; £945) **Stalls** Centre

Form — RPR
3-1 **1** **Aqlaam**[32] 2198 3-9-1 93 ...... RHills 12 — 119+
(W J Haggas) *lw: hld up in tch: led 2f out: edgd bdly lft: rdn out: readily holding runner-up fnl f* — **13/2**[2]
6-10 **2** *2* **Il Warrd (IRE)**[38] 2032 3-9-1 109 ...... LDettori 11 — 114
(Saeed Bin Suroor) *lw: stdd s: t.k.h and prom: chalng whn edgd away fr hanging wnr over 1f out: kpt on same pce* — **10/1**
16-5 **3** *nk* **Dream Eater (IRE)**[46] 1808 3-9-1 111 ......(t) FrancisNorton 6 — 113
(A M Balding) *hld up in rr: hdwy and hrd rdn over 2f out: styd on fnl f: nt rch first 2* — **7/1**[3]
-102 **4** *1/2* **Stimulation (IRE)**[25] 2409 3-9-1 110 ...... SteveDrowne 16 — 112
(H Morrison) *lw: t.k.h: sn prom: rdn over 2f out: kpt on fnl f* — **17/2**
4-50 **5** *2 3/4* **Strike The Deal (USA)**[46] 1808 3-9-6 110 ...... RyanMoore 8 — 109
(J Noseda) *mid-div: hdwy to chse ldrs 3f out: one pce appr fnl f* — **25/1**
1-4 **6** *nk* **Jupiter Pluvius (USA)**[25] 2418 3-9-4 0 ...... JMurtagh 15 — 106
(A P O'Brien, Ire) *lw: t.k.h: settled in rr of mid-div: effrt and hrd rdn over 2f out: styd on same pce: nvr able to chal* — **13/2**[2]
1-22 **7** *hd* **Generous Thought**[35] 2104 3-9-1 98 ...... JamieSpencer 3 — 103
(P Howling) *dwlt: sn rdn along and struggling in last pl: styd on u.p fnl 3f: nvr nrr* — **16/1**
3-1 **8** *shd* **War Officer (USA)**[50] 1712 3-9-1 0 ...... C-PLemaire 18 — 103
(J-C Rouget, France) *w'like: lw: hld up towards rr gng wl: sme hdwy 2f out: sn rdn and no imp* — **11/1**
1-1 **9** *nse* **Calming Influence (IRE)**[25] 2409 3-9-1 107 ......(t) KerrinMcEvoy 7 — 102
(Saeed Bin Suroor) *lw: mid-div: rdn 3f out: nt pce to chal* — **9/2**[1]
2-11 **10** *1 1/2* **Tawaash (USA)**[18] 2624 3-9-1 95 ...... MartinDwyer 5 — 98
(M A Jarvis) *b.hind: disp ld: led 1/2-way tl 2f out: btn whn hmpd over 1f out* — **33/1**
3-30 **11** *1 3/4* **Royal Confidence**[45] 1830 3-8-12 108 ...... MichaelHills 14 — 91
(B W Hills) *a towards rr: rdn and n.d fnl 3f* — **25/1**
4-33 **12** *3 1/2* **Red Alert Day**[25] 2409 3-9-1 105 ...... ShaneKelly 9 — 84
(S A Callaghan) *mid-div: effrt and hung rt over 2f out: sn btn* — **16/1**
0-25 **13** *2 1/4* **Bobs Surprise**[25] 2409 3-9-1 107 ...... WilliamBuick 17 — 78
(B W Hills) *swtg: disp ld tl 1/2-way: hrd rdn and wknd over 2f out* — **50/1**
0-10 **14** *10* **Georgebernardshaw (IRE)**[38] 2032 3-9-1 0 ...... JAHeffernan 2 — 51
(A P O'Brien, Ire) *in rr of mid-div: rdn and wknd 1/2-way: sn bhd* — **28/1**
33-6 **15** *1 3/4* **Billyford (IRE)**[16] 2684 3-9-1 0 ...... MJKinane 13 — 46
(Liam Roche, Ire) *tall: lengthy: t.k.h in midfield: rdn 3f out: sn wknd* — **66/1**
31-4 **16** *1* **Shallal**[60] 1471 3-9-1 100 ...... JimmyFortune 10 — 44
(P W Chapple-Hyam) *b: chsd ldrs: drvn along over 4f out: sn lost pl* — **33/1**

1m 26.98s (-1.02) **Going Correction** +0.125s/f (Good) — **16** Ran SP% **117.5**
Speed ratings (Par 109): **110,107,107,106,103 103,103,102,102,101 99,95,92,81,79 78**
toteswinger: 1&2 £17.40, 1&3 £9.90, 2&3 £15.30. CSF £62.58 CT £472.58 TOTE £8.90: £3.40, £3.40, £2.90; EX 82.60 Trifecta £557.60 Pool: £6,781.63. 9.00 winning units..
Owner Hamdan Al Maktoum **Bred** Granham Farm **Trained** Newmarket, Suffolk
FOCUS
A typically competitive renewal of a race that caters mainly for those unable to cut it over 1m at the top level, although it was rather disappointing to see only four horses from the Newmarket Classics taking their place in the line-up. A big step up from Aqlaam, who is not far behind the leading 3yo milers now, and Il Warrd built on his Polytrack form.
NOTEBOOK
Aqlaam ◆, supported strongly in the market beforehand, was evidently expected to step up markedly on his recent win in a Newbury maiden (form worked out extremely well with four of next five home having won subsequently) and he found plenty once hitting the front over a furlong out to win in the style of a very smart horse. Settling nicely, just a few lengths in behind the leaders, he was switched right to come with his challenge and seemed to relish this faster surface. The William Haggas yard has been in tremendous form of late, so this win certainly came as no surprise to connections, with his trainer stating afterwards he is probably the best horse in his care. He was still green under pressure and there should be plenty of improvement to come, with 1m likely to prove within his stamina range. There are reportedly no specific plans, although his trainer plans on keeping him to flat tracks as the horse has had knee problems. He is an exciting prospect. (op 7-1 tchd 8-1 in a place and 15-2)
Il Warrd(IRE), with Marcus Tregoning when bolting up inthe Easter Stakes at Kempton on his three-year-old debut, failed to get home having raced freely on his first start for Bin Suroor in the French 2000 Guineas, and this drop down to 7f was always likely to suit. He once again failed to settle, taking a good grip just in behind the leaders, but still looked a big player when coming through over a furlong out. He was always coming off second best to Aqlaam though and having the winner carry him slightly left made no difference to the outcome. The son of Pivotal is up to winning a race at this level, and may be even better next season, as he looks just the type to improve with age. (op 11-1 tchd 12-1 in a place)
Dream Eater(IRE) excelled himself to finish fifth at 50-1 behind Henrythenavigator in the 2000 Guineas at Newmarket (first-time tongue tie) and he too looked likely to be helped by the return to 7f. That may have been a premature assumption though as, having been held up towards the near side early, he lacked the basic speed of the front pair and the line came too soon for him to claim second. He shows a good attitude and his rider confirmed after the race that he will benefit from a return to further, but his winning record leaves a bit to be desired and he is not going to be the easiest to place. (op 15-2)

Stimulation(IRE), four lengths behind Dream Eater at Newmarket and a head behind Calming Influence last time, is a tough and consistent sort and was 4lb better off with the latter. Soon prominent, he started to come under pressure after three out and looked set to drop away with two to run, but dug in and stuck on willingly for fourth. On this showing he needs 1m, albeit he appeared not to stay in the Guineas, and he is likely to continue to give a good account at Listed/Group 3 level. (op 8-1 tchd 9-1)

Strike The Deal(USA), the third and final runner from the 2000 Guineas, was always likely to struggle under his Group 2 penalty and he ran above expectations back in fifth. He is not going to find winning easy this season.

Jupiter Pluvius(USA), a smart two-year-old who claimed the scalp of French 2000 Guineas runner-up Famous Name in a Group 3 at Leopardstown, had looked Ballydoyle's number one Guineas contender until being overtaken by Henrythenavigator and he ended up missing the race. He ran well to a point on his reappearance in the Irish equivalent, getting quite tired in the final furlong, and this drop back to 7f looked in his favour. The penalty was never going to make life easy though and he never looked likely to win at any stage, lacking a sufficient change of gear to challenge. He still seemed to be carrying condition before the race though, so it is probable we have not yet seen the best of him. (op 11-2 tchd 7-1 in a place)

Generous Thought has been shaping like a Pattern performer in handicaps and could easily have come into this on a five-timer had things gone his way in two starts this season (beaten a short head at Newbury without Spencer resorting to the whip and then coming from way back to finish second at York last time). He struggled to lay up early, being ridden along in last, but stayed on well inside the final quarter mile and looks in need of 1m now.

War Officer(USA), whose yard was responsible for last year's beaten favourite, US Ranger, has returned in France this year to win two Listed races and this faster going was expected to suit, according to connections. He travelled strongly through the race and few looked to be going better two out, but he was unable to go on with his effort from over a furlong out and faded. He clearly has an engine and perhaps returning to a slower surface will help.

Calming Influence(IRE), unbeaten in two previous starts, was 4lb worse off with his Newmarket victim Stimulation, but was still expected to confirm the form, even though it was interesting to see that he had seemingly been shunned by Dettori. However, he started to struggle from well over two out and could not muster a run, fading out in the final furlong. This was obviously disappointing and perhaps slower ground will be required in future for the son of King's Best. (tchd 5-1 in places)

Tawaash(USA), a recent handicap winner, ran well for a long way and was still third just over a furlong out, but in the end it all proved a bit much.

Royal Confidence could never get into it and failed to build on her 1000 Guineas effort.

Red Alert Day Official explanation: jockey said colt hung right

Georgebernardshaw(IRE) has finally got his act together this season and followed his easy maiden win with a rampant success in a Listed contest at the Curragh in April. Both those wins were in heavy ground though and he seemed to find the livelier conditions against him when a disappointing tenth in the French Guineas. This return to 7f was expected to suit, but he again had questions to answer regarding the ground and was beaten at just past halfway. He did not look great in his coat beforehand. (op 33-1)

Shallal Official explanation: jockey said colt hung right

3120 WINDSOR FOREST STKS (GROUP 2) (F&M) — 1m (S)

3:05 (3:08) (Class 1) 4-Y-O+

£79,478 (£30,128; £15,078; £7,518; £3,766; £1,890) **Stalls** Centre

Form	Pos	Dist	Horse	Jockey	RPR
31-1	**1**		**Sabana Perdida (IRE)**[39] 1993 5-8-12 0 (A De Royer-Dupre, France) *trckd ldrs: wnt 2nd 2f out: rdn and hung rt whn clsng ins fnl f: r.o to ld fnl 50yds* **4/1**[2]	(t) C-PLemaire 8	115
3-11	**2**	*3/4*	**Heaven Sent**[46] 1807 5-8-12 111 (Sir Michael Stoute) *midfield: hdwy over 3f out: rdn to ld ent fnl 2f out: r.o u.p: worn down fnl 50yds* **9/4**[1]	RyanMoore 7	113+
-051	**3**	*1 3/4*	**Grecian Dancer**[25] 2420 5-8-12 0 (Charles O'Brien, Ire) *str: midfield: rdn and hdwy over 2f out: sn denied a run: swtchd lft over 1f out whn nt pce of ldrs: styd on wl towards fin* **8/1**	JMurtagh 9	109+
-005	**4**	*nk*	**Majestic Roi (USA)**[12] 2788 4-9-3 115 (M R Channon) *racd keenly in midfield: hdwy whn nt clr run and swtchd rt over 2f out: sn chsd ldrs: styd on u.p fnl f* **16/1**	DarryllHolland 1	113
4-13	**5**	*nk*	**Enforce (USA)**[11] 2827 5-8-12 105 (Mrs L Wadham) *in tch: effrt 2f out: nt qckn over 1f out: sn edgd rt: styd on ins fnl f: one pce cl home* **25/1**	WilliamBuick 5	108
-300	**6**	*2 1/4*	**Barshiba (IRE)**[11] 2827 4-8-12 108 (D R C Elsworth) *sn led: rdn and hdd ent fnl 2f: continued to chse ldrs: kpt on same pce fnl f* **25/1**	TQuinn 6	102
-341	**7**	*2 3/4*	**Nans Joy (IRE)**[27] 2347 4-8-12 97 (E J O'Neill) *stdd s: hld up: rdn and hdwy into midfield 2f out: no imp fr over 1f out* **40/1**	KerrinMcEvoy 3	96
1-32	**8**	*3 1/2*	**Fragrancy (IRE)**[23] 2465 4-8-12 91 (M A Jarvis) *led early: prom: pushed along and lost pl 2f out: n.d after* **25/1**	PhilipRobinson 2	88
-122	**9**	*3/4*	**Many Colours**[117] 672 4-8-12 105 (Saeed Bin Suroor) *prom and racd wd of field in centre of trck: grad c over fr 5f out: pressed ldrs 2f out: hung rt and wknd over 1f out* **15/2**	LDettori 13	86+
15-2	**10**	*1 1/2*	**Harvest Queen (IRE)**[46] 1807 5-8-12 110 (P J Makin) *midfield: hdwy over 3f out: pushed along 2f out: wknd over 1f out* **16/1**	SebSanders 10	83
46-4	**11**	*3/4*	**Selinka**[11] 2827 4-8-12 107 (R Hannon) *stdd s: hld up in rr: pushed along over 3f out: nvr on terms w ldrs* **25/1**	RichardHughes 4	81
50-4	**12**	*nk*	**Silca Chiave**[16] 2666 4-8-12 104 (M R Channon) *hld up: rdn over 2f out: wl btn over 1f out* **66/1**	TedDurcan 11	80
2015	**13**	*15*	**Baharah (USA)**[11] 2827 4-8-12 109 (G A Butler) *midfield: effrt whn n.m.r over 2f out: sn lost pl: eased whn btn over 1f out* **7/1**[3]	EddieAhern 12	46+

1m 39.73s (-0.87) **Going Correction** +0.125s/f (Good) **13** Ran SP% **117.2**

Speed ratings (Par 115): **109,108,106,106,105 103,100,97,96,95 94,94,79**

toteswinger: 1&2 £2.20, 1&3 £7.30, 2&3 £3.30. CSF £11.97 CT £68.75 TOTE £3.80: £1.20, £1.50, £2.30; EX 11.80 Trifecta £68.50 Pool: £7,921.87, 85.50 winning units..

Owner Scuderia Zaro **Bred** Musaed Abo Salim **Trained** Chantilly, France

FOCUS

Not the strongest of renewals, but the front pair look capable of mixing it at Group 1 level and the fourth is already a winner in that grade. The winning time was ordinary for a fillies' Group 2, 1/10th of a second slower than the Royal Hunt Cup and about a second quicker than the three-year-old fillies' Listed handicap, albeit they did not go much of a gallop. Sabana Perfida looks the best guide to the form.

NOTEBOOK

Sabana Perdida(IRE), third at 50/1 behind Nannina in last season's renewal, returned with a ready win at Lingfield on her seasonal return and looked a major player with a tongue tie on here. Always well placed, she got tapped for toe when Heaven Sent kicked into the lead inside the final furlong, but ran on strongly for pressure and it was clear from half a furlong out she was going to get up. A sound surface seems a must and the Group 1 Prix d'Astarte at Deauville is her next probable target. (op 7-2 tchd 9-2 in places)

Heaven Sent ◆, representing the Cheveley Park Stud, responsible for two of the last three winners of this contest, is a typical improver of Stoute's and she recorded a career-best when winning the Group 3 Dahlia Stakes at Newmarket last time. She showed a good change of pace to go into the lead inside the final furlong and looked all over the winner until run down close home. There is an argument to say she went too soon, her rider eager to secure his first ever Royal Ascot winner, but this still represented an improved effort and she looks capable of scoring at this level. (op 5-2)

Grecian Dancer, currently in-foal to Galileo, posted improved form when romping away with a Group 3 at the Curragh last month and looked a player. She did not get the splits though and may well have been a length or so closer had things gone her way. She just managed to grab third and this versatile mare is clearly on the top of her game right now. (op 10-1)

Majestic Roi(USA), shouldering a Group 1 penalty for last season's Sun Chariot Stakes win, has not been at her best this season, but ran a better race in the Diomed at Epsom last time and this represented another improved effort. She is steadily finding her form again, but the penalty will continue to make life tough for her at this level. (op 18-1 tchd 20-1)

Enforce(USA), an in-form filly who finished third behind Lady Gloria at Epsom recently, ran another solid race and was able to confirm form with several of these. She is not quite up to this level and will find easier opportunities to gain more black type. (tchd 40-1)

Barshiba(IRE) is very talented on her day, as shown when winning the Sandringham at last year's meeting and finishing fourth with a slipped saddle in the Group 1 Prix d'Astarte, but she has largely struggled this year and often spoils her chance by pulling. She was ridden differently on this occasion, going off the front end, but was always likely to prove vulnerable and in the end was found wanting for a change of gear.

Nans Joy(IRE), a Listed winner at Frankfurt last month, did not look that great in her coat beforehand, but she ran about as well as could have been expected in this grade and will find easier opportunities. (op 66-1)

Fragrancy(IRE) is a useful handicapper, but she did not look that good in her coat and stood little chance of making an impact in this company. (op 33-1)

Many Colours, a progressive filly in Dubai earlier in the season, went solo in the centre of the track until just before halfway before dropping out tamely in the final furlong. She needs to step up on this if she is to find a race at Group level. (op 10-1)

Harvest Queen(IRE), second to Heaven Sent in the Dahlia Stakes, should have done a lot better and evidently failed to run her race. (op 14-1)

Selinka pleased with her recent comeback in the Lady Gloria race at Epsom, but this faster ground was not in her favour and she struggled to get into it.

Silca Chiave had a lot to prove and duly strugggled.

Baharah(USA), unsuited by the track when only fifth behind Lady Gloria at Epsom, had earlier won well over course and distance and she looked one of the likelier winners. However, she was squeezed for room at a vital stage and soon dropped out, being eased from a furlong out. Her trainer speculated that this race had probably come too soon, but she is developing the profile of an inconsistent filly. Official explanation: trainer said race had probably come too soon (op 11-2)

3121 PRINCE OF WALES'S STKS (GROUP 1) — 1m 2f

3:45 (3:46) (Class 1) 4-Y-O+

£212,887 (£80,700; £40,387; £20,137; £10,087; £5,062) **Stalls** High

Form	Pos	Dist	Horse	Jockey	RPR
3-11	**1**		**Duke Of Marmalade (IRE)**[24] 2432 4-9-0 0 (A P O'Brien, Ire) *lw: chsd ldrs: drvn along over 2f out: led jst over 1f out: sn drew clr* **1/1**[1]	JMurtagh 13	130+
1-12	**2**	*4*	**Phoenix Tower (USA)**[32] 2193 4-9-0 116 (H R A Cecil) *hld up in rr of midfield: outpcd and rdn whn hung rt ent st: rallied over 1f out: styd on wl to snatch 2nd on line* **7/1**[2]	TedDurcan 8	121
1-33	**3**	*shd*	**Pipedreamer**[20] 2543 4-9-0 110 (J H M Gosden) *mid-div: rdn and hdwy 2f out: chsd wnr ins fnl f: a comf hld: lost 2nd on line* **11/1**	JimmyFortune 9	121
11-2	**4**	*1 1/2*	**Pressing (IRE)**[31] 2230 5-9-0 116 (M A Jarvis) *prom: led briefly wl over 1f out: sn outpcd by wnr* **10/1**	NCallan 3	118
12-1	**5**	*nk*	**Ask**[54] 1596 5-9-0 119 (Sir Michael Stoute) *b. nr fore: lw: in tch: drvn along ent st: one pce: btn whn n.m.r 2f out* **7/1**[2]	RyanMoore 6	119+
1-55	**6**	*hd*	**Stotsfold**[41] 1921 5-9-0 110 (W R Swinburn) *s.s: hld up in last pl: hdwy on rail 2f out: swtchd lft over 1f out: r.o: nrst fin* **100/1**	AdamKirby 5	117
3-13	**7**	*1 1/4*	**Loup Breton (IRE)**[31] 2238 4-9-0 0 (E Lellouche, France) *hld up in rr: rdn over 2f out: nvr rchd ldrs* **20/1**	C-PLemaire 11	114
-036	**8**	*5*	**Petara Bay (IRE)**[20] 2543 4-9-0 105 (T G Mills) *chsd ldr: drvn to chal 2f out: wknd over 1f out* **100/1**	JimCrowley 10	104
1200	**9**	*5*	**Hattan (IRE)**[20] 2543 6-9-0 113 (C E Brittain) *dwlt and swtchd to ins rail: hld up towards rr: mod effrt over 2f out: n.d* **66/1**	SebSanders 7	94
-014	**10**	*4 1/2*	**Regime (IRE)**[20] 2543 4-9-0 112 (M L W Bell) *lw: hld up in rr: rdn over 2f out: nvr trbld ldrs* **40/1**	JamieSpencer 1	85
23-3	**11**	*1*	**Red Rock Canyon (IRE)**[24] 2432 4-9-0 0 (A P O'Brien, Ire) *lw: led tl wknd wl over 1f out* **66/1**	JAHeffernan 2	83
0-21	**12**	*1 1/2*	**Sixties Icon**[27] 2325 5-9-0 114 (J Noseda) *lw: hld up in tch: rdn over 2f out: sn wknd* **8/1**[3]	LDettori 12	80

2m 5.35s (-4.45) **Going Correction** 0.0s/f (Good) **12** Ran SP% **115.7**

Speed ratings (Par 117): **117,113,113,112,112 112,111,107,103,99 98,97**

toteswinger: 1&2 £1.60, 1&3 £4.60, 2&3 £12.90. CSF £7.62 CT £49.29 TOTE £1.80: £1.02, £2.60, £4.70; EX 7.30 Trifecta £37.60 Pool: £10,871.03, 213.92 winning units..

Owner Mrs John Magnier & M Tabor **Bred** Southern Bloodstock **Trained** Ballydoyle, Co Tipperary

FOCUS

This did not look the strongest of renewals in terms of depth (of the three Group 1 winners in the field only Duke Of Marmalade's carried any real substance) but the winner confirmed himself to be the leading 1m2f performer in Europe with an impressive display. He is rated up 4lb and only 3lb behind Manduro's winning perfomance in this event last year. The form looks solid with Lockinge runner-up Phoenix Tower staying on for second and last year's fifth Pressing going one better this time.

NOTEBOOK

Duke Of Marmalade(IRE) consistently performed to a high-class level in Group 1 company at three without gaining any success, but he was reportedly running with pain most of the time, the pins he had in his front joint apparently catching a ligament and resulting in him being semi-lame all the time. A few procedures over the winter have seemingly sorted things out though and he has looked a much happier horse this term. Workmanlike winner of the Prix Ganay on his reappearance, he did not have to be at his best to beat Finsceal Beo in the Tattersalls Gold Cup and the way he was backed before the race suggested defeat was out of the question. Always well placed, he edged out rounding for home and quickly settled the issue over a furlong out, showing a bright turn of foot. This was an impressive performance from Europe's leading 1m2f performer, but he has already shown himself to be fully effective at 1m and he shapes as though 1m4f will be within his range. Therefore races such as the Eclipse, Irish Champion Stakes, King George and Arc are all likely to come under consideration, but with Henrythenavigator and Soldier Of Fortune also likely to enter calculations for those events, O'Brien will have some juggling to do. (op 11-8 tchd 6-4 in places)

Phoenix Tower(USA), narrow winner of the Earl Of Sefton on reappearance (head and a neck in front of Pipedreamer) improved on that to fill second spot behind Creachadoir in the Lockinge and it was interesting he was lining up in this contest, as opposed to the Queen Anne where there appeared to be no outstanding performer. Restrained early on, he did not pick up immediately, but stuck on really well inside the final furlong and just managed to confirm earlier form with Pipedreamer. He was no match for the easy winner, but gives the form a solid look and is more than capable of winning at this level. Races such as the Eclipse, Juddmonte International and Champion Stakes are likely to fall under consideration. (op 5-1)

Pipedreamer, a highly progressive three-year-old who looked a horse of real quality when romping away with the Cambridgeshire, was unsuited by the slow gallop on his reappearance when just denied in the Earl Of Sefton, and then got too far back in soft ground when third in the Brigadier Gerard Stakes at Sandown last time. The good gallop here really suited though and he was able to show his true capabilities, despite getting warm beforehand, emerging as the winner's main challenger, only to get run out of second close home. He certainly has the ability to win races at Group 2 level, but connections are going to have to change tactics on the horse when returning to smaller-field events, as he usually has to give up too much ground off a steady gallop. (op 10-1)

Pressing(IRE), fifth in a stronger renewal last year, gained his first win at the top level at the Capannelle last November and returned there with a improved effort to just get touched off by Saddex last month. Edgy beforehand, he was soon prominent and ran well, but could not quicken when asked and found the winner in a different league. He has not won as much as he should have done for a horse of his ability though and is always likely to fall short in top Group 1 company, but should find other opportunities as he is likely to be campaigned. (tchd 11-1)

Ask stood only three races last season, winning two Group 3s and finishing up with a fine second on firm ground in the Woodbine International. Dropped back down to 1m2f for his reappearance at Sandown, he made quite hard work of winning, but had been kept fresh for this and he looked a danger if getting a decent gallop. He did, but still lacked the pace on this fast ground and could only stay on at the one pace. A return to further is evidently needed and connections must now be rueing the fact they chose this contest over the Hardwicke, a race he would have held very strong claims in. (tchd 15-2)

Stotsfold, a Group 3 winner who has struggled a bit in that grade this year, excelled himself back in sixth and was arguably unlucky not to finish closer, coming from last turning in. He is another who needs a good gallop to be seen to best effect.

Loup Breton(IRE), third behind Sageburg and Darjina in the Prix d'Ispahan last time, had won a Group 2 over this distance on his reappearance, but he lacked the basic speed on this faster ground and could never challenge. (op 16-1)

Petara Bay(IRE), around four lengths behind Pipedreamer in the Brigadier Gerard, was always going to struggle in this grade and he ran about as well as could have been expected.

Hattan(IRE) was always going to fall short at this level and he never looked like making a run. (op 100-1)

Regime(IRE) needs softer ground to be at his best and could not pick up from the rear. (tchd 50-1)

Red Rock Canyon(IRE) performed his pace-making duties admirably. He is a smart performer in his own right and surely deserves another chance in maiden company to finally win a race.

Sixties Icon coped really well with this trip when winning tidily at Goodwood last time, but he failed to run to form here and trailed in a disappointing last. His stable have not been in the best of form and perhaps he can be given another chance, but he is unlikely to be winning at this level again. (op 9-1)

3122 ROYAL HUNT CUP (HERITAGE H'CAP) — 1m (S)

4:20 (4:23) (Class 2) 3-Y-O+

£62,310 (£18,660; £9,330; £4,670; £2,330; £1,170) **Stalls** Centre

Form					RPR
2120	**1**		**Mr Aviator (USA)**[12] [2790] 4-9-5 **102** (R Hannon) *trckd ldrs: rdn and str chal fr over 1f out: r.o gamely to ld fnl 75yds* **25/1**	RichardHughes 4	112
6-44	**2**	*nk*	**Docofthebay (IRE)**[23] [2465] 4-9-6 **103** (b[1]) (J A Osborne) *racd keenly in midfield: hdwy 4f out: rdn to ld over 2f out: hrd pressed fnl f: hdd fnl 75yds* **10/1**	ShaneKelly 1	113+
0-36	**3**	*nk*	**Royal Power (IRE)**[12] [2789] 5-8-12 **95** (D Nicholls) *hld up: hdwy 1/2-way: chsd ldrs over 2f out: str chal fnl f: nt qckn cl home* **25/1**	AdrianTNicholls 5	104
0114	**4**	*3/4*	**Kavachi (IRE)**[19] [2582] 5-8-4 **87** (G L Moore) *hld up: hdwy over 3f out: nt clr run over 2f out: swtchd lft over 1f out: rn and clsd bhd ldrs ins fnl f: nt quite pce to get there* **33/1**	FrancisNorton 6	94
1-11	**5**	*3 1/4*	**Bankable (IRE)**[18] [2600] 4-9-2 **99** 5ex (L M Cumani) *lw: edgy in stalls: hld up in rr on outside: hdwy over 3f out: styd on fnl f: nvr trbld nr side ldrs* **13/8**[1]	LDettori 25	99+
6144	**6**	*3/4*	**Ballinteni**[20] [2545] 6-8-10 **93** (Miss Gay Kelleway) *midfield: pushed along 1/2-way: hdwy over 1f out: styd on u.p ins fnl f: nt pce to chal ldrs* **100/1**	C-PLemaire 24	91+
-020	**7**	*1 1/4*	**Diamond Tycoon (USA)**[19] [2580] 4-9-8 **105** (B J Meehan) *prom: led over 3f out: hdd over 2f out: edgd rt u.p over 1f out: styd on same pce fnl f* **33/1**	NCallan 8	100
03-0	**8**	*1*	**Humungous (IRE)**[39] [1982] 5-9-2 **99** (p) (C R Egerton) *lw: midfield: nt clr run over 2f out: sn swtchd rt: styd on over 1f out: nvr able to rch ldrs* **50/1**	SteveDrowne 12	92
0010	**9**	*1/2*	**Orchard Supreme**[20] [2545] 5-8-5 **88** (R Hannon) *lw: hld up in mdfield: rdn and hdwy over 3f out: chsd ldrs and edgd rt fr 2f out: kpt on u.p fnl f* **50/1**	MartinDwyer 2	80
0212	**10**	*2*	**Extraterrestrial**[40] [1942] 4-8-11 **94** (R A Fahey) *lw: midfield: rdn 1/2-way: plugged on at one pce fnl f: nvr able to chal* **16/1**	PaulHanagan 9	81
0030	**11**	*nk*	**Dream Lodge (IRE)**[12] [2789] 4-8-10 **93** (J G Given) *lw: chsd ldrs: outpcd and lost pl 1/2-way: rallying whn nt clr run under 2f out: styd on over 1f out: no imp on ldrs ins fnl f* **100/1**	TPQueally 10	79
14/4	**12**	*3*	**Overturn (IRE)**[13] [2762] 4-8-4 **87** (W R Swinburn) *trckd ldrs: rdn over 3f out: wknd over 2f out* **25/1**	SaleemGolam 3	67
5250	**13**	*2 1/4*	**Yarqus**[23] [2465] 5-8-7 **90** (bt) (C E Brittain) *midfield: effrt to try and chse ldrs over 3f out: wknd over 1f out* **50/1**	HayleyTurner 18	64
33-4	**14**	*nk*	**We'll Come**[39] [1982] 4-8-10 **93** (b[1]) (M A Jarvis) *lw: midfield: rdn over 1f out: no imp* **8/1**[3]	PhilipRobinson 27	67+
1012	**15**	*1 1/4*	**Ansells Pride (IRE)**[8] [2913] 5-8-3 **86** (B Smart) *prom: rdn 1/2-way: wknd 2f out* **66/1**	WMLordan 16	57
0-04	**16**	*3 3/4*	**Flipando (IRE)**[18] [2595] 7-8-11 **94** (T D Barron) *midfield: nvr able to get competitive* **16/1**	JamieSpencer 20	56+
2400	**17**	*nk*	**Dubai's Touch**[39] [1989] 4-9-7 **104** (M Johnston) *slowly int stride: trckd ldrs: rdn 1/2-way: wknd 2f out* **40/1**	JoeFanning 7	66
1206	**18**	*1 1/4*	**Crocodile Bay (IRE)**[6] [2969] 5-7-11 **87** (D W Barker) *led: rdn and hdd over 3f out: wknd over 2f out* **100/1**	DavidProbert(7) 13	46
0650	**19**	*1 1/4*	**Final Verse**[18] [2600] 5-9-3 **100** (Jane Chapple-Hyam) *chsd ldrs: rdn over 3f out: sn wknd* **100/1**	JohnEgan 11	56
2-25	**20**	*1*	**Oceana Gold**[32] [2200] 4-8-5 **88** (A M Balding) *in tch on outside: rdn and wknd over 1f out* **16/1**	WilliamBuick 26	41+
6-12	**21**	*3 1/4*	**Lang Shining (IRE)**[34] [2132] 4-9-4 **101** (Sir Michael Stoute) *hld up: hdwy on outside over 2f out: wknd over 1f out* **7/1**[2]	RyanMoore 22	47+
3-15	**22**	*3/4*	**Emerald Wilderness (IRE)**[12] [2789] 4-8-12 **95** (b[1]) (A King) *chsd ldrs: rdn over 3f out: wknd 2f out* **40/1**	TedDurcan 17	39
1120	**23**	*2*	**Mujood**[12] [2789] 5-8-8 **91** (Eve Johnson Houghton) *in tch: rdn over 4f out: wknd over 3f out* **100/1**	StephenCarson 19	31+
0-50	**24**	*2 1/4*	**Pride Of Nation (IRE)**[111] [745] 6-9-9 **106** (J W Hills) *hld up on outside: rdn 3f out: nvr on terms* **100/1**	EddieAhern 29	40+
0040	**25**	*3*	**Samarinda (USA)**[14] [2711] 5-8-5 **88** (Mrs P Sly) *awkward s: sn prom: rdn 1/2-way: wknd 3f out* **100/1**	PaulDoe 14	16
0-06	**26**	*7*	**Sir Xaar (IRE)**[18] [2595] 5-8-7 **90** (v[1]) (B Smart) *midfield: pushed along 1/2-way: wknd over 3f out* **100/1**	TomEaves 23	—+
60-5	**27**	*9*	**Secret World (IRE)**[21] [2503] 5-9-10 **107** (J Noseda) *stdd s: a bhd: eased whn no ch over 1f out* **66/1**	AlanMunro 21	—+
0060	**28**	*35*	**Fajr (IRE)**[12] [2789] 6-9-8 **105** (p) (Miss Gay Kelleway) *stdd s: a bhd: eased whn no ch over 2f out* **66/1**	JMurtagh 28	—+
45/0	**29**	*15*	**Fight Club (GER)**[20] [2543] 7-9-8 **105** (R Brotherton) *in tch: lost pl 1/2-way: eased whn wl bhd over 2f out* **40/1**	SebSanders 15	—

1m 39.63s (-0.97) **Going Correction** +0.125s/f (Good) **29** Ran SP% **131.5**

Speed ratings (Par 109): **109,108,108,107,104 103,102,101,100,98 98,95,93,93,91 88,87,86,85,84 81,80,78,76,73 66,57,22,**

toteswinger: 1&2 £43.40, 1&3 £652.30, 2&3 £30.10. CSF £240.03 CT £3381.79 TOTE £31.30: £5.10, £1.90, £7.50, £9.90; EX 304.50 Trifecta £6220.80 Part won. Pool: £8,406.60, 0.70 winning units..

Owner Mrs Sue Brendish **Bred** Dr Tom Keenan & Dr H G White Jr **Trained** East Everleigh, Wilts

FOCUS

A highly competitive handicap won by a horse officially rated between 91 and 105 for the tenth consecutive year, but this was a massive draw race, with those in low stalls at a huge advantage, and the form needs treating with caution although it is solid enough as it stands. The first three in the market all had no chance from their draws. The whole field tacked over towards the stands' rail and those drawn middle to high had no chance. It defies belief that with so many fancied horses drawn in the high numbers they did not go across to the far rail, as they surely could not have done any worse than they did being stranded out in the centre of the track.

NOTEBOOK

Mr Aviator(USA) got the better of a good battle with Docofthebay and Royal Power throughout the last quarter-mile. An improver on Polytrack through the winter whose best form was at around 1m2f, he put his stamina to good use to wear down his rivals. He may now go for a Listed race back over 1m2f. (op 50-1)

Docofthebay(IRE), who is well suited by fast ground, has now been runner-up in both the Cambridgeshire and this race as well as being in the frame in several other good handicaps. Fitted with blinkers for the first time, he got himself in a bit of a lather beforehand, but ran a terrific race. He deserves to win a big race before long and will reportedly attempt to gain compensation in Friday's Buckingham Palace Handicap. (op 12-1)

Royal Power(IRE), who finished half a length ahead of Docofthebay at York last month, is another whose best form is on fast ground and he ran pretty close to his Knavesmire mark with the runner-up. He came through to have every chance before the quarter-mile pole and stuck to his task, but was run out of it late on. He has not won since taking the German 2000 Guineas in May 2006, but looks to have found form again for his new connections.

Kavachi(IRE), who has a mainly progressive profile at around 1m2f since last autumn, having risen from a mark of 64 to his current rating of 87, finished best of all. He came home really strongly, having been near the rear after halfway and not getting the clearest of passages, and was on the heels of the principals passing the line, so his improvement has not finished yet.

Bankable(IRE), raised 19lb for winning a Goodwood Listed race easily from a subsequent winner in that grade, had just a 5lb penalty to carry in this contest, so in theory was a stone well in. He went off extremely well backed, but was quite excitable, playing up before leaving the paddock and then getting restless in the stalls, having to have the hood re-fitted. These were ominous signs for his supporters but things got worse when the stalls opened as, not only did he miss the break, but the whole field came over towards the stands' rail, leaving those drawn high somewhat isolated in the centre. He ran a massive race in the circumstances and would surely have won had there not been such a draw bias. (op 7-4 tchd 2-1 in places and 15-8 in places)

Ballinteni, yet another that stays 1m2f, had a question mark over his ability to handle the ground, but put up a terrific effort from his number 24 stall, staying on well late, although never troubling the leading group.

Diamond Tycoon(USA) looked a potential Classic winner when winning a Newbury maiden early last season but has had his problems since. He was in the leading group throughout and this effort showed that a good deal of his ability still remains.

Humungous(IRE) handles fast ground well and, with the cheekpieces back on, was staying on late from well back without reaching a challenging position.

Orchard Supreme, a stablemate of the winner, showed up until fading inside the last two furlongs.

Extraterrestrial, raised 8lb for his win in the Thirsk version of this race, seemed to handle this faster surface and finished his race quite well without ever looking likely to get involved.

Dream Lodge(IRE) was staying on again after losing his place despite not looking altogether happy on the fast going.

We'll Come, fitted with blinkers for the first time, did at least show up in the centre of the track for a good way, but he would have preferred more cover and was another done no favours by the draw. (tchd 17-2 in a place)

Oceana Gold had a good chance judged on last September's form with the favourite, plus he had conditions to suit and his stable has been in good form, but he could never really get involved from his draw. (op 20-1 tchd 25-1 in a place)

Lang Shining(IRE) was poorly drawn in stall 22 as things turned out and can be given another chance. (op 15-2 tchd 8-1 in places)

Emerald Wilderness(IRE) Official explanation: jockey said gelding had no more to give

Pride Of Nation(IRE) Official explanation: trainer said horse was unsuited by the good to firm (firm in places) ground

3123 QUEEN MARY STKS (GROUP 2) (FILLIES) — 5f

4:55 (4:57) (Class 1) 2-Y-O

£45,416 (£17,216; £8,616; £4,296; £2,152; £1,080) **Stalls** Centre

Form					RPR
12	**1**		**Langs Lash (IRE)**[33] [2167] 2-8-12 (M G Quinlan) *racd stands' side: mde virtually all towards centre: hld on wl fnl f* **25/1**	AlanMunro 6	98
3	**2**	*nk*	**Shyrl**[16] [2677] 2-8-12 (S A Callaghan) *str: lw: wnt rt s: chsd ldrs stands' side: hrd rdn over 1f out: kpt on wl and clsd fnl f: jst hld* **12/1**	LDettori 2	97
	3	*hd*	**Connie Mac (IRE)**[11] [2851] 2-8-12 (Andrew Oliver, Ire) *w'like: racd stands' side: w wnr thrght: hrd rdn fnl f: jst outpcd nr fin* **25/1**	SebSanders 1	96
1	**4**	*nk*	**Lucky Leigh**[37] [2035] 2-8-12 (M R Channon) *unf: in rr far side: hdwy 2f out: led gp and ev ch 1f out: kpt on* **14/1**	DarryllHolland 15	95
	5	*hd*	**Sugar Free (IRE)**[24] [2431] 2-8-12 (T Stack, Ire) *w'like: scope: dwlt: towards rr stands' side: rdn and hdwy over 1f out: nrst fin* **7/1**[3]	WMLordan 4	94

The Form Book, Raceform Ltd, Compton, RG20 6NL

6 1 **Nubar Lady (IRE)**[13] 2767 2-8-12 ....(t) JamieSpencer 10 91
(T Stack, Ire) *w'like: swtchd to r far side: w ldrs: hrd rdn over 1f out: kpt on same pce* **25/1**

1 7 2 **Baileys Cacao (IRE)**[30] 2253 2-8-12 .... RichardHughes 8 84
(R Hannon) *w'like: lw: chsd ldrs stands' side: hrd rdn over 1f out: wknd fnl f* **7/1**[3]

05 8 ½ **Sweet Applause (IRE)**[13] 2759 2-8-12 .... DarrenWilliams 17 82
(A P Jarvis) *sn in tch far side: effrt 2f out: one pce appr fnl f* **100/1**

21 9 nk **Rebecca De Winter**[41] 1924 2-8-12 .... RyanMoore 16 81
(R Hannon) *lw: racd far side: w ldrs tl wknd over 1f out* **16/1**

111 10 ½ **Bahamian Babe**[33] 2167 2-8-12 .... HayleyTurner 11 81+
(M L W Bell) *swtchd to r stands' side: towards rr: effrt and hrd rdn 2f out: no imp* **10/1**

41 11 ¾ **Beat Seven**[51] 1680 2-8-12 .... MickyFenton 7 76
(Miss Gay Kelleway) *racd stands' side: in tch: outpcd and dropped to rr 1/2-way: kpt on again fnl f* **25/1**

1310 12 ½ **White Shift (IRE)**[21] 2497 2-8-12 .... StephenDonohoe 14 74
(P D Evans) *in tch far side tl wknd 2f out* **66/1**

4023 13 1 ¼ **Amosite**[30] 2253 2-8-12 ....(b[1]) JimCrowley 5 73+
(J R Jenkins) *dwlt: bhd stands' side: rdn and sme hdwy 2f out: sn wknd* **100/1**

14 ½ **Heart Shaped (USA)**[25] 2416 2-8-12 .... JMurtagh 3 71+
(A P O'Brien, Ire) *leggy: scope: hmpd s: bhd stands' side: mod effrt 1/2-way: sn hrd rdn and btn* **9/2**[2]

13 15 shd **Glamorous Spirit (IRE)**[33] 2147 2-8-12 .... MJKinane 9 73+
(J Noseda) *racd stands' side: chsd ldrs 3f* **16/1**

21 16 11 **Excellent Show**[19] 2574 2-8-12 .... TedDurcan 13 28+
(B Smart) *str: mid-div at best far side: wknd over 2f out: sn bhd* **20/1**

11 17 1 ¾ **Danehill Destiny**[16] 2677 2-8-12 .... JimmyFortune 12 22+
(W J Haggas) *lw: racd far side: bmpd s: a towards rr: no ch fnl 2f* **7/2**[1]

60.87 secs (0.37) **Going Correction** +0.125s/f (Good) **17 Ran SP% 124.2**
Speed ratings (Par 102): **102,101,101,100,100 98,95,94,94,93 92,91,89,88,88 70,68**
toteswinger: 1&2 £65.80, 1&3 £105.50, 2&3 £62.00. CSF £287.44 CT £3970.89 TOTE £26.90: £7.30, £3.40, £8.30; EX 447.00 Trifecta £3392.50 Part won. Pool: £4,584.54, 0.30 winning units..

Owner John Hanly **Bred** Cathal Ryan **Trained** Newmarket, Suffolk

■ The first Royal Ascot winner for trainer Mick Quinlan.

■ Stewards' Enquiry : Alan Munro three-day ban: used whip with excessive frequency without giving filly time to respond (Jul 2-4)

FOCUS

The first five finished in a heap and this looked like a modest renewal of the Queen Mary. The first three home emerged from low stalls, but the draw did not seem to play as significant a part as in some races this week. They spilt into two groups, although the majority of runners tended to avoid the rails, and there was not much between the two sides at the line.

NOTEBOOK

Langs Lash(IRE) looked to have something to find in this company having been beaten half a length into second by Bahamian Babe in a Listed event at York on her previous start, but she stepped up significantly on that effort with a game effort from the front. She showed decent speed to lead the near-side group pretty much from the start, but was well off the stands' rail and looked vulnerable when coming under strong pressure fully two furlongs from the finish. However, she kept finding for pressure and just held on in a bunch finish. She may now be stepped up to 6f for the Lowther Stakes at York and, while it's not obvious from this effort that she will get the extra furlong, it would be folly to stay she definitely won't stay, as she was under pressure a fair way out this time, so the extra furlong will allow her to travel for longer, and there is stamina on the dam's side of her pedigree.

Shyrl ◆ looked a nice prospect when third under a sympathetic ride behind Danehill Destiny and Prolific in a novice event on her debut at Windsor and she confirmed that promise with a fine second. She travelled well, but was left with ground to make up when the race got serious and just failed to reel in Langs Lash. This was probably just an ordinary renewal, but she still appeals as a filly to take from the race. She has the option of going for a maiden or sticking to this sort of company.

Connie Mac(IRE) improved massively on the form she showed when a well-held second at 33/1 over 6f on her debut at the Curragh. Having shown bags of speed, she was just run out of it late on, although she did end up racing tight against the stands' rail and may have been at a slight advantage. (op 50-1)

Lucky Leigh, a clear-cut winner of an ordinary maiden on her debut at Redcar, ran a fine race on this significant step up in class, coming out on top in the slightly smaller group towards the far side of the track. There should be more to come. (op 12-1)

Sugar Free(IRE) ◆, third on her debut in a good race over 6f at the Curragh, promised to be suited by this drop back in trip on breeding, but she just found things happening a little too quickly for her and was doing all her best work at the finish. She is still learning and can do better again. (tchd 9-1 in a place and 15-2 in a place)

Nubar Lady(IRE), runner-up to Windsor Castle second Bushranger at Tipperary on her previous start, came into this as one of the more experienced in the line up and she ran well from a far-from-ideal draw in stall ten. (op 33-1)

Baileys Cacao(IRE) won well on her debut at Windsor, but this was tougher and she just came up short. She was not given too hard a time once her chance had gone and could be capable of better in time. (op 6-1)

Sweet Applause(IRE) had shown just moderate form in a couple of maidens, but she clearly appreciated the switch to quick ground and this was a much-improved effort. Drawn highest of all in stall 17, she got a good lead on the far side of the track and stayed on again after getting outpaced when coming under pressure about two furlongs out. She should go close if returned to maiden company next time, but is unlikely to represent much value.

Rebecca De Winter, off the mark at Chester on her second start, found this a lot harder and finished up well held. She looks all speed.

Bahamian Babe had today's winner behind when landing a Listed event at York on her latest start, her third straight success, but she did not have things go her way this time. Not ideally drawn in stall 11, she was late in switching over to the stands' side and was always playing catch-up thereafter. (op 12-1)

Beat Seven, a well regarded type who won a Windsor maiden on her previous start, failed to land a blow on this significant step up in class. (op 20-1)

Heart Shaped(USA) came into this off the back of a Listed race success at the Curragh, but she struggled to get involved after being slightly hampered on leaving the stalls. (op 6-1)

Glamorous Spirit(IRE) has not progressed in two runs since winning a course-and-distance maiden on her debut. (tchd 20-1)

Excellent Show was a Musselburgh maiden winner on her previous start, but she ran no sort of race this time. Official explanation: jockey said filly had no more to give (op 16-1)

Danehill Destiny looked a smart prospect when winning on her debut at Newmarket and following up in a good novice event at Windsor (Shyrl third), but the ground was much quicker this time and she failed to run a race. She probably requires a little further and a bit of give underfoot. Official explanation: trainer had no explanation for the poor form shown (tchd 4-1, 5-1 in a place and 9-2 in places)

3124 SANDRINGHAM H'CAP (LISTED RACE) (FILLIES) 1m (S)

5:30 (5:32) (Class 1) (0-110,100) 3-Y-O

£34,062 (£12,912; £6,462; £3,222; £1,614; £810) **Stalls** Centre

Form RPR

5-33 1 **Festivale (IRE)**[33] 2170 3-9-1 **94**.................................. KerrinMcEvoy 13 101
(J L Dunlop) *hld up: hdwy whn nt clr run briefly over 2f out: rdn over 1f out: r.o ins fnl f to ld fnl strides* **10/1**

310 2 nk **Illusion**[11] 2819 3-8-7 **86** oh3.. SebSanders 2 92
(J H M Gosden) *lw: a.p: rdn to ld over 2f out: running wl appr fnl f: hdd and hld fnl strides* **7/1**[3]

1-02 3 1 ½ **Shabiba (USA)**[32] 2196 3-8-11 **90**.................................. MartinDwyer 1 93
(M P Tregoning) *lw: w ldr: n.m.r and hmpd wl over 6f out: continued to trck ldrs: rdn over 1f out: styd on ins fnl f but a hld* **7/1**[3]

0-56 4 ½ **Shaker (IRE)**[33] 2149 3-9-1 **94**....................................... JamieSpencer 5 96
(M L W Bell) *stdd s: hld up: nt clr run over 2f out: hdwy and swtchd rt to r on outside over 1f out: r.o ins fnl f: nvr gng to rch ldrs* **18/1**

-410 5 nk **Rosaleen (IRE)**[28] 2305 3-9-2 **95**.. LDettori 10 96
(B J Meehan) *lw: hld up: effrt and hdwy over 2f out: nt clr run over 1f out: styd on ins fnl f: nt pce to chal ldrs* **16/1**

5-20 6 ¾ **Comeback Queen**[35] 2105 3-8-12 **91**......................... RichardHughes 8 90
(S Kirk) *lw: settled in tch: rdn and nt qckn over 2f out: styd on and clsd towards fin: nt pce to go w ldrs* **20/1**

100- 7 nk **Dellini (IRE)**[270] 5614 3-8-9 **88**.................................... DarryllHolland 15 87
(M R Channon) *lw: hld up: rdn over 2f out: hdwy on outside over 1f out: one pce ins fnl f* **50/1**

100S 8 ¾ **Tathkaar**[17] 2655 3-8-11 **90**.. NCallan 12 87
(C E Brittain) *midfield: hdwy to chse ldrs over 2f out: rdn over 1f out: no ex ins fnl f* **25/1**

-506 9 nk **Eva's Request (IRE)**[11] 2827 3-9-7 **100**............................... MJKinane 9 96
(M R Channon) *in tch: effrt to chal over 2f out: fdd ins fnl f* **20/1**

0-00 10 nk **Insaaf**[33] 2170 3-8-9 **88**...(v[1]) JMurtagh 11 84+
(W J Haggas) *hld up: rdn 2f out: hung lft over 1f out: nt clr run ins fnl f: sn eased* **16/1**

-016 11 1 **Amanjena**[39] 1991 3-8-7 **86**... WilliamBuick 6 79
(A M Balding) *prom: rdn over 2f out: wknd over 1f out* **16/1**

10-4 12 1 **Makaaseb (USA)**[33] 2170 3-9-4 **97**.......................................(p) RHills 4 88
(M A Jarvis) *lw: led: edgd over towards rail over 6f out: rdn and hdd over 2f out: losing pl whn n.m.r over 1f out: sn wknd* **11/2**[2]

413- 13 nk **Maramba (USA)**[235] 6498 3-9-2 **95**................................ RyanMoore 7 90+
(Sir Michael Stoute) *in tch: rdn and lost pl over 3f out: n.m.r whn struggling whn n.m.r and hmpd over 1f out: eased whn btn ins fnl f* **5/1**[1]

2-15 14 2 ¼ **Jazz Jam**[28] 2305 3-9-2 **95**... TQuinn 14 80
(P F I Cole) *in tch: rdn 3f out: wknd over 1f out: sn eased* **14/1**

1-26 15 ¾ **Cruel Sea (USA)**[35] 2105 3-9-2 **95**................................. MichaelHills 3 78
(B W Hills) *racd keenly: hld up in midfield: rdn and lost pl over 2f out: eased whn btn ins fnl f* **8/1**

456- 16 39 **Pretty Ballerina (USA)**[17] 2646 3-8-7 **86** oh4................... WMLordan 16 —
(John Joseph Murphy, Ire) *midfield on outside: rdn and wknd 3f out: t.o* **40/1**

1m 40.75s (0.15) **Going Correction** +0.125s/f (Good) **16 Ran SP% 124.6**
Speed ratings (Par 104): **104,103,102,101,101 100,100,99,99,99 98,97,96,94,93 54**
toteswinger: 1&2 £19.70, 1&3 £16.00, 2&3 £10.80. CSF £75.13 CT £558.99 TOTE £13.50: £2.70, £2.50, £2.10, £6.40; EX 116.70 Trifecta £1548.50 Place 6: £1,856.09, Place 5: £693.57. Pool: £5,650.00. 2.70 winning units..

Owner Prince A A Faisal **Bred** Nawara Stud Co Ltd **Trained** Arundel, W Sussex

FOCUS

An ordinary renewal of the Sandringham Stakes, but still quite competitive. Solid form despite the improvement from the winner, who is up 10lb, plus the second and fourth. All the action took place towards the stands'-side rail. The winning time was around a second slower than both the Windsor Forest Stakes and the Hunt Cup.

NOTEBOOK

Festivale(IRE), third in the Nell Gwyn before filling the same position in a Listed event at York on her first run over 1m, did not look too harshly treated off a mark of 94 on her handicap debut and gained a narrow success. She looked to have it all to do when Illusion held a clear lead passing the furlong pole, but she produced a sustained effort to get up close home. Her sire was a sprinter, but her dam stayed beyond 1m6f and, on this evidence, she looks as though she will get 1m2f. (op 9-1 tchd 12-1 in a place)

Illusion, a Windsor maiden winner, was probably unsuited by easy ground when only seventh at Doncaster on her latest start, but this faster surface was more suitable and she was just denied from 3lb out of the handicap. She looked the winner when clear passing the furlong pole, but tired late on and was just pegged back. (op 8-1)

Shabiba(USA), Hamdan Al Maktoum's second string according to jockey bookings, ran a good race on this step up to 1m, despite racing keenly. She found herself caught on heels after taking a grip around six furlongs out, but recovered quickly and kept on for pressure in the closing stages. There should be more to come, but it will have to be hoped she can settle better in future. (op 15-2)

Shaker(IRE) ◆, dropped back in trip, looked unlucky not to finish much closer as she was continually denied a clear run and had to switch wide with her effort, eventually getting in the clear with just a furlong to run. (op 25-1)

Rosaleen(IRE) travelled well, but she was another denied a clear run when beginning to make her move. She was not unlucky, but can be considered a little better than the bare form.

Comeback Queen, who beat just one home in the Musidora over 1m2f on her previous start, lacked the pace of some of these, but this was a respectable effort in defeat. (op 25-1)

Dellini(IRE), stepped up from 6f and with the visor left off on her return from 270 days off, ran well for a long way until getting tired. It's possible this trip stretched her, but she should strip fitter next time. (op 66-1)

Tathkaar, who slipped up in the German Guineas on her previous start, never really looked a threat, but this was a reasonable effort. (op 33-1)

Eva's Request(IRE) had no easy task conceding weight all round and she ran with credit.

Insaaf was unproven over this trip and was far from guaranteed to stay on breeding, but nothing went her way in any case. She got no run at all in the first-time visor, but was also inclined to hang and might not be straightforward. (op 20-1)

Amanjena is probably more of a 1m2f filly. (op 20-1)

Makaaseb(USA) was the pick of Richard Hills over Shabiba and Insaaf, but she was well held in first-time cheekpieces. (op 9-2 tchd 4-1 in a place)

Maramba(USA), upped in trip on her return from 235 days off, failed to justify market support, but she met trouble when dropping out of contention, exaggerating the beaten distance. (tchd 11-2)

T/Jkpt: Not won. T/Plt: £2,938.20 to a £1 stake. Pool: £467,304.84. 116.10 winning tickets. T/Qpdt: £209.40 to a £1 stake. Pool: £17,607.19. 62.20 winning tickets. LM

[2936]HAMILTON (R-H)

Wednesday, June 18

OFFICIAL GOING: Good to firm (good in places)

Wind: Almost nil Weather: Overcast

3125 LANARKSHIRE CHAMBER OF COMMERCE MAIDEN AUCTION STKS 6f 5y

2:10 (2:11) (Class 6) 2-Y-O **£1,942** (£578; £288; £144) **Stalls** Low

Form RPR

42 **1** **Reve De Soleil (FR)**[19] 2584 2-8-12 0........................ ChrisCatlin 5 71
(E J O'Neill) *in tch: hdwy 1/2-way: led over 1f out: rdn and edgd lft ins fnl f: hld on wl* **4/6**[1]

0 **2** *3/4* **Digit**[9] 2887 2-8-4 0........................ RoystonFfrench 3 61
(B Smart) *led to over 1f out: swtchd rt and rallied ins fnl f: kpt on: hld nr fin* **33/1**

3 *1/2* **Noble Storm (USA)** 2-8-13 0........................ RichardMullen 2 68
(E S McMahon) *cl up: effrt and ch over 1f out: kpt on same pce wl ins fnl f* **7/2**[2]

5 **4** *9* **Royal Muwasim**[22] 2485 2-8-7 0........................ TPO'Shea 4 35
(M R Channon) *prom: drvn and outpcd over 2f out: n.d after* **6/1**[3]

5 **5** *2 1/4* **Jobekani (IRE)**[19] 2569 2-8-11 0........................ TolleyDean(3) 8 36
(Mrs L Williamson) *cl up: rdn over 2f out: wknd wl over 1f out* **12/1**

0 **6** *1* **Sweet Virginia (USA)**[12] 2775 2-8-8 0........................ AndrewElliott 6 27
(K R Burke) *prom tl rdn and wknd over 2f out* **66/1**

7 *6* **Dark Velvet (IRE)** 2-8-5 0........................ DO'Donohoe 1 6
(E J Alston) *rn green towards rr: struggling 1/2-way: sn btn* **40/1**

0 **8** *2 1/2* **Royal Premium**[23] 2443 2-8-9 0........................ DavidAllan 7 2
(H A McWilliams) *s.i.s: nvr wnt pce* **100/1**

1m 11.4s (-0.80) **Going Correction** -0.25s/f (Firm) 8 Ran SP% **112.1**

Speed ratings (Par 91): **95,94,93,81,78 77,69,65**

toteswinger: 1&2 £5.90, 1&3 £1.70, 2&3 £10.60. CSF £31.64 TOTE £1.60: £1.02, £6.80, £1.30; EX 8.40.

Owner G A Lucas & A Solomon **Bred** Mme Annie Delarue **Trained** Averham Park, Notts

FOCUS

An ordinary bunch but a fair gallop and the first three pulled clear in the last quarter mile. The form seems sound enough.

NOTEBOOK

Reve De Soleil(FR), who had shaped with promise on his two starts at York, took the eye in the paddock and did not have to improve to get off the mark in workmanlike fashion. He should prove suited by 7f and may be capable of better. (op 8-13 tchd 8-11 in places)

Digit, who hung badly when well beaten on her debut, turned in a much improved effort this time. While vulnerable to the more progressive sorts in this grade, she looks capable of picking up a minor event in due course.

Noble Storm(USA) ◆, a half-brother to several winners from sprint to middle distances, attracted support on this racecourse debut and showed more than enough to suggest he can win an ordinary event. He has scope for physical improvement and should have no problems with 7f. (tchd 4-1 in a place)

Royal Muwasim, a leggy type, ran to a similar level of form as on her racecourse debut. She is going to improve for the step up to 7f but is likely to continue to look vulnerable in this type of event. (op 8-1)

Jobekani(IRE), just in front of a subsequent winner on his debut, took the eye in the preliminaries as a strong sort with scope but he was easy to back and proved a bit of a disappointment. Modest nurseries may be the way forward with him. (op 10-1)

Sweet Virginia(USA), well beaten on her debut at Catterick, fared little better this time and is going to remain vulnerable in this type of event. (op 50-1)

3126 HAMILTON-PARK.CO.UK H'CAP 1m 65y

2:45 (2:45) (Class 6) (0-60,60) 3-Y-O **£1,942** (£578; £288; £144) **Stalls** High

Form RPR

-063 **1** **Willkandoo (USA)**[8] 2915 3-8-13 55........................ FergalLynch 13 76
(K A Ryan) *prom: swtchd lft and hdwy to ld wl over 1f out: drifted to stands' rail: drew clr* **9/2**[1]

0350 **2** *10* **Natural Rhythm (IRE)**[15] 2704 3-8-5 50..........(b) MichaelJStainton(3) 15 48
(Mrs R A Carr) *led after 1f to wl over 1f out: kpt on: no ch w wnr* **20/1**

0001 **3** *3 1/2* **Grit (IRE)**[8] 2922 3-9-3 59 6ex........................ TPO'Shea 9 49
(M R Channon) *midfield on ins: drvn and outpcd over 3f out: rallied over 1f out: nrst fin* **6/1**[2]

54 **4** *nk* **Willyn (IRE)**[37] 2041 3-8-12 59........................ GaryBartley(5) 11 48
(J S Goldie) *midfield: drvn over 3f out: no imp fr 2f out* **8/1**

60-6 **5** *1 3/4* **Brandane (IRE)**[22] 2488 3-9-4 60........................ RoystonFfrench 14 45
(Mrs A Duffield) *chsd ldrs tl wknd fr 2f out* **18/1**

5634 **6** *1 1/4* **Zaplamation (IRE)**[13] 2750 3-8-1 46........................ AndrewMullen(3) 1 28
(D W Barker) *t.k.h: hld up: drvn over 3f out: no imp fr 2f out* **16/1**

0-00 **7** *3/4* **Harlequinn Danseur (IRE)**[23] 2463 3-8-0 47 oh1 ow1 KellyHarrison(5) 12 28
(N Tinkler) *led 1f: cl up: ev ch over 3f out: sn rdn and wknd* **40/1**

-403 **8** *hd* **Medici Time**[8] 2911 3-8-12 54........................(b[1]) DavidAllan 8 34
(T D Easterby) *dwlt: t.k.h and sn prom: chal over 3f to 2f out: sn wknd* **9/2**[1]

000 **9** *3/4* **Profumo Affair**[68] 1295 3-8-6 48........................ AndrewElliott 7 26
(M L W Bell) *bhd: drvn over 3f out: nvr rchd ldrs* **25/1**

0656 **10** *3/4* **Zabougg**[8] 2911 3-9-0 56........................ TonyHamilton 3 33
(D W Barker) *bhd: drvn over 3f out: nvr on terms* **14/1**

000 **11** *4* **Mytexie (FR)**[15] 2700 3-8-10 52........................ GregFairley 2 20
(M Johnston) *bhd: checked and swtchd outside 5f out: shortlived effrt over 3f out: sn btn* **50/1**

2223 **12** *5* **Just Sam (IRE)**[11] 2833 3-9-4 60........................(v) DNolan 4 16
(D Carroll) *towards rr: hdwy u.p over 3f out: wknd 2f out* **13/2**[3]

00-0 **13** *4* **Graze On And On**[46] 1817 3-8-6 48 ow1........................ GrahamGibbons 10 —
(J J Quinn) *in tch: lost pl 4f out: n.d after* **66/1**

2500 **14** *3 1/2* **Supporting Role (IRE)**[17] 2639 3-8-13 55........................(p) RichardMullen 5 —
(E S McMahon) *sn towards rr on outside: drvn and wknd fr 1/2-way* **16/1**

056- **15** *16* **Safari Dancer (IRE)**[272] 5550 3-9-4 60........................ DO'Donohoe 6 —
(Miss L A Perratt) *plld hrd on outside: in tch 3f: sn lost pl* **14/1**

1m 46.8s (-1.60) **Going Correction** -0.25s/f (Firm) 15 Ran SP% **120.0**

Speed ratings (Par 97): **98,88,84,84,82 81,80,80,79,78 74,69,65,62,46**

toteswinger: 1&2 £23.70, 1&3 £4.20, 2&3 £46.10. CSF £101.00 CT £565.47 TOTE £5.90: £2.40, £5.70, £2.00; EX 122.80.

Owner M Forsyth,J Turner And M F Logistics Ltd **Bred** Craig Singer **Trained** Hambleton, N Yorks

FOCUS

A modest event but a fair pace and a much improved effort from the winner who would take some beating under a penalty. The form is rated through the second.

Safari Dancer(IRE) Official explanation: jockey said bit slipped through gelding's mouth

3127 RAEBURN BRICK FILLIES' H'CAP (A QUALIFIER FOR THE RBS SCOTTISH TROPHY HANDICAP SERIES FINAL) 1m 1f 36y

3:20 (3:21) (Class 5) (0-70,70) 3-Y-O+ **£3,238** (£963; £481; £240) **Stalls** High

Form RPR

0560 **1** **Grethel (IRE)**[16] 2662 4-8-7 48........................ DanielleMcCreery(5) 1 55
(A Berry) *hld up: hdwy to ld over 1f out: hld on wl fnl f* **25/1**

0240 **2** *hd* **Papa's Princess**[12] 2782 4-8-13 49........................ FergalLynch 4 56
(J S Goldie) *hld up: hdwy over 2f out: ev ch fnl f: jst hld* **9/2**[3]

2305 **3** *3 1/4* **Dream Sea**[15] 2695 3-9-5 66........................ TPO'Shea 6 65
(M R Channon) *set stdy pce: rdn 3f out: hdd over 1f out: no ex* **3/1**[2]

04-6 **4** *1/2* **Annaliesse (IRE)**[15] 2699 3-9-2 70........................ BMcHugh(7) 8 67
(R A Fahey) *hld up ins: hdwy 3f out: rdn 2f out: sn no imp* **11/4**[1]

6505 **5** *3/4* **Carefree**[10] 2870 4-9-2 52........................ GregFairley 3 49
(Mrs R A Carr) *prom: drvn over 2f out: one pce over 1f out* **20/1**

040 **6** *3/4* **Mystical Ayr (IRE)**[40] 1953 6-9-12 62........................ RoystonFfrench 9 57
(Miss L A Perratt) *hld up: effrt over 3f out: one pce over 1f out* **9/1**

6040 **7** *1 1/2* **Vanatina (IRE)**[12] 2781 4-8-6 49........................ DeanHeslop(7) 7 40
(W M Brisbourne) *t.k.h: cl up: lost pl 3f out: n.d after* **9/1**

156 **F** **Lizzie Wiggins**[21] 2496 3-9-7 68........................ RichardMullen 2 63?
(M L W Bell) *t.k.h: cl up: rdn 3f out: wkng whn clipped heels and fell over 1f out* **9/2**[3]

1m 59.55s (-0.15) **Going Correction** -0.25s/f (Firm)

WFA 3 from 4yo+ 11lb 8 Ran SP% **116.6**

Speed ratings (Par 100): **90,89,86,86,85 85,83,—**

toteswinger: 1&2 £16.70, 1&3 £10.50, 2&3 £3.80. CSF £136.02 CT £447.97 TOTE £33.10: £7.00, £2.00, £1.30; EX 198.70.

Owner Mrs Linda White **Bred** Liam Queally **Trained** Cockerham, Lancs

FOCUS

A modest event but, although the pace was on the steady side and the time was moderate, those held up came to the fore in the closing stages. The winner is rated to this year's form.

Grethel(IRE) Official explanation: trainer's rep had no explanation for the apparent improvement in form.

3128 HAMILTON PARK SUPER SIX CLAIMING STKS 5f 4y

4:00 (4:00) (Class 6) 3-Y-O+ **£1,942** (£578; £288; £144) **Stalls** Low

Form RPR

-401 **1** **Luloah**[22] 2474 5-8-6 50........................ LukeMorris(3) 5 51
(J G M O'Shea) *cl up: led 1/2-way: rdr dropped whip cl home: jst hld on* **9/2**[3]

506 **2** *nse* **Obe One**[7] 2936 8-8-10 43........................ FergalLynch 8 52
(A Berry) *bhd and outpcd: hdwy 2f out: chsd wnr ins fnl f: kpt on wl nr fin: jst hld* **9/1**

0220 **3** *3* **Blackheath (IRE)**[12] 2780 12-8-5 58........................ KellyHarrison(5) 2 41
(S T Mason) *trckd ldrs: effrt and edgd rt wl over 1f out: nt qckn fnl f* **10/3**[2]

2252 **4** *nk* **Lethal**[37] 2040 5-9-10 75........................ TonyHamilton 7 54
(R A Fahey) *trckd ldrs: drvn 1/2-way: one pce appr fnl f* **10/11**[1]

005 **5** *4 1/2* **La Guancha**[19] 2576 3-8-2 52 ow10........................(tp) PaulPickard(7) 6 29
(D A Nolan) *bhd: drvn and outpcd 1/2-way: n.d after* **25/1**

6040 **6** *3* **Fly Time**[57] 1529 4-8-9 35........................(v[1]) ChrisCatlin 9 12
(Mrs L Williamson) *racd wd in rr: drvn and outpcd 1/2-way: sn btn* **25/1**

-006 **7** *1 1/4* **Howards Prince**[19] 2576 5-8-9 40........................ GaryBartley(5) 4 12
(D A Nolan) *led to 1/2-way: sn rdn and btn* **66/1**

59.10 secs (-0.90) **Going Correction** -0.25s/f (Firm)

WFA 3 from 4yo+ 6lb 7 Ran SP% **112.8**

Speed ratings (Par 101): **97,96,92,91,84 79,77**

toteswinger: 1&2 £3.60, 1&3 £3.00, 2&3 £3.30. CSF £40.22 TOTE £5.80: £2.40, £2.80; EX 41.80.

Owner W R Baddiley **Bred** Mrs S M Lee **Trained** Elton, Gloucs

FOCUS

A modest event and a race that took less winning than seemed likely with the two market leaders disappointing.

3129 RECTANGLE GROUP H'CAP 6f 5y

4:35 (4:35) (Class 5) (0-75,71) 3-Y-O+ **£3,238** (£963; £481; £240) **Stalls** Low

Form RPR

0-00 **1** **No Grouse**[47] 1775 8-8-12 53........................ DavidAllan 2 64
(E J Alston) *trckd ldrs: rdn to ld ins fnl f: kpt on strly* **20/1**

/00- **2** *nk* **Forzarzi (IRE)**[377] 2393 4-8-7 53........................ GaryBartley(5) 4 63
(H A McWilliams) *hld up in tch: hdwy and ev ch ent fnl f: kpt on wl* **40/1**

6013 **3** *3 1/4* **Botham (USA)**[2] 3079 4-9-0 55 6ex........................ FergalLynch 3 55
(J S Goldie) *hld up: hdwy appr fnl f: r.o: nt rch first two* **2/1**[1]

0456 **4** *1/2* **Coleorton Dancer**[13] 2751 6-9-13 68........................ RobertWinston 8 66
(K A Ryan) *wtih ldrs: led over 1f out to ins fnl f: no ex* **11/2**

0634 **5** *3 1/2* **Yorkshire Blue**[7] 2938 9-9-10 65........................ DanielTudhope 7 52
(J S Goldie) *hld up wd: drvn and outpcd over 2f out: n.d after* **5/2**[2]

-401 **6** *nk* **Opal Noir**[13] 2751 4-9-13 68........................ DO'Donohoe 6 54
(Miss L A Perratt) *t.k.h: w ldrs tl wknd appr fnl f* **7/2**[3]

1005 **7** *4 1/2* **Brut**[12] 2777 6-10-0 69........................(p) TonyHamilton 1 40
(D W Barker) *led to over 1f out: sn wknd* **12/1**

1m 10.87s (-1.33) **Going Correction** -0.25s/f (Firm)

WFA 3 from 4yo+ 7lb 7 Ran SP% **114.4**

Speed ratings (Par 103): **98,97,93,92,87 87,81**

toteswinger: 1&2 £16.40, 1&3 £7.80, 2&3 £16.40. CSF £497.68 CT £2299.97 TOTE £21.30: £5.20, £10.30; EX 201.90.

Owner The Grumpy Old Geezers **Bred** Zubieta Ltd **Trained** Longton, Lancs

FOCUS

A modest handicap in which the pace was only moderate and one in which the two outsiders dominated the finish. The winner is rated to last year's best.

3130 JOIN THE SCOTTISH RACING BUSINESS CLUB MEDIAN AUCTION MAIDEN STKS 1m 1f 36y

5:10 (5:11) (Class 6) 3-5-Y-O **£2,047** (£604; £302) **Stalls** High

Form RPR

0-32 **1** **Shady Gloom (IRE)**[12] 2779 3-9-1 75........................ FergalLynch 6 78+
(K A Ryan) *mde all: pushed along 2f out: edgd lft and styd on strly to go clr fnl f* **4/5**[1]

46 **2** *7* **Bocciani (GER)**[19] 2573 3-9-1 0........................ GregFairley 2 63
(M Johnston) *cl up: effrt over 3f out: chsd wnr over 1f out: no imp fnl f* **13/2**[3]

02 **3** *2* **Dream Esteem**[11] 2847 3-8-10 0........................ ChrisCatlin 1 54
(E J O'Neill) *plld hrd early: chsd wnr to over 1f out: no ex u.p* **5/2**[2]

4 *5* **Chatanoogachoochoo** 3-8-10 0........................ RobertWinston 3 43
(G A Swinbank) *in tch: drvn and outpcd over 3f out: n.d after* **14/1**

The Form Book, Raceform Ltd, Compton, RG20 6NL

060- **5** *nk* **Smart Pick**[184] 7169 5-9-7 44 TonyHamilton 4 43
(Mrs L Williamson) *bhd: drvn over 3f out: edgd rt: nvr on terms* **33/1**

6 **6** *3 1/4* **Ayrpassionata**[30] 2246 3-8-10 0 DO'Donohoe 5 36
(Miss L A Perratt) *in tch: drvn over 4f out: btn over 2f out* **28/1**

1m 57.11s (-2.59) **Going Correction** -0.25s/f (Firm)
WFA 3 from 5yo 11lb 6 Ran SP% **110.5**
Speed ratings (Par 101): **101,94,93,88,88 85**
toteswinger: 1&2 £1.80, 1&3 £1.10, 2&3 £1.60. CSF £6.55 TOTE £1.80: £1.30, £2.10; EX 6.30.
Owner Brendan P Hayes **Bred** Kilfrush Stud **Trained** Hambleton, N Yorks

FOCUS
An uncompetitive event in which the pace was on the steady side. The winner faced a straightforward task.

3131 TURFTV IN YOUR BETTING SHOP APPRENTICE H'CAP (ROUND 1) 1m 4f 17y
5:45 (5:46) (Class 6) (0-60,59) 4-Y-0+ **£2,047** (£604; £302) **Stalls** High

Form RPR

-002 **1** **Bolckow**[15] 2707 5-8-8 48 PatrickDonaghy 4 59
(J T Stimpson) *chsd ldr: led 4f out: styd on strly: unchal* **14/1**

50-6 **2** *3 3/4* **Fistral**[27] 189 4-8-2 45 AshleyMorgan(3) 5 50
(P D Niven) *bhd tl styd on fnl 2f: tk 2nd cl home: no ch w wnr* **4/1**[2]

0-04 **3** *1/2* **Jane Of Arc (FR)**[13] 2752 4-8-4 51 (p) PaulPickard(7) 2 55
(J S Goldie) *led and clr: hdd 4f out: rallied 2f out: no ex and lost 2nd cl home* **11/1**

0000 **4** *2* **Jalamid (IRE)**[20] 2535 6-8-5 45 (t) SophieDoyle 11 46
(M A Barnes) *in tch: effrt over 2f out: no ex ins fnl f* **18/1**

0121 **5** *1* **Wizard Looking**[9] 2884 7-9-5 59 6ex MatthewDavies 12 58
(D E Cantillon) *hld up: stdy hdwy over 4f out: rdn and one pce fnl 2f* **2/1**[1]

5015 **6** *3 1/2* **Wulimaster (USA)**[13] 2752 5-9-0 54 ClGillies 6 48
(D W Barker) *hld up: drvn over 3f out: nvr rchd ldrs* **9/1**

-062 **7** *2 3/4* **Psycho Cat**[14] 2731 5-8-5 48 DeanHeslop(3) 7 37
(W M Brisbourne) *bhd: rdn and hung to stands' rail fr over 3f out: nvr rchd ldrs* **12/1**

50-0 **8** *1/2* **Surdoue**[10] 2863 8-8-2 45 (p) DeclanCannon(3) 13 34
(J G M O'Shea) *chsd ldrs tl rdn and wknd over 2f out* **33/1**

0/66 **9** *4 1/2* **Nelson Vettori**[33] 2143 4-8-11 54 BMcHugh(3) 1 35
(Miss L A Perratt) *prom: drvn 3f out: sn wknd* **16/1**

/000 **10** *15* **Donna's Double**[19] 2578 13-8-5 45 (p) RobbieEgan 8 2
(Karen McLintock) *bhd: pushed along 4f out: sn btn* **40/1**

0-04 **11** *2 1/4* **Dr Light (IRE)**[7] 2957 4-8-11 54 SimonPearce(3) 10 8
(M A Peill) *midfield: struggling over 4f out: sn btn* **11/2**[3]

062- **12** *22* **Pugnacity**[348] 3274 4-8-6 49 StacyRenwick(3) 9 —
(K W Hogg) *unruly bef s: dwlt: bhd: rdn over 4f out: wkng whn hung to stands rail fr over 3f out* **28/1**

2m 36.52s (-2.08) **Going Correction** -0.25s/f (Firm) 12 Ran SP% **121.4**
Speed ratings (Par 101): **96,93,93,91,91 88,87,86,83,73 72,57**
toteswinger: 1&2 £13.80, 1&3 £19.70, 2&3 £10.40. CSF £70.02 CT £661.81 TOTE £16.00: £3.40, £2.20, £3.70; EX 70.40 Place 6: £1,806.90, Place 5: £1,461.61..
Owner J T Stimpson **Bred** Khorshed And Ian Deane **Trained** Newcastle-Under-Lyme, Staffs

FOCUS
A modest event in which the gallop seemed sound but only two horses got into the race and this bare form may not prove entirely reliable. The race is rated around the third.
T/Plt: £13,700.30 to a £1 stake. Pool: £40,350.38. 2.15 winning tickets. T/Qpdt: £1,505.30 to a £1 stake. Pool: £2,034.29. 0.10 winning tickets. RY

2943 KEMPTON (A.W) (R-H)
Wednesday, June 18

OFFICIAL GOING: Standard
Wind: Brisk, across Weather: Fine but cloudy

3132 WEATHERBYS BLOODSTOCK SERVICES APPRENTICE H'CAP (ROUND 3) 1m 2f (P)
6:15 (6:15) (Class 4) (0-80,78) 4-Y-0+ **£4,209** (£1,252; £625; £312) **Stalls** High

Form RPR

4263 **1** **Prime Number (IRE)**[36] 2071 6-9-3 71 JackMitchell 3 79
(J Akehurst) *rousted along fr s: pressed ldr: led 1/2-way: drvn clr fr 3f out: at least 8 l clr over 1f out: hld on* **9/1**

/025 **2** *1 3/4* **Show Winner**[18] 2599 5-9-4 75 DavidProbert(3) 8 80+
(A M Balding) *hld up in midfield: prog over 2f out: chsd clr wnr wl over 1f out: clsd fnl f but unable to chal* **11/4**[1]

6401 **3** *8* **Artreju (GER)**[26] 2374 5-9-2 73 JemmaMarshall(3) 10 62
(G L Moore) *dwlt: hld up in midfield: effrt over 2f out: wnt modest 3rd over 1f out: fnd little but jst hld on for 3rd* **11/2**[3]

2060 **4** *hd* **Man Of Gwent (UAE)**[19] 2582 4-9-7 78 RichardEvans(3) 2 66
(P D Evans) *hld up in rr: effrt on wd outside 3f out: no ch of rching ldng pair but kpt on* **15/2**

401/ **5** *nse* **Accompanist**[31] 2226 5-8-0 59 oh1 (v) BACurtis(5) 1 47
(T G McCourt, Ire) *stdd s and dropped in fr wd draw: hld up in last pair: no ch fr 2f out: styd on fr over 1f out* **25/1**

122 **6** *3 3/4* **Uig**[5] 2990 7-8-8 65 MCGeran(3) 6 46
(H S Howe) *hld up in rr: rdn and struggling 3f out: plugged on fr over 1f out* **10/1**

-102 **7** *1 1/4* **Ryedale Ovation (IRE)**[22] 2476 5-9-0 68 JamieJones 7 46
(M Hill) *dwlt: hld up in rr: nvr on terms and no ch fnl 2f* **4/1**[2]

5652 **8** *5* **Happy As Larry (USA)**[60] 1486 6-9-0 71 (t) JackDean(3) 9 39
(J S Moore) *chsd clr ldng pair over 2f out: sn wknd* **16/1**

335- **9** *3 1/2* **Stargazer Jim (FR)**[186] 7160 6-9-6 77 WilliamCarson(3) 5 38
(W J Haggas) *prom in chsng gp: no imp 3f out: wknd sn after 2f out* **10/1**

005 **10** *6* **Tinnarinka**[14] 2718 4-9-4 72 (b[1]) HaddenFrost 4 21
(R Hannon) *racd freely: led to 1/2-way: chsd wnr tl wknd wl over 1f out* **14/1**

02-3 **11** *42* **Touch Of Style (IRE)**[166] 47 4-9-1 72 HarryPoulton(3) 11 —
(J R Boyle) *chsd ldng pair: hit rail after 2f: sn lost pl: bhd 3f out: virtually p.u fnl 2f* **12/1**

2m 6.96s (-1.04) **Going Correction** +0.025s/f (Slow) 11 Ran SP% **126.1**
Speed ratings (Par 105): **105,103,97,97,97 94,93,89,86,81 47**
toteswinger: 1&2 £12.80, 1&3 £12.50, 2&3 £4.70. CSF £36.50 CT £159.06 TOTE £9.50: £2.90, £1.20, £2.70; EX 24.60.
Owner A D Spence **Bred** Ballylinch Stud **Trained** Epsom, Surrey

FOCUS
A fair handicap run at a very strong pace thanks to a contested lead between the eventual winner Prime Number and Tinnarinka.
Uig Official explanation: jockey said mare was never travelling
Tinnarinka Official explanation: jockey said filly had lost her action
Touch Of Style(IRE) Official explanation: jockey said gelding had ducked into the rail

3133 EDWIN COE LLP MAIDEN FILLIES' STKS 1m 2f (P)
6:45 (6:47) (Class 5) 3-Y-0+ **£2,590** (£770; £385; £192) **Stalls** High

Form RPR

30 **1** **Albarouche**[23] 2454 3-8-12 0 (b[1]) PhilipRobinson 5 72
(M A Jarvis) *awkward s: sn trckd ldrs: wnt 3rd 1/2-way: effrt 2f out: led jst ins fnl f: cajoled along and drew clr* **4/1**[2]

2 *2 1/4* **Mumayeza** 3-8-12 0 RHills 4 70+
(Sir Michael Stoute) *t.k.h: pressed ldr: led 2f out: rdn and hdd jst ins fnl f: outpcd* **8/1**

5-3 **3** *1 1/2* **Signora (IRE)**[21] 2500 3-8-12 0 DarryllHolland 8 64
(M Johnston) *wl in tch bhd ldrs: prog 2f out: shkn up fnl f: tk 3rd nr fin* **7/1**[3]

4- **4** *shd* **Sensible**[220] 6777 3-8-12 0 PatCosgrave 6 64
(M J Wallace) *wl in tch bhd ldrs: effrt over 2f out: rdn to chse ldng pair over 1f out: kpt on but no imp: lost 3rd nr fin* **10/1**

5 *4 1/2* **Opera De Luna** 3-8-12 0 DaneO'Neill 14 55+
(J R Fanshawe) *hld up wl in rr: stdy prog fr over 2f out: shkn up 1f out: kpt on: nvr nrr* **18/1**

6 *1/2* **Taminas Desert** 3-8-12 0 JohnEgan 11 54+
(M Botti) *hld up in midfield: sme prog whn rn wd bnd 2f out: reminder sn after: eased whn hld fnl f* **8/1**

0 **7** *2* **Liberally (IRE)**[7] 2955 3-8-12 0 RichardHughes 9 53+
(B J Meehan) *chsd ldng pair to 1/2-way: rdn over 3f out: steadily fdd fnl 2f* **10/1**

8 *hd* **Oops Another Act** 3-8-12 0 AdamKirby 2 59+
(W R Swinburn) *dwlt: rn green in rr: sme prog over 2f out: stl gaining but no ch whn rn into trble 1f out and eased* **33/1**

9 *2 1/2* **Ivona** 3-8-12 0 TedDurcan 10 44+
(Saeed Bin Suroor) *hld up towards rr: sme prog whn v wd bnd 2f out: hanging bdly and sn btn* **7/1**[3]

0-3 **10** *2 3/4* **Fortunella**[33] 2156 3-8-12 0 JimmyQuinn 7 39
(P Howling) *nvr bttr than midfield: wknd wl over 1f out* **40/1**

0-3 **11** *1 3/4* **Basanti (USA)**[14] 2716 3-8-12 0 MichaelHills 3 35+
(B W Hills) *sn led: rdn and hdd 2f out: wknd rapidly* **3/1**[1]

12 *30* **Dalayla (IRE)**[80] 4-9-10 0 LPKeniry 12 —
(J W Mullins) *in tch to 1/2-way: t.o over 2f out* **100/1**

13 *2 3/4* **Nyumba (IRE)** 3-8-12 0 JimCrowley 13 —
(P R Chamings) *s.s: a in last trio: t.o 3f out* **20/1**

14 *16* **Ardkilly Belle (IRE)** 3-8-5 0 BACurtis(7) 1 —
(Ruaidhri Joseph Tierney, Ire) *s.v.s: a t.o* **66/1**

2m 8.35s (0.35) **Going Correction** +0.025s/f (Slow)
WFA 3 from 4yo 12lb 14 Ran SP% **128.3**
Speed ratings (Par 100): **99,97,96,95,92 91,90,90,88,85 84,60,58,45**
toteswinger: 1&2 £6.00, 1&3 £10.60, 2&3 £6.70. CSF £37.52 TOTE £5.70: £1.90, £4.30, £2.40; EX 52.90.
Owner Mrs Barbara Facchino **Bred** Miss K Rausing & Globe Bloodstock **Trained** Newmarket, Suffolk

■ Stewards' Enquiry : Pat Cosgrave caution: careless riding

FOCUS
Some big stables were represented in this ordinary fillies' maiden and even though the winning time was much slower than the two handicaps over the same trip, a few of these attracted market support and one or two are very likely to progress from this. The principals all raced handily.
Taminas Desert ◆ Official explanation: jockey said filly had no more to give
Oops Another Act ◆ Official explanation: jockey said filly had run green
Basanti(USA) Official explanation: jockey said filly had stopped quickly

3134 DIGIBET H'CAP 1m 2f (P)
7:15 (7:18) (Class 4) (0-85,85) 3-Y-O **£4,209** (£1,252; £625; £312) **Stalls** High

Form RPR

11-5 **1** **Tomintoul Flyer**[18] 2610 3-9-3 81 TedDurcan 11 94+
(H R A Cecil) *trckd ldrs: gap appeared 2f out and shkn up to chal over 1f out: trying to hang but led last 150yds and sn clr* **2/1**[1]

60-1 **2** *2* **Reclamation (IRE)**[37] 2052 3-8-9 73 SebSanders 9 82
(Sir Mark Prescott) *led: kicked on over 2f out: hdd 1f out: kpt on but easily outpcd by wnr* **4/1**[2]

212 **3** *1 1/2* **Ocean Legend (IRE)**[57] 1540 3-8-9 73 JohnEgan 12 79
(Miss J Feilden) *pressed ldr to 4f out: renewed effrt on inner to chal over 1f out: narrow ld 1f out: sn hdd and fdd* **8/1**

11-0 **4** *3 3/4* **Hilbre Court (USA)**[105] 799 3-9-7 85 IanMongan 6 84
(B J Meehan) *bolted nrly a m on way to post: t.k.h: hld up in midfield: prog and rdn over 2f out: v wd bnd sn after: one pce u.p* **16/1**

11-0 **5** *nk* **City Of The Kings (IRE)**[54] 1600 3-9-4 85 PatrickHills(3) 8 83
(R Hannon) *hld up wl in rr: last over 2f out: sme prog over 1f out: nt clr run briefly 1f out: kpt on: nvr nrr* **16/1**

-214 **6** *shd* **Martyr**[48] 1746 3-9-6 84 RichardHughes 4 82
(R Hannon) *hld up towards rr: shkn up 2f out: sme prog over 1f out but nvr on terms* **6/1**[3]

1-00 **7** *2* **Cuban Missile**[11] 2819 3-9-6 84 SteveDrowne 10 78
(R Charlton) *hld up in midfield: rdn over 2f out: no imp over 1f out: wknd* **14/1**

1 **8** *1* **Rowan Rio**[124] 570 3-9-1 79 MichaelHills 5 71
(W J Haggas) *hld up wl in rr: sme prog on inner over 2f out: struggling over 1f out* **12/1**

1-20 **9** *1 1/4* **Bushy Dell (IRE)**[34] 2118 3-8-1 72 AmyBaker(7) 1 62
(Miss J Feilden) *mostly racd wd: hld up: a wl in rr* **50/1**

1- **10** *hd* **Jadaara**[298] 4796 3-9-7 85 DarryllHolland 7 74
(M Johnston) *t.k.h: trckd ldng pair: chal for 2nd 3f out: wd bnd 2f out and wknd* **8/1**

16-0 **11** *14* **Port Quin**[35] 2109 3-8-11 75 DaneO'Neill 3 36
(G Wragg) *hld up and a wl in rr: wknd rapidly 2f out: t.o* **40/1**

2m 6.47s (-1.53) **Going Correction** +0.025s/f (Slow) 11 Ran SP% **120.4**
Speed ratings (Par 101): **107,105,104,101,100 100,99,98,97,97 86**
toteswinger: 1&2 £1.60, 1&3 £8.80, 2&3 £10.40. CSF £9.80 CT £54.35 TOTE £3.10: £1.40, £1.90, £3.00; EX 15.00.
Owner Angus Dundee Distillers plc **Bred** Whitsbury Manor Stud **Trained** Newmarket, Suffolk

FOCUS
This was a decent handicap, the pace was strong and the winning time was around half a second faster than the older horses in the opener and nearly two seconds faster than the maiden. The front three pulled clear and look progressive, and the form should work out.

3135 DIGIBET.COM E B F MAIDEN FILLIES' STKS — 7f (P)
7:45 (7:46) (Class 5) 2-Y-O — £3,885 (£1,156; £577; £288) Stalls High

Form — RPR

02 **1** **Misdaqeya**[26] 2368 2-9-0 0 ... RHills 2 — 82+
(B W Hills) *trckd ldr: led over 1f out: shkn up and sn clr: readily* **11/8**[1]

2 3 **Good Again** 2-9-0 0 ... HayleyTurner 4 — 74+
(G A Butler) *hld up in 8th: plld out and effrt jst over 2f out: prog over 1f out: wnt 2nd ins fnl f and r.o wl: no ch to trble wnr* **20/1**

05 **3** 3 1/4 **Meydan Groove**[37] 2048 2-9-0 0 ... TQuinn 1 — 64
(P F I Cole) *racd wd: in tch: rdn over 2f out: kpt on same pce to chal fr over 1f out* **10/1**

4 hd **Lady Cottingham** 2-9-0 0 ... DaneO'Neill 6 — 64
(R Hannon) *cl up: rdn to chse ldng pair wl over 2f out: no imp on wnr: one pce* **16/1**

4 **5** 2 1/4 **Moonburst**[26] 2368 2-9-0 0 ... SebSanders 10 — 58
(E A L Dunlop) *hld up in midfield: rdn over 2f out: no prog* **15/8**[2]

04 **6** 1/2 **Balladiene (IRE)**[15] 2691 2-9-0 0 ... JimmyQuinn 5 — 57
(M H Tompkins) *in tch: rdn and wl outpcd over 2f out: no ch after* **14/1**

54 **7** nse **Redhead (IRE)**[14] 2713 2-9-0 0 ... RichardHughes 7 — 57
(R Hannon) *led to over 1f out: sn wknd* **8/1**[3]

8 1 1/4 **Red Reef** 2-9-0 0 ... TedDurcan 3 — 53
(D J Coakley) *dwlt: hld up in last: pushed along over 2f out: no prog* **33/1**

00 **9** 9 **Four Green Fields (IRE)**[18] 2614 2-8-7 0 ... GabrielHannon(7) 8 — 31
(B W Duke) *t.k.h early: chsd ldng pair to wl over 2f out: wknd* **100/1**

1m 28.28s (2.28) **Going Correction** +0.025s/f (Slow) — **9 Ran SP% 118.3**
Speed ratings (Par 90): **87,83,79,79,77 76,76,75,64**
toteswinger: 1&2 £7.00, 1&3 £6.10, 2&3 £106.10. CSF £34.59 TOTE £1.80: £1.10, £2.80, £3.50; EX 22.60.
Owner Hamdan Al Maktoum **Bred** D J And Mrs Deer **Trained** Lambourn, Berks

FOCUS
An ordinary fillies' maiden and a two-horse race according to the market, but with one running moderately it may not have taken much winning. The first two are both rated a bit better than the bare form and a couple of the others are entitled to improve.

NOTEBOOK
Misdaqeya, who had given the impression that she would appreciate this longer trip in her previous starts, was always in the ideal place to strike and found a tidy turn of foot to settle it when asked. She may not have beaten much here especially with her only serious market rival disappointing, but she continues to improve. (op 15-8 tchd 5-4, 2-1 in a place)
Good Again ◆, a 40,000gns half-sister to 7f winner Ink Spot, was ridden with plenty of patience but found her way blocked when she tried to get closer and by the time she was switched out wide the favourite had got away. She made up a great deal of late ground though and looks to have a future. (op 16-1)
Meydan Groove, well beaten in her two previous starts over the minimum, showed a bit more over this longer trip and was staying on at the end. There should be a small race in her. (op 11-1 tchd 14-1)
Lady Cottingham, a 45,000gns half-sister to a winning juvenile over 7f, swerved away to her left as the stalls opened but still took a handy position and kept plugging away to the end. She looked to be the stable's second string according to the market so this was a perfectly satisfactory debut. (op 14-1 tchd 12-1)
Moonburst, three lengths behind Misdaqeya on her Newmarket debut, was backed to get closer here with that experience under her belt, but she never looked that happy and was beaten much further this time. Perhaps she did not take to the surface. (op 9-4)
Balladiene(IRE), trying sand for the first time after showing a little ability on turf, was completely friendless in the market and was one of the first beaten. (op 17-2)
Redhead(IRE) had her own way out in front, but patently failed to see out the extra furlong. (op 7-1)

3136 DIGIBET CASINO H'CAP — 6f (P)
8:15 (8:15) (Class 4) (0-80,77) 3-Y-O — £4,209 (£1,252; £625; £312) Stalls High

Form — RPR

-213 **1** **Honey Monster (IRE)**[7] 2945 3-9-5 75 ... PatCosgrave 4 — 82
(A J McCabe) *trckd ldng trio: rdn and effrt over 2f out: wnt 2nd over 1f out: drvn ahd ins fnl f: styd on dourly* **7/4**[1]

1102 **2** 3/4 **Lieutenant Pigeon**[19] 2555 3-9-5 75 ... PaulEddery 5 — 80
(G D Blake) *led: drvn over 2f out: hdd ins fnl f: kpt on wl but hld after* **3/1**[2]

2356 **3** 1/2 **Caprio (IRE)**[7] 2945 3-9-0 70 ... RichardKingscote 2 — 73
(Tom Dascombe) *hld up in last: prog on inner fr 2f out: wnt 3rd fnl f and kpt on wl: nvr able to chal* **8/1**

425 **4** 1 1/2 **Wynberg (IRE)**[5] 3000 3-9-0 70 ... SebSanders 1 — 68
(S A Callaghan) *stdd s and dropped in fr wd draw: hld up in 8th: prog fr 2f out: disp 3rd 1f out: one pce after* **9/1**

1206 **5** 2 **Liberty Valance (IRE)**[9] 2883 3-9-6 76 ... RichardHughes 7 — 68
(S Kirk) *hld up in 6th: rdn over 2f out: sme prog u.p over 1f out: nt rch ldrs and eased ins fnl f* **6/1**[3]

1036 **6** 3/4 **Kinout (IRE)**[20] 2529 3-8-13 74 ... NeilBrown(5) 6 — 63
(K A Ryan) *trckd ldng pair: wnt 2nd over 2f out to over 1f out: wknd* **10/1**

-140 **7** 2 3/4 **Emperors Jade**[57] 1546 3-9-3 73 ... TedDurcan 9 — 54
(A P Jarvis) *mostly in 5th: rdn 2f out: no real prog: fdd fnl f* **9/1**

-160 **8** 1/2 **What Katie Did (IRE)**[5] 2998 3-9-0 77 ... DTDaSilva(7) 3 — 56
(P F I Cole) *chsd ldr to over 2f out: sn lost pl u.p* **20/1**

1m 13.4s (0.30) **Going Correction** +0.025s/f (Slow) — **8 Ran SP% 120.6**
Speed ratings (Par 101): **99,98,97,95,92 91,88,87**
toteswinger: 1&2 £1.50, 1&3 £5.10, 2&3 £7.80. CSF £7.55 CT £33.97 TOTE £2.90: £1.30, £1.60, £3.10; EX 9.90.
Owner Brian Morton & Ray Standring **Bred** Michael O'Mahony **Trained** Babworth, Notts

FOCUS
An ordinary sprint handicap and it paid to race up with the pace. The winner continues to progress and the form looks sound overall.

3137 ANNE AYRES 55TH BIRTHDAY CELEBRATION H'CAP — 2m (P)
8:45 (8:45) (Class 6) (0-65,63) 4-Y-O+ — £2,047 (£604; £302) Stalls High

Form — RPR

05/2 **1** **Rainbow Dash (IRE)**[28] 2320 9-9-6 62 ... (p) PatCosgrave 4 — 73
(T G McCourt, Ire) *buried away in midfield: prog on inner 3f out: drvn to chal over 1f out: briefly outpcd by runner-up: rallied to ld ins fnl f: styd on wl* **8/1**

2320 **2** 1 1/2 **Leyte Gulf (USA)**[19] 2572 5-9-3 59 ... DaneO'Neill 7 — 68
(C C Bealby) *stdd s: hld up wl in rr: smooth prog fr 4f out: shkn up and effrt over 2f out: led over 1f out and looked certain wnr: hdd and nt qckn ins fnl f* **6/1**[2]

055- **3** 3 1/2 **Moonshine Beach**[197] 7012 10-9-0 56 ... JimCrowley 8 — 61
(P W Hiatt) *pressed ldr: led over 2f out: drvn and hdd over 1f out: one pce* **12/1**

05 **4** hd **Foreign King (USA)**[29] 546 4-9-3 59 ... LPKeniry 11 — 64
(J W Mullins) *trckd ldrs: rdn over 3f out: plugged on fnl 2f but nvr pce to trble ldrs* **16/1**

6450 **5** 1 1/4 **Mister Completely (IRE)**[19] 2567 7-9-3 59 ... (v) JamesDoyle 5 — 62
(Ms J S Doyle) *hld up in last: prog on wd outside over 2f out: kpt on but nvr pce to rch ldrs* **15/2**[3]

6P/0 **6** 7 **Fiddlers Ford (IRE)**[44] 1856 7-8-13 55 ... JimmyQuinn 9 — 50
(T Keddy) *trckd ldrs: rdn wl over 3f out: stl chsng 2f out: wknd over 1f out* **20/1**

6 **7** 2 **Pepito Collonges (FR)**[36] 2073 5-8-8 50 ... (b[1]) PaulDoe 12 — 42
(Mrs L J Mongan) *prom: pressed ldng pair 3f out: stl cl up 2f out: wknd over 1f out* **28/1**

0-62 **8** 6 **Pochard**[17] 2643 5-9-3 59 ... RichardHughes 10 — 44
(J M P Eustace) *led to over 2f out: eased whn btn over 1f out* **6/1**[2]

0165 **9** 1 3/4 **Synonymy**[17] 2643 5-9-2 58 ... (b) SteveDrowne 6 — 41
(M Blanshard) *trckd ldrs on outer: rdn over 3f out: sn lost pl and btn* **8/1**

4630 **10** 1 1/2 **Title Deed (USA)**[23] 2467 4-9-5 61 ... (v) TedDurcan 1 — 42
(A P Jarvis) *mostly in midfield: u.p and nt on terms 3f out: no ch fnl 2f* **16/1**

000/ **11** 4 **Left Hand Drive**[13] 3017 5-8-6 55 ow2 ... (bt) GabrielHannon(7) 3 — 31
(B W Duke) *rdn in last bef 1/2-way: a struggling after* **66/1**

2025 **12** nse **Kanisorn (SWE)**[10] 2867 6-9-7 63 ... (vt) VinceSlattery 14 — 39
(Mike Hammond) *dwlt: a wl in rr and nvr gng wl: wl btn over 2f out* **25/1**

200- **13** 9 **Ganymede**[37] 3448 7-8-6 53 ... (b) JackDean(5) 13 — 19
(Mark Gillard) *hld up in midfield on inner: effrt over 3f out: wknd over 2f out* **16/1**

5313 **14** 27 **Whaxaar (IRE)**[19] 2567 4-9-5 61 ... RobertHavlin 2 — —
(R Ingram) *prog on outer to press ldng pair after 6f: rdn over 4f out: sn wknd: t.o* **7/2**[1]

3m 30.32s (0.22) **Going Correction** +0.025s/f (Slow) — **14 Ran SP% 123.7**
Speed ratings (Par 101): **100,99,97,97,96 93,92,89,88,87 85,85,81,67**
toteswinger: 1&2 £11.20, 1&3 £70.00, 2&3 £113.50. CSF £54.85 CT £590.75 TOTE £12.50: £2.80, £3.30, £4.60; EX 118.50.
Owner Niall Mellon **Bred** Airlie Stud & Thomas Pilkingto **Trained** Stamullen, Co Meath

FOCUS
A modest staying handicap and the pace was ordinary, but still quite a competitive race and several were in with a chance rounding the home turn. Straightforward form.
Whaxaar(IRE) Official explanation: vet said gelding finished distressed

3138 DAY TIME, NIGHT TIME, GREAT TIME H'CAP — 7f (P)
9:15 (9:15) (Class 4) (0-85,85) 3-Y-O+ — £4,209 (£1,252; £625; £312) Stalls High

Form — RPR

6304 **1** **Bomber Command (USA)**[7] 2947 5-9-12 83 ... (v) TQuinn 4 — 92
(J W Hills) *sn trckd ldr: rdn to take narrow ld 2f out: jnd over 1f out: battled on wl u.p: jst hld on* **5/2**[2]

3321 **2** nse **Cha Cha Cha**[7] 2947 4-9-2 78 6ex ... NeilBrown(5) 5 — 87
(K A Ryan) *t.k.h early: hld up bhd ldrs: gng easily over 2f out: effrt to chal and jnd wnr over 1f out: drvn and limited rspnse fnl f: jst pipped* **8/11**[1]

6604 **3** 1 1/4 **Chjimes (IRE)**[40] 1954 4-8-10 67 ... LPKeniry 3 — 73
(C R Dore) *led: narrowly hdd 2f out: cl up bhd ldng pair fnl f but a hld* **12/1**[3]

-160 **4** 1 **Rankayo Hitam (USA)**[16] 2665 3-8-13 79 ... JohnEgan 7 — 79
(P F I Cole) *hld up in last pair: rdn over 2f out: kpt on fr over 1f out: nvr able to chal* **22/1**

1060 **5** hd **Millfield (IRE)**[14] 2722 5-9-0 71 ... JimCrowley 9 — 73
(P R Chamings) *plld hrd early: hld up: rdn over 2f out: kpt on fr over 1f out: nvr able to chal* **12/1**[3]

0-06 **6** 6 **Starlight Gazer**[19] 2565 5-9-2 76 ... TravisBlock(3) 6 — 62
(J A Geake) *plld hrd early: trckd ldng pair to over 2f out: sn btn* **12/1**[3]

3506 **7** 1/2 **Crystal Gazer (FR)**[16] 2679 4-9-9 85 ... HaddenFrost(5) 8 — 70
(R Hannon) *t.k.h early: hld up in last pair: rdn over 2f out: wknd wl over 1f out* **14/1**

1m 27.22s (1.22) **Going Correction** +0.025s/f (Slow)
WFA 3 from 4yo+ 9lb — **7 Ran SP% 120.6**
Speed ratings (Par 105): **94,93,92,91,91 84,83**
toteswinger: 1&2 £1.10, 1&3 £5.30, 2&3 £3.10. CSF £5.02 CT £16.96 TOTE £4.10: £2.10, £1.30; EX 7.20 Place 6 £54.07, Place 5 £29.71.
Owner Gary & Linnet Woodward (2) **Bred** Jeffrey B Feins **Trained** Upper Lambourn, Berks

FOCUS
An unusual handicap in that they went 12-1 bar two in a seven-horse race. They dawdled early and it developed into a sprint, but the finish was still dominated by the two market principals, the winner turning around recent form with the second. The winning time was understandably slow.
T/Plt: £168.60 to a £1 stake. Pool: £43,955.15. 190.25 winning tickets. T/Qpdt: £20.60 to a £1 stake. Pool: £3,947.18. 141.70 winning tickets. JN

2730 RIPON (R-H)
Wednesday, June 18

OFFICIAL GOING: Good to firm (good in places) changing to good after race 3 (7.55)
Wind: Virtually nil Weather: Overcast - heavy showers

3139 HIGH MOOR APPRENTICE (S) STKS — 6f
6:55 (6:57) (Class 6) 3-4-Y-O — £2,590 (£770; £385; £192) Stalls Low

Form — RPR

-400 **1** **Jaconet (USA)**[16] 2660 3-8-9 57 ... (b[1]) AdamCarter 12 — 49
(T D Barron) *mde all far side: clr over 2f out: rdn over 1f out: jst hld on* **13/2**

0-00 **2** nse **Missus Molly Brown**[51] 1675 4-9-2 42 ... FrederikTylicki 8 — 51
(R A Fahey) *hld up in tch stands' side: hdwy over 2f out: rdn wl over 1f out: styd on strly ins fnl f: jst failed* **6/1**[3]

3463 **3** 1 3/4 **Jevington Star (IRE)**[23] 2463 3-8-9 44 ... (b) AnthonyBetts(5) 7 — 48
(B Ellison) *in rr stands' side: pushed along 1/2-way: rdn and hdwy 2f out: styd on strly ins fnl f: nrst fin* **4/1**[1]

0-40 **4** 1/2 **Mandalay King (IRE)**[15] 2704 3-9-0 45 ... JohnCavanagh 3 — 47
(Mrs Marjorie Fife) *cl up stands' side: rdn to ld that gp 2f out: sn drvn and wknd ent fnl f* **33/1**

5000 **5** 5 **Only A Splash**[7] 2936 4-9-2 42 ... (p) MJMurphy(5) 4 — 33
(Mrs R A Carr) *cl up stands' side: led that gp 1/2-way: rdn and hdd 2f out: sn drvn and kpt on same pce* **25/1**

The Form Book, Raceform Ltd, Compton, RG20 6NL

000- **6** ¾ **Terandeil**[254] 6062 4-9-2 30 .... KrishGundowry 2 25
(J G M O'Shea) *dwlt and in rr stands' side: hdwy 1/2-way: rdn over 2f out and plugged on same pce* **66/1**

-000 **7** ¾ **Caught In Paradise (IRE)**[29] 2268 3-9-0 48 .... (p) TobyAtkinson 11 26
(D W Thompson) *in tch far side: effrt over 2f out: sn rdn and kpt on same pce* **22/1**

-200 **8** 2 **Maahe (IRE)**[16] 2661 3-8-4 46 .... AndreaAtzeni(5) 9 14
(R A Fahey) *dwlt and in rr stands' side: hdwy 1/2-way: rdn along 2f out and sn no imp* **14/1**

-000 **9** ¾ **Best Suited**[16] 2661 3-8-9 54 .... JamieKyne 6 12
(J J Quinn) *towards rr stands' side: rdn along over 2f out: nvr a factor* **11/2**[2]

000- **10** 1¼ **Carlton Mac**[225] 6698 3-8-9 48 .... JonathanHinch(5) 16 13
(N Bycroft) *in tch far side: rdn along 1/2-way: sn drvn and no imp* **33/1**

0-03 **11** 1¼ **Bungie**[13] 2748 4-9-2 45 .... RyanClark(5) 14 11
(Paul Green) *dwlt and towards rr far side: hdwy and in tch 1/2-way: rdn over 2f out and n.d* **7/1**

4-06 **12** 3¾ **Mill Creek**[16] 2661 3-8-9 42 .... JamesRogers 1 —
(Jedd O'Keeffe) *led stands' side: hdd 1/2-way: sn rdn along and wknd 2f out* **9/1**

05-0 **13** 2½ **Joint Agency (IRE)**[6] 2966 3-8-9 45 .... SamuelDrury 10 —
(N Wilson) *chsd wnr far side: rdn along over 2f out: sn wknd* **28/1**

0000 **14** 4½ **Stir Crazy (IRE)**[16] 2658 4-9-7 41 .... (v[1]) BradleyRoper 5 —
(D W Barker) *chsd ldrs stands' side: rdn over 2f out and sn wknd* **18/1**

00-0 **15** 10 **Splendidio**[16] 2676 4-8-11 47 .... MatthewLawson(5) 15 —
(A Crook) *a towards rr far side* **16/1**

0400 **16** 18 **Cryptic Clue (USA)**[7] 2936 4-9-7 43 .... (b) NBazeley 17 —
(Mrs R A Carr) *chsd ldrs far side: rdn along 1/2-way and sn wknd* **22/1**

0005 **17** *dist* **Hapi**[12] 2803 3-9-0 45 .... (t) DebraEngland 18 —
(S C Williams) *a bhd far side* **25/1**

1m 13.25s (0.25) **Going Correction** -0.15s/f (Firm)
WFA 3 from 4yo 7lb **17** Ran SP% **130.5**
Speed ratings (Par 101): **92,91,89,88,82 81,80,77,76,74 73,68,64,58,45 21,—**
toteswinger: 1&2 £6.60, 1&3 £4.50, 2&3 £4.20. CSF £43.64 TOTE £7.50: £3.30, £2.30, £2.70; EX 42.30.There was no bid for the winner.
Owner R G Toes **Bred** Team Block **Trained** Maunby, N Yorks
■ Stewards' Enquiry : Matthew Lawson one-day ban: failing to ride to draw (Jul 2)
Adam Carter one-day ban: failing to ride to draw (Jul 2)
Debra England one-day ban: failing to ride to draw (Jul 2)

FOCUS
This was a desperately poor affair even by selling standards and most of these would be more at home contesting the erstwhile "banded" events. They split into two groups, stalls nine and below coming stands' side and ten and above going far side. The first four home came well clear and the form makes sense among the principals. No bids or claims were received.
Hapi Official explanation: jockey said gelding lost its action

3140 METEOR MEDIAN AUCTION MAIDEN STKS 5f
7:25 (7:29) (Class 5) 2-Y-O £2,914 (£867; £433; £216) Stalls Low

Form RPR

522 **1** **Rievaulx World**[19] 2574 2-9-3 0 .... PaulMulrennan 2 89+
(K A Ryan) *qckly away: mde all: qcknd clr over 1f out: styd on wl* **5/4**[1]

0 **2** 4½ **Ishe Mac**[9] 2887 2-8-9 0 .... MarkLawson(3) 9 67
(N Bycroft) *chsd ldrs: effrt to chse wnr 2f out: sn rdn and no imp ent fnl f* **40/1**

00 **3** 1¾ **Kheylide (IRE)**[9] 2893 2-8-12 0 .... ShaneCreighton(5) 7 66
(Miss V Haigh) *chsd wnr: rdn along over 2f out: kpt on same pce appr fnl f* **66/1**

4 **4** 3¾ **Abu Derby (IRE)**[16] 2657 2-9-3 0 .... J-PGuillambert 3 52
(J G Given) *chsd ldrs: rdn along 2f out: kpt on same pce* **11/2**[3]

5 **5** ½ **Miss Moloney (IRE)**[15] 2702 2-8-9 0 .... PJMcDonald(3) 5 45
(Mrs S Lamyman) *in tch: rdn along over 2f out: kpt on same pce* **50/1**

4 **6** 3¼ **Rio Cobolo (IRE)**[18] 2608 2-9-3 0 .... LiamJones 4 39
(Paul Green) *chsd ldrs: rdn along 2f out: grad wknd* **4/1**[2]

020 **7** ¾ **El Bobby (IRE)**[23] 2462 2-9-3 0 .... DeanMcKeown 11 36
(J R Weymes) *in tch on outer: rdn along 1/2-way: sn wknd* **14/1**

8 3½ **Cosmic Sun** 2-8-10 0 .... FrederikTylicki(7) 12 23
(R A Fahey) *sn outpcd and bhd tl sme late hdwy* **33/1**

00 **9** ½ **Ba Globetrotter**[8] 2916 2-9-3 0 .... SamHitchcott 10 21
(M R Channon) *reminders after s and a in rr* **25/1**

10 ½ **Blackwater Fort (USA)** 2-9-3 0 .... PaulFessey 6 20
(T D Barron) *a in rr* **20/1**

11 1¾ **Ishiquick** 2-8-9 0 .... DuranFentiman(3) 1 8
(T D Easterby) *sn outpcd and a in rr* **33/1**

12 2¼ **Royal Max (IRE)** 2-9-0 0 .... JamieMoriarty(3) 14 5
(R A Fahey) *wnt bdly rt s: a bhd* **20/1**

13 6 **Rebelwithoutacause (IRE)** 2-9-0 0 .... TolleyDean(3) 13 —
(George Baker) *in tch on outer: rdn along after 2f: sn wknd* **6/1**

59.25 secs (-1.45) **Going Correction** -0.15s/f (Firm) **13** Ran SP% **125.9**
Speed ratings (Par 93): **105,97,95,89,88 83,81,76,75,74 71,68,58**
toteswinger: 1&2 £48.80, 1&3 Not won, 2&3 Not won. Pool of £165.01 carried over to Friday. CSF £84.26 TOTE £1.90: £1.30, £11.50, £23.60; EX 57.00.
Owner Rievaulx Racing Syndicate **Bred** Grovewood Stud & Padraid O'Neill **Trained** Hambleton, N Yorks

FOCUS
A modest maiden that did not take a lot of winning, but it was won in a very smart winning time for a race like this. Rievaulx World built on his previous good form.

NOTEBOOK
Rievaulx World was unlucky to bump into a smart horse in Excellent Show at Musselburgh last time, but he had shown plenty to suggest that a race like this was within his ability, and he made easy work of this lot, showing good speed from his low draw and coming home nicely clear of the runner-up. His future probably lies in nursery company. (op 4-6 tchd 6-4 in places)
Ishe Mac, a cheap 3,000gns purchase, is a half-sister to Jade's Promise, a 1m2f winner, Boy Express, a dual 1m-1m2f winner in Italy and Kitope, a dual sprint winner in Italy. She stepped up on her debut effort over this shorter trip and looks to be going the right way. (tchd 33-1)
Kheylide(IRE) ran his best race to date, staying on for third, and he should pay his way in modest nursery company.
Abu Derby(IRE) was better behaved this time but he finished ten lengths behind the winner and probably did not improve as much as his supporters, who backed him in from 16-1, had expected. (op 16-1)
Miss Moloney(IRE), a cheap purchase, is a half-sister to Onenightinlisbon, who won twice over 5f at two and has since won at up to a mile. (op 100-1)
Rio Cobolo(IRE) may do better when he can get his toe in. (op 11-1)
Blackwater Fort(USA) Official explanation: jockey said colt hung right
Rebelwithoutacause(IRE) is a half-brother to Festive Affair, a triple 6f winner, Night Runner, a dual sprint winner, and Signor Panettiere, a 5f winner at two, and one would expect him to do better with this debut run under his belt. (op 7-1 tchd 5-1)

3141 NORMAN WELLS MEMORIAL CHALLENGE TROPHY H'CAP 6f
7:55 (7:55) (Class 3) (0-95,88) 3-Y-O £7,885 (£2,360; £1,180; £590; £293) Stalls Low

Form RPR

-042 **1** **Wise Melody**[9] 2896 3-8-11 **78** .... LiamJones 8 89
(W J Haggas) *cl up: led 2f out: rdn clr whn hung rt ent fnl f: styd on strly* **13/2**[2]

1131 **2** 3¾ **Great Charm (IRE)**[14] 2732 3-9-2 **83** .... PaulMulrennan 3 82
(M L W Bell) *trckd ldng pair: hdwy to chse wnr wl over 1f out: sn rdn and kpt on same pce ins fnl f* **11/4**[1]

2310 **3** 2¼ **Tawzeea (IRE)**[22] 2481 3-8-12 **79** .... RoystonFfrench 6 71
(M Johnston) *chsd ldrs: rdn along 2f out: drvn and one pce appr fnl f* **8/1**

5405 **4** 1¾ **Mister Hardy**[25] 2410 3-9-1 **85** .... JamieMoriarty(3) 2 71
(R A Fahey) *chsd ldrs: rdn along 2f out: sn drvn and no imp* **11/4**[1]

-060 **5** 1¼ **Anosti**[39] 1999 3-9-1 **82** .... PaulFessey 4 64
(K A Ryan) *towards rr: effrt and sme hdwy 1/2-way: nvr a factor* **16/1**

0-02 **6** ¾ **La Chicaluna**[16] 2674 3-8-12 **79** .... J-PGuillambert 7 59
(J G Given) *led: rdn along and hdd 2f out: sn wknd* **7/1**[3]

1-30 **7** 2¾ **Quest For Success (IRE)**[25] 2410 3-9-4 **85** .... DaleGibson 5 56
(D J G Murray Smith) *dwlt: a towards rr* **20/1**

6150 **8** 1¾ **Jonny Lesters Hair (IRE)**[16] 2674 3-8-2 **72** .... DuranFentiman(3) 9 37
(T D Easterby) *dwlt: hdwy on outer and in tch 1/2-way: sn rdn and wknd 2f out* **20/1**

0-00 **9** 10 **Calmdownmate (IRE)**[45] 1837 3-9-7 **88** .... (v[1]) FergusSweeney 1 21
(K R Burke) *t.k.h: chsd ldrs on inner: rdn along 1/2-way: sn wknd* **9/1**

1m 11.53s (-1.47) **Going Correction** -0.15s/f (Firm) **9** Ran SP% **115.7**
Speed ratings (Par 103): **103,98,95,92,91 90,86,84,70**
toteswinger: 1&2 £1.10, 1&3 £4.90, 2&3 £3.40. CSF £24.78 CT £143.86 TOTE £5.20: £1.20, £1.60, £2.60; EX 8.90.
Owner Wise Move UK Limited **Bred** I A Southcott **Trained** Newmarket, Suffolk

FOCUS
A useful bunch of three-year-old sprinters on show. The winner is still relatively unexposed and progressive.

NOTEBOOK
Wise Melody was due to go up 2lb anyway after getting touched off over the minimum trip at Windsor last Monday but she now faces a much more serious hike after blowing these rivals away in convincing fashion. Lightly raced, she can improve again. (op 5-1)
Great Charm(IRE) has been on a great run of late and but for being unlucky at Hamilton on his penultimate start might well have come into this race on a five-timer. He met a seriously progressive filly here, and the likelihood is that he is up to defying his current mark too long, maybe over the extra furlong which he seems sure to stay on this evidence. (tchd 2-1)
Tawzeea(IRE) was returning to the trip over which he won his maiden at Hamilton but though he ran a solid enough race he had nowhere near the firepower of the front two and looks handicapped out of things at the moment. (op 17-2 tchd 7-1)
Mister Hardy was sent off as joint-favourite but looks in the Handicapper's grip. (op 7-2 tchd 4-1)
Anosti is paying the price for some consistently good juvenile efforts and needs some respite from the Handicapper. (op 20-1 tchd 25-1)
Calmdownmate(IRE) Official explanation: jockey said gelding lost its action

3142 BOROUGHBRIDGE RACES CUP (H'CAP) 1m 1f 170y
8:25 (8:26) (Class 4) (0-85,83) 4-Y-O+ £4,857 (£1,445; £722; £360) Stalls High

Form RPR

3003 **1** **Wigwam Willie (IRE)**[14] 2733 6-9-4 **80** .... (p) PaulMulrennan 8 86
(K A Ryan) *in tch: hdwy and rdn along 3f out: swtchd ins and drvn appr fnl f: styd on to ld last 50yds* **9/2**[2]

2030 **2** *nk* **Intersky Charm (USA)**[19] 2582 4-8-13 **75** .... DeanMcKeown 5 80
(R M Whitaker) *hld up in rr: hdwy on outer over 2f out: rdn to chal over 1f out: drvn and led briefly ins fnl f: hdd and nt qckn last 50yds* **4/1**[1]

42/3 **3** ½ **Sculastic**[26] 2379 5-9-4 **80** .... RobertWinston 3 84
(J Howard Johnson) *sn led: rdn along over 2f out: drvn over 1f out: hdd ins fnl f: nt qckn last 100yds* **9/1**

6060 **4** ¾ **Bed Fellow (IRE)**[12] 2795 4-8-0 **67** oh1 ow3 .... KellyHarrison(5) 9 70
(Paul Murphy) *chsd ldng pair: hdwy 3f out: rdn to chal 2f out: sn drvn and ev ch tl no ex jst ins fnl f* **40/1**

4320 **5** 3¼ **Rosbay (IRE)**[19] 2582 4-9-4 **83** .... DuranFentiman(3) 1 79
(T D Easterby) *trckd ldrs: effrt 3f out: rdn along 2f out: drvn over 1f out and one pce* **5/1**[3]

12-0 **6** 1 **Prince Noel**[16] 2672 4-7-12 **65** .... DanielleMcCreery(5) 2 59
(N Wilson) *trckd ldr: effrt 3f out: rdn along 2f out and grad wknd* **8/1**

0500 **7** *nk* **Nuit Sombre (IRE)**[25] 2397 8-8-12 **74** .... (p) SilvestreDeSousa 6 68
(G A Harker) *t.k.h: in tch: hdwy whn nt clr run over 2f out: sn rdn and wknd over 1f out* **14/1**

0003 **8** *nk* **Minority Report**[6] 2969 8-9-7 **83** .... AdrianTNicholls 7 76+
(D Nicholls) *hld up and bhd: hdwy 3f out: effrt and n.m.r over 1f out: wknd and eased ins fnl f* **11/2**

0031 **R** **Claret And Amber**[16] 2658 6-8-9 **74** .... JamieMoriarty(3) 4 —
(R A Fahey) *blind removed late and ref to r: tk no part* **11/2**

2m 4.59s (-0.81) **Going Correction** +0.05s/f (Good) **9** Ran SP% **115.8**
Speed ratings (Par 105): **105,104,104,103,101 100,100,99,—**
toteswinger: 1&2 £7.20, 1&3 £16.70, 2&3 £94.10. CSF £22.95 CT £155.33 TOTE £5.60: £1.80, £2.70, £2.20; EX 28.90.
Owner Neil & Anne Dawson Partnership **Bred** Mrs Margaret Christie **Trained** Hambleton, N Yorks
■ Stewards' Enquiry : Dean McKeown five-day ban: used whip with excessive frequency and without giving colt time to respond (Jul 3-7)

FOCUS
A fair handicap, but the early pace was steady and the race developed into something of a sprint. The form is thus not that solid.

3143 BRENTWOOD DESIGN PARTNERSHIP H'CAP 1m 4f 10y
8:55 (8:55) (Class 5) (0-75,72) 4-Y-O+ £2,914 (£867; £433; £216) Stalls High

Form RPR

5211 **1** **Hits Only Vic (USA)**[3] 3059 4-9-4 **69** .... DavidAllan 7 87+
(D Carroll) *hld up: hdwy on bit 3f out: led 2f out: sn clr* **8/11**[1]

-542 **2** 1¼ **Demolition**[18] 2591 4-9-2 **72** .... AshleyHamblett(5) 2 84
(N Wilson) *racd wd: a.p: effrt 3f out: sn rdn and ev ch tl drvn and one pce appr fnl f* **8/1**

0-04 **3** 8 **Fascinatin Rhythm**[34] 2125 4-9-5 **70** .... SamHitchcott 1 69
(M R Channon) *towards rr: hdwy 3f out: rdn over 2f out: drvn over 1f out: styd on to take 3rd pl ins fnl f* **25/1**

0326 **4** 1¾ **Valdan (IRE)**[12] 2782 4-8-7 **58** .... (t) DeanMcKeown 4 54
(M A Barnes) *prom: led after 3f: hdd 2f out and wknd* **16/1**

-003 **5** 1¼ **Tcherina (IRE)**[11] 2822 6-9-1 **69** .... DuranFentiman(3) 3 63
(T D Easterby) *hld up in tch: effrt 3f out: sn rdn along and no imp* **7/1**[3]

3-00 **6** *10* **Campli (IRE)**^{26} 2365 6-8-7 **58** ow1 .... PaulMulrennan 10 36
(Micky Hammond) *hld up: a towards rr* **20/1**

363- **7** *1 1/2* **Edas**^{297} 4843 6-8-6 **64** .... JamieKyne(7) 6 40
(J J Quinn) *led 3f: cl up tl rdn along 3f and wkng whn hung bdly rt 2f out* **20/1**

3123 **8** *2 1/2* **Pee Jay's Dream**^{15} 2701 6-9-3 **68** .... DaleGibson 9 40
(M W Easterby) *dwlt: sn prom: rdn along over 3f out and sn wknd* **9/2**^{2}

2m 37.37s (0.67) **Going Correction** +0.05s/f (Good) **8** Ran SP% **118.9**
Speed ratings (Par 103): **99,98,92,91,90 84,83,81**
toteswinger: 1&2 £6.00, 1&3 £6.40, 2&3 £4.40. CSF £7.64 CT £87.07 TOTE £1.70: £1.60, £1.60, £3.90; EX 11.00.
Owner Kell-Stone & Watson **Bred** Peter E Blum **Trained** Sledmere, E Yorks

FOCUS
Just a fair handicap for older horses which revolved around the winner's attempt to run up a quick hat-trick, which he achieved easily. He is rated a bit better than the bare form, but there was not much strength in depth to this race.
Edas Official explanation: jockey said horse hung right

3144 COVERDALE MAIDEN STKS 6f
9:25 (9:26) (Class 5) 3-Y-O **£2,914** (£867; £433; £216) **Stalls** Low

Form RPR

-235 **1** **Everything**^{46} 1817 3-8-9 65 .... JamieMoriarty(3) 3 73
(P T Midgley) *chsd ldrs: sltly outpcd 1/2-way: carried rt 2f out: sn rdn and hdwy over 1f out: styd on ins fnl f to ld last 100yds* **7/2**^{2}

322 **2** *4* **Great Knight (IRE)**^{36} 2067 3-9-3 74 ....(b1) LiamJones 11 65
(W J Haggas) *wnt rt s: sn chsng ldrs: led after 2f: rdn 2f out: drvn ent fnl f: hdd and no ex last 100yds* **6/4**^{1}

350- **3** *3/4* **Pintano**^{265} 5745 3-9-3 75 .... RobertWinston 7 63
(J Howard Johnson) *cl up: rdn and ch 2f out: drvn over 1f out and kpt on same pce ins fnl f* **13/2**^{3}

0 **4** *2 1/2* **First Swallow**^{12} 2786 3-8-10 0 .... FrederikTylicki(7) 10 55+
(R A Fahey) *wnt rt s and bhd tl styd on fnl 2f: nrst fin* **16/1**

635- **5** *1 3/4* **Do As I Say**^{366} 2710 3-9-0 70 .... DuranFentiman(3) 1 49
(T D Easterby) *chsd ldrs: rdn along over 2f out: sn one pce* **20/1**

0433 **6** *nse* **Bertie Vista**^{23} 2466 3-9-3 65 ....(b) DavidAllan 9 49
(T D Easterby) *chsd ldrs: rdn over 2f out: sn one pce* **8/1**

0 **7** *3 3/4* **Dubai To Barnsley**^{20} 2546 3-9-3 0 .... PaulMulrennan 2 37
(Garry Moss) *led 2f: rdn along and wkng whn hung bdly rt 2f out: sn lost pl* **66/1**

05 **8** *2 1/4* **Great Destination**^{56} 1556 3-9-3 0 .... RoystonFfrench 6 30
(B Smart) *a in rr* **8/1**

6 **9** *nk* **Mrs Bun**^{11} 2823 3-8-12 0 .... FergalLynch 5 24
(K A Ryan) *dwlt: a bhd* **9/1**

00 **10** *1 1/4* **Lovely Lilling**^{37} 2038 3-8-12 0 .... PaulFessey 4 20
(P T Midgley) *in tch: rdn along 1/2-way and bhd fr 1/2-way* **80/1**

1m 13.36s (0.36) **Going Correction** +0.05s/f (Good) **10** Ran SP% **121.1**
Speed ratings (Par 99): **99,93,92,89,87 86,81,78,78,76**
toteswinger: 1&2 £1.60, 1&3 £5.90 , 2&3 £3.50. CSF £9.43 TOTE £5.50: £1.40, £1.60, £2.10; EX 14.20 Place 6 £15.44, Place 5 £6.63.
Owner Anthony D Copley **Bred** Jim Cockburn **Trained** Westow, N Yorks

FOCUS
A modest maiden won by an exposed performer, who is rated to the best view of her 2yo form.
T/Plt: £13.40 to a £1 stake. Pool: £57,246.12. 3,114.93 winning tickets. T/Qpdt: £5.70 to a £1 stake. Pool: £4,766.09. 612.10 winning tickets. JR

3145 - 3151a (Foreign Racing) - See Raceform Interactive

3119 ASCOT (R-H)
Thursday, June 19

OFFICIAL GOING: Good to firm
Dolling out added 12yards to race distances on the round course.
Wind: Fresh, against Weather: Fine

3152 NORFOLK STKS (GROUP 2) 5f
2:30 (2:31) (Class 1) 2-Y-O
£45,416 (£17,216; £8,616; £4,296; £2,152; £1,080) **Stalls** Centre

Form RPR

1 **1** **South Central (USA)**^{17} 2657 2-9-1 0 .... RobertWinston 5 107
(J Howard Johnson) *w'like: str: mde all: rdn over 1f out: edgd lft ins fnl f: gamely hld on fnl strides* **11/4**^{1}

511 **2** *hd* **Spin Cycle (IRE)**^{12} 2838 2-9-1 0 .... TedDurcan 3 106
(B Smart) *cmpt: str: hld up: pushed along and hdwy 1/2-way: rdn to chse wnr over 1f out: edgd rt and r.o strly ins fnl f: gaining qckly at fin: jst failed* **7/1**^{3}

12 **3** *1* **Prolific (IRE)**^{17} 2677 2-9-1 0 .... RichardHughes 11 103
(R Hannon) *lengthy: lw: in tch: effrt 2f out: sn chsd ldrs: r.o ins fnl f but nt pce of front pair* **6/1**^{2}

331 **4** *hd* **Flashmans Papers**^{2} 3105 2-9-1 0 .... SteveDrowne 13 102
(J R Best) *lw: hld up in rr: swtchd lft and hdwy under 2f out: r.o ins fnl f: nvr quite got to ldrs* **10/1**

4 **5** *2 3/4* **Elegant Cad (CAN)**^{12} 2838 2-9-1 0 .... LPKeniry 6 92
(J R Best) *w'like: scope: trckd ldrs: rdn 2f out: kpt on same pce fr over 1f out* **14/1**

1 **6** *1 1/4* **Cerito**^{36} 2098 2-9-1 0 .... DarryllHolland 7 88
(M R Channon) *leggy: athletic: lw: pressed wnr tl rdn over 1f out: wknd ins fnl f* **6/1**^{2}

6421 **7** *2* **Klynch**^{15} 2709 2-9-1 0 .... JamieSpencer 1 80
(B J Meehan) *in tch: rdn and wanted to hang rt 2f out: wknd over 1f out* **20/1**

22 **8** *nk* **Servoca (CAN)**^{20} 2569 2-9-1 0 .... MichaelHills 12 80+
(B W Hills) *lw: hld up: hdwy to trck ldrs 3f out: rdn over 1f out: sn wknd* **16/1**

331 **9** *hd* **Sun Ship (IRE)**^{35} 2124 2-9-1 0 .... RyanMoore 4 79+
(R Hannon) *lw: in tch: pushed along 1/2-way: sn wknd* **14/1**

26 **10** *1 3/4* **Skid Solo (IRE)**^{50} 1714 2-9-1 0 ....(t) AlanMunro 15 72
(P W Chapple-Hyam) *towards rr: pushed along and outpcd fnl 2f* **40/1**

11 **11** *2 3/4* **Baycat (IRE)**^{50} 1714 2-9-1 0 .... JamesDoyle 10 62
(J G Portman) *lw: bustled along leaving stalls to r in midfield: rdn and wknd over 1f out* **8/1**

61.83 secs (1.33) **Going Correction** +0.15s/f (Good) **11** Ran SP% **114.4**
Speed ratings (Par 105): **95,94,93,92,88 86,83,82,82,79 75**
toteswinger: 1&2 £4.30, 1&3 £3.50, 2&3 £9.50. CSF £20.87 TOTE £3.50: £1.50, £2.30, £2.00; EX 22.80 Trifecta £167.40 Pool: £6085.89 - 26.89 winning units.
Owner Transcend Bloodstock LLP **Bred** Tony Holmes & Walter Zent **Trained** Billy Row, Co Durham
■ A second Norfolk win for connections in four years, following Masta Plasta at York in 2005.
■ Stewards' Enquiry : Robert Winston two-day ban: used whip in incorrect place (Jul 3-4)

FOCUS
A very moderate winning time for a Norfolk, nearly a second slower than the previous day's Queen Mary and well over a second slower than Tuesday's Windsor Castle. However, the runners were racing into a headwind. A solid renewal.

NOTEBOOK
South Central(USA) had looked a Norfolk colt after his 13-length winning debut at Carlisle last month. Smartly away, he made every yard but looked in trouble when coming under pressure with over a furlong to run, edging to his left and appearing uncomfortable on the fast ground. To his credit, having looked like getting caught he stuck his neck out to hold on. Easier ground and an extra furlong will suit him and he is clearly a smart juvenile, but he is for sale and has no immediate targets. (op 5-2 tchd 3-1)
Spin Cycle(IRE), bidding for a hat-trick, ran a fine race on this big rise in grade. Held up at the rear, he improved on the near side of the bunch before going after the winner. He looked sure to get up for much of the final furlong, but South Central just pulled out that bit extra to deny him. Goodwood's Molecomb Stakes is his immediate target. (op 8-1)
Prolific(IRE) ◆ had his colours lowered at Windsor by subsequent Queen Mary Stakes disappointment Danehill Dancer. He ran a big race and the way he stuck on strongly suggests that he has improvement in him over 6f, with the July Stakes at Newmarket and the Gimcrack at York looking the obvious targets. (op 5-1 tchd 13-2 in places)
Flashmans Papers, a 100/1 winner of the Windsor Castle Stakes two days earlier, ran up to form on this quick reappearance although the edge might just have been taken off him. He ran on late when switched out and just failed to get up for third.
Elegant Cad(CAN) ◆, who was fourth to today's runner-up on his Musselburgh debut, finished one place behind his stablemate here. He did not find quite as much when let down as he had promised to, but is clearly a very useful colt who will have no problem winning a maiden. (op 12-1)
Cerito, who made a winning debut at Bath, rmatched that form in defeat but, after chasing the winner for three and a half furlongs, he had nothing more to give at the business end. (op 5-1)
Klynch, who was the most experienced member of the field, ran about as well as could be expected but did look to be feeling the ground. (op 33-1 tchd 18-1)
Servoca(CAN), runner-up to impressive Coventry winner Art Connoisseur on his debut at Newmarket, filled the same position over 6f next time. Back down in trip, he ran well up to a point but was on the retreat when short of room approaching the final furlong. The fast ground might have been against him.
Sun Ship(IRE), the Hannon second string, was in trouble by halfway. (op 20-1)
Skid Solo(IRE), representing the connections of last year's winner Winker Watson, was out of his depth but did finish in front of Baycat this time. (tchd 33-1)
Baycat(IRE), winner of his first two starts, including a decent conditions event over course and distance last time, failed to run his race on this sounder surface. Official explanation: jockey said colt hung left (op 12-1)

3153 RIBBLESDALE STKS (GROUP 2) (FILLIES) 1m 4f
3:05 (3:05) (Class 1) 3-Y-O
£85,155 (£32,280; £16,155; £8,055; £4,035; £2,025) **Stalls** High

Form RPR

-010 **1** **Michita (USA)**^{13} 2792 3-8-12 109 .... JimmyFortune 5 111+
(J H M Gosden) *swtg: hld up in tch: rdn to ld 2f out: drew clr over 1f out: comf* **10/3**^{1}

5-31 **2** *3 1/2* **Arthur's Girl**^{35} 2123 3-8-12 84 .... SteveDrowne 1 104
(G Wragg) *stmbld sltly s: hld up in rr of midfield: swtchd outside and hdwy over 2f out: wnt 2nd 1f out: no ch w wnr* **7/1**

20-3 **3** *2 1/2* **Hobby**^{34} 2149 3-8-12 95 .... SebSanders 8 100
(R M Beckett) *lw: led and set modest pce: rdn and hdd 2f out: one pce* **11/1**

21 **4** *3/4* **Icon Project (USA)**^{28} 2336 3-8-12 84 .... RichardHughes 6 102+
(B J Meehan) *lw: stdd s: hld up in 2nd last: effrt whn ct in scrimmaging ins fnl 2f: styd on fnl f: nvr nrr* **12/1**

2-51 **5** *hd* **Elmaleeha**^{15} 2716 3-8-12 0 .... RHills 10 98+
(J L Dunlop) *chsd ldrs: n.m.r over 2f out: hrd rdn and outpcd ins fnl 2f* **16/1**

3-23 **6** *2* **Changing Skies (IRE)**^{43} 1915 3-8-12 100 .... LDettori 4 95
(B J Meehan) *lw: chsd ldr: rdn 3f out: disputing 3rd and btn whn bmpd over 1f out* **11/2**^{3}

6-45 **7** *hd* **Sovereign's Honour (USA)**^{36} 2105 3-8-12 97 .... RyanMoore 7 95
(Sir Michael Stoute) *lw: hld up in rr of midfield: effrt whn bmpd and n.m.r over 2f out: sn rdn and btn* **10/1**

-000 **8** *2 1/4* **Kitty Matcham (IRE)**^{11} 2877 3-8-12 0 .... JMurtagh 2 91
(A P O'Brien, Ire) *lw: s.s and dropped in last: shkn up and no prog over 1f out: hrd rdn ins fnl f: nvr a factor* **13/2**

1-26 **9** *3 1/2* **Cape Amber (IRE)**^{13} 2792 3-8-12 104 .... AlanMunro 9 85
(P W Chapple-Hyam) *plld hrd: chsd ldng pair towards outside: pushed along over 3f out: wknd over 2f out* **9/2**^{2}

2m 31.87s (-3.63) **Going Correction** -0.10s/f (Good) **9** Ran SP% **113.5**
Speed ratings (Par 108): **108,105,104,103,103 102,101,100,98**
toteswinger: 1&2 £5.60, 1&3 £7.60, 2&3 £16.60. CSF £26.34 TOTE £3.50: £1.40, £2.90, £3.60; EX 18.10 Trifecta £333.70 Pool: £ 6850.52 - 15.59 winning units.
Owner Stonerside Stable Llc **Bred** Stonerside Stable **Trained** Newmarket, Suffolk
■ Stewards' Enquiry : Richard Hughes two-day ban: careless riding (Jul 3-4)

FOCUS
A mix of profiles contested this Group 2, with a couple of maidens at one end of the spectrum and at the other, three fillies who have mixed it in the very highest company. Despite this, no filly was sent off at bigger than 16-1 as there were plenty of doubts surrounding those to have run in the Classics while the more unexposed types had potential. The pace was sound. The winner looked different class, but there were much-improved performances too from the second, fourth and fifth.

NOTEBOOK
Michita(USA) ran out a resounding winner. She had failed to act around Epsom in the Oaks but on this flatter track she settled beautifully off the sound gallop set by Hobby, sitting one off the rail in the mid-division. Merely shaken up to range alongside the leader, once her jockey gave her a crack she lengthened right away, and was impressive. Her trainer put up the Yorkshire Oaks as a target, indicating that he wanted to keep her racing against her own sex for this year. It would be no surprise to see her provide the Epsom heroine Look Here with a severe test if they reoppose on the flat Yorkshire track, while if last year's winner Peeping Fawn comes back to contest the race it would take on something of an unmissable air. (op 3-1 tchd 7-2, 4-1 in places)
Arthur's Girl seemed to stumble slightly leaving the gates, but her jockey seemed more than happy to hold her up at the rear anyway, so it had little bearing on the result. A daughter of Hernando, sire of the Oaks winner Look Here, she travelled well throughout the race. She picked up well to come out of the pack and give chase to the winner in the straight without ever looking like getting to her. A minor Group race should be hers before too long. (op 13-2 tchd 15-2 in a place)
Hobby set a sound gallop from the off, and picked up well off the home turn to get everything bar the first two home on the stretch. Not able to go with the winner, she kept on well for third. The level of form she showed here ought to put her in as a good thing for something like a Listed contest, but her style of racing does set her up as something of a sitting duck. She will stay further, however, and has Doncaster's Park Hill Stakes as a long-term target. (op 16-1)
Icon Project(USA) found herself travelling well in behind a couple of horses into the straight before suffering a hefty barge from Sovereign's Honour as she attempted to pull around them. Still enjoying little daylight, she kept on well to the line and, as this was just her third start, there should be more improvement. (op 16-1)

Elmaleeha improved substantially on the basic form of her maiden win. Out of a sister to top miler Bahri, she saw the trip out all right, despite not enjoying the clearest of passages. (op 20-1)
Changing Skies(IRE) sat closest to the leader through the early stages and was the cause of the scrimmaging as she weakened out of things. In fairness, she didn't get beaten by as far as she looked like being at one stage and a maiden would be a formality. (op 6-1 tchd 7-1 in a place)
Sovereign's Honour(USA) already looked beaten when she got involved in a bit of a bumping match with Icon Project about two furlongs out. Having now taken in Group company on her last two starts, she might be better off thrown back into a maiden for a confidence boost. (tchd 11-1, 12-1 in a place)
Kitty Matcham(IRE) has now disappointed on all four starts this term, albeit in exalted company. She was stuck in behind a wall of horses turning into the straight, but didn't pick up once in the clear and is beginning to run out of excuses. It is starting to look as though she simply hasn't trained on. (op 7-1 tchd 15-2)
Cape Amber(IRE), who had finished one place in front of the winner at Epsom, refused to settle in the early stages despite the pace being sound enough. Still throwing her head around after they had turned out of Swinley Bottom, she unsurprisingly had nothing left in the tank at the business end. This was only her fourth start, and she deserves more chances to show just how good she is, but she won't do so unless she becomes a little more tractable. Official explanation: jockey said filly ran too free (op 4-1 tchd 5-1 in a place)

3154 GOLD CUP (GROUP 1) — 2m 4f

3:45 (3:45) (Class 1) 4-Y-O+

£141,925 (£53,800; £26,925; £13,425; £6,725; £3,375) **Stalls** High

Form — RPR

13-1 **1** **Yeats (IRE)**[53] 1655 7-9-2 0 .... JMurtagh 4 124
(A P O'Brien, Ire) *lw: in tch: clsd over 5f out: disp ld over 4f out: rdn over 2f out: sn slt advantage but hrd pressed: styd on gamely to draw clr fnl 100yds* **11/8**[1]

22-1 **2** *5* **Geordieland (FR)**[34] 2169 7-9-2 117 .... ShaneKelly 9 119
(J A Osborne) *racd keenly: hld up: hdwy over 5f out: chsd ldrs over 3f out: rdn to move upsides to chal strly 2f out: lugged rt and no answer to wnr fnl 100yds* **15/2**[3]

1-11 **3** *4 1/2* **Coastal Path**[32] 2236 4-9-0 0 .... SPasquier 2 115
(A Fabre, France) *lengthy: tall: racd keenly: trckd ldrs: wnt 2nd after 4f: disp ld over 4f out: rdn over 2f out: sn hdd: lost grnd on front pair ent fnl 1f: wknd fnl 100yds* **2/1**[2]

31-0 **4** *1 3/4* **Allegretto (IRE)**[21] 2542 5-8-13 113 .... RyanMoore 1 110+
(Sir Michael Stoute) *hld up in rr: rdn and hdwy over 2f out: styd on fr over 1f out: nvr able to trble ldrs* **16/1**

23-0 **5** *shd* **Sagara (USA)**[13] 2797 4-9-0 122 .... KerrinMcEvoy 5 113
(Saeed Bin Suroor) *b.hind: lw: racd keenly: hld up: nt clr run over 3f out: effrt and hdwy to chse clr ldrs over 2f out: no imp: styd on at one pce fnl f* **25/1**

4-23 **6** *1/2* **Regal Flush**[19] 2625 4-9-0 112 .... LDettori 6 112+
(Saeed Bin Suroor) *lw: hld up: nt clr run over 2f out: sn mde hdwy wout troubling ldrs: no ex ins fnl f* **11/1**

00 **7** *1 1/2* **Thundering Star (SAF)**[21] 2542 5-9-2 0 .... (p) KShea 3 111
(M F De Kock, South Africa) *str: midfield: lost pl 4f out: plugged on appr fnl f: n.d* **33/1**

-030 **8** *27* **Diamond Quest (SAF)**[105] 816 7-9-2 0 .... MartinDwyer 11 84
(A M Balding) *racd keenly: midfield: pushed along to chse clr front trio but no imp over 3f out: wknd 2f out: eased whn btn fnl f* **50/1**

4-64 **9** *38* **Le Miracle (GER)**[32] 2236 7-9-2 0 .... DBoeuf 7 46
(W Baltromei, Germany) *led: hdd over 4f out: wknd 3f out: eased whn btn fnl f: t.o* **28/1**

35-1 **10** *3 3/4* **Finalmente**[21] 2542 6-9-2 110 .... (p) MJKinane 10 42
(S A Callaghan) *trckd ldr for 4f: remained prom: losing pl whn tightened up over 3f out and again sn after: sn n.d: eased whn btn fnl f: t.o* **28/1**

4m 21.14s (0.34) **Going Correction** -0.10s/f (Good)
WFA 4 from 5yo+ 2lb — **38** Ran SP% **117.1**
Speed ratings (Par 117): **95,93,91,90,90 90,89,78,63,62**
toteswinger: 1&2 £2.10, 1&3 £1.10, 2&3 £2.30. CSF £11.87 TOTE £2.40: £1.10, £1.80, £1.20; EX 7.90 Trifecta £17.80 Pool: £16173.50 - 669.91 winning units.
Owner Mrs John Magnier & Mrs David Nagle **Bred** Barrowsdale Stud & Orpendale **Trained** Ballydoyle, Co Tipperary
■ Yeats was emulating the great French stayer Sagaro, the only previous triple winner of the race.

FOCUS
A memorable and historic Gold Cup. Although it was run in a very modest time for a Group 1 it rates the best of Yeats's three wins in the race. The form is rated through the runner-up.

NOTEBOOK
Yeats(IRE) put up a fine display of class and courage to become only the second horse, after Sagaro in 1975-1977, to win the Gold Cup three times. Coming here after a single prep race this time, he was always handily placed and, when his market rival Coastal Path eased past the pacesetting Le Miracle with over half a mile to run, Murtagh was quick to cover the move. The French raider was travelling marginally the better of the two turning into the straight, with Geordieland stalking the pair in third. The three were in line with two furlongs to run and Yeats was under pressure, but Coastal Path soon cracked and the reigning champion was left to fight it out with Geordieland. Battling on, he was in command entering the final furlong and pulled away inside the last. It remains to be seen whether he will back next year. (tchd 13-8, 7-4 in places)
Geordieland(FR), beaten a length and a half by Yeats in last year's renewal, came here following a memorable Yorkshire Cup win. He closed to track the two favourites into the home straight, travelling characteristically strongly, and threw down his challenge at the two pole. He was soon engaged in a straight fight with Yeats, but had to give best entering the final furlong. There was no disgrace in this and Kelly did not deserve the criticism levelled at him that he had committed his mount too soon. He could drop back in trip for the King George here next month. (op 9-1)
Coastal Path, whose half-brother Reefscape was runner-up to Yeats in the 2006 Gold Cup, experienced his first defeat on his seventh career start. Tackling fast ground for the first time, he moved past the leader at the same time as Yeats and looked to be going the better of the pair entering the straight, but he could not race on with Yeats or Geordieland from the two pole and he was being caught for third at the end as his stamina ran out. He had raced rather keenly and will have better prospects of staying this trip if he can learn to settle better as he matures. (op 15-8 tchd 9-4 in places)
Allegretto(IRE) failed to get home in last year's Gold Cup but did not settle that day when equipped with a visor. Last of ten in a muddling race on her reappearance at Sandown, she showed more on this better ground, despite not looking great in her coat. However, having been held up at the back of the field until approaching the straight she could only stay on for fourth without ever threatening the big players.
Sagara(USA), who was gelded after joining Godolphin, was stepping up a mile in trip. He ran a respectable race, despite proving rather keen again, but although staying on he never really promised to take a hand in the finish. (op 20-1)
Regal Flush ran respectably and probably stayed this longer trip, but was another for whom fourth place was the best he could ever hope for the way the race developed. (op 16-1)
Thundering Star(SAF), tried in cheekpieces, probably stayed the longer trip but the fast ground may not have suited him.
Diamond Quest(SAF) has returned to Andrew Balding after a spell in Dubai with Herman Brown. He turned into the home straight in fourth place before his stamina started to wane. He needed to settle better if he was to stay. (op 66-1 tchd 40-1)
Le Miracle(GER), last year's third, set the pace but weakened quite tamely not long after being headed. He has not recaptured his form this term. (op 33-1 tchd 25-1, 40-1 in a place)
Finalmente, given a fine tactical ride from the front to land the Henry II Stakes at Sandown, is a pretty consistent performer who finished fourth in this last year, but he was well below form here. After racing prominently, he was already beginning to drop away when encountering trouble on the home turn. (op 25-1 tchd 33-1)

3155 BRITANNIA STKS (HERITAGE H'CAP) (C&G) — 1m (S)

4:20 (4:26) (Class 2) (0-105,104) 3-Y-O

£62,310 (£18,660; £9,330; £4,670; £2,330; £585) **Stalls** Centre

Form — RPR

10-0 **1** **Fifteen Love (USA)**[62] 1441 3-8-10 93 .... (p) SteveDrowne 4 104+
(R Charlton) *lw: leapt s and s.i.s: hld up in rr stands' side: gd hdwy 2f out: led gp ins fnl f: jst prevailed fr runner-up on far side* **28/1**

-312 **2** *1/2* **Masaalek**[26] 2412 3-8-11 94 .... RHills 22 104+
(M P Tregoning) *lw: hld up in rr far side: gd hdwy 2f out: led gp over 1f out: r.o wl: jst pipped by stands' side wnr* **20/1**

1-21 **3** *1 1/2* **Yaddree**[26] 2412 3-8-12 95 .... PhilipRobinson 30 101
(M A Jarvis) *lw: prom far side: rdn to chal over 2f out: nt qckn ins fnl f: 2nd of 11 in gp* **12/1**

-500 **4** *hd* **Dubai Dynamo**[19] 2594 3-8-10 93 .... JohnEgan 7 99
(P F I Cole) *in tch stands' side: effrt over 2f out: led gp over 1f out tl ins fnl f: one pce: 2nd of 17 in gp* **33/1**

5-15 **5** *hd* **Lazy Days**[12] 2819 3-8-5 88 .... HayleyTurner 26 94+
(D R C Elsworth) *swtg: chsd ldrs far side: rdn over 2f out: kpt on fnl f: 3rd of 11 in gp* **25/1**

0-24 **6** *nk* **Flawed Genius**[26] 2403 3-8-13 96 .... RyanMoore 25 101+
(Sir Michael Stoute) *lw: dwlt: towards rr far side: hdwy 2f out: chsd ldrs over 1f out: one pce fnl f: 4th of 11 in gp* **9/1**[3]

5-60 **6** *dht* **Jedediah**[26] 2403 3-8-4 94 .... DavidProbert[(7)] 18 99+
(A M Balding) *chsd ldrs stands' side: led gp over 2f out: sn hdd: one pce fnl f: 3rd of 17 in gp* **25/1**

2120 **8** *nk* **Fathsta (IRE)**[5] 3047 3-8-10 93 .... LPKeniry 6 97+
(S Kirk) *lw: hld up in rr stands' side: swtchd rt and sme hdwy over 3f out: swtchd lft over 1f out: r.o: 4th of 17 in gp* **33/1**

4113 **9** *3/4* **Slugger O'Toole**[13] 2794 3-8-7 90 .... MichaelHills 21 92
(B W Hills) *hld up in rr far side: swtchd lft and hdwy over 2f out: drvn to chse ldrs over 1f out: one pce: 5th of 11 in gp* **40/1**

101 **10** *1/2* **Throne Of Power (USA)**[33] 2189 3-8-12 95 .... KerrinMcEvoy 24 96
(M A Magnusson) *chsd ldrs far side: rdn and no hdwy fnl 2f: 6th of 11 in gp* **14/1**

-600 **11** *4 1/2* **Solent Ridge (IRE)**[12] 2825 3-8-6 89 .... MartinDwyer 20 80
(J S Moore) *mid-div far side: hrd rdn and btn over 2f out: 7th of 11 in gp* **100/1**

4-13 **12** *shd* **Perks (IRE)**[47] 1806 3-8-8 91 .... JimmyQuinn 19 82
(J L Dunlop) *in rr of mid-div stands' side: effrt and sme hdwy over 2f out: edgd lft and btn wl over 1f out: 5th of 17 in gp* **16/1**

1- **13** *1 1/2* **Amazing Star (IRE)**[17] 2683 3-8-6 89 .... RPCleary 5 76
(M Halford, Ire) *towards rr stands' side: rdn over 2f out: nvr rchd ldrs: 6th of 17 in gp* **66/1**

41-1 **14** *1 1/4* **Redford (IRE)**[12] 2819 3-8-10 93 .... JamieSpencer 27 77+
(M L W Bell) *lw: hld up in midfield far side: hdwy over 3f out: led gp over 2f out tl over 1f out: btn whn hmpd jst ins fnl f: 8th of 11 in gp* **15/2**[2]

22-1 **15** *1 1/4* **Rattan (USA)**[33] 2199 3-8-7 90 .... TedDurcan 16 72
(H R A Cecil) *lw: hld up in tch stands' side: trckd ldrs over 3f out: rdn and wknd 2f out: 7th of 17 in gp* **12/1**

1112 **16** *nk* **Commander Cave (USA)**[26] 2403 3-9-1 98 .... RichardHughes 2 79
(R Hannon) *led stands' side gp against rail tl over 2f out: wknd over 1f out: 8th of 17 in gp* **12/1**

2-13 **17** *1 1/2* **Virtual**[21] 2544 3-9-3 100 .... JimmyFortune 12 77
(J H M Gosden) *hld up in midfield stands' side: effrt over 2f out: sn btn: 9th of 17 in gp* **14/1**

1-40 **18** *nse* **Billion Dollar Kid**[26] 2412 3-8-6 89 .... WilliamBuick 29 66
(S A Callaghan) *led far side gp after 1f tl over 2f out: sn wknd: 9th of 11 in gp* **66/1**

12-2 **19** *1/2* **Hurricane Hymnbook (USA)**[45] 1875 3-9-0 97 .... MJKinane 1 73
(B J Meehan) *towards rr stands' side: n.d fnl 3f: 10th of 17 in gp* **7/1**[1]

-121 **20** *1/2* **Fervent Prince**[26] 2405 3-8-5 91 .... PatrickHills[(3)] 23 66
(H Morrison) *rrd stalls and s.s: sn in tch far side: rdn and wknd over 2f out: 10th of 11 in gp* **33/1**

2-32 **21** *4 1/2* **Fateh Field (USA)**[20] 2580 3-9-7 104 .... LDettori 14 69
(Saeed Bin Suroor) *hld up towards rr stands' side: hdwy and in tch over 2f out: wknd wl over 1f out: 11th of 17 in gp* **16/1**

2111 **22** *1 1/2* **Thebes**[89] 967 3-8-5 88 .... RoystonFfrench 28 49
(M Johnston) *lw: led far side gp 1f: w ldrs tl hrd rdn and wknd 2f out: last of 11 in gp* **25/1**

-113 **23** *4 1/2* **Jaser**[26] 2403 3-8-10 93 .... AlanMunro 11 44
(P W Chapple-Hyam) *chsd ldrs stands' side over 5f: 12th of 17 in gp* **25/1**

-061 **24** *nk* **Bellomi (IRE)**[13] 2794 3-8-9 92 .... EddieAhern 13 42
(W J Haggas) *w ldrs stands' side 5f: sn wknd: 13th of 17 in gp* **33/1**

1-23 **25** *nk* **Love Galore (IRE)**[25] 2425 3-8-7 90 .... RobertWinston 15 39
(M Johnston) *w ldrs stands' side over 5f: wkng whn hmpd over 1f out: 14th of 17 in gp* **20/1**

4454 **26** *3/4* **Siberian Tiger (IRE)**[12] 2825 3-9-1 98 .... DarryllHolland 9 46
(M R Channon) *lw: w ldrs stands' side over 5f: sn wknd: 15th of 17 in gp* **20/1**

4 **27** *33* **Badger Or Bust (IRE)**[53] 1652 3-9-0 97 .... PJSmullen 10 —
(Liam Roche, Ire) *mid-div stands' side: wknd 3f out: sn bhd and eased: 16th of 17 in gp* **50/1**

40-4 **28** *50* **Proud Linus (USA)**[30] 2283 3-8-7 93 ow3 .... StephenDonohoe 3 —
(D Carroll) *stdd s and s.i.s: plld hrd stands' side and wandered abt in last pl: wl bhd fnl 4f: last of 17 in gp* **100/1**

1m 40.1s (-0.50) **Going Correction** +0.15s/f (Good) — **33** Ran SP% **136.7**
Speed ratings (Par 105): **108,107,106,105,105 105,105,105,104,103 99,99,97,96,95 94,93,93,92,92 87,86,81,81,81 80,47,E**
toteswinger: 1&2 £991.30, 1&3 £116.60, 2&3 £50.40. CSF £512.89 CT £6989.76 TOTE £40.80: £8.50, £7.20, £4.70, £8.70; EX 1098.00 Trifecta £6652.00 Part won. Pool: £8989.28 - 0.20 winning units..
Owner K Abdulla **Bred** Juddmonte Farms Inc **Trained** Beckhampton, Wilts
■ Stewards' Enquiry : John Egan two-day ban: used whip with excessive frequency (Jul 3-4)

FOCUS

The prize money for this race was given a big boost this year. This was a typical Britannia, featuring a number of lightly raced and unexposed three-year-olds. The bias towards those drawn on the extremes in big-field straight-course handicaps which existed at this meeting prior to the redevelopment has continued, and following on from Sir Gerard (drawn 2) and Eddie Jock (29) winning the last two renewals, Fifteen Love won here from stall 4. The field split into three initially, but the group in the centre steadily moved over to join the stands'-side bunch while a smaller, 11-strong group raced up the far-side rail. The usual strong form for the grade, and some of these will prove better than handicappers.

NOTEBOOK

Fifteen Love(USA) ◆, completely unsuited by soft ground in the Horris Hill on his final start at two, also found the ground on the easy side when down the field on his reappearance at Newbury back in April. Aimed at this race ever since in the expectation of getting the quicker ground he needs, he came through strongly from off the pace to edge the result from the far-side 'winner' Masaalek. He wore cheekpieces for the first time here because he had apparently been working lazily, and the headgear, coupled with the strong pace in this big field suited him. He will probably have to step up to Listed company after reassessment, but he should be able to hold his own provided the ground remains fast. (op 25-1)

Masaalek had a 4lb pull with Yaddree compared with when they met at Newmarket last time, and that proved enough to see him reverse the form. A son of Green Desert, he is at home on a fast surface and stayed on well to win his race on the far side. (op 16-1 tchd 25-1 in a place)

Yaddree had the best of the draw on the far side and confirmed himself a progressive sort. His 9lb rise in the weights for his Newmarket win just found him out, but he is open to further improvement, perhaps over further, as he is by Singspiel out of a Nashwan mare. (op 16-1)

Dubai Dynamo, for whom stamina was the worry beforehand as he is by Kyllachy, had never raced over 1m before, but he saw it out surprisingly well up the stands' rail. He remains quite high in the handicap, though. (op 50-1 tchd 80-1 in a place)

Lazy Days ◆ only got into the race as a reserve - the first time on-the-day reserves had been allowed in Britain - and he ran a blinder on the far side considering that the ground was probably on the fast side for him. He is open to further improvement and appeals as the type to win a decent handicap this season.

Jedediah, unlucky in running in the Silver Bowl at Haydock last time, was representing an in-form stable. He ran well considering he was drawn in the middle and it cost him ground crossing over to race with the stands'-side bunch. (op 10-1)

Flawed Genius has gone up 9lb in the handicap this season without winning and, while he reversed Haydock form with Commander Cave and Jaser, the Handicapper appears to be keeping up with him. (op 10-1)

Fathsta(IRE) takes his racing extremely well but usually races over shorter. He was not beaten for stamina but rather it is simply a case of the Handicapper knowing plenty about him now. (tchd 40-1, 50-1 in a place)

Slugger O'Toole, whose Newmarket win was gained in a tactical race, has looked held since. He did not see this mile out quite as strongly as one or two either.

Throne Of Power(USA), raised 10lb for his Doncaster win, may have appreciated more cut in the ground.

Solent Ridge(IRE) is fairly exposed and ran about as well as could be expected.

Perks(IRE) was another who would probably have appreciated easier ground.

Amazing Star(IRE) did not run too badly considering that he did not look well handicapped based on his Irish form.

Redford(IRE) ◆, who is highly regarded, won his prep race for this in good style 12 days earlier and was only 6lb higher. He travelled strongly at Doncaster, and that was the case again, as he looked to be going best of the far-side group two furlongs out, but he did not find a great deal off the bridle and was weakening when hampered. This ground was probably plenty fast enough for him and he can return to winning ways on an easier surface. One could see him proving as effective over shorter. (op 7-1 tchd 8-1, 9-1 in a place)

Rattan(USA) had been raised 12lb for winning his maiden by five lengths, and that probably did for his chances.

Commander Cave(USA) may also now be high enough in the weights. (tchd 14-1 in places)

Virtual is by Pivotal and his good third in Listed company last time came on soft ground, so it was always likely that he would find conditions too quick. Official explanation: jockey said colt was unsuited by the good to firm (firm in places) ground

Billion Dollar Kid found the trip beyond him and will surely be dropped back to 7f or even 6f now.

Hurricane Hymnbook(USA) was disappointing as he gave subsequent Silver Bowl winner Staying On a race at Windsor on his reappearance, and was well drawn in stall one. He is surely better than this run suggests. (op 8-1)

Fervent Prince, who reared up as the stalls opened, is another who appears to have stamina limitations. Official explanation: jockey said gelding reared as stalls opened

Fateh Field(USA) had a lot on his plate under top weight. Official explanation: jockey said colt was unsuited by the good to firm (firm in places) ground (op 14-1)

Thebes did not get home and will appreciate dropping back in trip.

Bellomi(IRE) may have found the race coming too soon after his Epsom win on Oaks day.

Love Galore(IRE) holds an Irish Derby entry but has struggled to get home over 1m2f plus this season. He was interesting dropped back to the trip over which he won his maiden at Hamilton last year, for while he is by Galileo, he is a half-brother Nell Gwyn winner Lil's Jessy. However, having shown early speed, he dropped right out. (op 22-1 tchd 25-1)

3156 HAMPTON COURT STKS (LISTED RACE) 1m 2f

4:55 (5:02) (Class 1) 3-Y-O

£34,062 (£12,912; £6,462; £3,222; £1,614; £810) **Stalls** High

Form RPR

1-61 **1** **Collection (IRE)**[36] 2109 3-9-2 93 KerrinMcEvoy 5 113+
(W J Haggas) *lw: swtchd rt s: hld up: rapid prog ent fnl 2f: swtchd rt over 1f out: str run to ld ins fnl f: pushed out whn wl in command towards fin* **13/2**[2]

-411 **2** *1 ½* **Staying On (IRE)**[26] 2403 3-9-2 99 AdamKirby 11 108
(W R Swinburn) *lw: led: rdn over 2f out: edgd rt whn pressed over 1f out: edgd lft and hdd ins fnl f: nt pce of wnr towards fin* **9/1**

-520 **3** *½* **King Of Rome (IRE)**[12] 2829 3-9-2 0 JMurtagh 10 107+
(A P O'Brien, Ire) *lw: midfield: pushed along and outpcd over 2f out: swtchd lft and hdwy over 1f out: hung rt and r.o ins fnl f: gaining towards fin: nvr gng to get there* **8/1**

214 **4** *¾* **Khateeb (IRE)**[21] 2544 3-9-2 98 (t) MartinDwyer 4 105+
(M A Jarvis) *lw: hld up: hdwy ent fnl 2f: nt clr run over 1f out: r.o ins fnl f: nt quite get to ldrs* **33/1**

3-01 **5** *½* **Without A Prayer (IRE)**[35] 2121 3-9-2 105 SebSanders 7 104
(R M Beckett) *in tch: effrt to press ldrs 2f out: edgd rt over 1f out: flattened out towards fin* **22/1**

15-0 **6** *nk* **Alfathaa**[47] 1808 3-9-2 107 (b[1]) RHills 12 103
(W J Haggas) *racd keenly: hld up: hdwy over 1f out: styd on ins fnl f: nt pce of ldrs towards fin* **25/1**

3 **7** *½* **Central Station (IRE)**[25] 2435 3-9-2 0 (b[1]) PJSmullen 15 102
(D K Weld, Ire) *racd keenly: trckd ldrs: rdn over 2f out: kpt on same pce fnl 100yds* **16/1**

-121 **8** *nk* **Unnefer (FR)**[26] 2408 3-9-7 111 TedDurcan 13 107
(H R A Cecil) *lw: racd keenly: hld up in midfield: rdn over 2f out: styng on whn hung rt over 1f out: kpt on ins fnl f but unable to chal ldrs* **15/2**[3]

21-1 **9** *hd* **Dr Faustus (IRE)**[47] 1811 3-9-2 99 MJKinane 1 101
(Sir Michael Stoute) *racd keenly: hld up: rdn over 2f out: kpt on fr 1f out: nvr able to chal* **8/1**

132 **10** *hd* **Pampas Cat (USA)**[26] 2408 3-9-2 103 JimmyFortune 3 101
(J H M Gosden) *prom: rdn to chal ent fnl 2f: no ex fnl 100yds* **10/1**

3-34 **11** *2 ½* **Feared In Flight (IRE)**[42] 1922 3-9-2 103 MichaelHills 2 96
(B W Hills) *racd keenly: prom: rdn 2f out: wknd ins fnl f* **16/1**

2054 **12** *1* **Whitcombe Minister (USA)**[19] 2600 3-9-2 100 JohnEgan 14 94
(Jamie Poulton) *midfield: pushed along 3f out: wknd over 1f out* **20/1**

-360 **13** *1 ¾* **Latin Lad**[41] 1943 3-9-2 99 PatDobbs 16 91
(R Hannon) *midfield: rdn over 2f out: wknd over 1f out* **50/1**

-1 **14** *4 ½* **Kensington Oval**[14] 2763 3-9-2 94 RyanMoore 8 82
(Sir Michael Stoute) *lw: missed break: racd in last pl: rdn 2f out: nvr on terms* **4/1**[1]

41-6 **15** *6* **Moynahan (USA)**[47] 1808 3-9-2 104 TQuinn 9 70
(P F I Cole) *racd keenly: trckd ldrs: rdn over 2f out: n.m.r whn wkng over 1f out* **12/1**

2m 7.55s (-2.25) **Going Correction** -0.10s/f (Good) **15** Ran SP% **123.7**
Speed ratings (Par 107): **105,103,103,102,102 102,101,101,101,101 99,98,97,93,88**
toteswinger: 1&2 £14.00, 1&3 £14.00, 2&3 £17.80. CSF £61.10 TOTE £9.40: £3.00, £3.70, £2.80; EX 98.30 Trifecta £1237.90 Pool: £5185.93 - 3.10 winning units.
Owner Highclere Thoroughbred Racing (Brunel) **Bred** P D Savill **Trained** Newmarket, Suffolk

FOCUS

A very competitive Listed contest but the early pace was not strong and it turned into something of a sprint from the turn in. Nevertheless, the finish was fought out by a good mix of prominent racers and hold-up horses. Much improved form from the winner and fourth in particular, but no fluke about it.

NOTEBOOK

Collection(IRE) ◆ looked to have a bit to do on this step up in grade having only won a handicap off 80 last time - he was the lowest rated horse in the field - but he has always been well regarded and showed himself to be a highly progressive colt here. He got a nice run through between horses in the straight and stayed on strongly to win fairly comfortably in the end. Fast ground clearly suits him well, and another two furlongs will pose him few problems. He looks well capable of holding his own in Group company. (op 11-2)

Staying On(IRE), who won the Silver Bowl last time out off 93, was stepping up in trip. He enjoys being out in front and once again got the run of the race. He set a muddling early pace and was well positioned when they turned for home and the sprint began, but even allowing for that, this was another excellent effort. (op 12-1)

King Of Rome(IRE), down the field in the Derby when he was Murtagh's pick from five O'Brien horses in the race, had less to do in this company. The fairly ordinary early pace would not have suited him, though, and he got outpaced when the sprint for home began. He was staying on well at the finish, though, and will appreciate a return to 1m4f. (op 9-1)

Khateeb(IRE) ◆ proved suited by the step up in trip on his first try on fast ground, but he would have been seen to better effect off a stronger gallop. He looks up to winning at this level, so if he were to make the cut in the John Smith's Cup he would look well handicapped off 98.

Without A Prayer(IRE), who was stepping up to 1m2f for the first time, had every chance but did not seem to see the trip out as well as a few of the others. (op 20-1 tchd 25-1 in a place)

Alfathaa raced keenly off the fairly modest early gallop in the first-time blinkers and, while he kept on next to the far rail, he was never close enough to threaten the principals.

Central Station(IRE) was another who had blinkers on for the first time, and he would not settle in the early stages off the ordinary pace. He should not be judged too harshly on this effort as he might well do much better in a stronger-run race. (op 25-1)

Unnefer(FR) had a task on under his 5lb penalty and he hung on this fast ground. Although successful at Newmarket last time on quick ground, he is by Danehill Dancer and is probably happiest with some give. Official explanation: jockey said colt had no more to give (op 8-1 tchd 9-1 in places)

Dr Faustus(IRE) could have done with a stronger pace. He will get 1m4f in time so a steady early gallop over this trip on ground which may be on the fast side for him did not see him at his best. (op 13-2)

Pampas Cat(USA) was disappointing as he was running over his best trip and well placed towards the front end in what was something of a tactical affair. (op 14-1)

Feared In Flight(IRE) did not get any cover and was keen in the early stages. (op 20-1 tchd 25-1 in a place)

Kensington Oval made a good impression when winning his maiden at Sandown, but this demanded a lot more and he was not up to it at this stage of his career. He still has the makings of a very useful performer, though. Official explanation: trainer said colt missed the break (op 7-2 tchd 9-2, 5-1 in a place)

Moynahan(USA), for whom this longer trip was a concern, gave himself little chance of getting home because he failed to settle in the early stages. Official explanation: jockey said colt ran too free (op 11-1)

3157 KING GEORGE V STKS (HERITAGE H'CAP) 1m 4f

5:30 (5:35) (Class 2) (0-105,96) 3-Y-O

£37,386 (£11,196; £5,598; £2,802; £1,398; £702) **Stalls** High

Form RPR

1-13 **1** **Colony (IRE)**[33] 2194 3-8-12 **87** RyanMoore 7 99+
(Sir Michael Stoute) *hld up in midfield: rdn and hdwy 2f out: led ent fnl f: drvn and styd on wl* **11/2**[1]

-616 **2** *1 ¾* **Savarain**[29] 2303 3-9-7 **96** LDettori 1 105+
(L M Cumani) *pressed ldr: rdn to ld briefly over 1f out: nt qckn ins fnl f* **16/1**

621 **3** *¾* **Moonquake (USA)**[12] 2847 3-9-1 **90** JimmyFortune 9 98
(J H M Gosden) *lw: towards rr and wd: rdn and r.o fnl 2f: nrst fin* **12/1**

113 **4** *nse* **Dream Desert (IRE)**[63] 1424 3-8-10 **85** EdwardCreighton 3 93
(M R Channon) *s.s: bhd: fnd clr passage nr ins rail and gd hdwy fr 2f out: styd on fnl f* **9/1**

1254 **5** *½* **Drill Sergeant**[26] 2408 3-9-4 **93** RobertWinston 14 100
(M Johnston) *led: rdn over 2f out: hdd over 1f out: one pce* **20/1**

-002 **6** *1 ¾* **Trenchtown (IRE)**[19] 2610 3-8-11 **86** SteveDrowne 10 91+
(R Charlton) *lw: hld up towards rr: nt clr run and swtchd outside over 2f out: styd on appr fnl f: nvr nrr* **12/1**

-221 **7** *hd* **Indian Days**[24] 2464 3-8-13 **88** J-PGuillambert 18 92+
(J G Given) *trckd ldrs: hemmed in on rail ent st tl swtchd lft over 1f out: no ex* **9/1**

8 *1 ¼* **Ghimaar**[22] 2518 3-9-0 **89** (b[1]) PJSmullen 5 91
(D K Weld, Ire) *s.s: bhd: sme hdwy whn hung rt ins fnl 2f: nvr rchd ldrs* **16/1**

-212 **9** *2 ½* **Fiulin**[33] 2201 3-9-3 **92** TedDurcan 19 90
(M Botti) *plld hrd: in tch on rail: pushed along over 3f out: hrd rdn and wknd 2f out* **14/1**

4242 **10** *nk* **Ramona Chase**[12] 2825 3-9-6 **95** DPMcDonogh 11 93
(S Kirk) *t.k.h in midfield: rdn over 2f out: sn wknd* **14/1**

6304 **11** *¾* **Better Hand (IRE)**[25] 2425 3-9-4 **93** (v[1]) DarryllHolland 16 89
(M R Channon) *t.k.h towards rr: hmpd 7f out: rdn and n.d fnl 3f: wl btn whn hmpd over 1f out* **40/1**

0233 **12** ½ **The Betchworth Kid**[12] 2840 3-8-11 86........................ HayleyTurner 15 82
(M L W Bell) *on and off the bridle: bhd: rdn 4f out: modest late hdwy* **33/1**

0-21 **13** ¾ **Daraahem (IRE)**[43] 1918 3-9-5 94........................ RHills 6 88
(B W Hills) *chsd ldrs tl n.m.r and bmpd over 2f out: sn wknd* **15/2**[3]

-212 **14** 1 **Missioner (USA)**[10] 2889 3-8-10 85........................ AlanMunro 13 78
(M Johnston) *lw: hld up in tch: rdn 4f out: wknd 3f out* **13/2**[2]

2312 **15** 3 ½ **Woolfall Treasure**[25] 2425 3-8-12 87........................ JohnEgan 17 74
(G G Margarson) *rdn 3f out: a bhd* **20/1**

61-1 **16** 17 **Strategic Mission (IRE)**[33] 2194 3-9-6 95........................ TQuinn 12 55
(P F I Cole) *prom: drvn along and starting to weaken whn bmpd over 2f out: sn lost pl* **8/1**

2m 30.62s (-4.88) **Going Correction** -0.10s/f (Good) **16** Ran SP% **127.0**
Speed ratings (Par 105): **112,110,110,110,109 108,108,107,106,105 105,105,104,103,101 90**
toteswinger: 1&2 £24.10, 1&3 £15.90, 2&3 £47.00. CSF £93.73 CT £1045.63 TOTE £4.70: £1.80, £4.90, £3.10, £3.00; EX 127.80 Trifecta £848.10 Pool: £5501.39 - 4.80 winning units. Place 6 £220.89, Place 5 £149.36..
Owner Highclere Thoroughbred Racing (Delilah) **Bred** Barronstown Stud And Orpendale **Trained** Newmarket, Suffolk

■ A first Royal Ascot winner for Ryan Moore at the 83rd attempt.

FOCUS
A competitive handicap, and although the early pace appeared ordinary, with a number not settling, the winning time was smart for a race like this, 1.25 seconds faster than the Ribblesdale. The usual strong form for this race, and it should work out well, with some going on to prove themselves in pattern races in due course, and others paying their way in decent handicaps.

NOTEBOOK
Colony(IRE) ◆, who shaped as though he would be suited by this longer trip when third at Newbury last time, stayed on strongly down the outside in the final two furlongs and was well on top at the finish. He is clearly just as effective on fast ground as he is on an easier surface and could well strengthen his trainer's hand even further in middle-distance Group races as the season progresses, although in the shorter term another big handicap looks likely to be targeted. (op 9-2 tchd 6-1 in places)
Savarain ◆ was given a more positive ride this time from an unfavourable draw and he ran really well under top weight. The return to fast ground probably helped him and he looks the type who will just keep improving as he gets stronger. (tchd 14-1)
Moonquake(USA) ◆, who won a nothing race at Newcastle last time, is by Mr Greeley so it should not have come as a big surprise that he improved for his first encounter with fast ground. He is still relatively unexposed and open to further improvement. (op 16-1 tchd 20-1 in a place)
Dream Desert(IRE) ◆, third to Bronze Cannon and Doctor Fremantle in a hot handicap at the Craven meeting, had not been out since and got to race here off a very attractive mark, just 2lb higher than at Newmarket. The worry was the longer trip as he is by the sprinter Elnadim, but he dispelled stamina doubts with a decent staying-on effort, weaving a way between horses to make the frame inside the last. This was only his fourth ever start and he can do better again. (op 12-1)
Drill Sergeant was not sure to appreciate the extra two furlongs and, having led for most of the way he did not quite get home. A drop back to 1m2f will suit him but he is likely to continue to bump into one or two less-exposed rivals in the good handicaps. (op 22-1)
Trenchtown(IRE), runner-up to Patkai at Haydock last time, stayed on once switched to the outside, but he looks a bit one-paced and is likely to do better as he steps up in trip even further. (op 14-1 tchd 16-1 in a place)
Indian Days, raised 9lb for his Redcar win, was kept in on the rail by the eventual runner-up but, once switched and in the clear, he failed to pick up as expected. The trip may well have stretched his stamina a touch and it is too early to say that the Handicapper has his measure. (op 14-1)
Ghimaar, blinkered for the first time, kept on in the straight like a horse who will improve for an even longer trip. He remains fairly unexposed.
Fiulin did not do himself any favours by failing to settle in the early stages. Official explanation: jockey said colt hung left all the way (op 12-1)
Ramona Chase, who was stepping up in distance, was another who did not help her chances of getting home by racing keenly off the ordinary early gallop. (op 16-1 tchd 20-1 in a place)
Better Hand(IRE), who has looked exposed off this sort of mark, was another keen enough in first-time heagear. Official explanation: jockey said colt ran too free (op 66-1)
The Betchworth Kid came into the race as one of the more exposed three-year-olds in the race.
Daraahem(IRE) looked to be one of the more interesting contenders, having beaten Moonquake in a maiden at Chester last time. He did not see the trip out, though, having given the outside to no-one throughout the first half of the race. (op 7-1 tchd 8-1)
Missioner(USA) did not get home over this longer trip. (op 6-1 tchd 7-1 in a place)
Woolfall Treasure Official explanation: jockey said colt suffered interference in running
Strategic Mission(IRE) probably found the ground too fast. (op 10-1)
T/Jkpt: £167,346.30 to a £1 stake. Pool: £353,548.59. 1.50 winning tickets. T/Plt: £295.80 to a £1 stake. Pool: £451,626.62. 1,114.39 winning tickets. T/Qpdt: £140.00 to a £1 stake. Pool: £21,515.82. 113.70 winning tickets. DO

2528 GREAT LEIGHS (A.W) (L-H)
Thursday, June 19

OFFICIAL GOING: Standard
Wind: Moderate, behind.

3158 CURLEW CALLING MAIDEN AUCTION STKS 6f (P)
6:30 (6:30) (Class 6) 2-Y-O **£2,388** (£705; £352) **Stalls** Low

Form RPR

05 **1** **Striding Edge (IRE)**[41] 1955 2-8-11 0........................ RichardThomas 1 66+
(W R Muir) *prom: led wl over 3f out: shkn up and in command over 1f out: readily* **3/1**[2]

00 **2** 2 ½ **Swingfire (USA)**[48] 1778 2-8-8 0........................ TravisBlock(3) 6 59
(R M H Cowell) *prom: chsd wnr over 3f out: rdn over 2f out: kpt on same pce last 2f* **11/1**

00 **3** 1 **Lislin**[38] 2048 2-8-4 0........................ DavidKinsella 2 49
(S Kirk) *hld up in tch: rdn and effrt on inner 2f out: kpt on same pce* **9/1**

4 2 ¾ **Terracotta Warrior** 2-8-11 0........................ NeilPollard 3 47
(J Jay) *in tch: sn pushed along: rdn 2f out: hung lft over 1f out: no imp* **9/1**

5 1 **Fajita** 2-8-11 0........................ TPO'Shea 4 44
(M G Quinlan) *awkward s: sn rcvrd and led: hdd over 3f out: styd handy: rdn over 2f out: wknd 1f out* **11/4**[1]

00 **6** 1 ½ **Mr Melodious**[14] 2754 2-9-1 0........................ RobertHavlin 8 44
(B W Hills) *bhd: struggling and rdn 4f out: n.d* **7/1**

7 14 **Chantilly Dancer (IRE)** 2-8-8 0 ow2........................ StephenCarson 5 —
(M J Wallace) *rrd s and v.s.a: a wl detached in last pl* **7/2**[3]

1m 14.23s (0.53) **Going Correction** +0.10s/f (Slow) **7** Ran SP% **114.7**
Speed ratings (Par 91): **100,96,95,91,90 88,69**
toteswinger: 1&2 £2.70, 1&3 £6.40, 2&3 £16.10. CSF £34.80 TOTE £4.10: £1.30, £3.60; EX 15.90.
Owner Linkslade Racing and Knightley Williams **Bred** G Prendergast **Trained** Lambourn, Berks

FOCUS
Probably not the strongest of maidens as four of these had run in a total of eight races between them prior to this and none of them had even been placed.

NOTEBOOK
Striding Edge(IRE) had been well held in two outings on turf coming into this, but he had attracted market support which suggested he was thought to possess some ability. This switch to sand and the extra furlong saw him finally produce it and he was well in command all the way down the home straight. As his dam scored over 1m4f, it is fair to assume that the best of him will be seen over much further in due course. (tchd 11-4 and 7-2)
Swingfire(USA), well beaten in a couple of maidens on turf and Fibresand, showed a bit more here having been up with the pace throughout but was in vain pursuit of the winner over the last couple of furlongs. This was an improvement, but he may not have achieved that much. (op 12-1 tchd 14-1)
Lislin, another whose form in two previous outings has been moderate, plugged on up the home straight but never looked like winning. She will need to progress again if she is to win a race. (op 7-1)
Terracotta Warrior, an 11,000gns colt whose dam is from the family of Legal Case and Love Divine, showed up for a long way and did best of the newcomers, though that may not be saying much. He is likely to appreciate further in due course, but will need to improve to make him competitive. (op 10-1)
Fajita, a 10,000gns half-brother to a couple of juvenile winners over this trip, showed to the fore for much of the way but did not get home. The market support suggests he is thought capable of better. (tchd 3-1)
Mr Melodious was never in the race at any stage and he is running out of excuses. (tchd 15-2)
Chantilly Dancer(IRE), a 15,000gns half-sister to a winning sprinter in the US, almost sent her rider into orbit leaving the stalls and then continued in a tailed-off last. Her prominent position in the market would suggest she is thought capable of an awful lot better. Official explanation: jockey said filly missed the break (op 11-4)

3159 KERSEY H'CAP 5f (P)
7:00 (7:01) (Class 6) (0-65,64) 4-Y-O+ **£2,266** (£674; £337; £168) **Stalls** Low

Form RPR

0410 **1** **Blessed Place**[5] 3042 8-8-9 56........................ BillyCray(7) 9 68
(D J S Ffrench Davis) *mde all: pushed along over 1f out: kpt on wl* **11/4**[2]

3312 **2** 1 ½ **Thoughtsofstardom**[8] 2934 5-9-5 64 6ex........................ KellyHarrison(5) 3 71
(M Wigham) *stdd s: hld up in tch: hdwy 1/2-way: rdn over 1f out: chsd wnr ins fnl f: no imp last 50yds* **9/4**[1]

0410 **3** nk **Perlachy**[54] 1634 4-8-13 56........................(v) TravisBlock(3) 5 62
(Mrs N Macauley) *chsd wnr: rdn over 2f out: kpt on same pce u.p fnl f: lost 2nd ins fnl f* **8/1**

5400 **4** 1 ¼ **Ela Aleka Mou**[21] 2547 4-8-2 47........................(b) MCGeran(5) 7 48
(Miss D Mountain) *s.i.s: in tch: rdn wl over 1f out: plugged on same pce* **25/1**

2050 **5** nk **El Potro**[44] 1901 6-9-1 55........................ FrancisNorton 4 55
(J R Holt) *chsd ldrs: rdn and outpcd 1/2-way: kpt on same pce u.p fr over 1f out* **10/1**

0434 **6** hd **Azygous**[10] 2881 5-9-7 61........................(p) IanMongan 6 61
(J Akehurst) *chsd ldrs: rdn and nt qckn 2f out: kpt on same pce fnl f* **7/2**[3]

5156 **7** 4 ½ **Gone'N'Dunnett (IRE)**[11] 2869 9-8-7 52........................(v) JackMitchell(5) 2 35
(Mrs C A Dunnett) *s.i.s: bhd: detached and rdn over 3f out: n.d* **11/1**

630/ **8** 1 ½ **Repeat (IRE)**[911] 6649 8-7-12 45........................ AmyBaker(7) 8 23
(M Wellings) *s.i.s: in tch: rdn and struggling over 2f out: wl bhd 1f out* **25/1**

60.61 secs (0.41) **Going Correction** +0.10s/f (Slow) **8** Ran SP% **115.9**
Speed ratings (Par 101): **100,97,97,95,94 94,87,84**
toteswinger: 1&2 £1.10, 1&3 £21.70, 2&3 £21.70. CSF £9.53 CT £41.06 TOTE £5.00: £1.30, £1.20, £1.70; EX 6.90.
Owner S J Edwards **Bred** Mrs W H Gibson Fleming **Trained** Lambourn, Berks

FOCUS
An ordinary sprint handicap and early speed proved crucial. The form seems sound with the winner running just about his best race on the All-Weather.

3160 MR TUMNUS H'CAP 1m 6f (P)
7:30 (7:30) (Class 5) (0-70,70) 4-Y-O+ **£2,590** (£770; £385; £192) **Stalls** Low

Form RPR

224- **1** **Tavalu (USA)**[49] 3653 6-9-2 65........................(b) GeorgeBaker 4 72
(G L Moore) *chsd ldrs tl led over 2f out: rdn over 1f out: kpt on and a doing enough fnl f* **7/2**[3]

3652 **2** nk **Medieval Maiden**[8] 2949 5-8-7 56........................ IanMongan 1 62+
(Mrs L J Mongan) *trckd ldrs: swtchd off rail 3f out: rdn to chse ldng pair wl over 1f out: kpt on to go 2nd nr fin* **3/1**[2]

-132 **3** nk **Josh You Are**[97] 886 5-9-7 70........................ FrancisNorton 7 76
(M Wigham) *hld up in tch: chsd wnr over 2f out: rdn wl over 1f out: unable qck u.p fnl f: lost 2nd nr fin* **7/4**[1]

-455 **4** 3 ¾ **Wild Pitch**[17] 2667 7-8-13 67........................(b) JackMitchell(5) 2 68
(Stef Liddiard) *awkward s and slowly away: hld up bhd: hdwy on inner 4f out: drvn to chse ldng trio over 1f out: no imp fnl f* **10/1**

5645 **5** 1 ¾ **Savannah**[9] 2921 5-9-2 65........................(b) TPO'Shea 6 63
(Luke Comer, Ire) *hld up in last trio: hdwy on outer over 3f out: no imp wl over 1f out* **15/2**

4020 **6** 10 **Mandalay Prince**[19] 2621 4-9-0 63........................ NeilPollard 5 47
(W J Musson) *hld up in last pair: hdwy 5f out: drvn over 2f out: wknd 2f out and sn wl btn* **10/1**

00/6 **7** ½ **Plain Champagne (IRE)**[22] 2512 6-8-2 51 oh6........................ RichardThomas 3 35
(Dr J R J Naylor) *led tl over 2f out: sn rdn and dropped out* **50/1**

33-0 **8** 48 **Ballad Maker (IRE)**[14] 2753 4-9-0 63........................ DaneO'Neill 8 —
(Mrs S J Humphrey) *chsd ldrs: rdn 4f out: sn wknd: eased fr wl over 1f out: t.o* **33/1**

3m 5.60s (2.40) **Going Correction** +0.10s/f (Slow) **8** Ran SP% **118.4**
Speed ratings (Par 103): **97,96,96,94,93 87,87,60**
toteswinger: 1&2 £10.90, 1&3 £3.10, 2&3 £2.60. CSF £15.08 CT £24.18 TOTE £4.60: £1.40, £1.50, £1.30; EX 15.00.
Owner Mrs Christine Painting **Bred** Gainsborough Farm Llc **Trained** Woodingdean, E Sussex

FOCUS
An ordinary staying handicap run at just a fair pace, but a close finish and the winner was the third on the night to race closest to the inside rail in the home straight. Modest form, but sound.
Savannah Official explanation: jockey said horse hung badly left
Ballad Maker(IRE) Official explanation: jockey said gelding had no more to give

3161 MALLARD MEDIAN AUCTION MAIDEN STKS 1m (P)
8:00 (8:07) (Class 6) 3-5-Y-O **£2,266** (£674; £337; £168) **Stalls** Low

Form RPR

0-4 **1** **Paint The Town Red**[37] 2079 3-8-8 0 ow1........................ JackMitchell(5) 11 79
(H J Collingridge) *hld up bhd: stl plenty to do over 2f out: hdwy wl over 1f out: r.o to ld nr fin* **25/1**

6-0 **2** nk **Sacrilege**[166] 58 3-8-9 0........................ MarcHalford(3) 14 77
(D R C Elsworth) *s.i.s: dropped in bhd: rdn and hdwy 3f out: chsd ldrs over 1f out: led ins fnl f: hdd and no ex nr fin* **14/1**

4-0 **3** *2 ¾* **Rum Jungle**[42] 1926 4-9-8 0 .... DaneO'Neill 13 73+
(H Candy) *chsd ldr tl led 2f out: sn rdn: hdd ins fnl f: fdd last 50yds* **11/1**[3]

00 **4** *shd* **Dr Brass**[33] 2197 3-8-12 0 .... RobertHavlin 2 70+
(H J L Dunlop) *chsd ldrs: rdn and outpcd 3f out: kpt on u.p fr over 1f out: nvr gng pce to rch ldrs* **12/1**

2 **5** *¾* **Buddhist Monk**[21] 2546 3-8-12 0 .... SebSanders 3 69
(Sir Mark Prescott) *racd in midfield: rdn wl over 3f out: hdwy 3f out: hung lft fr wl over 1f out: chsd ldrs ent fnl f: wknd last 100yds* **8/11**[1]

30-3 **6** *3 ½* **Dea Caelestis (FR)**[10] 2885 3-8-7 0 .... DavidKinsella 15 56
(H R A Cecil) *in tch: rdn wl over 3f out: wknd u.p over 1f out* **11/4**[2]

7 *1 ¾* **Lady Brora** 3-8-7 0 .... FrancisNorton 5 52
(A M Balding) *wl bhd: styd on steadily fr over 1f out: nvr nr ldrs* **25/1**

06P- **8** *nk* **Muharjam**[238] 6451 3-8-5 0 ....(b) PatrickDonaghy(7) 1 56
(C E Brittain) *chsd ldrs: rdn over 2f out: hung lft and wknd over 1f out* **40/1**

0-0 **9** *2 ¾* **Lilburn (IRE)**[22] 2509 3-8-12 0 .... TPO'Shea 7 50
(J R Fanshawe) *s.i.s: t.k.h: hld up towards rr: nvr trbld ldrs* **12/1**

0056 **10** *1* **Lady Florence**[21] 2552 3-8-7 51 .... RichardKingscote 4 42
(A B Coogan) *led tl rdn and hdd 2f out: wknd qckly over 1f out* **50/1**

6-0 **11** *1* **Toballa**[8] 2954 3-8-7 0 ....(t) SimonWhitworth 8 40
(H J Collingridge) *a towards rr* **50/1**

12 *3 ½* **Johnny McGurk** 3-8-12 0 .... NeilPollard 12 37
(M E Rimmer) *chsd ldrs: drvn over 2f out: wknd 2f out* **40/1**

00- **13** *3* **Where To Now**[240] 6411 3-8-7 0 .... RichardThomas 16 25
(Mrs C A Dunnett) *bhd: reminders 5f out: wl bhd last 3f* **66/1**

14 *23* **Steady Gaze** 3-8-9 0 .... TravisBlock(3) 6 —
(M A Allen) *s.i.s: a wl bhd: t.o last 2f* **40/1**

000P **15** *1* **Too Much To Do**[21] 2528 3-8-12 37 .... SaleemGolam 9 —
(T D McCarthy) *racd in midfield: rdn and struggling 1/2-way: t.o and virtually p.u fnl f* **100/1**

1m 40.78s (0.88) **Going Correction** +0.10s/f (Slow)
WFA 3 from 4yo 10lb **15 Ran SP% 136.4**
Speed ratings (Par 101): **99,98,95,95,95 91,89,89,86,85 84,81,78,55,54**
toteswinger: Not won. Pool carried forward to Saturday 21st June. CSF £357.24 TOTE £33.90: £8.80, £7.50, £3.60; EX 1161.30.
Owner Miss C Fordham **Bred** Snailwell Stud Co Ltd **Trained** Exning, Suffolk

FOCUS
Just an ordinary maiden, and with the favourite disappointing there was little previous form to go on . The first two came from off the pace.

3162 TRUDI H'CAP — 1m (P)
8:30 (8:37) (Class 6) (0-60,66) 4-Y-0+ **£2,266** (£674; £337; £168) **Stalls** Low

Form RPR

-501 **1** **Sularno**[11] 2870 4-9-7 66 6ex .... TravisBlock(3) 4 73
(H Morrison) *chsd ldr tl led over 4f out: rdn 3f out: kpt on u.p: jst lasted* **11/10**[1]

004/ **2** *hd* **Mystic Roll**[564] 6693 5-8-11 53 .... JohnEgan 8 59+
(Jane Chapple-Hyam) *hld up in tch: shuffled bk 3f out: sn swtchd rt and rdn: r.o wl fnl f: wnt 2nd towards fin: nt quite rch wnr* **12/1**

5260 **3** *hd* **Postmaster**[8] 2943 6-8-9 51 .... RobertHavlin 14 57
(R Ingram) *hld up wl in rr: hdwy over 2f out: rdn over 1f out: edgd lft but r.o wl fnl f: nt quite rch ldng pair* **12/1**

5000 **4** *1 ¼* **The Graig**[24] 2449 4-8-5 47 .... DavidKinsella 15 50
(J R Holt) *in tch: hdwy to chse wnr over 2f out: drvn and tried to chal over 1f out: btn last 50yds: lost 2 pls nr fin* **20/1**

5054 **5** *¾* **Upstairs**[5] 3037 4-9-0 59 .... MarcHalford(3) 11 60
(D R C Elsworth) *t.k.h: hld up in midfield: hdwy 3f out: rdn and sltly outpcd 2f out: kpt on u.p fnl f: nt pce to rch ldrs* **7/1**[3]

0002 **6** *2 ½* **Zorn**[5] 3037 9-8-1 46 oh1 .... LukeMorris(3) 9 42
(P Howling) *chsd ldrs: chsd wnr 4f out tl over 2f out: sn outpcd: plugged on fnl f* **12/1**

5500 **7** *½* **Ruffie (IRE)**[13] 2795 5-7-11 46 .... AmyBaker(7) 5 40
(Miss J Feilden) *t.k.h: hld up in midfield: rdn and effrt over 2f out: no imp fr wl over 1f out* **25/1**

6000 **8** *¾* **To The Max (IRE)**[5] 3034 4-8-8 55 ....(v[1]) JackMitchell(5) 7 48
(Mrs C A Dunnett) *wnt lft s and slowly away: t.k.h and sn in midfield: rdn and hdwy on outer over 2f out: no prog last 2f* **33/1**

4524 **9** *2 ¾* **Not Now Lewis (IRE)**[27] 2352 4-9-0 56 .... SebSanders 12 42
(Miss Gay Kelleway) *hld up bhd: hdwy and swtchd rt 3f out: sn rdn: wknd over 1f out: eased ins fnl f* **4/1**[2]

0-10 **10** *1 ¾* **High Class Problem (IRE)**[14] 2758 5-9-0 56 .... NeilPollard 16 38
(D C O'Brien) *hld up in midfield: rdn and unable qck 3f out: n.d after* **14/1**

0000 **11** *2 ¾* **Golden Brown (IRE)**[15] 2722 4-8-10 52 ....(b) DaneO'Neill 2 28
(David Pinder) *hld up towards rr: rdn 4f out: edgd rt 3f out: wl bhd last 2f* **20/1**

00-0 **12** *5* **Sorrel Point**[130] 517 5-8-11 53 .... SimonWhitworth 13 17
(H J Collingridge) *t.k.h: hld up in rr: n.d* **25/1**

05-0 **13** *11* **Granakey (IRE)**[169] 13 5-8-11 53 .... FrancisNorton 1 —
(M Wigham) *led tl over 4f out: sn dropped out: wl bhd last 2f* **16/1**

6300 **14** *9* **Club Captain (USA)**[8] 2949 5-8-4 46 oh1 ....(p) SaleemGolam 3 —
(T D McCarthy) *racd in midfield: lost pl and rdn 4f out: bhd and sltly hmpd 3f out: t.o and eased over 1f out* **40/1**

000- **15** *5* **Caj (IRE)**[327] 3948 4-8-13 55 ....(b) TPO'Shea 10 —
(Luke Comer, Ire) *t.k.h: hld up bhd: hdwy on outer 5f out: rdn and wknd 3f out: t.o and eased over 1f out* **66/1**

1m 41.16s (1.26) **Going Correction** +0.10s/f (Slow) **15 Ran SP% 139.8**
Speed ratings (Par 101): **97,96,96,95,94 92,91,90,88,86 83,78,67,58,53**
toteswinger: 1&2 - Not won . Pool carried forward to Saturday 21st June. 1&3 £9.30, 2&3 - Not won . Pool carried forward to Saturday 21st June. CSF £2.30 CT £1.88 TOTE £2.60: £1.80, £1.80, £2.40; EX 49.60.
Owner Miss B Swire **Bred** Miss B Swire **Trained** East Ilsley, Berks
■ Welcome Releaf was withdrawn with a broken bridle. Deduct 5p in the £ under Rule 4. New market formed.

FOCUS
A moderate handicap. Sularno was 5lb off his recent Fibresand form and the race is rated through the third.

3163 FOX AND HOUND FILLIES' H'CAP — 1m 2f (P)
9:00 (9:04) (Class 4) (0-85,80) 4-Y-0+ **£4,533** (£1,348; £674; £336) **Stalls** Low

Form RPR

255- **1** **Algarade**[301] 4735 4-9-1 73 .... SebSanders 4 86+
(Sir Mark Prescott) *t.k.h: disp 2nd tl chsd ldr over 5f out: led on bit over 2f out: rdn clr wl over 1f out: readily* **3/1**[2]

3404 **2** *2 ½* **Bavarica**[7] 2978 6-8-0 65 .... AmyBaker(7) 2 72
(Miss J Feilden) *stdd s: hld up in last pair: hdwy wl over 2f out: rdn and effrt on outer 2f out: chsd wnr ins fnl f: nvr threatened wnr* **14/1**

1116 **3** *2 ¼* **Stringsofmyheart**[6] 2990 4-9-7 79 .... DarryllHolland 5 81
(Miss Gay Kelleway) *sn led: drvn 3f out: sn hdd: no ch w wnr after: lost 2nd ins fnl f* **7/2**[3]

4043 **4** *hd* **Montrachet**[12] 2820 4-9-4 79 .... TravisBlock(3) 3 81
(M L W Bell) *restless in stalls: disp 2nd tl over 5f out: rdn 4f out: wknd 2f out* **11/4**[1]

1-11 **5** *3 ½* **Auntie Mame**[13] 2770 4-8-4 62 .... TPO'Shea 7 57
(D J Coakley) *in tch: rdn 3f out: drvn 2f out: wknd wl over 1f out* **11/4**[1]

/40- **6** *5* **Seaflower Reef (IRE)**[309] 4505 4-7-12 63 .... DavidProbert(7) 6 48
(A M Balding) *stdd s: bhd: reminders 6f out: wl bhd last 3f* **8/1**

00 **7** *59* **Baby Princess (BRZ)**[132] 496 4-9-5 80 .... GeorgeBaker 1 —
(J W Hills) *hld up in tch: rdn 4f out: wl bhd last 3f: virtually p.u last 2f* **20/1**

2m 6.48s (-2.12) **Going Correction** +0.10s/f (Slow) **7 Ran SP% 123.1**
Speed ratings (Par 102): **112,110,108,108,105 101,54**
toteswinger: 1&2 £4.30, 1&3 £3.40, 2&3 £6.30. CSF £46.08 TOTE £5.10: £3.30, £5.30; EX 80.20 Place 6 £309.75, Place 5 £100.05..
Owner Miss K Rausing **Bred** Miss K Rausing And Mrs S M Rogers **Trained** Newmarket, Suffolk

FOCUS
The pace was sound in this fillies' handicap. The form is rated through the third and fourth and there could be more to come from the winner.
Montrachet Official explanation: jockey said filly hung right
Baby Princess(BRZ) Official explanation: jockey said filly had no more to give
T/Plt: £1,114.30 to a £1 stake. Pool: £36,942.88. 24.20 winning tickets. T/Qpdt: £243.90 to a £1 stake. Pool: £2,373.30. 7.20 winning tickets.

3026 LEICESTER (R-H)
Thursday, June 19

OFFICIAL GOING: Good to firm (firm in places)
Wind: Fresh, half-behind. Weather: Cloudy with sunny spells

3164 NELSON RESTAURANT MAIDEN STKS (C&G) — 7f 9y
6:50 (6:51) (Class 4) 2-Y-0 **£4,533** (£1,348; £674; £336) **Stalls** Low

Form RPR

632 **1** **Jazacosta (USA)**[6] 3001 2-9-0 0 .... JimCrowley 1 76
(Mrs A J Perrett) *mde virtually all: rdn over 2f out: styd on* **1/4**[1]

0 **2** *¾* **Threestepstoheaven**[19] 2592 2-9-0 0 .... ChrisCatlin 2 74
(B W Hills) *sn pushed along in rr: hdwy over 1f out: r.o* **11/1**[3]

6 **3** *nk* **Tropical Blue**[19] 2608 2-9-0 0 .... SamHitchcott 6 73
(Jennie Candlish) *chsd ldrs: wnt 2nd 1/2-way: rdn over 2f out: unable qck towards fin* **20/1**

0 **4** *1 ¼* **Supernoverre (IRE)**[7] 2972 2-9-0 0 .... JamesDoyle 7 70
(Mrs A J Perrett) *a.p: shkn up 1/2-way: styd on* **40/1**

5 *6* **Mannlichen** 2-9-0 0 .... JoeFanning 4 55
(M Johnston) *s.s: hdwy 4f out: edgd lft over 1f out: wknd fnl f* **5/1**[2]

6 *4 ½* **Spring Secret** 2-9-0 0 .... CatherineGannon 5 44
(B Palling) *w wnr 3f: sn rdn: wknd over 2f out* **33/1**

1m 25.04s (-1.16) **Going Correction** -0.275s/f (Firm) **6 Ran SP% 115.1**
Speed ratings (Par 95): **95,94,93,92,85 80**
toteswinger: 1&2 £1.10, 1&3 £5.50, 2&3 £5.30. CSF £4.34 TOTE £1.10: £1.02, £5.40; EX 3.70.
Owner John Connolly **Bred** William L S Landes Iii **Trained** Pulborough, W Sussex
■ Stewards' Enquiry : Sam Hitchcott caution: used whip down shoulder in forehand position

FOCUS
A moderate bunch of juveniles aside from the winner, who didn't have to be at his best to win.

NOTEBOOK
Jazacosta(USA) had run with credit in some of the best juvenile maidens seen so far this season, and didn't have to reproduce that form in order to gain a workmanlike victory. He well be lumped with plenty of weight in nurseries. (op 2-7)
Threestepstoheaven improved significantly on his debut effort over this extra furlong, and while he would be one of his yard's lesser lights, he should find a little race at some point. (op 12-1)
Tropical Blue was another to show a lot more in this than he had done on debut, and isn't totally without ability.
Supernoverre(IRE), a stablemate of the winner, shaped with a good deal of promise in keeping on well under tender handling. He looks like doing better over further in time. (op 33-1)
Mannlichen, a drifter in the marker beforehand, was slowly away and did little to suggest that he is going to be winning any time soon. (op 7-2)

3165 VALLEY H'CAP — 7f 9y
7:20 (7:20) (Class 5) (0-75,75) 4-Y-0+ **£4,857** (£1,445; £722; £360) **Stalls** Low

Form RPR

-013 **1** **Bold Cross (IRE)**[18] 2642 5-8-12 66 .... PaulFitzsimons 4 66
(E G Bevan) *trckd ldrs: plld hrd: shkn up and edgd rt fr over 1f out: rdn to ld ins fnl f: r.o* **2/1**[1]

0000 **2** *¾* **Lap Of Honour (IRE)**[12] 2818 4-9-7 75 .... JimmyQuinn 2 73
(Jennie Candlish) *sn led: rdn and edgd rt over 1f out: hdd ins fnl f: styd on* **7/2**[3]

350- **3** *½* **Littleton Telchar (USA)**[234] 6553 8-9-1 69 .... TGMcLaughlin 1 66
(S W Hall) *hld up: rdn over 1f out: r.o ins fnl f: nt rch ldrs* **18/1**

1240 **4** *nk* **Unlimited**[11] 2860 6-8-10 67 .... KirstyMilczarek(3) 5 63
(A W Carroll) *stdd s: plld hrd: hdwy to trck ldr over 5f out: rdn over 1f out: no ex ins fnl f* **85/40**[2]

00-0 **5** *nk* **Yerevan**[17] 2679 4-8-11 65 ....(t) JimCrowley 3 60
(R T Phillips) *trckd ldrs: racd keenly: rdn and nt clr run over 1f out: swtchd lft: styd on* **25/1**

0-60 **6** *15* **Torquemada (IRE)**[12] 2837 7-8-11 65 .... PaulDoe 6 20
(M J Attwater) *prom: rdn over 1f out: sn wknd and eased* **11/2**

1m 25.68s (-0.52) **Going Correction** -0.275s/f (Firm) **6 Ran SP% 112.0**
Speed ratings (Par 103): **91,90,89,89,88 71**
toteswinger: 1&2 £2.20, 1&3 £12.00, 2&3 £4.00. CSF £9.37 CT £90.83 TOTE £2.70: £1.50, £2.40; EX 12.40.
Owner E G Bevan **Bred** M Hosokawa **Trained** Ullingswick, H'fords

FOCUS
Just a modest bunch of older handicappers, the winning time being two-thirds of a second slower than the juveniles clocked in the preceding maiden. They finished in a bit of a heap and the form looks ordinary.
Torquemada(IRE) Official explanation: jockey said gelding had a breathing problem

3166 TOWN HALL (S) STKS — 1m 1f 218y
7:50 (7:51) (Class 6) 3-Y-0 **£1,942** (£578; £288; £144) **Stalls** High

Form RPR

5500 **1** **Landikhaya (IRE)**[18] 2639 3-9-3 56 ....(p) PatCosgrave 12 54
(D K Ivory) *a.p: led over 2f out: drvn out* **7/2**[3]

6040 **2** *½* **Coral Shores**[30] 2288 3-9-3 54 ....(v) ChrisCatlin 1 53
(P W Hiatt) *trckd ldrs: plld hrd: rdn over 1f out: styd on* **10/1**

The Form Book, Raceform Ltd, Compton, RG20 6NL

2413 **3** 3 1/4 **One Called Alice**[13] 2801 3-9-0 56 .... KirstyMilczarek(3) 3 47
(A W Carroll) *hld up in tch: rdn over 2f out: no ex ins fnl f* **11/4**[2]

0306 **4** 1 **Balais Folly (FR)**[23] 2475 3-9-3 47 ....(v1) CatherineGannon 10 45
(B Palling) *s.i.s: hdwy over 8f out: chsd ldr 7f out: rdn and n.m.r 3f out: sn lost pl: hung rt over 1f out: nt run on* **10/1**

0040 **5** nse **Fortunes Maid (IRE)**[27] 2352 3-8-12 41 .... JimmyQuinn 8 39
(M H Tompkins) *hld up: hdwy over 3f out: styd on u.p* **16/1**

0445 **6** 6 **Awesome Light (IRE)**[115] 698 3-9-3 65 ....(t) JamesDoyle 6 32
(W R Muir) *hld up: hdwy u.p over 2f out: hung rt and wknd fnl f* **5/2**[1]

0000 **7** 1 **Marramed**[9] 2915 3-8-12 48 .... TGMcLaughlin 5 25
(J O'Reilly) *hld up: rdn over 3f out: n.d* **33/1**

0-55 **8** 1/2 **Never Sold Out (IRE)**[71] 1274 3-9-3 48 ....(v) AndrewElliott 11 29
(J G M O'Shea) *led: rdn and hdd over 2f out: wknd fnl f* **16/1**

9 32 **Lassie Goes West (IRE)**[293] 5021 3-8-12 0 .... SamHitchcott 2 —
(E J Creighton) *s.i.s: a in rr: rdn and wknd over 3f out* **66/1**

00-P **10** nse **Tagula King (IRE)**[17] 2669 3-9-3 0 ....(b1) DNolan 7 —
(D Carroll) *chsd ldrs: rdn 1/2-way: wknd 4f out* **40/1**

000- **11** 3 **Jolly Tipsy**[380] 2344 3-8-6 39 ow1 .... StevenCorrigan(7) 9 —
(S W Hall) *s.i.s: a in rr: rdn and wknd over 3f out* **66/1**

2m 9.16s (1.26) **Going Correction** -0.025s/f (Good) **11** Ran SP% **115.8**
Speed ratings (Par 97): **93,92,90,89,89 84,83,83,57,57 55**
toteswinger: 1&2 £2.70, 1&3 £1.40, 2&3 £18.50. CSF £36.89 TOTE £4.10: £1.60, £3.20, £1.50; EX 38.40.There was no bid for the winner.
Owner K T Ivory **Bred** Holborn Trust Co **Trained** Radlett, Herts

FOCUS
A very weak seller, with the clear top-rated on official ratings coming into the contest completely unproven on turf and not running his race. The form has been rated negatively
Awesome Light(IRE) Official explanation: jockey said colt had a breathing problem

3167 WINDMILL H'CAP 1m 60y
8:20 (8:20) (Class 3) (0-90,85) 4-Y-0- **£7,885** (£2,360; £1,180; £590; £293) **Stalls** High

Form RPR

4340 **1** **Bahar Shumaal (IRE)**[21] 2545 6-9-0 83 .... AhmedAjtebi(5) 5 95
(C E Brittain) *chsd ldr 3f: led over 2f out: edgd rt and hdd over 1f out: rdn to ld ins fnl f: r.o wl* **5/2**[1]

3433 **2** 2 1/2 **Den's Gift (IRE)**[40] 2013 4-9-3 81 ....(b) ChrisCatlin 6 87
(C G Cox) *led: rdn and hdd over 2f out: rallied to ld over 1f out: hdd and unable qck ins fnl f* **7/2**[2]

0-04 **3** 2 1/4 **The Fifth Member (IRE)**[16] 2693 4-8-12 76 .... PatCosgrave 7 77
(J R Boyle) *prom: rdn over 2f out: styd on same pce fnl f* **7/2**[2]

06-4 **4** 4 1/2 **Jo'Burg (USA)**[20] 2565 4-9-5 83 ....(b) JimCrowley 3 74
(Mrs A J Perrett) *s.i.s and hmpd s: effrt over 2f out: nt trble ldrs* **9/2**[3]

02-0 **5** 1 1/2 **Baizically (IRE)**[31] 2264 5-9-4 82 .... DO'Donohoe 1 69
(George Baker) *hld up in tch: rdn and hmpd over 2f out: hung rt and wknd over 1f out* **8/1**

3120 **6** 20 **Dado Mush**[21] 2531 5-8-12 79 ....(p) KirstyMilczarek(3) 2 20
(T T Clement) *hld up: racd keenly: rdn and wknd over 3f out* **14/1**

/056 **7** 2 **Clipperdown (IRE)**[35] 2132 7-9-7 85 ....(t) SamHitchcott 4 22
(E J Creighton) *s.i.s and hung lft s: hdwy to chse ldr 5f out: rdn: hung lft and wknd over 2f out* **25/1**

1m 42.52s (-2.58) **Going Correction** -0.025s/f (Good) **7** Ran SP% **112.8**
Speed ratings (Par 107): **111,108,106,101,100 80,78**
toteswinger: 1&2 £9.60, 1&3 £4.60, 2&3 £4.60. CSF £11.11 TOTE £3.90: £1.80, £1.80; EX 8.50.
Owner Saeed Manana **Bred** Airlie Stud And Sir Thomas Pilkington **Trained** Newmarket, Suffolk

FOCUS
This handicap for older horses was contested by some useful animals, and they clocked a very fast time. It seemed to pay to race handy. Solid form.

NOTEBOOK
Bahar Shumaal(IRE) enjoyed not having to cut out the donkey work for once with the runner-up giving him a nice tow along. This was his first win since the end of 2006, and now it is clear that he's happiest with a lead, he might be able to go on from this. (op 7-2 tchd 4-1)
Den's Gift(IRE) is a victim of his own consistency. Never out of the frame in eight starts since he returned to the track last November following over a year off with injury, he is unlikely to get any respite from the Handicapper any time soon, while his style of running makes him a sitting target for any hold-up horses against him. (op 3-1)
The Fifth Member(IRE) was close enough if good enough but he hasn't really gone on from a couple of wins at Lingfield and Folkestone last year. (op 4-1 tchd 3-1)
Jo'Burg(USA) was hampered at the start as Clipperdown came out sidweways but had plenty of time to gather himself and showed nothing to suggest that he is off the regressive curve he has been following since his first few juvenile runs. (op 4-1 tchd 5-1)

3168 LEICESTER RACECOURSE CONFERENCE CENTRE MAIDEN STKS 1m 3f 183y
8:50 (8:50) (Class 5) 3-Y-0+ **£3,238** (£963; £481; £240) **Stalls** High

Form RPR

522 **1** **Maria Di Scozia**[17] 2669 3-8-5 77 .... AlanMunro 3 75+
(P W Chapple-Hyam) *w ldr tl led 7f out: rdn over 1f out: edgd lft ins fnl f: styd on* **5/6**[1]

0 **2** 1 1/2 **Lemonesse (USA)**[30] 2291 3-8-5 0 .... JimmyQuinn 1 71
(H R A Cecil) *a.p: rdn over 2f out: styd on towards fin* **28/1**

42-5 **3** nk **Mushtaaq (USA)**[17] 2668 3-8-10 83 ....(p) NCallan 5 76
(M A Jarvis) *a.p: chsd wnr 5f out: rdn and hung rt over 1f out: no ex towards fin* **15/8**[2]

6-25 **4** 5 **Spiritonthemount (USA)**[28] 2336 3-8-10 69 ....(b1) ChrisCatlin 9 68
(B W Hills) *trckd ldrs: plld hrd: rdn over 2f out: sn hung rt: wknd fnl f* **15/2**[3]

06 **5** 21 **Waarid**[17] 2669 3-8-10 0 ....(b) LiamJones 6 34
(W J Haggas) *s.s: plld hrd: hdwy 4f out: sn rdn: hung rt and wknd over 2f out* **18/1**

6 11 **Herculaneum** 3-8-10 0 .... JoeFanning 4 17
(M Johnston) *sn pushed along in rr: bhd fr 1/2-way* **10/1**

50- **7** 51 **Minjim**[274] 5541 3-8-5 0 .... AhmedAjtebi(5) 11 —
(C E Brittain) *led 5f: rdn and wknd over 3f out* **40/1**

R **Tot Hill**[25] 5-9-5 0 .... SamHitchcott 2 —
(C N Kellett) *ref to r: tk no part* **150/1**

2m 33.73s (-0.17) **Going Correction** -0.025s/f (Good)
WFA 3 from 4yo+ 14lb **8** Ran SP% **122.0**
Speed ratings (Par 103): **99,98,97,94,80 73,39,—**
toteswinger: 1&2 £2.90, 1&3 £1.10, 2&3 £17.70. CSF £33.82 TOTE £2.10: £1.10, £4.10, £1.10; EX 32.20.
Owner Miss K Rausing **Bred** Miss K Rausing **Trained** Newmarket, Suffolk

FOCUS
No strength in depth to this maiden and the finish was fought out by a trio from top Newmarket yards. The winner did not need to improve.

3169 WALTHAM-ON-THE-WOLDS H'CAP 5f 218y
9:20 (9:21) (Class 5) (0-75,73) 3-Y-0+ **£3,238** (£963; £481; £240) **Stalls** Low

Form RPR

0612 **1** **Dickie Le Davoir**[10] 2891 4-9-9 68 .... StephenDonohoe 5 81+
(John A Harris) *s.i.s: hld up: hdwy to ld over 1f out: r.o* **9/4**[1]

2430 **2** 1 **Mandarin Spirit (IRE)**[5] 3033 8-9-0 59 .... OscarUrbina 3 66
(G C H Chung) *hld up: hdwy and n.m.r over 1f out: sn rdn: r.o* **8/1**

3156 **3** 1 1/4 **Hart Of Gold**[13] 2798 4-9-5 67 .... KevinGhunowa(3) 4 70+
(R A Harris) *chsd ldrs: rdn over 1f out: styd on* **11/1**

0644 **4** hd **Rainbow Bay**[5] 3024 5-8-10 55 ....(v) PatCosgrave 2 57
(P D Evans) *hld up: rdn over 1f out: r.o ins fnl f: nt rch ldrs* **10/3**[2]

-205 **5** 1/2 **Bertie Swift**[23] 2484 4-8-13 58 .... JimCrowley 6 59
(J Gallagher) *chsd ldrs: rdn over 1f out: no ex ins fnl f* **22/1**

/041 **6** 1 1/4 **Danzili Bay**[9] 2923 6-8-8 60 .... StacyRenwick(7) 1 57
(A W Carroll) *racd alone towards stands' side: hung rt fr 1/2-way: rdn over 1f out: nt trble ldrs* **9/2**[3]

0506 **7** 6 **Tag Team (IRE)**[8] 2950 7-8-9 54 oh3 ....(b) ChrisCatlin 7 32
(John A Harris) *awkward leaving stalls: sn chsng ldr: led over 4f out: rdn: hdd and edgd lft over 1f out: wknd ins fnl f* **20/1**

0600 **8** 15 **Dakota Rain (IRE)**[24] 2445 6-10-0 73 .... JimmyQuinn 8 3
(Jennie Candlish) *sn led: hdd over 4f out: rdn and wknd over 1f out* **5/1**

1m 12.21s (-0.79) **Going Correction** -0.275s/f (Firm) **8** Ran SP% **117.3**
Speed ratings (Par 103): **94,92,91,90,90 88,80,60**
toteswinger: 1&2 £20.10, 1&3 £8.70, 2&3 £3.40. CSF £21.91 CT £166.32 TOTE £3.20: £1.30, £3.00, £2.90; EX 9.50 Place 6 £10.56, Place 5 £8.70..
Owner Stan Wright Shaun Taylor **Bred** P And Mrs A G Venner **Trained** Eastwell, Leics
■ Stewards' Enquiry : Oscar Urbina one-day ban: started from incorrect stall (Jul 3)
Kevin Ghunowa one-day ban: started from incorrect stall (Jul 3)

FOCUS
Mostly modest older handicappers on show, and it seemed to be an advantage to be held up off the pace. The winner was well treated and the form is rated through the runner-up.
T/Plt: £7.80 to a £1 stake. Pool: £37,011.54. 3,421.64 winning tickets. T/Qpdt: £4.20 to a £1 stake. Pool: £2,956.10. 512.40 winning tickets. CR

3139 RIPON (R-H)
Thursday, June 19

OFFICIAL GOING: Soft (8.1)
Wind: Moderate, half across Weather: Sunny and blustery

3170 E B F INGHAM UNDERWRITING MAIDEN STKS 6f
2:10 (2:10) (Class 5) 2-Y-0 **£4,209** (£1,252; £625; £312) **Stalls** Low

Form RPR

0 **1** **Keeptheboatafloat (USA)**[20] 2584 2-9-3 0 .... DarrenWilliams 6 75
(K R Burke) *chsd ldrs: hdwy whn hung rt 2f out: sn rdn and styd on to ld ent fnl f: sn drvn and kpt on* **25/1**

26 **2** 1/2 **Cutting Comments**[20] 2584 2-9-3 0 .... TonyHamilton 4 74
(M Dods) *cl up: led 1/2-way: rdn wl over 1f out: drvn and hdd ent fnl f: kpt on u.p* **5/2**[2]

5 **3** 2 **Grand Stitch (USA)**[25] 2424 2-9-3 0 .... DeanMcKeown 1 68
(P A Blockley) *led: pushed along and hdd 1/2-way: rdn 2f out and kpt on same pce* **13/8**[1]

4 8 **Artesium** 2-9-3 0 .... PatCosgrave 2 44
(D J G Murray Smith) *chsd ldng pair: rdn along 1/2-way: sn outpcd* **14/1**

5 1/2 **Lost In Paris (IRE)** 2-9-3 0 .... DavidAllan 7 42
(T D Easterby) *wnt rt s and bhd tl styd on fnl 2f* **8/1**

6 20 **Final Salute** 2-9-3 0 .... TomEaves 5 —
(B Smart) *dwlt: a outpcd in rr* **7/2**[3]

1m 15.01s (2.01) **Going Correction** +0.025s/f (Good) **6** Ran SP% **110.5**
Speed ratings (Par 93): **87,86,83,73,72 45**
CSF £83.99 TOTE £15.00: £4.60, £1.80; EX 64.40.
Owner Cyril Wall **Bred** Barronstown Stud **Trained** Middleham Moor, N Yorks

FOCUS
The bare form of this juvenile maiden looks modest. The winning time was 1.51 seconds slower than the later older-horse claimer.

NOTEBOOK
Keeptheboatafloat(USA) beat just two home on his debut at York, but he left that form behind with a decisive success, despite holding his head awkwardly and trying to hang to his right. He's by Fusaichi Pegasus, so he might be even better suited by quicker ground. (op 20-1)
Cutting Comments had every chance but he was unable to confirm recent York form with the much-improved winner. (op 11-4 tchd 10-3)
Grand Stitch(USA) shaped well on his debut over 5f on good ground at Newmarket, but he was unable to build on that under these different conditions and was a little disappointing. (op 9-4 tchd 5-2 tchd 6-4 in places)
Artesium, £37,000 son of Haafhd, half-brother to Unlicensed, finished up well held on his racecourse debut. (op 18-1 tchd 12-1)
Lost In Paris(IRE), a 26,000gns son of Elusive City, half-brother to among others the smart Meanya, a multiple 5f-1m winner in Italy, out of a mare who was placed over 5f-6f at two, dived to his right from his wide berth and was never involved. (op 9-1 tchd 7-1)
Final Salute, a 58,000gns son of Royal Applause, half-brother to among others Wilde, a 5f-7f winner in the UAE, out of an Ayr Gold Cup winner, was slowly away and was never seen with a chance. He is surely capable of a lot better. (op 5-2)

3171 KNARESBOROUGH H'CAP 5f
2:45 (2:45) (Class 5) (0-75,75) 3-Y-0+ **£2,914** (£867; £433; £216) **Stalls** Low

Form RPR

3-21 **1** **Wotashirtfull (IRE)**[12] 2850 3-9-11 75 ....(p) NCallan 3 85
(K A Ryan) *sn led: rdn 2f out: drvn ent fnl f and styd on wl* **4/1**[2]

0-06 **2** 1 1/2 **Never Without Me**[10] 2892 8-9-2 60 .... TPQueally 1 67
(J F Coupland) *cl up: rdn 2f out and ev ch tl drvn and nt qckn ins fnl f* **9/1**

3002 **3** nk **Highland Warrior**[14] 2760 9-10-0 72 .... MickyFenton 8 78+
(P T Midgley) *wnt rt s: hld up: hdwy on outer over 2f out: rdn and ch over 1f out: drvn and one pce ins fnl f* **4/1**[2]

6010 **4** 3/4 **Windjammer**[3] 3080 4-9-10 68 .... DavidAllan 4 71
(T D Easterby) *chsd ldrs: effrt 2f out: sn rdn and kpt on same pce ent fnl f* **5/1**[3]

6231 **5** 1/2 **Timber Treasure (USA)**[7] 2968 4-10-1 73 6ex ....(b) FrancisNorton 5 74+
(Paul Green) *chsd ldrs: rdn along over 2f out: sn drvn and no imp* **7/2**[1]

0640 **6** hd **Fast Freddie**[21] 2551 4-9-6 64 .... GrahamGibbons 6 65
(S Parr) *chsd ldres: rdn along 2f out: drvn and wknd over 1f out* **16/1**

3300 7 2 1/4 **Steel City Boy (IRE)**[10] 2891 5-8-11 60......................(p) AnnStokell(5) 2 53
(Miss A Stokell) *in tch: rdn along 1/2-way and sn wknd* 12/1

0144 8 3 1/4 **Mandurah (IRE)**[14] 2751 4-9-10 68.............................. AdrianTNicholls 7 49
(D Nicholls) *hld up: a in rr* 7/1

60.36 secs (-0.34) **Going Correction** +0.025s/f (Good)
WFA 3 from 4yo+ 6lb **8** Ran SP% **115.0**
Speed ratings (Par 103): **103,100,100,98,98 97,94,89**
toteswinger: 1&2 £12.30, 1&3 £3.00, 2&3 £5.40. CSF £39.51 CT £153.98 TOTE £4.50: £1.60, £3.30, £1.60; EX 39.00.
Owner Sporting Gunners Syndicate Two **Bred** Luke O'Reilly **Trained** Hambleton, N Yorks
■ Stewards' Enquiry : N Callan caution: used whip in incorrect place

FOCUS
A modest sprint handicap in which the first two were always to the fore. The form seems sound enough.
Mandurah(IRE) Official explanation: jockey said gelding was unsuited by the soft ground

3172 GO RACING IN YORKSHIRE CLAIMING STKS 6f
3:20 (3:20) (Class 5) 3-Y-0+ **£2,914** (£867; £433; £216) **Stalls** Low

Form RPR

0456 1 **Caribbean Coral**[9] 2906 9-9-6 81.............................. GrahamGibbons 4 78
(J J Quinn) *trckd ldrs: hdwy and cl up 2f out: rdn to ld ins fnl f: drvn and jst hld on* 5/2[1]

4226 2 *nse* **Guest Connections**[5] 3050 5-9-2 70......................(v) AdrianTNicholls 7 74
(D Nicholls) *chsd ldrs: rdn along on outer 1/2-way: hdwy wl over 1f out: drvn to chal ins fnl f: kpt on: jst failed* 5/2[1]

1100 3 2 3/4 **Harry Up**[33] 2212 7-9-5 80.............................. NCallan 5 69
(K A Ryan) *led: rdn 2f out: drvn and hdd jst ins fnl f: one pce* 7/2[2]

3-05 4 3 **Mister Fips (IRE)**[51] 1707 3-9-1 82.............................. TGMcLaughlin 3 61
(Jane Chapple-Hyam) *prom: rdn along 2f out: sn one pce* 7/1[3]

60/0 5 1/2 **Bigalo's Banjo**[13] 2806 5-8-9 52.............................. DuranFentiman(3) 10 51
(L A Mullaney) *wnt rt s and towards rr tl styd on appr fnl f: n.d* 33/1

3000 6 6 **Captain Turbot (IRE)**[17] 2661 3-8-3 41.............................. PaulHanagan 9 29
(D W Barker) *prom: rdn along over 2f out and grad wknd* 25/1

000- 7 12 **Bold Haze**[258] 5966 6-8-11 50......................(v) MickyFenton 6 —
(Miss S E Hall) *sn rdn along in rr: bhd fr 1/2-way* 8/1

-060 8 3 3/4 **Mis Chicaf (IRE)**[17] 2658 7-8-7 45 ow1.............................. DavidAllan 1 —
(D Carroll) *in tch: rdn along 1/2-way: sn wknd* 16/1

1m 13.5s (0.50) **Going Correction** +0.025s/f (Good)
WFA 3 from 4yo+ 7lb **8** Ran SP% **115.6**
Speed ratings (Par 103): **97,96,93,89,88 80,64,59**
toteswinger: 1&2 £1.50, 1&3 £1.60, 2&3 £1.70 CSF £8.89 TOTE £3.60: £1.30, £1.30, £1.70; EX 10.80.The winner was claimed by A. B. Haynes for £16,000.
Owner Dawson And Quinn **Bred** P And C Scott **Trained** Settrington, N Yorks

FOCUS
A good claimer in which the form horses finished to the fore. Sound form, rated through the runner-up. The winning time was 1.51 seconds faster than opening juvenile maiden.

3173 LADIES DAY H'CAP 1m 1f
4:00 (4:00) (Class 3) (0-90,89) 4-Y-0+ **£8,723** (£2,612; £1,306) **Stalls** High

Form RPR

0-11 1 **Ben Chorley**[19] 2619 4-9-5 87.............................. TPQueally 3 98+
(D R Lanigan) *cl up: led after 1f: rdn over 1f out: edgd lft ent fnl f and styd on wl* 10/11[1]

25-2 2 1 1/4 **Observatory Star (IRE)**[15] 2733 5-8-10 78......................(p) DavidAllan 2 85
(T D Easterby) *t.k.h: hld up: hdwy and nt clr run on inner appr fnl f: swtchd lft and kpt on same pce* 7/4[2]

-430 3 9 **My Paris**[20] 2582 7-9-4 89.............................. AndrewMullen(3) 6 77
(Ollie Pears) *led 1f: cl up: rdn along 3f out: drvn 2f out and wknd appr fnl f* 4/1[3]

1m 58.07s (3.37) **Going Correction** +0.175s/f (Good) **3** Ran SP% **108.7**
Speed ratings (Par 107): **92,90,82**
CSF £2.82 TOTE £1.90; EX 1.90.
Owner Diamond Racing Ltd **Bred** Mrs A Yearley **Trained** Newmarket, Suffolk
■ Stewards' Enquiry : T P Queally caution: careless riding

FOCUS
The feature race on the card cut up to just three runners with five taken out, three because the ground had turned soft. The progressive winner improved again.

NOTEBOOK
Ben Chorley has been a revelation this season after a lengthy spell on the sidelines and he completed the hat-trick after making most of the running, defying a 7lb rise for his recent Newbury success. His jockey reported that he disliked the tacky ground, but he was always bossing this field. (op 4-5 tchd 6-5)
Observatory Star(IRE), who went for a run up the inside as the race developed, was briefly short of room and may have lost his momentum for a stride or two as the winner went for home. He kept on pretty well under hands and heels riding, but he was never able to get to the winner. (op 9-4)
My Paris had the ground was in his favour, but he faded out of it inside the last two furlongs. He probably needs some respite from the Handicapper. (op 10-3 tchd 9-4)

3174 HARROGATE H'CAP 1m 4f 10y
4:35 (4:36) (Class 4) (0-85,81) 3-Y-0 **£4,857** (£1,445; £722; £360) **Stalls** High

Form RPR

3-10 1 **Jabal Tariq**[33] 2194 3-9-7 81.............................. NCallan 2 90+
(B W Hills) *cl up: led over 4f out: sn clr: unchal* 1/1[1]

0-61 2 4 1/2 **Smarterthanuthink (USA)**[14] 2750 3-8-10 70......................(p) PaulHanagan 4 63
(R A Fahey) *led: pushed along and hdd over 4f out: sn rdn and outpcd* 6/4[2]

060P 3 14 **St Johns Wood**[17] 2675 3-8-8 68......................(b[1]) GrahamGibbons 3 38
(M W Easterby) *in tch: sn pushed along: rdn 4f out: plugged on for remote 3rd* 16/1

0-30 4 33 **Pondapie (IRE)**[34] 2173 3-8-10 70.............................. DeanMcKeown 5 —
(R M Whitaker) *trckd ldng pair: rdn along over 4f out: sn outpcd and bhd* 13/2[3]

2m 40.89s (4.19) **Going Correction** +0.175s/f (Good) **4** Ran SP% **109.2**
Speed ratings (Par 101): **93,90,80,58**
CSF £2.81 TOTE £1.80; EX 3.00.
Owner Mohamed Obaida **Bred** Gainsborough Stud Management Ltd **Trained** Lambourn, Berks

FOCUS
Just the four runners and an easy opportunity for Jabal Tariq, who is rated up 8lb. The winning time was 0.98 seconds slower than the closing 46-65 amateur riders' handicap.

3175 RACING AT REDCAR TOMORROW AND SATURDAY H'CAP 1m
5:10 (5:12) (Class 6) (0-65,65) 4-Y-0+ **£2,590** (£770; £385; £192) **Stalls** High

Form RPR

6-06 1 **San Antonio**[16] 2697 8-9-7 65......................(b) MickyFenton 14 75+
(Mrs P Sly) *mde all: clr 1/2-way: rdn wl over 2f out: styd on wl* 8/1

2105 2 1 3/4 **West End Lad**[16] 2703 5-8-9 53......................(b) DeanMcKeown 4 58
(S R Bowring) *chsd ldrs: hdwy over 3f out: rdn over 2f out: sn drvn and kpt on u.p ins fnl f: nt rch wnr* 28/1

6040 3 *nse* **Silly Gilly (IRE)**[8] 2936 4-8-4 48.............................. TWilliams 10 53
(R E Barr) *chsd wnr: rdn along wl over 2f out: drvn over 1f out: kpt on ins fnl f* 33/1

6006 4 2 3/4 **Nufoudh (IRE)**[13] 2780 4-8-7 51 ow1.............................. GrahamGibbons 7 50
(Miss Tracy Waggott) *chsd ldrs: rdn along wl over 2f out: kpt on same pce u.p* 16/1

6500 5 3/4 **Messiah Garvey**[10] 2891 4-8-13 60.............................. PJMcDonald(3) 12 57
(D Nicholls) *midfield: hdwy 4f out: rdn to chse ldrs over 2f out: sn drvn and one pce* 15/2[3]

400- 6 3/4 **Volaticus (IRE)**[261] 5525 7-8-7 51 ow1.............................. DavidAllan 8 46
(A D Brown) *towards rr: hdwy 3f out: sn rdn and kpt on same pce appr fnl f* 20/1

2564 7 3/4 **King Of The Moors (USA)**[12] 2841 5-9-2 65.............................. NeilBrown(5) 9 59
(T D Barron) *hld up in rr: hdwy on outer over 2f out: sn rdn and kpt on appr fnl f: nrst fin* 7/1[2]

0040 8 1/2 **Kingsholm**[22] 2510 6-9-4 62.............................. TonyHamilton 20 54
(I W McInnes) *hld up towards rr on inner: swtchd lft and hdwy over 2f out: sn rdn and no imp appr fnl f* 10/1

0400 9 1 3/4 **Cool Sands (IRE)**[6] 2927 6-8-0 47 oh1 ow1.........(v) AndrewMullen(3) 19 35
(J G Given) *in rr: sme late hdwy: nvr a factor* 14/1

0503 10 1 1/4 **Apache Nation (IRE)**[17] 2662 5-8-13 57.............................. TomEaves 16 42
(M Dods) *hld up in midfield: effrt 4f out: sn rdn along and no hdwy* 7/4[1]

0- 11 3/4 **Desert Rat (IRE)**[14] 6552 4-9-0 58......................(p) PaulHanagan 18 42
(Micky Hammond) *chsd ldrs: rdn along 1/2-way: sn wknd* 14/1

435- 12 *nse* **Thornaby Green**[181] 7214 7-8-9 60.............................. DeanHeslop(7) 3 44
(T D Barron) *prom on outer: rdn along 3f out: sn drvn and wknd over 2f out* 20/1

0400 13 2 1/4 **Apres Ski (IRE)**[27] 2375 5-8-9 53.............................. TPQueally 13 31+
(J F Coupland) *t.k.h: hld up in rr: rdr lost irons 1/2-way: nvr a factor* 25/1

6040 14 36 **Kadia**[24] 2463 5-8-2 46 oh1.............................. PaulFessey 6 —
(P T Midgley) *chsd ldrs: rdn along 4f out: sn wknd* 33/1

1m 42.51s (1.11) **Going Correction** +0.175s/f (Good) **14** Ran SP% **122.7**
Speed ratings (Par 101): **101,99,99,96,95 94,94,93,91,90 89,89,87,51**
toteswinger: 1&2 £29.00, 1&3 £39.70, 2&3 £59.60 CSF £226.52 CT £6990.31 TOTE £10.50: £3.10, £5.00, £5.90; EX 236.70.
Owner R Brazier **Bred** G Reed **Trained** Thorney, Cambs

FOCUS
A moderate handicap in which the principals were always prominent. The third and fourth seem the best guide.
Apache Nation(IRE) Official explanation: trainer had no explanation for the poor form shown
Apres Ski(IRE) Official explanation: jockey said saddle slipped
Kadia Official explanation: jockey said mare finished distressed

3176 BEAUMONT ROBINSON LADIES' DERBY H'CAP (LADY AMATEUR RIDERS) 1m 4f 10y
5:40 (5:40) (Class 6) (0-65,65) 4-Y-0+ **£2,810** (£871; £435; £217) **Stalls** High

Form RPR

432- 1 **Master Nimbus**[26] 5389 8-9-5 47.............................. MissADeniel 1 68+
(J J Quinn) *hld up in midfield: smooth hdwy over 3f out: led wl over 2f out: pushed clr wl over 1f out: unchal* 3/1[1]

040- 2 10 **Mister Pete (IRE)**[222] 6732 5-9-6 48............ MissGDGracey-Davison 11 52
(W Storey) *in tch: hdwy over 3f out: rdn 2f out: drvn over 1f out: kpt on ins fnl f: tk 2nd nr line* 7/1

5363 3 *shd* **Court Of Appeal**[13] 2776 11-10-5 61......................(tp) MissLEllison 8 65
(B Ellison) *prom: led 1/2-way: rdn along and ehaded wl over 2f out: sn drvn and kpt on same pce: lost 2nd nr line* 9/2[2]

-452 4 6 **Gamesters Lady**[9] 2908 5-10-3 62......................(p) MissMSowerby(3) 2 56+
(W M Brisbourne) *hld up and bhd: hdwy on wd outside over 2f out: sn rdn and plugged on same pce fnl f* 13/2

0651 5 1/2 **Fenners (USA)**[13] 2804 5-10-5 64.............................. MissJCoward(3) 4 57
(M W Easterby) *chsd ldrs: rdn along over 3f out: drvn over 2f out and sn btn* 11/2[3]

66-0 6 *shd* **Bollin Freddie**[27] 2364 4-9-0 47.............................. MissWGibson(5) 3 40
(A J Lockwood) *chsd ldrs: rdn along 3f out: sn drvn: edgd rt and wknd* 8/1

000/ 7 6 **Bramantino (IRE)**[40] 5960 8-9-5 52.............................. MissHCuthbert(5) 10 36
(T A K Cuthbert) *a towards rr* 20/1

0031 8 3 3/4 **Shenandoah Girl**[16] 2694 5-10-0 56......................(p) MissEJJones 14 34
(Miss Gay Kelleway) *dwlt: keen and sn chsng ldrs: prom on inner 1/2-way: rdn along and wkng whn n.m.r 3f out* 15/2

5-40 9 9 **Finnegans Rainbow**[24] 2207 6-8-13 46 oh1.............................. MissZoeLilly(5) 12 9
(M C Chapman) *prom: rdn along 1/2-way: wknd over 4f out* 33/1

001/ 10 6 **Barman (USA)**[271] 5105 9-10-4 65......................(t) MissMMullineaux(5) 9 19
(M Mullineaux) *s.i.s: a towards rr* 14/1

000- 11 39 **Missouri (USA)**[258] 5087 5-8-13 46 oh1.........(t) MissAngelaBarnes(5) 7 —
(M A Barnes) *led to 1/2-way: rdn along 4f out and sn wknd* 50/1

2m 39.91s (3.21) **Going Correction** +0.175s/f (Good) **11** Ran SP% **123.6**
Speed ratings (Par 101): **96,89,89,85,84 84,80,78,72,68 42**
toteswinger: 1&2 £5.10, 1&3 £5.40, 2&3 £10.30 CSF £25.44 CT £97.77 TOTE £4.60: £1.70, £3.10, £2.00; EX 34.00 Place 6 £233.48, Place 5 £80.70..
Owner J H Hewitt **Bred** A H Bennett **Trained** Settrington, N Yorks

FOCUS
A modest handicap for lady amateurs' which was turned into a procession by Master Nimbus, who was very well treated if transferring his jumps form. The overall form is pretty sound. The winning time was 0.98 seconds faster than earlier three-year-old 66-85 handicap.
T/Plt: £123.60 to a £1 stake. Pool: £40,095.10. 236.70 winning tickets. T/Qpdt: £23.00 to a £1 stake. Pool: £2,577.89. 82.70 winning tickets. JR

3084 WARWICK (L-H)
Thursday, June 19

OFFICIAL GOING: Firm
The jockeys reported that the ground was very fast after only 1.6mm of the predicted 6mm fell the previous day. 19 horses were taken out due to ground.
Wind: Moderate behind Weather: Fine

3177 WARWICKRACECOURSE.CO.UK MAIDEN FILLIES' STKS 6f
2:20 (2:21) (Class 5) 3-Y-0+ **£3,238** (£963; £481; £240) **Stalls** Centre

Form RPR

5-52 1 **Arabian Art (USA)**[38] 2038 3-9-0 68.............................. IanMongan 8 74+
(H R A Cecil) *mde all: in command whn shkn up 1f out: pushed out* 7/4[1]

The Form Book, Raceform Ltd, Compton, RG20 6NL

5-0 **2** *3* **Lady Carollina**[41] 1960 3-9-0 0 .... SaleemGolam 7 64
(Rae Guest) *s.i.s: sn hld up in tch: pushed along over 1f out: chsd wnr fnl f: no imp* **11/1**
P- **3** *1 ½* **Laureldean Dream (USA)**[356] 3055 3-8-9 0 ....(t) AshleyHamblett(5) 1 59
(P W Chapple-Hyam) *a.p: rdn over 1f out: one pce* **7/2**[2]
-0 **4** *3* **Siren Party**[28] 2341 3-9-0 0 .... NickyMackay 13 50+
(L M Cumani) *t.k.h in tch: sddle slipped after 2f: awkward and hung rt bnd over 2f out: no real prog fnl f* **17/2**[3]
44- **5** *nk* **Tittle**[253] 6105 3-9-0 0 .... DaneO'Neill 10 49
(H Candy) *s.i.s: sn prom: rdn and edgd rt over 1f out: wknd ins fnl f* **9/1**
- **6** *¾* **Dancing Belle** 3-9-0 0 .... OscarUrbina 4 46
(J A R Toller) *s.i.s: towards rr: pushed along and swtchd lft 2f out: sme hdwy over 1f out: n.d* **12/1**
0-40 **7** *nk* **Night Rainbow (IRE)**[19] 2622 5-9-7 49 .... FergalLynch 12 47
(Mrs S Leech) *prom tl wknd over 1f out* **33/1**
8 *¾* **More Applause** 3-9-0 0 .... JimCrowley 6 43
(Pat Eddery) *hld up in tch: pushed along and wknd 2f out* **12/1**
00 **9** *2* **Frosty's Gift**[9] 2917 4-9-7 0 .... RichardSmith 2 38
(J C Fox) *a towards rr* **50/1**
0 **10** *½* **Lekezia (IRE)**[12] 2834 3-8-7 0 .... GabrielHannon(7) 16 35
(J W Hills) *s.i.s and wnt rt: a in rr* **40/1**
0 **11** *5* **Groundhog Day**[12] 2823 4-9-7 0 .... PatrickMathers 14 21
(J Balding) *t.k.h: in tch on outside: rn green 3f out: wknd 2f out* **33/1**
P **Ashbys Dance** 3-8-11 0 .... KirstyMilczarek(3) 15 —
(M Botti) *wnt rt s: a in rr: p.u lame wl ins fnl f: dead* **10/1**

1m 10.17s (-1.63) **Going Correction** -0.25s/f (Firm) course record
WFA 3 from 4yo+ 7lb **12 Ran SP% 122.2**
Speed ratings (Par 100): **100,96,94,90,89 88,88,87,84,83 77,—**
toteswinger: 1&2 £6.10, 1&3 £2.00, 2&3 £11.80. CSF £23.24 TOTE £2.20: £1.40, £3.80, £1.60; EX 29.60.
Owner Malih L Al Basti **Bred** Kidder, Cole & Robenalt **Trained** Newmarket, Suffolk

FOCUS
The combination of quick ground and a tail wind led to the course record being lowered by 0.77 seconds over what is still a comparatively new layout for 6f at Warwick. This was just a modest maiden, with an improved run from the winner.
Laureldean Dream(USA) Official explanation: jockey said filly was unsuited by the firm ground
Siren Party ◆ Official explanation: jockey said saddle slipped
Dancing Belle Official explanation: jockey said filly was unsuited by the firm ground

3178 RACING UK MEDIAN AUCTION MAIDEN STKS 5f
2:55 (2:57) (Class 5) 2-Y-O **£2,914** (£867; £433; £216) **Stalls** Centre

Form RPR
42 **1** **Countrywide City (IRE)**[9] 2909 2-8-12 0 .... AshleyHamblett(5) 5 69
(P W Chapple-Hyam) *t.k.h: chsd ldr: led over 1f out: hrd rdn fnl f: jst hld on* **2/5**[1]
2 *hd* **Red Rosanna** 2-8-9 0 .... RussellKennemore(3) 7 63
(R Hollinshead) *a.p: rdn and wnt 2nd 1f out: edgd rt wl ins fnl f: r.o: jst failed* **20/1**
5 **3** *1 ½* **Coleorton Choice**[41] 1967 2-9-3 0 .... FergalLynch 2 63
(K A Ryan) *s.i.s: sn chsng ldrs: edgd rt bnd over 2f out: rdn over 1f out: hung rt ins fnl f: kpt on* **4/1**[2]
400 **4** *¾* **Bethie**[19] 2608 2-8-12 0 .... PaulMulrennan 6 55
(R Brotherton) *led: rdn 2f out: hdd over 1f out: no ex ins fnl f* **100/1**
5 *1* **Pressed For Time (IRE)**[34] 2178 2-8-12 0 .... ChrisCatlin 1 52
(E J Creighton) *t.k.h in tch: rdn over 1f out: no hdwy* **22/1**
03 **6** *½* **Scrapper Smith (IRE)**[15] 2709 2-9-3 0 .... DaneO'Neill 4 55
(E F Vaughan) *s.i.s: hld up: rdn over 1f out: no rspnse* **12/1**[3]
03 **7** *3 ¾* **Bold Rose**[11] 2865 2-8-12 0 ....(t) RichardSmith 8 36
(M D I Usher) *s.i.s: hung rt over 1f out: a in rr* **28/1**

59.43 secs (-0.17) **Going Correction** -0.25s/f (Firm) **7 Ran SP% 112.7**
Speed ratings (Par 93): **91,90,88,87,85 84,78**
toteswinger: 1&2 £4.00, 1&3 £1.30, 2&3 £5.90. CSF £13.67 TOTE £1.40: £1.10, £6.60; EX 13.60.
Owner Countrywide Steel & Tubes Ltd **Bred** T Cahalan & S Hayley **Trained** Newmarket, Suffolk

FOCUS
Almost certainly modest form with the winner making hard work of what looked an easy opportunity.

NOTEBOOK
Countrywide City(IRE) made really hard work of landing the odds on this return to the minimum trip and would probably have been overhauled had the runner-up not come off a true line. (op 1-2 tchd 8-15)
Red Rosanna ◆ is a half-sister to a couple of winners including Fibresand specialist Preskani. She may well have made a winning debut but for showing signs of inexperience. A similar event is there for the taking and she will get further in due course. (tchd 12-1)
Coleorton Choice could have been feeling the ground when starting to lug right at halfway. To his credit he did stick to his task. (tchd 5-1)
Bethie again made the running and lasted a lot longer than she had done in better company last time when getting unsettled in the stalls. (op 66-1)
Pressed For Time(IRE), an Irish import, had not shown a lot in a couple of Dundalk maidens either side of a run in soft ground. (op 20-1 tchd 28-1)

3179 BOTT LTD H'CAP 1m 6f 213y
3:30 (3:30) (Class 5) (0-75,75) 4-Y-O+ **£3,238** (£963; £481; £240) **Stalls** Low

Form RPR
3262 **1** **Alnwick**[45] 1856 4-8-12 **66** .... DaneO'Neill 1 77+
(P D Cundell) *sn hld up in tch: led over 1f out: sn rdn: comf* **5/1**[3]
0442 **2** *2 ½* **Plane Painter (IRE)**[21] 2525 4-9-4 **72** .... AndrewElliott 2 79
(M Johnston) *led: rdn over 2f out: hdd over 1f out: nt qckn* **13/8**[1]
6-22 **3** *¾* **Right Option (IRE)**[124] 588 4-8-13 **70** .... TolleyDean(3) 11 76
(J L Flint) *s.i.s: in rr: rdn and hdwy on ins wl over 1f out: sn edgd rt: kpt on same pce fnl f* **9/1**
0/04 **4** *2* **Emile Zola**[8] 2952 6-8-9 **63** .... JimCrowley 4 66
(Miss Venetia Williams) *chsd ldr tl rdn 2f out: no ex fnl f* **7/2**[2]
-166 **5** *1 ¾* **Dansilver**[31] 2245 4-7-13 **60** ow2 .... PatrickDonaghy(7) 7 61
(D J Wintle) *prom: rdn over 3f out: btn whn rdr dropped reins over 1f out* **9/1**
-320 **6** *5* **Command Marshal (FR)**[28] 2332 5-9-1 **74** .... JackDean(5) 9 69
(M J Scudamore) *hld up: sme hdwy 3f out: rdn and wknd over 1f out* **15/2**
V-03 **7** *1 ¾* **L'Oiseau De Feu (USA)**[18] 2643 4-8-2 **56** oh2 .... CatherineGannon 6 48
(Mrs K Waldron) *hld up: pushed along over 3f out: hdwy over 2f out: sn rdn: wknd over 1f out* **20/1**

3m 13.85s (-5.15) **Going Correction** -0.25s/f (Firm) **7 Ran SP% 113.5**
Speed ratings (Par 103): **103,101,101,100,99 96,95**
toteswinger: 1&2 £2.10, 1&3 £3.10, 2&3 £3.10. CSF £13.38 CT £69.54 TOTE £6.00: £2.90, £1.50; EX 16.90.
Owner Entre Nous and P D Cundell **Bred** Roden House Stud **Trained** Compton, Berks

FOCUS
A modest staying handicap run at an average pace. The bare form is pretty ordinary.
Right Option(IRE) Official explanation: jockey said gelding was unsuited by the firm ground

3180 MIDSUMMER MEDIAN AUCTION MAIDEN STKS 7f 26y
4:10 (4:14) (Class 5) 3-5-Y-O **£2,914** (£867; £433; £216) **Stalls** Low

Form RPR
2 **1** **Monaadema (IRE)**[24] 2466 3-8-12 0 .... LiamJones 8 79+
(W J Haggas) *a.p: led over 1f out: sn edgd rt: comf* **8/13**[1]
00-6 **2** *4 ½* **Rondeau (GR)**[14] 2756 3-9-3 65 .... JimCrowley 14 68
(P R Chamings) *a.p: rdn over 1f out: wnt 2nd ins fnl f: nt trble wnr* **20/1**
2-04 **3** *1 ¾* **Penchesco (IRE)**[17] 2673 3-9-3 72 .... PaulEddery 7 63
(Pat Eddery) *hld up in tch: rdn over 1f out: r.o one pce fnl f* **10/3**[2]
0 **4** *¾* **Coup De Torchon (FR)**[37] 2084 3-8-12 0 .... SamHitchcott 9 56
(J A Osborne) *led: rdn and hdd over 1f out: wknd wl ins fnl f* **40/1**
0- **5** *hd* **Gambling Jack**[394] 1919 3-9-3 0 .... CatherineGannon 13 61
(A W Carroll) *t.k.h: chsd ldr to 2f out: sn rdn: wknd ins fnl f* **33/1**
66 **6** *2 ¼* **Cheney Manor**[45] 1854 3-9-3 0 .... ChrisCatlin 1 55+
(B W Hills) *hld up and bhd: shkn up over 1f out: nvr trbld ldrs* **9/1**[3]
00- **7** *4* **Carole Os (IRE)**[272] 5603 3-8-5 0 .... StevenCorrigan(7) 10 39
(S W Hall) *s.i.s: sn hld up in mid-div: lost pl over 4f out: bhd fnl 2f* **25/1**
8 *13* **Global Glory (IRE)** 3-9-3 0 .... OscarUrbina 5 9
(J A R Toller) *s.i.s: a in rr* **14/1**
9 *¾* **Bluebird Chariot** 5-9-9 0 .... TolleyDean(3) 11 7
(J M Bradley) *dwlt: sn mid-div: pushed along over 3f out: wknd over 2f out* **66/1**
10 *7* **Wendy Craig** 3-8-12 0 .... PatrickMathers 12 —
(J Balding) *s.s: a in rr* **66/1**

1m 23.26s (-1.34) **Going Correction** -0.25s/f (Firm)
WFA 3 from 5yo 9lb **10 Ran SP% 118.6**
Speed ratings (Par 103): **97,91,89,89,88 86,81,66,65,57**
toteswinger: 1&2 £5.20, 1&3 £1.30, 2&3 £8.60. CSF £21.93 TOTE £1.70: £1.10, £3.40, £1.30; EX 17.80.
Owner Hamdan Al Maktoum **Bred** Shadwell Estate Company Limited **Trained** Newmarket, Suffolk

FOCUS
An uncompetitive maiden and ordinary form, but the winner is capable of better.
Rondeau(GR) ◆ Official explanation: jockey said colt was unsuited by the firm ground
Penchesco(IRE) Official explanation: jockey said colt was unsuited by the firm ground

3181 WARWICKRACECOURSE.CO.UK H'CAP 1m 22y
4:45 (4:45) (Class 5) (0-75,75) 4-Y-O+ **£3,238** (£963; £481; £240) **Stalls** Low

Form RPR
315- **1** **Red Birr (IRE)**[183] 5889 7-9-7 **75** .... ChrisCatlin 3 83
(P R Webber) *broke wl: hld up in tch: hdwy on ins over 1f out: led ins fnl f: rdn and r.o wl* **15/2**
3400 **2** *1 ¼* **Garden Party**[19] 2615 4-9-0 **68** .... FrankieMcDonald 10 73
(Jane Chapple-Hyam) *a.p: wnt 2nd 4f out: rdn to ld jst over 1f out: hdd and nt qckn ins fnl f* **14/1**
3440 **3** *¾* **Blacktoft (USA)**[14] 2764 5-9-5 **73** ....(e) SaleemGolam 4 76
(S C Williams) *hld up towards rr: hung lft whn swtchd rt and hdwy over 1f out: sn rdn: kpt on ins fnl f* **3/1**[1]
040 **4** *2* **Under Fire (IRE)**[18] 2642 5-8-3 **60** .... KirstyMilczarek(3) 6 59
(A W Carroll) *chsd ldr: led 2f out: rdn and hdd jst over 1f out: no ex wl ins fnl f* **6/1**
5600 **5** *1 ¼* **Golden Prospect**[10] 2897 4-8-11 **72** .... GabrielHannon(7) 1 68
(J W Hills) *s.s: hld up in rr: rdn and hdwy over 1f out: one pce ins fnl f* **9/2**[3]
0055 **6** *1 ¾* **Outer Hebrides**[9] 2917 7-8-3 **57** ....(v) CatherineGannon 5 49
(J M Bradley) *t.k.h: in mid-div: hdwy over 3f out: rdn over 1f out: wknd ins fnl f* **14/1**
50-3 **7** *3 ½* **Regal Curtsy**[15] 2718 4-8-3 **57** .... NickyMackay 9 41
(P R Chamings) *hld up: sn in tch: wknd wl over 1f out* **9/1**
0433 **8** *1 ¼* **Lordship (IRE)**[16] 2693 4-8-4 **61** .... LukeMorris(3) 7 42
(A W Carroll) *hld up: c wd st: rdn wl over 1f out: no rspnse* **10/3**[2]
000- **9** *12* **Feeling (IRE)**[112] 6235 4-8-9 **66** ....(v[1]) RussellKennemore(3) 8 19
(W Clay) *led: hdd 2f out: sn rdn and wknd* **50/1**

1m 37.63s (-3.37) **Going Correction** -0.25s/f (Firm) **9 Ran SP% 117.6**
Speed ratings (Par 103): **106,104,104,102,100 99,95,94,82**
toteswinger: 1&2 £12.70, 1&3 £4.90, 2&3 £13.00. CSF £107.08 CT £388.92 TOTE £10.30: £1.40, £4.70, £1.50; EX 109.10.
Owner John Nicholls (Trading) Ltd **Bred** Mrs Ellen Lyons **Trained** Mollington, Oxon

FOCUS
Modest form, and perhaps not the most solid. The pace was reasonable.

3182 TURFTV H'CAP 1m 2f 188y
5:20 (5:20) (Class 6) (0-55,55) 4-Y-O+ **£2,047** (£604; £302) **Stalls** Low

Form RPR
0-06 **1** **Laish Ya Hajar (IRE)**[13] 2795 4-9-0 **55** .... ChrisCatlin 10 66
(P R Webber) *plld hrd: w ldr: led after 2f: rdn over 1f out: r.o wl u.p ins fnl f* **13/2**
00-5 **2** *1 ¼* **Faith And Reason (USA)**[8] 2957 5-8-7 **55** .... MJMurphy(7) 17 64
(A P Stringer) *hld up in rr: hdwy on ins wl over 1f out: rdn and nt qckn wl ins fnl f* **10/1**
4066 **3** *1 ¼* **Skye But N Ben**[15] 2731 4-8-5 **46** oh1 ....(p) DO'Donohoe 8 53
(G A Harker) *hld up in mid-div: hdwy over 1f out: rdn and nt qckn ins fnl f* **5/1**[2]
6-54 **4** *1* **Giddywell**[16] 2707 4-8-7 **51** .... RussellKennemore(3) 2 56
(R Hollinshead) *hld up in mid-div: hdwy 4f out: rdn wl over 1f out: one pce fnl f* **11/4**[1]
0350 **5** *1* **Magic Warrior**[8] 2943 8-8-9 **50** .... PaulFitzsimons 1 53
(J C Fox) *stdd s: hld up in rr: hdwy on ins over 3f out: rdn 2f out: no ex wl ins fnl f* **11/2**[3]
0504 **6** *2 ¾* **Viscount Rossini**[13] 2770 6-8-5 **49** .... LukeMorris(3) 7 47
(A W Carroll) *prom: rdn 3f out: wkng whn hit rail wl ins fnl f* **7/1**
0-00 **7** *2 ¼* **Icansingarainbow**[20] 2572 4-8-11 **52** .... CatherineGannon 12 46
(R Hollinshead) *awkward leaving stalls: hld up in rr: nvr nr ldrs* **20/1**
00-0 **8** *5* **Ardent Prince**[11] 2870 5-8-1 **49** .... StacyRenwick(7) 6 34
(A J McCabe) *stdd s: plld hrd: sn prom: stmbld sltly over 7f out: wnt 2nd 6f out: ev ch over 2f out: rdn and wknd over 1f out* **18/1**
0000 **9** *1* **General Flumpa**[3] 3084 7-8-6 **54** .... SoniaEaton(7) 16 37
(Miss Tor Sturgis) *t.k.h: led 2f: prom tl wknd over 3f out* **10/1**

050 **10** *70* **Brutus Maximus**[24] 2456 5-8-5 **46** oh1....................(b) PatrickMathers 11 —
(I W McInnes) *s.i.s: hld up in mid-div: hung rt and reminders over 6f out: bhd 4f out: t.o fnl 2f* **20/1**

2m 18.09s (-3.01) **Going Correction** -0.25s/f (Firm) **10** Ran SP% **117.5**
Speed ratings (Par 101): **100,99,98,97,96 94,93,89,88,37**
toteswinger: 1&2 £7.40, 1&3 £5.80, 2&3 £13.90. CSF £70.20 CT £349.22 TOTE £8.50: £2.10, £1.90, £2.30; EX 54.60.
Owner The Auctionair Racing Partnership **Bred** Gainsborough Stud Management Ltd **Trained** Mollington, Oxon
■ Stewards' Enquiry : Sonia Eaton one-day ban: careless riding (Jul 3)

FOCUS
Not a great contest with several of the field apparently on the decline. The pace was steady and this is moderate form.
Brutus Maximus Official explanation: jockey said horse was unsuited by the firm ground and lost two shoes

3183 TURFTV APPRENTICE H'CAP — 1m 22y
5:50 (5:50) (Class 6) (0-65,65) 3-Y-0 — **£2,047** (£604; £302) **Stalls** Low

Form — RPR

60 **1** **Titfer (IRE)**[23] 2475 3-8-5 **51**.. BMcHugh[(5)] 1 56
(A W Carroll) *a.p: hrd rdn fnl f: r.o to ld last strides* **14/1**

0-00 **2** *hd* **Charming Tale (USA)**[20] 2566 3-8-9 **55**...............................(b[1]) KMay[(5)] 3 59
(B J Meehan) *hld up in mid-div: hdwy over 4f out: rdn wl over 1f out: led cl home: hdd last strides* **16/1**

6000 **3** *nk* **Duneen Dream (USA)**[23] 2475 3-8-3 **51**.................... DebraEngland[(7)] 5 54
(W J Musson) *a.p: rdn to ld over 1f out: hdd cl home* **20/1**

43-2 **4** *½* **The Willowy Wigeon**[18] 2639 3-9-5 **60**............................. TolleyDean 2 62
(P Winkworth) *hld up in tch: rdn over 2f out: kpt on ins fnl f* **5/1**[2]

-162 **5** *nk* **Metal Madness (IRE)**[7] 2982 3-9-7 **65**............................ JamieJones[(3)] 7 66
(M G Quinlan) *hld up in mid-div: hdwy over 1f out: sn rdn: nt qckn ins fnl f* **11/4**[1]

03-0 **6** *½* **Rampant Ronnie (USA)**[41] 1962 3-9-0 **60**.................. GaryBartley[(5)] 12 60+
(P W D'Arcy) *fly-jmpd leaving stalls: hld up in rr: rdn over 1f out: r.o ins fnl f: nt rch ldrs* **16/1**

-064 **7** *shd* **Star Pattern (USA)**[54] 1622 3-9-1 **63**......................... CharlesEddery[(7)] 9 63+
(J H M Gosden) *wnt rt s: hld up in rr: c wd st: edgd lft over 1f out: nvr able to chal* **11/2**[3]

50-0 **8** *nk* **Stage Acclaim (IRE)**[17] 2678 3-9-7 **65**........................ JamesMillman[(3)] 8 64
(B R Millman) *hld up towards rr: rdn over 1f out: sme late hdwy* **8/1**

30-4 **9** *½* **Space Pirate**[133] 464 3-8-9 **55**.................................... SimonPearce[(5)] 6 53
(J Pearce) *hld up in rr: rdn 2f out: hdwy on ins over 1f out: one pce ins fnl f* **12/1**

-003 **10** *2¾* **Bahamian Blue (IRE)**[35] 2126 3-8-12 **53**..........(v[1]) RussellKennemore 4 45
(P G Murphy) *led: hung rt bnd over 2f out: rdn and hdd over 1f out: wknd ins fnl f* **16/1**

6-00 **11** *5* **Robbmaa (FR)**[24] 2451 3-9-4 **59**.. LukeMorris 14 39
(A W Carroll) *hld up: rdn over 3f out: a towards rr* **33/1**

5334 **12** *7* **Casino Night**[12] 2842 3-9-3 **61**.................................. AshleyHamblett[(3)] 11 25
(J R Weymes) *hld up in mid-div: bhd fnl 2f* **10/1**

0-00 **13** *3¼* **Purple Ransom (IRE)**[13] 2805 3-8-7 **51**.............................(t) NicolPolli[(3)] 16 8
(D J Wintle) *chsd ldr over 3f: wknd over 2f out* **40/1**

1m 39.57s (-1.43) **Going Correction** -0.25s/f (Firm) **13** Ran SP% **121.1**
Speed ratings (Par 97): **97,96,96,96,95 95,95,94,94,91 86,79,76**
toteswinger: 1&2 £56.20, 1&3 £56.50, 2&3 £99.80 CSF £218.56 CT £2615.32 TOTE £19.80: £5.50, £8.40, £8.50; EX 418.20 Place 6 £17.57, Place 5 £11.79..
Owner J T Billson **Bred** C M Farrell **Trained** Cropthorne, Worcs
■ Stewards' Enquiry : K May two-day ban: used whip with excessive frequency (Jul 3-4)

FOCUS
A bunch finish to this low-grade affair with less than four lengths covering the first nine. The form is modest, but sound enough.
Bahamian Blue(IRE) Official explanation: jockey said gelding tried to duck out on final bend
Casino Night Official explanation: jockey said filly was unsuited by the firm ground
T/Plt: £20.80 to a £1 stake. Pool: £43,690.02. 1,531.85 winning tickets. T/Qpdt: £18.10 to a £1 stake. Pool: £1,738.50. 70.90 winning tickets. KH

3184 - 3190a (Foreign Racing) - See Raceform Interactive

3052 LONGCHAMP (R-H)
Thursday, June 19

OFFICIAL GOING: Good

3191a PRIX DU LYS (GROUP 3) (C&G) — 1m 4f
2:20 (2:26) 3-Y-0 — **£29,412** (£11,765; £8,824; £5,882; £2,941)

RPR

1 **Montmartre (FR)**[18] 2654 3-8-11 .... CSoumillon 4 107
(A De Royer-Dupre, France) *a cl up: 5th st: led 1 1/2f out: r.o wl* **6/4**[1]

2 *2* **Zack Dream (FR)**[18] 2654 3-8-11 .... IMendizabal 8 104
(M Delzangles, France) *hld up in rr: last st: hdwy on outside 2f out: chal over 1f out: one pce fnl f* **15/1**

3 *snk* **Watar (IRE)**[19] 2636 3-8-11 .... DBonilla 6 104
(F Head, France) *hld up: 8th st: hdwy 2f out: nt clr run 1 1/2f out: styd on steadily fnl f* **62/10**

4 *4* **Mount Helicon**[44] 3-8-11 .... OPeslier 9 97
(A Fabre, France) *a.p: 3rd st: ev ch 1 1/2f out: one pce* **9/2**[3]

5 *½* **Hello Morning (FR)**[18] 2654 3-8-11 .... AlexisBadel 5 97
(Mme C Head-Maarek, France) *hld up in rr: hdwy on ins and 7th st: tried for run on rails and blocked jst over 2f out: moved lft: styd on fnl f* **11/1**

6 *2½* **Cinq Cinq (FR)**[25] 2441 3-8-11 .... FBlondel 1 93
(J P Sabatino, France) *a cl up: 4th st: led 2f out to 1 1/2f out: rdn and wknd appr fnl f* **23/1**

7 *2½* **Weald**[19] 2636 3-8-11 .... TThulliez 7 89
(P Bary, France) *9th st: nvr a factor* **3/1**[2]

8 *3* **Ripple (FR)**[38] 2064 3-8-11 .... C-PLemaire 3 84
(J-C Rouget, France) *disp ld early: 2nd st: ev ch 1 1/2f out: sn wknd* **6/4**[1]

9 *8* **Beret Rouge (IRE)**[37] 3-8-11 .... FDiFede 2 71
(A De Royer-Dupre, France) *s.s: pushed along to ld after 2f: hdd 2f out: sn wknd* **6/4**[1]

10 *2* **Cabaretune (FR)**[28] 3-8-11 .... MGuyon 10 68
(F Doumen, France) *disp ld early: 6th st: btn 2f out* **79/1**

2m 28.9s (-2.30) **Going Correction** +0.15s/f (Good) **10** Ran SP% **197.1**
Speed ratings: **113,111,111,108,108 106,105,103,97,96**
PARI-MUTUEL: WIN 2.50 (coupled with Beret Rouge & Ripple); PL 1.80, 3.50, 2.30; DF 22.00.
Owner H H Aga Khan **Bred** Snc Lagardere Elevage **Trained** Chantilly, France

NOTEBOOK
Montmartre(FR) was always going well within himself off a workmanlike pace set by his stablemate. Two furlongs out he was asked to make his move up the centre of the track and by the furlong pole he had engaged top gear and accelerated impressively away from the other nine runners. Galloping strongly to the line to win by two lengths, he clearly appreciated this longer distance, and connections have now marked him down for the Grand Prix de Paris on July 14.
Zack Dream(FR), held up at the back of the field, began to make his move at the two-furlong marker and showed good acceleration but never looked like troubling the winner. He just held on for second and is an immature sort who can only improve from this. Connections are unsure of future plans for the moment.
Watar(IRE), another who was held up for much of the race, got squeezed by the eventual second and fourth a furlong and a half out and had to be checked. When he saw daylight he fairly flew through the last furlong and was only just touched off for second place. He does not hold an entry in the Grand Prix de Paris so will have to be supplemented into the Group 1 event. Connections are undecided at this stage.
Mount Helicon, who was always well up, was given every chance but was one-paced in the closing stages.

3152 ASCOT (R-H)
Friday, June 20

OFFICIAL GOING: Firm (good to firm in places)
Despite 8mm of water being put on the track since the previous day's racing, the ground continued to dry out and was riding really quick.
Wind: Moderate, against

3192 ALBANY STKS (GROUP 3) (FILLIES) — 6f
2:30 (2:32) (Class 1) 2-Y-0
£39,739 (£15,064; £7,539; £3,759; £1,883; £945) **Stalls** Centre

Form — RPR

1 **1** **Cuis Ghaire (IRE)**[18] 2686 2-8-12 0................................... KJManning 4 101+
(J S Bolger, Ire) *w'like: str: trckd ldrs: rdn wl over 1f out: r.o wl to ld ins fnl f: wl on top towards fin* **8/11**[1]

311 **2** *1¾* **Penny's Gift**[7] 2987 2-8-12 0... RyanMoore 7 96
(R Hannon) *str: in tch: hdwy over 2f out: rdn to ld wl over 1f out: hdd ins fnl f: hld cl home* **12/1**[3]

01 **3** *hd* **Danidh Dubai (IRE)**[41] 1987 2-8-12 0................................... ChrisCatlin 3 95
(M R Channon) *hld up: hdwy whn nt clr run over 2f out: edgd rt whn proging ins fnl f: fin wl* **25/1**

2 **4** *½* **African Skies**[20] 2627 2-8-12 0... NCallan 13 94+
(K A Ryan) *w'like: racd keenly: hld up: swtchd lft and hdwy under 2f out: styd on wl towards fin: nt quite pce to shake-up ldrs* **20/1**

122 **5** *½* **April Pride**[35] 2147 2-8-12 0... RichardHughes 5 92
(R Hannon) *lw: led: rdn and hdd wl over 1f out: styd on same pce towards fin* **20/1**

61 **6** *hd* **Ares Choix**[24] 2485 2-8-12 0... KerrinMcEvoy 6 92
(P C Haslam) *str: racd keenly: pressed ldr: rdn over 1f out whn stl chalng: kpt on same pce fnl 100yds* **50/1**

21 **7** *1* **Art Princess (USA)**[42] 1961 2-8-12 0...................................... MichaelHills 11 89
(B W Hills) *lw: hld up: hdwy 1/2-way: rdn on outside to chse ldrs over 1f out: no ex fnl 75yds* **16/1**

1233 **8** *nk* **Aspen Darlin (IRE)**[23] 2497 2-8-12 0.. JMurtagh 1 88
(A Bailey) *racd keenly: hld up: rdn 1/2-way: hdwy over 2f out: one pce ins fnl f*

2 **9** *nk* **Salsa Star (USA)**[28] 2377 2-8-12 0... PaulHanagan 12 87
(R A Fahey) *w'like: hld up: hdwy over 2f out: no imp on ldrs whn flashed tail ins fnl f* **25/1**

10 *½* **Jet D'Eau (FR)**[18] 2-8-12 0..(b) LDettori 15 85
(R Pritchard-Gordon, France) *leggy: awkward s: sn pushed along towards rr: sme prog ins fnl f: nvr gng pce to get competitive* **14/1**

1 **11** *9* **Please Sing**[24] 2479 2-8-12 0... DarryllHolland 9 58
(M R Channon) *unf: scope: lw: fractious at s: in tch: rdn 2f out: wknd over 1f out* **6/1**[2]

1 **12** *8* **Foxtrot Alpha (IRE)**[13] 2835 2-8-12 0... StephenCarson 8 34
(P Winkworth) *swtg: midfield: effrt and hdwy over 2f out to chse ldrs: wknd over 1f out* **50/1**

24 **13** *11* **Aahaygirl (IRE)**[23] 2497 2-8-12 0.. FergusSweeney 14 —
(K R Burke) *w'like: swtg: wnt rt s: in tch on outside: rdn 1/2-way: wknd 2f out* **66/1**

1 **14** *7* **Daisy Moses (IRE)**[48] 1794 2-8-12 0.. JimmyFortune 2 —
(D Nicholls) *tall: leggy: scope: racd keenly: pressed ldrs: nudged along 1/2-way: wknd over 2f out* **33/1**

1m 15.72s (1.32) **Going Correction** +0.125s/f (Good) **14** Ran SP% **122.8**
Speed ratings (Par 100): **96,93,93,92,92 91,90,90,89,89 77,66,51,42**
toteswinger: 1&2 £3.90, 1&3 £8.20, 2&3 £44.10. CSF £8.69 CT £143.60 TOTE £1.80: £1.10, £3.60, £6.00; EX 12.40 Trifecta £215.70 Pool: £4592.33 - 15.75 winning units.
Owner Mrs J S Bolger **Bred** J S Bolger **Trained** Coolcullen, Co Carlow

FOCUS
There have been only six previous runnings of the Albany Stakes - it was upgraded from Listed status in 2005 - and the race has yet to have much impact on the domestic Classics, but it often produces its share of good fillies. A field of 14 was down on last year, when 20 lined up, and the overall quality seemed relatively ordinary. Indeed the classy winner did not need to reproduce her previous level. They raced towards the stands' side, but rather surprisingly the jockeys seemed happy to avoid the near rail. They didn't go as quick early on as one might have expected.

NOTEBOOK
Cuis Ghaire(IRE) ◆'s maiden win over 6f at Naas hasn't really worked out this week, but she had shown herself to be a smart filly when winning the Group 3 Swordlestown Sprint Stakes on her next start, and escaped a penalty for that success. The only real concern was that as a daughter of Galileo she might not have the pace to cope with such a speed test. As it turned out, the early gallop was surprisingly modest, and she ended up taking a bit of a grip passing the four-furlong pole. She was much happier once switched to the left of early-leader April Pride, but was flat footed when the pace began to increase approaching the two-furlong pole and briefly looked in trouble before her stamina kicked in and she kept finding to get on top in the final furlong. The bare form does not look anything special at this stage, but as she is bred to appreciate trips of 1m-plus she is potentially high class. She is likely to be aimed at the Debutante Stakes at the Curragh, a 7f Group 2 in August, and, if all goes according to plan, she would then go for the Moyglare Stud Stakes, a Group 1 over the same course and distance which her stable landed last year with Saoirse Abu. (op 10-11 tchd Evens in places)
Penny's Gift, aimed at this event since landing the second of two races at Chepstow, ran well in defeat. She was given every chance by Ryan Moore, but was simply beaten by a better filly. She may be aimed at the Super Sprint, a race in which her stable has a great record. (op 11-1 tchd 14-1, 16-1 in a place)

Danidh Dubai(IRE) ◆, whose trainer won this race with Silca's Gift in 2003 and last year with Nijoom Dubai, came here off the back of a success in a 6f maiden at Haydock and ran a solid race in third. She struggled to get a good position early on, and had to come from further back than the front two, but she finished well and might have got second in a few more strides. She looks the type to run well in something like the Cherry Hinton, with the Newmarket July course's stiff finish almost sure to suit, and the winner of that race has come out of the Albany in three of the last four years.

African Skies ◆ was said by Kevin Ryan to have improved a lot since running second over this trip at York on her debut and produced a very good effort considering she did not get the run of things. She was dropped in from her wide draw, with Neil Callan presumably keen not to let her get stuck out towards the centre of the track, but she was soon well back and took a grip off the ordinary early pace. She was struggling to make up the lost ground when the race got serious, but kept plugging away and looks pretty smart. Like the third home, something like the Cherry Hinton could be a suitable target, although she also has the option of returning to maiden company. (op 16-1)

April Pride took them along at a sensible pace on this step up in trip, with Richard Hughes looking to save a bit, and she is possibly a touch flattered. Still, there was a lot to like about the way she stuck to her task and she has an entry in the Redcar Two-Year-Old Trophy.

Ares Choix, a winner over this trip at Redcar on her previous start, showed bags of speed but did not quite see out her race. Her dam was a 1m2f winner, but she is by Choisir and, on this evidence, she would not mind a drop back to 5f. Slightly easier ground may also suit better. (op 40-1)

Art Princess(USA), targeted at this race since winning over 5f at Nottingham on her second start (Ares Choix sixth), was stuck out wide towards the middle of the track for much of the way and made only a short-lived effort. (op 14-1)

Aspen Darlin(IRE) did not help her chances by racing keenly.

Salsa Star(USA) is held in high regard by Richard Fahey, but she failed to land a telling blow and flashed her tail when hit with the whip. (op 28-1)

Jet D'Eau(FR) had won her first two starts on easier ground, but she was never going this time. (op 12-1)

Please Sing, a stablemate of the third and winner of a 5f maiden at Leicester on her debut, was the only one backed against the favourite, but she played up beforehand, getting rid of her rider at the start and needing a blanket for stalls entry, and she ran no race. (op 8-1 tchd 10-1 in a place)

Daisy Moses(IRE) Official explanation: jockey said filly ran too free

3193 KING EDWARD VII STKS (GROUP 2) (C&G) 1m 4f

3:05 (3:06) (Class 1) 3-Y-O

£134,317 (£50,916; £25,481; £12,705; £6,364; £3,194) **Stalls** High

Form / RPR

-113 **1** **Campanologist (USA)**[41] 1992 3-8-12 107 ..... LDettori 2 110
(Saeed Bin Suroor) *lw: mde all: shkn up and qcknd wl over 2f out: r.o wl* **9/1**

1-31 **2** ¾ **Conduit (IRE)**[13] 2825 3-8-12 98 ..... RyanMoore 4 112+
(Sir Michael Stoute) *lw: hld up in midfield: hdwy 5f out: bmpd and rdn 3f out: unable qck tl hdwy over 1f out: swtchd lft jst ins fnl f: r.o strly to go 2nd wl ins fnl f: nt rch wnr* **11/4**[1]

143 **3** 1 **Top Lock**[30] 2303 3-8-12 100 ..... MartinDwyer 1 107
(A M Balding) *lw: chsd wnr: hdwy to press wnr 4f out: ev ch and rdn wl over 2f out: keeping on same pce whn hung lft ent fnl f: lost 2nd wl ins fnl f* **40/1**

1-12 **4** nk **All The Aces (IRE)**[43] 1922 3-8-12 111 ..... PhilipRobinson 8 107
(M A Jarvis) *swtg: chsd ldrs: rdn 3f out: outpcd 2f out: rallied fnl f: styd on but nt pce to threaten wnr* **13/2**

213 **5** 2 **Moiqen (IRE)**[40] 2023 3-8-12 0 ..... DPMcDonogh 7 103
(Kevin Prendergast, Ire) *w'like: tall: chsd ldrs: rdn and effrt wl over 2f out: kpt on same pce fr over 1f out* **16/1**

2-61 **6** 2 **City Leader (IRE)**[30] 2303 3-8-12 111 ..... JamieSpencer 6 100
(B J Meehan) *stdd and jostled s: t.k.h: hld up in rr: hdwy 3f out: sn rdn and swtchd lft: no imp fr over 1f out* **8/1**

1-11 **7** nse **Bronze Cannon (USA)**[26] 2425 3-8-12 94 ..... JimmyFortune 3 100+
(J H M Gosden) *s.i.s: hld up in last: stl last 3f out: plld out and rdn wl over 2f out: kpt on but nvr pce to trble ldrs* **10/3**[2]

8 1 ½ **Winchester (USA)**[13] 2854 3-8-12 0 ..... PJSmullen 5 98
(D K Weld, Ire) *w'like: scope: wnt rt and jostled rival s: hld up in tch: plld out and bmpd rival wl over 2f out: sn rdn and unable qck: short of room over 1f out: wl hld and wandering after* **14/1**

321 **9** nse **Hebridean (IRE)**[26] 2435 3-8-12 0 ..... JMurtagh 9 98
(A P O'Brien, Ire) *w'like: str: t.k.h: hld up in last trio: rdn and effrt wl over 2f out: no prog* **9/2**[3]

2m 31.24s (-4.26) **Going Correction** -0.05s/f (Good) **9** Ran SP% **117.4**
Speed ratings (Par 111): **112,111,110,110,109 107,107,106,106**
toteswinger: 1&2 £6.00, 1&3 £29.40, 2&3 £886.80. CSF £34.61 CT £963.41 TOTE £9.10: £2.20, £1.50, £8.00; EX 46.50 Trifecta £886.80 Pool: £6699.10 - 5.59 winning units.
Owner Godolphin **Bred** Darley **Trained** Newmarket, Suffolk

■ Europe's richest Group 2 contest following two supplementary entries of £20,000.

FOCUS

Despite the Epsom Derby form going unrepresented, on paper this still looked like a reasonable renewal, with some sort of case to be made for almost the entire field. However, the form needs treating with caution as the winner, Campanologist, was able to dictate a most gallop for much of the way. They were still reasonably well bunched at the top of the straight and it proved hard to make up significant amounts of ground. The winner was given a great ride by Frankie Dettori, and the runner-up was probably the best horse in the race.

NOTEBOOK

Campanologist(USA), a progressive type for Mark Johnston who was acquired by Godolphin after winning the Listed Fielden Stakes at Newmarket in April, was not quite at his best when third on his debut for his new connections in the Lingfield Derby Trial but, upped to his furthest trip to date, he took full advantage of having the run of the race. Having set an ordinary gallop for much of the way, he caught most of his rivals flat footed when going for home early in the straight and was just able to hold off the fast-finishing Conduit. It would be difficult to see him confirming form with the runner-up in a stronger-run race, but his connections said he is still on the weak side and expect him to make a better four-year-old. It remains to be seen where he will go next, but the Great Voltigeur Stakes at York is a possible target. (op 12-1)

Conduit(IRE) ◆ was supplemented at a cost of £20,000 after running out a mightily impressive winner of a hot 1m2f Epsom handicap off a mark of 85 on Derby day and he can probably be considered a little unlucky as, not only did he not have the race run to suit, but he was also bumped off the home bend. Stepped up to 1m4f for the first time, the modest pace was totally against him and he just got going too late, having unsurprisingly failed to quicken in the straight after being held up a little way off the ordinary pace set by Campanologist. He was motoring at the finish, suggesting he would have won off a stronger gallop, and he is quickly progressing into a very smart colt. He has had two quick races, so could well be given a short break, and is another who could well go for something like the Great Voltigeur later in the season. (op 3-1 tchd 10-3, 7-2 in places)

Top Lock was only third behind City Leader in a Listed race at Goodwood on his previous start and, while this was obviously better, he looks a little flattered. He was well placed considering the lack of early pace and stuck on for third in a race few were able to make up ground. He is apparently being aimed at the German Derby. (op 50-1)

All The Aces(IRE), another supplemented at a cost of £20,000, could not match the form he showed when beaten only half a length by Derby fourth Doctor Fremantle in the Chester Vase on his previous start. However, he did not have the race run to suit and probably found this ground plenty quick enough as well. (op 6-1)

Moiqen(IRE), third in the Derrinstown Stud Derby Trial on his previous start, was trying 1m4f for the first time, but he failed to land a blow.

City Leader(IRE) had Top Lock behind when winning a Listed race at Goodwood on his previous start, so this could be considered disappointing, but he was basically too keen for his own good and would have preferred a stronger pace to run at. (op 9-1 tchd 10-1 in a place)

Bronze Cannon(USA), a most progressive handicapper who just held Doctor Fremantle off level weights over 1m2f at Newmarket two starts back, came here instead of a tilt at the Derby, but he failed to run a race. He was held up last, so the ordinary pace would have been totally against him, and he failed to make any impression in the straight. (op 7-2 tchd 4-1 in places)

Winchester(USA), an athletic sort stepping up in trip, had something to find in this company and was well held. (op 11-1)

Hebridean(IRE), the only gelding in the line up, has progressed nicely to win his last two starts, including a Group 3 at the Curragh on his latest outing, but he was well beaten this time. He was keen enough early, suggesting the steady pace was against him. (tchd 5-1)

3194 CORONATION STKS (GROUP 1) (FILLIES) 1m (R)

3:45 (3:47) (Class 1) 3-Y-O

£154,698 (£58,642; £29,348; £14,633; £7,330; £3,678) **Stalls** High

Form / RPR

0615 **1** **Lush Lashes**[14] 2792 3-9-0 0 ..... KJManning 3 121+
(J S Bolger, Ire) *lw: a.p: rdn to chal 2f out: led over 1f out: sn strly pressed: r.o to draw away ins fnl 100yrds* **5/1**[2]

1-14 **2** 3 ¼ **Infallible**[47] 1830 3-9-0 110 ..... JimmyFortune 11 112+
(J H M Gosden) *lw: hld up: hdwy and swtchd lft 2f out: rdn to move upsides wnr over 1f out: no ex ins fnl 100yrds* **11/2**[3]

-114 **3** ¾ **Carribean Sunset (IRE)**[26] 2433 3-9-0 0 ..... PJSmullen 5 110
(D K Weld, Ire) *lengthy: trckd ldrs: rdn 2f out: edgd lft sltly over 1f out whn unable qck: kpt on u.p ins fnl f but a hld* **16/1**

11-2 **4** ½ **Spacious**[47] 1830 3-9-0 112 ..... JamieSpencer 9 109
(J R Fanshawe) *bmpd sn after s: hld up in midfield: rdn and nt qckn 2f out: hdwy 1f out: styng on whn edgd rt ins fnl f: swtchd lft whn flattened out towards fin* **9/4**[1]

1-10 **5** ½ **Muthabara (IRE)**[47] 1830 3-9-0 107 ..... RHills 8 108
(J L Dunlop) *bustled along leaving stalls: racd keenly in midfield: rdn 2f out: styd on ins fnl f but nt gng pce to threaten ldrs* **10/1**

-050 **6** 2 **Nahoodh (IRE)**[26] 2433 3-9-0 112 ..... LDettori 10 103
(M Johnston) *led: rdn and hdd over 1f out: wknd ins fnl f* **10/1**

06 **7** hd **Psalm (IRE)**[40] 2033 3-9-0 0 ..... JMurtagh 1 102
(A P O'Brien, Ire) *str: in midfield: pushed along over 2f out: hung rt over 1f out: plugged on at one pce ins fnl f: eased whn no imp towards fin* **9/1**

31-1 **8** 1 ½ **Raymi Coya (CAN)**[35] 2170 3-9-0 102 ..... KerrinMcEvoy 7 99
(M Botti) *bmpd sn after s: towards rr: rdn over 2f out: nvr able to trble ldrs* **25/1**

23-2 **9** 6 **Tuscan Evening (IRE)**[26] 2433 3-9-0 0 ..... MJKinane 6 85
(John Joseph Murphy, Ire) *midfield: stdd after 2f to r in rr: struggling over 2f out: n.d* **25/1**

-241 **10** 2 ½ **Modern Look**[19] 2651 3-9-0 0 ..... SPasquier 4 79+
(D Smaga, France) *lw: prom: rdn whn chalng over 2f out: 4th and struggling to hold pl whn n.m.r and squeezed out over 1f out: sn eased* **7/1**

6013 **11** 3 ¼ **Love Of Dubai (USA)**[19] 2655 3-9-0 106 .....(p) DarryllHolland 2 72
(C E Brittain) *racd keenly in midfield: rdn over 2f out: wknd over 1f out* **33/1**

1m 39.23s (-1.57) **Going Correction** -0.05s/f (Good) **11** Ran SP% **120.0**
Speed ratings (Par 110): **105,101,101,100,100 98,97,96,90,87 84**
toteswinger: 1&2 £5.70, 1&3 £14.80, 2&3 £16.80. CSF £32.71 CT £422.93 TOTE £6.30: £2.50, £2.60, £4.10; EX 35.30 Trifecta £714.20 Pool: £12836.56 - 13.30 winning units.
Owner Mrs J S Bolger **Bred** Mrs A M Jenkins **Trained** Coolcullen, Co Carlow

FOCUS

Unusually, this did not attract the winner of the 1,000 Guineas or its Irish and French equivalents. However, the form of those races was well represented, with five of the first eight from Newmarket, two of the first six from Longchamp, and three of the first seven from the Curragh. It was a decent renewal, and it was run in a time only just outside the record set by Nannina in the race two years ago. Lush Lashes saw out the finish much more strongly than Infallible. Carribean Sunset seemed to run pretty much to her Irish Guineas form.

NOTEBOOK

Lush Lashes was a real eye-catcher when a fast-finishing sixth in the 1000 Guineas at Newmarket, and confirmed that promise with an impressive success over 1m2f in the Musidora at York, but she was a beaten favourite in the Oaks at Epsom, not appearing to handle the track and possibly failing to see out the trip. Dropped back in distance, her rider seemed keen not to let her get too far back and she travelled well for much of the way. Produced with her challenge in the straight, she momentarily looked vulnerable when Infallible ranged upsides, but she ran on really strongly, pulling away for a most decisive success. Having shown her versatility with big wins over both 1m and 1m2f, she will bid to make up for the disappointment of Epsom in the Irish Oaks but, while the more conventional track will suit, she will have her stamina to prove. (op 7-1)

Infallible ◆, the 1000 Guineas fourth, was held up early on and there was a danger she might get trapped starting up the straight, but Jimmy Fortune extricated her in good time and she showed good tactical speed between the 2f and 1f markers to get almost upsides Lush Lashes. However, the final furlong of this stiffish mile found her out and she was basically outstayed by Lush Lashes. She handled the quick ground surprisingly well for a daughter of Pivotal, but an easier surface will probably suit her best. She is likely to be better suited by 7f too, and probably even has the speed for 6f. (op 7-2)

Carribean Sunset(IRE), the winner of two Group 3 contests before being promoted into third in the Irish Guineas, was up there all the way and ran well. Dermot Weld, who has done so well on the international scene, is considering stepping her up in trip for the American Oaks at Hollywood Park, a race he won in 2003 with Dimitrova. The Falmouth Stakes is also an option. (tchd 20-1 in a place)

Spacious, runner-up in the 1000 Guineas at Newmarket on her reappearance, could only manage fourth this time. Unable to quicken and inclined to lug to the right, away from the whip, the big, rangy filly was probably not suited by such a quick surface. Her connections felt she lacked her usual spark, but she is very much the type to come into her own in the latter part of this year, and next season. She should be better suited by slightly easier ground and may also benefit from a step up in trip in time. (op 11-4 tchd 3-1, 7-2 in a place)

Muthabara(IRE) has taken time getting her coat and still wasn't among the more attractive members of the field. She was a bit keen early but kept on for a respectable fifth. She looks worth a try over further and is another who probably wants slightly easier ground. (op 11-1)

Nahoodh(IRE), having her first start since leaving Mick Channon, had very different tactics employed this time having looked unlucky under a hold-up ride in the 1000 Guineas, and run below form in the Irish version. She was taken straight to the front, but once joined in the straight she had little more to offer. (tchd 11-1)

Psalm(IRE) looked much better than the bare form of her recent sixth behind Zarkava in the French Guineas, but she was unable to build on that effort with this ground probably much quicker than ideal. She is still a maiden, but is very talented and can do better when there is more give underfoot. Official explanation: jockey said filly hung right. (op 8-1)

Raymi Coya(CAN) won a Group 3 at Newmarket on her final start and two and landed a Listed race at York on her reappearance, but this represented a big step up in class and she was well held. (op 33-1)

Tuscan Evening(IRE), second past the post in the Irsh Guineas but demoted to fourth, was well below that form this time. Official explanation: trainer later said filly met interference at the start and finished sore post-race (op 28-1 tchd 33-1)

Modern Look, a Group 2 winner at Chantilly since her French Guineas fourth, was struggling to hold her place when she was tightened up between the winner and Carribean Sunset. She was also reported to have lost her action. Official explanation: jockey said filly lost her action (op 8-1 tchd 13-2)

Love Of Dubai(USA), the Italian Guineas winner, has had a very busy time and trailed the field. (op 40-1)

3195 WOLFERTON H'CAP STKS (LISTED RACE) — 1m 2f

4:20 (4:23) (Class 1) (0-110,110) 4-Y-0+

£34,062 (£12,912; £6,462; £3,222; £1,614; £810) **Stalls** High

Form				RPR
0-43	**1**		**Supaseus**^{37} 2103 5-8-11 **100** .... SteveDrowne 10 (H Morrison) *mde all: rdn over 2f out: battled on gamely* **12/1**	110
-022	**2**	*1*	**Many Volumes (USA)**^{23} 2503 4-9-5 **108** .... TedDurcan 13 (H R A Cecil) *lw: chsd wnr for 1f: chsd ldng pair after: nt clr run jst over 2f out: sn swtchd lft and forced way out: chsd wnr u.p after: edgd rt and unable qck fnl f* **17/2**	116
3-44	**3**	*shd*	**Pinpoint (IRE)**^{23} 2503 6-9-2 **105** .... AdamKirby 3 (W R Swinburn) *hld up in rr: hdwy and rdn over 2f out: edgd rt briefly over 1f out: r.o wl: nt rch wnr* **16/1**	113+
11-0	**4**	*hd*	**Buccellati**^{22} 2543 4-8-12 **101** .... (v) WilliamBuick 16 (A M Balding) *t.k.h: hld up in midfield: hdwy 3f out: swtchd rt and unable qck u.p over 1f out: styng on whn nt clr run ins fnl f: unable to chal wnr* **13/2**^{3}	108+
5004	**5**	*nk*	**Halicarnassus (IRE)**^{26} 2432 4-9-5 **108** .... (v^{1}) DarryllHolland 12 (M R Channon) *plld hrd: hld up in last: c wd and rdn wl over 2f out: stl last 2f out: r.o strly fnl f: nt rch ldrs* **8/1**	115+
16-3	**6**	*¾*	**Monte Alto (IRE)**^{25} 2465 4-8-11 **100** .... JMurtagh 4 (L M Cumani) *t.k.h: hld up in last pair: plld out and rdn wl over 2f out: r.o but nvr pce to rch ldrs* **3/1**^{1}	105+
0250	**7**	*¾*	**Illustrious Blue**^{17} 2708 5-9-4 **107** .... (v^{1}) RichardKingscote 11 (W J Knight) *t.k.h: hld up in midfield: rdn over 2f out: swtchd rt over 1f out: kpt on but nvr pce to threaten ldrs* **16/1**	111
0115	**8**	*3*	**Watamu (IRE)**^{35} 2168 7-9-1 **104** .... (v) SebSanders 7 (P J Makin) *plld hrd: hld up in midfield: hdwy 4f out: chsd ldrs and rdn over 2f out: wknd wl over 1f out* **14/1**	102
56-1	**9**	*4 ½*	**Emirates Skyline (USA)**^{14} 2790 5-9-6 **109** .... LDettori 9 (Saeed Bin Suroor) *lw: chsd wnr after 1f: rdn over 2f out: bmpd and lost position 2f out: wknd over 1f out* **4/1**^{2}	98
-022	**10**	*12*	**Under The Rainbow**^{27} 2402 5-9-1 **104** .... (b^{1}) NCallan 6 (B W Hills) *t.k.h: chsd ldrs: rdn over 2f out: sn wknd: eased ins fnl f* **14/1**	69

2m 6.81s (-2.99) **Going Correction** -0.05s/f (Good) **10** Ran SP% **112.8**
Speed ratings (Par 111): **109,108,108,107,107 107,106,104,100,90**
toteswinger: 1&2 £20.30, 1&3 £26.20, 2&3 £19.70. CSF £101.04 CT £1413.73 TOTE £15.80: £3.80, £3.00, £5.70; EX 102.20 Trifecta £1699.20 Pool: 4156.30 - 1.81 winning units.

Owner Ben & Sir Martyn Arbib **Bred** Arbib Bloodstock Partnership **Trained** East Ilsley, Berks

■ Soapy Danger was withdrawn at the start (10/1, deduct 5p in the £ under rule 4).

FOCUS

A solid-looking Listed handicap but the early pace was modest, meaning many horses were pulling very hard. The last five runnings had been won by four-year-olds and that age group provided four of the remaining ten contestants following six withdrawals. However, this time the race went to the five-year-old Supaseus, who dictated a modest early-gallop and won under a canny ride. The form is rated through the second and fourth.

NOTEBOOK

Supaseus prevailed under a well-judged front-running ride from Steve Drowne. He had run well to finish third off a 4lb lower mark on his first try at this trip at York last month and, in a race in which nothing else wanted to go on, he was able to dictate at his own pace, which caused several of his rivals to take a grip. Having stacked the opposition up, he quickened off the final bend and had enough in reserve to hold the challengers. He may go for the John Smith's Cup at York next month under a 5lb penalty. (tchd 14-1)

Many Volumes(USA) was one of quite a few to race keenly early on, but he was always in a good position just behind the leader. Although briefly short of room when hemmed in by the weakening Emirates Skyline passing the two-furlong pole, he got out in plenty of time and had every chance. This was his third consecutive second placing and he deserves a change of luck (op 10-1)

Pinpoint(IRE) returned to something close to his best form after a couple of modest efforts this season. He looked as though he might even win at one stage when produced with his effort from off the pace, but he was making little impression on the winner in the last half-furlong despite staying on well. (op 20-1 tchd 22-1)

Buccellati ◆, with the visor back on, pulled harder than most in the early stages just behind the leaders. He did not have a great deal of room on a couple of occasions inside the last two furlongs, otherwise he may well have finished second. This was a decent effort under the circumstances and he can win a nice race. The John Smith's Cup next month, where a strong pace is almost guaranteed, could well be made for him. (tchd 6-1 and 7-1, 15-2 in places)

Halicarnassus(IRE), back in handicap company after finishing fourth to Duke Of Marmalade in the Tattersalls Gold Cup at the Curragh last month, got badly messed about when the field crowded in towards the inside rail after the start and then took a fierce hold out the back, which may have been due to the first-time visor he wore. He was still last passing the two-furlong pole and was switched very wide in order to make his effort, but although he finished very strongly he was never going to get there. (op 10-1)

Monte Alto(IRE), the well-backed favourite, was forced to make his effort down the middle of the straight after being towards the rear early. For a moment, he looked like bridging the gap to the leaders but his effort soon flattened out and he never really got involved. He undoubtedly would have wanted a stronger pace, so can easily be given another chance. (tchd 7-2, 4-1 in places)

Illustrious Blue stayed on quite well but ruined his chance by pulling too hard in the early stages. He is much more effective off a strong pace. (op 18-1 tchd 20-1)

Watamu(IRE) was pulling his jockey's arms out in the early stages, so it did not come as a shock when he had nothing left when asked to quicken. (tchd 16-1)

Emirates Skyline(USA) was disappointing considering he was well placed throughout. Perhaps this race came too soon after his recent successful return to action at Epsom following an 11-month absence. Official explanation: jockey said gelding ran flat (op 7-2 tchd 9-2 in a place)

Under The Rainbow pulled too hard in the first-time blinkers and ran no sort of race. (op 20-1)

3196 QUEEN'S VASE (GROUP 3) — 2m

4:55 (4:55) (Class 1) 3-Y-0

£34,062 (£12,912; £6,462; £3,222; £1,614; £810) **Stalls** High

Form				RPR
-321	**1**		**Patkai (IRE)**^{20} 2610 3-9-1 104 .... RyanMoore 7 (Sir Michael Stoute) *lw: a shade keen early: hld up: hdwy 5f out: qcknd up on outside to ld wl over 1f out: sn edgd rt and clr: impressive* **6/4**^{1}	103+
0-11	**2**	*7*	**Amerigo (IRE)**^{30} 2310 3-9-1 93 .... PhilipRobinson 1 (M A Jarvis) *lw: trckd ldrs: effrt over 2f out: chalng for pls whn wnr had flown appr fnl f: tk 2nd post* **14/1**	94
541	**3**	*shd*	**Gravitation**^{18} 2669 3-8-12 80 .... AlanMunro 10 (W Jarvis) *racd keenly in midfield: hdwy 1/2-way: rdn and hung rt whn chsd ldrs over 2f out: continued to chal for pls appr fnl f: no ch w wnr* **33/1**	91
20	**4**	*½*	**Tiffany Diamond (IRE)**^{14} 2792 3-8-12 0 .... JMurtagh 3 (A P O'Brien, Ire) *hld up: rdn and hdwy 2f out: styd on u.p appr fnl f whn chalng for plcs: no ch w wnr* **8/1**^{3}	91+
-121	**5**	*¾*	**Enroller (IRE)**^{34} 2201 3-9-1 94 .... MartinDwyer 13 (W R Muir) *trckd ldrs: pushed along 3f out: outpcd and lost pl over 2f out: kpt on u.p ins fnl f: no ch* **20/1**	93
-150	**6**	*1 ½*	**Judgethemoment (USA)**^{18} 2675 3-9-1 75 .... JohnEgan 8 (Jane Chapple-Hyam) *midfield: nudged along 5f out: rdn and lost pl over 2f out: styd on ins fnl f: nvr able to chal* **50/1**	91
0551	**7**	*nk*	**Moment's Notice**^{20} 2603 3-9-1 76 .... GeorgeBaker 5 (S Kirk) *swtchd rt s: hld up: rdn over 2f out: kpt on u.p fnl f: nvr able to chal* **66/1**	91
46-5	**8**	*¾*	**Donegal (USA)**^{43} 1922 3-9-1 100 .... WilliamBuick 9 (A M Balding) *racd keenly: prom: wnt 2nd 11f out: sn w ldr: rdn whn chalng over 2f out: outpcd over 1f out: wknd fnl f* **25/1**	90
1151	**9**	*½*	**Captain Webb**^{35} 2142 3-9-1 96 .... JoeFanning 11 (M Johnston) *lw: led: rdn over 2f out: hdd wl over 1f out: wknd fnl f* **9/2**^{2}	89
5-11	**10**	*nk*	**Unleashed (IRE)**^{9} 2948 3-9-1 82 .... TedDurcan 4 (H R A Cecil) *hld up: rdn on outside 2f out: edgd rt appr fnl f: eased whn no imp wl ins fnl f* **16/1**	89
1-13	**11**	*¾*	**Age Of Reason (UAE)**^{27} 2408 3-9-1 101 .... KerrinMcEvoy 2 (M Johnston) *w ldr tl 11f out: rdn 2f out: keeping on u.p whn n.m.r over 1f out: nt clr run but nt pce to chal whn eased ins fnl f* **12/1**	92+
	12	*nk*	**Ebadiyan (IRE)**^{47} 1846 3-9-1 0 .... (p) MJKinane 12 (John M Oxx, Ire) *lw: w'like: midfield: lost pl over 3f out: outpcd after: eased whn n.d wl ins fnl f* **9/2**^{2}	88

3m 27.86s (-4.74) **Going Correction** -0.05s/f (Good) **12** Ran SP% **122.7**
Speed ratings (Par 109): **109,105,105,105,104 104,103,103,103,103 102,102**
toteswinger: 1&2 £6.50, 1&3 £18.80, 2&3 £51.10. CSF £25.95 CT £531.57 TOTE £2.60: £1.30, £3.40, £9.60; EX 25.20 Trifecta £731.50 Pool; £5842.34 - 5.91 winning units.

Owner Ballymacoll Stud **Bred** Ballymacoll Stud Farm Ltd **Trained** Newmarket, Suffolk

FOCUS

A tough test for mainly inexperienced three-year-olds. The last two winners, Mahler and Soapy Danger, have gone on to prove themselves at a similar level and above, and Patkai looks sure to follow in their footsteps after a impressive success. However, he stood out on pre-race form and with his main dangers below form it would be hard to rate this race highly.

NOTEBOOK

Patkai(IRE) ◆ won in great style on his first attempt at 2m, quickening clear in a matter of strides just over a furlong out. Pushed out to the line, he was full value for the wide margin, confirming that he is progressing with every run. Related to Islington and Greek Dance, who got better with maturity, the omens are good for this colt and wherever his trainer decides to send him, he is very much a horse to follow until beaten. The owner already has two possible contenders for the St Leger in current market leader Tartan Bearer and Conduit, but he would be an able deputy for either if running in the final Classic of the season. (op 11-8 tchd 13-8 in places)

Amerigo(IRE), who has improved with every run, lacked the finishing kick of the winner, but outstayed the rest of his rivals in grim style throughout the final furlong. Connections are eyeing the Doncaster Cup, in which there are favourable terms for three-year-olds, but he is seen as a potential Cup horse next year as he strengthens up physically and mentally. (op 12-1)

Gravitation, stepping up in trip by half a mile, just got mugged for second, but this was another progressive effort, especially as she was incredibly keen for the first half of the contest. She looks to have improved for quicker ground and connections mentioned the Park Hill Stakes as a target. (op 28-1 tchd 50-1 in a place)

Tiffany Diamond(IRE), who was heavily eased in the Oaks after failing to get involved, travelled strongly at the rear of the field and briefly looked threatening about two furlongs from home. However, Patkai had already flown (she tracked him in the early stages) and her effort flattened out a touch in the final half a furlong. She is a tough sort who should win again this season if not given impossible tasks. (op 12-1 tchd 16-1 in a place)

Enroller(IRE) was a little short of room as they entered the final bend but he had more than enough time to get going up the home straight. The increase in tempo caught him out and he was always going to struggle to get involved after being outpaced.

Judgethemoment(USA), who was well beaten last time over 1m4f, got niggled along down the back straight and looked in big trouble as the pace kept increasing. However, he responded well to pressure and kept on in dour style up the home straight. (op 66-1)

Moment's Notice, who took a good grip to post, was dropped in last and pulled very hard in the middle part of the race. He stayed on quite well, considering how keenly he raced, but was readily held. (op 50-1)

Donegal(USA) raced alongside Captain Webb in the early stages and dropped away with him when the race got serious. (op 33-1)

Captain Webb set only modest fractions in front, so it was slightly disappointing to see him so easily brushed aside when challenged. (op 5-1 tchd 11-2 in places)

Unleashed(IRE) was still travelling strongly as they entered the home straight but found nothing when asked to quicken. The rise in class and trip seemed to find him out. (tchd 20-1 in a place)

Age Of Reason(UAE), who was taking a big step up in trip, tracked the leaders going well but had absolutely nowhere to go up the home straight on quite a few occasions. With a clear passage, it would not be too unfair to suggest that he would have been challenging for one of the place positions. (tchd 16-1)

Ebadiyan(IRE), who was stepping up in trip by half a mile and wearing cheekpieces for the first time, showed a reasonable level of form in Ireland but was most disappointing in this. However, there must be a suspicion that he is a bit better than this effort suggests, as he was not well positioned turning in and kept on in the manner of a stayer rather than a horse with a finishing kick. (op 5-1 tchd 11-2)

3197 BUCKINGHAM PALACE STKS (HERITAGE H'CAP) — 7f

5:30 (5:34) (Class 2) (0-105,105) 3-Y-0+

£37,386 (£11,196; £5,598; £2,802; £1,398; £702) **Stalls** Centre

Form				RPR
2226	**1**		**Regal Parade**^{42} 1942 4-8-6 **92** .... AhmedAjtebi$^{(5)}$ 3 (D Nicholls) *racd on stands side: chsd ldrs: hdwy to ld over 1f out: edgd rt but r.o wl* **25/1**	104

0501 **2** ½ **Dhaular Dhar (IRE)**[20] 2595 6-9-0 **95**......................... DanielTudhope 28 106
(J S Goldie) *racd far side: hld up in tch: hdwy 2f out: rdn to ld far side ins fnl f: r.o: no quite rch wnr: 1st of 14 in gp* **25/1**

0-05 **3** *nk* **Jedburgh**[28] 2371 7-8-5 **86**..(b) JimmyQuinn 5 96
(J L Dunlop) *racd stands side: stdd s: hld up bhd: hdwy 3f out: chsd wnr over 1f out: edgd rt u.p: kpt on* **16/1**

66-2 **4** ½ **Border Music**[41] 1985 7-8-12 **93**................................(b) FrancisNorton 17 102
(A M Balding) *lw: racd on far side: t.k.h: hld up towards rr: hdwy 3f out: gng wl 2f out:led ent fnl f: sn hdd: kpt on same pce 2nd of 14 in gp* **16/1**

6U16 **5** ½ **Laa Rayb (USA)**[20] 2600 4-9-8 **103**..................................... JoeFanning 25 110
(M Johnston) *racd on far side: hld up in midfield: hdwy over 2f out: chsd ldrs 1f out: r.o: nt quite rch ldrs: 3rd of 14 in gp* **25/1**

0-00 **6** ¾ **South Cape**[41] 1982 5-8-6 **87**.. SamHitchcott 24 92+
(M R Channon) *racd on far side: hld up towards rr: hdwy over 1f out: running on and swtchd rt ins fnl f: nt rch ldrs: 4th of 14 in gp* **33/1**

4-15 **7** 1½ **Celtic Sultan (IRE)**[21] 2580 4-9-8 **103**.............................. MickyFenton 6 104
(T P Tate) *racd on stand side: overall ldr tl rdn and hdd over 1f out: wknd jst ins fnl f: 3rd of 14 in gp* **20/1**

3000 **8** 1 **Lovelace**[20] 2607 4-9-9 **104**... MJKinane 16 103
(M Johnston) *racd on far side: hld up in rr: plld out and gd hdwy 3f out: led 2f out: hdd ent fnl f: wknd last 100yds: 5th of 14 in gp* **20/1**

506 **9** ½ **Meydan Dubai (IRE)**[14] 2794 3-7-12 **88** oh4......... MohammedSaeed 21 82+
(J R Best) *racd on far side: in tch: n.m.r and lost pl over 2f out: swtchd lft over 1f out: r.o fnl f: nt rch ldrs: 6th of 14 in gp* **50/1**

0206 **10** *nk* **Buxton**[7] 2995 4-7-13 **80** oh1 ow1...........................(t) FrankieMcDonald 20 76
(R Ingram) *racd on far side:s.i.s: racd in midfield tl rdn and struggling 1/2-way: stdy on past btn horses fnl f: nvr trbld ldrs: 7th of 14 in gp* **100/1**

1626 **11** *nk* **Racer Forever (USA)**[41] 1989 5-9-10 **105**..........(b) JimmyFortune 29 101
(J H M Gosden) *racd on far side: chsd ldrs: rdn and effrt jst over 2f out: wknd ent fnl f: 8th of 14 in gp* **16/1**

0021 **12** ½ **Our Faye**[7] 2993 5-8-9 **90** 5ex..................................... RichardHughes 14 84
(S Kirk) *racd on stand side: hld up bhd: hdwy 3f out: chsd ldrs and rdn 2f out: wknd over 1f out: 4th of 14 in gp* **20/1**

-442 **13** 1 **Docofthebay (IRE)**[2] 3122 4-9-8 **103**..........................(b) ShaneKelly 12 95
(J A Osborne) *lw: racd on stands' side: t.k.h:hld up bhd : hedawy 3f out: chsd ldrs and swtchd rt 2f out: sn hanging rt and btn: 5th of 14 in gp* **5/1**[1]

00-0 **14** ¾ **Prince Of Light (IRE)**[14] 2789 5-8-12 **93**........................ MartinDwyer 7 82
(M Johnston) *racd on stands side: chsd ldrs: rdn over 2f out: wknd wl over 1f out: 6th of 14 in gp* **28/1**

0625 **15** *nk* **Count Ceprano (IRE)**[7] 2995 4-7-7 **81** ow1................... BillyCray(7) 9 70
(M D I Usher) *racd on stands side: racd in midfield: rdn over 2f out: wknd 2f out: hung rt fnl f: 7th of 14 in gp* **50/1**

0025 **16** *nk* **Captain Jacksparra (IRE)**[10] 2905 4-8-7 **88**.......................... NCallan 2 76
(K A Ryan) *swtg: racd on stands side: chsd overall ldr tl 2f out: sn wknd: 8th of 14 in gp* **25/1**

0400 **17** 1 **Vortex**[20] 2595 9-9-2 **97**..(t) JohnEgan 23 82
(Miss Gay Kelleway) *swtg: racd on far side: hld up towards rr: rdn and hdwy jst over 2f out: chsd ldrs over 1f out: wknd fnl f: 9th of 14 in gp* **33/1**

2512 **18** 1 **King's Bastion (IRE)**[13] 2818 4-8-5 **86**......................... HayleyTurner 8 68
(M L W Bell) *racd on stands side: hld up bhd: rdn 2f out: no prog: 10th of 14 in gp* **33/1**

3041 **19** *nk* **Bomber Command (USA)**[2] 3138 5-8-7 **88** 5ex ow9...(v) TedDurcan 11 70
(J W Hills) *racd on stands' side: racd in midfield tl lost pce 5f out: n.d after: 11th of 14 in gp* **33/1**

0-05 **20** *shd* **Giganticus (USA)**[20] 2595 5-9-4 **99**............................... WilliamBuick 26 80
(B W Hills) *swtg: racd on far side: chsd ldrs : rdn and struggling whn hmpd 2f out: no ch after: 10th of 14 in gp* **12/1**[2]

0-02 **21** ¾ **Binanti**[6] 3040 8-8-9 **90**.. JimCrowley 10 69
(P R Chamings) *lw: racd on stand side: in tch: rdn over 2f out: wknd 2f out: 12th of 14 in gp* **14/1**[3]

-106 **22** 4½ **Dabbers Ridge (IRE)**[21] 2580 6-9-5 **100**.....................(p) MichaelHills 18 67
(B W Hills) *lw: racd on far side: chsd ldrs: rdn jst over 2f out: wknd qckly over 1f out: 11th of 14 in gp* **33/1**

4032 **23** *nk* **Hinton Admiral**[20] 2595 4-9-2 **97**................................... PaulHanagan 27 63
(R A Fahey) *racd far side: led that gp tl 2f out: sn hung lft and wknd: 12th of 14 in gp* **14/1**[3]

2-03 **24** 4½ **Berbice (IRE)**[22] 2530 3-8-10 **100**................................... RyanMoore 22 51
(R Hannon) *racd far side: t.k.h: hld up in rr: rdn over 2f out: sn btn: eased ins fnl f: 13th of 14 in gp* **25/1**

3006 **25** 4½ **Trafalgar Square**[35] 2163 6-8-3 **84**.......................... NelsonDeSouza 15 26
(M J Attwater) *swtg: racd on stands' side: racd in midfield: rdn and no prog over 2f out: hung rt over 1f out: 12th of 14 in gp* **50/1**

65-3 **26** 3¾ **Carnivore**[13] 2818 6-8-1 **82** ow1..................................... RichardThomas 1 14
(T D Barron) *racd stands' side: chsd ldrs: rdn over 4f out: sn struggling: wl bhd last 2f: 13th of 14 in gp* **16/1**

-321 **27** 10 **Iguazu Falls (USA)**[14] 2793 3-8-13 **103**................................... LDettori 19 5
(Saeed Bin Suroor) *racd far side: chsd ldrs: rdn and hung rt 2f out: sn wknd: heavily eased ins fnl f: 14th of 14 in gp* **5/1**[1]

-005 **28** 15 **Prior Warning**[26] 2426 4-9-3 **98**.................................(t) EddieAhern 13 —
(Miss D Mountain) *racd stands' side: stdd s: bhd: lost tch 3f out: eased fr over 1f out: t.o: 14th of 14 in gp* **28/1**

1m 27.17s (-0.83) **Going Correction** +0.125s/f (Good)
WFA 3 from 4yo+ 9lb **28 Ran SP% 139.9**
Speed ratings (Par 109): **109,108,108,107,106 106,104,103,102,102 101,101,100,99,99 98,97,96,96,95 95,89,89,84,79 75,63**
toteswinger: 1&2 £259.30, 1&3 £77.00, 2&3 £168.00. CSF £552.16 CT £9966.13 TOTE £49.50: £8.60, £7.90, £3.50, £5.40; EX 1226.20 TRIFECTA Not won. Place 6 £906.29, Place 5 £648.15..
Owner Dab Hand Racing **Bred** Highclere Stud And Harry Herbert **Trained** Sessay, N Yorks
■ A winner for Dubaian apprentice Ahmed Ajtebi on his first ride at the Royal meeting.

FOCUS
Most of these were pretty exposed, and of all the week's handicaps this one is the hardest from which to draw positives for the future.They split into two equal groups and, just as in Thursday's Britannia, there was nothing in it at the finish. Personal bests from Regal Parade and Dhaular Dhar, and not too many hard luck stories behind them.

NOTEBOOK
Regal Parade, who has been running well all year, tracked Captain Jacksparra down the stands'-side rail before coming through to lead over a furlong out. He did more than enough once in front and held on well despite hanging right. He had crept back up the handicap but the 5lb claimed by Ahmed Ajtebi, who was champion apprentice in the UAE this year, made the difference. (op 33-1)
Dhaular Dhar(IRE) 'won' the race on the far side of the track but could not get to the winner, who came down the stands' side. This appeared to be a career-best effort off a lofty handicap mark, so he will need to improve a bit to go one better next time.
Jedburgh pressed the winner strongly through the final furlong after coming off the pace. He had not won a handicap since he took the corresponding race off 99 in 2005, when it was run at York, but a Group 3 win in Ireland had kept him on a high enough mark until recently. This was more like his old self and he proved that he can still be competitive over 7f on fast ground. (op 14-1)
Border Music travelled strongly, which he often does, but failed to really quicken once his jockey went for him. Most of his wins have come on the All-Weather, some off higher marks, but this was another fine effort on turf. He usually runs well at Goodwood, so it is not hard to see him running well in one of the big handicaps at the Glorious meeting if sent there. (op 14-1)
Laa Rayb(USA) ran a fine race off a career-high mark, keeping on well down the far-side without quite getting to the front. He is the right type for these big-field handicaps, although his official mark will always make him vulnerable.
South Cape ran an almost identical race to the one he ran in this race last season. He wins in his turn and is not badly handicapped.
Celtic Sultan(IRE) led the stands' side, racing on the wide outside of his group, and was clear at one point. Front-running tactics are not easy to pull off in big field handicaps, so this effort was not a bad one by any means. (op 25-1)
Lovelace, having his first start in handicap company since last September, came from the back of the far-side group to lead that bunch for about a furlong before weakening quickly inside the final stages. He desperately needs to come down the weights. (op 25-1)
Meydan Dubai(IRE), who has yet to win a race, finished well enough after being behind but was never going to trouble the principals. He shaped as if another furlong will help.
Buxton ran really well considering he had nowhere to go up the far-side rail about three furlongs from home. (op 100-1)
Racer Forever(USA), dropped 5lb since his last run, travelled really strongly, as he often does, but could not accelerate once asked to quicken. (op 20-1 tchd 22-1)
Our Faye came to have every chance after weaving her way through the stands'-side group, but she found little for pressure and never got on terms with the leaders. (op 16-1 tchd 25-1 in a place)
Docofthebay(IRE) was still travelling well about a couple of furlongs from home but failed to quicken when asked to. His effort in the Hunt Cup on Wednesday probably took the edge of him. (op 13-2 tchd 7-1 in places)
Giganticus(USA) went strongly until losing his pitch three furlongs from home. He has yet to hit form this season. (op 16-1)
Hinton Admiral led the far-side group in the early stages but dropped away tamely under pressure. Official explanation: jockey said gelding hung left (op 16-1)
Carnivore Official explanation: jockey said gelding was never travelling
Iguazu Falls(USA) travelled very strongly in the early stages but emptied out alarmingly when asked for an effort. After winning most impressively last time, this cannot be a true reflection of his ability. Official explanation: jockey said colt was unsuited by the firm (good to firm in places) ground (tchd 11-2, 13-2 in a place and 6-1 in places)
T/Jkpt: Not won. T/Plt: £2,514.70 to a £1 stake. Pool: £441,743.53. 128.23 winning tickets. T/Qpdt: £211.30 to a £1 stake. Pool: £20,853.59. 73.02 winning tickets. DO

2521 AYR (L-H)
Friday, June 20

OFFICIAL GOING: Good to firm
Wind: Fresh, half against Weather: Overcast

3198 NATWEST LIFE APPRENTICE H'CAP — 1m 5f 13y
6:10 (6:10) (Class 5) (0-75,74) 4-Y-0+ **£3,412** (£1,007; £504) **Stalls** Low

Form RPR

-443 **1** **Forrest Flyer (IRE)**[13] 2849 4-8-2 **55** oh5.............................. LanceBetts(3) 2 63
(Miss L A Perratt) *set stdy pce: rdn clr fr over 2f out: unchal* **3/1**[3]

1060 **2** 8 **Calzaghe (IRE)**[6] 3045 4-9-7 **71**.. RobbieEgan 5 67
(K R Burke) *hld up in tch: hdwy to chse wnr over 1f out: kpt on: no imp fnl f* **9/2**

/ **3** *nk* **Summer Soul (IRE)**[19] 4956 6-9-10 **74**...............................(b) ClGillies 3 69
(Miss Lucinda V Russell) *prom: drvn and outpcd 3f out: rallied over 1f out: no imp* **11/4**[2]

4-00 **4** 2¼ **Jordan's Light (USA)**[13] 2848 5-8-7 **60**.........................(v) BMcHugh(3) 1 52
(P Monteith) *t.k.h: chsd wnr: rdn over 2f out: no ex and lost 2nd over 1f out* **11/1**

-041 **5** *hd* **Kyber**[13] 2844 7-8-8 **58**... GaryBartley 4 50
(J S Goldie) *cl up: stmbld bdly after 3f: outpcd over 2f out: n.d after* **7/4**[1]

2m 51.5s (-5.10) **Going Correction** -0.475s/f (Firm) **5 Ran SP% 114.5**
Speed ratings (Par 103): **96,91,90,89,89**
CSF £16.88 TOTE £4.50: £2.10, £2.50; EX 29.10.
Owner Mrs Camille Macdonald **Bred** Philip Lau **Trained** Carluke, S Lanarks

FOCUS
A messy race in which the winner was allowed to poach a healthy advantage in the straight. This bare form does not look reliable.

3199 ROYAL BANK OF SCOTLAND MAIDEN AUCTION STKS — 6f
6:40 (6:42) (Class 5) 2-Y-0 **£3,885** (£1,156; £577; £288) **Stalls** High

Form RPR

1 **Prize Point** 2-8-13 0.. FergalLynch 3 77+
(K A Ryan) *blkd s: sn led: shkn up and edgd lft over 1f out: kpt on strly* **11/8**[2]

2 1¾ **Saif Al Fahad (IRE)** 2-8-11 0.................................... RoystonFfrench 1 66
(E J O'Neill) *cl up: rdn 2f out: kpt on ins fnl f: nt pce of wnr* **7/1**[3]

23 **3** ¾ **Woolston Ferry (IRE)**[14] 2796 2-8-11 0.................................. TPO'Shea 2 64
(M R Channon) *in tch: stdy hdwy 1/2-way: rdn 2f out: rallied appr fnl f: one pce ins fnl f* **1/1**[1]

4 4 **Igneous** 2-8-7 0.. PaulFessey 5 48
(K R Burke) *bhd and drvn along: outpcd 1/2-way: n.d after* **14/1**

0 **5** 1¾ **Jack Jicaro**[10] 2903 2-8-5 0 ow1...................................... TolleyDean(3) 6 44
(Mrs L Williamson) *chsd ldrs tl rdn and wknd over 2f out* **50/1**

6 13 **Captain Cromby (IRE)** 2-8-7 0.......................................(p) DO'Donohoe 4 4
(J R Weymes) *cl up tl rdn and wknd fr over 2f out: t.o* **25/1**

1m 12.53s (-1.07) **Going Correction** -0.475s/f (Firm) **6 Ran SP% 117.1**
Speed ratings (Par 93): **88,85,84,79,77 59**
toteswinger: 1&2 £2.10, 1&3 £1.10, 2&3 £1.80. CSF £12.22 TOTE £3.00: £1.50, £2.90; EX 7.30.
Owner J C Fretwell **Bred** Mrs B Skinner **Trained** Hambleton, N Yorks

FOCUS
The market leader proved disappointing but nevertheless this was a pleasing debut run from Prize Point, who is the type to hold his own in stronger company.

NOTEBOOK
Prize Point ◆, out of a dam who is a half-sister to a couple of 1m winners, is entered up a couple of the valuable sales races and he created a favourable impression on this racecourse debut for his in-form yard. He has physical scope for further improvement and is very much the type to win more races. (op 9-4)
Saif Al Fahad(IRE), a 19,000gns half brother to winners from sprint distances to 1m4f, was easy to back but ran creditably on this racecourse debut. He should be suited by 7f and is capable of picking up a minor event. (tchd 8-1)
Woolston Ferry(IRE), who had shaped well on his first two starts, was again below the form of his debut run on this first start on ground as quick as this. He will be suited by the step up to 7f and, although starting to look exposed, is capable of winning a similar event. (op 4-5 tchd 8-11 tchd 11-10 in places)

Igneous, a half-brother to a 1m winner in Italy, shaped as though a stiffer test than this one was required on this racecourse debut. He is going to have to improve a fair bit to win in this grade, though.
Jack Jicaro, well beaten from a wide draw after a slow start on his debut, again offered little immediate promise.
Captain Cromby(IRE), out of a multiple 1m-1m2f winner, was fitted with cheekpieces for this racecourse debut and was soundly beaten. (op 18-1)

3200 THISTLE SYSTEMS GROUP MAKINGWORKSPACEWORK MAIDEN STKS 7f 50y
7:15 (7:15) (Class 5) 3-Y-O+ **£3,885** (£1,156; £577; £288) **Stalls** Low

Form RPR
4023 **1** **Ninefineirishmen (IRE)**[22] 2539 3-9-3 75................(p) DarrenWilliams 4 71
(K R Burke) *pressed ldr: rdn to ld over 1f out: edgd lft: kpt on wl fnl f* **7/4**[2]
0323 **2** *1 ¾* **August Gale (USA)**[9] 2929 3-9-3 82.......................... RoystonFfrench 2 66
(M Johnston) *led: rdn over 2f out: hdd over 1f out: one pce fnl f* **5/4**[1]
00 **3** *3 ¼* **Important News**[18] 2673 3-9-3 0.................................... DO'Donohoe 6 58+
(M Johnston) *hld up in tch: pushed along over 2f out: kpt on fnl f: nt rch first 2* **10/1**
6-03 **4** *1 ½* **Nayarna**[23] 2500 3-8-12 70.. TonyHamilton 3 49
(R A Fahey) *trckd ldrs: rdn over 2f out: one pce over 1f out* **7/2**[3]
00-0 **5** *hd* **Warm Tribute (USA)**[32] 2246 4-9-9 38.............. PJMcDonald(3) 5 56?
(A G Foster) *prom: drvn over 2f out: no ex over 1f out* **50/1**
00-0 **6** *14* **Senora Lenorah**[89] 980 4-9-0 35.................................(t) PaulPickard(7) 1 13
(D A Nolan) *in tch tl wknd over 2f out* **100/1**
0-0 **7** *3 ½* **Endeavor**[13] 2847 3-9-3 0... PaulFessey 8 —
(P Monteith) *s.i.s: a bhd* **33/1**
000- **8** *18* **Wolf Pack**[260] 5935 6-9-7 33..(t) GaryBartley(5) 7 —
(D A Nolan) *missed break: nvr on terms* **100/1**

1m 30.44s (-2.96) **Going Correction** -0.475s/f (Firm)
WFA 3 from 4yo+ 9lb **8** Ran SP% **119.0**
Speed ratings (Par 103): **97,95,91,89,89 73,69,48**
toteswinger: 1&2 £1.10, 1&3 £11.80, 2&3 £3.90. CSF £4.52 TOTE £2.90: £1.10, £1.10, £2.80; EX 3.90.
Owner Cyril Wall **Bred** Thomas Hassett **Trained** Middleham Moor, N Yorks
■ Stewards' Enquiry : Darren Williams caution: careless riding

FOCUS
A moderate maiden in which the pace was just fair. The two market leaders pulled clear in the closing stages but the form is dubious.

3201 RBS BANCASSURANCE H'CAP 1m
7:45 (7:47) (Class 6) (0-55,55) 4-Y-O+ **£3,070** (£906; £453) **Stalls** Low

Form RPR
5003 **1** **Chin Wag (IRE)**[18] 2672 4-9-0 55..................................(p) FergalLynch 3 64
(J S Goldie) *trckd ldrs: rdn over 2f out: rallied to ld appr fnl f: carried hd high and edgd rt ins fnl f: kpt on* **3/1**[2]
4030 **2** *2* **Ensign's Trick**[14] 2781 4-8-13 54.. TPO'Shea 4 58
(W M Brisbourne) *t.k.h: in tch: effrt and ev ch over 1f out: kpt on same pce ins fnl f* **33/1**
0045 **3** *1 ¾* **Muncaster Castle (IRE)**[25] 2446 4-8-5 53 ow1............ LanceBetts(7) 8 53
(R F Fisher) *w ldr: ev ch tl one pce fnl f* **16/1**
20-0 **4** *1 ¼* **Monsieur Dumas (IRE)**[39] 2053 4-8-11 52...........(p) DarrenWilliams 12 49
(R Bastiman) *midfield: effrt 2f out: kpt on u.p fnl f* **8/1**
2-32 **5** *½* **Lady Valentino**[22] 2523 4-8-11 52...................................... TonyHamilton 5 48
(M Dods) *led tl rdn and hdd appr fnl f: no ex* **9/4**[1]
0200 **6** *1* **Moverra (IRE)**[6] 3034 4-8-11 52...................................(p) NickyMackay 7 46
(M Wigham) *prom: drvn over 2f out: no imp over 1f out* **14/1**
6-00 **7** *hd* **Baylaw Star**[14] 2806 7-8-12 53................................. RoystonFfrench 10 46
(I W McInnes) *cl up tl rdn and no ex over 1f out* **28/1**
00-2 **8** *nk* **Reddy Ronnie (IRE)**[18] 2662 4-8-2 50............................ PaulPickard(7) 6 42+
(D Carroll) *sn bhd: drvn 1/2-way: sme late hdwy: nvr rchd ldrs* **6/1**[3]
3300 **9** *¾* **Time To Regret**[56] 1605 8-8-9 55.................................(p) GaryBartley(5) 11 46
(I W McInnes) *hld up: rdn and hung lft 3f out: nvr rchd ldrs* **33/1**
R-6 **10** *nk* **Polish Star**[15] 2747 4-8-10 51.. DO'Donohoe 2 41
(Miss L A Perratt) *hld up: drvn over 3f out: sn n.d* **25/1**
006- **11** *½* **Whittinghamvillage**[259] 5964 7-8-3 51............................ BMcHugh(7) 1 40
(Mrs H O Graham) *bhd: shortlived effrt over 2f out: sn btn* **18/1**
4130 **12** *¾* **King Of Legend (IRE)**[20] 2597 4-8-9 53........................ PJMcDonald(3) 13 40
(A G Foster) *in tch to 1/2-way: sn lost pl* **8/1**
-000 **13** *3 ½* **Ulysees (IRE)**[9] 2940 9-8-7 48... PaulFessey 14 27
(J Barclay) *bhd on outside: rdn 3f out: sn btn* **25/1**
0064 **14** *4 ½* **Hollywood George**[14] 2806 4-8-11 52...................(b[1]) PatrickMathers 9 21
(Miss M E Rowland) *midfield: struggling wl over 2f out: sn btn* **16/1**

1m 39.67s (-4.13) **Going Correction** -0.475s/f (Firm) **14** Ran SP% **133.0**
Speed ratings (Par 101): **101,99,97,96,95 94,94,94,93,92 92,91,88,83**
toteswinger: 1&2 £9.90, 1&3 £26.10, 2&3 Not won CSF £119.07 CT £1456.06 TOTE £4.20: £2.00, £10.50, £5.00; EX 64.50.
Owner Fyffees **Bred** R N Auld **Trained** Uplawmoor, E Renfrews

FOCUS
A run-of-the-mill handicap. The pace was sound but those attempting to come from the back of the field were at a disadvantage. The runner-up and third set the level of the form.

3202 WALTER SCOTT SAINTS & SINNERS CHALLENGE CUP H'CAP 6f
8:20 (8:20) (Class 4) (0-80,77) 3-Y-O **£5,828** (£1,734; £866; £432) **Stalls** High

Form RPR
4-52 **1** **Pavershooz**[22] 2526 3-9-0 70.. DO'Donohoe 7 76
(N Wilson) *mde all: rdn over 1f out: drifted lft ins fnl f: kpt on wl* **3/1**[2]
2620 **2** *¾* **Leading Edge (IRE)**[8] 2976 3-9-4 74...................................... TPO'Shea 6 78
(M R Channon) *trckd ldrs: effrt and wnt 2nd over 1f out: kpt on fnl f: nt rch wnr* **11/2**
0-00 **3** *1* **Peter's Storm (USA)**[43] 1925 3-9-0 70............................... FergalLynch 5 71
(K A Ryan) *cl up: rdn over 2f out: rallied over 1f out: one pce ins fnl f* **13/2**
0-42 **4** *2 ¼* **Tyfos**[11] 2883 3-9-7 77.. DarrenWilliams 3 71
(W M Brisbourne) *t.k.h: prom: effrt 2f out: sn one pce* **9/2**[3]
0-55 **5** *nk* **Bahamian Ballad**[27] 2399 3-8-4 60................................. RoystonFfrench 4 53
(J D Bethell) *bhd: hdwy over 2f out: rdn and no imp appr fnl f* **16/1**
6413 **6** *1 ½* **Atlantic Beach**[27] 2407 3-9-2 72.................................... TonyHamilton 2 60
(R A Fahey) *bhd: rdn and shortlived effrt on outside over 2f out: sn btn* **2/1**[1]
-230 **7** *4 ½* **Flying Sommelier (USA)**[58] 1556 3-8-10 66........................ PaulFessey 1 39
(T D Barron) *chsd ldrs tl rdn and wknd over 2f out* **16/1**

1m 10.47s (-3.13) **Going Correction** -0.475s/f (Firm) **7** Ran SP% **117.0**
Speed ratings (Par 101): **101,100,98,95,95 93,87**
toteswinger: 1&2 £4.00, 1&3 £3.30, 2&3 £9.10. CSF £20.56 TOTE £3.90: £2.30, £2.90; EX 23.20.
Owner Mrs Michael John Paver **Bred** Exors Of The Late M J Paver **Trained** Flaxton, N Yorks

FOCUS
An ordinary sprint in which the market leader disappointed, but it was still an improved effort from the winner, who is the type to win more races. The race has been rated through the fifth.
Atlantic Beach Official explanation: trainer's representative had no explanation for the improved form shown.

3203 ROYAL BANK OF SCOTLAND H'CAP 7f 50y
8:50 (8:50) (Class 4) (0-85,85) 4-Y-O+ **£6,476** (£1,927; £963; £481) **Stalls** Low

Form RPR
2334 **1** **Flying Bantam (IRE)**[9] 2925 7-8-6 70.............................. TonyHamilton 5 78
(R A Fahey) *prom: led and edgd lft over 1f out: hld on wl fnl f* **6/1**[3]
-410 **2** *¾* **Flores Sea (USA)**[41] 2005 4-8-5 69...................................... PaulFessey 4 75
(T D Barron) *led to 1/2-way: rallied: rdn and ev ch over 1f out: kpt on ins fnl f* **16/1**
0232 **3** *½* **Esoterica (IRE)**[3] 3108 5-7-12 67...............................(b) KellyHarrison(5) 3 76+
(J S Goldie) *plld hrd: prom: no room fr over 2f out: effrt and cl 3rd whn hmpd ins fnl f: nt rcvr* **10/11**[1]
0000 **4** *½* **Distant Sun (USA)**[9] 2938 4-8-13 77...................................... DO'Donohoe 6 80
(Miss L A Perratt) *hld up: rdn over 2f out: hdwy over 1f out: kpt on fnl f* **14/1**
-261 **5** *nk* **Abbondanza (IRE)**[21] 2578 5-9-2 85...............................(p) NeilBrown(5) 2 87
(Miss L A Perratt) *t.k.h: hld up: hdwy over 1f out: r.o fnl f* **7/2**[2]
4426 **6** *20* **H Harrison (IRE)**[4] 3087 8-8-8 77.................................... GaryBartley(5) 8 25
(I W McInnes) *cl up: led 1/2-way to over 1f out: wkng whn hmpd ins fnl f* **9/1**
0205 **U** **Red Romeo**[38] 2083 7-8-7 74.. AndrewMullen(3) 7 78
(N Wilson) *trckd ldrs: rdn whn nt clr run over 1f out: 4th and keeping on whn clipped heels, stmbld bdly and uns rdr ins fnl f* **9/1**

1m 29.16s (-4.24) **Going Correction** -0.475s/f (Firm) **7** Ran SP% **121.4**
Speed ratings (Par 105): **105,104,103,103,102 79,—**
toteswinger: 1&2 £20.30, 1&3 £2.10, 2&3 £4.80. CSF £95.14 CT £167.10 TOTE £5.60: £1.60, £10.80; EX 182.10.
Owner The Matthewman Partnership **Bred** Robinski Bloodstock Limited **Trained** Musley Bank, N Yorks
■ Stewards' Enquiry : Kelly Harrison eight-day ban: careless riding (Jul 4-10, Aug 12)

FOCUS
Exposed sorts in this ordinary handicap but a steady gallop means this bare form is not reliable.

3204 NATWEST H'CAP 1m 2f
9:20 (9:24) (Class 6) (0-65,65) 4-Y-O+ **£3,070** (£906; £453) **Stalls** Low

Form RPR
0630 **1** **Shy Glance (USA)**[15] 2749 6-8-10 59.................................. NeilBrown(5) 4 71+
(P Monteith) *hld up in tch: hdwy to ld over 1f out: kpt on wl fnl f* **3/1**[1]
-640 **2** *1 ¼* **Grandad Bill (IRE)**[9] 2940 5-8-5 49.................................. FergalLynch 10 59+
(J S Goldie) *hld up: hdwy over 2f out: chsd wnr ins fnl f: r.o* **4/1**[3]
00/- **3** *1 ¼* **Inch High**[6] 5838 10-7-12 47 oh1 ow1.......................(p) KellyHarrison(5) 7 54
(J S Goldie) *led to over 1f out: kpt on same pce fnl f* **7/1**
0051 **4** *1 ½* **Malguru**[22] 2523 4-8-4 48..(p) PaulFessey 8 52
(A G Foster) *chsd ldrs: effrt and ch 2f out: one pce fnl f* **7/1**
2425 **5** *1 ½* **Black Falcon (IRE)**[4] 3077 8-9-1 59................................... RoystonFfrench 11 60
(John A Harris) *dwlt: sn cl up: ev ch over 3f out to over 1f out: sn no ex* **7/2**[2]
4-00 **6** *1 ½* **Marieschi (USA)**[32] 2249 4-9-0 58..................................... TonyHamilton 3 56
(R F Fisher) *hld up: rdn 3f out: nvr rchd ldrs* **16/1**
6-00 **7** *shd* **Templet (USA)**[12] 2867 8-8-2 46 oh1.............................(v) NickyMackay 2 44
(W G Harrison) *hld up in tch: drvn and over 2f out: sn n.d* **33/1**
042- **8** *21* **Always Best**[233] 6590 4-8-4 48... DO'Donohoe 1 4
(R Allan) *trckd ldrs to over 2f out: t.o* **9/2**

2m 7.80s (-4.20) **Going Correction** -0.475s/f (Firm) **8** Ran SP% **119.2**
Speed ratings (Par 101): **97,96,95,93,92 91,91,74**
toteswinger: 1&2 £3.40, 1&3 £7.10, 2&3 £4.30. CSF £16.06 CT £78.71 TOTE £5.10: £1.50, £1.70, £1.50; EX 21.20 Place 6 £ 710.39, Place 5 £ 212.77.
Owner Walcal Property Development Ltd **Bred** R D Hubbard And Constance Sczesny **Trained** Rosewell, Midlothian

FOCUS
A modest handicap in which the pace was just fair.
T/Plt: £456.50 to a £1 stake. Pool: £36,459.84. 58.30 winning tickets. T/Qpdt: £68.40 to a £1 stake. Pool: £3,532.58. 38.20 winning tickets. RY

2993 GOODWOOD (R-H)
Friday, June 20

OFFICIAL GOING: Good to firm (good in places; 9.0)
Rail realignment added approx. 20 metres to race distances on the round course.
Wind: Moderate, half against

3205 CHICHESTER CITY MAIDEN STKS 1m 1f
6:20 (6:25) (Class 5) 3-Y-O+ **£3,238** (£963; £481; £240) **Stalls** High

Form RPR
4- **1** **Asfurah's Dream (IRE)**[252] 6138 3-8-9 0................................ LPKeniry 5 85
(M P Tregoning) *mde all: rdn over 1f out: kpt on wl* **6/1**[3]
04 **2** *1 ½* **Mohathab (IRE)**[43] 1926 3-9-0 0.. SebSanders 3 86
(J H M Gosden) *hld up: hdwy 4f out: rdn and wnt 2nd over 1f out: got nrr to wnr ins fnl f but a hld* **8/13**[1]
56-0 **3** *8* **Pretty Ballerina (USA)**[2] 3124 3-8-9 0...................... EdwardCreighton 6 64
(John Joseph Murphy, Ire) *trckd wnr: rdn over 2f out: lost 2nd over 1f out and one pce after* **8/1**
36 **4** *6* **Mazloma (USA)**[42] 1946 3-8-9 0.................................... CatherineGannon 1 52
(M R Channon) *racd in 3rd pl: rdn over 3f out: wknd over 1f out* **4/1**[2]
5 *1 ¼* **Katy Kitten (UAE)** 3-8-9 0.. FergusSweeney 2 49
(G L Moore) *hld up: rdn 3f out: lost tch wl over 1f out* **14/1**
6 *5* **Lady Marguerite** 3-8-9 0.. PatDobbs 4 38
(M P Tregoning) *s.i.s: a in rr: rdn 3f out: lost tch 2f out* **12/1**

1m 57.99s (1.69) **Going Correction** +0.125s/f (Good) **6** Ran SP% **121.7**
Speed ratings (Par 103): **97,95,88,83,82 77**
toteswinger: 1&2 £1.70, 1&3 £5.10, 2&3 £2.30. CSF £11.24 TOTE £8.90: £3.80, £1.20; EX 17.50.
Owner Hadi Al-Tajir **Bred** Hadi Al Tajir **Trained** Lambourn, Berks

The Form Book, Raceform Ltd, Compton, RG20 6NL

FOCUS
A steadily run race in which the winner was able to dominate throughout. Far from solid form rated around the runner-up.

3206 PAUL SMITH ASSOCIATES 10TH ANNIVERSARY STKS (H'CAP) 1m 1f 192y
6:50 (6:57) (Class 5) (0-70,68) 3-Y-O £3,238 (£963; £481; £240) Stalls High

Form RPR

-020 1 **Addwaitya**[20] 2613 3-9-2 63 JimCrowley 6 77
(C F Wall) *mde all: rdn clr over 1f out: r.o wl* 7/1[3]

00-0 2 2 3/4 **Cosmea**[21] 2563 3-9-0 61 FergusSweeney 13 69
(A King) *in tch: rdn over 2f out: styd on to go 2nd nr fin* 14/1

1-1 3 1 1/4 **Mission Control (IRE)**[107] 803 3-9-6 67 SebSanders 3 73
(J R Boyle) *prom on outside: chsd wnr 2f out tl lost 2nd towards fin* 3/1[2]

4465 4 2 **Tamasou (IRE)**[26] 2429 3-9-3 64 SaleemGolam 5 66+
(Garry Moss) *mid-div: rdn over 2f out: styd on: nvr nrr* 11/1

006- 5 1 3/4 **Ever Dreaming (USA)**[189] 7145 3-9-4 65 LPKeniry 10 63
(A M Balding) *chsd ldrs: rdn 3f out: wknd appr fnl f* 20/1

34-4 6 2 1/4 **Addikt (IRE)**[18] 2678 3-9-7 68 RichardHughes 2 62+
(S Kirk) *hld up and c over to ins fr wd draw: hdwy whn short of room and swtchd lft over 2f out: nvr able to chal* 5/2[1]

3200 7 1/2 **King Bathwick (IRE)**[15] 2763 3-9-3 67 (t) KevinGhunowa(3) 8 60
(B R Millman) *plld hrd: prom: rdn 3f out: wknd appr fnl f* 12/1

0000 8 1 1/4 **Ruby Delta**[5] 3065 3-8-8 55 (b) SimonWhitworth 11 45
(P D Cundell) *towards rr: rdn and hdwy over 2f out: sn one pce* 33/1

0-50 9 3 3/4 **Teadancer (IRE)**[16] 2719 3-8-7 54 ow1 JamesDoyle 14 37
(J G Portman) *hld up in mid-div: swtchd rt and rdn 3f out: wknd over 1f out* 50/1

0-50 10 nk **Better In Heaven**[39] 2047 3-9-5 66 IanMongan 4 48+
(H J L Dunlop) *towards rr: hdwy on outside over 4f out: rdn and wknd over 1f out* 14/1

5-00 11 1 **House Of Tudor**[42] 1962 3-9-1 62 (b[1]) AdamKirby 16 42
(David Pinder) *towards rr: rdn on ins 4f out: wkng whn bmpd over 1f out: eased ins fnl f* 33/1

000- 12 3 1/4 **Pinnacle Point**[260] 5937 3-8-13 60 StephenCarson 7 43+
(G L Moore) *t.k.h: prom: rdn and hung rt over 2f out* 10/1

0-00 13 3/4 **Empire Seeker (USA)**[25] 2449 3-9-2 63 DarryllHolland 12 35
(J W Hills) *a in rr* 10/1

6004 14 1 **King's Alchemist**[20] 2603 3-8-11 58 EdwardCreighton 9 28
(M D I Usher) *a bhd* 12/1

0406 15 1 **Blur**[50] 1740 3-8-8 55 RichardSmith 1 23
(R Hannon) *mid-div: bhd fnl 3f* 33/1

060- 16 hd **Lenouska (IRE)**[252] 6150 3-8-9 56 HayleyTurner 15 24
(J W Hills) *s.i.s: sn trckd ldrs: rdn 4f out: wknd 2f out* 33/1

2m 8.52s (0.52) **Going Correction** +0.125s/f (Good) **16 Ran SP% 139.8**
Speed ratings (Par 99): **102,99,98,97,95 94,93,92,89,89 88,85,85,84,83 83**
toteswinger: 1&2 £51.50, 1&3 £6.30, 2&3 £22.40. CSF £109.73 CT £376.47 TOTE £11.60: £2.70, £4.90, £1.40, £2.30; EX 283.30.
Owner Les McLaughlin **Bred** L McLaughlin **Trained** Newmarket, Suffolk

FOCUS
An ordinary handicap but solid enough form. The first two have been rated as improving and the fourth 5lb off his Newmarket run.
Addikt(IRE) Official explanation: jockey said, regarding running and riding, his orders were to drop colt out to get the trip, adding that it was not bred to stay, it ran freely, dropped back further than intended in order to get settled, didn't handle the downhill well and finished with the bit through its mouth; trainer's rep added colt sustained some cuts to his legs
House Of Tudor Official explanation: jockey reported gelding hung both ways.
Pinnacle Point Official explanation: jockey said gelding ran too free and hung right.
Empire Seeker(USA) Official explanation: jockey reported colt was slowly away.

3207 INCHCAPE RENAULT MASTER MAIDEN AUCTION FILLIES' STKS 6f
7:25 (7:26) (Class 4) 2-Y-O £3,885 (£1,156; £577; £288) Stalls Low

Form RPR

2 1 **Aunt Nicola**[17] 2702 2-8-10 0 HayleyTurner 9 76
(M L W Bell) *t.k.h: trckd ldrs: led 2f out: pushed out fnl f* 11/2[3]

2 1 1/4 **Spanish Cygnet (USA)** 2-8-13 0 JimCrowley 8 75
(Mrs A J Perrett) *a.p on outside: chsd wnr fnl f* 10/1

42 3 1 **Gal Aloud (USA)**[13] 2821 2-8-13 0 RichardHughes 4 72
(R Hannon) *trckd ldr: rdn 2f out: nt qckn fnl f* 7/4[2]

4 1 **Russian Rave** 2-8-12 0 JamesDoyle 10 68+
(J G Portman) *hld up on outside: hdwy 1/2-way: ev ch over 1f out: nt qckn ins fnl f* 14/1

4 5 nk **Deyas Dream**[20] 2618 2-8-8 0 FrancisNorton 2 63
(A M Balding) *led tl hdd 2f out: one pce after* 5/4[1]

6 3/4 **Now** 2-8-5 0 SaleemGolam 1 58
(P Winkworth) *in tch: rdn over 2f out: nt qckn fr over 1f out* 25/1

0 7 1 3/4 **Nun Today (USA)**[20] 2618 2-8-6 0 SimonWhitworth 7 54
(J S Moore) *t.k.h: rdn 1/2-way: wknd over 1f out* 33/1

8 1 **Val De Flores** 2-8-12 0 LPKeniry 11 57
(E F Vaughan) *s.i.s: a bhd* 12/1

00 9 4 1/2 **Flawless Diamond (IRE)**[35] 2146 2-8-6 0 FergusSweeney 5 37
(J S Moore) *outpcd and a bhd* 33/1

00 10 1/2 **Sienna Lake (IRE)**[42] 1961 2-8-7 0 CatherineGannon 6 37
(S Kirk) *in tch: rdn 1/2-way: wknd 2f out* 33/1

1m 13.37s (1.17) **Going Correction** 0.0s/f (Good) **10 Ran SP% 132.3**
Speed ratings (Par 92): **92,90,89,87,87 86,83,82,76,75**
CSF £64.41 TOTE £6.50: £1.70, £2.90, £1.20; EX 45.40.
Owner R P B Michaelson, J Thompson & M Caine **Bred** Bearstone Stud **Trained** Newmarket, Suffolk

FOCUS
Average form for the grade, with the third the best guide to the level.

NOTEBOOK
Aunt Nicola stepped up on her debut, which was on Fibresand, and while she acted well enough on that surface, she looks even better on turf. Staying the extra furlong really well, she should improve again. (op 11-1)
Spanish Cygnet(USA), a $100,000 daughter of the high-class American dirt miler El Corredor, and from a speedy US family, made a promising debut. Turf clearly holds no problems for her, and she is good enough to win a routine maiden. However, given her breeding, she may well prove a bit better than that.
Gal Aloud(USA) had done reasonably well in her three races to date and, while capable of landing a run-of-the-mill maiden, she looks an obvious sort for nurseries from now on. (op 2-1)
Russian Rave, a 45,000gns daughter of Danehill Dancer out of a speedy dam, has plenty of pace in her extended family as well. She made an encouraging debut here, and should improve enough to win races. (op 10-1 tchd 16-1)
Deyas Dream adopted front-running tactics this time, but has yet to prove that this is the ideal way to ride her. She had shown more promise than this on her debut, and is worth another chance. (op 11-8 tchd 6-4)
Now, whose sire Where Or When progressed into a high-class miler, has plenty of winners in her family up to 2m, and longer trips will suit in due course. Her dam won three times from 1m-1m2f, and she will really come into her own when able to tackle trips at least two furlongs farther than this satisfactory debut. (op 28-1 tchd 33-1)

3208 SMC RENAULT GROUP TRAFIC STKS (H'CAP) 1m
7:55 (7:57) (Class 5) (0-70,70) 4-Y-O+ £3,412 (£1,007; £504) Stalls High

Form RPR

5115 1 **Paraguay (USA)**[18] 2662 5-9-3 66 EdwardCreighton 7 73
(Miss V Haigh) *hld up in rr: hdwy on outside 2f out: r.o wl to ld ins fnl f* 9/2[2]

1234 2 1 **Follow The Flag (IRE)**[20] 2615 4-9-6 69 GeorgeBaker 5 74
(C F Wall) *hld up in mid-div: hdwy 3f out: sn rdn: led appr 1f out: hdd ins fnl f: jst hld on for 2nd* 15/2

3151 3 nk **Silver Blue (IRE)**[7] 2990 5-9-1 64 6ex CatherineGannon 10 68+
(W K Goldsworthy) *hld up: short of room on ins fr over 2f out tl got clr run and r.o ins fnl f* 5/2[1]

2551 4 hd **Onenightinlisbon (IRE)**[9] 2943 4-9-0 63 FergusSweeney 9 67+
(J R Boyle) *mid-div: short of room fr 2f out: kpt on ins fnl f* 6/1[3]

0134 5 nk **Napoletano (GER)**[12] 2860 7-8-13 62 (p) SebSanders 6 65+
(S Dow) *in rr: hdwy 2f out: r.o fnl f: nvr nrr* 8/1

3203 6 1/2 **Recalcitrant**[9] 2943 5-7-13 55 SophieDoyle(7) 11 57
(S Dow) *prom: rdn over 3f out: ev ch appr 1f out: no ex ins fnl f* 12/1

05-0 7 nk **Eastern Emperor**[11] 2897 4-9-7 70 (p) AdamKirby 4 71+
(W R Swinburn) *hld up in rr: nt clr run and swtchd lft over 2f out: kpt on fnl f* 7/1

31-4 8 2 1/4 **Quaglino Way (GR)**[11] 2897 4-9-4 67 JimCrowley 8 63
(P R Chamings) *led: rdn 2f out: hdd & wknd appr fnl f* 15/2

0-00 9 4 1/2 **Ken's Girl**[36] 2128 4-9-3 66 (p) LPKeniry 2 51
(W S Kittow) *t.k.h: prom tl rdn and wknd 2f out* 28/1

-040 10 1/2 **Mythical Charm**[14] 2795 9-8-2 51 oh3 (t) HayleyTurner 3 35
(J J Bridger) *in tch tl rdn and wknd 2f out* 33/1

3044 11 6 **Binnion Bay (IRE)**[13] 2837 7-8-2 54 ow2 (b) MarcHalford(3) 1 25
(J J Bridger) *t.k.h: prom: rdn over 2f out: sn wknd: eased fnl f* 20/1

1m 40.81s (0.91) **Going Correction** +0.125s/f (Good) **11 Ran SP% 127.0**
Speed ratings (Par 103): **100,99,98,98,98 97,97,95,90,90 84**
toteswinger: 1&2 £5.80, 1&3 £5.90, 2&3 £5.80. CSF £40.80 CT £108.95 TOTE £6.50: £2.10, £2.70, £1.70; EX 43.70.
Owner R J Budge **Bred** Nutbush Farm **Trained** Wiseton, Notts

FOCUS
A steadily run handicap and messy form to rate. The well-in third and fourth got little luck in running but hardly flew home when in the clear.
Silver Blue(IRE) Official explanation: jockey said gelding was denied a clear run.

3209 RENAULT MASTER VANS STKS (H'CAP) 1m 6f
8:30 (8:30) (Class 2) (0-100,95) 4-Y-O+ £12,462 (£3,732; £1,866; £934; £466; £234) Stalls Low

Form RPR

-343 1 **Ollie George (IRE)**[5] 3060 5-8-12 84 LPKeniry 2 91
(A M Balding) *led tl hdd 2f out: rallied and battled bk to ld wl ins fnl f: hld on* 5/1

2124 2 shd **Fregate Island (IRE)**[21] 2577 5-8-6 78 FergusSweeney 6 85
(A G Newcombe) *trckd ldrs: rdn to ld 2f out: hdd wl ins fnl f but kpt on to press wnr* 12/1

0251 3 2 **Formax (FR)**[20] 2599 6-9-4 90 PatDobbs 8 94
(M P Tregoning) *hld up in rr: hdwy over 3f out: rdn and styd on fr over 1f out: nvr nrr* 9/2

-533 4 1/2 **Shela House**[28] 2372 4-8-13 85 RichardHughes 1 89
(J R Fanshawe) *hld up: hdwy 3f out: swtchd rt over 2f out: ev ch ins fnl f: no ex towards fin* 7/2[3]

20-2 5 1 1/4 **Bandama (IRE)**[13] 2830 5-9-5 91 JimCrowley 5 93
(Mrs A J Perrett) *mid-div: effrt over 3f out: rdn and one pce fr over 1f out* 10/3[2]

6-04 6 14 **Lepido (ITY)**[20] 2593 4-9-0 86 SebSanders 3 68
(L M Cumani) *hld up: effrt 3f out: sn btn* 14/1

0-30 7 8 **Swan Queen**[29] 2346 5-9-2 88 EddieAhern 4 59
(J L Dunlop) *trckd ldr tl rdn and wknd 2f out* 3/1[1]

5/0- 8 32 **Tusculum (IRE)**[438] 990 5-9-9 95 ShaneKelly 7 21
(A P Stringer) *in tch tl lost pl 5f out: steadily wknd: t.o* 12/1

3m 4.42s (0.82) **Going Correction** +0.125s/f (Good) **8 Ran SP% 127.2**
Speed ratings (Par 109): **102,101,100,100,99 91,87,68**
toteswinger: 1&2 £16.60, 1&3 £4.20, 2&3 £11.30. CSF £68.84 CT £301.01 TOTE £7.20: £1.70, £2.70, £1.90; EX 95.50.
Owner Peter R Grubb **Bred** Lawrence Walsh **Trained** Kingsclere, Hants

FOCUS
A fair handicap not run at a great early pace. The runner-up looks high enough in the weights and the third ran close to recent course form.

NOTEBOOK
Ollie George(IRE) showed tremendous courage to snatch the race back after appearing beaten a furlong from home. This was his highest winning mark, but he has been in fine form of late and this longer trip clearly played to his strengths. (op 13-2)
Fregate Island(IRE) looked better suited by this trip than the 2m he tackled last time, only to be run out of it on the line by the rallying winner. He had looked the likely winner for much of the home straight, and is unexposed at these extended distances, so looks capable of finding a similar event off his current mark. (tchd 14-1)
Formax(FR) has to be held up like this, but the exaggerated tactics can cause problems in running and he did look as if he might have gone close if things had gone more his way. This trip is no problem to him, and he can win again given a stronger pace and luck in running. Official explanation: jockey said gelding was denied a clear run. (op 4-1)
Shela House just about got the longer trip, though a return to 1m4f would not be a problem. She has been going well this season, and looks capable of finding a handicap, particularly if dropped a pound or two. (op 5-1)
Bandama(IRE) had every chance of staying this trip, but the jury is still out after his effort near the centre of the track petered out a bit in the last furlong. At his best he is certainly capable of winning a decent handicap around 1m4f. (op 7-2)
Swan Queen Official explanation: trainer's representative said the mare was unsuited by the ood to firm (good in places) going.

3210 TAURUS WASTE RECYCLING FILLIES' STKS (H'CAP) 7f
9:00 (9:04) (Class 4) (0-85,84) 3-Y-O+ £4,533 (£1,011; £1,011; £336) Stalls High

Form RPR

2016 1 **Rydal Mount (IRE)**[9] 2947 5-9-12 82 FergusSweeney 3 91
(W S Kittow) *hld up: hdwy 3f out: led 2f out: hld on wl* 12/1

031 2 3/4 **Naughty Frida (IRE)**[16] 2714 3-9-2 81 JohnEgan 5 85
(M Botti) *a.p: rdn over 1f out: kpt on to share 2nd post* 5/1

-562 **2** *dht* **Just Like A Woman**[8] 2976 3-8-8 **73** ow1 RichardHughes 9 77
(M L W Bell) *t.k.h: trckd ldr: ev ch ins fnl f: jnd for 2nd post* **7/4**[1]

4102 **4** *1 1/2* **Love On Sight**[17] 2692 4-8-13 **69** SebSanders 8 72
(J R Boyle) *hld up: hdwy on ins 2f out: nvr nr to chal* **9/1**

-245 **5** *3/4* **Nice To Know (FR)**[7] 2993 4-9-10 **80** GeorgeBaker 1 81+
(G L Moore) *hld up: and c towards centre fr outside draw: short of room 2f out: kpt on fnl f: nvr nr to chal* **7/2**[2]

5-02 **6** *5* **Medicea Sidera**[9] 2947 4-10-0 **84** LPKeniry 4 71
(E F Vaughan) *led tl hdd 2f out: sn wknd* **4/1**[3]

0-60 **7** *4* **Ivory Lace**[15] 2762 7-10-0 **84** JimCrowley 6 61
(S Woodman) *hld up: rdn and swtchd lft over 2f out: n.d* **10/1**

4504 **8** *3* **Bookish**[9] 2930 3-8-4 **69** (b) CatherineGannon 2 35
(Jamie Poulton) *prom tl wknd 2f out* **33/1**

1m 27.76s (0.36) **Going Correction** +0.125s/f (Good)
WFA 3 from 4yo+ 9lb **8** Ran SP% **125.0**
Speed ratings (Par 102): **102,101,101,99,98 92,88,84**
Place 6 £ 69.84, Place 5 £ 50.96; toteswinger: RM&NF £6.70, RM&JLAW £8.00, NF&JLAW £3.10. TOTE £16.70: £3.70 TRIFECTA 2nd Pl NF 1.60, JLAW 1.50; Ex: RM-NF 61.80, RM-JLAW 24.80; CSF: RM-NF 38.55, RM-JLAW 18.37; T/C: RM-NF-JLAW 81.54, RM-JLAW-NF 65.59.

FOCUS
Another steadily run race, and not the most solid of form as a result.
Medicea Sidera Official explanation: jockey said filly was struck into.
T/Plt: £60.90 to a £1 stake. Pool: £50,328.40. 602.36 winning tickets. T/Qpdt: £13.40 to a £1 stake. Pool: £3,604.69. 198.10 winning tickets. JS

2838 MUSSELBURGH (R-H)

Friday, June 20

OFFICIAL GOING: Good to firm (firm in places; 8.5)
Wind: Moderate, half against Weather: Dry and sunny

3211 SCOTMAT CARPETS AND MAPEI UK H'CAP 7f 30y
2:10 (2:13) (Class 6) (0-65,65) 4-Y-0+ **£2,590** (£770; £385; £192) **Stalls** High

Form RPR

1152 **1** **Zabeel Tower**[13] 2846 5-9-2 **60** (p) TonyHamilton 14 71
(R Allan) *trckd ldrs on inner: smooth hdwy over 2f out: rdn to ld ent fnl f: styd on* **11/4**[1]

-000 **2** *1 1/4* **Joshua's Gold (IRE)**[15] 2365 7-9-3 **61** (v) DNolan 4 68
(D Carroll) *cl up on outer: effrt 3f out: rdn to ld wl over 1f out: drvn and hdd ent fnl f: kpt on* **5/1**[3]

3000 **3** *2 3/4* **Attacca**[4] 3079 7-8-4 **48** PaulFessey 13 48
(J R Weymes) *chsd ldrs: hdwy wl over 2f out: sn rdn anmd styd on u.p ins fnl f* **18/1**

-020 **4** *hd* **Grand Diamond (IRE)**[20] 2597 4-9-2 **60** (p) FergalLynch 8 59
(J S Goldie) *led: rdn along 3f out: hdd wl over 1f out: sn drvn and one pce ent fnl f* **8/1**

0-04 **5** *1/2* **Beaumont Boy**[15] 2747 4-8-9 **56** (p) PJMcDonald(3) 7 54
(A G Foster) *in tch: hdwy 3f out: rdn over 2f out and no imp appr fnl f* **25/1**

1403 **6** *1 1/2* **Shunkawakhan (IRE)**[14] 2806 5-8-13 **57** (p) DO'Donohoe 3 55+
(Miss L A Perratt) *in tch: effrt on inner whn n.m.r over 2f out: sn swtchd lft and rdn: no imp* **12/1**

0020 **7** *1/2* **Kunte Kinteh**[14] 2782 4-9-2 **63** AndrewMullen(3) 10 56
(D Nicholls) *prom: rdn along 3f out: sn wknd* **8/1**

6004 **8** *1* **Royal Challenge**[11] 2891 7-9-4 **62** PatrickMathers 6 52
(I W McInnes) *a towards rr* **20/1**

-000 **9** *1/2* **Fan Club**[22] 2523 4-7-13 **48** oh1 ow2 (b) KellyHarrison(5) 12 41+
(Mrs R A Carr) *s.i.s: hdwy whn nt clr run on inner 2f out: nt rcvr* **33/1**

2663 **10** *2 1/4* **A Big Sky Brewing (USA)**[11] 2891 4-8-10 **59** NeilBrown(5) 11 42
(T D Barron) *midfield: effrt wl over 2f out: sn rdn along and btn* **7/2**[2]

2-60 **11** *1/2* **Motu (IRE)**[9] 2925 7-9-7 **65** (v) RoystonFfrench 5 46
(I W McInnes) *a in rr* **20/1**

-000 **12** *4 1/2* **Baaher (USA)**[60] 1521 4-8-12 **63** (p) BMcHugh(7) 2 32
(T J Pitt) *a towards rr* **20/1**

1m 29.48s (-0.82) **Going Correction** -0.075s/f (Good) **12** Ran SP% **123.3**
Speed ratings (Par 101): **101,99,96,96,95 93,93,92,91,89 88,83**
toteswinger: 1&2 £4.10, 1&3 £11.00, 2&3 £24.80. CSF £15.46 CT £217.44 TOTE £3.30: £1.60, £1.70, £5.60; EX 20.40.
Owner R. H. I. Ltd **Bred** Gainsborough Stud Management Ltd **Trained** Duns, Scottish Borders

FOCUS
A low-grade handicap won by one of the few in-form horses in the race. He is rated back to his best old form.
Shunkawakhan(IRE) Official explanation: jockey said gelding was denied a clear run
Royal Challenge Official explanation: jockey said gelding was denied a clear run

3212 BRYANT HOMES HOPEFIELD MEADOWS (S) STKS 5f
2:45 (2:46) (Class 6) 3-Y-0+ **£2,266** (£674; £337; £168) **Stalls** Low

Form RPR

3642 **1** **Whinhill House**[4] 3080 8-9-4 61 (v) TonyHamilton 9 72
(D W Barker) *sn led: rdn clr appr fnl f: kpt on* **6/4**[1]

5300 **2** *2 1/2* **Fire Up The Band**[10] 2906 9-9-10 82 FergalLynch 5 69
(A Berry) *cl up: rdn 2f out: drvn ent fnl f and kpt on same pce* **7/2**[2]

0040 **3** *5* **Alfie Lee (IRE)**[13] 2843 11-8-11 48 (tp) PaulPickard(7) 7 45
(D A Nolan) *prom: rdn along wl over 1f out: drvn and kpt on ins fnl f* **66/1**

0135 **4** *2* **Angelofthenorth**[9] 2928 6-9-0 51 KellyHarrison(5) 1 39+
(C J Teague) *dwlt and rr: swtchd rt and hdwy 2f out: nt clr run over 1f out: kpt on ins fnl f: nrst fin* **9/1**

015- **5** *nk* **Elijah Pepper (USA)**[227] 6699 3-8-12 73 PaulFessey 8 35
(T D Barron) *towards rr: hdwy whn n.m.r over 1f out: swtchd lft and rdn: styd on ins fnl f: nrst fin* **5/1**[3]

3200 **6** *1 3/4* **Baileys Outshine**[18] 2676 4-9-5 66 (b[1]) DO'Donohoe 4 31
(J G Given) *chsd ldrs: rdn and edgd lft wl over 1f out: sn wknd* **12/1**

0060 **7** *1/2* **Howards Prince**[2] 3128 5-8-13 40 GaryBartley(5) 6 29
(D A Nolan) *in rr tl styd on appr fnl f: nrst fin* **150/1**

3502 **8** *1/2* **Princess Charlmane (IRE)**[21] 2576 5-8-10 43 (t) PJMcDonald(3) 11 22
(C J Teague) *prom: rdn along 2f out: sn wknd* **14/1**

6600 **9** *3/4* **Percy Douglas**[14] 2777 8-8-13 37 AnnStokell(5) 12 24
(Miss A Stokell) *chsd ldrs: rdn 2f out and sn wknd* **100/1**

0-64 **10** *2 1/2* **Best Lead**[32] 2248 9-8-11 50 (b) DeclanCannon(7) 10 15
(Ian Emmerson) *in tch towards outer: rdn along 2f out and sn btn* **11/1**

0-00 **11** *3/4* **Sokoke**[31] 2283 7-9-4 40 PatrickMathers 3 12
(D A Nolan) *chsd ldrs to 1/2-way* **100/1**

0005 **12** *9* **Dotty's Daughter**[127] 562 4-8-10 38 (p) AndrewMullen(3) 2 —
(B Storey) *nvr nr ldrs* **66/1**

0000 **13** *1 3/4* **Notforloveormoney**[21] 2576 3-8-7 33 RoystonFfrench 14 —
(A G Foster) *in tch on wd outside: rdn along and bhd fr 1/2-way* **125/1**

59.86 secs (-0.54) **Going Correction** -0.075s/f (Good)
WFA 3 from 4yo+ 6lb **13** Ran SP% **118.0**
Speed ratings (Par 101): **101,97,89,85,85 82,81,80,79,75 74,60,57**
toteswinger: 1&2 £2.30, 1&3 £19.60, 2&3 £38.40. CSF £6.38 TOTE £2.70: £1.20, £1.60, £9.60; EX 8.00.There was no bid for the winner.
Owner Destiny Racing Club **Bred** W R And Mrs Arblaster **Trained** Scorton, N Yorks

FOCUS
The 'classier' and in-form pair dominated and came clear of the proper selling-grade horses. The winner is rated to his best form of last year but could be vulnerable if he goes up in the weights for this.

3213 BUCK CONSULTANTS H'CAP 7f 30y
3:20 (3:21) (Class 6) (0-65,65) 3-Y-0 **£2,590** (£770; £385; £192) **Stalls** High

Form RPR

0200 **1** **Dnata Flyer (USA)**[28] 2366 3-9-2 **60** RoystonFfrench 7 67
(M Johnston) *chsd ldrs: rdn along and hung lft over 2f out: styng on whn swtchd rt ent fnl f: drvn and led last 50yds* **8/1**

0-04 **2** *3/4* **Forrest Star**[42] 1951 3-8-12 **56** DO'Donohoe 9 61
(Miss L A Perratt) *t.k.h: led: jnd 3f out: rdn 2f out: hung lft ent fnl f: hdd and no ex last 50yds* **8/1**

0-56 **3** *3 1/2* **Ride A White Swan**[49] 1781 3-9-6 **64** DarrenWilliams 8 60
(K R Burke) *trckd ldrs: hdwy on bit and cl up 1/2-way: rdn 2f out and ev ch tl drvn and one pce appr fnl f* **11/4**[1]

4633 **4** *2 1/4* **Jevington Star (IRE)**[2] 3139 3-7-13 **46** oh1 (b) AndrewMullen(3) 1 35
(B Ellison) *in rr: hdwy on outer over 2f out: sn rdn and styd on ins fnl f: nt rch ldrs* **4/1**[3]

-405 **5** *3 1/4* **Low Flyer (USA)**[10] 2911 3-8-8 **57** (b[1]) NeilBrown(5) 3 38
(T D Barron) *chsd ldrs: rdn along wl over 2f out: sn wknd* **3/1**[2]

0-40 **6** *1* **Princess Rhianna (IRE)**[14] 2781 3-8-12 **59** PJMcDonald(3) 5 37
(Mrs G S Rees) *hld up: a towards rr* **8/1**

000 **7** *2* **Ceduna Roadhouse (IRE)**[15] 2750 3-8-4 **48** ow1 PatrickMathers 4 21
(A M Crow) *a in rr* **40/1**

0 **8** *5* **Distant Rock**[18] 2660 3-9-7 **65** DNolan 6 24
(D Carroll) *trckd ldrs: hdwy over 3f out: rdn over 2f out: sn drvn and wknd* **10/1**

1m 29.52s (-0.78) **Going Correction** -0.075s/f (Good) **8** Ran SP% **116.5**
Speed ratings (Par 97): **101,100,96,93,89 88,86,80**
toteswinger: 1&2 £7.20, 1&3 £6.30, 2&3 £6.40. CSF £70.64 CT £200.98 TOTE £11.00: £3.30, £2.10, £1.20; EX 51.10.
Owner Sheikh Hamdan Bin Mohammed Al Maktoum **Bred** L And D Farms **Trained** Middleham Moor, N Yorks

FOCUS
A very moderate handicap, probably best rated through the second and third. Few winners are likely to emerge from the race.
Dnata Flyer(USA) Official explanation: trainer's representative had no explanation for the improved form shown.
Ceduna Roadhouse(IRE) Official explanation: jockey said filly was unsuited by the firm (good to firm in places) going.

3214 DM HALL H'CAP 1m
4:00 (4:00) (Class 4) (0-80,75) 4-Y-0+ **£6,476** (£1,927; £963; £481) **Stalls** High

Form RPR

0-41 **1** **Sunnyside Tom (IRE)**[13] 2841 4-9-4 **72** TonyHamilton 1 81
(R A Fahey) *cl up: rdn to ld 2f out: drvn ins fnl f: edgd lft and kpt on wl towards fin* **6/4**[1]

0520 **2** *nk* **Fiefdom (IRE)**[8] 2969 6-9-2 **70** (p) RoystonFfrench 2 78
(I W McInnes) *trckd ldng pair: effrt 3f out: sn rdn and chal ent fnl f: ev ch whn rdr dropped whip and nt qckn last 50yds* **11/2**

-600 **3** *1 1/4* **Frank Crow**[15] 2749 5-8-6 **65** GaryBartley(5) 4 70
(J S Goldie) *in tch: hdwy on outer over 2f out: rdn and edgd rt over 1f out: drvn and kpt on ins fnl f* **10/1**

-165 **4** *1* **Dispol Isle (IRE)**[18] 2672 6-8-11 **70** NeilBrown(5) 5 73+
(T D Barron) *trckd ldng pair: effrt on inner whn nt clr 2f out: swtchd lft and rdn over 1f out: nt qckn ins fnl f* **7/2**[3]

25-0 **5** *2 1/4* **Emerald Bay (IRE)**[154] 218 6-9-7 **75** DO'Donohoe 3 73
(Miss L A Perratt) *led: rdn along 3f out: hdd 2f out and sn wknd* **10/3**[2]

1m 40.58s (-0.62) **Going Correction** -0.075s/f (Good) **5** Ran SP% **109.8**
Speed ratings (Par 105): **100,99,98,97,95**
CSF £9.99 TOTE £1.90: £1.20, £2.90; EX 9.40.
Owner The Sunnyside Racing Partnership **Bred** S W D McIlveen **Trained** Musley Bank, N Yorks

FOCUS
A muddling affair, and ordinary form for the grade. The winner is improving but possibly benefited from Dispol Isle having nowhere to go for much of the home straight.

3215 SCOTTISH RACING CLAIMING STKS 5f
4:35 (4:37) (Class 6) 2-Y-0 **£2,266** (£674; £337; £168) **Stalls** Low

Form RPR

325 **1** **Faraway Sound (IRE)**[18] 2657 2-9-8 0 LeeEnstone 1 70
(P C Haslam) *cl up: led 2f out: rdn clr ins fnl f: kpt on* **4/6**[1]

6432 **2** *2 1/4* **Lady Fantasie**[8] 2965 2-8-7 0 RoystonFfrench 2 47
(Mrs A Duffield) *led: rdn along and hdd 2f out: sn drvn and kpt on same pce* **2/1**[2]

5 **3** *1 1/2* **Chicken Momo**[45] 1889 2-9-2 0 DarrenWilliams 4 51
(K R Burke) *s.i.s: in rr tl hdwy 1/2-way: rdn to chse ldng pair over 1f out: sn no imp* **7/1**[3]

4 *12* **Moomoo** 2-9-0 0 DO'Donohoe 3 5
(J R Weymes) *wnt rt s: chsd ldng pair: rdn along 1/2-way and sn outpcd* **14/1**

61.69 secs (1.29) **Going Correction** -0.075s/f (Good) **4** Ran SP% **112.5**
Speed ratings (Par 91): **86,82,80,60**
CSF £2.42 TOTE £1.60; EX 2.20.
Owner Middleham Park Racing XXXIX **Bred** Yeomanstown Stud **Trained** Middleham Moor, N Yorks

FOCUS
An uncompetitive claimer but straightforward form to rate.

NOTEBOOK
Faraway Sound(IRE) had the cheekpieces left off on this drop in grade and comfortably got off the mark at the fourth time of asking. He should be able to go on from this. (op Evens)
Lady Fantasie continues to run well, but she found the winner too strong. There is not a lot of her and she may not have a lot of scope for improvement. (tchd 5-2)
Chicken Momo, slowly into stride, ran a fair race under the circumstances. This was his second run and he may prove capable of better. (op 9-2)

Moomoo, a daughter of Kheleyf out of a dual 5f-7f juvenile winner, showed nothing on her debut. (op 18-1)

3216 CRUDEN GROUP H'CAP — 2m 2f 37y
5:10 (5:10) (Class 5) (0-70,74) 4-Y-0+ — £4,209 (£1,252; £625; £312) Stalls High

Form				RPR
2121	1		**Directa's Digger (IRE)**[4] 3083 4-9-9 **74** 6ex ....(v) JackDean[(5)] 4 (M J Scudamore) *trckd ldr: hdwy 3f out: rdn to chal on outer over 2f out and sn hung rt: drvn to ld ins fnl f: jst hld on* **2/5**[1]	63
4266	2	hd	**Easibet Dot Net**[15] 2752 8-8-5 **50** oh2 ....(b) DO'Donohoe 1 (Miss L A Perratt) *hld up: hdwy on inner over 2f out: rdn to ld wl over 1f out: sn edgd lft: drvn and hdd ins fnl f: kpt on u.p: jst hld* **10/3**[2]	39
-060	3	6	**Asrar**[15] 2752 6-8-2 **50** oh5 .... AndrewMullen[(3)] 5 (Miss Lucinda V Russell) *in rr: hdwy over 2f out: rdn to chse ldrs over 1f out: kpt on same pce ent fnl f* **33/1**	33
-600	4	1 ½	**Stravonian**[15] 2752 8-8-2 **54** oh5 ow4 .... DeanHeslop[(7)] 3 (D A Nolan) *cl up: led 1/2-way: rdn along 3f out: drvn and hdd wl ov er 1f out: stl cl up whan hmpd over 1f out: sn wknd* **100/1**	35
/05-	5	1 ¾	**Act Sirius (IRE)**[62] 3379 4-9-10 **70** .... TonyHamilton 2 (A Crook) *led to 1/2-way: clsd up: rdn 2f out and ev ch tl hmpd over 1f out and sn wknd* **10/1**[3]	49

4m 12.72s (252.72)
WFA 4 from 6yo+ 1lb — 5 Ran SP% **107.5**
CSF £1.87 TOTE £1.40: £1.10, £1.10; EX 1.80.
Owner I J Anderson **Bred** J Dorrian **Trained** Bromsash, Herefordshire

FOCUS
A moderate handicap run over a marathon trip and they did not look to at all quick early on. The form is virtually worthless with the third and fourth well out of the weights.

3217 TURFTV APPRENTICE H'CAP — 5f
5:40 (5:40) (Class 6) (0-65,70) 3-Y-0 — £2,266 (£674; £337; £168) Stalls Low

Form				RPR
6211	1		**Speedy Senorita (IRE)**[12] 2864 3-9-11 **70** 6ex .... DeclanCannon[(5)] 2 (K R Burke) *mde all: rdn over 1f out: hung rt ins fnl f: drvn and styd on wl towards fin* **6/4**[1]	76
-634	2	½	**Grudge**[13] 2850 3-9-10 **64** .... AndrewMullen 3 (D W Barker) *chsd ldrs: rdn over 1f out: styd on to chal ins fnl f: drvn and nt qckn towards fin* **4/1**[2]	68
5000	3	nk	**Thomas Malory (IRE)**[18] 2660 3-9-0 **54** .... DNolan 4 (Miss V Haigh) *in tch whn sltly hmpd after 1f and towards rr: hdwy 2f out: rdn and styd on ins fnl f: nrst fin* **13/2**[3]	57
6004	4	1 ¼	**Paddy Jack**[22] 2527 3-9-5 **62** ....(p) NeilBrown[(3)] 8 (J R Weymes) *prom: rdn along and ev ch over 1f out: drvn and wknd ins fnl f* **12/1**	60
-530	5	nk	**Miss Sunshine**[22] 2527 3-8-5 **48** .... KellyHarrison[(3)] 5 (J S Goldie) *towards rr: hdwy 2f out: sn rdn and styd on ins fnl f: nrst fin* **12/1**	45
0003	6	½	**Andrasta**[15] 2747 3-8-9 **54** .... DanielleMcCreery[(5)] 6 (A Berry) *chsd ldrs: rdn along 2f out: drvn and kpt on same pce appr fnl f* **14/1**	49
0556	7	3 ¼	**Extreme North (USA)**[24] 2490 3-9-1 **60** ....(b) ShaneCreighton[(5)] 1 (Miss V Haigh) *chsd ldrs on inner: rdn along 2f out: drvn over 1f out and no imp ins fnl f* **13/2**[3]	43
603	8	1 ¾	**Champagne Lawn (USA)**[13] 2823 3-9-3 **62** ....(b[1]) DeanHeslop[(5)] 7 (T D Barron) *dwlt and a towards rr* **14/1**	39
055	9	¾	**La Guancha**[2] 3128 3-8-1 **48** ow3 ....(tp) JamesRogers[(7)] 9 (D A Nolan) *chsd ldrs and swtchd lft after 1f: rdn along 1/2-way: sn lost pl and rr* **33/1**	22

60.08 secs (-0.32) **Going Correction** -0.075s/f (Good) — 9 Ran SP% **118.3**
Speed ratings (Par 97): **99,98,97,95,95 94,89,86,85**
toteswinger: 1&2 £2.30, 1&3 £3.60, 2&3 £6.50. CSF £7.58 CT £30.59 TOTE £2.30: £1.10, £1.80; EX 5.80 Place 6 £9.04, Place 5 £4.81..
Owner Market Avenue Racing Club Ltd **Bred** R McEnery And Vincent Millett **Trained** Middleham Moor, N Yorks

■ Stewards' Enquiry : Andrew Mullen one-day ban: used whip with frequency and down the shoulder in the forehand position (Jul 4)

FOCUS
A modest sprint handicap but sound enough form for the grade, with the runner-up rated close to his recent level.
Andrasta Official explanation: jockey said filly's saddle slipped.
T/Plt: £7.10 to a £1 stake. Pool: £37,676.54. 3,821.90 winning tickets. T/Qpdt: £4.80 to a £1 stake. Pool: £1,765.99. 267.20 winning tickets. JR

2423 NEWMARKET (R-H)
Friday, June 20

OFFICIAL GOING: Good to firm (9.3)
Wind: Light across Weather: Overcast

3218 NEWMARKET NIGHTS APPRENTICE H'CAP — 1m
6:00 (6:01) (Class 5) (0-70,70) 4-Y-0+ — £3,885 (£1,156; £577; £288) Stalls Low

Form				RPR
0340	1		**Sintenis Mac (GER)**[9] 2949 5-8-4 **55** ....(b[1]) AshleyMorgan[(5)] 8 (P J O'Gorman) *s.i.s: hld up: hdwy over 3f out: led over 1f out: rdn and edgd rt ins fnl f: r.o* **12/1**	64
-421	2	1 ¾	**Isphahan**[7] 2992 5-9-4 **67** 6ex .... DavidProbert[(3)] 10 (A M Balding) *a.p: rdn over 1f out: edgd rt: styd on* **7/2**[2]	72
-564	3	shd	**Sonny Parkin**[9] 2943 6-9-5 **70** ....(v) SimonPearce[(5)] 12 (J Pearce) *hld up: swtchd lft and hdwy over 1f out: rdn and ev ch ins fnl furlong: nt run on* **10/3**[1]	75
66-5	4	2 ½	**Samahir (USA)**[23] 2513 4-8-3 **52** .... MCGeran[(3)] 13 (T T Clement) *hld up: hdwy over 2f out: rdn over 1f out: hung lft ins fnl f: styd on same pce* **8/1**	51
5501	5	2 ¼	**Batchworth Blaise**[28] 2355 5-8-0 **51** oh2 .... RossAtkinson[(5)] 6 (E A Wheeler) *hld up: plld hrd: hdwy over 2f out: rdn over 1f out: wknd ins fnl f* **8/1**	45
0650	6	½	**Sir Liam (USA)**[9] 2933 4-9-1 **61** .... AshleyHamblett 14 (R A Teal) *sn led: hdd 5f out: rdn over 2f out: wknd ins fnl f* **13/2**[3]	54
6000	7	1 ½	**Louisiade (IRE)**[11] 2897 7-8-9 **60** ....(p) NBazeley[(5)] 3 (M C Chapman) *chsd ldr tl led 5f out: rdn and hdd over 2f out: wknd fnl f* **33/1**	49
0210	8	hd	**Mick Is Back**[14] 2795 4-8-10 **59** ....(vt) JPHamblett[(3)] 11 (G G Margarson) *hld up: hdwy and hung lft over 2f out: sn rdn: wknd fnl f* **9/1**	48
0-00	9	3 ¼	**Peak Seasons (IRE)**[8] 2983 5-8-2 **51** oh6 ....(v) AmyBaker[(3)] 5 (M C Chapman) *chsd ldrs: rdn over 3f out: wknd over 1f out* **66/1**	32
-560	10	1 ¼	**Espejo (IRE)**[43] 1938 4-8-2 **53** .... DebraEngland[(5)] 2 (W J Musson) *hld up in tch: wknd over 2f out* **20/1**	31
45-4	11	½	**Astroangel**[38] 2070 4-8-11 **57** ....(p) NicolPolli 4 (M H Tompkins) *s.i.s: sn prom: rdn and wknd over 1f out* **8/1**	34
0-50	12	6	**Rasmani**[9] 2929 4-8-0 **51** oh6 .... RosieJessop[(5)] 1 (Miss Gay Kelleway) *chsd ldrs: rdn over 2f out: wknd over 1f out* **40/1**	14

1m 40.35s (0.35) **Going Correction** +0.075s/f (Good) — 12 Ran SP% **121.3**
Speed ratings (Par 103): **101,99,99,96,94 93,92,92,88,87 87,81**
toteswinger: 1&2 £10.90, 1&3 £11.60, 2&3 £2.80. CSF £53.59 CT £178.76 TOTE £16.40: £3.30, £1.70, £2.00; EX 85.60.
Owner Michael McDonnell **Bred** B Fassbender **Trained** Newmarket, Suffolk

FOCUS
A moderate handicap, confined to apprentice riders, run at a fair pace. The placed horses set the level.

3219 CORPORATEFX FOREIGN CURRENCY MAIDEN STKS — 6f
6:30 (6:31) (Class 4) 2-Y-0 — £5,180 (£1,541; £770; £384) Stalls Low

Form				RPR
4	1		**Rose Diamond (IRE)**[13] 2821 2-8-12 0 .... ChrisCatlin 10 (R Charlton) *a.p: shkn up over 1f out: rdn to ld and hung lft wl ins fnl f* **1/1**[1]	80
50	2	¾	**Head Down**[21] 2562 2-9-3 0 .... DaneO'Neill 3 (R Hannon) *a.p: chsd ldr over 2f out: rdn to ld and hung lft ins fnl f: sn hdd styd on* **8/1**[3]	83
2	3	1 ½	**Green Beret (IRE)**[11] 2893 2-9-3 0 .... RobertHavlin 1 (J H M Gosden) *led: rdn over 1f out: hdd ins fnl f: styng on same pce whn hmpd towards fin* **5/2**[2]	79+
	4	½	**Desert Icon (IRE)** 2-9-3 0 .... PaulDoe 12 (W J Knight) *hld up: hdwy over 2f out: rdn over 1f out: hung lft ins fnl f: r.o* **20/1**	77
	5	2 ½	**Wannabe King** 2-9-3 0 .... TPQueally 2 (D R Lanigan) *chsd ldr over 3f: sn rdn: wknd fnl f* **14/1**	69+
	6	shd	**Flintlock (IRE)** 2-9-3 0 ....(b[1]) DavidKinsella 9 (J H M Gosden) *s.i.s: sn drvn along in rr: r.o u.p ins fnl f: nt trble ldrs* **25/1**	69+
	7	1 ¼	**Swiss Diva** 2-8-12 0 .... TQuinn 13 (D R C Elsworth) *hld up: effrt over 1f out: n.d* **16/1**	60
	8	½	**Zaffaan** 2-9-3 0 .... StephenDonohoe 5 (E A L Dunlop) *chsd ldrs 4f* **20/1**	64
5	9	1 ½	**Charismatic Charli (IRE)**[29] 2331 2-9-3 0 .... LiamJones 11 (P W D'Arcy) *mid-div: sn pushed along: lost pl 4f out: wknd over 2f out* **50/1**	59
	10	1 ½	**Red Humour (IRE)** 2-9-0 0 .... PatrickHills[(3)] 4 (B W Hills) *chsd ldrs: rdn over 2f out: wknd over 1f out* **16/1**	55
	11	3 ½	**Sericus (IRE)** 2-9-3 0 .... KShea 7 (W Jarvis) *s.i.s: sme hdwy over 2f out: sn wknd* **25/1**	44

1m 13.16s (0.66) **Going Correction** +0.075s/f (Good) — 11 Ran SP% **127.3**
Speed ratings (Par 95): **98,97,95,94,91 90,89,88,86,84 79**
toteswinger: 1&2 £2.90, 1&3 £1.40, 2&3 £3.30. CSF £10.52 TOTE £2.20: £1.10, £3.10, £1.40; EX 15.80.
Owner B E Nielsen **Bred** Bjorn Nielsen **Trained** Beckhampton, Wilts

FOCUS
This has proved to be a good juvenile maiden in the past and this year's running looks a fair event. The form is set by the first three.

NOTEBOOK
Rose Diamond(IRE), very well backed, confirmed the promise of her debut fourth at Doncaster 13 days previously and just did enough to repel the runner-up where it mattered. While her dam was a smart sprinter for the stable, this filly is bred to appreciate a stiffer test and should really relish another furlong or so in due course. She looks a useful perfomer in the making. (op 11-8 tchd 13-8)
Head Down showed by far his best form to date, only just going down, and enjoyed the switch to a quicker surface. He has a maiden in him on similar ground, but does look a more likely type for nurseries. (op 9-1 tchd 7-1)
Green Beret(IRE), second on his debut at Windsor 11 days previously, was given a positive ride and had his chance from the front. He was held prior to being hampered late in the day and this was only a slight improvement on his initial run, but there is still likely more to come from him. (op 11-4 tchd 3-1)
Desert Icon(IRE), whose dam was a 5f winner at three, posted a pleasing debut effort and fared best of the newcomers. This experience will certainly not be lost on him and he has a future. (op 22-1)

3220 WALKER TRANSPORT SERVICES H'CAP — 1m 4f
7:05 (7:05) (Class 5) (0-75,75) 4-Y-0+ — £3,885 (£1,156; £577; £288) Stalls Centre

Form				RPR
3322	1		**Bassinet (USA)**[21] 2558 4-9-1 **70** .... KirstyMilczarek[(3)] 9 (J A R Toller) *hld up: swtchd lft and hdwy over 2f out: rdn to ld ins fnl f: r.o: edgd lft towards fin* **4/1**[2]	80
-124	2	1	**Summer Of Love (IRE)**[10] 2921 4-9-1 **67** ....(b) StephenDonohoe 5 (Mrs S J Humphrey) *s.s: sn prom: led over 2f out: sn edgd rt: rdn and hdd ins fnl f: styd on same pce* **6/1**[3]	76
4-11	3	3 ½	**Susie May**[28] 2354 4-9-3 **69** .... TPQueally 4 (G L Moore) *a.p: rdn over 2f out: no ex fnl f* **15/8**[1]	72
3463	4	¾	**Just Intersky (USA)**[8] 2456 5-8-7 **59** ....(p) ChrisCatlin 8 (V Smith) *hld up: plld hrd: hdwy over 3f out: rdn over 1f out: no ex* **20/1**	61
3055	5	1	**Is It Me (USA)**[10] 2908 5-9-0 **66** .... KShea 10 (A W Carroll) *led: hdd over 2f out: sn rdn: wknd ins fnl f* **9/1**	66
1016	6	½	**Apache Fort**[15] 2304 5-8-8 **67** .... AshleyMorgan[(7)] 3 (T Keddy) *hld up: hdwy over 3f out: rdn over 1f out: wknd ins fnl f* **14/1**	67
5-24	7	3	**Spanish Diva**[76] 1205 4-9-4 **70** .... DaneO'Neill 7 (S C Williams) *trckd ldrs: plld hrd: rdn over 2f out: wknd fnl f* **8/1**	65
-440	8	1 ½	**Pretty Demanding (IRE)**[7] 3003 4-9-0 **71** .... JamieJones[(5)] 2 (M G Quinlan) *hld up: outpcd over 2f out: n.d after* **9/1**	63
-604	9	3 ½	**Royal Jasra**[11] 2895 4-9-9 **75** ....(b[1]) TQuinn 1 (E A L Dunlop) *chsd ldr tl rdn over 2f out: wkng whn n.m.r over 1f out* **14/1**	62

2m 32.11s (-0.79) **Going Correction** +0.075s/f (Good) — 9 Ran SP% **118.3**
Speed ratings (Par 103): **105,104,102,101,100 100,98,97,95**
toteswinger: 1&2 £6.40, 1&3 £2.20, 2&3 £3.70. CSF £29.04 CT £59.36 TOTE £5.50: £2.00, £2.10, £1.10; EX 26.00.
Owner John Drew **Bred** Juddmonte Farms Inc **Trained** Newmarket, Suffolk

FOCUS
A modest handicap run at a steady early pace. The form is set by the second and third.

3221 PORTLAND PLACE PROPERTIES H'CAP 1m
7:35 (7:37) (Class 5) (0-75,74) 3-Y-O **£3,885** (£1,156; £577; £288) **Stalls** Low

Form RPR

0-50 **1** **Yathreb (USA)**[35] 2151 3-9-1 **66**................(b) RHills 6 81
(J L Dunlop) *chsd ldrs: led over 2f out: rdn and hung rt fr over 1f out: styd on* **9/2**[3]

4005 **2** *2* **Mr Hichens**[18] 2678 3-9-4 **69**................RobertHavlin 8 81+
(B J Meehan) *a.p: rdn to chse wnr and hung rt over 1f out: sn hung lft: ev ch whn hit rails wl ins fnl f: no ex* **7/1**

3042 **3** *7* **Jollyhockeysticks**[17] 2700 3-8-10 **66**................MCGeran(5) 7 60
(M R Channon) *hld up in tch: rdn over 3f out: edgd lft and wknd over 1f out* **8/1**

431- **4** *nk* **Southpaw Lad**[226] 6714 3-9-9 **74**................DaneO'Neill 13 67
(J R Best) *dwlt: hld up: plld hrd: hdwy u.p and hung lft fr over 1f out: wknd fnl f* **12/1**

0-04 **5** *1* **Reve Vert (FR)**[10] 2922 3-8-1 **55** oh3................KirstyMilczarek(3) 3 46
(A W Carroll) *led: rdn and hdd over 1f out: wkng whn hung lft ins fnl f* **12/1**

2303 **6** *2 1/4* **Christophers Quest**[26] 2429 3-9-1 **66**................LiamJones 10 52
(A W Carroll) *hld up: rdn over 2f out: hung lft and wknd over 1f out* **3/1**[1]

4-33 **7** *4* **Jafra (IRE)**[39] 2041 3-8-8 **59**................KShea 1 36
(R M Whitaker) *mid-div: hdwy over 3f out: sn rdn: wknd over 1f out* **9/1**

0-60 **8** *2 3/4* **Cinerama (IRE)**[25] 2449 3-8-13 **64**................TPQueally 5 34
(M P Tregoning) *hld up: racd keenly: hdwy over 3f out: sn rdn: wknd over 1f out* **14/1**

0-64 **9** *1 1/4* **Augmentation**[8] 2982 3-8-7 **58**................(p) ChrisCatlin 11 25
(P W D'Arcy) *s.i.s: hdwy 6f out: rdn: hung lft and wknd over 2f out* **16/1**

0142 **10** *8* **Challow Hills (USA)**[25] 2451 3-9-4 **69**................MichaelHills 9 18
(B W Hills) *prom: rdn 1/2-way: hung lft and wknd over 2f out* **4/1**[2]

3060 **11** *1/2* **Reprieved**[8] 2982 3-8-0 **58**................CharlotteKerton(7) 12 6
(M C Chapman) *s.s: plld hrd: hdwy over 6f out: rdn: hung lft and wknd over 2f out* **40/1**

1m 38.73s (-1.27) **Going Correction** +0.075s/f (Good) **11** Ran SP% **127.2**
Speed ratings (Par 99): **109,107,100,99,98 96,92,89,88,80 79**
toteswinger: 1&2 £10.50, 1&3 £10.60, 2&3 £12.30. CSF £39.47 CT £257.21 TOTE £7.10: £2.70, £3.00, £1.80; EX 52.50.
Owner Hamdan Al Maktoum **Bred** Shadwell Farm LLC **Trained** Arundel, W Sussex

FOCUS
A modest handicap run at a sound pace. It has been rated around the runner-up, with the third and fifth 5lb off their recent form.
Yathreb(USA) Official explanation: trainer's representative said, regarding the running, that the gelding was inconsistent and appeared to benefit for the drop down to a mile.
Reve Vert(FR) Official explanation: jockey said colt ran too free.
Challow Hills(USA) Official explanation: jockey said filly was unsuited by the good to firm ground.

3222 CORPORATEFX PRIVATE CLIENTS H'CAP 7f
8:10 (8:11) (Class 3) (0-95,94) 3-Y-O+ **£9,066** (£2,697; £1,348; £673) **Stalls** Low

Form RPR

5410 **1** **Masai Moon**[22] 2545 4-9-2 **87**................JamesMillman(5) 11 98
(B R Millman) *mde all: rdn over 1f out: edgd lft: r.o wl* **14/1**

-015 **2** *2 1/4* **Aye Aye Digby (IRE)**[8] 2967 3-9-1 **90**................DaneO'Neill 14 92
(H Candy) *hld up: hdwy over 1f out: rdn to chse wnr and edgd lft ins fnl f: styd on* **9/1**[2]

4-40 **3** *1/2* **Presumptive (IRE)**[41] 1982 8-9-7 **94**................DavidProbert(7) 9 98+
(R Charlton) *s.i.s: hld up: rdn over 1f out: swtchd rt and r.o ins fnl f: edgd lft nr fin: nt rch ldrs* **10/1**[3]

1-62 **4** *1/2* **Kal Barg**[27] 2405 3-9-5 **94**................PhilipRobinson 6 93
(M A Jarvis) *hld up in tch: rdn over 2f out: styd on same pce ins fnl f* **5/6**[1]

5120 **5** *1* **Obezyana (USA)**[5] 3054 6-8-7 **78**................JackMitchell(5) 10 78
(A Bailey) *chsd ldrs: rdn over 1f out: no ex ins fnl f* **10/1**[3]

-061 **6** *2* **Southandwest (IRE)**[35] 2158 4-9-8 **89**................SteveDrowne 13 83
(J S Moore) *chsd ldrs: rdn and hung lft 2f out: wknd fnl f* **10/1**[3]

-056 **7** *nse* **Jeninsky (USA)**[20] 2605 3-8-13 **88**................TPQueally 7 79
(P J McBride) *hld up: hdwy 2f out: sn rdn: wknd fnl f* **28/1**

05-1 **8** *1 1/2* **Perfect Treasure (IRE)**[12] 2860 5-8-13 **79** 6ex................AlanMunro 5 69
(J A R Toller) *s.i.s: hld up: rdn over 2f out: nvr trbld ldrs* **12/1**

2016 **9** *nk* **Compton's Eleven**[6] 3040 7-9-2 **87**................MCGeran(5) 1 76
(M R Channon) *hld up in tch: racd keenly: rdn and nt clr run over 2f out: wknd over 1f out* **16/1**

1100 **10** *1* **Silver Hotspur**[10] 2905 4-9-9 **89**................StephenDonohoe 15 75
(M Wigham) *hld up: rdn over 2f out: a in rr* **33/1**

0000 **11** *3/4* **Moonlight Man**[13] 2818 7-8-12 **78**................(t) LiamJones 12 62
(C R Dore) *chsd ldrs: rdn 1/2-way: wknd over 1f out* **33/1**

5004 **12** *2 1/4* **Purus (IRE)**[28] 2371 6-8-13 **84**................AshleyHamblett(5) 2 62
(R A Teal) *plld hrd and prom: rdn over 2f out: wknd over 1f out* **11/1**

1m 25.31s (-0.39) **Going Correction** +0.075s/f (Good)
WFA 3 from 4yo+ 9lb **12** Ran SP% **129.7**
Speed ratings (Par 107): **105,102,101,101,100 97,97,96,95,94 93,91**
toteswinger: 1&2 £13.60, 1&3 £24.60, 2&3 £5.90. CSF £144.55 CT £1363.82 TOTE £19.80: £4.20, £2.20, £3.70; EX 245.90.
Owner C Roper **Bred** Mrs B A Matthews **Trained** Kentisbeare, Devon

FOCUS
A very useful handicap which included a trio of three-year-olds who were not quite able to take advantage of the weight-for-age allowance at this stage of the season. It has been rated around the runner-up and third to around their best form.

NOTEBOOK
Masai Moon was only 2lb higher than when winning at Southwell on his penultimate start and proved that he is just as good on turf with a convincing success. He did benefit from being handed a soft lead on this occasion, though, and it might be that he was just a tad flattered. Official explanation: trainer said, regarding the apparent improvement in form, gelding benefitted from being in a calmer state of mind today (op 11-1)
Aye Aye Digby(IRE) won over 6f at Nottingham on his penultimate start and proved himself just as effective over this intermediate trip by staying on well to the line. It is not always easy for a three-year-old to beat older horses at this time of the year and the son of Captain Rio lost little caste in defeat. (op 17-2 tchd 8-1)
Presumptive(IRE) was probably done no favours by the steady early pace, as he was slowly away and held up at the rear. He finished well enough to suggest that when things fall his way he will go very close off his current mark. (op 8-1)
Kal Barg kept rarified company as a juvenile, including getting within three-and-a-half lengths of subsequent Group 1 winner Ibn Khaldun in a nursery at Ascot in receipt of just 7lb, and having run creditably in a couple of hot handicaps so far this year, it was no surprise to see him go off a short-priced favourite on his first start against his elders. On this performance, however, he looks a shade one-paced to defy such a high handicap mark. (op 6-5 tchd 4-5, 5-4 in places)
Obezyana(USA), having his third race in eight days, is due to go up another 3lb in the handicap from the weekend for a fair effort on the first of those, and as he already looks too high in the weights, his immediate future appears grim. (op 14-1)
Purus(IRE) Official explanation: jockey said gelding was unsuited by the good to firm ground.

3223 NEWMARKETRACECOURSES.CO.UK MAIDEN STKS 1m 2f
8:40 (8:41) (Class 4) 3-Y-O **£5,180** (£1,541; £770; £384) **Stalls** Centre

Form RPR

1 **Le Brocquy** 3-9-3 0................AlanMunro 8 84
(M G Quinlan) *chsd ldrs: swtchd lft over 3f out: rdn to chse ldr and hung lft fr over 1f out: led ins fnl f: r.o u.p* **14/1**[3]

03 **2** *1/2* **Schopenhauer (USA)**[27] 2413 3-9-3 0................DaneO'Neill 3 83
(L M Cumani) *chsd ldr tl led over 2f out: sn rdn and hung lft: hdd ins fnl f: styd on* **1/3**[1]

25-3 **3** *4 1/2* **Moville (IRE)**[9] 2955 3-9-3 83................MichaelHills 2 74
(B W Hills) *led: rdn and hdd over 2f out: hung lft fr over 1f out: wknd fnl f* **3/1**[2]

4 *1/2* **Pebble Rock (IRE)** 3-9-3 0................(t) TPQueally 5 73?
(J R Jenkins) *hld up: racd keenly: rdn and hung lft fr over 2f out: wknd fnl f* **20/1**

2m 7.01s (1.51) **Going Correction** +0.075s/f (Good) **4** Ran SP% **111.4**
Speed ratings (Par 101): **96,95,92,91**
CSF £20.89 TOTE £10.10; EX 21.60.
Owner Plantation Stud **Bred** Plantation Stud **Trained** Newmarket, Suffolk
■ Stewards' Enquiry : Alan Munro one-day ban: used whip forehanded down the shoulder and without allowing colt time to respond (Jul 6)

FOCUS
A few more-than useful sorts took part in this maiden which cut up badly numbers-wise. It was slowly run and the third is not the most reliable guide to the level, despite being exposed.

3224 CORPORATEFX ONLINE PAYMENTS H'CAP 5f
9:10 (9:11) (Class 5) (0-75,75) 3-Y-O **£3,885** (£1,156; £577; £288) **Stalls** Low

Form RPR

0-03 **1** **First Trim (IRE)**[7] 3000 3-9-2 **75**................KMay(7) 4 79
(B J Meehan) *chsd ldrs: rdn to ld wl ins fnl f: edgd rt: r.o* **13/2**[3]

1602 **2** *3/4* **Orpen's Art (IRE)**[23] 2506 3-9-1 **74**................HollyHall(7) 9 75
(S A Callaghan) *trckd ldrs: plld hrd: led over 3f out: rdn: edgd rt and hdd wl ins fnl f* **16/1**

4240 **3** *shd* **Diademas (USA)**[6] 3021 3-7-13 **58**................TobyAtkinson(7) 12 59+
(M J Gingell) *s.i.s: hld up: r.o wl ins fnl f* **33/1**

2610 **4** *shd* **Magical Speedfit (IRE)**[25] 2460 3-9-9 **75**................DaneO'Neill 8 75
(G G Margarson) *hld up: hdwy over 1f out: r.o* **14/1**

5-43 **5** *1 1/4* **Mandelieu (IRE)**[17] 2690 3-9-3 **69**................LiamJones 7 65
(W J Haggas) *hld up in tch: rdn and nt clr run over 1f out: styd on* **2/1**[1]

313 **6** *3/4* **Jane's Payoff (IRE)**[20] 2602 3-9-2 **68**................RichardThomas 13 61
(Mrs L C Jewell) *hld up: rdn over 1f out: r.o: nt trble ldrs* **10/1**

0062 **7** *1* **Shatter Resistant (IRE)**[12] 2864 3-8-4 **56** oh2................(e) ChrisCatlin 3 45
(M D Squance) *led: hdd over 3f out: rdn over 1f out: wknd ins fnl f* **8/1**

-010 **8** *hd* **Liberty Belle (IRE)**[7] 3000 3-9-7 **73**................SteveDrowne 2 62
(J R Best) *chsd ldrs: rdn over 1f out: wknd fnl f* **8/1**

-030 **9** *1/2* **Rough Rock (IRE)**[8] 2983 3-8-10 **69**................(b) AntiocoMurgia(7) 5 56
(Miss Gay Kelleway) *prom: rdn and hung lft over 1f out: wknd ins fnl f* **20/1**

00-4 **10** *1 1/4* **Ramblin Bob**[169] 23 3-8-7 **59**................StephenDonohoe 11 41
(W J Musson) *broke wl: lost pl over 3f out: n.d after* **14/1**

43-3 **11** *nk* **Town And Gown**[150] 261 3-9-3 **69**................AlanMunro 10 50
(S C Williams) *trckd ldrs: rdn over 1f out: wknd fnl f* **10/1**

1561 **12** *1 1/4* **Yankee Storm**[23] 2506 3-9-8 **74**................JoeFanning 6 51
(M Johnston) *s.i.s: hld up: rdn over 1f out: n.d* **9/2**[2]

59.96 secs (0.86) **Going Correction** +0.075s/f (Good) **12** Ran SP% **132.2**
Speed ratings (Par 99): **96,94,94,94,92 91,89,89,88,86 86,84**
toteswinger: 1&2 £21.00, 1&3 £40.00, 2&3 £148.10. CSF £118.37 CT £3321.54 TOTE £9.50: £2.70, £4.00, £12.00; EX 168.50 Place 6 £ 533.83, Place 5 £ 283.93.
Owner Kennet Valley Thoroughbreds II **Bred** Catridge Farm Stud And Burgage Stud **Trained** Manton, Wilts
■ Stewards' Enquiry : Antioco Murgia four-day ban: used whip down shoulder in the forehand position and without allowing gelding time to respond (Jul 4, 6-8)

FOCUS
A fair bunch of three-year-old sprinters in action, with the horses finishing in third, fourth, fifth and sixth undoubtedly disadvantaged by being held up in an event in which it paid to race handily. The fourth has been used to rate the race.
T/Plt: £9,389.70 to a £1 stake. Pool: £44,376.44. 3.45 winning tickets. T/Qpdt: £830.90 to a £1 stake. Pool: £3,143.99. 2.80 winning tickets. CR

2909 REDCAR (L-H)
Friday, June 20

OFFICIAL GOING: Good to firm changing to firm (good to firm in places) after race 3 (3.30)
The ground was described as 'very firm but no jar'.
Wind: strong 1/2 against Weather: fine but very breezy and becoming overcast

3225 OPTIMUMRACING.CO.UK (S) STKS 7f
2:20 (2:21) (Class 6) 2-Y-O **£1,683** (£501; £250; £125) **Stalls** Centre

Form RPR

65 **1** **Cherry Belle (IRE)**[8] 2980 2-8-7 0 ow1................(v1) TomEaves 6 52
(P D Evans) *wnt lft and bmpd s: hld up: hdwy over 2f out: styd on to ld wl ins fnl f* **3/1**[1]

0 **2** *1 1/4* **Hold The Bucks (USA)**[4] 3091 2-8-11 0................RobertWinston 3 53
(J S Moore) *chsd ldr: led over 1f out: hdd and no ex fnl 75yds* **9/1**

610 **3** *1* **Dispol Diva**[7] 3008 2-8-9 0................JamieMoriarty(3) 2 51
(P T Midgley) *chsd ldrs on wd outside: rdn and hung lft over 2f out: kpt on fnl f* **6/1**[3]

30 **4** *nk* **Inca Slew (IRE)**[10] 2910 2-8-11 0................(b1) PaulMulrennan 5 49
(P C Haslam) *hmpd s: sn trcking ldrs: hung lft over 1f out: kpt on ins fnl f* **4/1**[2]

3633 **5** *4 1/2* **Kheley (IRE)**[4] 3091 2-8-3 0................DuranFentiman(3) 9 33
(W M Brisbourne) *trckd ldrs: effrt over 2f out: hung lft over 1f out: wknd ins fnl f* **3/1**[1]

6 **6** *1 3/4* **Charly's Rose**[8] 2980 2-7-13 0................PatrickDonaghy(7) 8 28
(P C Haslam) *led tl hdd & wknd over 1f out* **16/1**

606 **7** *3* **Transformation (IRE)**[9] 2924 2-8-6 0................GrahamGibbons 4 20
(J R Weymes) *wnt rt s: sn trcking ldrs: wknd over 1f out* **20/1**

The Form Book, Raceform Ltd, Compton, RG20 6NL

56 **8** *9* **Quadrifolio**[57] 1574 2-8-11 0 KimTinkler 7 2
(N Tinkler) *mid-div: rdn and outpcd 3f out: sn bhd* **12/1**
0 **9** *7* **Willin Dillon (IRE)**[18] 2671 2-8-11 0 TWilliams 1 —
(W Storey) *in rr: bhd fnl 3f* **66/1**
1m 26.98s (2.48) **Going Correction** 0.0s/f (Good) 9 Ran SP% **114.1**
Speed ratings (Par 91): **85,83,82,82,76 74,71,61,53**
toteswinger: 1&2 £6.60, 1&3 £8.00, 2&3 £21.40. CSF £30.73 TOTE £3.50: £1.50, £2.90, £2.00; EX 23.10.There was no bid for the winner.
Owner Mrs I M Folkes **Bred** Brook Stud Bloodstock Ltd **Trained** Pandy, Monmouths

FOCUS
A poor race even by selling race standards.

NOTEBOOK
Cherry Belle(IRE), who is only small, came off a straight line and took a bump exiting the stalls. Given a patient ride, she came with a sustained effort to take charge. (op 4-1)
Hold The Bucks(USA), who started on terms this time, found the filly too strong in the closing stages. (op 12-1)
Dispol Diva, the only previous winner in the field, found herself racing on the wide outside. She appeared to be feeling the very firm ground but her stamina was coming into play at the end. (op 5-1 tchd 15-2)
Inca Slew(IRE), in first-time blinkers, took a bump at the start. He proved a tricky ride but was persuaded to put in some good work near the line. (op 5-1 tchd 7-2)
Kheley(IRE), who is only small, wanted to hang left and in the end the extra furlong proved beyond her. Official explanation: jockey said filly hung left throughout (op 5-2 tchd 9-4 and 10-3 in a place)
Charly's Rose, with the headgear left off, took them along but did not see it out. (op 14-1)

3226 JACKSONS-CPL SOLICITORS WE-CAN-WORK-IT-OUT H'CAP 1m 2f
2:55 (2:55) (Class 5) (0-70,68) 4-Y-0+ **£2,331** (£693; £346; £173) **Stalls** Low

Form RPR
0300 **1** **Holiday Cocktail**[17] 2697 6-8-10 **57** (p) GrahamGibbons 5 65
(J J Quinn) *sn chsng ldrs: drvn and outpcd 5f out: hdwy over 2f out: led 1f out: hld on* **5/1**[2]
004 **2** *1* **Seyaadi**[13] 2848 6-8-12 **59** (p) DeanMcKeown 4 65+
(Miss Tracy Waggott) *s.i.s: hld up in rr: hdwy and nt clr run 3f out: sn swtchd wd: hdwy over 1f out: styd on: nt rch wnr* **8/1**
6660 **3** *1 3/4* **Treetops Hotel (IRE)**[39] 2053 9-8-2 **49** AndrewElliott 2 52
(L R James) *hld up in rr: hdwy over 3f out: styd on same pce fnl f* **20/1**
000- **4** *nk* **Garibaldi (GER)**[205] 6969 6-8-2 **49** PaulQuinn 8 51
(N Wilson) *hld up in rr: stdy hdwy 4f out: led over 2f out: hdd 1f out: kpt on same pce* **7/1**
6520 **5** *1 3/4* **Bramcote Lorne**[6] 3029 5-7-12 **52** (p) CharlesEddery[(7)] 7 50
(R C Guest) *led tl over 2f out: one pce* **8/1**
6600 **6** *hd* **College Land Boy**[13] 2846 4-8-2 **49** oh4 (v[1]) TWilliams 10 47
(A Kirtley) *hld up in rr: effrt over 3f out: one pce fnl 2f* **50/1**
0060 **7** *1/2* **Bright Sun (IRE)**[9] 2957 7-8-11 **58** KimTinkler 6 55
(N Tinkler) *trckd ldrs: one pce fnl 2f* **12/1**
-030 **8** *1/2* **Alberts Story (USA)**[18] 2662 4-8-7 **57** ow2 JamieMoriarty[(3)] 1 53
(R A Fahey) *mid-div: outpcd 3f out: kpt on appr fnl f* **11/2**[3]
-044 **9** *1 1/2* **Penang Cinta**[21] 2568 5-9-7 **68** TomEaves 3 61
(P D Evans) *trckd ldrs: drvn over 3f out: lost pl over 1f out* **3/1**[1]
-520 **10** *1 1/2* **Titinius (IRE)**[13] 2848 8-9-3 **64** PaulMulrennan 9 54
(Micky Hammond) *chsd ldrs: hung lft and lost pl over 1f out* **10/1**
2m 6.12s (-0.98) **Going Correction** 0.0s/f (Good) 10 Ran SP% **115.3**
Speed ratings (Par 103): **103,102,100,100,99 99,98,98,97,95**
toteswinger: 1&2 £8.40, 1&3 £22.80, 2&3 £7.40. CSF £44.15 CT £734.07 TOTE £6.60: £2.00, £3.10, £3.80; EX 51.10.
Owner Estio Racing **Bred** Mrs W H Gibson Fleming **Trained** Settrington, N Yorks

FOCUS
A modest handicap with the runner-up out of luck. The form looks weak.
Titinius(IRE) Official explanation: jockey said gelding hung left-handed in straight

3227 H JARVIS 130TH ANNIVERSARY MAIDEN STKS 1m 2f
3:30 (3:31) (Class 5) 3-Y-0+ **£2,331** (£693; £346; £173) **Stalls** Low

Form RPR
-224 **1** **Prince Kalamoun (IRE)**[28] 2366 3-9-0 70 RobertWinston 10 79
(G A Swinbank) *hld up towards rr: hdwy over 3f out: hrd rdn and led ins fnl f: hld on wl* **5/1**[3]
03- **2** *1* **Elliwan**[233] 6593 3-9-0 0 AndrewElliott 11 77
(M Johnston) *chsd ldrs: reminders over 4f out: rdn to ld over 3f out: hdd over 1f out: rallied ins fnl f* **10/1**
252- **3** *1/2* **Altitude**[261] 5914 3-8-9 77 J-PGuillambert 7 71
(Sir Mark Prescott) *trckd ldrs: upsides over 1f out: kpt on same pce ins fnl f* **9/4**[2]
3/2 **4** *hd* **Alqaahir (USA)**[16] 2735 6-9-12 0 TomEaves 1 76
(J S Wainwright) *hld up in midfield: hdwy over 4f out: led over 1f out: hdd ins fnl f: no ex* **14/1**
4 **5** *3 1/4* **Kidlat**[23] 2509 3-9-0 0 PatCosgrave 3 69
(L M Cumani) *chsd ldrs: effrt over 3f out: kpt on one pce: nvr able to chal* **11/10**[1]
05 **6** *14* **Linby (IRE)**[13] 2847 3-9-0 0 DaleGibson 8 41
(N Tinkler) *s.i.s: in rr and sn pushed along: nvr nr ldrs* **50/1**
03 **7** *1/2* **Ducal Regancy Duke**[10] 2912 4-9-12 0 DavidAllan 4 40
(C J Teague) *led tl 7f out: lost pl 3f out* **50/1**
8 *12* **Divvys Dream**[23] 6-9-12 0 PaulMulrennan 6 16
(P Beaumont) *s.s: t.o 5f out* **50/1**
0- **9** *1 1/2* **Fleetway (IRE)**[324] 4076 3-8-6 0 DuranFentiman[(3)] 9 8
(F Watson) *in rr: drvn 4f out: sn bhd* **200/1**
05 **10** *1 1/2* **Micallef**[16] 2735 3-8-7 0 ow1 JamieMoriarty[(3)] 2 6
(R A Fahey) *chsd ldrs: reminders over 4f out: lost pl 3f out* **100/1**
11 *7* **I Feel Fine**[15] 5-9-7 0 PAspell 5 —
(A Kirtley) *w ldr: led 7f out tl over 3f out: sn lost pl* **200/1**
2m 5.67s (-1.43) **Going Correction** 0.0s/f (Good)
WFA 3 from 4yo+ 12lb 11 Ran SP% **118.7**
Speed ratings (Par 103): **105,104,103,103,101 89,89,79,78,77 71**
toteswinger: 1&2 £7.90, 1&3 £2.50, 2&3 £5.70. CSF £52.40 TOTE £6.70: £1.10, £3.10, £1.10; EX 57.70.
Owner Jonathan Dixon **Bred** Michael Pitt **Trained** Melsonby, N Yorks

FOCUS
A fair maiden which should throw up a winner or two. The form looks sound rated through the fourth.
Divvys Dream Official explanation: jockey said gelding missed the break

3228 JACKSONS-CPL SOLICITORS - ELEANOR RIGBY H'CAP 6f
4:10 (4:10) (Class 3) (0-95,94) 3-Y-0+ **£6,799** (£2,023; £1,011; £505) **Stalls** Centre

Form RPR
6040 **1** **Tabaret**[7] 3009 5-9-7 **87** (p) DeanMcKeown 10 98
(R M Whitaker) *w ldrs: styd on fnl f: led last strides* **11/1**
-412 **2** *nk* **Total Impact**[7] 3009 5-8-11 **80** JamieMoriarty[(3)] 4 90
(R A Fahey) *w ldrs: led over 1f out: hdd nr fin* **15/8**[1]
2-14 **3** *1 1/4* **Solar Spirit (IRE)**[34] 2189 3-8-8 **81** RobertWinston 9 85+
(G A Swinbank) *trckd ldrs: t.k.h: effrt over 2f out: kpt on same pce fnl f* **3/1**[2]
60-0 **4** *1/2* **Guertino (IRE)**[98] 3-9-2 **89** TomEaves 8 91
(B Smart) *stdd s: hld up in rr: effrt 2f out: styd on wl ins fnl f* **25/1**
1-60 **5** *nse* **Dig Deep (IRE)**[14] 2778 6-9-4 **84** GrahamGibbons 11 88
(J J Quinn) *sn trcking ldrs: effrt over 2f out: kpt on same pce fnl f* **12/1**
3120 **6** *nk* **Obe Gold**[13] 2831 6-9-12 **92** (v) SilvestreDeSousa 1 95
(D Nicholls) *chsd ldrs: drvn and outpcd over 3f out: kpt on fnl 2f* **9/1**
2026 **7** *3/4* **High Curragh**[17] 2698 5-9-5 **85** (p) PaulMulrennan 5 86
(K A Ryan) *led tl over 1f out: fdd ins fnl f* **9/2**[3]
222/ **8** *7* **Libor (IRE)**[647] 5265 5-8-13 **79** PatCosgrave 2 58
(L M Cumani) *s.i.s: t.k.h: hdwy to trck ldrs 3f out: lost pl over 1f out: sn bhd* **11/1**
1m 10.87s (-0.93) **Going Correction** 0.0s/f (Good)
WFA 3 from 4yo+ 7lb 8 Ran SP% **116.2**
Speed ratings (Par 107): **106,105,103,103,103 102,101,92**
toteswinger: 1&2 £6.20, 1&3 £10.40, 2&3 £2.80. CSF £32.65 CT £80.99 TOTE £15.20: £3.80, £1.50, £1.20; EX 42.60.
Owner T L Adams **Bred** The P B T Group And G F Pemberton **Trained** Scarcroft, W Yorks
■ Stewards' Enquiry : Dean McKeown caution: using whip without giving mount time to respond.

FOCUS
A sprint not run at a strong pace to halfway. There was little between the first seven at the line and the form should be taken with a pinch of salt.

NOTEBOOK
Tabaret, on a long losing run, appreciated the very fast ground and, helped by first-time cheekpieces, put his head in front almost on the line. Official explanation: trainer's representative said, regarding the improved form shown, that the gedling appreciated today's faster ground and appeared to respond well to first-time cheekpieces. (op 10-1 tchd 12-1)
Total Impact, stepping up to six, saw far too much daylight on the wide outside and, after travelling best, in the end he was just picked off. He should continue to give a good account of himself. (op 7-4 tchd 6-4 and 2-1 in places)
Solar Spirit(IRE), suited by the drop back to six, took a fierce hold in a sprint not run at a strong pace. Sticking on at the finish, this will have completed his education and he can surely find another race. (op 7-2 tchd 5-1)
Guertino(IRE), out of luck in three starts in Dubai, is now a gelding. Taken very quietly to post and dropped in, he was putting in some solid late work and his former trainer will have been pleased with this effort.
Dig Deep(IRE) ran easily his best race for his new trainer on his third start. Though he stays further, the minimum trip seems to suit him best nowadays. (tchd 11-1)
Obe Gold, 9lb higher than his last success, is a lazy individual and the way this race was run did not play to his strengths. (op 10-1)

3229 BODDINGTONS REDCAR STRAIGHT-MILE CHAMPIONSHIP H'CAP (QUALIFIER) 1m
4:45 (4:45) (Class 5) (0-75,73) 3-Y-0+ **£2,331** (£693; £346; £173) **Stalls** Centre

Form RPR
-055 **1** **Ezdeyaad (USA)**[13] 2846 4-9-13 **70** RobertWinston 2 82+
(G A Swinbank) *led: wl clr after 2f: pushed out fnl f: unchal* **5/1**[3]
0242 **2** *1* **Just Bond (IRE)**[7] 3006 6-9-9 **71** SladeO'Hara[(5)] 7 78+
(G R Oldroyd) *hld up gng wl: hdwy to chse wnr jst ins fnl f: fin wl: nt rch wnr* **2/1**[1]
-050 **3** *1 3/4* **Chicken George (IRE)**[27] 2406 4-9-11 **68** SilvestreDeSousa 3 71
(D Nicholls) *chsd ldrs: kpt on same pce fnl f* **10/1**
024 **4** *nk* **King Fingal (IRE)**[24] 2488 3-9-6 **73** GrahamGibbons 8 73
(J J Quinn) *in rr: hdwy over 2f out: styd on same pce* **11/4**[2]
0024 **5** *1 1/2* **Aussie Blue (IRE)**[14] 2787 4-9-4 **61** DeanMcKeown 9 60
(R M Whitaker) *hld up: effrt 3f out: wnt 2nd over 1f out: wknd ins fnl f* **9/1**
00-0 **6** *11* **Kaymich Perfecto**[18] 2672 8-8-9 **55** MichaelJStainton[(3)] 6 29
(R M Whitaker) *chsd ldrs: lost pl over 1f out* **22/1**
0205 **7** *2 1/2* **Bailieborough (IRE)**[5] 3054 9-9-10 **67** (p) TomEaves 4 35
(B Ellison) *sn chsng ldrs on outer: drvn over 3f out: lost pl 2f out* **8/1**
0501 **8** *8* **Gee Ceffyl Bach**[13] 2846 4-8-12 **55** DaleGibson 5 4
(R C Guest) *t.k.h: trckd ldrs: wknd 2f out* **14/1**
1m 37.5s (-0.50) **Going Correction** 0.0s/f (Good)
WFA 3 from 4yo+ 10lb 8 Ran SP% **117.9**
Speed ratings (Par 103): **102,101,99,98,97 86,83,75**
toteswinger: 1&2 £4.10, 1&3 £5.30, 2&3 £6.20. CSF £15.98 CT £98.36 TOTE £6.30: £1.60, £1.20, £2.90; EX 16.40.
Owner Elsa Crankshaw, G Allan M Wane B Boanson **Bred** Caldara Farm **Trained** Melsonby, N Yorks
■ Stewards' Enquiry : Slade O'Hara seven-day ban: breach of rule 156 - rode an ill-judged race (Jul 4-10)

FOCUS
The headstrong winner was gifted a long lead and the form looks highly dubious as a result.

3230 OPTIMUMRACING.CO.UK CLAIMING STKS 1m 2f
5:20 (5:20) (Class 6) 3-Y-0+ **£2,047** (£604; £302) **Stalls** Low

Form RPR
0536 **1** **Intersky Melody (USA)**[10] 2915 3-8-6 55 DeanMcKeown 4 58
(R M Whitaker) *rrd at s: sn trcking ldrs: drvn 3f out: styd on to ld last 75yds* **5/1**[3]
1034 **2** *nk* **Rowan Lodge (IRE)**[4] 3077 6-9-3 64 (b) JamieMoriarty[(3)] 2 60
(Ollie Pears) *trckd ldr: chal on bit over 2f out: rdn to take narrow advantage over 1f out: hung lft: rdr dropped whip: hdd and no ex last 75yds* **11/4**[2]
0040 **3** *1/2* **Roman History (IRE)**[4] 3077 5-9-6 55 (p) SilvestreDeSousa 8 59
(Miss Tracy Waggott) *mde most: hdd over 1f out: edgd rt: no ex wl ins fnl f* **12/1**
5141 **4** *2 1/2* **Boundless Prospect (USA)**[18] 2667 9-9-1 70 RichardEvans[(7)] 11 56+
(Ollie Pears) *hld up in rr: effrt on outer over 3f out: hung lft: kpt on: nt rch ldrs* **9/4**[1]
0-00 **5** *10* **Rotuma (IRE)**[88] 989 9-8-11 44 (b) JohnCavanagh[(7)] 13 32
(M Dods) *mid-div: hdwy 3f out: sn rdn and hung lft: wknd over 1f out* **16/1**
5600 **6** *1* **Mchepple**[50] 1754 3-8-1 37 TWilliams 6 25
(W Storey) *hld up in midfield: effrt 3f out: nvr a threat* **80/1**
0663 **7** *2 1/4* **Skye But N Ben**[1] 3182 4-9-2 45 (tp) PaulMulrennan 7 23
(G A Harker) *s.i.s: nvr on terms* **13/2**
060- **8** *1* **Moving Story**[30] 6452 5-9-2 44 TomEaves 9 21
(M E Sowersby) *sn trcking ldrs: effrt 3f out: sn wknd* **20/1**
50-0 **9** *10* **Starlight Girl**[31] 2269 3-8-9 65 DavidAllan 10 6
(T D Easterby) *chsd ldrs: drvn over 3f out: lost pl over 2f out: bhd whn eased ins fnl f* **14/1**

0 **10** *5* **Cabb City (IRE)**[55] 1636 5-8-8 34 DuranFentiman(3) 5 —
(W M Brisbourne) *chsd ldrs: lost pl over 2f out* **66/1**

205- **11** *nk* **Namarian (IRE)**[7] 5698 4-8-4 42 (b) NSLawes(7) 12 —
(M E Sowersby) *in rr: bhd fnl 4f* **50/1**

000/ **12** *1 1/4* **Distinctlythebest**[648] 5241 8-9-4 35 PAspell 3 —
(F Watson) *s.i.s: a in rr: bhd fnl 4f* **100/1**

2m 6.04s (-1.06) **Going Correction** 0.0s/f (Good)
WFA 3 from 4yo+ 12lb **12** Ran SP% **118.1**
Speed ratings (Par 101): **104,103,103,101,93 92,90,89,81,77 77,76**
toteswinger: 1&2 £4.40, 1&3 £10.00, 2&3 £10.60. CSF £18.59 TOTE £7.10: £2.30, £2.10, £4.70; EX 21.80.
Owner Intersky Bloodstock I **Bred** Emory A Hamilton **Trained** Scarcroft, W Yorks

FOCUS
A modest claimer and the overall form is anchored by the winner and the third.
Skye But N Ben Official explanation: jockey said gelding ran flat

3231 "LADIES-DAY" TOMORROW MAIDEN H'CAP 5f
5:50 (5:53) (Class 5) (0-70,69) 3-Y-0+ **£2,331** (£693; £346; £173) **Stalls** Centre

Form RPR

4-04 **1** **Le Toreador**[27] 2396 3-9-4 **63** (t) JamieMoriarty(3) 12 69
(K A Ryan) *w ldrs: led jst ins fnl f: hld on wl* **4/1**[2]

0-00 **2** *nk* **The Cube**[13] 2824 4-8-10 **46** (b) PaulMulrennan 14 53
(J Balding) *w ldrs: hung lft and led over 1f out: hdd ins fnl f: no ex towards fin* **12/1**

026 **3** *3/4* **Tangerine Trees**[25] 2466 3-9-13 **69** (v) TomEaves 8 71
(B Smart) *effrt over 2f out: trckd ldrs: kpt on wl fnl f* **10/3**[1]

5-20 **4** *nk* **Tugalu (IRE)**[63] 1454 3-9-12 **68** (p) SilvestreDeSousa 9 70+
(K A Ryan) *trckd ldrs: nt clr run and swtchd lft 1f out: kpt on wl* **11/2**[3]

00/0 **5** *shd* **She Who Dares Wins**[24] 2491 8-8-9 **45** TWilliams 11 48
(L R James) *mid-div: hdwy over 1f out: kpt on wl ins fnl f* **25/1**

-060 **6** *1 3/4* **Tumbleweed Di**[9] 2928 4-8-8 **49** SladeO'Hara(5) 13 46
(G R Oldroyd) *dwlt: sn mid-div: styd on fnl f* **10/1**

-035 **7** *hd* **Recent Times**[13] 2824 3-9-5 **61** DavidAllan 6 55
(T D Easterby) *sn outpcd in rr: kpt on fnl 2f: nt rch ldrs* **6/1**

-005 **8** *3/4* **Violet's Pride**[24] 2491 4-8-9 **45** (p) KimTinkler 5 38
(N Tinkler) *mid-div: drvn over 2f out: hung lft: nvr trbld ldrs* **16/1**

2563 **9** *3/4* **High Window (IRE)**[24] 2491 8-8-4 **47** ow2 NSLawes(7) 2 37
(G P Kelly) *sn outpcd in rr: kpt on fnl 2f: nvr a factor* **8/1**

6600 **10** *nse* **Jabraan (USA)**[9] 2936 6-8-2 **45** (v) AdeleRothery(7) 4 35
(Mrs R A Carr) *s.i.s: in rr tl kpt on fnl f* **22/1**

4000 **11** *4 1/2* **Cryptic Clue (USA)**[2] 3139 4-8-6 **45** (b) DuranFentiman(3) 3 19
(Mrs R A Carr) *sn clr ld: wknd and hdd over 1f out* **25/1**

0-00 **12** *1 1/2* **Keeparryappy (IRE)**[32] 2260 3-9-6 **62** (p) AndrewElliott 10 29
(K R Burke) *chsd ldrs: rdn over 2f out: lost pl over 1f out* **20/1**

58.43 secs (-0.17) **Going Correction** 0.0s/f (Good)
WFA 3 from 4yo+ 6lb **12** Ran SP% **123.3**
Speed ratings (Par 103): **101,100,99,98,98 95,95,94,93,93 85,83**
toteswinger: 1&2 £13.30, 1&3 £5.10, 2&3 £11.60. CSF £50.56 CT £182.90 TOTE £4.60: £2.20, £3.60, £1.50; EX 59.40 Place 6 £62.20, Place 5 £31.19..
Owner Guy Reed **Bred** G Reed **Trained** Hambleton, N Yorks

FOCUS
A maiden handicap contested by horses that had run almost 150 times between them beforehand. The winner has the pedigree and the potential to rate higher but a large blanket would have covered the first five at the line.
High Window(IRE) Official explanation: trainer said gelding was found to be coughing after race
T/Plt: £86.80 to a £1 stake. Pool: £39,472.36. 331.80 winning tickets. T/Qpdt: £7.90 to a £1 stake. Pool: £2,600.69. 242.30 winning tickets. WG

3232 - 3242a (Foreign Racing) - See Raceform Interactive

2875 CHANTILLY (R-H)
Friday, June 20

OFFICIAL GOING: Soft

3243a PRIX HAMPTON (LISTED RACE) 5f
4:00 (3:59) 3-Y-0+ **£19,118** (£7,647; £5,735; £3,824; £1,912)

RPR

1 **Stern Opinion (USA)**[40] 2034 3-8-13 TThulliez 9 112
(P Bary, France)

2 *shd* **Masta Plasta (IRE)**[13] 2828 5-9-2 AdrianTNicholls 1 111
(D Nicholls) *led: hrd rdn over 1f out: ct last stride (39/10)* **39/10**[1]

3 *2* **Mariol (FR)**[19] 2652 5-9-5 SMaillot 7 107
(Robert Collet, France)

4 *1* **Day By Day**[18] 2685 4-8-12 (b) OPeslier 5 96
(B J Meehan) *pressed ldr: rdn and ev ch wl over 1f out: one pce fr appr fnl f (51/10)* **51/10**[2]

5 *1/2* **Avanguardia (GER)**[31] 3-8-8 CSoumillon 2 94
(Y De Nicolay, France)

6 *nk* **Val Jaro (FR)**[231] 6633 5-9-5 TJarnet 3 101
(S Morineau, France)

7 *1 1/2* **Lumiere Noire (FR)**[15] 4-8-12 TRicher 6 88
(R Gibson, France)

8 *1* **Mood Music**[19] 2652 4-9-5 (b) DBoeuf 10 92
(Mario Hofer, Germany)

9 *8* **Fantastica (GER)**[607] 6121 5-8-12 C-PLemaire 4 56
(Frau K Haustein, Germany)

10 *3* **Arc De Triomphe (GER)**[57] 1593 6-9-2 JVictoire 8 49
(D Fechner, Germany)

11 **Saint Stan (FR)**[246] 10-9-2 (b) TGillet 11 49
(Mlle A De Clerck, France)

57.90 secs (-0.20) **Going Correction** +0.25s/f (Good)
WFA 3 from 4yo+ 6lb **11** Ran SP% **36.8**
Speed ratings: **111,110,107,106,105 104,102,100,87,83 83**
PARI-MUTUEL: WIN 3.80; PL 1.70, 1.90, 2.50; DF 10.50.
Owner K Abdulla **Bred** Juddmonte Farms **Trained** Chantilly, France

NOTEBOOK
Masta Plasta(IRE) showed his usual speed and was only denied right on the line. He was clear of the rest and can win at this level on a sharp or flat track.
Day By Day did not run badly but her best form is on a quicker surface.

3244 - (Foreign Racing) - See Raceform Interactive

3192 ASCOT (R-H)
Saturday, June 21

OFFICIAL GOING: Good to firm (firm in places)
Wind: Light, across Weather: Overcast

3245 CHESHAM STKS (LISTED RACE) 7f
2:30 (2:34) (Class 1) 2-Y-O
£34,062 (£12,912; £6,462; £3,222; £1,614; £810) **Stalls** Centre

Form RPR

1 **1** **Free Agent**[19] 2663 2-9-3 0 RichardHughes 12 98+
(R Hannon) *str: lw: dropped in bhd after s: sltly squeezed and dropped to last 5f out: stl last over 2f out: swtchd rt: rdn and gd hdwy wl over 1f out: led ins fnl f: edgd rt but r.o strly and sn clr* **7/2**[1]

22 **2** *2 1/4* **Seaway**[21] 2592 2-9-3 0 JimmyFortune 10 92
(J H M Gosden) *t.k.h: hld up towards rr: hdwy over 2f out: rdn to ld over 1f out: sn edgd lft: hdd ins fnl f: nt pce of wnr* **7/2**[1]

4 **3** *1 1/2* **Markyg (USA)**[10] 2937 2-9-3 0 FergusSweeney 6 89
(K R Burke) *leggy: in tch: hdwy over 2f out: chsd ldrs and hung rt 2f out: led wl over 1f out: sn hdd: outpcd ins fnl f* **22/1**

4 **4** *1* **Tudor Key (IRE)**[36] 2146 2-9-3 0 JimCrowley 7 86
(Mrs A J Perrett) *hld up wl in tch: rdn and effrt wl over 1f out: keeping on same pce whn squeezed for room jst ins fnl f: plugged on* **33/1**

4 **5** *3/4* **Flying Lady (IRE)**[12] 2887 2-8-12 0 TPO'Shea 8 79
(M R Channon) *unf: t.k.h: hld up towards rr: hdwy 3f out: swtchd rt and rdn jst over 2f out: sn edging lft and no hdwy: styd on again last 100yds* **25/1**

0104 **6** *nse* **Bad Beat**[35] 2204 2-9-3 0 NCallan 1 84
(V Smith) *chsd ldrs: wnt 2nd over 3f out: rdn to ld 2f out: sn hdd: wknd ent fnl f* **33/1**

3 **7** *2 1/4* **Pegasus Lad (USA)**[10] 2937 2-9-3 0 JoeFanning 4 79+
(M Johnston) *w'like: scope: led tl hdd and rdn 2f out: wkng whn hung rt and short of room jst over 1f out: eased ins fnl f* **7/1**[2]

4 **8** *6* **Dr Smart (IRE)**[21] 2592 2-9-3 0 RoystonFfrench 2 64
(B Smart) *w'like: leggy: stdd s: plld hrd: sn in tch: rdn 3f out: wknd qckly 2f out* **20/1**

41 **9** *7* **Imperial Guest**[24] 2507 2-9-3 0 JMurtagh 5 46
(G G Margarson) *w'like: hanging rt thrght: chsd ldr tl 1/2-way: rdn 3f out: wkng whn short of room over 1f out: eased fnl f* **7/1**[2]

10 *1* **Quatermain** 2-9-3 0 TomEaves 11 44
(B Smart) *w'like: s.i.s: t.k.h: hld up in rr: hdwy 3f out: rdn and wknd qckly over 2f out: sn wl bhd* **20/1**

2 **11** *3 3/4* **Johnny Rook (GER)**[36] 2150 2-9-3 0 LDettori 9 34+
(E A L Dunlop) *in tch: rdn and effrt 2f out: sn btn and nt pushed: eased fnl f* **8/1**[3]

1m 29.59s (1.59) **Going Correction** +0.25s/f (Good) **11** Ran SP% **104.2**
Speed ratings (Par 101): **100,97,95,94,93 93,91,84,76,75 70**
toteswinger: 1&2 £1.80, 1&3 £19.70, 2&3 £23.20 CSF £10.19 CT £162.28 TOTE £2.90: £1.30, £1.20, £10.80; EX 7.70 Trifecta £100.60 Pool: £7,835.66 - 57.59 winning units..
Owner The Queen **Bred** The Queen **Trained** East Everleigh, Wilts
■ Free Agent was the Queen's first winner at the Royal meeting since Blueprint in 1999.
■ Stewards' Enquiry : Fergus Sweeney one-day ban: careless riding (Jul 6)

FOCUS
A weak Chesham on pre-race figures but the first two built on their previous promising efforts and popular winner Free Agent is capable of better still. Swindler was withdrawn after getting upset in the stalls (6/1, deduct 10p in the £ under rule 4).

NOTEBOOK
Free Agent ◆, successful on his debut over 6f at Leicester, duly improved for the extra frulong and ran out a decisive winner in the end. He found himself at the back of the field after being squeezed out early on, but after tacking over to the stands' side of the group he came through strongly to show ahead inside the last and stayed on very well. Sure to improve over further, he will be given a break now and it could be that he will not run again this season. He is a nice prospect. (op 10-3 tchd 4-1)
Seaway was also runner-up on his first two starts, in a Haydock maiden which has been working out well and at Doncaster behind this week's Coventry fourth Himalya. He again found one too good, just lacking the winner's pace late on having come through to hold every chance. There seems no reason to doubt his attitude and he should soon get a win under his belt. Official explanation: jockey said colt ran too free (op 10-3 tchd 4-1)
Markyg(USA) stepped up considerably on what he showed on his debut over 6f at Hamilton and turned around form from that race with Pegasus Lad. After improving from off the pace he showed in front briefly before the first two pulled away from him inside the last. He will be hard to beat if reverting to maiden company. (op 50-1)
Tudor Key(IRE) improved considerably for his debut experience at Newbury and was keeping on quite well at the end after being tightened up entering the last. (op 40-1)
Flying Lady(IRE), upped in trip for this second start, was the only filly in the race. She took time to settle but ran respectably, staying on again in the latter stages. (tchd 20-1)
Bad Beat, the most exposed runner in the field, was taking a rise both in class and trip. Showing with a slender advantage with two to run, he did not hold on to his lead for long but this was improved form. (op 40-1)
Pegasus Lad(USA), who finished one place ahead of today's fourth when they made their respective debuts at Hamilton, made the running for five furlongs but was already on the retreat when he was a little short of room approaching the furlong pole. (op 8-1 tchd 9-1)
Imperial Guest Official explanation: jockey said colt hung right

3246 HARDWICKE STKS (GROUP 2) 1m 4f
3:05 (3:07) (Class 1) 4-Y-0+
£85,155 (£32,280; £16,155; £8,055; £4,035; £2,025) **Stalls** High

Form RPR

-013 **1** **Macarthur**[15] 2791 4-9-0 0 JMurtagh 7 121
(A P O'Brien, Ire) *trckd ldrs: rdn to chse ldr 2f out: wanted to lug rt ins fnl f: styd on wl for press to ld towards fin* **11/8**[1]

-440 **2** *nk* **Multidimensional (IRE)**[15] 2791 5-9-0 111 TedDurcan 4 120
(H R A Cecil) *racd keenly: sn led: hdd after 2f: continued to trck ldr: led and kicked on over 2f out: sn rdn and hung rt: styd on: worn down and hdd towards fin* **25/1**

0-22 **3** *5* **Maraahel (IRE)**[23] 2543 7-9-0 117 (b) RHills 5 112
(Sir Michael Stoute) *awkward leaving stalls: racd in midfield: hdwy 2f out: rdn to chse front pair wl over 1f out: no imp ins fnl f* **5/1**[3]

51-3 **4** *1* **Speed Gifted**[15] 2797 4-9-0 102 DaneO'Neill 11 110
(L M Cumani) *towards rr: nudged along after 4f: hdwy u.p over 1f out: edgd rt ins fnl f: no imp whn edgd lft towards fin* **14/1**

0-00 **5** 3 1/4 **Yellowstone (IRE)**[48] 1829 4-9-0 105.................................(p) JohnEgan 3 105
(Jane Chapple-Hyam) *trckd ldrs: rdn over 2f out: one pce fr over 1f out* **33/1**

/6-1 **6** 3 1/2 **Spanish Moon (USA)**[42] 1980 4-9-0 108.......................... RyanMoore 8 99
(Sir Michael Stoute) *lw: racd keenly: hld up: pushed along over 3f out: swtchd lft 2f out: sn btn* **3/1**[2]

10 **7** 1/2 **Happy Boy (BRZ)**[23] 2543 5-9-0 0.. LDettori 9 99
(Saeed Bin Suroor) *led early: stdd after 2f: pushed along over 2f out: no imp: wl btn over 1f out* **9/1**

26-0 **8** 4 1/2 **Shahin (USA)**[15] 2797 5-9-0 112.....................................(v) SebSanders 2 91
(M P Tregoning) *prom: led after 2f: rdn and hdd over 2f out: wknd wl over 1f out* **50/1**

111- **9** *hd* **Hi Calypso (IRE)**[282] 5352 4-9-0 108.................................. MJKinane 10 91
(Sir Michael Stoute) *hld up in rr: pushed along over 5f out: nvr on terms* **11/1**

2m 31.29s (-4.21) **Going Correction** +0.025s/f (Good) **9** Ran SP% **117.5**
Speed ratings (Par 115): **115,114,111,110,108 106,105,102,102**
toteswinger: 1&2 £11.10, 1&3 £2.20, 2&3 £28.30 CSF £44.83 CT £144.73 TOTE £2.80: £1.30, £5.60, £1.60; EX 50.30 Trifecta £173.70 Pool: £8,442.93 - 35.96 winning units..
Owner D Smith, Mrs J Magnier, M Tabor **Bred** Deerfield Farm **Trained** Ballydoyle, Co Tipperary

FOCUS
The pace was not strong and not many were able to get involved. Macarthur pretty much confirmed his Epsom mark and the second improved to the tune of 5lb. They finished clear of Maraahel, who was 5lb off this year's form.

NOTEBOOK
Macarthur, a good third to stablemate Soldier Of Fortune in the Coronation Cup, had earlier taken Chester's Ormonde Stakes in convincing style. Always well placed and sent after the leader with a quarter of a mile left, he showed an ungainly head carriage but certainly battled and eventually got on top close home. Capable of further improvement, he may come back here for the King George but he is unlikely to be the stable first string in that Group 1. (tchd 5-4 and 6-4, 13-8 in places)
Multidimensional(IRE), always in the first two, moved back into the lead entering the home straight and tried to kick clear, only conceding defeat in the final 50 yards. The stiff 1m4f just found him out, but this was still his best ever run and he got a lot closer to Macarthur than he had at Epsom. He was evidently fitted with a different bit here, and that may help explain his improvement.
Maraahel(IRE) was successful in the last two editions of this event and was runner-up when it was run at York in 2005. He followed the eventual winner through entering the straight, travelling well, but although keeping on for third he never looked like catching the first two. Without a win since this race last year, he is still capable of adding to his tally. (op 15-2)
Speed Gifted, stepping up in grade, never travelled particularly well but did stay on in the home straight without ever promising to be involved in the finish. This race was not run to suit and he is probably worth another chance, but he does not look entirely straightforward and might not be one to trust too much. (op 8-1)
Yellowstone(IRE), with the headgear back on, ran a pretty solid race with no obvious excuses. (op 50-1)
Spanish Moon(USA), winner of a Listed race over course and distance last month, raced rather keenly and did not have much to offer when brought under pressure before the home turn. He will need to settle better to fulfil his potential. (op 11-4 tchd 7-2)
Happy Boy(BRZ), back up in trip and faced with very different ground to his British debut at Sandown, ran a bit better without ever promsing to get involved. (op 16-1)
Hi Calypso(IRE), whose four-timer last season culminated in the Park Hill Stakes at Doncaster, was always at the rear of the field on this belated reappearance. (op 14-1)

3247 GOLDEN JUBILEE STKS (BRITISH LEG OF THE GLOBAL SPRINT CHALLENGE) (GROUP 1) 6f

3:45 (3:45) (Class 1) 3-Y-O+

£212,887 (£80,700; £40,387; £20,137; £10,087; £5,062) **Stalls** Centre

Form RPR

12-0 **1** **Kingsgate Native (IRE)**[4] 3101 3-8-11 118..................... SebSanders 3 123
(J R Best) *t.k.h: hld up in bhd ldrs: rdn to chal over 1f out: led last 100yds: edgd sltly lft and flashed tail but r.o strly* **33/1**

262 **2** 1 1/4 **War Artist (AUS)**[38] 2106 5-9-4 116.............................. KerrinMcEvoy 1 120
(J M P Eustace) *lw: prom: chsd ldr 1/2-way: ev ch and rdn over 1f out: chsd wnr ins fnl f: kpt on same pce* **8/1**

-013 **3** 3/4 **Sir Gerry (USA)**[20] 2652 3-8-11 112........................... JamieSpencer 4 116
(J R Fanshawe) *hld up in midfield: swtchd lft and rdn wl over 1f out: chsd ldng trio jst over 1f out: wnt 3rd wl ins fnl f: r.o wl but nvr quite getting to ldng pair* **20/1**

2-12 **4** 2 1/4 **Takeover Target (AUS)**[4] 3101 9-9-4 0.................................. JayFord 2 111
(J Janiak, Australia) *lw: chsd ldr tl led 1/2-way: hrd pressed and rdn over 1f out: hdd last 100yds: fdd towards fin* **4/1**[1]

4-34 **5** 1 **US Ranger (USA)**[38] 2106 4-9-4 0....................................... JMurtagh 5 108
(A P O'Brien, Ire) *lw: wl bhd: rdn wl over 2f out: r.o wl fr over 1f out: nvr threatened ldrs* **6/1**

36-1 **6** 1/2 **Marchand D'Or (FR)**[20] 2652 5-9-4 0.................................. DBonilla 12 106+
(F Head, France) *lw: taken down early and walked to s: t.k.h: hld up towards rr: bmpd and n.m.r wl over 2f out: sn rdn: styd on fr over 1f out: nvr threatened ldrs* **9/2**[2]

0-01 **7** 3/4 **Astronomer Royal (USA)**[28] 2417 4-9-4 0................. CO'Donoghue 10 104
(A P O'Brien, Ire) *bhd: rdn over 2f out: styd on fr over 1f out: nvr trbld ldrs* **25/1**

0-15 **8** *nk* **Zidane**[48] 1831 6-9-4 109.. RobertWinston 6 103
(J R Fanshawe) *hld up in rr: rdn and effrt 2f out: chsd ldrs and rdn over 1f out: sn no imp* **25/1**

-325 **9** 3 **Dark Missile**[21] 2606 5-9-1 103.. WilliamBuick 19 90
(A M Balding) *hld up in tch: effrt 2f out: chsd ldrs and rdn over 1f out: wknd fnl f* **40/1**

-001 **10** 3/4 **Balthazaar's Gift (IRE)**[19] 2680 5-9-4 112.................. JimmyFortune 11 91
(L M Cumani) *a in rr: rdn and effrt jst over 2f out: nvr trbld ldrs* **20/1**

-211 **11** 1/2 **Fat Boy (IRE)**[21] 2605 3-8-11 112.................................... RyanMoore 14 87
(P W Chapple-Hyam) *lw: led tl 1/2-way: rdn over 2f out: wknd over 1f out* **16/1**

66 **12** 4 1/2 **Seachange (NZ)**[84] 1090 6-9-1 0.. TedDurcan 18 72
(G Sanders, New Zealand) *chsd ldrs: rdn jst over 2f out: wknd qckly wl over 1f out* **22/1**

1133 **13** 4 **Snaefell (IRE)**[19] 2685 4-9-4 0.. PJSmullen 13 62
(M Halford, Ire) *hld up in midfield: rdn and effrt jst over 2f out: wknd over 1f out: sn wl btn* **100/1**

0-21 **14** 1/2 **Assertive**[38] 2106 5-9-4 112.. RichardHughes 15 60+
(R Hannon) *lw: chsd ldrs: rdn over 2f out: wknd over 1f out: eased ins fnl f* **25/1**

0-03 **15** 5 **Aeroplane**[42] 1989 5-9-4 100.. AlanMunro 7 44+
(P W Chapple-Hyam) *racd in midfield tl lost pl over 3f out: struggling whn edgd rt wl over 2f out and bmpd rival: sn wl btn: eased fnl f* **40/1**

/410 **16** 1 1/2 **Diabolical (USA)**[84] 1089 5-9-4 117.. LDettori 8 39+
(Saeed Bin Suroor) *chsd ldrs tl wknd qckly 2f out: virtually p.u ins fnl f* **33/1**

15-2 **17** 4 **Sakhee's Secret**[48] 1831 4-9-4 120.................................. SteveDrowne 9 27+
(H Morrison) *lw: racd in tch in midfield: rdn and losing pl whn bmpd wl over 2f out: sn wl bhd: virtually p.u fnl f* **5/1**[3]

1m 13.33s (-1.07) **Going Correction** +0.25s/f (Good)
WFA 3 from 4yo+ 7lb **17** Ran SP% **123.3**
Speed ratings (Par 117): **117,115,114,111,110 109,108,107,103,102 102,96,90,90,83 81,76**
toteswinger: 1&2 £48.00, 1&3 £51.40, 2&3 £28.30 CSF £250.50 CT £3087.54 TOTE £48.00: £11.00, £3.90, £7.30; EX 452.50 Trifecta £4015.80 Pool: £14,652.49 - 2.70 winning units..
Owner John Mayne **Bred** Peter McCutcheon **Trained** Hucking, Kent
■ Kingsgate Native was this race's first three-year-old winner since Atraf in 1996, when it was a mere Group 3.
■ Stewards' Enquiry : Jay Ford one-day ban: used whip without giving gelding time to respond (Jul 6)

FOCUS
A fine renewal of this Group 1 sprint, but the draw played a major role with the first five all coming from the lowest five stalls. They all raced in a group of six that raced slightly apart from the main group until the groups merged with around two to run. The form is weakened by the below-par showings of Marchand D'Or and Sakhee's Secret, but Kingsgate Native confirmed himself one of the top European sprinters. Last year's winner Soldier's Tale was a late withdrawal and may not race again.

NOTEBOOK
Kingsgate Native(IRE) was only tenth in the King's Stand on the opening day, but he had raced with the choke out and was better drawn this time near the stands' rail. Held up racing keenly, just off the pace set by Takeover Target, he challenged at the furlong pole and ran on well to secure victory, despite giving a couple of tail flashes late on. This confirmed that his fine juvenile form was not largely down to a generous weight-for-age allowance, and he got the extra furlong well on his first attempt at the trip. He will go for the July Cup next before attempting a repeat victory in the Nunthorpe.
War Artist(AUS) has improved with each run since coming to Britain and he ran another big race, albeit from the best draw of all. Having shown speed throughout he came through to win his race at the furlong pole but could not quite get his head in front. He will take on Kingsgate Native again in the July Cup. (op 9-1)
Sir Gerry(USA) appreciated the extra furlong after finishing third to Marchand D'Or over the minimum trip at Chantilly. Another favourably drawn, he was slightly outpaced by the three in front of him over a furlong out but ran on well inside the last, moving into third past the weakening Takeover Target. The July Cup could be next for him too.
Takeover Target(AUS), third in this event two years ago and runner-up last year, had finished just under four lengths in front of today's winner when second to Equiano in the King's Stand earlier in the week. He again showed fine pace, leading the near-side bunch and showing ahead overall at halfway, but he could not hold on in the last half-furlong. Connections had felt that he may have been feeling the effects of his race earlier in the week, but post-race scans revealed a slight tear in his nearside suspensory tendon. He will therefore miss the July Cup and return to Australia to be prepared for the 2008 Victoria Spring Carnival. (op 5-1)
US Ranger(USA) certainly had no excuses on account of the draw this time but he was outpaced and under pressure some way out, only finding his stride approaching the final furlong and finishing well without threatening to reach a place. This trip looks a bit sharp for him now. Official explanation: jockey said colt was hampered at start (tchd 11-2, 13-2 in places)
Marchand D'Or(FR), who beat King's Stand winner Equiano at Chantilly last time, with Sir Gerry third, was back over his optimum trip. Held up, he was left with an awful lot to do when running into trouble past halfway but he found himself carried over to the stands' side where the ground was better and finished to good effect. He is to bid for a third successive win in Deauville's Prix Maurice de Gheest, over an extra half-furlong. (op 11-2)
Astronomer Royal(USA), the Ballydoyle second string, had won a Curragh Group 3 over this trip last time but in this top company the 6f proved insufficient and he was only really getting going when it was too late. (tchd 22-1)
Zidane, whose usual rider partnered his stablemate Sir Gerry instead, ran a decent race on this return to 6f but could not capitalise on what was a pretty favourable draw.
Dark Missile, never out of the first two in four previous visits to Ascot, including a win in last year's Wokingham, ran another good race from what turned out to be the worst draw of all. (op 50-1)
Balthazaar's Gift(IRE), runner-up to Les Arcs two years ago when a 50/1 chance, could never get involved.
Fat Boy(IRE), taking a big step up in class, showed his by now familiar pace to lead the field overall until Takeover Target went past at halfway. Official explanation: jockey said colt hung left (op 20-1)
Seachange(NZ) had a wide draw to contend with on her British debut and is capable of better. She is in the July Cup, but she also holds an entry in the Falmouth Stakes and she has won at up to 1m in New Zealand. (op 16-1 tchd 25-1)
Sakhee's Secret, unsuited by the rain which loosened the ground on top, ran no sort of race and was already beaten when getting buffeted about just after halfway. He ought to be a different proposition if the ground is on top when he bids to repeat last year's July Cup win. Official explanation: jockey said colt lost a front shoe and suffered interference (op 4-1 tchd 11-2 in a place)

3248 WOKINGHAM STKS (HERITAGE H'CAP) 6f

4:25 (4:26) (Class 2) (0-110,109) 3-Y-O+

£62,310 (£18,660; £9,330; £4,670; £2,330; £585) **Stalls** Centre

Form RPR

2202 **1** **Big Timer (USA)**[21] 2607 4-9-2 **100**..................................... TomEaves 28 111
(Miss L A Perratt) *racd on far side: chsd ldrs: rdn over 1f out: overall ld ins fnl f: edgd lft and r.o towards fin* **20/1**

4000 **2** 1/2 **Beaver Patrol (IRE)**[27] 2426 6-9-2 **100**..........................(v) MJKinane 2 109
(Eve Johnson Houghton) *racd on stands' side: hld up: rdn and hdwy 2f out: r.o to ld gp ins fnl f: hld by wnr on other side towards fin: 1st of 18 in gp* **16/1**

11-5 **3** *nse* **King's Apostle (IRE)**[49] 1809 4-9-0 **98**............................ LiamJones 23 107
(W J Haggas) *racd on far side: hld up: hdwy and swtchd lft over 1f out: edgd lft and gaining when running on towards fin: 2nd of 9 in gp* **11/1**

2005 **4** 1 1/2 **Knot In Wood (IRE)**[28] 2401 6-9-0 **98**.............................. PaulHanagan 6 102
(R A Fahey) *racd on stands' side: midfield: rdn and hdwy over 2f out: chalng over 1f out: r.o ins fnl f: hld towards fin: 2nd of 18 in gp* **10/1**

11-2 **5** 3/4 **Tamagin (USA)**[23] 2530 5-9-3 **101**.. NCallan 5 103
(K A Ryan) *racd on stands' side: led gp: hung rt fr 1/2-way: hdd ins fnl f whn in centre of trck: r.o same pce towards fin: 3rd of 18 in gp* **14/1**

3004 **6** *hd* **Capricorn Run (USA)**[23] 2530 5-9-7 **105**.....................(p) JamesDoyle 26 106
(A J McCabe) *racd on far side: w ldr: pushed along 1/2-way: led gp over 2f out: hdd ins fnl f: styd on same pce towards fin: dead-heated for 3rd of 9 in gp* **40/1**

0-16 **6** *dht* **Bentong (IRE)**[50] 1765 5-9-5 **103**.......................................(t) TQuinn 22 104
(P F I Cole) *racd on far side: hld up: rdn and hdwy over 2f out: sn chsd ldrs: one pce towards fin: dead-heated for 3rd of 9 in gp* **66/1**

-140 **8** *hd* **Northern Fling**[21] 2626 4-9-4 **102**.............................. GrahamGibbons 21 103+
(D Nicholls) *s.i.s: racd on far side: towards rr: hdwy 1/2-way: pushed along whn n.m.r and lost pl over 2f out: rallied and fin wl: 5th of 9 in gp* **66/1**

-135 **9** *nk* **New Freedom (BRZ)**[84] 1089 7-9-7 **105**.......................... TedDurcan 20 105
(D R Lanigan) *swtg: racd on far side: midfield: rdn and hung rt fr 1/2-way: r.o u.p ins fnl f: gaining towards fin: nt quite pce of ldrs: 6th of 9 in gp* **66/1**

00-2 **10** *nk* **Intrepid Jack**[28] 2401 6-9-7 **105**.. RyanMoore 7 109+
(H Morrison) *racd on stands' side: hld up: hdwy 1f out: running on whn nt clr run ins fnl f: sn swtchd rt: unable to rcvr: 4th of 18 in gp* **6/1**[1]

20-2 **11** *hd* **Lipocco**[19] 2680 4-9-4 **102**.. SebSanders 11 100
(R M Beckett) *racd on stands' side: a.p: rdn and chalng over 1f out: nt qckn towards fin: 5th of 18 in gp* **12/1**

2400 **12** *1/2* **Machinist (IRE)**[14] 2831 8-9-1 **99**....................................... JoeFanning 8 96+
(D Nicholls) *s.i.s: racd on stands' side: in rr: hdwy over 1f out: styd on ins fnl f: nt pce to chal ldrs: 6th of 18 in gp* **33/1**

0005 **13** *1 3/4* **Conquest (IRE)**[21] 2598 4-9-1 **99**..................................... ShaneKelly 27 90
(W J Haggas) *racd on far side: led gp: rdn and hdd over 2f out: wknd ins fnl f: 7th of 9 in gp* **50/1**

0154 **14** *1/2* **Vitznau (IRE)**[15] 2789 4-9-4 **102**.................................... JimmyFortune 24 91
(R Hannon) *lw: racd on far side: bhd: rdn over 1f out: styd on and prog ins fnl f: nt pce to rch ldrs: 8th of 9 in gp* **33/1**

4-00 **15** *1/2* **Sunrise Safari (IRE)**[120] 670 5-9-2 **100**..................(p) KerrinMcEvoy 12 88
(R A Fahey) *racd on stands' side: midfield: rdn 2f out: kpt on fnl f: no imp on ldrs: 7th of 18 in gp* **50/1**

-016 **16** *hd* **Off The Record**[28] 2404 4-9-1 **99**.. TPQueally 17 86
(J G Given) *swtg: racd on stands' side: prom: drifted rt w rival fr 1/2-way: wknd whn in centre of trck ins fnl f: 8th of 18 in gp* **16/1**

-330 **17** *2* **Fullandby (IRE)**[28] 2404 6-9-2 **103**............................ PJMcDonald(3) 15 84
(T J Etherington) *missed break: racd on stands' side: in rr: hdwy over 2f out: kpt on ins fnl f: nvr able to chal: 9th of 18 in gp* **20/1**

0-01 **18** *shd* **Viking Spirit**[21] 2598 6-8-12 **103** 5ex........................... DavidProbert(7) 25 83
(W R Swinburn) *racd on far side: midfield: n.m.r and hmpd over 2f out: sn lost pl: n.d after: 9th of 9 in gp* **33/1**

4003 **19** *nk* **Prime Defender**[19] 2680 4-9-8 **106**..............................(p) MichaelHills 10 85
(B W Hills) *swtg: racd on stands' side: midfield: effrt over 2f out: wknd fnl f: 10th of 18 in gp* **22/1**

-020 **20** *1 1/2* **Abraham Lincoln (IRE)**[4] 3101 4-9-9 **107**.......................... JMurtagh 4 82
(A P O'Brien, Ire) *racd on stands' side: bhd: sn pushed along: nvr on terms: 11th of 18 in gp* **13/2**[2]

-030 **21** *2 1/4* **Something (IRE)**[22] 2580 6-9-2 **100**.................................. DaneO'Neill 3 67
(D Nicholls) *racd on stands' side: hld up: effrt over 1f out: no imp on ldrs: wknd ins fnl f: 12th of 18 in gp* **16/1**

5512 **22** *1 1/2* **Dark Islander (IRE)**[35] 2214 5-9-10 **108**......................... EddieAhern 18 71
(J W Hills) *racd on stands' side: sn pushed along: a bhd: 13th of 18 in gp* **33/1**

1-03 **23** *3* **Biniou (IRE)**[17] 2712 5-9-4 **102**.. AlanMunro 13 55
(R M H Cowell) *racd on stands' side: chsd ldrs: rdn 1/2-way: wknd 2f out: 14th of 18 in gp* **100/1**

0406 **24** *nse* **Indian Trail**[21] 2626 8-9-4 **102**...(v) LDettori 16 55
(D Nicholls) *racd on stands' side: midfield: rdn over 2f out: sn wknd: 15th of 18 in gp* **33/1**

14-1 **25** *3 1/4* **Tombi (USA)**[36] 2172 4-9-4 **102**.................................... RobertWinston 9 45
(J Howard Johnson) *lw: racd on stands' side: prom tl rdn and wknd over 1f out: 16th of 18 in gp* **12/1**

00-1 **26** *8* **Nota Bene**[23] 2530 6-9-4 **102** 5ex.................................... JamieSpencer 1 19
(D R C Elsworth) *lw: racd on stands' side: in tch: rdn and wknd over 1f out: eased whn btn ins fnl f: 17th of 18 in gp* **9/1**[3]

1261 **27** *4* **Edge Closer**[6] 3063 4-9-11 **109** 5ex............................ RichardHughes 14 13
(R Hannon) *racd on stands' side: prom tl rdn and wknd over 2f out: 18th of 18 in gp* **14/1**

1m 14.37s (-0.03) **Going Correction** +0.25s/f (Good) **27** Ran SP% **141.8**
Speed ratings (Par 109): **110,109,109,107,106 106,106,105,105,104 104,104,101,101,100 100,97,97,96,94 91,89,85,85,81 70**
toteswinger: 1&2 £82.00, 1&3 £46.40, 2&3 £91.30 CSF £307.68 CT £3766.79 TOTE £35.20: £6.90, £4.60, £3.20, £3.10; EX 1048.78 Trifecta £18785.00 Pool: £93,925.15 - 3.70 winning units..
Owner Gordon McDowall **Bred** Mt Brilliant Farm Llc **Trained** Carluke, S Lanarks
■ The first Royal Ascot winner for both Linda Perratt and Tom Eaves.

FOCUS
The usual solid form in this highly competitive event. They split into two groups and the winner, drawn 28 of 28 in complete contrast to the Golden Jubilee result, was one of nine to race down the far side. The runner-up raced up the opposite flank and the form makes sense down the two sides.

NOTEBOOK
Big Timer(USA) showed high-class form when runner-up in a 7f Group 3 last time. Racing from the highest draw, he tracked the pace in the smaller far-side group and hit the front once pulled off the rail, edging to his left under pressure and getting the verdict from his closest pursuer who raced on the opposite flank. This might be the end of handicaps for him. (op 25-1 tchd 28-1, 33-1 in a place)
Beaver Patrol(IRE) is a smart sprinter when on song and he has run well in these big-field handicaps plenty of times. He improved from the rear to hit the front in the 18-strong group on the stands' side but was just held by the winner who raced on the opposite wing. (op 25-1)
King's Apostle(IRE) ◆, whose yard has enjoyed a successful week at Ascot, maintained his progressive profile with another fine effort. Running on late down the far side, he would have been second overall in another stride or two. There should be more to come from him, perhaps back over an extra furlong. (op 10-1 tchd 14-1 in a place and 12-1 in a place)
Knot In Wood(IRE), back over 6f, came through to lead the larger stands'-side group briefly and kept on for fourth. He remains capable of picking up a big handicap. (op 8-1 tchd 11-1 in a place)
Tamagin(USA), back on turf, once again showed blistering pace although he edged over from the stands' side to race down the centre. He only relinquished the overall lead inside the last. (op 16-1)
Bentong(IRE) ran a sound race back down in trip on turf and with the tongue tie refitted. (op 66-1)
Capricorn Run(USA), running on turf for the first time this year, had cheekpieces back on in place of the visor. He disputed the lead in the far-side group and, although unable to counter when the winner went by, he stuck on under pressure for a share of sixth. (op 66-1)
Northern Fling, back up in trip, made late progress to reach the best placing of the four Nicholls runners.
New Freedom(BRZ) made a pleasing British debut at long odds over a trip his form in Brazil and Dubai suggested might stretch him. (op 50-1)
Intrepid Jack ◆, 5lb higher than when runner-up a year ago, was in the process of running on when he was stopped in his tracks inside the final furlong, but for which he would have gone close to making the frame. He remains in good heart. (op 8-1)
Lipocco was ahead of the Handicapper following his good conditions race second at Windsor, but the faster the ground the better, so overnight rain did not help. He still showed bright pace until inside the final furlong. (tchd 14-1 in places)
Machinist(IRE), who could do with a bit of help from the handicapper, was noted putting in some decent late work. (op 28-1)
Conquest(IRE) matched strides with Capricorn Run down the far side until fading out of it.
Off The Record showed pace to go with Tamagin down the centre before his exertions told inside the last.
Fullandby(IRE), out of his depth in a Group 2 last time, ran better than his finishing position suggests. (tchd 22-1)
Abraham Lincoln(IRE), ninth in the King's Stand earlier in the week, was well supported on this handicap debut but was never in the hunt. (op 8-1 tchd 10-1 in places and 9-1)
Dark Islander(IRE) Official explanation: jockey said horse was unsuited by the good to firm (firm in places) ground
Nota Bene, successful at Great Leighs last time, was not far from the pace on the stands' side for over half a mile and was eased right down when beaten. Official explanation: jockey said gelding was unsuited by the good to firm (firm in places) ground (op 11-1)

3249 DUKE OF EDINBURGH STKS (HERITAGE H'CAP) 1m 4f

5:00 (5:01) (Class 2) (0-105,105) 3-Y-O+

£37,386 (£11,196; £5,598; £2,802; £1,398; £702) **Stalls** High

Form RPR

3-13 **1** **Sugar Ray (IRE)**[36] 2168 4-9-0 **95**..................................(t) RyanMoore 14 106
(Sir Michael Stoute) *mde all: rdn wl over 2f out: hld on gamely: all out* **8/1**[3]

22-2 **2** *nk* **Mad Rush (USA)**[29] 2372 4-9-2 **97**.............................. JimmyFortune 10 108
(L M Cumani) *hld up wl in tch: chsd ldrs and rdn over 2f out: chsd wnr jst over 1f out: str chal ins fnl f: kpt on but nt quite rch wnr* **5/2**[1]

0335 **3** *1 3/4* **King Charles**[38] 2103 4-9-2 **97**...................................... KerrinMcEvoy 17 105+
(E A L Dunlop) *hld up in midfield: shuffled bk and towards rr 6f out: swtchd lft over 2f out: r.o wl to go 3rd nr fin: nt rch ldng pair* **18/1**

-000 **4** *1/2* **Young Mick**[15] 2797 6-9-5 **100**....................................(v) RobertWinston 2 107
(G G Margarson) *hld up in midfield: hdwy 5f out: chsd ldrs and drvn over 2f out: kpt on same pce fnl f* **20/1**

1-24 **5** *1/2* **Furmigadelagiusta**[36] 2168 4-9-3 **98**..................................... JMurtagh 7 105
(K R Burke) *swtchd rt and dropped in bhd after s: stl plenty to do and swtchd lft over 2f out: r.o wl fr over 1f out: nt rch ldrs* **20/1**

6-41 **6** *nk* **Proponent (IRE)**[48] 1828 4-9-2 **97**.................................. SteveDrowne 4 103+
(R Charlton) *lw: chsd wnr tl over 7f out: rdn to chse wnr again over 2f out tl jst over 1f out: wknd last 100yds* **8/1**[3]

05-2 **7** *3/4* **Camps Bay (USA)**[49] 1812 4-9-3 **98**................................. JimCrowley 1 103+
(Mrs A J Perrett) *hld up and bhd: stl plenty to do and swtchd lft over 2f out: r.o wl fr over 1f out: grad edging rt fnl f: nt rch ldrs* **11/1**

3-44 **8** *1 3/4* **Night Crescendo (USA)**[36] 2144 5-9-2 **97**.......................... MJKinane 9 99
(Mrs A J Perrett) *t.k.h: hld up and bhd: hdwy on outer 6f out: rdn over 2f out: kpt on but nvr pce to threaten ldrs* **16/1**

0-02 **9** *3/4* **Pevensey (IRE)**[36] 2168 6-9-0 **95**................................ GrahamGibbons 3 98+
(J J Quinn) *hld up in midfield tl shuffled bk towards rr 6f out: rdn and no prog whn nt clr run and swtchd lft over 1f out: plugged on but n.d* **14/1**

-454 **10** *1 3/4* **Smart Instinct (USA)**[15] 2790 4-8-13 **94**....................... PaulHanagan 13 92
(R A Fahey) *hld up wl in tch: rdn wl over 2f out: wknd over 1f out* **20/1**

3-11 **11** *hd* **Ezdiyaad (IRE)**[21] 2593 4-9-5 **100**... RHills 15 98
(M P Tregoning) *t.k.h: chsd ldrs tl wnt 2nd over 7f out rdn to press wnr 3f out tl over 2f out: sn wknd* **7/1**[2]

000- **12** *3 3/4* **Strategic Mount**[203] 6994 5-9-1 **96**.. TQuinn 8 88
(P F I Cole) *t.k.h: hld up in rr: nvr trbld ldrs* **33/1**

3010 **13** *1/2* **Capable Guest (IRE)**[14] 2830 6-9-0 **95**....................(v) RichardHughes 6 86
(M R Channon) *t.k.h: hld up towards rr: hdwy into midfield 6f out: swtchd lft and effrt 3f out: no prog whn sltly hmpd over 2f out: no ch after* **33/1**

0232 **14** *1 3/4* **Pinch Of Salt (IRE)**[17] 2711 5-8-13 **94**........................ WilliamBuick 11 82
(A M Balding) *hld up in midfield on outer: rdn 3f out: sn struggling and btn* **33/1**

3-00 **15** *nk* **Players Please (USA)**[14] 2830 4-9-0 **95**............................ JohnEgan 16 83
(M Johnston) *chsd ldrs: rdn 3f out: wknd over 2f out* **33/1**

-000 **16** *12* **Coeur De Lionne (IRE)**[121] 652 4-9-2 **97**....................... TedDurcan 12 66
(E A L Dunlop) *hld up towards rr: hdwy over 4f out: wknd over 2f out: wl btn and eased fnl f* **33/1**

05-0 **17** *5* **Jadalee (IRE)**[43] 1944 5-9-10 **105**... NCallan 18 66
(G A Butler) *taken down early: hld up in midfield: rdn 3f out: sn struggling: wl btn and eased fnl f* **50/1**

1-00 **18** *1 1/2* **Gulf Express (USA)**[38] 2103 4-9-1 **96**........................ JamieSpencer 19 54+
(Sir Michael Stoute) *hmpd and snatched up after s: a bhd: wl btn and eased fnl f* **16/1**

1-20 **19** *hd* **Evident Pride (USA)**[98] 906 5-9-0 **95**.............................. DaneO'Neill 5 53
(B R Johnson) *t.k.h: hld up in midfield: rdn and wknd over 3f out: wl btn and eased fnl f* **33/1**

2m 32.95s (-2.55) **Going Correction** +0.025s/f (Good) **19** Ran SP% **129.2**
Speed ratings (Par 109): **109,108,107,107,106 106,106,105,104,103 103,100,100,99,99 91,87,86,86**
toteswinger: 1&2 £3.60, 1&3 £36.80, 2&3 £13.90 CSF £25.73 CT £378.43 TOTE £7.30: £1.60, £1.50, £5.20, £3.60; EX 28.00 Trifecta £653.20 Pool: £5,040.50 - 5.71 winning units..
Owner Philip Newton **Bred** Barronstown Stud And Pacelco S A **Trained** Newmarket, Suffolk

FOCUS
This was not as strongly run as usual, the winner making all, but the pace was still fair. The front pair were unexposed and the form is sound enough, without being quite as strong as one would normally expect.

NOTEBOOK
Sugar Ray(IRE) went up another couple of pounds for his good run in defeat at York but the handicapper had obviously not got to him. Racing in a tongue tie for the first time, he dictated the pace under a good ride from Moore and stayed on well under pressure to hold off a determined challenge from the runner-up. (tchd 15-2)
Mad Rush(USA), who made such a promising reappearance at Newmarket, became a little warm before the off. Always well placed, he was ridden on the home turn and threw down a strong challenge to the leader in the straight, but could never quite get past. He will go up a few pounds for this but has only run six times in his life and there should still be improvement in him. (op 11-4 tchd 3-1 in places)
King Charles lost his pitch at around halfway but stayed on well down the outside in the home straight for third. He continues to battle against the handicapper but this sound run proves that he is fully effective over this longer trip. (op 20-1)
Young Mick, winner of this race two years ago, was back down to the same mark as when last running in a handicap in the 2006 Ebor. On a course that he likes, he ran his best race of the season, one of four battling for the lead in the straight but unable to produce a change of gear. He raced on the outside of the bunch for much of the way and emerges with plenty of credit. (op 25-1 tchd 33-1 in a place)
Furmigadelagiusta ◆ had a lot of ground to make up turning into the home straight but came home in eye-catching fashion for fifth. (op 16-1)
Proponent(IRE) ◆, who had today's third behind when winning over 1m1f at Newmarket, ran every bit as well but his stamina just gave out in the final half-furlong. The John Smith's Cup at York looks an ideal race for him. (op 15-2)
Camps Bay(USA), raised 6lb and racing from a career-high mark, was held up as usual but was putting in some good late work. (op 12-1)

Pevensey(IRE), successful in last year's renewal from a 5lb lower mark, showed a return to form at York last time. He never really threatened to land this race for a second time but would have finished closer than he did had he enjoyed luck in running. (op 12-1 tchd 11-1)
Ezdiyaad(IRE) compromised his chance of getting this longer trip by racing too keen. (op 9-1)
Gulf Express(USA) was snatched up leaving the stalls and could never get into the race. This can be ignored. Official explanation: jockey said colt suffered interference in running (op 10-1)

3250 QUEEN ALEXANDRA STKS (CONDITIONS RACE) 2m 5f 159y

5:35 (5:38) (Class 2) 4-Y-0+

£37,386 (£11,196; £5,598; £2,802; £1,398; £702) **Stalls** High

Form / RPR

30-4 **1** **Honolulu (IRE)**[36] 2169 4-9-5 0 JMurtagh 4 117
(A P O'Brien, Ire) *hld up: hdwy over 4f out: chal 2f out: narrowly led whn carried hd high wl over 1f out: hrd pressed tl asserted fnl 100yds* **7/4**[1]

14-3 **2** *1 1/2* **Distinction (IRE)**[52] 1717 9-9-7 107 RyanMoore 3 115
(Sir Michael Stoute) *lw: midfield: hdwy over 4f out: chal 2f out: upsides wnr tl no ex fnl 100yds* **8/1**

336- **3** *11* **Metaphoric (IRE)**[76] 5952 4-9-0 100 (t) JamieSpencer 15 99
(M L W Bell) *lw: racd keenly: in tch: lost pl 5f out: n.m.r and hmpd over 4f out: nt clr run over 3f out: hdwy whn swtchd lft 2f out: sn chsd ldrs: no ch over 1f out* **14/1**

05-1 **4** *hd* **Bulwark (IRE)**[45] 1916 6-9-2 103 (v) JimCrowley 16 99
(Ian Williams) *lw: midfield: hdwy 3f out: rdn to chse ldrs over 2f out but no ch: plugged on for pls* **8/1**

4-11 **5** *13* **Ajaan**[35] 2202 4-9-0 102 (b) TedDurcan 8 93+
(H R A Cecil) *lw: midfield: hdwy 4f out: upsides over 3f out: led over 2f out: sn hung rt: hdd wl over 1f out: sn wknd: eased whn wl btn ins fnl f* **7/2**[2]

212- **6** *1* **Caracciola (GER)**[56] 6335 11-9-2 99 EddieAhern 11 85
(N J Henderson) *midfield: rdn and hung rt over 1f out whn no imp: nvr able to trble ldrs* **20/1**

4/0- **7** *3 3/4* **Merveilles**[24] 2517 5-9-2 0 (p) PJSmullen 6 81
(Mrs John Harrington, Ire) *racd keenly: in tch: upsides over 3f out: rdn over 2f out: wknd over 1f out* **25/1**

06/ **8** *1/2* **Bahrain Storm (IRE)**[24] 2517 5-9-2 0 (b) MJKinane 5 81
(Patrick J Flynn, Ire) *racd keenly: stdd to run off the pce after 2f: effrt over 3f out: no imp: nvr on terms* **25/1**

-500 **9** *hd* **Baddam**[4] 3104 6-9-2 91 RichardHughes 17 80
(Ian Williams) *midfield: rdn and hdwy 5f out: chal on outside over 3f out tl 2f out: wknd over 1f out* **16/1**

0-44 **10** *4* **Kayf Aramis**[21] 2628 6-9-2 71 SteveDrowne 14 76
(Miss Venetia Williams) *chsd ldrs: rdn and losing pl whn n.m.r over 3f out: n.d whn n.m.r again over 2f out* **66/1**

362 **11** *29* **Ashmolian (IRE)**[60] 1538 5-9-2 52 SamHitchcott 2 47
(Miss Z C Davison) *dwlt: bhd: struggling 3f out: nvr on terms* **80/1**

40-6 **12** *8* **Enjoy The Moment**[23] 2542 5-9-5 105 ShaneKelly 9 42
(J A Osborne) *s.i.s: racd keenly: hld up: hdwy over 3f out: rdn and wknd over 2f out* **6/1**[3]

0-13 **13** *10* **Noddies Way**[37] 2135 5-9-2 62 LiamJones 7 29
(J F Panvert) *chsd ldrs: wnt 2nd 10f out tl 7f out: sn rdn: wknd 3f out* **40/1**

101/ **14** *10* **Hasanpour (IRE)**[21] 2634 8-9-2 0 RobertWinston 10 19
(K J Burke) *midfield: hdwy to chse ldrs 10f out: wnt 2nd 7f out: led over 3f out: hdd over 2f out: wkng whn hmpd over 1f out: fin tired* **66/1**

0030 **15** *10* **Invasian (IRE)**[23] 2531 7-9-2 86 JohnEgan 12 9
(P W D'Arcy) *led: clr after 7f: reduced advantage 10f out: rdn over 4f out: hdd over 3f out: sn wknd* **66/1**

0026 **16** *93* **Basalt (IRE)**[4] 3104 4-9-0 80 KerrinMcEvoy 1 —
(T J Pitt) *sn chsd ldr: lost 2nd 10f out: pushed along 7f out: wknd 6f out: t.o* **25/1**

4m 49.07s (-7.43) **Going Correction** +0.025s/f (Good)
WFA 4 from 5yo+ 2lb **16** Ran SP% **132.1**
Speed ratings (Par 109): **114,113,109,109,104 104,102,102,102,101 90,87,84,80,76 43**
toteswinger: 1&2 £4.00, 1&3 £9.10, 2&3 £19.50 CSF £16.81 CT £172.24 TOTE £2.90: £1.60, £2.30, £4.90; EX 18.60 Trifecta £259.20 Pool: £6,983.19 - 19.93 winning units. Place 6 £428.47, Place 5 £235.64.
Owner D Smith, Mrs J Magnier, M Tabor **Bred** Kilfrush Stud **Trained** Ballydoyle, Co Tipperary
■ The sixth winner of the week for Aidan O'Brien and Johnny Murtagh.

FOCUS

A classy renewal of the Queen Alexandra and they finished well strung out behind the first two. The pace was not that strong. Honolulu is the best winner of the race on RPRs for a number of years.

NOTEBOOK

Honolulu(IRE) was running over the best part of a mile further than he had tackled before, but he was the class act in this field based on his form last term in the Ebor and the St Leger. Only put into the race in the straight, he had to fight off a sustained challenge from the runner-up before getting on top in the last half-furlong. The yard also has Yeats and Septimus in the staying division, and no plans have been made for him yet. (tchd 6-4 and 15-8)
Distinction(IRE), twice placed in the Gold Cup, made his move at the same time as the winner and the pair were locked together for a time up the straight before the younger horse proved the stronger late on. He loses nothing in defeat. (tchd 15-2)
Metaphoric(IRE) has won twice over hurdles, including his most recent start in April, since his last Flat appearance back in October. He endured something of a nightmare passage, losing a decent pitch and finding himself with only two behind him straightening up for home. He did stay on under pressure but the first two had already flown, although third was probably the best he could have hoped for in any case. Official explanation: jockey said gelding hung right (op 12-1 tchd 16-1)
Bulwark(IRE), the Chester Cup winner, ran respectably and plugged on to almost claim third, finishing a long way clear of the rest. (op 12-1)
Ajaan, a very progressive handicapper, had never run over further than 1m7f. After racing keenly, he showed in front entering the straight but he soon came under pressure and his stamina ebbed away. (op 4-1 tchd 9-2)
Caracciola(GER), having his first run on the Flat since finishing second in last year's Cesarewitch, has plenty of stamina and was plugging on in the straight. (op 16-1)
Merveilles, third in a 1m6f Listed event at Leopardstown last time, was right there turning for home but did not stay. (op 20-1)
Baddam, making a quick reappearance like he did when winning this two years ago, weakened out of things in the straight. (op 25-1)
Enjoy The Moment, who enjoyed the soft ground when successful in an inferior edition of this race twelve months previously, could never make his presence felt. (op 13-2 tchd 7-1 and 15-2 in a palce)
Noddies Way Official explanation: trainer said gelding was found to have a virus
Basalt(IRE) Official explanation: jockey said gelding ran flat
T/Jkpt: Not won. T/Plt: £283.00 to a £1 stake. Pool: £470,703.91. 1,213.95 winning tickets. T/Qpdt: £107.70 to a £1 stake. Pool: £16,920.09. 116.24 winning tickets. SP

[3198] AYR (L-H)

Saturday, June 21

OFFICIAL GOING: Good to firm (9.6)
Wind: Fresh, half-behind Weather: Overcast

3251 SCOTTISH SUN H'CAP 1m

2:35 (2:37) (Class 2) (0-100,92) 3-Y-0

£15,577 (£4,665; £2,332; £1,167; £582; £292) **Stalls** Low

Form / RPR

-611 **1** **Summon Up Theblood (IRE)**[35] 2209 3-9-0 **85** DarryllHolland 3 97
(M R Channon) *prom: hdwy over 3f out: led over 1f out: rdn clr* **11/4**[1]

11 **2** *3* **Underworld**[91] 975 3-9-7 **92** AdrianTNicholls 6 98
(M Johnston) *led: rdn over 2f out: hdd over 1f out: kpt on: nt pce of wnr* **4/1**[2]

23-1 **3** *2 1/4* **Slam**[39] 2079 3-9-6 **91** DO'Donohoe 2 91
(B W Hills) *plld hrd early: cl up: effrt over 2f out: sn one pce* **9/2**[3]

31-0 **4** *3/4* **Midnight Muse (USA)**[43] 1943 3-8-10 **81** FergalLynch 4 80+
(T D Barron) *hld up: shkn up over 2f out: kpt on fnl f: nvr rchd ldrs* **20/1**

112- **5** *hd* **Points Of View**[225] 6750 3-9-1 **86** J-PGuillambert 5 84
(Sir Mark Prescott) *prom: drvn over 2f out: kpt on same pce* **7/1**

-023 **6** *shd* **Bere Davis (FR)**[35] 2189 3-8-10 **81** StephenDonohoe 7 79
(P D Evans) *midfield: drvn 3f out: kpt on fnl f: nt pce to chal* **11/1**

1-30 **7** *1 1/2* **Traphalgar (IRE)**[57] 1595 3-9-3 **88** NelsonDeSouza 1 83
(P F I Cole) *trckd ldrs tl rdn and outpcd fr over 2f out* **12/1**

-500 **8** *1/2* **Oasis Wind**[28] 2410 3-9-3 **91** TolleyDean(3) 8 84
(P F I Cole) *hld up: rdn over 2f out: n.d* **12/1**

221- **9** *2 1/4* **Hold The Gold (IRE)**[195] 7084 3-8-10 **81** ChrisCatlin 10 69
(E J O'Neill) *bhd: drvn over 3f out: nvr on terms* **17/2**

4-60 **10** *10* **Jim Martin**[16] 2747 3-8-2 **73** oh2 PaulFessey 9 38
(Miss L A Perratt) *t.k.h in rr: rdn and struggling fr 3f out* **33/1**

1m 38.8s (-5.00) **Going Correction** -0.50s/f (Hard) **10** Ran SP% **119.3**
Speed ratings (Par 105): **105,102,99,99,98 98,97,96,94,84**
toteswinger: 1&2 £1.20, 1&3 £3.80, 2&3 £5.60 CSF £13.86 CT £48.74 TOTE £3.80: £1.40, £2.00, £2.60; EX 13.20 Trifecta £25.00 Pool: £70.64 - 2.09 winning units..
Owner Derek And Jean Clee **Bred** D D And Mrs Jean P Clee **Trained** West Ilsley, Berks

FOCUS

A decent handicap, but one in which the pace was only fair to the straight and those held up were at a disadvantage. There were enough unexposed/progressive horses in the field to suggest the form is good for the grade. It has been rated largely around the fourth.

NOTEBOOK

Summon Up Theblood(IRE) ◆ is a progressive sort who turned in his best effort yet from this 6lb higher mark. He is thriving at present on a sound surface and, as he has only had 8 runs, may well be capable of further improvement. (op 7-2)
Underworld ◆, unbeaten in two starts over 7f on Polytrack, had the run of the race but nevertheless turned in a useful performance on this turf and handicap debut over this longer trip. He still looked as though this experience would do him good and is sure to win more races. (op 7-2)
Slam, who did not have to improve to win on his All-Weather debut last time, was not disgraced against a couple of progressive sorts but he is really going to have to settle better if he is to win a race of this nature. (op 11-2)
Midnight Muse(USA), tailed off in a Group 3 on his reappearance, shaped better than the bare form suggests as he fared best of the hold-up horses in a race that suited prominent racers. He is worth another try over 1m2f and is one to keep an eye on. (op 16-1)
Points Of View, a dual Polytrack winner up to this trip last year, was not disgraced on his reappearance. He left the impression that the step up to 1m2f would be in his favour. (op 13-2)
Bere Davis(FR), returned to this longer trip, was not disgraced in a race where the leaders did not stop. He is another in this field who shaped as though a stiffer test of stamina would have been in his favour. (op 14-1)

3252 SCOTTISH NEWS OF THE WORLD EBF LAND O'BURNS FILLIES' STKS (LISTED RACE) (F&M) 5f

3:10 (3:10) (Class 1) 3-Y-0+

£17,031 (£6,456; £3,231; £1,611; £807; £405) **Stalls** High

Form / RPR

-411 **1** **Look Busy (IRE)**[28] 2390 3-8-11 100 DanielTudhope 3 93
(A Berry) *hld up: gd hdwy on outside fr 2f out: styd on wl fnl f to ld cl home* **5/2**[1]

0041 **2** *shd* **Princess Ellis**[14] 2843 4-9-3 75 DavidAllan 9 95
(E J Alston) *led: rdn and drifted lft fnl f: hdd cl home* **18/1**

0-50 **3** *1/2* **How's She Cuttin' (IRE)**[21] 2626 5-9-3 83 (v[1]) DarryllHolland 1 93
(T D Barron) *bhd stands' side tl gd hdwy over 1f out: styd on wl towards fin* **18/1**

1-22 **4** *3/4* **Eastern Romance**[17] 2738 3-9-1 105 FergalLynch 6 92
(K A Ryan) *trckd ldrs: drvn over 2f out: kpt on same pce fnl f* **5/2**[1]

-610 **5** *3/4* **Manzila (FR)**[17] 2738 5-9-3 104 AdrianTNicholls 10 88
(D Nicholls) *prom: drvn 2f out: kpt on same pce fnl f* **7/2**[2]

61 **6** *1 3/4* **Mondovi**[29] 2359 4-9-3 89 ChrisCatlin 4 81
(N J Vaughan) *towards rr: drvn 1/2-way: kpt on fnl f: no imp* **12/1**

5-36 **7** *3 1/2* **The Loan Express (IRE)**[19] 2685 3-8-11 0 WJLee 5 67
(T Stack, Ire) *in tch: drvn and outpcd 1/2-way: n.d after* **10/1**[3]

-100 **8** *hd* **Morinqua (IRE)**[14] 2828 4-9-7 93 J-PGuillambert 2 72
(J G Given) *trckd ldrs tl rdn and wknd over 1f out* **12/1**

-000 **9** *1/2* **Loch Jipp (USA)**[7] 3041 3-8-11 90 DO'Donohoe 8 64
(J S Wainwright) *hld up in tch: drvn 1/2-way: wknd over 1f out* **33/1**

55.68 secs (-4.42) **Going Correction** -0.675s/f (Hard) course record
WFA 3 from 4yo+ 6lb **9** Ran SP% **117.3**
Speed ratings (Par 108): **108,107,107,105,104 101,96,95,95**
toteswinger: 1&2 £4.00, 1&3 £10.60, 2&3 £39.40 CSF £51.87 TOTE £3.70: £1.30, £3.50, £2.90; EX 51.60 TRIFECTA Not won..
Owner A Underwood **Bred** Tom And Hazel Russell **Trained** Cockerham, Lancs
■ Stewards' Enquiry : David Allan two-day ban: careless riding (Jul 6-7)

FOCUS

A strongly run race and, although there was a fair tailwind, it was remarkable that every horse in the race broke the longstanding 5f track record. It is not easy to get a definite handle on the form, though, with the runner-up rated only 75 and third rated 83. It has been rated tentatively around the third to the best view of her handicap form.

NOTEBOOK

Look Busy(IRE) is thriving, and she extended her winning sequence in a strongly run race when getting up late to beat a 75-rated rival, in the process smashing the 5f track record that had stood since 1993. How much she had to improve to beat a 75-rated rival is debatable but she is clearly in rude health and should continue to give a good account. (op 11-4 tchd 3-1)

Princess Ellis is all about speed and, although she looked to have a stiff task at the weights, she ran a blinder for her in-form yard, especially as she set and sustained a strong pace throughout. Her tendency to drift left arguably cost her the race and, even though this was a career-best run, life is going to be tougher after reassessment. (op 20-1)

How's She Cuttin'(IRE) has not been the most reliable but, even though she had a bit to find at the weights, she returned to form in the first-time visor. Although she has raced almost exclusively over 5f, she looks worth another try over 6f, but it remains to be seen whether the headgear will have the desired effect next time. (tchd 20-1)

Eastern Romance, from a bang in-form yard, had a good chance at the weights and the run of the race but, while not at her very best, she left the impression that the return to 6f would have been more to her liking. (op 7-2)

Manzila(FR), a useful sprinter who had a decent chance at the weights, was not at her best in a race that was a thorough test of speed. She may prove better suited by 6f but may not be the easiest to place successfully. (tchd 3-1)

Mondovi, a triple 7f winner in Germany who notched her first win for current connections at Haydock, had a bit to find at the weights and was another to shape as though the step up to 6f would have been more suitable. (op 15-2)

3253 SCOTTISH SUN MISS SCOTLAND H'CAP — 1m 5f 13y

3:50 (3:50) (Class 3) (0-95,94) 4-Y-O+ **£11,009** (£3,275; £1,637; £817) **Stalls** Low

Form	Pos	Dist	Horse / Trainer / Comment	Jockey	SP	RPR
1030	1		**Birkside**^{14} 2830 5-8-8 **81** (D Carroll) *prom: rdn to ld wl over 1f out: edgd lft ins fnl f: r.o wl*	DavidAllan 5	**6/1^{3}**	91+
00-1	2	1 1/4	**Record Breaker (IRE)**^{14} 2839 4-9-5 **92** (M Johnston) *led to wl over 1f out: rdr dropped reins ins fnl f: kpt on nr fin*	DarryllHolland 2	**2/1^{1}**	99
0-33	3	2	**Acropolis (IRE)**^{21} 2609 7-9-7 **94** (Miss L A Perratt) *prom: effrt over 2f out: one pce over 1f out*	(v) PaulFessey 1	**11/1**	98
41-0	4	nk	**Night Hour (IRE)**^{134} 493 6-9-4 **91** (Saeed Bin Suroor) *t.k.h: chsd ldr: effrt over 2f out: one pce over 1f out*	DO'Donohoe 3	**9/2^{2}**	95
0002	5	hd	**Gordonsville**^{10} 2939 5-8-2 **75** (J S Goldie) *t.k.h: hld up in last: effrt over 2f out: kpt on: nvr able to chal*	ChrisCatlin 6	**2/1^{1}**	78+
	6	24	**Gray Mountain (USA)**^{38} 5-8-2 **75** (Miss Lucinda V Russell) *dwlt: hld up: hdwy and cl up 1/2-way: rdn and wknd over 2f out: eased whn no ch fnl f*	(v^{1}) AdrianTNicholls 4	**20/1**	42

2m 50.81s (-5.79) **Going Correction** -0.50s/f (Hard) **6** Ran SP% **112.2**
Speed ratings (Par 107): **97,96,95,94,94 79**
toteswinger: 1&2 £3.80, 1&3 £2.20, 2&3 £7.70 CSF £18.46 TOTE £7.20: £3.30, £1.20; EX 19.90.

Owner J M Walsh & R Glynn **Bred** Pendley Farm **Trained** Sledmere, E Yorks

FOCUS
A fair handicap run at a modest early pace, and the form looks ordinary rated through the third.

NOTEBOOK
Birkside has been a revelation in the last 12 months and turned in his best effort to win with more in hand than the official margin suggests. He will be up in the weights for this but, in view of his record, may well be capable of further progress. (op 15-2 tchd 8-1)

Record Breaker(IRE), 4lb higher than his Musselburgh win, had the run of the race and seemed to give it his best shot. He is a relatively lightly raced sort who is well worth a try over 2m and is the type to win again for this yard. (op 9-4 tchd 15-8)

Acropolis(IRE), back in trip, ran creditably in terms of form but, not for the first time, did not look the most enthusiastic under pressure. He will be suited by a much stiffer test of stamina but remains one to tread carefully with. (op 8-1)

Night Hour(IRE), a fair middle distance handicapper for John Gosden last year, had the run of the race and bettered the form of his first run for the yard on dirt at Nad Al Sheba. A stronger overall gallop may help but he has little margin for error from his current mark in handicaps. (op 4-1)

Gordonsville, who shaped well at Hamilton on his previous start, was not seen to best effect in a race that was not run to suit. An end-to-end gallop suits him ideally and he is worth another chance back in ordinary company. (op 5-2)

Gray Mountain(USA), a dual US winner who scored on his hurdling debut and first run for the yard last month, dropped away tamely in the first-time visor. He will have to show a good deal more before he is a betting proposition in this type of event. (op 12-1)

3254 SUBWAY EUROPEAN BREEDERS' FUND MAIDEN STKS — 6f

4:20 (4:21) (Class 5) 2-Y-O **£3,885** (£1,156; £577; £288) **Stalls** High

Form	Pos	Dist	Horse / Trainer / Comment	Jockey	SP	RPR
543	1		**Senatorial**^{19} 2663 2-9-3 0 (B W Hills) *in tch: hdwy 1/2-way: rdn to ld over 1f out: drvn out*	ChrisCatlin 2	**6/4^{1}**	71
63	2	3/4	**Jimwil (IRE)**^{15} 2783 2-9-3 0 (M Dods) *cl up: effrt over 1f out: kpt on u.p fnl f*	DavidAllan 7	**4/1^{3}**	69
60	3	1 1/4	**Herring Senior (IRE)**^{22} 2584 2-9-3 0 (P F I Cole) *trckd ldrs: effrt 2f out: kpt on same pce*	NelsonDeSouza 3	**25/1**	65
6030	4	2	**Premier Krug (IRE)**^{18} 2691 2-8-12 0 (P D Evans) *led to over 1f out: kpt on same pce*	StephenDonohoe 1	**16/1**	54
0	5	nk	**Daanaat (IRE)**^{35} 2206 2-8-12 0 (M R Channon) *in tch: effrt over 1f out: keeping on u.p whn n.m.r ins fnl f: no ex*	DarryllHolland 4	**9/1**	54+
	6	1/2	**Bella's Story** 2-8-7 0 (J S Goldie) *bhd: pushed along over 2f out: kpt on fnl f: n.d*	GaryBartley$^{(5)}$ 6	**14/1**	52
2	7	2 1/4	**Becausewecan (USA)**^{17} 2730 2-9-3 0 (M Johnston) *prom: lost pl after 2f: n.d after*	AdrianTNicholls 5	**2/1^{2}**	50

69.74 secs (-3.86) **Going Correction** -0.675s/f (Hard) **7** Ran SP% **119.7**
Speed ratings (Par 93): **98,97,95,92,92 91,88**
toteswinger: 1&2 £1.60, 1&3 £9.20, 2&3 £13.00 CSF £8.68 TOTE £2.60: £1.50, £2.20; EX 7.40.

Owner K Abdulla **Bred** Juddmonte Farms Ltd **Trained** Lambourn, Berks

FOCUS
Not the strongest of maidens and one in which the second favourite proved disappointing. The winner and runner-up look the best benchmarks to the form.

NOTEBOOK
Senatorial had shown fair form in three previous starts and probably did not have to improve too much to open his account in workmanlike fashion. He is a reliable sort who should continue to give a good account. (op 7-4 tchd 2-1)

Jimwil(IRE) is a steadily progressive sort who turned in his best effort yet to chase home a reliable yardstick. He should be suited by the step up to 7f and is likely to be winning races for this yard before very long. (tchd 9-2)

Herring Senior(IRE) had not shown much in his first two starts but turned in an improved effort. He will be better suited by 7f and is the type to win in ordinary nursery company in due course.

Premier Krug(IRE) is an exposed sort who was not disgraced but failed to confirm recent York placings with Herring Senior. He is likely to remain vulnerable in this type of event but may do better if dropped in grade.

Daanaat(IRE), soundly beaten on her debut at Thirsk, fared much better this time and would have finished closer but for meeting trouble at a crucial stage. She may be able to pick up a small nursery in due course. (op 12-1 tchd 8-1)

Bella's Story, who has winning sprinters in her pedigree, only hinted at ability on this racecourse debut. Modest handicaps will be the way forward with her. (op 20-1)

Becausewecan(USA), who shaped well in soft ground on his debut, proved a big disappointment under these much quicker conditions. A stiffer test of stamina may suit and he would not be one to write off just yet. (op 7-4 tchd 9-4)

3255 ROBB REINSTATEMENT LTD H'CAP — 6f

4:55 (4:56) (Class 5) (0-70,74) 4-Y-O+ **£3,238** (£963; £481; £240) **Stalls** High

Form	Pos	Dist	Horse / Trainer / Comment	Jockey	SP	RPR
3440	1		**Maison Dieu**^{5} 3079 5-8-6 **55** ow1 (E J Alston) *trckd ldrs: effrt and swtchd lft over 1f out: led ins fnl f: kpt on wl*	DavidAllan 9	**11/2^{3}**	65
5023	2	1/2	**Circuit Dancer (IRE)**^{7} 3042 8-9-5 **68** (D Nicholls) *w ldrs: rdn 2f out: kpt on towards fin*	AdrianTNicholls 5	**7/2^{1}**	76
5300	3	1/2	**Red Cape (FR)**^{7} 3050 5-9-5 **68** (Mrs R A Carr) *slt ld to ins fnl f: kpt on same pce*	(b) ChrisCatlin 11	**9/1**	74
0040	4	1/2	**Royal Challenge**^{1} 3211 7-8-8 **62** (I W McInnes) *hld up in tch: effrt on outside over 1f out: kpt on same pce ins fnl f*	GaryBartley$^{(5)}$ 2	**9/1**	67
-031	5	1	**John Keats**^{4} 3111 5-9-11 **74** 6ex (J S Goldie) *hld up: hdwy 2f out: sn rdn: no imp fnl f*	DanielTudhope 4	**9/2^{2}**	76
0302	6	1	**Obe Royal**^{9} 2983 4-9-0 **70** (P D Evans) *prom tl rdn and no ex over 1f out*	(b) RichardEvans$^{(7)}$ 7	**15/2**	68
0-25	7	nse	**Quicks The Word**^{10} 2936 8-8-9 **58** (T A K Cuthbert) *w ldrs tl rdn and no ex over 1f out*	FergalLynch 8	**13/2**	56
0000	8	1 3/4	**Welcome Approach**^{12} 2892 5-8-9 **58** (J R Weymes) *bhd tl sme late hdwy: nvr rchd ldrs*	DarryllHolland 3	**11/1**	51
0005	9	5	**Howards Tipple**^{16} 2748 4-8-13 **62** (Miss L A Perratt) *bhd: shortlived effrt over 2f out: eased whn btn fnl f*	DO'Donohoe 1	**16/1**	39
0000	10	1 1/2	**Ulysees (IRE)**^{1} 3201 9-8-2 **51** oh3 (J Barclay) *dwlt: a bhd*	PaulFessey 6	**33/1**	23
00-6	11	2	**Alexia Rose (IRE)**^{128} 562 6-7-11 **53** oh6 ow2 (A Berry) *s.s: nvr on terms*	SophieDoyle$^{(7)}$ 10	**50/1**	18

68.37 secs (-5.23) **Going Correction** -0.675s/f (Hard) course record **11** Ran SP% **120.0**
Speed ratings (Par 103): **107,106,105,105,103 102,102,99,93,91 88**
toteswinger: 1&2 £5.30, 1&3 £10.70, 2&3 £9.20 CSF £25.61 CT £178.10 TOTE £7.10: £2.10, £1.70, £3.30; EX 34.60.

Owner Whitehills Racing Syndicate **Bred** Andy Miller **Trained** Longton, Lancs

FOCUS
A strongly run race and another course record. Those racing up with the pace again held the edge. It has been rated through the winner to his best form and the second, third and fourth to their recent efforts.

Howards Tipple Official explanation: jockey said gelding hung left-handed throughout

3256 REAL RADIO H'CAP — 5f

5:30 (5:30) (Class 4) (0-85,82) 3-Y-O **£6,476** (£1,927; £963; £481) **Stalls** High

Form	Pos	Dist	Horse / Trainer / Comment	Jockey	SP	RPR
-413	1		**Discanti (IRE)**^{22} 2570 3-8-11 **72** (T D Easterby) *t.k.h: mde all: rdn and edgd lft fr 2f out: kpt on strly*	DavidAllan 6	**4/7^{1}**	81+
0320	2	2	**Killer Class**^{5} 3080 3-8-3 **64** (J S Goldie) *in tch: effrt 2f out: chsd wnr ins fnl f: kpt on*	AdrianTNicholls 4	**6/1^{2}**	60
60	3	1/2	**I Confess**^{11} 2906 3-9-0 **82** (P D Evans) *bhd and sn pushed along: hdwy over 1f out: nrst fin*	RichardEvans$^{(7)}$ 2	**10/1**	76
1-25	4	1 1/2	**Maryolini**^{10} 2945 3-9-1 **76** (N J Vaughan) *cl up tl rdn and no ex over 1f out*	ChrisCatlin 5	**7/1**	65
0604	5	2	**Barraland**^{12} 2896 3-8-12 **73** (M R Channon) *cl up: drvn 1/2-way: no ex over 1f out*	DarryllHolland 3	**13/2^{3}**	55
300-	6	7	**Rocking**^{288} 5207 3-9-2 **77** (Miss L A Perratt) *sn bhd and outpcd: struggling fr 1/2-way*	DO'Donohoe 1	**25/1**	33

56.62 secs (-3.48) **Going Correction** -0.675s/f (Hard) course record **6** Ran SP% **116.7**
Speed ratings (Par 101): **100,96,96,93,90 79**
toteswinger: 1&2 £1.90, 1&3 £2.40, 2&3 £6.50 CSF £5.02 TOTE £1.60: £1.30, £2.30; EX 5.50.

Owner The Lapin Blanc Racing Partnership **Bred** Glending Bloodstock **Trained** Great Habton, N Yorks

FOCUS
Only six runners but another decent gallop and another very quick time. It has been rated through the runner-up to her fast-ground form and the third to his Irish juvenile form.

3257 BIG HEARTED SCOTLAND H'CAP — 1m 2f

6:00 (6:02) (Class 5) (0-75,74) 4-Y-O+ **£4,533** (£1,348; £674; £336) **Stalls** Low

Form	Pos	Dist	Horse / Trainer / Comment	Jockey	SP	RPR
3044	1		**Supercast (IRE)**^{16} 2749 5-8-13 **66** (N J Vaughan) *trckd ldrs: rdn to ld over 1f out: edgd lft ins fnl f: hld on wl*	ChrisCatlin 4	**4/1^{3}**	75
5220	2	1/2	**King Of Rhythm (IRE)**^{8} 3006 5-9-5 **72** (D Carroll) *hld up in tch: effrt over 2f out: ev ch whn n.m.r ins fnl f: kpt on*	DavidAllan 8	**7/4^{1}**	80
2-06	3	3 1/2	**Hawkit (USA)**^{23} 2524 7-9-5 **72** (P Monteith) *hld up: rdn over 2f out: hdwy over 1f out: kpt on: nt rch first two*	DarryllHolland 9	**6/1**	73
0-54	4	1/2	**Darfour**^{10} 2942 4-8-7 **65** (J S Goldie) *in tch: drvn and outpcd over 2f out: kpt on fnl f*	GaryBartley$^{(5)}$ 6	**7/2^{2}**	65
26-0	5	1 3/4	**Dragon Slayer (IRE)**^{140} 409 6-9-7 **74** (John A Harris) *led to over 2f out: sn no ex*	StephenDonohoe 1	**10/1**	71
3264	6	1	**Valdan (IRE)**^{3} 3143 4-8-5 **58** (M A Barnes) *chsd ldr: led over 2f out to over 1f out: sn btn*	(t) AdrianTNicholls 7	**9/2**	53
060-	7	30	**Second Reef**^{226} 6732 6-8-2 **55** oh10 (T A K Cuthbert) *hld up: drvn over 3f out: sn lost tch*	PaulFessey 2	**33/1**	—

2m 8.35s (-3.65) **Going Correction** -0.50s/f (Hard) **7** Ran SP% **123.1**
Speed ratings (Par 103): **94,93,90,90,89 88,64**
toteswinger: 1&2 £2.10, 1&3 £5.00, 2&3 £2.80 CSF £12.64 CT £43.69 TOTE £5.20: £2.20, £2.00; EX 5.50 Place 6 £15.21, Place 5 £11.38.

Owner Bould & Walker Racing **Bred** J Egan, J Corcoran And J Judd **Trained** Hampton, Cheshire

■ Stewards' Enquiry : Chris Catlin one-day ban: careless riding (Jul 6)

FOCUS
A run-of-the-mill handicap in which the pace was only fair. The runner-up has been rated as running a personal best, and the third has been rated to last year's fast ground form.

T/Plt: £36.00 to a £1 stake. Pool: £64,203.73. 1,300.05 winning tickets. T/Qpdt: £8.10 to a £1 stake. Pool: £2,802.19. 255.90 winning tickets. RY

2965 HAYDOCK (L-H)

Saturday, June 21

OFFICIAL GOING: Good (8.3)

Just 4mm rain before racing but the heavy showers turned the ground on the round course for the final three races to 'genuine good to soft'.

Wind: Light, half-behind Weather: overcast, damp, showers, rain last 2

3258 RUSHTON HINCHY SOLICITORS APPRENTICE H'CAP 1m 2f 120y

6:45 (6:46) (Class 5) (0-75,75) 4-Y-0+ **£2,590** (£770; £385; £192) **Stalls** High

Form RPR

000 **1** **Moment Of Clarity**[10] 2927 6-8-5 59 (p) StacyRenwick(3) 11 66
(R C Guest) *hood removed v late: dwlt: t.k.h in rr: hdwy over 3f out: led 1f out: styd on* **10/1**

6306 **2** ¾ **Cheshire Prince**[11] 2904 4-9-0 68 DeanHeslop 1 73
(W M Brisbourne) *trckd ldr: t.k.h: led 7f out tl 1f out: no ex* **4/1**[1]

5601 **3** 3 ¼ **Grethel (IRE)**[3] 3127 4-8-5 56 6ex oh2 DanielleMcCreery 7 55
(A Berry) *t.k.h in rr: hdwy on outer 4f out: sltly hmpd 2f out: kpt on same pce appr fnl f* **7/1**[3]

21-4 **4** ½ **Vanquisher (IRE)**[9] 2970 4-9-2 70 SimonPearce(3) 10 68
(Ian Williams) *trckd ldrs: nt clr run over 2f out: kpt on same pce over 1f out* **4/1**[1]

6050 **5** 1 ¼ **Longspur**[14] 2822 4-9-2 72 (t) NSLawes(5) 5 68+
(M W Easterby) *hld up in rr: effrt over 3f out: nt clr run on inner 2f out: hung lft and kpt on fnl f* **9/1**

2405 **6** hd **Pitbull**[7] 3029 5-8-3 61 (p) IanCraven(7) 3 56
(Mrs G S Rees) *s.s: hdwy on outside over 3f out: hung lft 2f out: one pce* **9/2**[2]

6-00 **7** 1 ¼ **Robert The Brave**[5] 3090 4-9-10 75 PatrickDonaghy 2 68
(P R Webber) *mid-div: hdwy 6f out: drvn 4f out: outpcd fnl 2f* **9/1**

2/ **8** 2 **Herakles (GER)**[94] 7-9-5 70 MichaelO'Connell 8 59
(M Mullineaux) *trckd ldrs: drvn 4f out: wknd over 1f out* **14/1**

3-06 **9** 2 ½ **Montrose Man**[12] 2886 4-9-1 66 KMay 9 50
(B J Meehan) *t.k.h: led tl 7f out: wknd over 1f out* **12/1**

42/0 **10** 3 ½ **Prince Of Love (IRE)**[18] 2701 5-8-5 61 ow4 BradleyRoper(5) 4 39
(Jedd O'Keeffe) *t.k.h: trckd ldrs: lost pl over 1f out* **14/1**

5300 **11** 2 ¾ **Bobering**[22] 2568 8-8-2 56 oh11 SoniaEaton(3) 6 28
(B P J Baugh) *in rr: drvn over 6f out: lost pl over 3f out* **28/1**

2m 19.19s (2.49) **Going Correction** +0.325s/f (Good) **11** Ran SP% **124.2**

Speed ratings (Par 103): **103,102,100,99,98 98,97,96,94,91 89**

toteswinger: 1&2 £11.60, 1&3 £17.60, 2&3 £22.10 CSF £52.72 CT £311.92 TOTE £12.90: £3.30, £1.90, £2.50; EX 51.10.

Owner Andrew Shedden **Bred** Lordship Stud **Trained** Carburton, Notts

■ Stewards' Enquiry : Patrick Donaghy caution: used whip above shoulder height

FOCUS

They went a very steady pace here and the form looks modest rated through the placed horses.

3259 CHAMPAGNE LANSON MAIDEN AUCTION STKS 5f

7:15 (7:16) (Class 5) 2-Y-0 **£2,590** (£770; £385; £192) **Stalls** Centre

Form RPR

2 **1** **Sunset Crest**[14] 2845 2-8-7 0 RoystonFfrench 11 75
(Mrs A Duffield) *w ldrs: led 2f out: edgd rt: jst hld on* **7/2**[2]

2 shd **Evelyn May (IRE)** 2-8-4 0 FrancisNorton 3 72
(B W Hills) *s.i.s: hld up in rr: hdwy over 2f out: swtchd lft 1f out: r.o wl: jst hld* **3/1**[1]

3 1 ¾ **Queen Sally (IRE)** 2-8-6 0 ow2 TolleyDean(3) 10 70
(J L Spearing) *chsd ldrs: kpt on wl fnl f* **33/1**

4 3 ¼ **Rainy Night** 2-8-12 0 RussellKennemore(3) 2 65
(R Hollinshead) *mid-div: hdwy 2f out: kpt on fnl f* **10/1**

5 1 ¼ **Isabella Grey** 2-8-7 0 FergalLynch 4 54+
(K A Ryan) *outpcd and sn drvn along: hdwy over 1f out: styd on ins fnl f* **4/1**[3]

0 **6** 3 ¼ **Jaslyn (IRE)**[23] 2534 2-8-4 0 DaleGibson 1 37
(J R Weymes) *swvd lft s: sn chsng ldrs: lost pl over 1f out* **25/1**

7 3 **Meydan Style (USA)** 2-8-12 0 PatrickMathers 5 35
(J Balding) *dwlt: mid-div: effrt over 2f out: wknd over 1f out* **25/1**

00 **8** ½ **Josiah Bartlett (IRE)**[30] 2324 2-9-1 0 J-PGuillambert 8 36
(J W Hills) *swvd rt s: trckd ldrs: edgd lft and wknd over 1f out* **7/1**

4 **9** 2 **Mo Mhuirnin (IRE)**[18] 2696 2-8-7 0 JamieMoriarty(3) 9 31+
(R A Fahey) *s.v.s: a bhd* **6/1**

0 **10** 3 ¾ **Ballarina**[91] 957 2-8-3 0 PatrickDonaghy(7) 6 10
(E J Alston) *led tl 2f out: sn lost pl* **16/1**

61.41 secs (0.91) **Going Correction** -0.025s/f (Good) **10** Ran SP% **119.6**

Speed ratings (Par 93): **91,90,88,82,80 75,70,70,66,60**

toteswinger: 1&2 £1.20, 1&3 £121.90, 2&3 £121.90 CSF £14.56 TOTE £3.90: £1.70, £1.60, £5.40; EX 10.10.

Owner H G D Partnership **Bred** Bearstone Stud **Trained** Constable Burton, N Yorks

FOCUS

An ordinary maiden which is not easy to rate accurately at this stage.

NOTEBOOK

Sunset Crest, who looked in fine form, dived right in front and in the end it was a very close call. (op 5-2)

Evelyn May(IRE), a bargain-basement buy, is bred for speed. On the leg and narrow, she had to switch when the winner went across her bows. Upsides inside the last, in the end she only just missed out. (op 9-2)

Queen Sally(IRE), a May foal, ran well on her introduction and will be better suited by six.

Rainy Night, a tall newcomer, showed ability and did quite well considering he found himself rather isolated towards the far side. (op 12-1)

Isabella Grey was clueless but showed ability, picking up nicely late in the day. She is crying out for further. (op 9-2)

Mo Mhuirnin(IRE) blew her chance with a very slow start. Official explanation: jockey said filly missed the break (op 5-1 tchd 9-2)

3260 LAMBRINI FILLIES' H'CAP 6f

7:45 (7:49) (Class 5) (0-75,75) 3-Y-0+ **£2,590** (£770; £385; £192) **Stalls** Centre

Form RPR

3256 **1** **Dorn Dancer (IRE)**[15] 2781 6-9-1 67 DanielleMcCreery(5) 6 79
(D W Barker) *sn outpcd and in rr: gd hdwy 2f out: styd on strly to ld wl ins fnl f* **9/1**

0-41 **2** 1 ¾ **Overwing (IRE)**[7] 3026 5-9-6 67 MartinDwyer 3 73
(R M H Cowell) *led: hdd 2f out: kpt on gamely: regained 2nd and no ex last 75yds* **13/2**[3]

3335 **3** ½ **Poppy's Rose**[9] 2968 4-9-2 63 RoystonFfrench 1 68
(I W McInnes) *trckd ldrs: led 2f out: edgd lft: hdd wl ins fnl f* **6/1**[2]

0-40 **4** ¾ **Hansomis (IRE)**[16] 2751 4-8-9 56 oh4 DaleGibson 5 58
(B Mactaggart) *mid-div: effrt 2f out: kpt on same pce fnl f* **25/1**

3000 **5** ½ **Feelin Foxy**[12] 2892 4-9-12 73 J-PGuillambert 4 74
(J G Given) *trckd ldrs: styd on same pce fnl 2f* **12/1**

0-05 **6** 2 ¼ **Misphire**[14] 2818 5-10-0 75 (b) FergalLynch 11 69
(M Dods) *stmbld sltly s: hld up in rr: effrt 2f out: kpt on: nvr nr ldrs* **4/1**[1]

-001 **7** 3 **Metal Guru**[10] 2928 4-9-0 64 (p) RussellKennemore(3) 8 48+
(R Hollinshead) *hld up in midfield: hdwy over 2f out: wknd over 1f out* **9/1**

2062 **8** ¾ **Lambency (IRE)**[10] 2936 5-8-2 56 oh1 DeanHeslop(7) 9 38+
(J S Goldie) *hld up in rr: sme hdwy 2f out: nvr on terms* **6/1**[2]

01 **9** 2 **Royal Grace**[14] 2823 3-8-8 65 DuranFentiman(3) 10 40
(T D Easterby) *s.s: hdwy on far side over 2f out: wknd over 1f out* **14/1**

150/ **10** 4 **Namu**[258] 5-9-0 64 JamieMoriarty(3) 12 26
(Miss T Spearing) *chsd ldrs: lost pl over 1f out* **22/1**

0 **11** 5 **Yatir (FR)**[30] 2341 3-9-2 70 (v[1]) FrancisNorton 7 16
(E F Vaughan) *mid-div: effrt over 2f out: lost pl over 1f out* **33/1**

0004 **12** 2 ¼ **Miacarla**[4] 3112 5-8-9 56 oh9 PatrickMathers 13 —
(H A McWilliams) *w ldrs: t.k.h: wknd over 1f out* **25/1**

00/0 **13** 16 **Frill A Minute**[28] 2399 4-8-9 56 oh11 TWilliams 2 —
(Miss L C Siddall) *dwlt: bhd whn eased over 3f out: sn detached* **100/1**

1m 13.74s (-0.26) **Going Correction** -0.025s/f (Good)

WFA 3 from 4yo+ 7lb **13** Ran SP% **112.2**

Speed ratings (Par 100): **100,97,97,96,95 92,88,87,84,79 72,69,48**

toteswinger: 1&2 £11.50, 1&3 £13.80, 2&3 £8.50 CSF £53.21 CT £287.44 TOTE £10.60: £2.60, £2.10, £2.00; EX 36.40.

Owner The Ebor Partnership **Bred** Timothy Coughlan **Trained** Scorton, N Yorks

FOCUS

They went very fast in the deteriorating ground and the winner came from way off the pace. The form looks very solid at this level rated through the runner-up and third.

3261 JOSEPH, JAKE AND ELLA WOODS H'CAP 1m 30y

8:15 (8:15) (Class 3) (0-90,89) 3-Y-0+ **£9,714** (£2,890; £1,444; £721) **Stalls** Low

Form RPR

1-13 **1** **Wasan**[44] 1923 3-9-2 88 MartinDwyer 4 104+
(E A L Dunlop) *led: qcknd 3f out: styd on strly: readily* **4/5**[1]

-041 **2** 1 ¾ **Goodbye Mr Bond**[8] 3006 8-9-10 86 J-PGuillambert 7 93
(E J Alston) *hld up in rr: stdy hdwy over 2f out: styd on same pce ins fnl f* **11/2**[2]

4600 **3** shd **Wovoka (IRE)**[36] 2155 5-8-11 73 RoystonFfrench 1 80
(D W Barker) *tk fierce hold: trckd ldrs: edgd rt over 2f out: styd on same pce appr fnl f* **33/1**

26 **4** hd **Goodbye**[42] 2013 4-9-9 85 PaulMulrennan 6 91
(G A Swinbank) *trckd ldrs: t.k.h: chal over 3f out: styd on same pce fnl f* **7/1**[3]

1000 **5** ½ **Blue Spinnaker (IRE)**[8] 3006 9-8-8 77 BradleyRoper(7) 8 82
(M W Easterby) *hld up in rr: effrt 3f out: kpt on: nvr trbld ldrs* **20/1**

-024 **6** 1 ¾ **Prince Golan (IRE)**[14] 2846 4-8-8 70 PatrickMathers 5 71
(J W Unett) *trckd ldrs on outer: hdwy over 3f out: edgd lft and fdd fnl f* **25/1**

1-00 **7** nk **Fitzroy Crossing (USA)**[14] 2825 3-8-10 82 JoeFanning 10 83+
(M Johnston) *w wnr: chal over 3f out: edgd lft over 1f out: 5th whn eased last 75yds* **25/1**

1100 **8** hd **The Osteopath (IRE)**[49] 1816 5-9-7 83 FergalLynch 9 83+
(M Dods) *stdd and swtchd lft s: t.k.h in rr: stdy hdwy and n.m.r 2f out: kpt on: nvr trbld ldrs* **10/1**

-620 **9** 1 ¼ **Danehillsundance (IRE)**[21] 2595 4-9-13 89 FrancisNorton 2 86
(S Parr) *hld up in rr: hdwy on ins 4f out: wknd over 1f out* **9/1**

-000 **10** 2 **Fort Amhurst (IRE)**[8] 3006 4-8-8 70 DaleGibson 3 63
(M W Easterby) *t.k.h in mid-div: lost pl 2f out* **66/1**

1m 47.58s (3.78) **Going Correction** +0.325s/f (Good)

WFA 3 from 4yo+ 10lb **10** Ran SP% **119.4**

Speed ratings (Par 107): **94,92,92,91,91 89,89,89,87,85**

toteswinger: 1&2 £1.50, 1&3 £22.90, 2&3 £42.70 CSF £5.16 CT £88.15 TOTE £1.70: £1.10, £2.20, £5.00; EX 6.30.

Owner Hamdan Al Maktoum **Bred** Belgrave Bloodstock **Trained** Newmarket, Suffolk

FOCUS

The heavily supported winner was given his own way in front but looked very much the best horse on the night anyway. The veteran runner-up gave his running but overall the lack of pace puts a slight question mark over the overall form.

NOTEBOOK

Wasan, running of the same mark as at Chester, had everything in his favour this time. Allowed to set his own pace, he quickened it up from the front and in the end scored in most convincing fashion. Still on the weak side, there should be even better to come. (tchd 10-11)

Goodbye Mr Bond, 6lb higher, was running over a shorter trip and the old boy came across an unexposed and improving youngster. (op 8-1)

Wovoka(IRE), struggling to find form since joining this yard, pulled like a train. He won from a mark of 81 at Ascot last year and this was much more encouraging. (op 28-1)

Goodbye, again running from a career-high mark, took a keen grip due to the lack of any pace.The ground had come in her favour and she ran right up to her best. (op 11-2)

Blue Spinnaker(IRE), slipping down the ratings once more, ran better than of late, the ground having come in his favour.

Prince Golan(IRE), suited by a return to a mile, has slipped to a lenient mark, but he has lost the winning habit. (tchd 28-1)

Fitzroy Crossing(USA), down 6lb after being asked a stiff question on his first two starts, looked a real danger at one stage but in the end his rider eased him off as if he had developed a problem. Official explanation: jockey said colt lost its action

The Osteopath(IRE), with the ground in his favour, had an outside draw to overcome. He enjoyed no luck at all when looking for racing room and is clearly back on song. Official explanation: jockey said gelding was denied a clear run (op 9-1 tchd 11-1)

3262 TYLDESELEY MAIDEN STKS 1m 30y

8:45 (8:46) (Class 5) 3-Y-0+ **£2,590** (£770; £385; £192) **Stalls** Low

Form RPR

020- **1** **Jack Junior (USA)**[246] 6298 4-9-12 107 JoeFanning 10 83+
(B J Meehan) *trckd ldrs: t.k.h: wnt 2nd over 5f out: led over 1f out: drvn rt out* **10/11**[1]

2 ¾ **Istiqdaam** 3-9-2 0 RobertHavlin 6 81+
(J H M Gosden) *trckd ldrs: effrt over 3f out: edgd lft fnl f: tk 2nd ins fnl f: kpt on* **9/2**[3]

604 **3** 2 ½ **Gulf Stream Lady (IRE)**[15] 2786 3-8-11 73 FrancisNorton 7 70
(B W Hills) *led tl over 1f out: kpt on same pce* **7/2**[2]

0 **4** 9 **Ghufa (IRE)**[24] 2509 4-9-12 0 MartinDwyer 9 57
(E A L Dunlop) *hld up in rr: hdwy over 3f out: sn chsng ldrs: wknd over 1f out* **5/1**

6-0 **5** 2 **Rascasse**[18] 2700 3-9-2 0 ... TWilliams 8 50
(Bruce Hellier) *dwlt: sn chsng ldrs: drvn over 3f out: wknd over 1f out* **100/1**

6 13 **Iraschko** 3-8-8 0 ... TolleyDean(3) 4 15
(J L Spearing) *drvn along in rr: lost pl over 3f out: sn bhd* **33/1**

00- **7** 2 1/4 **Ugly Betty**[261] 5931 3-8-11 0 ... RoystonFfrench 5 10
(Bruce Hellier) *in tch: shkn up over 6f out: lost pl over 3f out: sn bhd* **100/1**

8 2 1/4 **Gulnaz** 3-8-11 0 ... DaleGibson 3 5
(Mrs G S Rees) *in rr: drvn over 4f out: lost pl over 3f out: sn bhd* **33/1**

1m 47.18s (3.38) **Going Correction** +0.325s/f (Good)
WFA 3 from 4yo 10lb **8** Ran SP% **117.3**
Speed ratings (Par 103): **96,95,92,83,81 68,66,64**
toteswinger: 1&2 £1.50, 1&3 £1.50, 2&3 £3.90 CSF £5.67 TOTE £2.10: £1.10, £1.90, £1.40; EX 4.60.
Owner Roldvale Limited **Bred** Marablue Farm **Trained** Manton, Wilts

FOCUS
33-1 bar four, and the 107-rated winner struggled in the end. Significantly, the third is rated just 73.

3263 MTB GROUP H'CAP — 1m 30y
9:15 (9:16) (Class 4) (0-80,80) 3-Y-O £4,533 (£1,348; £674; £336) Stalls Low

Form RPR

2314 **1** **Marning Star**[11] 2913 3-9-4 **75** ... MartinDwyer 14 83
(D Nicholls) *mde all: hld on gamely* **8/1**

0-04 **2** nk **Giant Love (USA)**[23] 2539 3-9-5 **76** ... J-PGuillambert 11 83
(M Johnston) *chsd ldrs: hrd rdn over 2f out: hung lft ins fnl f: styd on towards fin* **12/1**

0-53 **3** 1 1/4 **Dark Prospect**[19] 2678 3-8-13 **70** ... FergalLynch 5 74
(M A Jarvis) *sn chsng ldrs: styd on same pce ins fnl f* **5/2**[1]

12-6 **4** 2 **Reel Buddy Star**[51] 1750 3-8-12 **72** ... RussellKennemore(3) 8 71
(G M Moore) *in tch: effrt over 2f out: kpt on same pce* **10/1**

26-1 **5** 3/4 **Art Currency (USA)**[32] 2269 3-9-9 **80** ... PaulMulrennan 10 78
(M J Wallace) *w ldrs: styd on same pce fnl f* **7/1**[3]

221 **6** 1 1/2 **San Jose City (IRE)**[19] 2673 3-9-9 **80** ... DNolan 1 74
(D Carroll) *hld up in rr: checked bnd over 4f out: hdwy 3f out: edgd lft: kpt on same pce fnl f* **9/2**[2]

16-6 **7** 2 3/4 **Brasingaman Hifive**[30] 2333 3-9-4 **75** ... DaleGibson 4 63
(Mrs G S Rees) *in rr: hdwy over 2f out: wknd appr fnl f* **9/1**

05-0 **8** 5 **Shanafarahan (IRE)**[30] 2333 3-8-10 **67** ... MickyFenton 7 43
(T P Tate) *hld up in rr: hmpd bnd over 4f out: nvr a factor afterwards* **14/1**

3-10 **9** 1/2 **We'Re Delighted**[19] 2674 3-8-13 **73** ... JamieMoriarty(3) 3 48
(T D Walford) *in rr: lost pl over 2f out* **11/1**

1330 **10** 3 3/4 **Royal Applord**[58] 1576 3-9-1 **72** ... RoystonFfrench 13 39
(K A Ryan) *hld up in rr: lost pl 4f out* **33/1**

250- **11** 4 1/2 **Aboriginie (USA)**[262] 5919 3-9-4 **75** ... RobertHavlin 9 31
(J H M Gosden) *in tch: hdwy 3f out: wknd over 1f out* **14/1**

-000 **12** 6 **Miesko (USA)**[47] 1852 3-9-9 **80** ... JoeFanning 12 22
(M Johnston) *stdd s: t.k.h in rr: sme hdwy over 2f out: sn lost pl* **20/1**

1m 46.88s (3.08) **Going Correction** +0.325s/f (Good) **12** Ran SP% **126.5**
Speed ratings (Par 101): **97,96,95,93,92 91,88,83,82,79 74,68**
toteswinger: 1&2 £24.80, 1&3 £13.20, 2&3 £17.00 CSF £107.22 CT £321.27 TOTE £10.20: £3.00, £5.40, £1.80; EX 150.30 Place 6 £28.76, Place 5 £10.54.
Owner N Martin **Bred** P And Mrs A G Venner **Trained** Sessay, N Yorks
■ Stewards' Enquiry : Robert Havlin caution: used whip down shoulder in forehand position

FOCUS
They went a strong pace and the winner deserves full marks. The race has been rated around the third and fourth and could be a shade higher.
Shanafarahan(IRE) Official explanation: jockey said gelding ran too free
T/Plt: £28.20 to a £1 stake. Pool: £62,182.35. 1,605.46 winning tickets. T/Qpdt: £7.20 to a £1 stake. Pool: £4,201.57. 429.10 winning tickets. WG

3032 LINGFIELD (L-H)
Saturday, June 21

OFFICIAL GOING: Turf course - good to firm (8.7); all-weather - standard
The stands' rail on the turf course was a huge advantage.
Wind: Moderate, behind Weather: Overcast

3264 SEVENOAKS (S) STKS — 1m 4f (P)
5:55 (5:56) (Class 6) 3-Y-O £1,774 (£523; £262) Stalls Low

Form RPR

00-0 **1** **Casual Garcia**[26] 2468 3-8-12 39 ... (b) SebSanders 12 56
(Sir Mark Prescott) *led after 1f: mde rest: drvn clr over 1f out: unchal* **11/2**[3]

5600 **2** 4 1/2 **Royal Soverin**[32] 2273 3-8-12 50 ... (v[1]) PatCosgrave 7 49
(M J Wallace) *hld up in midfield: gng wl 4f out: prog 3f out: drvn to chse wnr jst over 1f out: no imp* **10/1**

6054 **3** 2 1/4 **Lady Jinks**[6] 3065 3-8-0 45 ... BillyCray(7) 5 40
(M D I Usher) *mostly in midfield: effrt 3f out: drvn and kpt on fnl 2f to take 3rd nr fin* **6/1**

3064 **4** 1/2 **Balais Folly (FR)**[2] 3166 3-8-12 47 ... (v) CatherineGannon 6 44
(B Palling) *hld up in midfield: prog on outer over 3f out: rdn wl over 2f out: chsd clr ldng pair fnl f: lost 3rd nr fin* **6/1**

0-05 **5** 3 1/4 **Golddigging (IRE)**[12] 2894 3-8-7 42 ... JamesDoyle 8 34
(J G Portman) *led 1f: styd prom: rdn 3f out: outpcd and btn over 2f out* **40/1**

0-64 **6** 3/4 **Has To Be Abacus (IRE)**[21] 2611 3-8-9 52 ... KevinGhunowa(3) 9 38
(A B Haynes) *t.k.h: prom: chsd wnr 3f out: no imp over 1f out: sn wknd* **3/1**[1]

-500 **7** 1 **Pay The Grey**[12] 2894 3-8-0 36 ... CharlesEddery(7) 4 31
(R Hannon) *towards rr: rdn and lost tch 5f out: nrly t.o 3f out: plugged on fr over 1f out* **25/1**

00 **8** shd **Owain James**[37] 2126 3-8-12 0 ... (p) TGMcLaughlin 10 36
(M Salaman) *dwlt: hld up wl in rr and racd wd: rdn 4f out: sn struggling* **20/1**

0-00 **9** nse **Two Imposters (USA)**[14] 2833 3-8-12 55 ... MohammedSaeed 1 36
(J R Best) *a in rr: rdn and no prog over 3f out* **14/1**

006 **10** nk **Toon Army**[21] 2611 3-8-7 44 ... (t) PaulEddery 11 30
(Miss D Mountain) *dwlt: rousted along and chsd ldr after 2f: drvn and wknd 3f out* **33/1**

5400 **11** 21 **Thankuforthemusic (IRE)**[21] 2613 3-8-12 53 ... FergusSweeney 3 2
(C Tinkler) *sn lost pl and in rr: wknd 4f out: t.o* **4/1**[2]

0 **12** 73 **Sevenovus (IRE)**[114] 734 3-8-9 0 ... TravisBlock(3) 2 —
(Peter Grayson) *dwlt: a in last pair: wknd 1/2-way: wl t.o* **20/1**

2m 32.82s (-0.18) **Going Correction** -0.10s/f (Stan) **12** Ran SP% **123.5**
Speed ratings (Par 97): **96,93,91,91,89 88,87,87,87,87 73,24**
toteswinger: 1&2 £8.60, 1&3 £3.40, 2&3 £45.50 CSF £57.36 TOTE £8.20: £2.40, £4.00, £2.20; EX 45.40.The winner was bought in for 6,400gns.
Owner Ne'Er Do Wells Ii **Bred** Miss K Rausing **Trained** Newmarket, Suffolk

FOCUS
A typical seller featuring mostly unreliable horses who are on the downgrade. It has been rated roughly around the runner-up, third and fourth to their recent marks.

3265 MARSH GREEN H'CAP — 1m 2f (P)
6:25 (6:27) (Class 6) (0-60,60) 4-Y-O+ £2,047 (£604; £302) Stalls Low

Form RPR

0000 **1** **Prince Charlemagne (IRE)**[4] 3113 5-9-1 **57** ... (b[1]) DaneO'Neill 4 67
(R M Stronge) *stdd s: hld up in rr: smooth prog fr 3f out: rdn to chse ldr over 1f out: styd on to ld last 150yds* **14/1**

3200 **2** 3/4 **Mix N Match**[37] 1528 4-8-7 **52** ... TravisBlock(3) 6 60
(R M Stronge) *taken down early: s.v.s: t.k.h and hld up in last: stl there over 2f out: rdn and gd prog over 1f out: wnt 2nd nr fin* **25/1**

5462 **3** 1/2 **Lunar River (FR)**[10] 2957 5-9-2 **58** ... (t) FergusSweeney 7 65
(David Pinder) *hld up in midfield: smooth prog 3f out: rdn to ld wl over 1f out: hdd and one pce last 150yds* **4/1**[2]

0005 **4** 1 3/4 **Green Pirate**[7] 3037 6-8-13 **55** ... (v) LPKeniry 13 59
(C R Dore) *stdd s: hld up in last trio: stl there over 2f out: rdn and kpt on same pce: nvr nrr* **14/1**

2220 **5** 2 3/4 **Kings Topic (USA)**[47] 1853 8-9-4 **60** ... (p) TGMcLaughlin 5 58
(A B Haynes) *reluctant to enter stalls: trckd ldrs: effrt on outer to try to chal over 2f out: sn nt qckn and btn* **5/2**[1]

00-4 **6** hd **Tenement (IRE)**[7] 3036 4-8-6 **48** ... SimonWhitworth 8 46
(Jamie Poulton) *hld up in midfield: pushed along 1/2-way: struggling 2f out: one pce* **11/2**[3]

40-5 **7** 3/4 **Bundle Up**[10] 2949 5-8-13 **55** ... IanMongan 9 51
(Mrs L J Mongan) *trckd ldrs: gng wl 3f out: rdn 2f out: wknd over 1f out* **8/1**

6000 **8** 2 1/4 **Competitor**[14] 2832 7-8-13 **58** ... (t) KirstyMilczarek(3) 14 50
(J Akehurst) *prog to press ldng pair 7f out: nrly upsides 2f out: rdn and wknd over 1f out* **16/1**

6600 **9** 4 1/2 **Thermidor (USA)**[21] 2597 5-8-13 **55** ... (b) RichardKingscote 2 38
(Lady Herries) *mde most to wl over 2f out: wknd wl over 1f out* **7/1**

5640 **10** 1 3/4 **Bowl Of Cherries**[13] 2870 5-8-6 **48** ... (v) JamesDoyle 1 27
(I A Wood) *trckd ldrs tl rdn and wknd over 2f out* **10/1**

4006 **11** hd **Film Queen (IRE)**[13] 2861 4-8-6 **48** ... PaulDoe 3 27
(Mrs L J Mongan) *trckd ldr: led wl over 2f out to wl over 1f out: wknd rapidly* **33/1**

0200 **12** 1 3/4 **Convallaria (FR)**[47] 1853 5-8-13 **55** ... (t) StephenCarson 10 30
(G Wragg) *a in rr and struggling in last 2f out* **8/1**

2m 5.20s (-1.40) **Going Correction** -0.10s/f (Stan) **12** Ran SP% **133.8**
Speed ratings (Par 101): **101,100,100,98,96 96,95,93,90,88 88,87**
toteswinger: 1&2 £84.50, 1&3 £13.80, 2&3 £76.80 CSF £355.72 CT £1692.30 TOTE £14.90: £4.60, £10.80, £1.90; EX 294.70.
Owner Tim Whiting **Bred** Michael O'Mahony **Trained** Beedon Common, Berks

FOCUS
A moderate handicap run at a good pace. It has been rated around the runner-up.
Mix N Match Official explanation: jockey said gelding missed the break
Kings Topic(USA) Official explanation: jockey said gelding hung right

3266 C.I.G. H'CAP — 7f 140y
6:55 (6:55) (Class 5) (0-75,70) 3-Y-O+ £2,331 (£693; £346; £173) Stalls High

Form RPR

3206 **1** **Tina's Best (IRE)**[9] 2974 3-9-6 **70** ... DaneO'Neill 8 79
(R Hannon) *racd against nr side rail: w ldrs: disp ld 1/2-way tl shkn up and led 2f out: pushed clr fnl f* **4/1**[2]

1543 **2** 3 1/4 **Golden Penny**[32] 2288 3-9-3 **70** ... TravisBlock(3) 6 71
(H Morrison) *racd two wd of nr side rail: w ldrs: disp ld 1/2-way to 2f out: drvn and no ch w wnr fnl f* **11/8**[1]

-000 **3** 2 1/2 **Registrar**[7] 3033 6-8-9 **49** oh1 ... (p) TGMcLaughlin 9 46
(Mrs C A Dunnett) *stdd s: racd against nr side rail: hld up in rr: effrt over 2f out: chsd ldng pair over 1f out: nt qckn and no imp* **16/1**

-004 **4** 2 **Gazboolou**[8] 2992 4-10-0 **68** ... FergusSweeney 5 60+
(David Pinder) *awkward s: hld up bhd ldrs and racd away fr rail: rdn and outpcd fr 2f out* **7/1**

5650 **5** hd **Double Valentine**[16] 2758 5-8-10 **53** ... KirstyMilczarek(3) 7 45
(R Ingram) *racd away fr nr side rail: hld up bhd ldrs: gng strly 3f out: outpcd 2f out* **11/1**

0000 **6** 1 1/2 **Briannsta (IRE)**[12] 2897 6-8-10 **55** ... NataliaGemelova(5) 2 43
(J E Long) *racd away fr nr side rail: w ldrs: disp ld 1/2-way to 2f out: wknd* **14/1**

1303 **7** 6 **Silca Destination**[6] 3065 3-8-13 **63** ... EdwardCreighton 4 36
(M R Channon) *racd towards outer: in tch to 3f out: sn wl btn* **13/2**[3]

2000 **8** 4 **Last Of The Line**[17] 2714 3-9-4 **68** ... (b) WilliamBuick 1 31
(H J L Dunlop) *racd wd: led to 1/2-way: sn wknd* **10/1**

000- **9** 8 **Gunner's View**[204] 6971 4-9-6 **67** ... HarryPoulton(7) 3 10
(R H York) *racd on wd outside: struggling fr 1/2-way: t.o* **28/1**

1m 30.75s (-1.55) **Going Correction** -0.15s/f (Firm)
WFA 3 from 4yo+ 10lb **9** Ran SP% **121.4**
Speed ratings (Par 103): **101,97,95,93,93 91,85,81,73**
toteswinger: 1&2 £1.70, 1&3 £46.00, 2&3 £37.20 CSF £10.44 CT £82.31 TOTE £5.90: £1.60, £1.20, £5.20; EX 11.10.
Owner Con Harrington **Bred** Mrs Chris Harrington **Trained** East Everleigh, Wilts
■ Stewards' Enquiry : T G McLaughlin one-day ban: used whip with excessive frequency (Jul 6)

FOCUS
A moderate handicap in which the favoured stands' rail heavily influenced the result. The race has been rated around the third.

3267 EDENBRIDGE MAIDEN AUCTION STKS — 7f
7:25 (7:26) (Class 6) 2-Y-O £2,266 (£674; £337; £168) Stalls Centre

Form RPR

2323 **1** **Firth Of Fifth (IRE)**[7] 3049 2-8-10 0 ... RichardKingscote 2 87+
(Tom Dascombe) *fast away: sn crossed to nr side rail: mde all: drew rt away fr over 2f out: eased ins fnl f* **2/1**[1]

0 **2** 7 **Flute Magic**[38] 2098 2-9-1 0 ... FergusSweeney 12 73
(W S Kittow) *racd against nr side rail: chsd wnr: lft bhd fr over 2f out but kpt on for clr 2nd* **9/1**

0 **3** 2 **Fong's Alibi**[21] 2618 2-8-5 0 SimonWhitworth 14 58
(J S Moore) *prom but racd off nr side rail: drvn and outpcd fr over 2f out: kpt on* **22/1**

65 **4** 1¾ **Black N Brew (USA)**[22] 2562 2-8-12 0 DaneO'Neill 3 60+
(J R Best) *dwlt: sn chsd ldrs but racd on outer: lft bhd fr over 2f out* **11/4**[2]

0 **5** 1 **Indian Blade (IRE)**[38] 2098 2-8-11 0 RichardSmith 6 57
(M D I Usher) *swtchd to r against nr side rail over 4f out: in rr of ldng gp: outpcd fr over 2f out* **33/1**

6 ¾ **Blazing Buck** 2-8-13 0 IanMongan 4 57+
(H J L Dunlop) *dwlt: racd wd: outpcd and wl bhd: effrt and sme prog 3f out: no ch of rching ldrs but kpt on* **16/1**

00 **7** 5 **Forster Island**[42] 2011 2-8-9 0 JamesDoyle 5 40+
(M Blanshard) *outpcd and struggling in rr over 4f out: modest late prog* **20/1**

8 hd **Reel Ale** 2-8-10 0 StephenCarson 13 41
(P Winkworth) *sltly hmpd after 150yds: prom but racd off nr side rail: wknd over 2f out* **12/1**

0 **9** nk **Vien (IRE)**[16] 2759 2-8-8 0 PatrickHills(3) 8 41
(R Hannon) *chsd ldrs but racd off nr side rail: wknd wl over 2f out* **12/1**

10 2½ **Positive Opinion** 2-8-7 0 AlanMunro 15 31
(B R Millman) *dwlt: rn green and mostly in last: styd on fnl f* **4/1**[3]

00 **11** 1½ **Leaf Hollow**[43] 1955 2-8-6 0 JimmyQuinn 9 26
(M Madgwick) *outpcd and struggling in rr over 4f out: nvr a factor* **66/1**

12 2¼ **Hassadin** 2-9-1 0 TGMcLaughlin 11 29
(A B Haynes) *outpcd and struggling in rr over 4f out: nvr a factor* **20/1**

13 2¼ **Honorable Endeavor** 2-9-1 0 LPKeniry 7 24
(E F Vaughan) *outpcd and struggling in rr over 4f out: nvr a factor* **14/1**

0 **14** ½ **The Beat Is On**[61] 1523 2-7-11 0 DavidProbert(7) 1 12
(J M Bradley) *prom but racd on outer: wknd rapidly fr 3f out* **100/1**

1m 22.21s (-1.09) **Going Correction** -0.15s/f (Firm) **14** Ran SP% **137.2**
Speed ratings (Par 91): **100,92,89,87,86 85,80,79,79,76 74,72,69,69**
toteswinger: 1&2 £10.60, 1&3 £35.80, 2&3 £44.80 CSF £23.62 TOTE £2.80: £1.40, £2.50, £6.60; EX 29.20.
Owner Daniel Perchard **Bred** Peter Savill **Trained** Lambourn, Berks
■ Stewards' Enquiry : Richard Kingscote one-day ban: failed to ride to draw (Jul 6); two-day ban: careless riding (Jul 7-8)

FOCUS
A seriously uncompetitive maiden and the stands' rail was again favoured. The form looks fairly solid, though.

NOTEBOOK
Firth Of Fifth(IRE), up in trip, quickly overcame his low draw and grabbed the much-favoured stands' rail. The manner of this success suggests he is decent, but there was not a lot in behind and he was racing on by far the quickest ground, so it would be unwise to get carried away. (op 13-8 tchd 9-4)
Flute Magic improved on the form he showed on his debut over 5f at Bath, but he had the benefit of the near-side rail. (op 14-1)
Fong's Alibi stepped up on the form she showed when well held over 6f on soft ground on her debut at Newbury, but she was still beaten a long way. (op 33-1)
Black N Brew(USA) was well held on this step up in trip, but he is better than he showed as he did not have the benefit of the faster strip of ground against the stands' rail. (op 4-1)
Positive Opinion, a 10,000gns daughter of Observatory, half-sister to quite useful dual 1m-1m2f winner Furia Ceca, was well backed beforehand, but that probably had a lot to do with her draw against the favoured rail. As it turned out, she was far too green to do herself justice. (op 15-2)

3268 FRANCESCA MCGARRY 50TH BIRTHDAY MAIDEN STKS 6f
7:55 (7:56) (Class 5) 3-Y-0+ **£2,331** (£693; £346; £173) **Stalls** High

Form RPR

4-2 **1** **Credit Swap**[11] 2919 3-9-0 0 DaneO'Neill 12 71+
(L M Cumani) *pressed ldr and racd off nr side rail: rdn 2f out: kpt on to ld ins fnl f: hld on* **1/3**[1]

25- **2** nk **Desert Pride**[175] 7264 3-9-0 0 FergusSweeney 15 70
(W S Kittow) *led and racd against nr side rail: rdn over 1f out: hdd ins fnl f: kpt on wl* **11/1**[3]

-004 **3** 2 **Sweet Kiss (USA)**[9] 2981 3-8-9 73 PaulEddery 14 59+
(B J Meehan) *trckd ldrs and racd against nr side rail: effrt 2f out: kpt on but nvr able to chal* **4/1**[2]

30 **4** 2¾ **Gioacchino (IRE)**[25] 2480 3-8-11 0 KevinGhunowa(3) 13 55
(R A Harris) *racd off nr side rail: hld up at rr of main gp: effrt over 2f out: styd on fr over 1f out: n.d* **66/1**

0 **5** hd **Celtic Spring (IRE)**[21] 2620 3-8-9 0 PatCosgrave 6 50
(J R Boyle) *stdd s: swtchd to r against nr side rail: hld up bhd ldrs: in tch 2f out: swtchd lft over 1f out and no prog after* **33/1**

4000 **6** 7 **Djalalabad (FR)**[9] 2983 4-9-2 48 (v) TGMcLaughlin 1 29
(Mrs C A Dunnett) *racd on wd outside: prom: stl in tch 2f out: sn lft bhd* **66/1**

04/ **7** nk **Prix Masque (IRE)**[99] 4-9-7 40 SaleemGolam 7 33
(Christian Wroe) *racd on outer: wl in tch tl wknd jst over 2f out* **100/1**

60 **8** 2 **Rockfield Rose**[6] 3061 3-8-9 0 SamHitchcott 5 20
(J A Osborne) *racd on outer: a struggling and nvr on terms* **33/1**

9 ¾ **The Young Fella** 3-9-0 0 WilliamBuick 8 22
(S A Callaghan) *dwlt: sn outpcd: a struggling and off the pce* **14/1**

50 **10** hd **Al Gillani (IRE)**[16] 2756 3-9-0 0 AmirQuinn 4 22
(J R Boyle) *hld up at rr of main gp: effrt towards outer over 2f out: sn no prog: wknd over 1f out* **33/1**

5 **11** nk **High Coincidence**[32] 2279 3-9-0 0 AlanDaly 2 21
(Andrew Turnell) *s.s: sn detached in last: nvr a factor* **66/1**

60 **12** 7 **Azzaamm**[14] 2823 3-9-0 0 JimmyQuinn 3 —
(C A Dwyer) *prom on outer tl wknd rapidly over 2f out* **50/1**

33 **13** 4½ **Micheals Boy (IRE)**[140] 413 3-9-0 0 AlanMunro 9 —
(J R Boyle) *a wl in rr and struggling* **14/1**

0- **14** 2 **Petomic (IRE)**[185] 7191 3-9-0 0 RichardThomas 11 —
(Christian Wroe) *pressed ldrs to 1/2-way: wkng rapidly whn stmbld over 2f out* **33/1**

1m 10.38s (-0.82) **Going Correction** -0.15s/f (Firm)
WFA 3 from 4yo 7lb **14** Ran SP% **135.9**
Speed ratings (Par 103): **99,98,95,92,92 82,82,79,78,78 77,68,62,59**
toteswinger: 1&2 £2.00, 1&3 £2.00, 2&3 £11.60 CSF £6.97 TOTE £1.40: £1.02, £3.00, £1.60; EX 6.80.
Owner Mrs Angie Silver **Bred** Jeremy Green And Sons **Trained** Newmarket, Suffolk

FOCUS
A modest maiden dominated by those racing towards the stands' rail. The close proximity of Gioacchino in fourth means the form is probably worth little.

Petomic(IRE) Official explanation: trainer said colt lost a front shoe and cut a hind leg

3269 SEAMUS AND ISABEL GOLDEN WEDDING ANNIVERSARY H'CAP 5f
8:25 (8:25) (Class 5) (0-75,74) 3-Y-0+ **£2,331** (£693; £346; £173) **Stalls** High

Form RPR

-566 **1** **Nusoor (IRE)**[15] 2777 5-8-5 55 (v) KirstyMilczarek(3) 7 66
(Peter Grayson) *fastest away: mde all and racd against nr side rail: clr and in command fr 2f out: rdn out* **10/1**

4323 **2** 2 **Desperate Dan**[11] 2923 7-9-9 70 TGMcLaughlin 8 74
(A B Haynes) *dwlt: outpcd in last: prog against nr side rail wl over 1f out: styd on to take 2nd last 50yds* **3/1**[2]

2421 **3** ½ **Misaro (GER)**[11] 2906 7-9-9 73 (b) KevinGhunowa(3) 6 75
(R A Harris) *chsd wnr but racd abt three wd of nr side rail: rdn and no imp 2f out: lost 2nd last 50yds* **4/7**[1]

-030 **4** 3½ **Our Fugitive (IRE)**[15] 2798 6-9-3 64 SamHitchcott 1 53
(C Gordon) *racd towards outer: chsd ldrs: hd high and reluctant fr 1/2-way: outpcd wl over 1f out* **14/1**

530- **5** 4½ **Hucking Harmony (IRE)**[263] 5887 3-8-9 62 LPKeniry 5 35
(J R Best) *outpcd and sn pushed along: effrt against nr side rail 2f out: sn wknd* **16/1**

4-00 **6** 1½ **Bluebok**[6] 3062 7-9-9 70 (t) WilliamBuick 2 38
(J M Bradley) *racd wd: outpcd and nvr on terms* **7/1**[3]

000- **7** 9 **Daddy Cool**[285] 5278 4-9-6 72 JackDean(5) 4 7
(W G M Turner) *racd towards outer: prom 2f: sn wknd* **16/1**

57.28 secs (-0.92) **Going Correction** -0.15s/f (Firm)
WFA 3 from 4yo+ 6lb **7** Ran SP% **128.7**
Speed ratings (Par 103): **101,97,97,91,84 81,67**
toteswinger: 1&2 £5.20, 1&3 £3.30, 2&3 £1.10 CSF £45.72 CT £47.23 TOTE £16.30: £8.00, £1.80; EX 46.00 Place 6 £159.61, Place 5 £47.59.
Owner R Teatum And Mrs S Grayson **Bred** Shadwell Estate Company Limited **Trained** Formby, Lancs

FOCUS
A low-quality contest in which once again the stands' rail played a huge part in the outcome.
T/Plt: £52.80 to a £1 stake. Pool: £42,640.77. 588.69 winning tickets. T/Qpdt: £9.90 to a £1 stake. Pool: £4,517.10. 336.30 winning tickets. JN

3218 NEWMARKET (R-H)
Saturday, June 21

OFFICIAL GOING: Good to firm (8.9)
Wind: Light, becoming fresher across Weather: Overcast

3270 PLAY BLACKJACK AT INTERCASINO.CO.UK H'CAP 7f
2:15 (2:15) (Class 4) (0-85,85) 3-Y-0 **£6,476** (£1,927; £963; £481) **Stalls** High

Form RPR

416- **1** **Relative Order**[281] 5374 3-9-3 79 LPKeniry 2 94
(J R Best) *racd centre: hld up: hdwy 2f out: rdn to ld and edgd rt ins fnl f: r.o wl* **33/1**

11-1 **2** 1¾ **High Standing (USA)**[32] 2276 3-9-6 82 OscarUrbina 9 92
(S A Callaghan) *racd stands' side: hld up: hdwy and nt clr run over 1f out: rdn: hung lft and ev ch ins fnl f: styd on same pce* **11/4**[1]

5-65 **3** 1½ **Noble Citizen (USA)**[28] 2412 3-9-5 81 SaleemGolam 13 87
(D M Simcock) *w ldr stands' side tl overall ldr and hung lft fr over 2f out: hdd and bmpd ins fnl f: no ex* **10/1**

1331 **4** 2¾ **Oceana Blue**[26] 2452 3-8-10 72 (t) FrancisNorton 6 71
(A M Balding) *racd centre: chsd ldrs: rdn and ev ch over 1f out: hmpd and wknd ins fnl f* **16/1**

2201 **5** 1¼ **Ink Spot**[25] 2481 3-9-5 81 HayleyTurner 12 76
(M L W Bell) *racd stands' side: trckd ldrs: rdn and hung lft over 1f out: styd on same pce* **8/1**[3]

-412 **6** nk **Dubai Meydan (IRE)**[15] 2794 3-9-8 84 GeorgeBaker 4 78
(Miss Gay Kelleway) *racd centre: hld up: hdwy 2f out: hung lft and nt clr run over 1f out: no ex* **3/1**[2]

51 **7** 1 **Sir Boss (IRE)**[14] 2824 3-9-1 77 MickyFenton 7 69
(D E Cantillon) *led centre: rdn and hdd that gp over 1f out: wknd ins fnl f* **11/1**

2-3 **8** 3½ **Bailey (IRE)**[70] 1336 3-9-3 79 (b[1]) RobertHavlin 11 61
(B J Meehan) *racd stands' side: trckd ldrs: rdn and hung lft 2f out: wknd over 1f out* **14/1**

3-00 **9** 1½ **Harlech Castle**[28] 2412 3-9-9 85 AdamKirby 8 63
(P F I Cole) *racd centre: chsd ldr: rdn over 2f out: ev ch over 1f out: sn wknd* **33/1**

015 **10** 1 **East Drive (IRE)**[15] 2794 3-9-9 85 PhilipRobinson 5 60
(M A Jarvis) *racd centre: prom: racd keenly: wknd wl over 1f out* **12/1**

22-0 **11** hd **Regal Bird (USA)**[17] 2714 3-9-0 76 IanMongan 1 51
(M A Magnusson) *racd centre: hld up: rdn over 2f out: n.d* **50/1**

1-10 **12** 1 **Debonnaire**[35] 2196 3-9-0 76 MartinDwyer 10 48
(M Johnston) *overall ldr stands' side over 4f: edgd lft and wknd over 1f out* **16/1**

-005 **13** 7 **Hunt The Bottle (IRE)**[28] 2407 3-8-9 71 JimmyQuinn 3 24
(B W Hills) *s.i.s: racd centre: hld up: plld hrd: rdn over 2f out: sn wknd* **14/1**

1m 25.57s (-0.13) **Going Correction** +0.15s/f (Good) **13** Ran SP% **120.8**
Speed ratings (Par 101): **106,104,102,99,97 97,96,92,90,89 89,88,80**
toteswinger: 1&2 £24.50, 1&3 £62.30, 2&3 £7.60. CSF £122.83 CT £1057.83 TOTE £52.40: £10.10, £1.50, £3.50; EX 220.00 TRIFECTA Not won..
Owner Heading For The Rocks Partnership **Bred** John And Mrs Caroline Penny **Trained** Hucking, Kent
■ Stewards' Enquiry : Saleem Golam four-day ban: careless riding (Jul 6-8, 10)

FOCUS
A fair, competitive three-year-old handicap. They split into two groups early on, with five sticking towards the stands' rail, but they merged as one in the closing stages and the main action took place up the centre of the track. Straightforward form, the winner up 11lb.
High Standing(USA) Official explanation: jockey said gelding hung left
Dubai Meydan(IRE) Official explanation: jockey said gelding ran too free
East Drive(IRE) Official explanation: jockey said colt was keen early
Debonnaire Official explanation: jockey said filly lost its action

3271 £800 FREE AT INTERCASINO.CO.UK H'CAP 6f
2:50 (2:51) (Class 4) (0-80,79) 3-Y-0+ **£6,476** (£1,927; £963; £481) **Stalls** High

Form RPR

0-0 **1** **Brunelleschi**[35] 2205 5-9-7 72 (b) GeorgeBaker 2 82
(P L Gilligan) *hld up: hdwy over 1f out: r.o to ld wl ins fnl f* **12/1**

4400 **2** nk **Resplendent Alpha**[14] 2837 4-9-3 **68** .... JimmyQuinn 3 77
(P Howling) *hld up: hdwy over 1f out: rdn and ev ch ins fnl f: edgd lft: r.o* **16/1**

0116 **3** 3/4 **Mango Music**[24] 2504 5-10-0 **79** .... FrancisNorton 7 86
(M Quinn) *led: rdn over 1f out: edgd rt and hdd wl ins fnl f* **10/1**

3112 **4** 1 1/4 **Best One**[11] 2906 4-9-7 **75** .... KevinGhunowa(3) 1 78
(R A Harris) *chsd ldrs: rdn and ev ch ins fnl f: no ex* **11/2**[2]

-545 **5** shd **Makshoof (IRE)**[15] 2778 4-9-10 **75** .... MartinDwyer 5 77
(K A Ryan) *hld up: hdwy over 1f out: rdn and hung lft ins fnl f: nt run on* **11/2**[2]

0062 **6** nk **Steel Blue**[9] 2968 8-8-10 **61** .... KShea 8 62
(R M Whitaker) *chsd ldrs: rdn over 2f out: edgd rt over 1f out: styd on same pce fnl f* **9/2**[1]

0532 **7** 3 3/4 **Tilly's Dream**[8] 2993 5-9-13 **78** .... AdamKirby 12 67
(G C Bravery) *hld up: hdwy over 1f out: wknd ins fnl f* **7/1**[3]

3122 **8** 1 1/2 **Thoughtsofstardom**[2] 3159 5-8-7 **65** .... TobyAtkinson(7) 13 50
(M Wigham) *hld up: racd keenly: rdn over 1f out: wknd ins fnl f* **12/1**

0000 **9** 1/2 **Diane's Choice**[7] 3042 5-9-6 **71** .... MickyFenton 4 54
(Miss Gay Kelleway) *hld up: hdwy over 1f out: hung rt and wknd fnl f* **25/1**

6301 **10** 1/2 **Applesnap (IRE)**[9] 2983 3-8-8 **73** .... AmyBaker(7) 10 54
(Mrs C A Dunnett) *chsd ldrs: rdn over 2f out: wknd fnl f* **20/1**

2246 **11** nk **Millfields Dreams**[20] 2644 9-8-5 **63** ....(p) WilliamCarson(7) 9 43
(P Leech) *chsd ldrs over 4f out: nt clr run and wknd over 1f out* **16/1**

50-0 **12** 7 **Minnis Bay (CAN)**[47] 1857 4-9-10 **75** ....(v1) LPKeniry 6 33
(E F Vaughan) *chsd ldr: rdn 2f out: wknd over 1f out* **14/1**

6-00 **13** 8 **Brother Barry (USA)**[35] 2199 3-8-11 **69** .... PhilipRobinson 11 1
(W J Musson) *prom: edgd rt and wknd over 2f out: sn hung lft* **9/1**

1m 12.42s (-0.08) **Going Correction** +0.15s/f (Good)
WFA 3 from 4yo+ 7lb **13 Ran SP% 123.0**
Speed ratings (Par 105): **106,105,104,102,102 102,97,95,94,94 93,84,73**
toteswinger: 1&2 £48.00, 1&3 £22.50, 2&3 £32.10. CSF £195.83 CT £2006.94 TOTE £16.10: £4.40, £6.20, £4.00; EX 276.60 Trifecta £297.30 Part won..
Owner Dr Susan Barnes **Bred** Dr Susan Barnes **Trained** Newmarket, Suffolk

FOCUS
A fair sprint handicap run at a good pace, and solid form. They raced up the middle of the track.
Tilly's Dream Official explanation: jockey said mare ran flat

3272 INTERCASINO.CO.UK EBF FILLIES' H'CAP 1m
3:25 (3:26) (Class 4) (0-85,83) 3-Y-0+ **£6,476** (£1,927; £963; £481) **Stalls** High

Form RPR

0124 **1** **Aphrodisia**[25] 2483 4-9-3 **69** .... GeorgeBaker 11 82
(S C Williams) *hld up: hdwy over 1f out: rdn to ld ins fnl f: r.o* **11/1**

4352 **2** 1 1/2 **Sam's Secret**[6] 3054 6-9-11 **77** .... PatCosgrave 8 87
(G A Swinbank) *s.i.s and wnt rt s: hld up: hdwy over 1f out: r.o u.p ins fnl f* **5/1**[3]

1-0 **3** 1/2 **Hip**[35] 2196 3-9-7 **83** .... KShea 9 90
(E A L Dunlop) *hmpd s: chsd ldrs: rdn to ld over 1f out: edgd lft: hdd and unable qck ins fnl f* **11/1**

3201 **4** 3/4 **Oat Cuisine**[29] 2373 4-9-4 **70** .... HayleyTurner 3 77
(M L W Bell) *chsd ldrs: ev ch over 1f out: sn rdn: styd on same pce ins fnl f* **3/1**[1]

01-0 **5** 3 **Albaraari**[44] 1930 3-8-10 **72** .... MartinDwyer 1 70
(Sir Michael Stoute) *chsd ldrs: rdn and ev ch over 1f out: wknd ins fnl f* **16/1**

01- **6** 3/4 **La Coveta (IRE)**[231] 6648 3-9-0 **76** .... NickyMackay 2 73
(B J Meehan) *hld up in tch: racd keenly: rdn and hung lft over 1f out: wknd ins fnl f* **12/1**

-640 **7** 3 1/2 **Sahaadi**[11] 2920 3-8-8 **70** .... PatDobbs 4 58
(R Hannon) *led over 6f: wknd fnl f* **16/1**

3-51 **8** 1 1/4 **Portodora (USA)**[43] 1946 3-9-3 **79** .... JimmyQuinn 7 65
(H R A Cecil) *hld up in tch: rdn over 1f out: sn edgd lft and wknd* **4/1**[2]

0000 **9** 3 3/4 **Dalkey Girl (IRE)**[34] 2231 3-9-3 **79** ....(p) PhilipRobinson 5 56
(V Smith) *mid-div: rdn 1/2-way: hung lft over 2f out: sn wknd* **20/1**

2534 **10** 1 **Paradise Dancer (IRE)**[51] 1742 4-9-2 **68** .... AdamKirby 6 45
(J A R Toller) *chsd ldrs: rdn over 2f out: wknd over 1f out* **16/1**

4053 **11** 5 **Fleuret**[8] 2995 4-10-0 **80** .... StephenCarson 10 45
(Eve Johnson Houghton) *hld up: rdn over 3f out: wknd 2f out* **9/1**

1m 40.46s (0.46) **Going Correction** +0.15s/f (Good)
WFA 3 from 4yo+ 10lb **11 Ran SP% 118.4**
Speed ratings (Par 102): **103,101,101,100,97 96,93,91,88,87 82**
toteswinger: 1&2 £14.20, 1&3 £24.70, 2&3 £14.20. CSF £65.71 CT £476.92 TOTE £12.30: £3.50, £2.10, £3.90; EX 88.30 Trifecta £231.10 Part won..
Owner bellhouseracing.com **Bred** Theobalds Stud **Trained** Newmarket, Suffolk

FOCUS
A fair fillies' handicap run at an ordinary pace early on. Sound form. The winning time was 0.93 seconds quicker than the later three-year-old maiden. They raced up the middle of the track.
Paradise Dancer(IRE) Official explanation: jockey said filly ran too free
Fleuret Official explanation: jockey said filly hung right and never travelled

3273 INTERCASINO.CO.UK H'CAP 5f
4:00 (4:01) (Class 2) (0-100,103) 3-Y-0
£12,462 (£3,732; £1,866; £934; £466; £234) **Stalls** High

Form RPR

-460 **1** **Dubai Princess (IRE)**[7] 3047 3-9-1 **92** .... GeorgeBaker 7 98
(J A Osborne) *hld up: hdwy and nt clr run over 1f out: swtchd lft: sn rdn and hung lft: r.o to ld wl ins fnl f* **14/1**

-111 **2** nk **Befortyfour**[7] 3028 3-9-12 **103** .... PhilipRobinson 9 108+
(M A Jarvis) *led: rdn over 1f out: hung lft and hdd wl ins fnl f* **11/10**[1]

-312 **3** 1 1/4 **Little Pete (IRE)**[7] 3028 3-8-11 **88** .... FrancisNorton 5 89+
(A M Balding) *trckd ldrs: racd keenly: rdn over 1f out: edgd lft: styd on same pce* **4/1**[2]

4-62 **4** 1/2 **Royal Intruder**[23] 2529 3-8-11 **88** .... PatDobbs 4 87
(R Hannon) *trckd ldr: rdn over 1f out: no ex wl ins fnl f* **12/1**

0-23 **5** 2 1/4 **Piscean (USA)**[43] 1945 3-8-4 **81** oh2 .... JimmyQuinn 2 72
(T Keddy) *hld up: hdwy u.p over 1f out: wknd ins fnl f* **16/1**

6200 **6** hd **Bosun Breese**[7] 3028 3-8-4 **81** .... HayleyTurner 1 71
(P W D'Arcy) *wnt lft s: sn chsng ldrs: rdn over 1f out: wknd ins fnl f* **33/1**

5022 **7** 1 **Chartist**[43] 1945 3-8-13 **90** .... LPKeniry 3 77
(R Hannon) *chsd ldrs: rdn over 1f out: wknd ins fnl f* **13/2**[3]

0130 **8** 4 1/2 **Cross Fell (USA)**[15] 2794 3-8-7 **84** ....(p) PatCosgrave 6 54
(J R Boyle) *prom: nt clr run and lost pl over 1f out: sn btn* **33/1**

20-6 **9** 24 **Vive Les Rouges**[21] 2606 3-9-4 **95** .... IanMongan 8 —
(C F Wall) *trckd ldrs: rdn and wknd over 1f out: eased ins fnl f* **16/1**

59.11 secs (0.01) **Going Correction** +0.15s/f (Good) **9 Ran SP% 113.0**
Speed ratings (Par 105): **105,104,102,101,98 97,96,89,50**
toteswinger: 1&2 £3.80, 1&3 £10.30, 2&3 £1.80. CSF £29.23 CT £76.71 TOTE £16.80: £4.10, £1.10, £1.70; EX 34.50 Trifecta £250.60 Part won. Pool: £338.67 - 0.60 winning units..
Owner A F O'Callaghan **Bred** Darley **Trained** Upper Lambourn, Berks

FOCUS
A good sprint handicap. They raced towards the stands' side for much of the way, but the principals drifted off the rail late on. Pretty sound form, the winner back to her 2yo best.

NOTEBOOK
Dubai Princess(IRE) made little impression when pitched into a handicap for the first time in a more competitive race than this over 6f at York last time, but she was dropped 3lb and returned to form to take advantage. Held up last of all early on, she got a dream gap around a furlong out and found enough to deny the favourite, despite initially edging left once in the clear. (tchd 12-1)
Befortyfour has progressed well since winning his maiden on the Polytrack at Lingfield earlier in the year, winning off 90 at Great Leighs and defying a mark of 95 at Leicester on his latest start, but he was just denied the four-timer after a further 8lb hike in the weights. He had the benefit of the strands' rail for much of the way, but drifted to his left late on and found one too strong. (op 6-5 tchd 10-11)
Little Pete(IRE) came into this in good form, but he proved no match for the front two. (tchd 9-2)
Royal Intruder was 12lb better off with Befortyfour for a length-and-a-quarter defeat at Great Leighs, but he was beaten even further this time. (op 9-1)
Piscean(USA), 2lb out of the handicap, is better than the bare form suggests as he was stuck out very wide, more towards the centre of the track for most of the way.
Bosun Breese was another caught wide.
Vive Les Rouges Official explanation: vet said filly bled from the nose

3274 INTERCASINO.CO.UK MAIDEN STKS 7f
4:35 (4:36) (Class 4) 2-Y-0 **£5,180** (£1,541; £770; £384) **Stalls** High

Form RPR

1 **Jazz Police** 2-9-3 0 .... PatDobbs 6 79+
(R Hannon) *hld up in tch: rdn to ld and edgd rt ins fnl f: r.o* **5/2**[1]

2 3/4 **Seminole (IRE)** 2-9-3 0 .... RobertHavlin 2 77
(J H M Gosden) *chsd ldrs: rdn to ld and hung lft over 1f out: hdd and bmpd ins fnl f: styd on same pce* **7/2**[3]

5 **3** 2 3/4 **Auld Arty (FR)**[21] 2592 2-9-3 0 .... PhilipRobinson 1 70
(T G Mills) *led: rdn and hdd over 1f out: edgd lft and no ex ins fnl f* **11/4**[2]

4 1 1/4 **Mefraas (IRE)** 2-9-3 0 .... KShea 3 67+
(E A L Dunlop) *s.i.s: hld up: hdwy over 1f out: no ex ins fnl f* **15/2**

5 10 **Congregation** 2-9-3 0 .... DavidKinsella 4 42
(J H M Gosden) *chsd ldrs: rdn over 2f out: sn hung lft and wknd* **8/1**

6 7 **State General (IRE)** 2-9-3 0 .... MickyFenton 5 25
(Miss J Feilden) *chsd ldrs: rdn 1/2-way: wknd wl over 1f out* **8/1**

1m 28.79s (3.09) **Going Correction** +0.15s/f (Good) **6 Ran SP% 111.4**
Speed ratings (Par 95): **88,87,84,82,71 63**
toteswinger: 1&2 £1.60, 1&3 £1.50, 2&3 £2.40. CSF £11.37 TOTE £3.60: £1.80, £2.10; EX 10.00.
Owner Michael Pescod **Bred** Mrs D O Joly **Trained** East Everleigh, Wilts
■ Stewards' Enquiry : Pat Dobbs one-day ban: careless riding (Jul 6)

FOCUS
Not many runners, and only one had run before, but this looked a reasonable juvenile maiden. They raced up the centre of the track.

NOTEBOOK
Jazz Police ◆, a 26,000gns son of Beat Hollow, out of a 7f three-year-old winner, was good enough to make a winning debut, justifying favouritism in the process. He responded well to pressure, but did not do much once in front, edging left and bumping the eventual runner-up, and he is open to a fair amount of improvement. (op 9-4 tchd 10-3)
Seminole(IRE) ◆, a 140,000gns son of Indian Ridge, half-brother to among others high-class 7f-1m performer Le Vie Dei Colori, out of a triple 6f winner at two and three, was just found out by his inexperience. Running green, he edged left when first coming under pressure, bumping Auld Arty, and was then nudged himself by the eventual winner when beginning to stay on again inside the final furlong, although he was probably just held at the time. He should know a lot more next time and ought to prove hard to beat in similar company. (op 9-2)
Auld Arty(FR) did not build on the form he showed when a staying-on fifth in a reasonable maiden over 6f on his debut at Doncaster, although he was probably beaten by a couple of useful types. (op 5-2)
Mefraas(IRE), by King's Best, half-brother to dual 1m winner Maghya, out of a quite useful 7f winner, struggled to make an impression and might need a little more time. Official explanation: jockey said colt was very green and slowly away (op 6-1 tchd 5-1)
Congregation, by Cape Cross, first foal of a 7f juvenile winner, is another who looks to need more time. (tchd 9-1)
State General(IRE), by Statute Of Liberty, half-brother to among others 2m winner Spectested, who has also been successful over hurdles, attracted some interesting market support, but he weakened very tamely in the closing stages. Presumably he is thought to be capable of better. Official explanation: trainer said that the colt was unsuited to the good to firm ground (op 10-1 tchd 13-2)

3275 PLAY BLACKJACK AT INTERCASINO.CO.UK MAIDEN STKS 1m
5:10 (5:11) (Class 4) 3-Y-0 **£5,180** (£1,541; £770; £384) **Stalls** High

Form RPR

6- **1** **Harald Bluetooth (IRE)**[345] 3462 3-9-3 0 .... GeorgeBaker 2 76+
(J R Fanshawe) *hld up: hdwy over 1f out: rdn to ld and edgd rt ins fnl f: r.o* **5/1**[2]

-400 **2** 1 **Talayeb**[31] 2302 3-9-3 72 .... PatDobbs 1 73
(M P Tregoning) *led: rdn over 1f out: hdd ins fnl f: styd on* **14/1**

3 shd **Meydan City (USA)** 3-9-3 0 .... PhilipRobinson 9 73+
(Saeed Bin Suroor) *s.i.s: sn prom: rdn and ev ch over 1f out: styd on* **5/6**[1]

43 **4** shd **Arts Guild (USA)**[63] 1467 3-9-3 0 .... KShea 3 73+
(W J Musson) *chsd ldrs: rdn over 1f out: r.o* **7/1**[3]

5 1 1/4 **I'm Sensational** 3-8-12 0 .... JimmyQuinn 4 65
(H R A Cecil) *s.i.s: hld up: hdwy over 1f out: styd on same pce ins fnl f* **16/1**

03-0 **6** 4 **Kinnego Bay (IRE)**[47] 1875 3-9-3 76 .... AdamKirby 10 61
(B W Hills) *hld up: hdwy over 2f out: rdn and lft over 1f out: wknd fnl f* **14/1**

00- **7** 5 **Bluejain**[247] 6281 3-9-3 0 .... MickyFenton 8 49
(Miss Gay Kelleway) *s.s: a in rr* **33/1**

8 nk **Cwm Rhondda (USA)** 3-8-12 0 .... HayleyTurner 6 44
(P W Chapple-Hyam) *s.i.s: hld up: rdn 1/2-way: wknd over 1f out* **11/1**

6-3 **9** nk **Robert Burns (IRE)**[10] 2954 3-9-3 0 .... RobertHavlin 7 48
(J H M Gosden) *chsd ldr tl rdn over 1f out: sn wknd* **9/1**

1m 41.39s (1.39) **Going Correction** +0.15s/f (Good) **9 Ran SP% 124.2**
Speed ratings (Par 101): **99,98,97,97,96 92,87,87,86**
toteswinger: 1&2 £7.80, 1&3 £3.20, 2&3 £5.50. CSF £77.17 TOTE £7.10: £1.90, £4.50, £1.10; EX 132.60.
Owner Mr & Mrs Duncan Davidson **Bred** Airlie Stud And Sir Thomas Pilkington **Trained** Newmarket, Suffolk
■ A 14,039/1 four-timer for George Baker.
■ Stewards' Enquiry : George Baker caution: careless riding

FOCUS
An ordinary maiden run at a steady early pace. The winner, third and fourth should prove better than this. The winning time was 0.93 seconds slower than the earlier 66-85 fillies' handicap. They raced up the middle of the track.

3276 PLAY ROULETTE AT INTERCASINO.CO.UK H'CAP 1m 6f 175y
5:40 (5:42) (Class 5) (0-75,73) 4-Y-0+ **£3,885** (£1,156; £577; £288) **Stalls** Centre

Form RPR
4-04 **1** **Kasban**[21] 2621 4-9-9 **73** AdamKirby 5 81
(Jane Chapple-Hyam) *chsd clr ldr: tk clsr order 1/2-way: rdn to ld ins fnl f: styd on* **9/2**[3]
4-25 **2** *nk* **Daylami Dreams**[21] 2628 4-9-7 **71** (b[1]) MickyFenton 6 78
(T P Tate) *led and sn clr: stdd 1/2-way: hdd over 2f out: styd on u.p* **9/2**[3]
3452 **3** *3/4* **Rose Bien**[6] 3059 6-8-5 **60** (p) JackMitchell[(5)] 4 66
(P J McBride) *chsd clr ldrs: rdn over 3f out: led 2f out: hdd and edgd rt ins fnl f: styd on* **5/2**[1]
2122 **4** *1 1/4* **Danzatrice**[17] 2734 6-9-4 **68** SaleemGolam 1 72
(C W Thornton) *dwlt: hld up: hdwy over 2f out: sn rdn: styd on same pce ins fnl f* **10/1**
541 **5** *6* **Lapina (IRE)**[10] 2952 4-9-1 **65** (b) PatDobbs 3 61
(Pat Eddery) *hld up: hdwy 1/2-way: rdn over 2f out: wknd over 1f out* **9/2**[3]
1323 **6** *15* **Josh You Are**[2] 3160 5-9-1 **65** OscarUrbina 8 40
(M Wigham) *s.i.s: hld up: rdn and wknd over 2f out* **4/1**[2]
0100 **7** *10* **Royal Audition**[12] 2884 7-8-4 **54** oh4 (p) HayleyTurner 2 15
(T T Clement) *hld up: hdwy 1/2-way: rdn and wknd over 2f out* **28/1**

3m 12.38s (1.08) **Going Correction** +0.15s/f (Good) **7** Ran SP% **115.7**
Speed ratings (Par 103): **103,102,102,101,98 90,85**
toteswinger: 1&2 £4.40, 1&3 £3.00, 2&3 £2.10. CSF £25.46 CT £61.17 TOTE £6.00: £3.80, £2.10; EX 28.20 Place 6 £176.88, Place 5 £65.21.
Owner Michael H Watt **Bred** Ardenode Stud **Trained** Lambourn, Berks

FOCUS
A pretty modest staying handicap. The pace was good early, but slowed mid-race. The main action took place up the centre of the track.
Lapina(IRE) Official explanation: jockey said filly ran too keenly
T/Plt: £482.90 to a £1 stake. Pool: £89,883.90. 135.85 winning tickets. T/Qpdt: £14.10 to a £1 stake. Pool: £4,174.38. 218.11 winning tickets. CR

[3225]REDCAR (L-H)
Saturday, June 21

OFFICIAL GOING: Good to firm (firm in places) changing to good to firm after race 4 (4.10)
Wind: Virtually nil Weather: Overcast and raining

3277 MARKET CROSS JEWELLERS MAIDEN STKS 7f
2:25 (2:25) (Class 5) 2-Y-0 **£2,331** (£693; £346; £173) **Stalls** Centre

Form RPR
624 **1** **Liturgical (USA)**[9] 2972 2-9-3 0 SilvestreDeSousa 9 77
(M A Magnusson) *trckd ldrs: hdwy 1/2-way: rdn to ld wl over 1f out: edgd lft ins fnl f: r.o wl* **7/2**[2]
2 *nk* **Yorgunnabelucky (USA)** 2-9-3 0 AndrewElliott 2 76
(M Johnston) *prom: effrt 2f out: sn rdn and ev ch: drvn and hung bdly lft ins fnl f: no ex towards fin* **5/4**[1]
3 **3** *1 1/2* **Hel's Angel (IRE)**[19] 2657 2-8-9 0 AndrewMullen[(3)] 11 68
(Mrs A Duffield) *led: rdn along 2f out: sn hdd: kpt on u.p ins fnl f* **9/1**
3 **4** *3 1/2* **Night Of Fortune**[23] 2521 2-9-3 0 PaulMulrennan 1 64+
(Sir Mark Prescott) *cl up: effrt over 2f out: sn rdn and ev ch tl drvn and one pce ent fnl f* **7/1**
5 *6* **Reigning In Rio (IRE)** 2-8-12 0 LeeEnstone 7 44
(P C Haslam) *chsd ldrs: rdn along over 2f out: sn drvn and wknd over 1f out* **28/1**
6 *1 1/4* **King's Counsel (IRE)** 2-9-3 0 NeilPollard 12 46
(B Smart) *green and towards rr: pushed along 1/2-way: sn rdn and sme late hdwy* **6/1**[3]
0 **7** *4 1/2* **Dark Oasis**[21] 2592 2-9-0 0 JamieMoriarty[(3)] 4 34
(K A Ryan) *a towards rr* **33/1**
5 **8** *1 1/2* **The Canny Dove (USA)**[16] 2746 2-8-12 0 NeilBrown[(5)] 5 31
(T D Barron) *chsd ldrs: rdn along 1/2-way: grad wknd* **20/1**
9 *1 1/4* **Aven Mac (IRE)** 2-8-9 0 MarkLawson[(3)] 6 23
(N Bycroft) *s.i.s: a in rr* **66/1**
10 *1/2* **Without Equal** 2-8-12 0 DaleGibson 3 21
(A Dickman) *s.i.s: a in rr* **50/1**
11 *12* **Darknstormy** 2-9-3 0 DeanMcKeown 10 —
(J R Weymes) *a in rr* **33/1**
12 *15* **Eborbrav** 2-9-3 0 TonyHamilton 8 —
(T D Easterby) *dwlt: a in rr* **28/1**

1m 25.33s (0.83) **Going Correction** +0.05s/f (Good) **12** Ran SP% **124.4**
Speed ratings (Par 93): **97,96,94,90,84 82,77,75,74,73 60,42**
toteswinger: 1&2 £2.80, 1&3 £6.70, 2&3 £5.10. CSF £8.13 TOTE £3.90: £1.30, £1.10, £2.40; EX 10.10.
Owner Eastwind Racing Ltd and Martha Trussell **Bred** R B Trussell Jr & J T L Jones III **Trained** Upper Lambourn, Berks

FOCUS
Three of the four runners with experience promised to improve on their previous placed efforts and a couple of the newcomers had attractive profiles so this was potentially a fair contest, and the way the first four pulled clear - with the rest fairly well strung out - was encouraging.

NOTEBOOK
Liturgical(USA), who had shown a reasonable level of form in three previous efforts, put his experience to good use by overpowering the well-bred Yorgunnabelucky in the latter stages. He saw this 7f out well, despite edging across the course with the runner-up, and has the makings of a fair juvenile. (op 10-3)
Yorgunnabelucky(USA) ◆ showed definite signs of greenness early but picked up well and only narrowly failed to hold on, despite edging badly left under pressure. A brother to top-class Shamardal, he is a late foal who will improve for this experience. (op 15-8)
Hel's Angel(IRE) was unlucky to bump into Royal Ascot winner South Central on her debut at Carlisle and may have run into another couple of above-average colts in this. After sharing the lead, she finished clear of the rest and is certainly up to winning in ordinary company. (op 12-1 tchd 8-1)
Night Of Fortune travelled really strongly in front with Hel's Angel but did not get home inside the final furlong. (tchd 13-2 and 8-1)
Reigning In Rio(IRE) was up with the leaders in the early stages but could not stay with them when the race got serious. (op 20-1)
King's Counsel(IRE) was not the usual sharp two-year-old you would associate with the stable, and only got the hang of things very late on. The experience will not have been lost on him and he should be much straighter next time. (tchd 5-1)

3278 SGW CONSTRUCTION GROUP ALICE WILLIAMS MEMORIAL H'CAP 1m
3:00 (3:00) (Class 2) (0-100,97) 4-Y-0+ **£10,361** (£3,083; £1,540; £769) **Stalls** Centre

Form RPR
0354 **1** *nse* **Billy Dane (IRE)**[8] 3006 4-8-2 **78** (p) DaleGibson 4 80
(R A Fahey) *t.k.h: sn led: rdn along and hdd over 2f out: remained cl up: rdn and ev ch whn hmpd ins fnl f and nr fin: jst hld: fin 2nd, nse: awrdd r* **7/2**[3]
/5-6 **2** **Scartozz**[49] 1816 6-9-7 **97** (b) NeilPollard 1 99
(M Botti) *a cl up: rdn to ld over 2f out: drvn and edgd rt ins fnl f: jst hld on fin 1st: disq: plcd 2nd* **15/2**
2422 **3** *1* **Just Bond (IRE)**[1] 3229 6-8-2 **78** oh4 SilvestreDeSousa 2 78
(G R Oldroyd) *trckd ldrs: effrt 2f out: sn rdn and ev ch ins fnl f: drvn and nt qckn last 100yds* **5/2**[1]
411- **4** *3/4* **Webbow (IRE)**[309] 4566 6-8-10 **89** DuranFentiman[(3)] 3 87
(T D Easterby) *hld up: smooth hdwy over 2f out: rdn over 1f out and ev ch tl edgd lft and one pce ins fnl f* **3/1**[2]
2110 **5** *14* **First Buddy**[26] 2465 4-9-7 **97** PaulMulrennan 5 63
(G A Swinbank) *trckd ldng pair: pushed along over 2f out: sn rdn and wknd wl over 1f out* **3/1**[2]

1m 36.55s (-1.45) **Going Correction** +0.05s/f (Good) **5** Ran SP% **112.6**
Speed ratings (Par 109): **108,109,107,107,93**
CSF £27.31 TOTE £5.30: £2.60, £3.90; EX 31.30.
Owner I Davies & Exors of the Late K Lee **Bred** Brian Killeen **Trained** Musley Bank, N Yorks
■ Stewards' Enquiry : Neil Pollard one-day ban: careless riding (July 6); one-day ban: used whip down shoulder in forehand position (Jul 7)

FOCUS
Only five runners but all of them had positives. Four of them produced a close finish and this form, while ordinary for the grade, should not be underestimated, though they did not go a great pace early.

NOTEBOOK
Billy Dane(IRE), with the cheekpieces left on, just got the worse of a tussle with Scartozz throughout the final furlong but got the verdict in the stewards' room. The drop in trip may have helped him, but this was only his second career victory in 17 runs, so he cannot be relied upon to go close next time. (op 9-2 tchd 10-3)
Scartozz passed the post first but was demoted to second for causing some minor-looking interference in the latter stages (the margin of victory probably meant the stewards had little option, but the jockey intends to appeal). A tricky-looking ride, he is not one to trust quite yet to do his best under pressure. (op 6-1)
Just Bond(IRE), who had shaped well over this course 24 hours earlier, kept on well down the stands'-side rail but could never quite get to the front. He will surely win on turf soon (every one of his seven victories has come at Wolverhampton). (op 7-2 tchd 9-4)
Webbow(IRE), who was most progressive in 2007, did not shape badly on his seasonal debut, considering that he would have been suited by a stronger pace. He has something to prove off his current handicap mark and will be better judged after his next run. (op 11-4 tchd 10-3)
First Buddy ran his second lacklustre race in a row after a good start to the season. The rise up the handicap this season will probably anchor him for a while. (op 11-4)

3279 TOTESWINGER H'CAP 1m 6f 19y
3:40 (3:42) (Class 6) (0-60,60) 4-Y-0+ **£1,942** (£578; £288; £144) **Stalls** Low

Form RPR
/113 **1** **Silver Seeker (USA)**[14] 2844 8-9-3 **59** TonyHamilton 3 67
(Miss P Robson) *hld up in tch: hdwy over 3f out: rdn along over 2f out: styd on appr last to ld last 100yds* **11/4**[1]
10-0 **2** *1* **Mcqueen (IRE)**[9] 2572 8-8-13 **58** RussellKennemore[(3)] 15 65
(J T Stimpson) *led: rdn along 3f out: drvn over 1f out: hdd and no ex last 100yds* **14/1**
-004 **3** *3* **Let It Be**[14] 2849 7-9-0 **56** PaulMulrennan 8 59
(K G Reveley) *trckd ldrs: hdwy 3f out: rdn over 2f out: drvn and one pce over 1f out* **6/1**[3]
-043 **4** *1 1/2* **Parchment (IRE)**[11] 2914 6-8-4 **49** (b) AndrewMullen[(3)] 9 50
(A J Lockwood) *hld up towards rr: hdwy 3f out: rdn along 2f out: styd on u.p ent fnl f: nrst fin* **8/1**
5000 **5** *1/2* **Able Dara**[26] 2467 5-8-4 **46** oh1 DaleGibson 14 46
(N Bycroft) *chsd ldr: rdn along over 3f out: drvn 2f out: wknd appr fnl f* **20/1**
0156 **6** *3/4* **Wulimaster (USA)**[3] 3131 5-8-9 **54** MarkLawson[(3)] 13 53+
(D W Barker) *hld up: hdwy on outer 4f out: rdn to chse ldr 2f out: sn drvn and wknd appr fnl f* **10/1**
-642 **7** *1* **Hi Dancer**[26] 2467 5-8-8 **57** PatrickDonaghy[(7)] 12 55
(P C Haslam) *hld up in midfield: hdwy 3f out: rdn along over 2f out: drvn and no imp appr fnl f* **3/1**[2]
0-01 **8** *1* **Sendali (FR)**[14] 2849 4-8-9 **51** AndrewElliott 10 47
(J D Bethell) *in tch on inner: effrt 3f out: sn rdn along and outpcd: kpt on u.p fnl 2f: n.d* **9/1**
06-0 **9** *2 1/4* **Compton Commander**[31] 1892 10-7-11 **46** oh1 JamieKyne[(7)] 6 39
(E W Tuer) *alwasys towards rr* **33/1**
6-5F **10** *nk* **Dance Sauvage**[26] 2467 5-8-6 **48** DeanMcKeown 2 41
(C W Thornton) *a towards rr* **8/1**
0-65 **11** *16* **Firestorm (IRE)**[5] 3083 4-8-1 **46** oh1 DuranFentiman[(3)] 4 16
(C W Fairhurst) *chsd ldng pair: rdn along 4f out: sn wknd* **40/1**
000 **12** *5* **Osteopathic Care (IRE)**[14] 2847 4-8-7 **54** ow2 NeilBrown[(5)] 11 17
(Miss Tracy Waggott) *a in rr* **25/1**
000 **13** *7* **Monte Pattino (USA)**[22] 2573 4-8-4 **46** oh1 (t) TWilliams 1 —
(C J Teague) *s.i.s: a bhd* **100/1**

3m 6.11s (1.41) **Going Correction** +0.05s/f (Good) **13** Ran SP% **128.9**
Speed ratings (Par 101): **97,96,94,93,93 93,92,92,90,90 81,78,74**
toteswinger: 1&2 £43.80, 1&3 £2.40, 2&3 £10.10. CSF £44.50 CT £231.33 TOTE £4.20: £1.70, £4.60, £1.90; EX 70.60 Trifecta £98.00 Pool: £264.90 - 2.00 winning units..
Owner Michael H Watt **Bred** Darley Stud Management, L L C **Trained** Kirkharle, Northumberland

FOCUS
A generally exposed bunch for this modest staying handicap, with the notable exception of the winner. The race is best rated through the runner-up and Silver Seeker did not need to run up to his best.

3280 SPORTING LODGE INNS H'CAP 6f
4:10 (4:10) (Class 5) (0-70,75) 3-Y-0 **£2,331** (£693; £346; £173) **Stalls** Centre

Form RPR
-050 **1** **Actabou**[26] 2466 3-8-7 **60** NeilBrown[(5)] 3 68
(M Dods) *mde all: rdn 2f out: drvn ent fnl f and styd on gamely towards fin* **25/1**

0001 **2** ½ **Royal Acclamation (IRE)**[15] 2780 3-9-3 **65** SilvestreDeSousa 2 71
(G A Harker) *prom: effrt 2f out: rdn to chal over 1f out: drvn ins fnl f and ev ch tl nt qckn towards fin* **4/1**[2]

223 **3** ¾ **Strawberry Moon (IRE)**[19] 2673 3-9-5 **67** PaulMulrennan 10 71
(B Smart) *trckd ldrs: hdwy on outer wl over 1f out: rdn to chal ins fnl f: nt qckn last 100yds* **5/1**[3]

2511 **4** *nk* **Filligree (IRE)**[4] 3118 3-9-6 **75** 6ex JPHamblett(7) 4 78
(Rae Guest) *cl up: rdn and ev ch over 1f out: drvn and one pce ins fnl f* **4/5**[1]

0016 **5** *nk* **Moonage Daydream (IRE)**[19] 2660 3-9-2 **64** (b) LeeEnstone 1 66
(T D Easterby) *chsd ldrs on outer: rdn along 2f out: drvn and one pce ins fnl f* **16/1**

4040 **6** *1* **Infinity Bond**[11] 2911 3-8-12 **65** SladeO'Hara(5) 8 63
(G R Oldroyd) *trckd ldrs: hdwy over 1f out: rdn and n.m.r ent fnl f: one pce* **28/1**

6-00 **7** *nk* **Horatio Carter**[59] 1556 3-9-3 **71** (p) JamieMoriarty(3) 7 66
(K A Ryan) *dwlt: hld up: hdwy 2f out: sn rdn and n.m.r ins fnl f: kpt on* **18/1**

0404 **8** 1½ **Legendary Guest**[23] 2526 3-9-6 **68** (v) TonyHamilton 5 61
(D W Barker) *hld up in rr: hdwy 2f out: rdn along over 1f out: wknd ins fnl f* **16/1**

0320 **9** *10* **Dolly No Hair**[12] 2891 3-9-0 **65** MarkLawson(3) 11 26
(D W Barker) *chsd ldrs: rdn along 1/2-way: sn wknd* **20/1**

1m 11.83s (0.03) **Going Correction** +0.05s/f (Good) 9 Ran SP% **121.3**
Speed ratings (Par 99): **101,100,99,98,98 97,96,94,81**
toteswinger: 1&2 £16.50, 1&3 £20.50, 2&3 £2.50. CSF £125.89 CT £610.68 TOTE £25.40: £4.60, £1.50, £1.30; EX 278.90.
Owner J Ellis **Bred** John Ellis **Trained** Denton, Co Durham

FOCUS
A modest but competitive three-year-old handicap. Quick ground made it difficult to come from behind, and a prominent early position proved crucial. The winner was potentially well treated on his 2yo form.
Filligree(IRE) Official explanation: jockey said he could not ride more vigorously late on for fear of clipping the heels of a rival
Legendary Guest Official explanation: jockey said gelding hung right
Dolly No Hair Official explanation: jockey said gelding hung right-handed

3281 SGW CONSTRUCTION GROUP ABIGAIL CLAIMING STKS 7f
4:45 (4:46) (Class 5) 3-Y-0+ **£2,331** (£693; £346; £173) **Stalls** Centre

Form RPR

2112 **1** **Royal Dignitary (USA)**[22] 2578 8-9-3 **83** AhmedAjtebi(5) 13 80
(D Nicholls) *mde all: rdn clr over 1f out: styd on strly* **11/4**[1]

0-10 **2** 3¼ **Lewis Lloyd (IRE)**[14] 2846 5-8-6 **52** (v[1]) BMcHugh(7) 8 62
(R E Barr) *s.i.s and bhd: hdwy 2f out: sn rdn and styd on strly ins fnl f: tk 2nd nr line* **16/1**

2050 **3** *nk* **Green Lagonda (AUS)**[17] 2710 6-9-1 **61** DeanMcKeown 10 63
(J G Given) *trckd ldrs: hdwy to chse wnr 2f out: sn rdn and one pce ins fnl f* **12/1**

2364 **4** ¾ **Swinbrook (USA)**[18] 2698 7-9-11 **75** (v) TonyHamilton 5 71
(R A Fahey) *towards rr: hdwy 1/2-way: rdn to chse ldrs 2f out: sn drvn and kpt on same pce* **3/1**[2]

0-00 **5** 2¾ **Borodinsky**[21] 2597 7-8-8 **55** (p) NeilBrown(5) 12 52
(R E Barr) *s.i.s and bhd tl sme late hdwy* **25/1**

-000 **6** *1* **Neon Blue**[23] 2535 7-9-0 **64** MichaelJStainton(3) 6 53
(R M Whitaker) *hld up: pushed along 1/2-way: sn rdn and n.d* **15/2**

-304 **7** 2½ **Angaric (IRE)**[14] 2818 5-9-8 **70** PaulMulrennan 3 51
(B Smart) *stmbld s: sn trcking ldrs: effrt 2f out: sn rdn and wknd* **7/2**[3]

0005 **8** *1* **General Feeling (IRE)**[21] 2597 7-8-5 **52** (p) DeclanCannon(7) 2 39
(S T Mason) *s.i.s: a in rr* **16/1**

-600 **9** *nk* **Veronicas Way**[15] 2781 3-8-1 **50** (p) AndrewElliott 7 33
(G M Moore) *chsd ldrs: rdn along 3f out: sn wknd* **20/1**

3400 **10** 3¼ **Sir Bond (IRE)**[84] 1086 7-8-8 **48** ow1 SladeO'Hara(5) 11 30
(G R Oldroyd) *a in rr* **20/1**

-500 **11** *6* **Bretwalda (IRE)**[42] 2009 5-8-13 **50** LeeEnstone 1 14
(P T Midgley) *prom on outer: rdn along over 2f out: sn wknd* **25/1**

0-50 **12** *hd* **Susiedil (IRE)**[19] 2658 7-8-2 **35** (p) KellyHarrison(5) 4 7
(S T Mason) *prom: rdn along over 2f out and sn wknd* **66/1**

1m 25.13s (0.63) **Going Correction** +0.05s/f (Good)
WFA 3 from 5yo+ 9lb 12 Ran SP% **123.8**
Speed ratings (Par 103): **98,94,93,93,89 88,85,84,84,80 73,73**
toteswinger: 1&2 £6.90, 1&3 £10.00, 2&3 £26.10. CSF £46.74 TOTE £3.30: £1.50, £3.30, £3.70; EX 48.40.
Owner Middleham Park Racing XXXVI **Bred** Bentley Smith, J Michael O'Farrell Jr , Joan Thor **Trained** Sessay, N Yorks

FOCUS
Just a handful with serious chances at the weights for this claimer and the winner outclassed his rivals. He is rated to his recent best but the overall form is not that solid.

3282 ARYM FLOWERS MAIDEN STKS 6f
5:20 (5:24) (Class 5) 3-Y-0+ **£2,331** (£693; £346; £173) **Stalls** Centre

Form RPR

6 **1** **Muftarres (IRE)**[15] 2786 3-8-7 **0** JPHamblett(7) 8 73+
(Sir Michael Stoute) *chsd ldrs: rdn along over 2f out: swtchd lft and hdwy over 1f out: styd on u.p to ld last 100yds* **15/8**[1]

0-0 **2** 1¾ **Ubenkor (IRE)**[15] 2786 3-9-0 **0** PAspell 1 67
(B Smart) *cl up: rdn to ld wl over 1f out: drvn ins fnl f: hdd and nt qckn last 100yds* **50/1**

3-50 **3** *1* **President Elect (IRE)**[45] 1911 3-8-9 **74** NeilBrown(5) 17 64+
(T D Barron) *in rr and rdn along 1/2-way: hdwy 2f out: styd on wl u.p ins fnl f* **9/2**[3]

6046 **4** 2½ **Buzbury Rings**[39] 2075 4-9-4 **49** MichaelJStainton(3) 7 58
(R E Barr) *in tch: hdwy 1/2-way: rdn wl over 1f out: kpt on same pce fnl f* **25/1**

04 **5** 1¼ **Beat The Bell**[9] 2966 3-8-11 **0** DominicFox(3) 10 52
(A Bailey) *hld up towards rr: hdwy 1/2-way: rdn and edgd lft over 1f out: kpt on ins fnl f: nrst fin* **16/1**

53 **6** *1* **Admiral Bond (IRE)**[14] 2824 3-8-9 **0** SladeO'Hara(5) 9 49
(G R Oldroyd) *midfield: rdn and hdwy 2f out: edgd lft and no imp fnl f* **16/1**

0 **7** ½ **Braille**[9] 2966 3-9-0 **0** TonyHamilton 3 47
(T D Walford) *cl up: rdn along 2f out: sn drvn and grad wknd* **33/1**

0-55 **8** ¾ **Alsadeek (IRE)**[12] 2883 3-9-0 **72** NeilPollard 14 45
(J L Dunlop) *towards rr: hdwy 2f out: sn rdn and no imp appr fnl f* **7/2**[2]

5000 **9** ¾ **Molly Ann (IRE)**[11] 2911 3-8-9 **57** (b) LeeEnstone 16 37
(T D Easterby) *racd wd: sn led: rdn along and hdd wl over 1f out: sn wknd* **18/1**

33 **10** 4½ **Devinius (IRE)**[49] 1817 3-8-9 **0** PaulMulrennan 15 23
(G A Swinbank) *a towards rr* **11/2**

11 *nse* **Mr Toshiwonka** 4-9-7 **0** SilvestreDeSousa 2 30
(D Nicholls) *midfield: towards rr fr 1/2-way* **16/1**

2 **12** 1¼ **Safaseef (IRE)**[14] 2823 3-8-6 **0** AndrewMullen(3) 5 30
(K A Morgan) *a towards rr* **10/1**

13 *4* **Singing Lion** 3-8-7 **0** JohnCavanagh(7) 6 11
(M Dods) *bhd fr 1/2-way* **33/1**

14 *shd* **Ourbelle** 3-8-9 **0** DeanMcKeown 13 6
(Miss Tracy Waggott) *s.i.s: a in rr* **80/1**

15 *10* **Supremely Blessed** 4-8-11 **0** KellyHarrison(5) 12 —
(B Storey) *chsd ldrs to 1/2-way: sn wknd* **100/1**

1m 12.25s (0.45) **Going Correction** +0.05s/f (Good)
WFA 3 from 4yo 7lb 15 Ran SP% **136.5**
Speed ratings (Par 103): **99,96,95,92,90 89,88,87,86,80 80,78,73,73,59**
toteswinger: 1&2 £37.10, 1&3 £3.70, 2&3 £33.10. CSF £147.20 TOTE £3.20: £2.00, £16.70, £2.50; EX 235.90.
Owner Hamdan Al Maktoum **Bred** Shadwell Estate Company Limited **Trained** Newmarket, Suffolk

FOCUS
The usual mixed bag for this sprint maiden and the form is unlikely to prove much out of the ordinary, although the winner is a fair prospect. The proximity of Buzbury Rings, who seemed to run well, is very worrying, as he is rated only 49.
Safaseef(IRE) Official explanation: jockey said filly lost its action

3283 THE COMMITMENTS ARE HERE SATURDAY 23RD AUGUST H'CAP 5f
5:50 (5:54) (Class 6) (0-60,60) 3-Y-0 **£2,047** (£604; £302) **Stalls** Centre

Form RPR

-000 **1** **Ursus**[29] 2367 3-8-5 **47** SilvestreDeSousa 1 54
(C R Wilson) *trckd ldrs: hdwy 2f out: rdn to chse ldr ent fnl f: drvn and styd on to ld nr fin* **33/1**

5222 **2** *nk* **Kyzer Chief**[14] 2850 3-8-13 **60** NeilBrown(5) 7 66
(R E Barr) *cl up: led 1/2-way: rdn over 1f out: drvn ins fnl f: edgd rt and hdd nr fin* **15/8**[1]

0430 **3** *2* **Handsinthemist (IRE)**[19] 2661 3-8-10 **52** (p) LeeEnstone 3 51
(P T Midgley) *chsd ldrs: hdwy 2f out: rdn over 1f out and kpt on same pce ins fnl f* **6/1**[3]

503 **4** *1* **Many Welcomes**[63] 1489 3-8-7 **49** AndrewElliott 4 44+
(B P J Baugh) *hmpd s and rr: swtchd rt 1/2-way: sn rdn and styd on fnl f: nrst fin* **20/1**

5046 **5** *nk* **Mujahope**[7] 3030 3-8-2 **51** (v) AdeleRothery(7) 2 45
(C J Teague) *s.i.s and bhd tl styd on appr fnl f: nrst fin* **8/1**

-050 **6** 1¾ **Foreign Rhythm (IRE)**[19] 2661 3-8-13 **55** KimTinkler 12 43
(N Tinkler) *in tch: effrt 2f out: sn rdn and no imp* **12/1**

-001 **7** ½ **Red River Boy**[19] 2661 3-8-6 **53** KellyHarrison(5) 13 39
(C W Fairhurst) *chsd ldrs: rdn 2f out and sn btn* **3/1**[2]

-006 **8** *3* **Abitofafath (IRE)**[14] 2824 3-9-4 **60** (b[1]) DeanMcKeown 8 35
(J G Given) *led to 1/2-way: sn rdn and wknd* **14/1**

0-50 **9** 1¾ **Cool Fashion (IRE)**[19] 2661 3-8-7 **49** (v) NeilPollard 14 18
(Ollie Pears) *t.k.h: in tch: swtchd lft and rdn along 1/2-way: sn wknd* **16/1**

3214 **10** 1¾ **Orange Square (IRE)**[123] 614 3-9-4 **60** TonyHamilton 11 23
(D W Barker) *chsd ldrs: rdn along 1/2-way: sn wknd* **8/1**

58.96 secs (0.36) **Going Correction** +0.05s/f (Good) 10 Ran SP% **124.2**
Speed ratings (Par 97): **99,98,95,93,93 90,89,84,82,79**
toteswinger: 1&2 £23.90, 1&3 £59.30, 2&3 £5.10. CSF £101.28 CT £464.42 TOTE £53.10: £10.70, £1.50, £1.30; EX 212.20 Place 6 £217.44, Place 5 £162.14.
Owner David Bartlett **Bred** Mrs Andrea Bartlett **Trained** Manfield, N Yorks
■ Stewards' Enquiry : Neil Brown two-day ban: careless riding (Jul 6-7)

FOCUS
A moderate handicap, where a horse with very little form popped up. Overall, it looked a very weak contest, although the form reads as sound enough.
Ursus Official explanation: trainer said, regarding the improved form shown, gelding appreciated the drop in trip to 5f for the first time
T/Plt: £222.20 to a £1 stake. Pool: £53,705.15. 176.40 winning tickets. T/Qpdt: £50.90 to a £1 stake. Pool: £3,100.20. 45.00 winning tickets. JR

3232 DOWN ROYAL (R-H)
Saturday, June 21

OFFICIAL GOING: Good to firm changing to good after race 4 (4.05)

3286a WILLIAM EWART PROPERTIES LTD RATED RACE 7f
3:30 (3:32) 3-Y-0+ **£6,351** (£1,479; £652; £376)

RPR

1 **Striking Force (IRE)**[22] 2590 6-9-7 **76** FMBerry 5 80+
(V C Ward, Ire) *racd mainly in 4th: tk clsr order under 2f out: squeezed through on rail to ld under 1f out: kpt on wl* **9/4**[2]

2 ½ **Invincible Joe (IRE)**[15] 2810 3-8-12 **78** KLatham 2 76
(G M Lyons, Ire) *hld up in rr: rdn into 3rd under 1f out: sn chal: no ex cl home* **9/1**

3 1½ **Torch Of Freedom (IRE)**[222] 6800 3-8-12 DPMcDonogh 4 72
(Sir Mark Prescott) *chsd ldr in 2nd: impr to ld 2f out: rdn and hdd under 1f out: no ex: kpt on same pce* **6/4**[1]

4 2½ **Kiss N Run**[12] 2899 3-8-12 NGMcCullagh 3 65
(Andrew Oliver, Ire) *chsd ldrs in 3rd: rdn 1 1/2f out: sn no ex: kpt on same pce* **4/1**[3]

5 *8* **Dubburg (USA)**[31] 2317 3-8-12 **76** (b[1]) JAHeffernan 1 44
(David Marnane, Ire) *led: rdn and hdd 2f out: wkng whn sltly hmpd over 1f out* **7/1**

1m 26.31s (-2.19)
WFA 3 from 6yo 9lb 5 Ran SP% **113.3**
CSF £20.98 TOTE £3.40: £1.60, £4.90; DF 23.70.
Owner Last Out Syndicate **Bred** Moyglare Stud Farm Ltd **Trained** Kilcock, Co Meath

NOTEBOOK
Torch Of Freedom(IRE), who showed fair form at two, was representing a trainer/jockey combination with a decent past record when teaming up in Ireland. He fly jumped the start, but that made little difference to his challenge and it was more likely a case of him proving fresh on this seasonal return that cost him. Entitled to come on for the run, he should now also be seen to better effect when faced with another furlong. (op 5/4)

3287 - 3291a (Foreign Racing) - See Raceform Interactive

2887 PONTEFRACT (L-H)

Sunday, June 22

OFFICIAL GOING: Good to firm (7.8)

Just 10mm rain over five days resulted in 'quick ground but with a very good covering of grass'.

Wind: strong, 1/2 behind Weather: fine but very windy

3292 EBF TOTEPLACEPOT MAIDEN FILLIES' STKS 6f

2:10 (2:11) (Class 5) 2-Y-0 **£3,885** (£1,156; £577; £288) **Stalls** Low

Form				RPR
52	1		**Harriet's Girl**[26] [2485] 2-9-0 0 ... AndrewElliott 2 (K R Burke) *chsd ldrs: styd on on ins fnl f to ld fnl 75yds* **7/1**[3]	73
4	2	1	**Desert Sunset**[30] [2357] 2-9-0 0 ... NCallan 11 (M Johnston) *w ldrs: kpt on same pce ins fnl f* **17/2**	70
5	3	nk	**Mutually Mine (USA)**[24] [2534] 2-9-0 0 ... MickyFenton 8 (Mrs P Sly) *led until hdd and no ex ins fnl f* **3/1**[1]	69
5	4	1	**Wohaida (IRE)**[19] [2691] 2-9-0 0 ... DarryllHolland 9 (M R Channon) *chsd ldrs: kpt on same pce appr fnl f* **3/1**[1]	66
4	5	1/2	**Pacific Bay (IRE)**[26] [2485] 2-9-0 0 ... RoystonFfrench 4 (Mrs A Duffield) *chsd ldrs: kpt on same pce appr fnl f* **16/1**	65
53	6	nk	**Gower Valentine**[41] [2035] 2-9-0 0 ... AdrianTNicholls 12 (D Nicholls) *chsd ldrs: effrt on outside over 2f out: kpt on same pce appr fnl f* **16/1**	64
0	7	1 1/4	**Tamarah**[30] [2368] 2-9-0 0 ... (t) TPQueally 7 (Miss D Mountain) *in rr: styd on over 1f out: nvr on terms* **40/1**	60
	8	nk	**Lock 'N' Load (IRE)** 2-9-0 0 ... TomEaves 1 (B Smart) *sn outpcd: sme hdwy over 1f out: nvr a factor* **16/1**	59
	9	1	**Jessica Mary (IRE)** 2-9-0 0 ... DavidAllan 10 (D Carroll) *outpcd and bhd: edgd lft and kpt on appr fnl f* **40/1**	56
33	10	2 1/4	**Gassal**[19] [2691] 2-9-0 0 ... (b[1]) RHills 5 (W J Haggas) *prom: drvn 2f out: edgd lft and wknd over 1f out* **7/2**[2]	49
00	11	4 1/2	**Sonett**[15] [2821] 2-9-0 0 ... DeanMcKeown 13 (A J McCabe) *swvd rt s: t.k.h in midfield: effrt on outer 2f out: wandered and sn wknd* **33/1**	36
0	12	3	**Senora Verde**[41] [2035] 2-8-11 0 ... JamieMoriarty(3) 3 (P T Midgley) *mid-div: wkng on ins whn sltly hmpd 1f out* **100/1**	27

1m 19.01s (2.11) **Going Correction** -0.025s/f (Good) 12 Ran SP% **121.7**

Speed ratings (Par 90): **84,82,82,80,80 79,78,77,76,73 67,63**

toteswinger: 1&2 £9.30, 1&3 £7.50, 2&3 £6.20 CSF £65.83 TOTE £8.50: £2.50, £2.70, £1.60; EX 66.00.

Owner Joe Sankey & Ray Bailey **Bred** J Sankey **Trained** Middleham Moor, N Yorks

FOCUS

An ordinary maiden fillies' race with the first nine stacked up at the line. The race has been rated through the winner's upgraded second.

NOTEBOOK

Harriet's Girl, drawn on the inside, stuck to the rail and the gap came at just the right time. (tchd 8-1)

Desert Sunset, drawn in double figures, stuck on in willing fashion but in the end was held. She will be suited by a step up to seven and should find a race. (op 12-1 tchd 14-1)

Mutually Mine(USA), a decent type, was well supported and had clearly improved for her debut effort. She fought off several challengers but had to settle for third spot in the end. She will improve again. (op 11-2)

Wohaida(IRE), a narrow type, is not the best of walkers. Drawn wide, she was found lacking comong to the final furlong. (op 9-4)

Pacific Bay(IRE), who is not that big, did not look right in her coat. She ran her race to the pound on Redcar form with the winner. (op 14-1)

Gower Valentine, drawn towards the outside, was always having to race wide. At least this opens up the nursery route. (op 14-1)

Tamarah, who had two handlers, stayed on late in the day and is crying out for a step up to seven. (tchd 33-1)

Gassal, who finished ahead of the fourth at Folkestone, was on her toes in the paddock in first-time blinkers. She was flat out going into the home turn and soon dropped away. Official explanation: trainer had no explanation for the poor form shown

Sonett Official explanation: jockey said filly hung right

3293 TOTEEXACTA FILLIES' H'CAP 1m 4y

2:40 (2:40) (Class 5) (0-70,68) 3-Y-0+ **£3,238** (£963; £481; £240) **Stalls** Low

Form				RPR
2-02	1		**Luck Will Come (IRE)**[24] [2533] 4-9-2 **61** ... JackMitchell(5) 5 (H J Collingridge) *trckd ldr: styd on to ld fnl 75yds* **9/2**[2]	67
-330	2	3/4	**Flying Time**[34] [2244] 3-9-4 **68** ... DarryllHolland 6 (M R Channon) *led: qcknd over 3f out: hdde and no ex ins fnl f* **6/1**	70
510	3	1	**Shosolosa (IRE)**[15] [2846] 6-8-7 **54** ... StacyRenwick(7) 4 (R C Guest) *s.s: hdwy on wd outside over 2f out: styd on wl ins fnl f* **7/1**	56
1244	4	nk	**Granary**[18] [2718] 4-10-0 **68** ... DaneO'Neill 1 (H Candy) *trckd ldrs: effrt over 1f out: kpt on same pce ins fnl f* **2/1**[1]	69
-056	5	1 1/4	**Onatopp (IRE)**[11] [2925] 4-9-6 **60** ... DavidAllan 3 (T D Easterby) *prom: shkn up over 4f out: effrt on ins over 1f out: kpt on same pce* **11/2**[3]	58
0555	6	3/4	**Malinsa Blue (IRE)**[15] [2841] 6-8-11 **58** ... LanceBetts(7) 9 (B Ellison) *w ldrs on outer: t.k.h: drvn 3f out: outpcd over 1f out: styd on ins fnl f* **15/2**	54
0-66	7	12	**The Hoofer (IRE)**[12] [2922] 3-8-2 **52** ow2 ... RoystonFfrench 7 (J L Dunlop) *chsd ldrs: outpcd over 2f out: sn lost pl and bhd* **11/1**	19

1m 48.41s (2.51) **Going Correction** -0.025s/f (Good)

WFA 3 from 4yo+ 10lb 7 Ran SP% **113.8**

Speed ratings (Par 100): **86,85,84,83,82 81,69**

toteswinger: 1&2 £3.40, 1&3 £4.80, 2&3 £5.40 CSF £30.79 CT £184.82 TOTE £4.20: £2.20, £3.00; EX 21.20.

Owner Greenstead Hall Racing **Bred** Mull Enterprises Ltd **Trained** Exning, Suffolk

FOCUS

A modest fillies-only handicap run at a steady pace with all but one of the seven runners in with a shout in the home straight.

3294 TOTEQUADPOT H'CAP 1m 2f 6y

3:10 (3:12) (Class 3) (0-90,90) 3-Y-0+

£9,346 (£2,799; £1,399; £700; £349; £175) **Stalls** Low

Form				RPR
16-	1		**Envisage (IRE)**[239] [6490] 4-9-10 **86** ... JamieSpencer 4 (Saeed Bin Suroor) *trckd ldrs: effrt over 3f out: hrd rdn and styd on to ld cl home* **7/2**[2]	100+
21-2	2	1/2	**Kaateb (IRE)**[38] [2120] 5-9-11 **87** ... RHills 5 (W J Haggas) *trckd ldrs: bmpd and led wl ins fnl f: hdd fnl strides* **4/5**[1]	100
21-	3	3/4	**Detonator (IRE)**[227] [6737] 3-8-13 **87** ... RoystonFfrench 11 (M Johnston) *led: edgd rt and hdd wl ins fnl f: no ex* **12/1**	98
0024	4	4 1/2	**Peruvian Prince (USA)**[16] [2784] 6-9-5 **84** ... JamieMoriarty(3) 8 (R A Fahey) *in rr: effrt over 2f out: kpt on: nvr nr ldrs* **7/1**[3]	86+
6150	5	1/2	**Veiled Applause**[8] [3046] 5-9-3 **86** ... BMcHugh(7) 10 (J J Quinn) *mid-div: hdwy to chse ldrs 4f out: one pce fnl 2f* **12/1**	87
050-	6	5	**Persian Peril**[309] [4617] 4-8-12 **74** ... PaulMulrennan 9 (G A Swinbank) *trckd ldrs: effrt over 2f out: wknd over 1f out* **50/1**	65
03-4	7	1 1/4	**Dium Mac**[30] [2379] 7-8-9 **76** ... NeilBrown(5) 7 (N Bycroft) *awkward to load: stdd s: hdwy on outside 6f out: lost pl 2f out* **28/1**	65
21-0	8	5	**Abydos**[17] [2764] 4-9-2 **78** ... TPQueally 3 (A P Stringer) *hld up in rr: brief effrt over 2f out: sn lost pl* **25/1**	57
1-00	9	21	**Fantastic Morning**[13] [2895] 4-8-12 **74** ... TomEaves 12 (F Jordan) *trckd ldrs: lost pl 3f out: sn bhd* **66/1**	11

2m 14.74s (1.04) **Going Correction** -0.025s/f (Good)

WFA 3 from 4yo+ 12lb 9 Ran SP% **116.4**

Speed ratings (Par 107): **94,93,93,89,89 85,84,80,63**

toteswinger: 1&2 £2.40, 1&3 £5.10, 2&3 £2.90 CSF £6.53 CT £28.27 TOTE £4.50: £1.30, £1.20, £2.00; EX 8.00.

Owner Godolphin **Bred** Kilfrush Stud **Trained** Newmarket, Suffolk

FOCUS

A good-class handicap with the runner-up dividing two less exposed types.

NOTEBOOK

Envisage(IRE), a debut winner at Nottingham in October on the first of his two starts at three, is a grand, big type who is now a gelding. Looking really well, he had to dig very deep, his rider changing his whip hand no less than three times in a blink of the eye, but in the end he got there. He will be suited by a step up to 1m4f and should continue to give a good account of himself. (tchd 5-1)

Kaateb(IRE), who like so many of his stablemates at present looked a picture of health, was racing from a 2lb higher mark. He got into a bumping match with Detonator on his inside and they were both mugged on their outside by Envisage. (op Evens tchd 8-11)

Detonator(IRE), off the mark with a wide-margin success on his second start on the All-Weather at Wolverhampton in November, made his handicap debut from a stiff-looking mark. He set the pace but his inexperience showed as he rolled off the rail inside the last, bumping Kaateb and gifting Envisage a golden opportunity. This should have taught him plenty. (op 15-2)

Peruvian Prince(USA), 3lb higher, had the quick ground he needs but he never entered the argument. (op 10-1)

Veiled Applause, 7lb higher than his last success, was simply not up to the task. (op 11-1 tchd 10-1)

3295 TOTESWINGER PONTEFRACT CASTLE STKS (LISTED RACE) 1m 4f 8y

3:40 (3:40) (Class 1) 4-Y-0+ **£16,824** (£6,405; £3,207; £1,602; £801) **Stalls** Low

Form				RPR
0412	1		**Tranquil Tiger**[22] [2625] 4-9-4 116 ... TPQueally 6 (H R A Cecil) *led: qcknd 3f out: sn clr: rdn ins fnl f: styd on* **1/3**[1]	106+
0-20	2	1 1/2	**Dunaskin (IRE)**[22] [2625] 8-9-1 99 ... TomEaves 2 (B Ellison) *trckd ldrs: drvn over 4f out: wnt 2nd over 1f out: kpt on wl ins fnl f* **12/1**[3]	101
3-36	3	16	**Alfie Flits**[37] [2169] 6-9-1 105 ... JimCrowley 4 (G A Swinbank) *trckd wnr: drvn over 4f out: wknd over 1f out* **7/2**[2]	75
-000	4	21	**Hanella (IRE)**[22] [2625] 5-8-10 80 ... NickyMackay 3 (S C Williams) *trckd ldrs: pushed along over 5f out: wl outpcd 3f out: sn lost tch* **50/1**	37
63-0	5	74	**Lost Soldier Three (IRE)**[22] [2625] 7-9-1 100 ... AdrianTNicholls 8 (D Nicholls) *hld up: jnd ldrs after 2f: drvn over 5f out: sn lost pl: t.o 2f out: virtually p.u* **25/1**	—

2m 37.12s (-3.68) **Going Correction** -0.025s/f (Good) 5 Ran SP% **110.7**

Speed ratings (Par 111): **111,110,99,85,36**

toteswinger: 1&2 £4.70 CSF £5.76 TOTE £1.30: £1.10, £3.20; EX 4.60.

Owner K Abdulla **Bred** Juddmonte Farms Ltd **Trained** Newmarket, Suffolk

FOCUS

The winner had a clear chance in this depleted field but in the end he had to be kept right up to his work.

NOTEBOOK

Tranquil Tiger, who really took the eye beforehand, had things his own way. He was at least eight lengths clear once in line for home but, idling, he had to be ridden out near the line. (op 1-2)

Dunaskin(IRE), who had 8lb to find, adopted different tactics than usual with the winner determined to lead. He really knuckled down and, sent in pursuit of the clear leader, he was closing the gap all the way to the line. (op 14-1)

Alfie Flits, who took this in 2006, again disappointed and in the end struggled to cross the finishing line. (op 11-4 tchd 4-1)

Hanella(IRE), asked a stiff question in three previous starts for this stable this year, was again totally out of her class but she did manage to achieve some black type. (tchd 66-1)

Lost Soldier Three(IRE) again ran badly on just his second start for this yard. He stopped completely going into the home turn and must surely have a major problem. (op 14-1)

3296 TOTETRIFECTA PONTEFRACT CUP (H'CAP) 2m 1f 216y

4:10 (4:10) (Class 4) (0-85,77) 4-Y-0+ **£5,180** (£1,541; £770; £384) **Stalls** Low

Form				RPR
3-02	1		**Aphorism**[13] [2888] 5-9-9 **75** ... JamieSpencer 8 (J R Fanshawe) *hld up in rr: hdwy 5f out: effrt over 2f out: hung lft over 1f out: kpt on to ld towards fin* **11/4**[1]	83
0004	2	1/2	**Thewhirlingdervish (IRE)**[13] [2888] 10-9-2 **68** ... DavidAllan 4 (T D Easterby) *trckd ldrs: chal 3f out: led over 1f out: crowded ins fnl f: hdd towards fin* **4/1**[2]	75
0-24	3	3	**Go Amwell**[23] [2567] 5-8-5 **57** oh1 ... LiamJones 2 (J R Jenkins) *in rr: hdwy 3f out: edgd lft and styd on appr fnl f* **9/2**[3]	61
142-	4	1 3/4	**Estate**[40] [6875] 6-9-9 **75** ... DaneO'Neill 3 (E J O'Neill) *mid-div: effrt 4f out: sltly hmpd 2f out: one pce* **11/2**	77
2210	5	7	**Mister Arjay (USA)**[22] [2628] 8-9-8 **74** ... TonyHamilton 5 (B Ellison) *led tl 10f out: led again 3f out tl over 1f out: sn wknd* **10/1**	69
000/	6	1	**Keelung (USA)**[604] [5942] 7-9-2 **68** ... PaulMulrennan 9 (R Ford) *trckd ldrs: t.k.h: led 10f out: sn clr: hdd 3f out: wknd over 1f out* **50/1**	61
101	7	21	**Rock 'N' Roller (FR)**[13] [2888] 4-9-10 **77** ... DO'Donohoe 11 (W R Muir) *hld up in rr: hdwy 6f out: drvn 4f out: wknd over 1f out: eased* **4/1**[2]	47
5000	8	7	**Great As Gold (IRE)**[13] [2888] 9-8-10 **62** ... (b) FergalLynch 7 (B Ellison) *in rr: drvn 5f out: nvr on terms* **18/1**	25

2/03 9 6 **Stolen Light (IRE)**[24] 2525 7-8-10 **62**..........(b) TomEaves 10 18
(A Crook) *chsd ldrs: lost pl over 2f out: sn bhd* **66/1**

4m 4.87s (0.97) **Going Correction** -0.025s/f (Good)
WFA 4 from 5yo+ 1lb 9 Ran SP% **118.0**
Speed ratings (Par 105): **96,95,94,93,90 90,80,77,75**
toteswinger: 1&2 £3.70, 1&3 £4.00, 2&3 £4.60 CSF £14.22 CT £48.26 TOTE £3.60: £1.60, £1.50, £2.10; EX 13.20 Trifecta £51.20 Pool: £374.04 - 5.40 winning units..
Owner Dr Catherine Wills **Bred** St Clare Hall Stud **Trained** Newmarket, Suffolk
■ Stewards' Enquiry : Jamie Spencer one-day ban: careless riding (Jul 6)

FOCUS
A sound gallop and a true test of stamina. The form looks sound at this level.
Keelung(USA) Official explanation: jockey said gelding ran too free

3297 BET TOTEPOOL ON ALL UK RACING MAIDEN STKS 1m 4f 8y
4:40 (4:41) (Class 5) 3-Y-O **£3,238** (£963; £481; £240) **Stalls** Low

Form RPR
-525 1 **Dalhaan (USA)**[20] 2669 3-9-3 **90**.......... RHills 1 82
(J L Dunlop) *trckd ldrs: effrt and swtchd rt 3f out: hung lft and led over 1f out: drvn clr ins fnl f* **4/5**[1]
4 2 3 1/2 **Motarid (USA)**[23] 2573 3-9-3 0.......... PaulMulrennan 8 76
(T D Walford) *hld up in mid-div: hdwy 4f out: styd on to go 2nd ins fnl f: no imp* **11/1**
3 2 3/4 **Boucheron** 3-8-12 0.......... TonyHamilton 2 67
(R A Fahey) *in rr: sn pushed along: hdwy over 3f out: styd on fnl f: tk 3rd nr fin* **20/1**
0-2 4 1 **Cherokee Star**[23] 2573 3-9-3 0.......... SamHitchcott 6 70
(C C Bealby) *led tl over 1f out: one pce* **9/1**[3]
0 5 4 1/2 **Ask Nicely**[20] 2681 3-8-12 0.......... DO'Donohoe 5 58
(W R Muir) *stdd s: t.k.h in rr: hdwy over 5f out: sn chsng ldrs: hung rt and wknd over 1f out* **14/1**
3 6 9 **Indian Groom (IRE)**[36] 2207 3-9-3 0.......... TomEaves 4 48
(J Howard Johnson) *s.i.s: sn chsng ldrs: drvn 4f out: wknd over 1f out* **5/2**[2]
0 7 29 **Faraway Bay**[7] 3058 3-8-12 0.......... DaneO'Neill 7 —
(E J O'Neill) *in rr: hdwy to chse ldrs over 5f out: lost pl over 3f out: sn bhd* **66/1**
0- 8 1 **Panamar Besar (IRE)**[365] 2888 3-9-3 0.......... PaulFessey 3 —
(J Howard Johnson) *w ldr: wknd over 3f out: sn bhd* **100/1**
0-F0 9 1 1/4 **Jontobel**[35] 2221 3-9-3 0.......... AndrewElliott 9 —
(Jedd O'Keeffe) *trckd ldrs: reminders 5f out: lost pl 3f out: sn bhd* **150/1**

2m 40.8s **Going Correction** -0.025s/f (Good) 9 Ran SP% **117.0**
Speed ratings (Par 99): **99,96,94,94,91 85,65,65,64**
toteswinger: 1&2 £3.10, 1&3 £6.50, 2&3 £13.70 CSF £11.76 TOTE £1.70: £1.10, £3.10, £3.60; EX 12.60.
Owner Hamdan Al Maktoum **Bred** Shadwell Farm LLC **Trained** Arundel, W Sussex
■ Stewards' Enquiry : R Hills one-day ban: careless riding (Jul 6)

FOCUS
A modest maiden and the winner ran nowhere near his official mark of 90.
Ask Nicely Official explanation: jockey said filly hung right-handed throughout

3298 PAUL BINGLEY MEMORIAL H'CAP 6f
5:10 (5:12) (Class 5) (0-75,74) 3-Y-O **£3,238** (£963; £481; £240) **Stalls** Low

Form RPR
3330 1 **Koraleva Tectona (IRE)**[28] 2429 3-8-11 **64**.......... PaulEddery 8 79
(Pat Eddery) *hld up: gd hdwy on wd outside 2f out: led jst ins fnl f: pushed clr* **3/1**[1]
1-50 2 5 **Gainshare**[43] 1988 3-8-9 **67**.......... NeilBrown(5) 4 64
(T D Barron) *led tl hdd jst ins fnl f: no ex* **20/1**
5421 3 1/2 **Leonid Glow**[6] 3086 3-9-3 **70** 6ex.......... FergalLynch 2 65
(M Dods) *trckd ldrs: chal over 1f out: kpt on same pce* **9/2**[3]
6433 4 3 3/4 **Splash The Cash**[30] 2366 3-8-7 **60**.......... DO'Donohoe 5 43
(K A Ryan) *wnt rt s: mid-div: effrt over 2f out: kpt on fnl f* **8/1**
2212 5 3/4 **Rio Sands**[18] 2732 3-9-2 **72**.......... MichaelJStainton(3) 7 53
(R M Whitaker) *chsd ldrs: one pce appr fnl f* **4/1**[2]
-204 6 3 **Connor's Choice**[10] 2976 3-9-7 **74**.......... AlanDaly 10 45
(Andrew Turnell) *prom: wknd appr fnl f* **10/1**
02- 7 6 **Red Skipper (IRE)**[232] 6635 3-8-2 **60**.......... DanielleMcCreery(5) 9 12
(N Wilson) *rrd s: hld up in rr: nvr a factor* **25/1**
300- 8 3 3/4 **Warners Bay (IRE)**[221] 6813 3-8-10 **63**.......... DarrenWilliams 3 3
(R Bastiman) *s.i.s: mid-div: lost pl 2f out* **40/1**
2351 9 5 **Everything**[4] 3144 3-9-1 **71** 6ex.......... JamieMoriarty(3) 1 —
(P T Midgley) *in rr: drvn and sme hdwy 2f out: sn wknd* **13/2**
0240 10 1/2 **Tanley**[8] 3030 3-8-5 **58** ow1..........(p) AdrianTNicholls 11 —
(J F Coupland) *chsd ldrs on outside: hung lft and lost pl over 1f out* **50/1**
60-3 11 13 **Planet Queen**[26] 2490 3-8-4 **57**..........(v[1]) AndrewElliott 6 —
(K R Burke) *hmpd s: in rr: bhd fnl 2f* **13/2**

1m 17.2s (0.30) **Going Correction** -0.025s/f (Good) 11 Ran SP% **123.1**
Speed ratings (Par 99): **97,90,89,84,83 79,71,66,60,59 42**
toteswinger: 1&2 £31.60, 1&3 £7.10, 2&3 £28.10 CSF £71.41 CT £284.08 TOTE £4.50: £1.80, £3.40, £2.30; EX 77.90 Place 6 £17.40,Place 5 £7.37.
Owner Pat Eddery Racing (Ramruma) **Bred** Cathal Ryan **Trained** Nether Winchendon, Bucks

FOCUS
A weak, low-grade sprint handicap but a ready and much improved winner.
Tanley Official explanation: jockey said gelding lost its action
Planet Queen Official explanation: jockey said filly lost its action
T/Plt: £22.60 to a £1 stake. Pool: £74,923.00. 2,418.05 winning tickets. T/Qpdt: £3.00 to a £1 stake. Pool: £6,860.00. 1,665.15 winning tickets. WG

3299 - 3305a (Foreign Racing) - See Raceform Interactive

DORTMUND (R-H)
Sunday, June 22

OFFICIAL GOING: Good

3306a GROSSER PREIS DER WIRTSCHAFT (GROUP 3) 1m 2f
4:15 (4:28) 3-Y-O+ **£23,529** (£7,353; £3,676; £2,206)

RPR
1 **Wiesenpfad (FR)**[35] 5-9-5.......... ADeVries 7 113
(W Hickst, Germany) *hld up: last st: hdwy on outside to ld 1f out: rdn out* **2/1**[1]
2 1 **Redolent (IRE)**[24] 2544 3-8-3.......... JimmyQuinn 1 107
(R Hannon) *led to 1f out: kpt on one pce u.p* **32/10**[3]
3 1 1/4 **Shrek (GER)**[35] 2230 4-9-5.......... EPedroza 5 109
(A Wohler, Germany) *hld up: hdwy and 4th st: r.o same pce fnl f* **3/1**[2]
4 1/2 **Rosenreihe (IRE)**[21] 2655 3-7-13.......... FilipMinarik 2 100
(P Schiergen, Germany) *disp 2nd fr 1 1/2-way: 2nd st: one pce fnl 2f* **2/1**[1]
5 nk **Allanit (GER)**[35] 4-9-1.......... ShaneKelly 6 103
(J Hirschberger, Germany) *racd in 4th to st: one pce fr over 1f out* **15/1**
6 13 **Estejo (GER)**[42] 2027 4-9-1.......... DPorcu 4 77
(R Rohne, Germany) *5th st: bhd fr over 1f out* **19/1**
7 32 **Lord Hill (GER)**[28] 2440 4-9-3.......... J-PCarvalho 8 15
(C Zeitz) *trckd ldr: 3rd st: sn wknd: t.o* **24/1**

2m 4.53s (124.53)
WFA 3 from 4yo+ 12lb 7 Ran SP% **130.7**
TOTE: WIN 30; PL 14, 17, 16; SF 134.
Owner Frau Heide Harzheim **Bred** Gestut Ravensberg **Trained** Germany

NOTEBOOK
Redolent(IRE) tried to make every yard and picked up well from the turn in, but he was caught inside the last. Softer ground would have suited him.

2880 MUNICH (L-H)
Sunday, June 22

OFFICIAL GOING: Good

3307a GROSSER CANON-PREIS - RIEMER STEHER TROPHY (LISTED RACE) 1m 6f
4:35 (4:42) 4-Y-O+ **£8,824** (£3,235; £1,765; £882)

RPR
1 **Sereth (IRE)**[31] 2346 5-9-4.......... OPeslier 1 103
(J Hirschberger, Germany)
2 1/2 **Ryan (IRE)**[50] 5-9-4.......... DMoffatt 8 102
(J Hanacek, Czech Republic)
3 1 1/2 **Sapiranga (GER)**[294] 4-8-7.......... RPiechulek 6 89
(Frau Marion Rotering, Germany)
4 1/2 **Alleviate (IRE)**[24] 2525 4-8-10.......... HayleyTurner 3 91
(Sir Mark Prescott) *trckd ldr: rdn 2f out: ev ch 1f out: wknd clsng stages* **18/10**[1]
5 hd **Emporio (GER)**[31] 2346 4-9-4.......... ASchikora 7 99
(P Schiergen, Germany)
6 1 **Prince Troy (GER)**[1008] 9-8-8.......... BClos 5 88
(Werner Glanz, Germany)
7 hd **Romanoff (GER)**[28] 2442 5-9-1..........(b) SteveDrowne 2 94
(M Weiss, Switzerland)

3m 1.80s (181.80) 7 Ran SP% **35.7**
TOTE: WIN 23; PL 14, 13, 16; SF 100.
Owner Gestut Schlenderhan **Bred** Gestut Schlenderhan **Trained** Germany

NOTEBOOK
Alleviate(IRE), who won a handicap off 80 last time out, came close to gaining some black type and is likely to continue to be campaigned with that target in mind.

3308 - (Foreign Racing) - See Raceform Interactive

2987 CHEPSTOW (L-H)
Monday, June 23

OFFICIAL GOING: Good to firm (9.5)
Wind: Nil Weather: Fine

3309 JENKINSONS CATERERS (S) STKS 5f 16y
6:50 (6:51) (Class 6) 2-Y-O **£1,748** (£520; £260; £129) **Stalls** High

Form RPR
1 **Royal Raider** 2-8-6 0.......... FergusSweeney 3 63+
(W S Kittow) *led for 2f: w ldr: led wl over 1f out: edgd lft ins fnl f: rdn and r.o* **17/2**[3]
2 1 1/4 **Mythical Blue (IRE)** 2-8-11 0.......... DeanMcKeown 9 64+
(P A Blockley) *w ldr: led 3f out tl wl over 1f out: sn rdn: kpt on ins fnl f* **8/15**[1]
4230 3 6 **Dazzling Dust (IRE)**[28] 2450 2-8-4 0.......... WilliamCarson(7) 10 42
(W G M Turner) *hld up in tch: rdn and one pce fnl 2f* **11/2**[2]
4 2 1/4 **Lavender Girl** 2-8-6 0.......... LiamJones 6 29
(P Winkworth) *mid-div: pushed along 3f out: no real prog fnl 2f* **20/1**
5205 5 1/2 **Syrup (IRE)**[28] 2459 2-8-6 0.......... CatherineGannon 7 27
(P D Evans) *hld up in rr: pushed along over 2f out: rdn wl over 1f out: kpt on same pce fnl f* **16/1**
0050 6 1/2 **Forzando Bloom**[7] 3091 2-8-11 0.......... TGMcLaughlin 4 30
(R A Harris) *hld up in mid-div: rdn and wknd over 1f out* **33/1**
0 7 3/4 **Miss Leona**[9] 3019 2-8-6 0.......... PaulFitzsimons 2 23
(J M Bradley) *w ldrs: rdn over 2f out: wknd over 1f out* **50/1**
62 8 shd **Inn Swinger (IRE)**[19] 2720 2-7-13 0.......... AshleyMorgan(7) 8 22
(W G M Turner) *hld up and bhd: hdwy over 3f out: rdn and wknd over 1f out* **16/1**
9 4 1/2 **Frame And Cover** 2-8-3 0.......... KevinGhunowa(3) 5 6
(R A Harris) *s.i.s: a in rr: rdn and no ch whn flashed tail over 1f out* **50/1**
10 11 **Rahzeena** 2-8-6 0.......... PatrickDonaghy(5) 1 —
(P Leech) *s.i.s: a in rr* **14/1**

60.10 secs (0.80) **Going Correction** -0.475s/f (Firm) 10 Ran SP% **121.2**
Speed ratings (Par 91): **74,72,62,58,58 57,56,55,48,31**
toteswinger: 1&2 £3.80, 1&3 £12.10, 2&3 £2.20 CSF £13.65 TOTE £9.90: £3.00, £1.10, £1.60; EX 38.90.The winner was sold to David Evans for 7,200gns. Mythical Blue was claimed by S C Williams for £6,000
Owner K B Hodges **Bred** Mrs Shelley Dwyer **Trained** Blackborough, Devon

FOCUS
Two came clear in a race lacking depth, with the poor sixth holding down the form. A very slow time, even for a two-year-old seller.

NOTEBOOK
Royal Raider, a cheap daughter of Piccolo, comes from a yard who introduced a newcomer to score recently and she looked one of the hot favourite's biggest dangers. Quickly into stride, she showed tons of early pace and started to pull away from the favourite over a furlong out. The fact the pair were clear bodes well and she looks capable of winning at a higher level. David Evans bought her for 7,200gns. (op 8-1 tchd 15-2 and 11-1)
Mythical Blue(IRE) is related to plenty of winners and it looked significant that he was gambled into 8/15 on this racecourse debut. He knew his job and soon had the rail, but the filly was simply too fast for him and he could not match her. He was clear of the third though and will now race for Stuart Williams, having been claimed for £6,000. (op 10-11 after evens in places and 11-10 in a place)
Dazzling Dust(IRE) is exposed and it was no surprise two newcomers proved too good. He is going to continue to struggle. (op 4-1 tchd 13-2)

Lavender Girl, who cost just £600, was introduced at the right level and she made some late headway. The experience should not be lost on her. (op 16-1)

Syrup(IRE) is another exposed at this level and winning is not going to be easy for her. (op 14-1 tchd 18-1)

3310 DIGIBET.CO.UK MAIDEN STKS — 1m 4f 23y

7:20 (7:21) (Class 5) 3-Y-0+ — **£2,590** (£770; £385; £192) **Stalls** Low

Form				RPR
-242	1		**Manyriverstocross (IRE)**[28] 2454 3-8-12 87 ..... EddieAhern 6 (A King) *mde all: shkn up over 1f out: pushed clr fnl f: comf* **4/11**[1]	86
06	2	6	**Nisaal (IRE)**[37] 2191 3-8-12 0 ..... FergusSweeney 10 (J L Dunlop) *hld up and bhd: hdwy over 3f out: rdn and chsd wnr over 2f out: no imp* **13/2**[2]	76
0-	3	2 ¾	**Special Branch Ami (IRE)**[285] 5337 3-8-12 0 ..... ShaneKelly 8 (C R Egerton) *hld up and bhd: sme hdwy on ins over 3f out: rdn over 2f out: styd on fnl f: nvr nrr* **25/1**	72
06	4	2 ¾	**Requia**[21] 2668 3-8-7 0 ..... DaneO'Neill 9 (H Candy) *prom: chsd wnr after 3f: rdn 3f out: wknd over 1f out* **25/1**	62
56-	5	2	**Manalito**[236] 6592 3-8-12 0 ..... DarryllHolland 5 (M R Channon) *prom: rdn 3f out: sn wknd* **15/2**[3]	64
	6	4 ½	**Yes Sir (IRE)**[68] 9-9-12 0 ..... VinceSlattery 12 (P Bowen) *s.s: rcvrd to join ldrs after 2f: rdn over 3f out: sn wknd* **12/1**	57
600-	7	5	**No Nukes**[228] 6737 3-8-12 43 ..... TGMcLaughlin 13 (P D Evans) *hld up and bhd: struggling whn rdn over 5f out* **50/1**	49?
0/	8	2 ¼	**Lockstone Lad (USA)**[56] 1439 5-9-12 0 ..... SimonWhitworth 2 (M S Saunders) *s.i.s: rdn over 3f out: a in rr* **100/1**	45?
-360	9	shd	**Snake Hips**[149] 322 4-9-12 38 ..... CatherineGannon 7 (B Palling) *chsd wnr 2f: prom tl rdn and wknd over 3f out* **40/1**	45?

2m 35.73s (-3.27) **Going Correction** -0.275s/f (Firm)
WFA 3 from 4yo+ 14lb — **9** Ran SP% **119.2**
Speed ratings (Par 103): **99,95,93,91,90 87,83,82,82**
toteswinger: 1&2 £1.50, 1&3 £5.80, 2&3 £31.70 CSF £3.28 TOTE £1.50: £1.02, £1.60, £6.30; EX 3.90.

Owner Mrs M C Sweeney **Bred** Crone Stud Farms Ltd **Trained** Barbury Castle, Wilts

FOCUS

A modest maiden which was not strongly run. The winner faced a straightforward task and the form makes a lot of sense amongst the first four.

3311 ROBERT PRICE BUILDERS MERCHANTS LTD H'CAP — 1m 2f 36y

7:50 (7:50) (Class 5) (0-75,75) 4-Y-0+ — **£3,238** (£963; £481; £240) **Stalls** Low

Form				RPR
3223	1		**Friends Hope**[28] 2453 7-9-4 75 ..... KevinGhunowa(3) 6 (P A Blockley) *s.i.s: hld up and bhd: stdy hdwy over 4f out: wnt 2nd over 2f out: sn rdn and edgd lft: led jst over 1f out: r.o* **3/1**[2]	83
44-4	2	1 ½	**Adorabella (IRE)**[22] 2641 5-8-8 62 ..... FergusSweeney 1 (A King) *hld up in tch: chsd ldr over 3f out tl over 2f out: swtchd rt over 1f out: chsd wnr fnl f: kpt on* **5/2**[1]	67
-500	3	2 ¼	**Garafena**[21] 2682 5-8-11 65 ..... TQuinn 2 (B G Powell) *hld up and bhd: hdwy over 3f out: rdn over 2f out: styd on same pce fnl f* **6/1**	65
-164	4	nk	**Celticello (IRE)**[10] 2990 6-9-5 73 ..... StephenDonohoe 3 (P D Evans) *hld up and bhd: rdn over 2f out: hdwy over 1f out: styd on same pce fnl f* **5/1**[3]	72
4150	5	4	**Davenport (IRE)**[14] 2897 6-9-1 74 .....(p) JamesMillman(5) 8 (B R Millman) *hld up and bhd: rdn over 2f out: nvr trbld ldrs* **11/2**	65
20/0	6	¾	**Spence Appeal (IRE)**[10] 2990 6-8-2 56 oh4 ..... FrancisNorton 7 (C Roberts) *t.k.h: chsd ldr tl over 3f out: rdn and wknd over 2f out* **16/1**	46
-620	7	hd	**Queen Excalibur**[10] 2990 9-7-9 56 oh1 ..... DavidProbert(7) 5 (C Roberts) *led: clr over 5f out: rdn and hdd over 1f out: wknd ins fnl f* **16/1**	46
000-	8	26	**Lights Of Vegas**[348] 3429 4-8-5 59 ..... CatherineGannon 4 (S Kirk) *prom: pushed along over 4f out: wknd over 3f out: t.o* **28/1**	—

2m 9.39s (-1.21) **Going Correction** -0.275s/f (Firm) — **8** Ran SP% **115.1**
Speed ratings (Par 103): **93,91,90,89,86 85,85,65**
toteswinger: 1&2 £5.50, 1&3 £3.00, 2&3 £2.70 CSF £11.04 CT £41.01 TOTE £4.20: £1.40, £1.50, £2.00; EX 15.50.

Owner Mrs Joanna Hughes **Bred** Huish Bloodstock **Trained** Lambourn, Berks

FOCUS

A modest handicap. The winner defied a career-high mark to beat a couple of disappointing types.

3312 JENKINSONS CATERERS MAIDEN STKS — 1m 14y

8:20 (8:22) (Class 5) 3-Y-0+ — **£2,590** (£770; £385; £192) **Stalls** High

Form				RPR
33	1		**Light From Mars**[28] 2449 3-9-2 0 ..... DarryllHolland 1 (B R Millman) *a.p: led over 4f out: rdn over 1f out: hld on wl ins fnl f* **7/2**[2]	78
0-23	2	nk	**Victoria Reel**[24] 2566 3-8-11 78 ..... PatDobbs 4 (R Hannon) *hld up in tch: chsd wnr over 2f out: rdn over 1f out: kpt on ins fnl f but a hld* **4/5**[1]	72
46	3	4	**Addiena**[12] 2954 4-9-7 0 ..... CatherineGannon 5 (B Palling) *led: hdd over 4f out: rdn over 2f out: one pce* **25/1**	65
4-35	4	2 ¼	**Barliffey (IRE)**[19] 2714 3-9-2 75 ..... EddieAhern 8 (D J Coakley) *hld up: hdwy over 3f out: rdn over 2f out: one pce* **7/2**[2]	63
60	5	12	**Trireme (IRE)**[12] 2954 4-9-12 0 ..... GeorgeBaker 9 (K A Morgan) *t.k.h in rr: pushed along over 3f out: nvr nr ldrs: b.b.v* **33/1**	37
3-03	6	2 ½	**Street Devil (USA)**[17] 2786 3-8-13 75 ..... KevinGhunowa(3) 2 (P A Blockley) *plld hrd: chsd ldr over 3f: rdn and wknd over 2f out* **14/1**[3]	29
000-	7	2 ½	**Break Out**[312] 4533 4-9-12 42 .....(b[1]) StephenDonohoe 3 (J M Bradley) *sn wl in rr* **100/1**	26
060-	8	19	**Danjoe**[259] 6062 4-9-12 43 ..... VinceSlattery 6 (R Brotherton) *prom tl rdn and wknd over 3f out: t.o* **100/1**	—

1m 33.95s (-2.25) **Going Correction** -0.475s/f (Firm)
WFA 3 from 4yo 10lb — **8** Ran SP% **115.4**
Speed ratings (Par 103): **92,91,87,85,73 70,68,49**
toteswinger: 1&2 £1.10, 1&3 £11.90, 2&3 £3.20 CSF £6.69 TOTE £5.10: £1.30, £1.10, £3.00; EX 9.20.

Owner R K Arrowsmith **Bred** Harts Farm And Stud **Trained** Kentisbeare, Devon

FOCUS

Two came clear in what was a modest maiden, run at a steady pace. The winner and third are better guides to this than the runner-up.

Trireme(IRE) Official explanation: jockey said gelding bled from the nose

Street Devil(USA) Official explanation: jockey said colt ran too free

3313 JENKINSONS CATERERS H'CAP — 6f 16y

8:50 (8:52) (Class 5) (0-70,70) 3-Y-0+ — **£3,076** (£915; £457; £228) **Stalls** High

Form				RPR
6242	1		**Farthermost (IRE)**[10] 2991 3-9-7 70 ..... PatDobbs 8 (R Hannon) *a.p: hrd rdn fnl f: led last strides* **7/2**[1]	79
-325	2	hd	**Shakespeare's Son**[9] 3030 3-8-4 56 ..... DuranFentiman(3) 2 (H J Evans) *chsd ldr: rdn to ld over 1f out: hdd last strides* **16/1**	64
2460	3	¾	**Millfields Dreams**[2] 3271 9-9-2 63 .....(p) PatrickDonaghy(5) 4 (P Leech) *hld up and bhd: rdn and hdwy 2f out: r.o ins fnl f* **16/1**	71
1030	4	½	**Trinculo (IRE)**[12] 2950 11-9-4 65 .....(b) HaddenFrost(5) 17 (R A Harris) *led: rdn and hdd over 1f out: kpt on* **11/1**	71
6604	5	½	**Linda Green**[9] 3026 7-9-3 59 ..... DarryllHolland 1 (M R Channon) *hld up in mid-div: rdn over 3f out: hdwy over 1f out: kpt on ins fnl f* **10/1**[3]	64
0/01	6	shd	**Boldinor**[21] 2664 5-8-13 55 ..... FergusSweeney 7 (M R Bosley) *hld up in tch: rdn over 1f out: nt qckn ins fnl f* **14/1**	59
4553	7	¾	**Memphis Man**[10] 2992 5-9-7 70 ..... RichardEvans(7) 12 (P D Evans) *hld up in mid-div: rdn and hdwy over 1f out: nvr able to chal* **8/1**[2]	72
0550	8	1	**Harrison's Flyer (IRE)**[14] 2881 7-9-3 59 .....(p) HayleyTurner 3 (J M Bradley) *hld up in mid-div: hdwy over 1f out: rdn and one pce ins fnl f* **22/1**	58
004-	9	nk	**Castano**[258] 6083 4-9-1 62 ..... JamesMillman(5) 15 (B R Millman) *prom: rdn over 2f out: fdd ins fnl f* **20/1**	60
4514	10	¾	**Marko Jadeo (IRE)**[9] 3021 10-9-3 62 ..... KevinGhunowa(3) 5 (R A Harris) *hld up in mid-div: pushed along over 3f out: rdn 2f out: no rspnse* **14/1**	57
2151	11	½	**Shot To Fame (USA)**[9] 3033 9-10-0 70 ..... GeorgeBaker 11 (S Kirk) *hld up and bhd: shortlived effrt over 1f out* **7/2**[1]	64
60-0	12	½	**The Cayterers**[10] 2992 6-9-11 67 ..... DaneO'Neill 14 (J M Bradley) *s.i.s: bhd: pushed along whn nt clr run and swtchd lft wl over 1f out: nvr nr ldrs* **20/1**	59+
0-00	13	¾	**The Name Is Frank**[11] 2974 3-9-2 65 ..... EddieAhern 9 (J W Mullins) *rrd s: in rr: rdn 2f out: eased whn no ch ins fnl f* **28/1**	53
0520	14	½	**Exit Strategy (IRE)**[17] 2798 4-8-6 55 .....(b) DavidProbert(7) 10 (R A Harris) *hld up in mid-div: lost pl over 3f out: sn bhd* **11/1**	43
0300	15	½	**Nordic Light (USA)**[11] 2968 4-9-11 67 .....(b) WilliamBuick 13 (J M Bradley) *prom tl wknd 3f out* **33/1**	54
00-0	16	10	**High Ridge**[12] 2950 9-8-13 55 .....(p) ShaneKelly 16 (J M Bradley) *hld up and bhd: sme hdwy on stands' rail over 3f out: swtchd rt over 2f out: sn wknd* **33/1**	10

1m 10.55s (-2.35) **Going Correction** -0.475s/f (Firm)
WFA 3 from 4yo+ 7lb — **16** Ran SP% **129.6**
Speed ratings (Par 103): **96,95,94,94,93 93,92,90,90,89 88,88,87,86,85 72**
toteswinger: 1&2 £18.90, 1&3 £30.20, 2&3 £30.20 CSF £64.25 CT £831.22 TOTE £5.50: £1.40, £4.10, £4.00, £3.20; EX 92.10.

Owner Mill House Partnership **Bred** Myra Stud **Trained** East Everleigh, Wilts

FOCUS

A moderate handicap sprint with not much getting into it from the rear. The first two home were 3yos and the form seems sound.

The Name Is Frank Official explanation: jockey said gelding reared as stalls opened

3314 JENKINSONS FIRST CHOICE FOR HOSPITALITY FILLIES' H'CAP — 1m 14y

9:20 (9:23) (Class 5) (0-70,70) 3-Y-0 — **£3,076** (£915; £457; £228) **Stalls** High

Form				RPR
0-54	1		**Oriental Girl**[24] 2563 3-8-9 58 .....(p) DavidKinsella 4 (J A Geake) *a.p: led over 3f out: rdn over 1f out: r.o wl* **11/1**	68
000-	2	¾	**Sarah Park (IRE)**[282] 5423 3-8-7 56 ..... WilliamBuick 2 (B J Meehan) *hld up in rr: hdwy over 2f out: wnt 2nd over 1f out: sn rdn: kpt on ins fnl f: nt trble wnr* **10/1**	65+
-640	3	3 ¾	**Betonart**[18] 2756 3-8-5 54 ..... NelsonDeSouza 5 (R M Beckett) *hld up in tch: lost pl over 3f out: rdn and rallied wl over 1f out: kpt on one pce fnl f: tk 3rd nr fin* **12/1**	54
-046	4	nk	**Mrs Summersby (IRE)**[31] 2367 3-8-8 60 ..... TravisBlock(3) 1 (H Morrison) *hld up in mid-div: hdwy over 3f out: rdn and one pce fnl 2f: lost 3rd nr fin* **11/4**[1]	59
2404	5	2 ½	**Milanollo**[12] 2956 3-9-1 64 ..... HayleyTurner 7 (M L W Bell) *t.k.h: led: hdd over 3f out: rdn and wknd ins fnl f* **7/2**[3]	58
-040	6	1 ¼	**Croeso Cusan**[17] 2774 3-7-11 53 oh4 ow2 ..... SophieDoyle(7) 13 (J L Spearing) *prom tl rdn and wknd wl over 1f out* **66/1**	44
-003	7	hd	**Garland**[9] 3023 3-9-2 65 .....(t) PatDobbs 12 (R Hannon) *t.k.h early: hld up in mid-div: hdwy 3f out: rdn and wknd over 1f out* **3/1**[2]	55
45-0	8	2 ¼	**Gower Belle**[45] 1958 3-9-2 65 ..... DaneO'Neill 3 (W R Muir) *prom tl rdn and wknd over 1f out* **14/1**	50
030-	9	2 ½	**Ambrose Princess (IRE)**[187] 7182 3-8-0 56 ..... DavidProbert(7) 9 (R A Harris) *prom: pushed along and lost pl over 3f out: bhd fnl 2f* **25/1**	35
0316	10	5	**Carry On Cleo**[58] 1614 3-8-11 60 .....(vt) FrancisNorton 10 (D E Pipe) *a bhd* **14/1**	28
30-0	11	1 ¼	**Hawk Eyed Lady (IRE)**[18] 2757 3-9-7 70 ..... ShaneKelly 14 (J A Osborne) *a bhd* **25/1**	35

1m 33.17s (-3.03) **Going Correction** -0.475s/f (Firm) — **11** Ran SP% **121.5**
Speed ratings (Par 96): **96,95,91,91,88 87,87,85,82,77 76**
toteswinger: 1&2 £10.80, 1&3 not won, 2&3 £24.60 CSF £117.73 CT £1360.18 TOTE £12.80: £2.40, £4.10, £3.70; EX 100.30 Place 6 £ 29.33, Place 5 £ 26.17.

Owner Kimpton Down Partnership **Bred** Aston Mullins Stud And D J Erwin **Trained** Kimpton, Hants

FOCUS

An average contest in which the winner is rated up 8lb and the runner-up similar.

T/Plt: £76.30 to a £1 stake. Pool: £74,464.93. 712.40 winning tickets. T/Qpdt: £33.80 to a £1 stake. Pool: £4,273.29. 93.50 winning tickets. KH

3264 LINGFIELD (L-H)

Monday, June 23

OFFICIAL GOING: Standard

Wind: very modest half against Weather: partly cloudy, bright spells

3315 REGISTER NOW @ BETDAQPOKER.CO.UK MAIDEN STKS — 5f (P)

2:15 (2:16) (Class 5) 2-Y-0 — **£3,238** (£963; £481; £240) **Stalls** High

Form				RPR
	1		**Art Preview (USA)** 2-9-3 0 ..... GeorgeBaker 6 (G L Moore) *trckd ldrs: wnt 2nd over 2f out: led 1f out: sn in command: readily* **9/4**[2]	80+

62 **2** 2 ¾ **Timeteam (IRE)**[9] 3019 2-9-3 0 .... JamieSpencer 4 70
(S Kirk) *sn led: rdn 2f out: hdd 1f out: no ch w wnr* **4/7**[1]

00 **3** 4 **Mean Mr Mustard (IRE)**[10] 2999 2-9-3 0 .... ShaneKelly 3 56
(J A Osborne) *s.i.s: racd in midfield: rdn over 2f out: kpt on to go 3rd nr fin: nvr trbld ldng pair* **33/1**

4 ½ **Edith's Boy (IRE)** 2-9-3 0 .... IanMongan 1 54
(S Dow) *chsd ldrs on inner: chsd ldng pair wl over 1f out: wknd ent fnl f: lost 3rd nr fin* **33/1**

5 ¾ **Good Buy Dubai (USA)** 2-9-3 0 .... LPKeniry 7 51
(J R Best) *s.i.s: bhd: pushed along 1/2-way: rdn 2f out: nvr trbld ldrs* **12/1**[3]

00 **6** ½ **Mr Willis**[7] 3092 2-9-3 0 .... MohammedSaeed 8 49
(J R Best) *s.i.s: bhd: nvr trbld ldrs* **25/1**

0 **7** 1 ¾ **Usual Suspects**[13] 2903 2-8-12 0 .... AdamKirby 10 38
(Peter Grayson) *chsd ldr tl over 2f out: wd bnd 2f out: sn wknd* **33/1**

8 5 **Luvmedo (IRE)** 2-8-12 0 .... RichardSmith 2 20
(R Hannon) *v.s.a: a wl bhd* **16/1**

59.15 secs (0.35) **Going Correction** +0.075s/f (Slow) **8** Ran SP% **120.7**
Speed ratings (Par 93): **100,95,89,88,87 86,83,75**
toteswinger: 1&2 £4.40, 1&3 £11.20, 2&3 £4.90. CSF £3.97 TOTE £4.00: £1.20, £1.02, £6.00; EX 4.60 Trifecta £47.50 Pool: £694.95 - 10.82 winning units..
Owner R A Green **Bred** Ponchartrain Stud **Trained** Woodingdean, E Sussex

FOCUS
An uncompetitive maiden and a two-horse race according to the market. The pair dominated throughout and little else got into it, but the time was very good and the winner looks above average and capable of better.

NOTEBOOK
Art Preview(USA) ◆, a $40,000 yearling but a 50,000gns two-year-old, is a half-brother to five winners including some in France and Italy. The market suggested he was expected to run a big race against the odds-on favourite and he did just that, travelling supremely well up with the pace before finding plenty when asked to go and win his race. This was a smart debut and he should be capable of going on to better things. (op 2-1)
Timeteam(IRE), who already had form on the board, bounced out of the stalls and travelled strongly in front, but once his market rival was unleashed he was made to look very leaden-footed. He undoubtedly came up against a decent newcomer and it is probably best to measure this effort by how far he pulled clear of the others. (op 4-6 tchd 8-11 in places)
Mean Mr Mustard(IRE), well beaten in a couple of turf maidens, stayed on late to finish a remote third but was never going to get anywhere near the two market leaders. He has badly missed the break in all three of his starts now, so he may be capable of a bit more when he manages to hit the gates running especially as he has now shown that he does possess a modicum of ability.
Edith's Boy(IRE), a 6,000euros yearling but a 26,400euros two-year-old, is out of a half-sister to the useful juvenile sprinter Amazing Bay. He showed quite a bit of early pace before appearing to blow up and should come on a fair degree for the experience. (op 50-1)
Good Buy Dubai(USA), a $35,000 half-brother to three winning sprinters in the US, took a while to realise what was required but did show a small amount of ability late on. (op 16-1 tchd 20-1)
Luvmedo(IRE), a 125,000euros half-sister to two winners including Dress To Impress, lost all chance at the start on this debut and it is probably best to give her another chance. (op 20-1)

3316 MAUREEN BROOKER BIRTHDAY H'CAP 6f (P)
2:45 (2:45) (Class 6) (0-60,61) 3-Y-0+ **£2,047** (£604; £302) **Stalls** Low

Form RPR

2003 **1** **Regal Royale**[14] 2881 5-9-5 **54** .... (v) AdamKirby 10 65
(Peter Grayson) *sn rdn: chsd ldr over 4f out: led over 3f out: hld on gamely u.p fnl f: all out* **16/1**

2001 **2** *hd* **Forced Upon Us**[17] 2806 4-9-6 **60** .... (b) JackMitchell(5) 7 70
(P J McBride) *in tch: drvn and unable qck 2f out: r.o last 100yds: nt quite rch wnr* **9/2**[2]

0062 **3** ¾ **Arfinnit (IRE)**[9] 3033 7-9-0 **52** .... (v) KirstyMilczarek(3) 9 60
(Mrs A L M King) *chsd ldr tl over 4f out: rdn to chse wnr wl over 1f out: unable qck fnl f: lost 3rd towards fin* **8/1**

5540 **4** *nk* **Mine Behind**[53] 1739 8-9-8 **57** .... LPKeniry 11 64
(J R Best) *dropped in bhd after s: wl bhd tl gd hdwy over 1f out: chsd ldrs ins fnl f: no imp last 50yds* **16/1**

4600 **5** 1 **Quality Street**[32] 2337 6-9-11 **60** .... (p) RichardThomas 1 63
(P Butler) *sn bustled along in rr: rdn 1/2-way: styd on fnl f: nvr rchd ldrs* **12/1**

6200 **6** ¾ **Rhapsilian**[18] 2758 4-9-7 **59** .... TravisBlock(3) 3 60
(J A Geake) *t.k.h: wnt sltly rt s: hld up in bhd ldrs: edgd lft over 4f out: hit rail over 2f out: sn rdn: chsd ldrs ent fnl f: no ex last 100yds* **7/1**[3]

3060 **7** 1 **Monashee Prince (IRE)**[20] 2692 6-9-10 **59** .... (v) JimmyQuinn 8 57
(J R Best) *hld up towards rr: rdn and effrt jst over 2f out: nvr pce to trble ldrs* **12/1**

2235 **8** *nk* **Kyllachy Storm**[10] 2991 4-8-13 **53** .... PatrickDonaghy(5) 2 50
(R J Hodges) *midfield whn clipped heels and stmbld over 4f out: towards rr after: kpt on fr over 1f out: nvr pce to rch ldrs* **8/1**

4133 **9** 3 ¾ **Duke Of Milan (IRE)**[12] 2936 5-9-4 **53** .... RyanMoore 6 38
(G C Bravery) *squeezed out and stmbld after s: a bhd* **15/8**[1]

0-35 **10** 4 ½ **Half A Tsar (IRE)**[9] 3021 4-8-10 **50** .... JackDean(5) 5 20
(Mark Gillard) *led tl over 3f out: chsd wnr after tl wl over 1f out: sn wknd* **25/1**

1m 12.09s (0.19) **Going Correction** +0.075s/f (Slow) **10** Ran SP% **118.7**
Speed ratings (Par 101): **101,100,99,99,98 97,95,95,90,84**
toteswinger: 1&2 £19.10, 1&3 £30.50, 2&3 £8.20 CSF £88.22 CT £635.93 TOTE £12.90: £3.80, £1.70, £2.50; EX 117.70 Trifecta £178.70 Part won. Pool: £241.52 - 0.90 winning units..
Owner S Kamis And Mrs S Grayson **Bred** Cheveley Park Stud Ltd **Trained** Formby, Lancs

FOCUS
A moderate sprint handicap and one or two met trouble in running, including the favourite which may have rendered this even less competitive. The form is solid for the grade though.
Duke Of Milan(IRE) Official explanation: jockey said gelding suffered interference immediately after start and resented the kickback.

3317 CROWHURST H'CAP 7f (P)
3:15 (3:15) (Class 4) (0-80,79) 4-Y-0+ **£5,180** (£1,541; £770; £384) **Stalls** Low

Form RPR

6043 **1** **Chjimes (IRE)**[5] 3138 4-8-9 **67** .... RyanMoore 8 78
(C R Dore) *t.k.h: trckd ldr tl led 1f out: rdn out* **7/2**[2]

6250 **2** ¾ **Count Ceprano (IRE)**[3] 3197 4-9-0 **79** .... GabrielHannon(7) 4 88
(M D I Usher) *hld up wl in tch in last trio: hdwy wl over 1f out: n.m.r and jostled over 1f out: r.o to go 2nd nr fin: nt rch wnr* **2/1**[1]

-001 **3** *hd* **Glencalvie (IRE)**[19] 2722 7-9-4 **76** .... (p) IanMongan 5 84
(J Akehurst) *led: rdn 2f out: hdd 1f out: kpt on same pce: lost 2nd nr fin* **7/1**

-000 **4** 1 ¾ **Wavertree Warrior (IRE)**[10] 2995 6-9-3 **78** .... (b) KirstyMilczarek(3) 7 81
(N P Littmoden) *s.i.s: in tch: rdn and edging lft over 1f out: kpt on same pce* **15/2**

6450 **5** *nse* **Royal Island (IRE)**[12] 2947 6-9-7 **79** .... VinceSlattery 6 82
(M G Quinlan) *hld up wl in tch in last trio: hdwy on outer wl over 2f out: kpt on but nvr pce to rch ldrs* **6/1**[3]

5420 **6** *shd* **Cativo Cavallino**[21] 2679 5-9-3 **75** .... RichardThomas 3 78
(J E Long) *t.k.h: in tch chsd ldrs and rdn 2f out: kpt on same pce fnl f* **11/1**

1046 **7** ½ **Cinnamon Hill**[28] 2457 4-8-11 **69** .... StephenCarson 1 71
(Eve Johnson Houghton) *chsd ldrs: rdn 2f out: wknd ins fnl f* **33/1**

2123 **8** 2 ¼ **Teasing**[74] 1286 4-9-4 **76** .... JimmyQuinn 2 70
(J Pearce) *s.i.s: bhd: effrt on inner 2f out: wknd over 1f out* **12/1**

1m 25.21s (0.41) **Going Correction** +0.075s/f (Slow) **8** Ran SP% **113.1**
Speed ratings (Par 105): **100,99,98,96,96 96,96,93**
toteswinger: 1&2 £2.80, 1&3 £6.60, 2&3 £2.90 CSF £10.65 CT £44.64 TOTE £4.60: £1.40, £1.10, £2.50; EX 15.50 Trifecta £59.00 Pool: £398.30 - 4.99 winning units..
Owner Sean J Murphy **Bred** Morgan O'Flaherty **Trained** West Pinchbeck, Lincs

FOCUS
A routine handicap of its type for the track and the pace was ordinary. Modest form, rated through the second and third.

3318 LOOK FOR BETTER ODDS AT BETDAQ MAIDEN FILLIES' STKS 1m (P)
3:45 (3:47) (Class 5) 3-Y-0+ **£2,729** (£806; £403) **Stalls** High

Form RPR

1 **Nice Matin (USA)** 3-8-9 0 .... KirstyMilczarek(3) 12 70
(J A R Toller) *s.i.s: flashed tail thrght: hld up in tch towards rr: hdwy over 2f out: chsd ldr over 1f out: led ins fnl f: r.o* **40/1**

2 ½ **Emirates Lady (USA)** 3-8-12 0 .... KerrinMcEvoy 1 69
(Saeed Bin Suroor) *s.i.s: chsd ldrs after 1f: led 5f out: edgd rt over 1f out: hdd and unable qck ins fnl f* **3/1**[2]

3 2 ¼ **St Trinians** 3-8-12 0 .... LPKeniry 10 64
(E F Vaughan) *v.s.a: in tch in rr: hdwy on inner 2f out: kpt on steadily: wnt 3rd wl ins fnl f: nt rch ldng pair* **50/1**

4-0 **4** ½ **Paradise Island (IRE)**[17] 2786 3-8-12 0 .... SteveDrowne 11 63
(E A L Dunlop) *in tch towards rr: rdn jst over 2f out: hdwy over 1f out: kpt on same pce fnl f* **10/1**

03- **5** *shd* **Shindy (FR)**[219] 6847 3-8-12 0 .... OscarUrbina 3 63
(J A R Toller) *chsd ldrs: wnt 2nd 2f out tl over 1f out: kpt on one pce fnl f* **9/2**[3]

0 **6** 2 ¼ **Citron Presse (USA)**[17] 2800 3-8-12 0 .... RobertHavlin 4 58
(J H M Gosden) *chsd ldrs: rdn jst over 2f out: wknd ent fnl f* **12/1**

0 **7** ¾ **Russian Empress (USA)**[35] 2257 3-8-12 0 .... RyanMoore 6 56
(Sir Michael Stoute) *chsd ldr tl 2f out: wknd u.p over 1f out* **6/4**[1]

8 3 ½ **Virginias Best** 3-8-12 0 .... TedDurcan 5 48
(M Botti) *s.i.s: t.k.h: sn wl in tch in midfield: rdn 2f out: sn wknd* **12/1**

0- **9** 3 ¼ **Rahaan (USA)**[264] 5913 3-8-7 0 .... AhmedAjtebi(5) 7 40
(C E Brittain) *led on outer tl 5f out: chsd ldrs after tl wknd 2f out* **20/1**

0 **10** 1 ½ **Savanna's Gold**[25] 2546 4-9-8 0 .... DMylonas 8 37
(G Prodromou) *in tch towards rr on outer: sme hdwy over 3f out: struggling and bhd over 2f out* **100/1**

0 **11** 17 **Miss Riviera Chic**[8] 3061 3-8-12 0 .... JoeFanning 2 —
(G Wragg) *s.i.s: in tch in midfield tl rdn and lost pl 3f out: t.o and eased fnl f* **40/1**

1m 38.96s (0.76) **Going Correction** +0.075s/f (Slow)
WFA 3 from 4yo 10lb **11** Ran SP% **120.2**
Speed ratings (Par 100): **99,98,96,95,95 93,92,89,85,84 67**
toteswinger: 1&2 £13.30, 1&3 £105.30, 2&3 £35.60 CSF £157.87 TOTE £52.10: £10.80, £1.40, £9.70; EX 272.50 TRIFECTA Not won..
Owner G B Partnership **Bred** Clovelly Farms **Trained** Newmarket, Suffolk

FOCUS
An ordinary fillies' maiden and the pace was only ordinary, but the first three were all newcomers and a few of these did suggest they were capable of improvement. Not an easy race to rate accurately though.

3319 ASHURST WOOD H'CAP 1m (P)
4:15 (4:16) (Class 3) (0-90,89) 3-Y-0+
£7,477 (£2,239; £1,119; £560; £279; £140) **Stalls** High

Form RPR

-111 **1** **Master Of Arts (USA)**[24] 2563 3-8-10 **82** .... DarryllHolland 1 96+
(Sir Mark Prescott) *trckd ldng pair on inner: swtchd off rail and nt clr run over 1f out: gap opened and qcknd to ld nr fin: cosily* **4/5**[1]

-152 **2** *nk* **The Snatcher (IRE)**[24] 2565 5-9-11 **87** .... RyanMoore 9 96
(R Hannon) *led for 2f: chsd ldr after: rdn and ev ch 2f out: led 1f out: hdd towards fin* **3/1**[2]

0430 **3** 1 ½ **Zero Cool (USA)**[18] 2762 4-9-1 **77** .... GeorgeBaker 2 83
(G L Moore) *in tch: rdn over 2f out: chsd ldrs ent fnl f: kpt on same pce* **12/1**

3010 **4** 1 ¼ **Salient**[9] 3040 4-9-12 **88** .... PaulDoe 7 91
(M J Attwater) *chsd ldr tl led 6f out: rdn over 2f out: hdd 1f out: wknd last 100yds* **10/1**

1000 **5** ½ **Silver Hotspur**[3] 3222 4-9-13 **89** .... ShaneKelly 8 91
(M Wigham) *t.k.h: chsd ldrs: rdn 2f out: kpt on same pce fnl f* **33/1**

1104 **6** 3 ½ **My Shadow**[53] 1745 3-8-7 **79** ow1 .... SteveDrowne 6 70
(S Dow) *stdd after s: hld up in last pair: rdn and effrt jst over 2f out: wknd over 1f out* **20/1**

6546 **7** 1 **Bahiano (IRE)**[54] 1723 7-9-7 **83** .... KerrinMcEvoy 4 74
(C E Brittain) *hld up in last trio: rdn over 2f out: sn struggling* **16/1**

0461 **8** ¾ **Twilight Star (IRE)**[18] 2762 4-9-4 **80** .... (t) TedDurcan 5 69
(R A Teal) *stdd s: hld up in tch: hdwy 3f out: drvn jst over 2f out: wknd wl over 1f out* **6/1**[3]

1m 37.66s (-0.54) **Going Correction** +0.075s/f (Slow)
WFA 3 from 4yo+ 10lb **8** Ran SP% **125.2**
Speed ratings (Par 107): **105,104,103,101,101 97,96,96**
toteswinger: 1&2 £1.50, 1&3 £4.40, 2&3 £5.70 CSF £3.91 CT £18.66 TOTE £2.30: £1.10, £1.20, £3.30; EX 5.40 Trifecta £24.70 Pool: £831.23 - 24.88 winning units..
Owner Eclipse Thoroughbreds-Osborne House III **Bred** Cyril Humphris **Trained** Newmarket, Suffolk

FOCUS
A fair little handicap and the pace sent by Salient was solid enough. The form looks reliable and the progressive Master Of Arts has been rated value for 3l.

NOTEBOOK
Master Of Arts(USA), bidding for a four-timer off a 12lb higher mark and 24lb higher than when successful on his most recent Polytrack start, raced keenly enough behind the leaders but looked in trouble when he found his path blocked behind Salient and The Snatcher starting up the home straight. However, with Salient dropping away soon after he made full use of the resulting gap and got up the inside of the runner-up to win with a degree of comfort. We have been here before with improvers from the yard and there is no telling how much further he can go. (op 11-10)

The Snatcher(IRE) continues to climb the weights and found himself off an 11lb higher mark than when last on sand. He was always up with the pace and had every chance, but the favourite managed to extricate himself in time and snuck up his inside to collar him near the line. He has won off a higher mark than this on turf and this effort suggests he is not yet handicapped out of things. (op 7-2 tchd 4-1)
Zero Cool(USA), 3lb lower than when last on sand, was weak in the market but he ran a very creditable race after holding every chance. He is not very consistent, but looks capable of winning a race off this sort of mark. (op 8-1)
Salient had to do a bit of work early in order to establish his favourite position out in front. He tried his best to see it out, but had nothing more to offer once headed inside the last furlong. (tchd 14-1)
Silver Hotspur has won on the Wolverhampton Polytrack, but all six of his wins since have come on Fibresand. This was better, especially as he raced very keenly early, but he will still need to find more in order to defy this stiff-looking mark.
Twilight Star(IRE), settled in behind his rivals, took quite a grip and although he tried to get into the race around the wide outside on the home bend, his earlier exertions then took their toll. Official explanation: jockey said gelding ran too free (tchd 15-2)

3320 ASHDOWN FOREST H'CAP — 5f (P)
4:45 (4:45) (Class 3) (0-90,89) 3-Y-0+

£7,477 (£2,239; £1,119; £560; £279; £140) **Stalls** High

Form — RPR

600- **1** **Little Edward**[199] 7053 10-9-13 **88** .... SteveDrowne 2 — 96
(R J Hodges) *taken down early: stdd after s: t.k.h: hld up towards rr: hdwy on outer 2f out: r.o wl to ld wl ins fnl f* **16/1**

-123 **2** *3/4* **Safari Mischief**[16] 2828 5-9-10 **88** .... TolleyDean(3) 9 — 93
(P Winkworth) *chsd ldrs: hdwy to press ldrs 2f out: rdn over 1f out: led ins fnl f: hdd and unable qck wl ins fnl f* **9/4**[1]

1400 **3** *nse* **Hereford Boy**[16] 2828 4-9-4 **79** .... RobertHavlin 4 — 84
(D K Ivory) *in tch in midfield: rdn over 2f out: hdwy u.p over 1f out: ev ch ins fnl f: kpt on* **9/1**

6010 **4** *nk* **Elhamri**[23] 2626 4-10-0 **89** .... RichardKingscote 7 — 93
(S Kirk) *stmbld sn after s: chsd ldrs: wnt 2nd over 3f out: ev ch and rdn 2f out: led jst over 1f out: hdd and kpt on same pce ins fnl f* **9/2**[2]

0500 **5** *2* **Magic Glade**[16] 2828 9-9-2 **77** .... AdamKirby 6 — 74
(Peter Grayson) *taken down early: led tl 4f out: chsd ldrs after: rdn and kpt on same pce fr over 1f out* **14/1**

3051 **6** *2 1/4* **Almaty Express**[26] 2501 6-9-10 **85** ....(b) JoeFanning 8 — 74
(J R Weymes) *chsd ldr tl led 4f out: rdn 2f out: hdd jst over 1f out: wknd ins fnl f* **11/1**

4450 **7** *shd* **Style Award**[10] 3009 3-9-2 **83** .... RyanMoore 5 — 71
(W J H Ratcliffe) *bhd on outer: struggling and rdn 1/2-way: modest late hdwy: n.d* **11/2**[3]

-600 **8** *nk* **Garstang**[41] 2082 5-8-6 **70** oh1....(b) KirstyMilczarek(3) 3 — 57
(Peter Grayson) *dwlt: t.k.h and sn chsng ldrs: rdn and tried to chal over 1f out: wknd jst ins fnl f* **14/1**

6100 **9** *1/2* **Halsion Chancer**[7] 3093 4-9-12 **87** .... LPKeniry 1 — 73
(J R Best) *in rr: rdn and effrt 2f out: n.d* **9/2**[2]

58.36 secs (-0.44) **Going Correction** +0.075s/f (Slow)
WFA 3 from 4yo+ 6lb — **9** Ran SP% **120.1**
Speed ratings (Par 107): **106,104,104,104,101 97,97,96,96**
toteswinger: 1&2 £10.50, 1&3 £24.40, 2&3 £9.40 CSF £54.36 CT £366.13 TOTE £16.60: £3.50, £1.50, £3.00; EX 67.30 Trifecta £212.70 Pool: £776.16 - £2.70 winning units..
Owner J W Mursell **Bred** J W Mursell **Trained** Charlton Mackrell, Somerset

FOCUS
A decent sprint handicap and with an established trailblazer in the field there was never going to be any hanging about. The form is pretty solid.

NOTEBOOK
Little Edward may be ten now, but there is little sign of age catching up with him and he has plenty of winning form around here. Freshened up by a six-month break, he was forced out wide rounding the home turn as he tried to get closer, but he still had enough time to put in a sustained run down the middle of the track. There is no reason why he cannot add to this. (tchd 20-1)
Safari Mischief, a stone higher than when successful over course and distance nearly a year ago, was always close to the pace and had every chance, but the veteran's late surge down the outside proved too much for him. He continues to run consistently well. (op 5-2 tchd 11-4)
Hereford Boy, well behind Safari Mischief in the big sprint at Epsom on Derby day, made his effort wide off the final bend but the winner made his move at the same time and saw his race out that much better. This was a decent effort, but he does look weighted right up to his best just now. (tchd 10-1)
Elhamri, well beaten in his only previous try on sand, ran much better this time and had every chance after having raced up with the pace throughout. The performance was probably even better than it looked too as he came back without his off-hind shoe. Official explanation: jockey said gelding lost his off-hind shoe (op 11-2 tchd 13-2)
Magic Glade, behind both Safari Mischief and Hereford Boy in the big sprint handicap at Epsom on Derby day, was backed at long prices and showed good early pace, but he was put in his place in the home straight. (op 22-1 tchd 25-1)
Almaty Express, raised 4lb for his Great Leighs victory, was having only his second try here. He showed his usual early dash even though he had to work a bit to get the early lead, but he did not get home. (op 8-1)
Style Award, a winner over course and distance in her only previous try on sand, barely went a yard this time and was disappointing. Official explanation: jockey said filly resented kick kickback (tchd 5-1)
Halsion Chancer, who has such a fine record over this trip around here, was in trouble a long way out and did not run his race at all. Official explanation: jockey said gelding never travelled (op 11-2)

3321 BET EURO 2008 - BETDAQ H'CAP — 1m 5f (P)
5:15 (5:17) (Class 6) (0-65,65) 4-Y-0+ — **£1,942** (£578; £288; £144) **Stalls** Low

Form — RPR

4303 **1** **Looks The Business (IRE)**[18] 2755 7-8-6 **55** ....(tp) JackDean(5) 13 — 64
(W G M Turner) *t.k.h: hld up towards rr: hdwy over 3f out: chsd ldr gng wl 2f out: led over 1f out: styd on wl* **12/1**

5/4- **2** *1* **Colophony (USA)**[212] 747 8-9-0 **63** .... JackMitchell(5) 9 — 70
(K A Morgan) *stdd s: t.k.h: hld up wl bhd: hdwy outer 3f out: chsd wnr jst ins fnl f: no imp last 100yds* **16/1**

0/63 **3** *2* **Greenwich Village**[13] 2921 5-9-4 **62** .... AmirQuinn 6 — 66
(W J Knight) *t.k.h: chsd ldrs: rdn over 2f out: hanging lft over 1f out: kpt on same pce fnl f* **4/1**[1]

00-1 **4** *1 3/4* **Trigger's Friend**[16] 2832 4-8-2 **49** .... KirstyMilczarek(3) 2 — 50
(Jamie Poulton) *in tch: bustled along 6f out: edgd lft jst over 2f out: chsd ldrs and drvn over 1f out: outpcd fnl f* **12/1**

5335 **5** *hd* **Abounding**[128] 588 4-8-13 **64** .... HarryPoulton(7) 11 — 65
(M J Attwater) *bmpd s: t.k.h: hld up in rr: hdwy on outer over 2f out: rdn wl over 1f out: kpt on same pce fnl f* **8/1**[3]

240 **6** *nk* **Jafaru**[24] 2567 4-9-7 **65** ....(p) JoeFanning 1 — 69+
(G A Butler) *pressed ldr: pushed along 4f out: nt clr run and shuffled bk to rr over 2f out: swtchd rt wl over 1f out: styd on but nvr able to rch ldrs* **6/1**[2]

0001 **7** *1/2* **Camera Shy (IRE)**[18] 2755 4-8-7 **51** .... SteveDrowne 12 — 51
(K A Morgan) *wnt lft s: in tch: hdwy to ld 3f out: rdn over 2f out: hdd over 1f out: wknd fnl f* **4/1**[1]

2460 **8** *1 1/2* **Beech Games**[9] 3025 4-8-7 **51** .... LPKeniry 5 — 49+
(F Jordan) *hld up in midfield: rdn 4f out: keeping on same pce whn hmpd over 2f out: no ch after* **16/1**

0000 **9** *1* **Dushstorm (IRE)**[9] 3036 7-9-4 **62** .... AdamKirby 3 — 58
(C R Dore) *hld up towards rr: drvn 4f out: n.d* **14/1**

0500 **10** *1* **Eddystone (IRE)**[20] 2694 4-8-2 **46** ....(v) JimmyQuinn 4 — 41
(Mrs L C Jewell) *t.k.h: hld up in midfield: rdn over 4f out: bhd last 3f* **33/1**

00 **11** *10* **L'Homme De Nuit (GER)**[38] 2153 4-9-2 **60** ....(b[1]) GeorgeBaker 14 — 40
(G L Moore) *reminders sn after s: in tch: rdn over 3f out: chsd ldr briefly over 2f out: sn btn: eased fnl f* **6/1**[2]

5000 **12** *8* **Princely Ted (IRE)**[7] 3084 7-8-6 **50** .... PaulEddery 8 — 18
(W Clay) *led: rdn 4f out: hdd 3f out: wknd over 2f out: eased fnl f* **16/1**

13 *10* **Tapaellya (IRE)**[210] 4-9-4 **62** .... RichardThomas 10 — 15
(J E Long) *hld up in midfield: rdn 4f out: sn bhd: t.o and eased fnl f* **50/1**

2m 45.4s (-0.60) **Going Correction** +0.075s/f (Slow) — **13** Ran SP% **124.3**
Speed ratings (Par 101): **104,103,102,101,100 100,100,99,98,98 92,87,81**
toteswinger: 1&2 £22.20, 1&3 £9.30, 2&3 £19.20 CSF £197.85 CT £919.53 TOTE £10.90: £4.10, £5.30, £1.70; EX 184.40 Trifecta £397.00 Part won. Pool: £536.58 - 0.51 winning units. Place 6: £52.59 Place 5: £46.53.
Owner M J B Racing **Bred** Mrs M O'Callaghan **Trained** Sigwells, Somerset

FOCUS
A modest staying handicap, but quite competitive nonetheless and the time was respectable enough. The form is sound for the grade and should prove pretty reliable.
Jafaru Official explanation: jockey said mare was denied a clear run
T/Plt: £43.20 to a £1 stake. Pool: £71,806.88. 1,210.70 winning tickets. T/Qpdt: £8.10 to a £1 stake. Pool: £4,137.68. 377.80 winning tickets. SP

3090 WINDSOR (R-H)
Monday, June 23

OFFICIAL GOING: Good to firm (good in places)
Wind: Almost nil Weather: Sunny, warm

3322 TOTESPORT.COM FILLIES' H'CAP — 1m 2f 7y
6:40 (6:41) (Class 5) (0-70,70) 3-Y-0+ — **£2,729** (£806; £403) **Stalls** Centre

Form — RPR

4630 **1** **Saraba (FR)**[24] 2567 7-9-6 **62** .... IanMongan 3 — 70
(Mrs L J Mongan) *hld up in midfield: prog over 2f out: drvn to ld jst over 1f out: hld on wl fnl f* **25/1**

-045 **2** *nk* **Danamight (IRE)**[11] 2982 3-8-6 **60** ow1.... RichardMullen 15 — 65
(J L Dunlop) *dwlt: hld up towards rr: gd prog wl over 1f out: pressed wnr fnl f: styd on but hld nr fin* **13/2**[2]

04-5 **3** *1/2* **Neve Lieve (IRE)**[8] 3057 3-8-11 **65** .... TedDurcan 2 — 69
(M Botti) *mde most: racd on inner in st: hrd pressed fr 3f out: hdd jst over 1f out: kpt on nr fin* **12/1**

0-30 **4** *1/2* **Rowan River**[60] 1577 4-9-13 **69** .... RichardKingscote 7 — 74
(Tom Dascombe) *wl in tch: rdn and effrt over 2f out: hanging lft fr over 1f out: styd on: unable to chal* **12/1**

4-60 **5** *1/2* **La Troupe (IRE)**[11] 2971 3-9-1 **69** .... RobertHavlin 5 — 71
(J H M Gosden) *hld up in midfield: prog 4f out: drvn to chal over 1f out: fdd ins fnl f* **14/1**

00-2 **6** *nk* **Politeia (USA)**[21] 2678 3-9-1 **69** .... RyanMoore 6 — 70
(R Hannon) *hld up towards rr: pushed along 4f out: effrt on outer over 2f out: nvr rchd ldrs: kpt on but n.d* **5/4**[1]

-500 **7** *1 3/4* **Jelly Mo**[12] 2956 3-8-5 **59** .... MartinDwyer 8 — 57
(J W Hills) *mostly in midfield: eased off rail and effrt over 1f out: nt pce to trble ldrs* **20/1**

6002 **8** *nk* **Miss Phoebe (IRE)**[8] 3065 3-8-11 **65** .... JamieSpencer 4 — 62
(S Kirk) *hld up in last trio: prog on outer 3f out: hrd rdn and no hdwy 2f out: one pce* **14/1**

0-06 **9** *nse* **Muffett's Dream**[31] 2353 4-8-10 **52** oh5.... StephenCarson 14 — 51
(J J Bridger) *hld up in last trio: pushed along 3f out and virtually last: sme prog over 1f out: reminders ins fnl f: nvr nr ldrs* **50/1**

0-00 **10** *3/4* **Turfani (IRE)**[24] 2566 3-8-6 **60** .... PaulDoe 1 — 56
(W J Knight) *pressed ldr to 2f out: wknd fnl f* **40/1**

1005 **11** *3/4* **Harvest Joy (IRE)**[21] 2682 4-10-0 **70** .... TPO'Shea 11 — 66
(J Gallagher) *dwlt: hld up in last: prog on wd outside 3f out: nt rch ldrs u.p wl over 1f out: fdd* **20/1**

3430 **12** *1* **Georgie The Fourth (IRE)**[45] 1962 3-8-7 **64** ....(v[1]) TolleyDean(3) 12 — 56
(George Baker) *sn trckd ldrs: lost pl over 3f out: toiling in rr after* **9/1**[3]

60-0 **13** *2* **Marchpane**[50] 1839 3-9-2 **70** .... KerrinMcEvoy 13 — 58
(R M Beckett) *cl up on inner: lost pl 3f out: in rr and struggling 2f out* **12/1**

5-64 **14** *1/2* **Spectrana**[12] 2931 3-8-8 **62** ....(b) JimCrowley 10 — 49
(Mrs A J Perrett) *reluctant to go to post: dwlt: sn prom: pressed ldng pair 4f out tl lost pl qckly over 2f out* **40/1**

2m 8.41s (-0.29) **Going Correction** -0.075s/f (Good)
WFA 3 from 4yo+ 12lb — **14** Ran SP% **124.4**
Speed ratings (Par 100): **98,97,97,96,96 96,94,94,94,94 93,92,91,90**
toteswinger: 1&2 Not won, 1&3 £91.30, 2&3 £19.00 CSF £175.75 CT £2095.28 TOTE £41.70: £7.80, £2.70, £3.80; EX 439.90.
Owner Mrs P J Sheen **Bred** S A Aga Khan **Trained** Epsom, Surrey

FOCUS
A modest fillies' handicap and, with the pace steady for much of the way, they finished in a bit of a heap. The form is rated through the first two.
Saraba(FR) Official explanation: trainer said, regarding apparent improvement in form, that the mare probably did not stay two miles on soft ground previously.

3323 PERTEMPS MAIDEN AUCTION STKS — 6f
7:10 (7:12) (Class 5) 2-Y-0 — **£2,729** (£806; £403) **Stalls** High

Form — RPR

1 **Portugese Caddy (IRE)** 2-8-9 0.... JimCrowley 6 — 72
(P Winkworth) *sn prom: rdn to dispute ld ent fnl f: kpt on wl to ld fnl strides* **50/1**

0 **2** *hd* **Campbeltown Trader (IRE)**[27] 2473 2-8-9 0.... RichardKingscote 5 — 71
(Tom Dascombe) *sn prom: rdn to dispute ld ent fnl f: upsides wnr after: jst pipped* **9/1**

3 *1* **Rumble Of Thunder (IRE)** 2-8-11 0.... AlanMunro 2 — 70
(D W P Arbuthnot) *racd on wd outside in midfield: stdy prog over 1f out: chsd ldng pair ins fnl f: nvr able to chal* **25/1**

4 *1 1/4* **Defector (IRE)** 2-8-13 0.... MartinDwyer 4 — 69+
(W R Muir) *hld up towards rr: sme prog over 2f out: shkn up and kpt on fnl f: nvr rchd ldrs* **9/2**[2]

5 1 **Ray Of Joy** 2-8-4 0 .... JimmyQuinn 11 57+
(J R Jenkins) *sn pushed along in last trio: prog over 2f out: styd on steadily fr over 1f out: nrst fin* **50/1**

5 **6** nse **Barnezet (GR)**[7] 3092 2-8-11 0 .... RyanMoore 3 64
(R Hannon) *fast away: led and crossed fr low draw to nr side rail: hdd & wknd ent fnl f* **7/2**[1]

7 1 **Jewelled Reef (IRE)** 2-8-11 0 .... StephenCarson 13 61
(Eve Johnson Houghton) *towards rr: pushed along fr 1/2-way: prog to chse ldrs over 1f out: no imp fnl f* **25/1**

8 nk **Wave Aside** 2-8-13 0 .... TedDurcan 9 62+
(B J Meehan) *dwlt: rn green in last trio: no prog tl styd on fr 2f out: bttr for experience* **16/1**

9 1¼ **Black Skirt** 2-8-4 0 .... RichardSmith 10 49+
(R Hannon) *hld up wl in rr: stmbld over 2f out: rn green but styd on fnl f* **25/1**

10 hd **Jeremiah (IRE)** 2-8-11 0 .... RichardMullen 15 55
(J G Portman) *dwlt: nvr beyond midfield: hanging and wknd over 1f out* **25/1**

0 **11** 1 **Duchess Of Doom (IRE)**[23] 2618 2-8-6 0 .... KerrinMcEvoy 7 47
(B W Hills) *mostly chsd ldr to wl over 1f out: wknd* **25/1**

5 **12** 3 **River Captain (IRE)**[12] 2944 2-8-11 0 .... JamieSpencer 16 43
(S Kirk) *prom tl lost pl and btn wl over 1f out* **7/2**[1]

13 1¼ **Kayceebee** 2-8-11 0 .... AdamKirby 8 40
(R M Beckett) *dwlt: t.k.h and hld up in last trio: nvr on terms* **8/1**[3]

14 ½ **Miss Kadee** 2-8-4 0 .... SaleemGolam 1 31
(P D Evans) *dwlt: a struggling in rr* **50/1**

15 3¼ **Nothing To Worry (IRE)** 2-8-13 0 .... TPO'Shea 14 30
(M R Channon) *prom to 1/2-way: wknd rapidly* **8/1**[3]

1m 13.47s (0.47) **Going Correction** -0.075s/f (Good) **15** Ran SP% **125.8**
Speed ratings (Par 93): **93,92,91,89,88 88,87,86,84,84 83,79,77,77,72**
toteswinger: not won CSF £442.64 TOTE £37.70: £7.40, £4.40, £8.00; EX 1315.90.
Owner Mrs Tessa Winkworth **Bred** N H Bloodstock Ltd **Trained** Chiddingfold, Surrey

FOCUS
They finished in something of a heap and the bare form of this maiden looks ordinary, but the race should produce its share of winners.

NOTEBOOK
Portugese Caddy(IRE), a £2,200 gelded son of Great Palm, first foal of a mare placed over 7f at three, belied his massive odds with a narrow success on his racecourse debut. He ran as though he will get another furlong and there could be more to come. (op 66-1 tchd 40-1)
Campbeltown Trader(IRE) improved massively on the form he showed when down the field on his debut over 5f on easy ground at Chepstow. He looked the winner just yards from the finish, only to be run out of it literally on the line. He could progress again and should win a similar race. (tchd 10-1)
Rumble Of Thunder(IRE) ◆, a 15,000gns son of Fath, half-brother to triple 7f-1m winner Coalpark, out of a 1m winner, looks one to take from the race. He was caught out really wide pretty much throughout, but kept staying on for pressure. He should know a lot more next time and might take a bit of beating in similar company. (op 40-1)
Defector(IRE) ◆, a 21,000gns son of Fasliyev, half-brother to the Group-class Stubbs Art, who was third in this year's English and Irish Guineas, out of a mare who was placed over 1m2f, attracted good market support during the day, but looked to be found out by his inexperience. He is another who should benefit a good deal from this experience. (op 5-1)
Ray Of Joy, an 8,000gns daughter of Tobougg, half-sister to among others 1m2f winner Tybalt, could not go the pace early, but finished nicely and this was a pleasing debut. She should stay further and slightly easier ground may also suit better.
Barnezet(GR)'s debut fifth over 5f here the previous week didn't really amount to much and she failed to justify favouritism on this step up in trip. She had to use up energy early to get across from her low draw and might be happier back over the minimum distance for the time being. Official explanation: jockey said filly hung left (tchd 10-3)
Wave Aside, a 24,000gns gelded son of Reset, half-brother to dual 6f winner Mr Sandicliffe, gave the impression he can improve significantly with the benefit of this experience. (tchd 25-1)
Black Skirt, a 5,000gns daughter of Kyllachy, out of a multiple 6-7f winner, did not help her chance with a stumble around two furlongs out and she looked in need of the experience, but still showed some ability. (op 33-1)
River Captain(IRE) ran a disappointing race, failing to confirm the ability he showed when fifth on his debut over this trip on the Polytrack at Kempton. Official explanation: jockey said colt had no more to give (op 9-2)

3324 REDBURN PARTNERS H'CAP — 6f
7:40 (7:42) (Class 4) (0-85,85) 3-Y-O — **£5,180** (£1,541; £770; £384) **Stalls** High

Form — RPR

-346 **1** **Lodi (IRE)**[10] 2998 3-8-8 **72** ....(t) IanMongan 2 86
(J Akehurst) *hld up in last trio: prog over 2f out: led over 1f out: sn wl in command: drvn out* **15/2**

2-10 **2** 2¼ **Dunn'o (IRE)**[50] 1837 3-9-0 **78** .... PhilipRobinson 5 85
(C G Cox) *bmpd s: sn w ldrs on outer: rdn over 1f out: chsd wnr fnl f: styd on but no imp* **4/1**[2]

5004 **3** 2¾ **Tadalavil**[14] 2883 3-8-11 **75** .... TPO'Shea 8 73
(M R Channon) *chsd ldrs: rdn 2f out: kpt on to take 3rd fnl f: no ch w ldng pair* **12/1**

30-0 **4** 2¾ **Sam's Cross (IRE)**[11] 2967 3-9-7 **85** .... KerrinMcEvoy 1 74
(K R Burke) *hld up in last trio: pushed along 2f out: sn outpcd: shkn up to take 4th fnl f: no ch w ldng trio* **8/1**

011 **5** 3¼ **Onceaponatime (IRE)**[12] 2945 3-9-6 **84** .... AlanMunro 6 63
(P W Chapple-Hyam) *w ldrs 1f: lost pl: rdn and nt qckn 2f out: no ch after: fin lame* **7/4**[1]

2511 **6** ½ **We Have A Dream**[14] 2883 3-9-5 **83** .... MartinDwyer 7 60
(W R Muir) *w ldr: upsides 2f out: wknd over 1f out* **5/1**[3]

033- **7** hd **Mudhish (IRE)**[199] 7052 3-8-6 **75** ....(b) AhmedAjtebi(5) 9 52
(C E Brittain) *racd against nr side rail: mde most to over 1f out: sn btn* **12/1**

-000 **8** hd **Just A Dancer (IRE)**[20] 2690 3-8-8 **72** .... MichaelHills 3 48
(B W Hills) *a in last trio: pushed along bef 1/2-way: no prog* **25/1**

0-00 **9** 10 **Westwood**[9] 3041 3-9-7 **85** .... TedDurcan 4 29
(D Haydn Jones) *racd on wd outside: chsd ldrs: wknd 2f out: heavily eased* **33/1**

1m 11.65s (-1.35) **Going Correction** -0.075s/f (Good) **9** Ran SP% **118.1**
Speed ratings (Par 101): **106,103,99,95,91 90,90,90,76**
toteswinger: 1&2 £15.40, 1&3 £39.80, 2&3 £5.80 CSF £38.49 CT £366.12 TOTE £10.20: £2.50, £1.80, £3.50; EX 40.70.
Owner Tattenham Corner Racing 3 **Bred** Allevamento Gialloblu S R L **Trained** Epsom, Surrey

FOCUS
A fair three-year-old sprint handicap. The winner showed improved form and the runner-up was 2lb off his best figure, which was posted over 5f.

Onceaponatime(IRE) Official explanation: vet said gelding returned lame in front

3325 WALTER SWINBURN RACING H'CAP — 1m 67y
8:10 (8:11) (Class 4) (0-85,85) 3-Y-O — **£5,180** (£1,541; £770; £384) **Stalls** High

Form — RPR

2245 **1** **Brave Hawk**[11] 2974 3-8-8 **72** ....(p) PhilipRobinson 2 77
(M A Jarvis) *led or disp thrght: def advantage 3f out: drvn out fnl f and a holding on* **10/1**

-213 **2** 1 **Glorious Gift (IRE)**[30] 2412 3-9-7 **85** .... AlanMunro 5 88
(P W Chapple-Hyam) *t.k.h: hld up bhd ldrs: rdn and prog over 2f out: styd on fnl f to snatch 2nd on line* **5/1**[3]

-034 **3** nse **Border Owl (IRE)**[19] 2714 3-8-13 **77** .... RyanMoore 10 80
(R Hannon) *trckd ldrs: effrt to chse wnr wl over 1f out: kpt on but a hld fnl f: lost 2nd on post* **9/1**

04-1 **4** nk **Slip**[8] 3065 3-8-3 **67** oh1 ow1 .... MartinDwyer 7 69+
(M P Tregoning) *hld up in last trio: sme prog 3f out: rdn and nt qckn 2f out: styd on wl last 150yds: nrst fin* **5/4**[1]

610 **5** 1½ **Irish Mayhem (USA)**[30] 2412 3-9-7 **85** ....(b[1]) JamieSpencer 13 84
(B J Meehan) *hld up in last: c wdst of all and effrt 3f out: styd on fnl 2f: nvr rchd ldrs* **9/2**[2]

1000 **6** ½ **Rehabilitation**[11] 2974 3-8-5 **69** ....(p) SaleemGolam 9 67
(W R Swinburn) *hld up towards rr: rdn 3f out: kpt on fnl 2f: nvr rchd ldrs* **25/1**

-515 **7** 4 **Dancer's Legacy**[25] 2532 3-9-1 **79** ....(t) TedDurcan 6 67
(E A L Dunlop) *rousted along early: led or disp ld to 3f out: wknd over 1f out* **20/1**

21-6 **8** 1¾ **Howdigo**[10] 3002 3-9-1 **79** .... LPKeniry 1 63
(J R Best) *hld up in midfield: drvn and struggling over 2f out: eased whn no ch ins fnl f* **25/1**

61- **9** nk **Bauhaus Bourbon (USA)**[196] 7097 3-8-9 **73** ....(t) JosedeSouza 12 57
(P F I Cole) *a in rr: lost tch 3f out: hanging lft but styd on u.p fnl f* **33/1**

2546 **10** 4½ **Amylee (IRE)**[18] 2761 3-9-1 **79** ....(b) AdamKirby 3 52
(C G Cox) *chsd ldng pair 5f out tl wknd u.p 2f out* **16/1**

301- **11** 10 **Loyal Knight (IRE)**[249] 6289 3-8-12 **76** .... KerrinMcEvoy 4 26
(S Kirk) *trckd ldrs tl wknd rapidly over 2f out* **25/1**

1m 42.81s (-1.89) **Going Correction** -0.075s/f (Good) **11** Ran SP% **123.5**
Speed ratings (Par 101): **106,105,104,104,103 102,98,96,96,92 82**
toteswinger: 1&2 £11.10, 1&3 £13.50, 2&3 £5.60 CSF £58.19 CT £494.35 TOTE £13.90: £3.10, £2.20, £2.30; EX 73.50.
Owner Mr & Mrs K Watts & Mr & Mrs S Bamber **Bred** Mount Coote Stud, Richard Pegum & M Bell Racing **Trained** Newmarket, Suffolk

FOCUS
A fair three-year-old handicap. It lacked really progressive types, but the form looks very solid. The winning time was 3.96 seconds quicker than the following maiden.
Dancer's Legacy Official explanation: jockey said colt had no more to give
Amylee(IRE) Official explanation: jockey said filly hung left

3326 COOLMORE DYLAN THOMAS MAIDEN STKS — 1m 67y
8:40 (8:41) (Class 5) 3-Y-O — **£2,729** (£806; £403) **Stalls** High

Form — RPR

4 **1** **Cave Lion (USA)**[16] 2834 3-9-3 0 .... RobertHavlin 10 85+
(J H M Gosden) *hld up in 3rd: swift move on inner to ld 2f out: clr whn hung lft fr over 1f out: eased nr fin* **3/1**[3]

30-5 **2** 2½ **Crystal Rock (IRE)**[47] 1918 3-9-3 80 .... MichaelHills 9 72
(B W Hills) *led: rdn and hdd 2f out: no ch w wnr after* **11/4**[2]

5-0 **3** ½ **Kingdom Of Fife**[17] 2786 3-9-3 0 .... RyanMoore 11 71+
(Sir Michael Stoute) *hld up in 5th: shkn up and outpcd over 2f out: hanging lft but styd on to take 3rd fnl f and cl on runner-up nr fin* **7/4**[1]

0-66 **4** 2 **Sterope (FR)**[17] 2800 3-8-12 69 .... TedDurcan 2 61
(H R A Cecil) *trckd ldr to over 2f out: sn outpcd and btn* **10/1**

00 **5** 1 **Road To Hucking (GER)**[42] 2056 3-9-3 0 .... LPKeniry 4 64?
(J R Best) *t.k.h: hld up in 4th: rdn over 2f out: sn outpcd* **50/1**

0- **6** hd **Bet Noir (IRE)**[241] 6470 3-8-12 0 .... AdamKirby 7 58
(W R Swinburn) *hld up in rr: pushed along over 3f out: nvr rchd ldrs but styd on fnl f* **14/1**

0 **7** ¾ **Island Treasure**[16] 2834 3-9-3 0 .... SteveDrowne 1 62
(H Morrison) *settled in 6th: rdn over 3f out: outpcd over 2f out: plugged on* **33/1**

00 **8** 9 **Testimonial**[11] 2973 3-8-12 0 .... MartinDwyer 6 36
(E A L Dunlop) *a in last trio: rdn and no rspnse over 3f out* **16/1**

00 **9** hd **Wivny (USA)**[12] 2955 3-8-12 0 .... J-PGuillambert 5 35
(P A Blockley) *s.s: hld up in last trio: lost tch and nudged along over 3f out: nvr nr ldrs after: eased over 1f out* **66/1**

10 10 **Alabjar** 3-9-3 0 .... JimCrowley 3 17
(J R Jenkins) *a in rr: wknd 3f out: t.o* **50/1**

1m 46.77s (2.07) **Going Correction** -0.075s/f (Good) **10** Ran SP% **118.0**
Speed ratings (Par 99): **86,83,83,81,80 79,79,70,69,59**
toteswinger: 1&2 £1.60, 1&3 £1.50, 2&3 £1.10 CSF £11.69 TOTE £4.00: £1.50, £1.40, £1.20; EX 12.30.
Owner H R H Princess Haya Of Jordan **Bred** Darley **Trained** Newmarket, Suffolk

FOCUS
An ordinary maiden, and they went steady early on, resulting in a winning time 3.96 seconds slower than the previous 66-85 three-year-old handicap. the form may not prove reliable but it seems to make sense and the winner, rated value for 6l, looks decent.
Island Treasure Official explanation: jockey said colt hung left
Wivny(USA) Official explanation: jockey said, regarding running and riding, his orders were to keep handy without force, but having missed the break was unable to do so, adding that he was able to get the filly back into the race due to the slow early pace, but became outpaced after crossing the junction

3327 RAB CAPITAL H'CAP — 1m 3f 135y
9:10 (9:11) (Class 5) (0-75,75) 3-Y-O — **£3,070** (£906; £453) **Stalls** Centre

Form — RPR

4400 **1** **Dancing Dik**[10] 2997 3-8-6 **60** ....(p) JimCrowley 8 70
(Mrs A J Perrett) *trckd ldr: led over 1f out: rdn clr* **7/2**[1]

-232 **2** 3 **Shy**[15] 2862 3-9-7 **75** .... StephenCarson 6 80
(P Winkworth) *led at gd pce: clr w wnr 2f out: hdd over 1f out: swtchd lft ent fnl f: no imp* **8/1**

-456 **3** ½ **Rock Peak (IRE)**[24] 2564 3-9-4 **72** .... KerrinMcEvoy 12 76
(H Morrison) *chsd ldng trio: wnt 3rd over 3f out: outpcd over 2f out: kpt on* **7/2**[1]

0030 **4** 1¼ **Sabancaya**[17] 2785 3-8-6 **60** .... AlanMunro 13 62
(W J Haggas) *chsd ldrs: rdn and outpcd over 2f out: kpt on fnl f* **14/1**

2145 **5** shd **Dubai Petal (IRE)**[11] 2977 3-9-4 **72** .... MartinDwyer 9 74
(J S Moore) *chsd ldng pair to over 3f out: sn rdn: outpcd over 2f out: kpt on u.p* **7/1**[3]

The Form Book, Raceform Ltd, Compton, RG20 6NL

0001 **6** *1/2* **World Time**[11] [2984] 3-9-5 **73**.. RichardMullen 10 74+
(J H M Gosden) *hld up wl in rr: pushed along over 3f out: nt qckn over 2f out: kpt on fr over 1f out: nrst fin* **4/1**[2]

500 **7** *1 1/2* **Benhego**[28] [2455] 3-8-8 **62**.. SaleemGolam 4 60+
(S C Williams) *hld up wl in rr: shkn up over 2f out: styd on fnl f: no ch* **33/1**

1403 **8** *nse* **Title Role**[10] [2996] 3-9-2 **73**.. TolleyDean(3) 2 71
(P F I Cole) *t.k.h early: hld up in rr: prog on outer over 3f out: chsng ldrs but nt on time over 1f out: fdd* **8/1**

65-5 **9** *1 1/4* **General Tufto**[83] [1128] 3-8-11 **65**..(p) TedDurcan 3 61
(R Charlton) *nvr beyond midfield: rdn and struggling wl over 2f out: sn btn* **16/1**

3100 **10** *1 3/4* **Oberlin (USA)**[34] [2280] 3-8-8 **62**.. JimmyQuinn 5 55
(T Keddy) *settled in midfield: lost pl over 3f out: wl in rr after: pushed along and no imp on ldrs* **33/1**

05-0 **11** *4* **Mystic Art (IRE)**[11] [2974] 3-8-13 **67**.. SteveDrowne 1 54
(C R Egerton) *dwlt: hld up in midfield: effrt on outer over 3f out: no prog over 2f out: wknd over 1f out* **25/1**

5121 **12** *1/2* **An Scaribh**[14] [2894] 3-8-13 **70**.. KirstyMilczarek(3) 11 56
(Mrs L C Jewell) *lost pl on outer after 1f: a in last trio after: wd and no prog 3f out* **10/1**

2m 28.76s (-0.74) **Going Correction** -0.075s/f (Good) **12** Ran SP% **130.5**
Speed ratings (Par 99): **99,97,96,95,95 95,94,94,93,92 89,89**
CSF £35.34 CT £111.14 TOTE £6.10: £1.80, £2.20, £2.00; EX 55.40 Place 6 £1895.30, Place 5 £ 382.34.
Owner Sir John Ritblat,David & Jennifer Sieff **Bred** Usk Valley Stud **Trained** Pulborough, W Sussex

FOCUS
A fair three-year-old handicap and the form is pretty solid with the right horses to the fore.
World Time Official explanation: jockey said colt was unsuited by the good to firm (firm in places) ground
T/Jkpt: Not won. T/Plt: £3,531.60 to a £1 stake. Pool: £98,693.96. 20.40 winning tickets. T/Qpdt: £18.50 to a £1 stake. Pool: £6,892.58. 275.00 winning tickets. JN

2801 WOLVERHAMPTON (A.W) (L-H)
Monday, June 23

OFFICIAL GOING: Standard
Wind: Light across Weather: Cloudy with sunny spells

3328 BETDAQ THE BETTING EXCHANGE AMATEUR RIDERS' (S) STK$m 4f 50y(P)
2:30 (2:30) (Class 6) 4-Y-0+ **£1,977** (£608; £304) **Stalls** Low

Form RPR

250/ **1** **Dandygrey Russett (IRE)**[6] [2892] 7-10-2 60........ MissSallyRandell(7) 6 66
(D L Williams) *mde all: shkn up fnl f: styd on* **11/1**

323- **2** *1 1/4* **Drizzi (IRE)**[194] [7123] 7-11-0 65.. MrSWalker 4 69
(P T Midgley) *hld up: hdwy over 4f out: chsd wnr over 2f out: styd on u.p ins fnl f* **4/6**[1]

-404 **3** *8* **York Cliff**[17] [2776] 10-10-11 51.. MrBenBrisbourne(3) 3 56
(W M Brisbourne) *s.i.s: hld up: styd on appr fnl f: nvr trbld ldrs* **11/2**[2]

4 *nk* **Classy Affair**[43] 4-10-4 0.. MrBMMorris(5) 9 51
(D Morris) *s.i.s: hld up: hdwy over 4f out: rdn and hung lft over 1f out: sn wknd* **9/1**

10-0 **5** *3 1/4* **Converti**[7] [3084] 4-10-7 52.. MrDRBass(7) 10 51
(H J Manners) *prom: chsd wnr over 4f out to over 2f out: wknd over 1f out* **25/1**

-040 **6** *2 1/2* **Soldiers Quest**[9] [3036] 4-10-7 58.. MrCEllingham(7) 5 47
(Peter Grayson) *hld up: hdwy over 3f out: wknd over 1f out* **8/1**[3]

2100 **7** *9* **Key Partners (IRE)**[20] [2707] 7-11-5 55.. MissADeniel 8 37
(P A Blockley) *plld hrd and prom: rdn and wknd over 2f out* **10/1**

8 *2 1/2* **Evianne**[11] 4-10-6 0.. MrsMarieKing(3) 11 23
(P W Hiatt) *prom: rdn and wknd over 2f out* **66/1**

9 *5* **Golly (IRE)**[36] 12-11-0 0.. MissLHorner 7 20
(D L Williams) *s.s: hdw2ay over 6f out: wknd over 3f out* **25/1**

0- **10** *3* **Bold Josr**[299] [4948] 4-10-9 0.. MrAshleePrice(5) 1 15
(D J S Ffrench Davis) *chsd wnr over 7f: wknd over 3f out* **50/1**

2m 46.16s (5.06) **Going Correction** +0.125s/f (Slow) **10** Ran SP% **125.1**
Speed ratings (Par 101): **88,87,81,81,79 77,71,70,66,64**
toteswinger: 1&2 £3.80, 1&3 £7.50, 2&3 £1.60 CSF £19.85 TOTE £16.90: £3.80, £1.10, £1.70; EX 31.60.There was no bid for the winner. Drizzi was claimed by J. J. Best for £6000.
Owner P M Rich **Bred** Haras Du Gazon **Trained** Great Shefford, Berks
■ A first winner under Rules for Sally Randell, on her first ride on the Flat.

FOCUS
A very modest bunch contested this selling race for amateur riders. The winner benefited from an uncontested lead and the form is dubious, rated through the third.

3329 BET WIMBLEDON TENNIS - BETDAQ H'CAP 7f 32y(P)
3:00 (3:01) (Class 6) (0-60,60) 3-Y-0+ **£2,388** (£705; £352) **Stalls** High

Form RPR

2042 **1** **Bentley**[9] [3034] 4-9-4 **56**.. TPQueally 8 68
(J G Given) *chsd ldr: rdn over 2f out: styd on u.p to ld wl ins fnl f* **7/2**[2]

-005 **2** *1 3/4* **All You Need (IRE)**[17] [2806] 4-9-6 **58**..(v[1]) NCallan 11 65
(R Hollinshead) *chsd ldrs: led 1/2-way: rdn clr over 1f out: hdd wl ins fnl f* **13/2**[3]

52-0 **3** *2 1/4* **Towy Girl (IRE)**[10] [2991] 4-9-6 **58**.. CatherineGannon 9 59
(A W Carroll) *prom: outpcd over 2f out: styd on u.p fnl f* **16/1**

4202 **4** *nk* **Guildenstern (IRE)**[17] [2806] 6-9-6 **58**.. TGMcLaughlin 5 58
(P Howling) *hld up: hdwy 1/2-way: rdn over 1f out: styd on same pce* **11/4**[1]

0652 **5** *nk* **Swift Cut (IRE)**[10] [2988] 4-8-10 **55**..(p) DavidProbert(7) 10 54
(D Burchell) *chsd ldrs: rdn over 2f out: styd on same pce appr fnl f* **14/1**

5300 **6** *1/2* **Tanforan**[12] [2925] 6-9-6 **58**..(p) DavidAllan 6 56
(B P J Baugh) *hld up: rdn 1/2-way: styd on ins fnl f* **15/2**

4306 **7** *1* **Playtotheaudience**[17] [2806] 5-9-4 **59**..(v) JamieMoriarty(3) 7 54
(R A Fahey) *hld up: hdwy 1/2-way: rdn over 1f out: wknd fnl f* **15/2**

2300 **8** *2 1/2* **Bens Georgie (IRE)**[17] [2806] 6-8-13 **54**.. DuranFentiman(3) 4 43
(D K Ivory) *wnt lft s: prom: rdn 1/2-way: wknd over 2f out* **14/1**

5000 **9** *4* **Newgate (UAE)**[16] [2846] 4-9-3 **55**..(b) DeanMcKeown 2 33
(Mrs R A Carr) *s.i.s and hmpd s: hdwy on outside over 2f out: sn wknd* **25/1**

0600 **10** *2 1/4* **Gramm**[21] [2672] 5-9-8 **60**.. PaulMulrennan 1 32
(M W Easterby) *led to 1/2-way: wkng whn nt clr run over 2f out* **16/1**

1m 30.13s (0.53) **Going Correction** +0.125s/f (Slow) **10** Ran SP% **122.4**
Speed ratings (Par 101): **101,99,96,96,95 95,94,91,86,84**
toteswinger: 1&2 £1.30, 1&3 £11.40, 2&3 £15.80 CSF £25.10 CT £237.56 TOTE £4.30: £2.00, £1.70, £5.40; EX 22.90.
Owner Danethorpe Racing Partnership **Bred** Paul Blows And Jenny Hall **Trained** Willoughton, Lincs
■ Bessemer was withdrawn on vet's advice (12/1, deduct 5p in the £ under rule 4).

FOCUS
The winner is in good form and can go on from this and the runner-up looks on a handy mark, but those behind them are a motley bunch who rarely get their heads in front. The form seems sound enough for the grade.
Newgate(UAE) Official explanation: jockey said gelding was reluctant to race

3330 BET EURO 2008 - BETDAQ CLAIMING STKS 5f 216y(P)
3:30 (3:30) (Class 6) 3-Y-0 **£2,914** (£867; £433; £216) **Stalls** Low

Form RPR

4405 **1** **Bertbrand**[11] [2983] 3-8-13 70.. NCallan 5 69
(M Botti) *a.p: led over 1f out: rdn and hung rt fnl f: r.o* **2/1**[1]

1201 **2** *2 3/4* **Copperbottomed (IRE)**[17] [2803] 3-8-9 66..(e) PatCosgrave 6 57
(J R Boyle) *hld up: hdwy and hung rt over 2f out: rdn over 1f out: styd on same pce fnl f* **10/3**[2]

10-4 **3** *hd* **Blue Zenith (IRE)**[40] [2099] 3-8-10 69.. DeanMcKeown 8 57
(J S Moore) *chsd ldrs: led over 2f out: rdn and hdd over 1f out: no ex ins fnl f* **7/1**[3]

4210 **4** *1/2* **Valhillen**[10] [2998] 3-9-5 72..(p) HayleyTurner 4 64
(M D I Usher) *chsd ldrs: nt clr run over 2f out: rdn over 1f out: styd on* **2/1**[1]

3663 **5** *1* **Bahamarama (IRE)**[17] [2803] 3-8-2 53..(p) WilliamBuick 2 44
(R A Harris) *chsd ldrs: lost pl over 4f out: hdwy u.p over 1f out: no imp fnl f* **12/1**

004 **6** *4 1/2* **Flying Seasons**[17] [2771] 3-8-12 50.. JamesMillman(5) 1 45
(B R Millman) *hld up: rdn over 2f out: hung lft fr over 1f out: n.d* **22/1**

-636 **7** *5* **Cherished Song**[127] [597] 3-7-13 43.. DominicFox(3) 7 14
(M G Quinlan) *led: hdd over 3f out: rdn and wknd over 2f out* **33/1**

0-00 **8** *1* **Jimmy Dean**[35] [2259] 3-8-7 40..(b) LiamJones 3 16
(M Wellings) *w ldr tl led over 3f out: hdd over 2f out: rdn and wknd over 1f out* **66/1**

1m 15.92s (0.92) **Going Correction** +0.125s/f (Slow) **8** Ran SP% **118.7**
Speed ratings (Par 97): **98,94,94,93,92 86,79,78**
toteswinger: 1&2 £2.00, 1&3 £5.00, 2&3 £5.30 CSF £9.31 TOTE £3.90: £1.10, £1.40, £1.80; EX 14.30.Bertbrand was claimed by D. J. Flood for £9000. Copperbottomed was claimed by Ms P. M. Marks for £7000.
Owner Giuliano Manfredini **Bred** R F And S D Knipe **Trained** Newmarket, Suffolk

FOCUS
A modest claimer. A few of these had some fair pieces of form to their credit at some point but not all of them came here in the best of heart. The form is weak.
Bahamarama(IRE) Official explanation: vet said filly pulled up lame

3331 BETDAQ.CO.UK EBF MAIDEN STKS 5f 216y(P)
4:00 (4:01) (Class 5) 2-Y-0 **£3,626** (£1,079; £539; £269) **Stalls** Low

Form RPR

22 **1** **Predict**[9] [3027] 2-8-12 0.. J-PGuillambert 7 79+
(Sir Mark Prescott) *a.p: chsd ldr over 3f out: led 2f out: rdn clr over 1f out: hung lft fnl f: idled towards fin* **4/11**[1]

0 **2** *1/2* **Talking Hands**[38] [2146] 2-8-12 0.. HaddenFrost(5) 1 82+
(S Kirk) *chsd ldrs: outpcd over 2f out: edgd lft and r.o wl ins fnl f* **7/1**[3]

3 *8* **Highland Storm** 2-9-3 0.. TPQueally 5 58+
(J G Given) *s.s: outpcd: r.o ins fnl f: nvr nrr* **16/1**

45 **4** *3/4* **Street Of Hope (USA)**[33] [2309] 2-8-12 0.. WilliamBuick 6 51
(J W Hills) *led: rdn and hdd 2f out: wknd fnl f* **6/1**[2]

430 **5** *2 3/4* **Entrancer (IRE)**[40] [2098] 2-9-3 0.. DO'Donohoe 4 48
(W R Muir) *hld up in tch: rdn and wknd over 2f out* **16/1**

6 *1/2* **Shaws Diamond (USA)** 2-8-12 0.. PatrickMathers 8 41
(D Shaw) *s.s: outpcd: nvr nrr* **40/1**

7 *3 1/2* **Der Rosenkavalier (IRE)** 2-9-3 0.. FrancisNorton 3 36
(A M Balding) *prom: rdn over 3f out: wknd over 2f out* **7/1**[3]

8 *3/4* **Iliketoboogie** 2-8-12 0.. PatCosgrave 9 28
(A J McCabe) *s.s: effrt over 2f out: a in rr* **25/1**

0 **9** *6* **Craft (FR)**[12] [2944] 2-9-3 0.. NCallan 2 15
(B J Meehan) *prom over 3f* **25/1**

1m 15.63s (0.63) **Going Correction** +0.125s/f (Slow) **9** Ran SP% **134.5**
Speed ratings (Par 93): **100,99,88,87,84 83,78,77,69**
toteswinger: 1&2 £3.30, 1&3 £4.20, 2&3 £17.20 CSF £5.19 TOTE £1.30: £1.02, £2.70, £6.00; EX 7.70.
Owner Faisal Salman **Bred** Belgrave Bloodstock Ltd **Trained** Newmarket, Suffolk

FOCUS
The front two aside, these appeared a distinctly moderate bunch of juveniles. The winner, however, clocked a decent winning time, around a third-of-a-second faster than the preceding three-year-old claimer. A big step up from the runner-up.

NOTEBOOK
Predict had run to a decent standard in finishing runner-up on both her previous starts and was unsurprisngly sent off as a very warm order to make it third time lucky. She looked set for an easy success when she passed the pacesetting Street Of Hope, but idled badly close home and her victory margin was rapidly diminishing at the line. Her future is in the hands of the Handicapper. (op 1-2)
Talking Hands was nibbled at in the market before his racecourse bow at Newbury last month, where he stayed on without ever threatening the principals. He again proved that stamina is going to be more his forte by running on strongly after getting a touch outpaced on the home turn. He will do much better still over the extra furlong. (op 6-1)
Highland Storm shaped with some promise on his first sight of a racecourse, running on well once he began to realise what was required of him after being slowly away and outpaced in the early stages. He should improve, but is probably only modest.
Street Of Hope(USA) took them along for the first half-mile but folded very tamely when challenged and looks modest. (op 7-1)

3332 BET MULTIPLES - BETDAQ H'CAP 5f 20y(P)
4:30 (4:31) (Class 5) (0-70,67) 3-Y-0 **£3,070** (£906; £453) **Stalls** Low

Form RPR

500 **1** **Stoneacre Pat (IRE)**[41] [2074] 3-8-8 **54**.. PatrickMathers 6 57
(Peter Grayson) *s.i.s: hdwy over 1f out: rdn: edgd lft and r.o to ld wl ins fnl f* **20/1**

1-32 **2** *3/4* **Heaven**[17] [2774] 3-9-7 **67**.. TPQueally 7 73+
(P J Makin) *s.i.s: hld up: hdwy 1/2-way: nt clr fr run over 1f out tl gap appeared wl ins fnl f: r.o wl: no ch w wnr* **3/1**[1]

0463 **3** *nk* **Our Kally**[17] [2774] 3-7-9 **48**.. DavidProbert(7) 8 47
(M D I Usher) *mid-div: sn pushed along: outpcd over 3f out: r.o wl ins fnl f* **14/1**

2400 **4** *1/2* **Jalons Bridewell**[15] [2864] 3-9-3 **63**..(v) FrancisNorton 2 60
(M Quinn) *led: rdn and hung lft fr over 1f out: hdd ins fnl f: styd on same pce* **6/1**[3]

32-0 **5** *shd* **Mystickhill (IRE)**[17] 2803 3-9-1 **61**..............................(t) PaulMulrennan 1 58
(J Balding) *s.i.s: sn chsng ldrs: ev ch whn hmpd over 1f out: rdn to ld ins fnl f: sn hdd and no ex* **11/1**

0620 **6** *½* **Shatter Resistant (IRE)**[3] 3224 3-8-10 **56** ow1....(e) StephenDonohoe 5 51
(M D Squance) *chsd ldr: rdn: hung lft and ev ch over 1f out: hung rt and nt run on wl ins fnl f* **7/2**[2]

-645 **7** *1 ¼* **Richardthesecond (IRE)**[25] 2527 3-8-13 **59**................ TGMcLaughlin 9 50
(W M Brisbourne) *prom: rdn and hung lft over 1f out: styd on same pce* **9/1**

6040 **8** *½* **Planet Paradise (IRE)**[9] 3030 3-8-2 **48** oh3........... CatherineGannon 10 37
(D Shaw) *s.i.s: outpcd: styd on ins fnl f: nt trble ldrs* **33/1**

2250 **9** *1* **Seductive Witch**[73] 1315 3-9-0 **60**.................................. DavidAllan 3 45
(J Balding) *chsd ldrs: rdn 1/2-way: wknd fnl f* **12/1**

0-66 **10** *3 ¾* **Laa Baas (IRE)**[11] 2981 3-9-2 **62**... NCallan 4 34
(M A Jarvis) *chsd ldrs to 1/2-way* **3/1**[1]

63.17 secs (0.87) **Going Correction** +0.125s/f (Slow) **10** Ran SP% **126.9**
Speed ratings (Par 99): **98,96,96,95,95 94,92,91,90,84**
toteswinger: 1&2 £14.60, 1&3 £37.60, 2&3 £3.80 CSF £86.56 CT £924.43 TOTE £34.00: £9.30, £1.80, £3.80; EX 199.80.
Owner R Teatum And Mrs S Grayson **Bred** J Kinsella **Trained** Formby, Lancs

FOCUS
This was a fairly weak handicap for modest three-year-old speedsters and they finished in something of a heap to suggest that if they met again the result would be somewhat different. The runner-up was unlucky and has been rated a length winner.
Heaven Official explanation: jockey said filly was denied a clear run

3333 TRY BETDAQ FOR AN EXCHANGE MEDIAN AUCTION MAIDEN STKS — 1m 141y(P)
5:00 (5:02) (Class 6) 3-Y-O — **£2,388** (£705; £352) **Stalls** Low

Form — RPR

2400 **1** **Themwerethedays**[21] 2678 3-8-12 70.......................... HaddenFrost(5) 4 69
(S Kirk) *s.i.s: hld up: hdwy over 2f out: rdn and hung lft fr over 1f out: led ins fnl f: all out* **15/8**[1]

004 **2** *hd* **Scary Movie (IRE)**[17] 2772 3-9-3 65.............................. PatCosgrave 7 69
(D J Coakley) *chsd ldrs: nt clr run over 1f out: rdn and ev ch ins fnl f: hung lft towards fin: r.o* **14/1**

00-4 **3** *nse* **Princess Gee**[25] 2528 3-8-12 70...................................... HayleyTurner 9 63
(B J McMath) *hld up: rdn over 3f out: hdwy over 2f out: rdn over 1f out: ev ch whn hmpd ins fnl f: edgd lft nr fin: r.o* **8/1**

6- **4** *3 ¾* **Beggars End (USA)**[234] 6616 3-9-3 0.......................... NCallan 11 60
(E F Vaughan) *s.i.s: sn prom: rdn to ld over 1f out: hdd: hung lft and no ex ins fnl f* **9/4**[2]

00 **5** *3 ¼* **Bramalea**[12] 2954 3-8-12 0.. TPQueally 5 47
(B W Duke) *sn led: hdd over 6f out: led again over 2f out: rdn and hdd over 1f out: wknd ins fnl f* **25/1**

4 **6** *2 ¾* **Hydrophonic**[12] 2929 3-8-9 0.. JamieMoriarty(3) 3 41
(R A Fahey) *hld up: rdn over 2f out: a in rr* **7/1**[3]

3224 **7** *3 ¼* **Zeffirelli**[17] 2805 3-9-3 61.. FrancisNorton 10 39
(M Quinn) *chsd ldr: led over 6f out: hdd over 2f out: hung lft and wknd fnl f* **7/1**[3]

0 **8** *2 ¾* **Snake Catcher**[13] 2912 3-9-3 0.................................. PaulMulrennan 8 32
(M W Easterby) *chsd ldrs: lost pl 6f out: wknd over 2f out* **66/1**

04 **9** *2 ¾* **Coup De Torchon (FR)**[4] 3180 3-8-12 0........................ SamHitchcott 2 21
(J A Osborne) *chsd ldrs: rdn 1/2-way: wknd wl over 1f out* **16/1**

-000 **10** *13* **Amber Ridge**[25] 2549 3-9-3 51..(p) DAllen 1 —
(B P J Baugh) *hld up: rdn and wknd over 2f out* **33/1**

1m 52.71s (2.21) **Going Correction** +0.125s/f (Slow) **10** Ran SP% **122.5**
Speed ratings (Par 97): **95,94,94,91,88 86,83,80,78,66**
toteswinger: 1&2 £8.50, 1&3 £5.70, 2&3 £14.80 CSF £31.68 TOTE £2.80: £1.10, £4.30, £2.00; EX 37.80 Place 6: £27.62 Place 5: £21.46.
Owner Mike & Maureen Browne **Bred** Plantation Stud **Trained** Upper Lambourn, Berks

FOCUS
A distinctly modest maiden. It was steadily run and has been rated through the winner and third.
T/Plt: £19.30 to a £1 stake. Pool: £60,678.05. 2,286.25 winning tickets. T/Qpdt: £5.10 to a £1 stake. Pool: £3,167.78. 453.20 winning tickets. CR

2924 BEVERLEY (R-H)
Tuesday, June 24

OFFICIAL GOING: Good to firm (firm in places)
Wind: Virtually nil Weather: Dry and sunny

3334 PADDOCK BAR MAIDEN AUCTION STKS — 7f 100y
2:15 (2:16) (Class 5) 2-Y-O — **£2,331** (£693; £346; £173) **Stalls** High

Form — RPR

0 **1** **Fastnet Storm (IRE)**[24] 2592 2-9-1 0............................ MickyFenton 10 75+
(T P Tate) *t.k.h: sn led: rdn along 2f out: drvn ins fnl f: styd on gamely* **9/4**[2]

4 **2** *nk* **Inheritor (IRE)**[8] 3078 2-9-3 0...................................... TomEaves 8 76
(B Smart) *t.k.h: cl up: effrt over 2f out: sn rdn and ev ch: drvn ins fnl f: no ex towards fin* **11/8**[1]

00 **3** *2 ¼* **Pride Of Kings**[38] 2186 2-8-13 0.................................... JoeFanning 3 67
(M Johnston) *t.k.h: sn stdd and hld up in tch: hdwy on outer 3f out: rdn to chal and ch whn edgd rt over 1f out: drvn and kpt on same pce ins fnl f* **20/1**

255 **4** *¾* **Yokozuna**[12] 2979 2-8-13 0..(b[1]) TPQueally 11 65
(E A L Dunlop) *stdd s and hld up in rr: hdwy 1/2-way: rdn 2f out: drvn and edgd rt over 1f out: kpt on u.p ins fnl f* **11/2**[3]

0 **5** *3 ½* **Victorian Tycoon (IRE)**[27] 2502 2-8-11 0.......................... NCallan 7 54
(E J O'Neill) *chsd ldng pair: rdn along over 2f out: sn drvn and wknd* **17/2**

00 **6** *7* **Ten Cents A Dance**[14] 2909 2-9-1 0................................ DavidAllan 5 42
(T D Easterby) *in tch: effrt 3fr out: sn rdn and no hdwy* **50/1**

0 **7** *2* **Smoke Me A Kipper (IRE)**[15] 2887 2-8-6 0.............. RoystonFfrench 1 28
(Mrs A Duffield) *a in rr* **20/1**

8 *¾* **Imperial Angel (IRE)** 2-8-8 0...................................... TonyHamilton 9 28
(D Carroll) *chsd ldng pair: rdn along 3f out: wknd over 2f out* **28/1**

0 **9** *9* **Davana**[14] 2909 2-7-13 0.. KellyHarrison(5) 2 —
(W J H Ratcliffe) *a in rr* **100/1**

00 **10** *shd* **Angela Tee (IRE)**[15] 2887 2-8-3 0............................ DuranFentiman(3) 4 —
(T D Easterby) *a in rr* **100/1**

1m 34.8s (1.00) **Going Correction** -0.225s/f (Firm) **10** Ran SP% **115.7**
Speed ratings (Par 93): **85,84,82,81,77 69,66,66,55,55**
toteswinger: 1&2 £2.00, 1&3 £10.20, 2&3 £8.50. CSF £5.27 TOTE £3.00: £1.20, £1.20, £2.50; EX 5.50.
Owner The Kittywake Partnership **Bred** Norelands Bloodstock **Trained** Tadcaster, N Yorks

FOCUS
An ordinary juvenile maiden run in a moderate time. The pace was steady early on and the first two home were in the first two throughout. The fourth helps govern the level.

NOTEBOOK
Fastnet Storm(IRE) confirmed the promise he showed when staying on late in a good 6f maiden at Doncaster, despite racing keenly early on. He probably would have been better off getting a lead in a stronger-run race, but he battled on well when challenged by the favourite to justify a big market move - he was around 5/1 in the morning. There should be more to come. (op 2-1 tchd 15-8)
Inheritor(IRE), a keeping-on fourth over just short of 6f on his debut at Carlisle, improved on that form on this step up in trip but was just held. Like the winner, he was a touch keen early and probably would have preferred a stronger pace, but he still pulled well clear of the remainder. (op 13-8)
Pride Of Kings showed very little in two runs over 5f, but this was much better. Having raced wide throughout from his low draw, he moved into contention travelling well in the straight, but was ultimately outstayed by the front pair, who had charted a much shorter route. On this evidence, he has the speed to cope with a drop back to 6f, but should stay 7f on an easier track. (tchd 22-1)
Yokozuna, upped in trip, was ridden surprisingly negatively considering he was fitted with blinkers for the first time and had the rails draw. He was doing all his best work at the finish, but was never a danger and did not offer a great deal of encouragement. (op 4-1)
Victorian Tycoon(IRE) did not beat a rival when well backed on his debut over 6f at Great Leighs and he again failed to justify a market move, although this was a little better. (op 16-1)

3335 RACING UK ON SKY 432 CLAIMING STKS — 1m 4f 16y
2:45 (2:45) (Class 6) 3-Y-O+ — **£2,331** (£693; £346; £173) **Stalls** High

Form — RPR

4255 **1** **Black Falcon (IRE)**[4] 3204 8-9-5 59.................................... NCallan 3 58
(John A Harris) *hld up towards rr: hdwy 4f out: swtchd lft and effrt 2f out: rdn to ld jst ins fnl f: drvn out* **9/4**[1]

-510 **2** *1 ¼* **Elite Land**[13] 2927 5-8-13 50...................................... NeilBrown(5) 7 55
(N Bycroft) *hld up towards rr: hdwy over 3f out: rdn wl over 1f out: styd on u.p ins fnl f* **9/2**[2]

/56- **3** *1 ½* **Dimashq**[205] 6325 6-8-13 43.. MickyFenton 5 48
(P T Midgley) *s.i.s and in rr: stdy hdwy over 3f out: ridden wl over 1f out: kpt on wl u.p ins fnl f* **14/1**

1002 **4** *¾* **Kryptonite (IRE)**[15] 2894 3-8-13 64........................(p) WilliamBuick 2 61
(J W Hills) *in tch: hdwy 3f out: rdn wl over 1f out: drvn and no imp ent fnl f* **5/1**[3]

40-4 **5** *1* **Cecina Marina**[20] 2731 5-8-9 44.................................. KellyHarrison(5) 4 46
(Mrs K Walton) *trckd ldr: effrt to ld over 2f out: rdn wl over 1f out: drvn and hdd jst ins fnl f: wknd* **9/1**

0000 **6** *2* **Ellies Faith**[20] 2731 4-8-13 35.................................... AndrewElliott 8 42
(L R James) *led: rdn along 3f out: hdd over 2f out: drvn and wknd over 1f out* **66/1**

60P3 **7** *3 ¾* **St Johns Wood**[5] 3174 3-8-8 68..................................(b) PaulMulrennan 9 45
(M W Easterby) *chsd ldrs: rdn along over 4f out and sn wknd* **6/1**

00-0 **8** *2 ¼* **Fadansil**[8] 3077 5-9-5 48.. TomEaves 11 38
(J Wade) *in rr tl sme late hdwy* **20/1**

/06- **9** *1 ¼* **Cottam Grange**[107] 965 8-9-8 37.................................. DaleGibson 12 39
(M W Easterby) *prom on inner: rdn along over 3f out and sn wknd* **50/1**

-600 **10** *10* **Welcome Cat (USA)**[32] 2364 4-9-8 49..............(p) SilvestreDeSousa 10 23
(A D Brown) *a in rr* **12/1**

4044 **11** *42* **Indecision**[42] 2080 3-8-6 48......................................(b[1]) BradleyRoper(7) 6 —
(M W Easterby) *chsd ldrs: sddle slipped after 2f: sn lost pl and t.o fr 1/2-way* **20/1**

2m 37.58s (-3.32) **Going Correction** -0.225s/f (Firm)
WFA 3 from 4yo+ 14lb **11** Ran SP% **117.2**
Speed ratings (Par 101): **102,101,100,99,99 97,95,93,92,86 58**
toteswinger: 1&2 £4.00, 1&3 £12.40, 2&3 £20.50. CSF £11.44 TOTE £3.60: £1.50, £1.80, £4.80; EX 13.50.
Owner Shaun Taylor **Bred** Gainsborough Stud Management Ltd **Trained** Eastwell, Leics
■ Stewards' Enquiry : Paul Mulrennan caution: used whip when out of contention

FOCUS
A moderate claimer in which the first three home were held up. The form appears sound rated through the next four home behind the winner, although that one did not need to run to his recent best.
Welcome Cat(USA) Official explanation: trainer said gelding finished lame

3336 LEVY BOARD H'CAP — 5f
3:15 (3:17) (Class 3) (0-95,95) 3-Y-O+ — **£7,123** (£2,119; £1,059; £529) **Stalls** High

Form — RPR

-324 **1** **Everymanforhimself (IRE)**[11] 3009 4-9-8 **90**................ NCallan 11 101
(K A Ryan) *chsd ldrs: rdn along 1/2-way: drvn and hdwy appr last: kpt on u.p to ld on line* **5/2**[1]

4000 **2** *hd* **Strike Up The Band**[17] 2828 5-9-9 **91**................ AdrianTNicholls 13 101
(D Nicholls) *led: rdn over 1f out: drvn ins fnl f: ct on line* **11/2**[3]

0-30 **3** *1 ¼* **Johannes (IRE)**[26] 2538 5-8-12 **80**............................ DeanMcKeown 9 86+
(E J O'Neill) *hmpd s and in rr: hdwy on outer over 1f out: sn rdn and styd on strly ins fnl f: nrst fin* **14/1**

0101 **4** *nk* **Namir (IRE)**[15] 2892 6-8-5 **76** oh1........................(vt) DuranFentiman(3) 7 81
(D Shaw) *trckd ldrs: rdn along and outpcd wl over 1f out: kpt on u.p ins fnl f: nrst fin* **14/1**

000- **5** *hd* **Handsome Cross (IRE)**[281] 5481 7-8-8 **76**............. RoystonFfrench 14 80
(Mrs A Duffield) *chsd ldr: rdn to chal over 1f out: sn drvn and one pce ins fnl f* **14/1**

3010 **6** *nk* **Fyodor (IRE)**[24] 2626 7-9-13 **95**................................ PaulMulrennan 6 98+
(W J Haggas) *stdd s and swtchd lft to inner: hdwy 2f out: swtchd lft and rdn over 1f out: styd on ins fnl f: nrst fin* **18/1**

-150 **7** *1 ¼* **Pacific Pride**[17] 2818 5-8-8 **79**................................ JamieMoriarty(3) 12 77
(J J Quinn) *in tch: rdn along 2f out: sn drvn and no imp* **20/1**

1233 **8** *nk* **Lord Of The Reins (IRE)**[11] 3009 4-8-12 **80**.................. TPQueally 17 77+
(J G Given) *mid div: n.m.r 2f out: swtchd lft 1f out: kpt on same pce* **5/1**[2]

0610 **9** *nk* **Steelcut**[17] 2828 4-8-8 **76**.. TonyHamilton 2 72
(R A Fahey) *qckly away and sn cl up: rdn along 1/2-way: sn wknd* **25/1**

250- **10** *1 ½* **Thunder Bay**[255] 6167 3-8-4 **85**.................................. BMcHugh(7) 10 76
(R A Fahey) *wnt lft and bmpd s: a towards rr* **22/1**

2550 **11** *shd* **Canadian Danehill (IRE)**[17] 2828 6-9-6 **93**..............(p) NeilBrown(5) 15 83
(R M H Cowell) *in tch: rdn along 2f out and sn wknd* **14/1**

00-0 **12** *nk* **Jack Rackham**[11] 3009 4-9-0 **82**................................ TomEaves 4 71
(B Smart) *a towards rr* **18/1**

000- **13** *¾* **The Tatling (IRE)**[241] 6487 11-9-8 **90**.......................... WilliamBuick 16 77
(J M Bradley) *a in rr* **12/1**

6200 **14** 15 **King Of Swords (IRE)**[11] 3009 4-8-10 78 JoeFanning 8 11
(N Tinkler) *wnt rt and bmpd s: a in rr* **40/1**

60.95 secs (-2.55) **Going Correction** -0.325s/f (Firm)
WFA 3 from 4yo+ 6lb **14** Ran SP% **120.9**
Speed ratings (Par 107): **107,106,104,104,103 103,101,100,100,98 97,97,96,72**
toteswinger: 1&2 £3.40, 1&3 £9.60, 2&3 £17.40. CSF £14.25 CT £165.76 TOTE £2.90: £1.40, £2.50, £5.10; EX 18.10.
Owner J Duddy B McDonald & A Heeney **Bred** Denis McDonnell **Trained** Hambleton, N Yorks
■ Stewards' Enquiry : Adrian T Nicholls one-day ban: used whip with excessive frequency (Jul 8)

FOCUS
A good handicap but, as is usually the case in sprints at Beverley, those drawn low were at a disadvantage. The winning time was 1.22 seconds quicker than the closing 46-55 apprentice handicap and the form looks decent rated around the runner-up and fourth.

NOTEBOOK
Everymanforhimself(IRE) had run well on all three of his starts since joining Kevin Ryan and he confirmed the promise of those efforts with a narrow success, staying on late to grab long-time leader Strike Up The Band on the line. He went without his usual blinkers this time, and fair enough he managed to win, but he was under pressure some way out and it would be no surprise to see some sort of headgear fitted again in future, just to help him concentrate. (op 10-3)
Strike Up The Band was on a handy mark - he was once rated 108 - and came into this in decent order judged on his close-up effort from a bad draw in the Dash at Epsom on his previous start. Nicely drawn, he went from the front and was only pegged back almost on the line, just failing to end a losing run stretching back to a Listed success gained in France in 2006. He will go back up in the weights, but might be able to pick up a similar race if turned out before he is reassessed. (op 5-1)
Johannes(IRE), racing off a career-low mark, was soon well out the back and never looked a danger, but he stayed on strongly when the race was all over to grab third. This was obviously encouraging, and he is clearly on a very favourable mark, but his only previous success was gained in a maiden back in 2005 and it would probably be unwise to get too carried away. (op 16-1)
Namir(IRE), 4lb higher than when winning at Pontefract on his previous start, and 7lb higher than when successful over course and distance three starts back, was far from ideally drawn in stall seven, but he was soon well placed. He kept on, but is at his best when the leaders fall away.
Handsome Cross(IRE) ◆ was backed at big prices on his debut for a new trainer and ran well for a long way after 281 days off. He should last a bit longer next time with the benefit of this run. (op 25-1 tchd 12-1)
Fyodor(IRE), without the visor this time, was dropped in from his low stall and cut all the way across to the inside rail. As a result, he needed luck in the straight, but got going too late in a race in which the pace held up. (op 16-1)
Lord Of The Reins(IRE) ◆ is a hold-up horse, so he could not take advantage of his draw against the rails, and he got no run at all from the quarter-mile to the furlong pole in the straight. He could not confirm recent York form with today's winner, but is better than he showed. Official explanation: jockey said gelding was denied a clear run (op 4-1)
King Of Swords(IRE) Official explanation: jockey said colt hung left-handed throughout

3337 ST JOHN AMBULANCE H'CAP 1m 1f 207y
3:45 (3:45) (Class 4) (0-80,80) 4-Y-0+ **£4,209** (£1,252; £625; £312) **Stalls** High

Form RPR
0-04 **1** **Piper's Song (IRE)**[14] 2904 5-9-3 76 PatCosgrave 3 84
(D J G Murray Smith) *trckd ldng pair: effrt wl over 1f out: rdn and swtchd lft ins fnl f: styd on strly to ld nr fin* **12/1**
2334 **2** ½ **Princess Cocoa (IRE)**[24] 2623 5-8-9 71 JamieMoriarty(3) 6 78
(R A Fahey) *trckd ldr: smooth hdwy to chal 2f out: rdn and slt ld ins fnl f: hdd and nt qckn nr fin* **11/4**[3]
002 **3** ½ **Mister Fizzbomb (IRE)**[13] 2927 5-8-3 62 (v) RoystonFfrench 1 68
(J S Wainwright) *led: pushed along and qcknd 3f out: rdn over 1f out: drvn and hdd ins fnl f: no ex towards fin* **9/2**
0-51 **4** 3¼ **Riley Boys (IRE)**[13] 2927 7-8-12 71 TPQueally 4 71
(J G Given) *hld up in tch: effrt and hdwy over 2f out: sn rdn and no imp appr fnl f* **7/4**[1]
22-0 **5** ½ **Del Mar Sunset**[11] 3003 9-9-3 76 LiamJones 5 75
(W J Haggas) *dwlt: t.k.h and hld up in rr: sme hdwy 2f out: rdn and no imp appr fnl f* **5/2**[2]

2m 9.53s (2.53) **Going Correction** -0.225s/f (Firm) **5** Ran SP% **117.5**
Speed ratings (Par 105): **80,79,79,76,76**
CSF £46.78 TOTE £18.50: £4.10, £2.30; EX 53.30.
Owner Rob Lloyd Racing Limited **Bred** Patrick M Ryan **Trained** Spurstow, Cheshire
■ A first winner for David Murray Smith since he returned to training.

FOCUS
A modest handicap and, with the pace very steady for much of the way, the time was very slow and the form needs treating with caution despite appearing to make some sense.

3338 TOMRODS STEEL STOCKHOLDERS MAIDEN STKS 1m 100y
4:15 (4:17) (Class 5) 3-Y-0 **£2,331** (£693; £346; £173) **Stalls** High

Form RPR
0-3 **1** **Wikaala (USA)**[17] 2834 3-9-3 0 DaleGibson 5 77+
(M P Tregoning) *dwlt: pushed along and hdwy to ld after 1f: rdn along 2f out: drvn ins fnl f and hld on gamely* **7/4**[2]
0-4 **2** ½ **Filigree Lace (USA)**[36] 2257 3-8-12 0 TomEaves 6 71+
(Sir Michael Stoute) *t.k.h: led 1f: cl up: rdn 2f out and sltly outpcd over 1f out: rallied wl u.p and ev ch ins fnl f tl no ex towards fin* **4/6**[1]
0 **3** 5 **Offshore Anna (IRE)**[91] 1019 3-8-12 0 PaulMulrennan 1 60
(J J Quinn) *hld up: hdwy on inner 3f out: rdn 2f out: styd on wl fnl f: nrst fin* **18/1**[3]
0 **4** 2½ **Mill Beattie**[28] 2488 3-8-12 0 AndrewElliott 3 54
(G M Moore) *chsd ldrs on outer: rdn along over 3f out: drvn and one pce fnl 2f* **80/1**
0 **5** 11 **Anna Lane**[13] 2929 3-8-7 0 KellyHarrison(5) 4 28
(W J H Ratcliffe) *chsd ldng pair: rdn along 3f out: sn drvn and wknd 2f out* **66/1**
0 **6** 8 **Willaby Lad**[18] 2786 3-9-3 0 PatrickMathers 9 15
(D Shaw) *in tch: rdn along over 3f out: sn wknd* **50/1**
7 hd **Aspendale (IRE)** 3-9-3 0 DavidAllan 7 15
(D Carroll) *hld up in rr: hdwy over 3f out: sn rdn and wknd fnl 2f* **20/1**
8 4½ **Lighting Shadow** 3-9-3 0 DNolan 2 4
(N Wilson) *in tch: rdn along over 3f out and sn wknd* **50/1**
9 ½ **Bandoran** 3-9-0 0 RussellKennemore(3) 8 3
(J R Holt) *a bhd* **50/1**

1m 47.04s (-0.56) **Going Correction** -0.225s/f (Firm) **9** Ran SP% **114.3**
Speed ratings (Par 99): **93,92,87,85,74 66,65,61,60**
toteswinger: 1&2 £1.30, 1&3 £2.60, 2&3 £2.20. CSF £3.08 TOTE £2.60: £1.10, £1.10, £2.60; EX 3.20.
Owner Hamdan Al Maktoum **Bred** Shadwell Farm LLC **Trained** Lambourn, Berks

FOCUS
This maiden only concerned two horses and they are probably a class above the opposition despite the fact it has been rated at something like face value for now.

3339 RACING AGAIN ON 4 JULY H'CAP 7f 100y
4:45 (4:46) (Class 5) (0-70,69) 3-Y-0+ **£2,914** (£867; £433; £216) **Stalls** High

Form RPR
-006 **1** **Mister Jingles**[7] 3108 5-9-0 57 MichaelJStainton(3) 14 66
(R M Whitaker) *chsd ldr: effrt over 2f out: rdn over 1f out: styd on to ld ins fnl f: drvn and hld on gamely towards fin* **11/2**[3]
0022 **2** hd **March Mate**[13] 2940 4-8-12 52 TomEaves 4 61
(B Ellison) *chsd ldrs: hdwy 2f out: rdn and ev ch ent fnl f tl drvn and no ex towards fin* **15/2**
6250 **3** 2¼ **Zennerman (IRE)**[22] 2662 5-9-4 58 (b) NCallan 3 61
(G A Swinbank) *hld up in tch: hdwy 3f out: rdn to chse ldng pair whn edgd rt ins fnl f and sn one pce* **13/2**
2-21 **4** 1½ **Shotley Mac**[13] 2925 4-9-9 68 NeilBrown(5) 2 67
(N Bycroft) *midfield: hdwy over 2f out: sn rdn and kpt on same pce ins fnl f* **4/1**[1]
-300 **5** ¾ **Northern Boy (USA)**[13] 2925 5-9-6 60 PaulMulrennan 7 57
(M W Easterby) *led: rdn along 2f out: drvn over 1f out: hdd & wknd ins fnl f* **20/1**
0-03 **6** 5 **Tough Love**[45] 2003 9-9-8 62 (p) DavidAllan 6 47
(T D Easterby) *t.k.h: in tch on inner: effrt over 2f out: sn rdn and no imp* **9/2**[2]
3001 **7** 2½ **Avontuur (FR)**[8] 3079 6-9-8 62 6ex (b) DaleGibson 11 41
(Mrs R A Carr) *s.i.s and bhd tl styd on fnl 2f: nt rch ldrs* **17/2**
3-00 **8** 6 **Sedge (USA)**[87] 1084 8-9-10 64 MickyFenton 1 28
(P T Midgley) *a towards rr* **16/1**
4250 **9** 1¼ **Kirkie (USA)**[7] 3117 3-9-6 69 (bt[1]) DarrenWilliams 9 27
(S Parr) *plld hrd: chsd ldng pair: rdn along 3f out and sn wknd* **16/1**
4000 **10** 5 **Ace Of Spies (IRE)**[11] 3004 3-8-2 58 MarieLussiana(7) 5 3
(M Johnston) *a towards rr* **12/1**
066- **11** 1¾ **Topazleo (IRE)**[321] 4283 4-9-1 55 TonyHamilton 12 —
(J Wade) *s.i.s: a in rr* **40/1**
600- **12** 19 **Leonard Charles**[290] 5238 4-9-2 59 JamieMoriarty(3) 8 —
(C R Dore) *in tch: rdn along over 3f out: sn wknd* **33/1**

1m 31.53s (-2.27) **Going Correction** -0.225s/f (Firm)
WFA 3 from 4yo+ 9lb **12** Ran SP% **118.8**
Speed ratings (Par 103): **103,102,100,98,97 91,89,82,80,75 73,51**
toteswinger: 1&2 £9.50, 1&3 £8.40, 2&3 £8.80. CSF £45.63 CT £281.46 TOTE £6.70: £2.10, £2.70, £2.70; EX 47.10.
Owner James Marshall & Mrs Susan Marshall **Bred** Catridge Farm Stud Ltd **Trained** Scarcroft, W Yorks

FOCUS
A moderate handicap run at a fair pace and a solid handicap for the grade.
Northern Boy(USA) Official explanation: jockey said gelding ran too free early stages
Avontuur(FR) Official explanation: jockey said gelding missed the break

3340 YORKSHIRE RACING FESTIVAL APPRENTICE H'CAP 5f
5:15 (5:22) (Class 6) (0-55,61) 3-Y-0+ **£2,331** (£693; £346; £173) **Stalls** High

Form RPR
5051 **1** **Kings College Boy**[8] 3080 8-9-11 61 6ex (b) FrederikTylicki 17 74
(R A Fahey) *cl up: hld wl over 1f out: rdn ins fnl f and kpt on wl* **4/1**[1]
1020 **2** ¾ **Jun Fan (USA)**[18] 2777 6-9-4 54 LanceBetts 1 64+
(B Ellison) *qckly away and sn led: rdn and hdd wl over 1f out: sn drvn and hung rt ent fnl f: ev ch tl no ex last 50yds* **16/1**
0230 **3** 2¼ **Whozart (IRE)**[7] 3112 5-8-10 50 MJMurphy(4) 13 52
(A Dickman) *chsd ldrs: rdn wl over 1f out: hung lft ins fnl f and kpt on same pce* **6/1**[2]
0606 **4** 3¼ **Tumbleweed Di**[4] 3231 4-8-11 47 SimonPearce 5 37+
(G R Oldroyd) *towards rr: hdwy wl over 1f out: swtchd rt and styd on ins fnl f: nrst fin* **16/1**
6546 **5** hd **Falmassim**[12] 2983 5-8-10 46 (v[1]) BMcHugh 10 35
(Miss J A Camacho) *chsd ldrs: rdn over 1f out: kpt on same pce ins fnl f* **8/1**[3]
0056 **6** ½ **Peopleton Brook**[13] 2934 6-9-2 52 (p) AshleyMorgan 12 39
(J M Bradley) *chsd ldrs: rdn wl over 1f out: hung lft and one pce ins fnl f* **22/1**
0-00 **7** 1¾ **Jellytot (USA)**[8] 3079 5-8-10 46 oh1 (be) JamieKyne 7 27
(J O'Reilly) *midfield: hdwy u.p on inner fnl 2f: nvr rch ldrs* **50/1**
5-66 **8** ¾ **Valiant Romeo**[15] 2881 8-8-11 47 AdeleRothery 11 25+
(R Bastiman) *prom: rdn along 2f out: grad wknd* **11/1**
2-42 **9** ½ **Smirfys Gold (IRE)**[18] 2802 4-9-2 52 AdamCarter 4 29+
(E S McMahon) *chsd ldrs: rdn wl over 1f out: wknd appr fnl f* **10/1**
00 **10** nse **Phinerine**[8] 3079 5-8-11 47 (e) StacyRenwick 16 24
(Miss J E Foster) *a towards rr* **33/1**
00-0 **11** hd **Mr Forthright**[66] 1476 4-8-12 48 DeanHeslop 9 24
(J M Bradley) *dwlt: a towards rr* **50/1**
0-40 **12** nk **Miss Mujahid Times**[16] 2869 5-8-10 46 oh1 (b) JamesRogers 8 21
(A D Brown) *a towards rr* **40/1**
363- **13** 2¾ **Piccolo Diamante (USA)**[187] 7207 4-8-10 50 AJSmith(4) 6 15
(S Parr) *rrd at s: plld hrd in rr: a bhd* **18/1**

62.17 secs (-1.33) **Going Correction** -0.325s/f (Firm) **13** Ran SP% **93.5**
Speed ratings (Par 101): **97,95,92,87,86 85,83,81,81,81 80,80,75**
toteswinger: 1&2 £8.30, 1&3 £4.10, 2&3 £14.70. CSF £38.18 CT £167.41 TOTE £3.20: £1.20, £4.60, £2.40; EX 39.10 Place 6: £42.72 Place 5: £32.12.
Owner The Cosmic Cases **Bred** Lady Jennifer Green **Trained** Musley Bank, N Yorks
■ The first winner in Britain following one in Ireland for German-born Frederik Tylicki.

FOCUS
A moderate sprint handicap restricted to apprentices who had not ridden more than ten winners. A high box is a big advantage over this course and distance although that was not totally obvious this time. The winning time 1.22 seconds slower than the earlier 76-95 handicap but the form looks solid.\n\x\x Angelofthenorth (12/1, upset in stalls) & Orotund (4/1, ref to enter stalls) were withdrawn. Deduct 25p in the £ under rule 4.)

T/Plt: £41.80 to a £1 stake. Pool: £72,240.84. 1,260.60 winning tickets. T/Qpdt: £21.50 to a £1 stake. Pool: £3,392.38. 116.50 winning tickets. JR

2930 BRIGHTON (L-H)

Tuesday, June 24

OFFICIAL GOING: Firm

Wind: Moderate, half behind

3341 MERCEDES-BENZ OF BRIGHTON MAIDEN VOYAGE MAIDEN AUCTION STKS 5f 213y

2:30 (2:31) (Class 5) 2-Y-O **£2,849** (£847; £423; £211) **Stalls** Low

Form				RPR
0232	1		**Souter's Sister (IRE)**[19] 2759 2-8-6 0 RyanMoore 3 (R Hannon) *led for 1f: swtchd rt over 3f out: led 2f out: sn clr: easily* **2/7**[1]	75+
36	2	6	**Sonhador**[46] 1955 2-9-1 0 JimCrowley 5 (P Winkworth) *led after 1f: hdd 2f out: sn outpcd by wnr* **11/2**[2]	65
00	3	1 1/2	**Calypso Prince**[13] 2944 2-8-10 0 (v[1]) HayleyTurner 4 (M D I Usher) *trckd first 2 thrght: carried rt over 3f out: rdn 2f out: one pce after* **33/1**	55
	4	2	**Rockinit (IRE)** 2-8-7 0 TPO'Shea 2 (M R Channon) *t.k.h: carried rt over 3f out: nvr on terms* **11/1**[3]	46
050	5	6	**Noworneva**[25] 2562 2-8-10 0 LPKeniry 1 (S Kirk) *s.i.s: last whn hmpd over 3f out: wl btn whn eased ins fnl f* **16/1**	31

1m 10.11s (-0.09) **Going Correction** -0.125s/f (Firm) **5 Ran SP% 110.3**

Speed ratings (Par 93): **95,87,85,82,74**

CSF £2.34 TOTE £1.20: £1.10, £1.60; EX 2.10.

Owner P D Merritt **Bred** John Cullinan **Trained** East Everleigh, Wilts

FOCUS

Just a modest selection of juveniles and an easy win for the most experienced filly in the line-up, who did not need to improve to score.

NOTEBOOK

Souter's Sister(IRE) had run with credit in better maidens than this and never came off the bridle in accounting for her rivals. She isn't really progressing with her racing though and may struggle against less-exposed sorts in nurseries. (op 1-3 tchd 4-11 in places)

Sonhador started off his racing career with a third to Langs Lash at Folkestone but while that one went on to win the Queen Mary Stakes at the Royal meeting last week, this son of Compton Place hasn't really progressed. On the basis of that debut run he may find himself harshly treated when the nurseries start. (op 8-1)

Calypso Prince didn't really improve much for the first-time visor he sported, although he did get caught up in the ripple effect of the winner's move right at halfway. (op 40-1)

Rockinit(IRE), a debutant daughter of Rock Of Gibraltar, looked green and was all over the place on the undulations. She should leave this form behind in time. (op 6-1)

Nowornevawas slowly away and coming to challenge wide up the centre of the course when getting a hefty bump from the rolling-around fourth home. He is already exposed as modest though. (tchd 14-1)

3342 BRAKES FRESH IDEAS MEDIAN AUCTION MAIDEN STKS 7f 214y

3:00 (3:01) (Class 6) 3-4-Y-O **£2,266** (£674; £337; £168) **Stalls** Low

Form				RPR
404	1		**Zaarmit (IRE)**[29] 2455 3-9-3 65 RyanMoore 6 (D M Simcock) *hld up in rr: hdwy on outside over 2f out: strly rdn and edgd lft bef led wl ins fnl f: all out* **10/11**[1]	67
0	2	nk	**Shadayid Khanum (IRE)**[19] 2756 3-8-12 0 HayleyTurner 3 (M P Tregoning) *hld up: hdwy to ld 2f out: hrd rdn and edgd lft bef hdd wl ins fnl f* **10/1**	61
00	3	7	**Burry Green**[40] 2123 3-8-9 0 ow2 HaddenFrost(5) 4 (R Hannon) *in tch: rdn over 2f out: wknd 1f out* **10/1**	47
6	4	1/2	**Zantic**[18] 2772 3-9-3 0 JimCrowley 2 (P R Chamings) *t.k.h: trckd ldr: wknd over 1f out* **9/2**[2]	49
4430	5	shd	**Bye Baby Bunting**[57] 1671 3-8-12 58 EddieAhern 5 (B R Johnson) *led until hdd 2f out: rdn and wknd appr fnl f* **5/1**[3]	44
00-0	6	13	**Veras Joy**[13] 2932 3-8-12 20 SamHitchcott 1 (B R Johnson) *chsd ldrs: rdn over 3f out: sn wknd and lost tch* **50/1**	14
6000	P		**Sweet Refrain**[19] 2756 3-8-9 45 (p) KirstyMilczarek(3) 7 (M J Attwater) *t.k.h: lost tch wl over 2f out: p.u over 1f out* **28/1**	—

1m 35.6s (-0.40) **Going Correction** -0.125s/f (Firm) **7 Ran SP% 110.8**

Speed ratings (Par 101): **97,96,89,89,89 76,—**

toteswinger: 1&2 £2.90, 1&3 £3.60, 2&3 £10.30. CSF £10.52 TOTE £1.90: £1.10, £4.30; EX 9.90.

Owner Khalifa Dasmal **Bred** Stone Ridge Farm **Trained** Newmarket, Suffolk

FOCUS

A very poor maiden, even by Brighton standards. The first two home pulled well clear of the rest and the winner, along with the third, sets a modest standard.

Sweet Refrain Official explanation: jockey said filly lost its action

3343 RACING ETC CLAIMING STKS 1m 1f 209y

3:30 (3:31) (Class 6) 3-Y-O+ **£1,748** (£520; £260; £129) **Stalls** High

Form				RPR
-341	1		**Ogre (USA)**[18] 2801 3-8-10 68 JimCrowley 3 (J R Boyle) *stdd s: hld up in hdwy to ld on bit 2f out: a in command after: hrd hld* **11/10**[1]	73+
300	2	2 1/4	**Fairly Honest**[43] 2053 4-8-8 49 WilliamCarson(7) 2 (P W Hiatt) *led tl hdd 2f out: rdn and kpt on but no ch w wnr after* **14/1**	57
25-5	3	16	**Shrewd Dude**[13] 2930 4-9-2 51 (p) NelsonDeSouza 1 (Carl Llewellyn) *trckd ldrs: rdn over 2f out: kpt on to retain poor 3rd ins fnl f* **7/1**	28
6033	4	nk	**Karmei**[13] 2930 3-9-1 60 EddieAhern 5 (J W Hills) *in rr: effrt on outside over 3f out: nvr on terms* **10/3**[2]	38
4032	5	1/2	**Split The Wind (USA)**[13] 2930 4-8-11 55 DavidProbert(7) 7 (Miss Sheena West) *trckd ldr tl rdn over 2f out: sn btn* **9/2**[3]	28
500-	6	30	**Valassini**[35] 6238 8-8-10 40 LPKeniry 6 (J W Mullins) *in tch: tl rdn over 4f out: sn wknd: t.o* **33/1**	—

2m 0.89s (-2.71) **Going Correction** -0.125s/f (Firm)

WFA 3 from 4yo+ 12lb **6 Ran SP% 111.0**

Speed ratings (Par 101): **105,103,90,90,89 65**

toteswinger: 1&2 £3.50, 1&3 £2.30, 2&3 £4.90. CSF £17.73 TOTE £2.00: £1.40, £5.20; EX 21.80.Ogre was claimed by P. D. Evans for £11000.

Owner M Khan X2 **Bred** Gulf Coast Farms LLC **Trained** Epsom, Surrey

FOCUS

A weak claimer. Ogre had every right to win on official figures and did so with her head in her chest. The front two pulled miles clear of the remainder but there is nothing solid about the rest.

3344 DIGIBET.CO.UK H'CAP 1m 3f 196y

4:00 (4:01) (Class 6) (0-65,62) 4-Y-O+ **£2,266** (£674; £337; £168) **Stalls** High

Form				RPR
054	1		**Foreign King (USA)**[6] 3137 4-9-4 59 LPKeniry 2 (J W Mullins) *mde all: rdn clr wl over 1f out: unchal* **7/2**[2]	66
4022	2	4	**Hester Brook (IRE)**[13] 2932 4-8-6 47 HayleyTurner 7 (J G M O'Shea) *hld up in tch: rdn and hdwy to go 2nd over 2f out: kpt on but no ch w wnr after* **4/1**[3]	48
0310	3	1/2	**Shenandoah Girl**[5] 3176 5-9-1 56 (tp) RyanMoore 5 (Miss Gay Kelleway) *hld up in rr: hdwy on outside 2f out: rdn and styd on to go 3rd ins fnl f* **7/2**[2]	56
-551	4	1 1/4	**African Pursuits (USA)**[13] 2932 4-9-7 62 (b[1]) JohnEgan 1 (Jamie Poulton) *trckd ldrs: rdn over 4f out: one pce fnl 2f* **11/4**[1]	60
0-45	5	hd	**Makai**[19] 2755 5-8-3 47 ow2 KevinGhunowa(3) 8 (M R Hoad) *t.k.h in mid-div: no hdwy fnl 2f* **8/1**	44
6504	6	1 1/4	**Bothar Brugha (IRE)**[29] 2456 4-8-1 45 KirstyMilczarek(3) 3 (J G M O'Shea) *unruly bef s and rrd up leaving stalls: bhd tl effrt on outside over 3f out: sn btn* **9/1**	40
0/0	7	8	**Drombeg Pride (IRE)**[21] 2694 4-8-5 46 ow1 PaulDoe 6 (G P Enright) *trckd wnr tl rdn and wknd qckly over 2f out* **33/1**	29
00-0	8	10	**Our Glenard**[19] 2755 9-7-13 45 NataliaGemelova(5) 4 (J E Long) *slowly away: a bhd: eased over 1f out* **33/1**	12

2m 32.2s (-0.50) **Going Correction** -0.125s/f (Firm) **8 Ran SP% 118.1**

Speed ratings (Par 101): **96,93,93,92,92 91,85,79**

toteswinger: 1&2 £3.80, 1&3 £3.40, 2&3 £3.80. CSF £18.64 CT £51.75 TOTE £4.30: £1.60, £1.50, £1.80; EX 23.10 Trifecta £52.80 Pool: £72240.84 - 1260.60 winning units..

Owner John Collins **Bred** Jayeff 'B' Stables **Trained** Wilsford-Cum-Lake, Wilts

FOCUS

Another singularly uncompetitive affair, the winner not hard pressed to break his duck on the level. The form is weak rated around the placed horses.

3345 BET365 BEST ODDS ON EVERY H'CAP 6f 209y

4:30 (4:32) (Class 5) (0-75,76) 3-Y-O+ **£2,849** (£847; £423; £211) **Stalls** Low

Form				RPR
013	1		**Choreography**[10] 3033 5-9-12 70 (p) PaulDoe 3 (Jim Best) *trckd ldrs: hdwy over 1f out: edgd lft and rdn to ld ins fnl f* **3/1**[2]	81
2061	2	2 1/4	**Tina's Best (IRE)**[3] 3266 3-9-9 76 6ex RyanMoore 5 (R Hannon) *trckd ldr: rdn to ld 2f out: no ex: sltly hmpd and hdd ins fnl f* **13/8**[1]	79+
46-1	3	3/4	**Imperial Lucky (IRE)**[10] 3034 5-9-0 58 ShaneKelly 6 (M J Wallace) *hld up: hdwy over 1f out: r.o fnl f: nvr nrr* **11/2**[3]	61
0565	4	1 3/4	**Star Strider**[32] 2350 4-9-5 63 (b[1]) JimCrowley 1 (Miss Gay Kelleway) *led tl rdn and hdd 2f out: one pce fnl f* **12/1**	61
1554	5	1	**Landucci**[14] 2917 7-10-0 72 (p) EddieAhern 4 (J W Hills) *hld up in tch: rdn over 2f out: no hdwy after* **11/2**[3]	67
5040	6	3 1/4	**Bookish**[4] 3210 3-8-6 62 (b) KirstyMilczarek(3) 7 (Jamie Poulton) *outpcd: racd wd: nvr on terms* **16/1**	46
4000	7	9	**Ile Royale**[20] 2721 3-8-0 53 CatherineGannon 2 (B R Johnson) *swvd bdly rt s and wl bhd: in tch after 2f: wknd over 2f out* **16/1**	12

1m 21.55s (-1.55) **Going Correction** -0.125s/f (Firm)

WFA 3 from 4yo+ 9lb **7 Ran SP% 113.3**

Speed ratings (Par 103): **103,100,99,97,96 92,82**

toteswinger: 1&2 £1.60, 1&3 £2.40, 2&3 £2.30. CSF £8.13 TOTE £3.70: £2.20, £1.10; EX 9.10.

Owner Bill Wallace **Bred** Cheveley Park Stud Ltd **Trained** Lewes, E Sussex

■ Stewards' Enquiry : Paul Doe caution: careless riding

FOCUS

A couple of fair sorts on show in this handicap, and with the first three home in good form coming into the race, the form looks fairly solid.

Ile Royale Official explanation: jockey said filly ran too free

3346 LORD'S TAVERNERS H'CAP 5f 59y

5:00 (5:00) (Class 6) (0-65,65) 3-Y-O+ **£2,266** (£674; £337; £168) **Stalls** Low

Form				RPR
0623	1		**Arfinnit (IRE)**[1] 3316 7-9-0 52 (p) KirstyMilczarek(3) 6 (Mrs A L M King) *wnt lft leaving stalls: trckd ldr: led jst over 2f out: rdn out fnl f* **13/2**[2]	63
0322	2	3/4	**Rocker**[33] 2330 4-9-13 62 RyanMoore 7 (G L Moore) *chsd ldr: styd prom: hung lft over 1f out: rdn and r.o wl ins fnl f* **13/8**[1]	70
0402	3	nk	**Fastrac Boy**[15] 2881 5-9-0 49 LPKeniry 2 (J R Best) *led tl hdd jst over 2f out: kpt on ins fnl f* **15/2**[3]	56
004-	4	1/2	**Make My Dream**[195] 7119 5-9-13 62 JimCrowley 11 (J Gallagher) *mid-div on outside: hdwy 2f out: kpt on fnl f* **9/1**	67
3263	5	1/2	**Night Prospector**[10] 3021 8-9-2 56 (p) HaddenFrost(5) 3 (R A Harris) *prom on ins: effrt whn n.m.r appr fnl f: nt qckn ins fnl f* **17/2**	59
6520	6	2	**Jayanjay**[10] 3033 9-9-8 57 SamHitchcott 8 (B R Johnson) *mid-div: rdn over 1f out: one pce after* **16/1**	53
6653	7	shd	**Spic 'n Span**[36] 2240 3-9-10 65 TGMcLaughlin 13 (R A Harris) *slowly away: hdwy and swtchd rt over 1f out: rdn and nt qckn after* **25/1**	59
5003	8	3/4	**Racing Stripes (IRE)**[13] 2934 4-8-13 48 CatherineGannon 5 (K O Cunningham-Brown) *stdd s: mid-div: rdn over 2f out: no hdwy after* **8/1**	41
-000	9	1 3/4	**Edge End**[13] 2930 4-8-11 46 (b[1]) PaulDoe 12 (R A Farrant) *chsd ldrs: rdn over 2f out: wknd over 1f out* **33/1**	33
0600	10	6	**Vlasta Weiner**[71] 1370 8-8-7 45 (b) KevinGhunowa(3) 9 (J M Bradley) *v.s.a: a bhd* **66/1**	10
0250	11	5	**Ben**[16] 2864 3-9-7 62 RobertHavlin 10 (P G Murphy) *a in rr* **25/1**	7
0552	12	nk	**One Way Ticket**[32] 2351 8-9-9 61 (p) TolleyDean(3) 4 (J M Bradley) *in rr: wl btn whn eased ent fnl f* **12/1**	7

61.56 secs (-0.74) **Going Correction** -0.125s/f (Firm)

WFA 3 from 4yo+ 6lb **12 Ran SP% 120.5**

Speed ratings (Par 101): **100,98,98,97,96 93,93,92,89,79 71,71**

toteswinger: 1&2 £3.20, 1&3 £8.00, 2&3 £4.60. CSF £17.11 CT £86.71 TOTE £6.60: £2.20, £1.30, £3.00; EX 17.10 Trifecta £140.50 Pool: £550.86 - 2.90 winning units. Place 6: £5.71 Place 5: £5.35.

Owner All The Kings Horses **Bred** Robert De Vere Hunt **Trained** Wilmcote, Warwicks

■ Stewards' Enquiry : Kirsty Milczarek two-day ban: careless riding (Jul 8,10)

FOCUS
A bunch of fully exposed familiar faces contested this handicap sprint, with the winner making a quick reappearance after a third placing at Lingfield 24 hours earlier. The form is modest but looks sound enough.
Night Prospector Official explanation: jockey said gelding was denied a clear run
Vlasta Weiner Official explanation: jockey said gelding reared as stalls opened
T/Plt: £8.50 to a £1 stake. Pool: £61,160.34. 5,226.68 winning tickets. T/Qpdt: £6.50 to a £1 stake. Pool: £3,515.77. 399.50 winning tickets. JS

2971 **NEWBURY** (L-H)
Tuesday, June 24

OFFICIAL GOING: Good to firm
Wind: modest across Weather: warm, muggy

3347 PUMP TECHNOLOGY APPRENTICE H'CAP — 1m 3f 5y
6:20 (6:21) (Class 5) (0-70,69) 4-Y-O+ **£2,590** (£770; £385; £192) **Stalls** Low

Form RPR
0304 **1** **Princess Flame (GER)**[16] 2863 6-8-9 **57** ow2........... KylieManser(3) 10 63
(B G Powell) *t.k.h: chsd ldr after 2f: led 7f out tl 6f out: chsd ldr after tl led again 2f out: edgd lft but hld on gamely fnl f* **10/1**
2201 **2** ½ **Wee Charlie Castle (IRE)**[7] 3113 5-8-9 **57** 6ex...... WilliamCarson(3) 14 64
(G C H Chung) *lw: t.k.h: hld up in midfield: rdn 3f out: edgd lft and swtchd rt over 2f out: styd on u.p fnl f: wnt 2nd nr fin* **5/2**[1]
0021 **3** shd **Double Spectre (IRE)**[14] 2921 6-9-8 **67**........................ JackMitchell 1 74+
(Jean-Rene Auvray) *rrd at s and v.s.a: sn in tch in rr: swtchd rt and hdwy 2f out: r.o wl fnl f: wnt 3rd nr fin* **13/2**[2]
-152 **4** ½ **Compton Charlie**[21] 2694 4-8-7 **55**.............................. JackDean(3) 13 61
(J G Portman) *bit bkwd: t.k.h: chsd ldrs: disp 2nd and hung lft 2f out: kpt on same pce u.p fnl f* **8/1**
3322 **5** shd **Alexander Guru**[20] 2715 4-8-11 **59**.............................. KMay(3) 11 65
(M Blanshard) *t.k.h: chsd ldr for 2f out: disp 2nd and rdn 2f out: kpt on same pce fnl f* **10/1**
05-6 **6** 3¼ **Golden Alchemist**[11] 2617 5-8-1 **51**.............................. BillyCray(5) 9 51
(M D I Usher) *t.k.h: hld up in tch: lost pl and bhd 4f out: styd on u.p fr over 1f out: nt threaten ldrs* **17/2**
1400 **7** ½ **Hatch A Plan (IRE)**[120] 697 7-8-10 **58**.................... DavidProbert(3) 15 57
(Mouse Hamilton-Fairley) *swtg: t.k.h: chsd ldrs tl hdwy to ld 6f out: clr 4f out: hdd and rdn 2f out: sn wknd* **16/1**
000- **8** ½ **Darghan (IRE)**[226] 6780 8-8-10 **60**.......................... DebraEngland(5) 12 59+
(W J Musson) *b.bkwd: s.i.s: t.k.h: hld up in midfield: stdd to rr 6f out: hdwy 3f out: chsd ldrs and rdn over 2f out: wknd ent fnl f* **10/1**
1020 **9** nse **Ryedale Ovation (IRE)**[6] 3132 5-9-3 **65**......................... AmyBaker(3) 7 64
(M Hill) *lw: s.i.s: hld up in tch: swtchd rt and rdn 2f out: nvr pce to trble ldrs* **15/2**[3]
4104 **10** nse **King Of Connacht**[7] 3113 5-8-5 **55**.......................(p) SamuelDrury(5) 8 53
(M Wellings) *t.k.h: chsd ldrs tl lost pl 5f out: effrt and rdn 2f out: sn hung lft and no imp* **12/1**
4-00 **11** 13 **Dr McFab**[12] 2978 4-9-8 **67**.............................. JamieJones 4 43
(Miss Tor Sturgis) *t.k.h: hld up wl in tch: rdn over 3f out: bhd last 2f* **40/1**
0-00 **12** 7 **Silver Surprise**[32] 2354 4-8-2 **50** oh5........................ MCGeran(3) 5 14
(J J Bridger) *led tl 7f out: rdn 4f out: sn wknd* **66/1**
000- **13** 24 **Danehill Folly (IRE)**[267] 5864 5-8-1 **50** oh5 ow3.......... SeanPalmer(7) 2 —
(M D I Usher) *s.i.s: in tch tl lost pl 5f out: t.o last 2f* **66/1**
2m 23.58s (2.38) **Going Correction** -0.10s/f (Good) **13** Ran SP% **121.6**
Speed ratings (Par 103): **87,86,86,86,86 83,83,83,83,82 73,68,50**
toteswinger: 1&2 £4.80, 1&3 £14.50, 2&3 £3.10. CSF £35.55 CT £183.07 TOTE £9.20: £2.90, £1.70, £2.80; EX 29.00.
Owner Mr & Mrs D A Gamble **Bred** V Kaufling **Trained** Upper Lambourn, Berks
■ Stewards' Enquiry : Jack Mitchell two-day ban: used whip with excessive frequency (Jul 8,10)
FOCUS
A moderate handicap for apprentice riders run in a very slow time. There was no early pace and the first five were closely covered at the death so the form is messy and relatively weak.

3348 WIN RACES WITH JONATHAN PORTMAN MAIDEN AUCTION FILLIES' STKS — 6f 8y
6:50 (6:52) (Class 4) 2-Y-O **£4,533** (£1,348; £674; £336) **Stalls** High

Form RPR
2 **1** **Pyrrha**[12] 2979 2-8-4 0.............................. MartinDwyer 12 82
(C F Wall) *w'like: scope: chsd ldr tl led 4f out: mde rest: pushed clr jst over 1f out: readily* **7/2**[2]
2 **2** 3½ **Qalahari (IRE)**[23] 2638 2-8-8 0.............................. TPO'Shea 13 75
(D J Coakley) *unf: lw: chsd ldrs tl wnt 2nd 2f out: sn rdn: nt pce of wnr fnl f* **9/4**[1]
3 **3** 1¼ **Blue Arctic**[12] 2979 2-8-6 0.............................. RichardMullen 4 69
(J M P Eustace) *str: in tch: hdwy jst over 2f out: chsd ldng pair and rdn over 1f out: kpt on same pce* **14/1**
4 1 **Solitary** 2-8-8 0.............................. DaneO'Neill 14 68
(H Candy) *unf: bit bkwd: chsd ldrs: rdn 2f out: edgd lft and kpt on same pce fnl f* **10/1**
5 ½ **Rioliina (IRE)** 2-8-6 0.............................. JamesDoyle 7 65
(J G Portman) *leggy: in tch in midfield: hdwy and rn green 2f out: hung lft but kpt on steadily fnl f: nvr threatened ldrs* **25/1**
6 shd **Oscar Silk** 2-8-8 0.............................. EdwardCreighton 10 66
(M R Channon) *w'like: leggy: in tch in midfield: rdn over 2f out: kpt on but nvr pce to threaten ldrs* **22/1**
0 **7** 1¾ **Barcode**[45] 2011 2-8-4 0.............................. RichardSmith 15 58+
(R Hannon) *leggy: in rr: rdn wl over 2f out: styd on past betaen horses fnl f: n.d* **50/1**
8 ½ **Golden Destiny (IRE)** 2-8-4 0.............................. FrancisNorton 16 56
(P J Makin) *w'like: bit bkwd: bhd: pushed along 3f out: kpt on steadily fnl f: nvr trbld ldrs* **40/1**
3 **9** hd **Damassin**[14] 2916 2-8-6 0.............................. StephenCarson 2 57
(Eve Johnson Houghton) *lw: chsd ldrs: rdn 2f out: wknd ent fnl f* **8/1**
10 1 **Bold Ring** 2-8-6 0.............................. AlanMunro 6 54
(D W P Arbuthnot) *leggy: hld up towards rr: hanging lft fr 1/2-way: nvr nr ldrs* **25/1**
11 ½ **Haafhd Time (IRE)** 2-8-6 0.............................. RichardKingscote 9 53
(Tom Dascombe) *w'like: s.i.s: sn in tch in midfield: rdn and lost pl 1/2-way: no ch after* **22/1**
12 1¼ **Our Day Will Come** 2-8-10 0.............................. RichardHughes 5 53+
(R Hannon) *w'like: hld up towards rr on outer: hdwy 3f out: swtchd rt 2f out: nvr on terms* **4/1**[3]
0 **13** 2½ **Accomplishment (IRE)**[15] 2887 2-8-8 0.............................. TedDurcan 3 43+
(A P Jarvis) *w'like: led for 2f: chsd wnr after tl wknd qckly 2f out* **50/1**
14 1¾ **Kaada** 2-8-3 0.............................. AhmedAjtebi(5) 11 38
(C E Brittain) *leggy: s.i.s: a bhd: rdn and struggling 1/2-way* **40/1**
15 10 **Queens Forester** 2-8-8 0.............................. NelsonDeSouza 1 8
(P F I Cole) *w'like: str: in tch on outer tl wknd qckly over 2f out: t.o* **33/1**
1m 12.75s (-0.25) **Going Correction** -0.10s/f (Good) **15** Ran SP% **128.0**
Speed ratings (Par 92): **97,92,90,89,88 88,86,85,85,83 83,81,78,75,62**
toteswinger: 1&2 £1.60, 1&3 £9.50, 2&3 £6.80. CSF £11.14 TOTE £5.50: £1.70, £1.60, £4.90; EX 13.60.
Owner Lady Juliet Tadgell **Bred** Hong Kong Breeders Club **Trained** Newmarket, Suffolk
FOCUS
An average juvenile fillies' maiden. A high draw was a plus, but the form looks sound and the winner impressed.
NOTEBOOK
Pyrrha ◆, drawn 12, quickly came over to the near rail and ultimately ran out a clear-cut winner, confirming the promise of her debut second at Yarmouth. She was in front long enough here, looking to idle a touch, and can be rated value for further than the bare margin suggests. A filly with scope, she should improve again for this experience and it will be interesting to see where she goes next. Another furlong should also be within her range. (tchd 10-3 and 4-1)
Qalahari(IRE), pipped on her debut at Bath, was unable to go with the winner when she went for home. This was another solid effort and she should not be long in finding an opening, but a return to one of the smaller tracks could be a wise move. (tchd 2-1 and 5-2)
Blue Arctic ran close to the level of her debut form with the winner and turned in another respectable effort. She is one for nurseries, but should win a maiden at one of the smaller tracks. (tchd 12-1)
Solitary bred for speed, knew her job and was soon handy from her decent draw. She lacked the pace when push came to shove, but is entitled to improve for this and looks to have a future. (op 15-2 tchd 7-1)
Rioliina(IRE), a half-sister to her stable's 6f juvenile winner Cheap Street, proved too green to do herself justice on this debut. She will be sharper for the run. (op 16-1)
Oscar Silk, a half-sister to a 1m winner in Italy, looked better the further she went and posted a fair debut. She will get longer trips and ought to improve for the experience. (op 25-1)
Our Day Will Come, a chunky filly who is out of a mare who was useful over further, never looked like getting into the race from off the pace. She was not helped by having to race wide, and her rider was not hard on her when her fate became apparent. (op 11-1 tchd 12-1)

3349 PUMPMATIC PUMP STATIONS BY PUMP TECHNOLOGY MAIDEN FILLIES' STKS — 7f (S)
7:25 (7:29) (Class 4) 2-Y-O **£5,828** (£1,734; £866; £432) **Stalls** High

Form RPR
4 **1** **Samara Valley (IRE)**[24] 2614 2-9-0 0.............................. TedDurcan 11 78+
(H R A Cecil) *w'like: attr: racd stands' side: led stands' side gp: chsd overall ldr 1/2-way: led wl over 1f out: rdn and edgd lft ent fnl f: styd on wl* **5/2**[1]
6 **2** 2¼ **Rose Cheval (USA)**[17] 2821 2-9-0 0.............................. DarryllHolland 1 72
(M R Channon) *leggy: attr: racd in centre gp: in tch: rdn 3f out: hdwy to chse ldrs 2f out: kpt on u.p* **12/1**
3 ½ **Triple Cee (IRE)** 2-9-0 0.............................. EdwardCreighton 6 71
(M R Channon) *leggy: racd in centre gp: in rr and bustled along early: hdwy over 2f out: chsd ldrs u.p over 1f out: kpt on* **33/1**
2 **4** 2¼ **Sterling Sound (USA)**[17] 2835 2-9-0 0.............................. MartinDwyer 3 66+
(M P Tregoning) *w'like: cl cpld: racd in centre gp: overall ldr tl wl over 1f out: wknd fnl f* **4/1**[2]
5 1¾ **Key Signature** 2-9-0 0.............................. ShaneKelly 12 61
(Pat Eddery) *w'like: str: bit bkwd: racd stands' side: t.k.h: chsd ldrs: rdn and no prog last 2f* **16/1**
6 1½ **Zaaqya** 2-9-0 0.............................. RHills 15 57+
(J L Dunlop) *w'like: athletic: racd stands' side: midfield: shkn up 3f out: nvr pce to threaten ldrs* **6/1**[3]
7 1½ **Peace Concluded** 2-9-0 0.............................. AlanMunro 2 54+
(B R Millman) *unf: bit bkwd: racd in centre gp: s.i.s: racd in midfield: outpcd over 2f out: n.d after* **66/1**
8 1½ **Le Grand Amour (IRE)** 2-9-0 0.............................. MichaelHills 10 50
(B W Hills) *w'like: racd in centre gp: a towards rr: no ch last 2f* **20/1**
6 **9** 2¼ **Give (IRE)**[14] 2916 2-9-0 0.............................. RyanMoore 8 44
(R Hannon) *lw: racd in centre gp: chsd overall ldr tl 1/2-way: wknd 2f out* **4/1**[2]
10 ½ **Winterfell** 2-9-0 0.............................. IanMongan 9 43
(C F Wall) *w'like: str: bit bkwd: racd in centre gp: rdn and struggling 3f out: sn wl btn* **50/1**
11 1 **Baheeya** 2-8-9 0.............................. AhmedAjtebi(5) 5 41+
(C E Brittain) *w'like: scope: str: racd in centre gp: in tch tl 3f out: sn struggling* **66/1**
6 **12** 2½ **Refuse To Decline**[32] 2368 2-9-0 0.............................. RichardMullen 4 34
(D M Simcock) *racd in centre gp: a bhd: lost tch 3f out* **66/1**
13 1 **Persian Memories (IRE)** 2-9-0 0.............................. DaneO'Neill 14 32
(J L Dunlop) *w'like: chunky: racd stands' side: a bhd: lost tch 1/2-way* **25/1**
14 16 **Tinkerbelle (IRE)** 2-9-0 0.............................. EddieAhern 13 —
(J L Dunlop) *w'like: bit bkwd: racd stands' side: a wl bhd: t.o fr 1/2-way* **33/1**
1m 25.66s (-0.04) **Going Correction** -0.10s/f (Good) **14** Ran SP% **117.4**
Speed ratings (Par 92): **96,93,92,90,88 86,84,83,80,80 78,76,74,56**
toteswinger: 1&2 £8.20, 1&3 £38.10, 2&3 £3.30. CSF £30.13 TOTE £3.60: £1.50, £2.90, £7.80; EX 39.20.
Owner Gestut Ammerland **Bred** Azienda Agricola Valle Falcone Srl **Trained** Newmarket, Suffolk
■ Ballyalla (11/1) was withdrawn (ref to enter stalls). Deduct 5p in the £ under rule 4.
FOCUS
This has often been a decent maiden in the past. The form should work out.
NOTEBOOK
Samara Valley(IRE) opened her account at the second time of asking with a professional display and looks a filly capable building on this as she steps up in trip. She showed a decent attitude under pressure and looked to find this ground plenty quick enough, so the step up to another furlong on easier going now looks sure to bring about further improvement. (op 11-4 tchd 10-3)
Rose Cheval(USA), sixth on debut at Doncaster 17 days previously, showed the benefit of that experience and eventually fared the best of those to race mid-track. She got the extra furlong well and is clearly going the right way. (tchd 11-1 and 14-1)
Triple Cee(IRE) ◆, who cost 90,000euros, turned in an eyecatching debut effort, running on well inside the final furlong and doing more than enough to suggest she can be found an opening with this debut experience under her belt.
Sterling Sound(USA), narrowly beaten into second on debut at Lingfield 17 days previously, was soon into her stride and leading down the middle of the track. She was still going nicely enough passing the two-furlong pole, but her response when push came to shove was limited and she probably found this extra furlong against her at this stage. She can do better again when reverting to 6f. (op 5-1)
Key Signature, a 100,000gns purchase, knew her job yet paid for racing too freely through the early parts. She is bred to do better in time and should come on for the run. (op 20-1 tchd 25-1)

Zaaqya cost 300,000gns and was representing the owner/trainer/jockey combination which had sent out the last two winners of this race. She proved easy to back for this debut and never really got into contention, looking green for most of the race. (op 9-2)
Give(IRE) met some support in the betting ring, but proved unable build on her debut effort at Salisbury last time and failed to get home over the extra furlong. (op 9-2 tchd 3-1)

3350 JUNG PUMPEN & PUMP TECHNOLOGY PARTNERSHIP MAIDEN FILLIES' STKS 1m 4f 5y

7:55 (7:57) (Class 4) 3-Y-0+ **£5,828** (£1,734; £866; £432) **Stalls** Low

Form RPR
0 **1** **Colourways (IRE)**[20] 2716 3-8-12 0 JimCrowley 9 80
(Mrs A J Perrett) *lw: chsd ldr tl led wl over 2f out: styd on wl u.p fnl f* **10/1**
3 **2** *1 ¾* **Solar Dance (USA)**[12] 2973 3-8-12 0 RobertHavlin 12 77
(J H M Gosden) *b. hind: lw: hld up in tch: hdwy over 3f out: chsd wnr over 2f out: unable qckn u.p fnl f* **1/1**[1]
00 **3** *2 ½* **Pure Song**[39] 2164 3-8-12 0 TedDurcan 10 73
(J L Dunlop) *w'like: leggy: on toes: stdd after s: t.k.h: hld up in tch: hdwy to chse ldng pair wl over 1f out: no imp* **14/1**
3 **4** *6* **Beauchamp Wonder**[10] 3035 3-8-12 0 EddieAhern 11 63
(G A Butler) *stdd after s: hld up bhd: hdwy on outer over 3f out: rdn over 2f out: wknd over 1f out* **8/1**[3]
0-32 **5** *2 ¼* **Ethereal Flame**[11] 2989 3-8-12 75 RichardHughes 3 60
(H R A Cecil) *lw: led tl hdd and rdn wl over 2f out: sn wknd* **5/2**[2]
00 **6** *hd* **Lovespell (USA)**[29] 2454 3-8-9 0 (b[1]) TravisBlock(3) 7 59
(H Morrison) *w'like: hld up in tch: rdn and effrt 3f out: sn edging lft: wl btn last 2f* **66/1**
00 **7** *2 ¾* **Let Me Pass (USA)**[12] 2971 3-8-12 0 JohnEgan 2 55
(Jane Chapple-Hyam) *w'like: str: flashed tail thrght: in tch: bhd and rdn wl over 3f out: sn wl btn* **50/1**
8 *6* **La Rochette** 3-8-12 0 AlanMunro 5 45
(P W Chapple-Hyam) *leggy: chsd ldng pair: rdn 3f out: wknd qckly over 2f out* **10/1**

2m 34.6s (-0.90) **Going Correction** -0.10s/f (Good)
WFA 3 from 4yo+ 14lb **8** Ran SP% **118.0**
Speed ratings (Par 102): **99,97,96,92,90 90,88,84**
toteswinger: 1&2 £8.00, 1&3 £28.90, 2&3 £3.60. CSF £21.21 TOTE £13.90: £2.50, £1.10, £3.20; EX 24.80.
Owner Lady Clague **Bred** Newberry Stud Company **Trained** Pulborough, W Sussex

FOCUS
Hand-timed. A fair fillies' maiden, run at a sound pace. The first three came clear and the third is probably the best guide with the first two improving from their debuts.
Ethereal Flame Official explanation: jockey said filly was unsuited by the good to firm ground
Let Me Pass(USA) Official explanation: jockey said filly was unsuited by the good to firm ground

3351 ENJOY THE GAME AT TADLEY RUGBY CLUB FILLIES' H'CAP 1m 2f 6y

8:30 (8:30) (Class 4) (0-85,80) 3-Y-0 **£4,533** (£1,348; £674; £336) **Stalls** Low

Form RPR
-210 **1** **Suzi's Decision**[17] 2840 3-9-6 79 JohnEgan 7 82+
(P W D'Arcy) *hld up wl in tch: hdwy 3f out: rdn over 2f out: drvn to ld jst ins fnl f: rdr dropped reins nr fin: hld on wl* **7/2**[2]
65-5 **2** *½* **Berry Baby (IRE)**[17] 2833 3-8-2 61 oh1 HayleyTurner 5 63+
(G A Butler) *s.i.s: hld up in rr: hdwy on outer 2f out: rdn and r.o to press wnr ins fnl f: hld towards fin* **14/1**
-440 **3** *nk* **Lush (IRE)**[33] 2328 3-9-1 74 RyanMoore 9 75
(R Hannon) *hld up in rr: hdwy over 1f out: r.o wl ins fnl f: nt quite rch ldng pair* **20/1**
0-35 **4** *1 ¼* **Moon Sister (IRE)**[25] 2560 3-9-5 78 AlanMunro 3 77
(W Jarvis) *lw: t.k.h: hld up in tch: swtchd lft and effrt on inner 2f out: pressed ldrs ins fnl f: no ex towards fin* **11/1**
3421 **5** *1 ¼* **Black Dahlia**[9] 3057 3-8-12 71 6ex PatCosgrave 10 67
(A J McCabe) *lw: hld up in tch: rdn and effrt 2f out: kpt on same pce u.p fnl f* **5/2**[1]
1-64 **6** *¾* **La Columbina**[14] 2920 3-9-5 78 RichardHughes 2 73
(R Hannon) *lw: led: hrd prssed 3f out: drvn over 2f out: hdd over 1f out: wknd ent fnl f* **5/1**[3]
41 **7** *1* **Ever Rigg**[63] 1542 3-9-2 75 SteveDrowne 6 68
(E A L Dunlop) *chsd ldrs: rdn and unable qckn jst over 2f out: kpt on same pce after* **8/1**
-006 **8** *nse* **Dusty Moon**[27] 2505 3-9-3 76 PaulDoe 8 69
(W J Knight) *t.k.h: chsd ldrs: hdwy to press ldrs over 3f out: rdn over 2f out: led over 1f out tl hdd jst ins fnl f: wknd* **25/1**
0-56 **9** *½* **Rockellio (IRE)**[20] 2717 3-8-5 64 MartinDwyer 11 58+
(B W Hills) *chsd ldr after 1f: upsides ldr 4f out: rdn over 2f out: wkng whn short of room over 1f out* **66/1**
1-0 **10** *1* **Malibu Girl (USA)**[54] 1746 3-9-7 80 TedDurcan 1 70
(E A L Dunlop) *hld up in tch in rr: rdn 2f out: no hdwy* **33/1**
-022 **11** *1 ¼* **Miss Jolyon (USA)**[13] 2931 3-9-4 77 PhilipRobinson 4 64
(M A Jarvis) *chsd ldr for 1f: styd handy: rdn jst over 2f out: wknd fnl f* **8/1**

2m 8.39s (-0.41) **Going Correction** -0.10s/f (Good) **11** Ran SP% **117.7**
Speed ratings (Par 98): **97,96,96,95,94 93,92,92,92,91 90**
toteswinger: 1&2 £7.60, 1&3 £17.50, 2&3 £83.60. CSF £49.08 CT £864.59 TOTE £4.50: £1.80, £3.10, £3.00; EX 60.10.
Owner Greenstead Hall Racing **Bred** David And Mrs Vicki Fleet **Trained** Newmarket, Suffolk

FOCUS
A fair fillies' handicap, run at a sound pace but the form is not as strong as it might have been rated around the winner and fourth.
La Columbina Official explanation: jockey said filly hung right
Miss Jolyon(USA) Official explanation: jockey said filly was unsuited by the good to firm ground

3352 PUMP TECHNOLOGY H'CAP 5f 34y

9:00 (9:02) (Class 5) (0-70,70) 3-Y-0+ **£3,238** (£963; £481; £240) **Stalls** High

Form RPR
6005 **1** **Bertie Southstreet**[21] 2692 5-9-8 65 (b) MartinDwyer 7 78
(J R Best) *stdd s: t.k.h: hld up in tch: hdwy 2f out: swtchd lft over 1f out: led last 100yds: sn in command* **12/1**
4422 **2** *1 ¾* **Comptonspirit**[24] 2596 4-9-9 66 SteveDrowne 11 73
(B P J Baugh) *chsd ldrs: rdn 2f out: led over 1f out: hdd and nt pce of wnr last 100yds* **6/1**
6-50 **3** *¾* **Brandywell Boy (IRE)**[14] 2923 5-9-8 65 RichardThomas 3 69
(D J S Ffrench Davis) *chsd ldrs: rdn 2f out: pressed ldrs ent fnl f: no ex last 100yds* **20/1**
0-60 **4** *2* **Bold Minstrel (IRE)**[26] 2551 6-9-2 59 FrancisNorton 16 56
(M Quinn) *led tl rdn and hdd over 1f out: fdd last 100yds* **25/1**
-005 **5** *½* **Pic Up Sticks**[9] 3062 9-9-11 68 RyanMoore 10 63
(B G Powell) *stdd s: bhd: hdwy over 1f out: kpt on steadily but nvr threatened ldrs* **9/2**[2]
6514 **6** *hd* **Equuleus Pictor**[10] 3042 4-9-4 66 JackDean(5) 15 60
(J L Spearing) *s.i.s: sn prom: chsd ldr after 2f tl over 1f out: wknd ins fnl f* **3/1**[1]
0512 **7** *1* **Doubtful Sound (USA)**[22] 2664 4-9-8 68 (b) KevinGhunowa(3) 1 59
(R A Harris) *bhd: rdn 1/2-way: sme late hdwy: nvr nr ldrs* **16/1**
-151 **8** *nk* **Bold Argument (IRE)**[13] 2950 5-9-2 64 JackMitchell(5) 12 54
(Mrs P N Dutfield) *in tch in midfield: rdn 2f out: hld hd high over 1f out: kpt on same pce* **5/1**[3]
005- **9** *2 ½* **Back In The Red (IRE)**[179] 7261 4-9-8 70 HaddenFrost(5) 4 51
(R A Harris) *in tch on outer: effrt and rdn 2f out: wknd over 1f out* **25/1**
0435 **10** *2 ¼* **Gleaming Spirit (IRE)**[54] 1739 4-9-7 64 EddieAhern 2 37
(A P Jarvis) *chsd ldrs: rdn 1/2-way: wknd wl over 1f out* **16/1**
0005 **11** *¾* **Gwilym (GER)**[10] 3042 5-9-13 70 (p) TedDurcan 5 40
(D Haydn Jones) *in tch in midfield: rdn over 2f out: sn struggling* **11/1**
0050 **12** *2* **Spanish Ace**[9] 3062 7-9-7 64 (p) PaulFitzsimons 9 27
(J M Bradley) *sn rdn along in midfield: struggling fr 1/2-way: wl bhd over 1f out* **33/1**
0540 **13** *hd* **Bateleur**[14] 2923 4-9-8 65 (v) SamHitchcott 13 27
(M R Channon) *v.s.a: a bhd* **16/1**
-206 **14** *30* **Don't Tell Sue**[97] 939 5-9-10 67 (e[1]) AlanMunro 14 —
(D W P Arbuthnot) *chsd ldr for 2f: sn dropped out: virtually p.u ins fnl f* **12/1**

60.46 secs (-0.94) **Going Correction** -0.10s/f (Good)
WFA 3 from 4yo+ 6lb **14** Ran SP% **130.9**
Speed ratings (Par 103): **103,100,99,95,95 94,93,92,88,85 83,80,80,32**
toteswinger: 1&2 £14.30, 1&3 £141.40, 2&3 £26.90. CSF £86.03 CT £1522.22 TOTE £16.80: £4.60, £1.50, £7.50; EX 111.80 Place 6: £203.52 Place 5: £120.45.
Owner G G Racing **Bred** B Whitehouse **Trained** Hucking, Kent

FOCUS
A competitive sprint handicap for the grade. The form looks solid and the placed horses set the standard.
Bold Minstrel(IRE) Official explanation: jockey said gelding bled from the nose
T/Jkpt: Not won. T/Plt: £171.10 to a £1 stake. Pool: £89,558.75. 382.05 winning tickets. T/Qpdt: £67.90 to a £1 stake. Pool: £5,281.91. 57.50 winning tickets. SP

3191 LONGCHAMP (R-H)

Tuesday, June 24

OFFICIAL GOING: Good

3356a PRIX DAPHNIS (GROUP 3) (C&G) 1m 1f

2:50 (2:54) 3-Y-0 **£29,412** (£11,765; £8,824; £5,882; £2,941)

RPR
1 **Indian Daffodil (IRE)**[61] 1594 3-8-11 C-PLemaire 5 109
(J-C Rouget, France) *prom: 2nd st: pushed along to ld 2f out: rdn over 1f out: jnd by Farrel 100yds out: led narrowly on line*
2 *1 ½* **In Chambers**[18] 2817 3-8-11 CSoumillon 3 106
(M Delzangles, France) *hld up: disputing 5th st: pushed along to go 3rd 1f out: short of room ins fnl f: styd on for 3rd: fin 3rd, nse & 1 ½l: plcd 2nd* **47/10**[3]
3 *nse* **Farrel (IRE)**[44] 2028 3-8-11 TThulliez 4 106
(B Grizzetti, Italy) *3rd st: pressed ldr 2f out: jinked rt over 1f out squeezing up runners bhd: jnd wnr 100yds out: hdd narrowly on line: fin 2nd, nse: plcd 3rd* **6/1**
4 *hd* **World Ruler**[18] 3-8-11 SPasquier 2 105
(A Fabre, France) *prom: 4th st: pushed along over 2f out: disputing 3rd 1f out: kpt on* **44/10**[2]
5 *1* **Murcielago (FR)**[16] 2875 3-8-11 TCastanheira 6 103
(P Demercastel, France) *hld up: disputing 5th st: pushed along on outside over 1 1/2f out: rdn 1f out: nvr nrr* **10/1**
6 *8* **Starlish (IRE)**[23] 2654 3-8-11 ACrastus 1 87
(E Lellouche, France) *led: pushed along st: hdd 2f out: sn rdn and one pce* **33/10**[1]
7 *20* **Maille Le Nelois (FR)**[24] 3-8-11 ACardine 7 45
(V Greco, France) *towards rr: last on outside st: sn pushed along and unable qck* **60/1**

1m 49.7s (-6.80) **7** Ran SP% **84.3**
PARI-MUTUEL: WIN 3.10; PL 1.80, 2.40; SF 15.50.
Owner Baron E De Rothschild **Bred** Ecurie De Meautry **Trained** Pau, France

NOTEBOOK
Indian Daffodil(IRE) is a useful performer over this distance and this victory gave a boost to the Jockey-Club form. He came with a run from one and a half out and stayed on gamely to win by inches. He has now won four of his six races and has been the runner-up in the other two. It would be no surprise if he was now brought back to a mile and races like the Prix Messidor and Prix Quincey will now be taken into consideration.
In Chambers, a very consistent individual, was slightly hampered in the closing stages and as a result was promoted to second position. His run began one and a half out before trying to go for a gap between the winner and runner-up but there was probably not enough room for him to make his final effort in that way. Judging by this performance this colt may stay a little further.
Farrel(IRE) was only beaten by inches after a ding-dong battle with the winner throughout the final furlong. Connections were upset after this colt was disqualified from second place, and it looked a harsh decision by the Stewards, especially as his substitute jockey was not given any suspension. It would be no surprise if this colt came back for the Prix Jean Prat.
World Ruler was another to not have had a much luck in running. He made his run up the far rail but had nowhere to go halfway up the straight and was running on at the end.

3357a PRIX DE LA PORTE MAILLOT (GROUP 3) 7f

3:20 (3:23) 3-Y-0+ **£29,412** (£117,654; £8,824; £5,882; £2,941)

RPR
1 **Vertigineux (FR)**[32] 4-9-1 PSogorb 2 106
(Mme C Dufreche, France) *prom on rail: 3rd st: sn pushed along: rdn to go 2nd 2f out: chal over 1f out: led 150yds out: drvn out* **37/1**
2 *shd* **Chantra (GER)**[33] 2347 4-8-12 JVictoire 7 103
(P Rau, Germany) *led: rdn over 2f out: hdd narrowly 150yds out: styd on* **35/1**
3 *1 ½* **Snow Key (USA)**[16] 2876 4-8-12 C-PLemaire 1 99
(J E Pease, France) *mid-div: disputing 6th st: hdwy on rail 1 1/2f out: rchd 3rd 1f out: kpt on* **73/10**
4 *snk* **African Rose**[33] 2348 3-8-4 SPasquier 4 100
(Mme C Head-Maarek, France) *hld up: 8th st: hdwy on outside over 1f out: fin wl to jst miss 3rd* **7/2**[2]

5 ¾ **Bertranicus (FR)**[50] 1885 5-9-1 .... CSoumillon 3 100
(L Urbano-Grajales, France) *in tch: 5th st: rdn & disputing 3rd 1f out: styd on at one pce* **76/10**

6 *hd* **Athanor (FR)**[16] 2876 6-9-1 .... DBonilla 6 99
(F Head, France) *prom: 2nd st: pushed along 2f out: outpcd fr 1f out* **9/5**[1]

7 2 **Belliflore (FR)**[24] 2637 4-8-12 .... TJarnet 5 91
(Mlle S-V Tarrou, France) *mid-div: disputing 6th st: pushed along on outside over 1 1/2f out: brief hdwy tl no ex fnl 150yds* **66/10**[3]

8 1½ **King Jock (USA)**[16] 2876 7-9-9 .... RMBurke 9 98
(R J Osborne, Ire) *hld up: last st: pushed along over 2f out: n.d* **29/1**

9 *hd* **Elusif (FR)**[56] 1712 3-8-8 ow1.. OPeslier 8 91
(A Fabre, France) *prom: 4th st: pushed along 2f out: sn wknd* **66/10**[3]

1m 19.9s (-1.00)
WFA 3 from 4yo+ 9lb **9** Ran SP% **116.7**
PARI-MUTUEL: WIN 37.70; PL 9.90, 8.70, 3.60; DF 207.30.
Owner Mme C & P Dufreche **Bred** Patrick Dufreche **Trained** France

NOTEBOOK
Vertigineux(FR), a rank outsider, was brought with a finely-timed late challenge and he took the lead literally on the line. Trained in the provinces, he was winning his first Group event and showed much improved form. This is his optimum trip and he is now back to his very best after a training setback last August. It will be no surprise to see him being aimed at the Prix du Prim and then the Prix de la Foret which are both run over this specialized track and distance.
Chantra(GER) made a brave effort to go from pillar to post. She still had a big advantage halfway up the straight before just failing to hold off the winner in the final strides. An individual who likes good ground, it was a fine run and her best performance so far this season.
Snow Key(USA), held up in the early part of this race, she was outpaced early in the straight before staying on in the final stages. She was a supplementary entry into the race and more than covered her late entry fee. A longer trip could be beneficial in the future.
African Rose, who was given a waiting ride, had to bide her time before finding an opening to make her final challenge. She was putting in her best work at the finish and would have been third in a few more strides and is one worth keeping an eye on next time out.

3019 BATH (L-H)
Wednesday, June 25

OFFICIAL GOING: Firm (good to firm in places; 10.1)
Wind: Fresh, against. Weather: Sunny

3358 E.B.F./HIGOS INSURANCE MAIDEN STKS 5f 161y
6:40 (6:43) (Class 5) 2-Y-O **£3,367** (£1,002; £500; £250) **Stalls** Centre

Form RPR

040 **1** **Blushing Maid**[24] 2638 2-8-9 0.. KirstyMilczarek(3) 11 66
(H S Howe) *chsd ldr: led over 1f out: hrd rdn ins fnl f: r.o* **20/1**

5 **2** *shd* **Flyit (IRE)**[14] 2937 2-9-3 0.. DarrylIHolland 1 71
(M R Channon) *led: hdd over 1f out: hrd rdn fnl f: r.o* **7/2**[2]

4 **3** *hd* **Hail Promenader (IRE)**[20] 2759 2-9-3 0.. MichaelHills 10 70
(B W Hills) *a.p: rdn fnl f: r.o towards fin* **4/7**[1]

5 **4** 3½ **Dalepak Flyer (IRE)**[21] 2709 2-9-3 0.. PaulEddery 8 59
(G D Blake) *chsd ldrs: pushed along over 2f out: rdn and one pce fnl f* **16/1**

5 ¾ **Hum Cat (IRE)** 2-8-10 0.. RichardEvans(7) 6 56
(J S Moore) *a.p: rdn and one pce fnl f* **50/1**

6 **6** 1½ **Yeoman Blaze**[16] 2893 2-9-3 0.. FrancisNorton 13 51
(A M Balding) *mid-div: hdwy over 1f out: sn rdn: edgd rt ins fnl f: one pce* **12/1**

44 **7** 2½ **Minder**[15] 2916 2-9-0 0.. TolleyDean(3) 12 43
(J G Portman) *s.i.s: in rr: rdn and hdwy 2f out: no further prog fnl f* **9/1**[3]

0 **8** *shd* **Benetti (IRE)**[13] 2979 2-9-3 0.. ChrisCatlin 2 43
(M R Channon) *chsd ldrs tl pushed along and wknd over 1f out* **50/1**

9 4 **Definite Honey** 2-8-12 0.. DavidKinsella 3 25
(A B Haynes) *s.i.s: a in rr* **100/1**

10 1¼ **Spiritual Bond** 2-8-12 0.. JohnEgan 9 20
(R A Harris) *mid-div: rdn wl over 1f out: sn wknd* **66/1**

0 **11** 2½ **Zaftil (IRE)**[24] 2638 2-8-12 0.. AlanDaly 7 12
(H S Howe) *hld up: hmpd and lost pl 4f out: bhd fnl 2f* **200/1**

0 **12** 5 **Colin Staite**[30] 2458 2-9-3 0.. CatherineGannon 5 —
(R Brotherton) *s.i.s: a in rr* **200/1**

0 **13** ¾ **Lucky Bid**[15] 2916 2-9-3 0.. StephenDonohoe 14 —
(J M Bradley) *wnt rt s: hld up on outside: pushed along over 2f out: sn bhd* **150/1**

0 **14** 2½ **Gilbertian**[19] 2769 2-9-3 0.. JamesDoyle 4 —
(R M Beckett) *hld up: hmpd on ins 4f out: sn bhd* **33/1**

1m 13.35s (2.15) **Going Correction** +0.125s/f (Good) **14** Ran SP% **125.2**
Speed ratings (Par 93): **90,89,89,84,83 81,78,78,73,71 68,61,60,57**
toteswinger: 1&2 £6.90, 1&3 £7.50, 2&3 £1.20. CSF £91.61 TOTE £21.80: £4.50, £1.60, £1.10; EX 104.70.
Owner Roly Roper **Bred** Kevin Daniel Crabb **Trained** Oakford, Devon

FOCUS
A modest juvenile maiden with a close finish and the winner is rated to his pre-race mark.

NOTEBOOK
Blushing Maid was well beaten over course and distance last time, but she had previously shown plenty of ability when fourth in a conditions event at Salisbury on her second start and confirmed the promise of that effort with a narrow success. She showed good speed to get a nice lead off Flyit, but did just the bare minimum when narrowly passing that rival inside the final two furlongs. On this evidence she will be even better over a bare 5f on an easier track. Official explanation: trainer said, regarding the improved form shown, filly seemed better suited by the faster ground on this occasion (op 25-1 tchd 16-1)
Flyit(IRE), fifth of six on his debut over 6f at Hamilton, showed good speed and kept on really well when headed well over a furlong out. (tchd 9-2)
Hail Promenader(IRE) did not build on the form he showed when fourth on soft ground at Sandown on his debut. He took an age to pick up and it would probably be unwise to make too many excuses. (op 4-6)
Dalepak Flyer(IRE), fifth on his debut on the Polytrack at Kempton, was under pressure a fair way out, but he stuck on. He should find his level in low-grade nurseries later in the season. (op 20-1)
Hum Cat(IRE), a 60,000euros son of One Cool Cat, travelled nicely to a point, but he was left behind when it mattered. (op 40-1)
Minder Official explanation: jockey said colt was unsuited by the firm, good to firm in places ground
Definite Honey Official explanation: jockey said filly was unsuited by the firm, good to firm in places ground

3359 HIGOS CHIPPING SODBURY (S) H'CAP 1m 5y
7:10 (7:12) (Class 6) (0-60,60) 3-Y-O **£1,780** (£529; £264; £132) **Stalls** Low

Form RPR

3030 **1** **Lancaster Lad (IRE)**[33] 2352 3-8-5 **47**..(p) DavidKinsella 12 50
(A B Haynes) *hld up in mid-div: hdwy on outside over 4f out: led over 2f out: edgd rt over 1f out: rdn out* **9/1**[3]

2266 **2** 1¾ **Fly In Johnny (IRE)**[20] 2753 3-9-2 **58**.. DaneO'Neill 4 57
(M R Hoad) *a.p: rdn whn sltly hmpd and swtchd lft jst over 1f out: kpt on ins fnl f* **6/1**[2]

60-0 **3** *nk* **Ochenvay**[19] 2772 3-8-7 **52**.. TolleyDean(3) 7 51
(C J Down) *hld up in rr: pushed along 3f out: hdwy on outside fnl f: fin wl* **9/1**[3]

4304 **4** *nk* **Yakama (IRE)**[12] 2988 3-8-6 **48**.. SamHitchcott 5 46
(D J S Ffrench Davis) *s.i.s: hld up and bhd: hdwy on ins over 2f out: rdn and swtchd rt wl over 1f out: kpt on one pce ins fnl f* **5/2**[1]

-000 **5** 1 **Charlie Be (IRE)**[25] 2611 3-8-4 **46** oh1.. AlanDaly 8 42
(Mrs P N Dutfield) *hld up towards rr: hdwy 2f out: rdn over 1f out: one pce fnl f* **20/1**

-000 **6** 1 **Bewdley**[12] 2988 3-8-4 **46** oh1.. CatherineGannon 3 39
(Mrs K Waldron) *led: rdn and hdd over 2f out: wknd ins fnl f* **33/1**

60-6 **7** 1¾ **Daisy Nook**[24] 2639 3-8-8 **50**.. SteveDrowne 11 39
(S Kirk) *sn chsng ldr: ev ch over 2f out: sn rdn: wknd fnl f* **5/2**[1]

0005 **8** 4 **Poppy Red**[14] 2932 3-7-11 **46** oh1..(b[1]) RossAtkinson(7) 2 26
(Miss J R Tooth) *s.s: hld up: hdwy 4f out: rdn and wknd over 1f out* **12/1**

000- **9** 4 **Les Allues (IRE)**[234] 6664 3-8-1 **46** oh1.. DominicFox(3) 1 17
(H S Howe) *s.v.s: in rr: rdn 2f out: no ch whn n.m.r on ins ins fnl f* **40/1**

-004 **10** *nk* **Fraamington**[8] 3118 3-8-4 **46** oh1.. ChrisCatlin 10 16
(M R Channon) *hld up and bhd: nt clr run and swtchd rt over 2f out: sn rdn: no rspnse* **9/1**[3]

-000 **11** 5 **Whenineedyou**[22] 2704 3-8-4 **46** oh1..(t) FrancisNorton 6 5
(I A Wood) *hld up in tch: lost pl over 2f out: no ch whn lost action and stmbld ins fnl f* **33/1**

1m 42.64s (1.84) **Going Correction** 0.0s/f (Good) **11** Ran SP% **122.2**
Speed ratings (Par 97): **90,88,87,87,86 85,83,79,75,75 70**
toteswinger: 1&2 £3.90, 1&3 £25.70, 2&3 £23.70. CSF £62.31 CT £523.28 TOTE £11.60: £2.80, £2.20, £3.70; EX 65.30.The winner was bought in for 5,000gns. Fly In Johnny was the subject of a friendly claim of £5,400. Yakama was claimed by Mr George Prodromou for £5,400.
Owner Mrs S M Maine **Bred** Tom Foley **Trained** Limpley Stoke, Bath

FOCUS
A poor seller, and weak form. The winning time was 2.59 seconds slower than the following 51-70 handicap for older horses.
Les Allues(IRE) Official explanation: jockey said filly missed the break
Whenineedyou Official explanation: jockey said filly lost her action

3360 OAK H'CAP 1m 5y
7:40 (7:40) (Class 5) (0-70,68) 4-Y-O+ **£3,561** (£1,059; £529; £264) **Stalls** Low

Form RPR

1003 **1** **Wahoo Sam (USA)**[14] 2933 8-8-8 **62**.. RichardEvans(7) 5 73
(P D Evans) *a.p: wnt 2nd over 2f out: rdn over 1f out: led ins fnl f: r.o* **7/1**[3]

2300 **2** *nk* **Wrighty Almighty (IRE)**[21] 2722 6-9-5 **66**.. GeorgeBaker 4 76
(P R Chamings) *hld up and bhd: hdwy whn swtchd rt 2f out: sn rdn: r.o towards fin* **7/1**[3]

-641 **3** *nk* **April Fool**[11] 3037 4-9-0 **61**..(v) DaneO'Neill 11 70
(J A Geake) *sn led: rdn over 1f out: hdd ins fnl f: kpt on* **7/2**[2]

0-44 **4** 2¾ **The Iron Giant (IRE)**[43] 2072 6-8-4 **51** oh1 ow2..(b[1]) AlanDaly 8 54
(Dr J R J Naylor) *hld up and bhd: rdn and hdwy over 1f out: one pce ins fnl f* **22/1**

404 **5** 1¾ **Under Fire (IRE)**[6] 3181 5-8-10 **60**.. KirstyMilczarek(3) 13 59
(A W Carroll) *prom: rdn over 2f out: wknd over 1f out* **8/1**

4-03 **6** *hd* **Trevian**[11] 3025 7-8-8 **55** ow5.. SteveDrowne 12 54
(J M Bradley) *led early: prom: rdn over 2f out: wknd over 1f out* **17/2**

4030 **7** *nk* **The Gaikwar (IRE)**[11] 3025 9-8-4 **51**..(b) RichardKingscote 9 49
(R A Harris) *hld up towards rr: hdwy on outside 2f out: rdn and no further prog fnl f* **12/1**

0232 **8** *nk* **Magroom**[9] 3087 4-9-2 **68**.. PatrickDonaghy(5) 10 65
(R J Hodges) *hld up in mid-div: hdwy over 2f out: rdn over 1f out: wknd ins fnl f* **3/1**[1]

4000 **9** 1 **Cantique (IRE)**[12] 2988 4-7-9 **49** oh4.. DavidProbert(7) 2 44
(R J Price) *hld up in mid-div: rdn over 1f out: no hdwy* **50/1**

-065 **10** ½ **Crosby Jemma**[14] 2940 4-7-13 **49** oh3.. DominicFox(3) 3 43
(J R Weymes) *a in rr* **16/1**

0040 **11** 18 **Coup D'Etat**[12] 2992 6-9-2 **63**..(b) JohnEgan 7 15
(R A Harris) *sn chsng ldr: rn wd bnd over 4f out: rdn and lost 2nd over 2f out: wknd and eased wl over 1f out* **12/1**

00-0 **12** 1¼ **Clewer**[14] 2934 4-8-3 **50**.. DavidKinsella 1 —
(A B Haynes) *a bhd: eased whn no ch fnl f* **66/1**

6000 **13** 15 **Golden Square**[102] 898 6-8-2 **49** oh4.. CatherineGannon 6 —
(A W Carroll) *hld up in mid-div: pushed along over 3f out: wknd over 2f out: eased whn no ch over 1f out* **66/1**

1m 40.05s (-0.75) **Going Correction** 0.0s/f (Good) **13** Ran SP% **124.4**
Speed ratings (Par 103): **103,102,102,99,97 97,97,97,96,95 77,76,61**
toteswinger: 1&2 £4.60, 1&3 £2.70, 2&3 £6.00. CSF £56.74 CT £211.33 TOTE £7.00: £2.30, £3.10, £1.90; EX 33.70.
Owner Premier Cru Racing **Bred** Stonereath Farms Inc **Trained** Pandy, Monmouths

FOCUS
A moderate handicap but the form is solid for the grade. The winning time was 2.59 seconds quicker than three-year-old 46-60 selling handicap.
Golden Square Official explanation: jockey said gelding had been unsuited by the firm, good to firm in places ground

3361 BRISTOL PORT COMPANY H'CAP 1m 2f 46y
8:10 (8:11) (Class 6) (0-65,62) 4-Y-O+ **£2,388** (£705; £352) **Stalls** Low

Form RPR

022 **1** **Sceilin (IRE)**[9] 3089 4-8-9 **50**..(t) SteveDrowne 10 62+
(J Mackie) *prom: led over 7f out: rdn fnl f: r.o wl* **9/4**[1]

1243 **2** 3 **Our Kes (IRE)**[14] 2957 6-9-6 **61**.. DarrylIHolland 12 67
(P Howling) *hld up towards rr: smooth hdwy over 2f out: rdn and chsd wnr jst ins fnl f: no imp* **7/2**[2]

0-06 **3** *nk* **Gallego**[9] 3089 6-9-4 **62**.. KirstyMilczarek(3) 11 67
(R J Price) *stdd s: hld up in rr: smooth hdwy on outside over 2f out: rdn and one pce fnl f* **9/1**

06-5 **4** ½ **Dancing Jest (IRE)**[43] 2070 4-9-3 **58**.. DaneO'Neill 9 62
(Rae Guest) *a.p: chsd wnr over 2f out tl jst ins fnl f: no ex* **7/2**[2]

-050 5 1 **Theatre Royal**[24] 2641 5-8-4 **45**.................. FrancisNorton 13 49+
(Mouse Hamilton-Fairley) *hld up towards rr: hdwy over 2f out: rdn wl over 1f out: one pce fnl f* **14/1**

0000 6 1 ½ **Fateful Attraction**[11] 3036 5-8-5 **46**..................(t) RichardThomas 5 45
(I A Wood) *prom: pushed along over 3f out: fdd fnl f* **33/1**

-502 7 ½ **Beckenham's Secret**[11] 3025 4-8-0 **48**.................. StacyRenwick(7) 8 46
(A W Carroll) *hld up and bhd: hdwy on outside over 1f out: sn wknd* **8/1**[3]

504 8 8 **Meohmy**[11] 3025 5-7-13 **45**.................. MCGeran(5) 7 27
(M R Channon) *hld up and bhd: rdn whn sme hdwy and n.m.r on ins 2f out: sn wknd* **14/1**

0000 9 ½ **The Grey One (IRE)**[11] 3025 5-8-5 **46**..................(p) PaulFitzsimons 3 27
(J M Bradley) *stdd s: plld hrd: hdwy over 7f out: pushed along whn nt clr run over 2f out and wl over 1f out: n.d after* **20/1**

000- 10 13 **Juce Of Hearts**[375] 2652 4-8-4 **45**.................. CatherineGannon 1 —
(John R Upson) *fly-jmpd s: sn rcvrd and jnd ldrs after 2f: rdn and wknd over 2f out* **50/1**

00/0 11 4 **Ath Tiomain (IRE)**[100] 916 5-8-5 **46** ow1..................(b[1]) AlanDaly 4 —
(D J S Ffrench Davis) *led: hdd over 7f out: wknd over 2f out* **80/1**

-400 12 10 **Eastern Princess**[78] 1259 4-8-1 **45**.................. DominicFox(3) 6 —
(G H Yardley) *bhd fnl 6f* **40/1**

2m 9.60s (-1.40) **Going Correction** 0.0s/f (Good) **12** Ran SP% **123.0**
Speed ratings (Par 101): **105,102,102,101,101 99,99,93,92,82 79,71**
toteswinger: 1&2 £2.50, 1&3 £3.00, 2&3 £5.00. CSF £9.95 CT £62.40 TOTE £3.60: £1.60, £1.70, £2.80; EX 11.20.
Owner W I Bloomfield **Bred** J S Bolger **Trained** Church Broughton , Derbys

FOCUS
A modest handicap, but the pace was decent and much of that was down to the successful favourite. There is more to come from her. The second and third were close to form.

3362 OAK MAIDEN STKS 1m 3f 144y
8:40 (8:42) (Class 5) 3-Y-O+ **£2,719** (£809; £404; £202) **Stalls** Low

Form RPR

4030 1 **Green Wadi**[12] 3004 3-8-13 **72**.................. DarryllHolland 3 73
(M R Channon) *hld up in tch: led over 1f out: rdn out* **2/1**[2]

2 ½ **Ragdollianna**[15] 4-9-8 **0**.................. GeorgeBaker 5 67
(Norma Twomey) *hld up and bhd: hdwy over 3f out: rdn and ev ch 1f out: kpt on* **12/1**[3]

4-63 3 1 ½ **Belotto (IRE)**[39] 2197 3-8-8 **78**.................. SteveDrowne 4 65
(R Charlton) *set stdy pce: qcknd 3f out: rdn and hdd over 1f out: no ex wl ins fnl f* **8/15**[1]

4-00 4 5 **Sparkling Montjeu (IRE)**[34] 2340 3-8-8 **61**..................(p) FrancisNorton 7 56
(J W Hills) *chsd wnr to 4f out: rdn and wknd wl over 1f out* **22/1**

0/0 5 4 ½ **Lockstone Lad (USA)**[2] 3310 5-9-13 **0**.................. SimonWhitworth 6 53?
(M S Saunders) *hld up: outpcd wl over 2f out: n.d after* **100/1**

6 5 **Bathwick Minstrel** 3-8-8 **0**.................. JohnEgan 9 40
(A B Haynes) *hld up in rr: rdn and struggling 3f out* **33/1**

00 7 64 **Daarth**[23] 2668 3-8-13 **0**.................. StephenCarson 2 —
(B W Duke) *prom: lost pl 6f out: t.o fnl 4f* **100/1**

2m 33.7s (3.10) **Going Correction** 0.0s/f (Good)
WFA 3 from 4yo+ 14lb **7** Ran SP% **115.5**
Speed ratings (Par 103): **89,88,87,84,81 78,35**
toteswinger: 1&2 £3.80, 1&3 £1.02, 2&3 £2.80. CSF £22.68 TOTE £3.40: £1.40, £2.70; EX 15.90.
Owner Jaber Abdullah **Bred** Mrs P A Clark **Trained** West Ilsley, Berks

FOCUS
A very uncompetitive maiden and just a two-horse race according to the market. It was rendered even less satisfactory by a dawdling early gallop which resulted in a very slow winning time for the grade. The form is rated around the winner, but looks pretty shaky.

3363 SACO SERVICED APARTMENTS H'CAP 5f 161y
9:10 (9:13) (Class 5) (0-75,74) 3-Y-O+ **£2,914** (£867; £433; £216) **Stalls** Centre

Form RPR

1351 1 **Dressed To Dance (IRE)**[9] 3093 4-9-4 **71** 6ex..........(v) RichardEvans(7) 4 83+
(P D Evans) *hld up in rr: pushed along and plenty to do over 2f out: hdwy over 1f out: r.o wl to ld cl home* **10/3**[1]

0143 2 1 **Just Joey**[9] 3080 4-9-2 **62**..................(b) AlanDaly 14 70
(J R Weymes) *chsd ldrs: led 1f out: sn rdn: hdd cl home* **8/1**[3]

0-00 3 1 ¾ **Loyal Royal (IRE)**[11] 3024 5-9-5 **65**.................. PaulFitzsimons 7 68
(J M Bradley) *mid-div: rdn over 2f out: hdwy 1f out: r.o u.p to take 3rd last strides* **33/1**

0024 4 nk **Alfresco**[9] 3093 4-9-12 **72**..................(v) GeorgeBaker 2 74
(I A Wood) *s.i.s: hdwy over 2f out: rdn over 1f out: no ex wl ins fnl f* **9/2**[2]

40-0 5 hd **Summer Recluse (USA)**[14] 2933 9-8-11 **57**..................(t) SteveDrowne 10 58
(J M Bradley) *hld up and bhd: nt clr run and swtchd lft jst over 1f out: sn rdn: hdwy fnl f: nvr nrr* **25/1**

0-00 6 2 ½ **High Ridge**[2] 3313 9-8-9 **55**..................(b) DaneO'Neill 12 47
(J M Bradley) *s.i.s: towards rr: pushed along over 3f out: hrd rdn and kpt on ins fnl f: n.d* **28/1**

4104 7 shd **Judge 'n Jury**[20] 2760 4-10-0 **74**..................(t) JohnEgan 16 66
(R A Harris) *sn w ldrs: led over 2f out: rdn and hdd 1f out: wknd wl ins fnl f* **9/2**[2]

1020 8 nk **Caustic Wit (IRE)**[11] 3024 10-9-3 **63**.................. SimonWhitworth 5 54
(M S Saunders) *s.i.s: in rr: sme hdwy on outside over 1f out: sn rdn: wknd ins fnl f* **9/1**

00-0 9 hd **Who's Winning (IRE)**[19] 2798 7-9-0 **60**.................. RichardKingscote 13 50
(B G Powell) *chsd ldrs: pushed along over 3f out: rdn over 2f out: wknd wl over 1f out* **11/1**

5066 10 hd **Diminuto**[25] 2616 4-8-9 **62**.................. DavidProbert(7) 15 52
(M D I Usher) *w ldr: rdn whn n.m.r over 1f out: wknd ins fnl f* **33/1**

404- 11 2 ½ **Jucebabe**[245] 6424 5-8-8 **57**..................(p) TolleyDean(3) 1 38
(J L Spearing) *chsd ldrs: rdn over 2f out: wknd over 1f out* **14/1**

0000 12 ½ **Willhewiz**[11] 3021 8-8-6 **55** oh5.................. KirstyMilczarek(3) 11 34
(M S Saunders) *led: hdd over 2f out: wknd and eased ins fnl f* **12/1**

2005 13 8 **Hobson**[22] 2690 3-9-3 **70**.................. StephenCarson 3 22
(Eve Johnson Houghton) *mid-div: rdn and wknd over 2f out* **8/1**[3]

3000 14 1 ¼ **Nordic Light (USA)**[2] 3313 4-9-7 **67**..................(b) StephenDonohoe 17 15
(J M Bradley) *mid-div: pushed along over 3f out: sn wknd* **33/1**

1m 11.47s (0.27) **Going Correction** +0.125s/f (Good)
WFA 3 from 4yo+ 7lb **14** Ran SP% **130.5**
Speed ratings (Par 103): **103,101,99,98,98 95,95,94,94,94 90,90,79,77**
toteswinger: 1&2 £3.80, 1&3 £5.80, 2&3 £9.80. CSF £31.64 CT £796.47 TOTE £3.90: £2.00, £2.10, £11.30; EX 28.80 Place 6 £90.64, Place 5 £75.03..
Owner Premier Cru Racing **Bred** John Doyle **Trained** Pandy, Monmouths

FOCUS
An ordinary but competitive sprint handicap and the pace was generous. Modest form, and sound, with the winner confirming her recent improvement.
Willhewiz Official explanation: jockey said gelding hung right-handed

T/Plt: £54.40 to a £1 stake. Pool: £74,142.65. 994.87 winning tickets. T/Qpdt: £18.70 to a £1 stake. Pool: £4,073.90. 161.00 winning tickets. KH

3077 CARLISLE (R-H)
Wednesday, June 25
OFFICIAL GOING: Soft (good to soft in places in home straight)
Wind: Stiff, half against Weather: Overcast

3364 EUROPEAN BREEDERS' FUND MAIDEN STKS 5f 193y
2:00 (2:00) (Class 5) 2-Y-O **£3,885** (£1,156; £577; £288) **Stalls** High

Form RPR

1 **Firebet (IRE)** 2-9-3 **0**.................. RoystonFfrench 6 76+
(Mrs A Duffield) *trckd ldrs: led over 1f out: pushed out fnl f* **14/1**

4 2 2 **Tepmokea (IRE)**[11] 3049 2-9-3 **0**.................. AndrewElliott 4 70
(K R Burke) *led to over 1f out: kpt on same pce ins fnl f* **7/4**[1]

3 ¾ **Mister Fantastic** 2-9-3 **0**.................. DaleGibson 10 68+
(M Dods) *dwlt: bhd: hdwy and green over 2f out: styd on ins fnl f: nrst fin* **40/1**

4 4 3 ¼ **Little Tokyo (USA)**[20] 2746 2-9-3 **0**.................. TonyHamilton 1 58
(J Howard Johnson) *cl up: drvn 2f out: sn one pce* **11/2**[3]

5 2 **Capo Regime** 2-9-3 **0**.................. AdrianTNicholls 3 52+
(D Nicholls) *s.i.s: hdwy over 2f out: hung rt over 1f out: sn no ex* **8/1**

6 1 ¼ **Ryedon Bye** 2-9-3 **0**.................. DavidAllan 8 48
(T D Easterby) *s.i.s: bhd: pushed along 1/2-way: nvr rchd ldrs* **25/1**

7 ¾ **Come And Go (UAE)** 2-9-3 **0**.................. PaulMulrennan 11 46
(G A Swinbank) *prom: effrt over 2f out: wknd over 1f out* **20/1**

0 8 hd **Olympic Dream**[95] 957 2-9-3 **0**.................. PaulHanagan 7 45
(R A Fahey) *towards rr: drvn along 1/2-way: n.d* **12/1**

4 9 3 ¼ **Visterre (IRE)**[30] 2443 2-8-12 **0**.................. TomEaves 5 31
(B Smart) *cl up tl rdn and wknd fr 2f out* **9/1**

10 4 **Abuelito John (IRE)** 2-9-3 **0**.................. DNolan 2 24
(D Carroll) *s.i.s: nvr wnt pce* **50/1**

6 11 11 **Damselfly**[25] 2627 2-8-12 **0**.................. JoeFanning 9 —
(M Johnston) *cl up tl wknd qckly fr 2f out* **5/1**[2]

1m 17.64s (3.94) **Going Correction** +0.60s/f (Yiel) **11** Ran SP% **116.9**
Speed ratings (Par 93): **97,94,93,89,86 84,83,83,79,73 59**
toteswinger: 1&2 £6.30, 1&3 £34.80, 2&3 £13.40. CSF £37.36 TOTE £17.20: £4.20, £1.10, £7.30; EX 39.60.
Owner Mrs H Steel **Bred** Derek Veitch And Saleh Ali Hammadi **Trained** Constable Burton, N Yorks

FOCUS
A modest juvenile maiden, but with not much to go on, the form rated through the runner-up, looks fair for the class.

NOTEBOOK
Firebet(IRE), a 65,000gns bred to be suited by longer distances in time, hails from a stable with a decent record with its juveniles at this track. He eventually ran out a ready debutant winner, responding to pressure after running green around 2f out, and handling the soft ground without much fuss. Given his dam's stamina influence it is very encouraging that he was able to win first-time-up over this trip and, with the promise of more to come on a sounder surface in due course, he looks one to follow as he steps up in trip this term. (op 16-1 tchd 12-1)
Tepmokea(IRE), fourth on debut at York 11 days previously, broke much better this time and showed a more professional attitude from the front. It was clear nearing the final furlong he was in trouble, however, and while he did little wrong in defeat he may well have just found this ground a bit too soft for his liking. It could also be that he found it coming a little too soon and no doubt he is capable of winning races in due course. (op 6-4 tchd 5-4)
Mister Fantastic, the first foal of a 10f winner at three, got himself behind after a tardy start and then looked distinctly green when asked to make up his ground. The penny dropped with him nearing the final furlong, however, and he caught the eye doing his best work at the finish. This was a pleasing debut effort. (op 20-1 tchd 50-1 in a place)
Little Tokyo(USA), green on debut at Hamilton 20 days previously, ran close enough to that level on this switch to softer ground. He looks to need more time and is one for nuseries. (op 17-2)
Capo Regime, bred to be suited by this sort of trip, lost ground with a tardy start and ultimately ran as though this debut experience was much needed. (op 10-1)
Damselfly dropped out sharply after showing up early on and something looked to go amiss with her. Her pedigree would suggest she may need quicker ground, however, and it could be that this surface was all too much for her. (op 4-1 tchd 11-2)

3365 TURFTV MAIDEN AUCTION STKS 5f
2:30 (2:34) (Class 5) 2-Y-O **£3,238** (£963; £481; £240) **Stalls** High

Form RPR

1 **Laahig** 2-9-2 **0**.................. TomEaves 12 79+
(G A Butler) *s.i.s: bhd: hdwy over 2f out: weaved through ins fnl f: kpt on wl to ld post* **9/2**[3]

26 2 nse **Sloop Johnb**[44] 2035 2-8-11 **0**.................. PaulHanagan 13 74
(R A Fahey) *w ldrs: rdn and led ins fnl f: kpt on: ct post* **6/4**[1]

3 ¾ **Tori's Secret (IRE)** 2-8-11 **0**.................. PaulMulrennan 1 71
(G A Swinbank) *prom: led appr fnl f tl hdd ins fnl f: kpt on u.p* **14/1**

4 hd **Blue Dagger (IRE)** 2-8-13 **0**.................. LeeEnstone 5 73
(P C Haslam) *bhd and sn pushed along: hdwy over 1f out: kpt on wl fnl f* **33/1**

2 5 ½ **What A Fella**[23] 2657 2-8-9 **0**.................. RoystonFfrench 4 67
(Mrs A Duffield) *prom: effrt and swtchd rt over 1f out: kpt on same pce fnl f* **3/1**[2]

6 2 **Suzie Quw** 2-8-6 **0**.................. AndrewElliott 3 57
(K R Burke) *slt ld to appr fnl f: sn no ex* **16/1**

00 7 1 ½ **Dispol Grand (IRE)**[15] 2909 2-8-7 **0** ow1.................. JamieMoriarty(3) 6 55
(P T Midgley) *w ldrs tl rdn and no ex 1f out* **40/1**

6 8 3 **Captain Cromby (IRE)**[5] 3199 2-8-9 **0**.................. DeanMcKeown 7 43
(J R Weymes) *chsd ldrs tl lost pl over 2f out: n.d after* **100/1**

004 9 hd **Port Ronan (USA)**[10] 3055 2-8-11 **0**.................. TonyHamilton 10 45
(J S Wainwright) *prom tl rdn and wknd over 2f out* **14/1**

10 17 **Iorek Byrnison** 2-8-9 **0**.................. AdrianTNicholls 8 —
(D Nicholls) *sn pushed along in rr: struggling fr 1/2-way* **20/1**

11 ¾ **Pennine Rose** 2-7-13 **0**.................. DanielleMcCreery(5) 11 —
(A Berry) *s.v.s: t.o thrght* **25/1**

65.20 secs (4.40) **Going Correction** +0.60s/f (Yiel) **11** Ran SP% **117.4**
Speed ratings (Par 93): **88,87,86,86,85 82,80,75,74,47 46**
toteswinger: 1&2 £2.30, 1&3 £17.20, 2&3 £8.60. CSF £11.02 TOTE £6.80: £1.80, £1.30, £4.10; EX 15.20.
Owner Fawzi Abdulla Nass **Bred** Chippenham Lodge Stud Ltd **Trained** Newmarket, Suffolk

FOCUS
An average juvenile maiden. The first five were closely covered at the finish and the winner is value for further. The runner-up is rated 8lb below his debut effort.

NOTEBOOK

Laahig, bred to be suited by around 1m in time, met support in the betting ring for this racecourse debut. He looked in trouble after losing ground with a slow start, but it was clear nearing the final furlong pole that he was still full of running and he eventually came through horses to just get up right on the line. He would have been an unlucky loser and rates value for further than the bare margin. Improvement looks assured for this experience. (op 7-2 tchd 6-1)

Sloop Johnb really set the standard on the level of his two previous outings and it looked very likely that he was going to do the business on entering the final furlong. His stride started to shorten as he idled close home, however, and he eventually just got mugged by the smallest of margins. It looks as though he is happier on a softer surface and he certainly deserves compensation. (op 11-8 tchd 13-8 tchd 7-4 in a place)

Tori's Secret(IRE), who has a deal of speed in his pedigree, showed up really well under a positive ride and was not beaten at all far. He should come on nicely for this debut run and clearly has a future. (op 33-1)

Blue Dagger(IRE) ◆, a half-brother to three soft-ground winning sprinters, posted a decent debut effort and may well have done the business had he not proved so green through the early parts. It is fair to expect a bundle of improvement from this and he could be found an opening in the coming weeks. (tchd 25-1)

What A Fella, a distant third to subsequent Norfolk winner South Central on his debut over course and distance 23 days previously, had his chance and stepped up on his initial effort. He was not too fussed by the deeper surface and now looks ready to tackle a sixth furlong. (op 4-1 tchd 5-2)

3366 LLOYD BMW CARLISLE BELL CONSOLATION RACE (H'CAP) 7f 200y

3:00 (3:02) (Class 4) (0-80,76) 3-Y-0+ £5,180 (£1,541; £770; £384) Stalls High

Form RPR

3343 **1** **Wind Shuffle (GER)**[9] 3082 5-8-8 **60** JoeFanning 8 71
(J S Goldie) *w ldr: led 3f out: hld on wl fnl f* **8/1**[3]

4330 **2** *1* **Lordship (IRE)**[6] 3181 4-8-3 **62** ow1 BMcHugh(7) 1 71
(A W Carroll) *hld up: hdwy over 2f out: sn rdn: kpt on fnl f: tk 2nd nr fin* **14/1**

5550 **3** *hd* **Charlie Tipple**[8] 3108 4-9-8 **74** (p) GrahamGibbons 4 83
(T D Easterby) *midfield: effrt and swtchd rt 2f out: kpt on ins fnl f* **8/1**[3]

2313 **4** *nk* **Hula Ballew**[5] 3109 8-9-5 **76** NeilBrown(5) 9 84
(M Dods) *trckd ldrs: effrt and ev ch over 1f out: no ex and lost two pls cl home* **9/2**[1]

4351 **5** *3* **Shadowtime**[28] 2496 3-8-10 **72** DeanMcKeown 6 71
(Miss Tracy Waggott) *prom: effrt over 2f out: no imp wl over 1f out* **16/1**

6600 **6** *nk* **Regent's Secret (USA)**[14] 2939 8-8-12 **64** (p) DanielTudhope 16 64
(J S Goldie) *bhd: rdn 3f out: kpt on fnl f: nrst fin* **12/1**

340- **7** *¾* **Silk Drum (IRE)**[272] 5749 3-8-6 **68** PaulFessey 17 65
(J Howard Johnson) *t.k.h: prom: outpcd over 3f out: rallied over 1f out: no imp* **14/1**

00-5 **8** *nk* **Packers Hill (IRE)**[14] 2942 4-9-6 **72** PaulMulrennan 11 70
(G A Swinbank) *midfield: drvn and outpcd over 2f out: sn n.d* **20/1**

225 **9** *1 ¾* **Ours (IRE)**[14] 2925 5-8-10 **62** AndrewElliott 14 56
(John A Harris) *hld up: drvn over 2f out: nvr rchd ldrs* **8/1**[3]

4060 **10** *1 ¾* **Middlemarch (IRE)**[27] 2535 8-9-5 **76** (v) GaryBartley(5) 10 66
(J S Goldie) *bhd: drvn over 3f out: nvr on terms* **28/1**

2200 **11** *nse* **Always Brave**[12] 3004 3-8-9 **71** RoystonFfrench 5 59
(M Johnston) *bhd: pushed along over 3f out: nvr rchd ldrs* **16/1**

-042 **12** *1 ½* **Giant Love (USA)**[4] 3263 3-9-0 **76** GregFairley 13 60
(M Johnston) *prom: rdn over 2f out: sn btn* **6/1**[2]

5000 **13** *½* **Social Rhythm**[9] 3079 4-8-5 **60** AndrewMullen(3) 12 45
(A C Whillans) *dwlt: a bhd* **50/1**

0450 **14** *2 ½* **Scotty's Future (IRE)**[14] 2927 10-7-7 **50** oh1 DanielleMcCreery(5) 7 29
(A Berry) *s.i.s: sn rdn along: nvr on terms* **28/1**

0-06 **15** *4 ½* **Hypnotic**[13] 2968 6-8-13 **65** AdrianTNicholls 15 34
(D Nicholls) *led to 3f out: wknd 2f out: eased whn no ch* **12/1**

1m 45.07s (5.07) **Going Correction** +0.60s/f (Yiel)
WFA 3 from 4yo+ 10lb **15** Ran SP% **119.9**
Speed ratings (Par 105): **98,97,96,96,93 93,92,92,90,88 88,87,86,84,79**
toteswinger: 1&2 £28.80, 1&3 £13.60, 2&3 £30.70. CSF £109.23 CT £934.96 TOTE £9.90: £2.50, £4.70, £2.60; EX 156.70.
Owner Mrs S E Bruce **Bred** Gestut Elsetal **Trained** Uplawmoor, E Renfrews
■ Stewards' Enquiry : Adrian T Nicholls caution: allowed gelding to coast home with no assistance

FOCUS

A fair handicap for those who missed out on a run in the following Carlisle Bell. It was a modest winning time, 1.59 seconds slower than the main event, but the form looks reasonable rated through the consistent fourth.

3367 LLOYD BMW CARLISLE BELL (H'CAP) 7f 200y

3:35 (3:37) (Class 4) (0-80,80) 3-Y-0+ £19,428 (£5,781; £2,889; £1,443) Stalls High

Form RPR

0011 **1** **Osteopathic Remedy (IRE)**[27] 2524 4-9-4 **79** TomEaves 1 90
(M Dods) *midfield: hdwy 2f out: led ins fnl f: styd on wl* **9/1**[3]

0100 **2** *1 ¼* **Bold Marc (IRE)**[12] 3006 6-9-3 **78** AndrewElliott 11 86
(K R Burke) *w ldr: led briefly 3f out and appr fnl f to ins fnl f: kpt on same pce* **9/1**[3]

-050 **3** *1 ½* **Rainbow Mirage (IRE)**[28] 2504 4-9-4 **79** GrahamGibbons 2 84
(E S McMahon) *prom: drvn 3f out: styd on wl ins fnl f* **28/1**

-411 **4** *½* **Sunnyside Tom (IRE)**[5] 3214 4-9-3 **78** 6ex PaulHanagan 3 81+
(R A Fahey) *trckd ldrs: led over 2f out to appr fnl f: no ex ins fnl f* **12/1**

5-22 **5** *1 ¼* **Observatory Star (IRE)**[6] 3173 5-9-3 **78** (p) DavidAllan 12 79+
(T D Easterby) *hld up: effrt whn nt clr run over 2f out: swtchd rt over 1f out: no imp ins fnl f* **8/1**[2]

0-16 **6** *2 ¾* **Motafarred (IRE)**[30] 2445 6-9-2 **77** JoeFanning 4 71
(Micky Hammond) *midfield: drvn and outpcd over 3f out: rallied fnl f: no imp* **33/1**

-066 **7** *¾* **Vicious Warrior**[21] 2733 9-9-5 **80** DeanMcKeown 10 72
(R M Whitaker) *led to 3f out: no ex fnl 2f* **22/1**

-053 **8** *2 ¼* **Hartshead**[15] 2913 9-9-5 **80** PaulMulrennan 7 67
(G A Swinbank) *hld up: pushed along over 2f out: nvr rchd ldrs* **14/1**

0030 **9** *shd* **Countdown**[18] 2818 6-9-3 **78** MickyFenton 13 65
(T D Easterby) *s.i.s: bhd: pushed along over 3f out: n.d* **22/1**

0006 **10** *nk* **Ella Woodcock (IRE)**[34] 2334 4-9-5 **80** TonyHamilton 9 66
(E J Alston) *hld up: rdn 3f out: nvr on terms* **20/1**

6 **11** *nk* **Lend A Grand (IRE)**[37] 2262 4-9-0 **78** TravisBlock(3) 15 64
(Miss Jo Crowley) *bhd: rdn on outside 3f out: sn btn* **33/1**

45-2 **12** *2 ¼* **Summer Dancer (IRE)**[19] 2787 4-9-2 **80** MarcHalford(3) 6 61
(D R C Elsworth) *t.k.h: hld up: pushed along over 2f out: sn btn* **11/1**

2112 **13** *nk* **Carlitos Spirit (IRE)**[20] 2762 4-8-11 **77** JamesMillman(5) 8 57
(B R Millman) *hld up: rdn over 2f out: eased whn no ch fnl f* **5/1**[1]

1 **14** *1* **Summer Gold (IRE)**[40] 2155 4-9-4 **79** ShaneKelly 14 57
(E J Alston) *prom: rdn over 2f out: sn wknd* **10/1**

1466 **15** *2 ¼* **Full Victory (IRE)**[20] 2762 6-9-3 **78** GregFairley 5 50
(R A Farrant) *midfield: rdn 3f out: wknd fr 2f out* **12/1**

0523 **16** *1 ¼* **Nevada Desert (IRE)**[12] 3006 8-8-13 **77** MichaelJStainton(3) 17 46
(R M Whitaker) *prom: checked after 3f: rdn and wknd 3f out* **8/1**[2]

1m 43.48s (3.48) **Going Correction** +0.60s/f (Yiel) **16** Ran SP% **121.2**
Speed ratings (Par 105): **106,104,103,102,101 98,98,95,95,95 95,92,92,91,89 88**
toteswinger: 1&2 £23.80, 1&3 £32.60, 2&3 £66.20. CSF £78.62 CT £2269.09 TOTE £9.90: £2.60, £2.70, £6.30, £2.70; EX 144.60.
Owner Kevin Kirkup **Bred** Airlie Stud **Trained** Denton, Co Durham
■ Stewards' Enquiry : Graham Gibbons two-day ban: careless riding (Jul 10,12)
Paul Hanagan two-day ban: careless riding (Jul 14,15)

FOCUS

A really competitive handicap for the class, with just 3lb covering the field. It was run at a solid pace and the form looks sound and should work out.

Hartshead Official explanation: jockey said gelding never travelled

Carlitos Spirit(IRE) Official explanation: jockey said gelding never travelled

3368 COLLIER HILL CUMBERLAND PLATE (H'CAP) 1m 3f 107y

4:05 (4:08) (Class 4) (0-80,79) 3-Y-0+ £19,428 (£5,781; £2,889; £1,443) Stalls Low

Form RPR

1210 **1** **Lochiel**[14] 2939 4-8-11 **71** NeilBrown(5) 11 82
(Mrs S C Bradburne) *hld up: last 4f out: hdwy over 2f out: swtchd rt over 1f out: led ent fnl f: styd on wl* **25/1**

2111 **2** *½* **Hits Only Vic (USA)**[7] 3143 4-9-6 **75** 6ex DavidAllan 6 85
(D Carroll) *midfield: hdwy to ld over 2f out: hdd ent fnl f: kpt on u.p* **3/1**[1]

0-00 **3** *1 ¼* **Wind Star**[26] 2582 5-9-9 **78** ShaneKelly 13 86+
(G A Swinbank) *hld up in midfield: hdwy whn nt clr run over 2f out to over 1f out: kpt on fnl f* **16/1**

131 **4** *¾* **Cotton Eyed Joe (IRE)**[18] 2822 7-9-7 **78** DeanMcKeown 3 85
(G A Swinbank) *chsd ldrs: effrt over 2f out: ch over 1f out: one pce ins fnl f* **8/1**[3]

600- **5** *4 ½* **Clueless**[243] 6475 6-9-8 **77** NeilPollard 9 77+
(A J McCabe) *cl up: disp ld over 2f out: rdn and no ex whn hmpd ins fnl f* **25/1**

1424 **6** *¾* **Inspirina (IRE)**[12] 3010 4-9-5 **74** RoystonFfrench 2 72
(R Ford) *prom: drvn 3f out: one pce fr 2f out* **17/2**

-313 **7** *hd* **La Vecchia Scuola (IRE)**[14] 2939 4-9-10 **79** DanielTudhope 7 76
(J S Goldie) *towards rr: drvn over 3f out: plugged on fnl f: nvr able to chal* **10/1**

1323 **8** *6* **Hue**[18] 2839 7-9-8 **77** TomEaves 17 64
(B Ellison) *hld up: drvn over 3f out: nvr rchd ldrs* **12/1**

3223 **9** *3 ¼* **Bazart**[11] 3045 6-9-10 **79** AndrewElliott 15 60
(K R Burke) *hld up: hdwy and in tch over 2f out: sn rdn and wknd* **10/1**

-066 **10** *hd* **Nur Tau (IRE)**[25] 2591 4-9-7 **79** (b[1]) TravisBlock(3) 8 60
(H Morrison) *racd wd towards rr: struggling over 4f out: nvr on terms* **18/1**

5142 **11** *¾* **Charlotte Vale**[8] 3110 7-9-6 **75** JoeFanning 4 54
(Micky Hammond) *prom: rdn whn n.m.r and lost pl over 3f out: n.d after* **25/1**

0-06 **12** *shd* **Olimpo (FR)**[20] 2764 7-9-3 **77** JamesMillman(5) 5 56
(B R Millman) *prom: led over 3f out to over 2f out: sn wknd* **25/1**

22-4 **13** *2 ½* **Sin City**[14] 2939 5-9-7 **76** PaulHanagan 10 51
(R A Fahey) *s.i.s: drvn in rr 4f out: nvr on terms* **13/2**[2]

-133 **14** *16* **Harry The Hawk**[26] 2585 4-9-2 **71** GrahamGibbons 1 19
(T D Walford) *t.k.h: led to over 3f out: sn wknd* **9/1**

0202 **15** *3 ½* **Key Decision (IRE)**[30] 2447 4-9-9 **78** PaulMulrennan 16 20
(G A Swinbank) *plld hrd in midfield: wknd over 4f out: eased whn no ch* **40/1**

2m 31.05s (7.95) **Going Correction** +0.60s/f (Yiel) **15** Ran SP% **124.8**
Speed ratings (Par 105): **95,94,93,93,89 89,89,84,82,81 81,81,79,67,65**
toteswinger: 1&2 £28.50, 1&3 £136.10, 2&3 £19.40. CSF £97.07 CT £1309.73 TOTE £33.40: £9.20, £1.70, £5.20; EX 199.50 TRIFECTA Not won..
Owner A Campbell **Bred** D W Barker **Trained** Cunnoquhie, Fife
■ The name of former northern-trained globetrotter Collier Hill has been added to the race title.
■ Stewards' Enquiry : Shane Kelly two-day ban: careless riding (Jul 10,12)

FOCUS

A fair but competitive-looking renewal of this traditional handicap. Solid form. They went a fair gallop and once again came stands' side.

Key Decision(IRE) Official explanation: jockey said gelding ran too free early

3369 EUROPEAN BREEDERS' FUND FILLIES' H'CAP 6f 192y

4:35 (4:39) (Class 4) (0-85,85) 3-Y-0+ £6,476 (£1,927; £963; £481) Stalls High

Form RPR

0-61 **1** **Medici Pearl**[19] 2781 4-9-1 **72** DavidAllan 1 87+
(T D Easterby) *hld up in tch: smooth hdwy over 2f out: led and edgd lft 1f out: kpt on wl u.p* **13/2**

51-3 **2** *2* **Lady Rangali (IRE)**[18] 2819 3-9-3 **83** RoystonFfrench 3 88
(Mrs A Duffield) *chsd ldrs: effrt over 2f out: wnt 2nd ins fnl f: nt rch wnr* **11/4**[1]

4-22 **3** *6* **Orpen Fire (IRE)**[19] 2781 3-8-11 **77** GrahamGibbons 8 66
(E S McMahon) *led to 1f out: sn outpcd* **7/2**[3]

31 **4** *1* **Celtic Lynn (IRE)**[53] 1795 3-8-9 **75** TomEaves 4 61
(M Dods) *t.k.h: prom: effrt over 2f out: no ex whn checked wl over 1f out* **5/1**

64 **5** *1 ½* **Goodbye**[4] 3261 4-10-0 **85** PaulMulrennan 7 70
(G A Swinbank) *pressed ldr tl no ex fr 2f out* **3/1**[2]

136- **6** *1* **Destinys Dream (IRE)**[266] 5914 3-8-7 **73** TonyHamilton 2 52
(D W Barker) *bhd: drvn 1/2-way: nvr on terms* **28/1**

0-66 **7** *4 ½* **Passion Fruit**[16] 2890 7-9-12 **83** DeanMcKeown 6 53
(C W Fairhurst) *missed break: nvr on terms* **16/1**

1m 31.05s (3.95) **Going Correction** +0.60s/f (Yiel)
WFA 3 from 4yo+ 9lb **7** Ran SP% **113.2**
Speed ratings (Par 102): **101,98,91,90,89 87,82**
toteswinger: 1&2 £4.20, 1&3 £4.60, 2&3 £2.10. CSF £24.21 CT £72.20 TOTE £7.70: £3.30, £1.70; EX 22.20.
Owner Ryedale Partners No 3 **Bred** Larkwood Stud **Trained** Great Habton, N Yorks
■ Stewards' Enquiry : David Allan caution: careless riding
Graham Gibbons three-day ban: careless riding (Jul 13-15)

FOCUS

A decent fillies' handicap in which two highly progressive sorts came clear. The pace set by the third looked over-strong so there is a doubt over how literally this form should be taken.

3370 EDMUNDSON ELECTRICAL H'CAP 5f

5:10 (5:10) (Class 4) (0-85,85) 3-Y-0+ £5,180 (£1,541; £770; £384) Stalls High

Form RPR

2306 **1** **Angus Newz**[12] 2993 5-9-13 **85** (v) ShaneKelly 2 96
(M Quinn) *mde virtually all: hrd pressed fnl f: all out* **7/1**[3]

0030 **2** *shd* **He's A Humbug (IRE)**[11] 3050 4-9-5 **77** (p) JoeFanning 1 88
(K A Ryan) *dwlt: sn prom: rdn to dispute ld ins fnl f: kpt on: jst hld* **8/1**

-100 **3** *2* **Sandwith**[18] 2843 5-8-10 **68** .... PaulHanagan 3 71
(R Johnson) *prom: effrt 2f out: kpt on u.p ins fnl f* **9/1**

00-4 **4** *nk* **Foxy Music**[15] 2906 4-9-8 **80** .... DavidAllan 5 82
(E J Alston) *w wnr tl rdn and no ex ins fnl f* **9/1**

0023 **5** *1 ¾* **Highland Warrior**[6] 3171 9-9-0 **72** .... MickyFenton 12 68+
(P T Midgley) *hld up: hdwy over 1f out: nt clr run and swtchd rt ins fnl f: nrst fin* **7/1**[3]

-000 **6** *1 ¾* **Prospect Court**[36] 2292 6-8-12 **73** .... AndrewMullen(3) 9 63+
(A C Whillans) *bhd: drvn over 2f out: kpt on fnl f: n.d* **11/1**

-423 **7** *2 ¼* **Glasshoughton**[20] 2760 5-9-6 **83** .... NeilBrown(5) 7 65
(M Dods) *trckd ldrs: effrt 2f out: sn no ex* **9/2**[1]

3360 **8** *3 ¼* **Deserted Dane (USA)**[12] 3009 4-9-3 **75** .... PaulMulrennan 13 45
(G A Swinbank) *prom tl rdn and wknd wl over 1f out* **15/2**

00-0 **9** *3 ½* **Katie Boo (IRE)**[14] 2938 6-9-3 **75** .... DanielTudhope 6 32
(A Berry) *prom: drvn and outpcd over 2f out: n.d after* **14/1**

11-0 **10** *1 ¼* **Divine Spirit**[12] 3009 7-9-13 **85** .... RoystonFfrench 8 38
(M Dods) *hld up: rdn 1/2-way: nvr on terms* **18/1**

0005 **11** *1 ¾* **Ice Planet**[28] 2501 7-9-10 **82** .... AdrianTNicholls 10 29
(D Nicholls) *pckd sn after s: a bhd* **13/2**[2]

56-0 **12** *23* **Tom Tower (IRE)**[53] 1818 4-8-8 **66** oh4 .... TWilliams 14 —
(A C Whillans) *bhd: struggling 1/2-way: t.o* **50/1**

62.97 secs (2.17) **Going Correction** +0.60s/f (Yiel) **12 Ran SP% 121.6**
Speed ratings (Par 105): **106,105,102,102,99 96,92,87,82,80 77,40**
toteswinger: 1&2 £15.00, 1&3 £17.50, 2&3 £20.30. CSF £63.78 CT £390.55 TOTE £9.30: £2.90, £3.80, £3.50; EX 84.10 Place 6: £251.11, Place 5: £120.10..
Owner M J Quinn **Bred** Henry And Mrs Rosemary Moszkowicz **Trained** Newmarket, Suffolk
■ Stewards' Enquiry : Paul Hanagan two-day ban: careless riding (Jul 10,12)

FOCUS
A fair handicap and solid form, with the first two close to their best.
Highland Warrior Official explanation: jockey said gelding was denied a clear run
T/Jkpt: Not won. T/Plt: £267.70 to a £1 stake. Pool: £75,198.99. 205.00 winning tickets. T/Qpdt: £125.30 to a £1 stake. Pool: £4,335.26. 25.60 winning tickets. RY

3132 KEMPTON (A.W) (R-H)
Wednesday, June 25

OFFICIAL GOING: Standard
Wind: Breezy, across.

3371 WEATHERBYS V.A.T. SERVICES APPRENTICE H'CAP (ROUND 4) 1m (P)
6:20 (6:22) (Class 6) (0-65,65) 4-Y-0+ **£2,047** (£604; £302) **Stalls** High

Form RPR

3-05 **1** **Parthenope**[11] 3034 5-8-5 **49** .... JackDean(3) 8 61
(J A Geake) *chsd ldng pair: rdn and effrt 2f out: led over 1f out: clr ins fnl f: idled towards fin* **7/1**[3]

344 **2** *3 ¼* **Million Percent**[17] 2861 9-9-4 **62** .... WilliamCarson(3) 2 67
(C R Dore) *stdd and dropped in after s: racd off the pce in midfield: hdwy over 3f out: styd on u.p to go 2nd ins fnl f: no ch w wnr* **6/1**[2]

4000 **3** *1 ¼* **Trivia (IRE)**[10] 3064 4-9-7 **62** .... AshleyHamblett 12 64
(Ms J S Doyle) *chsd ldrs: rdn to chal over 2f out: led 2f out: hdd over 1f out: outpcd fnl f* **16/1**

-004 **4** *1* **Crafty Fox**[17] 2866 5-8-0 **46** oh1 .... (v) SoniaEaton(5) 11 46
(John A Harris) *racd off the pce in midfield: hdwy on inner 3f out: swtchd lft over 1f out: edgd lft but styd on fnl f: nvr rchd ldrs* **20/1**

6402 **5** *nk* **Eagle Nebula**[14] 2943 4-9-7 **65** .... MarkCoumbe(3) 1 64
(B R Johnson) *sn wl bhd in last: reminders 6f out: c wd 3f out: r.o last 2f: nvr able to chal* **4/1**[1]

0026 **6** *1* **Zorn**[6] 3162 9-8-0 **46** oh1 .... CharlesEddery(5) 7 43
(P Howling) *pressed ldr: ev ch and rdn over 2f out tl fdd ent fnl f* **14/1**

3600 **7** *1* **Hollow Jo**[14] 2947 8-9-9 **64** .... HaddenFrost 6 59
(J R Jenkins) *racd off the pce in midfield: hdwy 3f out: kpt on same pce fnl f* **10/1**

203 **8** *¾* **Hits Only Cash**[28] 2510 6-9-5 **65** .... SimonPearce(5) 14 58
(J Pearce) *alwys bhd: rdn over 4f out: nvr trbld ldrs* **4/1**[1]

110 **9** *2 ¼* **Sion Hill (IRE)**[14] 2933 7-9-9 **64** .... (p) KellyHarrison 10 52
(John A Harris) *set fast pce tl hdd 2f out: wknd over 1f out* **4/1**[1]

4610 **10** *1 ¼* **Hey Presto**[55] 1747 8-8-0 **46** .... RichardRowe(5) 4 31
(R Rowe) *racd wd: a bhd* **25/1**

0-00 **11** *2* **Barley Moon**[14] 2933 4-8-0 **46** oh1 .... AshleyMorgan(5) 5 26
(T Keddy) *s.i.s: bhd: rdn and edgd rt 3f out: n.d* **50/1**

000- **12** *11* **Sir Mikeale**[196] 7124 5-8-0 **46** oh1 .... JosephineBruning(5) 3 —
(J Pearce) *chsd ldrs: struggling 1/2-way: t.o last 2f* **66/1**

1m 42.06s (2.26) **Going Correction** +0.175s/f (Slow) **12 Ran SP% 120.5**
Speed ratings (Par 101): **95,91,90,89,89 88,87,86,84,82 80,69**
toteswinger: 1&2 £9.60, 1&3 £14.20, 2&3 £19.00. CSF £47.90 CT £669.37 TOTE £7.80: £2.50, £2.90, £4.80; EX 55.30.
Owner Dr and Mrs John Merrington **Bred** Theakston Stud **Trained** Kimpton, Hants

FOCUS
A weak race with not many turning up in much form. The winner was confirming the return to form of the Geake yard after a long spell in the doldrums. The form is quite fluid and has been rated through the regressive third. The early pace was strong.

3372 DAVID LLOYD EPSOM MAIDEN STKS 7f (P)
6:50 (6:52) (Class 4) 2-Y-0 **£3,885** (£1,156; £577; £288) **Stalls** High

Form RPR

44 **1** **Roly Boy**[18] 2826 2-9-3 0 .... RichardHughes 11 74
(R Hannon) *trckd ldng pair: effrt to chal wl over 1f out: rdn to ld and edgd rt ins fnl f: hld on* **2/5**[1]

2 *hd* **Celtic Spur (IRE)** 2-9-3 0 .... WilliamBuick 3 74+
(A M Balding) *s.i.s: wl bhd: swtchd rt jst over 2f out: gd hdwy over 1f out: pressed wnr wl ins fnl f: hld last strides* **25/1**

536 **3** *¾* **Duke Of Aquitaine (USA)**[23] 2663 2-9-3 0 .... JosedeSouza 13 72
(P F I Cole) *led: hrd pressed over 2f out: rdn wl over 1f out: hdd ins fnl f: no ex last 100yds* **14/1**

60 **4** *2 ½* **Northumberland**[23] 2657 2-9-3 0 .... J-PGuillambert 5 65
(M Johnston) *chsd ldr: ev ch 2f out tl over 1f out: outpcd fnl f* **33/1**

5 *shd* **Fisher Hill (USA)** 2-9-3 0 .... NCallan 4 65+
(K A Ryan) *awkward leaving stalls: t.k.h: sn in tch: rdn and effrt 2f out: kpt on same pce fr over 1f out* **12/1**[3]

6 *5* **Mister Dee Bee (IRE)** 2-9-3 0 .... RHills 9 53
(B W Hills) *in tch in midfield: effrt and rdn jst over 2f out: sn wknd* **8/1**[2]

5 **7** *¾* **Killmarnock**[19] 2796 2-9-3 0 .... TedDurcan 6 51
(R A Teal) *sn pushed along in midfield: rdn and hanging rt wl over 2f out: nvr threatened ldrs* **16/1**

8 *1* **Oil Man (IRE)** 2-9-3 0 .... JimCrowley 2 48
(P Winkworth) *bhd: sn pushed along: rn wd bnd wl over 4f out: n.d* **20/1**

6 **9** *nk* **Astroleo**[55] 1736 2-9-3 0 .... JimmyQuinn 7 48
(M H Tompkins) *a bhd: rdn over 3f out: n.d* **50/1**

10 *1* **Corredor Sun (USA)** 2-9-3 0 .... TPQueally 8 45
(Carl Llewellyn) *sn pushed along in midfield: struggling 3f out: wl btn after* **16/1**

0 **11** *3* **My Kingdom (IRE)**[13] 2972 2-9-3 0 .... (t) EdwardCreighton 1 38
(H Morrison) *wnt rt s: t.k.h: sn chsng ldrs: rdn and wknd over 2f out* **50/1**

12 *2 ¾* **Rockfella** 2-9-3 0 .... TPO'Shea 10 31
(D J Coakley) *s.i.s: a struggling in last* **33/1**

1m 28.24s (2.24) **Going Correction** +0.175s/f (Slow) **12 Ran SP% 127.1**
Speed ratings (Par 95): **94,93,92,90,89 84,83,82,81,80 77,74**
toteswinger: 1&2 £3.80, 1&3 £3.20, 2&3 £11.30. CSF £24.11 TOTE £1.40: £1.02, £5.30, £2.90; EX 16.50.
Owner The Calvera Partnership No 2 **Bred** Miss G Abbey **Trained** East Everleigh, Wilts
■ Stewards' Enquiry : Richard Hughes caution: careless riding

FOCUS
A decent juvenile maiden, the front three all being likeable sorts. The third sets the level for now and the race could rate higher.

NOTEBOOK
Roly Boy, who improved from his debut to run fourth in the Woodcote at Epsom on Derby day, made hard work of landing some prohibitive odds. Already hard ridden to repel the eventual third home, he did, in fairness, pick up close to the line to ward off the thrust of the fast-finishing runner-up. His future lies in handicaps. (op 8-13 tchd 4-6)
Celtic Spur(IRE) ◆ came from a different parish to grab the runner's-up spot. Slowly away, he only had one behind him turning in and looks almost certain to win a maiden in the near future. (op 20-1 tchd 16-1)
Duke Of Aquitaine(USA) had finished behind subsequent Royal Ascot winners on two of his three previous starts and it was only in the last 50 yards that he really gave way. His form is solid but that will be factored into his handicap mark. (op 12-1)
Northumberland, an own brother to Group 1-winning juvenile Donna Blini, showed pace but, as his pedigree suggested, this trip seemed to stretch him. (op 25-1)
Fisher Hill(USA) showed strong signs of ability after a sluggish start and can only do better with this experience under his belt. (op 10-1 tchd 9-1)
Mister Dee Bee(IRE), a debutant son of Orpen, showed up well for a long way and will improve for this. (tchd 13-2)

3373 EUROPEAN BREEDERS' FUND MAIDEN FILLIES' STKS 6f (P)
7:20 (7:21) (Class 5) 2-Y-O **£3,885** (£1,156; £577; £288) **Stalls** High

Form RPR

5 **1** **Ahla Wasahl**[18] 2821 2-8-9 0 .... AhmedAjtebi(5) 10 78+
(D M Simcock) *in tch: nt clr run and swtchd lft over 1f out: rdn to ld ins fnl f: r.o strly* **2/1**[1]

66 **2** *2* **Deal Clincher**[24] 2638 2-9-0 0 .... JimCrowley 7 72
(P Winkworth) *pressed ldr: rdn and unable qck 2f out: kpt on u.p fnl f* **16/1**

0 **3** *shd* **Today's The Day**[22] 2691 2-9-0 0 .... PhilipRobinson 6 72
(M A Jarvis) *in tch: sltly hmpd over 1f out: swtchd rt ins fnl f: flashed tail u.p kpt on* **20/1**

2 **4** *hd* **Sparkling Crystal (IRE)**[19] 2769 2-9-0 0 .... WilliamBuick 4 71
(B W Hills) *in tch: rdn and effrt on outer over 2f out: kpt on u.p fnl f: nvr gng pce to trble wnr* **2/1**[1]

5 **5** *2 ½* **Azwa**[35] 2306 2-9-0 0 .... RHills 9 64
(E A L Dunlop) *led: rdn and qcknd 2f out: hdd ins fnl f: wknd rapidly last 100yds* **8/1**[3]

6 *½* **Minor Vamp (IRE)** 2-9-0 0 .... PatDobbs 8 62
(R Hannon) *s.i.s: in tch in rr: effrt and rn green over 2f out: kpt on but nvr trbld ldrs* **25/1**

5 **7** *½* **Polly's Choice (IRE)**[11] 3027 2-9-0 0 .... RichardHughes 3 63+
(R Hannon) *s.i.s: t.k.h: hld up in tch in rr: rdn jst over 2f out: no imp* **9/2**[2]

63 **8** *6* **Innactualfact**[25] 2614 2-9-0 0 .... PaulDoe 5 43
(L A Dace) *chsd ldrs: rdn over 2f out: edgd lft and wknd 2f out* **14/1**

0 **9** *2 ¼* **Prima Fonteyn**[16] 2893 2-9-0 0 .... TPO'Shea 2 36
(M R Channon) *rrd in stalls and v.s.a: a wl bhd* **50/1**

1m 14.74s (1.64) **Going Correction** +0.175s/f (Slow) **9 Ran SP% 119.1**
Speed ratings (Par 90): **96,93,93,92,89 88,88,80,77**
toteswinger: 1&2 £47.20, 1&3 £58.50, 2&3 £58.50. CSF £39.88 TOTE £3.20: £1.10, £4.00, £4.00; EX 44.30.
Owner Sultan Ali **Bred** Dachel Stud **Trained** Newmarket, Suffolk
■ Stewards' Enquiry : Ahmed Ajtebi two-day ban: careles riding (Jul 10,12)

FOCUS
Another decent maiden, especially for one confined to fillies. The winner looks the type to keep progressing and trhe form should work out.

NOTEBOOK
Ahla Wasahl ◆ built on the promise of her debut at Doncaster by running out a convincing winner. She had to be switched around the weakening Azwa, but once in the clear showed a real turn of foot that will stand her in good stead in better company. (op 9-4 tchd 5-2)
Deal Clincher was always up in the firing-line and looked like she was going to finish well beaten when swamped with a quarter-mile left, so deserves a bit of credit for staying on again to the line. She shouldn't be overburdened in nurseries. (op 14-1)
Today's The Day didn't get much daylight at a crucial stage but at best it cost her second place. She showed a bit of temperament under pressure and is obviously one of the yard's lesser lights, but there may be a little race in her nonetheless. (op 16-1)
Sparkling Crystal(IRE) is from a family that has thrown up its fair share of disappointments among some undoubtedly classy types. This latest representative held every chance of improving on her debut second at Bath when challenging two furlongs out, but her finishing effort was tame. She could prove hard to win with. (op 6-4 tchd 9-4 in places)
Azwa showed plenty of speed but stopped as if shot once challenged inside the final furlong. If everything is all right with her, she would prove hard to beat dropped to the minimum in similar grade. (op 12-1)
Minor Vamp(IRE), a debutante daughter of Hawk Wing, made some minor headway from the rear after a slow start and should leave this form behind her in due course. (op 16-1)
Polly's Choice(IRE), like her stablemate one place in front of her, could never get competitive after a slow start. She had the advantage of a previous run and this was a disappointment. (op 15-2)

3374 SALLY NICHOLLS (I AM BACK) H'CAP 6f (P)
7:50 (7:51) (Class 4) (0-80,80) 3-Y-O+ **£4,209** (£1,252; £625; £312) **Stalls** High

Form RPR

-511 **1** **Whiskey Junction**[19] 2773 4-9-11 **77** .... LPKeniry 11 86
(A M Balding) *mde all: rdn and qcknd jst over 2f out: hld on gamely fnl f* **3/1**[1]

1324 **2** *nk* **Dvinsky (USA)**[44] 2058 7-9-9 **75** .... (b) JimmyQuinn 12 83
(P Howling) *t.k.h: chsd ldrs: effrt on inner to chse wnr 2f out: sn swtchd lft: str chal fnl f: nt qckn last 100yds* **4/1**[2]

0-40 **3** *nk* **Sheriff's Silk**[19] 2798 4-8-11 **63**........(b) OscarUrbina 9 70
(G D Blake) *wnt lft and bmpd s: bhd: rdn over 1f out: r.o strly fnl f: nt quite rch ldng pair* **25/1**

5540 **4** *3/4* **Hucking Hill (IRE)**[51] 1853 4-8-12 **64**........(b) TedDurcan 7 69
(J R Best) *in tch in midfield: rdn and unable qck jst over 1f out: styd on u.p fnl f* **6/1**[3]

3000 **5** *1/2* **Steel City Boy (IRE)**[6] 3171 5-9-1 **72**........ AnnStokell(5) 6 75
(Miss A Stokell) *chsd ldrs: rdn 2f out: kpt on same pce after: lost 2 pls wl ins fnl f* **25/1**

-034 **6** *nk* **Replicator**[14] 2945 3-8-12 **71**........ PatDobbs 8 71
(Pat Eddery) *hld up in tch: effrt and rdn 2f out: drvn over 1f out: plugged on same pce* **14/1**

236 **7** *1 1/2* **Spoof Master (IRE)**[21] 2710 4-9-4 **70**........ LiamJones 10 67
(C R Dore) *hld up in rr: effrt and rdn over 2f out: nvr threatened ldrs* **12/1**

2600 **8** *nk* **Adantino**[23] 2679 9-9-2 **68**........(b) TGMcLaughlin 4 64
(B R Millman) *stdd after s: t.k.h: hld up in rr: rdn over 1f out: no hdwy* **20/1**

1315 **9** *2 3/4* **Diriculous**[20] 2760 4-10-0 **80**........ JimCrowley 5 68
(T G Mills) *racd keenly: chsd ldr: hanging lft bnd 1/2-way: hung bdly lft ent fnl f: eased whn btn ins fnl f* **3/1**[1]

1m 13.8s (0.70) **Going Correction** +0.175s/f (Slow)
WFA 3 from 4yo+ 7lb **9** Ran SP% **111.1**
Speed ratings (Par 105): **102,101,101,100,99 99,97,96,93**
toteswinger: 1&2 £1.70, 1&3 £19.40, 2&3 £43.50. CSF £13.87 CT £233.85 TOTE £2.20: £1.20, £2.20, £6.20; EX 12.00.
Owner Kingsclere Racing CLub **Bred** Mrs I A Balding **Trained** Kingsclere, Hants
■ Stewards' Enquiry : Jimmy Quinn one-day ban: used whip with excessive frequency (Jul 10)
L P Keniry one-day ban: used whip with excessive frequency (Jul 10)
Oscar Urbina one-day ban: used whip without allowing sufficient time to respond (Jul 10)

FOCUS
A fair bunch of sprint handicappers on show. The form looks particularly solid, with the front three home in particular likely to remain highly competitive.
Diriculous Official explanation: jockey said gelding hung left

3375 DIGIBET.COM H'CAP 1m 4f (P)
8:20 (8:20) (Class 4) (0-85,85) 4-Y-O+ **£4,209** (£1,252; £625; £312) **Stalls** Centre

Form RPR
1223 **1** **Buster Hyvonen (IRE)**[46] 1984 6-9-7 **85**........ JamieSpencer 6 101+
(J R Fanshawe) *stdd after s: hld up in last trio: smooth hdwy jst over 2f out: stalked ldr on bit over 1f out: cruised into ld ins fnl f: hrd hld* **7/2**[2]

-353 **2** *3/4* **Jagger**[64] 1547 8-9-4 **82**........(p) EddieAhern 5 94
(G A Butler) *taken down early: hld up in midfield: rdn and hdwy to ld 2f out: clr w wnr 1f out: hdd and no ch w wnr ins fnl f* **8/1**

-531 **3** *6* **Cleaver**[25] 2621 7-9-2 **80**........ RichardHughes 4 82
(Lady Herries) *racd wd: chsd ldrs: rdn and hld hd high over 2f out: pressed ldrs 2f out: sn outpcd by ldng pair* **4/1**[3]

0166 **4** *shd* **Apache Fort**[5] 3220 5-8-8 **72**........ JimmyQuinn 7 74
(T Keddy) *hld up in tch: swtchd ins and hdwy over 2f out: ev ch 2f out: sn outpcd by ldng pair* **14/1**

-020 **5** *2 1/4* **Bold Adventure**[25] 2621 4-8-3 **67**........ TPO'Shea 3 66
(W J Musson) *s.i.s: hld up bhd: effrt and hanging rt 2f out: nvr nr ldrs* **12/1**

-000 **6** *3* **Birkspiel (GER)**[25] 2599 7-8-9 **73**........(t) IanMongan 9 67
(S Dow) *chsd ldr: upside ldr and rdn wl over 2f out: wknd wl over 1f out* **25/1**

10-4 **7** *4* **Dustoori**[12] 3003 4-9-2 **80**........ RHills 8 67
(E A L Dunlop) *chsd ldng pair: rdn to chal over 2f out: wknd qckly wl over 1f out* **5/2**[1]

200 **8** *8* **Mister Right (IRE)**[10] 3060 7-8-11 **75**........ NCallan 1 50
(D J S Ffrench Davis) *t.k.h: hld up in tch: rdn and effrt wl over 2f out: wknd wl over 1f out: eased wl ins fnl f* **33/1**

3-52 **9** *10* **Awatuki (IRE)**[99] 927 5-9-3 **81**........ TPQueally 10 40
(J R Boyle) *led tl rdn and hdd 2f out: wknd rapidly: eased fnl f* **5/1**

01-0 **10** *13* **Eva Soneva So Fast (IRE)**[33] 1857 6-9-7 **85**........ VinceSlattery 2 23
(G F Bridgwater) *s.i.s: bhd: rdn and lost tch 4f out: t.o and eased fnl f* **33/1**

2m 34.74s (0.24) **Going Correction** +0.175s/f (Slow) **10** Ran SP% **122.7**
Speed ratings (Par 105): **106,105,101,101,99 97,95,89,83,74**
toteswinger: 1&2 £3.00, 1&3 £1.02, 2&3 £2.80. CSF £32.94 CT £118.95 TOTE £4.60: £1.50, £2.20, £2.10; EX 34.10.
Owner Simon Gibson **Bred** Hollington Stud **Trained** Newmarket, Suffolk

FOCUS
A fair handicap, run at a modest early pace. The first pair came clear and, with the form looking sound enough, the easy winner rates value for a lot further.
Dustoori Official explanation: trainer's rep said colt was unsuited by the polytrack
Awatuki(IRE) Official explanation: jockey said gelding had no more to give

3376 DIGIBET CASINO H'CAP (LONDON MILE QUALIFIER) 1m (P)
8:50 (8:51) (Class 4) (0-80,78) 3-Y-O+ **£4,209** (£1,252; £625; £312) **Stalls** High

Form RPR
2202 **1** **Totally Focussed (IRE)**[20] 2756 3-9-1 **75**........ IanMongan 8 87+
(S Dow) *hld up in last trio: gd hdwy over 2f out: ev ch 1f out: r.o wl to ld last strides* **7/2**[1]

0312 **2** *hd* **Willow Dancer (IRE)**[9] 3090 4-9-7 **71**........(p) SaleemGolam 14 84
(W R Swinburn) *chsd ldrs: on inner: rdn to ld 2f out: edgd lft ins fnl f but r.o wl tl hdd and no ex last strides* **7/2**[1]

2605 **3** *3 1/4* **Murrin (IRE)**[21] 2722 4-9-9 **73**........ JimCrowley 9 79
(T G Mills) *hld up in tch: effrt and rdn over 2f out: chsd ldng pair ins fnl f: no imp* **6/1**[2]

1036 **4** *1* **Phluke**[15] 2905 7-10-0 **78**........ NCallan 13 82
(Eve Johnson Houghton) *led for 1f: chsd ldr after: ev ch and rdn wl over 2f out: outpcd by ldng pair fnl f* **10/1**

60-1 **5** *3/4* **Practicallyperfect (IRE)**[27] 2537 4-9-8 **72**........ JamieSpencer 12 74
(M J Wallace) *in tch: rdn and hung rt 2f out: one pce after* **9/1**[3]

51-0 **6** *2* **Sister Act**[33] 2373 4-9-11 **75**........ OscarUrbina 4 72
(J R Fanshawe) *hld up towards rr: hdwy into midfield 3f out: rdn over 2f out: no imp last 2f* **9/1**[3]

6516 **7** *1 1/4* **Billy One Punch**[12] 3006 6-9-6 **70**........ RichardMullen 2 65
(D Shaw) *hld up in midfield: rdn over 2f out: no imp last 2f* **10/1**

-000 **8** *nk* **Mountain Cat (IRE)**[25] 2619 4-9-10 **74**........ TPO'Shea 5 68+
(W J Musson) *hld up bhd: pushed along over 2f out: kpt on but nvr trbld ldrs* **33/1**

-600 **9** *1* **Sofia's Star**[64] 1546 3-9-1 **75**........ LiamJones 1 65
(P Winkworth) *a bhd* **33/1**

-625 **10** *2 3/4* **Cupid's Glory**[19] 2799 6-9-6 **70**........(p) RichardHughes 3 55
(Mrs L C Jewell) *chsd ldr tl led after 1f: hdd 2f out: wknd wl over 1f out* **14/1**

5505 **11** *4* **Desert Clover (USA)**[20] 2761 3-8-13 **73**........ NelsonDeSouza 6 47
(P F I Cole) *a bhd: rdn and struggling 3f out* **16/1**

6060 **12** *3* **Smokin Joe**[33] 2355 7-9-7 **71**........(b) LPKeniry 11 40
(J R Best) *t.k.h: hld up towards rr: n.d* **25/1**

2001 **13** *12* **Bartercard (USA)**[15] 2917 7-9-9 **73**........ EddieAhern 7 14
(Stef Liddiard) *stdd s: a last: lost tch 3f out: virtually p.u fnl f: sddle slipped* **20/1**

1m 39.66s (-0.14) **Going Correction** +0.175s/f (Slow)
WFA 3 from 4yo+ 10lb **13** Ran SP% **124.0**
Speed ratings (Par 105): **107,106,103,102,101 99,98,98,97,94 90,87,75**
toteswinger: 1&2 £3.80, 1&3 £5.80, 2&3 £9.80. CSF £14.22 CT £73.20 TOTE £4.50: £1.60, £1.50, £3.00; EX 15.90.
Owner The St Cloud Partnership **Bred** Fintan Doran **Trained** Epsom, Surrey
■ Stewards' Enquiry : Saleem Golam two-day ban: used whip with excessive frequency (Jul 12,13)

FOCUS
A fair handicap, run at a strong pace. The first pair came clear and the winner showed improved form.
Cupid's Glory Official explanation: jockey said gelding lost its action
Bartercard(USA) Official explanation: jockey said saddle slipped

3377 MIX BUSINESS WITH PLEASURE H'CAP 2m (P)
9:20 (9:21) (Class 6) (0-65,60) 4-Y-O+ **£2,047** (£604; £302) **Stalls** High

Form RPR
55-3 **1** **Moonshine Beach**[7] 3137 10-9-3 **56**........ JimCrowley 6 64
(P W Hiatt) *chsd ldr: led 5f out: 4 l clr 2f out: hld on gamely: all out* **17/2**

3202 **2** *3/4* **Leyte Gulf (USA)**[7] 3137 5-9-6 **59**........ LPKeniry 14 66
(C C Bealby) *t.k.h: hld up towards rr: plenty to do over 3f out: plld out over 2f out and rdn: chsd wnr 1f out: styd on u.p but nvr quite getting to wnr* **11/4**[1]

6440 **3** *3/4* **Adage**[14] 2952 5-9-2 **55**........(t) SaleemGolam 8 61
(David Pinder) *hld up in midfield: hdwy and rdn over 2f out: sn hanging rt: disp 2nd wl over 1f out: styd on but nvr rchd wnr* **12/1**

P/06 **4** *1/2* **Fiddlers Ford (IRE)**[7] 3137 7-9-2 **55**........ JimmyQuinn 10 61
(T Keddy) *chsd ldrs: rdn over 4f out: chsd wnr 2f out: kpt on u.p but nvr gng pce to rch wnr* **16/1**

-243 **5** *2* **Critical Stage (IRE)**[21] 2715 9-8-13 **57**........ HaddenFrost(5) 5 60
(J D Frost) *chsd ldrs: rdn 4f out: disp 2nd u.p 2f out: no imp and eased wl ins fnl f* **15/2**[3]

/005 **6** *6* **Senor Set (GER)**[22] 2707 7-8-7 **46**........ PatrickMathers 2 42
(D Shaw) *hld up towards rr: rdn over 3f out: kpt on u.p last 2f: nvr nr ldrs* **33/1**

4505 **7** *1 3/4* **Mister Completely (IRE)**[7] 3137 7-9-6 **59**........(v) EdwardCreighton 13 53
(Ms J S Doyle) *t.k.h: hld up towards rr: rdn 3f out: nvr nr ldrs* **8/1**

4031 **8** *10* **Arabian Sun**[24] 2643 4-9-4 **57**........(v) NCallan 9 39
(M J Attwater) *sn led: hdd and rdn 5f out: chsd wnr after tl 2f out: eased whn wl btn fnl f* **10/3**[2]

10-0 **9** *1/2* **Colwyn Bay (IRE)**[16] 2888 6-9-7 **60**........(bt[1]) JamieSpencer 11 41
(R M Stronge) *hld up bhd: c wd and rdn 3f out: n.d* **8/1**

5000 **10** *2 3/4* **Eddystone (IRE)**[2] 3321 4-8-7 **46**........(v) TPQueally 3 24
(Mrs L C Jewell) *in tch in midfield: hdwy 7f out: rdn over 4f out: wknd over 3f out: wl bhd last 2f* **33/1**

5203 **11** *5* **Chiff Chaff**[12] 544 4-8-10 **49**........ LiamJones 12 21
(C R Dore) *in tch: rdn over 3f out: wknd 3f out: t.o and eased fnl f* **16/1**

000- **12** *63* **Best Warning**[12] 4172 4-8-6 **45**........ RichardMullen 4 —
(J Ryan) *s.i.s: a bhd: t.o and virtually p.u last 2f* **80/1**

3m 33.0s (2.90) **Going Correction** +0.175s/f (Slow) **12** Ran SP% **120.8**
Speed ratings (Par 101): **99,98,98,98,97 94,93,88,87,86 84,52**
toteswinger: 1&2 £19.30, 1&3 £24.30, 2&3 £15.20. CSF £32.38 CT £292.32 TOTE £10.20: £3.50, £1.60, £3.00; EX 44.60 Place 6 £65.83, Place 5 £11.33..
Owner Mrs Kerry Lewis **Bred** Lawrence Shepherd **Trained** Hook Norton, Oxon

FOCUS
A weak staying handicap. The form looks straightforward enough, if modest.
Best Warning Official explanation: vet said filly pulled up lame
T/Plt: £90.30 to a £1 stake. Pool: £59,662.23. 482.06 winning tickets. T/Qpdt: £15.70 to a £1 stake. Pool: £4,227.60. 198.80 winning tickets. SP

3060 SALISBURY (R-H)
Wednesday, June 25
OFFICIAL GOING: Good to firm changing to firm after race 3 (3.15)
Wind: Fresh, against Weather: Sunny spells

3378 PETER GRIGG MEMORIAL EBF MAIDEN FILLIES' STKS 5f
2:10 (2:13) (Class 4) 2-Y-O **£4,371** (£1,300; £650; £324) **Stalls** High

Form RPR
5 **1** **Sea Of Leaves (USA)**[47] 1961 2-9-0 0........(t) JimmyFortune 6 82
(J H M Gosden) *sn stdd bk into mid-div: hdwy and edgd rt 2f out: r.o to ld fnl 50yds* **2/1**[1]

2 *hd* **Raedah (USA)** 2-9-0 0........ RHills 5 81
(M A Jarvis) *str: prom: led wl over 1f out: rdn and kpt on: hdd fnl 50yds* **11/1**

220 **3** *2 3/4* **Our Wee Girl (IRE)**[18] 2826 2-9-0 0........ RyanMoore 1 71
(S Kirk) *lw: hdwy to ld after 1f: hdd wl over 1f out: one pce* **9/4**[2]

4 *3/4* **Princess Hannah** 2-9-0 0........ PatDobbs 3 71+
(R Hannon) *unf: scope: bit bkwd: missed break and wnt lft s: rn green and sn wl bhd: rdn and r.o encouragingly fr 2f out: gng on wl at fin* **20/1**

5 *1 1/4* **Danzadil (IRE)** 2-9-0 0........ DaneO'Neill 7 64
(R A Teal) *w'like: leggy: chsd ldrs: rdn 3f out: outpcd fnl 2f: btn whn edgd rt fnl f* **20/1**

25 **6** *1/2* **Straitjacket**[18] 2835 2-9-0 0........ RichardHughes 4 62
(R Hannon) *lw: t.k.h: chsd ldrs: rdn 2f out: wknd fnl f* **10/3**[3]

7 *3/4* **Brer Rabbit** 2-9-0 0........ MichaelHills 2 60
(B W Hills) *leggy: s.i.s and bmpd s: bhd: rdn 1/2-way: nvr rchd ldrs* **16/1**

0 **8** *1/2* **Piste**[37] 2253 2-8-7 0........ GemmaElford(7) 11 59+
(B J Meehan) *w'like: s.s: bhd: sme hdwy whn nt clr run on far rail and swtchd lft over 1f out: unable to chal* **66/1**

9 *1* **On The Feather** 2-9-0 0........ StephenCarson 10 54
(P Winkworth) *w'like: bit bkwd: str: in tch on far rail: nt clr run ins fnl 2f: swtchd lft and rt: sn wknd* **33/1**

60 **10** *1 1/4* **August Days (IRE)**[30] 2458 2-9-0 0........ JamesDoyle 9 50
(R M Beckett) *led 1f: w ldr tl wknd 2f out* **66/1**

0 **11** *2* **Goodenough Magic**[24] 2638 2-9-0 0 .... AlanDaly 8 43
(Andrew Turnell) *w'like: mid-div tl rdn and wknd over 2f out* **100/1**
61.60 secs (0.80) **Going Correction** -0.125s/f (Firm) **11** Ran SP% **117.8**
Speed ratings (Par 92): **88,87,83,82,80 79,78,77,75,73 70**
toteswinger: 1&2 £4.60, 1&3 £1.90, 2&3 £3.10. CSF £23.27 TOTE £3.00: £1.30, £2.60, £1.20; EX 25.50.
Owner K Abdulla **Bred** Juddmonte Farms Inc **Trained** Newmarket, Suffolk

FOCUS
A fair sprint maiden with the front two clear of the third. It could be overrated with the time moderate but worth chancing for the present.

NOTEBOOK
Sea Of Leaves(USA) ◆, with a tongue-tie fitted this time, improved on the form she showed when fifth on her debut over this trip at Nottingham. She probably did well to win this, as she had plenty of ground to make up inside the final two furlongs on the positively ridden Raedah, a rival who could turn out to be quite decent. She looks a useful prospect and her rider apparently thinks she will benefit from another furlong. (op 5-2 tchd 11-4)
Raedah(USA) ◆, a daughter of Elusive Quality, half-sister to dual 1m2f winner Chant De Guerre, out of a smart 6f winner at three, was easy to back, but she knew her job and was only just denied. Having shown good speed from the off, she was only picked up late on by a useful type in the making, and she finished clear of the remainder. She is likely to be hard to beat in similar company next time. (op 13-2)
Our Wee Girl(IRE), runner-up in a couple of maidens before beating just one home in the Listed Woodcote Stakes at Epsom on Derby day, was far from ideally drawn in stall one and proved no real match for two useful fillies. (op 2-1 tchd 5-2, 11-4 in a place)
Princess Hannah, a 37,000gns daughter of Royal Applause, out of a 1m winner, was friendless in the market, but she shaped with real promise on her debut. She was too inexperienced to pose a serious threat, but was noted doing some good late work and will know more next time. (op 33-1)
Danzadil(IRE), a 30,000gns daughter of Mujadil, first foal of a 5f winner on her two-year-old debut, showed ability on her debut and is open to improvement. (tchd 25-1)
Straitjacket, a beaten favourite on her first two starts over 6f, raced keenly, despite dropping back to the minimum trip, and again disappointed. (op 11-2)
On The Feather ◆, a daughter of Josr Algarhoud, is better than the bare result suggests and looks to have plenty of ability. She was denied a clear run when beginning to stay on and was by no means given a hard time once her chance had gone. (op 25-1 tchd 22-1)

3379 SMITH & WILLIAMSON MAIDEN FILLIES' STKS 6f 212y
2:40 (2:46) (Class 5) 3-Y-O **£3,885** (£1,156; £577; £288) **Stalls** High

Form RPR
63 **1** **Profitability (USA)**[15] 2918 3-9-0 .... JimmyFortune 8 70
(J H M Gosden) *lw: hld up in tch: effrt over 2f out: led and edgd lft ins fnl f: maintained narrow advantage to line: drvn out* **10/3**[1]
32-0 **2** *hd* **Deira Dubai**[47] 1946 3-9-0 71 .... RHills 7 70
(B W Hills) *t.k.h: stdd in midfield: hdwy over 2f out: slt ld over 1f out tl ins fnl f: kpt on wl: narrowly hld* **7/2**[2]
4- **3** *1 ¾* **Wusuul**[280] 5524 3-9-0 .... RyanMoore 11 68+
(C E Brittain) *unf: in rr of midfield: rdn 3f out: hdwy 2f out: cl 3rd and styng on whn bmpd and snatched up ins fnl f* **5/1**[3]
0- **4** *1* **Perfect Silence**[235] 6649 3-9-0 .... PhilipRobinson 10 62
(C G Cox) *awkward leaving stalls: led after 1f tl over 1f out: no ex fnl f* **13/2**
0 **5** *2 ½* **Miss Clarice (USA)**[69] 1423 3-9-0 .... RichardHughes 4 56+
(B J Meehan) *s.s: bhd: swtchd outside 2f out: rdn and styd on: edgd lft: nt rch ldrs* **17/2**
5-0 **6** *¾* **World View (IRE)**[20] 2756 3-9-0 .... PatDobbs 6 54+
(M P Tregoning) *dwlt: bhd: rdn 3f out: swtchd outside over 2f out: carried lft: sme late hdwy* **40/1**
00- **7** *½* **Todber**[268] 5856 3-9-0 .... MartinDwyer 1 52+
(M P Tregoning) *in tch: shkn up and sltly outpcd 3f out: nt clr run over 2f out tl over 1f out: nt knocked abt whn btn* **16/1**
- **8** *1 ¾* **Encore Belle** 3-8-7 .... DavidProbert(7) 9 47
(Mouse Hamilton-Fairley) *w'like: leggy: dwlt: towards rr: sme hdwy in centre over 2f out: no imp over 1f out* **66/1**
9 *½* **Poyle Dee Dee** 3-9-0 .... JamesDoyle 12 46
(R M Beckett) *w'like: chsd ldrs: rdn over 3f out: wknd wl over 1f out* **16/1**
3-0 **10** *2* **La Famiglia**[10] 3061 3-9-0 .... DaneO'Neill 3 41
(H Candy) *lw: led 1f: w ldrs after: sing to weaken whn squeezed for room 2f out: sn lost pl* **7/1**
0- **11** *26* **Amber Bamber**[283] 5442 3-9-0 .... TQuinn 5 —
(D Haydn Jones) *neat: bit bkwd: chsd ldrs: rdn after 2f: wknd over 3f out: eased whn no ch fnl 2f* **80/1**
00 **12** *16* **Alutando (IRE)**[19] 2772 3-9-0 .... CatherineGannon 2 —
(B Palling) *leggy: w ldrs: drvn along over 3f out: sn wknd* **50/1**
1m 28.7s (-0.30) **Going Correction** -0.125s/f (Firm) **12** Ran SP% **117.2**
Speed ratings (Par 96): **96,95,93,92,89 88,88,86,85,83 53,35**
toteswinger: 1&2 £2.70, 1&3 £3.10, 2&3 £3.60. CSF £14.69 TOTE £3.80: £1.50, £1.70, £1.90; EX 10.20.
Owner H R H Princess Haya Of Jordan **Bred** Darley **Trained** Newmarket, Suffolk

FOCUS
An ordinary fillies' maiden. The runner-up is the best guide to the form with the winner to her latest course and distance form and backed up by the third.

3380 DOCCOMBE EUROPEAN BIBURY CUP (H'CAP) 1m 4f
3:15 (3:16) (Class 3) (0-95,85) 3-Y-O
£7,477 (£2,239; £1,119; £560; £279; £140) **Stalls** High

Form RPR
-031 **1** **Resplendent Light**[18] 2840 3-9-4 82 .... MartinDwyer 7 94
(W R Muir) *hld up mainly 5th and off the pce: rdn and hdwy over 2f out: slt ld 1f out: hld on gamely* **8/1**[3]
-241 **2** *nk* **Warringah**[13] 2977 3-9-7 85 .... RyanMoore 3 97
(Sir Michael Stoute) *led: rdn and hdd over 1f out: galloped on relentlessly to press wnr fnl f: nt quite able to get bk up* **8/13**[1]
-031 **3** *1 ¼* **Any Given Day (IRE)**[34] 2340 3-8-10 74 .... RichardMullen 4 84
(D M Simcock) *cl up bhd ldng pair: rdn and hung rt 3f out: slt ld over 1f out: sn hdd: nt qckn fnl f* **11/2**[2]
3155 **4** *7* **Seattle Storm (IRE)**[11] 3038 3-8-13 77 .... TQuinn 1 76
(D R C Elsworth) *t.k.h: stdd in 4th: pushed along 4f out: drvn and wknd 2f out* **16/1**
0-14 **5** *nk* **Killcara Boy**[37] 2256 3-9-2 80 .... DaneO'Neill 2 78
(H Candy) *lw: pressed ldr: hrd rdn over 3f out: wknd 2f out* **12/1**
0-10 **6** *2 ¾* **It's A Date**[23] 2665 3-9-4 82 .... ChrisCatlin 6 76
(A King) *hld up in rr: rdn 7f out: n.d fnl 4f* **12/1**
2m 33.65s (-4.35) **Going Correction** -0.125s/f (Firm) **6** Ran SP% **109.7**
Speed ratings (Par 103): **109,108,107,103,103 101**
toteswinger: 1&2 £1.90, 1&3 £3.30, 2&3 £1.70. CSF £12.91 TOTE £8.00: £2.90, £1.40; EX 15.00.
Owner Middleham Park Racing XLIX **Bred** Usk Valley Stud **Trained** Lambourn, Berks

FOCUS
Just the six runners, but the positive tactics employed by the favourite meant that this was truly run and the front three pulled miles clear of the other trio. There is more to come from the first two.

NOTEBOOK
Resplendent Light ◆, raised 4lb for his narrow Musselburgh victory, had conditions in his favour and the decent pace would have helped him too. Indeed he was struggling a little to stay in touch starting up the long home straight, but he is obviously not short of stamina and once the gaps appeared for him to come through and take the lead, he then battled on really well to hold the rallying favourite. He shapes as though he will get further and as he only just does enough the Handicapper should not be too hard on him. There should be more decent handicaps in him.
Warringah ◆, raised 10lb for his Newbury victory, attempted the same positive tactics here but this would have been the fastest ground he had encountered and he did not look that comfortable on it. He came off the bridle some way out, but fought back very bravely after the winner headed him and it is probably safe to assume that he will resume winning ways when he can get his toe in again. He remains a colt of some promise. (op 4-6 tchd 4-7, 8-11 in a place)
Any Given Day(IRE), another raised 10lb for his easy victory in similar conditions over course and distance last month, was never far away and looked a possible winner when challenging down the outside inside the last couple of furlongs, but he did not appear to quite see it out this time. (op 9-2 tchd 13-2)
Seattle Storm(IRE), trying this trip for the first time, had been shaping as though he would appreciate it but he took quite a grip early and probably expended too much energy which counted against him later on. He is worth another try over the trip in the hope that he settles better.
Killcara Boy, raised 2lb despite only finishing fourth of seven last time, could not get the lead this time thanks to the favourite and his efforts to keep tabs on him eventually told. He was the least exposed in the field, but he does not look at all well handicapped at present. (op 11-1)
It's A Date was never travelling at any stage and it is very possible that he did not like this ground at all, but he has also to prove that he deserves to be on this sort of mark. (op 16-1)

3381 RACING UK FILLIES' H'CAP 6f
3:45 (3:49) (Class 5) (0-70,70) 3-Y-O **£3,238** (£963; £481; £240) **Stalls** High

Form RPR
10-4 **1** **Candela Bay (IRE)**[16] 2898 3-9-3 66 .... RyanMoore 4 78+
(W J Haggas) *lw: hld up in rr: plld outside and hdwy over 2f out: led 1f out: rdn clr: qcknd wl* **11/4**[1]
3000 **2** *3 ½* **Ivory Silk**[13] 2976 3-9-7 70 .... ChrisCatlin 5 71
(D K Ivory) *mid-div: rdn and hdwy 2f out: wnt 2nd 1f out: nt pce of wnr* **33/1**
0031 **3** *¾* **Presto Levanter**[11] 3030 3-8-12 61 .... RichardHughes 12 59
(R Hannon) *lw: chsd ldr: slt ld over 1f out: sn hdd and comf outpcd by wnr* **11/4**[1]
-046 **4** *½* **Apple Pie Order (IRE)**[12] 3000 3-9-3 66 .... SteveDrowne 9 63
(R J Hodges) *s.i.s: sn in midfield: drvn to chse ldrs over 1f out: kpt on fnl f* **12/1**[3]
6-50 **5** *shd* **Tea Cake (IRE)**[16] 2898 3-8-13 62 .... JamesDoyle 1 58+
(H J L Dunlop) *hld up in rr: clipped heels & stmbld over 4f out: plld outside wl over 1f out: r.o: nrst fin* **12/1**[3]
1050 **6** *¾* **Khazina (USA)**[33] 2378 3-9-4 67 .... NCallan 2 61
(C E Brittain) *bhd: hdwy and n.m.r 2f out: drvn to chse ldrs over 1f out: styd on same pce* **16/1**
0-45 **7** *5* **Belle Bellino (FR)**[15] 2922 3-9-0 63 .... DaneO'Neill 13 41
(B R Millman) *chsd ldrs over 4f* **7/1**[2]
05 **8** *1* **Ma Vie En Rose (IRE)**[15] 2918 3-9-0 63 .... (t) LPKeniry 10 38
(A M Balding) *prom over 3f* **16/1**
3-35 **9** *4* **Midnight Fling**[20] 2757 3-9-5 68 .... RichardKingscote 7 30
(R Charlton) *sn pushed along towards rr: mod effrt whn sltly hmpd over 2f out: n.d* **12/1**[3]
0300 **10** *6* **Infinite Patience**[15] 2922 3-8-8 57 .... (b[1]) MartinDwyer 6 —
(J S Moore) *sn led: hdd & wknd rapidly over 1f out* **16/1**
0-43 **11** *¾* **Blue Zenith (IRE)**[2] 3330 3-8-11 65 .... NataliaGemelova(5) 8 5
(J S Moore) *chsd ldrs: rdn over 3f out: wknd over 2f out: no ch whn hmpd wl over 1f out* **16/1**
003 **12** *3* **Milldown Bay**[34] 2341 3-9-5 68 .... AlanMunro 3 —
(B R Millman) *a in rr gp: hrd rdn and n.d fnl 3f* **14/1**
1m 15.61s (0.81) **Going Correction** -0.125s/f (Firm) **12** Ran SP% **122.0**
Speed ratings (Par 96): **89,84,83,82,82 81,74,73,68,60 59,55**
toteswinger: 1&2 £18.30, 1&3 £2.10, 2&3 £22.10. CSF £122.37 CT £285.61 TOTE £3.60: £1.90, £6.10, £1.50; EX 119.80.
Owner Mrs A Goddard & M Hawkes **Bred** Piercetown Stud **Trained** Newmarket, Suffolk

FOCUS
An ordinary fillies' handicap and although the early pace looked strong, the final time was slow suggesting they went too quick at the start of the contest. The fourth is the best guide to the form.
Tea Cake(IRE) ◆ Official explanation: jockey said filly was denied a clear run
Belle Bellino(FR) Official explanation: jockey said filly had no more to give

3382 COORS BREWERS NOEL CANNON MEMORIAL TROPHY H'CAP 1m
4:15 (4:23) (Class 2) (0-100,98) 3-Y-O+
£10,281 (£3,078; £1,539; £770; £384; £193) **Stalls** High

Form RPR
/01- **1** **Military Cross**[221] 6852 5-10-0 98 .... DaneO'Neill 1 104
(L M Cumani) *stdd s: hld up in rr: swtchd outside and hdwy over 2f out: led wl over 1f out: hld on wl ins fnl f: rdn out nr fin* **6/1**[3]
0100 **2** *¾* **Orchard Supreme**[7] 3122 5-9-4 88 .... JimmyFortune 2 94+
(R Hannon) *hld up in rr: hdwy on far rail whn nt clr run 2f out: fnd gap and rdn to chse ldng pair over 1f out: hung lft fnl f: kpt on* **7/2**[2]
1042 **3** *nk* **Hustle (IRE)**[11] 3038 3-8-7 87 .... RichardHughes 4 88
(R Hannon) *lw: trckd ldng pair: rdn and swtchd lft over 2f out: chal over 1f out: nt qckn fnl 75yds* **7/2**[2]
1200 **4** *9* **Mujood**[7] 3122 5-9-8 92 .... StephenCarson 5 75
(Eve Johnson Houghton) *w ldr tl wknd wl over 1f out* **8/1**
136- **5** *2 ¾* **Officer**[143] 4-9-1 85 .... RyanMoore 6 61
(G L Moore) *lw: sn led: hdd & wknd wl over 1f out* **2/1**[1]
620 **6** *26* **Prince Of Thebes (IRE)**[19] 2789 7-9-1 85 .... PaulDoe 3 1
(M J Attwater) *in tch: rdn 3f out: sn wknd* **6/1**[3]
1m 43.25s (-0.25) **Going Correction** -0.125s/f (Firm)
WFA 3 from 4yo+ 10lb **6** Ran SP% **117.5**
Speed ratings (Par 109): **96,95,94,85,83 57**
toteswinger: 1&2 £4.70, 1&3 £3.80, 2&3 £2.50. CSF £28.42 TOTE £7.50: £2.90, £2.20; EX 36.20.
Owner R Thompson & A Bengough **Bred** Cheveley Park Stud Ltd **Trained** Newmarket, Suffolk

FOCUS
A tight little handicap, but although the favourite was sent straight into the lead he set only a modest pace once there and this developed into something of a sprint. There was not much separating the front three at the line, but the other trio were spread out over Wiltshire. The winner continues to progress but the runner-up was a little unlucky.

NOTEBOOK

Military Cross, up 5lb and not seen since winning on the Lingfield Polytrack last November, was returning from a five-month layoff then so fitness was unlikely to have been a problem here. The way he drifted in the market did look ominous, but he belied his weakness with a thoroughly professional performance, coming from virtually last down the outside and keeping on well once in front. He has had his problems, but there were no signs of them here and it will be a brave man that says he cannot complete the hat-trick. (op 4-1 tchd 7-1)

Orchard Supreme, ninth in the Royal Hunt Cup seven days earlier, like the winner was switched off out the back early but crucially he had to wait for Officer to drift off the inside rail in order to get a run through whilst the winner was enjoying a clear run down the outside. He stayed on well, but his rival had got first run and he could never get to him. (tchd 3-1)

Hustle(IRE), up another 2lb and therefore 8lb above his last winning mark, was always in a good position and he tried his hardest, but he could not match the finishing pace of the front two. His ideal trip has still not really been established. (op 10-3 tchd 3-1)

Mujood, who ran poorly in the Hunt Cup the previous week and was a long way adrift of Orchard Supreme, kept Officer company for a long way but they both dropped away very tamely once challenged. He looks to have gone right off the boil after his purple patch last month.

Officer, well backed on this debut for the yard on this return from eight months off, soon found himself in front and although he was given no peace by Mujood it was still disappointing to see him fade so tamely. He was without the visor he had worn in his previous five outings including both his wins, but it is hard to say whether that had any relevance. (op 7-2)

Prince Of Thebes(IRE) came off the bridle a long way out and dropped right away. He is without a win in almost two years and the Handicapper has him nailed to the floor, but even so this was too bad to be true. (op 8-1 tchd 17-2)

3383 NEW FOREST FARM MACHINERY/JOHN DEERE H'CAP 6f 212y

4:50 (4:58) (Class 6) (0-65,65) 4-Y-0+ £2,914 (£867; £433; £216) Stalls High

Form RPR

4212 1 **Isphahan**[5] 3218 5-9-0 65 .... DavidProbert(7) 8 78
(A M Balding) *hld up in midfield: hdwy to ld 2f out: drvn to hold off runner-up fnl f* 2/1[1]

1345 2 ¾ **Napoletano (GER)**[5] 3208 7-9-4 62 .... (p) NCallan 7 73
(S Dow) *stdd s: t.k.h in rr: hdwy and weaved through 2f out: pressed wnr fnl f: hld fnl 100yds* 13/2[3]

0-20 3 2½ **Moves Goodenough**[37] 2243 5-9-4 62 .... RyanMoore 5 66
(Andrew Turnell) *hld up in midfield: hdwy to press ldrs 2f out: one pce appr fnl f* 5/1[2]

-000 4 ¾ **Grizedale (IRE)**[12] 2995 9-9-1 59 .... (tp) PaulDoe 10 61
(M J Attwater) *hld up in midfield: clsd on ldrs on far rail 2f out: hrd rdn over 1f out: one pce* 25/1

5105 5 1 **Contented (IRE)**[19] 2798 6-9-0 58 .... (p) LPKeniry 3 57
(Mrs L C Jewell) *t.k.h towards rr: hdwy and n.m.r 2f out: rdn and styd on same pce* 25/1

-000 6 hd **Leptis Magna**[16] 2897 4-9-0 58 .... TQuinn 11 57
(D R C Elsworth) *chsd ldrs: rdn over 2f out: no ex ins fnl f* 14/1

5056 7 nk **Goose Green (IRE)**[12] 2992 4-8-13 57 .... SteveDrowne 1 55
(R J Hodges) *hld up in rr: swtchd outside and gd hdwy to chse ldrs 2f out: hrd rdn over 1f out: no imp* 22/1

-000 8 2¾ **Bidable**[42] 2097 4-8-10 54 .... CatherineGannon 2 45
(B Palling) *bhd: rdn along 3f out: hdwy on outside and in tch 2f out: wknd over 1f out* 66/1

-045 9 2¾ **Finsbury**[12] 2992 5-9-4 62 .... GeorgeBaker 14 45
(J M Bradley) *s.s: bhd: sme hdwy over 2f out: sn rdn and wknd* 16/1

6-00 10 nk **Doctor's Cave**[14] 2933 6-8-12 56 .... (b) PatDobbs 6 38
(K O Cunningham-Brown) *stmbld s: qckly rcvrd to ld at gd pce tl wknd 2f out* 50/1

-003 11 3¾ **Takitwo**[15] 2917 5-8-12 56 .... SimonWhitworth 12 28
(P D Cundell) *in tch: rdn over 3f out: sn wknd* 10/1

0-01 12 8 **Pragmatist**[26] 2556 4-9-4 62 .... StephenCarson 4 13
(P Winkworth) *prom tl squeezed for room and wknd 2f out* 11/1

4-34 13 2 **Shaded Edge**[20] 2758 4-9-1 59 .... AlanMunro 9 4
(D W P Arbuthnot) *mid-div: rdn and wknd 3f out: sn bhd* 13/2[3]

010- 14 ¾ **Ten To The Dozen**[229] 6749 5-8-11 55 .... ChrisCatlin 13 —
(P W Hiatt) *prom 4f* 16/1

1m 27.98s (-1.02) **Going Correction** -0.125s/f (Firm) 14 Ran SP% 128.0

Speed ratings (Par 101): **100,99,96,95,94 94,93,90,87,87 82,73,71,70**

toteswinger: 1&2 £8.00, 1&3 £6.30, 2&3 £5.90. CSF £14.98 CT £63.44 TOTE £3.30: £1.40, £2.60, £2.50; EX 22.40.

Owner Mohamad Rafique **Bred** J H Wall **Trained** Kingsclere, Hants

FOCUS

There was a decent pace on here and the form looks sound with the form horses coming to the fore.

3384 DANCO MARQUEES H'CAP 1m 1f 198y

5:20 (5:26) (Class 5) (0-75,75) 3-Y-0 £3,238 (£963; £481; £240) Stalls High

Form RPR

2334 1 **Kyrie Eleison (IRE)**[9] 3095 3-8-10 67 .... PatrickHills(3) 6 73
(R Hannon) *hld up in rr: hdwy on outside 3f out: rdn to ld 1f out: hld on wl fnl f* 11/1

-442 2 ½ **Mizooka**[34] 2342 3-9-2 70 .... GeorgeBaker 10 75+
(R M Beckett) *hld up in rr: rdn and hdwy 2f out: pressed wnr ins fnl f: kpt on* 11/2[1]

0003 3 1 **Palmerin**[13] 2974 3-9-3 71 .... RichardHughes 7 74
(R Hannon) *in rr of midfield: hdwy 3f out: led ins fnl 2f: hung rt and hdd 1f out: one pce ins fnl f* 6/1[2]

1-00 4 1¾ **Fair Gale**[23] 2665 3-9-6 74 .... LPKeniry 8 74
(S Kirk) *led briefly after 1f: t.k.h and chsd ldrs after: rdn 3f out: ch on far rail whn nt clr run and swtchd lft 1f out: drifted further lft: one pce* 33/1

000 5 hd **Quinzey's Best (IRE)**[26] 2560 3-8-5 59 ow1 .... PaulDoe 5 58
(W J Knight) *s.s: towards rr: effrt whn nt clr run over 2f out: styd on appr fnl f: nvr nrr* 33/1

3305 6 3 **Colorado Blue (IRE)**[23] 2665 3-9-7 75 .... (bt[1]) SteveDrowne 12 68
(R Charlton) *led 1f: chsd ldrs after: rdn over 3f out: btn whn carried rt over 1f out* 6/1[2]

-032 7 nk **Latin Scholar (IRE)**[9] 3095 3-8-11 65 .... DaneO'Neill 4 58
(A King) *chsd ldrs: chal 3f out: btn whn squeezed for room over 1f out* 7/1

0-23 8 ½ **Sinbad The Sailor**[15] 2907 3-9-2 70 .... EddieAhern 11 62
(J W Hills) *bhd: drvn along over 3f out: mod effrt over 1f out: nvr able to chal* 8/1

-600 9 nse **Prince Desire (IRE)**[21] 2714 3-9-5 73 .... (b) RichardKingscote 9 64
(Tom Dascombe) *t.k.h: in tch and wd: rdn to press ldrs 2f out: n.m.r and wknd over 1f out* 13/2[3]

0-55 10 14 **Shesha Bear**[16] 2885 3-9-2 70 .... MartinDwyer 1 33
(W R Muir) *chsd ldr: led over 3f out tl wknd ins fnl 2f: btn whn hmpd and eased over 1f out* 25/1

05-0 11 16 **Red Twist**[25] 2603 3-9-1 69 .... JimmyFortune 2 —
(H Morrison) *led over 8f out tl over 3f out: wknd over 2f out* 20/1

2m 9.99s (0.09) **Going Correction** -0.125s/f (Firm) 11 Ran SP% 103.7

Speed ratings (Par 99): **94,93,92,91,91 88,88,88,88,76 64**

toteswinger: 1&2 £6.60, 1&3 £8.20, 2&3 £8.80. CSF £50.77 CT £251.05 TOTE £11.20: £3.20, £2.20, £2.50; EX 73.90.

Owner Mrs J Wood **Bred** And Mrs B Firestone **Trained** East Everleigh, Wilts

■ Stewards' Enquiry : Richard Hughes two-day ban: careless riding (Jul 10,12)

FOCUS

They only went an ordinary gallop this time but the first two came from well off the pace. The form, rated through the fourth, is not as strong as it might have been.

Shesha Bear Official explanation: trainer said filly was unsuited by the firm ground

Red Twist Official explanation: tariner's rep said gelding was unsuited by the firm ground

T/Plt: £12.90 to a £1 stake. Pool: £58,485.03. 3,307.99 winning tickets. T/Qpdt: £9.70 to a £1 stake. Pool: £2,315.18. 174.90 winning tickets. LM

3385 - 3391a (Foreign Racing) - See Raceform Interactive

3158 GREAT LEIGHS (A.W) (L-H)

Thursday, June 26

OFFICIAL GOING: Standard

Wind: medium across Weather: bright, sunny

3392 RIOJA MEDIAN AUCTION MAIDEN STKS 6f (P)

2:10 (2:11) (Class 6) 2-Y-0 £1,942 (£578; £288; £144) Stalls Low

Form RPR

5 1 **Sapphire Prince (USA)**[21] 2754 2-9-3 0 .... MohammedSaeed 4 78
(J R Best) *s.i.s: hld up bhd: hdwy on outer 2f out: nudged along and r.o wl to ld ins fnl f* 14/1

5 2 1¼ **Special Cuvee**[24] 2663 2-9-3 0 .... DO'Donohoe 6 74
(Sir Mark Prescott) *s.i.s: sn chsng ldr: rdn over 2f out: carried rt over 1f out: led ins fnl f: sn hdd and one pce* 6/4[2]

003 3 ¾ **Kheylide (IRE)**[8] 3140 2-9-3 0 .... EdwardCreighton 5 72
(Miss V Haigh) *chsd ldrs: rdn 2f out: ev ch ent fnl f: edgd lft and one pce fnl f* 12/1

32 4 1½ **Sir Geoffrey (IRE)**[15] 2944 2-9-3 0 .... PatCosgrave 7 68
(A J McCabe) *restless in stalls: racd keenly: led: rdn jst over 2f out: hung rt fr wl over 1f out: hdd ins fnl f: wknd last 100yds* 5/4[1]

5 1½ **Mabait** 2-9-3 0 .... KerrinMcEvoy 2 63
(L M Cumani) *sn bustled along: in tch in rr: rdn over 2f out: no imp fr over 1f out* 10/1[3]

0 6 3½ **Catenaccio (IRE)**[21] 2754 2-9-3 0 .... JimCrowley 1 53
(P Winkworth) *chsd ldrs: rdn 1/2-way: drvn 2f out: wknd over 1f out* 40/1

002 7 11 **Elusive Ronnie (IRE)**[28] 2548 2-9-3 0 .... SaleemGolam 3 20
(R A Teal) *s.i.s: sn rdn along: lost tch 1/2-way* 33/1

1m 15.0s (1.30) **Going Correction** +0.10s/f (Slow) 7 Ran SP% 113.3

Speed ratings (Par 91): **95,93,92,90,88 83,69**

toteswinger: 1&2 £6.70, 1&3 £6.20, 2&3 £5.20. CSF £34.98 TOTE £17.50: £5.30, £1.20; EX 54.90.

Owner Ian Beach & John Fletcher **Bred** Bruce Moriarty & Jill Moriarty **Trained** Hucking, Kent

■ A first winner in Britain on his fourth ride for Dubai-based jockey Mohammed Saeed.

FOCUS

An ordinary maiden and a two-horse race according to the market, but neither of them were good enough despite both getting the run of the race. The third is rated just above his previous Ripon form.

NOTEBOOK

Sapphire Prince(USA), from a stable in blinding form, had been weak in the market on his debut but the opposite was true here despite his starting price. Settled off the pace early whilst the two market leaders got on with it, he was brought out widest rounding the home bend to make his effort and he stayed on particularly strongly to land the prize. He should progress again and ought to get another furlong or so without any difficulty. (op 20-1)

Special Cuvee, backed to step up from his Leicester debut, kept the favourite company for much of the way and had every chance but the winner's turn of foot down his outside proved too much for him. He still did not look quite the finished article and should be up to winning a race like this. (op 2-1)

Kheylide(IRE), one of the most experienced in the field, stuck closer to the inside rail than the other principals and kept on to show that he does stay this trip. He lacks the scope of the front pair, but the nurseries are just around the corner and that may be where his future lies. (op 11-1 tchd 10-1)

Sir Geoffrey(IRE), placed in his two previous starts both on Polytrack, soon managed to get across from the outside stall in front. However, after taking quite a grip he was then inclined to hang away to his right once into the home straight and was ultimately swamped. This was a step backwards and perhaps he will appreciate the arrival of nurseries too. (op 6-5 tchd 6-4)

Mabait, a 27,000gns foal but a 70,000gns yearling, is out of a half-sister to winners in Germany and Italy. The only newcomer in the field, he was weak in the market which is not good news for one from the yard and he ran accordingly. It would be no surprise to see him come on for the experience, but he will need to. Official explanation: jockey said colt did not face kickback (op 13-2)

3393 BAROSSA H'CAP 1m 6f (P)

2:40 (2:43) (Class 5) (0-75,75) 3-Y-0 £2,590 (£770; £385; £192) Stalls Low

Form RPR

-423 1 **Tasheba**[14] 2977 3-9-4 72 .... AlanMunro 7 91
(P W Chapple-Hyam) *chsd ldr: wnt 2nd 6f out: rdn to ld and hld hd high over 2f out: hrd pressed ent fnl f: hld on wl: all out* 6/4[1]

00-0 2 shd **Askar Tau (FR)**[31] 2449 3-8-3 57 .... JimmyQuinn 10 76
(M P Tregoning) *in tch: hdwy to chse ldrs 4f out: chsd wnr wl over 1f out: str chal ent fnl f: a jst hld* 14/1

641 3 20 **Novestar (IRE)**[18] 2867 3-8-2 63 .... StacyRenwick(7) 11 54
(G J Smith) *t.k.h: chsd ldr tl led over 7f out: rdn and hdd wl over 1f out: sn wknd* 10/1

000 4 1¼ **Ultimate Quest (IRE)**[155] 265 3-8-4 58 .... DO'Donohoe 15 47
(Sir Mark Prescott) *s.i.s: sn rdn along to chse ldrs: reminders 8f out: rdn 4f out: wknd over 2f out* 6/1[2]

0-00 5 ½ **Rivington Pike (IRE)**[29] 2495 3-8-5 59 .... GrahamGibbons 6 48
(J J Quinn) *hld up towards rr: hdwy 6f out: rdn wl over 3f out: sn wknd* 25/1

005 6 hd **Seedless**[12] 3035 3-8-9 70 .... DavidProbert(7) 1 58
(A M Balding) *hld up in midfield: hdwy on inner 6f out: chsd ldrs and rdn 3f out: wknd over 2f out* 16/1

0-30 7 6 **Colorado Springs**[14] 2984 3-8-6 60 ow1 .... (p) KerrinMcEvoy 5 40
(W Jarvis) *s.i.s: hld up towards rr: hdwy 7f out: rdn wl over 3f out: wknd over 2f out* 16/1

263 8 14 **Ben Ami**[26] 2612 3-9-7 75 .... OscarUrbina 8 35
(Miss J R Gibney) *hld up in midfield: hdwy 7f out: chsd ldrs and rdn over 3f out: wknd qckly over 2f out: t.o* 16/1

-41P **9** *shd* **Caffari (GER)**[29] 2495 3-8-3 **57** .... LiamJones 12 17
(K R Burke) *sn rdn along: bhd: hdwy on outer 6f out: wknd over 3f out: t.o* **12/1**

2-00 **10** *12* **Funseeker (UAE)**[35] 2327 3-8-8 **62** .... FrancisNorton 3 5
(Jamie Poulton) *a towards rr: rdn 9f out: lost tch 5f out: t.o last 2f* **50/1**

0-65 **11** *hd* **Hellzapoppin**[11] 3058 3-9-4 **72** .... TedDurcan 13 15
(D R Lanigan) *hld up in midfield: effrt over 4f out: rdn and wknd over 3f out: t.o* **16/1**

-410 **12** *3 1/4* **Crimson Mitre**[48] 1962 3-9-4 **72** .... ShaneKelly 4 11
(J Jay) *t.k.h: hld up in midfield: wknd over 4f out: sn wl btn: t.o* **33/1**

-654 **13** *1* **Flash Of Fire (USA)**[14] 2984 3-7-11 **56** oh1 .... AhmedAjtebi(5) 14 —
(J M P Eustace) *stdd and dropped in after s: a wl bhd: lost tch over 4f out: t.o* **16/1**

-305 **14** *62* **Tamrai Dancer**[26] 2603 3-8-6 **60** .... JamesDoyle 9 —
(R M Beckett) *a bhd: rdn over 7f out: t.o last 3f: virtually p.u last 2f* **25/1**

2302 **15** *32* **Maximus Aurelius (IRE)**[16] 2907 3-9-4 **72** .... PatCosgrave 2 —
(J Jay) *led tl over 7f out: rdn and dropped out 5f out: sn t.o: virtually plld last 3f* **15/2**[3]

3m 1.87s (-1.33) **Going Correction** +0.10s/f (Slow) **15** Ran SP% **131.5**
Speed ratings (Par 99): **107,106,95,94,94 94,90,82,82,76 75,74,73,38,19**
toteswinger: 1&2 £10.40, 1&3 £3.60, 2&3 £69.20. CSF £26.90 CT £185.04 TOTE £2.90: £1.10, £3.80, £5.90; EX 38.90.
Owner Terry Benson **Bred** C R Mason **Trained** Newmarket, Suffolk

FOCUS
This proved quite a test for these three-year-olds and very few proved up to it with an astonishing margin between the front pair and the others considering the size of the field. This was the fastest time for a race over the trip to date, though of course it is still early days, but the first two still deserve a lot of credit.
Crimson Mitre Official explanation: vet said colt finished lame
Tamrai Dancer Official explanation: jockey said filly did not face the kickback

3394 LOIRE H'CAP — 6f (P)
3:10 (3:11) (Class 3) (0-90,87) 3-Y-0+ **£6,623** (£1,982; £991; £495; £246) **Stalls** Low

Form RPR

2131 **1** **Honey Monster (IRE)**[8] 3136 3-9-1 **81** 6ex .... JamesDoyle 2 89
(A J McCabe) *chsd ldr: rdn to ld over 1f out: hld on gamely fnl f* **5/2**[1]

5610 **2** *nk* **Yankee Storm**[6] 3224 3-8-8 **74** .... J-PGuillambert 7 81
(M Johnston) *s.i.s: chsd ldrs on outer: rdn 2f out: chsd wnr over 1f out: ev ch ins fnl f: unable qckn last 100yds* **6/1**

3566 **3** *4* **Distinctly Game**[34] 2358 6-9-9 **82** .... DO'Donohoe 6 77
(K A Ryan) *sn led and crossed to rail: rdn 2f out: hdd over 1f out: wknd ins fnl f* **9/2**[3]

1364 **4** *1 1/4* **Hammer Of The Gods (IRE)**[29] 2501 8-9-0 **73** .... IanMongan 3 64
(G C Bravery) *hmpd s: bhd: effrt on inner wl over 1f out: nvr trbld ldrs* **7/1**

2121 **5** *1* **Benllech**[100] 925 4-10-0 **87** .... SimonWhitworth 1 74
(M Wigham) *t.k.h: hld up bhd ldrs on inner: rdn and effrt wl over 1f out: wknd fnl f* **7/2**[2]

2300 **6** *1 3/4* **The Game**[20] 2794 3-9-2 **82** .... PatCosgrave 4 61
(J R Boyle) *awkward s and slowly away: hld up in last pair: swtchd rt and rdn over 1f out: no imp* **10/1**

113- **7** *6* **Imprimis Tagula (IRE)**[435] 1099 4-9-7 **80** .... FrancisNorton 5 39
(A Bailey) *t.k.h: chsd ldrs: rdn over 2f out: wknd wl over 1f out* **8/1**

1m 14.38s (0.68) **Going Correction** +0.10s/f (Slow)
WFA 3 from 4yo+ 7lb **7** Ran SP% **116.0**
Speed ratings (Par 107): **99,98,93,91,90 87,79**
toteswinger: 1&2 £3.50, 1&3 £2.60, 2&3 £6.70. CSF £18.48 TOTE £3.60: £2.10, £2.20; EX 19.70.
Owner Brian Morton & Ray Standring **Bred** Michael O'Mahony **Trained** Babworth, Notts

FOCUS
A decent little handicap, but the early pace was surprisingly ordinary. Despite that the front pair came right away late on and the runner-up sets the standard.

NOTEBOOK
Honey Monster(IRE), carrying a 6lb penalty for his recent Kempton victory and well backed to follow up, travelled nicely just behind the leaders and found just about enough when asked to get the better of a protracted battle with the runner-up. He is in great order just now and may not have stopped winning yet. (op 7-2)
Yankee Storm, 4lb higher than when winning over the minimum trip here two starts ago, is just as effective over this distance. Brought widest into the home straight, he tried very hard to get on top of the favourite and went down with all guns blazing. He looks so much better on sand than on turf. (op 13-2)
Distinctly Game soon managed to gain an easy lead against the inside rail, but once the front pair were delivered down his outside in the home straight he was quickly left behind. He is gradually edging back down to a more feasible mark, but needs to drop a bit further. (tchd 5-1)
Hammer Of The Gods(IRE) got into a spot of bother with those drawn either side of him after leaving the stalls which left him further off the pace than he usually likes to be. He tried to get into the contest in the home straight, but his effort came to little and it may be best to put a line through this. (op 8-1)
Benllech, returning from a three-month break off a 3lb higher mark, was weak in the market which suggested he was thought to need it. The way he ran seemed to back that up, though his trainer was inclined to blame the deep surface. Official explanation: trainer said gelding was unsuited by the all-weather surface (op 9-4)
The Game, back on Polytrack after a couple of dire efforts on turf, jumped right up in the air as the stalls opened and lost a lot of ground. Even though the modest early pace meant that he was soon able to get back in touch, it was not long before he was left behind again. (op 12-1)
Imprimis Tagula(IRE), whose two wins to date have been on Fibresand, had not been seen since finishing third behind Sakhee's Secret in a Newmarket handicap 14 months ago. He was fairly steady in the market which did not suggest he was thought likely to blow up, but the way he ran suggests he might have. (tchd 7-1)

3395 PENEDES H'CAP — 6f (P)
3:40 (3:42) (Class 6) (0-55,55) 3-Y-0 **£1,942** (£578; £288; £144) **Stalls** Low

Form RPR

5000 **1** **Minwir (IRE)**[14] 2982 3-9-0 **55** ....(v[1]) PatCosgrave 12 59
(M Quinn) *hld up in midfield: hdwy over 2f out: styd on wl u.p to ld last 100yds* **25/1**

-000 **2** *3/4* **Swift Acclaim (IRE)**[10] 3086 3-8-10 **51** .... JimCrowley 11 53
(K R Burke) *pressed ldr tl led 2f out: sn rdn: edgd rt fr over 1f out: hdd and no ex last 100yds* **20/1**

0-02 **3** *shd* **Bilboa**[12] 3030 3-9-0 **55** .... AlanMunro 10 57+
(B R Millman) *t.k.h: hld up in midfield: hung rt and lost pl bnd 4f out: bhd 2f out: hung lft fr over 1f out: r.o strly fnl f: snatched 3rd on line* **9/2**[2]

6002 **4** *hd* **Kannon**[17] 2898 3-9-0 **55** ....(v) ShaneKelly 3 56
(W J Knight) *chsd ldrs: drvn and effrt 2f out: kpt on same pce u.p fnl f* **6/1**

4323 **5** *1 1/2* **Peas In A Pod**[16] 2922 3-8-13 **54** .... JamieSpencer 4 50
(J R Fanshawe) *hld up in midfield: hdwy over 2f out: chsd ldrs and hrd drvn over 1f out: one pce ins fnl f* **2/1**[1]

06-0 **6** *1/2* **Fantasy Fighter (IRE)**[54] 1817 3-8-9 **50** .... JimmyQuinn 2 45
(J J Quinn) *s.i.s: bhd: hdwy on inner 3f out: chsd ldrs over 1f out: flashed tail u.p: no prog ins fnl f* **16/1**

60-0 **7** *nse* **Cryptonite Diamond (USA)**[28] 2549 3-8-13 **54** ....(t) SaleemGolam 13 48
(W R Swinburn) *s.i.s: sn wl in tch: rdn and unable qck 2f out: kpt on again ins fnl f* **11/1**

0560 **8** *nk* **Lady Florence**[7] 3161 3-8-10 **51** .... FrancisNorton 5 45
(A B Coogan) *led tl rdn and hdd 2f out: wknd ent fnl f* **25/1**

-100 **9** *4* **King Of Cadeaux (IRE)**[12] 3030 3-8-13 **54** ....(b) KerrinMcEvoy 9 35
(M A Magnusson) *s.i.s: bhd: sme hdwy and hung lft 1f out: n.d* **11/2**[3]

-600 **10** *1/2* **Expediter**[38] 2260 3-8-13 **54** .... FergusSweeney 6 33
(H Candy) *towards rr: rdn and struggling 3f out: n.d after* **16/1**

-345 **11** *1* **Run From Nun**[131] 583 3-8-4 **48** .... KirstyMilczarek(3) 16 24
(John Berry) *pressed ldrs tl rdn 2f out: sn wknd* **16/1**

030 **12** *shd* **Klarity**[13] 2991 3-8-10 **51** .... TedDurcan 15 27
(J Pearce) *t.k.h: hld up in rr: no ch whn sltly hmpd 1f out* **20/1**

5454 **13** *1* **Gelert (IRE)**[24] 2661 3-8-9 **50** .... PatrickMathers 7 22
(Peter Grayson) *chsd ldr: rdn and struggling 3f out: no ch last 2f* **14/1**

5000 **14** *1/2* **Little Cee (IRE)**[15] 2946 3-9-0 **55** .... TQuinn 8 26
(D R C Elsworth) *towards rr: rdn and struggling 4f out: n.d* **25/1**

500- **15** *2 1/4* **Midnight Oasis**[239] 6595 3-8-8 **49** .... J-PGuillambert 14 13
(Rae Guest) *a bhd: sltly hmpd bnd 4f out: nvr on terms* **16/1**

1m 15.11s (1.41) **Going Correction** +0.10s/f (Slow) **15** Ran SP% **140.8**
Speed ratings (Par 97): **94,93,92,92,90 89,89,89,84,83 82,82,80,80,77**
toteswinger: 1&2 £83.70, 1&3 £60.20, 2&3 £6.90. CSF £494.43 CT £2688.61 TOTE £59.80: £13.20, £8.60, £2.50; EX 1647.60.
Owner Steven Astaire **Bred** Shadwell Estate Company Limited **Trained** Newmarket, Suffolk

FOCUS
A big field, but a very modest handicap and the time was nothing special compared with the earlier races over the same trip and the form looks pretty limited. Again those that made their efforts out in the centre of the track seemed to hold the advantage.
Fantasy Fighter(IRE) ◆ Official explanation: jockey said gelding was bumped at the start
Lady Florence Official explanation: jockey said filly missed the break
Gelert(IRE) Official explanation: jockey said colt did not handle the bend

3396 TAY CONDITIONS STKS — 1m (P)
4:10 (4:12) (Class 3) 3-Y-0 **£6,799** (£2,023; £1,011; £505) **Stalls** Low

Form RPR

-216 **1** **Tasdeer (USA)**[33] 2409 3-9-8 92 .... PhilipRobinson 1 103
(M A Jarvis) *mde all: rdn 2f out: styng on wl whn lft wl clr over 1f out: in n.d after* **9/2**[2]

2455 **2** *4 1/2* **Gaspar Van Wittel (USA)**[28] 2544 3-9-3 96 ....(p) JamieSpencer 2 93
(S A Callaghan) *chsd ldr: 1 1/2l down and keeping on same pce whn veered bdly rt over 1f out: hung lft but kpt on fnl f: no ch w wnr fnl f* **11/2**[3]

213- **3** *5* **Dauberval (IRE)**[285] 5414 3-9-3 97 .... PatDobbs 6 77
(S Kirk) *hld up in last pair: hdwy to chse ldng pair 3f out: sn rdn and outpcd* **14/1**

15- **4** *3 1/4* **Almajd (IRE)**[243] 6495 3-9-3 101 .... KerrinMcEvoy 3 69
(Sir Michael Stoute) *hld up in tch: shkn up 3f out: sn btn* **4/9**[1]

050- **5** *1/2* **Dry Speedfit (IRE)**[265] 5974 3-9-3 87 .... AlanMunro 4 68
(G G Margarson) *chsd ldrs: rdn over 3f out: sn outpcd and wl btn* **20/1**

00 **6** *nk* **Lightning Squall (USA)**[29] 2509 3-9-3 0 .... TedDurcan 5 67?
(M Botti) *stdd s: hld up in last: lost tch 1/2-way* **100/1**

1m 40.22s (0.32) **Going Correction** +0.10s/f (Slow) **6** Ran SP% **115.2**
Speed ratings (Par 103): **102,97,92,89,88 88**
toteswinger: 1&2 £1.50, 1&3 £2.00, 2&3 £2.20. CSF £29.45 TOTE £5.30: £1.60, £2.00; EX 22.10.
Owner Hamdan Al Maktoum **Bred** Shadwell Farm LLC **Trained** Newmarket, Suffolk

FOCUS
Further proof that Great Leighs has no problem attracting a good quality of horse, despite not being allowed to stage Class 1 events while the course is bedding in. The favourite flopped badly and, while the winner handed weight and a beating to his rivals, three were making belated seasonal bows, one is wayward, and the other outclassed, so it is difficult to know what the winner achieved.

NOTEBOOK
Tasdeer(USA) was able to make all for a third career success, defying a 5lb penalty for his win in a Class 2 conditions event at Doncaster which, until now, had worked out abysmally. A son of Irish 1000 Guineas winner Mehthaaf, he is going to have to keep cracking away at Listed company, for all that it has proved beyond him thus far, as his handicap mark is going to be punitive now. (op 7-2)
Gaspar Van Wittel(USA) is very useful but fully exposed, and would have a hard task in handicaps. This sort of race should be meat and drink for him, but he is temperamental even with the cheekpieces fitted, and he veered violently to his right when in with every chance over a furlong out. It is a testament to his natural ability that he still finished five lengths in front of the third horse. (op 5-1 tchd 9-2 and 13-2)
Dauberval(IRE) was making a belated seasonal reappearance and had signed off his juvenile season with a fine effort in the Listed Stardom Stakes at Goodwood. The mark of 97 he earned that day makes it difficult for him to be taken along the handicap route, and judged on this effort, for all that he may come on for it, he isn't up to Listed/Pattern company. (op 12-1 tchd 10-1)
Almajd(IRE), a half-brother to the top-class Alhaarth among numerous winners, was the recipient of Classic quotes after making a winning debut at the Cambridgeshire meeting. Beaten favourite (though far from disgraced) in the Group Three Horris Hill Stakes on his only other start, he has obviously had his problems. This was not his true form, and whether it was the configuration of the track, the surface, him not being the same horse as he was last year, or a combination of all three, he is best watched for the time being. Official explanation: trainer's rep said, regarding running, that the colt lost its action on the final bend and was not suited by the all-weather track (op 8-13 tchd 4-6 in places)
Dry Speedfit(IRE) had it all to do on the figures and on his first race for nine months. He will be better off in handicaps. (op 22-1 tchd 25-1)

3397 LAWYERS SILK H'CAP — 1m (P)
4:40 (4:42) (Class 6) (0-60,60) 3-Y-0 **£1,942** (£578; £288; £144) **Stalls** Low

Form RPR

400 **1** **Deep Winter**[34] 2380 3-9-3 **59** .... KerrinMcEvoy 4 64+
(R A Fahey) *bhd: rdn and hdwy on inner over 2f out: chsd ldr over 1f out: led ins fnl f: comf* **6/4**[1]

650- **2** *1 1/4* **Rowan Dancer**[238] 6601 3-8-12 **54** .... PatCosgrave 5 56
(J R Boyle) *towards rr: rdn over 4f out: hdwy u.p 2f out: chsd ldng pair 1f out: wnt 2nd ins fnl f: no ch w wnr* **50/1**

0060 **3** *3/4* **Tallest Peak (USA)**[19] 2833 3-8-11 **53** .... VinceSlattery 13 54
(M G Quinlan) *chsd ldr tl led over 4f out: clr over 2f out: rdn and hung rt over 1f out: edgd lft ent fnl f: hdd ins fnl f: fdd towards fin* **8/1**[3]

-000 **4** *3 3/4* **Townkab (IRE)**[14] 2982 3-9-3 **59** ....(b[1]) TGMcLaughlin 10 51
(N P Littmoden) *s.i.s: bhd: hdwy u.p on inner 2f out: plugged on but nvr nr ldrs* **16/1**

005 **5** *1 ¼* **Isabella's Fancy**^{28} 2546 3-9-1 **57**........................ JamieSpencer 11 46
(J R Fanshawe) *hld up in midfield: rdn and unable qckn 3f out: plugged on u.p fr over 1f out: nvr trbld ldrs* **8/1**^{3}

-440 **6** *1 ¼* **Evenstorm (USA)**^{85} 1149 3-8-7 **56**........................ DavidProbert$^{(7)}$ 16 42
(B Gubby) *in tch: hdwy to chse ldrs and rdn 3f out: wnt 2nd 2f out: no imp and lost 2nd over 1f out: wknd* **33/1**

0030 **7** *1* **Hla Tun (USA)**^{25} 2639 3-9-0 **56**........................(p) SaleemGolam 14 40
(W R Swinburn) *racd in midfield: rdn and struggling over 3f out: no ch last 2f* **8/1**^{3}

310 **8** *3* **Tapas Lad (IRE)**^{26} 2613 3-8-8 **57**........................(v) StacyRenwick$^{(7)}$ 8 34
(G J Smith) *t.k.h: chsd ldrs: rdn jst over 2f out: wknd l over 1f out* **10/1**

0-66 **9** *nk* **Payne Relief (IRE)**^{63} 1586 3-9-0 **56**........................ LiamJones 12 32
(M L W Bell) *a towards rr: n.d* **16/1**

-220 **10** *nk* **Waterloo Dock**^{45} 2041 3-9-3 **59**........................ ShaneKelly 6 35
(M Quinn) *racd in midfield: rdn and struggling 3f out: no ch last 2f* **14/1**

0-04 **11** *2 ¾* **Coloratura (IRE)**^{61} 1637 3-9-2 **58**........................ TQuinn 9 27
(E A L Dunlop) *t.k.h: prom: chsd ldr over 2f out tl 2f out: wknd qckly* **14/1**

6-00 **12** *nse* **Istria (USA)**^{26} 2622 3-9-2 **58**........................(b^{1}) JamesDoyle 7 27
(R M Beckett) *bhd: rdn and no hdwy over 2f out: no ch whn hmpd and eased ins fnl f* **50/1**

400 **13** *4* **Llab Nala**^{45} 2041 3-9-0 **56**........................ EdwardCreighton 2 16
(M R Channon) *led tl over 4f out: chsd ldr after tl over 2f out: wknd qckly wl over 1f out* **25/1**

3-24 **14** *7* **The Willowy Wigeon**^{7} 3183 3-9-4 **60**........................(p) JimCrowley 1 4
(P Winkworth) *chsd ldrs tl lost pl qckly 5f out: bhd last 3f: virtually p.u fnl f* **5/1**^{2}

1m 42.45s (2.55) **Going Correction** +0.10s/f (Slow) **14** Ran SP% **134.9**
Speed ratings (Par 97): **91,89,89,85,84 82,81,78,78,78 75,75,71,64**
toteswinger: 1&2 £31.00, 1&3 £9.50, 2&3 £66.10. CSF £131.00 CT £558.71 TOTE £2.30: £1.90, £12.30, £5.60; EX 166.20.
Owner R A Fahey **Bred** Gainsborough Stud Management Ltd **Trained** Musley Bank, N Yorks

FOCUS
A moderate handicap for three-year-olds and the finish was fought out by a couple of unexposed sorts who were upped in trip after the bare three qualifying runs in maidens. The form is not solid but the winner is an interesting prospect.
Isabella's Fancy Official explanation: jockey said filly hung left
Istria(USA) Official explanation: jockey said filly was squeezed out at start
The Willowy Wigeon Official explanation: jockey said filly never travelled

3398 CORNISH HALL H'CAP — 1m 2f (P)
5:10 (5:12) (Class 3) (0-95,95) 4-Y-0+ **£6,623** (£1,982; £991; £495; £246) **Stalls** Low

Form RPR

14- **1** **Moon Quest (IRE)**^{365} 2999 4-8-13 **87**........................ KerrinMcEvoy 7 96+
(Saeed Bin Suroor) *chsd ldr tl over 6f out and again 3f out: led 2f out: hld on gamely fnl f: all out* **5/2**^{2}

2142 **2** *hd* **Trans Siberian**^{13} 3003 4-8-10 **84**........................ TQuinn 1 93
(P F I Cole) *led tl hdd 2f out: rallied gamely u.p: no ex last strides* **8/1**

-340 **3** *1 ½* **Rayhani (USA)**^{41} 2168 5-9-3 **91**........................ PatDobbs 10 97
(M P Tregoning) *trckd ldrs: rdn and hung lft in bhd ldrs over 1f out: nt qckn fnl f* **11/2**^{3}

-330 **4** *1 ¼* **Heaven Knows**^{53} 1828 5-9-7 **95**........................(v^{1}) LiamJones 3 99+
(W J Haggas) *s.i.s: hld up in last pair: shkn up and hdwy 3f out: rdn 2f out: hung rt and nt qckn over 1f out: kpt on ins fnl f: nvr rchd ldrs* **9/4**^{1}

-355 **5** *5* **Bid For Glory**^{26} 2593 4-8-13 **90**........................(v^{1}) KirstyMilczarek$^{(3)}$ 9 84
(H J Collingridge) *stdd s: hld up in last trio: nt clr run 3f out: effrt and nt clr run wl over 1f out: sn rdn and no imp* **14/1**

1-25 **6** *4* **Kay Gee Be (IRE)**^{57} 1723 4-9-7 **95**........................ JamieSpencer 5 81
(M J Wallace) *stdd s: hld up in rr: c wd over 6f out: rdn and effrt over 2f out: no hdwy over 1f out: eased ins fnl f* **13/2**

-504 **7** *1* **Beauchamp Viceroy**^{22} 2711 4-9-4 **92**........................ ShaneKelly 6 76
(G A Butler) *t.k.h: hld up in tch: rdn over 2f out: wknd wl over 1f out: eased ins fnl f* **16/1**

2314 **8** *8* **Curzon Prince (IRE)**^{28} 2531 4-8-11 **85**........................ AlanMunro 2 53
(C F Wall) *hld up in midfield: rdn 4f out: wl bhd last 2f* **14/1**

1001 **9** *1 ¾* **Safari Sundowner (IRE)**^{22} 2711 4-8-7 **81**........................ JimCrowley 8 45
(P Winkworth) *racd in midfield: reminder 5f out: rdn 4f out: wknd over 2f out: eased ins fnl f* **8/1**

00 **10** *4* **Free Tussy (ARG)**^{118} 4-9-4 **95**........................ FergusSweeney 4 48
(G L Moore) *chsd ldrs: wnt 2nd over 6f out tl 3f out: sn wknd: eased ins fnl f* **40/1**

2m 6.62s (-1.98) **Going Correction** +0.10s/f (Slow) **10** Ran SP% **131.9**
Speed ratings (Par 107): **111,110,109,108,104 101,100,94,92,89**
toteswinger: 1&2 £5.50, 1&3 £3.80, 2&3 £8.90. CSF £26.98 CT £112.11 TOTE £3.60: £1.60, £2.40, £2.20; EX 31.80 Place 6: £285.25 Place 5: £125.58.
Owner Godolphin **Bred** Darley **Trained** Newmarket, Suffolk

FOCUS
A very useful handicap, and the winner, if he can stay clear of the problems which have obviously beset him, can go on to much better things. The third and fourth were close to recent form and set the level.

NOTEBOOK
Moon Quest(IRE) has obviously had his fair share of problems and was all out to make it two wins from three career starts. Having gone off at even-money to make a winning debut in a Windsor maiden, he ran in a warm renewal of the Bibury Cup, where he wasn't beaten far. Turning up here for his next start, fully one year on, he obviously lacked nothing in fitness, so while he won't be improving on that score, he should still be doing so mentally, which could leave him a step in front of the Handicapper if he turns up to contest one of the decent prizes on offer at somewhere such as Goodwood. (tchd 3-1)
Trans Siberian went up a couple of pounds in the handicap for chasing home Crete at Sandown a fortnight previously and is likely to go up again for a bold attempt to make all here. He won't always run into as unexposed a sort as the winner in these older-horse affairs, however. (tchd 15-2)
Rayhani(USA) seemed to be travelling a little bit better than the first two home when they were the only two in front of him on the crown of the home bend, but all the way up the straight his inclination was to lug in behind them under pressure. He needs a career-best to defy his current mark. (op 8-1)
Heaven Knows was strongly supported in the market to continue the good run of the William Haggas stable, which can do little wrong at present. Held up right out the back in a first-time visor, he took an age to get balanced in the straight, and once he picked up the leaders had flown. He continues to give the impression that he is better than he has shown, but is running out of excuses. (op 7-2)
Bid For Glory was stopped in his run a couple of times and deserves rating a fair bit better than the bare form. Official explanation: jockey said colt was denied a clear run (op 12-1)
Kay Gee Be(IRE) didn't appear to be facing the kickback early on and Spencer took him wide around the bends as a result, losing many lengths in the process. Eventually eased when he had no chance, this run is best forgiven. Official explanation: jockey said gelding did not face the kickback (op 7-1 tchd 11-2 and 8-1 in a place)
T/Plt: £655.30 to a £1 stake. Pool: £42,375.92. 47.20 winning tickets. T/Qpdt: £209.10 to a £1 stake. Pool: £2,742.08. 9.70 winning tickets. SP

3125 HAMILTON (R-H)
Thursday, June 26

OFFICIAL GOING: Good
Wind: Fresh, half behind Weather: Fine

3399 SECRETARIAL LADY AMATEUR H'CAP — 1m 5f 9y
7:00 (7:03) (Class 6) (0-65,64) 4-Y-0+ **£1,977** (£608; £304) **Stalls** High

Form RPR

500- **1** **Front Rank (IRE)**^{25} 5087 8-9-0 **49**........................ MissECSayer$^{(7)}$ 9 61
(Mrs Dianne Sayer) *mde all: rdn over 2f out: styd on strly* **16/1**

4431 **2** *1* **Forrest Flyer (IRE)**^{6} 3198 4-9-8 **50**........................ MissSBrotherton 12 60
(Miss L A Perratt) *pressed wnr: rdn over 2f out: kpt on ins fnl f* **2/1**^{2}

5-00 **3** *1 ¼* **Spume (IRE)**^{29} 2510 4-10-3 **59**........................(t) MissRDavidson 4 67
(S Parr) *trckd ldrs: effrt over 2f out: kpt on same pce fnl f* **16/1**

32-1 **4** *9* **Master Nimbus**^{7} 3176 8-9-11 **53** 6ex........................ MissADeniel 11 48
(J J Quinn) *hld up in tch: effrt over 2f out: edgd rt: sn outpcd* **1/1**^{1}

00/0 **5** *3 ¼* **Bramantino (IRE)**^{7} 3176 8-9-5 **52**........................ MissHCuthbert$^{(5)}$ 6 42
(T A K Cuthbert) *midfield: outpcd over 4f out: rallied fnl f: n.d* **66/1**

6-00 **6** *¾* **Compton Commander**^{5} 3279 10-8-10 **45**........................ MissAMcCullagh$^{(7)}$ 8 34
(E W Tuer) *bhd tl sme late hdwy: nvr on terms* **40/1**

-000 **7** *¾* **Hunting Haze**^{59} 1679 5-8-10 **45**........................(p) MrsDWilkinson$^{(7)}$ 2 33
(Miss S E Hall) *hld up: struggling after 5f: plugged on fnl f: nvr on terms* **50/1**

/400 **8** *½* **Mt Desert**^{17} 2888 6-10-8 **64**........................ MissLHorner 1 51
(E W Tuer) *in tch: drvn and lost pl 1/2-way: n.d after* **40/1**

/00- **9** *7* **Bollin Thomas**^{23} 3501 10-10-3 **59**........................ MrsCBartley 5 36
(R Allan) *hld up on ins: drvn over 4f out: sn wknd* **40/1**

066 **10** *1 ½* **Besi**^{10} 3083 6-8-13 **46**........................ MissWGibson$^{(5)}$ 3 20
(A Berry) *prom tl wknd over 3f out* **40/1**

0021 **11** *nk* **Bolckow**^{8} 3131 5-9-1 **48**........................ MissMMullineaux$^{(5)}$ 10 22
(J T Stimpson) *in tch tl wknd over 2f out* **9/1**^{3}

0604 **12** *8* **Bed Fellow (IRE)**^{8} 3142 4-10-0 **63**........................ MissJKWilson$^{(7)}$ 7 25
(Paul Murphy) *missed break: bhd: shortlived effrt on outside 1/2-way: sn wknd* **25/1**

2m 55.63s (1.73) **Going Correction** +0.025s/f (Good) **12** Ran SP% **122.2**
Speed ratings (Par 101): **95,94,93,88,86 85,85,84,80,79 79,74**
toteswinger: 1&2 £15.50, 1&3 £63.00, 2&3 £13.70. CSF £48.21 CT £559.11 TOTE £27.90: £4.50, £1.40, £3.70; EX 101.70.
Owner Andrew Sayer **Bred** Ballymacoll Stud Farm Ltd **Trained** Hackthorpe, Cumbria

FOCUS
A low-quality event in which three drew well clear of the favourite and the form is best rated through the third.

3400 E B F "HAPPY 16TH BIRTHDAY JANETTE" MAIDEN STKS — 6f 5y
7:30 (7:31) (Class 4) 2-Y-O **£4,857** (£1,445; £722; £360) **Stalls** Low

Form RPR

1 **Mister Laurel** 2-9-0 0........................ PaulHanagan 4 77+
(R A Fahey) *mde all: pushed along and edgd rt over 1f out: hld on wl fnl f* **15/8**^{1}

42U **2** *¾* **Verinco**^{21} 2746 2-9-3 0........................(b^{1}) TomEaves 1 78
(B Smart) *covered up bhd ldrs: effrt and plld out over 1f out: rdn and pressed wnr ins fnl f: hld whn hesitated nr fin* **15/8**^{1}

25 **3** *2* **Taazur**^{23} 2696 2-9-3 0........................ JoeFanning 5 72
(M Johnston) *pressed wnr to ins fnl f: no ex* **7/2**^{2}

4 *9* **Montmartre (USA)** 2-8-9 0........................ NeilBrown$^{(5)}$ 2 42
(K A Ryan) *dwlt: rn green in rr: nvr on terms* **9/2**^{3}

1m 13.3s (1.10) **Going Correction** +0.15s/f (Good) **4** Ran SP% **110.0**
Speed ratings (Par 95): **98,97,94,82**
CSF £5.72 TOTE £3.10; EX 6.40.
Owner The Cosmic Cases **Bred** Mrs M Bryce **Trained** Musley Bank, N Yorks
■ Stewards' Enquiry : Tom Eaves two-day ban: used whip with excessive force (Jul 10,12)

FOCUS
A modest maiden rated through the third and backed up by the time.

NOTEBOOK
Mister Laurel, a half-brother to the yard's useful juvenile Mister Hardy, knew his job and was quick to bag the rail. He found plenty when pressed by Taazur and kept on strongly close home to hold Verinco. This was a promising start and he holds a couple of entries in sales races, so it would come as no surprise to see him take his chance in one of those. (op 13-8 tchd 6-4)
Verinco, who had the race in the bag when jinking right and unshipping his rider over course and distance last time, had first-time blinkers on here and his rider was keen to get him plenty of early cover. He came to have his chance, but again did not look straightforward under pressure and was always being held. There is a small race in him, but he is evidently not one to take a short price about. (op 5-2 tchd 11-4)
Taazur flopped badly in soft ground at Ripon last time and he seemed to appreciate the sounder surface. This was more like his debut form, but the sixth furlong seemed beyond him and perhaps a 5f nursery would be ideal at this stage. (op 5-2 tchd 4-1)
Montmartre(USA), whose yard can ready a newcomer, looked clueless on this racecourse debut and he was always struggling. The experience should not be lost on him, but he will need to raise his game significantly. (op 8-1)

3401 FIRST TRANSPENNINE EXPRESS SPRINT H'CAP — 5f 4y
8:00 (8:02) (Class 4) (0-80,80) 3-Y-0+ **£6,476** (£1,927; £963; £481) **Stalls** Centre

Form RPR

6230 **1** **The Nifty Fox**^{13} 3009 4-9-9 **77**........................ DavidAllan 1 87
(T D Easterby) *hld up in tch: hdwy 2f out: led ins fnl f: kpt on wl* **10/3**^{1}

0511 **2** *hd* **Kings College Boy**^{2} 3340 8-8-7 **61** 6ex........................(b) PaulHanagan 9 71
(R A Fahey) *led to ins fnl f: rallied u.p: jst hld* **7/2**^{2}

5000 **3** *2 ¾* **Yungaburra (IRE)**^{40} 2188 4-9-2 **70**........................(t) LeeEnstone 4 70
(S Parr) *trckd ldrs: effrt over 1f out: hmpd ent fnl f: r.o wl to take 3rd nr fin* **33/1**

-000 **4** *½* **Blazing Heights**^{19} 2843 5-9-4 **77**........................ GaryBartley$^{(5)}$ 8 75
(J S Goldie) *hld up: hdwy over 1f out: kpt on same pce ins fnl f* **16/1**

2550 **5** *3 ½* **Rothesay Dancer**^{19} 2843 5-8-11 **65**........................ DanielTudhope 5 50
(J S Goldie) *hld up: hdwy over 1f out: wknd ins fnl f* **15/2**^{3}

2300 **6** *½* **Hawaii Prince**^{9} 3112 4-8-7 **61** oh1........................ RoystonFfrench 2 45
(S T Mason) *cl up tl rdn and wknd ent fnl f* **40/1**

0050 **7** *nse* **Brut**^{8} 3129 6-9-1 **69**........................(p) TonyHamilton 11 52
(D W Barker) *prom: drvn over 2f out: wknd ins fnl f* **20/1**

-020 **8** *3 ½* **My Gacho (IRE)**^{9} 3111 6-9-9 **77**........................(b) JoeFanning 3 48
(M Johnston) *prom: rdn and lost pl: bhd: c to stands' side after 2f: nvr on terms* **8/1**

0021 9 *13* **Ronnie Howe**[21] 2748 4-8-7 **66**.......... NeilBrown(5) 7 —
(M Dods) *chsd ldrs to 2f out: sn struggling* **7/2**[2]

60.69 secs (0.69) **Going Correction** +0.15s/f (Good) **9** Ran SP% **106.4**
Speed ratings (Par 105): **100,99,95,94,88 88,88,82,61**
toteswinger: 1&2 £1.50, 1&3 £48.40, 2&3 £15.00. CSF £12.46 CT £231.81 TOTE £3.90: £1.50, £1.40, £5.20; EX 13.30.
Owner Roy Peebles **Bred** Mrs Norma Peebles **Trained** Great Habton, N Yorks

FOCUS
A modest handicap sprint but solid form with the winner to his best and the second close to his mark from earlier in the week.
Hawaii Prince Official explanation: jockey said gelding became upset in stalls
Ronnie Howe Official explanation: jockey said gelding became upset in stalls

3402 HAMILTON PARK SUPER SIX MAIDEN STKS 1m 1f 36y
8:30 (8:31) (Class 5) 3-4-Y-O **£3,238** (£963; £481; £240) **Stalls** High

Form RPR
3546 1 **King Kenny**[41] 2173 3-9-0 74.......... LeeEnstone 9 79+
(S Parr) *hld up in tch: hdwy to ld over 2f out: sn clr: eased cl home* **5/2**[2]
2 *2* **Woody Waller** 3-9-0 0.......... RoystonFfrench 7 75+
(J Howard Johnson) *rn green in rr: bhd tl hdwy 2f out: wnt 2nd ins fnl f: no ch w wnr* **14/1**
024- 3 *2 ¾* **Ceka Dancer (IRE)**[195] 7145 3-8-9 74.......... PaulHanagan 5 64
(E J O'Neill) *plld hrd 4f: chsd ldrs: effrt over 2f out: sn chsng wnr: hung rt over 1f out: lost 2nd and no ex ins fnl f* **9/2**
3-40 4 *2* **Green Diamond**[23] 2699 3-9-0 75.......... JoeFanning 3 65
(M Johnston) *cl up: led over 3f out to over 2f out: no ex over 1f out* **2/1**[1]
6 5 *9* **Circus Clown (IRE)**[19] 2847 3-9-0 0.......... TomEaves 4 46
(Miss L A Perratt) *midfield: drvn and outpcd 1/2-way: no imp fr 2f out* **4/1**[3]
-030 6 *shd* **Wilmington**[28] 2524 4-9-8 58.......... AndrewMullen(3) 1 47
(Mrs J C McGregor) *led to over 3f out: sn wknd* **14/1**
7 *¾* **Setareh** 4-9-8 0.......... PJMcDonald(3) 6 45
(J S Wainwright) *s.s: nvr on terms* **20/1**
0- 8 *19* **Barashi**[340] 3761 3-8-7 0.......... RobbieEgan(7) 2 4
(J Howard Johnson) *trckd ldrs tl wknd fr 3f out* **40/1**
9 *24* **Cadeaux Singer** 4-9-11 0.......... TonyHamilton 8 —
(J Barclay) *missed break: nvr on terms* **100/1**

2m 0.11s (0.41) **Going Correction** +0.025s/f (Good)
WFA 3 from 4yo 11lb **9** Ran SP% **121.6**
Speed ratings (Par 103): **99,97,94,93,85 84,84,67,46**
toteswinger: 1&2 £10.50, 1&3 £2.40, 2&3 £13.40. CSF £38.46 TOTE £3.70: £1.60, £3.20, £1.10; EX 39.50.
Owner Gordon Crawford & Willie McKay **Bred** D P Martin **Trained** Bawtry, S Yorks
■ Stewards' Enquiry : Lee Enstone one-day ban: used whip down shoulder in forehand position (Jul 10)

FOCUS
A moderate maiden with the runner-up not progressive and fourth coming into this off a poor run.

3403 EUROPEAN BREEDERS' FUND FILLIES' CONDITIONS STKS 1m 65y
9:00 (9:00) (Class 3) 3-Y-O+ **£9,969** (£2,985; £1,492; £747; £372) **Stalls** High

Form RPR
1432 1 **Flying Clarets (IRE)**[17] 2890 5-9-0 100.......... PaulHanagan 4 89
(R A Fahey) *led to 3f out: sn drvn and rallied: led wl ins fnl f: styd on wl* **1/2**[1]
3522 2 *1* **Sam's Secret**[5] 3272 6-9-0 77.......... TomEaves 5 87
(G A Swinbank) *prom: smooth hdwy over 2f out: led appr fnl f: sn rdn: hdd and no ex wl ins fnl f* **6/1**[3]
5141 3 *3 ¼* **Magic Echo**[20] 2784 4-8-9 89.......... NeilBrown(5) 3 80
(M Dods) *trckd wnr: led 3f out to appr fnl f: kpt on same pce* **4/1**[2]
2231 4 *3* **Friends Hope**[3] 3311 7-9-0 75.......... DanielTudhope 2 73
(P A Blockley) *prom: effrt over 2f out: wknd over 1f out* **11/1**
0 5 *45* **Spabreaksdotcom (IRE)**[20] 2786 3-8-4 0.......... RoystonFfrench 1 —
(J S Wainwright) *in tch tl wknd fr over 3f out: t.o* **200/1**

1m 47.79s (-0.61) **Going Correction** +0.025s/f (Good)
WFA 3 from 4yo+ 10lb **5** Ran SP% **109.8**
Speed ratings (Par 104): **104,103,99,96,51**
CSF £4.07 TOTE £1.30: £1.20, £2.30; EX 4.40.
Owner The Matthewman Partnership **Bred** Gabriel Bell **Trained** Musley Bank, N Yorks

FOCUS
This was not the most competitive of races with the runner-up setting the level.

NOTEBOOK
Flying Clarets(IRE) has been in really good form this season, winning at Pontefract back in March and running with great credit in Pattern contests the last twice. This represented a big drop in grade and she was expected to score well, but in the end made rather hard work of it. She was on top at the line though and this hardy mare will again take her chance under a 5lb penalty in the John Smith's Cup, a race she was second in a year ago. (op 4-9 tchd 4-7 in a place)
Sam's Secret has been running well without reward and this was another case in point. She travelled up strongly and briefly looked the winner, but Flying Clarets rallied well and she was held close home. A race deserves to fall her way. (tchd 13-2)
Magic Echo, raised 9lb for her recent Doncaster romp, was up there throughout and always held a good position. She could not quicken under pressure though and, despite plugging on, could not trouble the front pair. (op 11-2)
Friends Hope is a highly consistent mare who won readily at Chepstow the other night, but this represented a much stiffer task and she ran about as well as could have been expected. (op 10-1 tchd 12-1)

3404 BOOK NOW FOR LADIES NIGHT H'CAP 6f 5y
9:30 (9:36) (Class 6) (0-65,65) 4-Y-O+ **£2,047** (£604; £302) **Stalls** Centre

Form RPR
6630 1 **Ingleby Princess**[12] 3050 4-9-5 **63**.......... PaulFessey 1 74
(T D Barron) *hld up in tch: hdwy to ld over 1f out: kpt on strly* **13/2**[3]
1004 2 *1 ½* **Kenmore**[12] 3033 6-8-13 **62**.......... ShaneCreighton(5) 5 68
(I W McInnes) *bhd: drvn 1/2-way: hdwy appr fnl f: wnt 2nd ins fnl f: nt rch wnr* **5/1**[2]
0050 3 *½* **Howards Tipple**[5] 3255 4-8-13 **62**..........(v) NeilBrown(5) 3 67
(Miss L A Perratt) *cl up: ev ch over 1f out: one pce fnl f* **7/1**
1000 4 *2* **Cheery Cat (USA)**[14] 2968 4-9-4 **62**..........(p) TonyHamilton 2 60
(D W Barker) *chsd ldrs: rdn over 2f out: nt qckn fnl f* **5/1**[2]
5062 5 *2* **Obe One**[8] 3128 8-8-2 **46** oh1.......... RoystonFfrench 9 38
(A Berry) *prom: drvn over 2f out: no ex fnl f* **7/1**
5-35 6 *3 ¼* **Distant Vision (IRE)**[9] 3112 5-7-13 **46** oh1.......... DuranFentiman(3) 10 27
(H A McWilliams) *cl up tl rdn and no ex over 1f out* **20/1**
6406 7 *nk* **Fast Freddie**[7] 3171 4-9-6 **64**..........(e) LeeEnstone 4 44
(S Parr) *led to over 1f out: sn wknd* **14/1**
00-0 8 *5* **Bold Haze**[7] 3172 6-8-3 **50**..........(v) AndrewMullen(3) 8 14
(Miss S E Hall) *bhd and drvn along: nvr on terms* **25/1**

1320 9 *2 ¼* **Mineral Rights (USA)**[10] 3080 4-9-7 **65**..........(v) TomEaves 11 22
(Miss L A Perratt) *w ldrs tl wknd fr 2f out* **7/2**[1]

1m 12.9s (0.70) **Going Correction** +0.15s/f (Good) **9** Ran SP% **109.2**
Speed ratings (Par 101): **101,99,98,95,93 88,88,81,78**
CSF £33.52 CT £175.68 TOTE £7.60: £2.10, £2.30, £2.60; EX 22.80 Place 6 £85.24, Place 5 £35.62.
Owner Dave Scott **Bred** Wheelersland Stud **Trained** Maunby, N Yorks

FOCUS
A moderate, yet competitive handicap and the form looks sound rated around the first three.
T/Plt: £141.10 to a £1 stake. Pool: £66,318.40. 342.99 winning tickets. T/Qpdt: £12.50 to a £1 stake. Pool: £4,879.19. 286.70 winning tickets. RY

3164 LEICESTER (R-H)
Thursday, June 26

OFFICIAL GOING: Good to firm (firm in places) (meeting abandoned after race 4 (8.15) due to unsafe ground)
Last 2 races abandoned - unsafe ground.
Wind: Fresh, behind Weather: Light rain

3405 GUARDSMAN LTD LADIES' H'CAP (LADY AMATEUR RIDERS) 5f 2y
6:45 (6:46) (Class 5) (0-70,69) 3-Y-O+ **£2,498** (£774; £387; £193) **Stalls** Low

Form RPR
3256 1 **Town House**[96] 971 6-9-4 **50** oh4.......... MissAWallace(5) 6 57
(B P J Baugh) *led 1f: w ldr: rdn and edgd rt over 1f out: r.o to ld nr fin* **66/1**
-006 2 *¾* **Roman Quintet (IRE)**[10] 3079 8-9-9 **55**..........(b) MissABevan(5) 14 59
(A J McCabe) *led 4f out: rdn over 1f out: edgd lft and hdd nr fin* **9/1**
1316 3 *1 ½* **Bayshambles (IRE)**[26] 2596 4-10-4 **66**.......... MissVBarr(7) 9 65
(R E Barr) *chsd ldrs: rdn 1/2-way: styd on* **7/1**[2]
0122 4 *hd* **Miss Daawe**[15] 2928 4-10-8 **63**.......... MissLEllison 2 61
(B Ellison) *s.i.s: hdwy over 3f out: rdn 1/2-way: sn edgd rt: styd on* **15/8**[1]
6505 5 *1 ¾* **Dancing Mystery**[15] 2934 14-9-9 **57**..........(b) MissCNosworthy(7) 8 49
(E A Wheeler) *chsd ldrs: rdn 1/2-way: styd on same pce fnl f* **28/1**
1220 6 *1 ½* **Thoughtsofstardom**[5] 3271 5-10-3 **65**.......... MrsLHarris(7) 15 51
(M Wigham) *chsd ldrs: rdn and edgd lft over 1f out: styd on same pce* **15/2**[3]
0000 7 *½* **Rasaman (IRE)**[14] 2968 4-10-13 **68**..........(t) MissARyan 4 53
(K A Ryan) *hld up: rdn 1/2-way: r.o ins fnl f: nvr trbld ldrs* **15/2**[3]
2600 8 *hd* **Guto**[26] 2596 5-10-7 **67**.......... MissKellyBurke(5) 1 51
(W J H Ratcliffe) *stmbld s: chsd ldrs: outpcd 1/2-way: n.d after* **11/1**
4142 9 *1 ¾* **Maggie Kate**[13] 3000 3-9-13 **67**.......... MissSSawyer(7) 13 45
(R Ingram) *chsd ldrs over 3f* **10/1**
2050 10 *1 ¾* **White Ledger (IRE)**[18] 2869 9-9-2 **50** oh5.......... MissSPeacock(7) 5 21
(R E Peacock) *sn outpcd* **33/1**
-400 11 *nse* **Night Rainbow (IRE)**[7] 3177 5-9-9 **50** oh1... MissGDGracey-Davison 16 21
(Mrs S Leech) *sn pushed along in rr: wknd 1/2-way: bhd whn edgd lft towards fin* **33/1**
5-00 12 *¾* **City For Conquest (IRE)**[21] 2748 5-9-9 **50** oh5..........(b) MrsMMorris 10 18
(John A Harris) *s.i.s: hld up: rdn and wknd 1/2-way: bhd whn hung rt rt wl ins fnl f* **40/1**
2355 13 *nk* **Time Share (IRE)**[28] 2547 4-9-2 **50** oh3..........(be) MissMHugo(7) 12 17
(M Wigham) *sn outpcd: bhd whn hmpd towards fin* **33/1**

59.46 secs (-0.54) **Going Correction** -0.525s/f (Hard)
WFA 3 from 4yo+ 6lb **13** Ran SP% **114.4**
Speed ratings (Par 103): **83,81,79,79,76 73,73,72,69,67 67,65,65**
toteswinger: 1&2 £55.30, 1&3 £27.60, 2&3 £5.00. CSF £542.36 CT £4800.89 TOTE £29.10: £7.90, £3.80, £3.00; EX 799.40.
Owner J H Chrimes **Bred** J H Chrimes **Trained** Audley, Staffs
■ Stewards' Enquiry : Mrs M Morris two-day ban: careless riding (Jul 12,15)

FOCUS
A weak sprint handicap, confined to lady amateur riders, in which few got involved from off the pace. It moderate winning time, even for a race like this, and the form is worth treating with caution.

3406 RAINBOWS CHILDRENS HOSPICE (S) STKS 7f 9y
7:15 (7:16) (Class 6) 3-Y-O **£1,942** (£578; £288; £144) **Stalls** Low

Form RPR
0226 1 **Rockfield Lodge (IRE)**[9] 3116 3-9-0 75.......... NeilPollard 2 58+
(M E Rimmer) *s.s: hdwy over 4f out: nt clr run over 1f out: r.o to ld wl ins fnl f* **13/8**[1]
4640 2 *1* **Lord Deevert**[12] 3021 3-8-9 50..........(p) JackDean(5) 5 55
(W G M Turner) *hld up: hdwy over 4f out: chsd ldr over 2f out: rdn and edgd lft over 1f out: styd on same pce ins fnl f* **16/1**
-540 3 *shd* **Samurai Warrior**[65] 1530 3-9-0 66..........(be[1]) EddieAhern 4 55
(P J Makin) *chsd ldr tl led over 2f out: rdn over 1f out: hdd wl ins fnl f* **13/2**[3]
6000 4 *6* **Where's Dids**[12] 3030 3-8-9 49.......... ChrisCatlin 1 34
(M R Channon) *chsd ldrs: rdn over 2f out: wknd fnl f* **20/1**
0050 5 *2 ¼* **Hapi**[8] 3139 3-8-7 45..........(t) WilliamCarson(7) 3 33
(S C Williams) *led: rdn and hdd over 2f out: wknd fnl f* **66/1**
0030 6 *4* **Flight Plan**[9] 3108 3-8-11 65..........(e) JamieMoriarty(3) 7 22
(R A Fahey) *s.s: hld up: rdn 4f out: nt run on* **11/4**[2]
0000 7 *¾* **Caught In Paradise (IRE)**[8] 3139 3-8-7 48..........(p) TobyAtkinson(7) 6 20
(D W Thompson) *hld up: bhd fr 1/2-way* **50/1**
4133 8 *5* **One Called Alice**[7] 3166 3-9-0 56.......... TedDurcan 9 7
(A W Carroll) *hld up: rdn and wknd 1/2-way* **13/2**[3]
0030 9 *4* **Bahamian Blue (IRE)**[7] 3183 3-9-0 53..........(v) SteveDrowne 8 —
(P G Murphy) *chsd ldrs to 1/2-way* **12/1**

1m 24.47s (-1.73) **Going Correction** -0.525s/f (Hard) **9** Ran SP% **113.2**
Speed ratings (Par 97): **88,86,86,79,77 72,71,66,61**
toteswinger: 1&2 £9.90, 1&3 £3.60, 2&3 Not won. CSF £29.22 TOTE £2.60: £1.30, £4.10, £2.50; EX 32.60.The winner was bought in for 8,000gns
Owner M Ioannou **Bred** John And Sarah Kelly **Trained** Newmarket, Suffolk

FOCUS
A moderate winning time, even for a seller and the winner did no more than he was entitled to. The race could rate higher at face value but looks a contest to treat negatively.

3407 FUNDAMENTAL ASSET MANAGEMENT H'CAP 1m 60y
7:45 (7:45) (Class 5) (0-75,80) 3-Y-O **£3,238** (£963; £481; £240) **Stalls** Low

Form RPR
0631 1 **Willkandoo (USA)**[8] 3126 3-8-8 **61** 6ex.......... FrancisNorton 5 71+
(K A Ryan) *trckd ldrs: plld hrd: hmpd 5f out: rdn over 1f out: r.o to ld nr fin* **10/11**[1]

0140 **2** 1/2 **Desiderio**[23] 2695 3-8-10 **70**..........(b) CharlesEddery(7) 1 77
(R Hannon) *led: clr 1/2-way: rdn and hdd nr fin* **12/1**

1-1 **3** 2 **Avertis**[9] 3116 3-9-13 **80** 6ex.......... TedDurcan 9 82
(M Botti) *s.i.s: sn prom: outpcd over 3f out: rallied and hung rt fr over 1f out* **7/1**[3]

-040 **4** 6 **Seventh Hill**[24] 2678 3-9-2 **69**.......... JamesDoyle 2 58
(M Blanshard) *hld up in tch: racd keenly: chsd ldr over 2f out: sn rdn and hung rt: wknd fnl f* **16/1**

01 **5** 2 **Titfer (IRE)**[7] 3183 3-8-2 **55** oh4.......... JimmyQuinn 10 39
(A W Carroll) *chsd ldrs: rdn 3f out: wknd over 1f out* **14/1**

-304 **6** 3/4 **Hellfire Bay**[132] 572 3-8-6 **59**.......... AdrianTNicholls 7 41
(J Mackie) *s.i.s: hld up: rdn over 3f out: a in rr* **40/1**

-060 **7** 7 **Tamara Moon (IRE)**[26] 2622 3-9-2 **69**.......... ChrisCatlin 3 35
(M R Channon) *dwlt: hdwy to chse ldr 6f out: slipped on bnd 5f out: rdn over 2f out: wknd over 1f out* **20/1**

5-42 **8** 3 1/2 **Wise Hawk**[9] 3117 3-9-3 **70**.......... JimmyFortune 6 28
(W J Haggas) *hld up: slipped on bnd 6f out: a bhd* **7/2**[2]

1260 **9** 3 3/4 **Hawa Khana (IRE)**[121] 704 3-8-8 **61**..........(p) SteveDrowne 4 11
(N P Littmoden) *hld up: plld hrd: rdn and wknd over 3f out* **40/1**

1m 44.12s (-0.98) **Going Correction** -0.125s/f (Firm) **9** Ran SP% **117.0**
Speed ratings (Par 99): **99,98,96,90,88 87,80,77,73**
toteswinger: 1&2 £4.40, 1&3 £1.20, 2&3 £14.80. CSF £13.83 CT £51.79 TOTE £1.90: £1.10, £4.10, £2.50; EX 16.50.
Owner M Forsyth,J Turner And M F Logistics Ltd **Bred** Craig Singer **Trained** Hambleton, N Yorks

FOCUS
A fair handicap rated around the placed horses. The form should be treated with some caution as a few slipped on the bend, but the winner remains progressive.
Wise Hawk Official explanation: jockey said gelding slipped on bend

3408 CHARLEY MILL SHOOT MAIDEN AUCTION STKS 5f 218y
8:15 (8:15) (Class 5) 2-Y-O **£3,238** (£963; £481; £240) **Stalls** Low

Form RPR

23 **1** **Lucky Redback (IRE)**[31] 2458 2-8-11 0.......... RichardHughes 5 81+
(R Hannon) *mde all: shkn up over 1f out: r.o wl: hung rt and eased wl ins fnl f* **5/2**[1]

5 **2** 2 3/4 **Cavendish Road (IRE)**[16] 2916 2-8-11 0.......... RichardMullen 1 70+
(W R Muir) *prom: rdn over 2f out: chsd wnr over 1f out: styd on same pce* **9/2**[3]

5 **3** 5 **Churchills Victory (IRE)**[15] 2951 2-9-2 0.......... AlanMunro 2 60
(W Jarvis) *trckd wnr: racd keenly: rdn over 2f out: wknd fnl f* **11/4**[2]

0 **4** 3 1/2 **Extremely So**[19] 2835 2-8-6 0.......... ChrisCatlin 3 39
(P J McBride) *sn outpcd* **16/1**

0 **5** 2 3/4 **Siciliando**[14] 2979 2-8-11 0.......... EddieAhern 4 36
(M L W Bell) *prom: rdn 1/2-way: wknd 2f out* **5/1**

0 **6** 6 **Milly Rose**[26] 2618 2-8-6 0.......... SteveDrowne 6 13
(M Blanshard) *wnt rt s: sn prom: rdn over 2f out: sn wknd* **6/1**

1m 10.86s (-2.14) **Going Correction** -0.525s/f (Hard) **6** Ran SP% **110.3**
Speed ratings (Par 93): **93,89,82,78,74 66**
toteswinger: 1&2 £5.40, 1&3 £1.10, 2&3 £5.10. CSF £13.46 TOTE £3.00: £1.80, £2.70; EX 12.30 Place 6 £22.89, Place 5 £4.11.
Owner Amblestock Partnership **Bred** M J Wiley **Trained** East Everleigh, Wilts

FOCUS
An ordinary little juvenile maiden which saw the field come home fairly strung out. The winner was stepping up on previous form and is value for further.

NOTEBOOK
Lucky Redback(IRE), placed on his previous two outings, deservedly got his head in front over this longer trip with a decisive display from the front. He again did not really convince with his attitude late on, but was always in control here and rates value for further than the bare margin. He should make his mark in nurseries. (op 11-4 tchd 3-1)
Cavendish Road(IRE), fifth on debut at Salisbury, showed the benefit of that experience and posted a respectable effort. He found the winner too classy, but was clear of the remainder at the finish and is going the right way. (op 13-2 tchd 7-1)
Churchills Victory(IRE), fifth on his debut at Nottingham 15 days previously, was admittedly giving away weight to his rivals yet it was more a case of him refusing to settle which hampered his cause. (tchd 9-4 and 3-1)
Extremely So was always struggling to go the pace, yet still improved a touch on the level of her Lingfield debut. (op 18-1)

3409 NICHOLAS HUMPHRIES ESTATE AGENTS H'CAP 1m 1f 218y
() (Class 4) (0-85,) 3-Y-O £

3410 SANDICLIFFE H'CAP 1m 3f 183y
() (Class 5) (0-75,) 4-Y-O+ £

T/Plt: £28.00 to a £1 stake. Pool: £77,966.84. 2,029.21 winning tickets. T/Qpdt: £1.80 to a £1 stake. Pool: £4,528.49. 1,853.90 winning tickets. CR

[2845] NEWCASTLE (L-H)
Thursday, June 26

OFFICIAL GOING: Good to soft (7.0)
After 4mm rain during the monring the ground was described as 'good to soft, softer than that from the 3f marker in the home straight to 1 1/2f out'.
Wind: strong 1/2 against Weather: overcast with heavy showers at first

3411 GUINNESS MAIDEN AUCTION STKS 6f
2:30 (2:32) (Class 4) 2-Y-O **£4,209** (£1,252; £625; £312) **Stalls** High

Form RPR

32 **1** **On Offer (IRE)**[17] 2887 2-8-11 0.......... DavidAllan 3 79+
(T D Easterby) *overall ldr far side: qcknd over 2f out: styd on strly: 1st of 6 that gp* **10/3**[2]

4 **2** 1 1/2 **Snow Bay**[48] 1948 2-8-11 0.......... TomEaves 9 74+
(B Smart) *racd stands' side: trckd ldrs: led that gp 2f out: r.o wl fnl f: unable to trble wnr* **5/1**[3]

2 **3** 1/2 **Kyllachy Star**[10] 3078 2-9-2 0.......... PaulHanagan 8 78+
(R A Fahey) *racd stands' side: chsd ldrs: effrt over 2f out: styd on wl fnl f* **2/1**[1]

4 hd **Lakeman (IRE)** 2-8-13 0.......... GregFairley 2 74
(B Ellison) *racd far side: chsd ldrs: wnt 2nd after 2f: kpt on same pce fnl 2f: 2nd of 6 that gp* **40/1**

5 hd **Tapis Wizard** 2-8-9 0.......... PaulMulrennan 15 69+
(M W Easterby) *in rr stands' side and sn drvn along: hdwy 2f out: styd on ins fnl f* **33/1**

6 nk **Sharp Sovereign (USA)** 2-8-9 0.......... PaulFessey 12 68+
(T D Barron) *s.s: racd in last stands' side tl hdwy over 1f out: fin wl* **25/1**

7 1 **Captain Imperial (IRE)** 2-8-13 0.......... MickyFenton 5 69
(T P Tate) *bmpd s: racd sfar side: chsd ldrs: outpcd over 2f out: kpt on fnl f: 3rd of 6 that gp* **20/1**

0 **8** 3/4 **Dark Moment**[9] 3107 2-8-13 0.......... DaleGibson 1 67
(A Dickman) *racd far side: chsd wnr over 2f out: fdd fnl f: 4th of 6 that gp* **33/1**

9 1/2 **Welcome Applause (IRE)** 2-8-11 0.......... TPO'Shea 11 64
(M G Quinlan) *s.s: racd stands' side: hdwy to trck ldrs 3f out: wknd over 1f out* **10/1**

6 **10** 3/4 **Hill Cross (IRE)**[19] 2845 2-8-13 0.......... RoystonFfrench 13 63
(Mrs A Duffield) *racd stands' side: chsd ldrs: wknd over 1f out* **20/1**

044 **11** 1/2 **Another Luke (IRE)**[71] 1390 2-8-6 0.......... PJMcDonald(3) 14 58
(T J Etherington) *racd stands' side: a towards rr* **16/1**

63 **12** shd **Aegean Warning**[11] 3055 2-8-11 0.......... NCallan 7 60
(K A Ryan) *led stands' side tl 2f out: sn wknd* **8/1**

13 3 1/4 **Dispol Kintie (IRE)** 2-8-4 0.......... FrankieMcDonald 6 43
(P T Midgley) *s.i.s: racd far side: sn in rr: bhd fnl 2f: 5th of 6 that gp* **50/1**

14 2 **Shadows Lengthen** 2-8-4 0 ow2.......... BradleyRoper(7) 10 44
(M W Easterby) *s.s: racd stands' side: hdwy to chse ldrs 3f out: lost pl wl over 1f out* **50/1**

15 1/2 **Haulage Lady (IRE)** 2-8-1 0.......... AndrewMullen(3) 4 35
(Karen McLintock) *swvd rt s: in rr far side: bhd fnl 2f: last of 6 that gp* **40/1**

1m 17.52s (2.32) **Going Correction** +0.275s/f (Good) **15** Ran SP% **127.2**
Speed ratings (Par 95): **95,93,92,92,91 91,90,89,88,87 86,86,82,79,78**
toteswinger: 1&2 £4.40, 1&3 £1.90, 2&3 £3.60. CSF £19.17 TOTE £4.20: £1.70, £2.20, £1.30; EX 21.90 TRIFECTA Pool: £575.33 - 9.68 winning units.
Owner Mrs Jennifer E Pallister **Bred** James Waldron **Trained** Great Habton, N Yorks

FOCUS
They split into two groups with six including the winner racing on the far side. Just a fair maiden auction race rated through the placed horses.

NOTEBOOK
On Offer(IRE) knew her job this time and, relishing getting her toe in, she dominated throughout on the far side and never really looked in any danger. She seems ideal nursery material. (op 3-1 tchd 11-4)
Snow Bay, absent for seven weeks, was on his toes and looked very fit. He took charge on the stands' side but the winner on the other wing always had this under control. (op 7-1 tchd 15-2)
Kyllachy Star, involved in a bit of scrimmaging at the halfway mark, put in some solid late work to claim second spot on the stands' side. He should improve again. (tchd 7-4 and 9-4)
Lakeman(IRE), a March foal, is a close-coupled newcomer. He came out second best on the far side and should improve and find a similar event.
Tapis Wizard, a cheap purchase, is out of a mare who won three times at up to 1m1fs. On the leg and very inexperienced, he picked up in encouraging fashion late in the day.
Sharp Sovereign(USA) ◆, a March foal, was very noisy beforehand and was keen to post. After a slow start he really picked up late in the day and looks sure to improve and find a race.
Captain Imperial(IRE), a hollow-backed newcomer, took a bump at the start. He stuck to his work in pleasing fashion late on and this will have taught him plenty.
Aegean Warning, who took them along on the stands' side, got involved in some scrimmaging at the halfway mark and in the end dropped right away. At least this opens up the nursery route for him. (op 11-1)

3412 WEATHERBYS BANK NOVICE STKS 6f
3:00 (3:01) (Class 5) 2-Y-O **£4,209** (£1,252; £625; £312) **Stalls** High

Form RPR

0162 **1** **Saxford**[41] 2154 2-9-5 0.......... TomEaves 4 95
(Mrs L Stubbs) *mde all: clr over 1f out: rdn rt out* **7/1**

2 7 **Raise All In (IRE)** 2-8-7 0.......... RyanMoore 6 67+
(R Hannon) *hld up on ins: stdy hdwy over 2f out: wnt 2nd over 1f out: r.o: no ch w wnr* **8/1**

31 **3** 5 **Uramazin (IRE)**[15] 2951 2-9-2 0.......... PJMcDonald(3) 2 59+
(G A Swinbank) *chsd ldrs: effrt 3f out: hung rt: wknd over 1f out* **7/2**[3]

16 **4** 1/2 **Full Of Nature**[19] 2826 2-9-0 0.......... NCallan 5 53+
(K A Ryan) *trckd ldrs: effrt over 2f out: wknd appr fnl f* **2/1**[1]

31 **5** hd **Dubai's Gazal**[25] 2638 2-8-9 0.......... TPO'Shea 1 47+
(M R Channon) *chsd ldrs on outside: effrt over 2f out: wknd over 1f out* **9/4**[2]

5 **6** 15 **Teneo Vestri**[34] 2349 2-8-12 0.......... TPQueally 3 —
(A B Haynes) *chsd wnr: sn drvn along: lost pl 2f out and bhd* **50/1**

1m 16.28s (1.08) **Going Correction** +0.275s/f (Good) **6** Ran SP% **111.9**
Speed ratings (Par 93): **103,93,87,86,86 66**
toteswinger: 1&2 £4.80, 1&3 £3.30, 2&3 £5.30. CSF £57.20 TOTE £7.70: £2.60, £3.50; EX 44.00.
Owner D Arundale **Bred** Malih L Al Basti **Trained** Norton, N Yorks

FOCUS
The winning time was decent for a race like this, 1.24 seconds quicker than the opener. The much improved winner dominated and ran out a wide-margin scorer. He is ready for a step up in grade now.

NOTEBOOK
Saxford, on his toes beforehand, led them a merry dance. He opened up a clear lead yet his rider persisted in using his whip inside the last. He deserves a crack in Listed company after this. (op 10-1)
Raise All In(IRE), a May foal, is a close-coupled type. She went in pursuit of the winner but had but a distant view of him. She can certainly find a maiden race. (op 7-1 tchd 6-1)
Uramazin(IRE) tended to hang right and in the end proved no match for the first two. (tchd 11-4)
Full Of Nature was disappointing, like the third and fifth getting left well behind by the first two. Official explanation: jockey said filly ran flat (op 11-4 tchd 3-1 in a place)
Dubai's Gazal, who is not that big, wore a blanket for stalls entry. Drawn on the outside, she dropped away coming to the final furlong. (op 13-8)

3413 NATIONAL EXPRESS SEATON DELAVAL TROPHY H'CAP 1m 3y(S)
3:30 (3:30) (Class 2) (0-100,100) 4-Y-O+
£15,577 (£4,665; £2,332; £1,167; £582; £292) **Stalls** High

Form RPR

-600 **1** **Kingsdale Orion (IRE)**[20] 2789 4-8-3 **82**.......... TPO'Shea 10 93
(B Ellison) *chsd ldrs: drvn along over 4f out: led on ins 2f out: hld on towards fin* **10/1**

4400 **2** nk **Rio Riva**[54] 1816 6-9-3 **96**.......... TomEaves 9 106+
(Miss J A Camacho) *hld up in rr: nt clr run over 2f out: hdwy to chal ins fnl f: no ex towards fin* **11/1**

0-2 **3** 2 **Zero Tolerance (IRE)**[50] 1910 8-8-3 **82**.......... PaulFessey 5 91+
(T D Barron) *mid-div: nt clr run over 2f out: kpt on wl fnl f: nt rch 1st 2* **7/1**

040 **4** 1/2 **Flipando (IRE)**[8] 3122 7-8-10 **94**.......... NeilBrown(5) 4 98+
(T D Barron) *hld up in rr: nt clr run over 2f out: styd on same pce fnl f* **16/1**

1504 **5** 1 3/4 **Collateral Damage (IRE)**[39] 2218 5-8-1 **83**..........(t) DuranFentiman(3) 8 83+
(T D Easterby) *stl had hood on whn stalls opened: dwlt: hld up in rr: swtchd wd 3f out: kpt on same pce fnl f* **16/1**

2122 **6** *6* **Benandonner (USA)**[42] 2133 5-9-7 **100**........................ PaulHanagan 3 86
(R A Fahey) *trckd ldrs: effrt 3f out: wknd over 1f out* **9/2**[2]
22-1 **7** *1 1/4* **Tazeez (USA)**[29] 2509 4-9-1 **94**........................ MartinDwyer 2 78
(J H M Gosden) *trckd ldrs on outer: effrt 2f out: wknd appr fnl f* **7/4**[1]
00-5 **8** *14* **Striving Storm (USA)**[42] 2133 4-9-2 **95**........................(b[1]) TPQueally 1 46
(P W Chapple-Hyam) *led over 6f out: hung lft and hdd 2f out: nt run on* **20/1**
3010 **9** *11* **Plum Pudding (IRE)**[26] 2595 5-9-5 **98**........................(p) RyanMoore 6 24
(R Hannon) *trckd ldrs on outer: stdy hdwy over 2f out: lost pl over 1f out: eased* **16/1**
5-61 **10** *17* **Scartozz**[5] 3278 6-9-4 **97**........................(b) NCallan 7 —
(M Botti) *led over 1f: effrt 3f out: wknd 2f out: sn bhd and eased* **6/1**[3]

1m 43.43s (0.03) **Going Correction** +0.275s/f (Good) **10** Ran SP% **121.2**
Speed ratings (Par 109): **110,109,107,107,105 99,98,84,73,56**
toteswinger: 1&2 £23.60, 1&3 £13.90, 2&3 £13.50. CSF £118.75 CT £849.25 TOTE £14.00: £3.20, £3.20, £2.00; EX 134.00 TRIFECTA Part won. Pool: £581.78 - 0.20 winning units..
Owner Mr & Mrs D A Gamble **Bred** Myles And Mrs Joan Doyle **Trained** Norton, N Yorks
■ Stewards' Enquiry : Paul Hanagan one-day ban: careless riding (Jul 13)

FOCUS
A messy race with the winner enjoying the rub of the green. The runner-up is rated in line with his Lincoln form.

NOTEBOOK
Kingsdale Orion(IRE), dropped 8lb after three previous outings this time, made quite hard work of it and was pushed to the limit in the end. (op 11-1 tchd 12-1 in a place)
Rio Riva, who took this a year ago from a 1lb lower mark, had the ground to suit and this was one of his much better efforts. Left short of room when trying to improve, he got to within a neck of the winner inside the last but was being held at the line. (op 9-1)
Zero Tolerance(IRE), who has started the season on a lenient mark, had to wait for an opening. He stuck on in willing fashion in the final furlong but had given the first two too much rope. He can surely end his drought from this sort of mark. (op 15-2)
Flipando(IRE), who took this two years ago from a 5lb lower mark, looked at his very best. He too ran out of room at a crucial stage and is clearly in very good heart at present.
Collateral Damage(IRE), drawn two from the stands'-side rail, still had the hood on when the stalls opened and as a result he had to make his way to the outside to find racing room. On ground that suits him nowadays, he did well to finish as close as he did. (op 20-1 tchd 12-1)
Benandonner(USA), raised 8lb after York, did not look at his very best and ran below form. (op 11-2 tchd 6-1)
Tazeez(USA), making his handicap debut, tended to race towards the centre in a race the leaders went off very fast. He stopped to nothing in the end but is well worth another chance. (tchd 9-4)
Striving Storm(USA), in blinkers for the first time, was soon setting strong fractions but he hung badly when collared and looks to one to have severe reservations about. (op 33-1)

3414 WEATHERBYS FINANCE H'CAP — 2m 19y
4:00 (4:00) (Class 4) (0-80,77) 4-Y-0+ **£5,361** (£1,604; £802; £401; £199) **Stalls** Low

Form RPR
-26 **1** **Winged D'Argent (IRE)**[26] 2628 7-9-5 **75**........................(b) NCallan 1 85+
(B J Llewellyn) *chsd ldrs: led over 1f out: drvn clr: eased towards fining* **6/1**
6-43 **2** *3 1/2* **Bollin Felix**[13] 3007 4-9-5 **75**........................(b) DavidAllan 6 80
(T D Easterby) *hld up in mid-div: effrt 4f out: wnt 2nd appr fnl f: no imp* **9/4**[1]
41/0 **3** *6* **Burnt Oak (UAE)**[19] 2822 6-9-5 **75**........................ DeanMcKeown 9 73
(C W Fairhurst) *dwlt: hld up in rr: hdwy and hung lft over 2f out: styd on fnl f* **18/1**
-216 **4** *1 3/4* **Nero West (FR)**[15] 2939 7-9-1 **71**........................(b) TomEaves 5 67
(Miss L A Perratt) *trckd ldr: led over 2f out: hdd over 1f out: sn wknd* **7/1**
1224 **5** *shd* **Danzatrice**[5] 3276 6-8-12 **68**........................ RyanMoore 3 64
(C W Thornton) *hld up in last: drvn over 4f out: rdn and hung lft over 2f out: styd on fnl f* **5/1**[3]
03/1 **6** *3* **Ritsi**[22] 2734 5-8-11 **67**........................ PaulHanagan 4 59
(Grant Tuer) *trckd ldrs: effrt over 4f out: wknd over 1f out* **11/1**
5203 **7** *3 1/4* **Hugs Destiny (IRE)**[10] 3083 7-8-2 **58** oh5........................(t) WilliamBuick 10 46
(M A Barnes) *chsd ldrs: drvn 5f out: lost pl over 2f out* **33/1**
6-46 **8** *2 1/2* **Dr Sharp (IRE)**[26] 2609 8-9-7 **77**........................ MickyFenton 7 62
(T P Tate) *led tl over 2f out: sn lost pl* **4/1**[2]
0000 **9** *2* **Great As Gold (IRE)**[4] 3296 9-8-6 **62**........................ TonyHamilton 2 44
(B Ellison) *mid-div: drvn over 4f out: lost pl 3f out* **33/1**

3m 40.59s (4.39) **Going Correction** +0.275s/f (Good) **9** Ran SP% **113.7**
Speed ratings (Par 105): **100,98,95,94,94 92,90,89,88**
toteswinger: 1&2 £3.80, 1&3 £17.00, 2&3 £14.50. CSF £19.55 CT £225.25 TOTE £6.60: £1.70, £1.40, £3.50; EX 23.30 Trifecta £372.50 Part won. Pool: £503.41 - 0.79 winning units..
Owner Terry Warner **Bred** Daniel A Couper And George Hosie **Trained** Fochriw, Caerphilly

FOCUS
A very moderate winning time for the class despite a fair gallop. The winner turned back the years, and the placed horses ran to their marks.

3415 EUROPEAN BREEDERS' FUND/NATIONAL EXPRESS HOPPINGS STKS (LISTED RACE) (F&M) — 1m 2f 32y
4:30 (4:33) (Class 1) 3-Y-0+
£17,031 (£6,456; £3,231; £1,611; £807; £405) **Stalls** Low

Form RPR
452 **1** **Classic Remark (IRE)**[26] 2612 3-8-7 83........................ MickyFenton 1 100
(H J L Dunlop) *trckd ldrs: t.k.h: styd on fnl 2f: led last 75yds: r.o* **40/1**
44-5 **2** *1 3/4* **Sell Out**[42] 2130 4-9-5 100........................ WilliamBuick 11 96+
(G Wragg) *hld up in rr: hdwy over 4f out: styd on fnl 2f: tk 2nd nr fin* **10/1**
-221 **3** *hd* **Wood Chorus**[22] 2735 3-8-7 78........................ TPQueally 8 96
(M L W Bell) *trckd ldrs: led over 1f out: hdd wl ins fnl f: one pce* **22/1**
5-64 **4** *shd* **Pentatonic**[33] 2402 5-9-5 97........................ JoeFanning 4 96
(L M Cumani) *led tl over 1f out: rallied ins fnl f: styd on* **12/1**
-150 **5** *3* **Jamboretta (IRE)**[19] 2827 4-9-5 96........................ RyanMoore 7 90+
(Sir Michael Stoute) *stdd s: hld up in rr: effrt over 2f out: kpt on: nvr rchd ldrs* **7/2**[2]
21 **6** *1 3/4* **Ghaidaa (IRE)**[14] 2973 3-8-7 91........................ MartinDwyer 9 86
(M A Jarvis) *hld up in midfield: effrt 3f out: kpt on: nvr a threat* **5/4**[1]
-206 **7** *3 3/4* **Comeback Queen**[8] 3124 3-8-7 91........................ TomEaves 6 79
(S Kirk) *mid-div: rdn over 2f out: nvr nr ldrs* **20/1**
5-00 **8** *1 1/2* **Miss Bootylishes**[19] 2825 3-8-7 83........................ GregFairley 3 76
(A B Haynes) *mid-div: drvn over 3f out: hung lft over 1f out: nvr a factor* **100/1**
-653 **9** *3/4* **Steam Cuisine**[17] 2890 4-9-5 94........................ TPO'Shea 2 74
(M G Quinlan) *hld up in rr: bried effrt 3f out: sn wknd* **14/1**
-050 **10** *3 1/2* **Rinterval (IRE)**[54] 1801 3-8-7 90........................ PaulHanagan 5 67
(R Hannon) *hld up in mid-div: effrt on ins over 2f out: lost pl over 1f out* **25/1**
0220 **11** *3/4* **Under The Rainbow**[6] 3195 5-9-5 104........................ NCallan 10 66
(B W Hills) *trckd ldrs: effrt 3f out: wknd over 1f out: eased* **6/1**[3]

2m 12.7s (0.80) **Going Correction** +0.275s/f (Good)
WFA 3 from 4yo+ 12lb **11** Ran SP% **120.8**
Speed ratings (Par 111): **107,105,105,105,102 101,98,97,96,93 93**
toteswinger: 1&2 £32.40, 1&3 £21.50, 2&3 £14.40. CSF £387.79 TOTE £35.60: £5.50, £2.70, £3.90; EX 435.90 Trifecta £621.62 Part won. Pool: £624.61 - 0.10 winning units..
Owner Hesmonds Stud **Bred** Hesmonds Stud Ltd **Trained** Lambourn, Berks

FOCUS
A Listed race but not easy to rate with the runner-up and the fourth the best guides. The much-improved winner is rated just 83, the third only 78.

NOTEBOOK
Classic Remark(IRE), from a family, which includes Bulaxie and Claxon, that has done well for the owners, seemingly suited by the give in the ground, broke her duck at the fourth attempt in this Listed race. (op 33-1)
Sell Out, another suited by the rain-softened ground, came from a different parish to snatch second spot on the line. (op 11-1 tchd 14-1)
Wood Chorus, a modest maiden winner and rated just 78, ran out of her skin but this will have blown a lenient handicap mark out of the water at the expense of some black type. (op 28-1)
Pentatonic, her stamina provne, took them along. She came back for more inside the last and would have finished second with a bit further to go. (tchd 11-1 and 16-1)
Jamboretta(IRE), last to leave the paddock and taken down early, was dropped in at the start. She was set a very stiff task and her rider elected to come wide on the slower ground in the home straight. In the circumstances she did well to finish as close as she did. (op 4-1 tchd 9-2)
Ghaidaa(IRE), a Group 1 entry, is not that big. Settled in midfield she never threatened to enter the argument. Her trainer does not mistake his geese for swans and she must be worth another chance at this level. (op 11-10 tchd 10-11 and 11-8)
Under The Rainbow, with the blinkers left off, ran a very tame race and, with all chance gone, she was allowed to coast home. Five year old now, she seems to have developed her own ideas.
Official explanation: jockey said mare ran flat (op 15-2)

3416 NATIONAL EXPRESS H'CAP — 7f
5:00 (5:01) (Class 5) (0-75,78) 3-Y-O **£4,533** (£1,348; £674; £336) **Stalls** High

Form RPR
33-0 **1** **Borasco (USA)**[16] 2911 3-9-1 **67**........................ PaulFessey 11 80
(T D Barron) *mde all: qcknd clr over 2f out: r.o strly: v readily* **17/2**
1551 **2** *4 1/2* **Yamal (IRE)**[9] 3108 3-9-12 **78** 6ex........................ JoeFanning 7 79+
(M Johnston) *dwlt: sn mid-div: effrt over 2f out: wnt 2nd over 1f out: no ch w wnr* **2/1**[1]
3213 **3** *hd* **Young Gladiator (IRE)**[9] 3118 3-8-10 **65**........................ AndrewMullen[(3)] 12 65
(Miss J A Camacho) *trckd ldrs: wnt 2nd over 2f out: styd on same pce* **13/2**[2]
-060 **4** *3 3/4* **Irving Place**[14] 2967 3-9-7 **73**........................ TonyHamilton 2 63
(R A Fahey) *swtchd rt after s: hld up: hdwy on ins over 2f out: kpt on: nvr nr ldrs* **10/1**
6-05 **5** *1/2* **Earlsmedic**[31] 2449 3-8-13 **65**........................ TPQueally 8 54+
(S C Williams) *t.k.h in midfield: nt clr run over 2f out: kpt on steadily fnl f* **13/2**[2]
4-06 **6** *4 1/2* **La Fortalesa (IRE)**[24] 2673 3-9-1 **67**........................ NCallan 5 44+
(K A Ryan) *mid-div: effrt over 2f out: lost pl over 1f out* **16/1**
-056 **7** *1/2* **Lady Benjamin**[24] 2674 3-8-10 **67**........................ PatrickDonaghy[(5)] 6 42+
(P C Haslam) *chsd ldrs: lost pl over 1f out* **7/1**[3]
6000 **8** *1* **Baronovici (IRE)**[47] 1988 3-9-2 **68**........................ PaulMulrennan 3 41+
(D W Barker) *t.k.h on outer: stdd: eased ins and dropped bk 4f out: no ch after* **16/1**
-000 **9** *7* **Strictly Elsie (IRE)**[10] 3081 3-8-5 **57**........................ RoystonFfrench 1 11
(J R Norton) *dwlt: in rr and pushed along: nvr on terms* **66/1**
0-10 **10** *14* **Berrymead**[65] 1548 3-8-10 **62**........................ DaleGibson 10 —
(M W Easterby) *trckd ldrs: t.k.h: hung lft: wknd 2f out: sn bhd* **20/1**
4336 **11** *5* **Bertie Vista**[8] 3144 3-8-10 **65**........................ DuranFentiman[(3)] 4 —
(T D Easterby) *chsd ldrs on outer: lost pl over 2f out* **33/1**
5-00 **12** *3* **Shanafarahan (IRE)**[5] 3263 3-9-1 **67**........................ MickyFenton 9 —
(T P Tate) *dwlt: sn trcking ldrs: hung ledft and lost pl over 2f out: sn bhd and eased* **10/1**

1m 29.22s (1.82) **Going Correction** +0.275s/f (Good) **12** Ran SP% **122.2**
Speed ratings (Par 99): **100,94,94,90,89 84,84,82,74,58 53,49**
toteswinger: 1&2 £7.20, 1&3 £12.90, 2&3 £3.70. CSF £26.15 CT £127.32 TOTE £13.00: £3.60, £1.80, £2.60; EX 41.90 Trifecta £269.20 Pool: £578.54 - 1.59 winning units. Place 6: £3447.15 Place 5: £2838.88.
Owner Patrick Toes & R G Toes **Bred** Kidder, Cole & J K & Linda Griggs **Trained** Maunby, N Yorks

FOCUS
A modest handicap but a very decisive winner Borasco who was almost certainly racing on the better ground hard against the stands'-side rail. Earlsmedic did best of those racing wide and is a bit better than the bare form.
Borasco(USA) Official explanation: trainer had no explanation for the apparent improvement in form
Berrymead Official explanation: jockey said filly hung left throughout
T/Jkpt: Not won. T/Plt: £1,665.80 to a £1 stake. Pool: £84,661.16. 37.10 winning tickets. T/Qpdt: £101.60 to a £1 stake. Pool: £4,737.45. 34.50 winning tickets. WG

3177 WARWICK (L-H)
Thursday, June 26

OFFICIAL GOING: Good to firm
Fast ground and a brisk tailwind led to two new track records on the straight course at a meeting that was a something of a front-runners benefit.
Wind: Fresh behind Weather: Fine

3417 COMMSCOPE AND BAILEY TESWAINE MAIDEN AUCTION STKS — 5f
2:20 (2:22) (Class 5) 2-Y-0 **£3,070** (£906; £453) **Stalls** Centre

Form RPR
0 **1** **Amour Propre**[21] 2759 2-8-9 0........................ DaneO'Neill 5 87+
(H Candy) *mde all: rdn and edgd lft jst over 1f out: r.o wl* **2/1**[1]
2 *3* **Deposer (IRE)** 2-8-12 0........................ LPKeniry 4 79
(J R Best) *chsd ldrs: rn green over 1f out: chsd wnr fnl f: no imp* **11/4**[2]
4 **3** *4* **Green Poppy**[7] 3020 2-8-10 0........................ RichardHughes 9 63
(Eve Johnson Houghton) *racd wd most of way: w ldrs: rdn over 1f out: wknd ins fnl f* **11/2**
00 **4** *1* **Song Of Praise**[15] 2944 2-8-7 0........................ SteveDrowne 2 56
(M Blanshard) *wnt rt s: towards rr: rdn over 1f out: hdwy fnl f: n.d* **40/1**
5 *3/4* **Chimbonda** 2-8-12 0........................ JohnEgan 3 59
(S Parr) *s.i.s: sn chsng ldrs: rdn over 1f out: wknd ins fnl f* **20/1**
3 **6** *3/4* **Tillers Satisfied (IRE)**[16] 2903 2-8-4 0........................ CatherineGannon 1 48
(R Hollinshead) *w wnr tl rdn and wknd wl over 1f out* **7/2**[3]

The Form Book, Raceform Ltd, Compton, RG20 6NL

0 **7** *6* **Hi Shinko**[16] 2916 2-8-9 0 ChrisCatlin 8 31
(B R Millman) *chsd ldrs over 2f* **16/1**

64 **8** *4* **Captain Kallis (IRE)**[24] 2677 2-8-2 0 BillyCray(7) 7 17
(D J S Ffrench Davis) *rdn over 2f out: a bhd* **66/1**

00 **9** *11* **Haulit**[13] 2987 2-8-9 0 RichardMullen 6 —
(R A Harris) *s.i.s: outpcd* **33/1**

57.95 secs (-1.65) **Going Correction** -0.375s/f (Firm) 2y crse rec **9** Ran SP% **115.1**
Speed ratings (Par 93): **98,93,86,85,84 82,73,66,49**
toteswinger: 1&2 £3.10, 1&3 £3.30, 2&3 £4.30. CSF £7.34 TOTE £2.80: £1.30, £1.50, £1.70; EX 8.50.

Owner Simon Broke And Partners **Bred** Mrs Sheila Oakes **Trained** Kingston Warren, Oxon

FOCUS
The juvenile course record which had stood since 1990 was broken by 0.45 seconds.

NOTEBOOK
Amour Propre ◆ found the conditions totally different to his soft-ground debut at Sandown. Showing plenty of speed, he can go on from here if the admittedly wind-assisted time is anything to go by. (op 11-4 tchd 3-1)
Deposer(IRE) ◆ showed signs of inexperience on his debut and could well have been feeling the ground. He will not always meet one so good as the winner and normal improvement should see him off the mark. (op 10-3)
Green Poppy broke much better this time and raced wide from the outside stall apart from cutting the corner at the elbow. She will require further in due course. (op 3-1)
Song Of Praise, reverting to the minimum trip, had less use made of her after going right at the start and did her best work in the closing stages. (op 66-1)
Chimbonda was not disgraced on his debut and should be better for the experience. (tchd 25-1)
Tillers Satisfied(IRE), in total contrast to her initial run at Chester, had the inside stall and showed plenty of speed. (op 3-1)

3418 COMMSCOPE AND PTC SYSTEMS H'CAP 6f
2:50 (2:51) (Class 4) (0-85,86) 3-Y-O+ **£6,476** (£1,927; £963; £481) **Stalls** Centre

Form RPR

0-64 **1** **Peter Island (FR)**[14] 2968 5-8-12 **68** (v) ChrisCatlin 1 81
(J Gallagher) *mde all: rdn jst over 1f out: drvn out* **5/1**[3]

5116 **2** *1* **Toms Laughter**[12] 3042 4-9-10 **83** (p) KevinGhunowa(3) 3 93
(R A Harris) *a chsng wnr: rdn and edgd lft ins fnl f: nt qckn* **7/2**[1]

342 **3** *2 1/4* **China Cherub**[10] 3093 5-9-5 **75** (v[1]) RichardHughes 9 78
(S Dow) *hld up: hdwy 3f out: swtchd rt wl over 1f out: sn rdn: kpt on towards fin* **5/1**[3]

2230 **4** *1* **Stamford Blue**[10] 3093 7-9-5 **80** (b) HaddenFrost(5) 4 80
(R A Harris) *wnt sltly rt s: prom: rdn wl over 1f out: one pce fnl f* **10/1**

-511 **5** *3/4* **Seamus Shindig**[35] 2339 6-9-7 **84** AmyScott(7) 6 81
(H Candy) *hld up and bhd: hdwy wl over 1f out: sn rdn: one pce fnl f* **9/2**[2]

1060 **6** *2* **Bombardier Wells**[14] 2974 3-8-7 **70** (b[1]) StephenCarson 5 61
(Eve Johnson Houghton) *bmpd s: bhd: rdn over 1f out: n.d* **20/1**

6351 **7** *nk* **Lunces Lad (IRE)**[12] 3024 4-9-7 **77** (v) DarryllHolland 7 67
(M R Channon) *bhd: rdn 2f out: nvr nr ldrs* **8/1**

4561 **8** *10* **Caribbean Coral**[7] 3172 9-10-2 **86** 6ex GeorgeBaker 2 44
(A B Haynes) *hld up and bhd: rdn wl over 1f out: sn struggling* **8/1**

-353 **9** *10* **Chinese Temple (IRE)**[119] 737 3-9-2 **82** JerryO'Dwyer(3) 8 8
(M G Quinlan) *sn prom: wkng whn n.m.r briefly 2f out* **25/1**

69.44 secs (-2.36) **Going Correction** -0.375s/f (Firm) course record
WFA 3 from 4yo+ 7lb **9** Ran SP% **113.7**
Speed ratings (Par 105): **100,98,95,94,93 90,90,76,63**
toteswinger: 1&2 £4.70, 1&3 £5.20, 2&3 £4.00. CSF £22.46 CT £91.39 TOTE £6.20: £1.80, £1.60, £2.00; EX 22.50.

Owner C R Marks (banbury) **Bred** E A R L Elevage De La Source **Trained** Moreton-in-Marsh, Gloucs

FOCUS
The course record which was only set in similar conditions last week was beaten by 0.73 seconds.
Caribbean Coral Official explanation: jockey said gelding was unsuited by to the good to firm ground

3419 COMMSCOPE AND REDSTONE CONVERGED SOLUTIONS MAIDEN STKS 7f 26y
3:20 (3:20) (Class 5) 3-Y-O+ **£2,914** (£867; £433; £216) **Stalls** Low

Form RPR

003- **1** **Manhattan Dream (USA)**[279] 5595 3-8-12 74 MichaelHills 2 75
(B W Hills) *mde all: rdn ins fnl f: r.o* **7/4**[1]

5404 **2** *1 3/4* **Polmaily**[16] 2918 3-9-3 75 (b[1]) RichardHughes 6 75
(B J Meehan) *dropped out s: hdwy over 3f out: chsd wnr wl over 1f out: rdn and nt qckn fnl f* **15/8**[2]

3 **3** *11* **Saintly Gaze**[31] 2455 3-9-3 0 RichardMullen 5 46
(W R Swinburn) *hld up in tch: rdn and wknd over 1f out* **11/4**[3]

0 **4** *hd* **Harryana To**[14] 2981 3-8-12 0 DaneO'Neill 3 40
(B J McMath) *hld up: dropped to rr 3f out: sn rdn: sme late prog* **33/1**

5 *1 3/4* **Soviet Cat (IRE)** 3-9-3 0 ChrisCatlin 4 40
(D W P Arbuthnot) *rn green: chsd wnr tl wl over 1f out: sn wknd* **12/1**

00 **6** *1 1/4* **King Of Sparta (USA)**[15] 2929 3-9-0 0 JamieMoriarty(3) 7 37
(T J Fitzgerald) *t.k.h: a bhd: no ch fnl 2f* **33/1**

0-05 **7** *shd* **Hill Of Clare (IRE)**[51] 1896 6-9-4 47 JerryO'Dwyer(3) 1 32
(G H Jones) *prom tl rdn and wknd 2f out* **40/1**

1m 23.61s (-0.99) **Going Correction** -0.15s/f (Firm)
WFA 3 from 6yo 9lb **7** Ran SP% **113.8**
Speed ratings (Par 103): **99,97,84,84,82 80,80**
toteswinger: 1&2 £41.80, 1&3 £1.70, 2&3 £1.50. CSF £5.29 TOTE £3.20: £1.70, £1.40; EX 5.90.

Owner Lady Richard Wellesley **Bred** Vallee Des Reves Syndicate **Trained** Lambourn, Berks

FOCUS
The first two drew clear in this modest maiden.

3420 COMMSCOPE ENTERPRISE SOLUTIONS WELCOMES OUR GUESTS ETERNAL STKS (LISTED RACE) (FILLIES) 7f 26y
3:50 (3:50) (Class 1) 3-Y-O
£14,760 (£5,595; £2,800; £1,396; £699; £351) **Stalls** Low

Form RPR

0-51 **1** **Clifton Dancer**[40] 2196 3-8-12 88 RichardKingscote 6 98
(Tom Dascombe) *mde all: rdn and edgd rt wl over 1f out: sn edgd lft: drvn out* **11/2**[3]

-521 **2** *nk* **Lesson In Humility (IRE)**[26] 2594 3-8-12 96 AndrewElliott 3 97
(K R Burke) *t.k.h: chsd wnr tl over 4f out: n.m.r on ins over 3f out: rdn and ev ch ins fnl f: nt qckn* **9/2**[2]

1-23 **3** *2 1/4* **Kylayne**[47] 1993 3-8-12 100 JohnEgan 5 91
(P W D'Arcy) *hld up: n.m.r sn after s: hdwy 3f out: rdn over 1f out: one pce ins fnl f: sddle slipped* **11/8**[1]

-056 **4** *3/4* **Highland Daughter (IRE)**[26] 2594 3-8-12 90 RichardMullen 2 89+
(C G Cox) *hld up: hmpd sn after s: rdn over 1f out: kpt on towards fin* **25/1**

4-15 **5** *1/2* **Frivolous (IRE)**[75] 1332 3-8-12 85 JimmyFortune 8 88
(J H M Gosden) *prom: edgd lft sn after s: chsd wnr over 4f out tl rdn wl over 1f out: swtchd rt jst over 1f out: no ex ins fnl f* **9/1**

-033 **6** *3 1/2* **Kay Es Jay (FR)**[24] 2666 3-8-12 92 MichaelHills 1 78
(B W Hills) *hld up: hmpd on ins sn after s: bhd fnl 3f* **8/1**

030- **7** *16* **Lady Aquitaine (USA)**[265] 5973 3-8-12 101 RichardHughes 4 35
(B J Meehan) *hmpd sn after s: racd awkwardly: in tch tl wknd over 2f out* **10/1**

1m 21.8s (-2.80) **Going Correction** -0.15s/f (Firm) **7** Ran SP% **109.7**
Speed ratings (Par 104): **110,109,107,106,105 101,83**
toteswinger: 1&2 £4.80, 1&3 £2.70, 2&3 £2.00. CSF £27.68 TOTE £7.00: £3.20, £1.80; EX 32.70.

Owner Clifton Partners **Bred** Redmyre Bloodstock And Stuart McPhee **Trained** Lambourn, Berks

FOCUS
This unofficially hand-timed event was not a great race by Listed standards and proved to be very messy shortly after the start.

NOTEBOOK
Clifton Dancer, described by her trainer as one who gives her all, held on well under pressure after running about a bit in the short home straight. The black type earned for this Listed success considerably enhances her value and she is a credit to her trainer. (op 15-2)
Lesson In Humility(IRE) ran her race on this first try at 7f despite proving difficult to settle but found that the winner would not be denied. (op 11-2)
Kylayne was one of several who got interfered with just after the start. Her rider subsequently reported that his saddle slipped although that did not stop him putting his filly under pressure. Official explanation: jockey said filly suffered interference shortly after start, and that saddle slipped (tchd 6-5 and 6-4)
Highland Daughter(IRE), on the quickest ground she has encountered so far, finished around three and a half lengths closer to the runner-up than she had done over 6f at Doncaster at the end of last month.
Frivolous(IRE), dropping back to 7f, caused a chain reaction when drifting across from the outside draw soon after the start. She could well have found the ground a bit lively. Official explanation: jockey said filly hung left on leaving stalls (op 15-2)

3421 COMMSCOPE AND ROYCE COMMUNICATIONS H'CAP 1m 2f 188y
4:20 (4:20) (Class 5) (0-75,75) 3-Y-O **£3,238** (£963; £481; £240) **Stalls** Low

Form RPR

0631 **1** **Amicable Terms**[16] 2915 3-8-4 **58** ow1 JohnEgan 4 63
(Rae Guest) *hld up in tch: rdn and edgd lft whn hit rail jst over 1f out: led jst ins fnl f: r.o wl* **9/4**[1]

-061 **2** *1* **Houri (IRE)**[15] 2956 3-9-5 **73** (p) GeorgeBaker 3 76
(R M Beckett) *chsd ldr tl 5f out: rdn to ld jst over 1f out: hdd jst ins fnl f: nt qckn* **11/4**[2]

51-0 **3** *1 1/4* **Wing Play (IRE)**[24] 2665 3-9-4 **75** TravisBlock(3) 9 76
(H Morrison) *hld up in tch: carried rt over 1f out: sn rdn: kpt on ins fnl f* **5/1**[3]

-000 **4** *1/2* **Cossack Prince**[10] 3095 3-9-2 **70** (p) RichardHughes 6 70
(B J Meehan) *led: rdn 3f out: hdd jst over 1f out: no ex ins fnl f* **7/1**

0500 **5** *2 3/4* **De Facto**[10] 3095 3-8-13 **67** (b) JimmyFortune 8 62
(J H M Gosden) *hld up: hdwy over 6f out: chsd ldr 5f out tl rdn and hung rt over 1f out: wknd ins fnl f* **15/2**

00-0 **6** *3/4* **Amwell House**[14] 2984 3-7-9 **56** oh11 BillyCray(7) 1 50?
(J R Jenkins) *hld up and bhd: pushed along over 5f out: nvr nr ldrs* **33/1**

34-0 **7** *5* **Red Cauldron**[13] 2996 3-9-1 **69** ChrisCatlin 2 54
(E J O'Neill) *t.k.h in rr: rdn and struggling wl over 1f out* **11/1**

2m 19.87s (-1.23) **Going Correction** -0.15s/f (Firm) **7** Ran SP% **109.6**
Speed ratings (Par 99): **98,97,96,96,94 93,89**
toteswinger: 1&2 £2.10, 1&3 £4.00, 2&3 £2.10. CSF £7.83 CT £23.50 TOTE £2.90: £1.70, £2.70; EX 6.40.

Owner Sentinel Bloodstock **Bred** Brook Stud Bloodstock Ltd **Trained** Newmarket, Suffolk

FOCUS
This slowly-run minor handicap developed into a sprint from the home turn with the wind behind them.

3422 BOLLINGER CHAMPAGNE CHALLENGE SERIES H'CAP (FOR GENTLEMAN AMATEUR RIDERS) 1m 22y
4:50 (4:51) (Class 5) (0-70,70) 4-Y-O+ **£3,123** (£968; £484; £242) **Stalls** Low

Form RPR

3323 **1** **El Dececy (USA)**[9] 3116 4-11-3 **68** MrJoshuaMoore(5) 6 81
(S Parr) *led 2f: w ldr: led 3f out: hung rt fnl f: pushed out* **2/1**[1]

-061 **2** *1 3/4* **Laish Ya Hajar (IRE)**[7] 3182 4-10-8 **61** 6ex MrDHannig(7) 12 70
(P R Webber) *led after 2f to 3f out: nt qckn fnl f* **11/2**[3]

-000 **3** *1 1/4* **Just Oscar (GER)**[20] 2782 4-10-2 **51** oh4 MrBenBrisbourne(3) 5 57+
(W M Brisbourne) *sn stdd into mid-div: rdn and hdwy over 1f out: swtchd rt ins fnl f: r.o* **15/2**

4042 **4** *1 1/2* **Bavarica**[7] 3163 6-10-12 **63** MrRBirkett(5) 7 66
(Miss J Feilden) *hld up in mid-div: hdwy over 3f out: rdn wl over 1f out: one pce fnl f* **9/2**[2]

0-46 **5** *2 1/4* **Semi Detached (IRE)**[38] 2243 5-10-4 **57** AlexEdwards(7) 10 55
(J W Unett) *t.k.h: prom: wknd ins fnl f* **15/2**

/500 **6** *3/4* **Banjo Patterson**[14] 2978 6-10-11 **64** (b) MrJMQuinlan(7) 1 60
(M G Quinlan) *hld up towards rr: hmpd on ins over 3f out: hrd rdn and hdwy over 1f out: no further prog fnl f* **14/1**

-660 **7** *nse* **Lopinot (IRE)**[22] 2722 5-10-5 **58** (p) MrDPeters(7) 9 54
(M R Bosley) *hld up and bhd: rdn and sme hdwy over 1f out: no imp fnl f* **9/1**

0000 **8** *8* **Passato (GER)**[15] 2957 4-10-6 **52** MrSDobson 11 29
(R A Harris) *s.i.s: a bhd* **20/1**

000- **9** *1/2* **A One (IRE)**[319] 4418 9-9-12 **51** oh6 MrDRBass(7) 2 27
(H J Manners) *a towards rr* **66/1**

0500 **10** *3/4* **Temtation (IRE)**[51] 1906 4-10-0 **51** oh6 MrBJToomey(5) 3 25
(J A Pickering) *t.k.h: prom tl wknd wl over 1f out* **40/1**

160 **11** *4 1/2* **Busy Man (IRE)**[19] 770 9-10-0 **53** oh6 ow2 MrCAHarris(7) 8 17
(R C Guest) *s.s: a wl in rr* **33/1**

1m 39.61s (-1.39) **Going Correction** -0.15s/f (Firm) **11** Ran SP% **118.7**
Speed ratings (Par 103): **100,98,97,95,93 92,92,84,83,83 78**
toteswinger: 1&2 £3.80, 1&3 £5.20, 2&3 £7.50. CSF £12.64 CT £71.84 TOTE £3.00: £1.60, £2.10, £3.00; EX 16.30 Place 6: £10.28 Place 5: £7.50.

Owner Willie McKay **Bred** Shadwell Farm LLC **Trained** Bawtry, S Yorks

FOCUS
A typically modest amateur's event.
T/Plt: £31.50 to a £1 stake. Pool: £55,788.00. 1,292.65 winning tickets. T/Qpdt: £7.40 to a £1 stake. Pool: £2,511.89. 248.20 winning tickets. KH

3429 - 3430a (Foreign Racing) - See Raceform Interactive

^{2903}CHESTER (L-H)

Friday, June 27

OFFICIAL GOING: Good (good to soft in places)
Rail realignment added 10yards per circuit to advertised distances.
Wind: Moderate, across Weather: Overcast

3431 BETFAIR APPRENTICE TRAINING SERIES H'CAP — 7f 122y
6:45 (6:50) (Class 5) (0-70,70) 4-Y-0+ £3,561 (£1,059; £529; £264) Stalls Low

Form / RPR

1521 **1** **Zabeel Tower**^{7} 3211 5-9-3 66 6ex (p) LanceBetts(3) 10 — 74
(R Allan) *a.p: led over 1f out: sn rdn: hrd pressed and jst hld on cl home* **5/1^{2}**

0003 **2** *hd* **Just Oscar (GER)**^{1} 3422 4-8-2 51 oh4 RossAtkinson(3) 2 — 58+
(W M Brisbourne) *hld up: sn in midfield: hdwy whn nt clr run and swtchd rt over 1f out: str run ins fnl f: jst failed* **6/1^{3}**

0-03 **3** *1 1/2* **Reveur**^{13} 3037 5-8-5 51 oh5 KMay 12 — 54
(M Mullineaux) *stmbld s: racd keenly chsng ldrs: rdn over 1f out: wnt 2nd briefly ins fnl f but no imp on wnr: nt qckn* **20/1**

1541 **4** *nk* **Mountain Pass (USA)**^{16} 2930 6-9-2 62 (p) KylieManser 14 — 65+
(B J Llewellyn) *rrd s and missed break: hld up: nt clr run over 1f out tl hdwy and swtchd lft ent fnl f: r.o wl towards fin: nrst fin* **14/1**

500- **5** *1/2* **Derricks Dotty**^{250} 6361 4-8-11 60 SimonPearce(3) 7 — 61
(N J Vaughan) *hld up in midfield: hdwy whn nt clr run over 1f out: one pce ins fnl f* **16/1**

3006 **6** *nse* **Tanforan**^{4} 3329 6-8-9 58 BillyCray(3) 6 — 59+
(B P J Baugh) *in tch: n.m.r and hmpd over 6f out: sn lost pl: towards rr: hdwy over 1f out: styd on ins fnl f* **8/1**

0302 **7** *nse* **Ensign's Trick**^{7} 3201 4-8-8 54 JackDean 5 — 55
(W M Brisbourne) *midfield: effrt whn n.m.r and bmpd over 1f out: styd on ins fnl f: nt pce to chal ldrs* **8/1**

0200 **8** *3 1/4* **Sands Of Barra (IRE)**^{16} 2925 5-9-7 67 DonnaCaldwell 9 — 60
(I W McInnes) *chsd ldrs: pushed along 2f out: losing pl whn bmpd over 1f out: n.d after* **12/1**

0100 **9** *1* **Komreyev Star**^{17} 2904 6-8-12 58 JPHamblett 16 — 48
(R E Peacock) *prom: led 2f out: rdn and hdd over 1f out: wknd ins fnl f* **22/1**

60-5 **10** *1* **Smart Pick**^{9} 3130 5-8-5 51 oh6 RobbieEgan 1 — 39
(Mrs L Williamson) *s.i.s: in rr: rdn 2f out: kpt on wout troubling ldrs ins fnl f* **25/1**

6-00 **11** *1 1/2* **Mangano**^{11} 3082 4-8-3 54 ow2 KrishGundowry(5) 13 — 38
(A Berry) *hld up towards rr: hdwy on outside 3f out: wknd wl over 1f out* **40/1**

234- **12** *3/4* **Beck**^{181} 7275 4-8-3 52 AshleyMorgan(3) 4 — 34
(W M Brisbourne) *racd keenly: hld up: rdn wl over 1f out: no imp* **12/1**

0660 **13** *1* **Mister Benji**^{63} 1602 9-8-2 51 oh5 (p) SoniaEaton(3) 11 — 31
(B P J Baugh) *led: rdn and hdd 2f out: wknd over 1f out* **40/1**

0031 **14** *18* **Wahoo Sam (USA)**^{2} 3360 8-9-8 68 6ex RichardEvans 3 — 3
(P D Evans) *rdr late to remove blindfold: missed break and swvd bdly rt s: hdwy on wd outside to chse ldrs 6f out: rdn and wknd 3f out* **7/2^{1}**

1m 36.22s (2.42) **Going Correction** +0.25s/f (Good) **14 Ran SP% 121.2**
Speed ratings (Par 103): **97,96,95,95,94 94,94,91,90,89 87,86,85,67**
toteswinger: 1&2 £7.80, 1&3 £56.30, 2&3 £114.20. CSF £32.93 CT £574.19 TOTE £5.50: £2.20, £3.20, £10.70; EX 56.60.

Owner R. H. I. Ltd **Bred** Gainsborough Stud Management Ltd **Trained** Duns, Scottish Borders

■ Stewards' Enquiry : Kylie Manser three-day ban: careless riding (Jul 12-14)
Lance Betts three-day ban: careless riding (Jul 12-14)

FOCUS
A modest handicap but a messy and rough race, with the favourite losing all chance at the start and numerous cases of scrimmaging throughout. The form is limited but the proximity of the placed horses, who were both racing from out of the handicap.

Wahoo Sam(USA) Official explanation: jockey said gelding missed the break

3432 ARNOLD CLARK RENAULT MAIDEN AUCTION FILLIES' STKS — 7f 2y
7:15 (7:17) (Class 5) 2-Y-0 £3,561 (£1,059; £529; £264) Stalls Low

Form / RPR

5 **1** **Cornish Rose (IRE)**^{42} 2160 2-7-12 0 AshleyMorgan(7) 3 — 69+
(M H Tompkins) *trckd ldrs: nt clr run over 1f out: sn swtchd lft: qcknd to ld ins fnl f: edgd rt whn running on and in command towards fin* **4/6^{1}**

3 **2** *1 1/2* **Musical Maze**^{14} 3008 2-8-1 0 DuranFentiman(3) 4 — 63
(W M Brisbourne) *pressed ldr: pushed along 3f out: stl ev ch and chalng ent fnl f: nt qckn fnl 75yds* **11/2^{3}**

0 **3** *1* **Lady Salama**^{27} 2627 2-8-9 0 AndrewElliott 2 — 66
(K R Burke) *racd keenly: led: rdn and hdd ins fnl f: no ex towards fin* **9/2^{2}**

0 **4** *4* **Lunar Romance**^{55} 1813 2-7-12 0 RossAtkinson(7) 6 — 52
(T J Pitt) *hld up bhd ldrs: effrt on outside 2f out: lugged lft and outpcd by ldrs ins fnl f* **16/1**

5 *9* **Our Apolonia (IRE)** 2-7-13 0 DanielleMcCreery(5) 7 — 28
(A Berry) *missed break: a outpcd and bhd* **28/1**

1m 30.6s (4.10) **Going Correction** +0.25s/f (Good) **5 Ran SP% 114.6**
Speed ratings (Par 90): **86,84,83,78,68**
toteswinger: 1&2 £2.70. CSF £3.94 TOTE £1.40: £1.10, £1.70; EX 3.70.

Owner M Winter **Bred** D And Mrs D Veitch **Trained** Newmarket, Suffolk

FOCUS
A moderate maiden for the course, in terms of quality and quantity and both placed horses had shaped with promise.

NOTEBOOK
Cornish Rose(IRE)'s debut form read better than anything else coming into the race, and she was accordingly backed into odds-on favouritism. Denied room early in the straight, she eventually quickened up to win quite decisively, but she is no world beater. (op Evens)

Musical Maze started off in a far-above average selling race at York where she shaped with a deal of promise, and built on it to give the favourite quite a fright, only giving second-best at the very death. She should find a little race or two before the year is out. (op 7-1 tchd 15-2)

Lady Salama raced a bit too freely to see out the extra furlong but built on the form of her debut effort at York all the same. (op 4-1 tchd 5-1)

Lunar Romance didn't improve a great deal on her last place finish in a better race on debut. (tchd 12-1)

Our Apolonia(IRE) Official explanation: jockey said filly missed the break

3433 RENAULT LIVERPOOL E B F FILLIES' H'CAP — 1m 2f 75y
7:45 (7:46) (Class 3) (0-95,84) 3-Y-0+ £10,037 (£2,986; £1,492; £745) Stalls High

Form / RPR

55-1 **1** **Algarade**^{8} 3163 4-9-9 79 6ex SebSanders 4 — 94+
(Sir Mark Prescott) *hld up: hdwy 2f out: r.o to ld ent fnl f: pushed out and in command after* **4/1^{2}**

-056 **2** *2* **Prelude**^{17} 2908 7-8-10 66 oh1 TGMcLaughlin 7 — 73
(W M Brisbourne) *led: rdn over 1f out: hdd ent fnl f: nt pce of wnr after* **25/1**

-113 **3** *hd* **Storyland (USA)**^{17} 2920 3-8-8 76 KerrinMcEvoy 3 — 83
(W J Haggas) *hld up: hdwy on outside wl over 1f out: styd on ins fnl f:* **7/4^{1}**

2-05 **4** *1/2* **Free Offer**^{13} 3046 4-9-9 84 AshleyHamblett(5) 5 — 90+
(J L Dunlop) *sn stdd in rr and racd keenly: rdn and hdwy over 1f out: styd on ins fnl f: one pce and no further prog towards fin* **4/1^{2}**

01 **5** *1 1/4* **Calakanga**^{14} 2989 3-8-12 80 RichardMullen 6 — 83
(C E Brittain) *chsd ldrs: pushed along over 2f out: one pce ins fnl f* **8/1**

3342 **6** *1 1/4* **Princess Cocoa (IRE)**^{3} 3337 5-8-7 71 BMcHugh(7) 1 — 72
(R A Fahey) *chsd ldrs: wnt 2nd 2f out tl rdn over 1f out: wknd ins fnl f* **8/1**

0-03 **7** *5* **Casa Catalina (IRE)**^{13} 3048 3-8-13 81 EddieAhern 2 — 72
(M Johnston) *chsd ldr tl rdn 2f out: wkng whn n.m.r over 1f out* **7/1^{3}**

2m 13.83s (1.63) **Going Correction** +0.25s/f (Good)
WFA 3 from 4yo+ 12lb **7 Ran SP% 114.9**
Speed ratings (Par 104): **103,101,101,100,99 98,94**
toteswinger: 1&2 £56.40, 1&3 £2.40, 2&3 £10.00. CSF £86.42 TOTE £4.60: £2.80, £4.70; EX 166.70.

Owner Miss K Rausing **Bred** Miss K Rausing And Mrs S M Rogers **Trained** Newmarket, Suffolk

FOCUS
A disappointing turnout for a handicap with a theoretical top-weight ceiling of 95 but in reality a horse rated 84 shouldered the highest burden. Still, the winner looks a progressive sort andn the runner-up is rated back to his best.

NOTEBOOK
Algarade had only made her reappearance eight days ago when she was a comfortable scorer at Great Leighs, and she only had to be pushed out to defy a 6lb penalty. She is a likely sort to remain one step ahead of the Handicapper. (op 5-2 tchd 9-2)

Prelude looked at the mercy of some far less-exposed rivals on paper but she loves it round here and again put up an honourable display from the front, over a trip short of her best. (op 20-1 tchd 14-1)

Storyland(USA) didn't pick up as well as she might have done. The race as it was run obviously wasn't unsuited to hold-up performers - the winner came from a similar position - and the Handicapper might just have her measure for now. (op 11-4 tchd 3-1)

Free Offer raced freely enough in the first half of the race considering the welter burden she was asked to hump, and it is to her credit that she ran on to the line. A return to winning ways might not be too far away. (tchd 9-2)

Calakanga pulled off something of a shock when winning a maiden at Chepstow and for all that she was very strongly supported in the market beforehand, is going to find her handicap mark tough to overcome on this evidence. (op 25-1)

3434 RENAULT MANCHESTER CLAIMING STKS — 6f 18y
8:15 (8:15) (Class 5) 3-Y-0 £3,238 (£963; £481) Stalls Low

Form / RPR

045 **1** **Beat The Bell**^{6} 3282 3-9-7 0 FrancisNorton 4 — 72
(A Bailey) *last to break: hdwy to ld after 1f: mde rest: rdn clr ent fnl f: eased towards fin* **13/8^{2}**

0036 **2** *7* **Andrasta**^{7} 3217 3-7-13 54 DanielleMcCreery(5) 3 — 33
(A Berry) *racd keenly: dropped to rr after 1f: swtchd rt over 1f out: kpt on u.p to take 2nd 100yds out: no ch w wnr* **10/3^{3}**

6-32 **3** *1 3/4* **Fast Feet**^{21} 2771 3-9-2 70 (p) PaulMulrennan 1 — 39
(K A Ryan) *led for 1f: racd in 2nd pl: pushed along over 2f out: outpcd by wnr over 1f out: wknd ins fnl f and lost 2nd 100yds out* **11/10^{1}**

1m 15.5s (1.70) **Going Correction** +0.25s/f (Good) **3 Ran SP% 108.8**
Speed ratings (Par 99): **98,88,86**
CSF £6.27 TOTE £2.50; EX 7.40.

Owner D J P Turner **Bred** D J P Turner **Trained** Newmarket, Suffolk

FOCUS
A singularly uninspiring contest and the form, with the favourite flopping, is dubious.

3435 LOOKERS GROUP RENAULT H'CAP — 7f 2y
8:50 (8:50) (Class 4) (0-85,83) 4-Y-0+ £5,180 (£1,541; £770; £384) Stalls Low

Form / RPR

0-14 **1** **Barons Spy (IRE)**^{13} 3040 7-9-8 82 SebSanders 3 — 94
(R J Price) *hld up: hdwy over 2f out: led over 1f out: pushed out and in command ins fnl f* **9/4^{1}**

4500 **2** *2 1/4* **The Kiddykid (IRE)**^{17} 2905 8-9-9 83 TGMcLaughlin 7 — 89
(P D Evans) *trckd ldrs: led wl over 1f out: sn rdn and hdd: edgd rt whn nt pce of wnr towards fin* **9/2^{2}**

-001 **3** *1 1/4* **No Grouse**^{9} 3129 8-8-4 64 6ex oh5 FrancisNorton 6 — 67
(E J Alston) *bhd: hdwy and swtchd lft over 1f out: styd on to chse ldrs: one pce fnl 100yds* **13/2**

230 **4** *4 1/2* **Methaaly (IRE)**^{51} 1917 5-8-9 69 RichardMullen 5 — 59
(M Mullineaux) *towards rr: hdwy on outside to chse ldrs over 2f out: edgd lft and wknd 1f out* **10/1**

5265 **5** *2 1/2* **Prince Namid**^{10} 3111 6-9-0 74 AndrewElliott 2 — 58
(Mrs A Duffield) *led: hdd 3f out: rdn 2f out: wknd over 1f out* **11/2^{3}**

205U **6** *1 1/4* **Red Romeo**^{7} 3203 7-9-0 74 PaulMulrennan 4 — 54
(N Wilson) *chsd ldrs: nt clr run under 3f out: n.m.r and shuffled bk over 2f out: n.d after* **7/1**

4266 **7** *3 1/4* **H Harrison (IRE)**^{7} 3203 8-8-10 77 BMcHugh(7) 8 — 49
(I W McInnes) *prom: led 3f out: rdn and hdd wl over 1f out: sn wknd* **9/2^{2}**

1m 27.98s (1.48) **Going Correction** +0.25s/f (Good) **7 Ran SP% 117.4**
Speed ratings (Par 105): **101,98,97,91,89 87,83**
toteswinger: 1&2 £2.40, 1&3 £2.40, 2&3 £4.40. CSF £13.17 CT £57.69 TOTE £2.60: £1.90, £2.90; EX 11.00.

Owner Barry Veasey **Bred** Tally-Ho Stud **Trained** Ullingswick, H'fords

FOCUS
Not many came into this heat in much form, winner excepted, and he proved himself in grand heart by running out a ready winner. The solid runner-up sets the level.

Red Romeo Official explanation: jockey said gelding was denied a clear run

3436 SUNWIN BRADFORD RENAULT H'CAP 1m 2f 75y
9:20 (9:20) (Class 5) (0-70,69) 3-Y-O **£3,561** (£1,059; £529; £264) **Stalls** High

Form				RPR
4240	1		**Highland Love**[21] 2785 3-9-2 **62** PaulMulrennan 2 (Jedd O'Keeffe) *pressed ldr: hung rt fr 5f out: strly rdn fr over 2f out: led over 1f out: kpt up to work thrght fnl f* **7/1**	67
3502	2	¾	**Natural Rhythm (IRE)**[9] 3126 3-8-4 **50** (b) AndrewElliott 1 (Mrs R A Carr) *racd keenly: led: rdn 2f out: hdd over 1f out: kpt on u.p and continued to chal thrght fnl f: hld towards fin* **14/1**	54
40-0	3	½	**Bigalo's Magic (UAE)**[21] 2785 3-9-4 **64** FrancisNorton 3 (E J O'Neill) *trckd ldrs: rdn 2f out: edgd rt fr over 1f out: styd on ins fnl f: nt quite pce of front pair* **7/2**[2]	67
-302	4	1 ¾	**Locum**[21] 2801 3-9-7 **67** SebSanders 9 (M H Tompkins) *hld up: rdn over 2f out: hdwy over 1f out: kpt on ins fnl f wout landing blow* **7/2**[2]	66
0151	5	1 ½	**Sabre Light**[10] 3115 3-8-11 **64** 6ex (p) BMcHugh(7) 6 (A Bailey) *midfield: effrt and hdwy to chse ldrs 2f out: no ex ins fnl f* **11/2**[3]	60
-002	6	½	**The Last Bottle (IRE)**[21] 2805 3-9-6 **66** TGMcLaughlin 5 (W M Brisbourne) *racd keenly: trckd ldrs: rdn 3f out: wknd over 1f out* **8/1**	61
4001	7	1 ¼	**Always Certain (USA)**[17] 2907 3-9-9 **69** EddieAhern 4 (M Johnston) *hld up: rdn over 4f out: no imp* **11/4**[1]	62
-600	8	nse	**Madame Rio (IRE)**[56] 1777 3-7-13 **50** oh5 DanielleMcCreery(5) 7 (M Mullineaux) *s.i.s: racd keenly: hld up: effrt 3f out: no imp on ldrs: wknd wl over 1f out* **40/1**	42

2m 13.9s (1.70) **Going Correction** +0.25s/f (Good) **8 Ran SP% 119.2**
Speed ratings (Par 99): **103,102,102,100,99 99,98,97**
toteswinger: 1&2 £26.40, 1&3 £19.10, 2&3 £23.90. CSF £100.40 CT £405.02 TOTE £9.60: £2.40, £3.70, £1.60; EX 120.90 Place 6 £175.60, Place 5 £68.46.
Owner Ken And Delia Shaw-KGS Consulting LLP **Bred** Farmers Hill Stud **Trained** Middleham Moor, N Yorks

FOCUS
Modest types on show in this handicap for three-year-olds and very few got into the race, the first two occupying the same postions throughout. Not a race to be with.
T/Plt: £688.20 to a £1 stake. Pool: £61,662.72. 65.40 winning tickets. T/Qpdt: £202.00 to a £1 stake. Pool: £3,331.30. 12.20 winning tickets. DO

3054 DONCASTER (L-H)
Friday, June 27

OFFICIAL GOING: Good (8.1)
10mm overnight rain resulted in ground 'just on the quick side but with an excellent covering of grass' with the running rail on the round course in place.
Wind: fresh half against Weather: fine and sunny, showers races 2 and 3

3437 EBF SOCIETY LIFESTYLE AND LEISURE MAGAZINE MAIDEN FILLIES' STKS 6f
2:20 (2:22) (Class 5) 2-Y-O **£3,561** (£1,059; £529; £264) **Stalls** High

Form				RPR
	1		**Faraway Flower (USA)** 2-9-0 0 MichaelHills 2 (B W Hills) *dwlt: hdwy on outer over 2f out: led over 1f out: r.o wl* **9/4**[2]	87+
	2	2 ½	**Moonlight Affair (IRE)** 2-9-0 0 GrahamGibbons 6 (E S McMahon) *chsd ldrs: styd on to take 2nd ins fnl f: no ch w wnr* **25/1**	74
6	3	2 ½	**Exceedingly Good (IRE)**[13] 3027 2-9-0 0 TomEaves 5 (B Smart) *hld up in rr: nt clr run 2f out: swtchd lft: styd on to take 3rd ins fnl f* **17/2**	66
60	4	3 ½	**Adozen Dreams**[14] 3005 2-8-9 0 SladeO'Hara(5) 1 (G R Oldroyd) *w ldrs: wknd fnl f* **50/1**	56
	5	1 ½	**Dream In Waiting** 2-9-0 0 SebSanders 9 (P F I Cole) *w ldr: hmpd and lost pl over 3f out: bmpd over 1f out: kpt on towards fin* **7/2**[3]	57+
3	6	¾	**Peter's Gift (IRE)**[20] 2821 2-9-0 0 NCallan 4 (K A Ryan) *trckd ldrs: led over 3f out tl over 1f out: edgd rt and sn wknd* **7/4**[1]	49
0	7	1 ½	**Claphands**[20] 2821 2-9-0 0 JamesDoyle 7 (A J McCabe) *led: dived rt and hdd over 3f out: wkng whn hmpd over 1f out* **11/1**	44

1m 15.11s (1.51) **Going Correction** +0.225s/f (Good) **7 Ran SP% 114.0**
Speed ratings (Par 90): **98,94,91,86,84 83,81**
toteswinger: 1&2 £10.20, 1&3 £4.10, 2&3 £10.20. CSF £50.99 TOTE £3.20: £1.80, £5.20; EX 66.50 Trifecta £343.00 Part won. Pool: £463.59. 0.50 winning units..
Owner K Abdulla **Bred** Juddmonte Farms Inc **Trained** Lambourn, Berks
■ Stewards' Enquiry : N CallanA two-day ban: careless riding (Jul 12-13)

FOCUS
Probably a very average maiden fillies' race in which only two had run before but the winner has real potential.

NOTEBOOK
Faraway Flower(USA) ◆, whose dam is a sister to Xaar, is quite a big filly. After missing a beat at the start she came there full of running and made this look very simple. She looks a good prospect. (op 2-1 tchd 5-2)
Moonlight Affair(IRE), a neat newcomer, finished clear second best and can surely be placed to advantage at a modest level. (op 33-1)
Exceedingly Good(IRE), who had two handlers including her trainer in the paddock, found herself shut in on the inner. She had to wait for an opening and did just enough in the end to secure third spot. (op 14-1 tchd 16-1)
Adozen Dreams, having her third start, showed plenty of toe and a 5f nursery looks a better option. (op 40-1)
Dream In Waiting, out of Sun Chariot Stakes winner, is a good-quartered filly. She had a most unhappy debut meeting serious interference twice. To her credit she was coming back for more at the line. (op 3-1 tchd 4-1)
Peter's Gift(IRE), who took the eye beforehand, was disappointing coming off a straight line and dropping right away. (op 2-1 tchd 6-4)

3438 ROYAL BRITISH LEGION NATIONAL VETERANS DAY MAIDEN STKS 6f
2:50 (2:51) (Class 5) 3-Y-O+ **£3,238** (£963; £481; £240) **Stalls** High

Form				RPR
62/	1		**Amicus Meus (IRE)**[608] 6207 4-9-7 0 DominicFox(3) 3 (A Bailey) *restless in stalls: in rr on outer: hdwy over 2f out: sddle slipped: edgd rt and styd on to ld ins fnl f* **25/1**	70+
60	2	1 ¼	**Virtuality (USA)**[48] 2008 3-8-12 0 TomEaves 8 (B Smart) *trckd ldrs: hrd rdn over 1f out: sltly hmpd and swtchd lft wl ins fnl f: kpt on* **28/1**	60+
50-2	3	hd	**Silvanus (IRE)**[15] 2981 3-9-3 79 EddieAhern 9 (W J Haggas) *trckd ldr: upsides 1f out: sn rdn and no ex* **2/5**[1]	63
00	4	shd	**Braille**[6] 3282 3-9-3 0 GrahamGibbons 2 (T D Walford) *led tl hdd ins fnl f: eased fnl strides and lost 3rd pl* **66/1**	63
4-	5	½	**Royal Encore**[293] 5231 4-9-5 0 OscarUrbina 4 (J R Fanshawe) *hld up towards rr: hdwy over 2f out: swtchd lft ins fnl f: hmpd nr fin* **10/1**[3]	58+
5	6	¾	**Tump Mac**[17] 2912 4-9-7 0 MarkLawson(3) 7 (N Bycroft) *outpcd and in rr: styd on fnl 2f: nt rch ldrs* **40/1**	61
30	7	3 ½	**Hardanger (IRE)**[15] 2966 3-9-0 0 JamieMoriarty(3) 6 (T J Fitzgerald) *t.k.h in rr: nvr nr ldrs* **25/1**	48+
0-	8	¾	**Tendulkar's Diva (IRE)**[252] 6306 3-8-7 0 DanielleMcCreery(5) 10 (A Berry) *s.i.s: short lived effrt and swtchd lft over 1f out: sn wknd* **100/1**	40
3000	9	3 ½	**Mollyatti**[32] 2452 3-8-12 59 SteveDrowne 5 (Miss V Haigh) *mid-div: effrt over 2f out: sn wknd* **50/1**	29
-036	10	¾	**Rowaad**[17] 2918 3-9-3 70 RHills 1 (M P Tregoning) *chsd ldrs on outer: lost pl over 1f out* **4/1**[2]	32

1m 14.97s (1.37) **Going Correction** +0.225s/f (Good)
WFA 3 from 4yo 7lb **10 Ran SP% 118.5**
Speed ratings (Par 103): **99,97,97,96,96 95,90,89,84,83**
toteswinger: 1&2 £20.60, 1&3 £4.90, 2&3 £7.00. CSF £509.75 TOTE £31.20: £4.30, £6.40, £1.02; EX 488.80 Trifecta £569.00 Part won. Pool: £768.99. 0.40 winning units..
Owner North Cheshire Trading & Storage Ltd **Bred** John Egan **Trained** Newmarket, Suffolk
■ Stewards' Enquiry : Eddie Ahern caution: used whip down shoulder in forehand position.
Graham Gibbons 21-day ban (takes into acocunt previous offences): failed to ride out for third place (Jul 11-31)

FOCUS
A weak maiden with little to choose between the first six at the line. The winner is well regarded but the third did not run anywhere near his official 79-rating.

3439 GREAT BRITISH GOLF SHOW DONCASTER 2008 NOVICE STKS 7f
3:25 (3:26) (Class 3) 2-Y-O **£6,476** (£1,927; £963; £481) **Stalls** High

Form				RPR
1	1		**Wildcat Wizard (USA)**[13] 3049 2-9-5 0 JoeFanning 2 (P F I Cole) *t.k.h: trckd ldrs on outer: edgd rt and led over 1f out: narrowly hdd wl ins fnl f: led post* **6/4**[1]	87
1	2	nse	**Prime Spirit (IRE)**[42] 2154 2-9-5 0 TomEaves 4 (B Smart) *t.k.h: hdwy and swtchd lft over 2f out: hrd rdn edgd rt and tk slt advantage 50yds out: hdd post* **5/2**[2]	87
031	3	5	**Motor Home**[10] 3107 2-9-2 0 WilliamBuick 5 (A M Balding) *led: hdd and sltly hmpd over 1f out: one pce* **11/4**[3]	71
1	4	¾	**Mister Green (FR)**[30] 2502 2-9-2 0 FergalLynch 1 (M J Wallace) *swvd lft s: sn trcking ldrs: n.m.r over 1f out: kpt on same pce* **7/1**	70
41	5	1 ½	**Calley Ho**[22] 2746 2-9-0 0 TonyHamilton 6 (Mrs L Stubbs) *trckd ldrs: effrt 3f out: outpcd over 1f out* **16/1**	64

1m 29.23s (2.93) **Going Correction** +0.225s/f (Good) **5 Ran SP% 113.6**
Speed ratings (Par 97): **92,91,86,85,83**
CSF £5.80 TOTE £2.30: £1.40, £1.90; EX 6.70.
Owner A D Spence **Bred** Gulf Coast Farms LLC **Trained** Whatcombe, Oxon
■ Stewards' Enquiry : Joe Fanning one-day ban: careless riding (Jul 12)

FOCUS
A very steady pace but in the end the first two came right away and they look well above average, with the form solid and possibly worth a little more.

NOTEBOOK
Wildcat Wizard(USA), who has plenty of size and scope, ran with the choke out on the outside. He came across to the stands'-side rail once in front and grabbed the prize out of the fire in the very last stride. (tchd 15-8)
Prime Spirit(IRE), who pipped a subsequent runaway winner on his debut at Newcastle, really took the eye in the paddock. He didn't settle but dug deep to take a narrow advantage well inside the last only to miss out by a pixel on the line. He will be suited by a stronger gallop and is well worth a try at Listed level. (op 4-1)
Motor Home, on a round track this time, took them along but his chance had slipped when the winner went across his bows. (op 9-4)
Mister Green(FR), drawn one, had nothing on his outside and went left leaving the stalls. His chance was fast slipping when tightened up and 6f seems to suit him better. (tchd 6-1)
Calley Ho, really only third-best when opening his account on his second start at Hamilton, found this task beyond him at this stage. (tchd 18-1)

3440 SECURITAS SECURITY SERVICES H'CAP 1m 4f
4:00 (4:03) (Class 4) (0-85,87) 4-Y-O+ **£4,857** (£1,445; £722; £360) **Stalls** Low

Form				RPR
3112	1		**Sir Duke (IRE)**[20] 2839 4-9-2 **78** EddieAhern 7 (P W D'Arcy) *trckd ldrs: led over 1f out: hld on wl* **15/8**[1]	85+
-006	2	¾	**New Beginning (IRE)**[14] 3007 4-9-2 **78** JimmyQuinn 3 (Mrs S Lamyman) *trckd ldrs: t.k.h: styd on to chal appr fnl f: no ex ins fnl f* **10/1**	84
0301	3	1	**Birkside**[6] 3253 5-9-11 **87** 6ex DavidAllan 6 (D Carroll) *hld up in mid-div: effrt over 2f out: chal appr fnl f: kpt on same pce* **11/4**[2]	91
6-06	4	2 ¼	**Stretton (IRE)**[14] 3010 10-8-5 **67** WilliamBuick 8 (J D Bethell) *hld up in mid-div: effrt on outer 4f out: one pce fnl 2f* **10/1**	68
3462	5	1 ¼	**Sporting Gesture**[14] 3010 11-8-9 **71** PaulMulrennan 2 (M W Easterby) *chsd ldrs: one pce appr fnl f* **15/2**[3]	70
-105	6	¾	**Robustian**[55] 1799 5-9-7 **83** FergalLynch 4 (George Baker) *hld up in midfield: hdwy on ins over 3f out: one pce fnl 2f* **14/1**	81
-210	7	4	**Maneki Neko (IRE)**[16] 2939 6-8-8 **70** TonyHamilton 1 (E W Tuer) *led: qcknd over 3f out: hdd over 1f out: sn wknd* **15/2**[3]	61
-255	8	35	**Shake On It**[21] 2790 4-9-7 **83** (t) StephenCarson 5 (Eve Johnson Houghton) *sed v slow: t.k.h in last: hrd rdn: effrt on outside over 2f out: sn wknd and eased: t.o* **8/1**	18

2m 35.17s (0.07) **Going Correction** +0.225s/f (Good) **8 Ran SP% 120.9**
Speed ratings (Par 105): **108,107,106,105,104 104,101,78**
toteswinger: 1&2 £5.80, 1&3 £1.90, 2&3 £7.10. CSF £23.60 CT £53.83 TOTE £2.60: £1.20, £3.10, £1.40; EX 27.50 Trifecta £120.10 Pool: £805.64. 4.96 winning units..
Owner Mrs Jan Harris **Bred** Southern Bloodstock **Trained** Newmarket, Suffolk
■ Stewards' Enquiry : Stephen Carson two-day ban: used whip with excessive force (Jul 12-13)

FOCUS
A fair handicap run at just a steady early pace but overall time was decent and the form has a very solid look about it.

Shake On It Official explanation: trainer had no explanation for the poor form shown

3441 WAKEFIELD HOSPICE H'CAP — 6f
4:35 (4:35) (Class 5) (0-70,70) 3-Y-O — **£3,238** (£963; £481; £240) **Stalls** High

Form — RPR

0654 **1** **Averoo**[13] 3030 3-8-9 **58**....(p) JimmyQuinn 7 — 71
(M D Squance) *hld up in rr: hdwy: nt clr run and swtchd lft over 1f out: str run to ld ins fnl f: rdn clr* **11/4**[2]

5-02 **2** *2 3/4* **Pretty Bonnie**[11] 3086 3-7-11 **51** oh1.... NataliaGemelova(5) 10 — 55
(A E Price) *chsd ldr: led over 4f out: hdd and no ex ins fnl f* **8/1**

-035 **3** *2 1/4* **Embra (IRE)**[20] 2850 3-8-7 **59**.... PJMcDonald(3) 2 — 56
(T J Etherington) *chsd ldrs: hmpd and edgd rt over 1f out: kpt on same pce* **8/1**

0003 **4** *nse* **Thomas Malory (IRE)**[7] 3217 3-8-5 **54**.... WilliamBuick 4 — 51
(Miss V Haigh) *mid-div: effrt on outer over 2f out: kpt on same pce fnl f* **5/1**[3]

0-00 **5** *hd* **Writingonthewall (IRE)**[42] 2161 3-9-7 **70**.... EddieAhern 5 — 66
(M L W Bell) *hld up in rr: smooth hdwy over 2f out: rdn over 1f out: kpt on same pce* **5/2**[1]

5305 **6** *1 1/4* **Miss Sunshine**[7] 3217 3-8-2 **51** oh3.... NickyMackay 8 — 46+
(J S Goldie) *in tch: nt clr run: swtchd lft and hmpd over 1f out: nt rcvr* **25/1**

0020 **7** *3 3/4* **Helping Hand (IRE)**[28] 2570 3-9-4 **67**.... TPO'Shea 3 — 47
(R Hollinshead) *chsd ldrs: wkng whn sltly hmpd over 1f out* **16/1**

-300 **8** *4* **Saranome (IRE)**[14] 2991 3-9-4 **67**....(b[1]) SteveDrowne 1 — 34
(R Charlton) *swvd lft s: hdwy on outer to join ldr 4f out: wkng whn sltly hmpd over 1f out* **18/1**

0-66 **9** *2 1/4* **Oxbridge**[16] 2935 3-8-9 **58**.... RoystonFfrench 6 — 18
(J M Bradley) *chsd ldrs: drvn 3f out: sn lost pl* **18/1**

-040 **10** *3 1/4* **Solemn**[14] 2991 3-8-13 **62**.... PaulMulrennan 9 — 12
(J M Bradley) *led over 1f: lost pl over 2f out* **25/1**

1m 14.99s (1.39) **Going Correction** +0.225s/f (Good) — **10** Ran SP% **118.2**
Speed ratings (Par 99): **99,95,92,92,92 90,85,80,77,72**
toteswinger: 1&2 £5.40, 1&3 £4.71, 2&3 £8.60. CSF £25.74 CT £159.90 TOTE £4.60: £1.50, £2.80, £2.50; EX 29.70 Trifecta £91.50 Pool: £383.53. 3.10 winning units..
Owner Troon Partnership **Bred** Mrs H Johnson Houghton & Mrs R F Johnson Hought **Trained** Newmarket, Suffolk
■ Stewards' Enquiry : Nicky Mackay two-day ban: careless riding (Jul 12,13)

FOCUS
A moderate handicap and a messy race rated through the placed horses but in the end the winner, despite an awkward head carriage, came right away.

3442 CROWNHOTEL-BAWTRY.COM H'CAP — 7f
5:05 (5:08) (Class 4) (0-80,80) 3-Y-O — **£4,857** (£1,445; £722; £360) **Stalls** High

Form — RPR

-551 **1** **Spirit Of A Nation (IRE)**[57] 1750 3-9-7 **80**.... WilliamBuick 2 — 91+
(S Parr) *hld up in rr: gd hdwy on outside to ld appr fnl f: edgd rt: r.o wl* **6/1**[2]

-425 **2** *1 3/4* **Astrodonna**[14] 3002 3-9-1 **74**.... JimmyQuinn 11 — 80+
(M H Tompkins) *hld up in rr: hdwy on ins whn nt clr run 2f: str run and chal jst ins fnl f: styd on same pce* **5/1**[1]

-432 **3** *2* **Flower**[17] 2922 3-8-6 **65**....(v) TPO'Shea 4 — 66
(W J Haggas) *t.k.h in mid-div on outer: hdwy over 2f out: hung rt and kpt on same pce fnl f* **5/1**[1]

1040 **4** *1 1/2* **Opus Maximus (IRE)**[13] 3050 3-9-3 **76**.... JoeFanning 5 — 73+
(M Johnston) *trckd ldrs: nt clr run and lost pl 2f out: kpt on wl fnl f* **6/1**[2]

6205 **5** *1/2* **Rossini's Dancer**[20] 2842 3-8-2 **61** oh2.... RoystonFfrench 6 — 56+
(R A Fahey) *hld up in rr: styd on wl fnl f: nrst fin* **16/1**

10-3 **6** *2 3/4* **Non Sucre (USA)**[22] 2761 3-9-4 **77**.... FergalLynch 9 — 65
(P A Blockley) *w ldrs: led 2f out: edgd lft and hdd appr fnl f: sn wknd* **8/1**[3]

6212 **7** *nk* **Admirals Way**[13] 3031 3-8-4 **63**.... NickyMackay 3 — 50
(C N Kellett) *chsd ldrs: n.m.r appr fnl f: kpt on same pce appr fnl f* **8/1**[3]

3355 **8** *1/2* **Asian Lady**[16] 2946 3-8-7 **66**.... SteveDrowne 7 — 52
(R Charlton) *hld up in mid-div: effrt over 2f out: nvr trbld ldrs* **8/1**[3]

410 **9** *hd* **Milton Of Campsie**[33] 2433 3-8-12 **71**.... LeeEnstone 10 — 66+
(S Parr) *hld up in rr: effrt 2f out: styng on on ins whn sltly hmpd ins fnl f* **17/2**

-560 **10** *nse* **Outside Edge (IRE)**[13] 3031 3-8-9 **68**....(v[1]) SaleemGolam 8 — 53
(W R Swinburn) *chsd ldrs: nt clr run ins fnl f* **25/1**

5030 **11** *hd* **Atheer Dubai (IRE)**[41] 2189 3-9-2 **75**.... J-PGuillambert 1 — 59
(C E Brittain) *led tl 2f out: wknd appr fnl f* **14/1**

1m 27.56s (1.26) **Going Correction** +0.225s/f (Good) — **11** Ran SP% **122.2**
Speed ratings (Par 101): **101,99,96,95,94 91,90,90,90,90 89**
toteswinger: 1&2 £7.80, 1&3 £7.30, 2&3 £4.60. CSF £37.63 CT £168.71 TOTE £7.60: £2.40, £1.90, £2.10; EX 53.50 Trifecta £96.60 Pool: £469.01. 3.59 winning units..
Owner Bezwell Fixings Limited **Bred** J P Hardiman **Trained** Bawtry, S Yorks
■ Stewards' Enquiry : Joe Fanning two-day ban: careless riding (Jul 13,14)
T P O'Shea two-day ban: careless riding (Jul 12,13)

FOCUS
A rough race and a bit messy but the fast-improving winner was definitely the best horse on the day and should progress further.

3443 BUSINESS YORKSHIRE EXHIBITION AND CONFERENCE H'CAP — 7f
5:35 (5:36) (Class 4) (0-85,77) 4-Y-O+ — **£4,857** (£1,445; £722; £360) **Stalls** High

Form — RPR

-053 **1** **Sadeek**[29] 2535 4-9-6 **76**.... RoystonFfrench 7 — 83
(B Smart) *in rr: sn drvn along: hdwy on outer over 2f out: led over 1f out: sddle slipped and rdr almost uns wl ins fnl f: hld on* **5/1**[3]

6345 **2** *hd* **Yorkshire Blue**[9] 3129 9-8-9 **65**.... NickyMackay 2 — 72
(J S Goldie) *sn detached in rr: gd hdwy on outside over 2f out: kpt on same pce ins fnl f* **8/1**

2244 **3** *nk* **Violent Velocity (IRE)**[10] 3108 5-8-8 **71**.... JamieKyne(7) 4 — 77+
(J J Quinn) *dwlt and swtchd rt after s: hdwy whn nt clr run over 2f out: nt clr run and swtchd ins over 1f out: r.o strly ins fnl f* **8/1**

0551 **4** *3* **Ezdeyaad (USA)**[7] 3229 4-9-6 **76** 6ex.... TPO'Shea 10 — 74+
(G A Swinbank) *trckd ldrs: chal over 1f out: edgd lft and kpt on same pce* **3/1**[1]

0006 **5** *3 1/2* **Neon Blue**[6] 3281 7-8-8 **64**.... J-PGuillambert 9 — 52
(R M Whitaker) *chsd ldrs: wknd over 1f out* **16/1**

0-05 **6** *1/2* **Viva Volta**[29] 2535 5-9-0 **73**....(b) JamieMoriarty(3) 6 — 60
(T D Easterby) *led tl over 1f out: sn wknd* **12/1**

0-00 **7** *hd* **Trimlestown (IRE)**[56] 1771 5-9-3 **73**....(p) FergalLynch 3 — 60
(K A Ryan) *chsd ldrs: one pce fnl 2f* **7/1**

-310 **8** *8* **Royal Storm (IRE)**[16] 2925 9-9-2 **77**.... JamesMillman(5) 8 — 42
(B R Millman) *trckd ldrs: lost pl over 1f out* **12/1**

0115 **9** *15* **My Learned Friend (IRE)**[13] 3040 4-9-7 **77**.... WilliamBuick 1 — 1
(A M Balding) *mid-div on outer: wknd over 2f out: sn bhd and eased* **7/2**[2]

-000 **10** *23* **Thabaat**[48] 2013 4-9-3 **73**.... SteveDrowne 5 — —
(J M Bradley) *chsd ldrs: lost pl over 2f out: sn bhd and eased: t.o* **33/1**

1m 27.79s (1.49) **Going Correction** +0.225s/f (Good) — **10** Ran SP% **122.8**
Speed ratings (Par 105): **100,99,99,96,92 91,91,82,64,38**
toteswinger: 1&2 £5.90, 1&3 £7.60, 2&3 £8.40. CSF £47.35 CT £329.84 TOTE £6.70: £2.00, £2.10, £2.40; EX 61.20 Trifecta £390.40 Part won. Pool: £527.68. 0.70 winning units. Place 6£29.05, Place 5 £7.44.
Owner Mrs Patricia Brown **Bred** T K & Mrs P A Knox **Trained** Hambleton, N Yorks

FOCUS
A fair handicap notable for a remarkable effort from Royston ffrench, who looked certain to hit the deck when the saddle on Sadeek slipped right round. They can give him the award for ride of the year at the Lesters now! The first three came from off the pace and there is a question over the reliability of this form.
Royal Storm(IRE) Official explanation: jockey said horse had no more to give
My Learned Friend(IRE) Official explanation: jockey said gelding ran flat
T/Plt: £53.60 to a £1 stake. Pool: £61,117.44. 831.27 winning tickets. T/Qpdt: £5.50 to a £1 stake. Pool: £4,097.06. 542.20 winning tickets. WG

2881 FOLKESTONE (R-H)
Friday, June 27

OFFICIAL GOING: Good to firm (good in places)
Wind: fresh across Weather: overcast

3444 EUROPEAN BREEDERS' FUND MEDIAN AUCTION MAIDEN STKS — 7f (S)
2:30 (2:30) (Class 6) 2-Y-O — **£2,817** (£838; £418; £209) **Stalls** Low

Form — RPR

2542 **1** **Rio Royale (IRE)**[19] 2859 2-9-3 0.... JimCrowley 1 — 78
(Mrs A J Perrett) *mde virtually all: rdn wl over 1f out: kpt on u.p: all out* **15/8**[1]

03 **2** *hd* **Zebrano**[22] 2754 2-9-3 0.... AlanMunro 13 — 78
(Miss E C Lavelle) *racd keenly: sn crossed over towards stands' rail and pressed wnr: ev ch and rdn wl over 1f out: unable qck fnl 100yds* **9/2**[2]

3 *hd* **Wilbury Star (IRE)** 2-9-3 0.... PatDobbs 4 — 77
(R Hannon) *hld up in midfield: shkn up and hdwy 1/2-way: chsd ldrs and swtchd rt jst ins fnl f: r.o wl and clsng towards fin* **12/1**[3]

054 **4** *7* **Blusher**[10] 3107 2-8-12 0.... CatherineGannon 7 — 55
(M R Channon) *chsd ldng pair: rdn and effrt 2f out: wknd qckly 1f out* **14/1**

5 *5* **Lahaleeb (IRE)** 2-8-12 0.... SamHitchcott 5 — 42
(M R Channon) *s.i.s: sn rdn along in rr: styd on past btn horses 2f out: swtchd rt 1f out: n.d* **16/1**

0 **6** *nk* **Cashed Up**[21] 2796 2-9-3 0.... LiamJones 8 — 46
(P Winkworth) *t.k.h: in tch: rdn 1/2-way: wknd 2f out: sn wl btn* **66/1**

00 **7** *2* **Paymaster In Chief**[16] 2944 2-9-3 0.... RichardSmith 2 — 44+
(M D I Usher) *sn rdn along in rr: lost tch 1/2-way: nvr nr ldrs* **100/1**

354 **8** *6* **Desire To Excel (IRE)**[32] 2458 2-9-3 0.... TQuinn 11 — 26
(P F I Cole) *chsd ldrs: rdn and hanging lft 1/2-way: wknd rapidly 2f out: eased ins fnl f* **9/2**[2]

4 **9** *3* **Temperence Hall (USA)**[22] 2754 2-9-3 0.... LPKeniry 10 — 19
(J R Best) *stdd s and dropped in bhd: lost tch and no ch fr 1/2-way* **9/2**[2]

10 *2 3/4* **Starlight Wish** 2-9-3 0.... FergusSweeney 3 — 12
(E F Vaughan) *t.k.h: hld up in midfield: rdn and struggling 1/2-way: no ch fnl 2f* **16/1**

0 **11** *13* **Indian Fiesta (IRE)**[27] 2592 2-9-3 0.... RichardKingscote 6 — —
(B G Powell) *sn rdn and struggling: lost tch 1/2-way: t.o and eased fnl f* **33/1**

000 **12** *6* **Ba Globetrotter**[9] 3140 2-9-3 0.... ChrisCatlin 9 — —
(M R Channon) *sn rdn along in rr: lost tch 1/2-way: t.o and eased fnl f* **33/1**

1m 26.13s (-1.17) **Going Correction** -0.375s/f (Firm) — **12** Ran SP% **123.8**
Speed ratings (Par 91): **91,90,90,82,76 76,74,67,63,60 45,39**
toteswinger: 1&2 £3.00, 1&3 £8.70, 2&3 £13.80. CSF £10.49 TOTE £2.70: £1.10, £2.00, £4.80; EX 10.90.
Owner Mrs Amanda Perrett **Bred** Glending Bloodstock **Trained** Pulborough, W Sussex

FOCUS
A modest juvenile As usual here on the straight course, the rail was the place to be.

NOTEBOOK
Rio Royale(IRE), who held obvious claims on form, had the huge advantage of the stands' side rail and he looked ready for this first try at 7f. Soon on the pace, he was strongly pressed from two out, but kept finding and just managed to hold on. He is only modest, but consistent enough and should pay his way in nurseries. (op 2-1 tchd 9-4 and 7-4)
Zebrano, who briefly had his field on the stretch when finishing third at Lingfield last time, again showed plenty of speed from a disadvantageous draw, albeit probably racing a little too freely. That did not stop him running a blinder though, finding plenty for pressure and just getting run out of it. He is now qualified for a handicap mark and should find a race at some stage. (op 13-2 tchd 7-1)
Wilbury Star(IRE), whose yard took this last year, had a decent draw and looked a big threat when switched wide with his challenge, but the line came too soon. He cost 25,000gns and a small race looks set to come his way on this evidence. (op 11-1)
Blusher, having her fourth start, ran well to a point, but weakened late on and again gave the impression this 7f stretches her stamina at the moment.
Lahaleeb(IRE), a 70,000gns daughter of Redback, was green following a slow start and only really got going in the final quarter mile. This was not a strong race and she was well held, but can improve. (tchd 14-1)
Desire To Excel(IRE) has not progressed and this was a most disconcerting effort, the horse hanging and stopping as if shot. One to avoid. Official explanation: jockey said colt hung left (op 4-1)
Temperence Hall(USA) comes from a yard enjoying a tremendous spell at present, but he went the wrong way from his promising debut effort and may now be more of a nursery type. (op 13-2 tchd 7-1)

3445 REDEC REFURBISHMENT MEDIAN AUCTION MAIDEN STKS — 7f (S)
3:05 (3:06) (Class 6) 3-5-Y-O — **£2,388** (£705; £352) **Stalls** Low

Form — RPR

2224 **1** **Autumn Blades (IRE)**[48] 1995 3-9-0 72....(b[1]) TQuinn 7 — 49+
(J W Hills) *stdd s: t.k.h: hld up in tch: n.m.r and swtchd lft over 1f out: upsides ldr on bit 1f out: nudged ahd fnl strides* **2/7**[1]

0-0 **2** *shd* **Station Place**[139] 500 3-8-2 0.... PNolan(7) 2 — 44
(A B Haynes) *led: rdn over 1f out: jnd 1f out: hdd fnl strides* **66/1**

0 **3** *4 1/2* **Bluebird Chariot**[8] 3180 5-9-6 0.... TolleyDean(3) 5 — 40
(J M Bradley) *stdd s: bhd and sn rdn along: hdwy over 2f out: chsd ldng pair ent fnl f: wknd ins fnl f* **33/1**

00-0 **4** 2 1/4 **Bakers Boy**[66] 1535 4-9-9 35 .... RichardThomas 3 34
(J E Long) *racd in midfield tl lost pl and rdn 1/2-way: hung rt and hdwy over 2f out: no prog fr over 1f out* **66/1**

0 **5** 1 1/4 **Global Glory (IRE)**[8] 3180 3-9-0 0 .... SimonWhitworth 8 28
(J A R Toller) *s.i.s: sn pushed along in rr: hdwy over 2f out: no prog fr over 1f out* **14/1**[3]

0-0 **6** 2 **Silver Diamond**[22] 2756 3-8-9 0 .... TPQueally 6 17
(W Jarvis) *chsd ldrs: wnt 2nd and rdn 2f out tl 1f out: sn wknd* **7/1**[2]

0006 **7** 2 1/4 **Joe Rich**[32] 1347 4-9-9 45 ....(b[1]) LPKeniry 1 19
(Mrs L C Jewell) *chsd ldr tl 2f out: wkng whn bmpd over 1f out* **40/1**

6400 **8** 11 **Pajada**[19] 2866 4-8-11 40 ....(v) JustinaKay(7) 4 —
(M D I Usher) *racd wd: in tch tl wknd over 2f out: t.o* **16/1**

1m 28.5s (1.20) **Going Correction** -0.375s/f (Firm)
WFA 3 from 4yo+ 9lb **8** Ran SP% **111.2**
Speed ratings (Par 101): **78,77,72,70,68 66,63,51**
toteswinger: 1&2 £8.80, 1&3 £5.00, 2&3 £54.90. CSF £39.73 TOTE £1.20: £1.02, £12.20, £6.20; EX 17.60.
Owner J W Hills **Bred** Dr D Crone & P Lafarge & P Johnston **Trained** Upper Lambourn, Berks

FOCUS
A desperate contest in which hot favourite Autumn Blade had to be kidded into victory. The time was pedestrian, 2.37 seconds slower than the two-year-olds in the opener, and the form is worthless.
Bakers Boy Official explanation: trainer said gelding spread a plate post-race

3446 TRAVIS PERKINS HIRE CLAIMING STKS 6f
3:40 (3:49) (Class 6) 3-Y-O+ **£2,047** (£604; £302) **Stalls** Low

Form RPR
0-00 **1** **Who's Winning (IRE)**[2] 3363 7-9-4 60 .... RichardKingscote 4 64
(B G Powell) *hld up in tch: hdwy 1/2-way: chsd ldr 2f out: drvn to ld wl ins fnl f* **9/4**[1]

0056 **2** 1/2 **Music Box Express**[39] 2263 4-8-3 61 ....(t) ThomasO'Brien(7) 5 54
(George Baker) *restless in stalls: led: rdn over 1f out: kpt on wl tl hdd and no ex wl ins fnl f* **3/1**[2]

0150 **3** 1 3/4 **Midnite Blews (IRE)**[13] 3021 3-8-2 64 ow4 .... PNolan(7) 1 54+
(A B Haynes) *v.s.a: in tch after 2f: hdwy on stands rail 1/2-way: chsd ldng pair and hanging rt wl over 1f out: one pce ins fnl f* **8/1**

0-00 **4** 1 3/4 **Inwaan (IRE)**[35] 2355 5-9-6 49 ....(tp) ChrisCatlin 8 53
(P R Webber) *wnt rt and bmpd rival s: t.k.h: hld up in midfield: effrt 2f out: hung rt and no imp 1f out* **12/1**

6001 **5** 1/2 **Currency**[13] 3021 11-8-7 54 .... TolleyDean(3) 7 41
(J M Bradley) *chsd ldrs on outer: rdn 4f out: drvn 2f out: wknd over 1f out* **7/1**

0- **6** 1/2 **Hennalaine (IRE)**[352] 3417 3-8-2 0 .... LiamJones 9 37+
(P Winkworth) *bmpd and v awkward s: lost many lengths and sn crossed to stands' rail: clsd and in tch after 2f: rdn and kpt on same pce fr over 1f out* **13/2**[3]

0650 **7** 3/4 **Fun In The Sun**[17] 2917 4-9-2 52 .... SamHitchcott 6 43
(A B Haynes) *sn bustled along to chse ldr tl 2f out: sn rdn: wknd over 1f out* **10/1**

/0P- **8** 6 **Panadin (IRE)**[304] 4914 6-8-10 40 ....(p) FrankieMcDonald 3 18
(Mrs L C Jewell) *sn pushed along: in tch tl struggling 1/2-way: n.d after* **66/1**

00-0 **9** 3 1/2 **Peruvian Style (IRE)**[13] 3021 7-8-12 47 .... LPKeniry 10 9
(J M Bradley) *hld up in tch: rdn over 2f out: wknd wl over 1f out* **20/1**

-000 **10** 7 **Santa Clara**[90] 1081 3-8-2 55 .... CatherineGannon 2 —
(P Leech) *bolted bef s: chsd ldrs tl wknd 1/2-way: sn bhd* **20/1**

1m 11.41s (-1.29) **Going Correction** -0.375s/f (Firm)
WFA 3 from 4yo+ 7lb **10** Ran SP% **120.5**
Speed ratings (Par 101): **93,92,90,87,87 86,85,77,72,63**
toteswinger: 1&2 £6.00, 1&3 £6.00, 2&3 £5.50. CSF £9.07 TOTE £3.40: £1.70, £2.00, £1.90; EX 13.40.
Owner Tony Head and Caroline Andrus **Bred** Colin Kennedy **Trained** Upper Lambourn, Berks

FOCUS
A weak contest. The first two had not been in particularly good form in handicaps lately and probably did not run to their best. The winning time was moderate.
Hennalaine(IRE) Official explanation: jockey said filly missed the break

3447 PROFILE MAIDEN STKS 5f
4:15 (4:17) (Class 5) 3-Y-O+ **£2,590** (£770; £385; £192) **Stalls** Low

Form RPR
0000 **1** **Lithaam (IRE)**[66] 1529 4-8-13 41 ....(p) PietroRomeo(7) 2 61
(J M Bradley) *led tl over 2f out: chsd ldr and hung rt over 1f out: led fnl 100yds: r.o strly and sn clr* **66/1**

3222 **2** 2 1/4 **Great Knight (IRE)**[9] 3144 3-9-0 74 ....(b) LiamJones 7 51
(W J Haggas) *chsd ldrs: wnt 2nd over 2f out: led 2f out: drvn and hung rt ent fnl f: hdd fnl 100yds: immediately btn* **6/5**[1]

3-30 **3** 3/4 **Town And Gown**[7] 3224 3-8-2 69 .... WilliamCarson(7) 1 43
(S C Williams) *s.i.s: t.k.h: hld up in tch: hdwy 2f out: nt qckn over 1f out: plugged on to go 3rd ins fnl f* **3/1**[2]

60-6 **4** 1 3/4 **Miss Poppy**[21] 2774 3-8-9 68 .... FergusSweeney 3 37
(P R Chamings) *sn bustled along and struggling to go pce: sme hdwy and edging rt over 2f out: nvr trbld ldrs* **6/1**

20 **5** nse **Filemot**[7] 2981 3-8-9 0 .... ChrisCatlin 5 37
(John Berry) *prom: led over 2f out tl 2f out: sn wknd* **5/1**[3]

40 **6** 3 3/4 **In Toto**[20] 2823 3-9-0 0 .... SimonWhitworth 6 28
(M Wigham) *s.i.s: a wl bhd* **33/1**

30-5 **7** 6 **Hucking Harmony (IRE)**[6] 3269 3-8-9 62 .... LPKeniry 4 1
(J R Best) *wnt rt s: sn pressing ldr tl over 2f out: sn wknd* **10/1**

59.22 secs (-0.78) **Going Correction** -0.375s/f (Firm)
WFA 3 from 4yo 6lb **7** Ran SP% **114.9**
Speed ratings (Par 103): **91,87,86,83,83 77,67**
toteswinger: 1&2 £10.30, 1&3 £11.60, 2&3 £1.70. CSF £148.41 TOTE £54.10: £10.40, £1.50; EX 108.70.
Owner JMB Racing.co.uk **Bred** Shadwell Estate Company Limited **Trained** Sedbury, Gloucs

FOCUS
A shock result with Lithaam bagging the stands' rail and winning at 66/1. Another race run in a moderate time.
Lithaam(IRE) Official explanation: trainer had no explanation for the apparent improvement in form
Filemot Official explanation: trainer said filly lost off-fore plate

3448 FGS PLANT/SOUTHERN PLANT H'CAP 1m 4f
4:45 (4:45) (Class 6) (0-60,65) 4-Y-O+ **£2,047** (£604; £302) **Stalls** Low

Form RPR
0406 **1** **Granary Girl**[10] 3113 6-8-6 47 .... LiamJones 12 59
(J Pearce) *hld up towards rr: swtchd lft 3f out: gd hdwy on outer over 2f out: led 1f out: edgd rt but sn in command* **16/1**

2312 **2** 3 **Astrolibra**[10] 3113 4-8-13 **54** .... TPQueally 3 61
(M H Tompkins) *in tch: drvn to chse ldr over 1f out: kpt on same pce u.p: wnt 2nd nr fin* **9/2**[1]

-050 **3** nk **Icannshift (IRE)**[18] 2884 8-8-11 **52** .... FrankieMcDonald 5 59
(T M Jones) *led: rdn jst over 2f out: hdd 1f out: kpt on same pce: lost 2nd nr fin* **11/1**

5504 **4** 1 1/2 **Songmaster (USA)**[11] 3084 5-9-3 **58** .... FergusSweeney 7 62
(A King) *chsd ldr: rdn 3f out: lost 2nd over 1f out: one pce* **11/2**[2]

4445 **5** 1 1/2 **Sand Repeal (IRE)**[12] 3059 6-8-9 **57** ....(v) AmyBaker(7) 4 59
(Miss J Feilden) *hld up in midfield: hdwy to chse ldrs 4f out: wd and rdn bnd 2f out: no prog after* **10/1**

0541 **6** 1/2 **Foreign King (USA)**[3] 3344 4-9-10 **65** 6ex .... LPKeniry 8 66
(J W Mullins) *chsd ldrs: rdn over 2f out: wknd wl over 1f out* **9/2**[1]

0242 **7** 3/4 **Mid Valley**[18] 2884 5-8-13 **54** .... SimonWhitworth 9 54
(J R Jenkins) *stdd s: t.k.h: hld up in rr: hdwy 3f out: rdn and no prog over 1f out* **12/1**

0-54 **8** 2 1/2 **Capistrano**[24] 2694 5-8-12 **53** .... PaulEddery 2 49
(G D Blake) *hld up in rr: hdwy on outer 6f out: drvn 4f out: wknd wl over 2f out* **10/1**

5-00 **9** hd **Sweet Request**[14] 2990 4-9-2 **57** .... RichardThomas 6 53
(Dr J R J Naylor) *in tch: lost pl 4f out: rdn 3f out: no ch w ldrs after* **40/1**

0-56 **10** nse **Prime Contender**[56] 451 6-8-11 **55** .... TolleyDean(3) 11 51
(George Baker) *stdd s: hld up in rr: effrt on outer 3f: no hdwy u.p 2f out* **11/1**

2230 **11** 7 **Ruling Reef**[68] 1505 6-8-6 **47** .... RichardSmith 10 31
(M R Bosley) *hld up towards rr: rdn 3f out: n.d* **14/1**

060- **12** 3 1/2 **Mighty Kitchener (USA)**[31] 7273 5-8-4 **45** .... ChrisCatlin 13 24
(P Howling) *t.k.h: chsd ldr tl stdd into midfield after 2f: wkng whn hmpd 3f out: no ch after* **17/2**[3]

006 **13** 1 1/2 **Black Cloud**[19] 2862 5-8-2 **50** ow1 .... ThomasO'Brien(7) 1 26
(A Ennis) *stdd and dropped in after s: a bhd* **50/1**

2m 39.35s (-1.55) **Going Correction** -0.05s/f (Good) **13** Ran SP% **121.8**
Speed ratings (Par 101): **103,101,100,99,98 98,97,96,96,96 91,89,88**
toteswinger: 1&2 £15.70, 1&3 £32.70, 2&3 £9.50. CSF £88.22 CT £853.50 TOTE £18.60: £5.60, £2.00, £4.10; EX 128.80.
Owner Mrs P O'Shea **Bred** Barry Minty **Trained** Newmarket, Suffolk

FOCUS
A moderate handicap, but run at a sound pace thanks to course specialist Icannshift. The winner was back to her best, and the other principals were close to their recent marks.

3449 BSS BOSS CENTENARY H'CAP 1m 1f 149y
5:15 (5:15) (Class 5) (0-75,75) 3-Y-O+ **£2,590** (£770; £385; £192) **Stalls** Centre

Form RPR
-004 **1** **Press The Button (GER)**[21] 2799 5-9-6 **74** .... HarryPoulton(7) 8 86
(J R Boyle) *mde all: stdd pce after 2f: shkn up and qcknd wl over 1f out: clr 1f out: pushed out* **3/1**[2]

31-0 **2** 2 **Flying Applause**[15] 2976 3-8-12 **71** .... FergusSweeney 2 79
(A King) *taken down early: s.i.s: sn pushed up to chse wnr: rdn over 2f out: outpcd by wnr over 1f out: hld on for 2nd fnl f* **15/2**

2653 **3** nse **Aegean Prince**[18] 2895 4-10-0 **75** .... PatDobbs 4 83+
(R Hannon) *stdd s: hld up in rr: plld hrd and rdn over 1f out: disp 2nd and edgd rt ent fnl f: no imp on wnr* **3/1**[2]

0061 **4** 3 1/2 **Shabahar (IRE)**[18] 2886 4-9-9 **70** .... TPQueally 6 71
(M J McGrath) *stdd s: t.k.h: hld up in last pair: nt clr run over 2f out tl over 1f out: sn rdn and no hdwy* **6/1**[3]

2631 **5** 1 **Prime Number (IRE)**[9] 3132 6-9-0 **66** .... JackMitchell(5) 5 65
(J Akehurst) *broke wl but sn pushed along and lost pl: hdwy on outer 4f out: chsd ldrs and drvn 3f out: wknd over 1f out* **11/4**[1]

6100 **6** 1 1/4 **Saviour Sand (IRE)**[14] 1520 4-9-11 **72** ....(b[1]) LPKeniry 7 68
(D R C Elsworth) *t.k.h: chsd ldng pair: rdn over 2f out: wknd over 1f out* **12/1**

5401 **7** 1 **Night Orbit**[15] 2978 4-9-5 **66** .... ChrisCatlin 1 60
(Miss J Feilden) *racd in midfield: rdn 3f out: wknd 2f out* **12/1**

2m 3.98s (-0.92) **Going Correction** -0.05s/f (Good)
WFA 3 from 4yo+ 12lb **7** Ran SP% **118.1**
Speed ratings (Par 103): **101,99,99,96,95 94,93**
toteswinger: 1&2 £6.00, 1&3 £3.30, 2&3 £6.00. CSF £26.64 CT £73.82 TOTE £4.40: £2.70, £3.30; EX 32.40 Place 6 £43.08, Place 5 £24.18.
Owner Brian McAtavey **Bred** Gestut Sommerberg **Trained** Epsom, Surrey

FOCUS
A modest handicap. The winner was well treated and was allowed an easy lead.
T/Plt: £109.70 to a £1 stake. Pool: £51,182.53. 340.50 winning tickets. T/Qpdt: £53.80 to a £1 stake. Pool: £2,844.90. 39.10 winning tickets. SP

[3411] NEWCASTLE (L-H)
Friday, June 27

OFFICIAL GOING: Good to soft changing to soft after race 3 (7.55)
Wind: Almost nil Weather: Overcast, raining

3450 GDBS & KB SHEET METAL H'CAP 1m 2f 32y
6:55 (6:58) (Class 5) (0-70,66) 4-Y-O+ **£4,209** (£1,252; £625; £312) **Stalls** Low

Form RPR
6142 **1** **Keisha Kayleigh (IRE)**[24] 2697 5-9-7 **66** ....(v) NCallan 13 79
(B Ellison) *dwlt: hld up: hdwy over 2f out: led 1f out: drvn out* **11/2**[1]

0252 **2** 1 3/4 **Calcutta Cup (UAE)**[20] 2848 5-9-0 **59** .... TonyHamilton 5 68
(Karen McLintock) *prom: smooth hdwy to ld over 2f out: hdd 1f out: kpt on same pce* **13/2**[2]

6402 **3** 3/4 **Grandad Bill (IRE)**[7] 3204 5-8-4 **49** .... PaulHanagan 14 57
(J S Goldie) *hld up: hdwy 2f out: kpt on fnl f: nrst fin* **7/1**[3]

6235 **4** 2 **Dan Tucker**[14] 3010 4-9-7 **66** .... DO'Donohoe 6 70
(N Tinkler) *midfield: hdwy over 2f out: cl up over 1f out: one pce fnl f* **12/1**

0310 **5** 3 **Dechiper (IRE)**[20] 2848 6-9-2 **66** .... PatrickDonaghy(5) 11 64
(R Johnson) *dwlt: hld up: plenty to do over 2f out: hdwy over 1f out: nrst fin* **16/1**

0042 **6** 1 1/4 **Seyaadi**[7] 3226 6-9-0 **59** ....(p) DeanMcKeown 9 54
(Miss Tracy Waggott) *hld up on outside: hdwy over 2f out: no imp fnl f* **8/1**

001 **7** 1 1/2 **Moment Of Clarity**[6] 3258 6-8-7 **59** ....(p) StacyRenwick(7) 15 51
(R C Guest) *hld up: hdwy over 2f out: no imp over 1f out* **12/1**

5055 **8** 2 1/2 **Carefree**[7] 3127 4-8-5 **50** ....(b[1]) SilvestreDeSousa 10 37
(Mrs R A Carr) *cl up: led 4f to over 2f out: sn wknd* **50/1**

3510 **9** 3 3/4 **Moonstreaker**[16] 2927 5-9-2 **64** .... MichaelJStainton(3) 1 44
(R M Whitaker) *plld hrd: cl up: outpcd over 3f out: n.d after* **7/1**[3]

400 **10** 3/4 **Getrah**[40] 2220 4-9-6 65 GrahamGibbons 8 37
(N Wilson) *midfield: drvn and outpcd over 2f out: sn btn* 9/1
4601 **11** 2 **Trouble Mountain (USA)**[20] 2848 11-9-6 65 (t) DaleGibson 4 33
(M W Easterby) *in tch: drvn over 4f out: btn fnl 2f* 12/1
0235 **12** 1 3/4 **Tizzy May (FR)**[21] 2782 8-8-12 57 (b[1]) TomEaves 3 22
(B Ellison) *hld up ins: drvn over 2f out: sn btn* 12/1
06-0 **13** 1 3/4 **Whittinghamvillage**[7] 3201 7-8-6 51 TWilliams 17 12
(Mrs H O Graham) *cl up on outside tl rdn and wknd over 2f out* 33/1
-450 **14** 1/2 **Trans Sonic**[16] 2927 5-8-11 59 AndrewMullen(3) 7 19
(A J Lockwood) *led to 4f out: sn lost pl* 20/1
35-0 **15** shd **Thornaby Green**[8] 3175 7-8-8 60 DeanHeslop(7) 2 20
(T D Barron) *cl up tl rdn and wknd over 3f out* 20/1

2m 14.9s (3.00) **Going Correction** +0.225s/f (Good) 15 Ran SP% **125.9**
Speed ratings (Par 103): **97,95,95,93,91 90,88,86,83,80 79,77,76,76,75**
toteswinger: 1&2 £23.50, 1&3 £8.00, 2&3 £9.90. CSF £39.67 CT £263.96 TOTE £7.00: £2.90, £3.40, £2.70; EX 58.20.
Owner C E Sherry **Bred** Ronnie Boland **Trained** Norton, N Yorks

FOCUS
A run-of-the-mill handicap in which the pace was fair but the form looks pretty sound, rated mainly around the third and fourth.

3451 ESH GROUP GOSFORTH PARK CUP (H'CAP) 5f
7:25 (7:27) (Class 2) (0-105,105) 3-Y-0+
£18,693 (£5,598; £2,799; £1,401; £699; £351) Stalls High

Form RPR
3550 **1** **Buachaill Dona (IRE)**[42] 2172 5-9-12 98 AdrianTNicholls 2 110+
(D Nicholls) *led far side quartet: rdn and drifted to stands' side gp over 1f out: led that gp ins fnl f: r.o wl* 12/1
-210 **2** 1 **Hamish McGonagall**[13] 3047 3-8-12 90 DavidAllan 12 97
(T D Easterby) *cl up stands' side: led that gp over 1f out to ins fnl f: kpt on towards fin* 13/2[1]
1030 **3** hd **Pusey Street Lady**[33] 2426 4-9-4 90 DO'Donohoe 15 98
(J Gallagher) *in tch stands' side: drvn after 2f: hdwy fnl f: nrst fin* 16/1
503 **4** 1 1/2 **How's She Cuttin' (IRE)**[6] 3252 5-8-11 83 (v) DarryllHolland 9 86+
(T D Barron) *bhd and sn rdn stands' side: gd hdwy fnl f: nrst fin* 13/2[1]
0-36 **5** 1/2 **Fathom Five (IRE)**[20] 2828 4-9-11 97 TomEaves 13 98
(B Smart) *led stands' side to over 1f out: kpt on same pce* 17/2[3]
-605 **6** nk **Dig Deep (IRE)**[7] 3228 6-8-12 84 GrahamGibbons 1 84
(J J Quinn) *cl up far side: lft w one other that side over 1f out: no imp fnl f* 12/1
000 **7** nk **Bond City (IRE)**[14] 3009 6-9-4 90 SilvestreDeSousa 14 89
(G R Oldroyd) *chsd ldrs: drvn 1/2-way: effrt over 1f out: one pce fnl f* 14/1
/50- **8** hd **Steve's Champ (CHI)**[12] 8-10-5 105 6ex (b) JacobJohansen 17 103
(Rune Haugen, Norway) *w stands' side ldr tl no ex wl over 1f out* 25/1
-235 **9** hd **Ishetoo**[12] 3056 4-9-7 93 DaleGibson 16 90+
(A Dickman) *dwlt: bhd and sn rdn stands' side: nvr rchd ldrs* 7/1[2]
0001 **10** 3/4 **Barney McGrew (IRE)**[29] 2538 5-9-8 94 TonyHamilton 8 89
(M Dods) *towards rr stands' side: drvn 1/2-way: nvr rchd ldrs* 16/1
0013 **11** 1/2 **Luscivious**[38] 2292 4-9-4 90 (b) TGillet 3 83
(A J McCabe) *cl up far side: drifted to stands' side gp over 1f out: sn btn* 25/1
50-0 **12** 1 1/4 **Efistorm**[14] 3009 7-9-0 86 ShaneKelly 5 74
(C R Dore) *in tch on outside of stands' side gp tl rdn and wknd appr fnl f* 18/1
0320 **13** nk **River Falcon**[27] 2626 8-9-8 94 DanielTudhope 11 81
(J S Goldie) *bhd and sn drvn along stands' side: nvr on terms* 14/1
4200 **14** 3/4 **Green Park (IRE)**[27] 2626 5-9-1 87 PaulHanagan 4 71
(R A Fahey) *in tch far side: effrt whn lft w one other that side over 1f out: n.d* 17/2[3]
0050 **15** nk **Special Day**[27] 2626 4-9-1 87 PhilipRobinson 6 70
(B W Hills) *hld up outside of stands' side gp: drvn over 2f out: nvr on terms* 14/1
2240 **16** 3 1/4 **Northern Empire (IRE)**[20] 2828 5-9-7 93 NCallan 7 65
(K A Ryan) *hld up towards rr stands' side: pushed along 1/2-way: btn over 1f out* 16/1

60.68 secs (-0.02) **Going Correction** +0.225s/f (Good)
WFA 3 from 4yo+ 6lb 16 Ran SP% **126.2**
Speed ratings (Par 109): **109,107,107,104,103 103,102,102,102,101 100,98,97,96,96 90**
toteswinger: 1&2 £39.80, 1&3 £60.00, 2&3 £34.70. CSF £90.82 CT £1327.21 TOTE £12.90: £2.50, £2.30, £3.20, £1.90; EX 111.60.
Owner Mike Browne **Bred** John O Browne **Trained** Sessay, N Yorks
■ Stewards' Enquiry : Adrian T Nicholls one-day ban: careless riding (Jul 12); caution: used whip down shoulder in forehand position.

FOCUS
A useful sprint but mainly featuring exposed sorts and a race in which the winner, who set out on the far side, drifted to the stands' side in the last quarter mile. The pace was sound throughout and this form, rated through the third, should stand up.

NOTEBOOK
Buachaill Dona(IRE)'s form has been patchy since his last win but he turned in a career best effort dropped in trip and back on easier ground, despite hanging across the course. Although he stays 6f, has so much speed that this looks his best trip and he is sure to win more races when the mood takes. (op 10-1)
Hamish McGonagall ◆, who did not get home returned to 6f at York last time, fared much better back over the minimum trip taking on his elders for the first time. He may be even more effective returned to a sound surface and is the sort to win a decent handicap over this trip this year. (op 11-1)
Pusey Street Lady, a soft-ground reappearance winner over 6f, ran her best race since but did shape as though the return to that longer trip would have been more to her liking. She will be vulnerable to the more progressive sorts in this grade, though. (op 20-1)
How's She Cuttin'(IRE) had run as well as she ever had done in a Listed event at Ayr at the weekend and she showed that was no fluke on this easier surface. Life will be tougher in future handicaps as she is due to go up 3lb but she remains worth another try over 6f.
Fathom Five(IRE) is all about speed and was not disgraced after his solid Epsom run. Although effective on soft, he may be more effective when able to dominate on a sound surface but his current mark is going to leave him vulnerable to an improver. (op 11-1)
Dig Deep(IRE), dropped in distance, may be a shade better than the bare form as he was left in front a long way out on the far side when the winner started his drift to the stands' side. He is ideally suited by coming off a decent gallop and he remains the type to win races for this yard. (op 10-1)
Bond City(IRE) was far from disgraced back on an easy surface but, as he has yet to win for his current yard and has only scored once in just over three years, he is likely to remain vulnerable from his current mark in this type of event. (op 20-1)
Steve's Champ(CHI), a multiple winner in Scandanavia, had the run of the race against the near side rail but was found out under his penalty. The return to non-handicap company may well be in his favour. (op 33-1)
Ishetoo Official explanation: jockey said gelding was denied a clear run
Efistorm Official explanation: jockey said gelding hung left-handed throughout

Special Day Official explanation: jockey said filly was unsuited by the good to soft ground

3452 PHOENIX SECURITY & PHOENIX EYE MAIDEN FILLIES' STKS 7f
7:55 (7:55) (Class 5) 3-Y-0+
£4,533 (£1,348; £674; £336) Stalls High

Form RPR
33 **1** **Persian Sea (UAE)**[28] 2571 3-8-12 0 PhilipRobinson 5 88
(M A Jarvis) *pressed ldr: led appr 2f out: pushed clr over 1f out: readily* 8/11[1]
0- **2** 6 **Rhadegunda**[223] 6847 3-8-12 0 ShaneKelly 6 72
(J H M Gosden) *hld up in tch: stdy hdwy 2f out: chsd wnr wl ins fnl f: no imp* 20/1
 3 1/2 **Lake Windermere (IRE)** 3-8-12 0 PaulHanagan 11 71
(J H M Gosden) *led: hung lft and hdd appr 2f out: no ex fnl f: lost 2nd wl ins fnl f* 11/4[2]
0-52 **4** 2 1/4 **Romantic Destiny**[30] 2500 3-8-12 75 NCallan 3 65
(K A Ryan) *trckd ldrs: effrt over 2f out: one pce fnl f* 8/1[3]
-404 **5** 3 **Hansomis (IRE)**[6] 3260 4-9-7 52 DaleGibson 7 59
(B Mactaggart) *towards rr: drvn and hdwy over 2f out: no imp over 1f out* 22/1
 6 13 **Ceili Mor (IRE)** 3-8-12 0 JoeFanning 8 21
(M Johnston) *dwlt: bhd and green: short-lived effrt 3f out: sn btn* 16/1
00 **7** 3 3/4 **Dalla Finestra**[29] 2546 3-8-12 0 TomEaves 9 11
(C F Wall) *t.k.h: in tch tl wknd fr 2f out* 25/1
0 **8** 40 **Ourbelle**[6] 3282 3-8-12 0 DeanMcKeown 1 —
(Miss Tracy Waggott) *in tch on outside tl wknd fr 1/2-way: t.o* 200/1
 9 12 **Born To Frill** 3-8-9 0 ow2 SladeO'Hara(5) 10 —
(Miss L C Siddall) *t.k.h: prom 3f: sn lost tch* 66/1

1m 28.66s (1.26) **Going Correction** +0.225s/f (Good)
WFA 3 from 4yo 9lb 9 Ran SP% **116.5**
Speed ratings (Par 100): **101,94,93,91,87 72,68,22,9**
toteswinger: 1&2 £2.90, 1&3 £1.20, 2&3 £2.50. CSF £23.66 TOTE £1.90: £1.10, £3.60, £1.30; EX 14.50.
Owner Sheikh Ahmed Al Maktoum **Bred** Darley **Trained** Newmarket, Suffolk
■ Stewards' Enquiry : N Callan one-day ban: failed to ride to draw (Jul 14)
Philip Robinson one-day ban: failed to ride to draw (Jul 12)

FOCUS
A race lacking anything in the way of strength but an emphatic performance by the winner, who is surely the type to win more races.

3453 DELOITTE & TOUCHE LLP H'CAP 1m 3y(S)
8:25 (8:25) (Class 4) (0-85,76) 3-Y-0+
£6,231 (£1,866; £933; £467; £233; £117) Stalls High

Form RPR
1-21 **1** **Spinning**[70] 1450 5-9-9 76 (b) NeilBrown(5) 7 87+
(T D Barron) *hld up: hdwy to chse wnr over 1f out: kpt on wl fnl f: led towards fin* 2/1[1]
0060 **2** 1/2 **Moody Tunes**[27] 2619 5-10-0 76 NCallan 8 86
(K R Burke) *set modest pce: qcknd clr over 1f out: kpt on fnl f: hdd towards fin* 2/1[1]
-544 **3** 9 **Darfour**[6] 3257 4-9-3 65 DanielTudhope 1 54
(J S Goldie) *cl up tl rdn and outpcd fr 2f out* 9/1[3]
0010 **4** 1/2 **Handsome Falcon**[20] 2818 4-9-10 72 PaulHanagan 2 60
(R A Fahey) *hld up in tch: drvn and outpcd over 2f out: n.d after* 11/2[2]
4656 **5** 1 1/2 **Jamieson Gold (IRE)**[20] 2841 5-10-0 76 (p) TomEaves 4 61
(Miss L A Perratt) *prom tl rdn and no ex fr over 2f out* 9/1[3]
2001 **6** 28 **Dnata Flyer (USA)**[7] 3213 3-8-8 66 6ex JoeFanning 3 —
(M Johnston) *hld up in tch: drvn 3f out: sn lost tch* 9/1[3]

1m 43.11s (-0.29) **Going Correction** +0.225s/f (Good)
WFA 3 from 4yo+ 10lb 6 Ran SP% **112.1**
Speed ratings (Par 105): **110,109,100,100,98 70**
toteswinger: 1&2 £1.90, 1&3 £5.30, 2&3 £4.10. CSF £5.91 CT £25.61 TOTE £2.80: £2.10, £1.70.

Owner Mrs J Hazell **Bred** Cheveley Park Stud **Trained** Maunby, N Yorks

FOCUS
A fair handicap in which the pace was sound and the winner did well considering the position he was in when the tempo increased. The form could be slightly underrated.
Dnata Flyer(USA) Official explanation: trainer had no explanation for the poor form shown

3454 KEVIN LEE MEMORIAL H'CAP 6f
8:55 (8:55) (Class 5) (0-75,73) 3-Y-0+ £4,209 (£1,252; £625; £312) Stalls High

Form RPR
0001 **1** **Ursus**[6] 3283 3-8-2 54 6ex oh1 SilvestreDeSousa 2 63
(C R Wilson) *hld up far side: hdwy 2f out: styd on to ld wl ins fnl f: r.o: 1st of 8 in gp* 40/1
5444 **2** nk **Ancient Cross**[13] 3050 4-9-7 66 GrahamGibbons 12 76
(M W Easterby) *trckd stands' side ldrs: effrt 2f out: led that gp ins fnl f: kpt on: jst hld by far side: 1st of 8 in gp* 5/1[1]
0142 **3** shd **The Bear**[22] 2751 5-9-6 68 PJMcDonald(3) 6 78
(R Johnson) *led far side to wl ins fnl f: no ex nr fin: 2nd of 8 in gp* 6/1[2]
0626 **4** 1 **Steel Blue**[6] 3271 8-9-2 61 DeanMcKeown 11 67
(R M Whitaker) *racd stands' side: led after 1f to ins fnl f: kpt on same pce: 2nd of 8 in gp* 11/1
0060 **5** 1 1/2 **Balakiref**[29] 2535 9-9-12 71 NCallan 15 73+
(M Dods) *hld up stands' side: hdwy over 1f out: kpt on fnl f: 3rd of 8 in gp* 9/1
-001 **6** nk **Rabbit Fighter (IRE)**[77] 1312 4-9-12 71 (v) PatrickMathers 3 72
(D Shaw) *trckd far side ldrs: drvn over 2f out: kpt on same pce ins fnl f: 3rd of 8 in gp* 11/1
0031 **7** hd **Bid For Gold**[18] 2891 4-9-6 65 PaulHanagan 8 65
(Jedd O'Keeffe) *prom far side: drvn fr 1/2-way: rallied: one pce fnl f: 4th of 8 in gp* 13/2[3]
2253 **8** nk **Rainbow Fox**[16] 2938 4-9-1 67 FrederikTylicki(7) 7 66
(R A Fahey) *chsd far side ldrs: effrt over 2f out: one pce fnl f: 5th of 8 in gp* 9/1
00-2 **9** 1 **Forzarzi (IRE)**[9] 3129 4-8-7 57 oh1 ow3 GaryBartley(5) 4 53
(H A McWilliams) *bhd far side: hdwy over 1f out: nvr rchd ldrs: 6th of 8 in gp* 25/1
-410 **10** 1 **Staked A Claim (IRE)**[16] 2936 4-8-12 57 DarryllHolland 16 50
(T D Barron) *t.k.h: bhd stands' side tl sme late hdwy: nvr rchd ldrs: 4th of 8 in gp* 14/1
5026 **11** 4 1/2 **Darcy's Pride (IRE)**[11] 3080 4-9-5 64 TonyHamilton 13 42
(D W Barker) *led 1f: cl up stands' side tl wknd fr 2f out: 5th of 8 in gp* 22/1
0202 **12** 3/4 **Jun Fan (USA)**[3] 3340 6-8-9 54 JoeFanning 5 30
(B Ellison) *cl up far side tl wknd over 1f out: 7th of 8 in gp* 8/1

The Form Book, Raceform Ltd, Compton, RG20 6NL

04-6 **13** *1* **Lake Chini (IRE)**[94] 1015 6-9-9 **68**..........................(b) DaleGibson 9 41
(M W Easterby) *prom stands' side tl rdn and wknd fr 2f out: 6th of 8 in gp* **33/1**

0040 **14** *6* **Rue Soleil**[21] 2777 4-8-9 **54** oh2.......................... PaulFessey 14 8
(J R Weymes) *prom stands' side: drvn 1/2-way: wknd wl over 1f out: 7th of 8 in gp* **40/1**

0600 **15** *3 1/4* **Paris Bell**[21] 2778 6-10-0 **73**.......................... DavidAllan 1 16
(T D Easterby) *towards rr far side: shortlived effrt over 2f out: sn btn: last of 8 in gp* **14/1**

5-30 **16** *24* **Cross Of Lorraine (IRE)**[22] 2751 5-9-3 **62**..........(b) TomEaves 10 —
(C Grant) *bhd stands' side: rdn and lost tch 1/2-way: t.o: last of 8 in gp* **20/1**

1m 15.7s (0.50) **Going Correction** +0.225s/f (Good)
WFA 3 from 4yo+ 7lb **16** Ran SP% **126.2**
Speed ratings (Par 103): **105,104,104,103,101 100,100,100,98,97 91,90,89,81,76 44**
toteswinger: 1&2 £83.40, 1&3 £18.20, 2&3 £5.90. CSF £225.76 CT £1471.99 TOTE £49.20: £6.30, £1.90, £1.70, £2.50; EX 404.50.
Owner David Bartlett **Bred** Mrs Andrea Bartlett **Trained** Manfield, N Yorks

FOCUS
An ordinary sprint in which the field split into two even groups and there was no advantage in the draw. Despite the shock winner the form looks pretty solid with the time reasonable and not much between the two sides.

3455 FRIENDS OF KEVIN LEE CELEBRATION H'CAP 5f
9:30 (9:30) (Class 5) (0-75,73) 3-Y-O **£4,209** (£1,252; £625; £312) **Stalls** High

Form RPR

4000 **1** **Select Committee**[20] 2850 3-8-4 **56**..........(v[1]) PaulHanagan 4 63
(J J Quinn) *trckd ldr far side: led that gp ins fnl f: drvn out nr fin: 1st of 5 in gp* **16/1**

2125 **2** *1 1/4* **Rio Sands**[5] 3298 3-9-3 **72**.......................... MichaelJStainton(3) 1 76+
(R M Whitaker) *trckd far side ldrs: effrt over 1f out: one pce whn n.m.r nr fin: 2nd of 5 in gp* **7/1**[3]

3202 **3** *shd* **Killer Class**[6] 3256 3-8-12 **64**.......................... DanielTudhope 3 66
(J S Goldie) *prom far side: effrt over 1f out: kpt on u.p ins fnl f: 3rd of 5 in gp* **9/2**[2]

3204 **4** *1 1/4* **Supermassive Muse (IRE)**[14] 3000 3-9-6 **72**......(p) GrahamGibbons 10 69+
(E S McMahon) *in tch stands' side: hdwy to ld that gp ins fnl f: no ch w far side: 1st of 7 in gp* **7/1**[3]

00-2 **5** *2 3/4* **Cheshire Rose**[27] 2602 3-9-0 **66**.......................... PaulFessey 5 53
(T D Barron) *led far side to ins fnl f: sn checked and no ex: 4th of 5 in gp* **8/1**

6342 **6** *1/2* **Grudge**[7] 3217 3-8-12 **64**.......................... TonyHamilton 7 49
(D W Barker) *w ldr stands' side: led that gp over 1f out to ins fnl f: no ex: 2nd of 7 in gp* **8/1**

1 **7** *nk* **Mayoman (IRE)**[34] 2396 3-9-4 **73**.......................... RussellKennemore(3) 12 57
(Paul Green) *dwlt: bhd and rdn stands' side: effrt and hung lft 2f out: sn non imp: 3rd of 7 in gp* **8/1**

0010 **8** *3/4* **Revue Princess (IRE)**[25] 2676 3-9-2 **68**..........(b[1]) DavidAllan 8 50
(T D Easterby) *prom: effrt over 2f out: no ex over 1f out: 4th of 7 in gp* **25/1**

1-00 **9** *1/2* **Well Informed**[25] 2676 3-9-4 **70**.......................... NCallan 2 50
(K A Ryan) *sn bhd far side: nvr on terms: last of 5 in gp* **25/1**

1453 **10** *hd* **Mac Dalia**[45] 2074 3-8-1 **60**.......................... StacyRenwick(7) 9 39
(A J McCabe) *chsd stands' side ldrs: effrt over 1f out: sn no ex: 5th of 7 in gp* **22/1**

50-2 **11** *4* **Ridge Wood Dani (IRE)**[29] 2527 3-9-4 **70**.......................... ShaneKelly 6 35
(E J Alston) *led stands' side to over 1f out: sn wknd: 6th of 7 in gp* **7/2**[1]

0263 **12** *1 3/4* **Tangerine Trees**[7] 3231 3-9-3 **69**..........(b[1]) TomEaves 11 27
(B Smart) *sn wl bhd stands' side: no ch fr 1/2-way: last of 7 in gp* **14/1**

61.96 secs (1.26) **Going Correction** +0.225s/f (Good) **12** Ran SP% **123.3**
Speed ratings (Par 99): **98,96,95,93,89 88,88,86,86,85 79,76**
toteswinger: 1&2 £20.80, 1&3 £73.10, 2&3 £34.80. CSF £125.93 CT £468.02 TOTE £25.60: £7.00, £3.00, £2.20; EX 272.10 Place 6 £43.99, Place 5 £21.08.
Owner Which Bits Mine Syndicate **Bred** Llety Stud **Trained** Settrington, N Yorks
■ Stewards' Enquiry : Paul Hanagan two-day ban: careless riding (Jul 16,17)
Michael J Stainton one-day ban: careeless riding (Jul 12)

FOCUS
A moderate sprint in which the smaller far-side group held the edge in the closing stages. The third is the best guide to the level.
Grudge Official explanation: jockey said gelding hung left-handed
Mayoman(IRE) Official explanation: jockey said colt was unsuited by the soft ground
Ridge Wood Dani(IRE) Official explanation: jockey said gelding was unsuited by the soft ground
T/Jkpt: Not won. T/Plt: £169.20 to a £1 stake. Pool: £111,097.10. 479.08 winning tickets. T/Qpdt: £20.90 to a £1 stake. Pool: £5,796.40. 205.10 winning tickets. RY

3270 NEWMARKET (R-H)
Friday, June 27

OFFICIAL GOING: Good to firm (good in places)
Wind: Fresh, across Weather: Overcast

3456 EUROPEAN BREEDERS' FUND MAIDEN FILLIES' STKS 6f
6:00 (6:01) (Class 4) 2-Y-O **£5,180** (£1,541; £770; £384) **Stalls** Low

Form RPR

1 **Dove Mews** 2-9-0 0.......................... HayleyTurner 10 73
(M L W Bell) *chsd ldrs: led over 1f out: drvn out* **25/1**

2 *nk* **Arctic Freedom (USA)** 2-9-0 0.......................... JimmyFortune 2 72
(E A L Dunlop) *a.p: rdn and ev ch ins fnl f: r.o* **11/2**[3]

4 **3** *nk* **Izzi Mill (USA)**[16] 2951 2-9-0 0.......................... TQuinn 11 71
(D R C Elsworth) *chsd ldrs: rdn over 1f out: edgd rt ins fnl f: r.o* **9/2**[2]

0 **4** *nk* **Bobbie Soxer (IRE)**[20] 2835 2-9-0 0.......................... TedDurcan 12 70
(J L Dunlop) *hld up: hdwy 1/2-way: rdn and edgd lft fr over 1f out: r.o* **10/1**

5 *1/2* **Resort** 2-9-0 0.......................... RyanMoore 4 71+
(Sir Michael Stoute) *trckd ldrs: rdn over 1f out: r.o* **10/3**[1]

6 *1 1/4* **Stylish Dream (USA)** 2-9-0 0.......................... JamieSpencer 9 68+
(J R Fanshawe) *broke wl: stdd and lost pl whn n.m.r over 4f out: swtchd rt and hdwy over 1f out: r.o* **10/1**

6 **7** *hd* **Miss Fritton (IRE)**[37] 2309 2-9-0 0.......................... RichardHughes 16 64
(R Hannon) *chsd ldrs: rdn over 1f out: styng on same pce whn hmpd ins fnl f* **9/1**

0 **8** *1/2* **Gemini Jive (IRE)**[12] 3055 2-9-0 0.......................... AlanMunro 14 63
(M G Quinlan) *led: racd keenly: rdn and hdd over 1f out: wknd wl ins fnl f* **25/1**

9 *1* **First Queen** 2-9-0 0.......................... DaneO'Neill 3 60
(L M Cumani) *hld up: rdn over 1f out: nt trble ldrs* **14/1**

10 *1* **Sapphire Rose** 2-9-0 0.......................... PatCosgrave 15 57
(J G Portman) *s.i.s: nvr nrr* **25/1**

11 *3/4* **It's Toast (IRE)** 2-9-0 0.......................... JamesDoyle 7 55
(R M Beckett) *mid-div: rdn over 3f out: n.d* **11/2**[3]

0 **12** *1* **Hosanna**[42] 2160 2-9-0 0.......................... JimCrowley 5 52
(B J Meehan) *hld up in tch: rdn and wknd over 1f out* **16/1**

13 *1* **Stellarina (IRE)** 2-9-0 0.......................... StephenDonohoe 6 49
(W J Musson) *hld up: bhd fr 1/2-way* **66/1**

14 *2* **Elsie Jo (IRE)** 2-8-7 0.......................... TobyAtkinson(7) 13 43+
(M Wigham) *s.s: hld up: plld hrd: a bhd: hung rt ins fnl f* **50/1**

15 *24* **Hayley's Girl** 2-8-11 0.......................... MarcHalford(3) 1 —
(J Ryan) *s.i.s: outpcd* **33/1**

1m 14.31s (1.81) **Going Correction** -0.025s/f (Good) **15** Ran SP% **130.7**
Speed ratings (Par 92): **86,85,85,84,84 82,82,81,80,78 77,76,75,72,40**
toteswinger: 1&2 £45.90, 1&3 £35.60, 2&3 £5.30. CSF £161.90 TOTE £39.30: £8.90, £2.60, £2.40; EX 306.90.
Owner Sir Thomas Pilkington **Bred** Sir Thomas Pilkington **Trained** Newmarket, Suffolk

FOCUS
A big field of maiden juvenile fillies, but although the time was modest and little covered the first five at the line, this race is still likely to provide its share of winners.

NOTEBOOK
Dove Mews, out of a triple winner over 5f to 7f, did this nicely as she was always in a good position behind the leaders and reponded well when asked up the final hill. The yard is doing well with its two-year-olds this season and there should be more to come from her. (op 20-1)
Arctic Freedom(USA), a 52,000gns half-sister to four winners including the useful trio Ocean Ridge, Polar Circle and Fokine, stuck to the inside rail throughout and she responded well to pressure to fight all the way to the line. She should improve, but she has a speedy pedigree so is unlikely to get much further than this. (op 8-1)
Izzi Mill(USA) put in some decent late work down the outside without ever quite managing to get there, but she did have the benefit of a previous run. The form of her Nottingham debut is yet to really work out, but there should still be an ordinary maiden in her.
Bobbie Soxer(IRE), not unbacked, saw more daylight on the wide outside than most, but she did stay on in pleasing style and was not beaten far at the line. She was another who held the benefit of a previous run, but this was an improvement on her debut effort and the dam's side of her pedigree suggests she may improve for a bit further. (op 16-1)
Resort, whose stable has produced the likes of Enthused and Russian Rhythm to win this race on their debuts within the past ten years, is a half-sister to four winners including the smart pair Byron and Gallantry. She was always there or thereabouts and appeared to have every chance, but although she may not have been beaten far and may improve, performance did not suggest she is anything special. (op 3-1 tchd 7-2)
Stylish Dream(USA) ◆, out of a useful half-sister to the likes of Playful Act, Percussionist and Echoes In Eternity, was probably the biggest eye-catcher of the contest. She did not enjoy the smoothest of passages and had to be brought out wide in order to see daylight, but she stayed on in decent style over the last furlong or so and was still going forward under considerate handling at the line. She should be a different proposition next time, but is likely to need further in order to show her true ability. (tchd 12-1)
Miss Fritton(IRE), a well-backed favourite when unplaced in a Sandown maiden on her debut that has not worked out that well, was weak in the market this time. She was not disgraced though and would have been a bit closer had she not become short of room on a couple of occasions between Izzi Mill and Bobbie Soxer inside the last furlong. (op 11-2)

3457 NGK SPARK PLUGS H'CAP 1m
6:35 (6:36) (Class 5) (0-75,75) 3-Y-O+ **£3,885** (£1,156; £577; £288) **Stalls** Low

Form RPR

5643 **1** **Sonny Parkin**[7] 3218 6-9-8 **69**..........(v) PatCosgrave 6 82
(J Pearce) *dwlt: hld up: hdwy over 1f out: shkn up to ld ins fnl f: styd on: put hd in air towards fin* **8/1**

3-60 **2** *1 1/4* **Palmetto Point**[21] 2795 4-9-3 **67**..........(tp) TravisBlock(3) 11 76
(H Morrison) *chsd ldrs: rdn to ld and edgd lft over 1f out: hdd and unable qck ins fnl f* **14/1**

0-32 **3** *3/4* **Hannicean**[22] 2764 4-9-10 **71**.......................... RyanMoore 3 78
(M A Jarvis) *hld up in tch: rdn over 1f out: no ex ins fnl f* **10/3**[1]

3053 **4** *1/2* **Aggravation**[11] 3090 6-9-9 **70**.......................... JimmyFortune 8 76
(D R C Elsworth) *hld up: r.o ins fnl f: nt rch ldrs* **6/1**[2]

-436 **5** *4* **Game Park (USA)**[23] 2714 3-9-4 **75**.......................... JamieSpencer 9 70
(J R Fanshawe) *prom: rdn and edgd rt over 1f out: styd on same pce* **6/1**[2]

100 **6** *nk* **Rock Anthem (IRE)**[22] 2762 4-9-11 **72**.......................... GeorgeBaker 12 68
(Mike Murphy) *hld up: hdwy over 2f out: rdn over 1f out: wknd ins fnl f* **9/1**

4012 **7** *hd* **Josr's Magic (IRE)**[58] 1725 4-8-8 **58**.......................... KirstyMilczarek(3) 1 54
(H J Collingridge) *chsd ldrs: rdn and ev ch over 1f out: wknd ins fnl f* **12/1**

3-30 **8** *1 1/4* **Bikini**[46] 2043 3-8-8 **72**.......................... AmyScott(7) 7 63
(H Candy) *led: hdd over 6f out: chsd ldr tl led again 3f out: rdn and hdd over 1f out: wknd ins fnl f* **10/1**

000- **9** *3 1/4* **Tyzack (IRE)**[237] 6646 7-9-10 **71**.......................... MickyFenton 4 56
(Stef Liddiard) *hld up: plld hrd: rdn over 2f out: wkng whn hung lft over 1f out* **25/1**

3401 **10** *hd* **Sintenis Mac (GER)**[7] 3218 5-8-9 **56** oh3..........(b) AlanMunro 5 41
(P J O'Gorman) *hld up: hdwy over 2f out: sn rdn: wknd over 1f out* **13/2**[3]

003/ **11** *2 1/2* **Berkeley Castle (USA)**[219] 4-10-0 **75**.......................... DaneO'Neill 10 54
(E F Vaughan) *hld up: rdn over 2f out: sn hung lft and wknd* **33/1**

054- **12** *4* **Spanish Don**[326] 4234 10-9-10 **74**.......................... MarcHalford(3) 2 44
(D R C Elsworth) *chsd ldr tl led over 6f out: hdd 3f out: sn edgd rt: wknd wl over 1f out* **22/1**

1m 39.16s (-0.84) **Going Correction** -0.025s/f (Good)
WFA 3 from 4yo+ 10lb **12** Ran SP% **120.7**
Speed ratings (Par 103): **103,101,101,100,96 96,96,94,91,91 88,84**
toteswinger: 1&2 £43.80, 1&3 £4.00, 2&3 £28.20. CSF £113.82 CT £458.69 TOTE £10.40: £3.10, £4.70, £1.60; EX 221.70.
Owner Fran O'Brien **Bred** Blenheim Bloodstock **Trained** Newmarket, Suffolk

FOCUS
An ordinary handicap, but the pace was a solid one and that suited the hold-up horses. The front four pulled clear and the form looks reliable through te third and fourth.

3458 EURO 08 FINAL AT BETINTERNET.COM CLAIMING STKS 1m
7:05 (7:06) (Class 4) 3-Y-O **£4,533** (£1,348; £674; £336) **Stalls** Low

Form RPR

1-05 **1** **City Of The Kings (IRE)**[9] 3134 3-9-8 85.......................... HaddenFrost(5) 10 92
(R Hannon) *chsd ldr tl led over 4f out: rdn over 1f out: edgd lft: r.o wl* **9/2**[3]

-400 **2** *7* **Billion Dollar Kid**[8] 3155 3-9-5 89.......................... JamieSpencer 2 68
(S A Callaghan) *stdd s: hld up: hdwy over 2f out: rdn to chse wnr and hung lft fr over 1f out: wknd ins fnl f* **15/8**[1]

1600 **3** *1 1/4* **Vettorenjoy**[57] 1746 3-9-2 77.......................... JohnEgan 6 62
(M Botti) *prom: rdn over 2f out: wknd fnl f* **6/1**

-506 **4** 1 1/2 **King Hafhafah**[16] 2953 3-9-3 85............ JimCrowley 5 60
(I A Wood) *chsd ldrs: rdn over 1f out: sn wknd* **3/1**[2]

5040 **5** 2 **Artsu**[23] 2714 3-9-1 73............ RyanMoore 3 53
(M L W Bell) *s.i.s: hld up: hdwy u.p over 1f out: wknd fnl f* **6/1**

6-00 **6** 2 3/4 **Gainsborough's Art (IRE)**[30] 2509 3-9-5 59............ TQuinn 8 51
(D R C Elsworth) *plld hrd and prom: rdn over 2f out: wknd over 1f out* **33/1**

52 **7** 2 1/2 **Near The Front**[56] 1777 3-8-9 0............ MickyFenton 9 35
(Miss Gay Kelleway) *s.i.s: hld up: rdn 1/2-way: sme hdwy over 1f out: sn wknd* **16/1**

4626 **8** 21 **Una Auroraborealis**[17] 2907 3-8-4 46............(p) DavidKinsella 4 —
(J Ryan) *led over 3f: rdn and wknd over 2f out* **40/1**

1m 39.4s (-0.60) **Going Correction** -0.025s/f (Good) 8 Ran SP% **117.8**
Speed ratings (Par 101): **102,95,93,92,90 87,85,64**
toteswinger: 1&2 £1.40, 1&3 £8.80, 2&3 £3.70. CSF £13.83 TOTE £5.00: £1.60, £1.30, £2.10; EX 10.00.
Owner T Hyde **Bred** Tom McDonald **Trained** East Everleigh, Wilts

FOCUS
A fair claimer but with the favourite looking less than enthusiastic it probably took little winning.

3459 ARISTOCRACY RACING CLUB H'CAP 1m 4f
7:35 (7:37) (Class 4) (0-80,79) 3-Y-O **£5,180** (£1,541; £770; £384) **Stalls** Centre

Form RPR

0113 **1** **Excape (IRE)**[25] 2665 3-9-7 77............(b) JimmyFortune 6 89
(D R C Elsworth) *mde all: rdn over 1f out: styd on gamely* **8/1**

-440 **2** 1 **Celt**[20] 2840 3-9-7 77............ DaneO'Neill 9 87
(L M Cumani) *a.p: rdn: edgd rt and ev ch over 1f out: unable qckn towards fin* **7/4**[1]

6452 **3** 1 1/2 **Dramatic Solo**[15] 2985 3-8-9 65............(v[1]) PatCosgrave 2 73
(K R Burke) *chsd wnr tl rdn 2f out: styd on u.p* **20/1**

0-01 **4** 2 3/4 **Mon Plaisir (USA)**[36] 2342 3-9-5 75............ TedDurcan 12 79
(J L Dunlop) *hld up: nt clr run and lost pl over 2f out: styd on ins fnl f* **15/2**[3]

6-65 **5** 3/4 **Spell Caster**[17] 2920 3-9-8 78............ GeorgeBaker 10 80
(R M Beckett) *hld up: plld hrd: hdwy over 1f out: sn rdn and edgd lft: no ex ins fnl f* **13/2**[2]

40-6 **6** 1/2 **Highland Laddie**[65] 1556 3-9-0 70............ RichardHughes 11 72
(C R Egerton) *prom: rdn and hung lft fr over 1f out: wknd ins fnl f* **14/1**

4104 **7** 1/2 **Yes Mr President (IRE)**[20] 2840 3-9-9 79............(b) GregFairley 5 80
(M Johnston) *chsd ldrs: rdn and ev ch over 1f out: edgd lft and wknd ins fnl f* **12/1**

-012 **8** 3 1/2 **Celtic Dragon**[16] 2948 3-9-7 77............(t) JimCrowley 1 72
(Mrs A J Perrett) *hld up: hdwy over 3f out: rdn over 1f out: wknd fnl f* **15/2**[3]

0664 **9** 5 **Lady Sorcerer**[21] 2785 3-8-12 68............ JamieSpencer 7 55
(A P Jarvis) *s.i.s: hld up and bhd: plld hrd: hdwy on outside over 3f out: rdn and hung lft over 1f out: wknd fnl f* **16/1**

051 **10** 3 **Totoman**[45] 2090 3-9-7 77............ RyanMoore 3 59
(G G Margarson) *hld up: rdn and swtchd lft over 2f out: wknd over 1f out* **8/1**

-060 **11** 4 1/2 **Lavender And Lace**[12] 3057 3-7-13 60 oh3............(p) KellyHarrison(5) 8 35
(T Keddy) *hld up: plld hrd: rdn over 2f out: sn wknd* **50/1**

2m 30.97s (-1.93) **Going Correction** -0.025s/f (Good) 11 Ran SP% **122.4**
Speed ratings (Par 101): **105,104,103,101,101 100,100,98,94,92 89**
toteswinger: 1&2 £6.30, 1&3 £25.60, 2&3 £20.30. CSF £23.24 CT £289.00 TOTE £9.20: £2.50, £1.50, £4.20; EX 28.40.
Owner Raymond Tooth **Bred** Kildaragh Stud **Trained** Newmarket, Suffolk

FOCUS
Quite a decent middle-distance handicap for three-year-olds and despite the solid pace there were still several in with a chance passing the two-furlong pole with the runners spread right across the track. It may be significant that the first three home were always handy and they were also the ones who stayed closest to the stands' rail when the charge for home began. The form appears solid and looks worth treating positively.
Lady Sorcerer Official explanation: jockey said filly had run too freely

3460 BETINTERNET.COM E B F FILLIES' CONDITIONS STKS 6f
8:05 (8:07) (Class 3) 3-Y-O+ **£9,066** (£2,697; £1,348; £673) **Stalls** Low

Form RPR

3061 **1** **Angus Newz**[2] 3370 5-8-12 85............ TPQueally 7 93
(M Quinn) *mde all: edgd lft fnl f: rdn out* **7/2**[2]

4-60 **2** 1 1/2 **Sophie's Girl**[34] 2410 3-8-6 89 ow1............ AlanMunro 6 87
(B J Meehan) *a.p: rdn to chse wnr and edgd lft over 1f out: styd on same pce* **7/2**[2]

210- **3** 2 1/4 **Bastakiya (IRE)**[373] 2756 3-8-5 93............ DavidKinsella 5 79
(J H M Gosden) *trckd ldrs: rdn over 1f out: no ex ins fnl f* **5/1**

3453 **4** 2 1/4 **Tia Mia**[14] 2993 3-8-5 89............ JohnEgan 1 72
(M Botti) *sn pushed along and prom: rdn and nt clr run over 1f out: swtchd rt: wknd fnl f* **5/2**[1]

22-0 **5** 3 1/2 **Sakhee's Song (IRE)**[27] 2606 4-9-8 100............ JimmyFortune 3 73
(D R C Elsworth) *plld hrd: w wnr tl rdn over 1f out: sn wknd* **9/2**[3]

-050 **6** 3 1/2 **Wickedish**[10] 3113 4-8-5 47............(t) TobyAtkinson(7) 2 51
(M J Gingell) *hld up: wknd over 1f out* **100/1**

3550 **7** 4 1/2 **Time Share (IRE)**[1] 3405 4-8-7 47............ KellyHarrison(5) 9 37
(M Wigham) *hld up: wknd over 1f out: eased ins fnl f* **40/1**

1m 12.09s (-0.41) **Going Correction** -0.025s/f (Good)
WFA 3 from 4yo+ 7lb 7 Ran SP% **111.3**
Speed ratings (Par 104): **101,99,96,93,88 83,77**
toteswinger: 1&2 £2.50, 1&3 £3.60, 2&3 £6.70. CSF £15.23 TOTE £4.00: £2.30, £2.50; EX 19.20.
Owner M J Quinn **Bred** Henry And Mrs Rosemary Moszkowicz **Trained** Newmarket, Suffolk
■ Stewards' Enquiry : Toby Atkinson caution: used whip when out of contention

FOCUS
Rather a messy affair for this fillies' conditions event, with the early pace surprisingly modest for a sprint, and the final time was ordinary. The form is ordinary for the grade.

NOTEBOOK
Angus Newz was by no means well treated at these weights, but she is in decent form just now and was always in a good position up with the leaders. She found plenty when asked to stretch and is a credit to the yard, this being her 11th career victory. She will make some broodmare in due course. (op 5-2)
Sophie's Girl, not at her best in her two previous starts this term, ran better here even though her brave efforts to get on terms with the winner were in vain. She does not look the easiest to place, however. (op 11-2 tchd 13-2)
Bastakiya(IRE), last seen finishing unplaced in last year's Queen Mary, was best in at the weights but that was probably less relevant given her long absence. She did not perform badly under the circumstances and she was by far the least-exposed in this field. (op 7-2)
Tia Mia went off the well-backed favourite despite not having won since her racecourse debut. She did not enjoy the clearest of runs and had to be switched out wide in order to see daylight, but once in the clear she did not exactly take off and she looks another that will remain difficult to place. (op 3-1)
Sakhee's Song(IRE), having her second start for the yard since arriving from Italy and down in class, looked a very reluctant leader as she pulled very hard against the far rail and once the winner went for home she had nothing left. (op 5-1 tchd 4-1)

3461 SIGN-UP BONUS AT BETINTERNET.COM H'CAP 1m 2f
8:40 (8:40) (Class 4) (0-85,85) 3-Y-O+
£4,984 (£1,492; £746; £373; £186; £93) **Stalls** Centre

Form RPR

01- **1** **Hawaass (USA)**[282] 5538 3-9-0 83............ GregFairley 3 96+
(M Johnston) *mde all: shkn up fnl f: r.o wl* **3/1**[1]

-152 **2** 3 3/4 **Taken (IRE)**[114] 799 3-8-8 77............ JamieSpencer 6 79
(J R Fanshawe) *a.p: rdn to chse wnr fnl f: styd on same pce* **11/2**[3]

4410 **3** 1 **Ross Moor**[14] 3003 6-8-13 70............ JimCrowley 2 70
(Mike Murphy) *s.s: hld up: hdwy over 2f out: rdn over 1f out: sn hung rt: no ex fnl f* **11/2**[3]

5-32 **4** nk **Dawn Sky**[39] 2264 4-10-0 85............(b[1]) TedDurcan 4 84
(D R Lanigan) *chsd wnr: rdn and edgd lft over 1f out: no ex fnl f* **5/1**[2]

-534 **5** 1 **Zaif (IRE)**[22] 2764 5-9-7 78............ GeorgeBaker 1 75
(Simon Earle) *hld up: hdwy and hmpd over 1f out: n.d after* **6/1**

0001 **6** 1/2 **Quince (IRE)**[13] 3029 5-9-9 80............(v) JimmyQuinn 9 76
(J Pearce) *prom: rdn 2f out: styd on same pce appr fnl f* **6/1**

1050 **7** 3/4 **Folio (IRE)**[14] 3003 8-9-9 80............ StephenDonohoe 7 75
(W J Musson) *hld up: hdwy over 3f out: rdn over 1f out: wkng whn hmpd ins fnl f* **16/1**

40-0 **8** 1 3/4 **Kestrel Cross (IRE)**[22] 2762 6-9-11 82............ DaneO'Neill 5 73
(L M Cumani) *hld up: racd keenly: rdn and wknd over 1f out* **10/1**

2m 7.10s (1.60) **Going Correction** -0.025s/f (Good)
WFA 3 from 4yo+ 12lb 8 Ran SP% **116.0**
Speed ratings (Par 105): **92,89,88,87,87 86,86,84**
toteswinger: 1&2 £12.80, 1&3 £13.00, 2&3 £9.90. CSF £19.99 CT £86.39 TOTE £3.40: £1.50, £1.70, £2.40; EX 10.80.
Owner Sheikh Ahmed Al Maktoum **Bred** Darley **Trained** Middleham Moor, N Yorks

FOCUS
A very unsatisfactory handicap thanks to a very moderate early pace and the favourite was basically gifted it. The form behind the winner looks ordinary.

3462 HUGHES H'CAP 5f
9:10 (9:10) (Class 4) (0-85,83) 3-Y-O **£5,180** (£1,541; £770; £384) **Stalls** Low

Form RPR

-050 **1** **Hadaf (IRE)**[14] 2998 3-9-8 82............ RHills 7 94
(M P Tregoning) *hld up: hdwy 1/2-way: led 1f out: drvn out* **8/1**

2111 **2** hd **Speedy Senorita (IRE)**[7] 3217 3-8-1 68............ DeclanCannon(7) 11 79
(K R Burke) *led: hdd over 3f out: led again over 1f out: sn rdn and hdd: r.o* **11/2**[3]

0521 **3** 2 **Monsieur Reynard**[18] 2896 3-9-3 77............ RyanMoore 4 81
(B J Meehan) *hld up: hdwy over 1f out: sn rdn: styd on same pce ins fnl f* **3/1**[1]

-235 **4** 1 **Piscean (USA)**[6] 3273 3-9-5 79............ MickyFenton 1 79+
(T Keddy) *s.i.s: outpcd: edgd rt and r.o ins fnl f: nrst fin* **8/1**

-321 **5** nse **Superduper**[14] 2991 3-9-2 76............ RichardHughes 12 76
(R Hannon) *chsd ldrs: rdn over 1f out: styd on same pce* **9/2**[2]

1341 **6** 1 3/4 **Requisite**[14] 3000 3-9-6 80............ JimCrowley 6 74
(I A Wood) *chsd ldrs: rdn and nt clr run over 1f out: wknd ins fnl f* **9/2**[2]

6104 **7** hd **Magical Speedfit (IRE)**[7] 3224 3-9-1 75............ TPQueally 5 68
(G G Margarson) *hld up: rdn over 1f out: nvr trbld ldrs* **14/1**

1100 **8** 1 1/4 **Ten Down**[29] 2529 3-9-0 81............ AntiocoMurgia(7) 2 70
(Miss Gay Kelleway) *led over 3f out: rdn and hdd over 1f out: wknd ins fnl f* **33/1**

-430 **9** nk **Another Socket**[18] 2896 3-8-13 73............ StephenDonohoe 9 60
(E S McMahon) *hood removed late: bhd: hdwy u.p 2f out: wknd fnl f* **20/1**

05-0 **10** 5 **Regal Step**[39] 2258 3-9-9 83............ TedDurcan 3 52
(R M H Cowell) *trckd ldr: rdn over 1f out: wknd fnl f* **20/1**

5256 **11** 1 **Baytown Blaze**[45] 2068 3-8-8 73............ KellyHarrison(5) 8 39
(M Wigham) *hld up: rdn and wknd over 1f out* **33/1**

59.09 secs (-0.01) **Going Correction** -0.025s/f (Good) 11 Ran SP% **121.0**
Speed ratings (Par 101): **99,98,95,93,93 91,90,88,88,80 78**
toteswinger: 1&2 £10.80, 1&3 £5.70, 2&3 £2.70. CSF £50.68 CT £167.19 TOTE £11.90: £3.00, £1.80, £1.70; EX 52.90 Place 6 £56.93, Place 5 £16.03.
Owner Hamdan Al Maktoum **Bred** Shadwell Estate Company Limited **Trained** Lambourn, Berks

FOCUS
A fair handicap sprint and the form looks pretty solid rated around the placed horses.
Regal Step Official explanation: jockey said filly had no more to give
T/Plt: £125.10 to a £1 stake. Pool: £57,077.95. 332.95 winning tickets. T/Qpdt: £27.60 to a £1 stake. Pool: £3,654.00. 97.90 winning tickets. CR

2851 CURRAGH (R-H)
Friday, June 27

OFFICIAL GOING: Good to yielding

3466a SAOIRE STKS (LISTED RACE) (FILLIES) 6f
7:30 (7:30) 2-Y-O **£26,327** (£7,724; £3,680; £1,253)

RPR

1 **Shimah (USA)**[20] 2851 2-8-12............ DPMcDonogh 4 104+
(Kevin Prendergast, Ire) *trckd ldrs: 3rd 1/2-way: impr to ld under 2f out: rdn clr fr 1f out: kpt on strly* **6/4**[1]

2 3 **Chintz (IRE)**[16] 2958 2-8-12............ JMurtagh 2 95
(David Wachman, Ire) *chsd ldr in cl 2nd: rdn to dispute under 2f out: 2nd and no ex 1f out whn swtchd: kpt on same pce fnl f* **9/4**[2]

3 6 **What's Up Pussycat (IRE)**[12] 3066 2-8-12............ WMLordan 6 77
(David Wachman, Ire) *hld up: rdn into 4th 2f out: no ex in mod 3rd over 1f out: kpt on same pce* **8/1**[3]

4 2 **Pasar Silbano (IRE)**[34] 2416 2-8-12............ KLatham 1 71
(G M Lyons, Ire) *dwlt: sn chsd ldrs: 4th 1/2-way: rdn in 5th 2f out: no ex: kpt on same pce* **11/1**

5 1 3/4 **Cool Tarifa (IRE)**[25] 2686 2-8-12............ FMBerry 7 66
(J G Burns, Ire) *towards rr: sme late hdwy to mod 6th over 1f out: kpt on same pce* **14/1**

6 ¾ **Excelente (IRE)**[5] 3302 2-8-12 .... WJSupple 3 64
(Mrs John Harrington, Ire) *chsd ldrs early: 6th 1/2-way: rdn in 7th over 2f out and no imp: kpt on one pce* **16/1**

7 1¼ **Sky Mystic (IRE)**[12] 3067 2-8-12 .... KJManning 8 60
(J S Bolger, Ire) *chsd ldrs: 5th 1/2-way: rdn and wknd 2 1/2f out* **12/1**

8 nk **Ceist Eile (IRE)** 2-8-12 .... DJMoran 5 59
(J S Bolger, Ire) *led: rdn and hdd under 2f out: no ex: wknd over 1f out* **33/1**

1m 12.97s (-1.53) **Going Correction** -0.225s/f (Firm) **8** Ran SP% **113.4**
Speed ratings: **101,97,89,86,84 83,81,80**
CSF £4.83 TOTE £2.00: £1.10, £1.50, £2.10; DF 4.10.
Owner Hamdan Al Maktoum **Bred** Shadwell Farm LLC **Trained** Friarstown, Co Kildare
■ Stewards' Enquiry : D P McDonogh caution: careless riding

NOTEBOOK
Shimah(USA) ◆ had run out an impressive maiden winner on her debut over course and distance 20 days previously and that form has been given a big boost when the runner-up, Connie Mac, went on to finish third in the Queen Mary at Royal Ascot. She was faced with much easier ground this time, but she handled it without fuss and ultimately made it two wins from as many starts with another clear-cut display. There was an awful lot to like about the gear change she showed when asked to win the race and is clearly a smart filly, with this trip looking perfect for her at present. Her trainer - holds her in very high regard - now intends to bring her back for the Group 1 Phoenix Stakes next month, again over the course and distance, where she will meet the colts for the first occasion. She was later given quotes of around 16/1 for next year's 1,000 Guineas. (op 9/10 tchd 7/4)
Chintz(IRE), a debut maiden winner at Leopardstown 16 days previously, got backed into clear second-favourtism and was the only one to give the eventual winner a serious time through the race. She was firmly put in her place when that rival quickened for home, but still finished nicely clear of the remainder and is evidently an improving filly. She looks well up to making her mark in this sort of class before the year is out and, seeing as her dam was a smart middle distance performer, will likely be helped by the return to a stiffer test now. (op 9/4 tchd 7/4)

3467 - 3469a (Foreign Racing) - See Raceform Interactive

3431
CHESTER (L-H)
Saturday, June 28

OFFICIAL GOING: Good (8.3)
Rail realignment added 12yards per circuit to advertised distances.
Wind: Moderate, across Weather: Overcast with bright spells developing

3470 TESSUTI NOVICE STKS 5f 16y
2:15 (2:16) (Class 4) 2-Y-O £4,727 (£1,406; £702; £351) **Stalls** Low

Form RPR

222 1 **Every Second**[15] 3005 2-8-12 0.......... RichardMullen 3 83+
(E S McMahon) *mde all: qcknd away over 1f out: r.o wl fnl f and a in command* **6/4**[1]

421 2 3¼ **Countrywide City (IRE)**[9] 3178 2-8-11 0.......... AshleyHamblett[(5)] 7 75
(P W Chapple-Hyam) *chsd wnr tl over 3f out: rdn over 1f out: styd on to take 2nd ins fnl f: nt trble wnr* **5/1**

4125 3 ¾ **Mazzola**[21] 2826 2-9-5 0.......... ChrisCatlin 5 75
(M R Channon) *chsd ldrs: wnt 2nd over 3f out: rdn and outpcd by wnr over 1f out: lost 2nd ins fnl f: styd on same pce after* **9/2**[3]

513 4 hd **River Rye (IRE)**[36] 2377 2-8-11 0.......... PatrickHills[(3)] 2 70
(R Hannon) *hld up: effrt over 1f out: styd on ins fnl f: nvr able to chal* **9/4**[2]

00 5 13 **Ballarina**[7] 3259 2-8-7 0.......... DavidAllan 1 16
(E J Alston) *chsd ldrs: pushed along 1/2-way: wknd over 1f out* **16/1**

66 6 4½ **That Boy Ronaldo**[18] 2903 2-8-4 0.......... AndrewMullen[(3)] 4 —
(A Berry) *missed break: a outpcd and bhd* **28/1**

62.22 secs (1.22) **Going Correction** +0.25s/f (Good) **6** Ran SP% **114.9**
Speed ratings (Par 95): **100,94,93,93,72 65**
toteswinger: 1&2 £1.60, 1&3 £1.20, 2&3 £3.90. CSF £9.96 TOTE £2.40: £1.60, £2.60; EX 9.70.
Owner J C Fretwell **Bred** Mrs Fiona Denniff **Trained** Lichfield, Staffs

FOCUS
A creditable winning time for what was just a fair contest with the runner-up to his mark the best guide.

NOTEBOOK
Every Second, runner-up on all three previous attempts, had finished behind River Rye at Windsor in May, but was 4lb better off this time and he simply had too much speed for his rivals. Soon in front, he settled things quickly off the home bend and was always in control. A positive ride clearly suits him best and he should continue to improve, while ground no faster than good also seems to suit. (op 11-8 tchd 9-4, 5-2 in a place)
Countrywide City(IRE), who made hard work of justifying odds of 2/5 at Warwick the previous week, stepped up on that effort and ran on well under pressure to take second. He was never in with a chance against the winner, but may have more to offer in nurseries. (op 6-1 tchd 4-1)
Mazzola ran an improved race to take fifth in the Woodcote Stakes at Epsom, but there was a big doubt as to whether this drop in trip was required and he was readily done for toe by the winner. This was a fair effort considering he was giving upward of 7lb all round and a return to further will help. (op 7-2)
River Rye(IRE) was disappointing. She beat the winner at Windsor in May and looked a big danger on this return to 5f, having finished third behind Shampagne over 6f at Pontefract last time. However, she lacked the speed to get involved and in hindsight her rider would probably have had her closer to the pace. (op 3-1 tchd 2-1)

3471 DEE 106.3 H'CAP 1m 4f 66y
2:50 (2:51) (Class 4) (0-85,82) 3-Y-O £5,180 (£1,541; £770; £384) **Stalls** Low

Form RPR

2104 1 **Sweet Lightning**[26] 2665 3-9-9 82.......... LiamJones 3 93+
(W R Muir) *n.m.r sn after s: stdd in midfield: clsd over 3f out: led over 1f out: sn qcknd clr: pushed out* **11/4**[1]

1403 2 6 **Kiribati King (IRE)**[16] 2985 3-8-9 68.......... ChrisCatlin 1 70
(M R Channon) *hld up: rdn and hdwy over 1f out: styd on to take 2nd wl ins fnl f: no ch w wnr* **5/1**[3]

1-14 3 ½ **Relative Strength (IRE)**[17] 2948 3-9-5 78.......... LPKeniry 5 79
(A M Balding) *hld up in rr: u.p fr over 5f out: hung lft fr over 1f out: styd on ins fnl f: nt pce to get competitive* **15/2**

-212 4 ¾ **Criterion**[38] 2310 3-9-8 81.......... (v) DeanMcKeown 6 81
(Sir Michael Stoute) *sn led: rdn and hdd over 1f out: sn edgd lft: one pce fnl f* **3/1**[2]

4 5 2¾ **London Times (IRE)**[26] 2668 3-9-5 78.......... GregFairley 7 73
(M Johnston) *prom: pushed along 4f out: pressed ldr: rdn whn stl chalng over 1f out: wknd ins fnl f* **9/1**

-213 6 5 **Top Ticket (IRE)**[37] 2327 3-9-7 80.......... RichardMullen 2 67
(D M Simcock) *trckd ldrs: pushed along over 4f out: rdn over 2f out: wknd over 1f out* **3/1**[2]

2m 39.9s **Going Correction** +0.25s/f (Good) **6** Ran SP% **115.1**
Speed ratings (Par 101): **110,106,105,105,103 100**
toteswinger: 1&2 £3.30, 1&3 £5.60, 2&3 £7.80. CSF £17.30 TOTE £3.90: £2.10, £3.00; EX 18.90.
Owner A J De V Patrick & M J Caddy **Bred** Mrs M Lavell **Trained** Lambourn, Berks

FOCUS
Just a fair handicap, but Sweet Lightning won in the style of a very useful sort. The winning time was also decent and the form looks solid with the next four home behind the winner close to their marks.
Top Ticket(IRE) Official explanation: jockey said colt was unable to handle the track

3472 BALANCE WINES H'CAP 5f 16y
3:30 (3:33) (Class 3) (0-90,91) 3-Y-O+ £8,831 (£2,643; £1,321; £660; £329) **Stalls** Low

Form RPR

066 1 **Bo McGinty (IRE)**[15] 3009 7-8-11 80.......... (b) FrederikTylicki[(7)] 2 89
(R A Fahey) *bmpd sn after s: in tch: effrt over 1f out: r.o to ld ins fnl f: pushed out towards fin* **13/2**[3]

0015 2 ¾ **Stolt (IRE)**[15] 3009 4-9-6 87.......... AshleyHamblett[(5)] 4 93
(N Wilson) *led: rdn over 1f out: hdd ins fnl f: nt qckn* **4/1**[1]

3123 3 hd **Little Pete (IRE)**[7] 3273 3-9-6 88.......... LPKeniry 7 92
(A M Balding) *midfield: rdn and hdwy over 1f out: r.o and gaining at fin* **4/1**[1]

2400 4 1½ **Carcinetto (IRE)**[15] 2993 6-9-7 83.......... StephenDonohoe 5 83
(P D Evans) *bhd: pushed along 1/2-way: styd on ins fnl f: nt pce to chal ldrs* **20/1**

U00- 5 hd **Kay Two (IRE)**[222] 6876 6-9-7 86.......... (p) PatrickHills[(3)] 1 85
(R J Price) *trckd ldrs: nt clr run on inner over 1f out: sn rdn: no ex fnl 100yds* **8/1**

4-05 6 ¾ **Golden Dixie (USA)**[37] 2326 9-10-0 90.......... TGMcLaughlin 10 87+
(R A Harris) *midfield: pushed along 1/2-way: styd on ins fnl f: nt pce to rch ldrs* **25/1**

0412 7 1 **Princess Ellis**[7] 3252 4-9-11 87.......... DavidAllan 8 80+
(E J Alston) *prom: rdn and edgd lft over 1f out: wknd fnl 100yds* **4/1**[1]

016 8 1 **Not My Choice (IRE)**[35] 2390 3-9-6 88.......... LiamJones 3 76
(S Parr) *s.i.s: towards rr: pushed along 1/2-way: nvr on terms* **9/2**[2]

0440 9 shd **Malapropism**[13] 3062 8-9-3 79.......... ChrisCatlin 6 68
(M R Channon) *prom: squeezed out 2f out: wknd over 1f out* **14/1**

61.33 secs (0.33) **Going Correction** +0.25s/f (Good)
WFA 3 from 4yo+ 6lb **9** Ran SP% **117.9**
Speed ratings (Par 107): **107,105,105,103,102 101,99,98,98**
toteswinger: 1&2 £7.00, 1&3 £4.50, 2&3 £2.80. CSF £33.43 CT £119.78 TOTE £7.60: £2.10, £2.10, £1.50; EX 31.20.
Owner Paddy McGinty & Bo Turnbull **Bred** Stephen Breen **Trained** Musley Bank, N Yorks

FOCUS
A decent little sprint rated around the first two and likely to produce winners.

NOTEBOOK
Bo McGinty(IRE), back on his last winning mark, got bumped coming out of the stalls, but it did not knock him off his game and he came with a strong run inside the final furlong to score, just having to be pushed out under hands and heels riding. He will need to find more to follow up, but it is not hard to see him going well after a small rise. (op 17-2)
Stolt(IRE), 7lb higher than when winning at York back in May, ran well for a long way off this mark last time and that was again the case here, just getting run out of it inside the final furlong. He is holding his form well and is clearly capable of winning off this mark. (tchd 5-1)
Little Pete(IRE), one of two three-year-olds in the field, has been running well in decent contests, winning one himself back in May, and he looked a player off the same mark as when finishing third at Newmarket last week. He came with his challenge, but got going a little too late and found the line coming too soon. This was another sterling effort though and he looks more than capable of lifting a similar race. (op 5-1 tchd 7-2)
Carcinetto(IRE), having her first start over 5f since November 2006, remains 2lb higher than when last winning, but this was certainly a more promising display. She was struggling early, but really came home well and this may set her up for a return to winning form.
Kay Two(IRE), having his first outing since November, was always likely to be found wanting and it was encouraging he ran so well back in fifth, meeting some trouble before emptying out inside the final half a furlong. One can expect an improved showing next time. (op 15-2 tchd 9-1)
Golden Dixie(USA), who had the worst of the draw, made a little late headway, but could do with some further assistance from the Handicapper. (op 16-1)
Princess Ellis, just denied in a Listed contest at Ayr the other day, has been stuck up 12lb and she could make no impact, using up too much gas from her wide draw. (tchd 7-2)
Not My Choice(IRE), a winner here at the May meeting, led throughout that day, but he was slowly away on this occasion and could never get into it. (op 5-1 tchd 7-1)

3473 PETER GILDING MAIDEN STKS 1m 2f 75y
4:00 (4:01) (Class 4) 3-Y-O+ £5,180 (£1,541; £770; £384) **Stalls** High

Form RPR

-432 1 **My Aunt Fanny**[18] 2920 3-8-10 79.......... LPKeniry 2 72+
(A M Balding) *racd keenly: a handy: chsd ldr 2f out: r.o to ld ent fnl f: sn clr: readily* **4/7**[1]

43 2 3½ **Maha Dubai (USA)**[30] 2536 3-8-10 0.......... GregFairley 1 65
(M Johnston) *led: hdd 7f out: remained prom: regained ld wl over 2f out: rdn over 1f out: hdd ent fnl f: sn no ch w wnr* **11/2**[3]

3 2 **Elbistan (IRE)** 3-9-1 0.......... StephenDonohoe 9 66
(Evan Williams) *s.i.s: hld up: hdwy over 2f out: wnt 3rd over 1f out: kpt on fnl f wout pce to trble front pair* **25/1**

60 4 2 **Lisbon Lion (IRE)**[21] 2847 3-8-8 0.......... SimonPearce[(7)] 8 62
(N J Vaughan) *racd keenly: hld up: hdwy 7f out: lost pl 3f out: n.d after* **20/1**

2 5 4½ **Akarshan (IRE)**[33] 2449 3-9-1 0.......... ChrisCatlin 7 54
(Evan Williams) *in tch: carried wd on bnd and lost pl after 2f: pushed along over 4f out: hdwy u.p over 2f out: sn wknd* **9/2**[2]

6/5- 6 nk **Hernando Cortes**[118] 6369 4-9-13 76.......... PAspell 3 53
(D McCain Jnr) *prom tl rdn and wknd over 4f out* **12/1**

6000 7 8 **Wee Ellie Coburn**[16] 2966 4-9-5 37.......... LeeVickers[(3)] 5 33
(M Mullineaux) *plld hrd: hld up: hdwy after 2f: hung rt and rn v wd rnd 1st bnd: hung rt thereafter: led 7f out: hdd wl over 2f out: wknd wl over 1f out* **66/1**

2m 14.43s (2.23) **Going Correction** +0.25s/f (Good)
WFA 3 from 4yo 12lb **7** Ran SP% **115.0**
Speed ratings (Par 105): **101,98,96,95,91 91,84**
toteswinger: 1&2 £1.40, 1&3 £14.20, 2&3 £32.70. CSF £4.23 TOTE £1.60: £1.20, £2.20; EX 3.60.
Owner J C & S R Hitchins **Bred** J C , J R And S R Hitchins **Trained** Kingsclere, Hants

FOCUS
Not a particularly competitive heat with the winner not needing to run to previous form to score, although the second ran to her mark.

Wee Ellie Coburn Official explanation: jockey said filly hung right-handed throughout

3474 STIRLING FIBRE CLAIMING STKS — 1m 2f 75y

4:30 (4:31) (Class 5) 3-Y-0+ **£3,432** (£1,021; £510; £254) **Stalls** High

Form RPR

0055 **1** **Lucayan Dancer**[18] 2904 8-9-1 67 AndrewMullen(3) 3 77
(D Nicholls) *racd keenly in midfield: pushed along 5f out: hdwy over 2f out: r.o to ld wl ins fnl f: on top towards fin* **9/2**[3]

3062 **2** 1 ¼ **Cheshire Prince**[7] 3258 4-9-6 71 LiamJones 8 76
(W M Brisbourne) *led: rdn over 1f out: hdd wl ins fnl f: nt qckn cl home* **4/1**[2]

1644 **3** 1 **Celticello (IRE)**[5] 3311 6-9-4 73 StephenDonohoe 4 72
(P D Evans) *midfield: hdwy 3f out: rdn over 1f out: styd on ins fnl f: nt rch front pair* **9/2**[3]

1405 **4** hd **Gold Prospect**[16] 2970 4-9-5 76 RichardMullen 5 73
(M L W Bell) *in tch: nt clr run over 1f out: sn swtchd lft: styd on ins fnl f: no further prog on ldrs nr fin* **5/1**

252- **5** 2 ½ **Torrens (IRE)**[245] 6501 6-9-3 76 TGMcLaughlin 2 66
(Ollie Pears) *in tch: wnt 2nd 2f out: sn rdn: wknd wl ins fnl f* **7/2**[1]

1225 **6** 2 ¼ **Sun Of The Sea**[81] 1256 4-9-11 74 RichardThomas 7 69
(N P Littmoden) *s.i.s: bhd: kpt on ent fnl f: nvr in contention* **12/1**

3004 **7** nk **Sweet World**[17] 2932 4-9-3 55 LPKeniry 6 61
(B J Llewellyn) *trckd ldrs: wnt 2nd over 5f out tl rdn 2f out: wknd ins fnl f* **33/1**

0106 **8** 3 ¼ **Sawwaah (IRE)**[93] 1041 11-8-10 70 PaulPickard(7) 11 54
(D Carroll) *bhd: rdn 2f out: hung lft over 1f out: no imp* **25/1**

00 **9** 11 **Cabb City (IRE)**[8] 3230 5-8-7 30 AshleyHamblett(5) 10 27
(W M Brisbourne) *prom: rdn and lost pl over 4f out: hung rt whn toiling wl over 2f out* **100/1**

0-00 **10** nk **Temple Place (IRE)**[6] 1920 7-9-9 92 PAspell 9 37
(D McCain Jnr) *rel to r and v.s.a: bhd: hdwy 6f out: wknd over 3f out* **11/1**

2m 14.58s (2.38) **Going Correction** +0.25s/f (Good) **10** Ran SP% **119.1**
Speed ratings (Par 103): **100,99,98,98,96 94,94,91,82,82**
toteswinger: 1&2 £5.10, 1&3 £4.90, 2&3 £4.30. CSF £23.14 TOTE £5.70: £1.80, £1.50, £2.00; EX 21.10.
Owner Racegoers Club Owners Group **Bred** The National Stud Owner Breeders Club Ltd **Trained** Sessay, N Yorks
■ Stewards' Enquiry : Ashley Hamblett one-day ban: used whip when out of contention (Jul 12)

FOCUS
A competitive race for the grade and rated around the first two, although the form is not totally solid.
Sun Of The Sea Official explanation: jockey said gelding never travelled

3475 CRUISE NIGHTSPOT H'CAP — 7f 2y

5:05 (5:06) (Class 3) (0-90,89) 3-Y-0 **£8,831** (£2,643; £1,321; £660; £329) **Stalls** Low

Form RPR

-250 **1** **Adversity**[14] 3039 3-9-3 83 RichardMullen 5 98+
(Sir Michael Stoute) *trckd ldr: led over 1f out: qcknd clr ins fnl f: comf* **6/4**[1]

4054 **2** 5 **Mister Hardy**[10] 3141 3-8-10 83 FrederikTylicki(7) 4 85
(R A Fahey) *wnt lft s: midfield: swtchd rt and hdwy 2f out: styd on to take 2nd ins fnl f: no ch w wnr* **8/1**

2-21 **3** 1 ½ **Ramaad**[17] 2929 3-9-4 84 LiamJones 2 81
(W J Haggas) *wnt rt s: in tch: n.m.r after 1f: rdn to chse ldrs over 1f out: kpt on u.p ins fnl f* **9/2**[3]

0-00 **4** 1 ¼ **Danzig Fox**[32] 2490 3-8-4 70 oh5 TWilliams 1 64
(M Mullineaux) *hld up: rdn along over 2f out: hdwy 1f out: styd on ins fnl f: nt pce to chal ldrs* **33/1**

34-1 **5** nk **Transfer**[23] 2756 3-9-3 83 LPKeniry 3 76
(A M Balding) *bmpd s: chsd ldrs: rdn over 1f out: wknd ins fnl f* **10/3**[2]

603 **6** ¾ **I Confess**[7] 3256 3-9-2 82 StephenDonohoe 8 73
(P D Evans) *wnt lft s: sn bmpd and racd keenly: in rr: rdn and hdwy over 1f out: one pce ins fnl f* **12/1**

2-40 **7** 2 **Zakhaaref**[35] 2403 3-9-9 89 GregFairley 6 75
(M Johnston) *in tch: rdn and wknd over 1f out* **9/1**

-000 **8** 4 ½ **Calmdownmate (IRE)**[10] 3141 3-9-3 83 (b[1]) TGMcLaughlin 9 57
(K R Burke) *rdn to sn ld: rdn and hdd over 1f out: wknd ins fnl f* **25/1**

0-00 **9** 8 **Jebel Tara**[14] 3039 3-9-0 87 (t) DebraEngland(7) 7 39
(C E Brittain) *bmpd s: towards rr: nigged along over 4f out: toiling and n.d over 2f out* **33/1**

-000 **10** 25 **Seeking Star (IRE)**[14] 3047 3-9-8 88 ChrisCatlin 11 —
(M R Channon) *bhd: pushed along over 4f out: lost tch over 3f out* **22/1**

1m 27.59s (1.09) **Going Correction** +0.25s/f (Good) **10** Ran SP% **124.1**
Speed ratings (Par 103): **103,97,95,94,93 92,90,85,76,47**
toteswinger: 1&2 £4.00, 1&3 £2.50, 2&3 £7.90. CSF £15.31 CT £47.94 TOTE £2.70: £1.30, £2.40, £1.90; EX 20.90 Place 6 £16.91, Place 5 £8.75.
Owner Sir Alex Ferguson **Bred** Branston Stud Ltd **Trained** Newmarket, Suffolk
■ Stewards' Enquiry : T G McLaughlin seven-day ban: careless riding (Jul 12-18)

FOCUS
A decent handicap with a clear-cut winner and the placed horses close to recent form, although the fourth from 5lb wrong raises doubts.

NOTEBOOK
Adversity has had little go right for him in his last two starts, being drawn terribly here at the May meeting and then not getting a run at Sandown last time, but connections opted to make a bit more use of him on this occasion and this galloping sort spurted clear in the straight. This was more like it and he remains capable of further improvement now, getting his head in front again, although the Handicapper looks sure to hit him hard. (op 2-1)
Mister Hardy has been shaping as though worth another try at this trip and he ran on well from the home turn to claim second. He found himself running off a career-low mark here and it should not be long before this once useful two-year-old is winning again. (tchd 15-2)
Ramaad, representing an in-form yard, did the job well enough at Beverley last time and he looked a player on this handicap debut, despite an opening mark of 84 looking a shade harsh. He did not have much room to operate in on the inside though and, having got in the clear, could only stay on at the one pace. This was still a good effort and he remains capable of better. (op 4-1 tchd 5-1)
Danzig Fox had the best of the draw and ran easily his best race of the season so far, and from 5lb out of the handicap as well. He will find easier opportunities than this. (op 28-1)
Transfer, ready winner of his maiden at Lingfield the other day, looked potentially well-weighted, having beaten a fair sort there, but he found disappointingly little for pressure and folded from a furlong out. He is clearly better than this, but has a bit to prove now. (tchd 7-2)
I Confess did not shape without promise, making a little late headway. (tchd 9-1)
Zakhaaref is a disappointing sort and clearly needs further assistance from the Handicapper. (op 11-1 tchd 12-1)
Calmdownmate(IRE) ran well for a long way in the first-time blinkers, but it remains to be seen whether he can build on it. (op 20-1)
T/Plt: £33.60 to a £1 stake. Pool: £75,419.87. 1,637.18 winning tickets. T/Qpdt: £6.30 to a £1 stake. Pool: £4,263.19. 497.50 winning tickets. DO

3437 DONCASTER (L-H)

Saturday, June 28

OFFICIAL GOING: Good to firm (9.4)
The ground had dried out from the previous day and was described as 'very nearly firm'. The running rail was again in position on the round course.
Wind: light, half against Weather: overcast

3476 SOCIETY LIFESTYLE AND LEISURE MAGAZINE MAIDEN STKS — 7f

6:40 (6:40) (Class 5) 2-Y-0 **£3,238** (£963; £481; £240) **Stalls** High

Form RPR

1 **Doctor Crane (USA)** 2-9-3 0 RobertHavlin 6 82+
(J H M Gosden) *trckd ldrs: swtchd lft over 1f out: led ins fnl f: edgd rt: r.o wl* **15/8**[2]

0 **2** 1 ¾ **Royal Executioner (USA)**[18] 2916 2-9-3 0 AlanMunro 1 75
(P W Chapple-Hyam) *w ldrs: sltly hmpd and nt qckn ins fnl f* **7/1**

0 **3** ½ **Thunderball**[28] 2592 2-9-3 0 DanielTudhope 4 73
(A J McCabe) *w ldr: led over 2f out tl ins fnl f: no ex* **5/1**[3]

4 7 **Pilot Light** 2-9-3 0 DavidAllan 2 56
(T D Easterby) *dwlt and swvd lft s: hdwy to chse ldrs over 4f out: lost pl over 1f out* **14/1**

5 1 **Tarzan (IRE)** 2-9-3 0 JoeFanning 5 53
(M Johnston) *led: hung lft thrght: hdd over 2f out: sn lost pl* **7/4**[1]

6 9 **Ruud Revenge (USA)** 2-8-12 0 ShaneCreighton(5) 3 31
(Miss V Haigh) *chsd ldrs: outpcd and lost pl over 3f out: sn bhd* **20/1**

1m 28.61s (2.31) **Going Correction** +0.025s/f (Good) **6** Ran SP% **111.7**
Speed ratings (Par 93): **87,85,84,76,75 65**
toteswinger: 1&2 £27.80, 1&3 £7.00, 2&3 £5.90. CSF £14.95 TOTE £2.70: £1.40, £2.50; EX 16.50.
Owner Ms Rachel D S Hood **Bred** Weldon R Johnson Jr **Trained** Newmarket, Suffolk

FOCUS
This did not look the most competitive of maidens and the time was modest. The race is almost impossible to rate with any accuracy.

NOTEBOOK
Doctor Crane(USA), a $25,000 yearling but a 52,000gns two-year-old, is a half-brother to three winners in the US. He was the paddock pick and, after taking time to get into full stride, he was right on top at the finish. A mile will not be a problem, this will have taught him plenty and he will go on from here. (op 11-4 tchd 13-8)
Royal Executioner(USA), with the benefit of a previous outing, mastered the pacesetter only for the winner to crowd him and shoot past inside the last. This was still a step in the right direction. (op 6-1)
Thunderball, another with previous experience, improved on his debut effort, showing ahead coming to the final quarter-mile and sticking on all the way to the line. He will improve again. (op 4-1)
Pilot Light, out of a winning sprinter at two from the family of Bollin Joanne, looked very much in need of the experience and should progress with racing. (op 9-1)
Tarzan(IRE), a 135,000gns half-brother to a 7f winner at two, disputed favouritism with the winner, but he hung left throughout and dropped right away 2f out. He has plenty of size about him and can surely do a lot better. (op 15-8 tchd 2-1)

3477 MOSSPM.CO.UK H'CAP — 6f

7:10 (7:10) (Class 4) (0-85,83) 4-Y-0+ **£4,857** (£1,445; £722; £360) **Stalls** High

Form RPR

0315 **1** **John Keats**[7] 3255 5-8-10 72 DanielTudhope 5 84
(J S Goldie) *hld up: hdwy on outside over 2f out: styd on to ld ins fnl f* **5/1**[2]

0260 **2** 1 ¼ **High Curragh**[8] 3228 5-9-7 83 FergalLynch 3 91
(K A Ryan) *chsd ldrs: upsides 1f out: no ex ins fnl f* **9/2**[1]

2411 **3** nk **Punching**[54] 1872 4-8-0 67 NicolPolli(5) 4 74
(Miss Gay Kelleway) *hld up: hdwy on outside over 2f out: upsides 1f out: kpt on same pce* **6/1**[3]

0232 **4** 1 **Circuit Dancer (IRE)**[7] 3255 8-8-7 69 AdrianTNicholls 6 73
(D Nicholls) *trckd ldrs: effrt and swtchd ins 2f out: kpt on same pce fnl f* **5/1**[2]

3003 **5** 1 ½ **Red Cape (FR)**[7] 3255 5-8-6 68 (b) JoeFanning 2 67
(Mrs R A Carr) *racd wd: w ldrs: led over 2f out: hung lft and hdd 1f out: wknd towards fin* **14/1**

-600 **6** 2 **Wyatt Earp (IRE)**[13] 3056 7-9-4 80 PaulHanagan 7 73
(R A Fahey) *sn outpcd: kpt on fnl 2f: nvr trbld ldrs* **5/1**[2]

0-00 **7** 2 ¼ **Baltimore Jack (IRE)**[14] 3050 4-8-6 68 GrahamGibbons 1 53
(M W Easterby) *chsd ldrs on outer: wknd over 1f out* **20/1**

0353 **8** 7 **Bel Cantor**[11] 3111 5-9-0 79 (p) AndrewMullen(3) 9 42
(W J H Ratcliffe) *w ldrs: lost pl over 1f out* **15/2**

-015 **9** 5 **Charles Darwin (IRE)**[27] 2644 5-9-7 83 (b) FrancisNorton 10 30
(M Blanshard) *mde most: hdd over 2f out: sn lost pl* **7/1**

1m 12.9s (-0.70) **Going Correction** +0.025s/f (Good) **9** Ran SP% **118.2**
Speed ratings (Par 105): **105,103,102,101,99 96,93,84,77**
toteswinger: 1&2 £36.40, 1&3 £4.60, 2&3 £5.10. CSF £28.50 CT £139.83 TOTE £6.70: £1.80, £1.80, £1.90; EX 39.20.
Owner Tough Construction Ltd **Bred** R Preece **Trained** Uplawmoor, E Renfrews

FOCUS
The pace was decent enough in this handicap, but despite that there was still five in a line passing the furlong pole. The form looks solid at this level rated around the first three.
Red Cape(FR) Official explanation: jockey said gelding became unbalanced final furlong

3478 URBAN-I LIVE MUSIC NIGHTS H'CAP — 1m (R)

7:45 (7:45) (Class 4) (0-80,78) 4-Y-0+ **£4,857** (£1,445; £722; £360) **Stalls** Low

Form RPR

1151 **1** **Paraguay (USA)**[8] 3208 5-9-0 71 PaulHanagan 3 78
(Miss V Haigh) *hld up: hdwy on ins over 2f out: styd on to ld fnl 75yds: hld on wl* **11/4**[2]

6441 **2** nk **It's A Dream (FR)**[23] 2749 5-8-5 62 (t) GrahamGibbons 6 68
(M W Easterby) *t.k.h: hdwy on inner to trck ldr over 3f out: led 2f out: edgd rt 1f out: hdd and no ex wl ins fnl f* **5/2**[1]

-153 **3** shd **Mumbleswerve (IRE)**[24] 2722 4-9-4 75 AlanMunro 2 81
(W Jarvis) *trckd ldrs: ev ch jst ins fnl f: edgd lft and no ex nr fin* **15/2**

/505 **4** hd **Emirate Isle**[12] 3082 4-8-9 66 FergalLynch 5 71
(C Grant) *trckd ldrs: styd on to have ev ch ins fnl f: hld whn crowded nr fin* **14/1**

302 **5** 4 **Intersky Charm (USA)**[10] 3142 4-9-7 78 DeanMcKeown 1 76
(R M Whitaker) *sn chsng ldrs: one pce whn hmpd 1f out: sn wknd* **11/2**

50-1 **6** 2 ½ **Cool Ebony**[45] 2101 5-9-6 77 SebSanders 4 67
(P J Makin) *led tl 2f out: wknd fnl f* **7/2**[3]

5600 **7** 1 ½ **Ninth House (USA)**[11] 3108 6-8-11 **68**............................(b) JoeFanning 7 55
(Mrs R A Carr) *s.i.s: effrt on outside over 3f out: lost pl over 1f out* **28/1**
14/0 **8** 1 ½ **Penryn**[15] 3006 5-8-13 **70**.. MickyFenton 9 53
(P T Midgley) *t.k.h in mid-div: effrt 3f out: wknd over 1f out* **40/1**
1m 40.2s (-0.80) **Going Correction** +0.025s/f (Good) 8 Ran SP% **117.2**
Speed ratings (Par 105): **105,104,104,104,100 97,96,94**
toteswinger: 1&2 £1.10, 1&3 £4.50, 2&3 £5.00. CSF £10.39 CT £45.85 TOTE £3.80: £1.50, £1.30, £1.90; EX 8.70.
Owner R J Budge **Bred** Nutbush Farm **Trained** Wiseton, Notts
■ Stewards' Enquiry : Graham Gibbons one-day ban: used whip down the shoulder in forehand position (Aug 5)
Alan Munro six-day ban: used whip with excessive frequency and without giving colt time to respond (Jul 12-17)
Fergal Lynch two-day ban: used whip down the shoulder in forehand position (Jul 12-13)
FOCUS
A modest handicap with the runners tending to get in each other's way. It has been rated through the in-form runner-up backed up by the third and fourth and looks reasonably solid.

3479 CROWNHOTEL-BAWTRY.COM MAIDEN FILLIES' STKS 1m 2f 60y
8:15 (8:17) (Class 4) 3-Y-O+ **£5,180** (£1,541; £770; £384) **Stalls** Low

Form RPR
2 **1** **Caprivi (IRE)**[16] 2971 3-8-12 0.................................... JimmyFortune 9 64+
(J H M Gosden) *mde all: drvn over 2f out: styd on wl* **5/6**[1]
0-55 **2** 1 ¼ **Saleima (IRE)**[26] 2675 3-8-12 73................................ AlanMunro 12 61+
(P W Chapple-Hyam) *trckd wnr: chal over 3f out: kpt on same pce appr fnl f* **9/2**[3]
0- **3** 1 ¼ **Time Control**[344] 3706 3-8-12 0.............................. JamieSpencer 3 59+
(L M Cumani) *restless in stalls and reloaded: chsd ldrs: drvn over 3f out: edgd rt over 1f out: kpt on same pce* **11/4**[2]
4 1 ¼ **Garra Molly (IRE)** 3-8-12 0.............................. PaulMulrennan 6 57+
(G A Swinbank) *sn prom: effrt over 3f out: styd on fnl f* **10/1**
0-0 **5** 4 **Shraayef**[24] 2717 3-8-12 0.................................... MickyFenton 5 49
(M Botti) *chsd ldrs: drvn over 4f out: one pce fnl 2f* **40/1**
6 nk **Can Can Dancer** 3-8-7 0.............................. ShaneCreighton(5) 7 48
(J G Given) *s.i.s: sn prom: effrt 3f out: hung lft and kpt on fnl f* **25/1**
0 **7** 2 ¼ **I Feel Fine**[8] 3227 5-9-10 0.. PAspell 1 44
(A Kirtley) *s.i.s: hdwy over 3f out: nvr a factor* **80/1**
000- **8** 1 **Lady Grantley**[351] 3510 3-8-12 39.................................. DaleGibson 8 42?
(M W Easterby) *mid-div: effrt over 3f out: nvr nr ldrs* **66/1**
9 ¾ **Unawatuna** 3-8-12 0.. TomEaves 11 41
(Mrs K Walton) *s.s: hdwy and edgd lft 3f out: nvr on terms* **66/1**
00- **10** 12 **Reel Classy**[274] 5770 3-8-12 0.................................... GregFairley 2 18
(T J Pitt) *in rr: sme hdwy 4f out: rdn and lost pl over 2f out: sn bhd* **33/1**
2m 12.84s (1.64) **Going Correction** +0.025s/f (Good)
WFA 3 from 5yo 12lb 10 Ran SP% **121.9**
Speed ratings (Par 102): **94,93,92,91,87 87,85,84,84,74**
toteswinger: 1&2 £1.10, 1&3 £1.10, 2&3 £2.30. CSF £5.25 TOTE £1.90: £1.10, £1.40, £1.50; EX 5.80.
Owner H R H Princess Haya Of Jordan **Bred** Darley **Trained** Newmarket, Suffolk
FOCUS
A modest maiden and the proximity of a 39-rated filly in eighth holds down the overall value of the form.
Can Can Dancer Official explanation: jockey said filly hung left in straight

3480 DONCASTER SPONSORSHIP CLUB H'CAP 1m 6f 132y
8:50 (8:50) (Class 4) (0-85,85) 4-Y-O+ **£4,857** (£1,445; £722; £360) **Stalls** Low

Form RPR
-664 **1** **Rajeh (IRE)**[14] 3044 5-9-1 **79**.. LiamJones 2 87
(J L Spearing) *led 1f: trckd ldrs: swtchd rt over 3f out: led over 2f out: edgd rt and styd on fnl f* **9/2**[3]
-201 **2** 1 ¼ **Four Miracles**[15] 3007 4-9-1 **79**.............................. PaulMulrennan 8 85
(M H Tompkins) *hld up: effrt 4f out: styd on to take 2nd appr fnl f: no real imp* **2/1**[1]
0310 **3** 1 ½ **Crossbow Creek**[13] 3060 10-9-7 **85**............................ JamieSpencer 9 89
(M G Rimell) *hld up in rr: hdwy and swtchd wd 2f out: hung rt and styd on to take 3rd on line* **9/1**
-244 **4** nk **Natural Action**[29] 2585 4-8-10 **74**..............................(p) AlanMunro 4 78
(W Jarvis) *trckd ldrs: effrt over 3f out: wnt 3rd appr fnl f: one pce* **4/1**[2]
54-3 **5** 5 **Industrial Star (IRE)**[24] 2734 7-8-5 **69**........................(p) DO'Donohoe 7 66
(Micky Hammond) *chsd ldrs: chal over 5f out: sn rdn and hung lft: wknd ins fnl f* **20/1**
1010 **6** hd **Chocolate Caramel (USA)**[14] 3045 6-9-2 **80**................ PaulHanagan 6 76
(R A Fahey) *led after 1f: hdd over 2f out: wknd ins fnl f* **9/2**[3]
1032 **7** 9 **Red Wine**[21] 2822 9-8-8 **79**.................................... StacyRenwick(7) 5 63
(A J McCabe) *s.v.s: sme hdwy on wd outside 3f out: sn wknd: eased ins fnl f* **5/1**
3m 9.93s (3.23) **Going Correction** +0.025s/f (Good) 7 Ran SP% **121.1**
Speed ratings (Par 105): **92,91,90,90,87 87,82**
toteswinger: 1&2 £2.40, 1&3 £7.40, 2&3 £6.90. CSF £15.10 CT £80.57 TOTE £7.70: £3.60, £2.60; EX 21.00.
Owner Miss C Ive **Bred** Mrs C S Acham **Trained** Kinnersley, Worcs
■ Stewards' Enquiry : Liam Jones one-day ban: careless riding (Jul 12)
FOCUS
A sound early gallop, but ultimately a moderate winning time for the grade. The form looks sound at this level though with the first four all running to their pre-race marks.
Crossbow Creek Official explanation: jockey said gelding hung right-handed throughout
Red Wine Official explanation: trainer said gelding was unsuited by the good to firm ground

3481 YORKSHIRE BUSINESS EXHIBITION & CONFERENCE FILLIES' H'CAP 7f
9:20 (9:23) (Class 5) (0-70,70) 3-Y-O+ **£3,238** (£963; £481; £240) **Stalls** High

Form RPR
0-00 **1** **Slip Star**[12] 3079 5-8-12 **48**.. GregFairley 1 56
(T J Etherington) *chsd ldr: led over 2f out: hld on wl* **25/1**
6003 **2** ¾ **Loveinanelevator**[17] 2946 3-9-7 **66**.............................. JamieSpencer 4 69
(M L W Bell) *hld up in rr: gd hdwy and swtchd rt over 1f out: styd on wl to take 2nd fnl strides: nt rch wnr* **11/4**[2]
-602 **3** shd **Welcome Return (IRE)**[12] 3081 3-9-6 **65**.....................(b) DavidAllan 7 68
(T D Easterby) *chsd ldrs: effrt over 2f out: kpt on wl fnl f* **7/1**
3040 **4** 2 **Jessica Wigmo**[14] 3023 5-8-9 **50**.............................. MarkCoumbe(5) 9 50
(A W Carroll) *hld up: hdwy over 2f out: wnt 2nd over 1f out: kpt on same pce ins fnl f* **20/1**
3353 **5** 4 **Poppy's Rose**[7] 3260 4-9-13 **63**.............................. RoystonFfrench 12 53
(I W McInnes) *hld up in rr: effrt over 2f out: edgd lft: nvr nr ldrs* **5/1**[3]

2-51 **6** ¾ **Navene (IRE)**[31] 2510 4-9-12 **62**.. AlanMunro 11 49
(C F Wall) *trckd ldrs: effrt over 3f out: wknd and hung bdly lft over 1f out* **7/4**[1]
4/ **7** ¾ **Bon News (IRE)**[243] 6552 4-10-0 **64**.................................. TomEaves 5 49
(B Smart) *s.i.s: hld up: effrt over 2f out: hung lft: nvr trbld ldrs* **12/1**
-050 **8** 2 **Miss Taboo (IRE)**[31] 2500 4-9-0 **50**.............................. MickyFenton 3 30
(P T Midgley) *hld up: hdwy to chse ldrs over 2f out: wknd over 1f out* **25/1**
66-0 **9** 1 ½ **Lady Zabeen (IRE)**[18] 2920 3-9-11 **70**...................... RichardMullen 6 43
(D M Simcock) *hld up in rr: effrt over 2f out: nvr a factor* **33/1**
000- **10** 1 ½ **Ducal Pip Squeak**[238] 6638 4-9-12 **62**.......................... PaulHanagan 2 34
(A B Haynes) *led tl over 2f out: sn wknd* **33/1**
-630 **11** 18 **Pennygee**[40] 2261 4-9-8 **58**.. PAspell 8 —
(S R Bowring) *trckd ldrs: lost pl over 3f out: bhd fnl 2f* **40/1**
1m 27.44s (1.14) **Going Correction** +0.025s/f (Good)
WFA 3 from 4yo+ 9lb 11 Ran SP% **120.7**
Speed ratings (Par 100): **94,93,93,90,86 85,84,82,80,78 58**
toteswinger: 1&2 £68.30, 1&3 £9.40, 2&3 £1.60. CSF £90.32 CT £571.11 TOTE £38.80: £6.30, £1.40, £2.20; EX 99.10 Place 6: £29.87, Place 5: £9.51.
Owner Russell Bradley **Bred** Sir Tatton Sykes **Trained** Norton, N Yorks
FOCUS
A low-grade handicap with the top-weight rated just 64 and a modest winning time but the form still looks reasonably sound.
Navene(IRE) Official explanation: jockey said filly hung left
T/Plt: £39.60 to a £1 stake. Pool: £80,509.24. 1,481.95 winning tickets. T/Qpdt: £6.20 to a £1 stake. Pool: £6,085.99. 725.50 winning tickets. WG

3315 LINGFIELD (L-H)
Saturday, June 28

OFFICIAL GOING: All-weather - standard; turf course - firm
Racing near the stands' rail still appeared to be an advantage on the turf course.
Wind: Brisk, half behind Weather: Sunny, warm

3482 BET EURO 2008 FINAL - BETDAQ (S) STKS 1m 4f (P)
5:50 (5:50) (Class 6) 3-Y-O+ **£1,774** (£523; £262) **Stalls** Low

Form RPR
143 **1** **Bridgewater Boys**[29] 2558 7-9-6 69............................ JemmaMarshall(7) 7 62+
(G L Moore) *dwlt: sn in midfield: prog 3f out: rdn to chse ldr wl over 1f out: led 1f out: idled but a holding on* **10/11**[1]
0-03 **2** 1 **Soundbyte**[28] 2611 3-8-8 55.. ShaneKelly 8 56
(J Gallagher) *hld up in last trio: prog on outer over 3f out: led jst over 2f out: hdd 1f out: kpt on wl u.p but a hld* **10/1**
0406 **3** 9 **Soldiers Quest**[5] 3328 4-9-8 58.................................. PatrickMathers 1 41
(Peter Grayson) *t.k.h: trckd ldng pair: cl up 2f out: sn outpcd: plugged on* **10/1**
000/ **4** 2 **Ello Lucky (IRE)**[545] 6852 6-9-3 34.......................... FrankieMcDonald 9 33
(J L Flint) *trckd ldrs: prog to ld wl over 3f out: hdd jst over 2f out: wknd over 1f out* **66/1**
-453 **5** 2 ¼ **Missie Baileys**[21] 2832 6-9-3 53..(p) PaulDoe 3 29
(Mrs L J Mongan) *a in midfield: outpcd fr 3f out: no ch fnl 2f* **6/1**[2]
6000 **6** ¾ **Thermidor (USA)**[7] 3265 5-9-8 53.............................. RichardKingscote 2 33
(Lady Herries) *hld up in last trio: rdn and struggling 3f out: no ch after* **8/1**
/20- **7** 16 **Kyles Prince (IRE)**[138] 593 6-9-1 78............................ AshleyMorgan(7) 4 8
(V Smith) *hld up in last trio: rdn and btn 3f out: fin lame* **15/2**[3]
00 **8** 24 **Thirtyfourthstreet (IRE)**[37] 2328 3-8-3 0......................(b[1]) HayleyTurner 5 —
(W R Muir) *sn chsd ldr: rdn and wknd rapidly 4f out: t.o* **33/1**
0000 **9** 21 **Competitor**[7] 3265 7-9-13 55..(vt) IanMongan 10 —
(J Akehurst) *sn led: drvn and hdd wl over 3f out: wknd rapidly wl over 2f out: eased: t.o* **12/1**
2m 35.79s (2.79) **Going Correction** +0.275s/f (Slow)
WFA 3 from 4yo+ 14lb 9 Ran SP% **119.9**
Speed ratings (Par 101): **101,100,94,93,91 91,80,64,50**
toteswinger: 1&2 £3.90, 1&3 £5.20, 2&3 £5.20. CSF £12.12 TOTE £1.80: £1.10, £2.80, £2.50; EX 11.60.The winner was bought in for 9,200gns. Soundbyte was claimed by O Pears for £6,000.
Owner Matthew Green & Richard Green **Bred** Southill Stud **Trained** Woodingdean, E Sussex
FOCUS
The winner is better than average at this grade, and the runner-up showed promise, but the rest looked very modest.
Kyles Prince(IRE) Official explanation: vet said gelding returned lame right-fore
Thirtyfourthstreet(IRE) Official explanation: jockey said filly hung right throughout
Competitor Official explanation: jockey said horse had a breathing problem

3483 11TH YEAR OF THE DAVID WOODHOUSE BIRTHDAY H'CAP 1m 4f (P)
6:20 (6:21) (Class 6) (0-60,60) 3-Y-O **£2,047** (£604; £302) **Stalls** Low

Form RPR
6504 **1** **Tripod Molly (IRE)**[31] 2495 3-9-0 **56**..............................(t) IanMongan 13 71
(P J McBride) *trckd ldrs: prog to go 2nd over 3f out: led wl over 2f out: sn drew wl clr: rdn rt out* **16/1**
0401 **2** 12 **Borrowdale**[21] 2833 3-9-3 **59**.. ShaneKelly 3 54
(J A Osborne) *trckd ldrs: effrt over 3f out: wl outpcd over 2f out: kpt on fnl f to take 2nd nr fin* **11/2**[2]
2-05 **3** ½ **Bobal Girl**[28] 2613 3-8-11 **58**.................................... JackMitchell(5) 10 53
(E F Vaughan) *hld up in rr: niggled along over 5f out: prog over 3f out: chsd ldrs over 2f out but wl outpcd: looked reluctant but plugged on to snatch 3rd nr fin* **16/1**
2104 **4** nse **Gunnadoit (USA)**[20] 2868 3-9-3 **59**..........................(p) HayleyTurner 4 53
(M L W Bell) *wl in rr: pushed along 5f out: prog over 3f out: styd on fr 2f out to chal for 2nd fnl f* **7/1**[3]
-056 **5** nk **Orbital Orchid**[21] 2833 3-8-11 **56**.............................(b[1]) TravisBlock(3) 7 50
(W S Kittow) *rousted along to go prom: effrt to ld wl over 3f out: hdd and outpcd wl over 2f out: no ch w wnr after: lost 3 pls nr fin* **5/1**[1]
3204 **6** 8 **Lord's Bidding**[15] 2997 3-9-4 **60**..............................(v) DavidKinsella 9 41
(R Ingram) *drvn in last after 2f and nt at all keen: prog u.p over 3f out to chse clr ldrs over 2f out: no ch* **11/2**[2]
6433 **7** 1 ¾ **Arniecoco**[65] 1586 3-9-3 **59**.. OscarUrbina 16 37
(Miss J R Gibney) *settled in rr: rdn and outpcd over 3f out: no ch after: plugged on* **10/1**
660 **8** ¾ **Code Violation**[24] 2716 3-9-3 **59**.............................. FrankieMcDonald 11 36
(Jean-Rene Auvray) *hld up wl in rr: pushed along in last pair over 4f out: trapped bhd rivals 3f out: 12th over 1f out: kpt on* **66/1**
-050 **9** 4 ½ **Darley Star**[11] 3117 3-8-10 **57**.................................... AhmedAjtebi(5) 6 27
(C E Brittain) *mde most to wl over 3f out: sn wknd* **20/1**
00-0 **10** 1 ¾ **Iron Cross (IRE)**[37] 2340 3-9-2 **58**.............................. J-PGuillambert 2 25
(Sir Mark Prescott) *rousted along firmly early on: nvr beyond midfield: shkn up over 3f out: sn lost tch* **10/1**

06-6 **11** *1 3/4* **Bosamcliff (IRE)**[33] 2454 3-9-1 **60** .... KevinGhunowa(3) 14 24
(A B Haynes) *racd wd in midfield: rdn over 4f out: wknd over 3f out: sn bhd* **15/2**

0000 **12** *6* **Daddy's Boy**[16] 2984 3-9-1 **57** .... (b) SimonWhitworth 5 12
(Mrs A J Perrett) *w ldr to 4f out: sn wknd* **20/1**

-000 **13** *15* **It's Josr**[25] 2695 3-9-2 **58** .... PaulDoe 1 —
(I A Wood) *nvr beyond midfield: outpcd and losing pl whn n.m.r over 2f out: t.o* **25/1**

00-0 **14** *10* **Lady Selkirk**[29] 2566 3-9-4 **60** .... RichardKingscote 8 —
(R Charlton) *prom: rdn 5f out: wknd over 3f out: eased whn no ch fnl 2f: t.o* **16/1**

405 **15** *58* **Princess Raya**[85] 1176 3-9-4 **60** .... NeilPollard 15 —
(M E Rimmer) *hld up towards rr: wknd 5f out: wl t.o over 3f out* **33/1**

2m 35.04s (2.04) **Going Correction** +0.275s/f (Slow) **15** Ran SP% **125.3**
Speed ratings (Par 97): **104,96,95,95,95 90,88,88,85,84 83,79,69,62,23**
toteswinger: 1&2 £38.50, 1&3 not won, 2&3 £11.00. CSF £99.14 CT £1475.77 TOTE £21.00: £5.10, £2.40, £5.30; EX 127.10.
Owner Tripod Partnership **Bred** Sheila Morrissey **Trained** Newmarket, Suffolk

FOCUS
A moderate handicap little better than a seller, but a creditable winning time for the type of race. The winner's wide-margin victory is hard to explain given earlier performances, although the placed horses and the fifth give the form some credibility.
Bosamcliff(IRE) Official explanation: jockey said filly never travelled
Princess Raya Official explanation: jockey said filly felt wrong behind

3484 BET IRISH DERBY - BETDAQ MEDIAN AUCTION MAIDEN STKS 1m 2f (P)
6:50 (6:51) (Class 6) 3-4-Y-O **£2,266** (£674; £337; £168) **Stalls** Low

Form RPR

5220 **1** **Mezzanisi (IRE)**[29] 2564 3-9-2 74 .... HayleyTurner 10 72+
(M L W Bell) *hld up in rr: smooth prog 3f out: hemmed in and forced way out over 1f out: led ins fnl f: hung rt and idled: urged along to hold on* **5/4**[1]

2 *nk* **Miss Carlotta** 3-8-11 0 .... PatDobbs 1 67+
(M P Tregoning) *cl up: lost pl on inner over 3f out: renewed effrt on outer 2f out: prog to chse wnr fnl 100yds: clsd but jst hld* **20/1**

53-6 **3** *1 1/2* **Soggy Dollar**[19] 2885 3-9-2 72 .... SaleemGolam 6 69
(M H Tompkins) *trckd ldng pair: prog to ld wl over 3f out: drvn over 1f out: hdd and one pce ins fnl f* **8/1**[3]

35 **4** *2 3/4* **Kimbolton**[42] 2207 3-8-11 0 .... IanMongan 9 58
(H R A Cecil) *hld up in midfield: prog to chse ldr over 3f out: to over 1f out: fdd* **14/1**

5 **5** *nse* **Marie Louise**[63] 1621 3-8-11 0 .... TedDurcan 8 58
(H R A Cecil) *hld up towards rr: prog 3f out: drvn and nt qckn over 2f out: holding wnr in over 1f out: fdd* **11/8**[2]

0 **6** *1 1/2* **One Oi**[28] 2612 3-9-2 0 .... SimonWhitworth 3 60
(D W P Arbuthnot) *trckd ldrs: effrt 3f out: cl enough 2f out: sn outpcd and btn* **50/1**

0-0 **7** *3 1/2* **Harting Hill**[15] 2994 3-8-9 0 .... KatiaScallan(7) 5 53+
(M P Tregoning) *trckd ldr to 4f out: gng wl enough but trapped on inner and lost pl bdly: stl cl enoughh 2f out: nudged along and fdd* **33/1**

8 *7* **Sponge** 3-9-2 0 .... PaulDoe 11 39
(P R Chamings) *s.s: mostly in last pair: outpcd fr 3f out* **50/1**

-000 **9** *10* **Eau Sauvage**[23] 2756 4-9-6 37 .... (v) KirstyMilczarek(3) 4 14
(M J Attwater) *led to wl over 3f out: sn wknd: bhd fnl 2f* **100/1**

00 **10** *30* **Ubiquitous**[19] 2885 3-8-11 0 .... RichardHughes 7 —
(S Dow) *a in last pair: wknd over 4f out: t.o* **66/1**

2m 9.75s (3.15) **Going Correction** +0.275s/f (Slow)
WFA 3 from 4yo 12lb **10** Ran SP% **118.4**
Speed ratings (Par 101): **98,97,96,94,94 93,90,84,76,52**
toteswinger: 1&2 £29.00, 1&3 £2.70, 2&3 £8.20. CSF £32.77 TOTE £2.70: £1.20, £4.10, £1.80; EX 51.50.
Owner T Redman And P Philipps **Bred** Knocklong House Stud **Trained** Newmarket, Suffolk
■ Stewards' Enquiry : Hayley Turner four-day ban: careless riding (Jul 12-15)

FOCUS
A routine maiden and not form to take too literally, with the pace steady and the winner 9lb below his mark from a solid handicap.

3485 E B F LOOK FOR BETTER ODDS AT BETDAQ MAIDEN STKS 5f
7:20 (7:23) (Class 5) 2-Y-O **£3,626** (£1,079; £539; £269) **Stalls** High

Form RPR

2 **1** **Mrs Kipling (IRE)**[17] 2951 2-8-12 0 .... DaneO'Neill 8 77+
(S A Callaghan) *sn pressed ldr: shkn up to ld 1f out: pushed out: comf* **4/7**[1]

03 **2** *2* **Pocket's Pick (IRE)**[15] 2999 2-9-3 0 .... RichardHughes 7 75+
(G L Moore) *led and racd against nr side rail: rdn and hdd 1f out: readily hld by wnr* **3/1**[2]

3 *6* **Ziggy Lee** 2-9-3 0 .... SaleemGolam 3 52
(S C Williams) *outpcd after 2f and racd on outer: shkn up and styd on again fnl f to take 3rd last strides* **50/1**

5232 **4** *hd* **Dedante**[18] 2903 2-8-9 0 .... KirstyMilczarek(3) 2 46
(D K Ivory) *wnt bdly lft s but sn pressed ldng pair: outpcd 2f out: wknd and lost 3rd fnl strides* **8/1**[3]

00 **5** *3/4* **Russian Art**[15] 2999 2-8-12 0 .... JackMitchell(5) 6 49
(R M Beckett) *sn outpcd and pushed along: a struggling: kpt on fnl f* **25/1**

4 **6** *3 3/4* **Battle Of Hastings**[26] 2663 2-9-3 0 .... HayleyTurner 9 35
(M L W Bell) *outpcd and sn bhd: nvr a factor* **10/1**

7 *1/2* **Minenotyours (IRE)** 2-9-3 0 .... IanMongan 5 33
(D E Cantillon) *chsd ldng trio: hung lft fr 1/2-way: wknd 2f out* **50/1**

8 *15* **Orangeleg** 2-9-3 0 .... J-PGuillambert 10 —
(S C Williams) *s.s: rn green: outpcd and a bhd: t.o* **20/1**

57.20 secs (-1.00) **Going Correction** -0.25s/f (Firm) **8** Ran SP% **121.4**
Speed ratings (Par 93): **98,94,85,84,83 77,76,52**
toteswinger: 1&2 £1.20, 1&3 £17.40, 2&3 £43.70. CSF £2.67 TOTE £1.60: £1.10, £1.20, £5.80; EX 3.20.
Owner Sangster Family & M Green **Bred** J Osborne **Trained** Newmarket, Suffolk

FOCUS
The first two home, who admittedly had the benefit of racing near the rail, set a decent standard at this level. However, the rest were well beaten.

NOTEBOOK
Mrs Kipling(IRE) stepped up on her promising debut by winning at the second attempt with a bit to spare. She looks effective at both 5f and 6f, and should continue to make her mark, with connections mentioning the Cherry Hinton and Dragon Stakes as possible targets. (op 4-6 tchd 8-11)
Pocket's Pick(IRE) had been sent to Sandown for his first two outings, which suggests he is highly rated at home, and this was a solid effort behind the odds-on favourite with the rest well beaten. He sets a decent standard at this level, and is certainly good enough to win races. (op 7-2 tchd 4-1)
Ziggy Lee attracted little interest as a yearling, and was sent off at a big price, so this encouraging staying-on debut was probably better than expected. This Lujain colt has winners in the family at up to 1m5f, and he is not without hope once he has established his best trip. Official explanation: jockey said colt hung right in final furlong
Dedante lost ground when swerving left at the start, and did not quite run up to the level of form she had shown in previous maidens. Though capable of winning at this level at his best, she is probably now ready for the switch to nurseries. (op 7-1)
Russian Art is an obvious candidate for nurseries following three modest runs in maiden company. He looks as if he will be suited by longer trips when he makes the switch. (op 20-1)
Battle Of Hastings does not have the speed for 5f, and found the drop in trip all too much. He should be given a chance to show what he can do at 7f. (op 8-1)
Minenotyours(IRE), a Tagula newcomer out of the triple 7f-1m2f winner Holly Rose, needs at least 6f even at this stage of his career, and should improve a bit with racing. (op 40-1 tchd 33-1)

3486 CGG VERITAS H'CAP 5f
7:55 (7:56) (Class 5) (0-75,74) 3-Y-O+ **£2,331** (£693; £346; £173) **Stalls** High

Form RPR

-354 **1** **Pretty Miss**[13] 3062 4-9-12 **70** .... FrankieMcDonald 4 79
(H Candy) *trckd ldng pair: wnt 2nd 1/2-way: rdn to chal over 1f out: fnlly gained upper hand fnl strides* **9/2**[3]

5661 **2** *shd* **Nusoor (IRE)**[7] 3269 5-9-0 **61** .... (v) KirstyMilczarek(3) 5 70
(Peter Grayson) *led and racd against nr side rail: rdn over 1f out: worn down fnl strides* **3/1**[2]

22-6 **3** *1 3/4* **Even Bolder**[13] 3062 5-9-12 **70** .... StephenCarson 7 73
(E A Wheeler) *hld up bhd ldrs: effrt 2f out: swtchd to outer over 1f out: hanging lft and nt qckn* **11/4**[1]

6022 **4** *3 3/4* **Orpen's Art (IRE)**[8] 3224 3-9-10 **74** .... HayleyTurner 8 61+
(S A Callaghan) *v awkward s and sn adrift: nvr on terms: modest prog against nr side rail fnl f* **5/1**

-001 **5** *shd* **Fairfield Princess**[24] 2710 4-9-2 **60** .... DaneO'Neill 3 49
(M S Saunders) *racd wd: nvr on terms w ldrs: struggling fnl 2f* **12/1**

-046 **6** *1 3/4* **Billy Red**[30] 2550 4-9-2 **60** .... (b) RichardHughes 6 43
(J R Jenkins) *hld up: pushed along briefly 2f out: sn lost tch w ldrs* **13/2**

5520 **7** *1* **One Way Ticket**[4] 3346 8-8-12 **61** .... (p) JackMitchell(5) 2 40
(J M Bradley) *w wnr 2f: rdn 1/2-way: put hd in air and gave up* **16/1**

56.46 secs (-1.74) **Going Correction** -0.25s/f (Firm)
WFA 3 from 4yo+ 6lb **7** Ran SP% **113.4**
Speed ratings (Par 103): **103,102,100,94,93 91,89**
toteswinger: 1&2 £1.60, 1&3 £4.50, 2&3 £3.70. CSF £18.08 CT £42.90 TOTE £5.80: £3.00, £3.10; EX 20.80.
Owner Mrs J E L Wright **Bred** Wheelersland Stud **Trained** Kingston Warren, Oxon

FOCUS
A fair handicap, if lacking a little in numbers, but the speedy Nusoor ensured a good gallop and he looks the best guide to the form.

3487 TAKE A LOOK AT BETDAQ FILLIES' H'CAP 7f
8:25 (8:25) (Class 5) (0-75,75) 3-Y-O **£2,331** (£693; £346; £173) **Stalls** High

Form RPR

-301 **1** **Candle Sahara (IRE)**[11] 3117 3-9-4 **72** .... TPO'Shea 8 77
(M R Channon) *racd towards nr side: hld up: pushed along fr 1/2-way: swtchd lft and rdn over 1f out: sustained effrt to ld fnl strides* **3/1**[2]

012- **2** *hd* **Polar Annie**[241] 6584 3-9-4 **72** .... DaneO'Neill 5 77
(M S Saunders) *t.k.h: led after 2f and crossed towards nr side rail: rdn and hanging lft fnl 2f: hdd fnl strides* **7/1**

-404 **3** *1 3/4* **Fly Kiss**[15] 2993 3-9-0 **73** .... AhmedAjtebi(5) 3 73
(C E Brittain) *cl up: chsd ldr and edgd rt over 2f out: nt qckn over 1f out: one pce and lost 2nd fnl f* **6/1**

1424 **4** *1 1/4* **Top Draw (USA)**[25] 2705 3-9-4 **72** .... HayleyTurner 6 69+
(M L W Bell) *dwlt: hld up in last pair: effrt over 2f out: taken towards outer and nt clr run wl over 1f out: one pce* **4/1**[3]

5 *1 3/4* **Zulu Princess (IRE)**[43] 2183 3-8-9 **63** .... TedDurcan 2 55+
(J S Moore) *hld up and racd wd: no prog over 2f out: n.d after* **12/1**

-103 **6** *1 1/4* **Fifty (IRE)**[13] 3064 3-9-7 **75** .... RichardHughes 1 64
(R Hannon) *racd on outer: hld up: rdn wl over 2f out: no prog: wl btn over 1f out* **5/2**[1]

30-0 **7** *2 1/4* **Deal Flipper**[16] 2976 3-9-0 **68** .... StephenCarson 7 50
(P Winkworth) *led 2f: chsd ldr to over 2f out: hmpd sn after and wknd tamely* **16/1**

1m 21.42s (-1.88) **Going Correction** -0.25s/f (Firm) **7** Ran SP% **113.9**
Speed ratings (Par 96): **100,99,97,96,94 92,90**
toteswinger: 1&2 £3.10, 1&3 £6.90, 2&3 £7.60. CSF £23.76 CT £117.25 TOTE £4.00: £2.20, £3.90; EX 25.90 Place 6: £71.25, Place 5: £45.48..
Owner Jaber Abdullah **Bred** John Cullinan **Trained** West Ilsley, Berks

FOCUS
A fair handicap, but short on numbers and modest form. The runner-up's nursery form is the best guide to the level.
Fly Kiss Official explanation: jockey said filly hung very badly right
Fifty(IRE) Official explanation: trainer's rep said filly was unsuited by the firm ground
T/Plt: £56.30 to a £1 stake. Pool: £56,147.68. 726.89 winning tickets. T/Qpdt: £10.30 to a £1 stake. Pool: £4,596.28. 327.80 winning tickets. JN

3450 NEWCASTLE (L-H)
Saturday, June 28

OFFICIAL GOING: Soft (good to soft in places; 6.6)
Wind: Fresh, half against Weather: Cloudy

3488 JOURNAL CHIPCHASE STKS (GROUP 3) 6f
2:10 (2:10) (Class 1) 3-Y-O+
£28,385 (£10,760; £4,035; £4,035; £1,345; £675) **Stalls** High

Form RPR

104 **1** **Utmost Respect**[35] 2390 4-9-3 105 .... PaulHanagan 4 116
(R A Fahey) *prom: shkn up over 2f out: led appr fnl f: drifted rt u.p ins fnl f: styd on wl* **11/4**[1]

-150 **2** *2 1/4* **Zidane**[7] 3247 6-9-3 109 .... JamieSpencer 2 113+
(J R Fanshawe) *hld up last pl: nt clr run fr 1/2-way tl swtchd rt and gd hdwy over 1f out: keeping on whn hmpd wl ins fnl f: kpt on to take 2nd post* **9/2**[2]

5360 **3** *shd* **Beckermet (IRE)**[13] 3063 6-9-3 110 .... RoystonFfrench 6 108
(R F Fisher) *w ldr: drvn 1/2-way: kpt on u.p ins fnl f* **25/1**

0-20 **3** *dht* **Burnwynd Boy**[35] 2403 3-8-10 98 .... TomEaves 1 106
(Miss L A Perratt) *sn bhd on outside: hdwy u.p 2f out: kpt on fnl f: nrst fin* **50/1**

010 **5** *3/4* **Reverence**[27] 2652 7-9-3 105 TPQueally 10 106
(E J Alston) *led stands' rail tl edgd lft and hdd appr fnl f: kpt on same pce* **10/1**

0-64 **6** *1 3/4* **Confuchias (IRE)**[26] 2680 4-9-3 106 NCallan 5 100
(K R Burke) *trckd ldrs tl rdn and no ex over 1f out* **15/2**

115- **7** *2 3/4* **Greek Renaissance (IRE)**[231] 6758 5-9-7 113 (t) DO'Donohoe 3 96+
(Saeed Bin Suroor) *sn pushed along towards rr: hdwy over 2f out: edgd rt and wknd over 1f out* **8/1**

4-03 **8** *1 1/2* **Philario (IRE)**[14] 3041 3-9-0 105 FergusSweeney 7 89
(K R Burke) *chsd ldrs tl rdn and wknd over 1f out* **16/1**

0041 **9** *nse* **Brave Prospector**[14] 3047 3-8-10 105 (t) AlanMunro 8 85
(P W Chapple-Hyam) *trckd ldrs tl edgd lft and wknd over 1f out* **5/1**[3]

061 **10** *1 3/4* **Lady Grace (IRE)**[14] 3040 4-9-0 102 (t) DarryllHolland 9 78
(W J Haggas) *dwlt: rdn in rr 1/2-way: nvr on terms* **10/1**

1m 16.23s (1.03) **Going Correction** +0.35s/f (Good)
WFA 3 from 4yo+ 7lb **10** Ran SP% **114.3**
Speed ratings (Par 113): **107,104,103,103,102 100,96,94,94,92**toteswinger: 1&2 £2.40, 1&3 (5-2) £8.20, 1&3 (5-10), 2&3 (2-6) £10.00, 2&3 (6-10) £21.40. CSF £14.36 TOTE £3.70; EX 14.00 TRIFECTA PL £1.60, £1.70, Beckermet £2.80, Burnwynd Boy £4.90. Trifecta: 5-6-2 £206.30 (0.60 w/u), 5-6-10 £79.30 (2.627 Owner.
■ Stewards' Enquiry : Paul Hanagan two-day ban: careless riding (Jul 18,19)

FOCUS

A decent renewal of this Group 3 event and a decent gallop, though the time was 0.24 seconds slower than the following Class 2 handicap. The form looks ordinary for the grade with the dead-heating third rated 98 casting doubts over the form. The field raced stands' side.

NOTEBOOK

Utmost Respect ◆, back on his favoured soft ground and at this more suitable trip, got a good tow and turned in a career-best effort. He remains worth another try over 7f and this lightly raced sort may well be capable of further progress when getting his ground. (op 3-1 tchd 10-3 in a place)

Zidane's style of racing means he needs things to drop into place and he would have gone very close in this contest had they done so. He is a smart sort who handles much quicker ground and has the ability to win in this grade when getting the rub of things. (op 5-1)

Burnwynd Boy, not for the first time this year, seemed to excel himself in the face of a very stiff task dropped back to this more suitable trip. He will be up in the weights for his exertions here, though, so is going to find life tougher back in handicaps.

Beckermet(IRE) has not been very reliable since his last win but he returned to something like his best back on soft ground. He is a smart performer but is likely to remain vulnerable to the younger, more progressive sorts in this grade.

Reverence, back over 6f and with conditions to suit, was far from disgraced after cutting out much of the running against the stands' rail. However, he was again a fair way below the pick of his form in 2006 and he is likely to remain vulnerable in this grade. (op 9-1 tchd 11-1)

Confuchias(IRE), the winner of this race on heavy ground the previous year, had run well on his first start for the yard but was below that level on this occasion. He is worth another chance. (tchd 7-1)

Greek Renaissance(IRE), who looked in tremendous shape, had a bit to find conceding weight all round and was not at his best on this seasonal reappearance. He handles quicker ground and is worth another chance this term. (op 13-2)

Philario(IRE) Official explanation: trainer said gelding lost some teeth when knocking into stalls

Brave Prospector Official explanation: jockey said colt was unsuited by the soft (good to soft places) ground

3489 TOTESCOOP6 H'CAP — 6f

2:45 (2:46) (Class 2) (0-100,99) 3-Y-0+

£18,693 (£5,598; £2,799; £1,401; £699; £351) **Stalls** High

Form RPR

1000 **1** **Geojimali**[13] 3056 6-8-9 80 JohnEgan 7 89
(J S Goldie) *dwlt: hld up far side: gd hdwy over 1f out: styd on wl to ld post: 1st of 9 in gp* **16/1**

4420 **2** *hd* **Pawan (IRE)**[21] 2831 8-8-11 87 ow4 (b) AnnStokell(5) 6 95
(Miss A Stokell) *prom far side: drvn and led that gp ins fnl f: kpt on: jst ct: 2nd of 9 in gp* **25/1**

4220 **3** *3/4* **Damika (IRE)**[43] 2172 5-9-11 99 MichaelJStainton(3) 1 108+
(R M Whitaker) *midfield far side: nt clr run over 2f: shuffled bk over 1f out: swtchd rt: gd hdwy and hung rt ins fnl f: nrst fin: 3rd of 9 in gp* **8/1**

001 **4** *1/2* **Rising Shadow (IRE)**[25] 2698 7-9-12 97 NCallan 9 101
(N Wilson) *hld up: hdwy over 1f out: kpt on fnl f: no imp towards fin: 4th of 9 in gp* **9/2**[1]

6414 **5** *1* **Baby Strange**[34] 2426 4-9-8 93 PaulMulrennan 14 94
(D Shaw) *led stands' side: rdn over 2f out: kpt on fnl f: nt rch far side: 1st of 5 in gp* **9/1**

4-40 **6** *1/2* **Burning Incense (IRE)**[28] 2595 5-9-3 88 JamieSpencer 16 88
(M Dods) *hld up stands' side: hdwy over 1f out: kpt on fnl f: no imp: 2nd of 5 in gp* **8/1**

5660 **7** *1/2* **Ingleby Arch (USA)**[17] 2938 5-9-0 85 PaulFessey 8 83
(T D Barron) *chsd clr ldr far side: drvn over 2f out: one pce fnl f: 5th of 9 in gp* **16/1**

-002 **8** *3/4* **Trojan Flight**[14] 3050 7-8-9 80 oh2 PaulHanagan 3 83+
(R A Fahey) *midfield far side: effrt over 1f out: keeping on whn no room ins fnl f: nt rcvr: 6th of 9 in gp* **10/1**

2112 **9** *3/4* **Valery Borzov (IRE)**[25] 2698 4-9-9 94 (v) AdrianTNicholls 4 87
(D Nicholls) *led and clr far side: hdd & wknd ins fnl f: 7th of 9 in gp* **6/1**[2]

-240 **10** *4 1/2* **Joseph Henry**[21] 2831 6-9-5 90 SilvestreDeSousa 15 69
(D Nicholls) *trckd stands' side ldrs: drvn and edgd lft over 2f out: sn no ex: 3rd of 5 in gp* **9/1**

-000 **11** *2 1/4* **Obe Brave**[13] 3056 5-9-0 92 BMcHugh(7) 5 64
(R A Fahey) *cl up far side tl rdn and wknd fr 2f out: 8th of 9 in gp* **40/1**

1-34 **12** *1 1/4* **Signor Peltro**[42] 2195 5-9-3 88 (v) FergusSweeney 17 56
(H Candy) *chsd stands' side ldrs: effot over 2f out: wknd appr fnl f: 4th of 5 in gp* **7/1**[3]

-406 **13** *15* **Curtail (IRE)**[17] 2938 5-8-11 82 SebSanders 12 2
(Miss L A Perratt) *chsd ldrs stands' side tl wknd appr 2f out: last of 5 in gp* **25/1**

14 *6* **Greco Tom (ARG)**[364] 4-9-11 96 JacobJohansen 11 —
(Rune Haugen, Norway) *hld up far side: rdn over 2f out: sn btn: last of 9 in gp* **16/1**

1m 15.99s (0.79) **Going Correction** +0.35s/f (Good)
WFA 3 from 4yo+ 7lb **14** Ran SP% **124.1**
Speed ratings (Par 109): **108,107,106,106,104 104,103,102,101,95 92,90,70,62**
toteswinger: 1&2 £118.50, 1&3 £40.10, 2&3 £35.40. CSF £379.44 CT £3430.39 TOTE £19.80: £5.40, £6.50, £3.20; EX 313.70 Trifecta £627.40 Part won. Pool: £847.94. 0.30 winning units..
Owner Fyffees 2 **Bred** Jim Goldie **Trained** Uplawmoor, E Renfrews
■ Stewards' Enquiry : N Callan one-day ban: careless riding (Jul 15)

FOCUS

A decent handicap in which the larger far-side group held the edge over the stands'-side bunch. The pace was sound and this form looks solid rated around the winner and fourth.

NOTEBOOK

Geojimali had not been at his best on quick ground but proved suited by these easier conditions and he ran as well as he ever has done. Whether this will be reproduced next time remains to be seen, though. (op 20-1)

Pawan(IRE), whose losing run stretches back nearly two years, ran a blinder with his rider putting up 4lb of overweight. He is a fair sort who should continue to give a good account either on turf or back on sand. (op 33-1)

Damika(IRE) ◆ was not at his best at York on his previous start but looked the unlucky horse in the race here. He was shuffled back when the leaders were quickening away from him, and once in the clear drifted from the far rail over towards the stands' side, so he did really well to get as close as he did at the finish. He is very much one to keep an eye on in the near future. (tchd 15-2 and 9-1)

Rising Shadow(IRE), back to winning ways in heavy ground on his previous start, shaped with plenty of credit from this 4lb higher mark. There are more races to be won with him, especially when there is plenty of give in the ground. (op 13-2)

Baby Strange, a useful and largely consistent sort, fared the best of those to race on the stands' side and he looks a bit better than the bare form. He goes well with cut in the ground and is worth another chance over 7f. (op 8-1 tchd 15-2)

Burning Incense(IRE), from a stable that has been in good heart this term, ran his best race of the year on the unfavoured side. He has not won for some time and has little margin for error from this mark but would not be one to write off yet. (op 13-2)

Ingleby Arch(USA), whose form has been patchy since his last win on Fibresand, had the run of the race and was not disgraced for a yard among the winners. He is worth another try over 7f.

Trojan Flight, who was just touched off at York on his previous start, was 2lb out of the handicap but is a fair bit better than the bare form of this race suggests.He was denied room at a crucial stage and he remains capable of winning races this term. Official explanation: jockey said gelding was denied a clear run (op 16-1)

Valery Borzov(IRE), a progressive sprinter this year, did too much too soon and not surprisingly had little to offer in the closing stages. He should be seen to best effect when the emphasis is more on speed. (tchd 11-2)

Joseph Henry Official explanation: jockey said gelding hung left from halfway

3490 JOHN SMITH'S NORTHUMBERLAND PLATE (HERITAGE H'CAP) — 2m 19y

3:20 (3:20) (Class 2) 3-Y-0+

£123,300 (£37,120; £18,560; £9,260; £4,640; £2,340) **Stalls** Low

Form RPR

0/1- **1** **Arc Bleu (GER)**[52] 1319 7-8-2 85 AdrianTNicholls 6 92+
(A J Martin, Ire) *hld up ins: hdwy whn swtchd lft wl over 1f out: swtchd rt appr fnl f: kpt on wl fnl f: led cl home* **14/1**

0-02 **2** *hd* **Halla San**[42] 2202 6-8-10 93 PaulHanagan 12 100
(R A Fahey) *midfield: hdwy over 2f out: rdn to ld ins fnl f: kpt on wl: ct cl home* **16/1**

2-52 **3** *3/4* **Bogside Theatre (IRE)**[63] 1625 4-8-4 87 DO'Donohoe 5 93
(G M Moore) *led: rdn clr 2f out: hdd ins fnl f: kpt on u.p* **10/1**

4-20 **4** *nk* **Akarem**[17] 2939 7-8-6 89 ow1 FergusSweeney 18 95
(K R Burke) *hld up in tch: effrt over 2f out: styd on ins fnl f* **50/1**

1-51 **5** *1 1/2* **Gee Dee Nen**[28] 2609 5-8-7 90 TPQueally 16 94
(M H Tompkins) *hld up: effrt over 2f out: kpt on fnl f: nrst fin* **20/1**

51-0 **6** *1/2* **Bollin Derek**[21] 2822 5-8-1 84 PaulFessey 19 87
(T D Easterby) *in tch: drvn fr over 5f out: rallied: kpt on same pce over 1f out* **28/1**

050- **7** *1/2* **Mudawin (IRE)**[72] 6335 7-8-7 90 JohnEgan 13 93
(J S Goldie) *bhd tl styd on fr 2f out: nrst fin* **40/1**

-041 **8** *1/2* **Missoula (IRE)**[11] 3104 5-8-7 90 5ex SamHitchcott 4 92
(Miss Suzy Smith) *midfield: rdn over 4f out: outpcd over 2f out: kpt on fnl f: nt pce to chal* **16/1**

9 *1/2* **Far From Old (IRE)**[23] 5-9-0 97 TGillet 9 99
(J E Hammond, France) *hld up: effrt on outside over 2f out: no ex ins fnl f* **10/1**

1-00 **10** *shd* **Inchnadamph**[52] 1916 8-8-6 89 (t) PaulMulrennan 7 90
(T J Fitzgerald) *chsd ldrs: effrt over 2f out: no ex ins fnl f* **50/1**

4-23 **11** *3/4* **Tilt**[52] 1916 6-8-10 93 (p) TomEaves 11 94
(B Ellison) *in tch: rdn 3f out: no ex over 1f out* **9/1**[3]

2-14 **12** *6* **Double Banded (IRE)**[52] 1916 4-8-10 93 SebSanders 14 86
(J L Dunlop) *hld up: rdn 3f out: btn over 1f out* **10/1**

0/33 **13** *10* **Carte Diamond (USA)**[50] 1944 7-9-9 106 JoeFanning 17 87
(B Ellison) *sn w ldr: rdn 3f out: sn wknd* **12/1**

2114 **14** *16* **Bukit Tinggi (IRE)**[11] 3104 4-8-4 87 PhilipRobinson 3 49
(M A Jarvis) *cl up: rdn over 2f out: wknd wl over 1f out* **11/2**[2]

10-1 **15** *18* **Desert Sea (IRE)**[14] 3044 5-8-7 90 5ex AlanMunro 15 31
(D W P Arbuthnot) *hld up: struggling 5f out: sn btn* **14/1**

63-5 **16** *9* **Whispering Death**[17] 2939 6-8-5 88 (p) RoystonFfrench 20 18
(J Howard Johnson) *bhd and sn pushed along: no ch fnl 4f* **25/1**

-133 **17** *13* **Rationale (IRE)**[22] 2790 5-8-2 85 WilliamBuick 8 —
(S C Williams) *bhd: lost tch fr over 4f out* **20/1**

1-15 **18** *3 1/2* **Highland Legacy**[52] 1916 4-8-12 95 JamieSpencer 2 5
(M L W Bell) *in tch on ins: effrt whn hmpd twice over 2f out: sn btn and eased* **4/1**[1]

3m 37.71s (1.51) **Going Correction** +0.35s/f (Good) **18** Ran SP% **128.6**
Speed ratings (Par 109): **110,109,109,109,108 108,108,107,107,107 107,104,99,91,82 77,71,69**
toteswinger: 1&2 £354.50, 1&3 £39.20, 2&3 £47.40. CSF £214.39 CT £2364.37 TOTE £15.80: £3.80, £5.70, £2.40, £9.60; EX 604.20 Trifecta £9085.80 Part won. Pool: £12,278.12. 0.50 winning units..
Owner P J McGee **Bred** Frau J Mayer **Trained** Summerhill, Co. Meath

FOCUS

The richest staying handicap in Europe and not surprisingly a competitive event. The pace was sound and the form should prove reliable.

NOTEBOOK

Arc Bleu(GER) ◆ is a progressive sort both on the Flat and over hurdles and, despite proving very easy to back before the off, turned in a career-best. This test of stamina clearly suits him and, while of obvious interest on the Flat in future handicaps granted a decent gallop, he will be one to keep a very close eye on when returned to hurdles. (op 10-1)

Halla San, from a stable going tremendously well at present, confirmed himself an improved performer on the Flat with a career-best effort. He handles quicker ground, is effective over shorter and is the type to win a decent handicap either on the Flat or over hurdles this year. (op 25-1)

Bogside Theatre(IRE) ◆, from a stable that has a good record in this race, proved suited by this test of stamina and turned in her best effort. She is a relatively lightly raced sort who has only had two races over this trip and appeals strongly as the type to win a fair handicap on the Flat when there is give in the ground this term. (op 12-1)

Akarem, having his first run over this trip on the Flat, belied his starting price with a solid effort returned to a soft surface. He is a versatile sort who should continue to give a good account.

Gee Dee Nen is an improved performer over this trip this year and he ran creditably on much softer ground than at Haydock. He is all about stamina and is the type to win more races when he gets a suitable test.

Bollin Derek had obviously come on for his reappearance run and, although one of the first off the bridle, he kept responding to pressure to register a solid effort. He is suited by a thorough test of stamina and he seems particularly well suited to a soft surface. (op 33-1 tchd 25-1)

Mudawin(IRE), the 2006 Ebor winner, ran creditably returned to the Flat after this short break on this first start for Jim Goldie. He is all about stamina but he leaves the impression that he may not be one to place maximum faith in. (op 50-1)

Missoula(IRE), a 2m4f winner at the Royal meeting earlier this month, was far from disgraced under her penalty but left the impression that an extreme test of stamina is going to be more to her liking. A race like the Cesarewitch may see her in an even better light. (op 18-1)

Far From Old(IRE), a progressive middle-distance performer in France, failed to get home over this trip as well as the principals. However, he ran well to a point and there are more races to be won with him over shorter. (tchd 11-1)

Bukit Tinggi(IRE) looked to have fair claims in this company after a solid Royal Ascot run but he proved a disappointment. Although he has won with cut, this ground was almost certainly too testing and he will be seen to best effect back on decent going. Official explanation: jockey said gelding was unsuited by the soft (good to soft places) ground (op 13-2)

Whispering Death Official explanation: jockey said gelding was unsuited by the soft (good to soft places) ground

Rationale(IRE) Official explanation: jockey said gelding was unsuited by the soft (good to soft places) ground

Highland Legacy, who looked sure to be better suited to this track than Chester, was not given a hard time after meeting trouble at a crucial stage. It is probably best to forgive him this below-par effort and he is worth another chance in decent handicap company granted suitable conditions. Official explanation: jockey said colt was hampered inside 3f mark (op 5-1)

3491 TOTESWINGER H'CAP — 7f

3:55 (3:56) (Class 2) (0-100,99) 3-Y-O+

£12,462 (£3,732; £1,866; £934; £466; £234) **Stalls** High

Form				RPR
1-10	1		**Redford (IRE)**[9] 3155 3-8-13 93 ... JamieSpencer 4	108+
			(M L W Bell) *hld up far side: smooth hdwy whn no room and swtchd sharply rt over 1f out: qckd to ld ins fnl f: rdn out: 1st of 9 in gp* **7/4**[1]	
1000	2	1 1/4	**The Osteopath (IRE)**[7] 3261 5-8-11 82 ... RoystonFfrench 8	92
			(M Dods) *stdd far side: hdwy on outside to ld that gp over 1f out to ins fnl f: nt pce of wnr: 2nd of 9 in gp* **14/1**	
50-0	3	3 1/2	**Game Lad**[28] 2595 6-9-0 85 ... PaulHanagan 2	86
			(T D Easterby) *in tch far side: effrt and ev ch that gp over 1f out: one pce fnl f: 3rd of 9 in gp* **10/1**	
1	4	nse	**Against The Grain**[91] 1069 5-8-12 83 ... JoeFanning 1	84
			(L Lungo) *in tch far side: nt clr run 2f to 1f out: kpt on fnl f: 4th of 9 in gp* **7/1**[3]	
-500	5	nk	**Maze (IRE)**[14] 3047 3-9-1 95 ... TomEaves 6	95
			(B Smart) *led far side to over 1f out: no ex: 5th of 9 in gp* **22/1**	
3523	6	1 1/4	**Stevie Gee (IRE)**[14] 3040 4-9-5 90 ... NCallan 9	87
			(G A Swinbank) *hld up far side: hdwy and ch that gp over 1f out: wknd ins fnl f: 6th of 9 in gp* **13/2**[2]	
-060	7	hd	**Sir Xaar (IRE)**[10] 3122 5-8-9 85 ...(v) NeilBrown(5) 3	81+
			(B Smart) *hld up towards rr far side: drvn over 2f out: keeping on whn n.m.r wl ins fnl f: no imp: 7th of 9 in gp* **20/1**	
-000	8	2 1/4	**Zomerlust**[43] 2172 6-9-2 87 ... SebSanders 11	77
			(J J Quinn) *prom stands' side: led and edgd lft that gp over 2f out: kpt on fnl f: no ch w far side: 1st of 5 in gp* **18/1**	
00-2	9	1 1/4	**Miyasaki (CHI)**[13] 6-9-11 96 ...(v[1]) JacobJohansen 5	83
			(Rune Haugen, Norway) *cl up far side tl rdn and wknd over 1f out: 8th of 9 in gp* **33/1**	
1411	10	3 3/4	**Daaweitza**[18] 2905 5-9-4 89 ... DO'Donohoe 17	66
			(B Ellison) *hld up stands' side: drvn over 2f out: sn no imp: 2nd of 5 in gp* **12/1**	
-363	11	6	**Royal Power (IRE)**[10] 3122 5-10-0 99 ... AdrianTNicholls 10	59
			(D Nicholls) *prom stands' side: drvn over 2f out: btn fnl f: 3rd of 5 in gp* **9/1**	
0-00	12	3 3/4	**Steenberg (IRE)**[21] 2818 9-9-2 87 ... PaulMulrennan 16	37
			(M H Tompkins) *cl up stands' side tl rdn and wknd fr 2f out: 4th of 5 in gp* **33/1**	
2060	13	2 1/2	**Crocodile Bay (IRE)**[10] 3122 5-9-0 85 ... TonyHamilton 14	28
			(D W Barker) *led stands' side to over 2f out: sn wknd: last of 5 in gp* **20/1**	
00-0	14	22	**Lone Wolfe**[14] 3040 4-9-7 92 ... JohnEgan 7	—
			(Jane Chapple-Hyam) *prom far side tl wknd over 2f out: eased whn no ch: last of 9 in gp* **28/1**	

1m 29.49s (2.09) **Going Correction** +0.35s/f (Good)
WFA 3 from 4yo+ 9lb 14 Ran SP% **124.1**
Speed ratings (Par 109): **102,100,96,96,96 94,94,91,90,86 79,75,72,47**
toteswinger: 1&2 £10.40, 1&3 £7.50, 2&3 £38.50. CSF £26.57 CT £209.38 TOTE £2.80: £1.70, £3.80, £3.20; EX 35.00 Trifecta £153.00 Pool: £618.21. 2.99 winning units..
Owner Highclere T'bred Racing (Housemaster) **Bred** T J Rooney **Trained** Newmarket, Suffolk

FOCUS

A good handicap won by a progressive colt and the form looks pretty solid for the conditions. The pace was sound and the larger far-side group held a big advantage over those that raced stands' side.

NOTEBOOK

Redford(IRE) ◆, back in trip and on much easier ground than at Royal Ascot, created a very favourable impression after being short of room. He is a grand sort on looks who is the type to hold his own in stronger company over this trip or over 1m when there is give in the ground. (op 2-1 tchd 9-4)

The Osteopath(IRE), back on soft ground, had a good tow on the favoured far-side group and returned to his best. He is a fair sort when he gets his conditions, has no problems with 1m and is the sort to win again away from progressive sorts. (op 16-1 tchd 12-1)

Game Lad, the winner of this race on heavy ground last year, is still 4lb higher but ran his best race since on only his second start of this year. He is particularly well suited by plenty of cut and may be capable of building on this. (op 12-1 tchd 9-1)

Against The Grain, whose two wins have been with give underfoot, including on his first run for the yard last time, had conditions to suit and shaped as though better than the bare form. He should be able to win again when he gets his ground. (op 8-1)

Maze(IRE), last year's Chesham winner, had the run of the race on the favoured far side but, while running his best race for some time, he underlined his vulnerability from his current mark in this type of event. (op 33-1)

Stevie Gee(IRE), a consistent sort up to this trip on all types of ground this year, ran creditably but left the impression that an extended 6f would be more to his liking. (tchd 11-2 and 7-1)

Zomerlust ◆, who has slipped in the weights, had conditions to suit and ran as though better than the bare form after finishing clear of those on the unfavoured side. A strongly run race over either this trip or over 6f suits and he is one to keep an eye on. (op 16-1 tchd 20-1)

Lone Wolfe Official explanation: jockey said colt was unsuited by the soft (good to soft places) ground

3492 E.B.F./TARMAC MAIDEN STKS — 6f

4:25 (4:25) (Class 4) 2-Y-O

£5,919 (£1,772; £886; £443; £221; £111) **Stalls** High

Form				RPR
	1		**Elmfield Boy (USA)** 2-9-3 0 ... PaulHanagan 4	86
			(R A Fahey) *mde all: rdn over 1f out: kpt on strly fnl f* **4/1**[2]	
0	2	2 1/2	**Dubai Hills**[17] 2951 2-9-3 0 ... TomEaves 10	79
			(B Smart) *trckd ldrs: effrt and chsd wnr over 1f out: kpt on same pce ins fnl f* **3/1**[1]	
	3	6	**Parisian Pyramid (IRE)** 2-9-3 0 ... SilvestreDeSousa 6	61
			(D Nicholls) *chsd wnr: rdn and hung lft over 1f out: sn outpcd* **10/1**	
	4	1 3/4	**Castle Myth (USA)** 2-9-3 0 ... SebSanders 9	55
			(B Ellison) *hld up: effrt over 2f out: no imp over 1f out* **8/1**[3]	
0	5	hd	**Royal Max (IRE)**[10] 3140 2-9-3 0 ... TonyHamilton 8	55
			(R A Fahey) *t.k.h: bhd: drvn and outpcd over 2f out: r.o ins fnl f* **18/1**	
6	6	7	**Red Max (IRE)**[14] 3049 2-9-3 0 ... PaulMulrennan 7	34
			(T D Easterby) *t.k.h: cl up tl rdn: edgd lft and wknd wl over 1f out* **3/1**[1]	
	7	4	**Moon Lightning (IRE)** 2-9-3 0 ... TPQueally 5	32+
			(M H Tompkins) *hld up in tch: effrt over 2f out: edgd lft and wknd over 1f out* **4/1**[2]	

1m 17.74s (2.54) **Going Correction** +0.35s/f (Good) 7 Ran SP% **115.5**
Speed ratings (Par 95): **97,93,85,83,83 73,68**
toteswinger: 1&2 £3.00, 1&3 £8.60, 2&3 £5.60. CSF £16.77 TOTE £4.60: £2.40, £1.80; EX 13.70.
Owner Mike Browne **Bred** Hill 'N' Dale Farm & N E T P **Trained** Musley Bank, N Yorks

FOCUS

A race that has often produced decent types in the past but, the first two apart, lacking strength in depth although that pair should go on from this.

NOTEBOOK

Elmfield Boy(USA), a $100,000 half-brother to a juvenile winner in the US, had the run of the race and showed a pleasing attitude on this racecourse debut. On this evidence he is likely to stay 7f and is the sort to win more races. (op 3-1)

Dubai Hills, who did not get the run of the race on his debut, fared better on this softer ground. His stable has a strong hand in the juvenile department and he is more than capable of picking up an ordinary maiden. (op 5-2, tchd 7-2)

Parisian Pyramid(IRE), a half-brother to winners from 7f to 1m2f She's Our Lass and King Of Rhythm, failed to keep straight under pressure on this debut but showed ability at an ordinary level. He is entitled to improve for the experience. (op 12-1 tchd 14-1)

Castle Myth(USA), a gelded half-brother to winners in Canada, was not totally disgraced on this racecourse debut. He left the impression that a stiffer test of stamina would have been in his favour and should improve for this outing. (op 9-2)

Royal Max(IRE), soundly beaten over 5f on quick ground on his debut, fared a little better over this longer trip on easier ground. He should do better over further still once qualified for handicaps. (op 25-1 tchd 14-1)

Red Max(IRE), who shaped like a stayer in a race that has thrown up winners on his debut, failed to settle and proved disappointing. He may do better on quicker ground and is worth another chance. (op 10-3 tchd 7-2)

Moon Lightning(IRE), who is related to winners over sprint distances and over middle distances, looked in tremendous shape and attracted support on this racecourse debut. He proved disappointing but would be worth another chance on better ground. Official explanation: jockey said colt lost its action (op 11-1)

3493 TOTESPORT.COM H'CAP — 1m 2f 32y

5:00 (5:01) (Class 4) (0-85,84) 3-Y-O+

£6,231 (£1,866; £933; £467; £233; £117) **Stalls** Centre

Form				RPR
0-10	1		**Tarkheena Prince (USA)**[21] 2819 3-8-11 79 ... NCallan 10	88+
			(G A Swinbank) *hld up: effrt over 2f out: str run fnl f: led nr fin* **6/1**[2]	
-063	2	3/4	**Hawkit (USA)**[7] 3257 7-8-9 70 ... NeilBrown(5) 3	78
			(P Monteith) *hld up: gd hdwy 2f out: led wl ins fnl f: ct nr fin* **12/1**	
3205	3	nk	**Rosbay (IRE)**[10] 3142 4-9-9 82 ... DuranFentiman(3) 8	89
			(T D Easterby) *in tch: effrt over 2f out: ev ch ins fnl f: hld nr fin* **14/1**	
-431	4	1 1/2	**Shaloo Diamond**[25] 2699 3-8-6 77 ... MichaelJStainton(3) 1	81
			(R M Whitaker) *t.k.h: led 3f: cl up: led over 2f out to wl ins fnl f: no ex* **9/2**[1]	
-303	5	5	**Celtic Change (IRE)**[29] 2582 4-9-11 81 ... TonyHamilton 13	75
			(M Dods) *hld up in midfield: pushed along over 3f out: effrt 2f out: sn outpcd* **6/1**[2]	
210-	6	hd	**Graceful Descent (FR)**[267] 5974 3-8-10 78 ... TPQueally 14	72
			(R A Fahey) *in tch tl drvn and outpcd fr 2f out* **16/1**	
-066	7	1/2	**Sadler's Kingdom (IRE)**[63] 1625 4-8-13 76 ... BMcHugh(7) 5	69+
			(R A Fahey) *hld up: pushed along over 2f out: sme late hdwy: nvr rchd ldrs* **7/1**[3]	
-265	8	1 3/4	**Toto Skyllachy**[17] 2953 3-9-2 84 ... MickyFenton 11	73
			(T P Tate) *t.k.h: led after 3f to over 2f out: wknd over 1f out* **8/1**	
6003	9	2 1/2	**Wovoka (IRE)**[7] 3261 5-9-3 73 ... RoystonFfrench 9	57
			(D W Barker) *in tch: stdy hdwy and cl up over 2f out: rdn and wknd over 1f out* **12/1**	
0606	10	5	**Fever**[22] 2787 4-8-11 74 ... BradleyRoper(7) 7	48
			(M W Easterby) *dwlt: bhd: drvn over 3f out: nvr on terms* **33/1**	
0-00	11	1	**Fort Churchill (IRE)**[21] 2830 7-9-6 83 ...(p) LanceBetts(7) 12	55
			(B Ellison) *hld up: drvn along over 2f out: sn wknd* **25/1**	
00-3	12	3 3/4	**Dar Es Salaam**[16] 2970 4-9-3 73 ... JohnEgan 6	38
			(J S Goldie) *towards rr on ins: pushed along over 3f out: nvr on terms* **14/1**	
1/34	13	1 1/4	**Marvo**[54] 1874 4-9-2 72 ... PaulMulrennan 2	34
			(M H Tompkins) *trckd ldrs tl rdn and wknd fr over 2f out* **7/1**[3]	

2m 13.56s (1.66) **Going Correction** +0.35s/f (Good)
WFA 3 from 4yo+ 12lb 13 Ran SP% **124.3**
Speed ratings (Par 105): **107,106,106,104,100 100,100,99,97,93 92,89,88**
toteswinger: 1&2 £3.00, 1&3 £5.60, 2&3 £8.60. CSF £79.51 CT £989.67 TOTE £8.90: £2.60, £3.30, £4.40; EX 118.80.
Owner G H Bell **Bred** Whitewood Stable Inc **Trained** Melsonby, N Yorks

FOCUS

An ordinary handicap but one run at a decent gallop throughout. The placed horses are exposed but set a reliable standard.

3494 GRAPHITE RESOURCES H'CAP — 1m (R)

5:35 (5:35) (Class 4) (0-85,84) 3-Y-O

£6,231 (£1,866; £933; £467; £233; £117) **Stalls** Centre

Form				RPR
1241	1		**Stevie Thunder**[14] 3039 3-9-7 84 ... PaulMulrennan 10	94+
			(G A Swinbank) *in tch: rdn to ld appr fnl f: hld on wl* **3/1**[1]	

1112 **2** *nk* **Topazes**[23] 2761 3-9-1 **78** .... JamieSpencer 11 87
(M L W Bell) *hld up in last pl: stdy hdwy over 2f out: rdn to press wnr ins fnl f: edgd lft u.p: kpt on* **7/2**[2]

3235 **3** *1 1/4* **Bowder Stone (IRE)**[34] 2427 3-8-9 **72** .... TPQueally 5 78
(M H Tompkins) *t.k.h: in tch: effrt 2f out: kpt on ins fnl f* **20/1**

2-64 **4** *3/4* **Reel Buddy Star**[7] 3263 3-8-9 **72** .... DarryllHolland 13 77
(G M Moore) *chsd ldrs: rdn over 2f out: led briefly over 1f out: no ex ins fnl f* **11/1**

10-4 **5** *2 1/4* **Resounding Glory (USA)**[19] 2889 3-8-10 **80** .... BMcHugh(7) 14 80
(R A Fahey) *hld up outside: effrt over 2f out: no imp over 1f out* **14/1**

1-04 **6** *1 1/2* **Boy Blue**[51] 1923 3-9-4 **81** .... NCallan 4 77
(D W Barker) *led to over 1f out: sn no ex* **9/1**

-060 **7** *hd* **Doon Haymer (IRE)**[14] 3048 3-8-11 **74** ....(v) PaulFessey 6 70
(Miss L A Perratt) *hld up: hdwy whn nt clr run over 2f out: sn rdn: kpt on fnl f: no imp* **22/1**

0130 **8** *3/4* **Bourse (IRE)**[21] 2840 3-8-3 **66** .... SilvestreDeSousa 3 60
(R Johnson) *hld up in tch: drvn over 2f out: btn over 1f out* **20/1**

2-10 **9** *5* **The Oil Magnate**[28] 2624 3-9-7 **84** .... TonyHamilton 1 66
(M Dods) *prom tl rdn and wknd fr 2f out* **10/1**

06-6 **10** *4* **Nine Stories (IRE)**[14] 3046 3-9-0 **82** .... NeilBrown(5) 2 55
(J Howard Johnson) *trckd ldrs tl rdn and wknd 2f out* **11/2**[3]

3-41 **11** *6* **Tourist**[17] 2954 3-9-2 **79** .... WilliamBuick 8 38
(B W Hills) *cl up tl rdn and wknd qckly 2f out* **8/1**

1m 45.58s (1.88) **Going Correction** +0.35s/f (Good) 11 Ran SP% **121.7**
Speed ratings (Par 101): **104,103,102,101,99 97,97,97,92,88 82**
toteswinger: 1&2 £2.00, 1&3 £15.80, 2&3 £14.90. CSF £13.41 CT £183.66 TOTE £3.80: £1.60, £1.90, £5.20; EX 14.20 Place 6 £1,031.53, Place 5 £551.52.
Owner Steve Gray **Bred** Sir Eric Parker **Trained** Melsonby, N Yorks

FOCUS
A fair handicap but this bare form is not totally reliable, despite the third and fourth running to their marks.
Boy Blue Official explanation: jockey said colt hung right-handed final furlong
Tourist Official explanation: vet said colt lost a hind shoe
T/Jkpt: Not won. T/Plt: £958.90 to a £1 stake. Pool: £192,580.41. 146.60 winning tickets. T/Qpdt: £73.50 to a £1 stake. Pool: £9,057.99. 91.10 winning tickets. RY

3456 NEWMARKET (R-H)
Saturday, June 28

OFFICIAL GOING: Firm (9.0)
Wind: Fresh, across Weather: Cloudy with sunny spells

3495 SIGN-UP BONUS AT BETINTERNET.COM MAIDEN STKS 7f
1:55 (1:58) (Class 4) 2-Y-O **£5,180** (£1,541; £770; £384) **Stalls** High

Form RPR

2 **1** **Weald Park (USA)**[35] 2411 2-9-3 0 .... RichardHughes 1 84+
(R Hannon) *mde all: shkn up over 1f out: r.o wl* **1/1**[1]

2 *3* **Imaam** 2-9-3 0 .... RHills 4 78+
(J L Dunlop) *gd sort: stdd s: hld up: nt clr run over 1f out: edgd rt and r.o wl ins fnl f: no ch w wnr* **7/1**[2]

3 *1 1/2* **Reaction** 2-9-3 0 .... TedDurcan 6 72
(M R Channon) *gd sort: bkwd: dwlt: hdwy over 4f out: rdn over 1f out: styd on same pce fnl f* **12/1**[3]

6 **4** *nse* **Africa's Star (IRE)**[43] 2160 2-8-12 0 .... JimmyFortune 11 67
(M A Jarvis) *bit bkwd: lw: hld up in tch: rdn over 1f out: styd on same pce fnl f* **7/1**[2]

5 *3/4* **Ocean's Minstrel** 2-9-0 0 .... JerryO'Dwyer(3) 3 70
(J Ryan) *leggy: scope: lw: chsd ldrs: rdn over 2f out: no ex fnl f* **50/1**

6 *1 3/4* **Howard** 2-9-3 0 .... EddieAhern 9 66
(J L Dunlop) *neat: hld up: styd on ins fnl f: nvr trbld ldrs* **16/1**

7 *3/4* **Dazinski** 2-9-3 0 .... MichaelHills 8 64
(M H Tompkins) *scope: sn pushed along in rr: n.m.r 1/2-way: styd on ins fnl f: nvr nrr* **25/1**

8 *1/2* **Al Mukaala (IRE)** 2-9-3 0 .... HayleyTurner 7 62
(C E Brittain) *w'like: scope: prom 5f* **16/1**

9 *2 3/4* **Are Can (USA)** 2-9-3 0 .... FergalLynch 5 55
(J S Wainwright) *w'like: scope: chsd ldrs: rdn over 2f out: edgd rt and wknd ins fnl f* **50/1**

0 **10** *hd* **Silent Hero**[39] 2275 2-9-3 0 .... ShaneKelly 2 55
(M A Jarvis) *trckd ldrs: racd keenly: wknd over 1f out: hmpd ins fnl f* **25/1**

11 *2* **Worth A King's** 2-9-3 0 .... KerrinMcEvoy 10 50
(Sir Michael Stoute) *w'like: scope: hld up: pushed along 1/2-way: wknd over 1f out* **7/1**[2]

1m 27.61s (1.91) **Going Correction** -0.125s/f (Firm) 11 Ran SP% **118.6**
Speed ratings (Par 95): **84,80,78,78,77 75,75,74,71,71 68**
toteswinger: 1&2 £2.20, 1&3 £4.50, 2&3 £8.20. CSF £8.05 TOTE £1.70: £1.10, £2.50, £3.10; EX 7.90.
Owner The Heffer Syndicate **Bred** George Strawbridge & London Thoroughbred Services **Trained** East Everleigh, Wilts

FOCUS
A fair maiden on paper but the winning time was very moderate for a race of this type and the level is fluid at this stage.

NOTEBOOK
Weald Park(USA), one of only three in the race with the benefit of previous experience, promised to be suited by this extra furlong. Up front from the off, he had the rail to help and pulled nicely clear in the closing stages. His stable has now won this race four times in the last five years. (op 5-4 tchd 6-4 in a place and 11-8 in places)
Imaam, a half-brother to Kashoof, a 5f winner at two, is out of Nell Gwyn winner Khulood. He did not get the clearest of runs on his debut but ran on to some purpose in the closing stages and looks sure to go one better soon. (op 15-2 tchd 8-1)
Reaction is a half-brother to Power Elite, a useful multiple winner between 7f and 1m2f, Nans Best, a 1m winner, and 5f winner La Sylvia. He ran green on his debut but will come on for this and will know a lot more next time. (tchd 10-1)
Africa's Star(IRE), who shaped alright on her debut despite showing signs of greenness, had an edge in experience over a number of her rivals this time. She may find things easier back against her own sex, although handicaps will soon be an option for her too. Official explanation: jockey said filly ran too free (op 13-2 tchd 15-2)
Ocean's Minstrel, whose dam is a half-sister to high-class 1m-1m4f performer Tamayaz, is a half-brother to Ming Vase, a modest 1m2f-1m3f winner. He ran a creditable race on this debut and will find things easier in handicap company in due course.
Howard, a half-brother to smart stayer Samuel, was running on at the finish as one would expect. (op 12-1)
Dazinski, whose dam is a half-sister to very useful middle-distance performer Hazeymm, is bred to want the same next year. He was getting the hang of things at the finish and should improve for this debut. (tchd 33-1)

Worth A King'S, the first foal of Oh So Sharp Stakes winner Top Romance, was a bit disappointing in the end but softer ground might help him. (op 11-2)

3496 BETINTERNET.COM EMPRESS STKS (LISTED RACE) (FILLIES) 6f
2:25 (2:25) (Class 1) 2-Y-O

£12,489 (£4,734; £2,369; £1,181; £591; £297) **Stalls** High

Form RPR

10 **1** **Baileys Cacao (IRE)**[10] 3123 2-8-12 0 .... RichardHughes 2 95+
(R Hannon) *mde all: shkn up and edgd rt fr over 1f out: r.o* **7/4**[1]

6 **2** *2* **Select (IRE)**[21] 2835 2-8-12 0 .... JimmyFortune 10 89
(P W Chapple-Hyam) *hld up in tch: jnd wnr over 2f out: rdn over 1f out: styd on same pce fnl f* **13/2**

21 **3** *1 1/4* **Aunt Nicola**[8] 3207 2-8-12 0 .... HayleyTurner 11 85
(M L W Bell) *chsd ldrs: rdn over 1f out: styd on same pce* **5/1**[2]

4 **4** *1 1/4* **Peper Harow (IRE)**[21] 2835 2-8-12 0 .... TQuinn 9 82
(M D I Usher) *sn pushed along in rr but in tch: edgd rt over 2f out: rdn over 1f out: styd on same pce* **28/1**

1 **5** *hd* **Madame Trop Vite (IRE)**[18] 2903 2-8-12 0 .... TedDurcan 5 81
(K A Ryan) *lw: s.i.s: sn prom: rdn over 2f out: edgd lft over 1f out: no ex fnl f* **6/1**[3]

521 **6** *2* **Harriet's Girl**[6] 3292 2-8-12 0 .... AndrewElliott 8 75
(K R Burke) *prom: racd keenly: rdn over 1f out: styd on same pce* **14/1**

331 **7** *1 3/4* **Barbee (IRE)**[30] 2534 2-8-12 0 .... ShaneKelly 6 70
(E A L Dunlop) *chsd ldrs: rdn over 1f out: sn wknd* **6/1**[3]

41 **8** *2 1/2* **Skruton (IRE)**[28] 2614 2-8-12 0 .... JerryO'Dwyer 3 62+
(M G Quinlan) *lw: w wnr tl rdn over 2f out: wkng whn nt clr run over 1f out* **14/1**

1m 11.66s (-0.84) **Going Correction** -0.125s/f (Firm) 8 Ran SP% **111.7**
Speed ratings (Par 98): **100,97,95,94,93 91,88,85**
toteswinger: 1&2 £2.40, 1&3 £3.00, 2&3 £6.40. CSF £12.83 TOTE £2.50: £1.20, £1.40, £2.10; EX 16.10 Trifecta £109.60 Pool: £266.72 - 1.80 winning units..
Owner William Durkan **Bred** Miss Mary Davison **Trained** East Everleigh, Wilts
■ Stewards' Enquiry : Ted Durcan caution: careless riding

FOCUS
Probably not the strongest of Listed races with those immedaitely behind the winner appearing to step up on previous form, and not a race to be with at this stage.

NOTEBOOK
Baileys Cacao(IRE), seventh in the Queen Mary, showed good early speed and made every yard, battling on well once they hit the rising ground. The extra furlong suited her and she did it well, but Group company will test her further. She is likely to go for the Moyglare or Goffs Million next, but might come back here for the Cherry Hinton. (op 15-8)
Select(IRE) only finished in mid-division on her debut in a Lingfield maiden so this looked like a stiff task on the face of it. She acquitted herself very well, though, and came up the stands' rail to chase the winner home. She has clearly improved on her debut effort and, providing she continues going the same way, a maiden should be a formality before a return to this sort of level. (op 4-1)
Aunt Nicola, a Goodwood maiden winner last time, showed good speed but was found wanting in the closing stages. Nurseries could offer her better options. (op 6-1)
Peper Harow(IRE), fourth on her debut in the Lingfield maiden in which Select was sixth, was unable to confirm that form but still shaped well enough on this step up in class. She did have the stands' rail to help, though. (op 33-1)
Madame Trop Vite(IRE), a winner on her debut at Chester, looked likely to be suited by the extra furlong. She challenged widest of all, which was probably not an advantage, but in the end did not see it out as well as some. (op 15-2 tchd 8-1)
Harriet's Girl, a winner over this trip at Pontefract last time, is another who should find her level in nursery company. (op 12-1 tchd 16-1 in a place)

3497 BETINTERNET.COM FRED ARCHER STKS (LISTED RACE) 1m 4f
3:00 (3:00) (Class 1) 4-Y-O+ **£17,031** (£6,456; £3,231; £1,611; £807) **Stalls** Centre

Form RPR

1-54 **1** **Lion Sands**[28] 2625 4-9-3 110 .... RichardHughes 1 115
(L M Cumani) *hld up: hdwy over 2f out: rdn and ev ch whn bmpd wl over 1f out: r.o u.p to ld post* **10/3**[2]

4121 **2** *hd* **Tranquil Tiger**[6] 3295 4-9-3 116 .... TedDurcan 6 116+
(H R A Cecil) *chsd ldrs: nt clr run fr over 2f out tl swtchd lft wl over 1f out: rdn to ld and hung rt sn after: hdd post* **8/11**[1]

-545 **3** *2 1/2* **Red Gala**[28] 2625 5-9-0 107 .... JimmyFortune 3 108
(Sir Michael Stoute) *lw: chsd ldr tl led over 2f out: rdn and hdd over 1f out: styd on same pce fnl f* **9/2**[3]

0-00 **4** *4* **Classic Punch (IRE)**[30] 2543 5-9-0 108 .... TQuinn 5 102
(D R C Elsworth) *led over 9f: sn edgd lft: rdn and ev ch over 1f out: wknd ins fnl f* **16/1**

100- **5** *5* **Group Captain**[49] 5618 6-9-0 108 .... RichardKingscote 2 94
(A King) *lw: hld up: rdn over 2f out: wknd wl over 1f out* **16/1**

2m 27.73s (-5.17) **Going Correction** -0.125s/f (Firm) 5 Ran SP% **110.9**
Speed ratings (Par 111): **112,111,110,107,104**
toteswinger: 1&2 £6.70. CSF £6.28 TOTE £4.00: £1.90, £1.10; EX 6.70.
Owner Stronach Stables **Bred** Fittocks Stud **Trained** Newmarket, Suffolk

FOCUS
A solid Listed contest and sound form for the grade with the first three close to recent York form.

NOTEBOOK
Lion Sands was almost four lengths behind Tranquil Tiger at York last time and looked destined to be beaten by him again, but the Cecil horse stopped in front and he was able to get up on the line. Perhaps he was a bit lucky but he is an honest individual who will not mind a return to 1m6f. (op 7-2 tchd 3-1)
Tranquil Tiger, who had everything his own way at Pontefract last time, had previously finished nicely in front of Lion Sands at York, and he looked sure to confirm that form when going on a furlong and a half out. However, as it turned out he took it up way too early and, idling in the closing stages, was collared on the line, to the cost of his 1.01 backers. He would have won had his challenge been delayed a little longer. (op 4-5 tchd 5-6 tchd 10-11in a place)
Red Gala has struggled somewhat since moving out of handicap company and simply keeps running into one or two too good for him in Pattern company. His performance is a good benchmark for the level of the form, though. (tchd 5-1)
Classic Punch(IRE), who sprang a 12-1 shock in this race last year, had his own way out in front but went a good gallop and simply set it up for the first two. (op 14-1 tchd 12-1)
Group Captain, having his first run back on the Flat following a successful campaign over hurdles, was held up at the back of the field and never really got in a blow. He probably needs softer ground to be seen at his best. (op 20-1 tchd 14-1)

3498 BETINTERNET.COM CRITERION STKS (GROUP 3) 7f
3:35 (3:35) (Class 1) 3-Y-O+ **£26,681** (£10,114; £5,061; £2,523; £1,264) **Stalls** High

Form RPR

6260 **1** **Racer Forever (USA)**[8] 3197 5-9-3 105 ....(b) JimmyFortune 5 111
(J H M Gosden) *mde all: rdn over 1f out: r.o gamely* **6/1**[3]

131 **2** *hd* **King Of Dixie (USA)**[29] 2580 4-9-3 109 .... RichardHughes 2 110+
(W J Knight) *trckd ldrs: rdn over 1f out: r.o* **10/11**[1]

4531 **3** ¾ **Blythe Knight (IRE)**[22] 2788 8-9-8 110 .... GrahamGibbons 6 113
(J J Quinn) *lw: chsd wnr: rdn over 1f out: unable qckn nr fin* **13/2**

0513 **4** ¾ **Appalachian Trail (IRE)**[28] 2607 7-9-3 112 ....(b) FergalLynch 1 106
(Miss L A Perratt) *hld up: plld hrd: hdwy over 1f out: rdn and no ex towards fin* **3/1**[2]

4000 **5** 2¼ **Vortex**[8] 3197 9-9-3 97 ....(t) TedDurcan 4 100
(Miss Gay Kelleway) *b. prom: rdn over 1f out: eased whn btn ins fnl f* **25/1**

1m 25.41s (-0.29) **Going Correction** -0.125s/f (Firm) 5 Ran SP% **108.8**
Speed ratings (Par 113): **96,95,94,94,91**
toteswinger: 1&2 £5.80. CSF £11.83 TOTE £8.00: £2.70, £1.10; EX 14.20.

Owner Mohamed Obaida **Bred** Gainsborough Farm Llc **Trained** Newmarket, Suffolk

FOCUS
Something of a tactical affair and the winning time was very slow indeed for a Group 3, 0.09 seconds slower than the later Class 5 apprentice handicap. Not the most reliable of form.

NOTEBOOK
Racer Forever(USA), who did not run too badly under top weight in the Buckingham Palace Stakes, finds winning opportunities difficult to come by, but he was racing over his best trip and enjoyed the run of things here, being given a fine front-running ride by Fortune, who dictated things next to the stands' rail. He held on gamely when strongly challenged close home. (op 7-1 tchd 8-1)

King Of Dixie(USA), a convincing winner of a conditions race at York last time, looked to have plenty in his favour, but Racer Forever was given a fine ride from the front and just held off his late challenge. He remains a lightly raced and progressive colt, though, and can make his mark at this level. (op Evens)

Blythe Knight(IRE), who had to give 5lb all round, has done all his winning over 1m plus so he was always going to need a strong pace over this shorter distance. It was something of a tactical affair, though, so in the circumstances he ran quite well. (op 8-1)

Appalachian Trail(IRE) had the best chance simply at the weights, but he relishes a strong pace and he did not get that here. He took a grip in the early stages and was just not suited to the way the race was run. (op 9-4)

Vortex, the lowest-rated runner in the field, appears to be finally regressing at the age of nine. (op 20-1)

3499 PLAY LIVE CASINO AT BETINTERNET.COM H'CAP 6f
4:10 (4:10) (Class 4) (0-80,76) 3-Y-O £5,180 (£1,541; £770; £384) Stalls High

Form RPR

36-3 **1** **Danish Art (IRE)**[16] 2981 3-9-8 75 .... KerrinMcEvoy 6 77
(J A R Toller) *lw: sn pushed along in rr: swtchd lft over 1f out: r.o to ld last strides* **4/1**

4144 **2** nse **Blue Jack**[14] 3028 3-9-8 75 .... JimmyFortune 7 77+
(W R Muir) *hld up in tch: nt clr run and stmbld over 1f out: swtchd rt 1f out: r.o u.p* **3/1**[1]

-010 **3** shd **Castles In The Air**[14] 3050 3-9-9 76 ....(v[1]) PaulEddery 4 77
(Pat Eddery) *w ldr tl led over 2f out: rdn and edgd lft over 1f out: edgd rt ins fnl f: hdd last strides* **10/3**[2]

1040 **4** shd **Magical Speedfit (IRE)**[1] 3462 3-9-8 75 .... EddieAhern 1 76
(G G Margarson) *hld up: hdwy over 2f out: rdn and ev ch ins fnl f: r.o* **12/1**

0005 **5** 1 **Nawaaff**[29] 2555 3-8-9 67 .... MCGeran(5) 2 65
(M R Channon) *w ldrs: rdn and edgd rt over 1f out: no ex wl ins fnl f* **16/1**

10 **6** ¾ **Hazelrigg (IRE)**[56] 1819 3-9-8 75 .... TedDurcan 3 70+
(T D Easterby) *hld up in tch: nt clr run over 1f out: sn rdn: styd on same pce* **7/2**[3]

1-00 **7** 6 **Blues Minor (IRE)**[23] 2761 3-9-9 76 .... RichardHughes 8 52
(R Hannon) *lw: led: rdn and hdd over 2f out: wknd fnl f* **14/1**

1m 12.57s (0.07) **Going Correction** -0.125s/f (Firm) 7 Ran SP% **110.5**
Speed ratings (Par 101): **94,93,93,93,92 91,83**
toteswinger: 1&2 £2.60, 1&3 £3.10, 2&3 £2.60. CSF £15.26 CT £40.46 TOTE £4.70: £2.10, £2.30; EX 18.10.

Owner Matthew Green **Bred** John Costello **Trained** Newmarket, Suffolk

FOCUS
A bit of a messy race which ended up in a bunched finish. The form does not look that reliable.

3500 BEST ODDS AT BETINTERNET.COM E B F FILLIES' H'CAP 1m
4:40 (4:40) (Class 3) (0-95,94) 3-Y-O+ £9,714 (£2,890; £1,444; £721) Stalls High

Form RPR

2112 **1** **Maghya (IRE)**[11] 3109 3-8-7 83 .... RHills 4 94
(W J Haggas) *chsd ldrs: led over 1f out: sn rdn and edgd lft: r.o* **9/4**[1]

1 **2** 1½ **Baby Houseman**[38] 2307 3-8-12 88 .... JimmyFortune 3 96
(J H M Gosden) *lw: s.i.s: sn trcking ldrs: rdn and ev ch fr over 1f out: edgd lft: no ex towards fin* **3/1**[2]

1241 **3** 1¼ **Aphrodisia**[7] 3272 4-8-9 75 oh1 .... KerrinMcEvoy 2 82
(S C Williams) *s.i.s: hld up: rdn over 1f out: styd on: nt rch ldrs* **6/1**

0-21 **4** nk **Princess Taylor**[11] 3109 4-9-3 83 ....(t) TedDurcan 1 89
(M Botti) *led: rdn and hdd over 1f out: styd on same pce* **10/3**[3]

6530 **5** 1½ **Steam Cuisine**[2] 3415 4-9-11 94 .... JerryO'Dwyer(3) 5 97
(M G Quinlan) *lw: hld up: rdn over 1f out: n.d* **9/1**

4-56 **6** 1½ **Star Of Gibraltar**[18] 2920 3-8-2 78 .... PaulEddery 6 75
(J L Dunlop) *sn chsng ldr: rdn over 2f out: wknd fnl f* **12/1**

1m 41.1s (1.10) **Going Correction** -0.125s/f (Firm)
WFA 3 from 4yo 10lb 6 Ran SP% **110.8**
Speed ratings (Par 104): **89,87,86,85,84 82**
toteswinger: 1&2 £1.70, 1&3 £3.00, 2&3 £2.90. CSF £8.96 TOTE £3.30: £1.70, £2.10; EX 6.50.

Owner Hamdan Al Maktoum **Bred** Shadwell Estate Company Limited **Trained** Newmarket, Suffolk

FOCUS
A fair fillies' handicap featuring a couple of progressive types, but the winning time was very slow for a race of this type. However, the form appears to make sense and looks sound.

NOTEBOOK
Maghya(IRE), who did not really have the race run to suit at Thirsk last time, travelled best and quickened up well from a furlong out. She only had to be nudged out to score comfortably, comprehensively reversed Thirsk form with Princess Taylor, and looks to be very much an improving filly. (op 5-2 tchd 11-4)

Baby Houseman, making her handicap debut, was the only one who could give the winner a race but even she gave best inside the final half-furlong. This was only her second start and she bumped into a progressive rival, so there was no disgrace in this, and one would expect her to improve again. (op 11-4)

Aphrodisia, 6lb higher than when winning over this course and distance a week earlier, stayed on to chase the two lightly raced, progressive rivals home. She probably ran as well as could be expected. (op 7-1)

Princess Taylor beat Maghya at Thirsk last time but she was 2lb worse off with that rival here and this more galloping track suited the other filly better. (op 9-2)

Steam Cuisine, back in handicap company for the first time since she won on the Rowley Mile in October, remains on a career-high mark and is probably happier on easier ground. (op 7-1)

3501 CELEBRATING 10 YEARS AT BETINTERNET.COM APPRENTICE H'CAP 7f
5:15 (5:15) (Class 5) (0-70,69) 4-Y-O+ £3,885 (£1,156; £577; £288) Stalls High

Form RPR

-412 **1** **Charlie Delta**[18] 2923 5-9-4 68 ....(b) WilliamCarson(5) 6 78
(J G M O'Shea) *a.p: led over 1f out: rdn out* **4/1**[2]

4010 **2** ¾ **Sintenis Mac (GER)**[1] 3457 5-8-8 58 ....(b) RossAtkinson(5) 11 66
(P J O'Gorman) *s.s: hld up: hdwy over 1f out: rdn to chse wnr ins fnl f: r.o* **7/2**[1]

0054 **3** 1 **Cornerstone**[14] 3034 4-8-2 50 ....(vt) KellyHarrison(3) 4 55
(S C Williams) *chsd ldrs: rdn over 2f out: styd on* **5/1**[3]

4246 **4** 2½ **Marmooq**[14] 3034 5-8-9 54 ....(e) TolleyDean 3 53
(M J Attwater) *lw: hld up: hdwy u.p over 1f out: styd on same pce ins fnl f* **5/1**[3]

1056 **5** ¾ **Arctic Desert**[46] 2069 8-8-11 63 ....(t) AntiocoMurgia(7) 8 60
(Miss Gay Kelleway) *dwlt: hld up: hdwy u.p over 1f out: styd on same pce fnl f* **16/1**

-504 **6** 1½ **Life's A Whirl**[11] 3116 6-8-0 50 oh1 ....(p) AmyBaker(5) 1 42
(Mrs C A Dunnett) *chsd ldrs: rdn over 2f out: wknd fnl f* **16/1**

5410 **7** ½ **Limonia (GER)**[20] 2869 6-8-1 53 .... JamieKyne(7) 9 44
(Mike Murphy) *half-rrd s: racd keenly and sn trcking ldr: rdn and ev ch over 1f out: wknd ins fnl f* **12/1**

50-3 **8** nk **Littleton Telchar (USA)**[9] 3165 8-9-3 69 .... StevenCorrigan(7) 7 59
(S W Hall) *chsd ldrs over 5f* **11/1**

0305 **9** 1½ **Grey Boy (GER)**[30] 2550 7-8-10 60 .... MarkCoumbe(5) 5 46
(A W Carroll) *plld hrd: led: rdn and hdd over 1f out: wknd fnl f* **5/1**[3]

6650 **10** 2 **Border Artist**[14] 3034 9-8-1 53 .... JosephineBruning(7) 12 34
(J Pearce) *lw: hld up: pushed along 1/2-way: wknd wl over 1f out* **20/1**

1m 25.5s (-0.20) **Going Correction** -0.125s/f (Firm) 10 Ran SP% **124.8**
Speed ratings (Par 103): **96,95,94,91,90 88,88,87,85,83**
toteswinger: 1&2 £2.90, 1&3 £6.20, 2&3 £4.40. CSF £19.94 CT £76.59 TOTE £3.00: £1.60, £2.20, £2.00; EX 14.60 Place 6 £5.48, Place 5 £3.91.

Owner The Lovely Jubbly's **Bred** P K Gardner **Trained** Elton, Gloucs

FOCUS
A moderate handicap run at a fair gallop and the form looks sound rated around the first three.
T/Plt: £8.50 to a £1 stake. Pool: £7,222.64. 7,222.64 winning tickets. T/Qpdt: £4.70 to a £1 stake. Pool: £3,317.57. 512.99 winning tickets. CR

3322 WINDSOR (R-H)
Saturday, June 28

OFFICIAL GOING: Good to firm (good in places) changing to good to firm after race 3 (3.40)
Wind: breezy behind Weather: bright, partly cloudy

3502 TOTEPLACEPOT MAIDEN STKS 6f
2:35 (2:36) (Class 5) 3-4-Y-O £2,729 (£806; £403) Stalls High

Form RPR

5-6 **1** **Lekita**[28] 2620 3-8-12 0 .... SaleemGolam 3 77
(W R Swinburn) *chsd ldrs: wnt 2nd over 2f out: rdn wl over 1f out: styd on wl to ld fnl 100yds* **3/1**[3]

2020 **2** 1 **North South Divide (IRE)**[17] 2947 4-9-10 78 ....(p) DaneO'Neill 7 81
(R A Teal) *taken down early: led: rdn 2f out: hdd and no ex fnl 100yds* **2/1**[2]

2-30 **3** 3 **Bailey (IRE)**[7] 3270 3-9-3 77 ....(b) RobertHavlin 9 69
(B J Meehan) *in tch: hdwy to chse ldng pair jst over 2f out: sn rdn and nt qckn: plugged on same pce* **7/4**[1]

4-0 **4** 3¼ **Kenton Street**[50] 1960 3-9-0 0 .... KirstyMilczarek(3) 10 59+
(J A R Toller) *t.k.h: hld up wl in tch: rdn 2f out: sn outpcd and no ch w ldrs* **10/1**

0 **5** 5 **The Young Fella**[7] 3268 3-8-10 0 .... HollyHall(7) 5 43
(S A Callaghan) *v.s.a: wl bhd: edgd rt over 2f out: styd on fr over 1f out: nvr on terms* **16/1**

0-6 **6** 1¼ **Warden Fizz**[65] 1581 3-9-0 0 .... MarcHalford(3) 4 39
(D R C Elsworth) *racd in midfield: rdn and struggling 3f out: no ch after* **33/1**

0 **7** 2 **Flipacoin**[13] 3061 3-8-12 0 .... IanMongan 1 28
(S Dow) *w ldr tl over 2f out: sn wknd* **66/1**

0 **8** 2¾ **Summer Rose**[16] 2981 3-8-12 0 ....(p) JimCrowley 6 19
(R M H Cowell) *s.i.s: a bhd* **25/1**

00-0 **9** 5 **Didntcomeback**[45] 2099 3-8-10 47 .... JakePayne(7) 2 8
(M S Saunders) *racd on outer in midfield: rdn and struggling 1/2-way: no ch fnl 2f* **66/1**

10 7 **Professor Malone** 3-9-0 0 .... TravisBlock(3) 8 —
(J C Tuck) *v.s.a: a bhd* **50/1**

1m 11.16s (-1.84) **Going Correction** -0.20s/f (Firm)
WFA 3 from 4yo 7lb 10 Ran SP% **121.4**
Speed ratings (Par 103): **104,102,98,94,87 86,83,79,73,63**
toteswinger: 1&2 £1.80, 1&3 £1.40, 2&3 £1.10. CSF £9.62 TOTE £4.50: £1.60, £1.30, £1.30; EX 13.10 Trifecta £22.20 Pool: £503.51. 16.76 winning units..

Owner Mrs A M Richards **Bred** Berkshire Equestrian Services Ltd **Trained** Aldbury, Herts

■ Stewards' Enquiry : Holly Hall 14-day ban: breach of Rule 157 (Jul 12-25)
Saleem Golam caution: used whip down shoulder in forehand position

FOCUS
A moderate pace on paper as races like this often are - even more so as the season progresses - but the pace was decent, they finished well spread out, and the official marks of the second and third probably provide a reliable guide to the merit of the form.

The Young Fella ◆ Official explanation: jockey said, regarding running and riding, her orders were to jump out and then drop in, adding that the colt missed the break and ran very green; 40-day suspension: (Jul 1-Aug 9)

3503 TOTEEXACTA MIDSUMMER STKS (LISTED RACE) 1m 67y
3:05 (3:06) (Class 1) 3-Y-O+
£14,760 (£5,595; £2,800; £1,396; £699; £351) Stalls High

Form RPR

0-20 **1** **Dunelight (IRE)**[22] 2788 5-9-4 109 ....(v) IanMongan 5 112
(C G Cox) *mde all: qcknd 4f out: clr 3f out: styd on wl: readily* **2/1**[1]

-515 **2** 2½ **Ordnance Row**[28] 2600 5-9-7 106 .... DaneO'Neill 6 109
(R Hannon) *hld up wl in tch: rdn to dispute 2nd over 2f out: kpt on but no imp on wnr: wnt 2nd post* **5/2**[2]

The Form Book, Raceform Ltd, Compton, RG20 6NL

50-4 **3** *nse* **Banknote**47 2044 6-9-4 108............................ FrancisNorton 1 106
(A M Balding) *t.k.h: hld up wl in tch: disp 2nd and rdn over 2f out: kpt on but no imp on wnr* **10/3**3

1446 **4** *3 1/4* **Ballinteni**10 3122 6-9-4 93............................ PaulDoe 2 99
(Miss Gay Kelleway) *sn bustled up to chsd wnr: rdn 3f out: wknd 2f out* **11/2**

3401 **5** *1/2* **Bahar Shumaal (IRE)**9 3167 6-9-4 83............................ AhmedAjtebi 3 98
(C E Brittain) *hld up in last pair: rdn and edgd lft 2f out: no hdwy* **10/1**

313- **6** *1/2* **Mount Hadley (USA)**288 5378 4-9-4 100............................ StephenCarson 4 96
(G A Butler) *t.k.h: hld up in last: lost tch qckly 4f out: hanging lft last 3f: n.d after* **20/1**

1m 41.4s (-3.30) **Going Correction** -0.125s/f (Firm) **6** Ran SP% **114.2**
Speed ratings (Par 111): **111,108,108,105,104 104**
toteswinger: 1&2 £1.30, 1&3 £1.10, 2&3 £1.60. CSF £7.50 TOTE £3.30: £1.90, £2.00; EX 9.70.
Owner Mr And Mrs P Hargreaves **Bred** D And B Egan **Trained** Lambourn, Berks

FOCUS
Not the most competitive Listed race in the world, but an interesting one nonetheless and a classic case of an habitual front-runner getting his own way. The winner is rated to his best.

NOTEBOOK
Dunelight(IRE) was 7lb better off with Ordnance Row for a half-length beating over course and distance last month, but more relevant was that he was making his seasonal reappearance then whilst his rival had the benefit of a previous run. Soon able to establish his favoured position out in front and allowed his own way, he appeared to be thoroughly enjoying himself and when asked to find a bit more to fend off his rivals, the response was more than adequate. He is likely to return to Glorious Goodwood next month for the Betfair Cup in which he finished third behind Tariq last year. (op 9-4 tchd 5-2 in places)
Ordnance Row was always likely to find it tough confirming last month's course form with Dunelight on 7lb worse terms and with his old rival likely to be fitter this time. He managed to get himself within striking distance, but on this occasion found the favourite was not for catching. He probably still ran up to form though. (tchd 9-4 and 11-4)
Banknote had been firmly put in his place by Ordnance Row and Dunelight here last month, but like the favourite he was making his seasonal reappearance then. He was 3lb better off with the former, but 4lb worse off with the latter and after racing keenly yet holding every chance, he battled right to the line and probably ran right up to his best. (op 7-2 tchd 4-1 and 3-1)
Ballinteni, back in Listed company after his cracking effort from a high draw in the Hunt Cup and very well supported in the market, appeared to race quite lazily despite being handy for much of the way, but he was eventually left behind. To be fair to him he faced a huge task at these weights and may also still have been feeling the effects of his Ascot exertions. Provided the Handicapper leaves him alone, his best chances of winning another race in the near future are probably still in handicap company. (op 10-1)
Bahar Shumaal(IRE), from a yard renowned for pitching them in at the deep end, faced an impossible task at the weights and was never seen with a chance. (op 11-1 tchd 9-1)
Mount Hadley(USA), ex-Godolphin and making his debut for the yard off the back of a nine-month absence, was detached and struggling by halfway but although he managed to fight his way back to finish on the heels of the stragglers he also looked very ill-at-ease on the track. He was an intended runner in the Wolferton at Royal Ascot until withdrawn on account of the fast ground, and this effort may help explain why. Official explanation: jockey said gelding was unsuited by the good to firm (good in places) ground (op 14-1 tchd 11-1)

3504 TOTESWINGER HERITAGE H'CAP 6f
3:40 (3:41) (Class 2) (0-105,104) 3-Y-O+
£31,155 (£9,330; £4,665; £2,335; £1,165; £585) **Stalls** High

Form RPR

325- **1** **Hitchens (IRE)**259 6167 3-9-1 102............................ PatDobbs 11 111
(G L Moore) *chsd ldrs: rdn to chse ldr 1f out: r.o wl to ld fnl stride* **15/2**3

0266 **2** *nse* **Hoh Hoh Hoh**49 1986 6-9-6 100............................ J-PGuillambert 14 111
(R J Price) *led: rdn 2f out: kpt on wl tl hdd fnl stride* **14/1**

64-5 **3** *1 3/4* **Siren's Gift**28 2626 4-9-1 95............................ FrancisNorton 2 100
(A M Balding) *chsd ldrs: wnt 2nd 2f out tl 1f out: kpt on same pce u.p fnl f* **8/1**

0-01 **4** *nse* **Mac Gille Eoin**21 2831 4-9-6 100............................ JimCrowley 10 105
(J Gallagher) *chsd ldr tl 2f out: kpt on same pce u.p after* **8/1**

00-3 **5** *nk* **Ashdown Express (IRE)**13 3063 9-9-6 100............................ PaulDoe 16 104+
(W J Knight) *hld up towards rr: bhd 1/2-way: hdwy over 1f out: grad edgd out lft but r.o wl fnl f: nt rch ldrs* **9/1**

0-10 **6** *3/4* **Nota Bene**7 3248 6-9-7 104............................ MarcHalford(3) 8 106
(D R C Elsworth) *in tch: rdn and effrt over 2f out: kpt on same pce fr over 1f out* **10/1**

0050 **7** *3 1/4* **Conquest (IRE)**7 3248 4-9-3 97............................ DaneO'Neill 7 88
(W J Haggas) *t.k.h: hld up in rr: rdn and hld hd high 2f out: swtchd rt over 1f out: sme late hdwy: n.d* **12/1**

0002 **8** *2* **Beaver Patrol (IRE)**7 3248 6-9-10 104............................(v) StephenCarson 12 89+
(Eve Johnson Houghton) *racd in midfield: rdn and no prog over 2f out: nt clr run and swtchd lft over 1f out: nvr trbld ldrs* **4/1**1

1400 **9** *nk* **Excusez Moi (USA)**28 2607 6-9-1 100............................ AhmedAjtebi(5) 13 84
(C E Brittain) *s.i.s: bhd: swtchd to outer 1/2-way: n.d* **16/1**

-006 **10** *4 1/2* **Judd Street**24 2712 6-9-8 102............................ IanMongan 6 72
(Eve Johnson Houghton) *t.k.h: hld up towards rr: rdn and brief effrt 1/2-way: n.d fnl 2f* **20/1**

4131 **11** *1/2* **Orpsie Boy (IRE)**112 836 5-9-3 100............................ KirstyMilczarek(3) 15 68
(N P Littmoden) *chsd ldrs for 2f: grad dropped to rr: bhd and no ch fnl 2f* **11/2**2

2421 **12** *1/2* **Ceremonial Jade (UAE)**57 1765 5-9-1 95............................(t) OscarUrbina 4 62
(M Botti) *hld up towards rr: rdn and effrt over 2f out: sn btn* **15/2**3

5-00 **13** *nk* **Pivotal Point**13 3063 8-9-4 98............................ RichardSmith 9 64
(P J Makin) *t.k.h: chsd ldrs tl wknd 2f out: wl btn whn hung rt over 1f out: b.b.v* **33/1**

00 **14** *3/4* **Mocha Java (SAF)**24 2712 6-8-13 96............................(b) TravisBlock(3) 3 59
(E F Vaughan) *stdd s: hld up towards rr on outer: rdn and sme hdwy over 2f out: wknd 2f out* **66/1**

1m 10.4s (-2.60) **Going Correction** -0.20s/f (Firm)
WFA 3 from 4yo+ 7lb **14** Ran SP% **129.7**
Speed ratings (Par 109): **109,108,106,106,106 105,100,98,97,91 91,90,90,89**
toteswinger: 1&2 £16.80, 1&3 £14.20, 2&3 £32.70. CSF £115.08 CT £911.97 TOTE £10.10: £3.50, £3.20, £3.50; EX 147.60 TRIFECTA Not won..
Owner R A Green **Bred** Curragh Bloodstock Agency Ltd **Trained** Woodingdean, E Sussex
■ Stewards' Enquiry : Richard Smith two-day ban: careless riding (Jul 12,13)

FOCUS
A fiercely competitive sprint handicap as it should be for the money, but although there was not a lot covering the front six at the line they pulled well clear of the others. It was crucial to race up with the pace here as the first four home were handy throughout, and those that stuck closest to the stands' rail also appeared to hold an advantage, which included the front pair. Those in the frame behind the winner set the standard.

NOTEBOOK
Hitchens(IRE), last seen finishing fifth behind Captain Gerrard in the Group 3 Cornwallis Stakes at Ascot last October, attracted significant market support on this return to action. Never far off the pace, a lovely gap appeared for him against the stands' rail coming to the last furlong and he made full use of it to storm home and snatch the race right on the line. This was a decent piece of training. (op 11-1)
Hoh Hoh Hoh, another that has been keeping decent company in his recent starts, managed to get to the front from his decent draw and set them all a merry dance. Unfortunately for him, he failed to stick close enough to the stands' rail which provided an opening for the winner and, despite giving his all, he agonisingly had the prize snatched from him right on the line. (op 16-1)
Siren's Gift ran a blinder from a bad draw having always been close to the pace on the wide outside. All her best form has been over the minimum trip, but lack of stamina was not the issue here and she is well worth another chance when more favourably berthed. (tchd 10-1)
Mac Gille Eoin, bumped up 7lb for his victory at Epsom on Derby day, raced up with the pace throughout and kept on all the way to the line. This effort suggests he is not handicapped out of things just yet. (op 10-1)
Ashdown Express(IRE), not quite the horse he was, had the plum draw but for a hold-up horse like him that probably made little difference. He did stay on in the latter stages on this second start for his new yard and he may now be able to end a losing run stretching back to September 2005. (op 12-1)
Nota Bene, never far away, kept on to not be beaten far and this was certainly better than his aweful effort in the Wokingham seven days earlier. It seems that you cannot quite be sure what you are likely to get from him these days. (op 12-1 tchd 9-1)
Conquest(IRE), gradually edging down the weights, gave himself plenty to do by being out the back early in a race dominated by prominent horses, and when he was eventually asked to close he looked very unenthusiastic. He cannot be backed with any confidence at the moment. (op 16-1)
Beaver Patrol(IRE), raised 4lb for his cracking effort in the Wokingham, went off a well-backed favourite but he may have been feeling the effects of his Ascot exertions as he was already under the whip and going nowhere when murdered against the stands' rail over a furlong from home. Official explanation: jockey said gelding ran flat (op 5-1 tchd 11-2)
Pivotal Point Official explanation: vet said gelding bled from the nose

3505 BET TOTEPOOL ON ALL UK RACING H'CAP 1m 3f 135y
4:15 (4:16) (Class 2) (0-100,94) 3-Y-~~O£10,092~~ (£3,020; £1,510; £755; £376) **Stalls** Centre

Form RPR

-056 **1** **Sahrati**44 2120 4-9-2 87............................(b1) AhmedAjtebi(5) 4 98
(C E Brittain) *chsd ldrs early: hld up and grad dropped towards rr: plld out and hdwy 3f out: str run on outer to ld fnl 100yds* **16/1**

/400 **2** *1 1/2* **Come On Jonny (IRE)**21 2830 6-9-8 88............................ NelsonDeSouza 8 96
(R M Beckett) *t.k.h: hld up in tch: hdwy on inner 3f out: rdn to ld 2f out: hdd and outpcd by wnr fnl 100yds* **12/1**

4300 **3** *nse* **John Terry (IRE)**21 2830 5-9-9 89............................ JimCrowley 5 97
(Mrs A J Perrett) *hld up in midfield: hdwy 4f out: chsd ldr 2f out: ev ch u.p over 1f out: one pce fnl 100yds* **17/2**

-251 **4** *3/4* **Paktolos (FR)**13 3060 5-9-8 88............................(b) DaneO'Neill 1 95
(A King) *s.i.s: stdy hdwy and midfield 1/2-way: rdn to chse ldrs 2f out: hung rt u.p jst ins fnl f: one pce* **4/1**1

0625 **5** *1/2* **Prince Sabaah (IRE)**36 2372 4-9-2 87............................(p) HaddenFrost(5) 11 93
(R Hannon) *t.k.h: chsd ldr tl 7f out: styd handy: rdn and unable qckn wl over 1f out: kpt on* **7/1**2

0/65 **6** *1/2* **Profit's Reality (IRE)**95 1018 6-9-5 88............................ KevinGhunowa(3) 9 94+
(P A Blockley) *t.k.h: hld up wl in tch: rdn and chsd ldrs 2f out: keeping on same pce whn n.m.r jst ins fnl f* **33/1**

-431 **7** *shd* **Coyote Creek**28 2591 4-9-3 86............................(v) TravisBlock(3) 6 91
(E F Vaughan) *t.k.h: chsd ldr tl wnt 2nd over 3f out tl 2f out: one pce u.p fnl f* **15/2**3

3236 **8** *3/4* **Grande Caiman (IRE)**42 2202 4-9-11 91............................(p) PatDobbs 2 95
(R Hannon) *hld up bhd: grad edgd out and hdwy over 2f out: no imp fnl f* **16/1**

130- **9** *3 3/4* **Royal Jet**448 940 6-9-13 93............................ TPO'Shea 12 91
(M R Channon) *stdd s: hld up bhd: nt clr run and swtchd lft 2f out: n.d* **25/1**

20-2 **10** *5* **Zonergem**47 2059 10-9-6 89............................ KirstyMilczarek(3) 3 78
(Lady Herries) *t.k.h: hld up towards rr: swtchd rt and effrt on rail 2f out: wknd jst over 1f out* **12/1**

/466 **11** *3 1/4* **Frank Sonata**31 2503 7-10-0 94............................ SaleemGolam 13 78
(M G Quinlan) *stdd s: hld up bhd: rdn and brief effrt 3f out: nvr nr ldrs* **25/1**

0643 **12** *29* **Kayak (SAF)**24 2711 6-9-10 90............................ J-PGuillambert 7 24
(D M Simcock) *led tl 6f out: led again over 3f out tl 2f out: sn wknd: eased fnl f: t.o* **8/1**

-061 **13** *17* **Step This Way (USA)**14 3045 3-8-8 88............................ IanMongan 10 —
(M Johnston) *chsd ldrs: wnt 2nd 7f out: led 6f out tl over 3f out: sn dropped out and bhd: virtually p.u fr over 1f out: t.o* **4/1**1

2m 26.44s (-3.06) **Going Correction** -0.125s/f (Firm)
WFA 3 from 4yo+ 14lb **13** Ran SP% **123.7**
Speed ratings (Par 109): **105,104,103,103,103 102,102,102,99,96 94,74,63**
toteswinger: 1&2 £28.40, 1&3 £52.50, 2&3 £15.80. CSF £198.20 CT £1764.54 TOTE £23.20: £5.30, £3.90, £2.60; EX 333.00 Trifecta £409.50 Part won. Pool: £553.43. 0.50 winning units..
Owner Saeed Manana **Bred** Darley **Trained** Newmarket, Suffolk

FOCUS
A decent competitive handicap, but the pace was ordinary as can be seen by the fact that a large blanket would have covered the second to eighth horses at the line. The form looks solid rated around the fourth, fifth and seventh.

NOTEBOOK
Sahrati, back on his last winning mark, found that the step back up in trip compensated for the lack of early pace. He was eventually produced with his effort down the centre of the track and came home very strongly, but he also deserves extra credit for this as up until this race there seemed to be a major advantage to those that stuck closest to the stands' rail. (tchd 20-1)
Come On Jonny(IRE) ◆, down another 6lb, got a dream run against the favoured stands' rail and looked like scoring until the winner was unleashed down the centre. He is much better handicapped now and this was a decent effort on ground that would have been plenty fast enough for him. (op 16-1 tchd 10-1)
John Terry(IRE), back on the same mark as when successful on Polytrack in February, looked much happier here than at Epsom last time and was brought through to hold every chance. He went down with all guns blazing and looks more than capable of winning again off this sort of mark. (tchd 8-1 and 9-1)
Paktolos(FR) had been bumped up 8lb for winning in first-time blinkers at Salisbury last time and there was always a question as to whether they would work so well a second time. Well backed beforehand, he stayed on well from off the pace over the last couple of furlongs, but for a proven stayer like him the lack of early pace was probably his biggest handicap. (op 11-2 tchd 6-1)
Prince Sabaah(IRE) had been raised 5lb for finishing fifth behind the useful Punjabi at Newmarket last time and that race has worked out well with the pair that finished either side of him going on to win their next starts, but he was beaten over 15 lengths by the winner, so the rise did look a bit harsh. Always there or thereabouts, he plugged on against the favoured stands' rail, but was never doing quite enough. He is another that would probably have preferred a stronger gallop. (op 8-1 tchd 9-1)

Profit's Reality(IRE), back off the same mark as when last successful in handicap company, stayed on quite nicely late on and this was by far his best effort on his third outing since returning from a long layoff in February. He is worth keeping an eye on.
Coyote Creek, raised 10lb for getting off the mark at the 12th attempt in the first-time visor at Doncaster last month, had every chance and was not disgraced, but will need to find improvement in order to defy this sort of mark. (op 9-1)
Grande Caiman(IRE), in first-time cheekpieces and yet to show much on grass, stays further than this so being held up out the back in a steadily run race was far fom ideal and he probably achieved as much as could have been expected under the circumstances. (op 14-1)
Zonergem Official explanation: jockey said gelding lost off-fore shoe
Kayak(SAF) Official explanation: jockey said gelding lost its action
Step This Way(USA), raised 8lb for her win in the big ladies' race at York earlier this month, showed to the fore early and was in front crossing the intersection, but she then dropped right out as though something was amiss. (op 9-2 tchd 5-1)

3506 BET TOTEPOOL ON ALL IRISH RACING H'CAP 6f
4:50 (4:51) (Class 5) (0-70,79) 3-Y-0+ **£2,729** (£806; £403) **Stalls High**

Form				RPR
3511	1		**Dressed To Dance (IRE)**[3] 3363 4-10-2 **79** 6ex...(v) RichardEvans(7) 16 (P D Evans) *s.i.s: hld up in midfield on inner: grad edgd out off rail and hdwy 3f out: carried lft over 1f out: wnt 2nd 1f out: led ins fnl f: r.o strly* **4/1**[1]	93
2421	2	1	**Farthermost (IRE)**[5] 3313 3-9-13 **76** 6ex.... PatDobbs 15 (R Hannon) *chsd ldrs: rdn and edgd lft over 1f out: chsd ldr briefly over 1f out: kpt on u.p fnl f* **11/2**[3]	85
-641	3	1 ½	**Peter Island (FR)**[2] 3418 5-10-4 **74** 6ex....(v) JimCrowley 9 (J Gallagher) *wnt lft s: sn led: clr over 2f out: rdn over 1f out: hdd ins fnl f: fdd fnl 100yds* **5/1**[2]	80
4262	4	1 ¾	**Prince Of Delphi**[14] 3024 5-9-8 **69**.... JackMitchell(5) 8 (R M Beckett) *bdly hmpd s: bhd: rdn 2f out: styd on but nvr pce to rch ldrs* **4/1**[1]	69+
4205	5	½	**Louphole**[66] 1567 6-9-13 **69**.... RichardSmith 3 (P J Makin) *bhd: hdwy 3f out: nt clr run over 1f out: sn swtchd rt and rdr dropped reins: styd on fnl f: nvr rchd ldrs* **25/1**	68+
6045	6	2 ¼	**Linda Green**[5] 3313 7-9-3 **59**.... TPO'Shea 10 (M R Channon) *wnt rt s: sn in tch: rdn and struggling over 2f out: n.d after* **8/1**	51
-500	7	nk	**Bobby Rose**[54] 1872 5-9-4 **65**.... DanielleMcCreery(5) 14 (D K Ivory) *hld up: hdwy over 2f out: chsd ldrs and carried lft over 1f out: wknd fnl f* **20/1**	56
6000	8	hd	**Hollow Jo**[3] 3371 8-8-12 **59**....(p) HaddenFrost(5) 6 (J R Jenkins) *chsd ldrs: rdn over 2f out: carried lft over 1f out: sn wknd* **33/1**	49
0040	9	1	**Jimmy The Guesser**[19] 2892 5-9-7 **66**....(b) KirstyMilczarek(3) 2 (N P Littmoden) *hmpd s: racd in midfield on outer: hdwy and rdn over 2f out: wknd over 1f out* **25/1**	53
4504	10	nk	**Norcroft**[16] 2983 6-8-6 **51** oh1....(v[1]) MarcHalford(3) 11 (Mrs C A Dunnett) *chsd ldrs: wnt 2nd briefly over 2f out: rdn and short of room 2f out: sn wknd* **12/1**	37
0600	11	4 ½	**Monashee Prince (IRE)**[5] 3316 6-8-11 **53**....(v) DaneO'Neill 13 (J R Best) *hld up towards rr: rdn and effrt over 2f out: nvr trbld ldrs* **12/1**	24
4300	12	shd	**Cracking Nick (IRE)**[15] 2991 3-9-5 **68**....(p) SaleemGolam 1 (W R Swinburn) *wnt rt s: sn chsd ldr tl over 2f out: edgd lft and sn wknd* **33/1**	37
000	13	1 ¾	**Trees Of Green (USA)**[46] 2081 4-9-4 **60**.... OscarUrbina 12 (M Wigham) *racd in midfield tl lost pl and bhd over 3f out: no ch after* **25/1**	26
3026	14	hd	**Obe Royal**[7] 3255 4-9-13 **69**....(b) CatherineGannon 7 (P D Evans) *a bhd* **25/1**	34
0460	15	2 ¼	**Cinnamon Hill**[5] 3317 4-9-13 **69**....(p) StephenCarson 5 (Eve Johnson Houghton) *chsd ldrs tl 1/2-way: sn dropped out: wl bhd fnl 2f* **40/1**	27

1m 11.2s (-1.80) **Going Correction** -0.20s/f (Firm)
WFA 3 from 4yo+ 7lb **15 Ran SP% 127.0**
Speed ratings (Par 103): **104,102,100,98,97 94,94,94,92,92 86,86,83,83,80**
toteswinger: 1&2 £5.60, 1&3 £5.20, 2&3 £7.60. CSF £24.00 CT £121.20 TOTE £4.20: £2.00, £2.80, £2.70; EX 21.00 Trifecta £113.70 Pool: £733.15. 4.77 winning units..
Owner Premier Cru Racing **Bred** John Doyle **Trained** Pandy, Monmouths

FOCUS
A competitive sprint handicap, but very few ever got into it. The race was dominated by in-form horses with the first three home all carrying 6lb penalties for recent successes and the third sets the level.
Cinnamon Hill Official explanation: jockey said filly ran flat

3507 BET TOTEPOOL AT TOTESPORT.COM FILLIES' H'CAP 1m 67y
5:25 (5:27) (Class 5) (0-75,75) 3-Y-0+ **£3,070** (£906; £453) **Stalls High**

Form				RPR
25-4	1		**Shanzu**[61] 1671 3-8-11 **68**.... DaneO'Neill 14 (H Candy) *chsd ldr tl led 6f out: hdd over 4f out: drvn to ld again 1f out: hdd ins fnl f: rallied gamely to ld again fnl stride* **12/1**	74
5514	2	shd	**Onenightinlisbon (IRE)**[8] 3208 4-9-0 **68**.... HarryPoulton(7) 1 (J R Boyle) *led for 2f: chsd ldr tl over 4f out: drvn and ev ch 1f out: led ins fnl f: hdd fnl stride* **12/1**	75
0-04	3	1 ½	**Selsey**[22] 2800 3-8-12 **69**.... TPO'Shea 10 (Sir Michael Stoute) *in tch in midfield: rdn and effrt jst over 2f out: kpt on u.p fnl f: nt rch ldng pair* **13/2**[2]	71+
3305	4	½	**Cape Velvet (IRE)**[14] 3023 4-9-7 **68**.... TQuinn 8 (J W Hills) *t.k.h: chsd ldrs: pushed along and sltly outpcd 3f out: kpt on u.p fnl f: nt rch ldrs* **12/1**	71
-240	4	dht	**Spanish Diva**[8] 3220 4-9-6 **67**.... SaleemGolam 12 (S C Williams) *hld up in midfield: lost pl and bhd over 4f out: rdn over 1f out: r.o wl fnl f: nt rch ldrs* **16/1**	70+
2014	6	½	**Oat Cuisine**[7] 3272 4-9-2 **70**.... RichardEvans(7) 13 (M L W Bell) *towards rr: rdn and struggling 4f out: hdwy and hung lft u.p over 1f out: kpt on: nvr rchd ldrs* **13/8**[1]	72+
505	7	shd	**Shamrock Lady (IRE)**[13] 3064 3-9-2 **73**.... StephenCarson 4 (J Gallagher) *t.k.h: hld up towards rr: hdwy on outer 2f out: kpt on fnl f: nt rch ldrs* **25/1**	72
2-03	8	2	**Towy Girl (IRE)**[5] 3329 4-8-11 **58**.... CatherineGannon 7 (A W Carroll) *plld hrd: hld up in midfield tl plld way into ld over 4f out: sn clr: rdn and hld hd high over 1f out: hdd 1f out: sn wknd* **33/1**	55
3213	9	nse	**Support Fund (IRE)**[44] 2128 4-9-7 **75**.... DanielBlackett(7) 3 (Eve Johnson Houghton) *hld up in tch: hdwy 4f out: chsd ldrs and rdn over 2f out: wknd 1f out* **15/2**[3]	72
506	10	¾	**Plum Asset (USA)**[33] 2455 3-8-7 **64**.... NelsonDeSouza 9 (R M Beckett) *s.i.s: bhd: rdn 3f out: kpt on u.p ins fnl f: n.d* **33/1**	57
4-30	11	shd	**Silky Steps (IRE)**[14] 3023 3-8-8 **65**.... RichardSmith 11 (P J Makin) *s.i.s: hld up in midfield: hdwy over 3f out: chsd ldrs and rdn over 2f out: wknd jst over 1f out* **10/1**	58
3006	12	nk	**Geestring (IRE)**[17] 2956 3-8-12 **69**....(b) PatDobbs 5 (R Hannon) *v.s.a: hld up in rr: hdwy on outer over 2f out: wknd over 1f out* **14/1**	61
034-	13	nk	**Welsh Opera**[201] 7097 3-8-9 **66**.... JimCrowley 6 (Mrs A J Perrett) *in tch: hdwy over 2f out: chsd ldrs and rdn 2f out: wknd jst over 1f out* **14/1**	57

1m 43.78s (-0.92) **Going Correction** -0.125s/f (Firm)
WFA 3 from 4yo+ 10lb **13 Ran SP% 124.3**
Speed ratings (Par 100): **99,98,97,96,96 96,96,94,94,93 93,93,92**
toteswinger: 1&2 £21.40, 1&3 £13.40, 2&3 £12.40. CSF £151.58 CT £1058.81 TOTE £15.80: £3.30, £3.00, £2.30; EX 158.40 TRIFECTA Not won. Place 6 £250.23, Place 5 £227.66..
Owner Baraka Partnership **Bred** Lakin Bloodstock And H And W Thornton **Trained** Kingston Warren, Oxon

FOCUS
An ordinary fillies' handicap run at a rather stop-start pace and the front pair were to the fore throughout. Again those that stayed closer to the stands' rail held the advantage and the runner-up is rated to the best of this year's form.
T/Plt: £709.90 to a £1 stake. Pool: £76,193.42. 78.35 winning tickets. T/Qpdt: £323.50 to a £1 stake. Pool: £3,147.79. 7.20 winning tickets. SP

3508 - (Foreign Racing) - See Raceform Interactive

3463 CURRAGH (R-H)
Saturday, June 28

OFFICIAL GOING: Yielding

3509a BARRONSTOWN STUD MAIDEN 6f
2:40 (2:42) 2-Y-0 **£8,637** (£2,012; £887; £512)

			RPR
1		**Westphalia (IRE)**[34] 2431 2-9-3.... JMurtagh 17 (A P O'Brien, Ire) *trckd ldrs: clsr in 2nd over 1f out: sn rdn to chal: led and styd on wl ins fnl f* **2/5**[1]	88+
2	1 ¼	**Douze Points (IRE)**[38] 2315 2-9-0.... DJMoran(3) 4 (Joseph G Murphy, Ire) *a.p: led under 2f out: strly pressed and hdd ins fnl f: kpt on wout matching wnr* **25/1**	84+
3	5	**Halaziya (IRE)** 2-8-12.... RPCleary 19 (M Halford, Ire) *sn mid-div: hdwy into 3rd over 1f out: sn no imp u.p: kpt on same pce* **33/1**	64+
4	2 ½	**Palazzone (IRE)** 2-9-3.... KLatham 9 (G M Lyons, Ire) *mid-div: rdn to go 7th over 1f out: sn no imp: kpt on same pce* **25/1**	62
5	¾	**Kilmagner (IRE)**[8] 3235 2-9-3.... WJSupple 16 (William Coleman O'Brien, Ire) *in rr of mid-div: rdn to go 9th over 1f out: sn no imp: kpt on one pce* **50/1**	60
6	½	**Fresca (IRE)**[17] 2958 2-8-12.... NGMcCullagh 3 (P J Prendergast, Ire) *chsd ldrs: 5th and no imp u.p fr over 1f out* **50/1**	53
7	2	**Call Me Alice (USA)** 2-8-12....(t) WMLordan 13 (David Wachman, Ire) *s.i.s: towards rr: rdn to go 8th over 1f out: sn no imp* **16/1**	47
8	nk	**Born To Be King (USA)** 2-9-3.... JAHeffernan 10 (A P O'Brien, Ire) *in rr of mid-div: kpt on same pce u.p fr under 2f out* **10/1**[3]	51
9	shd	**Gold Blossom (IRE)** 2-8-12.... DMGrant 6 (David Wachman, Ire) *towards rr: kpt on same pce fr 2f out* **25/1**	46
10	½	**Optimal Power (IRE)**[57] 1782 2-9-3.... WJLee 2 (Edward Lynam, Ire) *in rr of mid-div: no imp fr under 2f out* **33/1**	49
11	¾	**Happy Larry** 2-9-3.... CDHayes 8 (Andrew Oliver, Ire) *sn led: hdd under 2f out: wknd* **50/1**	47
12	2	**Uvpaintedupyurlips (IRE)** 2-8-12.... MCHussey 5 (Peter Henley, Ire) *towards rr for most: nvr a factor* **50/1**	36
13	nk	**Proud Catch (IRE)**[15] 3011 2-9-3.... FMBerry 15 (J G Burns, Ire) *cl up: dropped to 4th and rdn 1f out: sn btn and sltly hmpd* **33/1**	40
14	1 ¾	**John Veale (USA)** 2-9-3....(t) KJManning 1 (J S Bolger, Ire) *cl up: rdn fr 1/2-way: wknd fr under 2f out* **10/1**[3]	35
15	3 ½	**Partner (IRE)** 2-8-10.... EJMcNamara(7) 12 (David Marnane, Ire) *a towards rr* **40/1**	24
16	2	**Ajsaam** 2-9-3.... DPMcDonogh 11 (Kevin Prendergast, Ire) *mid-div: no ex u.p fr under 2f out* **13/2**[2]	18
17	2 ½	**Paddys Lad (IRE)**[10] 3145 2-8-7.... GinaMangan(10) 7 (Francis Ennis, Ire) *chsd ldrs: lost pl and wknd fr 2f out* **50/1**	—
18	¾	**Wild And Innocent (IRE)** 2-9-3.... PShanahan 18 (J T Gorman, Ire) *s.i.s and a trailing* **50/1**	—

1m 14.18s (-0.32) **Going Correction** -0.15s/f (Firm) **19 Ran SP% 143.4**
Speed ratings: **96,94,87,84,83 82,80,79,79,78 77,75,74,72,67 65,61,60**
CSF £25.04 TOTE £1.50: £1.10, £10.00, £5.60, £14.20; DF 33.40.
Owner Michael Tabor **Bred** Lynch Bages Ltd & Samac Ltd **Trained** Ballydoyle, Co Tipperary
■ Stewards' Enquiry : R P Cleary caution: careless riding

NOTEBOOK
Westphalia(IRE), who just lost out to Intense Focus, the subsequent Coventry runner-up and Railway Stakes third, on debut over course and distance in May, was representing leading connections with an excellent past record in this event. Backed to the exception of anything else, he duly got off the mark, but was workmanlike in doing so and still looks to be very much learning his trade. Later given quotes of around 20/1 for next season's 2,000 Guineas, that looks a touch hasty, yet no doubt he will now be upped in class to further test his credentials. He could be a likely sort for the Vintage Stakes ovr an extra furlong at Goodwood next month. (op 4/9 tchd 4/11)

3511a AUDI PRETTY POLLY STKS (GROUP 1) (F&M) 1m 2f
3:45 (3:45) 3-Y-0+
£110,294 (£34,926; £16,544; £5,514; £3,676; £1,838)

			RPR
1		**Promising Lead**[44] 2130 4-9-9.... RyanMoore 1 (Sir Michael Stoute) *chsd ldr in mod 2nd: clsd st: chal and led under 2f out: styd on wl u.p* **2/1**[1]	117
2	1 ¼	**Mad About You (IRE)**[34] 2433 3-8-11 **111**.... PJSmullen 7 (D K Weld, Ire) *chsd ldrs: mod 3rd 1/2-way: clsd and wnt 2nd travelling wl fr under 2f out: kpt on u.p wout matching wnr fnl f* **9/2**[3]	114
3	4 ½	**Anna Pavlova**[22] 2791 5-9-9.... JamieMoriarty 9 (R A Fahey) *chsd ldrs: sn mod 4th: rdn 3f out: sn no imp: kpt on into 3rd wout threatening fr 1f out* **10/1**	105

The Form Book, Raceform Ltd, Compton, RG20 6NL

4 4 1/2 **Beach Bunny (IRE)**[13] 3070 3-8-11 101 .... CDHayes 3 96
(Kevin Prendergast, Ire) *racd in mod 6th for much: rdn st: sn no imp: kpt on wout threatening* **40/1**

5 1/2 **She's Our Mark**[35] 2420 4-9-9 104 .... DMGrant 8 95
(Patrick J Flynn, Ire) *towards rr: mod 8th 1/2-way: no imp u.p and kpt on wout threatening st* **40/1**

6 1 1/4 **Ice Queen (IRE)**[13] 3070 3-8-11 104 .... JAHeffernan 2 93+
(A P O'Brien, Ire) *led and sn wl clr: swished tail: reduced ld fr 3f out: strly pressed and hdd under 2f out: wknd fr 1f out* **33/1**

7 4 **Sail (IRE)**[22] 2792 3-8-11 105 .... JMurtagh 4 85
(A P O'Brien, Ire) *sn settled in poor last: no imp u.p fr 3f out* **6/1**

8 8 **Marjalina (IRE)**[45] 2113 3-8-11 108 .... DPMcDonogh 6 69
(Kevin Prendergast, Ire) *chsd ldrs: dropped to mod 7th 3f out: sn no imp u.p* **16/1**

9 2 1/2 **Finsceal Beo (IRE)**[11] 3100 4-9-9 117 .... KJManning 5 92+
(J S Bolger, Ire) *wl off pce towards rr: rdn to go mod 5th 3f out: sn no imp: eased fr over 1f out* **5/2**[2]

2m 6.82s (-2.68) **Going Correction** +0.10s/f (Good)
WFA 3 from 4yo+ 12lb **9 Ran SP% 117.2**
Speed ratings: **114,113,109,105,105 104,101,94,92**
CSF £11.50 TOTE £3.10: £1.10, £1.70, £4.30; DF 9.20.
Owner K Abdulla **Bred** Juddmonte Farms Ltd **Trained** Newmarket, Suffolk

NOTEBOOK
Promising Lead ◆, an easy winner in Group 3 company at York on her seasonal bow, bagged her first Group 1 success with a battling display. She was always well placed behind the pacemaker and showed battling qualities to fend off the runner-up inside the final furlong. The type her trainer has few peers with, this scopey daughter of Danehill now looks set to go in search of further glory at this level against her own sex, and should really have a little more to offer still. The Nassau at Goodwood in early August looks an ideal next step for her. (op 2/1 tchd 9/4)
Mad About You(IRE) ◆ confirmed the promise of her seasonal-debut second in the Irish 1,000 Guineas and posted her best effort to date on this step up in trip. She was the only one to really push the winner from the final furlong marker and finished nicely clear of the remainder. This was the first time she had taken on her elders and it was a really solid effort, so she richly deserves to find another opening now. She also looks the type to really come into her own as she matures further and this could well be her race next season, providing she is kept in training as a four-year-old. (op 5/1)
Anna Pavlova, back against her own sex, was given her chance and simply lacked the gears to go with the front pair when it mattered most. This was more like it from her, on ground she still would have found likely enough, and there will still be other days for this likeable filly, especially when she is faced with really soft ground again. (op 7/1)
Finsceal Beo(IRE), a gallant third in the Queen Anne nine days previously, proved easy to back on this step back up in trip and ultimately failed to run her race. She was beaten before the 2f out and her rider accepted the situation passing the final furlong pole, easing her right off. Her excellent second to Duke Of Marmalade over slightly further than this in the Tattersalls Gold Cup last month showed she is fully effective over 10f and it was probably more a case of her having had a hard race at Ascot previously which resulted in her lifeless display. Indeed she was found to be clinically abnormal post race. Official explanation: vet said filly was found to be clinically abnormal post-race (op 2/1 tchd 3/1)

3513a AT THE RACES CURRAGH CUP (GROUP 3) 1m 6f
4:45 (4:46) 3-Y-0+
£33,088 (£10,477; £4,963; £1,654; £1,102; £551)

RPR

1 **Septimus (IRE)**[288] 5376 5-10-0 122 .... JMurtagh 3 118+
(A P O'Brien, Ire) *racd in 5th: rdn to go 2nd under 2f out: led over 1f out: styd on wl to draw clr ins fnl f* **1/2**[1]

2 2 1/2 **Mores Wells**[21] 2854 4-10-0 110 ....(t) WJSupple 6 114
(Kevin Prendergast, Ire) *racd mainly in 4th: clsr in 3rd under 3f out: kpt on same pce u.p fr over 1f out: 2nd cl home* **12/1**

3 nk **Peppertree Lane (IRE)**[22] 2797 5-10-0 .... RyanMoore 4 114
(M Johnston) *sn trckd ldr in 2nd: led under 3f out: strly pressed and hdd over 1f out: sn no imp: dropped to 3rd cl home* **5/1**[2]

4 1 **Red Moloney (USA)**[8] 3238 4-9-11 110 .... DPMcDonogh 7 109
(Kevin Prendergast, Ire) *sn in rr: clsr in 4th and rdn whn swtchd over 1f out: sn no imp: kpt on same pce* **10/1**

5 5 **Hasanka (IRE)**[31] 2517 4-9-8 106 .... MJKinane 2 99
(John M Oxx, Ire) *sn trckd ldrs in 3rd: 4th under 3f out: no imp u.p in 5th fr over 1f out* **9/1**[3]

6 2 1/2 **Nick's Nikita (IRE)**[13] 3070 5-9-11 105 .... RPCleary 1 99
(M Halford, Ire) *towards rr: mainly 6th: no imp u.p fr 1 1/2f out* **25/1**

7 2 **Mikhail Fokine (IRE)**[253] 6321 3-8-10 93 .... JAHeffernan 5 98
(A P O'Brien, Ire) *sn led: hdd under 3f out: wknd fr under 2f out* **40/1**

3m 7.17s (2.47) **Going Correction** +0.10s/f (Good)
WFA 3 from 4yo+ 17lb **7 Ran SP% 116.4**
Speed ratings: **97,95,95,94,91 90,89**
CSF £8.64 TOTE £1.40: £1.20, £5.80; DF 15.30.
Owner Derrick Smith **Bred** Barronstown Stud & Orpendale **Trained** Ballydoyle, Co Tipperary

NOTEBOOK
Septimus(IRE) ◆ has taken time to come to himself this season and missed out on the Gold Cup this month, allowing his stable companion Yeats a greater chance of a third win at Ascot. He looked to have a fairly straightforward task to get his season off to a winning note and duly obliged with a comfortable display. Despite yet to taste success at the highest level, it would come as a surprise were he not to make his mark in Group 1 company this term, and the Irish St Leger in September really appeals as his race this year. (op 8/13 tchd 4/6)
Mores Wells, officially rated 12lb the winner's inferior, had finished third to Yeats in last season's Irish St Leger and confirmed heren he is happier when faced with a true test of stamina. This was certainly his best effort of the current campaign. (op 10/1)
Peppertree Lane(IRE), back up in trip, was given his usual promient ride and ran very close to the level of his Listed success at Goodwood 22 days previously.

3512 - 3514a (Foreign Racing) - See Raceform Interactive

HAMBURG (R-H)
Saturday, June 28
OFFICIAL GOING: Good

3515a JAXX-POKAL (EX HAMBURGER MEILE) (GROUP 3) 1m
4:15 (4:27) 3-Y-0+ £23,529 (£7,353; £3,676; £2,206)

RPR

1 **Sehrezad (IRE)**[47] 2066 3-8-8 .... JiriPalik 5 111
(Andreas Lowe, Germany) *in tch: 3rd st: qcknd up over 1f out: led 100yds out: pushed out* **115/10**

2 1 3/4 **Santiago (GER)**[41] 6-9-4 .... ASuborics 4 107
(H Blume, Germany) *towards rr: 5th and styng on st: fin strly cl home to take 2nd nr fin* **1/1**[1]

3 1/2 **Contat (GER)**[20] 2878 5-9-4 .... RJuracek 9 106
(P Vovcenko, Germany) *led: r.o 1 1/2f out: hdd 100yds out: nt pce of wnr* **83/10**[3]

4 shd **Konig Concorde (GER)**[47] 2066 3-8-8 .... WPanov 8 106
(C Sprengel, Germany) *mid-div: 6th st: pushed along and styd on fr over 1f out to take 4th* **26/10**[2]

5 2 1/2 **Beltanus (GER)**[20] 2878 4-9-2 .... THellier 2 98
(F Willenbrock, Germany) *prom: 4th st: shkn up 2f out: styd on at one pce* **9/1**

6 1 1/2 **Smokejumper (GER)**[20] 2878 4-9-2 .... J-PCarvalho 1 95
(Frau E Mader, Germany) *towards rr: effrt early st: nvr a threat* **31/1**

7 3/4 **Balios (GER)**[20] 2875 3-8-10 ow1 .... EPedroza 3 97
(A Wohler, Germany) *hld up: n.d* **147/10**

8 5 **Willingly (GER)**[54] 1885 9-9-4 .... ADeVries 6 84
(M Trybuhl, Germany) *missed break and racd towards rr: n.d* **137/10**

9 7 **Mharadono (GER)**[41] 5-9-4 .... AStarke 7 69
(P Hirschberger, Germany) *prom: 2nd st: wknd 1 1/2f out* **11/1**

1m 38.24s (98.24)
WFA 3 from 4yo+ 10lb **9 Ran SP% 131.2**
(Including 10 Euros stake): WIN 125; PL 20, 11, 17; SF 374.
Owner Stall Phillip **Bred** Stall Phillip **Trained** Germany

3378 SALISBURY (R-H)
Sunday, June 29
OFFICIAL GOING: Good to firm (firm in places; 9.5)
Wind: Moderate,across. Weather: dry

3518 KEITH HUTCHINGS 60TH BIRTHDAY H'CAP 1m 1f 198y
1:55 (1:56) (Class 5) (0-70,68) 4-Y-0+ £3,238 (£963; £481; £240) Stalls High

Form RPR

1412 1 **Western Roots**[17] 2978 7-8-1 55 .... DavidProbert(7) 8 63+
(A M Balding) *a.p: led 5f out: shkn up over 1f out: idled sltly but a hd enough in hand: pushed out* **10/3**[2]

-404 2 1 1/2 **Follow The Colours (IRE)**[20] 2886 5-9-0 61 .... LiamJones 6 66
(J W Hills) *hld up towards rr: hdwy 4f out: rdn to chse wnr fr 3f out: sn hung rt: kpt on but a hld* **11/1**

-004 3 1 1/4 **Wester Ross (IRE)**[33] 2482 4-9-5 66 .... HayleyTurner 2 69
(J M P Eustace) *hld up towards rr: nudged along 6f out: stdy prog u.p fr over 2f out: wnt 3rd over 1f out: nvr threatened ldrs* **12/1**

0360 4 1 1/2 **Master Mahogany**[13] 3090 7-9-4 65 .... JimCrowley 1 65
(R J Hodges) *hld up and bhd: rdn over 3f out: styd on same pce fnl 2f out: wnt 4th ins fnl f: nt rch ldrs* **20/1**

0000 5 1/2 **Siena Star (IRE)**[13] 3089 10-8-9 56 .... MickyFenton 3 55
(Stef Liddiard) *hld up towards rr: rdn over 3f out: swtchd to centre over 2f out: styd on: nvr trbld ldrs* **18/1**

-060 6 2 1/2 **Muffett's Dream**[6] 3322 4-8-2 49 oh2 .... DavidKinsella 5 43
(J J Bridger) *prom: rdn 4f out: kpt on tl fdd ins fnl f* **40/1**

5-06 7 11 **Balnagore**[16] 3003 4-9-7 68 .... MartinDwyer 9 40
(J L Dunlop) *chsd ldrs: rdn 4f out: wknd 2f out: eased whn btn* **7/4**[1]

-400 8 1 **Red Current**[17] 2978 4-8-12 62 .... KevinGhunowa(3) 4 32
(R A Harris) *chsd ldrs: rdn over 3f out: wknd over 1f out* **20/1**

6622 9 4 **Zach's Harmoney (USA)**[21] 2863 4-9-4 65 .... ChrisCatlin 10 27
(P W Hiatt) *led tl 5f out: rdn over 3f out: wknd 2f out* **9/2**[3]

2m 9.00s (-0.90) **Going Correction** -0.15s/f (Firm) **9 Ran SP% 110.9**
Speed ratings (Par 103): **97,95,94,93,93 91,82,81,78**
toteswinger: 1&2 £4.90, 1&3 £6.40, 2&3 £13.20. CSF £36.22 CT £371.70 TOTE £3.10: £1.40, £2.70, £3.50; EX 30.20.
Owner I A Balding **Bred** Stratford Place Stud **Trained** Kingsclere, Hants

FOCUS
A modest handicap, but run at a fair pace. Not form to get excited about, but the winner will still be well treated on his All Weather form when reassessed and can do better again.
Balnagore Official explanation: jockey said colt was unsuited by the good to firm (firm in places) ground

3519 HERBERT AND GWEN BLAGRAVE E B F MAIDEN STKS (C&G) 6f 212y
2:25 (2:27) (Class 4) 2-Y-0 £4,371 (£1,300; £650; £324) Stalls High

Form RPR

0 1 **Oratory (IRE)**[18] 2951 2-9-0 0 .... DaneO'Neill 1 80+
(R Hannon) *carried lft s: hld up: hdwy over 3f out: sn rdn to chal: led ent fnl f: edgd rt towards fin: rdn out* **7/2**[2]

2 1 1/4 **Dreamwalk (IRE)** 2-9-0 0 .... RichardKingscote 8 77
(R M Beckett) *led: narrowly hdd over 3f out: sn rdn: kpt on and ev ch ent fnl f: no ex fnl 100yds* **12/1**[3]

62 3 1/2 **Mohanad (IRE)**[15] 3049 2-9-0 0 .... DarryllHolland 3 76
(M R Channon) *prom: tk narrow advantage over 3f out: sn rdn and hrd pressed: hdd ent fnl f: 3rd and hld whn n.m.r briefly towards fin* **2/5**[1]

4 3 1/2 **Perfect Shot (IRE)** 2-9-0 0 .... IanMongan 5 67
(J L Dunlop) *s.i.s: hld up: rdn 3f out: styd on to go 4th over 1f out but nt pce to trble ldrs* **40/1**

04 5 2 1/2 **Supernoverre (IRE)**[10] 3164 2-9-0 0 .... JimCrowley 2 61
(Mrs A J Perrett) *wnt lft s: sn chsng ldrs: rdn 3f out: wknd ent fnl f* **14/1**

6 1/2 **Spit And Polish** 2-9-0 0 .... MartinDwyer 7 59+
(J L Dunlop) *trckd ldrs: rdn 3f out: wknd ent fnl f* **33/1**

0 7 8 **Captain Walcot**[17] 2972 2-8-9 0 .... HaddenFrost(5) 4 39
(R Hannon) *chsd ldrs tl 3f out: sn btn* **33/1**

8 3 1/4 **Crystallize** 2-9-0 0 .... DavidKinsella 9 31
(A B Haynes) *s.i.s: towards rr: rdn over 2f out: wknd over 1f out* **100/1**

1m 30.55s (1.55) **Going Correction** +0.125s/f (Good) **8 Ran SP% 117.3**
Speed ratings (Par 95): **96,94,94,90,87 86,77,73**
toteswinger: 1&2 £4.70, 1&3 £1.10, 2&3 £3.80. CSF £41.20 TOTE £4.10: £1.20, £3.00, £1.10; EX 70.80.
Owner Highclere Thoroughbred Racing (Munnings) **Bred** Lynch Bages Ltd & Samac Ltd **Trained** East Everleigh, Wilts

FOCUS
A fair juvenile maiden and the form looks sound, with the first three coming clear.

NOTEBOOK
Oratory(IRE) relished the step up to this extra furlong and opened his account at the second attempt. This 90,000euros purchase has clearly come on a bundle since his debut run and looks sure to improve again for this experience, with the likelihood of easier ground suiting him better as well. On this evidence he will also get 1m without much fuss. (op 5-2)

Dreamwalk(IRE) ◆, a half-brother to his stable's smart 7f/1m winner Celtic Slipper, knew his job and was soon on the early lead. He kept on once headed and this rates a very pleasing debut effort, so he should prove hard to reel in next time granted the normal improvement. (op 20-1 tchd 25-1)

Mohanad(IRE) got the longer trip well enough, but probably failed to run up to the level of his previous second to Wildcat Wizard and has to rate as somewhat disappointing. He was in turn clear of the remainder, and has ability, but does now look more of one for nuseries. (op 8-13 tchd 4-6 in places)

Perfect Shot(IRE), half-brother to six winners, including the high-class Atlantic Prince, was always out the back after a sluggish start yet still showed some ability late in the day. He should prove a deal sharper for this debut experience. (op 50-1 tchd 33-1)

3520 K J PIKE & SONS LTD SENIORS' SPRINT H'CAP 5f

2:55 (2:57) (Class 4) (0-80,77) 6-Y-0+ **£6,476** (£1,927; £963; £481) **Stalls** High

Form				RPR
4213	1		**Misaro (GER)**[8] 3269 7-8-12 **73**....(b) HaddenFrost(5) 1 (R A Harris) *chsd ldrs: rdn over 2f out: led over 1f out: r.o: drvn out* **5/2**[1]	84
-040	2	½	**Bahamian Ballet**[16] 3009 6-9-7 **77**.... GrahamGibbons 7 (E S McMahon) *hld up: nt clr run on rails over 2f out: sn swtchd lft and bmpd: rdn and r.o ins fnl f: wnt 2nd towards fin* **4/1**[3]	86
3430	3	1¾	**Digital**[15] 3042 11-9-6 **76**....(v) ChrisCatlin 2 (M R Channon) *sn pushed along in rr: rdn over 3f out: no imp tl r.o wl fnl f: wnt 3rd nr fin: nvr on terms* **5/1**	79
3232	4	½	**Desperate Dan**[8] 3269 7-9-0 **70**....(b) DaneO'Neill 9 (A B Haynes) *chsd ldrs: rdn whn bmpd over 2f out: ev ch ent fnl f: no ex fnl 75yds* **7/2**[2]	71
5500	5	nk	**Harrison's Flyer (IRE)**[6] 3313 7-8-3 **62** ow3....(p) KevinGhunowa(3) 8 (J M Bradley) *towards rr: struggling 3f out: r.o ins fnl f: nvr threatened ldrs* **14/1**	62
4101	6	nk	**Blessed Place**[10] 3159 8-7-13 **62**.... BillyCray(7) 3 (D J S Ffrench Davis) *prom: led after 1f: rdn and hrd pressed fr over 2f out: hdd over 1f out: one pce after* **8/1**	61
0500	7	1¾	**Spanish Ace**[5] 3352 7-8-6 **62**....(b) PaulFitzsimons 6 (J M Bradley) *sn pumped into ld: narrowly hdd after 1f: rdn and ev ch over 2f out: wknd over 1f out* **28/1**	55
-006	8	3½	**Bluebok**[8] 3269 7-8-8 **67**....(t) TolleyDean(3) 5 (J M Bradley) *mid-div: rdn over 2f out: wknd over 1f out* **14/1**	47

61.45 secs (0.65) **Going Correction** +0.125s/f (Good) **8 Ran SP% 115.4**
Speed ratings: **99,98,95,94,94 93,90,85**
toteswinger: 1&2 £3.90, 1&3 £3.40, 2&3 £4.10. CSF £12.81 CT £45.87 TOTE £3.20: £1.10, £1.60, £2.40; EX 14.10.
Owner Messrs Criddle Davies Dawson & Villa **Bred** Wilhelm Fasching **Trained** Earlswood, Monmouths

■ Stewards' Enquiry : Graham Gibbons three-day ban: used whip with excessive frequency and without giving gelding time to respond (Aug 6-8)

FOCUS
Just a fair sprint handicap, run at a sound pace. The winner was well in and the runner-up met trouble.

3521 ARMISHAWS REMOVALS AND STORAGE MAIDEN STKS 1m 1f 198y

3:30 (3:30) (Class 5) 3-Y-0+ **£3,885** (£1,156; £577; £288) **Stalls** High

Form				RPR
40-2	1		**Craigstown**[15] 3043 3-9-0 77.... DarryllHolland 2 (Saeed Bin Suroor) *qcknd pce to ld after 2f: rdn and hrd pressed fr 3f out: styd on strly to assert ins fnl f: rdn out* **7/2**[2]	83
2220	2	3	**Special Reserve (IRE)**[22] 2825 3-9-0 81.... DaneO'Neill 7 (R Hannon) *chsd ldrs: rdn to chal fr 3f out: ev ch ent fnl f: no ex* **4/5**[1]	77
06-	3	4½	**Sinaaf**[225] 6847 3-8-9 0.... MartinDwyer 1 (M P Tregoning) *hld up in tch: rdn and effrt 3f out: kpt on same pce fnl 2f* **14/1**	63
04	4	2¼	**Purely By Chance**[16] 2989 3-8-9 0.... RichardKingscote 6 (R M Beckett) *s.i.s: sn pushed along in rr: rdn and stdy prog fr 3f out: styd on* **12/1**	59
	5	1½	**Chioroscuro** 3-9-0 0.... IanMongan 3 (J L Dunlop) *slowly away: bhd: sme prog over 3f out: sn rdn: styd on but nvr trbld ldrs* **16/1**	61
50-	6	5	**Lobby**[338] 3896 3-9-0 0....(t) JimCrowley 8 (Mrs A J Perrett) *chsd ldrs: rdn 3f out: wknd over 1f out* **7/1**[3]	51
	7	22	**Kijani (IRE)** 3-9-0 0.... EdwardCreighton 4 (M R Channon) *a towards rr* **25/1**	7
0	8	8	**Age Of Miracles (IRE)**[23] 2772 3-9-0 0.... MickyFenton 5 (G A Ham) *led for 2f: chsd ldr: struggling 4f out: sn bhd* **66/1**	—

2m 7.62s (-2.28) **Going Correction** -0.15s/f (Firm) **8 Ran SP% 115.9**
Speed ratings (Par 103): **103,100,97,95,94 90,72,66**
toteswinger: 1&2 £1.20, 1&3 £5.90, 2&3 £4.10. CSF £6.72 TOTE £4.10: £1.40, £1.10, £2.10; EX 8.80.
Owner Godolphin **Bred** Peter Player **Trained** Newmarket, Suffolk

FOCUS
A fair maiden for three-year-olds, run at an uneven pace. The field came home strung out behind the comfortable winner, who seemed to improve, and the form is not that solid.

3522 K J PIKE & SONS LTD AUCTION STKS (CONDITIONS RACE) 6f

4:05 (4:05) (Class 2) 2-Y-0 **£8,723** (£2,612; £1,306; £653; £326) **Stalls** High

Form				RPR
41	1		**Classic Blade (IRE)**[23] 2783 2-8-5 0.... RichardKingscote 3 (Tom Dascombe) *wnt rt s: mde all: kpt on gamely: rdn out* **9/4**[2]	93
31	2	2	**Measurement (IRE)**[19] 2916 2-8-6 0.... MartinDwyer 2 (R Hannon) *trckd wnr tl over 3f out: sn rdn: kpt on to regain 2nd ent fnl f but a hld by wnr* **7/2**[3]	88
611	3	4	**Northern Tour**[43] 2204 2-8-9 0.... ChrisCatlin 4 (P F I Cole) *hld up in cl 5th: rdn 3f out: one pce fnl 2f* **7/1**	79
3	4	1½	**Young Dottie**[20] 2893 2-7-12 0.... CatherineGannon 1 (P M Phelan) *hld up in cl 4th: rdn over 2f out: kpt on same pce* **14/1**	64
261	5	1½	**Agente Parmigiano (IRE)**[17] 2979 2-8-8 0.... HayleyTurner 5 (G A Butler) *t.k.h: trckd ldrs: wnt 2nd over 3f out: rdn and ev ch 2f out: wknd ins fnl f* **13/8**[1]	69

1m 14.97s (0.17) **Going Correction** +0.125s/f (Good) **5 Ran SP% 110.3**
Speed ratings (Par 99): **103,100,95,93,91**
CSF £10.38 TOTE £3.10: £2.00, £2.00; EX 12.30.
Owner The Classic Strollers Partnership **Bred** Ballybrennan Stud Ltd **Trained** Lambourn, Berks

FOCUS
An interesting little conditions event, and a taking winner. It was run at a solid pace and, while the favourite failed to run his race, the form still looks decent.

NOTEBOOK
Classic Blade(IRE), off the mark at Doncaster 23 days previously, confirmed himself a progressive juvenile and ran out a very ready winner from the front. He found plenty when the eventual runner-up emerged with his challenge, showing a game attitude, and really looking better the further he went. Where goes from here is uncertain, but he would not look out of place in Listed company. (op 7-2)

Measurement(IRE), who took his maiden over course and distance 19 days previously, was unable to get to the winner despite giving his all under pressure. He finished nicely clear of the rest and this was still another improved effort in defeat, so there will likely be other days. (op 4-1 tchd 3-1)

Northern Tour was bidding for a hat-trick on this first try over the extra furlong, but it was the fastest ground he had encountered and he looked to save a bit for himself when put under maximum pressure. (op 13-2 tchd 6-1)

Agente Parmigiano(IRE) was not surprisingly warm in the betting ring on the strength of his display at Yarmouth 17 days previously, but he was in trouble before the final furlong and evetually dropped right out. He did take time to settle, but this was really too bad to be true. Official explanation: trainer had no explanation for the poor form shown (op 5-4 tchd 7-4 in a place)

3523 H S LESTER MEMORIAL H'CAP 1m 6f 21y

4:40 (4:41) (Class 4) (0-85,82) 4-Y-0+ **£4,371** (£1,300; £650; £324) **Stalls** Far side

Form				RPR
-503	1		**Hawridge King**[38] 2332 6-8-10 **76**.... JamesMillman(5) 4 (W S Kittow) *trckd ldrs: rdn to ld wl over 1f out: drifted rt wl ins fnl f: styd on strly* **10/3**[2]	82
3503	2	1¼	**They All Laughed**[18] 2952 5-8-12 **73**.... DaneO'Neill 2 (P W Hiatt) *hld up and bhd: rdn 4f out: hdwy 3f out: styd on v strly ins fnl f: snatched 2nd fnl stride* **7/1**	77
2121	3	hd	**Trachonitis (IRE)**[36] 2414 4-9-6 **81**.... DarryllHolland 1 (J R Jenkins) *hld up towards rr: hdwy to trck ldrs 3f out: w.w: swtchd rt to chal and rdn ent fnl f: kpt on but no ex: lost 2nd fnl stride* **15/8**[1]	85
004-	4	nk	**Trew Style**[215] 6961 6-8-7 **68**.... SaleemGolam 3 (M H Tompkins) *led at stdy pce tl qcknd after 2f: sn 5 l clr: rdn and hdd wl over 1f out: rallied: 3rd and hld whn n.m.r and swtchd lft towards fin* **16/1**	72
-043	5	1½	**Fascinatin Rhythm**[11] 3143 4-8-4 **65**.... ChrisCatlin 6 (M R Channon) *mid-div: hdwy 4f out: rdn and ch 2f out: kpt on same pce* **10/1**	66
403/	6	6	**Wise Owl**[17] 5991 6-9-7 **82**.... MartinDwyer 8 (D E Pipe) *prom: rdn 4f out: sn one pce* **5/1**[3]	75
333	7	3	**King's Fable (USA)**[23] 2804 5-8-3 **64**....(p) CatherineGannon 7 (Karen George) *mid-div: rdn 4f out: sn btn* **14/1**	53
5-05	8	1	**Optimus (USA)**[22] 2304 6-9-4 **79**.... JimCrowley 5 (B G Powell) *reminders sn after s: mid-div: rdn over 4f out: sn btn* **10/1**	66

3m 12.7s (5.30) **Going Correction** -0.15s/f (Firm) **8 Ran SP% 117.8**
Speed ratings (Par 105): **78,77,77,77,76 72,71,70**
toteswinger: 1&2 £5.10, 1&3 £2.20, 2&3 £3.60. CSF £27.74 CT £55.92 TOTE £4.30: £1.50, £2.20, £1.40; EX 28.30.
Owner Eric Gadsden **Bred** Old Mill Stud **Trained** Blackborough, Devon

FOCUS
A fair staying handicap on paper, but the early pace was almost non-existent and it proved a messy affair. The time was poor and the form should be treated with caution.

3524 AXMINSTER CARPETS APPRENTICE H'CAP (WHIPS SHALL BE CARRIED BUT NOT USED) 1m

5:15 (5:21) (Class 6) (0-60,60) 3-Y-0 **£2,914** (£867; £433; £216) **Stalls** High

Form				RPR
5200	1		**Jemiliah**[17] 2984 3-8-9 **53**.... RossAtkinson(3) 7 (B G Powell) *mid-div: rdn and hdwy 2f out: led jst ins fnl f: kpt on wl* **25/1**	59
0054	2	1¼	**Mganga**[19] 2915 3-8-13 **54**.... MatthewDavies 16 (M R Channon) *hld up towards rr: hdwy 3f out: sn rdn: ev ch ent fnl f: no ex* **2/1**[1]	57
002	3	1½	**Charming Tale (USA)**[10] 3183 3-9-2 **57**....(b) KMay 3 (B J Meehan) *trckd ldrs: led 3f out: sn rdn: hdd jst ins fnl f: no ex* **7/1**[2]	57
6005	4	1	**Bon Ton Roulet**[28] 2639 3-8-6 **52**.... CharlesEddery(5) 11 (R Hannon) *s.i.s: sn mid-div: hdwy 3f out: ch ent fnl f: kpt on same pce* **10/1**	49
00-6	5	1	**Pretty Officer (USA)**[14] 3065 3-8-3 **47**.... BillyCray(3) 13 (Rae Guest) *trckd ldrs: rdn 3f out: kpt on same pce fnl f* **10/1**	42
0003	6	2	**Duneen Dream (USA)**[10] 3183 3-8-6 **52**.... DebraEngland(5) 10 (W J Musson) *in tch: rdn 3f out: kpt on same pce* **15/2**[3]	42
3550	7	4½	**Bold Diva**[16] 2991 3-9-0 **55**....(v) StacyRenwick 2 (A W Carroll) *hld up and bhd: sme late prog: nvr a factor* **20/1**	35
4-60	8	nk	**Karate Queen**[19] 2922 3-9-0 **55**.... DavidProbert 1 (A M Balding) *in tch: sltly hmpd 4f out: rdn 3f out: wknd ent fnl f* **16/1**	34
060-	9	nk	**Bathwick Icon (IRE)**[264] 6074 3-8-10 **56**.... PNolan(5) 8 (A B Haynes) *nvr bttr than mid-div* **40/1**	35
3040	10	2	**Rhode Island Red (USA)**[30] 2559 3-8-9 **50**.... JemmaMarshall 6 (H J L Dunlop) *mid-div: rdn 4f out: no imp* **20/1**	24
0-00	11	2	**Bathwick Man**[16] 3004 3-9-5 **60**.... WilliamCarson 15 (B R Millman) *led tl 3f out: sn wknd* **10/1**	29
06-0	12	¾	**Medici Gold**[15] 3023 3-8-10 **51**.... KylieManser 5 (B G Powell) *mid-div tl 3f out* **10/1**	19
-330	13	3¼	**Ray Diamond**[19] 2922 3-8-11 **52**.... AlanRutter 4 (M Madgwick) *a towards rr* **18/1**	12
600	14	2¼	**Heroic Lad**[29] 2612 3-8-6 **50**.... SimonPearce(3) 9 (A B Haynes) *trckd ldrs: veered lft 4f out: sn rdn: wknd over 2f out* **33/1**	5
0000	15	12	**Rosy Dawn**[18] 2932 3-8-2 **48**....(be) RichardRowe(5) 12 (Ms J S Doyle) *uns rdr gng to s and rn loose: prom tl wknd over 2f out* **25/1**	—

1m 45.17s (1.67) **Going Correction** +0.125s/f (Good) **15 Ran SP% 127.7**
Speed ratings (Par 97): **96,94,93,92,91 89,84,84,84,82 80,79,76,73,61**
toteswinger: 1&2 £19.40, 1&3 £30.20, 2&3 £5.00. CSF £73.60 CT £435.59 TOTE £29.40: £7.00, £1.50, £2.30; EX 119.10 Place 6 £14.39, Place 5 £3.56..
Owner Nigel Stafford **Bred** John And Susan Davis **Trained** Upper Lambourn, Berks

FOCUS
A typically weak handicap for apprentice riders, but it was run at a sound enough pace and the form, though limited, looks reliable enough.

Medici Gold Official explanation: jockey said filly was never travelling

T/Plt: £14.40 to a £1 stake. Pool: £60,369.29. 3,053.94 winning tickets. T/Qpdt: £6.10 to a £1 stake. Pool: £3,524.19. 422.10 winning tickets. TM

3502 WINDSOR (R-H)

Sunday, June 29

OFFICIAL GOING: Good to firm (good in places; 8.1)

Wind: Breezy, behind. Weather: overcast

3525 TOTESPORT BETXTRA H'CAP 1m 67y

2:35 (2:35) (Class 5) (0-70,74) 3-Y-0 £2,729 (£806; £403) Stalls High

Form RPR

1000 **1** **Coole Dodger (IRE)**[15] 3039 3-8-12 **68**.................... GabrielHannon(7) 7 75
(M D I Usher) *hld up towards rr: hdwy on rail over 2f out: chsd ldrs over 1f out: led ins fnl f: r.o wl* **33/1**

0052 **2** 1 1/4 **Mr Hichens**[9] 3221 3-9-11 **74**..............................(b1) AlanMunro 3 78
(B J Meehan) *t.k.h: chsd ldrs: hdwy to ld over 1f out: sn rdn and hung rt: nt run on and hdd ins fnl f* **6/1[2]**

55-0 **3** 2 1/4 **Stormbeam (USA)**[17] 2981 3-9-2 **65**.............................. NCallan 5 64
(G A Butler) *hld up towards rr: hdwy over 1f out: hung rt but styd on fnl f: wnt 3rd last 100yds: nt rch ldrs* **20/1**

1402 **4** 1 **Desiderio**[3] 3407 3-9-0 **70**..............................(b) CharlesEddery(7) 4 67
(R Hannon) *led: hrd pressed and rdn 2f out: hdd over 1f out: hung lft and wknd fnl f* **8/1[3]**

6311 **5** 1/2 **Willkandoo (USA)**[3] 3407 3-9-6 **74** 6ex.................... NeilBrown(5) 13 70
(K A Ryan) *chsd ldrs: rdn wl over 2f out: unable qck 2f out: kpt on same pce fnl f* **2/1[1]**

4-05 **6** 1 **Driven (IRE)**[17] 2976 3-9-7 **70**.............................. TPQueally 8 63
(Mrs A J Perrett) *t.k.h: hld up in midfield on outer: rdn 3f out: keeping on same pce and wl hld whn hmpd ins fnl f* **16/1**

3053 **7** 1 3/4 **Dream Sea**[11] 3127 3-9-2 **65**..............................(v1) TPO'Shea 1 54
(M R Channon) *chsd ldr: drvn to chal 2f out: wknd ent fnl f: wl hld whn hmpd ins fnl f* **25/1**

6010 **8** 1 3/4 **Nikolaievich (IRE)**[19] 2922 3-9-2 **65**....................(b) NelsonDeSouza 10 50
(P F I Cole) *t.k.h: hld up towards rr: nvr trbld ldrs* **40/1**

6036 **9** 6 **Feasible**[27] 2678 3-9-3 **66**.............................. RichardMullen 11 37
(J G Portman) *hmpd sn after s: hld up in last pair: nvr trbld ldrs* **8/1[3]**

-440 **10** 1 1/4 **Mahadee (IRE)**[68] 1543 3-9-5 **68**..............................(b1) WilliamBuick 6 37
(C E Brittain) *hld up towards rr: hdwy on outer over 3f out: rdn over 2f out: wknd over 1f out: eased wl ins fnl f* **40/1**

6-55 **11** 1/2 **Charmel's Lad**[59] 1743 3-9-1 **64**.............................. AdamKirby 14 31
(W R Swinburn) *short of room and swtchd lft sn after s: t.k.h: hld up in midfield: rdn wl over 2f out: sn wknd* **9/1**

-001 **12** 3/4 **Monashee Rock (IRE)**[14] 3064 3-9-9 **72**.................... TGMcLaughlin 9 38
(M Salaman) *hld up in midfield: rdn 3f out: sn lost pl: no ch last 2f* **12/1**

0640 **13** 1 3/4 **Star Pattern (USA)**[10] 3183 3-9-0 **63**.................... SteveDrowne 12 25
(J H M Gosden) *s.i.s: hmpd sn after s: hld up in rr: nvr trbld ldrs* **8/1[3]**

1m 44.41s (-0.29) **Going Correction** +0.025s/f (Good) **13** Ran SP% **121.0**
Speed ratings (Par 99): **102,100,98,97,97 96,94,92,86,85 84,84,82**
toteswinger: 1&2 £55.60, 1&3 £111.30, 2&3 £45.20. CSF £215.04 CT £4083.41 TOTE £38.00: £6.70, £2.40, £4.60; EX 467.90 TRIFECTA Not won..
Owner R H Brookes **Bred** Hyde Park Stud & Stephen Hillen **Trained** Upper Lambourn, Berks

FOCUS
A modest handicap, but the winning time was 0.95 seconds quicker than 71-90 handicap. It was a going day for the winner, who is hardly progressive, and the runner-up ran close to recent Newmarket form.

3526 TOTESPORT BETXTRA WIN ONLY H'CAP 5f 10y

3:05 (3:07) (Class 5) (0-70,69) 3-Y-0 £2,729 (£806; £403) Stalls High

Form RPR

-322 **1** **Heaven**[6] 3332 3-9-5 **67**.............................. NCallan 2 76+
(P J Makin) *stdd s: t.k.h: hld up in tch: hdwy to chse ldr over 1f out: led ins fnl f: sn clr: readily* **4/5[1]**

4303 **2** 2 1/2 **Handsinthemist (IRE)**[8] 3283 3-8-4 **52**..................(p) FrankieMcDonald 5 52
(P T Midgley) *bhd and sn bustled along: swtchd lft over 2f out: styd on u.p to go 2nd nr fin: no ch w wnr* **9/1**

-053 **3** 1/2 **Kalligal**[20] 2896 3-9-3 **65**.............................. SteveDrowne 1 63
(R Ingram) *taken down early: led: rdn jst over 1f out: hdd ins fnl f: no ch w wnr: lost 2nd nr fin* **15/2[3]**

-205 **4** 1/2 **Rathmolyon**[23] 2774 3-9-1 **63**.............................. TQuinn 9 59
(D Haydn Jones) *pressed ldr tl over 1f out: kpt on same pce u.p fnl f* **9/2[2]**

5040 **5** nk **Enodoc**[16] 3000 3-9-3 **65**..............................(t) DO'Donohoe 4 60
(W R Muir) *t.k.h: hld up in tch: rdn and effrt over 1f out: unable qckn and no imp fnl f* **14/1**

00-0 **6** 1 **Archilini**[22] 2824 3-8-10 **63**.............................. JackMitchell(5) 10 55
(K A Morgan) *v awkward leaving stalls and slowly away: reminder and veered lft sn after s: detached in last: hdwy u.p 1/2-way: in tch in midfield over 1f out: no prog fnl f* **22/1**

3060 **7** 2 1/2 **Lady Vibeeka**[64] 1635 3-8-4 **52**.............................. WilliamBuick 3 35
(Mrs H Sweeting) *chsd ldrs: rdn and hung lft over 1f out: wknd qckly fnl f* **33/1**

6406 **8** 1 1/2 **Penrice Castle**[29] 2602 3-8-13 **61**.............................. PatDobbs 6 38
(R Hannon) *stdd s: t.k.h: sn in midfield: lost pl 2f out: no ch fnl f* **16/1**

60.50 secs (0.20) **Going Correction** -0.05s/f (Good) **8** Ran SP% **115.3**
Speed ratings (Par 99): **96,92,91,90,89 88,84,81**
toteswinger: 1&2 £2.00, 1&3 £1.90, 2&3 £3.20. CSF £9.24 CT £34.46 TOTE £1.70: £1.10, £1.90, £1.70; EX 6.60 Trifecta £22.10 Pool: £409.17 - 13.70 winning tickets..
Owner Wedgewood Estates **Bred** Mrs D O Joly **Trained** Ogbourne Maisey, Wilts

FOCUS
An uncompetitive sprint handicap, and the winning time was 0.58 seconds slower than the later juvenile conditions race. The winner stood out on his recent unlucky All Weather second. Sound enough form behind.
Kalligal Official explanation: jockey said saddle slipped

3527 TOTESPORT BETXTRA SHOW ONLY H'CAP 1m 2f 7y

3:40 (3:40) (Class 3) (0-95,88) 3-Y-0 £9,714 (£2,890; £1,444; £721) Stalls Low

Form RPR

14 **1** **Swinging Sixties (IRE)**[15] 3048 3-9-4 **85**.................... PhilipRobinson 6 96+
(M A Jarvis) *mde all: rdn 2f out: styd on wl: readily* **15/8[1]**

0160 **2** 2 1/2 **Amanjena**[11] 3124 3-9-2 **83**.............................. WilliamBuick 7 89
(A M Balding) *t.k.h: chsd wnr thrght: rdn 3f out: kpt on same pce u.p fnl 2f* **16/1**

0332 **3** 1 **Ellemujie**[16] 2996 3-9-0 **81**.............................. TPQueally 5 85
(D K Ivory) *stdd s: hld up towards rr: hdwy over 4f out: chsd ldrs and rdn 3f out: kpt on same pce fr over 2f out* **14/1**

-215 **4** 1 1/2 **Mega Watt (IRE)**[39] 2311 3-8-11 **78**.............................. AlanMunro 4 79+
(W Jarvis) *hld up in last trio: hdwy on outer over 2f out: drvn and kpt on same pce fr over 1f out* **14/1**

1350 **5** 1 1/4 **No To Trident**[29] 2610 3-9-0 **81**.............................. TGMcLaughlin 1 80
(P D Evans) *t.k.h: hld up in tch: drvn and unable qck over 2f out: kpt on same pce* **66/1**

1-23 **6** 3/4 **Maxwil**[15] 3038 3-9-5 **86**..............................(b1) GeorgeBaker 2 83
(G L Moore) *stdd s: hld up in last trio: hdwy 3f out: drvn 2f out: no prog fr over 1f out* **8/1**

2264 **7** 2 1/4 **Higgy's Boy (IRE)**[16] 2996 3-8-10 **77**.............................. PatDobbs 8 70
(R Hannon) *hld up bhd: rdn 4f out: nvr gng pce to threaten ldrs* **33/1**

5060 **8** shd **Meydan Dubai (IRE)**[9] 3197 3-9-3 **84**.................... MohammedSaeed 10 76
(J R Best) *hld up in midfield: lost pl and pushed along 4f out: wl hld whn edgd rt ent fnl f* **15/2[3]**

3-1 **9** 13 **Porthole (USA)**[27] 2681 3-9-7 **88**.............................. MichaelHills 9 80
(B W Hills) *stmbld s and s.i.s: sn in tch: drvn 3f out: wknd 2f out: wl btn whn hmpd ent fnl f: virtually p.u after* **5/2[2]**

1-04 **10** 3/4 **Hilbre Court (USA)**[11] 3134 3-9-4 **85**.............................. JamieSpencer 3 50
(B J Meehan) *chsd ldrs: rdn over 3f out: wknd qckly over 2f out: virtually p.u ins fnl f* **20/1**

2m 7.86s (-0.84) **Going Correction** +0.025s/f (Good) **10** Ran SP% **114.6**
Speed ratings (Par 103): **104,102,101,100,99 98,96,96,86,85**
toteswinger: 1&2 £6.80, 1&3 £4.60, 2&3 £21.40. CSF £32.99 CT £329.18 TOTE £2.50: £1.40, £3.20, £2.90; EX 40.30 Trifecta £471.80 Pool: £637.62 - 1.00 winning ticket..
Owner Sheikh Ahmed Al Maktoum **Bred** Darley **Trained** Newmarket, Suffolk

FOCUS
A fair handicap on paper, but very few got involved. The winner was well on top at the end and has more improvement in him. It was a good effort from the second too, and the third was to recent form

NOTEBOOK
Swinging Sixties(IRE) failed to build on his debut success at Newmarket when a beaten favourite in a handicap at York on his latest start, racing keenly under a hold-up ride, but he was ridden from the front this time and, very much allowed the run of the race, he made no mistake. It's fair to say everything went his way, but he is back on track now and can continue to progress. (op 2-1 tchd 13-8 and 85-40 in a place)
Amanjena appreciated the return to 1m2f and ran her race, but the winner was far too good.
Ellemujie fared best of those held up, although he did make up some ground before the race got serious, and this was a respectable effort. He is in good form, but is plenty high enough in the weights and continues to find one or two too good. (op 16-1)
Mega Watt(IRE), stepped up from 1m, was given a lot to do in a race in which it proved hard to make up ground and could never get involved after being taken very wide in the straight. He is better than he showed and will probably appreciate a more positive ride in future. (op 11-1 tchd 16-1)
No To Trident has struggled since winning a Doncaster maiden in March. Official explanation: jockey said gelding hung right in final furlong
Porthole(USA) made all when an impressive winner in maiden company over course and distance on his previous start, but he struggled to get a position this time after starting awkwardly, and he was never going. He was beaten a long way out and was continuing to drop back when hampered against the rail around a furlong out. Official explanation: jockey said colt lost a front shoe and suffered overreach (tchd 9-4)
Hilbre Court(USA) Official explanation: jockey said colt moved badly and never travelled

3528 E B F BETXTRA AT TOTESPORT.COM FILLIES' CONDITIONS STKS 5f 10y

4:15 (4:15) (Class 2) 2-Y-0

£12,462 (£3,732; £1,866; £934; £466; £234) Stalls High

Form RPR

4333 **1** **Kerrys Requiem (IRE)**[15] 3020 2-8-9 0.............................. TPO'Shea 5 81
(M R Channon) *stdd s: sn pushed along in midfield: swtchd lft over 1f out: styd on wl u.p to ld towards fin* **6/1[3]**

3100 **2** 3/4 **White Shift (IRE)**[11] 3123 2-9-5 0.............................. StephenDonohoe 2 88
(P D Evans) *led and set fast pce: rdn 2f out: hdd ins fnl f: kpt on gamely to regain 2nd last stride* **15/2**

10 **3** shd **To The Point**[44] 2167 2-8-12 0.............................. RichardMullen 1 81
(E S McMahon) *chsd ldr: hdwy to chal 2f out: wanting to hang lft after: led ins fnl f: hdd and lost 2 plcs towards fin* **5/4[1]**

1342 **4** 2 **Doughnut**[15] 3020 2-8-12 0.............................. RichardSmith 4 74
(R Hannon) *chsd ldrs: rdn over 2f out: edgd lft fnl f: no imp* **2/1[2]**

0 **5** 5 **Val De Flores**[9] 3207 2-8-9 0.............................. LPKeniry 6 53
(E F Vaughan) *a in last pair: struggling bef 1/2-way* **14/1**

0 **6** 3 3/4 **Rapanui Belle**[16] 2999 2-8-9 0.............................. FergusSweeney 3 39
(G L Moore) *a last and outpcd* **50/1**

59.92 secs (-0.38) **Going Correction** -0.05s/f (Good) **6** Ran SP% **112.5**
Speed ratings (Par 96): **101,99,99,96,88 82**
toteswinger: 1&2 £3.20, 1&3 £1.80, 2&3 £2.00. CSF £47.49 TOTE £7.60: £2.40, £3.10; EX 21.90.
Owner Mrs M Findlay **Bred** Mrs T V Ryan **Trained** West Ilsley, Berks

FOCUS
An ordinary conditions contest, but they went off very quickly and the winning time was good, 0.58 seconds quicker than the earlier three-year-old 51-70 handicap. Improved form from the winner.

NOTEBOOK
Kerrys Requiem(IRE) looked to have something to find in this company, but she proved well suited by the furious pace and stayed on strongest of all, although it has to be said she looked to carry her head at a slight angle under strong pressure. (op 11-2 tchd 9-2)
White Shift(IRE), down the field in the Queen Mary, found this easier and ran a really game race in defeat. Having set a strong pace, she looked set to drop away when headed inside the final furlong, but she kept plugging away and regained second near the line. (op 8-1)
To The Point, a winner on her debut at Warwick but a beaten favourite in Listed company next time, seemed to have her chance but she was run out of it in the closing stages. Her maiden win was gained on easy ground, so perhaps this really quick surface was not ideal. (op 13-8 tchd 7-4)
Doughnut was below form and the way she hung to her left late on suggests she may have found the ground quicker than ideal. (op 7-4)
Val De Flores should find things easier in nurseries later in the season. (op 20-1 tchd 25-1)

3529 BETXTRA AT TOTESPORT 0800 221 221 H'CAP 1m 67y

4:50 (4:50) (Class 3) (0-90,87) 3-Y-0+ £7,123 (£2,119; £1,059; £529) Stalls High

Form RPR

6045 **1** **Rambling Light**[13] 3090 4-8-13 **72**..............................(p) LPKeniry 1 79
(A M Balding) *chsd ldr: rdn over 2f out: led jst over 1f out: edgd rt ins fnl f: hld on: all out* **9/2[2]**

2253 **2** nk **Guilded Warrior**[19] 2905 5-10-0 **87**.............................. FergusSweeney 8 94+
(W S Kittow) *led: rdn over 2f out: hdd jst over 1f out: swtchd lft ins fnl f: rallied gamely wl ins fnl f: nt quite get bk up* **7/4[1]**

00-0 **3** 3/4 **Cape Of Luck (IRE)**[16] 2995 5-9-3 **76**..............................(p) JohnEgan 2 81
(P M Phelan) *chsd ldng trio: clsd 4f out: drvn 2f out: ev ch ins fnl f: unable qck last 100yds* **16/1**

2060 **4** 1/2 **Buxton**[9] 3197 4-9-3 **76**..............................(t) PatDobbs 4 79
(R Ingram) *hld up off the pce in midfield: hdwy over 3f out: rdn 2f out: chsd ldrs ent fnl f: one pce last 100yds* **12/1**

6340 **5** *3* **Red Somerset (USA)**[31] 2540 5-9-9 **82**.......................... SteveDrowne 7 79
(R J Hodges) *chsd ldng pair: rdn 3f out: wknd 2f out* **5/1**[3]

4610 **6** *1 1/2* **Twilight Star (IRE)**[6] 3319 4-9-7 **80**.......................(t) GeorgeBaker 5 73
(R A Teal) *stdd s and v.s.a: hld up wl bhd: hdwy over 2f out: rdn and little rspnse over 1f out* **7/1**

1- **7** *22* **Hucking Heist**[292] 5315 4-9-4 **77**.......................... JamieSpencer 6 19
(J R Best) *stdd after s: bhd: pushed along over 5f out: drvn and hdwy 3f out: wknd 2f out: virtually p.u fnl f* **9/2**[2]

1m 45.36s (0.66) **Going Correction** +0.025s/f (Good) **7** Ran SP% **115.5**
Speed ratings (Par 107): **97,96,95,95,92 90,68**
toteswinger: 1&2 £2.50, 1&3 £11.90, 2&3 £7.80. CSF £13.10 CT £114.27 TOTE £6.10: £3.10, £1.90; EX 14.90 TRIFECTA Not won..
Owner Another Bottle Racing **Bred** George Strawbridge **Trained** Kingsclere, Hants

FOCUS
Quite competitive, but the bare form looks ordinary for the grade and the winning time was 0.95 seconds slower than the opening 51-70 three-year-old handicap.

NOTEBOOK
Rambling Light took well to the fitting of cheekpieces and stepped up on his recent efforts with a determined success. This looked a soft race for the grade, but he should remain competitive off higher marks if the headgear continues to have a positive effect. (op 6-1 tchd 7-1)
Guilded Warrior stuck to his task most gamely once headed. This was a fine effort considering he has always looked at his best on soft ground. (op 9-4 tchd 5-2 in a place)
Cape Of Luck(IRE) has not won since June 2006, but this was a respectable effort in first-time cheekpieces. (tchd 18-1 and 20-1 in places)
Buxton, who ran well in the Buckingham Palace Handicap on his previous start, would have found this easier, but he still found a few too good. (tchd 8-1)
Red Somerset(USA) could not justify market support and looks plenty high enough in the weights. (op 9-1)
Twilight Star(IRE) Official explanation: jockey said gelding missed the break
Hucking Heist Official explanation: jockey said gelding ran green

3530 BET ON US RACING AT TOTESPORT.COM MAIDEN STKS — 1m 3f 135y
5:25 (5:27) (Class 5) 3-5-Y-O — **£2,729** (£806; £403) **Stalls** Low

Form — RPR

30 **1** **Dance The Star (USA)**[27] 2669 3-9-0 0.......................... RichardMullen 4 76
(D M Simcock) *hld up in midfield: outpcd wl over 3f out: rdn to chse clr ldng pair 3f out: edgd lft: styd on* **25/1**

0-0 **2** *2* **Trawlerman (IRE)**[108] 867 3-8-7 0.......................... AshleyMorgan(7) 10 73
(M H Tompkins) *hld up towards rr: outpcd wl over 3f out: modest 5th and rdn over 3f out: kpt on to chse wnr ins fnl f: hung lft: kpt on but nt chal wnr* **66/1**

6 **3** *4* **Optimus Maximus (IRE)**[13] 3094 3-9-0 0.......................... TQuinn 2 67
(P F I Cole) *t.k.h: chsd ldr over 8f out: clr w ldr and rdn wl over 3f out: ev ch over 1f out: wknd ins fnl f* **9/2**[2]

4 *nk* **Starburst** 3-8-9 0.......................... LPKeniry 7 61
(A M Balding) *v.s.a: bhd: hdwy over 4f out: rdn over 3f out: chsd ldrs over 1f out: kpt on same pce fnl f* **25/1**

2-3 **5** *4* **French Riviera**[69] 1526 3-9-0 0.......................... JamieSpencer 9 60
(Sir Michael Stoute) *led: rdn clr w one rival wl over 3f out: drvn wl over 1f out: hdd 1f out: sn btn: eased towards fin* **1/2**[1]

6 *25* **Masettos Fun** 3-9-0 0.......................... JohnEgan 6 20
(M Botti) *in tch in midfield: rdn 5f out: wl bhd last 3f: t.o* **25/1**

0-0 **7** *nse* **Royal Tartan (USA)**[16] 2994 3-8-9 0.......................... SteveDrowne 3 15
(G L Moore) *t.k.h: hld up towards rr: rdn and lost tch over 3f out: t.o* **50/1**

64 **8** *7* **April's Daughter**[27] 2681 3-8-9 0.......................... AlanMunro 1 3
(B R Millman) *t.k.h: chsd ldrs tl rdn and wknd qckly wl over 3f out: t.o and eased over 1f out* **8/1**[3]

0 **9** *23* **Upstart (IRE)**[62] 1669 3-9-0 0.......................... TPQueally 8 —
(H R A Cecil) *chsd ldrs: rdn and wknd qckly over 3f out: t.o last 2f* **16/1**

0 **10** *1 3/4* **Unique (IRE)**[24] 2763 3-8-11 0.......................... KirstyMilczarek(3) 5 —
(N P Littmoden) *chsd ldr tl over 8f out: chsd ldrs after tl wknd qckly wl over 3f out: t.o last 2f* **66/1**

11 *35* **Kavatcha (FR)**[175] 5-9-11 0.......................... TravisBlock(3) 11 —
(Miss Tor Sturgis) *a bhd: lost tch 5f out: wl t.o last 3f* **33/1**

2m 29.81s (0.31) **Going Correction** +0.025s/f (Good)
WFA 3 from 5yo 14lb **11** Ran SP% **121.3**
Speed ratings (Par 103): **99,97,95,94,92 75,75,70,55,54 30**
toteswinger: 1&2 £19.40, 1&3 £30.20, 2&3 £5.00. CSF £1067.51 TOTE £26.30: £5.20, £15.60, £1.10; EX 838.40 TRIFECTA Not won..
Owner Sultan Ali **Bred** B M Kelley And B P Walden **Trained** Newmarket, Suffolk

FOCUS
Little strength in depth, and with the first two in the betting being asked to do too much too soon the form looks shaky, although it was still a much improved effort from the winner.
T/Jkpt: Not won. T/Plt: £525.80 to a £1 stake. Pool: £94,732.17. 131.50 winning tickets. T/Qpdt: £61.70 to a £1 stake. Pool: £5,181.89. 62.10 winning tickets. SP

3508 CURRAGH (R-H)
Sunday, June 29

OFFICIAL GOING: Good to yielding

3531a LADBROKES.COM H'CAP (PREMIER HANDICAP) — 1m
1:30 (1:31) 3-Y-O+ — **£47,867** (£14,044; £6,691; £2,279)

RPR

1 **Settigano (IRE)**[36] 2419 5-9-12 99.......................(p) JAHeffernan 9 104
(Michael Joseph Fitzgerald, Ire) *chsd ldrs: rdn to dispute ld 1 1/2f out: led under 1f out: kpt on wl* **10/1**[2]

2 *hd* **Zero Tolerance (IRE)**[3] 3413 8-8-9 82.......................... RyanMoore 19 89+
(T D Barron) *chsd ldrs: rdn on inner 2f out: short of room and swtchd to outer 1f out: kpt on wl cl home* **9/2**[1]

3 *1/2* **Ridge Boy (IRE)**[18] 2962 7-8-12 85.......................(b) WJSupple 17 89
(Mrs John Harrington, Ire) *led: rdn and jnd 2f out: hdd 1 1/2f out: kpt on same pce fnl f* **12/1**

4 *3/4* **Slam Dunk (USA)**[16] 3014 3-9-0 97.......................... JMurtagh 15 97
(G M Lyons, Ire) *prom: rdn to dispute ld fr 2f out: hdd under 1f out: no ex* **11/1**[3]

5 *1* **Celtic Dane (IRE)**[77] 1357 4-9-7 94.......................... DPMcDonogh 18 94
(Kevin Prendergast, Ire) *mid-div on inner: 7th 2f out: kpt on wl fnl f* **12/1**

6 *nk* **Reload (IRE)**[7] 3303 5-8-6 86.......................... DEMullins(7) 11 85
(Thomas Mullins, Ire) *mid-div: 8th 2f out: kpt on same pce* **10/1**[2]

7 *nk* **Ahoy (IRE)**[239] 6660 4-8-7 80.......................... WMLordan 16 79
(David Wachman, Ire) *mid-div on inner: nt clr run 2f out: styd on fnl f* **14/1**

8 *3/4* **Monteriggioni (IRE)**[70] 1511 6-9-7 97.......................... PBBeggy(3) 2 94
(John Geoghegan, Ire) *towards rr: prog fr 2 1/2f out: rdn in 4th 1f out: no ex* **20/1**

9 *1 1/4* **No Strings (IRE)**[86] 1200 3-8-9 92.......................(b) PJSmullen 13 84
(D K Weld, Ire) *towards rr: prog 3f out: kpt on same pce fr 1 1/2f out* **12/1**

10 *shd* **Tango Foxtrot (IRE)**[36] 2421 6-8-4 77.......................... CDHayes 10 71
(W P Mullins, Ire) *nvr bttr than mid-div* **25/1**

11 *hd* **Belle Noverre (IRE)**[18] 2962 4-8-9 82.......................(p) KJManning 12 76
(J S Bolger, Ire) *chsd ldrs: rdn fr 2 1/2f out: no ex fr 1 1/2f out: eased fnl f* **12/1**

12 *nk* **Worldly Wise**[18] 2962 5-9-4 91.......................... DMGrant 14 84
(Patrick J Flynn, Ire) *towards rr: no imp fr 2f out* **20/1**

13 *3/4* **Rain Rush (IRE)**[18] 2962 5-9-6 93.......................... FMBerry 8 84
(David Marnane, Ire) *in rr: no imp fr 2f out* **10/1**[2]

14 *1* **Little Eye (IRE)**[18] 2962 7-8-9 82.......................... PShanahan 5 71
(D K Weld, Ire) *in rr of mid-div: no imp fr 3f out* **33/1**

15 *shd* **Regaleya (IRE)**[22] 2856 5-8-2 82.......................(bt) MHarley(7) 4 71
(H Rogers, Ire) *mid-div: clsr in 6th 2f out: rdn and kpt on same pce* **33/1**

16 *1 1/4* **Dynamo Dancer (IRE)**[18] 2962 5-9-4 98.......................... EJMcNamara(7) 1 84
(G M Lyons, Ire) *chsd ldrs: wknd fr 2f out* **25/1**

17 *3/4* **Chevie (IRE)**[18] 2960 3-8-8 91.......................(p) MJKinane 7 74
(T Hogan, Ire) *a towards rr* **10/1**[2]

18 *nk* **Dont Cross Tina (IRE)**[4] 3388 4-7-11 77 oh5.......................... SFoley(7) 6 61
(Seamus Fahey, Ire) *chsd ldrs: rdn and wknd fr 2f out* **33/1**

1m 39.93s (-1.97) **Going Correction** -0.025s/f (Good)
WFA 3 from 4yo+ 10lb **19** Ran SP% **126.4**
Speed ratings: **109,108,108,107,106 106,105,105,103,103 103,103,102,101,101 100,99,99**
CSF £50.65 CT £576.65 TOTE £8.70: £1.70, £1.70, £3.20, £2.00; DF 57.90.
Owner Andrew Farnan **Bred** Western Bloodstock **Trained** Gowran, Co. Kilkenny

NOTEBOOK
Zero Tolerance(IRE) ◆ motored home inside the final furlong but the line came just too soon. He looked unlucky, having met some trouble, and he deserves to go one better again now. (op 11/2)

3532a NETJETS SCURRY H'CAP (PREMIER HANDICAP) — 6f 63y
2:05 (2:06) 3-Y-O+ — **£47,867** (£14,044; £6,691; £2,279)

RPR

1 **Rock Moss (IRE)**[3] 3425 3-8-11 96.......................... DJMoran(3) 3 109
(J S Bolger, Ire) *mid-div: prog fr 2f out: disp ld over 1f out: led ins fnl f: kpt on wl* **20/1**

2 *1 1/2* **Northern Dare (IRE)**[31] 2538 4-8-12 87.......................... AdrianTNicholls 6 97
(D Nicholls) *led and disp: rdn along 2f out: hdd ins fnl f: kpt on wl* **13/2**[2]

3 *3 1/2* **Miss Gorica (IRE)**[23] 2808 4-9-13 102.......................... DPMcDonogh 9 102
(Ms Joanna Morgan, Ire) *chsd ldrs: rdn in 3rd 2f out: kpt on same pce fnl f* **16/1**

4 *nk* **Epic Odyssey**[22] 2852 3-8-6 88.......................... KLatham 14 85
(G M Lyons, Ire) *prom: rdn in 4th 1f out: kpt on same pce* **10/1**[3]

5 *1 1/4* **Kingsdale Ocean (IRE)**[14] 3069 5-9-4 93.......................... PJSmullen 13 89
(D K Weld, Ire) *mid-div: 8th u.p 1 1/2f out: kpt on wout threatening* **14/1**

6 *shd* **College Scholar (GER)**[18] 2962 4-8-4 79.......................(t) MCHussey 19 74
(Liam McAteer, Ire) *led and disp: rdn fr 2f out: hdd over 1f out: no ex* **25/1**

7 *nk* **Croi Mo Ri (IRE)**[3] 3425 3-9-6 102 5ex.......................... WJSupple 5 94
(P D Deegan, Ire) *chsd ldrs: rdn in 6th 1f out: no ex* **14/1**

8 *1/2* **Over The Tylery (IRE)**[4] 3387 4-8-4 79 oh16.......................... NGMcCullagh 22 72
(Eamon Tyrrell, Ire) *nvr bttr than mid-div* **50/1**

9 *hd* **Flash McGahon (IRE)**[14] 3069 4-9-9 98.......................(b) MJKinane 10 90
(John M Oxx, Ire) *towards rr: prog fr 1/2-way: 8th 1f out: kpt on same pce* **16/1**

10 *nk* **Port Of Spain (USA)**[23] 2808 4-8-5 80.......................... DavidMcCabe 17 71
(A P O'Brien, Ire) *nvr bttr than mid-div* **20/1**

11 *1 1/4* **Cuilaphuca (IRE)**[14] 3069 4-9-6 95.......................... PShanahan 4 83
(Tracey Collins, Ire) *prom: no imp fr 1 1/2f out* **12/1**

12 *1 1/4* **Aine (IRE)**[29] 2606 3-9-4 100.......................... WMLordan 2 82
(T Stack, Ire) *mid-div: rdn and no imp fr 2f out* **5/2**[1]

13 *1* **Mutamared (USA)**[44] 2172 8-9-6 95.......................... FergalLynch 15 76
(K A Ryan) *chsd ldrs: short of room over 2f out: rdn and sn no imp* **16/1**

14 *shd* **Benwilt Breeze (IRE)**[16] 3012 6-9-5 101.......................(t) EJMcNamara(7) 7 82
(G M Lyons, Ire) *mid-div: kpt on same pce fr 2f out* **20/1**

15 *1/2* **Alocin (IRE)**[7] 3301 5-7-12 80 oh19 ow1.......................(b) BACurtis(7) 11 60
(Mrs A M O'Shea, Ire) *a bhd* **50/1**

16 *nk* **Alone He Stands (IRE)**[71] 1497 8-8-11 86.......................... FMBerry 1 65
(J C Hayden, Ire) *a towards rr* **20/1**

17 *1* **Majestic Times (IRE)**[18] 2962 8-8-13 95.......................... SFoley(7) 8 71
(Liam McAteer, Ire) *chsd ldrs: no imp fr 1 1/2f out* **33/1**

18 *2* **Nastrelli (IRE)**[14] 3069 5-8-11 86.......................(p) JMurtagh 18 56
(M Halford, Ire) *chsd ldrs: no imp fr 2f out* **12/1**

19 *1* **An Tadh (IRE)**[27] 2685 5-9-5 101.......................(p) MJLane(7) 16 68
(G M Lyons, Ire) *s.i.s: sn chsd ldrs on outer: wknd fr 2f out* **25/1**

20 *nk* **Insiyaabi (USA)**[71] 1497 4-7-13 81.......................... JamesPSullivan(7) 24 47
(J G Burns, Ire) *nvr a factor* **25/1**

21 *4* **Controvento (IRE)**[63] 1651 6-8-4 79 oh23.......................(b) RPCleary 20 34
(Eamon Tyrrell, Ire) *a bhd* **66/1**

22 *9* **Bunsen Burner (IRE)**[46] 2111 3-8-11 93.......................... KJManning 12 20
(J S Bolger, Ire) *a bhd* **16/1**

1m 15.62s (-2.38) **Going Correction** -0.275s/f (Firm)
WFA 3 from 4yo+ 7lb **24** Ran SP% **142.2**
Speed ratings: **105,103,98,97,96 96,95,95,94,94 92,91,89,89,88 88,87,84,83,82 77,65**
CSF £146.05 CT £2228.74 TOTE £37.60: £6.80, £2.40, £5.60, £3.70; DF 359.10.
Owner Fiona Bolger **Bred** James F Hanly **Trained** Coolcullen, Co Carlow

NOTEBOOK
Northern Dare(IRE) ran a super race and ran all the way to the line as you would expect of a Dandy Nicholls trained horse in a race like this. He was prominent throughout towards the stands' side and, after briefly looking as though he would back-pedal a furlong out, found a bit extra. He kept going well up the hill but the winner was just too good. (op 7/1 tchd 15/2)
Mutamared(USA) needs quicker ground than this to be seen at his best.

3533a WILLIAM FRY SAPPHIRE STKS (GROUP 3) — 5f
2:40 (2:40) 3-Y-O+ — **£47,794** (£13,970; £6,617; £2,205)

RPR

1 **Tax Free (IRE)**[27] 2685 6-9-7.......................... AdrianTNicholls 3 121
(D Nicholls) *trckd ldrs in 3rd: rdn in 2nd over 1f out: led ins fnl f: kpt on wl* **4/1**[2]

2 *1 1/4* **Benbaun (IRE)**[12] 3101 7-9-9.......................(b) FMBerry 6 118
(M J Wallace) *trckd ldr in 2nd: rdn to ld 1 1/2f out: hdd ins fnl f: kpt on same pce* **5/2**[1]

The Form Book, Raceform Ltd, Compton, RG20 6NL

3 2 **Desert Lord**^{28} 2652 8-9-4 ....(b) FergalLynch 1 106
(K A Ryan) *led: pushed along fr 1/2-way: hdd 1 1/2f out: no ex fnl f* **7/1**

4 1/2 **Le Cadre Noir (IRE)**^{49} 2029 4-9-7 110.................... PJSmullen 7 107
(D K Weld, Ire) *hld up in rr: rdn in 5th 2f out: kpt on wout threatening fnl f* **12/1**

5 1 1/2 **Myboycharlie (IRE)**^{36} 2417 3-9-3 120.................... JMurtagh 2 102
(T Stack, Ire) *mid-div: rdn along after 1/2-way: sn no imp* **5/2**^{1}

6 1 **Elletelle (IRE)**^{55} 1880 3-9-0 105.................... KLatham 8 95
(G M Lyons, Ire) *s.i.s and in rr: no imp fr 2f out* **20/1**

7 1/2 **Contest (IRE)**^{27} 2685 4-9-4 106.................... WMLordan 5 93
(David Wachman, Ire) *chsd ldrs: rdn in 4th 2f out: sn no ex* **6/1**^{3}

8 2 1/2 **Senor Benny (USA)**^{58} 1783 9-9-4 101.................... DPMcDonogh 4 84
(M McDonagh, Ire) *mid-div: wknd fr 2f out* **33/1**

59.03 secs (-3.37) **Going Correction** -0.275s/f (Firm)
WFA 3 from 4yo+ 6lb **8** Ran SP% **119.3**
Speed ratings: **116,114,110,110,107 106,105,101**
CSF £15.18 TOTE £4.90: £1.60, £1.50, £2.60; DF 21.10.
Owner Ian Hewitson **Bred** Denis & Mrs Teresa Bergin **Trained** Sessay, N Yorks

NOTEBOOK
Tax Free(IRE), second in this event last season, showed his now typically resolute attitude when asked for maximumm effort and followed up his Naas Listed win 27 days previously with a career-best display. He is evidently still improving at the age of six and could now head back to Goodwood next month in search of further glory. (op 6/1)
Benbaun(IRE), seventh to Equiano in the King's Stand 12 days previously, was given every chance to enhance his course-and-distance record but found the concession of 2lb to the winner beyond him. He was a clear second-best, however, and again just left the impression he ideally wants a sixth furlong now. (op 2/1)
Desert Lord was given his customary trail-blazing ride and showed improved form, but was still well held at the finish. (op 10/1)
Myboycharlie(IRE), having his first outing over the minimum, failed to improve on the level of his seasonal comeback and looked to lack the pace for this trip. He has yet to truly prove he has fully trained on, but it may be more a case of him coming into his own again later in the year, and all of his winning as a juvenile was achieved on much easier ground. (op 9/4 tchd 7/2)

3534a ONE 51 RAILWAY STKS (GROUP 2) 6f
3:10 (3:12) 2-Y-O
£55,147 (£17,463; £8,272; £2,757; £1,838; £919)

RPR

1 **Mastercraftsman (IRE)**^{55} 1878 2-9-1 .... JMurtagh 3 107+
(A P O'Brien, Ire) *trckd ldrs in 5th: cl 3rd 1 1/2f out: rdn to narrowly ld ins fnl f: kpt on wl: all out* **8/11**^{1}

2 shd **Alhaban (IRE)**^{77} 1351 2-9-1 .... DPMcDonogh 2 107
(Kevin Prendergast, Ire) *disp ld bef 1/2-way: hdd 1 1/2f out: disp ld briefly 1f out: narrowly hdd ins fnl f: kpt on wl: jst failed* **13/2**^{3}

3 nk **Intense Focus (USA)**^{12} 3103 2-9-1 .... KJManning 5 106
(J S Bolger, Ire) *chsd ldrs in 3rd: led briefly 1 1/2f out: narrowly hdd ins fnl f: kpt on* **11/4**^{2}

4 7 **Sea Of Marmara (USA)**^{11} 3145 2-9-1 .... JAHeffernan 6 85
(A P O'Brien, Ire) *led: jnd bef 1/2-way: hdd 2f out: sn no imp* **12/1**

5 10 **Beauthea (IRE)**^{46} 2110 2-8-12 .... CDHayes 4 52+
(H Rogers, Ire) *slowly away and trailing: sn eased: pushed out to take 5th cl home* **66/1**

6 1 1/4 **Egypt**^{18} 2959 2-9-1 .... CO'Donoghue 1 51
(A P O'Brien, Ire) *chsd ldrs in 4th: rdn after 1/2-way: wknd fr 1 1/2f out* **25/1**

1m 13.32s (-1.18) **Going Correction** -0.275s/f (Firm) **6** Ran SP% **110.9**
Speed ratings: **97,96,96,87,73 72**
CSF £6.07 TOTE £1.50: £1.20, £2.30; DF 6.00.
Owner Derrick Smith **Bred** Lynch Bages Ltd **Trained** Ballydoyle, Co Tipperary
■ Stewards' Enquiry : D P McDonogh two-day ban: excessive use of the whip (Jul 14-15)

NOTEBOOK
Mastercraftsman(IRE) ◆, a course-and-distance maiden winner on debut back in May, proved all the rage in the betting ring to enhance to connections' outstanding previous record in the race. He was hardly impressive and just did enough, but he shaped as if he is crying out for a stiffer test now and remains a potential star as he has bundles of scope. Time may tell he did very well to win this and further improvement looks assured. Wherever he turns up next, he will likely take a world of beating. (op 4/5 tchd 4/6)
Alhaban(IRE), a debut winner over 5f at Navan in May, showed a game attitude to fend off the eventual third inside the final furlong only to be mugged by the winner on the line. He had the benefit of the rail, but this was still a bold effort and he handled the quicker ground without fuss. (op 8/1)
Intense Focus(USA), second in the Coventry last time, was given a positive ride and only just lost out in a driving finish. He is a solid benchmark for the form, and can score in this class. (op 7/4 tchd 3/1)

3535a DUBAI DUTY FREE IRISH DERBY (GROUP 1) (ENTIRE COLTS & FILLIES) 1m 4f
3:50 (3:53) 3-Y-O
£619,852 (£211,764; £101,470; £35,294; £24,264; £13,235)

RPR

1 **Frozen Fire (GER)**^{22} 2829 3-9-0 114.................... JAHeffernan 1 123+
(A P O'Brien, Ire) *dwlt sltly: in rr: prog into 8th 2f out: swtchd to outer and hdwy 1 1/2f out: carried sltly lft ins fnl f: sn led: r.o strly cl home* **16/1**

2 2 **Casual Conquest (IRE)**^{22} 2829 3-9-0 118.................... PJSmullen 6 119
(D K Weld, Ire) *towards rr: prog into 8th 3f out: rdn in 6th 2f out: kpt on fnl f: wnt 2nd cl home* **4/1**^{2}

3 1/2 **Tartan Bearer (IRE)**^{22} 2829 3-9-0 .... RyanMoore 5 120+
(Sir Michael Stoute) *mid-div: prog into 3rd 2 1/2f out: rdn to dispute ld whn carried sharply lft 1f out: sn hdd and nt rcvr: fin 4th, 2l, shd and 1/2l: plcd 3rd* **1/1**^{1}

4 shd **Alessandro Volta**^{22} 2829 3-9-0 114.................... JMurtagh 8 119+
(A P O'Brien, Ire) *trckd ldrs: led on inner 4f out: clr 2f out: reduced ld and strly pressed whn veered sharply lft 1f out: sn hdd and nt rcvr: fin 3rd, 2l & shd: plcd 4th* **7/1**^{3}

5 2 **Curtain Call (FR)**^{22} 2829 3-9-0 .... FMBerry 4 115+
(L M Cumani) *in rr of mid-div: prog bef st: rdn in cl 3rd whn bdly hmpd 1f out: nt rcvr and kpt on one pce* **8/1**

6 shd **Bashkirov**^{8} 3289 3-9-0 90.................... SMLevey 10 115?
(A P O'Brien, Ire) *trckd ldrs: rdn fr 4f out: no imp fr 3f out: 6th and kpt on same pce on inner fnl f* **150/1**

7 8 **Winchester (USA)**^{9} 3193 3-9-0 105.................... PShanahan 2 102
(D K Weld, Ire) *in rr of mid-div: 8th on outer 3f out: sn no ex* **40/1**

8 1 **Centennial (IRE)**^{45} 2131 3-9-0 .... SebSanders 9 100
(J H M Gosden) *mid-div: 4th 3f out: rdn in 5th 2f out: sn no ex* **25/1**

9 12 **Upton Grey (IRE)**^{18} 2953 3-9-0 .... TedDurcan 12 81
(J H M Gosden) *trckd ldrs: rdn and wknd fr 4f out* **300/1**

10 1/2 **Hindu Kush (IRE)**^{22} 2854 3-9-0 106.................... DavidMcCabe 11 80
(A P O'Brien, Ire) *led: pushed along bef 1/2-way: hdd 4f out: sn no imp* **66/1**

11 12 **Washington Irving (IRE)**^{22} 2829 3-9-0 114.................... CO'Donoghue 7 61
(A P O'Brien, Ire) *prom: rdn and wknd fr 5f out: sn trailing* **12/1**

2m 31.96s (-5.54) **Going Correction** -0.025s/f (Good) **12** Ran SP% **116.0**
Speed ratings: **117,115,115,115,113 113,108,107,99,99 91**
CSF £77.12 TOTE £21.40: £4.30, £1.50, £1.10; DF 84.00.
Owner Michael Tabor **Bred** J U W Hoyer **Trained** Ballydoyle, Co Tipperary

FOCUS
This had looked an intriguing renewal, but the late defection of Epsom Derby winner New Approach with a bruised foot took away a fair amount of its interest. There was also plenty of trouble in the home straight, with the winner, third, fourth and fifth all inconvenienced to varying degrees. Frozen Fire, one of five from the O'Brien stable, looked a worthy winner nevertheless, proving his Epsom run to be all wrong. The form is rated through the runner-up, and there was a personal best from the progressive yet wayward Alessandro Volta.

NOTEBOOK
Frozen Fire(GER), who reportedly did not handle the track at Epsom, showed his true colours on this more galloping circuit and came home a ready winner under a very patient ride. He was nigh on last turning for home but found a willing turn of foot when asked to make up his ground up the outside in the home straight and won going away. His Dante run showed he possessed a real engine and this was obviously by far his best effort to date, on just his fifth career start. While several of his main rivals met trouble, he looked a worthy winner and he will be a force to reckon with over this sort of distance now. He could be campaigned similarly to his connections' 2007 winner Soldier Of Fortune, who won the Prix Niel on his way to the Arc (fifth behind stable companion Dylan Thomas), but his trainer would not rule out a crack at the St Leger. With stamina on both sides of his pedigree and a relaxed style of racing one could see him having a big say at Doncaster. Official explanation: trainer said, regarding the apparent improvement in form, owing to the nature of the track at Epsom and lack of pace at crucial stages, the horse was unable to make up ground last time (op 20/1)
Casual Conquest(IRE), the Epsom third, was also ridden patiently and was produced with every chance in the home straight. He ran very close to his previous level in defeat, going some way to helping set the standard of this form, and remains a progressive colt. This trip is well within his range now and perhaps he could find some further improvement for being ridden more aggressively, as he looks to lack the turn of foot displayed by the winner. It will be very interesting to see where this lightly-raced colt turns up next. Connections may consider an Arc bid later in the year, but he is also entered in the King George at Ascot next month and the Irish St Leger back at this venue in September. (op 7/2)
Tartan Bearer(IRE), the clear second at Epsom, looked to have outstanding prospects of going one better after the late defection of New Approach. He was another given time to find his stride from off the pace and emerged with his challenge at the top of the home straight. He was bang there when carried badly wide by Alessandro Volta passing the furlong marker and that certainly cost him momentum. Whether he would have been able to fend off the late challenge of the eventual winner one can not be sure, but he is obviously better than the bare result.
Alessandro Volta, in contrast to his main rivals, was ridden more prominently than had been the case at Epsom and hit the front at the top of the home straight. He began to show real signs of inexperience thereafter, however, and eventually veered badly left, hampering Curtain Call and carrying Tartan Bearer across the track with him. He was predictably demoted from third by the stewards after the race, but the decision to keep him fourth ahead of Curtain Call is surprising. The fact he was preferred here by Murtagh suggests he was the number one hope for his connections and had he not run so green when out in front, he would have probably taken some catching. This still rates as his best effort to date and, considering he would never have been in front so early before, he deserves the benefit of the doubt to show he does not have temperament issues. (op 7/1 tchd 8/1)
Curtain Call(FR) had appeared not to handle the undulations of Epsom last time, where he ran well below expectations. He confirmed that effort to be wrong with a much-improved effort on this more conventional track, travelling sweetly for most of the race, and being produced with every chance turning for home. While he would not have won, he would have been significantly closer but for being badly hampered when Alessandro Volta went left. (op 8/1 tchd 7/1)
Bashkirov, finally off the mark in maiden company last time, has always looked a stayer in the making and confirmed that here with a vastly-improved display. His proximity at the finish raises a doubt as to the overall form, but he too could be an improving sort and his next outing should reveal even more on that front.
Centennial(IRE), fourth in the Dante last time out, was unable to raise his game on this step up in trip and never seriously threatened. A drop back in class now looks a must for him.
Upton Grey(IRE), a stable companion of Centennial, is in the same ownership as New Approach and had been supplemented for this with pacemaking duties in mind. After the defection of the ante-post favourite his participation was somewhat meaningless, as he has been exposed in handicap company previously this term and was faced with an impossible task here.
Hindu Kush(IRE) Official explanation: jockey said colt was checked on home turn when dropping back
Washington Irving(IRE) Official explanation: jockey said colt lost its action at halfway

3536a WOODIES D.I.Y. CELEBRATION STKS (LISTED RACE) 1m
4:35 (4:37) 3-Y-O+ **£47,867** (£14,044; £6,691; £2,279)

RPR

1 **Lisvale (IRE)**^{22} 2854 3-9-2 106.................... WMLordan 2 115
(David Wachman, Ire) *mid-div: prog into mod 4th 3f out: rdn in 2nd 2f out: impr to ld ins fnl f: kpt on wl* **4/1**^{1}

2 3 **Jumbajukiba**^{11} 3148 5-10-0 114....................(b) FMBerry 9 112
(Mrs John Harrington, Ire) *led and sn clr: rdn fr 2f out: reduced advantage 1f out: hdd and no ex ins fnl f* **4/1**^{1}

3 shd **Capt Chaos (IRE)**^{55} 1879 3-9-4 106.................... CDHayes 6 110
(Edward Lynam, Ire) *trckd ldrs: rdn in mod 4th 2f out: btn in 3rd whn rdr lost whip under 1f out: kpt on* **10/1**

4 1 3/4 **Plan (USA)**^{57} 1808 3-8-13 100.................... JAHeffernan 12 101+
(A P O'Brien, Ire) *in rr: 9th 2 1/2f out: rdn and styd on strly fnl f: nvr nrr* **6/1**^{3}

5 1/2 **Jalmira (IRE)**^{25} 2740 7-9-9 98.................... PJSmullen 11 102
(C F Swan, Ire) *trckd ldrs in mod 3rd: rdn in mod 5th 2f out: no ex* **20/1**

6 2 **Lucifer Sam (USA)**^{49} 2032 3-8-13 100.................... CO'Donoghue 8 95
(A P O'Brien, Ire) *trckd ldr in mod 2nd: rdn in 3rd 2f out: sn no imp* **25/1**

7 1 **Summit Surge (IRE)**^{18} 2961 4-10-0 109....................(t) KLatham 5 100
(G M Lyons, Ire) *trckd ldrs: rdn and no imp fr 2f out* **8/1**

8 2 1/2 **Danehill Music (IRE)**^{56} 1847 5-9-9 100.................... DPMcDonogh 7 90
(David Wachman, Ire) *a towards rr: rdn and no imp st* **16/1**

9 1 3/4 **Crooked Throw (IRE)**^{11} 3148 9-9-9 108.................... WJLee 10 86
(C F Swan, Ire) *a towards rr: rdn and no imp st* **16/1**

10 shd **One Great Cat (USA)**^{11} 3148 3-8-13 103.................... JMurtagh 4 84
(A P O'Brien, Ire) *in rr of mid-div thrght: no imp st* **9/2**^{2}

11 1 3/4 **Prince Shaun (IRE)**[18] 2961 3-8-13 104................................ DMGrant 3 80
(Patrick J Flynn, Ire) *trckd ldrs: rdn in 5th whn drifted lft 2 1/2f out: wknd fr 2f out* **12/1**

1m 36.95s (-4.95) **Going Correction** -0.025s/f (Good) 12 Ran SP% **120.7**
WFA 3 from 4yo+ 10lb
Speed ratings: **124,121,120,119,118 116,115,113,111,111 109**
CSF £20.30 TOTE £4.80: £1.80, £2.10, £2.70; DF 21.40.
Owner Mrs Moira McNamara **Bred** Grangecon Stud **Trained** Goolds Cross, Co Tipperary

One Great Cat(USA) Official explanation: jockey said colt lost a shoe at the start

3537 - 3539a (Foreign Racing) - See Raceform Interactive

3515 HAMBURG (R-H)
Sunday, June 29

OFFICIAL GOING: Good

3540a IDEE HANSA-PREIS (GROUP 2) 1m 4f
4:05 (4:11) 3-Y-0+ **£44,118** (£15,441; £8,088; £4,044; £1,838)

RPR

1 **Egerton (GER)**[35] 2440 7-9-2 .... TMundry 3 117
(P Rau, Germany) *racd in 4th to 1/2-way: 6th st: str run fr dist to ld wl ins fnl f* **19/2**

2 3/4 **It's Gino (GER)**[35] 2440 5-9-4 .... KerrinMcEvoy 5 118
(P Vovcenko, Germany) *hld up in 7th: hdwy to go 2nd 1/2-way: w ldr fr over 3f out: led 2f out tl ct wl ins fnl f* **9/10**[1]

3 1 **Adlerflug (GER)**[63] 1662 4-9-6 .... THellier 6 118
(J Hirschberger, Germany) *hld up in 3rd: 5th st: trckd ldr wl over 1f out: ev ch 1f out: one pce* **28/10**[2]

4 1 3/4 **Poseidon Adventure (IRE)**[35] 2440 5-9-2 ....(b) AHelfenbein 1 112
(W Figge, Germany) *hld up: 7th st: last 2f out: r.o u.p: nrest at fin* **25/1**

5 1/2 **Prince Flori (GER)**[17] 5-9-2 .... FilipMinarik 9 111
(S Smrczek, Germany) *trckd ldr to over 5f out: 3rd st: one pce fr over 1f out* **7/1**

6 2 **Anton Chekhov**[38] 2346 4-9-2 .... ADeVries 4 108
(W Hickst, Germany) *hld up in mid-div: 6th st: one pce fnl 2f* **28/1**

7 nse **Dickens (GER)**[14] 3075 5-9-2 .... ASuborics 2 108
(H Blume, Germany) *hld up in rr: last st: nvr a factor* **69/10**[3]

8 7 **Prinz (GER)**[329] 4-9-2 .... EPedroza 7 96
(A Wohler, Germany) *mid-div: hdwy and 4th st: wknd wl over 1f out* **113/10**

9 6 **Sommersturm (GER)**[254] 4-9-2 .... MCadeddu 8 87
(J Hirschberger, Germany) *led to 2f out* **52/1**

2m 34.53s (-0.02) 9 Ran SP% **130.9**
(including ten euro stakes): WIN 105; PL 16, 12, 14; SF 301.
Owner Stall Reckendorf **Bred** Gestut Rottgen **Trained** Germany

2902 SAINT-CLOUD (L-H)
Sunday, June 29

OFFICIAL GOING: Good to soft

3542a GRAND PRIX DE SAINT-CLOUD - 10 ANS DE LA LNR (GROUP 1) 1m 4f
3:28 (3:30) 4-Y-0+ **£168,059** (£67,235; £33,618; £16,794; £8,412)

RPR

1 **Youmzain (IRE)**[23] 2791 5-9-2 .... RichardHughes 4 127
(M R Channon) *in tch: 5th st: hdwy to press ldrs 2f out: qcknd to ld appr fnl f: r.o wl: rdn out* **7/1**

2 1/2 **Soldier Of Fortune (IRE)**[23] 2791 4-9-2 .... CSoumillon 7 126
(A P O'Brien, Ire) *mid-div: 6th and drvn st: rdn to chal 1 1/2f out: wnt 2nd 1f out: nt pce of wnr* **10/11**[1]

3 3 **Doctor Dino (FR)**[28] 2653 6-9-2 .... OPeslier 9 121
(R Gibson, France) *hld up: last st: rdn and styd on fr 1 1/2f out: wnt 3rd 100yds out* **6/1**[3]

4 1 1/2 **Zambezi Sun**[28] 2653 4-9-2 .... SPasquier 3 119
(P Bary, France) *in tch: 4th and rdn st: wnt 2nd briefly over 1 1/2f out: no ex u.p after* **12/1**

5 2 **Getaway (GER)**[23] 2791 5-9-2 .... TThulliez 6 116
(A Fabre, France) *hld up: 8th st: last 1 1/2f out: styd on at one pce fnl f: n.d* **11/4**[2]

6 snk **Lucarno (USA)**[31] 2543 4-9-2 .... JimmyFortune 5 116
(J H M Gosden) *prom: 3rd 1/2-way: pushed along over 2f out to ld 1 1/2f out: hdd appr fnl f: one pce* **14/1**

7 hd **Not Just Swing (IRE)**[28] 2653 4-9-2 .... JVictoire 8 115
(A Fabre, France) *towards rr: 7th st: n.d* **33/1**

8 10 **Sommertag (GER)**[287] 5467 5-9-2 .... JAuge 2 99
(J Hirschberger, Germany) *led: drvn st: hdd 1 1/2f out: eased* **250/1**

9 8 **Song Of Hiawatha**[23] 2791 4-9-2 .... TGillet 1 86
(A P O'Brien, Ire) *racd in 2nd: pushed along to press ldr 3f out: no ex over 1 1/2f out: eased* **250/1**

2m 28.2s (-12.20) **Going Correction** -0.575s/f (Hard) 9 Ran SP% **123.9**
Speed ratings: **117,116,114,113,112 112,112,105,100**
PARI-MUTUEL: WIN 6.70; PL 1.30, 1.10, 1.20; DF 3.90.
Owner Jaber Abdullah **Bred** Frank Dunne **Trained** West Ilsley, Berks

NOTEBOOK
Youmzain(IRE) looked in magnificent condition in the paddock and won this race with authority, although he did idle inside the final furlong. In mid-division early on, he was cruising halfway up the straight and took control running into the final furlong. It was his first victory for 21 months and he did it in style, with a strong early pace certainly helping, and he will now have another tilt at the King George VI and Queen Elizabeth Stakes at Ascot, where he looks the one they all have to beat.
Soldier Of Fortune(IRE) was given every possible chance and lost nothing in defeat. He moved up to challenge a furlong and a half out, went to the head of affairs shortly after but could not quicken like the winner. He ran on but was slightly flattered as the winner stopped when hitting the front, although it was another sound performance.
Doctor Dino(FR) was dropped back last from his outside draw and remained in that position until the straight. He made a forward move from a furlong and a half out but never had a chance of catching either the winner or the runner-up, although it was another decent performance.
Zambezi Sun was given every chance. He was asked to quicken two furlongs out and then stayed on one-paced to the line.
Getaway(GER) was perhaps overrated following his impressive Newmarket success, but he did not handle the track at Epsom and his defeat here was put down to the ground being on the fast side, despite the official description, and him losing a near-fore shoe.
Lucarno(USA), well up from the start in what was a strongly run race, still ran a little bit free early on. He had every chance coming into the straight but was one-paced when things really quickened up. He seems to have taken time to come to himself and may need a fast surface to produce his best.

3543a PRIX DE MALLERET (GROUP 2) (FILLIES) 1m 4f
4:00 (4:02) 3-Y-0 **£54,485** (£21,029; £10,037; £6,691; £3,346)

RPR

1 **Treat Gently**[28] 2650 3-8-9 .... SPasquier 3 106
(A Fabre, France) *racd in cl 2nd: pushed along to ld over 2f out: rdn and r.o 1 1/2f out: fnd more whn pressed ins fnl f: hld on wl cl home* **11/10**[1]

2 nse **Leo's Starlet (IRE)**[21] 2877 3-8-9 .... C-PLemaire 4 106
(A De Royer-Dupre, France) *hld up: 4th st: pushed along and 3rd 2f out: rdn to chal 1f out: r.o and ev ch cl home: jst failed* **5/2**[2]

3 hd **Dar Re Mi**[46] 2105 3-8-9 .... JimmyFortune 5 106
(J H M Gosden) *racd in last: pushed along over 2f out: sn rdn and styd on down outside: chal 150yds out: ev ch cl home: r.o* **7/2**[3]

4 2 **Miracle Seeker**[23] 2792 3-8-9 .... OPeslier 2 103
(C G Cox) *led: pushed along st: hdd over 2f out: rdn and sn disputing ld again: no ex fr over 1f out* **9/1**

5 2 1/2 **Myakoda (FR)**[28] 2650 3-8-9 .... CSoumillon 1 99
(Y De Nicolay, France) *racd in 3rd: pushed along 1 1/2f out: rdn and one pce fnl f* **16/1**

2m 31.1s (-9.30) **Going Correction** -0.575s/f (Hard) 5 Ran SP% **114.3**
Speed ratings: **108,107,107,106,104**
PARI-MUTUEL: WIN 2.00; PL 1.20, 1.30; SF 5.40.
Owner K Abdulla **Bred** Juddmonte Farms **Trained** Chantilly, France
■ Stewards' Enquiry : Jimmy Fortune €200 fine: whip abuse
C-P Lemaire €200 fine: whip abuse

NOTEBOOK
Treat Gently put up a very brave performance and really stuck her head down when it mattered. She took up the running two out and then fended off some desperate late challenges to win by inches. A progressive filly, her next target will be the Prix Vermeille, although she could have an outing before in the Prix Nonette at Deauville.
Leo's Starlet(IRE) took some time to quicken in the straight and only engaged top gear at the furlong marker, but she only just lost on the nod. She will now be rested and will probably be prepared for an autumn campaign in the States.
Dar Re Mi, held up last early on, made her run up the centre of the straight. She quickened well from a furlong out but did not quite make it to the head of affairs. She would have won had she been subjected to a more positive ride and could come back to France for something like the Prix Minerve at Deauville in August.
Miracle Seeker tried to make every yard of the running but came under pressure at the two-furlong marker. She just stayed on one-paced to the line afterwards. There are no plans for her at the moment.

3211 MUSSELBURGH (R-H)
Monday, June 30

OFFICIAL GOING: Good to firm (good in places)
Wind: Fresh, half behind Weather: Cloudy, bright

3545 BOLLINGER CHAMPAGNE CHALLENGE SERIES H'CAP (FOR GENTLEMAN AMATEUR RIDERS) 2m
6:55 (6:56) (Class 6) (0-65,65) 4-Y-0+ **£2,498** (£774; £387; £193) **Stalls** Low

Form RPR

0415 1 **Kyber**[10] 3198 7-10-11 57................................ MrPNorton(5) 6 64
(J S Goldie) *trckd ldrs: led gng wl over 2f out: hrd pressed fnl f: hld on wl* **2/1**[1]

5505 2 1 **Merrymaker**[21] 2888 8-11-4 62................................ MrBenBrisbourne(3) 1 68
(W M Brisbourne) *hld up: hdwy and prom after 6f: effrt over 2f out: ev ch ins fnl f: kpt on: hld nr fin* **4/1**[2]

-5F0 3 1 3/4 **Dance Sauvage**[9] 3279 5-10-5 46 oh1................................ MrSDobson 7 50
(C W Thornton) *hld up in tch: effrt 3f out: edgd rt and one pce ins fnl f* **9/2**[3]

201/ 4 6 **Spring Breeze**[64] 4681 7-11-3 65................................(v) MrGRSmith(7) 9 62
(M Dods) *led to over 2f out: sn rdn: btn over 1f out* **8/1**

0603 5 3 3/4 **Asrar**[10] 3216 6-10-5 46 oh1................................ MrSWalker 3 38
(Miss Lucinda V Russell) *hld up: hdwy over 4f out: drvn and outpcd fr over 2f out* **25/1**

6 shd **Harcas (IRE)**[254] 5398 6-11-5 65................................ MrJoshuaMoore(5) 8 57
(M Todhunter) *towards rr: rdn 4f out: n.d* **7/1**

2662 7 7 **Easibet Dot Net**[10] 3216 8-10-2 50................................(b) MrRossSmith(7) 4 34
(Miss L A Perratt) *hld up: drvn over 3f out: sn btn* **7/1**

40-0 8 14 **Mycenean Prince (USA)**[22] 1116 5-9-13 47 oh1 ow1(b) MrCAHarris(7) 2 14
(R C Guest) *prom: lost pl over 6f out: sn btn* **28/1**

6004 9 6 **Stravonian**[10] 3216 8-10-5 51 oh1 ow5................................ MrGCrow(5) 5 11
(D A Nolan) *trckd ldrs: rdn over 4f out: wknd 3f out* **50/1**

3m 31.67s (-4.43) **Going Correction** -0.25s/f (Firm) 9 Ran SP% **116.9**
Speed ratings (Par 101): **101,100,99,96,94 94,91,84,81**
toteswinger: 1&2 £2.80, 1&3 £2.80, 2&3 £5.00. CSF £9.94 CT £32.06 TOTE £3.30: £1.40, £1.30, £1.30; EX 11.00.
Owner Great Northern Partnership **Bred** P B Holmes **Trained** Uplawmoor, E Renfrews
■ Stewards' Enquiry : Mr Ben Brisbourne one-day ban: careless riding (Jul 25)

FOCUS
A low-grade staying event and modest form..

3546 NCB STOCKBROKERS H'CAP 5f
7:25 (7:25) (Class 6) (0-65,64) 4-Y-0+ **£2,590** (£770; £385; £192) **Stalls** Low

Form RPR

3453 1 **Raccoon (IRE)**[13] 3112 8-9-7 64................................(v) NCallan 2 71
(Mrs R A Carr) *mde all: rdn over 1f out: kpt on wl fnl f: jst lasted* **7/4**[1]

040 2 shd **Wicked Wilma (IRE)**[19] 2928 4-8-8 51 ow1........................ TomEaves 3 58
(A Berry) *bhd: hdwy over 1f out: str run fnl f: jst hld* **20/1**

2430 3 1/2 **Bond Becks (IRE)**[13] 3112 8-8-12 55................................ SilvestreDeSousa 4 60
(G R Oldroyd) *in tch: hdwy to chse wnr over 1f out to ins fnl f: kpt on: hld nr fin* **20/1**

-000 4 1 1/4 **Ryedane (IRE)**[42] 2263 6-8-12 58................................(b) DuranFentiman(3) 11 59+
(T D Easterby) *hld up: hdwy outside over 1f out: kpt on fnl f: nrst fin* **20/1**

5020 5 nk **Princess Charlmane (IRE)**[10] 3212 5-8-0 48 ow3..(t) KellyHarrison(5) 6 48
(C J Teague) *hld up: effrt on outside over 1f out: kpt on ins fnl f: no imp* **40/1**

0400 6 nk **Spirit Of Coniston**[13] 3112 5-8-10 56................................ JamieMoriarty(3) 5 55
(P T Midgley) *prom: effrt over 2f out: one pce fnl f* **9/1**

The Form Book, Raceform Ltd, Compton, RG20 6NL

0000 **7** *1 1/4* **Mutayam**[13] 3112 8-8-2 **52** ow7........(t) PaulPickard(7) 14 46
(D A Nolan) *trckd ldrs: drvn over 2f out: no ex appr fnl f* **80/1**
0-65 **8** *hd* **Jojesse**[22] 2869 4-8-2 **45**........ DaleGibson 7 38
(G A Swinbank) *hld up: nt clr run over 1f out: nvr rchd ldrs* **8/1**
-460 **9** *1* **Melandre**[110] 857 6-8-2 **45**........ TWilliams 1 35
(M Brittain) *chsd wnr to over 1f out: sn no ex* **66/1**
2562 **10** *nse* **Highland Song (IRE)**[57] 1827 5-8-0 **46**........ AndrewMullen(3) 10 36
(R F Fisher) *dwlt: rdn in rr 1/2-way: n.d* **13/2**[3]
0000 **11** *1 1/4* **Welcome Approach**[9] 3255 5-8-12 **55**........(b) RobertWinston 13 40
(J R Weymes) *bhd: drvn along 1/2-way: nvr on terms* **15/2**
3501 **12** *8* **Toy Top (USA)**[13] 3112 5-9-1 **63**........(b) NeilBrown(5) 9 19
(M Dods) *prom tl rdn and wknd wl over 1f out* **5/1**[2]

59.01 secs (-1.39) **Going Correction** -0.25s/f (Firm) 12 Ran SP% **118.7**
Speed ratings (Par 101): **101,100,100,98,97 97,95,94,93,93 91,78**
toteswinger: 1&2 £17.40, 1&3 £14.60, 2&3 £61.20. CSF £47.13 CT £475.85 TOTE £2.50: £1.20, £5.30, £4.80; EX 29.90.
Owner P D Savill **Bred** P D Savill **Trained** Stillington, N Yorks
■ Stewards' Enquiry : Kelly Harrison one-day ban: careless riding (Jul 14)

FOCUS
A moderate sprint handicap.
Jojesse Official explanation: jockey said gelding was denied a clear run
Welcome Approach Official explanation: jockey said gelding was denied a clear run
Toy Top(USA) Official explanation: trainer said regarding running, that the mare was unable to dominate

3547 MACMILLAN CANCER SUPPORT/E.B.F. MEDIAN AUCTION MAIDEN STKS 5f
7:55 (7:55) (Class 5) 2-Y-O £3,238 (£963; £481; £240) Stalls Low

Form RPR
40 **1** **Visterre (IRE)**[5] 3364 2-8-12 0........ TomEaves 6 68
(B Smart) *wnt rt s: towards rr on outside: hdwy 2f out: edgd lft and styd on wl to ld nr fin* **9/1**
44 **2** *3/4* **Eldorado Days (IRE)**[17] 3005 2-9-3 0........ RobertWinston 4 70
(K R Burke) *trckd ldrs: led and rdn over 1f out: flashed tail ins fnl f: hdd nr fin* **7/2**[3]
35 **3** *1* **Mesyaal**[24] 2769 2-9-3 0........ SamHitchcott 2 66
(M R Channon) *prom: drvn 1/2-way: effrt over 1f out: one pce ins fnl f* **3/1**[2]
45 **4** *nse* **Blow Your Mind**[38] 2362 2-9-3 0........ PaulMulrennan 3 66
(Karen McLintock) *cl up: rdn and ev ch over 1f out: one pce ins fnl f* **8/1**
06 **5** *3* **Compton Ford**[35] 2462 2-9-3 0........ DaleGibson 1 55
(M Dods) *led to over 1f out: sn wknd* **22/1**
5 **6** *3/4* **Mintoe**[16] 3049 2-9-3 0........ NCallan 7 53
(K A Ryan) *carried rt s: sn in tch: effrt 1/2-way: btn fnl f* **11/8**[1]
7 *21* **Wee Bizzom** 2-8-9 0 ow2........ SladeO'Hara(5) 5 —
(A Berry) *missed break: sn wl bhd* **40/1**

59.78 secs (-0.62) **Going Correction** -0.25s/f (Firm) 7 Ran SP% **117.2**
Speed ratings (Par 93): **94,92,91,91,86 85,51**
toteswinger: 1&2 £17.00, 1&3 £8.40, 2&3 £1.80. CSF £41.94 TOTE £15.10: £4.10, £2.40; EX 59.00.
Owner Prime Equestrian **Bred** Miss Eileen Farrelly **Trained** Hambleton, N Yorks
■ Stewards' Enquiry : Tom Eaves caution: careless riding

FOCUS
This was not the strongest of maidens, but it should produce winners.

NOTEBOOK
Visterre(IRE), who failed to get home over 6f in soft ground at Carlisle last time, was seen to much better effect on this faster surface and she came with a strong late charge to get up close home. She still showed signs of greenness and may well be capable of better still in nurseries. (tchd 10-1)
Eldorado Days(IRE) has improved with each run and he looked the winner racing inside the final furlong, but could not repel the late surge of the winner. He is now qualified for nurseries and looks capable of winning a race at two. (op 5-2)
Mesyaal showed speed and ran well on this drop in trip, but lacked a change of pace when it mattered. He is another likely to fare better once handicapping. (op 7-2)
Blow Your Mind seemed to find 6f too far at Newcastle last time, but he ran on right to the line here and clearly has the ability to win races. (op 16-1)
Mintoe, who showed tons of speed before failing to get home over 6f on debut (decent race at York) was expected to be suited by this drop in trip, but he was carried right at the start and was never travelling with the same zest. This was disappointing and it leaves him with a bit to prove. (op 13-8 tchd 15-8)

3548 "GOOD LUCK CLAIRE" H'CAP 7f 30y
8:25 (8:26) (Class 4) (0-85,85) 3-Y-O+ £6,476 (£1,927; £963; £481) Stalls High

Form RPR
51-4 **1** **Kings Point (IRE)**[20] 2905 7-9-6 **82**........ AhmedAjtebi(5) 6 90
(D Nicholls) *prom: effrt over 2f out: led ins fnl f: pushed out* **9/2**[3]
2615 **2** *1 1/4* **Abbondanza (IRE)**[10] 3203 5-10-0 **85**........(p) RobertWinston 1 90
(Miss L A Perratt) *trckd ldr: rdn and led briefly 2 out: kpt on u.p fnl f* **8/1**
3212 **3** *3/4* **Cha Cha Cha**[12] 3138 4-9-11 **82**........ NCallan 7 85
(K A Ryan) *chsd ldrs: led over 1f out to ins fnl f: no ex* **2/1**[1]
155 **4** *2 1/4* **Stoic Leader (IRE)**[18] 2969 8-9-2 **73**........ PaulMulrennan 2 70
(R F Fisher) *hld up in tch: drvn over 2f out: kpt on fnl f: nvr trbld ldrs* **14/1**
-112 **5** *5* **Stellite**[23] 2841 8-8-13 **70**........ DanielTudhope 5 53
(J S Goldie) *hld up: drvn 3f out: no imp fr 2f out* **9/2**[3]
204 **6** *1 3/4* **Al Wasef (USA)**[16] 3051 3-8-7 **73**........ JoeFanning 4 52
(M Johnston) *dwlt: hld up: rdn and edgd rt over 2f out: sn wknd* **8/1**
0-22 **7** *1/2* **Il Castagno (IRE)**[45] 2158 5-9-12 **83**........ TomEaves 3 60
(B Smart) *taken early to post: uns rdr bef s: led to 2f out: sn wknd* **4/1**[2]

1m 27.46s (-2.84) **Going Correction** -0.25s/f (Firm)
WFA 3 from 4yo+ 9lb 7 Ran SP% **118.6**
Speed ratings (Par 105): **106,104,103,101,95 93,92**
toteswinger: 1&2 £4.90, 1&3 £3.10, 2&3 £4.30. CSF £41.20 TOTE £6.70: £3.80, £4.60; EX 45.10.
Owner WRB 61 (The Claire King Syndicate) **Bred** John Costello **Trained** Sessay, N Yorks

FOCUS
A fair handicap run at a decent pace and the form looks sound.

3549 SCOTTISH RACING YOUR BETTER BET H'CAP 7f 30y
8:55 (8:56) (Class 6) (0-55,55) 3-Y-O £2,266 (£674; £337; £168) Stalls High

Form RPR
0000 **1** **Molly Ann (IRE)**[9] 3282 3-9-0 **55**........ TomEaves 7 56
(T D Easterby) *prom: smooth hdwy over 2f out: led over 1f out: drvn out* **7/2**[2]
0600 **2** *2* **Lucky Character**[16] 3030 3-8-6 **47** oh1 ow1........(t) SamHitchcott 6 42
(N J Vaughan) *hld up in tch: effrt over 2f out: rallied over 1f out: chsd wnr wl ins fnl f: kpt on* **4/1**[3]
000- **3** *1/2* **Personal Choice**[326] 4328 3-8-9 **50**........ TWilliams 2 44
(M Brittain) *trckd ldr: rdn over 2f out: one pce fnl f* **18/1**
0000 **4** *shd* **Your Golf Travel**[19] 2946 3-8-0 **46** oh1........ KellyHarrison(5) 5 40
(J S Wainwright) *led to over 1f out: kpt on same pce* **12/1**
00-0 **5** *2* **Trojan Hero (IRE)**[28] 2673 3-8-5 **46** oh1........ DaleGibson 8 34
(A Dickman) *t.k.h: trckd ldrs tl rdn and no ex over 1f out* **25/1**
0-60 **6** *3/4* **Kiwi Princess**[34] 2490 3-8-11 **52**........ JoeFanning 4 38
(M Brittain) *dwlt: hld up: effrt on outside 2f out: no imp appr fnl f* **13/2**
5000 **7** *1 1/4* **Saafend Geezer**[25] 2753 3-9-0 **55**........ RobertWinston 3 38
(A Berry) *hld up in tch: rdn over 2f out: hung rt and sn btn* **6/1**
4055 **8** *1 1/2* **Low Flyer (USA)**[10] 3213 3-9-0 **55**........ SilvestreDeSousa 1 34
(T D Barron) *hld up: rdn over 2f out: sn n.d* **5/2**[1]

1m 30.48s (0.18) **Going Correction** -0.25s/f (Firm) 8 Ran SP% **115.2**
Speed ratings (Par 97): **88,85,85,85,82 81,80,78**
toteswinger: 1&2 £3.90, 1&3 £8.40, 2&3 £8.40. CSF £18.10 CT £219.65 TOTE £3.70: £1.60, £2.10, £3.10; EX 23.20.
Owner Dale And Ann Wilsdon **Bred** Peter Hill **Trained** Great Habton, N Yorks

FOCUS
A very moderate winning time for a race of its type and the form looks weak.
Kiwi Princess Official explanation: jockey said filly missed the break and hung left-handed on bend turning in
Saafend Geezer Official explanation: jockey said gelding was unsuited by the good to firm (good in places) ground

3550 TARTAN TURF GUIDE H'CAP 1m 4f
9:25 (9:25) (Class 5) (0-70,65) 4-Y-O+ £3,885 (£1,156; £577; £288) Stalls High

Form RPR
054- **1** **Chookie Hamilton**[203] 7104 4-8-13 **57**........ TomEaves 8 64+
(Miss L A Perratt) *hld up in tch: hdwy over 2f out: styd on wl u.p fnl f: led nr fin* **4/1**[2]
-043 **2** *3/4* **Jane Of Arc (FR)**[12] 3131 4-8-6 **50**........(p) JoeFanning 2 56
(J S Goldie) *t.k.h: cl up: led over 2f out: rdn and edgd rt over 1f out: kpt on: hdd nr fin* **2/1**[1]
0453 **3** *3 1/4* **Muncaster Castle (IRE)**[10] 3201 4-8-8 **52**........ PaulMulrennan 6 53
(R F Fisher) *led to over 2f out: one pce over 1f out* **5/1**[3]
0-00 **4** *2 3/4* **Bond Casino**[38] 2364 4-8-9 **53**........ SilvestreDeSousa 7 49
(G R Oldroyd) *prom: effrt over 2f out: wknd over 1f out* **9/1**
12-0 **5** *1/2* **Sir Sandicliffe (IRE)**[20] 2908 4-8-10 **57**........ DuranFentiman(3) 1 53
(W M Brisbourne) *hld up: drvn over 2f out: nvr able to chal* **8/1**
2400 **6** *2 1/2* **Evelith Regent (IRE)**[14] 3083 5-9-7 **65**........ RobertWinston 4 57
(G A Swinbank) *t.k.h: hld up: effrt on outside over 2f out: hung rt and sn btn* **7/1**
0/02 **7** *hd* **Channel Crossing**[28] 2667 6-9-7 **65**........ NCallan 5 56
(S Wynne) *prom: pushed along over 2f out: wkng whn n.m.r over 1f out* **8/1**

2m 35.82s (-3.88) **Going Correction** -0.25s/f (Firm) 7 Ran SP% **114.7**
Speed ratings (Par 103): **102,101,99,97,97 95,95**
toteswinger: 1&2 £2.20, 1&3 £1.60, 2&3 £4.10. CSF £12.54 CT £39.76 TOTE £3.70: £2.10, £2.00; EX 13.40 Place 6: £242.86, Place 5: £189.25..
Owner Raeburn Brick Limited **Bred** D And J Raeburn **Trained** Carluke, S Lanarks

FOCUS
A moderate handicap.
Channel Crossing Official explanation: jockey said gelding lost its action
T/Plt: £125.20 to a £1 stake. Pool: £82,659.67. 481.80 winning tickets. T/Qpdt: £30.00 to a £1 stake. Pool: £4,432.55. 109.18 winning tickets. RY

3292 PONTEFRACT (L-H)
Monday, June 30

OFFICIAL GOING: Good (good to firm in places; 7.3)
After 30mm rain and 5mm watering over the previous five days the ground was described as 'spot on, just on the quick side of good'.
Wind: Light half behind Weather: mainly fine

3551 PONTEFRACT LADIES' H'CAP (FOR LADY AMATEUR RIDERS) 1m 2f 6y
2:15 (2:17) (Class 5) (0-70,70) 3-Y-O+ £3,123 (£968; £484; £242) Stalls Low

Form RPR
0402 **1** **Coral Shores**[11] 3166 3-8-12 **59** ow4........(v) MrsMarieKing(3) 3 68
(P W Hiatt) *t.k.h: trckd ldrs: led over 2f out: kpt on wl* **11/1**
0002 **2** *1 1/4* **Gala Sunday (USA)**[30] 2617 8-9-12 **58**........(bt) MissSBrotherton 8 64
(M W Easterby) *prom: wnt 2nd over 1f out: kpt on same pce ins fnl f* **11/2**[1]
3001 **3** *2* **Holiday Cocktail**[10] 3226 6-10-1 **61**........(p) MissADeniel 10 63+
(J J Quinn) *mid-div: effrt whn hmpd over 2f: styd on wl to take 3rd ins fnl f* **11/2**[1]
0-04 **4** *1 1/4* **Gulf Coast**[33] 2496 3-8-7 **58**........ MissERamstrom(7) 2 58
(T D Walford) *chsd ldrs: edgd lft 2f out: kpt on same pce* **8/1**[3]
-320 **5** *3 1/2* **Society Venue**[23] 2840 3-9-12 **70**........ MrsCBartley 17 63
(Jedd O'Keeffe) *mid-div: hdwy on outer 4f out: one pce fnl 2f* **6/1**[2]
4500 **6** *2 3/4* **Scotty's Future (IRE)**[5] 3366 10-9-0 **51** oh2........ MissMMullineaux(5) 15 38+
(A Berry) *swtchd lft after s: bhd: kpt on fnl 2f: nvr nr ldrs* **50/1**
0-00 **7** *3/4* **Golden Dagger (IRE)**[24] 2784 4-10-10 **70**........ MissARyan 14 56
(K A Ryan) *mid-div: hdwy over 1f out: kpt on* **10/1**
2503 **8** *1 1/2* **Ming Vase**[22] 2870 6-9-0 **51** oh3........ MissWGibson(5) 1 34
(P T Midgley) *chsd ldrs: one pce whn hmpd over 2f out* **18/1**
400- **9** *1 1/4* **Paparaazi (IRE)**[254] 6325 6-9-5 **58** ow6........(p) MissKSharp(7) 11 38
(I W McInnes) *s.s: nvr on terms* **28/1**
450 **10** *1 1/4* **Kylkenny**[30] 2617 13-9-2 **53** ow1........(t) MissVCartmel(5) 9 31
(H Morrison) *mid-div: effrt over 2f out: nvr nr ldrs* **9/1**
6060 **11** *shd* **Galley Slave (IRE)**[3] 2549 3-8-8 **52** oh1 ow1........ MrsSMoore 12 29
(M C Chapman) *chsd ldrs: fdd 2f out* **40/1**
0-06 **12** *nk* **Cameroonéy**[23] 2848 5-9-1 **52** oh5 ow1........ MissBeverleyKendall(5) 7 29
(A D Brown) *t.k.h: w ldr: led 3f out: sn hdd & wknd* **25/1**
0-00 **13** *7* **Take To The Skies (IRE)**[16] 3037 4-9-1 **52**........ MissLEBurke(5) 4 15
(A P Jarvis) *s.i.s: sme hdwy over 3f out: lost pl 2f out* **50/1**
36-5 **14** *9* **Reel Buddy Blaze**[35] 2464 3-9-3 **68**........ MissKECooper(7) 13 13
(T P Tate) *in rr: bhd whn rn wd bnd 2f out* **16/1**
1060 **15** *1* **Sawwaah (IRE)**[2] 3474 11-10-10 **70**........ MissGDGracey-Davison 6 13
(D Carroll) *mid-div: lost pl over 2f out* **18/1**
600- **16** *3 1/2* **Abbey Express**[23] 6305 3-8-8 **57** ow5........(t) MissAngelaBarnes(5) 5 —
(M A Barnes) *t.k.h: led tl 3f out: wandered and sn wkng whn hmpd 2f out* **100/1**

1013 **17** ½ **Hucking Heat (IRE)**[20] 2908 4-9-11 **62**....................(p) MissRKneller(5) 16 —
(R Hollinshead) *in rr-div: hdwy on outside 6f out: lost pl and hung 2f out* **9/1**

2m 14.71s (1.01) **Going Correction** +0.125s/f (Good)
WFA 3 from 4yo+ 12lb **17** Ran SP% **124.6**
Speed ratings (Par 103): **100,99,97,96,93 91,90,89,88,87 87,87,81,74,73 70,70**
toteswinger: 1&2 £10.90, 1&3 £15.10, 2&3 £4.40. CSF £68.34 CT £382.45 TOTE £14.60: £2.80, £1.50, £1.90, £2.70; EX 84.90.
Owner P W Hiatt **Bred** Cheveley Park Stud Ltd **Trained** Hook Norton, Oxon
■ Stewards' Enquiry : Miss E Ramstrom three-day ban: careless riding (Jul 15,25,28)

FOCUS
A modest handicap for lady amateur riders and the early pace was not strong.

3552 JAMES THADDEUS BOURKE - A LIFETIME IN RACING FILLIES' H'CAP 1m 4y
2:45 (2:46) (Class 5) (0-70,70) 3-Y-O+ **£3,238** (£963; £481; £240) **Stalls** Low

Form RPR
041 **1** **Flying Valentino**[14] 3082 4-9-7 **65**.................................. PJMcDonald(3) 1 83
(G A Swinbank) *trckd ldrs: wnt 2nd over 2f out: led on bit over 1f out: sn rdn clr* **7/2**[1]
-063 **2** 8 **Striving (IRE)**[14] 3095 3-8-11 **62**..............................(v) KerrinMcEvoy 10 60
(Sir Michael Stoute) *hld up: hdwy on wd outside 3f out: wnt 2nd over 1f out: no ch w wnr* **5/1**[2]
1654 **3** 2½ **Dispol Isle (IRE)**[10] 3214 6-9-9 **69**.................................. NeilBrown(5) 2 63
(T D Barron) *t.k.h: trckd ldrs: stdd and dropped bk after 3f: hdwy over 2f out: kpt on ins fnl f* **6/1**[3]
2402 **4** hd **Papa's Princess**[12] 3127 4-8-6 **52**.................................. GaryBartley(5) 6 49+
(J S Goldie) *rrd s: hld up in rr: hdwy whn nt clr run 1f out: styd on ins fnl f* **11/1**
6013 **5** shd **Grethel (IRE)**[9] 3258 4-8-8 **54**.................... DanielleMcCreery(5) 12 47
(A Berry) *dwlt: hdwy over 2f out: kpt on same pce appr fnl f* **22/1**
0550 **6** 1¾ **Carefree**[3] 3450 4-8-9 **50** oh1..............................(b) SilvestreDeSousa 3 39
(Mrs R A Carr) *reluctant to load: set str pce: hdd over 1f out: sn btn* **20/1**
1-00 **7** 1½ **Harlem Shuffle (UAE)**[20] 2911 3-9-5 **70**.............................. GregFairley 9 54
(M Johnston) *chsd ldrs on outer: one pce fnl 2f* **14/1**
0041 **8** 1 **Society Music (IRE)**[19] 2942 6-9-7 **69**.......................... BMcHugh(7) 8 53
(M Dods) *s.i.s: hdwy over 3f out: rdn 2f out: one pce* **13/2**
60-0 **9** ¾ **Bunny Hug**[70] 1519 3-8-3 **54**..(b[1]) ChrisCatlin 4 34
(T D Easterby) *in rr: hdwy over 3f out: nvr nr ldrs* **50/1**
3302 **10** 4½ **Flying Time**[8] 3293 3-9-3 **68**.. DarryllHolland 7 37
(M R Channon) *sn chsng ldrs: lost pl appr fnl f* **15/2**
521- **11** 5 **River Bounty**[208] 7030 3-8-13 **64**...................................... AndrewElliott 5 22
(A P Jarvis) *w ldrs: wknd over 1f out* **16/1**
-150 **12** 22 **Twilight Dawn**[23] 2848 4-9-12 **67**...................................... PaulHanagan 11 —
(L Lungo) *in rr: rdn and lost pl over 2f out: sn bhd: eased ins fnl f* **20/1**

1m 45.94s (0.04) **Going Correction** +0.125s/f (Good)
WFA 3 from 4yo+ 10lb **12** Ran SP% **115.0**
Speed ratings (Par 100): **104,96,93,93,93 91,89,88,88,83 78,56**
toteswinger: 1&2 £2.40, 1&3 £6.40, 2&3 £7.00. CSF £18.35 CT £102.30 TOTE £4.70: £2.00, £1.40, £2.50; EX 19.30.
Owner Adrian Butler **Bred** Helshaw Grange Stud Ltd **Trained** Melsonby, N Yorks

FOCUS
This looked a competitive if modest fillies' handicap beforehand, but the pace was strong and nothing could live with Flying Valentino.
Flying Time Official explanation: trainer had no explanation for the poor form shown

3553 SPINDRIFTER CONDITIONS STKS 6f
3:15 (3:15) (Class 3) 2-Y-O **£6,476** (£1,927; £963; £481) **Stalls** Low

Form RPR
421 **1** **Reve De Soleil (FR)**[12] 3125 2-8-10 0.................................. ChrisCatlin 2 91+
(E J O'Neill) *hld up: effrt and swtchd outside over 1f out: led jst ins fnl f: drvn out* **15/2**[3]
01 **2** 2 **Keeptheboatafloat (USA)**[11] 3170 2-9-1 0.................... AndrewElliott 5 90
(K R Burke) *w ldrs: led and qcknd 2f out: hdd jst ins fnl f: no ex* **16/1**
412 **3** 3½ **Indian Art (IRE)**[23] 2826 2-8-13 0... PatDobbs 1 77
(R Hannon) *set modest pce: hdd 2f out: one pce* **5/6**[1]
5431 **4** 1¾ **Senatorial**[9] 3254 2-9-1 0.. MichaelHills 3 74
(B W Hills) *trckd ldrs: effrt over 1f out: edgd lft: nvr able to chal* **10/3**[2]
1233 **5** 1½ **In Transit (IRE)**[17] 2987 2-8-8 0.. MCGeran(5) 4 67
(M R Channon) *w ldrs outpcd 2f out: sn btn* **15/2**[3]

1m 19.07s (2.17) **Going Correction** +0.125s/f (Good) **5** Ran SP% **107.0**
Speed ratings (Par 97): **90,87,82,80,78**
CSF £84.01 TOTE £7.20: £2.80, £4.70; EX 80.10.
Owner G A Lucas & A Solomon **Bred** Mme Annie Delarue **Trained** Averham Park, Notts

FOCUS
This long-standing conditions race for juveniles numbers the likes of Timeless Times and Lucky Story among its roll of honour. While this year's winner is not in their league, he is progressing well.

NOTEBOOK
Reve De Soleil(FR) started off in the good maiden at York won by the subsequent Coventry Stakes third Lord Shanakill, and while he had to be dropped into maiden auction company to get off the mark at Hamilton, that would have done his confidence the world of good and he came home a decisive winner. He is by little-known sire Dyhim Diamond, who stands in France and whose best progeny thus far has been Turtle Bowl, a close third behind Ramonti in last year's Queen Anne Stakes. (op 8-1)
Keeptheboatafloat(USA) finished some 17 lengths behind the winner on debut at York, but has improved by leaps and bounds since, going in on heavy ground at Ripon at 25-1 on his next start and improving again here. Indeed, he looked a real threat when leading off the turn, this despite being caught out wide and not handling the bend that well, and was probably only worn down by an above-average sort. He will be heavily burdened in nurseries now, though. (op 14-1)
Indian Art(IRE) proved a most disappointing favourite, despite having the run of the race and the advantage of the inside rail around the turn during his mid-race battle with the runner-up. The jury is out on him now. (tchd 4-5 tchd 10-11 in places and evens in a place)
In Transit(IRE) is a fair sort, but he is not really improving and was found wanting here. (op 13-2)

3554 E B F CHRIS DEUTERS MEMORIAL FILLIES' H'CAP 6f
3:45 (3:46) (Class 3) (0-90,83) 3-Y-O+
£9,346 (£2,799; £1,399; £700; £349; £175) **Stalls** Low

Form RPR
1163 **1** **Mango Music**[9] 3271 5-9-10 **79**.. FrancisNorton 10 91
(M Quinn) *led: swtchd lft after 110yds: shkn up over 1f out: kpt on wl: unchal* **3/1**[1]
-010 **2** 3½ **Swift Princess (IRE)**[30] 2598 4-10-0 **83**....................(v) AndrewElliott 6 84+
(K R Burke) *checked after 110yds: hdwy and swtchd outside over 1f out: styd on wl to take 2nd ins fnl f: nt rch wnr* **9/1**
0-00 **3** 2 **Katie Boo (IRE)**[5] 3370 6-9-6 **75**................................... PaulMulrennan 1 69
(A Berry) *chsd ldrs: wnt 2nd over 1f out: styd on same pce* **16/1**
10-0 **4** ¾ **Cat Whistle**[37] 2405 3-9-4 **80**.. TonyHamilton 5 70+
(R A Fahey) *in rr: hdwy on wd outside 2f out: hung-rt: styd on wl ins fnl f* **16/1**
5505 **5** ½ **Woodnook**[32] 2530 5-9-11 **80**.. PatDobbs 8 70
(J A R Toller) *trckd ldrs: kpt on same pce appr fnl f* **8/1**[3]
2561 **6** nk **Dorn Dancer (IRE)**[9] 3260 6-8-13 **73**................... DanielleMcCreery(5) 7 62
(D W Barker) *prom on outer: kpt on same pce appr fnl f* **9/1**
5100 **7** hd **Valley Of The Moon (IRE)**[15] 3056 4-9-9 **78**................. PaulHanagan 4 67
(R A Fahey) *hld up in midfield: effrt 2f out: kpt on: nvr trbld ldrs* **10/1**
-056 **8** nk **Misphire**[9] 3260 5-9-5 **74**..(b) DarryllHolland 9 62
(M Dods) *s.i.s: hdwy on outside over 4f out: rdn and one pce over 1f out* **4/1**[2]
-032 **9** 2½ **Shes Minnie**[48] 2077 5-9-9 **78**.. ChrisCatlin 2 58
(P A Blockley) *checked after 110yds: nvr nr ldrs* **10/1**
0605 **10** 2½ **Anosti**[12] 3141 3-9-2 **78**..(b[1]) DO'Donohoe 3 48
(K A Ryan) *s.i.s: nvr on terms* **10/1**
0123 **11** 5 **Loose Caboose (IRE)**[53] 1934 3-9-3 **79**.........................(p) NeilPollard 11 33
(A J McCabe) *chsd ldrs: lost pl over 1f out* **20/1**

1m 17.01s (0.11) **Going Correction** +0.125s/f (Good)
WFA 3 from 4yo+ 7lb **11** Ran SP% **119.9**
Speed ratings (Par 104): **104,99,96,95,95 94,94,93,90,87 80**
toteswinger: 1&2 £5.60, 1&3 £15.70, 2&3 £36.50. CSF £31.34 CT £386.38 TOTE £4.00: £1.80, £3.20, £5.30; EX 29.80.
Owner Brian Morton **Bred** A G Antoniades **Trained** Newmarket, Suffolk
■ Stewards' Enquiry : Francis Norton one-day ban: failed to ride to draw (Jul 14)

FOCUS
Some very useful sprinting fillies turned up for this handicap, won by the in-form and enterprisingly-ridden Mick Quinn representative, who was continuing the resurgence of that yard.

NOTEBOOK
Mango Music is clearly thriving at the moment, and this was her third success in five starts since the beginning of May. Despite this she was still racing off a rating 3lb lower than her highest winning mark, which she carried to victory at Sandown in the September of her three-year-old year, and while this victory owed much to the enterprising tactics of Norton, she still will not be badly handicapped once reassessed. (tchd 10-3 tchd 7-2 in places)
Swift Princess(IRE) came from well off the pace with a strong run and was unlucky to come up against an obviously well-handicapped mare who had the run of things to boot. She will not be long in adding to her Redcar gains if she keeps running to this standard. (op 8-1)
Katie Boo(IRE), who is in foal, tends to stay in form once she hits it, and after a period in the doldrums this effort perhaps gave notice that she is finally coming to hand. (tchd 18-1)
Cat Whistle had to come widest of all around the home turn but performed easily the best of the trio of three-year-olds on show. She will do better still when she learns to settle. Official explanation: jockey said filly hung right-handed
Woodnook is pretty harshly handicapped for what she has achieved on turf, hence her frequent appearances in Listed company, and while this was a perfectly respectable effort, she needs to drop a few pounds if she is going to get her head in front. (tchd 15-2)
Misphire, who had shaped as though comng to hand on her last two starts, could never get into the race on this occasion. (op 9-2)

3555 WAYNE CONWAY MEMORIAL H'CAP 1m 4f 8y
4:15 (4:17) (Class 5) (0-70,70) 3-Y-O **£3,238** (£963; £481; £240) **Stalls** Low

Form RPR
1104 **1** **Cape Colony**[18] 2977 3-9-7 **70**.. PatDobbs 7 80
(R Hannon) *hld up in rr: hdwy over 3f out: led 1f out: hld on wl* **8/1**[3]
5640 **2** nk **My Mate Max**[18] 2977 3-9-7 **70**..................................... DarryllHolland 13 79
(R Hollinshead) *mid-div: hdwy 3f out: wnt cl 2nd jst ins fnl f: kpt on towards fin* **10/1**
40-6 **3** 7 **Hawk Mountain (UAE)**[27] 2700 3-8-6 **55** ow2......... GrahamGibbons 14 53+
(J J Quinn) *rr-div: hdwy 3f out: kpt on fnl f* **14/1**
-003 **4** ½ **Marie Tempest**[22] 2868 3-8-2 **51** oh1................................ FrancisNorton 4 48
(B W Hills) *t.k.h in rr: hdwy on ins over 3f out: one pce fnl 2f* **20/1**
0002 **5** 1 **Golden Bishop**[18] 2984 3-8-13 **62**.................................. JamieSpencer 5 58
(M L W Bell) *trckd ldrs: led and rdn 2f out: hdd 1f out: wknd* **7/4**[1]
00-0 **6** 5 **Jackday (IRE)**[33] 2496 3-8-10 **59**...................................... DavidAllan 16 47
(T D Easterby) *hld up in rr: sme hdwy 3f out: nvr nr ldrs* **20/1**
-103 **7** 5 **Mista Rossa**[41] 2280 3-9-4 **70**...................................... TravisBlock(3) 15 50
(H Morrison) *rr-div: effrt over 3f out: wknd over 1f out* **9/2**[2]
6346 **8** 6 **Zaplamation (IRE)**[12] 3126 3-7-11 **51** oh5.......... DanielleMcCreery(5) 10 21
(D W Barker) *hld up in rr: hdwy over 3f out: plld wd 2f out: sn wknd* **33/1**
006 **9** 15 **Royal Avenue (IRE)**[41] 2269 3-8-9 **58**................................ MickyFenton 1 4
(T D Easterby) *mid-div: short-lived effrt 3f out: wknd* **50/1**
350 **10** 8 **Boy Racer (IRE)**[44] 2207 3-9-4 **67**...................................... GregFairley 8 —
(M Johnston) *mid-div: effrt over 3f out: lost pl over 2f out* **20/1**
0-01 **11** 3 **Patthepainter (GER)**[19] 2926 3-8-7 **56**.....................(b) AndrewElliott 11 —
(K R Burke) *set str pce: hdd & wknd 2f out: sn bhd* **12/1**
0-30 **12** 2½ **Fortunella**[12] 3133 3-8-2 **51**.. ChrisCatlin 6 —
(P Howling) *bhd and sn pushed along: nvr on terms* **33/1**
-000 **13** 8 **Harlequinn Danseur (IRE)**[12] 3126 3-8-2 **51** oh6............ KimTinkler 12 —
(N Tinkler) *in tch: rdn and lost pl 3f out* **100/1**
-153 **14** 1½ **Sheer Fantastic**[52] 1950 3-8-12 **66**....................(b) PatrickDonaghy(5) 3 —
(P C Haslam) *chsd ldrs: wknd qckly over 2f out* **11/1**
0-00 **15** 19 **Mathool (IRE)**[35] 2468 3-8-2 **51** oh6.................................... PaulEddery 9 —
(C W Thornton) *prom: reminders over 5f out: lost pl 4f out: t.o 2f out* **100/1**
-040 **16** 19 **Princess Maria (USA)**[18] 2984 3-8-2 **51** oh4..................... PaulHanagan 2 —
(R A Fahey) *chsd ldrs: lost pl over 3f out: t.o 2f out* **40/1**

2m 39.2s (-1.60) **Going Correction** +0.125s/f (Good) **16** Ran SP% **124.0**
Speed ratings (Par 99): **110,109,105,104,104 100,97,93,83,78 76,74,69,68,55 42**
toteswinger: 1&2 £18.70, 1&3 £26.30, 2&3 £29.40. CSF £78.34 CT £1122.88 TOTE £9.90: £1.90, £2.80, £2.90, £3.70; EX 71.70.
Owner P D Merritt **Bred** Allan Merritt **Trained** East Everleigh, Wilts

FOCUS
Only a fair handicap, but the first two home pulled well clear and with the pace strong they clocked a decent winning time to boot.

3556 WILFRED UNDERWOOD MEMORIAL MAIDEN FILLIES' STKS 1m 2f 6y
4:45 (4:45) (Class 5) 3-4-Y-O **£3,238** (£963; £481; £240) **Stalls** Low

Form RPR
32 **1** **Lee Miller (IRE)**[24] 2800 3-9-0 0.. JamieSpencer 2 83
(L M Cumani) *trckd ldrs: chal over 2f out: sn rdn: wnt lft ins fnl f: led last 50yds: all out* **8/11**[1]
-622 **2** nk **Siyasa (USA)**[18] 2973 3-9-0 77..............................(p) KerrinMcEvoy 1 82
(Saeed Bin Suroor) *led: qcknd 3f out: rdn and hung lft over 1f out: bmpd ins fnl f: hdd towards fin* **9/4**[2]

00 3 13 **Miss Serena**[15] 3058 3-9-0 0 .... MickyFenton 5 56
(Mrs P Sly) *hld up in rr: shkn up to chse ldrs 6f out: one pce fnl 2f* **66/1**

4 ½ **Proficiency** 3-9-0 0 .... GrahamGibbons 7 55
(T D Walford) *sn chsng ldrs: one pce fnl 2f* **66/1**

5 5 **Etta Place** 3-9-0 0 .... AlanMunro 3 45
(P W Chapple-Hyam) *mid-div: effrt 4f out: lost pl over 2f out* **20/1**

0- 6 11 **Ghizlaan (USA)**[261] 6184 3-9-0 0 .... GregFairley 4 23
(M Johnston) *trckd ldrs: drvn over 5f out: lost pl over 2f out: sn bhd* **8/1**[3]

00 7 10 **Faraway Bay**[8] 3297 3-9-0 0 .... ChrisCatlin 6 —
(E J O'Neill) *in rr: effrt and hung rt 4f out: sn lost pl* **100/1**

2m 14.74s (1.04) **Going Correction** +0.125s/f (Good) **7 Ran SP% 108.5**
Speed ratings (Par 100): **100,99,89,88,84 76,68**
toteswinger: 1&2 £1.10, 1&3 £9.60, 2&3 £7.10. CSF £2.17 TOTE £1.80: £1.20, £1.10; EX 2.50.
Owner Scuderia Rencati Srl **Bred** Razza Della Sila S R L **Trained** Newmarket, Suffolk
■ Stewards' Enquiry : Jamie Spencer caution: careless riding

FOCUS
No strength in depth to this weak fillies' maiden which boiled down to a two-horse race, though the two concerned are useful sorts.

3557 BEST UK RACECOURSES ON TURFTV H'CAP — 1m 4y
5:15 (5:15) (Class 5) (0-75,75) 3-Y-O+ **£3,238** (£963; £481; £240) **Stalls** Low

Form RPR

0245 1 **Aussie Blue (IRE)**[10] 3229 4-9-0 **59** .... MichaelJStainton(3) 4 69
(R M Whitaker) *hld up towards rr: gd hdwy over 1f out: styd on wl ins fnl f: led last stride* **9/2**[2]

-061 2 shd **San Antonio**[11] 3175 8-10-0 **70** .... (b) MickyFenton 8 80
(Mrs P Sly) *chsd ldr: led over 2f out: clr over 1f out: hdd post* **8/1**

-030 3 1¼ **Myfrenchconnection (IRE)**[19] 2925 4-9-3 **59** .... FrankieMcDonald 3 66
(P T Midgley) *trckd ldrs: hung lft and wnt 2nd over 1f out: styd on same pce* **5/1**[3]

2641 4 3¼ **Pianoforte (USA)**[19] 2940 6-9-8 **64** .... (b) DavidAllan 10 64
(E J Alston) *swtchd lft after s: hld up in rr: gd hdwy over 1f out: kpt on: nvr trbld ldrs* **14/1**

02-0 5 1¾ **Thanxforthat (USA)**[44] 2208 3-8-2 **61** .... JamieKyne(7) 5 55
(J J Quinn) *chsd ldrs on outer: effrt over 2f out: hung lft: one pce fnl 2f* **20/1**

0014 6 2¾ **Boy Dancer (IRE)**[14] 3082 5-9-0 **56** .... GrahamGibbons 9 45
(J J Quinn) *hld up in rr: effrt 3f out: kpt on appr fnl f: nvr nr ldrs* **7/1**

1204 7 ¾ **Kildare Sun (IRE)**[42] 2262 6-9-8 **67** .... PJMcDonald(3) 11 54
(J Mackie) *hld up in rr: hdwy 3f out: kpt on: edgd lft ins fnl f nvr nr ldrs* **14/1**

4-06 8 4 **Very Well Red**[138] 537 5-9-13 **69** .... ChrisCatlin 2 47
(P W Hiatt) *t.k.h in midfield: effrt over 3f out: wknd over 1f out* **18/1**

000/ 9 1½ **Super King**[930] 6573 7-8-9 **51** oh6 .... AndrewElliott 1 26
(A D Brown) *in rr: kpt on fnl 2f: nvr on terms* **100/1**

0031 10 ½ **Chin Wag (IRE)**[10] 3201 4-9-4 **60** .... (p) PaulHanagan 6 34
(J S Goldie) *chsd ldrs: effrt over 2f out: hung lft over 1f out: wkng whn sltly hmpd ins fnl f* **7/2**[1]

0000 11 25 **Provost**[19] 2925 4-8-13 **62** .... BradleyRoper(7) 12 —
(M W Easterby) *set str pce: hdd over 2f out: wknd over 1f out: sn bhd: t.o* **33/1**

1-5 12 40 **River Ardeche**[52] 1949 3-9-9 **75** .... JamieSpencer 7 —
(P C Haslam) *hld up: hdwy on outer to trck ldrs 6f out: hung bdly rt and lost pl over 2f: sn t.o and virtually p.u* **15/2**

1m 46.17s (0.27) **Going Correction** +0.125s/f (Good)
WFA 3 from 4yo+ 10lb **12 Ran SP% 119.7**
Speed ratings (Par 103): **103,102,101,98,96 93,93,89,87,87 62,22**
toteswinger: 1&2 £8.70, 1&3 £5.30, 2&3 £11.90. CSF £40.29 CT £193.02 TOTE £5.70: £2.00, £3.60, £2.00; EX 35.90 Place 6: £313.48 Place 5: £154.49.
Owner T L Adams **Bred** T L Adams & G F Pemberton **Trained** Scarcroft, W Yorks

FOCUS
A modest handicap though the pace was sound enough..
River Ardeche Official explanation: jockey said gelding hung violently right
T/Plt: £580.50 to a £1 stake. Pool: £88,750.68. 111.60 winning tickets. T/Qpdt: £123.20 to a £1 stake. Pool: £3,496.29. 21.00 winning tickets. WG

3525 WINDSOR (R-H)
Monday, June 30

OFFICIAL GOING: Good to firm (8.1)
Wind: Light, half behind Weather: Sunny, warm

3558 PLAY VIDEO POKER AT TOTESPORTCASINO.COM FILLIES' MEDIAN AUCTION MAIDEN STKS — 5f 10y
6:40 (6:41) (Class 5) 2-Y-O **£2,729** (£806; £403) **Stalls** High

Form RPR

1 **Queen Of Thebes (IRE)** 2-9-0 0 .... SteveDrowne 4 75+
(G L Moore) *pressed ldr: hung lft over 1f out: sn led: in command ins fnl f* **13/2**

333 2 1¾ **Like For Like (IRE)**[14] 3092 2-9-0 0 .... RichardHughes 8 69
(R Hannon) *led: hung bdly lft and hdd jst over 1f out: continued to hang and nt qckn* **11/10**[1]

3 ½ **Touching (IRE)** 2-9-0 0 .... RyanMoore 5 67+
(R Hannon) *trckd ldrs: prog to chal over 1f out: one pce fnl f* **5/1**[3]

4 4½ **Ruby Tallulah** 2-8-11 0 .... KirstyMilczarek(3) 1 51
(N P Littmoden) *veered lft s: bhd in last pair: stdy prog fr 1/2-way: outpcd wl over 1f out: kpt on* **33/1**

0 5 nk **Anjuna (USA)**[16] 3027 2-9-0 0 .... JimmyFortune 10 50
(J H M Gosden) *trckd ldng pair: outpcd fr 2f out: edgd lft and fdd* **9/2**[2]

6 1½ **Imaginary Diva** 2-9-0 0 .... DaneO'Neill 2 45
(G G Margarson) *dwlt: rcvrd to chse ldrs: rdn 1/2-way: wknd wl over 1f out* **20/1**

7 2¼ **Dancing Delta** 2-9-0 0 .... MartinDwyer 6 36
(W R Muir) *chsd ldrs but sn pushed along: outpcd bef 1/2-way: toiling after* **20/1**

8 2¾ **Southoffrance (IRE)** 2-8-9 0 .... JackDean(5) 7 27
(W G M Turner) *chsd ldrs 2f: sn rdn and lost tch* **66/1**

9 1 **Silver Salsa** 2-9-0 0 .... JimCrowley 9 23+
(J R Jenkins) *s.s: outpcd and a in last pair* **20/1**

60.67 secs (0.37) **Going Correction** -0.10s/f (Good) **9 Ran SP% 114.5**
Speed ratings (Par 90): **93,90,89,82,81 79,75,71,69**
toteswinger: 1&2 £3.00, 1&3 £4.40, 2&3 £1.10. CSF £13.15 TOTE £8.00: £1.80, £1.10, £1.70; EX 17.60.
Owner The Horse Players **Bred** Michael Dalton **Trained** Woodingdean, E Sussex

FOCUS
An ordinary juvenile fillies' maiden. The runner-up sets the level.

NOTEBOOK
Queen Of Thebes(IRE), a half-sister to five winners at up to 1m3f, got her career off to a perfect start and ran out a ready winner. She ran green when asked to get to the lead nearing the final furlong, tending to edge left, but was soon on top thereafter. She looked suited by the quick surface and this bodes well for her future as her breeding suggests she will come into her own over a longer trip. (op 7-1 tchd 6-1, 15-2 in places)
Like For Like(IRE), third on her previous three outings, showed early dash yet tended to hang pretty much throughout and she could not go with the winner at the business end. She has ability, but is becoming exposed now and a switch to nurseries may be her best option. Official explanation: jockey said filly lost a front shoe (op 5-4 tchd 11-8 in places)
Touching(IRE), who cost 45,000gns, proved easy to back ahead of this racecourse bow as the money came for her stable companion. She ran accordingly, finishing just off that rival, and left the impression she would get closer next time out. Another furlong now looks a wise move too. (op 4-1 tchd 7-2)
Ruby Tallulah, a cheap purchase whose pedigree suggests both speed and stamina, proved distinctly green through the first half of the race. She began to get the hang of things in the final two furlongs, however, and did more than enough to suggest she would improve for the experience. (op 25-1)
Anjuna(USA) showed a more professional attitude this time, but was unable to raise her game from the two-furlong pole. She needs more time and probably easier ground than this. (tchd 5-1)

3559 TOTESPORTGAMES.COM (S) STKS — 6f
7:10 (7:11) (Class 6) 3-Y-O+ **£2,047** (£604; £302) **Stalls** High

Form RPR

6400 1 **Game Lady**[34] 2474 4-8-12 51 .... RyanMoore 16 62
(I A Wood) *pressed ldrs: swtchd off rail 2f out: effrt to ld jst over 1f out: rdn clr* **11/1**

3306 2 2¾ **High Reach**[16] 3021 8-9-8 55 .... (p) JimCrowley 10 63
(J G M O'Shea) *t.k.h: sn pressed ldr: rdn to ld briefly over 1f out: outpcd fnl f* **11/1**

0503 3 ½ **Green Lagonda (AUS)**[9] 3281 6-9-3 60 .... RichardHughes 12 56
(J G Given) *taken down early: trckd ldrs: effrt 2f out: styd on to press for 2nd ins fnl f: no ch w wnr* **13/8**[1]

6000 4 2 **Monashee Prince (IRE)**[2] 3506 6-9-3 53 .... (v) MartinDwyer 13 50
(J R Best) *pressed ldrs: rdn over 2f out: fdd fnl f* **10/1**

2350 5 1 **Mr Rooney (IRE)**[13] 3112 5-9-3 55 .... AdrianTNicholls 3 47
(D Nicholls) *led and sn crossed to nr side rail: drvn and hdd over 1f out: fdd* **6/1**[2]

-350 6 ¾ **Half A Tsar (IRE)**[7] 3316 4-8-12 50 .... JackDean(5) 4 44+
(Mark Gillard) *racd on outer: wl in rr: rdn over 2f out: kpt on fr over 1f out: nvr on terms* **40/1**

7 ½ **Lauras Joy (IRE)**[282] 5651 5-8-12 40 .... DaneO'Neill 8 38+
(G P Enright) *hld up in last pair: rdn over 2f out: no prog whn nt clr run over 1f out: picked up fnl 150yds and fin wl* **66/1**

5140 8 ½ **Marko Jadeo (IRE)**[7] 3313 10-9-5 62 .... KevinGhunowa(3) 7 46
(R A Harris) *taken down early: mostly in midfield: pushed along 1/2-way: effrt towards outer 2f out: one pce and no imp* **8/1**

-000 9 ½ **Indian Lady (IRE)**[34] 2474 5-8-9 40 .... (b) KirstyMilczarek(3) 9 35
(Mrs A L M King) *trckd ldrs: stl cl enough u.p over 1f out: wknd rapidly fnl f* **66/1**

3104 10 ¾ **Jal Music**[22] 2864 3-9-1 67 .... MohammedSaeed 5 40
(R A Harris) *racd on outer: prom: wkng whn rdr unbalanced 1f out* **7/1**[3]

0-00 11 ½ **Peruvian Style (IRE)**[3] 3446 7-9-3 47 .... (p) SteveDrowne 6 36
(J M Bradley) *a wl in rr: no ch whn edgd lft over 1f out* **33/1**

0015 12 1 **Currency**[3] 3446 11-9-8 54 .... StephenCarson 14 37
(J M Bradley) *a wl in rr: no prog fnl 2f* **14/1**

-000 13 1 **Jimmy Dean**[7] 3330 3-8-10 40 .... (b) LiamJones 1 27
(M Wellings) *racd on outer: nvr on terms: struggling over 2f out* **100/1**

000/ 14 shd **Neat 'n Tidy**[144] 5563 4-8-13 49 ow1 .... AdamKirby 2 25
(A E Jones) *racd on wd outside: in tch: reminder wl over 1f out: sn eased* **100/1**

0006 15 1½ **Scarlett Heart (IRE)**[24] 2802 4-8-12 51 .... (b[1]) PaulDoe 11 19
(S Curran) *s.s: wl in rr: effrt u.p 1/2-way: sn btn* **14/1**

1m 12.65s (-0.35) **Going Correction** -0.10s/f (Good)
WFA 3 from 4yo+ 7lb **15 Ran SP% 125.4**
Speed ratings (Par 101): **98,94,93,91,89 88,88,87,86,85 85,83,82,82,80**
toteswinger: 1&2 £1.10, 1&3 £1.80, 2&3 £3.80. CSF £128.48 TOTE £13.70: £3.40, £4.70, £1.40; EX 276.00.Green Lagonda was claimed by Stef Liddiard for £6,000. There was no bid for the winner.
Owner C S Tateson **Bred** The Hon Mrs E J Wills **Trained** Upper Lambourn, Berks

FOCUS
A moderate, yet open seller. The form is rated around the third and fourth.
Lauras Joy(IRE) Official explanation: jockey said mare hung right on the good to firm ground
Jal Music Official explanation: jockey said gelding hung left

3560 TOTESPORTCASINO.COM H'CAP — 1m 67y
7:40 (7:40) (Class 4) (0-85,85) 3-Y-O **£5,504** (£1,637; £818; £408) **Stalls** High

Form RPR

-212 1 **Lindelaan (USA)**[19] 2953 3-9-7 **85** .... (v) RyanMoore 1 97
(Sir Michael Stoute) *hld up early off fierce pce: clsd fr 1/2-way: rdn 2f out: sn chalng: led ins fnl f: drew away* **5/6**[1]

2451 2 4 **Brave Hawk**[7] 3325 3-9-0 **78** 6ex .... (p) PhilipRobinson 4 81
(M A Jarvis) *trckd ldng pair at str pce: rdn to ld 2f out: hdd & wknd ins fnl f* **5/2**[2]

3141 3 1 **Marning Star**[9] 3263 3-9-1 **79** .... AdrianTNicholls 5 80
(D Nicholls) *led at v str pce but pressed: hdd 2f out: plugged on but outpcd fnl f* **8/1**[3]

U350 4 3¾ **Ten Pole Tudor**[34] 2481 3-8-10 **77** .... KevinGhunowa(3) 6 69
(R A Harris) *hld up off fierce early pce: clsd 1/2-way: taken towards outer and cl enough 2f out: sn wknd* **33/1**

2630 5 3½ **Rich Kid (IRE)**[18] 2974 3-8-7 **71** .... (p) LiamJones 3 55
(R A Harris) *s.i.s: hld up off fierce early pce: rdn to cl over 3f out: in tch on wd outside 2f out: sn wknd* **11/1**

0600 6 nk **Meydan Dubai (IRE)**[1] 3527 3-9-6 **84** .... MohammedSaeed 2 67
(J R Best) *pressed furious early pce: wknd over 2f out* **10/1**

1m 43.62s (-1.08) **Going Correction** -0.025s/f (Good) **6 Ran SP% 114.6**
Speed ratings (Par 101): **104,100,99,95,91 91**
toteswinger: 1&2 £1.10, 1&3 £1.80, 2&3 £3.80. CSF £3.23 TOTE £1.90: £1.20, £2.00; EX 3.50.
Owner Mrs R J Jacobs **Bred** Kinsman Farm **Trained** Newmarket, Suffolk
■ Stewards' Enquiry : Ryan Moore two-day ban: careless riding (Jul 14,15)

FOCUS
A fair little handicap for three-year-olds. It was run at a very strong early pace which suited the winner and she posted a personal-best.

3561 PLAY BLACKJACK AT TOTESPORTCASINO.COM H'CAP 1m 2f 7y
8:10 (8:10) (Class 4) (0-80,80) 3-Y-0+ **£4,533** (£1,348; £674; £336) **Stalls** Low

Form RPR
-034 **1** **Australia Day (IRE)**[14] 3090 5-9-2 **68** MartinDwyer 5 86+
(P R Webber) *racd freely: mde all: qcknd clr over 3f out: unchal after: eased fnl 100yds* **6/1**[3]
320- **2** *8* **Beverly Hill Billy**[332] 3590 4-9-13 **79** RichardHughes 6 79+
(A King) *hld up in last pair and wl bhd: stl in last pair over 2f out: prog on outer and nt clr run over 1f out: styd on to take 2nd ins fnl f: hopeless task* **14/1**
2165 **3** *1* **Emperor Court (IRE)**[17] 3003 4-10-0 **80** RyanMoore 7 78+
(P J Makin) *plld hrd early: hld up in last pair and wl bhd: stl in last pair over 2f out: swtchd to wd outside and prog wl over 1f out: disp 2nd fr 1f out: hopeless task* **7/2**[2]
-030 **4** *1 1/4* **Good Effect (USA)**[20] 2921 4-9-3 **69** DaneO'Neill 9 65
(C P Morlock) *hld up towards rr: prog over 3f out: drvn to chse clr wnr over 1f out: no ch: one pce fnl f* **10/1**
1200 **5** *2 1/2* **Proper (IRE)**[17] 3010 4-9-8 **74** WilliamBuick 10 65
(C J Mann) *prom in chsng gp: rdn over 3f out: disp 2nd 2f out but no ch w wnr: fdd fnl f* **14/1**
3604 **6** *hd* **Harry Gee**[27] 2699 3-8-11 **75** SteveDrowne 8 65
(G Wragg) *in tch in chsng gp: rdn over 3f out: no imp fnl 2f* **10/3**[1]
2-30 **7** *2 1/4* **Touch Of Style (IRE)**[12] 3132 4-9-5 **71** (p) AmirQuinn 4 57
(J R Boyle) *chsd wnr after 2f: rdn and outpcd over 3f out: wknd wl over 1f out* **25/1**
2/4- **8** *4* **Golden Feather**[43] 4184 6-9-12 **78** GeorgeBaker 12 56
(O Sherwood) *prom in chsng gp: u.p over 3f out: steadily wknd* **14/1**
0-50 **9** *hd* **Risque Heights**[148] 417 4-9-10 **76** PatCosgrave 11 53
(J R Boyle) *hld up in rr: effrt whn nt clr run over 2f out: shkn up and no prog after* **14/1**
4-26 **10** *12* **Jill Dawson (IRE)**[26] 2718 5-8-9 **64** KirstyMilczarek(3) 3 17
(John Berry) *chsd wnr 2f: prom after: rdn 4f out: wknd rapidly 2f out* **12/1**
1336 **11** *6* **Scamperdale**[32] 2531 6-10-0 **80** TPQueally 2 21
(B P J Baugh) *hld up towards rr: rdn and prog 3f out: disp 2nd 2f out but no ch w wnr: wknd rapidly over 1f out* **8/1**

2m 6.50s (-2.20) **Going Correction** -0.025s/f (Good)
WFA 3 from 4yo+ 12lb **11 Ran SP% 118.0**
Speed ratings (Par 105): **107,100,99,98,96 96,94,91,91,81 77**
toteswinger: 1&2 £6.70, 1&3 £4.00, 2&3 £31.70. CSF £87.07 CT £341.11 TOTE £7.60: £2.30, £3.70, £2.10.
Owner Samantha & Emma McQuiston Partnership **Bred** Kenilworth House Stud **Trained** Mollington, Oxon

FOCUS
A fair handicap which saw the winner score easily having been gifted an uncontested lead.
Scamperdale Official explanation: trainer said gelding was unsuited by the good to firm ground

3562 PLAY ROULETTE AT TOTESPORTCASINO.COM FILLIES' H'CAP 1m 3f 135y
8:40 (8:40) (Class 5) (0-70,69) 3-Y-0+ **£2,729** (£806; £403) **Stalls** Low

Form RPR
0-02 **1** **Cosmea**[10] 3206 3-8-10 **64** DaneO'Neill 7 73
(A King) *hld up in midfield: prog over 3f out: led 2f out: rdn clr over 1f out: readily* **5/1**[2]
-113 **2** *2 3/4* **Susie May**[10] 3220 4-10-0 **68** RyanMoore 5 73
(G L Moore) *hld up in last trio: prog u.p fr over 3f out: styd on grimly to take 2nd ins fnl f: no ch w wnr* **11/4**[1]
5101 **3** *1* **Naughty Thoughts (IRE)**[17] 3010 4-9-4 **65** RossAtkinson(7) 4 68
(Tom Dascombe) *hld up in rr: stdy prog over 3f out: rdn to chal 2f out: nt qckn wl over 1f out: lost 2nd ins fnl f* **5/1**[2]
0304 **4** *1* **Sabancaya**[7] 3327 3-8-6 **60** LiamJones 12 61
(W J Haggas) *w ldr: led 6f out to 2f out: one pce u.p* **8/1**
3336 **5** *hd* **Sea Chorus**[24] 2785 3-9-0 **68** (t) HayleyTurner 9 69
(M L W Bell) *hld up wl in rr: stdy prog over 3f out: rdn and nt qckn 2f out: kpt on fnl f: n.d* **7/1**[3]
0002 **6** *3* **Kijivu**[30] 2611 3-7-10 **57** ow4 SophieDoyle(7) 1 53
(A J Lidderdale) *led to 6f out: lost pl over 3f out: stl cl up over 2f out: hanging lft and fdd* **50/1**
0-00 **7** *3* **Zia Zabel (IRE)**[28] 2668 3-8-12 **66** TPO'Shea 8 57
(J L Dunlop) *t.k.h: trckd ldrs: rdn and nt qckn 3f out: struggling fnl 2f* **25/1**
1-00 **8** *nk* **Trinkila (USA)**[20] 2920 3-8-8 **69** DTDaSilva(7) 3 59
(P F I Cole) *pressed ldrs: bmpd along over 2f out: wknd rapidly over 1f out* **40/1**
5600 **9** *4 1/2* **Spiritofthestorm (USA)**[15] 3065 3-8-3 **60** KirstyMilczarek(3) 14 43
(R A Teal) *t.k.h: trckd ldrs: effrt over 3f out: cl enough over 2f out: wknd wl over 1f out: eased* **33/1**
323- **10** *1/2* **Alecia (IRE)**[18] 7247 4-9-10 **64** TQuinn 10 46
(B G Powell) *a towards rr: rdn over 3f out: no prog over 2f out: fdd* **20/1**
6522 **11** *1 1/4* **Medieval Maiden**[11] 3160 5-8-12 **52** oh1 IanMongan 2 32
(Mrs L J Mongan) *trckd ldrs: effrt to chal over 3f out: wknd rapidly 2f out* **8/1**
000 **12** *6* **Poppy Gregg**[18] 2971 3-8-0 **54** ow2 DavidKinsella 6 23
(Dr J R J Naylor) *a in last trio: pushed along over 4f out: sn no ch* **66/1**
01 **13** *3 3/4* **Ericarrow (IRE)**[30] 2611 3-8-1 **62** DavidProbert(7) 13 25
(M F Harris) *a wl in rr: struggling fnl 3f* **16/1**
4-00 **14** *4 1/2* **Appointment**[17] 2997 3-8-8 **62** JimCrowley 11 17
(Mrs A J Perrett) *trckd ldrs tl wknd rapidly 3f out* **20/1**

2m 29.0s (-0.50) **Going Correction** -0.025s/f (Good)
WFA 3 from 4yo+ 14lb **14 Ran SP% 122.8**
Speed ratings (Par 100): **100,98,97,96,96 94,92,92,89,89 88,84,81,78**
toteswinger: 1&2 £5.70, 1&3 £8.30, 2&3 £1.20. CSF £18.05 CT £75.49 TOTE £6.50: £2.20, £1.80, £2.00; EX 22.20.
Owner Four Mile Racing **Bred** T R Lock **Trained** Barbury Castle, Wilts

FOCUS
A modest fillies' handicap, run at a sound pace, and the form looks reliable for the class.
Spiritofthestorm(USA) Official explanation: jockey said filly ran too free.

3563 OVER 100 GAMES AT TOTESPORTCASINO.COM H'CAP 1m 67y
9:10 (9:10) (Class 5) (0-70,70) 3-Y-0+ **£2,729** (£806; £403) **Stalls** High

Form RPR
5-00 **1** **Eastern Emperor**[10] 3208 4-9-13 **69** (p) AdamKirby 2 78
(W R Swinburn) *t.k.h early: cl up: effrt to chal 3f out: disp ld and drvn wl over 1f out: gained upper hand and styd on wl* **4/1**[2]
2342 **2** *1 1/4* **Follow The Flag (IRE)**[10] 3208 4-10-0 **70** GeorgeBaker 12 76
(C F Wall) *chsd ldrs: 5th and rdn over 2f out: hanging lft but styd on u.p over 1f out to take 2nd ins fnl f* **7/2**[1]
5015 **3** *1* **Batchworth Blaise**[10] 3218 5-8-9 **51** oh2 StephenCarson 7 55
(E A Wheeler) *dwlt: hld up in last pair: wl adrift 4f out: prog fr 3f out: drvn and styd on to take 3rd nr fin: nvr nrr* **16/1**
0-22 **4** *3/4* **Stand In Flames**[16] 3023 3-8-13 **65** ShaneKelly 8 65
(Pat Eddery) *t.k.h: prom: effrt 3f out: drvn to dispute ld wl over 1f out: fdd fnl f* **7/2**[1]
-036 **5** *hd* **Trevian**[5] 3360 7-8-9 **51** oh1 RyanMoore 10 53
(J M Bradley) *mde most at str pce to wl over 1f out: fdd* **14/1**
6-50 **6** *4 1/2* **Thunder Gorge (USA)**[18] 2976 3-9-4 **70** JimCrowley 1 59
(Mouse Hamilton-Fairley) *stdd s: hld up in last pair: wl adrift over 3f out: reminder 2f out: styd on fr over 1f out: nvr nr ldrs* **20/1**
0503 **7** *1 1/2* **Chicken George (IRE)**[10] 3229 4-9-12 **68** AdrianTNicholls 9 56
(D Nicholls) *dwlt: a off the pce towards rr: outpcd 3f out: v modest late prog* **11/2**[3]
-665 **8** *1* **Timber Creek**[17] 2994 3-9-2 **68** (v[1]) DaneO'Neill 11 52
(H Candy) *hld up in midfield: outpcd by ldrs over 3f out: tried to cl over 2f out but nt qckn: wknd over 1f out* **16/1**
00-0 **9** *2 1/4* **Rosentraub**[68] 1573 3-9-1 **67** SteveDrowne 4 46
(H J L Dunlop) *hld up in rr: brief effrt over 3f out: sn btn* **33/1**
-000 **10** *1 3/4* **Black Or Red (IRE)**[35] 2451 3-8-11 **63** RichardThomas 6 38
(I A Wood) *nvr on terms: rdn and struggling 4f out* **50/1**
1205 **11** *1 1/2* **Glenridding**[13] 3108 4-9-10 **66** TPQueally 5 39
(J G Given) *w ldr to over 2f out: wknd rapidly* **10/1**

1m 44.24s (-0.46) **Going Correction** -0.025s/f (Good)
WFA 3 from 4yo+ 10lb **11 Ran SP% 117.0**
Speed ratings (Par 103): **101,99,98,98,97 93,91,90,88,86 85**
toteswinger: 1&2 £5.50, 1&3 £104.20, 2&3 £112.10. CSF £17.94 CT £205.99 TOTE £5.60: £2.10, £1.70, £5.40; EX 19.90 Place 6: £9.47, Place 5: £7.13..
Owner The "A" Team **Bred** Alan Parker **Trained** Aldbury, Herts

FOCUS
A modest handicap, but run at a decent pace. The second and fourth set the standard.
Stand In Flames Official explanation: trainer's rep said filly was unsuited by the good to firm ground
T/Jkpt: £43,033.10 to a £1 stake. Pool: £333,355.56. 5.50 winning tickets. T/Plt: £13.10 to a £1 stake. Pool: £145,053.94. 8,054.21 winning tickets. T/Qpdt: £6.30 to a £1 stake. Pool: £5,965.10. 696.40 winning tickets. JN

3328 WOLVERHAMPTON (A.W) (L-H)
Monday, June 30

OFFICIAL GOING: Standard
Wind: Light, half behind Weather: Fine

3564 AT-TOOLCENTRE.CO.UK H'CAP 5f 216y(P)
2:30 (2:32) (Class 6) (0-65,65) 3-Y-0 **£2,388** (£705; £352) **Stalls** Low

Form RPR
0-36 **1** **Bishopbriggs (USA)**[37] 2396 3-9-7 **65** LeeEnstone 12 71
(S Parr) *mde all: rdn wl over 1f out: r.o* **16/1**
1-63 **2** *1 1/4* **Romantic Verse**[14] 3086 3-9-4 **62** LiamJones 1 64
(W J Haggas) *chsd ldrs: pushed along over 2f out: edgd lft jst over 1f out: r.o u.p to take 2nd cl home* **4/1**[2]
4334 **3** *1/2* **Splash The Cash**[8] 3298 3-9-2 **60** TedDurcan 8 60
(K A Ryan) *a.p: chsd wnr over 2f out: rdn over 1f out: nt qckn: lost 2nd cl home* **5/1**[3]
3400 **4** *1/2* **Imperial Djay (IRE)**[28] 2674 3-9-7 **65** (v[1]) DNolan 9 64
(D Carroll) *hld up in mid-div: rdn and hdwy whn hung lft 1f out: kpt on ins fnl f* **10/1**
0-60 **5** *nk* **Bohobe (IRE)**[20] 2911 3-9-7 **65** TPQueally 10 63
(J G Given) *a.p: rdn over 2f out: nt qckn ins fnl f* **16/1**
0-63 **6** *1 1/2* **Sir Ike (IRE)**[17] 2991 3-9-5 **63** FergusSweeney 11 56+
(W S Kittow) *hld up in mid-div: pushed along and hdwy on outside over 2f out: no imp fnl f* **5/2**[1]
-560 **7** *shd* **Annes Rocket (IRE)**[25] 2760 3-9-5 **63** LPKeniry 3 56
(J C Fox) *hld up and bhd: hdwy on ins wl over 1f out: sn rdn and n.m.r: no further prog fnl f* **20/1**
0000 **8** *5* **Young Ivanhoe**[36] 2429 3-9-6 **64** JohnEgan 5 41
(C A Dwyer) *chsd wnr tl rdn over 2f out: wkng whn n.m.r jst over 1f out* **14/1**
-216 **9** *hd* **Straight (IRE)**[69] 1548 3-9-0 **61** MarkLawson(3) 6 37
(M Brittain) *chsd ldrs over 2f* **12/1**
64-0 **10** *1/2* **Wreningham**[17] 3000 3-9-4 **65** JerryO'Dwyer(3) 7 39
(T Keddy) *hld up in mid-div: rdn over 2f out: sn bhd* **16/1**
2100 **11** *1 3/4* **Flying Indian**[23] 2850 3-9-1 **62** TolleyDean(3) 2 31
(J Balding) *s.i.s: a in rr* **16/1**
0-30 **12** *3* **Towy Boy (IRE)**[69] 1548 3-9-4 **62** SebSanders 4 21
(I A Wood) *s.i.s: a towards rr* **8/1**

1m 15.9s (0.90) **Going Correction** +0.075s/f (Slow) **12 Ran SP% 128.1**
Speed ratings (Par 97): **97,95,94,94,93 91,91,84,84,83 81,77**
toteswinger: 1&2 £8.40, 1&3 £9.00, 2&3 £4.40. CSF £85.39 CT £392.09 TOTE £20.90: £5.40, £1.50, £2.30; EX 110.40 Trifecta £286.30 Part won..
Owner Willie McKay **Bred** Sycamore Hall Farm Llc **Trained** Bawtry, S Yorks
■ Stewards' Enquiry : Liam Jones caution: careless riding

FOCUS
A very modest sprint handicap run at an ordinary pace and very few ever got into it. The third is the best guide to the form.
Towy Boy(IRE) Official explanation: jokey said the colt had no more to give.

3565 BETDAQ THE BETTING EXCHANGE (S) STKS 5f 20y(P)
3:00 (3:00) (Class 6) 3-Y-0+ **£2,047** (£604; £302) **Stalls** Low

Form RPR
2231 **1** **Hurricane Hen**[105] 917 3-9-4 67 PatCosgrave 3 74
(P D Evans) *mde all: shkn up and wnt clr over 1f out: pushed out* **2/1**[1]
2635 **2** *3 1/4* **Night Prospector**[6] 3346 8-9-2 56 (p) KevinGhunowa(3) 7 59
(R A Harris) *a.p: chsd wnr over 1f out: sn rdn: no imp* **4/1**[2]
-000 **3** *3/4* **City For Conquest (IRE)**[4] 3405 5-9-0 43 StephenDonohoe 10 51
(John A Harris) *hld up towards rr: rdn and hdwy over 1f out: kpt on to take 3rd cl home* **20/1**
460 **4** *3/4* **Monte Major (IRE)**[51] 2010 7-9-2 64 TolleyDean(3) 5 54
(D Shaw) *hld up towards rr: pushed along 3f out: rdn and hdwy over 1f out: one pce fnl f* **4/1**[2]

The Form Book, Raceform Ltd, Compton, RG20 6NL

0030 **5** ½ **Racing Stripes (IRE)**[6] 3346 4-9-5 48.........................(b) RichardSmith 9 56+
(K O Cunningham-Brown) *s.i.s: hld up and bhd: nt clr run on ins and stmbld ent st: hdwy whn switchd lft ins fnl f: nt rch ldrs* **16/1**
0000 **6** *hd* **Willhewiz**[5] 3363 8-9-5 50..(v) FergusSweeney 11 51
(M S Saunders) *a.p: rdn and one pce fnl f* **10/1**
6000 **7** 3 ¼ **Percy Douglas**[10] 3212 8-9-0 36......................................(b) AnnStokell(5) 2 39
(Miss A Stokell) *prom: rdn over 1f out: wknd ins fnl f* **33/1**
0510 **8** ½ **Montzando**[52] 1966 5-9-5 58...(v) JamesMillman(5) 8 43
(B R Millman) *sn outpcd* **15/2**
2006 **9** 1 ¼ **Baileys Outshine**[10] 3212 4-9-5 62..............................(b) TPQueally 4 33
(J G Given) *w wnr tl rdn over 1f out: wknd fnl f* **6/1**[3]
00-3 **10** *10* **Rose De Rita**[24] 2771 3-8-8 36.................................... SimonWhitworth 12 —
(L P Grassick) *a towards rr: eased ins fnl f* **40/1**
5-00 **11** 1 ¼ **Joint Agency (IRE)**[12] 3139 3-8-9 39 ow1.............................(b[1]) DNolan 6 —
(N Wilson) *s.i.s: hdwy after 1f: wknd wl over 1f out: eased ins fnl f* **28/1**

62.52 secs (0.22) **Going Correction** +0.075s/f (Slow)
WFA 3 from 4yo+ 6lb 11 Ran SP% **127.9**
Speed ratings (Par 101): **101,95,94,93,92 92,87,86,84,68 66**
toteswinger: 1&2 £8.40, 1&3 £9.00, 2&3 £4.40. CSF £10.56 TOTE £3.30: £1.50, £1.90, £7.70; EX 16.70 Trifecta £199.20 Pool: £401.26 - 1.49 winning units..There was no bid for the winner.
Owner Mrs I M Folkes **Bred** Aston Mullins Stud **Trained** Pandy, Monmouths

FOCUS
A modest seller, though the pace was good thanks to the favourite. As in the opener, the winner, who is a bit better than this grade, made all and few got into it.
Night Prospector Official explanation: jockey said gelding hung right throughout.
Racing Stripes(IRE) Official explanation: jockey said the gelding stumbled turning into the home straight.
Percy Douglas Official explanation: jockey said the gelding hung right from the home turn.

3566 PWM GROUP H'CAP — 1m 4f 50y(P)
3:30 (3:30) (Class 5) (0-75,75) 3-Y-O **£3,238** (£963; £481; £240) **Stalls** Low

Form RPR
6111 **1** **Precision Break (USA)**[24] 2785 3-9-4 72.............................. JohnEgan 8 84
(P F I Cole) *sn chsng ldr: led over 2f out: rdn clr 2f out: r.o wl* **6/4**[1]
000 **2** *7* **Don't Stop Me Now (IRE)**[32] 2528 3-8-8 62........................ TPQueally 5 63
(J W Hills) *hld up in tch: chsd wnr over 2f out: sn rdn: no imp* **22/1**
0-04 **3** 1 ¼ **All Lit Up**[26] 2719 3-8-2 56 oh4..................................... WilliamBuick 4 55
(A King) *in rr: hdwy 2f out: sn rdn: hung lft ins fnl f: one pce* **15/2**
2230 **4** 2 ½ **Love Empire (USA)**[25] 2750 3-8-9 63.......................(b) RoystonFfrench 6 58
(M Johnston) *hld up and bhd: hdwy over 3f out: rdn over 2f out: one pce* **10/1**
4100 **5** 3 ¾ **Boy On A Swing (USA)**[40] 2310 3-9-7 75.........................(t) ShaneKelly 3 64
(J A Osborne) *prom: rdn over 2f out: wknd fnl f* **15/2**
-505 **6** *1* **Ministerofinterior**[14] 3095 3-8-5 64.............................. JackMitchell(5) 7 51
(C F Wall) *hld up in rr: pushed along 5f out: rdn and short-lived effrt over 2f out* **9/2**[3]
413 **7** *8* **Novestar (IRE)**[4] 3393 3-8-6 63.................................... KevinGhunowa(3) 1 38
(G J Smith) *led: rdn and hdd over 3f out: wknd over 2f out* **11/4**[2]

2m 40.01s (-1.09) **Going Correction** +0.075s/f (Slow) 7 Ran SP% **121.8**
Speed ratings (Par 99): **106,101,100,98,96 95,90**
toteswinger: 1&2 £7.80, 1&3 £3.10, 2&3 £12.90. CSF £40.28 CT £208.61 TOTE £2.20: £1.20, £7.60; EX 33.20 Trifecta £266.50 Pool: £641.26 - 1.78 winning units..
Owner JMH Lifestyle Ltd **Bred** Gainesway Thoroughbreds Ltd **Trained** Whatcombe, Oxon

FOCUS
Not a bad little middle-distance handicap and a few of these were unexposed. The pace seemed quite uneven on the first circuit, but things certainly quickened up when the favourite hit the front, and the final time was decent. The form has been rated around the third to his best.
Novestar(IRE) Official explanation: jockey said colt ran flat.

3567 BETDAQ.CO.UK APPRENTICE CLAIMING STKS — 7f 32y(P)
4:00 (4:01) (Class 6) 4-Y-O+ **£2,729** (£806; £403) **Stalls** High

Form RPR
3621 **1** **One More Round (USA)**[25] 2753 10-8-11 71.......(b) RichardEvans(3) 11 72+
(Ollie Pears) *s.i.s: hld up towards rr: hdwy over 3f out: swtchd rt ent st: rdn to ld ins fnl f: edgd lft towards fin: drvn out* **5/2**[1]
60-0 **2** ¾ **Le Chiffre (IRE)**[14] 3090 6-9-1 68..........................(p) RossAtkinson(5) 10 73
(S Curran) *a.p: rdn over 2f out: rdr lost whip jst over 1f out: kpt on to take 2nd cl home* **10/1**
-600 **3** ¾ **Motu (IRE)**[10] 3211 7-8-9 62..(v) LanceBetts(5) 7 65
(I W McInnes) *tried to anticipate s: t.k.h in mid-div: hdwy over 3f out: led wl over 1f out: sn rdn and edgd lft: hdd ins fnl f: nt qckn* **16/1**
0050 **4** ¾ **General Feeling (IRE)**[9] 3281 7-8-7 56................(p) DeclanCannon(3) 6 59
(S T Mason) *s.i.s: hld up towards rr: hdwy over 3f out: hrd rdn over 1f out: kpt on same pce fnl f* **16/1**
2524 **5** 2 ¼ **Lethal**[12] 3128 5-8-11 73.. FrederikTylicki(5) 9 59
(R A Fahey) *led over 3f: led over 2f out tl wl over 1f out: wknd wl ins fnl f* **3/1**[2]
4235 **6** ¾ **Moayed**[25] 2753 9-8-11 63...(b) MarkCoumbe(3) 5 55
(N P Littmoden) *s.i.s: hld up in rr: hdwy over 2f out: rdn over 1f out: no further prog* **8/1**
3124 **7** ½ **Kingsmaite**[19] 2950 7-9-2 62...(b) NicolPolli 1 56
(S R Bowring) *w ldr: bmpd sn after s: led over 3f out: rdn and hdd over 2f out: wknd over 1f out* **6/1**[3]
-000 **8** *10* **Doctor's Cave**[5] 3383 6-9-2 68...................................(b) JamieJones 4 29
(K O Cunningham-Brown) *prom tl wknd over 2f out: sddle slipped* **18/1**
4500 **9** *6* **Alucica**[16] 3026 5-8-6 52...(v) DavidProbert(3) 2 5
(D Shaw) *prom: hmpd and lost pl sn after s: sn mid-div: bhd fnl 4f* **18/1**
0050 **10** *5* **Copper King**[16] 3037 4-9-1 50.. BillyCray(5) 3 3
(Miss Tor Sturgis) *prom: bmpd and lost pl sn after s: sn mid-div: rdn over 3f out: sn bhd* **20/1**
0306 **11** *12* **Kabis Amigos**[28] 2658 6-9-5 62................................(t) AdeleRothery(5) 8 —
(S T Mason) *hld up in tch: swtchd rt over 4f out: rdn and wknd over 3f out* **9/1**

1m 30.77s (1.17) **Going Correction** +0.075s/f (Slow) 11 Ran SP% **125.1**
Speed ratings (Par 101): **96,95,94,93,90 90,89,78,71,65 51**
toteswinger: 1&2 £7.50 1&3 £12.70, 2&3 £31.50. CSF £31.01 TOTE £3.10: £1.60, £3.00, £6.20; EX 37.40 Trifecta £375.70 Pool: £655.01 - 1.29 winning units..
Owner Diamond Racing Ltd **Bred** Kenneth L Ramsey And Sarah K Ramsey **Trained** Norton, N Yorks

■ Stewards' Enquiry : Adele Rothery two-day ban: careless riding (Jul 14,15)
Frederik Tylicki four-day ban: careless riding (Jul 14-17)

FOCUS
A modest claimer and, with several vying for the lead on the first bend, there was bound to be problems for a few. The form is unlikely to mean a lot outside of this level.
Motu(IRE) Official explanation: jockey said gelding missed the break.
Doctor's Cave Official explanation: jockey said gelding's saddle slipped.

3568 E B F REGISTER NOW @ BETDAQPOKER.CO.UK MAIDEN STKS — 7f 32y(P)
4:30 (4:33) (Class 5) 2-Y-O **£3,626** (£1,079; £539; £269) **Stalls** High

Form RPR
02 **1** **Talking Hands**[7] 3331 2-9-3 0.. SebSanders 1 78
(S Kirk) *led after 1f: hrd rdn fnl f: jst hld on* **1/2**[1]
6 **2** *shd* **Shaws Diamond (USA)**[7] 3331 2-8-12 0.......................... TGMcLaughlin 4 73
(D Shaw) *hld up in tch: wnt 2nd 2f out: rdn 1f out: r.o wl towards fin: jst failed* **28/1**
3 *1* **Sunny Future (IRE)** 2-9-3 0.. FergusSweeney 7 75+
(M S Saunders) *hld up in tch: rdn over 2f out: r.o one pce fnl f* **20/1**
4 *3* **Stirling Castle** 2-9-3 0.. TedDurcan 10 68
(M J Wallace) *hld up in mid-div: hdwy over 2f out: one pce fnl f* **3/1**[2]
5 **5** 2 ¾ **Congregation**[9] 3274 2-9-3 0.. DavidKinsella 8 61
(J H M Gosden) *prom: rdn wl over 1f out: sn edgd lft: wknd fnl f* **14/1**
4 **6** *9* **Artesium**[11] 3170 2-9-3 0...(t) PatCosgrave 6 39
(D J G Murray Smith) *led 1f: w wnr: rdn and ev ch 2f out: sn wknd* **28/1**
0 **7** 3 ¼ **Abuelito John (IRE)**[5] 3364 2-9-3 0................................... DNolan 2 31
(D Carroll) *rdn over 3f out: a bhd* **50/1**
4 **8** *4* **Scarth Hill (IRE)**[26] 2730 2-9-3 0................................ RoystonFfrench 3 21
(Mrs A Duffield) *bhd fnl 5f* **11/1**[3]
0 **9** 1 ½ **Bella Olympia**[23] 2821 2-8-12 0.. TPQueally 9 13
(A J McCabe) *prom tl wknd over 3f out* **50/1**
10 *6* **Amazing Blue Sky** 2-9-3 0... J-PGuillambert 12 —
(K J Burke) *s.i.s: sn swtchd lft: in rr: rdn over 3f out: sn struggling* **33/1**
0 **11** *16* **Blushing Bertie**[35] 2458 2-9-3 0.................................... PatrickMathers 5 —
(J W Unett) *nvr gng wl: a in rr: lost tch fnl 3f* **50/1**

1m 31.11s (1.51) **Going Correction** +0.075s/f (Slow) 11 Ran SP% **127.1**
Speed ratings (Par 93): **94,93,92,89,86 75,72,67,65,59 40**
toteswinger: 1&2 £8.20, 1&3 £6.10, 2&3 £36.40. CSF £30.10 TOTE £1.50: £1.02, £7.10, £6.50; EX 23.90 Trifecta £509.90 Pool: £820.00 - 1.19 winning units..
Owner Deauville Daze Partnership **Bred** Wood Hall Stud Limited **Trained** Upper Lambourn, Berks

FOCUS
A very uncompetitive maiden with them going 11-1 bar two. The pace was solid enough and they finished very well spread out, but it seems likely that this race very much lacked strength in depth.

NOTEBOOK
Talking Hands, who had suggested that he would appreciate further when runner-up over 6f here last time, was duly given a positive ride and it looked as though he would win easily when kicking off the final bend, but in the end he had to fight very hard and he would have been caught in another stride. Even though he won, this was a bit disappointing and it may be that he is more suited by getting a lead.
Shaws Diamond(USA), 12 lengths behind Talking Hands on her debut over 6f here, though her rival did have the benefit of a previous run, improved on that no-end and her strong late run only just failed. She should give her connections some fun in the coming months. (op 20-1)
Sunny Future(IRE) ◆, a 40,000euros half-brother to eight winners in Italy, ran a most encouraging debut. Racing very wide throughout, he stayed on nicely down the outside in the home straight to finish right on the heels of the front pair. Normal progression should see him win a race like this.
Stirling Castle, a 55,000gns half-brother to four winners at up to 1m3f, moved into contention on the home turn but lacked the foot to take him any closer to the leaders. He will be suited by further in due course. (op 7-2)
Congregation had every chance, but he did not get home and did not improve much from his Newmarket debut. Official explanation: jockey said colt hung left. (op 12-1)
Scarth Hill(IRE) Official explanation: jockey said gelding was never travelling.

3569 TRY BETDAQ FOR AN EXCHANGE H'CAP — 1m 141y(P)
5:00 (5:01) (Class 6) (0-60,62) 3-Y-O+ **£2,388** (£705; £352) **Stalls** Low

Form RPR
22 **1** **Willie Ever**[34] 2491 4-9-6 51.. J-PGuillambert 2 72+
(B Ellison) *t.k.h in tch: wnt 2nd wl over 1f out: led ins fnl f: pushed out* **2/1**[1]
0-00 **2** 2 ¾ **Ardent Prince**[11] 3182 5-9-2 47.. SebSanders 11 57
(A J McCabe) *hld up towards rr: stdy hdwy on outside over 4f out: led over 2f out: rdn wl over 1f out: hdd and nt qckn ins fnl f* **20/1**
5000 **3** 2 ½ **Supporting Role (IRE)**[12] 3126 3-8-11 53...............(b[1]) RichardMullen 9 56
(E S McMahon) *bhd: hdwy on outside over 3f out: rdn and hung rt over 1f out: hung lft ins fnl f: one pce* **11/1**
0421 **4** 3 ¾ **Bentley**[7] 3329 4-10-3 62 6ex.. TPQueally 5 57
(J G Given) *led early: chsd ldr: led 3f out: sn hdd and rdn: wknd fnl f* **10/3**[2]
0004 **5** *nk* **The Graig**[11] 3162 4-9-2 47... DavidKinsella 8 42
(J R Holt) *hld up and bhd: hdwy over 2f out: hung lft fr wl over 1f out: no imp* **14/1**
6634 **6** ¾ **Solo River**[23] 2833 3-9-0 56.. FergusSweeney 4 48
(P J Makin) *towards rr: n.m.r bnd 7f out: styd on fr over 1f out: n.d* **8/1**
0-10 **7** 1 ¾ **Wogan's Sister**[42] 2247 3-9-1 57.. ShaneKelly 7 45
(I A Wood) *sltly hmpd s: hld up: sn mid-div: swtchd rt over 2f out: nvr nr ldrs* **16/1**
6-60 **8** *2* **Kansas Gold**[42] 2243 5-10-0 59.................................... RoystonFfrench 1 43
(J Mackie) *prom tl rdn and wknd over 2f out* **15/2**[3]
0-00 **9** ½ **Kimono My House**[30] 2597 4-9-4 49................................... PatCosgrave 3 32
(J G Given) *hld up towards rr: sme hdwy over 2f out: sn rdn: no further prog* **22/1**
4-06 **10** *7* **Fair Sailing (IRE)**[16] 3025 4-9-8 53.............................. WilliamBuick 6 20
(J W Hills) *wnt rt s: prom: rdn and ev ch over 2f out: sn wknd* **10/1**
1415 **11** 1 ¾ **Montemayorprincess (IRE)**[83] 1258 4-9-9 54............(p) TedDurcan 10 17
(D Haydn Jones) *hld up in mid-div: rdn over 3f out: sn struggling* **8/1**
0000 **12** *7* **Passato (GER)**[4] 3422 4-9-7 52.......................................(b[1]) LPKeniry 12 —
(R A Harris) *sn led: hdd 3f out: sn wknd* **33/1**
3044 **13** 1 ½ **Rambling Socks**[22] 2869 5-9-4 49........................(p) StephenDonohoe 13 —
(S R Bowring) *hld up in tch: rdn and wknd over 3f out* **22/1**

1m 51.1s (0.60) **Going Correction** +0.075s/f (Slow)
WFA 3 from 4yo+ 11lb 13 Ran SP% **136.8**
Speed ratings (Par 101): **100,97,95,92,91 91,89,87,87,81 79,73,71**
toteswinger: 1&2 £16.50, 1&3 £12.20, 2&3 £42.40. CSF £57.50 CT £422.33 TOTE £3.80: £1.20, £6.40, £4.30; EX 97.40 TRIFECTA Not won..
Owner Black and White Diamond Partnership **Bred** G Russell **Trained** Norton, N Yorks

FOCUS
An ordinary handicap run at an average pace, but they did finish well spread out. The form looks sound rated through the runner-up.

T/Plt: £27.20 to a £1 stake. Pool: £68,276.33. 1,829.59 winning tickets. T/Qpdt: £8.60 to a £1 stake. Pool: £4,186.37. 357.75 winning tickets. KH

3341 BRIGHTON (L-H)

Tuesday, July 1

OFFICIAL GOING: Firm

Wind: Moderate, half against

3570 HORSEMART.CO.UK CLAIMING STKS — 5f 213y

2:30 (2:31) (Class 6) 2-Y-O — **£2,072** (£616; £308; £153) **Stalls** Low

Form — RPR

4 **1** **Time For Old Time**[15] 3091 2-8-5 0 .... PaulDoe 4 — 59
(I A Wood) *stdd s: t.k.h: sn trckd ldr: led over 4f out: hdd appr fnl f: swished tail but rallied to ld again ins fnl f* **4/1**[2]

4055 **2** ½ **Readily**[17] 3032 2-8-9 0 .... RyanMoore 1 — 61
(J G Portman) *led: hdd over 4f out: rdn to ld appr fnl f: no ex and hdd ins fnl f* **4/7**[1]

2303 **3** 4 **Dazzling Dust (IRE)**[8] 3309 2-8-2 0 ....(t) JackDean(5) 2 — 47
(W G M Turner) *in tch: rdn 3f out: effrt 2f out but hung lft after and sn btn* **6/1**[3]

00 **4** 3½ **Benetti (IRE)**[6] 3358 2-8-10 0 .... DarryllHolland 3 — 40
(M R Channon) *in tch: rdn 1/2-way: wknd over 2f out* **9/1**

1m 11.58s (1.38) **Going Correction** -0.15s/f (Firm) **4 Ran SP% 107.9**
Speed ratings (Par 92): **84,83,78,73**
CSF £6.88 TOTE £5.00; EX 7.80.
Owner C S Tateson **Bred** C S Tateson **Trained** Upper Lambourn, Berks

FOCUS
A weak claimer that only really concerned two horses. The winning time was very moderate.

NOTEBOOK
Time For Old Time ran green when fourth on her debut in a seller at Windsor, but she clearly learnt from that and just proved too strong for the odds-on favourite. After recovering from a slow start, she raced a little keenly early on, but was sensibly allowed to bowl along and battled on well for pressure in the straight, despite flashing her tail. This is moderate form, but there could be a little more to come and she looks the type to win a small nursery. (op 3-1 tchd 9-2)
Readily has not progressed since running well when fourth in a Windsor maiden on her debut in April and she found one too strong on this drop in grade. (op 8-11)
Dazzling Dust(IRE) did not really improve for a first-time tongue-tie. (op 13-2)

3571 LESTIES GOING TO GRACELANDS H'CAP — 6f 209y

3:00 (3:01) (Class 5) (0-70,70) 3-Y-O — **£2,775** (£830; £415; £207; £103) **Stalls** Low

Form — RPR

4-10 **1** **Vigano (IRE)**[20] 2945 3-9-7 **70** .... RyanMoore 2 — 73
(S Kirk) *a in tch on ins: led over 1f out: rdn: jst hld on* **9/2**[2]

3563 **2** nse **Caprio (IRE)**[13] 3136 3-9-7 **70** .... RichardKingscote 3 — 73
(Tom Dascombe) *hld up: hdwy on outside over 1f out: r.o strly to go 2nd cl home and jst failed to catch wnr* **3/1**[1]

3530 **3** nk **Benedetto**[20] 2945 3-9-3 **66** ....(p) JimCrowley 6 — 68
(Mrs A J Perrett) *hld up: hdwy over 2f out: wnt 2nd over 1f out: hung lft and lost 2nd cl home* **5/1**[3]

3224 **4** 3 **Regal Veil**[15] 3086 3-7-9 **51** oh5 .... DavidProbert(7) 4 — 45
(S C Williams) *a.p: rdn over 2f out: one pce fr over 1f out* **9/1**

-503 **5** hd **Seeking The Star (CAN)**[14] 3117 3-8-11 **65** ....(p) AhmedAjtebi(5) 7 — 58
(D M Simcock) *mid-div: rdn over 2f out: one pce after* **13/2**

0300 **6** 2¾ **Rough Rock (IRE)**[11] 3224 3-9-4 **67** ....(b) DaneO'Neill 5 — 53
(Miss Gay Kelleway) *led tl rdn and hdd over 1f out: wknd ins fnl f* **9/1**

-405 **7** 5 **Doric Lady**[24] 2836 3-9-2 **65** .... EddieAhern 1 — 38
(J A R Toller) *a in rr* **5/1**[3]

-000 **8** 11 **Moluccella**[31] 2613 3-8-4 **53** ....(t) NickyMackay 8 — —
(H Morrison) *racd wd: prom tl wknd over 2f out: eased fnl f* **25/1**

1m 22.12s (-0.98) **Going Correction** -0.15s/f (Firm) **8 Ran SP% 113.7**
Speed ratings (Par 100): **99,98,98,95,94 91,86,73**
toteswinger: 1&2 £3.70, 1&3 £3.20, 2&3 £2.40. CSF £18.19 CT £69.15 TOTE £4.20: £1.50, £1.50, £1.70; EX 15.40 Trifecta £47.40 Pool: £644.37 - 10.04 winning units..
Owner Norman Ormiston **Bred** John Bernard O'Connor **Trained** Upper Lambourn, Berks

FOCUS
A modest but competitive sprint handicap.

3572 MACCONVILLES SURVEYING (S) STKS — 7f 214y

3:30 (3:30) (Class 6) 3-4-Y-O — **£1,942** (£578; £288; £144) **Stalls** Low

Form — RPR

0301 **1** **Lancaster Lad (IRE)**[6] 3359 3-8-13 47 ....(p) SebSanders 1 — 60
(A B Haynes) *hld up: hdwy on ins 2f out: led jst ins fnl f: r.o wl* **6/1**

002 **2** 2¼ **Fairly Honest**[7] 3343 4-8-10 49 .... WilliamCarson(7) 2 — 52
(P W Hiatt) *led tl rdn and hdd jst ins fnl f: nt pce of wnr* **10/3**[2]

1120 **3** 2¼ **Straight Face (IRE)**[67] 1602 4-9-8 55 .... RyanMoore 4 — 52
(Miss Gay Kelleway) *hld up in rr: hdwy on outside over 1f out: styd on to go 3rd ins fnl f* **7/2**[3]

6402 **4** 1 **Lord Deevert**[5] 3406 3-8-3 50 ....(b) JackDean(5) 6 — 42
(W G M Turner) *t.k.h: hld up: hdwy on outside 3f out: hung bdly lft wl over 1f out: one pce and lost 3rd ins fnl f* **11/4**[1]

0325 **5** 3¾ **Split The Wind (USA)**[7] 3343 4-8-12 55 ....(b) HayleyTurner 3 — 31
(Miss Sheena West) *trckd ldrs: rdn and short of room wl over 1f out: nvr on terms after* **5/1**

000 **6** 2½ **Llab Nala**[5] 3397 3-8-9 56 ow1 ....(v) DarryllHolland 5 — 29
(M R Channon) *trckd ldr tl rdn and bdly hmpd wl over 1f out: nt rcvr* **14/1**

-006 **7** 1¾ **Whodouthinkur (IRE)**[14] 3115 3-8-8 48 .... CatherineGannon 7 — 24
(Mrs C A Dunnett) *mid-div: rdn 3f out: wknd 2f out* **50/1**

1m 34.98s (-1.02) **Going Correction** -0.15s/f (Firm)
WFA 3 from 4yo 9lb **7 Ran SP% 111.5**
Speed ratings (Par 101): **99,96,94,93,89 87,85**
toteswinger: 1&2 £7.70, 1&3 £8.60, 2&3 £2.00. CSF £24.91 TOTE £8.20: £3.10, £2.40; EX 28.00.The winner was bought in for 8,800gns.
Owner Mrs S M Maine **Bred** Tom Foley **Trained** Limpley Stoke, Bath

FOCUS
A standard seller.
Lord Deevert Official explanation: jockey said gelding hung left

3573 DGH RECRUITMENT MAIDEN STKS — 1m 1f 209y

4:00 (4:02) (Class 5) 3-Y-O+ — **£2,775** (£830; £415; £207; £103) **Stalls** High

Form — RPR

06 **1** **Zuwaar**[31] 2612 3-9-1 0 ....(t) RHills 5 — 76
(J H M Gosden) *w.w: hdwy whn edgd rt over 1f out: rn green and wnt lft bef led ins fnl f: kpt on* **16/1**

-533 **2** 1¾ **Dark Prospect**[10] 3263 3-9-1 70 .... DarryllHolland 3 — 73
(M A Jarvis) *in tch: led over 3f out: rdn and hung rt over 1f out: hung left and hdd ins fnl f* **7/2**[3]

55 **3** 2¼ **Hendersyde (USA)**[15] 3094 3-9-1 0 .... AdamKirby 6 — 68
(W R Swinburn) *trckd ldrs: carried rt over 1f out and sltly hmpd ins fnl f: one pce* **11/4**[2]

04 **4** 1¼ **Day Trip (IRE)**[17] 3043 3-9-1 0 .... EddieAhern 4 — 66
(B J Meehan) *hld up: rdn oer 3f out: effrt over 1f out: wknd fnl f* **25/1**

00 **5** 7 **Dixie Dean (USA)**[15] 3094 3-9-1 0 .... RyanMoore 2 — 52
(Sir Michael Stoute) *a in rr* **14/1**

-500 **6** 30 **Rasmani**[11] 3218 4-9-0 46 ....(t) RosieJessop(7) 7 — —
(Miss Gay Kelleway) *t.k.h: w ldr tl lost pl over 4f out: sn bhd: t.o* **100/1**

3-43 **P** **Gingham**[20] 2956 3-8-10 75 .... DaneO'Neill 1 — —
(L M Cumani) *mde most tl hdd over 3f out: lost action 2f out: p.u and dismntd ins fnl f* **11/10**[1]

2m 0.02s (-3.58) **Going Correction** -0.15s/f (Firm)
WFA 3 from 4yo 11lb **7 Ran SP% 113.9**
Speed ratings (Par 103): **108,106,104,103,98 74,—**
toteswinger: 1&2 £7.70, 1&3 £8.60, 2&3 £2.00. CSF £70.36 TOTE £18.80: £4.30, £2.20; EX 58.50.
Owner Hamdan Al Maktoum **Bred** Shadwell Estate Company Limited **Trained** Newmarket, Suffolk

FOCUS
Some big stables represented, but this was a very ordinary maiden. The winning time was decent, though.

3574 MACCONVILLES H'CAP — 1m 3f 196y

4:30 (4:32) (Class 5) (0-70,70) 3-Y-O+ — **£2,775** (£830; £415; £207; £103) **Stalls** High

Form — RPR

4661 **1** **Sea Admiral**[20] 2931 3-9-4 **70** ....(b) RyanMoore 4 — 77
(R Charlton) *sn trckd ldr: led over 2f out: hung lft over 1f out: styd on wl ins fnl f* **11/8**[1]

-463 **2** 3¼ **Loveofmylife**[35] 2475 3-7-10 **55** .... DavidProbert(7) 7 — 57
(R M Beckett) *flyj. leaving stalls: hdwy on outside 2f out: hung lft but ev ch ent fnl f: one pce after* **6/1**

4-04 **3** 1¾ **Vincenzio (IRE)**[17] 3029 4-10-0 **67** ....(b) ShaneKelly 2 — 66
(C R Egerton) *a in tch on ins: hung lft over 1f out: kpt on one pce ins fnl f* **5/1**[3]

6506 **4** ¾ **Sir Liam (USA)**[11] 3218 4-8-13 **57** .... AshleyHamblett(5) 5 — 60+
(R A Teal) *hld up in tch: hdwy whn hmpd on ins over 1f out: rallying whn short of room again ins fnl f* **10/1**

0660 **5** 3 **Threestoneburn (USA)**[28] 2695 3-8-8 **60** ow2 .... SteveDrowne 1 — 53
(J R Boyle) *trckd ldrs: rdn and ev ch 2f out: wknd appr fnl f* **16/1**

0-01 **6** 1½ **Casual Garcia**[10] 3264 3-8-7 **59** ow1 ....(b) SebSanders 6 — 50
(Sir Mark Prescott) *led tl rdn and hdd over 2f out: sn btn* **4/1**[2]

0203 **7** 22 **Persian Wish (IRE)**[20] 2931 3-8-8 **60** .... LPKeniry 3 — 15
(J W Mullins) *a towards rr: rdn 3f out: sn wl bhd: eased ins fnl f* **25/1**

2m 30.78s (-1.92) **Going Correction** -0.15s/f (Firm)
WFA 3 from 4yo 13lb **7 Ran SP% 111.9**
Speed ratings (Par 103): **100,97,96,96,94 93,78**
toteswinger: 1&2 £2.80, 1&3 £2.30, 2&3 £3.70. CSF £9.66 TOTE £2.30: £1.70, £2.30; EX 11.50.
Owner Axom (IV) **Bred** Stratford Place Stud **Trained** Beckhampton, Wilts
■ Stewards' Enquiry : David Probert two-day ban: careless riding (Jul 15,16)

FOCUS
A messy race and modest form. The field bunched up early in the straight and then it all got a little tight against the far rail inside the final two furlongs, with the first three home all hanging left.
Vincenzio(IRE) Official explanation: jockey said gelding hung left
Persian Wish(IRE) Official explanation: trainer said colt was unsuited by the firm ground

3575 BRIGHTON'S JUICE 107.2 H'CAP — 5f 59y

5:00 (5:02) (Class 5) (0-70,70) 3-Y-O+ — **£2,775** (£830; £415; £207; £103) **Stalls** Low

Form — RPR

0000 **1** **Diane's Choice**[10] 3271 5-9-10 **67** ....(t) DaneO'Neill 9 — 74
(Miss Gay Kelleway) *a.p on outside: str run u.p fnl f to ld cl home* **13/2**

2003 **2** shd **Cosmic Destiny (IRE)**[39] 2351 6-9-12 **69** .... LPKeniry 3 — 76
(E F Vaughan) *in tch: rdn to ld appr fnl f: kpt on hdd post* **5/1**[3]

4023 **3** hd **Fastrac Boy**[7] 3346 5-8-7 **50** oh1 .... MohammedSaeed 8 — 56
(J R Best) *led tl strly rdn and hdd appr fnl f: nt qckn cl home* **7/2**[2]

1432 **4** 1½ **Just Joey**[6] 3363 4-9-5 **62** ....(b) DarryllHolland 5 — 63
(J R Weymes) *in tch: ev ch over 2f out tl no ex ins fnl f* **11/8**[1]

1560 **5** shd **Gone'N'Dunnett (IRE)**[12] 3159 9-8-7 **50** oh1 ....(v) CatherineGannon 6 — 50
(Mrs C A Dunnett) *prom: ev ch 2f out: tl no ex ins fnl f* **25/1**

5055 **6** ¾ **Dancing Mystery**[5] 3405 14-9-0 **57** ....(b) StephenCarson 4 — 55
(E A Wheeler) *s.i.s: sn in tch: hung lft over 1f out and no hdwy ins fnl f* **11/1**

0156 **7** 14 **Swindon Town Flyer (IRE)**[28] 2690 3-9-1 **70** ....(b) PNolan(7) 1 — 17
(A B Haynes) *v.s.a and a bhd* **20/1**

62.58 secs (0.28) **Going Correction** -0.15s/f (Firm)
WFA 3 from 4yo+ 5lb **7 Ran SP% 111.3**
Speed ratings (Par 103): **91,90,90,88,87 86,64**
toteswinger: 1&2 £3.70, 1&3 £4.40, 2&3 £2.70. CSF £36.35 CT £127.60 TOTE £7.60: £3.20, £2.10; EX 40.40 Trifecta £479.90 Pool: £ 1232.35 - 1.90 winning units. Place 6: £1118.05 Place 5: £202.60.
Owner The Dark Side **Bred** Green Pastures Farm **Trained** Exning, Suffolk

FOCUS
A modest sprint handicap and the winning time was very ordinary for the grade.
T/Plt: £676.30 to a £1 stake. Pool: £81,111.21. 87.55 winning tickets. T/Qpdt: £82.90 to a £1 stake. Pool: £4,596.69. 41.00 winning tickets. JS

3399 HAMILTON (R-H)

Tuesday, July 1

OFFICIAL GOING: Good (good to firm in places)

Wind: Light, half behind Weather: Cloudy

3576 GARRY OWEN NURSERY — 6f 5y

2:15 (2:15) (Class 5) 2-Y-O — **£3,885** (£1,156; £577; £288) **Stalls** Low

Form — RPR

032 **1** **Johnmanderville**[55] 1907 2-8-9 **65** .... AndrewElliott 1 — 74+
(K R Burke) *trckd ldrs: rdn to ld over 1f out: rdn and drifted rt: hld on wl* **10/3**[2]

2166 **2** 3½ **Veronicas Boy**[25] 2775 2-9-3 **73** .... DanielTudhope 2 — 71
(G M Moore) *prom: drvn over 2f out: rallied to chse wnr ins fnl f: no imp* **17/2**

203 **3** 1½ **Carmanjoe**[28] 2702 2-8-12 **68** .... PaulMulrennan 6 — 62
(M W Easterby) *pressed ldr: effrt over 2f out: kpt on same pce over 1f out* **25/1**

51 **4** 1¼ **Elaine's Folly**[21] 2910 2-8-5 **61** .... PaulHanagan 3 — 51
(P C Haslam) *in tch: effrt over 2f out: hung rt: no ex over 1f out* **7/2**[3]

The Form Book, Raceform Ltd, Compton, RG20 6NL

426 **5** *7* **Raimond Ridge (IRE)**[78] 1363 2-8-12 **68** SamHitchcott 5 37
(M R Channon) *blkd s: sn led: hdd over 1f out: sn btn* **2/1**[1]

41 **6** *54* **Sweet Smile (IRE)**[27] 2730 2-9-7 **77** DO'Donohoe 4 —
(K A Ryan) *nvr gng wl: sn detached: eased whn no ch fnl 2f* **9/2**

1m 13.38s (1.18) **Going Correction** -0.10s/f (Good) **6** Ran SP% **111.2**
Speed ratings (Par 94): **88,83,81,79,70** —
toteswinger: 1&2 £4.20, 1&3 £6.40, 2&3 £18.00. CSF £29.29 TOTE £3.80: £1.60, £4.40; EX 29.90.

Owner Jet Racing Partnership **Bred** Natton House Thoroughbreds & Mark Woodall **Trained** Middleham Moor, N Yorks

■ The first nursery handicap of the season.

FOCUS
The opening nursery of the season and it was a modest affair. The 'official' ratings shown next to each horse are estimated and for information purposes only.

NOTEBOOK
Johnmanderville, placed in maiden company on his last two outings, has been gelded since his last run and showed his true colours to score on this nursery bow. He did the job comfortably in the end and, while he probably would not want to be going up too much for this, he does possess the scope to rate a little higher. (op 7-2 tchd 3-1 and 4-1 in a place)

Veronicas Boy enjoyed the return to this stiffer test and ran a fair race in defeat. He may even be worth trying over 7f now on this evidence. (op 15-2 tchd 7-1)

Carmanjoe posted an improved effort on the step back up to this trip and showed he can be just as effective on turf. (op 16-1)

Elaine's Folly, off the mark in claiming company 21 days previously, met a good deal of support in the betting ring for this step up in class. She ran a little below her previous level and looks to have been overrated by the assessor. (op 6-1 tchd 13-2)

Raimond Ridge(IRE), returning from a 78-day break, showed up quickly to bag the early lead yet he eventually had no more to give when the challengers emerged. He now has a good deal to prove. Official explanation: jockey said gelding pulled up lame right-fore (op 9-4 tchd 15-8)

Sweet Smile(IRE), a maiden winner at Ripon on softer ground 27 days previously, was in trouble soon after the start and something clearly went wrong with him. Official explanation: jockey said colt lost its action (op 3-1)

3577 SCOTTISH RACING CLAIMING STKS 5f 4y
2:45 (2:45) (Class 6) 3-5-Y-O **£2,388** (£705; £352) **Stalls** Centre

Form RPR

0503 **1** **Howards Tipple**[5] 3404 4-8-13 59 (p) TomEaves 5 64
(Miss L A Perratt) *trckd ldrs: effrt over 1f out: carried lft and led ins fnl f: drvn out* **7/4**[1]

4011 **2** *1 1/2* **Luloah**[13] 3128 5-8-7 50 LukeMorris(3) 1 56
(J G M O'Shea) *w ldrs: led 2f out: hung lft and hdd ins fnl f: kpt on same pce* **9/2**[2]

15-5 **3** *2 1/4* **Elijah Pepper (USA)**[11] 3212 3-8-11 67 NeilBrown(5) 6 57
(T D Barron) *dwlt: bhd tl hdwy over 1f out: kpt on: nt rch first two* **11/2**

3460 **4** *1/2* **The Little Fizzer (IRE)**[18] 3000 3-8-4 58 AndrewElliott 2 43
(K R Burke) *led to 2f out: sn rdn and no ex* **9/2**[2]

6000 **5** *3 1/4* **Guto**[5] 3405 5-8-13 67 AndrewMullen(3) 3 40
(W J H Ratcliffe) *w ldrs tl edgd rt and wknd fr 2f out* **5/1**[3]

-000 **6** *3 1/4* **Stormy Journey**[15] 3079 3-8-1 48 KellyHarrison(5) 7 21
(Mrs K Walton) *prom: rdn 1/2-way: wknd over 1f out* **40/1**

0-06 **7** *nse* **Senora Lenorah**[11] 3200 4-8-10 35 ow9 (t) GaryBartley(5) 4 27
(D A Nolan) *towards rr: drvn 1/2-way: nvr rchd ldrs* **100/1**

0362 **8** *1 1/4* **Andrasta**[4] 3434 3-8-0 54 (p) DanielleMcCreery(5) 9 16
(A Berry) *midfield on outside: rdn 1/2-way: sn btn* **16/1**

000 **9** *17* **Deer Park Lord**[26] 2747 4-8-6 1 (t) DeclanCannon(7) 8 —
(D A Nolan) *towards rr: struggling 1/2-way: sn btn* **200/1**

59.34 secs (-0.66) **Going Correction** -0.10s/f (Good)
WFA 3 from 4yo+ 5lb **9** Ran SP% **114.6**
Speed ratings (Par 101): **101,98,95,94,89 83,83,81,54**
toteswinger: 1&2 £1.90, 1&3 £3.40, 2&3 £4.60. CSF £9.75 TOTE £2.10: £1.40, £1.20, £1.80; EX 11.00.

Owner Gordon McDowall **Bred** New Hall Stud **Trained** Carluke, S Lanarks

■ Stewards' Enquiry : Luke Morris five-day ban (includes two deferred days): careless riding (Jul 15-19)

FOCUS
A typically weak claimer. The form looks fair for the grade.

Guto Official explanation: jockey said gelding hung right-handed throughout

3578 WEATHERBYS BANK H'CAP 1m 65y
3:15 (3:15) (Class 5) (0-70,65) 3-Y-O **£3,238** (£963; £481; £240) **Stalls** High

Form RPR

4001 **1** *shd* **Deep Winter**[5] 3397 3-9-8 **65** 6ex PaulHanagan 6 72+
(R A Fahey) *prom: effrt and edgd lft over 1f out: carried lft ins fnl f: kpt on: jst failed: fin 2nd: awrdd the r* **4/6**[1]

0423 **2** **Jollyhockeysticks**[11] 3221 3-9-7 **64** SamHitchcott 8 71
(M R Channon) *trckd ldrs: pushed along over 3f out: effrt 2f out: hung lft and led wl ins fnl f: all out: fin first: disqualified and plcd 2nd* **7/2**[2]

-132 **3** *3/4* **Johnny Friendly**[95] 1060 3-8-13 **63** DeclanCannon(7) 1 68
(K R Burke) *led tl hdd and no ex wl ins fnl f* **11/1**

3340 **4** *7* **Casino Night**[12] 3183 3-8-12 **60** NeilBrown(5) 7 49
(J R Weymes) *prom tl edgd lft and outpcd fr 2f out* **20/1**

44 **5** *4 1/2* **Willyn (IRE)**[13] 3126 3-8-9 **57** GaryBartley(5) 3 36
(J S Goldie) *hld up in tch: drvn along over 3f out: outpcd over 2f out* **17/2**[3]

56-0 **6** *1 1/2* **Safari Dancer (IRE)**[13] 3126 3-9-1 **58** TomEaves 4 33
(Miss L A Perratt) *hld up: rdn over 3f out: nvr on terms* **25/1**

6020 **7** *3 1/2* **Chaenomeles (USA)**[15] 3081 3-9-3 **60** GregFairley 2 27
(M Johnston) *towards rr: drvn 1/2-way: btn fnl 2f* **22/1**

00-6 **8** *2 1/2* **Halton Castle**[21] 2912 3-8-11 **57** PJMcDonald(3) 5 18
(G M Moore) *hld up: drvn and outpcd 3f out: sn btn* **80/1**

1m 47.21s (-1.19) **Going Correction** -0.10s/f (Good) **8** Ran SP% **115.3**
Speed ratings (Par 100): **100,101,100,93,89 88,85,81**
toteswinger: 1&2 £1.20, 1&3 £3.10, 2&3 £4.10. CSF £2.99 CT £12.47 TOTE £1.80: £1.10, £1.20, £2.20; EX 2.70.

Owner R A Fahey **Bred** Gainsborough Stud Management Ltd **Trained** Musley Bank, N Yorks

■ Stewards' Enquiry : Sam Hitchcott one-day ban: careless riding (Jul 15)

Paul Hanagan caution: used whip with excessive frequency

FOCUS
A modest handicap for three-year-olds which saw the first three come clear. The first two placings were later reversed by the stewards.

3579 TRADESTYLE CABINETS H'CAP (A QUALIFIER FOR THE RBS SCOTTISH TROPHY HANDICAP SERIES FINAL) 1m 1f 36y
3:45 (3:45) (Class 5) (0-75,71) 3-Y-0+ **£3,885** (£1,156; £577; £288) **Stalls** High

Form RPR

0441 **1** **Supercast (IRE)**[10] 3257 5-10-0 **70** SamHitchcott 2 79
(N J Vaughan) *mde all: rdn 2f out: hld on wl fnl f* **7/1**[3]

3140 **2** *1/2* **Fujin Dancer (FR)**[36] 2464 3-9-5 **71** PaulHanagan 7 80+
(R A Fahey) *hld up in tch: hdwy whn nt clr run over 2f out: swtchd rt over 1f out: sn chsng wnr: kpt on fnl f* **9/4**[1]

0632 **3** *4 1/2* **Hawkit (USA)**[3] 3493 7-9-9 **70** NeilBrown(5) 3 68
(P Monteith) *hld up: effrt over 2f out: edgd rt: kpt on fnl f: no imp* **7/2**[2]

6006 **4** *1/2* **Regent's Secret (USA)**[6] 3366 8-9-3 **64** (p) GaryBartley(5) 6 61
(J S Goldie) *bhd tl hdwy over 1f out: nrst fin* **7/1**[3]

50-2 **5** *hd* **Bold Indian (IRE)**[20] 2942 4-9-6 **62** PatCosgrave 1 59
(Miss L A Perratt) *plld hrd: cl up tl rdn and no ex over 1f out* **8/1**

0060 **6** *7* **Farne Island**[15] 3082 5-8-11 **53** PaulMulrennan 5 35
(Micky Hammond) *cl up tl rdn and wknd over 1f out* **14/1**

5640 **7** *2 1/4* **King Of The Moors (USA)**[12] 3175 5-9-6 **62** RobertWinston 4 39
(T D Barron) *t.k.h in rr: rdn over 2f out: sn btn* **7/1**[3]

406 **8** *1 1/4* **Mystical Ayr (IRE)**[13] 3127 6-9-2 **58** RoystonFfrench 9 33
(Miss L A Perratt) *chsd ldrs: outpcd over 2f out: sn btn* **14/1**

1m 59.23s (-0.47) **Going Correction** -0.10s/f (Good)
WFA 3 from 4yo+ 10lb **8** Ran SP% **114.9**
Speed ratings (Par 103): **98,97,93,93,92 86,84,83**
toteswinger: 1&2 £3.40, 1&3 £5.10, 2&3 £1.90. CSF £23.31 CT £65.01 TOTE £10.70: £2.50, £1.20, £1.30; EX 29.90.

Owner Bould & Walker Racing **Bred** J Egan, J Corcoran And J Judd **Trained** Hampton, Cheshire

FOCUS
Just a modest handicap with the favourite, the only three-year-old in the line-up, possibly an unlucky loser.

Farne Island Official explanation: jockey said gelding hung right

King Of The Moors(USA) Official explanation: jockey said gelding hung right-handed coming down the hill

3580 DAILY RECORD H'CAP 1m 4f 17y
4:15 (4:16) (Class 6) (0-65,60) 3-Y-O **£2,266** (£674; £337; £168) **Stalls** Low

Form RPR

0-55 **1** **Aleatricis**[27] 2719 3-8-6 **45** DO'Donohoe 2 55
(Sir Mark Prescott) *cl up: rdn over 4f out: led over 2f out: kpt on wl fnl f: jst lasted* **9/4**[1]

605- **2** *nse* **Next Of Kin (IRE)**[282] 5663 3-9-7 **60** RobertWinston 5 70
(G A Swinbank) *hld up in tch: rdn over 3f out: rallied 2f out: chsd wnr ins fnl f: kpt on wl: jst hld* **12/1**

-256 **3** *3 1/4* **Livvy Inn (USA)**[26] 2750 3-8-10 **54** NeilBrown(5) 1 59
(Miss Lucinda V Russell) *midfield: effrt on outside over 2f out: chsd wnr over 1f out to ins fnl f: no ex* **6/1**[3]

-542 **4** *4* **Jemima's Art**[26] 2750 3-8-8 **47** (b) PaulMulrennan 4 46
(M W Easterby) *cl up: led 4f out to over 2f out: no ex over 1f out* **11/4**[2]

00-6 **5** *2* **Marie Camargo**[29] 2659 3-8-6 **45** PaulHanagan 10 40
(R A Fahey) *unruly in stalls: hld up in tch: drvn over 3f out: outpcd fnl 2f* **10/1**

6006 **6** *2 1/2* **Mchepple**[11] 3230 3-8-1 **45** KellyHarrison(5) 3 36
(W Storey) *t.k.h: hld up: rdn over 3f out: nvr able to chal* **66/1**

-002 **7** *2 1/2* **Blazing Mask (IRE)**[20] 2941 3-8-11 **50** RoystonFfrench 8 37
(Mrs A Duffield) *prom tl rdn and wknd over 2f out* **12/1**

0001 **8** *2 1/2* **Hoar Frost**[20] 2941 3-8-13 **52** SamHitchcott 7 35
(M R Channon) *in tch tl rdn and wknd over 2f out* **14/1**

00-5 **9** *3 3/4* **Elusive Deal (USA)**[21] 2907 3-9-1 **54** PatCosgrave 6 31
(D J G Murray Smith) *hld up: rdn over 3f out: nvr on terms* **16/1**

-506 **10** *7* **Lady In Chief**[20] 2926 3-8-8 **50** PJMcDonald(3) 9 16
(Miss J A Camacho) *bhd: pushed along over 3f out: sn btn* **20/1**

-405 **11** *2 1/2* **Northgate Maisie**[20] 2926 3-8-6 **45** (p) AndrewElliott 11 7
(Jedd O'Keeffe) *led to 4f out: wknd over 2f out* **50/1**

2m 40.3s (1.70) **Going Correction** -0.10s/f (Good) **11** Ran SP% **117.0**
Speed ratings (Par 98): **90,89,87,85,83 82,80,78,76,71 69**
toteswinger: 1&2 £7.90, 1&3 £3.90, 2&3 £9.80. CSF £30.21 CT £146.21 TOTE £3.60: £1.50, £3.80, £2.00; EX 36.50.

Owner The Green Door Partnership **Bred** Miss K Rausing **Trained** Newmarket, Suffolk

■ Stewards' Enquiry : D O'Donohoe two-day ban: used whip down shoulder in forehand and with excessive frequency (Jul 15,16)

FOCUS
Low-grade fare, reflected by a moderate winning time.

3581 WEATHERBYS BLOODSTOCK INSURANCE H'CAP 5f 4y
4:45 (4:45) (Class 5) (0-75,74) 3-Y-O+ **£3,238** (£963; £481; £240) **Stalls** Centre

Form RPR

1605 **1** **Invincible Lad (IRE)**[15] 3080 4-8-8 **56** oh3 ow1 PatCosgrave 3 70
(E J Alston) *mde all: rdn over 1f out: kpt on strly fnl f* **15/2**[3]

5505 **2** *1 1/4* **Rothesay Dancer**[5] 3401 5-8-12 **65** KellyHarrison(5) 2 74
(J S Goldie) *hld up: hdwy over 1f out: chsd wnr wl ins fnl f: r.o* **8/1**

5112 **3** *nk* **Kings College Boy**[5] 3401 8-8-13 **61** (b) PaulHanagan 4 69
(R A Fahey) *t.k.h bhd ldrs: effrt over 1f out: kpt on same pce ins fnl f* **6/4**[1]

0366 **4** *1* **Kinout (IRE)**[13] 3136 3-9-5 **72** DO'Donohoe 6 74
(K A Ryan) *cl up: drvn over 2f out: one pce appr fnl f* **18/1**

0-00 **5** *2 3/4* **Elkhorn**[45] 2210 6-9-12 **74** (b) PaulMulrennan 7 68
(Miss J A Camacho) *hld up: hdwy over 1f out: edgd rt: nvr rchd ldrs* **7/2**[2]

0402 **6** *nse* **Wicked Wilma (IRE)**[1] 3546 4-8-2 **55** oh5 DanielleMcCreery(5) 10 49
(A Berry) *cl up on outside tl wknd over 1f out* **9/1**

-040 **7** *nk* **Bahama Baileys**[36] 2463 3-8-3 **56** GregFairley 9 47
(M Johnston) *cl up tl rdn and wknd over 1f out* **20/1**

4016 **8** *3/4* **Opal Noir**[13] 3129 4-9-6 **68** RobertWinston 5 58
(Miss L A Perratt) *chsd ldrs: rdn over 2f out: wknd over 1f out* **9/1**

-000 **9** *13* **Sokoke**[11] 3212 7-8-10 **63** oh10 ow8 GaryBartley(5) 8 7
(D A Nolan) *prom tl wknd qckly fr 2f out* **125/1**

58.93 secs (-1.07) **Going Correction** -0.10s/f (Good)
WFA 3 from 4yo+ 5lb **9** Ran SP% **115.9**
Speed ratings (Par 103): **104,102,101,99,95 95,94,93,72**
toteswinger: 1&2 £9.80, 1&3 £3.20, 2&3 £3.90. CSF £66.01 CT £137.88 TOTE £9.10: £2.00, £2.50, £1.30; EX 49.10.

Owner Con Harrington **Bred** Mrs Chris Harrington **Trained** Longton, Lancs

FOCUS
Just a fair sprint handicap, and with it being a definite advantage to be drawn low, the form could be shaky.

3582 THE SUNDAY MAIL FAMILY NIGHT NEXT WEEK H'CAP 6f 5y
5:15 (5:17) (Class 6) (0-65,62) 3-Y-0+ £2,388 (£705; £352) Stalls Centre

Form RPR
0-23 1 **Optical Illusion (USA)**81 1313 4-9-6 55........................ PaulHanagan 2 67
(R A Fahey) *trckd ldrs: led ent fnl f: hld on wl* 7/2[1]
2310 2 ½ **Imperial Sword**26 2751 5-9-1 55..............................(b) NeilBrown(5) 11 65
(T D Barron) *prom: led appr fnl f to ent fnl f: kpt on u.p: hld nr fin* 11/2
0S-0 3 2 **Orphan (IRE)**15 3079 6-9-5 57.. PJMcDonald(3) 6 61
(G M Moore) *towards rr: hdwy over 1f out: kpt on fnl f: nt pce of first two* 14/1
0003 4 ¾ **Mormeatmic**28 2706 5-9-5 54.. PaulMulrennan 7 55
(M W Easterby) *led to appr fnl f: kpt on same pce* 18/1
0133 5 ½ **Botham (USA)**13 3129 4-9-1 55.................................... GaryBartley(5) 12 55
(J S Goldie) *bhd and outpcd: hdwy over 1f out: nvr rchd ldrs* 5/1[3]
4401 6 1 **Maison Dieu**10 3255 5-9-9 58.. PatCosgrave 10 54
(E J Alston) *in tch: effrt over 1f out: edgd rt: sn no ex* 9/2[2]
0200 7 1 ¾ **Desert Hunter (IRE)**15 3079 5-8-10 45.......................... DO'Donohoe 8 36
(Micky Hammond) *bhd: drvn and outpcd over 2f out: n.d after* 20/1
-060 8 7 **Mill Creek**13 3139 3-8-4 45.. AndrewElliott 4 13
(Jedd O'Keeffe) *chsd ldr tl wknd over 1f out* 50/1
0-60 R **Alexia Rose (IRE)**10 3255 6-8-5 45...................(t) DanielleMcCreery(5) 1 —
(A Berry) *s.v.s: ref to r* 80/1

1m 11.39s (-0.81) **Going Correction** -0.10s/f (Good)
WFA 3 from 4yo+ 6lb 9 Ran SP% **92.3**
Speed ratings (Par 101): **101,100,97,96,96 94,92,83,—**
toteswinger: 1&2 £3.30, 1&3 £7.70, 2&3 £11.10. CSF £13.63 CT £97.96 TOTE £3.20: £1.30, £1.90, £2.80; EX 14.80 Place 6: £14.34 Place 5: £3.27.
Owner James Gaffney **Bred** Arthur I Appleton **Trained** Musley Bank, N Yorks

FOCUS
A moderate bunch of sprint handicappers in action, but the winner might have found his trip now that he is in the care of the Fahey yard and could be one to follow.
T/Plt: £15.90 to a £1 stake. Pool: £75,533.54. 3,447.78 winning tickets. T/Qpdt: £3.30 to a £1 stake. Pool: £4,803.99. 1,062.30 winning tickets. RY

3482 LINGFIELD (L-H)
Tuesday, July 1

OFFICIAL GOING: Standard
Wind: Moderate, behind Races 1-4; almost nil Races 5-6 Weather: Sunny, very warm

3583 SURREY ROYAL BRITISH LEGION VETERANS TA-100 CENTENARY H'CAP 1m (P)
6:00 (6:00) (Class 6) (0-65,65) 3-Y-0+ £2,590 (£770; £385; £192) Stalls High

Form RPR
-000 1 **Kaballero (GER)**33 2533 7-9-4 62.................................... JamieJones(5) 8 74
(S Gollings) *led for 1f: styd prom: led again wl over 2f out and sn kicked on: hung rt and idled fr over 1f out: hld on* 14/1
0-05 2 ¾ **Run For Ede'S**26 2758 4-9-8 61.......................................(p) IanMongan 3 71
(P M Phelan) *hld up in midfield: prog fr 3f out: rdn to chse wnr jst over 1f out: tried to chal fnl f: hanging rt and nt qckn* 12/1
0001 3 2 ¾ **Prince Charlemagne (IRE)**10 3265 5-9-9 62.............(b) GeorgeBaker 2 66
(R M Stronge) *hld up wl in rr: stdy prog fr 3f out: rdn and styd on to take 3rd ins fnl f: no threat to wnr* 5/1[1]
-203 4 1 ¼ **Moves Goodenough**6 3383 5-9-9 62..........................(b) HayleyTurner 9 63
(Andrew Turnell) *led after 1f: rdn and hdd wl over 2f out: wknd fnl f* 5/1[1]
050 5 1 ½ **Calistos Quest**29 2678 3-9-2 64.......................................(t) JohnEgan 4 62
(M Botti) *prom: rdn 3f out: outpcd over 2f out: no imp over 1f out: fdd ins fnl f* 8/1
3442 6 1 ¼ **Million Percent**6 3371 9-9-9 62.. LiamJones 11 57
(C R Dore) *hld up towards rr: shkn up over 2f out: modest prog fr over 1f out: nvr on terms* 13/2[2]
3050 7 1 ½ **Shouldntbethere (IRE)**26 1049 4-8-11 55.................. JackMitchell(5) 10 46
(Mrs P N Dutfield) *stdd s: hld up in last trio but sn nt gng wl: drvn over 3f out: modest late prog* 33/1
0030 8 1 ½ **Garland**8 3314 3-9-3 65...(t) RyanMoore 1 53
(R Hannon) *dwlt: rushed up on inner to chse ldrs: nt qckn over 2f out: wknd fnl f* 7/1[3]
0/0- 9 nk **Plush**326 4351 5-9-0 60.. RobbieEgan(7) 5 47
(D Flood) *stdd s: t.k.h and hld up in last trio: nt look keen and struggling on outer 3f out* 50/1
-400 10 11 **Sky Quest (IRE)**25 2795 10-9-2 62............................. HarryPoulton(7) 7 24
(J R Boyle) *plld hrd: hld up in midfield: wknd rapidly 2f out: eased* 16/1
0003 11 6 **Trivia (IRE)**6 3371 4-9-7 60.. JamesDoyle 12 8
(Ms J S Doyle) *chsd ldr after 2f to over 3f out: wknd rapidly* 12/1
410- 12 26 **Blue Space**303 5068 4-9-12 65.. SebSanders 6 —
(P J Makin) *chsd ldrs: wknd rapidly over 3f out: virtually p.u 2f out* 5/1[1]

1m 39.86s (1.66) **Going Correction** +0.225s/f (Slow)
WFA 3 from 4yo+ 9lb 12 Ran SP% **119.8**
Speed ratings (Par 101): **100,99,96,95,93 92,91,89,89,78 72,46**
toteswinger: 1&2 £21.80, 1&3 £19.40, 2&3 £8.30. CSF £173.47 CT £979.85 TOTE £19.40: £5.70, £2.90, £1.60; EX 147.20.
Owner John Crow Holdings Ltd **Bred** Stiftung Gestut Fahrhof **Trained** Scamblesby, Lincs
■ Stewards' Enquiry : James Doyle two-day ban: careless riding (Jul 15,16)

FOCUS
A very modest handicap though quite competitive with three 5-1 co-favourites. The race has been rated around the winner to last year's form in this country and the runner-up to a personal best.
Moves Goodenough Official explanation: jockey said gelding ran too free
Blue Space Official explanation: jockey said filly was hampered soon after start and never travelled

3584 TALACRE BEACH LEISURE GROUP MAIDEN FILLIES' STKS 6f (P)
6:30 (6:35) (Class 5) 2-Y-0 £3,238 (£963; £481; £240) Stalls Low

Form RPR
0 1 **Luxuria (IRE)**43 2253 2-9-0 0.. RyanMoore 2 67+
(R Hannon) *mde virtually all: rdn and styd on wl fr over 1f out* 5/4[1]
40 2 2 ¼ **Kitty Allen**14 3114 2-9-0 0.. JohnEgan 6 60
(M Botti) *reluctant to enter stalls: trckd ldrs: gng strly over 2f out: chsd wnr wl over 1f out: sn nt qckn and no imp* 7/2[2]
0 3 3 ¼ **Mistress Mary**39 2368 2-9-0 0.. AdamKirby 7 50
(G G Margarson) *w wnr tl jst over 2f out: sn outpcd and btn* 25/1
4 1 ½ **Carina Nebula (USA)** 2-9-0 0.. JimCrowley 8 46
(T G Mills) *dwlt: swishing tail early but trckd ldrs after 2f: effrt over 2f out: fdd over 1f out* 6/1[3]
00 5 1 **Betoula**27 2709 2-9-0 0.. AmirQuinn 4 43
(Mrs A L M King) *fractious bef gng in stalls: trckd ldrs: rdn over 2f out: sn btn* 50/1
2 6 1 ½ **Coconut Shy**34 2508 2-9-0 0.. DMylonas 9 38
(G Prodromou) *s.s: a struggling in rr: no ch fnl 2f* 8/1
0 7 3 ½ **Into My Arms**25 2769 2-9-0 0.. LPKeniry 5 28
(M S Saunders) *nvr on terms w ldrs: struggling fr 1/2-way* 50/1
00 8 19 **Duchess Of Doom (IRE)**8 3323 2-9-0 0.............................. MichaelHills 1 —
(B W Hills) *dwlt: t.k.h: hld up in midfield: stmbld after 1f: nt rcvr: t.o* 20/1
0 9 1 ¼ **Halaak (USA)**24 2821 2-8-9 0.................................... AhmedAjtebi(5) 10 —
(D M Simcock) *fractious bef gng in stalls: a bhd: t.o* 6/1[3]
U **Royal Acclaim** 2-9-0 0.. TPQueally 3 —
(M H Tompkins) *trckd ldrs: cl 5th whn broke leg and uns rdr jst ins fnl 2f* 14/1

1m 15.49s (3.59) **Going Correction** +0.225s/f (Slow) 10 Ran SP% **125.5**
Speed ratings (Par 91): **85,82,77,75,74 72,67,42,40,—**
toteswinger: 1&2 £2.10, 1&3 £9.70, 2&3 £16.20. CSF £5.99 TOTE £2.40: £1.20, £1.30, £4.80; EX 7.70.
Owner Mrs J Wood **Bred** Calley House Uk **Trained** East Everleigh, Wilts
■ Stewards' Enquiry : D Mylonas two-day ban: careless riding (Jul 15,16)

FOCUS
A race marred by the tragic accident that befell Royal Acclaim. The pace was ordinary and not many ever got into it whilst the winning time was also moderate, almost three seconds slower than the later all-aged handicap. The form probably does not amount to a great deal.

NOTEBOOK
Luxuria(IRE), ninth in a Windsor maiden on her debut that has produced a couple of winners, was a different proposition this time and was well backed to show improvement. Positively ridden from the start, she showed a good attitude to keep her rivals at bay and the race was in safe keeping all the way down the home straight. The form looks modest and she will need to progress a good deal again in order to follow up, but that is a possibility. (op 7-4)
Kitty Allen, awkward beforehand, was suited by the return to Polytrack over this extra furlong and looked a danger to the favourite on the home turn, but she was soon put in her place. With the nursery season now upon us she has a few more options. Official explanation: jockey said filly ran too free (op 9-2 tchd 5-1)
Mistress Mary, a well-beaten last of eight on her Newmarket debut, was much more professional this time and showed up for a long way. She is bred to stay and the best of her is likely to be seen in handicap company over further in due course. (tchd 20-1)
Carina Nebula(USA), a $50,000 yearling and retained for 16,000gns as a two-year-old, is a half-sister to a winning juvenile sprinter on dirt in the US. She looked very much in need of this initial experience, but did show a little ability and is entitled to improve. (op 17-2)
Betoula, beaten a long way in her two previous outings, played up before the start and, although she showed up for a fair way, it is debatable as to whether she improved much.
Halaak(USA), who beat just one home on her Doncaster debut, though a couple of winners have come out of that race, attracted quite a bit of market support, but having played up beforehand she showed nothing at all in the race. Obviously someone considers her capable of much better. (op 11-1 tchd 14-1)

3585 TINDLE NEWSPAPERS H'CAP 5f (P)
7:00 (7:01) (Class 6) (0-65,71) 3-Y-0+ £2,590 (£770; £385; £192) Stalls High

Form RPR
0005 1 **Coconut Moon**21 2906 6-9-0 60.. RobbieEgan(7) 3 77+
(D Flood) *v fast away: led for 150yds: 3rd whn n.m.r over 2f out: swtchd rt and rallied to ld 1f out: drvn clr* 5/1[3]
1016 2 3 ¼ **Blessed Place**2 3520 8-9-9 62.. DarryllHolland 4 67
(D J S Ffrench Davis) *rousted along to ld after 150yds: drvn and jnd 2f out: hdd 1f out: no ex but hld on for 2nd* 7/1
6612 3 1 **Nusoor (IRE)**3 3486 5-9-5 61..............................(v) KirstyMilczarek(3) 5 62
(Peter Grayson) *chsd ldng pair: wnt 2nd 1/2-way and jnd ldr 2f out: upsides 1f out: sn btn* 6/1
0051 4 ½ **Bertie Southstreet**7 3352 5-10-4 71 6ex....................(b) MartinDwyer 6 71
(J R Best) *settled in midfield: nvr gng pce of ldrs: effrt 2f out: kpt on one pce fnl f: n.d* 11/4[1]
1000 5 1 ¼ **The Magic Blanket (IRE)**27 2710 3-9-2 60.................(t) JamesDoyle 8 53+
(Stef Liddiard) *outpcd in last: kpt on fr over 1f out: no ch* 50/1
600- 6 ¾ **Kindallachan**235 6747 5-9-4 57.. SebSanders 1 49
(G C Bravery) *chsd ldrs: outpcd whn n.m.r over 2f out: no imp over 1f out: eased whn btn* 25/1
3222 7 1 ½ **Rocker**7 3346 4-9-9 62...(be) RyanMoore 10 49+
(G L Moore) *racd wd in rr: a struggling to go the pce* 7/2[2]
55-0 8 ½ **Tous Les Deux**49 2082 5-9-10 63.................................... GeorgeBaker 7 48
(Peter Grayson) *a in last trio: struggling to stay in tch fr 1/2-way: nvr a factor* 12/1
0015 9 2 ¼ **Fairfield Princess**3 3486 4-9-7 60................................ AdamKirby 9 37
(M S Saunders) *a outpcd in rr: nvr a factor* 8/1

59.94 secs (1.14) **Going Correction** +0.225s/f (Slow)
WFA 3 from 4yo+ 5lb 9 Ran SP% **117.0**
Speed ratings (Par 101): **99,93,92,91,89 88,85,85,81**
toteswinger: 1&2 £9.70, 1&3 £2.70, 2&3 £4.00. CSF £40.34 CT £216.09 TOTE £6.30: £2.30, £2.10, £1.50; EX 39.50.
Owner Valley Paddocks Racing Limited **Bred** Mrs R D Peacock **Trained** Wollerton, Shropshire
■ A first winner since regaining his licence for trainer David Flood.

FOCUS
They went a very strong early pace in this, but the final time was pretty average. Very few ever got into it and the race is best rated through the runner-up to his All-Weather mark.
The Magic Blanket(IRE) Official explanation: vet said gelding was struck into in front
Tous Les Deux Official explanation: jockey said gelding hung right under pressure

3586 BARCLAYS COMMERCIAL BANKING H'CAP 1m 5f (P)
7:30 (7:30) (Class 4) (0-85,81) 3-Y-0 £5,046 (£1,510; £755; £377; £188) Stalls Low

Form RPR
5-12 1 **Inchwood (IRE)**19 2977 3-9-7 81.................................... DarryllHolland 3 93+
(M A Jarvis) *hld up in last: shkn up 3f out and looking for spce: squeezed through to go 2nd over 1f out: led jst ins fnl f: drvn clr* 10/11[1]
0-12 2 2 ¼ **Reclamation (IRE)**13 3134 3-9-4 78.................................... SebSanders 4 87+
(Sir Mark Prescott) *hld up in 3rd: rdn 3f out: wd bnd 2f out: styd on u.p fnl f to take 2nd nr fin* 11/4[2]
2110 3 ½ **Leamington (USA)**55 1919 3-9-5 79.................................... RyanMoore 1 87
(M Johnston) *led: tried to kick on fr 3f out: hdd jst ins fnl f: one pce and lost 2nd nr fin* 10/1
2105 4 2 ¾ **Flash Of Colour**53 1962 3-9-0 74.................................... JimCrowley 5 78
(Mrs A J Perrett) *trckd ldr: rdn over 2f out: nt qckn and lost 2nd over 1f out: fdd fnl f* 7/1[3]

6616 **5** 3 ¾ **Love And Glory (FR)**[18] 3004 3-8-7 **67**.......................... SteveDrowne 2 65
(G L Moore) *hld up in 4th: rdn and effrt over 2f out: nt qckn wl over 1f out: wknd fnl f* **8/1**

2m 47.59s (1.59) **Going Correction** +0.225s/f (Slow) **5** Ran SP% **111.8**
Speed ratings (Par 102): **104,102,102,100,98**
CSF £3.71 TOTE £1.60: £1.10, £1.70; EX 3.50.

Owner Sheikh Ahmed Al Maktoum **Bred** Woodcote Stud Ltd **Trained** Newmarket, Suffolk

■ Stewards' Enquiry : Darryll Holland one-day ban: careless riding (Jul 15)

FOCUS
Probably quite a decent staying handicap for three-year-olds with all five having won at least once already this year. The early pace was modest, but the final time was solid enough and the first two home were the first to come off the bridle. It has been rated through the third.

3587 MAYO WYNNE BAXTER SOLICITORS H'CAP 6f (P)
8:00 (8:01) (Class 4) (0-85,83) 3-Y-0+ **£5,046** (£1,510; £755; £377; £188) **Stalls** Low

Form RPR

5111 **1** **Whiskey Junction**[6] 3374 4-10-3 **83** 6ex.............................. LPKeniry 6 94+
(A M Balding) *pressed ldr: led over 1f out: over a l clr fnl f: a holding on nr fin* **3/1**[2]

1005 **2** ½ **Vintage (IRE)**[20] 2947 4-9-1 **67**.............................. IanMongan 5 76
(J Akehurst) *trckd ldrs: wnt 3rd and rdn over 1f out: hanging and nt qckn: consented to run on fnl f and clsd on wnr nr fin* **8/1**

6102 **3** 2 ¼ **Yankee Storm**[5] 3394 3-9-2 **74**.............................. RyanMoore 1 74+
(M Johnston) *sn last: plenty to do 2f out: picked up ent fnl f: r.o to take 3rd last 75yds: nvr nrr* **11/4**[1]

0400 **4** 1 ½ **Woodcote (IRE)**[16] 3062 6-9-10 **76**..............................(tp) JimCrowley 3 73
(P R Chamings) *trckd ldng pair: rdn and nt qckn wl over 1f out: fdd ins fnl f* **10/1**

100 **5** nse **Pha Mai Blue**[20] 2945 3-9-8 **80**.............................. RichardKingscote 4 75
(W J Knight) *led: drvn and hdd over 1f out: wknd ins fnl f* **16/1**

2000 **6** ½ **Lucayos**[24] 2831 5-9-6 **79**.............................. KylieManser(7) 2 74
(Mrs H Sweeting) *hld up bhd ldrs on inner: effrt 2f out: pressing for a pl whn nt clr run jst ins fnl f: no ch after* **7/1**

4051 **7** nse **Bertbrand**[8] 3330 3-8-11 **76** 6ex..............................(b[1]) RobbieEgan(7) 7 69
(D Flood) *stdd s: hld up in rr but in tch: rdn wl over 1f out: no imp: kpt on nr fin* **20/1**

423 **8** 6 **China Cherub**[5] 3418 5-9-10 **76**..............................(v) SebSanders 8 52
(S Dow) *trckd ldrs and racd wd: rdn 2f out: wknd jst over 1f out* **9/2**[3]

1m 12.54s (0.64) **Going Correction** +0.225s/f (Slow)
WFA 3 from 4yo+ 6lb **8** Ran SP% **113.2**
Speed ratings (Par 105): **104,103,100,98,98 97,97,89**
toteswinger: 1&2 £6.80, 1&3 £1.40, 2&3 £4.30. CSF £26.49 CT £71.98 TOTE £4.20: £1.50, £2.50, £1.10; EX 40.70.

Owner Kingsclere Racing CLub **Bred** Mrs I A Balding **Trained** Kingsclere, Hants

FOCUS
A fair little sprint handicap run at a solid pace. It has been rated through the runner-up to the best view of his earlier form.

3588 RONALD LINGLEY'S 65TH BIRTHDAY H'CAP 1m 2f (P)
8:30 (8:31) (Class 6) (0-55,55) 3-Y-0+ **£2,590** (£770; £385; £192) **Stalls** Low

Form RPR

20-0 **1** **Lilac Moon (GER)**[52] 2001 4-9-6 **55**.............................. RichardKingscote 11 67+
(N J Vaughan) *pushed up to ld: mde all: had most in trble 3f out and sn kicked at least 3l clr: drvn over 1f out: hung rt ins fnl f: hld on* **4/1**[1]

35-0 **2** ¾ **Papradon**[22] 2884 4-9-5 **54**..............................(v) GeorgeBaker 7 62
(J R Best) *hld up towards rr: prog on outer over 2f out: drvn and styd on to take 2nd last 100yds: nvr quite rchd wnr* **9/2**[2]

3100 **3** 1 ½ **Formidable Guest**[17] 3036 4-9-4 **53**.............................. SebSanders 4 58
(J Pearce) *trckd ldrs: prog over 2f out: chsd wnr wl over 1f out: hld ins fnl f and lost 2nd last 100yds* **6/1**[3]

2002 **4** ¾ **Mix N Match**[10] 3265 4-9-3 **55**.............................. TravisBlock(3) 10 59
(R M Stronge) *hld up wl in rr: drvn on outer and struggling 3f out: prog over 1f out: styd on on fnl f: nrst fin* **7/1**

1000 **5** 1 ½ **Oasis Sun (IRE)**[30] 2641 5-9-6 **55**..............................(b) LPKeniry 1 56
(J R Best) *hld up in midfield: effrt over 2f out: hanging and nt qckn u.p over 1f out: kpt on* **22/1**

2603 **6** ½ **Postmaster**[12] 3162 6-9-4 **53**.............................. RobertHavlin 6 53
(R Ingram) *hld up wl in rr: pushed along over 2f out: sme prog fr over 1f out: kpt on: n.d* **8/1**

-040 **7** hd **Dr Light (IRE)**[13] 3131 4-9-4 **53**.............................. JimCrowley 9 52
(M A Peill) *hld up wl in rr: rdn 3f out: no prog tl styd on fr over 1f out: nrst fin* **17/2**

2036 **8** 3 ¾ **Recalcitrant**[11] 3208 5-9-5 **54**.............................. JamesDoyle 3 46+
(S Dow) *mostly chsd wnr: drvn over 3f out: wknd wl over 1f out* **9/1**

0054 **9** nk **Green Pirate**[10] 3265 6-9-0 **54**..............................(v) JackMitchell(5) 5 45
(C R Dore) *hld up in midfield: u.p and struggling 3f out: lost pl 2f out: n.d after* **14/1**

01/0 **10** 1 **Danish Monarch**[25] 2795 7-9-3 **52**.............................. SaleemGolam 8 41
(David Pinder) *chsd ldng trio: drvn over 3f out: steadily wknd fr 2f out* **33/1**

50 **11** ½ **Nil Bleu (USA)**[125] 722 4-9-3 **55**.............................. KirstyMilczarek(3) 13 43
(Noel T Chance) *hld up in last pair: rdn and struggling 3f out: no prog* **22/1**

05-6 **12** 1 **Mamichor**[20] 2930 5-9-3 **52**.............................. RichardSmith 2 38
(B R Johnson) *trckd ldng pair: drvn to dispute 2nd 2f out: wknd rapidly jst over 1f out* **16/1**

4100 **13** 29 **Balerno**[17] 3034 9-9-3 **52**.............................. IanMongan 12 —
(Mrs L J Mongan) *a in rr: wknd 3f out: t.o* **16/1**

2m 7.84s (1.24) **Going Correction** +0.225s/f (Slow) **13** Ran SP% **126.7**
Speed ratings (Par 101): **104,103,102,101,100 100,99,96,96,95 95,94,71**
toteswinger: 1&2 £4.20, 1&3 £6.50, 2&3 £3.10 CSF £22.40 CT £113.20 TOTE £6.50: £1.80, £2.90, £2.80; EX 29.10 Place 6 £ 25.33, Place 5 £ 7.19.

Owner A Black **Bred** Graf Und Grafin Von Stauffenberg **Trained** Hampton, Cheshire

FOCUS
A modest handicap, but quite a competitive one and a fair pace was set by the eventual winner. The overall form looks solid, with the third the best guide to the level, and the fourth rated to his latest effort.

Recalcitrant Official explanation: jockey said gelding had no more to give

T/Plt: £57.50 to a £1 stake. Pool: £76,145.44. 965.85 winning tickets. T/Qpdt: £10.70 to a £1 stake. Pool: £6,394.51. 440.20 winning tickets. JN

3106 THIRSK (L-H)
Tuesday, July 1

OFFICIAL GOING: Good to firm (10.6)
The ground was described as 'good to firm, a good covering of grass and no jar whatsoever'.
Wind: moderate 1/2 against Weather: fine and sunny

3589 WHITE SWAN AMPLEFORTH H'CAP 2m
6:20 (6:21) (Class 6) (0-60,60) 4-Y-0+ **£3,139** (£926; £463) **Stalls** Low

Form RPR

34-3 **1** **Squirtle (IRE)**[170] 152 5-8-4 **49**.............................. LukeMorris(3) 2 62+
(W M Brisbourne) *trckd ldrs gng wl: led on bit over 2f out: rdn clr 1f out: readily* **13/2**[3]

36-2 **2** 3 ¾ **Park's Prodigy**[165] 67 4-8-3 **50**..............................(t) PatrickDonaghy(5) 16 56
(P C Haslam) *mid-div: hdwy 5f out: wnt 2nd 1f out: edgd lft: kpt on same pce* **11/1**

3633 **3** 1 ½ **Court Of Appeal**[12] 3176 11-8-11 **60**..............................(tp) LanceBetts(7) 5 64
(B Ellison) *in tch: effrt 3f out: keeping on same pce whn n.m.r on inner ins fnl f* **10/1**

5102 **4** 1 ¾ **Elite Land**[7] 3335 5-8-7 **49**.............................. GrahamGibbons 12 51
(N Bycroft) *bhd: hdwy over 2f out: styd on same pce* **11/1**

000/ **5** 2 ¾ **Pilca (FR)**[12] 663 8-8-4 **46** oh1.............................. AdrianTNicholls 6 45
(D Carroll) *hld up in midfield: effrt 3f out: nvr nr ldrs* **13/2**[3]

0/23 **6** 7 **Bad Boy Al (IRE)**[26] 2752 4-9-3 **59**.............................. JoeFanning 9 58
(N J Vaughan) *w ldrs: led 3f out: sn hdd: wknd and eased ins fnl f* **5/2**[1]

2030 **7** 1 ½ **Chiff Chaff**[6] 3377 4-8-7 **49**.............................. TonyHamilton 1 38
(C R Dore) *mid-div: effrt over 3f out: wknd over 1f out* **20/1**

0434 **8** ½ **Parchment (IRE)**[10] 3279 6-8-2 **47**..............................(b) AndrewMullen(3) 8 35
(A J Lockwood) *hld up towards rr: hdwy 3f out: sn rdn: nvr nr ldrs* **6/1**[2]

-425 **9** nk **El Dee (IRE)**[55] 461 5-8-0 **49** oh1 ow3.............................. PaulPickard(7) 3 37
(D Carroll) *led tl 3f out: lost pl over 1f out* **16/1**

5065 **10** 8 **Qaasi (USA)**[25] 2804 6-8-9 **54** ow3.............................. MarkLawson(3) 14 32
(M Brittain) *hld up in rr: hdwy 4f out: hrd rdn and wknd over 2f out* **16/1**

0-00 **11** 3 **Vice Admiral**[56] 1892 5-8-4 **46** oh1.............................. DaleGibson 4 20
(M W Easterby) *trckd ldrs: drvn over 3f out: wknd over 1f out: eased* **12/1**

-400 **12** 6 **Finnegans Rainbow**[12] 3176 6-7-11 **46** oh1......... CharlotteKerton(7) 11 13
(M C Chapman) *midfield: drvn on outer 6f out: nvr a factor* **66/1**

0000 **13** 4 ½ **Monte Pattino (USA)**[10] 3279 4-8-4 **46** oh1..............................(t) PatrickMathers 15 8
(C J Teague) *s.i.s: in rr: drvn 6f out: bhd fnl 4f* **100/1**

-650 **14** 1 ¼ **Firestorm (IRE)**[10] 3279 4-8-1 **46** oh1.............................. DuranFentiman(3) 13 6
(C W Fairhurst) *in rr: drvn over 4f out: nvr on terms: eased ins fnl f* **66/1**

0-00 **15** 25 **Into Action**[40] 1136 4-8-7 **52** ow2..............................(tp) MichaelJStainton(3) 7 —
(Mrs Marjorie Fife) *trckd ldrs: drvn over 5f out: sn lost pl and bhd: t.o* **50/1**

-545 **16** nk **Gavanello**[34] 348 5-7-11 **46** oh1..............................(bt) RichardRowe(7) 10 —
(M C Chapman) *in rr: t.o 5f out* **100/1**

3m 28.13s (-5.27) **Going Correction** -0.125s/f (Firm) **16** Ran SP% **126.4**
Speed ratings (Par 101): **108,106,105,104,103 99,98,98,98,94 92,89,87,87,74 74**
toteswinger: 1&2 £25.40, 1&3 £8.80, 2&3 £32.90. CSF £76.96 CT £729.41 TOTE £8.20: £1.50, £3.00, £2.40, £3.10; EX 96.20.

Owner J Jones Racing Ltd **Bred** Ballygallon Stud Limited **Trained** Great Ness, Shropshire

■ Stewards' Enquiry : Richard Rowe one-day ban: used whip when out of contention (Jul 15)
Patrick Donaghy double caution: careless riding

FOCUS
A low-grade handicap run at a sound pace in a decent time and a very ready winner. The form looks modest but sound enough rated through the runner-up, third and fourth.

Vice Admiral Official explanation: trainer said after scoping gelding was found to have mucus on its lungs

3590 ANTHONY FAWCETT MEMORIAL MAIDEN STKS 6f
6:50 (6:50) (Class 5) 2-Y-0 **£4,274** (£1,271; £635; £317) **Stalls** High

Form RPR

1 **Prime Delivery (USA)** 2-9-3 0.............................. TedDurcan 8 79+
(R M H Cowell) *hld up in tch: effrt over 2f out: led last 75yds: jst hld on* **8/1**

0 **2** shd **Cosmic Sun**[13] 3140 2-8-10 0.............................. FrederikTylicki(7) 16 79
(R A Fahey) *chsd ldrs: drvn 3f out: chal ins fnl f: jst failed* **33/1**

22 **3** 2 ½ **Secret Venue**[16] 3055 2-9-3 0.............................. TonyHamilton 7 71
(Jedd O'Keeffe) *swtchd rt after s: led tl 2f out: ev ch ins fnl f: no ex* **4/1**[2]

4 2 ½ **Sirenuse (IRE)** 2-8-12 0.............................. TomEaves 14 59
(B Smart) *trckd ldrs: led 2f out: hung lft: hdd ins fnl f: wknd* **3/1**[1]

5 ½ **Aahaygran (USA)** 2-8-12 0.............................. FergusSweeney 15 57+
(K R Burke) *mid-div: styd on fnl 2f: nvr rchd ldrs* **14/1**

6 2 **Mary Mason** 2-8-9 0.............................. AndrewMullen(3) 10 51+
(Mrs A Duffield) *dwlt: kpt on fnl 2f: nvr nr ldrs* **40/1**

0 **7** nk **Acclaben (IRE)**[17] 3049 2-9-3 0.............................. TPO'Shea 12 55
(G A Swinbank) *chsd ldrs: lost pl over 2f out* **10/1**

53 **8** 2 ¼ **Coleorton Choice**[12] 3178 2-9-3 0.............................. NCallan 9 48
(K A Ryan) *chsd ldrs: hung lft and lost pl over 1f out* **6/1**

9 nse **Sardan Dansar (IRE)** 2-8-12 0.............................. MickyFenton 3 43
(Mrs A Duffield) *nvr bttr than mid-div* **33/1**

6 **10** ½ **Gems Star**[28] 2696 2-9-3 0.............................. GrahamGibbons 4 47
(J J Quinn) *in rr: sme hdwy 2f out: nvr on terms* **100/1**

5 **11** nk **Monsieur Jourdain (IRE)**[80] 1324 2-9-3 0.............................. DavidAllan 5 46
(T D Easterby) *in rr: sme hdwy fnl 2f: nvr a factor* **14/1**

46 **12** 2 **Rio Cobolo (IRE)**[13] 3140 2-9-3 0.............................. StephenDonohoe 1 40
(Paul Green) *a towards rr* **50/1**

13 nse **Off Hand** 2-8-9 0.............................. DuranFentiman(3) 6 35
(T D Easterby) *dwlt: a in rr* **66/1**

50 **14** 1 ½ **The Canny Dove (USA)**[10] 3277 2-8-10 0.............................. DeanHeslop(7) 17 35
(T D Barron) *chsd ldrs: rdn and lost pl over 2f out* **10/1**

20 **15** ¾ **Black Attack (IRE)**[20] 2951 2-9-0 0.............................. RussellKennemore(3) 11 33
(Paul Green) *chsd ldrs: hung lft over 2f out: sn lost pl* **9/2**[3]

00 **16** 10 **Ennovy**[21] 2910 2-8-12 0.............................. KimTinkler 2 —
(N Tinkler) *t.k.h on outer: trckd ldrs: lost pl 3f out* **125/1**

1m 12.26s (-0.44) **Going Correction** -0.075s/f (Good) **16** Ran SP% **127.5**
Speed ratings (Par 94): **99,98,95,92,91 88,88,85,85,84 84,81,81,79,78 65**
toteswinger: 1&2 £69.50, 1&3 £19.00, 2&3 £25.70. CSF £265.18 TOTE £12.50: £3.90, £11.20, £2.60; EX 433.40.

Owner Prestige Racing **Bred** London Thoroughbred Services Ltd **Trained** Six Mile Bottom, Cambs

FOCUS
A fair maiden rated through the third. The fourth is the likely big improver.

NOTEBOOK

Prime Delivery(USA), a robust newcomer, travelled strongly just off the pace. He picked up in good style to take a narrow advantage well inside the last and he can improve on this debut effort. (op 11-1 tchd 12-1)

Cosmic Sun, well beaten on his first outing two weeks earlier, was soon being rousted along. He stuck to his guns and, upsides inside the last, was only just denied. He will improve again, especially over seven. (op 50-1)

Secret Venue, drawn in single figures, was soon setting the fractions hard against the stands'-side rail. In the end the first two proved much stronger. (op 7-2 tchd 3-1)

Sirenuse(IRE) ◆, a narrow newcomer, was drawn high yet was soon racing away from the favoured rail. She went on running away but her inexperience showed and, ending up towards the centre, she ran out of fuel near the finish. This will have taught her plenty. (op 4-1)

Aahaygran(USA), very green to post, picked up in encouraging fashion in the second half of the contest. There should be plenty of improvement from this $110,000 purchase. (op 12-1 tchd 16-1)

Mary Mason, a May foal, looked very burly and she made a pleasing debut after a tardy start.

3591 HARES OF SNAPE H'CAP — 7f

7:20 (7:21) (Class 5) (0-75,75) 3-Y-O+ — **£4,274** (£1,271; £635; £317) **Stalls** Low

Form — RPR

2443 **1** **Violent Velocity (IRE)**[4] 3443 5-9-2 **70** JamieKyne(7) 5 — 83
(J J Quinn) *s.i.s: hld up in rr: hdwy and swtchd rt over 1f out: str run to ld nr fin* **7/2**[2]

2323 **2** ½ **Esoterica (IRE)**[11] 3203 5-9-9 **70** (b) DanielTudhope 4 — 82
(J S Goldie) *trckd ldrs: effrt over 1f out: edgd rt: no ex last strides* **7/4**[1]

6213 **3** ½ **Micky Mac (IRE)**[129] 686 4-8-10 **57** GrahamGibbons 3 — 67
(T D Walford) *led: hdd and no ex towards fin* **16/1**

5420 **4** 1¾ **Hiccups**[15] 3087 8-10-0 **75** TomEaves 9 — 81
(M Dods) *hld up towards rr: hdwy over 2f out: kpt on fnl f* **12/1**

0004 **5** nse **Cheery Cat (USA)**[5] 3404 4-8-8 **62** (p) BMcHugh(7) 1 — 67
(D W Barker) *trckd ldrs: styd on same pce appr fnl f* **16/1**

6330 **6** 1¼ **Oeuf A La Neige**[15] 3082 8-8-7 **57** JamieMoriarty(3) 7 — 59
(Miss L A Perratt) *mid-div: effrt over 2f out: kpt on same pce* **16/1**

0203 **7** 1½ **Soto**[25] 2780 5-9-2 **63** DaleGibson 6 — 61
(M W Easterby) *trckd ldrs: t.k.h: hung lft and one pce fnl 2f* **20/1**

00-0 **8** 5 **Multitude (IRE)**[15] 3082 4-8-9 **56** (b) DavidAllan 8 — 41
(T D Easterby) *chsd ldrs: wknd 1f out* **40/1**

5011 **9** 8 **Wisdom's Kiss**[33] 2533 4-9-7 **68** (b) TedDurcan 10 — 31
(J D Bethell) *in rr: bhd fnl 2f* **15/2**[3]

0000 **10** ½ **Louisiade (IRE)**[11] 3218 7-8-6 **56** oh1 RussellKennemore(3) 12 — 18
(M C Chapman) *hld up in midfield: effrt on outer over 3f out: sn wknd* **50/1**

2262 **11** 7 **Guest Connections**[12] 3172 5-9-7 **68** (v) AdrianTNicholls 11 — 11
(D Nicholls) *mid-div: drvn over 4f out: lost pl over 1f out* **10/1**

4-00 **12** 6 **Jerry Hamilton (USA)**[14] 3117 3-8-10 **65** (b[1]) JoeFanning 2 — —
(M Johnston) *s.i.s: t.k.h in rr: swtchd rt after 2f: bhd and eased 2f out* **40/1**

1m 25.67s (-1.53) **Going Correction** -0.125s/f (Firm)
WFA 3 from 4yo+ 8lb — **12** Ran SP% **116.4**
Speed ratings (Par 103): **103,102,101,99,99 98,96,90,81,81 73,66**
toteswinger: 1&2 £2.00, 1&3 £13.40, 2&3 £6.80. CSF £9.39 CT £84.51 TOTE £4.90: £1.70, £1.40, £4.40; EX 12.00.
Owner Mrs S Quinn **Bred** Miss Jill Finegan **Trained** Settrington, N Yorks

FOCUS

A tight-knit handicap and the winner did well to overcome traffic problems. The form looks pretty solid with the runner-up performing to his recent level.

Wisdom's Kiss Official explanation: jockey said gelding never travelled

Guest Connections Official explanation: jockey said gelding hung both ways throughout

Jerry Hamilton(USA) Official explanation: jockey said gelding lost its action

3592 RECTANGLE GROUP H'CAP — 1m

7:50 (7:51) (Class 4) (0-85,80) 3-Y-O — **£5,569** (£1,657; £828; £413) **Stalls** Low

Form — RPR

0244 **1** **King Fingal (IRE)**[11] 3229 3-8-13 **72** GrahamGibbons 4 — 79
(J J Quinn) *in rr: hdwy on wd outside 3f out: styd on to ld last stride* **7/2**[2]

1-06 **2** shd **Almoutaz (USA)**[37] 2425 3-9-7 **80** WilliamBuick 1 — 87
(B W Hills) *led: edgd rt over 1f out: hdd post* **5/1**

4123 **3** 2 **Montiboli (IRE)**[25] 2781 3-9-0 **73** NCallan 6 — 75
(K A Ryan) *trckd ldrs: effrt over 2f out: no ex ins fnl f* **10/3**[1]

500 **4** 3½ **Merrion Tiger (IRE)**[39] 2380 3-8-2 **61** oh1 DaleGibson 2 — 55
(K R Burke) *hld up towards rr: hdwy on ins over 3f out: sn chsng ldrs: kpt on same pce appr fnl f* **7/1**

-130 **5** shd **Blindspin**[31] 2624 3-9-6 **79** TonyHamilton 3 — 73
(M Dods) *hld up in rr: effrt on ins 3f out: kpt on same pce appr fnl f* **11/2**

6-23 **6** 3½ **Elk Trail (IRE)**[17] 3031 3-9-4 **77** MickyFenton 5 — 63
(T P Tate) *chsd ldrs: sn drvn along: outpcd 3f out: no threat after* **4/1**[3]

003 **7** 15 **Important News**[11] 3200 3-8-8 **67** JoeFanning 7 — 18
(M Johnston) *chsd ldrs: lost pl over 1f out: eased and sn bhd* **16/1**

-600 **8** 31 **Jim Martin**[10] 3251 3-8-10 **69** TomEaves 8 — —
(Miss L A Perratt) *hld up in last on outer: lost pl over 3f out: sn bhd: virtually p.u: t.o* **16/1**

1m 38.66s (-1.44) **Going Correction** -0.125s/f (Firm) — **8** Ran SP% **121.6**
Speed ratings (Par 102): **102,101,99,96,96 92,77,46**
toteswinger: 1&2 £3.80, 1&3 £2.00, 2&3 £5.50. CSF £22.97 CT £65.60 TOTE £6.40: £1.90, £1.70, £1.50; EX 23.90.
Owner Geoffrey Van Cutsem **Bred** The Lavington Stud **Trained** Settrington, N Yorks

FOCUS

A fair handicap won by an improving sort. The runner-up has been rated 4lb up on the best of his two-year-old form.

3593 TURFTV H'CAP — 1m

8:20 (8:22) (Class 6) (0-55,57) 3-Y-O+ — **£3,139** (£926; £463) **Stalls** Low

Form — RPR

0306 **1** **Emperor's Well**[15] 3082 9-9-4 **53** (b) PaulMulrennan 8 — 61+
(M W Easterby) *mde all: kpt on fnl 2f: jst lasted* **8/1**

0006 **2** ½ **Anduril**[56] 1902 7-8-13 **48** (p) PatrickMathers 7 — 55
(I W McInnes) *hld up in rr: effrt over 2f out: hung lft: styd on wl fnl f: jst hld* **50/1**

0403 **3** hd **Silly Gilly (IRE)**[12] 3175 4-9-0 **49** PaulHanagan 13 — 55
(R E Barr) *chsd ldrs: styd on fnl f: no ex towards fin* **16/1**

3000 **4** ½ **Time To Regret**[17] 3201 8-9-5 **54** (p) DanielTudhope 3 — 59
(I W McInnes) *in tch: effrt over 2f out: kpt on wl fnl f* **40/1**

0-20 **5** nk **Reddy Ronnie (IRE)**[11] 3201 4-9-1 **50** DavidAllan 4 — 55
(D Carroll) *in tch: effrt over 2f out: kpt on wl fnl f* **11/2**[2]

0064 **6** 2 **Nufoudh (IRE)**[12] 3175 4-9-0 **49** GrahamGibbons 9 — 49
(Miss Tracy Waggott) *trckd wnr: effrt over 2f out: wknd ins fnl f* **11/1**

2450 **7** 1¼ **Silidan**[31] 2597 5-9-0 **52** MarkLawson(3) 1 — 49
(M Brittain) *chsd ldrs: one pce fnl 2f* **22/1**

00-6 **8** 1½ **Barataria**[52] 2009 6-9-5 **54** RobertWinston 17 — 48
(R Bastiman) *s.i.s: hld up in rr: hdwy over 2f out: put hd in air and hung lft over 1f out: nt keen* **10/1**

4000 **9** ½ **Franksalot (IRE)**[17] 3034 8-9-5 **54** RoystonFfrench 5 — 47
(I W McInnes) *mid-div: effrt over 2f out: nvr nr ldrs* **28/1**

-102 **10** 2½ **Lewis Lloyd (IRE)**[10] 3281 5-8-13 **55** BMcHugh(7) 15 — 42
(R E Barr) *reminders after s: in rr: sme hdwy over 2f out: nvr on terms* **16/1**

0000 **11** ½ **Sea Land (FR)**[36] 2444 4-9-3 **52** TomEaves 10 — 38
(B Ellison) *midfield: effrt 3f out: sn rdn: wknd over 1f out* **9/4**[1]

3020 **12** 1¾ **Ensign's Trick**[4] 3431 4-9-2 **54** LukeMorris(3) 6 — 36
(W M Brisbourne) *chsd ldrs: hung bdly rt over 1f out: sn lost pl* **7/1**[3]

000- **13** 7 **Ignition**[270] 5964 6-9-4 **53** PAspell 14 — 19
(A Kirtley) *in rr: bhd fnl 3f* **100/1**

0566 **14** 1¾ **Contemplation**[15] 3077 5-9-6 **55** (t) TPO'Shea 12 — 16
(G A Swinbank) *in rr: effrt over 2f out: sn wknd and eased* **11/1**

-005 **15** 1¼ **Borodinsky**[10] 3281 7-9-1 **53** (p) AndrewMullen(3) 16 — 12
(R E Barr) *sn drvn along in rr: bhd fnl 2f* **33/1**

1m 39.61s (-0.49) **Going Correction** -0.125s/f (Firm) — **15** Ran SP% **123.4**
Speed ratings (Par 101): **97,96,96,95,95 93,92,90,90,87 87,85,78,76,75**
toteswinger: 1&2 £61.30, 1&3 £6.30, 2&3 £122.00. CSF £384.78 CT £6144.67 TOTE £8.00: £2.40, £23.50, £2.30; EX 610.10.
Owner M W Easterby **Bred** M W Easterby And K Hodgson **Trained** Sheriff Hutton, N Yorks

FOCUS

A seller in all but name. It was rather gifted to the winner but in the end the post came just in time with the next four home fast closing him down at the line. The form is rated around the third and sixth.

Barataria Official explanation: jockey said gelding became unbalanced in home straight

3594 RECTANGLE H'CAP — 5f

8:50 (8:53) (Class 4) (0-85,85) 3-Y-O+ — **£5,569** (£1,657; £828; £413) **Stalls** High

Form — RPR

3163 **1** **Baybshambles (IRE)**[5] 3405 4-8-7 **66** RoystonFfrench 16 — 76
(R E Barr) *chsd ldrs on ins: styd on wl fnl f: led post* **11/4**[1]

0000 **2** shd **Rasaman (IRE)**[5] 3405 4-8-9 **68** (tp) JoeFanning 6 — 78
(K A Ryan) *w ldrs: led jst ins fnl f: edgd rt: hdd post* **16/1**

6362 **3** 1½ **River Thames**[14] 3111 5-9-7 **80** NCallan 9 — 85
(K A Ryan) *hld up on stands' side: hdwy over 1f out: nt clr run ins fnl f: swtchd rt and kpt on towards fin* **4/1**[2]

4040 **4** ½ **First Order**[24] 2843 7-9-6 **79** (v) TomEaves 1 — 82
(Miss L A Perratt) *trckd ldrs on wd outside: hung lft and kpt on fnl f* **7/1**

3006 **5** 1½ **Hawaii Prince**[5] 3401 4-8-7 **66** oh8 SilvestreDeSousa 14 — 63
(S T Mason) *w ldr: led on ins 2f out: hdd jst ins fnl f: hmpd and fdd* **25/1**

0500 **6** 1 **Brut**[5] 3401 6-8-2 **68** (p) AdeleRothery(7) 10 — 62
(D W Barker) *prom: outpcd after 2f: kpt on fnl f* **12/1**

0104 **7** hd **Windjammer**[12] 3171 4-8-8 **67** DavidAllan 11 — 60
(T D Easterby) *chsd ldrs: fdd appr fnl f* **11/2**[3]

6600 **8** hd **Cape Royal**[16] 3062 8-9-7 **80** (bt) StephenDonohoe 8 — 72
(J M Bradley) *prom: outpcd and lost pl after 2f* **20/1**

3000 **9** 1¼ **Classic Encounter (IRE)**[40] 2326 5-9-12 **85** FergusSweeney 3 — 73
(D M Simcock) *led overall in centre: hdd 2f out: wknd appr fnl f* **22/1**

59.21 secs (-0.39) **Going Correction** -0.075s/f (Good)
WFA 3 from 4yo+ 5lb — **9** Ran SP% **92.9**
Speed ratings (Par 105): **100,99,97,96,94 92,92,92,90**
toteswinger: 1&2 £11.30, 1&3 £1.60, 2&3 £11.70. CSF £27.19 CT £87.25 TOTE £2.90: £1.10, £5.50, £1.40; EX 33.20 Place 6 £256.01, Place 5 £84.01.
Owner Miss S Haykin **Bred** Mrs H F Mahr **Trained** Seamer, N Yorks
■ Stewards' Enquiry : Joe Fanning caution: careless riding

FOCUS

A depleted field with four non-runners and three withdrawn at the stalls. The winner continues on the upgrade. The third and fourth are the guide to the form.

T/Jkpt: Not won. T/Plt: £105.30 to a £1 stake. Pool: £95,828.17. 663.93 winning tickets. T/Qpdt: £17.10 to a £1 stake. Pool: £6,889.85. 296.95 winning tickets. WG

2775 CATTERICK (L-H)

Wednesday, July 2

OFFICIAL GOING: Good to firm (good in places; 8.6)

Wind: light, half- behind Weather: fine and sunny

3597 EUROPEAN BREEDERS' FUND ZETLAND MEDIAN AUCTION MAIDEN STKS — 7f

2:30 (2:32) (Class 5) 2-Y-O — **£3,691** (£1,098; £548; £274) **Stalls** Low

Form — RPR

44 **1** **Watergate (IRE)**[26] 2783 2-9-3 0 SebSanders 7 — 84+
(Sir Mark Prescott) *mde all: clr 1f out: eased towards fin* **4/5**[1]

63 **2** 7 **Tropical Blue**[13] 3164 2-9-3 0 TPO'Shea 6 — 69+
(Jennie Candlish) *trckd ldrs: wnt 2nd over 2f out: eased whn no ch w wnr ins fnl f* **5/1**[2]

3 2¾ **Digger Derek (IRE)** 2-9-3 0 PaulHanagan 5 — 56
(R A Fahey) *chsd ldrs: outpcd and lost pl 4f out: hdwy on outside over 2f out: edgd lft: kpt on fnl f* **16/1**

4 ½ **Across The Rhine (USA)** 2-9-3 0 RBurke 3 — 54
(R J Osborne, Ire) *s.i.s: hld up: chceked bnd over 4f out: hdwy over 2f out: nvr a threat* **7/1**

260 **5** 3½ **Woteva**[34] 2534 2-8-12 0 GrahamGibbons 1 — 41
(J J Quinn) *sn chsng ldrs: drvn over 2f out: wknd over 1f out* **6/1**[3]

45 **6** 5 **Pacific Bay (IRE)**[10] 3292 2-8-12 0 RoystonFfrench 8 — 28
(Mrs A Duffield) *chsd ldrs: drvn over 3f out: wknd 2f out* **10/1**

0 **7** 2 **Kingaroo (IRE)**[19] 3008 2-9-0 0 MarkLawson(3) 4 — 28
(Garry Moss) *s.i.s: sn drvn along: nvr on terms* **100/1**

8 nse **Franali (IRE)** 2-8-12 0 TonyHamilton 2 — 23
(R F Fisher) *s.s: a in rr* **40/1**

1m 27.22s (0.22) **Going Correction** +0.10s/f (Good) — **8** Ran SP% **117.4**
Speed ratings (Par 94): **102,94,90,90,86 80,78,78**
toteswinger: 1&2 £2.00, 1&3 £4.30, 2&3 £9.30. CSF £5.44 TOTE £2.10: £1.10, £1.50, £3.90; EX 6.50.
Owner Charles C Walker-Osborne House III **Bred** Irish National Stud **Trained** Newmarket, Suffolk
■ Sir Mark Prescott has now won this maiden four times since 1999. His '05 winner, Confidential Lady, later won the French Oaks.

FOCUS

An ordinary maiden, but an above-average winner. The winning time was very decent for a race of its type, only around half a second slower than the later older-horse 61-80 handicap.

NOTEBOOK

Watergate(IRE) ◆ failed to build on the promise he showed in a good maiden at Haydock on his debut when only fourth at Doncaster last time, but that race probably came a little too soon and, in any case, the form has worked out much better than one might have expected. The only horse from the Prescott yard entered in the Group 1 National Stakes, he is clearly held in high regard and confirmed that initial promise on this step up in trip, getting to the front soon after the start and drawing right away in the straight. He looks very useful and there should be more to come as he continues to strengthen up. (op Evens tchd 5-4, 11-8 in places)

Tropical Blue confirmed the improved form he showed when third at Leicester on his latest start, but he still proved no match for the very useful winner. He is now eligible for nurseries. (op 9-2 tchd 4-1)

Digger Derek(IRE), an 18,000euros son of Key Of Luck and half-brother to Mistress Bailey, a dual winner at around 7f at two, proved easy to back but showed ability. He is entitled to come on for this. (op 14-1 tchd 12-1)

Across The Rhine(USA) ◆, a son of Cuvee, a high-class juvenile on the dirt in the US and half-brother to five winners, including multiple middle-distance winner Trick Or Treat, was brought over from Ireland for his racecourse debut and was well backed against the favourite in the morning, but he was found out by his inexperience. Having proved reluctant to load, he missed the break and ran green, but showed definite signs of ability. He can improve a ton for this experience. (op 11-2 tchd 9-2)

Woteva failed to prove her stamina on this first run over 7f. (op 10-1)

3598 EUROPEAN BREEDERS' FUND MAIDEN FILLIES' STKS 5f

3:00 (3:02) (Class 5) 2-Y-O **£3,885** (£1,156; £577; £288) **Stalls** Low

Form RPR

32 **1** **Shyrl**[14] 3123 2-9-0 0 ... JamieSpencer 3 89
(S A Callaghan) *mde all: shkn up and edgd rt over 1f out: readily* **1/4**[1]

0 **2** *3 ½* **Minotaurious (IRE)**[35] 2497 2-9-0 0 ... FergusSweeney 6 76
(K R Burke) *chsd ldrs: wnt 2nd appr fnl f: no ch w wnr* **28/1**[3]

40 **3** *1 ½* **Mo Mhuirnin (IRE)**[11] 3259 2-9-0 0 ... PaulHanagan 7 71
(R A Fahey) *outpcd after 2f: hdwy over 1f out: tk 3rd ins fnl f* **33/1**

2 **4** *2 ½* **Hysterical Lady**[37] 2443 2-9-0 0 ... AdrianTNicholls 4 62
(D Nicholls) *sn chsng ldrs: wknd fnl f* **9/2**[2]

4 **5** *1 ¼* **Impressible**[22] 2903 2-9-0 0 ... DavidAllan 8 58
(E J Alston) *sn w wnr: wknd appr fnl f* **28/1**[3]

55 **6** *6* **First Choice (IRE)**[16] 3085 2-9-0 0 ... FergalLynch 2 36
(K A Ryan) *sn outpcd: nvr on terms* **40/1**

7 *1 ½* **Wotatomboy** 2-8-11 0 ... MichaelJStainton(3) 1 31
(R M Whitaker) *s.i.s: nvr wnt pce* **50/1**

8 *1 ¾* **Carhue Princess (IRE)** 2-8-11 0 ... MarkLawson(3) 5 24
(N Bycroft) *s.s: a outpcd and bhd* **100/1**

59.40 secs (-0.40) **Going Correction** -0.30s/f (Firm) **8** Ran SP% **113.4**

Speed ratings (Par 91): **91,85,83,79,77 67,65,62**

toteswinger: 1&2 £3.60, 1&3 £4.60, 2&3 £21.10. CSF £15.50 TOTE £1.30: £1.02, £3.90, £3.80; EX 10.30.

Owner Saleh Al Homaizi & Imad Al Sagar **Bred** Cromlech Bloodstock **Trained** Newmarket, Suffolk

FOCUS

This revolved around Queen Mary runner-up Shyrl and she duly obliged by outclassing her rivals without having to run near to her previous level.

NOTEBOOK

Shyrl ◆, the Queen Mary second, came here for a confidence-booster and she duly obliged without really having to come out of third gear. Given a no-nonsense ride, she still looked a little green when asked to stamp her authority on the race and will likely come on again for this experience. Fast ground looks important to her cause, which is not that surprising given her sire's influence, and a return to Group company is now n the cards for her. The Prix Robert Papin at Maisons-Laffitte (won by Natagora last year) or the Molecomb at Goodwood later this month both rate as possible targets. (tchd 2-7 in places)

Minotaurious(IRE), out the back in the Hilary Needler at Beverley on debut last time, was ridden with greater restraint on this drop into maiden company and stepped up nicely on her initial run. She found the winner in a different league, but still finished nicely enough clear in second and is now going the right way. (op 25-1)

Mo Mhuirnin(IRE) showed her best form to date on this switch to a quicker surface and left the impression that she probably wants a stiffer test now. She is also now eligible for nurseries.

Hysterical Lady failed to confirm the promise of her debut second at Carlisle in May and dropped out disappointingly from the final-furlong marker. This was a backwards step, but it is too soon to write her off and she will have the option of nurseries after her next assignment. (tchd 5-1)

3599 5TH REGIMENT ROYAL ARTILLERY H'CAP 7f

3:30 (3:31) (Class 4) (0-80,78) 3-Y-O+ **£4,727** (£1,406; £702; £351) **Stalls** Low

Form RPR

6122 **1** **Gap Princess (IRE)**[18] 3026 4-9-1 65 ... PaulHanagan 8 74
(R A Fahey) *chsd ldrs: wnt 2nd over 1f out: styd on to ld towards fin* **8/1**[3]

5000 **2** *nk* **Nuit Sombre (IRE)**[14] 3142 8-9-6 70 ... (p) SilvestreDeSousa 6 78
(G A Harker) *led: kpt on wl fnl f: hdd nr fin* **14/1**

0300 **3** *nse* **Countdown**[7] 3367 6-10-0 78 ... (b) DavidAllan 11 86+
(T D Easterby) *in rr: hdwy on outside over 2f out: styd on wl fnl f* **10/1**

4204 **4** *shd* **Hiccups**[1] 3591 8-9-11 75 ... TomEaves 4 83
(M Dods) *edgd lft sn after s: trckd ldrs: kpt on wl fnl f* **5/1**[1]

1604 **5** *2* **Al Samha (USA)**[18] 3031 3-9-6 78 ... JoeFanning 5 77
(M Johnston) *prom: drvn 3f out: kpt on same pce appr fnl f* **12/1**

6-13 **6** *½* **Turn Me On (IRE)**[21] 2925 5-8-10 65 ... KellyHarrison(5) 14 66+
(T D Walford) *in rr: hdwy and nt clr run over 1f out: styd on ins fnl f* **11/2**[2]

0002 **7** *¾* **Joshua's Gold (IRE)**[12] 3211 7-9-0 64 ... (v) DNolan 7 63
(D Carroll) *chsd ldrs: wknd fnl 150yds* **11/2**[2]

2-24 **8** *¾* **Carmenero (GER)**[16] 3087 5-9-11 75 ... DO'Donohoe 10 72
(W R Muir) *s.i.s: sme hdwy over 2f out: n.m.r: nvr nr ldrs* **9/1**

554 **9** *½* **Stoic Leader (IRE)**[2] 3548 8-9-9 73 ... RoystonFfrench 9 68
(R F Fisher) *mid-div on outer: effrt over 2f out: nvr trbld ldrs* **14/1**

0230 **10** *½* **Champain Sands (IRE)**[16] 3087 9-9-3 67 ... GrahamGibbons 1 61
(E J Alston) *s.i.s: a towards rr* **11/1**

0200 **11** *1 ¾* **Kunte Kinteh**[12] 3211 4-8-12 62 ... AdrianTNicholls 12 51
(D Nicholls) *dwlt: in rr: sme hdwy on ins over 2f out: n.m.r: sn wknd* **18/1**

0002 **12** *9* **Lap Of Honour (IRE)**[13] 3165 4-9-12 76 ... TPO'Shea 3 41
(Jennie Candlish) *mid-div: lost pl over 2f out: eased* **12/1**

030 **13** *1* **Ducal Regancy Duke**[12] 3227 4-8-7 60 ... AndrewMullen(3) 2 22
(C J Teague) *hmpd sn after s: mid-div: lost pl over 2f out: sn bhd* **50/1**

1m 26.76s (-0.24) **Going Correction** +0.10s/f (Good)

WFA 3 from 4yo+ 8lb **13** Ran SP% **121.9**

Speed ratings (Par 105): **105,104,104,104,102 101,100,99,99,98 96,86,85**

toteswinger: 1&2 £18.80, 1&3 £9.60, 2&3 £47.00. CSF £117.49 CT £1146.56 TOTE £5.60: £2.10, £5.10, £3.50; EX 106.00.

Owner Dr W D Ashworth **Bred** D Veitch And Musagd Abo Salim **Trained** Musley Bank, N Yorks

■ Stewards' Enquiry : Tom Eaves one-day ban: careless riding (July 16)

FOCUS

A fair, competitive handicap and average form for the grade rated around the fourth and fifth.

Carmenero(GER) Official explanation: jockey said gelding was denied a clear run

Kunte Kinteh Official explanation: jockey said gelding was denied a clear run

3600 WE RACE AGAIN NEXT WEDNESDAY MEDIAN AUCTION MAIDEN STKS 5f 212y

4:00 (4:01) (Class 6) 3-4-Y-O **£2,047** (£604; £302) **Stalls** Low

Form RPR

0465 **1** **Mujahope**[11] 3283 3-8-12 49 ... (v) KellyHarrison(5) 2 58
(C J Teague) *s.i.s: t.k.h in rr: hdwy on ins over 2f out: styd on to ld ins fnl f: drvn clr* **18/1**

2 *2 ½* **Naias (IRE)** 3-8-5 0 ... FrederikTylicki(7) 10 45+
(R A Fahey) *chsd ldrs on outer: edgd lft 2f out: upsides jst ins fnl f: styd on same pce* **12/1**

00 **3** *½* **Dubai To Barnsley**[14] 3144 3-9-3 0 ... SebSanders 5 48
(Garry Moss) *led: t.k.h: hdd and hmpd over 4f out: led over 1f out tl ins fnl f: no ex* **33/1**

0 **4** *¾* **Billy Bowmore**[20] 2966 3-9-3 0 ... TonyHamilton 4 46
(M Dods) *in rr: hdwy 2f out: styd on ins fnl f* **11/1**

2240 **5** *¾* **Walragnek**[19] 2991 4-9-9 58 ... AndrewElliott 7 46
(J G M O'Shea) *sn trcking ldrs: effrt over 2f out: sn hmpd: kpt on same pce fnl f* **9/1**

2222 **6** *½* **Kyzer Chief**[11] 3283 3-9-3 65 ... RoystonFfrench 8 42
(R E Barr) *chsd ldrs on outer: effrt over 2f out: hung lft: kpt on same pce fnl f* **5/4**[1]

50-0 **7** *6* **Champagne Sue**[39] 2399 4-9-1 32 ... PJMcDonald(3) 1 20
(D W Barker) *mid-div: effrt over 2f out: sn btn* **66/1**

0- **8** *1* **Uncle Harry**[379] 2739 3-9-3 0 ... GrahamGibbons 3 20
(J J Quinn) *mid-div: drvn over 2f out: sn lost pl* **33/1**

220- **9** *2 ¾* **Lavande**[254] 6386 3-8-12 65 ... JamieSpencer 9 6
(M J Wallace) *unruly leaving paddock: trckd ldrs: led over 4f out tl over 1f out: sn wknd and eased* **9/2**[2]

56 **10** *½* **Tump Mac**[5] 3438 4-9-6 0 ... MarkLawson(3) 6 11
(N Bycroft) *dwlt: a in rr* **6/1**[3]

1m 15.07s (1.47) **Going Correction** +0.10s/f (Good)

WFA 3 from 4yo 6lb **10** Ran SP% **115.6**

Speed ratings (Par 101): **94,90,90,89,88 87,79,78,74,73**

toteswinger: 1&2 £22.10, 1&3 £35.30, 2&3 £42.60. CSF £210.07 TOTE £20.90: £3.70, £3.00, £6.00; EX 184.70.

Owner Collins Chauffeur Driven Executive Cars **Bred** R W Huggins **Trained** Station Town, Co Durham

■ Stewards' Enquiry : Frederik Tylicki two-day ban: careless riding (July 18-19)

FOCUS

A very weak sprint maiden with the winner rated just 49.

3601 TELEPHONE 01748 810165 FOR RACEDAY HOSPITALITY H'CAP 5f 212y

4:30 (4:30) (Class 4) (0-80,79) 3-Y-O+ **£4,727** (£1,406; £702; £351) **Stalls** Low

Form RPR

3103 **1** **Tawzeea (IRE)**[14] 3141 3-9-5 77 ... JoeFanning 3 86
(M Johnston) *chsd ldr: led over 1f out: r.o strly* **7/2**[2]

651- **2** *2 ¾* **Seta Pura**[246] 6557 3-8-10 68 ... RoystonFfrench 1 68
(Mrs A Duffield) *chsd ldrs: styd on fnl f: tk 2nd nr fin* **8/1**

4030 **3** *nk* **Dark Champion**[15] 3111 8-8-8 60 oh1 ... (v) PaulHanagan 4 61
(R E Barr) *led: hdd over 1f out: no ex* **10/1**

4040 **4** *1 ¼* **Legendary Guest**[11] 3280 3-8-8 66 ... (p) TomEaves 2 61
(D W Barker) *trckd ldrs: effrt over 2f out: kpt on fnl f* **10/1**

1210 **5** *nk* **Expensive Art (IRE)**[39] 2398 4-9-13 79 ... GrahamGibbons 5 75
(S A Callaghan) *rrd s: hdwy over 4f out: rdn over 2f out: kpt on same pce* **11/2**

2-63 **6** *½* **Hotham**[18] 3050 5-9-9 75 ... DNolan 6 69
(N Wilson) *trckd ldrs: outpcd over 2f out: kpt on fnl f* **5/2**[1]

0035 **7** *1 ¼* **Red Cape (FR)**[4] 3477 5-9-2 68 ... (b) SebSanders 7 58
(Mrs R A Carr) *s.i.s: in rr: kpt on fnl 2f: nvr a factor* **4/1**[3]

1m 13.68s (0.08) **Going Correction** +0.10s/f (Good)

WFA 3 from 4yo+ 6lb **7** Ran SP% **115.5**

Speed ratings (Par 105): **103,99,98,97,96 96,94**

toteswinger: 1&2 £4.00, 1&3 £5.10, 2&3 £11.00. CSF £31.48 CT £255.67 TOTE £5.30: £2.20, £3.30; EX 35.70.

Owner Hamdan Al Maktoum **Bred** Shadwell Estate Company Limited **Trained** Middleham Moor, N Yorks

FOCUS

A modest sprint handicap with the first two improvers and the third the best guide.

3602 STOCKTON H'CAP 1m 3f 214y

5:00 (5:00) (Class 6) (0-65,62) 4-Y-O+ **£2,047** (£604; £302) **Stalls** Low

Form RPR

0-62 **1** **Fistral**[14] 3131 4-8-4 45 ... PaulHanagan 2 53
(P D Niven) *mid-div: drvn over 5f out: hdwy over 3f out: chal over 1f out: edgd lft: led post* **5/2**[1]

023 **2** *shd* **Mister Fizzbomb (IRE)**[8] 3337 5-9-7 62 ... (v) GrahamGibbons 10 70
(J S Wainwright) *sn chsng ldrs: rdn over 4f out: led over 1f out: crowded ins fnl f: hdd post* **10/3**[2]

6-06 **3** *6* **Bollin Freddie**[13] 3176 4-8-1 45 ... AndrewMullen(3) 6 43
(A J Lockwood) *sn chsng ldrs: effrt over 3f out: kpt on same pce fnl 2f* **15/2**

0-45 **4** *1 ¼* **Cecina Marina**[8] 3335 5-7-13 45 ... KellyHarrison(5) 7 41
(Mrs K Walton) *chsd ldrs: one pce fnl 2f* **12/1**

604 **5** *½* **Funky Town (IRE)**[22] 2914 6-8-7 48 ... TomEaves 8 44
(Grant Tuer) *led after 2f tl over 1f out: fdd* **16/1**

015 **6** *2 ¾* **Saluscraggie**[29] 2701 6-9-2 62 ... DanielleMcCreery(5) 4 53
(R E Barr) *s.i.s: sme hdwy 3f out: nvr nr ldrs* **7/1**[3]

/006 **7** *2 ½* **Toss The Caber (IRE)**[37] 2467 6-8-4 45 ... RoystonFfrench 5 32
(K G Reveley) *chsd ldrs: drvn over 3f out: wknd 2f out* **8/1**

6-00 **8** *2* **Intavac Boy**[19] 3010 7-8-6 47 ... JoeFanning 1 31
(S P Griffiths) *led 2f: chsd ldrs: wknd 2f out* **16/1**

6006 **9** *½* **College Land Boy**[12] 3226 4-8-4 45 ... TWilliams 9 28
(A Kirtley) *in rr: reminders 5f out: nvr a factor* **50/1**

0004 **10** *1* **Jalamid (IRE)**[5] 3131 6-7-11 45 ... (bt[1]) SophieDoyle(7) 11 27
(M A Barnes) *s.v.s: hdwy on outside 4f out: rdn and hung lft 2f out: sn wknd* **16/1**

0-0 **11** *13* **Desert Rat (IRE)**[13] 3175 4-9-0 55 ... (p) SebSanders 3 16
(Micky Hammond) *hld up in rr: drvn over 4f out: no rspnse: bhd and eased ins fnl f* **18/1**

2m 37.95s (-0.95) **Going Correction** +0.10s/f (Good) **11** Ran SP% **119.6**

Speed ratings (Par 101): **107,106,102,102,101 99,98,96,96,95 87**

toteswinger: 1&2 £2.80, 1&3 £6.20, 2&3 £7.60. CSF £10.72 CT £55.73 TOTE £3.80: £1.70, £1.60, £2.60; EX 11.60 Place 6: £897.02 Place 5: £656.45.

Owner Hale Racing Limited **Bred** Mrs Wendy Miller **Trained** Barton-le-Street, N Yorks

■ Stewards' Enquiry : Graham Gibbons caution: using whip down shoulder in forehand position

FOCUS
A poor handicap, run at a solid pace, in which the first pair came well clear. It was a decent winning time for the grade.
T/Plt: £993.20 to a £1 stake. Pool: £61,009.50. 44.84 winning tickets. T/Qpdt: £734.90 to a £1 stake. Pool: £2,880.08. 2.90 winning tickets. WG

3309 CHEPSTOW (L-H)
Wednesday, July 2

OFFICIAL GOING: Good to firm (8.8)
Wind: Light, against Weather: Fine

3603 JOHN SMITH'S/E.B.F. MAIDEN STKS — 6f 16y
6:40 (6:43) (Class 5) 2-Y-O — £3,561 (£1,059; £529; £264) Stalls High

Form — RPR
6 **1** **Gallagher**[47] 2150 2-9-3 0 .... RichardHughes 11 — 89+
(B J Meehan) *a.p: led wl over 1f out: pushed clr ins fnl f: comf* **10/11**[1]
52 **2** 4½ **My Sweet Georgia (IRE)**[16] 3092 2-8-12 0 .... WilliamBuick 8 — 68
(B W Hills) *a.p: rdn over 2f out: wnt 2nd ins fnl f: no ch w wnr* **11/4**[2]
0 **3** 1¼ **My Best Man**[22] 2916 2-9-3 0 .... TGMcLaughlin 10 — 69
(B R Millman) *hld up in tch: rdn and edgd rt over 1f out: kpt on same pce fnl f* **80/1**
4 shd **Hand Painted** 2-9-0 0 .... TravisBlock(3) 17 — 70+
(P J Makin) *dwlt: hld up in rr: hdwy over 2f out: carried rt and n.m.r briefly over 1f out: kpt on ins fnl f: bttr for r* **40/1**
5 nk **Piazza San Pietro** 2-9-3 0 .... SteveDrowne 1 — 68
(C G Cox) *a chsng ldrs: one pce fnl f* **33/1**
23 **6** ½ **Lesley's Choice**[36] 2473 2-9-0 0 .... KevinGhunowa(3) 12 — 67
(P A Blockley) *led: hdd wl over 1f out: sn rdn: wknd ins fnl f* **11/2**[3]
0 **7** 7 **Join Up**[21] 2951 2-9-3 0 .... AdamKirby 16 — 46
(W R Swinburn) *hld up towards rr: stdy hdwy over 3f out: rdn over 1f out: wknd fnl f* **16/1**
8 3½ **Jimwasright (IRE)** 2-8-10 0 .... RichardEvans(7) 6 — 35
(P D Evans) *mid-div: rdn and lost pl over 2f out: n.d after* **50/1**
9 1½ **Cash In The Attic** 2-8-12 0 .... EdwardCreighton 15 — 26
(M R Channon) *dwlt: outpcd: nvr nr ldrs* **28/1**
0 **10** 1¾ **Endofmytether**[22] 2916 2-8-12 0 .... ShaneKelly 4 — 20
(P D Evans) *s.i.s: short-lived effrt over 3f out* **100/1**
0 **11** 1½ **Hollow Green (IRE)**[44] 2253 2-8-12 0 .... JamesDoyle 9 — 16
(P D Evans) *a in rr* **66/1**
05 **12** hd **Indian Blade (IRE)**[11] 3267 2-9-3 0 .... RichardSmith 13 — 20
(M D I Usher) *mid-div: lost pl over 3f out: sn bhd* **66/1**
04 **13** shd **Twos And Eights (IRE)**[63] 1722 2-9-3 0 .... PaulEddery 14 — 20
(G D Blake) *w ldr tl rdn and wknd over 2f out* **66/1**
14 1¾ **Conakry** 2-9-3 0 .... CatherineGannon 5 — 15
(M R Channon) *pushed along over 3f out: a towards rr* **66/1**
5 **15** nk **Meirig's Dream (IRE)**[51] 2042 2-9-3 0 .... RichardKingscote 3 — 14
(B G Powell) *chsd ldrs 3f* **50/1**
0 **16** 7 **Lady Aoy (IRE)**[16] 3085 2-8-12 0 .... VinceSlattery 7 — —
(D J Wintle) *s.i.s: rdn over 3f out: a in rr* **200/1**

1m 10.88s (-2.02) **Going Correction** -0.275s/f (Firm) — **16** Ran SP% **121.8**
Speed ratings (Par 94): **102,96,94,94,93 93,83,79,77,74 72,72,72,70,69 60**
toteswinger: 1&2 £1.02, 1&3 £10.40, 2&3 Not won. CSF £3.06 TOTE £2.20: £1.10, £1.50, £12.60; EX 4.40.
Owner Brimacombe, McNally, Rickman & Sangster **Bred** Ptarmigan Bloodstock Limited **Trained** Manton, Wilts

FOCUS
A very decent winning time for a race like this, 0.22 seconds faster than the later handicap for older horses.

NOTEBOOK
Gallagher ◆ showed why he started favourite when not living up to market expectations in a stronger race than this at Newbury last month. Well regarded by his trainer, he scored in the style of one who seems sure to go on to better things. (tchd 11-10, 6-5 in a place)
My Sweet Georgia(IRE) did not mind being back up to 6f but proved no match for the convincing winner. (op 3-1 tchd 2-1)
My Best Man, a half-brother to three winners, had shown nothing when starting at 40/1 for his Salisbury debut last month. His starting price suggests that connections will be delighted by this much-improved effort. (tchd 66-1)
Hand Painted ◆, a half-brother to several winners, made a highly promising debut despite doubling in price in the ring. He will know more next time. (op 20-1)
Piazza San Pietro made a satisfactory debut and could well have been at a disadvantage being out in the centre of the course thanks to his low draw. (op 28-1 tchd 25-1)
Lesley's Choice, a big drifter in the market, again had plenty of use made of him and got found out by the step up to 6f. (op 12-1)
Twos And Eights(IRE) Official explanation: jockey said colt lost its action

3604 JOHN SMITH'S PREMIER CLUB CLAIMING STKS — 1m 14y
7:10 (7:13) (Class 6) 3-Y-O+ — £2,072 (£616; £308; £153) Stalls High

Form — RPR
3411 **1** **Ogre (USA)**[8] 3343 3-8-8 68 .... TGMcLaughlin 4 — 59
(P D Evans) *hld up in mid-div: hdwy 3f out: led over 1f out: drvn ins fnl f: jst hld on* **1/1**[1]
2424 **2** hd **Wizby**[126] 711 5-8-10 45 ow1 .... RichardHughes 16 — 54
(P D Evans) *hld up in mid-div: hdwy 3f out: rdn and ev ch over 1f out: rdn and r.o towards fin: jst failed* **12/1**
1000 **3** 5 **Mrs Jefferson (IRE)**[32] 2603 3-8-1 63 ow1 .... JackDean(5) 11 — 46
(J G Portman) *a.p: wnt 2nd 3f out: shkn up to ld wl over 1f out: sn hdd: rdn and wknd ins fnl f* **22/1**
0300 **4** 1½ **The Gaikwar (IRE)**[7] 3360 9-8-12 51 ....(b) HaddenFrost(5) 13 — 46
(R A Harris) *hld up towards rr: swtchd rt ins fnl f: kpt on to take 4th nr fin* **8/1**[3]
0350 **5** ½ **Personify**[24] 2863 6-8-12 48 ....(p) KevinGhunowa(3) 14 — 43
(R A Harris) *hld up in tch: rdn and ev ch 2f out: wknd over 1f out* **10/1**
00/0 **6** shd **Follow The Buzz**[30] 2667 4-9-0 0 .... AdamKirby 2 — 42
(M Wellings) *carried rt s: hdwy over 3f out: sn rdn: wknd wl over 1f out* **200/1**
0/60 **7** 2 **The Plainsman**[30] 2667 6-8-12 42 .... LukeMorris(3) 1 — 38
(P W Hiatt) *wnt rt s: hld up towards rr: rdn 3f out: nvr trbld ldrs* **66/1**
560- **8** hd **Psychic Star**[20] 1890 5-9-0 67 .... VinceSlattery 10 — 37
(Mrs A M Thorpe) *rdn over 3f out: a towards rr* **33/1**
000- **9** 2 **Foxy Diplomat**[147] 6873 4-8-12 45 .... KirstyMilczarek(3) 15 — 33
(R Dickin) *led: hdd wl over 1f out: sn wknd* **50/1**
0556 **10** nse **Outer Hebrides**[13] 3181 7-9-4 55 ....(v) SteveDrowne 7 — 36
(J M Bradley) *chsd ldr 5f: wknd 2f out* **18/1**
-000 **11** 6 **Robbmaa (FR)**[13] 3183 3-8-8 55 .... BMcHugh(7) 3 — 26
(A W Carroll) *s.i.s: nvr nr ldrs* **50/1**
4000 **12** 2 **Eastern Princess**[7] 3361 4-8-6 45 ....(b) DominicFox(3) 5 — 8
(G H Yardley) *prom tl wknd 3f out* **100/1**
0-04 **13** 17 **Sekula Pata (NZ)**[83] 1286 9-9-0 50 ....(v) EdwardCreighton 12 — —
(E J Creighton) *a in rr: eased whn no ch fnl f* **50/1**
0 **14** 7 **Berry Pomeroy**[57] 1896 3-8-8 0 .... SamHitchcott 9 — —
(A G Newcombe) *hld up in tch: lost pl over 5f out: sn bhd: eased whn no ch fnl f* **150/1**
5111 **U** **One Night In Paris (IRE)**[37] 2456 5-8-8 70 .... RichardEvans(7) 6 — —
(P D Evans) *hld up in mid-div: stmbld and uns rdr after 2f: broke leg: dead* **7/2**[2]

1m 34.86s (-1.34) **Going Correction** -0.275s/f (Firm)
WFA 3 from 4yo+ 9lb — **15** Ran SP% **122.2**
Speed ratings (Par 101): **95,94,89,88,87 87,85,85,83,83 77,75,58,51,—**
toteswinger: 1&2 £1.70, 1&3 £8.20, 2&3 £20.50. CSF £14.83 TOTE £2.10: £1.30, £2.80, £8.20; EX 20.60.The winner was subject to a friendly claim. Wizby was claimed by H. J. Manners for £5,000.
Owner Diamond Racing Ltd **Bred** Gulf Coast Farms LLC **Trained** Pandy, Monmouths
■ Stewards' Enquiry : Jack Dean one-day ban: careless riding (Jul 16); one-day ban: failing to keep straight leaving stalls (Jul 17)

FOCUS
There were plenty available at fancy prices in this ordinary claimer. The form is best rated around the runner-up and seventh rather that the much higher-rated winner and third
Follow The Buzz Official explanation: jockey said gelding hung right-handed
Foxy Diplomat Official explanation: jockey said gelding ran too free

3605 JOHN SMITH'S (S) STKS — 7f 16y
7:40 (7:44) (Class 6) 3-Y-O — £1,942 (£578; £288; £144) Stalls High

Form — RPR
30-0 **1** **Ambrose Princess (IRE)**[9] 3314 3-8-6 56 .... KevinGhunowa(3) 16 — 48
(R A Harris) *bhd: rdn and hdwy on stands' side over 1f out: str run u.p to ld post* **11/2**[2]
-550 **2** shd **Never Sold Out (IRE)**[13] 3166 3-8-11 47 ....(v) LukeMorris(3) 2 — 53
(J G M O'Shea) *s.i.s: hdwy over 3f out: rdn to ld over 2f out: edgd rt ins fnl f: ct post* **8/1**[3]
0050 **3** 2 **Poppy Red**[7] 3359 3-8-9 45 .... PaulFitzsimons 15 — 42
(Miss J R Tooth) *s.i.s: hld up and bhd: stdy hdwy over 3f out: rdn and ev ch over 2f out: hrd rdn and nt qckn ins fnl f* **16/1**
04-5 **4** 1¼ **New Balls Please (IRE)**[21] 2935 3-9-0 51 ....(p) ShaneKelly 1 — 44
(P M Phelan) *hld up in tch: rdn and ev ch over 2f out: one pce ins fnl f* **4/1**[1]
6360 **5** nk **Cherished Song**[9] 3330 3-8-6 46 .... DominicFox(3) 14 — 38
(M G Quinlan) *hld up and bhd: rdn over 2f out: hdwy over 1f out: one pce fnl f* **20/1**
0046 **6** ¾ **Flying Seasons**[9] 3330 3-8-10 50 ow1 .... JamesMillman(5) 8 — 42
(B R Millman) *s.i.s: sn hld up in tch: rdn and ev ch over 2f out: no ex ins fnl f* **11/2**[2]
0006 **7** 3¼ **Nestor Protector (IRE)**[49] 2099 3-9-0 45 .... SamHitchcott 12 — 32
(A B Haynes) *hld up in tch: rdn and ev ch over 2f out: wknd ins fnl f* **12/1**
0000 **8** nk **Rosy Dawn**[3] 3524 3-9-0 48 ....(be) JamesDoyle 5 — 32
(Ms J S Doyle) *w ldrs: hrd rdn 3f out: wknd fnl f* **14/1**
3600 **9** 1 **Mama Leo**[21] 2935 3-8-9 50 ....(b) PaulEddery 6 — 24
(J G M O'Shea) *hld up: sn wl in rr: rdn and hdwy whn hung lft over 1f out: n.d* **25/1**
0040 **10** ½ **Fraamington**[7] 3359 3-8-9 43 .... MCGeran(5) 3 — 27
(M R Channon) *hld up in mid-div: rdn over 2f out: no hdwy* **20/1**
0 **11** 2 **Lassie Goes West (IRE)**[13] 3166 3-8-4 0 .... ShaneCreighton(5) 11 — 17
(E J Creighton) *hld up in mid-div: hung lft over 2f out: wknd over 1f out* **66/1**
56-0 **12** 1¾ **La Varrosa**[175] 92 3-8-10 44 ow6 .... HaddenFrost(5) 10 — 18
(J D Frost) *prom 4f* **16/1**
0000 **13** 2 **Marysedge**[16] 3086 3-8-10 42 ow1 .... PaulMulrennan 9 — 8
(R Brotherton) *w ldrs: led after 2f: rdn and hdd over 2f out: wknd wl over 1f out* **66/1**
00-0 **14** 5 **Defnikov**[24] 2864 3-9-0 45 .... EdwardCreighton 7 — —
(A B Haynes) *led 2f: rdn over 3f out: wknd over 2f out* **50/1**
000 **15** 4 **Alutando (IRE)**[7] 3379 3-8-9 0 ....(p) CatherineGannon 4 — —
(B Palling) *s.s: a in rr* **12/1**
040- **16** 8 **Little Evie**[274] 5887 3-8-9 55 .... SteveDrowne 13 — —
(R J Hodges) *a bhd* **9/1**

1m 25.5s (2.30) **Going Correction** -0.275s/f (Firm) — **16** Ran SP% **124.0**
Speed ratings (Par 98): **75,74,72,71,70 69,66,65,64,64 61,59,57,51,47 38**
toteswinger: 1&2 £13.00, 1&3 £44.50, 2&3 £40.50. CSF £46.47 TOTE £5.70: £2.20, £3.40, £5.40; EX 65.60.The winner was bought in for 4,200gns.
Owner Brian Hicks **Bred** Tally-Ho Stud **Trained** Earlswood, Monmouths

FOCUS
A pedestrian winning time for this poor seller. The form looks weak rated around the third and fourth.

3606 JOHN SMITH'S EXTRA SMOOTH H'CAP — 1m 4f 23y
8:10 (8:12) (Class 6) (0-65,65) 4-Y-O+ — £2,428 (£722; £361; £180) Stalls Low

Form — RPR
240- **1** **Soviet Sceptre (IRE)**[15] 5188 7-8-9 **53** ....(tp) FergusSweeney 4 — 62+
(Tim Vaughan) *s.i.s: hld up and bhd: stdy hdwy 4f out: nt clr run and swtchd rt over 2f out: rdn to ld wl ins fnl f: r.o* **9/1**
/633 **2** ½ **Greenwich Village**[9] 3321 5-9-4 **62** .... PaulDoe 7 — 70
(W J Knight) *led: rdn and hdd 2f out: led 1f out: hdd and no ex wl ins fnl f* **5/1**[1]
5 **3** 2 **Sonnengold (GER)**[26] 2776 7-8-3 **50** .... LukeMorris(3) 1 — 55
(B J Llewellyn) *a.p: rdn over 2f out: hung lft over 1f out: styd on to take 3rd last strides* **20/1**
3304 **4** nk **Floodlight Fantasy**[16] 2715 5-8-5 **56** ....(b) BMcHugh(7) 16 — 60
(Dr R D P Newland) *hld up in tch: rdn wl over 1f out: styd on ins fnl f* **6/1**[2]
1/0- **5** hd **Awash (USA)**[16] 3099 6-8-7 **51** ....(p) PaulFitzsimons 12 — 55
(D Broad, Ire) *hld up in tch: jnd ldr gng wl over 3f out: shkn up to ld 2f out: sn rdn: hdd 1f out: no ex towards fin* **11/1**
-540 **6** 2¾ **Capistrano**[5] 3448 5-8-6 **50** ....(b) PaulEddery 6 — 50
(G D Blake) *hld up and bhd: hdwy over 2f out: rdn over 1f out: nvr trbld ldrs* **25/1**
3025 **7** nk **Bob's Your Uncle**[33] 2567 5-8-13 **57** .... JamesDoyle 2 — 56
(J G Portman) *s.i.s: sn hld up in mid-div: hdwy over 2f out: sn rdn: wknd over 1f out* **6/1**[2]
4400 **8** 1 **Pretty Demanding (IRE)**[12] 3220 4-9-4 **65** .... DominicFox(3) 11 — 63+
(M G Quinlan) *s.i.s: hld up and bhd: sme hdwy whn nt clr run over 2f out: n.d after* **12/1**

256- 9 shd My Legal Eagle (IRE)[262] 6200 14-7-13 48 ow2 MCGeran(5) 5 45
(E G Bevan) hld up and bhd: sme hdwy over 4f out: rdn over 2f out: sn wknd 33/1
0035 10 6 Summer Bounty[16] 3084 12-8-4 48 WilliamBuick 10 36
(F Jordan) s.s: a bhd 14/1
331- 11 ½ Master At Arms[13] 2415 5-9-7 65 SteveDrowne 14 52
(Daniel Mark Loughnane, Ire) hld up in mid-div: rdn over 2f out: sn wknd 8/1[3]
540/ 12 4½ Resplendent Star (IRE)[15] 1021 11-8-13 57 (bt) VinceSlattery 17 37
(Mrs L J Young) prom: rdn over 3f out: sn wknd 66/1
000/ 13 1¾ Triple Bluff[68] 5911 5-8-10 59 ow3 HaddenFrost(5) 15 36
(J D Frost) hld up in mid-div: rdn over 3f out: bhd fnl 2f 25/1
0-00 14 1½ Le Corvee (IRE)[17] 6-9-7 65 RichardHughes 3 40
(A W Carroll) hld up in mid-div: eased and virtually p.u ins fnl f: reins snapped 8/1[3]
500/ 15 14 Out Of This Way[562] 6860 5-8-10 54 CatherineGannon 8 6
(Mrs N S Evans) chsd ldr to 4f out: rdn and wknd 3f out 50/1

2m 37.24s (-1.76) **Going Correction** -0.10s/f (Good) 15 Ran SP% 119.0
Speed ratings (Par 101): **101,100,99,99,99 97,96,96,96,92 91,88,87,86,77**
toteswinger: 1&2 £23.40, 1&3 £31.20, 2&3 £27.80. CSF £48.70 CT £892.00 TOTE £10.00: £3.30, £2.80, £5.70; EX 77.50.
Owner The Welsh Valleys Syndicate **Bred** Barnane Stud **Trained** Aberthin, Vale of Glamorgan

FOCUS
A weak handicap that looksmsound enough rated around the third, fourth and fifth.

3607 JOHN SMITH'S "NO NONSENSE" RACING H'CAP 1m 14y
8:40 (8:42) (Class 5) (0-75,75) 3-Y-0+ **£3,885** (£1,156; £577; £288) **Stalls** High

Form RPR
5124 1 Ermine Grey[32] 2597 7-8-10 58 KirstyMilczarek(3) 8 66
(A W Carroll) slipped leaving stalls: hld up and sn detached in rr: hdwy over 2f out: rdn over 1f out: edgd rt ins fnl f: led nr fin: r.o 9/1
-501 2 hd Yathreb (USA)[12] 3221 3-9-6 74 (b) MartinDwyer 5 80
(J L Dunlop) hld up and bhd: swtchd rt and hdwy 2f out: rdn to ld ins fnl f: hdd nr fin 15/8[1]
1- 3 1¾ Hallingdal (UAE)[260] 6254 3-9-7 75 J-PGuillambert 7 77+
(M Johnston) hld up and bhd: hdwy over 3f out: rdn to ld over 1f out: hdd ins fnl f: nt qckn 11/2
0360 4 ½ Kensington (IRE)[16] 3093 7-10-0 73 JamesDoyle 3 75
(P D Evans) w ldr: led over 3f out tl over 1f out: no ex towards fin 22/1
1-02 5 hd Flying Applause[5] 3449 3-9-3 71 FergusSweeney 2 71
(A King) led: hdd over 3f out: rdn over 1f out: one pce 3/1[2]
0131 6 2¼ Bold Cross (IRE)[13] 3165 5-9-10 69 PaulFitzsimons 4 66
(E G Bevan) t.k.h: sn in tch: rdn and ev ch wl over 1f out: wknd ins fnl f 5/1[3]
0400 7 3½ Coup D'Etat[7] 3360 6-9-4 63 RichardKingscote 1 52
(R A Harris) t.k.h: w ldrs: rdn 3f out: sn wknd 20/1
056- 8 ¾ Road To Recovery[240] 2110 4-8-9 54 SamHitchcott 6 41
(D J Wintle) hld up in tch: n.m.r and lost pl 3f out: rdn over 2f out: wknd wl over 1f out 50/1

1m 33.99s (-2.21) **Going Correction** -0.275s/f (Firm)
WFA 3 from 4yo+ 9lb 8 Ran SP% 112.9
Speed ratings (Par 103): **100,99,98,97,97 95,91,90**
toteswinger: 1&2 £4.90, 1&3 £8.00, 2&3 £1.40. CSF £25.52 CT £102.74 TOTE £10.40: £2.50, £1.30, £1.50; EX 30.80.
Owner L M Baker **Bred** D Brocklehurst **Trained** Cropthorne, Worcs
■ Stewards' Enquiry : Kirsty Milczarek two-day ban: careless riding (July 16-17)

FOCUS
Quite a competitive little handicap with the winner rated to his recent best.
Coup D'Etat Official explanation: jockey said gelding ran too free

3608 JOHN SMITH'S EXTRA COLD H'CAP 6f 16y
9:10 (9:12) (Class 6) (0-65,65) 3-Y-0+ **£2,428** (£722; £361; £180) **Stalls** High

Form RPR
000- 1 Danjet (IRE)[335] 4103 5-9-1 53 JamesDoyle 15 67
(P D Evans) a.p: rdn to ld over 1f out: r.o wl 7/1[3]
0- 2 1¾ First In Command (IRE)[13] 3186 3-9-7 65 (t) PaulFitzsimons 6 72
(Daniel Mark Loughnane, Ire) hmpd s: hld up: hdwy 2f out: rdn and r.o to take 2nd towards fin: nt trble wnr 33/1
0-05 3 ½ Summer Recluse (USA)[7] 3363 9-9-5 57 (t) SteveDrowne 17 64
(J M Bradley) s.i.s: in rr: swtchd rt and hdwy on stands' side over 1f out: sn rdn: r.o wl to take 3rd cl home: nrst fin 8/1
0304 4 1 Trinculo (IRE)[9] 3313 11-9-8 65 (b) HaddenFrost(5) 14 69
(R A Harris) led: rdn and hdd over 1f out: no ex wl ins fnl f 9/2[2]
0200 5 nse Caustic Wit (IRE)[7] 3363 10-9-11 63 (p) FergusSweeney 3 67
(M S Saunders) hld up in tch: rdn over 1f out: one pce fnl f 11/1
300 6 ½ Stormburst (IRE)[18] 3033 4-8-9 47 VinceSlattery 12 49
(A J Chamberlain) hld up and bhd: rdn over 2f out: hdwy over 1f out: no ex towards fin 28/1
00-2 7 2 Miracle Baby[27] 2753 6-8-9 50 TravisBlock(3) 4 46
(J A Geake) prom: rdn over 2f out: eased whn btn towards fin 16/1
/016 8 nk Boldinor[9] 3313 5-9-3 55 SamHitchcott 5 50+
(M R Bosley) wnt rt s: hld up in mid-div: nt clr run over 1f out tl ins fnl f: nvr able to chal 10/1
0500 9 1¼ Lady Fas (IRE)[132] 634 5-8-5 46 oh1 LukeMorris(3) 8 37
(A W Carroll) stdd s: hld up towards rr: rdn over 2f out: hdwy over 1f out: no imp whn nt clr run briefly ins fnl f 66/1
0000 10 3½ Tadlil[20] 2968 6-9-5 57 (v[1]) RichardKingscote 10 36
(J M Bradley) hld up and bhd: short-lived effrt over 1f out 25/1
0303 11 1¼ Cyfrwys (IRE)[19] 2988 7-8-10 48 (v) CatherineGannon 9 23
(B Palling) prom tl rdn and wknd over 2f out 11/1
4000 12 ¾ Night Rainbow (IRE)[6] 3405 5-8-11 49 MartinDwyer 7 22
(Mrs S Leech) wnt rt s: a bhd fnl 3f 25/1
6530 13 2¼ Spic 'n Span[8] 3346 3-9-7 65 TGMcLaughlin 1 29
(R A Harris) prom: rdn 2f out: sn wknd 11/1
30/0 14 1½ Repeat (IRE)[13] 3159 8-8-3 46 oh1 NicolPolli(5) 13 7
(M Wellings) prom tl wknd over 2f out 66/1
3312 15 2 Blakeshall Quest[24] 2869 8-9-8 60 (b) PaulMulrennan 2 15
(R Brotherton) prom tl wknd over 2f out 12/1
40-0 16 14 Stagnite[18] 3021 8-8-8 46 oh1 WilliamBuick 16 —
(D L Williams) sn outpcd 22/1
5415 17 94 Tilsworth Charlie[18] 3026 5-9-7 59 (b) RichardHughes 11 —
(J R Jenkins) prom over 3f: eased over 1f out 10/3[1]

1m 11.1s (-1.80) **Going Correction** -0.275s/f (Firm)
WFA 3 from 4yo+ 6lb 17 Ran SP% 134.0
Speed ratings (Par 101): **101,98,98,96,96 95,93,92,91,86 84,83,80,78,76 57,—**
toteswinger: 1&2 £31.30, 1&3 £31.30, 2&3 £31.30. CSF £242.23 CT £1998.16 TOTE £11.20: £3.50, £9.60, £2.40, £1.10; EX 527.90 Place 6 £101.76, Place 5 £81.30.
Owner E A R Morgans **Bred** David Maher **Trained** Pandy, Monmouths

FOCUS
A typically wide-open minor sprint handicap in which the form looks sound rated around the fourth and fifth.
Boldinor Official explanation: jockey said gelding was denied a clear run
Tilsworth Charlie Official explanation: jockey said mare lost her action and lost a right hind shoe
T/Jkpt: Not won. T/Plt: £72.20 to a £1 stake. Pool: £84,199.47. 851.26 winning tickets. T/Qpdt: £37.90 to a £1 stake. Pool: £5,363.10. 104.50 winning tickets. KH

3371 KEMPTON (A.W) (R-H)
Wednesday, July 2

OFFICIAL GOING: Standard
Wind: Light, behind Weather: Fine

3609 DAY TIME, NIGHT TIME, GREAT TIME H'CAP 5f (P)
6:20 (6:24) (Class 5) (0-75,74) 3-Y-0 **£2,590** (£770; £385; £192) **Stalls** High

Form RPR
-041 1 Le Toreador[12] 3231 3-9-0 67 (t) NCallan 4 83
(K A Ryan) mde all: rdn clr wl over 1f out: unchal after 2/1[1]
0224 2 3¾ Orpen's Art (IRE)[4] 3486 3-9-7 74 HayleyTurner 6 76
(S A Callaghan) bmpd s: t.k.h: hld up in 4th: hanging and nt qckn over 1f out: kpt on to take 2nd ins fnl f 3/1[3]
043- 3 ½ Fabuleux Cherie[207] 7072 3-9-2 69 RichardMullen 3 69
(W R Muir) chsd wnr: nt qckn and outpcd wl over 1f out: no imp after: lost 2nd ins fnl f 8/1
2065 4 ½ Liberty Valance (IRE)[14] 3136 3-9-6 73 (t) RyanMoore 5 71
(S Kirk) bmpd s: settled in last: outpcd wl over 1f out: kpt on one pce after: nrst fin 5/2[2]
0136 5 3 Stoneacre Sarah[34] 2527 3-8-9 62 LPKeniry 1 50
(Peter Grayson) dropped in fr wd draw: a in last pair: no prog over 1f out 12/1
001 6 nk Stoneacre Pat (IRE)[9] 3332 3-8-7 60 6ex PatrickMathers 7 47
(Peter Grayson) chsd ldng pair to wl over 1f out: wknd 12/1

60.89 secs (0.39) **Going Correction** +0.05s/f (Slow) 6 Ran SP% 113.4
Speed ratings (Par 100): **98,92,91,90,85 85**
toteswinger: 1&2 £1.10, 1&3 £4.40, 2&3 £4.80. CSF £8.49 TOTE £2.20: £1.10, £2.20; EX 7.70.
Owner Guy Reed **Bred** G Reed **Trained** Hambleton, N Yorks

FOCUS
A modest handicap dominated throughout by the speedy and improving winner. The form looks sound rated through the pretty solid runner-up.

3610 FRESHEYEMARKETING E B F MAIDEN FILLIES' STKS 7f (P)
6:50 (6:52) (Class 5) 2-Y-0 **£3,885** (£1,156; £577; £288) **Stalls** High

Form RPR
4 1 Lady Cottingham[14] 3135 2-9-0 0 DaneO'Neill 9 66
(R Hannon) trckd ldr 2f: wnt 2nd again over 2f out: clsd to ld narrowly ins fnl f: asserted last 75yds 11/4[1]
0P4 2 1¼ Misty Glade[29] 2702 2-9-0 0 JimmyFortune 1 63
(B J Meehan) crossed fr wd draw to ld: set modest pce tl kicked on jst over 2f out: hdd ins fnl f: one pce last 75yds 8/1
3 hd Black Nun 2-9-0 0 RyanMoore 6 62+
(R Hannon) dwlt: settled in last pair and rn green: stl in last pair 2f out: picked up wl jst over 1f out: r.o to take 3rd last stride: bttr for experience 4/1[2]
4 hd Nashmiah (IRE) 2-9-0 0 NCallan 2 62
(C E Brittain) dwlt: t.k.h early: hld up and wd: rn v green most of way: gd prog to chse ldng pair over 1f out: styd on but lost 3rd last stride: bttr for experience 18/1
4 5 5 Casting Couch (IRE)[26] 2769 2-9-0 0 RHills 4 49+
(B W Hills) rn in snatches: chsd ldrs: readily outpcd fr wl over 1f out 11/4[1]
6 1¾ Heaven Knows When (IRE) 2-9-0 0 ChrisCatlin 7 45
(B W Hills) t.k.h: chsd ldr after 2f to over 2f out: wknd 16/1
000 7 ½ Herecomesbella[18] 3032 2-9-0 0 PatCosgrave 3 44
(Stef Liddiard) t.k.h: trckd ldrs on outer: rdn over 2f out: sn wl outpcd and btn 66/1
8 ¾ Protiva 2-9-0 0 JimCrowley 10 42
(A P Jarvis) hld up towards rr: effrt on inner over 2f out: wknd over 1f out 11/2[3]
9 1 Efficiency 2-9-0 0 LPKeniry 8 39
(M Blanshard) dwlt: a in last pair: pushed along and no prog 2f out 28/1

1m 30.57s (4.57) **Going Correction** +0.05s/f (Slow) 9 Ran SP% 115.9
Speed ratings (Par 91): **75,73,73,73,67 65,64,63,62**
toteswinger: 1&2 £4.20, 1&3 £2.20, 2&3 £6.60. CSF £26.09 TOTE £3.80: £1.40, £2.30, £1.60; EX 33.60.
Owner J R May **Bred** The Duke Of Devonshire **Trained** East Everleigh, Wilts

FOCUS
They went no pace in this modest maiden and that resulted in a very slow winning time indeed for a race like this.

NOTEBOOK
Lady Cottingham, always well placed in a race that lacked early pace, took the leader's advantage inside the last and was nicely on top at the finish. She had the run of things here and the form looks nothing special, but she should pay her way in ordinary nursery company. (op 9-4 tchd 3-1)
Misty Glade, running on Polytrack for the first time, showed good early speed to cross over from the one box and lead on the rail, but once there her rider was able to slow things down and dictate a slow pace. Needless to say, she was very well postioned for when the sprint began, and while she was eventually overhauled inside the last, she ran to her very best in defeat. (op 9-1 tchd 12-1)
Black Nun, a half-sister to Night Kiss, a two-time winner over 7f, including as a juvenile, raced out the back off the steady early pace. While she ran on well once in the clear in the straight, she was never going to catch the winner, who was in the best position throughout. She showed definite signs of inexperience here and will know a lot more next time. (op 5-1)
Nashmiah(IRE), a half-sister to four winners, including Streets Ahead, a useful dual 7f-1m winner at two, is another who looks sure to derive plenty from this debut experience. She raced wide throughout and ran on but was green when asked to make up ground in the straight. She can do better. (op 16-1 tchd 20-1)

Casting Couch(IRE) was expected to appreciate the step up to 7f, but she was easily seen off by the principals. A stronger pace will suit her in future. (op 5-2 tchd 2-1)

3611 DIGIBET MAIDEN FILLIES' STKS — 1m 3f (P)

7:20 (7:22) (Class 5) 3-Y-0+ — **£2,590** (£770; £385; £192) **Stalls** High

Form				RPR
043-	**1**		**Armure**^{277} 5812 3-8-12 76 .... NCallan 6 (M A Jarvis) *trckd ldrs: prog to go 2nd 2f out: narrow ld ent fnl f: urged along and fnd enough to assert nr fin* **$4/1^{2}$**	77+
3-30	**2**	½	**Amhooj**^{22} 2920 3-8-12 70 .... RHills 7 (M P Tregoning) *trckd ldr: led over 2f out: drvn and narrowly hdd ent fnl f: fought on but hld nr fin* **$5/1^{3}$**	76
4-02	**3**	4	**Stormy View (USA)**^{21} 2956 3-8-12 73 .... JimmyFortune 10 (J H M Gosden) *s.s: rchd midfield 7f out: prog u.p to take 3rd over 1f out: easily outpcd by ldng pair* **$11/4^{1}$**	69
4403	**4**	5	**Lush (IRE)**^{8} 3351 3-8-12 74 .... RyanMoore 8 (R Hannon) *towards rr: rdn and effrt wl over 2f out: nvr on terms but styd on fnl f* **$11/4^{1}$**	61
24	**5**	½	**Beautiful Lady (IRE)**^{71} 1542 3-8-12 0 .... TQuinn 9 (P F I Cole) *trckd ldrs: cl enough over 2f out: sn wl outpcd* **16/1**	60
	6	1	**Kritzia** 3-8-12 0 .... TedDurcan 3 (H R A Cecil) *wl in rr and rn green: hanging whn asked for effrt over 2f out: styd on fr over 1f out* **20/1**	58
0-0	**7**	1¼	**Siena**^{35} 2509 3-8-12 0 .... PatCosgrave 13 (Mrs C A Dunnett) *trckd ldrs: cl enough over 2f out: sn rdn and wknd* **100/1**	56
66	**8**	2	**Alzaroof (USA)**^{20} 2971 3-8-12 0 .... DaneO'Neill 11 (E A L Dunlop) *nvr beyond midfield: outpcd fr over 2f out: no imp after* **16/1**	53
5	**9**	¾	**Sacred Flame (USA)**^{20} 2973 3-8-12 0 .... EddieAhern 1 (B J Meehan) *plld hrd in midfield early: prog to chse ldng pair 3f out: wnt 2nd briefly over 2f out: sn wknd* **14/1**	52
5	**10**	1½	**Katy Kitten (UAE)**^{12} 3205 3-8-5 0 .... JemmaMarshall(7) 14 (G L Moore) *trckd ldrs: rdn and outpcd over 2f out: wknd over 1f out* **50/1**	49
05	**11**	8	**One Oak (USA)**^{20} 2971 3-8-5 0 .... GemmaElford(7) 2 (B J Meehan) *a bhd: last 3f out: nudged along and passed 3 rivals fnl f* **66/1**	35
	12	4½	**Rumline** 3-8-12 0 .... ChrisCatlin 4 (S A Callaghan) *s.s: mostly in last: brief effrt 4f out: wknd over 2f out* **50/1**	28
-000	**13**	1½	**In Decorum**^{17} 3065 3-8-12 37 .... LPKeniry 5 (J A Geake) *dwlt: a in last trio: rdn and struggling 3f out* **100/1**	25
000-	**14**	1¼	**Bellalatino (IRE)**^{310} 4903 3-8-12 51 .... JimCrowley 12 (Norma Twomey) *led to over 2f out: wknd rapidly* **80/1**	23

2m 22.41s (0.51) **Going Correction** +0.05s/f (Slow) **14** Ran SP% **121.8**
Speed ratings (Par 100): **100,99,96,93,92 92,91,89,89,88 82,78,77,76**
toteswinger: 1&2 £3.80, 1&3 £2.50, 2&3 £6.20. CSF £24.01 TOTE £6.20: £1.80, £2.60, £1.50; EX 28.50.

Owner Sarah J Leigh and Robin S Leigh **Bred** Sarah J Leigh And Robin S Leigh **Trained** Newmarket, Suffolk

FOCUS
The third is a solid benchmark for the form of this fair fillies' handicap.
Stormy View(USA) Official explanation: jockey said filly missed the break

3612 DIGIBET LONDON MILE H'CAP (LONDON MILE QUALIFIER) — 1m (P)

7:50 (7:51) (Class 4) (0-80,80) 3-Y-0+ — **£4,727** (£1,406; £702; £351) **Stalls** High

Form				RPR
-043	**1**		**The Fifth Member (IRE)**^{13} 3167 4-9-4 **70** .... PatCosgrave 3 (J R Boyle) *trckd ldng pair: wnt 2nd 2f out: drvn to ld jst over 1f out: styd on wl and drew clr* **10/1**	85
123	**2**	3¾	**Ocean Legend (IRE)**^{14} 3134 3-8-11 **75** .... JerryO'Dwyer(3) 14 (Miss J Feilden) *led: drvn 2f out: edgd lft over 1f out: sn hdd: no ch w wnr fnl f but hld on for 2nd* **$5/1^{1}$**	79
-060	**3**	½	**Eternal Luck (IRE)**^{21} 2953 3-9-5 **80** .... (b1) NCallan 8 (M A Jarvis) *hld up towards rr: hrd rdn and prog over 2f out: styd on to take 3rd ins fnl f and closed on runner-up nr fin* **11/1**	83
-245	**4**	¾	**Indy Driver**^{29} 2699 3-8-13 **74** .... DaneO'Neill 1 (J R Fanshawe) *dropped in fr wd draw and hld up wl in rr: rdn over 2f out: prog wl over 1f out: styd on: nrst fin* **$17/2^{3}$**	75+
20-0	**5**	1¾	**Mr Garston**^{81} 1334 5-9-7 **80** .... HarryPoulton(7) 11 (J R Boyle) *pressed ldr to 2f out: grad fdd* **20/1**	79
5600	**6**	1¼	**Cross The Line (IRE)**^{19} 3006 6-10-0 **80** .... JimCrowley 13 (A P Jarvis) *trckd ldrs on inner: rdn 2f out: no rspnse and sn btn* **$17/2^{3}$**	76
0-00	**7**	5	**Networker**^{29} 2693 5-9-6 **72** .... JimmyFortune 7 (P J McBride) *settled wl in rr: rdn and outpcd by ldrs over 2f out: modest late prog: nvr a factor* **16/1**	57
-015	**8**	nk	**Hasty Retreat**^{15} 3116 3-8-11 **72** .... (t) RyanMoore 6 (E A L Dunlop) *trckd ldrs on outer: rdn and nt qckn over 2f out: sn lost tch* **$5/1^{1}$**	54
2-10	**9**	1½	**Thannaan (USA)**^{41} 2333 3-9-3 **78** .... RHills 12 (B W Hills) *hld up bhd ldrs: rdn and nt qckn over 2f out: btn after* **$5/1^{1}$**	57
41/1	**10**	2½	**Benfleet Boy**^{92} 1126 4-9-13 **79** .... TedDurcan 4 (B G Powell) *nvr beyond midfield: u.p and struggling over 2f out: wknd over 1f out* **$7/1^{2}$**	54
0010	**11**	1¾	**Sun Catcher (IRE)**^{34} 2533 5-9-11 **77** .... (p) RobertHavlin 10 (P G Murphy) *a towards rr: rdn and lft bhd fr over 2f out* **25/1**	48
030-	**12**	15	**St Petersburg**^{244} 6603 8-9-6 **72** .... AmirQuinn 5 (J R Boyle) *t.k.h: racd wd and hld up: lost tch u.p over 2f out: t.o* **33/1**	8
0000	**13**	½	**To The Max (IRE)**^{13} 3162 4-8-9 **61** oh9 .... (v) DMylonas 2 (Mrs C A Dunnett) *hld up on wd outside and sn wl in rr: t.o* **80/1**	—

1m 38.99s (-0.81) **Going Correction** +0.05s/f (Slow)
WFA 3 from 4yo+ 9lb **13** Ran SP% **119.6**
Speed ratings (Par 105): **106,102,101,101,99 98,93,92,91,88 86,71,71**
toteswinger: 1&2 £19.10, 1&3 £21.50, 2&3 £14.30. CSF £57.40 CT £591.59 TOTE £12.60: £3.20, £2.00, £4.30; EX 82.20.

Owner Chris Simpson, Miss Elizabeth Ross **Bred** Ms Amy Mulligan **Trained** Epsom, Surrey

FOCUS
A competitive handicap with three 5-1 co-favourites and the pace was a good one too. Those that raced handily were at an advantage with the front pair right up with the pace from the start. The form is rated around those in the frame behind the winner.
Networker Official explanation: jockey said gelding hung left in the straight
Benfleet Boy Official explanation: jockey said gelding ran flat
St Petersburg Official explanation: jockey said gelding hung left

3613 DIGIBET.COM H'CAP — 2m (P)

8:20 (8:20) (Class 3) (0-90,86) 4-Y-0+ — **£7,352** (£2,201; £1,100; £551; £274; £138) **Stalls** High

Form				RPR
6355	**1**		**Salute (IRE)**^{32} 2621 9-8-10 **75** .... RobertHavlin 3 (P G Murphy) *trckd ldr: effrt to ld 3f out: sn rdn at least 2l clr: kpt on u.p fnl 2f* **12/1**	82
5050	**2**	2	**Mister Completely (IRE)**^{7} 3377 7-7-9 **67** oh9 ...... (v) DavidProbert(7) 11 (Ms J S Doyle) *trckd ldrs: prog 4f out: wnt 2nd over 2f out: drvn and no imp on wnr after* **16/1**	72
2022	**3**	2¾	**Leyte Gulf (USA)**^{7} 3377 5-8-2 **67** oh4 .... ChrisCatlin 4 (C C Bealby) *hld up in midfield: prog 4f out: drvn 3f out: chsd ldng pair 2f out: one pce and no real imp* **13/2**	68
-223	**4**	5	**Right Option (IRE)**^{13} 3179 4-8-4 **72** ow2 .... TolleyDean(3) 1 (J L Flint) *trckd ldng pair: rdn 5f out: lft bhd fr over 2f out: jst hld on for 4th* **16/1**	67
244	**5**	hd	**Alonso De Guzman (IRE)**^{26} 2804 4-8-3 **68** .... LiamJones 8 (J R Boyle) *led: clr w wnr 4f out: hdd 3f out: wknd fnl 2f* **$5/1^{3}$**	63
1300	**6**	2¼	**Calculating (IRE)**^{18} 3044 4-9-7 **86** .... HayleyTurner 7 (M D I Usher) *t.k.h: hld up in midfield: lost pl and rdn wl over 4f out: toiling in rr 3f out: n.d after* **$7/2^{2}$**	78
-450	**7**	2½	**Ursis (FR)**^{19} 2822 7-8-8 **73** ow1 .... EddieAhern 6 (S Gollings) *hld up in midfield: brief prog on outer 5f out: rdn and nt rspnse 4f out: wknd over 2f out* **12/1**	62
000/	**8**	2½	**Hippodrome (IRE)**^{8} 6-9-1 **80** .... (b) RyanMoore 2 (G L Moore) *hld up in last pair: nvr on terms: struggling over 3f out* **11/1**	66
-066	**9**	4½	**Irish Quest (IRE)**^{18} 3044 4-8-12 **77** .... (p) NCallan 9 (M A Jarvis) *trckd ldng pair: rdn 5f out: wknd over 2f out* **$3/1^{1}$**	58
2405	**10**	7	**Kames Park (IRE)**^{25} 2822 6-8-8 **78** .... MarkCoumbe(5) 5 (R C Guest) *dwlt: hld up in rr: nvr on terms: struggling over 3f out* **16/1**	51
040-	**11**	4½	**William's Way**^{214} 6995 6-9-1 **80** .... GeorgeBaker 10 (I A Wood) *stdd s: plld hrd and hld up in last trio: wknd over 3f out: wl bhd* **20/1**	47

3m 30.29s (0.19) **Going Correction** +0.05s/f (Slow) **11** Ran SP% **123.3**
Speed ratings (Par 107): **101,100,98,96,96 94,93,92,90,86 84**
toteswinger: 1&2 £18.70, 1&3 £17.10, 2&3 £25.00. CSF £197.24 CT £1373.94 TOTE £6.70: £2.70, £6.10, £2.40; EX 227.40.

Owner The Golden Anorak Partnership **Bred** Ahmed M Foustok **Trained** East Garston, Berks

FOCUS
This was a proper test of stamina thanks to the pace set by Alonso De Guzman and it found out a few.

NOTEBOOK
Salute(IRE), fifth and fourth in the last two runnings of this contest, also has winning form over this course and distance. Ridden close to the pace, he was committed starting up the home straight and his undoubted stamina then saw him through.
Mister Completely(IRE) had it all to do from 9lb wrong, but like the winner he also has winning form over this course and distance. Brought with his effort starting up the home straight, he tried hard to get to the winner but found him too determined. Hopefully for his sake the Handicapper does not take this effort at face value. (tchd 14-1)
Leyte Gulf(USA), 4lb wrong, was probably helped and hindered by the strong pace in equal measure. Whilst it did enable him to settle, it also asked a serious question of his still as yet unproven stamina and, although he looked dangerous when produced with his effort down the outside entering the last quarter-mile, he had flattened out by the time he reached the furlong pole. (tchd 11-2)
Right Option(IRE), runner-up in his last two tries over this course and distance, raced handily for a long way before getting left behind. He has plenty of form over the trip, but it does seem that a strongly run race over it is right on the limit of his stamina. However, with the overweight he was 11lb above his last winning mark here and that was at least as big a problem.
Alonso De Guzman(IRE), trying half a mile further than he had ever attempted before, was not ridden as though stamina was thought to be a problem. He tried to break clear with the eventual winner rounding the home bend, but could not go with him and had run his race by the time he reached the two-furlong pole. (op 11-2 tchd 6-1)
Calculating(IRE), well beaten in two outings on turf following a highly successful period on the sand, was in trouble a long way out and this return to Polytrack did not produce the renaissance that the market suggested it might. (op 9-2)
Irish Quest(IRE), very disappointing in a couple of outings, including one here, earlier this year before an improved effort at Sandown, was not for the first time well backed to return to form, but again he dropped out quickly over the last couple of furlongs and cannot be trusted at present. (op 4-1 tchd 9-2)
William's Way Official explanation: jockey said gelding ran too free

3614 "BEST OF BRITISH NIGHT" NEXT WEDNESDAY H'CAP — 1m 4f (P)

8:50 (8:56) (Class 6) (0-65,66) 3-Y-0+ — **£2,047** (£604; £302) **Stalls** Centre

Form				RPR
4060	**1**		**Hadron Collider (FR)**^{19} 2997 3-9-1 **64** .... RyanMoore 12 (R Hannon) *settled in rr: rdn and prog fr over 2f out: sustained effrt to ld ins fnl f: sn clr* **$4/1^{2}$**	76
4001	**2**	2¾	**Dancing Dik**^{9} 3327 3-9-3 **66** 6ex .... (p) JimCrowley 2 (Mrs A J Perrett) *trckd ldr to 1/2-way: styd cl up: effrt 3f out: clsd u.p to ld over 1f out: hdd and no ex ins fnl f* **$4/1^{2}$**	73
000	**3**	1¼	**L'Homme De Nuit (GER)**^{9} 3321 4-9-10 **60** .... (t) GeorgeBaker 10 (G L Moore) *hld up in last pair: reminder 6f out: rdn and sme prog over 2f out: styd on wl fnl f to take 3rd nr fin* **20/1**	65
5041	**4**	¾	**Tripod Molly (IRE)**^{4} 3483 3-8-13 **62** 6ex .... (t) NCallan 7 (P J McBride) *trckd ldrs: effrt 3f out: clsd u.p and w ldr over 1f out: fdd fnl f* **$7/4^{1}$**	66
6004	**5**	2½	**Nothingtodeclaire**^{21} 2949 4-9-6 **56** .... (p) ChrisCatlin 8 (V Smith) *reluctant to enter stalls and v restless in them: s.s: rcvrd and prom after 2f: chsd ldr 4f out to over 2f out: fdd over 1f out* **$10/1^{3}$**	56
5-00	**6**	hd	**Ocean Avenue (IRE)**^{22} 2921 9-9-12 **62** .... TedDurcan 9 (C A Horgan) *hld up wl in rr: sme prog on wd outside over 2f out: no imp over 1f out: fdd fnl f* **40/1**	62
2020	**7**	1¾	**One To Follow**^{22} 2921 4-10-0 **64** .... EddieAhern 1 (C G Cox) *hld up in midfield: effrt over 3f out: tried to cl on ldrs u.p over 2f out: fdd over 1f out* **$10/1^{3}$**	61
3220	**8**	3½	**Director's Chair**^{34} 2528 3-8-12 **64** .... (b) JerryO'Dwyer(3) 4 (Miss J Feilden) *rapid prog fr midfield to ld 1/2-way: at least 3l clr 3f out: hanging and rel after: hdd & wknd over 1f out* **20/1**	55
-040	**9**	4½	**Ostinata (IRE)**^{64} 1710 3-8-2 **51** .... LiamJones 6 (B W Duke) *nvr beyond midfield: struggling in rr over 4f out* **50/1**	35
60-0	**10**	3	**Mighty Kitchener (USA)**^{5} 3448 5-8-13 **52** .... TolleyDean(3) 13 (P Howling) *a in rr: struggling wl over 4f out* **33/1**	31
-003	**11**	2¾	**Brave Quest (IRE)**^{23} 2884 4-9-9 **59** .... IanMongan 11 (Mrs L J Mongan) *drvn up to ld: hdd 1/2-way: wknd over 3f out* **12/1**	33

010 **12** *2 1/2* **Ericarrow (IRE)**[2] [3562] 3-8-6 **62**.............................. DavidProbert(7) 3 32
(M F Harris) *nvr beyond midfield: struggling in rr over 4f out* **20/1**

0655 **13** *37* **Love Angel (USA)**[32] [2617] 6-9-0 **50**..............................(v) DaneO'Neill 14 —
(J J Bridger) *virtually ref to r: t.o* **50/1**

2m 35.15s (0.65) **Going Correction** +0.05s/f (Slow)
WFA 3 from 4yo+ 13lb **13** Ran SP% **125.8**
Speed ratings (Par 101): **99,97,96,95,94 94,92,90,87,85 83,82,57**
toteswinger: 1&2 £6.60, 1&3 £26.60, 2&3 £26.90. CSF £19.91 CT £297.71 TOTE £5.80: £1.80, £2.00, £5.10; EX 27.10.
Owner Mrs J Wood **Bred** Serpentine Bloodstock Ltd Et Al **Trained** East Everleigh, Wilts

FOCUS
A moderate handicap, but competitive nonetheless and sound form.
Director's Chair Official explanation: jockey said colt hung right in the straight
Brave Quest(IRE) Official explanation: jockey said gelding had no more to give
Love Angel(USA) Official explanation: jockey said gelding was reluctant to race

3615 WEATHERBYS BANK APPRENTICE H'CAP (ROUND 5) 6f (P)
9:20 (9:22) (Class 5) (0-75,75) 3-Y-0+ **£2,590** (£770; £385; £192) **Stalls** High

Form RPR

6400 **1** **Sahaadi**[11] [3272] 3-8-9 **67**.............................. CharlesEddery(5) 9 78
(R Hannon) *hld up: sn outpcd in rr: pushed along 1/2-way: gd prog 2f out: led jst ins fnl f: sn clr* **12/1**

4042 **2** *2 1/4* **Westport**[54] [1969] 5-10-0 **75**.............................. NeilBrown 7 81
(K A Ryan) *off the pce in midfield: rdn in 6th and plenty to do over 2f out: styd on to cl fr 2f out: wnt 2nd ins fnl f: n.d to wnr* **5/1**[3]

5040 **3** *3/4* **Norcroft**[4] [3506] 6-8-13 **63**.............................. DonnaCaldwell(3) 5 67
(Mrs C A Dunnett) *dwlt: hld up: sn outpcd and wl bhd: rdn bef 1/2-way: styd on fnl 2f to take 3rd nr fin* **10/1**

3242 **4** *hd* **Dvinsky (USA)**[7] [3374] 7-10-0 **75**..............................(b) AshleyHamblett 6 78+
(P Howling) *pressed ldng pair at furious pce: wnt 2nd over 2f out to over 1f out: kpt on and ch ent fnl f: no ex* **15/8**[1]

0012 **5** *1/2* **Forced Upon Us**[9] [3316] 4-8-13 **60**..............................(b) JackMitchell 4 61
(P J McBride) *chsd clr ldng trio: rdn 1/2-way: swtchd to inner and clsd to chal over 1f out: fdd ins fnl f* **9/2**[2]

1024 **6** *nk* **Joy And Pain**[89] [1182] 7-8-12 **62**.............................. HarryPoulton(3) 1 62
(M J Attwater) *outpcd and last of main gp: a struggling: kpt on as ldrs tired fnl 2f* **20/1**

2104 **7** *nk* **Valhillen**[9] [3330] 3-9-2 **72**..............................(p) DavidProbert(3) 3 69
(M D I Usher) *chsd clr ldrs: outpcd in 5th pl over 3f out: tried to cl u.p fr 2f out: no ex fnl f* **20/1**

-065 **8** *1* **Scarlet Oak**[16] [3093] 4-8-9 **59**..............................(p) BillyCray(3) 8 55
(D J S Ffrench Davis) *pressed v fast pce set by ldr: led wl over 2f out: hdd & wknd rapidly jst ins fnl f* **9/1**

-060 **9** *7* **Minaash (USA)**[30] [2679] 4-9-4 **70**.............................. ChrisHough(5) 2 44
(D M Simcock) *s.v.s and lost all ch: a t.o* **20/1**

2325 **10** *1/2* **Mambazo**[23] [2881] 6-8-11 **61**..............................(p) WilliamCarson(3) 10 33
(S C Williams) *fast away: set furious pce but pressed: hdd wl over 2f out: wknd rapidly* **13/2**

1m 12.92s (-0.18) **Going Correction** +0.05s/f (Slow)
WFA 3 from 4yo+ 6lb **10** Ran SP% **124.0**
Speed ratings (Par 103): **103,100,99,98,98 97,97,95,86,85**
toteswinger: 1&2 £63.00, 1&3 £63.00, 2&3 £19.50. CSF £73.38 CT £628.50 TOTE £19.40: £3.70, £1.90, £3.10; EX 129.70 Place 6 £199.68, Place 5 £113.69.
Owner Mrs James Wigan **Bred** Mrs James Wigan **Trained** East Everleigh, Wilts

FOCUS
An interesting race in that the three leaders went off far too fast, eventually finishing fourth, eighth and a well-beaten last. As a result the form may not be totally reliable.
T/Plt: £159.30 to a £1 stake. Pool: £68,884.10. 315.62 winning tickets. T/Qpdt: £71.80 to a £1 stake. Pool: £4,274.50. 44.00 winning tickets. JN

3616 - 3618a (Foreign Racing) - See Raceform Interactive

3145 LEOPARDSTOWN (L-H)
Wednesday, July 2

OFFICIAL GOING: Good

3619a IRISH STALLION FARMS EUROPEAN BREEDERS FUND BROWNSTOWN STKS (GROUP 3) (F&M) 7f
7:30 (7:31) 3-Y-0+ **£43,014** (£12,573; £5,955; £1,985)

RPR

1 **Cheyenne Star (IRE)**[39] [2420] 5-9-6 **106**.............................. JAHeffernan 10 108+
(Ms F M Crowley, Ire) *trckd ldrs: 6th 1/2-way: rdn to chal 1f out: disp ins fnl f: asserted cl home* **9/2**[3]

2 *1 1/2* **Age Of Chivalry (IRE)**[28] [2738] 3-9-1 **106**.............................. MJKinane 4 104
(John M Oxx, Ire) *trckd ldrs: 4th 1/2-way: rdn to chal 1f out: led and disp ins fnl f: no ex cl home* **7/2**[2]

3 *1 1/4* **Dimenticata (IRE)**[30] [2684] 4-9-6 **97**..............................(b) CDHayes 11 101
(Kevin Prendergast, Ire) *hld up: 9th 2f out: hdwy in 7th over 1f out: kpt on wl fnl f* **14/1**

4 *1 3/4* **Mystical Lady (IRE)**[4] [3510] 3-8-12 **90**.............................. CO'Donoghue 9 93
(A P O'Brien, Ire) *towards rr: hdwy in 8th on inner 2f out: rdn into 5th 1f out: kpt on fnl f* **20/1**

5 *1 1/2* **My Girl Sophie (USA)**[28] [2738] 3-8-12 **98**.............................. DJMoran 8 89
(J S Bolger, Ire) *disp early: sn chsd ldr in 2nd: impr to ld under 2f out: rdn and strly pressed over 1f out: hdd ins fnl f and no ex* **10/1**

6 *1/2* **Aleagueoftheirown (IRE)**[28] [2738] 4-9-6 **101**.............................. WMLordan 5 91
(David Wachman, Ire) *mid-div: 10th bef st: rdn in 9th over 1f out: kpt on same pce fnl f* **8/1**

7 *1/2* **Emily Blake (IRE)**[28] [2738] 4-9-6 **100**.............................. PTownend 3 90
(J C Hayden, Ire) *chsd ldrs: 3rd 1/2-way: rdn 2f out: no ex in 6th 1f out: kpt on one pce* **14/1**

8 *3/4* **Queen Jock (USA)**[4] [3510] 3-8-12 **85**.............................. PShanahan 2 85
(Tracey Collins, Ire) *sn led: rdn and hdd under 2f out: wknd fr 1f out* **16/1**

9 *nk* **Joshua's Princess**[430] [1323] 4-9-6 **88**.............................. NGMcCullagh 1 87
(John M Oxx, Ire) *mid-div: rdn into 6th 2f out: sn no ex: wknd over 1f out* **10/1**

10 *shd* **Royal Confidence**[14] [3119] 3-8-12 .... MichaelHills 12 83
(B W Hills) *mid-div: 7th 1/2-way: rdn in 6th bef st: sn no ex and wknd* **10/3**[1]

11 *1* **Forthefirstime**[28] [2738] 3-8-12 **99**.............................. FMBerry 7 81
(John M Oxx, Ire) *a towards rr* **8/1**

12 *3 1/2* **Subtle Shimmer**[4] [3510] 4-9-6 **87**.............................. DPMcDonogh 6 74
(Ms Joanna Morgan, Ire) *chsd ldrs: 5th 1/2-way: rdn and wknd over 2f out* **25/1**

1m 27.3s (-3.00) **Going Correction** -0.15s/f (Firm)
WFA 3 from 4yo+ 8lb **12** Ran SP% **131.7**
Speed ratings: **111,109,107,105,104 103,103,102,101,101 100,96**
CSF £23.20 TOTE £6.20: £2.40, £1.70, £3.30; DF 18.30.
Owner Mrs Jacqueline Alder **Bred** Roland H Alder **Trained** Curragh, Co Kildare

FOCUS
Sound enough form for the grade, with the third rated to her best.

NOTEBOOK
Cheyenne Star(IRE), third in the Group 3 Ridgewood Pearl Stakes at the Curragh last time, showed the benefit of that outing to land this in impressive fashion. Having been settled in mid-division, she came with her challenge out wide soon after turning into the straight and responded to her jockey's urgings to show a neat turn of foot soon after. She got her head in front 150 yards out and then extended her lead from there onwards. This was her fourth Pattern-race success and her trainer reported that a crack at the Group 1 Matron Stakes back at Leopardstown in September is the long-term target, with a trip to Goodwood for another Group 3 race on the cards before then. (op 5/1 tchd 6/1)
Age Of Chivalry(IRE), the other horse in this race to have previously tasted Group-race success, was stepping up to 7f having landed the 6f Ballyogun Stakes on her previous start. Tracking the leaders, she looked short of room when the pace quickened at the top of the straight, but soon found room to hit the front over a furlong out. She held every chance at that stage but had no answer to the finishing kick of the winner. This was still a fine effort, though, possibly a slight improvement on her recent course win, and she looks capable of adding another Pattern-race success later in the campaign. (op 4/1)
Dimenticata(IRE) has proved frustrating since finishing second in last season's Irish 1,000 Guineas but she may appreciate a return to 1m after this staying-on effort. Last out of the stalls, she was doing her best work at the end and could still reach her full potential on favourable ground over 1m. (op 12/1)
Mystical Lady(IRE), another who was doing her best work at the finish, appeared to be hampered at the halfway stage before having her path blocked again up the straight. She was motoring home inside the final furlong and could possibly have troubled the first two home if enjoying a clearer run. (op 25/1)
Royal Confidence, who represented 2006 winning trainer Barry Hills, was the disappointment of the race. She was back competing against her own sex having failed to enter calculations in the Jersey Stakes, but her previous seventh behind Natagora in the 1,000 Guineas at Newmarket appeared to give her every chance. She could never get involved, though, after racing on the outside of the main group. (op 3/1 tchd 4/1)

3620 - 3622a (Foreign Racing) - See Raceform Interactive

3596 HAMBURG (R-H)
Wednesday, July 2

OFFICIAL GOING: Good

3623a PREIS DER SPIELBANK HAMBURG (GROUP 3) (F&M) 1m
6:45 (6:53) 3-Y-0+ **£23,529** (£7,353; £3,676; £2,206)

RPR

1 **Peace Royale (GER)**[51] [2065] 3-8-9 .... EPedroza 4 102
(A Wohler, Germany) *led over 2f: 2nd st: led again wl over 1f out: drvn out* **1/1**[1]

2 *shd* **Flashing Colour (GER)**[11] 4-9-6 .... THellier 2 104
(J Hirschberger, Germany) *trckd ldrs: 3rd st: ev ch fnl 150yds: r.o wl: jst failed* **5/1**[2]

3 *1 3/4* **Nolas Lolly (IRE)**[24] [2879] 4-9-4 .... FilipMinarik 1 98
(M Botti) *hld up: hdwy on ins and 5th st: hrd rdn over 1f out: r.o one pce* **188/10**

4 *3/4* **Waky Love (GER)**[45] 4-9-4 .... ASuborics 6 96
(Frau J Meyer, Germany) *towards rr tl hdwy and 6th st: kpt on one pce to take 4th cl home* **62/10**[3]

5 *1/2* **Impetious**[23] [2890] 4-9-6 ....(b) StephenDonohoe 5 97
(Eamon Tyrrell, Ire) *led over 5f out to wl over 1f out: styd on u.p: lost 4th cl home* **35/1**

6 *2* **Vinea Federspiel (IRE)**[17] 4-9-6 ....(b) GBocskai 3 93
(C Bocksai, Germany) *cl up on outside: 4th st: one pce fr wl over 1f out* **16/1**

7 *1 1/2* **Themelie Island (IRE)**[31] [2655] 3-8-9 .... ADeVries 9 87
(A Trybuhl, Germany) *hld up in rr: last st: hdwy on rails 2f out: nvr nr to chal* **73/10**

8 *hd* **Ledicea**[41] [2347] 4-9-4 .... TMundry 7 87
(P Rau, Germany) *trckd ldrs: 7th and wkng st* **15/1**

9 *1 1/4* **Now Forever (GER)**[17] 3-8-9 .... AStarke 10 84
(P Schiergen, Germany) *a in rr* **106/10**

10 *7* **Masako (IRE)**[39] 3-8-9 .... J-PCarvalho 8 68
(W Hickst, Germany) *cl up to over 3f out: bhd fnl 2f* **124/10**

11 *18* **New Fee (GER)**[248] 4-9-4 .... JiriPalik 11 26
(Andreas Lowe, Germany) *cl up to over 3f out: wl bhd fnl 2f* **36/1**

1m 36.81s (96.81)
WFA 3 from 4yo 9lb **11** Ran SP% **131.4**
TOTE (including ten euro stakes): WIN 20; PL 14, 21, 32; SF 121.
Owner Filly Syndicate **Bred** Gestut Etzean **Trained** Germany

NOTEBOOK
Nolas Lolly(IRE) was expected to appreciate the drop back to a mile, but this was a higher grade of race than that which she ran in at Krefeld last time. She ran a solid race.

3258 HAYDOCK (L-H)
Thursday, July 3

OFFICIAL GOING: Good changing to good (good to soft in places) after race 3 (3.40)
Rail realignment added 16yards to advertised race distances on round course.
Wind: Light, across Weather: Showers

3624 VISTA PANELS FILLIES' H'CAP 1m 3f 200y
1:40 (1:41) (Class 5) (0-75,73) 3-Y-0+ **£3,238** (£963; £481; £240) **Stalls** High

Form RPR

0035 **1** **Tcherina (IRE)**[15] [3143] 6-9-6 **67**.............................. DuranFentiman(3) 12 79
(T D Easterby) *a.p: led 3f out: edgd lft over 1f out: kpt on wl whn pressed towards fin* **7/1**

306 **2** ½ **Sphere (IRE)**[29] 2716 3-8-8 65 .... JamieSpencer 13 76
(J R Fanshawe) *a.p: rdn to chse wnr ent fnl 2f: edgd lft ins fnl f: styd on towards fin but a looked hld* **9/2**[1]

0562 **3** ¾ **Prelude**[6] 3433 7-9-7 65 .... TGMcLaughlin 7 71
(W M Brisbourne) *midfield: rdn over 3f out: hdwy over 2f out: styd on u.p ins fnl f: nt pce to trble front pair* **10/1**

3103 **4** nk **Shenandoah Girl**[9] 3344 5-8-11 55 oh2 .... (tp) NCallan 1 60
(Miss Gay Kelleway) *hld up: rdn over 2f out: hdwy over 1f out: styd on ins fnl f: no imp towards fin* **14/1**

-435 **5** 2¼ **Its Moon (IRE)**[34] 2572 4-9-9 67 .... GrahamGibbons 4 69
(T D Walford) *led: hdd 3f out: sn rdn: kpt on u.p tl wknd ins fnl f* **5/1**[2]

0005 **6** 1½ **Snow Dancer (IRE)**[22] 2927 4-9-1 64 ow2 .... (p) PBradley(5) 5 63
(H A McWilliams) *hld up: rdn over 2f out: nt clr run over 1f out: kpt on ins fnl f: nvr able to chal* **20/1**

1 **7** 1¼ **Eventide**[19] 3035 3-9-2 73 .... PaulDoe 11 70
(W J Knight) *in tch: rdn 4f out: hung lft over 1f out: wknd ins fnl f* **7/1**

4260 **8** shd **Sudden Impulse**[19] 3029 7-9-7 72 .... LanceBetts(7) 10 69
(A D Brown) *midfield: rdn and hdwy over 2f out: one fnl f* **25/1**

-430 **9** 2¼ **Kalokairi (IRE)**[38] 2468 3-8-4 61 .... ChrisCatlin 6 60+
(J L Dunlop) *broke wl: stdd after 2f to r off pce: niggled along over 4f out: effrt w plenty to do whn n.m.r and hmpd ins fnl f: n.d* **6/1**[3]

6350 **10** ¾ **Sforzando**[21] 2978 7-9-5 63 .... TomEaves 9 51
(Mrs L Stubbs) *midfield: rdn and lost pl over 2f out: n.d after* **9/1**

0400 **11** 9 **Vanatina (IRE)**[15] 3127 4-8-4 55 oh10 .... DeanHeslop(7) 8 29
(W M Brisbourne) *trckd ldrs: rdn 4f out: wknd over 2f out* **66/1**

0-00 **12** nse **Syriana**[18] 3058 3-8-1 58 ow1 .... FrancisNorton 3 32
(A Bailey) *niggled along 5f out: a bhd* **16/1**

2m 34.98s (1.78) **Going Correction** +0.20s/f (Good)
WFA 3 from 4yo+ 13lb **12 Ran SP% 115.9**
Speed ratings (Par 100): **102,101,99,99,97 96,95,95,94,92 86,86**
toteswinger: 1&2 £7.40, 1&3 £18.20, 2&3 £7.60. CSF £36.80 CT £317.07 TOTE £9.80: £3.10, £1.70, £2.90; EX 32.50.
Owner Mr & Mrs W J Williams **Bred** Ken Carroll **Trained** Great Habton, N Yorks
■ Stewards' Enquiry : Paul Doe caution: careless riding

FOCUS
A modest fillies' handicap run at a decent pace. Solid enough form for the grade.

3625 E B F GLASS TIMES NOVICE FILLIES' STKS 6f
2:10 (2:13) (Class 4) 2-Y-O **£6,476** (£1,927; £963; £481) **Stalls** Centre

Form RPR

5 **1** **Isabella Grey**[12] 3259 2-8-10 0 .... FergalLynch 4 86+
(K A Ryan) *in tch: pushed along 1/2-way: prog to chse ldr over 1f out: r.o to ld fnl strides* **18/1**

2122 **2** hd **Caranbola**[36] 2497 2-9-0 0 .... TWilliams 1 89
(M Brittain) *led: rdn over 1f out: worn down fnl strides* **9/2**[2]

3 3½ **Zuzu (IRE)** 2-8-7 0 ow1 .... NCallan 6 72+
(M A Jarvis) *trckd ldrs: rdn to chal 4f out and ev ch ent fnl 2f: kpt on same pce and n.d to front pair fnl f* **3/1**[1]

1 **4** 1½ **Anglezarke (IRE)**[77] 1425 2-9-3 0 .... DavidAllan 2 77
(T D Easterby) *hld up: hdwy after 2f: rdn whn chalng 2f out: no ex appr fnl f* **11/2**

031 **5** 3½ **Common Diva**[24] 2887 2-9-0 0 .... SebSanders 8 64
(A J McCabe) *prom: rdn 2f out: wknd over 1f out* **13/2**

6 4½ **Super Midge** 2-8-8 0 ow2 .... JamieSpencer 5 44
(B J Meehan) *hld up: rdn over 1f out: hung lft whn no imp ins fnl f* **14/1**

146 **7** 2 **Fuaigh Mor (IRE)**[47] 2204 2-8-10 0 .... FrancisNorton 7 40
(A Bailey) *in tch: pushed along 1/2-way: wknd 2f out* **20/1**

8 1 **Game Roseanna** 2-8-6 0 .... LiamJones 9 33+
(W M Brisbourne) *missed break: rn green and sn outpcd* **50/1**

1 **9** 2 **Vintage Steps (IRE)**[78] 1390 2-9-0 0 .... PaulHanagan 10 35+
(R A Fahey) *stmbld s: in tch: rdn and wknd 2f out* **5/1**[3]

10 50 **Silk Meadow (IRE)** 2-8-6 0 .... ChrisCatlin 3 —
(B J Meehan) *missed break: a bhd: t.o* **20/1**

1m 14.76s (0.76) **Going Correction** +0.10s/f (Good) **10 Ran SP% 112.0**
Speed ratings (Par 93): **98,97,93,91,86 80,77,76,73,7**
toteswinger: 1&2 £17.00, 1&3 £13.40, 2&3 £3.40. CSF £91.31 TOTE £18.20: £3.00, £1.80, £1.50; EX 127.10.
Owner T G & Mrs M E Holdcroft **Bred** Goldford Stud And P E Clinton **Trained** Hambleton, N Yorks

FOCUS
A competitive little heat and solid enough form with the most experienced filly in the race pulling clear with the winner in the closing stages. The winner built significantly on her debut form.

NOTEBOOK
Isabella Grey, a half-sister to four winners over various distances, showed promise here on her debut over 5f, and stepped up significantly on that in this better race - there were five previous winners in opposition. The extra furlong suited her very well as she was outpaced at halfway but came home well. Indeed, another furlong will probably not go amiss in time. (tchd 20-1)
Caranbola, narrowly beaten by her stable-companion in the Hilary Needler last time, kept on well to pull clear of the rest but she was just denied by the lightly raced Ryan filly close home. She got the extra furlong well, and it was a good effort as she was conceding 4lb to the winner. (op 4-1)
Zuzu(IRE), who cost 90,000gns, is a half-sister to multiple winning Italian sprinter Green Band, three-time winning sprinter Tappit, juvenile 5f winner Bohobe, and Agilis, a dual 7f-1m winner at two. Her rider put up 1lb overweight but she was favoured in the market in receipt of weight from her more experienced rivals. Doing best of the four newcomers, she shaped well and, being by Acclamation, will probably be suited by quicker ground. (tchd 10-3 in places)
Anglezarke(IRE), who beat Caranbola by half a length on her debut at Ripon back in April, was asked to give weight all round here, including 3lb to Mel Brittain's filly. She may have just needed the run and was not given too hard a time by her rider, so there should be better to come from her. (op 6-1)
Common Diva showed speed for a long way and was not disgraced on this step up in class, but nurseries are likely to offer her better opportunities in the near future. (op 15-2)
Super Midge, who cost 80,000gns, is a sister to Tremar, a Group 3 winner over 6f at two, and a half-sister to three other sprint winners. Her rider put up 2lb overweight on her on this debut and she struggled to get involved, although the main action was away from her towards the other side of the track. (op 10-1)
Vintage Steps(IRE), of whom better was no doubt expected, stumbled leaving the stalls and failed to show her best. Official explanation: jockey said filly stumbled leaving stalls (op 9-2 tchd 11-2)

3626 BOHLE H'CAP 6f
2:40 (2:45) (Class 4) (0-80,78) 3-Y-O+ **£5,504** (£1,637; £818; £408) **Stalls** Centre

Form RPR

5455 **1** **Makshoof (IRE)**[12] 3271 4-9-10 73 .... NCallan 8 82
(K A Ryan) *midfield: rdn and hdwy over 2f out: r.o to ld wl ins fnl f: hld on wl cl home* **5/1**[1]

1-00 **2** nk **Kashimin (IRE)**[18] 3056 3-9-9 78 .... KerrinMcEvoy 15 84
(G A Swinbank) *hld up in midfield: rdn and hdwy whn hung lft over 1f out: r.o and gaining towards fin* **12/1**

3151 **3** shd **John Keats**[5] 3477 5-10-1 78 6ex .... DanielTudhope 14 86
(J S Goldie) *midfield: rdn and hdwy over 1f out: r.o wl and gaining towards fin* **13/2**[3]

-014 **4** 2¼ **Witchry**[23] 2923 6-9-1 64 .... DaneO'Neill 4 65
(A G Newcombe) *in tch: pushed along over 2f out: kpt on u.p ins fnl f* **16/1**

0050 **5** nk **Hunt The Bottle (IRE)**[12] 3270 3-8-13 68 .... WilliamBuick 16 66
(B W Hills) *towards rr: rdn over 2f out: styd on wl fnl f: nrst fin* **14/1**

0-00 **6** nk **Pearl Dealer (IRE)**[34] 2570 3-8-10 72 .... SimonPearce(7) 11 69
(N J Vaughan) *s.i.s: hld up racing keenly: hdwy 1/2-way: nt clr run 2f out: styd on ins fnl f: nt pce to chal ldrs* **66/1**

1200 **7** hd **My Kaiser Chief**[19] 3050 3-9-2 71 .... FergalLynch 9 67
(W J H Ratcliffe) *towards rr: rdn over 1f out: styd on ins fnl f: nt pce to chal ldrs* **33/1**

060 **8** hd **Tudor Prince (IRE)**[56] 1928 4-10-0 77 .... JoeFanning 13 75
(A W Carroll) *chsd ldrs: rdn over 1f out: no ex fnl 100yds* **20/1**

-500 **9** 2 **Sir Nod**[19] 3050 6-9-9 72 .... (v) TomEaves 6 63
(Miss J A Camacho) *led: rdn over 1f out: hdd and wl ins fnl f: sn wknd* **22/1**

14-4 **10** nk **Feeling Fresh (IRE)**[176] 102 3-8-8 63 .... LiamJones 10 51
(Paul Green) *s.i.s: outpcd: sme hdwy over 1f out: one pce fnl f* **20/1**

5245 **11** ¾ **Lethal**[3] 3567 5-9-10 73 .... PaulHanagan 1 61
(R A Fahey) *prom: rdn over 1f out: wknd ins fnl f* **12/1**

3066 **12** nse **Cornus**[18] 3054 6-9-9 77 .... (be) JackMitchell(5) 2 65
(A J McCabe) *midfield: pushed along 1/2-way: nvr able to chal* **16/1**

304 **13** 1½ **Methaaly (IRE)**[6] 3435 5-9-6 69 .... (be) SebSanders 5 52
(M Mullineaux) *dwlt: hld up in midfield: rdn 2f out: fdd ins fnl f* **20/1**

0605 **14** 2¼ **Balakiref**[6] 3454 9-9-8 71 .... JamieSpencer 17 47
(M Dods) *s.i.s: a bhd* **13/2**[3]

2315 **15** ¾ **Timber Treasure (USA)**[14] 3171 4-9-12 75 .... (b) FrancisNorton 7 48
(Paul Green) *midfield: pushed along 1/2-way: wknd over 1f out* **6/1**[2]

1432 **16** 5 **Prime Factor**[22] 2945 3-9-7 76 .... ChrisCatlin 3 31
(B W Hills) *a bhd* **12/1**

00-0 **17** 17 **Top Bid**[19] 3050 4-9-4 67 .... (b) DavidAllan 12 —
(T D Easterby) *prom tl rdn and wknd over 2f out* **40/1**

1m 14.69s (0.69) **Going Correction** +0.10s/f (Good)
WFA 3 from 4yo+ 6lb **17 Ran SP% 124.6**
Speed ratings (Par 105): **99,98,98,95,95 94,94,94,91,91 90,90,88,85,84 77,54**
toteswinger: 1&2 £14.10, 1&3 £6.80, 2&3 £16.30. CSF £59.68 CT £420.30 TOTE £6.80: £2.10, £3.50, £2.10, £4.80; EX 69.50.
Owner F Gillespie **Bred** J Egan **Trained** Hambleton, N Yorks

FOCUS
A competitive sprint handicap and, thanks to Sir Nod, they went a good pace. The form looks sound although those drawn 1-6 initially raced a bit away from the main pack so could have been slightly inconvenienced.
Balakiref Official explanation: jockey said gelding hit his head on the stalls

3627 TUFFX H'CAP 1m 30y
3:10 (3:12) (Class 3) (0-95,88) 3-Y-O+ **£9,714** (£2,890; £1,444; £721) **Stalls** Low

Form RPR

1122 **1** **Topazes**[5] 3494 3-8-10 78 .... JamieSpencer 5 89+
(M L W Bell) *hld up in rr: hdwy and swtchd rt over 2f out: edgd lft over 1f out: sn led: r.o: a doing enough towards fin* **4/1**[2]

-21 **2** ½ **Just Lille (IRE)**[36] 2499 5-9-11 87 .... (p) AndrewMullen(3) 8 96
(Mrs A Duffield) *in tch: pushed along over 4f out: chsd ldrs u.p and nt qckn whn sltly short of room over 1f out: styd on to snatch 2nd post* **14/1**

0652 **3** shd **Suits Me**[21] 2970 5-9-11 84 .... NCallan 10 93
(T P Tate) *a.p: led 2f out: rdn and hdd 1f out: styd on u.p ins fnl f but a hld* **11/2**[3]

5045 **4** 2 **Collateral Damage (IRE)**[7] 3413 5-9-10 83 .... (t) DavidAllan 9 87
(T D Easterby) *in rr: rdn over 2f out: styd on ins fnl f: nvr gng pce to chal ldrs* **10/1**

1002 **5** nk **Bold Marc (IRE)**[8] 3367 6-8-12 78 .... DeclanCannon(7) 7 81
(K R Burke) *led: rdn and hdd 2f out: no ex ins fnl f* **7/1**

0602 **6** 1½ **Moody Tunes**[6] 3453 5-9-3 76 .... TomEaves 2 76
(K R Burke) *trckd ldrs: pushed along over 2f out: wknd over 1f out* **6/1**

21-1 **7** 2¼ **Axiom**[27] 2787 4-10-0 87 .... DaneO'Neill 1 82
(L M Cumani) *midfield: effrt and hdwy over 2f out: wknd fnl f* **11/4**[1]

021- **8** nse **Miss Emma May (IRE)**[254] 6411 3-9-3 85 .... (v) FrancisNorton 3 78
(D R C Elsworth) *hld up in midfield and racd keenly: rdn 3f out: wknd ins fnl f* **33/1**

-400 **9** 9 **Arctic Cape**[22] 2953 3-9-0 82 .... JoeFanning 6 54
(M Johnston) *midfield: pushed along and lost pl over 4f out: n.d after* **18/1**

1m 44.52s (0.72) **Going Correction** +0.20s/f (Good)
WFA 3 from 4yo+ 9lb **9 Ran SP% 112.8**
Speed ratings (Par 107): **104,103,103,101,101 99,97,97,88**
toteswinger: 1&2 £8.30, 1&3 £4.60, 2&3 £13.60. CSF £56.32 CT £307.78 TOTE £4.40: £1.80, £3.50, £1.90; EX 40.60.
Owner R A Pegum **Bred** Baron F Von Oppenheim **Trained** Newmarket, Suffolk
■ Stewards' Enquiry : Jamie Spencer caution: careless riding

FOCUS
They went a decent gallop in this well-contested handicap. A good race for the grade and solid form, with the progressive winner value for 2l.

NOTEBOOK
Topazes had the race run to suit this time and he came with a good challenge down the outside. He did not win by far, which should ensure he does not go up too much in the weights, but he was comfortably on top at the finish and there could yet be even better to come from this progressive son of Cadeaux Genereux. (op 7-2)
Just Lille(IRE) would probably not have appreciated the rain softening the ground but it did make it a bit more of a test of stamina, which was handy as she was dropping back in trip. She stayed on late for second after not enjoying the best of runs, but she never quite looked like winning, and a return to further will suit her. (op 10-1)
Suits Me travelled up well early in the straight but may have been sent on plenty soon enough as things turned out. He was there to be shot at by the eventual winner inside the last two furlongs. (op 9-1)
Collateral Damage(IRE) was another who had the race run to suit but he remains above his last winning mark and is better on proper soft ground. (op 12-1)
Bold Marc(IRE), twice a winner in four previous starts over this course and distance, tried to make all, just has he did on his last start here in April, but he probably set a pace which was a tad too strong for his own good. (tchd 13-2)
Moody Tunes is on a mark he should be competitive off, but he proved disappointing. (op 7-1 tchd 11-2)

The Form Book, Raceform Ltd, Compton, RG20 6NL

Axiom was 7lb higher than when successful on his seasonal reappearance, but that does not explain this disappointing effort. (tchd 10-3 in places)

3628 SCHUCO INTERNATIONAL MAIDEN STKS (DIV I) 1m 30y
3:40 (3:41) (Class 5) 3-Y-0+ **£2,752** (£818; £409; £204) **Stalls** Low

Form RPR
2 **1** **Tanto Faz (IRE)**[19] 3051 3-9-0 0........................ KerrinMcEvoy 10 89+
(W J Haggas) *trckd ldrs: wnt 2nd over 2f out: r.o ins fnl f to ld towards fin* **4/7**[1]
3 **2** *nk* **French Art**[36] 2509 3-9-0 80........................ SebSanders 4 88
(D R C Elsworth) *led: abt 4 l clr 1/2-way: rdn over 1f out: hdd and hld towards fin* **4/1**[2]
23 **3** *8* **Hippolytus**[44] 2269 3-9-0 0........................ NCallan 9 70
(J J Quinn) *midfield: hdwy to chse ldrs over 3f out: one pce appr fnl f* **12/1**
34 **4** *nk* **Times Vital (IRE)**[23] 2912 3-9-0 0........................ ChrisCatlin 8 69
(E J O'Neill) *midfield: pushed along over 3f out: hdwy over 2f out: one pce appr fnl f* **33/1**
35 **5** *nk* **Presvis**[31] 2673 4-9-2 0........................ MJMurphy[(7)] 1 70
(L M Cumani) *stdd s: hld up and racd keenly: swtchd lft and sme hdwy 2f out: no imp on ldrs* **15/2**[3]
04 **6** *8* **Ghufa (IRE)**[12] 3262 4-9-9 0........................ JoeFanning 2 52
(E A L Dunlop) *hld up: effrt over 2f out: sn eased briefly: no imp on ldrs* **40/1**
0- **7** *1* **Confide In Me**[428] 1398 4-9-9 0........................ DavidAllan 11 50
(G A Butler) *bhd: kpt on fnl f: nvr on terms w ldrs* **50/1**
8 *10* **Dream Of Olwyn (IRE)** 3-8-9 0........................ J-PGuillambert 5 20
(J G Given) *chsd ldrs: pushed along over 4f out: wknd over 2f out* **50/1**
9 *2 ¾* **Our Nations** 3-9-0 0........................ DNolan 7 18
(D Carroll) *s.i.s: a bhd* **100/1**
10 *3* **Middle Of Nowhere (USA)** 3-9-0 0........................ TomEaves 6 11
(M A Magnusson) *s.i.s: hld up: pushed along over 3f out: rn green: nvr on terms* **20/1**
5-0 **11** *2* **Double Duty (IRE)**[21] 2971 3-8-9 0........................ JamieSpencer 3 —
(B J Meehan) *chsd ldr over 5f out tl over 2f out: sn wknd: eased whn btn ins fnl f* **20/1**

1m 44.65s (0.85) **Going Correction** +0.20s/f (Good)
WFA 3 from 4yo 9lb 11 Ran SP% **122.9**
Speed ratings (Par 103): **103,102,94,94,94 86,85,75,72,69 67**
toteswinger: 1&2 £1.60, 1&3 £2.90, 2&3 £4.20. CSF £2.98 TOTE £1.70: £1.10, £1.70, £2.90; EX 3.80.
Owner Tanto Faz Partnership **Bred** Neville O'Byrne **Trained** Newmarket, Suffolk

FOCUS
A fair maiden and the quicker of the two divisions by 1.15sec. The form has been rated positively with the winner showing nice improvement.

3629 SCHUCO INTERNATIONAL MAIDEN STKS (DIV II) 1m 30y
4:10 (4:12) (Class 5) 3-Y-0+ **£2,752** (£818; £409; £204) **Stalls** Low

Form RPR
3-22 **1** **Tatbeeq (IRE)**[22] 2954 3-8-9 73........................ NCallan 1 71
(M A Jarvis) *mde all: rdn over 1f out: r.o wl fnl f and a in command* **2/1**[2]
00 **2** *1 ½* **Liberally (IRE)**[15] 3133 3-8-9 0........................ WilliamBuick 8 67
(B J Meehan) *racd keenly: trckd ldrs: dropped into midfield 5f out: rdn over 2f out: prog appr fnl f: styd on to take 2nd towards fin: nt trble wnr* **50/1**
6-30 **3** *½* **Robert Burns (IRE)**[12] 3275 3-9-0 70........................ PaulHanagan 6 71
(J H M Gosden) *plld hrd: in tch: rdn over 2f out: styd on to chse wnr ent fnl f but no imp: lost 2nd towards fin* **14/1**
0-6 **4** *1 ¾* **Holden Eagle**[23] 2919 3-9-0 0........................ FergalLynch 2 67+
(A G Newcombe) *s.i.s: hld up in rr: hdwy over 1f out: styd on ins fnl f: nt rch ldrs: one to nte* **40/1**
00 **5** *¾* **Into The Light**[22] 2954 3-9-0 0........................ StephenDonohoe 10 65+
(E S McMahon) *hld up: pushed along over 2f out: edgd lft and hdwy over 1f out: styd on ins fnl f: no imp on ldrs* **50/1**
05 **6** *3* **Soviet (IRE)**[22] 2955 3-9-0 0........................ JoeFanning 7 58
(M Johnston) *w wnr tl rdn over 2f out: wknd fnl f* **20/1**
55 **7** *1 ¾* **Dolcetto (IRE)**[36] 2509 3-8-9 0........................ JamieSpencer 5 49+
(J R Fanshawe) *trckd ldrs: rdn over 1f out: sn wknd: eased whn btn ins fnl f* **3/1**[3]
6 **8** *½* **Ateesh**[19] 3051 3-9-0 0........................ DaneO'Neill 4 53+
(L M Cumani) *s.i.s: sn in midfield: pushed along 3f out: wknd over 1f out* **40/1**
9 *2 ¾* **Shaylee** 3-8-9 0........................ GrahamGibbons 11 42
(T D Walford) *towards rr: outpcd 3f out* **100/1**
2 **10** *½* **Applaude**[27] 2786 3-9-0 0........................ KerrinMcEvoy 9 46
(G A Swinbank) *racd keenly: prom on outside: rdn and wknd 2f out: edgd rt over 1f out: eased whn btn ins fnl f* **13/8**[1]
00 **11** *27* **Bountiful Bay**[34] 2560 3-8-2 0........................ GemmaElford[(7)] 3 —
(B J Meehan) *a bhd* **100/1**

1m 45.8s (2.00) **Going Correction** +0.20s/f (Good) 11 Ran SP% **118.6**
Speed ratings (Par 103): **98,96,96,94,93 90,88,88,85,85 58**
toteswinger: 1&2 £16.20, 1&3 £5.20, 2&3 £37.10. CSF £106.78 TOTE £2.80: £1.20, £8.80, £2.20; EX 96.10.
Owner Hamdan Al Maktoum **Bred** Patrick Jones **Trained** Newmarket, Suffolk

FOCUS
They went a steady early pace here and the final time was 1.15sec slower than the first division. It is only ordinary maiden form using the winner and third as a guide.
Holden Eagle ◆ Official explanation: jockey said colt missed the break
Applaude Official explanation: jockey said gelding hung right

3630 SELECTA SYSTEMS STAYERS' H'CAP 1m 6f
4:40 (4:40) (Class 4) (0-85,85) 4-Y-0+ **£5,180** (£1,541; £770; £384) **Stalls** Low

Form RPR
3130 **1** **La Vecchia Scuola (IRE)**[8] 3368 4-9-1 79........................ DanielTudhope 7 87+
(J S Goldie) *chsd ldrs: wnt 2nd over 3f out: led 2f out: rdn ins fnl f: hld on wl towards fin* **11/4**[1]
45-0 **2** *¾* **Yossi (IRE)**[26] 2822 4-8-12 76........................ NCallan 3 83
(M H Tompkins) *chsd ldrs: rdn over 1f out: wnt 2nd ins fnl f: pressed wnr ins fnl 100yds: hld fnl strides* **9/2**[2]
163 **3** *1 ¼* **Stringsofmyheart**[14] 3163 4-8-13 77........................ KerrinMcEvoy 2 82
(Miss Gay Kelleway) *led: rdn and hdd 2f out: continued to chal: no ex towards fin* **9/1**
4133 **4** *3 ¼* **Pass The Port**[19] 3044 7-9-3 81........................ PaulHanagan 4 82
(D Haydn Jones) *hld up: hdwy over 2f out: rdn whn chsd ldrs over 1f out: one pce fnl 100yds* **9/2**[2]
1-44 **5** *nse* **Vanquisher (IRE)**[12] 3258 4-8-4 68........................ WilliamBuick 5 69
(Ian Williams) *midfield: rdn 3f out: styd on appr fnl f: no imp on ldrs* **14/1**
4200 **6** *1 ¾* **Cruise Director**[19] 3045 8-8-11 75........................ StephenDonohoe 1 73
(Ian Williams) *midfield: rdn and hdwy over 3f out: chsd ldrs over 2f out: wknd ins fnl f* **22/1**
2500 **7** *1 ¼* **Clear Reef**[16] 3104 4-8-12 76........................ TGMcLaughlin 8 72
(Jane Chapple-Hyam) *missed break: in rr: effrt over 2f out: edgd lft over 1f out: no imp on ldrs* **10/1**
4-20 **8** *17* **Rudry World (IRE)**[23] 2908 5-8-5 69........................ FergalLynch 6 42
(M Mullineaux) *hld up: rdn over 3f out: nvr on terms* **15/2**[3]
/0-0 **9** *18* **Tusculum (IRE)**[13] 3209 5-9-7 85........................ JamieSpencer 9 32
(A P Stringer) *chsd ldr tl rdn over 3f out: wknd over 2f out: sn eased* **12/1**

3m 8.25s (3.95) **Going Correction** +0.20s/f (Good) 9 Ran SP% **112.6**
Speed ratings (Par 105): **96,95,94,93,92 91,91,81,71**
toteswinger: 1&2 £3.90, 1&3 £7.80, 2&3 £8.40. CSF £14.35 CT £94.68 TOTE £3.60: £1.50, £2.10, £2.10; EX 18.10 Place 6 £72.23, Place 5 £31.26..
Owner John Connor Graham Brown **Bred** Maurice Craig **Trained** Uplawmoor, E Renfrews

FOCUS
A fair handicap and solid enough form using the second and third as a guide.
T/Jkpt: Not won. T/Plt: £66.20 to a £1 stake. Pool: £79,414.00. 874.87 winning tickets. T/Qpdt: £14.00 to a £1 stake. Pool: £3,922.96. 206.60 winning tickets. DO

3347 NEWBURY (L-H)
Thursday, July 3

OFFICIAL GOING: Good to firm (8.4)
Wind: Moderate, against. Strong headwind for 2nd race. Weather: Dry. Heavy shower before 2nd race.

3631 WINDSOR INSURANCE APPRENTICE H'CAP 1m 3f 5y
5:50 (5:50) (Class 5) (0-70,70) 4-Y-0+ **£2,590** (£770; £385; £192) **Stalls** Low

Form RPR
4-51 **1** **Constant Cheers (IRE)**[17] 3089 5-9-7 70........................ DavidProbert[(3)] 9 87
(W R Swinburn) *lw: confidently rdn: trckd ldrs: led over 2f out: kpt on wl whn pressed fr over 1f out: pushed out* **1/1**[1]
2 *½* **Blakfrankisch (IRE)**[422] 5-8-13 64........................ RossAtkinson[(5)] 2 80
(Tom Dascombe) *hld up: hdwy and nt clr run 3f out: chsd wnr fr 2f out: sn rdn: kpt on but a jst hld but wl clr of remainder* **10/1**
1455 **3** *16* **Rising Force (IRE)**[11] 2394 5-9-5 65........................(b) JackDean 7 52
(J L Spearing) *hld up: rdn over 4f out: wandered u.p and wnt 3rd over 1f out: no ch w ldng pair* **9/2**[2]
00-1 **4** *¾* **It's No Problem (IRE)**[58] 1895 4-8-2 51 oh2........................ ThomasO'Brien[(3)] 5 37
(Mrs N S Evans) *trckd ldrs: rdn over 3f out: wknd over 1f out* **12/1**
40-3 **5** *1* **Daring Racer (GER)**[24] 2886 5-9-1 61........................ AshleyHamblett 8 45
(Mrs L J Mongan) *led tl over 5f out: rdn over 3f out: wknd over 1f out* **15/2**[3]
0505 **6** *nk* **Theatre Royal**[8] 3361 5-8-2 51 oh6........................ AmyBaker[(3)] 6 35
(Mouse Hamilton-Fairley) *mid-div: hdwy over 3f out: sn rdn: disp 3rd 2f out: wknd over 1f out* **16/1**
0-60 **7** *¾* **Goldan Jess (IRE)**[17] 1890 4-8-0 51 oh1........................ RichardRowe[(5)] 3 33
(A W Carroll) *n.m.r on rails after 1f: mid-div: rdn over 3f out: sn btn* **18/1**
5003 **8** *2 ¼* **Garafena**[10] 3311 5-9-2 65........................ KylieManser[(3)] 1 43
(B G Powell) *t.k.h w ldr: led over 5f out: rdn and hdd over 2f out: sn wknd* **14/1**
0/60 **9** *3 ½* **Plain Champagne (IRE)**[14] 3160 6-8-2 55 oh6 ow4 MatthewCosham[(7)] 4 27
(Dr J R J Naylor) *s.i.s: a bhd* **66/1**

2m 21.12s (-0.08) **Going Correction** +0.075s/f (Good) 9 Ran SP% **116.0**
Speed ratings (Par 103): **103,102,91,90,89 89,88,87,84**
toteswinger: 1&2 £5.40, 1&3 £2.60, 2&3 £5.10. CSF £12.45 CT £33.79 TOTE £2.10: £1.10, £2.70, £1.70; EX 14.70.
Owner Mr & Mrs W R Swinburn **Bred** Pendley Farm **Trained** Aldbury, Herts

FOCUS
A modest handicap run at no great pace. Interesting form with the first two pulling a long way clear, and their efforts have been rated at face value.

3632 TOTESPORT.COM E B F MAIDEN FILLIES' STKS 6f 8y
6:20 (6:22) (Class 4) 2-Y-O **£5,828** (£1,734; £866; £432) **Stalls** Centre

Form RPR
02 **1** **Starlarks (IRE)**[19] 3032 2-9-0 0........................ ShaneKelly 10 78
(W J Knight) *lw: mde all on stands' side: battled on and hrd pressed fr over 1f out: hld on gamely: all out* **5/1**[2]
2 *shd* **Acquiesced (IRE)** 2-9-0 0........................ JimmyFortune 5 78+
(R Hannon) *w'like: mid-div in centre: rdn and hdwy wl over 1f out: edgd sltly lft but r.o strly fnl f: jst hld* **16/1**
2 **3** *nk* **Evelyn May (IRE)**[12] 3259 2-9-0 0........................ MichaelHills 1 77
(B W Hills) *w'like: lw: prom in centre: rdn and ev ch fr over 1f out: kpt on but no ex towards finsish* **9/4**[1]
4 **4** *5* **Russian Rave**[13] 3207 2-9-0 0........................ JamesDoyle 13 62
(J G Portman) *leggy: lw: t.k.h trcking ldr on stands' side: rdn over 2f out: kpt on same pce fnl f* **8/1**[3]
05 **5** *nk* **Abby Belle (IRE)**[24] 2887 2-9-0 0........................ RichardKingscote 11 61
(J G Portman) *unf: chsd ldng pair on stands' side: effrt 2f out: kpt on same pce fnl f* **50/1**
6 *½* **Evaluation** 2-9-0 0........................ RyanMoore 8 62+
(R Hannon) *leggy: rn green towards rr of centre gp: styd on fr over 1f out: nvr gng pce to get on terms* **8/1**[3]
7 *shd* **Always There (IRE)** 2-9-0 0........................ RichardSmith 7 59
(R Hannon) *w'like: tall: led centre gp tl wl over 1f out: wknd ins fnl f* **33/1**
8 *½* **Perfect Pride (USA)** 2-9-0 0........................ PhilipRobinson 2 58
(C G Cox) *unf: mid-div in centre: bmpd over 2f out: sn rdn: kpt on same pce fnl f* **8/1**[3]
9 *1 ¼* **Dream Huntress** 2-9-0 0........................ MartinDwyer 3 54
(B J Meehan) *leggy: s.i.s: towards rr of centre gp: hdwy and swtchd lft over 2f out: no further imp fr over 1f out* **33/1**
4 **10** *1* **Snoqualmie Girl (IRE)**[17] 3092 2-9-0 0........................ TQuinn 6 51
(D R C Elsworth) *w'like: prom in centre: rdn 3f out: grad fdd* **5/1**[2]
0 **11** *6* **Sicilian Pink**[26] 2821 2-9-0 0........................ EddieAhern 9 33
(J L Dunlop) *unf: scope: mid-div of centre gp tl 2f out* **20/1**
12 *¾* **Fly Butterfly** 2-8-11 0........................ PatrickHills[(3)] 12 31
(B J Meehan) *s.i.s: sn swtchd to centre gp: mainly in rr* **16/1**

13 2 ½ **Amatara (IRE)** 2-9-0 0 .... SteveDrowne 4 23
(B G Powell) *w'like: prom in centre tl 3f out: sn hung lft and wknd* **50/1**

1m 15.36s (2.36) **Going Correction** +0.20s/f (Good) **13** Ran SP% **123.8**
Speed ratings (Par 93): **92,91,91,84,84 83,83,82,81,79 71,70,67**
toteswinger: 1&2 £21.50, 1&3 £1.70, 2&3 £8.60. CSF £80.59 TOTE £6.40: £2.10, £4.20, £1.50; EX 107.50.
Owner Mrs W W Fleming **Bred** Stourbank Stud **Trained** Patching, W Sussex

FOCUS
A competitive maiden on paper, but three drew clear. The race should produce its share of winners but the modest time holds down the form.

NOTEBOOK
Starlarks(IRE), who improved on her debut effort when finishing second over 5f at Lingfield last time, shaping as though this step back up to 6f was needed, was sharply into stride and led the group of three who elected to race towards the stands' side. She looked vulnerable approaching the final furlong, seemingly likely to finish third at one stage, but kept battling away and her head was down at the right time as they crossed the line. This was a fully deserved win and she may well be capable of further improvement in nurseries, with a further step up to 7f likely to suit. (op 4-1 tchd 11-2)
Acquiesced(IRE) ◆, a 150,000euros daughter of Refuse To Bend, comes from a yard always to be feared in juvenile events and it was a surprise she was allowed to go off at such a big price. She came with a strong challenge from a furlong out, looking the likely winner, but went slightly left under pressure and that ultimately cost her. This was a highly pleasing start to her career and it would be a surprise were she not winning before long. A step up to 7f will suit and the fact the first three were clear bodes well for the form. (tchd 20-1)
Evelyn May(IRE), who would probably have won on debut but for a slow start, just failing to get up, looked the one to beat on this step up to 6f and she ran well, but was unable to pull out any extra close home. She was clear of the fourth and should find a small maiden, possibly back at 5f, before going into nurseries. (tchd 5-2 and 11-4 in a place)
Russian Rave showed plenty of ability when fourth on her recent debut at Goodwood and she tracked the winner through in the stands'-side trio. However, she lacked a change of gear and could only keep on at the one pace under pressure. She will be qualified for a handicap mark following one more run and should fare better in that sphere. (op 17-2 tchd 15-2)
Abby Belle(IRE) ◆ has improved with each outing and this was easily her best effort so far. She was the other to race in the stands'-side trio and will make plenty of appeal once contesting nurseries, for which she is now qualified. (tchd 66-1)
Evaluation comes from a decent family, but she was certainly in need of this debut experience, running green and not quite looking sure of what is required. She stuck on for pressure though and should be much wiser next time over 7f. (tchd 17-2)
Always There(IRE), a 185,000euros daughter of Bachelor Duke, was the outsider of the Hannon trio and she knew her job, but in the end it all proved a bit much. This was a fair enough start and she should improve.
Perfect Pride(USA), a $55,000 American-bred, comes from a yard who can ready a useful newcomer, but this one looked in need of it. Much better can be expected next time.
Dream Huntress, a 40,000gns daughter of Dubai Destination, was immediately on the back foot having been slow away, but she made a brief forward move and there is definitely ability there.
Snoqualmie Girl(IRE) shaped much better than expected on her recent debut over 5f, considering she is bred for middle-distances, but she could not go on from that here and was the diappointment of the race. It would be unwise to hold it against her though and she will be interesting once qualified for nurseries. Official explanation: jockey said filly slipped on leaving stalls (op 10-1 tchd 11-1)
Sicilian Pink was unable to improve on her recent debut effort, but she is a half-sister to the stable's dual Group 3 winner Scarlet Runner, and it is hard to believe she will not do much better in time.
Fly Butterfly, a 37,000gns daughter of Bahamian Bounty, did not offer a great deal on this racecourse debut, but may improve. (tchd 20-1)
Amatara(IRE), a cheap purchase compared to most of these, showed up well to a point and will stand more of a chance at a lesser track.

3633 CHEVIOT ASSET MANAGEMENT H'CAP 1m 4f 5y
6:50 (6:51) (Class 4) (0-85,88) 3-Y-O **£5,180** (£1,541; £770; £384) **Stalls** Low

Form RPR
-134 1 **Downhiller (IRE)**[43] 2310 3-9-7 **84** .... EddieAhern 1 92
(J L Dunlop) *mde all: qcknd pce 3f out: styd on wl: edgd rt towards fin: rdn out* **12/1**
1-33 2 1 ¼ **First Avenue**[26] 2825 3-9-5 **82** .... PhilipRobinson 7 88
(M A Jarvis) *restrained in rr: hdwy over 3f out: sn rdn to chse wnr: edgd lft fr over 1f out: hld whn carried rt towards fin* **2/1**[1]
1041 3 1 ¾ **Sweet Lightning**[5] 3471 3-9-11 **88** 6ex .... MartinDwyer 4 91
(W R Muir) *lw: trckd ldrs: lost pl sltly and nt clr run over 3f out: sn swtchd rt and rdn: hung lft but kpt on fr over 1f out* **7/2**[3]
511 4 1 ½ **Casilda (IRE)**[23] 2920 3-9-4 **81** .... PaulDoe 8 82
(W J Knight) *trckd ldrs: rdn to dispute 2nd 3f out: kpt on same pce fnl 2f* **10/1**
3-15 5 *hd* **Monterrico**[60] 1839 3-8-12 **75** .... RyanMoore 5 75
(G Wragg) *hld up: rdn over 3f out: kpt on same pce: nvr able to mount chal* **15/2**
2-25 6 ½ **West With The Wind**[26] 2840 3-9-5 **82** .... MickyFenton 6 82
(T P Tate) *lw: sn trcking ldrs: rdn 3f out: kpt on but nvr gng pce to mount a chal* **9/4**[2]
0000 7 9 **Ruff Diamond (USA)**[26] 2840 3-9-4 **81** .... (b[1]) LPKeniry 2 66
(J R Best) *w wnr: rdn and hung rt 3f out: sn btn* **50/1**

2m 35.56s (0.06) **Going Correction** +0.075s/f (Good) **7** Ran SP% **116.8**
Speed ratings (Par 102): **102,101,100,99,98 98,92**
toteswinger: 1&2 £4.80, 1&3 £63.00, 2&3 £3.90. CSF £37.77 CT £106.35 TOTE £14.70: £4.40, £2.30; EX 42.00.
Owner Windflower Overseas Holdings Inc **Bred** Windflower Overseas Holdings Inc **Trained** Arundel, W Sussex

FOCUS
This looked a good handicap on paper and, although the form is not trustworthy as a result of the slow pace, the race should still produce winners. The winner had the run of the race but is not flattered and remains progressive.

3634 LADBROKES.COM ROSE BOWL STKS (LISTED RACE) 6f 8y
7:25 (7:25) (Class 1) 2-Y-O **£17,031** (£6,456; £3,231; £1,611; £807; £405) **Stalls** Centre

Form RPR
1621 1 **Saxford**[7] 3412 2-9-0 0 .... ShaneKelly 7 95+
(Mrs L Stubbs) *lw: sddle slipped leaving stalls: led after 1f: mde rest: shkn up and r.o wl fnl 150yds: readily* **4/1**[2]
15 2 2 **Saucy Brown (IRE)**[16] 3105 2-9-0 0 .... RyanMoore 5 89
(R Hannon) *lw: t.k.h: led for 1f: w wnr: rdn 2f out: kpt on but hld fnl 150yds: jst hld on for 2nd* **6/4**[1]
510 3 *hd* **Dabbers Chief (USA)**[16] 3105 2-9-0 0 .... MichaelHills 6 88
(B W Hills) *lw: little slowly away: towards rr: rdn and hdwy wl over 1f out: r.o fnl f: wnt 3rd nr fin* **16/1**
1 4 ½ **Oasis Breeze**[19] 3027 2-8-9 0 .... PaulEddery 3 82
(G D Blake) *w'like: leggy: hld up: hdwy and swtchd lft 2f out: sn rdn: kpt on ins fnl f* **8/1**
3310 5 *nse* **Sun Ship (IRE)**[14] 3152 2-9-0 0 .... JimmyFortune 2 87
(R Hannon) *lw: trckd ldrs: effrt 2f out: kpt on same pce fnl f* **11/1**
16 6 4 ½ **Cerito**[14] 3152 2-9-0 0 .... EdwardCreighton 8 73
(M R Channon) *lw: trckd ldrs: rdn over 2f out: sn btn* **5/1**[3]
2110 7 2 ¼ **Shampagne**[16] 3103 2-9-5 0 .... TQuinn 4 72
(P F I Cole) *t.k.h early: trckd ldrs: rdn over 2f out: sn btn* **15/2**

1m 13.83s (0.83) **Going Correction** +0.20s/f (Good) **7** Ran SP% **113.8**
Speed ratings (Par 102): **102,99,99,98,98 92,89**
toteswinger: 1&2 £2.40, 1&3 £13.50, 2&3 £5.50. CSF £10.32 TOTE £5.30: £2.40, £1.50; EX 11.40.
Owner D Arundale **Bred** Malih L Al Basti **Trained** Norton, N Yorks

FOCUS
A good Listed contest largely made up of Royal Ascot also-rans. The winner more than confirmed his excellent Newcastle effort and the standard looks solid overall.

NOTEBOOK
Saxford, a progressive sort who routed the opposition in a novice event at Newcastle last week, is clearly thriving on racing and he took another big step forward by winning this Listed prize in authoritative fashion. The 6f trip has clearly been the making of him and the impressive thing about this victory was that his saddle had slipped leaving the stalls, making things a shade awkward. He may well head to Glorious Goodwood next and it is not hard to see him running above expectations, on a course that will suit his aggressive style. (op 11-2 tchd 6-1 and 7-2 in places)
Saucy Brown(IRE), a winner on debut who shaped as though this 6f trip would suit when fifth in the Windsor Castle Stakes at Royal Ascot, comes from a yard who have won this prize three times in the last four years and he set a decent standard. He did himself no favours by taking a keen grip early though and was unable to match Saxford for speed from a furlong out. He remains capable of better, without suggesting he can become a Group winner. (op 5-4)
Dabbers Chief(USA), a Haydock maiden winner who ran no sort of race in the Windsor Castle, was soon in rear having been a bit sluggish out of the gate, but he came with a good run inside the final quarter mile and only just missed out on second. He has plenty of scope and looks capable of winning a race at this level. (tchd 25-1)
Oasis Breeze, a narrow winner at Leicester on debut, shaped well in the face of a much stiffer task and looks a useful filly. A late foal, she still has improving to do and should go on to gain more black type this season, with a step up to 7f unlikely to inconvenience her. (tchd 15-2)
Sun Ship(IRE), a Salisbury maiden winner who struggled to make an impact in the Norfolk Stakes, looked vulnerable to a couple of these and he failed to improve for the extra furlong. He may do better in nurseries, depending on what sort of mark he gets. (op 9-1 tchd 14-1)
Cerito, another maiden winner who found himself outclassed in the Norfolk, ran most disappointingly and does not seem to have progressed. He was beaten before stamina could be become an issue and looks one to have reservations over for the time being. (tchd 4-1 and 11-2)
Shampagne, a progressive sort until getting completely outclassed in the Coventry Stakes, looked vulnerable conceding weight all round and he ran poorly. It was later reported he had run too free. Official explanation: jockey said colt had run freely to halfway (op 10-1)

3635 MOUNTGRANGE STUD CONDITIONS STKS 7f (S)
7:55 (7:58) (Class 3) 3-Y-O+ **£7,477** (£2,239; £1,119; £560; £279; £140) **Stalls** Centre

Form RPR
16- 1 **Atlantic Sport (USA)**[292] 5406 3-8-5 103 .... EdwardCreighton 6 106+
(M R Channon) *lw: in tch: nt clr run jst over 2f out: burst through gap over 1f out: r.o wl to ld ins fnl f: rdn out* **1/1**[1]
152- 2 ½ **Al Muheer (IRE)**[271] 6001 3-8-5 97 .... MartinDwyer 8 104
(C E Brittain) *lw: sn led: rdn and hdd ins fnl f: rallied gamely: hld nr fin* **25/1**
-330 3 ½ **Red Alert Day**[15] 3119 3-8-5 105 .... ShaneKelly 2 103
(S A Callaghan) *hld up: hdwy over 2f out: rdn and ev ch ent fnl f: no ex* **7/2**[2]
1540 4 2 ½ **Vitznau (IRE)**[12] 3248 4-8-13 100 .... RyanMoore 3 99
(R Hannon) *restrained s: rdn and hdwy over 1f out: kpt on but nvr trbld ldrs* **6/1**[3]
0-30 5 4 ½ **Eisteddfod**[31] 2680 7-9-2 106 .... NelsonDeSouza 1 90
(P F I Cole) *broke wl: prom: rdn and ev ch over 1f out: one pce fnl f* **7/1**
0214 6 3 ¼ **Raptor (GER)**[54] 1989 5-9-6 101 .... FergusSweeney 4 85
(K R Burke) *trckd ldr: rdn over 2f out: wknd fnl f* **14/1**
7 ¾ **Rubacuori (BRZ)**[46] 4-8-13 0 .... LukeMorris[(3)] 7 79
(J M P Eustace) *w'like: lw: in tch: punched along fr 1/2-way: nvr gng pce to chal* **50/1**
0005 8 19 **Vortex**[5] 3498 9-8-13 95 .... (t) MickyFenton 5 25
(Miss Gay Kelleway) *chsd ldrs: rdn over 2f out: wknd over 1f out: eased whn btn: dismntd after line* **25/1**

1m 25.53s (-0.17) **Going Correction** +0.20s/f (Good)
WFA 3 from 4yo+ 8lb **8** Ran SP% **115.3**
Speed ratings (Par 107): **108,107,106,104,98 95,94,72**
toteswinger: 1&2 £7.60, 1&3 £1.60, 2&3 £22.50. CSF £34.27 TOTE £2.00: £1.20, £3.30, £1.50; EX 29.40.
Owner Jaber Abdullah **Bred** Gainsborough Farm Llc **Trained** West Ilsley, Berks

FOCUS
A decent conditions contest in which the three younger horses dominated. It was steadily run and the runner-up, who set the pace, could be flattered. The winner looks a smart prospect.

NOTEBOOK
Atlantic Sport(USA), a highly regarded two-year-old who had not been seen since finishing sixth in the Champagne Stakes at Doncaster, has been kept off the track with several niggling problems, but he looked to have been found a suitable starting point for this seasonal debut. Very solid at the head of the market, he had to wait to make his run, but picked up well between runners and was always doing enough inside the final furlong. A half-brother to the yard's formerly high-class miler Zafeen, he will reportedly avoid very firm ground and it will be interesting to see where he turns up next. (op 11-10 tchd 6-5 in place & 5-4 in a place)
Al Muheer(IRE), a generally progressive sort at two, was another making his seasonal debut and he ran way above market expectation. Soon in front, he was challenged strongly a furlong out, but battled back gamely and ensured the winner did not have it easy. This was a promising reappearance, but he is not going to be at all easy to place. (op 28-1 tchd 33-1)
Red Alert Day could make no impact in the Jersey Stakes at Royal Ascot, but he had earlier been running well in Listed/Group 3 contests and he gives the form a solid look back in third. He continues to give the impression he will be happier back on a slower surface, but he is another who is not going to find winning easy this season. (tchd 10-3 and 4-1)
Vitznau(IRE), who finished in mid-division on his recent return to sprinting in the Wokingham, looked vulnerable to the three-year-olds on this step back up in trip and he could make no impression inside the final furlong. A faster pace would have helped. (op 11-2 tchd 5-1)
Eisteddfod is still capable on his day, but he was was always going to struggle against these, especially with the ground riding faster than ideal. (op 8-1 tchd 9-1)
Raptor(GER) was conceding weight all round and he struggled on ground he would have found too fast. (op 16-1)
Rubacuori(BRZ), a Brazilian import, struggled for pace and was never travelling. He is entitled to come on for this and will appreciate a return to further.

Vortex finished tailed-off and was reported to have been struck into from behind. Official explanation: vet said gelding had been struck into right hind (op 20-1)

3636 COOLMORE EXCELLENT ART FILLIES' H'CAP 7f (S)
8:30 (8:30) (Class 4) (0-80,78) 3-Y-0+ **£4,857** (£1,445; £722; £360) **Stalls** Centre

Form RPR
01-6 **1** **La Coveta (IRE)**[12] 3272 3-9-4 **76**........................ GabrielHannon(5) 6 82
(B J Meehan) *trckd ldrs: rdn over 2f out: r.o ent fnl f: led fnl 75yds: jst hld on* **6/1**
1535 **2** *shd* **Secret Night**[17] 3087 5-9-13 **72**........................(p) PhilipRobinson 5 81
(C G Cox) *broke wl: tk v t.k.h: sn restrained in rr: smooth hdwy on bridle 2f out: shkn up and r.o strly fnl f: jst failed* **11/2**[3]
-020 **3** *3/4* **The Jostler**[33] 2624 3-9-10 **77**........................ MichaelHills 3 81
(B W Hills) *lw: in tch: tk clsr order over 2f out: rdn to ld over 1f out: hdd fnl 75yds: no ex* **8/1**
1- **4** *1 1/2* **Fantasy Princess (USA)**[229] 6847 3-9-11 **78**............... HayleyTurner 4 78
(G A Butler) *restrained s: rdn over 2f out: no imp tl r.o fnl f: nrst fin* **5/1**[2]
-600 **5** *1/2* **Cinerama (IRE)**[13] 3221 3-8-9 **62**........................ MartinDwyer 10 61
(M P Tregoning) *trckd ldr: rdn and ev ch over 1f out: sn edgd rt: no ex ins fnl f* **10/1**
-202 **6** *1/2* **Danseuse Volante (IRE)**[18] 3064 3-9-7 **74**................ EddieAhern 8 71
(J W Hills) *lw: hld up: swtchd rt and effrt 2f out: kpt on same pce* **4/1**[1]
6202 **7** *1 3/4* **Leading Edge (IRE)**[13] 3202 3-9-8 **75**................ EdwardCreighton 1 68
(M R Channon) *led: rdn and hdd over 1f out: fdd fnl f* **10/1**
1024 **8** *1 1/4* **Love On Sight**[13] 3210 4-9-10 **69**........................ PatCosgrave 2 61
(J R Boyle) *hld up: rdn over 2f out: no imp* **8/1**
-100 **9** *3/4* **Debonnaire**[12] 3270 3-9-8 **75**........................ JimmyFortune 9 62
(M Johnston) *chsd ldrs: rdn over 2f out: wknd over 1f out* **10/1**

1m 26.69s (0.99) **Going Correction** +0.20s/f (Good)
WFA 3 from 4yo+ 8lb **9** Ran SP% **115.8**
Speed ratings (Par 102): **102,101,101,99,98 98,96,94,93**
toteswinger: 1&2 £8.70, 1&3 £5.90, 2&3 £8.30. CSF £39.04 CT £266.77 TOTE £7.00: £2.00, £2.50, £2.90; EX 48.10.
Owner Mrs Wendy English **Bred** Mrs Noelle Walsh **Trained** Manton, Wilts

FOCUS
Just a fair fillies' handicap, which was steadily run. The form is pretty ordinary but sound enough.
Debonnaire Official explanation: jockey said filly moved poorly throughout

3637 KINGWOOD HOUSE STABLES MAIDEN STKS 1m 4f 5y
9:00 (9:00) (Class 5) 3-Y-0+ **£4,209** (£1,252; £625; £312) **Stalls** Low

Form RPR
2 **1** **Ordination (IRE)**[66] 1690 3-9-0 0........................ JimmyFortune 8 73+
(B J Meehan) *lw: w'like: rangy: scope: trckd ldr: led over 4f out: styd on wl: drvn out* **7/4**[2]
3 **2** *1 1/4* **Dazzling Light (UAE)**[21] 2971 3-8-9 0........................ SteveDrowne 10 66+
(R Charlton) *lw: mid-div: gd hdwy over 3f out: wnt 2nd over 2f out: sn rdn: kpt on but a hld by wnr* **9/2**[3]
00 **3** *2 1/2* **Filun**[31] 2669 3-9-0 0........................ DaneO'Neill 5 67+
(L M Cumani) *hld up: hdwy over 3f out: sn rdn: wnt 3rd over 2f out: styd on same pce* **20/1**
4 *1 3/4* **Darksideofthemoon (IRE)**[21] 6-9-13 0........................ PaulDoe 2 64
(N J Gifford) *awkward leaving stalls: bhd: rdn and stdy prog fr over 3f out but nt pce to get on terms* **100/1**
5 **5** *1* **Go On Ahead (IRE)**[26] 2832 8-9-13 0........................ FergusSweeney 6 63
(W S Kittow) *sn led: hdd over 4f out: sn rdn: one pce fr over 2f out* **100/1**
6 **6** *1 1/2* **Lady Marguerite**[13] 3205 3-8-9 0........................ MartinDwyer 7 55
(M P Tregoning) *trckd ldrs: rdn to chal over 3f out: one pce fnl 2f* **50/1**
0 **7** *3/4* **Solar Max (IRE)**[47] 2191 3-9-0 0........................ ShaneKelly 1 59
(C R Egerton) *a towards rr* **50/1**
3 **8** *6* **Dancer In Demand (IRE)**[47] 2191 3-9-0 0........................ RyanMoore 3 49
(Sir Michael Stoute) *lw: s.i.s: struggling ent st: a bhd* **10/11**[1]
-00 **9** *1/2* **Kennyboy**[38] 2454 3-8-7 0........................ KylieManser(7) 9 49
(Mrs H Sweeting) *trckd ldrs: rdn and hung lft over 3f out: sn wknd* **100/1**

2m 38.43s (2.93) **Going Correction** +0.075s/f (Good)
WFA 3 from 6yo+ 13lb **9** Ran SP% **118.6**
Speed ratings (Par 103): **93,92,90,89,88 87,87,83,82**
toteswinger: 1&2 £1.80, 1&3 £8.30, 2&3 £12.80. CSF £9.96 TOTE £3.20: £1.10, £1.50, £3.80; EX 8.50 Place 6 £ 17.30, Place 5 £13.71.
Owner Catesby W Clay **Bred** Runnymede Farm Inc And Catesby W Clay **Trained** Manton, Wilts

FOCUS
An ordinary maiden that was slowly run, and the close proximity of hurdlers in fourth and fifth holds down the form, as does the poor showing of hot favourite Dancer In Demand.
Dancer In Demand(IRE) Official explanation: trainer said colt never travelled; vet said colt was found to be lame behind
T/Plt: £26.70 to a £1 stake. Pool: £65,560.16. 1,788.73 winning tickets. T/Qpdt: £12.70 to a £1 stake. Pool: £3,369.50. 195.15 winning tickets. TM

3277 REDCAR (L-H)
Thursday, July 3

OFFICIAL GOING: Good to firm (firm in places; 9.1)
The ground was described as ;genuine firm'.
Wind: Moderate, half-behind. Weather: Mainly fine

3638 MARKET CROSS JEWELLERS APPRENTICE H'CAP 6f
6:10 (6:44) (Class 6) (0-60,58) 3-Y-0+ **£2,388** (£705; £352) **Stalls** Centre

Form RPR
-404 **1** **Mandalay King (IRE)**[15] 3139 3-8-3 **45**........................ KellyHarrison(3) 9 54
(Mrs Marjorie Fife) *trckd ldrs: led appr fnl f: styd on wl* **12/1**
0464 **2** *1 3/4* **Buzbury Rings**[12] 3282 4-9-5 **55**........................ NeilBrown(3) 2 60
(R E Barr) *chsd ldrs on outer: styd on same pce ins fnl f* **8/1**
5630 **3** *hd* **High Window (IRE)**[13] 3231 8-8-5 **45**........................ BradleyRoper(7) 5 49
(G P Kelly) *hld up in midfield: hdwy 2f out: styd on wl ins fnl f* **33/1**
-003 **4** *nk* **Greek Secret**[22] 2950 5-9-5 **52**........................ MichaelJStainton 14 55
(J O'Reilly) *mid-div: drvn over 2f out: styd on wl ins fnl f* **6/1**[2]
503 **5** *nk* **Foxy Jane**[44] 2268 3-8-7 **53**........................ AdamCarter(7) 1 53
(M Brittain) *hld up: hdwy on wd outside over 2f out: hung bdly lft: styd on fnl f* **33/1**
0362 **6** *1 1/4* **Wiltshire (IRE)**[17] 3079 6-9-9 **56**........................(v) JamieMoriarty 12 54
(P T Midgley) *slowly away: hdwy over 3f out: one pce fnl 2f* **13/2**[3]
0620 **7** *nk* **Lambency (IRE)**[12] 3260 5-9-3 **55**........................ GaryBartley(5) 8 52
(J S Goldie) *hld up in rr: hdwy on inner 2f out: styd on wl ins fnl f* **6/1**[2]
2303 **8** *1/2* **Whozart (IRE)**[9] 3340 5-8-12 **50**........................ PatrickDonaghy(5) 10 46
(A Dickman) *led tl hdd appr fnl f: fdd* **13/2**[3]
5465 **9** *1 1/2* **Falmassim**[9] 3340 5-8-8 **46**........................(p) BMcHugh(5) 6 37
(Miss J A Camacho) *unruly in stalls: hld up: hdwy and swtchd rt 2f out: nvr nr ldrs* **8/1**
0001 **10** *shd* **Avoncreek**[36] 2511 4-9-5 **57**........................ JemmaMarshall(5) 3 48
(B P J Baugh) *hld up in rr: effrt 2f out: nvr nr ldrs* **16/1**
0004 **11** *1/2* **Ryedane (IRE)**[3] 3546 6-9-11 **58**........................(b) DuranFentiman 13 47
(T D Easterby) *chsd ldrs: wknd appr fnl f* **5/1**[1]
0-05 **12** *3* **Warm Tribute (USA)**[13] 3200 4-8-7 **45**........................ RobbieEgan(5) 7 25
(A G Foster) *chsd ldrs: rdn over 2f out: lost pl over 1f out* **25/1**
0/05 **13** *1/2* **She Who Dares Wins**[13] 3231 8-8-12 **45**........................ RussellKennemore 11 23
(L R James) *chsd ldrs: sn drvn along: lost pl over 1f out* **28/1**

1m 11.29s (-0.51) **Going Correction** -0.15s/f (Firm)
WFA 3 from 4yo+ 6lb **13** Ran SP% **120.9**
Speed ratings (Par 101): **97,94,94,94,93 91,91,90,88,88 88,84,83**
toteswinger: 1&2 £32.90, 1&3 £100.60, 2&3 £100.60. CSF £102.17 CT £3174.35 TOTE £16.30: £4.50, £2.90, £12.10; EX 172.50.
Owner Green Lane **Bred** Forenaghts Stud And Dermot Cantillon **Trained** Stillington, N Yorks

FOCUS
A rock-bottom apprentice handicap which was delayed over half an hour due to Danielle McCreery having to be airlifted to hospital after a fall from Only A Splash (withdrawn) on the way to post. Very ordinary form rated through the third.

3639 O'GRADYS HOTEL REDCAR NURSERY 5f
6:40 (7:06) (Class 4) 2-Y-0 **£3,885** (£1,156; £577; £288) **Stalls** Centre

Form RPR
5221 **1** **Rievaulx World**[15] 3140 2-9-2 **84**........................ NeilBrown(5) 3 100+
(K A Ryan) *mde all: wnt clr appr fnl f: easily* **8/13**[1]
61 **2** *6* **Simple Rhythm**[35] 2548 2-8-10 **76**........................ DominicFox(3) 4 68
(M G Quinlan) *trckd ldr: effrt over 1f out: sn rdn and hung lft: no ch w wnr* **9/2**[2]
230 **3** *4 1/2* **Camelot Communion (IRE)**[35] 2534 2-8-11 **74**........ RoystonFfrench 1 50
(Mrs A Duffield) *trckd ldrs: rdn over 2f out: sn wl outpcd* **6/1**[3]
0304 **4** *1/2* **Premier Krug (IRE)**[12] 3254 2-7-13 **62**........................ CatherineGannon 2 36
(P D Evans) *sn drvn along: outpcd and lost pl 1/2-way: no ch after* **9/1**
620 **5** *14* **Jethro Bodine (IRE)**[23] 2909 2-7-13 **65** oh6 ow4..... DuranFentiman(3) 5 —
(W J H Ratcliffe) *in rr: drvn and wl outpcd over 2f out: hung lft: bhd whn eased ins fnl f* **11/1**

57.27 secs (-1.33) **Going Correction** -0.15s/f (Firm) **5** Ran SP% **112.7**
Speed ratings (Par 96): **104,94,87,86,64**
CSF £3.95 TOTE £1.60: £1.10, £1.80; EX 2.40.
Owner Rievaulx Racing Syndicate **Bred** Grovewood Stud & Padraid O'Neill **Trained** Hambleton, N Yorks

FOCUS
The 'official' ratings shown next to each horse are estimated and for information purposes only. A one-horse race and the speedy winner is a smart sort who is clearly going the right way.

NOTEBOOK
Rievaulx World, who is clearly thriving, showed a very willing attitude and proved much too speedy for this lot, and in the end came right away for a very easy win. He goes for the Molecomb at Goodwood now and should be respected there. (tchd 8-11 in places)
Simple Rhythm, expensive to retain at Yarmouth, kept tabs on the winner but in the end it proved very much a one-sided contest. (op 5-1)
Camelot Communion(IRE), closely matched with the winner on Haydock running, was dropping back in trip and was being run off her feet soon after the halfway mark.
Premier Krug(IRE), another dropping back in trip, was soon struggling to keep up. (tchd 10-1)
Jethro Bodine(IRE), 6lb out of the handicap and with his substitute rider putting up 4lb overweight, was soon out of the contest and in the end he completed in his own time. Official explanation: jockey said gelding hung left (op 14-1)

3640 SUBSCRIBE TO RACING UK (S) STKS 1m
7:10 (7:29) (Class 5) 3-4-Y-0 **£3,070** (£906; £453) **Stalls** Centre

Form RPR
4000 **1** **Hasty Lady**[22] 2946 3-8-2 65........................(p) CatherineGannon 3 53
(K A Ryan) *chsd ldrs: wnt 2nd over 4f out: led ins fnl f: hld on towards fin* **3/1**[1]
650- **2** *1/2* **Viscaya (IRE)**[268] 6074 3-8-2 55........................ RoystonFfrench 9 52
(Mrs A Duffield) *chsd ldrs: rdn and outpcd over 2f out: styd on wl fnl f* **12/1**
04-0 **3** *hd* **Manuka Bee**[31] 2675 3-8-7 67........................ PaulMulrennan 13 57
(J Howard Johnson) *chsd ldrs: rdn and outpcd 4f out: hdwy over 1f out: kpt on wl ins fnl f* **7/1**
1020 **4** *shd* **Ghafeer (USA)**[17] 3082 4-9-1 56........................(p) LanceBetts(7) 11 64
(B Ellison) *chsd ldr: chsd ldrs: outpcd over 2f out: kpt on wl fnl f* **7/2**[2]
6003 **5** *1 1/4* **Only A Grand**[22] 2940 4-8-11 49........................(b) DarrenWilliams 1 50
(R Bastiman) *led after 2f: edgd lft and hdd ins fnl f: wknd towards fin* **5/1**[3]
60-0 **6** *1 1/4* **Bond Scissorsister (IRE)**[23] 2915 3-8-2 48........................ SilvestreDeSousa 6 46
(G R Oldroyd) *chsd ldrs on outer: kpt on one pce fnl 2f* **10/1**
00-0 **7** *4 1/2* **Carlton Mac**[15] 3139 3-8-7 41........................ PaulFessey 2 40
(N Bycroft) *in rr: sme hdwy over 2f out: nvr nr ldrs: eased towards fin* **20/1**
00-0 **8** *10* **Motherwell**[89] 1222 3-8-2 43........................ TWilliams 7 12
(M Brittain) *in rr: effrt 3f out: sn lost pl* **33/1**
500 **9** *23* **Jayne Dean**[40] 2395 4-8-8 30........................ MichaelJStainton(3) 12 —
(A Crook) *chsd ldrs: t.k.h: edgd rt and lost pl 3f out: sn bhd* **33/1**
0 **10** *10* **Wendy Craig**[14] 3180 3-8-3 0 ow1........................ PatrickMathers 4 —
(J Balding) *s.i.s: sme hdwy 4f out: lost pl over 2f out: sn bhd* **50/1**
000 **11** *35* **Paris Hall**[27] 2803 3-8-0 44........................ DonnaCaldwell(7) 8 —
(I W McInnes) *reminders after s: sn detached in last: virtually p.u over 2f out: hopelessly t.o* **25/1**

1m 38.41s (0.41) **Going Correction** -0.15s/f (Firm)
WFA 3 from 4yo 9lb **11** Ran SP% **109.6**
Speed ratings (Par 103): **91,90,90,90,88 87,83,73,50,40 5**
toteswinger: 1&2 £12.30, 1&3 £1.40, 2&3 £14.80. CSF £32.37 TOTE £4.40: £1.80, £3.50, £1.90; EX 49.00.There was no bid for the winner
Owner Graham Frankland **Bred** N Poole And A Franklin **Trained** Hambleton, N Yorks

FOCUS
A weakish seller run in a slow time. The fourth is probably the best guide.
Wendy Craig Official explanation: jockey said filly ran green
Paris Hall Official explanation: jockey said gelding never travelled

3641 GO RACING IN YORKSHIRE SUMMER FESTIVAL H'CAP 1m 2f
7:45 (7:52) (Class 4) (0-85,84) 3-Y-0 **£6,476** (£1,927; £963; £481) **Stalls** Low

Form RPR
2241 **1** **Prince Kalamoun (IRE)**[13] 3227 3-8-12 **80**........................ NeilBrown(5) 9 94
(G A Swinbank) *hld up in rr: stdy hdwy on ins over 3f out: wnt 2nd 2f out: shkn up to ld jst ins fnl f: pushed out* **9/2**[3]
3-13 **2** *2 1/2* **Mangham (IRE)**[30] 2699 3-9-3 **80**........................ PaulMulrennan 2 89
(D H Brown) *led: hdd jst ins fnl f: kpt on same pce* **7/2**[2]

-405 **3** *5* **Joinedupwriting**[41] 2378 3-8-8 **71** .... DavidAllan 1 70
(R M Whitaker) *chsd ldrs: drvn over 4f out: one pce fnl 2f* **7/1**

0236 **4** *5* **Bere Davis (FR)**[12] 3251 3-9-3 **80** .... CatherineGannon 4 69
(P D Evans) *hld up: hdwy to chse ldrs over 4f out: one pce fnl 3f* **10/1**

1-22 **5** *5* **Inspector Clouseau (IRE)**[19] 3048 3-9-3 **80** .... TonyHamilton 6 59
(T P Tate) *trckd ldrs: wnt 2nd over 3f out: wknd 2f out* **15/8**[1]

20-0 **6** *11* **Madison Heights (IRE)**[37] 2488 3-8-3 **66** .... PaulFessey 8 23
(J Howard Johnson) *chsd ldrs: outpcd over 4f out: sn btn* **25/1**

-062 **7** *½* **Heart Of Dubai (USA)**[19] 3035 3-8-2 **70** .... AhmedAjtebi(5) 7 26
(C E Brittain) *hld up in rr: effrt 4f out: lost pl over 2f out: eased ins fnl f* **16/1**

3232 **8** *7* **August Gale (USA)**[13] 3200 3-8-11 **74** .... RoystonFfrench 5 16
(M Johnston) *chsd ldr: rdn over 4f out: lost pl 3f out: sn bhd* **8/1**

2m 4.92s (-2.18) **Going Correction** -0.15s/f (Firm) **8** Ran SP% **117.6**
Speed ratings (Par 102): **102,100,96,92,88 79,78,73**
toteswinger: 1&2 £4.00, 1&3 £6.40, 2&3 £8.20. CSF £21.32 CT £109.85 TOTE £5.10: £2.10, £1.40, £2.60; EX 29.50.
Owner Jonathan Dixon **Bred** Michael Pitt **Trained** Melsonby, N Yorks

FOCUS
A strongly-run race and in the end a very ready winner. The first two finished clear and this is good form for the grade.

3642 FAMILY FUN DAY SUNDAY 20TH JULY H'CAP 1m 6f 19y
8:15 (8:15) (Class 5) (0-70,67) 4-Y-0+ **£4,533** (£1,348; £674; £336) **Stalls** Low

Form RPR

6-04 **1** **Abstract Folly (IRE)**[38] 2467 6-9-5 **65** .... PaulFessey 4 70
(J D Bethell) *hld up in rr: hdwy 4f out: led 2f out: hld on towards fin* **13/2**

4523 **2** *nk* **Rose Bien**[12] 3276 6-8-11 **62** ....(p) JackMitchell(5) 5 67
(P J McBride) *hld up in mid-div: shkn up over 5f out: hdwy to chal 2f out: styd on towards fin* **5/2**[1]

0-00 **3** *3* **Apsara**[26] 2849 7-8-2 **48** oh3 .... CatherineGannon 3 48
(G M Moore) *chsd ldrs: outpcd 4f out: hdwy on wd outside over 2f out: styd on fnl f* **33/1**

3/16 **4** *nk* **Ritsi**[7] 3414 5-9-2 **67** .... NeilBrown(5) 9 67
(Grant Tuer) *hld up in rr: outpcd 5f out: hdwy over 3f out: kpt on fnl f* **5/1**[3]

0043 **5** *2 ½* **Let It Be**[12] 3279 7-8-10 **56** .... PaulMulrennan 1 52
(K G Reveley) *chsd ldrs: hrd rdn 3f out: one pce* **7/2**[2]

0-02 **6** *2 ¾* **Mcqueen (IRE)**[12] 3279 8-8-13 **62** .... RussellKennemore(3) 6 55
(J T Stimpson) *drvn to ld: hdd 2f out: fdd appr fnl f* **5/1**[3]

050- **7** *nk* **Riodan (IRE)**[114] 6186 6-8-12 **61** .... DuranFentiman(3) 7 53
(L A Mullaney) *chsd ldrs: drvn over 4f out: wknd over 1f out* **18/1**

6603 **8** *1 ½* **Treetops Hotel (IRE)**[13] 3226 9-8-3 **49** .... TWilliams 2 39
(L R James) *in rr-div: drvn 4f out: sn chsng ldrs: wknd over 1f out* **18/1**

2-00 **9** *47* **Bronze Dancer (IRE)**[58] 1892 6-9-2 **62** .... RoystonFfrench 8 —
(B Storey) *hld up in rr: lost pl over 3f out: sn wl bhd: t.o* **25/1**

3m 4.30s (-0.40) **Going Correction** -0.15s/f (Firm) **9** Ran SP% **114.8**
Speed ratings (Par 103): **95,94,93,92,91 89,89,88,62**
toteswinger: 1&2 £5.80, 1&3 Not won, 2&3 £42.10. CSF £22.96 CT £499.94 TOTE £8.40: £2.10, £1.30, £10.50; EX 14.80.
Owner Clarendon Thoroughbred Racing **Bred** John Neary **Trained** Middleham Moor, N Yorks
■ Stewards' Enquiry : Jack Mitchell two-day ban: used whip with excessive frequency (Jul 17,18)

FOCUS
A modest stayers' handicap run at a sound pace. The form makes sense among the front pair.
Mcqueen(IRE) Official explanation: jockey said gelding was unsuited by the good to firm (firm in places) ground

3643 TEES VALLEY COMMUNITY FOUNDATION CLAIMING STKS 7f
8:50 (8:50) (Class 5) 3-Y-0+ **£3,561** (£1,059; £529; £264) **Stalls** Centre

Form RPR

1121 **1** **Royal Dignitary (USA)**[12] 3281 8-9-6 83 .... AhmedAjtebi(5) 2 85
(D Nicholls) *mde all: shkn up over 3f out: edgd rt over 1f out: styd on* **4/7**[1]

3020 **2** *2 ½* **Efidium**[17] 3082 10-8-8 62 .... NeilBrown(5) 6 66
(N Bycroft) *sn chsng ldrs: kpt on same pce appr fnl f: no imp* **8/1**

0363 **3** *1 ½* **Inside Story (IRE)**[17] 3077 6-9-3 67 ....(b) DaleGibson 8 66
(M W Easterby) *chsd ldrs: rdn over 2f out: kpt on same pce* **11/2**[2]

-260 **4** *2 ¾* **Grand Opera (IRE)**[38] 2445 5-9-9 69 .... PaulMulrennan 9 65
(J Howard Johnson) *dwlt: sn chsng wnr: one pce appr fnl f* **15/2**[3]

0065 **5** *hd* **Neon Blue**[6] 3443 7-9-1 62 ....(v) MichaelJStainton(3) 1 59
(R M Whitaker) *hld up in rr: effrt over 2f out: sn rdn: one pce* **9/1**

4000 **6** *2* **Sir Bond (IRE)**[12] 3281 7-8-8 45 ow1 .... SladeO'Hara(5) 7 49
(G R Oldroyd) *s.i.s: sn chsng ldrs: one pce fnl 2f* **40/1**

5000 **7** *11* **Bretwalda (IRE)**[12] 3281 5-8-11 45 ....(v[1]) JamieMoriarty(3) 10 20
(P T Midgley) *w ldrs: t.k.h: lost pl over 2f out: sn bhd* **50/1**

0-0 **8** *3 ¼* **Calza Di Seta**[23] 2912 3-8-3 0 .... RoystonFfrench 3 8
(G M Moore) *sn chsng ldrs: lost pl 3f out: sn bhd* **66/1**

1m 24.19s (-0.31) **Going Correction** -0.15s/f (Firm)
WFA 3 from 5yo+ 8lb **8** Ran SP% **117.8**
Speed ratings (Par 103): **95,92,90,87,87 84,72,68**
toteswinger: 1&2 £1.90, 1&3 £1.30, 2&3 £6.80. CSF £6.41 TOTE £1.40: £1.10, £1.60, £1.90; EX 6.20.
Owner Middleham Park Racing XXXVI **Bred** Bentley Smith, J Michael O'Farrell Jr , Joan Thor **Trained** Sessay, N Yorks

FOCUS
The winner made all and is rated to this year's form, with the second also running to his mark.

3644 THE COMMITMENTS ARE HERE IN AUGUST FILLIES' H'CAP 1m 2f
9:20 (9:20) (Class 5) (0-70,69) 3-Y-0+ **£3,561** (£1,059; £529; £264) **Stalls** Low

Form RPR

55-4 **1** **Sweet Sara**[21] 2973 3-9-9 **69** .... AhmedAjtebi(5) 6 77+
(C E Brittain) *w ldr: led over 2f out: kpt on wl fnl f* **4/1**[2]

0221 **2** *2 ½* **Sceilin (IRE)**[8] 3361 4-9-13 **57** 6ex ....(t) DavidAllan 1 60
(J Mackie) *led: t.k.h: hdd over 3f out: styd on same pce fnl f* **8/11**[1]

5556 **3** *1* **Malinsa Blue (IRE)**[11] 3293 6-10-0 **58** .... J-PGuillambert 8 59
(B Ellison) *trckd ldrs: t.k.h: hung lft and and nt qckn appr fnl f* **7/1**[3]

0050 **4** *¾* **Mozayada (USA)**[22] 2927 4-9-4 **48** .... TWilliams 2 47
(M Brittain) *chsd ldrs: rdn 3f out: one pce appr fnl f* **33/1**

-320 **5** *¾* **Misplaced Fortune**[23] 2911 3-9-10 **65** .... KimTinkler 3 63
(N Tinkler) *chsd ldrs: outpcd and lost pl 5f out: rallied over 2f out: edgd rt: one pce* **14/1**

0-00 **6** *2 ½* **Honeycott (IRE)**[23] 2915 3-8-7 **48** ....(v[1]) PaulFessey 5 41
(J D Bethell) *t.k.h in rr: effrt 4f out: nvr nr ldrs* **33/1**

6004 **7** *2 ¾* **Miss Understanding**[17] 3081 3-8-2 **46** .... DuranFentiman(3) 4 33
(J R Weymes) *in rr: hdwy and drvn over 4f out: lost pl over 1f out* **20/1**

5-00 **8** *1 ½* **Awaken**[17] 3077 7-9-6 **50** .... RoystonFfrench 7 34
(Miss Tracy Waggott) *hld up: effrt on outer over 4f out: wknd 2f out* **10/1**

2m 8.37s (1.27) **Going Correction** -0.15s/f (Firm)
WFA 3 from 4yo+ 11lb **8** Ran SP% **116.8**
Speed ratings (Par 100): **88,86,85,84,84 82,79,78**
toteswinger: 1&2 £1.20, 1&3 £4.90, 2&3 £1.50. CSF £7.30 CT £17.99 TOTE £5.20: £1.30, £1.10, £2.30; EX 8.50 Place 6 £119.01, Place 5 £9.59..
Owner Dr Ali Ridha **Bred** Harts Farm And Stud **Trained** Newmarket, Suffolk

FOCUS
A low-grade fillies' handicap with doubts over the form, but a ready winner who completed a double for her rider.
T/Plt: £155.60 to a £1 stake. Pool: £61,224.69. 287.17 winning tickets. T/Qpdt: £7.60 to a £1 stake. Pool: £3,409.79. 331.10 winning tickets. WG

3417 WARWICK (L-H)
Thursday, July 3

OFFICIAL GOING: Good (good to firm in places; 8.2)
Wind: Almost nil. Weather: Fine

3645 EUROPEAN BREEDERS' FUND MEDIAN AUCTION MAIDEN STKS 7f 26y
6:30 (6:33) (Class 4) 2-Y-0 **£6,476** (£1,927; £963; £481) **Stalls** Low

Form RPR

6 **1** **Swift Chap**[27] 2769 2-8-12 0 .... JamesMillman(5) 9 66
(B R Millman) *mde virtually all: rdn and edgd lft wl over 1f out: drvn out* **15/2**

0 **2** *½* **Saharan Royal**[27] 2769 2-8-12 0 .... SamHitchcott 1 60
(M Salaman) *trckd ldrs: rdn to chse wnr over 1f out: edgd lft ins fnl f: r.o* **7/1**[3]

0 **3** *4 ½* **Arushore (IRE)**[27] 2796 2-9-3 0 .... PatDobbs 10 54
(R Hannon) *trckd ldrs: edgd lft wl over 1f out: sn rdn: one pce* **12/1**

0 **4** *1* **Kaada**[9] 3348 2-8-12 0 .... LiamJones 6 46
(C E Brittain) *dwlt: hld up: hdwy on ins over 2f out: nt clr run and swtchd rt wl over 1f out: no imp* **40/1**

2554 **5** *2 ½* **Yokozuna**[9] 3334 2-9-3 0 ....(b) JimCrowley 3 45
(E A L Dunlop) *w wnr: rdn 2f out: sn wknd* **9/2**[2]

60 **6** *5* **Astroleo**[8] 3372 2-9-3 0 .... SaleemGolam 8 32
(M H Tompkins) *hld up: struggling whn rdn wl over 1f out* **40/1**

0 **7** *1 ¼* **Daily Planet (IRE)**[48] 2146 2-8-12 0 .... GabrielHannon(5) 4 29
(B W Duke) *trckd ldrs: rdn over 2f out: hung lft wl over 1f out: sn wknd* **80/1**

06 **8** *1 ¾* **Samba Queen (IRE)**[16] 3114 2-8-9 0 .... TolleyDean(3) 7 20
(J L Spearing) *plld hrd: hung rt thrght: a in rr* **20/1**

9 *4 ½* **New Adventure** 2-8-10 0 .... WilliamCarson(7) 5 14
(P F I Cole) *dwlt: a in rr* **3/1**[1]

00 **10** *hd* **Craft (FR)**[10] 3331 2-9-3 0 .... TPO'Shea 2 13
(B J Meehan) *w ldrs tl wknd 2f out* **33/1**

1m 25.6s (1.00) **Going Correction** +0.075s/f (Good) **10** Ran SP% **89.0**
Speed ratings (Par 96): **97,96,91,90,87 81,80,78,73,72**
toteswinger: 1&2 £7.10, 1&3 £3.20, 2&3 £6.80. CSF £29.40 TOTE £6.50: £2.30, £2.10, £3.60; EX 33.50.
Owner M A Swift **Bred** D R Tucker **Trained** Kentisbeare, Devon
■ The Kyllachy Kid was withdrawn after proving unruly in the stalls (9/4F, deduct 30p in the £ under Rule 4).
■ Stewards' Enquiry : Gabriel Hannon one-day ban: used whip when out of contention (Jul 18); £290 fine: left weighing room too soon after race

FOCUS
A weak juvenile maiden. The first pair came clear and the winner improved by 7lb but this is limited form.

NOTEBOOK
Swift Chap showed the clear benefit of his debut experience at Bath and, relishing the longer distance, got off the mark with a gutsy display. He enjoyed being ridden positively and can now make his mark through the nursery ranks. (op 7-1 tchd 6-1)
Saharan Royal was the only one to give the winner a serious time of it late on and posted a much-improved effort. She finished clear of the rest, evidently enjoyed the step up to this stiffer test and will be eligible for nurseries after her next assignment. (op 8-1 tchd 6-1)
Arushore(IRE), seventh on his debut at Goodwood, stepped up on that effort without seriously threatening and got the longer trip well enough. He is one for nurseries after his next run. (op 14-1)
Kaada again took time to get going, but would have been a touch closer with a clearer passage when making her effort. She is another who will be eligible for nurseries after her next outing. (op 50-1 tchd 66-1)
Yokozuna is now exposed and in danger of going the wrong way. (tchd 5-1)
Samba Queen(IRE) Official explanation: jockey said filly ran too freely
New Adventure, related to numerous winners for this stable, met plenty of support ahead of this racecourse bow and a big run was evidently expected. He ran no sort of race in the end, however, and looked clueless for most of the contest. (op 5-1 tchd 11-2)

3646 ARDENCOTE MANOR HOTEL H'CAP 7f 26y
7:00 (7:02) (Class 4) (0-85,85) 3-Y-0+ **£5,180** (£1,541; £770; £384) **Stalls** Low

Form RPR

0-25 **1** **Kafuu (IRE)**[33] 2619 4-9-11 **82** ....(p) SebSanders 1 94
(S A Callaghan) *a.p: rdn to ld over 1f out: wnt clr u.p ins fnl f: r.o wl* **7/2**[1]

60-0 **2** *3 ½* **Woodcote Place**[19] 3040 5-9-9 **80** .... JimCrowley 6 83
(P R Chamings) *hld up in mid-div: hdwy over 2f out: rdn over 1f out: kpt on take 2nd towards fin: nt trble wnr* **8/1**

3100 **3** *¾* **Royal Storm (IRE)**[6] 3443 9-9-1 **77** .... JamesMillman(5) 2 78
(B R Millman) *led: rdn over 2f out: hdd over 1f out: no ex and lost 2nd towards fin* **11/1**

5002 **4** *1 ¼* **The Kiddykid (IRE)**[6] 3435 8-9-12 **83** .... SaleemGolam 5 80
(P D Evans) *hld up in tch: rdn over 2f out: one pce* **9/2**[2]

16-0 **5** *¾* **Shamayel**[26] 2819 3-9-4 **83** .... ChrisCatlin 3 80+
(B W Hills) *hld up in tch: hung rt and lost pl bnd over 3f out: hdwy over 1f out: nvr trbld ldrs* **6/1**[3]

-660 **6** *½* **Passion Fruit**[8] 3369 7-9-12 **83** .... AndrewElliott 9 77+
(C W Fairhurst) *hld up and bhd: rdn and sme hdwy on ins over 1f out: n.d* **25/1**

060 **7** *1 ½* **Overrule (USA)**[23] 2905 4-9-6 **77** .... TomEaves 10 67+
(B Ellison) *hld up and bhd: sme late prog: nvr nrr* **8/1**

2660 **8** *¾* **H Harrison (IRE)**[6] 3435 8-9-2 **76** .... PJMcDonald(3) 7 64
(I W McInnes) *hld up in tch: wknd over 2f out* **22/1**

6-00 **9** *1 ¼* **Namid Reprobate (IRE)**[17] 3090 5-9-2 **73** .... JoeFanning 11 57
(P F I Cole) *s.i.s: a bhd* **28/1**

4400 **10** *2 ½* **Dazed And Amazed**[28] 2760 4-9-7 **78** .... PatDobbs 4 56
(R Hannon) *chsd ldr over 4f: wknd 1f out* **11/1**

0021 **11** 2 3/4 **Gallantry**[17] 3087 6-9-11 **85** .... TolleyDean(3) 8 55
(P Howling) *s.i.s: pushed along over 2f out: a bhd* **15/2**

1m 23.66s (-0.94) **Going Correction** +0.075s/f (Good)
WFA 3 from 4yo+ 8lb **11** Ran SP% **117.0**
Speed ratings (Par 105): **108,104,103,101,100 100,98,97,96,93 90**
toteswinger: 1&2 £25.00, 1&3 £8.50, 2&3 £55.00. CSF £30.75 CT £286.21 TOTE £3.90: £1.70, £3.30, £5.10; EX 40.00.
Owner Saleh Al Homaizi & Imad Al Sagar **Bred** J Hanly **Trained** Newmarket, Suffolk

FOCUS
A fair handicap in which few really got into from off the pace. The winner is progressive, but the form should be treated with a little caution.
Shamayel Official explanation: jockey said filly failed to handle the bend
Gallantry Official explanation: trainer said, regarding running, that the gelding was unsuited by the good (good to firm places) ground.

3647 TURFTV H'CAP 6f
7:35 (7:35) (Class 3) (0-95,94) 3-Y-0+ **£7,771** (£2,312; £1,155; £577) **Stalls** Centre

Form RPR
4202 **1** **Pawan (IRE)**[5] 3489 8-8-12 **83** .... (b) AnnStokell(5) 8 95
(Miss A Stokell) *a gng wl: led 1f out: r.o* **7/1**[3]
0-30 **2** 1 3/4 **Phantom Whisper**[39] 2426 5-9-6 **91** .... JamesMillman(5) 5 97+
(B R Millman) *stdd s: hld up and bhd: rdn 3f out: hdwy over 1f out: r.o to take 2nd cl home* **5/1**[2]
-243 **3** 1/2 **Orpenindeed (IRE)**[18] 3056 5-9-9 **92** .... (t) KirstyMilczarek(3) 6 96
(M Botti) *a.p: ev ch jst over 1f out: rdn and nt qckn ins fnl f* **11/4**[1]
6003 **4** *shd* **Hurricane Spirit (IRE)**[33] 2598 4-9-13 **93** .... SebSanders 4 97
(J R Best) *led: rdn and hdd 1f out: no ex and lost 2nd cl home* **9/1**
-303 **5** 1/2 **Johannes (IRE)**[9] 3336 5-9-0 **80** .... ChrisCatlin 9 82
(E J O'Neill) *t.k.h towards rr: hdwy over 2f out: rdn and one pce fnl f* **7/1**[3]
00-1 **6** *hd* **Little Edward**[10] 3320 10-10-0 **94** 6ex .... JimCrowley 2 96
(R J Hodges) *hld up: hdwy over 1f out: rdn and one pce fnl f* **14/1**
-056 **7** 1 **Golden Dixie (USA)**[5] 3472 9-9-10 **90** .... TGMcLaughlin 1 89
(R A Harris) *prom: rdn 2f out: wknd ins fnl f* **7/1**[3]
5061 **8** 1/2 **Ajigolo**[39] 2426 5-9-13 **93** .... TPO'Shea 7 90
(M R Channon) *t.k.h in mid-div: shkn up 1f out: sn btn* **15/2**
3100 **9** 3 3/4 **Dubai Power**[20] 2998 3-8-10 **82** .... WilliamBuick 3 66
(C E Brittain) *s.i.s: a in rr* **16/1**

1m 11.05s (-0.75) **Going Correction** +0.075s/f (Good) course record
WFA 3 from 4yo+ 6lb **9** Ran SP% **115.1**
Speed ratings (Par 107): **108,105,105,104,104 103,102,101,96**
toteswinger: 1&2 £14.20, 1&3 £4.00, 2&3 £6.30. CSF £41.74 CT £119.77 TOTE £7.40: £1.80, £2.20, £1.40; EX 48.60.
Owner Ms Caron Stokell **Bred** Hadi Al Tajir **Trained** Brompton-on-Swale, N Yorks

FOCUS
A good handicap run at just a fair pace. The form looks sound enough with the well-in Pawan rated to his latest.

NOTEBOOK
Pawan(IRE), pipped in this race last season, had been narrowly denied at Newcastle five days previously and was able to race from the same mark on this quick reappearance. He travelled kindly through the race before taking it up nearing the final furlong and, once in front, he always looked like doing the business. This was much deserved, but he is certainly not one to be banking on when bidding to follow up and was already due to race from a 7lb higher future mark. (op 13-2 tchd 6-1)
Phantom Whisper was given a fair bit to do from off the pace and was always getting there too late. This was better from him, but he hardly looks well handicapped at present. (op 11-2 tchd 6-1)
Orpenindeed(IRE) was given every chance, yet again managed to find a couple too good. He rates a fair benchmark for the form. (op 11-2)
Hurricane Spirit(IRE) was given an aggressive ride, but ran below his previous level on this quicker surface and looks to really want a stiffer test than this. (op 13-2)
Dubai Power Official explanation: jockey said filly missed the break

3648 ARDENCOTE SPA CLAIMING STKS 1m 22y
8:05 (8:06) (Class 5) 3-Y-0+ **£3,412** (£1,007; £504) **Stalls** Low

Form RPR
10-0 **1** **Ten To The Dozen**[8] 3383 5-9-0 55 .... ChrisCatlin 3 63
(P W Hiatt) *chsd ldr: rdn over 2f out: led ins fnl f: drvn out* **16/1**
6000 **2** 1 1/2 **Casablanca Minx (IRE)**[19] 3023 5-8-9 53 .... (v) StephenDonohoe 6 55
(P D Evans) *hld up in rr: c wd st: rdn and gd hdwy fnl f: edgd rt and fin wl to take 2nd nr post* **14/1**
5610 **3** 1/2 **Steig (IRE)**[20] 2995 5-9-7 72 .... JimCrowley 4 65
(Carl Llewellyn) *hld up in tch: rdn over 2f out: kpt on one pce fnl f* **10/3**[2]
3126 **4** *nk* **The Jailer**[25] 2860 5-8-2 60 .... (p) WilliamCarson(7) 5 53
(J G M O'Shea) *led: clr after 2f: rdn over 1f out: hdd ins fnl f: no ex and lost 2nd nr fin* **3/1**[1]
0614 **5** 1 1/4 **Cap St Jean (IRE)**[22] 2933 4-8-9 65 .... (p) MarkCoumbe(5) 1 55
(R Hollinshead) *t.k.h in rr: pushed along over 3f out: rdn over 1f out: styd on ins fnl f* **3/1**[1]
-310 **6** 2 1/2 **Sistos Fascination**[37] 2480 3-8-4 65 .... KirstyMilczarek(3) 2 51
(M Botti) *hld up in tch: outpcd over 3f out: n.d after* **8/1**
0010 **7** 2 1/4 **Bartercard (USA)**[8] 3376 7-9-5 73 .... SebSanders 7 49
(Stef Liddiard) *t.k.h in rr: rdn over 2f out: no rspnse* **11/2**[3]

1m 40.86s (-0.14) **Going Correction** +0.075s/f (Good)
WFA 3 from 4yo+ 9lb **7** Ran SP% **112.1**
Speed ratings (Par 103): **103,101,101,100,99 96,94**
toteswinger: 1&2 £43.70, 1&3 £2.50, 2&3 £43.70. CSF £195.55 TOTE £13.70: £4.20, £4.20; EX 109.20.
Owner Clive Roberts Vince Walsh **Bred** S J Mear **Trained** Hook Norton, Oxon

FOCUS
A moderate affair, run at a strong early pace. The form is rated around the winner.
The Jailer Official explanation: jockey said mare ran too freely

3649 LANSON CHAMPAGNE H'CAP 1m 2f 188y
8:40 (8:40) (Class 4) (0-85,84) 3-Y-0+ **£6,476** (£1,927; £963; £481) **Stalls** Low

Form RPR
-555 **1** **Bencoolen (IRE)**[39] 2425 3-8-12 **80** .... (p) ChrisCatlin 4 88
(R Charlton) *t.k.h: mde all: set stdy pce after 2f: qcknd over 2f out: rdn 1f out: r.o wl* **11/4**[3]
-003 **2** 2 1/4 **Wind Star**[8] 3368 5-9-5 **78** .... PJMcDonald(3) 2 82
(G A Swinbank) *wnt rt and hit gate leaving stalls: hld up: hdwy over 1f out: rdn and chsd wnr fnl f: no imp* **9/4**[1]
1-0 **3** 1 1/4 **Jadaara**[15] 3134 3-9-0 **82** .... JoeFanning 3 84
(M Johnston) *awkward leaving stalls: hld up in rr: hdwy on ins 1f out: kpt on same pce* **8/1**
6035 **4** *nk* **Mustajed**[18] 3060 7-9-6 **81** .... JamesMillman(5) 6 82
(B R Millman) *hld up in tch: chsd wnr over 4f out: rdn over 1f out: lost 2nd and one pce fnl f* **10/1**
0244 **5** 1 1/4 **Peruvian Prince (USA)**[11] 3294 6-10-0 **84** .... PaulHanagan 1 83
(R A Fahey) *chsd wnr tl over 4f out: rdn over 1f out: wknd ins fnl f* **5/2**[2]
0102 **6** 3/4 **Given A Choice (IRE)**[51] 2073 6-8-11 **74** .... (p) SimonPearce(7) 5 72
(J Pearce) *t.k.h towards rr: edgd lft wl over 1f out: sn rdn: no rspnse* **14/1**

2m 23.9s (2.80) **Going Correction** +0.075s/f (Good)
WFA 3 from 5yo+ 12lb **6** Ran SP% **112.9**
Speed ratings (Par 105): **92,90,89,89,88 87**
toteswinger: 1&2 £1.50, 1&3 £5.00, 2&3 £2.30. CSF £9.49 TOTE £4.30: £2.50, £1.80; EX 8.80.
Owner De La Warr Racing **Bred** Darley **Trained** Beckhampton, Wilts

FOCUS
A decent little handicap, run at an uneven pace. The winner was allowed to dictate as he pleased and is rated in line with his 2yo form.

3650 RACING UK H'CAP 1m 4f 134y
9:10 (9:11) (Class 5) (0-75,75) 4-Y-0+ **£3,238** (£963; £481; £240) **Stalls** Low

Form RPR
0-52 **1** **Moonshine Creek**[28] 2755 6-8-2 **56** oh10 .... PaulHanagan 2 61
(P W Hiatt) *t.k.h: a.p: led wl over 1f out: edgd lft ins fnl f: rdn out* **14/1**
2356 **2** 1 1/4 **Urban Warrior**[18] 3060 4-8-10 **64** .... SebSanders 7 67
(Ian Williams) *chsd ldr: rdn and ev ch over 1f out: nt qckn ins fnl f* **7/1**
0555 **3** *nse* **Is It Me (USA)**[13] 3220 5-8-9 **63** .... ChrisCatlin 4 66
(A W Carroll) *led: rdn and hdd wl over 1f out: rallied towards fin* **7/1**
016- **4** 3/4 **Callisto Moon**[78] 1536 4-9-0 **68** .... StephenDonohoe 8 70
(Ian Williams) *hld up in tch: pushed along over 3f out: rdn wl over 1f out: swtchd and edgd lft ent fnl f: styd on* **4/1**[2]
0 **5** 3/4 **Atomic Winner (IRE)**[23] 2920 4-9-0 **71** .... TravisBlock(3) 1 72
(A King) *t.k.h in rr: rdn and hdwy 1f out: hld whn eased nr fin* **11/2**[3]
-250 **6** *hd* **Wyeth**[23] 2921 4-8-6 **60** .... WilliamBuick 5 61
(J R Fanshawe) *hld up and bhd: rdn wl over 1f out: sltly hmpd ent fnl f: styd on towards fin* **6/1**
5261 **7** *nk* **Thorny Mandate**[23] 2908 6-8-4 **58** .... LiamJones 6 58
(W M Brisbourne) *hld up and bhd: hdwy over 2f out: rdn over 1f out: one pce* **3/1**[1]
-610 **8** *nk* **Transvestite (IRE)**[18] 3060 6-9-4 **75** .... PatrickHills(3) 3 75
(J W Hills) *hld up in tch: rdn wl over 1f out: btn whn n.m.r wl ins fnl f* **12/1**

2m 45.17s (0.57) **Going Correction** +0.075s/f (Good) **8** Ran SP% **114.0**
Speed ratings (Par 103): **101,100,100,99,99 99,98,98**
toteswinger: 1&2 £3.10, 1&3 £39.10, 2&3 £3.20. CSF £106.39 CT £749.62 TOTE £12.60: £2.30, £2.10, £3.50; EX 153.40 Place 6 £2,666.10, Place 5 £867.96. .
Owner P W Hiatt **Bred** Lawrence Shepherd **Trained** Hook Norton, Oxon

FOCUS
A moderate handicap which saw a surprise winner from 10lb out of the handicap. The first three were always the leading trio. This is suspect form and the winner could well have been flattered.
T/Plt: £6,844.20 to a £1 stake. Pool: £55,316.78. 5.90 winning tickets. T/Qpdt: £225.60 to a £1 stake. Pool: £4,695.35. 15.40 winning tickets. KH

3113 YARMOUTH (L-H)
Thursday, July 3

OFFICIAL GOING: Good to firm (8.8)
Wind: fresh half against Weather: bright but overcast

3651 E.B.F./RACING WELFARE LIFETIME IN RACING SERIES MAIDEN STKS 6f 3y
2:30 (2:30) (Class 5) 2-Y-0 **£3,784** (£1,132; £566; £283; £141) **Stalls** High

Form RPR
30 **1** **Khor Dubai (IRE)**[16] 3105 2-9-3 0 .... LDettori 5 79
(Saeed Bin Suroor) *hld up in tch: swtchd lft and hdwy 2f out: led over 1f out: rdn and hld on wl fnl f* **4/9**[1]
2 *hd* **Magaling (IRE)** 2-9-3 0 .... PatCosgrave 8 78+
(L M Cumani) *t.k.h: hld up in tch: hdwy 2f out: chsd wnr 1f out: kpt on wl but a jst hld* **8/1**[3]
3 4 **Annapolis** 2-9-3 0 .... GregFairley 9 66+
(M Johnston) *towards rr: rdn 3f out: swtchd rt over 1f out: styd on steadily to go 3rd wl ins fnl f: nt trble ldng pair* **20/1**
05 **4** 1 **Siciliando**[7] 3408 2-9-3 0 .... RichardMullen 4 63
(M L W Bell) *towards rr: rdn 3f out: kpt on steadily fnl f: wnt 4th towards fin: nvr trbld ldrs* **33/1**
52 **5** *nk* **Flyit (IRE)**[8] 3358 2-9-3 0 .... DarryllHolland 10 63
(M R Channon) *pressed ldr: rdn jst over 2f out: outpcd fnl f* **5/1**[2]
0 **6** 1/2 **Sericus (IRE)**[13] 3219 2-9-3 0 .... TedDurcan 7 61
(W Jarvis) *s.i.s: hld up towards rr: rdn 3f out: kpt on steadily fnl f: nt trble ldrs* **28/1**
035 **7** *nk* **Magical Illusion**[19] 3020 2-8-12 0 .... AdrianMcCarthy 12 55
(P D Evans) *led: rdn jst over 2f out: hdd over 1f out: wknd fnl f* **22/1**
8 3/4 **River Dee (IRE)** 2-9-3 0 .... DO'Donohoe 11 58
(Miss Amy Weaver) *s.i.s: bhd and sn bustled along: kpt on fnl f but nvr competitive* **66/1**
9 1 1/2 **Jacobite Prince (IRE)** 2-9-3 0 .... GeorgeBaker 1 53+
(M H Tompkins) *v.s.a: bhd: sme prog 1/2-way: nvr trbld ldrs* **33/1**
00 **10** 2 **Clerical (USA)**[18] 3055 2-9-3 0 .... RobertHavlin 2 47
(M J Gingell) *chsd ldrs tl 2f out: sn rdn and wknd* **100/1**
11 *nk* **Lady Dinsdale (IRE)** 2-8-12 0 .... FrankieMcDonald 3 41
(T Keddy) *wnt rt s and slowly away: hdwy and in tch 1/2-way: rdn and hung rt 2f out: sn wknd* **66/1**
12 6 **Missou Maiden** 2-8-12 0 .... TPQueally 13 23
(M H Tompkins) *s.i.s: a wl bhd* **50/1**

1m 15.79s (1.39) **Going Correction** +0.075s/f (Good) **12** Ran SP% **121.4**
Speed ratings (Par 94): **93,92,87,86,85 85,84,83,81,78 78,70**
toteswinger: 1&2 £2.10, 1&3 £4.70, 2&3 £19.30. CSF £4.14 TOTE £1.60: £1.02, £3.40, £4.80; EX 6.20 Trifecta £60.40 Pool: £60.40. 4.39 winning units..
Owner Godolphin **Bred** K And Mrs Cullen **Trained** Newmarket, Suffolk

FOCUS
A decent maiden for juveniles which revolved around the Godolphin representative who hadn't been disgraced at the Royal meeting. He is the first juvenile winner for the yard this season.

NOTEBOOK
Khor Dubai(IRE) was backed as if success was a mere formality, having been ninth in the Windsor Castle on his last appearance, but landed the odds in workmanlike fashion having been made to fight all the way to the line. His future is in the hands of the Handicapper as he won't be good enough for Pattern company. (op 4-6)
Magaling(IRE) ◆ almost made a winning bow and gave the odds-on favourite quite a fright in the process. His trainer is only just getting going with his juveniles and this son of Medicean is a certain future winner. (op 11-1 tchd 12-1)
Annapolis ◆, a grandson of 1,000 Guineas runner-up Kerrera, made a pleasing debut. He picked up well for a few smacks inside the final furlong to secure a clear third and can only come on for the experience. (op 14-1 tchd 22-1)

Siciliando kept on steadily from the rear and looks the sort who could leave his maiden form behind thrown into nurseries, especially over longer trips.
Flyit(IRE) is a speedy sort who wouldn't be inconvenienced by a drop back to the bare 5f. (op 4-1 tchd 7-2)
Sericus(IRE) was again slowly away but this time made some late headway and looks as though he is being brought along with nurseries in mind. (op 25-1)
Magical Illusion showed plenty of speed on this occasion, and drop back to the bare minimum could be worth another try now that the penny seems to have dropped with her. (op 20-1 tchd 25-1)
Jacobite Prince(IRE) Official explanation: jockey said colt missed the break
Lady Dinsdale(IRE) Official explanation: jockey said filly missed the break

3652 PKF (UK) LLP (S) STKS — 6f 3y
3:00 (3:01) (Class 6) 2-Y-O — **£1,942** (£578; £288; £144) **Stalls** High

Form — RPR
0 **1** **Rocket Rob (IRE)**[20] 2999 2-8-11 0 .... TedDurcan 6 — 57
(S A Callaghan) *hld up in tch: hdwy to trck ldr over 2f out: chal over 1f out: rdn 1f out: led fnl 100yds: rdn out* **5/6**[1]
4132 **2** *nk* **Come On Buckers (IRE)**[17] 3091 2-9-2 0 .... (v) PatCosgrave 4 — 61
(P D Evans) *led: rdn over 1f out: hdd fnl 100yds: unable qck towards fin* **11/2**[3]
62 **3** *2* **Hip Hip Hooray**[25] 2865 2-8-6 0 .... RichardMullen 2 — 45
(E S McMahon) *restless in stalls: fly j. and slowly away: hld up in tch: rdn and nt qckn 2f out: hdwy and swtchd lft over 1f out: no imp fnl f* **15/8**[2]
00 **4** *2 1/4* **Kosama**[17] 3091 2-8-1 0 .... MCGeran(5) 1 — 38
(M R Channon) *chsd ldrs: rdn wl over 2f out: outpcd over 1f out: n.d fnl f* **40/1**
0 **5** *12* **Tillagirl**[16] 3114 2-8-6 0 .... AdrianMcCarthy 5 — 2
(G G Margarson) *a in last pair: rdn 4f out: wl bhd fnl 2f* **33/1**
0 **6** *5* **Redsetgo**[33] 2614 2-8-6 0 .... GregFairley 3 — —
(S W Hall) *chsd ldr tl over 2f out: sn racing awkwardly and btn* **66/1**

1m 15.82s (1.42) **Going Correction** +0.075s/f (Good) — **6** Ran SP% **111.6**
Speed ratings (Par 92): **93,92,89,86,70 64**
toteswinger: 1&2 £1.20, 1&3 £1.02, 2&3 £1.10. CSF £6.01 TOTE £1.60: £1.20, £2.00; EX 5.30.The winner was bought in for 16,000gns. Come On Buckers was claimed by Ms Trina Cornwell for £5,000. Hip Hip Hooray was claimed by Luke Dace £5,000.
Owner Bill Hinge, J Searchfield & N Callaghan **Bred** Mrs Marita Rogers **Trained** Newmarket, Suffolk

FOCUS
A very good race for the grade, reflected by the fact that both the second and third home were claimed, while the winner's connections went to 16,000gns to retain him.

NOTEBOOK
Rocket Rob(IRE) was backed into odds-on favouritism but, after travelling strongly, still looked green when given the office on what was, after all, just his second start. He will hold his own in much better grade than this. (op 5-4)
Come On Buckers(IRE) has already become something of a standing dish in this grade and ran right up to the best of his form (op 7-2)
Hip Hip Hooray looked a little uneasy on the fast ground and was slightly disappointing as a consequence. Her previous runs were on artificial surfaces but she should be all right on turf with a little more ease in it. (tchd 7-4 and 2-1)
Kosama ran about as well as could be expected, and there will plenty of much easier sellers for her to contest during the rest of the summer. (tchd 33-1)
Redsetgo Official explanation: jockey said filly ran green

3653 BET365 BEST ODDS GUARANTEED ON EVERY RACE H'CAP — 7f 3y
3:30 (3:31) (Class 5) (0-75,76) 3-Y-O+ — **£2,719** (£809; £404; £202) **Stalls** High

Form — RPR
0003 **1** **Registrar**[12] 3266 6-8-8 51 oh3 .... (p) PatCosgrave 8 — 60
(Mrs C A Dunnett) *stdd s: hld up in rr: swtchd rt and hdwy over 1f out: shkn up to ld ins fnl f: readily* **14/1**
-112 **2** *1* **Oh So Saucy**[20] 2992 4-9-13 70 .... GeorgeBaker 3 — 77
(C F Wall) *hld up towards rr: hdwy over 2f out: rdn to ld ent fnl f: sn hung rt: hdd ins fnl f: one pce* **13/8**[1]
4360 **3** *1 1/2* **Wodhill Schnaps**[26] 2837 7-9-1 58 .... TedDurcan 2 — 61
(D Morris) *hld up in last: outpcd over 2f out: swtchd lft over 1f out: r.o fnl f to go 3rd towards fin: nt rch ldng pair* **10/1**
-000 **4** *hd* **Semah Harold**[19] 3031 3-8-13 64 .... RichardMullen 7 — 63
(E S McMahon) *hld up in tch: rdn and edgd lft fr 2f out: styd on u.p fnl f: nt rch ldrs* **33/1**
4000 **5** *1 1/4* **Ike Quebec (FR)**[43] 2311 3-9-3 73 .... (b) HaddenFrost(5) 9 — 69
(J R Boyle) *led: qcknd and clr 3f out: rdn over 2f out: hdd ent fnl f: wknd ins fnl f* **16/1**
0000 **6** *nk* **Hazytoo**[22] 2947 4-9-7 64 .... LDettori 6 — 62
(S A Callaghan) *chsd ldrs: rdn over 2f out: drvn and nt qckn wl over 1f out: wl hld fnl f* **9/2**[3]
3010 **7** *1/2* **Applesnap (IRE)**[12] 3271 3-9-8 73 .... TPQueally 4 — 66
(Mrs C A Dunnett) *chsd ldr: rdn over 2f out: ev ch u.p over 1f out: wknd 1f out* **12/1**
0006 **8** *7* **Djalalabad (FR)**[12] 3268 4-8-5 51 oh3 .... (t) MarcHalford(3) 5 — 29
(Mrs C A Dunnett) *wl in tch in midfield: rdn over 2f out: wknd wl over 1f out* **33/1**
0131 **9** *3/4* **Choreography**[9] 3345 5-10-0 76 6ex .... (p) MCGeran(5) 1 — 52
(Jim Best) *t.k.h: chsd ldrs: rdn wl over 2f out: wknd qckly wl over 1f out* **10/3**[2]

1m 26.34s (-0.26) **Going Correction** +0.075s/f (Good)
WFA 3 from 4yo+ 8lb — **9** Ran SP% **114.6**
Speed ratings (Par 103): **104,102,101,100,99 99,98,90,89**
toteswinger: 1&2 £4.90, 1&3 £9.90, 2&3 £4.00. CSF £36.90 CT £245.84 TOTE £16.90: £2.50, £1.20, £2.90; EX 21.30 Trifecta £119.70 Pool: £566.16. 3.50 winning units..
Owner The Smart Syndicate **Bred** Cheveley Park Stud Ltd **Trained** Hingham, Norfolk

FOCUS
Just a fair handicap, and with the second filly setting a consistent standard this year, the form looks solid. The winner was close to his best. They went a good pace and the first four all came from the rear.
Choreography Official explanation: trainer had no explanation for the poor form shown; vet said gelding was found to be lame

3654 BOS MAGAZINE MAIDEN STKS — 1m 2f 21y
4:00 (4:01) (Class 5) 3-Y-O+ — **£2,775** (£830; £415; £207; £103) **Stalls** Low

Form — RPR
6- **1** **Angel Rock (IRE)**[295] 5321 3-9-2 0 .... DarryllHolland 11 — 82+
(M Botti) *stdd s: t.k.h: hld up in rr: gd hdwy on outer over 2f out: chsd wnr 1f out: r.o wl to ld fnl stride* **13/2**
2 *nse* **Skycap (IRE)** 3-9-2 0 .... LDettori 10 — 82+
(Saeed Bin Suroor) *s.i.s: hld up in midfield: gd hdwy over 3f out: led 2f out: rdn over 1f out: battled on wl tl hdd fnl stride* **15/2**
3 *3 3/4* **Almonafis (IRE)** 3-9-2 0 .... RHills 7 — 74+
(Sir Michael Stoute) *s.i.s: t.k.h: hld up in rr: hdwy over 3f out: chsd ldrs and hanging lft fr over 2f out: kpt on same pce fnl f* **13/8**[1]
03 **4** *3* **Capstan**[19] 3043 3-9-2 0 .... PatCosgrave 6 — 68
(L M Cumani) *t.k.h: chsd ldr: hung rt bnd 5f out: led 3f out: rdn and hdd 2f out: wknd fnl f* **7/2**[2]
0 **5** *2* **Spider Silk**[47] 2199 3-8-9 0 .... JPHamblett(7) 8 — 67+
(W Jarvis) *t.k.h: hld up in midfield: rdn and hung lft 3f out: nt clr run and swtchd rt over 2f out: no ch w ldrs after* **66/1**
6 *5* **Colourful Move** 3-9-2 0 .... TPQueally 4 — 54
(H R A Cecil) *led: rdn and hdd 3f out: wknd wl over 1f out* **14/1**
7 *11* **Coliseum** 3-9-2 0 .... RichardMullen 3 — 32
(Sir Michael Stoute) *bustled along in rr: rdn over 4f out: sn lost tch: t.o* **16/1**
00 **8** *1/2* **Zeeran**[47] 2199 3-9-2 0 .... GregFairley 1 — 31
(C E Brittain) *t.k.h: chsd ldrs: rdn over 3f out: wknd over 2f out: t.o* **100/1**
4 **9** *25* **Classy Affair**[10] 3328 4-9-8 0 .... (t) GeorgeBaker 2 — —
(D Morris) *stdd s: hld up in rr: hdwy over 4f out: sn struggling: t.o and eased wl over 1f out* **50/1**
0 **10** *2 1/4* **Renege The Joker**[159] 317 5-9-8 0 .... HaddenFrost(5) 9 — —
(S Regan) *chsd ldrs tl lost pl 5f out: wl bhd fnl 3f: t.o and eased wl over 1f out* **200/1**
6 **11** *nk* **Intercom**[28] 2763 3-9-2 0 .... TedDurcan 5 — —
(H R A Cecil) *in tch: rdn and btn wl over 2f out: t.o and eased fr wl over 1f out* **5/1**[3]

2m 9.20s (-1.30) **Going Correction** -0.05s/f (Good)
WFA 3 from 4yo+ 11lb — **11** Ran SP% **119.6**
Speed ratings (Par 103): **103,102,99,97,95 91,83,82,62,60 60**
toteswinger: 1&2 £10.40, 1&3 £5.00, 2&3 £3.10. CSF £55.34 TOTE £9.00: £2.20, £2.20, £1.30; EX 74.80 Trifecta £168.90 Pool: £662.17. 2.90 winning units..
Owner Tenuta Dorna Di Montaltuzzo SRL **Bred** Ascagnano S P A **Trained** Newmarket, Suffolk

FOCUS
This looked a decent maiden with some top yards from down the road in Newmarket represented. They finished quite well strung out behind the first two, and the form looks at least useful and should work out. The first three should all build on this.
Capstan Official explanation: jockey said colt hung left throughout
Colourful Move Official explanation: trainer's rep said colt was unsuited by the good to firm ground
Classy Affair Official explanation: jockey said filly had no more to give
Renege The Joker Official explanation: trainer said gelding had a breathing problem
Intercom Official explanation: trainer's rep had no explanation for the poor form shown

3655 WEATHERBYS PRINTING H'CAP — 1m 2f 21y
4:30 (4:32) (Class 5) (0-70,67) 3-Y-O+ — **£2,719** (£809; £404; £202) **Stalls** Low

Form — RPR
4223 **1** **Multicultural**[16] 3110 5-10-0 67 .... RichardMullen 3 — 77
(D M Simcock) *in tch: effrt on inner 3f out: rdn to chal 2f out: led 1f out: drvn out* **5/2**[1]
6-54 **2** *3/4* **Dancing Jest (IRE)**[8] 3361 4-9-5 58 .... DarryllHolland 2 — 66
(Rae Guest) *led: hrd pressed and drvn 3f out: hdd 1f out: unable qck u.p fnl f* **5/1**[3]
0022 **3** *2 1/4* **South Wales**[23] 2915 3-8-3 53 .... DO'Donohoe 6 — 57
(S C Williams) *s.i.s: hld up in midfield: rdn 3f out: hdwy u.p to chse ldng pair over 1f out: no imp fnl 100yds* **10/3**[2]
300 **4** *nse* **Star Grazer**[26] 2833 3-8-8 58 .... TPQueally 1 — 61
(C F Wall) *t.k.h: hld up towards rr: rdn and little rspnse 3f out: swtchd rt 2f out: hanging lft after: hdwy to chse ldrs 1f out: kpt on but nvr pce to trble ldrs* **20/1**
00-0 **5** *3 1/2* **Colton**[24] 2884 5-8-11 55 .... HaddenFrost(5) 8 — 51
(J M P Eustace) *hld up in rr: hdwy over 4f out: ev ch 3f out tl 2f out: wknd over 1f out* **12/1**
0016 **6** *3 1/4* **Dnata Flyer (USA)**[6] 3453 3-9-1 65 .... GregFairley 10 — 55
(M Johnston) *chsd ldr: evry ch and rdn over 3f out: wknd wl over 1f out* **12/1**
0-05 **7** *1 3/4* **Silent Applause**[24] 2886 5-9-10 63 .... GeorgeBaker 9 — 49
(Dr J D Scargill) *stdd after s and hld up in rr: stmbld and lost grnd 6f out: hdwy over 3f out: no imp and wl hld whn hung lft over 1f out* **6/1**
0623 **8** *8* **Iceman George**[21] 2978 4-9-7 60 .... TedDurcan 11 — 30
(D Morris) *hld up in midfield: hdwy 4f out: rdn and struggling 3f out: wl hld fnl 2f* **7/1**
060/ **9** *19* **Seattle Spy (USA)**[910] 49 5-8-12 51 .... DMylonas 7 — —
(Miss J Feilden) *chsd ldrs tl 4f out: wl bhd fnl 3f: t.o* **66/1**

2m 8.50s (-2.00) **Going Correction** -0.05s/f (Good)
WFA 3 from 4yo+ 11lb — **9** Ran SP% **116.7**
Speed ratings (Par 103): **106,105,103,103,100 98,96,90,75**
toteswinger: 1&2 £3.90, 1&3 £2.80, 2&3 £4.70. CSF £15.49 CT £42.09 TOTE £3.10: £1.30, £2.20, £1.70; EX 17.40 Trifecta £76.40 Pool: £441.62. 7.10 winning units..
Owner Tick Tock Partnership **Bred** Genesis Green Stud Ltd **Trained** Newmarket, Suffolk

FOCUS
Just a modest handicap, but the winner and third have been there or thereabouts all year so the form looks sound.
Silent Applause Official explanation: jockey said gelding slipped on the bend
Iceman George Official explanation: jockey said gelding lost a right front shoe

3656 WEATHERBYS BLOODSTOCK INSURANCE H'CAP — 1m 1f
5:00 (5:01) (Class 6) (0-70,70) 3-Y-O — **£2,719** (£809; £404; £202) **Stalls** Low

Form — RPR
60-1 **1** **Charlevoix (IRE)**[52] 2041 3-9-3 66 .... GeorgeBaker 1 — 78+
(C F Wall) *t.k.h: trckd ldrs: wnt 2nd 2f out: rdn to chal 1f out: led ins fnl f: r.o wl* **2/1**[1]
50-0 **2** *1* **Aboriginie (USA)**[12] 3263 3-9-7 70 .... RobertHavlin 3 — 80
(J H M Gosden) *led at stdy gallop: rdn and qcknd 2f out: hdd and no ex ins fnl f* **8/1**
6311 **3** *2 3/4* **Amicable Terms**[7] 3421 3-9-0 63 6ex .... TedDurcan 9 — 67
(Rae Guest) *hld up in tch towards rr: hdwy on outer 3f out: rdn and edgd lft over 1f out: chsd ldng pair jst over 1f out: no imp and eased towards fin* **5/2**[2]
0040 **4** *3* **Blandys Wood**[21] 2984 3-8-8 62 .... MCGeran(5) 6 — 59
(M R Channon) *s.i.s: t.k.h: hld up in tch in rr: hdwy on inner over 3f out: rdn 2f out: sn outpcd* **16/1**
4010 **5** *1 1/4* **Ramprakash**[20] 3004 3-9-3 66 .... AdamKirby 7 — 61
(M L W Bell) *chsd ldr: rdn 3f out: lost 2nd 2f out: wknd over 1f out* **6/1**[3]
50-0 **6** *18* **Minjim**[14] 3168 3-8-6 55 .... RichardMullen 4 — 10
(C E Brittain) *hld up in tch in 10: rdn 3f out: sn struggling and wl btn* **25/1**
505 **7** *hd* **Red Sonja (IRE)**[122] 773 3-8-2 51 oh3 .... AdrianMcCarthy 2 — 6
(D Morris) *t.k.h: hld up in tch: rdn over 2f out: sn wknd and wl btn* **14/1**

0-40 **8** *2* **Space Pirate**[14] 3183 3-8-5 **54** DO'Donohoe 8 4
(J Pearce) *chsd ldrs: rdn over 2f out: wknd over 1f out: wl hld whn heavily eased fnl 100yds* **13/2**

1m 57.91s (2.11) **Going Correction** +0.075s/f (Good) **8** Ran SP% **117.0**
Speed ratings (Par 98): **93,92,89,87,85 69,69,67**
toteswinger: 1&2 £5.30, 1&3 £1.70, 2&3 £5.80. CSF £19.48 CT £42.03 TOTE £3.30: £1.40, £2.20, £1.50; EX 22.30 Trifecta £59.90 Pool: 502.43. 6.20 winning units..
Owner M Sinclair **Bred** Farmers Hill Stud **Trained** Newmarket, Suffolk

FOCUS
Not much got into this race as they only went a very sedate pace. The form of those up front should be reliable though, with the winner and third following up recent successes and the runner-up coming from a top yard. There should be more to come from Charlevoix.
Ramprakash Official explanation: trainer's rep said colt was unsuited by the good to firm ground
Space Pirate Official explanation: jockey said colt lost its action

3657 PERTEMPS PEOPLE DEVELOPMENT "HANDS AND HEELS" APPRENTICE SERIES H'CAP — 1m 3f 101y
5:30 (5:30) (Class 6) (0-65,62) 4-Y-0+ **£1,942** (£578; £288; £144) **Stalls** Low

Form RPR
000- **1** **Credential**[246] 6598 6-8-12 **52** BillyCray 9 58
(John A Harris) *mde all: pushed along over 2f out: styd on wl* **16/1**
6/20 **2** *1 ¾* **Kangrina**[17] 3089 6-9-5 **62** FrederikTylicki(3) 6 66
(George Baker) *hld up in rr: hdwy 4f out: chsd wnr over 1f out: kpt on same pce fnl f* **5/2**[1]
0000 **3** *1 ¾* **Ruwain**[16] 3113 4-8-2 **45** DebraEngland(3) 4 46
(W J Musson) *s.i.s: t.k.h: sn chsng ldrs: pushed along and kpt on same pce fr over 1f out* **40/1**
3122 **4** *hd* **Astrolibra**[6] 3448 4-9-2 **56** AshleyMorgan 8 56
(M H Tompkins) *hld up towards rr: hdwy over 3f out: chsd ldrs over 1f out: kpt on same pce fnl f* **5/2**[1]
0305 **5** *1 ¾* **Dubai Shadow (IRE)**[19] 3036 4-8-10 **53** RosieJessop(3) 2 51
(C E Brittain) *chsd ldr: ev ch 3f out tl 2f out: wknd ent fnl f* **16/1**
-150 **6** *shd* **Chapter (IRE)**[17] 3084 6-8-7 **47** (p) AdeleRothery 7 44
(Mrs A L M King) *hld up in rr: nt clr run and swtchd rt over 2f out: kpt on fr over 1f out but nvr threatened ldrs* **6/1**[3]
0403 **7** *8* **Desert Hawk**[16] 3113 7-8-5 **48** KrishGundowry(3) 5 33
(W M Brisbourne) *hld up towards rr: hdwy 4f out: pushed along and outpcd over 2f out: no ch after* **11/2**[2]
065- **8** *hd* **Lady Suffragette (IRE)**[210] 2345 5-8-2 **45** CharlesEddery(3) 3 29
(John Berry) *chsd ldrs: rdn and edgd lft over 2f out: wknd 2f out* **16/1**
5020 **9** *hd* **Beckenham's Secret**[8] 3361 4-8-8 **48** StacyRenwick 1 32
(A W Carroll) *s.i.s: hld up in tch: rdn over 3f out: wknd over 2f out* **10/1**

2m 29.17s (0.47) **Going Correction** -0.05s/f (Good) **9** Ran SP% **116.0**
Speed ratings (Par 101): **96,94,93,93,92 91,86,86,85**
toteswinger: 1&2 £10.30, 1&3 £51.50, 2&3 £28.50. CSF £56.39 CT £1617.49 TOTE £22.90: £4.20, £1.30, £9.90; EX 70.10 TRIFECTA Not won. Place 6 £5.30, Place 5 £4.38..
Owner Mr Vijay Kara **Bred** Rockwell Bloodstock **Trained** Eastwell, Leics

FOCUS
A weak handicap for apprentice jockeys. The fourth has been running well all year though, so the overall standard of the form should prove dependable.
T/Plt: £7.20 to a £1 stake. Pool: £52,748.00. 5,342.00 winning tickets. T/Qpdt: £4.00 to a £1 stake. Pool: £2,833.90. 513.00 winning tickets. SP

3658 - 3661a (Foreign Racing) - See Raceform Interactive

3334 BEVERLEY (R-H)
Friday, July 4

OFFICIAL GOING: Good to firm (good in places)
Wind: Virtualy nil Weather: bright and mainly sunny

3662 HALL CONSTRUCTION (S) STKS — 7f 100y
6:45 (6:46) (Class 6) 3-Y-0+ **£2,266** (£674; £337; £168) **Stalls** High

Form RPR
5005 **1** **Messiah Garvey**[15] 3175 4-9-3 **57** SilvestreDeSousa 14 59
(D Nicholls) *in tch: swtchd lft and effrt 2f out: rdn to ld ins fnl f: all out* **3/1**[1]
264 **2** *nk* **Five Wishes**[32] 2658 4-8-12 **57** (be) TomEaves 10 54
(M Dods) *chsd ldrs: drvn and ev ch 2f out: led over 1f out: hdd ins fnl f: unable qck after* **4/1**[2]
5006 **3** *hd* **Scotty's Future (IRE)**[4] 3551 10-9-3 **49** FergalLynch 13 58+
(A Berry) *s.i.s: sn wl bhd: hdwy over 3f out: swtchd lft over 1f out: edging rt but r.o strly fnl f: nt quite rch ldrs* **14/1**
2230 **4** *1 ¼* **Penel (IRE)**[23] 2927 7-9-3 **55** (p) NCallan 4 55
(P T Midgley) *s.i.s and sn rdn along towards rr: hdwy 4f out: chsd ldrs over 2f out: kpt on u.p but nvr pce to rch ldrs* **11/2**[3]
0-50 **5** *1 ½* **Josephine Malines**[18] 3077 4-8-12 **65** RoystonFfrench 9 46
(Mrs A Duffield) *in tch: drvn 3f out: edgd lft over 1f out: kpt on u.p but nvr pce to rch ldrs* **8/1**
465- **6** *hd* **Gunner Fly (IRE)**[202] 7149 3-8-9 **62** PaulHanagan 12 48
(R A Fahey) *chsd ldr: clsd 3f out: rdn to ld 2f out: hdd over 1f out: one pce fnl f* **11/2**[3]
-000 **7** *nk* **Jellytot (USA)**[10] 3340 5-8-12 **45** (be) DavidAllan 2 45
(J O'Reilly) *in tch: effrt to chse ldrs over 2f out: bmpd over 1f out: kpt on same pce u.p after* **40/1**
130 **8** *3 ¼* **Blue Empire (IRE)**[31] 2703 7-9-8 **62** (p) TonyHamilton 6 46
(Ollie Pears) *racd in midfield: lost pl 3f out: no ch w ldrs after* **11/1**
300 **9** *1 ¼* **Jaassey**[39] 2463 5-9-3 **45** (t) PAspell 8 37
(J S Wainwright) *s.i.s: drvn over 3f out: modest late hdwy: nvr trbld ldrs* **33/1**
-000 **10** *2 ¼* **Baylaw Star**[14] 3201 7-8-12 **52** GaryBartley(5) 1 32
(I W McInnes) *hld up towards rr: effrt on outer 3f out: nvr trbld ldrs* **28/1**
4000 **11** *1 ¼* **Apres Ski (IRE)**[15] 3175 5-8-10 **53** NBazeley(7) 7 29
(J F Coupland) *v.s.a: c wd over 3f out: n.d* **40/1**
-000 **12** *14* **Convince (USA)**[24] 2917 7-9-3 **48** (b) GrahamGibbons 11 —
(J M Bradley) *led: clr over 4f out: rdn and hdd 2f out: sn fdd: eased ins fnl f* **40/1**
5000 **13** *2 ¼* **Moon Forest (IRE)**[21] 2988 6-9-0 **42** (b) KirstyMilczarek(3) 5 —
(J M Bradley) *chsd ldrs tl over 3f out: sn struggling: wl bhd and eased fnl f* **40/1**
4400 **14** *13* **Cabourg (IRE)**[26] 2866 5-9-3 **52** (b) PatCosgrave 3 —
(R Bastiman) *racd in midfield: lost pl and rdn over 3f out: t.o and eased fnl f* **22/1**

1m 33.82s (0.02) **Going Correction** +0.025s/f (Good)
WFA 3 from 4yo+ 8lb **14** Ran SP% **122.4**
Speed ratings (Par 101): **100,99,99,98,96 96,95,91,90,87 86,70,67,52**
toteswinger: 1&2 £3.60, 1&3 £2.20, 2&3 £19.40. CSF £13.74 TOTE £3.90: £1.40, £1.60, £3.80; EX 18.40.There was no bid for the winner.
Owner N Martin **Bred** Hascombe And Valiant Studs **Trained** Sessay, N Yorks

■ Stewards' Enquiry : Silvestre De Sousa two-day ban: careless riding (Jul 18-19)

FOCUS
Ordinary selling grade form, but fairly sound. The early pace was good.
Moon Forest(IRE) Official explanation: jockey said gelding ran too freely.

3663 E B F COTTINGHAM PARKS GOLF & COUNTRY CLUB NOVICE STKS — 5f
7:15 (7:17) (Class 4) 2-Y-0 **£4,695** (£1,397; £698; £348) **Stalls** High

Form RPR
1 **1** **Master Noverre (IRE)**[48] 2186 2-9-2 **0** PaulHanagan 9 91
(R A Fahey) *chsd ldr: rdn over 2f out: led jst over 1f out: sn hung lft: hdd ins fnl f: rallied to ld again last strides* **11/8**[1]
2 *shd* **Fitz Flyer (IRE)** 2-8-8 **0** RoystonFfrench 6 83
(D H Brown) *s.i.s: sn in tch in rr: plld out and hdwy over 1f out: ev ch and hung rt ent fnl f: led wl ins fnl f: hdd last strides* **33/1**
3421 **3** *3 ½* **Favourite Girl (IRE)**[18] 3078 2-8-11 **0** DavidAllan 5 76+
(T D Easterby) *t.k.h: trckd ldrs: swtchd lft over 1f out: pressing ldrs whn squeezed and hmpd jst ins fnl f: nt rcvr* **3/1**[2]
301 **4** *3 ½* **La Brigitte**[31] 2702 2-9-9 **0** PatCosgrave 8 61+
(A J McCabe) *sn led: rdn and hd hld high 2f out: hdd jst over 1f out: keeping on same pce but stl ev ch whn bdly hmpd jst ins fnl f: no ch after* **12/1**
310 **5** *nk* **Fivefootnumberone (IRE)**[27] 2826 2-9-2 **0** GrahamGibbons 4 64
(J J Quinn) *chsd ldrs: rdn over 2f out: wknd jst over 1f out* **4/1**[3]
4210 **6** *½* **Klynch**[15] 3152 2-9-0 **0** RobertHavlin 1 61
(B J Meehan) *chsd ldrs: rdn over 2f out: keeping on same pce whn hmpd jst ins fnl f: no ch after* **8/1**
7 *4* **Alexander Gulch (USA)** 2-8-8 **0** NCallan 2 40
(K A Ryan) *wnt lft s: a struggling in rr* **20/1**
1 **8** *1 ½* **Fathey (IRE)**[56] 1948 2-9-5 **0** TonyHamilton 7 46
(R A Fahey) *a struggling in rr* **12/1**

61.84 secs (-1.66) **Going Correction** -0.225s/f (Firm) **8** Ran SP% **121.3**
Speed ratings (Par 96): **104,103,98,92,92 91,84,82**
toteswinger: 1&2 £12.60, 1&3 £2.20, 2&3 £19.40. CSF £57.69 TOTE £1.90: £1.10, £6.90, £1.40; EX 36.60.
Owner Percy/Green Racing 1 **Bred** Barbara Prendergast **Trained** Musley Bank, N Yorks

FOCUS
A fair juvenile event featuring six previous winners. The winner is up 7lb and the form seems solid.

NOTEBOOK
Master Noverre(IRE), a shock winner on his debut, has been gelded since. He had the best of the draw here and raced towards the far rail throughout. Keeping on well for pressure, he rallied after being headed, and once again shaped very much as though another furlong would suit him. (op 5-6)
Fitz Flyer(IRE), whose price rose from 8,000gns as a foal to 55,000gns as a yearling, is out of a mare who won twice on soft ground, over 7f and 1m2f, but his sire is an influence for speed and his progeny tend to prefer a sound surface. The complete outsider of the field, he ran a blinder on his debut, running on strongly in the closing stages, and his Gimcrack entry was clearly not the fanciful engagement it looked on paper. (op 28-1 tchd 25-1)
Favourite Girl(IRE) was coming with her challenge between horses when the gap closed on her and she was hampered. She would have probably gone close with a clear run. (op 7-1)
La Brigitte was also hampered as the eventual runner-up edged right when challenging out wide, but in fairness she was weakening at the time. Nevertheless, she ran better than the beaten distance suggests. (tchd 14-1)
Fivefootnumberone(IRE), well held in the Woodcote Stakes last time out, looked to hold sound claims back in this company, but he dropped out tamely. Perhaps a sharper track will suit him. (op 13-2 tchd 7-2)
Klynch, the most experienced runner in the field, had less to do than in the Norfolk last time but he does not seem to be progressing. (op 7-1)

3664 AUNT BESSIE'S YORKSHIRE PUDDING H'CAP — 1m 100y
7:45 (7:45) (Class 4) (0-85,84) 4-Y-0+ **£4,727** (£1,406; £702; £351) **Stalls** High

Form RPR
123 **1** **Bustan (IRE)**[23] 2942 9-9-1 **78** PatCosgrave 6 88
(G C Bravery) *s.i.s: sn chsng ldrs: shkn up and clsd 3f out: swtchd lft 1f out: led wl ins fnl f: r.o wl* **11/2**
0002 **2** *1* **Mesbaah (IRE)**[20] 3046 4-9-7 **84** (v[1]) TonyHamilton 7 92
(R A Fahey) *racd keenly: clr w ldr: rdn wl over 2f out: unable qck ent fnl f: plugged on to go 2nd again nr fin* **4/1**[2]
-514 **3** *nk* **Riley Boys (IRE)**[10] 3337 7-8-8 **71** TPQueally 9 78
(J G Given) *led: clr w rival: rdn and edgd lft jst over 1f out: hdd wl ins fnl f: fdd and lost 2nd nr fin* **6/1**
-214 **4** *¾* **Shotley Mac**[10] 3339 4-8-5 **68** PaulHanagan 1 74
(N Bycroft) *chsd ldrs: rdn wl over 3f out: chsd ldrs u.p 1f out: kpt on same pce fnl f* **7/2**[1]
5230 **5** *½* **Nevada Desert (IRE)**[9] 3367 8-8-11 **77** MichaelJStainton(3) 5 81
(R M Whitaker) *hld up in midfield: plld out and effrt over 2f out: chsd ldrs 1f out: no imp last 100yds* **6/1**
5202 **6** *3 ¾* **Fiefdom (IRE)**[14] 3214 6-8-8 **71** RoystonFfrench 3 67
(I W McInnes) *hld up in midfield: swtchd lft and rdn over 2f out: chsd ldrs over 1f out: wknd fnl f* **14/1**
6114 **7** *5* **Daniel Thomas (IRE)**[28] 2795 6-8-11 **77** KirstyMilczarek(3) 8 61
(Mrs A L M King) *stdd s: hld up in rr: rdn and effrt over 2f out: n.d* **5/1**[3]
3/24 **8** *½* **Alqaahir (USA)**[14] 3227 6-9-0 **77** TomEaves 2 60
(J S Wainwright) *hld up in rr: rdn and hdwy over 2f out: hrd rdn and wknd over 1f out* **10/1**

1m 45.88s (-1.72) **Going Correction** +0.025s/f (Good) **8** Ran SP% **118.6**
Speed ratings (Par 105): **109,108,107,106,106 102,97,97**
toteswinger: 1&2 £5.80, 1&3 £7.00, 2&3 £3.10. CSF £28.89 CT £138.85 TOTE £7.80: £2.40, £2.00, £2.10; EX 29.40.
Owner Mrs J Morley **Bred** Sean Twomey **Trained** Cowlinge, Suffolk

FOCUS
A fair handicap race run at a sound gallop. The form, rated through the winner and fourth, should prove reliable.
Daniel Thomas(IRE) Official explanation: jockey said gelding was never travelling.

3665 WESTBRIDGE HOMES CLASSIC H'CAP — 5f
8:20 (8:22) (Class 6) (0-65,65) 3-Y-0+ **£2,590** (£770; £385; £192) **Stalls** High

Form RPR
4-00 **1** **Choisette**[18] 3080 3-9-7 **65** TomEaves 2 73
(B Smart) *in tch: rdn and hdwy over 1f out: led last 100yds: hld on wl nr fin* **33/1**
23-4 **2** *hd* **Royal Composer (IRE)**[45] 2270 5-9-5 **58** (b) DavidAllan 11 67
(T D Easterby) *taken down early: sn rdn along in midfield: hdwy u.p on outer over 1f out: wnt 2nd wl ins fnl f: hld towards fin* **5/1**[1]

2402 **3** 3/4 **Commander Wish**[37] 2511 5-9-4 **57**..........................(p) TGMcLaughlin 12 64
(Lucinda Featherstone) *in tch early: lost pl and midfield 3f out: rdn and hdwy over 1f out: r.o wl u.p to go 3rd nr fin: nt rch ldrs* **8/1**

0062 **4** 3/4 **Roman Quintet (IRE)**[8] 3405 8-9-0 **53**..........................(b) PatCosgrave 1 57
(A J McCabe) *prom on outer: grad crossed over and led after 1f: rdn over 1f out: hdd last 100yds: fdd towards fin* **14/1**

0302 **5** *nse* **Colorus (IRE)**[17] 3112 5-9-9 **65**.................................. JamieMoriarty(3) 8 69
(W J H Ratcliffe) *chsd ldrs: wnt 2nd 3f out: rdn to chal ent fnl f: unable qck last 100yds* **7/1**[3]

0404 **6** *nk* **Royal Challenge**[13] 3255 7-9-3 **61**.................................. GaryBartley(5) 9 64+
(I W McInnes) *taken down early: s.i.s: bhd: hdwy on far rail over 1f out: fin wl: nt rch ldrs* **9/1**

0566 **7** 3/4 **Peopleton Brook**[10] 3340 6-8-13 **52**..........................(p) PaulHanagan 17 52
(J M Bradley) *in tch: rdn and hdwy 2f out: chsd ldrs 1f out: wknd last 100yds* **8/1**

40-0 **8** 2 1/4 **Northern Chorus (IRE)**[17] 3112 5-8-13 **55**........(v) MichaelJStainton(3) 3 47
(J O'Reilly) *in tch: rdn and edging rt wl over 1f out: no imp after* **33/1**

6064 **9** 1/2 **Tumbleweed Di**[10] 3340 4-8-8 **47**.................................. GrahamGibbons 10 37
(G R Oldroyd) *racd in midfield: swtchd rt 2f out: nvr pce to trble ldrs* **22/1**

0-00 **10** 1/2 **Viewforth**[56] 1966 10-8-8 **47**..........................(b) RoystonFfrench 16 35
(M A Buckley) *led on far rail for 1f: rdn and struggling over 2f out: sn wknd* **14/1**

-000 **11** *nse* **Morristown Music (IRE)**[32] 2676 4-9-4 **57**.................. TonyHamilton 13 45
(J S Wainwright) *s.i.s: bhd: kpt on u.p over 1f out: nvr trbld ldrs* **25/1**

0260 **12** *hd* **Darcy's Pride (IRE)**[7] 3454 4-9-10 **63**.................................. FergalLynch 15 50
(D W Barker) *chsd ldrs tl 1/2-way: wkng whn n.m.r 2f out* **6/1**[2]

0-60 **13** 6 **Yorke's Folly (USA)**[23] 2928 7-8-9 **48**..........................(v) AndrewElliott 6 14
(C W Fairhurst) *a bhd* **33/1**

0460 **14** 1 1/4 **Dhahab (USA)**[21] 2991 3-8-13 **57**.................................. NCallan 4 16
(C E Brittain) *sn rdn along and outpcd in rr* **40/1**

63.14 secs (-0.36) **Going Correction** -0.225s/f (Firm)
WFA 3 from 4yo+ 5lb **14 Ran SP% 108.5**
Speed ratings (Par 101): **93,92,91,90,90 89,88,84,84,83 83,82,73,71**
toteswinger: 1&2 £16.20, 1&3 £46.00, 2&3 £7.60. CSF £163.55 CT £1362.00 TOTE £35.30: £8.40, £1.80, £3.30; EX 173.90.
Owner Pinnacle Choisir Partnership **Bred** M R M Bloodstock **Trained** Hambleton, N Yorks
■ Never Without Me (5/1JF) was withdrawn after refusing to enter the stalls. R4 applies, deduct 15p in the £.

FOCUS
An ordinary sprint handicap. The winner and second both raced on the outer of the main pack but the form seems sound enough at face value.
Choisette Official explanation: trainer had no explanation for the apparent improvement in form

3666 FERGUSON FAWSITT ARMS H'CAP 1m 4f 16y
8:50 (8:50) (Class 6) (0-60,60) 3-Y-O+ **£2,266** (£674; £337; £168) **Stalls** High

Form RPR

0406 **1** **Fossgate**[23] 2957 7-9-9 **55**.................................. NCallan 7 61
(J D Bethell) *hld up in midfield: hdwy over 4f out: rdn and qcknd to ld wl over 1f out: r.o wl fnl f* **9/2**[3]

1566 **2** 3/4 **Wulimaster (USA)**[13] 3279 5-9-6 **52**.................................. FergalLynch 5 57
(D W Barker) *s.i.s: hld up in last pair: hdwy over 3f out: chsd wnr wl over 1f out: ev ch 1f out: unable qck fnl f* **7/1**

0541 **3** *nk* **Trip The Light**[39] 2468 3-8-10 **55**.................................. PaulHanagan 10 65+
(R A Fahey) *racd in midfield: rdn over 3f out: outpcd over 2f out: nt clr run and shuffled bk 2f out: swtchd lft jst over 1f out: r.o wl fnl f: snatched 3rd last strides* **7/2**[2]

00-0 **4** *shd* **Banquet (IRE)**[27] 2847 3-8-11 **56**.................................. GrahamGibbons 12 60
(T D Walford) *hld up in last trio: rdn and effrt on outer over 2f out: outpcd 2f out: kpt on u.p fnl f* **12/1**

4340 **5** *nk* **Parchment (IRE)**[3] 3589 6-8-10 **47**..........................(b) GaryBartley(5) 1 51
(A J Lockwood) *s.i.s: clsd over 3f out: plld out and rdn over 1f out: r.o wl fnl f: nt rch ldrs* **9/2**[3]

5500 **6** 1/2 **Parkview Love (USA)**[23] 2957 7-9-8 **57**.................................. LeeVickers(3) 8 60
(J G Given) *trckd ldrs: nt clr run and lost pl jst over 2f out: swtchd lft over 1f out: kpt on u.p fnl f* **20/1**

0600 **7** 1 1/4 **Bright Sun (IRE)**[14] 3226 7-9-8 **54**.................................. KimTinkler 2 55
(N Tinkler) *t.k.h: hld up wl in tch: rdn and unable qck 2f out: plugged on same pce after* **20/1**

0522 **8** 5 **River Kent**[23] 2926 3-8-12 **57**..........................(p) RoystonFfrench 3 50
(Mrs A Duffield) *chsd ldr: led jst over 2f out: sn hung rt: hdd wl over 1f out: sn btn* **3/1**[1]

4-06 **9** 5 **Special Feature (IRE)**[31] 2694 3-8-2 **47**..........................(p) DO'Donohoe 4 32
(C R Egerton) *led tl rdn and hdd jst over 2f out: sn btn* **20/1**

2m 40.78s (-0.12) **Going Correction** +0.025s/f (Good)
WFA 3 from 4yo+ 13lb **9 Ran SP% 118.1**
Speed ratings (Par 101): **101,100,100,100,100 99,98,95,92**
toteswinger: 1&2 £4.30, 1&3 £2.10, 2&3 £5.60. CSF £35.39 CT £120.38 TOTE £5.80: £1.70, £2.10, £1.70; EX 33.10.
Owner Mrs James Bethell **Bred** Mrs P A Clark **Trained** Middleham Moor, N Yorks

FOCUS
A moderate handicap but the form looks sound for the level, although they did finish in a bit of a bunch. The second and third are relatively unexposed and capable of more.

3667 WILLIAM JACKSON BAKERY FILLIES' H'CAP 1m 1f 207y
9:20 (9:20) (Class 5) (0-70,69) 3-Y-O **£3,238** (£963; £481; £240) **Stalls** High

Form RPR

3012 **1** **Millie's Rock (IRE)**[27] 2833 3-8-10 **61**.................................. JamieMoriarty(3) 1 71+
(M J Wallace) *t.k.h: chsd ldr: chal 2f out: rdn to ld over 1f out: r.o wl fnl f* **13/8**[1]

2-00 **2** 1 1/2 **Broughtons Flight (IRE)**[18] 3095 3-9-1 **63**.................................. TPQueally 6 67
(W J Musson) *led at stdy gallop: rdn and qcknd over 2f out: hdd over 1f out: kpt on same pce fnl f* **9/2**[3]

4650 **3** 3 **Eureka Moment**[19] 3057 3-9-7 **69**.................................. TomEaves 2 67
(E A L Dunlop) *hld up in tch: rdn and chsd ldng pair 2f out: no imp u.p after* **9/2**[3]

20-0 **4** 4 1/2 **Artistic Light**[28] 2805 3-9-0 **62**.................................. DO'Donohoe 4 51
(W R Muir) *chsd ldrs: rdn 2f out: wknd over 1f out* **11/1**

-412 **5** 2 **Autumn Charm**[172] 156 3-8-11 **59**..........................(p) TGMcLaughlin 3 44
(Lucinda Featherstone) *awkward leaving stalls and s.i.s: t.k.h: hld up in last pair: rdn and effrt 2f out: no hdwy* **12/1**

4-64 **6** 98 **Annaliesse (IRE)**[16] 3127 3-9-7 **69**.................................. PaulHanagan 5 —
(R A Fahey) *plld hrd: hld up in last pair: sddle slipped after 3f: lost tch and eased over 3f out: virtually p.u last 2f* **11/4**[2]

2m 11.03s (4.03) **Going Correction** +0.025s/f (Good) **6 Ran SP% 117.2**
Speed ratings (Par 97): **84,82,80,76,75** —
toteswinger: 1&2 £3.30, 1&3 £3.50, 2&3 £5.40. CSF £10.02 CT £27.84 TOTE £2.20: £1.50, £2.90; EX 11.30 Place 6 £55.90, Place 5 £33.90.
Owner Mike & Denise Dawes **Bred** Mrs U Schwarzenbach **Trained** Newmarket, Suffolk

FOCUS
A very modest contest run at a slow early pace. The form is rated through the runner-up and looks very dubious.
Annaliesse(IRE) Official explanation: jockey said that the filly's saddle slipped
T/Plt: £22.10 to a £1 stake. Pool: £70,986.48. 2,337.94 winning tickets. T/Qpdt: £9.40 to a £1 stake. Pool: £3,482.10. 272.15 winning tickets. SP

3624 HAYDOCK (L-H)
Friday, July 4

OFFICIAL GOING: Good (7.8)
Rail realignment added 16yards to advertised race distances on round course.
Wind: Light, half behind Weather: Fine

3668 JOHN CARROLL APPRENTICE H'CAP 5f
6:55 (6:58) (Class 5) (0-75,73) 3-Y-0+ **£3,238** (£963; £481; £240) **Stalls** Centre

Form RPR

1440 **1** **Mandurah (IRE)**[15] 3171 4-9-8 **68**.................................. MarkCoumbe(3) 9 77
(D Nicholls) *mde most: rdn over 1f out: kpt on towards fin* **4/1**[2]

0536 **2** 1/2 **Niteowl Lad (IRE)**[17] 3112 6-8-12 **58**..........................(p) RobbieEgan(3) 4 65
(J Balding) *wnt rt s: racd keenly: chsd ldrs: outpcd 1/2-way: rallied over 1f out: r.o towards fin* **4/1**[2]

2236 **3** 1/2 **Alexander Huricane (IRE)**[28] 2773 4-10-0 **71**..........................(b[1]) NeilBrown 8 76
(K A Ryan) *hmpd s: hld up in midfield: rdn and hdwy over 1f out: r.o and gaining towards fin* **5/2**[1]

0-00 **4** 1 1/4 **Triple Shadow**[17] 3112 4-8-5 **55** ow3.................................. MJMurphy(7) 7 56
(M A Peill) *unruly bef s: missed break and hmpd s: in rr: rdn and hdwy to chse ldrs over 1f out: no ex fnl 50yds* **14/1**

4060 **5** 3/4 **Fast Freddie**[8] 3404 4-8-12 **62**.................................. AJSmith(7) 12 60
(S Parr) *chsd ldrs: rdn over 1f out: no ex ins fnl f* **20/1**

0003 **6** 2 1/4 **Yungaburra (IRE)**[8] 3401 4-9-8 **70**..........................(t) KrishGundowry(5) 3 60
(S Parr) *missed break: in rr: effrt and hdwy 2f out: no further prog fnl f* **13/2**[3]

0001 **7** *hd* **Lithaam (IRE)**[7] 3447 4-8-4 **52** 6ex oh1..........................(p) PietroRomeo(5) 5 41
(J M Bradley) *wnt rt s: midfield: rdn over 1f out: wknd ins fnl f* **9/1**

33-1 **8** 2 1/2 **Lambrini Lace (IRE)**[28] 2774 3-8-12 **63**.................................. MCGeran(3) 11 43
(Mrs L Williamson) *w wnr: rdn 2f out: wknd over 1f out* **10/1**

504- **9** 5 **Throw The Dice**[241] 6702 6-8-4 **52** oh3..........................(v) BMcHugh(5) 10 14
(A Berry) *racd keenly: prom: rdn 1/2-way: sn wknd* **25/1**

60.39 secs (-0.11) **Going Correction** -0.15s/f (Firm)
WFA 3 from 4yo+ 5lb **9 Ran SP% 116.3**
Speed ratings (Par 103): **94,93,92,90,89 85,85,81,73**
toteswinger: 1&2 £3.70, 1&3 £2.30, 2&3 £2.20. CSF £20.58 CT £47.90 TOTE £5.40: £2.00, £2.00, £1.10; EX 23.90.
Owner Martin Hignett **Bred** Michael Lyons **Trained** Sessay, N Yorks

FOCUS
A modest but open affair and straightforward form rated around the first two.

3669 MTB GROUP MAIDEN AUCTION STKS 6f
7:25 (7:28) (Class 5) 2-Y-O **£3,238** (£963; £481; £240) **Stalls** Centre

Form RPR

0 **1** **Pure Poetry (IRE)**[21] 3001 2-8-13 0.................................. PatDobbs 13 86+
(R Hannon) *a.p: led wl over 1f out: r.o: pushed out towards fin* **11/4**[1]

2 1 1/2 **Captain Ellis (USA)** 2-9-2 0.................................. FergusSweeney 8 85+
(K R Burke) *s.i.s: sn in midfield: hdwy over 2f out: chsd wnr 1f out: styd on: nt qckn and hld towards fin* **9/2**

0 **3** 3 **Tale Of Silver (IRE)**[53] 2035 2-8-11 0.................................. LeeEnstone 6 71
(G A Swinbank) *s.i.s: sn in midfield: pushed along 1/2-way: hdwy over 1f out: styd on ins fnl f: nt pce to rch front pair* **14/1**

02 **4** 3/4 **Digit**[16] 3125 2-8-4 0.................................. PaulFessey 10 61
(B Smart) *led: hung bdly lft fr 1/2-way: hdd wl over 1f out: no ex ins fnl f* **4/1**[3]

233 **5** 1 1/4 **Woolston Ferry (IRE)**[14] 3199 2-8-4 0.................................. MCGeran(5) 9 63
(M R Channon) *midfield: pushed along and hdwy 1/2-way: hung lft whn chsd ldrs fr 1f out: one pce fnl 100yds* **7/2**[2]

6 1 **When Doves Cry** 2-8-4 0.................................. FrancisNorton 3 61+
(B W Hills) *s.i.s: outpcd and bhd: styd on fr 1f out: nt clr run ins fnl f: nvr trbld ldrs: will improve* **12/1**

7 2 1/2 **Jul's Lad (IRE)** 2-8-11 0 ow5.................................. NeilBrown(5) 14 59
(Paul Green) *hld up: sme hdwy 1f out: kpt on wout troubling ldrs* **33/1**

0 **8** 2 **Buckers Beauty (IRE)**[35] 2569 2-8-4 0.................................. CatherineGannon 2 41
(P D Evans) *chsd ldrs: rdn 1/2-way: wknd 2f out* **33/1**

9 3 **Lucky Numbers (IRE)** 2-8-12 0 ow8.................................. MarkCoumbe(5) 5 45
(Paul Green) *s.i.s: midfield: hdwy to chse ldrs 1/2-way: wknd 1f out* **20/1**

05 **10** 4 1/2 **Pedregal**[24] 2909 2-8-4 0.................................. BMcHugh(7) 12 26
(R A Fahey) *a outpcd and bhd* **33/1**

5 **11** 3 **Reigning In Rio (IRE)**[13] 3277 2-7-13 0.................................. PatrickDonaghy(5) 7 10
(P C Haslam) *trckd ldrs tl rdn and wknd over 2f out* **40/1**

4 **12** 3 1/4 **Terracotta Warrior**[15] 3158 2-8-9 0.................................. PaulQuinn 11 5
(J Jay) *sn outpcd* **28/1**

13 1 **Paddyntrev Bakfavs (IRE)** 2-8-8 0.................................. DuranFentiman(3) 4 4
(T D Easterby) *s.i.s: towards rr: pushed along and outpcd fr 1/2-way* **40/1**

1m 12.67s (-1.33) **Going Correction** -0.15s/f (Firm) **13 Ran SP% 123.3**
Speed ratings (Par 94): **102,100,96,95,93 92,88,86,82,76 72,67,66**
toteswinger: 1&2 £3.60, 1&3 £9.50, 2&3 £83.80. CSF £14.56 TOTE £3.80: £2.00, £2.20, £3.70; EX 15.30.
Owner Mrs J Wood **Bred** R Collins And Jerry Kennedy **Trained** East Everleigh, Wilts

FOCUS
A fair maiden rated around the time, which was reasonably good for the grade, and the fourth.

NOTEBOOK
Pure Poetry(IRE) was suited by the drop in trip as he did not appear to last home over 7f when favourite first time out. He won decisively and did nothing to suggest that the longer trip would be a problem from now on. (op 3-1 tchd 7-2 in places)
Captain Ellis(USA), the first foal of a half-sister to Palace Episode, had to concede 3lb to the winner so there is very little between them. He came well clear of the third and did not have the benefit of a previous run, so there will be improvement to come. (op 7-2)
Tale Of Silver(IRE) had run green on his debut but knew a bit more about it this time, and he looks the type to improve again. He is sprint-bred but it would be no great surprise if he got further. (op 16-1)
Digit showed good speed but then did her cause no good by hanging left from halfway. She will be handicapped now and if the hanging was a one-off, she has done enough in her three races to suggest there is a nursery in her. Official explanation: jockey said filly hung left (op 6-1)
Woolston Ferry(IRE) looked as if he might get into it at halfway but then hung left and had no more to offer from the furlong marker. (tchd 4-1)

When Doves Cry, a half-brother to a jumper out of a mare that stayed well, was never able to get in a threatening blow but she was getting the hang of things in the latter stages and is one to keep an eye on. (op 16-1)

3670 HARVEY LANE (S) STKS — 6f
7:55 (8:04) (Class 4) 2-Y-O — £5,504 (£1,637; £818; £408) Stalls Centre

Form — RPR

1 **Fol Liam** 2-8-11 0 .... PaulQuinn 9 68+
(D Nicholls) *missed break: sn in midfield: wnt rt whn hdwy 1/2-way: chsd ldrs over 1f out: r.o to ld ins fnl 100yds: wl in command fnl strides* 16/1

6461 2 ½ **Smalljohn**[21] 3008 2-9-2 0 .... DNolan 1 72
(D Carroll) *led: rdn and hrd pressed fr 2f out: hdd ins fnl 100yds: stuck on wl but hld fnl strides* 5/1[3]

3 3 nse **Parisian Pyramid (IRE)**[6] 3492 2-8-11 0 .... FrancisNorton 10 66
(D Nicholls) *a.p: rdn and upsides ldrs fr 2f out: nt qckn fnl strides* 4/1[2]

2440 4 1 **Kingswinford (IRE)**[17] 3105 2-8-11 0 .... CatherineGannon 7 63
(P D Evans) *chsd ldrs: rdn to chal strly fr 2f out: no ex cl home* 7/2[1]

621 5 ½ **Scenic Pass**[17] 3106 2-8-6 0 .... MCGeran(5) 15 62
(M R Channon) *bmpd s: in tch: rdn 2f out: hung lft whn chsd ldrs fr 1f out: kpt on u.p ins fnl f wout chalng front quartet* 7/1

4344 6 1 ½ **Transcentral**[53] 2048 2-8-6 0 ow7 .... RobbieEgan(7) 8 59
(W M Brisbourne) *towards rr: hdwy 1/2-way: rdn over 2f out: drifted lft whn chsng ldrs fr 1f out: one pce fnl 75yds* 14/1

0 7 7 **Fashion Icon (USA)**[69] 1627 2-8-6 0 .... PaulFessey 6 31
(T D Barron) *bhd: hdwy over 2f out: edgd lft u.p over 1f out: one pce fnl f* 28/1

01 8 ½ **Anacaona (IRE)**[18] 3091 2-8-11 0 .... PatDobbs 3 35
(R Hannon) *in tch: rdn and outpcd over 2f out: carried sltly lft whn no imp over 1f out* 15/2

05 9 4 **Bold Account (IRE)**[21] 3008 2-8-11 0 .... FergusSweeney 11 23
(K R Burke) *prom tl rdn and wknd 2f out* 33/1

0 10 hd **Fathtastic (IRE)**[32] 2671 2-8-11 0 .... EdwardCreighton 14 22
(Miss V Haigh) *missed break and bmpd s: bhd: nvr able to trble ldrs* 100/1

4 11 1 **Blue Dagger (IRE)**[9] 3365 2-8-11 0 .... LeeEnstone 12 19
(P C Haslam) *racd keenly: prom: rdn and wknd over 2f out* 13/2

00 12 1 ¼ **Lucky Bid**[9] 3358 2-8-4 0 .... BMcHugh(7) 16 16
(J M Bradley) *midfield: rdn over 2f out: wknd over 1f out* 80/1

00 13 5 **One Cool Pet (IRE)**[17] 3106 2-8-1 0 .... PatrickDonaghy(5) 4 —
(P C Haslam) *missed break: a bhd* 100/1

00 14 6 **Baby Special**[44] 2309 2-8-3 0 .... DuranFentiman(3) 13 —
(C G Cox) *in tch: rdn 1/2-way: sn wknd* 33/1

4 15 1 **Incy Wincy**[25] 2882 2-8-4 0 .... PietroRomeo(7) 17 —
(J M Bradley) *midfield: lost pl 1/2-way: wnt lft whn n.d ins fnl f* 66/1

1m 13.69s (-0.31) **Going Correction** -0.15s/f (Firm) 15 Ran SP% 123.1
Speed ratings (Par 96): **96,95,95,93,93 91,81,81,75,75 74,72,66,58,56**
toteswinger: 1&2 £30.40, 1&3 £23.20, 2&3 £5.80. CSF £93.38 TOTE £24.20: £5.40, £2.20, £1.90; EX 228.40.The winner was sold to Dr Marwan Koukash for £26,000.
Owner Middleham Park Racing XXXVII **Bred** Adrian Smith **Trained** Sessay, N Yorks

FOCUS
A strong seller in which the first six finished clear of the rest and the form looks solid.

NOTEBOOK
Fol Liam took a bit of winding up but he kept responding to his rider's encouragement and held on well in a good finish. It was his racecourse bow so there may be some improvement to come. (op 20-1)
Smalljohn, one of the most experienced runners in the line-up having fared well in better company, ran his race again and should be able to win a nursery. (op 13-2)
Parisian Pyramid(IRE), a stable companion of the winner, had shown speed first time out at Newcastle and this represented improved form. (op 9-2 tchd 5-1 in places)
Kingswinford(IRE) had looked the form pick on early-season running but was unable to take advantage of this easier task, although it was only late on that he gave best. (op 4-1)
Scenic Pass has been running well, but not a lot went right for her. She was bumped at the start and, though never far away from the leader, she kept on despite hanging left.
Transcentral, dropped in class, did her cause no good by hanging left but she wasn't beaten all that far despite her substitute apprentice rider not being able to claim any of his 7lb allowance. (op 16-1 tchd 20-1)
Bold Account(IRE) Official explanation: jockey said colt ran too freely
Fathtastic(IRE) Official explanation: jockey said colt was never travelling
Blue Dagger(IRE) Official explanation: jockey said gelding ran too freely to post

3671 HARVEY NICHOLS H'CAP — 1m 6f
8:30 (8:31) (Class 5) (0-70,69) 3-Y-O — £3,238 (£963; £481; £240) Stalls Low

Form — RPR

0-02 1 **Askar Tau (FR)**[8] 3393 3-8-4 57 .... PatrickDonaghy(5) 16 72+
(M P Tregoning) *in tch: wnt 2nd 8f out: led over 3f out: sn kicked clr: styd on wl: eased down towards fin* 5/4[1]

-254 2 3 ¾ **Spiritonthemount (USA)**[15] 3168 3-9-7 69 .... (b) FrancisNorton 6 77
(B W Hills) *chsd ldr to 8f out: rdn over 3f out: wnt 2nd over 1f out: no imp on wnr* 20/1

6410 3 1 ¾ **Murcar**[22] 2977 3-9-7 69 .... EddieAhern 8 74
(C G Cox) *midfield: hdwy over 3f out: chsd wnr but no imp over 2f out: lost 2nd over 1f out: one pce fnl 100yds* 12/1

-041 4 2 ¾ **Mount Lavinia (IRE)**[20] 3022 3-9-1 63 .... JamesDoyle 9 64+
(R M Beckett) *hld up: hdwy on outside over 2f out: styd on appr fnl f: no imp on ldrs* 7/1[2]

00-0 5 5 **Rutba**[25] 2885 3-8-4 52 .... ChrisCatlin 14 46
(M P Tregoning) *chsd ldrs: pushed along and outpcd over 4f out: plugged on at one pce fnl 2f* 40/1

2130 6 ½ **Fantastic Lass**[19] 3057 3-8-4 59 .... BMcHugh(7) 4 53
(R A Fahey) *midfield: rdn over 2f out: one pce* 10/1

-542 7 3 **Smetana**[26] 2868 3-8-8 56 .... SteveDrowne 3 46
(H Morrison) *led: rdn and hdd over 3f out: sn outpcd by wnr: wknd over 1f out* 9/1[3]

3245 8 1 **Graylyn Ruby (FR)**[37] 2495 3-8-12 65 .... MarkCoumbe(5) 12 53
(J Jay) *midfield: hdwy to chse ldrs over 6f out: wknd over 1f out* 16/1

0652 9 ½ **Capal Dubh Alainn (IRE)**[39] 2468 3-8-7 62 .... (t) FrederikTylicki(7) 11 49
(T J Pitt) *in rr: sme hdwy over 1f out: nvr able to chal* 9/1[3]

0550 10 hd **Eddie Dowling**[28] 2785 3-9-3 65 .... EdwardCreighton 5 52
(M R Channon) *chsd ldrs: lost pl over 6f out: pushed along over 4f out: n.d after* 20/1

0040 11 1 ½ **King's Alchemist**[14] 3206 3-8-8 56 .... (v[1]) FergusSweeney 7 41
(M D I Usher) *racd keenly: in tch: rdn and wknd over 3f out* 40/1

4620 12 6 **Miss Mactango**[29] 2750 3-8-3 54 .... DuranFentiman(3) 1 31
(W M Brisbourne) *awkward s: a bhd* 66/1

4000 13 24 **Daraiym (IRE)**[24] 2907 3-8-7 55 .... DaleGibson 10 —
(Paul Green) *a bhd* 66/1

6-04 14 4 ½ **Harrison's Star**[23] 2926 3-8-3 51 .... PaulFessey 2 —
(G M Moore) *midfield: pushed along 6f out: wknd 4f out* 50/1

000 15 2 **Tank Commander**[18] 3094 3-9-0 62 .... PatDobbs 13 —
(W R Muir) *in tch: rdn and wknd over 3f out* 20/1

3m 2.92s (-1.38) **Going Correction** +0.05s/f (Good) 15 Ran SP% 123.7
Speed ratings (Par 100): **105,102,101,100,97 97,95,94,94,94 93,90,76,73,72**
toteswinger: 1&2 £8.10, 1&3 £8.30, 2&3 £31.70. CSF £36.00 CT £233.35 TOTE £2.00: £1.10, £5.70, £4.40; EX 33.10.
Owner Nurlan Bizakov **Bred** Gestut Zoppenbroich & Aerial Bloodstock **Trained** Lambourn, Berks

FOCUS
A modest handicap but the winner is improving although he did not need to match his previous effort to score. The race is rated around those immediately behind.

3672 CANTER, LEVIN & BERG SOLICITORS FILLIES' H'CAP — 1m 30y
9:00 (9:01) (Class 5) (0-75,75) 3-Y-O — £3,238 (£963; £481; £240) Stalls Low

Form — RPR

4-40 1 **Quirina**[43] 2328 3-9-7 75 .... SteveDrowne 11 83+
(J H M Gosden) *a.p: led over 1f out: r.o wl fnl f and a in command* 5/2[1]

6023 2 2 ¼ **Welcome Return (IRE)**[6] 3481 3-8-11 65 .... (b) ChrisCatlin 10 68
(T D Easterby) *towards rr: hdwy over 2f out: chsd wnr over 1f out: no imp towards fin* 6/1

0-26 3 1 ¼ **Finmore Queen (USA)**[43] 2328 3-9-4 72 .... EddieAhern 13 72+
(J R Fanshawe) *midfield: nt clr run 2f out: hdwy 1f out: styd on ins fnl f: nt pce of front pair* 11/2

-463 4 shd **Top Vision**[19] 3057 3-9-3 71 .... EdwardCreighton 2 71
(M R Channon) *hld up: swtchd rt 2f out: rdn and hdwy over 1f out: styd on ins fnl f: nvr able to chal ldrs* 4/1[2]

330 5 2 ¼ **Devinius (IRE)**[13] 3282 3-8-8 62 .... PaulFessey 4 57
(G A Swinbank) *racd keenly: prom: chal 2f out: sn rdn: wknd ins fnl f* 10/1

0-50 6 2 ¼ **Ma Al Salamah (IRE)**[42] 2376 3-8-6 60 .... JimmyQuinn 3 50
(C E Brittain) *led: rdn 2f out: hdd over 1f out: wkng whn n.m.r ins fnl f* 20/1

-034 7 1 ½ **Nayarna**[14] 3200 3-8-6 67 .... FrederikTylicki(7) 9 53
(R A Fahey) *in tch: rdn over 1f out: wknd ins fnl f* 12/1

1420 8 5 **Challow Hills (USA)**[14] 3221 3-9-1 69 .... FrancisNorton 5 44
(B W Hills) *trckd ldrs tl rdn and wknd 2f out* 5/1[3]

33-4 9 21 **Sempre Libera (IRE)**[165] 243 3-8-10 64 .... JamesDoyle 7 —
(R T Phillips) *bhd: pushed along over 3f out: nvr on terms* 33/1

1m 44.64s (0.84) **Going Correction** +0.05s/f (Good) 9 Ran SP% 119.4
Speed ratings (Par 97): **97,94,93,93,91 88,87,82,61**
toteswinger: 1&2 £2.50, 1&3 £2.20, 2&3 £4.80. CSF £18.68 CT £76.44 TOTE £3.00: £1.70, £1.60, £1.80; EX 24.90.
Owner Dr Ornella Carlini Cozzi **Bred** Dr Ornella Cozzi Carlini **Trained** Newmarket, Suffolk

FOCUS
A modest handicap in which the form looks sound with the runner-up and fourth to previous handicap form.
Ma Al Salamah(IRE) Official explanation: jockey said filly hung right
Challow Hills(USA) Official explanation: jockey said filly found the good ground too fast

3673 LAMBRINI H'CAP — 1m 3f 200y
9:30 (9:30) (Class 4) (0-80,79) 3-Y-O+ — £5,504 (£1,637; £818; £408) Stalls High

Form — RPR

0120 1 **Amanda Carter**[19] 3059 4-8-11 69 .... FrederikTylicki(7) 5 84
(R A Fahey) *led after 2f: mde rest: qcknd clr over 2f out: r.o wl and unchal after* 3/1[2]

14-3 2 7 **Merchant Of Dubai**[25] 2889 3-8-11 75 .... EddieAhern 3 78
(G A Swinbank) *racd keenly: led for 2f: chsd wnr tl over 5f out: outpcd over 3f out: kpt on to take 2nd over 1f out but no ch w wnr* 11/8[1]

0/45 3 2 ¾ **Markington**[43] 2332 5-9-1 66 .... (p) ChrisCatlin 2 65
(P Bowen) *in tch: lost pl over 5f out: wl outpcd over 4f out: styd on fnl f: tk 3rd fnl 100yds: nt rch front 2* 6/1

0131 4 4 ½ **Bull Market (IRE)**[22] 2970 5-9-13 78 .... StephenDonohoe 1 70
(Ian Williams) *chsd ldrs: wnt 2nd over 5f out: rdn and outpcd by wnr over 2f out: lost 2nd over 1f out: wknd ins fnl f* 7/2[3]

4/00 5 5 **High Command**[26] 2867 5-8-7 65 .... NSLawes(7) 9 49
(M W Easterby) *hld up: pushed along over 3f out: nvr on terms w ldrs: wl btn fnl f* 22/1

05-2 6 12 **Royal Flynn**[69] 1613 6-9-8 78 .... NeilBrown(5) 6 43
(Mrs K Walton) *missed break: a bhd: lft toiling fnl 2f* 12/1

2m 33.96s (0.76) **Going Correction** +0.05s/f (Good)
WFA 3 from 4yo+ 13lb 6 Ran SP% 115.7
Speed ratings (Par 105): **99,94,92,89,86 78**
toteswinger: 1&2 £1.90, 1&3 £3.10, 2&3 £2.40. CSF £7.89 CT £21.88 TOTE £4.70: £2.20, £1.50; EX 8.60 Place 6 £17.75, Place 5 £13.63.
Owner Mrs Janis Macpherson **Bred** James G Thom **Trained** Musley Bank, N Yorks

FOCUS
A fairly open handicap but they finished well strung out and perhaps the form should not be taken literally.
T/Plt: £26.10 to a £1 stake. Pool: £74,136.24. 2,073.13 winning tickets. T/Qpdt: £9.40 to a £1 stake. Pool: £4,172.80. 325.60 winning tickets. DO

3518 SALISBURY (R-H)
Friday, July 4

OFFICIAL GOING: Good to firm (firm in places; 9.1)
Wind: Moderate, half behind

3674 "COME SHOPPING AT CASTLEPOINT" BOURNEMOUTH MAIDEN AUCTION FILLIES' STKS — 6f 212y
6:35 (6:36) (Class 5) 2-Y-O — £3,885 (£1,156; £577; £288) Stalls High

Form — RPR

23 1 **Maid For Music (IRE)**[25] 2887 2-8-12 .... AdamKirby 11 82
(E S McMahon) *mde all: rdn out fnl f* 15/8[1]

5 2 1 ¾ **Bouggie Daize**[34] 2618 2-8-4 .... NeilPollard 8 69+
(C G Cox) *chsd wnr thrght: rdn and kpt on but no imp ins fnl f* 5/1[3]

03 3 ¾ **Fong's Alibi**[13] 3267 2-8-5 .... RichardThomas 18 69
(J S Moore) *a.p: styd on fnl f* 16/1

4 5 **Prophetise (USA)** 2-8-6 ow3 .... GabrielHannon(5) 6 62
(J W Hills) *mid-div: styd on one pce ins fnl 2f* 50/1

0 5 1 **Positive Opinion**[13] 3267 2-8-7 .... HayleyTurner 15 55
(B R Millman) *a in tch: rdn and one pce fnl 3f* 25/1

6 ½ **Order Order** 2-8-6 .... PaulDoe 9 53
(H J L Dunlop) *twrds rr until styd on one pce fnl 2f* 66/1

45 **7** ½ **Flying Lady (IRE)**[13] 3245 2-8-9 .... TPO'Shea 1 54+
(M R Channon) *swtchd rt fr outside draw after s: bhd whn bmpd over 4f out and nvr got into r* **11/4**[2]

00 **8** ¾ **Caressing**[53] 2048 2-8-5 .... PatrickHills(3) 17 51
(R Hannon) *chsd ldrs tl rdn and wknd over 1f out* **33/1**

9 *nse* **Sweet Possession (USA)** 2-8-10 .... DarrenWilliams 3 53
(A P Jarvis) *s.i.s: bhd tl swtchd outside and hdwy 3f out: wknd appr fnl f* **66/1**

00 **10** 3½ **Nun Today (USA)**[14] 3207 2-8-7 .... LPKeniry 7 41
(J S Moore) *in tch tl wknd over 1f out* **33/1**

00 **11** *nk* **Barcode**[10] 3348 2-8-5 .... RichardSmith 12 38
(R Hannon) *in tch tl rdn and wknd wl over 1f out* **14/1**

12 3 **Reel Hope** 2-8-5 .... MohammedSaeed 10 31
(J R Best) *mid-div: bhd fnl 2f* **50/1**

13 5 **Thewaytosanjose (IRE)** 2-8-9 ow1........ HaddenFrost(5) 16 27+
(S Kirk) *s.s: hmpd on rail over 4f out: a struggling in rr* **33/1**

14 ¾ **Eightdaysaweek** 2-8-12 .... MartinDwyer 13 23+
(S Kirk) *s.s: in rr whn bmpd over 4f out: nvr on terms* **8/1**

00 **15** 2¾ **The Beat Is On**[13] 3267 2-7-11 .... DavidProbert(7) 14 7
(J M Bradley) *bhd fr 1/2-way* **100/1**

16 *hd* **Highams Park (IRE)** 2-8-9 .... FrankieMcDonald 5 12
(J G Portman) *sn bhd* **66/1**

17 4 **Zaruschka** 2-8-5 .... JosedeSouza 4 —
(R M Beckett) *in tch tl wknd over 1f out: eased* **20/1**

1m 26.9s (-2.10) **Going Correction** -0.175s/f (Firm) **17 Ran SP% 128.6**
Speed ratings (Par 91): **105,103,102,96,95 94,94,93,93,89 88,85,79,78,75 75,70**
toteswinger: 1&2 £1.40, 1&3 £3.20, 2&3 £12.80. CSF £10.98 TOTE £3.30: £1.50, £1.50, £4.70; EX 14.00.
Owner J C Fretwell **Bred** Celbridge Estates Ltd **Trained** Lichfield, Staffs

FOCUS
An ordinary fillies' maiden but the time was decent and the winner scored in good style giving weight away all round. The first three were clear and the form looks solid.

NOTEBOOK
Maid For Music(IRE) pinged out of the stalls and was never headed. She had actually beaten the second favourite the previous month so it was no great surprise she collected and her future now lies in nurseries. (op 11-4)
Bouggie Daize chased the winner from the outset but was held when changing her legs in the final furlong and was probably feeling the ground. However, there is a race of this nature in her. (op 10-3)
Fong's Alibi seems to be progressing steadily with experience and was well clear of the rest. She is another for nurseries now. (op 20-1)
Prophetise(USA), who has an American dirt pedigree with plenty of sprinters on her dam's side, did best of those with no previous experience and she should derive some benefit for the outing.
Positive Opinion improved on her debut effort despite being well held and is another who will probably go the nursery route after another outing.
Order Order, who has a fair bit of speed in her pedigree despite her dam staying 1m2f, could muster just the one pace on her debut and like her mother should appreciate further, and possibly softer ground, in time. (op 50-1)
Flying Lady(IRE), who had finished fifth in the Chesham, had the worst of the draw and was immediately switched to the favoured far side at the rear of a big field. When she did look like getting a run she did not seem to relish going about her business as she carried her head quite high. The Ascot race on a fast surface appears to have left its mark and she has questions to answer now. (tchd 5-2 and 3-1)

3675 "COME SHOPPING AT CASTLEPOINT" EMPRISE SERVICES PLC CLAIMING STKS — 6f 212y
7:05 (7:06) (Class 5) 3-Y-0+ **£3,238** (£963; £481; £240) **Stalls High**

Form RPR

1003 **1** **Royal Storm (IRE)**[1] 3646 9-9-5 77........ JamesMillman(5) 8 75
(B R Millman) *mde all: rdn over 1f out: kpt up to work* **6/5**[1]

-054 **2** ½ **Mister Fips (IRE)**[15] 3172 3-9-4 78........ FrankieMcDonald 5 73
(Jane Chapple-Hyam) *chsd wnr thrght: r.o but no imp ins fnl f* **5/1**[3]

-000 **3** 4 **Blues Minor (IRE)**[6] 3499 3-9-3 76........ RyanMoore 4 61
(R Hannon) *chsd first 2 but one pce fr over 1f out* **11/4**[2]

0600 **4** 7 **Our Blessing (IRE)**[20] 3050 4-9-11 64........ DarrenWilliams 3 45
(A P Jarvis) *in tch tl wknd over 1f out* **8/1**

-400 **5** 7 **Christalini**[9] 915 4-9-3 44........ LPKeniry 2 18
(J C Fox) *slowly away: a bhd* **33/1**

0000 **6** 38 **Tagula Sands (IRE)**[36] 2528 4-9-3 37........ RichardSmith 1 —
(J C Fox) *racd on outside: bhd fr 1/2-way: t.o* **50/1**

45-6 **7** 6 **Unlicensed**[181] 58 3-8-11 70........ TedDurcan 6 —
(R Hannon) *in rr: lost tch fr 1/2-way: t.o* **8/1**

1m 27.19s (-1.81) **Going Correction** -0.175s/f (Firm)
WFA 3 from 4yo+ 8lb **7 Ran SP% 115.9**
Speed ratings (Par 103): **103,102,97,89,81 38,31**
toteswinger: 1&2 £1.70, 1&3 £2.40, 2&3 £2.20. CSF £8.08 TOTE £2.10: £1.50, £2.40; EX 5.40.
Owner Mrs H Brain **Bred** E Campion **Trained** Kentisbeare, Devon

FOCUS
This claimer went more or less with official figures, but there is some doubt about the current ability of the placed horses, which undermines the form.
Christalini Official explanation: trainer's representative said gelding bled from the nose
Unlicensed Official explanation: jockey said gelding had no more to give

3676 CASTLEPOINT SUPPORTS DORSET & SOMERSET AIR AMBULANCE H'CAP — 1m 1f 198y
7:35 (7:35) (Class 4) (0-85,85) 3-Y-0+ **£6,799** (£2,023; £1,011; £505) **Stalls High**

Form RPR

0041 **1** **Press The Button (GER)**[7] 3449 5-9-4 80 6ex........ HarryPoulton(7) 2 88
(J R Boyle) *led tl hdd over 3f out: rallied to ld again over 1f out: rdn out* **10/3**[2]

4-14 **2** ¾ **Mazaaya (USA)**[48] 2201 3-9-3 83........ TedDurcan 4 89
(D R Lanigan) *a in tch: t.k.h: kpt on to go 2nd ins fnl f* **4/1**[3]

0440 **3** ¾ **Penang Cinta**[14] 3226 5-8-11 66........(p) ShaneKelly 5 71
(P D Evans) *hld up in rr: styd on fr over 1f out: nvr nrr* **16/1**

13 **4** ¾ **Mission Control (IRE)**[14] 3206 3-7-9 68........ DavidProbert(7) 3 71
(J R Boyle) *a in tch: rdn over 1f out: nt qckn ins fnl f* **9/4**[1]

6135 **5** *nk* **Basra (IRE)**[30] 2711 5-10-0 83........ AdamKirby 1 85
(Miss Jo Crowley) *trckd ldr: led over 3f out: hdd over 1f out: no ex ins fnl f* **6/1**

2005 **6** *hd* **Proper (IRE)**[4] 3561 4-9-5 74........ MartinDwyer 6 76
(C J Mann) *hld up: rdn over 1f out: one pce after* **14/1**

10 **7** 2¼ **Tri Nations (UAE)**[50] 2121 3-9-5 85........ RyanMoore 7 83
(J W Hills) *hld up: swtchd lft over 2f out: sn rdn and nvr on terms* **11/2**

2m 8.63s (-1.27) **Going Correction** -0.175s/f (Firm)
WFA 3 from 4yo+ 11lb **7 Ran SP% 116.1**
Speed ratings (Par 105): **98,97,96,96,95 95,94**
toteswinger: 1&2 £1.70, 1&3 £8.90, 2&3 £7.00. CSF £17.58 TOTE £4.00: £2.20, £2.70; EX 17.30.
Owner Brian McAtavey **Bred** Gestut Sommerberg **Trained** Epsom, Surrey

FOCUS
There was a sedate gallop early on in this fair handicap and the time was moderate for the grade. The form is rated around the winner and third.

3677 "COME SHOPPING AT CASTLEPOINT" DOUGLAND SUPPORT SERVICES NURSERY — 6f
8:10 (8:12) (Class 5) 2-Y-0 **£3,885** (£1,156; £577; £288) **Stalls High**

Form RPR

465 **1** **Ridgeway Silver**[21] 2987 2-7-5 61 oh1........ DavidProbert(7) 8 64
(M D I Usher) *trckd ldr: led over 2f out: rdn out fnl f* **12/1**

341 **2** ¾ **Finnegan McCool**[18] 3092 2-9-5 82........ GeorgeBaker 4 83
(R M Beckett) *a.p: chsd wnr fnl 2f* **3/1**[2]

220 **3** 1¾ **Servoca (CAN)**[15] 3152 2-9-7 84........ RyanMoore 6 80
(B W Hills) *hld up in rr: rdn over 2f out: styd on to go 3rd ins fnl f* **6/4**[1]

540 **4** 2 **Redhead (IRE)**[16] 3135 2-8-5 68........ MartinDwyer 5 58
(R Hannon) *prom: rdn over 2f out: wknd ins fnl f* **9/2**[3]

214 **5** ¾ **Soul Sista (IRE)**[37] 2507 2-8-7 73........ TolleyDean(3) 3 60
(J L Spearing) *in tch: rdn 1/2-way: one pce fnl f* **10/1**

0505 **6** 5 **Noworneva**[10] 3341 2-7-5 61 oh5........ CharlesEddery(7) 7 33
(S Kirk) *a towards rr* **33/1**

054 **7** *hd* **Shadow Bay (IRE)**[78] 1425 2-8-3 66........ TPO'Shea 2 38
(M R Channon) *a outpcd in rr* **5/1**

5500 **8** 4½ **Madison Belle**[21] 2987 2-7-13 62........ DavidKinsella 1 20
(Mrs H Sweeting) *wnt lft s but sn led: hung bdly lft and hdd over 2f out: sn btn* **33/1**

1m 15.12s (0.32) **Going Correction** -0.175s/f (Firm) **8 Ran SP% 122.5**
Speed ratings (Par 94): **90,89,86,84,83 76,76,70**
toteswinger: 1&2 £8.70, 1&3 £8.70, 2&3 £1.10. CSF £51.58 CT £89.13 TOTE £21.00: £3.80, £1.80, £1.10; EX 57.40.
Owner The Ridgeway Bloodstock Company Ltd **Bred** B Mills **Trained** Upper Lambourn, Berks

FOCUS
A fair nursery with the winner stepping up and the runner-up performing to his mark backed up by the third, so the form looks solid. The 'official' ratings shown next to each horse are estimated and for information purposes only.

NOTEBOOK
Ridgeway Silver went on soon after halfway and stuck on gamely to fend off the attentions of the runner-up. She had shown hints of ability in her three previous efforts, but according to her trainer she was always going to be a nursery filly as she has been quite big and backward. If that is correct there might be a bit more to come as another furlong may well suit. (op 14-1 tchd 16-1)
Finnegan McCool had a decent chance on paper but did himself no favours when getting revved up in the preliminaries and actually crashed through a rail and came down soon after leaving the paddock. Obviously he was none the worse for the tumble, but it could not have done him any good so this has to go down as a fair effort. As long as his temperament does not get the better of him again he could well be up to winning in this company. (op 11-4 tchd 9-4)
Servoca(CAN) had not been beaten far in a Royal Ascot Group 2 last time so the form is not bad, but the Handicapper has not taken too many chances with his rating. (op 5-2)
Redhead(IRE) was dropping a furlong in trip but that previous race was on sand. She looked one-paced and a step back up to 7f on grass might suit better. (op 8-1 tchd 17-2)
Soul Sista(IRE) showed her best form on soft ground early in the spring. She will benefit from similar conditions in this grade. (op 8-1 tchd 15-2)
Madison Belle Official explanation: jockey said filly hung left badly throughout

3678 "COME SHOPPING AT CASTLEPOINT" H'CAP — 6f
8:40 (8:42) (Class 6) (0-65,70) 3-Y-0 **£2,914** (£867; £433; £216) **Stalls High**

Form RPR

4024 **1** **Lord Deevert**[3] 3572 3-8-6 50........ AlanDaly 18 59
(W G M Turner) *led tl hdd over 1f out: rallied to ld again ins fnl f* **12/1**

3252 **2** *hd* **Shakespeare's Son**[11] 3313 3-8-9 56........ TolleyDean(3) 15 64
(H J Evans) *trckd wnr: led over 1f out: rdn and hdd again ins fnl f* **8/1**

6541 **3** 1¼ **Averoo**[7] 3441 3-9-6 64 6ex........(p) GeorgeBaker 14 68+
(M D Squance) *towards rr: hdwy 2f out: swtchd rt ins fnl f: r.o to go 3rd towards fin* **10/3**[2]

-023 **4** ½ **Bilboa**[8] 3395 3-8-11 55........ HayleyTurner 11 57
(B R Millman) *mid-div: rdn and hdwy over 1f out: r.o: nvr nrr* **8/1**

0313 **5** *nk* **Presto Levanter**[9] 3381 3-9-3 61........ RyanMoore 4 62
(R Hannon) *racd on outside: hdwy 3f out: strly rdn over 1f out: kpt on* **15/2**[3]

304 **6** *nk* **Gioacchino (IRE)**[13] 3268 3-8-13 60........ KevinGhunowa(3) 2 60
(R A Harris) *racd on outside: hdwy 3f out: kpt on fr over 1f out* **40/1**

3301 **7** ¾ **Koraleva Tectona (IRE)**[12] 3298 3-9-12 70 6ex........ TedDurcan 8 68
(Pat Eddery) *hld up in mid-div: styd on fr over 1f out but nvr on terms* **2/1**[1]

0024 **8** 1 **Kannon**[8] 3395 3-8-11 55........(v) RichardKingscote 12 50
(W J Knight) *chsd ldrs tl hrd rdn and wknd over 2f out* **16/1**

2520 **9** ¾ **Too Grand**[35] 2563 3-8-0 51........(v) DavidProbert(7) 1 43
(J J Bridger) *a towards rr* **25/1**

-505 **10** 1¼ **Tea Cake (IRE)**[9] 3381 3-9-4 62........ MartinDwyer 13 50
(H J L Dunlop) *chsd ldrs: rdn 1/2-way: wknd 2f out* **14/1**

3-40 **11** 1 **Lullaby Lady**[50] 2118 3-8-13 60........(b[1]) PatrickHills(3) 7 45
(B W Hills) *dwlt: a bhd* **33/1**

-000 **12** 2¼ **The Name Is Frank**[11] 3313 3-9-7 65........ LPKeniry 16 43
(J W Mullins) *prom tl wknd wl over 1f out* **25/1**

600 **13** *nk* **Rockfield Rose**[13] 3268 3-8-8 52........ ShaneKelly 3 29
(J A Osborne) *hmpd after 1f: a struggling in rr* **66/1**

500 **14** 6 **Talamahana**[46] 2260 3-8-13 57........ DavidKinsella 17 15
(A B Haynes) *sn bhd* **40/1**

00-0 **15** 1¾ **Oronsay**[19] 3064 3-8-10 54........ TPO'Shea 9 6
(B R Millman) *bhd fr 1/2-way* **66/1**

00-0 **16** ½ **Bad Moon Rising**[181] 60 3-9-1 59........ IanMongan 10 10
(J Akehurst) *mid-div tl 1/2-way: sn bhd* **40/1**

1m 14.61s (-0.19) **Going Correction** -0.175s/f (Firm) **16 Ran SP% 131.6**
Speed ratings (Par 98): **94,93,92,91,91 90,89,88,87,85 84,81,80,72,70 69**
toteswinger: 1&2 £16.50, 1&3 £23.60, 2&3 £9.90. CSF £106.81 CT £332.05 TOTE £25.60: £4.80, £1.60, £2.10, £2.00; EX 139.00.
Owner Mrs M S Teversham **Bred** Mrs Monica Teversham **Trained** Sigwells, Somerset

FOCUS
A low-grade handicap in which those drawn high appeared to have an advantage, as the first three came from the five highest stalls. The runner-up, backed up by the next three home, give the race a sound feel.

Lullaby Lady Official explanation: jockey said filly was never travelling

3679 "COME SHOPPING AT CASTLEPOINT" A3060 BOURNEMOUTH FILLIES' H'CAP 1m
9:10 (9:11) (Class 4) (0-85,82) 3-Y-0+ £6,799 (£2,023; £1,011; £505) Stalls High

Form RPR
24-3 1 **Quotation**[50] 2123 3-10-0 82 RyanMoore 6 95+
(Sir Michael Stoute) *hld up in rr: swtchd lft 2f out: kpt on wl to ld ins fnl f: stretched clr* 4/7[1]
6210 2 3 ¾ **Mekong Melody (IRE)**[23] 2953 3-9-8 76 AdamKirby 3 77
(C G Cox) *in tch: rdn and kpt on to go 2nd ins fnl f: no ch w wnr* 5/1[2]
2-40 3 nk **Marraasi (USA)**[17] 3117 3-8-13 67 MartinDwyer 4 67
(M P Tregoning) *led: rdn and hdd ins fnl f: lost 2nd towards fin* 14/1
0612 4 4 **Tina's Best (IRE)**[10] 3345 3-9-3 76 HaddenFrost(5) 5 67
(R Hannon) *a same pl: one pce fr over 1f out* 6/1[3]
0-06 5 11 **Plumage**[19] 3061 3-8-10 64 LPKeniry 2 30
(M Blanshard) *trckd ldr: t.k.h: rdn and wknd 2f out* 33/1
-011 6 4 ½ **Maybe I Will (IRE)**[20] 3023 3-9-2 70 HayleyTurner 1 25
(S Dow) *in tch tl wknd 2f out* 10/1

1m 43.71s (0.21) **Going Correction** -0.175s/f (Firm) 6 Ran SP% **113.3**
Speed ratings (Par 102): **91,87,86,82,71 67**
toteswinger: 1&2 £1.20, 1&3 £4.00, 2&3 £31.40. CSF £3.98 TOTE £1.60: £1.30, £2.60; EX 3.60 Place £20.18, Place £11.63.
Owner Cheveley Park Stud **Bred** Cheveley Park Stud Ltd **Trained** Newmarket, Suffolk

FOCUS
A fair but slowly-run fillies' handicap that resulted in a clear-cut winner. The form looks messy but the winner is rated to previous course form with the placed horses to their marks from earlier in the season.
T/Plt: £16.10 to a £1 stake. Pool: £57,254.67. 2,580.43 winning tickets. T/Qpdt: £7.20 to a £1 stake. Pool: £2,948.00. 300.00 winning tickets. JS

3038 SANDOWN (R-H)
Friday, July 4

OFFICIAL GOING: Good to firm changing to good to firm (firm in places) after race 4 (4.00)
Dolling out added 5yds to advertised race distances on round course
Wind: Light, across Weather: Sunny, warm

3680 DELANCEY H'CAP 5f 6y
2:20 (2:22) (Class 3) (0-95,94) 3-Y-0+ £9,066 (£2,697; £1,348; £673) Stalls High

Form RPR
1213 1 **Crimson Fern (IRE)**[19] 3062 4-8-12 80 TGMcLaughlin 14 95+
(M S Saunders) *trckd ldrs on inner: eased off rail fr wl over 1f out: effrt on outer and r.o to ld last 100yds: sn clr* 7/1
0401 2 1 ¾ **Tabaret**[14] 3228 5-9-9 91 (p) PaulMulrennan 12 100
(R M Whitaker) *trckd ldng trio: rdn to chal 1f out: upsides fnl f: outpcd by wnr last 100yds* 17/2
30-1 3 ¾ **Osiris Way**[19] 3062 6-9-3 85 PhilipRobinson 8 91
(P R Chamings) *lw: pressed ldr: led jst over 1f out: hdd and no ex last 100yds* 13/2[3]
0002 4 1 ¼ **Strike Up The Band**[10] 3336 5-9-9 91 AdrianTNicholls 4 93
(D Nicholls) *led: drvn and hdd jst over 1f out: fdd ins fnl f* 7/1
0-52 5 hd **Playful**[19] 3062 5-8-12 80 AdamKirby 13 85+
(R M Beckett) *trckd ldng pair: cl up and waiting for gap over 1f out: nt clr run and snatched up jst ins fnl f: one pce after* 7/1
0-00 6 nk **Tony The Tap**[21] 3009 7-8-13 81 RichardMullen 2 81
(W R Muir) *s.i.s: settled in last pair but outpcd after 2f: styd on fr over 1f out: nrst fin* 33/1
20-1 7 nse **Sohraab**[21] 3009 4-9-11 93 JimmyQuinn 9 93+
(H Morrison) *lw: hld up in midfield: sme prog on inner 2f out: nt clr run briefly over 1f out: kpt on same pce fnl f* 10/3[1]
0600 8 2 ½ **Bazroy (IRE)**[34] 2595 4-9-11 93 (b) StephenDonohoe 10 84
(P D Evans) *b. warm: s.i.s: outpcd in last trio after 2f: kpt on fnl f: no ch* 50/1
3-04 9 2 ¾ **Sundae**[19] 3056 4-9-9 91 GeorgeBaker 11 72
(C F Wall) *nvr beyond midfield: rdn and no prog 2f out: sltly checked over 1f out: wknd fnl f* 9/2[2]
0-60 10 hd **The Jobber (IRE)**[19] 3056 7-9-10 92 DaneO'Neill 5 72
(M Blanshard) *nvr beyond midfield and a struggling to go the pce: rdn bef 1/2-way: no prog* 25/1
0-60 11 2 ¾ **Fantasy Believer**[62] 1809 10-9-5 87 DarryllHolland 3 57
(J J Quinn) *lw: a in last trio: struggling fr 1/2-way* 25/1

59.66 secs (-1.94) **Going Correction** -0.20s/f (Firm) 11 Ran SP% **115.2**
WFA 3 from 4yo+ 5lb
Speed ratings (Par 107): **107,104,103,101,100 100,100,96,91,91 87**
toteswinger: 1&2 £12.30, 1&3 £6.40, 2&3 £14.30. CSF £61.12 CT £413.78 TOTE £6.50: £2.10, £3.50, £2.40; EX 65.00.
Owner M S Saunders **Bred** David Brickley **Trained** Green Ore, Somerset

FOCUS
A competitive enough handicap, and with the far rail brought in three or four yards the usual high draw advantage ought to have been reduced at least. However, with the first three drawn 14 (of 14), 12, and eight, it certainly didn't hurt to be drawn near the fence. The time was decent and, although nothing came from far off the pace and the first four were in the first half dozen throughout, the form looks solid.

NOTEBOOK
Crimson Fern(IRE), who won over the course and distance in June, settled well in midfield before being produced with a winning surge inside the final furlong. She seems to be improving quickly (excuses can be made for her last run) and her trainer is hopeful of landing some black type with her if the right race can be found. (op 6-1)
Tabaret managed a win last time, after going a long time without success, when cheekpieces were applied for the first time. Raised 4lb for that success, he ran right up to his best again and is one to watch for if found a race at York soon, as he has run well there in the past. (op 8-1 tchd 9-1)
Osiris Way showed plenty of pace and led for a brief moment inside the final furlong. However, he could not hold off the strong-finishing filly, who he had beaten last time. This was still a very respectable performance and he confirmed he is going in the right direction. (op 12-1)
Strike Up The Band showed tremendous pace from a low draw but could not sustain that effort inside the final furlong. He has been in really good form recently and gives the race a solid look. (op 6-1 tchd 8-1)
Playful was never far way but got slightly hampered a couple of times when wanting to make a challenge. Her effort flattened right out once in the clear, but she is probably better than the bare form suggests. Official explanation: jockey said mare was denied a clear run (op 8-1)
Tony The Tap, well behind Sohraab and Tabaret last time, never threatened to challenge for a place but did keep on respectably inside the final furlong. (op 50-1)
Sohraab, who was raised 5lb for winning on seasonal debut last time, got behind early and was never able to get on terms after having his way blocked for a few strides up the inside rail. Trainer Hughie Morrison implied afterwards that the gelding might not be the most manoeuvrable and prefers to run hard and fast in a straight line. (op 11-4)
Sundae travelled well towards the middle of the pack but failed to pick up when his jockey asked him to quicken. He is shaping like a horse that needs a bit of help from the Handicapper as well as wanting some softer ground. (tchd 5-1)
The Jobber(IRE) was pushed along at the halfway point, towards the middle of the course, and failed to threaten the leaders. However, he has come down to a more realistic handicap mark, so his turn may not be far away.

3681 AAIM DRAGON STKS (LISTED RACE) 5f 6y
2:50 (2:52) (Class 1) 2-Y-0
£17,031 (£6,456; £3,231; £1,611; £807; £405) Stalls High

Form RPR
510 1 **Light The Fire (IRE)**[17] 3105 2-9-2 0 JimmyFortune 5 98+
(B J Meehan) *trckd ldrs: cruised through to ld jst over 2f out: edgd rt over 1f out: 2l clr fnl f: drvn out* 10/3[2]
1225 2 ¾ **April Pride**[14] 3192 2-8-11 0 RyanMoore 2 90
(R Hannon) *lw: settled in 5th or 6th: rdn and effrt 2f out: styd on to go 2nd ins fnl f: clsd on wnr but unable to chal* 9/4[1]
3110 3 ¾ **Moss Likely (IRE)**[17] 3105 2-8-11 0 DarryllHolland 3 87
(M R Channon) *lw: hld up in 5th or 6th: effrt 2f out: nt qckn over 1f out: rdn to dispute 2nd ins fnl f: one pce* 5/1[3]
2321 4 1 **Raggle Taggle (IRE)**[17] 3114 2-8-11 0 AdamKirby 6 84
(R M Beckett) *cl up: rdn to dispute ld jst over 2f out: hld whn short of room against rail over 1f out: one pce after and lost 2 pls ins fnl f* 9/1
1 5 2 **Royal Raider**[11] 3309 2-8-11 0 TGMcLaughlin 7 77
(P D Evans) *pushed along in last over 3f out: nvr on terms: kpt on fnl f: nrst fin* 22/1
1002 6 ¾ **White Shift (IRE)**[5] 3528 2-9-0 0 StephenDonohoe 4 77
(P D Evans) *mde most against rail to jst over 2f out: sn outpcd and btn* 7/1
4211 7 9 **Russet Reward**[20] 3020 2-9-2 0 DaneO'Neill 1 46
(Mrs L Stubbs) *w ldrs to 1/2-way: hung lft and lost pl rapidly sn after* 6/1

60.83 secs (-0.77) **Going Correction** -0.20s/f (Firm) 7 Ran SP% **111.6**
Speed ratings (Par 102): **98,96,95,94,90 89,75**
toteswinger: 1&2 £2.00, 1&3 £3.40, 2&3 £2.10. CSF £10.71 TOTE £4.40: £2.40, £1.90; EX 7.50.
Owner Joe L Allbritton **Bred** A Panetta **Trained** Manton, Wilts

FOCUS
A small but fair field for a Listed event in which the runner-up sets the standard. The first two home should be able to handle themselves in this sort of grade.

NOTEBOOK
Light The Fire(IRE), who did not run too badly in the Windsor Castle Stakes at Royal Ascot from a modest draw, travelled like a decent sort before quickening away from his rivals in a matter of strides. He should be competitive in similar company or a bit higher, so a race like the Molecomb Stakes at Goodwood could be the right race for him. (op 9-2 tchd 5-1 in a place)
April Pride, fifth in the Group 3 Albany Stakes last time, was held up in the early stages but kept on powerfully inside the final furlong to grab the runner-up spot. A step back up to 6f will definitely suit her. (tchd 5-2)
Moss Likely(IRE), who was about four lengths behind Light The Fire at Royal Ascot, was another to come from off the pace and pretty much had every chance. She had beaten April Pride earlier in the season, so it was slightly disappointing to see her readily held by that rival in this. (op 7-2)
Raggle Taggle(IRE) was not disgraced on this step up in grade and would have been a bit closer, without taking a place, had the winner not come across her about a furlong from home. (op 17-2)
Royal Raider, who only won a seller last time, got behind early and made some modest late headway. (op 20-1 tchd 25-1)
White Shift(IRE), who was making a fairly quick reappearance, showed plenty of early dash but was going backwards by the time the field hit the two-furlong pole. (op 11-2 tchd 5-1)
Russet Reward went a bit to his left at the start but was soon up in the lead, showing good pace. However, he was joined over two furlongs from home and dropped out of contention under pressure while edging to his left, something he has done before. Official explanation: trainer said gelding returned with torn back muscles (op 8-1 tchd 11-2)

3682 CUSHMAN & WAKEFIELD E B F MAIDEN STKS 7f 16y
3:25 (3:30) (Class 4) 2-Y-0 £6,476 (£1,927; £963; £481) Stalls High

Form RPR
1 **Zacinto** 2-9-3 0 RyanMoore 12 95+
(Sir Michael Stoute) *w'like: tall: leggy: scope: trckd ldng pair: plld out over 2f out: led over 1f out: sltly green but sn drew clr: pushed out to the fin: impressive debut* 5/6[1]
2 2 8 **Seminole (IRE)**[13] 3274 2-9-3 0 (b[1]) JimmyFortune 5 75
(J H M Gosden) *led: shkn up and hdd over 1f out: no ch w wnr after but in n.d of losing 2nd* 7/2[2]
00 3 1 ½ **Oasis Knight (IRE)**[22] 2972 2-9-3 0 RichardMullen 7 71
(M P Tregoning) *settled in midfield: shkn up and effrt over 2f out: hanging over 1f out: styd on fnl f to take 3rd nr fin* 33/1
6 4 1 ¼ **Flintlock (IRE)**[14] 3219 2-9-3 0 (b) DavidKinsella 6 68
(J H M Gosden) *chsd ldr to 2f out: hanging u.p: outpcd and no ch after: lost 3rd nr fin* 12/1
5 1 ¾ **Mt Kintyre (IRE)** 2-9-3 0 JimmyQuinn 11 64
(M H Tompkins) *w'like: lw: chsd ldng trio: pushed along and nt on terms fr 3f out: no imp after* 15/2[3]
0 6 2 ½ **Mons Calpe (IRE)**[22] 2972 2-9-3 0 TQuinn 1 58
(P F I Cole) *mostly in same pl and nvr on terms: pushed along fr 3f out and no prog* 33/1
0 7 ½ **Kyle Of Bute**[22] 2972 2-9-3 0 TedDurcan 2 56
(J L Dunlop) *mostly in same pl and nvr on terms: shkn up 2f out: no prog* 50/1
8 1 ½ **Appraisal** 2-9-3 0 DarryllHolland 4 53+
(R Hannon) *w'like: scope: bit bkwd: reluctant to enter stalls: s.v.s: wl bhd in last pair: nvr a factor* 12/1
9 2 ½ **Chiberta King** 2-9-3 0 WilliamBuick 9 46
(A M Balding) *w'like: immediately struggling in last pair: nvr a factor* 25/1
10 3 **Storm Mist (IRE)** 2-9-3 0 JoeFanning 8 39
(P F I Cole) *w'like: leggy: nvr bttr than 7th or 8th and nvr on terms: wknd 2f out* 16/1

1m 29.6s (0.10) **Going Correction** -0.10s/f (Good) 10 Ran SP% **121.5**
Speed ratings (Par 96): **95,85,84,82,80 77,77,75,72,69**
toteswinger: 1&2 £1.60, 1&3 £16.10, 2&3 £26.00. CSF £3.87 TOTE £1.90: £1.20, £1.30, £6.60; EX 4.00.
Owner K Abdulla **Bred** Juddmonte Farms Ltd **Trained** Newmarket, Suffolk

FOCUS
Those with previous form looked nothing special, so this was at the mercy of any half-decent newcomer. The winner looks potentially smart while the runner-up sets the level but the form could prove better than this in time.

NOTEBOOK

Zacinto, whose stable won the corresponding race with its last two runners, looked the part in the preliminaries and, although he was green, won so impressively that he was promoted to favourite for the 2,000 Guineas at just 10-1 with VCbet, and 14-1 elsewhere. The first foal of a dam that was smart at up to a mile, he was never far away as the Gosden pair cut out the running, but showed signs of greenness when pulled to the outside to challenge over a furlong out before powering right away in the manner of a smart prospect. One of the most impressive two-year-old maiden winners seen so far this season at any distance, something like the Champagne Stakes at Goodwood may be a suitable target for connections to aim at. (op Evens tchd 11-10 in places)

Seminole(IRE), wearing blinkers for the first time on only his second start, jumped straight out in front and made the running until outclassed by a highly promising Zacinto. He ought to win a race but has limitations. (op 11-4)

Oasis Knight(IRE), who had been well and truly thrashed on both his previous starts, improved for the stiffer test of stamina, putting in good late work to snatch third. He will find his level in handicaps. (op 50-1)

Flintlock(IRE), who was fitted with headgear after showing only modest promise on his debut, chased his stablemate for much of the race but could not quicken when asked to stay in touch. (op 16-1 tchd 20-1)

Mt Kintyre(IRE) was a springer in the market but never looked like making a successful debut. He must have been showing plenty on the home gallops, as his stable is not renowned for first-time-out juvenile winners. The experience will have done him good and he should be capable of winning a maiden. (op 13-2)

Mons Calpe(IRE) Official explanation: jockey said colt hung right all the way up the straight

Appraisalplayed up a bit before going into the stalls and then took a while to get organised once leaving them. He is one to treat with caution until showing less temperament. Official explanation: jockey said colt missed the break (op 14-1 tchd 16-1)

Chiberta King was very green and never looked like getting involved.

Storm Mist(IRE) is a nice-looking son of Giant's Causeway but, unfortunately, did not show much sparkle on his racecourse debut. (op 25-1)

3683 WILLIAM EWART PROPERTIES GALA STKS (LISTED RACE) 1m 2f 7y
4:00 (4:03) (Class 1) 3-Y-O+

£22,708 (£8,608; £4,308; £2,148; £1,076; £540) Stalls High

Form RPR

0222 1 **Many Volumes (USA)**[14] 3195 4-9-5 109 TedDurcan 10 116
(H R A Cecil) *trckd ldng pair: wnt 2nd 3f out: hrd rdn to ld over 1f out: edgd rt sn after: drvn clr* **9/2**[3]

311 2 3 **Bushman**[36] 2545 4-9-5 105 RichardMullen 6 110+
(D M Simcock) *hld up in last trio: rdn wl over 2f out: styd on fr 2f out: wnt 2nd last 100yds: no ch w wnr* **3/1**[2]

2U10 3 2 1/2 **Kandidate**[78] 1422 6-9-8 110 (t) DarryllHolland 3 108
(C E Brittain) *lw: led: drvn over 2f out: hdd over 1f out: wknd and lost 2nd last 100yds* **10/1**

110- 4 7 **Stage Gift (IRE)**[272] 6032 5-9-5 115 LDettori 5 91
(Saeed Bin Suroor) *t.k.h: hld up in last trio: rdn and nt qckn on outer over 2f out: 3rd briefly over 1f out but wl btn: fin slowly* **7/4**[1]

-545 5 2 3/4 **Tell**[34] 2607 5-9-5 106 KerrinMcEvoy 1 86
(J L Dunlop) *trckd ldr to 3f out: wknd rapidly over 2f out* **16/1**

5/00 6 5 **Fight Club (GER)**[16] 3122 7-9-5 102 (b[1]) PaulMulrennan 7 76
(R Brotherton) *s.i.s: t.k.h: hld up in last trio: wknd wl over 1f out* **66/1**

2m 6.72s (-3.78) **Going Correction** -0.10s/f (Good) **6** Ran SP% **96.0**
Speed ratings (Par 111): **111,108,106,101,98 94**
toteswinger: 1&2 £2.00, 1&3 £3.80, 2&3 £5.30. CSF £12.86 TOTE £5.20: £2.00, £1.80; EX 13.20.
Owner K Abdulla **Bred** Juddmonte Farms Inc **Trained** Newmarket, Suffolk
■ Spanish Moon (4/1) was withdrawn after proving unruly at the satlls. Deduct 20p in the £ under Rule 4).

FOCUS

Four non-runners and perhaps not the strongest of Listed races but the winner has been consistent this season and is probably the best guide to the level, backed up by the second.

NOTEBOOK

Many Volumes(USA), runner-up in five of his previous six starts, deserved a change of luck, and with conditions to suit - 1m2f on fast ground - he chalked up his first win in Pattern company. The form is probably not the most solid for Listed grade, though, and whether he can cut it at Group level remains to be seen. (op 11-2)

Bushman did not run at Royal Ascot because of the fast ground, and conditions here looked far from ideal, but presumably connections had decided they wanted him to run and he was allowed to take his chance. In the event he ran a terrific race despite never looking comfortable on the ground, and he can certainly win at this level when getting some dig. The Group 3 Strensall Stakes at York is apparently his next target. (op 4-1 tchd 9-2)

Kandidate, who won this race in 2006, had to give 3lb to the rest and he was returning from an enforced rest as a result of pulling a muscle. In the circumstances it was a solid effort. (op 14-1)

Stage Gift(IRE), who looked fit for this seasonal return, won two Group races last term but escaped a penalty. He was the highest-rated horse in the field but appeared to blow up on this seasonal return having threatened to challenge inside the final furlong and a half. A bit of give in the ground suits this son of Cadeaux Genereux best. (tchd 13-8 and 15-8 in places)

Tell, who is a difficult horse to place, was missing the usual blinkers. He has never convinced over this distance before and once again he patently failed to stay. (tchd 20-1)

Fight Club(GER) raced keenly in the first-time blinkers. He is another whose mark makes him difficult to place.

3684 HELICAL BAR H'CAP 1m 2f 7y
4:35 (4:37) (Class 2) (0-100,97) 3-Y-O+

£12,462 (£3,732; £1,866; £934; £466; £234) Stalls High

Form RPR

1-22 1 **Kaateb (IRE)**[12] 3294 5-9-4 87 (v[1]) RHills 7 101+
(W J Haggas) *lw: mde most: steadily increased tempo fr 3f out: clr and in command fr 2f out: rdn out* **4/1**[1]

-000 2 1 1/4 **Gulf Express (USA)**[13] 3249 4-9-13 96 (v[1]) RyanMoore 6 106+
(Sir Michael Stoute) *lw: hld up in rr early: sn in 5th or 6th: drvn on outer over 2f out: prog over 1f out: styd on to take 2nd last 75yds: wnr already home* **7/1**[3]

111- 3 1 1/2 **Caravel (IRE)**[284] 5696 4-9-8 91 PaulMulrennan 1 98
(Sir Mark Prescott) *reluctant to enter stalls: trckd ldng pair: rdn over 2f out: chsd wnr wl over 1f out: no real imp on wnr: lost 2nd last 75yds* **9/2**[2]

2125 4 1 1/2 **Jeer (IRE)**[20] 3045 4-9-9 92 JimmyFortune 2 96
(E A L Dunlop) *hld up in 5th or 6th: drvn over 2f out: tried to cl over 1f out: kpt on one pce fnl f* **12/1**

3-00 5 1 1/4 **Humungous (IRE)**[16] 3122 5-10-0 97 (p) KerrinMcEvoy 10 99
(C R Egerton) *t.k.h: hld up in 7th or 8th: rdn over 2f out: kpt on fr over 1f out: no ch to chal* **9/1**

0646 6 1 1/4 **Snoqualmie Boy**[39] 2465 5-9-11 94 LDettori 8 93
(Jane Chapple-Hyam) *trckd ldng pair: rdn over 2f out: disp 2nd over 1f out: no imp: one pce fnl f* **15/2**

0302 7 3/4 **Troubadour (IRE)**[65] 1724 7-9-7 90 (b) TedDurcan 12 88
(W Jarvis) *hld up in 9th: outpcd fr 3f out: reminders over 1f out: styd on fnl f but no ch: nvr nrr* **33/1**

2545 8 1 **Drill Sergeant**[15] 3157 3-9-0 94 JoeFanning 3 90
(M Johnston) *chsd wnr: drvn over 2f out: lost 2nd wl over 1f out: wknd fnl f* **9/2**[2]

5111 9 5 **Art Man**[36] 2531 5-9-6 89 GeorgeBaker 11 75
(G L Moore) *hld up in 10th: rdn 3f out: sn struggling and btn* **9/1**

0100 10 1 **Capable Guest (IRE)**[13] 3249 6-9-12 95 (v) DarryllHolland 9 79
(M R Channon) *dropped in last: rdn and detached 3f out: no ch after* **20/1**

-133 11 6 **Cactus King**[29] 2762 5-8-12 81 IanMongan 4 53
(P M Phelan) *t.k.h: hld up in 7th or 8th: rdn 3f out: sn wknd* **16/1**

2m 8.78s (-1.72) **Going Correction** -0.10s/f (Good)
WFA 3 from 4yo+ 11lb **11** Ran SP% **121.9**
Speed ratings (Par 109): **102,101,99,98,97 96,96,95,91,90 85**
toteswinger: 1&2 £6.20, 1&3 £4.40, 2&3 £9.00. CSF £33.48 CT £134.81 TOTE £4.20: £1.60, £3.20, £2.50; EX 28.30.
Owner Hamdan Al Maktoum **Bred** Shadwell Estate Company Limited **Trained** Newmarket, Suffolk

FOCUS

A decent handicap and a triumph for headgear, with the first two both wearing a visor for the first time.

NOTEBOOK

Kaateb(IRE), a beaten favourite in his last two starts, had a visor on for the first time and different tactics were employed, with Hills setting out to make all on this son of Alhaarth. He hugged the rail throughout and did what he does well, which is ride a good front-running race, but in truth he was probably on the best horse in the race anyway and this lightly raced five-year-old looks progressive. (op 7-2)

Gulf Express(USA), also visored for the first time, stayed on well down the outside without ever threatening to get to the winner. He remains on a stiff enough mark. (op 11-2)

Caravel(IRE), who racked up a five-timer last year, did not look too badly treated on this belated seasonal reappearance. He looked fit for this seasonal return, but ran well and should be a threat in similar company next time. (op 7-2)

Jeer(IRE) had conditions to suit but he is now on a mark 7lb higher than for his last win and he simply looks held. (op 16-1)

Humungous(IRE) remains difficult to place off his current mark despite having been dropped 7lb since August last year. (op 11-1 tchd 12-1)

Snoqualmie Boy, who has dropped 8lb since the beginning of the year, was clipped in from double-figure prices, but he failed to justify the support. It is over two years since he last won a race. (op 10-1)

Drill Sergeant, the only three-year-old in the field, was denied the lead by the eventual winner and was easily seen off in the closing stages. Softer ground probably suits him best, although his stable is struggling for winners at the moment. (op 8-1)

Art Man, a winner of five races on Polytrack earlier this year, failed to translate that form to fast turf. Perhaps he is simply an All-Weather specialist, but he is worth giving another chance to on easier ground. Official explanation: jockey said gelding was unsuited to the good to firm, firm in places ground (op 8-1 tchd 7-1)

3685 BEE BEE DEVELOPMENTS H'CAP 1m 6f
5:05 (5:07) (Class 4) (0-85,85) 3-Y-O+ £6,476 (£1,927; £963; £481) Stalls High

Form RPR

1506 1 **Judgethemoment (USA)**[14] 3196 3-8-13 85 LDettori 4 91
(Jane Chapple-Hyam) *led: kicked on over 3f out: jnd ins fnl f and edgd rt briefly: hld on gamely nr fin* **7/2**[3]

2122 2 hd **Spring Dream (IRE)**[23] 2952 5-9-2 73 JimmyFortune 10 79+
(A King) *trckd ldng trio: gng wl whn pce lifted 3f out: prog on inner to go 2nd over 1f out: jnd wnr but making hrd work of it whn bmpd 100yds out: jst hld after* **3/1**[2]

0430 3 1/2 **Swingkeel (IRE)**[21] 2997 3-8-2 74 DavidKinsella 5 79
(J L Dunlop) *lw: trckd ldng pair: rdn 3f out: styd chsng and cl up fr 2f out: kpt on wl fnl f: a jst hld* **7/1**

2621 4 1/2 **Alnwick**[15] 3179 4-9-0 71 DaneO'Neill 8 75
(P D Cundell) *chsd wnr: drvn 3f out: lost 2nd over 1f out but stl cl up: kpt on u.p fnl f: a jst hld* **11/4**[1]

3355 5 5 **Abounding**[11] 3321 4-8-9 66 oh2 WilliamBuick 1 63
(M J Attwater) *hld up in 5th: drvn 3f out: threatened to cl briefly over 1f out: nt look keen and sn btn* **14/1**

-050 6 3 1/4 **Optimus (USA)**[5] 3523 6-9-8 79 TQuinn 2 72
(B G Powell) *hld up in 6th: rdn 3f out: no rspnse and sn lft trailing* **16/1**

604- 7 1 1/2 **Simba Sun (IRE)**[152] 5870 4-9-7 78 DarryllHolland 3 69
(A King) *dwlt: hld up in detached last: rdn and no rspnse over 3f out: bhd after* **11/2**

3m 3.41s (-3.19) **Going Correction** -0.10s/f (Good)
WFA 3 from 4yo+ 15lb **7** Ran SP% **114.3**
Speed ratings (Par 105): **105,104,104,104,101 99,98**
toteswinger: 1&2 £2.80, 1&3 £6.20, 2&3 £4.00. CSF £14.44 CT £68.08 TOTE £5.30: £2.30, £1.60; EX 16.00 Place 6 £47.01, Place 5 £12.93.
Owner Gordon Li **Bred** Todd Graves & Michele Graves **Trained** Lambourn, Berks
■ Stewards' Enquiry : L Dettori three-day ban: careless riding (Jul 18-20)

FOCUS

Just a fair handicap, and a somewhat controversial finish, with the first past the post keeping the race in the Stewards' room despite causing interference to the second, who was only narrowly beaten. The form is rated around those in the frame behind the winner but is not totally convincing.
T/Jkpt: Not won. T/Plt: £30.90 to a £1 stake. Pool: £113,105.26. 2,669.35 winning tickets.
T/Qpdt: £5.00 to a £1 stake. Pool: £5,775.00. 848.70 winning tickets. JN

2865 SOUTHWELL (L-H)

Friday, July 4

OFFICIAL GOING: Standard to slow

Wind: Light, across Weather: Fine and sunny

3686 CARTWRIGHT KING H'CAP 5f (F)
2:30 (2:30) (Class 6) (0-65,63) 3-Y-O £1,978 (£584; £292) Stalls High

Form RPR

0-05 1 **Mr Funshine**[28] 2771 3-8-4 51 ow1 JackMitchell(5) 1 62
(Mrs P N Dutfield) *chsd ldr: led over 1f out: edgd rt ins fnl f: rdn out* **33/1**

4530 2 3 **Mac Dalia**[7] 3455 3-9-4 60 (p) SebSanders 3 60
(A J McCabe) *led over 3f: no ex ins fnl f* **9/2**[2]

00-3 3 hd **Carmine Rock**[67] 1674 3-8-7 52 RussellKennemore(3) 5 51
(R Hollinshead) *edgd rt s: sn chsng ldrs: rdn 1/2-way: styd on same pce fnl f* **4/1**[1]

4651 4 2 **Mujahope**[2] 3600 3-8-13 55 6ex (v) AndrewElliott 13 47+
(C J Teague) *s.s: outpcd: r.o ins fnl f: nrst fin* **5/1**[3]

4-50 5 1/2 **Westwood Dawn**[54] 1743 3-8-0 45 LukeMorris(3) 4 35
(Mrs N Macauley) *mid-div: hdwy u.p over 1f out: nt trble ldrs* **40/1**

The Form Book, Raceform Ltd, Compton, RG20 6NL

0500 **6** *4* **Acclimate**[28] 2774 3-8-13 **55** ... FergusSweeney 14 31
(W S Kittow) *mid-div: sn drvn along: n.d* **11/1**

4340 **7** *2* **Note Perfect**[31] 2704 3-8-8 **50** ...(b) DaleGibson 11 19
(M W Easterby) *chsd ldrs to 1/2-way* **10/1**

0000 **8** *½* **Santa Clara**[7] 3446 3-8-13 **55** ... NCallan 2 22
(P Leech) *dwlt: outpcd* **22/1**

050 **9** *½* **Wicksy Creek**[17] 3118 3-8-1 **48** ow3 ... PatrickDonaghy(5) 8 13
(G C H Chung) *s.i.s: outpcd* **33/1**

2-05 **10** *½* **Mystickhill (IRE)**[11] 3332 3-9-5 **61** ...(t) PatrickMathers 9 24
(J Balding) *chsd ldrs 3f* **10/1**

0060 **11** *½* **Abitofafath (IRE)**[13] 3283 3-9-2 **58** ...(b) TPQueally 12 20
(J G Given) *s.s: outpcd* **33/1**

0000 **12** *nk* **Lady Aviator**[23] 2928 3-8-0 **45** ... DuranFentiman(3) 6 —
(T D Easterby) *s.i.s and hmpd s: outpcd* **40/1**

4004 **13** *19* **Jalons Bridewell**[11] 3332 3-9-7 **63** ... FrancisNorton 10 —
(M Quinn) *chsd ldrs: rdn 1/2-way: sn hung lft and wknd* **5/1**[3]

61.73 secs (2.03) **Going Correction** +0.375s/f (Slow) 13 Ran SP% **116.1**
Speed ratings (Par 98): **98,93,92,89,88 82,79,78,77,76 76,75,45**
toteswinger: 1&2 £9.60, 1&3 £49.30, 2&3 £3.00. CSF £164.30 CT £605.50 TOTE £27.60: £4.40, £1.70, £1.80; EX 76.00 Trifecta £295.60 Part won. Pool: £399.59 - 0.20 winning tickets..
Owner Unity Farm Holiday Centre Ltd **Bred** Unity Farm Holiday Centre Ltd **Trained** Axmouth, Devon

FOCUS
A moderate sprint handicap and the draw played its part with the first three coming from the five lowest stalls. Very few ever got into it. The form looks pretty sound.
Jalons Bridewell Official explanation: jockey said colt never travelled

3687 LINCOLNSHIRE DEVELOPMENTS LTD CLAIMING STKS 1m 4f (F)
3:00 (3:00) (Class 6) 3-Y-O+ **£1,978** (£584; £292) **Stalls** Low

Form RPR

2551 **1** **Black Falcon (IRE)**[10] 3335 8-9-5 70 ... NCallan 14 63
(John A Harris) *a.p: led over 2f out: rdn and hung lft fr over 1f out: styd on* **11/8**[1]

040 **2** *2¾* **Persistent (IRE)**[42] 2367 3-8-5 55 ... DO'Donohoe 3 58
(P T Midgley) *trckd ldrs: ev ch 2f out: sn rdn: no ex fnl f* **20/1**

600- **3** *2½* **North Walk (IRE)**[16] 3922 5-9-4 57 ...(b) FrancisNorton 10 54
(Jennie Candlish) *sn led: rdn and hdd over 2f out: styd on same pce appr fnl f* **28/1**

0304 **4** *nk* **Starcross Maid**[26] 2867 6-8-9 51 ... MarkCoumbe(5) 13 50
(J F Coupland) *s.i.s: hld up: hdwy and n.m.r over 3f out: rdn over 2f out: no ex fnl f* **14/1**

0210 **5** *2½* **Nimello (USA)**[31] 2707 12-9-3 58 ... FergusSweeney 12 49
(A G Newcombe) *hld up: hdwy and edgd lft over 3f out: sn rdn: wknd fnl f* **8/1**

3551 **6** *4* **Shandelight (IRE)**[33] 2641 4-9-5 60 ...(p) RoystonFfrench 9 44
(Mrs A Duffield) *prom: chsd ldr over 4f out: rdn and wknd 2f out* **4/1**[2]

2300 **7** *½* **Matinee Idol**[73] 1551 5-8-11 38 ...(b) PJMcDonald(3) 7 38
(Mrs S Lamyman) *hld up: hdwy whn hmpd 3f out: nt rcvr* **66/1**

0060 **8** *9* **Toon Army**[13] 3264 3-7-10 40 ...(bt[1]) DominicFox(3) 2 22
(Miss D Mountain) *bhd fr 1/2-way* **100/1**

0 **9** *2* **Brathay (IRE)**[28] 2779 4-9-8 0 ... TPQueally 4 29
(M H Tompkins) *hld up: pushed along 8f out: bhd fr 1/2-way* **50/1**

-000 **10** *2* **Sibo Baggins (IRE)**[17] 3113 4-8-11 42 ... AmyBaker(7) 5 22
(Mrs C A Dunnett) *chsd ldr tl rdn over 4f out: edgd lft and wknd 3f out* **66/1**

1322 **11** *34* **Turner's Touch**[72] 1564 6-9-5 73 ...(b) JemmaMarshall(7) 8 —
(G L Moore) *s.i.s: hld up: a in rr: wknd 4f out: eased fnl f* **15/2**[3]

1402 **12** *2* **Paul The Carpet (UAE)**[66] 1710 3-8-13 49 ... SebSanders 1 —
(G L Moore) *stmbld s: plld hrd and prom: hmpd after 1f: sn lost pl: rdn and wknd wl over 4f out: eased fnl 2f* **8/1**

2m 44.39s (3.39) **Going Correction** +0.275s/f (Slow)
WFA 3 from 4yo+ 13lb 12 Ran SP% **116.9**
Speed ratings (Par 101): **99,97,95,95,93 90,90,84,83,81 59,57**
toteswinger: 1&2 £45.10, 1&3 £3.70, 2&3 Not won. CSF £37.56 TOTE £2.40: £1.30, £5.00, £5.60; EX 52.70 Trifecta £199.00 Part won. Pool: £269.02 - 0.10 winning tickets..Persistent was claimed by M. J. Gingell for £6,000.
Owner Shaun Taylor **Bred** Gainsborough Stud Management Ltd **Trained** Eastwell, Leics
■ Stewards' Enquiry : Francis Norton four-day ban: careless riding (Jul 18-21)

FOCUS
A typical Fibresand claimer and a wide range of abilities. As in the opener, not that many ever got competitive and it paid to race handily. The form is sound.

3688 JACKIE & JEANETTE MAIDEN STKS 1m 4f (F)
3:35 (3:35) (Class 5) 3-Y-O+ **£2,729** (£806; £403) **Stalls** Low

Form RPR

52-3 **1** **Altitude**[14] 3227 3-8-9 75 ... SebSanders 14 78
(Sir Mark Prescott) *chsd ldrs: led over 2f out: sn rdn: styd on u.p* **15/8**[1]

003- **2** *1* **Starfala**[314] 4796 3-8-9 77 ... NCallan 3 76
(P F I Cole) *a.p: rdn over 2f out: hung rt fr over 1f out: styd on* **13/2**[3]

02 **3** *¾* **Lemonesse (USA)**[15] 3168 3-8-9 0 ... TPQueally 9 75
(H R A Cecil) *led after 1f: rdn and hdd over 2f out: styd on same pce towards fin* **8/1**

34-3 **4** *12* **Blue Citadel (USA)**[32] 2669 3-9-0 79 ... JimCrowley 7 61
(Mrs A J Perrett) *prom: reminders sn after s: rdn over 4f out: wknd 3f out* **2/1**[2]

0 **5** *¾* **Winners Chant (IRE)**[30] 2717 3-8-4 0 ow2 ... JPHamblett(7) 4 57+
(Sir Michael Stoute) *prom: hmpd over 8f out: lost pl over 5f out: n.d after* **16/1**

05 **6** *16* **Ask Nicely**[12] 3297 3-8-9 0 ... DO'Donohoe 1 29
(W R Muir) *led 1f: chsd ldr tl rdn over 3f out: hung rt and wknd over 2f out* **28/1**

7 *13* **Suprendre Espere**[101] 8-9-13 0 ...(t) LiamTreadwell 10 13
(Jennie Candlish) *s.s: outpcd: effrt over 4f out: sn wknd* **66/1**

0 **8** *½* **Red Rock Prince (IRE)**[18] 3094 3-9-0 0 ... NelsonDeSouza 12 13
(P F I Cole) *hld up: plld hrd: hdwy 8f out: rdn over 6f out: wknd over 4f out* **20/1**

9 *1* **Beaujeu (IRE)** 3-9-0 0 ... RoystonFfrench 11 11
(M Johnston) *s.i.s: hdwy over 7f out: rdn 5f out: wknd over 3f out* **14/1**

10 *51* **Alright Chuck** 4-9-13 0 ... SaleemGolam 2 —
(P W Hiatt) *s.s: a in rr: bhd fr 1/2-way* **50/1**

0 **11** *1½* **Munlochy Bay**[20] 3035 4-9-8 0 ... FergusSweeney 8 —
(W S Kittow) *mid-div: edgd lft over 9f out: bhd fnl 5f* **66/1**

R **12** *11* **Tot Hill**[15] 3168 5-9-5 0 ... LeeVickers(3) 6 —
(C N Kellett) *mid-div: hmpd over 9f out: bhd fr 1/2-way* **100/1**

2m 42.98s (1.98) **Going Correction** +0.275s/f (Slow)
WFA 3 from 4yo+ 13lb 12 Ran SP% **119.3**
Speed ratings (Par 103): **104,103,102,94,94 83,75,74,74,40 39,31**
toteswinger: 1&2 £5.70, 1&3 £2.60, 2&3 £3.00. CSF £14.10 TOTE £3.20: £1.70, £2.70, £2.10; EX 14.70 Trifecta £28.80 Pool: £214.63 - 5.51 winning tickets..
Owner Miss K Rausing **Bred** Miss K Rausing **Trained** Newmarket, Suffolk

FOCUS
Not as competitive a race as the numbers would suggest and the front three proved different class to the others. Ordinary form, rated through the first two. The winning time was creditable enough though when compared to the preceding claimer. Yet again those that raced handily dominated.
Ask Nicely Official explanation: jockey said filly hung right
Munlochy Bay Official explanation: jockey said filly would not face the kickback

3689 C J PETTITT TRANSPORT LTD MEDIAN AUCTION MAIDEN STKS 6f (F)
4:10 (4:11) (Class 6) 2-Y-O **£1,978** (£584; £292) **Stalls** Low

Form RPR

52 **1** **Special Cuvee**[8] 3392 2-9-3 0 ... SebSanders 4 78+
(Sir Mark Prescott) *chsd ldrs: rdn to ld over 1f out: sn hung rt: r.o* **8/15**[1]

2 **2** *1¼* **Red Baron Dancer**[17] 3106 2-9-3 0 ... PatCosgrave 6 74
(J R Boyle) *led: rdn and hdd over 1f out: hung rt and styd on same pce fnl f* **3/1**[2]

002 **3** *5* **Swingfire (USA)**[15] 3158 2-9-0 0 ... TravisBlock(3) 7 59
(R M H Cowell) *sn chsng ldr: rdn over 2f out: wknd fnl f* **10/1**[3]

0 **4** *1¾* **Iliketoboogie**[11] 3331 2-8-12 0 ... TPQueally 11 49
(A J McCabe) *chsd ldrs: rdn over 2f out: hung lft and wknd over 1f out* **25/1**

55 **5** *1¼* **Miss Moloney (IRE)**[16] 3140 2-8-9 0 ... PJMcDonald(3) 1 45
(Mrs S Lamyman) *hld up: nt clr run over 4f out: hmpd over 3f out: nvr trbld ldrs* **33/1**

6 *1* **Coniston Wood** 2-8-5 0 ... BradleyRoper(7) 12 42
(M W Easterby) *sn pushed along in rr: hdwy 1/2-way: rdn over 2f out: sn wknd* **66/1**

7 *1½* **Manhattan Sunrise (USA)** 2-8-12 0 ... PaulEddery 9 38
(G D Blake) *mid-div: sn drvn along: wknd over 2f out* **12/1**

8 *¾* **Fawaz** 2-9-3 0 ... DMylonas 10 41
(Mrs C A Dunnett) *sn pushed along and prom: edgd lft over 4f out and over 3f out: sn wknd* **66/1**

00 **9** *nk* **Senora Verde**[12] 3292 2-8-9 0 ... JamieMoriarty(3) 2 35
(P T Midgley) *hld up in tch: racd keenly: wkng whn hung lft over 2f out* **100/1**

10 *1¾* **Curtain Up** 2-9-3 0 ... DaleGibson 8 34
(M W Easterby) *s.s: outpcd* **40/1**

0 **11** *3¼* **Moroccan Party**[24] 2909 2-8-10 0 ... NSLawes(7) 5 25
(M W Easterby) *sn outpcd* **80/1**

12 *6* **Hark Forrard** 2-9-0 0 ... MarcHalford(3) 3 —
(Miss J E Foster) *s.s: outpcd* **80/1**

1m 19.11s (2.61) **Going Correction** +0.275s/f (Slow) 12 Ran SP% **122.7**
Speed ratings (Par 92): **93,91,84,82,80 79,77,76,75,73 69,61**
toteswinger: 1&2 £1.30, 1&3 £1.10, 2&3 £5.30. CSF £2.28 TOTE £1.70: £1.02, £1.30, £2.10; EX 2.60 Trifecta £12.30 Pool: £422.81 - 25.26 winning tickets..
Owner John Brown & Megan Dennis **Bred** John Brown & Megan Dennis **Trained** Newmarket, Suffolk
■ Stewards' Enquiry : D Mylonas two-day ban: careless riding (Jul 18,19)

FOCUS
Another uncompetitive maiden and they finished very much as the market would have suggested. Yet again it was crucial to race close to the pace. The first two finished clear and the form is solid.

NOTEBOOK
Special Cuvee, who showed improved form at Great Leighs last time, was always in a great position and found plenty when asked to pick up the leader. He is bred to get another furlong and the way he won this suggested he should, so he may well be able to find an opportunity in a nursery. (op 8-11 tchd 4-5 in a place)
Red Baron Dancer, just pipped on his debut in a Thirsk seller for David Nicholls last month, ran a decent race from the front and although unable to cope with the winner still pulled nicely clear of the others. He was suited by the way the track was riding, but should still be able to find a small race. (op 5-2)
Swingfire(USA), runner-up in a weak-looking Great Leighs maiden on his third start last month, showed up for a long way but was firmly put in his place by the front pair and may need a drop in class if he is to break his duck. (op 17-2)
Iliketoboogie ran a bit better than on her Wolverhampton debut having been ridden much more prominently this time. She could improve further, but will need to. (op 20-1)
Miss Moloney(IRE) ran a bit better than her finishing position might suggest having met trouble in running. She only cost 800gns and has already shown enough to suggests she can recoup that.

3690 ROSEMARY HERON MEMORIAL H'CAP 1m (F)
4:45 (4:45) (Class 6) (0-65,65) 3-Y-O **£1,978** (£584; £292) **Stalls** Low

Form RPR

6053 **1** **Mr Fantozzi (IRE)**[22] 2982 3-9-0 **58** ...(b) SaleemGolam 3 66
(Miss J Feilden) *led 7f out: rdn clr fr over 2f out: all out* **6/1**

6-60 **2** *2¼* **Highland Homestead**[67] 1685 3-9-0 **61** ... PJMcDonald(3) 6 64+
(B R Millman) *sn outpcd: hdwy u.p fr over 1f out: styd on wl towards fin: nt rch wnr* **11/2**[3]

5355 **3** *8* **Double On Red**[42] 2376 3-8-11 **58** ...(b) LukeMorris(3) 8 42
(J M P Eustace) *prom: chsd wnr 5f out: rdn and edgd lft over 2f out: wknd fnl f* **9/2**[1]

0600 **4** *2½* **Reprieved**[14] 3221 3-8-8 **52** ... J-PGuillambert 9 31
(M C Chapman) *prom: rdn 1/2-way: wknd over 2f out* **12/1**

0-30 **5** *2¼* **Little Toto**[86] 1274 3-8-13 **62** ... JackMitchell(5) 7 36
(C G Cox) *chsd ldrs: lost pl 5f out: n.d after* **5/1**[2]

-563 **6** *3* **Ride A White Swan**[14] 3213 3-9-4 **62** ...(p) AndrewElliott 1 29
(K R Burke) *s.i.s: hdwy over 3f out: rdn and wknd 2f out* **7/1**

0000 **7** *nk* **So Sublime**[36] 2552 3-8-13 **60** ... LeeVickers(3) 5 26
(M C Chapman) *sn pushed along and prom: lost pl 6f out: n.d after* **25/1**

60-6 **8** *1½* **Sheik'N'Knotsterd**[23] 2929 3-8-13 **57** ... TPQueally 13 19
(J F Coupland) *led 1f: rdn and wknd 3f out* **22/1**

-640 **9** *7* **Spectrana**[11] 3322 3-9-4 **62** ...(b) JimCrowley 14 8
(Mrs A J Perrett) *hld up: rdn 1/2-way: sn wknd* **16/1**

-U00 **10** *20* **Miss Olivia**[36] 2549 3-8-3 **47** ... DO'Donohoe 10 —
(Ollie Pears) *sn outpcd* **20/1**

655 **11** *nk* **Cheeky Chilli**[28] 2786 3-9-7 **65** ... SebSanders 12 —
(A J McCabe) *prom 5f* **15/2**

0-06 12 8 **L'Art Du Silence (IRE)**[37] 2506 3-9-4 62......................(p) PatCosgrave 2 —
(J R Boyle) *sn outpcd* **10/1**

1m 48.26s (4.56) **Going Correction** +0.275s/f (Slow) **12** Ran SP% **124.4**
Speed ratings (Par 98): **88,85,77,75,73 70,69,68,61,41 40,32**
toteswinger: 1&2 £5.60, 1&3 £17.50, 2&3 £8.50. CSF £39.99 CT £168.57 TOTE £7.90: £2.80, £2.60, £2.40; EX 68.10 Trifecta £280.00 Part won. Pool: £378.39 - 0.20 winning tickets..
Owner Mrs Rita Cioffi **Bred** David Commins **Trained** Exning, Suffolk

FOCUS
A competitive handicap judged on the numbers, but yet again very few got into it and the very slow winning time puts a big question mark against the form. The first two came clear but the form is probably very ordinary.
Sheik'N'Knotsterd Official explanation: jockey said gelding had no more to give
Cheeky Chilli Official explanation: jockey said filly was enver travelling

3691 SHADES SCREEN PRINT LTD H'CAP — 7f (F)
5:15 (5:16) (Class 5) (0-70,70) 3-Y-0+ **£2,729** (£806; £403) **Stalls** Low

Form RPR

4462 1 **My Mentor (IRE)**[20] 3036 4-9-10 66......................(b) SebSanders 3 80
(Sir Mark Prescott) *hld up: hdwy 1/2-way: rdn to chse ldr over 1f out: led ins fnl f: styd on u.p* **4/1**[1]

6421 2 3 **Elusive Warrior (USA)**[26] 2866 5-9-10 66......................(p) TPQueally 5 71
(A J McCabe) *sn led: clr over 2f out: rdn over 1f out: hdd and unable qck ins fnl f* **8/1**

0000 3 4 **Autograph Hunter**[23] 2949 4-8-9 51 oh6...................... PatrickMathers 2 46+
(Peter Grayson) *s.s: outpcd: r.o u.p ins fnl f: nrst fin* **40/1**

-403 4 nk **Sheriff's Silk**[9] 3374 4-9-7 63......................(b) PaulEddery 12 57
(G D Blake) *prom: rdn 1/2-way: wknd over 1f out* **12/1**

-000 5 2 **Megalo Maniac**[31] 2706 5-8-10 55......................(p) JamieMoriarty(3) 11 43
(R A Fahey) *s.i.s: outpcd: hdwy u.p over 1f out: n.d* **7/1**[3]

6600 6 2 **Mister Benji**[7] 3431 9-8-9 51 oh5......................(p) AndrewElliott 8 34
(B P J Baugh) *chsd ldrs: lost pl 4f out: n.d after* **66/1**

256 7 nk **Surwaki (USA)**[36] 2533 6-9-8 64...................... JimCrowley 9 46
(R M H Cowell) *hld up: rdn over 4f out: sn lost pl: n.d after* **13/2**[2]

-341 8 hd **Dancing Deano (IRE)**[31] 2703 6-9-6 65...................... RussellKennemore(3) 6 47
(R Hollinshead) *mid-div: sn pushed along: rdn over 2f out: n.d* **4/1**[1]

0000 9 nse **Government (IRE)**[21] 2703 7-8-9 51 oh6...................... J-PGuillambert 1 33
(M C Chapman) *chsd ldrs: lost pl over 4f out: wknd 1/2-way* **66/1**

2133 10 5 **Young Gladiator (IRE)**[8] 3416 3-9-0 64......................(v[1]) DO'Donohoe 4 32
(Miss J A Camacho) *s.i.s: rdn over 2f out: a in rr* **11/1**

5011 11 3 **Sularno**[15] 3162 4-9-11 70...................... TravisBlock(3) 14 30
(H Morrison) *chsd ldrs over 4f* **4/1**[1]

0000 12 nk **Doctor's Cave**[4] 3567 6-9-7 68......................(b) JackMitchell(5) 13 27
(K O Cunningham-Brown) *sn pushed along and prom: wknd over 2f out* **25/1**

0306 13 12 **Union Jack Jackson (IRE)**[26] 2866 6-8-9 51 oh6.........(b) DaleGibson 7 —
(John A Harris) *chsd ldrs: rdn over 2f out: sn wknd* **33/1**

1m 31.48s (1.18) **Going Correction** +0.275s/f (Slow)
WFA 3 from 4yo+ 8lb **13** Ran SP% **125.2**
Speed ratings (Par 103): **104,100,96,95,93 91,90,90,90,84 81,80,67**
toteswinger: 1&2 £8.00, 1&3 Not won, 2&3 £57.40. CSF £37.72 CT £859.21 TOTE £6.00: £2.30, £2.80, £8.70; EX 43.10 Trifecta £218.30 Part won. Pool: £295.10 - 0.50 winning tickets. Place 6 £23.00, Place 5 £10.81.
Owner Mr And Mrs Arthur Finn **Bred** B D Burnett **Trained** Newmarket, Suffolk

FOCUS
A modest but competitive handicap and with so many pacesetters in the field a strong tempo was always likely. Despite that the winner became the first of the afternoon to win from off the pace. The second is the best guide.
Sularno Official explanation: jockey said gelding had no more to give
T/Plt: £57.80 to a £1 stake. Pool: £61,772.62. 779.80 winning tickets. T/Qpdt: £13.10 to a £1 stake. Pool: £3,323.40. 187.50 winning tickets. CR

3645 WARWICK (L-H)
Friday, July 4

OFFICIAL GOING: Good to firm (good in places)
Wind: Almost nil Weather: Fine

3692 CLEAN EVENT (S) STKS — 1m 2f 188y
2:10 (2:12) (Class 6) 3-Y-0 **£2,047** (£604; £302) **Stalls** Low

Form RPR

3-06 1 **Rampant Ronnie (USA)**[15] 3183 3-8-13 60...................... EddieAhern 6 59
(P W D'Arcy) *hld up in mid-div: hdwy 8f out: wnt 2nd over 3f out: rdn to ld 2f out: sn hung lft: drvn out* **11/10**[1]

01-4 2 3/4 **Berrynarbor**[172] 156 3-8-8 62...................... LPKeniry 13 52
(A G Newcombe) *wnt rt s: t.k.h towards rr: hdwy 4f out: rdn over 1f out: tk 2nd wl ins fnl f: nt rch wnr* **10/1**[3]

0543 3 1 1/4 **Lady Jinks**[13] 3264 3-8-1 43...................... BillyCray(7) 8 50
(M D I Usher) *hld up in tch: rdn over 2f out: kpt on same pce fnl f* **10/1**[3]

2230 4 1/2 **Just Sam (IRE)**[16] 3126 3-8-9 60 ow1...................... DNolan 10 50
(D Carroll) *hld up in mid-div: hdwy over 6f out: rdn and chsd wnr over 1f out: sn edgd lft: no ex wl ins fnl f* **5/2**[2]

0644 5 2 1/2 **Balais Folly (FR)**[13] 3264 3-8-6 47......................(b[1]) AshleyMorgan(7) 3 50
(B Palling) *s.i.s and stmbld: hld up towards rr: hdwy whn nt clr run briefly over 2f out: hung lft fr over 1f out: no imp* **10/1**[3]

0-06 6 11 **Illusionary**[25] 2894 3-8-8 42...................... JackDean(5) 2 30
(J G Portman) *stdd and fly-jmpd leaving stalls: hld up towards rr: nvr nr ldrs* **28/1**

0-00 7 1/2 **Mellifluous (IRE)**[39] 2456 3-8-8 45...................... MichaelHills 12 24
(J W Hills) *led: rdn and hdd 2f out: wknd over 1f out* **40/1**

8 4 **Atteme Bomb** 3-8-8 0...................... JamesDoyle 1 —
(S Curran) *hld up: sn mid-div: rdn over 3f out: sn bhd* **33/1**

-400 9 2 1/2 **Avian Flew**[92] 1169 3-8-1 38...................... StacyRenwick(7) 11 —
(J A Pickering) *prom tl wknd over 4f out* **66/1**

665 10 1 1/4 **Pure Inspiration**[17] 3115 3-8-8 43...................... ShaneKelly 4 —
(P Howling) *chsd ldr tl hung rt bnd over 3f out: wknd over 2f out* **33/1**

2m 20.55s (-0.55) **Going Correction** -0.05s/f (Good) **10** Ran SP% **116.7**
Speed ratings (Par 98): **100,99,98,98,96 88,88,85,83,82**
toteswinger: 1&2 £4.10, 1&3 £3.60, 2&3 £7.30. CSF £13.05 TOTE £2.10: £1.20, £2.40, £1.70; EX 16.80.The winner was bought in for 7,200gns.
Owner R Delnevo **Bred** Jodi Anderson **Trained** Newmarket, Suffolk

FOCUS
A weak seller in which the winner took advantage of the drop in grade. Poor form.
Illusionary Official explanation: jockey said gelding was fly leaping when he left the stalls
Pure Inspiration Official explanation: jockey said filly hung badly right handed on the bends

3693 CLEAN EVENT NOVICE AUCTION STKS — 7f 26y
2:40 (2:44) (Class 5) 2-Y-O **£3,885** (£1,156; £577; £288) **Stalls** Low

Form RPR

231 1 **Lucky Redback (IRE)**[8] 3408 2-9-1 0...................... PatDobbs 2 72+
(R Hannon) *t.k.h: mde all: hung rt fr jst over 1f out: bit slipped through mouth: comf* **1/5**[1]

4 2 2 **Rockinit (IRE)**[10] 3341 2-8-6 0...................... ChrisCatlin 3 52
(M R Channon) *chsd wnr: rdn 2f out: no imp fnl f* **17/2**[2]

006 3 nk **Fasalee (IRE)**[28] 2783 2-8-9 0...................... DarrenWilliams 5 54
(A P Jarvis) *t.k.h in tch: rdn and disp 2nd fnl f: one pce* **33/1**

00 4 10 **Super Fourteen**[25] 2893 2-8-12 0...................... RichardSmith 6 31
(R Hannon) *hld up in tch: pushed along over 3f out: sn bhd* **12/1**[3]

00 5 12 **Free To Choose (IRE)**[28] 2783 2-8-11 0...................... RichardThomas 1 —
(A P Jarvis) *hld up in tch: pushed along over 3f out: wknd wl over 1f out* **33/1**

1m 26.98s (2.38) **Going Correction** -0.05s/f (Good) **5** Ran SP% **107.4**
Speed ratings (Par 94): **84,81,81,69,56**
toteswinger: 1&2 £2.30. CSF £2.30 TOTE £1.20: £1.02, £2.40; EX 2.10.
Owner Amblestock Partnership **Bred** M J Wiley **Trained** East Everleigh, Wilts

FOCUS
A typically small field for one of these novice events. The winner probably did not need to match his best to score.

NOTEBOOK
Lucky Redback(IRE), a free-going sort, confirmed that he is not straightforward and caused the bit to go through his mouth when yet again hanging right. He still did not have too much difficulty in justifying being a red-hot favourite. (op 1-4)
Rockinit(IRE) had to be content to play second fiddle despite the antics of the winner. (op 10-1 tchd 8-1)
Fasalee(IRE) proved difficult to settle over this extra furlong after making the running last time. He just lost out in the battle for second after looking the main threat to the winner turning for home. (op 18-1)

3694 CHURCHILL OFFICE SOLUTIONS LTD MAIDEN STKS — 7f 26y
3:10 (3:12) (Class 5) 3-4-Y-O **£3,238** (£963; £481; £240) **Stalls** Low

Form RPR

06 1 **Nightjar (USA)**[63] 1763 3-9-3 0...................... GregFairley 6 82+
(M Johnston) *hld up towards rr: hdwy 2f out: rdn to ld jst over 1f out: hung rt ins fnl f: r.o wl* **20/1**[3]

20-0 2 5 **Storm Sir (USA)**[34] 2620 3-9-3 78......................(t) JamieSpencer 2 72+
(B J Meehan) *hld up in mid-div: hdwy over 2f out: sn swtchd rt: carried bdly rt over 1f out: r.o to take 2nd wl ins fnl f: no ch w wnr* **3/1**[1]

3- 3 3/4 **Mille Feuille (IRE)**[304] 5110 3-8-12 0...................... JamesDoyle 12 61
(R M Beckett) *a.p: rdn to ld over 1f out: sn swvd rt and hdd: one pce* **3/1**[1]

00-6 4 4 1/2 **Bid To The Beat**[46] 2259 3-9-3 51...................... MickyFenton 11 54
(H J Collingridge) *hld up in tch: lost pl over 3f out: kpt on same pce fnl f* **50/1**

04- 5 1/2 **Cigalas**[296] 5323 3-9-3 0...................... MichaelHills 3 53
(B W Hills) *sn led: hdd over 1f out: sn rdn and hung rt: wknd wl ins fnl f: sddle slipped* **3/1**[1]

420 6 1 1/4 **Marchingontogether (IRE)**[48] 2187 3-8-12 70...................... DNolan 1 44
(D Carroll) *a.p: rdn over 1f out: wknd ins fnl f* **4/1**[2]

00 7 2 **Lekezia (IRE)**[15] 3177 3-8-7 0...................... GabrielHannon(5) 7 39
(J W Hills) *hld up in tch: wknd over 2f out* **66/1**

6-0 8 1 3/4 **Our Dolly**[45] 2269 3-8-12 0...................... SamHitchcott 9 34
(Garry Moss) *hld up: a towards rr* **66/1**

50 9 shd **High Coincidence**[13] 3268 3-9-3 0...................... AlanDaly 10 39
(Andrew Turnell) *dwlt: a in rr* **66/1**

10 1 1/4 **Park Run** 3-8-5 0...................... StacyRenwick(7) 8 31
(A W Carroll) *a in rr* **66/1**

0- 11 7 **Man Appeal**[297] 5313 3-8-12 0...................... NickyMackay 5 12
(B J Meehan) *t.k.h: led early: chsd ldr to 2f out: sn wknd and eased: sddle slipped* **50/1**

1m 24.67s (0.07) **Going Correction** -0.05s/f (Good) **11** Ran SP% **109.7**
Speed ratings (Par 103): **97,91,90,85,84 83,81,79,78,77 69**
toteswinger: 1&2 £9.60, 1&3 £12.40, 2&3 £2.30. CSF £65.83 TOTE £21.50: £3.10, £1.30, £1.50; EX 46.40.
Owner Sheikh Hamdan Bin Mohammed Al Maktoum **Bred** Derry Meeting Farm & London Thoroughbred Services **Trained** Middleham Moor, N Yorks
■ Email was withdrawn after proving unruly at the stalls (9/1, deduct 10p in the £ under Rule 4).

FOCUS
An eventful affair which probably did not take much winning with several horses hanging. The winner showed big improvement but the modest fifth limits the form.
Cigalas Official explanation: jockey said his saddle slipped
Man Appeal Official explanation: jockey said his saddle slipped

3695 WARWICKRACECOURSE.CO.UK FILLIES' H'CAP — 5f 110y
3:45 (3:45) (Class 5) (0-70,69) 3-Y-0+ **£3,885** (£1,156; £577; £288) **Stalls** Centre

Form RPR

-022 1 **Pretty Bonnie**[7] 3441 3-8-0 53...................... NataliaGemelova(5) 11 65
(A E Price) *a.p: rdn to ld over 1f out: edgd rt ins fnl f: r.o wl* **15/2**

1-04 2 2 1/4 **Nomoreblondes**[18] 3080 4-9-11 67......................(p) MickyFenton 6 72
(P T Midgley) *led: rdn and hdd jst over 1f out: r.o one pce* **4/1**[3]

0032 3 1/2 **Cosmic Destiny (IRE)**[3] 3575 6-9-13 69...................... LPKeniry 2 72
(E F Vaughan) *hld up in tch: smooth hdwy over 1f out: rdn and nt qckn ins fnl f* **7/2**[2]

-412 4 nse **Overwing (IRE)**[13] 3260 5-9-12 68...................... EddieAhern 5 71
(R M H Cowell) *a.p: swtchd rt over 1f out: rdn and kpt on same pce fnl f* **3/1**[1]

5000 5 1 1/4 **Lady Fas (IRE)**[2] 3608 5-8-1 50 oh5...................... StacyRenwick(7) 8 49
(A W Carroll) *half-rrd and s.i.s: hld up in rr: c wd elbow over 2f out: r.o ins fnl f: nrst fin* **50/1**

0-00 6 1 1/2 **Safranine (IRE)**[32] 2676 11-8-6 53 oh2 ow3...................... AnnStokell(5) 9 47
(Miss A Stokell) *mid-div: no hdwy fnl 2f* **25/1**

0010 7 1 1/2 **Metal Guru**[13] 3260 4-9-8 64......................(p) SteveDrowne 4 53
(R Hollinshead) *hld up towards rr: rdn and hdwy on ins 2f out: wknd ins fnl f* **11/2**

0400 8 1 1/4 **Planet Paradise (IRE)**[11] 3332 3-8-2 50 oh5...................... AdrianMcCarthy 7 34
(D Shaw) *s.i.s: rdn over 1f out: a towards rr* **50/1**

50/0 9 1 **Namu**[13] 3260 5-9-4 60...................... ChrisCatlin 1 41
(Miss T Spearing) *sat down as stalls opened and s.s: sn outpcd: eased whn no ch ins fnl f* **20/1**

5-03 **10** *6* **Sofinella (IRE)**[52] 2088 5-9-1 **57**........................ CatherineGannon 3 18
(A W Carroll) *w ldr tl rdn wl over 1f out: sn wknd* **12/1**
65.47 secs (-0.43) **Going Correction** -0.05s/f (Good)
WFA 3 from 4yo+ 5lb **10** Ran SP% **114.6**
Speed ratings (Par 100): **100,97,96,96,94 92,90,88,87,79**
toteswinger: 1&2 £5.80, 1&3 £5.70, 2&3 £3.40. CSF £35.59 CT £126.68 TOTE £10.60: £2.50, £1.60, £1.70; EX 34.10.
Owner N Field **Bred** P And Mrs A G Venner & Alpha Bloodstock Ltd **Trained** Leominster, H'fords
FOCUS
There were several front-runners in this ordinary handicap. Modest fillies' form, limited by the fifth.
Namu Official explanation: jockey said his saddle slipped

3696 NEW TICKET HOTLINE ON 08445793013 H'CAP 6f
4:20 (4:20) (Class 4) (0-80,80) 3-Y-0 **£7,123** (£2,119; £1,059; £529) **Stalls** Centre

Form RPR
-005 **1** **Masada (IRE)**[21] 2998 3-9-7 **80**........................ JamieSpencer 6 90
(B J Meehan) *hld up in rr: swtchd lft and hdwy on ins over 1f out: hrd rdn and edgd rt ins fnl f: led last strides* **3/1**[2]
2-35 **2** *shd* **Oarsman**[73] 1535 3-8-12 **71**........................ SteveDrowne 3 81
(R Charlton) *hld up: hdwy on outside to ld jst over 1f out: hrd rdn ins fnl f: hdd last strides* **9/4**[1]
2216 **3** *1 1/4* **San Jose City (IRE)**[13] 3263 3-9-7 **80**........................ DNolan 1 86
(D Carroll) *hld up in tch: rdn to ld over 1f out: sn edgd rt and hdd: nt qckn wl ins fnl f* **6/1**
2006 **4** *2* **Bosun Breese**[13] 3273 3-9-5 **78**........................ EddieAhern 4 80+
(P W D'Arcy) *led: rdn and hdd over 1f out: sn bmpd and carried rt: no ex ins fnl f* **7/1**
0-00 **5** *3 1/2* **Meridian Line (IRE)**[28] 2773 3-8-13 **77**........................ JackDean(5) 8 65
(J G Portman) *prom: wknd fnl f* **22/1**
1022 **6** *shd* **Lieutenant Pigeon**[16] 3136 3-8-10 **76**........................ WilliamCarson(7) 7 64
(G D Blake) *prom: rdn over 2f out: wknd fnl f* **4/1**[3]
20-0 **7** *23* **The Real Guru**[78] 1426 3-8-11 **70**........................ ChrisCatlin 5 —
(Miss Tor Sturgis) *prom 3f* **22/1**
1m 11.08s (-0.72) **Going Correction** -0.05s/f (Good) course record **7** Ran SP% **111.3**
Speed ratings (Par 102): **102,101,100,97,92 92,62**
toteswinger: 1&2 £2.20, 1&3 £3.60, 2&3 £2.80. CSF £9.60 CT £34.48 TOTE £3.90: £2.30, £1.70; EX 5.60.
Owner Ballymacoll Stud **Bred** Ballymacoll Stud Farm Ltd **Trained** Manton, Wilts
■ Stewards' Enquiry : Steve Drowne one-day ban: used whip with excessive frequency (Jul 18)
FOCUS
A decent handicap. This was the only race of the day to beat the standard time and the form looks pretty sound.

3697 TURFTV H'CAP 1m 6f 213y
4:55 (4:55) (Class 5) (0-75,78) 3-Y-0+ **£3,885** (£1,156; £577; £288) **Stalls** Low

Form RPR
4231 **1** **Tasheba**[8] 3393 3-9-0 **78** 6ex........................ SteveDrowne 5 88
(P W Chapple-Hyam) *hld up in tch: wnt 2nd over 8f out: led wl over 1f out: rdn clr ent fnl f: comf* **4/6**[1]
0004 **2** *4 1/2* **Cossack Prince**[8] 3421 3-8-2 **66**........................ NickyMackay 8 70
(B J Meehan) *hdwy to ld over 10f out: rdn and hdd wl over 1f out: one pce* **17/2**
415 **3** *4 1/2* **Lapina (IRE)**[13] 3276 4-9-3 **64**........................(b) ShaneKelly 3 62
(Pat Eddery) *dropped out s: hdwy over 7f out: rdn wl over 1f out: nt run on fnl f* **8/1**[3]
-604 **4** *1 3/4* **Archimboldo (USA)**[5] 1408 5-8-12 **59**........................(b) GregFairley 1 55
(T Wall) *s.i.s: sn prom: lost pl over 6f out: n.d after* **25/1**
0065 **5** *1/2* **Teen Spirit (IRE)**[21] 2997 3-7-12 **62** oh6........................ AdrianMcCarthy 2 57
(J W Hills) *led: hdd over 10f out: chsd ldr tl over 8f out: rdn 6f out: wknd over 2f out* **10/1**
42-4 **6** *3 1/2* **Estate**[12] 3296 6-10-0 **75**........................ ChrisCatlin 9 66
(E J O'Neill) *hld up: hdwy over 7f out: pushed along over 3f out: wknd over 2f out* **5/1**[2]
-030 **7** *38* **Sister Agnes (IRE)**[30] 1856 4-8-13 **60**........................(v) MickyFenton 4 1
(M F Harris) *chsd ldr 3f: sn dropped to rr: struggling 2f out: eased whn no ch ins fnl f* **50/1**
3m 15.68s (-3.32) **Going Correction** -0.05s/f (Good)
WFA 3 from 4yo+ 17lb **7** Ran SP% **113.2**
Speed ratings (Par 103): **106,103,101,100,100 98,77**
toteswinger: 1&2 £2.40, 1&3 £2.30, 2&3 £4.80. CSF £7.15 CT £25.25 TOTE £1.70: £1.20, £3.10; EX 8.10.
Owner Terry Benson **Bred** C R Mason **Trained** Newmarket, Suffolk
FOCUS
An uncompetitive modest staying handicap. The winner was well-in and the second ran to form.

3698 RACING UK APPRENTICE H'CAP 1m 4f 134y
5:25 (5:25) (Class 6) (0-60,59) 4-Y-0+ **£2,047** (£604; £302) **Stalls** Low

Form RPR
0546 **1** **Opera Writer (IRE)**[18] 3084 5-9-1 **55**........................(p) SoniaEaton 10 61
(R Hollinshead) *a.p: led over 3f out: rdn out* **7/1**[3]
4000 **2** *1* **Sky Chart (IRE)**[19] 3059 4-8-4 **47**........................ SimonPearce(3) 13 51
(N J Vaughan) *plld hrd: hdwy after 2f: rdn over 1f out: wnt 2nd wl ins fnl f: nt trble wnr* **6/1**[2]
4433 **3** *1/2* **Barbirolli**[18] 3084 6-8-13 **53**........................ RossAtkinson 8 56
(W M Brisbourne) *hld up towards rr: hdwy over 3f out: rdn 1f out: kpt on one pce* **7/2**[1]
0000 **4** *1 1/2* **The Grey One (IRE)**[9] 3361 5-8-6 **46**........................(p) BillyCray 2 47+
(J M Bradley) *s.i.s: hld up and bhd: c wd st: hdwy on outside over 1f out: rdn and one pce ins fnl f* **11/1**
0360 **5** *hd* **Trysting Grove (IRE)**[23] 2949 7-9-0 **54**........................ AshleyMorgan 4 55
(E G Bevan) *hld up in mid-div: hdwy on ins over 7f out: wnt 2nd over 2f out: rdn wl over 1f out: fdd wl ins fnl f* **11/1**
0-00 **6** *4 1/2* **Orphina (IRE)**[27] 1643 5-8-1 **46** ow1........................(t) PaulPickard(5) 12 40
(B G Powell) *bhd: sn pushed along: hdwy on ins over 4f out: rdn over 2f out: wknd 1f out* **20/1**
0-05 **7** *2 1/2* **Converti**[11] 3328 4-8-5 **50**........................ GarryWhillans(5) 3 40
(H J Manners) *hld up in tch: wknd over 3f out* **25/1**
0- **8** *nk* **Baileys Best**[441] 1002 6-9-5 **59**........................ DeanHeslop 11 49
(M F Harris) *hld up in tch: lost pl over 8f out: bhd 6f out: n.d after* **25/1**
000- **9** *1* **Royal Tender (IRE)**[228] 4739 4-8-2 **45**........................ DebraEngland(3) 5 33
(V Smith) *hld up in mid-div: lost pl after 2f: sn bhd: n.d after* **25/1**
3033 **10** *10* **Still Dreaming**[19] 3059 4-8-4 **49**........................(b) CharlesEddery(5) 9 22
(R J Price) *w ldr: led over 6f out tl over 3f out: wknd wl over 1f out* **7/2**[1]
4130 **11** *11* **Sovietta (IRE)**[33] 2643 7-8-6 **49**........................(t) RichardRowe(3) 1 6
(Ian Williams) *led tl over 6f out: wknd over 5f out* **6/1**[2]

0-45 **12** *43* **Intersky Sports (USA)**[140] 569 4-8-7 **52**........................(t) SamuelDrury(5) 7 —
(Miss C Dyson) *s.i.s: a in rr: t.o fnl 4f* **33/1**
2m 44.34s (-0.26) **Going Correction** -0.05s/f (Good) **12** Ran SP% **121.4**
Speed ratings (Par 101): **98,97,97,96,96 93,91,91,90,84 78,51**
toteswinger: 1&2 £9.10, 1&3 £6.70, 2&3 £7.00. CSF £46.27 CT £176.08 TOTE £8.10: £3.10, £2.00, £1.70; EX 54.20 Place 6 £6.04, Place 5 £3.89.
Owner John L Marriott **Bred** J Davison **Trained** Upper Longdon, Staffs
■ Stewards' Enquiry : Dean Heslop one-day ban: used whip when out of contention (Jul 18)
FOCUS
A competitive if low-key event. It was steadily run and the form is modest, rated around the winner and third.
T/Plt: £10.30 to a £1 stake. Pool: £46,237.69. 3,255.63 winning tickets. T/Qpdt: £7.10 to a £1 stake. Pool: £2,001.00. 206.10 winning tickets. KH

3699 - 3704a (Foreign Racing) - See Raceform Interactive

3623 HAMBURG (R-H)
Friday, July 4

OFFICIAL GOING: Soft

3705a GROSSER PREIS DER JUNGHEINRICH GABELSTAPLER (GROUP 3) (FILLIES) 1m 3f
6:35 (6:39) 3-Y-0 **£23,529** (£7,353; £3,676; £2,206)

RPR
1 **Lady Marian (GER)**[22] 3-9-2........................ DBoeuf 9 107
(W Baltromei, Germany) *towards rear early, headway to go 3rd over 4f out, close 5th on outside straight, led well over 1f out, driven out*
2 *3* **Ashantee (GER)**[23] 3-9-2........................ EPedroza 6 102
(M Rulec, Germany) *held up, last & brought wide straight, good headway 2f out, chased winner, final f, kept on one pace & never able to challenge*
3 *1* **Umirage (GER)** 3-9-2........................ ASuborics 5 100
(H Blume, Germany) *held up, 8th straight, switched to outside 2f out, headway & tracking 2nd over 1f out, one pace*
4 *1* **Goathemala (GER)**[19] 3073 3-9-2........................ AStarke 2 99
(P Schiergen, Germany) *always prominent, 4th straight, every chance well over 1f out, one pace*
5 *1* **Salve Germania (IRE)** 3-9-2........................ LennartHammer-Hansen 8 97
(W Hickst, Germany) *always close up, 6th & ridden straight, soon one pace*
6 *3* **Yarastar**[30] 2743 3-9-2........................ JVictoire 1 92
(H-A Pantall, France) *always close up, 3rd on inside straight, driven to lead over 2f out, headed well over 1f out, soon weakened*
7 *hd* **Auentime (GER)**[19] 3073 3-9-2........................ THellier 3 91
(U Ostmann, Germany) *held up, closing up & 7th on inside straight, soon one pace*
8 *1* **Splash Mountain (IRE)**[19] 3073 3-9-2........................ ADeVries 4 90
(A Trybuhl, Germany) *tracked leader, 2nd straight, ridden & beaten 2f out*
9 *2 1/2* **Flure De Leise (IRE)**[12] 3300 3-9-2........................ JO'Dwyer 7 86
(Eamon Tyrrell, Ire) *led to over 2f out*
2m 32.09s (7.39) **9** Ran
(including ten euro stakes): WIN 548; PL 95, 37, 38; SF 5340.
Owner Rennstall Gestut Hachtsee **Bred** Count & Countess Von Stauffenberg **Trained** Germany

3662 BEVERLEY (R-H)
Saturday, July 5

OFFICIAL GOING: Good changing to good to soft after race 2 (2.55)
Wind: Virtually nil Weather: rain, clearing to showers

3706 AWARD WINNING COACHMAN CARAVANS CLAIMING STKS 7f 100y
2:20 (2:20) (Class 5) 2-Y-0 **£2,590** (£770; £385; £192) **Stalls** High

Form RPR
0544 **1** **Blusher**[8] 3444 2-8-4 0........................ TPO'Shea 1 64+
(M R Channon) *mde all: sn crossed to rail: pushed clr 2f out: r.o wl* **5/1**[3]
052 **2** *3 3/4* **Debbys Boy**[23] 2980 2-8-7 0........................(b) ChrisCatlin 2 58
(Miss Gay Kelleway) *a chsng wnr: rdn and unable qck over 2f out: kpt on same pce* **8/1**
02 **3** *1 1/4* **Hold The Bucks (USA)**[15] 3225 2-8-6 0........................ LukeMorris(3) 10 57
(J S Moore) *in tch: rdn and effrt over 2f out: chsd ldng pair 2f out: no imp* **8/1**
00 **4** *5* **Kingaroo (IRE)**[3] 3597 2-8-9 0........................ PatrickMathers 5 46
(Garry Moss) *s.i.s: bhd: hdwy 3f out: bmpd over 1f out: kpt on to go modest 4th 1f out: nvr nr ldrs* **80/1**
6150 **5** *4 1/2* **Kneesy Earsy Nosey**[22] 3008 2-8-2 0........................ KimTinkler 3 28
(N Tinkler) *t.k.h: hld up in midfield: rdn over 2f out: no prog after* **25/1**
6103 **6** *1/2* **Dispol Diva**[15] 3225 2-8-0 0 ow1........................ AndrewMullen(3) 11 28
(P T Midgley) *chsd ldrs: rdn over 3f out: wknd over 2f out* **6/1**
46 **7** *7* **Strictly Royal**[81] 1377 2-8-7 0........................ EdwardCreighton 6 15
(M R Channon) *racd in midfield: rdn and struggling over 3f out: n.d* **40/1**
651 **8** *nk* **Cherry Belle (IRE)**[15] 3225 2-8-2 0........................(v) CatherineGannon 8 10+
(P D Evans) *bmpd s: hmpd after 100yds: a towards rr: no ch whn short of room and hmpd over 1f out* **9/2**[2]
415 **9** *3/4* **Calley Ho**[8] 3439 2-9-5 0........................ TomEaves 12 25
(Mrs L Stubbs) *chsd ldng pair: rdn 3f out: wknd jst over 2f out: wl btn last 2f* **5/2**[1]
0 **10** *6* **Darknstormy**[14] 3277 2-8-7 0 ow1........................(b[1]) JamieMoriarty(3) 9 —
(J R Weymes) *s.i.s: a bhd* **66/1**
00 **11** *6* **Holst (IRE)**[18] 3107 2-8-6 0........................(b[1]) DuranFentiman(3) 4 —
(T D Easterby) *chsd ldrs: rdn and wknd over 2f out: no ch whn sltly hmpd over 1f out* **50/1**
554 **12** *32* **Scarlet Blade**[18] 3106 2-8-5 0........................(b[1]) RoystonFfrench 13 —
(Mrs A Duffield) *rn in snatches: stmbld after 1f: rdn and lost tch 4f out: wl t.o last 2f* **20/1**
03 **U** **Just Five (IRE)**[23] 2965 2-8-11 0........................ TonyHamilton 7 —
(M Dods) *bmpd s: midfield whn clipped heels, stmbld and uns rdr after 100yds* **16/1**
1m 37.61s (3.81) **Going Correction** +0.40s/f (Good) **13** Ran SP% **121.5**
Speed ratings (Par 94): **94,89,88,82,77 76,68,68,67,60 53,17,—**
.Blusher was claimed by Claes Bjorling for £10000.\n\x\x
Owner John Breslin **Bred** J Breslin **Trained** West Ilsley, Berks
FOCUS
A weak claimer rated around the placed horses. The form is sound enough.

NOTEBOOK

Blusher, one of the most experienced in the field, was quickly away from her low draw and crossed over to make the running. It was a decisive move, as she dominated the race from then on, quickening away inside the final two furlongs for a comfortable win. The drop in class helped but with this confidence boost under her belt it would not be a surprise to see her pay her way in nursery company. (op 4-1 tchd 7-2)

Debbys Boy, runner-up in a seller at Yarmouth last time when wearing blinkers for the first time, had the headgear on again. He was another who was poorly drawn but showed good early speed to cross over and race prominently from the off. In the end the winner was much too good for him, but he beat the rest well enough. (op 10-1)

Hold The Bucks(USA), a half-brother to five winners in the US, is another who finished runner-up in a seller last time. He was not disgraced on this easier ground. (op 16-1)

Kingaroo(IRE) has been slowly away on each of his three starts to date. This was his best performance to date, but that probably says more about the quality of the race than anything. (op 66-1)

Kneesy Earsy Nosey, who has not built on her win in a 6f seller at Ripon in May, finished up well held.

Dispol Diva did not seem to get home over this extended 7f on rain-softened ground. (op 7-1)

Calley Ho was disappointing on this drop in class, even allowing for the fact that he had to give at least 8lb all round. (op 11-4)

Scarlet Blade Official explanation: jockey said gelding suffered interference in running

3707 LEISURE FURNISHINGS MAIDEN STKS — 5f

2:55 (2:55) (Class 4) 2-Y-O — **£4,047** (£1,204; £601; £300) **Stalls** High

Form				RPR
26	**1**		**Total Gallery (IRE)**[18] 3105 2-9-3 0 .... TPO'Shea 2 (J S Moore) *hld up in bhd ldrs: plld out 2f out: led ent fnl f: sn in command: comf* **6/5**[1]	96+
	2	*3 1/2*	**Global City (IRE)** 2-8-13 0 ....(t) ChrisCatlin 10 (Saeed Bin Suroor) *led: rdn 2f out: edgd lft over 1f out: hdd ent fnl f: no ch w wnr* **9/2**[3]	78
23	**3**	*4 1/2*	**Carnaby Haggerston (IRE)**[22] 3005 2-8-12 0 .... NeilBrown(5) 6 (K A Ryan) *chsd ldrs: rdn and struggling 1/2-way: kpt on u.p to go modest 3rd nr fin* **4/1**[2]	66
5	**4**	*1*	**Lucky Art (USA)**[29] 2775 2-9-3 0 .... RoystonFfrench 8 (J Howard Johnson) *chsd ldr: rdn 2f out: wkng whn rdr dropped reins over 1f out: wl btn fnl f: lost 3rd nr fin* **10/1**	63
	5	*7*	**Gee Gina** 2-8-7 0 ow2 .... JamieMoriarty(3) 9 (P T Midgley) *chsd ldrs: rdn 3f out: sn outpcd: no ch last 2f* **66/1**	30
46	**6**	*2*	**Battle Of Hastings**[7] 3485 2-9-3 0 .... AndrewElliott 4 (M L W Bell) *racd off the pce in midfield: n.d* **33/1**	30
	7	*2*	**Sampower Rose (IRE)** 2-8-9 0 ow1 .... DNolan 7 (D Carroll) *s.i.s: nvr on terms* **66/1**	15
	8	*5*	**Arriva La Diva** 2-8-8 0 .... TonyHamilton 5 (J J Quinn) *s.i.s: sn rdn along in rr: nvr on terms* **33/1**	—
0	**9**	*5*	**Ishiquick**[17] 3140 2-8-9 0 .... DuranFentiman(3) 1 (T D Easterby) *sn rdn along in midfield: no ch fr 1/2-way: t.o* **66/1**	—
	10	*7*	**Indonesian Idol (IRE)** 2-8-13 0 .... TomEaves 11 (B Smart) *v.s.a: nvr gng and sn wl bhd: t.o 1/2-way* **7/1**	—
0	**11**	*1 1/4*	**Cleard For Action**[28] 2845 2-9-3 0 .... DaleGibson 3 (J R Weymes) *sn outpcd: t.o 1/2-way* **100/1**	—

64.03 secs (0.53) **Going Correction** +0.225s/f (Good) **11** Ran SP% **116.6**

Speed ratings (Par 96): **104,98,91,89,78 75,72,64,56,44 42**

toteswinger: 1&2 £1.50, 1&3 £1.50 2&3 £3.90. CSF £6.49 TOTE £2.00: £1.10, £2.10, £1.40; EX 8.00.

Owner Coleman Bloodstock Limited **Bred** Michael Woodlock And Seamus Kennedy **Trained** Upper Lambourn, Berks

FOCUS

A fair maiden in which very few got competitive. It has been rated positively with the third a good guide to the level.

NOTEBOOK

Total Gallery(IRE) had shown more than enough in his previous two starts, including when sixth in the Windsor Castle Stakes, to suggest that he could win a race like this, and the easing of the ground only served to help his chance, as he is by Namid. He won in good style in the end and will not mind a return to 6f. His trainer believes he is Group class and the Redcar Two-Year-Old Trophy is the long-term target. (op 13-8)

Global City(IRE), whose price rose from 12,000gns as a yearling to £200,000 as a two-year-old at the breeze-ups, is a half-brother to that very useful sprinter Sweet Afton. Showing good early pace from the gate, he shaped well on his debut, but whether this rain-softened ground was ideal for this son of Exceed And Excel is open to question. He should improve for a sounder surface. (op 3-1 tchd 11-4)

Carnaby Haggerston(IRE) never threatened the principals and only took third late on from the weakening Lucky Art, whose rider lost his reins inside the final two furlongs. He probably wants 6f now, and faster ground will suit him. He should pay his way in nursery company. (tchd 7-2 and 9-2)

Lucky Art(USA), who hassled the leader Global City on the front end, was plenty keen enough in the early stages, but he would probably still have finished third had his rider not dropped his reins inside the final two furlongs. (op 8-1 tchd 11-1)

Gee Gina, a half-sister to Green State, a prolific winner between 6f and 1m2f in Italy, was a late foal. She showed some early speed on her racecourse debut and is entitled to come on for this. (op 50-1)

Battle Of Hastings shapes as though he will be suited by further when moved into handicap company. (op 25-1)

Indonesian Idol(IRE) Official explanation: jockey said colt was unsuited by the good to soft ground

3708 COACHMAN CARAVANS QUALITY H'CAP — 5f

3:30 (3:30) (Class 4) (0-85,83) 3-Y-O+ — **£6,476** (£1,927; £963; £481) **Stalls** High

Form				RPR
0302	**1**		**He's A Humbug (IRE)**[10] 3370 4-9-4 **80** ....(p) NeilBrown(5) 3 (K A Ryan) *chsd ldrs: rdn over 1f out: led ins fnl f: styd on wl* **5/1**[3]	91
6000	**2**	*1 1/4*	**Winthorpe (IRE)**[21] 3050 8-8-3 **67** .... JamieKyne(7) 8 (J J Quinn) *hld up towards rr: hdwy and rdn over 1f out: r.o wl to go 2nd nr fin: nt trble wnr* **22/1**	74
-033	**3**	*hd*	**Mambo Spirit (IRE)**[25] 2906 4-9-9 **80** .... ChrisCatlin 9 (J G Given) *chsd ldrs: rdn 2f out: chsd ldr ins fnl f: no imp and lost 2nd nr fin* **7/2**[1]	86
3-40	**4**	*3/4*	**Hypnosis**[39] 2489 5-9-4 **75** .... TonyHamilton 4 (D W Barker) *chsd ldr: rdn to ld over 1f out: hdd ins fnl f: fdd towards fin* **20/1**	78
2301	**5**	*1/2*	**The Nifty Fox**[9] 3401 4-9-11 **82** .... TomEaves 10 (T D Easterby) *in tch: drvn ent fnl 2f: one pce fnl f* **5/1**[3]	83
4400	**6**	*nse*	**Malapropism**[7] 3472 8-9-6 **77** .... EdwardCreighton 1 (M R Channon) *led and styd wd: rdn and hdd over 1f out: no ex fnl f* **20/1**	78
1-00	**7**	*2*	**Divine Spirit**[10] 3370 7-9-11 **82** .... RoystonFfrench 11 (M Dods) *hld up in rr on far side: pushed along over 1f out: nvr trbld ldrs* **14/1**	76
1014	**8**	*3/4*	**Namir (IRE)**[11] 3336 6-9-1 **75** ....(vt) DuranFentiman(3) 5 (D Shaw) *hld up in rr: hdwy 2f out: rdn over 1f out: wknd ins fnl f* **15/2**	66
0661	**9**	*nk*	**Bo McGinty (IRE)**[7] 3472 7-9-5 **83** ....(b) BMcHugh(7) 7 (R A Fahey) *in tch: rdn and struggling 1/2-way: n.d after* **4/1**[2]	73
6056	**10**	*7*	**Dig Deep (IRE)**[8] 3451 6-9-9 **83** .... JamieMoriarty(3) 6 (J J Quinn) *a bhd* **15/2**	48

64.00 secs (0.50) **Going Correction** +0.225s/f (Good) **10** Ran SP% **119.6**

Speed ratings (Par 105): **105,103,102,101,100 100,97,96,95,84**

toteswinger: 1&2 £2.60, 1&3 £9.60, 2&3 £22.20. CSF £113.35 CT £450.55 TOTE £7.00: £2.10, £6.10, £2.00; EX 126.90.

Owner David Fravigar, Kathy Dixon **Bred** Denis McDonnell **Trained** Hambleton, N Yorks

FOCUS

A fair handicap sprint where, for once, the draw did not seem to have much of an effect. The form looks sound.

3709 C.G.I. H'CAP — 1m 100y

4:05 (4:05) (Class 4) (0-80,79) 3-Y-O — **£5,180** (£1,541; £770; £384) **Stalls** High

Form				RPR
0110	**1**		**Gala Casino Star (IRE)**[28] 2840 3-8-12 **73** .... JamieMoriarty(3) 5 (R A Fahey) *s.i.s: sn pushed up to chse ldr: led wl over 1f out: edgd rt but sn drvn clr: in n.d fnl f* **2/1**[1]	89
-234	**2**	*7*	**Cathedral Walk (USA)**[78] 1448 3-9-3 **75** .... AndrewElliott 6 (K R Burke) *led: rdn and hung lft jst over 2f out: hdd wl over 1f out: no ch w wnr fnl f* **5/1**[3]	75
515	**3**	*1 3/4*	**Shadowtime**[10] 3366 3-8-13 **71** .... TonyHamilton 1 (Miss Tracy Waggott) *chsd ldrs: rdn 2f out: sn outpcd by wnr: plugged on* **4/1**[2]	67
-333	**4**	*11*	**Atabaas Pride**[28] 2842 3-9-7 **79** .... TomEaves 7 (M Johnston) *in tch: rdn along 4f out: hung lft over 2f out: sn swtchd rt and drvn: wl btn over 1f out* **2/1**[1]	50
-203	**5**	*3/4*	**Safebreaker**[110] 920 3-9-2 **74** .... ChrisCatlin 4 (N Tinkler) *bhd: looked reluctant and lost tch 5f out: n.d after* **11/1**	43

1m 49.81s (2.21) **Going Correction** +0.40s/f (Good) **5** Ran SP% **111.7**

Speed ratings (Par 102): **104,97,95,84,83**

toteswinger: 1&2 £17.40 CSF £12.48 TOTE £2.40: £2.00, £3.70; EX 14.10.

Owner The Friar Tuck Racing Club **Bred** Glashare House Stud **Trained** Musley Bank, N Yorks

FOCUS

This looked a fair contest but the winner won in easy style. The form does not look very strong but it makes sense at face value.

Atabaas Pride Official explanation: trainer had no explanation for the poor fom shown

3710 ELTHERINGTON STKS (H'CAP) — 2m 35y

4:40 (4:40) (Class 5) (0-70,70) 3-Y-O+ — **£3,561** (£1,059; £529; £264) **Stalls** High

Form				RPR
/303	**1**		**Zeloso**[47] 2245 10-8-9 **51** oh6 ....(v) CatherineGannon 1 (M F Harris) *hld up wl in tch: rdn 3f out: drvn to ld ent fnl f: edgd rt: drvn out* **25/1**	57
1012	**2**	*2*	**Pegasus Prince (USA)**[19] 3083 4-9-7 **63** .... TomEaves 9 (Miss J A Camacho) *hld up in tch: rdn and unable qck jst over 2f out: swtchd lft ent fnl f: plugged on to go 2nd wl ins fnl f: nt rch wnr* **9/2**	67
0042	**3**	*3/4*	**Thewhirlingdervish (IRE)**[13] 3296 10-9-11 **70** .... DuranFentiman(3) 2 (T D Easterby) *chsd ldr: upsides ldr over 3f out: led over 2f out: rdn 2f out: hdd ent fnl f: wknd ins fnl f* **10/3**[3]	73
022	**4**	*1 3/4*	**Herrera (IRE)**[20] 3058 3-8-7 **68** .... TonyHamilton 8 (R A Fahey) *t.k.h: trckd ldrs: rdn 4f out: ev ch u.p over 1f out: sltly hmpd ent fnl f: wknd ins fnl f* **5/2**[1]	69
5-31	**5**	*2*	**Moonshine Beach**[10] 3377 10-9-2 **58** .... ChrisCatlin 4 (P W Hiatt) *led: rdn and hdd over 2f out: wkng whn short of room and hmpd 1f out: wl hld after* **11/4**[2]	57
-010	**6**	*2 1/2*	**Sendali (FR)**[14] 3279 4-8-9 **51** oh1 .... AndrewElliott 6 (J D Bethell) *hld up in last: rdn and effrt over 2f out: no imp* **8/1**	47
0056	**7**	*41*	**Senor Set (GER)**[10] 3377 7-8-9 **51** oh6 .... PatrickMathers 5 (D Shaw) *hld up in tch: wd and rdn bnd 4f out: wl bhd last 2f: t.o* **25/1**	—

3m 46.93s (7.13) **Going Correction** +0.40s/f (Good)

WFA 3 from 4yo+ 19lb **7** Ran SP% **115.3**

Speed ratings (Par 103): **98,97,96,95,94 93,73**

toteswinger: 1&2 £25.50, 1&3 £23.60, 2&3 £1.40. CSF £134.02 CT £479.93 TOTE £27.10: £7.70, £2.30; EX 100.30.

Owner M Harris **Bred** Coln Valley Stud **Trained** Edgcote, Northants

■ Stewards' Enquiry : Catherine Gannon caution: careless riding

FOCUS

A low-grade staying event, where the first and third were both aged ten. It was steadily run and the form looks limited.

3711 POWERPART H'CAP — 1m 1f 207y

5:15 (5:22) (Class 5) (0-75,75) 3-Y-O+ — **£3,561** (£1,059; £529; £264) **Stalls** High

Form				RPR
5143	**1**		**Riley Boys (IRE)**[1] 3664 7-9-4 **70** .... ShaneCreighton(5) 5 (J G Given) *hld up in midfield: hdwy 3f out: chsd ldr over 1f out: nudged into narrow ld last 100yds: kpt on* **8/1**	81
-044	**2**	*shd*	**Gulf Coast**[5] 3551 3-7-11 **58** .... DuranFentiman(3) 14 (T D Walford) *chsd ldrs: wnt 2nd wl over 2f out: rdn to ld over 1f out: narrowly hdd last 100yds: unable qck towards fin* **6/1**[2]	69
024	**3**	*3*	**Always Cruising (USA)**[28] 2847 3-8-13 **71** .... AndrewElliott 9 (M Johnston) *dwlt: hld up towards rr: pushed along 4f out: hdwy on inner over 3f out: chsd ldrs and drvn 2f out: kpt on same pce fnl f* **8/1**	76
113	**4**	*nk*	**Princelywallywogan**[24] 2927 6-9-3 **67** .... PJMcDonald(3) 12 (John A Harris) *dwlt: sn pushed up to ld: rdn over 2f out: hdd over 1f out: wknd ent fnl f* **10/3**[1]	71
0022	**5**	*4 1/2*	**Gala Sunday (USA)**[5] 3551 8-8-11 **58** ....(bt) DaleGibson 1 (M W Easterby) *hld up in midfield: rdn and hdwy to chse ldrs 3f out: wknd over 1f out* **7/1**[3]	53
2202	**6**	*11*	**King Of Rhythm (IRE)**[14] 3257 5-9-13 **74** .... DNolan 8 (D Carroll) *t.k.h: chsd ldrs: swtchd off rail and drvn jst over 2f out: wknd over 1f out* **7/1**[3]	47
50-6	**7**	*1/2*	**Persian Peril**[13] 3294 4-9-9 **70** .... TomEaves 3 (G A Swinbank) *prom: chsd ldr over 5f out tl over 2f out: wkng and wl hld whn hmpd over 1f out* **20/1**	42
3-00	**8**	*nse*	**John Dillon (IRE)**[94] 1159 4-9-4 **65** .... LeeEnstone 7 (P C Haslam) *hld up bhd: wl hld whn nt clr run and swtchd lft over 1f out: n.d* **20/1**	37
103-	**9**	*nk*	**Hurricane Thomas (IRE)**[118] 5839 4-9-4 **70** .... NeilBrown(5) 11 (R E Barr) *hld up in last: effrt on inner over 3f out: nvr nr ldrs* **16/1**	42

0-03 **10** *2* **Bigalo's Magic (UAE)**[8] 3436 3-8-6 **64** ChrisCatlin 6 32
(E J O'Neill) *t.k.h: hld up in tch: rdn and struggling over 3f out: sn bhd* **15/2**

4130 **11** *3* **Snowed Under**[29] 2784 7-9-7 **75** BMcHugh(7) 13 37
(J D Bethell) *chsd ldr tl over 5f out: rdn over 3f out: wknd over 2f out* **12/1**

6240 **12** *6* **Site Sentry (IRE)**[30] 1296 5-8-13 **60** EdwardCreighton 4 10
(M F Harris) *bhd: rdn over 4f out: wl bhd last 3f* **50/1**

2m 12.5s (5.50) **Going Correction** +0.40s/f (Good)
WFA 3 from 4yo+ 11lb **12** Ran SP% **121.4**
Speed ratings (Par 103): **94,93,91,91,87 78,78,78,78,76 74,69**
toteswinger: 1&2 £54.70, 1&3 £18.10, 2&3 £19.40. CSF £55.55 CT £406.65 TOTE £5.50: £2.20, £2.50, £3.70; EX 68.40.
Owner Paul Riley **Bred** P J Makin **Trained** Willoughton, Lincs

FOCUS
A competitive if steadily run handicap and sound enough form for the grade.
Persian Peril Official explanation: jockey said gelding was unsuited by the good to soft ground

3712 COACHMAN MAIDEN STKS 5f
5:45 (5:49) (Class 5) 3-Y-O+ **£2,914** (£867; £433; £216) **Stalls** High

Form RPR

622- **1** **Barbary Boy (FR)**[256] 6409 3-9-3 79 AndrewElliott 5 62
(M L W Bell) *chsd ldrs: rdn to ld over 1f out: hld on wl u.p ins fnl f* **7/4**[1]

0506 **2** *nk* **Foreign Rhythm (IRE)**[14] 3283 3-8-12 53 (v[1]) KimTinkler 11 56
(N Tinkler) *in tch: rdn over 2f out: swtchd rt over 1f out: r.o wl to press wnr wl ins fnl f: hld towards fin* **20/1**

0500 **3** *1/2* **Miss Taboo (IRE)**[7] 3481 4-9-0 48 JamieMoriarty(3) 9 56
(P T Midgley) *in tch: rdn and effrt 2f out: ev ch ins fnl f: unable qck last 100yds* **28/1**

60 **4** *1/2* **Mrs Bun**[17] 3144 3-8-7 0 NeilBrown(5) 8 52
(K A Ryan) *racd off the pce in midfield: hdwy over 1f out: styd on wl fnl f: nt quite rch ldrs* **20/1**

04 **5** *2 1/2* **First Swallow**[17] 3144 3-8-10 0 BMcHugh(7) 14 48
(R A Fahey) *outpcd and bhd: hdwy 2f out: styd on wl fnl f: nt rch ldrs* **7/1**[3]

254- **6** *1 1/4* **Nickel Silver**[275] 5931 3-9-3 73 TomEaves 3 44
(B Smart) *chsd ldrs: wnt 2nd over 1f out tl ins fnl f: wknd qckly last 100yds* **7/2**[2]

-002 **7** *2* **The Cube**[15] 3231 4-9-3 46 (b) JamieJones(5) 12 39
(J Balding) *chsd ldrs on far side: rdn and hung lft wl over 1f out: wknd fnl f* **9/1**

0 **8** *2 1/2* **Lydia's Legacy**[23] 2966 3-8-12 0 EdwardCreighton 2 23
(T J Etherington) *bhd: sme modest late hdwy: nvr nr ldrs* **100/1**

0 **9** *shd* **Aspendale (IRE)**[11] 3338 3-9-3 0 DNolan 13 27
(D Carroll) *s.i.s: racd off the pce in midfield: drvn 3f out: nvr trbld ldrs* **40/1**

0 **10** *1/2* **Portugal**[28] 2823 3-8-9 0 PJMcDonald(3) 1 20
(T J Etherington) *wnt lft s: wl bhd: sme modest late hdwy: nvr on terms* **40/1**

11 *1/2* **Molly Two** 3-8-12 0 CatherineGannon 4 19
(L A Mullaney) *led tl over 1f out: wknd rapidly fnl f* **50/1**

536 **12** *1 1/2* **Admiral Bond (IRE)**[14] 3282 3-9-3 69 LeeEnstone 7 18
(G R Oldroyd) *wnt lft s: racd off the pce in midfield: struggling 1/2-way: n.d* **10/1**

35-5 **13** *hd* **Do As I Say**[17] 3144 3-9-0 67 DuranFentiman(3) 10 18
(T D Easterby) *chsd ldrs tl 1/2-way: sn wknd* **7/1**[3]

00 **14** *1/2* **Groundhog Day**[16] 3177 4-9-3 0 PatrickMathers 6 13
(J Balding) *hmpd s: a bhd* **33/1**

000 **15** *1/2* **Lovely Lilling**[17] 3144 3-8-12 35 PAspell 15 9
(P T Midgley) *in tch for 2f: sn struggling: wl bhd last 2f* **80/1**

0-0 **16** *5* **Tendulkar's Diva (IRE)**[8] 3438 3-8-12 0 TWilliams 16 —
(A Berry) *s.i.s: a wl bhd* **33/1**

65.79 secs (2.29) **Going Correction** +0.225s/f (Good)
WFA 3 from 4yo 5lb **16** Ran SP% **130.6**
Speed ratings (Par 103): **90,89,88,87,83 81,78,74,74,73 72,70,70,69,68 60**
toteswinger: 1&2 £10.80, 1&3 £18.70, 2&3 £50.60. CSF £47.74 TOTE £2.50: £1.60, £7.80, £8.30; EX 46.80 Place 6: £425.51 Place 5: £137.53.
Owner Thurloe Thoroughbreds XX **Bred** Jean-Francois Gribomont **Trained** Newmarket, Suffolk

FOCUS
A weak maiden in which they were spread right across the track looking for the best ground. The second and third hold lowly ratings, suggesting that Barbary Boy has run well below his current mark despite winning.
Lydia's Legacy Official explanation: jockey said filly ran green
T/Plt: £1,032.40 to a £1 stake. Pool: £63,008.81. 44.55 winning tickets. T/Qpdt: £161.70 to a £1 stake. Pool: £3,082.56. 14.10 winning tickets.

3364 CARLISLE (R-H)
Saturday, July 5

OFFICIAL GOING: Good (good to soft in places; 8.3)
Just 5mm rain before racing but 'soft ground' and after the downpour it became 'very soft' with the stands'-side rail the place to be.
Wind: fresh, half - behind Weather: Mainly fine, occasional showers, heavy thunder storm race 4

3713 COORS GROLSCH APPRENTICE H'CAP 5f 193y
7:05 (7:05) (Class 5) (0-75,73) 4-Y-O+ **£3,070** (£906; £453) **Stalls** High

Form RPR

1224 **1** **Miss Daawe**[9] 3405 4-8-9 **63** LanceBetts(5) 1 74
(B Ellison) *w ldrs: hrd rdn and styd on styd on stands' side to ld nr fin* **9/4**[1]

0010 **2** *hd* **Avontuur (FR)**[11] 3339 6-8-8 **60** (b) MCGeran(3) 6 70
(Mrs R A Carr) *in rr: hdwy over 2f out: led over 1f out: wnt rt: hdd nr fin* **8/1**

-250 **3** *1/2* **Quicks The Word**[14] 3255 8-8-3 **57** DeanHeslop(5) 4 65
(T A K Cuthbert) *led 1f: chsd ldrs: kpt on same pce fnl f* **12/1**

4564 **4** *1* **Coleorton Dancer**[17] 3129 6-9-0 **66** ClGillies(3) 3 71
(K A Ryan) *trckd ldrs: styd on same pce appr fnl f* **7/2**[2]

6050 **5** *1* **Balakiref**[2] 3626 9-9-2 **70** JohnCavanagh(5) 12 72
(M Dods) *s.i.s: hung rt and kpt on fnl f* **8/1**

2655 **6** *hd* **Prince Namid**[8] 3435 6-9-6 **72** ThomasO'Brien(3) 2 73
(Mrs A Duffield) *chsd ldrs: kpt on same pce fnl 2f* **9/1**

0-20 **7** *nk* **Forzarzi (IRE)**[8] 3454 4-8-5 **57** PatrickDonaghy(3) 5 57
(H A McWilliams) *s.i.s: kpt on fnl 2f: nvr nr ldrs* **14/1**

-003 **8** *1 1/4* **Katie Boo (IRE)**[5] 3554 6-9-7 **73** GaryBartley(3) 9 69
(A Berry) *chsd ldrs: drvn over 3f out: sn outpcd* **7/1**[3]

6000 **9** *2* **Dakota Rain (IRE)**[16] 3169 6-9-1 **69** NSLawes(5) 8 59
(Jennie Candlish) *led after 1f: hdd over 1f out: sn wknd* **16/1**

1m 14.8s (1.10) **Going Correction** +0.30s/f (Good) **9** Ran SP% **119.9**
Speed ratings (Par 103): **104,103,103,101,100 100,99,98,95**
toteswinger: 1&2 £6.40, 1&3 £5.90, 2&3 £17.50. CSF £21.62 CT £181.90 TOTE £3.60: £1.50, £3.00, £3.20; EX 21.40.
Owner Mrs Andrea M Mallinson **Bred** N R C Trading Ltd **Trained** Norton, N Yorks
■ Stewards' Enquiry : Lance Betts three-day ban: used whip with excessive frequency (Jul 19-21)

FOCUS
A modest apprentice handicap and the winner had the benefit of the stands' side rail, the place to be all night. This took place on the best of the ground which goes some way to explaining the good time. The form is rated through the third.

3714 ANDERSONS DENTON HOLME LTD MAIDEN AUCTION STKS 5f
7:35 (7:35) (Class 5) 2-Y-O **£2,590** (£770; £385; £192) **Stalls** High

Form RPR

3523 **1** **Metroland**[19] 3078 2-8-8 0 JoeFanning 4 68+
(M Johnston) *stumbed s: sn led: hung rt fnl f: hld on towards fin* **6/5**[1]

2 *1/2* **Whispering Spirit (IRE)** 2-8-6 0 RoystonFfrench 1 64
(Mrs A Duffield) *chsd ldrs: kpt on stands' side ins fnl f: no ex towards fin* **20/1**

3 *1 1/4* **Paddy Bear** 2-8-9 0 PaulHanagan 6 63
(R A Fahey) *s.i.s: hdwy over 3f out: sn chsng ldrs: kpt on same pce ins fnl f* **10/1**[3]

3056 **4** *nk* **Fitzolini**[19] 3078 2-8-9 0 (p) SilvestreDeSousa 10 62
(A D Brown) *led early: chsd ldrs: kpt on same pce appr fnl f* **22/1**

5 *1* **Rio Pomba (IRE)** 2-8-6 0 DavidAllan 3 55
(D Carroll) *hld up: hdwy 2f out: shkn up and fdd appr fnl f* **28/1**

3 **6** *2 3/4* **Tori's Secret (IRE)**[10] 3365 2-8-11 0 RobertWinston 7 50+
(G A Swinbank) *chsd ldrs: effrt over 1f out: wknd last 150yds* **13/8**[2]

7 *9* **Miss Scarlet** 2-8-8 0 FrancisNorton 8 15
(K A Ryan) *sn outpcd and bhd* **12/1**

8 *2 1/2* **Nino Zachetti (IRE)** 2-8-12 0 ow1 DanielTudhope 9 10
(E J Alston) *hld up: hdwy 3f out: lost pl wl over 1f out* **50/1**

63.15 secs (2.35) **Going Correction** +0.30s/f (Good) **8** Ran SP% **114.9**
Speed ratings (Par 94): **93,92,90,89,88 83,69,65**
toteswinger: 1&2 £4.60, 1&3 £3.40, 2&3 £10.70. CSF £30.46 TOTE £2.30: £1.10, £2.80, £2.50; EX 36.10.
Owner J Shack **Bred** West Dereham Abbey Stud **Trained** Middleham Moor, N Yorks
■ Stewards' Enquiry : Robert Winston jockey said gelding was unsuited by the good (good to soft places) ground

FOCUS
Just an ordinary maiden auction race with the experienced winner setting the standard. The bare form is very modest.

NOTEBOOK
Metroland, a rangy individual typical of this stable's inmates, stumbled leaving the stalls. She tended to run lazily in front but in the end did just enough. (op 11-8 tchd 6-4)
Whispering Spirit(IRE), never far away, had the best of the ground on the stands'-side rail and was cutting back the winner at the line. She will be even better suited by six. (tchd 25-1)
Paddy Bear, quite a delicate type, did well on his debut considering he was racing towards the centre. He should have no difficulty finding a race. (tchd 9-1)
Fitzolini, over six lengths behind tonight's winner here last time, seemed suited by the much easier ground and the fitting of first-time cheekpieces. (op 16-1)
Rio Pomba(IRE) travelled strongly on her debut and looked a threat when moving up but in the end she did not get home. She will improve a fair bit for the outing. (op 16-1)
Tori's Secret(IRE), the biggest in the line-up, still looks on the weak side and he seemed to be found out by the soft ground. He may need a little more time yet. Official explanation: jockey said gelding was unsuited by the good (good to soft places) ground (op 7-4 tchd 15-8)

3715 STORY CONSTRUCTION (S) STKS 7f 200y
8:05 (8:06) (Class 6) 3-Y-O **£2,047** (£604; £302) **Stalls** High

Form RPR

00 **1** **One Night In May (IRE)**[23] 2973 3-8-7 0 FrancisNorton 4 46
(W R Muir) *in tch: drvn over 4f out: styd on stands' side to ld 1f out: hrd rdn and hld on towards fin* **12/1**[3]

0000 **2** *3/4* **Caught In Paradise (IRE)**[9] 3406 3-8-9 41 MarkLawson(3) 2 49
(D W Thompson) *sn chsng ldrs: rdn to leave 3f out: edgd rt and hdd 1f out: kpt on towards fin* **20/1**

-360 **3** *7* **Terracos Do Pinhal**[54] 2037 3-8-12 60 JoeFanning 7 33
(M Johnston) *led after 1f tl 3f out: one pce* **6/5**[1]

6334 **4** *5* **Jevington Star (IRE)**[15] 3213 3-8-5 43 (v[1]) LanceBetts(7) 3 21
(B Ellison) *dwlt: hld up detached in last: effrt over 3f out: nvr on terms* **11/4**[2]

6060 **5** *2* **Northwest**[24] 2941 3-8-12 43 DanielTudhope 6 17
(A Berry) *trckd ldrs: wknd 1f out* **16/1**

0066 **6** *23* **Mchepple**[4] 3580 3-8-4 37 DominicFox(3) 5 —
(W Storey) *bolded to post: led 1f: w ldr: lost pl over 2f out: sn bhd* **20/1**

1m 45.81s (5.81) **Going Correction** +0.70s/f (Yiel) **6** Ran SP% **95.2**
Speed ratings (Par 98): **98,97,90,85,83 60**
toteswinger: 1&2 £7.70, 1&3 £3.40, 2&3 £4.30. CSF £128.40 TOTE £9.00: £2.70, £4.60; EX 85.80.The winner was sold to W A Tinkler for 7,000gns.
Owner F Hope **Bred** Garry Chong **Trained** Lambourn, Berks
■ Stewards' Enquiry : Francis Norton three-day ban: used whip with excessive frequency (Jul 21-23)

FOCUS
A poor seller won all out by an unexposed filly with the runner-up, the best guide, rated just 41.
Mchepple Official explanation: trainer said filly bolted to post

3716 COORS FINE LIGHT H'CAP 7f 200y
8:35 (8:36) (Class 4) (0-80,80) 3-Y-O+ **£5,180** (£1,541; £770; £384) **Stalls** High

Form RPR

3431 **1** **Wind Shuffle (GER)**[10] 3366 5-8-12 **64** DanielTudhope 5 73
(J S Goldie) *w ldr: chal stands' side over 2f out: hrd rdn and styd on to ld post* **2/1**[1]

0220 **2** *shd* **Celtic Step**[22] 3006 4-9-9 **75** PaulHanagan 7 84
(P D Niven) *led: carried hd high: hdd post* **9/2**[2]

-330 **3** *2* **Major Magpie (IRE)**[44] 2334 6-10-0 **80** PaulFessey 1 84
(M Dods) *hld up in last: hdwy centre over 2f out: styd on fnl f* **5/1**[3]

005 **4** *3/4* **Feisty Royale**[18] 3109 3-8-13 **74** JoeFanning 2 75
(M Johnston) *chsd ldrs: kpt on wl ins fnl f* **10/1**

0530 **5** *1/2* **Hartshead**[10] 3367 9-9-12 **78** RobertWinston 10 80
(G A Swinbank) *trckd ldrs: chal 2f out: kpt on same pce appr fnl f* **8/1**

-040 **6** *1 3/4* **Bavarian Nordic (USA)**[33] 2675 3-8-8 **72** AndrewMullen(3) 4 68
(Mrs A Duffield) *in rr: hdwy on outer over 2f out: nvr trbld ldrs* **25/1**

4040 **7** *nk* **Moheebb (IRE)**[29] 2790 4-9-5 **74** (b) MichaelJStainton(3) 3 71
(Mrs R A Carr) *prom: effrt over 2f out: one pce* **6/1**

10-5 **8** *12* **Bonjour Allure (IRE)**[26] 2889 3-9-2 **77**........................ RoystonFfrench 8 44
(Mrs A Duffield) *sn chsng ldrs: lost pl over 2f out: sn bhd* **11/1**

6060 **9** *3 1/2* **Fever**[7] 3493 4-8-13 **72**.. BradleyRoper(7) 9 33
(M W Easterby) *s.i.s: sme hdwy centre over 2f out: sn lost pl and bhd* **25/1**

1m 45.05s (5.05) **Going Correction** +0.70s/f (Yiel)
WFA 3 from 4yo+ 9lb **9** Ran SP% **118.7**
Speed ratings (Par 105): **102,101,99,99,98 96,96,84,81**
toteswinger: 1&2 £3.40, 1&3 £2.30, 2&3 £7.20. CSF £11.28 CT £39.04 TOTE £3.00: £1.10, £2.50, £2.20; EX 17.60.
Owner Mrs S E Bruce **Bred** Gestut Elsetal **Trained** Uplawmoor, E Renfrews
■ Stewards' Enquiry : Daniel Tudhope two-day ban: used whip with excessive frequency (Jul 19-20)

FOCUS
This race was run in a downpour. Another winner who raced hard against the stands' side rail, he is rated up 4lb. Sound form.

3717 NORTHERN SECURITY LTD H'CAP 6f 192y
9:05 (9:06) (Class 5) (0-70,70) 3-Y-O **£3,238** (£963; £481; £240) **Stalls** High

Form RPR

-000 **1** **Horatio Carter**[14] 3280 3-9-2 **65**........................ RobertWinston 12 80
(K A Ryan) *trckd ldrs: led on far side over 3f out: sn swtchd to stands' side: clr 2f out: styd on strly* **12/1**

4213 **2** *3 1/2* **Leonid Glow**[13] 3298 3-9-6 **69**........................ FergalLynch 5 74
(M Dods) *mid-div: hdwy stands' side over 2f out: styd on to take 2nd ins fnl f* **5/1**[2]

0450 **3** *1 1/2* **Complete Frontline (GER)**[25] 2911 3-8-7 **56**.............. AndrewElliott 15 57
(K R Burke) *s.i.s: sn mid-div: effrt on outer over 2f out: drifted lft: wnt 2nd appr fnl f: kpt on same pce* **16/1**

-156 **4** *1/2* **Island Music (IRE)**[18] 3109 3-9-4 **70**........................ JamieMoriarty(3) 14 70+
(J J Quinn) *hld up in mid-div: effrt over 2f out: kpt on fnl f* **25/1**

0530 **5** *nk* **Dream Sea**[6] 3525 3-9-2 **65**........................ SamHitchcott 4 64
(M R Channon) *hld up in rr: hdwy on outer 2f out: kpt on fnl f* **12/1**

0001 **6** *1/2* **Molly Ann (IRE)**[5] 3549 3-8-12 **61** 6ex........................ DavidAllan 1 58
(T D Easterby) *mid-div: effrt over 2f out: styd on fnl f* **8/1**

2055 **7** *3/4* **Rossini's Dancer**[8] 3442 3-8-10 **59**........................ PaulHanagan 8 54
(R A Fahey) *hld up in rr: kpt on fnl 2f: nvr trbld ldrs* **3/1**[1]

5-01 **8** *3 1/4* **Umverti**[19] 3081 3-8-8 **60** ow1........................ MarkLawson(3) 2 47
(N Bycroft) *in rr: sn drvn along: kpt on fnl 2f: nvr a factor* **10/1**

04-0 **9** *5* **Rio Sabotini**[33] 2660 3-8-6 **58**........................ PJMcDonald(3) 9 31
(G A Swinbank) *chsd ldrs: effrt and hung rt over 2f out: lost pl on outer over 1f out* **33/1**

3200 **10** *1 3/4* **Dolly No Hair**[14] 3280 3-8-11 **63**........................ AndrewMullen(3) 6 31
(D W Barker) *chsd ldrs: effrt over 2f out: hung rt: wknd over 1f out* **25/1**

0-65 **11** *7* **Brandane (IRE)**[17] 3126 3-8-7 **56**........................(v) RoystonFfrench 10 6
(Mrs A Duffield) *t.k.h: trckd ldrs: lost pl on outer over 1f out* **25/1**

4-00 **12** *1 1/2* **Mick's Dancer**[75] 1524 3-9-4 **67**........................ FrancisNorton 7 13
(W R Muir) *hld up in midfield: effrt over f out: sn wknd* **20/1**

2412 **13** *3/4* **Party In The Park**[25] 2911 3-9-5 **68**........................ TomEaves 13 11
(Miss J A Camacho) *chsd ldrs: effrt on outer over 2f out: lost pl over 1f out* **11/2**[3]

5-00 **14** *15* **Top Man Dan (IRE)**[56] 2008 3-8-11 **60**........................ JoeFanning 11 —
(D Carroll) *mde most to over 3f out: sn wknd: bhd whn eased fnl f: sddle slipped* **16/1**

1m 31.87s (4.77) **Going Correction** +0.70s/f (Yiel) **14** Ran SP% **123.6**
Speed ratings (Par 100): **100,96,94,93,93 92,91,88,82,80 72,70,69,52**
toteswinger: 1&2 £13.40, 1&3 £76.90, 2&3 £19.50. CSF £68.10 CT £1018.88 TOTE £16.40: £4.20, £2.50, £7.30; EX 90.50.
Owner T Alderson **Bred** Mrs T Brudenell **Trained** Hambleton, N Yorks

FOCUS
A modest handicap but the winner took it in most convincing fashion, ending up racing on the better ground against the stands'-side rail. The next three home all ran close to this year's form.
Brandane(IRE) Official explanation: jockey said gelding failed to handle bend leaving back straight
Party In The Park Official explanation: jockey said gelding was unsuited by the soft (good to soft places) ground
Top Man Dan(IRE) Official explanation: jockey said saddle slipped

3718 CFM RADIO MAIDEN H'CAP 2m 1f 52y
9:35 (9:36) (Class 6) (0-65,65) 4-Y-0+ **£2,047** (£604; £302) **Stalls** High

Form RPR

40-2 **1** **Mister Pete (IRE)**[16] 3176 5-8-1 **48**........................ DominicFox(3) 16 56+
(W Storey) *hld up in mid-div: hdwy over 4f out: led over 2f out: styd on wl: readily* **11/2**[2]

0-35 **2** *2* **Blushing Hilary (IRE)**[25] 2914 5-8-8 **52** ow1..................(b) TomEaves 9 58
(Miss J A Camacho) *in tch: wnt prom 6f out: kpt on same pce appr fnl f* **8/1**

000- **3** *3/4* **Florentino**[100] 4771 4-8-1 **48** oh1 ow2........................ AndrewMullen(3) 7 53
(C W Thornton) *hld up in rr: hdwy on outer over 3f out: chsng ldrs 2f out: styd on same pce fnl f* **33/1**

55-0 **4** *2 3/4* **Follow On**[19] 1052 6-8-6 **50** ow1........................ DavidAllan 3 52
(M A Barnes) *hld up in rr: hdwy over 4f out: kpt on same pce fnl 2f* **7/1**

0435 **5** *6* **Fascinatin Rhythm**[6] 3523 4-9-7 **65**........................ SamHitchcott 6 60
(M R Channon) *hld up in rr: hdwy over 3f out: nvr rchd ldrs* **6/1**[3]

032/ **6** *12* **Nevsky Bridge**[38] 6494 6-8-2 **46** oh1........................ RoystonFfrench 11 26
(M Todhunter) *hld up in midfield: hdwy over 4f out: wknd over 1f out* **11/1**

0005 **7** *1/2* **Able Dara**[14] 3279 5-8-2 **46** oh1........................ DaleGibson 1 26
(N Bycroft) *hld up in tch: keen and jnd ldrs 10f out: hung rt and lost pl over 1f out* **10/1**

0040 **8** *3/4* **Stravonian**[5] 3545 8-8-1 **52** oh1 ow6........................ PaulPickard(7) 13 31
(D A Nolan) *midfield: effrt over 4f out: wknd 3f out* **50/1**

6-22 **9** *nk* **Park's Prodigy**[4] 3589 4-8-1 **50**........................(t) PatrickDonaghy(5) 15 28
(P C Haslam) *trckd ldrs: t.k.h: chal over 3f out: wknd over 1f out* **5/2**[1]

0000 **10** *2 1/2* **Monte Pattino (USA)**[4] 3589 4-8-3 **47** oh1 ow1......(vt[1]) AndrewElliott 12 22
(C J Teague) *drvn to ld: reminders 9f out: hdd over 3f out: sn lost pl* **100/1**

640- **11** *29* **Named At Dinner**[2] 5087 7-8-2 **46** oh1........................(v) PaulFessey 14 —
(Miss Lucinda V Russell) *chsd ldrs: lost pl over 3f out: sn bhd: virtually p.u: t.o* **11/1**

000/ **12** *35* **Tewitfield Lass**[19] 55 6-8-2 **46** oh1........................ PaulQuinn 8 —
(K W Hogg) *chsd ldrs: lost pl over 5f out: t.o 4f out: virtually p.u: t.o* **100/1**

450- **13** *47* **Modern Verse (USA)**[13] 2714 5-8-9 **56**....................(v[1]) PJMcDonald(3) 4 —
(Jennie Candlish) *chsd ldrs: wknd over 5f out: t.o 3f out: virtually p.u* **33/1**

0000 **14** *1 1/4* **Fardi (IRE)**[29] 2776 6-8-2 **46** oh1........................ TWilliams 5 —
(K W Hogg) *hld up in rr: bhd fnl 6f: t.o 4f out: virtually p.u* **100/1**

4m 3.98s (10.98) **Going Correction** +0.70s/f (Yiel) **14** Ran SP% **118.4**
Speed ratings (Par 101): **102,101,100,99,96 90,90,90,90,89 75,58,36,36**
toteswinger: 1&2 £11.40, 1&3 £55.80, 2&3 £68.10. CSF £46.99 CT £1325.74 TOTE £7.10: £2.10, £3.10, £6.40; EX 65.00 Place 6: £948.77 Place 5: £426.42.
Owner W Storey **Bred** Tom Radley **Trained** Muggleswick, Co Durham

FOCUS
A low-grade maiden handicap run at a strong pace with stamina at a premium in the very soft ground. Modest form but the winner should do better.
T/Plt: £1,621.20 to a £1 stake. Pool: £71,735.00. 32.30 winning tickets. T/Qpdt: £338.90 to a £1 stake. Pool: £4,031.00. 8.80 winning tickets. WG

3668 HAYDOCK (L-H)
Saturday, July 5

OFFICIAL GOING: Good (good to soft in places) changing to soft after race 1 (2.25)
Rail realignment added 21yards to race distances on round course.
Wind: Moderate, across Weather: Showery but bright

3719 BET365 BEST ODDS GUARANTEED H'CAP 1m 3f 200y
2:25 (2:27) (Class 2) (0-100,96) 3-Y-O **£25,904** (£7,708; £3,852; £1,924) **Stalls** High

Form RPR

1-16 **1** **Inventor (IRE)**[35] 2610 3-8-10 **85**........................ AlanMunro 10 100
(B J Meehan) *s.i.s: hld up: hdwy over 3f out: chsd ldr and edgd lft over 1f out: edgd rt ins fnl f: edgd lft and r.o to ld towards fin* **20/1**

-321 **2** *1* **Laterly (IRE)**[33] 2675 3-8-11 **86**........................ MickyFenton 3 99
(T P Tate) *led: rdn over 1f out: hdd and hld towards fin* **25/1**

-210 **3** *5* **Daraahem (IRE)**[16] 3157 3-9-4 **93**........................ MartinDwyer 1 98
(B W Hills) *in tch: effrt 4f out: edgd lft whn chsd ldrs over 2f out: one pce ins fnl f* **20/1**

111 **4** *4 1/2* **Allied Powers (IRE)**[50] 2151 3-9-1 **93**........................ TravisBlock(3) 4 91
(M L W Bell) *hld up in rr: hdwy over 3f out: rdn whn chsd ldrs over 2f out: wknd ins fnl f* **5/2**[1]

-321 **5** *1* **Full Speed (GER)**[50] 2173 3-8-11 **86**........................ RobertWinston 9 82
(G A Swinbank) *hld up: swtchd lft and hdwy over 3f out: rdn whn chsd ldrs over 2f out: wknd ins fnl f* **16/1**

0026 **6** *2 1/2* **Trenchtown (IRE)**[16] 3157 3-8-11 **86**........................ SteveDrowne 7 78
(R Charlton) *racd keenly in midfield: hdwy to chse ldrs over 4f out: wknd over 1f out: eased whn btn ins fnl f* **7/2**[3]

251 **7** *3 3/4* **Nemo Spirit (IRE)**[40] 2454 3-8-13 **88**........................ RichardMullen 6 74
(W R Muir) *hld up: rdn over 3f out: sn btn: eased ins fnl f* **33/1**

2-14 **8** *6* **Tighnabruaich (IRE)**[59] 1919 3-9-0 **89**........................ PhilipRobinson 2 66
(M A Jarvis) *chsd ldr: rdn over 3f out: lost 2nd 2f out: wknd over 1f out: eased whn btn ins fnl f* **10/3**[2]

12-3 **9** *13* **Planetarium**[73] 1557 3-8-12 **87**........................ GregFairley 8 43
(M Johnston) *in tch: pushed along and wknd over 3f out: eased whn btn fnl f* **18/1**

1510 **10** *21* **Captain Webb**[15] 3196 3-9-7 **96**........................ JoeFanning 5 18
(M Johnston) *prom tl rdn and wknd qckly 4f out: eased whn btn fnl f: t.o* **7/1**

2m 34.68s (1.48) **Going Correction** +0.30s/f (Good) **10** Ran SP% **113.8**
Speed ratings (Par 106): **107,106,103,100,99 97,95,91,82,68**
toteswinger: 1&2 £56.70, 1&3 £94.10 2&3 £111.60. CSF £407.23 CT £9662.61 TOTE £36.30: £7.10, £6.40, £4.70; EX 295.40 Trifecta £612.50 Part won..
Owner Highclere Thoroughbred Racing (Lake Con) **Bred** Brendan Holland And P Connell **Trained** Manton, Wilts

FOCUS
A strong three-year-old handicap, but they finished strung out on the easy ground, which was changed from 'good' to 'soft' after this race, despite there being no more rain. The first three are all progressive. The winning time was 0.08 seconds quicker than the Lancashire Oaks, but 0.87 seconds slower than the Old Newton Cup. They raced up the middle of the track in the straight.

NOTEBOOK
Inventor(IRE) was a touch disappointing when only sixth on much quicker ground over this course and distance on his previous start, but his trainer's horses have struck form with a vengeance since then and he stepped up on that effort with a determined success. The way he stayed on suggests he will benefit from a step up in trip and there ought to be more to come. (op 18-1 tchd 25-1)
Laterly(IRE), 6lb higher than when making all under similar conditions at Thirsk on his previous start, was again allowed his own way out in front and he held a clear lead at the top of the straight, but he was eventually just pegged back. He was well clear of the remainder and is progressing nicely. (op 20-1)
Daraahem(IRE), a St Leger entry, plugged on for pressure and improved on his recent Ascot effort, but he found a couple too good. (op 16-1)
Allied Powers(IRE), another entered in the St Leger, came into this bidding for a four-timer, but he was 11lb higher than when gaining his latest success at Newbury, and fully 25lb higher than when beginning his winning run. The ground should not have posed him any problems, but he was beaten a long way into fourth and proved rather disappointing. (tchd 3-1 in places)
Full Speed(GER) was 10lb higher than when winning on much quicker ground at York on his previous start. (op 10-1 tchd 9-1)
Trenchtown(IRE) took a bit of a grip early on and did not seem to handle the ground. (op 9-2 tchd 10-3)
Tighnabruaich(IRE) promised to be suited by the ground, but he dropped out tamely once beaten. (op 4-1 tchd 3-1)
Captain Webb Official explanation: jockey said colt never travelled

3720 BET365 LANCASHIRE OAKS (GROUP 2) (F&M) 1m 3f 200y
3:00 (3:03) (Class 1) 3-Y-0+
£56,770 (£21,520; £10,770; £5,370; £2,690; £1,350) **Stalls** High

Form RPR

6-03 **1** **Anna Pavlova**[7] 3511 5-9-8 112........................ PaulHanagan 10 114+
(R A Fahey) *hld up: nt clr run and hdwy over 2f out: led over 1f out: sn clr: edgd lft whn wl in command ins fnl f* **5/2**[1]

31-5 **2** *3 1/4* **Ezima (IRE)**[38] 2517 4-9-5 0........................ MJKinane 4 106
(J S Bolger, Ire) *racd keenly in midfield: hdwy over 3f out: led 2f out: sn edgd rt and carried hd high: hdd over 1f out: nt pce of wnr ins fnl f* **5/2**[1]

-146 **3** *1 1/2* **Queen Of Naples**[45] 2305 3-8-6 98........................(b) RichardMullen 5 104
(J H M Gosden) *chsd ldr for 2f: remained prom tl rdn over 3f out: sn outpcd: styd on fr 1f out: tk 3rd ins fnl f: nt rch front 2* **40/1**

3-11 **4** *3 3/4* **Folk Opera (IRE)**[42] 2402 4-9-5 107........................ KerrinMcEvoy 1 98
(Saeed Bin Suroor) *led: rdn and hdd 2f out: wknd fnl f* **9/2**[2]

0-20 **5** *2 1/4* **Turbo Linn**[29] 2791 5-9-5 110........................ NCallan 12 94
(G A Swinbank) *midfield: effrt over 3f out: sn no imp* **6/1**[3]

6 *1 3/4* **Dress Rehearsal (IRE)**[15] 3238 3-8-6 0........................(t) WMLordan 8 91
(David Wachman, Ire) *in tch: rdn to chal 3f out: wknd 2f out* **12/1**

015 **7** *1 1/2* **Calakanga**[8] 3433 3-8-6 80........................ GregFairley 9 89
(C E Brittain) *chsd ldr after 2f tl rdn and 3f out: wknd 2f out* **80/1**

0325 **8** 3 ¾ **Sweet Lilly**[19] 3088 4-9-5 102 RobertWinston 7 83
(M R Channon) *ref to settle in midfield: effrt 3f out: edgd rt and flashed tail whn btn over 1f out* **25/1**

113- **9** 2 ½ **Samira Gold (FR)**[266] 6168 4-9-5 106 SebSanders 6 79
(L M Cumani) *hld up: pushed along over 4f out: nvr on terms* **10/1**

2m 34.76s (1.56) **Going Correction** +0.30s/f (Good)
WFA 3 from 4yo+ 13lb **9** Ran SP% **113.9**
Speed ratings (Par 115): **106,103,102,100,98 97,96,94,92**
toteswinger: 1&2 £1.90, 1&3 £23.70 2&3 £22.90. CSF £8.23 TOTE £3.50: £1.30, £1.60, £4.70; EX 8.20 Trifecta £535.30 Part won..
Owner Galaxy Racing **Bred** Raymond Cowie **Trained** Musley Bank, N Yorks

FOCUS
Probably just an ordinary Group 2 for fillies and mares in which the first two ran to form. The winning time was 0.08 seconds slower than the opening three-year-old 81-100 handicap, and 0.95 seconds slower than the Old Newton Cup. They raced towards the stands' side in the straight.

NOTEBOOK
Anna Pavlova ◆ is up there with the best mares around when getting her favoured soft ground and she was in a different league to this lot, a fine effort turned out just a week after running third in the Group 1 Pretty Polly Stakes in Ireland. Having travelled well enough off the pace, she gradually worked her way to the front in the straight and drew nicely clear, despite edging left late on. She is now 4-4 over 1m4f on soft ground. Future targets very much depend on the going, but her connections have the Irish St Leger in mind as a possible long-term target. (op 11-4 tchd 9-4 and 3-1 in places)
Ezima(IRE), a triple Listed winner in Ireland, including on her latest start on quick ground over 1m6f at Leopardstown, did not help her chance by racing keenly early on and she also edged right under pressure, but she was basically beaten by a better one on the day. Like the winner, she has an Irish Leger entry. (op 9-2 tchd 9-4)
Queen Of Naples proved suited by the ground, the softest she has encountered to date, and she produced a career-best effort to pick up some valuable black type. She never looked likely to win, but did what was required to grab a place and this will have boosted her paddock value. (tchd 33-1)
Folk Opera(IRE)'s recent course-and-distance Listed success was gained on quick ground and this softer surface may not have suited. This was a tougher race, however. (tchd 4-1)
Turbo Linn won this race last year on the July Course at Newmarket, but she has struggled since following up in a Listed race at the same venue last summer. This ground may have been softer than she would have ideally liked, but she was still a little disappointing. She has apparently now been retired. (op 4-1 after early 7-2, tchd 13-2)
Dress Rehearsal(IRE) landed a Listed race on quick ground at Limerick last time, but this was tougher and the ground may not have suited. (op 14-1 tchd 10-1)
Calakanga, a Yorkshire Oaks entry, was well held but still ran above her official mark of 80, which is now likely to be revised. (op 100-1 tchd 66-1)
Sweet Lilly was far too keen for her own good. (op 18-1 tchd 12-1)

3721 BET365 OLD NEWTON CUP (HERITAGE H'CAP) 1m 3f 200y
3:35 (3:39) (Class 2) 4-Y-0+
£62,310 (£18,660; £9,330; £4,670; £2,330; £1,170) **Stalls** High

Form RPR

2-22 **1** **Mad Rush (USA)**[14] 3249 4-9-7 **102** SebSanders 1 117
(L M Cumani) *trckd ldrs: wnt 2nd over 3f out: led over 2f out: stormed clr ins fnl f: eged lft whn in full control towards fin* **5/2**[1]

0004 **2** 4 **Young Mick**[14] 3249 6-9-6 **101** (v) RobertWinston 14 109
(G G Margarson) *hld up: hdwy over 3f out: nt clr run whn chsd ldrs over 2f out: sn rdn: wnt 2nd over 1f out: no imp on wnr fnl f* **16/1**

5-20 **3** shd **Camps Bay (USA)**[14] 3249 4-9-3 **98** JimCrowley 7 106
(Mrs A J Perrett) *hld up: hdwy 3f out: rdn and edgd rt over 1f out: continued to chal for 2nd thrght fnl f: no imp on wnr* **8/1**[3]

-020 **4** 2 ½ **Pevensey (IRE)**[14] 3249 6-9-0 **95** GrahamGibbons 12 99
(J J Quinn) *missed break: in rr: hdwy 3f out: sn rdn: chsd ldrs over 1f out: kpt on same pce ins fnl f* **20/1**

1-04 **5** nk **Buccellati**[15] 3195 4-9-7 **102** (v) WilliamBuick 13 106
(A M Balding) *towards rr: swtchd lft over 3f out: hdwy whn hung lft over 2f out: swtchd lft over 1f out: styd on whn hung lft ins fnl f: nt pce to threaten ldrs* **13/2**[2]

3353 **6** 2 ¼ **King Charles**[14] 3249 4-9-4 **99** KerrinMcEvoy 4 99
(E A L Dunlop) *midfield: hdwy over 3f out: rdn over 2f out: one pce fr over 1f out* **8/1**[3]

-202 **7** 1 ¼ **Dunaskin (IRE)**[13] 3295 8-9-5 **100** PatCosgrave 9 98
(B Ellison) *prom: pressed ldr fr over 6f out: led over 4f out: rdn and hdd over 2f out: sn wknd* **20/1**

-363 **8** 1 ¾ **Alfie Flits**[13] 3295 6-9-7 **102** NCallan 10 97
(G A Swinbank) *midfield: nt clr run whn losing pl over 3f out: rdn over 2f out: no imp after* **20/1**

0-12 **9** ¾ **Record Breaker (IRE)**[14] 3253 4-9-0 **95** GregFairley 15 89
(M Johnston) *trckd ldrs: pushed along over 4f out: wknd over 2f out* **22/1**

0-P0 **10** 1 ½ **The Last Drop (IRE)**[57] 1944 5-9-0 **95** WJSupple 5 87
(B W Hills) *hld up: rdn over 2f out: no imp* **50/1**

10-6 **11** 4 **Pippa Greene**[50] 2168 4-9-0 **95** MartinDwyer 6 80
(P F I Cole) *racd keenly: trckd ldrs: rdn over 2f out: sn wknd* **8/1**[3]

01-4 **12** 2 ½ **Greek Envoy**[70] 1629 4-9-8 **103** MickyFenton 16 84
(T P Tate) *midfield: rdn over 4f out: wknd 2f out* **11/1**

2210 **13** 1 **Eradicate (IRE)**[29] 2790 4-9-7 **102** JoeFanning 11 82
(M Johnston) *prom: stdd into midfield after 2f: hdwy to chse ldrs over 3f out: wknd over 1f out* **16/1**

001- **14** 14 **Solent (IRE)**[279] 5829 6-9-10 **105** PaulHanagan 2 62
(J J Quinn) *led: hdd over 4f out: wknd over 2f out* **50/1**

/330 **R** **Carte Diamond (USA)**[7] 3490 7-9-9 **104** FrancisNorton 8 —
(B Ellison) *ref to r: tk no part* **12/1**

2m 33.81s (0.61) **Going Correction** +0.30s/f (Good) **15** Ran SP% **125.6**
Speed ratings (Par 109): **109,106,106,104,104 102,102,100,100,99 96,95,94,85,—**
toteswinger: 1&2 £11.60, 1&3 £5.80 2&3 £20.40. CSF £44.17 CT £296.64 TOTE £3.70: £1.80, £2.80, £2.90; EX 54.00 Trifecta £1180.80 Pool: £26170.99 - 16.40 winning units..
Owner The Honorable Earle I Mack **Bred** Avalon Farm **Trained** Newmarket, Suffolk
■ A fourth winner of this race in the last 11 years for Luca Cumani. His 2004 winner, Alkaased, later landed two Group 1s.

FOCUS
A competitive renewal of the Old Newton Cup, although the race lacked many progressive types. The first four all came from Ascot's Duke of Edinburgh Stakes with Mad Rush beating the second and third further than he had there. The winning time was 0.87 seconds quicker than the opening three-year-old 81-100 handicap, and 0.95 seconds quicker than the Lancashire Oaks. They tended to race towards the stands' side in the straight.

NOTEBOOK
Mad Rush(USA) ◆ had not really had things go his way in his first two runs this season, bumping into the extremely well handicapped Punjabi on his reappearance at Newmarket before not getting the run of the race when a close second in the Duke Of Edinburgh at Royal Ascot. He made no mistake this time, continuing his improvement in grand style. The return to soft ground did not cause him any problems and he stayed on really strongly for pressure to draw right away from some decent handicappers. Connections said afterwards he is now likely to be stepped up to Listed or Group 3 company and it would be no surprise to see him try and emulate his trainer's 2004 winner, Alkaased, who followed up in the Glorious Stakes at Goodwood, a race Cumani also won last year with Purple Moon. (op 10-3 tchd 7-2)
Young Mick returned to form when fourth in the Duke Of Edinburgh at Royal Ascot, but he had little chance in reversing placings with Mad Rush. He handled the soft ground well and emerges with plenty of credit. He was third in the Ebor in 2006 and it would be no surprise to see him have another crack at that race. (op 14-1)
Camps Bay(USA)'s two wins to date were both gained on quick ground, and this was the softest surface he has encountered so far, but he handled the conditions surprisingly well and ran a big race in third. He has yet to win this season, but is still progressing and could be another for the Ebor. (tchd 7-1 and 9-1 in places)
Pevensey(IRE) looked better than the bare form at Royal Ascot on his previous start, but he had his chance this time and ran well. (op 14-1)
Buccellati ◆ was not unlucky, but he can be rated a little better than the bare form as he was continually denied a clear run in the straight. There could be a decent race in him this season if things fall right. (tchd 7-1)
King Charles was less than two lengths behind today's winner at Royal Ascot on his previous start, but he was well below that form this time. He has won on good to soft, but perhaps this surface was too testing for his liking. (op 12-1)
Pippa Greene has apparently had some niggly problems, and he was keen enough after almost two months off, so he can be expected to do a little better with the benefit of this run. (tchd 15-2)

3722 BET365.COM CONDITIONS STKS 6f
4:10 (4:13) (Class 2) 3-Y-0+
£15,577 (£4,665; £2,332; £1,167; £582; £292) **Stalls** Centre

Form RPR

2203 **1** **Damika (IRE)**[7] 3489 5-8-11 99 JimCrowley 5 113
(R M Whitaker) *midfield: pushed along over 4f out: hdwy over 1f out: led ins fnl f: r.o* **6/1**[3]

0554 **2** ½ **Advanced**[36] 2580 5-8-11 104 NCallan 3 111
(K A Ryan) *chsd ldrs: rdn 2f out: led over 1f out: sn edgd rt: hdd ins fnl f: rallied gamely thrght clsng stages* **7/1**

-166 **3** 3 ¼ **Bentong (IRE)**[14] 3248 5-8-11 102 (t) JoeFanning 2 101
(P F I Cole) *midfield: hdwy to chse ldrs 2f out: nt pce of front pair fnl 100yds* **12/1**

0054 **4** 1 **Knot In Wood (IRE)**[14] 3248 6-8-11 98 PaulHanagan 6 98+
(R A Fahey) *midfield: nt clr run 2f out: rdn and hdwy over 1f out: styd on ins fnl f: run flattened out fnl 100yds* **7/2**[1]

014 **5** 4 **Rising Shadow (IRE)**[7] 3489 7-8-11 97 JimmyQuinn 8 85+
(N Wilson) *missed break: hld up in rr: nt clr run fr 2f out tl over 1f out: styd on wout troubling ldrs* **14/1**

1350 **6** hd **New Freedom (BRZ)**[14] 3248 7-8-11 104 (b[1]) SebSanders 1 84
(D R Lanigan) *led: hung rt fr 1/2-way: hung bdly rt whn hdd over 1f out: wknd and eased ins fnl f* **11/2**[2]

-106 **7** 3 ¼ **Nota Bene**[7] 3504 6-9-8 104 MarcHalford 4 85
(D R C Elsworth) *prom: upsides 1/2-way: sn rdn: n.m.r 2f out: wknd over 1f out* **33/1**

-250 **8** ½ **Bobs Surprise**[17] 3119 3-8-5 105 WilliamBuick 12 72+
(B W Hills) *midfield: effrt whn n.m.r and hmpd over 2f out: sn lost pl: swtchd lft over 1f out: sn n.m.r and hmpd: n.d after* **7/1**

500- **9** ¾ **Patavellian (IRE)**[246] 6633 10-8-11 103 (b) SteveDrowne 10 70
(R Charlton) *in rr: pushed along over 2f out: sn nt clr run: swtchd lft over 1f out: no imp* **25/1**

105 **10** 2 ½ **Reverence**[7] 3488 7-9-10 105 WJSupple 7 75
(E J Alston) *prom: upsides 1/2-way: rdn and losing pl whn n.m.r over 2f out: wknd over 1f out* **13/2**

0/0- **11** 3 ¼ **Les Arcs (USA)**[416] 1770 8-8-11 118 DarrenWilliams 13 52
(S Parr) *chsd ldrs: rdn and lost pl 2f out: n.d after* **14/1**

1m 13.5s (-0.50) **Going Correction** +0.15s/f (Good)
WFA 3 from 4yo+ 6lb **11** Ran SP% **118.0**
Speed ratings (Par 109): **109,108,104,102,97 97,92,92,91,87 83**
toteswinger: 1&2 £8.00, 1&3 £9.60 2&3 £21.80. CSF £47.89 TOTE £6.60: £2.00, £2.30, £3.70; EX 56.10.
Owner G B Bedford **Bred** Patrick J Monahan **Trained** Scarcroft, W Yorks

FOCUS
A good conditions sprint, but the winning time was only 0.24 seconds quicker than the following three-year-old 71-90 handicap. The form is not easy to pin down with most of these falling between handicaps and Pattern races these days. They raced towards the stands' side.

NOTEBOOK
Damika(IRE) had conditions very much in his favour and gained compensation for an unlucky defeat at Newcastle the previous week. This was a good effort considering he would have been 4lb better off with Advanced had this been a handicap and he will now be aimed at the Bunbury Cup, for which he has picked up a 6lb penalty, but he will probably need it on the soft side to be seen at his best. (op 9-2)
Advanced, last year's Ayr Gold Cup winner, found one too good but was well clear of the remainder. (op 13-2 tchd 9-2)
Bentong(IRE) has always looked at his best on decent ground, including when sixth in the Wokingham on his latest start, but he handled the soft conditions surprisingly well and ran a creditable race in third. (op 9-1 tchd 14-1)
Knot In Wood(IRE) often runs a big race in defeat - his latest fourth in the Wokingham being close to his best form - but he rarely wins and is in danger of becoming disappointing. (op 5-1 tchd 10-3)
Rising Shadow(IRE) can be rated a little better than bare form as he did not enjoy the clearest of runs. Official explanation: jockey said gelding was denied a clear run (op 12-1)
New Freedom(BRZ) ◆ showed good speed in first-time blinkers but he hung right, just as he did when ninth in the Wokingham on his British debut, and could not sustain his effort. There could be a good race in him over 5f, even if he is inclined to hang. Official explanation: jockey said gelding hung badly right (op 8-1)
Bobs Surprise ◆ was short of room against the stands' rail inside the final three furlongs and then got caught in behind the weakening Les Arcs, so he wants rating much better than the bare form. There ought to be a similar event in him. (op 11-1)
Patavellian(IRE) was another who was denied a clear run. (op 16-1)

3723 POKER AT BET365 H'CAP 6f
4:45 (4:49) (Class 3) (0-90,88) 3-Y-0 **£9,714** (£2,890; £1,444; £721) **Stalls** Centre

Form RPR

1312 **1** **Great Charm (IRE)**[17] 3141 3-9-2 **83** MickyFenton 2 95+
(M L W Bell) *mde all: rdn over 1f out: r.o ins fnl f: a doing enough cl home* **15/2**

-102 **2** ¾ **Dunn'o (IRE)**[12] 3324 3-8-13 **80** .... PhilipRobinson 8 88
(C G Cox) *chsd wnr thrght: rdn 2f out: edgd lft ins fnl f: r.o* **12/1**

0-00 **3** 2¼ **Errigal Lad**[30] 2761 3-8-11 **78** .... NCallan 15 78
(K A Ryan) *prom: rdn wl over 1f out: styd on same pce ins fnl f* **22/1**

1311 **4** *hd* **Honey Monster (IRE)**[9] 3394 3-9-4 **85** .... WJSupple 4 85
(A J McCabe) *chsd ldrs: pushed along 1/2-way: rdn over 2f out: one pce fnl 100yds* **10/1**

-220 **5** 1½ **Baldemar**[21] 3047 3-9-7 **88** .... FrancisNorton 10 83
(K R Burke) *trckd ldrs: rdn 2f out: one pce fnl f* **14/1**

113 **6** *nk* **Marvellous Value (IRE)**[50] 2171 3-9-7 **88** .... FergalLynch 7 82+
(M Dods) *swtchd rt sn after s: hld up: hdwy and swtchd rt over 2f out: rdn whn chsd ldrs over 1f out: hung lft ins fnl f: one pce* **6/1**[3]

-143 **7** 2¾ **Solar Spirit (IRE)**[15] 3228 3-9-0 **81** .... KerrinMcEvoy 5 66
(G A Swinbank) *prom: rdn 2f out: wknd ins fnl f* **11/2**[2]

033 **8** 2¾ **Captain Dunne (IRE)**[21] 3028 3-8-10 **77** .... DavidAllan 11 53
(T D Easterby) *prom: rdn over 2f out: wknd over 1f out* **16/1**

3-21 **9** *hd* **Muhajaar (IRE)**[23] 2966 3-8-13 **80** .... SebSanders 12 56
(L M Cumani) *in tch: rdn and wknd over 2f out* **2/1**[1]

6-30 **10** *1* **Montaquila**[33] 2674 3-9-1 **82** ....(t) RobertWinston 6 55
(J Howard Johnson) *sn outpcd: nvr on terms* **33/1**

50-5 **11** *6* **Dry Speedfit (IRE)**[9] 3396 3-9-4 **85** .... RichardMullen 16 38
(G G Margarson) *s.i.s: hld up: rdn over 2f out: nvr on terms w ldrs* **50/1**

1-56 **12** ½ **Lord Sandicliffe (IRE)**[56] 1999 3-8-13 **80** .... WilliamBuick 14 32
(B W Hills) *midfield: rdn over 2f out: wknd over 1f out: eased whn btn ins fnl f* **20/1**

0604 **13** 3¼ **Irving Place**[9] 3416 3-8-3 **70** .... PaulHanagan 3 11
(R A Fahey) *towards rr: toiling fnl 2f* **16/1**

-300 **14** *15* **Quest For Success (IRE)**[17] 3141 3-9-1 **82** ....(b[1]) PatCosgrave 1 —
(D J G Murray Smith) *s.i.s: in tch: bmpd after 1f: rdn and wknd 1/2-way: eased whn btn fr over 1f out* **33/1**

1m 13.74s (-0.26) **Going Correction** +0.15s/f (Good) 14 Ran SP% **126.9**
Speed ratings (Par 104): **107,106,103,102,100 100,96,93,92,91 83,82,78,58**
toteswinger: 1&2 £17.10, 1&3 £4.40 2&3 £46.40. CSF £93.83 CT £1978.08 TOTE £9.20: £2.60, £4.10, £7.00; EX 111.90.
Owner Mr & Mrs G Middlebrook **Bred** G And Mrs Middlebrook **Trained** Newmarket, Suffolk

FOCUS
A good three-year-old sprint handicap, but it paid to be on the pace. The winner remains progressive and the form is rated around the third. The winning time was only 0.24 seconds slower than the conditions contest. They raced middle to stands' side.

NOTEBOOK
Great Charm(IRE), second off this mark on quick ground at Ripon on his previous start, appreciated the return to a soft surface and posted a career best, confirming he is still very much on the up. He is quite versatile and appeals as one to keep on side. (op 10-1)
Dunn'o(IRE) ran better than when second in a lesser race at Windsor on his previous start, pulling well clear of all bar the progressive winner. He has the scope for further improvement. (op 10-1)
Errigal Lad ran his best race of the season so far on this drop back in trip and looks up to finding a similar event. (tchd 20-1)
Honey Monster(IRE), a triple winner on the Polytrack this year, including off a mark of 81 at Great Leighs on his previous start, showed himself of a similar level of ability on turf with a solid effort in defeat. (tchd 15-2)
Baldemar had no easy task under his big weight but he ran with credit. (op 10-1)
Marvellous Value(IRE) was not at his best, but he still fared best of those held up and can do better. (op 9-2)
Solar Spirit(IRE) promised to be suited by the ground, but he was well held. (tchd 6-1)
Captain Dunne(IRE) Official explanation: jockey said gelding ran without its off-fore plate
Muhajaar(IRE) should have handled the ground, but he was well below the form he showed when winning his maiden over course and distance on a quicker surface. (op 4-1)

3724 CASINO AT BET365.COM H'CAP 5f
5:20 (5:20) (Class 5) (0-75,75) 3-Y-0+ **£4,857** (£1,445; £722; £360) **Stalls** Centre

Form RPR

4321 **1** **Cheveton**[21] 3042 4-9-10 **73** .... JimCrowley 9 89
(R J Price) *a.p: led over 1f out: sn rdn: hung lft ins fnl f: r.o and wl in command towards fin* **3/1**[1]

-003 **2** *2* **Peter's Storm (USA)**[15] 3202 3-9-1 **69** .... NCallan 2 75
(K A Ryan) *a.p: rdn to chal fr over 1f out: nt qckn towards fin* **11/2**[3]

1400 **3** *hd* **Sands Crooner (IRE)**[18] 3112 5-8-13 **62** ....(v) SebSanders 3 70
(J G Given) *chsd ldrs: rdn to chal over 1f out: no ex fnl 100yds* **12/1**

0016 **4** ½ **Rabbit Fighter (IRE)**[8] 3454 4-9-6 **69** ....(v) PaulHanagan 11 75
(D Shaw) *in tch: nt qckn over 1f out: sn rdn: lugged lft ins fnl f: r.o towards fin* **6/1**

5005 **5** ½ **Harrison's Flyer (IRE)**[6] 3520 7-8-8 **57** ....(p) GregFairley 6 61
(J M Bradley) *chsd ldrs: rdn ins fnl f: styd on same pce* **9/1**

4440 **6** *1* **Charles Parnell (IRE)**[26] 2892 5-9-12 **75** .... FergalLynch 10 76+
(M Dods) *hld up: rdn and hdwy to chse ldrs over 1f out: one pce ins fnl f* **9/2**[2]

664 **7** ¾ **Desert Opal**[31] 2710 8-9-6 **69** ....(b) RobertWinston 16 67
(C R Dore) *chsd ldrs: rdn 2f out: sn outpcd* **16/1**

2561 **8** ½ **Town House**[9] 3405 6-8-0 **56** oh3........ SoniaEaton(7) 14 52
(B P J Baugh) *racd freely: led: rdn and hdd over 1f out: wkng whn hung lft ins fnl f* **20/1**

06-3 **9** ¾ **Pickering**[26] 2892 4-9-7 **70** .... WJSupple 12 63
(E J Alston) *hld up: hdwy to chse ldrs 1/2-way: rdn over 1f out: sn wknd* **11/2**[3]

0/0- **10** 1¼ **Jonny Ebeneezer**[295] 5391 9-8-11 **67** .... RobbieEgan(7) 15 56
(D Flood) *rdr lost irons briefly after rrd s and slowly away: bhd: shkn up over 1f out: nvr on terms w ldrs* **25/1**

0-00 **11** *6* **Mr Forthright**[11] 3340 4-8-7 **56** oh11........ WilliamBuick 4 23
(J M Bradley) *towards rr: outpcd 2f out: eased whn btn fnl f* **50/1**

60.94 secs (0.44) **Going Correction** +0.15s/f (Good)
WFA 3 from 4yo+ 5lb 11 Ran SP% **122.4**
Speed ratings (Par 103): **102,98,98,97,96 95,94,93,92,90 80**
toteswinger: 1&2 £4.80, 1&3 £10.10 2&3 £12.90. CSF £19.94 CT £180.08 TOTE £3.60: £1.80, £2.30, £4.60; EX 26.00.
Owner Mrs K Oseman **Bred** Miss K Rausing **Trained** Ullingswick, H'fords

FOCUS
A fair sprint handicap in which the form has been rated positively with the progressive Cheveton up another 7lb. There were two groups early, with some racing stands' side and a smaller group coming up the centre, but they merged as one up the middle in the closing stages.

Jonny Ebeneezer Official explanation: jockey said he lost stirrup irons on leaving stalls

3725 KEELSUPPLY H'CAP 1m 30y
5:50 (5:50) (Class 5) (0-75,75) 3-Y-0+ **£4,857** (£1,445; £722; £360) **Stalls** Low

Form RPR

6-02 **1** **Sacrilege**[16] 3161 3-8-13 **72** .... MarcHalford(3) 8 81+
(D R C Elsworth) *in tch: lost pl whn n.m.r over 3f out: sn nt clr run and rdn: prog ent fnl 2f: led 1f out: edgd lft ins fnl f: r.o* **9/2**[3]

4056 **2** *1* **Pitbull**[14] 3258 5-8-12 **59** ....(p) WJSupple 9 63
(Mrs G S Rees) *racd keenly: hld up: hdwy over 3f out: rdn and upsides fr 2f out: hung lft ins fnl f: nt qckn* **13/2**

-030 **3** ½ **Bonny Rose**[18] 3109 3-9-0 **70** .... GregFairley 1 71
(M Johnston) *racd keenly: led: rdn and edgd rt over 2f out: hdd 1f out: continued to chal tl no ex towards fin* **9/1**

0000 **4** *4* **Moonlight Man**[15] 3222 7-9-7 **75** ....(t) WilliamCarson(7) 7 69
(C R Dore) *trckd ldrs: rdn over 2f out: nt qckn whn rdr lost whip over 1f out: nt pce of front trio ins fnl f* **16/1**

5005 **5** 1¾ **Polish Corridor**[29] 2787 9-9-4 **65** .... FergalLynch 4 55
(M Dods) *hld up: rdn wl over 1f out: nvr able to chal* **11/2**

0246 **6** ½ **Prince Golan (IRE)**[14] 3261 4-9-7 **68** .... MartinDwyer 10 56
(J W Unett) *racd keenly: w ldr: rdn over 2f out: wknd appr fnl f* **7/2**[2]

3302 **7** 4½ **Lordship (IRE)**[10] 3366 4-9-3 **64** .... SebSanders 6 42
(A W Carroll) *midfield: hdwy 3f out: sn rdn: wknd over 1f out* **3/1**[1]

1206 **8** *7* **Dado Mush**[16] 3167 5-9-13 **74** ....(p) MickyFenton 5 36
(T T Clement) *trckd ldrs: rdn over 3f out: sn wknd* **11/1**

4000 **9** 3¾ **Mister Always**[84] 1338 4-8-2 **56** oh11........ RobbieEgan(7) 2 9
(D Flood) *a bhd: toiling fnl 2f* **33/1**

1m 47.22s (3.42) **Going Correction** +0.30s/f (Good)
WFA 3 from 4yo+ 9lb 9 Ran SP% **121.3**
Speed ratings (Par 103): **94,93,92,88,86 86,81,74,71**
CSF £35.71 CT £260.60 TOTE £4.80: £1.70, £2.70, £3.10; EX 33.00 Place 6: £4629.50 Place 5: £136.16.
Owner The National Stud 1 **Bred** The National Stud **Trained** Newmarket, Suffolk

FOCUS
A fair handicap, but they went a steady pace. The form is sound enough. They raced middle to stands' side in the straight.
T/Plt: £1,612.70 to a £1 stake. Pool: £147,691.31. 66.85 winning tickets. T/Qpdt: £65.90 to a £1 stake. Pool: £8,882.42. 99.60 winning tickets. DO

3405 LEICESTER (R-H)
Saturday, July 5

OFFICIAL GOING: Good to firm
Wind: Fresh behind Weather: Cloudy with sunny spells

3726 TOTEPLACEPOT (S) STKS 5f 218y
2:35 (2:35) (Class 6) 2-Y-O **£1,942** (£578; £288; £144) **Stalls** Low

Form RPR

053 **1** **Meydan Groove**[17] 3135 2-8-6 0........ ShaneKelly 7 69+
(P F I Cole) *mde all: shkn up over 1f out: sn clr* **2/5**[1]

2 *7* **Dean Iarracht (IRE)** 2-8-11 0........(bt[1]) DaneO'Neill 2 50
(John R Upson) *s.i.s: outpcd: hdwy over 2f out: rdn to chse wnr and edgd lft over 1f out: sn outpcd* **14/1**[3]

0 **3** 3¼ **Frame And Cover**[12] 3309 2-8-5 0 ow2........ KevinGhunowa(3) 8 37
(R A Harris) *s.i.s: rcvrd to chse wnr 6f out: rdn over 2f out: edgd rt over 1f out: sn wknd* **33/1**

0506 **4** *4* **Forzando Bloom**[12] 3309 2-8-11 0........ TGMcLaughlin 5 28
(R A Harris) *chsd ldrs: rdn 1/2-way: wknd 2f out* **33/1**

2 **5** *shd* **Gaborone**[77] 1480 2-8-6 0........ LiamJones 3 23
(J R Gask) *trckd ldrs: plld hrd: rdn and wknd wl over 1f out* **5/2**[2]

1m 11.53s (-1.47) **Going Correction** -0.425s/f (Firm) 5 Ran SP% **112.5**
Speed ratings (Par 92): **92,82,78,73,72**
toteswinger: 1&2 £4.50 CSF £8.13 TOTE £1.40: £1.10, £9.30; EX 8.40 Trifecta £65.00 Pool: £158.15 - 1.80 winning units.The winner was bought in for 15,000gns.
Owner Bigwigs Bloodstock XVIII **Bred** Darley **Trained** Whatcombe, Oxon

FOCUS
The jockeys described the going as perfect fast Flat-racing ground. This juvenile seller boiled down to just five runners due to the three non-runners and Meydan Groove was far too good for her rivals, rated to her maiden form.

NOTEBOOK
Meydan Groove, whose previous from was head and shoulders above the opposition, had little difficulty in opening her account over a trip that was probably on the short side for her. She was always in control and won as she pleased in the end. Nurseries are now the way forward with her as connections were keen to retain her at the subsequent auction, so obviously think there is more to come. (op 1-2 tchd 8-13 in a place)
Dean Iarracht(IRE) was beaten a fair way on this first taste of racecourse action. However, there was a worrying side to him as he was wearing a tongue-tie and blinkers, which suggests connections consider him to be far from straightforward. (op 16-1 tchd 12-1)
Frame And Cover, carrying 2lb overweight, was easily seen off. She was tailed-off in one of these on her debut, so she is modest. (op 22-1)
Forzando Bloom, very disappointing since showing a glimmer of ability on his debut, again ran moderately. (op 40-1)
Gaborone, having her first outing for her new trainer, was very disappointing and will have to step up considerably on this if she is going to win even in this grade. (op 9-4 tchd 15-8)

3727 STEFAN ADAMEK MEMORIAL FILLIES' H'CAP 5f 218y
3:10 (3:11) (Class 5) (0-70,70) 3-Y-O **£3,885** (£1,156; £577; £288) **Stalls** Low

Form RPR

5-02 **1** **Lady Carollina**[16] 3177 3-8-10 **59** .... DaneO'Neill 1 69+
(Rae Guest) *hld up in tch: nt clr run over 1f out: swtchd rt: led ins fnl f: r.o* **11/4**[1]

4323 **2** ½ **Flower**[8] 3442 3-9-2 **65** .... LiamJones 3 73
(W J Haggas) *hld up: hdwy over 1f out: edgd rt: rdn and swished tail ins fnl f: r.o* **11/4**[1]

450 **3** 2¼ **Red Amaryllis**[19] 3086 3-8-13 **62** .... RichardKingscote 8 63
(H J L Dunlop) *led: rdn over 1f out: edgd rt: hdd and unable qck ins fnl f* **12/1**

0002 **4** ¾ **Ivory Silk**[10] 3381 3-9-7 **70** .... HayleyTurner 7 69
(D K Ivory) *hld up: swtchd rt over 1f out: r.o ins fnl f: no imp towards fin* **6/1**[3]

-605 **5** ½ **Bohobe (IRE)**[5] 3564 3-9-2 **65** .... J-PGuillambert 2 62
(J G Given) *chsd ldr: rdn over 2f out: no ex ins fnl f* **12/1**

0043 **6** 2½ **Sweet Kiss (USA)**[14] 3268 3-9-5 **68** .... IanMongan 10 57
(B J Meehan) *prom: rdn over 2f out: wknd fnl f* **7/2**[2]

5-00 **7** 1 1/4 **Gower Belle**[12] 3314 3-9-0 63 ... DO'Donohoe 11 48
(W R Muir) *prom: rdn over 2f out: wknd fnl f* **14/1**

0002 **8** 8 **Ma Mirage (IRE)**[18] 3118 3-8-2 51 oh6 ... NickyMackay 4 11
(S C Williams) *chsd ldrs: rdn over 2f out: hung rt and wknd over 1f out* **28/1**

1m 10.33s (-2.67) **Going Correction** -0.425s/f (Firm) **8** Ran SP% **115.3**
Speed ratings (Par 97): **100,99,96,95,94 91,89,79**
toteswinger: 1&2 £1.30, 1&3 £4.60 2&3 £9.00. CSF £10.48 CT £75.92 TOTE £4.10: £1.10, £1.40, £2.70; EX 10.50 Trifecta £90.60 Pool: £160.45 - 1.31 winning units..
Owner L J Vaessen **Bred** Alwyn Moss & Leon Vaessen **Trained** Newmarket, Suffolk

FOCUS
Not surprisingly this fillies' handicap was won in a time over a second quicker than the seller. Just modes torm, but the winner is on the up.

3728 TOTESPORT BETXTRA H'CAP 5f 218y
3:45 (3:46) (Class 4) (0-85,85) 3-Y-0+
£6,854 (£2,052; £1,026; £513; £256; £128) **Stalls** Low

Form RPR

0200 **1** **My Gacho (IRE)**[9] 3401 6-9-2 **74** ... (b) J-PGuillambert 8 89
(M Johnston) *mde all: rdn clr over 1f out: eased nr fin* **11/1**

1162 **2** 3 3/4 **Toms Laughter**[9] 3418 4-9-10 **85** ... (p) KevinGhunowa(3) 6 88
(R A Harris) *chsd wnr: rdn over 1f out: styd on same pce* **3/1**[2]

6301 **3** 2 1/2 **Ingleby Princess**[9] 3404 4-8-9 **67** ... PaulFessey 9 62
(T D Barron) *chsd ldrs: rdn over 2f out: styd on same pce appr fnl f* **12/1**

6036 **4** 2 **I Confess**[7] 3475 3-9-3 **81** ... IanMongan 7 69
(P D Evans) *prom: outpcd 1/2-way: styd on ins fnl f* **12/1**

3-60 **5** 1 1/2 **Flying Goose (IRE)**[32] 2693 4-9-6 **78** ... TGMcLaughlin 4 62
(R A Harris) *s.i.s: hld up: rdn and hung lft fr over 2f out: n.d* **10/1**

-003 **6** shd **Gift Horse**[28] 2831 8-9-13 **85** ... (v) DaneO'Neill 5 68
(D Nicholls) *dwlt: hdwy over 4f out: rdn and wknd over 2f out* **11/4**[1]

2624 **7** nk **Prince Of Delphi**[7] 3506 5-8-11 **69** ... (p) JamesDoyle 3 52
(R M Beckett) *hld up in tch: rdn over 2f out: wknd over 1f out* **5/1**[3]

6121 **8** 3/4 **Dickie Le Davoir**[16] 3169 4-9-0 **77** ... MarkCoumbe(5) 1 57
(John A Harris) *sn outpcd* **11/2**

066- **9** 4 1/2 **River Kirov (IRE)**[224] 6938 5-8-12 **70** ... ShaneKelly 2 36
(M Wigham) *s.i.s: hld up: shkn up over 2f out: sn wknd* **25/1**

69.70 secs (-3.30) **Going Correction** -0.425s/f (Firm)
WFA 3 from 4yo+ 6lb **9** Ran SP% **120.4**
Speed ratings (Par 105): **105,100,96,94,92 91,91,90,84**
toteswinger: 1&2 £28.20, 1&3 £10.50, 2&3 £9.50. CSF £46.05 CT £419.27 TOTE £13.20: £2.40, £1.80, £3.10; EX 27.70 Trifecta £96.90 Pool: £264.57 - 2.02 winning units..
Owner Grant Mercer **Bred** Mount Coote Stud **Trained** Middleham Moor, N Yorks

FOCUS
A decent handicap sprint and the time was not far off the course record and obviously faster than the two previous contests over this trip. They all wanted to race down the centre of the track and the first four were in the same order throughout, so there are doubts over this form.
Gift Horse Official explanation: jockey said gelding never travelled

3729 TOTESPORT.COM EUROPEAN BREEDERS' FUND FILLIES' H'CAP 1m 1f 218y
4:20 (4:20) (Class 4) (0-80,83) 3-Y-0+
£6,854 (£2,052; £1,026; £513; £256; £128) **Stalls** High

Form RPR

2101 **1** **Suzi's Decision**[11] 3351 3-9-8 **83** ... ShaneKelly 7 94+
(P W D'Arcy) *trckd ldrs: racd keenly: nt clr run over 1f out: swtchd lft: r.o to ld wl ins fnl f* **5/6**[1]

56-3 **2** 1 **Flam**[27] 2862 3-8-12 **73** ... DaneO'Neill 5 75
(J R Fanshawe) *led: rdn over 2f out: hdd wl ins fnl f* **8/1**

6166 **3** nk **Snowdrop Princess**[20] 3057 3-8-10 **71** ... LiamJones 1 72
(W J Haggas) *s.i.s: hld up: pushed along 1/2-way: hdwy over 2f out: rdn and hung rt fr over 1f out: ev ch wl ins fnl f: unable qck* **20/1**

0-00 **4** 2 **Rabeera**[31] 2716 3-7-8 **62** ... (v[1]) DavidProbert(7) 6 59
(A M Balding) *hld up: rdn over 1f out: r.o ins fnl f* **22/1**

-602 **5** 1 3/4 **Red Icon**[20] 3057 3-9-0 **75** ... JamesDoyle 2 69
(R M Beckett) *chsd ldrs: rdn over 2f out: no ex ins fnl f* **9/2**[2]

3350 **6** 2 1/4 **Collette's Choice**[22] 3007 5-9-0 **64** ... (p) HayleyTurner 4 53
(R A Fahey) *chsd ldr: ev ch over 2f out: rdn over 1f out: hung rt and wknd ins fnl f* **7/1**[3]

00-2 **7** 2 3/4 **She's Our Lass (IRE)**[84] 1329 7-9-9 **73** ... DO'Donohoe 8 57
(D Carroll) *prom: rdn over 2f out: wknd fnl f* **14/1**

456 **8** 17 **Lisathedaddy**[28] 2820 6-9-7 **78** ... KylieManser(7) 3 28
(B G Powell) *s.s and rel to r: sme hdwy over 3f out: sn wknd* **16/1**

2m 7.90s **Going Correction** +0.05s/f (Good)
WFA 3 from 5yo+ 11lb **8** Ran SP% **118.0**
Speed ratings (Par 102): **102,101,100,99,97 96,93,80**
toteswinger: 1&2 £9.10, 1&3 £25.60, 2&3 £24.10. CSF £8.89 CT £82.63 TOTE £1.60: £1.10, £2.40, £5.30; EX 14.50 TRIFECTA Not won..
Owner Greenstead Hall Racing **Bred** David And Mrs Vicki Fleet **Trained** Newmarket, Suffolk
■ Stewards' Enquiry : Dane O'Neill caution: used whip down shoulder in forehand position

FOCUS
A modest fillies' handicap. It was steadily run and the bare form is a bit messy, but the favourite did it well enough. The form is rated through the placed fillies.
Lisathedaddy Official explanation: jockey said mare was reluctant to race

3730 TOTESPORT 0800 221 221 CLAIMING STKS 1m 1f 218y
4:55 (4:56) (Class 5) 3-Y-0 **£3,238** (£963; £481; £240) **Stalls** High

Form RPR

4336 **1** **Maddy**[61] 1870 3-7-12 58 ... (p) FrankieMcDonald 7 49
(George Baker) *led 2f: chsd ldr tl led 3f out: rdn over 1f out: r.o: eased nr fin* **2/1**[2]

6040 **2** 3 **Mouse White**[29] 2805 3-8-9 49 ... DaneO'Neill 5 54
(H Candy) *chsd ldr tl led 8f out: hdd 3f out: sn rdn: no ex ins fnl f* **14/1**

2304 **3** 2 **Just Sam (IRE)**[1] 3692 3-8-4 60 ... HayleyTurner 6 45
(D Carroll) *hld up: hdwy over 2f out: nt clr run and swtchd lft over 1f out: styd on same pce fnl f* **7/4**[1]

60-0 **4** 3 **Lenouska (IRE)**[15] 3206 3-8-5 54 ow1 ... SimonWhitworth 4 40
(J W Hills) *chsd ldrs: rdn over 3f out: wknd over 1f out* **20/1**

0604 **5** nk **Redsensor**[29] 2801 3-9-1 61 ... ShaneKelly 3 49
(M Quinn) *chsd ldrs: rdn and ev ch over 2f out: wknd over 1f out* **4/1**[3]

-064 **6** 7 **Howe's Jack (IRE)**[8] 2894 3-8-6 44 ... (t) RussellKennemore(3) 2 29
(M C Chapman) *stdd s: hld up: racd keenly: rdn and wknd 3f out* **25/1**

4456 **7** 13 **Awesome Light (IRE)**[16] 3166 3-8-3 63 ... (t) DO'Donohoe 1 —
(W R Muir) *hld up: pushed along 4f out: rdn and wknd over 2f out* **8/1**

2m 9.56s (1.66) **Going Correction** +0.025s/f (Good) **7** Ran SP% **116.1**
Speed ratings (Par 100): **94,91,90,87,87 81,71**
toteswinger: 1&2 £8.70, 1&3 £1.02, 2&3 £10.10. CSF £30.00 TOTE £2.80: £1.70, £4.10; EX 24.80 Trifecta £338.50.Maddy was subject to a friendly claim.
Owner Collings, Powner, Sword & Partners **Bred** P K Gardner **Trained** Moreton Morrell, Warwicks

FOCUS
A weak claimer run at a slowish pace, and form to be against.
Awesome Light(IRE) Official explanation: jockey said colt had a breathing problem

3731 TOTESPORTCASINO.COM RATING RELATED MAIDEN STKS 7f 9y
5:30 (5:30) (Class 5) 3-Y-0+ **£3,238** (£963; £481; £240) **Stalls** Low

Form RPR

0032 **1** **Loveinanelevator**[7] 3481 3-8-9 68 ... HayleyTurner 3 74+
(M L W Bell) *hld up: plld hrd: hdwy over 1f out: r.o to ld nr fin* **2/1**[1]

5020 **2** 1/2 **Bahamian Kid**[23] 2976 3-8-12 67 ... DO'Donohoe 11 73
(R Hollinshead) *hld up in tch: led over 2f out: hung lft over 1f out: rdn and hung lft ins fnl f: hdd nr fin* **16/1**

5-23 **3** 1 3/4 **El Fuser**[23] 2976 3-8-12 69 ... RichardSmith 1 68
(P J Makin) *led over 4f: sn rdn: styd on* **5/2**[2]

33-4 **4** nk **Tense (IRE)**[24] 2946 3-8-9 68 ... ShaneKelly 7 64
(J A Osborne) *chsd ldrs: rdn over 1f out: styd on* **12/1**

-550 **5** 1/2 **Alsadeek (IRE)**[14] 3282 3-8-12 70 ... (b[1]) DaneO'Neill 5 66
(J L Dunlop) *hld up: hdwy over 2f out: swtchd rt over 1f out: no ex wl ins fnl f* **11/2**

0-20 **6** 2 **Red Tarn**[25] 2911 3-8-12 70 ... (v[1]) PaulMulrennan 2 60
(B Smart) *chsd ldr: rdn over 2f out: wknd fnl f* **9/1**

5-33 **7** 12 **Signora (IRE)**[17] 3133 3-8-9 70 ... J-PGuillambert 8 25
(M Johnston) *s.i.s: outpcd: sme hdwy 3f out: sn wknd* **4/1**[3]

-440 **8** 4 1/2 **Billy Hot Rocks (IRE)**[25] 2922 3-8-12 64 ... JamesDoyle 6 16
(R M Beckett) *dwlt: plld hrd: hdwy over 4f out: rdn over 2f out: sn wknd* **16/1**

0-00 **9** 1 3/4 **Bagenalstown (IRE)**[20] 3065 3-8-12 30 ... RichardKingscote 9 11
(M Wellings) *prom over 4f* **100/1**

1m 24.14s (-2.06) **Going Correction** -0.425s/f (Firm)
WFA 3 from 4yo 8lb **9** Ran SP% **127.7**
Speed ratings (Par 103): **94,93,91,91,90 88,74,69,67**
toteswinger: 1&2 £20.40, 1&3 £2.40, 2&3 £30.10. CSF £41.48 TOTE £2.40: £1.60, £5.10, £1.40; EX 45.20 Trifecta £338.50 Part won..
Owner R L W Frisby **Bred** D D And Mrs Jean P Clee **Trained** Newmarket, Suffolk

FOCUS
One or two of these in this maiden had had quite a few chances in the past and are heading for the last chance saloon. The winner is probably a bit better than the bare form but this is not a race to be too positive about.
T/Plt: £24.90 to a £1 stake. Pool: £61,693.01. 1,805.13 winning tickets. T/Qpdt: £15.10 to a £1 stake. Pool: £2,752.29. 134.69 winning tickets. CR

2950 NOTTINGHAM (L-H)
Saturday, July 5

OFFICIAL GOING: Good to firm (firm on the straight course; 8.3)
Dolling out added 5yds to distances on the round course.
Wind: light against Weather: gloomy, some rain

3732 AMATEUR JOCKEYS ASSOCIATION INVESTING IN RACING LADY RIDERS' H'CAP 1m 2f 50y
6:20 (6:21) (Class 6) (0-60,61) 4-Y-0+ **£1,977** (£608; £304) **Stalls** Low

Form RPR

00-0 **1** **Paparaazi (IRE)**[5] 3551 6-9-6 **52** ... (p) MissKSharp(7) 12 62
(I W McInnes) *bhd: effrt over 3f out: plugged on to ld wl ins fnl f: rdr fell off wl after fin* **20/1**

3210 **2** 1/2 **Faraday (IRE)**[43] 2353 5-9-7 **51** ... MissFCumani(5) 10 60
(A P Stringer) *t.k.h in 2nd: lft in ld over 4f out: rdn 1f out: ct and no ex fnl 50yds* **2/1**[1]

6036 **3** 2 3/4 **Postmaster**[4] 3588 6-9-3 **49** ow2 ... MissSSawyer(7) 6 53
(R Ingram) *bhd: last 1/2-way: hdwy 3f out: hung lft: wnt 3rd ins fnl f: kpt on* **10/1**

0400 **4** 2 1/4 **Kingsholm**[16] 3175 6-10-7 **60** ... MissARyan 3 59
(I W McInnes) *chsd ldrs: drvn 3f out: one pce fnl 2f* **13/2**[2]

005- **5** hd **Uhuru Peak**[246] 6629 7-9-11 **50** ... (t) MissSBrotherton 11 49
(M W Easterby) *chsd ldrs: disp 3rd and rdn 2f out: one pce* **10/1**

4030 **6** 1 1/4 **Desert Hawk**[2] 3657 7-9-4 **48** ... MissRKneller(5) 13 44
(W M Brisbourne) *midfield: no imp fnl 2f* **13/2**[2]

05-0 **7** 2 3/4 **Centenary (IRE)**[59] 1913 4-9-13 **52** ... (b[1]) MissADeniel 9 43
(D E Cantillon) *s.s: bhd: rdn 4f out: sme prog to midfield but n.d and nt keen* **15/2**[3]

2100 **8** 3/4 **Mick Is Back**[15] 3218 4-9-12 **58** ... (vt) MissKMargarson(7) 5 47
(G G Margarson) *t.k.h in ld: sn 6 l clr: rn wd and hdd over 4f out: nt rdn whn losing pl fnl 2f* **16/1**

/0-0 **9** 21 **Monash Lad (IRE)**[19] 3084 6-10-1 **61** ow4 ... (p) MissMBryant(7) 8 8
(P Butler) *t.o fnl 3f* **66/1**

0-03 **10** 5 **Jiminor Mack**[29] 2782 5-9-2 **46** ... (p) MissKellyBurke(5) 15 —
(W J H Ratcliffe) *s.s: sn dashed up to ldrs: fdd over 3f out: sn t.o* **10/1**

5600 **11** 3/4 **Espejo (IRE)**[15] 3218 4-9-12 **51** ... MissEJJones 4 —
(W J Musson) *midfield: hmpd bnd bef st: t.o fnl 3f* **33/1**

1010 **P** **Jarvo**[24] 2957 7-10-4 **57** ... (v) MrsCBartley 16 —
(I W McInnes) *sddled sn slipped: p.u 1/2-way* **14/1**

2m 12.57s (0.07) **Going Correction** -0.075s/f (Good) **12** Ran SP% **120.8**
Speed ratings (Par 101): **96,95,93,91,91 90,88,87,70,66 66,—**
toteswinger: 1&2 £5.20, 1&3 £13.30, 2&3 £4.40. CSF £60.35 CT £454.96 TOTE £19.80: £5.00, £1.50, £1.70; EX 91.80.
Owner Mrs Jo Sharp **Bred** A R Nemazee **Trained** Catwick, E Yorks

FOCUS
A moderate handicap. The winner had slipped back to a good mark on last year's form and was close to that level here.
Jarvo Official explanation: jockey said saddle slipped

3733 RACING UK - ONLY £12.99 PER MONTH (S) STKS 6f 15y
6:50 (6:54) (Class 6) 3-4-Y-0 **£2,047** (£604; £302) **Stalls** High

Form RPR

300 **1** **Klarity**[9] 3395 3-8-5 49 ... (e) LiamJones 2 47
(J Pearce) *t.k.h towards rr: effrt over 2f out: led 100yds out: drvn and hld on wl* **10/1**

00-F **2** nk **Flamestone**[40] 2456 4-8-11 40 ... NataliaGemelova(5) 10 52
(A E Price) *towards rr: rdn and clsd over 1f out: ev ch and sustained chal through fnl f: jst hld* **50/1**

0305 **3** 1 1/4 **Racing Stripes (IRE)**[5] 3565 4-9-2 47 ... (b) RichardSmith 12 48
(K O Cunningham-Brown) *rrd at s: effrt 1/2-way: drvn over 2f out: nt qckn ins fnl f* **9/1**

0306 **4** ¾ **Flight Plan**[9] [3406] 3-8-10 60 .... TPQueally 9 45
(R A Fahey) *chsd ldrs: rdn and ev ch 1f out: wkng cl home* **5/2**[1]

1600 **5** shd **What Katie Did (IRE)**[17] [3136] 3-9-1 70 .... (b[1]) NelsonDeSouza 4 49
(P F I Cole) *swtchd to stands' rail and sn led: rdn and hdd 100yds out: wknd* **7/2**[2]

0000 **6** 1 ¼ **Nordic Light (USA)**[10] [3363] 4-9-2 63 .... (v[1]) SteveDrowne 11 41
(J M Bradley) *rdn and chsng ldrs 2f out: no imp over 1f out* **14/1**

000- **7** ½ **Come On Nellie (IRE)**[267] [6147] 4-8-4 41 .... AshleyMorgan(7) 5 35
(J G M O'Shea) *wl bhd early: hdwy over 2 out: sn rdn and no ex* **66/1**

0-00 **8** hd **Vogarth**[21] [3034] 4-8-11 53 .... JamesMillman(5) 3 39
(B R Millman) *bhd: sme late prog: no ch w ldrs* **8/1**

2055 **9** ¾ **Bertie Swift**[16] [3169] 4-9-2 56 .... ShaneKelly 8 37
(J Gallagher) *midfield and drvn 1/2-way: btn over 2f out* **4/1**[3]

00-0 **10** 4 **Minimum Fuss (IRE)**[177] [109] 4-8-5 40 ow1 .... NBazeley(7) 16 20
(M C Chapman) *prom: rdn over 2 out: sn lost pl* **66/1**

0-00 **11** 4 ½ **Fervent**[53] [2070] 4-8-13 42 .... (v[1]) TolleyDean(3) 7 9
(J M Bradley) *chsd ldrs: rdn and n.m.r over 2f out: sn btn* **33/1**

3000 **12** 5 **Marquis De Louvois (IRE)**[94] [1139] 3-8-5 54 .... (p) JackMitchell(5) 14 —
(Mrs A Duffield) *cl up: rdn over 2f out: sn fdd* **25/1**

00-0 **13** shd **Leonard Charles**[11] [3339] 4-9-2 53 .... (v[1]) DarrenWilliams 6 —
(C R Dore) *rdn and effrt on outside over 2f out: sn btn* **33/1**

0-56 **14** 12 **Capriccioso**[128] [734] 3-8-5 49 .... JimmyQuinn 15 —
(P Howling) *reluctant to go to s: prom over 4f: sn lost pl* **22/1**

1m 15.76s (0.66) **Going Correction** -0.15s/f (Firm) **14** Ran SP% **126.7**
WFA 3 from 4yo 6lb
Speed ratings (Par 101): **89,88,86,85,85 84,83,83,82,76 70,64,64,48**
toteswinger: 1&2 not won, 1&3 £55.40, 2&3 £50.40. CSF £455.44 TOTE £14.00: £3.50, £8.40, £3.70; EX 432.00.There was no bid for the winner.
Owner Jay Three Racing **Bred** Mill House Stud **Trained** Newmarket, Suffolk

FOCUS
A weak seller evidenced by the performance of the 40-rated runner-up. The form is rated through him.
Flight Plan Official explanation: jockey said gelding hung right throughout
Bertie Swift Official explanation: jockey said gelding was unsuited by the firm ground

3734 MIKE GARLAND LOACH CONSTRUCTION MAIDEN AUCTION FILLIES' STKS 5f 13y
7:20 (7:23) (Class 5) 2-Y-O **£2,914** (£867; £433; £216) **Stalls** High

Form RPR

5332 **1** **The Magic Of Rio**[18] [3114] 2-8-12 0 .... LiamJones 5 77
(W J Haggas) *prom: led over 1f out: sn tk decisive advantage: pushed out* **8/1**

3 **2** 1 ½ **Sills Vincero**[18] [3114] 2-8-8 0 .... AlanMunro 3 68
(P W Chapple-Hyam) *bhd and pushed along: effrt over 1f out: styd on wl but nt rch wnr: promising* **6/1**[3]

404 **3** hd **Amber Sunset**[24] [2944] 2-8-1 0 .... LukeMorris(3) 10 63
(J Jay) *cl up: rdn over 1f out: hung lft: nt qckn fnl 100yds* **12/1**

2 **4** ¾ **Red Rosanna**[16] [3178] 2-8-5 0 .... RussellKennemore(3) 1 65
(R Hollinshead) *chsd ldrs on outside: rdn and one pce fnl f* **8/1**

5 1 **Diggeratt (USA)** 2-8-8 0 .... DO'Donohoe 4 63+
(R A Fahey) *dwlt: last early: effrt whn hmpd over 1f out: rallied and kpt on ins fnl f* **50/1**

0230 **6** 2 **Amosite**[17] [3123] 2-8-4 0 .... (v) AdrianMcCarthy 9 50
(J R Jenkins) *rdn to ld: hdd over 1f out: sn gave up* **10/3**[1]

546 **7** 1 **Voulez Vous**[37] [2534] 2-8-12 0 .... ChrisCatlin 6 54
(E J O'Neill) *towards rr: rdn after 2f: btn wl over 1f out* **7/2**[2]

8 ¾ **Lady Master** 2-8-4 0 .... FrankieMcDonald 2 43
(H Candy) *unbalanced and hanging fr 1/2-way: no ch after and v green* **20/1**

4 **9** hd **One Cool Kitty**[23] [2979] 2-8-12 0 .... TPQueally 8 51
(M G Quinlan) *w ldr: rdn 1/2-way: wknd over 1f out* **7/2**[2]

00 **10** 4 **Miss Leona**[12] [3309] 2-8-4 0 .... NelsonDeSouza 7 28
(J M Bradley) *racd awkwardly in rr: hung lft and struggling 1/2-way* **150/1**

60.93 secs (0.23) **Going Correction** -0.15s/f (Firm) **10** Ran SP% **119.1**
Speed ratings (Par 91): **92,89,89,88,86 83,81,80,80,73**
toteswinger: 1&2 £8.00, 1&3 £11.70, 2&3 £34.30. CSF £55.94 TOTE £9.00: £2.00, £2.00, £3.40; EX 48.30.
Owner M Scotney/ D Asplin/ A Symonds **Bred** R F And S D Knipe **Trained** Newmarket, Suffolk

FOCUS
The form looks solid enough for the grade rated through the second, third and fourth.

NOTEBOOK
The Magic Of Rio had started to look exposed but she settled better off the decent gallop here and came through to win a shade comfortably. Her stable continues in fantastic form and there could be better to come from this daughter of Captain Rio in nursery company.
Sills Vincero, one place behind The Magic Of Rio at Yarmouth on her debut, again shaped with promise, staying on late to chase her old rival home. She is crying out for another furlong. (op 7-1 tchd 5-1)
Amber Sunset, who has not been getting home over 6f, appreciated this shorter distance and ran a sound enough race in third. (op 14-1)
Red Rosanna, stuck on the outside, boxed on well and was just run out of the places close home. She probably performed to a similar level as at Warwick. Official explanation: jockey said filly ran green (op 12-1 tchd 15-2)
Diggeratt(USA), a half-sister to a juvenile winner in Russia, did not enjoy the clearest of runs but was staying on at the finish. She should come on for the experience. Official explanation: jockey said filly was denied a clear run (op 22-1)
Amosite was below her best back down in grade having contested the Queen Mary Stakes last time out. (op 9-4 tchd 7-2)
Lady Master Official explanation: jockey said filly hung badly right under pressure
Miss Leona Official explanation: jockey said filly ran green

3735 RACINGUK.TV MEDIAN AUCTION MAIDEN STKS 5f 13y
7:50 (7:51) (Class 5) 2-Y-O **£3,070** (£906; £453) **Stalls** High

Form RPR

3 **1** **Jargelle (IRE)**[19] [3085] 2-8-12 0 .... LiamJones 6 82+
(W J Haggas) *stmbld sltly s and wnt lft: mde all: drew clr 1f out: pushed out* **8/15**[1]

2 1 ¼ **Leftontheshelf (IRE)** 2-8-9 0 .... TolleyDean(3) 8 78+
(J L Spearing) *chsd wnr: drvn over 1f out: kpt on but wl hld ins fnl f* **6/1**[2]

00 **3** 5 **Gemini Jive (IRE)**[8] [3456] 2-8-12 0 .... AlanMunro 7 60
(M G Quinlan) *chsd ldrs: rdn 1/2-way: no ch w first pair fnl f* **10/1**[3]

44 **4** nse **Abu Derby (IRE)**[17] [3140] 2-9-3 0 .... J-PGuillambert 5 64
(J G Given) *pushed lft s: cl up: drvn 1/2-way: btn over 1f out* **16/1**

50 **5** 4 ½ **Fyelehk (IRE)**[31] [2709] 2-8-12 0 .... JamesMillman(5) 2 48
(B R Millman) *rdn over 2f out: sn btn* **25/1**

0 **6** 10 **Meydan Style (USA)**[14] [3259] 2-9-3 0 .... PatrickMathers 3 12
(J Balding) *pressed ldrs over 3f: sn struggling* **66/1**

7 ¾ **Jiggalong** 2-8-12 0 .... AdrianMcCarthy 1 —
(G G Margarson) *immediately bdly outpcd: t.o* **10/1**[3]

8 10 **Iachimo** 2-9-3 0 .... DarrenWilliams 4 —
(K R Burke) *hmpd s: rdn over 2f out: fdd qckly: t.o: fin lame* **20/1**

60.64 secs (-0.06) **Going Correction** -0.15s/f (Firm) **8** Ran SP% **113.7**
Speed ratings (Par 94): **94,92,84,83,76 60,59,43**
toteswinger: 1&2 £1.30, 1&3 £3.60, 2&3 £6.10. CSF £3.93 TOTE £1.50: £1.02, £1.80, £2.60; EX 5.40.
Owner B Smith,A Duke,J Netherthorpe,G Goddard **Bred** Mrs A Robinson **Trained** Newmarket, Suffolk

FOCUS
Ordinary maiden form, with the winner improving from her debut effort.

NOTEBOOK
Jargelle(IRE), who had shaped with promise on her debut, recovered quickly after an early stumble and showed good speed to lead throughout. She could well make her mark in better grade. (op 4-5 tchd 1-2)
Leftontheshelf(IRE), a half-sister to Dearg, a winner over 6f at two, had the rail to help and kept on for a clear second. The winner had an edge in experience so it was a decent effort. (op 5-2)
Gemini Jive(IRE), dropped down to five, is a daughter of Namid and will likely do better on easier ground. (op 8-1)
Abu Derby(IRE) is finding life in maiden company a bit difficult and will have a better chance of success in modest handicaps. A longer trip will suit him, too. (op 18-1)
Fyelehk(IRE) might do better dropped into plating company. (tchd 28-1)
Iachimo Official explanation: jockey said colt finished lame

3736 MATTHEWS & TANNERT H'CAP 1m 2f 50y
8:20 (8:22) (Class 4) (0-80,79) 3-Y-O+ **£5,828** (£1,734; £866; £432) **Stalls** Low

Form RPR

424 **1** **Hunting Country**[19] [3094] 3-9-0 76 .... J-PGuillambert 5 86+
(M Johnston) *pressed ldr: rdn to ld 3f out: hld on wl cl home: a looked jst in command* **9/4**[1]

0-32 **2** hd **Nesno (USA)**[28] [2848] 5-8-10 61 .... AlanMunro 1 71
(J D Bethell) *t.k.h in 3rd: led briefly over 3f out: pressd wnr hrd after: drvn and no ex fnl 50yds* **11/2**[3]

2-05 **3** 1 ¼ **Del Mar Sunset**[11] [3337] 9-9-9 74 .... LiamJones 9 81
(W J Haggas) *s.i.s and pushed along: pulling hrd after 3f: bhd tl prog over 2f out: swtchd rt 1f out and brief effrt: sn no imp* **7/1**

-041 **4** 3 ¾ **Piper's Song (IRE)**[11] [3337] 5-9-13 78 .... PatCosgrave 3 78
(D J G Murray Smith) *t.k.h and chsd ldrs: rdn over 2f out: no imp after* **5/1**[2]

0-50 **5** ½ **Packers Hill (IRE)**[10] [3366] 4-9-5 70 .... ShaneKelly 10 69
(G A Swinbank) *towards rr: drvn and no rspnse and racd awkwardly fr 4f out: n.d but styd on cl home* **22/1**

0016 **6** 1 **Quince (IRE)**[8] [3461] 5-10-0 79 .... (v) JimmyQuinn 8 76
(J Pearce) *towards rr: drvn 4f out: edgd sltly lft and nvr able to chal* **10/1**

6-05 **7** ¾ **Dragon Slayer (IRE)**[14] [3257] 6-9-8 73 .... WilliamBuick 2 68
(John A Harris) *t.k.h in ld: rdn and hdd over 3f out: sn lost pl* **14/1**

4100 **8** 2 ½ **Stock Market (USA)**[21] [3038] 3-9-2 78 .... SteveDrowne 6 68
(E A L Dunlop) *chsd ldrs: rdn over 3f out: sn btn* **7/1**

-063 **9** nk **Gallego**[10] [3361] 6-8-7 61 .... KirstyMilczarek(3) 11 51
(R J Price) *s.s: a in rr* **14/1**

2m 10.27s (-2.23) **Going Correction** -0.075s/f (Good) **9** Ran SP% **114.6**
WFA 3 from 4yo+ 11lb
Speed ratings (Par 105): **105,104,103,100,100 99,99,97,96**
toteswinger: 1&2 £3.40, 1&3 £2.30, 2&3 £7.20. CSF £14.38 CT £73.82 TOTE £2.50: £1.40, £2.00, £2.30; EX 16.30.
Owner Sheikh Hamdan Bin Mohammed Al Maktoum **Bred** Floors Farming & London Thoroughbred Services Ltd **Trained** Middleham Moor, N Yorks

FOCUS
Solid form for the grade, with the first three nicely clear. The clear pick of the three C/D times.

3737 CITY LIFE AND COUNTY LIVING MAGAZINE H'CAP 1m 2f 50y
8:50 (8:50) (Class 5) (0-75,78) 3-Y-O **£3,238** (£963; £481; £240) **Stalls** Low

Form RPR

3056 **1** **Colorado Blue (IRE)**[10] [3384] 3-9-6 74 .... (b) SteveDrowne 8 79
(R Charlton) *mde all: drvn 3f out: racd rather idly but a holding rivals fnl f* **11/4**[2]

5-66 **2** 1 ¼ **Timbalier (USA)**[22] [2996] 3-8-11 65 .... StephenDonohoe 10 68
(D M Simcock) *sn drvn and lost tch: on and off bridle in last: cajoled to improve wl over 1f out: r.o to go 2nd ins fnl f: nt rch wnr* **12/1**

-235 **3** 1 ¼ **Brexca (IRE)**[24] [2948] 3-9-7 75 .... (v) RichardMullen 9 75
(C G Cox) *cl up: wnt 2nd 3f out: sn rdn: one pce after: lost 2nd ins fnl f* **6/1**

61-0 **4** 5 **Bauhaus Bourbon (USA)**[12] [3325] 3-9-2 70 .... (t) NelsonDeSouza 3 60
(P F I Cole) *bhd: btn wl over 2f out: plodded on* **14/1**

0432 **5** 1 ¾ **Castlebury (IRE)**[43] [2367] 3-8-11 65 .... ShaneKelly 6 52
(G A Swinbank) *chsd ldrs: rdn 3f out: wknd 2f out* **6/4**[1]

2600 **6** 4 ½ **Whaston (IRE)**[43] [2367] 3-8-2 56 oh2 .... (v[1]) JimmyQuinn 4 34
(J D Bethell) *t.k.h: cl up 7f: wl btn 2f out* **25/1**

0-21 **7** 3 ¼ **Might Be Magic**[131] [698] 3-9-3 71 .... AlanMunro 7 42
(P W Chapple-Hyam) *pressed ldr for 7f: sn lost pl and racd awkwardly* **11/2**[3]

2m 11.72s (-0.78) **Going Correction** -0.075s/f (Good) **7** Ran SP% **114.5**
Speed ratings (Par 100): **100,99,98,94,92 89,86**
toteswinger: 1&2 £11.90, 1&3 £4.80, 2&3 £11.40. CSF £34.35 CT £183.16 TOTE £4.40: £2.50, £5.80; EX 40.80.
Owner Michael Pescod **Bred** Duncan A McGregor **Trained** Beckhampton, Wilts

FOCUS
The winner dominated from the front and, with the third not progressing, the form looks ordinary for a race of this sort.
Whaston(IRE) Official explanation: jockey said gelding ran too free

3738 SUBSCRIBE TO RACING UK H'CAP 1m 75y
9:20 (9:20) (Class 5) (0-70,74) 3-Y-O+ **£3,238** (£963; £481; £240) **Stalls** Centre

Form RPR

3231 **1** **El Dececy (USA)**[9] [3422] 4-9-11 74 .... KrishGundowry(7) 2 94
(S Parr) *mde all at str pce: 4l clr 4f out: edgd lft under volley of reminders ins fnl f: all out* **5/1**[2]

4412 **2** hd **It's A Dream (FR)**[7] [3478] 5-9-6 62 .... (t) GrahamGibbons 4 82
(M W Easterby) *plld hrd and chsd ldrs: wnt 2nd over 2f out: drvn to chal 1f out: ch after: kpt on cl home* **1/1**[1]

0003 **3** 7 **Harare**[20] [3054] 7-9-8 64 .... (v) JimmyQuinn 7 67
(R J Price) *midfield: rdn 3f out: put hd in air: no imp after* **9/1**

6005 **4** ½ **Golden Prospect**[16] [3181] 4-9-13 69 .... JamesDoyle 9 71
(J W Hills) *nvr bttr than midfield: rdn 3f out: no imp: btn over 1f out* **15/2**[3]

The Form Book, Raceform Ltd, Compton, RG20 6NL

2-44 **5** shd **Flashy Max**[47] 2247 3-8-0 51 oh2 .... WilliamBuick 1 51
(Jedd O'Keeffe) *plld hrd: disp 2nd tl over 2f out: rdn and put hd in air: nt run on* **14/1**

050- **6** 1 **Stravita**[192] 7237 4-9-3 62 .... RussellKennemore(3) 6 62
(R Hollinshead) *bhd and sn rdn: effrt on rails wl over 2f out: v one pce: btn over 1f out* **40/1**

1052 **7** 8 **West End Lad**[16] 3175 5-8-12 54 .... (b) TPQueally 11 35
(S R Bowring) *t.k.h: disp 2nd for 5f: sn wknd* **9/1**

060- **8** 7 **Rocheport**[292] 5484 3-8-11 62 .... OscarUrbina 8 25
(G C H Chung) *nvr bttr than midfield: struggling wl over 2f out* **50/1**

0000 **9** 21 **Heartsanddiamonds**[19] 3084 4-8-9 51 oh3 .... ChrisCatlin 10 —
(A W Carroll) *immediately outpcd: t.o 1/2-way* **50/1**

5-03 **10** 2 ¾ **Eton Fable (IRE)**[32] 2700 3-9-0 65 .... (v1) DO'Donohoe 5 —
(W J H Ratcliffe) *immediately outpcd: t.o 1/2-way: eased fnl 3f* **16/1**

1m 44.65s (-0.75) **Going Correction** -0.075s/f (Good)
WFA 3 from 4yo+ 9lb **10** Ran SP% **117.3**
Speed ratings (Par 103): **100,99,92,92,92 91,83,76,55,52**
toteswinger: 1&2 £1.30, 1&3 £17.70, 2&3 £5.70. CSF £10.32 CT £43.34 TOTE £6.60: £2.00, £1.10, £2.90; EX 11.80 Place 6: £549.65 Place 5: £244.58.
Owner Willie McKay **Bred** Shadwell Farm LLC **Trained** Bawtry, S Yorks
■ Stewards' Enquiry : James Doyle one-day ban: careless riding (Jul 19)

FOCUS
They went a decent pace here and, with the second running to something like his best, the form looks sound enough.
Stravita Official explanation: jockey said filly hung right
West End Lad Official explanation: jockey said gelding hung right
T/Plt: £612.50 to a £1 stake. Pool: £64,566.00. 76.95 winning tickets. T/Qpdt: £43.30 to a £1 stake. Pool: £4,268.00. 72.80 winning tickets. IM

3680 SANDOWN (R-H)
Saturday, July 5

OFFICIAL GOING: Good to firm (firm in places)
Round course at innermost configuration.
Wind: Light, half against Weather: Fine

3739 CHAMPAGNE LANSON SPRINT STKS (GROUP 3) 5f 6y
2:10 (2:13) (Class 1) 3-Y-O+

£36,900 (£13,988; £7,000; £3,490; £1,748; £877) **Stalls** High

Form RPR

-613 **1** **Ancien Regime (IRE)**[21] 3047 3-8-12 105 .... LDettori 10 111
(M A Jarvis) *trckd ldng pair: effrt over 1f out: drvn to ld last 150yds: edgd rt u.p: hld on* **3/1**[2]

0030 **2** nk **Prime Defender**[14] 3248 4-9-3 104 .... MichaelHills 5 112
(B W Hills) *pushed along on outer in midfield after 2f: prog u.p fr wl over 1f out: styd on to chse wnr last 100yds: jst hld* **12/1**

-555 **3** ½ **Hoh Mike (IRE)**[18] 3101 4-9-3 112 .... JamieSpencer 9 110
(M L W Bell) *dwlt: hld up in last and wl off the pce: taken to outer and effrt wl over 1f out: drvn and r.o fnl f: nrst fin* **13/8**[1]

-350 **4** ½ **Wi Dud**[52] 2106 4-9-3 106 .... TedDurcan 12 108
(K A Ryan) *hld up in abt 7th: stdy prog fr 2f out: tried to cl on ldrs fr 1f out: lacked ex zip to chal* **8/1**

0160 **5** nk **Off The Record**[14] 3248 4-9-3 98 .... TPQueally 3 107
(J G Given) *trckd ldng pair: clsd to chal and nrly upsides 1f out: nt qckn fnl f* **25/1**

320- **6** nk **Peace Offering (IRE)**[272] 6039 8-9-3 110 .... AdrianTNicholls 7 109+
(D Nicholls) *taken down early: chsd ldr: rdn sn after 1/2-way: led wl over 1f out: hdd fnl 150yds: stl 3rd but hld whn hmpd 50yds out* **14/1**

0-20 **7** ¾ **Intrepid Jack**[14] 3248 6-9-3 104 .... RyanMoore 2 104
(H Morrison) *hld up in last pair fr low draw: drvn on outer over 1f out: styd on fnl f: nrst fin* **13/2**[3]

2-00 **8** ½ **Rowe Park**[31] 2712 5-9-7 107 .... LPKeniry 11 106
(Mrs L C Jewell) *trckd ldng pair on inner: cl up whn n.m.r wl over 1f out: and lost pl: nvr rcvrd* **22/1**

0050 **9** ¾ **Matsunosuke**[18] 3101 6-9-3 99 .... JimmyFortune 8 99
(A B Coogan) *s.i.s: hld up in 9th: stl at rr but clsd on ldrs over 1f out: fdd fnl f* **33/1**

6324 **10** 2 **Day By Day**[15] 3243 4-9-0 96 .... (b) DarryllHolland 4 89
(B J Meehan) *led to wl over 1f out: wknd* **25/1**

60.40 secs (-1.20) **Going Correction** -0.05s/f (Good)
WFA 3 from 4yo+ 5lb **10** Ran SP% **116.9**
Speed ratings (Par 113): **107,106,105,104,104 103,102,101,100,97**
toteswinger: 1&2 £7.40, 1&3 £1.80, 2&3 £5.00. CSF £36.29 TOTE £4.10: £1.70, £3.80, £1.10; EX 53.50 Trifecta £265.10 Pool: £1433.16 - 4.00 winning units..
Owner Sheikh Ahmed Al Maktoum **Bred** Deer Forest Stud **Trained** Newmarket, Suffolk
■ Stewards' Enquiry : Jamie Spencer one-day ban: used whip with excessive frequency (Jul 19)
L Dettori two-day ban: careless riding (Jul 21,22)

FOCUS
The far rail had been brought in four yards and there did not appear to be a bias towards those racing on the far side. Yet another Group-race success for a three-year-old in this division, and more proof that a decent generation of sprinters are finally coming through. They went a good pace throughout and the form looks solid, although it is anchored by the fifth and nothing special for the grade.

NOTEBOOK
Ancien Regime(IRE), the only three-year-old in the field, was representing a generation of sprinters that have been carrying all before them in the top sprints this year. Although he had a bit to find with one or two strictly on the ratings, he was understandably well backed, and when he quickened up a furlong out he always looked like holding off his late challengers. He coped well with the drop back to 5f on this stiff track, but he will be just as effective back over an easy six. His trainer now plans to send him to York for the Nunthorpe. (op 7-2 tchd 4-1, 9-2 in places)
Prime Defender was well below his best in cheekpieces in the Wokingham, but the headgear was discarded this time and he returned to form. He has shown his best in the past over 6f, but he too benefited from the strong pace over this stiff five and was keeping on really well at the death. A quick reappearance in the July Cup is possible, but he will surely find a few too good at Newmarket.
Hoh Mike(IRE) won this race last year and his fifth in the King's Stand last time out suggested he was as good as ever, but he is a hold-up type who needs his fair share of luck in running. Spencer avoided any trouble this time by switching him out wide with plenty of the race remaining and he enjoyed a clear run down the outside. He finished well but was never quite getting there, and it is possible that he simply prefers to weave between horses. Official explanation: jockey said colt missed the break (op 15-8)
Wi Dud found the trip, even on this stiff track, to be on the short side for him. He kept on well, challenging between horses, but the line was always going to come too soon for him. Winless since his Flying Childers success in 2006, he could do with a confidence booster in a small conditions race somewhere.
Off The Record, the second lowest rated horse in the field, was sixth in the Temple Stakes two starts back and he probably ran close to that form again. Now high in the weights for handicaps but a bit below the required standard to win in this sort of company, he threatens to become difficult to place.
Peace Offering(IRE) chased the strong pace set by Day By Day and unsurprisingly, given that this was his seasonal reappearance and this track would be stiffer than ideal, he faded inside the last, where he was hampered. It was a promising effort and he should be spot on next time. (op 12-1 tchd 11-1)
Intrepid Jack, stepping up in class from handicap company, is a popular horse for some reason but he just seems to cost his followers money. Since notching a hat-trick back in 2005, he has only won one race - a handicap at Bath at 4-1 - but he has been a beaten favourite or co-favourite nine times. (op 7-1)
Rowe Park had a stiff task as he had to carry a 4lb penalty for winning a Group 3 race at Newbury last year. He went well for much of the way and was still handy, though unlikely to figure, when short of room. (tchd 20-1 and 25-1)
Matsunosuke is another who is difficult to place off his current mark. (op 25-1)
Day By Day

3740 TOTESWINGER STKS (HERITAGE H'CAP) 1m 14y
2:40 (2:44) (Class 2) 3-Y-O+

£62,310 (£18,660; £9,330; £4,670; £2,330; £1,170) **Stalls** High

Form RPR

0000 **1** **Lovelace**[15] 3197 4-9-6 102 .... JimmyFortune 13 115
(M Johnston) *awkward s: t.k.h: hld up in abt 11th: bhd wall of rivals 2f out: gd run through over 1f out and again ent fnl f: drvn to ld last 150yds: r.o wl* **18/1**

0-42 **2** 1 ¼ **Ace Of Hearts**[49] 2200 9-8-6 93 .... JackMitchell(5) 4 103
(C F Wall) *trckd ldng trio: gng wl 3f out: effrt to ld narrowly over 1f out: hrd rdn and hdd last 150yds: kpt on* **16/1**

3122 **3** hd **Masaalek**[16] 3155 3-8-8 99 .... RHills 14 107
(M P Tregoning) *hld up in midfield: prog on inner fr over 2f out: drvn to chal over 1f out: upsides ins fnl f: one pce* **9/2**[1]

4000 **4** nk **Dubai's Touch**[17] 3122 4-9-4 100 .... DarryllHolland 1 109
(M Johnston) *trckd ldr: led 3f out: drvn and narrowly hdd jst over 1f out: styd on same pce* **25/1**

0-01 **5** ½ **Fifteen Love (USA)**[16] 3155 3-8-9 100 .... (p) RichardHughes 3 106
(R Charlton) *stdd s: hld up in abt 12th: tried to make prog over 2f out: kpt on fr over 1f out but nvr able to chal* **15/2**[3]

0404 **6** 1 **Flipando (IRE)**[9] 3413 7-8-11 93 .... JamieSpencer 10 98+
(T D Barron) *hld up in late trio: prog on outer 2f out: hanging bdly rt and nt qckn 1f out: kpt on* **11/1**

60-2 **7** ¾ **Unshakable (IRE)**[29] 2789 9-8-9 91 .... PaulEddery 16 95
(Bob Jones) *trckd ldng pair: lost pl and rdn over 2f out: grad shuffled bk over 1f out: kpt on ins fnl f* **16/1**

-120 **8** ½ **Lang Shining (IRE)**[17] 3122 4-9-5 101 .... RyanMoore 9 104+
(Sir Michael Stoute) *sn last and pushed along: u.p and gng nowhere wl over 2f out: grad styd on: nrst fin* **5/1**[2]

1144 **9** shd **Kavachi (IRE)**[17] 3122 5-8-8 90 .... FergusSweeney 15 92
(G L Moore) *hld up in midfield on inner: no prog u.p 2f out: kpt on same pce after* **14/1**

20-1 **10** nse **Jack Junior (USA)**[14] 3262 4-9-4 100 .... LDettori 17 102
(B J Meehan) *wl enough plcd bhd ldrs: lost pl wl over 1f out: one pce and no imp after* **10/1**

-443 **11** nse **Pinpoint (IRE)**[15] 3195 6-9-10 106 .... AdamKirby 8 108
(W R Swinburn) *t.k.h: hld up in abt 10th: drvn on outer and sme prog 2f out: no imp on ldrs 1f out: one pce* **10/1**

3011 **12** nk **Farley Star**[23] 2969 4-8-8 90 .... TQuinn 7 91
(R Charlton) *mostly in last pair: rdn 3f out: struggling after: styd on fr over 1f out: nrst fin* **16/1**

0-00 **13** nk **Prince Of Light (IRE)**[15] 3197 5-8-8 90 .... EddieAhern 11 91
(M Johnston) *trckd ldrs: tried to cl over 2f out: stl chsng 1f out: fdd last 150yds* **33/1**

4015 **14** 1 ¼ **Bahar Shumaal (IRE)**[7] 3503 6-8-1 88 .... AhmedAjtebi(5) 2 86
(C E Brittain) *t.k.h: trckd ldrs on outer: losing pl whn squeezed out wl over 1f out* **16/1**

-150 **15** hd **Celtic Sultan (IRE)**[15] 3197 4-9-6 102 .... TedDurcan 12 99
(T P Tate) *led to 3f out: wknd jst over 1f out* **14/1**

1m 40.31s (-2.99) **Going Correction** -0.05s/f (Good)
WFA 3 from 4yo+ 9lb **15** Ran SP% **122.0**
Speed ratings (Par 109): **112,110,110,110,109 108,108,107,107,107 107,107,106,105,105**
toteswinger: 1&2 £142.60, 1&3 £28.30, 2&3 £19.90. CSF £282.68 CT £1566.11 TOTE £24.70: £6.60, £5.20, £2.50; EX 475.30 TRIFECTA Not won..
Owner Hamad Suhail **Bred** Mrs Mary Taylor **Trained** Middleham Moor, N Yorks

FOCUS
A competitive handicap run at a good pace and the form looks sound. The winner has been rated a length or so up on his good 2007 form, and the third and fifth are up slightly on their Britannia runs.

NOTEBOOK
Lovelace has struggled somewhat since completing a four-timer in a Group 3 race last September, but he ran a decent race under a big weight in the Buckingham Palace Stakes last time out and had been dropped a couple of pounds since then. The step up to a mile suited him and he ran on well in the closing stages, weaving his way between horses, and is clearly back to his very best, something which can probably also be said for his stable, which has struggled in recent months. He will have more than one option at Glorious Goodwood. (op 25-1)
Ace Of Hearts, who won this race in 2005 and was second in it in 2006, ran a big race again on his favoured fast ground, travelling well into contention two and a half furlongs out and boxing on well under pressure. He is a consistent performer but has only won once in 24 starts since August 2005.
Masaalek, runner-up but the 'winner' on the far side in the Britannia, reversed Ascot form with Fifteen Love on 2lb better terms. He is steadily progressive and this was a good, solid effort against the older horses. (op 5-1)
Dubai's Touch underlined his stable's return to form with his best effort for some time. He has been dropped 10lb since this time last year and is another who will have one or two options at Glorious Goodwood, where he was a winner in Listed company last year. (op 20-1)
Fifteen Love(USA) could not confirm Britannia form with Masaalek on 2lb worse terms but he still ran a sound race in defeat. On the evidence of this run he will be worth a try over 1m2f. (op 8-1)
Flipando(IRE) hung as he tried to close in from the back of the field. Conditions were very quick here and perhaps a little ease in the ground suits him best these days. Official explanation: jockey said gelding hung right (op 9-1)
Unshakable(IRE), twice a winner and three times placed in his previous seven starts at this track, has never won off a mark in the 90s and needs a bit of give in the ground to be seen at his best. (op 12-1)
Lang Shining(IRE) is another who probably found conditions too quick. He was keeping on at the finish and is not one to write off when getting some ease. (tchf 11-2 in a place)

Kavachi(IRE), who ran really well in the Hunt Cup, was a bit disappointing off a 3lb higher mark. His pedigree suggests he should appreciate a bit of cut, and his wins have generally been with some ease, but he has plenty of form on faster, including at Ascot, so it is difficult to come up with an excuse for him. (op 12-1)

Jack Junior(USA), who made hard work of beating ordinary opposition in a maiden at Haydock last time, is poorly handicapped and needs some relief. (op 12-1 tchd 9-1)

Pinpoint(IRE), third in the Wolferton last time out, threatened to get involved down the outside approaching the two-furlong marker, but his effort flattened out. (op 11-1 tchd 12-1)

Farley Star, 5lb higher than for her latest win at Haydock and up in class, could never get in a blow from off the pace. (op 14-1)

Celtic Sultan(IRE), whose form is over shorter, set a strong pace and paid the price in the closing stages. (op 16-1 tchd 18-1)

3741 CORAL-ECLIPSE (GROUP 1) 1m 2f 7y

3:20 (3:21) (Class 1) 3-Y-0+

£283,850 (£107,600; £53,850; £26,850; £13,450; £6,750) **Stalls** High

Form RPR

-635 **1** **Mount Nelson**[18] [3100] 4-9-7 0 ... JMurtagh 1 123
(A P O'Brien, Ire) *hld up in 6th: prog on outer over 2f out: rdn and hanging rt over 1f out: chsd ldr ins fnl f: drvn and r.o gamely to ld last stride* **7/2**[2]

-122 **2** *shd* **Phoenix Tower (USA)**[17] [3121] 4-9-7 116 ... TedDurcan 2 122
(H R A Cecil) *settled in 5th: prog on outer over 2f out: led over 1f out: hrd rdn and styd on gamely fnl f: hdd post* **5/2**[1]

-333 **3** *1* **Pipedreamer**[17] [3121] 4-9-7 110 ... JimmyFortune 4 120
(J H M Gosden) *hld up in 6th: rdn over 2f out: prog over 1f out: hrd drvn and styd on to snatch 3rd last strides* **4/1**[3]

1131 **4** *nk* **Campanologist (USA)**[15] [3193] 3-8-10 107 ... LDettori 3 119
(Saeed Bin Suroor) *unable to ld and trckd ldng pair: effrt to ld 2f out: hdd and edgd rt over 1f out: stl ev ch ins fnl f: fdd nr fin* **13/2**

5/20 **5** *¾* **Rob Roy (USA)**[49] [2193] 6-9-7 110 ... RyanMoore 5 118
(Sir Michael Stoute) *hld up in last: stl there 2f out: efofrt and rdn over 1f out: styd on ins fnl f: nt rch ldrs* **14/1**

-556 **6** *1* **Stotsfold**[17] [3121] 5-9-7 110 ... AdamKirby 6 116
(W R Swinburn) *sn chsd ldng trio: rdn and nt qckn over 2f out and lost pl: kpt on again fnl f* **25/1**

4402 **7** *½* **Multidimensional (IRE)**[14] [3246] 5-9-7 105 ... TPQueally 7 115
(H R A Cecil) *pushed up to ld and set gd pce: rdn 3f out: hdd 2f out: grad fdd* **7/1**

-223 **8** *7* **Maraahel (IRE)**[14] [3246] 7-9-7 116 ... (v) RHills 9 101
(Sir Michael Stoute) *trckd ldr: moved up to chal over 2f out: wknd rapidly over 1f out* **12/1**

2m 5.56s (-4.94) **Going Correction** -0.05s/f (Good)
WFA 3 from 4yo+ 11lb **8** Ran SP% **114.8**
Speed ratings (Par 117): **117,116,116,115,115 114,114,108**
toteswinger: 1&2 £2.50, 1&3 £4.30, 2&3 £2.10. CSF £12.76 TOTE £4.50: £1.80, £1.10, £2.60; EX 15.00 Trifecta £43.80 Pool: £8021.52 - 135.29 winning units..

Owner D Smith, Mrs J Magnier, M Tabor **Bred** Cliveden Stud Ltd **Trained** Ballydoyle, Co Tipperary

FOCUS

A relatively weak renewal, featuring only one previous Group 1 winner in Mount Nelson, and a favourite and third favourite who had been stuffed by Duke Of Marmalade in the Prince Of Wales's Stakes. They went a good pace but a bunch finish only goes to underline the impression that, although sound, the form is ordinary for this level. The runner-up, third and sixth have all been rated within a pound of their Royal Ascot form. The proximity of Campanologist, who has been upped 9lb, raises a doubt over the form, but it could be seen as a pointer to the strength of the three-year-olds.

NOTEBOOK

Mount Nelson has had his problems since winning the Group 1 Criterium International as a juvenile, but he ran with plenty of promise when shaping better than his fifth position suggested in the Queen Anne last time out, and it looked significant that O'Brien, who had a good line to the principal dangers through Duke Of Marmalade, was happy to rely on him alone. Held up out the back tracking Phoenix Tower, he took a while to pick up and hung right under pressure, but Murtagh got enough out of him to edge ahead close to the line and just deny the favourite. The step up to 1m2f suited him and he probably won despite the ground, so there could be better to come on an easier surface. While this was probably a fairly average renewal, he will look a more than able substitute for Duke Of Marmalade in the top 1m2f events later in the season in which his stablemate does not compete. (op 3-1 tchd 5-2 tchd 4-1in a place)

Phoenix Tower(USA), who finished four lengths behind Duke Of Marmalade in the Prince Of Wales's Stakes, was backed into favouritism in what looked a weaker event. Sent for home from two and a half furlongs out and in front approaching the final furlong, he was just run out of it close home by Mount Nelson, who had stalked him throughout, but beat Pipedreamer slightly further than he had at Ascot. Some might criticize the rider for not holding onto him for a bit longer, but in truth he did little wrong. (op 7-2)

Pipedreamer, held up towards the back of the field, was expected to appreciate this stiffer track than Ascot, where he finished narrowly behind Phoenix Tower. He had the race run to suit, with the pace strong and stamina coming into play in the latter stages, but he was never making his ground up quick enough and was always being held by the first two close home. He does not look quite up to winning in this company, and the Group 3 Rose Of Lancaster Stakes was mentioned as a next possible target. His trainer suggested that ground a little easier will suit him in future. (op 5-1 tchd 11-2 in a place)

Campanologist(USA), the only three-year-old in the field, stole the King Edward VII Stakes from the front and on paper it was possible that he would get an easy lead again, but unfortunately for him Multidimensional was keen to get to the front and set a strong gallop, so he had to be settled in behind the pace instead. This was a fine effort back in trip - he had every chance a furlong out - and the most significant point about this performance is that it indicates that the top three-year-olds should be well up to taking on the best of the older horses over this sort of trip this season. (tchd 6-1 and 7-1 in a place)

Rob Roy(USA), who has never won over this far but was second in the Champion Stakes back in 2006, had the race run to suit as he was held up in last place off the strong pace. He stayed on but was never a threat to the principals and is simply not up to winning in this class these days. (tchd 12-1)

Stotsfold got the good gallop he needs but a stiff track like this is probably not ideal. He is another who was out of his depth in this grade, but will demand respect back in Listed or Group 3 company.

Multidimensional(IRE), who appreciated both a change of bit and tactics at Royal Ascot when only narrowly beaten in the Hardwicke Stakes, was again keen to lead. He ended up setting too strong a gallop for his own good, though, and paid the price over the final two furlongs. (op 6-1)

Maraahel(IRE) tracked the strong pace set by Multidimensional and probably did too much too soon, but the ground may also have been quicker than he likes these days. (tchd 14-1)

3742 AGFA HEALTHCARE STKS (REGISTERED AS THE DISTAFF STAKES) (LISTED RACE) (FILLIES) 1m 14y

3:55 (3:56) (Class 1) 3-Y-O

£22,708 (£8,608; £4,308; £2,148; £1,076; £540) **Stalls** High

Form RPR

4105 **1** **Rosaleen (IRE)**[17] [3124] 3-8-12 95 ... LDettori 6 98
(B J Meehan) *trckd ldrs: rdn to go 2nd over 1f out: r.o to ld last 150yds: drvn out* **9/1**

120- **2** *nk* **Visit**[274] [5973] 3-9-4 108 ... RyanMoore 8 104+
(Sir Michael Stoute) *hld up in abt 7th: prog fr 2f out: hrd rdn and r.o to take 2nd last 75yds: clsd on wnr but nvr gng to get there* **6/1**[2]

3102 **3** *¾* **Illusion**[17] [3124] 3-8-12 91 ... JimmyFortune 9 96
(J H M Gosden) *led and set mod pce: kpt on wl whn chal fr over 1f out: hdd and one pce last 150yds* **13/2**[3]

-120 **4** *1* **Sugar Mint (IRE)**[29] [2792] 3-8-12 103 ... MichaelHills 11 94+
(B W Hills) *dwlt and rousted along early to rch midfield: prog on inner 2f out: kpt on same pce fnl f and nvr able to chal* **7/1**

-023 **5** *¾* **Shabiba (USA)**[17] [3124] 3-8-12 92 ... RHills 5 94+
(M P Tregoning) *t.k.h: hld up in abt 8th: nt clr run over 2f out: effrt and styd on fr over 1f out: nt pce to rch ldrs* **8/1**

-212 **6** *nk* **Melodramatic (IRE)**[23] [2975] 3-8-12 101 ... RichardHughes 7 91
(R Charlton) *trckd ldrs: tried to chal 2f out: fdd over 1f out* **2/1**[1]

0-40 **7** *½* **Makaaseb (USA)**[17] [3124] 3-8-12 95 ... TedDurcan 3 90
(M A Jarvis) *hld up in last pair: taken to outer and rdn over 1f out: styd on ins fnl f: nvr nrr* **16/1**

2060 **8** *1 ½* **Comeback Queen**[9] [3415] 3-8-12 90 ... JamieSpencer 10 87
(S Kirk) *trckd ldrs on inner: lost pl over 1f out and sltly checked: n.d after* **25/1**

521 **9** *½* **Soft Shoe Shuffle (IRE)**[20] [3061] 3-8-12 83 ... AdamKirby 4 86
(W R Swinburn) *trckd ldrs: rdn over 2f out: fdd fr over 1f out* **12/1**

30-0 **10** *11* **Lady Aquitaine (USA)**[9] [3420] 3-8-12 101 ... EddieAhern 1 60
(B J Meehan) *hld up in last trio: brief effrt on outer over 2f out: wknd rapidly wl over 1f out: t.o* **33/1**

015 **11** *nk* **Kelowna (IRE)**[26] [2902] 3-8-12 92 ... TPQueally 2 60
(J L Dunlop) *stdd s: t.k.h and hld up in last pair: wknd 2f out: t.o* **22/1**

1m 41.98s (-1.32) **Going Correction** -0.05s/f (Good) **11** Ran SP% **119.3**
Speed ratings (Par 105): **104,103,102,101,101 100,100,98,98,87 87**
toteswinger: 1&2 £11.20, 1&3 £11.40, 2&3 £5.30. CSF £61.69 TOTE £10.70: £2.50, £2.70, £2.90; EX 73.60 Trifecta £622.30 Pool: £1093.28 - 1.30 winning units..

Owner F C T Wilson **Bred** Alan Dargan **Trained** Manton, Wilts

FOCUS

This featured four fillies who contested the Sandringham at Royal Ascot, similarly Listed status but a handicap. Back at level weights for this, the fifth Rosaleen gained revenge on both Illusion and Shabiba, who had been placed getting plenty of weight from her. Although the penalised Group 3 winner Visit chased her home, it was a muddling affair with the pace eased after the initial dash, and the form is nothing special by Listed standards.

NOTEBOOK

Rosaleen(IRE) sat much closer to the pace than she had in the Listed Sandringham handicap at Royal Ascot, and made her prominent position tell, as she got first run on her rivals in the final furlong. She seems to have two ways of running but, at her best, she is well up to winning again in this company. (op 10-1)

Visit, having her first run of the season despite being aimed at the Guineas earlier in the year, made a most pleasing comeback, strongly hinting that she is capable of adding to her Group-race success last year. Not very big, she followed the winner up the home straight and, after finding herself in a pocket for a few strides, kept on strongly to make Rosaleen really work hard for victory. There should be more to come from her. (op 5-1)

Illusion had an easy time of it out in the front but could not confirm her Royal Ascot form with the winner, on much worse terms. She is just the type to get better with age and follow in the footsteps of some of her owner's very talented fillies/mares of the past. (op 6-1 tchd 7-1)

Sugar Mint(IRE), taking a big drop in trip after a modest effort in the Oaks, stayed on really well from off the pace but was never getting to the leaders quickly enough to pose them a serious threat. She will easily stay another couple of furlongs at this level. Official explanation: jockey said filly was denied a clear run (op 10-1)

Shabiba(USA) did not have had the clearest of runs when required inside the two-furlong pole, so can be rated closer to Sugar Mint. Considering the way she pulled early, a drop back to seven or even 6f (a distance she won her only race over) may be worth trying again. (op 15-2 tchd 9-1 in a place)

Melodramatic(IRE) had every chance but faded inside the final furlong. She appeared to be outpaced by speedier types, so a step back up in trip may be needed. (op 9-4 tchd 11-4)

Makaaseb(USA), with the cheekpieces removed, was held up before making her move about two furlongs from home. She was manoeuvred from the inside rail to the centre of the track, and kept on in good style under pressure. This looked a promising effort and she might be returning to her best. (op 12-1)

Comeback Queen was always in about the same position throughout.

Soft Shoe Shuffle(IRE) had every chance but found the hike up in grade too much for her. (op 11-1)

3743 WEATHERBYS VAT SERVICES STKS (REGISTERED AS THE ESHER STAKES) (LISTED RACE) 2m 78y

4:30 (4:32) (Class 1) 4-Y-O+

£22,708 (£8,608; £4,308; £2,148; £1,076; £540) **Stalls** Centre

Form RPR

4-32 **1** **Distinction (IRE)**[14] [3250] 9-9-3 107 ... RyanMoore 7 116
(Sir Michael Stoute) *hld up in 5th and wl off the pce: clsd fr 3f out: wnt 2nd over 1f out: drvn to ld last 75yds and edgd rt: hld on* **7/2**[3]

0-31 **2** *shd* **Samuel**[35] [2625] 4-9-3 114 ... EddieAhern 4 116+
(J L Dunlop) *t.k.h at times: trckd ldng pair: wnt 2nd 3f out: rdn over 2f out: clsd to ld over 1f out: hdd last 75yds: bmpd sn after: jst hld* **11/4**[1]

40 **3** *6* **Tungsten Strike (USA)**[35] [2625] 7-9-0 107 ... DarryllHolland 6 106
(Mrs A J Perrett) *led after 2f and set gd pce: rdn over 2f out: hdd over 1f out: sn btn* **8/1**

5-10 **4** *2 ¼* **Finalmente**[16] [3154] 6-9-7 113 ... (p) LDettori 9 110
(S A Callaghan) *led 2f: chsd ldr: rdn 4f out: lost 2nd and btn 3f out: one pce* **16/1**

-105 **5** *2 ¼* **Raincoat**[29] [2797] 4-9-0 107 ... JimmyFortune 1 100
(J H M Gosden) *trckd ldng trio: wnt 3rd wl over 2f out: no hdwy wl over 1f out: wknd fnl f* **10/1**

-042 **6** *4* **Balkan Knight**[37] [2542] 8-9-0 112 ... JamieSpencer 10 95
(D R C Elsworth) *hld up in last pair and wl off the pce: rdn and no imp over 2f out* **6/1**

-115 **7** *19* **Ajaan**[14] 3250 4-9-0 101 (b) TedDurcan 3 73
(H R A Cecil) *hld up in last pair: hanging and reluctant over 2f out: sn t.o* **10/3**[2]

3m 34.73s (-4.77) **Going Correction** -0.05s/f (Good) **7** Ran SP% **112.3**
Speed ratings (Par 111): **109,108,105,104,103 101,92**
toteswinger: 1&2 £2.00, 1&3 £5.90, 2&3 £4.60. CSF £13.06 TOTE £4.30: £2.50, £2.10; EX 14.00.
Owner Highclere Thoroughbred Racing Ltd **Bred** Orpendale And Minch Bloodstock **Trained** Newmarket, Suffolk

FOCUS
A decent field for this Listed event. Tungsten Strike tried to steal the race over 3f out but he was unable to hold off the progressive Samuel and proven Distinction. The winner put up his best effort since returning from injury, while the runner-up and fourth were close to form.

NOTEBOOK
Distinction(IRE), taking a big drop in trip after running a great race in the 2m6f Queen Alexandra Stakes at Royal Ascot last time, came from off the pace down the outside to get past Samuel inside the final furlong and just hold on. The Stewards did look into possible interference he caused close to the line, but they were satisfied the result was unaffected. While he remains in this sort of form there are no plans to retire him, and the Goodwood Cup, which he won in 2005, will presumably be on the agenda again. (op 10-3 tchd 3-1)
Samuel ◆ has really got his act together this season and posted another sound effort. Having headed long-time leader Tungsten Strike well over a furlong out, he tried to hold off Distinction in the last furlong but failed narrowly to do so (the bump he got close to the line did not affect the final outcome). He is definitely one to follow for the rest of the season. (tchd 3-1)
Tungsten Strike(USA) tried to steal victory by quickening at the top of the home straight, but he soon came back to his field and was readily brushed aside, once again, by Samuel. He is still finding his way back to form, despite a fair effort on his seasonal debut, after a poor display in last season's Melbourne Cup. (op 10-1 tchd 11-1)
Finalmente looked to have plenty on under his penalty and unsurprisingly failed to make any impression. (op 14-1)
Raincoat, who was wearing a sheepskin noseband, was trying this sort of trip for the first time and gave the strong impression he was unsuited by it. (op 9-1)
Balkan Knight was given a patient ride that never threatened to trouble the leaders. On official ratings, he should have run much better. (op 8-1)
Ajaan never looked happy and his jockey confirmed after the race that his mount hated the quick ground. Official explanation: jockey said colt was unsuited by the good to firm ground (op 3-1)

3744 EMERALD STEEL H'CAP — 7f 16y
5:05 (5:07) (Class 3) (0-95,94) 3-Y-O

£9,346 (£2,799; £1,399; £700; £349; £175) Stalls High

Form RPR
1 **1** **Main Aim**[25] 2918 3-8-12 85 RyanMoore 11 96+
(Sir Michael Stoute) *t.k.h: hld up in last pair: stdy prog on outer fr over 2f out: pushed firmly into ld last 150yds: rdn out nr fin* **4/6**[1]
60-2 **2** *nk* **Firestreak**[49] 2189 3-9-5 92 RichardHughes 3 105+
(R Hannon) *hld up in 6th: plld out over 1f out and prog: wnt 2nd last 75yds and clsd but wnr already home* **9/1**
4103 **3** *1 1/2* **Brassini**[22] 2998 3-8-12 85 JamieSpencer 7 91
(B R Millman) *trckd ldr: led over 2f out and gng strly: rdn over 1f out: hdd and one pce last 150yds* **25/1**
0404 **4** *1 1/4* **Opus Maximus (IRE)**[8] 3442 3-8-3 76 AdrianTNicholls 10 79
(M Johnston) *uns rdr bef gng into stalls: hld up in 7th: effrt on inner over 2f out: sme prog over 1f out: styd on: no ch w ldrs* **16/1**
-001 **5** *nk* **Elysee Palace (IRE)**[44] 2333 3-8-7 80 MichaelHills 6 82
(M A Jarvis) *trckd ldrs: rdn 2f out: one pce and nvr able to mount a chal* **14/1**
2-22 **6** *1* **Smokey Rye**[171] 178 3-8-6 79 ow1 FergusSweeney 9 78
(G L Moore) *s.i.s: hld up in last: rdn over 2f out: styd on fnl f: nrst fin* **33/1**
1-30 **7** *nse* **Nezami (IRE)**[29] 2794 3-9-0 87 LDettori 2 86
(B J Meehan) *racd freely: led to over 2f out: styd chsng tl wknd ins fnl f* **12/1**
0312 **8** *1 1/2* **Lindoro**[21] 3039 3-9-5 92 AdamKirby 5 87
(W R Swinburn) *trckd ldrs: rdn 2f out: nt qckn sn after: wknd fnl f* **15/2**[3]
5004 **9** *4* **Dubai Dynamo**[16] 3155 3-9-7 94 JimmyFortune 1 78
(P F I Cole) *trckd ldrs: cl 3rd jst over 2f out: hanging and wknd bdly over 1f out* **6/1**[2]

1m 28.12s (-1.38) **Going Correction** -0.05s/f (Good) **9** Ran SP% **123.1**
Speed ratings (Par 104): **105,104,102,101,101 100,99,98,93**
toteswinger: 1&2 £3.60, 1&3 £6.20, 2&3 £20.30. CSF £8.72 CT £96.12 TOTE £1.80: £1.10, £1.90, £5.40; EX 7.60.
Owner K Abdulla **Bred** Juddmonte Farms Ltd **Trained** Newmarket, Suffolk

FOCUS
The pace looked even throughout and, although ordinary for the grade, the form should prove solid.

NOTEBOOK
Main Aim ◆ finished strongly from off the pace and just had enough in hand to withstand the late challenge of Firestreak. Unraced until June this year, and still unbeaten, he surely has plenty more to come and is a promising sort. (op 8-11 tchd 4-5 in places)
Firestreak ◆ gave away around a length while waiting for a gap to appear, so he was possibly unlucky not to have got his head in front (although the inexperienced winner may have been dossing in front). This track suits him well and he looks up to winning a similar contest this season. (tchd 8-1)
Brassini ran right up to his best over a trip he had never attempted before. However, it is worth noting that the winning time was ordinary and this may not have been a proper test at the distance.
Opus Maximus(IRE), who played up at the start, did not get the best of runs for the second time in a row and, without troubling the winner or runner-up, would have finished nearly upsides Brassini with a clear passage. His turn is not far away but he is starting to look a bit quirky.
Elysee Palace(IRE) had every chance, despite Lindoro pestering her for much of the race, but was not good enough. (op 12-1)
Smokey Rye made a very satisfactory return to the track after a long break, especially as she did not have her usual blinkers on. (op 50-1)
Lindoro pulled much too hard and had nothing left to give under pressure. (op 11-1)

3745 SODEXO PRESTIGE H'CAP — 1m 2f 7y
5:35 (5:42) (Class 4) (0-85,85) 3-Y-O £7,771 (£2,312; £1,155; £577) Stalls High

Form RPR
0033 **1** **Palmerin**[10] 3384 3-8-7 71 EddieAhern 9 81
(R Hannon) *led 1f: restrained bhd ldrs: effrt 3f out: rdn to ld 2f out: hrd pressed by runner-up after tl asserted last 75yds* **8/1**
-100 **2** *3/4* **American Art (IRE)**[42] 2405 3-9-2 80 (t) DarryllHolland 4 88
(B W Hills) *prom: wnt 2nd 1/2-way: rdn to ld over 2f out: hdd 2f out: pressed wnr after and clr of rest: no ex last 75yds* **25/1**
1430 **3** *2 1/2* **Greylami (IRE)**[22] 2996 3-9-2 80 MichaelHills 13 83+
(T G Mills) *t.k.h: hld up in last trio: tried to make prog but trbld passage fr 3f out to 2f out: styd on fnl f to take 3rd last stride* **16/1**
2312 **4** *hd* **St Jean Cap Ferrat**[40] 2464 3-9-1 79 RichardHughes 11 82
(G Wragg) *t.k.h: hld up bhd ldrs: outpcd over 3f out: chsd ldng pair over 1f out: nvr able to cl enough: lost 3rd last stride* **7/2**[1]
040 **5** *5* **Drum Major (IRE)**[20] 3058 3-8-10 74 RyanMoore 14 67+
(Sir Michael Stoute) *hld up in last trio: pushed along and hanging 3f out: wl bhd after: taken to outer and last over 1f out: passed 7 rivals fnl f* **14/1**
4104 **6** *1* **Master Spy**[22] 3002 3-9-7 85 (b[1]) JimmyFortune 10 76
(J H M Gosden) *t.k.h: hld up in midfield: outpcd fr over 3f out: nvr on terms after* **10/1**
-103 **7** *3/4* **Classical Rhythm (IRE)**[32] 2695 3-8-2 66 DavidKinsella 7 55
(J R Boyle) *led after 1f: qckmd 4f out: hdd over 2f out: wknd over 1f out* **33/1**
01-0 **8** *1 1/4* **Loyal Knight (IRE)**[12] 3325 3-8-9 73 LPKeniry 3 60
(S Kirk) *hld up in last: wl outpcd fr 4f out: modest prog fr 2f out: nvr on terms* **33/1**
1121 **9** *1/2* **Buddy Holly**[22] 3004 3-9-3 81 PatDobbs 8 67
(Pat Eddery) *trckd ldrs: lost grnd whn wd bnd over 4f out to over 3f out: struggling in rr over 2f out* **4/1**[2]
15-2 **10** *1 3/4* **King Columbo (IRE)**[31] 2714 3-9-2 83 JerryO'Dwyer[(3)] 15 65
(Miss J Feilden) *hld up towards rr: outpcd fr 4f out: no prog and btn wl over 2f out* **13/2**[3]
1522 **11** *2 1/2* **Taken (IRE)**[8] 3461 3-8-13 77 JamieSpencer 2 54
(J R Fanshawe) *t.k.h: trckd ldr to 1/2-way: outpcd 3f out: hanging and wknd 2f out* **13/2**[3]
51 **12** *nk* **Never Ending Tale**[35] 2612 3-9-7 85 TedDurcan 6 62
(W Jarvis) *t.k.h: trckd ldrs: shkn up 3f out: sn btn: eased whn no ch fnl f* **8/1**

2m 8.32s (-2.18) **Going Correction** -0.05s/f (Good) **12** Ran SP% **122.5**
Speed ratings (Par 102): **106,105,103,103,99 98,97,96,96,95 93,92**
toteswinger: 1&2 £46.89, 1&3 £39.90, 2&3 £27.00. CSF £199.13 CT £3108.34 TOTE £10.60: £2.70, £7.90, £5.00; EX 320.70 Place 6: £25.77 Place 5: £19.02.
Owner Mrs John Lee **Bred** London Thoroughbred S'Ces Ltd & West Blagdon Stud **Trained** East Everleigh, Wilts

FOCUS
A fair handicap but this was a nonsense of a race, as the early gallop was very moderate and around half the field pulled too hard for their own good. The first two home were never far off the leaders, so Greylami, along with the fourth, probably emerges with the most credit from the race.
T/Jkpt: Not won. T/Plt: £22.30 to a £1 stake. Pool: £209,883.39. 6,858.64 winning tickets. T/Qpdt: £6.50 to a £1 stake. Pool: £8,368.22. 942.95 winning tickets. JN

3746 - 3748a (Foreign Racing) - See Raceform Interactive

955 DEAUVILLE (R-H)
Saturday, July 5

OFFICIAL GOING: Turf course - soft; all-weather - standard

3749a PRIX YACOWLEF (LISTED RACE) (UNRACED) — 5f
2:05 (2:08) 2-Y-O £20,221 (£8,088; £6,066; £4,044; £2,022)

RPR
1 **Abbeyside** 2-9-2 CSoumillon 5 99
(P F I Cole) *prom: 4th 1/2-way: pushed along 1 1/2f out: 2nd and chalng 1f out: led 100yds out: pushed out* **6/5**[1]
2 *3/4* **Pure Joy** 2-8-13 SPasquier 10 93
(Mme C Head-Maarek, France)
3 *2 1/2* **Privalova (IRE)** 2-8-13 TJarnet 4 84
(R Pritchard-Gordon, France)
4 *shd* **Thorns Of Life (USA)** 2-8-13 OPeslier 7 84
(Robert Collet, France)
5 *3* **Antinea** 2-8-13 C-PLemaire 9 73
(P Bary, France)
6 *3/4* **Anyaar (IRE)** 2-8-13 DBonilla 2 70
(F Head, France)
7 *2* **Ribadesella** 2-8-13 MBlancpain 3 63
(C Laffon-Parias, France)
8 *2* **Island Home** 2-8-13 THuet 6 56
(J E Pease, France)
9 *2* **Sendama (FR)** 2-8-13 FLefebvre 8 49
(S Loeuillet, France)

58.40 secs (0.90) **9** Ran SP% **45.5**
PARI-MUTUEL: WIN 2.20; PL 1.40, 1.60, 3.20; DF 4.80.
Owner Mrs Carmen Burrell **Bred** Paulyn Limited **Trained** Whatcombe, Oxon

NOTEBOOK
Abbeyside, quickly settled just behind the leaders, produced his effort up the centre of the track from a furlong and a half out and dominated the final stages of the race to win by three-quarters of a length. The Prix Morny at Deauville in August will now be considered by connections.

3705 HAMBURG (R-H)
Saturday, July 5

OFFICIAL GOING: Soft

3751a CREDIT SUISSE-RENNEN - HANSHIN-CUP (LISTED RACE) (F&M) — 1m 3f
3:00 (3:06) 4-Y-0+ £11,029 (£4,044; £2,206; £1,103)

RPR
1 **Lilia (GER)**[27] 2879 4-8-12 J-PCarvalho 7 99
(Frau E Mader, Germany)
2 *6* **Foreign Music (FR)**[27] 2879 4-9-0 ASuborics 1 92
(H J Groschel, Germany)
3 *1/2* **Polyanta (GER)**[42] 6-8-12 AGoritz 6 89
(Markus Klug, Germany)
4 *1/2* **Now Again (GER)**[27] 2879 4-9-0 ADeVries 2 90
(W Hickst, Germany)
5 *1 1/4* **Lavana (GER)**[265] 6220 5-9-0 BClos 5 88
(Werner Glanz, Germany)
6 *1* **Lumen (FR)**[49] 6-9-0 LennartHammer-Hansen 3 87
(O Larsen, Sweden)
7 *2 1/2* **Algarade**[8] 3433 4-9-2 THellier 4 85
(Sir Mark Prescott) *racd in 4th on ins: swtchd outside over 3f out: 5th and followed wnr to outside rail ent st: wknd ins fnl f* **11/10**[1]
8 *6* **Spectra (IRE)**[42] 4-9-2 EPedroza 8 75
(M Rulec, Germany)

2m 27.46s (2.76) **8** Ran SP% **47.6**
(Including 10 Euros stake): WIN 136; PL 30, 18, 38; SF 870.

Owner Dr G Apel **Bred** H Pferdmenges **Trained** Germany

NOTEBOOK

Algarade bidding for a hat-trick having won her last two starts in handicaps, was taking a big step up in this search for black type but nevertheless started favourite. However, she weakened out of contention in the closing stages and possibly found the soft ground against her.

3752a LOTTO-HAMBURG-TROPHY (GROUP 3) 6f

4:30 (4:44) 3-Y-O+ **£29,418** (£13,235; £6,618; £3,676; £2,206)

RPR

1 **Overdose**[34] 3-8-8 .... ASuborics 6 111
(S Ribarszki, Hungary) *mde all: rdn out* **2/5**[1]

2 *1 1/2* **Abbadjinn (GER)**[49] 2214 4-9-4 .... TMundry 7 110
(P Rau, Germany) *racd in 4th: wnt 2nd 2f out: kpt on* **62/10**[3]

3 *3/4* **Mariol (FR)**[15] 3243 5-9-2 .... SMaillot 3 106
(Robert Collet, France) *midfield: pushed along bef 1/2-way: kpt on u.str.p fnl 2f* **17/2**

4 *nse* **Shinko's Best (IRE)**[20] 7-9-0 .... ADeVries 9 104
(A Kleinkorres, Germany) *hld up: styd on down outside rail fnl 1 1/2f* **23/1**

5 *1* **Calrissian (GER)**[32] 4-9-2 .... THellier 10 103
(L Kelp, Denmark) *hld up: 7th st: styd on at one pce fnl 2f* **24/1**

6 *nse* **Key To Pleasure (GER)**[20] 8-9-0 .... AHelfenbein 1 100
(Mario Hofer, Germany) *in rr: kpt on steadily fnl 2f* **23/1**

7 *1 1/4* **Alaska River (GER)**[69] 1660 4-9-2 .... AStarke 8 99
(P Schiergen, Germany) *racd in 2nd to over 2f out: one pce* **53/10**[2]

8 *8* **Matrix (GER)**[20] 7-9-0 .... DBoeuf 4 73
(W Baltromei, Germany) *racd in 3rd: wknd fr 2f out* **21/1**

9 *3* **Adamantinos**[49] 2214 4-9-0 .... EPedroza 2 64
(Frau E Mader, Germany) *a in rr* **31/1**

1m 12.19s (-0.50)
WFA 3 from 4yo+ 6lb **9** Ran SP% **131.7**
WIN 14; PL 11, 13, 13; SF 64.
Owner S C H Racing Team **Bred** Mr & Mrs G Robinson **Trained** Hungary

NOTEBOOK

Overdose, the best horse to come out of Hungary for a long time, retained his unbeaten record despite having had hoof problems in the run up to the race. He will return to Germany for a Group 2 and if all goes well the Prix de L'Abbaye could be on the cards.

3251 AYR (L-H)

Sunday, July 6

OFFICIAL GOING: Good to soft (good in places) changing to good on straight course after race 1 (2.20)

After a dry night and a damp day the ground was described as 'generally good, not good to soft anywhere'.

Wind: fresh 1/2 behind Weather: overcast, heavy shower race 4, then light rain.

3753 TOTEPLACEPOT H'CAP 6f

2:20 (2:22) (Class 6) (0-60,60) 3-Y-O **£2,590** (£770; £385; £192) **Stalls** Low

Form RPR

4001 1 **Jaconet (USA)**[18] 3139 3-8-12 **54** ....(b) PaulFessey 14 67
(T D Barron) *led 3 others on stands' side and overall ldr: kpt on wl ins fnl f: 1st of 4 in gp* **5/1**[2]

040 2 *1/2* **Bonne**[94] 1162 3-8-13 **55** .... HayleyTurner 11 66
(M L W Bell) *racd stands' side: sn outpcd: hdwy to chse wnr that side over 1f out: chal ins fnl f: no ex: 2nd of 4 that gp* **8/1**

4041 3 *1 3/4* **Mandalay King (IRE)**[3] 3638 3-8-4 **46** oh1 .... RoystonFfrench 6 52+
(Mrs Marjorie Fife) *chsd ldrs: led far side over 1f out: hung rt: no ex ins fnl f* **11/4**[1]

3620 4 *2 3/4* **Andrasta**[5] 3577 3-8-10 **52** .... FrancisNorton 9 49+
(A Berry) *led far side tl over 1f out: no ex* **12/1**

0-30 5 *1 1/2* **Planet Queen**[14] 3298 3-9-1 **57** ....(v) AndrewElliott 13 49
(K R Burke) *s.i.s: racd stands' side: sn chsng wnr: one pce fnl 2f: 3rd of 4 that gp* **12/1**

5034 6 *1/2* **Many Welcomes**[15] 3283 3-8-2 **47** .... DuranFentiman(3) 7 38
(B P J Baugh) *sn outpcd and in rr: styd on fnl f* **16/1**

6-06 7 *nse* **Fantasy Fighter (IRE)**[10] 3395 3-8-7 **49** .... PaulMulrennan 5 39
(J J Quinn) *chsd ldrs: kpt on same pce fnl 2f* **20/1**

-050 8 *3/4* **Orpen Bid (IRE)**[34] 2659 3-8-5 **47** oh1 ow1 .... PatrickMathers 12 35
(A M Crow) *racd stands' side: sn outpcd: last of 4 that gp* **40/1**

1153 9 *3 3/4* **Big Slick (IRE)**[29] 2850 3-9-4 **60** .... TWilliams 4 36
(M Brittain) *chsd ldrs: wknd over 1f out* **6/1**[3]

2-0 10 *3/4* **Red Skipper (IRE)**[14] 3298 3-9-1 **57** .... PaulHanagan 3 31
(N Wilson) *w ldrs: lost pl over 1f out* **8/1**

3056 11 *1 1/4* **Miss Sunshine**[9] 3441 3-8-4 **46** .... AdrianTNicholls 8 16
(J S Goldie) *chse ldrs: rdn 2f out: sn wknd* **10/1**

1-00 12 *3 1/2* **Paint Stripper**[66] 1750 3-8-12 **57** .... DominicFox(3) 1 15
(W Storey) *in rr: bhd fnl 2f* **20/1**

2200 13 *45* **Rich James (IRE)**[33] 2704 3-8-6 **48** .... JoeFanning 2 —
(J D Bethell) *chsd ldrs: lost pl over 4f out: sn bhd: t.o 2f out: virtually p.u* **20/1**

1m 10.16s (-3.44) **Going Correction** -0.60s/f (Hard) **13** Ran SP% **126.9**
Speed ratings (Par 98): **98,97,95,91,89 88,88,87,82,81 79,75,17**
toteswinger: 1&2 £8.00, 1&3 £3.50, 2&3 £6.20. CSF £45.38 CT £141.97 TOTE £6.20: £1.80, £3.60, £1.60; EX 58.20.
Owner R G Toes **Bred** Team Block **Trained** Maunby, N Yorks

FOCUS

A moderate sprint handicap, in which the winner was one of only four to race stands' side. He is rated to his best juvenile form backed up by the second.

Paint Stripper Official explanation: jockey said gelding was unsuited by the good to soft (good in places) ground

Rich James(IRE) Official explanation: jockey said gelding never travelled

3754 UNISON HEALTH 60TH NHS ANNIVERSARY MEDIAN AUCTION MAIDEN STKS 6f

2:50 (2:51) (Class 5) 2-Y-O **£3,238** (£963; £481; £240) **Stalls** Low

Form RPR

42 1 **Snow Bay**[10] 3411 2-9-3 0 .... TomEaves 3 74+
(B Smart) *t.k.h: led 1f: led jst ins fnl f: edgd rt: pushed out* **4/5**[1]

03 2 *1 3/4* **Hameildaeme**[22] 3032 2-8-12 0 .... J-PGuillambert 2 64
(S C Williams) *trckd ldrs: effrt 2f out: styd on to take 2nd ins fnl f: no imp* **7/1**[3]

632 3 *1 3/4* **Jimwil (IRE)**[15] 3254 2-9-3 0 .... TonyHamilton 6 64
(M Dods) *swvd rt s: led after 1f tl jst ins fnl f: no ex* **9/4**[2]

6 4 *3/4* **Bella's Story**[15] 3254 2-8-7 0 .... GaryBartley(5) 1 56
(J S Goldie) *chsd ldrs: outpcd over 1f out: kpt on ins fnl f* **10/1**

5 *1/2* **Katie Higgins** 2-8-9 0 .... TolleyDean(3) 5 55
(J L Spearing) *chsd ldrs: drvn over 2f out: kpt on same pce* **25/1**

0 6 *2 1/4* **Dougie Peel**[80] 1425 2-9-3 0 .... FergalLynch 4 53
(K A Ryan) *chsd ldrs: outpcd over 1f out* **50/1**

7 *34* **Liberty Trail (IRE)** 2-9-3 0 .... PaulMulrennan 8 —
(Miss L A Perratt) *dwlt and carried rt s: sn outpcd and in rr: bhd fnl 2f: t.o* **20/1**

1m 11.9s (-1.70) **Going Correction** -0.60s/f (Hard) **7** Ran SP% **118.5**
Speed ratings (Par 94): **87,84,82,81,80 77,32**
toteswinger: 1&2 £1.80, 1&3 £1.10, 2&3 £2.50. CSF £7.80 TOTE £1.50: £1.50, £2.10; EX 7.50.
Owner Pinnacle Bahamian Bounty Partnership **Bred** West Dereham Abbey Stud **Trained** Hambleton, N Yorks

FOCUS

A very lightweight maiden. The time of the race was almost 2secs slower than the preceding handicap but the form, although ordinary, looks reliable.

NOTEBOOK

Snow Bay was strongly backed into odds-on favouritism and the plunge was well founded as the son of Bahamian Bounty only had to be pushed out to get off the mark at the third time of asking. His future lies in the hands of the Handicapper. (op 13-8)

Hameildaeme briefly looked like giving the winner a real race entering the final furlong before her run flattened out and, while she is progresssing with each race, her ability hasn't been hidden from the Handicapper. (op 11-2)

Jimwil(IRE) took them along for much of the way but found disappointingly little at the business end of the race. He will need to find improvement for somewhere to win a nursery. (op 2-1 tchd 15-8)

Bella's Story looks like she is being brought along slowly with nurseries in mind. (op 9-1)

Katie Higgins made a perfectly respectable racecourse bow, showing plenty of pace for a long way. (op 16-1)

3755 TOTESWINGER H'CAP 1m 1f 20y

3:20 (3:22) (Class 6) (0-65,65) 4-Y-O+ **£2,590** (£770; £385; £192) **Stalls** Low

Form RPR

4024 1 **Papa's Princess**[6] 3552 4-8-8 **52** .... HayleyTurner 7 62
(J S Goldie) *trckd ldrs: styd on to ld ins fnl f: hld on towards fin* **10/1**

0310 2 *1/2* **Chin Wag (IRE)**[6] 3557 4-9-2 **60** ....(p) FergalLynch 14 69
(J S Goldie) *swtchd lft after s: hld up in rr: hdwy on inner and nt clr run over 1f out: swtchd rt ins fnl f: r.o: nt quite rch wnr* **7/1**[2]

2646 3 *3/4* **Valdan (IRE)**[15] 3257 4-8-11 **55** ....(t) AdrianTNicholls 12 62
(M A Barnes) *s.i.s: sn in tch: effrt 3f out: led 1f out: hdd and no ex ins fnl f* **14/1**

2-06 4 *3/4* **Prince Noel**[18] 3142 4-9-4 **62** .... DanielTudhope 6 68
(N Wilson) *mid-div: hdwy 3f out: kpt on wl fnl f* **14/1**

0-25 5 *1* **Bold Indian (IRE)**[5] 3579 4-9-4 **62** .... TomEaves 13 66
(Miss L A Perratt) *hld up in rr: effrt on outer over 2f out: styd on fnl f* **12/1**

6301 6 *shd* **Shy Glance (USA)**[16] 3204 6-9-0 **65** .... BMcHugh(7) 1 69
(P Monteith) *trckd ldrs: led over 2f out: hdd 1f out: kpt on same pce* **8/1**[3]

4023 7 *1 1/4* **Grandad Bill (IRE)**[9] 3450 5-8-7 **51** .... PaulHanagan 4 52
(J S Goldie) *hld up in rr: hdwy 3f out: kpt on: nvr rchd ldrs* **11/4**[1]

5030 8 *1 1/2* **Apache Nation (IRE)**[17] 3175 5-8-13 **57** .... RoystonFfrench 5 55
(M Dods) *mid-div: drvn over 3f out: nvr nr ldrs* **9/1**

0020 9 *3/4* **Joshua's Gold (IRE)**[4] 3599 7-8-13 **64** .... PaulPickard(7) 2 60
(D Carroll) *chsd ldrs: wknd 1f out* **11/1**

-600 10 *1 1/4* **Distant Pleasure**[25] 2957 4-8-9 **53** .... TonyHamilton 3 47
(M Dods) *chsd ldrs: wknd 1f out* **20/1**

0135 11 *9* **Grethel (IRE)**[6] 3552 4-8-10 **54** .... FrancisNorton 9 29
(A Berry) *chsd ldrs: lost pl over 1f out* **12/1**

1020 12 *nse* **Lewis Lloyd (IRE)**[5] 3593 5-8-8 **55** ....(v) MichaelJStainton(3) 10 30
(R E Barr) *s.v.s: a bhd* **25/1**

050 13 *1 1/4* **Border Fox**[29] 2847 5-9-0 **58** .... PaulMulrennan 8 30
(L Lungo) *t.k.h: led tl over 2f out: wkng whn hmpd over 1f out* **12/1**

0050 14 *9* **Borodinsky**[5] 3593 7-8-9 **53** ....(v) PatrickMathers 11 6
(R E Barr) *sn chsng ldrs on outer: drvn 4f out: lost pl over 2f out: sn bhd* **66/1**

1m 56.7s (-1.70) **Going Correction** -0.15s/f (Firm) **14** Ran SP% **124.2**
Speed ratings (Par 101): **101,100,99,99,98 98,97,95,95,94 86,85,84,76**
toteswinger: 1&2 £11.00, 1&3 £26.90, 2&3 £27.60. CSF £79.49 CT £1005.86 TOTE £11.50: £3.10, £2.60, £5.90; EX 92.50.
Owner Sutherland Five **Bred** The National Stud **Trained** Uplawmoor, E Renfrews

FOCUS

A very ordinary handicap producing a one-two for the Jim Goldie yard. The form looks modest but sound rated around the third and fifth.

Grandad Bill(IRE) Official explanation: jockey said gelding missed the break

Border Fox Official explanation: jockey said gelding hung right

3756 TOTESPORT 0800 221 221 H'CAP 1m 5f 13y

3:50 (3:50) (Class 5) (0-70,67) 4-Y-O+ **£3,238** (£963; £481; £240) **Stalls** Low

Form RPR

2021 1 **Bijou Dan**[30] 2776 7-8-12 **58** .... GregFairley 12 67
(G M Moore) *mid-div: stdy hdwy 6f out: styd on wl to ld wl ins fnl f* **13/2**[3]

6/3- 2 *1/2* **Inner Voice (USA)**[16] 1973 5-8-3 **49** ....(b) RoystonFfrench 13 57
(J J Lambe, Ire) *s.i.s: sn prom: hung lft and led 1f out: hdd and no ex ins fnl f* **9/2**[2]

4312 3 *1 3/4* **Forrest Flyer (IRE)**[10] 3399 4-8-9 **55** .... TomEaves 8 61
(Miss L A Perratt) *chsd ldrs: kpt on same pce fnl f* **3/1**[1]

2030 4 *2* **Hugs Destiny (IRE)**[10] 3414 7-8-6 **52** ....(t) JoeFanning 2 55
(M A Barnes) *chsd ldrs: led over 2f out: hdd 1f out: kpt same pce* **18/1**

3236 5 *6* **Josh You Are**[15] 3276 5-9-4 **64** .... FrancisNorton 9 58
(M Wigham) *s.i.s: hld up in rr: sme hdwy over 2f out: nvr nr ldrs* **9/1**

0/-3 6 *1* **Inch High**[16] 3204 10-8-2 **48** oh1 .... PaulHanagan 1 40
(J S Goldie) *led tl over 2f out: fdd over 1f out* **7/1**

0004 7 *shd* **Don Jose (USA)**[21] 3059 5-7-9 **48** oh3 ....(e) StacyRenwick(7) 10 40
(N J Vaughan) *hld up in rr: kpt on fnl 3f: nvr rchd ldrs* **12/1**

-004 8 *2 3/4* **Jordan's Light (USA)**[16] 3198 5-8-10 **56** .... PaulFessey 3 44
(P Monteith) *chsd ldrs: wknd over 1f out* **33/1**

0432 9 *3/4* **Jane Of Arc (FR)**[6] 3550 4-8-4 **50** .... AdrianTNicholls 4 37
(J S Goldie) *chsd ldrs: drvn 7f out: wknd over 1f out* **8/1**

2/0 10 *3/4* **Herakles (GER)**[15] 3258 7-9-7 **67** .... FergalLynch 5 53
(M Mullineaux) *in rr: drvn over 4f out: nvr on terms* **20/1**

0/05 11 *1 3/4* **Bramantino (IRE)**[10] 3399 8-8-3 **49** .... DaleGibson 11 32
(T A K Cuthbert) *mid-div: drvn over 4f out: nvr a threat* **50/1**

4151 12 *1 1/2* **Kyber**[6] 3545 7-8-12 **63** 6ex .... GaryBartley(5) 14 44
(J S Goldie) *hld up in rr: nvr on terms* **9/1**

00-0 **13** *63* **Jentris Girl (IRE)**[47] 2290 4-8-0 **49** AndrewMullen(3) 7 —
(A C Whillans) *in rr-div: lost pl 6f out: t.o 4f out* **66/1**
2U-0 **14** *4 1/2* **Danehill Silver**[35] 51 4-8-9 **58** PJMcDonald(3) 6 —
(B Storey) *in rr: bhd and reminders 7f out: t.o 4f out* **40/1**
2m 53.29s (-3.31) **Going Correction** -0.15s/f (Firm) **14** Ran SP% **126.7**
Speed ratings (Par 103): **104,103,102,101,97 97,97,95,94,94 93,92,53,50**
toteswinger: 1&2 £7.60, 1&3 £5.90, 2&3 £3.50. CSF £36.39 CT £110.86 TOTE £9.20: £1.80, £1.20, £2.00; EX 43.50.
Owner Bert Markey **Bred** James Thom And Sons **Trained** Middleham Moor, N Yorks

FOCUS
Another low-grade handicap, and the first four pulled well clear of the remainder off a strong early pace. The form looks sound rated around the first three.
Herakles(GER) Official explanation: jockey said gelding missed the break

3757 TOTESPORT.COM H'CAP 7f 50y
4:20 (4:24) (Class 5) (0-70,67) 3-Y-O+ **£3,238** (£963; £481; £240) **Stalls** Low

Form RPR
00-5 **1** **Derricks Dotty**[9] 3431 4-8-12 **58** (vt[1]) SimonPearce(7) 1 69
(N J Vaughan) *mde all: hld on towards fin* **16/1**
-055 **2** *3/4* **Earlsmedic**[10] 3416 3-9-1 **62** J-PGuillambert 9 68
(S C Williams) *trckd ldrs: wnt 2nd appr fnl f: carried hd high: styd on towards fin* **11/4**[1]
4045 **3** *1* **Hansomis (IRE)**[9] 3452 4-9-1 **54** DaleGibson 5 60
(B Mactaggart) *trckd wnr: hung lft over 1f out: kpt on same pce ins fnl f* **20/1**
0066 **4** *3/4* **Tanforan**[9] 3431 6-8-10 **56** BillyCray(7) 3 60
(B P J Baugh) *chsd ldrs: drvn 3f out: styd on same pce appr fnl f* **12/1**
3306 **5** *1/2* **Oeuf A La Neige**[5] 3591 8-9-4 **57** TomEaves 7 60
(Miss L A Perratt) *mid-div: effrt over 2f out: styd on same pce fnl f* **8/1**
-024 **6** *2 1/2* **Vesuvio**[30] 2782 4-9-0 **53** LeeEnstone 6 49
(C W Thornton) *chsd ldrs: effrt over 2f out: one pce* **8/1**
013 **7** *1 3/4* **Strabinios King**[24] 2983 4-10-0 **67** FrancisNorton 10 58
(M Wigham) *in tch: t.k.h: edgd lft 1f out: one pce* **13/2**[3]
-000 **8** *nk* **Mangano**[9] 3431 4-8-10 **49** PaulHanagan 8 39
(A Berry) *mid-div: effrt over 2f out: one pce whn sltly hmpd 1f out* **16/1**
3102 **9** *nk* **Imperial Sword**[5] 3582 5-9-2 **55** (b) PaulFessey 13 45
(T D Barron) *hld up in rr: hdwy on ins over 2f out: wknd appr fnl f* **13/2**[3]
006 **10** *1/2* **Battling Lil (IRE)**[25] 2955 4-8-13 **55** TolleyDean(3) 11 43
(J L Spearing) *mid-div: effrt on outside over 2f out: sn wknd* **20/1**
60-0 **11** *1/2* **Second Reef**[15] 3257 6-8-9 **48** oh3 GregFairley 4 35
(T A K Cuthbert) *hld up in rr: stdy hdwy on ins over 2f out: wknd appr fnl f* **66/1**
3452 **12** *1 3/4* **Yorkshire Blue**[9] 3443 9-10-0 **67** DanielTudhope 12 49
(J S Goldie) *hld up in rr: nvr on terms* **9/2**[2]
1m 32.03s (-1.37) **Going Correction** -0.15s/f (Firm)
WFA 3 from 4yo+ 8lb **12** Ran SP% **124.2**
Speed ratings (Par 103): **101,100,99,98,97 94,92,92,92,91 90,88**
toteswinger: 1&2 £14.80, 1&3 £51.60, 2&3 £15.10. CSF £61.53 CT £951.56 TOTE £19.80: £5.50, £1.40, £4.50; EX 77.90.
Owner Derricks Dotty Syndicate **Bred** Helshaw Grange Stud, E Kent & Mrs E Connelly **Trained** Hampton, Cheshire

FOCUS
Another ordinary handicap, and it proved to be an advantage to race prominently. The winner and runner-up are lightly raced and improving.
Yorkshire Blue Official explanation: jockey said gelding was unsuited by the slow early pace

3758 CAMPBELTOWN BAR STEWART SCOTT MEMORIAL H'CAP 1m
4:50 (4:50) (Class 4) (0-85,84) 3-Y-O+ **£6,476** (£1,927; £963; £481) **Stalls** Low

Form RPR
3232 **1** **Esoterica (IRE)**[5] 3591 5-9-0 **70** (v[1]) DanielTudhope 2 79+
(J S Goldie) *hld up: effrt over 2f out: nt clr run on inner and swtchd rt over 1f out: styd on to ld last 75yds* **10/3**[2]
0030 **2** *3/4* **Wovoka (IRE)**[8] 3493 5-9-3 **73** FergalLynch 1 80
(D W Barker) *trckd ldrs: led over 1f out: hdd and no ex wl ins fnl f* **9/1**
0031 **3** *1/2* **Wigwam Willie (IRE)**[18] 3142 6-9-7 **84** (p) BMcHugh(7) 8 90+
(K A Ryan) *hld up in rr: effrt on wd outside over 1f out: styd on ins fnl f: nt rch 1st 2* **5/1**
4311 **4** *3/4* **Wind Shuffle (GER)**[1] 3716 5-9-1 **71** 6ex PaulHanagan 4 75
(J S Goldie) *led tl over 1f out: kpt on same pce ins fnl f* **7/2**[3]
4 **5** *1 3/4* **Against The Grain**[8] 3491 5-9-13 **83** JoeFanning 6 83
(L Lungo) *trckd ldrs on outer: effrt over 2f out: kpt on same pce appr fnl f* **5/2**[1]
5-05 **6** *1 1/2* **Emerald Bay (IRE)**[16] 3214 6-9-3 **73** TomEaves 5 70
(Miss L A Perratt) *chsd ldr: fdd appr fnl f* **14/1**
0410 **7** *2 1/2* **Society Music (IRE)**[6] 3552 6-8-13 **69** (p) TonyHamilton 3 60
(M Dods) *chsd ldrs: lost pl over 1f out* **18/1**
1m 41.44s (-2.36) **Going Correction** -0.15s/f (Firm) **7** Ran SP% **112.5**
Speed ratings (Par 105): **105,104,103,103,101 99,97**
toteswinger: 1&2 £7.90, 1&3 £3.90, 2&3 £5.90. CSF £31.27 CT £145.81 TOTE £4.00: £1.90, £4.90; EX 40.30.
Owner Mrs S E Bruce **Bred** A Lyons Bloodstock **Trained** Uplawmoor, E Renfrews

FOCUS
A fair handicap run at a decent gallop but ordinary form rated around the runner-up and fourth.

3759 BET TOTEPOOL ON ALL UK RACING AMATEUR RIDERS' H'CAP 5f
5:20 (5:21) (Class 6) (0-65,65) 4-Y-O+ **£2,637** (£811; £405) **Stalls** Low

Form RPR
-004 **1** **Conjecture**[25] 2936 6-10-3 **52** MissRBastiman(5) 12 62
(R Bastiman) *chsd ldr stands' side: led that gp and overall 1f out: styd on wl* **3/1**[1]
-600 **2** *1 1/4* **The History Man (IRE)**[44] 2356 5-11-1 **64** (be) MissMMullineaux(5) 6 70
(M Mullineaux) *led far side: no ex ins fnl f: 1st of 6 that gp* **13/2**[3]
0625 **3** *3/4* **Obe One**[10] 3404 8-9-11 **46** oh1 MissBeverleyKendall(5) 3 49
(A Berry) *racd far side: chsd ldrs: kpt on same pce ins fnl f: 2nd of 6 that gp* **16/1**
6421 **4** *1 3/4* **Whinhill House**[16] 3212 8-11-7 **65** (v) MissARyan 11 62
(D W Barker) *led stands' side tl 1f out: kpt on same pce* **3/1**[1]
6200 **5** *1 1/2* **Lambency (IRE)**[3] 3638 5-10-6 **55** MrPNorton(5) 5 46
(J S Goldie) *hld up far side: effrt 2f out: kpt on fnl f: nt rch ldrs: 3rd of 6 that gp* **9/2**[2]
0000 **6** *1* **Strensall**[19] 3112 11-10-4 **55** MissVBarr(7) 4 43
(R E Barr) *dwlt: sn chsng ldrs far side: one pce appr fnl f: 4th of 6 that gp* **14/1**
0000 **7** *nse* **Percy Douglas**[6] 3565 8-9-9 **46** oh1 (p) MissKECooper(7) 10 34
(Miss A Stokell) *racd stands' side: prom: one pce fnl 2f* **40/1**
000- **8** *2* **Legal Set (IRE)**[233] 6826 12-10-2 **46** oh1 MissADeniel 9 26
(Miss A Stokell) *dwlt: sn outpcd stands' side: kpt on fnl 2f: nvr on terms* **25/1**
40-4 **9** *1/2* **Almost Married (IRE)**[105] 980 4-10-13 **57** MrsCBartley 2 36
(J S Goldie) *restless in stalls: chsd ldrs far side: lost pl over 1f out: 5th of 6 that gp* **8/1**
0-00 **10** *2* **Seafield Towers**[29] 2843 8-10-2 **46** oh1 MrSDobson 8 17
(D A Nolan) *prom stands' side: hung lft and lost pl over 1f out* **33/1**
003- **11** *9* **Astronomical Odds (USA)**[2] 3703 5-10-1 **52** (b) MissCVAnnan(7) 7 —
(J J Lambe, Ire) *racd far side: sn outpcd and bhd: last of 6 that gp* **16/1**
0-00 **12** *7* **She's Our Beauty (IRE)**[31] 2748 5-9-9 **46** oh1 (p) MissStephanieBowey(7) 13 —
(S T Mason) *swvd rt s: racd stands' side: sn bhd* **16/1**
58.85 secs (-1.25) **Going Correction** -0.60s/f (Hard) **12** Ran SP% **126.2**
Speed ratings (Par 101): **86,84,82,80,77 76,75,72,71,68 54,43**
toteswinger: 1&2 £6.60, 1&3 £10.40, 2&3 £16.20. CSF £24.22 CT £287.22 TOTE £4.60: £1.60, £2.30, £3.10; EX 29.70 Place 6: £135.85 Place 5: £75.78.
Owner The McMaster Springford Partnership **Bred** Darley **Trained** Cowthorpe, N Yorks

FOCUS
They split into two equal groups in this handicap for amateur riders, and as in the first race, the stands' side proved favoured. The form could be rated higher but looks more solid rated around the first two.
T/Jkpt: Not won. T/Plt: £739.50 to a £1 stake. Pool: £89,609.69. 88.45 winning tickets. T/Qpdt: £155.50 to a £1 stake. Pool: £4,729.50. 22.50 winning tickets. WG

3570 BRIGHTON (L-H)
Sunday, July 6

OFFICIAL GOING: Firm changing to good to firm after race 3 (3.30)
A strong headwind in the home straight would have had a detrimental effect on the race times. The last four races were hand-timed.
Wind: Strong, against Weather: Driving rain until race 2, then occasional sunshine

3760 E B F CATS PROTECTION MEDIAN AUCTION MAIDEN STKS 6f 209y
2:30 (2:30) (Class 6) 2-Y-O **£2,590** (£770; £385; £192) **Stalls** Low

Form RPR
632 **1** **Rapid Release (CAN)**[31] 2754 2-9-3 SebSanders 3 78
(Sir Mark Prescott) *trckd ldng pair: led and hung rt over 1f out: rdn to get on top fnl 100yds* **13/8**[2]
3 **2** *1 1/4* **Wilbury Star (IRE)**[9] 3444 2-9-3 RyanMoore 2 75
(R Hannon) *led or disp ld tl over 1f out: kpt on tl outpcd by wnr fnl 100yds* **8/15**[1]
0004 **3** *2* **Percys Corismatic**[24] 2980 2-8-12 TPQueally 1 65?
(J Gallagher) *disp ld tl 2f out: no ex fnl f* **33/1**[3]
6 **4** *dist* **Graysland**[44] 2349 2-8-7 JackDean(5) 5 —
(W G M Turner) *sn drvn along and bhd: t.o and eased fnl 2f* **66/1**
1m 25.48s (2.38) **Going Correction** 0.0s/f (Good) **4** Ran SP% **107.8**
Speed ratings (Par 92): **86,84,82,—**
CSF £2.82 TOTE £3.20; EX 2.70.
Owner W E Sturt - Osborne House III **Bred** Shyman Racing Stables **Trained** Newmarket, Suffolk

FOCUS
An unremarkable turnout both in terms of quality and numbers. The first two look roughly to form but the time was slow with the headwind a factor.

NOTEBOOK
Rapid Release(CAN) became a bit unbalanced on this tricky course as the runners raced into a strong headwind up the final hill, but he saw the trip out really well and was safely on top near the finish. (op 11-8)
Wilbury Star(IRE) was clearly only second-best despite going off long odds-on, but he ran respectably in defeat and cannot yet be ruled out in minor maiden company. (op 4-6)
Percys Corismatic ran in a seller last time and that, or a weak nursery, looks a more suitable home for her from now on.
Graysland, who will surely need longer trips in due course, cannot be seriously considered until she shows more than she has in her first two races.

3761 AGORA MANAGEMENT IN SUPPORT OF CATS PROTECTION H'CAP 6f 209y
3:00 (3:02) (Class 5) (0-75,75) 3-Y-O+ **£2,775** (£830; £415; £207; £103) **Stalls** Low

Form RPR
3022 **1** **Patavium Prince (IRE)**[25] 2933 5-8-12 **59** DaneO'Neill 2 67
(Miss Jo Crowley) *chsd ldr: drvn to ld over 1f out: edgd lft: kpt on u.p: jst hld on* **5/2**[1]
0605 **2** *shd* **Millfield (IRE)**[18] 3138 5-9-8 **69** GeorgeBaker 3 77
(P R Chamings) *stdd s: hld up in rr: rdn and hdwy 2f out: chsd wnr fnl f: clsd grad: jst failed* **7/2**[3]
1-05 **3** *nk* **Albaraari**[15] 3272 3-9-1 **70** (v[1]) RyanMoore 7 74
(Sir Michael Stoute) *hld up: hdwy on outside and rdn over 2f out: looked hld tl styd on wl fnl f: clsng at fin* **3/1**[2]
2261 **4** *3/4* **Rockfield Lodge (IRE)**[10] 3406 3-8-12 **74** TobyAtkinson(7) 4 76
(M E Rimmer) *hld up towards rr and gng wl: shkn up and hdwy over 1f out: styd on fnl f* **14/1**
-001 **5** *1* **Who's Winning (IRE)**[9] 3446 7-8-13 **60** CatherineGannon 6 62
(B G Powell) *chsd ldrs: rdn 3f out: kpt on gamely and briefly wnt 2nd 1f out: no ex fnl 100yds* **14/1**
240 **6** *4* **Carmenero (GER)**[4] 3599 5-10-0 **75** DO'Donohoe 5 67
(W R Muir) *chsd ldrs: rdn over 2f out: 4th and looking hld whn nt clr run and snatched up over 1f out: n.d after: eased fnl 100yds* **11/2**
0-00 **7** *3 1/2* **Minnis Bay (CAN)**[15] 3271 4-9-9 **70** (p) LPKeniry 1 52
(E F Vaughan) *led tl hrd rdn and hdd over 1f out: sn wknd* **10/1**
1m 23.96s (0.86) **Going Correction** 0.0s/f (Good)
WFA 3 from 4yo+ 8lb **7** Ran SP% **113.6**
Speed ratings (Par 103): **95,94,94,93,92 87,83**
toteswinger: 1&2 £3.10, 1&3 £1.30, 2&3 £2.60. CSF £11.36 CT £26.07 TOTE £3.70: £2.40, £2.00; EX 12.00 Trifecta £26.90 Pool: £386.36 - 10.13 winning units..
Owner Mrs Liz Nelson **Bred** J P Hardiman **Trained** Whitcombe, Dorset
■ Stewards' Enquiry : Dane O'Neill 11-day ban (inc nine deferred days): used whip with excessive frequency (Jul 20-30)

FOCUS
A close finish to a middling handicap and the form is ordinary rated around the first two.

3762 BARKING BRICKWORK MAIDEN STKS — 7f 214y
3:30 (3:34) (Class 5) 3-Y-O — **£2,775** (£830; £415; £207; £103) **Stalls** Low

Form — RPR

-232 **1** **Desert Chill (USA)**[23] 2994 3-8-12 80 ... DO'Donohoe 5 — 86
(Saeed Bin Suroor) *mde all: rdn and hung bdly rt across to stands' rail fnl 2f: pushed out fnl 100yds: comf* **2/5**[1]

0-0 **2** 8 **Certain Promise (USA)**[79] 1444 3-8-12 ... RyanMoore 3 — 68+
(Sir Michael Stoute) *cl 2nd: hung rt fr 2f out: drvn and btn whn wnt lft bhd wnr ins fnl f* **7/2**[2]

34 **3** 2 1/4 **Gulch's Rose (USA)**[38] 2536 3-8-12 ... TPQueally 1 — 62
(J Noseda) *t.k.h: trckd ldng pair: rdn 2f out: one pce* **7/1**[3]

4 48 **Barrashot** 3-9-3 ... JimmyQuinn 2 — —
(M J McGrath) *lft bhd whn tempo qcknd after 2f: no ch fnl 4f* **50/1**

5 dist **Kingdom Of Heaven (IRE)** 3-8-5 ... TobyAtkinson(7) 4 — —
(M J Gingell) *s.s: sn t.o* **50/1**

1m 35.9s (-0.10) **Going Correction** 0.0s/f (Good) **5** Ran SP% **110.1**
Speed ratings (Par 100): **100,92,89,—,—**
toteswinger: 1&2 £2.60. CSF £2.13 TOTE £1.40: £1.10, £2.10; EX 2.00.
Owner Godolphin **Bred** Darley **Trained** Newmarket, Suffolk

FOCUS
The first three all represented decent stables, but they looked to be among their trainers' lesser lights and overall the form is probably nothing special for the track. The form is rated around the placed horses to their previous marks.

3763 PETPLAN IN SUPPORT OF CATS PROTECTION H'CAP — 1m 1f 209y
4:00 (4:02) (Class 5) (0-70,68) 3-Y-O — **£2,775** (£830; £415; £207; £103) **Stalls** High

Form — RPR

0223 **1** **South Wales**[3] 3655 3-8-3 53 ... LukeMorris(3) 8 — 64
(S C Williams) *awkward s: sn in midfield: rdn 5f out: chsd ldr 2f out: styd on to ld ins fnl f: edgd rt: drvn clr* **15/8**[1]

4400 **2** 3 1/4 **Mahadee (IRE)**[7] 3525 3-9-2 68 ... (b) AhmedAjtebi(5) 4 — 72
(C E Brittain) *led: wnt 7l clr 1/2-way: hrd rdn over 1f out: hdd and no ex ins fnl f* **16/1**

6403 **3** 2 3/4 **Betonart**[13] 3314 3-8-5 52 ... (v[1]) NelsonDeSouza 7 — 51
(R M Beckett) *chsd ldrs: rdn and hung rt 2f out: one pce* **8/1**

0464 **4** 10 **Ba Dreamflight**[38] 2552 3-8-2 49 oh2 ... JimmyQuinn 9 — 28
(H Morrison) *chsd ldr: hrd rdn 3f out: wknd 2f out* **8/1**

-300 **5** 1 1/2 **Media Stars**[33] 2695 3-9-4 65 ... (b[1]) TPQueally 6 — 41
(J A Osborne) *dwlt: towards rr: rdn 5f out: nvr trbld ldrs* **33/1**

6-00 **6** 1 1/4 **Poppy Dean (IRE)**[32] 2719 3-8-3 55 ... JackDean(5) 2 — 28
(J G Portman) *chsd ldrs tl wknd 2f out* **20/1**

-035 **7** 29 **Looter (FR)**[22] 3022 3-8-13 60 ... (b[1]) SebSanders 3 — —
(J L Dunlop) *mainly mod 6th: rdn 5f out: no ch fnl 3f* **9/4**[2]

4041 **8** 2 1/2 **Zaarmit (IRE)**[12] 3342 3-9-6 67 ... RyanMoore 5 — —
(D M Simcock) *hld up in rr: hit by clod of earth and looked uncomfortable fr 1/2-way: no ch fnl 3f* **6/1**[3]

2m 2.90s (-0.70) **Going Correction** 0.0s/f (Good) **8** Ran SP% **115.6**
Speed ratings (Par 100): **102,99,97,89,88 87,63,61**
toteswinger: 1&2 £5.70, 1&3 £3.80, 2&3 £14.60. CSF £33.78 CT £199.29 TOTE £2.60: £1.30, £3.50, £1.90; EX 34.60 Trifecta £268.60 Pool: £472.03 - 1.30 winning units..
Owner K J Mercer **Bred** Usk Valley Stud **Trained** Newmarket, Suffolk

FOCUS
A low-grade handicap, with the pace looking good after the first 2f. The runner-up is rated to his best previous turf form with the winner progressing.
Zaarmit(IRE) Official explanation: jockey said colt was hit by a clod of turf and never travelled thereafter

3764 ARGUS H'CAP — 7f 214y
4:30 (4:33) (Class 6) (0-65,65) 3-Y-O+ — **£2,137** (£635; £317; £79; £79) **Stalls** Low

Form — RPR

3452 **1** **Napoletano (GER)**[11] 3383 7-10-0 65 ... (p) SebSanders 2 — 75
(S Dow) *plld hrd in rr: swtchd wd and hdwy over 2f out: str run u.p to ld nr fin* **9/4**[2]

5003 **2** 1/2 **Prince Valentine**[28] 2863 7-8-12 49 ... (p) RyanMoore 8 — 58
(G L Moore) *chsd ldrs: drvn to ld 1f out: kpt on u.p: hdd nr fin* **2/1**[1]

6600 **3** 1 3/4 **Lopinot (IRE)**[10] 3422 5-9-4 55 ... (p) GeorgeBaker 9 — 60
(M R Bosley) *in tch: hrd rdn over 2f out: drvn to chse ldrs over 1f out: styd on same pce* **8/1**

3505 **4** hd **Magic Warrior**[17] 3182 8-8-9 46 ... PaulFitzsimons 7 — 51
(J C Fox) *mid-div: rdn over 2f out: chsd ldrs over 1f out: kpt on same pce* **16/1**

1-40 **4** dht **Quaglino Way (GR)**[16] 3208 4-10-0 65 ... PaulDoe 1 — 70
(P R Chamings) *led: hrd rdn and hdd 1f out: one pce* **9/2**[3]

4250 **6** 3 1/2 **Convivial Spirit**[97] 1112 4-9-4 55 ... (t) LPKeniry 4 — 51
(E F Vaughan) *towards rr: rdn 3f out: nvr able to chal* **12/1**

-660 **7** 1/2 **The Hoofer (IRE)**[14] 3293 3-8-4 50 ... (b[1]) DO'Donohoe 3 — 43
(J L Dunlop) *chsd ldrs: hrd rdn 2f out: wknd 1f out* **20/1**

000- **8** 3/4 **Linden's Lady**[288] 5627 8-8-10 47 ... (v) TPQueally 5 — 41
(J R Weymes) *chsd ldr: rdn over 2f out: wknd over 1f out* **25/1**

0506 **9** 6 **Wickedish**[9] 3460 4-8-4 48 ... (t) TobyAtkinson(7) 6 — 28
(M J Gingell) *dwlt: bhd on outside: rdn and hung bdly lft to far rail 2f out: nvr a factor* **50/1**

1m 36.6s (0.60) **Going Correction** 0.0s/f (Good)
WFA 3 from 4yo+ 9lb **9** Ran SP% **117.5**
Speed ratings (Par 101): **97,96,94,94,94 91,90,89,83**
toteswinger: 1&2 £1.70, 1&3 £4.30, 2&3 £5.40. CSF £7.15 CT £29.51 TOTE £2.70: £1.10, £1.30, £2.90; EX 6.40 Trifecta £27.40 Pool: £480.71 - 12.97 winning units..
Owner Miss Helen Chamberlain **Bred** Gestut Hof Ittlingen **Trained** Epsom, Surrey

FOCUS
A typical Brighton handicap, moderate in quality but competitive enough, and run at a fair gallop. The form is ordinary with the runner-up rated to last year's form backed up by the fourth and fifth to recent form.

3765 DIGIBET.CO.UK H'CAP — 5f 59y
5:00 (5:02) (Class 6) (0-65,65) 3-Y-O — **£2,137** (£635; £317; £158) **Stalls** Low

Form — RPR

0405 **1** **Enodoc**[7] 3526 3-9-7 65 ... (t) DO'Donohoe 2 — 69
(W R Muir) *chsd ldr: slt ld over 1f out: hld on to narrow advantage thrght fnl f: all out* **6/1**

5036 **2** shd **Miss Firefly**[20] 3086 3-8-12 61 ... MCGeran(5) 8 — 65
(R J Hodges) *led tl over 1f out: rallied wl u.p and only narrowly hld thrght fnl f* **8/1**

4445 **3** 1 **Easy Wonder (GER)**[20] 3086 3-8-13 57 ... RyanMoore 6 — 57
(I A Wood) *dwlt: towards rr: rdn over 2f out: gd late hdwy* **3/1**[1]

44-5 **4** 1/2 **Tittle**[17] 3177 3-9-0 58 ... DaneO'Neill 4 — 56
(H Candy) *chsd ldrs: hrd rdn over 1f out: kpt on* **10/3**[2]

1503 **5** 2 **Midnite Blews (IRE)**[9] 3446 3-9-0 58 ... SebSanders 3 — 49+
(A B Haynes) *hld up in rr: effrt and in tch 2f out: hung bdly lft into rail and jockey unable to ride out fr over 1f out* **9/2**[3]

6206 **6** nk **Shatter Resistant (IRE)**[13] 3332 3-8-10 54 ... (e) TPQueally 7 — 44
(M D Squance) *dwlt: hdwy into 4th over 3f out: wknd over 1f out* **13/2**

2403 **7** hd **Diademas (USA)**[16] 3224 3-8-7 58 ... TobyAtkinson(7) 5 — 47
(M J Gingell) *hld up in 5th: effrt and hung lft over 1f out: sn wknd* **9/1**

63.10 secs (0.80) **Going Correction** 0.0s/f (Good) **7** Ran SP% **118.8**
Speed ratings (Par 98): **93,92,91,90,87 86,86**
toteswinger: 1&2 £7.20, 1&3 £5.10, 2&3 £9.50. CSF £52.06 CT £171.85 TOTE £8.40: £3.00, £4.20; EX 53.00 Trifecta £145.70 Pool: £512.24 - 2.60 winning units. Place 6: £98.69 Place 5: £24.73.
Owner Mrs D Edginton **Bred** Fonthill Stud **Trained** Lambourn, Berks
■ Stewards' Enquiry : D O'Donohoe caution: used whip with excessive frequency.

FOCUS
A moderate handicap with most of the runners either generally disappointing or not at their peak of late. The time was ordinary and the form looks weak.
Easy Wonder(GER) Official explanation: jockey said filly lost a front shoe
Midnite Blews(IRE) Official explanation: jockey said gelding hung both ways
T/Plt: £74.90 to a £1 stake. Pool: £73,003.21. 710.78 winning tickets. T/Qpdt: £20.70 to a £1 stake. Pool: £4,864.80. 173.70 winning tickets. LM

3751 HAMBURG (R-H)
Sunday, July 6

OFFICIAL GOING: Soft

3773a BMW 139TH DEUTSCHES DERBY (GROUP 1) (C&F) — 1m 4f
4:25 (4:30) 3-Y-O — **£236,029** (£78,676; £47,206; £23,603; £7,868)

RPR

1 **Kamsin (GER)**[28] 2880 3-9-2 ... AStarke 5 — 115
(P Schiergen, Germany) *w ldrs: led over 9f out: c to middle in st: rdn over 1f out: r.o wl* **66/10**

2 3 **Ostland (GER)**[45] 3-9-2 ... ADeVries 8 — 110
(P Schiergen, Germany) *led over 2f: 2nd st: hrd rdn 2f out: one pce and 3rd over 1f out: rallied to regain 2nd ins fnl f* **176/10**

3 1/2 **Top Lock**[16] 3193 3-9-2 ... MartinDwyer 14 — 109
(A M Balding) *a.p: disp 3rd 1/2-way: 6th st: sn drvn: styd on fnl f to take 3rd last strides* **101/10**

4 hd **Liang Kay (GER)**[21] 3074 3-9-2 ... THellier 2 — 109
(U Ostmann, Germany) *a in tch: 3rd st: rdn to go 2nd 1 1/2f out: no ex fnl f* **29/10**[1]

5 1/2 **Satier (FR)**[14] 3-9-2 ... KerrinMcEvoy 16 — 108
(Mario Hofer, Germany) *unruly bef s: last to st: gd hdwy wl over 1f out: nrest at fin* **41/1**

6 3 **King Of Rome (IRE)**[17] 3156 3-9-2 ... JMurtagh 10 — 103
(A P O'Brien, Ire) *in rr to st: hdwy on ins fr 2f out: drvn 1f out: one pce* **52/10**[2]

7 1 1/2 **Adelar (GER)**[31] 3-9-2 ... DBoeuf 9 — 101
(W Baltromei, Germany) *hld up: rdn ent st: styd on fr 2f out: no ex fnl f* **47/1**

8 2 1/2 **Soum (GER)**[31] 3-9-2 ... JVictoire 4 — 97
(A Fabre, France) *nvr nrr than mid-div* **19/2**

9 1 **Solapur (GER)**[14] 3-9-2 ... TMundry 7 — 95
(A Wohler, Germany) *mid-div: c wd st: hrd rdn and towards rr 2f out: sme late prog* **15/1**

10 3 **Il Divo (GER)**[28] 2880 3-9-2 ... EPedroza 13 — 91
(A Wohler, Germany) *nvr nr to chal* **127/10**

11 shd **Santero (GER)**[21] 3074 3-9-2 ... JLermyte 15 — 90
(N Sauer, Germany) *in rr to st: nvr a factor* **54/1**

12 1 1/2 **Narcisco (GER)**[29] 3-9-2 ... JiriPalik 17 — 88
(P Schiergen, Germany) *sn prom fr outside draw: 8th st: brought wdst: sn rdn and btn* **50/1**

13 4 **Akiem (IRE)**[21] 3074 3-9-2 ... ASuborics 12 — 82
(Andreas Lowe, Germany) *hdwy on ins to go 4th at 1/2-way: 7th st: sn rdn: eased whn btn fnl f* **15/2**

14 2 **Secundus (GER)** 3-9-2 ... J-PCarvalho 11 — 78
(H Blume, Germany) *a towards rr: last 2f out* **59/1**

15 4 **Walzertraum (USA)**[28] 2880 3-9-2 ... LDettori 6 — 72
(J Hirschberger, Germany) *cl up: disputing 3rd 1/2-way: 5th st: rdn and btn 2f out: eased* **6/1**[3]

16 2 **Agapanthus (GER)**[21] 3074 3-9-2 ... (p) FJohansson 1 — 69
(J Hirschberger, Germany) *trckd ldrs: 4th st: wknd 2f out* **41/1**

2m 39.29s (4.74) **16** Ran SP% **130.7**
TOTE: WIN 76; PL 28, 43, 41; SF 1258.
Owner Stall Blankenese **Bred** Gestut Karlshof **Trained** Germany
■ A thunderstorm broke during the parade and the race was run in heavy rain.

NOTEBOOK
Kamsin(GER), close up from the start, took up the running passing the stands and dominated the race from then on. Able to set a steady gallop, when he picked up the pace those in behind just could not catch him. It was a good tactical ride.
Ostland(GER) led early and remained handy once Kamsin went on. He got the trip well but was well placed throughout in something of a tactical affair.
Top Lock, third in the King Edward VII, would not have been suited by the easing of the ground, so in the circumstances he ran well. He was up with the pace throughout, though, in a race run at a steady early pace. The Great Voltigeur and St Leger could be on his agenda, although his trainer maintains he will be a better horse next year.
King Of Rome(IRE), down the field in the Derby but third in the Hampton Court Stakes, ought to have been suited by the return to 1m4f, but he was held up out the back in a steadily run race and could never get close enough to land a blow.

2986 MAISONS-LAFFITTE (R-H)

Sunday, July 6

OFFICIAL GOING: Good to soft

3774a PRIX DU BOIS (GROUP 3) 5f
2:45 (2:45) 2-Y-0 **£29,412** (£11,765; £8,824; £5,882; £2,941)

RPR

1 **Percolator**[22] 3052 2-8-8 .... CSoumillon 3 106+
(P F I Cole) *broke fast: mde all: pushed clr fr over 1f out: comf* **2/5**[1]

2 3 **Caparroso (FR)**[32] 2-8-8 .... C-PLemaire 2 95
(T Lemer, France) *disp 2nd: chsd wnr fr wl over 1f out: no imp* **27/1**

3 4 **Kenz (FR)**[44] 2-8-8 ....(b) OTrigodet 4 81
(C Baillet, France) *rrd s: in rr and rdn 2f out: kpt on u.p to take 3rd ins fnl f* **38/1**

4 1 **Bargouzine (USA)**[22] 3052 2-8-8 .... SPasquier 6 77
(A Fabre, France) *disp 2nd tl wkng over 1 1/2f out* **62/10**[3]

5 snk **Elegant Cad (CAN)**[17] 3152 2-8-11 .... SteveDrowne 1 79
(J R Best) *s.i.s: outpcd and rdn 1/2-way: kpt on one pce* **76/10**

6 ½ **Takyro (FR)**[20] 2-8-11 .... OPeslier 5 78
(J-P Pelat, France) *racd in 4th tl wkng wl over 1f out* **11/2**[2]

57.00 secs (57.00) **6** Ran SP% **118.5**
PARI-MUTUEL: WIN 1.40; PL 1.20, 4.20; SF 15.50.
Owner A H Robinson **Bred** A H And C E Robinson Partnership **Trained** Whatcombe, Oxon

NOTEBOOK
Percolator was winning her fourth race in a row, and in the process broke the track record over 5f. Quickly out of the stalls, she showed incredible speed, with her rivals struggling by halfway, and continued to go further clear as the race came to an end. She passed the post three lengths in front, and the Group 2 Prix Robert Papin (July 27) is now a likely target, while the Group 1 Nunthorpe Stakes at York could also be a possibility.
Caparroso(FR) followed the winner for much of the race and was the only runner able to go with her. In the closing stages she could only stay on one-paced, but her preference for a softer surface could benefit her later in the season.
Kenz(FR) was not helped by a slow departure from the stalls. She made up a lot of ground in the latter stages to stay on to take third position, though, and could go for a Listed event at Vichy next on July 26.
Bargouzine(USA), quickly into second position, raced prominently but could not go with the winner in the last furlong and a half.
Elegant Cad(CAN), tardy for much of the race, was outpaced from the start and being pushed along before halfway. His jockey reported that the ground was a little on the soft side for him, and his trainer will now look for a maiden race for him.

3775a PRIX CHLOE (GROUP 3) (FILLIES) (STRAIGHT) 1m (S)
3:15 (3:18) 3-Y-0 **£29,412** (£11,765; £8,824; £5,882; £2,941)

RPR

1 **Goldikova (IRE)**[28] 2877 3-8-12 .... OPeslier 9 116
(F Head, France) *trckd ldr: led over 2f out: sn clr: pushed out and r.o wl* **7/10**[1]

2 3 **Top Toss (IRE)**[28] 2877 3-9-1 .... C-PLemaire 2 112
(Y De Nicolay, France) *hld up in rr: hdwy 2f out: wnt 2nd over 1f out: no ch w wnr* **21/1**

3 3 **Proviso**[28] 2877 3-9-1 .... SPasquier 7 105
(A Fabre, France) *racd in 4th: cl 2nd 2f out: sn one pce* **39/10**[2]

4 4 **Caesarine (FR)**[47] 2294 3-8-12 .... RichardHughes 6 93
(A Fabre, France) *hld up: clsd up on outside over 2f out: sn rdn and btn* **33/1**

5 2½ **Azabara**[27] 2902 3-8-12 .... TThulliez 1 87
(A Fabre, France) *racd alone on rails: jnd main gp at 1/2-way and racing in 5th: rdn and btn over 2f out* **16/1**

6 8 **Pas Seule (FR)**[34] 3-8-12 .... DBonilla 3 69
(F Head, France) *led to over 2f out* **7/10**[1]

7 4 **Dariena (FR)**[40] 3-8-12 .... CSoumillon 8 60
(A De Royer-Dupre, France) *hld up: a in rr: eased fnl 2f* **71/10**[3]

8 1½ **Vattene (IRE)**[35] 3-8-12 .... ACrastus 5 56
(M Gasparini, Italy) *disp 2nd tl wkng wl over 2f out: sn wl bhd* **20/1**

1m 34.9s (-7.40) **8** Ran SP% **168.5**
PARI-MUTUEL: WIN 1.70 (coupled with Pas Seule); PL 1.10, 2.10, 1.40;DF 13.30.
Owner Wertheimer Et Frere **Bred** Wertheimer Et Frere **Trained** France

NOTEBOOK
Goldikova(IRE) ran away with this race in very impressive fashion, breaking the track record in the process. She was aided by a pacemaker who set a strong pace up front while she sat just in behind. She did not settle too well in the early stages but when asked to quicken almost two furlongs out, she did it in style, showing a classy turn of foot to pass the post three lengths clear of her nearest rival. Her next target will be the Prix d'Astarte at Deauville on August 3.
Top Toss(IRE) was held up towards the back of the field, came with her run from the two-furlong pole and stayed on for second without ever bothering the winner. This was her first run back over a mile since last September and her trainer feels this is her best distance. She now goes for the Prix d'Astarte.
Proviso, another dropping back to a mile, was never far from the leaders but could not quicken when the pace went up a gear. She stayed on for third without threatening the first two past the post and there are no plans for her at present.
Caesarine(FR), held up at the back of the field, seemed to be going as well as anything at the two-furlong pole but, as the tempo quickened, she found nothing and just stayed on to take fourth position.

3760 BRIGHTON (L-H)

Monday, July 7

OFFICIAL GOING: Good to firm (8.4)
In races 4 and 6, several runners came to the stands' rail. While there was not a huge amount in it, the result of the finale suggested that there had been no need.
Wind: Strong, half against Weather: Overcast

3778 EUROPEAN BREEDERS' FUND MEDIAN AUCTION MAIDEN STKS 5f 213y
2:30 (2:30) (Class 5) 2-Y-0 **£3,469** (£1,038; £519; £259) **Stalls** Low

Form RPR

54 1 **Wohaida (IRE)**[15] 3292 2-8-12 .... DarryllHolland 1 74
(M R Channon) *pressed ldr: led 3f out: drvn along ent fnl f: in control fnl 1/2f: rdn out* **13/8**[2]

34 2 2½ **Night Of Fortune**[16] 3277 2-9-3 .... SebSanders 3 71
(Sir Mark Prescott) *chsd ldng pair: hrd rdn 3f out: persistently lugging lft: wnt 2nd ins fnl f: one pce* **7/2**[3]

3332 3 5 **Like For Like (IRE)**[7] 3558 2-8-12 .... RichardHughes 4 51+
(R Hannon) *bit slipped early in r: led: hdd and hrd rdn 3f out: rallied u.p and disputing 1 l 2nd whn jockey stopped riding and veered rt 150yds out: eased* **5/4**[1]

6 4 2¾ **Imaginary Diva**[7] 3558 2-8-12 .... DaneO'Neill 2 43
(G G Margarson) *sltly s.i.s: in tch: shkn up over 2f out: wknd over 1f out* **25/1**

1m 12.94s (2.74) **Going Correction** +0.275s/f (Good) **4** Ran SP% **108.6**
Speed ratings (Par 94): **92,88,82,78**
CSF £7.37 TOTE £2.90; EX 4.80.
Owner Sheikh Ahmed Al Maktoum **Bred** Darley **Trained** West Ilsley, Berks

FOCUS
A weakly-contested maiden, made even less competitive by the favourite's bit slipping. Modest form, although the first two did step forward on their previous efforts.

NOTEBOOK
Wohaida(IRE) had been a shade disappointing in her first two races, and found an ideal opportunity here which was made even easier by the favourite's bit slipping early on and the runner-up not acting on the track. She did everything asked of her, and was safely on top at the finish, but did not achieve much in victory and needs to be kept to a modest level for the time being. (op 2-1)
Night Of Fortune did not look happy on the Brighton undulations in the home straight, and was never finding enough to overhaul the winner. He has enough ability to win a little nursery over 6f or 7f, but a flatter track will suit him much better. (tchd 5-2 and 9-2)
Like For Like(IRE)'s bit slipped through her mouth shortly after the start, and in the circumstances Hughes did well to keep her going for as long as he did around this tricky circuit. Though she lost it completely in the last 150 yards, veering badly to the middle of the track with her jockey sitting tight, she had again shown enough to suggest she can find a little race with better fortune. Official explanation: jockey said bit slipped through (op 11-10 tchd 13-8)
Imaginary Diva, who was again a bit sluggish out of the stalls, was not knocked about when held by the first three and is heading for handicaps after one more run.

3779 FRIDAY-AD (S) STKS 5f 213y
3:00 (3:00) (Class 6) 3-Y-0+ **£1,942** (£578; £288; £144) **Stalls** Low

Form RPR

0040 1 **Majestical (IRE)**[23] 3034 6-9-10 53 ....(p) WilliamBuick 6 65
(V Smith) *hld up in rr: hdwy on outside 2f out: led 1f out: sn clr* **15/2**

4305 2 4 **Bye Baby Bunting**[13] 3342 3-8-9 55 ow1 .... DaneO'Neill 3 43
(B R Johnson) *w ldrs: led wl over 1f out: hdd and nt pce of wnr 1f out* **5/1**[2]

2360 3 nk **Cleveland**[63] 1865 6-9-7 50 .... RussellKennemore(3) 9 51
(R Hollinshead) *towards rr: swtchd outside 3f out: hdwy and hrd rdn 2f out: one pce appr fnl f* **15/2**

0000 4 1 **Young Ivanhoe**[7] 3564 3-9-4 64 ....(b[1]) JimmyQuinn 1 48+
(C A Dwyer) *hld up in tch: effrt and swtchd to rail 2f out: 3rd and clsng whn hmpd and snatched up over 1f out: kpt on again fnl f* **10/1**

4001 5 2½ **Game Lady**[7] 3559 4-9-5 51 .... SebSanders 11 35
(I A Wood) *in tch on outside: effrt over 2f out: wknd over 1f out* **11/10**[1]

1040 6 1¼ **Jal Music**[7] 3559 3-9-4 67 .... LiamJones 7 35
(R A Harris) *slt ld tl over 2f out: wknd over 1f out* **6/1**[3]

4004 7 shd **Ela Aleka Mou**[18] 3159 4-8-9 45 ....(b) MCGeran(5) 4 26
(Miss D Mountain) *in tch: outpcd over 2f out: in rr and n.d after* **28/1**

3506 8 nk **Half A Tsar (IRE)**[7] 3559 4-9-0 47 .... JackDean(5) 10 30
(Mark Gillard) *w ldrs: led over 2f out tl wl over 1f out: sn wknd* **33/1**

1m 11.64s (1.44) **Going Correction** +0.275s/f (Good)
WFA 3 from 4yo+ 6lb **8** Ran SP% **117.6**
Speed ratings (Par 101): **101,95,95,93,90 88,88,88**
toteswinger: 1&2 £6.00, 1&3 £3.40, 2&3 £6.70. CSF £45.94 TOTE £9.20: £2.10, £2.20, £2.20; EX 56.50 Trifecta £262.40 Part won. Pool: £489.84, 0.40 winning units..The winner was sold to Ron Harris for 5,200gns
Owner V Smith **Bred** Sean Beston **Trained** Exning, Suffolk

FOCUS
A poor seller, but run at a decent pace with several vying for the early lead. The winner dictates the level.

3780 BETTERBET.COM H'CAP 1m 1f 209y
3:30 (3:32) (Class 6) (0-65,65) 3-Y-0+ **£2,137** (£635; £317; £158) **Stalls** High

Form RPR

003 1 **Ornella**[21] 3089 4-9-11 65 .... TravisBlock(3) 8 74
(H Morrison) *t.k.h: hld up in midfield: hdwy to ld over 3f out: jnd by runner-up fnl 2f: battled on gamely u.p to hold on narrowly* **5/2**[2]

0-65 2 nk **Pretty Officer (USA)**[8] 3524 3-7-13 47 .... JimmyQuinn 3 55
(Rae Guest) *chsd ldrs: rdn to join ldr ins fnl 2f: sustained chal u.p: kpt on gamely: narrowly hld* **9/1**[3]

0612 3 7 **Laish Ya Hajar (IRE)**[11] 3422 4-9-12 63 .... DaneO'Neill 4 58
(P R Webber) *prom: hrd rdn and edgd lft fr 2f out: nt pce of first 2* **7/4**[1]

-444 4 2½ **The Iron Giant (IRE)**[12] 3360 6-8-11 48 ....(b) AlanDaly 2 38
(Dr J R J Naylor) *stdd s: hld up in rr: hdwy 4f out: wnt fair 5th 3f out: no imp fnl 2f* **14/1**

-060 5 1 **Spent**[21] 3095 3-8-13 61 .... SebSanders 9 49
(Mouse Hamilton-Fairley) *hld up in rr of midfield: hdwy over 4f out: chsd ldrs over 2f out: hrd rdn and edgd lft: sn outpcd* **9/1**[3]

000- 6 17 **Halsion Challenge**[294] 5470 3-8-7 55 .... LPKeniry 5 11
(J R Best) *a towards rr: rdn and n.d fnl 3f* **20/1**

6605 7 6 **Threestoneburn (USA)**[6] 3574 3-8-10 58 .... EddieAhern 7 3
(J R Boyle) *prom: rdn and lost pl over 4f out: sn struggling in rr* **12/1**

0/00 8 7 **Drombeg Pride (IRE)**[13] 3344 4-8-9 46 oh1 .... PaulDoe 6 —
(G P Enright) *mid-div: rdn and wknd 3f out: sn bhd* **66/1**

-450 9 17 **General Knowledge (USA)**[59] 1954 5-9-11 62 ....(b[1]) PaulEddery 1 —
(G D Blake) *led: sn 7 l clr: hdd & wknd rapidly over 3f out: sn bhd* **12/1**

2m 5.95s (2.35) **Going Correction** +0.275s/f (Good)
WFA 3 from 4yo+ 11lb **9** Ran SP% **113.2**
Speed ratings (Par 101): **101,100,95,93,92 78,73,68,54**
CSF £24.83 CT £47.45 TOTE £3.20: £1.20, £2.40, £1.30; EX 32.70 Trifecta £111.30 Pool: £435.01, 2.89 winning units..
Owner Mrs M D Low **Bred** Hollington Stud **Trained** East Ilsley, Berks

FOCUS
A modest race, with the first two finishing clear of some pedestrian rivals. Not form to get excited about.

3781 VISIT BETTER ON QUEENS ROAD BRIGHTON MAIDEN H'CAP 1m 3f 196y
4:00 (4:00) (Class 5) (0-75,74) 3-Y-O £2,712 (£811; £405; £202; £101) Stalls High

Form RPR
55-0 1 **Tyrrells Wood (IRE)**[24] 3004 3-9-7 74 TedDurcan 1 77
(T G Mills) *dwlt: sn chsng ldrs on ins: hung bdly rt towards stands' side pair fr 2f out: drvn to ld ins fnl f* 11/4[2]
-500 2 1 3/4 **Tantris (IRE)**[46] 2340 3-8-10 63 ShaneKelly 4 63
(J A Osborne) *in tch: led over 3f out and c stands' side: hrd rdn and hdd ins fnl f: one pce* 6/1[3]
00-0 3 1 1/4 **Pinnacle Point**[17] 3206 3-8-2 55 WilliamBuick 6 54
(G L Moore) *chsd ldrs: c stands' side w wnr 3f out: sltly outpcd tl hrd rdn and rallied over 1f out: one pce fnl f* 20/1
-004 4 4 1/2 **Sparkling Montjeu (IRE)**[12] 3362 3-8-6 59 (p) LiamJones 8 51
(J W Hills) *sn rdn along in rr: c stands' side st: edgd lft bk towards centre 2f out: sme late hdwy* 20/1
462 5 hd **Bocciani (GER)**[19] 3130 3-9-0 67 J-PGuillambert 7 58
(M Johnston) *led: rdn 5f out: hdd over 3f out and styd centre to far side: no ex fnl 2f* 13/2
0-03 6 10 **Astrodome**[25] 2984 3-8-3 56 DO'Donohoe 5 39+
(Sir Mark Prescott) *prom: styd centre to far side st: hrd rdn and wknd over 1f out* 2/1[1]
-300 7 47 **Nino Cochise (IRE)**[25] 2977 3-9-0 67 SebSanders 2 —
(C R Egerton) *in tch: wnt centre st: edgd rt 2f out: wknd over 1f out: eased whn btn fnl f: sddle slipped* 7/1

2m 35.67s (2.97) **Going Correction** +0.275s/f (Good) 7 Ran SP% **109.6**
Speed ratings (Par 100): **101,99,99,96,96 89,56**
toteswinger: 1&2 £3.00, 1&3 £10.70, 2&3 £13.00. CSF £17.76 CT £245.01 TOTE £3.20: £2.50, £2.90; EX 17.60 Trifecta £188.30 Pool: £455.54, 1.79 winning units.
Owner P C Ryan **Bred** Kilfrush Stud **Trained** Headley, Surrey

FOCUS
The favourite failed to give his running and this was a moderate race overall, with the field fanning out from one side to the other off the final bend. However, Tyrrells Wood is a potential improver and might have won by even farther had he not drifted across the track to join the second and third near the stands' rail.
Bocciani(GER) Official explanation: jockey said gelding had no more to give
Nino Cochise(IRE) Official explanation: jockey said saddle slipped

3782 MARK, FRED AND RAY MEMORIAL H'CAP 5f 213y
4:30 (4:30) (Class 5) (0-75,75) 3-Y-O £2,784 (£828; £414; £206) Stalls Low

Form RPR
-435 1 **Mandelieu (IRE)**[17] 3224 3-9-0 68 LiamJones 2 73
(W J Haggas) *plld hrd in rr early: hdwy over 2f out: edgd lft and led over 1f out: drvn to hold on fnl f* 4/1[3]
0404 2 1/2 **Magical Speedfit (IRE)**[9] 3499 3-9-7 75 EddieAhern 3 78
(G G Margarson) *hld up in rr: effrt over 2f out: r.o u.p fr over 1f out: clsng at fin* 15/2
-521 3 1 1/4 **Arabian Art (USA)**[18] 3177 3-9-0 68 TedDurcan 6 67
(H R A Cecil) *prom: hrd rdn over 1f out: kpt on same pce* 11/10[1]
5300 4 1/2 **Spic 'n Span**[5] 3608 3-8-7 64 (b[1]) KevinGhunowa(3) 5 61
(R A Harris) *w ldrs: led 3f out tl over 1f out: no ex ins fnl f* 33/1
0043 5 3 **Tadalavil**[14] 3324 3-9-6 74 DarryllHolland 4 62
(M R Channon) *disp ld 3f: rdn and btn 2f out* 10/3[2]
3006 6 8 **Rough Rock (IRE)**[6] 3571 3-8-13 67 (b) DaneO'Neill 1 35+
(Miss Gay Kelleway) *disp ld 3f: hrd rdn and wknd wl over 1f out* 16/1

1m 11.36s (1.16) **Going Correction** +0.275s/f (Good) 6 Ran SP% **111.3**
Speed ratings (Par 100): **103,102,100,100,96 85**
toteswinger: 1&2 £3.20, 1&3 £1.40, 2&3 £2.70. CSF £31.64 TOTE £5.10: £2.10, £3.10; EX 27.60.
Owner L Palmer/ B Smith/ W Haggas **Bred** Rathbarry Stud **Trained** Newmarket, Suffolk

FOCUS
Just a fair race, with the favourite not reproducing her maiden form. All the runners came down the centre of the track until the winner drifted back to the far rail in the final furlong.
Spic 'n Span Official explanation: jockey said gelding lost front right shoe

3783 SOUTHERN FM H'CAP 5f 59y
5:00 (5:00) (Class 6) (0-65,58) 3-Y-O+ £2,137 (£635; £317; £158) Stalls Low

Form RPR
20-1 1 **Croeso Bach**[26] 2934 4-9-2 55 SophieDoyle(7) 1 66+
(J L Spearing) *mde virtually all: styd on far rail st: clr over 1f out: easily* 10/3[3]
0003 2 4 **City For Conquest (IRE)**[7] 3565 5-8-13 45 StephenDonohoe 4 42
(John A Harris) *chsd ldrs: c stands' side st: effrt over 2f out: drvn to go 2nd wl over 1f out: no ch w wnr on far side* 11/1
6352 3 1/2 **Night Prospector**[7] 3565 8-9-7 56 (b) KevinGhunowa(3) 6 51
(R A Harris) *w ldrs: c stands' side st: rdn and outpcd over 2f out: kpt on fnl f* 5/1
6231 4 1 1/2 **Arfinnit (IRE)**[13] 3346 7-9-6 55 (p) KirstyMilczarek(3) 3 44
(Mrs A L M King) *chsd ldrs: c stands' side st: rdn over 2f out: one pce* 9/4[1]
4453 5 1 1/4 **Easy Wonder (GER)**[1] 3765 3-9-6 57 SebSanders 2 42+
(I A Wood) *s.i.s: bhd: styd far side st: rdn 2f out: n.d* 3/1[2]
5600 6 16 **Signor Panettiere**[32] 2748 7-9-3 49 DaneO'Neill 5 —
(A D Brown) *w ldrs: c stands' side st: wknd over 2f out: eased whn no ch fnl f* 14/1

63.87 secs (1.57) **Going Correction** +0.275s/f (Good)
WFA 3 from 4yo+ 5lb 6 Ran SP% **110.5**
Speed ratings (Par 101): **98,91,90,88,86 60**
toteswinger: 1&2 £6.30, 1&3 £3.00, 2&3 £5.40. CSF £35.24 CT £169.65 TOTE £4.40: £1.70, £3.70; EX 45.30 Trifecta £138.80 Pool: £335.81, 1.79 winning units. Place 6 £ 476.13, Place 5 £ 165.16.
Owner Mrs Richard Evans **Bred** Richard Evans Bloodstock **Trained** Kinnersley, Worcs

FOCUS
A low-grade sprint handicap, but the easy winner is in fine form and was one of only two to stay on the far side, suggesting that had been the best place to be all afternoon.
Night Prospector Official explanation: jockey said gelding was hanging right
Easy Wonder(GER) Official explanation: trainer said filly never travelled
Signor Panettiere Official explanation: trainer's rep said gelding had a breathing problem
T/Plt: £562.30 to a £1 stake. Pool: £64,167.17. 83.30 winning tickets. T/Qpdt: £61.60 to a £1 stake. Pool: £5,374.58. 64.50 winning tickets. LM

[3545]MUSSELBURGH (R-H)
Monday, July 7

OFFICIAL GOING: Straight course - good to soft (good in places); round course - good (good to soft in places) (6.4)
Wind: Virtually nil Weather: Dry and overcast, sunny intervals

3784 WATCH 2008 OLYMPICS @ THE THORNTREE (S) STKS 5f
2:15 (2:16) (Class 6) 3-Y-O+ £1,942 (£578; £288; £144) Stalls Low

Form RPR
0235 1 **Highland Warrior**[12] 3370 9-9-4 71 MickyFenton 6 54+
(P T Midgley) *s.i.s and sn rdn along in rr: hdwy 2f out: rdn wl over 1f out: styd on u.p ins fnl f to ld last 75yds* 1/2[1]
3002 2 1/2 **Fire Up The Band**[17] 3212 9-9-9 70 DanielTudhope 10 57
(A Berry) *cl up: rdn over 1f out: led ent fnl f: drvn: hdd and no ex last 75yds* 7/2[2]
-660 3 1/2 **Valiant Romeo**[13] 3340 8-9-4 44 (v) RoystonFfrench 7 50
(R Bastiman) *prom: rdn along wl over 1f out: kpt on same pce ins fnl f* 14/1
3062 4 2 3/4 **High Reach**[7] 3559 8-9-9 55 (p) AndrewElliott 3 45
(J G M O'Shea) *cl up: led after 1f: rdn over 1f out: hdd ent fnl f: wknd* 15/2[3]
0600 5 nk **Howards Prince**[17] 3212 5-8-13 37 GaryBartley(5) 5 39
(D A Nolan) *towards rr tl styd on u.p appr fnl f: nrst fin* 150/1
0000 6 nk **Percy Douglas**[1] 3759 8-8-13 36 (p) AnnStokell(5) 11 38
(Miss A Stokell) *in tch: rdn along 1/2-way: kpt on u.p appr fnl f: nrst fin* 50/1
0550 7 7 **La Guancha**[17] 3217 3-8-8 41 (bt) GregFairley 12 8
(D A Nolan) *wnt rt s: a in rr* 50/1
00-0 8 7 **Compton Lad**[48] 2283 5-9-4 41 (p) PatrickMathers 1 —
(D A Nolan) *led 1f: cl up tl rdn and wknd wl over 1f out* 100/1
000/ 9 2 1/2 **One Trick Pony**[798] 1344 5-9-1 49 (p) PJMcDonald(3) 4 —
(B Storey) *sn outpcd and a bhd* 50/1

61.10 secs (0.70) **Going Correction** +0.175s/f (Good)
WFA 3 from 5yo+ 5lb 9 Ran SP% **114.9**
Speed ratings (Par 101): **101,100,99,95,94 94,82,71,67**
toteswinger: 1&2 £1.50, 1&3 £2.90, 2&3 £3.60. CSF £2.45 TOTE £1.50: £1.02, £1.10, £2.70; EX 2.70.There was no bid for the winner
Owner Frank & Annette Brady **Bred** Rowcliffe Stud **Trained** Westow, N Yorks

FOCUS
This looked a decent seller on paper, with the first two home posessing official marks in the 70s, but the proximity of the fifth and sixth horses, both of whom are officially rated in the mid-30s, casts grave doubts over the merit of the form. The first two were some way off their marks.

3785 GREGOR SHORE H'CAP 1m 6f
2:45 (2:45) (Class 5) (0-75,75) 4-Y-O+ £3,885 (£1,156; £577; £288) Stalls High

Form RPR
2164 1 **Nero West (FR)**[11] 3414 7-9-0 68 (b) TomEaves 6 78
(Miss L A Perratt) *mde all: rdn 2f out: styd on wl fnl f* 11/8[1]
0025 2 4 1/2 **Gordonsville**[16] 3253 5-9-7 75 DanielTudhope 7 79
(J S Goldie) *trckd ldng pair: hdwy 3f out and sn rdn along: chsd wnr 2f out: drvn wl over 1f out and sn no imp* 13/8[2]
4355 3 2 1/2 **Fascinatin Rhythm**[2] 3718 4-8-11 65 TPO'Shea 5 65
(M R Channon) *trckd ldrs: hdwy over 4f out: chal over 3f out and sn rdn: drvn 2f out and kpt on same pce* 6/1[3]
0-64 4 14 **Danish Rebel (IRE)**[20] 3110 4-9-1 69 (t) PaulMulrennan 4 49
(G A Charlton) *t.k.h: hld up: a in rr* 10/1
0540 5 9 **Wild Fell Hall (IRE)**[24] 3010 5-9-5 73 (b[1]) SilvestreDeSousa 2 41
(A D Brown) *cl up: rdn along over 4f out sn wknd* 25/1

3m 3.33s (-1.97) **Going Correction** +0.025s/f (Good) 5 Ran SP% **107.4**
Speed ratings (Par 103): **106,103,102,94,88**
toteswinger: 1&2 £2.50, CSF £3.66 TOTE £2.40: £1.10, £1.20; EX 3.60.
Owner Mr & Mrs Charles Villiers **Bred** Ecurie Pelder **Trained** Carluke, S Lanarks

FOCUS
A fair handicap, the first three home pulling miles clear of a pair hopelessly uncompetitive off their current marks. Fairly solid form, but limited.

3786 IME COST EFFECTIVE PROPERTY MEDIAN AUCTION MAIDEN STKS 7f 30y
3:15 (3:16) (Class 6) 3-5-Y-O £1,942 (£578; £288; £144) Stalls High

Form RPR
0406 1 **Infinity Bond**[16] 3280 3-9-3 63 SilvestreDeSousa 6 64
(G R Oldroyd) *chsd ldrs: hdwy to ld 2f out: sn rdn and edgd rt: drvn and kpt on ins fnl f* 7/2[3]
0222 2 2 **Hester Brook (IRE)**[13] 3344 4-9-6 45 (p) AndrewElliott 3 57
(J G M O'Shea) *led: rdn along 3f out: hdd 2f out: sn drvn and kpt on same pce* 7/1
-042 3 2 **Forrest Star**[17] 3213 3-8-12 59 TomEaves 4 49
(Miss L A Perratt) *t.k.h: prom: rdn along 3f out: drvn wl over 1f out: kpt on same pce* 13/8[1]
5-00 4 4 **Cranworth Blaze**[25] 2966 4-9-6 45 GregFairley 1 41
(T J Etherington) *dwlt: sn chsng ldrs: rdn along 1/2-way: sn one pce* 33/1
5 5 **Billy Cadiz** 3-9-3 0 ChrisCatlin 5 29
(E J O'Neill) *hld up: sn in rr: green and outpcd after 2f: sme late hdwy* 15/8[2]
6 6 **Cabin Gate (IRE)**[34] 5-9-8 0 PJMcDonald(3) 2 16
(R Johnson) *a in rr* 66/1
6-05 7 6 **Rascasse**[16] 3262 3-9-3 60 TWilliams 7 —
(Bruce Hellier) *chsd ldrs: rdn along over 3f out and sn outpcd* 33/1

1m 30.59s (0.29) **Going Correction** +0.025s/f (Good)
WFA 3 from 4yo+ 8lb 7 Ran SP% **115.0**
Speed ratings (Par 101): **99,96,94,89,84 77,70**
toteswinger: 1&2 £2.50, 1&3 £2.10, 2&3 £2.40. CSF £27.24 TOTE £4.90: £2.10, £2.80; EX 29.80.
Owner R C Bond **Bred** Yapham Mill Stud **Trained** Brawby, N Yorks

FOCUS
Surely one of the worse maidens that will be run this season. Little better than plating form.

3787 BETFAIR BETTING AS IT SHOULD BE/LE GARCON D'OR H'CAP 5f
3:45 (3:45) (Class 4) (0-80,76) 3-Y-O+ £6,476 (£1,927; £963; £481) Stalls Low

Form RPR
1003 1 **Sandwith**[12] 3370 5-9-0 **67** PJMcDonald(3) 3 78+
(R Johnson) *trckd ldrs: hdwy over 1f out: rdn ent fnl f: led last 100yds* **5/2**[1]
5052 2 2 1/4 **Rothesay Dancer**[6] 3581 5-8-13 **63** DanielTudhope 4 66
(J S Goldie) *trckd ldrs: hdwy 2f out: rdn and ev ch ent fnl f: sn drvn and nt qckn last 100yds* **7/2**[2]
00-5 3 hd **Handsome Cross (IRE)**[13] 3336 7-9-11 **75** RoystonFfrench 6 77
(Mrs A Duffield) *cl up: rdn wl over 1f out: drvn to ld briefly ent fnl f: hdd and no ex last 100yds* **13/2**
-000 4 1/2 **Seafield Towers**[1] 3759 8-8-7 **57** oh12 GregFairley 1 57
(D A Nolan) *towards rr: hdwy wl over 1f out: sn rdn and styd on ins fnl f: nrst fin* **100/1**
4-60 5 2 1/4 **Lake Chini (IRE)**[10] 3454 6-9-1 **65** (b) DaleGibson 7 57
(M W Easterby) *chsd ldrs: rdn along 2f out: kpt on same pce u.p appr fnl f* **14/1**
1040 6 1 1/4 **Windjammer**[6] 3594 4-9-3 **67** (b) PaulHanagan 9 55
(T D Easterby) *led: rdn wl over 1f out: drvn and hdd ent fnl f: wknd* **11/2**[3]
0004 7 1/2 **Blazing Heights**[11] 3401 5-9-7 **76** GaryBartley(5) 10 62
(J S Goldie) *in tch: rdn along 2f out: no imp* **6/1**
0000 8 1 **Mutayam**[7] 3546 8-8-7 **57** oh12 (t) PatrickMathers 2 39
(D A Nolan) *a towards rr* **66/1**
0-00 9 2 **Inspainagain (USA)**[21] 3080 4-9-2 **66** PaulFessey 11 41
(T D Barron) *chsd ldrs on outer: rdn along 2f out: sn drvn and wknd* **11/1**
00-0 10 42 **Mister Marmaduke**[38] 2576 7-8-7 **57** oh12 (p) TPO'Shea 5 —
(D A Nolan) *slowly away and wnt rt s: a wl bhd* **100/1**

60.64 secs (0.24) **Going Correction** +0.175s/f (Good) 10 Ran SP% **112.3**
Speed ratings (Par 105): **105,101,101,100,96 94,93,92,89,41**
toteswinger: 1&2 £2.20, 1&3 £4.60, 2&3 £4.40. CSF £10.64 CT £48.08 TOTE £3.10: £1.20, £1.90, £2.00; EX 12.00.
Owner M Sawers **Bred** R R Whitton **Trained** Newburn, Tyne & Wear

FOCUS
A fair handicap won in convincing style in a time half a second faster than the seller which kicked off the card. The winner looks back to his best.
Inspainagain(USA) Official explanation: jockey said gelding lost its action

3788 LADBROKES RACECOURSE TEAM - SECOND TO NONE NURSERY 5f
4:15 (4:16) (Class 5) 2-Y-O £2,520 (£2,520; £577; £288) Stalls Low

Form RPR
604 1 **Adozen Dreams**[10] 3437 2-8-11 **65** SilvestreDeSousa 5 62
(G R Oldroyd) *cl up: rdn to ld over 1f out: drvn ins fnl f: jnd on line* **9/1**
262 1 dht **Cutting Comments**[18] 3170 2-9-7 **75** TomEaves 2 72
(M Dods) *trckd ldrs: hdwy over 1f out and sn rdn: drvn ins fnl f: styd on to join ldr on line* **5/4**[1]
5511 3 1/2 **Just The Lady**[26] 2924 2-8-12 **66** TonyHamilton 4 61
(Ollie Pears) *led: rdn along 2f out: edgd rt and hdd over 1f out: sn drvn: rallied u.p and ev ch ins fnl f: no ex towards fin* **7/2**[3]
000 4 shd **Dispol Grand (IRE)**[12] 3365 2-8-6 **60** PaulFessey 6 55
(P T Midgley) *cl up: rdn wl over 1f out and ev ch: drvn ins fnl f: no ex towards fin* **16/1**
004 5 hd **Wigan Pier**[23] 3027 2-8-4 **58** PaulHanagan 3 52
(T D Easterby) *dwlt: sn chsng ldrs: swtchd rt and rdn over 1f out: sn ev ch tl drvn and nt qckn ins fnl f* **3/1**[2]
5554 6 3/4 **Kings House**[25] 2965 2-7-13 **53** ow1 DaleGibson 1 45
(M W Easterby) *hld up in rr: hdwy and nt clr run over 1f out: swtchd rt and nt clr run ent fnl f: rdn and hmpd last 100yds: nt rcvr* **16/1**

62.73 secs (2.33) **Going Correction** +0.175s/f (Good) 6 Ran SP% **113.4**
Speed ratings (Par 94): **88,88,87,87,86 85**
toteswinger: 1&2 £3.40, 1&3 £1.40, 2&3 £3.10. TRIFECTA Tote win: CC 1.10, AD 5.40, Pl: CC 1.40, AD 3.70; Ex: CC-AD 10.90, AD-CC 7.00; CSF: CC-AD 6.96, AD-CC 10.65.
Owner Brannon Dennis Dick Holden **Bred** J C S Wilson Bloodstock **Trained** Denton, Co Durham
Owner Impossible Dreams Racing Limited **Bred** Bond Thoroughbred Corporation **Trained** Brawby, N Yorks
■ Stewards' Enquiry : Silvestre De Sousa caution: careless riding; two-day ban: used whip with excessive frequency down shoulder in forehand position (Jul 21,22)

FOCUS
The 'official' ratings shown next to each horse are estimated and for information purposes only. A very messy nursery and a large blanket would have covered the six runners at the line. The time was modest and the form looks far from reliable.

NOTEBOOK
Adozen Dreams appreciated the return to the minimum and benefited from being given a positive ride in what turned into a messy affair. She battled on very bravely, but was forced to share the prize right on the line. (tchd 8-1)
Cutting Comments, another dropping back to the minimum trip, had to wait for a gap to appear next to the stands' rail and once it appeared he flew home to share the spoils right on the line. He handles easy ground well, but a return to 6f looks to be in order. (tchd 8-1)
Just The Lady, bidding for a hat-trick after winning a Lingfield seller and a Beverley claimer, both when long odds-on, pinged the gates and tried to make every yard. She kept plugging away, but was just not quite good enough at the weights and lacks the scope of the pair that beat her. (op 11-4 tchd 4-1)
Dispol Grand(IRE), seventh in all three of his starts in maidens, raced up with the pace the whole way but was short of finishing speed where it mattered. (op 14-1)
Wigan Pier missed the break and was forced to track the leaders. Dramatically switched to the wide outside to make her effort, she plugged on but was never doing enough. (op 10-3 tchd 11-4)
Kings House, already exposed as a poor performer, may have finished last here but he might arguably have won with better luck in running. He was repeatedly hampered and had whips flailing in his face when trying to find a route through his rivals, but the door was consistently slammed in his face. However, in view of his moderate previous form it may be a mistake to get too carried away. Official explanation: jockey said colt was denied a clear run (op 14-1)

3789 HILL, WILLIAMS, LOGAN - THE RAILS BOOKMAKERS H'CAP 7f 30y
4:45 (4:47) (Class 6) (0-60,59) 4-Y-O+ £2,590 (£770; £385; £192) Stalls High

Form RPR
0204 1 **Grand Diamond (IRE)**[17] 3211 4-9-4 **59** (p) DanielTudhope 13 66
(J S Goldie) *mde all: rdn clr wl over 1f out: drvn ins fnl f: jst hld on* **11/4**[1]
0000 2 hd **Fern House (IRE)**[21] 3080 6-8-4 **45** TPO'Shea 7 53+
(Bruce Hellier) *in tch: hdwy 3f out: nt clr run 2f out: sn swtchd lft and rdn: styng on whn edgd rt ins fnl f: jst failed* **25/1**
-052 3 2 1/4 **Anthemion (IRE)**[21] 3082 11-8-4 **48** AndrewMullen(3) 9 48
(Mrs J C McGregor) *chsd wnr: rdn 2f out: drvn over 1f out: kpt on same pce ins fnl f* **9/1**
-045 4 1 1/4 **Beaumont Boy**[17] 3211 4-8-13 **54** (p) RobertHavlin 12 51
(A G Foster) *trckd ldrs: hdwy 3f out: rdn 2f out: sn drvn and kpt on same pce fnl f* **12/1**
0000 5 1/2 **Fan Club**[17] 3211 4-8-4 **45** (b) DaleGibson 11 41
(Mrs R A Carr) *chsd ldrs: nt clr run and swtchd lft 2f out: sn rdn and kpt on on same pce* **16/1**
0003 6 1 **Autograph Hunter**[3] 3691 4-8-4 **45** PatrickMathers 14 38
(Peter Grayson) *s.i.s and bhd: hdwy 3f out: rdn 2f out and kpt on: nrst fin* **8/1**
1020 7 3/4 **Imperial Sword**[1] 3757 5-9-0 **55** (b) PaulFessey 6 46+
(T D Barron) *towards rr: pushed along and sme hdwy 3f out: rdn whn nt clr run wl over 1f out: sn no imp* **4/1**[2]
0 8 5 **Mugeba**[31] 2781 7-8-13 **54** (t) PaulHanagan 8 31
(Miss Gay Kelleway) *hld up towards rr on inner: effrt 3f out: sn rdn and no hdwy* **11/2**[3]
0003 9 3 3/4 **Attacca**[17] 3211 7-8-6 **47** ChrisCatlin 3 14
(J R Weymes) *hld up towards rr: hdwy on outer 3f out: rdn 2f out: sn drvn and wknd over 1f out* **13/2**
-400 10 5 **Miss Mujahid Times**[13] 3340 5-8-4 **45** (b) SilvestreDeSousa 10 —
(A D Brown) *chsd ldrs: rdn along 3f out: drvn over 2f out and sn wknd* **28/1**

1m 30.25s (-0.05) **Going Correction** +0.025s/f (Good) 10 Ran SP% **117.4**
Speed ratings (Par 101): **101,100,98,96,96 95,94,88,84,78**
toteswinger: 1&2 £18.20, 1&3 £5.90, 2&3 £25.10. CSF £77.61 CT £566.92 TOTE £3.70: £1.70, £7.30, £2.70; EX 105.60.
Owner Mrs M Craig **Bred** Newberry Stud Company **Trained** Uplawmoor, E Renfrews

FOCUS
A moderate handicap, but the pace was strong thanks to the favourite. The first two are rated to their best recent form.
Mugeba Official explanation: jockey said mare hung right
Miss Mujahid Times Official explanation: jockey said mare hung right-handed throughout

3790 SALWICK FLYER IRISH MAFIA H'CAP 1m
5:15 (5:15) (Class 6) (0-65,64) 3-Y-O £2,590 (£770; £385; £192) Stalls High

Form RPR
4654 1 **Tamasou (IRE)**[17] 3206 3-9-6 **63** DaleGibson 1 68
(Garry Moss) *cl up: chal 3f out: rdn to ld 2f out: drvn ent fnl f and styd on gamely* **5/2**[1]
0013 2 1 1/2 **Grit (IRE)**[19] 3126 3-9-5 **62** TPO'Shea 7 64
(M R Channon) *trckd ldng pair: hdwy 3f out: rdn over 2f out: chal over 1f out and ev ch tl drvn and nt qckn ins fnl f* **9/2**[2]
1300 3 1/2 **Bourse (IRE)**[9] 3494 3-9-4 **64** PJMcDonald(3) 6 64
(R Johnson) *trckd ldrs: hdwy over 2f out: rdn and ev ch over 1f out: sn drvn and one pce ins fnl f* **5/2**[1]
445 4 1 3/4 **Willyn (IRE)**[6] 3578 3-9-0 **57** (p) DanielTudhope 9 53
(J S Goldie) *in tch: hdwy 3f out: rdn to chse ldrs 2f out: sn drvn and kpt on same pce* **7/1**[3]
3404 5 5 **Casino Night**[6] 3578 3-9-3 **60** ChrisCatlin 2 45
(J R Weymes) *led: rdn along 3f out: hdd 2f out and sn wknd* **10/1**
630- 6 1 **Howards Hope**[259] 6388 3-9-6 **63** TomEaves 4 46
(Miss L A Perratt) *midfield: effrt 3f out: sn rdn and no imp fnl 2f* **18/1**
2300 7 3 **Flying Sommelier (USA)**[17] 3202 3-9-5 **62** PaulFessey 3 38
(T D Barron) *a towards rr* **20/1**
0-56 8 nk **Habbie Heights**[21] 3081 3-8-13 **56** RoystonFfrench 5 31
(R Bastiman) *a towards rr* **20/1**
00-0 9 3/4 **Midnight Oasis**[11] 3395 3-8-2 **45** PaulHanagan 10 18
(Rae Guest) *trckd ldrs on inner: pushed along 3f out: sn rdn and wknd* **16/1**

1m 43.01s (1.81) **Going Correction** +0.025s/f (Good) 9 Ran SP% **117.6**
Speed ratings (Par 98): **91,89,89,87,82 81,78,77,77**
toteswinger: 1&2 £2.90, 1&3 £2.40, 2&3 £3.90. CSF £14.17 CT £29.63 TOTE £3.70: £1.20, £2.00, £1.40; EX 15.90 Place 6 £ 22.43, Place 5 £ 19.19.
Owner Brooklands Racing **Bred** Garry Gleeson **Trained** Loughborough, Leics

FOCUS
A moderate handicap and not very competitive either judging by the market. The early pace was modest too and the final time was slow. Solid enough form, the winner rated to his best.
T/Plt: £27.80 to a £1 stake. Pool: £66,989.89. 1,753.25 winning tickets. T/Qpdt: £19.90 to a £1 stake. Pool: £2,773.10. 102.70 winning tickets. JR

3170 RIPON (R-H)
Monday, July 7

OFFICIAL GOING: Heavy
32mm of rain in three days resulted in 'very heavy ground'.
Wind: light 1/2 behind Weather: heavy showers before racing, becoming fine and dry

3791 MARKET PLACE (S) STKS 1m 1f 170y
6:50 (6:51) (Class 6) 3-Y-O £2,729 (£806; £403) Stalls High

Form RPR
3160 1 **Carry On Cleo**[10] 3314 3-8-12 57 (v) JohnEgan 11 56
(A Berry) *led after 1f: styd on wl fnl 2f* **10/1**
156F 2 1 1/2 **Lizzie Wiggins**[19] 3127 3-8-12 66 JamieSpencer 8 53
(M L W Bell) *trckd ldrs: wnt handy 2nd over 4f out: rdn over 1f out: kpt on same pce* **4/6**[1]
3043 3 6 **Just Sam (IRE)**[2] 3730 3-8-1 60 ow1 (v) PaulPickard(7) 1 36
(D Carroll) *t.k.h: wnt handy 3rd 4f out: one pce fnl 2f* **4/1**[2]
0002 4 3 1/4 **Caught In Paradise (IRE)**[2] 3715 3-8-11 41 ow2 MarkLawson(3) 9 35
(D W Thompson) *sn drvn along: lost pl 6f out: wnt modest 4th over 2f out: kpt on* **14/1**
-000 5 24 **Sun In Splendour (USA)**[41] 2486 3-8-12 45 DarrenWilliams 7 —
(A P Jarvis) *hld up: hdwy to chse ldrs over 5f out: wknd 3f out: eased ins fnl f* **40/1**
05 6 13 **Spabreaksdotcom (IRE)**[11] 3403 3-8-7 0 FergalLynch 2 —
(J S Wainwright) *sn chsng ldrs: edgd lft and lost pl 3f out: sn bhd: eased ins fnl f* **50/1**
000 7 1 3/4 **Jakam (IRE)**[27] 2915 3-8-12 48 JoeFanning 6 —
(E J O'Neill) *trckd ldrs: drvn over 4f out: wknd 3f out: eased ins fnl f* **6/1**[3]
00- 8 72 **Caffrey Kelly**[315] 4897 3-8-12 0 PAspell 10 —
(A Kirtley) *led 1f: w ldr: lost pl over 4f out: sn t.o: virtually p.u* **80/1**

2m 14.27s (8.87) **Going Correction** +0.85s/f (Soft) 8 Ran SP% **115.7**
Speed ratings (Par 98): **98,96,92,89,70 59,58,1**
toteswinger: 1&2 £2.40, 1&3 £1.60, 2&3 £1.20. CSF £17.44 TOTE £8.60: £1.90, £1.20, £1.30; EX 23.10.There was no bid for the winner. Lizzie Wiggins was claimed by Mrs Marjorie Fife for £6,000

Owner Alan Berry **Bred** J E Abbey **Trained** Cockerham, Lancs

FOCUS

A very modest seller in which stamina was crucial. The form is of little consequence.

Caught In Paradise(IRE) Official explanation: jockey said gelding was unsuited by the heavy ground

3792 SKELLGATE MAIDEN AUCTION FILLIES' STKS — 6f

7:20 (7:23) (Class 5) 2-Y-O — £2,914 (£867; £433; £216) Stalls Low

Form			Horse	Jockey	RPR
	1		**First City** 2-8-7 0 (D M Simcock) *mid-div on outer: hdwy over 2f out: edgd rt over 1f out: styd on to ld last 75yds* **4/1**[2]	RichardMullen 12	73+
050	2	1 ¼	**Sweet Applause (IRE)**[19] 3123 2-8-10 0 (A P Jarvis) *led: rdn and edgd rt 1f out: hdd wl ins fnl f* **4/5**[1]	DarrenWilliams 3	72
0	3	¾	**Rossett Rose (IRE)**[23] 3049 2-8-7 0 (M Brittain) *chsd ldrs: styd on ins fnl f* **22/1**	TWilliams 10	67
	4	1 ¾	**Identity** 2-8-4 0 (E J O'Neill) *chsd ldrs: kpt on fnl f* **8/1**	JoeFanning 1	59
0	5	2	**Jessica Mary (IRE)**[15] 3292 2-8-7 0 (D Carroll) *swtchd lft after s: chsd ldrs: one pce appr fnl f* **7/1**[3]	HayleyTurner 15	56
0	6	10	**Dispol Kintie (IRE)**[11] 3411 2-8-4 0 (P T Midgley) *chsd ldrs: lost pl over 1f out* **28/1**	FrankieMcDonald 11	23
04	7	2 ¾	**Lunar Romance**[10] 3432 2-8-7 0 (T J Pitt) *chsd ldrs: lost pl over 1f out* **12/1**	PaulMulrennan 6	18
0	8	¾	**Without Equal**[16] 3277 2-8-4 0 (A Dickman) *swvd rt s: a outpcd and in rr* **50/1**	MarcHalford(3) 14	15
0	9	4 ½	**Pennine Rose**[12] 3365 2-8-7 0 (A Berry) *dwlt: sn in mid-div: lost pl over 2f out: eased* **50/1**	JohnEgan 7	2
0	10	8	**Aven Mac (IRE)**[16] 3277 2-8-4 0 (N Bycroft) *drvn along in rr: bhd fnl 2f* **50/1**	AdrianTNicholls 8	—

1m 18.28s (5.28) **Going Correction** +0.70s/f (Yiel) — **10 Ran SP% 120.5**

Speed ratings (Par 91): **92,90,89,87,84 71,67,66,60,49**

toteswinger: 1&2 £5.10, 1&3 £13.40, 2&3 £8.00. CSF £7.56 TOTE £7.90: £1.70, £1.10, £4.20; EX 12.50.

Owner Saeed Misleh **Bred** Darley **Trained** Newmarket, Suffolk

FOCUS

A very ordinary maiden auction fillies' race with the runner-up nowhere near the form she showed over 5f on firm ground at Royal Ascot. The time and the principals set the level.

NOTEBOOK

First City, the paddock pick, ran in a rubber bit. She made her effort on the wide outside and stayed on in willing fashion to outstay the favourite in the closing stages. (op 5-1 tchd 15-2)

Sweet Applause(IRE), eighth in the Queen Mary, was encountering totally different ground. She has a long stride and, after taking them along, edged away from the stands'-side rail and the winner stayed the six much too well for her. (op 11-10 tchd 8-11 and 5-4 in a place)

Rossett Rose(IRE), out of a 5f winner, improved on her debut effort and was coming back for more at the line. (op 25-1 tchd 28-1)

Identity, a half-sister to six winners, was unable to find a buyer at the sales. Constantly swishing her tail beforehand, she stuck on in willing fashion and this was an encouraging debut. (op 11-2)

Jessica Mary(IRE), drawn widest of all, was soon showing bags of toe with the main bunch towards the stands'-side rail. (op 8-1 tchd 9-1)

3793 WORK INTERIORS H'CAP — 1m 4f 10y

7:50 (7:52) (Class 5) (0-75,78) 3-Y-O — £4,857 (£1,445; £722; £360) Stalls High

Form			Horse	Jockey	RPR
10	1		**Rowan Rio**[19] 3134 3-9-7 75 (W J Haggas) *w ldrs: led over 3f out: hld on wl* **16/1**	RHills 3	82+
2201	2	½	**Mezzanisi (IRE)**[9] 3484 3-9-7 75 (M L W Bell) *hld up in rr: smooth hdwy 4f out: chal over 1f out: hrd rdn: no ex wl ins fnl f* **8/1**	HayleyTurner 1	81
-024	3	2 ½	**Red Merlin (IRE)**[24] 3004 3-9-4 72 (C G Cox) *s.s: t.k.h: hdwy to trck ldrs after 3f: edgd rt over 1f out: kpt on same pce* **5/1**[3]	PhilipRobinson 6	74
6-42	4	9	**Red Lily (IRE)**[37] 2603 3-8-12 66 (J R Fanshawe) *trckd ldrs: drvn over 3f out: chal over 2f out: wknd appr fnl f* **15/8**[1]	JamieSpencer 7	55+
1000	5	¾	**Oberlin (USA)**[14] 3327 3-8-5 59 (T Keddy) *sn trcking ldrs: rdn 4f out: wknd over 2f out* **40/1**	FrankieMcDonald 4	47
-000	6	16	**Shanafarahan (IRE)**[11] 3416 3-8-8 62 (T P Tate) *restless in stalls: in rr: hung rt and lost pl 7f out: bhd fnl 3f* **33/1**	MickyFenton 5	26
1111	7	15	**Precision Break (USA)**[7] 3566 3-9-10 78 6ex (P F I Cole) *trckd ldrs: shkn up to ld over 7f out: hdd over 3f out: sn wknd and eased* **2/1**[2]	JohnEgan 2	19+
-113	8	18	**Ovthenight (IRE)**[31] 2785 3-9-4 72 (Mrs P Sly) *led: hdd over 7f out: lost pl over 3f out: sn bhd and eased* **15/2**	JoeFanning 8	—

2m 46.34s (9.64) **Going Correction** +0.85s/f (Soft) — **8 Ran SP% 118.9**

Speed ratings (Par 100): **101,100,99,93,92 81,71,59**

toteswinger: 1&2 £21.20, 1&3 £10.80, 2&3 £5.40. CSF £140.58 CT £745.52 TOTE £25.10: £2.70, £2.30, £2.10; EX 231.00.

Owner Rowan Stud Partnership 1 **Bred** Rowan Farm Stud **Trained** Newmarket, Suffolk

FOCUS

A very steady gallop for the first half-mile in very testing conditions. The unexposed winner stuck on too well for the strong-travelling Mezzanisi and they came home well strung out. Fair form, the winner stepping forward.

Precision Break(USA) Official explanation: jockey said colt was unsuited by the heavy ground

3794 COMMERCIAL FIRST MORTGAGES H'CAP — 6f

8:20 (8:21) (Class 2) (0-100,89) 3-Y-£11,354 (£3,398; £1,699; £849; £423) Stalls Low

Form			Horse	Jockey	RPR
2-14	1		**Maimoona (IRE)**[39] 2529 3-9-1 81 (W J Haggas) *trckd ldrs: hung rt and led appr fnl f: rdn clr ins fnl f* **2/1**[1]	RHills 2	93+
0-00	2	4	**Cristal Clear (IRE)**[54] 2104 3-9-7 87 (T D Easterby) *dwlt: hdwy over 2f out: hung rt and styd on fnl f: tk 2nd nr line* **12/1**	RobertWinston 5	86
-211	3	½	**Wotashirtfull (IRE)**[18] 3171 3-9-1 81 (K A Ryan) *led tl appr fnl f: no ex* **2/1**[1]	(p) NCallan 4	79
1440	4	½	**Mey Blossom**[25] 2967 3-9-4 87 (R M Whitaker) *dwlt: sn pushed along: kpt on fnl 2f: nvr a threat* **9/1**	(p) MichaelJStainton(3) 1	83
6-34	5	½	**Irish Pearl (IRE)**[52] 2148 3-9-7 87 (K R Burke) *chsd wnr: chal over 1f out: kpt on same pce* **9/2**[2]	DarrenWilliams 7	81
2354	6	4	**Piscean (USA)**[10] 3462 3-8-11 77 (T Keddy) *sn drvn along: hdwy on outer over 2f out: hung rt: lost pl over 1f out* **8/1**[3]	MickyFenton 3	59

1m 16.71s (3.71) **Going Correction** +0.70s/f (Yiel) — **6 Ran SP% 113.7**

Speed ratings (Par 106): **103,97,97,96,95 90**

toteswinger: 1&2 Not won, 1&3 £1.80, 2&3 £2.60. CSF £27.54 TOTE £2.90: £1.80, £4.90; EX 27.20.

Owner Hamdan Al Maktoum **Bred** Shadwell Estate Company Limited **Trained** Newmarket, Suffolk

FOCUS

A strong pace in the bad ground and in the end a most decisive success from the unexposed winner, with little to choose between the next four home at the line. Not form to go overboard about.

NOTEBOOK

Maimoona(IRE), 2lb lower than on her handicap debut, looked a picture of health. She found the testing conditions no problem and pulled clear in the end despite a tendency to hang away from the running rail. (op 15-8 tchd 9-4)

Cristal Clear(IRE), down 5lb after two previous outings this time, showed a return to her useful juvenile form. Her head carriage does not please everyone. (op 10-1)

Wotashirtfull(IRE), 9lb higher than Newcastle, took them along at a strong pace but he is all speed and 5f surely suits him better. (tchd 13-8 and 9-4)

Mey Blossom, proven on soft ground, stuck on in her own time and justified her trainer's decision to stick to 6f with her. (op 12-1 tchd 14-1)

Irish Pearl(IRE), highly tried, was making her handicap debut. She kept tabs on the pacesetter but in the end came up short. (op 13-2 tchd 7-1)

Piscean(USA) was never racing on an even keel. He looks tricky and 5f on fast ground is more his game. (tchd 9-1)

3795 BONDGATE H'CAP — 1m

8:50 (8:50) (Class 5) (0-70,70) 3-Y-O+ — £2,914 (£867; £433; £216) Stalls High

Form			Horse	Jockey	RPR
0612	1		**San Antonio**[7] 3557 8-10-0 70 (Mrs P Sly) *mde all: drvn over 3f out: clr over 1f out: rdn out* **1/2**[1]	(b) MickyFenton 9	81+
-004	2	2 ¾	**Hurlingham**[25] 2969 4-10-0 70 (M W Easterby) *trckd ldrs: styd on to go 2nd 1f out: no imp* **15/2**[3]	PaulMulrennan 2	75
5054	3	1	**Emirate Isle**[9] 3478 4-9-10 66 (C Grant) *chsd ldrs: drvn 5f out: wnt 2nd over 2f out: hung rt: kpt on same pce* **11/2**[2]	RobertWinston 5	69
5-P0	4	5	**Admiralcollingwood**[34] 2706 3-7-13 53 (T P Tate) *s.i.s: hdwy 4f out: kpt on one pce fnl 2f* **33/1**	DominicFox(3) 6	45
00-6	5	2 ¾	**Volaticus (IRE)**[18] 3175 7-8-4 51 oh3 (A D Brown) *hld up: effrt over 4f out: sn chsng ldrs: wknd over 1f out* **10/1**	PatrickDonaghy(5) 7	37
6-50	6	5	**Reel Buddy Blaze**[7] 3551 3-9-3 68 (T P Tate) *chsd wnr: wknd over 1f out* **16/1**	AdrianTNicholls 1	43
0400	7	½	**Kadia**[18] 3175 5-8-8 53 oh6 ow2 (P T Midgley) *in rr: effrt on outer over 3f out: sn wknd* **33/1**	(p) JamieMoriarty(3) 4	27
3000	8	nk	**Steel Grey**[103] 1032 7-8-9 51 oh6 (M Brittain) *chsd ldrs: drvn over 5f out: wknd over 3f out* **40/1**	TWilliams 8	24

1m 47.41s (6.01) **Going Correction** +0.85s/f (Soft)

WFA 3 from 4yo+ 9lb — **8 Ran SP% 117.1**

Speed ratings (Par 103): **103,100,99,94,91 86,86,85**

toteswinger: 1&2 £2.40, 1&3 £2.10, 2&3 £2.20. CSF £5.15 CT £11.89 TOTE £1.80: £1.20, £1.40, £1.30; EX 5.90.

Owner R Brazier **Bred** G Reed **Trained** Thorney, Cambs

FOCUS

A very modest handicap and the in-form winner was given his own way. He did not need to show his best.

3796 KIRKGATE MAIDEN STKS — 1m

9:20 (9:21) (Class 5) 3-Y-O+ — £2,914 (£867; £433; £216) Stalls High

Form			Horse	Jockey	RPR
542	1		**La Sarrazine (FR)**[38] 2566 3-8-12 78 (J R Fanshawe) *trckd ldrs: led over 2f out: styd on wl: drvn out* **4/5**[1]	JamieSpencer 6	85+
54	2	3	**Ainia**[38] 2560 3-8-12 0 (D M Simcock) *sn trcking ldrs: plld wd over 2f out: kpt on: no real imp* **3/1**[2]	RichardMullen 12	78
	3	5	**Stalking Shadow (USA)** 3-9-3 0 (Saeed Bin Suroor) *s.s and wnt lft s: t.k.h: sn trcking ldrs: hung lft over 2f out: one pce* **7/2**[3]	NCallan 9	72+
24	4	3 ¾	**Valferno (IRE)**[58] 2015 3-8-12 0 (Mrs P Sly) *led tl over 2f out: hung rt and wknd over 1f out* **16/1**	MickyFenton 11	59
03	5	6	**Offshore Anna (IRE)**[13] 3338 3-8-9 0 (J J Quinn) *in rr: drvn and wl outpcd over 3f out: no ch after* **22/1**	JamieMoriarty(3) 4	46
	6	17	**Amy's Mercedes** 4-9-4 0 (N Bycroft) *in rr-div: drvn over 5f out: bhd fnl 3f* **80/1**	MarkLawson(3) 10	9
-000	7	¾	**Naledi**[45] 2365 4-9-12 45 (J R Norton) *t.k.h: sn trcking ldrs: wknd over 2f out* **100/1**	(b) PaulMulrennan 3	12
00	8	7	**Snake Catcher**[14] 3333 3-8-10 0 (M W Easterby) *hld up in rr: drvn over 5f out: bhd fnl 3f* **100/1**	BradleyRoper(7) 7	—

1m 46.68s (5.28) **Going Correction** +0.85s/f (Soft)

WFA 3 from 4yo 9lb — **8 Ran SP% 116.2**

Speed ratings (Par 103): **107,104,99,95,89 72,71,64**

toteswinger: 1&2 £1.20, 1&3 £3.10, 2&3 £2.40. CSF £3.53 TOTE £1.90: £1.10, £1.50, £1.60; EX 3.80 Place 6 £ 10.02, Place 5 £ 8.35.

Owner Mr & Mrs Duncan Davidson **Bred** Benedikt Fassbender **Trained** Newmarket, Suffolk

FOCUS

Only three in serious consideration beforehand. The winner made quite hard work of taking this modest maiden but probably ran up to her mark.

T/Plt: £10.80 to a £1 stake. Pool: £72,408.09. 4,850.10 winning tickets. T/Qpdt: £7.30 to a £1 stake. Pool: £4,350.70. 437.30 winning tickets. WG

3558 WINDSOR (R-H)

Monday, July 7

OFFICIAL GOING: Soft

The course was dolled out to nearly its widest point, with the rail on the bends and the false rail up the straight out 12 yards.

Wind: Almost nil Weather: Torrential downpours in afternoon; sunshine and showers during meeting

3797 FAY WATTS 25TH BIRTHDAY APPRENTICE H'CAP — 6f

6:30 (6:31) (Class 5) (0-75,75) 4-Y-O+ — £2,729 (£806; £403) Stalls High

Form			Horse	Jockey	RPR
540	1		**Kelamon**[35] 2679 4-9-4 69 (M D I Usher) *hld up far side: prog 1/2-way: led gp 2f out: sn drvn and pressed: jnd ins fnl f: hld on wl* **3/1**[1]	WilliamBuick 1	80
4302	2	nk	**Mandarin Spirit (IRE)**[18] 3169 8-8-5 61 (G C H Chung) *hld up in rr far side: prog over 2f out: drvn to join wnr fnl f: jst hld nr fin* **16/1**	WilliamCarson(5) 5	71
5530	3	¾	**Memphis Man**[14] 3313 5-8-13 69 (P D Evans) *dwlt: towards rr far side: effrt 2f out: styd on u.p fnl f: nrst fin* **9/1**	SimonPearce(5) 3	76

0260 **4** 1/2 **Obe Royal**[9] 3506 4-9-3 **68**....................(b) LukeMorris 9 74
(P D Evans) *chsd far side ldrs: outpcd on outer of gp fr 2f out: styd on wl fnl f: gaining at fin* **16/1**

5-00 **5** 1 1/2 **Blue Java**[24] 2995 7-9-5 **70**.................... TravisBlock 2 71
(H Morrison) *pressed far side ldr: styd cl up fr 2f out: no ex ins fnl f* **12/1**

1510 **6** 1 **Bold Argument (IRE)**[13] 3352 5-8-10 **64**.................... JackMitchell(3) 10 62+
(Mrs P N Dutfield) *dwlt and hmpd s: in rr of far side gp: c to nr side 1/2-way: styd on to ld 2 rivals fnl f: nt on terms* **8/1**[3]

2404 **7** hd **Unlimited**[18] 3165 6-8-10 **66**.................... MarkCoumbe(5) 12 63
(A W Carroll) *chsd far side ldrs on outer of gp: spent last 2f alone in centre: one pce* **16/1**

1510 **8** hd **Shot To Fame (USA)**[14] 3313 9-9-2 **70**.................... HaddenFrost(3) 7 67
(S Kirk) *pressed far side ldrs: drvn over 1f out: fdd ins fnl f* **20/1**

0304 **9** 1 1/2 **Our Fugitive (IRE)**[16] 3269 6-8-6 **62**....................(p) JemmaMarshall(5) 8 54+
(C Gordon) *chsd clr ldr nr side: swtchd to r far side 1/2-way and w ldrs: wknd over 1f out* **25/1**

-305 **10** hd **Cheap Street**[35] 2679 4-9-4 **72**.................... JackDean(3) 11 63
(J G Portman) *chsd far side ldrs: struggling on outer of gp fr 2f out* **6/1**[2]

0003 **11** 1 1/4 **Makabul**[21] 3093 5-8-12 **66**.................... JamesMillman(3) 4 53+
(B R Millman) *trckd far side ldrs: lost pl 1/2-way and n.m.r sn after: struggling fnl 2f* **8/1**[3]

6006 **12** nk **Sailor King (IRE)**[55] 2085 6-9-10 **75**.................... TolleyDean 6 61
(D K Ivory) *led far side gp to over 2f out: sn lost pl and btn* **33/1**

0456 **13** 1 3/4 **Linda Green**[9] 3506 7-8-2 **58**.................... ThomasO'Brien(5) 14 39
(M R Channon) *racd on outer of far side gp: grad c across to nr side fr over 2f out: nvr on terms* **10/1**

0162 **14** 1 **Blessed Place**[6] 3585 8-8-6 **62**.................... BillyCray(5) 16 39+
(D J S Ffrench Davis) *overall ldr nr side and sn at least 6 l clr: wknd 2f out: lost overall ld over 1f out and hdd by nr side rivals fnl f* **14/1**

1m 14.7s (1.70) **Going Correction** +0.375s/f (Good) **14** Ran SP% **124.2**
Speed ratings (Par 103): **103,102,101,100,98 97,97,97,95,94 93,92,90,89**
toteswinger: 1&2 £88.80, 1&3 £17.40, 2&3 £44.40. CSF £56.01 CT £330.99 TOTE £5.30: £2.10, £4.30, £3.90; EX 110.60.
Owner Mr & Mrs Richard Hames And Friends **Bred** R And Mrs Hames **Trained** Upper Lambourn, Berks

FOCUS
A modest but competitive sprint handicap restricted to apprentices. The majority of these headed over to the far rail in the straight and that's where the main action took place. The winner was back to his best and the form is solid but of little consequence.

3798 EBF VISIT LONDON-IRISH.COM MAIDEN STKS 6f
7:00 (7:02) (Class 5) 2-Y-O **£3,885** (£1,156; £577; £288) **Stalls** High

Form RPR

4 **1** **Desert Icon (IRE)**[17] 3219 2-9-3 0.................... PaulDoe 14 78+
(W J Knight) *w ldrs: led over 2f out: hanging lft after but clr over 1f out: pushed out: comf* **3/1**[1]

2 2 3/4 **Whisky Jack** 2-9-3 0.................... DO'Donohoe 4 70+
(W R Muir) *pressed ldrs: hanging lft fr over 2f out: chsd wnr after: stmbld over 1f out: sn outpcd* **15/2**[3]

3 2 **Cawdor (IRE)** 2-9-3 0.................... DaneO'Neill 9 64
(H Candy) *w ldrs: upsides over 2f out: rn green and sn outpcd: one pce fr over 1f out* **3/1**[1]

4 2 **Mr Snowballs** 2-9-3 0.................... LPKeniry 3 58+
(R A Farrant) *dwlt: off the pce towards rr: sme prog against far side rail 2f out: nt clr run briefly 1f out: kpt on* **40/1**

5 shd **Bounty Reef** 2-8-12 0.................... PatCosgrave 15 52+
(P D Evans) *trckd ldrs: hanging bdly lft fr 2f out: snatched up 1f out: styd on again last 100yds* **28/1**

30 **6** 3/4 **Satwa Boy**[26] 2951 2-9-3 0.................... JimmyFortune 1 55
(E A L Dunlop) *mde most to over 2f out: wknd over 1f out* **11/1**

7 1 **Daily Double** 2-9-3 0.................... RyanMoore 6 52+
(R Hannon) *s.v.s: detached in last pair: pushed along 1/2-way: styd on steadily fr over 1f out: nrst fin* **5/1**[2]

54 **8** 1 3/4 **Dalepak Flyer (IRE)**[12] 3358 2-9-3 0.................... PaulEddery 8 47
(G D Blake) *chsd ldrs: rdn over 2f out: steadily wknd* **16/1**

9 2 1/2 **Silver Sceptre (IRE)** 2-9-3 0.................... SebSanders 7 39
(W J Musson) *dwlt: off the pce in rr: nvr on terms fr 1/2-way* **40/1**

10 shd **Celtic Commitment** 2-9-3 0.................... RichardHughes 11 39
(R Hannon) *w ldrs to over 2f out: steadily wknd* **16/1**

11 4 1/2 **West Leake (IRE)** 2-9-3 0.................... MichaelHills 5 26
(B W Hills) *s.i.s: off the pce in rr: nvr a factor* **8/1**

12 15 **Red Robert** 2-9-3 0.................... IanMongan 16 —
(J L Dunlop) *sn struggling in last pair: t.o* **20/1**

1m 15.9s (2.90) **Going Correction** +0.375s/f (Good) **12** Ran SP% **122.7**
Speed ratings (Par 94): **95,91,88,86,85 84,83,81,77,77 71,51**
toteswinger: 1&2 £16.20, 1&3 £1.10, 2&3 £19.80. CSF £26.31 TOTE £4.10: £1.70, £2.50, £2.40; EX 34.50.
Owner B & Mrs D Willis, B & Mrs M Pullin **Bred** Lynch Bages Ltd & Samac Ltd **Trained** Patching, W Sussex

FOCUS
Probably just an ordinary juvenile maiden. They all raced far side in the straight.

NOTEBOOK
Desert Icon(IRE) ◆, fourth on his debut on quick ground at Newmarket, handled these very different conditions well and ran out a clear-cut winner. He looks a nice type in the making and could now be aimed at a race at Goodwood. (tchd 11-4 and 7-2)

Whisky Jack ◆, a 16,000gns son of Bahamian Bounty, half-brother to multiple sprint winner Green Target, out of a 5f juvenile winner, made a pleasing introduction. He showed his inexperience by hanging left at around the intersection and also stumbled about a furlong out, suggesting he is still on the weak side. There should be much more to come. (op 16-1)

Cawdor(IRE), a £26,000 son of Kyllachy, half-brother to dual 7f-1m1f winner How's Things, out of a triple 5f-6f winner at two to three, was well supported on his racecourse debut, but he ran green and found a couple too good. He should learn from this and can make his mark. (op 11-4 tchd 10-3)

Mr Snowballs, a £1,800 gelded son of Monsieur Bond, half-brother to triple 6f-7f winner Middle Eastern, made a satisfactory introduction.

Bounty Reef, a 20,000gns daughter of Bahamian Bounty, half-sister to among others prolific 1m-1m2f winner Ottobre Rosso, out of a triple 1m winner, might have made the frame but for running into the heels of rivals and having to be reined in. She should learn from this and ought to stay further. (op 20-1)

Daily Double, a 36,000gns son of Needwood Blade, lost his race with a very slow start, but he did some good late work and can leave this form behind. (op 6-1 tchd 13-2)

3799 GET ON WITH HILLS - 0800 444040 H'CAP 1m 67y
7:30 (7:30) (Class 5) (0-70,74) 3-Y-O **£2,729** (£806; £403) **Stalls** High

Form RPR

-043 **1** **Penchesco (IRE)**[18] 3180 3-9-7 **70**.................... PaulEddery 9 74
(Pat Eddery) *t.k.h: trckd ldrs: lost pl 1/2-way: rdn over 2f out: str run on outer jst over 1f out: led last stride* **11/1**

5432 **2** nk **Golden Penny**[16] 3266 3-9-4 **70**.................... TravisBlock(3) 8 73
(H Morrison) *trckd ldr: led wl over 2f out: drvn and looked in command over 1f out: over a l clr 75yds out: ct last stride* **10/3**[1]

6P-0 **3** hd **Muharjam**[18] 3161 3-9-2 **65**....................(b) SebSanders 13 68
(C E Brittain) *n.m.r sn after s: t.k.h and hld up in rr: rdn and struggling wl over 2f out: str run on outer jst over 1f out: gaining fast on runner-up but jst outpcd by wnr* **25/1**

0-62 **4** 1 1/4 **Rondeau (GR)**[18] 3180 3-9-2 **65**.................... JimCrowley 2 65
(P R Chamings) *prom: chsd ldr over 2f out: no imp and hld over 1f out: lost 2 pls nr fin* **12/1**

0001 **5** 1/2 **Coole Dodger (IRE)**[8] 3525 3-9-6 **74** 6ex.................... GabrielHannon(5) 14 73
(M D I Usher) *stdd s: hld up towards rr: stdy prog fr over 3f out: looked awkward and nt qckn 2f out: shuffled along and styd on fnl f* **13/2**[3]

5001 **6** shd **Landikhaya (IRE)**[18] 3166 3-8-8 **57**.................... WilliamBuick 10 56
(D K Ivory) *prom: chsd ldng pair 2f out: rdn and fnd little: fdd ins fnl f* **8/1**

-300 **7** 1 1/2 **Silky Steps (IRE)**[9] 3507 3-9-0 **63**.................... LPKeniry 1 59
(P J Makin) *hld up in midfield: prog to press ldrs 3f out: drvn 2f out: fdd over 1f out* **14/1**

4001 **8** 2 1/2 **Themwerethedays**[14] 3333 3-9-7 **70**.................... RyanMoore 4 60
(S Kirk) *hld up in last pair: pushed along 1/2-way: swtchd towards far rail over 2f out: rdn over 1f out: no imp on ldrs* **6/1**[2]

0542 **9** hd **Mganga**[8] 3524 3-8-5 **54**.................... EdwardCreighton 6 44
(M R Channon) *chsd ldrs: rdn 3f out: steadily wknd fr over 2f out* **8/1**

000- **10** 4 **Epsom Salts**[235] 6820 3-8-8 **57**.................... IanMongan 7 38
(P M Phelan) *led to wl over 2f out: sn wknd* **50/1**

-300 **11** 2 **Karky Schultz (GER)**[28] 2891 3-8-13 **62**.................... RichardHughes 11 38
(J M P Eustace) *nvr beyond midfield: shkn up and no prog over 2f out: fdd* **20/1**

0360 **12** 4 **Feasible**[8] 3525 3-9-3 **66**.................... JimmyFortune 5 34+
(J G Portman) *dwlt: hld up in last pair: shkn up and no prog over 2f out: taken to outer and nt clr run over 1f out: no ch after* **11/1**

54-0 **13** hd **Astania**[26] 2956 3-9-7 **70**.................... ShaneKelly 3 37
(P W D'Arcy) *hld up in midfield: effrt over 3f out: lost pl and struggling over 2f out: sn btn* **16/1**

60-6 **14** 3 1/4 **Siryena**[25] 2982 3-8-7 **56** ow1....................(v[1]) SteveDrowne 12 16
(E A L Dunlop) *hld up in midfield: wknd over 2f out* **22/1**

1m 51.79s (7.09) **Going Correction** +0.825s/f (Soft) **14** Ran SP% **124.7**
Speed ratings (Par 100): **97,96,96,95,94 94,93,90,90,86 84,80,80,77**
toteswinger: 1&2 £17.70, 1&3 £58.10, 2&3 £45.60. CSF £47.18 CT £940.02 TOTE £11.50: £2.50, £1.90, £8.70; EX 56.80.
Owner Pat Eddery Racing (Sanglamore) **Bred** Patrick J Dempsey **Trained** Nether Winchendon, Bucks

FOCUS
A modest three-year-old handicap run at a steady pace. They raced middle to far side in the straight, with the front two making their challenges up the centre.
Coole Dodger(IRE) Official explanation: jockey said colt hung right-handed
Feasible Official explanation: jockey said gelding was unsuited by the soft ground

3800 GET A BONUS @ WILLIAMHILLCASINO.COM H'CAP 1m 2f 7y
8:00 (8:00) (Class 4) (0-85,85) 3-Y-O+ **£5,504** (£1,637; £818; £408) **Stalls** Centre

Form RPR

004- **1** **Sam Lord**[33] 2340 4-9-7 **78**.................... DaneO'Neill 7 87
(A King) *sn trckd ldrs: pushed along 3f out: rallied over 1f out: r.o wl ins fnl f to ld nr fin* **16/1**

0500 **2** 1/2 **Folio (IRE)**[10] 3461 8-9-6 **77**.................... StephenDonohoe 6 85
(W J Musson) *hld up: stl last 3f out: prog on outer 2f out: rdn to ld ins fnl f: hdd and nt qckn nr fin* **25/1**

051- **3** 1 **Samsons Son**[286] 5718 4-10-0 **85**.................... LPKeniry 9 91
(J R Best) *hld up in rr: smooth prog on outer fr 3f out: led over 1f out: rdn and fnd little: hdd ins fnl f: nt qckn* **20/1**

4401 **4** 1 1/4 **Closertobelieving**[21] 3095 3-8-10 **78**.................... TQuinn 3 83+
(D R C Elsworth) *hld up in tch: shkn up over 3f out: effrt 2f out: trying to cl whn squeezed out last 150yds: nt rcvr* **5/2**[2]

013 **5** 3/4 **Artreju (GER)**[19] 3132 5-9-1 **72**.................... RyanMoore 8 74
(G L Moore) *led after 2f: hrd pressed fr 3f out: hdd over 1f out: fdd* **11/1**

0611 **6** nse **Dear Maurice**[21] 3090 4-10-0 **85**.................... SebSanders 2 87+
(E A L Dunlop) *trckd ldrs: moved up to chal 3f out: upsides fr over 2f out to jst over 1f out: fdd ins fnl f* **5/4**[1]

3505 **7** 6 **No To Trident**[8] 3527 3-8-13 **81**.................... PatCosgrave 1 71
(P D Evans) *reluctant ldr for 2f: trckd ldr after: hrd rdn over 2f out: wknd over 1f out* **18/1**

1513 **8** 6 **Silver Blue (IRE)**[17] 3208 5-8-13 **70**.................... CatherineGannon 5 48
(W K Goldsworthy) *hld up in tch: effrt and cl up 3f out: wknd 2f out* **10/1**[3]

4505 **9** 5 **Royal Island (IRE)**[14] 3317 6-9-7 **78**.................... VinceSlattery 4 46
(M G Quinlan) *t.k.h: cl up tl wknd 3f out: eased whn no ch fnl f* **16/1**

2m 17.81s (9.11) **Going Correction** +0.825s/f (Soft)
WFA 3 from 4yo+ 11lb **9** Ran SP% **116.1**
Speed ratings (Par 105): **96,95,94,93,93 93,88,83,79**
toteswinger: 1&2 £58.20, 1&3 £23.90, 2&3 £23.90. CSF £343.19 CT £7755.10 TOTE £17.10: £2.80, £3.80, £3.90; EX 281.90.
Owner Winter Madness **Bred** Wickfield Farm Partnership **Trained** Barbury Castle, Wilts

FOCUS
A moderate winning time, even allowing for the conditions.
Silver Blue(IRE) Official explanation: jockey said gelding was unsuited by the soft ground

3801 NEW PLAYER BONUS @ WILLIAMHILLPOKER.COM MAIDEN FILLIES' STKS 1m 67y
8:30 (8:31) (Class 5) 3-4-Y-O **£2,729** (£806; £403) **Stalls** High

Form RPR

03 **1** **Fountains Abbey (USA)**[38] 2560 3-9-3 0.................... RyanMoore 4 76+
(Sir Michael Stoute) *mde all: shkn up and wandered briefly over 2f out: sn drew clr: pushed out* **8/11**[1]

3 **2** 5 **Suede**[31] 2800 3-9-3 0.................... PaulEddery 11 64
(Pat Eddery) *t.k.h early: hld up: nt qckn over 3f out: prog u.p over 2f out: kpt on to take 2nd ins fnl f* **5/2**[2]

0 **3** ¾ **Romiosini Way (GR)**[22] 3061 3-9-3 0 .... JimCrowley 1 62
(P R Chamings) *in tch: prog to dispute 2nd 3f out: kpt on same pce fr over 1f out* **50/1**

0- **4** ½ **Alto Singer (IRE)**[455] 972 3-9-0 0 .... JamesMillman(3) 3 61
(B R Millman) *prom: chsd wnr 5f out: no imp 2f out: one pce and lost 2 pls fnl f* **50/1**

06 **5** 1 ¾ **Citron Presse (USA)**[14] 3318 3-9-3 0 .... JimmyFortune 5 57
(J H M Gosden) *chsd wnr 3f: lost pl 3f out: rdn and one pce after* **8/1**[3]

0 **6** nse **Futurity**[24] 2994 3-9-3 0 .... StephenCarson 8 57
(Eve Johnson Houghton) *hld up in last pair: effrt 3f out: one pce fnl 2f* **16/1**

60- **7** 5 **Bianca Capello**[279] 5882 3-9-3 0 .... AdamKirby 6 46
(J R Fanshawe) *t.k.h early: hld up in tch: shkn up and wknd 2f out* **20/1**

5 **8** 5 **Circadian Rhythm**[168] 244 3-8-10 0 .... WilliamCarson(7) 10 35
(S C Williams) *hld up in last: wknd 2f out* **50/1**

1m 51.22s (6.52) **Going Correction** +0.825s/f (Soft) 8 Ran SP% **114.1**
Speed ratings (Par 100): **100,95,94,93,92 91,86,81**
toteswinger: 1&2 £1.10, 1&3 £32.10, 2&3 £8.60. CSF £2.55 TOTE £1.70: £1.10, £1.10, £8.60; EX 2.90.
Owner Gainsborough **Bred** Gainsborough Farm Llc **Trained** Newmarket, Suffolk

FOCUS
A modest maiden. The winner looks an interesting type for handicaps but the bare form is unlikely to prove any better than rated.

3802 EBF GILL PARTOS 60TH BIRTHDAY H'CAP — 1m 3f 135y
9:00 (9:00) (Class 4) (0-80,80) 3-Y-O+ **£5,375** (£1,599; £799; £399) **Stalls** Centre

Form RPR

6533 **1** **Aegean Prince**[10] 3449 4-9-9 **75** .... RichardHughes 5 86+
(R Hannon) *hld up towards rr: prog over 2f out: rdn to ld jst over 1f out: sn clr* **4/1**[2]

243 **2** 1 ¾ **Coin Of The Realm (IRE)**[35] 2668 3-8-13 **78** .... RyanMoore 2 86
(E A L Dunlop) *hld up in midfield: effrt 3f out: chal and upsides 2f out to jst over 1f out: kpt on same pce* **4/1**[2]

-435 **3** ¾ **Fourth Dimension (IRE)**[26] 2952 9-9-2 **68** .... AdamKirby 7 75
(Miss T Spearing) *trckd ldng trio: rdn to ld 2f out and wandered: hdd and nt qckn jst over 1f out* **16/1**

-210 **4** ½ **Dove Cottage (IRE)**[47] 2304 6-9-9 **75** .... FergusSweeney 4 81
(W S Kittow) *led: kicked on 3f out: hdd 2f out: steadily fdd* **7/2**[1]

0-05 **5** 2 ¼ **Know The Law**[28] 2895 4-9-10 **76** .... (b) JimmyFortune 11 78
(D R C Elsworth) *hld up in last pair: effrt 3f out: hrd rdn to chse ldrs over 1f out: no imp after* **14/1**

3-35 **6** 1 ½ **Spirit Of Adjisa (IRE)**[32] 2764 4-9-9 **75** .... (v[1]) ShaneKelly 6 75
(Pat Eddery) *s.v.s: t.k.h: sn in tch: effrt 3f out: no imp fr 2f out* **11/2**

5340 **7** 5 **Rapid City**[33] 2711 5-10-0 **80** .... GeorgeBaker 1 72
(Miss J Feilden) *hld up in last pair: shkn up and no prog over 2f out: no ch after* **20/1**

-060 **8** 16 **Olimpo (FR)**[12] 3368 7-9-5 **74** .... JamesMillman(3) 9 49+
(B R Millman) *t.k.h: trckd ldr to over 2f out: wknd rapidly and eased: t.o* **12/1**

41 **9** 6 **Bell Island**[29] 2862 4-10-0 **80** .... SebSanders 3 43+
(Lady Herries) *trckd ldng pair tl wknd rapidly over 2f out: eased: t.o* **5/1**[3]

2m 37.96s (8.46) **Going Correction** +0.825s/f (Soft)
WFA 3 from 4yo+ 13lb 9 Ran SP% **119.3**
Speed ratings (Par 105): **104,102,102,102,100 99,96,85,81**
toteswinger: 1&2 £4.60, 1&3 £12.00, 2&3 £7.30. CSF £21.20 CT £234.91 TOTE £5.70: £2.10, £2.20, £3.20; EX 24.40 Place 6 £ 549.44, Place 5 £ 213.60.
Owner Theobalds Stud **Bred** Theobalds Stud **Trained** East Everleigh, Wilts

FOCUS
A fair handicap, and pretty solid form.
Olimpo(FR) Official explanation: jockey said gelding had no more to give
Bell Island Official explanation: jockey said gelding was unsuited by the soft ground
T/Jkpt: Not won. T/Plt: £442.90 to a £1 stake. Pool: £123,993.42. 204.36 winning tickets. T/Qpdt: £54.50 to a £1 stake. Pool: £6,573.45. 89.10 winning tickets. JN

3803 - 3804a (Foreign Racing) - See Raceform Interactive

2899 ROSCOMMON (R-H)
Monday, July 7

OFFICIAL GOING: Soft (heavy in places)

3805a LENEBANE STKS (LISTED RACE) — 1m 4f
6:40 (6:43) 3-Y-O+ **£23,933** (£7,022; £3,345; £1,139)

RPR

1 **Raydiya (IRE)**[31] 2813 3-8-7 94 .... NGMcCullagh 12 98
(John M Oxx, Ire) *mde all: strly pressed fr 2f out: styd on wl fnl f* **10/1**

2 ¾ **Arkadina (IRE)**[54] 2113 4-9-6 96 .... JMurtagh 11 97+
(David Wachman, Ire) *mid-div: clsr in 6th into st: wnt 3rd u.p over 1f out: chal in 2nd and ev ch fnl f: kpt on same pce cl home* **11/2**[2]

3 1 ¾ **Honoria (IRE)**[10] 3469 3-8-7 .... SMLevey 10 94
(A P O'Brien, Ire) *towards rr: swtchd to outer and rdn st: wnt 6th over 1f out: styd on wl fnl f: nrst fin* **12/1**

4 hd **Simawa (IRE)**[17] 3238 3-8-7 98 .... MJKinane 14 94
(John M Oxx, Ire) *trckd ldrs: clsr in 2nd into st: chal fr 2f out: no imp u.p and kpt on same pce ins fnl f* **7/1**[3]

5 shd **Superius (IRE)**[10] 3469 3-8-10 90 .... WJLee 13 97
(T Stack, Ire) *chsd ldrs: 6th bef st: impr into 3rd and rdn fr 2f out: no imp in 4th and kpt on same pce fr over 1f out* **12/1**

6 2 ½ **Silk Affair (IRE)**[25] 2975 3-8-7 .... MCHussey 3 90
(M G Quinlan) *hmpd at s: towards rr: kpt on wout threatening u.p st* **12/1**

7 hd **Perihelion (IRE)**[2] 3746 3-8-7 68 .... CO'Donoghue 15 89
(A P O'Brien, Ire) *mid-div: rdn appr st: 8th fr 2f out: 7th and kpt on same pce fr over 1f out* **16/1**

8 nk **Red Moloney (USA)**[9] 3513 4-10-0 109 .... DPMcDonogh 1 97
(Kevin Prendergast, Ire) *wnt rt out of stalls: sn in mid-div: prog 4f out: 4th bef st: chal u.p 2f out: dropped to 5th and no ex fr over 1f out* **2/1**[1]

9 4 **Unwritten Rule (IRE)**[29] 2874 3-8-10 100 .... (b) PJSmullen 9 86
(D K Weld, Ire) *prom: rdn in 5th bef st: 6th fr 2f out: no ex fr over 1f out* **14/1**

10 6 **Hold Me Love Me (IRE)**[2] 3746 3-8-7 60 .... DavidMcCabe 6 73
(A P O'Brien, Ire) *trckd ldr in 2nd: lost pl 4f out and sn dropped to rr: kpt on same pce* **50/1**

11 3 ½ **Sweet Sixteen (IRE)**[54] 2113 3-8-8 ow1 .... JAHeffernan 7 68
(A P O'Brien, Ire) *in rr of mid-div: rdn and wd early st: sn no imp* **10/1**

12 3 **Majestic Eviction (IRE)**[50] 2227 4-9-6 87 .... (t) RPCleary 4 63
(M Halford, Ire) *chsd ldrs: 7th 1/2-way: no ex fr bef st* **50/1**

13 2 ½ **Angels Story (IRE)**[9] 3512 3-8-7 95 .... (p) DJMoran 2 59
(J S Bolger, Ire) *prom: rdn in 2nd bef st: sn 3rd and wknd: eased fr over 1f out* **9/1**

14 4 ½ **Bold Bibi (IRE)**[276] 5998 4-9-6 93 .... WMLordan 8 51
(M Halford, Ire) *a towards rr: nvr a factor* **33/1**

2m 49.9s (6.60)
WFA 3 from 4yo 13lb **15** Ran SP% **131.9**
CSF £69.91 TOTE £12.10: £4.30, £2.50, £5.20; DF 86.40.
Owner H H Aga Khan **Bred** H H The Aga Khan's Studs Sc **Trained** Currabeg, Co Kildare
■ Stewards' Enquiry : N G McCullagh caution: excessive use of the whip

FOCUS
The form is rated around the placed horses.

NOTEBOOK
Raydiya(IRE) did well to make all on this ground and should stay further.
Arkadina(IRE) came from off the pace to throw down her challenge and loses nothing in defeat. (op 13/2 tchd 7/1)
Honoria(IRE) was nearest at the finish having endured a troubled passage. (op 14/1)
Silk Affair(IRE) stayed on from an unpromising position in the straight.
Red Moloney(USA) disappointed again, finding nothing when let down. (op 9/4 tchd 13/8)

3806 - (Foreign Racing) - See Raceform Interactive

HOLLYWOOD PARK (L-H)
Saturday, July 5

OFFICIAL GOING: Turf course - firm; all-weather - fast

3807a AMERICAN OAKS INVITATIONAL STKS (GRADE 1) (FILLIES) (TURF) — 1m 2f
12:00 (12:36) 3-Y-O **£226,131** (£75,377; £45,226; £22,613; £7,538)

RPR

1 **Pure Clan (USA)**[21] 3-8-9 .... (b) JRLeparoux 1 116
(Robert E Holthus, U.S.A) **5/2**[1]

2 ¾ **Satan's Circus (USA)**[27] 2877 3-8-9 .... IMendizabal 3 115
(J-C Rouget, France) **29/2**

3 ½ **Clearly Foxy (USA)**[64] 3-8-9 .... GKGomez 5 114
(Mark Casse, Canada) **182/10**

4 2 ¾ **Carribean Sunset (IRE)**[15] 3194 3-8-9 .... PJSmullen 9 108
(D K Weld, Ire) *held up in mid-division, headway on outside 3f out, 6th straight, stayed on one pace* **31/10**[2]

5 nse **Missit (IRE)**[28] 3-8-9 .... VEspinoza 8 108
(B Cecil, U.S.A) **192/10**

6 1 **Magical Fantasy (USA)**[28] 3-8-9 .... ASolis 2 106
(Patrick Gallagher, U.S.A) **355/10**

7 hd **Backseat Rhythm (USA)**[98] 3-8-9 .... JJCastellano 10 106
(Patrick L Reynolds, U.S.A) **144/10**

8 ¾ **Raw Silk (USA)**[35] 3-8-9 .... (b) AGarcia 4 104
(Thomas Albertrani, U.S.A) **11/2**[3]

9 2 ¾ **Bel Air Sizzle (USA)**[28] 3-8-9 .... RBejarano 6 99
(Barry Abrams, U.S.A) **84/10**

10 4 **Zaskar**[22] 3018 3-8-9 .... DFlores 11 91
(Tom Dascombe) *mid-division, closed up 4f out, not much room and snatched up over 2f out, behind final 2f* **425/10**

11 ½ **Annie Skates (USA)**[23] 2975 3-8-9 .... JohnEgan 7 90
(Jane Chapple-Hyam) *in touch til weakening from 3f out* **235/10**

12 18 **My Baby Baby (USA)**[64] 3-8-9 .... BBlanc 12 54
(Kenneth McPeek, U.S.A) **114/10**

2m 0.50s (120.50) **12** Ran SP% **119.3**
PARI-MUTUEL: 7.00; PL (1-2) 4.00, 12.60; SHOW (1-2-3) 3.40, 10.00, 9.80;DF 59.80; SF 90.00.
Owner Lewis G Lakin IEAH Stable & Pegasus Holding Group **Bred** A Lakin And Sons Inc **Trained** North America

NOTEBOOK
Pure Clan(USA) is now unbeaten in four turf starts.
Satan's Circus(USA), who was fifth in the Prix de Diane, ran a game race following her long trip from the south of France.
Carribean Sunset(IRE), whose trainer won this race five years ago with Dimitrova, was a little disappointing on this step up in trip.
Zaskar will now continue her career in the USA.
Annie Skates(USA) was found wanting on this step up in grade.

3551 PONTEFRACT (L-H)
Tuesday, July 8

OFFICIAL GOING: Good
Wind: Fresh behind Weather: Dry and sunny

3809 DIANNE NURSERY — 6f
2:30 (2:35) (Class 4) 2-Y-O **£6,476** (£1,927; £963; £481) **Stalls** Low

Form RPR

535 **1** **Rosabee (IRE)**[46] 2357 2-8-1 **66** .... DuranFentiman(3) 10 80
(Miss V Haigh) *chsd ldrs on outer: effrt 2f out: rdn to ld appr fnl f: edgd lft and sn clr* **33/1**

0612 **2** 4 ½ **Madame Jourdain (IRE)**[27] 2924 2-7-9 **64** .... CharlotteKerton(7) 9 65
(N Wilson) *hung rt thrght: sn led: rdn 2f out: hdd over 1f out: kpt on same pce* **33/1**

041 **3** 1 **Tagula Breeze (IRE)**[28] 2909 2-9-4 **80** .... RoystonFfrench 6 78
(I W McInnes) *midfield: hdwy 2f out: rdn to chse ldrs whn hung lft ent fnl f: kpt on same pce* **15/2**[3]

0321 **4** 1 **Johnmanderville**[7] 3576 2-8-9 **71** 6ex .... AndrewElliott 1 66
(K R Burke) *in tch on inner: hdwy 2f out and sn rdn: drvn ent fnl f and sn one pce* **5/2**[2]

1300 **5** 1 ¾ **Lisburn (IRE)**[41] 2507 2-8-12 **74** .... TWilliams 12 63
(M Brittain) *cl up: rdn 2f out and ev ch tl drvn and wknd jst ins fnl f* **33/1**

42U2 **6** 4 **Verinco**[12] 3400 2-9-7 **83** .... (b) TomEaves 3 60
(B Smart) *towards rr tl styd on appr fnl f: nrst fin* **10/1**

221 **7** 11 **Predict**[15] 3331 2-9-4 **80** .... SebSanders 4 24
(Sir Mark Prescott) *hld up in rr: hdwy on inner 2f out: rdn to chse ldrs wl over 1f out: sn btn* **6/4**[1]

003 **8** 8 **Mean Mr Mustard (IRE)**[15] 3315 2-8-0 **62** .... DavidKinsella 5 —
(J A Osborne) *chsd ldrs: rdn along over 2f out and sn wknd* **12/1**

The Form Book, Raceform Ltd, Compton, RG20 6NL

215 **9** *2 ¼* **Red Cell (IRE)**[45] [2392] 2-8-8 **70**........................ ChrisCatlin 11 —
(E J O'Neill) *chsd ldrs: rdn along 1/2-way: sn wknd* **10/1**

1m 19.3s (2.40) **Going Correction** +0.40s/f (Good) **9** Ran SP% **115.0**
Speed ratings (Par 96): **100,94,92,91,89 83,69,58,55**
toteswinger: 1&2 £38.50, 1&3 £31.30, 2&3 £22.40. CSF £776.03 CT £8693.85 TOTE £39.50: £6.80, £4.50, £2.00; EX 355.80.

Owner R J Budge **Bred** J F Tuthill **Trained** Wiseton, Notts

FOCUS
A fair nursery on paper but a shock result, although no fluke. The 'official' ratings shown next to each horse are estimated and for information purposes only.

NOTEBOOK
Rosabee(IRE), who had hung left on her previous two starts, appreciated this sharp left-handed track. She came home a clear winner despite being sent off a big price and looks capable of better.
Madame Jourdain(IRE), in contrast, did not look happy on the track, hanging right throughout. A winner of a seller last month, she was easily seen off by the winner but appreciated the return to 6f. (op 25-1)
Tagula Breeze(IRE) appeared to have a bit to do at the weights based on his maiden form, but he stayed on after getting outpaced despite hanging left in the closing stages. (op 8-1)
Johnmanderville, carrying a 6lb penalty for winning the first nursery of the season a week earlier, was not disgraced in this stronger event. (tchd 9-4)
Lisburn(IRE), who has been highly tried since winning her maiden, showed more back down to handicap company, but 5f probably suits her better. (tchd 40-1)
Predict looked one to follow when winning her maiden on the Polytrack so this has to go down as a very disappointing effort. She clearly failed to show her true form for one reason or another.
Official explanation: trainer had no explanation for the poor fom shown (op 7-4 tchd 15-8 in a place)

3810 AEDAS ARCHITECTS MAIDEN STKS — 1m 2f 6y
3:00 (3:01) (Class 5) 3-Y-O+ **£3,885** (£1,156; £577; £288) **Stalls** Low

Form RPR
6 **1** **Hevelius**[25] [2994] 3-9-1 0........................ AdamKirby 5 91
(W R Swinburn) *hld up in midfield: pushed along over 3f out: swtchd ins and hdwy 2f out: rdn to ld ins fnl f: edgd rt and kpt on* **12/1**
5-02 **2** *nk* **Syvilla**[34] [2717] 3-8-10 82........................ JimCrowley 6 85
(Rae Guest) *trckd ldrs: hdwy on outer 2f out: rdn to ld and hung bdly lft over 1f out: drvn and hdd ins fnl f: kpt on* **1/1**[1]
22-4 **3** *13* **Siyabona (USA)**[26] [2971] 3-8-10 78........................ LDettori 2 62
(Saeed Bin Suroor) *trckd ldrs: effrt over 2f out and ev ch tl rdn and one pce appr fnl f* **2/1**[2]
4 *2 ¼* **London Bid (USA)** 3-8-10 0........................ RyanMoore 10 58+
(Sir Michael Stoute) *cl up: effrt 3f out: rdn and ev ch 2f out: wknd over 1f out* **10/1**
4 **5** *1 ½* **Gifted Leader (USA)**[27] [2955] 3-9-1 0........................ ShaneKelly 9 60
(Pat Eddery) *s.i.s: gd prog to ld after 2f: rdn along over 2f out: drvn and hdd over 1f out and sn wknd* **8/1**[3]
00 **6** *20* **I Feel Fine**[10] [3479] 5-9-7 0........................ PAspell 1 19
(A Kirtley) *s.i.s and a bhd* **100/1**
440- **7** *nk* **White Lightening (IRE)**[48] [4179] 5-9-12 72........................ RobertWinston 7 24
(J Wade) *led 2f: cl up tl rdn along and wkng whn n.m.r on inner 2f out* **33/1**
0 **8** *7* **Alright Chuck**[4] [3688] 4-9-12 0........................ DarrenWilliams 3 —
(P W Hiatt) *chsd ldrs: rdn along over 2f out and sn wknd* **200/1**
60- **9** *¾* **Glenisland**[365] [3365] 4-9-4 49........................ TolleyDean(3) 4 —
(Mrs L Williamson) *a bhd* **200/1**
10 *3 ¼* **Sweet Destiny** 3-8-10 0........................ JimmyQuinn 8 —
(M H Tompkins) *a bhd* **40/1**

2m 16.95s (3.25) **Going Correction** +0.40s/f (Good)
WFA 3 from 4yo+ 11lb **10** Ran SP% **118.6**
Speed ratings (Par 103): **103,102,92,90,89 73,73,67,66,64**
toteswinger: 1&2 £4.00, 1&3 £4.30, 2&3 £1.20. CSF £25.18 TOTE £11.60: £2.10, £1.20, £1.20; EX 33.40.

Owner The Warsaw Pact **Bred** W And R Barnett Ltd **Trained** Aldbury, Herts
■ Stewards' Enquiry : Jim Crowley caution: careless riding

FOCUS
No more than a fair maiden. The first two handled conditions better than the rest and came a long way clear. The third is becoming disappointing.
Gifted Leader(USA) Official explanation: jockey said colt hit its head on stalls

3811 HARWORTH ESTATES H'CAP — 5f
3:30 (3:31) (Class 5) (0-75,75) 3-Y-O **£3,885** (£1,156; £577; £288) **Stalls** Low

Form RPR
0411 **1** **Le Toreador**[6] [3609] 3-9-3 71 6ex........................(t) NCallan 5 82+
(K A Ryan) *mde all: rdn and hung rt ent fnl f: kpt on* **7/4**[1]
0044 **2** *2 ¾* **Paddy Jack**[18] [3217] 3-8-6 **60**........................(p) ChrisCatlin 4 61
(J R Weymes) *chsd ldrs: rdn 2f out: drvn over 1f out and kpt on u.p ins fnl f* **25/1**
4300 **3** *¾* **Another Socket**[11] [3462] 3-9-2 **70**........................ SebSanders 3 69
(E S McMahon) *towards rr: rdn along and hdwy 2f out: styd on u.p ins fnl f* **10/1**
6045 **4** *¾* **Barraland**[17] [3256] 3-9-4 **72**........................(v[1]) DarryllHolland 8 68
(M R Channon) *cl up: rdn along 2f out: drvn and one pce fr over 1f out* **9/1**
0001 **5** *nse* **Select Committee**[11] [3455] 3-8-6 **60**........................(v) PaulHanagan 7 56
(J J Quinn) *hld up in tch: hdwy 2f out: sn rdn and kpt on same pce* **7/1**[3]
0451 **6** *1 ½* **Beat The Bell**[11] [3434] 3-9-2 **70**........................ FrancisNorton 6 60
(A Bailey) *dwlt and sn pushed along: hdwy to chse ldrs 2f out: rdn and wandered over 1f out: sn btn* **7/2**[2]
3530 **7** *½* **Chinese Temple (IRE)**[12] [3418] 3-9-4 **75**........................ JerryO'Dwyer(3) 2 64
(M G Quinlan) *s.i.s: a in rr* **28/1**
3426 **8** *2 ½* **Grudge**[11] [3455] 3-8-10 **64**........................(p) TonyHamilton 9 44
(D W Barker) *chsd ldrs: rdn along 2f out and sn wknd* **15/2**
0100 **9** *1* **Revue Princess (IRE)**[11] [3455] 3-8-13 **67**........................(b) DavidAllan 1 43
(T D Easterby) *chsd ldrs on inner: rdn along 1/2-way: flashed tail and wknd wl over 1f out* **14/1**

65.20 secs (1.90) **Going Correction** +0.40s/f (Good) **9** Ran SP% **115.9**
Speed ratings (Par 100): **100,95,94,93,93 90,89,85,84**
toteswinger: 1&2 £8.20, 1&3 £3.80, 2&3 £23.40. CSF £52.08 CT £352.08 TOTE £2.40: £1.20, £4.20, £3.20; EX 49.50.

Owner Guy Reed **Bred** G Reed **Trained** Hambleton, N Yorks

FOCUS
A modest handicap dominated from the gate by the progressive winner, although he did not beat a great deal with the second helping anchor the form.

Chinese Temple(IRE) Official explanation: jockey said colt hung left

3812 KING RICHARD III H'CAP — 6f
4:00 (4:02) (Class 3) (0-90,88) 3-Y-O+
£9,346 (£2,799; £1,399; £700; £349; £175) **Stalls** Low

Form RPR
1210 **1** **Dickie Le Davoir**[3] [3728] 4-9-0 **77**........................ MarkCoumbe(5) 6 87
(John A Harris) *towards rr: gd hdwy on inner 2f out: rdn to ld and edgd rt ent fnl f: drvn out* **16/1**
-050 **2** *½* **Grazeon Gold Blend**[23] [3056] 5-9-0 **72**........................ RobertWinston 7 81
(J J Quinn) *midfield: gd hdwy on outer wl over 1f out: rdn and hung lft ent fnl f: sn drvn and kpt on* **22/1**
1513 **3** *2 ¼* **John Keats**[5] [3626] 5-9-6 **78**........................ DanielTudhope 11 80
(J S Goldie) *hld up: hdwy wl over 1f out: sn rdn and kpt on ins fnl f: nrst fin* **7/2**[1]
6000 **4** *hd* **Paris Bell**[11] [3454] 6-8-12 **70**........................ DavidAllan 8 71+
(T D Easterby) *rr: hdwy on inner wl over 1f out: rdn and styd on ins fnl f: nrst fin* **33/1**
0526 **5** *nk* **Mr Wolf**[21] [3111] 7-8-13 **71**........................(p) FergalLynch 3 72+
(D W Barker) *led: rdn and edgd lft over 1f out: hdd ent fnl f: sn drvn: n.m.r and wknd* **7/1**[3]
6600 **6** *1 ¼* **Ingleby Arch (USA)**[10] [3489] 5-9-11 **83**........................ PaulFessey 10 80
(T D Barron) *towards rr: hdwy on outer over 1f out: sn rdn and kpt on ins fnl f: nrst fin* **10/1**
6006 **7** *nse* **Wyatt Earp (IRE)**[10] [3477] 7-9-5 **77**........................(b) PaulHanagan 4 74
(R A Fahey) *chsd ldrs: rdn along wl over 1f out: kpt on same pce* **10/1**
4230 **8** *shd* **Glasshoughton**[13] [3370] 5-9-10 **82**........................ TonyHamilton 9 78
(M Dods) *hld up in rr: swtchd ins and rdn over 1f out: kpt on ins fnl f: nrst fin* **14/1**
0-04 **9** *nk* **Guertino (IRE)**[18] [3228] 3-9-10 **88**........................ TomEaves 1 83+
(B Smart) *prom: rdn along 2f out: drvn and wkng whn n.m.r ent fnl f* **8/1**
-000 **10** *1 ¼* **Steenberg (IRE)**[10] [3491] 9-9-11 **83**........................ JimmyQuinn 2 75
(M H Tompkins) *in tch: rdn along 2f out: sn wknd* **22/1**
2602 **11** *4 ½* **High Curragh**[10] [3477] 5-9-13 **85**........................ NCallan 14 63+
(K A Ryan) *prom: rdn along 2f out: sn wknd and eased ins fnl f* **6/1**[2]
6-30 **12** *9* **Pickering**[3] [3724] 4-8-12 **70**........................ ShaneKelly 12 21
(E J Alston) *chsd ldrs: rdn along wl over 1f out: sn edgd lft and wknd* **14/1**
462- **13** *9* **Mansii**[279] [5910] 3-9-3 **81**........................ RyanMoore 5 5
(C E Brittain) *chsd ldrs: rdn 2f out and sn wknd* **20/1**
-03L **R** **Gunfighter (IRE)**[27] [2938] 5-9-10 **85**........................(p) PJMcDonald(3) 13 —
(R Johnson) *ref to r* **10/1**

1m 18.41s (1.51) **Going Correction** +0.40s/f (Good)
WFA 3 from 4yo+ 6lb **14** Ran SP% **123.0**
Speed ratings (Par 107): **105,104,101,101,100 99,98,98,98,96 90,78,66,—**
toteswinger: 1&2 £62.10, 1&3 £12.90, 2&3 £18.90. CSF £339.55 CT £1525.41 TOTE £20.90: £5.70, £6.80, £1.70; EX 494.70.

Owner Stan Wright Shaun Taylor **Bred** P And Mrs A G Venner **Trained** Eastwell, Leics
■ Stewards' Enquiry : Mark Coumbe three-day ban: careless riding (Jul 22,23+1)

FOCUS
A fair sprint handicap run at a good pace. The winner is rated back towards his best, as is the second.

NOTEBOOK
Dickie Le Davoir never got competitive at Leicester last time, but he was not too badly away here, and the decent pace suited him. He got a good run through on the inside turning into the straight and came through to lead inside the last, always holding off Grazeon Gold Blend close home. A stiff finish seems to suit him.
Grazeon Gold Blend threatened to throw down a strong challenge to Dickie Le Davoir inside the last but in actual fact he was always being held. He has dropped to a very good mark, though, and this was a welcome return to form. (op 20-1)
John Keats again ran well despite being poorly drawn and having to challenge wide. He would not want the ground any softer than this.
Paris Bell has not been in much form this season but this was much more encouraging, and he is certainly on a fair enough mark at present, so he will be of interest when the ground is on the soft side.
Mr Wolf showed good early speed as usual but did not get home, and his losing run now stretches back 24 starts. (op 6-1)
Ingleby Arch(USA), another handicapped by a double-figure draw, was staying on at the finish but could never land a blow.
Wyatt Earp(IRE) Official explanation: jockey said gelding was denied a clear run
High Curragh Official explanation: jockey said gelding hung left

3813 BOOK ONLINE AT PONTEFRACT-RACES.CO.UK MAIDEN STKS — 1m 4f 8y
4:30 (4:33) (Class 5) 3-Y-O+ **£3,885** (£1,156; £577; £288) **Stalls** Low

Form RPR
3 **1** **Boucheron**[16] [3297] 3-8-8 0........................ PaulHanagan 5 83+
(R A Fahey) *mde all: rdn clr 2f out: styd on strly* **14/1**[3]
42 **2** *10* **Motarid (USA)**[16] [3297] 3-8-13 0........................ TonyHamilton 8 72
(T D Walford) *hld up towards rr: hdwy 3f out: rdn 2f out: styd on appr fnl f: no ch w wnr* **6/1**[2]
2-22 **3** *2 ½* **Heritage Coast (USA)**[25] [3004] 3-8-8 80........................ RyanMoore 9 63
(Sir Michael Stoute) *trckd ldrs: effrt 3f out: chsd wnr over 2f out: sn rdn and one pce* **4/9**[1]
0 **4** *1 ¾* **Lough Diver (IRE)**[36] [2669] 3-8-13 0........................ JimmyQuinn 7 65
(M H Tompkins) *hld up towards rr: hdwy 3f out: rdn along 2f out: kpt on fnl f: nrst fin* **16/1**
56-5 **5** *¾* **Manalito**[15] [3310] 3-8-13 75........................ DarryllHolland 2 64
(M R Channon) *prom: rdn along 3f out: drvn and wknd 2f out* **20/1**
6 *2 ¾* **Major Promise** 3-8-13 0........................ RobertWinston 1 59
(G G Margarson) *chsd ldrs: rdn along over 3f out: drvn and wknd 2f out* **66/1**
6 **7** *2* **Yes Sir (IRE)**[15] [3310] 9-9-12 0........................ VinceSlattery 11 56
(P Bowen) *s.i.s: a in rr* **66/1**
8 *8* **Bella Medici** 3-8-1 0........................ AshleyMorgan(7) 4 38
(M H Tompkins) *s.i.s: a in rr* **100/1**
0 **9** *10* **Tuxedo**[22] [3094] 3-8-13 0........................ DarrenWilliams 12 27
(P W Hiatt) *a in rr* **100/1**
062 **10** *4 ½* **Nisaal (IRE)**[15] [3310] 3-8-13 78........................ RHills 6 20
(J L Dunlop) *chsd wnr: rdn along 3f out: wknd over 2f out* **6/1**[2]
06 **11** *18* **Willaby Lad**[14] [3338] 3-8-13 0........................ PatrickMathers 10 —
(D Shaw) *a in rr* **100/1**

0- 12 17 **Kaichou (IRE)**[369] 3244 4-9-7 0 NCallan 3 —
(B J Meehan) *in tch: rdn along over 4f out and sn wknd* **66/1**

2m 43.34s (2.54) **Going Correction** +0.40s/f (Good)
WFA 3 from 4yo+ 13lb 12 Ran SP% **122.6**
Speed ratings (Par 103): **107,100,98,97,97 95,93,88,81,78 66,55**
toteswinger: 1&2 £4.20, 1&3 £2.90, 2&3 £2.10. CSF £96.84 TOTE £13.80: £2.90, £1.60, £1.10; EX 74.40.
Owner Dr Anne J F Gillespie **Bred** Falcon Assets Ltd **Trained** Musley Bank, N Yorks

FOCUS
Not a bad maiden and certainly an impressive performance from the improved winner, despite having the run of things up front.

3814 PONTEFRACT APPRENTICE SERIES (ROUND 3) H'CAP 1m 2f 6y
5:00 (5:02) (Class 5) (0-70,70) 4-Y-0+ **£3,238** (£963; £481; £240) **Stalls** Low

Form				RPR
0013	1		**Holiday Cocktail**[8] 3551 6-8-12 **61** (p) JamieKyne(3) 13	73+
			(J J Quinn) *in tch: hdwy on inner 2f out: swtchd rt and rdn ins fnl f: styd on to ld last 50yds: rdr dropped whip nr fin* **7/2**[1]	
1113	2	¾	**Annibale Caro**[39] 2579 6-9-10 **70** ClGillies 7	79
			(Grant Tuer) *trckd ldrs: hdwy 2f out: rdn and squeezsed through to ld jst ins fnl f: sn drvn: hdd and no ex last 50yds* **13/2**	
2354	3	2½	**Dan Tucker**[11] 3450 4-9-5 **65** AdeleRothery 1	69+
			(N Tinkler) *in tch: hdwy over 2f out: rdn wl over 1f out: kpt on ins fnl f* **9/2**[2]	
3105	4	hd	**Dechiper (IRE)**[11] 3450 6-9-0 **65** GarryWhillans(5) 6	69
			(R Johnson) *trckd ldrs: effrt and cl up 2f out: rdn to ld briefly over 1f out: hdd jst ins fnl f: one pce* **17/2**	
-005	5	1¼	**Rotuma (IRE)**[18] 3230 9-8-3 **54** oh6 ow3 (b) JohnCavanagh(5) 4	55
			(M Dods) *chsd ldng pair: hdwy on inner to ld 2f out: sn rdn and hdd over 1f out: kpt on same pce ins fnl f* **25/1**	
5-00	6	8	**Thornaby Green**[11] 3450 7-8-10 **56** DeanHeslop 3	41
			(T D Barron) *led: rdn along 3f out: hdd 2f out and sn wknd* **25/1**	
0-50	7	nk	**Betteras Bertie**[35] 2697 5-8-8 **54** BillyCray 8	38
			(M Brittain) *hld up: hdwy 3f out: rdn along over 2f out and sn no imp* **25/1**	
/306	8	2	**Three Strings (USA)**[27] 2927 5-8-9 **58** (p) FrederikTylicki(3) 9	38
			(P D Niven) *chsd ldr: rdn along 3f out: wknd 2f out* **5/1**[3]	
0300	9	7	**Alberts Story (USA)**[18] 3226 4-8-7 **53** (p) BMcHugh 14	19
			(R A Fahey) *a towards rr* **14/1**	
0010	10	½	**Moment Of Clarity**[11] 3450 6-9-4 **64** (p) StacyRenwick 12	29
			(R C Guest) *a towards rr* **20/1**	
00-4	11	¾	**Garibaldi (GER)**[18] 3226 6-8-5 **51** oh2 SimonPearce 5	15
			(N Wilson) *in tch: rdn along 3f out: sn wknd* **8/1**	
6-54	12	39	**Samahir (USA)**[18] 3218 4-8-5 **51** AshleyMorgan 11	—
			(T T Clement) *rrd s and v.s.a: a bhd* **9/1**	

2m 17.46s (3.76) **Going Correction** +0.40s/f (Good) 12 Ran SP% **125.0**
Speed ratings (Par 103): **100,99,97,97,96 89,89,88,82,82 81,50**
toteswinger: 1&2 £5.00, 1&3 £4.40, 2&3 £5.50. CSF £26.48 CT £104.83 TOTE £5.20: £2.00, £2.20, £1.90; EX 33.70 Place 6: £77.55 Place 5: £7.89 .
Owner Estio Racing **Bred** Mrs W H Gibson Fleming **Trained** Settrington, N Yorks
■ Stewards' Enquiry : Jamie Kyne one-day ban: careless riding (Jul 22)

FOCUS
Modest handicap form but sound enough for the grade, the winner close to his best.
Alberts Story(USA) Official explanation: jockey said gelding had no more to give
Samahir(USA) Official explanation: jockey said filly missed the break
T/Jkpt: Not won. T/Plt: £155.50 to a £1 stake. Pool: £115,831.72. 543.53 winning tickets. T/Qpdt: £4.30 to a £1 stake. Pool: £6,657.71. 1,132.60 winning tickets. JR

3686 SOUTHWELL (L-H)
Tuesday, July 8

OFFICIAL GOING: Standard
After rain the surface was back to normal, 'Standard' officially and confirmed by the riders.
Wind: fresh 1/2 behind Weather: overcast

3815 SOUTHWELL RACECOURSE BEST BET FOR CONFERENCES (S) STKS 5f (F)
6:40 (6:43) (Class 6) 2-Y-O **£1,978** (£584; £292) **Stalls** High

Form				RPR
05	1		**Silent Treatment (IRE)**[24] 3019 2-8-8 0 ow2 (t) SebSanders 1	54
			(R M Beckett) *mde all: hld on towards fin* **3/1**[2]	
0	2	½	**Iorek Byrnison**[13] 3365 2-8-11 0 SilvestreDeSousa 8	55
			(D Nicholls) *chsd ldrs: rdn over 2f out: styd on ins fnl f: jst hld* **12/1**	
	3	¾	**Forever's Girl** 2-8-6 0 RoystonFfrench 9	48
			(G R Oldroyd) *sn chsng ldrs: kpt on wl ins fnl f* **16/1**	
5306	4	½	**Dispol Mulofky (IRE)**[30] 2865 2-8-6 0 (p) PaulFessey 2	46
			(P T Midgley) *wnt rt s: sn chsng ldrs: hung lft and kpt on same pce fnl f* **11/4**[1]	
620	5	3¾	**Inn Swinger (IRE)**[15] 3309 2-8-3 0 LukeMorris(3) 4	32
			(W G M Turner) *chsd ldrs: outpcd appr fnl f* **11/1**	
005	6	1½	**Tyler**[22] 3091 2-8-11 0 TGMcLaughlin 3	32
			(W M Brisbourne) *hmpd s: hdwy to chse ldrs over 2f out: hung lft: wknd appr fnl f* **22/1**	
00	7	nk	**Hunch**[21] 3106 2-8-11 0 PatrickMathers 5	31
			(Garry Moss) *chsd ldrs: wknd appr fnl f* **40/1**	
3326	8	hd	**Makaluna**[22] 3091 2-8-6 0 JackDean(5) 6	30
			(W G M Turner) *w ldrs: wknd appr fnl f* **5/1**[3]	
0	9	9	**Maj William Martin**[40] 2548 2-8-11 0 PatCosgrave 10	—
			(M Quinn) *sn outpcd and in rr: bhd fnl 2f* **50/1**	
	10	shd	**Don't Go On (IRE)** 2-8-6 0 CatherineGannon 7	—
			(P D Evans) *dwlt: sn outpcd and in rr: bhd fnl 2f* **12/1**	
30	P		**Comghaire (IRE)**[28] 2910 2-8-6 0 JamesDoyle 11	—
			(P D Evans) *lame: p.u and dismntd after 1f* **7/1**	

60.76 secs (1.06) **Going Correction** +0.025s/f (Slow) 11 Ran SP% **119.2**
Speed ratings (Par 92): **92,91,90,89,83 80,80,80,65,65** —
toteswinger: 1&2 £24.80, 1&3 n/a, 2&3 £28.50. CSF £38.99 TOTE £3.90: £1.30, £6.20, £4.80; EX 63.20.The winner was sold to Gay Kelleway for 7,500gns.
Owner Mrs Ralph Beckett **Bred** Gerard And Yvonne Kennedy **Trained** Whitsbury, Hants

FOCUS
A poor race even by selling race standards. The exposed fourth sets the standard.

NOTEBOOK
Silent Treatment(IRE), an excitable type, made every yard, and under maximum assistance did just enough. Gay Kelleway took a fancy to her at the auction. (op 4-1)
Iorek Byrnison, a hollow-backed individual, stepped up on his turf debut and in the end made the winner pull out all the stops. (op 10-1 tchd 14-1)
Forever's Girl, fitted with a blanket for stalls entry, stuck on in willing fashion late in the day and should improve and find a similar event. (op 20-1 tchd 14-1)
Dispol Mulofky(IRE), fitted with cheekpieces on her first try in selling company, went sideways leaving the stalls and did not come home in a straight line. This was her sixth start and she is looking fully exposed. (op 7-2 after 4-1 in a place tchd 5-2)
Inn Swinger(IRE) was left behind in the closing stages and will be better suited by 6f. (op 12-1 tchd 10-1)
Tyler behaved himself better beforehand this time, but after taking a bump at the start he wanted to do nothing but go left-handed. (op 16-1)
Don't Go On(IRE) Official explanation: jockey said filly missed the break
Comghaire(IRE) injured her pelvis and was soon pulled up hopping lame. (op 7-2)

3816 BOOK YOUR TICKETS ONLINE MAIDEN FILLIES' H'CAP 1m (F)
7:10 (7:10) (Class 6) (0-65,64) 3-Y-0+ **£1,978** (£584; £292) **Stalls** Low

Form				RPR
-000	1		**Kimono My House**[8] 3569 4-8-13 **49** PatCosgrave 6	59
			(J G Given) *mid-div: hdwy over 3f out: sn chsaing ldrs: edgd lft and kpt on ins fnl f to ld nr fin* **22/1**	
-030	2	½	**Towy Girl (IRE)**[10] 3507 4-9-2 **57** MarkCoumbe(5) 1	66
			(A W Carroll) *hld up in rr: hdwy over 3f out: led 2f out: hdd and no ex nr fin* **8/1**[2]	
6225	3	3	**Juzilla (IRE)**[83] 1406 4-9-7 **64** DavidProbert(7) 7	66
			(W R Swinburn) *chsd ldrs: styd on same pce fnl f* **15/8**[1]	
-466	4	½	**Aquarian Dancer**[35] 2704 3-8-4 **49** AndrewElliott 8	48
			(Jedd O'Keeffe) *led tl 2f out: one pce* **8/1**[2]	
060	5	2½	**Poulaine Bleue**[43] 2455 3-8-2 **47** HayleyTurner 14	41
			(M L W Bell) *swtchd lft and lost pl after 1f: hdwy over 2f out: sn chsng ldrs: one pce* **9/1**[3]	
0005	6	1½	**Piverina (IRE)**[22] 3081 3-8-2 **50** AndrewMullen(3) 12	40
			(Miss J A Camacho) *rrd s: sn chsng ldrs on outside: hrd rdn over 3f out: wknd over 1f out* **10/1**	
5006	7	8	**Rasmani**[7] 3573 4-8-10 **46** (t) NCallan 4	21
			(Miss Gay Kelleway) *chsd ldrs: wknd over 1f out: eased ins fnl f* **16/1**	
-200	8	7	**Palais Polaire**[157] 402 6-8-11 **50** (p) TravisBlock(3) 3	9
			(J A Geake) *in rr: bhd fnl 3f* **8/1**[2]	
-050	9	2	**Pentandra (IRE)**[26] 2982 3-8-11 **56** TPQueally 2	9
			(J G Given) *hld up in rr: bhd fnl 3f* **16/1**	
40-0	10	2¼	**Madam Carwell**[23] 3057 3-8-10 **55** JamesDoyle 9	3
			(J G Given) *chsd ldrs: lost pl 3f out* **33/1**	
00-3	11	5	**Personal Choice**[6] 3549 3-8-5 **50** TWilliams 5	—
			(M Brittain) *chsd ldrs: lost pl 4f out* **20/1**	
6030	12	1½	**Champagne Lawn (USA)**[18] 3217 3-9-0 **59** PaulFessey 11	—
			(T D Barron) *chsd ldrs on outer: lost pl over 3f out: sn bhd* **25/1**	
0-30	13	11	**Regal Curtsy**[19] 3181 4-9-5 **55** DaneO'Neill 10	—
			(P R Chamings) *chsd ldrs on outside: lost pl over 3f out: sn bhd* **11/1**	

1m 45.36s (1.66) **Going Correction** +0.175s/f (Slow)
WFA 3 from 4yo+ 9lb 13 Ran SP% **123.2**
Speed ratings (Par 98): **98,97,94,94,91 90,82,75,73,70 65,64,53**
toteswinger: 1&2 £40.30, 1&3 £60.40, 2&3 £2.40. CSF £187.15 CT £519.88 TOTE £30.40: £7.40, £3.30, £1.10; EX 434.60.
Owner Beadle Booth Bloodstock Limited **Bred** G And Mrs Middlebrook **Trained** Willoughton, Lincs

FOCUS
A low-grade maiden fillies' handicap.
Piverina(IRE) Official explanation: trainer said filly was slowly away
Regal Curtsy Official explanation: jockey said filly never travelled

3817 ARENALEISUREPLC.COM CLAIMING STKS 1m (F)
7:40 (7:40) (Class 5) 3-Y-O **£2,729** (£806; £403) **Stalls** Low

Form				RPR
	1		**Blue Savannah (FR)** 3-8-4 0 WilliamBuick 6	56+
			(D J S Ffrench Davis) *s.i.s: hdwy on wd outside over 3f out: styd on wl to ld jst ins fnl f* **16/1**	
1330	2	2¼	**One Called Alice**[12] 3406 3-8-8 54 HayleyTurner 5	55
			(A W Carroll) *chsd ldrs: wnt 2nd 2f out: kpt on same pce ins fnl f* **7/1**[3]	
2240	3	1¼	**Zeffirelli**[15] 3333 3-9-1 59 PatCosgrave 1	59
			(M Quinn) *led tl over 4f out: led 3f out: hdd & wknd jst ins fnl f* **8/1**	
4-00	4	3	**Red Cauldron**[12] 3421 3-8-9 65 DaneO'Neill 4	47
			(E J O'Neill) *in tch: sn drvn along: one pce fnl 2f* **11/4**[2]	
0026	5	8	**The Last Bottle (IRE)**[11] 3436 3-9-0 65 TGMcLaughlin 2	34
			(W M Brisbourne) *chsd ldrs: rdn 3f out: hung rt: lost pl over 1f out* **15/8**[1]	
2600	6	½	**Hawa Khana (IRE)**[12] 3407 3-8-8 58 (p) StephenDonohoe 7	27
			(N P Littmoden) *t.k.h: w ldrs: led over 4f out tl 3f out: wknd over 1f out* **14/1**	
520	7	3½	**Near The Front**[11] 3458 3-8-13 57 MickyFenton 8	24
			(Miss Gay Kelleway) *chsd ldrs: drvn 4f out: lost pl over 2f out: sn bhd* **17/2**	
3044	8	7	**Yakama (IRE)**[13] 3359 3-8-13 47 (p) DMylonas 3	9
			(G Prodromou) *in tch: lost pl over 3f out: sn bhd* **12/1**	

1m 44.5s (0.80) **Going Correction** +0.175s/f (Slow) 8 Ran SP% **115.8**
Speed ratings (Par 100): **103,100,99,96,88 88,84,77**
toteswinger: 1&2 £8.10, 1&3 £33.60, 2&3 £2.60. CSF £123.33 TOTE £17.40: £4.30, £1.90, £1.60; EX 177.80.Blue Savannah was claimed by G Smith for £6000.
Owner Houghton Bloodstock **Bred** Hascombe And Valiant Studs **Trained** Lambourn, Berks

FOCUS
An ordinary claimer but an unraced winner of some potential provided she goes the right way.

3818 DINE IN THE QUEEN MOTHER RESTAURANT MAIDEN STKS 6f (F)
8:10 (8:10) (Class 5) 3-4-Y-O **£2,729** (£806; £403) **Stalls** Low

Form				RPR
-662	1		**To Bubbles**[56] 2084 3-8-7 63 NeilBrown(5) 1	67
			(T D Barron) *sn w ldrs on ins: styd on to ld last 100yds* **4/6**[1]	
5-2	2	1¼	**Frisbee**[142] 598 4-9-4 0 RobertWinston 4	64+
			(C J Teague) *w ldrs: led 3f out: hdd ins fnl f: no ex* **5/1**[2]	
	3	6	**Crataegus** 3-9-3 0 DaneO'Neill 7	49+
			(H Candy) *sn drvn along: outpcd over 3f out: styd on appr fnl f: tk modest 3rd nr line* **8/1**	
60	4	nse	**Sosostris Pitch (FR)**[36] 2673 3-9-3 0 (bt[1]) SebSanders 5	49
			(P C Haslam) *w ldrs on outer: drvn over 3f out: one pce fnl 2f* **10/1**	
	5	4	**Ellalucianna** 3-8-9 0 MichaelJStainton(3) 3	31
			(M Wigham) *s.i.s: outpcd and detached tl kpt on fnl 2f* **33/1**	
0-33	6	4½	**Carmine Rock**[4] 3686 3-8-9 52 RussellKennemore(3) 2	17
			(R Hollinshead) *mde most tl 3f out: wknd 2f out* **7/1**[3]	

The Form Book, Raceform Ltd, Compton, RG20 6NL

0- 7 22 **Lady Amy**[316] 4882 3-8-12 0 .... TPQueally 6 —
(Miss Amy Weaver) *outpcd and lost pl 4f out: sn bhd: t.o* **40/1**

1m 17.4s (0.90) **Going Correction** +0.175s/f (Slow)
WFA 3 from 4yo 6lb 7 Ran SP% **114.7**
Speed ratings (Par 103): **101,99,91,91,85 79,50**
toteswinger: 1&2 £2.40, 1&3 £2.70, 2&3 £15.40. CSF £4.49 TOTE £1.70: £1.10, £2.40; EX 4.40.
Owner Mrs J Hazell **Bred** Rainsbrook Bloodstock **Trained** Maunby, N Yorks

FOCUS
A weak sprint maiden won by a 63-rated animal. She probably did not have to run to that mark to achieve a tidy victory in the end.
Carmine Rock Official explanation: jockey said race came too soon

3819 SOUTHWELL-RACECOURSE.CO.UK H'CAP 6f (F)
8:40 (8:41) (Class 5) (0-70,71) 3-Y-0+ £2,729 (£806; £403) Stalls Low

Form RPR

5-01 1 **Elusive Hawk (IRE)**[154] 441 4-9-8 65 .... TPQueally 3 80+
(A P Stringer) *trckd ldrs: led 2f out: pushed out: readily* **7/2[2]**

4113 2 2 1/2 **Punching**[10] 3477 4-9-11 68 .... NCallan 10 73
(Miss Gay Kelleway) *trckd ldrs: wnt 2nd appr fnl f: edgd lft: no imp* **13/2[3]**

4212 3 5 **Elusive Warrior (USA)**[4] 3691 5-9-9 66 .... (p) JamesDoyle 1 56
(A J McCabe) *chsd ldrs: kpt on same pce fnl 2f* **11/4[1]**

4350 4 1 **Gleaming Spirit (IRE)**[14] 3352 4-9-5 62 .... DarrenWilliams 6 49
(A P Jarvis) *led tl 2f out: one pce whn sltly hmpd 1f out* **22/1**

3423 5 3 1/2 **Wiseman's Diamond (USA)**[22] 3081 3-9-3 66 .... MickyFenton 2 41
(P T Midgley) *dwlt: sn chsng ldrs: fdd over 1f out* **25/1**

3251 6 1 1/2 **Owed**[30] 2869 6-9-6 63 .... (tp) RobertWinston 4 35
(R Bastiman) *mid-div: rdn and outpcd over 3f out: hdwy on ins 2f out: sn wknd* **13/2[3]**

2160 7 shd **Straight (IRE)**[8] 3564 3-8-9 61 .... MarkLawson(3) 8 31
(M Brittain) *in rr: sn drvn along: sme hdwy over 2f out: nvr a factor* **50/1**

5060 8 hd **Tag Team (IRE)**[19] 3169 7-9-0 62 .... MarkCoumbe(5) 13 33
(John A Harris) *mid-div: effrt on wd outside over 2f out: nvr nr ldrs* **33/1**

0005 9 1 1/2 **Steel City Boy (IRE)**[13] 3374 5-9-8 70 .... AnnStokell(5) 9 36
(Miss A Stokell) *dwlt: sme hdwy over 3f out: sn btn* **20/1**

-361 10 1 **Bishopbriggs (USA)**[8] 3564 3-9-8 71 6ex .... LeeEnstone 11 33
(S Parr) *chsd ldrs: wknd over 2f out* **16/1**

004 11 1 1/4 **Triple Shadow**[4] 3668 4-8-6 52 .... DuranFentiman(3) 14 11
(M A Peill) *mid-div on outer: c v wd over 2f out: sn lost pl* **14/1**

0-05 12 3/4 **Tender Process (IRE)**[98] 1129 5-9-5 62 .... SebSanders 7 19
(E S McMahon) *mid-div: drvn 3f out: lost pl over 1f out: eased ins fnl f* **7/1**

0135 13 15 **Grand Palace (IRE)**[126] 786 5-9-9 66 .... (v) DeanMcKeown 12 —
(D Shaw) *t.k.h on outer: lost pl 4f out: bhd and eased fnl 2f* **22/1**

0400 14 20 **Solemn**[11] 3441 3-8-7 59 .... TolleyDean(3) 5 —
(J M Bradley) *bhd: detached and eased over 1f out: t.o* **66/1**

1m 16.18s (-0.32) **Going Correction** +0.175s/f (Slow)
WFA 3 from 4yo+ 6lb 14 Ran SP% **124.3**
Speed ratings (Par 103): **109,105,99,97,93 91,90,90,88,87 85,84,64,37**
toteswinger: 1&2 £11.80, 1&3 £2.10, 2&3 £2.30. CSF £25.25 CT £75.84 TOTE £5.20: £2.00, £3.40, £1.70; EX 43.60.
Owner Curley Leisure **Bred** J Fike **Trained** Newmarket, Suffolk

FOCUS
The unexposed winner and the progressive runner-up came clear in the end of a good yardstick.
Grand Palace(IRE) Official explanation: jockey said gelding suffered interference shortly after start

3820 PLAY GOLF AT SOUTHWELL GOLF CLUB H'CAP 1m 6f (F)
9:10 (9:10) (Class 6) (0-65,64) 4-Y-0+ £1,978 (£584; £292) Stalls Low

Form RPR

6-30 1 **Spanish Conquest**[35] 2707 4-9-0 57 .... SebSanders 9 65
(Sir Mark Prescott) *hld up towards rr: hdwy over 5f out: led over 1f out: hld on towards fin* **11/4[1]**

3054 2 3/4 **Victory Quest (IRE)**[118] 854 8-9-7 64 .... (v) RobertWinston 6 71+
(Mrs S Lamyman) *chsd ldrs: n.m.r on inner 3f out: swtchd rt over 1f out: edgd lft and styd on to take 2nd ins fnl f: no ex nr fin* **25/1**

5046 3 2 3/4 **Viscount Rossini**[19] 3182 6-8-4 47 .... HayleyTurner 2 50
(A W Carroll) *trckd ldrs gng wl: chal 2f out: kpt on same pce appr fnl f* **33/1**

1215 4 2 1/4 **Wizard Looking**[20] 3131 7-9-7 64 .... NCallan 14 64
(D E Cantillon) *hld up in midfield: hdwy over 4f out: led over 2f out tl over 1f out: one pce* **3/1[2]**

/00- 5 4 **Historic Place (USA)**[78] 6473 8-9-0 62 .... (p) HaddenFrost(5) 12 56
(J A Geake) *hld up in rr: hdwy on outer over 5f out: sn chsng ldrs: one pce fnl 2f* **25/1**

6343 6 3/4 **Amwell Brave**[42] 2290 7-8-7 50 .... JamesDoyle 1 43
(J R Jenkins) *hld up in rr: stdy hdwy over 4f out: chsng ldrs over 2f out: one pce* **6/1[3]**

264- 7 6 **Rule For Ever**[382] 2825 6-9-7 64 .... PatrickMathers 13 49
(I W McInnes) *rn in snatches: chsd ldrs: shkn up after 4f: n.m.r over 5f out: lost pl over 1f out* **20/1**

0013 8 12 **Tykie Two**[35] 2707 4-8-11 54 .... LiamJones 3 22
(S Wynne) *drvn to ld: hdd over 4f out: lost pl 2f out* **9/1**

6300 9 1 3/4 **Title Deed (USA)**[20] 3137 4-9-1 58 .... (v) DarrenWilliams 5 24
(A P Jarvis) *trckd ldrs: led over 4f out: hdd over 2f out: wknd over 1f out* **40/1**

0656 10 9 **Muntami (IRE)**[27] 2952 7-8-7 50 .... StephenDonohoe 7 3
(John A Harris) *in rr and sn pushed along: lost pl over 3f out: sn bhd* **6/1[3]**

510/ 11 1 1/4 **Jungle Lion**[1209] 639 10-8-2 45 .... (t) PaulFessey 10 —
(P A Kirby) *chsd ldrs: lost pl over 2f out* **50/1**

0/ 12 14 **My Trip (IRE)**[237] 1699 6-8-2 45 .... CatherineGannon 8 —
(Kieran P Cotter, Ire) *hld up in rr: hdwy 8f out: sn drvn along: lost pl over 4f out: bhd and eased 2f out* **33/1**

0560 13 16 **Senor Set (GER)**[3] 3710 7-7-13 45 .... (p) DuranFentiman(3) 11 —
(D Shaw) *in rr: sn pushed along: lost pl over 5f out: sn t.o* **14/1**

0040 14 18 **Kadouchski (FR)**[29] 2884 4-8-8 51 ow1 .... MickyFenton 4 —
(A B Coogan) *chsd ldrs: lost pl over 5f out: sn bhd: t.o 3f out* **16/1**

3m 11.76s (3.46) **Going Correction** +0.175s/f (Slow) 14 Ran SP% **125.5**
Speed ratings (Par 101): **97,96,95,93,91 91,87,80,79,74 73,65,56,46**
toteswinger: 1&2 £38.20, 1&3 £47.80, 2&3 n/a. CSF £82.72 CT £1958.30 TOTE £3.50: £2.20, £7.60, £4.10; EX 90.00 Place 6: £104.87 Place 5: £25.32.
Owner Neil Greig - Osborne House Ii **Bred** Miss K Rausing **Trained** Newmarket, Suffolk

FOCUS
A low-grade stayers' handicap rated around the first four.
Spanish Conquest Official explanation: trainer's rep said, regarding apparent improvement in form, that the ground was reported standard but after heavy rain became sloppy and the riding tactics were changed.
T/Plt: £278.10 to a £1 stake. Pool: £70,851.68. 185.95 winning tickets. T/Qpdt: £44.20 to a £1 stake. Pool: £5,475.49. 91.65 winning tickets. WG

3564 WOLVERHAMPTON (A.W) (L-H)
Tuesday, July 8

OFFICIAL GOING: Standard
Wind: Moderate half behind Weather: Fine

3821 HORIZONS RESTAURANT MAIDEN AUCTION STKS 7f 32y(P)
2:15 (2:18) (Class 5) 2-Y-0 £3,885 (£1,156; £577; £288) Stalls High

Form RPR

0 1 **City Diamond**[28] 2916 2-8-8 0 .... TravisBlock(3) 7 76
(P J Makin) *sn chsng ldr: led over 2f out: pushed clr wl over 1f out: rdn and r.o fnl f* **10/1**

2 1 1/4 **Learo Dochais (USA)** 2-8-12 0 .... EddieAhern 3 74+
(M J Wallace) *hld up in tch: rdn over 2f out: chsd wnr jst over 1f out: kpt on* **4/1[2]**

3 shd **Russian George (IRE)** 2-8-12 0 .... MickyFenton 6 76+
(T P Tate) *hld up in mid-div: c wd st: hdwy on outside over 1f out: kpt on ins fnl f* **9/4[1]**

04 4 6 **Extremely So**[12] 3408 2-8-7 0 .... SteveDrowne 1 54
(P J McBride) *a.p: rdn over 2f out: wknd ins fnl f* **11/1**

00 5 6 **Claphands**[11] 3437 2-8-8 0 .... (p) TPQueally 2 40
(A J McCabe) *led: hdd over 2f out: sn rdn wl over 1f out: wknd 1f out* **10/1**

55 6 3 **Old Father Zieten**[59] 1987 2-8-6 0 .... RossAtkinson(7) 9 37
(Tom Dascombe) *t.k.h in tch: rdn over 2f out: sn wknd* **5/1[3]**

0 7 1 1/4 **Strikemaster (IRE)**[53] 2150 2-8-13 0 .... AlanMunro 8 34
(J W Hills) *s.i.s: in rr: nvr nr ldrs* **33/1**

3 8 nk **Loched Up**[50] 2239 2-8-11 0 .... TPO'Shea 4 31
(P A Blockley) *a in rr* **40/1**

9 1 **Coral Point (IRE)** 2-8-9 0 .... LPKeniry 5 27
(S Kirk) *mid-div: outpcd after 2f: sn bhd* **20/1**

10 1 **Irish Joe (USA)** 2-8-9 0 .... PaulMulrennan 11 24
(T D Barron) *s.i.s: a in rr* **11/2**

0 11 2 1/2 **Dancing Delta**[8] 3558 2-8-4 0 .... MartinDwyer 10 13
(W R Muir) *hdwy over 5f out: rdn and wknd 3f out* **20/1**

12 18 **Julie Mill (IRE)** 2-8-4 0 .... RichardThomas 12 —
(P G Murphy) *dwlt: a in rr: t.o* **100/1**

1m 31.67s (2.07) **Going Correction** +0.25s/f (Slow) 12 Ran SP% **125.2**
Speed ratings (Par 94): **98,96,96,89,82 79,77,77,76,75 72,51**
toteswinger: 1&2 £10.00, 1&3 £5.40, 2&3 £3.30 CSF £50.25 TOTE £11.60: £2.80, £2.10, £1.20; EX 61.30 Trifecta £227.90 Part won. Pool: £307.99 - 0.40 winning units..
Owner D A Poole **Bred** Red House Stud **Trained** Ogbourne Maisey, Wilts

FOCUS
A modest maiden and they finished strung out.

NOTEBOOK
City Diamond ◆ confirmed the promise he showed when an eye-catcher over 6f on his debut at Salisbury, but he did not win as well as had looked likely at the top of the straight and gave the impression this extra furlong just stretched him. He was clear at the top of the straight and looked set to win convincingly, but his stride shortened as he got tired inside the final furlong and he very much gave the impression he will be better back over 6f for the time being. (op 11-1 tchd 8-1)
Learo Dochais(USA), a 16,000gns son of Mutakaddim, half-brother to Brush With Danger, a multiple winner at around 6f-1m1f in the US, and triple dirt sprint winners Brush The Law Agin and Yield With Caution, out of a smart prolific winner at 1m, made a pleasing debut in second. He was closing fast at the line and can build on this. (op 7-2 tchd 11-4)
Russian George(IRE), a 13,000gns son of Sendawar, brother to Mannsar, a 1m juvenile winner in France, was a well-backed favourite on his racecourse debut, but could only manage third. He has presumably been showing a bit at home, and he clearly has ability, so it would be no surprise to see improvement next time. (op 2-1 tchd 3-1)
Extremely So, upped in trip, fared best of the fillies. She is now qualified for a nursery mark and might do better back over shorter, but she probably needs her sights lowering a little.
Claphands did not prove her stamina on this step up in trip with cheekpieces on for the first time. (tchd 8-1)
Old Father Zieten proved rather disappointing on this step up in trip. (tchd 11-2)
Loched Up Official explanation: jockey said colt was hampered on 1st bend
Irish Joe(USA), a son of Graded winner Brahms, half-brother to two sprint winners on dirt in the US, out of a fairly useful multiple winner in the US, was backed in from big odds, but he was never competitive. (op 40-1)

3822 BOOK ONLINE AT WOLVERHAMPTON-RACECOURSE.CO.UK (S) STKS 1m 141y(P)
2:45 (2:45) (Class 6) 3-Y-0+ £1,978 (£584; £292) Stalls Low

Form RPR

0565 1 **Arctic Desert**[10] 3501 8-10-0 61 .... (t) HayleyTurner 2 67
(Miss Gay Kelleway) *dropped out s: hld up in rr: swtchd rt and carried rt ent st: hdwy over 1f out: rdn and r.o wl to ld towards fin* **9/1**

0002 2 nk **Casablanca Minx (IRE)**[5] 3648 5-9-9 53 .... (v) StephenDonohoe 4 61
(P D Evans) *hld up towards rr: hdwy over 2f out: rdn and chsd clr ldr over 1f out: r.o ins fnl f* **10/1**

0-02 3 1/2 **Le Chiffre (IRE)**[8] 3567 6-9-8 68 .... (p) PaulDoe 13 59+
(S Curran) *w ldr: led over 5f out: clr over 2f out: rdn wl over 1f out: ct towards fin* **2/1[1]**

0006 4 2 3/4 **Sir Bond (IRE)**[5] 3643 7-9-8 50 .... AlanMunro 3 53
(G R Oldroyd) *hld up in mid-div: hdwy 2f out: swtchd rt ent st: rdn over 1f out: one pce* **20/1**

0540 5 7 **Green Pirate**[7] 3588 6-10-0 54 .... (v) LPKeniry 8 42
(C R Dore) *stdd s: hld up in rr: pushed along over 2f out: rdn wl over 1f out: sme prog fnl f: nvr nr ldrs* **25/1**

0032 6 2 1/4 **Ugenius**[30] 2866 4-10-0 50 .... DMylonas 9 37
(G Prodromou) *t.k.h in tch: rdn over 2f out: wknd fnl f* **25/1**

4014 7 1 1/4 **Samuel Charles**[71] 1670 10-10-0 67 .... (b) LiamJones 1 34
(C R Dore) *hld up in mid-div: pushed along over 3f out: wknd 2f out* **13/2[3]**

4004 8 6 **Kingsholm**[3] 3732 6-9-8 65 .... PaulMulrennan 6 15
(I W McInnes) *prom: rdn over 2f out: wknd over 1f out* **13/2[3]**

4300 9 1 3/4 **Putra Laju (IRE)**[41] 2513 4-9-8 64 .... (v) EddieAhern 10 11
(J W Hills) *s.i.s: hld up in rr: sme hdwy over 3f out: rdn over 2f out: wknd wl over 1f out* **6/1[2]**

-000 10 1 **Jerry Hamilton (USA)**[7] 3591 3-8-12 74 .... GregFairley 5 8
(M Johnston) *led: hdd over 5f out: chsd ldr tl rdn over 2f out: wknd wl over 1f out* **14/1**

6525 11 18 **Swift Cut (IRE)**[15] 3329 4-9-8 55 .... (p) MickyFenton 11 —
(D Burchell) *prom tl wknd 3f out: eased whn no ch over 1f out* **25/1**

-000 **12** *3½* **Into Action**[7] 3589 4-9-8 53....................(tp) SteveDrowne 12 —
(Mrs Marjorie Fife) *mid-div: lost pl 5f out: rdn and lost tch 3f out* **66/1**

1m 52.4s (1.90) **Going Correction** +0.25s/f (Slow)
WFA 3 from 4yo+ 10lb **12 Ran SP% 117.8**
Speed ratings (Par 101): **101,100,100,97,91 89,88,83,81,80 64,61**
toteswinger: 1&2 £8.50, 1&3 £4.80, 2&3 £4.80. CSF £88.20 TOTE £8.30: £3.20, £3.20, £1.40; EX 122.60 Trifecta £111.30 Part won. Pool: £150.54 - 0.40 winning units..The winner was bought in for £6,500. Le Chiffre was claimed by S Taylor for £6000.
Owner Miss Gay Kelleway **Bred** Whatton Manor Stud **Trained** Exning, Suffolk

FOCUS
A standard seller run at a decent pace. The winning time was 0.84 seconds quicker than the following maiden.
Kingsholm Official explanation: jockey said gelding stopped quickly

3823 WOLVERHAMPTON-RACECOURSE.CO.UK MEDIAN AUCTION MAIDEN STKS 1m 141y(P)
3:15 (3:16) (Class 6) 3-4-Y-0 **£2,729** (£806; £403) **Stalls Low**

Form RPR
3 **1** **St Trinians**[15] 3318 3-8-12 0.................... LPKeniry 5 74+
(E F Vaughan) *hld up in mid-div: smooth hdwy 3f out: shkn up to ld jst over 1f out: clr ins fnl f: comf* **11/10[1]**
6 **2** *4* **Quail Landing**[31] 2834 3-8-12 0.................... MartinDwyer 6 65
(M P Tregoning) *a.p: led over 2f out: rdn and hdd jst over 1f out: btn whn edgd rt ins fnl f* **11/4[2]**
0 **3** *5* **Veni Bidi Vici**[115] 897 3-8-12 0.................... WilliamBuick 13 54
(A M Balding) *sn prom: rdn 2f out: edgd rt and wknd over 1f out* **12/1**
4 *5* **Manchestermaverick (USA)** 3-9-3 0.................... SteveDrowne 1 47
(H Morrison) *led: hdd over 6f out: chsd ldr tl over 3f out: rdn and edgd lft over 1f out: sn wknd* **4/1[3]**
5 *¾* **Painted Smile (IRE)** 4-9-8 0.................... MickyFenton 9 41
(Dr J D Scargill) *wnt rt s: hld up in mid-div: hdwy over 3f out: rdn and wknd over 2f out* **40/1**
00 **6** *2* **Age Of Miracles (IRE)**[9] 3521 3-9-3 0.................... StephenDonohoe 3 41
(G A Ham) *prom tl wknd over 3f out* **50/1**
7 *1* **Willridge** 3-8-10 0.................... RossAtkinson(7) 4 38
(Tom Dascombe) *hld up towards rr: pushed along over 2f out: no rspnse* **20/1**
8 *4* **Jayarbee (IRE)** 3-8-12 0.................... HayleyTurner 10 24
(P J McBride) *s.i.s and sltly hmpd s: bhd: rdn 3f out: sn struggling* **28/1**
0 **9** *hd* **Tycoon's Buddy**[68] 1751 3-9-3 0.................... DeanMcKeown 8 29
(E J O'Neill) *w ldr: led over 6f out tl over 2f out: wknd over 1f out* **66/1**
64 **10** *19* **Zantic**[14] 3342 3-9-3 0.................... AlanMunro 12 —
(P R Chamings) *a towards rr: t.o fnl 2f* **20/1**
11 *1¼* **Golondrina** 3-8-12 0.................... PaulMulrennan 2 —
(T J Fitzgerald) *s.i.s: a bhd: rdn 3f out: eased whn t.o 2f out* **66/1**
12 *15* **Karibu Blue** 4-9-8 0.................... GeorgeBaker 11 —
(C F Wall) *s.i.s and bmpd s: t.o fnl 3f* **20/1**

1m 53.24s (2.74) **Going Correction** +0.25s/f (Slow)
WFA 3 from 4yo 10lb **12 Ran SP% 127.1**
Speed ratings (Par 101): **97,93,89,84,83 82,81,77,77,60 59,46**
toteswinger: 1&2 £1.20, 1&3 £10.90, 2&3 £15.80. CSF £4.09 TOTE £2.50: £1.20, £1.10, £2.80; EX 5.10 Trifecta £64.50 Pool: £269.50 - 3.09 winning units..
Owner Hungerford Park Stud **Bred** Mrs E L Hunter **Trained** Newmarket, Suffolk

FOCUS
A very uncompetitive maiden and they finished strung out. The winning time was 0.84 seconds slower than the seller.

3824 STAY AT THE WOLVERHAMPTON HOLIDAY INN H'CAP 1m 4f 50y(P)
3:45 (3:45) (Class 5) (0-75,75) 3-Y-0+ **£2,729** (£806; £403) **Stalls Low**

Form RPR
4130 **1** **Novestar (IRE)**[8] 3566 3-8-3 66 ow5.................... KevinGhunowa(3) 9 73
(G J Smith) *mde all: stdd pce after 3f: qcknd 4f out: rdn 3f out: drvn out* **8/1**
1505 **2** *2¾* **Davenport (IRE)**[15] 3311 6-9-7 71....................(p) JamesMillman(3) 4 74
(B R Millman) *hld up in rr: hdwy over 3f out: rdn and chsd wnr over 2f out: no imp fnl f* **13/2**
-004 **3** *nk* **Fair Gale**[13] 3384 3-8-12 72.................... SteveDrowne 2 74
(S Kirk) *chsd wnr 3f: prom: rdn over 2f out: styd on ins fnl f* **7/4[1]**
0024 **4** *nk* **Kryptonite (IRE)**[14] 3335 3-8-6 66 ow2.................... EddieAhern 3 68
(J W Hills) *hld up: hdwy whn rdn and hung lft bnd over 2f out: styd on u.p ins fnl f* **5/1[3]**
04- **5** *6* **Manathon (FR)**[192] 7173 5-9-3 64.................... LPKeniry 1 56
(A E Jones) *hld up: hdwy on ins over 2f out: rdn over 1f out: wknd fnl f* **20/1**
6 *8* **Monfils Monfils (USA)**[52] 6-10-0 75.................... JamesDoyle 6 55
(A J McCabe) *prom: chsd wnr after 3f tl over 3f out: sn wknd* **10/1**
0010 **7** *10* **Inch Lodge**[22] 3089 6-9-10 71....................(t) PaulEddery 7 35
(Miss D Mountain) *hld up in tch: wknd 3f out: fin lame* **7/2[2]**

2m 42.52s (1.42) **Going Correction** +0.25s/f (Slow)
WFA 3 from 5yo+ 13lb **7 Ran SP% 113.5**
Speed ratings (Par 103): **105,103,102,102,98 93,86**
toteswinger: 1&2 £10.40, 1&3 £3.80, 2&3 £2.90. CSF £56.84 CT £131.37 TOTE £9.20: £2.40, £4.20; EX 46.60 Trifecta £138.50 Pool: £411.76 - 2.20 winning units..
Owner Graham Smith **Bred** Mrs Eithne Thompson **Trained** Six Hills, Leics

FOCUS
A modest handicap for the grade.
Inch Lodge Official explanation: vet said horse finished lame

3825 RINGSIDE SUITE 700 THEATRE STYLE CONFERENCE H'CAP 5f 216y(P)
4:15 (4:16) (Class 6) (0-60,60) 3-Y-0+ **£2,388** (£705; £352) **Stalls Low**

Form RPR
0660 **1** **Diminuto**[13] 3363 4-9-4 59.................... PatrickHills(3) 7 69
(M D I Usher) *a.p: rdn wl over 1f out: led wl ins fnl f: r.o* **28/1**
3343 **2** *½* **Splash The Cash**[8] 3564 3-8-9 58....................(p) NeilBrown(5) 3 65
(K A Ryan) *chsd ldr: ev ch over 2f out: rdn wl over 1f out: sn edgd rt: r.o ins fnl f* **11/2[3]**
0052 **3** *½* **All You Need (IRE)**[15] 3329 4-9-8 60....................(p) HayleyTurner 10 67
(R Hollinshead) *hld up in mid-div: rdn and hdwy wl over 1f out: sn swtchd lft: kpt on ins fnl f* **9/4[1]**
5150 **4** *hd* **Just Jimmy (IRE)**[24] 3030 3-9-0 58.................... StephenDonohoe 2 63+
(P D Evans) *s.i.s: in rr: rdn and hdwy over 1f out: fin wl* **16/1**
-060 **5** *hd* **Morse (IRE)**[32] 2798 7-9-8 60....................(p) TPQueally 13 65
(J A Osborne) *a.p: rdn 3f out: kpt on towards fin* **22/1**
4303 **6** *¾* **Bond Becks (IRE)**[8] 3546 8-9-3 55.................... AlanMunro 5 58
(G R Oldroyd) *led: rdn over 1f out: hdd and no ex wl ins fnl f* **8/1**

0102 **7** *¾* **Avontuur (FR)**[3] 3713 6-9-8 60....................(b) DaleGibson 4 61
(Mrs R A Carr) *s.i.s: hld up in rr: hdwy fnl f: nrst fin* **4/1[2]**
3000 **8** *1* **Bens Georgie (IRE)**[15] 3329 6-9-0 52.................... AdrianMcCarthy 12 49
(D K Ivory) *hld up: hdwy over 3f out: rdn over 2f out: no further prog* **14/1**
13-4 **9** *1* **Lujano**[36] 2660 3-9-2 60.................... PaulMulrennan 8 53+
(Ollie Pears) *hld up towards rr: rdn over 2f out: c wd st: edgd lft wl over 1f out: nvr nr ldrs* **8/1**
0000 **10** *2* **Trees Of Green (USA)**[10] 3506 4-9-5 57.................... OscarUrbina 6 45
(M Wigham) *a towards rr* **22/1**
00-0 **11** *3* **Ducal Pip Squeak**[10] 3481 4-9-3 55.................... EddieAhern 1 33
(A B Haynes) *mid-div: rdn over 3f out: wknd wl over 1f out: eased ins fnl f* **20/1**
4103 **12** *2¼* **Perlachy**[19] 3159 4-9-1 56....................(v) TravisBlock(3) 11 27
(Mrs N Macauley) *prom: hrd rdn over 2f out: wknd wl over 1f out* **20/1**

1m 16.51s (1.51) **Going Correction** +0.25s/f (Slow)
WFA 3 from 4yo+ 6lb **12 Ran SP% 122.6**
Speed ratings (Par 101): **99,98,97,97,97 96,95,93,92,89 85,82**
toteswinger: 1&2 £36.20, 1&3 £18.20, 2&3 £3.70. CSF £170.10 CT £508.70 TOTE £34.70: £10.80, £2.20, £1.20; EX 339.20 TRIFECTA Not won..
Owner R H Brookes **Bred** B Minty **Trained** Upper Lambourn, Berks

FOCUS
A competitive sprint handicap for the level.
Lujano Official explanation: jockey said gelding hung right

3826 SPONSOR A RACE BY CALLING 01902 390009 H'CAP 7f 32y(P)
4:45 (4:46) (Class 6) (0-65,64) 3-Y-0+ **£2,388** (£705; £352) **Stalls High**

Form RPR
21 **1** **Willie Ever**[8] 3569 4-9-4 57 6ex.................... J-PGuillambert 8 71+
(B Ellison) *hld up: hdwy after 2f: led over 1f out: r.o wl* **5/6[1]**
6630 **2** *2½* **A Big Sky Brewing (USA)**[18] 3211 4-9-2 60....................(b) NeilBrown(5) 6 67
(T D Barron) *a.p: sltly outpcd wl over 1f out: sn rdn: r.o to take 2nd post: nt trble wnr* **15/2[3]**
4214 **3** *shd* **Bentley**[8] 3569 4-9-9 62.................... TPQueally 7 69
(J G Given) *a.p: led over 2f out: hrd rdn and hdd over 1f out: nt qckn: lost 2nd post* **9/2[2]**
6003 **4** *¾* **Motu (IRE)**[8] 3567 7-9-2 62....................(v) LanceBetts(7) 2 67
(I W McInnes) *hld up: hdwy on ins wl over 1f out: sn rdn: kpt on same pce ins fnl f* **16/1**
2-42 **5** *2½* **The City Kid (IRE)**[33] 2758 5-9-6 62.................... JamieMoriarty(3) 10 60
(G D Blake) *hld up and bhd: hdwy on outside over 2f out: c wd st: sn rdn and hung lft: no imp* **8/1**
450- **6** *½* **Pride Of Northcare (IRE)**[273] 6088 4-9-6 59.................... DeanMcKeown 3 56
(D Shaw) *n.m.r s: hld up in rr: sme hdwy on ins over 1f out: n.d* **50/1**
544- **7** *nk* **Blitzen (IRE)**[252] 6572 3-8-10 64.................... RossAtkinson(7) 9 60
(Tom Dascombe) *s.i.s: in rr: rdn 4f out: nvr nr ldrs* **16/1**
2005 **8** *3* **Dasheena**[43] 2457 5-9-4 62....................(be) MCGeran(5) 5 50
(A J McCabe) *s.i.s: hld up towards rr: rdn 2f out: no rspnse* **25/1**
000- **9** *5* **Benny The Bus**[203] 6148 6-9-5 58.................... EddieAhern 1 32
(J R Weymes) *led: prom: rdn 3f out: wknd wl over 1f out* **20/1**
3005 **10** *½* **Northern Boy (USA)**[14] 3339 5-9-5 58.................... PaulMulrennan 4 31
(M W Easterby) *led after 1f: rdn and hdd over 2f out: wknd wl over 1f out* **10/1**

1m 31.06s (1.46) **Going Correction** +0.25s/f (Slow)
WFA 3 from 4yo+ 8lb **10 Ran SP% 127.0**
Speed ratings (Par 101): **101,98,98,97,94 93,93,89,84,83**
toteswinger: 1&2 £3.40, 1&3 £1.90, 2&3 £9.00. CSF £8.89 CT £23.37 TOTE £1.70: £1.10, £2.30, £2.30; EX 12.80 Trifecta £53.20 Pool: £649.80 - 9.03 winning units. Place 6: £48.09 Place 5: £29.74.
Owner Black and White Diamond Partnership **Bred** G Russell **Trained** Norton, N Yorks

FOCUS
A moderate handicap.
T/Plt: £169.10 to a £1 stake. Pool: £66,879.64. 288.56 winning tickets. T/Qpdt: £34.80 to a £1 stake. Pool: £4,260.70. 90.40 winning tickets. KH

3597 CATTERICK (L-H)
Wednesday, July 9

OFFICIAL GOING: Good (7.8)
Wind: Virtually nil Weather: Overcast, sunny periods, heavy shower before last race.

3830 GO RACING IN YORKSHIRE SUMMER FESTIVAL (S) STKS 5f
2:20 (2:22) (Class 6) 2-Y-O **£2,047** (£604; £302) **Stalls Low**

Form RPR
1 **Casual Style** 2-8-6 0.................... RichardMullen 1 74+
(E S McMahon) *trckd ldr on inner: swtchd rt and hdwy 2f out: led wl over 1f out: comf* **4/6[1]**
4322 **2** *6* **Lady Fantasie**[19] 3215 2-8-6 0.................... RoystonFfrench 2 51
(Mrs A Duffield) *led: rdn along 2f out: hdd wl over 1f out: kpt on same pce* **5/2[2]**
6205 **3** *4* **Jethro Bodine (IRE)**[6] 3639 2-8-8 0.................... AndrewMullen(3) 4 42
(W J H Ratcliffe) *cl up: rdn along 1/2-way: drvn wl over 1f out and sn one pce* **8/1[3]**
00 **4** *1½* **Ernies Keep**[22] 3106 2-8-8 0.................... DominicFox(3) 7 36
(W Storey) *racd wd: chsd ldrs: rdn 2f out: sn btn* **100/1**
3066 **5** *hd* **Dispol Toba**[22] 3106 2-8-6 0.................... PaulFessey 6 30
(P T Midgley) *chsd ldrs: rdn along 1/2-way: sn drvn and outpcd fnl 2f* **25/1**
00 **6** *2¾* **Cotton N Silk**[26] 3005 2-8-6 0....................(b[1]) DavidAllan 5 21
(T D Easterby) *cl up: rdn along 1/2-way: sn drvn and wknd wl over 1f out* **25/1**
6060 **7** *3½* **Transformation (IRE)**[19] 3225 2-8-6 0....................(p) AndrewElliott 8 8
(J R Weymes) *racd wd: prom tl rdn along 1/2-way and sn wknd* **66/1**
8 *21* **Rocking Laura** 2-8-7 0 ow1.................... TomEaves 3 —
(R Craggs) *v.s.i.s: rn green and a wl bhd* **40/1**

60.49 secs (0.69) **Going Correction** -0.05s/f (Good) **8 Ran SP% 112.3**
Speed ratings (Par 92): **92,82,76,73,73 68,63,29**
toteswinger: 1&2 £1.10, 1&3 £2.10, 2&3 £2.00. CSF £2.27 TOTE £1.50: £1.02, £1.40, £1.90; EX 2.30.The winner was sold to David Pipe for £14,000.
Owner J C Fretwell **Bred** Wyck Hall Stud Ltd **Trained** Lichfield, Staffs

FOCUS
A very moderate race, where only the first two home are worth any consideration next time. The winner was different class and was sold for 14,000gns after the race.

NOTEBOOK

Casual Style, making her debut in a race that took very little winning, was always ideally positioned and came right away from her mainly exposed rivals with ease when asked to quicken. It was not surprising that she attracted attention at the auction afterwards, and she was purchased by David Pipe for 14,000gns. (op 7-4)

Lady Fantasie, dropped into a seller after running in claimers recently, would have been a clear winner without the well-touted newcomer. She deserves to get her head in front soon. (op 11-10)

Jethro Bodine(IRE) never looked a threat to the front two and, while holding the outsiders, appears to be regressing. (tchd 11-1)

Ernies Keep kept plugging away but achieved virtually nothing.

Dispol Toba, one of the most experienced runners in the race, showed a bit of early toe but was readily brushed aside when this poor race got serious. (op 16-1 tchd 28-1)

Rocking Laura fell out of the stalls and did not have a clue what was going on. (op 33-1)

3831 BOOK TICKETS ON-LINE AT CATTERICKBRIDGE.CO.UK H'CAP — 7f

2:55 (2:55) (Class 5) (0-75,72) 3-Y-O — **£2,590** (£770; £385; £192) **Stalls** Low

Form — RPR

-413 **1** **Dream Express (IRE)**[37] 2674 3-9-2 **72** .... NeilBrown(5) 3 — 75
(M Dods) plld hrd: trckd ldrs: hdwy on outer wl over 1f out: rdn to ld ins fnl f: styd on **7/4**[1]

5636 **2** *nk* **Ride A White Swan**[5] 3690 3-8-11 **62** .... AndrewElliott 4 — 64
(D Shaw) t.k.h: hld up in rr: gd hdwy over 1f out: str run ent fnl f and sn ev ch: drvn and nt qckn towards fin **11/1**

1- **3** *2 1/4* **San Silvestro (IRE)**[246] 6698 3-9-4 **69** .... RoystonFfrench 5 — 65
(Mrs A Duffield) hld up in rr: pushed along and outpcd 1/2-way: rdn over 2f out: styd on appr fnl f: nrst fin **11/2**[3]

0012 **4** *1/2* **Royal Acclamation (IRE)**[18] 3280 3-9-2 **67** .... SilvestreDeSousa 1 — 62
(G A Harker) led: rdn along 2f out: drvn over 1f out: hdd & wknd ins fnl f **11/4**[2]

4004 **5** *3/4* **Imperial Djay (IRE)**[9] 3564 3-9-0 **65** .... (v) DNolan 2 — 58
(D Carroll) trckd ldrs on inner: hdwy over 2f out: rdn over 1f out: ev ch ins fnl f: drvn and wknd last 100yds **12/1**

4300 **6** *1 1/4* **Kyllis**[23] 3081 3-8-8 **59** .... TomEaves 6 — 48
(B Smart) cl up: effrt 2f out: sn rdn and ev ch tl drvn ent fnl f and sn wknd **12/1**

50-3 **7** *9* **Pintano**[21] 3144 3-9-3 **68** .... RobertWinston 7 — 33
(J Howard Johnson) cl up on outer: rdn along 3f out and sn wknd **9/1**

1m 27.86s (0.86) **Going Correction** +0.05s/f (Good) — 7 Ran SP% **112.1**

Speed ratings (Par 100): **97,96,94,93,92 91,80**

toteswinger: 1&2 £4.40, 1&3 £2.70, 2&3 £6.40. CSF £21.15 TOTE £2.10: £1.60, £4.50; EX 23.60.

Owner J A Wynn-Williams Les Waugh **Bred** Quay Bloodstock **Trained** Denton, Co Durham

FOCUS

An ordinary-looking handicap, which the most in-form horse won. The runner-up has proved to be a frustrating maiden, but the third is still capable of improvement.

3832 "TURMERIC" H'CAP — 1m 7f 177y

3:30 (3:30) (Class 4) (0-85,83) 3-Y-0+ — **£4,857** (£1,445; £722; £360) **Stalls** Low

Form — RPR

2105 **1** **Mister Arjay (USA)**[17] 3296 8-9-3 **72** .... TonyHamilton 3 — 81
(B Ellison) set stdy pce: qcknd 4f out: rdn along and qcknd 2f out: drvn ins fnl f and styd on gamely **12/1**

1112 **2** *3/4* **Hits Only Vic (USA)**[14] 3368 4-9-11 **80** .... DavidAllan 4 — 88
(D Carroll) t.k.h: hld up in tch: hdwy over 2f out: rdn over 1f out: drvn and ch ins fnl f: kpt on **13/8**[1]

162 **3** *hd* **Cavendish**[32] 2849 4-8-10 **68** .... (b) LukeMorris(3) 6 — 76
(J M P Eustace) trckd ldng pair: rdn along and sltly outpcd 3f out: styd on u.p fr over 1f out: drvn and no ex wl ins fnl f **9/2**[3]

3000 **4** *1 3/4* **Sphinx (FR)**[26] 3007 10-9-11 **80** .... (b) RobertWinston 8 — 86
(E W Tuer) t.k.h: hld up in rr: effrt 3f out: hdwy on outer wl over 1f out: sn rdn and kpt on same pce ins fnl f **16/1**

-000 **5** *1 1/4* **Golden Dagger (IRE)**[9] 3551 4-9-1 **70** .... FergalLynch 2 — 74?
(K A Ryan) hld up in rr: gd hdwy over 3f out: rdn to chse wnr 2f out: drvn over 1f out and wknd ent fnl f **25/1**

5614 **6** *nk* **Numero Due**[26] 3007 6-9-9 **83** .... NeilBrown(5) 7 — 87
(G M Moore) trckd wnr: effrt over 2f out and sn rdn along: drvn over 1f out and one pce appr fnl f **15/8**[2]

05-5 **7** *12* **Act Sirius (IRE)**[19] 3216 4-8-12 **67** .... TomEaves 1 — 57
(A Crook) chsd ldrs: rdn along over 3f out and sn wknd **33/1**

3m 39.4s (7.40) **Going Correction** +0.05s/f (Good) — 7 Ran SP% **111.4**

Speed ratings (Par 105): **83,82,82,81,81 80,74**

toteswinger: 1&2 £3.40, 1&3 £3.90, 2&3 £1.70. CSF £30.43 CT £101.32 TOTE £14.40: £3.20, £1.60; EX 33.70.

Owner Keith Middleton **Bred** Barbara Hunter **Trained** Norton, N Yorks

FOCUS

A modest staying event, that the winner looked to steal from the front.

3833 CALL 01748 810165 TO BOOK RACEDAY HOSPITALITY H'CAP — 5f 212y

4:05 (4:06) (Class 5) (0-75,74) 3-Y-0 — **£2,590** (£770; £385; £192) **Stalls** Low

Form — RPR

-521 **1** **Pavershooz**[19] 3202 3-9-7 **74** .... DO'Donohoe 7 — 85
(N Wilson) trckd ldrs on inner: smooth hdwy 2f out: shkn up to ld over 1f out: sn clr: comf **9/2**[3]

-616 **2** *3 1/2* **Capone (IRE)**[44] 2460 3-9-7 **74** .... JoeFanning 5 — 74
(Garry Moss) hld up in rr: hdwy on outer over 2f out: rdn wl over 1f out: styd on ins fnl f: tk 2nd nr line **9/1**

3664 **3** *nk* **Kinout (IRE)**[8] 3581 3-9-5 **72** .... FergalLynch 4 — 71
(K A Ryan) led: rdn 2f out: drvn and hdd over 1f out: sn one pce: lost 2nd nr line **6/1**

0011 **4** *5* **Ursus**[12] 3454 3-8-4 **57** .... SilvestreDeSousa 3 — 40
(C R Wilson) in tch: effrt to chse ldrs over 2f out: sn rdn and no imp over 1f out **2/1**[1]

-502 **5** *2 3/4* **Gainshare**[17] 3298 3-8-9 **67** .... NeilBrown(5) 6 — 41
(T D Barron) t.k.h: cl up: rdn along over 2f out and sn wknd **11/4**[2]

0000 **6** *nse* **Baronovici (IRE)**[13] 3416 3-8-11 **64** .... TonyHamilton 2 — 38
(D W Barker) hld up: a in rr **12/1**

3036 **7** *9* **Second Opinion (IRE)**[32] 2850 3-8-5 **61** .... LukeMorris(3) 1 — 6
(J M P Eustace) chsd ldrs: rdn along wl over 2f out and sn wknd **16/1**

1m 13.46s (-0.14) **Going Correction** +0.05s/f (Good) — 7 Ran SP% **116.0**

Speed ratings (Par 100): **102,97,96,90,86 86,74**

toteswinger: 1&2 £5.20, 1&3 £4.50, 2&3 £8.50. CSF £44.24 TOTE £5.70: £2.10, £3.50; EX 39.40.

Owner Mrs Michael John Paver **Bred** Exors Of The Late M J Paver **Trained** Flaxton, N Yorks

FOCUS

A fair sprint handicap for three-year-olds. The winner was the least exposed in the field and is progressing nicely.

Ursus Official explanation: trainer's rep said, regarding running, that the gelding ran flat after 3 runs in 21-days

3834 TURFTV.CO.UK H'CAP — 7f

4:40 (4:41) (Class 6) (0-65,65) 3-Y-0+ — **£2,217** (£654; £327) **Stalls** Low

Form — RPR

2133 **1** **Micky Mac (IRE)**[8] 3591 4-9-6 **57** .... SilvestreDeSousa 3 — 70
(T D Walford) mde all: rdn clr over 1f out: styd on strly **10/3**[1]

-136 **2** *1 3/4* **Turn Me On (IRE)**[7] 3599 5-9-11 **65** .... DuranFentiman(3) 13 — 73
(T D Walford) hld up in midfield: hdwy on outer 2f out: rdn over 1f out: styd on wl fnl f: nt rch wnr **7/1**[3]

6-13 **3** *1 1/4* **Imperial Lucky (IRE)**[15] 3345 5-9-7 **58** .... RobertWinston 10 — 63
(M J Wallace) chsd ldrs: effrt 2f out and sn rdn: swtchd ins and drvn ent fnl f: kpt on **5/1**[2]

-000 **4** *1* **Baltimore Jack (IRE)**[11] 3477 4-9-12 **63** .... (b[1]) PaulMulrennan 7 — 65
(M W Easterby) prom: hdwy to chse wnr over 2f out and sn rdn: drvn and edgd lft ent fnl f: one pce **20/1**

0005 **5** *1/2* **Megalo Maniac**[5] 3691 5-8-10 **47** .... (p) TonyHamilton 9 — 48
(R A Fahey) chsd ldrs on outer: rdn along 2f out: sn drvn and wknd appr fnl f **15/2**

0005 **6** *3 1/2* **Fan Club**[2] 3789 4-8-9 **46** oh1 .... (b) JoeFanning 1 — 37
(Mrs R A Carr) t.k.h: chsd ldrs on inner: rdn along 2f out and sn one pce **14/1**

0000 **7** *2 1/4* **Pay Time**[22] 3108 9-9-3 **54** .... PatrickMathers 4 — 39
(R E Barr) towards rr tl sme late hdwy **25/1**

-400 **8** *2* **Myriola**[28] 2928 3-8-3 **48** .... PaulFessey 2 — 25
(S Gollings) chsd ldrs: rdn along 2f out: grad wknd **40/1**

00-0 **9** *1 1/4* **Linden's Lady**[3] 3764 8-8-10 **47** .... (v) DO'Donohoe 11 — 24
(J R Weymes) a towards rr **33/1**

0222 **10** *1/2* **March Mate**[15] 3339 4-9-4 **55** .... TomEaves 5 — 30+
(B Ellison) rrd s w blindfold stl in pl and v.s.a: a bhd **10/3**[1]

-054 **11** *3 1/2* **Brigadore**[23] 3079 9-9-3 **54** .... DeanMcKeown 14 — 20
(J G Given) a in rr **14/1**

00-0 **12** *5* **Warners Bay (IRE)**[17] 3298 3-9-0 **59** .... RoystonFfrench 12 — 8
(R Bastiman) a in rr **50/1**

500 **13** *2 1/4* **Ticking**[71] 1700 5-8-2 **46** oh1 .... AshleyMorgan(7) 8 — —
(T Keddy) a in rr **66/1**

1m 27.13s (0.13) **Going Correction** +0.05s/f (Good)

WFA 3 from 4yo+ 8lb — 13 Ran SP% **117.9**

Speed ratings (Par 101): **101,99,97,96,95 91,89,87,85,85 81,75,72**

toteswinger: 1&2 £5.30, 1&3 £4.50, 2&3 £7.50. CSF £24.75 CT £120.17 TOTE £3.20: £1.90, £3.00, £1.40; EX 28.00.

Owner A M McArdle **Bred** Stephen O'Rourke **Trained** Sheriff Hutton, N Yorks

FOCUS

A moderate handicap saw Sheriff Hutton handler Tim Walford saddle the first two home.

March Mate Official explanation: jockey said gelding reared as stalls opened and was unable to remove blindfold immediately

Brigadore Official explanation: jockey said gelding lost its action on bend turn into home straight

3835 RACINGUK.TV MEDIAN AUCTION MAIDEN STKS — 1m 5f 175y

5:15 (5:15) (Class 5) 3-4-Y-0 — **£2,590** (£770; £385; £192) **Stalls** Low

Form — RPR

2 **1** **Woody Waller**[13] 3402 3-8-11 0 .... RobertWinston 7 — 75+
(J Howard Johnson) hld up in rr: hdwy over 4f out: rdn along and rn green 3f out: drvn to chse ldr over 1f out: styd on u.p to ld wl ins fnl f **13/8**[1]

23 **2** *1/2* **Hollins**[35] 2735 4-9-12 0 .... PaulMulrennan 4 — 74
(Micky Hammond) led: rdn along 3f out: drvn over 1f out: hdd and no ex wl ins fnl f **16/1**

023 **3** *8* **Dream Esteem**[21] 3130 3-8-6 71 .... DeanMcKeown 1 — 58
(E J O'Neill) trckd ldrs: hdwy to chse ldr over 2f out: rdn to chal wl over 1f out and ev ch until drvn and wknd appr fnl f **7/1**

0-24 **4** *3 3/4* **Cherokee Star**[17] 3297 3-8-11 75 .... RoystonFfrench 5 — 58
(C C Bealby) chsd ldrs: hdwy over 3f out: rdn over 2f out: drvn wl over 1f out and no imp **7/2**[3]

60 **5** *7* **Enderby Princess (IRE)**[24] 3058 3-8-6 0 .... DavidAllan 6 — 43
(D Carroll) hld up: hdwy over 4f out: rdn along over 2f out and nvr a factor **40/1**

55 **6** *1 3/4* **Marie Louise**[11] 3484 3-8-6 0 .... JoeFanning 3 — 41
(H R A Cecil) chsd ldr: effrt and cl up 4f out: rdn along 3f out and sn wknd **11/4**[2]

0- **7** *114* **Tiegan An Josh**[201] 7208 3-8-7 0 ow1 .... TomEaves 2 — —
(A Crook) chsd ldrs: rdn along 5f out: sn wknd and wl bhd **125/1**

3m 5.39s (1.79) **Going Correction** +0.05s/f (Good)

WFA 3 from 4yo 15lb — 7 Ran SP% **108.6**

Speed ratings (Par 103): **96,95,91,89,85 84,—**

toteswinger: 1&2 £3.40, 1&3 £2.50, 2&3 £4.30. CSF £26.39 TOTE £2.70: £1.80, £2.30; EX 21.30 Place 6 £49.34, Place 5 £48.70..

Owner J Howard Johnson **Bred** P M Hicks **Trained** Billy Row, Co Durham

FOCUS

No more than a fair maiden, and the first two pulled well clear of the remainder.

Marie Louise Official explanation: jockey said filly did not appear to stay 1m 6f

T/Plt: £56.70 to a £1 stake. Pool: £47,111.18. 606.05 winning tickets. T/Qpdt: £20.00 to a £1 stake. Pool: £2,480.90. 91.50 winning tickets. JR

3609 KEMPTON (A.W) (R-H)

Wednesday, July 9

OFFICIAL GOING: Standard

Wind: Virtually nil. Weather: raining

3836 HARNESS RACING HERE NEXT WEDNESDAY H'CAP — 1m 2f (P)

6:20 (6:25) (Class 4) (0-80,80) 3-Y-0+ — **£4,727** (£1,406; £702; £351) **Stalls** High

Form — RPR

-060 **1** **Jebel Ali (IRE)**[26] 3003 5-9-3 **69** .... (v) ChrisCatlin 2 — 78
(B Gubby) in tch: rdn wl over 2f out: hdwy u.p over 1f out: led wl ins fnl f: all out **66/1**

652- **2** *hd* **Vilna (USA)**[259] 6427 3-8-2 **65** .... NickyMackay 9 — 74
(S A Callaghan) s.i.s: hld up towards rr: rdn jst over 2f out: hdwy on outer u.p over 1f out: str chal wl ins fnl f: jst hld **7/1**[3]

-000 **3** *1/2* **Novikov**[41] 2540 4-9-13 **79** .... (tp) RobertHavlin 12 — 87
(J H M Gosden) led for 1f: chsd ldr after tl rdn to ld over 1f out: hdd wl ins fnl f: nt qckn towards fin **8/1**

6053 **4** *2* **Murrin (IRE)**[14] 3376 4-9-6 **72**........ JimCrowley 11 76
(T G Mills) *s.i.s: hld up in midfield: rdn and sltly outpcd 2f out: styd on u.p fnl f: nt pce to chal ldrs* **6/1**[2]

0200 **5** *shd* **Ryedale Ovation (IRE)**[15] 3347 5-8-10 **65**........ TravisBlock(3) 10 69
(M Hill) *chsd ldrs: drvn to chse ldr over 1f out tl ins fnl f: fdd last 100yds* **12/1**

4303 **6** *1 ½* **Zero Cool (USA)**[16] 3319 4-9-4 **77**........ JemmaMarshall(7) 1 78
(G L Moore) *chsd ldrs: rdn and lost pl wl over 2f out: kpt on again fnl f: nt pce to rch ldrs* **12/1**

0604 **7** *1 ½* **Man Of Gwent (UAE)**[21] 3132 4-9-11 **77**........(p) NCallan 4 75
(P D Evans) *s.i.s: in rr: rdn and effrt on inner wl over 1f out: no imp last 100yds* **8/1**

4-53 **8** *½* **Sign Of The Cross**[41] 2531 4-10-0 **80**........ JamieSpencer 7 77
(J R Fanshawe) *s.i.s: pushed up to ld after 1f: rdn and hung lft 2f out: hdd over 1f out: sn btn* **3/1**[1]

1500 **9** *hd* **Air Chief**[37] 2665 3-8-10 **73**........ RichardKingscote 5 69
(H J L Dunlop) *hld up in midfield: rdn and outpcd over 2f out: kpt on same pce u.p last 2f* **14/1**

-500 **10** *hd* **Risque Heights**[9] 3561 4-9-10 **76**........ DavidKinsella 6 72
(J R Boyle) *v.s.a: bhd: effrt on outer 2f out: nvr trbld ldrs* **20/1**

13-5 **11** *9* **Encores**[138] 660 4-9-1 **67**........ EddieAhern 8 45
(M G Quinlan) *stdd after s: hld up bhd: lost tch 2f out* **16/1**

2m 7.59s (-0.41) **Going Correction** +0.075s/f (Slow)
WFA 3 from 4yo+ 11lb **11** Ran SP% **108.2**
Speed ratings (Par 105): **104,103,103,101,101 100,99,98,98,98 91**
toteswinger: 1&2 £58.00, 1&3 £58.00, 2&3 £58.00. CSF £406.32 CT £3059.76 TOTE £24.20: £9.00, £3.00, £3.20; EX 316.50.
Owner Brian Gubby **Bred** C A Jennings And S G Collen **Trained** Bagshot, Surrey
■ Wikaala was withdrawn (6/1, unruly in stalls). R4 applies, deduct 10p in the £.
■ Stewards' Enquiry : Chris Catlin one-day ban: used whip with excessive force (Jul 23)
Jemma Marshall one-day ban: used whip above shoulder height (Jul 23)

FOCUS
Just an ordinary handicap.

3837 EUROPEAN BREEDERS' FUND MEDIAN AUCTION MAIDEN FILLIES' STKS 6f (P)
6:50 (6:55) (Class 5) 2-Y-O **£3,885** (£1,156; £577; £288) **Stalls** High

Form RPR

3 **1** **Touching (IRE)**[9] 3558 2-9-0 0........ EddieAhern 5 79
(R Hannon) *mde all: rdn over 2f out: edgd rt ent fnl f: r.o strly* **3/1**[1]

03 **2** *1 ¾* **Today's The Day**[14] 3373 2-9-0 0........ PhilipRobinson 12 74
(M A Jarvis) *chsd wnr thrght: rdn over 2f out: carried sltly rt ent fnl f: keeping on same pce whn swtchd lft ins fnl f* **4/1**

45 **3** *2 ¼* **Deyas Dream**[19] 3207 2-9-0 0........ NCallan 6 67
(A M Balding) *chsd ldng trio: rdn over 2f out: kpt on same pce under presuure fr over 1f out* **10/3**[2]

4 *1 ¾* **Happy Forever (FR)** 2-9-0 0........ JohnEgan 9 62
(M Botti) *t.k.h: chsd ldrs: rdn over 2f out: wknd ent fnl f* **9/2**

0 **5** *shd* **Sparkling Suzie**[23] 3085 2-9-0 0........ PatDobbs 11 62
(R Hannon) *stdd after s: racd in midfield: rdn and kpt on one pce fr over 2f out* **20/1**

6 *½* **Key To Love (IRE)** 2-9-0 0........ IanMongan 3 60+
(H J L Dunlop) *wnt rt and bmpd s: a midfield: rdn 3f out: nvr gng pce to trble ldrs* **66/1**

6 *dht* **Never Cry** 2-9-0 0........ LDettori 4 60
(Saeed Bin Suroor) *racd in midfield: rdn over 2f out: kpt on but nvr gng pce to trble ldrs* **7/2**[3]

8 *nk* **Athania (IRE)** 2-9-0 0........ DarrenWilliams 8 59
(A P Jarvis) *v.s.a: wl bhd: hdwy 4f out: swtchd lft and rdn over 2f out: no imp after* **66/1**

9 *3* **Handful Of Magic** 2-9-0 0........ RichardKingscote 10 50
(Tom Dascombe) *s.i.s: a bhd* **20/1**

30 **10** *19* **True Britannia**[25] 3032 2-9-0 0........ JamieSpencer 2 —
(S Kirk) *racd wd: sn outpcd and bhd: t.o last 2f* **28/1**

1m 13.86s (0.76) **Going Correction** +0.075s/f (Slow) **10** Ran SP% **124.4**
Speed ratings (Par 91): **97,94,91,89,89 88,88,88,84,58**
toteswinger: 1&2 £4.10, 1&3 £1.20, 2&3 £12.40. CSF £15.73 TOTE £4.90: £1.40, £1.40, £1.50; EX 21.60.
Owner T Hely-Hutchinson & Lord Donoughmore **Bred** D Veitch **Trained** East Everleigh, Wilts
■ Stewards' Enquiry : Eddie Ahern two-day ban: interference (Jul 23-24)

FOCUS
A fair maiden featuring a couple of interesting newcomers.

NOTEBOOK
Touching(IRE) had run really well to finish third at Windsor on her debut the previous week and responded gamely under a positive ride here to keep her rivals at bay, though she did hang away to her right in the home straight, doing the runner-up few favours. She was allowed to keep the race at the subsequent enquiry and should continue to progress. (op 11-4 tchd 7-2 tchd 4-1 in a place)
Today's The Day, whose third behind Ahla Wasahl over course and distance last time was boosted when the winner finished third in the Cherry Hinton earlier in the day, was always stalking the winner, and although she was intimidated a couple of times by her rival in the last furlong, she still seemed to have every chance to go past had she been good enough. She does not yet look quite the finished article. (op 11-2)
Deyas Dream had every chance and may have a few more options now that she qualifies for nurseries. (op 7-2 tchd 4-1)
Happy Forever(FR), whose yard do well at this course, did best of the newcomers and deserves credit as she raced quite keenly for most of the contest. She was well supported beforehand and is clearly thought to be capable of better. (op 7-1)
Sparkling Suzie, a stablemate of the winner, ran better than on her Warwick debut and looks another likely type for nurseries. (tchd 18-1)
Key To Love(IRE) did not perform too badly on this debut as she took quite a bump from Never Cry leaving the stalls. Better should be seen from her in due course. (tchd 9-2 and 5-1 in a place)
Never Cry, whose yard have yet to get going with their juveniles, never looked like winning and is obviously nothing special. (tchd 9-2 and 5-1 in a place)
Athania(IRE) Official explanation: jockey said filly missed the break
Handful Of Magic Official explanation: jockey said filly ran green

3838 DIGIBET.COM H'CAP 6f (P)
7:20 (7:25) (Class 4) (0-85,84) 3-Y-O **£4,727** (£1,406; £702; £351) **Stalls** High

Form RPR

-132 **1** **Fabreze**[26] 2998 3-9-6 **83**........ EddieAhern 8 96+
(P J Makin) *t.k.h: hld up in bhd ldrs: rdn and effrt on inner 2f out: led ins fnl f: r.o strly: readily* **15/8**[1]

1-00 **2** *1 ¾* **Street Star (USA)**[26] 2993 3-9-7 **84**........ JamieSpencer 6 87
(J R Fanshawe) *led: rdn and qcknd over 2f out: hung lft and hdd narrowly over 1f out: stl ev ch tl nt pce of wnr last 100yds: regained 2nd nr fin* **12/1**

2614 **3** *¾* **Rockfield Lodge (IRE)**[3] 3761 3-8-11 **74**........ NeilPollard 3 75
(M E Rimmer) *awkward s and slowly away: t.k.h: hld up in midfield: hdwy 4f out: chal u.p 2f out: led narrowly over 1f out: hdd and nt pce of wnr ins fnl f: lost 2nd nr fin* **12/1**

3244 **4** *3 ½* **Sparton Duke (IRE)**[27] 2967 3-9-3 **80**........(p) NCallan 7 70+
(K A Ryan) *stdd s: t.k.h: hld up toward rr: rdn and unable qck over 2f out: kpt on but nvr gng pce to trble ldrs* **2/1**[2]

1023 **5** *1 ½* **Yankee Storm**[8] 3587 3-9-0 **77**........ J-PGuillambert 9 62
(M Johnston) *chsd ldrs: rdn over 2f out: wknd wl over 1f out* **5/1**[3]

0050 **6** *½* **Miss Clonyn (IRE)**[33] 2800 3-9-7 **84**........ RichardThomas 4 67
(Christian Wroe) *chsd ldr: rdn and ev ch over 2f out: struggling to hold pl whn short of room over 1f out: n.d after* **50/1**

4210 **7** *2 ½* **Fools Gold**[29] 2922 3-8-10 **73**........ PaulEddery 1 48
(G D Blake) *bhd: rdn along 4f out: wknd 2f out* **18/1**

21-0 **8** *2 ¼* **Our Piccadilly (IRE)**[53] 2196 3-9-3 **80**........ FergusSweeney 10 48
(W S Kittow) *stdd s: t.k.h: hld up towards rr: rdn over 2f out: wknd wl over 1f out* **10/1**

1m 13.93s (0.83) **Going Correction** +0.075s/f (Slow) **8** Ran SP% **116.5**
Speed ratings (Par 102): **97,94,93,89,87 86,83,80**
toteswinger: 1&2 £5.80, 1&3 £10.40, 2&3 £36.00. CSF £25.92 CT £218.46 TOTE £3.20: £1.50, £2.50, £3.40; EX 16.60.
Owner Weldspec Glasgow Limited **Bred** D Brocklehurst **Trained** Ogbourne Maisey, Wilts

FOCUS
A fair handicap.
Street Star(USA) Official explanation: jockey said filly hung left
Miss Clonyn(IRE) Official explanation: jockey said filly suffered interference in running

3839 DIGIBET CASINO H'CAP 1m (P)
7:50 (7:51) (Class 6) (0-58,58) 3-Y-O+ **£2,047** (£604; £302) **Stalls** High

Form RPR

5000 **1** **Alucica**[9] 3567 5-9-2 **52**........(v) JimCrowley 10 61
(D Shaw) *hld up in midfield: rdn and hdwy over 2f out: led ins fnl f: hld on wl: jst prevailed: all out* **20/1**

0233 **2** *nse* **Brouhaha**[25] 3034 4-9-5 **55**........ TedDurcan 7 64
(B J McMath) *hld up in rr: hdwy on inner over 2f out: str run to join wnr ins fnl f: r.o wl but jst hld* **9/4**[1]

0363 **3** *2 ½* **Postmaster**[4] 3732 6-9-3 **53**........ RobertHavlin 5 56
(R Ingram) *hld up in rr: rdn and hdwy over 2f out: chsd ldrs ins fnl f: nt pce of ldng pair last 100yds: snatched 3rd nr fin* **9/1**

300- **4** *½* **Inquisitress**[226] 6945 4-9-6 **56**........ EddieAhern 14 58
(J J Bridger) *hld up towards rr: hdwy on inner over 2f out: rdn jst over 2f out: chsd ldr ent fnl f: ev ch briefly ins fnl f: outpcd last 100yds* **20/1**

04/2 **5** *1 ¼* **Mystic Roll**[20] 3162 5-9-6 **56**........ JohnEgan 11 55
(Jane Chapple-Hyam) *in tch: rdn and hdwy 3f out: chsd clr ldr over 2f out: clsd and ev ch jst ins fnl f: wknd last 100yds* **4/1**[2]

5-50 **6** *1 ¼* **Dr Synn**[26] 2995 7-9-1 **58**........ DavidProbert(7) 1 54
(M J Attwater) *hld up in midfield: swtchd lft and rdn over 2f out: kpt on but nvr gng pce to rch ldrs* **16/1**

1203 **7** *nk* **Straight Face (IRE)**[8] 3572 4-9-5 **55**........(b) NCallan 12 51
(Miss Gay Kelleway) *led for 1f: pressed ldr after tl led again 3f out: sn rdn clr: 3 l ld over 1f out: wknd qckly and hdd ins fnl f: sn btn* **6/1**[3]

2024 **8** *shd* **Guildenstern (IRE)**[16] 3329 6-9-8 **58**........ TGMcLaughlin 3 53
(P Howling) *racd wd: hld up in rr: rdn and effrt over 2f out: nvr trbld ldrs* **12/1**

000- **9** *10* **Sierra Rose**[291] 5647 4-9-5 **55**........ FrancisNorton 6 27
(P J McBride) *a towards rr: detached last over 3f out: no ch after* **50/1**

000- **10** *2* **Nashharry (IRE)**[308] 5136 4-9-2 **55**........ KevinGhunowa(3) 9 23
(R A Harris) *t.k.h: chsd ldrs: rdn 4f out: wknd 3f out: wl bhd last 2f* **33/1**

-000 **11** *5* **Take To The Skies (IRE)**[9] 3551 4-9-2 **52**........ DarrenWilliams 2 8
(A P Jarvis) *led after 1f tl 3f out: sn wknd: t.o* **33/1**

-051 **12** *6* **Parthenope**[14] 3371 5-9-1 **56**........ JackDean(5) 8 —
(J A Geake) *chsd ldrs: rdn and wknd qckly 3f out: wl bhd last 2f: t.o* **13/2**

0000 **13** *14* **Newgate (UAE)**[16] 3329 4-9-3 **53**........ LiamJones 4 —
(Mrs R A Carr) *chsd ldrs tl over 3f out: wl bhd last 2f: eased fnl f: t.o* **40/1**

1m 40.01s (0.21) **Going Correction** +0.075s/f (Slow) **13** Ran SP% **121.8**
Speed ratings (Par 101): **101,100,98,97,96 95,95,95,85,83 78,72,58**
toteswinger: 1&2 £38.50, 1&3 £44.60, 2&3 £6.10. CSF £62.74 CT £463.63 TOTE £26.60: £5.30, £1.70, £3.00; EX 114.10.
Owner Shakespeare Racing **Bred** D R Tucker **Trained** Danethorpe, Notts

FOCUS
A moderate handicap, though competitive enough. The pace looked ordinary and the principals all came from behind.
Nashharry(IRE) Official explanation: jockey said filly ran too free

3840 DIGIBET LONDON MILE H'CAP (LONDON MILE QUALIFIER) 1m (P)
8:20 (8:22) (Class 4) (0-80,80) 3-Y-O+ **£4,727** (£1,406; £702; £351) **Stalls** High

Form RPR

0431 **1** **The Fifth Member (IRE)**[7] 3612 4-9-10 **76** 6ex........ PatCosgrave 6 87
(J R Boyle) *hld up in tch: hdwy to ld 2f out: rdn and qcknd over 1f out: r.o wl fnl f* **2/1**[1]

1533 **2** *¾* **Mumbleswerve (IRE)**[11] 3478 4-9-9 **75**........ AlanMunro 8 84
(W Jarvis) *hld up in midfield: hdwy 3f out: chsd wnr over 1f out: kpt on same pce fnl f* **8/1**

232 **3** *shd* **Ocean Legend (IRE)**[7] 3612 3-8-11 **75**........ JerryO'Dwyer(3) 12 82
(Miss J Feilden) *hld up in midfield: hdwy and edgd out lft 2f out: swtchd lft over 1f out: r.o u.p fnl f* **7/1**[3]

2502 **4** *¾* **Count Ceprano (IRE)**[16] 3317 4-9-9 **80**........ GabrielHannon(5) 2 87
(M D I Usher) *hld up towards rr: effrt over 2f out: rdn and gd hdwy to chse ldrs ent fnl f: no imp last 100yds* **16/1**

010- **5** *2 ¾* **Danetime Panther (IRE)**[420] 1773 4-9-12 **78**........ JosedeSouza 13 79
(P F I Cole) *t.k.h: hld up wl in tch: rdn over 2f out: wknd ent fnl f* **20/1**

2004 **6** *hd* **Mujood**[14] 3382 5-9-13 **79**........(v) StephenCarson 14 79
(Eve Johnson Houghton) *sn bustled along to chse ldrs: led after 2f: drvn and hdd 2f out: wknd fnl f* **14/1**

0053 **7** *½* **Very Wise**[39] 2604 6-9-13 **79**........ JimmyFortune 10 78
(W J Haggas) *s.i.s: wl bhd: hdwy on inner jst over 2f out: nvr threatened ldrs* **11/2**[2]

6000 **8** *1* **Ninth House (USA)**[11] 3478 6-9-12 **78**........(b) LiamJones 7 75
(Mrs R A Carr) *s.i.s: t.k.h: hld up in midfield: rdn 3f out: plugged on same pce after* **50/1**

0-03 **9** *3 ¾* **Cape Of Luck (IRE)**[10] 3529 5-9-2 **68**........(p) JamieSpencer 11 61+
(P M Phelan) *hld up towards rr: swtchd rt onto rail and effrt jst over 2f out: nvr rchd ldrs: eased whn btn ins fnl f* **9/1**

60 **10** *nse* **Lend A Grand (IRE)**[14] 3367 4-9-6 **75**........ TravisBlock(3) 9 63
(Miss Jo Crowley) *stdd after s: hld up in rr: n.d* **33/1**

The Form Book, Raceform Ltd, Compton, RG20 6NL

-230 **11** *14* **Last Sovereign**[23] 3090 4-9-8 **74**........................ JohnEgan 3 30
(Jane Chapple-Hyam) *led for 2f: chsd ldr after tl wknd qckly jst over 2f out: eased ins fnl f: t.o* **16/1**
1046 **12** *6* **My Shadow**[16] 3319 3-9-2 **77**........................ IanMongan 4 17
(S Dow) *nvr travelling in rr: wl bhd last 2f: t.o and eased ins fnl f* **28/1**
0013 **13** *¾* **Glencalvie (IRE)**[16] 3317 7-9-11 **77**........................(p) NCallan 5 17
(J Akehurst) *chsd ldrs tl rdn and wknd 3f out: t.o and eased ins fnl f* **20/1**
0603 **14** *14* **Eternal Luck (IRE)**[7] 3612 3-9-5 **80**........................(b) PhilipRobinson 1 —
(M A Jarvis) *pressed ldrs tl 3f out: sn wknd: eased fr over 1f out* **12/1**

1m 39.63s (-0.17) **Going Correction** +0.075s/f (Slow)
WFA 3 from 4yo+ 9lb **14** Ran SP% **126.3**
Speed ratings (Par 105): **103,102,102,101,98 98,97,96,93,93 79,73,72,58**
toteswinger: 1&2 £7.70, 1&3 £5.20, 2&3 £9.40. CSF £17.74 CT £105.85 TOTE £3.30: £1.70, £3.60, £2.90; EX 28.40.
Owner Chris Simpson, Miss Elizabeth Ross **Bred** Ms Amy Mulligan **Trained** Epsom, Surrey

FOCUS
A good and competitive handicap for the class. The first four came clear.
Last Sovereign Official explanation: jockey said colt ran too free

3841 LEONARD CURTIS FILLIES' H'CAP 1m 3f (P)
8:50 (8:51) (Class 5) (0-75,75) 3-Y-0 **£2,590** (£770; £385; £192) **Stalls** High

Form RPR
-322 **1** **Pediment**[30] 2885 3-9-7 **75**........................ JamieSpencer 3 85+
(J R Fanshawe) *hld up in rr: swtchd lft and gd hdwy over 2f out: jnd ldrs gng wl 2f out: led over 1f out: sn clr: pushed out* **7/2**[2]
410 **2** *1 ½* **Ever Rigg**[15] 3351 3-9-7 **75**........................ TedDurcan 10 82
(E A L Dunlop) *in tch: rdn 3f out: chsd wnr 1f out: kpt on u.p but nvr gng pce to chal wnr* **7/1**
6640 **3** *2 ¾* **Lady Sorcerer**[12] 3459 3-9-0 **68**........................ DarrenWilliams 7 70
(A P Jarvis) *hld up towards rr: hdwy 3f out: sltly hmpd over 2f out: rdn to chse ldng pair jst ins fnl f: no imp after* **16/1**
24-3 **4** *¾* **Ceka Dancer (IRE)**[13] 3402 3-9-3 **71**........................ ChrisCatlin 6 72
(E J O'Neill) *stdd and dropped out last after s: sme hdwy 3f out: no prog and swtchd lft over 1f out: r.o fnl f: nvr trbld ldrs* **16/1**
2322 **5** *½* **Shy**[16] 3327 3-9-7 **75**........................ StephenCarson 9 75
(P Winkworth) *led: rdn over 2f out: hrd pressed 2f out: hdd over 1f out: sn outpcd by wnr: wknd ins fnl f* **10/3**[1]
-200 **6** *1 ½* **Bushy Dell (IRE)**[21] 3134 3-8-7 **68**........................ AmyBaker(7) 12 66
(Miss J Feilden) *in tch: sltly hmpd after 1f: effrt to chse ldrs 2f out: sn rdn: wknd ent fnl f* **12/1**
-023 **7** *½* **Stormy View (USA)**[7] 3611 3-9-5 **73**........................ JimmyFortune 4 70
(J H M Gosden) *sn pushed up to chse ldr: edgd rt after 1f: rdn over 2f out: ev ch 2f out: outpcd by wnr over 1f out: wknd ent fnl f* **4/1**[3]
51-6 **8** *3 ¾* **Brave Mave**[85] 1381 3-9-6 **74**........................ J-PGuillambert 14 64
(W Jarvis) *hld up in rr: rdn and effrt on inner over 2f out: n.d* **12/1**
06-5 **9** *4* **Ever Dreaming (USA)**[19] 3206 3-8-10 **64**........................ LPKeniry 13 48
(A M Balding) *chsd ldng pair: rdn wl over 2f out: wknd qckly 2f out* **12/1**
0550 **10** *2* **Tewin Green**[27] 2984 3-8-9 **63**........................ JohnEgan 2 43
(M Botti) *racd wd: racd in midfield: rdn over 4f out: bhd last 3f* **33/1**
0-00 **11** *14* **Bunty Malenoir**[41] 2552 3-7-9 **56** oh9........................(v) DavidProbert(7) 11 12
(Mrs C A Dunnett) *hmpd after 1f: dropped to rr over 4f out: t.o fnl f* **66/1**
00-0 **12** *1 ¼* **Flower Song**[39] 2603 3-8-3 **57**........................ DavidKinsella 5 11
(J Gallagher) *hmpd after 1f: in tch in midfield: rdn 4f out: wl bhd last 2f: t.o* **50/1**

2m 21.2s (-0.70) **Going Correction** +0.075s/f (Slow) **12** Ran SP% **119.0**
Speed ratings (Par 97): **105,103,101,101,101 99,99,96,93,92 82,81**
toteswinger: 1&2 £6.00, 1&3 £35.90, 2&3 £47.70. CSF £28.28 CT £352.07 TOTE £4.30: £1.80, £2.60, £6.50; EX 38.10.
Owner Cheveley Park Stud **Bred** Cheveley Park Stud Ltd **Trained** Newmarket, Suffolk
■ Stewards' Enquiry : Jimmy Fortune two-day ban: careless riding (Jul 23-24)
Jamie Spencer caution: careless riding

FOCUS
A modest fillies' handicap, run at a sound pace.

3842 WEATHERBYS PRINTING APPRENTICE H'CAP (ROUND 6) 7f (P)
9:20 (9:20) (Class 5) (0-70,70) 4-Y-0+ **£2,590** (£770; £385; £192) **Stalls** High

Form RPR
4603 **1** **Millfields Dreams**[16] 3313 9-9-1 **64**........................(p) MarkCoumbe(3) 10 72
(P Leech) *t.k.h: hld up towards rr: hdwy on inner over 2f out: swtchd lft over 1f out: sn rdn to chal: led wl ins fnl f: r.o wl* **14/1**
0004 **2** *½* **Grizedale (IRE)**[14] 3383 9-8-8 **57**........................(tp) DavidProbert(3) 11 64
(M J Attwater) *t.k.h: hld up in midfield: rdn 2f out: r.o fnl f: wnt 2nd nr fin: nvr quite getting to wnr* **13/2**
0060 **3** *hd* **Djalalabad (FR)**[6] 3653 4-8-2 **51** oh3........................(t) DonnaCaldwell(3) 4 57
(Mrs C A Dunnett) *s.i.s: hld up bhd: hdwy on inner over 2f out: drvn and swtchd lft over 1f out: r.o to press ldrs ins fnl f: no ex nr fin* **40/1**
0431 **4** *nk* **Chjimes (IRE)**[16] 3317 4-9-7 **70**........................ WilliamCarson(3) 7 76+
(C R Dore) *in tch: chsd ldr over 2f out: rdn to chal 2f out: led ent fnl f: hdd wl ins fnl f: lost 2 pls nr fin* **9/2**[2]
1264 **5** *3 ¼* **The Jailer**[6] 3648 5-8-11 **60**........................(p) MCGeran(3) 5 57
(J G M O'Shea) *led: rdn and hrd pressed 2f out: hdd ent fnl f: wknd* **6/1**
0543 **6** *1 ¾* **Cornerstone**[11] 3501 4-8-2 **51** oh1........................(vt) RobbieEgan(3) 6 44
(S C Williams) *bhd: hdwy on inner over 2f out: kpt on but nvr gng pce to trble ldrs* **11/2**[3]
0266 **7** *1 ¾* **Zorn**[14] 3371 9-8-0 **51** oh6........................ CharlesEddery(5) 3 40
(P Howling) *chsd ldr tl over 2f out: wknd u.p 2f out* **33/1**
623 **8** *½* **Valentino Swing (IRE)**[32] 2837 5-9-7 **67**........................ JackDean 1 54
(Miss T Spearing) *stdd s: hld up in midfield: rdn and hung rt wl over 2f out: n.d after* **9/1**
0-00 **9** *¾* **Sorrel Point**[20] 3162 5-8-0 **51** oh1........................ TobyAtkinson(5) 8 37
(H J Collingridge) *hld up towards rr: hdwy over 3f out: rdn and no prog over 2f out: wknd over 1f out* **20/1**
5000 **10** *1 ¾* **Ruffie (IRE)**[20] 3162 5-8-2 **51** oh6........................(e) AmyBaker(3) 2 32
(Miss J Feilden) *chsd ldrs: rdn over 3f out: wknd over 2f out* **25/1**
00-1 **11** *½* **Danjet (IRE)**[7] 3608 5-8-10 **59** 6ex........................ RichardEvans(3) 9 39
(P D Evans) *t.k.h: chsd ldrs: rdn and lost pl over 3f out: no ch last 2f* **7/2**[1]
0030 **12** *12* **Trivia (IRE)**[8] 3583 4-8-11 **60**........................ SophieDoyle(3) 12 10
(Ms J S Doyle) *chsd ldrs: rdn 3f out: sn wknd: virtually p.u ins fnl f* **16/1**

1m 26.07s (0.07) **Going Correction** +0.075s/f (Slow) **12** Ran SP% **119.9**
Speed ratings (Par 103): **102,101,101,100,97 95,93,92,91,89 89,75**
toteswinger: 1&2 £7.20, 1&3 £17.20, 2&3 £103.60. CSF £99.43 CT £3622.14 TOTE £16.90: £4.60, £2.60, £12.50; EX 143.20 Place 6 £120.17, Place 5 £22.98..
Owner Mrs Theresa Fitsall **Bred** T G Price **Trained** Newmarket, Suffolk

FOCUS
A moderate handicap, confined to apprentice riders. The form is rated around the fourth.
T/Plt: £323.20 to a £1 stake. Pool: £72,023.36. 162.67 winning tickets. T/Qpdt: £28.50 to a £1 stake. Pool: £7,193.30. 186.30 winning tickets. SP

3583 LINGFIELD (L-H)
Wednesday, July 9

OFFICIAL GOING: Turf course - good to firm changing to good (good to soft in places) after race 1 (2.10) changing to soft after race 2 (2.45); all-weather - standard
Wind: Moderate, half-behind Weather: raining

3843 REGINALD DE COBHAM FILLIES' H'CAP 1m 3f 106y
2:10 (2:11) (Class 5) (0-70,70) 3-Y-0+ **£2,590** (£770; £385; £192) **Stalls** High

Form RPR
4-53 **1** **Neve Lieve (IRE)**[16] 3322 3-9-6 **67**........................ JohnEgan 9 73
(M Botti) *led for 1f: w ldr: led 3f out: briefly hdd 2f out: battled on wl* **7/1**[3]
-664 **2** *1* **Sterope (FR)**[16] 3326 3-9-6 **67**........................ IanMongan 2 71
(H R A Cecil) *hld up: rdn over 3f out: styd on u.p fnl 2f: tk 2nd nr fin* **9/1**
1034 **3** *¾* **Shenandoah Girl**[6] 3624 5-9-4 **53**........................(bt[1]) NCallan 3 56
(Miss Gay Kelleway) *dwlt: hld up: gd prog 4f out: led briefly 2f out: hld fnl f: lost 2nd nr fin* **8/1**
3-04 **4** *nk* **Broken Moon**[24] 3057 3-9-9 **70**........................ PatCosgrave 8 72
(J R Fanshawe) *trckd ldrs: rdn and nt qckn 2f out: kpt on same pce* **11/4**[1]
0121 **5** *hd* **Millie's Rock (IRE)**[5] 3667 3-9-3 **67** 6ex........................ JamieMoriarty(3) 11 69+
(M J Wallace) *t.k.h: trckd ldrs: gng wl 3f out: sn rdn: n.m.r and hmpd 2f out: kpt on same pce* **11/4**[1]
4-42 **6** *½* **Adorabella (IRE)**[16] 3311 5-10-0 **63**........................ FergusSweeney 4 64
(A King) *trckd ldrs: rdn over 2f out: kpt on same pce* **4/1**[2]
000- **7** *1 ¼* **Miss Cruisecontrol**[328] 4547 3-8-0 **47**........................ MohammedSaeed 6 46
(J R Best) *dwlt: hld up: effrt on outer 3f out: nt qckn 2f out: kpt on fnl f* **33/1**
0-00 **8** *3* **Marchpane**[16] 3322 3-9-6 **67**........................(b[1]) JamesDoyle 10 61
(R M Beckett) *led after 1f tl 3f out: sn hanging and nt qckn: wknd fnl f* **25/1**
0005 **9** *17* **Oasis Sun (IRE)**[8] 3588 5-8-13 **48**........................(b) LPKeniry 5 15
(J R Best) *cl up tl wknd over 2f out: t.o* **25/1**
0000 **10** *4 ½* **Poppy Gregg**[9] 3562 3-8-5 **52**........................ RichardThomas 7 12
(Dr J R J Naylor) *a in rr: t.o* **66/1**

2m 33.67s (2.17) **Going Correction** +0.20s/f (Good)
WFA 3 from 5yo 12lb **10** Ran SP% **119.1**
Speed ratings (Par 100): **100,99,98,98,98 98,97,94,82,79**
toteswinger: 1&2 £11.60, 1&3 £3.90, 2&3 £10.90. CSF £66.57 CT £521.48 TOTE £8.20: £2.40, £3.50, £1.90; EX 54.10 Trifecta £373.60 Pool £600.81 - 1.19 winning units..
Owner The Great Partnership **Bred** Darley **Trained** Newmarket, Suffolk

FOCUS
A modest, yet fairly competitive fillies' handicap for the class. The third sets the level.

3844 EDENBRIDGE (S) STKS 1m 2f
2:45 (2:47) (Class 6) 3-Y-0+ **£2,047** (£604; £302) **Stalls** Low

Form RPR
-300 **1** **Colorado Springs**[13] 3393 3-8-4 57........................(b[1]) AdrianMcCarthy 14 54
(W Jarvis) *t.k.h: prom: wnt 2nd over 2f out: styd on u.p to ld fnl 100yds* **13/2**[3]
3- **2** *¾* **Check Up (IRE)**[56] 4256 7-9-3 0........................ KevinGhunowa(3) 5 58
(J L Flint) *s.i.s: hld up: rdn and prog 3f out: styd on to take 2nd nr fin* **7/1**
1/00 **3** *¾* **Danish Monarch**[8] 3588 7-9-6 52........................ FergusSweeney 12 56
(David Pinder) *led: drvn over 2f out: hdd and one pce fnl 100yds* **10/1**
0 **4** *1 ¾* **Wouldn'Titbenice**[26] 2994 3-8-4 0........................ FrancisNorton 13 48
(V Smith) *towards rr: rdn and prog to chse ldng pair 2f out: one pce fnl f* **7/4**[1]
0040 **5** *7* **Sweet World**[11] 3474 4-9-6 55........................ NCallan 3 39
(B J Llewellyn) *t.k.h: hld up in midfield: effrt 3f out: no prog and btn 2f out* **4/1**[2]
0020 **6** *¾* **Classic Hall (IRE)**[35] 2731 5-9-1 44........................ SimonWhitworth 9 32
(J Akehurst) *chsd ldrs tl grad wknd fr over 2f out* **11/1**
0620 **7** *1 ½* **Psycho Cat**[21] 3131 5-9-6 47........................ TGMcLaughlin 1 34
(W M Brisbourne) *t.k.h trcking ldrs: wkng whn hmpd over 1f out: fin lame* **14/1**
0-00 **8** *8* **Lady Lorins**[40] 2556 4-9-1 45........................ AlanDaly 6 13
(Andrew Turnell) *dwlt: a wl in rr* **25/1**
0000 **9** *3 ¾* **Rosy Dawn**[7] 3605 3-8-10 48........................(be) JamesDoyle 2 12
(Ms J S Doyle) *chsd ldng pair tl 3f out: wknd* **50/1**
-500 **10** *1 ¾* **Cobbold Point**[51] 2259 3-8-6 45 ow4........................ StevenCorrigan(7) 11 11
(S W Hall) *a wl in rr* **66/1**
11 *1 ½* **Just 'N' Casey (IRE)**[17] 5-9-6 0........................(t) LPKeniry 10 4
(Tim Vaughan) *s.s: a bhd* **33/1**
3-00 **12** *½* **Ballad Maker (IRE)**[20] 3160 4-9-3 60........................ JerryO'Dwyer(3) 8 3
(Mrs S J Humphrey) *a bhd* **33/1**
-040 **13** *2 ¾* **Sekula Pata (NZ)**[7] 3604 9-9-1 50........................(b) ShaneCreighton(5) 7 —
(E J Creighton) *chsd ldr tl 2f out: wknd rapidly* **33/1**

2m 14.22s (3.72) **Going Correction** +0.35s/f (Good)
WFA 3 from 4yo+ 11lb **13** Ran SP% **122.4**
Speed ratings (Par 101): **99,98,97,96,90 90,89,82,79,78 77,76,74**
toteswinger: 1&2 £13.80, 1&3 £15.70, 2&3 £12.60. CSF £49.87 TOTE £9.40: £2.60, £2.60, £3.20; EX 65.10 TRIFECTA Not won..The winner was bought in for 5,200gns.
Owner Tim Hedin **Bred** Mrs N Hedin **Trained** Newmarket, Suffolk

FOCUS
A typically weak seller.
Psycho Cat Official explanation: vet said gelding returned lame
Rosy Dawn Official explanation: jockey said filly had no more to give and lost its action

3845 RYDON GROUP H'CAP 1m 1f
3:20 (3:23) (Class 6) (0-65,65) 3-Y-0 **£2,047** (£604; £302) **Stalls** Low

Form RPR
0-00 **1** **Stage Acclaim (IRE)**[20] 3183 3-9-3 **64**........................(p) JamesMillman(3) 8 70
(B R Millman) *mde all: kpt on wl fnl 2f* **9/1**
-500 **2** *1 ¼* **Hawk Flight (IRE)**[26] 3004 3-9-7 **65**........................ EddieAhern 5 68
(W R Muir) *chsd wnr after 3f: rdn to chal 2f out: nt qckn* **8/1**[3]
50-2 **3** *1 ½* **Rowan Dancer**[13] 3397 3-8-12 **56**........................ PatCosgrave 13 56
(J R Boyle) *in tch: chsd ldng pair 2f out: one pce fnl f* **11/1**
-240 **4** *¾* **Tara's Garden**[23] 3095 3-9-5 **63**........................ FrancisNorton 4 61
(M Blanshard) *t.k.h: chsd wnr for 3f: one pce fnl 2f* **7/1**[2]
0005 **5** *½* **Quinzey's Best (IRE)**[14] 3384 3-8-13 **57**........................ PaulDoe 14 54+
(W J Knight) *rrd stalls: hld up in last trio: prog over 2f out: nt rch ldrs* **17/2**
0404 **6** *½* **Blandys Wood**[6] 3656 3-8-13 **62**........................ MCGeran(5) 6 58+
(M R Channon) *hld up in rr: effrt on outer over 2f out: styd on: nrst fin* **25/1**

-000 7 nk **Bainisteoir**[27] 2982 3-8-11 **55** PatDobbs 3 50
(S Kirk) *hld up in midfield: nt qckn over 2f out: one pce after* **33/1**

6601 8 ¾ **Caltire (GER)**[40] 2559 3-9-1 **64** (b) JamieJones(5) 12 58
(M G Quinlan) *dwlt: in midfield: no prog u.p 3f out: plugged on* **7/1**[2]

-440 9 nk **Where's Susie**[37] 2678 3-9-7 **65** RobertHavlin 2 58
(D K Ivory) *hld up in midfield: no prog 3f out: no ch whn nt clr run fnl f* **11/1**

-000 10 ½ **Havanavich**[23] 3095 3-9-3 **61** LPKeniry 10 53
(S Kirk) *trckd ldrs: fdd fnl 2f* **14/1**

000 11 2 **Janshe Gold**[41] 2528 3-8-11 **55** JamesDoyle 11 42
(J G Portman) *hld up in last pair: modest late prog: nvr nr ldrs* **50/1**

-550 12 7 **Driven Snow**[25] 3023 3-9-6 **64** NCallan 1 36
(E F Vaughan) *s.s: sn midfield: u.p 3f out: eased whn btn fnl f* **5/2**[1]

00-0 13 3 ½ **Carole Os (IRE)**[20] 3180 3-9-7 **65** TGMcLaughlin 9 29
(S W Hall) *dwlt: hld up: a in last pair* **40/1**

3-62 14 63 **Sharps Gold**[140] 623 3-8-12 **59** (bt) JerryO'Dwyer(3) 7 —
(P J McBride) *plld hrd: in tch tl 4f out: t.o* **25/1**

2m 1.37s (4.77) **Going Correction** +0.50s/f (Yiel) **14 Ran SP% 123.6**
Speed ratings (Par 98): **98,96,95,94,94 94,93,93,92,92 90,84,81,25**
toteswinger: 1&2 £27.60, 1&3 £20.40, 2&3 £32.40. CSF £77.54 CT £837.49 TOTE £13.50: £3.40, £3.00, £3.20; EX 105.90 TRIFECTA Not won..
Owner Horses for Causes **Bred** Oaks Stud **Trained** Kentisbeare, Devon

FOCUS
A moderate handicap, run at a fair pace. The third helps to set the level.
Janshe Gold Official explanation: trainer later said, according to jockey, filly was unsuited by the soft ground
Sharps Gold Official explanation: jockey said filly had a breathing problem

3846 TOWERGATE UNDERWRITING NURSERY 5f (P)
3:55 (3:56) (Class 5) 2-Y-O £3,238 (£963; £481; £240) Stalls High

Form RPR

0033 1 **Kheylide (IRE)**[13] 3392 2-8-9 **73** ow1 NCallan 3 77
(Miss V Haigh) *trckd ldrs: effrt on inner over 1f out: led last 150yds: hung bdly rt: styd on* **11/4**[2]

1630 2 1 **Kate The Great**[22] 3105 2-8-11 **75** EddieAhern 1 75
(M J Wallace) *led: drvn and hdd last 150yds: hld whn carried rt after* **4/1**[3]

150 3 1 ¼ **Missile Dodger (USA)**[22] 3105 2-9-8 **89** JamieMoriarty(3) 2 85
(R M Beckett) *pressed ldrs: chal over 1f out: fnd nil u.p* **5/2**[1]

030 4 1 **Bold Rose**[20] 3178 2-7-5 **62** oh2 (t) DavidProbert(7) 4 54
(M D I Usher) *awkward s: effrt fr rr 2f out: kpt on but unable to chal* **8/1**

004 5 hd **Speak The Truth (IRE)**[42] 2502 2-8-0 **64** DavidKinsella 8 55
(J R Boyle) *pressed ldng pair tl nt qckn over 1f out* **16/1**

000 6 1 ¾ **Josiah Bartlett (IRE)**[18] 3259 2-8-2 **66** FrancisNorton 7 51
(J W Hills) *sn rdn: nvr gng pce to trble ldrs* **12/1**

2324 7 3 **Dedante**[11] 3485 2-8-4 **68** AdrianMcCarthy 6 42
(D K Ivory) *mounted on crse: a in rr* **7/1**

046 8 5 **Taurus Twins**[44] 2458 2-7-12 **62** oh3 CatherineGannon 5 18+
(W G M Turner) *sn rdn to stay in tch: wkng whn hmpd 2f out* **33/1**

59.16 secs (0.36) **Going Correction** -0.075s/f (Stan) **8 Ran SP% 115.4**
Speed ratings (Par 94): **94,92,90,88,88 85,80,72**
toteswinger: 1&2 £1.80, 1&3 £1.20, 2&3 £1.90. CSF £14.41 CT £30.04 TOTE £3.50: £1.40, £1.60, £1.40; EX 15.60 Trifecta £35.30 Pool £816.86 - 17.10 winning units..
Owner R J Budge **Bred** Ged O'Leary **Trained** Wiseton, Notts
■ Stewards' Enquiry : N Callan one-day ban: careless riding (Jul 23)

FOCUS
A modest nursery.

NOTEBOOK
Kheylide(IRE), who went well for a long way in a decent 6f maiden at Great Leighs last month (second won next time) had earlier run well over this trip and, having held a nice early sit just in behind the speed, he picked up well when brought with his challenge on the inside. He was always on top inside the final furlong and was correctly allowed to keep the race following a Stewards' Enquiry, as the interference he caused to the runner-up late on did not affect the result. He is clearly going the right way, carried 1lb overweight here, and remains capable of better. (op 10-3 tchd 5-2 and 7-2 in places)
Kate The Great found the competition of the Windsor Castle Stakes too hot to handle at Royal Ascot, but she looked in with a chance here off a mark of 76 and it was no surprise to see her run well. Soon in front, she kept finding under pressure, but could not repel the winner inside the final furlong. There may be a similar race in her off this sort of mark. (op 10-3 tchd 9-2)
Missile Dodger(USA), several places ahead of the runner-up at Royal Ascot, looked vulnerable here considering he was conceding plenty of weight all round and he could find no extra for pressure. He is not going to be easy to place. (op 2-1)
Bold Rose, whose trainer/jockey combined for a nursery winner last week, was nibbled at in the market beforehand and she ran well, but never quite looked like reaching the front three. She may well want an extra furlong. (op 14-1)
Speak The Truth(IRE), another handicap debutant, showed up well to a point, but could not find an extra gear under pressure.
Josiah Bartlett(IRE) was always struggling for speed and will need an extra furlong on this evidence. (op 10-1)
Dedante is clearly not the easiest and she has limited scope for improvement. (tchd 6-1)

3847 ST PETER'S CROSS MEDIAN AUCTION MAIDEN STKS 6f (P)
4:30 (4:30) (Class 6) 3-4-Y-O £2,388 (£705; £352) Stalls Low

Form RPR

522 1 **Bahamian Bliss**[71] 1709 3-8-12 64 RobertHavlin 6 61+
(J A R Toller) *wnt rt s: trckd ldrs: cl up and nt clr run 1f out: swtchd rt: r.o wl to ld nr fin* **6/1**[3]

25-2 2 hd **Desert Pride**[18] 3268 3-9-3 73 FergusSweeney 5 62
(W S Kittow) *prom: wnt 2nd over 2f out: rdn to ld 1f out: hdd nr fin* **8/11**[1]

0000 3 ¾ **Edge End**[15] 3346 4-9-3 44 (p) PaulDoe 3 61
(R A Farrant) *pressed ldr: led 1/2-way: hdd 1f out: nt qckn* **50/1**

05 4 1 ½ **Celtic Spring (IRE)**[18] 3268 3-8-12 0 PatCosgrave 7 50
(J R Boyle) *bmpd s: prog on outer fr 1/2-way: hrd rdn and one pce fr over 1f out* **5/1**[2]

3/ 5 ¾ **Night Rocket (IRE)**[593] 6575 4-9-4 0 FrancisNorton 9 49+
(A M Balding) *t.k.h: hld up in tch: nt qckn 2f out: one pce after* **9/1**

0304 6 1 **Tiger Trail (GER)**[36] 2692 4-9-9 66 EddieAhern 2 51
(Mrs N Smith) *dwlt: prog fr rr over 2f out: shkn up and one pce fr over 1f out* **6/1**[3]

0- 7 1 **Too Hot To Handle (IRE)**[260] 6409 3-8-12 0 JohnEgan 8 42
(J M P Eustace) *dwlt: hld up in last pair: shkn up over 1f out: n.d* **20/1**

0 8 3 ½ **Professor Malone**[11] 3502 3-9-3 0 LPKeniry 4 36
(J C Tuck) *in tch tl wknd over 2f out* **100/1**

00 9 3 ¾ **Flipacoin**[11] 3502 3-8-12 0 IanMongan 1 19
(S Dow) *led tl 1/2-way: wknd* **100/1**

1m 12.82s (0.92) **Going Correction** -0.075s/f (Stan)
WFA 3 from 4yo 6lb **9 Ran SP% 121.8**
Speed ratings (Par 101): **90,89,88,86,85 84,83,78,73**
toteswinger: 1&2 £2.10, 1&3 £33.50, 2&3 £16.20. CSF £11.33 TOTE £7.40: £1.20, £1.20, £11.10; EX 16.60 Trifecta £208.70 Pool £674.08 - 2.39 winnning units..
Owner Ms Frances Dakers **Bred** Miss Frances Dakers **Trained** Newmarket, Suffolk

FOCUS
A modest maiden.

3848 PLAYSTOWE MAIDEN AUCTION STKS 6f (P)
5:05 (5:05) (Class 6) 2-Y-O £2,388 (£705; £352) Stalls Low

Form RPR

2 1 **Deposer (IRE)**[13] 3417 2-9-1 0 LPKeniry 4 85+
(J R Best) *t.k.h: pressed ldr: led wl over 1f out: rdn clr* **4/7**[1]

2 3 ½ **Shangani** 2-8-4 0 FrankieMcDonald 1 60
(H Candy) *led: clr w wnr 1/2-way: hdd wl over 1f out: sn outpcd* **20/1**

0 3 2 ¾ **Jeremiah (IRE)**[16] 3323 2-8-12 0 JamesDoyle 12 60
(J G Portman) *chsd ldng pair tl 1/2-way: sn outpcd: hanging lft and one pce after* **33/1**

4 1 ¼ **Importer (IRE)** 2-8-12 0 PatCosgrave 9 56
(W R Muir) *awkward s: chsd ldng trio: outpcd 1/2-way* **8/1**[3]

0 5 ½ **Golden Destiny (IRE)**[15] 3348 2-8-4 0 FrancisNorton 7 47+
(P J Makin) *dwlt: bhd: sme prog fr 1/2-way: n.d* **6/1**[2]

6 2 **Give Us A Song (USA)** 2-8-9 0 SimonWhitworth 6 46+
(J S Moore) *dwlt: hld up: wl bhd 1/2-way: sme late prog* **25/1**

03 7 1 ¾ **Mistress Mary**[8] 3584 2-8-4 0 AdrianMcCarthy 8 36
(G G Margarson) *chsd ldng trio: wknd over 1f out* **16/1**

0 8 hd **Starlight Wish**[12] 3444 2-8-12 0 FergusSweeney 11 43
(E F Vaughan) *a wl in rr* **33/1**

9 ¾ **Jubilee Juggins (IRE)** 2-8-10 0 MarkCoumbe(5) 5 44
(N P Littmoden) *chsd clr ldrs tl 1/2-way: wknd* **50/1**

10 1 ½ **True Decision** 2-8-10 0 ow3 HaddenFrost(5) 2 39
(S Kirk) *dwlt: a wl in rr* **25/1**

0 11 ½ **Rocksy**[29] 2916 2-8-7 0 CatherineGannon 10 30
(D J Coakley) *a bhd* **16/1**

0 U **Chantilly Dancer (IRE)**[20] 3158 2-8-7 0 JamieMoriarty(3) 3 —
(M J Wallace) *rrd stalls, sat down and uns rdr* **25/1**

1m 12.32s (0.42) **Going Correction** -0.075s/f (Stan) **12 Ran SP% 125.0**
Speed ratings (Par 92): **94,89,85,84,83 80,78,78,77,75 74,—**
toteswinger: 1&2 £5.90, 1&3 £11.40, 2&3 £80.20. CSF £20.86 TOTE £1.60: £1.10, £4.20, £7.10; EX 16.30 Trifecta £575.30 Part won. Pool £777.51 - 0.80 winning units. Place 6 £200.61, Place 5 £41.42..
Owner Kent Bloodstock **Bred** Mrs G P Booth And J Porteous **Trained** Hucking, Kent

FOCUS
An ordinary maiden.

NOTEBOOK
Deposer(IRE), who shaped with a good deal of promise to finish second over 5f on his recent Warwick debut, comes from a yard with a deal of juvenile talent and he was strong at the head of the market. Soon with the pace, he readily came clear from a furlong out and looks a useful horse in the making. There should be more to come and it will be interesting to see what mark he gets for nurseries. (op 8-11)
Shangani comes from a yard who can ready a newcomer and she certainly knew her job. Speed is clearly her thing and she stuck on well enough once headed, but was no match for the useful winner. A small maiden should come her way on this evidence, possibly in races restricted to her own sex. (op 16-1)
Jeremiah(IRE) shaped with only limited promise on his Windsor debut, but had clearly learned from that and this was a much improved performance. Official explanation: jockey said gelding hung left throughout (op 25-1)
Importer(IRE), nibbled at in the market beforehand, recovered from a sluggish start to show speed and he stuck on down the straight, but could not muster the speed. This was a promising start and he should come on for the experience. (op 12-1)
Golden Destiny(IRE) ran to a similar level as on her debut and is more of a nursery type. (op 5-1)
T/Plt: £143.90 to a £1 stake. Pool: £47,077.49. 238.72 winning tickets. T/Qpdt: £8.50 to a £1 stake. Pool: £3,852.10. 332.60 winning tickets. JN

3495 NEWMARKET (R-H)
Wednesday, July 9

OFFICIAL GOING: Good changing to good to soft after race 1 (1.30) and to soft after race 4 (3.10)
The quickest ground looked to be up the middle of the track.
Wind: Light, against Weather: Raining

3849 EUROPEAN BREEDERS' FUND FILLIES' H'CAP 7f
1:30 (1:33) (Class 2) (0-100,95) 3-Y-O
£31,155 (£9,330; £4,665; £2,335; £1,165; £585) Stalls Low

Form RPR

4-21 1 **Red Dune (IRE)**[33] 2800 3-8-11 **83** PhilipRobinson 6 98+
(M A Jarvis) *lw: mde all: racd keenly: rdn clr over 1f out: hung lft ins fnl f: styd on* **11/8**[1]

5622 2 ¾ **Just Like A Woman**[19] 3210 3-8-4 **76** oh1 HayleyTurner 7 86
(M L W Bell) *lw: hld up: hdwy u.p over 1f out: r.o* **12/1**

-000 3 1 ¾ **Insaaf**[21] 3124 3-9-1 **87** (v) MartinDwyer 5 92
(W J Haggas) *s.i.s: hld up: hdwy over 2f out: rdn over 1f out: styd on same pce ins fnl f: edgd rt nr fin* **14/1**

231- 4 2 ¼ **Sourire**[283] 5837 3-9-3 **89** SebSanders 8 88
(Sir Mark Prescott) *sn chsng wnr: rdn over 2f out: no ex fnl f* **11/1**[3]

4252 5 hd **Astrodonna**[12] 3442 3-8-4 **76** JimmyQuinn 13 74
(M H Tompkins) *lw: hld up: hdwy u.p over 1f out: edgd lft: styd on same pce* **12/1**

441 6 nse **Badweia (USA)**[39] 2620 3-8-6 **78** RHills 3 76
(J L Dunlop) *scope: chsd ldrs: rdn over 1f out: wknd ins fnl f* **6/1**[2]

3314 7 2 ¾ **Oceana Blue**[18] 3270 3-7-11 **76** oh5 (t) DavidProbert(7) 11 67
(A M Balding) *s.i.s: sn prom: rdn and wknd over 1f out* **12/1**

0-04 8 ¾ **Cat Whistle**[9] 3554 3-8-8 **80** PaulHanagan 4 69+
(R A Fahey) *plld hrd and prom: stdd and lost pl over 4f out: hmpd sn after: rdn over 1f out: no imp* **33/1**

116- 9 shd **Janina**[383] 2812 3-9-9 **95** MichaelHills 9 84
(B W Hills) *hld up: rdn over 1f out: n.d* **16/1**

0564 10 1 **Highland Daughter (IRE)**[13] 3420 3-9-4 **90** AdamKirby 1 76
(C G Cox) *chsd ldrs: rdn over 2f out: wknd over 1f out* **16/1**

0-06 **11** *1 3/4* **Gone Fast (USA)**[37] 2666 3-8-13 **90**............ AhmedAjtebi(5) 10 71
(D M Simcock) *hld up: rdn over 2f out: wknd over 1f out* **50/1**

00S0 **12** *1 3/4* **Tathkaar**[21] 3124 3-9-2 **88**............ KerrinMcEvoy 12 64
(C E Brittain) *lw: hld up in tch: rdn and wknd over 1f out* **18/1**

0-42 **13** *hd* **Filigree Lace (USA)**[15] 3338 3-8-4 **76** oh2............ WilliamBuick 2 52
(Sir Michael Stoute) *prom: rdn over 2f out: wknd sn after* **16/1**

1m 25.91s (0.21) **Going Correction** +0.125s/f (Good) **13** Ran SP% **122.3**
Speed ratings (Par 103): **103,102,100,97,97 97,94,93,93,92 90,88,87**
toteswinger: 1&2 £6.20, 1&3 £5.80, 2&3 £35.10. CSF £19.87 CT £179.89 TOTE £2.40: £1.50, £3.80, £3.60; EX 26.30 Trifecta £536.50 Part won. Pool £725.10 - 0.60 winning units..
Owner Sheikh Ahmed Al Maktoum **Bred** Ballymacoll Stud Farm Ltd **Trained** Newmarket, Suffolk

FOCUS
A valuable but somewhat one-sided fillies' handicap, with the short-priced winner dominating throughout and proving herself a class above.

NOTEBOOK
Red Dune(IRE), who won her maiden over a mile at Goodwood last time, looked potentially well handicapped off 83, and she proved very popular in the market. Soon well into her stride, she was very keen in front and it is to her credit that she had enough left in the tank to get home. That suggests that she is a very useful filly indeed, and it is no surprise that her connections are now planning to step her up in grade, with a return to Goodwood for the Group 3 Oak Tree Stakes on the cards. (op 6-4 tchd 5-4, 13-8 in places)
Just Like A Woman, who was 1lb out of the handicap, is building up a consistent profile. She finished well from off the pace but the winner was probably just idling and she is flattered to get so close to her. (op 16-1)
Insaaf, whose three previous runs this season did not look that good at first glance, had excuses on each start and this was an easier assignment than she has been set of late. Representing a stable in flying form, she came home well from off the pace and ran up to her recent best. (op 12-1 tchd 11-1)
Sourire, making a belated reappearance, chased the leader for most of the race. She was entitled to need this and should be dangerous in similar company next time. (op 14-1)
Astrodonna would have probably appreciated a stronger pace over this distance, as while she was staying on at the finish she was never getting there in time. (op 16-1)
Badweia(USA), a 6f soft-ground maiden winner, did not see this longer trip out on this stiff track. (op 11-2 tchd 13-2, 7-1 in a place)
Oceana Blue had a stiff task from 5lb out of the handicap and ran about as well as could be expected. (op 14-1)
Cat Whistle did not settle off the ordinary early gallop. (tchd 40-1)
Janina, is by a sprinter, out of a sprinter, and while any give in the ground was going to suit her, her stamina for this distance was always in question. Last seen finishing sixth in the Albany Stakes last year, she was entitled to need this seasonal reappearance. (tchd 18-1)

3850 TOTESWINGER STKS (HERITAGE H'CAP) 6f
2:00 (2:01) (Class 2) (0-105,104) 3-Y-O

£62,310 (£18,660; £9,330; £4,670; £2,330; £1,170) **Stalls** Low

Form RPR

-023 **1** **Spanish Bounty**[27] 2967 3-8-7 **90**............ TPQueally 13 98
(J G Portman) *lw: led 5f out: rdn over 1f out: edgd lft: r.o u.p* **33/1**

-205 **2** *3/4* **Spitfire**[25] 3047 3-8-12 **95**............ LDettori 9 101
(J R Jenkins) *hld up in tch: rdn over 1f out: r.o* **14/1**

-110 **3** *3/4* **Tawaash (USA)**[21] 3119 3-9-0 **97**............ RHills 7 101
(M A Jarvis) *chsd ldrs: rdn over 1f out: styd on* **8/1**[2]

6-6 **4** *hd* **Dohasa (IRE)**[25] 3047 3-9-7 **104**............ KJManning 16 107+
(G M Lyons, Ire) *hld up: edgd lft and r.o ins fnl f: nt rch ldrs* **25/1**

-624 **5** *nse* **Royal Intruder**[18] 3273 3-8-7 **90** ow2............ RyanMoore 10 93
(R Hannon) *lw: hld up: hdwy over 2f out: rdn over 1f out: r.o* **16/1**

-225 **6** *1 1/2* **Wigram's Turn (USA)**[56] 2104 3-8-3 **86**............(v[1]) WilliamBuick 12 84+
(A M Balding) *lw: mid-div: outpcd over 2f out: r.o ins fnl f* **20/1**

3121 **7** *shd* **Great Charm (IRE)**[4] 3723 3-8-6 **89** 6ex............ JamieSpencer 14 87
(M L W Bell) *lw: chsd ldrs: rdn and hung lft over 1f out: no ex ins fnl f* **7/1**[1]

1 **8** *nk* **Temple Of Thebes (IRE)**[45] 2428 3-8-5 **88**............ KerrinMcEvoy 18 85
(E A L Dunlop) *lw: hld up in tch: rdn over 1f out: styd on same pce fnl f* **9/1**[3]

-425 **9** *shd* **Cape Vale (IRE)**[46] 2405 3-8-4 **87**............ AdrianTNicholls 3 83
(D Nicholls) *prom: racd keenly: rdn over 2f out: no ex fnl f* **9/1**[3]

1110 **10** *1* **Thebes**[20] 3155 3-8-5 **88**............ GregFairley 6 81
(M Johnston) *chsd ldrs: rdn over 2f out: wknd ins fnl f* **12/1**

3114 **11** *nk* **Honey Monster (IRE)**[4] 3723 3-8-2 **85**............(p) ChrisCatlin 11 77
(A J McCabe) *lw: s.i.s: hdwy over 4f out: rdn over 1f out: wknd fnl f* **25/1**

0560 **12** *hd* **Jeninsky (USA)**[19] 3222 3-8-3 **86**............ JimmyQuinn 8 78
(P J McBride) *hld up: hdwy u.p 2f out: wknd fnl f* **50/1**

0314 **13** *hd* **Good Gorsoon (USA)**[25] 3047 3-8-8 **91**............ MichaelHills 17 82
(B W Hills) *hld up in tch: rdn over 1f out: wkng whn n.m.r ins fnl f* **12/1**

1210 **14** *1* **Fervent Prince**[20] 3155 3-8-7 **90**............ SteveDrowne 20 78
(H Morrison) *lw: hld up: rdn over 2f out: nvr trbld ldrs* **20/1**

0020 **15** *nk* **Carleton**[25] 3047 3-8-9 **92**............ StephenDonohoe 1 79
(W J Musson) *sn bhd: styd on ins fnl f: nvr nrr* **12/1**

1-20 **16** *1* **Kaldoun Kingdom (IRE)**[56] 2104 3-8-6 **89**............ PaulHanagan 2 73
(R A Fahey) *chsd ldrs: rdn over 2f out: wknd fnl f* **14/1**

0162 **17** *4* **Victorian Bounty**[25] 3047 3-8-11 **94**............ MickyFenton 4 65
(Stef Liddiard) *led 1f: remained handy tl rdn and wknd over 1f out* **16/1**

-602 **18** *3 1/2* **Sophie's Girl**[12] 3460 3-8-9 **92**............ AlanMunro 5 52
(B J Meehan) *hld up in tch: rdn over 2f out: sn wknd* **28/1**

5-U0 **19** *4* **Lytton**[25] 3047 3-8-10 **93**............ SebSanders 15 40
(W R Swinburn) *s.i.s: hld up: rdn over 2f out: sn wknd* **33/1**

0421 **20** *2 3/4* **Wise Melody**[21] 3141 3-8-4 **87**............ LiamJones 19 25
(W J Haggas) *chsd ldrs over 4f* **12/1**

1m 12.52s (0.02) **Going Correction** +0.175s/f (Good) **20** Ran SP% **128.0**
Speed ratings (Par 106): **106,105,104,103,103 101,101,101,101,99 99,99,98,97,97 95,90,85,80,76**
toteswinger: 1&2 £46.10, 1&3 £66.90, 2&3 £32.80. CSF £420.54 CT £4057.60 TOTE £37.40: £6.80, £3.00, £2.40, £5.70; EX 505.60 TRIFECTA Not won..
Owner The Farleigh Court Racing Partnership **Bred** Farleigh Court Racing Partnership **Trained** Compton, Berks
■ Stewards' Enquiry : Ryan Moore caution: careless riding

FOCUS
Persistent rain led to the official going being changed to good to soft before this race. A strong and competitive handicap and the action developed up the centre of the track, with those racing on the flanks seemingly at a bit of disadvantage. It also appeared to be an advantage to race prominently.

NOTEBOOK
Spanish Bounty, who does not mind a bit of cut in the ground, was up there from the start and, coming up the centre of the track, which appeared to be the place to be, was always holding off his challengers up the hill. He was probably quite strongly favoured by where he raced, but there can be no doubting that he had shaped well in his previous two starts and was underestimated by the market simply because he was from a small stable.
Spitfire, another who benefited from racing up the centre of the track, was suited by the stiff finish and ran on well once he hit the rising ground. He had looked fairly exposed beforehand and the difference in his price and the winner's can be explained by the presence of Dettori in the saddle. (op 16-1)
Tawaash(USA), who finished in midfield in the Jersey Stakes, had no easy task off 97 but he is lightly raced and, racing up the centre of the track, which appeared to be favoured, put his 7f stamina to good use in the closing stages. (op 9-1 tchd 10-1)
Dohasa(IRE), one place behind Spitfire at York last time, had a job on under top weight and ran respectably in the circumstances. He finished really well, and towards the stands' side too, which was not really the place to be. (op 33-1)
Royal Intruder appreciated the return to 6f and coped with the softer ground well. His rider put up 2lb overweight, which makes his performance even more creditable. (op 25-1)
Wigram's Turn(USA), visored for the first time on this drop back to 6f, raced up the centre but only got going once he hit the rising ground. He found this trip on the short side. (op 25-1)
Great Charm(IRE), carrying a 6lb penalty for his win at Haydock four days earlier, could have done with the rain starting earlier, but all in all he ran a satisfactory race. (tchd 15-2 and 8-1 in a place)
Temple Of Thebes(IRE) raced up the stands' side, which was not really the place to be. A lightly raced filly, she was perhaps not seen at her best here, but she is capable of further improvement. (op 8-1)
Cape Vale(IRE) was also at a disadvantage racing towards the far side as the best ground appeared more towards the centre. (op 12-1)
Thebes was a blatant non-stayer in the Britannia last time and was expected to appreciate the drop back to 6f, especially with his stable returning to form. He showed good pace, but was drawn low and raced towards the far side while the best ground was up the centre. (tchd 11-1)
Honey Monster(IRE), wearing cheekpieces for the first time, did not seem to have too many excuses. (op 33-1)
Good Gorsoon(USA) did not get home. This trip on easy ground on this stiff track just stretched his stamina.
Kaldoun Kingdom(IRE) was not well drawn as things turned out. (op 12-1)
Wise Melody, 9lb higher than when bolting up at Ripon last time, saw the ground go against her, and to cap it all she was drawn to race towards the stands' side while the best ground was up the centre. (op 9-1)

3851 IRISH THOROUGHBRED MARKETING CHERRY HINTON STKS (GROUP 2) (FILLIES) 6f
2:35 (2:36) (Class 1) 2-Y-O

£45,416 (£17,216; £8,616; £4,296; £2,152; £1,080) **Stalls** Low

Form RPR

10 **1** **Please Sing**[19] 3192 2-8-12 0............ EdwardCreighton 1 98+
(M R Channon) *chsd ldrs: lost pl over 3f out: sn outpcd: hdwy over 1f out: r.o to ld wl ins fnl f* **14/1**

210 **2** *3/4* **Art Princess (USA)**[19] 3192 2-8-12 0............ MichaelHills 7 96
(B W Hills) *led: rdn over 1f out: hdd wl ins fnl f* **10/1**

51 **3** *1* **Ahla Wasahl**[14] 3373 2-8-12 0............ AhmedAjtebi 4 93
(D M Simcock) *trckd ldr: racd keenly: rdn over 1f out: styd on same pce ins fnl f* **25/1**

0 **4** *3/4* **Heart Shaped (USA)**[21] 3123 2-8-12 0............ RyanMoore 8 91
(A P O'Brien, Ire) *lw: wnt rt s: sn prom: chsd ldr over 3f out: rdn over 1f out: edgd rt and no ex ins fnl f* **2/1**[1]

14 **5** *nk* **Lucky Leigh**[21] 3123 2-8-12 0............ DarryllHolland 6 90
(M R Channon) *stdd s: hld up: hdwy over 2f out: rdn over 1f out: hmpd ins fnl f: styd on* **3/1**[2]

51 **6** *1/2* **Sea Of Leaves (USA)**[14] 3378 2-8-12 0............(t) JimmyFortune 3 88
(J H M Gosden) *w'like: leggy: hld up: plld hrd: rdn over 2f out: r.o ins fnl f: nvr nrr* **13/2**

3331 **7** *hd* **Kerrys Requiem (IRE)**[10] 3528 2-8-12 0............ TPO'Shea 2 88
(M R Channon) *hld up: plld hrd: rdn over 2f out: nt much ins fnl f: nvr trbld ldrs* **20/1**

21 **8** *1 1/2* **Mrs Kipling (IRE)**[11] 3485 2-8-12 0............ LDettori 5 83
(S A Callaghan) *trckd ldrs: racd keenly: rdn over 1f out: hung rt and wknd ins fnl f* **5/1**[3]

1m 14.54s (2.04) **Going Correction** +0.175s/f (Good) **8** Ran SP% **112.7**
Speed ratings (Par 103): **93,92,90,89,89 88,88,86**
toteswinger: 1&2 £15.40, 1&3 £24.70, 2&3 £23.30. CSF £138.48 TOTE £17.90: £3.50, £2.40, £4.90; EX 128.10 Trifecta £775.50 Part won. Pool £1,048.05 - 0.10 winning units..
Owner Mrs Ann C Black **Bred** Mrs R D Peacock **Trained** West Ilsley, Berks

FOCUS
A weak renewal of this Group 2 event and it has been rated the equal worst of the last decade. They went steady early, with a few failing to settle.

NOTEBOOK
Please Sing had excuses when well beaten in the Albany, where she was a well-backed second favourite, but that had seemingly been forgotten by most as she was pretty friendless for this weaker event. She found a good turn of foot once switched and hitting the rising ground, and was well on top at the finish. Her trainer thinks she will get 7f in time, but whether she is up to taking on the best of her generation remains to be seen. The Lowther is the next logical step. Official explanation: trainer had no explanation for the improved form shown (tchd 12-1 and 16-1)
Art Princess(USA), seventh in the Albany, enjoyed the run of the race next to the far-side rail. She set only an ordinary gallop and was just unable to hold off the winner when she quickened up on hitting the rising ground. It was a good effort, but she is probably flattered by the bare form. (op 12-1)
Ahla Wasahl, clear-cut winner of an ordinary Kempton maiden last time out, was another who was well placed, chasing the leader next to the far rail. She had her chance once switched but was one-paced in the closing stages. The Princess Margaret Stakes at Ascot on King George day was apparently mentioned as her next possible target. (tchd 28-1)
Heart Shaped(USA), down the field in the Queen Mary, would not really have appreciated the softish ground as her pedigree suggests she should be happiest on a sound surface. She did not really pick up under pressure. (op 13-8 tchd 6-4)
Lucky Leigh, fourth in the Queen Mary, raced towards the outside of the pack. She took a while to pick up and was a bit disappointing, but the easier ground may not have suited her. (op 10-3 tchd 7-2)
Sea Of Leaves(USA) was running on at the finish, having failed to settle early and been caught out when the sprint for home began. She will do better in a stronger-run race, and over 7f. Official explanation: jockey said filly ran too free (op 8-1)
Kerrys Requiem(IRE) did not settle off the steady early pace, and she was hampered a furlong out, which did not help her cause, but she is probably not up to this class anyway. (op 16-1)
Mrs Kipling(IRE), by a sire whose progeny tend to prefer a fast surface, did not get home after racing keenly early. Official explanation: jockey said filly hung right (op 6-1)

3852 UAE HYDRA PROPERTIES FALMOUTH STKS (GROUP 1) (F&M) 1m
3:10 (3:13) (Class 1) 3-Y-O+

£113,540 (£43,040; £21,540; £10,740; £5,380; £2,700) **Stalls** Low

Form RPR

0506 **1** **Nahoodh (IRE)**[19] 3194 3-8-10 **112**............ LDettori 9 116
(M Johnston) *hld up: hdwy over 1f out: rdn to ld and hung lft wl ins fnl f: r.o* **10/1**

-142 **2** *1 ¾* **Infallible**[19] 3194 3-8-10 110........ JimmyFortune 1 112
(J H M Gosden) *lw: hld up in tch: led over 2f out: rdn: hdd and hung rt wl ins fnl f* **7/2**[2]

-112 **3** *¾* **Heaven Sent**[21] 3120 5-9-5 111........ RyanMoore 7 113+
(Sir Michael Stoute) *hld up: hdwy wl over 1f out: sn hrd rdn: styng on same pce whn hmpd wl ins fnl f* **3/1**[1]

660 **4** *3 ½* **Seachange (NZ)**[18] 3247 6-9-5 0........ TedDurcan 11 104
(G Sanders, New Zealand) *lw: trckd ldrs: rdn over 1f out: wknd ins fnl f* **7/1**

3-1 **5** *1 ¼* **Briseida**[38] 2655 3-8-10 0........ AStarke 2 99
(P Schiergen, Germany) *hld up: hdwy over 2f out: sn rdn: wknd fnl f* **8/1**

0054 **6** *shd* **Majestic Roi (USA)**[21] 3120 4-9-5 112........ DarryllHolland 5 101
(M R Channon) *lw: hld up: rdn over 1f out: nvr trbld ldrs* **16/1**

5230 **7** *½* **Finsceal Beo (IRE)**[11] 3511 4-9-5 0........(t) KJManning 8 100
(J S Bolger, Ire) *s.s: hdwy over 2f out: sn ev ch: rdn over 1f out: wknd ins fnl f* **5/1**[3]

-211 **8** *9* **Kasumi**[30] 2890 5-9-5 102........ TravisBlock 6 79
(H Morrison) *lw: chsd ldrs tl rdn and wknd wl over 1f out* **25/1**

-221 **9** *3 ½* **Lady Gloria**[32] 2827 4-9-5 106........ TPQueally 3 71
(J G Given) *led over 5f: wknd over 1f out* **12/1**

1-03 **10** *21* **Hip**[18] 3272 3-8-10 83........ RHills 12 21
(E A L Dunlop) *chsd ldrs: rdn over 2f out: sn wknd* **100/1**

0130 **11** *16* **Love Of Dubai (USA)**[19] 3194 3-8-10 106........(p) SebSanders 10 —
(C E Brittain) *prom 6f* **66/1**

1m 38.6s (-1.40) **Going Correction** +0.175s/f (Good) 11 Ran SP% **116.5**
WFA 3 from 4yo+ 9lb
Speed ratings (Par 117): **114,112,111,108,106 106,106,97,93,72 56**
toteswinger: 1&2 £7.50, 1&3 £7.80, 2&3 £2.50. CSF £44.23 TOTE £11.10: £3.30, £1.60, £1.20; EX 56.30 Trifecta £170.00 Pool £4,710.69 - 20.50 winning units..
Owner Sheikh Hamdan Bin Mohammed Al Maktoum **Bred** Petra Bloodstock Agency Ltd **Trained** Middleham Moor, N Yorks

FOCUS
By no means a strong Falmouth Stakes following the withdrawal of forecast favourite Darjina, but they went a good pace in the conditions, and the winning time was 3.05 seconds quicker than the closing handicap won by the 83-rated Habshan. The winner is rated 3lb above her Guineas mark and the form looks pretty solid. They raced up the middle of the track, avoiding both rails.

NOTEBOOK
Nahoodh(IRE) had proved disappointing in both the Irish Guineas and the Coronation Stakes (first start since leaving Mick Channon) since looking unlucky in the English Guineas at Newmarket, and she was well beaten on her only previous start on soft ground in the Fred Darling, so it was hard to make a convincing case for her beforehand but, full credit to her new trainer, she returned to her best in no uncertain terms. She was tried from the front on her debut for the Johnston team at Ascot, but proved well suited by the return to hold-up tactics and travelled strongly out the back. She moved into contention going well inside the final two furlongs and picked up nicely in the conditions to quickly leave the Cheveley Park pair behind inside the final furlong, although she was inclined to edge to left, coming across Heaven Sent close home. She is clearly high class on her day and races like the Matron Stakes and Sun Chariot are obvious targets, but there is also the Sussex Stakes at the end of the month if her connections are willing to test her against the colts. (op 8-1)
Infallible was faced with the softest ground she had encountered to date and, a daughter of Pivotal, it promised to suit much better than when a fine second under quick conditions in the Coronation Stakes on her previous start. The worry was whether she would see out this much stiffer 1m and, as it turned out, she found one too strong, a rival who she had beaten in both the Guineas and at Ascot. She is likely to remain vulnerable over this trip in top company and she looks worth a try over 6f or 7f. The Prix Maurice de Gheest over an extended 6f at Deauville in August could be a suitable target if she kept to Group 1 company, although that would be against the colts. (tchd 3-1, 4-1 in places)
Heaven Sent, runner-up in an ordinary renewal of the Group 2 Windsor Forest Stakes at Royal Ascot on her previous start, ran her race and looks the best guide to the strength of the form, although she was hampered close home and might have finished half a length closer. She is likely to continue to be campaigned in similar events. (op 11-4 tchd 5-2)
Seachange(NZ), a seven-time Group 1 winner in New Zealand, was stepping back up in trip after struggling from a poor draw over 6f in the Golden Jubilee, but she again ran below her best. She had plenty of easy-ground form to her name in her homeland, but soft ground in New Zealand is probably not as testing as it can be in this country and these conditions looked to find her out. She travelled strongly, but failed to pick up when asked. She has now been retired. (op 11-1)
Briseida, winner of the German 1000 Guineas on her previous start, had something to find in this company and found a few too good. (tchd 15-2)
Majestic Roi(USA) was below the pick of her form and probably wants better ground. (op 14-1 tchd 18-1, 20-1 in a place)
Finsceal Beo(IRE), turned out less than two weeks after failing to beat a rival over 1m2f in the Pretty Polly, had a tongue-tie on for the first time and she was well backed beforehand, but soft ground is not for her. She was slowly away, but recovered to have her chance before weakening. (op 13-2 tchd 8-1)
Kasumi has progressed nicely this season, winning a Listed race at Pontefract on her latest start, but had plenty to find at this level and paid for chasing a strong pace.
Lady Gloria, a Group 3 winner at Epsom on her previous start, looked to go off too quickly in the conditions.
Hip was entered as a pacemaker but never got to the front.

3853 STRUTT & PARKER E B F MAIDEN STKS 7f
3:45 (3:46) (Class 2) 2-Y-O **£9,714** (£2,890; £1,444; £360; £360) **Stalls** Low

Form RPR

4 **1** **Soul City (IRE)**[30] 2893 2-9-3 0........ JimmyFortune 7 80+
(R Hannon) *w'like: strong: swtg: mde virtually all: rdn over 1f out: hung lft ins fnl f: r.o u.p* **7/2**[1]

2 *nk* **Swindler (IRE)** 2-9-3 0........ WilliamBuick 11 79+
(A M Balding) *w'like: scope: tall: chsd ldrs: rdn over 1f out: edgd lft: r.o* **5/1**[3]

3 *hd* **Whispering Angel** 2-9-3 0........ AlanMunro 8 79+
(B J Meehan) *w'like: leggy: hld up in tch: rdn over 1f out: edgd lft: r.o* **8/1**

4 *½* **Derbaas (USA)** 2-9-3 0........ MartinDwyer 1 78+
(E A L Dunlop) *strong: bit bkwd: swtg: hld up: hdwy over 1f out: n.m.r ins fnl f: r.o* **33/1**

4 *dht* **Holyrood** 2-9-3 0........ RyanMoore 5 80+
(Sir Michael Stoute) *w'like: lengthy: mid-div: sn pushed along: outpcd 2f out: r.o ins fnl f* **11/1**

6 *shd* **Combat Zone (IRE)** 2-9-3 0........ LDettori 10 77+
(Saeed Bin Suroor) *w'like: leggy: hld up: hdwy u.p over 1f out: edgd lft: r.o* **11/2**

7 *½* **Cloudy Start** 2-9-3 0........ TedDurcan 4 76+
(H R A Cecil) *unf: scope: trckd ldrs: plld hrd: rdn and hung lft over 1f out: no ex towards fin* **12/1**

8 *nse* **Citizenship** 2-9-3 0........ JimCrowley 9 76+
(Pat Eddery) *strong: bit bkwd: hld up: r.o ins fnl f: nvr nrr* **22/1**

9 *¾* **Makhaaleb (IRE)** 2-9-3 0........ RHills 6 74+
(B W Hills) *w'like: scope: hmpd s: sn prom: chsd wnr 4f out: rdn and ev ch over 1f out: n.m.r ins fnl f: no ex* **9/2**[2]

10 *1 ¾* **Millharbour (IRE)** 2-9-3 0........ MichaelHills 2 70+
(B W Hills) *lw: s.i.s: hld up: swtchd lft over 1f out: n.d* **20/1**

0 **11** *2* **Topolski (IRE)**[32] 2845 2-9-3 0........ GregFairley 3 65
(M Johnston) *unf: chsd wnr 4f: rdn over 2f out: wknd over 1f out* **20/1**

1m 29.77s (4.07) **Going Correction** +0.35s/f (Good) 11 Ran SP% **116.4**
Speed ratings (Par 100): **90,89,89,88,88 88,88,88,87,85 82**
toteswinger: 1&2 £4.40, 1&3 £7.80, 2&3 £9.50. CSF £19.25 TOTE £4.00: £1.80, £2.40, £2.90; EX 19.80.
Owner Patrick J Fahey **Bred** Peter Thome **Trained** East Everleigh, Wilts

FOCUS
Traditionally a very good maiden. They finished in a heap and the bare form needs treating with some caution, but the race should still produce a few nice winners with many of these capable of improving on the bare form. The main action took place up the middle of the track.

NOTEBOOK
Soul City(IRE), fourth behind a potentially very useful Henry Candy two-year-old on his debut over 6f on quick ground at Windsor, improved on that form, putting his experience to good use to come out on top in a bunch finish. Being a son of Elusive City the soft ground had to be a slight concern, but he handled the conditions well and stayed on strongly after setting a modest gallop. His connections think there will be more improvement to come. (op 9-2 tchd 10-3)
Swindler(IRE) ◆, a 65,000gns son of Sinndar and a half-brother to a number of middle-distance three-year-old winners, had been well backed ahead of his intended debut in the Listed Chesham Stakes at Royal Ascot, but was withdrawn after being unruly at the start. He lined up here rather than in the Group 2 Superlative Stakes later in the week and very nearly made a winning debut. There should be improvement to come and this well-regarded type looks very useful in the making. (op 10-3)
Whispering Angel ◆, a 95,000euros son of Hawk Wing, half-brother to useful 1m winner Momix, out of a winner at around 1m in France, has been given a National Stakes entry and made a very pleasing debut. Settled off the leaders, he stayed on nicely and fared best of those held up. He can do better in a stronger-run race and could be very good. (op 5-1 tchd 9-1)
Derbaas(USA) ◆, a son of Seeking The Gold and a half-brother to 1m winner Jaleela, out of a sprint winner in the US, was his owner's second string and was friendless in the market, but he shaped with plenty of encouragement. Staying on nicely close home, he very much displayed a quick-ground action and should improve for a switch to a better surface. (tchd 40-1)
Holyrood ◆, a son of Falbrav and a half-brother to among others useful triple 7f-1m2f winner Portal, out of a lightly raced 1m juvenile winner, showed his inexperience beforehand, initially having to be led down by his trainer. In the race itself he was another doing some good late work and there should be much more to come. (tchd 40-1)
Combat Zone(IRE) ◆, a 280,000euros son of Refuse To Bend, is a half-brother to quite useful 7f juvenile Zut Alors out of a useful triple 6f-1m winner at two in France. He was unsuited by the steady pace and could not get on terms with the principals. He is another who should come on a bundle. (op 9-2)
Cloudy Start ◆, by Oasis Dream and a half-brother among others to useful dual 7f-1m3f winner Valentine Girl, who was also very smart at up to 1m6f, is out of a fairly useful 1m4f performer at three in France. He looks better than he was able to show, for he was too keen for his own good off the unsatisfactory early gallop and ended up racing against the unfavoured far rail in the closing stages. Much better can be expected next time.
Citizenship is by Beat Hollow and a brother to Triple Beat, who was placed over 7f-1m in France, as well as a half-brother to 7f juvenile winner Trilogy, who was later a 1m winner in the US. He ran green early and had to be niggled, but he stayed on encouragingly when the race was as good as over. (op 20-1 tchd 25-1)
Makhaaleb(IRE), a 190,000gns son of Haafhd, half-brother to 1m winner Seleet, out of a useful dual 6f winner at three, was soon close up but found disappointingly little at the business end. (op 8-1)

3854 XPLOR MAIDEN STKS 1m 2f
4:20 (4:21) (Class 3) 3-Y-O **£9,714** (£2,890; £1,444; £721) **Stalls** Centre

Form RPR

3 **1** **Meydan City (USA)**[18] 3275 3-9-3 0........ LDettori 6 92+
(Saeed Bin Suroor) *hld up: hdwy over 2f out: led 1f out: r.o: edgd lft and eased towards fin* **7/1**

0-3 **2** *¾* **Woodcutter (IRE)**[23] 3094 3-9-3 0........ JimmyFortune 9 90
(J H M Gosden) *led 2f: chsd ldr tl led 1/2-way: rdn and hdd 1f out: styd on* **8/1**

4 **3** *2 ¾* **King O'The Gypsies (IRE)**[84] 1398 3-9-3 0........ SteveDrowne 8 84
(R Charlton) *lw: chsd ldrs: outpcd over 1f out: styd on ins fnl f* **2/1**[1]

0 **4** *¾* **Finney Hill**[79] 1525 3-8-12 0........ DaneO'Neill 7 78
(H Candy) *w'like: neat: hld up: hdwy over 3f out: rdn over 1f out: no ex ins fnl f* **16/1**

522 **5** *3 ¾* **Eqbaal**[34] 2763 3-9-3 86........ RHills 3 75
(J L Dunlop) *prom: rdn over 1f out: sn wknd* **3/1**[2]

3 **6** *1 ½* **Hall Hee (IRE)**[26] 2994 3-8-12 0........ MartinDwyer 4 67
(M P Tregoning) *chsd ldrs: rdn and ev ch over 1f out: wknd ins fnl f* **9/2**[3]

4-3 **7** *8* **Wusuul**[14] 3379 3-8-12 0........ RyanMoore 5 51
(C E Brittain) *lw: half-rrd s: hld up: rdn over 2f out: sn wknd* **14/1**

20 **8** *7* **Applaude**[6] 3629 3-9-3 0........ KerrinMcEvoy 1 42
(G A Swinbank) *chsd ldr tl led 8f out: hdd 1/2-way: rdn and wknd over 2f out* **22/1**

4 **9** *8* **Pebble Rock (IRE)**[19] 3223 3-9-3 0........(t) TPQueally 2 26
(J R Jenkins) *hung lft s: hdwy to latch on to the rest over 8f out: rdn over 3f out: hung lft and wknd over 2f out* **66/1**

2m 8.99s (3.49) **Going Correction** +0.35s/f (Good) 9 Ran SP% **118.5**
Speed ratings (Par 104): **100,99,97,96,93 92,86,80,74**
toteswinger: 1&2 £5.80, 1&3 £3.80, 2&3 £5.00. CSF £63.20 TOTE £7.00: £1.80, £2.30, £1.40; EX 48.20.
Owner Godolphin **Bred** Jayeff 'B' Stables **Trained** Newmarket, Suffolk

FOCUS
A decent three-year-old maiden in which the first two pulled clear. The form should work out. They raced towards the near-side rail, but the winner made his move out wide, more towards the middle.

NOTEBOOK
Meydan City(USA) ◆, who looked a bit weak when failing to justify favouritism on his belated debut at this track 18 days previously, showed his true colours with that experience under his belt and did the job tidily. The longer distance no doubt helped his cause and, while he was at an advantage in being kept to the middle of the track in the final two furlongs, he does rate a worthy winner. Clearly he has an awfully long way to go if he is ever to justify his sky-high yearling price, but this late-maturing colt is evidently now coming good and promises to be better suited by a step up to 1m4f in due course. (op 5-1)
Woodcutter(IRE) ◆, who ran green on his reappearance at Windsor, just hit a flat spot at a crucial stage before coming right back at the winner near the finish. He was nicely clear of the remainder and looks as though he is ready to tackle a stiffer test now. He should improve again for this experience and also now has the option of handicaps, but his prospective mark in that sphere will be lofty enough. (tchd 15-2)

The Form Book, Raceform Ltd, Compton, RG20 6NL

King O'The Gypsies(IRE) ◆, who stayed on takingly over this trip on his debut at the Craven meeting back in April, proved popular in the betting ring for this return from nearly three months off. He again got going too late in the day, however, and was probably not helped by being kept towards the stands' side with his challenge on this easing ground. No doubt he has a future, but he looks to be crying out for a longer trip, or a more positive ride over this distance. (op 5-2)
Finney Hill, ninth on debut at Windsor in April, did not go unbacked for this step up in trip and showed improved form without seriously threatening. This looks her ideal trip at present and she ought to progress again for the run. (op 20-1)
Eqbaal set the standard with an official rating of 86, but he ran below his previous level and has to rate disappointing. He is better than he showed, but now has something to prove. Official explanation: trainer had no explanation for the poor form shown
Hall Hee(IRE) had every chance nearing the final furlong, but eventually dropped right out and failed to really confirm the promise of her debut third at Goodwood. (op 5-1 tchd 6-1)
Pebble Rock(IRE) Official explanation: jockey said gelding hung both ways throughout

3855 KATHY DENNISON BIRTHDAY H'CAP — 1m

4:55 (4:55) (Class 3) (0-90,88) 3-Y-0+ **£9,714** (£2,890; £1,444; £721) **Stalls** Low

Form — RPR

-464 **1** **Habshan (USA)**[24] 3054 8-9-10 **83** GeorgeBaker 12 — 90
(C F Wall) *hld up: hdwy u.p over 1f out: styd on to ld wl ins fnl f* **8/1**

4332 **2** 1 1/4 **Den's Gift (IRE)**[20] 3167 4-9-8 **81** (b) AdamKirby 9 — 85
(C G Cox) *led: rdn over 1f out: hdd wl ins fnl f* **7/1**[3]

3542 **3** 3/4 **Billy Dane (IRE)**[18] 3278 4-9-6 **79** (p) PaulHanagan 11 — 81
(R A Fahey) *chsd ldr: rdn and hung lft fr over 2f out: styd on* **9/1**

0420 **4** hd **Giant Love (USA)**[14] 3366 3-8-11 **79** GregFairley 2 — 79
(M Johnston) *hld up: rdn over 1f out: r.o ins fnl f: nt rch ldrs* **14/1**

0-00 **5** 3/4 **Heroes**[70] 1719 4-9-9 **82** AlanMunro 10 — 82
(C F Wall) *swtg: s.s: sn prom: racd keenly: rdn over 2f out: styd on same pce fnl f* **6/1**[2]

1-41 **6** 1 **Kings Point (IRE)**[9] 3548 7-9-10 **88** 6ex AhmedAjtebi(5) 14 — 86
(D Nicholls) *lw: chsd ldrs: rdn over 1f out: no ex ins fnl f* **6/1**[2]

0102 **7** 1/2 **Sintenis Mac (GER)**[11] 3501 5-8-2 **68** oh7 (b) RossAtkinson(7) 6 — 65
(P J O'Gorman) *s.s: hld up: hdwy over 1f out: styd on same pce fnl f* **14/1**

550- **8** 1 3/4 **Marajaa (IRE)**[305] 5221 6-9-10 **83** StephenDonohoe 17 — 76
(W J Musson) *hld up: hdwy over 1f out: wknd ins fnl f* **20/1**

0-55 **9** 1 1/4 **Tender The Great (IRE)**[154] 456 5-9-6 **79** DarryllHolland 3 — 69
(V Smith) *hld up: hung lft and hdwy 2f out: wknd ins fnl f* **25/1**

0412 **10** nse **Goodbye Mr Bond**[18] 3261 8-9-13 **86** JimmyQuinn 1 — 76
(E J Alston) *hld up: rdn and wknd over 1f out* **4/1**[1]

-014 **11** 3 3/4 **Burnbrake**[25] 3039 3-8-4 **72** MartinDwyer 8 — 51
(J A R Toller) *chsd ldrs: rdn over 2f out: hung lft and wknd over 1f out* **15/2**

1m 41.65s (1.65) **Going Correction** +0.35s/f (Good)
WFA 3 from 4yo+ 9lb **11** Ran SP% **115.9**
Speed ratings (Par 107): **105,103,103,102,102 101,100,98,97,97 93**
toteswinger: 1&2 £10.50, 1&3 £9.90, 2&3 £8.00. CSF £62.09 CT £517.24 TOTE £9.30: £2.80, £2.70, £3.60; EX 72.10 Place 6 £567.98, Place 5 £314.97..
Owner Alan & Jill Smith **Bred** Darley Stud Management, L L C **Trained** Newmarket, Suffolk

FOCUS

Just an ordinary handicap for the grade, with six non-runners owing to the ground. The winning time was 3.05 seconds slower than the Falmouth Stakes. Once again the main action took place up the middle.

NOTEBOOK

Habshan(USA) had excuses for his two defeats since running fourth behind Bankable on soft ground at Ascot on his reappearance, but he made no mistake this time. He travelled strongly, well off the pace early on, but needed strong driving to go through with his effort in the closing stages and a rise in the weights in tougher company should be enough to stop him following up. (tchd 9-1)
Den's Gift(IRE) was allowed his own way in front and kept on to the line, but he found one too good. (op 8-1 tchd 9-1)
Billy Dane(IRE), only 1lb higher than when winning on quick ground at Redcar, seemed to handle the very different ground and looked to run his race. (op 8-1)
Giant Love(USA) ◆ returned to form with a good effort on ground softer than ideal. He can build on this back on better ground.
Heroes, a stablemate of the winner, had conditions to suit and ran his best race since joining the Chris Wall yard. (op 8-1)
Kings Point(IRE) probably found the ground softer than ideal and could not defy a penalty for his recent Musselburgh success. (op 5-1 tchd 7-2)
Sintenis Mac(GER) ran with credit from 7lb out of the handicap and might be of interest if turned out of his correct mark before he is reassessed, but this was an ordinary race for the level. (op 16-1)
Goodbye Mr Bond came into this in good form and would not have minded the ground, but he failed to run his race. Official explanation: jockey said gelding was unsuited by the soft ground (op 7-2)
T/Jkpt: Not won. T/Plt: £721.10 to a £1 stake. Pool: £189,730.61. 192.06 winning tickets. T/Qpdt: £64.00 to a £1 stake. Pool: £9,310.90. 107.50 winning tickets. CR

3856 - 3860a (Foreign Racing) - See Raceform Interactive

3385 NAAS (L-H)

Wednesday, July 9

OFFICIAL GOING: Yielding

3861a THOROUGHBRED COUNTY MAIDEN — 1m 2f

8:30 (8:30) 3-Y-0+ **£5,588** (£1,302; £574; £331)

RPR

1 **Zulu Chief (USA)**[83] 1418 3-9-5 JMurtagh 13 — 106+
(A P O'Brien, Ire) *trckd ldrs: 4th 1/2-way: hdwy to 2nd over 2f out: led over 1 1/2f out: sn clr: v easily* **1/2**[1]

2 20 **Truxton King (IRE)** 3-9-0 PTownend(5) 14 — 54
(W P Mullins, Ire) *mid-div: hdwy to 6th 1/2-way: 5th 4f out: rdn into 3rd 2f out: 2nd over 1f out: no ch w wnr* **10/1**[3]

3 1 **Jettymarc (IRE)**[12] 3469 3-9-5 PShanahan 9 — 50
(Tracey Collins, Ire) *chsd ldrs early: lost pl bef 1/2-way: 8th 4f out: rdn over 2f out: styd on to mod 5th 1f out: kpt on same pce* **20/1**

4 1 3/4 **Nanuka (IRE)**[24] 3071 3-9-0 MCHussey 1 — 42
(T Stack, Ire) *mid-div: hdwy to mod 9th over 2f out: 6th 1f out: kpt on same pce* **16/1**

5 hd **Gunavira (IRE)**[11] 3514 3-9-5 (b[1]) PJSmullen 15 — 46
(D K Weld, Ire) *chsd ldrs: 2nd 1/2-way: rdn ent st: no ex in 4th over 2f out: kpt on one pce* **5/1**[2]

6 7 **Vignelaure Rose (IRE)**[14] 3390 3-9-0 FMBerry 10 — 27
(Charles O'Brien, Ire) *led: clr bef 1/2-way: reduced advantage over 2f out: hdd over 1 1/2f out: no ex* **25/1**

7 nk **Mel Del (IRE)** 3-9-0 RPCleary 6 — 27
(L Byrne, Ire) *in rr of mid-div: sme hdwy in 10th 2f out: kpt on one pce* **33/1**

8 1 1/4 **Belleshee Banshee (IRE)** 3-8-9 OCasey(5) 4 — 24
(Peter Casey, Ire) *towards rr: sme late hdwy fr under 2f out* **20/1**

9 1/2 **Royal Entourage**[286] 5759 3-9-5 KLatham 2 — 28
(G M Lyons, Ire) *chsd ldrs: 5th 1/2-way: rdn in mod 7th ent st: no ex and kpt on one pce* **16/1**

10 3 **Sand Rose (IRE)**[23] 3098 3-9-0 WJSupple 16 — 17
(S Slevin, Ire) *chsd ldrs: 4th 1/2-way: rdn in 7th 4f out: sn no ex and wknd* **50/1**

11 2 **Ballyvourney (IRE)**[254] 6550 3-9-5 NGMcCullagh 3 — 18
(M Halford, Ire) *mid-div: mod 7th 1/2-way: sn rdn and no ex* **25/1**

12 hd **Churchtown Star (IRE)**[11] 3514 4-9-13 KTColeman(3) 5 — 18
(P Budds, Ire) *chsd ldrs: 3rd 1/2-way: rdn in 5th ent st: wknd fr 2f out* **66/1**

13 3 **Karnak (IRE)**[13] 3429 6-9-9 CO'Farrell(7) 11 — 12
(J H Scott, Ire) *a towards rr* **25/1**

14 nk **Skiathos Queen (IRE)** 3-9-0 FFDaSilva 8 — 6
(William J Fitzpatrick, Ire) *a towards rr* **33/1**

15 1 1/4 **Beech View (IRE)** 3-9-0 JAHeffernan 12 — 4
(John Joseph Murphy, Ire) *mid-div: wknd 1/2-way* **25/1**

16 10 **Langkawi Breeze (IRE)**[38] 2646 3-9-5 WMLordan 7 — —
(T J O'Mara, Ire) *mid-div: wknd 1/2-way* **33/1**

2m 14.9s (-0.70)
WFA 3 from 4yo+ 11lb **16** Ran SP% **141.4**
CSF £7.04 TOTE £1.20: £1.10, £3.60, £4.80, £5.40; DF 9.10.
Owner Mrs John Magnier **Bred** Strategy Bloodstock **Trained** Ballydoyle, Co Tipperary

NOTEBOOK

Zulu Chief(USA) ◆, last seen finishing third in a division of the Wood Ditton on his debut back in April, was entitled to open his account without much fuss against this company yet he could hardly have done the job much more impressively in the end. The step up in trip was well within his range and, shooting clear when asked to win the race near the final furlong, he eventually came nearly a distance clear without ever coming out of third gear. This half-brother to Hawk Wing is evidently improving at a rate of knots, having taken time to mature, and has a host of Group race options available to him now. (op 4/7 tchd 4/9)

3862 - (Foreign Racing) - See Raceform Interactive

3476 DONCASTER (L-H)

Thursday, July 10

OFFICIAL GOING: Good (good to firm in places)
Rail realignment added 13yards to advertised distances on the round course.
Wind: Virtually nil Weather: Cloudy, sunny periods

3863 DONCASTER RACECOURSE SPONSORSHIP CLUB APPRENTICE H'CAP — 2m 110y

6:30 (6:32) (Class 6) (0-65,65) 4-Y-0+ **£2,729** (£806; £403) **Stalls** Low

Form — RPR

/65- **1** **That Look**[53] 3448 5-8-5 **51** RosieJessop(5) 3 — 62
(D E Cantillon) *cl up: led after 2f: rdn along wl over 2f out: drvn over 1f out: edgd rt ins fnl f: hld on gamely* **5/2**[1]

0435 **2** nk **Let It Be**[7] 3642 7-8-10 **56** FrederikTylicki(5) 8 — 67
(K G Reveley) *trckd ldrs: hdwy over 4f out: chsd wnr 3f out: rdn to chal 2f out and sn ev ch: drvn ins fnl f and kpt on: jst hld* **7/2**[2]

04/0 **3** 2 1/2 **Restart (IRE)**[41] 2585 7-8-6 **50** BillyCray(3) 5 — 58
(Lucinda Featherstone) *a.p: rdn along over 3f out: drvn 2f out and kpt on same pce appr fnl f* **11/1**

5-30 **4** 7 **Jenny Soba**[52] 2245 5-8-5 **46** oh1 (v) DavidProbert 10 — 45
(Lucinda Featherstone) *hld up in rr: gd hdwy on outer over 3f out: rdn to chse ldrs 2f out: sn one pce* **12/1**

5F03 **5** 2 3/4 **Dance Sauvage**[10] 3545 5-8-2 **46** oh1 LanceBetts(3) 7 — 42
(C W Thornton) *hld up towards rr: hdwy 1/2-way: rdn along 4f out: kpt on u.p fnl 2f: nvr rch ldrs* **5/1**[3]

01/4 **6** 2 3/4 **Spring Breeze**[10] 3545 7-9-5 **65** (v) JohnCavanagh(5) 6 — 58
(M Dods) *midfield: pushed along after 4f: reminders and in tch over 6f out: rdn 4f out and sn no imp* **17/2**

0/04 **7** 1 1/4 **Fair Spin**[36] 2734 8-8-9 **50** (p) GaryBartley 4 — 41
(Micky Hammond) *chsd ldrs: rdn along over 4f out: drvn over 3f out and grad wknd* **20/1**

-006 **8** 1 3/4 **Compton Commander**[14] 3399 10-8-0 **46** oh1 JamieKyne(5) 14 — 35
(E W Tuer) *dwlt: a towards rr* **28/1**

0/00 **9** 4 **Lodgician (IRE)**[33] 2849 6-8-6 **50** BMcHugh(3) 1 — 34
(K G Reveley) *in tch: rdn along over 4f out and sn wknd* **16/1**

004/ **10** 8 **Euro Route (IRE)**[1003] 5829 7-8-5 **46** oh1 StacyRenwick 9 — 21
(G J Smith) *chsd ldrs: rdn along 4f out: sn wknd* **33/1**

0-00 **11** 2 3/4 **Lawyer To World**[30] 1643 4-8-5 **46** oh1 (p) AmyBaker 2 — 17
(Mrs C A Dunnett) *a towards rr* **40/1**

-500 **12** 12 **Foxxy**[33] 2849 4-8-5 **46** oh1 (v[1]) MarkCoumbe 15 — 3
(J R Norton) *hld up towards rr: gd hdwy to join ldrs over 7f out: chsd wnr 4f out: rdn along over 3f out and sn wknd* **20/1**

-P00 **13** 1/2 **Bobansheil (IRE)**[13] 2914 4-8-0 **46** oh1 (b) JamesRogers(5) 11 — 2
(J S Wainwright) *led 2f: prom tl rdn along and wknd over 4f out* **66/1**

0-00 **14** 34 **Fadansil**[16] 3335 5-8-5 **46** oh1 WilliamCarson 13 — —
(J Wade) *a in rr* **40/1**

3m 37.42s (-2.98) **Going Correction** -0.075s/f (Good) **14** Ran SP% **122.2**
Speed ratings (Par 101): **104,103,102,99,98 96,96,95,93,89 88,82,82,66**
toteswinger: 1&2 £1.60, 1&3 £5.10, 2&3 £12.20. CSF £10.01 CT £84.58 TOTE £3.60: £1.50, £1.50, £3.90; EX 12.50.
Owner J W Orbell **Bred** P Askew **Trained** Newmarket, Suffolk
■ Stewards' Enquiry : Mark Coumbe two-day ban: careless riding (Jul 24-25)

FOCUS

Three came clear in a race very low on quality but the winner is improving and the placed horses offer the best guide to the level.
Compton Commander Official explanation: jockey said gelding was denied a clear run

3864 DIBCO PRECISION ENGINEERING H'CAP — 1m 4f

7:00 (7:00) (Class 4) (0-80,80) 3-Y-0+ **£5,180** (£1,541; £770; £384) **Stalls** Low

Form — RPR

3100 **1** **Boz**[40] 2591 4-9-13 **79** (v[1]) JamieSpencer 6 — 90+
(L M Cumani) *hld up: hdwy on bit 3f out: cruised up to ldrs over 1f out: shkn up and led ins fnl f* **7/1**[3]

-100 **2** 1 1/2 **The Oil Magnate**[12] 3494 3-9-0 **79** TonyHamilton 7 — 83
(M Dods) *hld up in rr: hdwy over 2f out: sn rdn: styd on fr over 1f out: tk 2nd ins fnl f: no ch w wnr* **14/1**

4625 **3** 1 1/4 **Sporting Gesture**[13] 3440 11-8-11 **70** ... BradleyRoper(7) 8 72
(M W Easterby) *in tch: hdwy over 3f out: rdn to chse ldr over 2f out: led over 1f out: drvn and hdd ins fnl f: one pce* **12/1**

0660 **4** 1 1/4 **Vicious Warrior**[15] 3367 9-9-12 **78** ... DeanMcKeown 3 78
(R M Whitaker) *t.k.h: hld up: hdwy to chse ldrs 3f out: rdn along 2f out and kpt on same pce* **14/1**

3035 **5** 1/2 **Celtic Change (IRE)**[12] 3493 4-10-0 **80** ... PaulMulrennan 10 79
(M Dods) *chsd clr ldr: rdn 3f out: drvn 2f out: sn one pce* **7/1**[3]

1201 **6** 1/2 **Amanda Carter**[6] 3673 4-9-2 **75** 6ex ... FrederikTylicki(7) 1 73
(R A Fahey) *led and sn clr: rdn along over 2f out: drvn and hdd over 1f out: sn wknd* **13/8**[1]

342- **7** 3 1/2 **Heathyards Pride**[245] 6739 8-9-11 **77** ... NCallan 4 70
(R Hollinshead) *hld up: hdwy 1/2-way: chsd ldrs 3f out: sn rdn and wknd 2f out* **7/1**[3]

00-5 **8** 34 **Clueless**[15] 3368 6-9-11 **77** ... JamesDoyle 9 15
(A J McCabe) *chsd ldng pair: pushed along over 5f out: rdn over 4f out and sn wknd* **9/2**[2]

2m 33.6s (-1.50) **Going Correction** -0.075s/f (Good)
WFA 3 from 4yo+ 13lb 8 Ran SP% **114.8**
Speed ratings (Par 105): **102,101,100,99,99 98,96,73**
toteswinger: 1&2 £21.40, 1&3 £20.90, 2&3 £32.40. CSF £96.79 CT £1152.19 TOTE £5.90: £2.40, £4.30, £2.40; EX 92.40.
Owner Aston House Stud **Bred** Aston House Stud **Trained** Newmarket, Suffolk

FOCUS
A fair handicap with the winner value for four lengths and the form rated around the second and fourth.
Clueless Official explanation: jockey said gelding never travelled

3865 WILLIAMS FASTENERS NOVICE FILLIES' STKS 5f
7:35 (7:35) (Class 4) 2-Y-O **£4,209** (£1,252; £625; £312) **Stalls High**

Form RPR

5351 **1** **Rosabee (IRE)**[2] 3809 2-9-3 0 ... EdwardCreighton 2 86
(Miss V Haigh) *chsd ldrs on outer: rdn along 1/2-way: styd on u.p to chal ent fnl f: drvn and led on wl to ld fnl 50yds* **9/1**

1 **2** shd **Maggie Lou (IRE)**[75] 1610 2-9-3 0 ... NCallan 3 86
(K A Ryan) *chsd ldr: hdwy 2f out: rdn to ld ent fnl f: sn drvn and hung rt: hdd and no ex fnl 50yds* **7/4**[1]

1 **3** hd **Excellerator (IRE)**[32] 2865 2-9-0 0 ... JamieSpencer 4 82+
(George Baker) *hld up: hdwy 2f out: rdn to chal whn hmpd jst ins fnl f: sn drvn and kpt on* **10/3**[3]

1 **4** 3/4 **Crystal Moments**[50] 2309 2-9-3 0 ... RyanMoore 1 82
(E A L Dunlop) *prom: effrt 2f out: sn rdn and ev ch tl drvn and nt qckn wl ins fnl f* **2/1**[2]

5 1 3/4 **Soviet Rhythm** 2-8-6 0 ... AndrewElliott 7 65
(G M Moore) *chsd ldrs: effrt 2f out: sn rdn and n.m.r wl over 1f out: sn swtchd lft and kpt on ins fnl f* **25/1**

410 **6** 1 1/4 **Skruton (IRE)**[12] 3496 2-9-0 0 ... JerryO'Dwyer(3) 6 71
(M G Quinlan) *led: rdn along 2f out: drvn and hdd ent fnl f: wknd* **20/1**

60.22 secs (-0.28) **Going Correction** +0.025s/f (Good) 6 Ran SP% **111.4**
Speed ratings (Par 93): **103,102,102,101,98 96**
toteswinger: 1&2 £2.30, 1&3 £4.20, 2&3 £1.30. CSF £24.90 TOTE £9.20: £2.30, £1.10; EX 29.40.
Owner R J Budge **Bred** J F Tuthill **Trained** Wiseton, Notts
■ Stewards' Enquiry : N Callan caution: careless riding; one-day ban: used whip with excessive frequency (Jul 24)

FOCUS
Just an ordinary novice event, but the time was smart, just 0.02 seconds slower than the later 56-79 handicap for older horses and the winner is progressing.

NOTEBOOK
Rosabee(IRE), who bolted up off a mark of 67 on her recent nursery debut, looked to face a much stiffer task in this company and had a bit to prove on this return to 5f. However, her stable are in really good form at present and, having been been outpaced, she came with a strong late run to get up. She is clearly progressing fast and it will be interesting to see where she turns up next. (op 15-2)
Maggie Lou(IRE), off since winning tidily on her debut at Haydock back in April, was solid at the head of the market and she made a good fist of it, but started to hang under pressure and she was eventually worn down. This was a pleasing return, but she has limited scope for improvement. (op 13-8 tchd 11-8, 15-8 in a place)
Excellerator(IRE), a strongly-supported favourite when winning nicely on debut at Southwell, had claims for being unlucky on this turf debut. She was running on well when slightly interfered with by the runner-up and should have at least finished second. She is another who remains capable of better. (op 3-1 tchd 4-1)
Crystal Moments, winner of a pretty ordinary Sandown maiden on debut, looked a big player, but her stable is hardly firing them in at present and she lacked the necessary pace to make a winning run. This was a shade disappointing, but she probably deserves another chance at 6f in nurseries. (op 11-4)
Soviet Rhythm, the only newcomer in the field, is related to plenty of winners and she made a pleasing debut back in fifth, keeping on well having been slightly interfered with. She will find easier opportunities in maidens. (op 40-1)
Skruton(IRE) could not handle the rise up to Listed level at Newmarket last time and she could have been expected to fare a lot better on this drop in grade. (op 16-1)

3866 BARIS GROUP FILLIES' H'CAP 1m (S)
8:05 (8:08) (Class 4) (0-80,79) 3-Y-O+ **£5,459** (£1,612; £806) **Stalls High**

Form RPR

10 **1** **Summer Gold (IRE)**[15] 3367 4-10-0 **79** ... DavidAllan 1 84
(E J Alston) *sn led at stdy pce: qcknd 3f out: rdn 2f out: drvn ent fnl f and styd on wl* **12/1**

0146 **2** 1 **Oat Cuisine**[12] 3507 4-9-5 **70** ... JamieSpencer 2 73+
(M L W Bell) *trckd ldrs: effrt on outer over 2f out and sn rdn: drvn ent fnl f: styd on to take 2nd nr line* **11/4**[2]

-021 **3** nk **Luck Will Come (IRE)**[18] 3293 4-8-11 **65** ... JerryO'Dwyer(3) 4 67
(H J Collingridge) *trckd ldng pair: hdwy to chse wnr 1/2-way: rdn wl over 2f out: drvn whn rdr dropped whip jst over 1f out: kpt on same pce: lost 2nd nr line* **10/1**[3]

36-6 **4** 2 **Destinys Dream (IRE)**[15] 3369 3-8-12 **72** ... TonyHamilton 7 67
(D W Barker) *chsd ldrs: rdn along wl over 2f out: kpt on same pce* **25/1**

0-02 **5** 2 3/4 **Lambda (USA)**[25] 3061 3-9-4 **78** ... RyanMoore 5 67
(Sir Michael Stoute) *hld up effrt 3f out: sn rdn and no hdwy* **4/6**[1]

-001 **6** shd **Slip Star**[12] 3481 5-8-9 **60** oh8 ... GregFairley 8 51
(T J Etherington) *chsd wnr: pushed along 1/2-way: rdn wl over 2f out: sn drvn and wknd* **20/1**

103 **7** 2 1/4 **Shosolosa (IRE)**[18] 3293 6-8-2 **60** oh6 ... StacyRenwick(7) 6 46
(R C Guest) *a in rr* **25/1**

1m 41.42s (2.12) **Going Correction** +0.025s/f (Good)
WFA 3 from 4yo+ 9lb 7 Ran SP% **115.9**
Speed ratings (Par 102): **90,89,88,86,83 83,81**
toteswinger: 1&2 £4.80, 1&3 £12.50, 2&3 £3.40. CSF £45.02 CT £345.89 TOTE £16.00: £4.30, £2.10; EX 67.90.
Owner J Stephenson **Bred** Rathbarry Stud **Trained** Longton, Lancs

FOCUS
A fair handicap but the pace was moderate and not form to take too literally.

3867 MOLLART COX MAIDEN STKS 6f
8:40 (8:44) (Class 5) 3-Y-O+ **£3,753** (£1,108; £554) **Stalls High**

Form RPR

1 **Chosen Forever** 3-9-3 0 ... SilvestreDeSousa 3 63
(G R Oldroyd) *chsd ldng pair: hdwy on outer 2f out: rdn over 1f out: led ins fnl f: sn drvn and jst hld on* **18/1**

04 **2** nse **Billy Bowmore**[8] 3600 3-9-3 0 ... TonyHamilton 5 63
(M Dods) *chsd ldrs: hdwy 2f out: rdn to ld over 1f out: drvn: edgd lft and hdd ins fnl f: rallied wl towards fin* **10/1**[3]

4-5 **3** 1 3/4 **Royal Encore**[13] 3438 4-9-4 0 ... JamieSpencer 6 58+
(J R Fanshawe) *hld up: hdwy 2f out: rdn whn n.m.r jst ins fnl f: one pce* **8/11**[1]

050 **4** nk **Ma Vie En Rose (IRE)**[15] 3381 3-8-12 **60** ... (t) NCallan 1 51
(A M Balding) *led: rdn along 2f out: hdd over 1f out and wknd ins fnl f* **5/1**[2]

5 8 **Haamesh (IRE)** 4-9-9 0 ... PAspell 8 30
(J S Wainwright) *v.s.a: hdwy 2f out: styd on appr fnl f* **33/1**

00 **6** 2 3/4 **Summer Rose**[12] 3502 3-8-12 0 ... (p) FergalLynch 4 17
(R M H Cowell) *closde up: rdn over 2f out: sn wknd* **33/1**

0- **7** 2 1/2 **Tara's Force (IRE)**[448] 1107 3-8-9 0 ... JamieMoriarty(3) 2 9
(J J Quinn) *wnt bdly lft s: a in rr* **12/1**

1m 13.91s (0.31) **Going Correction** +0.025s/f (Good)
WFA 3 from 4yo 6lb 7 Ran SP% **102.5**
Speed ratings (Par 103): **98,97,95,95,84 80,77**
toteswinger: 1&2 £19.10, 1&3 £4.10, 2&3 £4.10. CSF £130.61 TOTE £14.50: £4.70, £3.00; EX 151.60.
Owner R C Bond **Bred** R C Bond **Trained** Brawby, N Yorks
■ Top Tribute (5/1) was withdrawn after refusing to enter the stalls. Rule 4 applies, deduct 15p in the £.

FOCUS
A typically modest three-year-old plus sprint maiden. The form is potentially weak and best rated through the fourth.

3868 HAF POWER TOOLS STKS (H'CAP) 5f
9:10 (9:11) (Class 5) (0-75,79) 3-Y-O+ **£3,561** (£1,059; £529; £264) **Stalls High**

Form RPR

2131 **1** **Misaro (GER)**[11] 3520 7-9-11 **79** 6ex ... (b) HaddenFrost(5) 4 89
(R A Harris) *chsd ldrs: hdwy 2f out: rdn over 1f out: drvn ins fnl f: led fnl 100yds* **14/1**

3025 **2** 1/2 **Colorus (IRE)**[6] 3665 5-9-2 **65** ... NCallan 13 73
(W J H Ratcliffe) *a.p: effrt to chal 2f out: sn rdn and ev ch tl drvn ins fnl f and nt qckn fnl 75yds* **15/2**[3]

1124 **3** hd **Best One**[19] 3271 4-9-9 **75** ... (p) KevinGhunowa(3) 12 82
(R A Harris) *led: rdn along 2f out: drvn ent fnl f: hdd and no ex fnl 100yds* **6/1**[2]

4406 **4** 1 1/2 **Charles Parnell (IRE)**[5] 3724 5-9-12 **75** ... FergalLynch 5 77+
(M Dods) *bhd: hdwy 2f out: rdn over 1f out: styd on strly ins fnl f: nrst fin* **15/2**[3]

/0-0 **5** 1 1/2 **Jonny Ebeneezer**[5] 3724 9-8-11 **67** ... RobbieEgan(7) 7 64+
(D Flood) *hld up in rr: hdwy 2f out: rdn and styd on ins fnl f: nrst fin* **33/1**

4222 **6** nk **Comptonspirit**[16] 3352 4-9-4 **67** ... (p) PaulMulrennan 9 63
(B P J Baugh) *chsd ldrs: rdn along 2f out: drvn over 1f out and kpt on same pce* **9/1**

114- **7** 1/2 **Making Music**[287] 5747 5-9-1 **64** ... (b) DavidAllan 17 58
(T D Easterby) *racd on stands' rail: chsd ldrs: rdn along wl over 1f out: kpt on same pce appr fnl f* **16/1**

-042 **8** hd **Nomoreblondes**[6] 3695 4-9-4 **67** ... (p) MickyFenton 16 60
(P T Midgley) *chsd ldrs: rdn 2f out: drvn and no imp appr fnl f* **8/1**

100 **9** 3/4 **Steelcut**[16] 3336 4-9-9 **75** ... JamieMoriarty(3) 6 65
(R A Fahey) *chsd ldrs: rdn along wl over 1f out: wknd ins fnl f* **14/1**

1423 **10** hd **The Bear**[13] 3454 5-9-4 **70** ... PJMcDonald(3) 11 60
(R Johnson) *stmbld s and s.i.s: a in rr* **5/1**[1]

004 **11** shd **Braille**[13] 3438 3-8-13 **67** ... TonyHamilton 14 56
(T D Walford) *racd towards stands' rail: chsd ldrs: rdn along 2f out: wknd over 1f out* **12/1**

-062 **12** 1 **Never Without Me**[21] 3171 8-8-7 **61** ... ShaneCreighton(5) 15 47
(J F Coupland) *a towards rr* **16/1**

0036 **13** 3/4 **Yungaburra (IRE)**[6] 3668 4-9-0 **70** ... (t) KrishGundowry(7) 3 53
(S Parr) *chsd ldrs towards outer: rdn along 2f out: sn wknd* **16/1**

350- **14** nk **Haajes**[300] 5379 4-9-11 **74** ... DarrenWilliams 10 56
(S Parr) *in tch: rdn along 2f out and sn wknd* **25/1**

-503 **15** 2 1/2 **Brandywell Boy (IRE)**[16] 3352 5-9-2 **65** ... RichardThomas 2 38
(D J S Ffrench Davis) *chsd ldrs on wd outside: rdn along 2f out and sn wknd* **16/1**

0065 **16** 3 **Hawaii Prince**[9] 3594 4-8-9 **58** ... SilvestreDeSousa 8 20
(S T Mason) *cl up: rdn along over 2f out and sn wknd* **28/1**

000- **17** 6 **She's Our Dream**[245] 6736 3-8-2 **56** oh2 ... (t) PatrickMathers 1 —
(R C Guest) *a towards rr* **66/1**

60.20 secs (-0.30) **Going Correction** +0.025s/f (Good)
WFA 3 from 4yo+ 5lb 17 Ran SP% **131.9**
Speed ratings (Par 103): **103,102,101,99,97 96,95,95,94,93 93,92,91,90,86 81,72**
toteswinger: 1&2 £8.80, 1&3 £21.70, 2&3 £27.90. CSF £120.44 CT £748.46 TOTE £18.00: £3.50, £2.50, £2.10, £2.40; EX 205.20 Place 6: £1,869.77, Place 5: £1,225.51..
Owner Messrs Criddle Davies Dawson & Villa **Bred** Wilhelm Fasching **Trained** Earlswood, Monmouths

FOCUS
An ultra-competitive sprint and sound enough with the winner to last year's best and the placed horses to this season's form.
The Bear Official explanation: jockey said gelding slipped leaving stalls
T/Plt: £2,421.00 to a £1 stake. Pool: £75,615.11. 22.80 winning tickets. T/Qpdt: £264.40 to a £1 stake. Pool: £5,468.30. 15.30 winning tickets. JR

3444 FOLKESTONE (R-H)
Thursday, July 10

OFFICIAL GOING: Soft
There were 22 non-runners due to unsuitably soft conditions.
Wind: medium across Weather: bright, partly cloudy

3869 E B F LADBROKES ODDS ON LOYALTY CARD MEDIAN AUCTION MAIDEN FILLIES' STKS 7f (S)
2:10 (2:13) (Class 5) 2-Y-O £3,561 (£1,059; £529; £264) Stalls Low

Form				RPR
	1		**Ballantrae (IRE)** 2-9-0 0 ... HayleyTurner 3 (M L W Bell) *hld up in tch: pushed along over 2f out: swtchd rt over 1f out: chal on bit 1f out: sn shkn up to ld: readily* 1/1[1]	77+
0	2	1 1/2	**Peace Concluded**[16] 3349 2-8-11 0 ... JamesMillman(3) 8 (B R Millman) *led tl over 2f out: led again over 1f out: hdd 1f out: kpt on but nt pce of wnr fnl f* 7/1[2]	68
32	3	5	**Musical Maze**[13] 3432 2-9-0 0 ... LiamJones 5 (W M Brisbourne) *in tch in midfield: rdn 3f out: outpcd over 1f out: plugged on fnl f to go modest 3rd towards fin* 8/1[3]	56
	4	1	**Second To Nun (IRE)** 2-9-0 0 ... FrankieMcDonald 12 (Jean-Rene Auvray) *s.i.s and bmpd s: sn in midfield: hdwy to chse ldr 1/2-way: led over 2f out tl over 1f out: fdd fnl f* 20/1	53
	5	shd	**Premier Superstar** 2-9-0 0 ... TQuinn 1 (M H Tompkins) *sn outpcd in last: styd on fr over 1f out: nvr trbld ldrs* 25/1	53+
	6	nk	**Bright Enough** 2-9-0 0 ... FergusSweeney 10 (E J O'Neill) *squeezed out sn after s: sn in midfield: rdn 1/2-way: outpcd 2f out: n.d fnl f* 16/1	52
0	7	hd	**Heartsease**[39] 2638 2-9-0 0 ... J-PGuillambert 4 (J G Portman) *chsd ldr tl 1/2-way: wkng whn swtchd rt 2f out: n.d fnl f* 20/1	52
	8	hd	**Chadwell Spring (IRE)** 2-8-11 0 ... RussellKennemore(3) 11 (Miss J Feilden) *squeezed out after s: bhd: modest late hdwy: nvr on terms* 40/1	51
5	9	1 1/2	**Lahaleeb (IRE)**[13] 3444 2-9-0 0 ... TPO'Shea 7 (M R Channon) *v.s.a: rdn 1/2-way: plugging on whn nt clr run and swtchd rt ins fnl f: eased after: n.d* 7/1[2]	48+
0	10	5	**Tobizzy**[37] 2691 2-9-0 0 ... SimonWhitworth 13 (J R Jenkins) *t.k.h: chsd ldrs tl 1/2-way: sn rdn: wknd 2f out* 22/1	35
6	11	nk	**Now**[20] 3207 2-8-11 0 ... TolleyDean(3) 9 (P Winkworth) *sn rdn along in rr: wl bhd fr 1/2-way* 12/1	34

1m 28.27s (0.97) **Going Correction** 0.0s/f (Good) 11 Ran SP% 119.8
Speed ratings (Par 91): **94,92,86,85,85 84,84,84,82,77 76**
toteswinger: 1&2 £2.80, 1&3 £2.80, 2&3 £5.80. CSF £7.52 TOTE £1.80: £1.10, £1.90, £2.70; EX 8.50 Trifecta £70.80 Pool: £161.90. 1.69 winning units..
Owner Sheikh Marwan Al Maktoum **Bred** Darley **Trained** Newmarket, Suffolk

FOCUS
Few of these seemed fancied and this looked a fairly weak juvenile fillies' maiden, although the first two came clear and the winner was value for more than the actial margin. They all raced stands' side.

NOTEBOOK
Ballantrae(IRE), a daughter of Diktat, sister to quite useful 7f juvenile Fox, and a half-sister to a number of other winners, out of a quite useful multiple 1m winner, justified strong market support on her racecourse debut. She looked in trouble when getting trapped against the rail with about three to run, but she loomed up travelling strongly when getting a gap and only had to be pushed out inside the final furlong. She looks better than the bare result and clearly has plenty of ability, but this did look a very weak race. (op 15-8 tchd 10-11)
Peace Concluded built on the promise she showed when mid-division in a fair Newbury maiden on her debut, finishing clear all bar the well-backed winner. (op 8-1)
Musical Maze, third in a seller on her debut before running second in a weak Chester maiden, ran a respectable race in third. She might be able to find a small nursery, but is probably only selling/claiming class. (op 7-1 tchd 13-2)
Second To Nun(IRE), a daughter of Bishop Of Cashel, first foal of a 1m winner who was also successful over hurdles, looked dangerous when hitting the front over two furlongs out, but she could not sustain her challenge. She clearly has some ability. (op 16-1)
Premier Superstar, a 14,000euros daughter of Bertolini, half-sister to triple-sprint winner Windjammer, was unfancied and ran green. (tchd 28-1)
Lahaleeb(IRE) Official explanation: jockey said filly was denied a clear run

3870 LADBROKES ODDS ON CARD - GET FREE BETS MAIDEN STKS 7f (S)
2:45 (2:45) (Class 5) 3-Y-O £2,590 (£770; £385; £192) Stalls Low

Form				RPR
322	1		**Tableau Vivant (IRE)**[29] 2929 3-8-12 80 ... PatDobbs 8 (Sir Michael Stoute) *mde all: sn crossed to stands' rail: shkn up and drew clr 1f out: eased towards fin: v easily* 4/9[1]	72+
-250	2	1 1/2	**Sheer Bluff (IRE)**[42] 2532 3-9-3 72 ... HayleyTurner 5 (D R C Elsworth) *t.k.h: chsd ldrs: wnt 2nd 2f out: rdn: hung lft and reluctant over 1f out: no ch w wnr fnl f* 5/1[3]	66
2-02	3	4 1/2	**Deira Dubai**[15] 3379 3-8-12 71 ... TQuinn 6 (B W Hills) *t.k.h: hld up wl in tch: chsd ldng pair jst over 1f out: wl outpcd fnl f* 9/2[2]	49
-0	4	1	**Encore Belle**[15] 3379 3-8-12 0 ... VinceSlattery 2 (Mouse Hamilton-Fairley) *t.k.h: hld up in last pair: rdn 2f out: kpt on same pce fr over 1f out* 66/1	46
	5	1	**Carved Emerald** 3-8-12 0 ... TRicher 7 (R Gibson, France) *s.i.s: hld up in rr: effrt and hung rt jst 2f out: no prog over 1f out* 16/1	43
0-00	6	1	**Didntcomeback**[12] 3502 3-9-3 45 ... FergusSweeney 4 (M S Saunders) *chsd wnr tl 2f out: sn rdn: wknd over 1f out* 150/1	46
0	7	1 1/4	**Alabjar**[17] 3326 3-9-3 0 ... SimonWhitworth 3 (J R Jenkins) *chsd ldrs: rdn 1/2-way: wknd 2f out* 200/1	42

1m 27.98s (0.68) **Going Correction** 0.0s/f (Good) 7 Ran SP% 112.6
Speed ratings (Par 100): **96,94,89,88,86 85,84**
toteswinger: 1&2 £2.20, 1&3 £1.10, 2&3 £3.10. CSF £3.10 TOTE £1.30: £1.02, £3.30; EX 2.80 Trifecta £15.70 Pool: £250.55. 11.75 winning units..
Owner Ballymacoll Stud **Bred** Ballymacoll Stud Farm Ltd **Trained** Newmarket, Suffolk

FOCUS
A modest, uncompetitive maiden limited by the proximity of the fourth and sixth, although the winner is value for four lengths. They all raced stands' side.

3871 LADBROKES ODDS ON CARD - GET BIGGER PRICES H'CAP 2m 93y
3:20 (3:20) (Class 6) (0-60,57) 4-Y-O+ £2,047 (£604; £302) Stalls Low

Form				RPR
0-14	1		**Trigger's Friend**[17] 3321 4-8-6 48 ... TolleyDean(3) 4 (Jamie Poulton) *t.k.h: in tch: rdn 4f out: chsd ldr 3f out: led over 1f out: styd on wl* 7/1[3]	57
4455	2	1 1/2	**Sand Repeal (IRE)**[13] 3448 6-9-2 55 ... GeorgeBaker 9 (Miss J Feilden) *led: rdn jst over 2f out: hdd and hung lft over 1f out: kpt on same pce u.p fnl f* 6/4[1]	62
0300	3	1/2	**Chiff Chaff**[2] 3589 4-8-8 47 ... SimonWhitworth 10 (C R Dore) *in tch: chsd ldng pair wl over 2f out: kpt on same pce fnl f* 12/1	53
06-2	4	1	**Wotchalike (IRE)**[11] 1726 6-8-13 52 ... (p) RichardThomas 1 (Jim Best) *hld up in last: rdn 4f out: chsd ldng trio wl over 1f out: plugged on but nvr pce to chal* 7/4[2]	57
4043	5	1	**York Cliff**[17] 3328 10-9-1 54 ... LiamJones 6 (W M Brisbourne) *hld up in last pair: rdn over 2f out: edgd rt but r.o fnl f: nt rch ldrs* 9/1	58
00-0	6	7	**Royal Tender (IRE)**[6] 3698 4-7-13 45 ... AshleyMorgan(7) 14 (V Smith) *chsd ldrs: rdn and struggling 3f out: wl bhd over 1f out* 16/1	41
0/05	7	5	**Lockstone Lad (USA)**[15] 3362 5-9-4 57 ... PatDobbs 8 (M S Saunders) *chsd ldr: rdn over 4f out: lost 2nd 3f out: wknd 2f out* 25/1	47

3m 53.74s (16.54) **Going Correction** +0.20s/f (Good) 7 Ran SP% 116.3
Speed ratings (Par 101): **66,65,65,64,64 60,58**
toteswinger: 1&2 £2.30, 1&3 £15.30, 2&3 £14.00. CSF £18.58 CT £127.24 TOTE £7.40: £2.90, £1.50; EX 24.10 Trifecta £101.60 Part won..
Owner R W Huggins **Bred** R W Huggins **Trained** Lewes, E Sussex

FOCUS
A moderate staying handicap that took little winning and is best rated through the runner-up. They went a steady pace early on and the time was pedestrian. Half the declared field were taken out because of the ground.
Wotchalike(IRE) Official explanation: jockey said gelding hung right

3872 LADBROKES ODDS ON CARD - DOUBLE POINTS DAY H'CAP 5f
3:55 (3:55) (Class 5) (0-70,69) 3-Y-O+ £2,590 (£770; £385; £192) Stalls Low

Form				RPR
0031	1		**Regal Royale**[17] 3316 5-9-0 57 ... (v) AdamKirby 10 (Peter Grayson) *mde all: grad crossed onto rail after 1f: drvn over 1f out: hrd pressed 1f out: battled on gamely to assert towards fin* 2/1[1]	69
2-63	2	3/4	**Even Bolder**[12] 3486 5-9-12 69 ... LiamJones 5 (E A Wheeler) *chsd wnr thrght: chal over 1f out: rdn ent fnl f: nt qckn u.p and btn fnl 50yds* 7/2[3]	78
0055	3	1 1/2	**Harrison's Flyer (IRE)**[5] 3724 7-8-7 57 ... (p) RossAtkinson(7) 3 (J M Bradley) *outpcd in last and sn pushed along: styd on over 1f out: wnt 3rd fnl 100yds: nvr able to chal ldng pair* 9/4[2]	61
2005	4	1 1/4	**Caustic Wit (IRE)**[8] 3608 10-9-5 62 ... FergusSweeney 9 (M S Saunders) *chsd ldng pair: rdn wl over 1f out: no imp fnl f: lost 3rd fnl 100yds* 4/1	61
4660	5	2 1/4	**Heron (IRE)**[75] 1635 3-7-11 50 ... NicolPolli(5) 2 (M R Hoad) *racd in last pair: rdn wl over 1f out: no prog after* 20/1	41

59.61 secs (-0.39) **Going Correction** 0.0s/f (Good)
WFA 3 from 4yo+ 5lb 5 Ran SP% 111.1
Speed ratings (Par 103): **103,101,99,97,93**
toteswinger: 1&2 £8.70. CSF £9.40 TOTE £2.90: £2.10, £1.50; EX 11.70 Trifecta £30.30 Pool: £297.61. 7.26 winning units..
Owner S Kamis And Mrs S Grayson **Bred** Cheveley Park Stud Ltd **Trained** Formby, Lancs

FOCUS
A moderate, uncompetitive sprint handicap but the pace was decent. They all raced stands' side and the near rail looked a big advantage but the race has been rated at face value. There were five non-runners.

3873 LADBROKES ODDS ON CARD - JOIN TODAY H'CAP 1m 4f
4:30 (4:31) (Class 5) (0-70,70) 3-Y-O £2,590 (£770; £385; £192) Stalls Low

Form				RPR
3000	1		**Okafranca (IRE)**[26] 3035 3-8-4 53 ... TPO'Shea 6 (W R Muir) *mde all: hrd pressed and drvn over 2f out: forged clr 1f out: eased towards fin* 14/1	59+
-506	2	2 1/4	**Trenchant**[37] 2695 3-9-4 67 ... AdamKirby 3 (J R Fanshawe) *chsd wnr after 3f: drvn and ev ch wl over 1f out: btn jst ins fnl f: plugged on to hold 2nd* 3/1[2]	69
0-06	3	1 3/4	**Amwell House**[14] 3421 3-8-2 51 oh6 ... AdrianMcCarthy 13 (J R Jenkins) *hld up in midfield: rdn and effrt 3f out: wnt modest 3rd 1f out: styd on steadily but nvr trbld ldng pair* 33/1	50
03-0	4	1 1/4	**Valvigneres (IRE)**[38] 2681 3-9-7 70 ... TQuinn 4 (E A L Dunlop) *hld up bhd: hdwy over 5f out: rdn and outpcd 3f out: kpt on fnl f: nvr trbld ldrs* 12/1	67+
0012	5	1	**Dancing Dik**[8] 3614 3-9-3 66 ... (p) GeorgeBaker 11 (Mrs A J Perrett) *hld up in midfield: rdn to chse ldng pair over 3f out: no imp: wknd and lost 2 pls fnl f* 7/4[1]	61
6540	6	5	**Flash Of Fire (USA)**[14] 3393 3-8-4 53 ... HayleyTurner 8 (J M P Eustace) *hld up in midfield: rdn 3f out: sn btn* 8/1[3]	40
0004	7	1 3/4	**Ultimate Quest (IRE)**[14] 3393 3-8-7 56 ... J-PGuillambert 5 (Sir Mark Prescott) *v slwly away: sn rdn along: reminders after 2f: rn wd bnd 9f out: bhd: passed btn horses fr over 1f out: nvr nr ldrs* 8/1[3]	41
6334	8	1	**Sergeant Sharpe**[23] 3115 3-8-6 62 ... ThomasBubb(7) 2 (M H Tompkins) *stdd s: hld up in rr: lost tch 3f out* 16/1	45
005	9	8	**Road To Hucking (GER)**[17] 3326 3-9-1 64 ... MohammedSaeed 10 (J R Best) *in tch: lost pl 5f out: no ch fnl 3f* 16/1	34
-050	10	9	**Hawkstar Express (IRE)**[28] 2984 3-8-2 51 oh4 ... (v[1]) DavidKinsella 7 (J R Boyle) *s.i.s: chsd ldrs after 2f: rdn and wknd qckly 3f out: t.o* 33/1	7
000	11	2 1/4	**Squire Boldwood (IRE)**[38] 2668 3-8-10 62 ... (b) MarcHalford(3) 14 (D R C Elsworth) *t.k.h: chsd ldr for 3f: styd handy tl wknd qckly 3f out: t.o* 33/1	14

2m 43.21s (2.31) **Going Correction** +0.20s/f (Good) 11 Ran SP% 118.5
Speed ratings (Par 100): **100,98,97,96,95 92,91,90,85,79 77**
toteswinger: 1&2 £9.80, 1&3 £37.10, 2&3 £23.50. CSF £55.59 CT £1372.37 TOTE £17.70: £3.50, £1.40, £6.40; EX 59.20 TRIFECTA Not won..
Owner The Eastwood Partnership **Bred** B Kennedy **Trained** Lambourn, Berks

FOCUS
A modest three-year-old handicap in which the winner did not need to run to his early-season form to score. They went a steady pace and it proved hard to make up ground.

3874 LADBROKES ODDS ON CARD - GET REWARDED TODAY FILLIES' H'CAP — 1m 1f 149y

5:05 (5:06) (Class 5) (0-70,72) 3-Y-0+ — **£2,590** (£770; £385; £192) **Stalls** Centre

Form	Pos	Dist	Horse / Details	Jockey	RPR
-205	1		**Xtravaganza (IRE)**[25] 3065 3-8-9 **62** (J W Hills) *in tch: rdn and hdwy jst over 2f out: drvn and chal ent fnl f: led fnl 100yds: r.o wl* **7/2**[3]	TQuinn 9	68
000-	2	1/2	**Wicked Lady (UAE)**[360] 3595 5-8-9 **51** oh6 (B J McMath) *hld up in rr: hdwy 2f out: ev ch whn hung bdly lft fr over 1f out: r.o towards fin: nt rcvr* **33/1**	DavidKinsella 6	56
-502	3	2	**Italian Goddess**[41] 2559 3-8-11 **64** (M L W Bell) *stdd s: hld up in last: rdn jst over 2f out: styd on fnl f: wnt 3rd towards fin: nt rch ldng pair* **9/4**[2]	HayleyTurner 2	65
0-11	4	3/4	**Charlevoix (IRE)**[7] 3656 3-9-5 **72** 6ex (C F Wall) *s.i.s: sn chsng ldrs: hdwy to ld jst over 2f out: sn edgd rt onto rail: rdn over 1f out: hdd fnl 100yds: wknd* **11/8**[1]	GeorgeBaker 3	71
0020	5	7	**Miss Phoebe (IRE)**[17] 3322 3-8-12 **65** (S Kirk) *chsd ldr: hung lft bnd 4f out: rdn over 3f out: wknd wl over 1f out* **9/1**	AdamKirby 4	49
0000	6	1 1/2	**Cantique (IRE)**[15] 3360 4-8-6 **51** oh6 (R J Price) *led: rdn and hdd jst over 2f out: hrd rdn and hmpd ent fnl 2f: wl btn after* **28/1**	TolleyDean(3) 8	32
0406	7	1 3/4	**Bookish**[16] 3345 3-7-13 **57** (Jamie Poulton) *hld up in tch: rdn and struggling over 2f out: wl bhd fnl f* **20/1**	(b) NataliaGemelova(5) 5	35

2m 7.58s (2.68) **Going Correction** +0.20s/f (Good)
WFA 3 from 4yo+ 11lb — **7** Ran SP% **116.2**
Speed ratings (Par 100): **97,96,95,94,88 87,86**
toteswinger: 1&2 £8.90, 1&3 £1.90, 2&3 £11.00. CSF £102.57 CT £314.84 TOTE £4.80: £2.10, £6.70; EX 93.50 Trifecta £349.60 Part won. Pool: £472.50. 0.50 winning units. Place 6: £115.36, Place 5: £89.14..
Owner Mrs P De W Johnson **Bred** Crone Stud Farms Ltd **Trained** Upper Lambourn, Berks

FOCUS
A moderate fillies' handicap rated around the winner and third.
Wicked Lady(UAE) Official explanation: jockey said mare hung left
Miss Phoebe(IRE) Official explanation: jockey said filly hung left
Cantique(IRE) Official explanation: jockey said filly did not handle the final bend
T/Plt: £65.90 to a £1 stake. Pool: £53,171.73. 588.89 winning tickets. T/Qpdt: £38.60 to a £1 stake. Pool: £3,283.70. 62.80 winning tickets. SP

3849 NEWMARKET (R-H)

Thursday, July 10

OFFICIAL GOING: Soft changing to good to soft after race 1 (1.30)
A fine day and a drying wind meant conditions were not as soft as they had been the previous day.
Wind: Fresh, half behind Weather: Cloudy with sunny spells

3875 BAHRAIN TROPHY (LISTED RACE) — 1m 5f

1:30 (1:31) (Class 1) 3-Y-O — **£24,978** (£9,468; £4,738; £2,362; £1,183; £594) **Stalls** Centre

Form	Pos	Dist	Horse / Details	Jockey	RPR
6-50	1		**Donegal (USA)**[20] 3196 3-9-0 100 (A M Balding) *chsd ldrs: rdn over 3f out: styd on u.p to ld wl ins fnl f* **16/1**	WilliamBuick 10	100
5413	2	nk	**Gravitation**[20] 3196 3-8-9 95 (W Jarvis) *lw: hld up: rdn over 2f out: hdwy u.p over 1f out: styd on* **7/1**[3]	LDettori 7	95
1200	3	nk	**Bougureau**[33] 2829 3-9-0 111 (P W Chapple-Hyam) *lw: chsd ldrs: led 3f out: rdn, hdd and edgd lft fr 2f out: unable qck towards fin* **1/1**[1]	AlanMunro 8	99
-110	4	nk	**Unleashed (IRE)**[20] 3196 3-9-0 90 (H R A Cecil) *hld up: hdwy over 3f out: led 2f out: rdn over 1f out: edgd lft and hdd wl ins fnl f* **11/1**	TedDurcan 1	99+
3040	5	2 1/4	**Better Hand (IRE)**[21] 3157 3-9-0 90 (M R Channon) *hld up: rdn over 3f out: styd on: nt rch ldrs* **50/1**	SamHitchcott 11	95
1215	6	4 1/2	**Enroller (IRE)**[20] 3196 3-9-0 96 (W R Muir) *lw: chsd ldrs: led over 3f out: sn hdd: rdn and wknd over 1f out* **11/2**[2]	MartinDwyer 6	89
	7	5	**Fiery Lad (IRE)**[34] 2812 3-9-0 0 (G M Lyons, Ire) *strong: lw: hld up: rdn over 3f out: hdwy over 1f out: sn wknd* **11/1**	JMurtagh 3	81
5510	8	1 1/2	**Moment's Notice**[20] 3196 3-9-0 85 (S Kirk) *prom: racd keenly: rdn and wknd 2f out* **33/1**	NCallan 2	79
2213	9	43	**Wood Chorus**[14] 3415 3-8-9 97 (M L W Bell) *sn led: hdd over 3f out: sn rdn and wknd: eased over 1f out* **9/1**	JamieSpencer 9	9

2m 44.83s (1.03) **Going Correction** +0.10s/f (Good) — **9** Ran SP% **115.3**
Speed ratings (Par 108): **100,99,99,99,98 95,92,91,64**
toteswinger: 1&2 £14.00, 1&3 £8.00, 2&3 £2.70. CSF £122.76 TOTE £17.30: £4.00, £1.70, £1.30; EX 119.20 Trifecta £523.90 Part won..
Owner The Donegal Partnership **Bred** Arthur B Hancock III **Trained** Kingsclere, Hants

FOCUS
A decent Listed race. The field raced down the centre of the track once into the long home straight before gradually edging over towards the far side. The winner and second both come down the outside of the bunch, nearest to the centre. Not an easy race to assess with five of these including the winner coming from the Queen's Vase. The winner has been rated to his best.

NOTEBOOK
Donegal(USA), who failed to see out the 2m of the Queen's Vase at Ascot, was dropping back in both trip and grade. After coming under pressure some way out, he was still only third entering the final furlong but his rider's efforts were rewarded as he stayed on to lead near the finish. Already gelded, he is well at home in soft conditions and it would be no surprise to see him sold as a hurdling prospect before long.
Gravitation was third on firm ground in the Queen's Vase, where she finished just under four lengths in front of today's winner. Only fourth entering the final furlong, she was staying on best of all at the end, suggesting this trip is a bare minimum for her. (op 8-1)
Bougureau, a creditable ninth in the Derby last time, had every chance, but after battling to get the better of Unleashed he could not hold off a couple of late challengers. He was the form pick beforehand and the ground ought not to have been an issue, so this was slightly disappointing. (tchd 6-5, 5-4 in places)
Unleashed(IRE) was another to come from the Queen's Vase, where the 2m trip seemed to stretch him. He came through from the rear to take a slender lead, but could not shake off the favourite and had no more to give well inside the last. The fact that he raced nearest the inside rail might not have helped. (op 12-1)
Better Hand(IRE), without the visor for this step back up in class, stayed on in the latter stages without ever getting into the action. He might be worth trying over a little further still.
Enroller(IRE), who raced prominently before dropping away in the latter stages, could not confirm his Queen's Vase superiority over Donegal and Unleashed. (op 9-2)
Fiery Lad(IRE) has been in good form in Ireland this season, winning a couple of 1m2f handicaps on the sand at Dundalk and a similar event on firm ground at Navan on his latest start. This represented a very different test and he was not up to it, although he did make a little progress from the rear before weakening again in the final furlong as his stamina ran out. (op 16-1)
Moment's Notice, seventh in the Queen's Vase, again did nothing for his chances by racing too keenly. (op 40-1)
Wood Chorus was taking a sizeable step up in trip and, once headed, she dropped right away. She will not be easy to place now. (op 12-1)

3876 TNT JULY STKS (GROUP 2) (C&G) — 6f

2:00 (2:02) (Class 1) 2-Y-O — **£45,416** (£17,216; £8,616; £4,296; £2,152; £1,080) **Stalls** Low

Form	Pos	Dist	Horse / Details	Jockey	RPR
411	1		**Classic Blade (IRE)**[11] 3522 2-8-12 0 (Tom Dascombe) *w'like: mde all: rdn and edgd rt over 1f out: edgd lft insde fnl f: r.o* **6/1**	RichardKingscote 5	107
2	2	shd	**Sayif (IRE)**[52] 2254 2-8-12 0 (P W Chapple-Hyam) *w'like: scope: lw: edgd rt s: chsd wnr: rdn over 1f out: r.o u.p: hung rt towards fin* **3/1**[2]	AlanMunro 1	107
123	3	3	**Prolific (IRE)**[21] 3152 2-8-12 0 (R Hannon) *lw: hld up: hdwy and hung lft over 1f out: sn rdn: no ex ins fnl f* **2/1**[1]	RyanMoore 4	98
221	4	nk	**Viva Ronaldo (IRE)**[27] 3005 2-8-12 0 (R A Fahey) *wnt rt s: sn trcking ldrs: rdn over 1f out: styd on same pce* **8/1**	LDettori 6	97
230	5	1 3/4	**I Am The Best**[23] 3103 2-8-12 0 (D M Simcock) *bmpd s: sn prom: rdn over 2f out: wknd over 1f out* **16/1**	RoystonFfrench 2	92
1	6	shd	**Prime Delivery (USA)**[9] 3590 2-8-12 0 (R M H Cowell) *bmpd s: hld up: rdn over 2f out: wknd over 1f out* **14/1**	TedDurcan 3	91
124	7	1/2	**Effort**[23] 3105 2-8-12 0 (M Johnston) *hmpd s: hld up: rdn over 2f out: wknd over 1f out* **9/2**[3]	KerrinMcEvoy 7	90

1m 13.21s (0.71) **Going Correction** +0.10s/f (Good) — **7** Ran SP% **114.5**
Speed ratings (Par 106): **99,98,94,94,92 92,91**
toteswinger: 1&2 £4.40, 1&3 £3.00, 2&3 £1.80. CSF £24.36 TOTE £7.50: £3.40, £2.40; EX 27.50.
Owner The Classic Strollers Partnership **Bred** Ballybrennan Stud Ltd **Trained** Lambourn, Berks
■ A first Group winner for both Tom Dascombe and Richard Kingscote.

FOCUS
A slightly below par renewal of this historic Group 2 contest and the time was modest too. The winner is a likeable sort, and the runner-up is now the best two-year-old maiden in training. The third has provisionally been rated 7lb below his Norfolk Stakes form.

NOTEBOOK
Classic Blade(IRE), a progressive colt, completed the hat-trick on this step up in class. Smartly away to bowl along in front, he was let down passing the two pole and, finding plenty for pressure, always just looked to be holding the runner-up, although it was a close-run thing in the end. Well suited by easy ground, he has an admirable attitude but he may struggle to build on this as the season progresses. (op 7-1)
Sayif(IRE) ◆ has been given a break since his promising debut in a conditions event at Windsor in May. Upped in both trip and grade, he confirmed himself a very useful prospect and just missed out. Chasing the winner virtually throughout, he showed signs of immaturity and hung in behind his rival slightly before running on late, drifting right as he did so and needing another stride. He handled the ground but will probably be more at home back on a sound surface. He looks the best long-term prospect in this field. (op 9-4 tchd 2-1)
Prolific(IRE) was stepping up to 6f after finishing third in the Norfolk Stakes at Ascot. He improved on the outer to move into third place, but hung to his left and never really looked like threatening the first two. The ground had probably gone against him. (op 5-2 tchd 11-4 in a place)
Viva Ronaldo(IRE) was tackling easy ground for the first time on this step up in trip. He stayed well enough, but lacked a change of gear in the latter stages. He also gave the impression that he is not straightforward. (op 12-1)
I Am The Best travelled quite well but was unable to pick up when the race really began with over a quarter of a mile to run. He is a surefire maiden winner if connections choose to revert to that company. (op 20-1 tchd 25-1 in a place)
Prime Delivery(USA), taking a big step up in class after his recent winning debut on fast ground at Thirsk, was not up to the task.
Effort, fourth in the Windsor Castle at Ascot, was found out on this rise in grade. He should have been suited by the extra furlong but looked ill at ease coming down the hill and failed to offer much under pressure. (tchd 11-2)

3877 LADBROKES.COM HERITAGE H'CAP — 1m 2f

2:35 (2:39) (Class 2) (0-105,103) 3-Y-O — **£62,310** (£18,660; £9,330; £4,670; £2,330; £1,170) **Stalls** Centre

Form	Pos	Dist	Horse / Details	Jockey	RPR
-606	1		**Jedediah**[21] 3155 3-8-5 **94** (A M Balding) *s.s: hld up: hdwy over 3f out: led ins fnl f: hung lft: rdn out* **11/1**	(p) DavidProbert(7) 1	105
-121	2	1/2	**Steele Tango (USA)**[26] 3038 3-8-8 **90** (R A Teal) *lw: hld up: hdwy over 2f out: rdn and edgd lft over 1f out: sn ev ch: r.o* **16/1**	DaneO'Neill 20	100
2210	3	1/2	**Indian Days**[21] 3157 3-8-6 **88** (J G Given) *lw: hld up in tch: led over 2f out: rdn over 1f out: hdd and unable qck ins fnl f* **14/1**	AlanMunro 2	97
-230	4	1/2	**Love Galore (IRE)**[21] 3155 3-8-8 **90** (M Johnston) *stdd s: hld up: hdwy u.p over 1f out: r.o* **25/1**	JoeFanning 4	98
2-01	5	1 1/4	**Dona Alba (IRE)**[38] 2665 3-8-8 **90** (J L Dunlop) *hld up: hdwy over 1f out: sn rdn: styd on* **11/1**	KerrinMcEvoy 16	96
-051	6	1	**City Of The Kings (IRE)**[13] 3458 3-8-8 **90** (R Hannon) *hld up: hdwy over 3f out: rdn and ev ch over 1f out: wknd ins fnl f* **33/1**	EddieAhern 5	94
-131	7	1	**Wasan**[19] 3261 3-8-13 **95** (E A L Dunlop) *lw: prom: rdn over 1f out: wknd ins fnl f* **6/1**[1]	RHills 10	97
-155	8	1 1/2	**Lazy Days**[21] 3155 3-8-7 **89** (D R C Elsworth) *lw: hld up: hdwy u.p and edgd lft over 1f out: too much to do* **7/1**[2]	JamieSpencer 6	88
31-5	9	7	**Rochefort (IRE)**[33] 2825 3-8-3 **85** (J H M Gosden) *hld up in tch: rdn: hung lft and wknd over 1f out* **8/1**[3]	JimmyQuinn 14	70
2120	10	1 1/4	**Missioner (USA)**[21] 3157 3-8-3 **85** (M Johnston) *mid-div: rdn over 3f out: wknd over 1f out* **16/1**	RoystonFfrench 7	67

The Form Book, Raceform Ltd, Compton, RG20 6NL

-130 **11** *shd* **Age Of Reason (UAE)**[20] 3196 3-9-5 **101**.......................... GregFairley 9 83
(M Johnston) *led 1f: chsd ldrs: rdn over 3f out: wknd over 1f out* **16/1**

1-10 **12** *5* **Dr Faustus (IRE)**[21] 3156 3-9-7 **103**................................. RyanMoore 19 75
(Sir Michael Stoute) *trckd ldrs: plld hrd: rdn over 2f out: sn wknd* **7/1**[2]

1-51 **13** *2 1/2* **Tomintoul Flyer**[22] 3134 3-8-8 **90**............................... TedDurcan 11 57
(H R A Cecil) *hld up: rdn and nt clr run over 2f out: wknd over 1f out* **7/1**[2]

2420 **14** *1/2* **Ramona Chase**[21] 3157 3-8-13 **95**............................... DPMcDonogh 12 61
(S Kirk) *s.i.s: rcvrd to ld after 1f: rdn: hung lft and hdd over 2f out: wknd over 1f out* **22/1**

3-13 **15** *1 3/4* **Slam**[19] 3251 3-8-9 **91**.. WilliamBuick 3 53
(B W Hills) *sn chsng ldr: rdn over 3f out: hung lft and wknd over 2f out* **20/1**

-340 **16** *2 1/2* **Feared In Flight (IRE)**[21] 3156 3-9-6 **102**...................... MichaelHills 15 59
(B W Hills) *sn pushed along in rr: hdwy 1/2-way: rdn and wknd over 2f out* **20/1**

2m 4.98s (-0.52) **Going Correction** +0.10s/f (Good) **16** Ran SP% **124.5**
Speed ratings (Par 106): **106,105,105,104,103 103,102,101,95,94 94,90,88,87,86 84**
toteswinger: 1&2 £47.80, 1&3 £33.90, 2&3 £58.10. CSF £165.75 CT £2496.59 TOTE £12.40: £2.90, £4.00, £3.80, £4.80; EX 306.90 Trifecta £1551.20 Part won..

Owner Mr & Mrs P McMahon & Mr & Mrs Peter Pausewang **Bred** Dunchurch Lodge Stud Company **Trained** Kingsclere, Hants

FOCUS
Traditionally one of the season's strongest three-year-old handicaps and this year's renewal looks up to scratch. It was run at a solid pace, with the field electing to come up the middle of the track, and the first eight, who were a good mix of prominent racers and horses who had been held up, came home clear of the remainder. The first two both improved significantly.

NOTEBOOK
Jedediah, who ran really well from this mark under today's jockey when sixth in the Britannia at Royal Ascot last time, was having his first run over a trip this far and racing in first-time cheekpieces. Despite missing the kick from his outside stall, he emerged from off the pace nearing the 2f pole going easily and it was clear he was the one to beat. His rider delayed his winning move and he eventually came home to score with something up his sleeve. This was much deserved and the longer trip evidently helped, plus he is clearly versatile as regards underfoot conditions. Open to further improvement over this sort of trip, his connections now plan to aim him at a similar race at Goodwood later this month and he looks a pattern performer in the making for next year. (op 12-1)
Steele Tango(USA), officially raised 5lb for his Sandown success 26 days previously, was another to be housed in an outside stall and, also like the winner, was given a patient ride through the first half of the race. He improved to have every chance, posting another personal best in defeat, and is clearly suited by some cut underfoot. He too remains open to further progression over this sort of distance, despite another likely rise in the weights.
Indian Days, better than his finishing position suggested over 1m4f at Royal Ascot last time, was produced with his challenge passing the 2f marker and kept on to record a sterling effort in defeat. He goes on most ground and, while he will go up for this, still appeals as the sort to bag a decent handicap before the season is out.
Love Galore(IRE), well below par in the Britannia at Royal Ascot, showed that effort to be all wrong on this step back up in distance and ran right up to his best. He enjoyed the way this race was run and is still capable of some more improvement.
Dona Alba(IRE), 7lb higher than when scoring readily at Leicester, was the sole filly in the race and was ridden much more patiently in this higher grade. She looked a possible threat nearing the final furlong, but she could only muster the same pace when asked for maximum effort and a return to a more prominent ride over this trip now looks a wise move for her. (op 14-1)
City Of The Kings(IRE) ◆, officially raised 5lb after hacking up in a good claimer at this venue, showed himself to be at the top of his game at present with a solid effort in defeat. He just found this extra distance beyond him on this softer ground and does not look weighted out of winning in handicap company just yet. (tchd 40-1)
Wasan was given a positive ride but had no more to give soon after the final furlong marker. He looked potentially still well treated, despite having gone up 7lb since his Haydock success, so this could be deemed as somewhat disappointing, but an explanation emerged afterwards. Official explanation: jockey said colt lost its action
Lazy Days, fifth in the Britannia last time, looked a big player in this from a 1lb higher mark and back on an easier surface. The extra distance was also expected to suit, but having been raced out the back for most of the race he made his move too late in the day and was never going to reach the principals. He is better than he showed here and there could well be a big pot in him before the year is out. (op 8-1)
Rochefort(IRE) was unable to pick up from off the pace and again showed a tendency to hang when under pressure. He may just need a sounder surface, but could possibly do with his sights lowering. (op 13-2)
Dr Faustus(IRE) did himself no favours by refusing to settle early on and was beaten at the 2f pole. (op 13-2)
Tomintoul Flyer would have been a little closer with a clearer passage around 2f out, but he still ran below expectations, even allowing for having been upped 9lb for his All-Weather success. (tchd 15-2)
Slam Official explanation: trainer had no explanation for the poor form shown

3878 PRINCESS OF WALES'S WBX.COM STKS (GROUP 2) 1m 4f
3:10 (3:11) (Class 1) 3-Y-O+

£56,770 (£21,520; £10,770; £5,370; £2,690; £1,350) **Stalls** Centre

Form RPR

1-06 **1** **Lucarno (USA)**[11] 3542 4-9-7 **115**.................................. JimmyFortune 3 122
(J H M Gosden) *lw: mde all: sn clr: stdd over 4f out: rdn clr over 1f out: unchal* **6/1**

30-4 **2** *1 1/4* **Papal Bull**[34] 2791 5-9-2 **121**.. RyanMoore 5 115+
(Sir Michael Stoute) *hld up: nt clr run over 1f out: r.o ins fnl f: nt rch wnr* **2/1**[1]

0360 **3** *1 3/4* **Petara Bay (IRE)**[22] 3121 4-9-2 **105**..................................... JimCrowley 7 112
(T G Mills) *hld up: hung lft and r.o ins fnl f: nrst fin* **22/1**

-541 **4** *6* **Lion Sands**[12] 3497 4-9-2 **110**.. DaneO'Neill 8 102
(L M Cumani) *lw: chsd ldrs: rdn over 1f out: wknd fnl f* **8/1**

3-05 **5** *2* **Sagara (USA)**[21] 3154 4-9-2 **122**.. LDettori 1 99
(Saeed Bin Suroor) *chsd wnr: rdn and hung lft over 1f out: sn wknd* **7/2**[3]

031 **6** *3 1/2* **Anna Pavlova**[5] 3720 5-9-2 **112**.................................... JamieMoriarty 2 94
(R A Fahey) *hld up: hdwy 1/2-way: rdn and edgd rt over 1f out: sn hung lft and wknd* **5/2**[2]

2m 33.37s (0.47) **Going Correction** +0.10s/f (Good) **6** Ran SP% **113.9**
Speed ratings (Par 115): **102,101,100,96,94 92**
toteswinger: 1&2 £7.20, 1&3 £8.90, 2&3 £9.00. CSF £18.88 TOTE £7.20: £3.10, £1.60; EX 17.50 Trifecta £180.90 Pool: £1051.44. 4.30 winning units..

Owner George Strawbridge **Bred** Augustin Stable **Trained** Newmarket, Suffolk

FOCUS
There were five absentees on account of the ground, which in the event was nowhere near as bad as it had seemed likely to be. It turned into a tactical affair, with Lucarno's rider Jimmy Fortune getting an easy lead and to some extent stealing the race. The winning time was very moderate for a Group 2.

NOTEBOOK
Lucarno(USA), saddled with a Group 1 penalty for last year's St Leger win, made every yard under an astute ride from Fortune, who soon had him about six lengths clear before getting a breather in half a mile from home. Kicking away again over a furlong out, he was never going to be caught. Although he enjoyed a soft lead, this was still a smart performance and he is well worth his chance in the King George field later this month, as he should come on further for this run. (op 8-1)
Papal Bull had Lucarno back in fourth when winning this event last year. Held up, he was short of room between Sagara and Anna Pavlova with over a furlong to run and when he got in the clear the winner was long gone, but he was closing the gap at the line. He has the ability to land another decent prize when things go his way but will face a stiff task in the King George. (op 5-2 tchd 11-4)
Petara Bay(IRE) ran a big race on this return to 1m4f. Having travelled well at the back of the field, he came through to challenge for the places and might have even been second had he not hung to his left, although he was never going to pose a threat to the winner. He can win a Group race but will probably require a truer-run race than this was. (op 33-1)
Lion Sands won a Listed event on firm ground over course and distance on his latest start. He ran respectably in this better grade and was disputing a fairly modest second going to the furlong pole before fading. (op 7-1)
Sagara(USA), fifth in the Gold Cup at Ascot last time, had no problem with the drop back in trip but was not good enough. He has not recaptured the form he showed last year for Jonathan Pease. (op 4-1)
Anna Pavlova was making a quick reappearance after her impressive win in the Lancashire Oaks at Haydock five days earlier with Moriarty, who was unable to claim, replacing the suspended Paul Hanagan. The drying ground was against her, and after improving from the rear to show in second place at around halfway she dropped away rather disappointingly. This probably came too soon. Official explanation: trainer said race came too soon (op 2-1 tchd 11-4 in a place)

3879 EUROPEAN BREEDERS' FUND NOVICE STKS 6f
3:45 (3:45) (Class 2) 2-Y-O

£9,714 (£2,890; £1,444; £721) **Stalls** Low

Form RPR

32 **1** **Ouqba**[67] 1832 2-8-12 0.. RHills 5 92+
(B W Hills) *lw: chsd ldr: rdn to ld over 1f out: edgd lft: r.o* **7/4**[1]

2 *1 3/4* **Kentish Dream** 2-8-8 0.. DaneO'Neill 1 82
(S A Callaghan) *w'like: lw: hld up in tch: rdn over 1f out: chsd wnr ins fnl f: no imp* **10/1**

210 **3** *1 1/4* **Brae Hill (IRE)**[23] 3105 2-9-2 0.. JamieSpencer 2 87
(M L W Bell) *plld hrd: hld up in tch: rdn over 1f out: styd on same pce fnl f* **3/1**[2]

10 **4** *hd* **Versaki (IRE)**[23] 3103 2-9-5 0.. RyanMoore 4 89
(R Hannon) *led over 4f: no ex ins fnl f* **4/1**

5 *5* **Maxwell Hawke (IRE)** 2-8-8 0... AlanMunro 3 63
(P W Chapple-Hyam) *w'like: hld up: rdn and hung rt over 1f out: sn hung lft and wknd* **7/2**[3]

1m 14.88s (2.38) **Going Correction** +0.10s/f (Good) **5** Ran SP% **112.7**
Speed ratings (Par 100): **88,85,84,83,77**
CSF £19.05 TOTE £2.80: £1.50, £2.60; EX 21.70.

Owner Hamdan Al Maktoum **Bred** Highclere Stud **Trained** Lambourn, Berks

FOCUS
An interesting little novice event, run at a fair pace. Slight improvement from the winner, and a nice debut from the runner-up.

NOTEBOOK
Ouqba, placed on his first two outings, got off the mark in ready fashion on this return from a 67-day break. He had the form to take this, but does look to have improved for his time off the track and handled the easy ground well. Despite holding a Gimcrack entry his big target is reportedly the valuable DBS Sales race at York's Ebor meeting and he should really proved a big player in that. (op 2-1 tchd 9-4)
Kentish Dream ◆, a 75,000gns half-brother to a useful 1m winner in France, turned in a highly encouraging debut display and looks sure to improve a bundle for the run. He was nicely clear of the remainder and looks a sure-fire maiden winner in the coming weeks. (op 12-1 tchd 9-1)
Brae Hill(IRE), midfield in the Windsor Castle Stakes, did not help his chances of getting home on this first attempt over the extra furlong and on the softer ground by refusing to settle under restraint. He did well to finish so close in the circumstances and, while he is looking more one for the better nurseries at present, it is likely the best of him has quite still to be seen. (op 7-2 tchd 4-1 in a place)
Versaki(IRE) failed to raise his game as could have been expected on this return to softer ground and eventually proved a sitting duck for the principals, despite being given an easy enough lead. His future now looks to lie with the Handicapper. (op 7-2)
Maxwell Hawke(IRE), whose stable sent out the well-backed debut winner Hamoody in this event in 2006, is a 130,000gns half-brother to winning sprinters Oranmore Castle and Achilles Of Troy. He did not go without support on this racecourse bow, yet he looked anything but straightforward when put under some pressure and was eventually well beaten off. He was very coltish beforehand and may well need quicker ground than this. (op 3-1)

3880 SIX WHITING STREET CONDITIONS STKS 1m
4:20 (4:20) (Class 2) 3-Y-O

£12,462 (£3,732; £1,866; £934; £466; £234) **Stalls** Low

Form RPR

-220 **1** **Generous Thought**[22] 3119 3-8-12 **100**......................... RobertWinston 3 104+
(P Howling) *dwlt: hld up: hdwy and n.m.r 2f out: nt clr run and swtchd rt over 1f out: rdn to ld ins fnl f: r.o* **4/1**[2]

5-06 **2** *3/4* **Alfathaa**[21] 3156 3-8-12 **105**..(b) RHills 4 102
(W J Haggas) *led: racd freely: rdn and hdd ins fnl f: styd on* **11/2**[3]

1-02 **3** *1/2* **Choose Your Moment**[33] 2819 3-8-12 **98**..................... KerrinMcEvoy 1 101
(P C Haslam) *chsd ldr: rdn over 1f out: sn ev ch: edgd rt fnl f: unable qck towards fin* **11/4**[1]

3-40 **4** *3* **Alan Devonshire**[33] 2829 3-8-12 **102**................................. EddieAhern 6 94
(M H Tompkins) *swtg: hld up: racd keenly: hdwy over 1f out: sn rdn: wknd ins fnl f* **8/1**

2-10 **5** *1/2* **Rattan (USA)**[21] 3155 3-8-12 **88**.. TedDurcan 7 93
(H R A Cecil) *chsd ldrs: rdn over 2f out: wknd fnl f* **7/1**

3303 **6** *nk* **Red Alert Day**[7] 3635 3-8-12 **105**... LDettori 5 92
(S A Callaghan) *lw: hld up: rdn over 2f out: wknd fnl f* **4/1**[2]

0540 **7** *3/4* **Whitcombe Minister (USA)**[21] 3156 3-8-12 **100**................. JohnEgan 2 90
(Jamie Poulton) *prom: rdn over 2f out: hmpd sn after: wknd over 1f out* **10/1**

1m 39.44s (-0.56) **Going Correction** +0.10s/f (Good) **7** Ran SP% **114.8**
Speed ratings (Par 106): **106,105,104,101,101 100,100**
toteswinger: 1&2 £5.20, 1&3 £2.70, 2&3 £2.70. CSF £26.15 TOTE £5.20: £2.70, £2.70; EX 31.70.

Owner Liam Sheridan **Bred** Aston Mullins Stud **Trained** Newmarket, Suffolk
■ Stewards' Enquiry : Robert Winston one-day ban: careless riding (Jul 24)

FOCUS
A tight conditions event, run at an ordinary pace. The winner shaped better than the bare form with the second running to his Royal Lodge figure.

NOTEBOOK

Generous Thought, not disgraced in the Group 3 Jersey Stakes last time, is the type who needs things to fall just right in his races and, despite finding a troubled passage from off the pace here, just did enough to get on top late in the day. This was his first attempt over the extra furlong and it suited, as did the return to an easier surface. Better than his winning margin would suggest, this was a much-deserved first success of the season, and he would not look out of place in Listed company now. (op 11-4 tchd 9-2)

Alfathaa was given an aggressive ride on this drop back in trip and, despite racing freely early on, kept willingly to his task when challenged inside the final furlong. He is not that straightforward, but should win again when consenting to settle better. (op 9-2 tchd 4-1)

Choose Your Moment, pipped by Redford at Doncaster, had been raised 5lb for that effort and met good support in the betting ring to go one better. He was given every chance and did little wrong in defeat, yet just lacked the tactical pace when it mattered most. Despite his sire's speed influence, he has stamina on the dam's side of his pedigree and now looks well worth stepping up to around 1m2f. (op 3-1 tchd 10-3)

Alan Devonshire, who beat just three home in the Derby last time out, again spoilt his chances by running too freely on this drop back in grade and trip. He paid the price entering the final furlong and must learn to settle if he is to now progress, but the return to a longer trip should suit him better all the same. (op 12-1)

Rattan(USA) had a fair amount to find on official figures and was not really disgraced. (op 15-2 tchd 13-2)

Red Alert Day has to rate as disappointing and was well below his previous level with no apparent excuses. (op 5-1)

3881 HIGHLAND MERIDIAN GARDENS H'CAP — 5f

4:55 (4:57) (Class 3) (0-95,95) 3-Y-O+ **£9,714** (£2,890; £1,444; £721) **Stalls** Low

Form			Horse	Jockey	RPR
00-5	**1**		**Kay Two (IRE)**[12] 3472 6-9-3 **84** (p) JimCrowley 13 (R J Price) *lw: chsd ldr: rdn to ld ins fnl f: r.o* **9/1**		92
0050	**2**	¾	**Prior Warning**[20] 3197 4-9-9 **95** (t) MCGeran(5) 4 (Miss D Mountain) *hld up: rdn over 1f out: r.o wl ins fnl f: nt rch wnr* **25/1**		100
334	**3**	*hd*	**Ebraam (USA)**[40] 2598 5-9-13 **94** JimmyQuinn 3 (P Howling) *lw: chsd ldrs: led over 1f out: rdn and hdd ins fnl f: edgd rt: styd on* **11/1**		98
-610	**4**	*nse*	**Zowington**[35] 2760 6-9-3 **84** IanMongan 5 (C F Wall) *hld up: hdwy over 1f out: sn rdn: r.o* **16/1**		88
3042	**5**	*shd*	**Northern Dare (IRE)**[11] 3532 4-9-6 **87** AdrianTNicholls 6 (D Nicholls) *lw: trckd ldrs: racd keenly: hmpd 4f out: rdn over 1f out: nt clr run and swtchd lft ins fnl f: r.o* **7/4**[1]		91+
2330	**6**	*nk*	**Lord Of The Reins (IRE)**[16] 3336 4-8-13 **80** AlanMunro 11 (J G Given) *s.i.s: hld up: swtchd rt over 1f out: r.o wl ins fnl f: nt rch ldrs* **8/1**[3]		83+
5500	**7**	*nse*	**Canadian Danehill (IRE)**[16] 3336 6-9-10 **91** (p) MartinDwyer 9 (R M H Cowell) *led: rdn: edgd rt and hdd over 1f out: unable qck towards fin* **25/1**		93
0130	**8**	*nse*	**Luscivious**[13] 3451 4-9-6 **87** (b) WilliamBuick 7 (A J McCabe) *chsd ldrs: rdn over 1f out: styd on* **8/1**[3]		89
-600	**9**	3 ¾	**The Jobber (IRE)**[6] 3680 7-9-11 **92** DaneO'Neill 17 (M Blanshard) *hld up: rdn over 1f out: n.d* **16/1**		81
4303	**10**	*hd*	**Digital**[11] 3520 11-8-9 **76** (v) SamHitchcott 15 (M R Channon) *hld up: rdn over 1f out: n.d* **12/1**		64
-040	**11**	2 ½	**Sundae**[6] 3680 4-9-10 **91** TedDurcan 12 (C F Wall) *hld up: racd keenly: rdn and hung lft over 1f out: sn wknd* **5/1**[2]		70

59.82 secs (0.72) **Going Correction** +0.10s/f (Good) **11** Ran SP% **120.7**
Speed ratings (Par 107): **98,96,96,96,96 95,95,95,89,89 85**
toteswinger: 1&2 £42.90, 1&3 £16.30, 2&3 £36.30. CSF £215.05 CT £2523.18 TOTE £11.30: £2.90, £7.10, £3.50; EX 265.90 Place 6: £216.08, Place 5: £160.57..

Owner Hugh B McGahon **Bred** Roger A Ryan **Trained** Ullingswick, H'fords

■ Stewards' Enquiry : Martin Dwyer two-day ban: careless riding (Jul 24,25)

FOCUS

Despite six non-runners this was a competitive enough sprint for the class, but it was not run at the fastest early pace and it resulted in a moderate time for the grade. The first eight were very closely covered at the finish. The winner has been rated to the best of his form in the last two years, and the runner-up to his British level.

NOTEBOOK

Kay Two(IRE) showed the benefit of his recent reappearance fifth at Chester, for which he had generously been dropped 2lb, and opened his account for the year in resolute fashion. He enjoys this sort of surface and, seeing as he should still be open to some improvement for the run, should at least remain competitive in good handicaps after a likely rise in the weights. (op 8-1 tchd 7-1)

Prior Warning bounced right back to form on this return to 5f and an easier surface, doing all of his best work towards the finish. A more positive ride over this trip should see him in an even better light and this rates a solid effort under top weight from this former French Listed winner.

Ebraam(USA), returning from a 40-day break, was always up with the pace and showed improved form. He is a consistent performer, who deserves another winning turn, and helps to set the level of this form. Official explanation: jockey said gelding hung right (op 12-1 tchd 14-1)

Zowington emerged from off the pace to have his chance and ran one of his better races. He really needs to come from off a searching pace to be seen at best effect. (op 14-1)

Northern Dare(IRE) ran a little too freely early on, but was still coming with his challenge prior to finding trouble inside the final furlong and should rate a little better than the bare form. He ideally wants another furlong nowadays and is in good heart at present, but he was already due to race from a 5lb higher mark in the future so this was really a missed opportunity. (op 2-1 tchd 85-40)

Lord Of The Reins(IRE), making his debut for a new trainer, was motoring home inside the final furlong after missing the break yet was always getting there too late. He will probably go up for this, but still has more prizes within his compass this term. (op 10-1)

Canadian Danehill(IRE) had his chance from the front and, while finding just the same pace at the business end, was not beaten at all far. This was better from him.

Luscivious posted one of his better efforts in defeat and was another not beaten far on this suitably easy surface. (op 14-1)

Sundae Official explanation: jockey said gelding had no more to give

T/Jkpt: £267,447.81 to a £1 stake. Pool: £1,695,092.25. 4.50 winning tickets. T/Plt: £519.50 to a £1 stake. Pool: £198,767.91. 279.27 winning tickets. T/Qpdt: £98.70 to a £1 stake. Pool: £8,651.20. 64.80 winning tickets. CR

3732 NOTTINGHAM (L-H)

Thursday, July 10

OFFICIAL GOING: Good to soft (good in places; 6.9)

Rail realignment added 5yards to advertised distances on round course.

Wind: moderate, half against Weather: fine, light shower race 4

3882 WEATHERBYS BLOODSTOCK INSURANCE MAIDEN AUCTION STKS — 6f 15y

6:20 (6:21) (Class 5) 2-Y-O **£3,238** (£963; £481; £240) **Stalls** High

Form			Horse	Jockey	RPR
	1		**Rafiqa (IRE)** 2-8-8 0 StephenCarson 8 (C F Wall) *s.i.s: rn green: outpcd and lost pl 3f out: gd hdwy on stands' side rail over 1f out: r.o wl to ld towards fin* **25/1**		75+
02	**2**	1 ½	**Campbeltown Trader (IRE)**[17] 3323 2-8-11 0 RichardKingscote 9 (Tom Dascombe) *chsd ldrs: effrt 2f out: led ins fnl f: hdd fnl 75yds* **5/2**[2]		74
3	**3**	1	**Noble Storm (USA)**[22] 3125 2-8-11 0 DarryllHolland 6 (E S McMahon) *trckd ldr: t.k.h: led over 1f out: hdd and no ex ins fnl f* **6/4**[1]		71
2	**4**	1 ¾	**Saif Al Fahad (IRE)**[20] 3199 2-8-11 0 ChrisCatlin 1 (E J O'Neill) *led: qcknd 3f out: hdd over 1f out: one pce fnl f* **6/1**		65
252	**5**	4 ½	**Forward Feline (IRE)**[44] 2473 2-8-6 0 CatherineGannon 3 (B Palling) *chsd ldrs: effrt over 2f out: wknd fnl f* **4/1**[3]		47
	6	6	**Tax Dodger (IRE)** 2-8-9 0 FrancisNorton 2 (J L Spearing) *dwlt: sn wl outpcd and bhd* **40/1**		32
0	**7**	*nk*	**Spring Quartet**[31] 2893 2-8-13 0 (b[1]) RoystonFfrench 4 (Pat Eddery) *dwlt: reminders and wl outpcd 3f out: sn bhd* **22/1**		35

1m 15.96s (0.86) **Going Correction** +0.025s/f (Good) **7** Ran SP% **113.5**
Speed ratings (Par 94): **95,93,91,89,83 75,74**
toteswinger: 1&2 £47.00, 1&3 £20.40, 2&3 £1.10. CSF £85.76 TOTE £23.60: £9.10, £2.30; EX 139.80.

Owner The Equema Partnership **Bred** Lady Juliet Tadgell **Trained** Newmarket, Suffolk

FOCUS

A relatively small field for this maiden and for much of the way it looked as if those with experience would dominate, especially as they went clear from the halfway point. However, things changed dramatically in the final furlong. The form looks fair.

NOTEBOOK

Rafiqa(IRE), a 20,000gns filly out of a winner at up to 1m4f, missed the break and ran green in the early stages but suddenly got the hang of things and, helped by getting a clear passage up the inside rail, swept through to win with a little in hand. Something of a surprise to connections, she will probably run in nurseries before having a crack at the Watership Down Sales race at Ascot later in the season. (op 20-1 tchd 33-1)

Campbeltown Trader(IRE) had improved on his debut when narrowly beaten on fast ground next time and looked sure to win when going ahead entering the final furlong, but had no answer to the winner's late surge. He deserves to pick up a race and now qualifies for a handicap mark. (op 9-4)

Noble Storm(USA), a half-brother to four winners out of a multiple winner, was well backed to build on his promising debut, but spoilt his chance by running too free in the early stages and consequently had nothing in reserve for the business end. His rider subsequently reported that he had run too free. Official explanation: jockey said colt ran too free (op 3-1)

Saif Al Fahad(IRE) was another to have made a promising debut and made the early running, but was readily brushed aside when the runner-up went on. (op 11-2 tchd 13-2)

Forward Feline(IRE), who was stepping up in trip having run well in decent company at 5f, seemed to have every chance before fading and a return to the minimum trip, possibly in nurseries, looks on the cards. (op 11-4)

3883 WEATHERBYS BLOODSTOCK INSURANCE FILLIES' H'CAP — 6f 15y

6:55 (6:56) (Class 4) (0-80,85) 3-Y-O+ **£7,447** (£2,216; £1,107; £553) **Stalls** High

Form			Horse	Jockey	RPR
0650	**1**		**Scarlet Oak**[8] 3615 4-8-8 **60** oh1 (p) ChrisCatlin 12 (D J S Ffrench Davis) *sn in rr stands' side: swtchd lft and gd hdwy over 1f out: r.o wl to ld fnl 75yds* **10/1**		70
1-55	**2**	1	**Quaroma**[31] 2896 3-8-13 **71** PaulDoe 3 (Jane Chapple-Hyam) *prom: hdwy to ld apparoaching fnl f: hdd and no ex wl ins fnl f* **40/1**		77
5616	**3**	½	**Dorn Dancer (IRE)**[10] 3554 6-9-2 **73** NeilBrown(5) 7 (D W Barker) *in rr: detached over 2f out: swtchd stands' rails over 1f out: fin fast* **10/1**		79
5320	**4**	1 ½	**Tilly's Dream**[19] 3271 5-9-9 **78** LukeMorris(3) 2 (G C Bravery) *chsd ldrs: styd on same pce fnl f* **14/1**		79
3535	**5**	*nk*	**Poppy's Rose**[12] 3481 4-8-11 **63** RoystonFfrench 8 (I W McInnes) *rr-div: hdwy over 2f out: n.m.r over 1f out: kpt on same pce* **12/1**		63
1631	**6**	*nk*	**Mango Music**[10] 3554 5-10-5 **85** 6ex FrancisNorton 11 (M Quinn) *chsd ldrs: kpt on same pce appr fnl f* **9/2**[2]		84+
0005	**7**	2	**Feelin Foxy**[19] 3260 4-9-6 **72** SebSanders 1 (J G Given) *led in centre tl appr fnl f: sn wknd* **16/1**		65
4001	**8**	*nse*	**Sahaadi**[8] 3615 3-8-2 **67** CharlesEddery(7) 9 (R Hannon) *s.i.s: hdwy over 2f out: lost pl over 1f out* **6/1**[3]		58
4124	**9**	*nk*	**Overwing (IRE)**[6] 3695 5-9-2 **68** KerrinMcEvoy 4 (R M H Cowell) *chsd ldrs: wknd appr fnl f* **10/1**		59
-223	**10**	5	**Orpen Fire (IRE)**[15] 3369 3-9-4 **76** DarryllHolland 6 (E S McMahon) *swtchd rt after s: w ldrs: lost pl over 1f out* **10/3**[1]		50
314	**11**	2	**Celtic Lynn (IRE)**[15] 3369 3-9-2 **74** StephenCarson 5 (M Dods) *mid-div: hung rt and hmpd over 1f out: sn eased* **13/2**		42

1m 14.96s (-0.14) **Going Correction** +0.025s/f (Good)
WFA 3 from 4yo+ 6lb **11** Ran SP% **118.8**
Speed ratings (Par 102): **101,99,99,97,96 96,93,93,93,86 83**
toteswinger: 1&2 £70.90, 1&3 £35.10, 2&3 £35.40. CSF £342.21 CT £4136.08 TOTE £14.90: £3.70, £9.80, £4.00; EX 684.90.

Owner Miss A Jones **Bred** Juddmonte Farms Ltd **Trained** Lambourn, Berks

■ Stewards' Enquiry : Chris Catlin one-day ban: careless riding (Jul 24)

FOCUS

A fair fillies' handicap in which the leaders Orpen Fire and Feelin Foxy appeared to go too fast in the early stages as the first three all came from off the pace. The winner and third set the standard and the form looks more solid than most fillies' races

Sahaadi Official explanation: jockey said filly never travelled

Celtic Lynn(IRE) Official explanation: jockey said filly hung right

3884 WEATHERBYS BANK JUMP JOCKEYS H'CAP (TO BE RIDDEN BY NATIONAL HUNT JOCKEYS) 1m 6f 15y

7:25 (7:26) (Class 4) (0-80,76) 4-Y-0+ **£6,476** (£1,927; £963; £481) **Stalls** Low

Form RPR

1222 **1** **Spring Dream (IRE)**[6] 3685 5-11-7 **73**................(b[1]) ChristianWilliams 7 81
(A King) *trckd ldrs: nt clr run 2f out: burst through jst ins fnl f: r.o to ld nr fin* **11/2**[3]

05/1 **2** *nk* **Tomina**[36] 2715 8-11-6 **72**................ TimmyMurphy 2 80
(Miss E C Lavelle) *set mod pce: qcknd over 4f out: kpt on gamely: hdd nr fin* **7/1**

-432 **3** *3/4* **Bollin Felix**[14] 3414 4-11-10 **76**................(b) DougieCostello 3 83
(T D Easterby) *chsd ldr: chal 3f out: no ex wl ins fnl f* **3/1**[1]

104- **4** *nk* **Downing Street (IRE)**[18] 4893 7-11-9 **75**................(v) NoelFehily 4 82+
(Jennie Candlish) *hld up in rr: hdwy on ins over 3f out: trapped and nt clr run fr 2f out: nt rcvr* **14/1**

201- **5** *3/4* **Dark Energy**[16] 6258 4-11-4 **70**................(t) TomScudamore 9 76
(M J Scudamore) *hld up in rr: hdwy over 3f out: nt clr run over 1f out: kpt on* **10/1**

1664 **6** *3/4* **Apache Fort**[15] 3375 5-10-13 **65**................ SeanCurran 1 69
(T Keddy) *chsd ldrs: kpt on same pce appr fnl f* **10/1**

6443 **7** *nk* **Celticello (IRE)**[12] 3474 6-11-5 **71**................ TonyEvans 5 75
(P D Evans) *hld up in rr: hdwy over 3f out: nvr rchd ldrs* **11/1**

5-02 **8** *1 1/4* **Yossi (IRE)**[7] 3630 4-11-10 **76**................ JamieMoore 12 78
(M H Tompkins) *hld up in mid-div: effrt on outer over 2f out: nvr rchd ldrs* **4/1**[2]

423/ **9** *1/2* **Depraux (IRE)**[27] 6758 5-10-12 **64**................ AndrewTinkler 6 66
(G M Moore) *chsd ldrs: rdn over 2f out: one pce* **40/1**

5032 **10** *2 1/2* **They All Laughed**[11] 3523 5-11-7 **73**................ LiamTreadwell 11 71
(P W Hiatt) *hld up in last: effrt on outer 4f out: nvr a factor* **12/1**

/044 **11** *nse* **Emile Zola**[21] 3179 6-10-10 **62**................ SamThomas 10 60
(Miss Venetia Williams) *hld up in mid-div: effrt over 3f out: sn outpcd* **20/1**

3m 17.28s (9.98) **Going Correction** +0.10s/f (Good) **11** Ran SP% **121.0**
Speed ratings (Par 105): **75,74,74,74,73 73,73,72,72,70 70**
toteswinger: 1&2 £6.90, 1&3 £5.10, 2&3 £16.40. CSF £45.23 CT £139.63 TOTE £5.70: £2.20, £3.00, £1.70; EX 42.20.
Owner W H Ponsonby **Bred** R N Auld **Trained** Barbury Castle, Wilts

FOCUS
A novelty event with the runners ridden by jump jockeys, although a number of them had form over hurdles and fences. The early gallop was reminiscent of most bumpers and the final time was pedestrian. The form is rated around the placed horses.

3885 SIMPLY CARTONS CONDITIONS STKS 1m 2f 50y

7:55 (7:55) (Class 3) 3-Y-0+ **£8,723** (£2,612; £1,306; £653; £326) **Stalls** Low

Form RPR

14/ **1** **Hala Bek (IRE)**[768] 2228 5-9-0 0................ KerrinMcEvoy 2 115+
(Saeed Bin Suroor) *trckd ldrs: effrt over 3f out: led over 1f out: r.o strly to draw clr* **7/2**[2]

212- **2** *7* **Fairmile**[250] 6653 6-9-0 111................ LDettori 1 101
(Saeed Bin Suroor) *hld up: hdwy over 5f out: shkn up over 3f out: styd on to take 2nd ins fnl f: no ch w wnr* **1/2**[1]

314- **3** *1 1/2* **Soft Morning**[211] 7128 4-8-9 105................ SebSanders 6 93
(Sir Mark Prescott) *anticipated s: led: hdd narrowly over 2f out: hdd over 1f out: styd on same pce* **7/1**[3]

0-00 **4** *3/4* **Levera**[41] 2580 5-9-0 95................ DarryllHolland 3 96
(A King) *chsd ldr: led narrowly and briefly over 2f out: kpt on same pce* **28/1**

125- **5** *16* **Kinsya**[229] 6931 5-9-0 96................ JimmyQuinn 4 64
(M H Tompkins) *tried to jump w ldr and hit gate: hld up in last: effrt 4f out: no imp: eased* **18/1**

2m 10.41s (-2.09) **Going Correction** +0.10s/f (Good)
WFA 3 from 4yo+ 11lb **5** Ran SP% **110.1**
Speed ratings (Par 107): **112,106,105,104,91**
toteswinger: 1&2 £1.40. CSF £5.70 TOTE £3.90: £1.70, £1.10; EX 6.50.
Owner Godolphin **Bred** Cliveden Stud Ltd **Trained** Newmarket, Suffolk

FOCUS
A decent conditions stakes and a fine return to action by the winner. The winning time was solid given the size of the field.

NOTEBOOK
Hala Bek(IRE) ◆ had been off the track since a narrowly beaten fourth in the 2006 Derby, when trained by Michael Jarvis. After tracking the leaders, he briefly looked in trouble early in the straight, but he picked up so well when asked that he came right away from his stable-companion. There are no short-term plans for him, but he has plenty of opportunities at 1m2f to 1m4f, with the Juddmonte International and the Dubai Champion Stakes among a number of possibilities. (op 4-1)
Fairmile was held up well off the pace, but he moved up going well only to have no answer when his stable companion went for home. His trainer reported that like the winner the run was needed. (op 4-5)
Soft Morning appeared to burst the stalls and made the running, but she was being asked for everything a fair way out and had nothing more to offer when headed by the winner. (op 4-1)
Levera was stepping up in trip and kept the leader company before briefly going to the front halfway up the straight. However, his stamina appeared to ebb away from that point, and he had a difficult task on official ratings in any case. (op 20-1)
Kinsya was held up in the rear, but was being ridden early in the straight and dropped away somewhat disappointingly. His rider reported that he banged his head on the stalls so can be given another chance. Official explanation: jockey said gelding banged its head on stalls (op 12-1 tchd 20-1)

3886 WEATHERBYS PRINTING H'CAP 1m 2f 50y

8:30 (8:34) (Class 5) (0-70,69) 3-Y-0 **£3,561** (£1,059; £529; £264) **Stalls** Low

Form RPR

4-46 **1** **Addikt (IRE)**[20] 3206 3-9-6 **68**................ LDettori 11 78+
(S Kirk) *trckd ldrs: effrt over 2f out: squeezed out over 1f out: swtchd outside: r.o wl to ld ins fnl f: readily* **6/4**[1]

5-00 **2** *1 1/4* **Mystic Art (IRE)**[17] 3327 3-9-1 **63**................(p) KerrinMcEvoy 12 68
(C R Egerton) *led 1f: w ldr: hung lft and led appr fnl f: edgd rt and hdd ins fnl f* **40/1**

-305 **3** *1* **Hawk House**[27] 3004 3-9-0 **62**................ ChrisCatlin 10 65
(B W Hills) *w ldrs: led 4f out tl over 2f out: kpt on same pce ins fnl f* **15/2**[3]

1030 **4** *nk* **Classical Rhythm (IRE)**[5] 3745 3-9-4 **66**................ AmirQuinn 2 68
(J R Boyle) *chsd ldrs: led over 2f out: hdd appr fnl f: kpt on same pce* **14/1**

0-26 **5** *3 1/2* **Politeia (USA)**[17] 3322 3-9-7 **69**................ PatDobbs 16 64+
(R Hannon) *hld up in rr: effrt over 4f out: edgd lft and styd on ins fnl f* **7/1**[2]

-550 **6** *3/4* **Shesha Bear**[15] 3384 3-9-5 **67**................ FrancisNorton 6 63+
(W R Muir) *awkward to load: swvd rt s: mid-div: shkn up over 5f out: hdwy over 3f out: clr 5th whn eased ins fnl f* **33/1**

-000 **7** *2 1/4* **Sainglend**[28] 2974 3-9-5 **67**................ PaulDoe 8 56
(S Curran) *in rr: sme hdwy over 2f out: nvr nr ldrs* **25/1**

0010 **8** *1/2* **Always Certain (USA)**[13] 3436 3-9-6 **68**................ DarryllHolland 1 56
(M Johnston) *led after 1f: hung rt and hdd 4f out: sn outpcd* **12/1**

-330 **9** *1 3/4* **Jafra (IRE)**[20] 3221 3-8-7 **58**................ MichaelJStainton[(3)] 13 43
(R M Whitaker) *s.i.s: effrt on wd outside over 4f out: nvr a factor* **14/1**

0-00 **10** *1* **Lilburn (IRE)**[21] 3161 3-9-4 **66**................ RobertWinston 14 49
(J R Fanshawe) *trckd ldrs: t.k.h: effrt over 2f out: wknd over 1f out* **12/1**

-030 **11** *1* **Nordic Commander (IRE)**[24] 3095 3-9-2 **64**................ SebSanders 9 45
(E A L Dunlop) *mid-div: effrt on outer over 2f out: fdd over 1f out* **12/1**

6650 **12** *2* **Timber Creek**[10] 3563 3-8-13 **68**................ AmyScott[(7)] 4 45
(H Candy) *dwlt: hld up in rr: sme hdwy 3f out: nvr a factor* **25/1**

056 **13** *1 1/2* **Linby (IRE)**[20] 3227 3-8-13 **61**................ DaleGibson 3 35
(N Tinkler) *dwlt: hdwy to chse ldrs after 2f: lost pl 2f out* **33/1**

3046 **14** *2 1/2* **Hellfire Bay**[14] 3407 3-8-8 **56**................ AdrianTNicholls 5 25
(J Mackie) *mid-div: effrt over 3f out: sn btn* **33/1**

-000 **15** *2* **Creative (IRE)**[28] 2982 3-8-12 **60**................ JimmyQuinn 15 25
(M H Tompkins) *swvd rt s: in rr: drvn over 4f out: nvr on terms* **20/1**

-660 **16** *1 3/4* **Morocchius (USA)**[43] 2496 3-9-5 **67**................ DO'Donohoe 7 28
(Miss J A Camacho) *dwlt: in rr: effrt 4f out: sn bhd* **40/1**

2m 13.49s (0.99) **Going Correction** +0.10s/f (Good) **16** Ran SP% **126.8**
Speed ratings (Par 100): **100,99,98,97,95 94,92,92,90,90 89,87,86,84,82 81**
toteswinger: 1&2 £25.20, 1&3 £6.00, 2&3 £55.70. CSF £94.41 CT £388.89 TOTE £2.60: £1.20, £9.00, £1.80, £3.80; EX 74.10.
Owner The Par 6 **Bred** Deerpark Stud **Trained** Upper Lambourn, Berks

FOCUS
A modest handicap with a big field, but they went 12-1 bar three and it provided a first success for the well-backed favourite. The third ran close to recent Sandown form and the winner is value for more than the official margin.
Shesha Bear Official explanation: jockey said filly ducked out of stalls and had no more to give closing stages
Sainglend Official explanation: jockey said gelding finished distressed
Always Certain(USA) Official explanation: jockey said gelding hung right throughout

3887 IMPERIAL LEATHER H'CAP 1m 75y

9:00 (9:00) (Class 4) (0-85,84) 3-Y-0+ **£6,476** (£1,927; £963; £481) **Stalls** Centre

Form RPR

0503 **1** **Rainbow Mirage (IRE)**[15] 3367 4-9-9 **79**................ DarryllHolland 1 88
(E S McMahon) *t.k.h: effrt over 4f out: led over 1f out: readily* **5/2**[1]

644 **2** *nk* **Reel Buddy Star**[12] 3494 3-8-6 **71**................ RoystonFfrench 7 77
(G M Moore) *swvd rt s: sn trcking ldrs: chal over 1f out: nt qckn ins fnl f* **7/2**[2]

-116 **3** *2* **Grand Vizier (IRE)**[31] 2897 4-8-11 **72**................ JackMitchell[(5)] 4 76+
(C F Wall) *hld up in rr: drvn and outpcd over 3f out: swtchd wd over 1f out: styd on* **4/1**[3]

0364 **4** *1 3/4* **Phluke**[15] 3376 7-10-0 **84**................ StephenCarson 3 84
(Eve Johnson Houghton) *led tl over 6f out: led over 2f tl over 1f out: sn wknd* **11/1**

4660 **5** *nk* **Full Victory (IRE)**[15] 3367 6-9-6 **76**................ ChrisCatlin 5 75
(R A Farrant) *t.k.h: hdwy 3f out: kpt on: nvr a threat* **8/1**

3303 **6** *2 1/2* **Major Magpie (IRE)**[5] 3716 6-9-10 **80**................ RobertWinston 2 73
(M Dods) *dwlt: hdwy on ins 4f out: sn chsng ldrs: wknd over 1f out* **4/1**[3]

30-0 **7** *2 1/4* **St Petersburg**[8] 3612 8-9-12 **82**................ AmirQuinn 6 70
(J R Boyle) *r wd: hdwy to ld over 6f out: hdd over 2f out: lost pl over 1f out* **25/1**

1m 47.67s (2.27) **Going Correction** +0.10s/f (Good)
WFA 3 from 4yo+ 9lb **7** Ran SP% **114.1**
Speed ratings (Par 105): **92,91,89,87,87 85,82**
toteswinger: 1&2 £2.20, 1&3 £4.40, 2&3 £3.60. CSF £11.40 CT £32.74 TOTE £3.50: £1.80, £2.40; EX 14.10 Place 6: £103.82, Place 5: £24.12..
Owner R L Bedding **Bred** Neville O'Byrne And Roderick Ryan **Trained** Lichfield, Staffs

FOCUS
An ordinary contest, but another successful favourite. The winning time was moderate for the grade and the form is not the most solid, with the runner-up the best guide.
St Petersburg Official explanation: jockey said gelding ran too free
T/Plt: £156.60 to a £1 stake. Pool: £59,875.07. 279.05 winning tickets. T/Qpdt: £5.10 to a £1 stake. Pool: £5,125.80. 740.80 winning tickets. WG

3692 WARWICK (L-H)

Thursday, July 10

OFFICIAL GOING: Soft (6.6)
Wind: Moderate behind Weather: Shower before 4.05

3888 WARWICKRACECOURSE.CO.UK MAIDEN AUCTION STKS 7f 26y

1:50 (1:53) (Class 5) 2-Y-0 **£3,238** (£963; £481; £240) **Stalls** Low

Form RPR

56 **1** **Kings Troop**[29] 2951 2-8-13 0................ TPQueally 4 81+
(H R A Cecil) *hld up in tch: led wl over 1f out: sn edgd rt: shkn up and wnt clr ins fnl f: readily* **7/2**[2]

0222 **2** *3 3/4* **Hay Fever (IRE)**[27] 2987 2-8-11 0................ StephenCarson 9 68
(Eve Johnson Houghton) *a.p: c wd to stands' rail ent st: led briefly 2f out: one pce fnl f: jst hld on to 2nd* **5/4**[1]

0 **3** *shd* **Captain Imperial (IRE)**[14] 3411 2-8-11 0................ MickyFenton 7 67
(T P Tate) *led: hdd 3f out: rdn over 1f out: kpt on same pce fnl f* **4/1**[3]

0 **4** *1* **Rockfella**[15] 3372 2-8-13 0................ FergalLynch 1 67
(D J Coakley) *s.i.s: hld up and bhd: hdwy wl over 1f out: kpt on ins fnl f* **16/1**

000 **5** *2 1/4* **Forster Island**[19] 3267 2-8-9 0................ SteveDrowne 11 57
(M Blanshard) *hld up in mid-div: no real prog fnl 2f* **33/1**

000 **6** *1/2* **Paymaster In Chief**[13] 3444 2-8-9 0................ ChrisCatlin 2 56
(M D I Usher) *w ldr: led 3f out to 2f out: faltered path jst over 1f out: wknd ins fnl f* **20/1**

7 *4 1/2* **Sherman McCoy** 2-8-9 0................ TGMcLaughlin 13 45
(B R Millman) *wnt rt s: in rr: n.d* **28/1**

0 **8** *1 3/4* **Rebelwithoutacause (IRE)**[22] 3140 2-8-13 0................ DO'Donohoe 6 44
(George Baker) *hld up in mid-div: wknd wl over 1f out* **33/1**

56 **9** *1/2* **Call Me Courageous (IRE)**[82] 1474 2-8-11 0................ PatCosgrave 10 41
(A B Haynes) *hld up in tch: rdn and wkng whn hung rt to stands' rail over 1f out* **16/1**

10 *nse* **Red Eric** 2-8-9 0................ PatrickMathers 12 39
(W M Brisbourne) *hld up towards rr: pushed along 2f out: no rspnse* **50/1**

6 11 2½ **Ruud Revenge (USA)**[12] [3476] 2-8-11 0........................ PaulMulrennan 8 35
(Miss V Haigh) *s.i.s: rdn over 3f out: a in rr* 66/1

1m 28.11s (3.51) **Going Correction** +0.325s/f (Good) 11 Ran SP% **116.0**
Speed ratings (Par 94): **92,87,87,86,83 83,78,76,75,75 72**
toteswinger: 1&2 £2.50, 1&3 £2.70, 2&3 £2.30. CSF £7.55 TOTE £4.00: £1.40, £1.30, £1.50; EX 8.20.
Owner W H Ponsonby **Bred** Wickfield Stud And Hartshill Stud **Trained** Newmarket, Suffolk

FOCUS
No strength in depth to this juvenile maiden. The winner did it well though and looks to have a bright future.

NOTEBOOK
Kings Troop ♦ only needed to be shaken up to gain a ready success. Showing much improvement for the extra furlong, he looks the type to do very well in nurseries. (op 10-3 tchd 3-1 and 4-1 in places)
Hay Fever(IRE) now runner-up on his last four starts, was brought across to the stands' rail in the straight, in search of better ground, but it proved to no avail. Stepping up in trip on soft going probably just stretched his stamina beyond the limit at this stage of his career. (tchd 11-10 and 11-8)
Captain Imperial(IRE) showed up well for a long way, and will be winning races in due course. (op 5-1)
Rockfella ♦ showed nothing on debut but was nibbled at in the market beforehand and kept on nicely in the closing stages, shaping as though he will appreciate another furlong in due course. (op 50-1)
Forster Island is moderate and will do better in nurseries.
Paymaster In Chief showed his first signs of ability, briefly leading on the home turn. He might be of some interest in a small 6f nursery. (op 25-1)

3889 LEVY BOARD MAIDEN STKS 5f
2:20 (2:24) (Class 5) 2-Y-0 **£2,590** (£770; £385; £192) **Stalls** Centre

Form RPR
23 1 **Green Beret (IRE)**[20] [3219] 2-9-3 0........................ RobertHavlin 5 83+
(J H M Gosden) *w ldrs: led over 3f out: pushed clr ins fnl f: easily* 2/7[1]
03 2 5 **My Best Man**[8] [3603] 2-9-3 0........................ TGMcLaughlin 1 65
(B R Millman) *led over 1f: rdn and hung rt over 1f out: sn no ch w wnr* 13/2[2]
24 3 4½ **Grand Plan (USA)**[96] [1214] 2-8-12 0........................ TPQueally 2 44
(J A Osborne) *w ldrs: n.m.r briefly over 2f out: rdn and wknd over 1f out* 8/1[3]
0056 4 11 **Tyler**[2] [3815] 2-9-3 0........................ DavidAllan 4 9
(W M Brisbourne) *sn outpcd: rdn over 2f out: sn struggling* 50/1

60.73 secs (1.13) **Going Correction** +0.20s/f (Good) 4 Ran SP% **104.2**
Speed ratings (Par 94): **98,90,82,65**
CSF £2.24 TOTE £1.30; EX 2.20.
Owner H R H Princess Haya Of Jordan **Bred** Denis And Mrs Teresa Bergin **Trained** Newmarket, Suffolk

FOCUS
An uncompetitive maiden and a penalty kick for the Gosden representative.

NOTEBOOK
Green Beret(IRE) was handed a confidence booster here after two good efforts in maidens at Windsor and Newmarket. He will be running in the better nurseries. (op 3-10)
My Best Man left his debut form well behind when placing at 80-1 in a Chepstow maiden last week, and showed that was no fluke by running to a similar level of form here. (op 9-2)
Grand Plan(USA) was obviously a precocious sort as she was out very early on the All-Weather and being sent off at short prices to boot. She must have had some kind of problem to have had over three months off though, and didn't show much promise on this first start since. (tchd 15-2)
Tyler is poor and never went the pace.

3890 EAGLE OTTAWA H'CAP 6f
2:55 (2:55) (Class 4) (0-85,80) 3-Y-0+
£4,984 (£1,492; £746; £373; £186; £93) **Stalls** Centre

Form RPR
0050 1 **Steel City Boy (IRE)**[2] [3819] 5-8-5 63 oh5 ow2........................ AnnStokell(5) 2 72
(Miss A Stokell) *a.p: wnt 2nd 3f out: sustained chal fr over 1f out: rdn to ld towards fin* 11/1
6413 2 hd **Peter Island (FR)**[12] [3506] 5-9-6 73........................(v) ChrisCatlin 1 81
(J Gallagher) *led: rdn ins fnl f: hdd towards fin* 9/2[3]
5644 3 1¼ **Coleorton Dancer**[5] [3713] 6-8-13 66........................(b) FergalLynch 4 70
(K A Ryan) *hld up in tch: swtchd rt jst over 1f out: rdn and nt qckn ins fnl f* 5/2[2]
0004 4 1¼ **Paris Bell**[2] [3812] 6-9-3 70........................ DavidAllan 6 70
(T D Easterby) *s.i.s: in rr: rdn and kpt on ins fnl f: snatched 4th post* 2/1[1]
5610 5 shd **Caribbean Coral**[14] [3418] 9-9-13 80........................ TPQueally 3 80
(A B Haynes) *hld up: hdwy over 1f out: rdn and no ex ins fnl f* 8/1
0226 6 2½ **Lieutenant Pigeon**[6] [3696] 3-9-3 76........................ PaulEddery 7 68
(G D Blake) *w ldr 3f: sn rdn: wknd jst over 1f out* 10/1

1m 12.74s (0.94) **Going Correction** +0.20s/f (Good)
WFA 3 from 5yo+ 6lb 6 Ran SP% **108.6**
Speed ratings (Par 105): **101,100,99,97,97 93**
toteswinger: 1&2 £6.60, 1&3 £7.80, 2&3 £2.40. CSF £54.55 TOTE £13.20: £4.70, £2.20; EX 69.00.
Owner J Medley **Bred** Mrs A B McDonnell **Trained** Brompton-on-Swale, N Yorks
■ Stewards' Enquiry : Ann Stokell two-day ban: used whip in incorrect place (Jul 24-25)

FOCUS
A fair sprint handicap best rated around the placed horses to their latest marks. Ann Stokell was securing her second win in a week after a long barren spell.
Lieutenant Pigeon Official explanation: jockey said gelding was unsuited by the soft ground

3891 TURFTV H'CAP 1m 6f 213y
3:30 (3:32) (Class 5) (0-75,74) 3-Y-0+ **£3,238** (£963; £481; £240) **Stalls** Low

Form RPR
00/6 1 **Keelung (USA)**[18] [3296] 7-9-5 65........................ MickyFenton 3 83+
(R Ford) *mde all: clr after 3f: unchal* 6/1
6611 2 14 **Sea Admiral**[9] [3574] 3-8-11 74 6ex........................(b) SteveDrowne 1 71
(R Charlton) *a chsng wnr: rdn over 3f out: no imp* 6/4[1]
40-6 3 ½ **Mith Hill**[49] [2332] 7-10-0 74........................ StephenDonohoe 2 70
(Ian Williams) *hld up and bhd: rdn and hdwy to take modest 3rd wl over 1f out: styd on same pce fnl f* 4/1[3]
6060 4 12 **Corum (IRE)**[29] [2952] 5-9-9 72........................(p) LeeVickers(3) 5 52
(Mrs K Waldron) *hld up in tch in chsng gp: rdn over 2f out: wknd over 1f out* 16/1
5052 5 12 **Merrymaker**[10] [3545] 8-9-2 62........................ TGMcLaughlin 6 27
(W M Brisbourne) *s.i.s: rn in snatches: in rr: hdwy over 6f out: rdn and wknd over 3f out: eased wl over 1f out* 7/2[2]

-043 6 20 **Vincenzio (IRE)**[9] [3574] 4-9-7 67........................(b) PaulMulrennan 4 6
(C R Egerton) *hld up in tch in chsng gp: rdn and wknd over 3f out: eased fnl 2f* 6/1

3m 20.75s (1.75) **Going Correction** +0.325s/f (Good)
WFA 3 from 4yo+ 17lb 6 Ran SP% **116.7**
Speed ratings (Par 103): **108,100,100,93,87 76**
toteswinger: 1&2 £3.20, 1&3 £4.20, 2&3 £1.90. CSF £16.31 TOTE £7.00: £2.70, £1.40; EX 19.50.
Owner D W Watson **Bred** Norman Cheng And Tony Feng **Trained** Cotebrook, Cheshire

FOCUS
An extraordinary handicap, the winner going into a clear lead and nothing ever getting to within ten lengths. The form, as such, has to have a question mark over it.

3892 EUROPEAN BREEDERS' FUND FILLIES' H'CAP 7f 26y
4:05 (4:06) (Class 4) (0-80,78) 3-Y-0+ **£6,799** (£2,023; £1,011; £505) **Stalls** Low

Form RPR
0560 1 **Misphire**[10] [3554] 5-9-10 74........................ PaulMulrennan 4 84
(M Dods) *hld up: hdwy on ins 3f out: rdn to ld jst over 1f out: drvn out* 12/1
-000 2 1 **Ken's Girl**[20] [3208] 4-8-12 62........................ ChrisCatlin 3 69
(W S Kittow) *led: hdd jst over 1f out: rdn and nt qckn ins fnl f* 14/1
2130 3 1 **Support Fund (IRE)**[12] [3507] 4-9-11 75........................ StephenCarson 7 80
(Eve Johnson Houghton) *hld up in rr: hdwy 1f out: kpt on to take 3rd cl home* 10/3[2]
6543 4 hd **Dispol Isle (IRE)**[10] [3552] 6-9-5 69........................ PaulFessey 1 73
(T D Barron) *a.p: rdn and hung lft over 1f out: one pce fnl f* 9/2[3]
-611 5 ¾ **Medici Pearl**[15] [3369] 4-10-0 78........................ DavidAllan 8 80
(T D Easterby) *hld up: c wd to stands' rail st: hdwy whn rdn and hung lft jst over 1f out: one pce* 5/2[1]
000- 6 1½ **Princess Valerina**[232] [6900] 4-9-11 75........................ TPQueally 9 73
(H R A Cecil) *w ldr tl hung lft wl over 1f out: wknd fnl f* 10/1
-154 7 ¾ **Glencal**[25] [3064] 4-8-13 63........................ SteveDrowne 2 59
(H Morrison) *t.k.h early in tch: lost pl over 2f out: n.d after* 9/2[3]

1m 26.51s (1.91) **Going Correction** +0.325s/f (Good)
WFA 3 from 4yo+ 8lb 7 Ran SP% **111.5**
Speed ratings (Par 102): **102,100,99,99,98 96,96**
toteswinger: 1&2 £11.20, 1&3 £8.20, 2&3 £9.10. CSF £147.29 CT £673.82 TOTE £12.50: £5.10, £4.60; EX 114.80.
Owner Transpennine Partnership **Bred** P T Tellwright **Trained** Denton, Co Durham

FOCUS
No more than a fair handicap and they all finished in a bit of a heap. The form looks fair enough on paper with the winner to her best and the third to previous course form.

3893 WARWICKRACECOURSE.CO.UK H'CAP 7f 26y
4:40 (4:40) (Class 5) (0-75,75) 3-Y-0 **£3,238** (£963; £481; £240) **Stalls** Low

Form RPR
5303 1 **Benedetto**[9] [3571] 3-8-12 66........................(p) TPQueally 1 70+
(Mrs A J Perrett) *t.k.h early: hld up: hdwy over 1f out: led wl ins fnl f: r.o* 9/4[2]
0-00 2 nk **Secret Gem (IRE)**[56] [2118] 3-8-9 63........................ PhilipRobinson 8 66
(C G Cox) *led: rdn and hdd wl ins fnl f: kpt on* 15/2
-653 3 1 **Whiteoak Lady (IRE)**[45] [2452] 3-8-9 68........................ JackDean(5) 10 68
(J L Spearing) *jnd ldr after 2f: hrd rdn over 1f out: nt qckn ins fnl f* 13/2[3]
0000 4 3½ **Just A Dancer (IRE)**[17] [3324] 3-8-13 67........................ RobertHavlin 3 58
(B W Hills) *chsd ldr 2f: a.p: rdn over 1f out: wknd fnl f* 12/1
55-5 5 ½ **Dan Chillingworth (IRE)**[40] [2620] 3-9-4 72........................ PatCosgrave 2 62
(J R Fanshawe) *t.k.h early towards rr: effrt over 1f out: wknd ins fnl f* 2/1[1]
0-00 6 ½ **Jay Gee Wigmo**[26] [3022] 3-8-2 58 oh11 ow3........................ KevinGhunowa(3) 9 47?
(A W Carroll) *s.i.s: hld up: hdwy over 4f out: rdn over 1f out: wknd fnl f* 50/1
406 7 1¼ **In Toto**[13] [3447] 3-8-3 57........................ NickyMackay 5 42
(M Wigham) *hld up: shkn up over 1f out: hung lft ent fnl f: a bhd* 12/1
01 8 1¾ **Lucullus**[113] [936] 3-9-3 71........................ SteveDrowne 6 51
(M Blanshard) *plld hrd: prom tl wknd 2f out* 8/1

1m 29.08s (4.48) **Going Correction** +0.325s/f (Good) 8 Ran SP% **117.7**
Speed ratings (Par 100): **87,86,85,81,80 80,78,76**
toteswinger: 1&2 £4.20, 1&3 £4.20, 2&3 £7.50. CSF £20.34 CT £98.35 TOTE £3.20: £1.40, £1.90, £2.00; EX 20.70.
Owner Woodcote Stud Ltd **Bred** Woodcote Stud Ltd **Trained** Pulborough, W Sussex

FOCUS
Only a modest handicap for three-year-olds, run in a time 2.57 seconds slower than the preceding fillies' handicap. The runner-up is rated to his juvenile form with the third and fourth close to this year's form.

3894 RACING UK MAIDEN STKS 1m 2f 188y
5:15 (5:17) (Class 5) 3-Y-0+ **£3,238** (£963; £481; £240) **Stalls** Low

Form RPR
-354 1 **Moon Sister (IRE)**[16] [3351] 3-8-9 78........................ RobertHavlin 11 79
(W Jarvis) *a.p: wnt 2nd over 5f out: led 2f out: sn rdn: edgd lft ins fnl f: r.o* 7/2[2]
2 1¼ **Wild Rhubarb** 3-8-9 0........................ PhilipRobinson 6 76+
(C G Cox) *led early: hmpd after 1f: sn settled in mid-div: rdn and hdwy over 1f out: styd on wl to take 2nd cl home: nt trble wnr* 16/1
344 3 1¼ **Seventh Cavalry (IRE)**[26] [3035] 3-9-0 81........................ TPQueally 15 79
(H R A Cecil) *hld up in tch: chsd wnr wl over 1f out: rdn and nt qckn ins fnl f* 8/1[3]
4 1¼ **Interchange (IRE)** 3-8-9 0........................ PatCosgrave 8 72+
(J R Fanshawe) *hld up in mid-div: sltly hmpd after 1f: hdwy 3f out: rdn wl over 1f out: styd on towards fin* 8/1[3]
3-62 5 1¼ **E Major**[46] [2427] 3-8-7 80........................ JPHamblett(7) 7 75
(Sir Michael Stoute) *a.p: led over 8f out tl over 7f out: rdn over 1f out: one pce* 11/8[1]
6 nk **Fortune City (UAE)** 3-9-0 0........................ DO'Donohoe 4 74
(Saeed Bin Suroor) *hld up and bhd: stdy hdwy over 4f out: styd on same pce fnl f* 12/1
0 7 1½ **Look To This Day**[49] [2328] 3-8-9 0........................ SteveDrowne 1 66+
(R Charlton) *hld up and bhd: hdwy over 2f out: kpt on same pce fnl f: bttr for r* 12/1
0 8 4½ **Cwm Rhondda (USA)**[19] [3275] 3-8-4 0........................ JackMitchell(5) 9 58
(P W Chapple-Hyam) *s.i.s: bhd: pushed along over 3f out: rdn wl over 1f out: nvr nr ldrs* 14/1
0 9 2¾ **Civitas Filius (USA)**[38] [2681] 3-9-0 0........................ StephenDonohoe 5 58
(D M Simcock) *hld up towards rr: rdn over 2f out: nvr nr ldrs* 14/1

The Form Book, Raceform Ltd, Compton, RG20 6NL

10 *nk* **Street Crime** 3-9-0 0 ... MickyFenton 13 58
(A M Balding) *s.s: sn rcvrd and led: swvd lft to ins rail after 1f: hdd over 8f out: led over 7f out: sn hung rt: carried hd high and hdd 2f out: sn wknd* **28/1**

0 11 *9* **Kavatcha (FR)**[11] 3530 5-9-9 0 ... TravisBlock(3) 10 41
(Miss Tor Sturgis) *s.s: a in rr* **125/1**

6 12 *½* **Iraschko**[19] 3262 3-8-9 0 ... FergalLynch 2 36
(J L Spearing) *hld up in rr: rdn and effrt wl over 1f out: no hdwy whn jinked rt at path jst over 1f out: eased* **100/1**

6 13 *3 ¾* **Bathwick Minstrel**[15] 3362 3-8-9 0 ... TGMcLaughlin 14 29
(A B Haynes) *a towards rr* **100/1**

0 14 *3 ¼* **Steady Gaze**[21] 3161 3-9-0 0 ... (t) NickyMackay 12 28
(M A Allen) *hld up in tch: hmpd after 1f: pushed along over 5f out: rdn 3f out: sn wknd* **100/1**

2m 26.73s (5.63) **Going Correction** +0.325s/f (Good)
WFA 3 from 5yo+ 12lb **14 Ran SP% 128.4**
Speed ratings (Par 103): **92,91,90,89,88 88,87,83,81,81 75,74,71,69**
toteswinger: 1&2 £21.80, 1&3 £6.60, 2&3 £20.70. CSF £62.65 TOTE £4.80: £1.40, £4.50, £2.60; EX 101.90 Place 6: £962.64, Place 5: £867.33..
Owner Abdullah Saeed Belhab **Bred** Darley **Trained** Newmarket, Suffolk

FOCUS
A fair maiden, with a couple coming having official ratings in the low-80s although the form is ordinary rated arond the winner and third. There were a few taking perfomances behind and this race should throw up more than a couple of winners.
Street Crime Official explanation: jockey said gelding ran green
T/Plt: £1,311.80 to a £1 stake. Pool: £37,827.66. 21.05 winning tickets. T/Qpdt: £668.50 to a £1 stake. Pool: £1,626.20. 1.80 winning tickets. KH

3245
ASCOT (R-H)
Friday, July 11

OFFICIAL GOING: Good to soft (good in places)
Dolling out added 15yards to advertised distances on round course.
Wind: breezy half against Weather: overcast and breezy

3895 ICAP E B F MAIDEN STKS 6f
2:25 (2:28) (Class 3) 2-Y-O **£7,771** (£2,312; £1,155; £577) **Stalls** Low

Form RPR

0 1 **Zaffaan**[21] 3219 2-9-3 0 ... TQuinn 7 84+
(E A L Dunlop) *chsd ldrs: led wl over 1f out: clr 1f out: easily* **10/1**

2 *3 ¾* **Rileyskeepingfaith** 2-9-3 0 ... EdwardCreighton 6 73+
(M R Channon) *s.i.s: hld up in tch: hdwy and n.m.r over 2f out: edgd rt wl over 1f out: chsd ldng pair ent fnl f: wnt 2nd nr fin: no ch w wnr* **8/1**

3 *nk* **Doctor Parkes** 2-9-3 0 ... GeorgeBaker 4 72+
(E F Vaughan) *s.i.s: hld up in tch: hdwy jst over 2f out: chsd wnr over 1f out: no imp: lost 2nd nr fin* **14/1**

0 4 *2 ¾* **Pagan Force (IRE)**[29] 2972 2-9-3 0 ... JimCrowley 11 64
(Mrs A J Perrett) *s.i.s: hld up in tch: effrt on outer over 2f out: wl outpcd over 1f out: plugged on* **8/1**

44 5 *nk* **Party Cat (IRE)**[41] 2601 2-9-3 0 ... EddieAhern 12 63
(R Hannon) *in tch in midfield: rdn and effrt jst over 2f out: wknd over 1f out* **5/2**[1]

6 *1 ½* **Ruasgreyasme (USA)** 2-8-12 0 ... PatDobbs 2 53+
(R Hannon) *rrd s and slowly away: hld up in rr: n.d* **14/1**

7 *nk* **Alyarf (USA)** 2-9-3 0 ... MartinDwyer 3 57
(B W Hills) *w ldr: rdn over 2f out: wknd qckly 2f out* **7/1**[3]

66 8 *½* **Yeoman Blaze**[16] 3358 2-9-3 0 ... WilliamBuick 1 56
(A M Balding) *hld up in tch: rdn 3f out: swtchd rt over 2f out: no ch after* **10/1**

5 9 *¾* **Hum Cat (IRE)**[16] 3358 2-9-3 0 ... JamesDoyle 10 54
(J S Moore) *in tch: pushed along 4f out: rdn over 2f out and wkng whn n.m.r over 1f out* **25/1**

0 10 *5* **All Spin (IRE)**[27] 3049 2-9-3 0 ... DarrenWilliams 5 39
(A P Jarvis) *t.k.h: led: rdn 2f out: sn hdd & wknd* **40/1**

42 P **Desert Sunset**[19] 3292 2-8-12 0 ... GregFairley 9 —
(M Johnston) *p.u sn after s: lame* **5/1**[2]

1m 15.95s (1.55) **Going Correction** +0.225s/f (Good) **11 Ran SP% 117.8**
Speed ratings (Par 98): **98,93,92,88,88 86,86,85,84,77** —
toteswinger: 1&2 £28.40, 1&3 £36.90, 2&3 £23.10. CSF £87.76 TOTE £12.40: £3.80, £2.90, £4.70; EX 124.90 TRIFECTA Not won..
Owner Hamdan Al Maktoum **Bred** Bloomsbury Stud **Trained** Newmarket, Suffolk

FOCUS
Probably an average juvenile maiden for the track. The winner improved and can rate higher.

NOTEBOOK
Zaffaan, eighth on his debut at Newmarket three weeks ago, responded most positively when asked for maximum effort shortly after 2f out and eventually ran out a comfortable winner. He enjoyed this softer surface and, remembering his dam was high-class at up to 1m, should also prove happier as he steps up in trip. (op 12-1)
Rileyskeepingfaith, whose dam was a 1m2f winner on the level and also later over fences, was always playing catch-up after a slow start. He also proved distinctly green through the first half of the race, so it is taking that he finished as he did and he looks sure to come on a great deal for this debut experience. Another furlong would also not go amiss. (op 6-1)
Doctor Parkes, the sixth foal of a very smart 16-times 5f winner, emerged to join the leaders going easily around 2f out and looked a likely winner. However, he failed to go with Zaffaan when that rival kicked on for home and just tired out of second near the line. He should come on nicely for this experience and has a future, but perhaps a drop back to 5f would be best for him in the short term. (op 16-1)
Pagan Force(IRE) was nibbled at in the betting to improve on his debut ninth at Newbury 29 days previously and duly did so without ever seriously threatening. He stayed on after hitting a flat spot, suggesting another furlong will suit before that long, and will be eligible for a nursery mark after his next outing. (op 12-1)
Party Cat(IRE), fourth on both his previous outings, proved very one-paced when push came to shove and has to rate as disappointing. He is at least now eligible for nurseries. (op 9-2)
Ruasgreyasme(USA), whose pedigree suggests a mix of speed and stamina, fell out of the gates after rearing up. She was never in the hunt, but was still noted doing some fair late work and appeals as one who will prove a good deal sharper now she has this debut experience under her belt. (op 8-1)
Desert Sunset was in trouble almost as soon as the gates opened and clearly something went wrong with her. Official explanation: vet said filly was pulled up lame behind (op 3-1)

3896 LIVERPOOL UNIVERSITY EQUINE VETS H'CAP 1m 2f
3:00 (3:03) (Class 3) (0-90,90) 3-Y-O+ **£9,066** (£2,697; £1,348; £673) **Stalls** High

Form RPR

-041 1 **Goodwood Starlight (IRE)**[28] 2996 3-9-0 87 ... EddieAhern 2 97+
(J L Dunlop) *stdd and dropped in after s: hld up towards rr: rdn and hdwy 3f out: chsd ldr jst over 1f out: led and edgd rt ins fnl f: in command towards fin* **6/4**[1]

F-26 2 *1 ¾* **Redesignation (IRE)**[34] 2819 3-9-0 87 ... PatDobbs 10 92
(R Hannon) *t.k.h: hld up in midfield: effrt on inner wl over 2f out: n.m.r and swtchd lft jst ins fnl f: kpt on to go 2nd last 100yds* **11/2**[2]

1100 3 *hd* **William Blake**[41] 2610 3-9-1 88 ... GregFairley 1 93
(M Johnston) *led: rdn over 2f out: 3 l clr wl over 1f out: hdd ins fnl f: kpt on same pce* **9/1**

0-25 4 *½* **Bandama (IRE)**[21] 3209 5-10-0 90 ... JimCrowley 9 94
(Mrs A J Perrett) *t.k.h: hld up in midfield: rdn and hdwy 3f out: chsd ldr briefly over 1f out: disp 2nd after tl fdd towards fin* **10/1**

2421 5 *1 ¼* **Formation (USA)**[32] 2889 3-8-13 86 ... TQuinn 7 87
(E A L Dunlop) *stdd s: t.k.h: hld up in rr: effrt and rdn wl over 1f out: flashed tail u.p: chsd ldrs ins fnl f: hld whn eased towards fin* **8/1**[3]

5345 6 *1 ¼* **Zaif (IRE)**[14] 3461 5-9-1 77 ... GeorgeBaker 11 76
(Simon Earle) *stdd s: hld up in last: rdn and effrt over 2f out: nvr pce to trble ldrs* **12/1**

10 7 *3 ¾* **Vinces**[32] 2886 4-8-9 71 oh1 ... WilliamBuick 6 62
(T D McCarthy) *t.k.h: chsd ldrs: rdn to chse ldr 3f out tl over 1f out: sn wknd* **16/1**

35-0 8 *3 ¼* **Stargazer Jim (FR)**[23] 3132 6-9-0 76 ... MartinDwyer 8 61
(W J Haggas) *t.k.h: hld up in last trio: rdn and effrt 3f out: no prog* **16/1**

51-3 9 *12* **Samsons Son**[4] 3800 4-9-9 85 ... HayleyTurner 3 46
(J R Best) *t.k.h: chsd ldrs: rdn over 3f out: wkng whn carried lft over 2f out: wl bhd fnl f* **9/1**

3156 10 *7* **Tilapia (IRE)**[118] 908 4-9-11 87 ... ShaneKelly 5 34
(Miss Gay Kelleway) *t.k.h: chsd ldr tl 3f out: wkng whn edgd lft over 2f out: wl bhd and eased fnl f* **25/1**

2m 10.03s (0.23) **Going Correction** +0.225s/f (Good)
WFA 3 from 4yo+ 11lb **10 Ran SP% 118.9**
Speed ratings (Par 107): **108,106,106,106,105 104,101,98,88,83**
toteswinger: 1&2 £4.20, 1&3 £5.20, 2&3 £20.20. CSF £9.84 CT £57.59 TOTE £2.40: £1.20, £2.50, £2.40; EX 11.60 Trifecta £154.60 Pool: £501.44 - 2.40 winning units..
Owner Goodwood Racehorse Owners Group Fourteen **Bred** Lynn Lodge Stud **Trained** Arundel, W Sussex

FOCUS
A good handicap, run at a fair pace. The first three are progressive, especially the winner, and the form is rated around the fourth and fifth.

NOTEBOOK
Goodwood Starlight(IRE) followed up his Goodwood success with another ready effort despite racing from an 8lb higher mark. It was clear nearing the final furlong he was going to do the business and this again advertises his versatility as regards underfoot conditions. He has now won four of his six career starts and it will be fascinating to see how he copes with another rise in the weights. (op 7-4 tchd 15-8 and 2-1 in places)
Redesignation(IRE) played up before the start and then took time to settle though the first few furlongs. He still came through with his challenge, albeit when the winner had already flown, and this was a much more encouraging effort in defeat from him. He can be ridden more prominently over this trip now connections know he stays. (tchd 7-1)
William Blake had an uncontested lead and, despite eventually proving a sitting duck for the winner, kept on gamely once headed. He is just struggling to find his optimum trip at present and has little room for error from his current official mark. (op 16-1)
Bandama(IRE) did not help his rider by refusing to settle through the early stages and would have likely enjoyed a more positive ride on this drop back in trip. He just looks held by the Handicapper. (op 7-1 tchd 13-2)
Formation(USA) ran his usual sort of race, coming late on the scene having taken time to settle under restraint, and then flashing his tal again when put under any serious pressure. He is one to remain wary of, but does help to set the standard of this form. (tchd 15-2)

3897 ASCOT ANNUAL BADGEHOLDERS H'CAP 7f
3:35 (3:35) (Class 3) (0-90,89) 3-Y-O **£7,771** (£2,312; £1,155; £577) **Stalls** Low

Form RPR

3-22 1 **Carniolan**[31] 2918 3-8-12 80 ... AdamKirby 3 100
(W R Swinburn) *hld up in tch: gng wl and nt clr run 2f out: forced way through to ld over 1f out: hung lft but drew clr fnl f: rdn out* **9/2**[3]

3100 2 *5* **Keep Discovering (IRE)**[35] 2794 3-9-7 89 ... GregFairley 5 95
(M Johnston) *chsd ldr: rdn over 2f out: ev ch 2f out: outpcd by wnr fnl f: plugged on to go 2nd last 100yds* **12/1**

41- 3 *nk* **Roaring Forte (IRE)**[242] 6791 3-9-0 82 ... EddieAhern 6 87
(W J Haggas) *led: rdn over 2f out: hdd over 1f out: outpcd by wnr fnl f: lost 2nd last 100yds* **6/4**[1]

1 4 *nk* **Kalahari Gold (IRE)**[31] 2919 3-9-3 85 ... WilliamBuick 4 89
(A M Balding) *bmpd s: in tch: rdn over 2f out: pressing ldrs and bmpd over 1f out: nt pce of wnr fnl f: plugged on* **3/1**[2]

4126 5 *5* **Dubai Meydan (IRE)**[20] 3270 3-9-2 84 ... ShaneKelly 1 75
(Miss Gay Kelleway) *stdd s: hld up in last: effrt and rdn jst over 2f out: sn btn* **7/1**

6000 6 *7* **Solent Ridge (IRE)**[22] 3155 3-9-5 87 ... MartinDwyer 2 59
(J S Moore) *wnt rt s: in tch: rdn 3f out: wknd ent fnl 2f* **10/1**

1m 28.12s (0.12) **Going Correction** +0.225s/f (Good) **6 Ran SP% 112.5**
Speed ratings (Par 104): **108,102,101,101,95 87**
toteswinger: 1&2 £26.10. CSF £51.47 TOTE £5.50: £1.90, £3.90; EX 43.20.
Owner Exors Of The Late Mrs P W Harris **Bred** Jeremy Gompertz **Trained** Aldbury, Herts
■ Stewards' Enquiry : Adam Kirby four-day ban: careless riding (Jul 25, 27-29)

FOCUS
A good little three-year-old handicap, run at an average pace. The winner was up a stone on his maiden form and the form is sound.

NOTEBOOK
Carniolan ◆, placed on each of his three previous runs, had never raced on ground this soft before yet it evidently suited as he came right away from his rivals to score. He travelled sweetly through the race and, once coming between horses with his effort nearing the final furlong, it was clear there was only going to be one winner. He will likely take a hike in the ratings for this, but remains open to a deal of further progression and looks very useful. (op 7-2 tchd 10-3 and 5-1 in palces)
Keep Discovering(IRE) showed improved form on this return to a more conventional track and had his chance, but was made to look very one-paced when the winner asserted. This was better from him, but he again did not impress with his head carriage and does look held by the Handicapper on 89. (op 11-1)

Roaring Forte(IRE), making his belated seasonal return, was well backed and looked set to run a big race on this handicap bow. Ridden very positively, he was still going easily enough 2f out, but his stride began to shorten approaching the final furlong and he eventually tired out of things. This colt is well thought of by his in-form stable and, with the strong possibility of him coming on for the run, his next outing really should reveal more as to whether he is currently well handicapped on a mark of 82. (op 7-4 tchd 2-1)
Kalahari Gold(IRE), a debut winner at Salisbury a month previously, still looked inexperienced through the race and only managed to find the same pace from 2f out on this easier ground. He is still open to improvement and may be ready to tackle 1m now. (tchd 11-4)

3898 RUFFLER BANK H'CAP — 6f
4:10 (4:10) (Class 3) (0-90,89) 3-Y-0+ **£9,066** (£2,697; £1,348; £673) **Stalls** Low

Form — RPR
-341 **1** **Shifting Star (IRE)**[28] 2998 3-9-6 **88**.......... AdamKirby 10 — 96
(W R Swinburn) *hld up in midfield: hdwy 1/2-way: rdn to ld over 1f out: hld on wl fnl f* **5/1**[1]
4022 **2** *nk* **Dingaan (IRE)**[38] 2693 5-9-4 **80**.......... WilliamBuick 12 — 88
(A M Balding) *hld up in midfield: hdwy over 2f out: hrd rdn over 1f out: styd on u.p last 100yds to go 2nd nr fin* **6/1**[2]
5223 **3** *nk* **Golden Desert (IRE)**[25] 3087 4-9-6 **82**.......... ShaneKelly 2 — 89
(T G Mills) *chsd ldr: led over 2f out: rdn and wanting to hang fr wl over 1f out: hdd over 1f out: unable qck last 100yds* **9/1**
1132 **4** *2 1/4* **Punching**[3] 3819 4-8-8 **70** oh2.......... HayleyTurner 8 — 70
(Miss Gay Kelleway) *bmpd s: hld up towards rr: hdwy over 2f out: chsd ldng trio ent fnl f: kpt on but nvr pce to rch ldrs* **13/2**[3]
0-02 **5** *2 3/4* **Woodcote Place**[8] 3646 5-9-4 **80**.......... JimCrowley 3 — 71
(P R Chamings) *chsd ldrs: ev ch and rdn over 2f out: wknd over 1f out* **9/1**
0560 **6** *1/2* **Golden Dixie (USA)**[8] 3647 9-9-7 **88**.......... HaddenFrost(5) 11 — 77
(R A Harris) *half rrd s: hld up bhd: hdwy over 2f out: rdn and no imp over 1f out* **20/1**
5111 **7** *hd* **Dressed To Dance (IRE)**[13] 3506 4-9-4 **85**..........(v) RichardEvans(5) 9 — 74
(P D Evans) *hmpd s: bhd: rdn and effrt over 2f out: nvr nr ldrs* **7/1**
0150 **8** *2 1/4* **Charles Darwin (IRE)**[13] 3477 5-9-6 **82**..........(p) JamesDoyle 5 — 64
(M Blanshard) *led for 2f: rdn over 2f out: wkng whn hmpd over 1f out* **25/1**
0616 **9** *3/4* **Southandwest (IRE)**[21] 3222 4-9-13 **89**.......... MartinDwyer 7 — 68
(J S Moore) *wnt rt s: in tch: rdn 1/2-way: wknd 2f out* **16/1**
01 **10** *1/2* **Brunelleschi**[20] 3271 5-8-10 **75**..........(b) LukeMorris(3) 1 — 53
(P L Gilligan) *a bhd* **13/2**[3]
1622 **11** *1 1/2* **Toms Laughter**[6] 3728 4-9-6 **85**..........(p) KevinGhunowa(3) 6 — 58
(R A Harris) *awkward s: t.k.h: led after 2f tl over 2f out: sn wknd* **13/2**[3]

1m 14.96s (0.56) **Going Correction** +0.225s/f (Good)
WFA 3 from 4yo+ 6lb — **11** Ran SP% **117.9**
Speed ratings (Par 107): **105,104,104,101,97 96,96,93,92,91 89**
toteswinger: 1&2 £4.80, 1&3 £10.50, 2&3 £14.40. CSF £34.48 CT £270.33 TOTE £5.70: £2.00, £2.60, £3.20; EX 27.30 Trifecta £365.10 Part won. Pool: £493.40 - 0.40 winning units..
Owner Night Shadow Syndicate **Bred** Hardys Of Kilkeel Ltd **Trained** Aldbury, Herts
■ Stewards' Enquiry : Luke Morris caution: used whip when out of contention
Adam Kirby two-day ban: used whip with excessive frequency (Jul 31-Aug 1)

FOCUS
A good sprint handicap for the class but only ordinary for Goodwood. The form is rated around the placed horses.

NOTEBOOK
Shifting Star(IRE), 7lb higher than when scoring at Goodwood four weeks earlier, put the race to bed when quickening to the front at the furlong marker and followed up in gutsy style. He was tying up near the finish, but showed a willing attitude close home and is clearly back at the top of his game at present. (tchd 6-1)
Dingaan(IRE), back down in trip, came through with a strong late challenge but was never quite going to get there in time. He has developed a habit of finding one too good and is clearly very tricky, but does have the talent to win from this mark if consenting to put it all in. He is a solid benchmark for the form. (op 5-1)
Golden Desert(IRE) travelled nicely just off the early leaders and looked a big player nearing the final furlong, but he did not help himself by wanting to hang right under maximum pressure. He was still only just beaten and, while he is another who is tending to find one or two too good at present, his turn may not be that far off again now. (op 10-1 tchd 11-1)
Punching ran a solid enough race from 2lb out of the handicap, without having the tactical pace to land a telling blow, and has developed into a consistent sprinter this term. (op 8-1)
Woodcote Place was given a positive ride on this drop back a furlong and had his chance, but his fate was sealed passing the furlong pole. He is back in good form again now, but ideally looks happier when coming off a decent pace.

3899 ENVIRONMENTAL ENERGY H'CAP — 1m (R)
4:45 (4:48) (Class 3) (0-95,90) 3-Y-0+ **£9,066** (£2,697; £1,348; £673) **Stalls** Low

Form — RPR
-154 **1** **Cape Hawk (IRE)**[41] 2604 4-9-6 **87**.......... HaddenFrost(5) 7 — 97
(R Hannon) *trckd ldrs: swtchd ins and effrt 2f out: rdn to ld over 1f out: edgd lft but r.o wl fnl f* **11/2**[3]
6006 **2** *1 3/4* **Meydan Dubai (IRE)**[11] 3560 3-8-13 **84**..........(v[1]) MohammedSaeed 2 — 88
(J R Best) *t.k.h: chsd ldrs: rdn over 2f out: chsd wnr fr over 1f out: no imp* **14/1**
-166 **3** *3/4* **Motafarred (IRE)**[16] 3367 6-8-13 **75**.......... TQuinn 3 — 79
(Micky Hammond) *hld up in last: plld out and hdwy wl over 1f out: styd on fnl f: nvr pce to rch ldng pair* **8/1**
-006 **4** *1 1/2* **South Cape**[21] 3197 5-9-11 **87**.......... EddieAhern 6 — 88
(M R Channon) *hld up in tch in rr: rdn and effrt on inner 2f out: kpt on but nvr pce to threaten ldrs* **4/1**[2]
1522 **5** *1/2* **The Snatcher (IRE)**[18] 3319 5-9-11 **90**.......... PatrickHills(3) 4 — 90
(R Hannon) *hld up in rr: effrt and rdn wl over 2f out: styng on same pce whn n.m.r briefly over 1f out: nvr pce to rch ldrs* **7/2**[1]
21-0 **6** *1* **Flight To Quality**[74] 1686 3-8-8 **79**.......... GregFairley 1 — 74
(M Johnston) *a towards rr: rdn 3f out: no prog* **16/1**
206 **7** *2 1/4* **Prince Of Thebes (IRE)**[16] 3382 7-9-7 **83**.......... AdamKirby 9 — 75
(M J Attwater) *led tl rdn and hdd over 1f out: sn wknd* **10/1**
0104 **8** *4 1/2* **Salient**[18] 3319 4-9-8 **87**.......... TolleyDean(3) 8 — 69
(M J Attwater) *t.k.h: w ldr: rdn over 2f out: wknd over 1f out* **14/1**

1m 42.96s (2.16) **Going Correction** +0.225s/f (Good)
WFA 3 from 4yo+ 9lb — **8** Ran SP% **97.0**
Speed ratings (Par 107): **98,96,95,94,93 92,90,85**
toteswinger: 1&2 £12.40, 1&3 £5.60, 2&3 £11.90. CSF £52.83 CT £319.77 TOTE £5.80: £1.90, £3.30, £2.00; EX 74.20 TRIFECTA Not won..
Owner Thurloe Thoroughbreds XVII **Bred** John And Leslie Young **Trained** East Everleigh, Wilts
■ Oceana Gold was withdrawn after proving unruly at the stalls (4/1, deduct 20p in the £ under Rule 4).

FOCUS
Just a fair event for the class. It was a moderate winning time but the form looks solid enough.

NOTEBOOK
Cape Hawk(IRE) readily took full advantage of a 5lb drop in the weights and, showing a much more willing attitude under pressure, registered his first win on turf to date. This was his highest winning mark and, while he is probably still open to some more improvement on turf, a likely rise back up in the ratings will likely scupper a follow-up bid. (tchd 7-1)
Meydan Dubai(IRE) showed more for the application of a first-time visor, but still ran freely though the early parts and again did not look too willing at the business end of the race. He has talent, but is a frustrating performer. (op 12-1 tchd 16-1)
Motafarred(IRE) was given a very patient ride and, after travelling sweetly into the home straight, was switched out with his challenge approaching the final furlong. He did not find quite as much as could have been expected when asked for maximum effort, but this was still a better effort from him and he could still be placed to strike on one of the smaller tracks. (op 10-1)
South Cape, sixth in the Buckingham Palace Stakes at the Royal Meeting three weeks previously, was given a patient ride on this return to the extra furlong and never seriously looked like troubling the winner. He is really happier over 7f. (tchd 7-2)
The Snatcher(IRE), second on his last two starts, took too long to hit his full stride and never really got involved. This was a fair effort under top weight, but he does look to be held by the Handicapper now. Official explanation: jockey said horse was upset by misbehaviour in next stall (op 4-1 tchd 11-4)

3900 LANDSBANKI APPRENTICE H'CAP — 1m 4f
5:20 (5:20) (Class 4) (0-85,83) 4-Y-0+ **£7,123** (£2,119; £1,059; £529) **Stalls** High

Form — RPR
4111 **1** **Hatton Flight**[24] 3110 4-9-8 **81**..........(b) WilliamBuick 4 — 91+
(A M Balding) *t.k.h: chsd ldng pair: rdn to chse ldr over 2f out: led over 1f out: edgd lft but styd on wl fnl f* **5/2**[1]
1121 **2** *3/4* **Sir Duke (IRE)**[14] 3440 4-9-5 **83**.......... GaryBartley(5) 2 — 92
(P W D'Arcy) *hld up in midfield: hdwy over 2f out: pressed wnr over 1f out: unable qck fnl f* **11/4**[2]
1633 **3** *2 3/4* **Stringsofmyheart**[8] 3630 4-9-4 **77**.......... RussellKennemore 7 — 82
(Miss Gay Kelleway) *led: 6 l clr 1/2-way: rdn 3f over 3f out: hdd over 1f out: kpt on same pce fnl f* **7/1**
4140 **4** *hd* **Bienheureux**[31] 2908 7-8-2 **64** oh3..........(t) NicolPolli(3) 3 — 68
(Miss Gay Kelleway) *s.i.s: hld up in last pair: c wd and hdwy over 2f out: kpt on u.p but nt pce to rch ldrs* **16/1**
-162 **5** *hd* **Colonel Flay**[31] 2921 4-8-10 **72**.......... JackMitchell(3) 1 — 76
(Mrs P N Dutfield) *stdd and dropped out after s: hld up wl bhd: plld out and hdwy over 2f out: kpt on: nvr rchd ldrs* **7/1**
5461 **6** *3* **Opera Writer (IRE)**[7] 3698 5-8-0 **64** 6ex oh3..........(p) SoniaEaton(5) 6 — 63
(R Hollinshead) *t.k.h: hld up in midfield: rdn over 2f out: wknd over 1f out* **10/1**
-125 **7** *hd* **Brief Goodbye**[27] 3044 8-9-1 **74**.......... LukeMorris 5 — 73
(John Berry) *taken down early: chsd ldr tl over 2f out: wknd u.p over 1f out* **5/1**[3]

2m 36.12s (0.62) **Going Correction** +0.225s/f (Good) — **7** Ran SP% **111.9**
Speed ratings (Par 105): **106,105,103,103,103 101,101**
toteswinger: 1&2 £1.60, 1&3 £4.90, 2&3 £4.00. CSF £9.17 TOTE £3.10: £1.90, £2.00; EX 5.20 Place 6: £693.32 Place 5: £101.57.
Owner David Brownlow **Bred** Fittocks Stud Ltd **Trained** Kingsclere, Hants
■ Stewards' Enquiry : Nicol Polli two-day ban: used whip with excessive frequency (Jul 25,27)

FOCUS
A fair handicap and the form looks sound if nothing special for the grade. The winner remains progressive.
Brief Goodbye Official explanation: trainer said gelding was unsuited by the good to soft ground
T/Plt: £2,001.40 to a £1 stake. Pool: £74,164.36. 27.05 winning tickets. T/Qpdt: £50.60 to a £1 stake. Pool: £5,417.20. 79.15 winning tickets. SP

3603 CHEPSTOW (L-H)
Friday, July 11

OFFICIAL GOING: Soft (5.7)
Wind: Light, across Weather: Fine

3901 CROWN AT WHITEBROOK APPRENTICE H'CAP — 1m 4f 23y
6:30 (6:30) (Class 5) (0-70,66) 4-Y-0+ **£2,590** (£770; £385; £192) **Stalls** Low

Form — RPR
0045 **1** **Great View (IRE)**[47] 2423 9-9-10 **66**..........(p) KylieManser 1 — 74
(Mrs A L M King) *hld up in tch: swtchd rt over 2f out: led wl over 1f out: r.o wl* **13/2**
50-0 **2** *3 3/4* **Everyman**[29] 2978 4-8-8 **50**.......... MCGeran 9 — 52
(A W Carroll) *hld up in mid-div: hdwy 3f out: rdn and ev ch over 1f out: one pce fnl f* **9/2**[2]
56-0 **3** *2* **My Legal Eagle (IRE)**[9] 3606 14-8-2 **47** oh1.......... AshleyMorgan(3) 7 — 46
(E G Bevan) *hld up towards rr: hdwy on ins over 4f out: rdn 3f out: styd on one pce fnl 2f* **8/1**
53 **4** *2 1/2* **Sonnengold (GER)**[9] 3606 7-8-8 **50**.......... DavidProbert 8 — 45
(B J Llewellyn) *led: hdd 7f out: chsd ldr: led 4f out: rdn over 2f out: hdd wl over 1f out: sn wknd* **13/8**[1]
4005 **5** *1* **Backlash**[149] 544 7-8-5 **47** oh2.......... JemmaMarshall 11 — 41
(A W Carroll) *hld up towards rr: styd on fr over 1f out: n.d* **12/1**
-040 **6** *2 3/4* **Looktheotherway (IRE)**[26] 3059 4-8-10 **52**..........(p) WilliamCarson 3 — 42
(J G M O'Shea) *prom: ev ch 3f out: wknd 2f out* **6/1**[3]
06/0 **7** *5* **Robbie Can Can**[42] 1148 9-8-0 **47** oh2.......... RichardRowe(5) 2 — 29
(A W Carroll) *s.i.s: a in rr* **12/1**
00-0 **8** *3 1/4* **Break Out**[18] 3312 4-8-2 **47** oh2..........(b) BillyCray(3) 6 — 24
(J M Bradley) *wnt rt s: sn chsng ldr: led 7f out: rdn and hdd 4f out: sn wknd* **25/1**

2m 48.49s (9.49) **Going Correction** +0.875s/f (Soft) — **8** Ran SP% **114.2**
Speed ratings (Par 103): **103,100,99,97,96 95,91,89**
toteswinger: 1&2 £2.30, 1&3 £9.80, 2&3 £28.30. CSF £35.66 CT £237.25 TOTE £6.30: £2.00, £1.60, £2.30; EX 36.50.
Owner All The Kings Horses **Bred** Terry McGrath **Trained** Wilmcote, Warwicks

FOCUS
A poor contest. The winner is rated to the form he showed this time last year.
Break Out Official explanation: jockey said colt ran too free

3902 E B F / DIGIBET.CO.UK NOVICE STKS — 5f 16y
7:00 (7:01) (Class 4) 2-Y-0 **£5,018** (£1,493; £746; £372) **Stalls** Low

Form — RPR
5 **1** **Night Seed (IRE)**[41] 2608 2-8-7 0.......... PatDobbs 2 — 65
(R Hannon) *a.p: jnd ldr over 2f out: rdn to ld wl ins fnl f: r.o* **5/1**[3]
1253 **2** *nk* **Mazzola**[13] 3470 2-9-0 0.......... MCGeran(5) 1 — 76
(M R Channon) *led: rdn and hdd wl ins fnl f: kpt on* **15/8**[2]
622 **3** *1 1/2* **Timeteam (IRE)**[18] 3315 2-8-12 0.......... FergusSweeney 4 — 64
(S Kirk) *a.p: rdn over 1f out: edgd lft jst ins fnl f: nt qckn* **11/10**[1]

0 **4** *5* **Conakry**[9] 3603 2-8-12 0 .... CatherineGannon 3 46
(M R Channon) *in tch: rdn and wknd 2f out* **12/1**

00 **5** *7* **Colin Staite**[16] 3358 2-8-12 0 .... VinceSlattery 5 21
(R Brotherton) *hld up in tch: rdn over 2f out: sn wknd* **50/1**

62.76 secs (3.46) **Going Correction** +0.275s/f (Good) 5 Ran SP% **108.7**
Speed ratings (Par 96): **83,82,80,72,60**
CSF £14.43 TOTE £4.60: £2.10, £1.30; EX 13.90.
Owner Andrew Russell **Bred** Pier House Stud **Trained** East Everleigh, Wilts

FOCUS
A very moderate winning time for what was not a great race for its type. None of these had proven form in soft ground.

NOTEBOOK
Night Seed(IRE) failed to live up to market expectations on her debut but found what was required on this much softer surface. She should get further in due course. (op 11-4)
Mazzola has been kept busy since making his debut at the end of April. He lost little in defeat on this first run on soft ground. (op 11-4)
Timeteam(IRE) continues to disappoint and rather than dig deep he was inclined to lug in behind the runner-up. (op 6-5 tchd 6-4)
Conakry fared better than on his debut over 6f on the top of the ground here but that is not saying a lot. (op 14-1 tchd 8-1)

3903 JOHN SMITH'S H'CAP 1m 14y
7:35 (7:38) (Class 5) (0-70,69) 3-Y-0+ **£3,238** (£963; £481; £240) **Stalls** Low

Form RPR

3404 **1** **Libre**[25] 3089 8-9-0 **55** .... PaulFitzsimons 1 64
(F Jordan) *hld up towards rr: hdwy 3f out: rdn wl over 1f out: edgd rt and led wl ins fnl f: r.o* **11/1**

020 **2** *½* **Lordship (IRE)**[6] 3725 4-9-6 **64** .... JamesMillman(3) 3 72
(A W Carroll) *hld up in tch: led wl over 2f out: rdn jst over 1f out: hdd and edgd rt wl ins fnl f: r.o* **9/1**

-214 **3** *½* **Dancing Storm**[27] 3023 5-9-8 **63** .... FergusSweeney 10 70
(W S Kittow) *a.p: rdn and ev ch over 1f out: carried rt and nt qckn wl ins fnl f* **2/1**[1]

1241 **4** *2 ¼* **Ermine Grey**[9] 3607 7-9-4 **64** 6ex .... MarkCoumbe(5) 6 66
(A W Carroll) *hld up in rr: rdn 3f out: hdwy fnl 2f: nt rch ldrs* **13/2**[3]

5303 **5** *2 ¾* **Memphis Man**[4] 3797 5-9-9 **69** .... RichardEvans(5) 4 64
(P D Evans) *s.i.s: hld up in rr: rdn and hdwy 3f out: no imp fnl 2f* **9/2**[2]

030 **6** *1 ¼* **Hits Only Cash**[16] 3371 6-9-2 **64** .... (p) SimonPearce(7) 2 56
(J Pearce) *hld up towards rr: rdn over 2f out: hdwy over 1f out: no further prog fnl f* **12/1**

4560 **7** *1 ¼* **Indian Edge**[40] 2642 7-9-5 **65** .... JackDean(5) 8 55
(B Palling) *led over 5f: sn rdn: wknd wl over 1f out* **17/2**

463 **8** *4* **Addiena**[18] 3312 4-9-11 **66** .... CatherineGannon 9 46
(B Palling) *prom: rdn over 3f out: wknd 2f out* **14/1**

6200 **9** *shd* **Queen Excalibur**[18] 3311 9-8-6 **54** .... (p) DavidProbert(7) 11 34
(C Roberts) *prom: rdn over 2f out: wknd wl over 1f out* **22/1**

-060 **10** *6* **Very Well Red**[11] 3557 5-9-7 **69** .... WilliamCarson(7) 7 35
(P W Hiatt) *prom tl rdn and wkng whn edgd lft over 2f out* **28/1**

050 **11** *27* **Tinnarinka**[23] 3132 4-9-8 **63** .... (b) PatDobbs 5 —
(R Hannon) *hld up towards rr: rdn over 3f out: sn struggling: t.o* **28/1**

1m 38.67s (2.47) **Going Correction** +0.275s/f (Good) 11 Ran SP% **119.3**
Speed ratings (Par 103): **98,97,97,94,92 90,89,85,85,79 52**
toteswinger: 1&2 £24.20, 1&3 £9.00, 2&3 £41.60. CSF £105.11 CT £284.96 TOTE £12.00: £2.20, £3.80, £1.50; EX 50.80.
Owner On The Up Partnership **Bred** J C S Wilson Bloodstock **Trained** Adstone, Northants
■ Stewards' Enquiry : Richard Evans two-day ban: used whip down shoulder in forehand position (Jul 25,27)

FOCUS
A low-key handicap. The form is rated through the third and fourth.
Tinnarinka Official explanation: jockey said filly was unsuited by the soft ground

3904 CROWN AT CELTIC MANOR H'CAP 7f 16y
8:05 (8:09) (Class 4) (0-85,83) 3-Y-0+ **£5,180** (£1,541; £770; £384) **Stalls** Low

Form RPR

-525 **1** **Arabian Spirit**[38] 2705 3-9-3 **78** .... TPQueally 4 88+
(E A L Dunlop) *chsd ldr: led wl over 2f out: rdn over 1f out: r.o wl* **4/1**[2]

044- **2** *2 ¾* **Irony (IRE)**[301] 5383 9-9-2 **76** .... DavidProbert(7) 2 82
(A M Balding) *led over 4f: hrd rdn over 1f out: kpt on same pce* **7/2**[1]

600 **3** *1 ¾* **Tudor Prince (IRE)**[8] 3626 4-9-10 **77** .... FergusSweeney 3 78
(A W Carroll) *t.k.h in tch: ev ch over 2f out: rdn wl over 1f out: one pce* **4/1**[2]

-066 **4** *shd* **Starlight Gazer**[23] 3138 5-9-2 **74** .... (t) HaddenFrost(5) 1 75
(J A Geake) *dwlt: t.k.h: hdwy over 5f out: ev ch over 2f out: rdn over 1f out: one pce* **7/1**

4121 **5** *nk* **Charlie Delta**[13] 3501 5-8-13 **73** .... (b) WilliamCarson(7) 5 73
(J G M O'Shea) *hld up in rr: swtchd lft over 2f out: rdn jst over 1f out: nvr able to chal* **4/1**[2]

3050 **6** *hd* **Silver Wind**[48] 2405 3-9-8 **83** .... (v) PatDobbs 7 80
(P D Evans) *hld up in tch: rdn over 2f out: wknd ins fnl f* **11/2**[3]

1316 **7** *3* **Bold Cross (IRE)**[9] 3607 5-9-2 **69** .... PaulFitzsimons 6 61
(E G Bevan) *hld up: rdn over 2f out: sn bhd* **10/1**

1m 25.97s (2.77) **Going Correction** +0.275s/f (Good)
WFA 3 from 4yo+ 8lb 7 Ran SP% **119.2**
Speed ratings (Par 105): **95,91,89,89,89 89,85**
toteswinger: 1&2 £36.30, 1&3 £36.30, 2&3 £15.90. CSF £19.52 TOTE £6.30: £3.20, £2.40; EX 20.50.
Owner P A Deal A L Deal & G Holland-Bosworth **Bred** Malih Lahij Al Basti **Trained** Newmarket, Suffolk

FOCUS
A tightly-knit event. Some of these did not come here in much form but the less exposed winner is up 9lb.

3905 CROWN HOTELS & RESTAURANTS SPRINT STKS (H'CAP) 6f 16y
8:40 (8:41) (Class 2) (0-100,97) 3-Y-£11,354 (£3,398; £1,699; £849; £423) **Stalls** Low

Form RPR

-302 **1** **Phantom Whisper**[8] 3647 5-9-6 **91** .... JamesMillman(3) 11 99
(B R Millman) *hld up in rr: hdwy over 2f out: led jst ins fnl f: r.o wl* **11/2**[1]

6031 **2** *2 ½* **Millfields Dreams**[2] 3842 9-8-1 **76** 6h12 .... (p) DavidProbert(7) 8 76
(P Leech) *hld up in tch: rdn and ev ch 1f out: nt qckn* **6/1**[2]

-340 **3** *2 ¼* **Signor Peltro**[13] 3489 5-9-4 **86** .... FergusSweeney 6 79
(H Candy) *a.p: rdn to ld over 1f out: hdd jst ins fnl f: no ex* **11/2**[1]

4-50 **4** *2* **Edge Of Light**[72] 1718 3-9-9 **97** .... CatherineGannon 1 82
(B Palling) *led: rdn over 2f out: hdd over 1f out: wknd ins fnl f* **14/1**

06-4 **5** *nk* **King's Caprice**[56] 2163 7-9-8 **90** .... (t) RichardThomas 9 75
(J A Geake) *chsd ldr tl rdn over 2f out: sn wknd* **7/1**[3]

1620 **6** *2 ¼* **Jake The Snake (IRE)**[41] 2619 7-8-6 **79** .... MarkCoumbe(5) 7 57
(A W Carroll) *hld up and bhd: rdn and sme hdwy over 1f out: nvr nr ldrs* **10/1**

030 **7** *2 ¾* **Berbice (IRE)**[21] 3197 3-9-9 **97** .... (t) PatDobbs 4 65
(R Hannon) *hld up in tch: rdn over 2f out: sn wknd* **12/1**

2304 **8** *1* **Stamford Blue**[15] 3418 7-8-7 **78** .... (b) KevinGhunowa(3) 12 44
(R A Harris) *hld up in mid-div: rdn over 2f out: sn wknd* **9/1**

0320 **9** *1 ½* **Shes Minnie**[11] 3554 5-8-3 **78** .... SophieDoyle(7) 3 39
(P A Blockley) *hld up in mid-div: rdn and bhd fnl 2f* **20/1**

5520 **10** *2 ½* **Vhujon (IRE)**[27] 3047 3-9-2 **95** .... RichardEvans(5) 2 47
(P D Evans) *prom 3f* **25/1**

0500 **11** *4* **Conquest (IRE)**[13] 3504 4-9-13 **95** .... TPQueally 5 36
(W J Haggas) *stmbld and s.s: a in rr* **7/1**[3]

0210 **12** *6* **Esteem Machine (USA)**[62] 1985 4-9-7 **94** .... JackMitchell(5) 10 15
(R A Teal) *hld up in tch: rdn over 2f out: sn wknd* **9/1**

1m 13.06s (0.16) **Going Correction** +0.275s/f (Good)
WFA 3 from 4yo+ 6lb 12 Ran SP% **122.1**
Speed ratings (Par 109): **109,105,102,100,99 96,92,91,89,86 80,72**
toteswinger: 1&2 £27.70, 1&3 £15.70, 2&3 £10.00. CSF £39.05 CT £198.46 TOTE £4.30: £2.00, £3.40, £3.10; EX 64.60.
Owner Mrs Tina Ann Dormer **Bred** Robin Lawson **Trained** Kentisbeare, Devon

FOCUS
This wide-open affair was not the greatest of Class 2 handicaps. The winner is rated up a length with the runner-up, who was 12lb wrong, rated to the best view of his old form.

NOTEBOOK
Phantom Whisper built on his second to a horse in form at Warwick last week. Confirming that he handles the soft, he was certainly not stopping and connections are toying with stepping up to 7f. (op 4-1)
Millfields Dreams, who has been pretty consistent since being fitted with cheekpieces, was unpenalised for his Kempton win two days earlier and was 12lb 'wrong' here. The Handicapper is likely to take a dim view of this career-best effort. (op 11-1)
Signor Peltro had the visor left off having slipped to a mark only a pound higher than when successful at Newmarket nearly a year ago. (tchd 5-1 and 6-1)
Edge Of Light was making her handicap debut with some decent Group 3 and Listed form to her name. (op 22-1)
King's Caprice likes to dominate and there was always a possibility that he would be taken on for the lead by Edge Of Light. (tchd 15-2)
Jake The Snake(IRE) could not land a blow on this return to sprinting. (op 9-1)
Conquest(IRE) Official explanation: jockey said gelding stumbled badly on leaving stalls

3906 WATERCHEM, WATER TREATMENT FILLIES' H'CAP 1m 14y
9:10 (9:12) (Class 5) (0-70,69) 3-Y-0 **£3,238** (£963; £481; £240) **Stalls** Low

Form RPR

5 **1** **Zulu Princess (IRE)**[13] 3487 3-8-9 **60** .... LukeMorris(3) 4 69
(J S Moore) *a.p: wnt 2nd over 2f out: hrd rdn over 1f out: sustained chal fnl f: led last strides* **9/2**[3]

-300 **2** *nk* **Bikini**[14] 3457 3-9-7 **69** .... FergusSweeney 7 77
(H Candy) *led: rdn over 1f out: hdd last strides* **2/1**[2]

4231 **3** *8* **Jollyhockeysticks**[10] 3578 3-9-2 **64** .... CatherineGannon 3 54
(M R Channon) *chsd ldr tl rdn over 2f out: wknd wl over 1f out* **7/4**[1]

5500 **4** *6* **Bold Diva**[12] 3524 3-8-4 **57** ow2 .... (v) MarkCoumbe(5) 6 33
(A W Carroll) *hld up: rdn over 2f out: sn struggling* **22/1**

34-0 **5** *5* **Welsh Opera**[13] 3507 3-9-1 **63** .... PatDobbs 2 28
(Mrs A J Perrett) *hld up: short-lived effrt over 2f out* **5/1**

60-0 **6** *5* **Iamagrey (IRE)**[31] 2922 3-8-6 **57** .... TolleyDean(3) 8 10
(C J Down) *hld up in tch: rdn 3f out: sn struggling* **33/1**

0000 **U** **Dawn Wind**[26] 3065 3-7-10 **51** oh5 ow1 .... (v) SophieDoyle(7) 5 —
(I A Wood) *hld up in last: stmbld and uns rdr over 6f out* **33/1**

1m 39.11s (2.91) **Going Correction** +0.275s/f (Good) 7 Ran SP% **114.8**
Speed ratings (Par 97): **96,95,87,81,76 71,—**
toteswinger: 1&2 £3.00, 1&3 £3.40, 2&3 £1.60. CSF £13.95 CT £20.53 TOTE £6.10: £2.40, £2.00; EX 15.50 Place 6 £74.26, Place 5 £27.87.
Owner Clare Group **Bred** Mount Eaton Stud **Trained** Upper Lambourn, Berks

FOCUS
The first two came clear of the disappointing favourite in this moderate handicap.
Zulu Princess(IRE) Official explanation: trainer said, regarding apparent improvement in form, that the filly was better suited by the soft ground.
T/Plt: £210.00 to a £1 stake. Pool: £50,692.70. 176.20 winning tickets. T/Qpdt: £47.20 to a £1 stake. Pool: £4,272.00. 66.90 winning tickets. KH

3470 CHESTER (L-H)
Friday, July 11

OFFICIAL GOING: Good to soft (good in places)
Wind: Moderate, against Weather: Overcast with bright spells developing

3907 ETHEL AUSTIN PROPERTIES H'CAP 7f 122y
6:40 (6:41) (Class 4) (0-80,79) 3-Y-0 **£5,828** (£1,734; £866; £432) **Stalls** Low

Form RPR

5512 **1** **Yamal (IRE)**[15] 3416 3-9-6 **78** .... J-PGuillambert 2 95
(M Johnston) *trckd ldrs: led over 1f out: sn edgd lft and clr: eased down cl home* **6/4**[1]

-026 **2** *6* **La Chicaluna**[23] 3141 3-9-7 **79** .... TGMcLaughlin 5 81
(J G Given) *led: hdd 4f out: remained w ldr: regained ld over 2f out: rdn and hdd over 1f out: no ch w wnr fnl f* **3/1**[2]

-004 **3** *1* **Danzig Fox**[13] 3475 3-8-7 **65** .... TWilliams 4 64
(M Mullineaux) *in tch: effrt to chal and hung rt 2f out: one pce fnl f* **9/1**

3011 **4** *1 ¾* **Candle Sahara (IRE)**[13] 3487 3-9-4 **76** .... TPO'Shea 1 71
(M R Channon) *in rr: pushed along over 4f out: effrt 2f out: plugged on at one pce and nt trble ldrs fnl f* **4/1**[3]

5064 **5** *3 ¾* **King Hafhafah**[14] 3458 3-9-7 **79** .... (b[1]) PatCosgrave 6 64
(I A Wood) *racd keenly: w ldr: led 4f out: hdd over 2f out: sn rdn and looked awkward: n.m.r ent fnl 2f: wknd appr fnl f* **7/1**

-050 **6** *36* **Scanno (IRE)**[39] 2660 3-8-2 **60** oh5 .... AdrianMcCarthy 3 —
(M Mullineaux) *reminders leaving stalls: nvr gng wl and a bhd: lost tch 3f out: t.o* **33/1**

1m 34.96s (1.16) **Going Correction** +0.15s/f (Good) 6 Ran SP% **110.4**
Speed ratings (Par 102): **100,94,93,91,87 51**
toteswinger: 1&2 £1.10, 1&3 £3.70, 2&3 £3.40. CSF £5.96 TOTE £2.30: £1.50, £1.80; EX 6.70.
Owner Sheikh Hamdan Bin Mohammed Al Maktoum **Bred** Gainsborough Stud Management Ltd **Trained** Middleham Moor, N Yorks

FOCUS
A modest handicap for three-year-olds. The form can be rated through the runner-up and third and the progressive winner rates value for even further.

3908 MONEYSUPERMARKET.COM CONDITIONS STKS — 5f 16y
7:10 (7:10) (Class 2) 2-Y-O — **£9,462** (£2,832; £1,416; £708; £352) **Stalls** Low

Form — RPR

3424 **1** — **Doughnut**[12] 3528 2-8-9 0 .... PatCosgrave 2 — 86
(R Hannon) *mde all: shkn up and qcknd over 1f out: r.o wl and nvr in any danger fnl f* — **5/2[2]**

15 **2** *1 1/2* **Madame Trop Vite (IRE)**[13] 3496 2-8-9 0 .... TPO'Shea 1 — 81+
(K A Ryan) *hld up bhd ldrs: pushed along 2f out: rdn to take 2nd ins fnl f: sn edgd rt: styd on towards fin: nt pce to trble wnr* — **11/8[1]**

4212 **3** *2* **Countrywide City (IRE)**[13] 3470 2-8-11 0 .... AdrianMcCarthy 4 — 75
(P W Chapple-Hyam) *racd in 2nd: rdn and outpcd by wnr over 1f out: lost 2nd ins fnl f: no ex* — **15/2**

2203 **4** *2 1/2* **Our Wee Girl (IRE)**[16] 3378 2-8-6 0 .... LPKeniry 5 — 61
(S Kirk) *s.i.s and wnt rt s: in rr: pushed along 1/2-way: rdn and lugged lft over 1f out whn no imp* — **4/1[3]**

024 **5** *hd* **Digit**[7] 3669 2-8-7 0 ow1 .... TomEaves 3 — 62
(B Smart) *n.m.r sn after s: chsd ldrs: nt handle bnd 2f out: rdn and hung lft whn wkng over 1f out* — **9/1**

61.49 secs (0.49) **Going Correction** +0.15s/f (Good) — **5** Ran SP% **112.4**
Speed ratings (Par 100): **102,99,96,92,92**
CSF £6.54 TOTE £2.50: £1.60, £1.60; EX 4.50.
Owner Simon Leech & Des Anderson **Bred** R F And S D Knipe **Trained** East Everleigh, Wilts

FOCUS
A modest event for the class, run at a sound pace. Straightforward to rate with the principals close to form.

NOTEBOOK
Doughnut pinged out from the gates and was quickly into the lead. She eventually found plenty when her rider asked her to go and seal the race, never really looking in any serious trouble down the home straight. Her sire's progeny to date have shown a preference for faster ground, but she has now won her two races with some cut underfoot. This rates her best effort to date and, a filly blessed with real early pace, it was no real surprise that this tight track proved up her street. (op 9-4 tchd 11-4)
Madame Trop Vite(IRE) had won her maiden on her debut over course and distance and was not disgraced in Listed company over 6f on her previous outing. She struggled to really go the early pace on this return to the minimum, however, and by the time she eventually hit full stride the winner had flown. This was also the easiest surface she had raced on to date so she should not be written off in this sort of class when returning to a stiffer test on slightly better ground. (op 2-1)
Countrywide City(IRE), the only colt in the race, was taking a step up in class and was not disgraced, but never looked like playing a serious part. He will look better off in nurseries. (op 13-2 tchd 6-1)
Our Wee Girl(IRE) was always playing catch-up after missing the kick and then veering right out of the gates. She was also struggling to go the pace from halfway on this, the softest ground she has encountered to date. While she is now looking fairly exposed, a switch to a nurseries now seems logical and a return to 6f also could be a wise move. (op 7-2)

3909 9TH KATHLEEN B. CORBETT MEMORIAL H'CAP — 5f 16y
7:45 (7:47) (Class 3) (0-95,95) 3-Y-O **£9,462** (£2,832; £1,416; £708; £352) **Stalls** Low

Form — RPR

2102 **1** — **Hamish McGonagall**[14] 3451 3-9-3 **91** .... DavidAllan 1 — 102+
(T D Easterby) *mde all: shkn up and asserted over 1f out: r.o and in command fnl f* — **4/5[1]**

3416 **2** *1* **Requisite**[14] 3462 3-8-6 **80** .... TPO'Shea 3 — 87
(I A Wood) *in rr: swtchd rt wl over 1f out: hdwy sn after: hung lft and wnt 2nd ent fnl f: styd on towards fin: unable to rch wnr* — **8/1[3]**

1233 **3** *2 1/2* **Little Pete (IRE)**[13] 3472 3-9-0 **88** .... LPKeniry 7 — 86
(A M Balding) *chsd ldrs: rdn and edgd rt over 1f out: one pce ins fnl f* — **4/1[2]**

50-0 **4** *1 1/2* **Thunder Bay**[17] 3336 3-8-9 **83** .... PaulHanagan 5 — 76
(R A Fahey) *in rr: c wd on bnd 2f out: styd on fnl f: nt pce to chal* — **18/1**

-300 **5** *1/2* **Fol Hollow (IRE)**[48] 2410 3-9-7 **95** .... AdrianTNicholls 4 — 86
(D Nicholls) *w wnr: rdn and hung rt 1/2-way: outpcd by wnr over 1f out: wkng whn n.m.r ins fnl f* — **12/1**

0025 **6** *1 1/2* **Cake (IRE)**[27] 3041 3-9-7 **95** .... PatCosgrave 8 — 80
(R Hannon) *prom on outside: u.p and btn over 1f out* — **9/1**

5-00 **7** *17* **Regal Step**[14] 3462 3-8-7 **81** ow1 .... (v[1]) J-PGuillambert 6 — —
(R M H Cowell) *missed break: sn outpcd and nvr handled trck* — **40/1**

61.17 secs (0.17) **Going Correction** +0.15s/f (Good) — **7** Ran SP% **112.1**
Speed ratings (Par 104): **104,102,98,96,95 92,65**
toteswinger: 1&2 £1.50, 1&3 £1.10, 2&3 £3.90. CSF £7.71 CT £16.54 TOTE £1.70: £1.50, £3.10; EX 5.90.
Owner Reality Racing Syndicate No 1 **Bred** J P Coggan And Whitsbury Manor Stud **Trained** Great Habton, N Yorks

FOCUS
A good sprint handicap for three-year-olds. The form looks sound enough with the front pair progressive.

NOTEBOOK
Hamish McGonagall took full advantage of his excellent draw in stall 1 and came home a ready winner from the front on this return to racing against his own age group. This progressive sprinter rates value for a bit further than the winning margin and deserves another crack at a valuable pot again now, with the Hong Kong Sprint at Ascot later this month likely to be on his agenda. He now picks up a 5lb penalty for that after this win. (op Evens tchd 6-5)
Requisite fared best of those to come from off the pace and enjoyed this return to an easier surface. She finished nicely clear of the remainder and does have the ability to defy this sort of mark, but a return to a stiffer track is surely a wise move now for her. (op 9-1 tchd 7-1)
Little Pete(IRE) came into this in good heart and, not drawn nearly as well as the front pair, once again managed to fill a place. He is a little better than this and does deserve to find another winning turn now. (op 7-2)
Thunder Bay failed to really handle the final turn, but he finished his race well enough in the circumstances and this was a more encouraging effort. He could come on again a little for the run. (op 14-1 tchd 20-1)
Fol Hollow(IRE) tried to go with the winner early on, but he wanted to hang right at around the halfway stage and eventually tired out of things. (op 17-2)

3910 ASTBURY WREN NURSERY — 6f 18y
8:15 (8:15) (Class 4) 2-Y-O — **£5,828** (£1,734; £866; £432) **Stalls** Low

Form — RPR

3446 **1** — **Transcentral**[7] 3670 2-8-2 **64** .... TPO'Shea 5 — 69
(W M Brisbourne) *sn led: rdn over 1f out: edgd rt whn pressed ins fnl f: r.o: edgd lft towards fin* — **6/1**

051 **2** *nk* **Alphabeth**[62] 2004 2-7-12 **60** .... AdrianMcCarthy 2 — 64
(M R Channon) *chsd ldrs: wnt 2nd over 2f out: rdn over 1f out: str chal ins fnl f: r.o: hld fnl strides* — **4/1[3]**

51 **3** *5* **Cornish Rose (IRE)**[14] 3432 2-9-1 **77** .... PaulHanagan 3 — 66+
(M H Tompkins) *niggled along in rr: chsd ldng pair 2f out: no imp* — **13/8[1]**

210 **4** *13* **Officer Mor (USA)**[24] 3105 2-9-2 **78** .... AndrewElliott 1 — 28+
(K R Burke) *racd keenly: w wnr tl rdn over 2f out: sn wknd* — **15/8[2]**

1m 15.62s (1.82) **Going Correction** +0.15s/f (Good) — **4** Ran SP% **107.2**
Speed ratings (Par 96): **93,92,85,68**
CSF £26.18 TOTE £7.40; EX 30.30.
Owner D R B Racing **Bred** D R Botterill **Trained** Great Ness, Shropshire

■ Stewards' Enquiry : Adrian McCarthy one-day ban: used whip with excessive frequency (Jul 25)

FOCUS
A modest nursery which saw the first pair come well clear. Improved form drom the winner, but no fluke. The 'official' ratings are estimated and are intended as a guide.

NOTEBOOK
Transcentral, beaten in selling company a week previously, bounced right back to form with a game career-first success. She had looked to be going backwards after showing ability on her first two starts this year, but despite having very much the run of the race out in front there appeared to be little fluke about this effort. Easy ground suits her well and she is worthy of another chance to prove she is now coming good, despite a likely weight rise. (tchd 13-2)
Alphabeth, a winner in selling company last time, gave her all in defeat and only just gave best in the end. She handled the softer ground without fuss, finished well clear of the remainder in second, and is going the right way. (op 7-2)
Cornish Rose(IRE), a winner over 7f at this venue a fortnight previously, did not prove suited by the return to this sharper test and was well beaten off in the end. A return to an extra furlong will suit, but she looks to have begun life in this sphere on a tough mark all the same. Official explanation: jockey said filly hung right (op 15-8 tchd 6-4)
Officer Mor(USA), outclassed in the Windsor Castle 24 days previously, showed early dash from the inside stall yet eventually paid for racing too freely. It was a very disappointing effort, but he surely better than this and may need genuinely fast ground. (tchd 13-8 and 2-1)

3911 SHELL UK H'CAP — 1m 2f 75y
8:50 (8:51) (Class 4) (0-85,85) 3-Y-O — **£5,828** (£1,734; £866; £432) **Stalls** High

Form — RPR

4321 **1** — **My Aunt Fanny**[13] 3473 3-9-1 **79** .... LPKeniry 1 — 92
(A M Balding) *chsd ldrs: r.o to ld ins fnl f: won gng away* — **7/2[2]**

2353 **2** *1 3/4* **Bowder Stone (IRE)**[13] 3494 3-8-8 **72** .... DavidAllan 3 — 82
(M H Tompkins) *chsd ldrs: wnt 2nd over 2f out: rdn to ld over 1f out: hdd ins fnl f: no ex towards fin* — **8/1**

132 **3** *6* **Mangham (IRE)**[8] 3641 3-9-2 **80** .... PatCosgrave 4 — 78
(D H Brown) *racd keenly: helped set str pce: led over 3f out: rdn and hdd over 1f out: wknd ins fnl f* — **2/1[1]**

1402 **4** *3 3/4* **Fujin Dancer (FR)**[10] 3579 3-8-7 **71** .... PaulHanagan 8 — 61
(R A Fahey) *in rr: hdwy over 3f out: no imp on ldrs over 2f out: wknd over 1f out* — **4/1[3]**

0243 **5** *2 3/4* **Always Cruising (USA)**[6] 3711 3-8-7 **71** .... J-PGuillambert 5 — 56
(M Johnston) *in rr: niggled along early: rdn and edgd lft over 1f out: nvr on terms* — **7/1**

5-03 **6** *3 1/4* **Kingdom Of Fife**[18] 3326 3-8-8 **72** .... TomEaves 7 — 50
(Sir Michael Stoute) *towards rr: pushed along over 4f out: toiling wl over 2f out* — **11/2**

-040 **7** *7* **Hilbre Court (USA)**[12] 3527 3-9-7 **85** .... (b[1]) TPO'Shea 2 — 49
(B J Meehan) *led at str pce: hdd over 3f out: wknd 2f out* — **16/1**

2m 12.57s (0.37) **Going Correction** +0.15s/f (Good) — **7** Ran SP% **120.4**
Speed ratings (Par 102): **104,102,97,94,92 90,84**
toteswinger: 1&2 £7.40, 1&3 £2.50, 2&3 £3.80. CSF £33.10 CT £71.64 TOTE £3.40: £1.80, £4.30; EX 38.90.
Owner J C & S R Hitchins **Bred** J C , J R And S R Hitchins **Trained** Kingsclere, Hants

FOCUS
A fair handicap for three-year-olds, run at a decent early pace. The first two are progressing but the next two were baten a fair way so the form is not easy to pin down.
Mangham(IRE) Official explanation: jockey said gelding ran too keenly early

3912 LAMBERT SMITH HAMPTON CHESHIRE YEOMANRY H'CAP — 1m 4f 66y
9:20 (9:20) (Class 5) (0-75,66) 3-Y-0+ — **£4,094** (£1,209; £604) **Stalls** Low

Form — RPR

5623 **1** — **Prelude**[8] 3624 7-10-0 **66** .... TGMcLaughlin 7 — 76
(W M Brisbourne) *mde all: rdn over 1f out: edgd rt ent fnl f: r.o gamely* — **7/2[3]**

2-05 **2** *1 1/4* **Sir Sandicliffe (IRE)**[11] 3550 4-9-5 **57** .... TPO'Shea 1 — 65
(W M Brisbourne) *hld up: hdwy over 3f out: rdn over 1f out: styd on to take 2nd post: nt rch wnr* — **12/1**

2-14 **3** *shd* **Master Nimbus**[15] 3399 8-8-10 **55** .... JamieKyne(7) 9 — 63
(J J Quinn) *racd keenly: chsd ldrs: rdn over 2f out: wnt 2nd and nt clr run over 1f out: nt qckn ins fnl f: lost 2nd post* — **11/4[1]**

521 **4** *1 1/4* **Moonshine Creek**[8] 3650 6-9-0 **52** 6ex .... PaulHanagan 8 — 58
(P W Hiatt) *plld hrd: chsd wnr: rdn over 2f out: lost 2nd over 1f out: no ex fnl 75yds* — **3/1[2]**

4333 **5** *6* **Barbirolli**[7] 3698 6-8-8 **53** .... RossAtkinson(7) 10 — 49
(W M Brisbourne) *chsd ldrs: rdn 4f out: wknd 2f out: no ch whn lugged lft over 1f out* — **7/2[3]**

0002 **6** *9* **Sky Chart (IRE)**[7] 3698 4-8-4 **49** oh2 .... StacyRenwick(7) 3 — 31
(N J Vaughan) *missed break: racd keenly: hdwy after 4f: chsd ldrs on outside 6f out: wknd over 3f out* — **8/1**

2m 43.66s (3.76) **Going Correction** +0.15s/f (Good) — **6** Ran SP% **114.9**
Speed ratings (Par 103): **93,92,92,91,87 81**
CSF £41.89 CT £130.84 TOTE £3.60: £2.20, £3.80; EX 26.00 Place 6 £243.17, Place 5 £195.24.

Owner A P Burgoyne **Bred** Cheveley Park Stud Ltd **Trained** Great Ness, Shropshire

FOCUS
A moderate handicap which provided a one-two for the Mark Brisbourne stable. It was a very moderate winning time, due to the uneven pace, and the form, which is modest, should be treated with a little caution.

T/Plt: £288.90 to a £1 stake. Pool: £61,754.43. 156.00 winning tickets. T/Qpdt: £118.60 to a £1 stake. Pool: £3,223.10. 20.10 winning tickets. DO

3631 NEWBURY (L-H)

Friday, July 11

OFFICIAL GOING: Soft (6.2)
Wind: Virtually nil

3913 BETDAQ THE BETTING EXCHANGE E B F MAIDEN FILLIES' STKS — 7f (S)
6:20 (6:26) (Class 4) 2-Y-O — **£5,828** (£1,734; £866; £432) **Stalls** High

Form — RPR

6 **1** **Minor Vamp (IRE)**[16] 3373 2-9-0 0 ... RyanMoore 4 — 83+
(R Hannon) *in rr: pushed along 3f out: hdwy over 2f out: drvn and str run to ld appr fnl f: sn in command* — **8/1**

5 **2** 2½ **Key Signature**[17] 3349 2-9-0 0 ... ShaneKelly 3 — 77+
(Pat Eddery) *pushed lft s: sn rcvrd and in tch: rdn 2f out: styd on to chse wnr ins fnl f: readily hld whn hung rt fnl 100yds* — **15/2**

3 1½ **Polly's Mark (IRE)** 2-8-9 0 ... GabrielHannon(5) 12 — 73
(C G Cox) *s.i.s: in rr: rdn over 2f out: styd on ins fnl f: gng on cl home but nvr a threat* — **20/1**

5 **4** hd **Dream In Waiting**[14] 3437 2-9-0 0 ... TQuinn 11 — 73
(P F I Cole) *chsd ldrs: drvn along over 2f out: outpcd fnl f* — **13/2**[3]

5 1¾ **Miss Sophisticat** 2-9-0 0 ... JamieSpencer 8 — 69+
(W J Knight) *tardy s but sn qckncd to ld: rdn over 2f out but kpt narrow ld tl hdd appr fnl f: btn whn hmpd fnl 110yds* — **14/1**

0 **6** ½ **It's Toast (IRE)**[14] 3456 2-9-0 0 ... GeorgeBaker 6 — 67+
(R M Beckett) *chsd ldrs: rdn over 2f out: wkng whn hung rt ins fnl f* — **4/1**[1]

50 **7** 1¾ **Polly's Choice (IRE)**[16] 3373 2-9-0 0 ... JimmyFortune 1 — 63
(R Hannon) *chsd ldrs: rdn to chal ins fnl 2f: wknd fnl f* — **20/1**

0 **8** shd **Le Grand Amour (IRE)**[17] 3349 2-9-0 0 ... SteveDrowne 10 — 62
(B W Hills) *in tch: rdn over 2f out: wknd over 1f out* — **17/2**

9 hd **Ballyalla** 2-9-0 0 ... RichardHughes 7 — 62
(R Hannon) *stdd s: sn in tch: rdn over 2f out: wknd over 1f out* — **11/2**[2]

3 **10** 1¼ **Triple Cee (IRE)**[17] 3349 2-9-0 0 ... EdwardCreighton 14 — 59
(M R Channon) *chsd ldrs: rdn over 2f out: wknd qckly over 1f out* — **4/1**[1]

11 8 **Fleur De'Lion (IRE)** 2-9-0 0 ... StephenCarson 13 — 39
(S Kirk) *s.i.s: a in rr* — **40/1**

12 ½ **Anaasheed** 2-9-0 0 ... MartinDwyer 15 — 37+
(J L Dunlop) *a in rr* — **14/1**

13 5 **Lake Kalamalka (IRE)** 2-9-0 0 ... JimCrowley 2 — 25
(J L Dunlop) *bhd fr 1/2-way* — **28/1**

1m 29.91s (4.21) **Going Correction** +0.65s/f (Yiel) — **13** Ran SP% **130.9**
Speed ratings (Par 93): **101,98,96,96,94 93,91,91,91,89 80,80,74**
toteswinger: 1&2 £12.50, 1&3 £39.90, 2&3 £37.00. CSF £70.40 TOTE £11.00: £2.70, £2.70, £6.80; EX 83.40.
Owner Michael Pescod & Justin Dowley **Bred** Mrs Joan Murphy **Trained** East Everleigh, Wilts
■ Stewards' Enquiry : Shane Kelly caution: careless riding

FOCUS
A decent maiden where previous experience once again came to the fore. The first two both improved.

NOTEBOOK
Minor Vamp(IRE), who shaped with promise at Kempton behind Cherry Hinton third Ahla Wasahl on her debut, appreciated the extra furlong and came nicely clear in the closing stages. She looks a nice sort for nurseries, but could well go for the Goffs Fillies Million next month. (op 10-1)
Key Signature, racing on different ground from her debut over this course and distance, coped well and beat the rest well enough. She looks to be going the right way and has a maiden in her. (op 11-1 tchd 12-1)
Polly's Mark(IRE), a sister to Yab Adee, who placed in middle-distance maidens, did best of the newcomers. She was out the back and under pressure some way out but stayed on well to be nearest at the finish. Another furlong is going to suit her. (op 33-1)
Dream In Waiting, who was green and hampered on her debut, had a happier experience this time but may have found the ground softer than ideal. (op 10-1)
Miss Sophisticat, a half-sister to Swanky, a winner at 1m plus, showed good speed on her debut and was hampered when weakening in the closing stages, but for which she would have finished a bit closer. (op 25-1 tchd 28-1)
It's Toast(IRE), a half-sister to high-class Dream Eater, who was fifth in this year's 2000 Guineas, was well backed but well beaten on her debut. Again she came in for plenty of support, and while she showed pace, she dropped out of things inside the last. A drop back in trip might help her. (op 9-1)
Triple Cee(IRE) did not look as effective on this softer ground. Official explanation: jockey said filly was unsuited by the soft ground (op 5-2 tchd 9-4)

3914 RIDGEWAY VOLKSWAGEN H'CAP — 1m 2f 6y
6:50 (6:55) (Class 5) (0-70,68) 4-Y-O+ — **£3,238** (£963; £481; £240) **Stalls** Low

Form — RPR

032- **1** **Oldrik (GER)**[32] 2980 5-9-4 **65** ...(p) JamieSpencer 9 — 77+
(P J Hobbs) *s.i.s: rdn and nt keen early: hrd rdn bnd 5f out and stl bhd: c on bit over 2f out: travelling wl 1f out: rdn to ld and hung lft fnl 110yds: drvn out* — **4/1**[1]

2 ¾ **Action Impact (ARG)**[175] 4-8-11 **60** ... RyanMoore 8 — 69
(G L Moore) *t.k.h: in rr: rdn and hdwy fr 2f out: styd on to chal ins fnl f: sn hung rt u.p and a hld by wnr* — **4/1**[1]

1040 **3** 3½ **King Of Connacht**[17] 3347 5-8-5 **52** ...(p) MartinDwyer 11 — 56
(M Wellings) *t.k.h: hld up in rr: hdwy over 3f out: led over 1f out: hdd and wkng whn hmpd fnl 110yds* — **11/1**

4010 **4** 1 **Night Orbit**[14] 3449 4-9-5 **66** ... GeorgeBaker 6 — 68
(Miss J Feilden) *chsd ldrs: rdn to take slt ld 2f out: hdd over 1f out: wkng whn hmpd fnl 110yds* — **10/1**

6523 **5** 4½ **Nightspot**[28] 2990 7-9-7 **68** ... StephenCarson 5 — 61
(Eve Johnson Houghton) *led tl hdd 2f out: sn btn* — **7/1**

0606 **6** nse **Muffett's Dream**[12] 3518 4-8-2 **49** ... FrankieMcDonald 1 — 41
(J J Bridger) *chsd ldr 7f out to 3f out: sn rdn: wknd over 1f out* — **50/1**

2646 **7** 1¾ **Effigy**[25] 3090 4-8-10 **64** ... AmyScott(7) 4 — 53
(H Candy) *towards rr tl stdy hdwy on outside over 3f out to chal over 2f out: wknd qckly wl over 1f out* — **11/2**[2]

-060 **8** 1 **Balnagore**[12] 3518 4-9-7 **68** ... JimCrowley 3 — 55
(J L Dunlop) *chsd ldrs: rdn 3f out: wknd 2f out* — **9/1**

0-24 **9** 11 **The Wily Woodcock**[43] 2533 4-9-5 **66** ... SteveDrowne 2 — 31
(G Wragg) *chsd ldrs: rdn 3f out: sn wknd* — **6/1**[3]

0120 **10** 16 **Josr's Magic (IRE)**[14] 3457 4-8-11 **58** ow2 ... RichardHughes 7 — —
(H J Collingridge) *t.k.h towards rr: sme prog 4f out: sn wknd* — **16/1**

2m 14.37s (5.57) **Going Correction** +0.65s/f (Yiel) — **10** Ran SP% **117.4**
Speed ratings (Par 103): **103,102,99,98,95 95,93,92,84,71**
toteswinger: 1&2 £4.00, 1&3 £10.70, 2&3 £12.80. CSF £19.56 CT £164.04 TOTE £5.30: £2.30, £1.80, £4.40; EX 21.60.
Owner D J Jones **Bred** H Feldt **Trained** Withycombe, Somerset
■ Stewards' Enquiry : Jamie Spencer three-day ban (reduced from four days on appeal): careless riding (Jul 25, 27-28)
Ryan Moore caution: careless riding

FOCUS
They did not seem to go more than an ordinary pace but the first three home raced in the last three places for most of the race. Not easy form to pin down.
Action Impact(ARG) Official explanation: jockey said gelding hung right
Josr's Magic(IRE) Official explanation: trainer said gelding was unsuited by the soft ground and ran too free early

3915 GARDNER MECHANICAL SERVICES H'CAP — 1m (S)
7:25 (7:26) (Class 4) (0-80,80) 3-Y-O+ — **£5,828** (£1,734; £866; £432) **Stalls** High

Form — RPR

6-1 **1** **Harald Bluetooth (IRE)**[20] 3275 3-9-1 **78** ... JamieSpencer 6 — 87+
(J R Fanshawe) *tardy s: hld up in tch: hdwy fr 2f out: sn drvn: led 1f out: hung rt u.p wl ins fnl f: kpt on wl* — **7/4**[1]

1511 **2** 1 **Paraguay (USA)**[13] 3478 5-9-5 **73** ... EdwardCreighton 9 — 82+
(Miss V Haigh) *hld up in rr: rdn and hdwy ins fnl 2f: styd on wl fnl f to chse wnr cl home but a hld* — **5/1**[3]

2202 **3** ½ **Special Reserve (IRE)**[12] 3521 3-9-0 **77** ... RichardHughes 5 — 83
(R Hannon) *hld up in rr but in tch: gd hdwy to chal jst ins fnl f: one pce whn hmpd fnl 100yds and swtchd lft* — **9/2**[2]

0522 **4** 2½ **Mr Hichens**[12] 3525 3-8-11 **74** ...(b) TedDurcan 4 — 74
(B J Meehan) *chsd ldrs: rdn and hung rt ins fnl f: sn hmpd and again nr fin: nt enthusiastic* — **13/2**

1-00 **5** 1 **Naval Review (USA)**[28] 3002 3-8-10 **73** ... RyanMoore 7 — 71
(Sir Michael Stoute) *in tch: rdn and hdwy over 1f out: nvr gng pce to be competitive and sn btn* — **17/2**

0-62 **6** nk **Sotik Star (IRE)**[32] 2897 5-9-2 **70** ... JimmyFortune 2 — 69
(P J Makin) *sn led: rdn 2f out: hdd 1f out: wknd ins fnl f* — **10/1**

0-05 **7** 4 **Mr Garston**[9] 3612 5-9-5 **80** ... HarryPoulton(7) 3 — 70
(J R Boyle) *t.k.h: chsd ldr over 6f: sn wknd* — **25/1**

6-44 **8** 8 **Jo'Burg (USA)**[22] 3167 4-9-12 **80** ...(b) JimCrowley 1 — 52
(Mrs A J Perrett) *a towards rr: dropped away fnl 2f* — **12/1**

1m 46.52s (6.82) **Going Correction** +0.65s/f (Yiel)
WFA 3 from 4yo+ 9lb — **8** Ran SP% **115.7**
Speed ratings (Par 105): **91,90,89,87,86 85,81,73**
toteswinger: 1&2 £2.90, 1&3 £2.40, 2&3 £6.10. CSF £10.80 CT £33.70 TOTE £2.40: £1.60, £1.50, £1.50; EX 6.10.
Owner Mr & Mrs Duncan Davidson **Bred** Airlie Stud And Sir Thomas Pilkington **Trained** Newmarket, Suffolk
■ Stewards' Enquiry : Jamie Spencer one-day ban: careless riding (Jul 31)

FOCUS
No more than a fair handicap run at an ordinary gallop, and the winning time was modest. The form is rated through the third.
Sotik Star(IRE) Official explanation: jockey says gelding hung right
Jo'Burg(USA) Official explanation: jockey said gelding was unsuited by the soft ground

3916 HEATHERWOLD STUD MAIDEN STKS — 6f 8y
7:55 (7:57) (Class 4) 3-Y-O — **£5,828** (£1,734; £866; £432) **Stalls** High

Form — RPR

50 **1** **Myanmar (IRE)**[34] 2834 3-9-3 0 ... ShaneKelly 13 — 79+
(J Noseda) *s.i.s: in rr: rdn over 2f out: swtchd rt over 1f out but stl plenty to do: str run under hand riding ins fnl f to ld last strides: cosily* — **7/2**[1]

00 **2** nk **Diego Rivera**[31] 2919 3-9-3 0 ... RichardSmith 9 — 72
(P J Makin) *hld up towards rr but in tch: hdwy fr 2f out: drvn to ld fnl 110yds: sn in command tl collared by cheeeky wnr last strides* — **8/1**

0 **3** 2¾ **Sydneysider**[31] 2919 3-9-3 0 ... StephenCarson 1 — 63
(Eve Johnson Houghton) *chsd ldrs: drvn to ld appr fnl f: hdd fnl 110yds and sn btn* — **14/1**

00 **4** ½ **Seven Royals (IRE)**[41] 2620 3-9-3 0 ... AdamKirby 5 — 62
(Miss A M Newton-Smith) *s.i.s: sn chsng ldrs: rdn over 2f out: kpt on tl wknd fnl 110yds* — **11/2**[2]

00 **5** ½ **Star Acclaim**[85] 1423 3-8-12 0 ... SteveDrowne 4 — 55
(T Keddy) *chsd ldrs: rdn 3f out: styd on same pce fnl 2f* — **7/1**

0-5 **6** 1 **Gambling Jack**[22] 3180 3-9-3 0 ... JimCrowley 2 — 57
(A W Carroll) *led: rdn over 2f out: hdd appr fnl f: sn wknd* — **6/1**[3]

-6 **7** 2¼ **Dancing Belle**[22] 3177 3-8-12 0 ... OscarUrbina 11 — 45
(J A R Toller) *towards rr but in tch: drvn over 2f out: nvr gng pce to be competitive* — **6/1**[3]

0-0 **8** 3½ **Man Appeal**[7] 3694 3-8-12 0 ... TedDurcan 7 — 33
(B J Meehan) *chsd ldrs: rdn 1/2-way: wknd fr 2f out* — **22/1**

9 10 **Red Rani** 3-8-7 0 ... GabrielHannon(5) 8 — 1
(B W Duke) *chsd ldrs tl rdn and wknd fr 1/2-way* — **25/1**

05 **10** 11 **The Young Fella**[13] 3502 3-9-3 0 ... JamieSpencer 12 — —
(S A Callaghan) *s.i.s: swtchd lft to outside and hdwy to chse ldrs 1/2-way: sn wknd: eased whn no ch fnl f* — **7/1**

000- **11** 9 **Follow The Band**[259] 6478 3-9-3 **62** ... RichardHughes 10 — —
(R Hannon) *a towards rr: wknd 1/2-way: eased whn no ch fnl f* — **12/1**

1m 17.84s (4.84) **Going Correction** +0.65s/f (Yiel) — **11** Ran SP% **124.8**
Speed ratings (Par 102): **93,92,88,88,87 86,83,78,65,50 38**
toteswinger: 1&2 £8.10, 1&3 £17.30, 2&3 £35.30. CSF £34.26 TOTE £4.30: £1.90, £3.50, £5.80; EX 47.30.
Owner D Smith, Mrs J Magnier, M Tabor **Bred** Mrs Jacqueline Donnelly **Trained** Newmarket, Suffolk

FOCUS
An ordinary maiden. Not easy form to assess, with the winner perhaps the best guide at this stage.
Man Appeal Official explanation: jockey said filly hung right on leaving stalls
The Young Fella Official explanation: jockey said colt broke awkwardly and had no more to give

3917 BETDAQ.CO.UK H'CAP — 1m 5f 61y
8:30 (8:30) (Class 5) (0-75,74) 4-Y-O+ — **£3,238** (£963; £481; £240) **Stalls** Low

Form — RPR

4302 **1** **Pocketwood**[41] 2621 6-8-13 **66** ... StephenCarson 7 — 75
(Jean-Rene Auvray) *dictated pce: drvn along over 2f out: styd on strly thrght fnl f* — **3/1**[1]

60-0 **2** ½ **Act Three**[29] 2978 4-8-9 **62** ... TedDurcan 2 — 70
(Mouse Hamilton-Fairley) *hld up in rr: stdy hdwy fr 3f out: drvn to chse wnr over 1f out: styd on thrght fnl f but a hld* — **16/1**

-021 **3** 3½ **Kokkokila**[25] 3084 4-8-6 **62** ... KirstyMilczarek(3) 3 — 65
(Lady Herries) *in tch: c to outside: rdn and styd on fr over 2f out but nvr gng pce to trble ldng duo* — **10/3**[2]

0/00 **4** ½ **Climate Change (USA)**[27] 3044 6-9-7 **74** ... LiamTreadwell 6 — 76
(Miss Venetia Williams) *chsd wnr 6f out: rdn and no imp over 2f out: lost 2nd over 1f out and sn wknd* — **12/1**

150 **5** *hd* **Mae Cigan (FR)**[26] 3060 5-9-0 **67** .... SteveDrowne 5 69+
(M Blanshard) *hld up in rr: rdn fr 3f out: styd on same pce fr over 2f out and nvr in contention* **7/2**[3]

0644 **6** *1 ½* **Alfie Noakes**[26] 3060 6-9-6 **73** .... JimCrowley 8 73
(Mrs A J Perrett) *in rr: rdn and styd on same pce fnl 3f* **7/2**[3]

0161 **7** *42* **Royal Premier (IRE)**[45] 2482 5-9-0 **70** .... (v) JerryO'Dwyer(3) 1 11
(H J Collingridge) *chsd wnr to 6f out: rdn 3f out: wknd rapidly 2f out: eased whn no ch: t.o* **8/1**

3m 9.24s (17.24) **Going Correction** +0.65s/f (Yiel) **7** Ran SP% **117.2**
Speed ratings (Par 103): **72,71,69,69,69 68,—**
toteswinger: 1&2 £11.30, 1&3 £2.80, 2&3 £10.30. CSF £50.65 CT £170.64 TOTE £4.50: £2.10, £7.50; EX 75.20.
Owner Jean-Rene Auvray **Bred** M J Lewin **Trained** Upper Lambourn, Berks
■ Stewards' Enquiry : Stephen Carson one-day ban: used whip with excessive frequency (Jul 25)

FOCUS
A fairly steady early gallop was set by the winner and not surprisingly the winning time was pedestrian. The form makes sense at face value.
Royal Premier(IRE) Official explanation: jockey said gelding was unsuited by the soft ground

3918 AXMINSTER CARPETS FILLIES' H'CAP 7f (S)
9:00 (9:01) (Class 5) (0-75,75) 3-Y-O **£3,561** (£1,059; £529; £264) **Stalls** High

Form RPR

2-10 **1** **Divine Power**[45] 2481 3-9-7 **75** .... GeorgeBaker 8 82
(R M Beckett) *hld up in rr: gd hdwy over 2f out: drvn to ld ins fnl f: rdn out* **12/1**

500 **2** *nk* **Sir Kyffin's Folly**[42] 2566 3-8-11 **65** .... AdamKirby 5 71
(J A Geake) *s.i.s: in rr tl hdwy fr 2f out: styd on strly u.p fnl f: gng on cl home but nt quite rch wnr* **18/1**

03-5 **3** *2 ¼* **Shindy (FR)**[18] 3318 3-9-2 **70** .... OscarUrbina 4 70+
(J A R Toller) *chsd ldrs: drvn to take slt advantage 1f out: sn hdd and bmpd: styd on same pce* **12/1**

633 **4** *1* **Theory**[31] 2919 3-9-5 **73** .... (b[1]) JimmyFortune 3 71
(J H M Gosden) *chsd ldrs: chal fr 2f out: led briefly jst ins fnl f: hung rt and sn hdd: continued to hang and wknd nr fin* **5/1**[2]

0401 **5** *2 ½* **Priti Fabulous (IRE)**[30] 2946 3-9-5 **73** .... JamieSpencer 11 64
(W J Haggas) *hld up towards rr: gd hdwy to trck ldrs fr 2f out: effrt to chal over 1f out: wknd fnl f* **7/4**[1]

1036 **6** *2 ¼* **Fifty (IRE)**[13] 3487 3-9-7 **75** .... RichardHughes 1 60
(R Hannon) *chsd ldrs: led 2f out: rdn and hdd appraching fnl f: sn btn* **5/1**[2]

0-00 **7** *1* **Rescue Me**[56] 2161 3-8-9 **66** .... PatrickHills(3) 10 49
(R Hannon) *in rr tl styd on fnl f: nvr in contention* **14/1**

02 **8** *nk* **Duty Doctor**[74] 1671 3-8-10 **64** .... MartinDwyer 2 46
(S Kirk) *chsd ldrs: rdn over 2f out: wknd over 1f out* **12/1**

3553 **9** *14* **Double On Red**[7] 3690 3-8-8 **62** .... (b) ShaneKelly 14 7
(J M P Eustace) *racd alone stands' side and overall ldr tl hdd 2f out: sn wknd* **10/1**[3]

-330 **10** *nse* **Artistic License (IRE)**[69] 1819 3-9-4 **72** .... EdwardCreighton 13 17
(M R Channon) *a towards rr* **16/1**

362- **11** *hd* **Sakhacity**[270] 6237 3-8-12 **66** .... StephenCarson 9 11
(J R Jenkins) *led centre gp but 2nd to lone ldr: hdd in that gp 2f out and wknd rapidly* **12/1**

1m 30.39s (4.69) **Going Correction** +0.65s/f (Yiel) **11** Ran SP% **127.4**
Speed ratings (Par 97): **99,98,96,94,92 89,88,88,72,71 71**
toteswinger: 1&2 £41.60, 1&3 £13.80, 2&3 £52.70. CSF £224.42 CT £2671.55 TOTE £17.00: £3.70, £6.20, £4.60; EX 297.20 Place 6 £1,276.37, Place 5 £148.99.
Owner Mill House Stud Racing Partnership **Bred** Mill House Stud **Trained** Whitsbury, Hants

FOCUS
Ordinary form, with the third and fourth providing the guide to rating the race. An improved effort from Divine Power.
Divine Power Official explanation: trainer had no explanation for the apparent improvememrt in form
T/Plt: £1,189.70 to a £1 stake. Pool: £67,473.27. 41.40 winning tickets. T/Qpdt: £88.50 to a £1 stake. Pool: £4,894.90. 40.90 winning tickets. ST

3875 NEWMARKET (R-H)
Friday, July 11

OFFICIAL GOING: Good changing to good to soft after race 5 (3.45) and to soft after race 6 (4.20)
Wind: Fresh against Weather: Cloudy with sunny spells

3919 UNICORN ASSET MANAGEMENT H'CAP 1m
1:30 (1:31) (Class 2) (0-100,99) 3-Y-O
£31,155 (£9,330; £4,665; £2,335; £1,165; £585) **Stalls** Low

Form RPR

-216 **1** **Duntulm**[48] 2403 3-9-3 **93** .... DaneO'Neill 11 105+
(H Candy) *lw: chsd ldrs: rdn and hung lft fr over 1f out: r.o to ld nr fin* **7/1**

3323 **2** *shd* **Ellemujie**[12] 3527 3-8-5 **81** .... RichardKingscote 5 93
(D K Ivory) *chsd ldrs: led over 1f out: sn rdn: hdd nr fin* **40/1**

16-1 **3** *2 ¾* **Relative Order**[20] 3270 3-8-10 **86** .... LPKeniry 9 92
(J R Best) *hld up: plld hrd: rdn over 2f out: hdwy over 1f out: nt rch ldrs* **20/1**

2411 **4** *hd* **Stevie Thunder**[13] 3494 3-8-12 **88** .... TomEaves 15 93
(G A Swinbank) *lw: hld up: hdwy u.p over 1f out: edgd lft: nt rch ldrs* **12/1**

2103 **5** *½* **Silver Rime (FR)**[30] 2953 3-8-11 **87** .... RichardHughes 19 91
(R Hannon) *hld up: swtchd lft over 6f out: hdwy u.p over 1f out: styd on same pce ins fnl f* **16/1**

110 **6** *nk* **Huzzah (IRE)**[48] 2403 3-9-9 **99** .... MichaelHills 13 102
(B W Hills) *lw: chsd ldrs: rdn over 1f out: edgd rt ins fnl f: styd on same pce* **20/1**

-130 **7** *½* **Perks (IRE)**[22] 3155 3-9-1 **91** .... JimmyQuinn 10 93+
(J L Dunlop) *hld up: rdn over 1f out: swtchd rt and styd on ins fnl f: nvr nrr* **8/1**[3]

-441 **8** *nk* **Mukhber**[51] 2311 3-8-11 **87** .... RHills 14 89
(J H M Gosden) *lw: hld up in tch: rdn over 1f out: no ex* **15/2**[2]

1130 **8** *dht* **Slugger O'Toole**[22] 3155 3-9-0 **90** .... JamieSpencer 8 92
(B W Hills) *swtg: s.i.s: hld up: hdwy over 1f out: sn rdn: no ex ins fnl f* **12/1**

1214 **10** *shd* **Albaqaa**[34] 2819 3-8-8 **84** .... PaulHanagan 12 85
(R A Fahey) *swtg: hld up: rdn over 1f out: styd on ins fnl f: nt clr run towards fin: n.d* **14/1**

-246 **11** *¾* **Flawed Genius**[22] 3155 3-9-6 **96** .... (v[1]) RyanMoore 4 96
(Sir Michael Stoute) *trckd ldrs: led over 3f out: rdn: hung lft and hdd over 1f out: wknd ins fnl f* **8/1**[3]

6111 **12** *1 ¾* **Summon Up Theblood (IRE)**[20] 3251 3-9-5 **95** .... DarryllHolland 18 91
(M R Channon) *prom: rdn over 2f out: wknd fnl f* **16/1**

1-04 **13** *½* **Midnight Muse (USA)**[20] 3251 3-8-5 **81** .... DeanMcKeown 3 75
(T D Barron) *prom: rdn over 3f out: hung rt and wknd over 1f out* **33/1**

1-20 **14** *nk* **Unbreak My Heart (IRE)**[48] 2403 3-9-3 **93** .... SteveDrowne 2 87
(R Charlton) *lw: chsd ldrs: rdn over 3f out: sn hung lft: wknd over 1f out* **16/1**

2-21 **15** *½* **Timetable**[31] 2912 3-8-8 **84** .... TedDurcan 16 77
(H R A Cecil) *hld up: rdn over 1f out: n.d* **14/1**

52-2 **16** *2 ¾* **Al Muheer (IRE)**[8] 3635 3-9-7 **97** .... SebSanders 7 83
(C E Brittain) *lw: led over 4f: sn rdn: wknd over 1f out* **20/1**

1010 **17** *¾* **Throne Of Power (USA)**[22] 3155 3-9-5 **95** .... KerrinMcEvoy 17 80
(M A Magnusson) *lw: hld up: rdn and hung lft over 1f out: sn wknd* **12/1**

3600 **18** *2 ¾* **Latin Lad**[22] 3156 3-9-6 **96** .... JimmyFortune 1 74
(R Hannon) *racd alone far side: chsd ldrs: rdn over 3f out: wknd over 1f out* **50/1**

1200 **19** *½* **Fathsta (IRE)**[22] 3155 3-9-3 **93** .... LDettori 6 70
(S Kirk) *hld up: plld hrd: rdn over 2f out: wknd over 1f out* **16/1**

1m 38.94s (-1.06) **Going Correction** +0.10s/f (Good) **19** Ran SP% **128.1**
Speed ratings (Par 106): **109,108,106,105,105 105,104,104,104,104 103,101,101,100,100 97,96,94,93**
toteswinger: 1&2 £76.40, 1&3 £56.60, 2&3 £195.60. CSF £298.53 CT £5331.89 TOTE £9.00: £2.30, £8.40, £5.80, £2.60; EX 374.90 TRIFECTA Not won..
Owner Thomas Barr **Bred** W And R Barnett Ltd **Trained** Kingston Warren, Oxon
■ Stewards' Enquiry : Dane O'Neill one-day ban: used whip down shoulder in forehand position (Jul 31)

FOCUS
A strong and hugely competitive three-year-old handicap likely to produce its share of winners. Although a couple of outsiders finished second and third, the form looks solid.

NOTEBOOK
Duntulm, who put up a remarkable performance considering the ground he lost at the start when making a successful handicap debut at the Newmarket Guineas Meeting, had little go right off this 9lb higher mark in the Silver Bowl at Haydock and this slower surface was always likely to be more to his advantage. Never too far from the speed, he failed to show the same acceleration he did on the Rowley Mile course and did not make things easy for O'Neill by hanging left under pressure, but still just shaded the verdict in a tight finish. He shapes like a horse who will prove just as effective at 7f and his trainer confirmed this, adding he would not go for the Cambridgeshire as 1m is as far as he wants to run. He has pretentions to be a pattern performer when conditions are right. (tchd 15-2)
Ellemujie endured a hectic juvenile campaign and is again being kept busy, but he clearly thrives on it and put up a brave effort in defeat. His last couple of runs were over 1m2f and he saw this stiff 1m out strongly, only just failing to cause an upset. He has not won since his second start as a two-year-old and things will not be any easier following a rise, but a victory certainly deserves to fall his way.
Relative Order, a surprise 33/1 winner over 7f at this course on his recent return, had been raised 7lb for that success and was faced with much stiffer opposition here. He failed to settle early and one could have forgiven him for not getting home, but he stuck on willingly and just managed to hold third. There may be more to come from this progressive type.
Stevie Thunder, on a hat-trick following wins at Sandown and Newcastle, is proven with some ease in the ground and he ran a sound race off a 4lb higher mark. He is another holding his form well, but winning is only going to become harder for him. (op 14-1)
Silver Rime(FR), successful off a mark of 83 at Windsor earlier in the season, has twice run with credit off this mark subsequently and he again gave a sound performance back in fifth, keeping on without looking likely to trouble the principals. Winning will not be easy off this mark, but he can find less-competitive contests in future. (op 20-1)
Huzzah(IRE) returned with narrow back-to-back wins at Newbury and Chester earlier in the season, but he seemed to find this mark beyond him when finishing down the field in the Silver Bowl last time. He was unable to adopt his usual prominent position that day though and he ran much better here, keeping on well for pressure. Improvement will need to be found to win off this mark, but he is a very tough sort who may just find it.
Perks(IRE) looked good when winning in soft ground off a mark of 73 on his handicap debut back in April (had Silver Rime back in second) and he improved on that to finish third behind Duntulm at Newmarket. Quick conditions were against him at Royal Ascot, but the slower ground here enabled him to run better and he may be worth a try at 1m2f now. (op 7-1)
Slugger O'Toole has twice run good races in defeat since winning at Newmarket, most recently when finishing ninth in the Britannia at Royal Ascot, but he was never involved here. (op 20-1)
Mukhber was 4lb higher than when narrowly winning an ordinary Sandown handicap last time and he struggled to make an impact in this stronger contest. (op 20-1)
Albaqaa, fourth in a decent handicap behind Redford last time, should have been a length or two closer as he got going too late and was then denied a clear run close home. He may still have more to offer off his current rating. Official explanation: jockey said gelding hung right throughout (op 16-1)
Flawed Genius had lots of form that tied in with the winner (also looking a shade unlucky in the Silver Bowl) and he ran well when sixth in the Britannia at Royal Ascot. Sporting a first-time visor, he travelled strongly and was in front not long after halfway, but he was unable to find for strong pressure and ultimately dropped out. A drop back to 7f may help, but he is becoming frustrating.
Summon Up Theblood(IRE), bidding for a hat-trick following a couple of wins up north, was 10lb higher than last time and struggled.
Unbreak My Heart(IRE), another to come from the Silver Bowl ay Haydock, should have fared better with the ground more in his favour this time. (op 14-1)
Timetable, who has been a work companion for Twice Over, struggled to land odds of 2/9 at Redcar last time and he never posed a threat on this handicap debut. (op 12-1)
Al Muheer(IRE) was unable to build on his promising comeback run. Due to be raised 9lb, he will find things even tougher in future.
Throne Of Power(USA), beaten little more than four lengths in the Britannia, was one of the main disappointments of the race and appeared to have no obvious excuse.
Latin Lad was always going to struggle, racing alone on the far side.

3920 WEATHERBYS SUPERLATIVE STKS (GROUP 2) 7f
2:00 (2:04) (Class 1) 2-Y-O
£45,416 (£17,216; £8,616; £4,296; £2,152; £1,080) **Stalls** Low

Form RPR

3231 **1** **Firth Of Fifth (IRE)**[20] 3267 2-9-0 0 .... RichardKingscote 8 104
(Tom Dascombe) *trckd ldrs: hdwy 3f out: maintained advantage of over 1 length through fnl f: gamely* **8/1**

21 **2** *1 ¼* **Weald Park (USA)**[13] 3495 2-9-0 0 .... RichardHughes 5 101+
(R Hannon) *lw: plld hrd: chsd ldrs: drvn 2f out: wnt 2nd over 1f out: nvr making any imp fnl f* **9/2**[2]

310 **3** *nk* **Shaweel**[24] 3103 2-9-0 0 .... LDettori 7 100
(M Johnston) *swtg: bhd: drvn and prog over 1f out: kpt on but nvr looked like winning* **13/2**

	4	1	**Grand Ducal (IRE)**[22] 3185 2-9-0 0 JMurtagh 2	98
			(A P O'Brien, Ire) *w'like: scope: midfield: rdn over 2f out: one pce and no imp fnl f* **11/4**[1]	
1	5	½	**Deadly Secret (USA)**[30] 2937 2-9-0 0 PaulHanagan 1	96
			(R A Fahey) *t.k.h towards rr: rdn over 1f out: plugged on: n.d* **9/1**	
3	6	1	**Sanvean (IRE)**[41] 2627 2-8-11 0 TedDurcan 9	91
			(M R Channon) *unf: scope: last away and sn swtchd to far rails: rdn and effrt over 2f out: n.d and nt qckn over 1f out* **16/1**	
12	7	nk	**Prime Spirit (IRE)**[14] 3439 2-9-0 0 TomEaves 3	93
			(B Smart) *strong: lw: taken to post v early: chsd ldr: rdn 1/2-way: lost pl over 1f out: wknd ins fnl f* **6/1**[3]	
51	8	8	**Managua**[28] 3001 2-9-0 0 DarryllHolland 6	73
			(M R Channon) *chsd ldrs: rdn 1/2-way: disp 2nd briefly: fdd qckly wl over 1f out* **8/1**	
51	9	1	**Sapphire Prince (USA)**[15] 3392 2-9-0 0 SebSanders 4	71
			(J R Best) *stdd s: plld hrd towards rr: rdn over 2f out: sn wknd* **20/1**	

1m 26.15s (0.45) **Going Correction** +0.10s/f (Good) **9** Ran SP% **115.3**
Speed ratings (Par 106): **101,99,99,98,97 96,96,86,85**
toteswinger: 1&2 £5.50, 1&3 £11.00, 2&3 £6.50. CSF £43.82 TOTE £8.60: £2.40, £1.70, £2.60; EX 51.80 Trifecta £511.40 Part won. Pool: £691.20 - 0.10 winning units..
Owner Daniel Perchard **Bred** Peter Savill **Trained** Lambourn, Berks

FOCUS
This was a weak contest for the grade, the standard slightly below the average for this race, and the form is questionable, with Firth Of Fifth dictating at a modest gallop and then kicking from the front. This was much-improved form from him. The winning time was modest for a race of its status.

NOTEBOOK
Firth Of Fifth(IRE) completed a memorable week for the Dascombe/Kingscote partnership by making all at a modest tempo, just as his stablemate Classic Blade had done in the July Stakes the previous day. Like that race, this did not look a good race for the grade, but Firth Of Fifth had clearly been given a boost by his recent maiden win and kept finding under pressure throughout the final furlong. He clearly has the right attitude, but is not that big and is unlikely to make it at the top level. (op 7-1)
Weald Park(USA), a tidy winner of a course-and-distance maiden last month, is well regarded but did himself no favours by refusing to settle early and then giving the winner too much rope, but he still emerged second best, running on well too late in the day. There should be more to come from him and he will benefit from having a sounder pace in future. (op 5-1 tchd 4-1)
Shaweel ran well for a long way before fading into eighth in the Coventry (race not working out brilliantly) and he did not seem inconvenienced by the different tactics here, but looking at how the raced worked out, he would have been better off racing on the pace. He was another who kept on without looking likely to catch the winner. There may be a small Listed prize in him somewhere, but he is nothing more than that. (op 7-1)
Grand Ducal(IRE), a workmanlike winner on his debut before being beaten at Fairyhouse last time, is evidently not one of his powerful yard's top juveniles and he was found wanting for a change of pace. His best chance of winning a pattern race lies back home. (op 3-1)
Deadly Secret(USA), who knew his job when making a winning debut at Hamilton, was expected to improve for this extra furlong and he ran well enough considering he was held up in a steadily-run race. He will find easier opportunities at a lesser level. (op 12-1)
Sanvean(IRE), who looked as though the experience would do her good when third on her debut at York, was another trying to come from a difficult position, also not helped by racing towards the far rail, and she could never get into it. She will benefit from a drop in grade and can probably win a small maiden. (op 12-1)
Prime Spirit(IRE), narrowly denied at Doncaster last time, having earlier won at Newcastle on debut, should have relished the extra furlong here, but he was never really going and dropped out disappointingly. He is evidently thought to be capable of better, but has a bit to prove now. (op 5-1 tchd 13-2)
Managua, winner of an average Sandown maiden, was one of the first beaten and dropped right out. (op 11-1)
Sapphire Prince(USA), a fine, big sort who caused a minor surprise when winning at Great Leighs last time, needed to have made big strides to compete in this contest and he never really looked like getting into it after pulling hard. His yard have a good juvenile team and perhaps he needs more time before realising his potential. (op 33-1)

3921 LADBROKES BUNBURY CUP (HERITAGE H'CAP) 7f

2:35 (2:37) (Class 2) 3-Y-0+

£62,310 (£18,660; £9,330; £4,670; £2,330; £1,170) **Stalls** Low

Form				RPR
021	1		**Little White Lie (IRE)**[35] 2789 4-9-0 98 DarryllHolland 19	109
			(J R Jenkins) *chsd ldrs: rdn over 2f out: edgd lft over 1f out: kpt on to ld fnl 100yds: jst hld on* **14/1**	
0001	2	hd	**Lovelace**[6] 3740 4-9-10 108 6ex RyanMoore 13	118
			(M Johnston) *s.i.s: stl last wl over 2f out: str run fnl f: jst failed* **15/2**[2]	
2261	3	1	**Regal Parade**[21] 3197 4-8-8 97 AhmedAjtebi(5) 9	104
			(D Nicholls) *lw: prom: led over 2f out: drvn 1f out: hdd and nt qckn fnl 100yds* **12/1**[3]	
0-02	4	nk	**Mastership (IRE)**[26] 3056 4-8-11 95 RobertWinston 7	101
			(J J Quinn) *bmpd s: impr to midfield gng wl 1/2-way: checked by wnr over 1f out: hrd rdn and fin stoutly: lft w too much to do* **14/1**	
-050	5	½	**Giganticus (USA)**[21] 3197 5-8-13 97 TedDurcan 18	102
			(B W Hills) *cl up: drvn and looked to lose interest over 2 out: rallied u.p ins fnl f: styd on* **20/1**	
2031	6	hd	**Damika (IRE)**[6] 3722 5-9-8 106 6ex DeanMcKeown 12	111
			(R M Whitaker) *lw: bhd: prog stands' side over 1f out: r.o: unable to chal* **14/1**	
2601	7	hd	**Racer Forever (USA)**[13] 3498 5-9-10 108 (b) JimmyFortune 6	112
			(J H M Gosden) *midfield: hdwy over 1f out: ch and hrd drvn 100yds out: wkng cl home* **20/1**	
0200	8	1 ½	**Diamond Tycoon (USA)**[23] 3122 4-9-4 102 (t) RichardHughes 11	102
			(B J Meehan) *prom: drvn over 1f out: nt qckn ins fnl f* **12/1**[3]	
0046	9	¾	**Capricorn Run (USA)**[20] 3248 5-9-5 103 (p) SebSanders 10	101
			(A J McCabe) *hdwy u.p over 2f out: unable to chal* **33/1**	
5012	10	1 ¼	**Dhaular Dhar (IRE)**[21] 3197 6-9-1 99 DanielTudhope 4	94
			(J S Goldie) *hld up: effrt 2f out: no ex fnl f* **12/1**[3]	
-431	11	2	**Zaahid (IRE)**[62] 1982 4-9-0 98 RHills 1	87
			(B W Hills) *lw: cl up tl rdn and wknd over 1f out* **4/1**[1]	
0-35	12	hd	**Ashdown Express (IRE)**[13] 3504 9-9-1 99 PaulDoe 2	88
			(W J Knight) *wl bhd: effrt 2f out: nvr bttr than midfield* **33/1**	
3630	13	nk	**Royal Power (IRE)**[13] 3491 5-9-1 99 AdrianTNicholls 8	87
			(D Nicholls) *towards rr: rdn 2f out: nvr able to chal* **20/1**	
40-3	14	1 ¼	**Artimino**[41] 2595 4-9-2 100 JamieSpencer 20	84
			(J R Fanshawe) *lw: stdd s: a bhd* **15/2**[2]	
-660	15	½	**Smart Enough**[46] 2465 5-9-5 103 KerrinMcEvoy 3	86
			(M A Magnusson) *cl up: rdn and wknd wl over 1f out* **33/1**	
0320	16	½	**Hinton Admiral**[21] 3197 4-8-6 97 FrederikTylicki(7) 5	79
			(R A Fahey) *cl up: rdn and wknd wl over 1f out* **16/1**	
-600	17	8	**Mine (IRE)**[62] 1982 10-9-0 98 (v) LDettori 15	58
			(J D Bethell) *slowly away: a bhd* **12/1**[3]	
1060	18	2	**Dabbers Ridge (IRE)**[21] 3197 6-9-0 98 MichaelHills 16	53
			(B W Hills) *led: rdn and hdd over 2f out: eased whn btn* **20/1**	

1m 24.16s (-1.54) **Going Correction** +0.10s/f (Good) **18** Ran SP% **128.1**
Speed ratings (Par 109): **112,111,110,110,109 109,109,107,106,105 102,102,102,100,100 99,90,88**
toteswinger: 1&2 £18.90, 1&3 £35.80, 2&3 £22.70. CSF £108.37 CT £1355.94 TOTE £15.70: £3.10, £2.20, £3.50, £3.40; EX 143.80 Trifecta £1131.40 Pool: £2140.50 - 1.40 winning units..
Owner The Three Honest Men **Bred** J L Hassett **Trained** Royston, Herts

FOCUS
A typically competitive Bunbury Cup in which the runners came down the centre of the track as one group for the most part, though a couple did drift over to both rails towards the end of the race. The winning time was very solid for the grade. Solid form, with personal bests from the first two.

NOTEBOOK
Little White Lie(IRE), raised 4lb for his Epsom victory, stays further than this and likes to get his toe in so was understandably ridden close to the pace. Drawn one off the stands' rail, he gradually edged towards the centre of the track and showed a very game attitude to battle hard all the way to the line and just hold on by a narrow margin. He has been transformed since joining John Jenkins. (tchd 12-1)
Lovelace, carrying a 6lb penalty for his victory in a very valuable handicap at Sandown six days earlier, did not get the best of breaks. Held up off the pace, when asked for his effort he finished in great style but just failed to get there. This was a cracking effort off this mark, but it appears that he does prefer 1m now. (op 8-1 tchd 17-2)
Regal Parade, put up 5lb for his victory in the Buckingham Palace under today's rider, when he had several of these behind, was up there from the start and never stopped trying. He remains in top form. (op 16-1)
Mastership(IRE), 5lb lower than at this time last year, had appeared to show improved form for his new yard last time and confirmed it with another smashing effort. Tucked away in mid-division early, he was briefly checked between the eventual winner and the weakening Dabbers Ridge over a furlong from home, but stayed on very well up the final climb. He has bags of ability and deserves to end a losing run stretching back to February of last year. (op 10-1)
Giganticus(USA), 3lb higher than when taking this last year, had shown little in three starts so far this season and was well beaten in the Buckingham Palace last time. Racing close to the pace early, his prospects did not look bright when he came off the bridle at halfway, but he responded to the pressure to stay on again up the hill and looks to be on the way back.
Damika(IRE), carrying a 6lb penalty for a conditions race win at Haydock last time, had done all his racing over 6f this year but he does have winning form over this trip. He was brought through to hold every chance when hanging right over to the stands' rail, something he has done before, and kept on all the way to the line. (op 12-1)
Racer Forever(USA), raised 3lb for his victory in a very slowly run Group 3 over course and distance last month, was a doubtful runner due to the easing ground but was allowed to take his chance when it dried up somewhat. He ran well too and it looked as though he would be placed at least when brought with his effort towards the far side inside the last couple of furlongs, but he had nothing left in the last 100 yards. (op 25-1)
Diamond Tycoon(USA), tried in a tongue tie and dropped 3lb after a creditable effort in the Hunt Cup, was up with the pace throughout but had nothing more to offer in the last furlong. This was another creditable effort, but still well below what had once seemed likely.
Zaahid(IRE), 6lb higher then when winning the Victoria Cup in May and given a short break since, rather lurched out of the stalls and never looked that happy afterwards, though he did briefly look a threat when delivered with his effort towards the far side of the track. He is better than this. (op 5-1)
Ashdown Express(IRE) was having his first try at this trip in two years, though he did win over it and further in his younger days. He made an effort towards the far side of the track entering the last quarter-mile, but could not maintain it and needs a return to 6f.
Artimino, raised 3lb for his creditable return to action in May, missed the break from the stands'-rail draw but seemed to travel well enough off the pace. However, he failed to find that much off the bridle and this was rather disappointing. (op 9-1)
Mine(IRE), a three-time winner of this race, was making his final racecourse appearance off a 4lb lower mark than for his most recent win in it two years ago. There was no fairytale ending to an admirable career, but he retires the winner of 11 of his 66 races and more than £355,000.

3922 DARLEY JULY CUP (BRITISH LEG OF THE GLOBAL SPRINT CHALLENGE) (GROUP 1) 6f

3:10 (3:10) (Class 1) 3-Y-0+

£227,080 (£86,080; £43,080; £21,480; £10,760; £5,400) **Stalls** Low

Form				RPR
6-16	1		**Marchand D'Or (FR)**[20] 3247 5-9-5 DBonilla 9	122+
			(F Head, France) *hld up wl in rr: stl last 2f out: rapid hdwy up stands rail fnl f to ld post* **5/2**[1]	
-345	2	hd	**US Ranger (USA)**[20] 3247 4-9-5 JMurtagh 12	121
			(A P O'Brien, Ire) *lw: chsd ldrs: sn pushed along: rdn to ld wl ins fnl f: hdd post* **9/2**[2]	
2622	3	½	**War Artist (AUS)**[20] 3247 5-9-5 116 KerrinMcEvoy 7	119
			(J M P Eustace) *lw: led: rdn and edgd rt over 1f out: hdd wl ins fnl f* **11/2**[3]	
-010	4	nk	**Astronomer Royal (USA)**[20] 3247 4-9-5 RyanMoore 5	118
			(A P O'Brien, Ire) *hld up: rdn over 1f out: r.o wl ins fnl f* **16/1**	
2-01	5	½	**Kingsgate Native (IRE)**[20] 3247 3-8-13 118 SebSanders 15	117
			(J R Best) *hld up: hdwy over 2f out: rdn over 1f out: unable qck towards fin* **6/1**	
4100	6	hd	**Diabolical (USA)**[20] 3247 5-9-5 117 LDettori 6	116
			(Saeed Bin Suroor) *lw: trckd ldrs: racd keenly: nt clr run over 1f out: sn rdn: r.o* **33/1**	
0302	7	nk	**Prime Defender**[6] 3739 4-9-5 106 MichaelHills 3	115+
			(B W Hills) *hld up in tch: nt clr run and lost pl over 1f out: r.o wl ins fnl f* **40/1**	
-210	8	1 ½	**Assertive**[20] 3247 5-9-5 112 RichardHughes 4	110
			(R Hannon) *chsd ldrs: rdn over 1f out: no ex ins fnl f* **25/1**	
2110	9	nk	**Fat Boy (IRE)**[20] 3247 3-8-13 114 JimmyFortune 16	109
			(P W Chapple-Hyam) *lw: chsd ldrs: rdn over 1f out: no ex ins fnl f* **20/1**	
-502	10	½	**Benbaun (IRE)**[12] 3533 7-9-5 119 (v) FMBerry 1	108
			(M J Wallace) *hld up in tch: rdn over 1f out: no ex fnl f* **16/1**	
1502	11	hd	**Zidane**[13] 3488 6-9-5 109 RobertWinston 13	107
			(J R Fanshawe) *hld up: rdn over 1f out: n.d* **20/1**	
1605	12	2 ¼	**Off The Record**[6] 3739 4-9-5 99 TPQueally 11	100
			(J G Given) *chsd ldr tl rdn over 2f out: wknd fnl f* **100/1**	
0133	13	1 ¼	**Sir Gerry (USA)**[20] 3247 3-8-13 112 JamieSpencer 14	96
			(J R Fanshawe) *lw: hld up: rdn and wknd over 1f out* **7/1**	

1m 11.01s (-1.49) **Going Correction** +0.10s/f (Good)
WFA 3 from 4yo+ 6lb **13** Ran SP% **120.4**
Speed ratings (Par 117): **113,112,112,111,111 110,110,108,107,107 107,104,102**
toteswinger: 1&2 £3.40, 1&3 £3.90, 2&3 £6.40. CSF £12.13 TOTE £3.50: £1.20, £2.20, £2.00; EX 15.10 Trifecta £83.00 Pool: £4523.69 - 40.30 winning units..
Owner Mme J-L Giral **Bred** Mme C Giral **Trained** France
■ Marchand D'Or was the first French-trained winner of this race since his trainer rode Anabaa to victory in 1996.

■ Stewards' Enquiry : Michael Hills caution: careless riding; two-day ban: careless riding (Jul 25,27)

FOCUS

An ordinary renewal. The right horses filled the frame for this prestigious contest, but the front seven were separated by just two lengths and the 104-rated Prime Defender had claims of being unlucky not to place, which does cast a doubt or two over the form. The time was also slightly disappointing for such a major sprint. Marchand D'Or ended the three-year-old domination of the big sprints this season and is clearly the best European sprinter this term, although he was not quite at his best here.

NOTEBOOK

Marchand D'Or(FR), who beat subsequent King's Stand winner Equiano a neck on his seasonal return in a 5f Group 2 at Chantilly, was unable to make an impact in the Golden Jubilee, racing too keenly and meeting some trouble before keeping on for sixth, but he looked the one to beat here if back to his best and he was rightly made favourite. A slightly unlucky fourth in this a year ago, the slightly slower surface was to his advantage on this occasion and, having been dropped right out, he came with a storming late run against the stands' rail to get up right on the line. He looked to have been set too much to do, but his sheer speed got him out of trouble and he can probably be rated better than the bare form. It was a strange race and the form is probably not the strongest with so many finishing tightly packed at the line, but he is probably the best around on his day and will now bid for a third successive victory in the Prix Maurice de Gheest at Deauville next month. (op 3-1 tchd 10-3 in places)

US Ranger(USA) has always been about potential and he has twice caught the eye in top sprints at York and Ascot this season. That potential looked like being realised when he hit the front deep into the final furlong, but he failed to seal the deal and was chinned on the line by Marchand D'Or. He undoubtedly has tons of ability and is clearly high-class when things go right, but he gives the impression he is one of those who will always be a nearly horse. (op 6-1)

War Artist(AUS) has made a really smooth transition from South Africa, running a blinder under his Group 1 penalty in the Duke Of York and again going down fighting in the Golden Jubilee. He looked likely to be bang there again, and he was, but despite his gallant efforts, was unable to hold on. The five-year-old has plenty of pace and will be considered for the Nunthorpe, but his trainer seems keen to head out to the Far East for their legs of the Global Sprint Challenge. (op 6-1)

Astronomer Royal(USA) ◆, winner of last season's French 2000 Guineas, has successfully made the transition to sprinter this term. Winner of a Group 3 6f contest at the Curragh in May, he got going too late from a less than favourable position when one place behind Marchand D'Or in the Golden Jubilee and this represented a personal best. Again restrained in rear, he really finished with a rattle and might have won in another 100 yards, maybe less. He has a telling late burst and that could be seen to good effect once again if returned to slightly further, with races such as the Prix Maurice de Gheest and Prix de la Foret in France later this year looking ideal targets. (tchd 20-1)

Kingsgate Native(IRE), last season's top juvenile sprinter, continued the three-year-old domination of top sprints this year when winning the Golden Jubilee at Royal Ascot (having made his seasonal debut in the King's Stand only a few days earlier) and he again looked a major player. However, genuinely quick ground would have been preferable and, having made progress to look a major threat, he just lacked that telling burst of speed. This was another good effort, if not quite up to his Ascot standard, but he will need to bounce back to his very best if he is to win again at the top level this season. (op 5-1 tchd 13-2)

Diabolical(USA) ran a huge race back in sixth. An ex-American-trained sprinter, he won a Group 3 contest in Dubai earlier in the year, but was beaten out of sight in the Golden Jubilee on his British debut, stopping quickly and basically being pulled up. All was clearly not well on that occasion, but he showed what he can do here with a slightly unlucky effort in sixth, not getting the splits when he wanted, but sticking on really well under pressure. He could win a decent prize if going the right way from this, albeit not at the top level.

Prime Defender ◆ ran well above himself in being beaten only around two lengths in seventh, looking slightly unlucky in the process too. He ran really well in a 5f Group 3 at Sandown just a few days previously, but was expected to be outclassed here and it was a surprise to see him put up such a good show. He should have been even closer and ought to take the beating if taking up either of his handicap engagements (Hong Kong Sprint Stakes/Stewards' Cup) off a mark of 104 over the next few weeks.

Assertive, who beat War Artist in the Duke Of York back in May, made no impact in the Golden Jubilee and again came up short here, for all that he ran much better.

Fat Boy(IRE) has had a good season and ran well to a point, but was always likely to struggle against the best of these. (tchd 22-1)

Benbaun(IRE) did not have a good draw and, as was expected, he found the 6f trip beyond him at this level. (tchd 20-1)

Zidane, who found all sorts of trouble under Spencer when finishing second to Utmost Respect in the Chipchase at Newcastle the other day, never threatened in this much better contest. (tchd 18-1)

Off The Record was running out of his grade.

Sir Gerry(USA) was the disappointment of the race. Third behind Marchand D'Or and Equiano at Chantilly, he again ran a cracker to fill that spot in the Golden Jubilee, but having briefly made a move, he found nothing and was not given a hard time. He is not the only horse from the yard to have disappointed recently. (op 6-1)

3923 GCE HIRES WINNERS E B F MAIDEN FILLIES' STKS — 6f

3:45 (3:48) (Class 2) 2-Y-O — **£9,714** (£2,890; £1,444; £721) **Stalls** Low

Form — RPR

1 **Fantasia** 2-9-0 0 .... DaneO'Neill 5 — 86+
(L M Cumani) *rangy: bit bkwd: cl up in 3rd pl: rdn to ld over 1f out: sn in command: decisively* — **7/1**

2 — 3 1/4 — **Respite** 2-9-0 0 .... MichaelHills 9 — 73+
(W J Haggas) *w'like: athletic: lw: trckd ldrs: rdn and effrt 2f out: tk 2nd cl home: no ch w wnr* — **9/2**[1]

3 — 1/2 — **Sharpener (IRE)** 2-9-0 0 .... RyanMoore 1 — 72
(R Hannon) *w'like: strong: bit bkwd: led: rdn and hdd over 1f out: one pce: lost 2nd cl home* — **5/1**[2]

4 — 3 1/4 — **Evening Sunset (GER)** 2-9-0 0 .... DarryllHolland 11 — 62+
(M R Channon) *lengthy: bit bkwd: hld up in rr: no ch 1f out: kpt on steadily* — **17/2**

5 — 1/2 — **Helpmeronda** 2-9-0 0 .... HollyHall 4 — 61
(S A Callaghan) *w'like: bit bkwd: towards rr: rdn and btn wl over 1f out* — **33/1**

60 — 6 — 2 — **Give (IRE)**[17] 3349 2-9-0 0 .... RichardHughes 3 — 55+
(R Hannon) *pressed ldr: drvn over 2f out: fdd over 1f out: eased whn btn* — **7/1**

7 — 3 3/4 — **Lovely Thought** 2-9-0 0 .... KerrinMcEvoy 2 — 43
(W J Haggas) *w'like: lengthy: chsd ldrs: rdn over 2f out: wknd over 1f out* — **13/2**[3]

8 — 5 — **Xaaroon (IRE)** 2-9-0 0 ....(t) RobertWinston 10 — 28
(P J McBride) *w'like: bit bkwd: s.s: wl bhd fnl 2f* — **20/1**

1m 14.53s (2.03) **Going Correction** +0.275s/f (Good) — **8** Ran SP% **91.4**
Speed ratings (Par 97): **97,92,92,87,87 84,79,72**
toteswinger: 1&2 £4.20, 1&3 £3.80, 2&3 £2.80. CSF £23.85 TOTE £6.50: £1.70, £1.40, £1.70; EX 24.30.
Owner Fittocks Stud & Andrew Bengough **Bred** Ronchalon Racing Uk Ltd **Trained** Newmarket, Suffolk
■ Zelloof (7/2) and Al Sabaheya (10/1) were withdrawn after refusing to enter the stalls. Deduct 25p in the £ under Rule 4.

FOCUS

A race in which only one of these had seen the racecourse before and it was weakened further by two withdrawals at the start. It was also run in a monsoon, so a few of these fillies could be forgiven for not showing their best. The time was solid enough given the deteriorating conditions though, and the winner did it impressively.

NOTEBOOK

Fantasia ◆, a Sadler's Wells half-sister to a winning juvenile over 7f and from the family of Cheveley Park winner Blue Duster, is from the stable which took this with another debutante Gossamer in 2001. She was always travelling smoothly just behind the leaders and she picked up very well when asked, coming away to score by a decent margin. Her trainer reportedly does not expect her to stay further than 1m, but the dam won over 1m2f and so she should have little difficulty getting further than this. She looks an exciting prospect. (op 8-1)

Respite ◆, out of a half-sister to Nowhere To Exit, Cesare and Embraced, attracted some market support but took a while to realise what was required before staying on well to snatch second place late on without being given at all a hard ride. She should come on for this debut and will know more next time. (op 6-1 tchd 13-2)

Sharpener(IRE), a 75,000gns half-sister to Princess Cocoa and Lady Power, plus a winning sprinter in Italy, tried to make every yard, and although she was swept aside by the winner, she showed enough on this debut to suggest she is up to winning a race. (tchd 11-2)

Evening Sunset(GER), a 145,000euros half-sister to a winning juvenile over 6f, is out of a high-class performer in the US. She came from well back to reach her final position and although she was never a threat, she did hint at some ability. It would be no surprise to see her do better in time. (op 7-1)

Helpmeronda, a 42,000gns half-sister to a couple of winners including Dark Moon, showed a little bit of ability before weakening out of it. She may be one for later on when she has qualified for a mark.

Give(IRE), the only one in this field to have run before, tracked the leader for much of the way but failed to pick up at all under pressure and eventually dropped out. She is becoming disappointing.

Lovely Thought, a 28,000gns half-brother to Just James, looked the stable's second string according to the market. She showed up for a while before dropping out and although she is entitled to come on for this, she will need to. (op 7-1 tchd 8-1)

Xaaroon(IRE), an 85,000gns foal but only a 38,000gns yearling, is out of a half-sister to a couple of useful performers in Gypsy Moth and Heavenly Whisper. Tongue-tied for this debut, she was nonetheless backed at fancy prices but never managed to get involved. Someone must believe she has some ability. (op 33-1)

3924 ARISTOCRACY RACING CLUB NURSERY — 7f

4:20 (4:22) (Class 2) 2-Y-O — **£12,952** (£3,854; £1,926; £962) **Stalls** Low

Form — RPR

312 — 1 — **Measurement (IRE)**[12] 3522 2-9-4 **82** .... RichardHughes 2 — 92
(R Hannon) *lw: hld up: hdwy over 2f out: rdn over 1f out: styd on to ld wl ins fnl f* — **7/4**[1]

31 — 2 — 1/2 — **Fareer**[26] 3055 2-9-1 **79** .... RHills 5 — 87
(E A L Dunlop) *lw: chsd ldrs: led and hung lft fr over 1f out: hdd wl ins fnl f* — **4/1**[2]

1046 — 3 — 2 1/2 — **Bad Beat**[20] 3245 2-9-6 **84** .... DarryllHolland 1 — 86
(V Smith) *s.i.s: hld up: hdwy over 2f out: rdn and ev ch over 1f out: no ex ins fnl f* — **12/1**

410 — 4 — 1 1/4 — **Beat Seven**[23] 3123 2-9-7 **85** .... MickyFenton 6 — 85+
(Miss Gay Kelleway) *lw: led: rdn and hdd over 1f out: hmpd sn after: no ex* — **12/1**

6215 — 5 — 1 — **Scenic Pass**[7] 3670 2-8-0 **67** oh3 .... JimmyQuinn 3 — 60+
(M R Channon) *chsd ldr: rdn and ev ch wl over 1f out: hmpd sn after: styd on same pce* — **16/1**

423 — 6 — nk — **Gal Aloud (USA)**[21] 3207 2-9-4 **82** .... RyanMoore 4 — 78
(R Hannon) *hld up: rdn over 2f out: nvr trbld ldrs* — **12/1**

331 — 7 — nk — **Daddy's Gift (IRE)**[36] 2754 2-8-12 **76** .... DaneO'Neill 13 — 71
(R Hannon) *lw: hld up: hdwy over 2f out: sn rdn: styd on same pce appr fnl f* — **14/1**

0313 — 8 — 8 — **Motor Home**[14] 3439 2-9-5 **83** .... JimmyFortune 11 — 58
(A M Balding) *hld up: effrt over 2f out: wknd over 1f out* — **15/2**[3]

5363 — 9 — nk — **Duke Of Aquitaine (USA)**[16] 3372 2-8-5 **76** .... DTDaSilva(7) 9 — 50
(P F I Cole) *prom: rdn: hung rt and wknd over 1f out* — **20/1**

616 — 10 — 21 — **Haven't A Clue**[28] 2987 2-8-13 **77** .... SebSanders 10 — —
(Sir Mark Prescott) *chsd ldrs over 5f: eased* — **8/1**

1m 28.72s (3.02) **Going Correction** +0.275s/f (Good) — **10** Ran SP% **119.6**
Speed ratings (Par 100): **93,92,89,88,87 86,86,77,76,52**
toteswinger: 1&2 £2.20, 1&3 £7.60, 2&3 £11.70. CSF £8.63 CT £65.78 TOTE £2.60: £1.40, £1.80, £3.70; EX 9.40.
Owner B Bull **Bred** Donagh Killilea **Trained** East Everleigh, Wilts
■ Stewards' Enquiry : R Hills one-day ban: careless riding (Jul 25)

FOCUS

A good nursery all told, although the close proximity of selling winner Scenic Pass raises slight question marks over the form. A modest time, even allowing for the conditions. The 'official' ratings are estimated and are intended as a guide.

NOTEBOOK

Measurement(IRE), who looked in need of this extra furlong when finishing second to this week's Group 2 July Stakes winner Classic Blade in a conditions contest at Salisbury last time, had shown he coped with some ease in the ground when third on his debut and, having taken a while to hit top stride, he was well on top of Fareer at the line. His dam won over over 1m and judging by this win he should have little trouble staying that trip in time. There should be more to come. (op 6-4 tchd 2-1 in a place and 15-8 in places)

Fareer, winner of an ordinary maiden at Doncaster last time, has plenty of speed in his pedigree and there was a question over how well the extra furlong would suit. This was also the slowest ground he has tackled to date, but he gave a really good account of himself and made the winner work hard enough for his victory, despite hanging under pressure. He will have no trouble with a drop back in trip. (op 9-2 tchd 5-1)

Bad Beat ran well for a long way in the Chesham Stakes at Royal Ascot and this looked easier. He did himself no favours with a sluggish start, but got himself into the race and looked in with every chance, but in the end could find no more. A drop back in trip looks required.

Beat Seven, winner of a 5f maiden at Windsor earlier in the season, is well regarded by connections and she looked ready for a step up in trip, having found things happening too quickly in the Queen Mary at Royal Ascot. The two-furlong rise seemed to stretch her though as, having showed up well for a long way, she found herself running on empty in the closing stages. She was not helped by the runner-up and remains capable of better back in distance. (op 8-1)

Scenic Pass recorded her win at selling level and was beaten in that grade last time. She had a fair bit to find, especially from 3lb out of the handicap, but acquitted herself with credit and was another not done any favours by the runner-up. She could win a handicap. (tchd 20-1)

Gal Aloud(USA) never threatened to get into it and did not improve as much as expected for this rise in distance. (op 16-1)

Daddy's Gift(IRE) was another unable to make any headway from the rear, possibly finding the softened ground too slow. (tchd 16-1 in a place)

Motor Home was one of the main disappointments of the race, never really travelling and not looking as effective on this slower ground. (op 10-1)

Duke Of Aquitaine(USA) ran poorly and does not seem to be progressing. (op 33-1)

Haven't A Clue, hugely favoured by a bias when winning her maiden, struggled at Chepstow last time and this was a dismal effort. (op 10-1)

3925 EGERTON HOUSE STABLES H'CAP — 1m 4f

4:55 (4:57) (Class 3) (0-90,90) 3-Y-O+ £9,714 (£2,890; £1,444; £721) Stalls Centre

Form				RPR
/656	1		**Profit's Reality (IRE)**[13] 3505 6-9-11 87 DarrylHolland 14 (P A Blockley) *mde all: rdn 2f out: hrd pressed by two rivals through fnl f: hung on gamely* 14/1	99
1-04	2	½	**Candle**[41] 2599 5-9-12 88 DaneO'Neill 9 (H Candy) *lw: trckd ldrs: effrt 5f out: last of three gng clr 2f out: ev ch but no imp fnl f: snatched 2nd nr fin* 8/1[3]	99
1-12	3	shd	**Cool Judgement (IRE)**[39] 2665 3-9-1 90 PhilipRobinson 13 (M A Jarvis) *lw: trckd ldrs: wnt 2nd over 3f out: rdn and sustained effrt fr wl over 1f out: a jst hld: lost 2nd fnl strides* 13/8[1]	101+
-331	4	3¾	**Tifernati**[30] 2939 4-9-10 86 LiamJones 16 (W J Haggas) *bhd: last after 5f: effrt 5f out: rdn and outpcd by ldng trio over 2f out* 6/1[2]	91+
3221	5	5	**Bassinet (USA)**[21] 3220 4-8-11 76 KirstyMilczarek(3) 1 (J A R Toller) *hld up: hdwy 5f out: disp 4th but no ch w ldrs 2f out: wknd 1f out* 20/1	73
1430	6	shd	**Haarth Sovereign (IRE)**[28] 3003 4-9-3 79 SaleemGolam 11 (W R Swinburn) *lw: nvr bttr than midfield: btn 3f out* 33/1	76
0-00	7	5	**Mikao (IRE)**[41] 2599 7-9-8 84 MichaelHills 3 (M H Tompkins) *sn chsng ldrs: rdn 4f out: wkng whn edgd rt over 2f out* 28/1	73
60-2	8	2¾	**Horseford Hill**[26] 3060 4-9-10 86 SebSanders 17 (D R C Elsworth) *hld up: sme prog to trck ldrs over 4f out: sn shkn up and btn* 8/1[3]	70
0000	9	1¾	**Ruff Diamond (USA)**[8] 3633 3-8-6 81 (v[1]) RichardKingscote 6 (J R Best) *chsd wnr but often urged along and nvr looked happy: lost 2nd u.p over 3f out: eased wl over 1f out* 33/1	62
4002	10	3	**Come On Jonny (IRE)**[13] 3505 6-9-13 89 NelsonDeSouza 2 (R M Beckett) *plld hrd early: struggling 4f out: eased fnl f* 8/1[3]	66
0062	11	2	**New Beginning (IRE)**[14] 3440 4-9-4 80 JimmyQuinn 7 (Mrs S Lamyman) *lost handy pl after 4f: no ch after* 33/1	53
2360	12	32	**Grande Caiman (IRE)**[13] 3505 4-9-13 89 RichardHughes 15 (R Hannon) *towards rr: pushed along 6f out: no rspnse: sn btn: virtually p.u fnl f* 16/1	11
0045	13	hd	**Moon Mix (FR)**[60] 2060 5-8-11 73 oh4 (t) LDettori 4 (J R Jenkins) *bhd: effrt on outside 6f out: fdd 4f out: virtually p.u fnl f* 20/1	—
1-10	14	15	**Abandon (USA)**[48] 2402 5-9-10 86 RyanMoore 8 (W J Haggas) *chsd ldrs to 1/2-way: virtually p.u fnl f* 14/1	—
3000	15	¾	**Ainama (IRE)**[27] 3044 4-8-13 75 JamieSpencer 12 (M Wigham) *stdd s: plld hrd in rr: struggling 1/2-way: virtually p.u fnl 2f* 20/1	—

2m 33.9s (1.00) **Going Correction** +0.275s/f (Good)
WFA 3 from 4yo+ 13lb 15 Ran SP% **131.5**
Speed ratings (Par 107): **107,106,106,104,100 100,97,95,94,92 91,69,69,59,59**
toteswinger: 1&2 £18.90, 1&3 £15.50, 2&3 £6.50. CSF £121.33 CT £287.78 TOTE £19.50: £5.80, £2.60, £1.50; EX 177.60 Place 6: £109.56 Place 5: £25.48.
Owner Phones Direct Partnership **Bred** Michael Munnelly **Trained** Lambourn, Berks

FOCUS
A big field and a competitive handicap on paper, but several appeared to fail to cope with the deteriorating conditions. It paid to race handily and very few ever really got into it. The form has been rated reasonably positively.

NOTEBOOK
Profit's Reality(IRE), who has winning form on soft ground, had also been given a chance by the Handicapper. The real key to this success though, was that he was left alone in the lead and was given a very well-judged ride from the front. It looked on several occasions throughout the last couple of furlongs as though his two main challengers would come and get him, but he was having none of it. (op 16-1)
Candle, for whom the deteriorating conditions would have been welcome, was produced with her effort on the outside of the leaders entering the last couple of furlongs, but she just lacked a killer punch and was also up against a determined rival. She looks a stayer, and although 6lb higher than for her last win, this mark does not look beyond her. (op 11-1)
Cool Judgement(IRE), who relishes soft ground, was well backed and went off a short-enough price for a competitive handicap like this. Always stalking the winner, he did his level best to get past him but he could never quite manage it and had to be content with a close third, well ahead of the others. He was up another 5lb despite getting beaten last time, but he was much less exposed than the vast majority and will probably end up the best of this bunch. (op 9-4)
Tifernati, raised 4lb for his Hamilton win, did much the best of those held up, but he did seem to hang after being produced with his effort down the wide outside and was firmly put in his place by the leading trio. His best form has come on faster ground. (op 9-2)
Bassinet(USA), raised 6lb for her course-and-distance victory on faster ground last month, looked briefly like getting involved entering the last half-mile but she could not go through with it. She has run well on easy ground before, but that was in a slowly run event with just five runners and on this occasion it appeared that the deteriorating ground exposed a lack of stamina. Official explanation: trainer said filly was unsuited by the soft ground (op 25-1)
Haarth Sovereign(IRE) ran a bit better than at Sandown, but he was never in the race with a chance. He looks too high in the weights at present.
Horseford Hill looked a brief threat entering the last half-mile, but that was as good as it got and it appeared that the softening ground did him few favours.
Ruff Diamond(USA) was tried in a visor instead of blinkers, but despite racing handily early he looked rather awkward and eventually dropped right out. It appears that he did not take to this form of headgear either.
New Beginning(IRE) Official explanation: trainer said gelding was unsuited by the soft ground
Grande Caiman(IRE) Official explanation: trainer's rep said colt had a breathing problem
Abandon(USA) Official explanation: jockey said mare had no more to give
T/Jkpt: Not won. T/Plt: £90.20 to a £1 stake. Pool: £174,837.88. 1,414.46 winning tickets. T/Qpdt: £10.30 to a £1 stake. Pool: £9,668.40. 688.00 winning tickets. CR

3045 YORK (L-H)
Friday, July 11

OFFICIAL GOING: Heavy
Persistent heavy rain turned the ground from soft to heavy before racing. It became more testing as the afternoon wore on.
Wind: almost nil Weather: raining

3926 HOVIS E B F MAIDEN STKS — 7f

2:15 (2:16) (Class 3) 2-Y-O £7,641 (£2,273; £1,136; £567) Stalls Low

Form				RPR
	1		**Rising Prospect** 2-9-0 0 PJMcDonald(3) 1 (G M Moore) *wnt lft s: hdwy over 2f out: led appr fnl f: styd on wl* 20/1	73
3	2	1½	**Highland Storm**[18] 3331 2-9-3 0 PaulMulrennan 2 (J G Given) *w ldrs: led briefly over 1f out: kpt on same pce* 9/1[3]	70
4	3	1	**Mefraas (IRE)**[20] 3274 2-9-3 0 DO'Donohoe 4 (E A L Dunlop) *dwlt: hld up in rr: hdwy over 2f out: kpt on same pce appr fnl f* 9/1[3]	67
	4	1	**Blackstone Vegas** 2-9-3 0 TonyHamilton 8 (J Howard Johnson) *trckd ldrs on outside: effrt over 2f out: hung lft and kpt on same pce fnl f* 14/1	65
	5	1¾	**Gulf President** 2-9-3 0 SamHitchcott 3 (M R Channon) *trckd ldrs: effrt over 2f out: one pce* 10/1	60+
	6	4	**Sultans Way (IRE)** 2-9-3 0 ChrisCatlin 7 (P F I Cole) *w ldrs: led over 2f out: hdd over 1f out: sn wknd* 6/1[2]	50+
2	7	¾	**Yorgunnabelucky (USA)**[20] 3277 2-9-3 0 JoeFanning 5 (M Johnston) *set modest pce: qcknd over 3f out: hdd over 2f out: lost pl over 1f out* 8/11[1]	48+
4	8	10	**Pilot Light**[13] 3476 2-9-3 0 DavidAllan 6 (T D Easterby) *in rr: sn pushed along: lost pl over 2f out: sn bhd* 33/1	23

1m 33.68s (8.38) **Going Correction** +0.95s/f (Soft) 8 Ran SP% **115.7**
Speed ratings (Par 98): **90,88,87,86,84 79,78,67**
toteswinger: 1&2 £21.90, 1&3 £17.20, 2&3 £11.30. CSF £186.35 TOTE £26.60: £4.60, £2.00, £2.10; EX 309.80.
Owner Geoff & Sandra Turnbull **Bred** Geoff & Sandra Turnbull **Trained** Middleham Moor, N Yorks

FOCUS
Not an easy race to rate run at a very steady pace on bad ground with the third probably the best guide.

NOTEBOOK
Rising Prospect, out of a prolific winning mare, stands over plenty of ground but needs to fill to his frame. He did not go unbacked at long odds and in the end ran out a most decisive winner. He will be even better suited by a mile. (tchd 16-1)
Highland Storm, stepping up in trip and having his first try on turf, took it up for a few strides but was soon overwhelmed by the winner. (op 16-1)
Mefraas(IRE) knew a lot more this time and to his credit kept going all the way to the line in the very testing conditions. (tchd 8-1)
Blackstone Vegas, who cost 110,000gns at the breeze-up sales, has plenty of size and scope. He made a satisfactory debut and much less testing conditions will see him in a better light. (op 12-1)
Gulf President, an April foal, showed ability on his debut and is another who will improve on less testing ground. (op 11-1 tchd 9-1)
Sultans Way(IRE) went on but in the end came up some way short. (op 13-2 tchd 7-1)
Yorgunnabelucky(USA) stepped up the pace from the front but in the end dropped right out, totally unsuited by the bad ground. This is best put a line through. (op 4-6 tchd 4-5)

3927 CUISINE DE FRANCE SUMMER STKS (GROUP 3) (F&M) — 6f

2:45 (2:47) (Class 1) 3-Y-O+

£36,900 (£13,988; £7,000; £3,490; £1,748; £877) Stalls Low

Form				RPR
0210	1		**Our Faye**[21] 3197 5-9-2 88 NCallan 11 (S Kirk) *chsd ldrs: styd on to ld ins fnl f: hld on towards fin* 12/1	101
610	2	hd	**Lady Grace (IRE)**[13] 3488 4-9-2 102 (t) AlanMunro 10 (W J Haggas) *hld up in rr: hdwy and c outside over 2f out: hung lft and no ex towards fin* 9/2[2]	100
	3	1¼	**San Sicharia (IRE)**[49] 3-8-10 0 IMendizabal 9 (J-C Rouget, France) *bmpd s: sn chsng ldrs: effrt over 2f out: styd on fnl f* 12/1	96
4111	4	¾	**Look Busy (IRE)**[20] 3252 3-8-10 100 PaulMulrennan 4 (A Berry) *w ldr on inner: led over 2f out: hdd and no ex ins fnl f* 8/1	93
6105	5	½	**Manzila (FR)**[20] 3252 5-9-2 103 SilvestreDeSousa 12 (D Nicholls) *chsd ldrs: kpt on same pce appr fnl f* 9/1	93
-224	6	1¼	**Eastern Romance**[20] 3252 3-8-10 105 FergalLynch 3 (K A Ryan) *in rr: kpt on fnl 2f: nvr rchd ldrs* 8/1	88
1-50	7	2¾	**Spinning Lucy (IRE)**[68] 1830 3-8-10 100 ChrisCatlin 7 (B W Hills) *led tl over 2f out: wknd over 1f out* 7/1[3]	80
4004	8	1	**Ripples Maid**[26] 3063 5-9-2 92 RobertHavlin 2 (J A Geake) *chsd ldrs on inner: wknd over 1f out* 12/1	78
1-13	9	1½	**Cartimandua**[37] 2738 4-9-2 105 StephenDonohoe 8 (E S McMahon) *wnt rt s: chsd ldrs: effrt over 2f out: sn wknd* 4/1[1]	73
005-	10	½	**Vital Statistics**[266] 6300 4-9-2 94 JoeFanning 13 (D R C Elsworth) *trckd ldrs on outer: lost pl over 1f out* 22/1	72
0-14	11	½	**Salsa Steps (USA)**[62] 1993 4-9-2 100 (t) TravisBlock 6 (H Morrison) *in tch: lost pl over 2f out* 9/1	70

1m 16.9s (5.00) **Going Correction** +0.95s/f (Soft)
WFA 3 from 4yo+ 6lb 11 Ran SP% **120.3**
Speed ratings (Par 113): **104,103,102,101,100 98,95,93,91,91 90**
toteswinger: 1&2 £12.10, 1&3 £33.90, 2&3 £19.20. CSF £66.87 TOTE £16.40: £4.20, £2.10, £3.50; EX 45.70 TRIFECTA Pool: £429.30 - 3.00 winning units..
Owner J B J Richards **Bred** J B J Richards **Trained** Upper Lambourn, Berks
■ Stewards' Enquiry : N Callan two-day ban: used whip with excessive frequency (Jul 25, 27)

FOCUS
The winner had the least chance of official figures emphasising how tricky this Group 3 fillies' and mares' race is to rate accurately.

NOTEBOOK
Our Faye, who had the least chance on official figures, is proven on soft ground and in the end she did just enough on this return to 6f. (op 16-1)
Lady Grace(IRE), third in this last year, is in-foal. She proved a tricky ride but in the end was just held at bay. (op 6-1)
San Sicharia(IRE), a winner twice over 7f in France, has shown she stays a mile. She took a bump at the start and was closing down the first two at the line. (op 9-1)
Look Busy(IRE), whose five career wins have been over 5f, clung on to fourth place earning some more valuable black type. (op 7-1)
Manzila(FR), suited by the soft ground, ran right up to her best. (op 10-1)
Eastern Romance keeps running well at this level. (op 10-1)
Spinning Lucy(IRE), back over sprint distances, took them along but she could not see it out in these very testing conditions. (op 13-2 tchd 6-1)
Cartimandua was well below her best and connections put the blame at the door of the testing ground. Official explanation: jockey said filly was unsuited by the heavy ground (op 5-1 tchd 11-2)
Salsa Steps(USA) Official explanation: jockey said filly was unsuited by the heavy ground

3928 HEARTHSTEAD HOMES STKS (H'CAP) — 7f

3:20 (3:21) (Class 4) (0-85,85) 3-Y-O+ £6,799 (£2,023; £1,011; £505) Stalls Low

Form				RPR
2131	1		**Harrison George (IRE)**[27] 3050 3-9-1 83 JamieMoriarty(3) 11 (R A Fahey) *hld up in rr: pushed along and hdwy on outer 3f out: styd on wl to ld nr fin* 15/2[2]	93
2015	2	nk	**Ink Spot**[20] 3270 3-8-13 81 (v[1]) PJMcDonald(3) 7 (M L W Bell) *hld up: hdwy and nt clr run 2f out: led ins fnl f: hdd nr fin* 17/2	90

-000 **3** *5* **Trimlestown (IRE)**[14] 3443 5-8-13 **70**....(p) NCallan 8 69
(K A Ryan) *trckd ldrs: led 2f out: hdd ins fnl f: one pce* **10/1**

0-03 **4** *½* **Game Lad**[13] 3491 6-9-10 **84**.... DuranFentiman(3) 12 82
(T D Easterby) *mid-div: hdwy on outer over 2f out: styd on same pce appr fnl f* **8/1**[3]

3003 **5** *2¼* **Countdown**[9] 3599 6-9-5 **76**....(b) DavidAllan 10 68
(T D Easterby) *hld up in mid-div: effrt over 2f out: kpt on same pce* **11/4**[1]

5-30 **6** *nse* **Carnivore**[21] 3197 6-9-9 **80**....(t) PaulFessey 5 72
(T D Barron) *chsd ldrs: kpt on same pce appr fnl f* **12/1**

2000 **7** *2* **My Kaiser Chief**[8] 3626 3-8-6 **71**....(t) FergalLynch 6 55
(W J H Ratcliffe) *trckd ldrs: t.k.h: wknd over 1f out* **20/1**

3341 **8** *nk* **Flying Bantam (IRE)**[21] 3203 7-8-9 **73**.... BMcHugh(7) 9 59
(R A Fahey) *trckd ldrs: fdd fnl f* **14/1**

-045 **9** *1½* **Russian Epic**[36] 2762 4-9-5 **76**....(t) AlanMunro 15 58
(M A Jarvis) *in rr and sn pushed along: sme hdwy on outside 2f out: nvr nr ldrs* **10/1**

05U6 **10** *3¼* **Red Romeo**[14] 3435 7-8-12 **74**.... AshleyHamblett(5) 1 47
(N Wilson) *led on inner: hdd 2f out: wknd fnl f* **20/1**

2144 **11** *nk* **Shotley Mac**[7] 3664 4-8-7 **69** ow1.... NeilBrown(5) 13 42
(N Bycroft) *prom on outer: lost pl over 1f out* **10/1**

0/0- **12** *1½* **Spirit Of France (IRE)**[512] 477 6-10-0 **85**.... DNolan 3 54
(D Carroll) *trckd ldrs: lost pl 2f out* **25/1**

0531 **13** *hd* **Kiwi Bay**[31] 2911 3-9-6 **85**.... TonyHamilton 2 50
(M Dods) *chsd ldrs on inner: lost pl 2f out* **9/1**

1m 31.34s (6.04) **Going Correction** +0.95s/f (Soft)
WFA 3 from 4yo+ 8lb **13** Ran SP% **125.1**
Speed ratings (Par 105): **103,102,96,96,93 93,91,91,89,85 85,83,83**
toteswinger: 1&2 £12.40, 1&3 £19.10, 2&3 £22.60. CSF £71.31 CT £659.24 TOTE £7.80: £2.70, £3.50, £4.00; EX 102.70.
Owner P D Smith Holdings Ltd **Bred** R P Ryan **Trained** Musley Bank, N Yorks

FOCUS
The first two finished clear but quite how much improvement they showed is open to doubt on account of the very bad ground.
Red Romeo Official explanation: jockey said gelding was unsuited by the heavy ground

3929 CADBURY CUP STKS (H'CAP) 1m 4f
3:55 (3:55) (Class 2) (0-100,96) 3-Y-O+ **£11,656** (£3,468; £1,733; £865) **Stalls** Centre

Form RPR

31 **1** **Ella**[72] 1730 4-8-13 **81**.... FrancisNorton 8 95
(G A Swinbank) *t.k.h: led: clr over 1f out: kpt on wl: unchal* **6/1**[3]

6010 **2** *2¾* **Mull Of Dubai**[34] 2830 5-9-10 **92**.... JohnEgan 5 102
(T P Tate) *hld up towards rr: hdwy 4f out: sltly hmpd over 2f out: sn chsng wnr: edgd rt and styd on fnl f* **11/1**

11-0 **3** *9* **Black Rock (IRE)**[65] 1916 4-10-0 **96**.... NCallan 12 93
(M A Jarvis) *trckd ldrs: t.k.h: hmpd over 2f out: kpt on same pce* **15/2**

1-04 **4** *½* **Night Hour (IRE)**[20] 3253 6-9-9 **91**.... DO'Donohoe 17 87
(Saeed Bin Suroor) *sn chsng ldrs: hung bdly lft over 2f out: one pce* **12/1**

16-1 **5** *14* **Envisage (IRE)**[19] 3294 4-9-10 **92**.... ChrisCatlin 16 67
(Saeed Bin Suroor) *chsd ldrs: drvn over 4f out: wkng whn hmpd over 2f out* **9/2**[2]

0100 **6** *6* **Maslak (IRE)**[27] 3045 4-9-5 **87**.... RobertHavlin 6 53
(P W Hiatt) *chsd ldrs: wkng whn n.m.r over 2f out* **25/1**

0022 **7** *2¾* **Mesbaah (IRE)**[7] 3664 4-9-2 **84**....(p) TonyHamilton 11 46
(R A Fahey) *trckd ldrs: t.k.h: lost pl over 3f out* **16/1**

51/5 **8** *17* **Toldo (IRE)**[28] 3007 6-9-1 **86**.... PJMcDonald(3) 15 22
(G M Moore) *mid-div: drvn over 4f out: lost pl 3f out* **10/1**

32-0 **9** *3½* **Bergonzi (IRE)**[56] 2168 4-8-12 **85**.... NeilBrown(5) 14 16
(J Howard Johnson) *in rr: bhd fnl 4f* **18/1**

13-1 **10** *35* **Crete (IRE)**[28] 3003 6-9-7 **89**.... AlanMunro 9 —
(W J Haggas) *hld up in rr: rdn and lost pl over 3f out: sn bhd: t.o* **11/4**[1]

3013 **11** *½* **Birkside**[14] 3440 5-9-5 **87**.... DavidAllan 2 —
(D Carroll) *hld up in rr: rdn and lost pl 4f out: t.o* **12/1**

13-1 **12** *16* **Muhannak (IRE)**[31] 2904 4-9-8 **90**.... PaulMulrennan 7 —
(M W Easterby) *w wnr 2f: lost pl over 8f out: sn bhd: t.o 5f out* **16/1**

2m 41.79s (8.59) **Going Correction** +0.95s/f (Soft) **12** Ran SP% **124.6**
Speed ratings (Par 109): **109,107,101,100,91 87,85,74,72,48 48,37**
toteswinger: 1&2 £9.90, 1&3 £11.10, 2&3 £12.40. CSF £74.35 CT £516.15 TOTE £5.10: £1.70, £3.00, £2.50; EX 53.50.
Owner Guy Reed **Bred** G Reed **Trained** Melsonby, N Yorks

FOCUS
They finished well struing out. The winner dominated throughout and the runner-up finished well clear of the third and fourth. Not form to take literally.

NOTEBOOK
Ella, having just her sixth start, not having appeared at two or three, was racing from a 9lb higher mark. She set the fractions and, out on her own coming to the final furlong, had only to be kept up to her work. She is taking after her dam who won the November Handicap. (tchd 7-1)
Mull Of Dubai, suited by the flat track and easy ground, was cutting the winner back all the way to the line but as a result his rating will go up. (op 12-1)
Black Rock(IRE), out of sorts after failing to see out the trip in the Chester Cup, did well under his big weight and should continue to progress this year. (op 10-1)
Night Hour(IRE), expected to be suited by the conditions, gave his rider real problems, hanging violently left. (op 11-1 tchd 10-1)
Envisage(IRE), 6lb higher, was stepping up in trip and his chance had gone when he took a bump. (tchd 5-1)
Crete(IRE), 13lb higher, never figured in this bad ground and was afterwards found to have lost a shoe. This is best forgotten. Official explanation: jockey said gelding was unsuited by the heavy ground and lost a shoe (op 3-1)
Muhannak(IRE) Official explanation: jockey said gelding was unsuited by the heavy ground

3930 MR KIPLING EXCEEDINGLY GOOD STKS (H'CAP) 1m 6f
4:30 (4:30) (Class 3) (0-95,88) 3-Y-O **£9,714** (£2,890; £1,444; £721) **Stalls** Low

Form RPR

3242 **1** **Dolly Penrose**[28] 2997 3-8-8 **75**.... SamHitchcott 4 83
(M R Channon) *hld up last: hmpd and snatched up bnd over 4f out: led appr fnl f: shkn up: hung lft and wnt clr ins fnl f: readily* **11/4**[2]

1 **2** *4½* **Le Brocquy**[21] 3223 3-9-5 **86**.... AlanMunro 3 87
(M G Quinlan) *trckd ldrs: chal over 3f out: led over 2f out: edgd rt: hdd appr fnl f: sn wl outpcd* **7/1**

2331 **3** *3¾* **Victoria Montoya**[28] 2997 3-8-9 **76**.... FrancisNorton 1 72
(A M Balding) *w ldr: led 7f out: faltered and hdd over 4f out: chal 3f out: edgd lft 2f out: sn btn* **2/1**[1]

10-6 **4** *6* **Graceful Descent (FR)**[13] 3493 3-8-9 **76**.... TonyHamilton 6 64
(R A Fahey) *trckd ldrs: led over 4f out: hdd over 2f out: sn sueezed out and wknd* **9/2**[3]

0610 **5** *109* **Step This Way (USA)**[13] 3505 3-9-7 **88**.... JoeFanning 5 —
(M Johnston) *led: hdd 7f out: shkn up over 5f out: lost pl over 4f out: sn bhd: t.o and eased 3f out* **9/2**[3]

3m 19.84s (19.64) **Going Correction** +0.95s/f (Soft) **5** Ran SP% **108.9**
Speed ratings (Par 104): **81,78,76,72,—**
toteswinger: 1&2 £13.30. CSF £19.92 TOTE £4.10: £1.80, £2.60; EX 22.80.
Owner Geoffrey Rowe **Bred** Jethro Bloodstock **Trained** West Ilsley, Berks

FOCUS
A pedestrian time, even allowing for the conditions. The winner seemed to handle the ground better than her opponents and turned around Goodwood form with the third.

NOTEBOOK
Dolly Penrose, closely matched with Victoria Montoya on Goodwood running, was having just her sixth career start. Knocked back turning in, she again tended to hang but came clear in the end. (tchd 3-1)
Le Brocquy, stepping up in trip and encountering totally different ground after winning on his debut at Newmarket three weeks ago, worked hard to get in front but in the end the winner proved much too strong. (op 6-1 tchd 5-1)
Victoria Montoya, narow conqueror of the winner at Goodwood, was not the first runner here to prove reluctant to leave the stable area and go to the start at the end of the back straight. She seemed to drop anchor turning in but, after renewing her challenge, in the end she folded rather tamely. It may be best to put a line through this. (op 7-4)
Graceful Descent(FR), a winner on easy ground at two, found herself in front turning in but her chance had slipped when left short of room. She has yet to prove she truly stays this far. (op 6-1)
Step This Way(USA), again 8lb higher than her all-the-way win in a ladies' race here last month, ran badly for the second successive time. Something is clearly amiss even if her trainer stays mum. (op 5-1 tchd 11-2)

3931 WARBURTONS, BAKERS BORN & BRED STKS (APPRENTICE H'CAP) 5f
5:05 (5:05) (Class 3) (0-90,89) 3-Y-O+ **£8,095** (£2,408; £1,203; £601) **Stalls** Low

Form RPR

-000 **1** **Inspainagain (USA)**[4] 3787 4-8-5 **70** oh4.... DeanHeslop(4) 7 79
(T D Barron) *sn outpcd and detached in last: hdwy and edgd lft over 1f out: hrd rdn styd on wl to ld last 50yds* **10/1**

-063 **2** *½* **Invincible Force (IRE)**[48] 2401 4-10-0 **89**....(b) NeilBrown 8 96
(Paul Green) *led: hdd wl ins fnl f* **11/2**

4122 **3** *4½* **Total Impact**[21] 3228 5-9-4 **83**.... BMcHugh(4) 6 74
(R A Fahey) *trckd ldrs: drvn 2f out: fdd fnl f* **3/1**[2]

0000 **4** *3¼* **Bond City (IRE)**[14] 3451 6-9-13 **88**....(p) SladeO'Hara 4 67
(G R Oldroyd) *chsd ldrs: sn drvn along: wknd ins fnl f* **9/2**

0152 **5** *8* **Stolt (IRE)**[13] 3472 4-9-12 **87**.... AshleyHamblett 2 37
(N Wilson) *sn w ldrs: wknd 1f out* **11/4**[1]

1112 **6** *6* **Wibbadune (IRE)**[27] 3042 4-8-11 **74**.... PatrickDonaghy(2) 3 3
(D Shaw) *wnt rt s: trckd ldrs: wknd appr fnl f: eased towards fin* **7/2**[3]

63.11 secs (3.81) **Going Correction** +0.95s/f (Soft) **6** Ran SP% **116.5**
Speed ratings (Par 107): **107,106,99,93,81 71**
toteswinger: 1&2 £7.20, 1&3 £10.00, 2&3 £4.00. CSF £64.06 CT £208.17 TOTE £11.80: £2.80, £2.90; EX 73.20 Place 6: £7484.92 Place 5: £1554.94.
Owner Jim Beaumont & Douglas Pryde **Bred** Leon Millsap **Trained** Maunby, N Yorks
■ Stewards' Enquiry : Dean Heslop one-day ban: used whip with excessive frequency (Jul 25)

FOCUS
The leaders seemed to go off too strongly in the bad ground. The first two had not been at their best previously this year and the form has a doubtful look about it.

NOTEBOOK
Inspainagain(USA), having his second outing in five days after losing his action at Musselburgh, soon looked a lost cause and was matched for £12 at 999/1 on the exchanges. Given maximum assistance, he crept through on the leader's inside to snatch this quite valuable prize near the line. (op 9-1)
Invincible Force(IRE), with the blinkers retained, has slipped to a lenient mark, and after setting a very strong pace he was mugged naer the line. (op 8-1)
Total Impact, who prefers cover, has yet to shine on very soft ground. There is another win in the can. (op 7-2 tchd 4-1)
Bond City(IRE), running from a career-low mark, has tasted success just once in the last three years and here he was soon flat out. (tchd 4-1)
Stolt(IRE), going into this in the form of his life, faded badly and the ground was probably just too testing for him. (op 3-1 tchd 5-2)
Wibbadune(IRE), absent for four weeks, stopped to nothing and connections blamed the very testing ground. Official explanation: jockey said filly was unsuited by the heavy ground (op 10-3)
T/Plt: £2,746.40 to a £1 stake. Pool: £85,590.34. 22.75 winning tickets. T/Qpdt: £189.20 to a £1 stake. Pool: £5,447.40. 21.30 winning tickets. WG

3749 **DEAUVILLE** (R-H)
Friday, July 11
OFFICIAL GOING: Turf course - soft; all-weather - standard

3938a PRIX DE RIS-ORANGIS (GROUP 3) (STRAIGHT) 6f
3:00 (3:00) 3-Y-O+ **£29,412** (£11,765; £8,824; £5,882; £2,941)

RPR

1 **Mariol (FR)**[6] 3752 5-9-0.... SMaillot 2 111
(Robert Collet, France) *cl up: 3rd 1/2-way: pushed along to chse ldrs over 1 1/2f out: rdn to chal appr fnl f: r.o to ld 50yds out: rdn out* **19/2**

2 *1½* **Stern Opinion (USA)**[21] 3243 3-8-8.... SPasquier 7 105
(P Bary, France) *prom on outside: 2nd 1/2-way: pushed along to chal over 1 1/2f out: drvn to ld 1f out: hdd 50yds out* **43/10**[2]

3 *1* **Only Answer**[40] 2652 4-9-1.... OPeslier 9 104
(A Fabre, France) *hld up towards outside: disputing 7th 1/2-way: pushed along over 1 1 1/2f out: rdn to go 3rd appr fnl f: styd on* **7/1**[3]

4 *nk* **Tiza (SAF)**[41] 2637 6-9-4.... CSoumillon 5 106
(A De Royer-Dupre, France) *hld up towards outside: disputing 7th 1/2-way: effrt and r.o over 1f out: styd on: nrest at fin* **11/10**[1]

5 *½* **Gipson Dessert (USA)**[50] 2348 3-8-5.... C-PLemaire 1 97
(J-C Rouget, France) *hld up in last: pushed along 2f out: rdn and styd on fr over 1f out: nrest at fin* **83/10**

6 *1½* **Salut L'Africain (FR)**[50] 2348 3-8-8.... DBoeuf 4 95
(Robert Collet, France) *mid-div: cl 6th 1/2-way: rdn over 1f out: no imp on ldrs* **19/2**

7 *2* **Gesture**[26] 6-9-4.... SLandi 8 94
(E Russo, Italy) *mid-div: 5th 1/2-way: drvn 2f out: one pce fr over 1f out* **8/1**

8 *5* **Wilki (FR)**[41] 2637 3-8-5.... TThulliez 3 71
(A De Royer-Dupre, France) *led: pushed along whn pressed over 1 1/2f out: hdd 1f out: rdn and wknd* **19/1**

9 *15* **Val Jaro (FR)**[21] 3243 5-9-0 .... THuet 6 30
(S Morineau, France) *prom: 4th 1/2-way: pushed along over 2f out: sn wknd and dropped to last: eased fnl f* **43/1**

1m 10.6s (-0.60) **Going Correction** +0.225s/f (Good)
WFA 3 from 4yo+ 6lb **9** Ran SP% **127.2**
Speed ratings: **113,111,109,109,108 106,103,97,77**
PARI-MUTUEL: WIN 10.50 (coupled with Salut L'Africain); PL 5.50, 2.20,2.60; DF 52.00.
Owner P Vidal **Bred** Robert Collet & Sarl Classic Breeding **Trained** Chantilly, France

NOTEBOOK
Mariol(FR), third for much of the race, was a little short of room a furlong and a half out but eventually got some daylight and stayed on strongly to win by a length and a half. There are no plans for him at the moment.
Stern Opinion(USA), quickly out of the stalls, sat just behind the leader and looked the winner at the furlong pole. He battled well to the line but could not match the speed of the winner.
Only Answer, held up behind the main group, started to make ground on the outside a furlong and a half out but she could not accelerate with the first two and stayed on to take third.
Tiza(SAF), held up at the back of the field, had a wall of horses in front of him when things quickened up. Switched to the outside, he could not accelerate and looked very one-paced in the final stages.

3895 ASCOT (R-H)
Saturday, July 12

OFFICIAL GOING: Good to soft
Dolling out added 15yards to advertised distances on round course.
Wind: Moderate, ahead Weather: Fine

3939 EURO EARTHWORKS NOVICE STKS — 7f
2:20 (2:20) (Class 4) 2-Y-0 **£6,476** (£1,927; £963; £481) **Stalls** Low

Form RPR

1 **The Cheka (IRE)** 2-8-8 0 .... TQuinn 2 100+
(Eve Johnson Houghton) *trckd ldrs stands' side: qcknd to ld wl over 1f out: sn clr: easily* **8/1**[3]

30 2 *10* **Pegasus Lad (USA)**[21] 3245 2-8-12 0 .... RyanMoore 1 79
(M Johnston) *led stands' side gp: rdn over 2f out: hdd wl over 1f out: sn no ch w wnr: hld on wl for 2nd* **7/2**[2]

3 *nk* **Sixties Swinger (USA)** 2-8-8 0 .... KerrinMcEvoy 3 74
(M A Jarvis) *towards rr stands' side: rdn over 2f out: styd on wl fnl f to press for 2nd cl home but nvr any ch w v easy wnr* **7/2**[2]

43 4 *nk* **Markyg (USA)**[21] 3245 2-8-12 0 .... FergusSweeney 4 78
(K R Burke) *chsd ldrs stands' side: qcknd to chal ins fnl 2f: no ch w easy wnr fr 1f out and styd on one pce* **2/1**[1]

5 *12* **Rio Del Oro (USA)** 2-8-8 0 .... RichardHughes 5 44+
(R Hannon) *chsd sole companion in centre and no ch w stands' side fr 2f out: moved into wl btn 5th fnl f* **8/1**[3]

5 6 *3 3/4* **Fisher Hill (USA)**[17] 3372 2-8-12 0 .... JamieSpencer 6 38+
(K A Ryan) *s.i.s: led sole opponent in centre crse: upsides to 1/2-way: no ch fr 2f out and dropped bk to poor last fnl f* **9/1**

1m 31.08s (3.08) **Going Correction** +0.375s/f (Good) **6** Ran SP% **110.0**
Speed ratings (Par 96): **97,85,85,84,71 66**
toteswinger: 1&2 £6.20, 1&3 £6.60, 2&3 £1.70. CSF £34.18 TOTE £10.90: £2.80, £2.10; EX 46.20.
Owner Anthony Pye-Jeary And Mel Smith **Bred** James Robert Mitchell **Trained** Blewbury, Oxon

FOCUS
A decent contest on paper, with Chesham Stakes form represented, but it was newcomer The Cheka who blew them away, winning in the style of a very smart performer. Even with the Chesham runners assessed as having been below their best the winner emerges with an RPR nudging three figures, and he already looks capable of holding his own in Group races. Sixties Swinger can be rated second best.

NOTEBOOK
The Cheka(IRE) ◆, a 58,000gns son of Xaar, comes from a yard who have been enduring a dreadful run of form, but he ended the dry spell with a most impressive display. He clearly knew his job and, having been well positioned in the stands' side quartet, romped away with it once asked for his effort. With Chesham form represented in second and fourth there is every reason to believe this was a very smart effort, and the stable will no doubt be hoping it has on its hands another Tout Seul, who won the Dewhurst back in 2002. It will be fascinating to see where he turns out next, and he will merit respect what ever the company. (op 15-2)
Pegasus Lad(USA) did a bit too much too soon when fading into seventh in the Chesham, but he was more relaxed on this occasion and managed to reverse form with Markyg, although the winner proved to be in a different league. He has done enough to suggest a maiden will come his way, but connections will also now have the option of nurseries with him. (op 10-3 tchd 5-2)
Sixties Swinger(USA) ◆, a 200,000euros son of Refuse To Bend who is related to several useful winners, somehow managed to find trouble and can be rated clear second best. He showed definite signs of greenness, but spent a good furlong looking for a run and stayed on nicely close home. The winner apart, he is the one to take from the race, and winning a maiden should prove a formality. (op 9-2 tchd 5-1 in places)
Markyg(USA) ran a huge race to finish third in the Chesham and he looked the one to beat back over the same course and distance. However, he could not quicken when asked and was made to look paceless by the winner. It was disappointing he was unable to confirm previous form with the runner-up, but an ordinary maiden up north should come his way. (op 7-4)
Rio Del Oro(USA), an 88,000gns American-bred, has plenty of speed in his pedigree and it was a little surprising to see him follow the pace-setting Fisher Hill down the centre of the track. He kept on past that rival, but was well adrift of the main bunch and we will learn more about him next time. (tchd 15-2)
Fisher Hill(USA), a pleasing fifth on debut at Kempton, made the running down the centre of the track, but he dropped right out in the end and 'lost' his own private race with newcomer Rio Del Oro. (tchd 8-1 and 10-1)

3940 PLYMOUTH GIN SUMMER MILE STKS (GROUP 2) — 1m (R)
2:55 (2:55) (Class 1) 4-Y-0+
£56,770 (£21,520; £10,770; £5,370; £2,690; £1,350) **Stalls** High

Form RPR

0131 1 **Archipenko (USA)**[76] 1666 4-9-6 0 ....(bt) KShea 2 122+
(M F De Kock, South Africa) *chsd ldrs: led 2f out: hrd drvn fnl f and hld on wl* **11/1**

3006 2 *3/4* **Barshiba (IRE)**[24] 3120 4-8-12 105 .... TQuinn 7 112
(D R C Elsworth) *t.k.h: chsd ldr: rdn and one pce over 1f out: rallied wl to retake 2nd ins fnl f: no imp on wnr* **50/1**

-144 3 *nk* **Cesare**[25] 3100 7-9-1 118 .... JamieSpencer 6 114
(J R Fanshawe) *stdd s: hld up in rr: str run on outside fr over 1f out: disp 2nd ins fnl f but no imp on wnr: sn one pce* **6/4**[1]

1-24 4 *2* **Pressing (IRE)**[24] 3121 5-9-6 116 .... RyanMoore 3 115
(M A Jarvis) *hld up in rr: hdwy over 2f out: chsd wnr briefly appr fnl f: no imp and sn wknd* **4/1**[3]

211- 5 *2 3/4* **Ramonti (FR)**[216] 7092 6-9-6 123 ....(t) LDettori 1 108
(Saeed Bin Suroor) *t.k.h early: towards rr: hdwy 4f out: rdn and effrt on outside fr 3f out: nvr quite gng pce to rch ldrs and wknd over 1f out* **2/1**[2]

312 6 *2 3/4* **Elusive Warning (USA)**[105] 1087 4-9-1 111 .... KerrinMcEvoy 5 97
(Saeed Bin Suroor) *chsd ldrs: rdn 3f out and sn wknd* **20/1**

U103 7 *5* **Kandidate**[8] 3683 6-9-1 110 ....(t) RichardHughes 4 86
(C E Brittain) *led: rdn 3f out: hdd 2f out: sn wknd* **33/1**

1m 42.16s (1.36) **Going Correction** +0.375s/f (Good) **7** Ran SP% **111.3**
Speed ratings (Par 115): **108,107,106,104,102 99,94**
toteswinger: 1&2 £29.50, 1&3 £2.70, 2&3 £12.50. CSF £373.40 TOTE £10.70: £2.90, £5.60; EX 211.00.
Owner Sheikh Mohammed Bin Khalifa Al Maktoum **Bred** Eagle Holdings **Trained** South Africa
■ A first British winner for top South African trainer Mike De Kock, who has a team of 20 based in Newmarket.

FOCUS
This was all about the return of top-class performer Ramonti, but the pace was unsatisfactory and so was the result, with Archipenko stealing a march on his rivals two out and just holding off 50/1 chance Barshiba. It was a strong race for the grade on paper and a high-class effort from the winner, but the form may not be as good as it looks.

NOTEBOOK
Archipenko(USA), having his first run in Britain since finishing fifth in last season's Sussex Stakes, had earlier been sent off just 13/2 for the Derby, but he has progressed markedly since having the blinkers applied by De Kock and registered his first Group 1 win in the QE II Cup at Sha Tin in April. Equally effective at this trip, he was very weak in the market, but was well positioned to counter the steady gallop and sprinted into what turned out to be a winning lead two furlongs out, getting first run on his rivals. Remarkably, this was De Kock's first winner in Britain, and the highly progressive four-year-old now heads Stateside for the Arlington Million at Chicago, a race he seems sure to play a big part in. (op 8-1)
Barshiba(IRE) ran the race of her life. Things have not really gone right for this partially-sighted filly since winning the Sandringham Handicap at last season's Royal Ascot, for rarely does she get the decent pace she needs, and a change to front-running tactics did not help in the Windsor Forest Stakes last time. She had been beaten just over three lengths in the Lockinge earlier in the season, but had not matched that form since and was understandably dismissed here. However, despite again not getting a good gallop and racing keenly, she emerged as the winner's only danger inside the final furlong. She could not get to him, but held on for second and has gained some valuable black type. Winning with her will remain a challenge, but she looks sure to be on the premises in more good races. (op 40-1)
Cesare, a real Ascot specialist and cosy winner of this last season, found every bit of trouble going under Spencer in the Queen Anne and would probably have won with clear run throughout. This looked a perfect opportunity for him to gain compensation, getting 6lb from the three Group 1 winners and with his main market rival returning from injury, but being held up just off a steady gallop was not good to him and, try though he might, the winner was not for catching. This was another sound effort from the seven-year-old and he can once again be rated better than the bare form. His trainer seemed to think the slight ease in the ground was against him and he will no doubt bid to go one closer than last year in the Celebration Mile at Glorious Goodwood later this month. (op 11-8 tchd 5-4)
Pressing(IRE), down to 1m for first time since his three-year-old days, ran really well when fourth in the Prince Of Wales's Stakes at the Royal meeting, but he was rendered ineffective here by the steady pace and simply lacked the speed to challenge. He is probably worth another go at this trip. (op 11-2 tchd 7-2)
Ramonti(FR), very much the Godolphin flagbearer, confirmed himself as a top-class performer when winning three domestic Group 1s last season, and he confirmed the impression that he had been crying out for 1m2f when landing the Hong Kong Cup on his final start of the year. The nearest thing to an iron horse since Giant's Causeway, he had been kept off the course with a lingering leg infection and was expected to need the run quite badly. A steady pace would not have been ideal at this trip and he was not made anywhere near as much use of as usual, being held up out wide and racing keenly. He only briefly looked a threat and after becoming outpaced he was not given a hard time once his chance had gone. He can be expected to strip much fitter next time, and if returning to his best he can again take high rank over 1m2f on the world stage this season. He ought to give Duke Of Marmalade sterner opposition that he has faced so far in mopping up relatively soft Group 1 races. (op 9-4 tchd 5-2)
Elusive Warning(USA), second in the Godolphin Mile on his most recent outing and making his debut on turf, had it all to do against the best of these and he ran as well as could have been expected. We will learn more about him next time. (op 16-1)
Kandidate was responsible for the modest pace, but he was never going to make all and dropped out once headed. (op 40-1)

3941 KELLY GROUP NURSERY — 6f
3:25 (3:29) (Class 3) 2-Y-0 **£6,476** (£1,927; £963; £481) **Stalls** Low

Form RPR

021 1 **Talking Hands**[12] 3568 2-9-2 80 .... JamieSpencer 5 88+
(S Kirk) *hld up in rr: pushed along over 3f out: swtchd rt 2f out: qcknd wl to ld ins fnl f: edgd lft: easily* **4/1**[3]

246 2 *1 1/4* **Heliodor (USA)**[30] 2972 2-8-10 74 .... RyanMoore 6 75
(R Hannon) *in rr: hdwy fr 2f out: chal over 1f out: slt ld jst ins fnl f: sn hdd and outpcd* **7/2**[2]

004 3 *1 1/2* **Rich Red (IRE)**[53] 2275 2-7-13 63 .... JimmyQuinn 2 60
(R Hannon) *chsd ldrs: rdn to chal ins fnl 2f: led briefly appr fnl f: sn hdd: styd on same pce ins fnl f* **14/1**

2106 4 *1 1/2* **Klynch**[8] 3663 2-9-7 85 .... LDettori 1 77
(B J Meehan) *bhd: rdn 3f out: sme prog fnl 2f: nvr in contention* **8/1**

441 5 *1 3/4* **Roly Boy**[17] 3372 2-9-6 84 .... RichardHughes 4 71
(R Hannon) *slt advantage tl hdd over 2f out: wknd fnl f* **10/3**[1]

4651 6 *1* **Ridgeway Silver**[8] 3677 2-7-9 66 .... DavidProbert(7) 3 50
(M D I Usher) *chsd ldrs: rdn over 2f out: wknd appr fnl f* **7/1**

5421 7 *1* **Rio Royale (IRE)**[15] 3444 2-9-4 82 .... JimCrowley 7 63
(Mrs A J Perrett) *w ldr tl led over 2f out: hdd over 1f out and wknd qckly* **5/1**

1m 17.33s (2.93) **Going Correction** +0.375s/f (Good) **7** Ran SP% **112.2**
Speed ratings (Par 98): **95,93,91,89,87 85,84**
toteswinger: 1&2 £3.40, 1&3 £11.90, 2&3 £6.70. CSF £17.65 TOTE £4.50: £2.50, £2.20; EX 17.50.
Owner Deauville Daze Partnership **Bred** Wood Hall Stud Limited **Trained** Upper Lambourn, Berks

FOCUS
A fair nursery, and the form looks solid, with the winner's earlier Wolverhampton defeat looking better now, the runner-up close to form, and the third fitting in too. The leaders may have gone too quick though, as they occupied the last three places at the finish.

NOTEBOOK
Talking Hands ◆ only scraped home after making the running over 7f at Wolverhampton last time but proved a different proposition here dropped a furlong and held up. He came there travelling strongly under Spencer and showed a good change of pace to settle things inside the final furlong, winning easily despite edging left in front. This was a decent effort and he can win again. It would come as no surprise to see him go well in one of the valuable sales type races later in the season. (op 10-3)

Heliodor(USA), one of three runners representing the Hannon team, had shown promise on all three starts in maidens and looked fairly treated. Held up early, he came to have every chance and briefly looked the winner, but it soon became clear the winner had his move covered. He stuck on for second though and should get an extra furlong. (tchd 3-1)

Rich Red(IRE), the outsider of the Hannon trio, had not done much in three starts over 5f in maidens, but this trip was always likely to suit better and he gave it a bold go, but in the end lacked a change of gear. He can surely find a small race off his lowly rating. (op 16-1 tchd 12-1)

Klynch, who has been highly tried, was having his first start at 6f and he never really threatened to get involved, running on too late under different tactics. He is on a high enough mark, but may yet be capable of better. (op 17-2 tchd 9-1)

Roly Boy was the disappointment of the race. Fourth in the Woodcote Stakes on Derby Day, he shaped as though this drop back in trip would help when scraping home in a 7f maiden at Kempton last time. However, having been up there early, he found little for pressure and dropped out inside the final furlong. He may have gone too quick, as Rio Royale, who went with him, also dropped out. (op 3-1 tchd 7-2)

Ridgeway Silver faced tougher oppostion than at Salisbury and could not make an impact. (op 15-2 tchd 8-1)

Rio Royale(IRE), racing against the favoured stands' rail when scraping home at Folkestone last time, had it to do here and, having showed up prominently, he stopped to nothing once headed. He is likely to continue to struggle off this sort of mark. (op 13-2 tchd 9-2)

3942 EMIRATES MELBOURNE CUP CLOSES 4TH AUGUST STKS (HERITAGE H'CAP) 2m

4:00 (4:01) (Class 2) (0-105,104) 3-Y-0+

£24,924 (£7,464; £3,732; £1,868; £932; £468) **Stalls** High

Form				RPR
36-3	**1**		**Metaphoric (IRE)**[21] 3250 4-9-6 **100**.....(vt) JamieSpencer 2 (M L W Bell) *in rr: hdwy fr 4f out: str run to ld over 1f out: drvn out* **10/1**	111
1301	**2**	1 ¾	**La Vecchia Scuola (IRE)**[9] 3630 4-8-5 **85**..... JimmyQuinn 13 (J S Goldie) *chsd ldrs: rdn and outpcd 2f out: rallied u.p fnl f to take 2nd cl home but no ch w wnr* **10/1**	94
-523	**3**	¾	**Bogside Theatre (IRE)**[14] 3490 4-8-9 **89**..... RichardHughes 8 (G M Moore) *chsd ldr: rdn 3f out: led over 2f out: hdd u.p over 1f out: styd on same pce* **15/2**[3]	97
22-3	**4**	¾	**Sanbuch**[56] 2202 4-9-10 **104**..... RyanMoore 6 (L M Cumani) *bhd: rdn over 3f out: styd on wl on outside fr over 1f out: gng on cl home* **4/1**[1]	111+
11-2	**5**	½	**Whenever**[28] 3044 4-8-2 **82**..... FrancisNorton 7 (R T Phillips) *bhd: stl plenty to do over 2f out: str run fr over 1f out: fin wl* **9/2**[2]	89+
3006	**6**	nk	**Calculating (IRE)**[10] 3613 4-7-5 **78** oh1..... DavidProbert(7) 4 (M D I Usher) *t.k.h towards rr: hdwy fr 5f out: rdn to chse ldrs and edgd rt 2f out: styd on same pce* **33/1**	84
-300	**7**	shd	**Swan Queen**[22] 3209 5-8-6 **86**..... KerrinMcEvoy 9 (J L Dunlop) *bhd: sme prog whn n.m.r over 2f out: styd on ins fnl f but nvr gng pce to be competitive* **16/1**	92+
-515	**8**	¾	**Gee Dee Nen**[14] 3490 5-8-10 **90**..... ShaneKelly 3 (M H Tompkins) *chsd ldrs: chal fr 4f out: led over 3f out: hdd over 2f out: wknd fnl f* **12/1**	95
-230	**9**	nk	**Tilt**[14] 3490 6-8-12 **92**.....(p) LDettori 10 (B Ellison) *mid-div: drvn along fr 3f out: styd on fnl f: nvr in contention* **8/1**	97
61	**10**	½	**Winged D'Argent (IRE)**[16] 3414 7-8-0 **83**.....(b) LukeMorris(3) 12 (B J Llewellyn) *in rr: drvn along 10f out: moved into mid-div and rdn 5f out: styng on on ins whn n.m.r over 2f out: styd on again ins fnl f* **14/1**	87
-204	**11**	1 ½	**Akarem**[14] 3490 7-8-11 **91**..... FergusSweeney 14 (K R Burke) *chsd ldrs: rdn over 3f out: wknd fr 2f out* **10/1**	93
643/	**12**	3 ¼	**Self Defense**[147] 5018 11-9-5 **99**..... JimCrowley 11 (Miss E C Lavelle) *chsd ldrs: rdn 3f out: sn btn* **40/1**	97
4111	**13**	½	**Pocket Too**[10] 1501 5-7-12 **78** oh2.....(p) DavidKinsella 5 (M Salaman) *led tl hdd over 3f out: wknd over 2f out* **20/1**	76
-004	**14**	8	**Classic Punch (IRE)**[14] 3497 5-9-9 **103**..... TQuinn 1 (D R C Elsworth) *chsd ldrs: rdn 3f out: wknd over 2f out* **25/1**	91

3m 34.94s (2.34) **Going Correction** +0.375s/f (Good) **14** Ran SP% **122.6**

Speed ratings (Par 109): **109,108,107,107,107 106,106,106,106,106 105,103,103,99**

toteswinger: 1&2 £28.00, 1&3 £15.10, 2&3 £11.50. CSF £103.96 CT £807.92 TOTE £12.90: £2.70, £3.80, £2.70; EX 177.20 Trifecta £423.20 Pool: £1,429.75 - 2.50 winning units..

Owner The Royal Ascot Racing Club **Bred** Gerrardstown House Stud **Trained** Newmarket, Suffolk

FOCUS

A highly competitive staying handicap, but they went just an ordinary gallop and several were inclined to race too keenly. Improved efforts from the first three.

NOTEBOOK

Metaphoric(IRE), who developed into a useful hurdler last jumps season, returned to the Flat with a fine effort when third over almost 2m6f in the Queen Alexandra Stakes at the Royal meeting and he had no trouble with this drop back in trip. Waited with in rear, he crept into contention and ran on strongly once hitting the front over a furlong out to win well. Connections are now eyeing a Listed contest over this trip at Chester. (tchd 12-1)

La Vecchia Scuola(IRE), a battling winner at Haydock last time, was 6lb higher here, but she is a model of consistency and ran another storming race, finding under pressure and grabbing second close home. She has been similarly tough and progressive over hurdles and remains capable of better when faced with a good test.

Bogside Theatre(IRE), who ran a blinding race from the front when finishing third in the Northumberland Plate, again looked a big player off a 2lb higher mark and she ran well, just done for speed by the winner. She is another tough and progressive filly and is also likely to continue to pay her way. (op 8-1 tchd 7-1)

Sanbuch has yet to run a bad race in his relatively short career. A fine third behind Ajaan on his reappearance at Newbury, he again ran creditably under top weight, running on strongly having been given too much to do. He remains capable of better. (op 5-1 tchd 11-2)

Whenever ◆, a progressive four-year-old having just the fifth start of his career, won his final couple of starts at three and reappeared with a fine effort when finishing second at Sandown. The extra quarter mile here was expected to suit, but he got too far back and had to wait to see daylight in the straight. He finished well once in the clear and this long-striding son of Medicean would have gone close to winning had he had time to find momentum earlier. There is more to come from him. (op 5-1 tchd 4-1 and 11-2 in places)

Calculating(IRE) is back on a decent mark now, but he was another who got too far back and he could not make up the ground in time in the straight. He will find easier opportunities. (op 40-1)

Swan Queen did not get the clearest of runs and was going on close home. She was a progressive sort last season and this was easily her most promising run of the year so far.

Gee Dee Nen, a running-on fifth in the Northumberland Plate, ran well for a long way under more aggressive tactics, but he failed to get home. Official explanation: jockey said gelding hung right (op 10-1 tchd 9-1)

Tilt failed to settle and could not build on his Newcastle effort. (tchd 15-2)

Classic Punch(IRE) was trying a longer trip, but stamina issues could not alone account for another disappointing effort. (op 33-1)

3943 KELTBRAY CUP H'CAP 5f

4:35 (4:36) (Class 2) (0-105,100) 3-Y-0+

£11,215 (£3,358; £1,679; £840; £419; £210) **Stalls** Low

Form				RPR
2131	**1**		**Crimson Fern (IRE)**[8] 3680 4-9-0 **88**..... RichardHughes 10 (M S Saunders) *wnt rt s: stdd in rr: n.m.r over 1f out: swtchd lft and rapid hdwy ins fnl f: styd on wl to ld last strides: cosily* **11/4**[1]	101+
0024	**2**	nk	**Strike Up The Band**[8] 3680 5-9-3 **91**..... LDettori 2 (D Nicholls) *led: rdn and kpt on wl fnl f: nabbed last strides* **7/2**[2]	103
4-53	**3**	1 ¾	**Siren's Gift**[14] 3504 4-9-7 **95**..... FrancisNorton 3 (A M Balding) *chsd ldrs: wnt 2nd over 1f out but no imp on ldr u.p: sn one pce* **4/1**[3]	101
0500	**4**	3 ¾	**Evens And Odds (IRE)**[35] 2828 4-9-12 **100**.....(b) JamieSpencer 7 (K A Ryan) *chsd ldrs: rdn 1/2-way: wknd fnl f* **12/1**	92
2000	**5**	¾	**The Trader (IRE)**[27] 3063 10-9-10 **98**.....(b) FergusSweeney 5 (M Blanshard) *bhd: mod late prog* **20/1**	88
0500	**6**	1 ½	**Matsunosuke**[7] 3739 6-9-11 **99**..... KerrinMcEvoy 6 (A B Coogan) *bhd: rdn 2f out: nvr gng pce to be competitive* **12/1**	83
-014	**7**	2 ¼	**Mac Gille Eoin**[14] 3504 4-9-12 **100**..... JimCrowley 4 (J Gallagher) *chsd ldr to 1/2-way: wknd over 1f out* **12/1**	76
0060	**8**	1	**Judd Street**[14] 3504 6-9-12 **100**.....(v) TQuinn 9 (Eve Johnson Houghton) *chsd ldrs: rdn to dispute 2nd 1/2-way: wknd 1f out* **11/1**	72
0300	**9**	2	**Something (IRE)**[21] 3248 6-9-8 **96**..... SilvestreDeSousa 1 (D Nicholls) *chsd ldrs: rdn 1/2-way: wknd over 1f out* **8/1**	61

61.18 secs (0.68) **Going Correction** +0.375s/f (Good) **9** Ran SP% **116.2**

Speed ratings (Par 109): **109,108,105,99,98 96,92,90,87**

toteswinger: 1&2 £2.90, 1&3 £2.90, 2&3 £3.10. CSF £12.41 CT £37.77 TOTE £3.30: £1.50, £1.50, £1.80; EX 9.80 Trifecta £32.10 Pool: £1,305.01 - 30.03 winning units..

Owner M S Saunders **Bred** David Brickley **Trained** Green Ore, Somerset

FOCUS

A fair sprint handicap in which rapidly progressive filly Crimson Fern registered her sixth win of the campaign. Solid form.

NOTEBOOK

Crimson Fern(IRE) ◆, a rapidly progressive filly who registered her fifth win of the year when quickening smartly at Sandown last time, had an 8lb rise to contend with here, but she settled nicely in rear and was brought by Hughes with a perfectly-timed challenge. She again showed a nice change of pace and fully deserves a crack at a pattern contest now, with her trainer eyeing the Group 3 King George Stakes at Glorious Goodwood next. She has speed to burn and may well go close to winning that contest. (tchd 3-1 and 7-2 in places)

Strike Up The Band, beaten over three lengths by the winner at Sandown, made her work harder this time with the swing at the weights. He is back in really good form. (tchd 4-1 in places)

Siren's Gift, back down to 5f, has done all her winning on fast ground, but she came to have every chance towards the stands' side and ran well. She gives the impression there is improvement still to come. (op 7-2)

Evens And Odds(IRE), well beaten at Epsom on Derby Day, was struggling soon after halfway and continues to give the impression he is too high in the weights.

The Trader(IRE), a formerly smart sprinter, is not an easy horse to win with these days and, although making some moderate late gains, he never looked likely to win. (tchd 16-1)

Matsunosuke stuck on without threatening and remains a little below his best form. (tchd 14-1 in places)

Something(IRE) looked worth another go at this trip and he showed plenty of speed through the first couple of furlongs, but was in trouble well over two out and dropped away disappointingly. (op 11-1)

3944 NORMAN COURT STUD FILLIES' H'CAP 1m (S)

5:10 (5:10) (Class 3) (0-90,86) 3-Y-0+ **£7,771** (£2,312; £1,155; £577) **Stalls** High

Form				RPR
-320	**1**		**Nutkin**[57] 2152 4-9-2 **76**..... JamieSpencer 2 (J R Fanshawe) *hld up in rr: grad c to centre of crse 3f out: hdwy fr 2f out: led 1f out: pushed clr* **3/1**[2]	85
1-24	**2**	2	**Badalona**[25] 3109 3-8-13 **82**..... LDettori 3 (M L W Bell) *tardy s: sn chsng ldrs: grad moved to centre of crse 3f out: styd on fnl f but no ch w wnr* **15/8**[1]	84
12-2	**3**	1 ¼	**Polar Annie**[14] 3487 3-8-6 **75**..... KerrinMcEvoy 7 (M S Saunders) *wnt rt s: racd alone in centre of crse and overall ldr: shkn up 2f out: hdd 1f out: sn outpcd* **13/2**	74
-600	**4**	3 ¾	**Ivory Lace**[22] 3210 7-9-8 **82**..... JimCrowley 8 (S Woodman) *pushed rt s: bhd: hdwy and moved to centre of crse 3f out: sn rdn: no imp on ldrs* **20/1**	75
0161	**5**	1	**Rydal Mount (IRE)**[22] 3210 5-9-12 **86**..... FergusSweeney 1 (W S Kittow) *in rr: moved towards centre of crse 3f out: sn rdn and no imp* **6/1**[3]	76
3040	**6**	8	**Madame Hoi (IRE)**[43] 2560 3-8-6 **75**..... EdwardCreighton 6 (M R Channon) *chsd overall ldr 4f out: sn rdn: edgd towards centre of crse and wknd 2f out* **10/1**	45
-405	**7**	1	**Sayyedati Symphony (USA)**[38] 2717 3-9-1 **84**..... RyanMoore 4 (C E Brittain) *chsd ldrs and styd stands' side: wknd 2f out* **12/1**	52
226	**8**	½	**Uig**[24] 3132 7-8-6 **69**..... KirstyMilczarek(3) 5 (H S Howe) *racd stands' side: chsd overall ldr in centre tl over 4f out: sn wknd* **12/1**	37

1m 43.73s (3.13) **Going Correction** +0.375s/f (Good)

WFA 3 from 4yo+ 9lb **8** Ran SP% **116.6**

Speed ratings (Par 104): **99,97,95,92,91 83,82,81**

toteswinger: 1&2 £2.30, 1&3 £3.30, 2&3 £3.20. CSF £9.26 CT £33.26 TOTE £4.10: £1.60, £1.20, £1.80; EX 8.10 Trifecta £38.60 Pool: £1,081.73 - 20.73 winning units..

Owner Lord Vestey **Bred** Stowell Park Stud **Trained** Newmarket, Suffolk

FOCUS

Just an ordinary fillies' handicap. Most of the runners moved into the centre of the course before halfway, joining Polar Annie who had been racing alone until that point.

NOTEBOOK

Nutkin, an unlucky loser at odds of 4/7 at Folkestone two starts back, looked well worth a drop back in trip, having appeared not to last home over 1m2f at Newbury last time, and she ran out a ready winner. In front over a furlong out, she ran on strongly for pressure and was not for catching. There may well be more to come from her at this distance. (tchd 11-4 and 10-3 and 7-2 in places)

Badalona, expected to be suited by this slower ground, usually makes the running, but she was a bit sluggish out of the gates and ended up racing in behind the leaders. She had her chance and again ran well, but was never getting to the winner. She has yet to run a bad race in her short career, but that lack of a finishing kick will continue to leave her vulnerable at the end of her races, just as her five runner-up placings suggest. (tchd 7-4 and 2-1)

Polar Annie, narrowly denied on her recent return at Lingfield, was trying 1m for the first time and she opted to race alone down the centre of the track. The ground was slower here than at Lingfield, but she coped well enough and saw the trip out okay, without suggesting she is in need of it. She was racing here off a 12lb higher mark than when winning last season, but remains capable of better. (op 9-1)

Ivory Lace remains on a fair mark, but she was always going to struggle against younger rivals and ran about as well as could have been expected.

Rydal Mount(IRE), up 4lb for her recent Goodwood victory, was another having her first try at the 1m and she was a shade disappointing. Unable to get into the contest, she probably found this career-high mark beyond her. (op 5-1)

Madame Hoi(IRE), beaten just over a length in the Masaka Stakes earlier in the season, has not gone on from that and she was unable to make an impact on this handicap debut. (op 14-1)

Sayyedati Symphony(USA), another who started the season contesting pattern races, made no impact back in maiden company last time and on this evidence she is going to struggle in handicaps too. (op 10-1)

Uig does most of her racing over further and she ran even worse than she had done at Kempton last time. (op 14-1 tchd 16-1)

3945 CITYWIDE H'CAP — 5f

5:45 (5:45) (Class 4) (0-85,83) 3-Y-O+ — **£6,476** (£1,927; £963; £481) **Stalls** Low

Form — RPR

3211 **1** — **Cheveton**[7] 3724 4-9-8 **79** .... JimCrowley 2 — 89+
(R J Price) *sn trcking ldrs: drvn along over 2f out: led 1f out: styd on strly* **1/1**[1]

3030 **2** ½ **Digital**[2] 3881 11-9-5 **76** .... (v) JimmyQuinn 4 — 81
(M R Channon) *bhd: niggled along 1/2-way: stl jst last 1f out: rapid hdwy ins fnl f to take 2nd cl home: nt rch wnr* **10/1**

0-00 **3** ½ **Efistorm**[15] 3451 7-9-12 **83** .... IanMongan 9 — 86+
(C R Dore) *hld up in rr: hdwy on outside whn n.m.r wl over 1f out: rdn and styd on wl fnl f: gng on cl home* **11/2**[2]

4006 **4** ½ **Malapropism**[7] 3708 8-9-5 **76** .... KShea 3 — 78
(M R Channon) *chsd ldrs: rdn and outpcd 2f out: styd on again u.p ins fnl f but nvr quite gng pce to chal* **14/1**

4003 **5** 1 ¼ **Hereford Boy**[19] 3320 4-9-8 **79** .... RobertHavlin 1 — 76
(D K Ivory) *towards rr but in tch: hdwy fr 2f out: disp 2nd 1f out: wknd fnl 100yds* **11/1**

6000 **6** 1 ¼ **Cape Royal**[11] 3594 8-9-6 **77** .... (bt) JamieSpencer 10 — 70
(J M Bradley) *chsd ldrs: rdn 2f out: wknd ins fnl f* **12/1**

1620 **7** 1 ¼ **Blessed Place**[5] 3797 8-8-0 **64** oh2 .... (t) DavidProbert(7) 5 — 52
(D J S Ffrench Davis) *led tl hdd 1f out: wknd qckly* **16/1**

3110 **8** 3 ¼ **What Do You Know**[43] 2583 5-9-7 **78** .... (v) DavidKinsella 7 — 54
(A M Hales) *sn chsng ldrs: rdn over 2f out: wknd over 1f out* **9/1**[3]

100- **9** 2 ¼ **Calabaza**[229] 6946 6-8-5 **65** .... KirstyMilczarek(3) 6 — 32
(M J Attwater) *in tch to 1/2-way* **25/1**

62.28 secs (1.78) **Going Correction** +0.375s/f (Good) — **9** Ran SP% **116.9**

Speed ratings (Par 105): **100,99,98,97,95 93,91,86,82**

toteswinger: 1&2 £3.00, 1&3 £2.80, 2&3 £9.10. CSF £12.41 CT £40.61 TOTE £1.90: £1.10, £1.80, £2.30; EX 12.80 Trifecta £86.60 Pool: £1,397.38 - 11.93 winning units. Place 6 £846.74, Place 5 £257.61.

Owner Mrs K Oseman **Bred** Miss K Rausing **Trained** Ullingswick, H'fords

FOCUS

A fair sprint handicap but pretty ordinary form for the grade. Cheveton probably did not have to improve to land the hat-trick.

T/Plt: £584.90 to a £1 stake. Pool: £114,071.12. 142.36 winning tickets. T/Qpdt: £12.90 to a £1 stake. Pool: £7,393.80. 421.60 winning tickets. ST

3907 CHESTER (L-H)

Saturday, July 12

OFFICIAL GOING: Good (8.3)

Dolling out added 7yards per circuit to race distances

Wind: Fresh, against Weather: Bright intervals

3946 TOTESCOOP6 CITY PLATE (LISTED RACE) — 7f 2y

2:25 (2:26) (Class 1) 3-Y-O+

£24,978 (£9,468; £4,738; £2,362; £1,183; £594) **Stalls** Low

Form — RPR

5313 **1** — **Blythe Knight (IRE)**[14] 3498 8-9-7 110 .... PatCosgrave 6 — 116
(J J Quinn) *midfield: hdwy over 2f out: chsd ldr over 1f out: r.o ins fnl f: led fnl strides* **11/2**[2]

3603 **2** shd **Beckermet (IRE)**[14] 3488 6-9-5 108 .... ChrisCatlin 3 — 114
(R F Fisher) *led: qcknd away 3f out: edgd rt fr over 1f out: worn down fnl strides* **7/1**[3]

612- **3** 2 ½ **Army Of Angels (IRE)**[399] 2442 6-9-2 109 .... (t) DO'Donohoe 11 — 104+
(Saeed Bin Suroor) *towards rr: pushed along and hdwy over 2f out: styd on to chse front pair 100yds out: nt pce to threaten ldrs* **5/1**[1]

-204 **4** 1 ½ **Welsh Emperor (IRE)**[42] 2637 9-9-2 110 .... MickyFenton 7 — 100
(T P Tate) *prom: rdn over 2f out: no ex ins fnl f* **7/1**[3]

-330 **5** 1 ¼ **Vanderlin**[42] 2600 9-9-2 102 .... WilliamBuick 5 — 97
(A M Balding) *chsd ldrs: lost pl 4f out: rallied on outside to chse ldrs over 2f out: styd on same pce ins fnl f* **5/1**[1]

-300 **6** 3 ¼ **Azarole (IRE)**[112] 960 7-9-2 98 .... FrankieMcDonald 2 — 88
(Jane Chapple-Hyam) *s.i.s: towards rr: pushed along 3f out: n.m.r over 2f out: styd on u.p fnl f: nt pce to get competitive* **28/1**

4110 **7** nk **Daaweitza**[14] 3491 5-9-2 89 .... StephenDonohoe 9 — 87
(B Ellison) *in rr: pushed along over 2f out: styd on fnl f: nvr rchd ldrs* **33/1**

5104 **8** 2 ¼ **Captain Marvelous (IRE)**[31] 2961 4-9-5 105 .... DeanMcKeown 4 — 84
(B W Hills) *missed break: a towards rr: nvr a danger* **7/1**[3]

0510 **9** ½ **Bertbrand**[11] 3587 3-8-8 67 .... (b) RobbieEgan 1 — 77?
(D Flood) *racd keenly: chsd ldrs tl rdn and wknd over 1f out* **100/1**

1-25 **10** 10 **Tamagin (USA)**[21] 3248 5-9-2 100 .... EddieAhern 10 — 53
(K A Ryan) *prom on outside: rdn 4f out: wkng whn n.m.r over 2f out: eased whn btn over 1f out* **8/1**

2161 **11** 1 **Tasdeer (USA)**[16] 3396 3-8-8 105 .... DaneO'Neill 8 — 47
(M A Jarvis) *chsd ldrs: effrt over 2f out: sn wknd* **11/2**[2]

1m 25.5s (-1.00) **Going Correction** +0.125s/f (Good)

WFA 3 from 4yo+ 8lb — **11** Ran SP% **120.1**

Speed ratings (Par 111): **110,109,107,105,103 100,99,97,96,85 84**

toteswinger: 1&2 £9.40, 1&3 £2.40, 2&3 £8.10. CSF £44.30 TOTE £6.80: £2.10, £2.80, £1.70; EX 37.40 Trifecta £309.80 Part won. Pool: £418.70 - 0.60 winning units..

Owner Maxilead Limited **Bred** Gainsborough Stud Management Ltd **Trained** Settrington, N Yorks

■ The first running of this race since its promotion to Listed status.

FOCUS

A decent Listed event featuring several Pattern-class performers and a few of them have been around for quite a few years, with the ages of the front half-dozen ranging between six and nine. With a few established trailblazers in the field, a strong pace was assured and not that many ever really got into it, but the form looks sound rated around the principals to form.

NOTEBOOK

Blythe Knight(IRE), conceding weight all round, got the strong pace he needs this time over a trip short of his best. He travelled well as a result and when asked for his effort he put in a determined challenge up the inside of the pacemaker to snatch the race near the line. He is as good as ever and is a credit to all concerned. (op 6-1 tchd 7-1)

Beckermet(IRE), who had the same chance as the winner on adjusted official official ratings, is yet to win over this far but could hardly have come any closer to breaking that statistic. One of three vying for the early lead, he eventually won that battle and held a clear lead rounding the bend into the home straight. Hanging out towards the centre of the track, he kept on trying but agonisingly had the prize snatched from him near the line. It would be hard to blame lack of stamina for this defeat and he deserves compensation. (tchd 8-1)

Army Of Angels(IRE), with the tongue-tie back on, was returning from a 13-month absence but was one of those best treated at these weights. He seemed to find everything happening too quickly for him early, but his stamina eventually kicked in and he stayed on tight against the inside rail to finish a clear third. He should come on for this and will appreciate easier ground and stepping back up to 1m. (op 11-2 tchd 9-2)

Welsh Emperor(IRE), best in at the weights but who would probably have preferred softer ground, was up there early but the presence of Beckermet meant that he could not get the lead on his own and failed to find the required turn of foot from the home bend. (op 11-2)

Vanderlin, who has a good record here and won the equivalent event in 2004, rather ran in snatches but his biggest problem was that he was caught on the wide outside and covered more ground as a result. On a line throught those that beat him, he probably still ran close to his mark however. (op 15-2)

Azarole(IRE) had plenty on at these weights and was noted finishing well from off the pace, but it may have just been a case of running on past beaten horses. (op 33-1 tchd 25-1)

Daaweitza had little chance at the weights, but he has a very good record on tracks like this and that almost certainly helped him run above his official mark.

Captain Marvelous(IRE) blew the start and in a race like this run at a fast pace that was fatal. (op 8-1)

Tamagin(USA) loves to dominate, but he could never do so here and his wide draw meant that he was trapped out wide whilst involved in a three-way battle for the early lead. That was always likely to eventually count against him. (tchd 15-2)

3947 TOTESPORT 0800 221 221 H'CAP — 1m 2f 75y

3:00 (3:00) (Class 4) (0-80,79) 4-Y-O+ — **£5,828** (£1,734; £866; £432) **Stalls** High

Form — RPR

0622 **1** — **Cheshire Prince**[14] 3474 4-8-13 **71** .... EddieAhern 11 — 81
(W M Brisbourne) *racd keenly: trckd ldrs: led 5f out: rdn over 1f out: r.o and in command ins fnl f* **4/1**[1]

0416 **2** 3 ½ **New Star (UAE)**[30] 2970 4-8-11 **72** .... DuranFentiman(3) 8 — 75
(W M Brisbourne) *led early: prom: rdn to chal 2f out: nt pce of wnr ins fnl f* **10/1**

/340 **3** 1 ½ **Marvo**[14] 3493 4-9-0 **72** .... WilliamBuick 4 — 72
(M H Tompkins) *in tch: rdn over 2f out: chsd ldrs over 1f out: styd on same pce ins fnl f* **15/2**

0060 **4** nk **Ella Woodcock (IRE)**[17] 3367 4-9-6 **78** .... (p) MickyFenton 2 — 77+
(E J Alston) *racd keenly: trckd ldrs: hmpd under 5f out: rdn over 1f out: kpt on same pce ins fnl f* **7/1**[3]

33 **5** 1 ¼ **Erdeli (IRE)**[27] 3058 4-9-1 **73** .... ChrisCatlin 3 — 70+
(P R Webber) *in tch: shuffled bk 5f out: styd on fnl f: nt pce to rch ldrs* **7/1**[3]

0414 **6** ¾ **Piper's Song (IRE)**[7] 3736 5-9-6 **78** .... PatCosgrave 15 — 73
(D J G Murray Smith) *hld up: rdn over 1f out: styd on fnl f: unable to rch ldrs* **11/1**

1-32 **7** ½ **Drawn Gold**[32] 2904 4-8-9 **67** .... DaneO'Neill 14 — 61+
(R Hollinshead) *rrd s and missed break: in rr: rdn over 2f out: styd on ins fnl f: nrst fin* **9/2**[2]

054- **8** ½ **Royal Indulgence**[289] 5750 8-8-2 **63** ow1 .... MarcHalford(3) 12 — 56
(W M Brisbourne) *midfield: hdwy over 3f out: rdn to chse ldrs over 2f out: no imp over 1f out: wknd ins fnl f* **33/1**

63-0 **9** nk **Edas**[24] 3143 6-8-4 **62** .... DO'Donohoe 13 — 55
(J J Quinn) *hld up: rdn over 4f out: styd on ins fnl f: nvr able to chal* **22/1**

-000 **10** 1 **Fort Churchill (IRE)**[14] 3493 7-9-0 **79** .... (bt) AnthonyBetts(7) 7 — 70
(B Ellison) *racd keenly: hld up: pushed along 2f out: styd on fnl f: nvr able to chal* **16/1**

1340 **11** 1 ¼ **Kindlelight Blue (IRE)**[36] 2784 4-9-2 **74** .... StephenDonohoe 5 — 62
(N P Littmoden) *in tch: bmpd and forced wd under 5f out: rdn and wknd over 1f out* **16/1**

025 **12** ½ **Intersky Charm (USA)**[14] 3478 4-9-6 **78** .... DeanMcKeown 10 — 65
(R M Whitaker) *midfield: rdn over 2f out: wknd over 1f out* **8/1**

00-0 **13** 21 **Feeling (IRE)**[23] 3181 4-7-9 **60** .... RichardRowe(7) 9 — 5
(W Clay) *racd keenly: led after 1f: hdd 5f out: sn hmpd and wknd* **50/1**

0000 **14** dist **Wee Ellie Coburn**[14] 3473 4-8-2 **60** oh15 .... (be) FrankieMcDonald 6 — —
(M Mullineaux) *bhd: hung bdly rt fr over 6f out: sn lost tch: virtually p.u fnl f* **100/1**

2m 14.1s (1.90) **Going Correction** +0.125s/f (Good) — **14** Ran SP% **125.5**

Speed ratings (Par 105): **97,94,93,92,91 91,90,90,90,89 88,87,71,—**

toteswinger: 1&2 £10.20, 1&3 £4.20, 2&3 £46.60. CSF £45.47 CT £301.50 TOTE £3.80: £1.50, £3.50, £3.40; EX 36.20.

Owner D C Rutter & H Clewlow **Bred** The National Stud **Trained** Great Ness, Shropshire

FOCUS

A competitive handicap, but a steady pace meant that a few pulled hard early and it was also something of a rough race. It resulted in a one-two for trainer Mark Brisbourne with the form looking straightforward rated around the runner-up and fifth.

Ella Woodcock(IRE) Official explanation: jockey said gelding suffered interference in running

Edas Official explanation: jockey said horse kept changing its legs

Wee Ellie Coburn Official explanation: jockey said filly was unsteerable

3948 TOTESWINGER CITY WALL STKS (LISTED RACE) — 5f 16y

3:35 (3:36) (Class 1) 3-Y-O+

£24,978 (£9,468; £4,738; £2,362; £1,183; £594) **Stalls** Low

Form — RPR

5-63 **1** — **Green Manalishi**[38] 2712 7-9-0 98 .... EddieAhern 2 — 87
(K A Ryan) *sn stdd into midfield: rdn and hdwy over 1f out: r.o u.str driving ins fnl f to ld post* **9/2**[3]

-122 **2** nse **Borderlescott**[27] 3063 6-9-0 110 .... PatCosgrave 9 — 87
(R Bastiman) *chsd ldrs: effrt on outside to ld 1f out: r.o u.p: ct post* **11/4**[1]

0611 **3** 1 **Angus Newz**[15] 3460 5-8-9 95 .... (v) MickyFenton 1 — 78+
(M Quinn) *chsd ldrs: pushed along and losing pl whn n.m.r 2f out: trying to rally whn bmpd over 1f out: swtchd lft ins fnl f: r.o and gaining towards fin* **7/2**[2]

0-44 **4** *nk* **Foxy Music**[17] 3370 4-9-0 79 DeanMcKeown 4 82
(E J Alston) *led: edgd rt appr fnl f: rdn and hdd 1f out: sn edgd lft: nt qckn and edgd lft again towards fin* **28/1**

12-1 **5** *½* **Oldjoesaid**[85] 1442 4-9-0 107 DaneO'Neill 10 80
(H Candy) *midfield: rdn and hdwy over 1f out: r.o ins fnl f: nt quite pce to shake-up ldrs* **5/1**

0051 **6** *1* **Coconut Moon**[11] 3585 6-8-9 68 RobbieEgan 7 72+
(D Flood) *squeezed out s: towards rr: rdn and prog whn nt clr run and tightened up 1f out: nvr able to chal ldrs after* **33/1**

2662 **7** *nk* **Hoh Hoh Hoh**[14] 3504 6-9-0 104 ChrisCatlin 3 76
(R J Price) *s.i.s: in rr: rdn over 1f out: styd on ins fnl f: nt pce to chal* **9/2**[3]

0006 **8** *2½* **Willhewiz**[12] 3565 8-9-0 50 DuranFentiman 5 67?
(W M Brisbourne) *towards rr: outpcd wl over 1f out* **100/1**

3240 **9** *1¾* **Day By Day**[7] 3739 4-8-9 96 (b) WilliamBuick 6 55
(B J Meehan) *prom: rdn and losing grnd whn swtchd rt over 1f out: n.d after* **16/1**

0130 **10** *shd* **Bertoliver**[42] 2626 4-9-0 95 StephenDonohoe 8 60
(D K Ivory) *prom: wnt 2nd over 3f out: chal 2f out: rdn over 1f out: wknd ins fnl f* **20/1**

60.87 secs (-0.13) **Going Correction** +0.125s/f (Good) **10** Ran SP% **119.9**
Speed ratings (Par 111): **106,105,104,103,103 101,100,96,94,94**
toteswinger: 1&2 £6.70, 1&3 £5.30, 2&3 £3.60. CSF £17.29 TOTE £5.70: £2.00, £1.60, £1.40; EX 24.60 Trifecta £56.10 Pool: £926.00 - 12.20 winning units..

Owner Mrs S McCarthy, J Brennan & J Smith **Bred** E Aldridge **Trained** Hambleton, N Yorks

■ Stewards' Enquiry : William Buick two-day ban: careless riding (Jul 27-28)

FOCUS

A competitive enough Listed sprint and, although the early pace was strong, the final time was ordinary and there was not much covering the first five at the line. The draw played its part with the two inside stalls finishing in the first three and the form is dubious, with the fourth, sixth and eighth too close for comfort.

NOTEBOOK

Green Manalishi, successful the last time he visited this track though that was over an extra furlong, travelled well having been dropped in from his good draw. Produced with his effort soon after turning in, he once again timed his run to perfection and this was a decent effort considering he would have been getting 12lb from the runner-up in a handicap, even though he was by far the better drawn of the pair. (op 13-2)

Borderlescott was best in at these weights, but against that was his poor draw. Tracking the leaders on the outside for much of the way, it looked as though he might prevail when hitting the front soon after turning in, but he had the prize snatched from him right on the line. He has now finished runner-up in five of his last six starts, but deserves a much better record than just one win in almost two years. (tchd 10-3)

Angus Newz, who came into this in flying form, tried to hold her place from the plum draw but her chances looked very slim when she was chopped off against the rail by the eventual winner turning for home. However, despite getting a bump from the weakening Day By Day she flew up the far rail inside the last furlong and was still closing on the front pair at the line. She remains at the top of her game. (op 9-2 tchd 10-3)

Foxy Music had an awful lot to find at these weights and was also safely held by Angus Newz on recent Carlisle running, but he gave himself a chance by pinging the gates and it took quite an effort from his rivals to cut him down. He may have been flattered, however, and a record of one win from 18 starts is hardly impressive.

Oldjoesaid, given a three-month break since his successful return at Newbury, was up in class but was still second-best in at these weights. He faced a huge task from the outside stall and was always trapped out wide as a result, so under the circumstances this was not a bad effort at all. (op 4-1 tchd 11-2)

Coconut Moon, winner of a Class 6 handicap on the Polytrack last time, had no chance on these terms. She had to take evasive action to switch around the weakening Bertoliver entering the last furlong, but it did not make any difference to the result. Connections must be hoping that the Handicapper does not take this performance at face value.

Hoh Hoh Hoh was second-best in at the weights, but not for the first time he fluffed the start and in a race like this that was always going to prove difficult to overcome. (tchd 5-1)

3949 TOTESPORT.COM MAIDEN AUCTION STKS — 5f 16y

4:10 (4:11) (Class 5) 2-Y-O — **£4,209** (£1,252; £625; £312) **Stalls** Low

Form / RPR

22 **1** **Red Baron Dancer**[8] 3689 2-8-9 0 PatCosgrave 1 74
(J R Boyle) *mde all: rdn clr over 1f out: r.o wl and in command fnl f* **6/5**[1]

53 **2** *3¼* **Titus Andronicus (IRE)**[39] 2696 2-9-2 0 EddieAhern 3 70+
(K A Ryan) *trckd ldrs: wnt 2nd wl over 1f out: no imp on wnr* **7/2**[3]

3 *1½* **Say You Say Me** 2-8-6 0 FrankieMcDonald 4 54
(N J Vaughan) *s.i.s: midfield: hdwy 1f out: styd on ins fnl f: nt pce to trble front pair* **8/1**

0 **4** *nk* **Lucky Numbers (IRE)**[8] 3669 2-8-7 0 ow1 RussellKennemore(3) 10 57
(Paul Green) *pushed wd s: sn outpcd: hdwy on outside 1/2-way: styd on ins fnl f: nt pce to chal* **18/1**

3323 **5** *1¼* **Like For Like (IRE)**[5] 3778 2-8-6 0 WilliamBuick 8 49
(R Hannon) *prom on outside: rdn over 1f out: sn edgd lft: wknd ins fnl f: hld whn eased fnl 75yds* **3/1**[2]

00 **6** *¾* **Accomplishment (IRE)**[18] 3348 2-8-3 0 DuranFentiman(3) 5 46
(A P Jarvis) *trckd ldrs and lost pl wl over 1f out: no imp after* **50/1**

0 **7** *1¾* **Dark Velvet (IRE)**[24] 3125 2-8-4 0 ChrisCatlin 2 38
(E J Alston) *prom: rdn over 1f out: wknd ins fnl f* **20/1**

0 **8** *¾* **Peckforton**[61] 2048 2-8-2 0 ow1 MarcHalford(3) 7 36
(D J G Murray Smith) *rdn 2f out: a bhd* **50/1**

9 *hd* **Lemon Dash** 2-8-4 0 DO'Donohoe 9 34
(J J Quinn) *wnt rt s: racd keenly in midfield: outpcd over 1f out* **16/1**

62.25 secs (1.25) **Going Correction** +0.125s/f (Good) **9** Ran SP% **123.6**
Speed ratings (Par 94): **95,89,87,86,84 83,80,79,79**
toteswinger: 1&2 £1.70, 1&3 £3.50, 2&3 £6.70. CSF £6.11 TOTE £2.20: £1.20, £1.40, £1.90; EX 6.60.

Owner M Khan X2 **Bred** P M Hicks **Trained** Epsom, Surrey

FOCUS

Quite a straightforward maiden with the favourite making full use of the one stall and not many ever got into it. The form outside the winner looks modest though, with the second favourite disappointing, but solid enough.

NOTEBOOK

Red Baron Dancer, dropped to the minimum trip for the first time after finishing runner-up in his first two starts over 6f, pinged the gates from the plum draw and never really looked in much danger of defeat. The form probably amounts to little, but he stretched out nicely towards the end and should hold his own in sprint nurseries. (op 6-4 tchd 7-4)

Titus Andronicus(IRE) got a nice run through against the inside rail on the home bend and went in hot pursuit of the favourite, but was never anywhere near him. He may be able to find a opportunity now that he qualifies for nurseries, probably over another furlong. (op 4-1)

Say You Say Me, retained for 18,000gns as a yearling and out of a half-sister to the winning-sprinter Milly Fleur, made a little late progress and fared much the best of the two newcomers. She is entitled to improve from this. (tchd 15-2)

Lucky Numbers(IRE), beaten out of sight on his debut, had it all to do from the outside stall and was forced to race very wide, so he did not fare too badly under the circumstances. He will need to improve again to have a chance of winning a race, but may have more opportunities when he qualifies for a nursery mark after one more run. (op 14-1)

Like For Like(IRE), by far the most experienced in the field, showed up for a long way but did not get home and looks to be going the wrong way. (op 5-2)

3950 TOTESPORT BETXTRA H'CAP — 1m 7f 195y

4:45 (4:47) (Class 4) (0-85,76) 3-Y-O+ — **£5,828** (£1,734; £866; £432) **Stalls** Low

Form / RPR

0/61 **1** **Keelung (USA)**[2] 3891 7-9-9 71 6ex MickyFenton 6 79
(R Ford) *led: rdn and hdd 1f out: continued to chal: rallied gamely u.str driving to regain ld post* **1/1**[1]

3206 **2** *nse* **Command Marshal (FR)**[23] 3179 5-9-6 71 PatrickHills(3) 5 79
(M J Scudamore) *chsd ldr: rdn to ld 1f out: hdd post* **12/1**

0525 **3** *7* **Merrymaker**[2] 3891 8-9-0 62 EddieAhern 7 62
(W M Brisbourne) *bustled along s: sn hld up: rdn 4f out: outpcd 3f out: wnt 3rd 1f out: n.d to front pair* **5/1**[3]

-445 **4** *3¾* **Vanquisher (IRE)**[9] 3630 4-9-4 66 StephenDonohoe 2 61
(Ian Williams) *chsd ldrs: effrt over 3f out: outpcd by ldng pair over 2f out: wknd over 1f out* **13/2**

0040 **5** *25* **Don Jose (USA)**[6] 3756 5-8-2 57 oh12 (e) StacyRenwick(7) 8 22
(N J Vaughan) *in rr: rdn 4f out: lost tch over 3f out* **16/1**

02-0 **6** *58* **Lyon's Hill**[29] 1814 4-8-2 57 oh8 KMay(7) 4 —
(M Mullineaux) *racd off the pce: nigged along 9f out: lost tch 6f out: t.o* **33/1**

010 **7** *4½* **Rock 'N' Roller (FR)**[20] 3296 4-10-0 76 DO'Donohoe 3 —
(W R Muir) *chsd ldrs: rdn 7f out: wknd over 3f out: virtually p.u fnl f* **4/1**[2]

3m 28.65s (-1.25) **Going Correction** +0.125s/f (Good) **7** Ran SP% **116.5**
Speed ratings (Par 105): **108,107,104,102,90 61,58**
toteswinger: 1&2 £3.90, 1&3 £1.90, 2&3 £5.90. CSF £15.71 CT £44.96 TOTE £2.10: £1.40, £4.30; EX 16.40.

Owner D W Watson **Bred** Norman Cheng And Tony Feng **Trained** Cotebrook, Cheshire

FOCUS

A smallish field and the front pair held those positions virtually throughout, but this produced an enthralling finish. The favourite set a solid enough pace which made it a proper stamina test and it certainly proved too much for several of these. The form has been rated cautiously with little solid behind the front pair.

3951 TOTESPORTGAMES.COM APPRENTICE H'CAP — 7f 122y

5:20 (5:21) (Class 5) (0-70,65) 4-Y-O+ — **£3,885** (£1,156; £577; £288) **Stalls** Low

Form / RPR

0033 **1** **Harare**[7] 3738 7-9-7 62 (v) RussellKennemore 10 78
(R J Price) *hld up: hdwy on outside 2f out: edgd lft and led ins fnl f: drew clr towards fin* **8/1**

2050 **2** *4½* **Glenridding**[12] 3563 4-9-6 64 ShaneCreighton(3) 9 69
(J G Given) *sn led: rdn over 1f out: bmpd and hdd ins fnl f: no ex towards fin* **14/1**

0664 **3** *3¼* **Tanforan**[6] 3757 6-9-1 56 JamieJones 4 58+
(B P J Baugh) *midfield: n.m.r and hmpd over 2f out: swtchd rt over 1f out to make prog: r.o ins fnl f: nt rch front 2* **13/2**[3]

0000 **4** *¾* **Princely Ted (IRE)**[19] 3321 7-8-11 52 NicolPolli 7 47
(W Clay) *chsd ldrs: n.m.r over 2f out: bmpd over 1f out: styd on same pce ins fnl f* **22/1**

2000 **5** *2* **Sands Of Barra (IRE)**[15] 3431 5-9-5 65 ClGillies(5) 1 55
(I W McInnes) *broke wl: chsd ldr: rdn over 2f out: lost 2nd over 1f out: wknd ins fnl f* **8/1**

0032 **6** *1¾* **Just Oscar (GER)**[15] 3431 4-8-7 53 RossAtkinson(5) 6 38
(W M Brisbourne) *bmpd s: midfield: effrt over 2f out: one pce fr over 1f out* **10/3**[2]

4000 **7** *1* **Vanatina (IRE)**[9] 3624 4-8-5 46 oh1 MarcHalford 5 29
(W M Brisbourne) *chsd ldrs: rdn over 2f out: wknd ins fnl f* **22/1**

033 **8** *¾* **Reveur**[15] 3431 5-8-4 50 KMay(5) 13 31
(M Mullineaux) *hld up: pushed along over 2f out: carried sltly wd whn u.p over 1f out: nvr able to trble ldrs* **12/1**

4-00 **9** *½* **Regal Dream (IRE)**[31] 2950 6-8-9 50 DuranFentiman 16 30
(J W Unett) *hld up: n.m.r over 3f out: rdn over 2f out: plugged on wout troubling leraders fnl f* **33/1**

/0-0 **10** *¾* **Plush**[11] 3583 5-8-12 58 RobbieEgan(5) 14 36
(D Flood) *racd keenly in rr: shkn up 1f out: rdn ins fnl f: nvr on terms* **33/1**

0-50 **11** *4½* **Smart Pick**[15] 3431 5-8-3 49 (p) StacyRenwick(5) 17 16
(Mrs L Williamson) *s.i.s: bhd: rdn over 2f out: nvr on terms* **40/1**

0200 **12** *2¼* **Ensign's Trick**[11] 3593 4-8-8 52 JackDean(3) 8 13
(W M Brisbourne) *chsd ldrs: hung rt fr over 5f out: rdn and wknd over 1f out* **16/1**

6006 **13** *2¾* **Mister Benji**[8] 3691 9-8-0 46 oh1 SoniaEaton(5) 12 —
(B P J Baugh) *chsd ldrs on outside: lost pl over 4f out: sn bhd* **28/1**

0-51 **14** *½* **Derricks Dotty**[6] 3757 4-9-4 64 6ex (vt) SimonPearce(5) 3 17
(N J Vaughan) *chsd ldrs: rdn and wkng whn n.m.r 2f out* **11/4**[1]

1m 33.79s (-0.01) **Going Correction** +0.125s/f (Good) **14** Ran SP% **126.0**
Speed ratings (Par 103): **105,100,97,96,94 92,91,91,90,89 85,83,80,79**
toteswinger: 1&2 £16.10, 1&3 £9.30, 2&3 £20.70. CSF £110.10 CT £808.05 TOTE £10.70: £2.90, £4.90, £2.50; EX 122.00 Place 6 £47.52, Place 5 £21.02.

Owner Mrs P A Wallis **Bred** Limestone Stud **Trained** Ullingswick, H'fords

FOCUS

A modest but competitive apprentice handicap even with the three non-runners and a serious pace set by the eventual runner-up. Once again not that many ever got into it and the winner eventually dotted up. The winner was taking a big step forward but the solid runner-up and third suggest the form is sound.

Tanforan Official explanation: jockey said gelding was denied a clear run

Ensign's Trick Official explanation: jockey said filly hung badly right

T/Plt: £107.90 to a £1 stake. Pool: £103,323.62. 698.90 winning tickets. T/Qpdt: £24.90 to a £1 stake. Pool: £4,812.80. 142.55 winning tickets. DO

[3576] HAMILTON (R-H)

Saturday, July 12

OFFICIAL GOING: Good to soft

Rail realignment around the loop reduced advertised distances on round course by circa 25yards.

Wind: Almost nil Weather: Overcast

3952 LORD ADVOCATE APPRENTICE RIDERS' H'CAP (ROUND 2) 6f 5y

6:10 (6:13) (Class 6) (0-60,58) 3-Y-0+ **£2,388** (£705; £352) **Stalls** Centre

Form				RPR
0413	1		**Mandalay King (IRE)**[6] 3753 3-8-6 **50** JohnCavanagh(5) 3 (Mrs Marjorie Fife) *prom: led over 1f out: edgd lft ins fnl f: kpt on strly* **2/1**[1]	65
0200	2	2	**Imperial Sword**[5] 3789 5-9-8 **58** (b) DeanHeslop(3) 2 (T D Barron) *dwlt: t.k.h and sn in tch: effrt and chsd wnr over 1f out: kpt on same pce ins fnl f* **3/1**[2]	68
	3	5	**Rebecca's Pride (IRE)**[266] 6347 5-8-12 **45** PatrickDonaghy 6 (John C McConnell, Ire) *missed break: bhd tl kpt on fr 2f out: no ch w first two* **12/1**	39
6253	4	1	**Obe One**[6] 3759 8-8-7 **45** KrishGundowry(5) 9 (A Berry) *cl up tl rdn and no ex wl over 1f out* **5/1**[3]	36
000-	5	6	**Sydneyroughdiamond**[288] 5782 6-8-7 **45** GarryWhillans(5) 5 (M Mullineaux) *prom: outpcd 1/2-way: no imp fr 2f out* **20/1**	17
0600	6	2 ¾	**Spinning Game**[37] 2748 4-8-7 **47** ow2 (b) MJMurphy(7) 1 (Mrs R A Carr) *led to edgd rt and hdd over 1f out: sn btn* **14/1**	10
5050	7	nse	**Afton View (IRE)**[56] 2189 3-9-2 **58** ow1 RyanMania(3) 10 (S Parr) *unruly in paddock: cl up tl hung lft and wknd fr over 2f out* **10/1**	20
000-	8	1 ½	**Vondova**[286] 5836 6-8-7 **45** PaulPickard(5) 7 (D A Nolan) *prom to 1/2-way: sn rdn and btn* **25/1**	—
3060	9	3	**Union Jack Jackson (IRE)**[8] 3691 6-8-12 **45** (b) MarkCoumbe 4 (John A Harris) *sn shuffled towards rr: hung rt 1/2-way: nvr on terms* **7/1**	—
-060	10	2 ½	**Senora Lenorah**[11] 3577 4-8-7 **45** (t) JamesRogers(5) 12 (D A Nolan) *midfield: outpcd after 2f: no ch after* **100/1**	—
0-00	11	14	**Mister Marmaduke**[5] 3787 7-8-12 **45** GaryBartley 11 (D A Nolan) *dwlt: a bhd* **100/1**	—
5060	12	13	**Wickedish**[6] 3764 4-8-10 **48** (t) SamuelDrury(5) 13 (M J Gingell) *virtually ref to r: t.o thrght* **33/1**	—

1m 14.52s (2.32) **Going Correction** +0.40s/f (Good)
WFA 3 from 4yo+ 6lb 12 Ran SP% **124.5**
Speed ratings (Par 101): **100,97,90,89,81 77,77,75,71,68 49,32**
toteswinger: 1&2 £5.20, 1&3 £5.10, 2&3 £7.10. CSF £7.95 CT £60.08 TOTE £3.30: £1.50, £1.90, £2.30; EX 9.50.
Owner Green Lane **Bred** Forenaghts Stud And Dermot Cantillon **Trained** Stillington, N Yorks

FOCUS

A low-grade handicap in which the field fanned across the course but the two market leaders, who pulled clear, ended up on the stands' side. The runner-up sets the standard but not a race to be positive about.

3953 JOHN BANKS MAIDEN (S) STKS 5f 4y

6:40 (6:42) (Class 6) 3-Y-0+ **£2,388** (£705; £352) **Stalls** Centre

Form				RPR
3500	1		**Johnston's Glory (IRE)**[30] 2966 4-8-11 54 (p) AndrewMullen(3) 6 (E J Alston) *hld up: hdwy over 2f out: styd on u.p to ld nr fin* **9/4**[1]	54
0050	2	nk	**Violet's Pride**[22] 3231 4-9-0 43 KimTinkler 4 (N Tinkler) *sn prom: rdn to ld over 1f out: kpt on: hdd nr fin* **8/1**	53
03-	3	½	**Glenveagh (IRE)**[328] 4636 3-8-9 0 NeilBrown(5) 7 (K A Ryan) *prom: effrt and ev ch over 1f out: kpt on: no ex wl ins fnl f* **5/2**[2]	54
0000	4	4 ½	**Saafend Geezer**[12] 3549 3-9-0 52 (v) PaulMulrennan 1 (A Berry) *dwlt: bhd tl styd on fr 2f out: nvr rchd ldrs* **17/2**	38
4540	5	1 ¾	**Gelert (IRE)**[16] 3395 3-9-0 48 PatrickMathers 8 (Peter Grayson) *in tch: outpcd after 2f: rallied 2f out: no imp* **5/1**[3]	32
0	6	2	**Mensadil**[47] 2455 3-9-0 0 TonyHamilton 9 (Mrs L Stubbs) *midfield: outpcd and hung rt 1/2-way: sn no imp* **20/1**	24
0000	7	2 ½	**Sokoke**[11] 3581 7-9-0 35 (p) GaryBartley(5) 2 (D A Nolan) *led to over 1f out: hung rt and sn btn* **80/1**	17
00	8	5	**Ourbelle**[15] 3452 3-8-9 0 PaulFessey 12 (Miss Tracy Waggott) *prom far side 2f: sn struggling* **50/1**	—
60-0	9	1 ½	**Head To Head (IRE)**[39] 2703 4-9-5 47 (b) DanielTudhope 11 (A D Brown) *spd far side to 2f out: wknd qckly* **16/1**	—
00	10	¾	**Portugal**[7] 3712 3-8-5 0 ow1 MarkCoumbe(5) 13 (T J Etherington) *sn outpcd far side: nvr on terms* **28/1**	—
0000	11	16	**Deer Park Lord**[11] 3577 4-8-12 1 (t) PaulPickard(7) 10 (D A Nolan) *sn wl bhd: nvr on terms* **250/1**	—

62.59 secs (2.59) **Going Correction** +0.40s/f (Good)
WFA 3 from 4yo+ 5lb 11 Ran SP% **115.3**
Speed ratings (Par 101): **95,94,93,86,83 80,76,68,66,64 39**
toteswinger: 1&2 £7.80, 1&3 £2.30, 2&3 £7.80. CSF £19.72 TOTE £3.70: £1.20, £1.80, £1.50; EX 20.50.There was no bid for the winner.
Owner The Good Shepherds **Bred** Gerard Keane **Trained** Longton, Lancs

FOCUS

A weak event, even by selling standards. The pace was sound and the first three pulled clear but the form looks dubious although the winner is rated to her best post-juvenile form.

3954 CALL SCOTBET ON 0800 461061 CLAIMING STKS 1m 3f 16y

7:10 (7:10) (Class 6) 4-Y-0+ **£2,388** (£705; £352) **Stalls** High

Form				RPR
2431	1		**Little Jimbob**[26] 3077 7-8-12 73 TonyHamilton 7 (R A Fahey) *set modest pce: rdn 2f out: hld on wl fnl f* **4/6**[1]	58
134	2	½	**Princelywallywogan**[7] 3711 6-9-0 67 MarkCoumbe(5) 5 (John A Harris) *plld hrd: hld up in tch: effrt over 1f out: chsd wnr ins fnl f: kpt on towards fin* **9/4**[2]	64
42	3	1 ¾	**Pendragon (USA)**[36] 2776 5-8-8 0 AndrewMullen(3) 8 (Mrs L B Normile) *trckd ldrs: rdn over 3f out: rallied over 1f out: one pce ins fnl f* **6/1**[3]	53
0040	4	3 ¾	**Jordan's Light (USA)**[6] 3756 5-9-2 56 ow2 RyanMania(7) 1 (P Monteith) *pressed wnr: rdn over 2f out: wknd ins fnl f* **20/1**	59

2m 31.0s (5.40) **Going Correction** +0.275s/f (Good) 4 Ran SP% **109.8**
Speed ratings (Par 101): **91,90,89,86**
toteswinger: 1&2 £2.40. CSF £2.48 TOTE £1.70; EX 2.30.Pendragon was claimed by Brian Ellison for £10,000.
Owner Dale Scaffolding Co Ltd **Bred** D R Tucker **Trained** Musley Bank, N Yorks

FOCUS

An uncompetitive event with four non-runners and a steady pace resulted in a moderate winning time, even for a claimer. The form is dubious with the front pair below their best and the third and fourth better guides.

3955 THE SUNDAY MAIL MEDIAN AUCTION MAIDEN STKS 5f 4y

7:40 (7:42) (Class 6) 3-Y-O **£2,266** (£674; £337; £168) **Stalls** Centre

Form				RPR
5062	1		**Foreign Rhythm (IRE)**[7] 3712 3-8-12 53 (v) KimTinkler 8 (N Tinkler) *sn outpcd: hdwy over 1f out: led ins fnl f: pushed out* **5/1**[3]	56
0442	2	1 ¼	**Paddy Jack**[4] 3811 3-9-3 60 (p) TonyHamilton 2 (J R Weymes) *w ldrs: rdn and hung rt fr 2f out: chsd wnr ins fnl f: r.o* **5/1**[3]	57
0-02	3	¾	**Ubenkor (IRE)**[21] 3282 3-9-3 70 PaulMulrennan 4 (B Smart) *w ldrs tl rdn and nt qckn fnl f* **9/4**[2]	54
0-	4	1 ½	**Ridley Didley (IRE)**[296] 5550 3-9-3 0 DanielTudhope 1 (N Wilson) *t.k.h bhd ldrs: led 1/2-way to ins fnl f: sn no ex* **11/1**	48
-503	5	½	**President Elect (IRE)**[21] 3282 3-8-12 70 NeilBrown(5) 7 (T D Barron) *plld hrd: prom: drvn and outpcd 1/2-way: no imp fnl f* **15/8**[1]	47
00	6	10	**Lydia's Legacy**[7] 3712 3-8-7 0 MarkCoumbe(5) 3 (T J Etherington) *led to 1/2-way: sn struggling* **28/1**	6
	7	16	**Idle Court** 3-8-12 0 PatrickMathers 6 (Bruce Hellier) *s.s: nvr on terms* **50/1**	—
6-	8	10	**Becky Quick (IRE)**[292] 5675 3-8-7 0 GaryBartley(5) 5 (Bruce Hellier) *prom 2f: sn struggling* **50/1**	—

62.70 secs (2.70) **Going Correction** +0.40s/f (Good) 8 Ran SP% **114.6**
Speed ratings (Par 98): **94,92,90,88,87 71,46,30**
toteswinger: 1&2 £2.60, 1&3 £1.02, 2&3 £6.60. CSF £29.66 TOTE £5.80: £1.60, £1.80, £1.30; EX 28.00.
Owner Hard Times Partnership **Bred** Yeomanstown Stud **Trained** Langton, N Yorks

FOCUS

An uncompetitive maiden in which the two market leaders were disappointing to varying degrees. The runner-up to recent form looks the best guide.

Idle Court Official explanation: jockey said filly froze in the stalls

3956 THE SUNDAY MAIL H'CAP 5f 4y

8:15 (8:15) (Class 4) (0-80,82) 3-Y-0+ **£6,476** (£1,927; £963; £481) **Stalls** Centre

Form				RPR
0002	1		**Rasaman (IRE)**[11] 3594 4-9-0 **69** (t) NeilBrown(5) 8 (K A Ryan) *mde all: rdn over 1f out: hrd pressed ins fnl f: kpt on gamely* **7/1**	83
0522	2	¾	**Rothesay Dancer**[5] 3787 5-8-10 **65** KellyHarrison(5) 2 (J S Goldie) *t.k.h in tch: hdwy and edgd rt over 1f out: ev ch ins fnl f: no ex towards fin* **2/1**[1]	76
5031	3	3 ¼	**Howards Tipple**[11] 3577 4-8-11 **61** (p) TonyHamilton 6 (Miss L A Perratt) *prom: drvn and edgd lft over 1f out: kpt on fnl f: nt rch first two* **9/2**[2]	60
2101	4	1 ½	**Dickie Le Davoir**[4] 3812 4-9-13 **82** 6ex MarkCoumbe(5) 9 (John A Harris) *towards rr on outside: hdwy wl over 1f out: no imp fnl f* **9/2**[2]	76
000-	5	nk	**Chookie Heiton (IRE)**[313] 5083 10-9-11 **75** PaulFessey 3 (Miss L A Perratt) *w wnr tl rdn and no ex over 1f out* **16/1**	68
0040	6	1	**Blazing Heights**[5] 3787 5-9-7 **76** (p) GaryBartley(5) 5 (J S Goldie) *t.k.h: hld up: pushed along whn hmpd over 1f out: n.d after* **6/1**[3]	65+
040	7	nse	**Methaaly (IRE)**[9] 3626 5-8-9 **66** DeanHeslop(7) 7 (M Mullineaux) *prom tl rdn and wknd wl over 1f out* **12/1**	55
5-00	8	¾	**Tous Les Deux**[11] 3585 5-8-7 **57** oh1 PatrickMathers 1 (Peter Grayson) *prom tl rdn and outpcd fr over 2f out* **18/1**	43

61.30 secs (1.30) **Going Correction** +0.40s/f (Good) 8 Ran SP% **115.3**
Speed ratings (Par 105): **105,103,98,96,95 94,94,92**
toteswinger: 1&2 £3.00, 1&3 £7.10, 2&3 £1.40. CSF £21.65 CT £71.47 TOTE £8.30: £2.40, £1.30, £1.70; EX 18.40.
Owner Royston Vasey **Bred** Rasana Partnership **Trained** Hambleton, N Yorks

■ Stewards' Enquiry : Patrick Mathers one-day ban: failed to ride to draw (Jul 27)
Kelly Harrison caution: careless riding

FOCUS

A run-of-the-mill sprint in which the pace was fair and the solid runner-up sets the standard. The winner is the type to score again for Kevin Ryan.

3957 SCOTBET.COM H'CAP (QUALIFIER FOR THE RBS SCOTTISH TROPHY HANDICAP SERIES FINAL) 1m 65y

8:45 (8:46) (Class 5) (0-75,80) 3-Y-0+ **£3,885** (£1,156; £577; £288) **Stalls** High

Form				RPR
2311	1		**El Dececy (USA)**[7] 3738 4-9-12 **80** KrishGundowry(7) 4 (S Parr) *mde all: c to stands' side ent st: kpt on strly fnl 2f: unchal* **13/2**	92
0054	2	4 ½	**Feisty Royale**[7] 3716 3-9-2 **72** GregFairley 5 (M Johnston) *hld up in tch: rdn over 3f out: kpt on to take 2nd towards fin: no ch w wnr* **4/1**[2]	72
5211	3	½	**Zabeel Tower**[15] 3431 5-9-8 **69** (p) TonyHamilton 8 (R Allan) *prom: effrt and chsd wnr over 2f out: sn rdn: no ex fnl f: lost 2nd nr fin* **5/1**	70
3102	4	1 ¼	**Chin Wag (IRE)**[6] 3755 4-8-13 **60** (p) DanielTudhope 11 (J S Goldie) *hld up: effrt over 2f out: kpt on fnl f: nvr able to chal* **11/4**[1]	58
001-	5	¾	**Primo Way**[82] 4496 7-9-1 **67** (p) MarkCoumbe(5) 3 (Miss L A Perratt) *stdd s: hdwy over 2f out: nvr able to chal* **25/1**	63
-056	6	10	**Emerald Bay (IRE)**[6] 3758 6-9-12 **73** (p) PaulFessey 7 (Miss L A Perratt) *cl up: c to stands' side w wnr ent st: hung rt and wknd over 2f out* **12/1**	46
6323	7	1 ¼	**Hawkit (USA)**[11] 3579 7-9-6 **72** NeilBrown(5) 9 (P Monteith) *hld up: rdn 3f out: btn fnl 2f* **9/2**[3]	42
0426	8	18	**Seyaadi**[15] 3450 6-9-0 **61** (v) PaulMulrennan 1 (Miss Tracy Waggott) *cl up tl rdn and wknd over 2f out* **14/1**	—

1m 49.95s (1.55) **Going Correction** +0.275s/f (Good)
WFA 3 from 4yo+ 9lb 8 Ran SP% **113.1**
Speed ratings (Par 103): **103,98,98,96,96 86,84,66**
toteswinger: 1&2 £11.50, 1&3 £4.20, 2&3 £6.90. CSF £31.87 CT £139.89 TOTE £8.00: £2.50, £1.30, £2.00; EX 25.40.
Owner Willie McKay **Bred** Shadwell Farm LLC **Trained** Bawtry, S Yorks

FOCUS

A fair handicap run at a reasonable gallop and one in which the winner elected to race towards the stands' side in the home straight. He recorded a personal best with the placed horses to their latest marks.

Seyaadi Official explanation: jockey said gelding hung right

3958 FAIR FRIDAY IN THE DIARY H'CAP — 1m 65y
9:15 (9:17) (Class 6) (0-60,58) 3-Y-O — **£2,388** (£705; £352) **Stalls** High

Form — RPR

5022 **1** **Natural Rhythm (IRE)**[15] 3436 3-8-11 **51**.................(b) DanielTudhope 7 — 58
(Mrs R A Carr) *mde all: rdn 2f out: kpt on wl fnl f* — **2/1**[1]

4045 **2** 2 1/4 **Casino Night**[5] 3790 3-8-13 **58**.....................................(p) NeilBrown(5) 8 — 60
(J R Weymes) *cl up: effrt and chsd wnr over 2f out: one pce fnl f* — **9/2**[3]

0300 **3** 7 **Champagne Lawn (USA)**[4] 3816 3-8-10 **57**............(v[1]) DeanHeslop(7) 6 — 43
(T D Barron) *pressed wnr: outpcd over 3f out: rallied 2f out: sn no imp* — **16/1**

0000 **4** 4 **Ace Of Spies (IRE)**[18] 3339 3-9-0 **54**.................................. GregFairley 5 — 31
(M Johnston) *prom: drvn and outpcd 3f out: edgd rt and sn n.d* — **3/1**[2]

6-06 **5** nk **Safari Dancer (IRE)**[11] 3578 3-8-13 **53**.....................(b[1]) PaulMulrennan 4 — 29
(Miss L A Perratt) *t.k.h: in tch: effrt over 3f out: wknd fr 2f out* — **8/1**

0-50 **6** 3 1/2 **Noche De Reyes**[30] 2966 3-8-8 **53**............................. MarkCoumbe(5) 1 — 21
(E J Alston) *bhd: shortlived effrt over 3f out: wknd fr over 2f out* — **25/1**

000 **7** 3/4 **Jordi Roper (IRE)**[50] 2380 3-9-4 **58**........................... DarrenWilliams 2 — 24
(S Parr) *hld up: smooth hdwy over 3f out: rdn and wknd 2f out* — **7/1**

1m 50.85s (2.45) **Going Correction** +0.275s/f (Good) — **7** Ran SP% **123.2**
Speed ratings (Par 98): **98,95,88,84,84 80,80**
toteswinger: 1&2 £1.10, 1&3 £9.90, 2&3 £9.10. CSF £10.19 CT £81.45 TOTE £2.60: £2.00, £2.20; EX 11.90 Place 6 £18.34, Place 5 £12.03.
Owner Michael Hill **Bred** Mark Commins **Trained** Stillington, N Yorks
■ Marie Camargo was withdrawn after becoming upset in the stalls. Rule 4 applies, deduct 10p in the £.

FOCUS
A low-grade handicap in which the pace was just fair but the form is sound rated around the first two to their recent marks.
T/Plt: £13.10 to a £1 stake. Pool: £60,356.36. 3,340.26 winning tickets. T/Qpdt: £7.10 to a £1 stake. Pool: £4,498.80. 465.10 winning tickets. RY

3882 NOTTINGHAM (L-H)
Saturday, July 12

OFFICIAL GOING: Good to soft (soft in places; 6.9)
Dolling out added 5yards to advertised distances on round course.
Wind: Light, across Weather: Overcast

3959 EUROPEAN BREEDERS' FUND MAIDEN FILLIES' STKS — 6f 15y
2:00 (2:01) (Class 5) 2-Y-O — **£3,885** (£1,156; £577; £288) **Stalls** High

Form — RPR

3 **1** **Sneak Preview**[28] 3027 2-9-0 0.................................... RichardMullen 11 — 86+
(E S McMahon) *chsd ldrs tl led 2f out: rdn and hung lft fr over 1f out: styd on wl: eased nr fin* — **11/2**[2]

55 **2** 6 **Azwa**[17] 3373 2-9-0 0.. OscarUrbina 14 — 68
(E A L Dunlop) *prom: rdn over 1f out: wknd ins fnl f* — **33/1**

40 **3** 1/2 **One Cool Kitty**[7] 3734 2-8-11 0........................... DominicFox(3) 12 — 67
(M G Quinlan) *stdd s: hld up: hdwy 2f out: nt rch ldrs* — **40/1**

4 hd **Surprise Party** 2-8-9 0.. JackMitchell(5) 9 — 66
(C F Wall) *hld up: hdwy over 1f out: nrst fin* — **40/1**

26 **5** 3/4 **Coconut Shy**[11] 3584 2-9-0 0.. LPKeniry 2 — 64
(G Prodromou) *racd alone far side: w ldrs: rdn over 1f out: wknd ins fnl f* — **100/1**

6 3 1/2 **The Legal Blonde (IRE)** 2-9-0 0........................... RichardKingscote 1 — 53+
(Tom Dascombe) *sn outpcd: styd on ins fnl f: nvr nrr* — **28/1**

62 **7** 2 **Select (IRE)**[14] 3496 2-9-0 0.. TPQueally 17 — 47
(P W Chapple-Hyam) *led 4f: sn hung lft and wknd* — **4/7**[1]

5 **8** 1 1/2 **Kapowee**[31] 2924 2-9-0 0.. NeilPollard 13 — 43
(W J Musson) *hld up: nvr nr to chal* — **100/1**

9 nk **Ever Loved (USA)** 2-9-0 0..................................... RoystonFfrench 7 — 42
(Saeed Bin Suroor) *prom: rdn over 2f out: sn wknd* — **11/1**

0 **10** 3/4 **Franchesca's Gold**[28] 3027 2-8-11 0........................ JamesMillman(3) 8 — 40
(B R Millman) *chsd ldr: rdn and hung lft over 2f out: sn wknd* — **66/1**

11 1 1/2 **Prom** 2-9-0 0.. TWilliams 4 — 35
(M Brittain) *sn outpcd: in rr whn hung lft over 2f out* — **100/1**

12 1 1/4 **Red Kyte** 2-9-0 0... PatDobbs 10 — 31
(K A Ryan) *dwlt: hdwy over 3f out: hung lft and wknd fr 1/2-way* — **8/1**[3]

13 7 **Royal Superlative** 2-9-0 0.. SebSanders 3 — 10
(R M Beckett) *mid-div: sn pushed along: hung lft thrght: wknd fr 1/2-way* — **16/1**

05 **14** 2 **Daanaat (IRE)**[21] 3254 2-9-0 0..................................... SamHitchcott 15 — —
(M R Channon) *prom to 1/2-way* — **33/1**

1m 16.05s (0.95) **Going Correction** +0.075s/f (Good) — **14** Ran SP% **123.0**
Speed ratings (Par 91): **96,88,87,87,86 81,78,76,76,75 73,71,62,59**
toteswinger: 1&2 £23.60, 1&3 £47.10, 2&3 £47.10. CSF £180.35 TOTE £5.60: £2.00, £6.30, £6.40; EX 115.20.
Owner J C Fretwell **Bred** S Kimberley **Trained** Lichfield, Staffs

FOCUS
An average fillies' maiden which saw an easy winner, who produced a big step up and can rate higher. The favourite failed to run her race, so the form looks best rated around the runner-up.

NOTEBOOK
Sneak Preview confirmed the promise of her debut third at Leicester four weeks previously and eventually ran out a facile winner. She is clearly improving fast, looked well suited to this softer ground, and looks the sort her connections will now go in search of some valuable black type with. (op 5-1 tchd 4-1)
Azwa, fifth on his two previous outings, was ridden with a bit more patience this time and had her chance only to be firmly put in her place by the easy winner. This rates her best effort yet and she is now eligible for a nursery mark, where she may well enjoy a step up in trip. (op 28-1)
One Cool Kitty came back to form with a fair effort in defeat, doing her best work towards the finish on this return to 6f, and looks one to be more interested in again now that she is qualified for a mark.
Surprise Party, related to winners over various distances, showed ability on this racecourse debut without ever looking like getting seriously involved from off the pace. Her yard has made a bright start with the few juveniles they have run this term and she looks sure to come on a bundle for the experience. (tchd 50-1)
The Legal Blonde(IRE), related to winners at up to 1m, ran too green for her own good through the first half of the race yet caught the eye as the penny eventually dropped. She can be expected to prove a good bit sharper next time. Official explanation: jockey said filly ran very green (tchd 33-1)
Select(IRE), a runner-up in Listed company a fortnight previously, was given an aggressive ride yet it was clear soon after passing the 2f pole that she was in trouble. This was clearly not her true running and the much easier ground was probably to blame. Official explanation: trainer's rep said filly was unsuited by the good to soft (soft in places) ground (op evs tchd 11-10)

Red Kyte Official explanation: jockey said filly hung badly left

3960 LES STONE MEMORIAL H'CAP — 6f 15y
2:35 (2:35) (Class 6) (0-65,65) 3-Y-O — **£2,914** (£867; £433; £216) **Stalls** High

Form — RPR

-021 **1** **Lady Carollina**[7] 3727 3-9-7 **65**.................................. RichardMullen 10 — 73
(Rae Guest) *racd stands' side: mid-div: sn pushed along: hdwy 2f out: nt clr run and swtchd lft over 1f out: hung lft and r.o u.p to ld post* — **3/1**[1]

0165 **2** hd **Moonage Daydream (IRE)**[21] 3280 3-9-6 **64**...................(b) TPQueally 3 — 71
(T D Easterby) *racd far side: overall ldr: rdn and hung rt fr over 1f out: hdd post* — **10/1**

1504 **3** 1/2 **Just Jimmy (IRE)**[4] 3825 3-9-0 **58**........................... CatherineGannon 1 — 63
(P D Evans) *racd far side: chsd ldr: rdn over 2f out: hung rt fr over 1f out: r.o* — **10/1**

4400 **4** 3/4 **Billy Hot Rocks (IRE)**[7] 3731 3-9-2 **60**.............................. SebSanders 9 — 63
(R M Beckett) *racd stands' side: trckd ldrs: led that gp over 1f out: sn rdn and hung lft: styd on* — **8/1**[3]

602 **5** 4 **Virtuality (USA)**[15] 3438 3-9-4 **62**.............................. RoystonFfrench 17 — 52
(B Smart) *led stands' side gp over 4f: sn hung lft: wknd ins fnl f* — **9/2**[2]

-100 **6** 1 **Berrymead**[16] 3416 3-9-3 **61**...(b[1]) LPKeniry 2 — 48
(M W Easterby) *racd stands' side: chsd ldrs: rdn over 2f out: wknd fnl f* — **28/1**

0055 **7** nse **Nawaaff**[14] 3499 3-9-7 **65**.. SamHitchcott 6 — 52
(M R Channon) *racd stands' side: chsd ldrs: rdn over 1f out: wknd fnl f* — **10/1**

2500 **8** hd **Lujiana**[28] 3050 3-8-6 **57**..................................... MatthewLawson(7) 5 — 43
(M Brittain) *racd far side: chsd ldrs: rdn over 2f out: hung rt over 1f out: wknd fnl f* — **16/1**

0-06 **9** 1/2 **Archilini**[13] 3526 3-9-2 **60**.. VinceSlattery 13 — 45
(M Sheppard) *racd stands' side: prom: outpcd 1/2-way: swtchd lft and hdwy over 2f out: sn rdn: hung lft and wknd over 1f out* — **33/1**

5004 **10** shd **Merrion Tiger (IRE)**[11] 3592 3-8-8 **59**..................... DeclanCannon(7) 14 — 43
(K R Burke) *racd stands' side: hld up: n.d* — **8/1**[3]

0464 **11** 1 **Apple Pie Order (IRE)**[17] 3381 3-9-2 **65**........................ MCGeran(5) 15 — 46
(R J Hodges) *racd stands' side: hld up: rdn and wknd over 1f out* — **9/1**

6514 **12** 2 **Mujahope**[8] 3686 3-9-0 **58**..(v) OscarUrbina 11 — 33
(C J Teague) *racd stands' side: s.s: outpcd* — **12/1**

4000 **13** 1 1/4 **Solemn**[4] 3819 3-9-1 **59**.. J-PGuillambert 12 — 30
(J M Bradley) *racd stands' side: chsd ldrs over 4f* — **50/1**

1600 **14** 1 1/2 **Straight (IRE)**[4] 3819 3-9-2 **60**... TWilliams 7 — 26
(M Brittain) *racd stands' side: chsd ldrs: rdn over 1f out: sn wknd* — **33/1**

0-00 **15** 18 **Starlight Girl**[22] 3230 3-9-4 **62**......................................(b[1]) LeeEnstone 4 — —
(T D Easterby) *racd far side: wnt rt s: outpcd: eased fnl f* — **33/1**

1m 15.8s (0.70) **Going Correction** +0.075s/f (Good) — **15** Ran SP% **130.5**
Speed ratings (Par 98): **98,97,97,96,90 89,89,89,88,88 86,84,82,80,56**
toteswinger: 1&2 £12.70, 1&3 £13.90, 2&3 £30.30. CSF £35.35 CT £294.97 TOTE £4.00: £1.40, £4.40, £3.00; EX 47.00.
Owner L J Vaessen **Bred** Alwyn Moss & Leon Vaessen **Trained** Newmarket, Suffolk

FOCUS
A modest sprint for three-year-olds but the winner was one of few on the upgrade. The draw looked to hold no real advantage and the first four came clear.
Virtuality(USA) Official explanation: jockey said filly stopped very quickly
Merrion Tiger(IRE) Official explanation: jockey said colt was unsuited by the good to soft (soft in places) ground
Starlight Girl Official explanation: jockey said filly slipped leaving stalls and never travelled

3961 NOTTINGHAM EVENING POST NURSERY — 5f 13y
3:10 (3:12) (Class 5) 2-Y-O — **£3,238** (£963; £481; £240) **Stalls** High

Form — RPR

0512 **1** **Alphabeth**[1] 3910 2-7-13 **66** ow6................................... MCGeran(5) 4 — 66
(M R Channon) *led early: chsd ldr: rdn over 1f out: led ins fnl f: r.o* — **11/4**[2]

441 **2** 1 **Bahamian Ceilidh**[28] 3032 2-8-12 **77**........................ JamesMillman(3) 3 — 73
(B R Millman) *stmbld s: sn rcvrd to ld: rdn and hdd ins fnl f: styd on same pce* — **10/11**[1]

5134 **3** 5 **River Rye (IRE)**[14] 3470 2-9-0 **83**............................ CharlesEddery(7) 1 — 61
(R Hannon) *chsd ldrs: rdn over 1f out: hung rt and wknd fnl f* — **5/1**[3]

0350 **4** 1 1/2 **Magical Illusion**[9] 3651 2-8-2 **64**........................... CatherineGannon 7 — 37
(P D Evans) *sn outpcd* — **14/1**

62.22 secs (1.52) **Going Correction** +0.075s/f (Good) — **4** Ran SP% **102.4**
Speed ratings (Par 94): **90,88,80,78**
toteswinger: 1&2 £3.00 CSF £5.02 TOTE £3.60; EX 5.30.
Owner The Lord Ilsley Racing Club **Bred** A C M Spalding **Trained** West Ilsley, Berks

FOCUS
A modest nursery which saw the first pair come clear. The winner is rated to her Chester mark and the form looks limited. The 'official' ratings shown next to each horse are estimated and for information purposes only.

NOTEBOOK
Alphabeth, pipped at Chester 24 hours previously, was given a positive ride by her apprentice jockey - who actually carried 6lb overweight - and readily gained compensation on this quick re-appearance. She is improving and has a good attitude, but a likely weight rise will now make her life much tougher. (op 3-1 tchd 5-2)
Bahamian Ceilidh, off the mark at Lingfield 28 days previously, was not helped by stumbling at the start and was then rushed up to take the early lead. She paid for those exertions at the business end, but this still rates a sound start to life in nurseries and the easier ground was no bother. (op 6-4 tchd 13-8)
River Rye(IRE) had her chance under top weight, but did not prove that suited to the softer ground. (op 7-2 tchd 11-2)
Magical Illusion was never going the pace and may not have enjoyed the softer ground, but does really look in need of a step back up in trip all the same. (op 9-1 tchd 8-1)

3962 JPD CONTRACTS H'CAP — 1m 6f 15y
3:40 (3:40) (Class 4) (0-80,78) 3-Y-O — **£6,476** (£1,927; £963; £481) **Stalls** Low

Form — RPR

05-3 **1** **General Ting (IRE)**[31] 2948 3-8-9 **66**................................ SebSanders 5 — 74+
(Sir Mark Prescott) *hld up: plld hrd: hdwy over 2f out: rdn to ld wl over 1f out: styd on wl* — **11/4**[1]

1455 **2** 1 3/4 **Dubai Petal (IRE)**[19] 3327 3-8-13 **70**.................................. LPKeniry 8 — 76
(J S Moore) *hld up: hdwy over 2f out: rdn and ev ch over 1f out: edgd lft: styd on same pce ins fnl f* — **13/2**

4032 **3** hd **Kiribati King (IRE)**[14] 3471 3-8-11 **68**........................... SamHitchcott 3 — 74
(M R Channon) *hld up in tch: racd keenly: rdn over 2f out: styd on* — **4/1**[3]

2-53 **4** 1 1/4 **Mushtaaq (USA)**[23] 3168 3-9-6 **77**.....................(b[1]) J-PGuillambert 7 — 81
(M A Jarvis) *chsd ldrs: rdn over 2f out: outpcd over 1f out: edgd lft and styd on ins fnl f* — **10/1**

6-06 **5** 3 1/2 **Fearless Warrior**[53] 2280 3-8-5 **62**.............................. RichardMullen 4 — 61
(J L Dunlop) *hld up: rdn over 4f out: hdwy over 2f out: wknd fnl f* — **8/1**

4-34 **6** *1 1/4* **Blue Citadel (USA)**[8] 3688 3-9-7 **78** PatDobbs 1 75
(Mrs A J Perrett) *led 12f out: rdn and hdd over 4f out: wknd over 1f out* **8/1**

5221 **7** *4 1/2* **Maria Di Scozia**[23] 3168 3-9-6 **77** TPQueally 6 68
(P W Chapple-Hyam) *led: hdd 12f out: chsd ldr tl led over 4f out: rdn and hdd wl over 1f out: sn hung lft and wknd* **3/1**[2]

-000 **8** *11* **Leitmotif (USA)**[36] 2785 3-8-2 **59** oh4 RoystonFfrench 9 35
(J L Dunlop) *chsd ldrs: rdn over 4f out: wkng whn hmpd wl over 2f out* **40/1**

3m 8.05s (0.75) **Going Correction** +0.20s/f (Good) **8** Ran SP% **118.8**
Speed ratings (Par 102): **105,104,103,103,101 100,97,91**
toteswinger: 1&2 £6.70, 1&3 £2.90, 2&3 £6.60. CSF £22.14 CT £72.30 TOTE £3.60: £1.80, £2.60, £1.10; EX 22.20.
Owner Lady Katharine Watts **Bred** R N Auld **Trained** Newmarket, Suffolk

FOCUS
A modest staying handicap for three-year-olds. The form is rated around the second and third and looks solid.

3963 KONICA MINOLTA EAST (S) STKS 1m 75y
4:15 (4:16) (Class 6) 3-4-Y-0 **£2,388** (£705; £352) **Stalls** Centre

Form RPR

-505 **1** **Josephine Malines**[8] 3662 4-9-2 60 RoystonFfrench 9 53
(Mrs A Duffield) *prom: chsd ldr 6f out: led over 2f out: sn rdn: all out* **10/1**

6050 **2** *hd* **Moorside Diamond**[39] 2707 4-9-2 44 (b[1]) OscarUrbina 1 53
(A D Brown) *unruly in stalls: chsd ldr 2f: remained handy: rdn over 2f out: swtchd lft over 1f out: hrd rdn and ev ch ins fnl f: styd on* **33/1**

0440 **3** *2 3/4* **Yakama (IRE)**[4] 3817 3-8-12 47 (b[1]) DMylonas 6 50
(G Prodromou) *s.i.s: hld up: racd keenly: hdwy over 3f out: rdn over 1f out: edgd lft and styd on same pce fnl f* **20/1**

642 **4** *1* **Five Wishes**[8] 3662 4-8-13 55 (be) PJMcDonald[(3)] 2 44+
(M Dods) *s.i.s: hld up: rdn 1/2-way: hdwy over 2f out: rdn and nt clr run over 1f out: swtchd rt ins fnl f: styd on* **3/1**[2]

0234 **5** *1 3/4* **Bilboa**[8] 3678 3-8-9 55 (p) JamesMillman[(3)] 10 43
(B R Millman) *hld up: plld hrd: hdwy 1/2-way: hung lft over 2f out: sn rdn: hung lft and wknd ins fnl f* **4/1**[3]

U4-1 **6** *1/2* **Thompsons Walls (IRE)**[26] 1823 3-9-4 82 (t) LeeEnstone 4 48
(P C Haslam) *sn led: rdn and hdd over 2f out: wknd fnl f* **15/8**[1]

0000 **7** *1/2* **Golden Brown (IRE)**[23] 3162 4-9-7 50 LPKeniry 17 43
(David Pinder) *hld up: rdn over 3f out: styd on ins fnl f: nrst fin* **16/1**

0-00 **8** *9* **Desert Rat (IRE)**[10] 3602 4-9-7 52 (v[1]) RichardMullen 5 22
(Micky Hammond) *chsd ldrs 6f* **14/1**

0 **9** *21* **Kijani (IRE)**[13] 3521 3-8-12 0 SamHitchcott 3 —
(M R Channon) *chsd ldrs: rdn 1/2-way: wknd over 2f out* **20/1**

6000 **10** *nse* **Mama Leo**[10] 3605 3-8-0 47 (b) CharlesEddery[(7)] 11 —
(J G M O'Shea) *sn pushed along: a bhd* **40/1**

11 *23* **Dungleddy Star** 3-8-7 0 CatherineGannon 8 —
(J M Bradley) *s.s: a bhd* **33/1**

1m 48.31s (2.91) **Going Correction** +0.20s/f (Good)
WFA 3 from 4yo 9lb **11** Ran SP% **119.3**
Speed ratings (Par 101): **93,92,90,89,87 86,86,77,56,56 33**
toteswinger: 1&2 £32.10, 1&3 £38.60, 2&3 £110.60. CSF £284.45 TOTE £9.90: £2.60, £7.90, £8.10; EX 193.70.The winner was bought in for £5,200.
Owner Middleham Park Racing Ix **Bred** Old Peartree Stud **Trained** Constable Burton, N Yorks
■ Stewards' Enquiry : Oscar Urbina one-day ban: careless riding (Jul 27)

FOCUS
A moderate winning time, even for a seller but the form appears sound rated through the third to form.

3964 KONICA MINOLTA EAST H'CAP 1m 75y
4:50 (4:50) (Class 5) (0-70,64) 3-Y-0+ **£3,238** (£963; £481; £240) **Stalls** Centre

Form RPR

0520 **1** **West End Lad**[7] 3738 5-9-4 **54** (b) RoystonFfrench 9 68
(S R Bowring) *chsd ldrs: led over 3f out: rdn clr fnl f* **6/1**

-045 **2** *7* **Reve Vert (FR)**[22] 3221 3-8-5 **50** CatherineGannon 2 46
(A W Carroll) *plld hrd and prom: rdn to chse wnr and hung lft over 2f out: wknd fnl f* **8/1**

525- **3** *4* **Viable**[234] 6894 6-9-10 **60** RichardMullen 8 49
(Mrs P Sly) *led: hdd 6f out: chsd ldrs: rdn over 2f out: wknd over 1f out* **9/2**[3]

1030 **4** *shd* **Shosolosa (IRE)**[2] 3866 6-9-4 **54** PAspell 6 43
(R C Guest) *hld up: sme hdwy u.p 2f out: wknd over 1f out* **15/2**

005/ **5** *2 1/4* **Out Of India**[722] 3697 6-9-4 **57** PJMcDonald[(3)] 4 40
(P T Dalton) *racd keenly: trckd ldr tl led 6f out: rdn and hdd over 3f out: wknd over 1f out* **14/1**

3-00 **6** *hd* **Zain (IRE)**[87] 1394 4-9-2 **52** (t) TPQueally 1 39+
(J G Given) *hld up: rdn over 3f out: sn hung lft: n.d* **11/4**[1]

1600 **7** *11* **Busy Man (IRE)**[16] 3422 9-8-9 **45** NelsonDeSouza 3 3
(R C Guest) *hld up: rdn and wknd over 2f out* **20/1**

5600 **8** *20* **Rain Stops Play (IRE)**[41] 2642 6-9-12 **62** SebSanders 10 —
(M Quinn) *chsd ldrs 6f* **3/1**[2]

1m 47.26s (1.86) **Going Correction** +0.20s/f (Good)
WFA 3 from 4yo+ 9lb **8** Ran SP% **118.4**
Speed ratings (Par 103): **98,91,87,86,84 84,73,53**
toteswinger: 1&2 £12.40, 1&3 £7.10, 2&3 £6.10. CSF £54.48 CT £240.18 TOTE £8.50: £2.60, £3.00, £2.30; EX 59.80.
Owner K Nicholls **Bred** Keith Nicholls **Trained** Edwinstowe, Notts

FOCUS
A moderate handicap, run at a fair pace. The winner rates full value for the winning margin and is rated as having improved 7lb with the runner-up to his latest mark.
Zain(IRE) Official explanation: jockey said gelding had a breathing problem
Rain Stops Play(IRE) Official explanation: jockey said gelding never travelled

3965 PERTEMPS PEOPLE DEVELOPMENT "HANDS AND HEELS" APPRENTICE SERIES H'CAP 1m 2f 50y
5:25 (5:25) (Class 5) (0-75,75) 4-Y-0+ **£2,914** (£867; £433; £216) **Stalls** Low

Form RPR

-050 **1** **Dragon Slayer (IRE)**[7] 3736 6-9-2 **69** AshleyMorgan 7 77
(John A Harris) *hld up in tch: racd keenly: led over 2f out: shkn up and edgd lft over 1f out: r.o: eased nr fin* **7/1**

2012 **2** *1 1/4* **Wee Charlie Castle (IRE)**[18] 3347 5-8-2 **60** AndreaAtzeni[(5)] 8 65
(G C H Chung) *s.s: hld up: hdwy over 2f out: sn chsng wnr: edgd lft fr over 1f out: styd on* **5/2**[1]

0130 **3** *3 3/4* **Hucking Heat (IRE)**[12] 3551 4-8-7 **60** (p) RosieJessop 2 58
(R Hollinshead) *hld up: hdwy over 2f out: shkn up over 1f out: wknd ins fnl f* **13/2**

00-1 **4** *3/4* **Credential**[9] 3657 6-8-3 **56** BillyCray 5 52
(John A Harris) *led: racd keenly: hdd over 2f out: wknd over 1f out* **11/4**[2]

6 **5** *nk* **Monfils Monfils (USA)**[4] 3824 6-9-8 **75** (b) DeclanCannon 6 70
(A J McCabe) *chsd ldr tl shkn up over 3f out: styd on same pce fnl 2f* **20/1**

0463 **6** *3/4* **Viscount Rossini**[4] 3820 6-8-3 **56** oh9 JemmaMarshall 1 50
(A W Carroll) *hld up: a in rr* **7/1**

6010 **7** *7* **Trouble Mountain (USA)**[15] 3450 11-8-9 **65** (t) NSLawes[(3)] 3 45
(M W Easterby) *chsd ldrs: pushed along 1/2-way: wknd over 1f out* **11/2**[3]

03/0 **8** *9* **Berkeley Castle (USA)**[15] 3457 4-9-0 **72** StevenCorrigan[(5)] 4 34
(E F Vaughan) *chsd ldrs: pushed along over 3f out: wknd 2f out* **25/1**

2m 14.19s (1.69) **Going Correction** +0.20s/f (Good) **8** Ran SP% **117.6**
Speed ratings (Par 103): **101,100,97,96,96 95,89,82**
toteswinger: 1&2 £1.80, 1&3 £6.30, 2&3 £4.70. CSF £25.66 CT £122.06 TOTE £8.50: £1.90, £1.20, £2.40; EX 21.40 Place 6 £3,356.56, Place 5 £523.63.
Owner Carl Would **Bred** Arandora Star Syndicate **Trained** Eastwell, Leics

FOCUS
A modest "hands and heels" handicap for apprentice riders. The winner scored with something in hand and the form is set by the consistent runner-up, although the sixth from 9lb wrong raises doubts.
T/Plt: £2,992.40 to a £1 stake. Pool: £45,502.28. 11.10 winning tickets. T/Qpdt: £158.70 to a £1 stake. Pool: £2,938.50. 13.70 winning tickets. CR

3674 SALISBURY (R-H)
Saturday, July 12

OFFICIAL GOING: Good to soft (good in places; 8.0)
Wind: Mild, across Weather: Dry

3966 BATHWICK TYRES LADY RIDERS' SERIES H'CAP 6f
6:25 (6:25) (Class 5) (0-75,70) 3-Y-0+ **£3,123** (£968; £484; £242) **Stalls** High

Form RPR

21-0 **1** **River Bounty**[12] 3552 3-9-5 **62** MissLEBurke[(5)] 1 71
(A P Jarvis) *chsd ldrs: led over 2f out: kpt on wl: rdn out* **22/1**

04-0 **2** *1* **Castano**[19] 3313 4-10-0 **60** MissGDGracey-Davison 10 67
(B R Millman) *mid-div: rdn and stdy prog fr over 2f out: styd on to go 2nd ins fnl f* **7/1**

-005 **3** *3/4* **Blue Java**[5] 3797 7-10-10 **70** MissARyan 4 75
(H Morrison) *hld up: hdwy 3f out: sn rdn: kpt on same pce fnl f* **4/1**[1]

2604 **4** *1* **Obe Royal**[5] 3797 4-10-8 **68** (b) MissEFolkes 3 69
(P D Evans) *s.i.s: towards rr: rdn 3f out: styd on fnl f: wnt 4th towards fin: nt rch ldrs* **6/1**[3]

0000 **5** *nk* **Kempsey**[35] 2837 6-9-0 **51** oh1 (b) MissZoeLilly[(5)] 2 51
(J J Bridger) *mid-div: rdn and hdwy fr 2f out: kpt on same pce fnl f* **50/1**

4032 **6** *1* **Corlough Mountain**[34] 2861 4-9-12 **65** (p) MissMBryant[(7)] 6 62
(P Butler) *hld up: rdn 3f out: styd on fnl f: nvr a factor* **16/1**

5000 **7** *1/2* **Bobby Rose**[14] 3506 5-9-10 **63** MissECrossman[(7)] 8 59
(D K Ivory) *hld up towards rr: hdwy 3f out: rdn and ev ch whn edgd lft over 1f out: wknd ins fnl f* **11/1**

3040 **8** *1 1/2* **Our Fugitive (IRE)**[5] 3797 6-9-9 **62** (p) MissLGray[(7)] 7 53
(C Gordon) *prom: rdn over 2f out: sn one pce* **16/1**

0030 **9** *7* **Makabul**[5] 3797 5-10-6 **66** MissEJJones 5 34
(B R Millman) *chsd ldrs: rdn 3f out: sn btn* **8/1**

3044 **10** *hd* **Trinculo (IRE)**[10] 3608 11-10-5 **65** (b) MissSBrotherton 11 33
(R A Harris) *led tl over 2f out: sn wknd* **5/1**[2]

-310 **11** *2 3/4* **Vanadium**[51] 2337 6-10-1 **66** MissHayleyMoore[(5)] 9 25
(G L Moore) *mid-div tl 3f out* **5/1**[2]

1m 18.19s (3.39) **Going Correction** +0.35s/f (Good)
WFA 3 from 4yo+ 6lb **11** Ran SP% **117.6**
Speed ratings (Par 103): **91,89,88,87,86 85,84,82,73,73 69**
toteswinger: 1&2 £45.10, 1&3 £10.40, 2&3 £13.00. CSF £168.87 CT £768.24 TOTE £18.80: £5.50, £2.80, £2.40; EX 202.50.
Owner Mrs Ann Jarvis **Bred** Limestone And Tara Studs **Trained** Twyford, Bucks

FOCUS
A typically moderate handicap for lady amateurs. Ordinary, straightforward form.

3967 WESTOVER GROUP NOVICE AUCTION STKS 6f
6:55 (6:57) (Class 5) 2-Y-0 **£3,885** (£1,156; £577; £288) **Stalls** High

Form RPR

2145 **1** **Soul Sista (IRE)**[8] 3677 2-8-11 0 ow1 AdamKirby 4 77+
(J L Spearing) *a.p: led 2f out: sn rdn clr: readily* **13/2**[3]

0 **2** *7* **Black Skirt**[19] 3323 2-8-4 0 FrancisNorton 2 49
(R Hannon) *trckd ldrs: rdn over 2f out: wnt 2nd over 1f out: no ch w wnr* **8/1**

051 **3** *4* **Striding Edge (IRE)**[23] 3158 2-9-1 0 MartinDwyer 7 48
(W R Muir) *trckd ldrs: rdn over 2f out: one pce fr over 1f out* **6/1**[2]

021 **4** *1/2* **Starlarks (IRE)**[9] 3632 2-9-1 0 ShaneKelly 6 47
(W J Knight) *s.i.s: cl 5th: swtchd rt and rdn over 2f out: nt qckn: wknd fnl f* **8/13**[1]

65 **5** *10* **Buddy Marvellous (IRE)**[63] 2011 2-8-12 0 RichardHughes 1 14
(R Hannon) *led tl 2f out: sn wknd* **11/1**

1m 17.34s (2.54) **Going Correction** +0.35s/f (Good) **5** Ran SP% **109.0**
Speed ratings (Par 94): **97,87,82,81,68**
toteswinger: 1&2 £22.30. CSF £48.86 TOTE £6.10: £2.00, £3.10; EX 60.10.
Owner Living In The Saddle Syndicate **Bred** T Berwanger & Aaron Quinn **Trained** Kinnersley, Worcs

FOCUS
A weak race for the grade, and with the odds-on favourite flopping badly, the form looks suspect. That said, the winner showed improvement. Despite the ground drying out all the time, they came straight across to the stands'-side rail from the gates.

NOTEBOOK
Soul Sista(IRE) revelled in the return to an easy surface, showing an endearing turn of foot to come home a decisive winner. She could do very well in the autumn on proper soft ground. (op 9-2 tchd 7-1)
Black Skirt showed a little bit of promise on her debut at Windsor last month and confirmed it here with a good effort. She was getting plenty of weight though and will have to improve again to win an average maiden. (op 12-1)
Striding Edge(IRE) was well held. It was only a maiden auction he won at Great Leighs and he couldn't find the necessary improvement to get competitive here. (op 7-1 tchd 8-1)
Starlarks(IRE) was running away from fast ground for the first time and despite a tardy start this was a disappointing effort, the daughter of Mujahid singularly failing to pick up once asked. Official explanation: trainer said race came too soon for filly (op 5-6 tchd 10-11)

Buddy Marvellous(IRE) had never raced on going softer than good before and went out like a light after setting the pace for 4f. (op 8-1)

3968 E B F BATHWICK TYRES MAIDEN STKS — 6f 212y
7:25 (7:33) (Class 4) 2-Y-O — **£4,695** (£1,397; £698; £348) **Stalls** High

Form — RPR

1 **Prince Siegfried (FR)** 2-8-10 0 ... DavidProbert(7) 3 — 89+
(A M Balding) *mid-div in centre: smooth hdwy over 2f out: led over 1f out: pushed clr: easily* **9/1**

2 5 **Full Toss** 2-9-3 0 ... RichardHughes 10 — 77
(R Hannon) *trckd ldrs on far side: rdn to chal and edgd lft over 2f out: kpt on to take 2nd ins fnl f: no ch w easy wnr* **7/1**

33 3 hd **Canwinn (IRE)**[30] 2972 2-9-3 0 ... EdwardCreighton 1 — 76
(M R Channon) *prom in centre: rdn and ev ch over 1f out: kpt on but nt pce of wnr: lost 2nd ins fnl f* **11/4**[1]

4 2 1/4 **Silver Print (USA)** 2-9-3 0 ... AdamKirby 11 — 70
(W R Swinburn) *mid-div on far side: rdn and swtchd lft over 2f out: kpt on same pce* **11/2**

44 5 6 **Tudor Key (IRE)**[21] 3245 2-9-3 0 ... JimCrowley 4 — 55
(Mrs A J Perrett) *prom in centre: led over 2f out: sn rdn: hdd over 1f out: wknd fnl f* **7/2**[2]

6 3 1/4 **Granski (IRE)** 2-9-3 0 ... RyanMoore 2 — 47
(R Hannon) *hld up in centre: sme prog u.p over 2f out: wknd over 1f out* **5/1**[3]

7 2 1/2 **Dubai Crest** 2-9-3 0 ... JamesDoyle 12 — 41
(Mrs A J Perrett) *s.i.s: towards rr on far side: sme prog over 2f out: wknd over 1f out* **16/1**

8 6 **Kidson (USA)** 2-9-3 0 ... SteveDrowne 8 — 26
(George Baker) *s.i.s: a towards rr on far side* **25/1**

0 9 3 1/4 **Zaruschka**[8] 3674 2-8-12 0 ... MartinDwyer 6 — 13
(R M Beckett) *led tl over 2f out: wknd* **25/1**

00 10 7 **Into My Arms**[11] 3584 2-8-12 0 ... RichardThomas 7 — —
(M S Saunders) *chsd ldrs: rdn over 3f out: wknd over 2f out* **150/1**

50 11 1/2 **Meirig's Dream (IRE)**[10] 3603 2-9-3 0 ... TQuinn 9 — —
(B G Powell) *mid-div on far side tl wknd 2f out* **50/1**

12 6 **Bermondsey Bob (IRE)** 2-9-0 0 ... TolleyDean(3) 5 — —
(J L Spearing) *a bhd centre gp* **50/1**

1m 31.16s (2.16) **Going Correction** +0.35s/f (Good) **12 Ran SP% 121.6**
Speed ratings (Par 96): **101,95,95,92,85 81,79,72,68,60 59,53**
toteswinger: 1&2 £12.00, 1&3 £16.60, 2&3 £2.80. CSF £69.99 TOTE £13.80: £3.00, £1.90, £1.30; EX 50.90.
Owner David Brownlow **Bred** Haras Saint Pair Du Mont **Trained** Kingsclere, Hants

FOCUS
A much above-average maiden for the course, reflected in a decent winning time. The winner impressed. Stalls 1-5 came across to the stands'-side rail early on, while the remainder stayed far side.

NOTEBOOK
Prince Siegfried(FR) made a most impressive winning debut, drawing right away in the closing stages for a very easy success. His target is the Tattersalls Million race at Newmarket's Cambridgeshire meeting, and while he looks for all the world like a horse who is going places, it is only fair to note that Royal Applause has sired a few impressive juveniles in the past who have not gone on as they looked they might. (op 20-1)
Full Toss looks sure to come on for this initial experience, keeping on well all the way to the line while clearly not in the winner's league. A maiden, at least, should be a formality for the son of Nayef. (op 6-1 tchd 4-1)
Canwinn(IRE) has done little wrong on all three of his starts and has been unlucky to come up against some above-average types each time. It will be a travesty if he doesn't pick up a race before the end of the season, but he is liable to be asked to carry a fair bit of weight in nurseries. (op 10-3 tchd 4-1)
Silver Print(USA), from the family of Derby winner Henbit, made a promising debut, and should find a less exacting maiden well within his compass especially with normal improvement forthcoming. (op 15-2 tchd 8-1)
Tudor Key(IRE), fourth in the Chesham Stakes at the Royal meeting, was the second horse to let the form of that race down today, following the defeat of third-placed Markyg at Ascot earlier in the afternoon. He might struggle in nurseries for which he is sure to be lumbered with welter burdens. Official explanation: jockey said colt hung right-handed (tchd 10-3 and 4-1)
Meirig's Dream(IRE) Official explanation: jockey said colt ran too free

3969 TURFTV H'CAP — 1m
8:00 (8:02) (Class 4) (0-85,85) 3-Y-O — **£4,857** (£1,445; £722; £360) **Stalls** High

Form — RPR

1221 1 **Topazes**[9] 3627 3-9-4 82 ... JamieSpencer 2 — 91+
(M L W Bell) *hld up: swtchd to stands' side 4f out: nt clr run and swtchd rt over 1f out: r.o strly to ld jst ins fnl f: readily* **8/11**[1]

-300 2 2 1/2 **Traphalgar (IRE)**[21] 3251 3-9-7 85 ... RyanMoore 8 — 88
(P F I Cole) *prom: led 2f out: sn rdn: edgd lft and hdd jst ins fnl f: nt pce of wnr* **15/2**[3]

0343 3 1/2 **Border Owl (IRE)**[19] 3325 3-9-1 79 ... RichardHughes 5 — 81
(R Hannon) *hld up: swtchd to stands' side 4f out: hdwy 2f out: sn rdn: kpt on fnl f* **5/1**[2]

6305 4 2 1/4 **Rich Kid (IRE)**[12] 3560 3-7-12 69 ... DavidProbert(7) 1 — 66
(R A Harris) *prom: led briefly over 2f out: sn rdn: one pce fr over 1f out* **12/1**

2364 5 hd **Bere Davis (FR)**[9] 3641 3-9-0 78 ... JamesDoyle 3 — 74
(P D Evans) *led: swtchd to stands' side over 4f out: rdn and hdd over 2f out: kpt pressing ldrs tl fdd fnl f* **12/1**

3504 6 3 3/4 **Ten Pole Tudor**[12] 3560 3-8-8 75 ... KevinGhunowa(3) 7 — 63
(R A Harris) *awkward leaving stalls: sn chsng ldrs: effrt 3f out: btn 2f out* **18/1**

7 8 **Majority (IRE)**[265] 6362 3-8-11 75 ... MartinDwyer 4 — 44
(B J Meehan) *chsd ldrs: rdn 3f out: wknd 2f out* **16/1**

1m 45.87s (2.37) **Going Correction** +0.35s/f (Good) **7 Ran SP% 112.9**
Speed ratings (Par 102): **102,99,99,96,96 92,84**
toteswinger: 1&2 £2.90, 1&3 £1.20, 2&3 £3.60. CSF £6.69 CT £16.42 TOTE £1.60: £1.30, £3.00; EX 5.40.
Owner R A Pegum **Bred** Baron F Von Oppenheim **Trained** Newmarket, Suffolk

FOCUS
No strength in depth to this handicap, which, with the clear exception of the winner, featured mainly badly-treated sorts. Topazes probably did not have to show much improvement to score.
Traphalgar(IRE) Official explanation: jockey said colt hung left-handed
Bere Davis(FR) Official explanation: jockey said gelding hung both ways

3970 THEBESTOF.CO.UK/SALISBURY H'CAP — 1m 4f
8:30 (8:30) (Class 5) (0-75,76) 3-Y-O+ — **£3,238** (£963; £481; £240) **Stalls** High

Form — RPR

4422 1 **Mizooka**[17] 3384 3-8-13 72 ... JamesDoyle 10 — 79
(R M Beckett) *cl up: hdwy over 2f out: rdn to ld over 1f out: styd on wl: rdn out* **7/2**[2]

1041 2 1/2 **Cape Colony**[12] 3555 3-9-3 76 ... RichardHughes 2 — 82
(R Hannon) *cl up: rdn and hdwy over 2f out: ev ch over 1f out: styd on: hld towards fin* **3/1**[1]

0601 3 1 3/4 **Hadron Collider (FR)**[10] 3614 3-8-12 71 ... RyanMoore 4 — 74
(R Hannon) *hld up in midfield: rdn and hdwy 3f out: styd on but nt quite pce to chal* **13/2**

0/1- 4 nk **Master Wells (IRE)**[37] 3485 7-9-1 66 ... HaddenFrost(5) 3 — 69
(J D Frost) *led: rdn and hdd over 1f out: kpt on but no ex* **12/1**

16-0 5 1/2 **Mistress Eva**[32] 2920 3-8-12 71 ... JimCrowley 7 — 73
(P Winkworth) *hld up: rdn over 3f out: prog over 2f out: styd on: nt rch ldrs* **20/1**

-040 6 7 **Mount Hermon (IRE)**[29] 3003 4-9-11 74 ... (b[1]) TravisBlock(3) 9 — 65
(H Morrison) *trckd ldrs: rdn 3f out: grad fdd* **15/2**

6001 7 nk **Obrigado (USA)**[28] 3036 8-9-11 71 ... (t) GeorgeBaker 6 — 61
(G L Moore) *hld up towards rr: short lived effrt 2f out* **8/1**

0336 8 3 **Bold Bobby Be (IRE)**[32] 2921 4-9-5 65 ... KerrinMcEvoy 1 — 50
(J L Dunlop) *trckd ldrs: wkng whn short of room over 2f out* **5/1**[3]

5-43 9 3 1/4 **Clovis**[111] 982 3-9-0 73 ... JamieSpencer 8 — 53
(N P Mulholland) *hld up and a towards rr* **16/1**

2m 41.03s (3.03) **Going Correction** +0.35s/f (Good)
WFA 3 from 4yo+ 13lb **9 Ran SP% 118.4**
Speed ratings (Par 103): **103,102,101,101,100 96,96,94,91**
toteswinger: 1&2 £4.20, 1&3 £12.00, 2&3 £1.50. CSF £14.89 CT £65.93 TOTE £5.40: £1.90, £2.00, £2.00; EX 16.80.
Owner M S T Partnership **Bred** Catridge Farm Stud Ltd **Trained** Whitsbury, Hants

FOCUS
Just a fair middle-distance handicap. The front five, which included four of the five 3-y-os in the race, pulled well clear of the remainder and the form is sound overall.

3971 EUROPEAN BREEDERS' FUND LADIES EVENING FILLIES' H'CAP — 1m
9:00 (9:01) (Class 3) (0-95,95) 3-Y-O
£9,969 (£2,985; £1,492; £747; £372; £187) **Stalls** High

Form — RPR

3-11 1 **Scuffle**[31] 2953 3-9-4 92 ... SteveDrowne 2 — 103+
(R Charlton) *trckd ldrs: rdn to ld over 1f out: kpt on wl: rdn out* **10/11**[1]

-232 2 2 3/4 **Victoria Reel**[19] 3312 3-8-3 77 ow1 ... MartinDwyer 4 — 82
(R Hannon) *prom: led 2f out: rdn and hdd over 1f out: sn hld* **9/2**[2]

13-0 3 2 3/4 **Maramba (USA)**[24] 3124 3-9-7 95 ... RyanMoore 7 — 94
(Sir Michael Stoute) *hld up: clsd on ldrs over 3f out: sn rdn: kpt on same pce fnl 2f: wnt 3rd jst over 1f out* **5/1**[3]

-150 4 1 **Jazz Jam**[24] 3124 3-9-7 95 ... TQuinn 5 — 91
(P F I Cole) *trckd ldrs: rdn 3f out: one pce fnl 2f* **8/1**

-000 5 1 1/4 **Miss Bootylishes**[16] 3415 3-8-5 82 ow1 ... KevinGhunowa(3) 3 — 76
(A B Haynes) *led tl 2f out: sn one pce* **12/1**

00-0 6 4 1/2 **Dellini (IRE)**[24] 3124 3-8-13 87 ... EdwardCreighton 6 — 70
(M R Channon) *hld up: rdn over 2f out: wknd over 1f out* **16/1**

1m 45.72s (2.22) **Going Correction** +0.35s/f (Good) **6 Ran SP% 111.9**
Speed ratings (Par 101): **102,99,96,95,94 89**
toteswinger: 1&2 £1.20, 1&3 £1.80, 2&3 £1.10. CSF £5.29 TOTE £1.80: £1.30, £1.60; EX 4.30 Place 6 £67.71, Place 5 £27.69.
Owner K Abdulla **Bred** Juddmonte Farms Ltd **Trained** Beckhampton, Wilts

FOCUS
Light on numbers but some very useful fillies on show in this handicap, where they came up the centre of the course for the first half of the race before taking to the stands' side at halfway. The progressive winner looks Listed class at least.

NOTEBOOK
Scuffle started off with a promising effort in a maiden that has worked out well on her only start at two. She has now won all three subsequent starts in the manner of a most progressive filly and on a variety of goings. Drowne did not have to get truly serious with her for this latest success, and with subsequent reassessment likely to take her handicap mark into three figures, the daughter of Daylami is surely looking at Listed races next. (op Evens tchd 11-10 in places and 6-5 in a place)
Victoria Reel, a lightly raced maiden, was getting plenty of weight from the other principals but this was a creditable effort nonetheless, leading briefly over a furlong out and only going down to a most progressive filly. There must be a race or two in her. (op 4-1 tchd 7-2)
Maramba(USA) was sent off favourite for the Sandringham Handicap at Royal Ascot on just her fourth career start last time, and while she understandably found that all a bit much for her at this stage of her career, this has to go down as a slightly disappointing effort given that she was proven on the ground. The jury must be out on her for now. (op 4-1 tchd 11-2)
Jazz Jam, who won a very weak renewal of the Masaka Stakes at Kempton on her reappearance, found it tough in Listed company on two subsequent starts and this drop in grade wasn't enough to see her competitive. She could prove hard to place as she has a very tough handicap mark to overcome but is not good enough to go close in normal-standard Listed events. (tchd 10-1)
Dellini(IRE) Official explanation: jockey said filly was unsuited by the good to soft, good in places ground

T/Plt: £98.90 to a £1 stake. Pool: £60,508.82. 446.20 winning tickets. T/Qpdt: £3.20 to a £1 stake. Pool: £5,547.30. 1,268.10 winning tickets. TM

3926 YORK (L-H)
Saturday, July 12

OFFICIAL GOING: Heavy (soft in places; 5.0)
The ground was described as 'sticky, very testing especially in the final furlong'.
Wind: Moderate, half against Weather: Mainly fine but breezy

3972 JOHN SMITH'S FENCE GATE INN STKS (H'CAP) — 1m
2:10 (2:10) (Class 3) (0-90,90) 3-Y-O+ — **£10,361** (£3,083; £1,540; £769) **Stalls** Low

Form — RPR

0005 1 **Blue Spinnaker (IRE)**[21] 3261 9-8-8 77 ... BradleyRoper(7) 3 — 89
(M W Easterby) *hld up towards rr: hdwy over 2f out: swtchd rt and rdn over 1f out: styd on ins fnl f: edgd lft and led last 50yds* **12/1**

4431 2 3/4 **Violent Velocity (IRE)**[11] 3591 5-8-6 75 ... JamieKyne(7) 11 — 85
(J J Quinn) *in tch: hdwy 3f out: rdn to ld over 1f out: clr ins fnl f: drvn: hdd and no ex last 50yds* **16/1**

2532 3 2 1/4 **Guilded Warrior**[13] 3529 5-9-12 88 ... SteveDrowne 2 — 93
(W S Kittow) *a.p: effrt over 2f out: rdn wl over 1f out: kpt on same pce u.p ins fnl f* **7/1**[3]

6001 **4** 2 **Kingsdale Orion (IRE)**[16] 3413 4-9-11 **87**.................... RobertWinston 1 88
(B Ellison) *chsd ldrs: rdn along 1/2-way: drvn and outpcd 2f out: kpt on u.p ins fnl f* **9/2**[1]

0400 **5** *shd* **Moheebb (IRE)**[7] 3716 4-8-9 **71**.................................(b) GregFairley 15 71
(Mrs R A Carr) *dwlt: gd hdwy on outer 3f out: rdn to chse ldrs wl over 1f out: drvn and edgd lft ent fnl f: one pce* **25/1**

0323 **6** 1 1/4 **Vainglory (USA)**[36] 2789 4-9-7 **90**.............................. ChrisHough(7) 10 87
(D M Simcock) *sltly hmpd after 150yds and bhd: gd hdwy on outer over 2f out: rdn to chse ldrs over 1f out: edgd lft and one pce ent fnl f* **11/1**

4114 **7** 1/2 **Sunnyside Tom (IRE)**[17] 3367 4-9-2 **78**........................... TonyHamilton 8 74
(R A Fahey) *trckd ldrs: smooth hdwy 3f out: rdn to chse ldr 2f out: sn hung lft and wknd ent fnl f* **16/1**

-211 **8** 3/4 **Spinning**[15] 3453 5-9-1 **82**.................................(b) NeilBrown(5) 4 77
(T D Barron) *hld up in rr: effrt 3f out and sn rdn along: drvn whn nt clr run and swtchd rt wl over 1f out: sn no imp* **5/1**[2]

2161 **9** 1 1/2 **Exit Smiling**[38] 2733 6-9-6 **85**.............................. JamieMoriarty(3) 14 76
(P T Midgley) *in tch: hdwy 3f out: rdn along 2f out and sn wknd* **10/1**

0025 **10** 1/2 **Bold Marc (IRE)**[9] 3627 6-9-4 **80**.............................. AndrewElliott 5 70
(K R Burke) *led and sn clr: rdn over 2f out: drvn and hdd over 1f out: grad wknd* **18/1**

6026 **11** 1 3/4 **Moody Tunes**[9] 3627 5-9-3 **79**.............................. TedDurcan 17 65
(K R Burke) *chsd clr ldr: rdn along over 2f out: sn wknd* **12/1**

-225 **12** 1 1/4 **Observatory Star (IRE)**[17] 3367 5-9-1 **77**.......................(p) DavidAllan 7 60
(T D Easterby) *sltly hmpd aftere 150yds: a in rr* **11/1**

0050 **13** 3 1/4 **Fremen (USA)**[55] 2218 8-10-0 **90**.............................. PaulQuinn 6 66
(D Nicholls) *dwlt: a in rr* **14/1**

0004 **14** 19 **Wavertree Warrior (IRE)**[19] 3317 6-8-9 **74**..............(b) TravisBlock(3) 13 6
(N P Littmoden) *chsd ldrs: rdn along over 3f out: sn wknd* **25/1**

1m 44.91s (6.11) **Going Correction** +0.85s/f (Soft) **14** Ran SP% **119.9**
Speed ratings (Par 107): **103,102,100,98,97 96,96,95,93,93 91,90,87,68**
toteswinger: 1&2 £44.20, 1&3 £20.60, 2&3 £20.70. CSF £190.20 CT £1483.43 TOTE £13.90: £3.80, £4.00, £3.00; EX 175.80 Trifecta £400.40 Part won. Pool: £541.10 - 0.30 winning units..
Owner G Sparkes G Hart S Curtis & T Dewhirst **Bred** M3 Elevage And Haras D'Etreham **Trained** Sheriff Hutton, N Yorks

FOCUS
A modest winning time for the class, even allowing for the conditions. The first two finished clear and the race has been rated round the winner's form this year.

NOTEBOOK
Blue Spinnaker(IRE), having his 24th outing here, stuck on in gallant fashion to shade it near the line.
Violent Velocity(IRE), 5lb higher, struck the front plenty soon enough and, flagging inside the last, was picked off near the line.
Guilded Warrior, unable to dominate, is running well but he is still 4lb higher than his final win last term. (op 8-1)
Kingsdale Orion(IRE), 5lb higher, took an age to get going. He is well worth another try in blinkers and in the longer term hurdling may well prove his game. (tchd 5-1)
Moheebb(IRE), who had the worst of the draw, put two below-par efforts behind him after missing the break and coming widest of all. Official explanation: jockey said gelding missed the break

3973 JOHN SMITH'S EXTRA COLD STKS (H'CAP) 6f
2:40 (2:41) (Class 3) (0-95,93) 3-Y-O+ **£10,361** (£3,083; £1,540; £769) **Stalls** Low

Form RPR

0000 **1** **Zomerlust**[14] 3491 6-9-5 **85**.............................. RobertWinston 8 98
(J J Quinn) *trckd ldrs: effrt 2f out and sn rdn: drvn ent fnl f: styd on wl to ld last 100yds* **4/1**[1]

-200 **2** 1 **Kaldoun Kingdom (IRE)**[3] 3850 3-9-3 **89**.................. TonyHamilton 12 98
(R A Fahey) *in tch: gd hdwy on outer 2f out: rdn to chal appr fnl f and ev ch tl drvn and nt qckn last 100yds* **7/1**

0102 **3** 1/2 **Swift Princess (IRE)**[12] 3554 4-9-3 **83**.....................(v) AndrewElliott 14 91
(K R Burke) *trckd ldrs: hdwy over 2f out: rdn to ld over 1f out: drvn and edgd lft ins fnl f: hdd and no ex last 100yds* **8/1**

2350 **4** 1 **Ishetoo**[15] 3451 4-9-13 **93**.............................. JohnEgan 10 98
(A Dickman) *in rr: pushed along 1/2-way: hdwy on outer wl over 1f out: sn rdn and styd on strly ins fnl f: nrst fin* **9/1**

3530 **5** 1/2 **Bel Cantor**[14] 3477 5-8-10 **79**.............................(p) AndrewMullen(3) 13 83
(W J H Ratcliffe) *cl up: led over 2f out: rdn and hdd over 1f out: wknd ins fnl f* **16/1**

4145 **6** 2 1/4 **Baby Strange**[14] 3489 4-9-13 **93**.............................. PaulMulrennan 6 88
(D Shaw) *led: rdn along and hdd over 2f out: wknd over 1f out* **11/2**[3]

-636 **7** 3/4 **Hotham**[10] 3601 5-8-9 **75**.............................. DNolan 3 67
(N Wilson) *chsd ldrs: rdn along over 2f out: drvn and wknd over 1f out* **20/1**

6000 **8** 1/2 **Bazroy (IRE)**[8] 3680 4-9-5 **90**.............................(b) RichardEvans(5) 9 81
(P D Evans) *bhd and pushed along 1/2-way: styd on u.p appr fnl f: nvr a factor* **40/1**

0303 **9** 1/2 **Pusey Street Lady**[15] 3451 4-9-11 **91**.............................. SteveDrowne 1 80
(J Gallagher) *midfield: effrt over 2f out: sn rdn and no hdwy* **5/1**[2]

0000 **10** 2 1/2 **Obe Brave**[14] 3489 5-9-2 **89**.............................. BMcHugh(7) 2 70
(R A Fahey) *chsd ldrs: rdn along wl over 2f out and sn wknd* **25/1**

0034 **11** 6 **Hurricane Spirit (IRE)**[9] 3647 4-9-12 **92**.............................. MartinDwyer 7 54
(J R Best) *a in rr* **12/1**

-600 **12** 8 **Fantasy Believer**[8] 3680 10-9-2 **82**.............................. PaulFessey 11 18
(J J Quinn) *in tch: rdn along wl over 2f out and sn wknd* **16/1**

1000 **13** 3 **Valley Of The Moon (IRE)**[12] 3554 4-8-8 **77**.............. JamieMoriarty(3) 5 —
(R A Fahey) *a in rr* **25/1**

1m 16.19s (4.29) **Going Correction** +0.85s/f (Soft)
WFA 3 from 4yo+ 6lb **13** Ran SP% **120.0**
Speed ratings (Par 107): **105,103,103,101,101 97,96,95,95,91 83,73,69**
toteswinger: 1&2 £6.10, 1&3 £9.70, 2&3 £9.90. CSF £30.23 CT £225.65 TOTE £4.70: £2.00, £3.20, £2.10; EX 33.60 Trifecta £180.60 Pool: £634.70 - 2.60 winning units..
Owner Dawson And Quinn **Bred** The Lavington Stud **Trained** Settrington, N Yorks
■ Stewards' Enquiry : Robert Winston two-day ban: used whip with excessive frequency (Jul 27-28)

FOCUS
A competitive sprint handicap and the form looks very solid allowing for the ground.

NOTEBOOK
Zomerlust, who won a similar event in these conditions from a 9lb higher mark almost a year ago, had hinted at a return to form at Newcastle on his previous start. He is a lazy individual and Winston had to be at his strongest, yet his reward was a two day-whip ban.
Kaldoun Kingdom(IRE), who had run at Newmarket earlier in the week, has a very scratchy action and is suited by this sort of ground. In the end he just missed out. (op 13-2)
Swift Princess(IRE) ran right up to her best and was only edged out in the closing stages.
Ishetoo, 8lb higher than his last success, proved suited by a return to 6f. (op 17-2)
Bel Cantor is at his best on soft ground and put a poor effort last time behind him. (op 14-1)
Baby Strange did too much too soon and in these conditions was never going to see it out. Official explanation: jockey said colt ran too free (op 5-1)

3974 49TH JOHN SMITH'S CUP (HERITAGE H'CAP) 1m 2f 88y
3:15 (3:15) (Class 2) 3-Y-O+
£93,465 (£27,990; £13,995; £7,005; £3,495; £1,755) **Stalls** Low

Form RPR

4321 **1** **Flying Clarets (IRE)**[16] 3403 5-8-12 **105** 5ex.......... FrederikTylicki(7) 12 115
(R A Fahey) *mde all: rdn wl over 2f out: drvn over 1f out: styd on gamely ins fnl f* **12/1**

2100 **2** 1 3/4 **Eradicate (IRE)**[7] 3721 4-9-2 **102**.............................. GregFairley 1 108
(M Johnston) *hld up towards rr: stdy hdwy 3f out: rdn to chse wnr wl over 1f out: drvn and ev ch ent fnl f: sn edgd lft and no ex* **20/1**

-110 **3** *nk* **Ezdiyaad (IRE)**[21] 3249 4-9-0 **100**.............................. MartinDwyer 3 105
(M P Tregoning) *in tch: hdwy to chse ldrs 3f out: rdn 2f out: sn drvn and kpt on same pce ins fnl f* **9/2**[2]

0456 **4** 2 1/4 **Prince Forever (IRE)**[35] 2830 4-8-11 **97**.............................. TedDurcan 2 98
(M A Jarvis) *hld up in rr: hdwy wl over 2f out: sn rdn and kpt on wl u.p appr fnl f: nrst fin* **20/1**

2020 **5** 1 **Dunaskin (IRE)**[7] 3721 8-8-13 **99**.............................. DavidAllan 16 98
(B Ellison) *chsd wnr: rdn along 3f out: drvn 2f out: outpcd over 1f out: kpt on u.p ins fnl f* **16/1**

4400 **6** 3 **Charlie Tokyo (IRE)**[28] 3046 5-8-6 **95**....................(b) JamieMoriarty(3) 9 88
(R A Fahey) *hld up in rr: hdwy 3f out: rdn 2f out: styd on appr fnl f: nrst fin* **16/1**

1000 **7** 1 1/4 **Capable Guest (IRE)**[8] 3684 6-8-9 **95**.............................. RobertWinston 18 85
(M R Channon) *hld up towards rr: gd hdwy on outer 3f out: rdn and hung lft 2f out: drvn to chse ldrs whn edgd lft over 1f out: sn btn* **50/1**

1226 **8** 1 1/2 **Benandonner (USA)**[16] 3413 5-8-9 **100**.............................. NeilBrown(5) 13 87
(R A Fahey) *in tch on outer: smooth hdwy over 3f out: rdn over 2f out: sn drvn and hld whn n.m.r 2f out* **25/1**

3304 **9** 5 **Heaven Knows**[16] 3398 5-8-9 **95**.............................(v) MichaelHills 6 72
(W J Haggas) *hld up towards rr: hdwy 3f out: rdn along 2f out: drvn and no imp* **8/1**[3]

2120 **10** 8 **Extraterrestrial**[24] 3122 4-8-8 **94**.............................. TonyHamilton 20 55
(R A Fahey) *hld up towards rr: hdwy 3f out: rdn along over 2f out and nvr nr ldrs* **25/1**

2-21 **11** 3 1/4 **Mutajarred**[45] 2503 4-9-6 **106**.............................. RHills 11 61
(W J Haggas) *trckd ldrs: effrt 3f out: sn rdn and wknd over 2f out* **11/4**[1]

6-36 **12** 8 **Monte Alto (IRE)**[22] 3195 4-9-0 **100**.............................. GeorgeBaker 10 39
(L M Cumani) *in tch: smooth hdwy to chse ldrs over 4f out: rdn over 3f out and sn btn* **8/1**[3]

141 **13** 2 **Championship Point (IRE)**[65] 1921 5-9-10 **110**......... DarryllHolland 17 45
(M R Channon) *hld up: a in rr* **18/1**

0004 **14** 3 **Fishforcompliments**[28] 3046 4-8-2 **95**.............................. BMcHugh(7) 8 24
(R A Fahey) *in tch: rdn along 3f out: sn wknd* **18/1**

-431 **15** 2 **Supaseus**[22] 3195 5-9-2 **105** 5ex.............................. TravisBlock(3) 5 30
(H Morrison) *prom: rdn along over 3f out and sn wknd* **16/1**

6466 **16** *nk* **Snoqualmie Boy**[8] 3684 5-8-8 **94**.............................. JohnEgan 15 18
(Jane Chapple-Hyam) *hld up towards rr: gd hdwy on outer 3f out: rdn along 2f out and sn wknd* **33/1**

2m 17.61s (5.11) **Going Correction** +0.85s/f (Soft) **20** Ran SP% **125.1**
Speed ratings (Par 109): **113,111,111,109,108 106,105,104,100,93 91,84,83,80,79 78**
toteswinger: 1&2 £57.30, 1&3 £11.60, 2&3 £17.70. CSF £244.48 CT £1261.25 TOTE £10.20: £1.80, £5.40, £1.70, £5.50; EX 472.60 Trifecta £3360.40 Pool: £41,324.40 - 9.10 winning units..
Owner The Matthewman Partnership **Bred** Gabriel Bell **Trained** Musley Bank, N Yorks
■ The third success in this historic handicap in seven years for Richard Fahey, who was responsible for five of this field.
■ Stewards' Enquiry : Robert Winston one-day ban: careless riding (Aug 9); caution: used whip down shoulder in forehand position.
Jamie Moriarty caution: careless riding
Frederik Tylicki two-day ban: used whip with excessive frequency (Jul 27-28)

FOCUS
A personal best from the admirable winner with the placed horses running to their pre-race marks. The race contained a lot of 'twilight' horses and there were no three-year-olds in the line-up.

NOTEBOOK
Flying Clarets(IRE), runner-up a year ago when the race was run over about a furlong shorter, was racing from a 17lb higher mark. She made every yard and, very capably handled, simply would not be denied. She is a fine advert for her stable. (op 16-1)
Eradicate(IRE), a poor mover, bounced back after two below-par efforts on this very testing ground. He was almost upsides entering the last but was very much second best at the line. He has the same name as the winner of this race in 1990. (op 22-1 tchd 25-1)
Ezdiyaad(IRE), a big individual, looked very fit. He proved suited by the drop back in trip and a return to an easy surface. (op 11-2 tchd 6-1 in a place)
Prince Forever(IRE), who has run over 7f and 1m4f already this year, put in some solid late work and appears to be coming to hand after injury curtailed his three-year-old season. (op 16-1)
Dunaskin(IRE), having his 16th start here, was unable to dominate but to his credit was coming back for more at the line.
Charlie Tokyo(IRE), who took this a year ago when it was run over 1m1f, defeating Flying Clarets from a 3lb lower mark, has been largely out of sorts this time and this marked a return to form on his favoured bad ground. (op 12-1)
Capable Guest(IRE), with the visor left off, gave his rider a wretched time.
Benandonner(USA), rated to the limit, was at the end of his tether when tightened up.
Mutajarred, 6lb higher and back on turf, was one of the first on the retreat. (op 10-3 tchd 7-2)

3975 JOHN SMITH'S EXTRA SMOOTH SILVER CUP STKS (H'CAP) (LISTED RACE) 1m 6f
3:50 (3:52) (Class 1) (0-110,109) 3-Y-O+
£24,978 (£9,468; £4,738; £2,362; £1,183; £594) **Stalls** Low

Form RPR

-005 **1** **Yellowstone (IRE)**[21] 3246 4-9-9 **105**.............................(p) JohnEgan 12 116
(Jane Chapple-Hyam) *trckd ldrs: c wdst of all in st: led 2f out: styd on wl towards fin* **10/1**

5-15 **2** 1/2 **Gull Wing (IRE)**[57] 2144 4-9-0 **96**.............................. SteveDrowne 2 106
(M L W Bell) *hld up in rr: stdy hdwy over 3f out: chal jst ins fnl f: no ex towards fin* **9/4**[1]

-2 **3** 5 **Eastern Anthem (IRE)**[36] 2797 4-9-13 **109**.....................(t) TedDurcan 11 112
(Saeed Bin Suroor) *trckd ldrs: led over 2f out: sn hdd: fdd fnl f* **5/1**[2]

360 **4** 3 **Wing Collar**[42] 2609 7-8-13 **95**.............................(p) DavidAllan 4 94
(T D Easterby) *in rr: drvn over 4f out: styd on fnl 3f: tk 3rd jst ins fnl f* **11/2**[3]

1-40 **5** 6 **Greek Envoy**[7] 3721 4-9-4 **100**.............................. RobertWinston 10 90
(T P Tate) *trckd ldrs: led 3f out: sn hdd: wknd jst ins fnl f* **14/1**

313/ **6** 1 1/2 **Empire Day (UAE)**[608] 6456 4-9-6 **102**.............................. GeorgeBaker 9 90
(Saeed Bin Suroor) *chsd ldrs: wknd over 2f out* **7/1**

2-00 **7** *26* **Kasthari (IRE)**[66] 1916 9-8-13 **95** oh5 DarryllHolland 8 47
(J D Bethell) *led tl 3f out: wknd over 1f out* **33/1**

0-20 **8** *7* **Supersonic Dave (USA)**[42] 2625 4-9-10 **106** RHills 1 48
(B J Meehan) *hld up in rr: hdwy 10f out: lost pl over 2f out: eased and sn bhd* **9/1**

01-0 **9** *14* **Solent (IRE)**[7] 3721 6-9-6 **102** JamieMoriarty 5 25
(J J Quinn) *w ldrs: wknd 3f out* **25/1**

-440 **10** *19* **Night Crescendo (USA)**[21] 3249 5-9-0 **96** MartinDwyer 6 —
(Mrs A J Perrett) *in rr-div: drvn and lost pl over 4f out: sn wl bhd* **11/1**

3m 7.94s (7.74) **Going Correction** +0.85s/f (Soft) **10** Ran SP% **116.2**
Speed ratings (Par 111): **111,110,107,106,102 101,87,83,75,64**
toteswinger: 1&2 £6.60, 1&3 £10.10, 2&3 £6.60. CSF £32.65 CT £129.84 TOTE £10.30: £2.50, £1.50, £2.20; EX 42.50 Trifecta £356.40 Pool: £1,107.80 - 2.30 winning units..
Owner Mrs Fitri Hay **Bred** Tullamaine Castle Stud & Partn **Trained** Lambourn, Berks

FOCUS
A sound test in the conditions. The winner recaptured his best three-year-old form on this drop in grade and the runner-up continues on the upgrade.

NOTEBOOK
Yellowstone(IRE), bought for 520,000gns, was very noisy beforehand. He grabbed the stands' rail position and showed a very willing attitude to fight off the runner-up's determined challenge. His trainer has an eye on the Irish St Leger but his former trainer Aidan O'Brien is sure to have an even stronger hand as he attempts to make a clean sweep of this year's five Irish Classics. (op 14-1)
Gull Wing(IRE), whose dam took this on her final racecourse appearance in 2002, came with what looked a winning challenge but in the end Yellowstone would simply not be denied. She deserves plenty of credit for this. (op 11-4 tchd 2-1)
Eastern Anthem(IRE), banged up 8lb after Goodwood, showed ahead for a few strides but in the end the first two saw out the extended trip much too well for him. (op 10-3)
Wing Collar, winner of three of his previous seven starts here, stuck on in his own time and is well worth another try over even further. (op 5-1)
Greek Envoy, suited by the soft, travelled strongly but, after taking charge, in the end this trip stretched him to breaking point. (tchd 16-1)
Empire Day(UAE), who missed all last year, is now a gelding. He won over 1m2f at two but has yet to prove his stays this far. (op 9-1)
Kasthari(IRE) Official explanation: jockey said gelding was unsuited by the heavy (soft in places) ground
Night Crescendo(USA) Official explanation: jockey said gelding was unsuited by the heavy (soft in places) ground

3976 JOHN SMITH'S CELEBRATING 250 YEARS MEDIAN AUCTION MAIDEN STKS 6f
4:25 (4:25) (Class 4) 2-Y-O **£6,670** (£1,984; £991; £495) **Stalls** Low

Form RPR

4 **1** **Lakeman (IRE)**[16] 3411 2-9-3 0 RobertWinston 5 76
(B Ellison) *trckd ldrs: led over 1f out: hld on wl* **9/2**[2]

2 *nk* **Frontline Girl (IRE)** 2-8-12 0 AndrewElliott 3 70
(K R Burke) *trckd ldr: led over 2f out: edgd rt and hdd over 1f out: no ex towards fin* **20/1**

5 **3** *nk* **Tapis Wizard**[16] 3411 2-9-3 0 DaleGibson 14 76+
(M W Easterby) *wnt rt s: sn chsng ldrs: hung lft and bmpd ins fnl f: no ex* **5/1**[3]

4 *3/4* **Hajoum (IRE)** 2-9-3 0 TedDurcan 9 72+
(Saeed Bin Suroor) *hld up in midfield: smooth hdwy over 2f out: rdn over 1f out: wnt rt ins fnl f: kpt on same pce* **5/2**[1]

5 *2 1/2* **Antigua Sunrise (IRE)** 2-8-5 0 BMcHugh(7) 6 59+
(R A Fahey) *slowly away and rn green: bhd tl kpt on fnl 2f: improve* **16/1**

6 *3 3/4* **Winsome Hearts** 2-9-3 0 DNolan 10 53
(M W Easterby) *in rr: kpt on fnl 2f: nvr nr ldrs* **33/1**

56 **7** *12* **Mintoe**[12] 3547 2-9-3 0 DarryllHolland 12 17
(K A Ryan) *chsd ldrs: hung lft and lost pl over 1f out* **7/1**

8 *11* **Smelly Cat** 2-8-12 0 DavidAllan 4 —
(T D Easterby) *led: hdd over 2f out: edgd lft and wknd qckly over 1f out: sn bhd* **7/1**

9 *2 1/2* **Tilerium's Dream (IRE)** 2-9-3 0 JimmyFortune 2 —
(G A Swinbank) *s.i.s: sn chsng ldrs: wknd over 1f out* **12/1**

10 *9* **Dakota Two (IRE)** 2-8-5 0 FrederikTylicki(7) 8 —
(R A Fahey) *s.i.s: in rr: bhd fnl 2f* **9/1**

1m 17.58s (5.68) **Going Correction** +0.85s/f (Soft) **10** Ran SP% **119.7**
Speed ratings (Par 96): **96,95,95,94,90 85,69,55,51,39**
toteswinger: 1&2 £12.50, 1&3 £4.10, 2&3 £17.40. CSF £91.79 TOTE £5.80: £1.80, £4.00, £2.20; EX 103.80.
Owner The Country Stayers **Bred** Tally-Ho Stud **Trained** Norton, N Yorks

FOCUS
A fair maiden with the time helping set the level. The winner and third replicated their Newcastle debut form almost to the pound.

NOTEBOOK
Lakeman(IRE) is not that big but he is well put together and really took the eye. He showed a very willing attitude and should improve again. (op 6-1 tchd 4-1)
Frontline Girl(IRE), a half-sister to last year's John Smith's Cup winner Charlie Tokyo, is a medium-sized filly. She looked to be carrying plenty of condition and, after showing ahead, in the end she went down fighting. She thoroughly deserves to go one better. (op 10-1)
Tapis Wizard, just behind the winner at Newcastle, was being held when taking a bump off the third near the line. A seventh furlong will be in his favour. (op 9-1)
Hajoum(IRE) ◆, a half-brother to the smart and speedy Swiss Lake, is a good-bodied individual. He came there full of running but seemed to flounder in the bad ground and was held near the line. He should prove himself much better than this on decent ground. (op 2-1)
Antigua Sunrise(IRE), who looked badly in need of the outing, started slowly and looked clueless. The penny was starting to drop at the end and she will improve a good deal especially when stepped up to seven. (op 12-1)
Winsome Hearts, bred for stamina rather than speed, made a satisfactory debut but will need more time yet.
Smelly Cat Official explanation: jockey said filly hung left final furlong
Tilerium's Dream(IRE) Official explanation: jockey said gelding lost its action

3977 JOHN SMITH'S "NO NONSENSE RACING" MAIDEN FILLIES' STKS 7f
5:00 (5:01) (Class 4) 3-4-Y-O **£6,799** (£2,023; £1,011; £505) **Stalls** Low

Form RPR

0 **1** **Amber Queen (IRE)**[56] 2198 3-9-0 0 MichaelHills 8 87
(B W Hills) *w ldr: led over 2f out: edgd rt and rdn clr fnl f: readily* **3/1**[2]

0-2 **2** *4 1/2* **Rhadegunda**[15] 3452 3-9-0 0 JimmyFortune 6 74
(J H M Gosden) *trckd ldrs: drvn over 3f out: wnt 2nd over 1f out: no imp* **3/1**[2]

F-00 **3** *7* **Uace Mac**[42] 2597 4-9-5 52 JamieMoriarty(3) 1 58
(N Bycroft) *mde most tl over 2f out: one pce* **33/1**

30 **4** *1 1/2* **Rio Guru (IRE)**[66] 1915 3-9-0 0 DarryllHolland 2 51
(M R Channon) *chsd ldrs: drvn over 3f out: one pce fnl 2f* **5/2**[1]

5460 **5** *1 3/4* **Amylee (IRE)**[19] 3325 3-9-0 77 RobertWinston 7 47
(C G Cox) *chsd ldrs: one pce fnl 2f* **4/1**[3]

6 **6** *11* **Ceili Mor (IRE)**[15] 3452 3-9-0 0 GregFairley 4 17
(M Johnston) *dwlt: sn chsng ldrs: rdn over 3f out: lost pl 2f out: sn bhd* **12/1**

P-3 **7** *1* **Laureldean Dream (USA)**[23] 3177 3-9-0 0 AdrianMcCarthy 5 14
(P W Chapple-Hyam) *t.k.h: effrt over 2f out: sn rdn and wknd* **14/1**

1m 29.0s (3.70) **Going Correction** +0.85s/f (Soft)
WFA 3 from 4yo 8lb **7** Ran SP% **115.9**
Speed ratings (Par 102): **112,106,98,97,95 82,81**
toteswinger: 1&2 £2.60, 1&3 £21.00, 2&3 £12.70. CSF £12.84 TOTE £4.30: £2.10, £2.10; EX 13.40.
Owner Lady Richard Wellesley **Bred** R A Bonnycastle And Marston Stud **Trained** Lambourn, Berks

FOCUS
A very smart winning time for a race like this considering the conditions. The winner was having only her second start and should go on from here.

3978 JOHN SMITH'S "PREMIER CLUB" STKS (NURSERY H'CAP) 5f
5:35 (5:35) (Class 3) 2-Y-O **£7,771** (£2,312; £1,155; £577) **Stalls** Low

Form RPR

521 **1** **Mullglen**[53] 2281 2-8-10 **76** DavidAllan 5 83+
(T D Easterby) *hld up: smooth hdwy on wd outside over 2f out: led appr fnl f: pushed clr: readily* **9/2**[2]

3105 **2** *1 3/4* **Fivefootnumberone (IRE)**[8] 3663 2-9-0 **80** RobertWinston 9 81
(J J Quinn) *w ldrs: led over 2f out: hdd appr fnl f: kpt on: no imp* **11/2**[3]

3005 **3** *2 1/2* **Lisburn (IRE)**[4] 3809 2-8-8 **74** TWilliams 6 66
(M Brittain) *led tl over 2f out: styd on same pce appr fnl f* **9/1**

12 **4** *hd* **Polish Pride**[70] 1813 2-8-9 **75** DarryllHolland 4 66
(M Brittain) *w ldrs: kpt on same pce over 1f out* **7/4**[1]

1140 **5** *3* **She's A Shaw Thing**[25] 3105 2-9-2 **87** RichardEvans(5) 3 67
(P D Evans) *dwlt: sn w ldrs: edgd lft and wknd fnl f* **9/2**[2]

4612 **6** *hd* **Smalljohn**[8] 3670 2-8-8 **74** DNolan 2 54
(D Carroll) *chsd ldrs: outpcd and lost pl over 1f out: kpt on ins fnl f* **8/1**

2033 **7** *1* **Carmanjoe**[11] 3576 2-8-0 **66** (b[1]) DaleGibson 7 42
(M W Easterby) *s.i.s: sn drvn along: nvr a factor* **16/1**

63.61 secs (4.31) **Going Correction** +0.85s/f (Soft) **7** Ran SP% **115.1**
Speed ratings (Par 98): **99,96,92,91,87 86,85**
toteswinger: 1&2 £4.00, 1&3 £7.40, 2&3 £10.10. CSF £29.45 CT £213.08 TOTE £6.20: £2.90, £2.80; EX 30.70 Place 6 £203.77, Place 5 £66.18.
Owner Richard Taylor & Philip Hebdon **Bred** Rosyground Stud **Trained** Great Habton, N Yorks
■ Stewards' Enquiry : Darryll Holland one-day ban: failed to ride to draw (Jul 27)
D Nolan one-day ban: failed to ride to draw (Jul 27)

FOCUS
The 'official' ratings shown next to each horse are estimated and for information purposes only. The winner is clearly improving fast and the runner-up sets the standard.

NOTEBOOK
Mullglen ◆ is not that big but he is solidly made and he looks to have thrived in the seven weeks since his Musselburgh win. Confidently ridden, he was left to take the stands' rail position and he won with plenty to spare. A follow-up even from his revised mark looks a real possibility. (tchd 5-1)
Fivefootnumberone(IRE), having his second race in nine days, was in an excitable mood and had two handlers in the paddock. He took it up at halfway but the winner was simply waiting to pounce.
Lisburn(IRE), an excitable filly, had two handlers in the paddock. Suited by the drop back to five, in the end she was simply not up to the task. (op 11-1)
Polish Pride, whose Thirsk form has not worked out, was on her toes and needed two handlers. This may be as good as she is. Official explanation: trainer said filly was unsuited by the soft ground (op 5-2 tchd 13-8)
She's A Shaw Thing, back on her favoured soft ground, is not in the same form as she was when showing very useful form when winning on her first two starts. (op 4-1 tchd 5-1)
Smalljohn, already having his eighth start, has already been tried in a visor and is not straightforward. The drop back to five was not in his favour. (op 7-1 tchd 10-1)
T/Jkpt: Not won. T/Plt: £441.30 to a £1 stake. Pool: £197,482.52. 326.61 winning tickets. T/Qpdt: £34.20 to a £1 stake. Pool: £7,546.92. 163.18 winning tickets. JR

3979 - 3981a (Foreign Racing) - See Raceform Interactive

3531
CURRAGH (R-H)
Saturday, July 12

OFFICIAL GOING: Straight course - yielding; round course - good to yielding

3982a KEENELAND MINSTREL STKS (GROUP 3) 7f
4:00 (4:03) 3-Y-O+ **£35,845** (£10,477; £4,963; £1,654)

RPR

1 **Jumbajukiba**[13] 3536 5-9-12 114 (b) FMBerry 7 115
(Mrs John Harrington, Ire) *stmbld leaving stalls: sn led and mde rest: rdn and strly pressed 2f out: kpt on wl fnl f* **4/1**[3]

2 *1/2* **Al Qasi (IRE)**[56] 2193 5-9-10 MJKinane 8 112
(P W Chapple-Hyam) *trckd ldrs in 3rd: rdn along 2f out: 2nd 1f out: kpt on same pce* **9/4**[1]

3 *1* **Georgebernardshaw (IRE)**[24] 3119 3-8-13 110 JMurtagh 9 103
(A P O'Brien, Ire) *chsd ldrs: 4th 2 1/2f out: sn rdn: wnt 3rd 1f out: kpt on same pce* **10/3**[2]

4 *nk* **Capt Chaos (IRE)**[13] 3536 3-9-2 106 CDHayes 4 105+
(Edward Lynam, Ire) *hld up towards rr: 6th 1 1/2f out: r.o wl fnl f* **9/1**

5 *4 1/2* **Raptor (GER)**[9] 3635 5-9-7 DPMcDonogh 2 93
(K R Burke) *chsd ldrs on outer: 5th 2 1/2f out: sn rdn and no ex* **16/1**

6 *nk* **Hard Rock City (USA)**[83] 1508 8-9-7 106 NGMcCullagh 5 92
(M J Grassick, Ire) *chsd ldrs: rdn in 6th 2 1/2f out: no imp* **20/1**

7 *1 1/2* **Aleagueoftheirown (IRE)**[10] 3619 4-9-4 100 WMLordan 1 85
(David Wachman, Ire) *hld up in rr: rdn and no imp fr 2f out* **20/1**

8 *3/4* **Garnica (FR)**[42] 2637 5-9-12 PJSmullen 6 91
(D Nicholls) *prom: travelling wl in 2nd 2 1/2f out: sn rdn and no imp* **6/1**

9 *3 1/2* **Confuchias (IRE)**[14] 3488 4-9-7 WJSupple 3 77
(K R Burke) *hld up in rr: rdn and no imp fr 2f out* **14/1**

1m 26.2s (-0.90) **Going Correction** +0.225s/f (Good)
WFA 3 from 4yo+ 8lb **9** Ran SP% **120.2**
Speed ratings: **114,113,112,111,106 106,104,103,99**
CSF £14.05 TOTE £4.30: £2.00, £1.50, £1.30; DF 20.30.
Owner J P O'Flaherty **Bred** Woodcote Stud Ltd **Trained** Moone, Co Kildare

FOCUS
The form is rated through the winner who ran to his best.

The Form Book, Raceform Ltd, Compton, RG20 6NL

NOTEBOOK

Jumbajukiba more than justified his connections' decision to supplement him for this at a cost of 7,500euros and gamely registered his first win in Group company. He soon overcame a stumble out of the gates and showed real battling qualities when challenged at the business end. A trip to France for the Group 1 Prix Maurice de Gheest next month could now figure in his plans. (op 7/2 tchd 9/2)

Al Qasi(IRE) was having his first outing in Ireland since landing his last race, a Group 3 over 6f at the track last August, and was well supported. He just hit a flat spot before coming back at the winner near the finish and posted one of his better efforts in defeat. (op 5/2 tchd 3/1)

Raptor(GER) ran a better race for the return to an easier surface, but was never seriously in the hunt and is not an easy horse to place successfully.

Garnica(FR) moved nicely through the race until coming under pressure passing the 2f pole and eventually dropping out. He was later found to have scoped badly. Official explanation: trainer said horse was found to have mucus following a post-race endoscopic examination (op 7/1 tchd 5/1)

Confuchias(IRE) was a long way below his recent level on this return to his former homeland and is one to tread carefully with at present. (op 12/1)

3983a KEENELAND INTERNATIONAL STKS (GROUP 3) 1m 1f

4:30 (4:31) 3-Y-0+ **£38,235** (£11,176; £5,294; £1,764)

RPR

1 **Plan (USA)**[13] 3536 3-8-11 100 JMurtagh 1 113+
(A P O'Brien, Ire) *trckd ldrs: pushed along in 4th fr 4f out: 3rd 2f out: led ins fnl f: styd on wl* **11/4**[2]

2 *1* **Regime (IRE)**[24] 3121 4-9-10 PJSmullen 7 114
(M L W Bell) *trckd ldr in mod 2nd: led 2f out: rdn and hdd ins fnl f: no ex* **5/1**[3]

3 *2* **Mustameet (USA)**[38] 2740 7-9-7 111 DPMcDonogh 4 106
(Kevin Prendergast, Ire) *hld up in 5th: rdn in 4th 2f out: kpt on in 3rd fnl f* **11/2**

4 *2 1/2* **Lisvale (IRE)**[13] 3536 3-8-11 110 WMLordan 2 101
(David Wachman, Ire) *trckd ldrs in 3rd: rdn in 2nd 2f out: no ex fr 1f out* **11/8**[1]

5 *5 1/2* **Alarazi (IRE)**[68] 1882 4-9-7 106 (b) MJKinane 6 89
(John M Oxx, Ire) *led and sn clr: reduced advantage 4f out: rdn and hdd 2f out: sn wknd* **7/1**

6 *16* **Crooked Throw (IRE)**[13] 3536 9-9-7 106 WJLee 3 55
(C F Swan, Ire) *t.k.h in last: collided w rail briefly after 2f: rdn and no imp fr 3f out: sn trailing* **33/1**

1m 56.8s (1.90) **Going Correction** +0.45s/f (Yiel)
WFA 3 from 4yo+ 10lb 7 Ran SP% **116.3**
Speed ratings: **109,108,106,104,99 85**
CSF £17.43 TOTE £3.90: £1.90, £2.80; DF 36.20.
Owner Michael Tabor **Bred** Dromoland Farm **Trained** Ballydoyle, Co Tipperary

FOCUS

The winner is progressive and the form is rated through the runner-up.

NOTEBOOK

Plan(USA), re-routed here after it was apparent he would not make the cut in the John Smith's Cup at York, was asked for his effort before the turn into the home straight and took time to hit top gear. However, he responded most positively for pressure and eventually got on top to win readily. This was his first run beyond 1m and it no doubt helped him, so with further improvement looking assured from this lightly-raced colt, he should really be able to build on this career-best display now. (op 9/4 tchd 3/1)

Regime(IRE) raced handily from the off and was the last to come off the bridle in the home straight. He had every chance, but was unable to hold off his younger rival where it mattered and this was much more like it from him.

Mustameet(USA), who took this race in 2006, kept on willingly from off the pace and would have likely enjoyed a more truly-run affair. (op 5/1)

Lisvale(IRE), who beat the winner over 1m at this venue 13 days previously, had his chance yet failed to see out the extra distance anywhere near as well as that rival. He can better this again when reverting to a sharper test. (op 2/1 tchd 5/4)

3984 - 3994a (Foreign Racing) - See Raceform Interactive

2858 BELMONT PARK (L-H)

Saturday, July 12

OFFICIAL GOING: Firm

3995a MAN O'WAR STKS (GRADE 1) (TURF) 1m 3f (T)

10:15 (10:18) 3-Y-0+

£150,754 (£50,251; £25,126; £12,563; £7,538; £2,513)

RPR

1 **Red Rocks (IRE)**[36] 2791 5-8-4 (b) JJCastellano 6 121
(B J Meehan) *raced in 3rd behind clear leaders, closed up going well 3f out, switched outside 2f out, led inside final f, driven out* **62/10**[3]

2 *2* **Curlin (USA)**[28] 4-8-4 RAlbarado 7 118
(Steven Asmussen, U.S.A) **9/20**[1]

3 *1/2* **Better Talk Now (USA)**[35] 9-8-8 (b) RADominguez 1 121
(H Graham Motion, U.S.A) **56/10**[2]

4 *3/4* **Sudan (IRE)**[42] 5-8-8 JRVelazquez 5 120
(Robert Frankel, U.S.A) **128/10**

5 *nk* **True Cause (USA)**[23] 5-8-4 (b) RMaragh 4 115
(Saeed Bin Suroor) **29/1**

6 *hd* **Grand Couturier**[23] 5-8-8 CHBorel 2 119
(Robert Ribaudo, U.S.A) **113/10**

7 *21 1/2* **Mission Approved (USA)**[20] 4-8-4 DCohen 3 79
(Gary Contessa, U.S.A) **39/1**

2m 12.6s (-2.45) 7 Ran SP% **119.2**
PARI-MUTUEL (including $2 stakes): WIN 14.40; PL (1-2) 4.00, 2.50;SHOW (1-2-3) 2.90, 2.10, 2.70; SF 32.00.
Owner J Paul Reddam **Bred** Ballylinch Stud **Trained** Manton, Wilts

NOTEBOOK

Red Rocks(IRE), fitted with blinkers for the first time, returned to form with a famous defeat of two fellow Breeders' Cup winners. With two runners going clear early on, he led the main group and was always travelling well. Once in front he was always holding the favourite, who failed to reproduce his outstanding dirt form. A third appearance in the Breeders' Cup is his main target, and he now stays in the USA.

Curlin(USA), the Breeders' Cup Classic and Dubai World Cup winner, who is almost certainly the best dirt horse in the world at present, did not look anywhere near as effective on this switch to grass. He was close enough to the winner throughout but was not good enough to get past on this firm surface. He may be suited by more give, which he will almost certainly get if taking his chance in the Arc, but it remains to be seen if connections give him another chance on turf before coming to Europe. The Irish Champion Stakes is another possibility.

Better Talk Now(USA), another winner of the Breeders' Cup Turf, ran a creditable race but connections feel he is better with more give in the ground.

3719 HAYDOCK (L-H)

Sunday, July 13

OFFICIAL GOING: Heavy (soft in places; 6.4)

After a wet spell the ground had started to dry out and was described as 'very dead, tacky and sticky'. Dolling added 21yds to distances on round course.
Wind: Light, half-against Weather: fine and sunny

3996 MANCHESTER EVENING NEWS CLAIMING STKS 1m 2f 120y

2:20 (2:21) (Class 5) 3-4-Y-0 **£3,238** (£963; £481; £240) **Stalls** High

Form RPR

0-60 1 **Persian Peril**[8] 3711 4-9-8 68 TomEaves 3 76
(G A Swinbank) *trckd ldr: effrt over 3f out: hung lft and led over 2f out: styd on wl fnl f* **9/1**

4522 2 *2* **Just Rob**[40] 2699 3-9-2 77 DarryllHolland 1 79
(R Hollinshead) *hld up: effrt 3f out: styd on to take 2nd ins fnl f: no imp* **11/10**[1]

1350 3 *1/2* **Grethel (IRE)**[7] 3755 4-9-1 54 DanielTudhope 5 65
(A Berry) *t.k.h in rr: hdwy 3f out: wnt 2nd over 1f out: kpt on same pce* **12/1**

1601 4 *7* **Carry On Cleo**[6] 3791 3-8-1 57 (v) FrancisNorton 6 51
(A Berry) *led: hdd over 2f out: hung lft and lost pl over 1f out* **8/1**[3]

4054 5 *1* **Gold Prospect**[15] 3474 4-9-7 73 TPQueally 4 57
(M L W Bell) *hld up: effrt 3f out: wknd over 1f out* **7/2**[2]

0600 6 *1 1/4* **Fever**[8] 3716 4-9-7 67 PaulMulrennan 2 55
(M W Easterby) *trckd ldrs: effrt over 3f out: hung both ways: lost pl over 1f out* **12/1**

2m 23.96s (7.26) **Going Correction** +0.75s/f (Yiel)
WFA 3 from 4yo 12lb 6 Ran SP% **106.3**
Speed ratings (Par 103): **103,101,101,96,95 94**
toteswinger: 1&2 £3.50, 1&3 £9.50, 2&3 £3.30. CSF £17.50 TOTE £10.40: £3.10, £1.20; EX 24.10.The winner and Fever were subject to friendly claims.
Owner Mrs J Porter **Bred** Mrs P Lewis **Trained** Melsonby, N Yorks

FOCUS

A fair claimer run in testing ground.

Fever Official explanation: jockey said gelding hung both ways

3997 FIONA STRINGER MAIDEN STKS 6f

2:50 (2:54) (Class 5) 2-Y-0 **£3,238** (£963; £481; £240) **Stalls** Centre

Form RPR

1 **Desert Phantom (USA)** 2-9-3 0 RichardMullen 7 88+
(D M Simcock) *w ldrs: led over 1f out: styd on wl* **11/4**[1]

00 2 *2 3/4* **Olympic Dream**[18] 3364 2-9-3 0 TonyHamilton 11 80
(R A Fahey) *hld up: smooth hdwy over 2f out: chal over 1f out: kpt on same pce* **11/1**

3 3 *3 3/4* **Captain Scooby**[50] 2388 2-9-0 0 MichaelJStainton(3) 4 69
(R M Whitaker) *t.k.h: led after 1f: hdd over 1f out: fdd* **4/1**[2]

4 *3/4* **Striker Torres (IRE)** 2-9-3 0 TomEaves 6 66+
(B Smart) *t.k.h: trckd ldrs: rdn over 2f out: outpcd over 1f out: kpt on ins fnl f* **11/4**[1]

30 5 *3* **Secret City (IRE)**[26] 3114 2-9-3 0 DarrenWilliams 10 57
(R Bastiman) *unruly s: w ldrs: hung lft and lost pl over 1f out* **12/1**

0 6 *1 3/4* **Who Art Thou (USA)**[31] 2972 2-9-3 0 DarryllHolland 1 52
(P A Blockley) *sn outpcd and in rr: nvr on terms* **10/1**

7 *hd* **Real Dandy** 2-9-3 0 TPQueally 9 51
(J G Given) *rrd s: in rr: sme hdwy 3f out: sn wknd* **7/1**[3]

8 *14* **Toledo Gold (IRE)** 2-9-3 0 DavidAllan 2 —
(E J Alston) *sn chsng ldrs: lost pl over 2f out: bhd whn eased ins fnl f* **20/1**

1m 18.07s (4.07) **Going Correction** +0.625s/f (Yiel) 8 Ran SP% **115.7**
Speed ratings (Par 94): **97,93,88,87,83 81,80,62**
toteswinger: 1&2 £8.30, 1&3 £3.20, 2&3 £10.80. CSF £34.92 TOTE £3.70: £1.50, £2.60, £1.80; EX 35.60.
Owner Ahmad Al Shaikh **Bred** John R Penn & Frank Penn **Trained** Newmarket, Suffolk

FOCUS

Just a fair maiden race but the winner has plenty of potential and the runner-up ran easily his best race so far on his third start. The third sets the standard.

NOTEBOOK

Desert Phantom(USA), quite a big, well-made newcomer, is from a stable with a good line to juvenile form and he was a major mover on the morning line. He knew his job and scored in most decisive fashion. His actions suggests that he does not necessarily need soft ground. (op 3-1 tchd 10-3 and 7-2 in places)

Olympic Dream ◆, who had shown little in two previous starts, is a grand looker and he looked in tip-top condition. He travelled smoothly and did more than enough to finish clear second best without his rider once picking up his stick. He will not receive a lenient nursery mark now but he looks very interesting all the same. (op 10-1)

Captain Scooby took a fierce grip. He was soon taking them along but in the end the sixth furlong found him out. (op 5-2 tchd 9-2)

Striker Torres(IRE), who fetched 100,00gns at the breeze-up sales, is a good-topped colt but he continually swished his tail in the paddock. He pulled like a trooper but after showing his inexperience he was sticking on again at the death. This will have taught him plenty. (op 4-1 tchd 5-2 tchd 9-2 in places)

Secret City(IRE) was in a foul mood at the start. He dropped himself right out and hopefully is not going the wrong way.

3998 JOBSMINE H'CAP 6f

3:20 (3:23) (Class 4) (0-85,84) 4-Y-0+ **£5,504** (£1,637; £818; £408) **Stalls** Centre

Form RPR

0505 1 **Balakiref**[8] 3713 9-8-7 **70** ow1 TomEaves 10 77
(M Dods) *hld up in rr: hdwy 2f out: edgd lft and styd on wl fnl f: led post* **7/2**[2]

0164 2 *shd* **Rabbit Fighter (IRE)**[8] 3724 4-8-8 **71** ow2 (v) PaulMulrennan 4 77
(D Shaw) *w ldrs: led over 1f out: hdd post* **17/2**

060- 3 *3/4* **Topflightcoolracer**[237] 6876 4-9-3 **80** LiamJones 3 84
(Mrs G S Rees) *chsd ldrs on outside: outpcd over 2f out: kpt on wl fnl f* **40/1**

0001 4 *3/4* **Geojimali**[15] 3489 6-9-7 **84** JohnEgan 2 86
(J S Goldie) *in rr: hdwy over 1f out: styd on towards fin* **7/1**[3]

4551 5 *3/4* **Makshoof (IRE)**[10] 3626 4-8-13 **76** DarryllHolland 5 76
(K A Ryan) *midfield: effrt over 2f out: kpt on: nvr able to chal* **11/4**[1]

6264 6 *2 1/4* **Steel Blue**[16] 3454 8-7-11 **65** oh5 NataliaGemelova(5) 6 58
(R M Whitaker) *led tl over 2f out: wknd appr fnl f* **15/2**

1014 **7** *1* **Dickie Le Davoir**[1] 3956 4-9-0 82 6ex................................ MarkCoumbe(5) 1 72
(John A Harris) *swtchd rt after s: hdwy stands' side to ld over 2f out: hdd over 1f out: sn wknd* **8/1**

0100 **8** *½* **Bonnie Prince Blue**[57] 2195 5-9-6 83.........................(b) DeanMcKeown 7 71
(B W Hills) *chsd ldrs: wknd appr fnl f* **14/1**

003 **9** *6* **Tudor Prince (IRE)**[2] 3904 4-8-12 75................................ TPQueally 8 45
(A W Carroll) *chsd ldrs: lost pl over 1f out* **7/1**[3]

1m 17.81s (3.81) **Going Correction** +0.625s/f (Yiel) **9** Ran SP% **116.4**
Speed ratings (Par 105): **99,98,97,96,95 92,91,90,82**
toteswinger: 1&2 £9.00, 1&3 £31.30, 2&3 £55.80. CSF £33.60 CT £1022.15 TOTE £4.70: £1.70, £2.80, £8.20; EX 40.90.
Owner Septimus Racing Group **Bred** S R Hope And D Erwin **Trained** Denton, Co Durham
■ Stewards' Enquiry : Tom Eaves three-day ban: used whip with excessive frequency and with unreasonable force (Jul 27-29)
Paul Mulrennan caution: used whip with excessive frequency

FOCUS
The first five were stacked up at the line in this fair handicap.

3999 M.E.N. SPORT H'CAP 6f
3:50 (3:51) (Class 4) (0-85,85) 3-Y-O **£5,504** (£1,637; £818; £408) **Stalls** Centre

Form RPR

0405 **1** **Artsu**[16] 3458 3-8-8 70................................ TPQueally 8 82
(M L W Bell) *stdd s: hld up in rr: gd hdwy on wd outside to ld over 1f out: sn clr: rdn out* **7/1**

00-0 **2** *1¼* **Sudden Impact (IRE)**[43] 2605 3-9-6 85................ RussellKennemore(3) 7 93
(Paul Green) *chsd ldrs: wnt 2nd over 1f out: kpt on: nt rch wnr* **12/1**

-104 **3** *4* **Minus Fifteen (IRE)**[41] 2674 3-9-1 77................................ DarryllHolland 6 73
(K A Ryan) *led: edgd lft and hdd over 1f out: sn wl outpcd* **15/2**

-002 **4** *2¾* **Kashimin (IRE)**[10] 3626 3-9-4 80................................ PaulMulrennan 10 68
(G A Swinbank) *chsd ldrs: kpt on same pce fnl 2f* **7/2**[2]

3510 **5** *3½* **Everything**[21] 3298 3-8-9 71................................ MickyFenton 11 48
(P T Midgley) *chsd ldrs on inner: hmpd 4f out: lost pl over 1f out* **22/1**

0542 **6** *¾* **Mister Hardy**[15] 3475 3-9-1 84................................ FrederikTylicki(7) 2 59
(R A Fahey) *chsd ldrs: lost pl over 1f out* **4/1**[3]

-424 **7** *4½* **Tyfos**[23] 3202 3-9-2 78................................ JohnEgan 1 40
(W M Brisbourne) *sn chsng ldrs: lost pl over 1f out* **16/1**

41 **8** *1½* **Yahwudhee (FR)**[48] 2455 3-9-4 80................................ AdrianMcCarthy 3 37
(P W Chapple-Hyam) *chsd ldrs: edgd lft over 2f out: sn btn* **11/4**[1]

5116 **9** *2* **We Have A Dream**[20] 3324 3-9-7 83................................ FrancisNorton 5 34
(W R Muir) *chsd ldrs: lost pl over 1f out* **7/1**

1m 17.45s (3.45) **Going Correction** +0.625s/f (Yiel) **9** Ran SP% **123.6**
Speed ratings (Par 102): **102,100,95,91,86 85,79,77,75**
toteswinger: 1&2 £17.60, 1&3 £10.90, 2&3 £16.30. CSF £92.60 CT £662.73 TOTE £8.90: £2.40, £3.50, £3.00; EX 71.90.
Owner Mrs Moira Gershinson **Bred** Lady Whent **Trained** Newmarket, Suffolk
■ Stewards' Enquiry : Darryll Holland one-day ban: careless riding (Jul 28)

FOCUS
A return to form from Artsu in this fair handicap.
Tyfos Official explanation: jockey said gelding was unsuited by the heavy (soft in places) ground
Yahwudhee(FR) Official explanation: jockey said colt had no more to give
We Have A Dream Official explanation: jockey said colt stopped quickly

4000 RICKY HATTON H'CAP 5f
4:25 (4:25) (Class 4) (0-80,77) 3-Y-O **£5,504** (£1,637; £818; £408) **Stalls** Centre

Form RPR

2044 **1** **Supermassive Muse (IRE)**[16] 3455 3-9-2 72.......(p) StephenDonohoe 4 80
(E S McMahon) *hld up in rr: stdy hdwy 2f out: burst through to ld last 150yds: rdn clr* **11/2**

1-56 **2** *3¼* **Weet A Surprise**[29] 3028 3-9-3 73................................ LiamJones 1 69
(R Hollinshead) *racd wd: sn outpcd: hdwy over 1f out: styd on to take 2nd ins fnl f: no ch w wnr* **18/1**

1252 **3** *1¾* **Rio Sands**[16] 3455 3-8-13 72................................ MichaelJStainton(3) 5 62
(R M Whitaker) *chsd ldrs: chal over 1f out: kpt on same pce* **3/1**[2]

65 **4** *shd* **Our Acquaintance**[59] 2127 3-8-13 69.........................(b[1]) RichardMullen 8 58
(W R Muir) *w ldrs: led over 1f out: hdd and no ex jst ins fnl f* **12/1**

0032 **5** *1½* **Peter's Storm (USA)**[8] 3724 3-8-13 69................................ DarryllHolland 2 53
(K A Ryan) *chsd ldrs on outer: rdn over 2f out: one pce* **5/2**[1]

-06 **6** *3½* **Firenza Bond**[44] 2570 3-9-7 77................................ SilvestreDeSousa 7 48
(G R Oldroyd) *led tl hdd & wknd over 1f out* **12/1**

0-25 **7** *1¾* **Cheshire Rose**[16] 3455 3-8-9 65................................ PaulFessey 3 30
(T D Barron) *hood removed v late: dwlt: hdwy on outer to chse ldrs over 2f out: edgd lft and lost pl over 1f out* **10/1**

2023 **8** *4* **Killer Class**[16] 3455 3-8-8 64................................ JohnEgan 6 15
(J S Goldie) *w ldrs: wknd over 1f out* **5/1**[3]

64.63 secs (4.13) **Going Correction** +0.625s/f (Yiel) **8** Ran SP% **115.4**
Speed ratings (Par 102): **91,85,83,82,80 74,72,65**
toteswinger: 1&2 £13.30, 1&3 £4.20, 2&3 £10.80. CSF £95.00 CT £354.46 TOTE £6.50: £1.90, £4.30, £1.60; EX 56.30.
Owner Nick Hughes **Bred** Richard O' Hara **Trained** Lichfield, Staffs

FOCUS
The leaders seemed to go off very fast and the first two came from off the pace.
Cheshire Rose Official explanation: jockey said filly missed the break

4001 CHANNEL M H'CAP 1m 30y
5:00 (5:01) (Class 5) (0-75,74) 3-Y-O+ **£3,238** (£963; £481; £240) **Stalls** Low

Form RPR

0-20 **1** **She's Our Lass (IRE)**[8] 3729 7-9-13 73................................ DavidAllan 7 80
(D Carroll) *hld up in midfield: effrt over 2f out: led over 1f out: edgd rt ins fnl f: hld on towards fin* **4/1**[3]

-030 **2** *shd* **Prince Samos (IRE)**[65] 1947 6-9-10 70................................ StephenDonohoe 5 76
(E S McMahon) *hld up in midfield: drvn over 3f out: hung lft: styd on appr fnl f: sltly hmpd ins fnl f: kpt on nr fin: fin 3rd, 1/2l & shd: plcd 2nd* **10/1**

0150 **3** *½* **Don Pietro**[42] 2642 5-9-7 67................................ DarryllHolland 1 73
(P A Blockley) *led tl over 1f out: edgd rt and rallied ins fnl f: no ex nr fin: fin 2nd, 1/2l: disq: plcd 3rd* **7/1**

0562 **4** *5* **Pitbull**[8] 3725 5-9-0 60.........................(p) LiamJones 8 53
(Mrs G S Rees) *t.k.h in rr: hdwy over 4f out: chsng ldrs over 2f out: hung lft: wknd appr fnl f* **3/1**[1]

1000 **5** *5* **Komreyev Star**[16] 3431 6-8-9 55................................ PaulMulrennan 4 37
(R E Peacock) *trckd ldrs: effrt over 3f out: wknd over 1f out* **10/1**

0630 **6** *2½* **Gallego**[8] 3736 6-8-12 61................................ KirstyMilczarek(3) 2 37
(R J Price) *slowly away in last: reminders over 3f out: nvr on terms* **14/1**

0302 **7** *nk* **Wovoka (IRE)**[7] 3758 5-9-13 73................................ TonyHamilton 6 48
(D W Barker) *hld up in rr: hdwy over 3f out: wknd 2f out* **7/2**[2]

-356 **8** *3¾* **Musca (IRE)**[33] 2913 4-10-0 74................................ TomEaves 3 41
(C Grant) *chsd ldrs: drvn over 3f out: lost pl 2f out: eased towards fin* **7/1**

1m 49.66s (5.86) **Going Correction** +0.75s/f (Yiel) **8** Ran SP% **117.1**
Speed ratings (Par 103): **100,99,99,94,89 86,86,82**
toteswinger: 1&2 £9.30, 1&3 £6.80, 2&3 £12.00. CSF £44.01 CT £275.56 TOTE £5.50: £1.90, £3.40, £2.30; EX 51.70 Place 6 £ 378.55, Place 5 £ 238.70.
Owner John Walsh & Reuben Glynn **Bred** Illuminatus Investments **Trained** Sledmere, E Yorks

FOCUS
A modest handicap.
Pitbull Official explanation: jockey said gelding hung left
Komreyev Star Official explanation: trainer said that after examination vet said gelding had thumps
Musca(IRE) Official explanation: jockey said gelding moved poorly
T/Plt: £275.00 to a £1 stake. Pool: £81,105.16. 215.22 winning tickets. T/Qpdt: £196.20 to a £1 stake. Pool: £4,110.90. 15.50 winning tickets. WG

4002 - (Foreign Racing) - See Raceform Interactive

3979 CURRAGH (R-H)
Sunday, July 13

OFFICIAL GOING: Straight course - good to yielding; round course - good

4003a THALGO LADIES DERBY H'CAP 1m 4f
2:35 (2:35) (60-100,100) 3-Y-O+ **£12,924** (£3,791; £1,806; £615) **Stalls** Far side

RPR

1 **Miss Fancy Pants**[18] 3388 4-9-8 73................................ MissNCarberry 83+
(Noel Meade, Ire) *mid-div on inner: prog travelling wl into 5th 2 1/2f out: led 1f out: kpt on wl: comf* **10/3**[2]

2 *3½* **The Last Hurrah (IRE)**[14] 3537 8-9-10 80.................(b) MissFCumani(5) 82
(Mrs John Harrington, Ire) *trckd ldrs: 4th 2 1/2f out: rdn to ld 2f out: hdd 1f out: kpt on same pce* **8/1**[3]

3 *shd* **Indian Pace (IRE)**[25] 3150 7-10-3 82................................ MissEJJones 84+
(John E Kiely, Ire) *towards rr on inner: hdwy fr 3f out: mod 3rd 1f out: styd on strly wout troubling wnr: nvr nrr* **10/1**

4 *3* **Raise The Goblet (IRE)**[312] 5131 4-9-4 76................................ MissKJSeal(7) 73
(P Hughes, Ire) *mid-div: 7th 2 1/2f out: kpt on fr 2f out* **25/1**

5 *½* **Fantoche (BRZ)**[22] 3287 6-10-6 85.........................(b) MissPaulineRyan 81
(Mrs John Harrington, Ire) *prom: disp ld 1/2-way: rdn and hdd 2f out: sn no ex* **10/1**

6 *hd* **Darenjan (IRE)**[10] 3661 5-9-2 74................................ MissRO'Neill(7) 70
(John Joseph Hanlon, Ire) *led: jnd 1/2-way: rdn ld narrowly 2 1/2f out: hdd 2f out: sn no imp* **14/1**

7 *nk* **Ballygologue (IRE)**[15] 3512 3-9-7 85................................ MsKWalsh 80
(T Stack, Ire) *mid-div: rdn in 8th 2f out: sn no imp* **3/1**[1]

8 *5½* **Qassas**[16] 3464 6-9-2 72.........................(b) MissMMGannon(5) 59
(Michael David Murphy, Ire) *trckd ldrs: no imp fr 4f out* **33/1**

9 *2½* **Long Road (USA)**[19] 3355 7-9-10 75................................ MissNadineForde 58
(Niall Madden, Ire) *towards rr on inner: prog into mod 12th 1 1/2f out: kpt on same pce* **40/1**

10 *1¼* **Always The Groom (IRE)**[21] 3305 6-9-8 73................................ MissAFoley 54
(Patrick J Flynn, Ire) *prom: disp ld 1/2-way: hdd and no imp fr 2 1/2f out* **10/1**

11 *1* **Mutakarrim**[22] 3287 11-10-13 99................................ MissSCiccone(7) 78
(D K Weld, Ire) *towards rr: no imp fr 4f out* **50/1**

12 *nk* **Prince Erik**[81] 1291 4-11-2 100................................ MissJWalsh(5) 79
(D K Weld, Ire) *nvr bttr than mid-div* **14/1**

13 *½* **Polish Power (GER)**[62] 2059 8-11-0 93................................ MrsSMoore 71
(J S Moore) *nvr bttr than mid-div* **11/1**

14 *1* **Swift Sailing (USA)**[9] 3704 7-9-0 72 oh2.........................(tp) MsLO'Neill(7) 48
(Patrick Allen, Ire) *prom: disp ld 1/2-way: hdd & wknd fr 2 1/2f out* **33/1**

15 *2½* **Bobs Pride (IRE)**[111] 1008 6-10-12 94................................ MissCCashman(3) 66
(D K Weld, Ire) *mid-div on wd outside: no imp fr 3f out* **25/1**

16 *2½* **Klassy (IRE)**[24] 2649 6-9-10 75 oh3 ow3................................ MissLAHourigan 43
(Bryan F Murphy, Ire) *trckd ldrs: wknd fr 3f out* **25/1**

17 *nk* **Akimbo (USA)**[4] 3862 7-9-0 72 oh3.........................(t) MissNChadwick(7) 40
(James Leavy, Ire) *a towards rr* **25/1**

18 *12* **Lazio (GER)**[182] 4867 7-10-11 93................................ MissCJMacmahon(3) 41
(F G Hand, Ire) *trckd ldrs: dropped to mid-div on outer ent st: sn wknd* **33/1**

19 *½* **Visit Wexford (IRE)**[605] 3128 7-9-6 78................................ MissDMcCurtin(7) 26
(John E Kiely, Ire) *in rr of mid-div on wd outside: no imp fr 4f out* **33/1**

2m 38.4s (0.90) **Going Correction** +0.075s/f (Good)
WFA 3 from 4yo+ 13lb **19** Ran SP% **139.7**
Speed ratings: **100,97,97,95,95 95,94,91,89,88 88,87,87,86,85 83,83,75,75**
CSF £31.18 CT £270.11 TOTE £4.00: £1.30, £1.80, £2.30, £10.20; DF 24.20.
Owner KellyTierneyMcEvoy Partnership **Bred** Mrs M Lavell **Trained** Castletown, Co Meath

NOTEBOOK
Miss Fancy Pants won this with a bit in hand and has a choice of engagements at Galway. (op 4/1)
Polish Power(GER) came into this on a hat-trick but was racing off a mark a stone higher than for the first of those successes and failed to get involved. (op 10/1 tchd 12/1)
Akimbo(USA) Official explanation: trainer later said gelding was found to have burst a blood vessel post-race
Lazio(GER) Official explanation: trainer said gelding was found to have burst a blood vessel post-race

4004a LADBROKES ROCKINGHAM H'CAP 5f
3:05 (3:09) 3-Y-O+
£53,029 (£16,852; £8,029; £2,735; £1,852; £970)

RPR

1 **Masta Plasta (IRE)**[23] 3243 5-9-11 104................................ CDHayes 14 114
(D Nicholls) *a.p: disp ld on far side 1/2-way: clr ld 1 1/2f out: styd on strly fnl f* **9/2**[1]

2 *1¾* **Le Cadre Noir (IRE)**[14] 3533 4-10-0 107................................ PJSmullen 11 110
(D K Weld, Ire) *mid-div: rdn in 5th 1f out: kpt on wout threatening wnr fnl f* **7/1**[2]

3 *¾* **How's She Cuttin' (IRE)**[16] 3451 5-8-5 84.........................(b) WJSupple 17 85
(T D Barron) *prom: rdn in 3rd 1 1/2f out: kpt on same pce fnl f* **8/1**[3]

4 *hd* **Kingsdale Ocean (IRE)**[14] 3532 5-8-2 91................................ LFRoche(10) 15 91
(D K Weld, Ire) *chsd ldrs: rdn in 4th 1 1/2f out: no ex* **12/1**

5 *shd* **College Scholar (GER)**[14] 3532 4-7-11 83 oh6................................ SFoley(7) 2 83
(Liam McAteer, Ire) *chsd ldrs: rdn and kpt on same pce fr 1 1/2f out* **16/1**

6 *½* **La Sylvia (IRE)**[9] 3701 3-8-4 88 oh1................................ NGMcCullagh 10 84
(Desmond McDonogh, Ire) *led: jnd 1/2-way: rdn and hdd 1 1/2f out: sn no ex* **11/1**

7	hd	**Flash McGahon (IRE)**[14] [3532] 4-9-5 98.........................(b) MJKinane 18	95
		(John M Oxx, Ire) *mid-div: rdn in 6th 1f out: no ex* **14/1**	
8	1 1/2	**Teachers Choice (IRE)**[263] [6441] 5-7-11 83 oh6............ MHarley(7) 16	75
		(Adrian McGuinness, Ire) *mid-div: kpt on same pce fr 2f out* **33/1**	
9	3/4	**Senor Benny (USA)**[14] [3533] 9-9-8 101........................ DPMcDonogh 5	90
		(M McDonagh, Ire) *in rr: sme late hdwy* **20/1**	
10	1/2	**Nanotech (IRE)**[16] [3468] 4-8-5 84.....................(p) MCHussey 12	71
		(Jarlath P Fahey, Ire) *chsd ldrs: cl up 2f out: rdn and sn wknd* **14/1**	
11	hd	**Brave Falcon (IRE)**[38] [2768] 4-7-11 83 oh6...................(p) DEMullins(7) 1	70
		(Leo J Temple, Ire) *chsd ldrs: wknd fr 2f out* **25/1**	
12	hd	**Soap Wars**[9] [3701] 3-8-4 88.. RPCleary 8	72
		(M Halford, Ire) *a towards rr* **16/1**	
13	shd	**Baggio (IRE)**[30] [3012] 7-9-1 94..(p) FMBerry 7	79
		(Charles O'Brien, Ire) *a towards rr* **8/1**[3]	
14	nk	**Speed Dream (IRE)**[58] [2175] 4-9-3 96.......................... WMLordan 6	80
		(David Wachman, Ire) *a towards rr* **25/1**	
15	2 1/2	**Abraham Lincoln (IRE)**[22] [3248] 4-10-0 107.................... JMurtagh 9	82
		(A P O'Brien, Ire) *a bhd* **7/1**[2]	
16	hd	**Great Rumpuscat (USA)**[28] [3069] 3-8-8 92....................... JAHeffernan 3	65
		(A P O'Brien, Ire) *chsd ldrs: wknd fr 2f out* **14/1**	
17	12	**Russian Reel**[206] [7202] 3-8-1 88.. DJMoran(3) 13	17
		(Ms Joanna Morgan, Ire) *mid-div: wknd fr 2f out* **25/1**	
18	27	**Fly By Magic (IRE)**[16] [3468] 4-8-1 83.......................... SMGorey(3) 4	—
		(Patrick Carey, Ire) *sddle slipped and uns rdr leaving parade ring: bolted bef s: a bhd: wknd fr 1/2-way: t.o* **20/1**	

60.71 secs (-1.69) **Going Correction** -0.05s/f (Good)
WFA 3 from 4yo+ 5lb **18 Ran SP% 137.2**
Speed ratings: **111,108,107,106,106 105,105,103,101,101 100,100,100,99,95 95,76,33**
CSF £34.42 CT £266.36 TOTE £4.90: £1.60, £2.40, £2.20, £3.80; DF 33.40.
Owner Lady O'Reilly **Bred** Shane Doyle **Trained** Sessay, N Yorks

NOTEBOOK
Masta Plasta(IRE), pipped in Listed company in France 23 days previously, was given his now customary positive ride and resumed winning ways with a tenacious display. This rates as his best effort of the current campaign and this year he has been another great advertisement for his trainer's skills. (op 7/1)
Le Cadre Noir(IRE), a Group 3 winner in Italy, was having his second run in this country.
How's She Cuttin'(IRE) had the blinkers replacing a visor and did not go unbacked for this first overseas outing. She tracked Masta Plasta from the off, but ultimately lacked the tactical speed to go with that rival when he quickened up. She was a little below her previous best here, but again left the impression they may be more to come when upped to another furlong. (op 7/1 tchd 9/1)
Fly By Magic(IRE) Official explanation: jockey said filly ran very freely to start

4005a DUBAI DUTY FREE ANGLESEY STKS (GROUP 3) 6f 63y
3:35 (3:35) 2-Y-O £35,900 (£10,533; £5,018; £1,709)

			RPR
1		**Bushranger (IRE)**[26] [3105] 2-9-1 .... WMLordan 5	108+
		(David Wachman, Ire) *hld up in tch: prog travelling wl into cl 3rd 2f out: rdn to ld 1f out: kpt on wl: comf* **7/2**[2]	
2	2 1/2	**Westphalia (IRE)**[15] [3509] 2-9-1 .... JMurtagh 1	101+
		(A P O'Brien, Ire) *racd cl 4th on stands' side: rdn to ld 1 1/2f out: hdd and no ex fr 1f out* **4/5**[1]	
3	1/2	**Kamado**[36] [2851] 2-9-1 .... CDHayes 4	99
		(Edward Lynam, Ire) *hld up in tch: rdn in 6th 2f out: kpt on wout threatening over 1f out* **33/1**	
4	3	**Sea Of Marmara (USA)**[14] [3534] 2-9-1 89.................... CO'Donoghue 2	90
		(A P O'Brien, Ire) *sn led: rdn and jnd 2f out: hdd 1 1/2f out: sn no ex* **33/1**	
5	1	**Intense Focus (USA)**[14] [3534] 2-9-1 106......................(t) KJManning 7	87
		(J S Bolger, Ire) *in tch in 5th: rdn in 3rd 2f out: sn no ex* **4/1**[3]	
6	nk	**Heart Of Fire (IRE)**[28] [3067] 2-9-1 98.................... DPMcDonogh 6	86
		(Kevin Prendergast, Ire) *chsd ldrs in 3rd: rdn in 2nd briefly 2f out: sn no imp* **8/1**	
7	12	**Peter Tchaikovsky**[26] [3103] 2-9-1 .... JAHeffernan 3	50+
		(A P O'Brien, Ire) *settled 2nd: rdn and wknd fr 2f out: eased and trailing over 1f out* **14/1**	

1m 17.6s (-0.40) **Going Correction** -0.05s/f (Good) **7 Ran SP% 121.4**
Speed ratings: **100,96,96,92,90 90,74**
CSF £7.25 TOTE £5.20: £2.80, £1.40; DF 11.20.
Owner Derrick Smith **Bred** Tally-Ho Stud **Trained** Goolds Cross, Co Tipperary

FOCUS
A fair renewal at least which could be slightly better than rated. A decisive winner who progressed from Ascot.

NOTEBOOK
Bushranger(IRE) ◆, second in the Windsor Castle at Royal Ascot last time, relished the extra furlong and ran out a decisive winner. Ridden to get the trip, he raced wide and without any cover for most of the race, before showing a neat turn of foot to settle the issue before the final furlong. He is value for further than the bare margin and is a smart colt, with his trainer intending to keep him to sprinting this year. Bookmakers were quick to give him quotes of around 16/1 for next year's 2000 Guineas, but while there is some stamina on his dam's side he does look a sprinter in the making at this stage. The Gimcrack at York's Ebor meeting next month looks a very viable target for him. (op 4/1)
Westphalia(IRE), a maiden winner over the course and distance 15 days previously, was the number one hope from Ballydoyle and met strong market support on this big step up in class. Having been ridden with patience early on he got a dream run up the rail with his challenge and looked a big player 2f out. However, he failed to really find a turn of foot under maximum pressure and found the winner much too strong at the business end. It was still a step in the right direction from him and, while he may prove to be no real star, a step up to 7f should now suit him ideally. (op Evs)
Kamado ◆, third in a hot maiden over course and distance on debut in June, ran green through the early stages and got outpaced at the 2f pole. He ran on very encouragingly under pressure inside the final furlong, suggesting he will improve again for the experience, and is clearly a talented colt.
Intense Focus(USA), a narrowly-beaten third in the Railway Stakes over this course and distance a fortnight previously, was equipped with a first-time tongue tie and proved easy to back. He was in trouble before the final furlong and ultimately ran a long way below his previous level, so may well be in need of a break now.

4006a DARLEY IRISH OAKS (GROUP 1) (FILLIES) 1m 4f
4:10 (4:13) 3-Y-O £206,250 (£70,220; £33,455; £11,397; £7,720; £4,044)

			RPR
1		**Moonstone**[37] [2792] 3-9-0 111.. JMurtagh 10	118
		(A P O'Brien, Ire) *trckd ldrs: 3rd 2 1/2f out: rdn in 2nd 1 1/2f out: strly pressed ldr and carried sltly lft fnl f: led on line* **2/1**[1]	
2	shd	**Ice Queen (IRE)**[15] [3511] 3-9-0 104.................... CO'Donoghue 9	118
		(A P O'Brien, Ire) *prom: rdn to ld 2f out: strly pressed fnl f: drifted lft and swished tail fnl f: hdd on line* **66/1**	
3	2	**Gagnoa (IRE)**[35] [2877] 3-9-0 .... JAHeffernan 14	115
		(A Fabre, France) *mid-div: prog into 4th 2 1/2f out: rdn in 3rd 1 1/2f out: kpt on same pce fnl f* **4/1**[3]	
4	1 1/4	**Chinese White (IRE)**[37] [2792] 3-9-0 107......................(t) PShanahan 11	114+
		(D K Weld, Ire) *in rr of mid-div: rdn and sme prog 2f out: 5th 1 1/2f out: kpt on same pce* **9/1**	
5	3/4	**Katiyra (IRE)**[37] [2792] 3-9-0 107.. MJKinane 3	111
		(John M Oxx, Ire) *mid-div: prog fr 4f out: rdn in 5th on outer 3f out: no imp fr 2f out* **10/3**[2]	
6	1 1/4	**Adored (IRE)**[37] [2792] 3-9-0 102.................... DavidMcCabe 1	109
		(A P O'Brien, Ire) *trckd ldr in 2nd: rdn to ld 3f out: hdd 2f out: sn no ex* **33/1**	
7	hd	**Prima Luce (IRE)**[35] [2877] 3-9-0 102.................... KJManning 6	109
		(J S Bolger, Ire) *in rr of mid-div: rdn and prog 3f out: 8th 1f out: kpt on same pce* **50/1**	
8	shd	**Mad About You (IRE)**[15] [3511] 3-9-0 114.................... PJSmullen 13	109
		(D K Weld, Ire) *trckd ldrs: 6th 4f out: rdn in 5th 2 1/2f out: no imp* **5/1**	
9	2	**Honoria (IRE)**[6] [3805] 3-9-0 96.................... DPMcDonogh 5	106
		(A P O'Brien, Ire) *trckd ldrs: rdn in 5th 4f out: kpt on same pce fr 3f out* **40/1**	
10	5 1/2	**Gentle On My Mind (IRE)**[11] [3621] 3-9-0 .... FMBerry 8	97
		(A P O'Brien, Ire) *s.i.s and in rr: no imp fr 4f out* **20/1**	
11	7	**Perihelion (IRE)**[6] [3805] 3-9-0 90.................... SMLevey 4	86
		(A P O'Brien, Ire) *sn led: rdn and hdd 3f out: sn dropped towards rr: kpt on same pce* **200/1**	
12	3/4	**Rosa Grace**[31] [2975] 3-9-0 .... ChrisCatlin 2	85
		(Rae Guest) *a towards rr* **20/1**	
13	nk	**Festival Princess (IRE)**[77] [1656] 3-9-0 .... RPCleary 12	84
		(M Halford, Ire) *a towards rr* **100/1**	
14	2 1/2	**Silk Affair (IRE)**[6] [3805] 3-9-0 .... MCHussey 7	80
		(M G Quinlan) *a bhd* **100/1**	

2m 34.37s (-3.13) **Going Correction** +0.075s/f (Good) **14 Ran SP% 123.9**
Speed ratings: **113,112,111,110,110 109,109,109,107,104 99,99,98,97**
CSF £188.96 TOTE £2.90: £1.10, £11.10, £1.60; DF 115.50.
Owner Mrs John Magnier **Bred** Britton House Stud Ltd **Trained** Ballydoyle, Co Tipperary
■ Aidan O'Brien, responsible for the first two home, has now won the last seven Irish Classics.
■ Stewards' Enquiry : C O'Donoghue two-day ban: careless riding (Jul 28-29)

FOCUS
Just an average renewal of this fillies' classic, run at no more than a fair early pace. It suited those racing close to the pace and provided a thrilling finish, with Moonstone just getting up from her lesser-fancied stable companion. The form is set through the third and fifth, who ran close to her Epsom form.

NOTEBOOK
Moonstone, second in the Oaks at Epsom last time, confirmed herself the top staying Irish three-year-old filly with a last-gasp success. Ridden prominently, she was perfectly placed for her challenge in the home straight and, despite again showing inexperience, eventually just did enough to edge out her much-lesser fancied stable companion on the line. She still looks to be learning her trade so further improvement should really be forthcoming and she clearly stays very well. She became the first maiden to land this race since Olwyn in 1977 and this was her connections' third successive win in this event. The Yorkshire Oaks at York's Ebor meeting could represent her next challenge and she would likely meet her Epsom conqueror Look Here there. (op 11/4)
Ice Queen(IRE), who finished last in the Epsom Oaks, was well suited by racing on the early pace, but this was still by far her best effort to date and she only gave best to her stable companion right at the finish. She has now shown a tendency to flash her tail under maximum pressure the last twice, but there seems to be nothing really ungenuine about her and she is well worth a chance to prove this no fluke. That may now come in the Nassau Stakes at Goodwood early next month, back over 1m2f, which could well suit on this evidence. (op 50/1)
Gagnoa(IRE), a well-beaten second behind Zarkava in the Prix de Diane 35 days previously, ran right up to her previous level without ever seriously looking like getting to the front inside the final furlong. She got the trip without any real fuss, indeed she would have likely been seen to even better effect off a stronger early pace, and she rates a solid benchmark for the form. There will be other days for her. (op 7/2)
Chinese White(IRE), a slightly disappointing ninth at Epsom, raced in a first-time tongue tie and not that surprisingly was given a much more patient ride this time. She showed her previous outing to be wrong with a much more encouraging effort in defeat, but this does go some way to confirming her present limitations. It may be that she improves as she matures further, however, and she is set to be kept in training as a four-year-old. (op 10/1 tchd 11/1)
Katiyra(IRE) had run a massive race in the Epsom Oaks on just her third career start, when little went her way, and looked a big player on this return to a more conventional track. She eventually proved somewhat disappointing, however, racing a little freely under early restraint and then finding just the same pace when asked for her effort in the home straight. She now has a bit to prove, but this was her first time racing on a right-handed track and she is too lightly raced to write off just yet. (op 7/2 tchd 4/1)
Mad About You(IRE), the Pretty Polly second, raced a bit freely on this step up in trip and that cannot have helped her chances of getting home. She had every chance nearing 2f out, but could offer no more thereafter and a drop back in distance now looks firmly on the cards. It would be folly to write her off. (op 9/2)
Rosa Grace ran a long way below the level of her Listed win at Newbury a month previously and was beaten too far out for the longer trip to have been a factor. (op 25/1)
Silk Affair(IRE) was faced with an near-impossible task really, but she was still the first beaten and ran a fair way below her recent level.

4007a KILBOY ESTATE STKS (LISTED RACE) (FILLIES) 1m 1f
4:45 (4:48) 3-Y-O+ £28,720 (£8,426; £4,014; £1,367)

			RPR
1		**Navajo Moon (IRE)**[25] [3148] 4-9-10 103.................... WMLordan 18	109
		(David Wachman, Ire) *mid-div: prog into cl 3rd 2f out: rdn to ld over 1f out: kpt on wl fnl f* **12/1**	
2	nk	**Jalmira (IRE)**[14] [3536] 7-9-12 97.................... WJLee 17	110
		(C F Swan, Ire) *hld up: rdn in 6th 2f out: wnt 2nd over 1f out: kpt on wl fnl f* **20/1**	
3	1	**Indiana Gal (IRE)**[15] [3510] 3-8-11 101.................... DPMcDonogh 11	102
		(Patrick Martin, Ire) *mid-div: 6th 3f out: rdn fr 2f out: kpt on in 3rd fr 1f out* **12/1**	
4	nk	**Mystical Lady (IRE)**[11] [3619] 3-8-11 96.................... CO'Donoghue 10	101
		(A P O'Brien, Ire) *in rr of mid-div: prog into 7th 3f out: rdn to dispute ld 2f out: hdd over 1f out: sn no ex* **25/1**	
5	1 1/4	**Psalm (IRE)**[23] [3194] 3-8-11 108.................... JMurtagh 7	99
		(A P O'Brien, Ire) *trckd ldrs: 2nd 3f out: sn rdn and no imp* **7/4**[1]	
6	shd	**Zafayra (IRE)**[58] [2184] 3-8-11 98.................... MJKinane 12	99
		(John M Oxx, Ire) *chsd ldrs and t.k.h early: 4th 3f out: rdn and no imp fr 2f out* **7/1**[3]	
7	1/2	**Beach Bunny (IRE)**[15] [3511] 3-8-11 101.................... CDHayes 13	97
		(Kevin Prendergast, Ire) *trckd ldrs: 3rd 3f out: rdn 2f out: sn no ex* **9/2**[2]	

8 *hd* **Bahia Breeze**[36] 2827 6-9-7 .... ChrisCatlin 16 98
(Rae Guest) *trckd ldrs: led on inner 3f out: rdn and jnd 2f out: hdd over 1f out: wknd* **14/1**

9 *1* **Deauville Vision (IRE)**[91] 1353 5-9-10 105............ RPCleary 15 99
(M Halford, Ire) *mid-div: no imp fr 3f out* **12/1**

10 *5* **Tis Mighty (IRE)**[36] 2856 5-9-7 87............ PShanahan 4 85
(P J Prendergast, Ire) *in rr: no imp fr 3f out: eased ins fnl f* **20/1**

11 *3 1/2* **Crossing**[136] 745 7-9-7 ....(t) MCHussey 9 78
(William J Fitzpatrick, Ire) *mid-div on outer: no imp fr 3f out* **25/1**

12 *1 1/4* **She's Our Mark**[15] 3511 4-9-12 101............ CPGeoghegan 3 80
(Patrick J Flynn, Ire) *a towards rr* **16/1**

13 *1 1/4* **Allicansayis Wow (USA)**[60] 2113 3-8-11 101............(p) KJManning 6 72
(J S Bolger, Ire) *mid-div: no imp fr 3f out: eased ins fnl f* **20/1**

14 *1* **Joshua's Princess**[11] 3619 4-9-7 88............ FMBerry 20 71
(John M Oxx, Ire) *trckd ldr in 2nd: disp ld 4f out: carried wd and hdd 3f out: sn wknd: eased over 1f out* **20/1**

15 *1 3/4* **Danehill Music (IRE)**[14] 3536 5-9-10 97............ WJSupple 2 70
(David Wachman, Ire) *a bhd* **33/1**

16 *3 1/2* **Sedna (IRE)**[41] 2684 6-9-7 91............ NGMcCullagh 8 60
(W T Farrell, Ire) *reluctant to post: in rr of mid-div: wknd fr 3f out* **33/1**

17 *20* **My Dark Rosaleen**[4] 3860 3-8-11 75............ SMLevey 14 18
(A P O'Brien, Ire) *led: rdn and hdd 3f out: sn wknd* **50/1**

18 *dist* **Love To Dance (IRE)**[11] 3621 3-8-11 85............ JAHeffernan 5 —
(A P O'Brien, Ire) *a bhd: wknd after 1/2-way* **25/1**

U **Les Fazzani (IRE)**[75] 1713 4-9-10 .... PJSmullen 1 —
(M J Wallace) *rrd up leaving stalls and uns rdr* **12/1**

1m 53.75s (-1.15) **Going Correction** +0.075s/f (Good)
WFA 3 from 4yo+ 10lb **19** Ran SP% **148.8**
Speed ratings: **108,107,106,106,105 105,104,104,103,99 96,95,94,93,91 88,70,—,—**
CSF £255.55 TOTE £13.20: £2.80, £7.60, £2.50, £8.20; DF 784.30.
Owner Mrs John Magnier **Bred** Southern Bloodstock **Trained** Goolds Cross, Co Tipperary

NOTEBOOK
Navajo Moon(IRE), a ready winner over the trip in this class against the males at Leopardstown 25 days previously, narrowly followed up without needing to markedly improve on that effort to score.
Beach Bunny(IRE) Official explanation: jockey said filly did not get a clear run in straight
Bahia Breeze led the field into the home straight, but was unable to sustain her effort shortly after the 2f pole.
Les Fazzani(IRE) came home in front, but was riderless after rearing up and leaving her jockey in the gates. Official explanation: jockey said filly reared as stalls opened (op 10/1)

3243 CHANTILLY (R-H)
Sunday, July 13

OFFICIAL GOING: Good

4010a **ABU DHABI SOROUH PRIX JEAN PRAT (GROUP 1) (C&F)** **1m**
1:45 (1:48) 3-Y-O **£168,059** (£67,235; £33,618; £16,794; £8,412)

RPR

1 **Tamayuz**[63] 2032 3-9-2 .... DBonilla 12 123
(F Head, France) *trckd ldr: 3rd st: led wl over 2f out: drvn out* **14/1**

2 *1 1/2* **Raven's Pass (USA)**[26] 3102 3-9-2 .... JimmyFortune 13 119+
(J H M Gosden) *hld up towards rr: hdwy on ins and 7th st: disp 3rd wl over 1f out: kpt on to take 2nd cl home* **7/4**[1]

3 *1/2* **Rio De La Plata (USA)**[36] 2829 3-9-2 .... LDettori 6 118+
(Saeed Bin Suroor) *a in tch: 8th st: outpcd 2f out: drvn 1 1/2f out: styd on to take 3rd last strides* **4/1**[2]

4 *1/2* **Cat Junior (USA)**[26] 3102 3-9-2 .... RichardHughes 3 117
(B J Meehan) *sn cl up on ins: 4th st: sn trcking wnr: hrd rdn over 1f out: no ex and lost 2nd 50yds out* **14/1**

5 *nk* **Kandahar Run**[36] 2829 3-9-2 .... TedDurcan 8 116
(H R A Cecil) *a cl up: 6th st: 3rd 2f out: one pce fnl f* **20/1**

6 *1 1/2* **Trincot (FR)**[42] 2654 3-9-2 .... CSoumillon 16 113+
(P Demercastel, France) *hld up in rr: snatched up on turn over 3f out: last st: hdwy towards ins 2f out: swtchd rt over 1f out: one pce last 150yds* **20/1**

7 *2 1/2* **Winker Watson**[367] 3459 3-9-2 .... JamieSpencer 2 107
(P W Chapple-Hyam) *towards rr tl hdwy on ins over 2f out: 6th 2f out: one pce fr over 1f out* **10/1**

8 *1/2* **Farrel (IRE)**[19] 3356 3-9-2 .... DVargiu 1 106
(B Grizzetti, Italy) *mid-div: 11th st: kpt on one pce fnl 2f* **33/1**

9 *2* **Falco (USA)**[26] 3102 3-9-2 .... OPeslier 10 102
(C Laffon-Parias, France) *5th st: disp 3rd 2f out: btn 1 1/2f out* **5/1**[3]

10 *1 1/2* **Eustachione (IRE)**[21] 3-9-2 .... JVictoire 9 99
(M Gasparini, Italy) *10th st: swtchd outside over 2f out: one pce fnl 1 1/2f* **40/1**

11 *3/4* **Murcielago (FR)**[19] 3356 3-9-2 .... TCastanheira 5 97
(P Demercastel, France) *towards rr to st: swtchd out over 2f out: sn rdn and one pce* **40/1**

12 *1* **Yorktown (FR)**[35] 2875 3-9-2 .... RyanMoore 11 95
(J-C Rouget, France) *hld up in rr: last 2f out: nvr a factor* **20/1**

13 *shd* **Senlis (IRE)**[35] 2875 3-9-2 .... ASanna 4 95
(E Borromeo, Italy) *hld up: towards rr whn sltly hmpd appr st: rdn 2f out: nvr a factor* **33/1**

14 *6* **Arcadia's Angle (USA)**[35] 2875 3-9-2 .... C-PLemaire 14 81
(P Bary, France) *a in rr* **16/1**

15 *4* **Legislation**[29] 3038 3-9-2 ....(b) RobertHavlin 15 73
(J H M Gosden) *2nd st: wknd over 2f out* **200/1**

16 *10* **Poligold (IRE)**[12] 3-9-2 ....(b) MBlancpain 7 51
(C Laffon-Parias, France) *led to wl over 2f out* **150/1**

1m 37.6s (-0.20) **Going Correction** +0.325s/f (Good) **16** Ran SP% **127.5**
Speed ratings: **114,112,112,111,111 109,107,106,104,103 102,101,101,95,91 81**
PARI-MUTUEL: WIN 11.80; PL 3.20, 1.80, 2.30; DF 23.60.
Owner Hamdan Al Maktoum **Bred** Shadwell Estate Company Limited **Trained** France

NOTEBOOK
Tamayuz was given an outstanding tactical ride, as from his outside draw he was soon settled behind the pacemaker Poligold and stayed there until taking the advantage two furlongs from the line. From then on he hugged the rail and never looked like being beaten. He had previously never got into the hunt in the Poulains, which came after he had lifted the Fontainebleau, but this change of tactics had a positive effect. He will now take his chance in the Jacques Le Marois at Deauville next month.
Raven's Pass(USA), fitted with a hood when being loaded into the stalls, was towards the tail of the field during the early part of the race and still had a big task on his hands entering the straight. He ran on well throughout the final furlong and a half but never got a blow in at the winner, and is now likely to be aimed at the Sussex Stakes at Goodwood.
Rio De La Plata(USA) came with a progressive run up the centre of the track and was putting in his best work at the finish. He is now likely to be stepped up to 1m2f, and races like the Prix Guillaume d'Ornano at Deauville and the Juddmonte International at York will be taken into consideration.
Cat Junior(USA) was settled just behind the leaders and was the first to try and peg back the eventual winner, but he ran out of steam inside the final furlong. It was a good effort from this inexperienced colt and he is another who will probably be run over a longer distance next time out.
Kandahar Run, always prominent, was asked to make a forward move two out but was then one-paced inside the final furlong. There are no plans for this colt at the present moment.
Winker Watson put up a decent effort considering he had not been out for almost exactly a year and that he lost a shoe during the race. Running round a bend and over a mile for the first time, he was given a waiting ride and tried to follow the runner-up in the straight. Considerable progress can be expected.
Falco(USA), who was rather keen in the early stages, has now run poorly twice since his French Guineas win.
Legislation was in as pacemaker for Raven's Pass.

3753 AYR (L-H)
Monday, July 14

OFFICIAL GOING: Good
Wind: Fresh, half against Weather: Cloudy

4013 **DAWN CONSTRUCTION H'CAP** **5f**
2:10 (2:11) (Class 6) (0-65,65) 3-Y-0+ **£2,590** (£770; £385; £192) **Stalls** Low

Form RPR

6051 1 **Invincible Lad (IRE)**[13] 3581 4-9-7 **60**............ DavidAllan 1 72
(E J Alston) *trckd far side ldr: led over 1f out: styd on strly* **9/4**[1]

45-0 2 *1* **Until When (USA)**[39] 2749 4-9-12 **65**............(v[1]) TomEaves 5 73
(B Smart) *dwlt: hld up far side: hdwy to chse wnr ins fnl f: kpt on: 2nd of 6 in gp* **8/1**

0034 3 *1 1/2* **Mormeatmic**[13] 3582 5-8-13 **52**............ PaulMulrennan 9 55
(M W Easterby) *cl up stands' side: led that gp appr fnl f: kpt on: nt rch far side: 1st of 6 in gp* **4/1**[2]

0000 4 *3/4* **Welcome Approach**[14] 3546 5-8-10 **52**............ JamieMoriarty[(3)] 11 52
(J R Weymes) *in tch stands' side: drvn over 2f out: kpt on fnl f: 2nd of 6 in gp* **8/1**

2304 5 *nk* **Angel Voices (IRE)**[100] 1204 5-9-12 **65**............ DarrenWilliams 13 64
(K R Burke) *in tch stands' side: effrt whn nt clr run over 1f out: kpt on fnl f: 3rd of 6 in gp* **14/1**

026 6 *hd* **Wicked Wilma (IRE)**[13] 3581 4-8-13 **52**............ FergalLynch 14 50+
(A Berry) *hld up in tch stands' side: nt clr run over 1f out: r.o fnl f: 4th of 6 in gp* **15/2**[3]

0-40 7 *hd* **Almost Married (IRE)**[8] 3759 4-8-13 **57**............ GaryBartley[(5)] 2 54
(J S Goldie) *bhd and pushed along far side: hdwy over 1f out: nrst fin: 3rd of 6 in gp* **16/1**

6603 8 *3/4* **Valiant Romeo**[7] 3784 8-8-7 **46** oh1............(v) RoystonFfrench 6 41
(R Bastiman) *prom far side: drvn 1/2-way: one pce fnl f: 4th of 6 in gp* **8/1**

2140 9 *nk* **Orange Square (IRE)**[23] 3283 3-8-12 **56**............ TonyHamilton 12 48
(D W Barker) *led stands' side to appr fnl f: kpt on same pce: 5th of 6 in gp* **33/1**

0004 10 *1 1/4* **Seafield Towers**[7] 3787 8-8-7 **46** oh1............ GregFairley 4 35
(D A Nolan) *chsd far side ldrs tl wknd over 1f out: 5th of 6 in gp* **14/1**

0-00 11 *hd* **Compton Lad**[7] 3784 5-8-3 **49** oh1 ow3............(t) PaulPickard[(7)] 8 37
(D A Nolan) *led far side to over 1f out: sn btn: last of 6 in gp* **100/1**

0006 12 *1* **Percy Douglas**[7] 3784 8-8-5 **49** oh1 ow3............(p) AnnStokell[(5)] 10 34
(Miss A Stokell) *cl up stands' side tl edgd lft and wknd 1f out: last of 6 in gp* **50/1**

58.79 secs (-1.31) **Going Correction** -0.225s/f (Firm)
WFA 3 from 4yo+ 5lb **12** Ran SP% **121.0**
Speed ratings (Par 101): **101,99,97,95,95 95,94,93,93,91 90,89**
toteswinger: 1&2 £5.20, 1&3 £2.80, 2&3 £7.70. CSF £21.29 CT £72.16 TOTE £3.20: £1.50, £2.30, £1.70; EX 25.50.
Owner Con Harrington **Bred** Mrs Chris Harrington **Trained** Longton, Lancs

FOCUS
A moderate sprint handicap. The draw proved no real bias and the form looks fair for the class rated through the first two.

4014 **RENAULT MASTER MEDIAN AUCTION MAIDEN STKS** **6f**
2:40 (2:41) (Class 5) 2-Y-O **£3,238** (£963; £481; £240) **Stalls** Low

Form RPR

52 1 **Suruor (IRE)**[27] 3107 2-9-3 0............ GregFairley 4 72
(M Johnston) *prom: effrt 2f out: led ent fnl f: kpt on wl* **3/1**[3]

0 2 *3/4* **Liberty Trail (IRE)**[8] 3754 2-9-3 0............ PaulMulrennan 8 70
(Miss L A Perratt) *led: hrd pressed fr 1/2-way: hdd ent fnl f: kpt on towards fin* **66/1**

25 3 *2 1/4* **What A Fella**[19] 3365 2-9-3 0............ RoystonFfrench 5 63
(Mrs A Duffield) *cl up: disp ld 2f out to ins fnl f: sn no ex* **14/1**

4 *1/2* **Postman** 2-9-3 0............ TomEaves 6 62
(B Smart) *hld up in tch: effrt and reminders over 1f out: kpt on steadily fnl f: bttr for r* **8/1**

3 5 *2 1/2* **Mister Fantastic**[19] 3364 2-9-3 0............ DaleGibson 3 54
(M Dods) *trckd ldrs: rdn 1/2-way: wknd appr fnl f* **11/4**[2]

64 6 *2* **Bella's Story**[8] 3754 2-8-7 0............ GaryBartley[(5)] 1 43
(J S Goldie) *in tch on ins: rdn over 2f out: wknd over 1f out* **14/1**

7 *2 1/4* **Chief Red Cloud (USA)** 2-9-3 0............ DarrenWilliams 2 41
(K R Burke) *trckd ldrs: rdn 2f out: sn wknd* **2/1**[1]

8 *1 1/4* **Asserting** 2-8-9 0............ PJMcDonald[(3)] 7 33
(A G Foster) *missed break: a struggling* **50/1**

1m 13.07s (-0.53) **Going Correction** -0.225s/f (Firm) **8** Ran SP% **112.9**
Speed ratings (Par 94): **94,93,90,89,86 83,80,78**
toteswinger: 1&2 £15.80, 1&3 £5.00, 2&3 £27.10. CSF £141.23 TOTE £3.80: £1.40, £7.80, £2.80; EX 95.60.
Owner Hamdan Al Maktoum **Bred** Shadwell Estate Company Limited **Trained** Middleham Moor, N Yorks

FOCUS
An ordinary maiden, but one that should produce winners at the right level. The form is rated around the winner and third.

NOTEBOOK

Suruor(IRE), who did not quite last the 7f at Thirsk last time, having looked the winner a furlong out, was up there throughout on this drop back in trip and battled on well to score at the third attempt. He is progressing steadily and is now set to step back up in trip for nurseries. (op 9-4 tchd 2-1)

Liberty Trail(IRE) ran a huge race. A tailed-off last of seven over course and distance on debut, he certainly knew more this time and made the winner fight hard. This was a cracking effort at odds of 66/1 and he may well improve again. He should make his mark in low-grade nurseries this season. (op 40-1)

What A Fella has been shaping as though this trip would suit, but having showed good early speed, he could find no more in the final half-furlong. He has shown enough to suggest a small race can come his way and is now qualified for nurseries. (op 10-1)

Postman ◆, a 200,000gns son of Dr Fong, comes from a yard who can ready a newcomer, but many of theirs have been needing a run this term and he was relatively weak in the market. He shaped with a good deal of promise though, keeping on under hands and heels riding having been outpaced, and winning an ordinary maiden should prove a formality, especially once upped to 7f. (op 10-1 tchd 11-1)

Mister Fantastic was unable to build on his debut effort and may be more of a nursery type. (op 3-1)

Chief Red Cloud(USA), a $110,000 relation to a sprint winner in France, comes from a yard who have so far done well with their juveniles this year and he seemed to come with a reputation. A fine, big type, he seemed to find all this a bit too much, getting outpaced and looking a shade green still. He is evidently thought to be capable of a good deal better and deserves another chance. (op 11-4 tchd 3-1)

4015 WEATHERBYS BLOODSTOCK INSURANCE H'CAP — 1m 2f

3:10 (3:11) (Class 5) (0-70,70) 3-Y-0+ **£3,561** (£1,059; £529; £264) **Stalls** Low

Form — RPR

3016 **1** **Shy Glance (USA)**[8] 3755 6-9-4 **65** ... NeilBrown(5) 5 — 74
(P Monteith) *hld up: smooth hdwy to chse ldr over 1f out: sn rdn: styd on wl to ld nr fin* **8/1**[3]

1132 **2** ¾ **Annibale Caro**[6] 3814 6-9-11 **70** ... PJMcDonald(3) 2 — 78
(Grant Tuer) *trckd ldrs gng wl: led wl over 1f out: rdn and edgd lft: kpt on fnl f: hdd nr fin* **10/3**[2]

0-30 **3** 3¾ **Dar Es Salaam**[16] 3493 4-9-12 **68** ... DanielTudhope 3 — 68
(J S Goldie) *dwlt: hld up: rdn over 2f out: edgd lft and hdwy over 1f out: kpt on fnl f: nt rch first two* **10/1**

2000 **4** nk **Always Brave**[19] 3366 3-9-2 **69** ... GregFairley 1 — 68
(M Johnston) *led to wl over 1f out: kpt on same pce* **14/1**

5500 **5** hd **Wednesdays Boy (IRE)**[36] 2870 5-8-9 **51** oh2 ... (p) RoystonFfrench 7 — 50
(P D Niven) *prom: effrt and hung lft over 1f out: one pce fnl f* **22/1**

0055 **6** ¾ **Polish Corridor**[9] 3725 9-9-6 **62** ... DaleGibson 9 — 60
(M Dods) *hld up: rdn and hdwy over 1f out: no imp fnl f* **10/1**

0131 **7** 1 **Holiday Cocktail**[6] 3814 6-8-12 **61** ... (p) JamieKyne(7) 4 — 57
(J J Quinn) *in tch: drvn over 2f out: no ex over 1f out* **5/4**[1]

3503 **8** 4 **Grethel (IRE)**[1] 3996 4-8-12 **54** ... PaulMulrennan 10 — 42
(A Berry) *hld up in tch: hdwy and cl up over 2f out: edgd lft and wknd over 1f out* **25/1**

R-60 **9** 4 **Polish Star**[24] 3201 4-8-9 **51** oh3 ... TomEaves 6 — 31
(Miss L A Perratt) *cl up tl hung lft and wknd fr 2f out* **40/1**

2m 8.21s (-3.79) **Going Correction** -0.35s/f (Firm)
WFA 3 from 4yo+ 11lb — **9** Ran SP% **114.1**
Speed ratings (Par 103): **101,100,97,97,97 96,95,92,89**
toteswinger: 1&2 £4.20, 1&3 £7.60, 2&3 £6.90. CSF £33.72 CT £270.96 TOTE £7.90: £1.90, £1.20, £2.50; EX 34.10.
Owner Walcal Property Development Ltd **Bred** R D Hubbard And Constance Sczesny **Trained** Rosewell, Midlothian

FOCUS
A modest handicap, run at a fair pace. The first pair came clear with the winner back to something like his best and the second building a bit further on recent form.
Wednesdays Boy(IRE) Official explanation: jockey said gelding hung left-handed in straight
Polish Corridor Official explanation: jockey said gelding hung right-handed final 2f

4016 ARNOLD CLARK RENAULT FILLIES' H'CAP — 6f

3:40 (3:41) (Class 4) (0-85,79) 3-Y-0+
£5,607 (£1,679; £839; £420; £209; £105) **Stalls** Low

Form — RPR

5222 **1** **Rothesay Dancer**[2] 3956 5-8-12 **65** ... DanielTudhope 8 — 74
(J S Goldie) *hld up: smooth hdwy to ld over 1f out: rdn out fnl f* **4/1**[1]

6163 **2** ½ **Dorn Dancer (IRE)**[4] 3883 6-9-6 **73** ... FergalLynch 1 — 80
(D W Barker) *hld up: hdwy and swtchd over 1f out: chsd wnr ins fnl f: r.o* **4/1**[1]

0030 **3** 2¾ **Katie Boo (IRE)**[9] 3713 6-9-3 **70** ... PaulMulrennan 9 — 68
(A Berry) *cl up: led over 2f out: edgd lft and hdd over 1f out: kpt on same pce* **10/1**[3]

3013 **4** nse **Ingleby Princess**[9] 3728 4-9-0 **67** ... PaulFessey 6 — 65
(T D Barron) *in tch: drvn over 2f out: kpt on fnl f* **13/2**[2]

1221 **5** 2½ **Gap Princess (IRE)**[12] 3599 4-8-12 **68** ... JamieMoriarty(3) 5 — 58
(R A Fahey) *w ldrs tl rdn and wknd over 1f out* **4/1**[1]

4324 **6** 2½ **Just Joey**[13] 3575 4-8-7 **65** ... (b) NeilBrown(5) 3 — 47
(J R Weymes) *led to over 2f out: wknd over 1f out* **12/1**

2440 **7** 1 **Sweet Pickle**[31] 2993 7-9-12 **79** ... (e) GregFairley 7 — 58
(J R Boyle) *in tch: drvn over 2f out: sn wknd* **10/1**[3]

-006 **8** ½ **Safranine (IRE)**[10] 3695 11-8-5 **63** oh13 ow3 ... AnnStokell(5) 4 — 40
(Miss A Stokell) *dwlt: sn prom: drvn and wknd over 1f out* **66/1**

14-3 **9** 8 **Mafasina (USA)**[180] 178 3-8-13 **72** ... TomEaves 2 — 24
(B Smart) *chsd ldrs tl rdn and wknd fr 2f out* **13/2**[2]

1m 11.39s (-2.21) **Going Correction** -0.225s/f (Firm)
WFA 3 from 4yo+ 6lb — **9** Ran SP% **114.0**
Speed ratings (Par 102): **105,104,100,100,97 93,92,91,81**
toteswinger: 1&2 £3.20, 1&3 £11.10, 2&3 £10.10. CSF £19.18 CT £147.97 TOTE £4.40: £2.10, £1.70, £3.70; EX 14.40.
Owner Highland Racing **Bred** Frank Brady **Trained** Uplawmoor, E Renfrews

FOCUS
A modest sprint, run at a solid pace, which saw the first pair come clear. It is doubtful if the winner had to run up to her latest form here.

4017 RENAULT TRAFIC H'CAP — 1m

4:10 (4:10) (Class 4) (0-85,81) 3-Y-0 **£4,857** (£1,445; £722; £360) **Stalls** Low

Form — RPR

-046 **1** **Boy Blue**[16] 3494 3-9-5 **79** ... TonyHamilton 4 — 86
(D W Barker) *hld up: hdwy over 1f out: led wl ins fnl f: rdn out* **8/1**[2]

0231 **2** 2 **Ninefineirishmen (IRE)**[24] 3200 3-9-1 **75** ... (p) DarrenWilliams 1 — 77
(K R Burke) *led: rdn over 2f out: hdd and no ex wl ins fnl f* **14/1**

0600 **3** hd **Doon Haymer (IRE)**[16] 3494 3-8-12 **72** ... (v) TomEaves 5 — 74
(Miss L A Perratt) *pressed ldr: effrt and ev ch over 2f out: one pce fnl f* **17/2**[3]

0406 **4** hd **Bavarian Nordic (USA)**[9] 3716 3-8-9 **69** ... RoystonFfrench 2 — 70
(Mrs A Duffield) *prom: drvn over 2f out: rallied over 1f out: one pce fnl f* **25/1**

0551 **5** 2½ **Capucci**[32] 2974 3-9-7 **81** ... (t) RobertHavlin 3 — 77
(J H M Gosden) *t.k.h: trckd ldrs: effrt over 1f out: fnd little* **1/2**[1]

-000 **6** ¾ **Fitzroy Crossing (USA)**[23] 3261 3-9-6 **80** ... GregFairley 7 — 74
(M Johnston) *bhd: drvn over 3f out: kpt on fnl f: nvr able to chal* **16/1**

0-45 **7** 14 **Resounding Glory (USA)**[16] 3494 3-9-1 **78** ... JamieMoriarty(3) 6 — 40
(R A Fahey) *in tch tl wknd over 2f out: eased whn no ch fnl f* **12/1**

1m 40.59s (-3.21) **Going Correction** -0.35s/f (Firm) — **7** Ran SP% **112.4**
Speed ratings (Par 102): **102,100,99,99,97 96,82**
toteswinger: 1&2 £3.30, 1&3 £6.80, 2&3 £4.40. CSF £101.77 TOTE £8.10: £3.20, £2.80; EX 100.10.
Owner Ian Bishop **Bred** G Russell **Trained** Scorton, N Yorks

FOCUS
A fair handicap. The form is a bit muddling with the favourite disappointing.
Capucci Official explanation: trainer's rep said colt finished distressed
Resounding Glory(USA) Official explanation: jockey said colt lost its action

4018 PARKS RENAULT H'CAP — 7f 50y

4:40 (4:40) (Class 6) (0-65,65) 3-Y-0+ **£2,729** (£806; £403) **Stalls** Low

Form — RPR

0013 **1** **No Grouse**[17] 3435 8-9-9 **61** ... DavidAllan 10 — 68
(E J Alston) *hld up in tch: effrt 2f out: led 1f out: drvn out* **8/1**

0453 **2** ½ **Hansomis (IRE)**[8] 3757 4-9-2 **54** ... DaleGibson 2 — 59
(B Mactaggart) *led: drvn 2f out: hdd 1f out: rallied: hld towards fin* **12/1**

0246 **3** 1¼ **Vesuvio**[8] 3757 4-9-1 **53** ... LeeEnstone 4 — 55
(C W Thornton) *prom: effrt 2f out: kpt on same pce ins fnl f* **12/1**

S-03 **4** 1¾ **Orphan (IRE)**[13] 3582 6-9-0 **55** ... PJMcDonald(3) 12 — 52+
(G M Moore) *hld up: hdwy 2f out: hung lft: kpt on ins fnl f: nrst fin* **12/1**

605 **5** ½ **Charlie Allnut**[32] 2966 3-8-13 **59** ... DarrenWilliams 7 — 52+
(K R Burke) *prom: drvn and outpcd over 2f out: rallied fnl f: no imp* **7/2**[1]

0005 **6** ½ **Sands Of Barra (IRE)**[2] 3951 5-9-6 **65** ... ClGillies(7) 8 — 60
(I W McInnes) *cl up tl rdn and wknd fnl f* **12/1**

0523 **7** 1¼ **Anthemion (IRE)**[7] 3789 11-8-10 **48** ... PaulFessey 5 — 39
(Mrs J C McGregor) *missed break: bhd tl styd on fnl f: n.d* **10/1**

4100 **8** 1 **Staked A Claim (IRE)**[17] 3454 4-8-12 **55** ... NeilBrown(5) 9 — 44
(T D Barron) *midfield on outside: outpcd over 2f out: n.d after* **10/1**

1335 **9** 1½ **Botham (USA)**[13] 3582 4-9-2 **54** ... DanielTudhope 11 — 38
(J S Goldie) *hld up: drvn over 2f out: btn over 1f out* **7/1**[3]

056 **10** ½ **Soviet (IRE)**[11] 3629 3-9-5 **65** ... GregFairley 6 — 45
(M Johnston) *dwlt: sn cl up: effrt over 2f out: wknd over 1f out* **4/1**[2]

6-00 **11** 4 **Tom Tower (IRE)**[19] 3370 4-9-8 **60** ... (t) TonyHamilton 13 — 32
(A C Whillans) *towards rr: drvn over 2f out: sn btn* **66/1**

0000 **12** 2½ **Mangano**[8] 3757 4-8-11 **49** ... FergalLynch 3 — 15
(A Berry) *bhd: pushed along over 2f out: nvr on terms* **40/1**

45-0 **13** 4½ **Doric Dream**[168] 343 3-8-12 **58** ... TomEaves 14 — 8
(B Smart) *bhd on outside: rdn 3f out: sn btn* **33/1**

006- **14** 9 **Royal Citadel (IRE)**[180] 5678 5-8-10 **48** ... PaulMulrennan 1 — —
(Mrs L B Normile) *hld up ins: rdn 3f out: sn btn* **50/1**

1m 30.73s (-2.67) **Going Correction** -0.35s/f (Firm)
WFA 3 from 4yo+ 8lb — **14** Ran SP% **123.6**
Speed ratings (Par 101): **101,100,99,97,96 95,94,93,91,91 86,83,78,68**
toteswinger: 1&2 £10.70, 1&3 £20.70, 2&3 £18.80. CSF £101.38 CT £1202.27 TOTE £8.70: £3.00, £4.60, £4.50; EX 124.30 TRIFECTA Not won..
Owner The Grumpy Old Geezers **Bred** Zubieta Ltd **Trained** Longton, Lancs

FOCUS
A moderate handicap but the form among the principals is sound.
Anthemion(IRE) Official explanation: jockey said gelding missed the break

4019 WATERAID LADIES NIGHT 9TH AUGUST APPRENTICE H'CAP — 1m 2f

5:10 (5:10) (Class 6) (0-65,62) 3-Y-0 **£2,590** (£770; £385; £192) **Stalls** Low

Form — RPR

-551 **1** **Aleatricis**[13] 3580 3-8-9 **52** ... RosieJessop(5) 6 — 74+
(Sir Mark Prescott) *mde all: rdn and edgd rt 2f out: sn clr* **11/10**[1]

4454 **2** 9 **Willyn (IRE)**[7] 3790 3-9-3 **55** ... GaryBartley 1 — 59
(J S Goldie) *in tch: effrt and chsd wnr over 1f out: kpt on: no imp* **9/2**[2]

3460 **3** 2½ **Zaplamation (IRE)**[14] 3555 3-8-2 **45** ... JamieKyne(5) 7 — 44
(D W Barker) *in tch: effrt over 2f out: one pce over 1f out* **11/2**[3]

00-0 **4** nse **Lady Grantley**[16] 3479 3-8-3 **45** ow1 ... BradleyRoper(5) 5 — 45
(M W Easterby) *prom: drvn and outpcd 2f out: kpt on fnl f* **10/1**

0340 **5** 2¼ **Nayarna**[10] 3672 3-9-7 **62** ... (p) BMcHugh(3) 3 — 56
(R A Fahey) *cl up tl rdn and no ex over 1f out* **8/1**

400 **6** 1 **Phantom Serenade (IRE)**[34] 2912 3-9-2 **54** ... ClGillies 4 — 46
(M Dods) *hld up: rdn over 3f out: sn no imp* **14/1**

0000 **7** 21 **Ceduna Roadhouse (IRE)**[24] 3213 3-8-5 **45** ow3 ... GarryWhillans(5) 2 — —
(A M Crow) *bhd: struggling over 4f out: sn btn* **50/1**

0-00 **8** 2¾ **Endeavor**[24] 3200 3-8-2 **45** ... PaulPickard(5) 8 — —
(P Monteith) *bhd: rdn 5f out: sn btn* **40/1**

0-60 **9** 2½ **Prince's Decree**[55] 2272 3-9-3 **55** ... PatrickDonaghy 9 — —
(G M Moore) *hld up: rdn 5f out: sn wknd* **25/1**

2m 8.27s (-3.73) **Going Correction** -0.35s/f (Firm) — **9** Ran SP% **116.3**
Speed ratings (Par 98): **100,92,90,90,88 88,71,69,67**
toteswinger: 1&2 £2.10, 1&3 £2.10 2&3 £5.60. CSF £6.11 CT £19.25 TOTE £1.70: £1.10, £1.90, £1.70; EX 8.10 Place 6: £831.37 Place 5: £517.28.
Owner The Green Door Partnership **Bred** Miss K Rausing **Trained** Newmarket, Suffolk

■ Stewards' Enquiry : Jamie Kyne one-day ban: used whip with excessive frequency (Jul 28)
Patrick Donaghy caution: careless riding

FOCUS
A desperately uncompetitive heat in which the winner beat little but remains ahead of the handicapper.

T/Plt: £219.80 to a £1 stake. Pool: £64,783.39. 215.15 winning tickets. T/Qpdt: £59.50 to a £1 stake. Pool: £4,528.90. 56.30 winning tickets. RY

[3797]WINDSOR (R-H)

Monday, July 14

OFFICIAL GOING: Good (7.5)

Wind: Nil

4020 LADBROKES IN THE COMMUNITY CHARITABLE TRUST E B F MAIDEN STKS — 5f 10y

6:30 (6:31) (Class 4) 2-Y-O — £4,695 (£1,397; £698; £348) Stalls High

Form				RPR
24	1		**Red Rossini (IRE)**[31] 2999 2-9-3 0 .... RichardHughes 4 (R Hannon) *trckd ldr: led over 2f out: drvn and styd on strly thrght fnl f* **3/1**[2]	77
30	2	¾	**Court Approval (IRE)**[27] 3105 2-9-3 0 .... JimCrowley 6 (T G Mills) *chsd ldrs: wnt 2nd ins fnl 2f: kpt on wl fnl f but a hld by wnr* **4/1**[3]	74
	3	1	**Zelos Girl (IRE)** 2-8-12 0 .... SaleemGolam 3 (Rae Guest) *in rr but in tch: hdwy fr 2f out: kpt on fnl f but nvr quite gng pce to rch ldng duo* **16/1**	67+
	4	3 ¾	**Art Correspondent (IRE)** 2-9-3 0 .... GeorgeBaker 10 (G L Moore) *broke wl: outpcd after 1f: hdwy 2f out: n.m.r whn rdn and green over 1f out: styd on ins fnl f but nvr in contention* **5/2**[1]	61+
0	5	¾	**Kayceebee**[21] 3323 2-9-3 0 .... SebSanders 2 (R M Beckett) *sn chsng ldrs: effrt in centre crse 2f out: rdn and edgd lft over 1f out: wknd ins fnl f* **18/1**	55
06	6	hd	**Sericus (IRE)**[11] 3651 2-9-3 0 .... TedDurcan 11 (W Jarvis) *in rr and detached after 1f: hdwy and hung lft fr 2f out: styd on wl fnl f but nvr in contention* **12/1**	57+
40	7	1 ½	**Black Salix (USA)**[30] 3027 2-8-7 0 .... AhmedAjtebi(5) 5 (Mrs P Sly) *s.i.s: towards rr: sme hdwy and hung lft over 1f out: nvr nr ldrs* **25/1**	43
0	8	nk	**Silver Salsa**[14] 3558 2-8-12 0 .... AdrianMcCarthy 7 (J R Jenkins) *chsd ldrs 3f* **66/1**	42
	9	½	**My Dixie Darling (USA)** 2-8-12 0 .... PatDobbs 8 (R Hannon) *bhd fr 1/2-way* **20/1**	41+
0	10	2	**Brer Rabbit**[19] 3378 2-8-12 0 .... MichaelHills 1 (B W Hills) *chsd ldrs tl wknd fr 2f out* **13/2**	33
0	11	3	**Emerald Lass**[30] 3019 2-8-12 0 .... TPQueally 9 (D J Coakley) *led tl hdd & wknd qckly over 2f out* **50/1**	23

59.93 secs (-0.37) **Going Correction** -0.05s/f (Good) — **11** Ran SP% **117.8**

Speed ratings (Par 96): **100,98,97,91,90 89,87,86,86,82 78**

toteswinger: 1&2 £1.60, 1&3 £7.10, 2&3 £50.70. CSF £14.93 TOTE £3.40: £1.50, £1.90, £5.90; EX 15.40.

Owner Terry Neill **Bred** And Mrs P & S Martin **Trained** East Everleigh, Wilts

FOCUS

Probably an above-average two-year-old maiden, with the two with the best form in the book disputing the finish, both showing improvement. Two likeable newcomers filled the rest of the frame, while a couple of likely nursery types occupied the next two spots.

NOTEBOOK

Red Rossini(IRE) was always leading or disputing the lead and had plenty left in his tank to hold the late challengers. The yard have their usual exceptional array of talent amongst their juvenile speedsters, and this one obviously rates towards the top of the pecking order judging by his trainer's post-race comments. (op 7-2)

Court Approval(IRE) had been very highly tried in his first two starts and the son of Royal Applause appreciated the drop in grade, keeping on well all the way to the line. He should be breaking his duck soon. (op 3-1)

Zelos Girl(IRE) was the first juvenile representative of her yard this year and put up a promising debut by coming home strongly. Her sire is doing very well with his first crop.

Art Correspondent(IRE), backed into clear favouritism, is a big sort and looked awkward and green on what was his racecourse bow. He will do better over further and can leave this form behind in due course. (op 3-1)

Kayceebee improved greatly on an admittedly poor debut effort. Stuck out in the centre of the course for much of the way from his low draw, he wasn't given a hard time once it was clear he could not win. (op 16-1 tchd 12-1)

Sericus(IRE) stayed on steadily without troubling the leaders for the second consecutive race and his jockey must have only done just enough to avoid the attention of the stewards. He has obviously been brought along with nurseries in mind and it would be no surprise to see him stepped up in trip on his debut in that sphere. (op 14-1)

4021 ROYAL BANK OF SCOTLAND H'CAP — 1m 3f 135y

7:00 (7:01) (Class 4) (0-85,85) 3-Y-O — £5,504 (£1,637; £818; £408) Stalls Low

Form				RPR
1-60	1		**Howdigo**[21] 3325 3-8-13 77 .... SteveDrowne 5 (J R Best) *hld up in rr: hdwy over 2f out: swtchd rt to stands' rail over 1f out: str run ins fnl f to assert cl home* **33/1**	85
-332	2	½	**First Avenue**[11] 3633 3-9-5 83 .... PhilipRobinson 3 (M A Jarvis) *led: drvn and qcknd over 2f out: edgd lft u.p ins fnl f: no ex and ct cl home* **7/4**[1]	90
2012	3	½	**Mezzanisi (IRE)**[7] 3793 3-8-11 75 .... JamieSpencer 9 (M L W Bell) *hld up in rr: nt clr run over 2f out: n.m.r over 1f out: swtchd lft and rapid hdwy u.p ins fnl f: squeezed through cl home: fin fast: nt quite get up* **7/2**[2]	83+
2154	4	1	**Mega Watt (IRE)**[15] 3527 3-8-13 77 .... TPQueally 11 (W Jarvis) *hld up in rr: nt clr run over 2f out: swtchd lft to outside and hdwy over 1f out: str run ins fnl f but nvr quite gng pce to chal* **14/1**	81+
-106	5	nk	**It's A Date**[19] 3380 3-8-13 77 .... DaneO'Neill 1 (A King) *chsd ldrs: wnt 2nd and rdn over 1f out: nvr quite gng pce to chal and outpcd ins fnl f* **16/1**	81
2640	6	7	**Higgy's Boy (IRE)**[15] 3527 3-8-12 76 .... RichardHughes 6 (R Hannon) *in tch 1/2-way: rdn to chse ldr over 2f out: wknd qckly over 1f out* **16/1**	68
-101	7	1 ½	**Tarkheena Prince (USA)**[16] 3493 3-9-7 85 .... KerrinMcEvoy 7 (G A Swinbank) *chsd ldrs: rdn 3f out: sn btn* **11/2**[3]	74
-142	8	3 ¾	**Mazaaya (USA)**[10] 3676 3-9-7 85 .... TedDurcan 8 (D R Lanigan) *in tch: rdn 3f out: sn wknd* **25/1**	68
2-31	9	6	**Altitude**[10] 3688 3-9-2 80 .... SebSanders 4 (Sir Mark Prescott) *chsd ldr: rdn 3f out: sn btn* **9/1**	53
4104	10	2 ¼	**Benedict Spirit (IRE)**[59] 2173 3-8-6 70 .... JimmyQuinn 10 (M H Tompkins) *chsd ldrs: rdn 3f out: sn btn* **25/1**	39
-120	11	5	**Taikoo**[66] 1962 3-8-10 77 .... TravisBlock(3) 2 (H Morrison) *a in rr* **20/1**	37

2m 29.65s (0.15) **Going Correction** +0.075s/f (Good) — **11** Ran SP% **117.8**

Speed ratings (Par 102): **102,101,101,100,100 95,94,92,88,86 83**

toteswinger: 1&2 £15.30, 1&3 £15.30, 2&3 £1.40. CSF £88.02 CT £273.15 TOTE £41.70: £9.60, £1.20, £1.50; EX 304.50.

Owner G G Racing **Bred** J R Wills **Trained** Hucking, Kent

FOCUS

Some useful three-year-olds on show in this handicap, which looked pretty warm for the grade. The first five home pulled well clear of the remainder and the form should work out.

Mezzanisi(IRE) Official explanation: jockey said gelding was denied a clear run

4022 SUNLEY FILLIES' H'CAP — 1m 67y

7:30 (7:31) (Class 4) (0-80,80) 3-Y-O+ — £4,857 (£1,445; £722; £360) Stalls High

Form				RPR
-052	1		**Run For Ede's**[13] 3583 4-9-0 63 .... (p) JohnEgan 2 (P M Phelan) *hld up in rr: t.k.h: hdwy over 2f out: sn drvn and edging lft whn styng on to ld wl ins fnl f: drvn out* **25/1**	72
-402	2	hd	**Trumpet Lily**[32] 2974 3-9-4 76 .... JimCrowley 5 (J G Portman) *in rr tl gd hdwy fr 3f out: drvn to ld appr fnl f: hdd and no ex wl ins fnl f* **10/3**[1]	83
2102	3	1 ½	**Mekong Melody (IRE)**[10] 3679 3-9-4 76 .... PhilipRobinson 6 (C G Cox) *chsd ldr: rdn and ev ch 2f out: one pce fnl f* **9/2**[3]	79
2444	4	3	**Granary**[22] 3293 4-9-4 67 .... DaneO'Neill 3 (H Candy) *led: rdn over 2f out: hdd appr fnl f: wknd ins fnl f* **7/1**	65
0434	5	hd	**Montrachet**[25] 3163 4-9-13 76 .... JamieSpencer 10 (M L W Bell) *chsd ldrs tl rdn and outpcd over 2f out: kpt on again fnl f but n.d* **7/2**[2]	74
03-0	6	1 ¾	**Gentle Guru**[31] 2995 4-9-13 76 .... SteveDrowne 7 (R T Phillips) *in rr tl rdn and sme hdwy over 2f out: nvr in contention* **14/1**	70
1-61	7	1 ¾	**La Coveta (IRE)**[11] 3636 3-9-3 80 .... GabrielHannon(5) 8 (B J Meehan) *chsd ldrs: rdn 3f out: wknd fr 2f out* **17/2**	68
5142	8	1	**Onenightinlisbon (IRE)**[16] 3507 4-9-2 72 .... HarryPoulton(7) 1 (J R Boyle) *chsd ldrs: rdn fr 3f out and sn btn* **12/1**	59
050	9	½	**Shamrock Lady (IRE)**[16] 3507 3-9-0 72 .... TPO'Shea 9 (J Gallagher) *t.k.h: nvr in contention* **20/1**	56
311-	10	13	**Sweet Gale (IRE)**[405] 2335 4-9-7 77 .... DavidProbert(7) 4 (Mike Murphy) *t.k.h in rr: hdwy on outside to trck ldrs fr 3f out: wknd qckly over 2f out* **14/1**	33

1m 45.17s (0.47) **Going Correction** +0.075s/f (Good)

WFA 3 from 4yo 9lb — **10** Ran SP% **116.1**

Speed ratings (Par 102): **100,99,98,95,95 93,91,90,90,77**

toteswinger: 1&2 £59.40, 1&3 £59.40, 2&3 £1.40. CSF £106.73 CT £459.50 TOTE £28.00: £5.10, £2.00, £1.80; EX 89.50.

Owner Ede's (uk) Ltd **Bred** Mrs James Wigan & London Thoroughbred Services Ltd **Trained** Epsom, Surrey

■ Stewards' Enquiry : Dane O'Neill caution: careless riding

FOCUS

A fair fillies' handicap. The principals had all been in some kind of form beforehand, which gives the race a solid look, although the form is only ordinary.

4023 RENT A PUB FROM TRUST INNS (S) STKS — 1m 3f 135y

8:00 (8:01) (Class 6) 3-4-Y-O — £2,047 (£604; £302) Stalls Low

Form				RPR
5433	1		**Lady Jinks**[10] 3692 3-7-11 53 .... BillyCray(7) 3 (M D I Usher) *chsd ldrs: led 3f out: rdn over 2f out: hld on wl u.p fnl f* **6/1**[2]	53
2222	2	1 ¾	**Hester Brook (IRE)**[7] 3786 4-9-3 45 .... JimCrowley 6 (J G M O'Shea) *hld up in rr: hdwy over 2f out: swtchd rt to stands' rail over 1f out: str run to chse wnr ins fnl f but a jst hld* **3/1**[1]	50
6002	3	2 ½	**Royal Soverin**[23] 3264 3-8-9 50 .... (v) PatCosgrave 5 (M J Wallace) *in rr: hdwy 3f out: chsd ldrs and rdn 2f out: outpcd fnl f* **10/1**	51
-050	4	nk	**Converti**[10] 3698 4-9-8 45 .... GeorgeBaker 1 (H J Manners) *chsd ldr: rdn and styd on 3f out: one pce fnl 2f* **10/1**	50
4063	5	4	**Soldiers Quest**[16] 3482 4-9-8 55 .... AdamKirby 10 (Peter Grayson) *chsd ldrs: rdn 3f out: wknd fr 2f out* **15/2**	43
0405	6	½	**Sweet World**[5] 3844 4-9-5 55 .... (p) TravisBlock(3) 4 (B J Llewellyn) *in rr tl hdwy fr 3f out: no imp u.p fr 2f out* **7/1**	43
000-	7	6	**Stafford Will (IRE)**[39] 5347 4-9-1 45 .... (b[1]) WilliamCarson(7) 9 (J G M O'Shea) *mid-div whn rdn over 3f out: nvr in contention after* **40/1**	32
0-63	8	½	**Leprechaun's Gold (IRE)**[40] 2731 4-9-1 46 .... DavidProbert(7) 8 (B J Llewellyn) *s.i.s: nvr bttr than mid-div* **13/2**[3]	32
0-0	9	2 ¼	**Bold Josr**[21] 3328 4-9-3 0 .... GabrielHannon(5) 13 (D J S Ffrench Davis) *a towards rr* **66/1**	28
5060	10	1 ¾	**Art Of Being (IRE)**[58] 2207 4-9-5 37 .... (p) LeeVickers(3) 11 (M C Chapman) *led tl hdd 3f out: sn wknd* **50/1**	25
0646	11	2 ¾	**Howe's Jack (IRE)**[9] 3730 3-8-6 43 .... (t) DominicFox(3) 12 (M C Chapman) *chsd ldrs to 1/2-way: wknd 4f out* **25/1**	20
0405	12	11	**Fortunes Maid (IRE)**[25] 3166 3-8-4 43 .... JimmyQuinn 7 (M H Tompkins) *chsd ldrs 8f* **14/1**	—
35-3	13	4 ½	**Dr Dream (IRE)**[19] 273 4-9-8 47 .... (v) WilliamBuick 2 (J G M O'Shea) *prom early: bhd fr 1/2-way* **7/1**	—

2m 32.83s (3.33) **Going Correction** +0.075s/f (Good)

WFA 3 from 4yo 13lb — **13** Ran SP% **124.0**

Speed ratings (Par 101): **91,89,88,87,85 84,80,80,79,77 76,68,65**

toteswinger: 1&2 £5.40, 1&3 £24.80, 2&3 £26.80. CSF £24.73 TOTE £7.40: £2.10, £1.80, £3.00; EX 25.90.The winner was bought in for £3,600.

Owner The High Jinks Partnership **Bred** A B Barraclough **Trained** Upper Lambourn, Berks

■ Stewards' Enquiry : William Carson five-day ban: used whip with excessive frequency and when out of contention (Jul 28-31, Aug 1)

FOCUS

A poor race even by selling standards. The winner is rated to her latter 2-y-o form.

Soldiers Quest Official explanation: jockey said colt ran too free

Sweet World Official explanation: jockey said gelding ran too free

Bold Josr Official explanation: jockey said gelding hung right

4024 NEW FOOTBALL POOLS MAIDEN STKS — 6f

8:30 (8:33) (Class 5) 2-Y-O — £2,729 (£806; £403) Stalls High

Form				RPR
0	1		**Tartan Turban (IRE)**[44] 2592 2-9-3 0 .... PatDobbs 12 (R Hannon) *chsd ldrs: rdn to ld fnl 100yds: hld on wl* **33/1**	71
0	2	½	**Hawkspur (IRE)**[38] 2769 2-9-3 0 .... DaneO'Neill 5 (R Hannon) *in tch: gd hdwy fr 2f out: pressed wnr fnl 100yds but a jst hld* **25/1**	70
0	3	hd	**Goldvil (IRE)**[31] 2999 2-9-3 0 .... KerrinMcEvoy 11 (B J Meehan) *sn slt ld: rdn along 2f out: hdd and no ex fnl 100yds* **5/2**[1]	69
	4	1 ½	**Rocoppelia (USA)** 2-9-3 0 .... JimCrowley 14 (Mrs A J Perrett) *in tch: hdwy fr 2f out: styd on fnl f but nvr quite gng pce of ldng trio* **16/1**	64+
	5	1 ½	**Retro (IRE)** 2-9-3 0 .... RichardHughes 7 (R Hannon) *hld up towards rr but in tch: gd hdwy ins fnl 2f: styd on fnl f but nvr quite gng pce to be competitive* **13/2**[3]	60+

0 **6** *1 3/4* **West Leake (IRE)**[7] 3798 2-9-3 0 .... MichaelHills 6 55
(B W Hills) *pressed ldrs: rdn 2f out: wknd fnl f* **20/1**

7 *1 1/4* **Olynard (IRE)** 2-9-3 0 .... SebSanders 16 51
(R M Beckett) *plld hrd early: chsd ldrs to 2f out: sn btn* **11/4**[2]

8 *nse* **Tidal Force (USA)** 2-9-3 0 .... NelsonDeSouza 9 51+
(P F I Cole) *in tch: wkng whn hmpd appr fnl f* **20/1**

9 *1* **Lyonesse** 2-8-12 0 .... SteveDrowne 15 43
(R Hannon) *nvr bttr than mid-div* **28/1**

10 *1/2* **Nasri** 2-9-3 0 .... WilliamBuick 13 46
(B J Meehan) *s.i.s: outpcd tl mod late prog* **13/2**[3]

11 *1 1/2* **Tagula Night (IRE)** 2-9-3 0 .... AdamKirby 3 42+
(W R Swinburn) *wnt lft s: sme hdwy on outside whn hmpd over 1f out: nvr in contention* **14/1**

0 **12** *2 1/4* **Silver Sceptre (IRE)**[7] 3798 2-9-3 0 .... NeilPollard 2 35
(W J Musson) *pushed lft s: a in rr* **40/1**

13 *1/2* **Come On Toby** 2-9-3 0 .... TedDurcan 10 34
(E A L Dunlop) *a in rr* **20/1**

542 **14** *3 3/4* **Dancing Wave**[90] 1384 2-8-9 0 .... DominicFox(3) 8 17+
(M C Chapman) *w ldr 3f* **12/1**

1m 13.68s (0.68) **Going Correction** -0.05s/f (Good) **14** Ran SP% **129.1**
Speed ratings (Par 94): **93,92,92,90,88 85,84,84,82,82 80,77,76,71**
toteswinger: 1&2 £42.60, 1&3 Not won, 2&3 £42.60. CSF £695.44 TOTE £33.90: £7.30, £6.10, £2.00; EX 472.10.
Owner McKendrick Morecombe Anderson Mahal **Bred** Mrs Joan Browne **Trained** East Everleigh, Wilts

FOCUS
A decent juvenile maiden saw a couple of Hannon-trained colts leave their debut efforts well behind and fight out the finish. There was not much pre-race form to go on and this level could be a couple of lengths or more out either way.

NOTEBOOK
Tartan Turban(IRE) showed some early speed on his debut at Doncaster before fading badly and this effort was a revelation in comparison, as he needed all of the 6f trip to overhaul his stablemate. A half-brother to the yard's Group-winning colt Paco Boy, he wouldn't want the ground too fast and might be kept back for the autumn now. (tchd 28-1)
Hawkspur(IRE), out of Nunthorpe winner Lyric Fantasy, known affectionately to racing fans as the "pocket rocket", but who has yet to produce a winner in the British Isles from nine previous foals, left a poor debut effort at Bath behind and showed himself to have inherited plenty of his dam's toe. His trainer has a wealth of two-year-old talent and the son of Hawk Wing should have no trouble being found a winning opportunity soon. (op 28-1 tchd 33-1)
Goldvil(IRE) was heavily backed into favouritism and duly left his debut form behind over the extra furlong. He won't be long in breaking his duck. (op 4-1)
Rocoppelia(USA), a $150,000 purchase, stayed on well to the line to make a pleasing racecourse bow. The yard's juveniles usually come on significantly for their first run and the son of Hennessy should have no trouble landing one of these contests. (op 14-1)
Retro(IRE), easily the shortest price of his trainer's team of four but a drifter in the market nonetheless, ran well enough to suggest that he will be winning races before long. (op 5-1 tchd 4-1 and 7-1)
West Leake(IRE) showed much more than on his recent debut here, briefly disputing the lead over a furlong out. He might prove best at the minimum. (op 16-1)
Olynard(IRE), a half-brother to smart sprinter Pivotal Flame and holding an entry in the Gimcrack Stakes, was walloped in the market beforehand so must have been something of a disappointment to connections, not seeing out the trip after pulling hard in the early stages. (op 4-1 tchd 9-2 in places)
Tidal Force(USA) Official explanation: jockey said colt suffered interference
Dancing Wave Official explanation: jockey said filly lost its action

4025 PATTONAIR DERBY CHALLENGE & INNOVATE H'CAP 5f 10y
9:00 (9:00) (Class 5) (0-75,74) 3-Y-0+ **£3,070** (£906; £453) **Stalls** High

Form RPR

04-4 **1** **Make My Dream**[20] 3346 5-9-0 **62** .... TPO'Shea 4 73
(J Gallagher) *sn trcking ldrs: rdn over 1f out: styd on strly fnl f to ld fnl 50yds: hld on wl* **12/1**

401 **2** *shd* **Kelamon**[7] 3797 4-9-7 **69** .... WilliamBuick 8 80+
(M D I Usher) *broke wl: sn outpcd towards rr but in tch: hdwy and nt clr run whn swtchd lft appr fnl f: fin strly: jst failed* **7/2**[1]

4004 **3** *1 1/4* **Woodcote (IRE)**[13] 3587 6-9-12 **74** .... (tp) JimCrowley 2 81
(P R Chamings) *pressed ldrs: drvn to ld jst ins fnl f: hdd and outpcd fnl 50yds* **9/1**

0505 **4** *3/4* **El Potro**[25] 3159 6-8-10 **58** ow1 .... RichardHughes 6 62
(J R Holt) *chsd ldrs: rdn and n.m.r appr fnl f: styd on but nvr gng pce of ldng trio* **14/1**

0514 **5** *1/2* **Bertie Southstreet**[13] 3585 5-9-9 **71** .... (b) SebSanders 10 73
(J R Best) *t.k.h in mid-div: hdwy fnl f but nt rch ldrs* **4/1**[2]

640 **6** *1/2* **Desert Opal**[9] 3724 8-9-4 **66** .... (b) TedDurcan 11 66
(C R Dore) *chsd ldrs: rdn and edgd lft over 1f out: sn wknd* **16/1**

5206 **7** *1* **Jayanjay**[20] 3346 9-8-7 **55** .... (v) SteveDrowne 1 52
(B R Johnson) *chsd ldrs: styng on one pce whn pushed lft over 1f out and sn wknd* **20/1**

360 **8** *3/4* **Spoof Master (IRE)**[19] 3374 4-9-6 **68** .... JohnEgan 13 62
(C R Dore) *slt ld: rdn 2f out: hdd & wknd jst ins fnl f* **13/2**[3]

5146 **9** *shd* **Dualagi**[30] 3026 4-9-3 **65** .... GeorgeBaker 12 59
(M R Bosley) *s.i.s: in rr and nvr gng pce to get into contention* **10/1**

00 **10** *1/2* **Garstang**[21] 3320 5-9-3 **65** .... (b) AdamKirby 9 57
(Peter Grayson) *in tch to 1/2-way* **10/1**

0130 **11** *2* **Brazilian Brush (IRE)**[31] 3000 3-9-1 **71** .... (t) TravisBlock(3) 5 56
(H Morrison) *chsd ldrs: rdn and wknd over 1f out* **12/1**

-051 **12** *13* **Mr Funshine**[10] 3686 3-8-4 **62** ow2 .... JackMitchell(5) 3 —
(Mrs P N Dutfield) *slowly away: a bhd* **20/1**

40 **13** *12* **Compton Classic**[108] 1061 6-9-1 **63** .... (p) PatCosgrave 7 —
(J R Boyle) *chsd ldrs: wkng whn hmpd and snatched up over 1f out* **16/1**

59.56 secs (-0.74) **Going Correction** -0.05s/f (Good)
WFA 3 from 4yo+ 5lb **13** Ran SP% **127.1**
Speed ratings (Par 103): **103,102,100,99,98 98,96,95,95,94 91,70,51**
toteswinger: 1&2 £10.80, 1&3 £34.90, 2&3 £17.40. CSF £57.12 CT £426.51 TOTE £12.90: £3.50, £2.10, £4.10; EX 104.10 Place 6 £57.25, Place 5 £20.61.
Owner Mrs Irene Clifford **Bred** The Valentines **Trained** Moreton-in-Marsh, Gloucs
■ Stewards' Enquiry : William Buick four-day ban: careless riding (Jul 29,31,Aug 1,3)

FOCUS
A modest sprint handicap, which has been rated through the winner to last year's best.
T/Jkpt: Not won. T/Plt: £67.50 to a £1 stake. Pool: £100,837.44. 1,088.97 winning tickets. T/Qpdt: £15.60 to a £1 stake. Pool: £5,792.50. 273.10 winning tickets. ST

3821 WOLVERHAMPTON (A.W) (L-H)
Monday, July 14

OFFICIAL GOING: Standard
Wind: Light, behind Weather: Overcast

4026 HORIZONS RESTAURANT CLASSIFIED CLAIMING STKS 1m 4f 50y(P)
6:50 (6:50) (Class 6) 3-Y-0+ **£2,047** (£604; £302) **Stalls** Low

Form RPR

0435 **1** **York Cliff**[4] 3871 10-9-4 54 .... EddieAhern 7 51
(W M Brisbourne) *hld up: hdwy 1/2-way: led over 2f out: rdn clr over 1f out: eased nr fin* **9/2**[2]

0000 **2** *1 1/4* **Bainisteoir**[5] 3845 3-8-6 55 .... MartinDwyer 11 50
(S Kirk) *hld up: hdwy over 2f out: rdn to chse wnr and hung lft ins fnl f: hung rt towards fin: styd on* **11/1**

6445 **3** *1 1/2* **Balais Folly (FR)**[10] 3692 3-8-5 50 .... (b) CatherineGannon 6 47
(B Palling) *hmpd sn after s: hld up: hdwy over 5f out: edgd lft and hmpd over 2f out: rdn to chse wnr over 1f out: no ex fnl f* **20/1**

0020 **4** *7* **Blazing Mask (IRE)**[13] 3580 3-8-5 48 .... AndrewMullen(3) 4 38
(Mrs A Duffield) *sn pushed along in rr: styd on fnl f: nvr nrr* **33/1**

560- **5** *1 3/4* **Zalkani (IRE)**[198] 7273 8-9-2 53 .... SimonPearce(7) 1 38
(J Pearce) *hld up in tch: hmpd over 2f out: sn rdn and wknd* **15/2**

0000 **6** *2 3/4* **Dushstorm (IRE)**[21] 3321 7-9-8 59 .... (p) FergusSweeney 3 32
(C R Dore) *led 4f: chsd ldrs: ev ch over 2f out: sn rdn: wknd over 1f out* **7/1**

-032 **7** *27* **Soundbyte**[16] 3482 3-8-7 56 .... (v[1]) ShaneKelly 5 —
(Ollie Pears) *prom: led 8f out: hdd over 6f out: led again 4f out: hdd over 2f out: hmpd and wknd sn after* **9/4**[1]

0-50 **8** *15* **Bundle Up**[23] 3265 5-9-9 54 .... IanMongan 9 —
(Mrs L J Mongan) *chsd ldr: led over 6f out: hdd 4f out: sn rdn: wknd over 2f out* **10/1**

00-0 **9** *13* **Star Berry**[78] 778 5-8-12 42 .... (p) RichardRowe(7) 10 —
(T Wall) *chsd ldrs: rdn 1/2-way: sn wknd* **66/1**

0044 **10** *19* **Crafty Fox**[19] 3371 5-8-12 43 .... (v) MarkCoumbe(5) 12 —
(John A Harris) *hld up: bhd fnl 7f* **16/1**

150- **11** *28* **Singleb (IRE)**[257] 6598 4-8-13 56 .... (tp) TolleyDean(3) 2 —
(George Baker) *trckd ldrs: racd keenly: rdn 1/2-way: wknd wl over 3f out* **13/2**[3]

2m 43.67s (2.57) **Going Correction** +0.175s/f (Slow)
WFA 3 from 4yo+ 13lb **11** Ran SP% **119.1**
Speed ratings (Par 101): **98,97,96,91,90 88,70,60,51,39 20**
toteswinger: 1&2 £10.00, 1&3 Not won, 2&3 Not won. CSF £52.92 TOTE £5.00: £1.10, £3.60, £5.40; EX 77.30.Soundbyte was claimed by Oliver Parsons for £7,000.
Owner Mark Brisbourne **Bred** F Hinojosa **Trained** Great Ness, Shropshire
■ Stewards' Enquiry : Catherine Gannon two-day ban: careless riding (Jul 28,29)

FOCUS
A weak claimer run in a slow time and rated through the winner to his recent best.
Star Berry Official explanation: jockey said mare stopped quickly
Crafty Fox Official explanation: jockey said gelding never travelled

4027 STAY AT THE WOLVERHAMPTON HOLIDAY INN MAIDEN AUCTION STKS 5f 216y(P)
7:20 (7:25) (Class 5) 2-Y-0 **£3,070** (£906; £453) **Stalls** Low

Form RPR

20 **1** **Blown It (USA)**[27] 3103 2-9-1 0 .... ShaneKelly 12 79+
(J A Osborne) *trckd ldrs: carried wd ent st: rdn and hung lft fr over 1f out: r.o to ld wl ins fnl f* **5/4**[1]

2 *3/4* **Diddums** 2-8-9 0 .... LiamJones 5 69
(W J Haggas) *chsd ldrs: rdn over 1f out: hung lft ins fnl f: r.o* **10/1**

4 **3** *1* **Defector (IRE)**[21] 3323 2-8-13 0 .... MartinDwyer 13 70
(W R Muir) *chsd ldr: rn wd ent st: sn rdn: hung lft ins fnl f: styd on* **11/4**[2]

50 **4** *1/2* **Abhainn (IRE)**[61] 2098 2-8-13 0 .... CatherineGannon 8 68
(B Palling) *led: rdn clr and hung lft over 1f out: hdd wl ins fnl f* **66/1**

5 *2 1/2* **Spanish Baron (USA)** 2-8-13 0 .... (t) EddieAhern 2 61
(R M H Cowell) *s.i.s: hdwy over 2f out: sn rdn: styd on same pce fnl f* **7/1**[3]

6 *3 1/4* **Weet In Nerja** 2-8-11 0 .... LPKeniry 10 49
(R Hollinshead) *hld up: hdwy over 2f out: rdn and wknd over 1f out: hung lft fnl f* **50/1**

5 **7** *2* **Handcuff**[105] 1118 2-8-13 0 .... SamHitchcott 11 45
(J A Osborne) *s.s: in rr effrt over 2f out: n.d* **50/1**

8 *1/2* **Fantastic Fred (IRE)** 2-8-9 0 .... MickyFenton 1 40
(J A Osborne) *mid-div: hdwy over 2f out: sn rdn and wknd* **40/1**

5 **9** *1 1/2* **Bounty Reef**[7] 3798 2-8-8 0 .... JamesDoyle 9 34
(P D Evans) *hld up: nvr nr to chal* **16/1**

4 **10** *1 1/4* **Igneous**[24] 3199 2-8-9 0 .... AndrewElliott 3 31
(K R Burke) *s.i.s: hld up: sme hdwy over 2f out: sn wknd* **28/1**

11 *6* **Haafhds Delight (IRE)** 2-8-1 0 .... LukeMorris(3) 6 8
(W M Brisbourne) *mid-div: rdn over 3f out: sn wknd* **66/1**

00 **12** *13* **Premier Demon (IRE)**[67] 1924 2-8-9 0 ow1 .... StephenDonohoe 7 —
(P D Evans) *sn outpcd* **100/1**

13 *hd* **Senorita Mirasol** 2-8-6 0 .... RichardSmith 4 —
(R Hannon) *sn outpcd* **25/1**

1m 17.19s (2.19) **Going Correction** +0.175s/f (Slow) **13** Ran SP% **116.2**
Speed ratings (Par 94): **92,91,89,89,85 81,78,78,76,74 66,49,48**
toteswinger: 1&2 £3.30, 1&3 £1.10, 2&3 £3.30. CSF £14.00 TOTE £2.60: £1.10, £1.80, £1.50; EX 16.30.
Owner R Pegum,M Kerr-Dineen,R Tullett & Ptns **Bred** H & W Thoroughbreds & Adrian Regan **Trained** Upper Lambourn, Berks

FOCUS
Probably a fair maiden, rated through the winner and the third.

NOTEBOOK
Blown It(USA) ◆, runner-up on his debut at Salisbury before running with credit when tenth of 18 in an ordinary renewal of the Coventry Stakes at Royal Ascot, proved too good for this lot on his return to maiden company. This was a decent enough effort considering he was conceding weight all round and got taken wide by Defector off the home bend. (op 7-4 tchd 9-4)
Diddums ◆, an 8,000gns gelded son of Royal Applause, half-brother to 1m winner Getrah, out of a dual 5f-6f juvenile winner, made a pleasing debut in second. Having gone the shortest way round for much of the way, he stuck on right the way to the line and displayed a likeable attitude. He looks well up to winning a similar event. (tchd 8-1)
Defector(IRE) shaped well when fourth on his debut at Windsor, but a high draw did him no favours this time. Having been forced to use up energy to get across and race handy, he didn't help his chance by swinging wide into the straight. He can do better. (op 13-8 tchd 6-4)
Abhainn(IRE), gelded since he was last seen, showed loads of speed and gave the impression he will be worth another try back over 5f.

Spanish Baron(USA), a $40,000 son of Dixieland Band, half-brother to four sprint winners in the US, had a tongue-tie on but he was not unfancied. He struggled to get a decent position early and never threatened, but he showed definite signs of ability. (op 8-1)
Bounty Reef Official explanation: jockey said filly suffered interference in running
Senorita Mirasol Official explanation: jockey said filly never travelled

4028 HOTEL & CONFERENCING AT WOLVERHAMPTON (S) STKS — 5f 20y(P)
7:50 (7:51) (Class 6) 3-4-Y-O — £1,978 (£584; £292) Stalls Low

Form — RPR
2311 **1** **Hurricane Hen**[14] 3565 3-9-0 67 ..... RichardEvans[(5)] 9 — 76
(P D Evans) *chsd ldrs: led over 1f out: shkn up and r.o: comf* **7/4**[1]
-323 **2** 2 3/4 **Fast Feet**[17] 3434 3-9-0 64 ..... (p) SilvestreDeSousa 6 — 61
(K A Ryan) *led 3f: sn rdn: styd on same pce u.p ins fnl f* **11/2**[3]
4604 **3** hd **The Little Fizzer (IRE)**[13] 3577 3-9-0 55 ..... FergusSweeney 2 — 60
(K R Burke) *chsd ldrs: rdn over 1f out: styd on same pce ins fnl f* **14/1**
550 **4** 1 1/2 **New York Oscar (IRE)**[47] 2501 4-9-5 70 ..... (b) JamesDoyle 1 — 57
(A J McCabe) *w ldr tl led 2f out: sn rdn and hdd: nt run on* **5/1**[2]
4060 **5** hd **Penrice Castle**[15] 3526 3-8-9 57 ..... RichardSmith 12 — 49
(R Hannon) *hld up: styd on appr fnl f: nvr trbld ldrs* **33/1**
3004 **6** 1/2 **Spic 'n Span**[7] 3782 3-9-0 64 ..... (b) LiamJones 4 — 52
(R A Harris) *prom: rdn 1/2-way: hung lft ins fnl f: nt run on* **10/1**
035- **7** 1/2 **Sinead Of Aglish (IRE)**[220] 7052 3-8-9 70 ..... (b) LPKeniry 3 — 45
(Peter Grayson) *in rr: sn pushed along: effrt over 1f out: n.d* **16/1**
-500 **8** hd **Cool Fashion (IRE)**[23] 3283 3-8-9 46 ..... (b[1]) DO'Donohoe 5 — 44
(Ollie Pears) *hld up: styd on ins fnl f: n.d* **40/1**
5600 **9** 2 1/2 **Lady Florence**[18] 3395 3-8-9 48 ..... RichardKingscote 13 — 35
(A B Coogan) *chsd ldrs: rdn 1/2-way: wknd over 1f out: sn hung lft* **28/1**
0000 **10** 1/2 **Mister Always**[9] 3725 4-8-12 45 ..... RobbieEgan[(7)] 7 — 41
(D Flood) *s.i.s: rdn over 1f out: a in rr* **66/1**
6005 **11** 3/4 **What Katie Did (IRE)**[9] 3733 3-9-5 75 ..... ShaneKelly 10 — 41
(P F I Cole) *prom: rdn 1/2-way: sn wknd: hung rt ins fnl f* **11/2**[3]

62.69 secs (0.39) **Going Correction** +0.175s/f (Slow)
WFA 3 from 4yo 5lb — 11 Ran SP% **115.8**
Speed ratings (Par 101): **103,98,98,95,95 94,93,93,89,88 87**
toteswinger: 1&2 £2.50, 1&3 £44.00, 2&3 £14.20. CSF £10.71 TOTE £2.50: £1.20, £1.50, £5.10; EX 11.20.The winner was bought in for 10,500gns. The Little Fizzer was claimed by P. D. Evans for £6,000.
Owner Mrs I M Folkes **Bred** Aston Mullins Stud **Trained** Pandy, Monmouths

FOCUS
A reasonable seller and the form makes a fair bit of sense.

4029 BUY TICKETS ONLINE H'CAP — 1m 5f 194y(P)
8:20 (8:21) (Class 6) (0-65,62) 4-Y-0+ — £2,388 (£705; £352) Stalls Low

Form — RPR
4-31 **1** **Squirtle (IRE)**[13] 3589 5-8-6 50 ..... LukeMorris[(3)] 5 — 57
(W M Brisbourne) *s.s: hld up: hdwy u.p over 2f out: hmpd over 1f out: styd on to ld wl ins fnl f* **11/4**[1]
5406 **2** 1 **Capistrano**[12] 3606 5-8-7 48 ..... PaulEddery 11 — 54
(G D Blake) *hld up: hmpd over 3f out: hdwy 2f out: sn rdn: ev ch wl ins fnl f: unable qck nr fin* **28/1**
4403 **3** 1 1/4 **Adage**[19] 3377 5-9-0 55 ..... (t) FergusSweeney 3 — 59
(David Pinder) *hld up: hdwy over 3f out: rdn and ev ch ins fnl f: styd on same pce* **11/4**[1]
6324 **4** nk **Best Selection**[83] 1538 4-9-7 62 ..... IanMongan 10 — 66
(Mrs L J Mongan) *hld up: hdwy over 4f out: led over 2f out: rdn and hung rt over 1f out: hung lft and hdd wl ins fnl f* **11/1**
3555 **5** 1 1/4 **Abounding**[10] 3685 4-9-5 60 ..... JamesDoyle 6 — 62
(M J Attwater) *hld up: hdwy over 3f out: rdn over 1f out: styd on same pce ins fnl f* **15/2**[3]
3500 **6** 1 1/4 **Bobsleigh**[22] 2643 9-8-2 46 ..... KirstyMilczarek[(3)] 7 — 46
(H S Howe) *chsd ldrs: outpcd over 3f out: rallied u.p over 2f out: wknd ins fnl f* **16/1**
0-04 **7** 3 1/4 **Swords**[39] 2755 6-8-8 49 ..... EddieAhern 4 — 45
(R E Peacock) *hld up: hdwy over 5f out: chsd ldr over 3f out: rdn and hung lft over 1f out: wknd fnl f* **10/1**
3000 **8** 6 **Lord Laing (USA)**[35] 2884 5-8-4 45 ..... LiamJones 9 — 32
(H J Collingridge) *led 1f: chsd ldr: led again over 6f out: rdn and hdd over 2f out: hmpd over 1f out: sn wknd* **7/1**[2]
0-50 **9** 11 **Phoenix Hill (IRE)**[20] 585 6-8-4 45 ..... MartinDwyer 2 — 17
(D R Gandolfo) *prom: rdn over 4f out: wknd over 2f out* **25/1**
10 hd **Mean Machine (IRE)**[308] 5105 6-7-13 47 ow2 ..... (be) RobbieEgan[(7)] 12 — 19
(D Flood) *s.i.s: hld up: hdwy 3f out: wknd over 2f out* **14/1**
06-0 **11** 13 **Laughing Game**[39] 2755 4-8-6 47 ..... DavidKinsella 13 — 1
(A M Hales) *chsd ldrs: rdn over 5f out: wknd 3f out* **50/1**
-006 **12** 4 1/2 **Campli (IRE)**[26] 3143 6-9-0 55 ..... DO'Donohoe 1 — 2+
(Micky Hammond) *led after 1f: rdn clr 10f out: eased over 8f out: hdd over 6f out: wknd 3f out: rdr rode a fin a circ too sn* **16/1**

3m 7.07s (1.07) **Going Correction** +0.175s/f (Slow) — 12 Ran SP% **122.7**
Speed ratings (Par 101): **103,102,101,101,100 100,98,94,88,88 81,78**
toteswinger: 1&2 £1.20, 1&3 Not won, 2&3 Not won. CSF £103.00 CT £240.66 TOTE £3.40: £1.60, £7.20, £1.50; EX 93.80.
Owner J Jones Racing Ltd **Bred** Ballygallon Stud Limited **Trained** Great Ness, Shropshire
■ Stewards' Enquiry : D O'Donohoe 12-day ban: mistook distance of race (Jul 28-Aug 8)
Luke Morris four-day ban: careless riding (Jul 28,29,31,Aug 1)

FOCUS
A very moderate handicap but the form looks pretty sound.
Campli(IRE) Official explanation: jockey said, regarding running and riding, that his orders were to ride the gelding positively but the early pace was slow and he tried to establish a lead in home straight first circuit.

4030 A & A DUCTWORK SUPPLY & FIT H'CAP — 7f 32y(P)
8:50 (8:51) (Class 5) (0-75,73) 3-Y-0+ — £3,238 (£963; £481; £240) Stalls High

Form — RPR
400 **1** **Methaaly (IRE)**[2] 3956 5-9-10 66 ..... (be) EddieAhern 9 — 78+
(M Mullineaux) *hld up: plld hrd: hung lft and r.o u.p ins fnl f to ld post* **7/1**
0000 **2** shd **Gross Prophet**[40] 2710 3-9-4 68 ..... RichardKingscote 4 — 77
(Tom Dascombe) *sn led: rdn over 1f out: hdd post* **4/1**[3]
4314 **3** 3/4 **Chjimes (IRE)**[5] 3842 4-10-0 70 ..... LPKeniry 8 — 80
(C R Dore) *sn chsng ldr: rdn and ev ch whn edgd lft over 1f out: styng on same pce whn n.m.r nr fin* **7/2**[2]
6000 **4** 1 3/4 **Wadnagin (IRE)**[38] 2806 4-8-12 54 ..... JamesDoyle 7 — 59
(I A Wood) *hld up: rdn over 1f out: r.o ins fnl f: nt rch ldrs* **12/1**
435- **5** 1 1/4 **Ochre Bay**[249] 6735 5-9-11 70 ..... RussellKennemore[(3)] 2 — 72
(R Hollinshead) *led early: chsd ldrs: edgd lft 6f out: rdn over 1f out: no ex fnl f* **8/1**
3035 **6** 2 **Memphis Man**[3] 3903 5-9-8 69 ..... RichardEvans[(5)] 5 — 66
(P D Evans) *s.s: hld up: rdn over 1f out: n.d* **5/2**[1]
-000 **7** 2 3/4 **Sedge (USA)**[20] 3339 8-9-12 68 ..... (p) MickyFenton 3 — 57
(P T Midgley) *prom: rdn over 2f out: wkng whn hung lft fnl f* **18/1**
5100 **8** 1 **Bertbrand**[2] 3946 3-9-2 73 ..... (b) RobbieEgan[(7)] 1 — 56
(D Flood) *plld hrd and prom: n.m.r and lost pl 6f out: hdwy over 2f out: sn rdn: wknd fnl f* **10/1**

1m 30.47s (0.87) **Going Correction** +0.175s/f (Slow)
WFA 3 from 4yo+ 8lb — 8 Ran SP% **116.5**
Speed ratings (Par 103): **102,101,101,99,97 95,92,91**
toteswinger: 1&2 £4.10, 1&3 £9.90, 2&3 £17.50. CSF £35.78 CT £117.09 TOTE £8.20: £2.50, £1.80, £1.10; EX 110.40.
Owner The Bellflower Methaaly Partnership **Bred** Scuderia Golden Horse S R L **Trained** Alpraham, Cheshire

FOCUS
A modest handicap run at a steady pace early on. The form is fairly sound with the winner rated to his winter best.
Wadnagin(IRE) Official explanation: jockey said filly hung right

4031 PARADE RESTAURANT H'CAP — 1m 141y(P)
9:20 (9:20) (Class 6) (0-60,60) 3-Y-0+ — £2,388 (£705; £352) Stalls Low

Form — RPR
4623 **1** **Lunar River (FR)**[23] 3265 5-9-12 60 ..... (t) FergusSweeney 11 — 71
(David Pinder) *hld up: hdwy over 2f out: rdn over 1f out: edgd lft and led ins fnl f: r.o* **5/1**[3]
-002 **2** 1 1/2 **Ardent Prince**[14] 3569 5-9-1 49 ..... JamesDoyle 5 — 57
(A J McCabe) *chsd ldr tl led over 2f out: rdn clr and hung lft over 1f out: hdd and unable qck ins fnl f* **9/4**[1]
0-65 **3** 1 **Volaticus (IRE)**[7] 3795 7-9-6 54 ..... (b) SilvestreDeSousa 1 — 60
(A D Brown) *a.p: chsd ldr over 2f out: rdn over 1f out: no ex ins fnl f* **12/1**
50-6 **4** 6 **Stravita**[9] 3738 4-9-8 59 ..... RussellKennemore[(3)] 8 — 51
(R Hollinshead) *hld up in tch: rdn over 3f out: wknd 2f out* **10/1**
0022 **5** 1/2 **Casablanca Minx (IRE)**[6] 3822 5-9-7 55 ..... (v) StephenDonohoe 6 — 46
(P D Evans) *s.i.s: hld up: nt clr run and swtchd rt over 1f out: styd on ins fnl f: nvr nrr* **7/2**[2]
0504 **6** hd **General Feeling (IRE)**[14] 3567 7-9-1 56 ..... (p) DeclanCannon[(7)] 9 — 46
(S T Mason) *s.i.s: sn pushed along in rr: hdwy over 2f out: rn wd ent st: rdn: hung lft and wknd over 1f out* **8/1**
/00- **7** 1/2 **Hurricane Coast**[310] 5237 9-9-1 56 ..... RobbieEgan[(7)] 10 — 45
(D Flood) *hld up: rdn over 2f out: hung lft fnl f: n.d* **33/1**
30-3 **8** 1/2 **Red Contact (USA)**[174] 258 7-9-12 60 ..... (p) IanMongan 2 — 48
(A Dickman) *led: hdd over 2f out: sn rdn: wknd over 1f out* **10/1**
-000 **9** 6 **Desert Rat (IRE)**[2] 3963 4-9-4 52 ..... (v) DO'Donohoe 12 — 26
(Micky Hammond) *hld up in mid-div: hdwy over 3f out: rdn and wknd over 2f out* **33/1**
50 **10** 1 1/4 **Sendreni (FR)**[79] 1620 4-9-8 56 ..... ShaneKelly 4 — 27
(M Wigham) *chsd ldrs tl rdn and wknd 2f out* **16/1**
0-00 **11** 7 **Leonard Charles**[9] 3733 4-9-8 56 ..... (b) LPKeniry 3 — 11
(C R Dore) *hld up in tch: rdn and wknd over 3f out* **40/1**

1m 51.6s (1.10) **Going Correction** +0.175s/f (Slow)
WFA 3 from 4yo+ 10lb — 11 Ran SP% **120.8**
Speed ratings (Par 101): **102,100,99,94,94 93,93,92,87,86 80**
toteswinger: 1&2 £4.60, 1&3 £6.30, 2&3 £10.50. CSF £16.89 CT £135.81 TOTE £8.40: £2.30, £1.80, £3.70; EX 22.90 Place 6 £39.56, Place 5 £6.83.
Owner The Little Farm Partnership **Bred** M Daguzan-Garros & Rolling Hills Farm **Trained** Kingston Lisle, Oxon

FOCUS
This was not a good race.
Stravita Official explanation: jockey said filly hung right
T/Plt: £61.40 to a £1 stake. Pool: £63,158.11. 750.50 winning tickets. T/Qpdt: £12.20 to a £1 stake. Pool: £4,685.30. 283.50 winning tickets. CR

4032 - 4040a (Foreign Racing) - See Raceform Interactive

3356 LONGCHAMP (R-H)
Monday, July 14

OFFICIAL GOING: Good

4041a PRIX MAURICE DE NIEUIL (GROUP 2) — 1m 6f
6:45 (6:51) 4-Y-0+ — £54,485 (£21,029; £10,037; £6,691; £3,346)

RPR
1 **Incanto Dream**[70] 1888 4-8-11 ..... (p) YLerner 5 — 115
(C Lerner, France) *plld hrd: hld up towards rr: 7th st: swtchd outside and hrd rdn 1 1/2f out: str run to ld 150yds out: r.o wl* **16/1**
2 1 1/2 **Caudillo (GER)**[53] 2346 5-8-11 ..... J-PCarvalho 7 — 113
(Dr A Bolte, Germany) *hld up: 8th st on ins: swtchd lft 1 1/2f out: styd on wl fnl f to take 2nd fnl 60yds* **25/1**
3 1 1/2 **Noble Prince (GER)**[43] 2653 4-8-11 ..... SPasquier 8 — 111
(A Fabre, France) *hld up in 10th: kpt on u.p down outside fr over 1f out to take 3rd on line* **7/2**[1]
4 shd **Brisant (GER)**[32] 2986 6-8-11 ..... WMongil 9 — 111
(M Trybuhl, Germany) *dropped out in last: hdwy over 1f out: fin wl* **33/1**
5 shd **Speed Gifted**[23] 3246 4-8-11 ..... LDettori 6 — 111
(L M Cumani) *spread plate gng to s and unruly whn re-shod: midfield: 5th st: disp ld briefly ins fnl f: one pce: lost 3rd on line* **4/1**[2]
6 hd **Ponte Tresa (FR)**[57] 2236 5-8-8 ..... OPeslier 1 — 107
(Y De Nicolay, France) *trckd ldr in 3rd: disp ld briefly ins fnl f: one pce* **25/1**
7 3/4 **Orion Star (FR)**[57] 2236 6-8-11 ..... JVictoire 11 — 109
(H-A Pantall, France) *racd in 2nd: rdn to ld narrowly 2f out: hdd ins fnl f: no ex* **7/2**[1]
8 2 **First Stream (GER)**[43] 2653 4-8-11 ..... C-PLemaire 2 — 107
(Mario Hofer, Germany) *racd in 5th: 6th st: one pce fnl 2f* **16/1**
9 1/2 **Varevees**[43] 2653 5-8-8 ..... CSoumillon 3 — 103
(R Gibson, France) *racd in 4th: effrt and unable qck over 1f out* **4/1**[2]
10 1 1/2 **Avanti Polonia (GER)**[46] 2553 4-8-8 ..... DBonilla 10 — 101
(F Head, France) *led to 2f out: wknd 1f out* **12/1**[3]
11 **Poseidon Adventure (IRE)**[15] 3540 5-8-11 ..... (b) DBoeuf 12 — 104
(W Figge, Germany) *midfield on outside: 9th st: btn 2f out* **14/1**

2m 57.1s (177.10) — 11 Ran SP% **121.2**
PARI-MUTUEL: WIN 9.60; PL 2.90, 5.10, 2.10; DF 67.20.
Owner Mme L Calamari **Bred** Skymarc Farm Inc **Trained** France

The Form Book, Raceform Ltd, Compton, RG20 6NL

NOTEBOOK

Incanto Dream is very consistent and is going from strength to strength. He was given an excellent ride by the trainer's son, who employed waiting tactics before bringing the four-year-old with a perfectly timed late run. His main target this year is the Prix du Cadran in early October and he will have a trial in either the Prix Kergorlay, the Grand Prix de Deauville or the Prix Gladiateur.

Caudillo(GER), held up in the early part of the race, came with a late run and was putting in his best work at the finish, but he never looked like pegging back the winner.

Noble Prince(GER), rather strangely for a one-paced horse, was dropped out early on before coming under pressure at the two-furlong marker. He stayed on but could not quicken and gave the impression a return to a longer distances would suit. He may now go for the Kergorlay at Deauville.

Brisant(GER), another to be given a waiting ride, was outpaced early in the straight before staying on one-paced. A longer trip would be to the advantage of this gelding.

Speed Gifted had to be re-shod before the race and got rather worked up before going down to the start. He was towards the tail of the field in the early part of the race, but did quicken well at the entrance to the straight before being dominated inside the final furlong. He can do better.

4042a JUDDMONTE GRAND PRIX DE PARIS (GROUP 1) (C&F) 1m 4f

7:20 (7:28) 3-Y-O **£252,088** (£100,853; £50,246; £25,191; £12,618)

RPR

1 **Montmartre (FR)**[25] 3191 3-9-2 .... CSoumillon 9 126+
(A De Royer-Dupre, France) *racd in 4th: led 2f out: qcknd clr: eased cl home* **9/2[2]**

2 *4* **Prospect Wells (FR)**[43] 2654 3-9-2 .... OPeslier 3 118+
(A Fabre, France) *hld up in last: styd on down outside fr over 1 1/2f out to take 2nd last 50yds* **9/2[2]**

3 *1/2* **Magadan (IRE)**[43] 2654 3-9-2 .... ACrastus 7 117
(E Lellouche, France) *hld up in rr: 12th st: styd on down outside fr over 1 1/2f out to take 2nd ins fnl f: lost 2nd 50yds out* **20/1**

4 *2 1/2* **Doctor Fremantle**[37] 2829 3-9-2 .... RyanMoore 6 116+
(Sir Michael Stoute) *towards rr: 11th st: nt clr run and hmpd over 1 1/2f out: nt clr run and swtchd rt over 1f out: styd on fnl f* **3/1[1]**

5 *3/4* **Change The World (IRE)**[51] 2422 3-9-2 .... IMendizabal 8 112
(J-C Rouget, France) *hld up towards rr: 7th and hdwy st: swtchd rt 1 1/2f out: wnt 2nd briefly on ins rail 1f out: one pce* **20/1**

6 *nse* **Alessandro Volta**[15] 3535 3-9-2 .... JMurtagh 10 112
(A P O'Brien, Ire) *hld up: 9th st: rdn 2f out: kpt on at one pce* **9/2[2]**

7 *snk* **Cima De Triomphe (IRE)**[64] 2028 3-9-2 .... DVargiu 11 111
(B Grizzetti, Italy) *hld up: 10th st: rdn 2f out: kpt on same pce* **14/1**

8 *4* **Centennial (IRE)**[15] 3535 3-9-2 ....(b) JimmyFortune 4 105
(J H M Gosden) *racd in 5th: rdn and one pce fr over 2f out* **40/1**

9 *snk* **Bashkirov**[15] 3535 3-9-2 .... JAHeffernan 1 105
(A P O'Brien, Ire) *racd in 3rd: 2nd st: disp ld briefly 2f out: lost 2nd 1f out: wknd* **40/1**

10 *1/2* **Curtain Call (FR)**[15] 3535 3-9-2 .... LDettori 13 104
(L M Cumani) *racd in 6th: rdn to dispute 3rd 1 1/2f out: wknd* **6/1[3]**

11 *3* **Americain (USA)**[44] 2636 3-9-2 .... SPasquier 2 99+
(A Fabre, France) *midfield: 8th st: nvr a factor* **40/1**

12 *6* **Sindajan (IRE)**[38] 3-9-2 .... FDiFede 5 90
(A De Royer-Dupre, France) *racd in 2nd: led over 3f out to 2f out: wknd* **200/1**

13 *dist* **William Hogarth**[85] 1510 3-9-2 .... CO'Donoghue 12 —
(A P O'Brien, Ire) *led and sn clr: hdd over 3f out: wknd* **66/1**

2m 26.2s (-5.00) **Going Correction** -0.025s/f (Good) **13 Ran SP% 119.3**
Speed ratings: **115,112,112,110,109 109,109,107,106,106 104,100,—**
PARI-MUTUEL: WIN 3.40 (coupled with Sindajan); PL 1.60, 1.90, 3.00;DF 10.10.

Owner H H Aga Khan **Bred** Snc Lagardere Elevage **Trained** Chantilly, France

■ Stewards' Enquiry : D Vargiu €200 fine: whip abuse

FOCUS

A good renewal of the Grand Prix de Paris, and Montmartre was very impressive, but it has to be noted that many of his main rivals were given too much to do. He was value for 7l and is rated the equal of New Approach on RPRs now.

NOTEBOOK

Montmartre(FR) was immediately made favourite for the Arc de Triomphe after this performance, his second success over the course and distance of Europe's richest race, and the best in France this year by a middle-distance three-year-old colt. He got a little worked up during the parade but otherwise had a perfect race. With his pacemaker doing an excellent job, he was full of running at the two-furlong marker and sprinted clear when asked for his effort. His jockey spent most of the final furlong looking over his shoulders and he was value for even more than the winning margin, although it has to be noted that many of his main rivals were given far too much to do. He will now be rested until the Prix Niel, the traditional Arc trial.

Prospect Wells(FR), once again slowly into his stride, looked to have a hopeless task as he raced in last position for much of the early part of the race and, brought with a late run up the centre of the track, he made up many lengths in the final furlong and a half. He never looked like catching the winner but this was another decent effort. He will now be given a break and is likely to run next in the Niel.

Magadan(IRE) had beaten the winner when they met in the spring. Held up for a late run, he was another to come up the centre of the track in the straight and battled on well, only losing second well inside the final furlong. He is another who will have a rest until the autumn and a tilt at the Niel is not ruled out.

Doctor Fremantle did not have the best of luck after missing the break. Towards the tail of the field early on, he began to make a forward move halfway up the straight but was hampered and had to be rebalanced for his final effort. He was staying on nicely and the Great Voltigeur at York is now a possibility.

Alessandro Volta would have gone close to winning the Irish Derby had he not hung off a straight line, but he was unable to build on that this time. He is quite a big horse and looks the type to benefit from more time.

Centennial(IRE), fitted with blinkers for the first time, made his effort halfway up the straight but his run petered out inside the final furlong.

Curtain Call(FR) was rather disappointing, failing to build on an unlucky effort in the Irish Derby. Fifth rounding the bend before the straight, he was given every chance but was unable to take a hand in the finish. His connections felt that the ground might have been a little lively and he will probably be brought back in distance as well.

3706 BEVERLEY (R-H)

Tuesday, July 15

OFFICIAL GOING: Good

Those who raced towards the far rail in the straight looked to be at a disadvantage.
Wind: Fresh against Weather: Sunny periods

4043 RACING UK ON SKY 432 CLAIMING STKS 7f 100y

2:15 (2:16) (Class 5) 3-Y-O **£2,590** (£770; £385; £192) **Stalls** High

Form RPR

3300 **1** **Royal Applord**[24] 3263 3-9-2 67........ PaulMulrennan 2 66
(K A Ryan) *trckd ldng pair: hdwy 2f out: rdn to ld jst over 1f out: edgd rt and hdd wl ins fnl f: rallied to ld nr fin* **13/2[3]**

0433 **2** *nk* **Just Sam (IRE)**[8] 3791 3-8-2 55........ RoystonFfrench 9 51
(D Carroll) *hld up in tch: smooth hdwy on inner 2f out: swtchd lft and nt clr run over 1f out: squeezed through and rdn to ld wl ins fnl f: drvn and hdd nr line* **7/4[1]**

P04 **3** *2 3/4* **Admiralcollingwood**[8] 3795 3-8-3 53........ DominicFox[(3)] 5 48
(T P Tate) *s.i.s and bhd: hdwy wl over 1f out: styd on strly ins fnl f* **10/1**

6550 **4** *3/4* **Cheeky Chilli**[11] 3690 3-8-5 65........ AndrewElliott 11 45
(A J McCabe) *cl up: rdn to ld 2f out: hdd jst over 1f out: sn drvn and wknd ins fnl f* **3/1[2]**

3344 **5** *1 3/4* **Jevington Star (IRE)**[10] 3715 3-8-7 42........(p) TomEaves 1 43
(B Ellison) *trckd ldrs: hdwy on outer wl over 2f out: rdn along wl over 1f out: sn drvn and wknd appr fnl f* **7/1**

-000 **6** *3 1/4* **Bagenalstown (IRE)**[10] 3731 3-8-7 30........(p) LiamJones 8 35
(M Wellings) *led: rdn along 3f out: hdd 2f out and sn wknd* **66/1**

0-00 **7** *4* **Carlton Mac**[12] 3640 3-8-7 41........ PaulFessey 6 25
(N Bycroft) *a towards rr* **18/1**

0004 **8** *nk* **Your Golf Travel**[15] 3549 3-8-6 46........ JoeFanning 7 23
(J S Wainwright) *in tch: rdn along over 2f out and sn wknd* **12/1**

00-0 **9** *1* **Reel Classy**[17] 3479 3-8-2 37........ DaleGibson 4 17
(T J Pitt) *dwlt: a in rr* **40/1**

0605 **10** *3/4* **Northwest**[10] 3715 3-8-5 40........ FrancisNorton 10 18
(A Berry) *chsd ldrs: rdn along over 2f out: sn wknd* **20/1**

1m 35.83s (2.03) **Going Correction** +0.075s/f (Good) **10 Ran SP% 117.9**
Speed ratings (Par 100): **91,90,87,86,84 80,76,76,74,74**
toteswinger: 1&2 £2.90, 1&3 £11.50, 2&3 £3.70. CSF £18.22 TOTE £6.10: £1.60, £1.20, £3.80; EX 15.60.Just Sam was claimed by D. W. Barker for £6000.

Owner Bull & Bell Partnership **Bred** Brick Kiln Stud And V A D'Haens **Trained** Hambleton, N Yorks

FOCUS

A modest claimer and shaky form with none of the front three having run to their best recently. The winning time was a full second slower than the following 46-65 handicap.

4044 CERUTTIS@BEVERLEY RACECOURSE H'CAP 7f 100y

2:45 (2:45) (Class 6) (0-65,63) 3-Y-O **£2,428** (£722; £361; £180) **Stalls** High

Form RPR

-406 **1** **Princess Rhianna (IRE)**[25] 3213 3-8-13 **55**........ LiamJones 9 65
(Mrs G S Rees) *hld up in rr: swtchd outside and hdwy wl over 1f out: str run to ld ins fnl f: sn clr* **25/1**

0004 **2** *3 3/4* **Ace Of Spies (IRE)**[3] 3958 3-8-12 **54**........ JoeFanning 4 55
(M Johnston) *hld up towards rr: stdy hdwy on outer over 2f out: rdn to ld and hung rt over 1f out: drvn and hdd ins fnl f: kpt on same pce* **14/1**

0132 **3** *1 1/2* **Grit (IRE)**[8] 3790 3-9-6 **62**........ TPO'Shea 1 59+
(M R Channon) *hld up in midfield: hmpd 1/2-way: hdwy towards outer over 2f out: rdn to chse ldrs whn sltly hmpd over 1f out: kpt on same pce u.p ins fnl f* **13/2[3]**

-030 **4** *3/4* **Defies Logic**[35] 2915 3-8-12 **54**........ PaulMulrennan 10 49
(J G Given) *prom: effrt and ev ch over 2f out: sn rdn: drvn over 1f out and kpt on same pce* **10/1**

0-24 **5** *nk* **My Flame**[47] 2549 3-8-13 **55**........ StephenDonohoe 5 49
(J R Jenkins) *led: rdn along over 2f out: drvn and hdd appr fnl f: wknd* **11/2[2]**

6002 **6** *hd* **Lucky Character**[15] 3549 3-8-6 **48**........(vt[1]) PaulFessey 11 42
(N J Vaughan) *s.i.s and bhd: gd hdwy on outer 2f out: rdn to chse ldrs ent fnl f: sn drvn: edgd rt and one pce* **16/1**

-650 **7** *1 1/2* **Brandane (IRE)**[10] 3717 3-8-12 **54**........ RoystonFfrench 13 44
(Mrs A Duffield) *chsd ldrs: hdwy 3f out: rdn along 2f out: drvn and hld whn hmpd over 12f out* **25/1**

1330 **8** *1/2* **Young Gladiator (IRE)**[11] 3691 3-9-7 **63**........ TomEaves 8 52
(Miss J A Camacho) *chsd ldrs: rn wd bnd at 1/2-way: rdn along wl over 2f out and sn btn* **12/1**

660 **9** *3/4* **Carpe Diem**[33] 2981 3-9-1 **57**........ TonyHamilton 12 44
(W J Haggas) *trckd ldrs: effrt over 2f out and sn rdn: drvn and no imp whn n.m.r over 12f out: wknd* **6/5[1]**

0055 **10** *1* **Isabella's Fancy**[19] 3397 3-8-10 **55**........ JamieMoriarty[(3)] 7 39
(J R Fanshawe) *a towards rr* **20/1**

0-00 **11** *1 1/2* **Monte Cassino (IRE)**[29] 3079 3-8-7 **49** ow1........ DavidAllan 3 30
(J O'Reilly) *a towards rr* **100/1**

0-30 **12** *8* **Personal Choice**[7] 3816 3-8-8 **50**........ TWilliams 14 11
(M Brittain) *cl up: rdn along over 2f out: sn drvn and grad wknd* **50/1**

1m 34.83s (1.03) **Going Correction** +0.075s/f (Good) **12 Ran SP% 118.9**
Speed ratings (Par 98): **97,92,91,90,89 89,87,87,86,85 83,74**
toteswinger: 1&2 £25.00, 1&3 £13.50, 2&3 £7.90. CSF £323.92 CT £2577.34 TOTE £26.10: £4.90, £3.30, £1.90; EX 267.90.

Owner Aricabeau Racing Limited **Bred** Rathasker Stud **Trained** Sollom, Lancs

FOCUS

A moderate handicap in which the first two home made their moves up the middle of the track. The winning time was a full second quicker than the claimer and the form looks sound enough.

Young Gladiator(IRE) Official explanation: trainer said gelding didn't handle track

Carpe Diem Official explanation: jockey said gelding was denied a clear run

Monte Cassino(IRE) Official explanation: jockey said gelding was denied a clear run

4045 CASINO RED HUDDERSFIELD OPENS AUGUST MAIDEN AUCTION STKS 5f

3:15 (3:16) (Class 5) 2-Y-O **£3,238** (£963; £481; £240) **Stalls** High

Form RPR

1 **Noodles Blue Boy** 2-8-9 0........ FrancisNorton 4 72+
(Ollie Pears) *hld up towards rr: hdwy on outer 1/2-way: chsd ldrs over 1f out: sn rdn and styd on to ld ins fnl f: edgd rt and kpt on wl* **20/1**

2 3/4 **Positivity** 2-8-4 0 .... RoystonFfrench 5 65
(B Smart) *chsd ldrs: hdwy 2f out: rdn to chal ent fnl f and ev ch tl edgd lft and no ex last 50yds* **8/1**

53 3 1 **Desert Falls**[52] 2392 2-8-9 0 .... DeanMcKeown 2 66
(R M Whitaker) *led: rdn along and hdd wl over 1f out: kpt on u.p ins fnl f: n.m.r towards fin* **9/4**[2]

4 shd **Solo Act (IRE)** 2-8-7 0 .... TonyHamilton 7 64+
(R A Fahey) *cl up: effrt to ld wl over 1f out: rn green and sn rdn: hdd ins fnl f: no ex whn n.m.r towards fin* **85/40**[1]

65 5 3 **Sale Or Return (IRE)**[28] 3106 2-8-1 0 ....(b[1]) DuranFentiman(3) 3 50
(T D Easterby) *dwlt: sn chsng ldrs: rdn along 2f out: kpt on same pce* **40/1**

0 6 1/2 **Shadows Lengthen**[19] 3411 2-8-2 0 .... BradleyRoper(7) 6 53
(M W Easterby) *dwlt and outpcd in rr tl styd on appr fnl f: nrst fin* **20/1**

50 7 hd **Monsieur Jourdain (IRE)**[14] 3590 2-8-9 0 .... DavidAllan 12 52
(T D Easterby) *s.i.s and bhd tl sme late hdwy* **7/1**

8 1 1/4 **Noble Heart (IRE)** 2-8-10 0 .... TomEaves 11 49
(T D Barron) *a towards rr* **13/2**[3]

00 9 1/2 **Real Diamond**[59] 2206 2-8-4 0 .... PaulFessey 10 41
(A Dickman) *chsd ldrs: rdn along 2f out: sn wknd* **40/1**

2060 10 1 1/2 **Cool Sonata (IRE)**[32] 3008 2-8-4 0 .... TWilliams 1 36
(M Brittain) *chsd ldrs: rdn along over 2f out and sn wknd* **33/1**

11 17 **Future Gem** 2-8-4 0 .... DaleGibson 8 —
(A Dickman) *sn outpcd and bhd* **40/1**

65.92 secs (2.42) **Going Correction** +0.425s/f (Yiel) **11** Ran SP% **119.5**
Speed ratings (Par 94): **97,95,94,94,89 88,88,86,85,82 55**
toteswinger: 1&2 £25.00, 1&3 £13.50, 2&3 £7.90. CSF £162.22 TOTE £22.80: £4.20, £2.00, £1.40; EX 161.70.

Owner Ian Bishop **Bred** Fifehead Farms M C Denning **Trained** Norton, N Yorks

FOCUS
A moderate maiden run at a decent pace. Guessy form. The main action took place up the middle of the track.

NOTEBOOK
Noodles Blue Boy, a 6,500gns gelded son of Makbul, first foal of a 7f juvenile winner, struggled to go the early pace, but he responded well to pressure to stay on strongest of all. This looked an ordinary race, but he is entitled to improve for the experience and should be competitive in nurseries.
Positivity, a 5,000gns daughter of Monsieur Bond, half-sister to four winners, including quite useful dual 1m winner Peculiarity, made a satisfactory debut in second and is open to some improvement. (op 11-1 tchd 15-2)
Desert Falls kept on surprisingly well considering he had gone off pretty fast. He could have a nursery in him. (op 2-1 tchd 13-8)
Solo Act(IRE), a 20,000gns daughter of One Cool Cat, first foal of a dual 5f juvenile winner, was well fancied on her racecourse debut, but found a few too strong after showing good speed. She should know more next time and ought to be able to find a similar race. (op 6-4 tchd 11-4)
Sale Or Return(IRE) improved for the fitting of blinkers, but is still only moderate. (op 33-1)

4046 MARY ELIZABETH WESTWOOD CELEBRATION H'CAP (REGISTERED AS 123RD YEAR OF THE WATT MEMORIAL STKS) 2m 35y

3:45 (3:45) (Class 4) (0-85,84) 3-Y-0+ **£12,952** (£3,854; £1,926; £962) **Stalls** High

Form RPR

0106 1 **Chocolate Caramel (USA)**[17] 3480 6-9-1 **78** .... JamieMoriarty(3) 8 88
(R A Fahey) *hld up: smooth hdwy over 4f out: effrt over 2f out: rdn to ld appr fnl f: styd on wl* **20/1**

1122 2 1 1/2 **Hits Only Vic (USA)**[6] 3832 4-9-6 **80** .... DavidAllan 3 88
(D Carroll) *hld up: stdy hdwy 6f out: trckd ldrs over 3f out: rdn to ld briefly over 1f out: sn hdd and drvn: kpt on same pce* **3/1**[1]

2245 3 1/2 **Danzatrice**[19] 3414 6-8-6 **66** .... TomEaves 2 73
(C W Thornton) *hld up in rr: hdwy over 3f out: rdn to chse ldrs over 1f out: kpt on same pce u.p ins fnl f* **16/1**

6146 4 7 **Numero Due**[6] 3832 6-9-7 **84** .... PJMcDonald(3) 12 83
(G M Moore) *trckd ldrs: hdwy over 3f out: rdn over 2f out: drvn and one pce fr over 1f out* **8/1**

0423 5 1 **Thewhirlingdervish (IRE)**[10] 3710 10-8-7 **70** .... DuranFentiman(3) 1 68
(T D Easterby) *in tch: pushed along aqnd lost pl 7f out: hdwy 3f out and sn rdn: drvn along wl over 1f out and kpt on same pce* **7/1**[3]

0205 6 3/4 **Bold Adventure**[20] 3375 4-8-7 **67** .... StephenDonohoe 6 64
(W J Musson) *hld up in rr: stdy hdwy on inner over 3f out: rdn to chse ldrs 2f out: sn drvn and no imp appr fnl f* **8/1**

0122 7 3/4 **Pegasus Prince (USA)**[10] 3710 4-8-4 **64** .... RoystonFfrench 10 60
(Miss J A Camacho) *trckd ldrs: smooth hdwy over 3f out: led over 2f out and sn rdn: hdd & wknd wl over 1f out* **8/1**

/164 8 4 1/2 **Ritsi**[12] 3642 5-8-5 **65** .... PaulFessey 7 56
(Grant Tuer) *hld up towards rr: hdwy on outer 3f out: rdn along and in tch 2f out: sn drvn and wknd* **14/1**

50-0 9 4 **Riodan (IRE)**[12] 3642 6-7-13 **59** .... DaleGibson 11 45
(L A Mullaney) *in tch: hdwy on inner 4f out: rdn to chse ldrs 3f out: drvn 2f out and grad wknd* **33/1**

0000 10 23 **Ruff Diamond (USA)**[4] 3925 3-8-1 **80** ....(v) FrancisNorton 9 38
(J R Best) *t.k.h: cl up: led after 2f: rdn along 3f out: hdd over 2f out and sn wknd* **28/1**

1051 11 15 **Mister Arjay (USA)**[6] 3832 8-9-4 **78** 6ex .... TonyHamilton 4 18
(B Ellison) *led 2f: chsd ldrs: rdn along 4f out: drvn 3f out and sn wknd* **14/1**

2-00 12 4 1/2 **Duty Free (IRE)**[28] 3104 4-9-9 **83** ....(p) JoeFanning 5 18
(C R Egerton) *prom: rdn along over 3f out and sn wknd* **5/1**[2]

3m 38.98s (-0.82) **Going Correction** +0.075s/f (Good)
WFA 3 from 4yo+ 19lb **12** Ran SP% **117.9**
Speed ratings (Par 105): **105,104,104,100,100 99,99,97,95,83 76,73**
toteswinger: 1&2 £15.90, 1&3 £32.80, 2&3 £9.80. CSF £77.52 CT £1020.00 TOTE £19.40: £4.60, £1.80, £3.50; EX 100.80.

Owner Jonathan Gill **Bred** Sierra Thoroughbreds **Trained** Musley Bank, N Yorks

FOCUS
An ordinary staying handicap for the grade. They went steady early on, but the front three still finished clear. Straightforward form, the winner rated to his best. Once again, the middle of the track looked the place to be in the straight.
Duty Free(IRE) Official explanation: jockey said gelding hung left-handed throughout

4047 EAST YORKSHIRE BUSINESS EXPO 2ND OCTOBER H'CAP 5f

4:15 (4:16) (Class 6) (0-65,65) 3-Y-0+ **£2,266** (£674; £337; £168) **Stalls** High

Form RPR

4023 1 **Commander Wish**[11] 3665 5-9-4 **57** ....(p) LiamJones 8 71+
(Lucinda Featherstone) *in rr: pushed along 1/2-way: swtchd lft and hdwy wl over 1f out: str run ent fnl f to ld last 50yds* **9/1**

2030 2 1 1/4 **Soto**[14] 3591 5-9-9 **62** .... PaulMulrennan 14 70
(M W Easterby) *chsd ldr: rdn along wl over 1f out: drvn and hung lft ins fnl f: kpt on wl towards fin* **8/1**[3]

2020 3 1 **Jun Fan (USA)**[18] 3454 6-8-9 **55** .... LanceBetts(7) 16 59+
(B Ellison) *led: rdn clr over 1f out: drvn ins fnl f: hdd & wknd last 50yds* **13/2**[1]

1123 4 nse **Kings College Boy**[14] 3581 8-9-5 **65** ....(v) BMcHugh(7) 2 69
(R A Fahey) *chsd ldrs: hdwy 2f out: sn rdn: styd on strly ins fnl f: nrst fin* **9/1**

4003 5 1 1/4 **Sands Crooner (IRE)**[10] 3724 5-9-9 **62** ....(v) TomEaves 15 61
(J G Given) *chsd ldrs: hdwy wl over 1f out: rdn and kpt on same pce ins fnl f* **13/2**[1]

0041 6 3/4 **Conjecture**[9] 3759 6-9-0 **58** 6ex .... KellyHarrison(5) 9 55
(R Bastiman) *towards rr: hdwy 2f out: swtchd rt and rdn wl over 1f out: styd on ins fnl f: nrst fin* **15/2**[2]

0303 7 1 **Dark Champion**[13] 3601 8-9-6 **59** ....(v) RoystonFfrench 10 52
(R E Barr) *hld up: hdwy 2f out: sn rdn and kpt on ins fnl f: nrst fin* **9/1**

0200 8 2 **Helping Hand (IRE)**[18] 3441 3-9-0 **65** .... JamieKyne(7) 17 51
(R Hollinshead) *chsd ldrs: rdn along 2f out and sn one pce* **16/1**

2605 9 nk **Grimes Faith**[102] 1190 5-9-7 **65** ....(p) NeilBrown(5) 1 50
(K A Ryan) *midfield: hdweay to chse ldrs on wd outside 1/2-way: sn rdn and no imp* **25/1**

4604 10 3/4 **Monte Major (IRE)**[15] 3565 7-8-13 **52** ....(v) DeanMcKeown 11 34
(D Shaw) *chsd ldrs: ridden along over 2f out and sn wknd* **16/1**

0040 11 3 **Ryedane (IRE)**[12] 3638 6-9-2 **55** ....(b) DavidAllan 4 26
(T D Easterby) *nvr bttr than midfield* **18/1**

4006 12 nse **Spirit Of Coniston**[15] 3546 5-8-11 **53** .... JamieMoriarty(3) 7 24
(P T Midgley) *a towards rr* **25/1**

1-0 13 4 1/2 **No Worries Yet (IRE)**[66] 1997 4-9-7 **60** .... FrancisNorton 5 15
(J L Spearing) *prom: rdn along over 2f out and sn wknd* **16/1**

0005 14 2 1/4 **Guto**[14] 3577 5-8-13 **55** .... AndrewMullen(3) 3 2
(W J H Ratcliffe) *a towards rr* **16/1**

0000 15 13 **Morristown Music (IRE)**[11] 3665 4-9-0 **53** .... TonyHamilton 12 —
(J S Wainwright) *dwlt: a towards rr* **20/1**

400 16 1 **Rue Soleil**[18] 3454 4-8-12 **51** .... JoeFanning 13 —
(J R Weymes) *a in rr* **33/1**

65.83 secs (2.33) **Going Correction** +0.425s/f (Yiel)
WFA 3 from 4yo+ 5lb **16** Ran SP% **123.7**
Speed ratings (Par 101): **98,96,94,94,92 91,89,86,85,84 79,79,72,68,48 46**
toteswinger: 1&2 £18.40, 1&3 £14.00, 2&3 £15.30. CSF £76.57 CT £534.07 TOTE £11.90: £2.60, £2.20, £2.80, £1.40; EX 100.10.

Owner J Roundtree **Bred** P R Featherstone **Trained** Atlow, Derbyshire

FOCUS
A moderate sprint handicap which has been rated through the first two. They were spread out all over the place, but the middle again looked the quickest ground.

4048 LADY JANE BETHELL MEMORIAL LADY RIDERS H'CAP (FOR LADY AMATEUR RIDERS) 1m 1f 207y

4:45 (4:48) (Class 6) (0-65,65) 3-Y-0+ **£1,873** (£581; £290; £145) **Stalls** High

Form RPR

0442 1 **Gulf Coast**[10] 3711 3-9-7 **62** .... MissJCoward(3) 17 69
(T D Walford) *in tch: hdwy on inner to trckd ldrs 3f out: rdn wl over 1f out: swtchd lft and drvn ent fnl f: styd on u.p to ld nr line* **2/1**[1]

2350 2 nse **Tizzy May (FR)**[18] 3450 8-10-0 **55** ....(v) MissLEllison 16 62
(B Ellison) *midfield: hdwy 4f out: rdn to chse ldrs 2f out: drvn and styd on to have ev ch wl ins fnl f: kpt on: jst hld* **15/2**[3]

-544 3 1/2 **Giddywell**[26] 3182 4-9-4 **52** ow2 .... MissStefaniaGandola(7) 12 58
(R Hollinshead) *chsd ldr: effrt over 2f out and sn rdn: drvn and kpt on ent fnl f: led last 50yds: hdd and no ex nr line* **16/1**

0225 4 1/2 **Gala Sunday (USA)**[10] 3711 8-10-4 **59** ....(bt) MissSBrotherton 14 64
(M W Easterby) *midfield: hdwy 3f out: rdn wl over 1f out: kpt on ins fnl f: nrst fin* **7/1**[2]

3061 5 nk **Emperor's Well**[14] 3593 9-9-11 **57** ....(b) MissJoannaMason(5) 4 61
(M W Easterby) *led: rdn over 2f out: drvn and wandered ins fnl f: hdd & wknd last 50yds* **14/1**

0063 6 3 1/4 **Scotty's Future (IRE)**[11] 3662 10-9-4 **50** .... MissWGibson(5) 7 48
(A Berry) *dwlt and bhd: hdwy wl over 2f out: sn rdn and styd on appr fnl f: nt rch ldrs* **18/1**

5662 7 nk **Wulimaster (USA)**[11] 3666 5-9-12 **53** .... MissARyan 15 50
(D W Barker) *hld up towards rr: hdwy over 3f out: rdn over 2f out: kpt on appr fnl f: nt rch ldrs* **9/1**

-026 8 nse **Barathea Dreams (IRE)**[31] 3036 7-10-8 **63** .... MrsSMoore 13 60
(J S Moore) *hld up: swtchd outside and hdwy 3f out: rdn wl over 1f out: hung rt and kpt on ins fnl f: nrst fin* **11/1**

-030 9 2 3/4 **Jiminor Mack**[10] 3732 5-9-0 **46** ....(p) MissKellyBurke(5) 5 38
(W J H Ratcliffe) *s.i.s and bhd tl styd on fnl 2f* **33/1**

045- 10 1 1/4 **Amazing King (IRE)**[83] 4591 4-9-9 **57** .... MissSMStaveley(7) 2 46
(P A Kirby) *chsd ldrs: rdn along over 3f out: grad wknd* **16/1**

156 11 hd **Saluscraggie**[13] 3602 6-9-12 **60** .... MissVBarr(7) 8 49
(R E Barr) *nvr nr ldrs* **22/1**

4500 12 6 **Trans Sonic**[18] 3450 5-10-0 **55** ....(v) MissADeniel 10 32
(A J Lockwood) *chsd ldrs: rdn alongf over 3f out: sn wknd* **18/1**

4-54 13 3 1/2 **Superior Star**[113] 996 5-10-10 **65** .... MrsCBartley 9 35
(N Wilson) *a towards rr* **20/1**

0532 14 2 1/4 **Red Rouge**[28] 3115 3-8-13 **56** .... MissLEBurke(5) 11 21
(G J Smith) *chsd ldrs: rdn along 3f out: wknd 2f out* **16/1**

0000 15 4 **General Flumpa**[26] 3182 7-9-11 **52** .... MissEJJones 6 9
(Miss Tor Sturgis) *chsd ldrs: rdn along over 3f out and sn wknd* **28/1**

6040 16 16 **Bed Fellow (IRE)**[19] 3399 4-10-1 **63** .... MissJKWilson(7) 3 —
(Paul Murphy) *midfield: lost pl and bhd fr 1/2-way* **66/1**

2m 8.89s (1.89) **Going Correction** +0.075s/f (Good)
WFA 3 from 4yo+ 11lb **16** Ran SP% **127.8**
Speed ratings (Par 101): **95,94,94,94,93 91,91,91,88,87 87,82,80,78,75 62**
toteswinger: 1&2 £7.90, 1&3 £11.00, 2&3 £37.70. CSF £15.87 CT £207.14 TOTE £3.10: £1.30, £2.40, £4.00, £1.40; EX 30.00.

Owner Mrs Mary & David Longstaff **Bred** R J Turner **Trained** Sheriff Hutton, N Yorks

■ Stewards' Enquiry : Miss J Coward caution: used whip with excessive frequency

The Form Book, Raceform Ltd, Compton, RG20 6NL

FOCUS
The form in these types of races usually needs treating with caution although this race does seem to make sense. The principals raced far side to middle.

4049 BETFAIR APPRENTICE TRAINING SERIES H'CAP — 1m 100y
5:15 (5:15) (Class 6) (0-65,62) 3-Y-O — £1,942 (£578; £288; £144) Stalls High

Form — RPR

-445 **1** **Flashy Max**[10] 3738 3-8-10 **48** .... PatrickDonaghy 1 55
(Jedd O'Keeffe) *mde all: rdn 2f out: drvn and hung bdly lft ins fnl f: hld on wl* 13/2

-000 **2** 1 1/2 **Top Man Dan (IRE)**[10] 3717 3-8-13 **56** .... PaulPickard(5) 5 59
(D Carroll) *a.p: rdn along over 2f out: drvn over 1f out: styd on and ev ch ins fnl f: edgd rt no ex towards fin* 12/1

-400 **3** 1 **Space Pirate**[12] 3656 3-9-2 **54** .... (p) SimonPearce 2 55
(J Pearce) *in tch: hdwy on outer 3f out: rdn 2f out: styd on u.p ins fnl f* 12/1

0406 **4** 1/2 **Croeso Cusan**[22] 3314 3-8-7 **45** .... SophieDoyle 6 45
(J L Spearing) *t.k.h: chsd ldrs: hdwy over 2f out: rdn over 1f out: one pce ins fnl f* 11/1

5420 **5** 2 1/2 **Mganga**[8] 3799 3-9-5 **57** .... MCGeran 8 51
(M R Channon) *hmpd s and bhd: stdy hdwy 3f out: rdn to chse ldrs over 1f out: ch ent fnl f: sn drvn and wknd* 4/1[1]

503 **6** 4 1/2 **Roundthetwist (IRE)**[34] 2941 3-9-10 **62** .... DeclanCannon 3 46
(K R Burke) *trckd ldrs: hdwy over 2f out: sn chal and ev ch tl rdn and wknd appr fnl f* 6/1

015 **7** hd **Titfer (IRE)**[19] 3407 3-8-13 **54** .... BMcHugh(3) 10 37
(A W Carroll) *chsd ldrs: rdn along wl over 2f out and sn wknd* 5/1[3]

4125 **8** 1/2 **Autumn Charm**[11] 3667 3-9-1 **58** .... (p) JPFeatherstone(5) 4 40
(Lucinda Featherstone) *s.i.s: a in rr* 10/1

6560 **9** 1/2 **Zabougg**[27] 3126 3-8-11 **54** .... (v[1]) JamieKyne(5) 9 35
(D W Barker) *dwlt and hmpd s: a in rr* 9/2[2]

-000 **10** 20 **Premier Class (IRE)**[18] 2495 3-8-2 **45** .... (b) JamesRogers(5) 7 —
(J S Wainwright) *prom: rdn along 3f out and sn wknd* 40/1

1m 48.45s (0.85) **Going Correction** +0.075s/f (Good) — **10** Ran SP% **117.7**
Speed ratings (Par 98): **98,96,95,95,92 88,87,87,86,66**
toteswinger: 1&2 £25.70, 1&3 £13.00, 2&3 £15.40. CSF £82.22 CT £919.41 TOTE £9.00: £2.20, £4.10, £3.80; EX 70.60 Place 6: £229.32 Place 5: £149.08.
Owner W R B Racing 50 (wrbracing.com) **Bred** Bearstone Stud **Trained** Middleham Moor, N Yorks
■ Stewards' Enquiry : Paul Pickard three-day ban: used whip with excessive frequency (Jul 29,31,Aug 1)

FOCUS
A moderate handicap in which the winner ended up racing against the stands' rail. He is rated up 5lb and the race could have been rated a bit higher.
T/Jkpt: Not won. T/Plt: £24.70 to a £1 stake. Pool: £73,087.14. 2,156.38 winning tickets. T/Qpdt: £17.00 to a £1 stake. Pool: £4,669.80. 203.00 winning tickets. JR

3778 BRIGHTON (L-H)
Tuesday, July 15

OFFICIAL GOING: Good to firm (firm in places)
Wind: Moderate, against

4050 MATTHEW CLARK WINES & SPIRITS MEDIAN AUCTION MAIDEN STKS — 5f 213y
2:30 (2:31) (Class 6) 2-Y-O — £2,396 (£712; £356; £177) Stalls Low

Form — RPR

06 **1** **Cashed Up**[18] 3444 2-9-3 0 .... StephenCarson 2 66
(P Winkworth) *mde virtually all: shkn up ent fnl f: hld on wl* 25/1

20 **2** hd **Johnny Rook (GER)**[24] 3245 2-9-3 0 .... SteveDrowne 3 65
(E A L Dunlop) *trckd wnr thrght: rdn and led briefly ent fnl f: no ex cl home* 6/4[2]

0 **3** shd **Cash In The Attic**[13] 3603 2-8-12 0 .... EdwardCreighton 7 60
(M R Channon) *a in 3rd pce and in tch: rdn sn after s: nt qckn towards fin* 16/1[3]

4 **4** 2 3/4 **Hand Painted**[13] 3603 2-9-0 0 .... TravisBlock(3) 1 66+
(P J Makin) *t.k.h in tch: nt clr run appr fnl f: eased whn ch had gone ins fnl f* 8/11[1]

1m 11.68s (1.48) **Going Correction** +0.05s/f (Good) — **4** Ran SP% **107.6**
Speed ratings (Par 92): **92,91,91,87**
toteswinger: 1&2 £11.20. CSF £61.49 TOTE £18.10; EX 47.20.
Owner Badger's Second Set **Bred** Mrs A Blanchard **Trained** Chiddingfold, Surrey

FOCUS
A trappy contest in which favourite Hand Painted got no run and has been rated as finishing alongside the winner. The form is worth little.

NOTEBOOK
Cashed Up, who had shown little ability in two previous starts, was back a furlong in trip and made plenty of use of. He just managed to hold on in a cracking finish, but with Hand Painted not seeing daylight and Cash In The Attic not being given a particularly hard time in defeat, it is debatable what he achieved. He will need to go into nurseries now and how he gets on will very much depend on what mark the Handicapper gives him. (tchd 16-1)
Johnny Rook(GER), a well-beaten last in the Chesham, had earlier shaped with promise on his debut at Newbury and he ran better here, but it was still a shade disappointing he failed to get past the winner. He is another who is now qualified for nurseries. (op Evens)
Cash In The Attic, always outpaced on her debut at Chepstow, had clearly learned a good deal from that run and she came with a late challenge, but just failed to get there. She may well have won had Creighton got stuck into her and it is reasonable to expected more improvement next time. (op 12-1 tchd 10-1 and 18-1)
Hand Painted, a promising fourth at Chepstow on debut, several places ahead of Cash In The Attic, was always going best and, having been blocked once, it was strange why his rider failed to switch him. He was eased once his rider felt he could not win and it is safe to ignore this run. Official explanation: jockey said colt was denied a clear run (op 5-4 tchd 11-8)

4051 DOROTHY CROSSLAND H'CAP — 5f 213y
3:00 (3:00) (Class 5) (0-75,75) 3-Y-O+ — £2,775 (£830; £415; £207; £103) Stalls Low

Form — RPR

3022 **1** **Mandarin Spirit (IRE)**[8] 3797 8-9-0 **61** .... OscarUrbina 8 71
(G C H Chung) *a in tch: rdn to ld 1f out: drvn out* 4/1[1]

2055 **2** 1 1/4 **Louphole**[17] 3506 6-9-8 **69** .... RichardSmith 9 75
(P J Makin) *hld up towards rr: gd hdwy appr fnl f: r.o to go 2nd ins fnl f* 12/1

4230 **3** 3/4 **China Cherub**[14] 3587 5-9-8 **74** .... (b) JackMitchell(5) 10 78
(S Dow) *raded wd in tch: hdwy over 1f out: r.o ins fnl f* 7/1

6240 **4** 3/4 **Prince Of Delphi**[10] 3728 5-9-7 **68** .... (p) GeorgeBaker 12 69
(R M Beckett) *swtchd lft fr outside draw sn after s: in tch: nt qckn ins fnl f* 5/1[2]

6150 **5** 1 3/4 **Buy On The Red**[29] 3093 7-9-11 **72** .... (p) MartinDwyer 6 68
(W R Muir) *trckd ldrs: ev ch 1f out: nt qckn after* 12/1

400 **6** 1/2 **Bateleur**[21] 3352 4-9-0 **61** .... EdwardCreighton 7 55
(M R Channon) *nvr bttr than mid-div* 10/1

4042 **7** 1 1/2 **Magical Speedfit (IRE)**[8] 3782 3-9-8 **75** .... EddieAhern 11 64
(G G Margarson) *in tch: rdn over 1f out and sn fdd* 7/1

0001 **8** shd **Diane's Choice**[14] 3575 5-9-2 **68** .... (t) AhmedAjtebi(5) 5 57
(Miss Gay Kelleway) *trckd ldr tl rdn and wknd over 1f out* 13/2[3]

0-00 **9** 1 1/4 **The Cayterers**[22] 3313 6-9-4 **65** .... (b[1]) SteveDrowne 1 50
(J M Bradley) *v.s.a: sn wnt to outside: nvr on terms* 16/1

0-00 **10** 1 3/4 **Just Sort It**[34] 2945 3-8-10 **70** .... JPHamblett(7) 4 49
(W Jarvis) *tride to duck under gate leaving stalls: a bhd* 25/1

400- **11** 3/4 **Tarraburn (USA)**[321] 4940 4-9-1 **69** .... WilliamCarson(7) 3 46
(G C H Chung) *slowly away: a bhd* 33/1

00 **12** 1/2 **One Way Ticket**[17] 3486 8-8-11 **58** .... (p) WilliamBuick 2 33
(J M Bradley) *led tl rdn and hdd 1f out: wknd rapidly* 20/1

1m 10.0s (-0.20) **Going Correction** +0.05s/f (Good)
WFA 3 from 4yo+ 6lb — **12** Ran SP% **116.9**
Speed ratings (Par 103): **103,101,100,99,97 96,94,94,92,90 89,88**
toteswinger: 1&2 £11.40, 1&3 £8.20, 2&3 £14.80. CSF £50.80 CT £328.52 TOTE £5.40: £2.00, £4.20, £2.50; EX 54.40 TRIFECTA Not won..
Owner Peter Tsim **Bred** W Haggas And W Jarvis **Trained** Newmarket, Suffolk
■ Stewards' Enquiry : Oscar Urbina one-day ban: used whip with excessive frequency (Jul 29)

FOCUS
A moderate sprint handicap and ordinary if fairly sound form.
The Cayterers Official explanation: jockey said gelding missed the break
Just Sort It Official explanation: jockey said gelding missed the break
Tarraburn(USA) Official explanation: jockey said gelding missed the break

4052 CATERING SERVICES INTERNATIONAL (S) STKS — 6f 209y
3:30 (3:31) (Class 6) 3-Y-O+ — £1,942 (£578; £288; £144) Stalls Low

Form — RPR

0150 **1** **Mannello**[31] 3034 5-9-4 54 .... (b) RichardThomas 1 59
(Jim Best) *t.k.h: mid-div: hdwy 2f out: led ins fnl f: sn clr* 9/1[3]

6500 **2** 2 1/2 **Fun In The Sun**[18] 3446 4-9-9 48 .... GeorgeBaker 13 57
(A B Haynes) *mid-div: hdwy over 1f out: r.o to go 2nd towards fin* 12/1

0-05 **3** 1/2 **Yerevan**[26] 3165 4-8-13 63 .... (t) TPQueally 6 46
(R T Phillips) *a.p: led 2f out: rdn and hdd ins fnl f: lost 2nd towards fin* 6/1[2]

6500 **4** 1 1/4 **Border Artist**[17] 3501 9-9-1 50 .... JerryO'Dwyer(3) 3 51+
(J Pearce) *towards rr: making gd hdwy whn hmpd jst ins fnl f: swtchd rt: r.o* 12/1

30-0 **5** 1 1/2 **Marvin Gardens**[64] 2055 5-9-4 40 .... FergusSweeney 4 43
(P S McEntee) *led tl hdd 2f out: rdn and one pce ins fnl f* 40/1

-023 **6** shd **Le Chiffre (IRE)**[7] 3822 6-8-13 68 .... (p) MarkCoumbe(5) 12 43
(John A Harris) *in tch: rdn over 2f out: one pce after* 6/4[1]

3052 **7** 2 **Bye Baby Bunting**[8] 3779 3-8-5 55 .... RichardSmith 7 30
(B R Johnson) *mid-div: rdn over 2f out: no hdwy fr over 1f out* 10/1

3000 **8** 3/4 **Infinite Patience**[20] 3381 3-8-5 55 .... (p) MartinDwyer 9 28
(J S Moore) *slowly away: effrt over 1f out: nvr on terms* 12/1

5060 **9** 1 **Compulsion**[37] 2866 5-8-13 48 .... PaulEddery 5 28
(Pat Eddery) *stdd s: sn mid-div: no hdwy fr over 1f out* 16/1

0503 **10** 4 1/2 **Poppy Red**[13] 3605 3-8-5 47 .... PaulFitzsimons 15 13
(Miss J R Tooth) *slowly away: a bhd* 25/1

0 **11** 3/4 **Lauras Joy (IRE)**[15] 3559 5-8-13 40 .... (p) WilliamBuick 2 14
(G P Enright) *slowly away: a bhd* 20/1

-000 **12** 3 1/2 **Peruvian Style (IRE)**[15] 3559 7-9-4 43 .... (v[1]) RichardKingscote 8 9
(J M Bradley) *in tch tl wknd wl over 1f out* 40/1

00-0 **13** 1/2 **A One (IRE)**[19] 3422 9-8-13 43 .... JamieJones(5) 11 8
(H J Manners) *prom tl wknd 2f out* 66/1

0000 **14** 2 1/4 **Whenineedyou**[20] 3359 3-8-5 44 .... (t) PaulDoe 10 —
(I A Wood) *flyj. s: a bhd* 66/1

0006 **15** 29 **Nordic Light (USA)**[10] 3733 4-9-4 58 .... (b) SteveDrowne 14 —
(J M Bradley) *mid-div: lost tch 1/2-way: eased over 1f out: t.o* 20/1

1m 22.87s (-0.23) **Going Correction** +0.05s/f (Good)
WFA 3 from 4yo+ 8lb — **15** Ran SP% **123.6**
Speed ratings (Par 101): **103,100,99,98,96 96,94,93,92,86 86,82,81,78,45**
toteswinger: 1&2 £25.50, 1&3 £9.90, 2&3 £18.30. CSF £106.97 TOTE £10.70: £4.00, £4.40, £2.30; EX 140.70 TRIFECTA Not won..The winner was bought in for 3,500gns.
Owner Eagle Bloodstock & Racing **Bred** Richard Moses **Trained** Lewes, E Sussex

FOCUS
An ordinary seller with the winner perhaps the best guide to the form, which could have been rated a bit higher.
Peruvian Style(IRE) Official explanation: jockey said gelding ran too free
Nordic Light(USA) Official explanation: jockey said gelding moved poorly

4053 MATTHEW CLARK WINES & SPIRITS H'CAP — 7f 214y
4:00 (4:00) (Class 6) (0-60,60) 3-Y-O+ — £2,396 (£712; £356; £177) Stalls Low

Form — RPR

0032 **1** **Prince Valentine**[9] 3764 7-9-0 **49** .... (p) FergusSweeney 4 58
(G L Moore) *mid-div: led wl over 1f out: r.o wl fnl f* 4/1[2]

0153 **2** 1 1/4 **Batchworth Blaise**[15] 3563 5-9-2 **51** .... StephenCarson 15 57
(E A Wheeler) *hld up on outside: hdwy over 1f out: r.o wl fnl f to go 2nd cl home* 9/1

430- **3** nk **Night Wolf (IRE)**[199] 7268 8-9-9 **58** .... PaulDoe 3 63
(S Curran) *led tl hung rt and hdd wl over 1f out: rallied ent fnl f and edgd lft but kpt on wl* 20/1

5-40 **4** hd **Astroangel**[25] 3218 4-8-13 **55** .... AshleyMorgan(7) 9 60
(M H Tompkins) *s.i.s: hdwy to trck wnr wl over 1f out: no ex towards fin* 14/1

3050 **5** 1 **Grey Boy (GER)**[17] 3501 7-9-9 **58** .... TPQueally 14 61
(A W Carroll) *mid-div: rdn over 1f out and kpt on fnl f* 10/1

2034 **6** nk **Moves Goodenough**[14] 3583 5-9-11 **60** .... MartinDwyer 5 62
(Andrew Turnell) *in tch: rdn over 1f out: kpt on one pce ins fnl f* 7/2[1]

0360 **7** 3 1/4 **Recalcitrant**[14] 3588 5-9-4 **53** .... WilliamBuick 7 47
(S Dow) *trckd ldr to 2f out: wknd appr fnl f* 13/2[3]

0004 **8** nk **Townkab (IRE)**[19] 3397 3-8-8 **57** .... (b) MarkCoumbe(5) 11 49
(N P Littmoden) *slowly away: in rr: sme hdwy over 1f out: nvr on terms* 11/1

00-0 **9** 1 3/4 **Fantasy Crusader**[34] 2943 9-9-0 **49** .... ShaneKelly 10 39
(R M H Cowell) *a towards rr* 20/1

50-0 **10** 2 3/4 **Crimsonwing (IRE)**[46] 2559 3-8-11 **60** .... NicolPolli(5) 1 41
(A M Hales) *slowly away: sn in tch: wknd wl over 1f out* 16/1

56-0 **11** nse **Road To Recovery**[13] 3607 4-8-13 **48** .... VinceSlattery 13 31
(D J Wintle) *hld up in tch: rdn over 3f out: wknd 2f out* 40/1

3011 **12** *9* **Lancaster Lad (IRE)**[14] 3572 3-9-0 **58** DavidKinsella 16 19
(A B Haynes) *chsd ldrs tl rdn and wknd rapidly appr fnl f* **12/1**

5-60 **13** *½* **Mamichor**[14] 3588 5-9-1 **50** RichardSmith 6 11
(B R Johnson) *mid-div: bhd fnl 2f* **25/1**

2662 **14** *24* **Fly In Johnny (IRE)**[20] 3359 3-9-0 **58** SteveDrowne 8 —
(M R Hoad) *in tch to 1/2-way: t.o* **12/1**

1m 35.88s (-0.12) **Going Correction** +0.05s/f (Good)
WFA 3 from 4yo+ 9lb **14** Ran SP% **126.7**
Speed ratings (Par 101): **102,100,100,100,99 98,95,95,93,90 90,81,81,57**
toteswinger: 1&2 £7.70, 1&3 £14.10, 2&3 £26.70. CSF £40.36 CT £688.70 TOTE £4.30: £1.50, £2.90, £3.90; EX 34.10 Trifecta £209.60 Part won. Pool: 283.30 - 0.10 winning units..

Owner D R Hunnisett **Bred** Mrs E Y Hunnisett **Trained** Woodingdean, E Sussex

■ Stewards' Enquiry : Fergus Sweeney caution: careless riding

FOCUS
A very moderate handicap and straightforward form.

Night Wolf(IRE) Official explanation: jockey said gelding hung right

Astroangel Official explanation: jockey said filly was slowly away

Lancaster Lad(IRE) Official explanation: jockey said colt ran too free

4054 BRIGHTON & HOVE ALBION FC H'CAP 1m 1f 209y

4:30 (4:31) (Class 6) (0-60,60) 3-Y-O+ **£2,396** (£712; £356; £177) **Stalls** High

Form RPR

0-52 **1** **Faith And Reason (USA)**[26] 3182 5-9-9 **56** (v) TPQueally 6 73+
(A P Stringer) *hld up in rr: smooth hdwy over 2f out: led on bit appr fnl f: sn clr: v easily* **9/4**[1]

022 **2** *6* **Fairly Honest**[14] 3572 4-8-11 **51** WilliamCarson(7) 7 56
(P W Hiatt) *led tl hdd appr fnl f: kpt on but no ch w wnr* **10/1**

6346 **3** *1¼* **Solo River**[15] 3569 3-8-8 **55** TravisBlock(3) 4 57
(P J Makin) *t.k.h: in tch: kpt on one pce fnl f* **10/1**

1224 **4** *½* **Astrolibra**[12] 3657 4-9-2 **56** AshleyMorgan(7) 3 57
(M H Tompkins) *chsd ldrs: rdn 2f out: one pce after* **3/1**[2]

0565 **5** *2¼* **Orbital Orchid**[17] 3483 3-8-11 **55** (v) FergusSweeney 1 52
(W S Kittow) *towards rr: rdn 3f out: kpt on past btn horses fnl 2f* **8/1**

4012 **6** *3* **Borrowdale**[17] 3483 3-9-1 **59** ShaneKelly 12 50
(J A Osborne) *racd wd: nvr bttr than mid-div* **7/1**[3]

0006 **7** *2½* **Fateful Attraction**[20] 3361 5-8-13 **46** oh1 (t) PaulDoe 13 32
(I A Wood) *t.k.h: trckd ldr after 2f: wknd over 1f out* **20/1**

5000 **8** *12* **Jelly Mo**[22] 3322 3-8-9 **56** PatrickHills(3) 11 18
(J W Hills) *prom tl rdn and wknd over 2f out* **17/2**

6-00 **9** *2¾* **Medici Gold**[16] 3524 3-8-6 **50** MartinDwyer 8 6
(B G Powell) *a towards rr* **25/1**

60-0 **10** *1¼* **Ireland Dancer (IRE)**[20] 2755 4-8-12 **52** HarryPoulton(7) 9 6
(P M Phelan) *steadied s: sn in tch on ins: rdn and wknd over 2f out* **50/1**

0P-0 **11** *5* **Panadin (IRE)**[18] 3446 6-8-13 **46** oh1 (p) SteveDrowne 2 —
(Mrs L C Jewell) *prom early: wknd wl over 2f out* **66/1**

2m 4.21s (0.61) **Going Correction** +0.05s/f (Good)
WFA 3 from 4yo+ 11lb **11** Ran SP% **120.1**
Speed ratings (Par 101): **99,94,93,92,91 88,86,77,74,73 69**
toteswinger: 1&2 £7.30, 1&3 £8.20, 2&3 £19.10. CSF £25.81 CT £195.35 TOTE £3.40: £1.50, £3.10, £3.20; EX 27.30 Trifecta £103.20 Pool: £334.86 - 2.40 winning units..

Owner Curley Leisure **Bred** Gainsborough Farm Llc **Trained** Newmarket, Suffolk

■ Stewards' Enquiry : Ashley Morgan one-day ban: used whip above shoulder height (Jul 29)

FOCUS
This modest handicap was turned into a procession by Faith And Reason who is rated in line with last year's best but still a stone+ off the pick of his 3yo form.

4055 HARDINGS BAR & CATERING SERVICES APPRENTICE H'CAP 1m 3f 196y

5:00 (5:02) (Class 6) (0-65,71) 4-Y-0+ **£2,266** (£674; £337; £168) **Stalls** High

Form RPR

3605 **1** **Trysting Grove (IRE)**[11] 3698 7-8-7 **53** AshleyMorgan(5) 5 61
(E G Bevan) *stdd s: hdwy on outside over 1f out: r.o strly to ld post* **8/1**

1/00 **2** *shd* **Irish Ballad**[83] 1562 6-8-3 **49** ow2 (t) WilliamCarson(5) 7 56
(S Dow) *in tch: jnd ldrs over 3f out: rdn and led briefly cl home: jst tched off* **16/1**

4045 **3** *¾* **Under Fire (IRE)**[20] 3360 5-8-12 **58** MarkCoumbe(5) 11 64
(A W Carroll) *led after 1f: rdn 2f out: rdn and kpt on but lost first 2 pls cl home* **11/1**

0031 **4** *2* **Ornella**[8] 3780 4-10-2 **71** 6ex TravisBlock 12 74+
(H Morrison) *mid-div: jnd ldrs 3f out: rdn and nt qckn ins fnl f* **2/1**[1]

3055 **5** *¾* **Dubai Shadow (IRE)**[12] 3657 4-8-2 **50** DebraEngland(7) 3 52
(C E Brittain) *hld up in tch: rdn 2f out: one pce fnl f* **9/1**

5064 **6** *½* **Sir Liam (USA)**[14] 3574 4-8-13 **57** AshleyHamblett(3) 8 58
(R A Teal) *led for 1f: ev ch fr 2f out tl wknd fnl f* **7/2**[2]

455 **7** *2* **Makai**[21] 3344 5-8-1 **47** oh1 ow1 RossAtkinson(5) 2 45
(M R Hoad) *in rr whn short of room over 4f out: nvr on terms* **16/1**

0010 **8** *3* **Camera Shy (IRE)**[22] 3321 4-8-6 **50** JackMitchell(3) 1 43
(K A Morgan) *hld up: rdn over 2f out: a bhd* **5/1**[3]

0-00 **9** *40* **Break Out**[4] 3901 4-8-5 **46** oh1 (p) TolleyDean 9 —
(J M Bradley) *a in rr: lost tch 3f out: virtually p.u over 1f out: t.o* **50/1**

00-0 **10** *59* **Danehill Folly (IRE)**[21] 3347 5-8-0 **48** oh1 ow2 SeanPalmer(7) 10 —
(M D I Usher) *trckd ldr after 2f: wknd qckly 5f out: virtually p.u over 2f out: t.o* **66/1**

2m 33.79s (1.09) **Going Correction** +0.05s/f (Good) **10** Ran SP% **116.9**
Speed ratings (Par 101): **98,97,97,96,95 95,93,91,65,25**
toteswinger: 1&2 £16.90, 1&3 £14.00, 2&3 £18.70. CSF £127.31 CT £1410.74 TOTE £10.10: £2.80, £4.30, £3.90; EX 125.20 TRIFECTA Not won. Place 6: £11822.34 Place 5: £347.72.

Owner E G Bevan **Bred** Knocktoran Stud **Trained** Ullingswick, H'fords

■ Stewards' Enquiry : Ashley Morgan two-day ban: used whip with excessive frequency (Jul 31,Aug 1)

FOCUS
An exciting finish to this low-quality handicap. The winner and third ran to their turf best but the favourite disappointed.

Ornella Official explanation: jockey said filly ran too free

T/Plt: £13,077.70 to a £1 stake. Pool: £68,971.88. 3.85 winning tickets. T/Qpdt: £129.10 to a £1 stake. Pool: £6,982.10. 40.00 winning tickets. JS

3392 GREAT LEIGHS (A.W) (L-H)

Tuesday, July 15

OFFICIAL GOING: Standard

Wind: breezy across Weather: warm, humid

4056 ESSEX COUNTY CLAIMING STKS 6f (P)

6:10 (6:10) (Class 6) 3-Y-O **£2,914** (£867; £433; £216) **Stalls** Low

Form RPR

4002 **1** **Billion Dollar Kid**[18] 3458 3-8-8 **79** JamieSpencer 6 71
(S A Callaghan) *chsd ldr: shkn up to ld 1f out: hld hd high but sn in command: rdn out* **10/11**[1]

4-00 **2** *1¼* **Wreningham**[15] 3564 3-8-10 **63** EddieAhern 4 69
(T Keddy) *chsd ldng pair: rdn jst over 2f out: chsd wnr last 100yds: r.o but nvr trbld wnr* **20/1**

0500 **3** *2½* **Bazguy**[34] 2945 3-8-12 **70** (b) JohnEgan 10 63
(P D Evans) *led: sn bustled along: rdn over 2f out: hdd 1f out: sn btn: lost 2nd last 100yds* **9/4**[2]

-505 **4** *7* **Westwood Dawn**[11] 3686 3-8-8 **41** CatherineGannon 7 37
(Mrs N Macauley) *stdd s: hld up bhd: hdwy on outer 2f out: sltly hmpd over 1f out: wnt modest 4th and hung lft ins fnl f: nvr nr ldrs* **50/1**

2012 **5** *2¾* **Copperbottomed (IRE)**[22] 3330 3-8-11 **65** (e) TedDurcan 5 31
(P G Murphy) *s.i.s: bhd: rdn 2f out: no imp and sn wl btn* **7/1**[3]

0300 **6** *2¼* **Bahamian Blue (IRE)**[19] 3406 3-8-6 **51** (b) RussellKennemore(3) 8 22
(P G Murphy) *t.k.h: in tch: rdn over 2f out: outpcd and edgd rt over 1f out: wl btn fnl f* **33/1**

-000 **7** *8* **Rockjumper**[31] 3030 3-8-7 **49** ow2 (b[1]) EmmettStack(3) 9 —
(H Morrison) *racd wd: in tch tl rdn and struggling 1/2-way: t.o and eased fnl f* **25/1**

600 **8** *1½* **Azzaamm**[24] 3268 3-8-10 **52** JimmyQuinn 1 —
(C A Dwyer) *hld up in last trio: rdn jst over 2f out: sn wknd: t.o and eased fnl f* **33/1**

1m 14.96s (1.26) **Going Correction** +0.325s/f (Slow) **8** Ran SP% **112.1**
Speed ratings (Par 98): **104,102,99,89,86 83,72,70**
toteswinger: 1&2 £8.60, 1&3 £3.40, 2&3 £8.60. CSF £24.22 TOTE £2.40: £1.10, £3.60, £1.10; EX 22.20.Billion Dollar Kid was claimed by R. A. Harris for £8000.

Owner M Sines **Bred** Catridge Farm Stud And Mrs J Hall **Trained** Newmarket, Suffolk

FOCUS
A weakish claimer although the winning time compared favourably with the better races run over this trip later on the card. The fourth, rated just 41, holds down the form.

Westwood Dawn Official explanation: jockey said gelding hung left

Copperbottomed(IRE) Official explanation: jockey said gelding never travelled

4057 WHITE NOTLEY MEDIAN AUCTION MAIDEN STKS 1m 6f (P)

6:40 (6:40) (Class 5) 3-5-Y-O **£3,561** (£1,059; £529; £264) **Stalls** Low

Form RPR

0002 **1** **Don't Stop Me Now (IRE)**[15] 3566 3-8-7 **60** EddieAhern 7 64
(J W Hills) *chsd ldr tl led 9f out: mde rest: rdn over 2f out: styd on wl fnl f* **5/2**[2]

6 **2** *4* **Kritzia**[13] 3611 3-8-7 **0** TedDurcan 6 61+
(H R A Cecil) *stdd s: hld up in last pair: hdwy to chse ldng pair over 6f out: drvn to chse wnr jst over 2f out: ev ch over 1f out: btn and eased last 100yds* **15/8**[1]

3-5 **3** *8* **Foresight**[75] 1741 3-8-12 **0** (p) JimCrowley 2 52
(Mrs A J Perrett) *s.i.s: sn chsd ldng pair: chsd wnr over 6f out: rdn 4f out: lost 2nd jst over 2f: wknd over 1f out* **6/1**

0 **4** *35* **Sponge**[17] 3484 3-8-12 **0** LPKeniry 1 3
(P R Chamings) *s.i.s: hld up in tch: rdn and lost tch 4f out: t.o last 2f* **25/1**

0-0 **P** **Kaichou (IRE)**[7] 3813 4-9-8 **0** (b[1]) IanMongan 4 —
(B J Meehan) *led tl 9f out: rdn and qckly lost tch 5f out: hopelessly t.o and p.u 2f out* **25/1**

550 **P** **Solas Alainn (IRE)**[43] 2668 3-8-12 **71** JamieSpencer 5 —
(J R Fanshawe) *chsd ldrs: rdn over 8f out: lost tch qckly 7f out: t.o and p.u over 5f out* **11/4**[3]

3m 6.20s (3.00) **Going Correction** +0.325s/f (Slow)
WFA 3 from 4yo+ 15lb **6** Ran SP% **112.0**
Speed ratings (Par 103): **104,101,97,77,—, —**
toteswinger: 1&2 £1.10, 1&3 £1.10, 2&3 £11.60. CSF £7.58 TOTE £3.20: £1.20, £1.70; EX 9.80.

Owner Mrs Paul Shanahan **Bred** Miss Patricia Heavey O'Connell **Trained** Upper Lambourn, Berks

■ Stewards' Enquiry : Jamie Spencer one-day ban: used whip with excessive force (Aug 1)

FOCUS
A modest maiden over 1m6f that took plenty of getting. The form is best rated around the first two.

Solas Alainn(IRE) Official explanation: jockey said gelding was unsuited by the track

4058 CHELMSFORD H'CAP 6f (P)

7:10 (7:11) (Class 4) (0-85,85) 3-Y-O+ **£5,180** (£1,541; £770; £384) **Stalls** Low

Form RPR

3150 **1** **Diriculous**[20] 3374 4-9-7 **79** JimCrowley 1 93
(T G Mills) *hld up in tch: a gng wl: swtchd rt and chsd ldr wl over 1f out: led jst ins fnl f: sn in command: readily* **11/2**[3]

-046 **2** *3* **Whitbarrow (IRE)**[42] 2692 9-8-13 **74** (b) JamesMillman(3) 7 78
(B R Millman) *chsd ldr tl led over 3f out: rdn over 2f out: hdd ins fnl f: kpt on but no ch w wnr* **16/1**

4004 **3** *1½* **Carcinetto (IRE)**[17] 3472 6-9-5 **82** RichardEvans(5) 6 81+
(P D Evans) *sn bustled along in midfield: hdwy and edgd out rt over 1f out: wnt 3rd ins fnl f: r.o but nvr pce to rch ldng pair* **11/1**

4206 **4** *½* **Cativo Cavallino**[22] 3317 5-8-11 **74** NataliaGemelova(5) 4 72
(J E Long) *sn niggled along in rr: hdwy on outer 2f out: styd on steadily fnl f but nvr pce to rch ldrs* **12/1**

0102 **5** *1½* **Varadouro (BRZ)**[56] 2293 6-9-7 **79** SilvestreDeSousa 3 72
(D Nicholls) *chsd ldrs: rdn wl over 1f out: wknd ent fnl f* **7/2**[1]

2424 **6** *1* **Dvinsky (USA)**[13] 3615 7-9-5 **77** (b) JimmyQuinn 10 67
(P Howling) *hld up bhd: rdn over 3f out: styd on past btn horses fr over 1f out: n.d* **9/2**[2]

3644 **7** *3¼* **Hammer Of The Gods (IRE)**[19] 3394 8-8-13 **71** (bt) SebSanders 8 50
(G C Bravery) *led tl over 3f out: chsd ldr after tl wknd u.p over 1f out* **15/2**

1441 **8** *4* **Harbour Blues**[66] 1988 3-9-6 **84** (t) CatherineGannon 12 50
(A W Carroll) *a towards rr: rdn over 2f out: and no prog wl 2f out* **7/1**

5663 **9** *1* **Distinctly Game**[19] 3394 6-9-8 **80** FergalLynch 2 43
(K A Ryan) *chsd ldrs: rdn over 2f out: wknd over 1f out: wl btn and eased fnl f* **8/1**

2066 **10** 3 ¼ **Muktasb (USA)**[134] 782 7-8-7 **68** ow2.............(v) RussellKennemore(3) 9 21
(D Shaw) *rrd at s and v.s.a: a bhd* **33/1**

1m 14.62s (0.92) **Going Correction** +0.325s/f (Slow)
WFA 3 from 4yo+ 6lb **10** Ran SP% **116.0**
Speed ratings (Par 105): **106,102,100,99,97 96,91,86,85,80**
toteswinger: 1&2 £0.00, 1&3 £13.60, 2&3 £6.80. CSF £88.50 CT £953.90 TOTE £7.40: £2.60, £3.90, £4.00; EX 158.60.
Owner Sherwoods Transport Ltd **Bred** Sherwoods Transport Ltd **Trained** Headley, Surrey

FOCUS
A competitive sprint handicap on paper, but it was won easily by the improving Diriculous, rated up another 10lb.
Varadouro(BRZ) Official explanation: jockey said gelding ran too free
Muktasb(USA) Official explanation: jockey said gelding missed the break

4059 WETHERSFIELD CONDITIONS STKS 6f (P)
7:40 (7:41) (Class 3) 3-Y-0+
£7,788 (£2,332; £1,166; £583; £291; £146) **Stalls** Low

Form RPR
4210 **1** **Ceremonial Jade (UAE)**[17] 3504 5-9-2 107......................(t) JohnEgan 8 110
(M Botti) *stdd s: hld up in rr: nt clr run briefly over 1f out: chsd ldrs ent fnl f: r.o wl to ld nr fin* **4/1**[2]
15-0 **2** ½ **Greek Renaissance (IRE)**[17] 3488 5-9-2 112...............(t) LDettori 9 108
(Saeed Bin Suroor) *hld up in rr: hdwy on outer 2f out: sn drvn: pressed ldrs ins fnl f: kpt on to go 2nd nr fin* **7/4**[1]
461- **3** *hd* **Starlit Sands**[306] 5373 3-8-7 113 ow2................................ SebSanders 1 103
(Sir Mark Prescott) *led: rdn over 2f out: battled on wl tl hdd and no ex nr fin* **10/1**
-010 **4** *hd* **Viking Spirit**[24] 3248 6-9-2 102.. AdamKirby 6 107
(W R Swinburn) *chsd ldr: rdn over 2f out: kpt on wl u.p fnl f but nvr quite pce to rch ldrs* **7/1**
1060 **5** 2 **Nota Bene**[10] 3722 6-9-2 101.. MarcHalford(3) 3 103
(D R C Elsworth) *taken down early: stdd s: hld up bhd: hdwy on inner 2f out: rdn and one pce fr over 1f out* **12/1**
-030 **6** 4 **Aeroplane**[24] 3247 5-9-2 100.. JamieSpencer 2 88
(S A Callaghan) *dwlt: hld up in midfield: hdwy over 2f out: chsd ldrs and rdn 2f out: wknd ent fnl f* **9/2**[3]
1101 **7** ½ **Came Back (IRE)**[48] 2504 5-9-2 94.................................. FergalLynch 5 86
(K A Ryan) *chsd ldrs rdn over 2f out: wknd over 1f out* **10/1**
-233 **8** ½ **Kylayne**[19] 3420 3-8-5 102... WilliamBuick 7 79
(P W D'Arcy) *in tch: rdn 1/2-way: chsd ldrs and drvn 2f out: wknd ent fnl f* **12/1**

1m 14.14s (0.44) **Going Correction** +0.325s/f (Slow)
WFA 3 from 5yo+ 6lb **8** Ran SP% **120.6**
Speed ratings (Par 107): **110,109,109,108,106 100,100,99**
toteswinger: 1&2 £10.70, 1&3 £3.20, 2&3 £4.90. CSF £12.15 TOTE £4.00: £1.70, £1.50, £2.10; EX 10.60.
Owner Giuliano Manfredini **Bred** Darley **Trained** Newmarket, Suffolk

FOCUS
A decent conditions race run at a good pace. The winner, third and fourth were all close to form but the runner-up was not at his best.

NOTEBOOK
Ceremonial Jade(UAE) is a much better horse on the All-Weather than on turf and, back on his favoured surface following a down-the-field effort at Windsor, took advantage of the strong pace to come from the back of the field and run down the leader inside the last. His stamina for further - he has won four times over 7f plus - certainly came into play here. (op 7-2)
Greek Renaissance(IRE) always needs his first run of the season but he had won second time out for the past two years and he held a solid chance on the ratings, which explains his strength in the market. Drawn widest of all, he was stuck on the outside and towards the rear of the field for much of the race and did not have much go his way. Challenging widest in the straight, he stayed on really well and deserves credit as he must have covered a lot more ground during the race than the winner, but was only beaten half a length. Official explanation: trainer's rep said horse had a breathing problem (op 2-1 tchd 9-4)
Starlit Sands ◆, who finished off last season winning a French Group 3 race, had previously finished fourth in a very hot Molecomb Stakes and was representing a generation that is doing well in decent sprinting company this year. The betting suggested she was expected to need the run, though. Fast away, she looked as though she might be tough to catch entering the straight, but lack of a recent outing began to tell entering the final furlong and she did not quite get home. A drop back to 5f will not hurt her, but she will get this trip alright, and she will be one to look out for next time. (op 8-1)
Viking Spirit has yet to win on the All-Weather, but out of the eight previous times he had recorded a three-figure RPR, four of them were achieved on the All-Weather. He ran well but looks likely to remain difficult to place off his current mark. (op 11-1 tchd 12-1)
Nota Bene, who won on his reappearance here in May, ran a sound race, finishing well clear of the rest, but he too looks likely to have problems being placed to win off his current rating. (op 14-1 tchd 20-1)
Aeroplane, who ran in the Golden Jubilee last time out, was taking a drop in class on his first start for his new trainer. He never landed a blow on his All-Weather debut, though, and has not really lived up to his potential so far. (op 11-2 tchd 7-1)
Kylayne Official explanation: trainer said filly was found to be in season on return home

4060 HALSTEAD H'CAP 1m (P)
8:10 (8:11) (Class 3) (0-90,90) 3-Y-0+
£7,477 (£2,239; £1,119; £560; £279; £140) **Stalls** Low

Form RPR
0410 **1** **Bomber Command (USA)**[25] 3197 5-9-7 **86**..............(v) PatrickHills(3) 4 99
(J W Hills) *chsd ldr: rdn to ld over 1f out: edgd lft but styd on strly to go clr ins fnl f* **14/1**
1-12 **2** 3 ¾ **High Standing (USA)**[24] 3270 3-9-0 **85**........................ JamieSpencer 1 87+
(S A Callaghan) *stdd after s: t.k.h: hld up in tch: plld out over 1f out: sn chal on bit: rdn 1f out: fnd nil and immediately btn: jst hld on for 2nd* **11/8**[1]
-000 **3** *hd* **Prince Of Light (IRE)**[10] 3740 5-9-11 **87**........................ EddieAhern 7 91
(M Johnston) *stdd s: hld up in tch: rdn and effrt jst over 2f out: chsd ldng trio over 1f out: kpt on to go 3rd ins fnl f: no ch w wnr* **9/2**[2]
0250 **4** 1 ¼ **Captain Jacksparra (IRE)**[25] 3197 4-9-11 **87**............... FergalLynch 3 88
(K A Ryan) *led: rdn 2f out: hdd over 1f out: wknd ins fnl f* **8/1**
0 **5** 4 ½ **Rubacuori (BRZ)**[12] 3635 4-9-11 **87**............................. JohnEgan 6 78
(J M P Eustace) *t.k.h: hld up in midfield: rdn and lost pl wl over 2f out: no ch fnl f* **33/1**
0210 **6** 3 ½ **Gallantry**[12] 3646 6-10-0 **90**.. JimmyQuinn 8 73
(P Howling) *chsd ldrs: rdn and struggling over 2f out: wknd wl over 1f out* **11/1**
1-6 **7** 1 ½ **Fr Dominic (USA)**[47] 2544 3-9-2 **87**...............................(v[1]) SebSanders 2 66
(R M Beckett) *bhd: reminders sn after s: swtchd to outer and rdn 4f out: lost tch 2f out* **15/2**[3]
-020 **8** 12 **Binanti**[25] 3197 8-9-9 **85**.. GeorgeBaker 5 37
(P R Chamings) *t.k.h: hld up in last trio: rdn and effrt over 2f out: wknd wl over 1f out: eased ins fnl f* **8/1**

1m 42.27s (2.37) **Going Correction** +0.325s/f (Slow)
WFA 3 from 4yo+ 9lb **8** Ran SP% **112.2**
Speed ratings (Par 107): **101,97,97,95,91 87,86,74**
toteswinger: 1&2 £4.20, 1&3 £3.40, 2&3 £2.50. CSF £32.58 CT £104.86 TOTE £19.20: £4.20, £1.20, £1.70; EX 53.40.
Owner Gary & Linnet Woodward (2) **Bred** Jeffrey B Feins **Trained** Upper Lambourn, Berks

FOCUS
A fairly decent handicap run at an ordinary pace. The winner was back to something like his best and the form is rated through the runner-up.

NOTEBOOK
Bomber Command(USA), always well placed chasing the leader, was asked to go on approaching the final furlong and stretched nicely clear to win convincingly. He had done all his previous winning over 7f but he relished every yard of this mile, and this track brought about improvement out of him. (op 11-1 tchd 16-1)
High Standing(USA) travelled well and had every chance early in the straight, but he just could not get to grips with the eventual winner. This was a solid effort off another 3lb higher mark, but the impression left was that the extra furlong stretched his stamina a touch. (op 7-4 after 2-1 in places, tchd 5-4)
Prince Of Light(IRE) ◆ has struggled this year but he was running off an 11lb lower mark than he began the season off, and he was dropping into a class 3 race for the first time in years. His regular style of running, which is to be up with the pace, suits this track, but for some reason he was held up and, off an ordinary gallop, was staying on all too late. He is worth keeping in mind for a similar contest. (op 4-1 tchd 5-1)
Captain Jacksparra(IRE), who had not been out of the first two in four previous starts on the All-Weather, enjoyed the run of the race, and his only excuse can be that this trip stretches his stamina.
Rubacuori(BRZ), who has winning form in Brazil, has yet to shine in two starts over here and probably needs help from the Handicapper. (op 25-1 tchd 40-1)
Gallantry was well below his best as he raced handily but was beaten turning into the straight. (op 8-1)
Fr Dominic(USA), who was pulled out of his intended start at the Newmarket July meeting because of the softish ground, had a visor on for the first time and was weak in the market. Given reminders and switched wide rounding the turn into the straight, he failed to respond and finished up well beaten. He looks one to avoid. (op 5-1 tchd 8-1)

4061 DANBURY H'CAP 1m (P)
8:40 (8:42) (Class 5) (0-70,70) 3-Y-0 **£3,561** (£1,059; £529; £264) **Stalls** Low

Form RPR
030 **1** **Thumbs Up**[33] 2981 3-9-4 **67**.. JamieSpencer 4 77+
(L M Cumani) *s.i.s: t.k.h: hld up in midfield: drvn and hdwy over 2f out: chal and edgd lft ent fnl f: drvn to ld nr fin* **5/6**[1]
6300 **2** *hd* **Speyside (IRE)**[33] 2974 3-9-1 **67**.............................(v[1]) PatrickHills(3) 12 74
(J W Hills) *hld up towards rr: hdwy and rdn on outer 3f out: led narrowly over 1f out: hdd and no ex nr fin* **20/1**
0-00 **3** 1 ¾ **Suzi Spends (IRE)**[34] 2956 3-9-7 **70**................................ JohnEgan 16 76+
(H J Collingridge) *hld up in rr: stl plenty to do over 2f out: hdwy on inner 2f out: swtchd rt 1f out: r.o wl to go 3rd wl ins fnl f: nt rch ldrs* **16/1**
4400 **4** 1 ½ **Lawton**[50] 2451 3-9-2 **65**.. PaulFitzsimons 8 65
(Miss J R Tooth) *led: rdn over 2f out: hdd over 1f out: wknd wl ins fnl f* **33/1**
023 **5** *nk* **Charming Tale (USA)**[16] 3524 3-8-8 **57**.........................(b) IanMongan 2 56
(B J Meehan) *in tch: hdwy over 3f out: rdn and chsd ldrs over 1f out: wknd wl ins fnl f* **8/1**[2]
2120 **6** ¾ **Admirals Way**[18] 3442 3-8-8 **62**................................. MarkCoumbe(5) 10 59
(C N Kellett) *chsd ldr: rdn and ev ch wl over 1f out: wknd last 100yds* **16/1**
0006 **7** ¾ **Rehabilitation**[22] 3325 3-9-7 **70**....................................(v) AdamKirby 3 65
(W R Swinburn) *in tch in midfield: rdn wl over 2f out: kpt on u.p but nvr pce to rch ldrs* **8/1**[2]
3126 **8** ¾ **Bury Treasure (IRE)**[64] 2047 3-9-4 **67**.......................... MickyFenton 5 61+
(Miss Gay Kelleway) *t.k.h: hld up in rr: rdn and no prog wl over 3f out: kpt on steadily u.p: nvr trbld ldrs* **20/1**
0-00 **9** 13 **Harting Hill**[17] 3484 3-8-11 **60**...................................... JimmyQuinn 11 24
(M P Tregoning) *t.k.h: in tch: hdwy to chse ldrs 4f out: rdn and wknd qckly over 2f out: wl bhd after* **16/1**
006 **10** 14 **Lightning Squall (USA)**[19] 3396 3-9-2 **65**.................... WilliamBuick 1 —
(M Botti) *chsd ldrs: rdn and wknd qckly jst over 2f out: eased fnl f: t.o* **25/1**
330 **11** 13 **Micheals Boy (IRE)**[24] 3268 3-8-9 **58**............................ JimCrowley 6 —
(J R Boyle) *racd in midfield tl dropped to rr 4f out: lost tch 3f out: virtually p.u fnl f: t.o* **12/1**
0-36 **12** 6 **Dea Caelestis (FR)**[26] 3161 3-9-2 **65**............................ TedDurcan 15 —
(H R A Cecil) *bhd: rdn and lost tch over 3f out: virtually p.u fr over 1f out: t.o* **10/1**[3]

1m 43.42s (3.52) **Going Correction** +0.325s/f (Slow) **12** Ran SP% **127.5**
Speed ratings (Par 100): **95,94,93,91,91 90,89,89,76,62 49,43**
toteswinger: 1&2 £0.00, 1&3 £5.60, 2&3 £35.80. CSF £28.22 CT £202.40 TOTE £1.90: £1.40, £5.90, £3.00; EX 36.80 Place 6 £15.60 place 5: £13.55.
Owner Team Spirit **Bred** London Thoroughbred Services Ltd **Trained** Newmarket, Suffolk

FOCUS
A modest handicap run at a steady early pace, resulting in something of a sprint finish and questionable form. The winner looks open to further improvement, though.
Dea Caelestis(FR) Official explanation: trainer's rep said filly did not face kickback
T/Plt: £54.30 to a £1 stake. Pool: £54,409.15. 730.53 winning tickets. T/Qpdt: £16.30 to a £1 stake. Pool: £4,603.20. 207.90 winning tickets. SP

3651 YARMOUTH (L-H)
Tuesday, July 15

OFFICIAL GOING: Good to firm
Wind: nil Weather: muggy

4062 E B F TOTEPLACEPOT MAIDEN STKS 7f 3y
6:20 (6:26) (Class 5) 2-Y-0 **£3,784** (£1,132; £566; £283; £141) **Stalls** High

Form RPR
5 **1** **Wannabe King**[25] 3219 2-9-3 0...................................... ChrisCatlin 7 80
(D R Lanigan) *racd keenly: prom: led after 3f: rdn 2f out: battled on gamely fnl f* **9/2**
2 *hd* **Yorksters Girl (IRE)** 2-8-12 0..................................... RobertWinston 10 75
(M G Quinlan) *bhd early: prog to chse wnr over 2f out: rdn and persistent chal fnl f: a jst hld* **33/1**

6 **3** 2 ¾ **Andhaar**[32] 3001 2-9-3 0 .... RHills 3 73
(E A L Dunlop) *prom: rdn 2f out: wl hld by ldng pair fnl f* **11/4**[2]

4 nk **Poster (IRE)** 2-9-3 0 .... DaneO'Neill 1 72+
(L M Cumani) *wnt lft s: effrt on far side over 2f out: one pce and btn 1f out* **12/1**

0 **5** 2 ¼ **Highway Magic (IRE)**[33] 2972 2-9-3 0 .... DarrenWilliams 11 66
(A P Jarvis) *plld hrd: prom over 5f: rdn and edgd slightly lft after: sn btn* **100/1**

6 ½ **Mirrored** 2-9-3 0 .... KerrinMcEvoy 4 65+
(Sir Michael Stoute) *chsd ldrs: wknd tamely wl over 1f out* **5/2**[1]

50 **7** 2 ¾ **Bounty Reef**[1] 4027 2-8-9 0 .... KevinGhunowa(3) 6 53
(P D Evans) *chsd ldrs: rdn over 2f out: sn btn* **33/1**

8 hd **Beraimi (IRE)** 2-9-3 0 .... PhilipRobinson 9 58+
(M A Jarvis) *led tl 1/2-way: sn lost pl and struggling* **10/1**

9 ¾ **Tae Kwon Do (USA)** 2-9-3 0 .... RichardMullen 8 56
(E A L Dunlop) *uns rdr at s and rn loose: s.s and wnt lft: sn urged along: nvr on terms* **16/1**

10 hd **Morning Sir Alan** 2-9-3 0 .... PatCosgrave 2 55
(M J McGrath) *t.k.h early: chsd ldrs over 4f: sn unbalanced and racing awkwardly* **50/1**

11 1 **Achromatic** 2-9-3 0 .... SaleemGolam 5 53+
(W R Swinburn) *uns rdr at paddock: awkward at stalls: stdd s: struggling after 1/2-way* **4/1**[3]

1m 24.15s (-2.45) **Going Correction** -0.30s/f (Firm) **11** Ran SP% **124.9**
Speed ratings (Par 94): **102,101,98,98,95 95,92,91,90,90 89**
toteswinger: 1&2 £38.80, 1&3 £4.50. CSF £152.49 TOTE £6.50: £2.30, £10.90, £1.30; EX 199.70.
Owner Saif Ali & Saeed H Altayer **Bred** Chippenham Lodge Stud Ltd **Trained** Newmarket, Suffolk

FOCUS
This looked a good maiden and the winner set a decent standard. The winning time was respectable and winners ought to emerge from the race.

NOTEBOOK
Wannabe King, whose debut effort came in a maiden that has produced winners, showed a really good attitude when asked to win the race, finding more for pressure all the way to the line. Related to some very useful sorts, he can hold his own in a slightly higher grade. (op 8-1)
Yorksters Girl(IRE) was not fancied in the betting ring but she showed plenty of ability despite looking a little green. The winner is probably above average, so she should have little trouble winning a maiden, especially if kept to her own sex.
Andhaar, who showed some promise on his debut, was never far away throughout but lacked a change of gear when the pace increased. He will be effective at a mile this season. (op 4-1)
Poster(IRE), a 22,000gns half-brother to a dirt sprint winner in the US, was held up early before making his move about two furlongs from home. He kept on in good style without ever looking like winning. (op 9-1 tchd 8-1)
Highway Magic(IRE) failed miserably on his debut but showed a very good attitude under pressure in this, keeping on in exuberant style. Bred to stay middle distances, he is probably one to keep an eye on for handicaps next season.
Mirrored attracted plenty of market support in the morning but was allowed to drift on course. A 240,000gns son of Dansili, he showed up well for a lot of the race but gave the impression he was in need of the experience. (op 5-4 tchd 7-2)
Beraimi(IRE) broke well and was soon prominent, but he lost his position for no obvious reason about three furlongs from home before running on again inside the final furlong. He was not given a really hard time and will be of interest in a similar maiden next time. (op 16-1 tchd 8-1)
Tae Kwon Do(USA), who got loose before the race, did not break very well and ran green throughout. (op 25-1)
Achromatic, an expensive half-brother to a 1m2f Listed winner, threw his jockey off in the paddock and then was awkward to load at the stalls. Backed in from an early 10/1, he must have been showing something on the gallops but looked in need of the experience. (op 10-1 tchd 7-2)

4063 TOTEEXACTA (S) NURSERY 7f 3y
6:50 (6:57) (Class 6) 2-Y-O **£1,942** (£578; £288; £144) **Stalls** High

Form RPR

2421 **1** **Rose Of Coma (IRE)**[33] 2980 2-8-11 **56** .... ChrisCatlin 7 55
(Miss Gay Kelleway) *cl up: led over 2f out: rdn and hdd over 1f out: kpt on to regain advantage fnl strides* **9/4**[1]

5545 **2** hd **Yokozuna**[12] 3645 2-9-7 **66** .... (b) DaneO'Neill 2 65
(E A L Dunlop) *s.i.s: sn chsng ldrs: rdn to ld over 1f out: jst ct* **4/1**[2]

6510 **3** shd **Cherry Belle (IRE)**[10] 3706 2-8-12 **57** .... (v) PatCosgrave 8 55
(P D Evans) *sn urged along and nvr looked v willing: clsd to press ldrs over 1f out: ev ch 100yds out: no ex nr fin* **8/1**

004 **4** 1 ¾ **Kosama**[12] 3652 2-8-1 **45** ow1 .... AdrianTNicholls 1 40
(M R Channon) *sn getting reminders in rr: drvn to cl 2 fout: flattered 1f out: no ex fnl 100yds* **18/1**

0043 **5** ½ **Percys Corismatic**[9] 3760 2-8-3 **48** ow3 .... KevinGhunowa(3) 5 44
(J Gallagher) *prom: rdn over 2f out: nt qckn ins fnl f* **11/2**[3]

4001 **6** 2 ½ **Missy Que (IRE)**[48] 2508 2-8-10 **55** .... (b[1]) RichardMullen 6 41
(W R Muir) *midfield: rdn over 2f out: nt keen and no imp fnl f* **9/1**

000 **7** 3 ¼ **Nun Today (USA)**[11] 3674 2-9-1 **60** .... RobertWinston 10 38
(J S Moore) *last early: rdn after 3f: nvr on terms* **13/2**

6205 **8** ½ **Inn Swinger (IRE)**[7] 3815 2-8-4 **49** .... SaleemGolam 9 26
(W G M Turner) *stdd s: t.k.h in rr: bhd fnl 2f* **18/1**

460 **9** 8 **Strictly Royal**[10] 3706 2-8-0 **45** .... AdrianMcCarthy 4 2
(M R Channon) *led tl hdd and lost pl rapidly over 2f out* **20/1**

1m 25.9s (-0.70) **Going Correction** -0.30s/f (Firm) **9** Ran SP% **115.9**
Speed ratings (Par 92): **92,91,91,89,89 86,82,81,72**
toteswinger: 1&2 £2.80, 1&3 £11.00, 2&3 £13.20. CSF £11.10 CT £60.84 TOTE £2.70: £1.20, £1.80, £3.00; EX 14.80.The winner was bought in for £3,800. Yokozuna was claimed by Mrs R. Carr for £5000.
Owner Whispering Winds **Bred** Pier House Stud **Trained** Exning, Suffolk

FOCUS
The time was slow and this is weak form.

NOTEBOOK
Rose Of Coma(IRE), who won a course-and-distance seller last time for Richard Fahey, set a good standard for the grade and just prevailed under a very strong ride. This would look to be her level. (op 10-3)
Yokozuna found the concession of 10lb to the winner just too much and only narrowly failed to claim his first victory. He should win something similar and was claimed by Ruth Carr. (tchd 9-2)
Cherry Belle(IRE), who had finished behind the winner here three runs previously, came to have every chance but gave the impression she was always being held. (tchd 7-1)
Kosama does not look an easy ride and her jockey did well to get her so close. (op 14-1)
Percys Corismatic finished behind Rose Of Coma here last month and never really looked like reversing the form. (op 4-1)
Missy Que(IRE), in first-time blinkers, travelled well in midfield but lacked a turn of foot. (op 7-1)

4064 TOTESWINGER H'CAP 5f 43y
7:20 (7:23) (Class 5) (0-70,69) 3-Y-O+ **£2,719** (£809; £404; £202) **Stalls** High

Form RPR

3504 **1** **Gleaming Spirit (IRE)**[7] 3819 4-9-5 **62** .... (v[1]) DarrenWilliams 9 73
(A P Jarvis) *mde all at fast pce and qckly had rest at full stretch: wkng ins fnl f but a looked like holding on* **13/2**

6123 **2** ½ **Nusoor (IRE)**[14] 3585 5-9-3 **63** .... (v) KirstyMilczarek(3) 11 72
(Peter Grayson) *chsd ldrs: urged along over 2f out: wnt 2nd ins fnl f but nvr gng w as much zest as wnr: little imp cl home* **3/1**[1]

0/00 **3** 1 **Namu**[11] 3695 5-8-12 **55** .... DaneO'Neill 8 60
(Miss T Spearing) *s.i.s: pushed along in rr: stl 7th over 1f out: running on cl home* **16/1**

1030 **4** ¾ **Charlotte Grey**[31] 3033 4-8-4 **50** oh3 .... DominicFox(3) 6 53
(P J McBride) *wl bhd and pushed along: stl 8th over 1f out: styng on strly cl home* **10/1**

1330 **5** nk **Duke Of Milan (IRE)**[22] 3316 5-8-10 **53** .... PatCosgrave 5 55
(G C Bravery) *bhd early: effrt 3f out: outpcd and rdn 2f out: kpt on ins fnl f* **8/1**

-604 **6** ½ **Bold Minstrel (IRE)**[21] 3352 6-9-2 **59** .... ChrisCatlin 2 59
(M Quinn) *chsd wnr: hrd rdn over 1f out: wknd to lose four pls wl ins fnl f* **6/1**[3]

4531 **7** 3 ¼ **Raccoon (IRE)**[15] 3546 8-9-9 **66** .... (v) RobertWinston 1 54
(Mrs R A Carr) *cl up: hrd drvn 1/2-way: no rspnse: btn over 1f out* **4/1**[2]

4600 **8** 8 **Bookiesindex Boy**[47] 2551 4-9-8 **65** .... AdrianMcCarthy 7 24
(J R Jenkins) *chsd ldrs tl 1/2-way: nt run on* **12/1**

00-0 **9** ½ **Daddy Cool**[24] 3269 4-9-7 **69** .... (v[1]) JackDean(5) 4 27
(W G M Turner) *sn getting str reminders: racd w hd in air and reluctant thrght: btn wl over 1f out* **25/1**

1000 **10** 6 **Taboor (IRE)**[63] 2075 10-8-7 **50** .... RichardMullen 10 —
(R M H Cowell) *s.v.s and a t.o* **12/1**

61.00 secs (-1.20) **Going Correction** -0.30s/f (Firm) **10** Ran SP% **117.9**
Speed ratings (Par 103): **97,96,94,93,92 92,86,74,73,63**
toteswinger: 1&2 £4.70, 1&3 £48.80, 2&3 £9.00. CSF £26.63 CT £261.64 TOTE £7.70: £2.90, £1.60, £4.80; EX 41.20.
Owner Eurostrait Ltd **Bred** Rathasker Stud **Trained** Twyford, Bucks

FOCUS
Just a modest-looking sprint but a good winning time. The winner looked to be on a quicker strip of ground and just lasted home. He is rated close to the form he showed when winning here last year.
Namu ◆ Official explanation: jockey said mare was slowly away
Charlotte Grey Official explanation: jockey said filly had no pace early on
Taboor(IRE) Official explanation: jockey said gelding was slowly away

4065 TOTESPORT.COM H'CAP 1m 1f
7:50 (7:50) (Class 5) (0-70,69) 3-Y-O+ **£2,719** (£809; £404; £202) **Stalls** Low

Form RPR

-265 **1** **Riqaab (IRE)**[73] 1805 3-9-1 **66** .... RHills 3 74+
(E A L Dunlop) *hld up: rdn over 2f out: rousted along to chal over 1f out: led fnl 75yds: kpt on* **11/2**[3]

0614 **2** 1 **Shabahar (IRE)**[18] 3449 4-10-0 **69** .... PatCosgrave 2 76
(M J McGrath) *cl up: led over 1f out: sn drvn: hdd and no ex fnl 75yds* **7/2**[2]

-542 **3** 3 ¼ **Dancing Jest (IRE)**[12] 3655 4-9-6 **61** .... DaneO'Neill 7 61
(Rae Guest) *led: rdn over 2f out: hdd over 1f out: wknd ins fnl f* **1/1**[1]

0050 **4** nk **Harvest Joy (IRE)**[22] 3322 4-10-0 **69** .... ChrisCatlin 6 69
(J Gallagher) *chsd ldrs: rdn 4f out: no imp fnl 2f* **16/1**

0062 **5** ¾ **Anduril**[14] 3593 7-8-9 **50** .... (p) PatrickMathers 1 48
(I W McInnes) *stdd in rr: drvn and racd awkwardly fr 3f out: nvr making any imp* **9/1**

5046 **6** ½ **Life's A Whirl**[17] 3501 6-8-9 **50** oh2 .... (p) RobertWinston 8 47
(Mrs C A Dunnett) *t.k.h: pressed ldr: rdn over 2f out: wknd over 1f out* **8/1**

1m 54.85s (-0.95) **Going Correction** -0.30s/f (Firm)
WFA 3 from 4yo+ 10lb **6** Ran SP% **114.6**
Speed ratings (Par 103): **92,91,88,87,87 86**
toteswinger: 1&2 £2.80, 1&3 £1.20, 2&3 £2.80. CSF £25.47 CT £34.03 TOTE £6.80: £2.70, £2.40; EX 21.50.
Owner Hamdan Al Maktoum **Bred** Shadwell Estate Company Limited **Trained** Newmarket, Suffolk

FOCUS
Not the most competitive race but Riqaab looks decent and the form could rate higher. The winning time broke the course record, but this is a very new distance and in comparison with other races on the card, the time looked average.

4066 TOTESPORT 0800 221 221 CLAIMING STKS 1m 2f 21y
8:20 (8:20) (Class 6) 3-Y-O+ **£1,942** (£578; £288; £144) **Stalls** Low

Form RPR

1006 **1** **Saviour Sand (IRE)**[18] 3449 4-9-11 70 .... (b) RobertHavlin 8 76
(D R C Elsworth) *2nd and clr of rest tl led over 3f out: rdn over 1f out: a holding rival fnl f* **7/2**[2]

1515 **2** 1 ½ **Sabre Light**[18] 3436 3-8-6 67 .... (b[1]) DominicFox(3) 3 68
(A Bailey) *settled in 3rd pl but 6 l fr ldng pair st: wnt 2nd over 3f out: hanging lft and nvr looked like over taking fr over 1f out* **7/2**[2]

0551 **3** 1 ¼ **Lucayan Dancer**[17] 3474 8-9-13 71 .... AdrianTNicholls 10 72
(D Nicholls) *plld hrd in rr: effrt 3f out: wnt 3rd and rdn 2f out: nvr able to cl* **7/4**[1]

6-4 **4** 7 **Beggars End (USA)**[22] 3333 3-9-0 0 .... (b[1]) KShea 4 56
(E F Vaughan) *towards rr: rdn over 3f out: sn racing v awkwardly: wnt mod 4th over 1f out* **8/1**

04-5 **5** 1 ¾ **Manathon (FR)**[7] 3824 5-9-3 64 .... (t) RobertWinston 7 45
(A E Jones) *stdd s: plld hrd: nvr bttr than midfield: rdn 3f out: sn btn* **12/1**

010P **6** shd **Jarvo**[10] 3732 7-9-2 57 .... (v) PatrickMathers 2 43
(I W McInnes) *chsd ldrs: drvn 4f out: sn struggling* **7/1**[3]

0060 **7** hd **Whodouthinkur (IRE)**[14] 3572 3-8-9 35 .... ChrisCatlin 6 47?
(Mrs C A Dunnett) *bhd: rdn over 3f out: no rspnse* **50/1**

600 **8** 29 **Southwark Newsboy (IRE)**[28] 3118 3-8-6 30 .... (t) KevinGhunowa(3) 1 —
(Mrs C A Dunnett) *t.k.h in ld: hdd over 3f out: rapidly dropped out: t.o* **66/1**

2m 7.44s (-3.06) **Going Correction** -0.30s/f (Firm)
WFA 3 from 4yo+ 11lb **8** Ran SP% **116.5**
Speed ratings (Par 101): **100,98,97,92,90 90,90,67**
toteswinger: 1&2 £3.00, 1&3 £1.40, 2&3 £1.70. CSF £16.58 TOTE £5.50: £1.30, £1.60, £1.30; EX 28.70.
Owner The Save Your Sand Partnership **Bred** Michael Munnelly **Trained** Newmarket, Suffolk

FOCUS
This was an ordinary claimer run at a moderate pace early. The form makes sense at face value.
Jarvo Official explanation: jockey said gelding hung left

Southwark Newsboy(IRE) Official explanation: jockey said gelding ran too free

4067 TOTESPORTGAMES.COM H'CAP — 1m 6f 17y

8:50 (8:50) (Class 5) (0-70,69) 3-Y-0+ £2,719 (£809; £404; £202) Stalls High

Form RPR
5000 1 **Benhego**[22] 3327 3-8-4 59 .... SaleemGolam 8 68+
(S C Williams) *t.k.h: trckd ldrs: rdn to ld wl over 1f out: styd on gamely* 6/1

0040 2 1 1/2 **Ultimate Quest (IRE)**[5] 3873 3-8-1 56 .... ChrisCatlin 4 63+
(Sir Mark Prescott) *wnt 2nd after 4f: shkn up 1/2-way: rdn fnl 4f: ev ch over 1f out: nt qckn* 10/1

4353 3 1/2 **Fourth Dimension (IRE)**[8] 3802 9-10-0 68 .... DaneO'Neill 7 74
(Miss T Spearing) *bhd: rdn and effrt over 2f out: no imp fnl f* 4/1[2]

-565 4 1/2 **Hamsat Elqamar**[33] 2985 3-8-11 66 .... RHills 1 71
(J H M Gosden) *led: rdn 3f out: hdd wl over 1f out: v one pce fnl f* 5/1

4134 5 1/2 **Fairfield Flame (GER)**[33] 2985 3-8-13 68 ....(b) RobertHavlin 3 73
(D R C Elsworth) *midfield: pressed ldrs and rdn fnl 3f: v one pce fnl f* 9/2[3]

406 6 13 **Jafaru**[22] 3321 4-9-11 65 ....(p) RichardMullen 2 51
(G A Butler) *cl up: drvn along 3f out: wknd qckly 2f out* 8/1

0042 7 4 **Cossack Prince**[11] 3697 3-8-11 66 .... KShea 5 47
(B J Meehan) *midfield: rdn 3f out: fdd qckly 2f* 7/2[1]

60-4 8 22 **Blue Admiral**[63] 2090 3-9-0 69 .... RobertWinston 6 19
(M H Tompkins) *a last: rdn 4f out: t.o fnl 2f: eased clsng stages* 14/1

3m 1.96s (-5.64) **Going Correction** -0.30s/f (Firm)
WFA 3 from 4yo+ 15lb 8 Ran SP% 118.2
Speed ratings (Par 103): **104,103,102,102,102 94,92,80**
toteswinger: 1&2 £61.00, 1&3 £56.70, 2&3 £6.10. CSF £65.32 CT £271.28 TOTE £8.40: £2.20, £2.40, £1.60; EX 34.30 Place 6: £72.74 Place 5: £30.47.
Owner Essex Racing Club **Bred** Old Mill Stud **Trained** Newmarket, Suffolk

FOCUS
A modest staying event that appeared to be run at an even pace. However, only a few lengths covered the first five home. The front two were improvers and can do better still, with the next three giving the form a fairly solid look.
Jafaru Official explanation: trainer said gelding was unsuited by the good, good to firm ground
Blue Admiral Official explanation: trainer said gelding was unsuited by the good to firm ground
T/Plt: £82.60 to a £1 stake. Pool: £62,802.69. 554.44 winning tickets. T/Qpdt: £23.60 to a £1 stake. Pool: £5,494.56. 172.28 winning tickets. IM

4068 - 4071a (Foreign Racing) - See Raceform Interactive

3830 CATTERICK (L-H)

Wednesday, July 16

OFFICIAL GOING: Good to firm (good in places)
Wind: Light across Weather: Overcast

4072 RACING UK LIVE ON 432 NOVICE AUCTION STKS — 7f

2:30 (2:31) (Class 5) 2-Y-0 £2,590 (£770; £385; £192) Stalls Low

Form RPR
21 1 **Solo Attempt**[35] 2944 2-8-12 0 .... GregFairley 8 79+
(M Botti) *chsd ldng pair: hdwy to ld over 2f out: rdn wl over 1f out: drvn ins fnl f and kpt on* 5/2[2]

42 2 1 1/2 **Inheritor (IRE)**[22] 3334 2-8-13 0 .... PaulMulrennan 7 77+
(B Smart) *led 3f: cl up: rdn over 2f out: sn drvn and ev ch whn hung lft and hit rail ins fnl f: nt rcvr* 6/4[1]

44 3 6 **Little Tokyo (USA)**[21] 3364 2-8-13 0 .... RobertWinston 5 61
(J Howard Johnson) *cl up: led after 3f: rdn along and hdd over 2f out: sn drvn and kpt on same pce* 15/2[3]

0 4 nk **Sardan Dansar (IRE)**[15] 3590 2-8-3 0 .... AndrewMullen(3) 2 54
(Mrs A Duffield) *in tch: hdwy to chse ldrs whn rn wd home bnd: sn rdn and kpt on same pce appr fnl f* 14/1

3 5 1/2 **Digger Derek (IRE)**[14] 3597 2-8-11 0 .... TonyHamilton 3 57
(R A Fahey) *n.m.r and stdd after sn: sn outpcd and rdn along in rr: hdwy 2f out: swtchd ins over 1f out: kpt on ins fnl f: nrst fin* 17/2

1662 6 3/4 **Veronicas Boy**[15] 3576 2-8-12 0 .... PJMcDonald(3) 6 59
(G M Moore) *hld up in rr: effrt and sme hdwy 2f out: sn rdn and nvr rch ldrs* 8/1

00 7 1 3/4 **Dark Oasis**[25] 3277 2-8-13 0 .... FergalLynch 1 53
(K A Ryan) *a in rr* 33/1

00 8 nk **Smoke Me A Kipper (IRE)**[22] 3334 2-8-4 0 .... RoystonFfrench 4 43
(Mrs A Duffield) *chsd ldrs: rdn along 3f out: sn wknd* 50/1

1m 26.41s (-0.59) **Going Correction** -0.20s/f (Firm) 8 Ran SP% 113.5
Speed ratings (Par 94): **95,93,86,86,85 84,82,82**
toteswinger: 1&2 £1.70, 1&3 £5.10, 2&3 £3.60. CSF £6.51 TOTE £4.10: £1.60, £1.10, £2.40; EX 6.20.
Owner Mrs R J Jacobs **Bred** Newsells Park Stud Limited **Trained** Newmarket, Suffolk

FOCUS
Only a modest event, that was dominated by the two horses that headed the market.

NOTEBOOK
Solo Attempt, having her first start on turf, tracked the early pace before quickening away from her market rival inside the final two furlongs. She never looked like being caught after gaining the advantage and is progressing into a useful sort. (op 9-4 tchd 10-3)
Inheritor(IRE) broke smartly and was always up with the leaders. He started his effort at the same time as the winner but could not match her pace, and was ultimately well held. There was a moment of worry for the jockey close to the line, as his mount jinked at the rail and nearly unshipped him. (op 2-1 tchd 11-8)
Little Tokyo(USA), stepping up in trip, led the field until both Solo Attempt and Inheritor kicked on off the final bend. He managed to plug on for third but was completely outpaced. (op 8-1 tchd 7-1)
Sardan Dansar(IRE), a relatively cheap half-sister to the decent handicapper Monte Alto, did not look particularly happy rounding the bend but she stayed on quite well up the home straight despite looking green. She will improve with maturity. (op 20-1)
Digger Derek(IRE) got behind soon after leaving the stalls and never threatened to get involved. (tchd 8-1 and 10-1)

4073 GO RACING IN YORKSHIRE SUMMER FESTIVAL (S) STKS — 5f 212y

3:00 (3:00) (Class 6) 3-Y-0+ £2,047 (£604; £302) Stalls Low

Form RPR
2450 1 **Lethal**[13] 3626 5-8-11 70 .... JamieMoriarty(3) 11 61
(R A Fahey) *mde virtually all: rdn clr 2f out: drvn and kpt on ins fnl f* 4/1[1]

0051 2 3/4 **Messiah Garvey**[12] 3662 4-9-6 58 .... AdrianTNicholls 6 65
(D Nicholls) *in tch: hdwy and wd st: rdn to chse wnr over 1f out: drvn and ev ch whn hung lft ins fnl f: no ex towards fin* 4/1[1]

3030 3 2 1/2 **Whozart (IRE)**[13] 3638 5-9-0 48 .... DanielTudhope 4 51
(A Dickman) *trckd ldng pair: hdwy to chse wnr 2f out: sn rdn and kpt on same pce ins fnl f* 6/1[2]

6444 4 2 1/2 **Rainbow Bay**[27] 3169 5-9-0 55 ....(p) DeanMcKeown 10 43
(Miss Tracy Waggott) *trckd ldrs: effrt 2f out: sn rdn and kpt on same pce* 6/1[2]

3001 5 1/2 **Klarity**[11] 3733 3-8-10 50 ....(e) LiamJones 12 42
(J Pearce) *stdd and swtchd lft s: hld up in rr: hdwy 2f out: sn rdn and styd on ins fnl f: nrst fin* 9/1

16-0 6 1/2 **Zamalik (USA)**[34] 2968 5-9-0 62 .... RoystonFfrench 3 40
(Mrs A Duffield) *chsd ldrs: rdn along over 2f out: sn drvn and one pce* 13/2[3]

42-0 7 1/2 **Mickleberry (IRE)**[190] 79 4-8-9 52 ow3 .... MarkLawson(3) 8 36
(M Brittain) *in rr tl sme late hdwy* 20/1

00-0 8 1 1/2 **Benny The Bus**[8] 3826 6-9-0 53 ....(v[1]) RobertWinston 2 33
(J R Weymes) *in tch: rdn along 3f out: styng on whn n.m.r ins fnl f* 20/1

00-0 9 1 **Petite Mac**[67] 2009 8-8-6 50 .... PJMcDonald(3) 5 25
(N Bycroft) *a towards rr* 12/1

0000 10 1 **Apres Ski (IRE)**[12] 3662 5-8-7 50 .... NBazeley(7) 7 27
(J F Coupland) *s.i.s: a in rr* 40/1

600- 11 hd **Amanda's Lad (IRE)**[453] 1134 8-8-11 49 .... RussellKennemore(3) 9 26
(M C Chapman) *prom: rdn along 3f out: sn wknd* 40/1

0000 12 5 **Marquis De Louvois (IRE)**[11] 3733 3-8-6 50 .... AndrewMullen(3) 1 10
(Mrs A Duffield) *in rr fr 1/2-way* 40/1

1m 13.43s (-0.17) **Going Correction** -0.20s/f (Firm)
WFA 3 from 4yo+ 5lb 12 Ran SP% 116.4
Speed ratings (Par 101): **93,92,88,85,84 84,83,81,80,78 78,71**
toteswinger: 1&2 £4.10, 1&3 £6.80, 2&3 £6.10. CSF £17.45 TOTE £5.60: £1.40, £1.70, £2.90; EX 21.70.There was no bid for the winner.
Owner The Matthewman One Partnership **Bred** A S Reid **Trained** Musley Bank, N Yorks

FOCUS
A particularly weak seller.
Mickleberry(IRE) Official explanation: jockey said filly was unsuited by the course

4074 DARLINGTON OPERATIC SOCIETY'S "THE PIRATE KING" H'CAP — 5f

3:30 (3:30) (Class 4) (0-85,85) 3-Y-0 £4,857 (£1,445; £722; £360) Stalls Low

Form RPR
1-05 1 **Know No Fear**[47] 2570 3-8-8 72 .... RobertWinston 1 80
(J J Quinn) *hld up: hdwy 2f out: rdn over 1f out: styd on to ld ent fnl f: drvn out* 11/4[2]

0-02 2 hd **Sudden Impact (IRE)**[3] 3999 3-9-4 85 .... RussellKennemore(3) 5 92
(Paul Green) *hld up: hdwy on outer 2f out: rdn over 1f out: drvn to chal and ev ch whn hung lft ins fnl f: nt qckn nr fin* 15/2

4131 3 2 **Discanti (IRE)**[25] 3256 3-9-1 79 .... DavidAllan 6 79+
(T D Easterby) *cl up: effrt 2f out: rdn to ld briefly over 1f out: hdd ent fnl f and one pce* 5/2[1]

6643 4 1 3/4 **Kinout (IRE)**[7] 3833 3-8-7 71 .... FergalLynch 4 65
(K A Ryan) *led: rdn along 2f out: drvn and hdd appr fnl f: grad wknd* 3/1[3]

4500 5 nk **Style Award**[23] 3320 3-9-0 81 .... AndrewMullen(3) 3 73
(W J H Ratcliffe) *chsd ldrs: rdn and hdwy 2f out: drvn over 1f out: wknd ent fnl f* 13/2

066 6 2 1/2 **Firenza Bond**[3] 4000 3-8-13 77 .... SilvestreDeSousa 7 60
(G R Oldroyd) *cl up on wd outside: rdn 2f out: sn drvn and wknd* 12/1

2560 7 20 **Baytown Blaze**[19] 3462 3-8-1 70 ....(b[1]) KellyHarrison(5) 2 —
(P S McEntee) *cl up: rdn along and wknd 1/2-way: sn bhd* 33/1

60.49 secs (0.69) **Going Correction** +0.20s/f (Good) 7 Ran SP% 116.0
Speed ratings (Par 102): **102,101,98,95,95 91,59**
toteswinger: 1&2 £5.20, 1&3 £2.60, 2&3 £2.30. CSF £24.05 TOTE £4.90: £1.80, £3.30; EX 25.10.
Owner F D C Racing Club **Bred** B Bargh **Trained** Settrington, N Yorks
■ Stewards' Enquiry : Robert Winston caution: used whip with excessive frequency

FOCUS
A decent sprint handicap run at a sound gallop.
Baytown Blaze Official explanation: trainer's rep said filly finished sore behind

4075 SUBSCRIBE TO RACING UK CLAIMING STKS — 1m 3f 214y

4:00 (4:00) (Class 6) 3-Y-0+ £2,217 (£654; £327) Stalls Low

Form RPR
1024 1 **Elite Land**[15] 3589 5-9-7 49 .... NeilBrown(3) 6 58
(N Bycroft) *trckd ldrs: smooth hdwy on inner 3f out: swtchd rt and effrt wl over 1f out: rdn to ld appr fnl f: edgd rt ins fnl f: styd on strly* 9/2[2]

0436 2 4 **Vincenzio (IRE)**[6] 3891 4-10-0 66 ....(b) MickyFenton 7 56
(C R Egerton) *chsd ldrs: effrt 3f out: rdn and ch 2f out: sn drvn and kpt on same pce* 11/2

03 3 1 1/4 **Bonny Bright Eyes**[40] 2779 3-8-11 0 .... LeeEnstone 2 49
(P C Haslam) *a.p: effrt 3f out: rdn to ld wl over 1f out: drvn and hdd over 1f out: swtchd lft and kpt on same pce* 10/1

2240 4 6 **Tidy (IRE)**[86] 1521 8-9-6 52 ....(v) RobertWinston 15 36
(Micky Hammond) *hld up and bhd: gd hdwy 3f out: rdn to chse ldrs over 1f out: sn drvn and no imp* 14/1

4006 5 1/2 **Rehearsal**[38] 2867 7-10-0 70 ....(p) PaulMulrennan 10 43
(L Lungo) *led: rdn along 3f out: drvn and hdd wl over 1f out: sn wknd* 11/2

5516 6 4 **Shandelight (IRE)**[12] 3687 4-9-9 56 ....(p) RoystonFfrench 8 32
(Mrs A Duffield) *prom: rdn along 3f out: drvn and wknd 2f out* 3/1[1]

0300 7 nk **Nelsons Column (IRE)**[51] 2447 5-9-11 67 .... RussellKennemore(3) 5 36
(G M Moore) *hld up: rdn 1/2-wy: effrt over 5f out: sn rdn along and nvr a factor* 5/1[3]

0-0 8 6 **Barashi**[20] 3402 3-8-13 0 .... JamieMoriarty(3) 9 27
(J Howard Johnson) *chsd ldrs: rdn along 3f out: wknd over 2f out* 50/1

0-0 9 9 **Panamar Besar (IRE)**[24] 3297 3-8-12 0 .... PaulFessey 13 8
(J Howard Johnson) *a in rr* 50/1

10 2 1/4 **River Mint**[41] 4-10-0 0 .... TonyHamilton 11 9
(D W Barker) *dwlt: a in rr* 40/1

0600 11 26 **Sawwaah (IRE)**[16] 3551 11-9-10 67 ....(b[1]) DNolan 14 —
(D Carroll) *hld up in midfield: smooth hdwy to chse ldrs 3f out: rdn over 2f out and sn btn* 14/1

2m 38.92s (0.02) **Going Correction** -0.20s/f (Firm)
WFA 3 from 4yo+ 12lb 11 Ran SP% 119.4
Speed ratings (Par 101): **91,88,87,83,83 80,80,76,70,68 51**
toteswinger: 1&2 £6.40, 1&3 £6.50, 2&3 £9.00. CSF £29.79 TOTE £6.00: £2.20, £2.20, £2.80; EX 28.10.Elite Land was claimed by K A Ryan for £6,000. Rehearsal was subject to a friendly claim.
Owner Mrs J Dickinson **Bred** T Umpleby **Trained** Brandsby, N Yorks
■ Stewards' Enquiry : Neil Brown caution: careless riding

FOCUS
A poor claimer in which the early pace looked sound and the field finished fairly strung out. The winner is on the upgrade but the form is weak.
Shandelight(IRE) Official explanation: jockey said filly slipped on final bend and lost her action

Nelsons Column(IRE) Official explanation: jockey said gelding stumbled leaving the stalls

4076 TURFTV MEDIAN AUCTION MAIDEN STKS — 7f

4:30 (4:33) (Class 6) 3-Y-O — **£2,217** (£654; £327) **Stalls** Low

Form — RPR

00-0 **1** **Bluejain**[25] 3275 3-9-3 64 ... MickyFenton 10 — 65
(Miss Gay Kelleway) *s.i.s and bhd: j. path after 1f: gd hdwy on outer 3f out: rdn to chal ent fnl f: drvn and kpt on to ld nr line* **4/1**[3]

4 **2** *nk* **Manchestermaverick (USA)**[8] 3823 3-9-0 0 ... TravisBlock(3) 4 — 64
(H Morrison) *trckd ldrs: gd hdwy on inner 2f out: rdn to ld wl over 1f out: drvn ins fnl f: hdd and no ex nr fin* **7/2**[2]

3 *1 1/4* **Onebidkintymill (IRE)** 3-9-3 0 ... LiamJones 2 — 61
(M Mullineaux) *s.i.s and bhd: hdwy over 2f out: sn rdn and styd on wl fnl f: nrst fin* **40/1**

0045 **4** *hd* **Imperial Djay (IRE)**[7] 3831 3-9-3 64 ... (b[1]) DNolan 6 — 60
(D Carroll) *hld up in tch: hdwy to chse ldrs 2f out: sn rdn: drvn and kpt on same pce ins fnl f* **9/4**[1]

04 **5** *1/2* **Mill Beattie**[22] 3338 3-8-12 0 ... AndrewElliott 1 — 55+
(G M Moore) *hld up towards rr: stdy hdwy on inner 2f out: rdn to chse ldrs ent fnl f: drvn and kpt on same pce* **11/1**

0-60 **6** *3 3/4* **Sheik'N'Knotsterd**[12] 3690 3-9-3 55 ... DavidAllan 3 — 49
(J F Coupland) *prom: rdn along wl over 2f out and grad wknd* **16/1**

5400 **7** *1 1/4* **Mujada**[84] 1558 3-8-9 48 ... MarkLawson(3) 11 — 40
(M Brittain) *led: rdn along over 2f out: hdd wl over 1f out and sn wknd* **14/1**

2 **8** *3/4* **Naias (IRE)**[14] 3600 3-8-9 0 ... JamieMoriarty(3) 9 — 38
(R A Fahey) *chsd ldrs: rdn along over 2f out and sn wknd* **8/1**

00 **9** *nse* **Stormin Heart (USA)**[67] 2008 3-9-3 0 ... GregFairley 12 — 43
(M Johnston) *prom: rdn along 1/2-way and sn wknd* **12/1**

00-4 **10** *2 1/4* **Peltre**[51] 2466 3-8-12 50 ... TWilliams 5 — 32
(M Brittain) *bhd fr 1/2-way* **14/1**

00 **11** *17* **Tycoon's Buddy**[8] 3823 3-9-3 0 ... DeanMcKeown 8 — —
(E J O'Neill) *prom: hung rt and rn wd st: sn bhd* **33/1**

1m 27.13s (0.13) **Going Correction** -0.20s/f (Firm) — **11 Ran SP% 124.7**
Speed ratings (Par 98): **91,90,89,89,88 84,82,81,81,79 59**
toteswinger: 1&2 £6.40, 1&3 £6.50, 2&3 £9.00. CSF £19.71 TOTE £5.10: £1.70, £1.80, £9.20; EX 18.00.
Owner Countrywide Classics Limited **Bred** David Sugars And Bob Parker **Trained** Exning, Suffolk
■ Stewards' Enquiry : Jamie Moriarty one-day ban: careless riding (Jul 31)

FOCUS
A moderate maiden but the winner is value for more than the official margin.
Peltre Official explanation: jockey said filly was unsuited by the course
Tycoon's Buddy Official explanation: jockey said gelding hung badly right-handed off the final bend

4077 CATTERICKBRIDGE.CO.UK H'CAP — 1m 3f 214y

5:00 (5:00) (Class 5) (0-70,68) 3-Y-O — **£2,590** (£770; £385; £192) **Stalls** Low

Form — RPR

41P0 **1** **Caffari (GER)**[20] 3393 3-8-8 55 ... AndrewElliott 4 — 64+
(K R Burke) *trckd ldrs: rdn along 4f out: swtchd rt and drvn wl over 1f out: styd on u.p to ld ins fnl f: kpt on strly* **10/1**

05-2 **2** *2 1/4* **Next Of Kin (IRE)**[15] 3580 3-9-5 66 ... RobertWinston 8 — 71+
(G A Swinbank) *chsd ldrs: rdn along 4f out: hdwy u.p over 2f out: drvn and edgd lft wl over 1f out: ev ch tl hrd drvn and one pce wl ins fnl f* **5/4**[1]

0000 **3** *1/2* **Templetuohy Max (IRE)**[35] 2926 3-8-2 49 oh2 ... (v[1]) PaulFessey 6 — 53
(J D Bethell) *prom: rdn along 4f out: drvn 2f out: bmpd wl over 1f out: rallied wl u.p ins fnl f: no ex towards fin* **66/1**

0-06 **4** *1* **Jackday (IRE)**[16] 3555 3-8-8 55 ... DavidAllan 7 — 58
(T D Easterby) *hld up in tch: hdwy on outer over 4f out: chsd ldrs over 2f out: rdn to chal and ev ch over 1f out tl drvn and one pce ins fnl f* **9/2**[3]

40-0 **5** *3/4* **Silk Drum (IRE)**[21] 3366 3-9-5 66 ... PaulMulrennan 3 — 68+
(J Howard Johnson) *hld up towards rr: hdwy over 2f out: rdn and styd on to chse ldrs whn nt clr run ins fnl f: nt rcvr* **9/1**

-005 **6** *1* **Rivington Pike (IRE)**[20] 3393 3-8-9 56 ... (v[1]) TonyHamilton 5 — 56
(J J Quinn) *hld up: hdwy over 2f out: rdn wl over 1f out: kpt on ins fnl f: nrst fin* **16/1**

003 **7** *nk* **Miss Serena**[16] 3556 3-8-13 60 ... MickyFenton 9 — 59
(Mrs P Sly) *sn led: rdn along 4f out: drvn wl over 1f out: hdd & wknd ins fnl f* **25/1**

0-66 **8** *4 1/2* **Highland Laddie**[19] 3459 3-9-7 68 ... GregFairley 10 — 60
(C R Egerton) *trckd ldr: cl up 4f out: rdn along 2f out and sn btn* **4/1**[2]

-005 **9** *2 1/4* **Pequeno Dinero (IRE)**[38] 2868 3-7-13 51 ow1 ... KellyHarrison(5) 2 — 40
(C W Fairhurst) *a in rr* **33/1**

000- **10** *53* **Spooky**[256] 6634 3-8-1 51 ... DominicFox(3) 1 — —
(W Storey) *a in rr* **100/1**

2m 36.29s (-2.61) **Going Correction** -0.20s/f (Firm) — **10 Ran SP% 116.9**
Speed ratings (Par 100): **100,98,98,97,97 96,96,93,91,56**
toteswinger: 1&2 £4.70, 1&3 £51.50, 2&3 £28.50. CSF £22.69 CT £826.62 TOTE £11.70: £2.30, £1.30, £15.20; EX 38.40 Place 6: £55.31, Place 5: £46.04..
Owner Richards, Gittins, Burke **Bred** Gestut Gorlsdorf **Trained** Middleham Moor, N Yorks

FOCUS
A moderate handicap.
Silk Drum(IRE) ◆ Official explanation: jockey said gelding was denied a clear run
T/Plt: £47.40 to a £1 stake. Pool: £47,037.65. 723.63 winning tickets. T/Qpdt: £17.60 to a £1 stake. Pool: £2,366.10. 99.30 winning tickets. JR

3836 KEMPTON (A.W) (R-H)

Wednesday, July 16

OFFICIAL GOING: Standard
Wind: Light, against Weather: Fine but cloudy

4078 WEATHERBYS BLOODSTOCK SERVICES APPRENTICE H'CAP (ROUND 7) — 1m 3f (P)

6:20 (6:20) (Class 4) (0-80,80) 4-Y-O+ — **£4,727** (£1,406; £702; £351) **Stalls** High

Form — RPR

0010 **1** **Safari Sundowner (IRE)**[20] 3398 4-9-7 80 ... WilliamCarson(3) 5 — 89+
(P Winkworth) *hld up in last trio: prog on outer fr 4f out: rdn to ld over 2f out: edgd rt but in command over 1f out: styd on wl* **13/2**

0252 **2** *2 1/4* **Show Winner**[28] 3132 5-9-10 80 ... JackMitchell 1 — 85
(A M Balding) *t.k.h: trckd ldr after 3f: chal over 2f out: chsd wnr after: one pce and wl hld fnl f* **5/2**[1]

-104 **3** *1/2* **Aypeeyes (IRE)**[39] 2822 4-9-5 78 ... SimonPearce(3) 7 — 82
(A King) *trckd ldrs: nt qckn and outpcd over 2f out: bmpd along and kpt on fr over 1f out: pressed for 2nd nr fin* **4/1**[3]

3225 **4** *2* **Alexander Guru**[22] 3347 4-8-5 64 ... KMay(3) 8 — 65
(M Blanshard) *t.k.h: led after 2f to over 2f out: sn outpcd and btn* **10/1**

-511 **5** *1/2* **Constant Cheers (IRE)**[13] 3631 5-9-5 78 ... AlanRutter(3) 6 — 78
(W R Swinburn) *t.k.h: hld up bhd ldrs: outpcd over 2f out: n.d after* **7/2**[2]

530- **6** *1 1/2* **Yab Adee**[265] 6459 4-8-2 63 ... KatiaScallan(5) 2 — 61
(M P Tregoning) *dwlt: t.k.h: hld up in last trio: v wd bnd over 3f out: nudged along and kpt on steadily fr over 1f out* **16/1**

040/ **7** *1/2* **Towerofcharlemagne (IRE)**[38] 4708 5-8-8 64 ... (p) JamieJones 3 — 61
(Miss E C Lavelle) *led 2f: trckd ldrs tl wl outpcd fr over 2f out* **33/1**

4103 **8** *1 1/4* **Ross Moor**[19] 3461 6-8-10 69 ... MarkCoumbe(3) 4 — 64
(Mike Murphy) *s.v.s: mostly in last: in tch tl outpcd over 2f out* **8/1**

2m 23.76s (1.86) **Going Correction** +0.175s/f (Slow) — **8 Ran SP% 113.2**
Speed ratings (Par 105): **100,98,98,96,96 95,94,93**
CSF £22.65 CT £72.89 TOTE £9.70: £2.60, £1.80, £1.10; EX 33.00 TRIFECTA toteswinger: 1&2 £4.20, 1&3 £6.00, 2&3 £2.70.
Owner P Winkworth **Bred** Michael Phelan **Trained** Chiddingfold, Surrey

FOCUS
A fair handicap for apprentices, and with the first three home coming from the top of the handicap the form looks solid.
Safari Sundowner(IRE) Official explanation: trainer had no explanation for the improved form shown

4079 SPILLERS NURSERY — 7f (P)

6:50 (6:50) (Class 5) 2-Y-O — **£3,238** (£963; £481; £240) **Stalls** High

Form — RPR

1440 **1** **Grand Honour (IRE)**[39] 2826 2-9-7 83 ... JimmyQuinn 12 — 82
(P Howling) *hld up in midfield: prog on inner 2f out: chsd ldr jst over 1f out: rdn to ld narrowly ins fnl f: asserted nr fin* **9/1**

330 **2** *1/2* **Gassal**[24] 3292 2-8-8 70 ... RHills 11 — 68
(W J Haggas) *mde most: rdn and flashed tail fr 2f out: narrowly hdd ins fnl f: rallied but hld nr fin* **8/1**[3]

630 **3** *1 3/4* **Aegean Warning**[20] 3411 2-8-6 68 ... TedDurcan 13 — 62
(K A Ryan) *hld up in midfield: prog on inner over 2f out: nt qckn over 1f out: kpt on fnl f: no imp on ldng pair* **12/1**

2155 **4** *hd* **Scenic Pass**[5] 3924 2-8-2 64 ... TPO'Shea 4 — 57
(M R Channon) *wnt rt s: trckd ldrs: rdn and nt qckn 2f out: kpt on to dispute 3rd fnl f* **8/1**[3]

0063 **5** *nse* **Fasalee (IRE)**[12] 3693 2-8-5 67 ... NeilPollard 7 — 60
(A P Jarvis) *t.k.h: trckd ldrs: rdn over 2f out: nt qckn over 1f out: disp 3rd fnl f: one pce* **25/1**

221 **6** *1/2* **The Dial House**[38] 2859 2-9-6 82 ... ShaneKelly 6 — 74
(J A Osborne) *dwlt and bmpd s: hld up in last trio: gng wl 3f out: plenty to do whn nt clr run wl over 1f out: pushed along and r.o fnl f: no ch* **11/4**[1]

5404 **7** *1 1/2* **Redhead (IRE)**[12] 3677 2-8-4 66 ... ChrisCatlin 2 — 54
(R Hannon) *pressed ldr to 2f out: wknd jst over 1f out* **16/1**

0023 **8** *shd* **Swingfire (USA)**[12] 3689 2-7-12 60 ... FrankieMcDonald 5 — 48
(R M H Cowell) *nudged s: t.k.h: hld up in rr: brought wd and effrt over 2f out: no imp fnl f* **16/1**

0440 **9** *1 3/4* **Another Luke (IRE)**[20] 3411 2-8-2 64 ow1 ... HayleyTurner 3 — 47
(T J Etherington) *t.k.h: racd wd in midfield: rdn 3f out: btn 2f out* **28/1**

4305 **10** *nse* **Entrancer (IRE)**[23] 3331 2-8-5 67 ... MartinDwyer 9 — 50
(W R Muir) *plld hrd early and hld up in midfield: rdn and no rspnse over 2f out* **33/1**

662 **11** *nk* **Deal Clincher**[21] 3373 2-8-8 70 ... JimCrowley 10 — 53
(P Winkworth) *hld up wl in rr: rdn over 2f out: one pce and nvr on terms* **4/1**[2]

000 **12** *shd* **Barcode**[12] 3674 2-7-12 60 ... DavidKinsella 8 — 42
(R Hannon) *settled in last trio: rdn and no prog over 2f out* **16/1**

003 **13** *4* **Calypso Prince**[22] 3341 2-7-8 63 ow2 ... (v) BillyCray(7) 14 — 35
(M D I Usher) *nvr gng wl: drvn and lost pl on inner 1/2-way: sn toiling in rr* **20/1**

1m 28.35s (2.35) **Going Correction** +0.175s/f (Slow) — **13 Ran SP% 119.2**
Speed ratings (Par 94): **93,92,90,90,90 89,87,87,85,85 85,85,80**
toteswinger: 1&2 £61.30, 1&3 £19.50, 2&3 £30.60. CSF £75.36 CT £615.45 TOTE £11.00: £4.00, £3.60, £3.70; EX 70.40.
Owner Ajaz Ahmed **Bred** Mrs E Kent **Trained** Newmarket, Suffolk
■ Stewards' Enquiry : Shane Kelly one-day ban: careless riding (Jul 31)

FOCUS
A strong-looking juvenile handicap and the winner bore out the old adage about backing top-weights in nurseries. The 'official' ratings are estimated and are intended as a guide.

NOTEBOOK
Grand Honour(IRE), whose previous win came on Polytrack, defied top-weight to get up and win close home. He was fortunate that a gap appeared up the rail at just the right time, but showed a willing attitude to take it. The Group 3 Sirenia Stakes, run here in September, was rather optimistically put forward as a target by connections. (op 12-1)
Gassal ran by far her best race on turf with juice in the ground, and on this evidence she is perfectly suited by the Polytrack surface. She looked the most likely winner for a long way despite showing flashes of temperament, and should be up to winning soon. (tchd 15-2)
Aegean Warning ran a stinker on soft ground last time, but on this evidence has been allotted a workable handicap mark. (op 11-1 tchd 10-1)
Scenic Pass could only keep on at the one pace. She only has a selling win to her credit. (op 15-2)
Fasalee(IRE) appeared to have been flattered by his third to a long odds-on shot at Warwick last time, but this effort proves that there are races to be won with him. (op 20-1 tchd 18-1)
The Dial House, backed into clear favouritism, suffered a hefty barge leaving the stalls and couldn't find any daylight when obviously travelling strongly in the closing stages. There are races to be won with him. Official explanation: jockey said colt suffered interference in running at the start. (op 7-2 tchd 5-2)

4080 E B F EPSOM TRAINERS OPEN DAY THIS SUNDAY MAIDEN FILLIES' STKS — 7f (P)

7:20 (7:24) (Class 4) 2-Y-O — **£4,857** (£1,445; £722; £360) **Stalls** High

Form — RPR

2 **1** **Spanish Cygnet (USA)**[26] 3207 2-9-0 0 ... JimCrowley 7 — 81+
(Mrs A J Perrett) *mde all: rdn and styd on wl fnl 2f: readily hld rivals fnl f* **7/2**[1]

2 *1* **Vitoria (IRE)** 2-9-0 0 ... TedDurcan 14 — 79
(M J Wallace) *trckd ldng pair: wnt 2nd 3f out: kpt on wl enough but nvr quite able to chal wnr* **13/2**

3 *1/2* **Brief Candle** 2-9-0 0 ... AdamKirby 1 — 77+
(W R Swinburn) *hld up in last of main gp: gd prog jst over 2f out to chse ldng pair over 1f out and looked dangerous: shuffled along and effrt petered out fnl f: promising debut* **33/1**

4 *2 1/2* **Starry Sky** 2-9-0 0 ... SebSanders 6 — 71
(Sir Mark Prescott) *s.s: t.k.h and hld up: prog 2f out: to chse ldng trio over 1f out: pushed along and no imp* **8/1**

3 **5** *4* **Black Nun**[14] 3610 2-9-0 0 ... PatDobbs 5 61
(R Hannon) *trckd ldng trio: rdn wl over 2f out: sn outpcd and struggling: no imp after* **4/1**[2]

62 **6** *nk* **Rose Cheval (USA)**[22] 3349 2-9-0 0 ... EdwardCreighton 3 60
(M R Channon) *chsd wnr to 3f out: steadily outpcd* **6/1**[3]

7 *1* **Dubai Legend** 2-9-0 0 ... RichardMullen 13 58
(D M Simcock) *dwlt: sn in tch on inner: outpcd fr over 2f out: n.d after* **16/1**

8 *4 1/2* **Desert Fairy** 2-9-0 0 ... DarryllHolland 10 47
(P W D'Arcy) *lost pl into midfield after 2f: rdn over 2f out: brief effrt sn after: wknd over 1f out* **25/1**

9 *2 1/4* **Harquahala (IRE)** 2-9-0 0 ... ShaneKelly 8 41
(T G Mills) *s.s: in tch in rr tl wknd over 2f out* **14/1**

10 *2 3/4* **Red Stiletto** 2-9-0 0 ... ChrisCatlin 9 34
(Rae Guest) *v green and sn detached in last* **50/1**

0 **11** *nk* **Lady Norlela**[50] 2479 2-8-11 0 ... PatrickHills(3) 4 33
(R Hannon) *racd wd: wl in tch: lost grnd bnd over 3f out: wknd u.p over 2f out* **50/1**

1m 28.24s (2.24) **Going Correction** +0.175s/f (Slow) **11** Ran SP% **104.2**
Speed ratings (Par 93): **94,92,92,89,84 84,83,78,75,72 72**
toteswinger: 1&2 £4.30, 1&3 £15.00, 2&3 £37.60. CSF £19.33 TOTE £4.20: £1.30, £2.10, £6.90; EX 17.30.
Owner Cotton, James, Slade, Tracey **Bred** Mr & Mrs R David Randal **Trained** Pulborough, W Sussex

FOCUS
A useful maiden, featuring a number of promising two-year-old fillies.

NOTEBOOK
Spanish Cygnet(USA) showed the benefit of previous racecourse experience against a field of mostly newcomers by making all. While she looks a good prospect, especially on the sand surface she was bred for, she wouldn't be sure to confirm the form with some of those behind her if they met again. (tchd 4-1)
Vitoria(IRE) ◆, a daughter of leading first-season sire Exceed And Excel, looked to know her job on debut and, always in the vanguard, kept on really well to find only one with previous racecourse experience too good for her. She looks certain to win races. (op 10-1)
Brief Candle ◆ made a most eyecatching racecourse bow. Last of the main group having looked a touch green early, she showed a rare turn of foot to pass seven horses in a matter of strides halfway up the straight, and but for finding herself something of the meat in a sandwich close home might have been angled out to go even closer. Sure to get further, she is a most interesting prospect.
Starry Sky ◆, the first foal out of a smart 1m2f winner, made good progress from the rear to go after the leaders in the closing stages, and was not knocked about. She is sure to improve and will stay further. (op 10-1)
Black Nun who had shown so much promise on her debut here a fortnight ago, was soon left behind when the leaders quickened and might need further already. (op 11-4)
Rose Cheval(USA) was a little disappointing. Early indications are that the Newbury maiden in which she ran second last time is not working out that well. (op 11-2)

4081 DIGIBET.COM LONDON MILE H'CAP (LONDON MILE QUALIFIER) 1m (P)
7:50 (7:52) (Class 5) (0-70,75) 3-Y-0+ **£3,238** (£963; £481; £240) **Stalls** High

Form RPR

6052 **1** **Millfield (IRE)**[10] 3761 5-10-0 **69** ... GeorgeBaker 11 81+
(P R Chamings) *stmbld sn after s: hld up in last pair: gd prog and scythed through field fr 2f out: sustained effrt to ld last 100yds* **6/1**[1]

0001 **2** *1 1/2* **Kaballero (GER)**[15] 3583 7-9-6 **66** ... JamieJones(5) 7 75
(S Gollings) *sn prom: disp 2nd fr 4f out: led over 2f out: carried hd high: hdd and nt qckn last 100yds* **6/1**[1]

0044 **3** *1 1/2* **Gazboolou**[25] 3266 4-9-13 **68** ... FergusSweeney 3 73
(David Pinder) *cl up on outer: rdn over 2f out: styd on fr over 1f out to take 3rd last strides* **16/1**

-402 **4** *nk* **Idesia (IRE)**[42] 2718 4-10-0 **69** ... AdamKirby 14 73
(W R Swinburn) *trckd ldr after 2f: chal over 2f out: pressed new ldr after tl no ex jst ins fnl f: lost 2nd last strides* **13/2**[2]

0601 **5** *1* **Jebel Ali (IRE)**[7] 3836 5-10-6 **75** 6ex ... (v) ChrisCatlin 13 77
(B Gubby) *t.k.h: trckd ldr 2f: stdd: cl up and hrd rdn over 2f out: kpt on same pce: nvr able to chal* **8/1**

4025 **6** *3/4* **Eagle Nebula**[21] 3371 4-9-10 **65** ... (v[1]) DaneO'Neill 12 65
(B R Johnson) *t.k.h: hld up in midfield: effrt to chse ldrs over 1f out: no imp: fdd ins fnl f* **8/1**

6606 **7** *1 1/4* **Copperwood**[68] 1958 3-9-2 **65** ... SteveDrowne 8 61
(M Blanshard) *hld up in midfield on outer: shkn up over 2f out: one pce and no imp over 1f out: fdd* **33/1**

4521 **8** *1 1/2* **Napoletano (GER)**[10] 3764 7-10-2 **71** 6ex ... (p) NCallan 2 65
(S Dow) *stdd s: hld up towards rr: rdn over 2f out: modest prog fnl f: no imp on ldrs* **12/1**

6000 **9** *1/2* **Prince Desire (IRE)**[21] 3384 3-9-7 **70** ... RichardKingscote 5 61
(Tom Dascombe) *mde most to over 2f out: n.m.r sn after: wknd* **15/2**[3]

4002 **10** *1* **Garden Party**[27] 3181 4-10-0 **69** ... FrankieMcDonald 6 60
(Jane Chapple-Hyam) *hld up in midfield and racd wd: rdn over 2f out: no imp: fdd over 1f out* **12/1**

0-30 **11** *3/4* **Affrettando (IRE)**[29] 3116 4-9-9 **64** ... (v[1]) EddieAhern 4 53
(J A R Toller) *hld up but sn trckd ldrs on inner: reminders wl over 2f out: losing pl whn eased over 1f out* **14/1**

-260 **12** *1/2* **Jill Dawson (IRE)**[16] 3561 5-9-5 **60** ... TedDurcan 9 48
(John Berry) *hld up in last trio: brief effrt on inner 2f out: sn no prog and wknd* **14/1**

3002 **13** *3/4* **Wrighty Almighty (IRE)**[21] 3360 6-10-0 **69** ... JimCrowley 1 55
(P R Chamings) *a wl in rr: u.p and no prog wl over 2f out* **12/1**

0-30 **14** *13* **Littleton Telchar (USA)**[18] 3501 8-9-12 **67** ... TPO'Shea 10 23
(S W Hall) *hld up wl in rr and racd wd: u.p and wl btn over 2f out: t.o* **25/1**

1m 40.27s (0.47) **Going Correction** +0.175s/f (Slow)
WFA 3 from 4yo+ 8lb **14** Ran SP% **125.0**
Speed ratings (Par 103): **104,102,101,100,99 98,97,96,95,94 93,93,92,79**
toteswinger: 1&2 £11.70, 1&3 £12.70, 2&3 £44.10. CSF £42.39 CT £581.12 TOTE £6.50: £2.30, £3.00, £4.50; EX 44.90.
Owner Inhurst Players **Bred** Limestone Stud **Trained** Baughurst, Hants
■ Stewards' Enquiry : George Baker caution: careless riding

FOCUS
Mostly moderate types contested this handicap, and they tend to win in their turn.
Jill Dawson(IRE) Official explanation: trainer said, according to jockey, filly made a noise during latter stages

4082 DIGIBET CASINO FILLIES' H'CAP 1m (P)
8:20 (8:23) (Class 4) (0-85,82) 3-Y-0 **£4,727** (£1,406; £702; £351) **Stalls** High

Form RPR

1000 **1** **Dubai Power**[13] 3647 3-8-12 **78** ... AhmedAjtebi(5) 2 88
(C E Brittain) *mde all: gng strly 3f out: rdn and r.o wl fnl 2f: unchal* **16/1**

-221 **2** *2 1/4* **Tatbeeq (IRE)**[13] 3629 3-8-12 **73** ... RHills 1 78
(M A Jarvis) *trckd ldng pair: wnt 2nd 3f out: clr of rest but no imp fnl 2f* **5/2**[1]

1233 **3** *4* **Montiboli (IRE)**[15] 3592 3-8-12 **73** ... NCallan 7 69
(K A Ryan) *hld up bhd ldrs: rdn and hd to one side over 2f out: wnt 3rd over 1f out: no ch ldng pair* **9/2**[2]

2313 **4** *3/4* **Jollyhockeysticks**[5] 3906 3-8-0 **66** ... MCGeran(5) 8 60
(M R Channon) *pushed along on inner to stay in tch: outpcd over 2f out: kpt on u.p fr over 1f out* **5/1**[3]

5 *1 1/4* **Bois Joli (IRE)**[81] 3-9-6 **81** ... JohnEgan 3 72
(M Botti) *hld up in last pair: rdn and no prog over 2f out: n.d after: modest late hdwy* **11/1**

0060 **6** *1* **Dusty Moon**[22] 3351 3-8-13 **74** ... PaulDoe 10 63
(W J Knight) *chsd wnr to 3f out: sn outpcd: wknd fnl f* **9/1**

1 **7** *3* **Nice Matin (USA)**[23] 3318 3-8-11 **72** ... RobertHavlin 9 54
(J A R Toller) *dwlt: t.k.h: hld up in midfield: nt qckn and much tail swishing over 2f out: wknd* **13/2**

-226 **8** *2 1/4* **Smokey Rye**[11] 3744 3-9-2 **77** ... (b) GeorgeBaker 4 54
(G L Moore) *hld up in last pair: drvn and no prog on outer over 2f out* **13/2**

3100 **9** *12* **Centenerola (USA)**[60] 2196 3-9-7 **82** ... MichaelHills 5 31
(B W Hills) *reluctant to enter the stalls: trckd ldrs on outer: wknd over 2f out: eased over 1f out: t.o* **14/1**

1m 39.27s (-0.53) **Going Correction** +0.175s/f (Slow) **9** Ran SP% **121.0**
Speed ratings (Par 99): **109,106,102,102,100 99,96,94,82**
toteswinger: 1&2 £7.00, 1&3 £24.00, 2&3 £1.60. CSF £58.83 CT £223.61 TOTE £21.70: £6.40, £1.10, £1.40; EX 95.80.
Owner Dr Ali Ridha **Bred** Malih L Al Basti **Trained** Newmarket, Suffolk

FOCUS
A fair fillies' handicap in which the winner dictated under a good ride.
Smokey Rye Official explanation: jockey said his saddle slipped

4083 DIGIBET SPORTS BETTING H'CAP 7f (P)
8:50 (8:51) (Class 5) (0-75,75) 3-Y-0 **£3,238** (£963; £481; £240) **Stalls** High

Form RPR

2241 **1** **Autumn Blades (IRE)**[19] 3445 3-9-4 **72** ... TQuinn 12 80
(J W Hills) *hld up in midfield: clsd on ldrs over 2f out: effrt and snatched up wl over 1f out: got through to ld jst over 1f out: hung lft: a holding on* **15/2**[2]

0-21 **2** *hd* **Greystoke Prince**[98] 1274 3-9-2 **70** ... AdamKirby 11 77
(W R Swinburn) *hld up bhd ldrs: rdn and effrt over 2f out: pressed wnr 1f out: kpt on but a hld* **11/4**[1]

160 **3** *2 1/4* **Spin Again (IRE)**[34] 2974 3-9-2 **70** ... SebSanders 6 71
(R M Beckett) *hld up in midfield: rdn and prog on outer over 2f out: styd on to take 3rd nr fin: no imp on ldng pair* **11/4**[1]

1040 **4** *hd* **Valhillen**[14] 3615 3-9-3 **71** ... (p) HayleyTurner 13 71
(M D I Usher) *trckd ldrs: effrt on inner 2f out: cl up over 1f out: one pce u.p* **14/1**

6050 **5** *1* **Anosti**[16] 3554 3-9-7 **75** ... (p) NCallan 8 73
(K A Ryan) *chsd ldr: rdn over 2f out: led wl over 1f out: hdd jst over 1f out: wknd* **10/1**

-632 **6** *2 3/4* **Romantic Verse**[16] 3564 3-8-6 **63** ... PatrickHills(3) 5 53
(W J Haggas) *chsd ldrs: rdn over 2f out: stl chsng over 1f out: wknd ins fnl f* **15/2**[2]

5200 **7** *1 1/2* **Too Grand**[12] 3678 3-8-2 **56** oh6 ... ChrisCatlin 3 42
(J J Bridger) *dwlt: wl in rr and wd: modest late prog u.p: nvr a factor* **25/1**

-051 **8** *1 1/4* **Redarsene**[40] 2805 3-8-13 **72** ... JamieJones(5) 7 55
(M G Quinlan) *dwlt: towards rr: hanging bdly fr over 2f out: eased fnl f* **14/1**

2046 **9** *hd* **Connor's Choice**[24] 3298 3-9-3 **71** ... MichaelHills 10 53
(Andrew Turnell) *led at brisk pce to wl over 1f out: immediately btn* **8/1**[3]

00-6 **10** *2 1/2* **Starfinch**[62] 2126 3-8-2 **56** oh10 ... JimmyQuinn 9 32
(J J Bridger) *dwlt: wl in rr: brief effrt on inner over 2f out: sn no prog* **50/1**

-660 **11** *3/4* **Oxbridge**[19] 3441 3-7-13 **57** oh1 ow1 ... AhmedAjtebi(5) 4 32
(J M Bradley) *a wl in rr: rdn and struggling 3f out* **40/1**

0005 **12** *6* **Ike Quebec (FR)**[13] 3653 3-9-0 **75** ... (b) HarryPoulton(7) 1 32
(J R Boyle) *racd wd: in tch to 1/2-way: sn bhd: t.o* **20/1**

1m 26.85s (0.85) **Going Correction** +0.175s/f (Slow) **12** Ran SP% **123.4**
Speed ratings (Par 100): **102,101,99,98,97 94,92,91,91,88 87,80**
toteswinger: 1&2 £6.00, 1&3 £6.90, 2&3 £3.20. CSF £28.61 CT £75.46 TOTE £7.00: £3.00, £1.70, £1.20; EX 22.00.
Owner J W Hills **Bred** Dr D Crone & P Lafarge & P Johnston **Trained** Upper Lambourn, Berks
■ Stewards' Enquiry : T Quinn caution: used whip without allowing sufficient time to respond

FOCUS
A modest handicap.
Romantic Verse Official explanation: jockey said that filly hung left
Redarsene Official explanation: jockey said his saddle slipped

4084 METROPOLIS H'CAP 7f (P)
9:20 (9:23) (Class 6) (0-65,65) 3-Y-0+ **£2,047** (£453; £453) **Stalls** High

Form RPR

0420 **1** **Sovereignty (JPN)**[41] 2758 6-9-9 **61** ... DaneO'Neill 11 73
(D K Ivory) *hld up bhd ldrs: gng wl 3f out: plld out and effrt 2f out: rdn to ld 1f out: sn in command* **10/1**

0240 **2** *2* **Guildenstern (IRE)**[7] 3839 6-9-6 **58** ... JimmyQuinn 1 65
(P Howling) *bdly bmpd s: wl in rr: effrt on inner over 2f out: prog over 1f out: kpt on wl fnl f* **16/1**

0 **2** *dht* **Anthill**[48] 2533 4-9-7 **59** ... GeorgeBaker 7 66
(I A Wood) *pressed ldrs: rdn to chal over 2f out: upsides but hanging fr 2f out tl outpcd ins fnl f* **8/1**

0042 **4** *1 1/4* **Grizedale (IRE)**[7] 3842 9-9-5 **57** ... (tp) PaulDoe 10 62+
(M J Attwater) *trckd ldrs: chal fr 2f out: led briefly jst over 1f out: no ex* **5/1**[2]

2030 **5** *2 1/2* **Straight Face (IRE)**[7] 3839 4-9-3 **55** ... (b) DarryllHolland 9 51
(Miss Gay Kelleway) *led 2f: pressed ldr: led over 2f out: hdd jst over 1f out: wknd ins fnl f* **5/1**[2]

0605 **6** *3/4* **Morse (IRE)**[8] 3825 7-9-8 **60** ... SebSanders 5 54
(J A Osborne) *wnt bdly lft s: chsd ldrs but rdn after 2f: lost pl and struggling 3f out: plugged on* **10/1**

-404 **7** *1 1/4* **Quaglino Way (GR)**[10] 3764 4-9-13 **65** ... JimCrowley 13 56
(P R Chamings) *led after 2f to over 2f out: styd upsides to over 1f out: wknd rapidly fnl f* **10/3**[1]

0404 **8** *3/4* **Jessica Wigmo**[18] 3481 5-9-0 **57** ... MarkCoumbe(5) 4 46
(A W Carroll) *s.s: wl in rr: rdn to chse clr ldng gp over 2f out: no imp: fdd* **11/1**

0000 **9** 1 3/4 **Hollow Jo**[18] 3506 8-9-10 **62** ... TQuinn 8 46
(J R Jenkins) *struggling off the pce after 3f: nvr a factor* **20/1**

5000 **10** 3/4 **Mr Rev**[33] 2991 5-9-2 **54** ... SteveDrowne 12 36
(J M Bradley) *hld up wl in rr: nvr a factor* **33/1**

4426 **11** 3 1/4 **Million Percent**[15] 3583 9-9-2 **61** ... WilliamCarson(7) 14 35
(C R Dore) *pressed ldrs: hrd rdn wl over 2f out: wknd wl over 1f out* **7/1**[3]

3400 **12** 3 **Grand Assault**[32] 3034 5-9-2 **54** ... AdamKirby 3 19
(G C Bravery) *bdly bmpd s: a bhd: struggling fr 1/2-way* **20/1**

1m 27.1s (1.10) **Going Correction** +0.175s/f (Slow) **12** Ran SP% **124.9**
Speed ratings (Par 101): **100,97,97,96,93 92,91,90,88,87 83,80**
toteswinger: 1&2 £11.50, 1&3 £16690, 2&3 £25.50. TOTE £14.70: £3.50 TRIFECTA 2nd pl: A 3.00, G 5.40; Ex: S-A 61.80, S_G 64.50; CSF: S-A 45.10, S-G 81.48; T/C S-A-G 659.02, S-G-A 691.72. Place 6 £ 60.51, Place.
Owner Radlett Racing **Bred** Darley Stud Management, L L C **Trained** Radlett, Herts

FOCUS
A moderate handicap.
Guildenstern(IRE) ◆ Official explanation: jockey said gelding suffered interference at the start
Jessica Wigmo Official explanation: jockey said mare was lame
T/Jkpt: Not won. T/Plt: £130.20 to a £1 stake. Pool: £63,342.43. 355.13 winning tickets. T/Qpdt: £6.00 to a £1 stake. Pool: £5,705.40. 696.50 winning tickets. JN

3843

LINGFIELD (L-H)

Wednesday, July 16

OFFICIAL GOING: Turf course - good to firm (9.1); all-weather - standard
Wind: modest half against Weather: bright, partly overcast

4085 ASHURST WOOD MAIDEN STKS — 1m 1f
2:20 (2:21) (Class 5) 3-4-Y-O — £2,729 (£806; £403) Stalls Low

Form — RPR

0- **1** **Who's This (IRE)**[403] 2455 4-9-12 0 ... AdamKirby 8 83+
(W R Swinburn) *s.i.s: hld up in tch: hdwy to ld over 2f out: hung rt 2f out: clr ent fnl f: eased towards fin* **12/1**

0- **2** 4 **Plavius (USA)**[274] 6252 3-9-3 0 ... LDettori 9 74+
(Saeed Bin Suroor) *chsd ldr tl over 3f out: ev ch and carried rt 2f out: chsd wnr ent fnl f: one pce and no imp after* **5/4**[1]

4002 **3** 3 1/4 **Talayeb**[25] 3275 3-9-3 75 ... (p) RHills 7 65
(M P Tregoning) *led: hung rt bnd over 3f out: hdd over 2f out: wknd ent fnl f* **15/8**[2]

0 **4** 4 1/2 **Cape Roberto (IRE)**[36] 2919 3-9-3 0 ... JohnEgan 3 56
(Jamie Poulton) *t.k.h: hld up off the pce in midfield: hdwy on inner over 3f out: chsd ldng trio over 1f out: plugged on but n.d* **33/1**

5 2 1/4 **Magpie (IRE)** 3-9-3 0 ... TQuinn 6 51+
(B G Powell) *v.s.a: wl bhd: styd on past btn horse fnl 2f: swtchd rt ins fnl f: n.d* **16/1**

50 **6** 1 **Sacred Flame (USA)**[14] 3611 3-8-12 0 ... JamieSpencer 2 44
(B J Meehan) *taken down early and ponied to s: chsd ldrs: hung lft ent fnl f 2f out: sn wknd* **11/2**[3]

4065 **7** 11 **Ma Ridge**[41] 2756 4-9-5 47 ... HarryPoulton(7) 10 27
(T D McCarthy) *chsd ldrs: wnt 2nd and rn wd bnd over 3f out: hung lft and wknd fr 3f out* **50/1**

00 **8** 11 **Steady Gaze**[6] 3894 3-9-3 0 ... (t) PaulDoe 5 3
(M A Allen) *s.i.s: bhd: stmbld 7f out: rn v wd bnd over 3f out: t.o after* **100/1**

0-00 **9** 30 **Sarah's Boy**[83] 1586 3-9-3 47 ... HayleyTurner 1 —
(S Dow) *t.k.h: hld up in rr: lost tch over 4f out: wl t.o fnl 2f* **66/1**

00- **10** 45 **Al Mogeer (IRE)**[214] 7152 3-9-3 0 ... PatCosgrave 4 —
(P J McBride) *sn detached in last: hopelessly t.o fr 1/2-way* **66/1**

1m 55.01s (-1.59) **Going Correction** -0.10s/f (Good)
WFA 3 from 4yo 9lb **10** Ran SP% **117.1**
Speed ratings (Par 103): **103,99,96,92,90 89,79,70,43,3**
toteswinger: 1&2 £5.40, 1&3 £5.90, 2&3 £1.50. CSF £27.60 TOTE £18.80: £2.90, £1.10, £1.40; EX 39.10 Trifecta £157.70 Pool: £383.66. 1.80 winning units..
Owner Alan Le Herissier **Bred** L Montgomery And D Hyland **Trained** Aldbury, Herts

FOCUS
No strength in depth to this maiden but the first three home set at least a fair standard.
Sarah's Boy Official explanation: jockey said that gelding did not handle the final bend

4086 EDENBRIDGE H'CAP — 1m 2f
2:50 (2:51) (Class 6) (0-65,65) 3-Y-O — £2,047 (£604; £302) Stalls Low

Form — RPR

4002 **1** **Mahadee (IRE)**[10] 3763 3-9-7 **65** ... (b) NCallan 5 71
(C E Brittain) *t.k.h: hld up towards rr: swtchd rt and hdwy over 2f out: rdn and str chal ent fnl f: r.o to ld nr fin* **11/2**[1]

3113 **2** 1/2 **Amicable Terms**[13] 3656 3-9-4 **62** ... TedDurcan 4 67
(Rae Guest) *hld up in midfield: hdwy to chse ldrs over 2f out: chsd wnr over 1f out: ev ch fnl f: one pce nr fin* **7/1**[3]

-636 **3** 1/2 **Dusk**[30] 3095 3-9-4 **62** ... (b[1]) JimmyQuinn 7 66
(J L Dunlop) *t.k.h: hld up towards rr: gd hdwy 2f out: ev ch ins fnl f: nt qckn towards fin* **8/1**

0100 **4** hd **Nikolaievich (IRE)**[17] 3525 3-9-4 **62** ... LDettori 3 66
(P F I Cole) *sn pushed along to chse ldr: rdn to ld wl over 2f out: hrd pressed ent fnl f: hdd and lost 3 pls towards fin* **12/1**

-002 **5** 2 **Mystic Art (IRE)**[6] 3886 3-9-5 **63** ... (p) WilliamBuick 13 63
(C R Egerton) *chsd ldrs: stmbld appr bnd over 3f out: sn rdn and outpcd: styd on again u.p fnl f* **7/1**[3]

-602 **6** 1 1/2 **Highland Homestead**[12] 3690 3-9-1 **62** ... JamesMillman(3) 9 59+
(B R Millman) *s.i.s: hld up in rr: rdn and no hdwy 3f out: nt clr run briefly 2f out: styd on fnl f: nvr trbld ldrs* **7/1**[3]

5002 **7** nk **Tantris (IRE)**[9] 3781 3-9-5 **63** ... ShaneKelly 2 59
(J A Osborne) *t.k.h: chsd ldrs: rdn to chse ldr over 2f out tl over 1f out: wknd ins fnl f* **8/1**

4-05 **8** shd **Coach And Four (USA)**[29] 3117 3-9-7 **65** ... JamieSpencer 12 61
(S A Callaghan) *stdd s: hld up in rr: drvn and effrt over 3f out: kpt on but nvr pce to trble ldrs* **6/1**[2]

00-0 **9** 3/4 **Epsom Salts**[7] 3799 3-8-13 **57** ... IanMongan 8 51
(P M Phelan) *in tch: hdwy to chse ldrs and rdn 3f out: wknd ent fnl f* **33/1**

-000 **10** 3 1/2 **House Of Tudor**[26] 3206 3-8-13 **57** ... (p) FergusSweeney 11 44
(David Pinder) *s.i.s: a bhd: no ch fnl 2f* **50/1**

-600 **11** nk **Contrada**[34] 2977 3-9-4 **62** ... (b[1]) SteveDrowne 1 49
(R Charlton) *led: rdn and hdd wl over 2f out: wknd wl over 1f out: eased ins fnl f* **12/1**

0-26 **12** hd **Highly Regal (IRE)**[34] 2984 3-9-4 **62** ... GeorgeBaker 6 48
(R A Teal) *in tch: rdn and struggling 3f out: n.d fnl 2f* **12/1**

0016 **13** 9 **Landikhaya (IRE)**[9] 3799 3-8-13 **57** ... (p) PatCosgrave 10 25
(D K Ivory) *s.i.s: hld up towards rr: hdwy 4f out: rdn over 3f out: sn struggling: wl bhd and eased ins fnl f* **9/1**

2m 10.45s (-0.05) **Going Correction** -0.10s/f (Good) **13** Ran SP% **127.4**
Speed ratings (Par 98): **96,95,95,95,93 92,92,91,91,88 88,88,80**
toteswinger: 1&2 £5.80, 1&3 £10.00, 2&3 £6.30. CSF £46.46 CT £320.94 TOTE £7.70: £2.50, £1.90, £2.70; EX 30.50 Trifecta £162.50 Part won. Pool: £219.62. 0.20 winning units..
Owner Saeed Manana **Bred** Darley **Trained** Newmarket, Suffolk

FOCUS
A modest but very competitive three-year-old handicap. The pace seemed fair.
Mystic Art(IRE) Official explanation: jockey said that gelding stumbled on the final bend

4087 SMP SILVER ANNIVERSARY H'CAP — 2m
3:20 (3:20) (Class 5) (0-75,74) 3-Y-O+ — £2,590 (£770; £385; £192) Stalls Low

Form — RPR

4303 **1** **Swingkeel (IRE)**[12] 3685 3-8-11 **74** ... EddieAhern 3 86+
(J L Dunlop) *chsd ldr tl rdn to ld and qcknd appr bnd over 3f out: styd on wl and in command after: pushed out fnl f* **2/1**[1]

4-12 **2** 2 1/4 **Lady Dedlock**[47] 2567 4-9-8 **68** ... RobertHavlin 4 77
(Jamie Poulton) *chsd ldng pair: rdn to chse wnr over 2f out: no imp and wl hld fnl f* **3/1**[2]

0502 **3** 2 **Mister Completely (IRE)**[14] 3613 7-8-9 **55** oh2 ... (v) EdwardCreighton 2 62
(Ms J S Doyle) *in tch in midfield: rdn over 3f out: chsd ldng pair over 1f out: plugged on same pce u.p* **5/1**

2444 **4** 2 3/4 **Natural Action**[18] 3480 4-9-7 **74** ... (p) JPHamblett(7) 5 77
(W Jarvis) *hld up in last pair: outpcd downhill appr bnd over 3f out: no real imp u.p fnl 3f* **10/3**[3]

5416 **5** 3 3/4 **Foreign King (USA)**[19] 3448 4-9-5 **65** ... LPKeniry 1 64
(J W Mullins) *led tl over 3f out: lost 2nd over 2f out: steadily fdd* **10/1**

20 **6** 1/2 **Ashmolian (IRE)**[25] 3250 5-8-9 **55** oh5 ... SamHitchcott 6 53
(Miss Z C Davison) *a last: outpcd over 3f out: n.d* **20/1**

3m 38.99s (4.19) **Going Correction** -0.10s/f (Good)
WFA 3 from 4yo+ 17lb **6** Ran SP% **111.9**
Speed ratings (Par 103): **85,83,82,81,79 79**
toteswinger: 1&2 £2.10, 1&3 £2.80, 2&3 £2.80. CSF £8.19 TOTE £2.80: £1.50, £2.10; EX 8.20.
Owner Mrs M E Slade **Bred** R J Cornelius **Trained** Arundel, W Sussex

FOCUS
Just a fair staying handicap, John Dunlop's progressive three-year-old taking advantage of the huge weight-for-age allowance at this trip.
Mister Completely(IRE) Official explanation: jockey said gelding hung left

4088 EUROPEAN BREEDERS' FUND MAIDEN FILLIES' STKS — 6f (P)
3:50 (3:50) (Class 5) 2-Y-O — £3,561 (£1,059; £529; £264) Stalls Low

Form — RPR

4 **1** **Carina Nebula (USA)**[15] 3584 2-9-0 0 ... JimCrowley 3 69
(T G Mills) *led for 1f: chsd ldr after: rdn over 2f out: kpt on u.p to ld fnl 100yds: all out* **10/1**

24 **2** 3/4 **Sterling Sound (USA)**[22] 3349 2-9-0 ... MartinDwyer 6 67
(M P Tregoning) *chsd ldr tl led after 1f: rdn over 1f out: hdd and no ex fnl 100yds* **7/4**[1]

2 **3** 3/4 **Raise All In (IRE)**[20] 3412 2-9-0 0 ... RichardSmith 2 65
(R Hannon) *chsd ldrs: pushed along and outpcd 1/2-way: rallied on inner 2f out: kpt on same pce ins fnl f* **7/4**[1]

0 **4** 1/2 **On The Feather**[21] 3378 2-9-0 0 ... StephenCarson 7 63
(P Winkworth) *chsd ldrs: hdwy to press ldrs on outer over 2f out: rdn and unable qck wl over 1f out: kpt on again ins fnl f* **14/1**

5 5 **Bussell Along (IRE)** 2-9-0 0 ... JamieSpencer 8 48
(M L W Bell) *s.i.s: bhd: c wd bnd 2f out: sme late hdwy: nvr on terms* **15/2**[2]

6 3/4 **Ageebah** 2-9-0 0 ... SebSanders 1 46
(C E Brittain) *v.s.a: rn green and wl bhd: sme hdwy 1/2-way: n.d* **9/1**[3]

06 **7** 3/4 **Rapanui Belle**[17] 3528 2-9-0 0 ... FergusSweeney 4 44
(G L Moore) *t.k.h: chsd ldrs: rdn and wknd 2f out: fdd bdly fnl f* **33/1**

8 18 **All Angel** 2-9-0 0 ... SaleemGolam 5 —
(M D Squance) *s.i.s: a outpcd in rr: t.o fnl f* **50/1**

1m 13.58s (1.68) **Going Correction** +0.15s/f (Slow) **8** Ran SP% **115.2**
Speed ratings (Par 91): **94,93,92,91,84 83,82,58**
toteswinger: 1&2 £4.60, 1&3 £4.30, 2&3 £1.30. CSF £28.20 TOTE £11.00: £2.30, £1.10, £1.10; EX 24.30 Trifecta £95.30 Pool: £488.48. 3.79 winning units..
Owner Mrs L M Askew **Bred** Flaxman Holdings Ltd **Trained** Headley, Surrey

FOCUS
Just a modest fillies' maiden.

NOTEBOOK
Carina Nebula(USA)'s debut fourth over course and distance represented pretty moderate form, but she improved significantly on that effort to get off the mark. This was an ordinary race, but there might be a little more to come and she should be competitive in nurseries. (op 15-2)
Sterling Sound(USA), dropped back from 7f, showed good early speed, but she found one too strong in the straight and could not really build on the form of her first two efforts. She does not seem to be progressing, but might do better now she is qualified for nurseries. (op 15-8 tchd 13-8)
Raise All In(IRE), a seven-length second to subsequent Listed winner Saxford on her debut in a novice event at Newcastle, proved rather disappointing in only managing third in what was a modest maiden. She might want 7f. (op 2-1 tchd 9-4 in places)
On The Feather looked better than the bare form on her debut at Salisbury and this was a respectable effort. She could be one for an ordinary nursery later in the season. (op 12-1)
Bussell Along(IRE), a 28,000gns daughter of Mujadil, first foal of a 7f juvenile winner, offered little but she is entitled to come on a fair bit for the experience. Official explanation: jockey said filly ran green (op 13-2)
Ageebah ◆, a 40,000gns daughter of Acclamation, half-sister to sprint winners Twosheetstothewind and Azygous, was absolutely clueless and is open to significant improvement. (op 12-1 tchd 14-1)

4089 E B F PAUL KELLEWAY MEMORIAL CLASSIFIED STKS — 1m (P)
4:20 (4:20) (Class 3) 3-Y-O+ — £8,411 (£2,519; £1,259; £630; £314) Stalls High

Form — RPR

1111 **1** **Master Of Arts (USA)**[23] 3319 3-8-9 **89** ... SebSanders 5 103+
(Sir Mark Prescott) *chsd ldng pair: rousted along 4f out: led 2f out: sn rdn clr: easily* **4/6**[1]

-520 **2** 4 1/2 **Hazzard County (USA)**[36] 2905 4-9-3 **87** ... RichardMullen 1 95
(D M Simcock) *led briefly: chsd ldr tl over 2f out: rdn jst over 2f out: chsd wnr fr over 1f out: no imp* **7/1**[3]

304- **3** 2 **Furnace (IRE)**[369] 3503 4-9-3 **90** ... JamieSpencer 4 90
(M L W Bell) *stdd s: hld up in last pair: rdn over 2f out: modest 3rd and hanging lft fr over 1f out* **4/1**[2]

0050 **4** 7 **Vortex**[13] 3635 9-9-3 **90** ... (e) JimmyQuinn 2 74
(Miss Gay Kelleway) *hld up in last pair: rdn and effrt on inner 2f out: no prog and wl btn over 1f out* **7/1**[3]

1265 **5** 3/4 **Dubai Meydan (IRE)**[5] 3897 3-8-9 84..............................(b[1]) JohnEgan 3 64
(Miss Gay Kelleway) *dwlt: sn pushed up to ld: rdn and hdd 2f out: sn wknd* **12/1**

1m 37.14s (-1.06) **Going Correction** +0.15s/f (Slow)
WFA 3 from 4yo+ 8lb **5** Ran SP% **112.7**
Speed ratings (Par 107): **111,106,104,97,93**
CSF £6.25 TOTE £1.60: £1.10, £3.00; EX 6.50.
Owner Eclipse Thoroughbreds-Osborne House III **Bred** Cyril Humphris **Trained** Newmarket, Suffolk

FOCUS
A few useful types took part in a good little race for the grade, but the ultra-progressive winner turned it into something of a procession.

NOTEBOOK
Master Of Arts(USA) started his winning run off a mark of 58, completed his nap hand in grand style here, and is surely heading towards a three-figure rating before too long. Typically, he took a bit of rousting before he hit top gear, but once he did the race was over as a contest in a matter of strides.He is an archetypal product of the Prescott yard, having had three quiet runs as a backward two-year-old, and has grown physically into a quite imposing sort. He needs soft gound on turf, but acts perfectly well on Polytrack also. He could well be up to winning a major handicap an some stage in the near future. (tchd 4-5)
Hazzard County(USA) gained his only win in 15 starts round here and definitely seems better on Polytrack on turf. He won't always bump into horses as progressive as this winner and will get plenty of chances on this surface to go one better. (tchd 15-2)
Furnace(IRE) had not been seen since last summer's July meeting at Newmarket, and while in the cirumstances this was a satisfactory reappearance, he will need to come on plenty if he is to be competitive from his current mark. (op 5-1)
Vortex was running his last race in an event that honoured his trainer's late father. He was bought out of Sir Michael Stoute's yard where he had just four starts and Gay Kelleway managed to turn him into a true globe-trotter, winning 17 races. He goes down into the annals as a great credit to this connections. (tchd 6-1)
Dubai Meydan(IRE) was lit-up by first-time blinkers, and having set a strongish pace folded tamely once challenged. He has a stiff enough handicap mark for what he's achieved. (tchd 14-1)

4090 FOREST ROW H'CAP — 6f (P)
4:50 (4:50) (Class 5) (0-75,75) 3-Y-O — **£2,590** (£770; £385; £192) **Stalls** Low

Form RPR

0241 **1** **Lord Deevert**[12] 3678 3-8-3 57 ow1.............................. AlanDaly 4 64
(W G M Turner) *mde all: rdn 2f out: clr over 1f out: styd on wl* **7/1**[2]

500 **2** 1 1/4 **Al Gillani (IRE)**[25] 3268 3-8-2 56 oh1.............................. DavidKinsella 5 59
(J R Boyle) *t.k.h: chsd ldrs: rdn to chse wnr jst over 2f out: kpt on same pce fnl f* **20/1**

0-1 **3** nk **Valatrix (IRE)**[48] 2546 3-9-0 73.............................. JackMitchell(5) 1 75+
(C F Wall) *s.i.s: towards rr on inner: rdn and hdwy 2f out: chsd ldng pair and swtchd rt ins fnl f: r.o but nvr rchd ldng pair* **7/2**[1]

-430 **4** 1 **Blue Zenith (IRE)**[21] 3381 3-8-8 62.............................. LPKeniry 2 61
(J S Moore) *hld up in midfield: rdn and edgd out off rail wl over 1f out: styd on fnl f: nt rch ldrs* **25/1**

6004 **5** 1 1/2 **Balata**[33] 2991 3-8-12 66.............................. RobertHavlin 8 60+
(B R Millman) *s.i.s: bhd: rdn 2f out: r.o fnl f: nvr rchd ldrs* **12/1**

00-0 **6** 3/4 **Todber**[21] 3379 3-8-5 59.............................. MartinDwyer 7 51
(M P Tregoning) *racd in midfield: rdn and no prog over 2f out: plugged on ins fnl f: nvr pce to threaten ldrs* **8/1**[3]

0654 **7** nse **Liberty Valance (IRE)**[14] 3609 3-9-4 72..............................(t) SebSanders 10 63
(S Kirk) *racd wd: chsd wnr 4f out tl over 2f out: wknd ent fnl f* **8/1**[3]

0001 **8** nk **Minwir (IRE)**[20] 3395 3-8-4 58..............................(v) WilliamBuick 9 49
(M Quinn) *chsd ldrs: rdn and nt qckn over 2f out: no ch w ldrs after* **14/1**

10-6 **9** 1/2 **Dresden Doll (USA)**[32] 3031 3-9-7 75.............................. JamieSpencer 3 64
(M L W Bell) *chsd wnr tl 4f out: rdn 1/2-way: wknd over 1f out: wl btn and eased towards fin* **7/2**[1]

2-31 **10** 1 1/2 **Moon Bound (IRE)**[182] 183 3-9-5 73.............................. RichardMullen 12 57
(W R Muir) *stdd and dropped in bhd after s: t.k.h: hld up in rr: a bhd* **8/1**[3]

-040 **11** 1/2 **River N' Blues (IRE)**[30] 3086 3-8-5 59.............................. JimmyQuinn 11 42
(Dr J R J Naylor) *stdd after s: hld up in rr: n.d* **33/1**

0606 **12** 4 **Bombardier Wells**[20] 3418 3-9-6 74..............................(b) StephenCarson 6 44
(Eve Johnson Houghton) *squeezed s and slowly away: t.k.h and hld up in rr: rdn and struggling over 2f out: no ch after* **14/1**

1m 12.88s (0.98) **Going Correction** +0.15s/f (Slow) **12** Ran SP% **122.9**
Speed ratings (Par 100): **99,97,96,95,93 92,92,92,91,89 88,83**
toteswinger: 1&2 £31.40, 1&3 £4.20, 2&3 £19.60. CSF £144.97 CT £582.25 TOTE £11.00: £2.40, £8.80, £2.10; EX 240.10 Place 6: £8.60, Place 5 £7.12. Not won..
Owner Mrs M S Teversham **Bred** Mrs Monica Teversham **Trained** Sigwells, Somerset

FOCUS
A modest three-year-old sprint handicap in which few got involved.
T/Plt: £9.60 to a £1 stake. Pool: £52,794.02. 4,007.22 winning tickets. T/Qpdt: £5.40 to a £1 stake. Pool: £2,402.50. 325.10 winning tickets. SP

4091 - 4094a (Foreign Racing) - See Raceform Interactive

3616 LEOPARDSTOWN (L-H)
Wednesday, July 16

OFFICIAL GOING: Good

4095a SILVER FLASH STKS (GROUP 3) (FILLIES) — 7f
6:30 (6:30) 2-Y-O — **£33,507** (£9,830; £4,683; £1,595)

RPR

1 **Luminous Eyes (IRE)**[9] 3803 2-8-12..............................(t) PJSmullen 2 102
(D K Weld, Ire) *mde all: rdn over 1f out: kpt on strly fnl f* **9/2**[3]

2 2 1/2 **Chintz (IRE)**[19] 3466 2-8-12.............................. JMurtagh 3 96
(David Wachman, Ire) *trckd ldrs in 3rd: impr into 2nd 1 1/2f out: sn rdn: no imp on ldr fnl f* **8/11**[1]

3 3 1/2 **Mark Of An Angel (IRE)**[63] 2110 2-8-12.............................. DPMcDonogh 5 87
(Kevin Prendergast, Ire) *dwlt and in rr: rdn into 4th 2f out: styd on u.p to 3rd 1f out: no imp on same pce* **14/1**

4 hd **Lac A Dancer (IRE)**[19] 3465 2-8-12.............................. KLatham 4 87
(G M Lyons, Ire) *racd mainly 4th: reminder bef 1/2-way: dropped to rr ent st: kpt u.p fnl f* **14/1**

5 9 **Aaroness (USA)**[41] 2765 2-8-12.............................. KJManning 6 64
(J S Bolger, Ire) *chsd ldrs in 2nd: rdn 2f out: no ex in 3rd 1 1/2f out: sn wknd* **3/1**[2]

1m 29.65s (-0.65) **Going Correction** 0.0s/f (Good) **6** Ran SP% **114.4**
Speed ratings: **103,100,96,95,85**
CSF £8.70 TOTE £4.40: £2.00, £1.10; DF 8.50.
Owner Dr R Lambe **Bred** Ballylinch Stud **Trained** The Curragh, Co Kildare

NOTEBOOK
Luminous Eyes(IRE) had shown good improvement from her debut run to win by five and a half lengths over this trip on soft ground at Roscommon nine days previously, and she stepped up again here to land this Group 3 event in good style on appreciably quicker ground. The winner made virtually all, and after quickening up well under two furlongs out, she ran on well to the line. The Group 2 Debutante Stakes at the Curragh next month followed by the Group 1 Moyglare Stud Stakes is now the plan. (op 4/1)
Chintz(IRE), a course and distance winner on her debut before finishing second to the smart Shimah in a 6f Listed race at the Curragh, raced in third place and briefly looked as if she might get trapped for room two furlongs out. That did not happen and she was soon sent in pursuit of Luminous Eyes, only to make little impression inside the final furlong. (op 1/1)
Mark Of An Angel(IRE), fifth behind the very useful Cuis Ghaire on her debut over 6f at Naas, raced in rear until improving one place before the turn in. She kept on, but never posed a serious threat. (op 8/1)
Lac A Dancer(IRE), placed once from three previous attempts, was never able to mount a serious challenge, although she did keep plugging away. (op 12/1)
Aaroness(USA), a five-length winner at Tipperary on her second start, raced in second place. She was unable to hold her position on the outside of Chintz two furlongs out and her effort petered out tamely with her jockey easing her before the finish. (op 5/2 tchd 100/30)

4100a CHALLENGE STKS (LISTED RACE) — 1m 6f
9:00 (9:00) 3-Y-O+ — **£23,933** (£7,022; £3,345; £1,139)

RPR

1 **Profound Beauty (IRE)**[17] 3537 4-9-6 108.............................. PJSmullen 5 109+
(D K Weld, Ire) *trckd ldrs: 6th 1/2-way: impr to 4th 3f out: chal 1 1/2f out: led 1f out: kpt on strly fnl f* **5/2**[2]

2 4 1/2 **Galistic (IRE)**[17] 3537 5-9-9 98.............................. DPMcDonogh 11 103
(Patrick J Flynn, Ire) *hld up towards rr: hdwy to 7th 4f out: impr to 4th 2f out: chal 1 1/2f out: disp over 1f out: 2nd ins fnl f: kpt on same pce* **14/1**

3 hd **Peppertree Lane (IRE)**[18] 3513 5-9-12 110.............................. JoeFanning 6 106
(M Johnston) *trckd ldrs: 4th 1/2-way: impr to ld under 2f out: strly pressed 1 1/2f out: hdd 1f out: no ex: kpt on same pce u.p* **9/4**[1]

4 2 1/2 **Ebadiyan (IRE)**[26] 3196 3-8-10 98.............................. MJKinane 13 100
(John M Oxx, Ire) *mid-div: rdn into 6th 2f out: sn no ex: kpt on same pce u.p fr over 1f out* **8/1**

5 1 **Hold Me Love Me (IRE)**[5] 3935 3-8-7 70.............................. JAHeffernan 7 96
(A P O'Brien, Ire) *sn chsd ldr: led after 3f: rdn 3f out: hdd under 2f out: no ex: kpt on one pce* **20/1**

6 shd **Power Of Future (GER)**[29] 3104 5-9-6 82.............................. CDHayes 10 95
(Andrew Oliver, Ire) *chsd ldrs: 7th 1/2-way: rdn in 5th ent st: no ex fr over 1 1/2f out: kpt on same pce* **33/1**

7 6 **Perihelion (IRE)**[3] 4006 3-8-7 90.............................. DavidMcCabe 9 87
(A P O'Brien, Ire) *towards rr: late hdwy to go mod 7th over 1f out: no imp on ldrs* **20/1**

8 6 **Fabia (IRE)**[58] 2265 3-8-7.............................. WJSupple 1 79
(David Wachman, Ire) *chsd ldrs: 5th 1/2-way: rdn and lost pl 4f out: kpt on one pce st* **25/1**

9 1 1/2 **Merveilles**[25] 3250 5-9-9 101..............................(p) NGMcCullagh 3 79
(Mrs John Harrington, Ire) *towards rr: mod 10th 3f out: kpt on one pce st* **16/1**

10 2 1/2 **Sweet Sixteen (IRE)**[9] 3805 3-8-7.............................. SMLevey 2 73
(A P O'Brien, Ire) *nvr a factor* **33/1**

11 19 **Always Beautiful (USA)**[31] 3070 3-8-7.............................. WMLordan 4 47
(David Wachman, Ire) *chsd ldrs: 3rd 1/2-way: rdn in 6th 3f out: sn wknd* **6/1**[3]

12 3 **Raydiya (IRE)**[9] 3805 3-8-10 100.............................. FMBerry 12 45
(John M Oxx, Ire) *led: hdd after 3f: chsd ldr in 2nd: rdn in 3rd 3f out: sn wknd* **7/1**

2m 55.0s (-6.00) **Going Correction** 0.0s/f (Good)
WFA 3 from 4yo+ 14lb **13** Ran SP% **129.0**
Speed ratings: **117,114,114,112,112 112,108,105,104,103 92,90**
CSF £42.12 TOTE £2.30: £1.40, £5.40, £1.20; DF 78.70.
Owner Moyglare Stud Farm **Bred** Moyglare Stud Farms **Trained** The Curragh, Co Kildare

FOCUS
The clear-cut winner has been rated to her previous best, and likewise the runner-up and seventh.

NOTEBOOK
Profound Beauty(IRE), placed a couple of times in Group 3 events this season before defying a big weight in a 1m4f handicap at the Curragh on her previous start, was trying a new trip here and she won in good style, delivering her challenge well over a furlong out and leading entering the final furlong before stretching clear for a convincing victory. Her trainer is toying with the idea of entering her for the Melbourne Cup and also mentioned the Irish Field St Leger as a possible target.
Galistic(IRE), winner of this race a year ago, had finished behind Profound Beauty on her two previous starts this season and did so again here. Held up, she began to improve leaving the back straight and challenged on the inside to have every chance a furlong out. She was unable to make any impression on the winner inside the final furlong but kept on to win the battle for second place.
Peppertree Lane(IRE) tracked the leaders and hit the front under two furlongs out before failing to quicken with the winner over the final furlong. (op 5/2 tchd 2/1)
T/Jkpt: @288.40. Pool of @10,000.00 - 26 winning units. T/Plt: @10.00. Pool of @10,295.09. II

4096 - 4100a (Foreign Racing) - See Raceform Interactive

3358 BATH (L-H)
Thursday, July 17

OFFICIAL GOING: Good (good to firm in places; 8.8)
Wind: Moderate, ahead

4101 NESTLE PROFESSIONAL NURSERY — 5f 11y
6:20 (6:21) (Class 5) 2-Y-O — **£3,885** (£1,156; £577; £288) **Stalls** Centre

Form RPR

14 **1** **Fault**[59] 2254 2-9-7 82.............................. SteveDrowne 7 83+
(R Charlton) *t.k.h in tch: qcknd 2f: sn rdn: led appr fnl f: hld on wl* **11/4**[1]

540 **2** 1 **Nativity**[40] 2835 2-8-5 66.............................. LiamJones 2 63
(J L Spearing) *chsd ldrs: drvn to chal fr over 1f out: stl upsides jst ins fnl f: kpt on but nt pce of wnr* **4/1**[2]

362 **3** hd **Sonhador**[23] 3341 2-8-11 72.............................. JimCrowley 1 68
(P Winkworth) *w ldr tl slt ld 3f out: hdd appr fnl f: kpt on same pce u.p ins fnl f* **13/2**

353 **4** 1 **Mesyaal**[17] 3547 2-8-13 74.............................. DarryllHolland 5 67
(M R Channon) *chsd ldrs: rdn 1/2-way: wknd appr fnl f* **11/4**[1]

0045 **5** nk **Speak The Truth (IRE)**[8] 3846 2-8-3 64.............................. DavidKinsella 4 56
(J R Boyle) *in rr: rdn 1/2-way: styd on wl fnl f but nvr gng pce to be competitive* **12/1**

60 **6** *8* **Fuaigh Mor (IRE)**[14] 3625 2-7-12 **62**..........................(p) DominicFox(3) 3 25
(A Bailey) *sn outpcd* **5/1**[3]

4004 **7** *7* **Bethie**[28] 3178 2-8-4 **65**.................................. FrankieMcDonald 6 3
(R Brotherton) *led 2f: sn wknd* **33/1**

63.46 secs (0.96) **Going Correction** +0.20s/f (Good) **7** Ran SP% **114.0**
Speed ratings (Par 94): **100,98,98,96,96 83,72**
toteswinger: 1&2 £3.50, 1&3 £2.10, 2&3 £13.10. CSF £13.92 TOTE £2.60: £1.90, £3.80; EX 22.40.

Owner John Livock **Bred** Mrs A M Vestey **Trained** Beckhampton, Wilts

FOCUS
A fair nursery. The winner looks the kind of progressive sort that will do better in better company. The 'official' ratings shown next to each horse are estimated and for information purposes only.

NOTEBOOK
Fault is obviously useful and bounced back from defeat on fast going at Windsor last time (had made all there on debut) to give weight and a beating to some fair rivals. (op 5-2 tchd 9-4 and 3-1)

Nativity found the extra furlong beyond her reach when disappointing on the turf at Lingfield last time, but she is all about speed and was able to bounce back to her best here. (op 8-1)

Sonhador has bumped into some decent animals in his short career despite being kept to the southern gaffs. He is not short of pace and will be found easier openings than this to break his maiden tag. (tchd 6-1 and 7-1)

Mesyaal has proved a little disappointing since a promising debut at Salisbury back in May and probably found himself too high in the weights here. (op 10-3 tchd 7-2)

Speak The Truth(IRE) was outpaced early on but kept on well to finish on the heels of the leaders, and deserves another crack at 6f now that he is in nursery company. (tchd 14-1)

4102 COCA COLA CLASSIC CLAIMING STKS — 5f 161y
6:50 (6:51) (Class 5) 3-Y-O+ **£3,561** (£1,059; £529; £264) **Stalls** Centre

Form RPR

25/0 **1** **Valverde (IRE)**[50] 2513 5-8-8 50..........................(v[1]) DO'Donohoe 6 58
(George Baker) *s.i.s: in rr and sn drvn: hdwy over 2f out: str run to ld fnl 50yds: all out* **16/1**

-300 **2** *nk* **Towy Boy (IRE)**[17] 3564 3-8-13 60..........................(t) PaulDoe 2 66
(I A Wood) *in rr: rdn and hdwy fr 3f out: drvn to ld over 1f out: hdd and no ex fnl 50yds* **16/1**

2324 **3** *3 1/4* **Desperate Dan**[18] 3520 7-9-4 70.......................... ShaneKelly 9 56
(A B Haynes) *in rr: swtchd to outside over 2f out: sn rdn and hdwy to chse ldrs 1f out: no ex ins fnl f* **7/2**[1]

0015 **4** *1* **Who's Winning (IRE)**[11] 3761 7-9-2 60.................. RichardKingscote 7 51
(B G Powell) *chsd ldrs: rdn to chal ins fnl 2f: wknd fnl f* **7/2**[1]

3523 **5** *1 1/4* **Night Prospector**[10] 3783 8-8-9 54 ow2..................(b) HaddenFrost(5) 10 44
(R A Harris) *led tl hdd & wknd over 1f out* **7/1**

0000 **6** *6* **Convince (USA)**[13] 3662 7-8-9 48..........................(b) TravisBlock(3) 13 22
(J M Bradley) *chsd ldrs: rdn over 2f out: sn wknd* **33/1**

1400 **7** *nk* **Marko Jadeo (IRE)**[17] 3559 10-8-9 58.................. KevinGhunowa(3) 8 21
(R A Harris) *chsd ldr to 1/2-way: wknd sn after* **12/1**

-005 **8** *3 1/4* **Meridian Line (IRE)**[13] 3696 3-9-0 74.......................... JimCrowley 17 16
(J G Portman) *in tch to 1/2-way: sn in rr* **6/1**[3]

0000 **9** *4* **Peruvian Style (IRE)**[2] 4052 7-9-0 43..........................(v) MickyFenton 1 —
(J M Bradley) *early spd* **33/1**

-006 **10** *6* **High Ridge**[22] 3363 9-9-6 53..........................(b) SteveDrowne 16 —
(J M Bradley) *spd to 1/2-way* **22/1**

0-00 **11** *1 3/4* **Deal Flipper**[19] 3487 3-8-0 65.......................... LiamJones 14 —
(P Winkworth) *slowly away and rel to r* **11/2**[2]

1m 11.78s (0.58) **Going Correction** +0.20s/f (Good)
WFA 3 from 4yo+ 5lb **11** Ran SP% **116.3**
Speed ratings (Par 103): **104,103,99,97,96 88,87,83,78,70 67**
toteswinger: 1&2 £23.90, 1&3 £11.90, 2&3 Not Won. CSF £238.40 TOTE £23.50: £5.70, £4.10, £1.20; EX 331.50.The winner was subject to a friendly claim.

Owner Mrs C E S Baker **Bred** Gestut Sohrenhof **Trained** Moreton Morrell, Warwicks

FOCUS
Probably a weak claimer, but the form is hard to rate. The time was decent and the front five pulled well clear.

Night Prospector Official explanation: jockey said gelding ran too free
Deal Flipper Official explanation: jockey said filly missed the break

4103 SHIRES FAMOUS PIES H'CAP — 5f 161y
7:25 (7:25) (Class 4) (0-80,83) 3-Y-O+ **£6,572** (£1,967; £983; £491; £244) **Stalls** Centre

Form RPR

1311 **1** **Misaro (GER)**[7] 3868 7-9-10 **83** 6ex..........................(b) HaddenFrost(5) 8 96
(R A Harris) *bmpd over 3f sn trcking ldrs: led ins fnl 2f: c clr fnl f: easily* **9/2**[2]

0402 **2** *5* **Bahamian Ballet**[18] 3520 6-9-11 **79**.......................... GregFairley 4 75
(E S McMahon) *chsd ldrs: rdn and edgd lft over 1f out: chsd wnr sn after but nvr any ch* **3/1**[1]

0000 **3** *1 1/4* **Thabaat**[20] 3443 4-8-11 **68**..........................(b[1]) KevinGhunowa(3) 5 60
(J M Bradley) *in rr and rdn along 3f out: hdwy fr 2f out: stud on ins fnl f to cl on 2nd but nvr any ch w easy wnr* **40/1**

-006 **4** *1 3/4* **Don Pele (IRE)**[31] 3093 6-9-8 **76**..........................(p) ShaneKelly 3 62
(R A Harris) *slt ld tl hdd ins fnl 2f: wknd fnl f* **14/1**

6601 **5** *1/2* **Diminuto**[9] 3825 4-8-4 **65** 6ex.......................... DavidProbert(7) 1 49
(M D I Usher) *chsd ldrs: rdn over 2f out: sn outpcd* **12/1**

0516 **6** *hd* **Coconut Moon**[5] 3948 6-8-9 **70**.......................... RobbieEgan(7) 10 53
(D Flood) *t.k.h towards rr but in tch: hdwy on outside over 2f out: nt pce to rch ldrs and sn btn* **9/2**[2]

-003 **7** *3 1/4* **Loyal Royal (IRE)**[22] 3363 5-8-10 **64**.......................... SteveDrowne 2 36
(J M Bradley) *s.i.s: in rr tl mod prog fnl f* **12/1**

0055 **8** *1/2* **Pic Up Sticks**[23] 3352 9-8-12 **66**.......................... RichardKingscote 7 37
(B G Powell) *in rr tl sme hdwy over 2f out: nt rch ldrs and sn btn* **7/1**

3510 **9** *2* **Lunces Lad (IRE)**[21] 3418 4-9-9 **77**.......................... DarryllHolland 9 41
(M R Channon) *w ldr 3f: wkng whn hmpd over 1f out* **6/1**[3]

1m 11.75s (0.55) **Going Correction** +0.20s/f (Good) **9** Ran SP% **112.6**
Speed ratings (Par 105): **104,97,95,93,92 92,88,87,84**
toteswinger: 1&2 £2.20, 1&3 £41.40, 2&3 £34.50. CSF £17.84 CT £465.70 TOTE £5.40: £1.90, £1.50, £6.50; EX 15.50.

Owner Messrs Criddle Davies Dawson & Villa **Bred** Wilhelm Fasching **Trained** Earlswood, Monmouths

■ Stewards' Enquiry : Robbie Egan one-day ban: careless riding (Jul 31)

FOCUS
A fair bunch of sprint handicappers treated with ruthless disdain by a horse in the rudest of good health. It is hard to know how literally to take this but the form has rated through the winner to the best view of his previous form.

4104 ECHO FALLS H'CAP — 1m 5y
7:55 (7:56) (Class 4) (0-80,84) 3-Y-O+ **£6,572** (£1,967; £737; £737; £244) **Stalls** Low

Form RPR

5121 **1** **Yamal (IRE)**[6] 3907 3-9-10 **84** 6ex.......................... GregFairley 4 95
(M Johnston) *drvn along to take slt advantage sn after s: asserted 4f out: drvn along fr 2f out: hld on all out cl home* **9/4**[1]

3405 **2** *shd* **Red Somerset (USA)**[18] 3529 5-10-0 **80**.................. RichardKingscote 1 92
(R J Hodges) *chsd ldrs: wnt 2nd 1f out: str run thrght fnl f: clsng on wnr: jst failed* **12/1**

0-16 **3** *3 3/4* **Cool Ebony**[19] 3478 5-9-10 **76**.......................... DarryllHolland 5 79
(P J Makin) *w ldr 2f: styd in 2nd and hrd drvn but no imp over 2f out: lost 2nd 1f out and sn one pce* **12/1**

-224 **3** *dht* **Barricado (FR)**[35] 2974 3-9-1 **75**..........................(b[1]) SteveDrowne 9 76+
(R Charlton) *s.i.s and sn drvn in rr: plenty to do over 2f out: str run u.p over 1f out and hung bdly lft ins fnl f: fining wl but nt rch ldrs* **11/2**[3]

5024 **5** *1 1/2* **Count Ceprano (IRE)**[8] 3840 4-9-9 **80**.................. GabrielHannon(5) 8 80
(M D I Usher) *in rr: hdwy fr 2f out: kpt on ins fnl f but nt rch ldrs* **12/1**

3604 **6** *nk* **Kensington (IRE)**[15] 3607 7-9-7 **73**.......................... PaulDoe 7 72
(P D Evans) *chsd ldrs: rdn over 2f out: styd on one pce* **16/1**

5414 **7** *1 3/4* **Mountain Pass (USA)**[20] 3431 6-8-10 **62**..................(p) FrancisNorton 10 57
(B J Llewellyn) *in tch: rdn 3f out: no imp on ldrs 2f out: wknd fnl f* **20/1**

-354 **8** *1 1/2* **Barliffey (IRE)**[24] 3312 3-8-13 **73**.......................... JimCrowley 13 63
(D J Coakley) *in tch: rdn over 2f out and no imp: styd on same pce fnl f* **20/1**

-150 **9** *3/4* **Rockfield Tiger (IRE)**[43] 2714 3-9-5 **79**..........................(t) ShaneKelly 2 67
(J A Osborne) *in tch: rdn 3f out: wknd fr 2f out* **33/1**

4223 **10** *nk* **Just Bond (IRE)**[26] 3278 6-9-4 **77**.......................... DavidProbert(7) 11 66
(G R Oldroyd) *t.k.h in rr: sme prog on outside 3f out: nvr in contention* **9/2**[2]

0116 **11** *3 1/4* **Maybe I Will (IRE)**[13] 3679 3-8-9 **69**.......................... MickyFenton 16 49
(S Dow) *in rr: sme hdwy 3f out: nvr bttr than mid-div and sn wknd* **18/1**

2-05 **12** *nse* **Baizically (IRE)**[28] 3167 5-9-12 **78**.......................... DO'Donohoe 15 60
(George Baker) *chsd ldrs to 3f out: btn fr 2f out* **33/1**

00/ **13** *1 1/4* **Pugilist**[616] 6418 6-9-10 **76**.......................... NickyMackay 3 55
(B J Meehan) *chsd ldrs to 3f out: sn wknd* **20/1**

1205 **14** *1 3/4* **Obezyana (USA)**[27] 3222 6-9-10 **79**.......................... DominicFox(3) 14 54
(A Bailey) *in rr: effrt into mid-div over 3f out: n.d after* **16/1**

5250 **15** *1 1/4* **Seneschal**[95] 1345 7-8-6 **65**.......................... PNolan(7) 12 37
(A B Haynes) *in rr: sme prog on outside 3f out: nvr in contention and sn wknd* **33/1**

000/ **16** *27* **Superfling**[40] 2099 7-8-6 **61** oh16.......................... KevinGhunowa(3) 6 —
(H J Manners) *bhd fnl 4f* **100/1**

1m 40.66s (-0.14) **Going Correction** +0.05s/f (Good)
WFA 3 from 4yo+ 8lb **16** Ran SP% **128.5**
Speed ratings (Par 105): **102,101,98,98,96 96,94,93,92,92 88,88,87,85,84 57**
PL: Cool Ebony £3.00, Barricado £2.20; TRICAST: CE £125.56, B £2.20; toteswinger: 1&2 £10.00, 1&3 (CE) £7.80, 1&3 (B) £1.60, 2&3 (CE) £9.80, 2&3 (B) £10.60. CSF £30.24 TOTE £2.80: £1.10, £3.40; EX 30.60.

Owner Sheikh Hamdan Bin Mohammed Al Maktoum **Bred** Gainsborough Stud Management Ltd **Trained** Middleham Moor, N Yorks

FOCUS
A useful handicap. The winner, 5lb well in, just held the strong finish of the runner-up who himself has looked like a well-handicapped horse for some time now, and the form has a very solid feel to it.

Cool Ebony Official explanation: jockey said saddle slipped
Barricado(FR) Official explanation: jockey said colt hung left-handed closing stages
Mountain Pass(USA) Official explanation: jockey said gelding ran too free

4105 SOL BRING ON SUNSHINE H'CAP — 2m 1f 34y
8:30 (8:30) (Class 6) (0-65,60) 4-Y-O+ **£2,914** (£867; £433; £108; £108) **Stalls** Centre

Form RPR

-141 **1** **Trigger's Friend**[7] 3871 4-8-12 **54** 6ex.......................... TolleyDean(3) 11 63
(Jamie Poulton) *in tch: hrd drvn fr 5f out: styd on to press ldrs over 1f out: str run u.p ins fnl f to ld last strides* **8/1**

06 **2** *hd* **Stoop To Conquer**[75] 1798 8-9-7 **60**.......................... JimCrowley 10 69
(A W Carroll) *t.k.h in rr early: wnt after 5f: slt ld ins fnl 3f: drvn to assert over 2f out kpt on wl: ct last strides* **13/2**[3]

6-24 **3** *2 1/4* **Wotchalike (IRE)**[7] 3871 6-8-13 **52**..........................(p) PaulDoe 4 58
(Jim Best) *chsd ldrs: wnt 3rd over 3f out: chsd ldr 2f out: chal 1f out: outpcd ins fnl f* **7/1**

-243 **4** *2 1/4* **Go Amwell**[25] 3296 5-9-3 **56**.......................... LiamJones 9 60+
(J R Jenkins) *in rr: rdn over 3f out and styd on fr 3f out: kpt on fnl 2f but nvr gng pce to rch ldrs* **3/1**[1]

3016 **4** *dht* **Brave Bugsy (IRE)**[38] 2888 5-8-12 **58**.......................... DavidProbert(7) 6 62+
(A M Balding) *hld up in rr: stl plenty to do 3f out: styd on fnl 2f and gng on ins fnl f: nt rch ldrs* **10/3**[2]

000/ **6** *6* **Jomelamin**[15] 417 6-8-6 **45**..........................(t) FrancisNorton 7 41
(M Sheppard) *in rr: rdn over 3f out: mod prog fnl 2f* **20/1**

4/0- **7** *nk* **Irish Whispers (IRE)**[452] 775 5-8-13 **57**.............. GabrielHannon(5) 12 53
(B G Powell) *in rr: rdn 4f out: sme prog fnl 3f out: nvr in contention* **40/1**

0330 **8** *1 1/2* **Still Dreaming**[13] 3698 4-8-8 **47**.......................... SteveDrowne 8 41
(R J Price) *t.k.h in rr: sme prog 3f out but nvr in contention* **16/1**

0310 **9** *5* **Arabian Sun**[22] 3377 4-9-3 **56**..........................(p) MickyFenton 5 44
(M J Attwater) *drvn to ld: hdd ins fnl 3f and sn wknd* **14/1**

5044 **10** *7* **Songmaster (USA)**[20] 3448 5-9-5 **58**.......................... DarryllHolland 13 38
(A King) *chsd ldrs: wnt 3rd 9f out: rdn 5f out: wknd 3f out* **7/1**

-000 **11** *14* **Sweet Request**[20] 3448 4-8-13 **52**.......................... RichardThomas 1 15
(Dr J R J Naylor) *chsd ldrs tl wknd 4f out* **40/1**

0 **12** *1* **Mean Machine (IRE)**[3] 4029 6-8-6 **45**..........................(b) DavidKinsella 3 7
(D Flood) *t.k.h: in tch tl wknd u.p obver 3f out* **28/1**

36-0 **13** *23* **Lord Nellsson**[186] 152 12-8-1 **45**.......................... NataliaGemelova(5) 2 —
(A B Haynes) *a in rr* **50/1**

3m 51.46s (-0.44) **Going Correction** +0.05s/f (Good) **13** Ran SP% **125.1**
Speed ratings (Par 101): **103,102,101,100,100 97,97,97,94,91 84,84,73**
toteswinger: 1&2 £20.20, 1&3 £8.40, 2&3 £6.10. CSF £59.30 CT £395.23 TOTE £4.60: £2.10, £3.20, £3.10; EX 101.40.

Owner R W Huggins **Bred** R W Huggins **Trained** Lewes, E Sussex

■ Stewards' Enquiry : Jim Crowley caution: used whip in incorrect place

The Form Book, Raceform Ltd, Compton, RG20 6NL

FOCUS
A modest staying handicap feauturing plenty of inconsistent types, so while the form isn't too reliable, the winner is a genuine improver who was 4lb wrong here under the penalty. The form might have been rated a bit higher using the second and third's old form.

4106 LINDLEY CATERING FOR CONFERENCES H'CAP — 5f 11y

9:00 (9:02) (Class 5) (0-75,75) 3-Y-O+ **£4,403** (£1,310; £654; £327) **Stalls** Centre

Form — RPR

3221 **1** **Heaven**[18] 3526 3-9-7 **75** ... DarryllHolland 10 — 79
(P J Makin) *hld up towards rr but in tch: str run on outside over 1f out: swooped to ld last stride* **11/4**[2]

5360 **2** *nse* **Admiral Bond (IRE)**[12] 3712 3-8-4 **65** ... (v[1]) DavidProbert[(7)] 4 — 69
(G R Oldroyd) *in rr: hdwy and nt clr run appr fnl f: str run ins fnl f and edgd lft the led cl home: ct last stride* **20/1**

0001 **3** *nk* **Pennyspider (IRE)**[79] 1699 3-8-6 **60** ... RichardKingscote 2 — 63
(M S Saunders) *w ldr: led 3f out: drvn fr 2f out: kpt slt ld tl hdd cl home* **16/1**

1243 **4** *1 1/4* **Best One**[7] 3868 4-9-8 **75** ... (p) KevinGhunowa[(3)] 3 — 75
(R A Harris) *chsd ldrs: drvn 2f out: chal ins fnl f: wknd cl home* **5/2**[1]

-060 **5** *nse* **Archilini**[5] 3960 3-8-6 **60** ... (p) DO'Donohoe 1 — 60+
(M Sheppard) *in rr: hdwy over 1f out: styng on to chal whn hmpd cl home and nt rcvr* **40/1**

4-0 **6** *1 1/4* **Jucebabe**[22] 3363 5-8-6 **56** oh1 ... (p) LiamJones 6 — 51
(J L Spearing) *chsd ldrs: chal fr 3f out to 1f out: wknd fnl f* **8/1**

300- **7** *1 3/4* **Talcen Gwyn (IRE)**[267] 6424 6-8-7 **57** ... (v) FrancisNorton 5 — 46
(M F Harris) *s.i.s: in rr: hdwy over 1f out: kpt on but nt pce to rch ldrs* **16/1**

0-11 **8** *3/4* **Croeso Bach**[10] 3783 4-8-4 **61** 6ex ... SophieDoyle[(7)] 11 — 47
(J L Spearing) *led to 3f out: stl upsides 2f out: sn wknd* **5/1**[3]

6200 **9** *shd* **Blessed Place**[5] 3945 8-8-5 **62** ... BillyCray[(7)] 9 — 48
(D J S Ffrench Davis) *pressed ldrs: rdn 1/2-way: upsides 2f out: sn wknd* **14/1**

060 **10** *1 1/4* **Bluebok**[18] 3520 7-8-12 **62** ... (bt[1]) SteveDrowne 12 — 43
(J M Bradley) *chsd ldrs 3f* **16/1**

0010 **11** *hd* **Lithaam (IRE)**[13] 3668 4-8-10 **60** ... (p) JimCrowley 7 — 41
(J M Bradley) *chsd ldrs: edgd lft u.p and wknd ins fnl 2f* **25/1**

5660 **12** *3* **Peopleton Brook**[13] 3665 6-8-8 **58** oh6 ow2 ... (b) MickyFenton 8 — 28
(J M Bradley) *s.i.s: outpcd* **22/1**

63.43 secs (0.93) **Going Correction** +0.20s/f (Good)
WFA 3 from 4yo+ 4lb — **12** Ran SP% **122.7**
Speed ratings (Par 103): **100,99,99,97,97 95,92,91,91,89 88,84**
toteswinger: 1&2 £24.20, 1&3 £2.70, 2&3 £35.00. CSF £64.53 CT £785.07 TOTE £3.30: £1.90, £6.20, £4.50; EX 65.40 Place 6 £188.81, Place 5 £95.99.
Owner Wedgewood Estates **Bred** Mrs D O Joly **Trained** Ogbourne Maisey, Wilts
■ Stewards' Enquiry : David Probert three-day ban: careless riding (Aug 1,3,4)

FOCUS
A fair sprint handicap dominated by a trio of three-year olds. The form is tricky to pin down but pretty modest.
T/Jkpt: Not won. T/Plt: £26.90 to a £1 stake. Pool: £52,580.97. 1,423.97 winning tickets. T/Qpdt: £10.70 to a £1 stake. Pool: £4,248.54. 291.80 winning tickets. ST

3863 DONCASTER (L-H)

Thursday, July 17

OFFICIAL GOING: Good (good to firm in places) changing to good after race 2 (7.05)
Rail realignment added 13yards to advertised distances on round course.
Wind: Fresh, across Weather: Overcast

4107 SOCIETY AND LIFESTYLE MAGAZINE APPRENTICE H'CAP — 5f

6:30 (6:32) (Class 6) (0-60,59) 3-Y-O+ **£2,729** (£806; £403) **Stalls** High

Form — RPR

5000 **1** **Lujiana**[5] 3960 3-8-7 **57** ... MatthewLawson[(8)] 19 — 66
(M Brittain) *towards rr: rdn along over 2f out: swtchd lft and gd hdwy over 1f out: styd on wl to ld ins fnl f* **20/1**

2060 **2** *3/4* **Overstayed (IRE)**[52] 2448 5-8-12 **55** ... (t) AndreaAtzeni[(5)] 9 — 62
(P J McBride) *hld up in midfield: hdwy 2f out: swtchd rt and rdn over 1f out: styd on wl fnl f* **14/1**

0203 **3** *1/2* **Jun Fan (USA)**[2] 4047 6-8-9 **55** ... AnthonyBetts[(8)] 10 — 60
(B Ellison) *a.p: rdn wl over 1f out: led briefly jst ins fnl f: sn hdd: edgd lft and no ex last 100yds* **7/2**[1]

0032 **4** *1 1/4* **City For Conquest (IRE)**[10] 3783 5-8-6 **47** ow2 ... GarryWhillans[(3)] 12 — 48
(John A Harris) *chsd ldrs: rdn 2f out: drvn and kpt on u.p ins fnl f* **12/1**

0605 **5** *1 1/2* **Fast Freddie**[13] 3668 4-9-4 **59** ... CharlesEddery[(3)] 3 — 54
(S Parr) *cl up in centre: rdn along wl over 1f out: kpt on same pce ins fnl f* **14/1**

5302 **6** *nk* **Mac Dalia**[13] 3686 3-9-2 **58** ... (p) KrishGundowry 15 — 51
(A J McCabe) *led on stands' rail: riudden 2f out: drvn over 1f out: hdd jst ins fnl f: wknd* **10/1**[3]

0034 **7** *1/2* **Thomas Malory (IRE)**[20] 3441 3-8-8 **53** ... JPFeatherstone[(3)] 17 — 44
(Miss V Haigh) *chsd ldrs: rdn along and outpcd 1/2-way: kpt on u.p ins fnl f* **13/2**[2]

3045 **8** *nse* **Rann Na Cille (IRE)**[66] 2036 4-8-11 **52** ... PaulPickard[(3)] 4 — 44
(P T Midgley) *prom: rdn along wl over 2f out: grad wknd* **12/1**

0020 **9** *nse* **The Cube**[12] 3712 4-8-8 **46** ... (b) DebraEngland 6 — 38
(J Balding) *dwlt and in rr: hdwy 2f out: swtchd lft and rdn over 1f out: kpt on ins fnl f: nrst fin* **18/1**

0556 **10** *3/4* **Dancing Mystery**[16] 3575 14-8-11 **54** ... (b) DanielBlackett[(5)] 13 — 43
(E A Wheeler) *a in midfield* **16/1**

3036 **11** *nk* **Bond Becks (IRE)**[9] 3825 8-9-0 **55** ... JohnCavanagh[(3)] 8 — 43
(G R Oldroyd) *in tch: rdn along 2f out: grad wknd* **10/1**[3]

0500 **12** *nse* **Afton View (IRE)**[5] 3952 3-8-10 **57** ... (tp) StevenCorrigan[(5)] 5 — 44
(S Parr) *chsd ldrs: rdn along 2f out: sn drvn and wknd* **33/1**

0560 **13** *2 3/4* **Miss Sunshine**[11] 3753 3-8-1 **46** ... TobyAtkinson[(3)] 14 — 23
(J S Goldie) *hld up: a in rr* **18/1**

2516 **14** *1/2* **Owed**[9] 3819 6-9-0 **52** ... (tp) JamesRogers 16 — 28
(R Bastiman) *sn rdn along and a in rr* **12/1**

000 **15** *2 1/4* **Groundhog Day**[12] 3712 4-8-4 **45** ... BradleyRoper[(3)] 11 — 13
(J Balding) *s.i.s: a bhd* **50/1**

63-0 **16** *1 1/4* **Piccolo Diamante (USA)**[23] 3340 4-8-9 **47** ... (t) RichardRowe 18 — 11
(S Parr) *s.i.s: a bhd* **28/1**

4-54 **17** *hd* **Tittle**[11] 3765 3-8-13 **58** ... AmyScott[(3)] 1 — 20
(H Candy) *dwlt: a outpcd and bhd* **12/1**

61.16 secs (0.66) **Going Correction** +0.175s/f (Good)
WFA 3 from 4yo+ 4lb — **17** Ran SP% **127.4**
Speed ratings (Par 101): **101,99,99,97,94 94,93,93,93,91 91,91,87,86,82 80,80**
toteswinger: 1&2 £70.80, 1&3 Not won, 2&3 £71.40. CSF £279.24 CT £1275.62 TOTE £28.20: £6.20, £5.00, £1.60, £2.20; EX 1261.30.
Owner Mel Brittain **Bred** Bearstone Stud **Trained** Warthill, N Yorks
■ Matthew Lawson's first winner. He is the brother of fellow apprentice Mark Lawson.

FOCUS
A moderate sprint handicap restricted to apprentices who had not ridden more than five winners. They raced middle to stands' side and a high draw was no disadvantage. Modest but sound form.
Overstayed(IRE) Official explanation: vet said gelding lost a front plate
Bond Becks(IRE) Official explanation: jockey said gelding never travelled

4108 RECTANGLE GROUP NOVICE STKS — 6f

7:05 (7:06) (Class 4) 2-Y-O **£2,520** (£2,520; £577; £288) **Stalls** High

Form — RPR

60 **1** **Oriental Rose**[90] 1447 2-8-6 0 ... DavidAllan 5 — 74
(G M Moore) *hld up in rr: hdwy 1/2-way: rdn to chal over 1f out: drvn ins fnl f: led nr fin: jnd on line* **66/1**

1 **1** *dht* **Fol Liam**[13] 3670 2-8-11 0 ... StephenDonohoe 8 — 79
(Ian Williams) *hld up: hdwy 2f out: swtchd lft and rdn over 1f out: styd on to ld ins fnl f: drvn and hdd nr fin: rallied on line* **8/1**

1 **3** *1 1/2* **Mister Laurel**[21] 3400 2-9-1 0 ... JamieMoriarty[(3)] 2 — 81
(R A Fahey) *cl up: rdn to ld wl over 1f out: drvn and hdd ins fnl f: kpt on same pce* **15/2**[3]

0 **4** *2 3/4* **Al Mukaala (IRE)**[19] 3495 2-8-11 0 ... NCallan 3 — 66
(C E Brittain) *dwlt: sn trcking ldrs: swtchd lft and hdwy over 2f out: rdn wl over 1f out: wknd ent fnl f* **10/1**

1 **5** *nk* **Prize Point**[27] 3199 2-9-1 0 ... RichardMullen 6 — 69
(K A Ryan) *led: rdn along over 2f out: drvn and hdd wl over 1f out: wknd ins fnl f* **1/1**[1]

1 **6** *5* **Missus Christie**[35] 2965 2-8-7 0 ow1 ... FergusSweeney 7 — 46
(Ian Williams) *a in rr* **28/1**

1 **7** *55* **Queen Of Thebes (IRE)**[17] 3558 2-8-10 0 ... WilliamBuick 1 — —
(G L Moore) *cl up: rdn along 1/2-way: sn wknd: bhd and eased over 1f out* **5/2**[2]

1m 14.22s (0.62) **Going Correction** +0.175s/f (Good) — **7** Ran SP% **115.5**
Speed ratings (Par 96): **102,102,100,96,95 89,15**
WIN: Fol Liam £4.70, Oriental Rose £25.20; PL: FL £3.70, OR £9.40; EX: FL-OR £279.30, OR-FL £216.90; CSF: FL-OR £148.15, OR-FL £257.51. toteswinger: 1&2 £44.50, (FL) 1&3 £9.00, (OR) 1&3 £6.70..
Owner Dr Marwan Koukash **Bred** Adrian Smith **Trained** Portway, Worcs
Owner Ean Muller Associates **Bred** E A C Muller **Trained** Middleham Moor, N Yorks

FOCUS
A competitive novice event, with five of the seven winners successful on their debuts, but the leaders looked to go off too quickly, setting this up for those held up, so the form, probably no better than fair, needs treating with caution. They raced towards the stands' side.

NOTEBOOK
Oriental Rose had not offered much on her first two starts, but she was pitched into novice company on both occasions, suggesting she might have been showing something at home. Stepped up in trip and switched to better ground, she produced a much-improved effort, although like Fol Liam everything fell into place, as she was held up off a strong pace. (op 80-1 tchd 100-1)
Fol Liam, picked up out of David Nicholls' yard after winning a decent seller on his debut at Haydock, improved to share the spoils in this stronger heat. However, the race fell in his lap with the leaders going off too fast and the form is not what it might have been. (op 80-1 tchd 100-1)
Mister Laurel, off the mark in a four-runner maiden on his debut at Haydock, had no easy task under top weight and he probably went off a little too soon. A son of Diktat, he might appreciate a bit of cut in the ground. (op 4-1)
Al Mukaala(IRE), down the field on his debut over 7f at Newmarket, ran well in fourth considering he made his move out wide. (op 25-1)
Prize Point, a maiden winner at Ayr over this trip on his debut, has been given a Gimcrack entry, but he proved disappointing. The way the race unfolded suggests he went off too fast. (op 6-4)
Missus Christie, carrying 1lb overweight, found this tougher than the maiden claimer at Haydock she won on her debut. (op 20-1)
Queen Of Thebes(IRE) was nowhere near the form she showed when winning on her debut at Windsor. Official explanation: jockey said filly lost its action (tchd 9-4)

4109 E B F CASINO RED HUDDERSFIELD OPENS AUGUST MAIDEN FILLIES' STKS — 7f

7:35 (7:35) (Class 4) 2-Y-O **£5,459** (£1,612; £806) **Stalls** High

Form — RPR

6 **1** **Zaaqya**[23] 3349 2-9-0 0 ... RichardMullen 8 — 75+
(J L Dunlop) *chsd ldrs: rdn along and lost pl after 3f: sn towards rr: swtchd markedly lft to outer and rdn over 1f out: styd on wl u.p ins fnl f to ld last 50yds* **4/1**[3]

2 *3/4* **Plotting** 2-9-0 0 ... NCallan 7 — 71
(K A Ryan) *hld up: gd hdwy 2f out: rdn to chal over 1f out and ev ch tl drvn and nt qckn wl ins fnl f* **14/1**

24 **3** *nse* **Sparkling Crystal (IRE)**[22] 3373 2-9-0 0 ... MichaelHills 5 — 71
(B W Hills) *prominent: rdn to ld over 1f out: sn drvn: hdd and nt qckn wl ins fnl f* **10/3**[1]

0 **4** *shd* **Our Day Will Come**[23] 3348 2-9-0 0 ... PatDobbs 4 — 71
(R Hannon) *trckd ldrs: hdwy over 2f out: rdn to chal over 1f out: drvn and led briefly wl ins fnl f: hdd and no ex last 50yds* **16/1**

5 *2* **Atabaas Allure (FR)** 2-9-0 0 ... JoeFanning 3 — 66
(M Johnston) *chsd ldrs: rdn along 2f out: drvn over 1f out and kpt on same pce ins fnl f* **14/1**

6 *nk* **Enhancing** 2-9-0 0 ... NeilPollard 1 — 67+
(A J McCabe) *s.i.s and bhd: hdwy wl over 1f out: styd on ins fnl f: nrst fin* **50/1**

5 **7** *1 1/2* **Aahaygran (USA)**[16] 3590 2-9-0 0 ... FergusSweeney 11 — 61
(K R Burke) *trckd ldrs: hdwy to ld over 2f out: rdn: edgd lft and hdd over 1f out: sn drvn: edgd rt ent fnl f and wknd* **7/2**[2]

8 *hd* **Amethyst Dawn (IRE)** 2-9-0 0 ... DavidAllan 10 — 63+
(T D Easterby) *t.k.h: trckd ldrs: hdwy and nt clr run wl over 1f out: swtchd rt and effrt whn hmpd on inner ent fnl f: no ch after* **33/1**

60 **9** *1/2* **Well Of Echoes**[40] 2821 2-9-0 0 ... WilliamBuick 2 — 60
(A J McCabe) *hld up in tch: rdn along over 2f out: drvn and no imp over 1f out* **25/1**

0 **10** *13* **First Queen**[20] 3456 2-9-0 0 ... PatCosgrave 9 — 27
(L M Cumani) *chsd ldrs: rdn along wl over 2f out: sn wknd* **9/2**

00 **11** *15* **Bella Olympia**[17] 3568 2-9-0 0 .... StephenDonohoe 6 —
(A J McCabe) *led: rdn along and hdd over 2f out: sn wknd* **66/1**

1m 28.5s (2.20) **Going Correction** +0.175s/f (Good) **11** Ran SP% **112.9**
Speed ratings (Par 93): **94,93,93,92,90 90,88,88,87,72 55**
toteswinger: 1&2 £10.70, 1&3 £5.20, 2&3 £25.80. CSF £53.84 TOTE £4.90: £2.10, £4.10, £1.60; EX 64.20.
Owner Hamdan Al Maktoum **Bred** Launceston Stud **Trained** Arundel, W Sussex
■ Stewards' Enquiry : Fergus Sweeney one-day ban: careless riding (Jul 31)

FOCUS
A fillies' maiden that should produce a few winners, but probably not a strong race for the track. The winning time was only 0.22 seconds slower than the following older fillies' handicap won by the 82-rated Persian Sea. They raced towards the stands' side, although the winner made her move up the middle.

NOTEBOOK
Zaaqya ◆ improved on the form she showed when sixth on her debut at Newbury with quite a taking effort. She was still very green early on, losing her position and dropping well back after a couple of furlongs or so, and she was then denied a clear run when beginning to understand what was required in the second half of the contest. Once switched with her challenge she was stuck out very wide down the centre of the track, and still had a few lengths to find, but she sustained her challenge right the way to the line. There should be further significant improvement to come, so she should would be of real interest if going for a nursery next time, as she will have to be handicapped pretty much on the bare form. (op 5-1 tchd 11-2)
Plotting, a 10,000gns daughter of Medicean, out of a dual 5f winner, made a very pleasing debut in second. She was easy to back, but showed plenty of ability and, with the benefit of this experience, she should be up to winning a similar event. (op 11-1)
Sparkling Crystal(IRE) hardly improved a great deal on her debut effort over 5f at Bath when only fourth over 6f at Kempton last time and this further step up in trip failed to bring about much progression. She is now qualified for nurseries, but does not seem to be progressing. (op 11-4 tchd 9-4)
Our Day Will Come looked better than the bare form on her debut at Newbury and this was a creditable effort in fourth. She might be able to win a similar event, but will also have the option of nurseries after one more run. (op 12-1)
Atabaas Allure(FR), a daughter of Alhaarth, half-sister to 6f juvenile winner Atabaas Pride, out of a smart dual 1m winner at three in France, has been given an entry in the Group 1 Moyglare Stud Stakes. She should come on for this. (op 9-1 tchd 8-1)
Enhancing, a daughter of Hawk Wing, missed the break and ran green early, but she showed ability when beginning to get the hang of things. (op 40-1)
Aahaygran(USA) did not improve as one might have expected on the form she showed on her debut over 6f at Thirsk. (op 13-2)
Amethyst Dawn(IRE) Official explanation: jockey said filly was denied a clerar run
First Queen showed ability on her debut over 6f at Newmarket, but she ran no race this time after taking a bit of a grip early. (op 7-2)

4110 MOSS PROPERTIES FILLIES' H'CAP 7f
8:10 (8:14) (Class 3) (0-95,86) 3-Y-0+
£7,477 (£2,239; £1,119; £560; £279; £140) **Stalls** High

Form RPR
331 **1** **Persian Sea (UAE)**[20] 3452 3-9-3 **82** .... PhilipRobinson 8 89+
(M A Jarvis) *mde all: rdn and qcknd wl over 1f out: clr ins fnl f: rdn out* **6/5**[1]
0-00 **2** *1 ¼* **Musical Beat**[30] 3109 4-9-7 **79** .... EdwardCreighton 4 86
(Miss V Haigh) *hld up in tch: hdwy 2f out: sn rdn and styd on wl u.p ins fnl f: nt rch wnr* **40/1**
2123 **3** *¾* **Cha Cha Cha**[17] 3548 4-9-10 **82** .... NCallan 5 87
(K A Ryan) *trckd wnr: effrt over 2f out: sn rdn and ev ch tl drvn and one pce ent fnl f* **11/1**[3]
6222 **4** *nk* **Just Like A Woman**[8] 3849 3-8-10 **75** .... HayleyTurner 7 76
(M L W Bell) *trckd ldrs: hdwy over 2f out: rdn over 1f out: kpt on same pce ins fnl f* **11/4**[2]
-550 **5** *3* **Tender The Great (IRE)**[8] 3855 5-9-7 **79** .... RichardMullen 10 75
(V Smith) *hld up in rr: hdwy 2f out: sn rdn and no imp* **25/1**
6606 **6** *½* **Passion Fruit**[14] 3646 7-9-8 **80** .... DeanMcKeown 9 75
(C W Fairhurst) *trckd ldrs: effrt 2f out: sn rdn and wknd appr fnl f* **16/1**
5601 **7** *9* **Misphire**[7] 3892 5-9-6 **78** 6ex .... PaulMulrennan 2 48
(M Dods) *t.k.h: hld up: a towards rr* **22/1**
4645 **8** *6* **Folly Lodge**[38] 2890 4-10-0 **86** .... WilliamBuick 1 40
(G Wragg) *chsd ldng pair: rdn along wl over 2f out: sn wknd* **14/1**

1m 28.28s (1.98) **Going Correction** +0.175s/f (Good)
WFA 3 from 4yo+ 7lb **8** Ran SP% **103.6**
Speed ratings (Par 104): **95,93,92,92,88 88,78,71**
toteswinger: 1&2 £6.50, 1&3 £1.30, 2&3 £9.40. CSF £52.09 CT £257.70 TOTE £2.00: £1.10, £5.50, £1.80; EX 50.70.
Owner Sheikh Ahmed Al Maktoum **Bred** Darley **Trained** Newmarket, Suffolk
■ Naughty Frida (9/1, ref to ent stalls) & Debonnaire (33/1, broke out of stalls) were withdrawn. Deduct 10p in the £ under Rule 4.

FOCUS
A fair fillies' handicap, but the winner was allowed to set just an ordinary pace. The form is a bit questionable with the third perhaps the best guide. The winning time was only 0.22 seconds quicker than the juvenile fillies' maiden. They raced stands' side.

NOTEBOOK
Persian Sea(UAE), a six-length maiden winner at Newcastle on her previous start, was allowed her own way in front, settling just an ordinary pace, and always looked like following up on this switch to handicap company. She gives the impression she will be even better back on easier ground and can continue to progress. (op 11-10 tchd 5-4)
Musical Beat, from a stable in great form, was never a threat to the winner, but she fared best of those held up and is one to respect in similar company. (op 33-1)
Cha Cha Cha not for the first time gave the impression she could improve for a drop back to 6f and a bit of cut in the ground. (op 10-1 tchd 9-1)
Just Like A Woman was unsuited by the lack of pace and could not take advantage of a mark 4lb lower than in future. (op 7-2)
Tender The Great(IRE) was due to be dropped 2lb.

4111 URBAN-I CONTEMPORARY LIVING H'CAP 1m 2f 60y
8:40 (8:40) (Class 4) (0-85,86) 4-Y-0+ **£4,857** (£1,445; £722; £360) **Stalls** Low

Form RPR
1212 **1** **Sir Duke (IRE)**[6] 3900 4-9-6 **83** .... PhilipRobinson 12 95+
(P W D'Arcy) *hld up: swtchd outside and gd hdwy over 2f out: str run to ld wl over 1f out: rdn and hung lft ins fnl f: styd on* **3/1**[1]
1421 **2** *2* **Keisha Kayleigh (IRE)**[20] 3450 5-8-9 **72** ....(v) NCallan 10 80
(B Ellison) *dwlt and hld up in rr: stdy hdwy 3f out: effrt and hung lft wl over 1f out: sn rdn: swtchd rt and styd on ent fnl f: nrst fin* **11/1**
66-2 **3** *nk* **Nanton (USA)**[47] 2593 6-9-6 **83** .... DanielTudhope 2 90
(J S Goldie) *hld up in tch: hdwy on inner 3f out: rdn to ld briefly 2f out: sn drvn and hdd: kpt on same pce ins fnl f* **6/1**
0355 **4** *3 ¼* **Celtic Change (IRE)**[7] 3864 4-9-3 **80** ....(v[1]) PaulMulrennan 4 81
(M Dods) *t.k.h: chsd ldng pair: hdwy 3f out: led briefly over 2f out: sn rdn and hdd: wknd ent fnl f* **10/1**
250 **5** *2 ¼* **Intersky Charm (USA)**[5] 3947 4-9-1 **78** ....(p) DeanMcKeown 6 74
(R M Whitaker) *hld up: hdwy to chse ldrs 3f out: sn rdn along and no imp fnl 2f* **25/1**
0335 **6** *1* **Fongs Gazelle**[40] 2820 4-9-4 **81** .... JoeFanning 1 75
(M Johnston) *chsd ldrs: rdn along 3f out: drvn and grad wknd fnl 2f* **14/1**
0-50 **7** *1 ¾* **Clueless**[7] 3864 6-9-0 **77** ....(be) NeilPollard 7 68
(A J McCabe) *in tch: hdwy to chse ldrs 4f out: rdn along wl over 2f out: sn drvn: edgd rt and wknd* **25/1**
222- **8** *1* **Augustus John (IRE)**[433] 1621 5-8-12 **75** .... DarrenWilliams 9 64
(S Parr) *hld up: a in rr* **22/1**
363 **9** *3 ½* **Granston (IRE)**[33] 3046 7-9-7 **84** .... KerrinMcEvoy 11 66
(J D Bethell) *chsd ldr: rdn along over 3f out and sn wknd* **7/2**[2]
1314 **10** *5* **Bull Market (IRE)**[13] 3673 5-9-1 **78** .... StephenDonohoe 5 50
(Ian Williams) *tk keen: hld up: a in rr* **14/1**
3111 **11** *2 ½* **El Dececy (USA)**[5] 3957 4-9-2 **86** 6ex .... KrishGundowry[(7)] 8 53
(S Parr) *led: rdn along 3f out: hdd 2f out and sn wknd* **11/2**[3]

2m 11.23s (0.03) **Going Correction** +0.175s/f (Good) **11** Ran SP% **119.7**
Speed ratings (Par 105): **106,104,104,101,99 98,97,96,93,89 87**
toteswinger: 1&2 £3.70, 1&3 £5.10, 2&3 £9.30. CSF £36.83 CT £187.55 TOTE £3.40: £1.70, £3.30, £2.20; EX 41.80.
Owner Mrs Jan Harris **Bred** Southern Bloodstock **Trained** Newmarket, Suffolk

FOCUS
A decent handicap. The winning time was fully two seconds quicker than the following three-year-old 51-70 handicap. The third is the best guide to the form.

4112 RUTLANDHOTEL-SHEFFIELD.COM H'CAP 1m 2f 60y
9:10 (9:10) (Class 5) (0-70,74) 3-Y-0 **£3,412** (£1,007; £504) **Stalls** Low

Form RPR
-461 **1** **Addikt (IRE)**[7] 3886 3-9-13 **74** 6ex .... WilliamBuick 10 84+
(S Kirk) *held up in tch: hdwy on outer 3f out: chsd ldr over 1f out: rdn to ld ent fnl f: styd on wl* **6/4**[1]
0034 **2** *2* **Grey Command (USA)**[60] 2221 3-9-4 **68** .... MarkLawson[(3)] 4 73
(M Brittain) *chsd clr ldr: hdwy to ld 3f out: rdn clr wl over 1f out: drvn and hdd ent fnl f: kpt on* **25/1**
-662 **3** *nse* **Timbalier (USA)**[12] 3737 3-9-5 **66** .... RichardMullen 6 71
(D M Simcock) *hld up: hdwy over 3f out: rdn along on inner 2f out: styd on u.p ins fnl f: nrst fin* **7/2**[2]
054 **4** *1 ½* **Isle Of Capri**[32] 3061 3-9-5 **66** .... PatDobbs 5 68
(R Hannon) *trckd ldrs: effrt over 3f out: rdn along wl over 2f out: sn drvn and kpt on same pce* **13/2**
-024 **5** *4 ½* **Kiho**[37] 2907 3-9-6 **67** .... StephenCarson 9 60
(Eve Johnson Houghton) *hld up in rr: hdwy on inner over 2f out: sn rdn and styd on appr fnl f: nrst fin* **8/1**
3205 **6** *nk* **Misplaced Fortune**[14] 3644 3-9-3 **64** .... KimTinkler 7 56
(N Tinkler) *trckd ldrs: hdwy over 3f out: rdn to chse ldr 2f out: sn drvn and wknd* **25/1**
P-03 **7** *1 ¼* **Muharjam**[10] 3799 3-9-4 **65** ....(b) NCallan 11 55
(C E Brittain) *stdd and swtchd lft s: hld up in rr: hdwy on outer wl over 2f out: sn rdn and no imp* **11/2**[3]
0400 **8** *3* **King's Alchemist**[13] 3671 3-8-5 **52** ....(v) HayleyTurner 2 36
(M D I Usher) *trckd ldrs: hdwy to chse ldng pair 4f out: rdn along 3f out and sn wknd* **16/1**
0000 **9** *9* **Strictly Elsie (IRE)**[21] 3416 3-8-2 **52** .... DuranFentiman[(3)] 3 18
(J R Norton) *s.i.s: a bhd* **66/1**
-F00 **10** *1 ½* **Jontobel**[25] 3297 3-8-1 **53** oh4 ow4 .... PatrickDonaghy[(5)] 1 16
(Jedd O'Keeffe) *led and sn clr: rdn along 4f out: hdd & wknd 3f out* **100/1**

2m 13.23s (2.03) **Going Correction** +0.175s/f (Good) **10** Ran SP% **118.1**
Speed ratings (Par 100): **98,96,96,95,91 91,90,87,80,79**
toteswinger: 1&2 £14.70, 1&3 £2.70, 2&3 £20.20. CSF £50.18 CT £121.59 TOTE £2.80: £1.10, £4.60, £1.60; EX 47.10 Place 6 £288.30, Place 5 £108.38.
Owner The Par 6 **Bred** Deerpark Stud **Trained** Upper Lambourn, Berks

FOCUS
A modest three-year-old handicap run at an ordinary pace. The winner is on the up but the form is ordinary. The winning time was fully two seconds slower than the older-horse 66-85 handicap.
T/Plt: £214.70 to a £1 stake. Pool: £58,397.76. 198.55 winning tickets. T/Qpdt: £5.10 to a £1 stake. Pool: £4,418.04. 629.64 winning tickets. JR

3952 HAMILTON (R-H)
Thursday, July 17

OFFICIAL GOING: Good (7.8)
Rail realignment around the loop reduced advertised distances on the round course by about 25yards.
Wind: Fresh, across Weather: Cloudy, bright

4113 DAILY RECORD MAIDEN AUCTION STKS 5f 4y
2:20 (2:20) (Class 6) 2-Y-0 **£2,388** (£705; £352) **Stalls** Low

Form RPR
6 **1** **Suzie Quw**[22] 3365 2-8-7 0 .... AndrewElliott 5 77+
(K R Burke) *cl up: led over 1f out: rdn clr fnl f* **3/1**[3]
3 **2** *3 ½* **Paddy Bear**[12] 3714 2-8-10 0 .... TonyHamilton 3 67+
(R A Fahey) *t.k.h: trckd ldrs: rdn and chsd wnr over 1f out: kpt on: no imp* **7/4**[1]
54 **3** *6* **Royal Muwasim**[29] 3125 2-8-6 0 .... EdwardCreighton 2 42
(M R Channon) *led to over 1f out: edgd rt and sn outpcd* **8/1**
253 **4** *1 ¼* **What A Fella**[3] 4014 2-8-7 0 .... AndrewMullen[(3)] 1 41
(Mrs A Duffield) *cl up: drvn 1/2-way: no ex over 1f out* **2/1**[2]
0 **5** *2 ¾* **Wee Bizzom**[17] 3547 2-7-11 0 .... CharlotteKerton[(7)] 4 25
(A Berry) *sn outpcd: struggling 1/2-way: nvr on terms* **100/1**

60.65 secs (0.65) **Going Correction** +0.10s/f (Good) **5** Ran SP% **106.8**
Speed ratings (Par 92): **98,92,82,80,76**
toteswinger: 1&2 £5.30. CSF £8.13 TOTE £4.20: £2.20, £1.30; EX 9.20.
Owner Aricabeau Racing Limited **Bred** The National Stud **Trained** Middleham Moor, N Yorks

FOCUS
An ordinary bunch on looks but a fair pace and an improved performance from the winner.

NOTEBOOK
Suzie Quw, who showed ability on her debut at Carlisle, attracted support and turned in an improved display. She will have no problems with 6f and she is the type to progress again. (op 9-2)
Paddy Bear, from a stable that has done well with its juveniles this year, probably ran to a similar level as on his debut. He should improve for the step up to 6f, is in good hands and is sure to be placed to best advantage. (op 11-10 tchd 2-1 in places)

Royal Muwasim, a moderate maiden, is an unfurnished sort who again had her limitations exposed in this type of event back over a trip that was far from sure to suit. She may do better in low grade nursery company over further.

What A Fella had shown enough in his three previous starts to suggest he was a player in this company but he proved a disappointment. He is starting to look exposed but will be suited by the return to further. (op 9-4 tchd 5-2 in places)

Wee Bizzom, well beaten on her debut, offered no promise for the short-term future. (op 50-1)

4114 HAMILTON-PARK.CO.UK CLAIMING STKS — 5f 4y

2:50 (2:51) (Class 6) 3-Y-O+ **£2,266** (£674; £337; £168) **Stalls** Low

Form RPR

2620 **1** **Guest Connections**[16] 3591 5-9-4 68 ....(v) AdrianTNicholls 6 77
(D Nicholls) *sn outpcd: hdwy over 1f out: led wl ins fnl f: r.o* **4/1**[2]

1003 **2** 1 **Harry Up**[28] 3172 7-9-5 77 ....(b) NeilBrown(3) 5 77
(K A Ryan) *led: rdn over 1f out: hdd and no ex wl ins fnl f* **3/1**[1]

0022 **3** 2½ **Fire Up The Band**[10] 3784 9-9-5 70 .... FergalLynch 7 65
(A Berry) *trckd ldr: rdn 1/2-way: no ex appr fnl f* **11/2**

1234 **4** 1 **Kings College Boy**[2] 4047 8-9-3 65 ....(v) TonyHamilton 3 60
(R A Fahey) *chsd ldrs: drvn over 2f out: one pce over 1f out* **3/1**[1]

0313 **5** 1 **Howards Tipple**[5] 3956 4-9-1 61 ....(p) TomEaves 1 54
(Miss L A Perratt) *prom: rdn 1/2-way: no imp over 1f out* **5/1**[3]

0112 **6** 19 **Luloah**[16] 3577 5-8-12 50 ....(p) SebSanders 2 —
(J G M O'Shea) *s.s: t.o thrght* **10/1**

59.90 secs (-0.10) **Going Correction** +0.10s/f (Good) 6 Ran SP% **111.1**
Speed ratings (Par 101): **104,102,98,96,95 64**
toteswinger: 1&2 £3.30, 1&3 £4.60, 2&3 £3.10. CSF £15.98 TOTE £5.60: £2.50, £2.10; EX 13.20.
Owner Hall Farm Racing & D Nicholls **Bred** The Lavington Stud **Trained** Sessay, N Yorks

FOCUS
A fair event and one run at a decent gallop throughout. Despite that the form is not that solid so has not been rated too positively.

4115 BILL AND DAVID MCHARG MEMORIAL H'CAP — 1m 65y

3:25 (3:26) (Class 6) (0-65,65) 3-Y-O **£2,266** (£674; £337; £168) **Stalls** High

Form RPR

4451 **1** **Flashy Max**[2] 4049 3-8-1 48 .... AndrewMullen(3) 5 54
(Jedd O'Keeffe) *led 2f: pressed ldr: led over 2f out: hld on wl fnl f* **11/4**[1]

0001 **2** ¾ **Hasty Lady**[14] 3640 3-9-1 62 ....(p) NeilBrown(3) 8 66
(K A Ryan) *chsd ldrs: effrt and ev ch over 2f out: kpt on u.p fnl f* **7/1**

4325 **3** nk **Castlebury (IRE)**[12] 3737 3-9-7 65 .... RobertWinston 9 68
(G A Swinbank) *prom: drvn over 3f out: rallied over 1f out: kpt on fnl f* **7/2**[2]

4205 **4** nk **Mganga**[2] 4049 3-8-13 57 .... EdwardCreighton 4 60
(M R Channon) *hld up: effrt and edgd rt 2f out: kpt on ins fnl f: hld towards fin* **11/2**[3]

0040 **5** 2 **Miss Understanding**[14] 3644 3-8-2 46 oh1 ....(p) DaleGibson 7 44
(J R Weymes) *bhd: outpcd and plenty to do over 4f out: rallied 2f out: no ex wl ins fnl f* **33/1**

1323 **6** 1½ **Johnny Friendly**[16] 3578 3-9-5 63 .... AndrewElliott 6 58
(K R Burke) *cl up: led after 2f to over 2f out: wknd over 1f out* **11/4**[1]

-050 **7** 3¾ **Rascasse**[10] 3786 3-9-2 60 .... TWilliams 1 46
(Bruce Hellier) *hld up in tch: drvn over 2f out: sn wknd* **100/1**

30-6 **8** 10 **Howards Hope**[10] 3790 3-9-5 63 ....(b) TomEaves 2 26
(Miss L A Perratt) *hld up: drvn over 3f out: btn 2f out* **16/1**

1m 49.38s (0.98) **Going Correction** +0.10s/f (Good) 8 Ran SP% **113.3**
Speed ratings (Par 98): **99,98,97,97,95 94,90,80**
toteswinger: 1&2 £4.90, 1&3 £3.10, 2&3 £3.50. CSF £22.34 CT £68.38 TOTE £4.00: £1.60, £1.80, £1.30; EX 16.90.
Owner W R B Racing 50 (wrbracing.com) **Bred** Bearstone Stud **Trained** Middleham Moor, N Yorks
■ Stewards' Enquiry : Neil Brown caution: used whip with excessive frequency
Andrew Mullen three-day ban: used whip with excessive frequency (Jul 31, Aug 1,3)

FOCUS
A run-of-the-mill handicap in which the pace was ordinary and the form looks messy.

4116 DAILY RECORD MAIDEN STKS — 1m 3f 16y

4:00 (4:02) (Class 5) 3-Y-O+ **£3,238** (£963; £481; £240) **Stalls** High

Form RPR

2333 **1** **Wells Lyrical (IRE)**[45] 2675 3-9-2 77 .... TomEaves 3 80
(B Smart) *chsd wnr: niggled 1/2-way: rdn over 3f out: rallied and led ins fnl f: kpt on wl* **6/4**[1]

25 **2** ½ **Buddhist Monk**[28] 3161 3-9-2 0 .... SebSanders 5 82+
(Sir Mark Prescott) *t.k.h: led: hanging lft whn rdr dropped whip 2f out: sn drifted to stands' side: hdd ins fnl f: r.o* **15/8**[2]

30 **3** 1¼ **Deer Daylami (IRE)**[90] 1446 3-9-2 0 .... TonyCulhane 4 77
(M R Channon) *prom: effrt over 3f out: kpt on same pce fnl f* **7/2**[3]

65 **4** 9 **Circus Clown (IRE)**[21] 3402 3-9-2 0 .... PaulFessey 7 60
(Miss L A Perratt) *hld up: drvn and outpcd over 3f out: n.d after* **33/1**

4 **5** ½ **Garra Molly (IRE)**[19] 3479 3-8-11 0 .... RobertWinston 1 54
(G A Swinbank) *hld up in tch: hdwy and cl up over 3f out: wknd 2f out* **7/1**

6 63 **Robin De La Folie (FR)**[70] 6-9-10 0 .... PJMcDonald(3) 6 —
(James Moffatt) *missed break: bhd: lost tch fr 4f out* **80/1**

00- **7** 56 **Ronnies Girl**[356] 3917 4-9-3 0 .... KellyHarrison(5) 2 —
(C J Teague) *unruly bef s: chsd ldrs to 1/2-way: lost tch fnl 4f* **150/1**

2m 25.61s (0.01) **Going Correction** +0.10s/f (Good)
WFA 3 from 4yo+ 11lb 7 Ran SP% **114.3**
Speed ratings (Par 103): **103,102,101,95,94 49,8**
toteswinger: 1&2 £1.70, 1&3 £1.70, 2&3 £2.40. CSF £4.61 TOTE £2.70: £1.40, £1.70; EX 5.70.
Owner M Barber **Bred** Brittas House Stud **Trained** Hambleton, N Yorks

FOCUS
A race lacking much in the way of strength in depth. The pace looked sound and the first three finished clear, so the form is probably reasonable.

4117 DOROTHY AND ARTHUR BALDING STKS (H'CAP) — 6f 5y

4:35 (4:35) (Class 5) (0-75,75) 3-Y-O+ **£4,533** (£1,348; £674; £336) **Stalls** Low

Form RPR

0502 **1** **Grazeon Gold Blend**[9] 3812 5-9-9 72 .... RobertWinston 6 85
(J J Quinn) *t.k.h: hld up in tch: hdwy over 1f out: edgd lft and led wl ins fnl f: drvn out* **5/2**[1]

0501 **2** 1 **Steel City Boy (IRE)**[7] 3890 5-8-8 62 6ex .... AnnStokell(5) 8 72
(Miss A Stokell) *led and sn crossed over to stands' rail: hdd wl ins fnl f: r.o* **15/2**

0303 **3** 1 **Katie Boo (IRE)**[3] 4016 6-9-7 70 .... FergalLynch 4 77
(A Berry) *in tch: effrt and swtchd rt over 1f out: checked ins fnl f: r.o* **8/1**

0-53 **4** nk **Heureux (USA)**[30] 3108 5-9-2 65 ....(b) SebSanders 1 71
(J Howard Johnson) *hld up ins: hdwy and swtchd rt over 1f out: kpt on fnl f: no imp* **6/1**[3]

0160 **5** nk **Opal Noir**[16] 3581 4-9-0 66 .... NeilBrown(3) 3 71
(Miss L A Perratt) *prom: drvn over 1f out: kpt on u.p fnl f* **14/1**

-231 **6** nk **Optical Illusion (USA)**[16] 3582 4-8-11 60 .... TonyHamilton 9 67+
(R A Fahey) *cl up: drvn and outpcd wl over 1f out: rallying whn hmpd and snatched up ins fnl f: nt rcvr* **4/1**[2]

0422 **7** ½ **Westport**[15] 3615 5-9-5 75 .... ClGillies(7) 7 77
(K A Ryan) *cl up: effrt and ev ch over 1f out: no ex ins fnl f* **6/1**[3]

3350 **8** 2¼ **Botham (USA)**[3] 4018 4-8-7 56 oh2 .... PaulFessey 2 51
(J S Goldie) *bhd and sn pushed along: nvr rchd ldrs* **8/1**

4/0 **9** 2 **Bon News (IRE)**[19] 3481 4-8-13 62 .... TomEaves 5 51
(B Smart) *hld up: rdn over 2f out: nvr on terms* **25/1**

1m 12.41s (0.21) **Going Correction** +0.10s/f (Good) 9 Ran SP% **121.6**
Speed ratings (Par 103): **102,100,99,98,98 98,97,94,91**
toteswinger: 1&2 £8.10, 1&3 £6.70, 2&3 £11.40. CSF £23.48 CT £137.64 TOTE £3.00: £1.20, £3.00, £3.30; EX 27.30.
Owner J R Rowbottom **Bred** Mrs E McKee **Trained** Settrington, N Yorks
■ Stewards' Enquiry : Robert Winston four-day ban: used whip with excessive frequency down shoulder in forehand position, and in the incorrect place (Aug 3-6)
C I Gillies one-day ban: failed to ride to draw (Jul 31)

FOCUS
An ordinary handicap in which the pace was not overly strong in the first half of the contest. The form is fair rated around the winner and third, although not the most solid.

4118 HAMILTON PARK LADIES-NIGHT H'CAP — 6f 5y

5:10 (5:10) (Class 6) (0-60,60) 3-Y-O+ **£2,266** (£674; £252; £252) **Stalls** Low

Form RPR

3432 **1** **Splash The Cash**[9] 3825 3-9-0 60 ....(p) NeilBrown(3) 8 70
(K A Ryan) *mde all: rdn over 2f out: kpt on strly fnl f* **9/2**[1]

3065 **2** 2¼ **Oeuf A La Neige**[11] 3757 8-9-3 55 .... TomEaves 2 59
(Miss L A Perratt) *hld up: gd hdwy over 1f out: styd on to take 2nd towards fin: no ch w wnr* **6/1**[3]

0624 **3** shd **High Reach**[10] 3784 8-9-6 58 .... SebSanders 1 62
(J G M O'Shea) *hld up ins: effrt and hdwy over 1f out: kpt on ins fnl f* **10/1**

-400 **3** dht **Woqoodd**[58] 2270 4-9-7 59 .... TonyHamilton 12 63
(R A Fahey) *chsd wnr: drvn and outpcd 2f out: styd on u.p ins fnl f* **15/2**

0002 **5** ½ **Fern House (IRE)**[10] 3789 6-8-7 45 .... TWilliams 11 47
(Bruce Hellier) *hld up in tch: effrt over 1f out: no ex wl ins fnl f* **8/1**

6362 **6** nk **Ride A White Swan**[8] 3831 3-9-3 60 .... AndrewElliott 10 60
(D Shaw) *prom gng wl: effrt over 1f out: nt qckn fnl f* **5/1**[2]

2005 **7** shd **Lambency (IRE)**[11] 3759 5-8-11 54 .... GaryBartley(5) 6 55
(J S Goldie) *hld up: hdwy on outside over 1f out: nvr able to chal* **13/2**

0-00 **8** 1¾ **Resolute Defender (IRE)**[41] 2780 3-8-12 55 ....(b[1]) RobertWinston 3 49
(J Howard Johnson) *stdd s: hld up: effrt over 1f out: n.d* **28/1**

2534 **9** hd **Obe One**[5] 3952 8-8-7 45 .... FergalLynch 9 40
(A Berry) *hld up: rdn whn no room over 1f out: nvr rchd ldrs* **9/1**

356 **10** 6 **Distant Vision (IRE)**[21] 3404 5-8-7 45 .... PaulFessey 7 20
(H A McWilliams) *cl up tl rdn and wknd fr 2f out* **25/1**

4422 **11** ½ **Paddy Jack**[5] 3955 3-9-0 60 ....(p) PJMcDonald(3) 5 33
(J R Weymes) *chsd ldrs tl edgd rt and wknd over 1f out* **8/1**

1m 12.37s (0.17) **Going Correction** +0.10s/f (Good)
WFA 3 from 4yo+ 5lb 11 Ran SP% **122.8**
Speed ratings (Par 101): **102,99,98,98,98 97,97,95,95,87 86**PL: Woqoodd £1.70, High Reach £1.90. toteswinger: Splash The Cash & Oeuf A La Neige £10.00, STC & Woqoodd £6.80, STC & High Reach £4.80, OALN & W £8.00, OALN & HR £13.70. TRICAST: Woqoodd £104.20, High Reach £134.81 CSF £32.89 TOTE £5.20: £2.50, £2.60; E27 Owner Trifecta £The Armchair Jockeys Bred G B Turnbull.
■ Stewards' Enquiry : Robert Winston two-day ban: careless riding (Jul 31, Aug 1)

FOCUS
A low-grade handicap in which the pace was sound and the form looks solid enough rated around the placed horses.

T/Plt: £30.40 to a £1 stake. Pool: £41,616.30. 997.40 winning tickets. T/Qpdt: £16.20 to a £1 stake. Pool: £2,672.00. 121.60 winning tickets. RY

3726 LEICESTER (R-H)

Thursday, July 17

OFFICIAL GOING: Good
Wind: Light behind Weather: Light rain

4119 LADBROKES.COM NURSERY — 5f 218y

2:10 (2:12) (Class 4) 2-Y-O **£3,885** (£1,156; £577; £288) **Stalls** Low

Form RPR

3511 **1** **Rosabee (IRE)**[7] 3865 2-8-10 75 12ex .... DuranFentiman(3) 5 83
(Miss V Haigh) *hld up in tch: rdn to ld ins fnl f: edgd rt: r.o* **11/4**[2]

14 **2** ¾ **Mister Green (FR)**[20] 3439 2-9-7 83 .... JamieSpencer 7 89
(M J Wallace) *s.i.s: hld up: hdwy u.p over 1f out: edgd rt: r.o* **8/1**

0006 **3** 1 **Paymaster In Chief**[7] 3888 2-7-5 60 oh9 .... DavidProbert(7) 11 63
(M D I Usher) *wnt lft s: hld up: hdwy over 1f out: rdn and ev ch whn hung lft ins fnl f: styd on same pce* **22/1**

004 **4** 1½ **Song Of Praise**[21] 3417 2-8-1 63 .... FrancisNorton 8 61+
(M Blanshard) *hmpd s: hld up: hdwy over 1f out: rdn whn hmpd ins fnl f: no ex towards fin* **50/1**

005 **5** ¾ **Russian Art**[19] 3485 2-7-12 60 .... AdrianMcCarthy 3 56
(R M Beckett) *chsd ldrs: led 2f out: sn rdn and hdd: styd on same pce* **16/1**

51 **6** ¾ **Golden Rosie (IRE)**[40] 2821 2-9-7 83 .... MichaelHills 6 77+
(B W Hills) *hld up in tch: led over 1f out: rdn and hdd whn hmpd ins fnl f: wknd towards fin* **13/8**[1]

14 **7** 1½ **Ykikamoocow**[41] 2775 2-8-9 71 .... SilvestreDeSousa 4 63+
(G A Harker) *prom: rdn whn hmpd and lost pl over 2f out: styd on ins fnl f* **14/1**

0230 **8** ¾ **Heaven Or Hell (IRE)**[34] 3008 2-8-1 63 .... CatherineGannon 1 50
(P D Evans) *led: rdn and hdd 2f out: sn edgd rt: wknd fnl f: eased nr fin* **33/1**

2335 **9** nse **In Transit (IRE)**[17] 3553 2-9-7 83 .... TPO'Shea 10 70
(M R Channon) *hmpd s: hld up: rdn over 2f out: a in rr* **20/1**

01 **10** 4 **Luxuria (IRE)**[16] 3584 2-8-10 72 .... RyanMoore 2 47
(R Hannon) *stmbld s: trckd ldrs: rdn and edgd lft over 2f out: sn wknd* **15/2**[3]

1m 13.45s (0.45) **Going Correction** +0.10s/f (Good) 10 Ran SP% **114.2**
Speed ratings (Par 96): **101,100,98,96,95 94,92,91,91,86**
toteswinger: 1&2 £5.60, 1&3 £14.10, 2&3 £24.80. CSF £23.13 CT £412.43 TOTE £3.10: £1.30, £1.80, £5.10; EX 25.50 Trifecta £334.70 Part won. Pool: £452.33. 0.50 winning units..
Owner R J Budge **Bred** J F Tuthill **Trained** Wiseton, Notts

FOCUS
A modest nursery with the winner to previous form although there is some concern about improved efforts in behind. The 'official' ratings are estimated and are intended as a guide.

NOTEBOOK
Rosabee(IRE) defied a double penalty to complete a ten-day hat-trick. After taking a bump at the start, she came through to lead inside the last and battled on well. There could be more to come from her, especially when there is a bit of give in the ground. (tchd 9-4)
Mister Green(FR) was back down in trip for his nursery debut. Held up in rear following a tardy start, once switched to race towards the stands' side he ran on well for second but the filly was always holding him. (op 12-1)
Paymaster In Chief showed improvement at Warwick last time and duly ran well again on this drop back to 6f. He was 9lb out of the weights which makes this effort all the more creditable. (op 25-1 tchd 20-1)
Song Of Praise, returning to 6f for this nursery debut, ran a decent race but was held when tightened up inside the final furlong. She gives the impression she is not a straightforward ride. (op 33-1)
Russian Art was stepping up in trip for this nursery bow. He probably stayed but might prove more effective back at 5f. (op 22-1 tchd 14-1)
Golden Rosie(IRE) holds an entry in the Group 2 Lowther Stakes and was a non-runner in a Listed event last time. She looked like justifying market support when striking the front but did not last long in the lead and was held when hampered inside the last. This first run in 41 days might just have been needed. (op 11-8 tchd 7-4)
Ykikamoocow, upped in trip for her nursery debut, would have been closer had she not been stopped in her run near the stands' rail. (tchd 12-1)

4120 LADBROKES.COM (S) STKS — 5f 2y
2:40 (2:43) (Class 6) 2-Y-O — **£1,942** (£578; £288; £144) **Stalls** Low

Form — RPR
50 **1** **Time Loup**[42] 2754 2-8-4 0 ... DavidProbert(7) 8 — 58
(Miss E C Lavelle) *chsd ldr: rdn to ld 1f out: edgd lft wl ins fnl f: r.o* **9/2**[3]
03 **2** *1* **Frame And Cover**[12] 3726 2-8-3 0 ... KevinGhunowa(3) 1 — 49
(R A Harris) *s.i.s: outpcd: r.o u.p ins fnl f: nt rch wnr* **12/1**
3222 **3** *1 1/4* **Lady Fantasie**[8] 3830 2-8-6 0 ... RoystonFfrench 6 — 45
(Mrs A Duffield) *sn led: rdn and hdd 1f out: sn edgd lft: styng on same pce whn nt clr run wl ins fnl f* **1/1**[1]
04 **4** *shd* **Conakry**[6] 3902 2-8-11 0 ... TPO'Shea 2 — 50
(M R Channon) *outpcd: hdwy u.p over 1f out: styd on same pce ins fnl f* **10/3**[2]
3260 **5** *7* **Makaluna**[9] 3815 2-8-4 0 ... WilliamCarson(7) 5 — 24+
(W G M Turner) *prom: rdn and hung rt fr over 3f out: wknd wl over 1f out* **9/1**
00 **6** *11* **Maj William Martin**[9] 3815 2-8-11 0 ... PatCosgrave 7 — —
(M Quinn) *s.i.s: sn chsng ldrs: rdn over 1f out: wknd and eased fnl f* **40/1**

62.09 secs (2.09) **Going Correction** +0.10s/f (Good) — **6** Ran SP% **111.4**
Speed ratings (Par 92): **87,85,83,83,72 54**
toteswinger: 1&2 £5.50, 1&3 £1.80, 2&3 £2.10. CSF £50.52 TOTE £6.40: £2.10, £3.20; EX 61.50 Trifecta £263.90 Pool: £563.58. 1.58 winning units..The winner was sold to Roy Bowring for £4,400.
Owner Caloona Racing **Bred** D R Tucker **Trained** Wildhern, Hants
■ Stewards' Enquiry : David Probert one-day ban: careless riding (Jul 31)

FOCUS
A weak seller in which the leaders went too fast and the third is the best guide to the level.

NOTEBOOK
Time Loup, down in grade, showed decent pace to go with the favourite. He got on top with a furlong to run before drifting left, probably through greenness. He changed hands at the auction. (op 13-2 tchd 4-1)
Frame And Cover, third in a similar race here over 6f last time, shaped as if in need of a return to that trip, only really finding her stride late on. (tchd 11-1 and 16-1)
Lady Fantasie has become expensive to follow. She had too much pace from the gates for most of her rivals, but the exception was the eventual winner and when he got past her about a furlong out the game was up. (op 11-8)
Conakry, dropped in grade, shaped as if in need of a return to further. (op 2-1 tchd 7-2)

4121 LADBROKESCASINO.COM H'CAP — 7f 9y
3:15 (3:16) (Class 4) (0-80,80) 3-Y-O+ — **£4,857** (£1,445; £722; £360) **Stalls** Low

Form — RPR
44-2 **1** **Irony (IRE)**[6] 3904 9-9-2 **76** ... DavidProbert(7) 10 — 88
(A M Balding) *chsd ldr tl led over 2f out: rdn over 1f out: r.o* **13/2**[3]
4-03 **2** *2 1/2* **Rum Jungle**[28] 3161 4-9-1 **68** ... DaneO'Neill 14 — 73
(H Candy) *a.p: chsd wnr over 2f out: rdn and edgd lft over 1f out: sn ev ch: styd on same pce ins fnl f* **7/1**
3603 **3** *2 1/2* **Internationaldebut (IRE)**[33] 3051 3-9-4 **78** ... DarrenWilliams 15 — 73
(S Parr) *hld up: hdwy over 1f out: sn rdn: nt run on* **10/1**
2031 **4** *3/4* **Manchurian**[34] 2995 4-9-12 **79** ... (p) JamieSpencer 4 — 75
(M J Wallace) *stdd s: hld up and bhd: stl last and plenty to do wl over 1f out: sn rdn and hung lft: r.o u.p ins fnl f: edgd rt: eased nr fin* **10/3**[1]
3160 **5** *1* **Bold Cross (IRE)**[6] 3904 5-9-2 **69** ... PaulFitzsimons 2 — 62
(E G Bevan) *hld up: swtchd lft and hdwy over 1f out: no ex ins fnl f* **20/1**
30-5 **6** *1* **Papillio (IRE)**[37] 2919 3-9-6 **80** ... NCallan 13 — 68
(J R Fanshawe) *stdd s: hld up: rdn over 2f out: hdwy over 1f out: no imp ins fnl f* **16/1**
0103 **7** *1/2* **Castles In The Air**[19] 3499 3-9-2 **76** ... LDettori 3 — 62
(Pat Eddery) *hld up: hdwy and hung rt fr over 2f out: eased whn btn ins fnl f* **11/2**[2]
0-01 **8** *1 1/2* **Ten To The Dozen**[14] 3648 5-8-10 **63** ... ChrisCatlin 9 — 48
(P W Hiatt) *prom: racd keenly: rdn over 2f out: wknd fnl f* **33/1**
-001 **9** *1/2* **Eastern Emperor**[17] 3563 4-9-7 **74** ... (p) AdamKirby 8 — 58
(W R Swinburn) *hld up: hdwy over 2f out: sn rdn: nt clr run over 1f out: wknd fnl f* **13/2**[3]
0031 **10** *3/4* **Royal Storm (IRE)**[13] 3675 9-9-5 **75** ... JamesMillman(3) 12 — 57
(B R Millman) *led over 4f: sn rdn: wknd fnl f* **14/1**
2106 **11** *1* **Divertimenti (IRE)**[65] 2083 4-9-9 **76** ... (p) FergusSweeney 5 — 55
(C R Dore) *hld up: plld hrd: hdwy 2f out: sn rdn: wknd over 1f out* **40/1**
3022 **12** *6* **Dancing Maite**[59] 2260 3-8-7 **67** ... PaulEddery 7 — 27
(S R Bowring) *chsd ldrs: rdn over 2f out: wknd over 1f out* **14/1**
05-0 **13** *1 3/4* **Petrosian**[163] 443 4-8-4 **62** ... NicolPolli(5) 11 — 20
(W Clay) *plld hrd and prom: rdn over 2f out: wknd over 1f out* **66/1**

1m 25.94s (-0.26) **Going Correction** +0.10s/f (Good)
WFA 3 from 4yo+ 7lb — **13** Ran SP% **117.6**
Speed ratings (Par 105): **105,102,99,98,97 96,95,93,93,92 91,84,82**
toteswinger: 1&2 £7.50, 1&3 £15.50, 2&3 £15.10. CSF £48.99 CT £455.72 TOTE £7.50: £3.40, £3.10, £3.90; EX 38.70 TRIFECTA Not won..
Owner John Nicholls Ltd/mobley Homes **Bred** Mrs G Doyle **Trained** Kingsclere, Hants

FOCUS
A fair handicap run at a sound pace. The favourite disappointed and the winner is rated to last year's best backed up by the placed horses.
Castles In The Air Official explanation: jockey said colt hung right

4122 LADBROKES.COM MELTON MOWBRAY CONDITIONS STKS — 1m 1f 218y
3:50 (3:51) (Class 3) 3-Y-O — **£7,569** (£2,265; £1,132; £566) **Stalls** High

Form — RPR
1320 **1** **Pampas Cat (USA)**[28] 3156 3-9-3 103 ... JimmyFortune 5 — 108
(J H M Gosden) *trckd ldr: led over 1f out: sn hrd rdn: edgd rt ins fnl f: styd on* **8/11**[1]
-023 **2** *1 1/2* **Choose Your Moment**[7] 3880 3-9-3 98 ... KerrinMcEvoy 2 — 105
(P C Haslam) *led over 8f out: shkn up over 2f out: rdn and hdd over 1f out: styd on same pce ins fnl f* **11/4**[2]
1 **3** *33* **Ancient Lights**[55] 2370 3-9-3 95 ... TedDurcan 3 — 39
(H R A Cecil) *hld up: racd keenly: rdn and wknd 3f out* **7/2**[3]
00- **4** *4 1/2* **Dareios (GER)**[328] 4784 3-8-10 0 ... SimonPearce(7) 4 — 30
(G J Smith) *plld hrd: led: hdd over 8f out: rdn and wknd over 3f out* **200/1**

2m 8.43s (0.53) **Going Correction** +0.225s/f (Good) — **4** Ran SP% **107.3**
Speed ratings (Par 104): **106,104,78,74**
CSF £2.99 TOTE £1.60; EX 3.00.
Owner Carwell Equities Ltd **Bred** Carwell Equities Ltd **Trained** Newmarket, Suffolk

FOCUS
A decent conditions event run at a reasonable pace, and the first two finished clear. The form is rated through the runner-up.

NOTEBOOK
Pampas Cat(USA), a smart performer who has been placed in Group 3 company, had to work fairly hard to get the better of a persistent rival. This will have boosted his confidence but he might not be easy to place from now on. (op 5-4)
Choose Your Moment, soon in front, wound things up in the straight and proved a tough nut to crack, galloping on once headed to make the favourite work hard for victory. He is well worth another try at this sort of trip. (op 5-2)
Ancient Lights, off the track since his winning debut in May, failed to run his race and was left progressively behind by the first two up the straight. He will need to settle better. (op 9-4)
Dareios(GER) showed little in two maidens for Alan Swinbank last season and was predictably outclassed on this return. (op 250-1)

4123 LYME DISEASE ACTION CLAIMING STKS — 1m 3f 183y
4:25 (4:28) (Class 5) 4-Y-O+ — **£3,238** (£963; £481; £240) **Stalls** High

Form — RPR
2110 **1** **Nawamees (IRE)**[33] 3045 10-9-7 75 ... (p) FergusSweeney 1 — 72
(G L Moore) *sn chsng ldr: led over 2f out: rdn over 1f out: edgd rt ins fnl f: styd on* **9/4**[2]
0600 **2** *3 1/4* **Olimpo (FR)**[10] 3802 7-9-4 74 ... JamesMillman(3) 6 — 67
(B R Millman) *sn led: rdn and hdd over 2f out: no ex ins fnl f* **5/1**[3]
6630 **3** *1 3/4* **Skye But N Ben**[27] 3230 4-8-5 45 ... (p) RoystonFfrench 7 — 48+
(G A Harker) *hld up: hdwy over 2f out: rdn and nt clr run over 1f out: styd on* **9/1**
000/ **4** *1 1/4* **Lady Llanover**[1799] 4111 8-8-4 0 ... CatherineGannon 8 — 45
(P D Evans) *plld hrd and prom: rdn over 2f out: wkng whn hung rt fnl f* **80/1**
5511 **5** *1 1/4* **Black Falcon (IRE)**[13] 3687 8-8-11 56 ... NCallan 12 — 50
(John A Harris) *hld up in tch: rdn over 2f out: wknd ins fnl f* **15/8**[1]
3044 **6** *1 1/4* **Starcross Maid**[13] 3687 6-8-6 41 ... ChrisCatlin 3 — 43+
(J F Coupland) *hld up: rdn over 2f out: styd on ins fnl f: nt trble ldrs* **16/1**
0 **7** *1* **Evianne**[24] 3328 4-8-2 0 ... NickyMackay 16 — 37
(P W Hiatt) *chsd ldrs: rdn over 4f out: wknd over 1f out* **80/1**
04/0 **8** *3/4* **Euro Route (IRE)**[7] 3863 7-8-6 45 ... StacyRenwick(7) 14 — 47
(G J Smith) *hld up in tch: plld hrd: n.m.r over 3f out: sn rdn: wknd wl over 1f out* **66/1**
-000 **9** *3* **Grafty Green (IRE)**[33] 3025 5-8-11 50 ... TedDurcan 10 — 40
(W M Brisbourne) *hld up: effrt over 3f out: wknd over 2f out* **40/1**
050 **10** *1/2* **Hill Of Clare (IRE)**[21] 3419 6-8-8 47 ow3 ... RussellKennemore(3) 11 — 40
(G H Jones) *prom: rdn over 3f out: wknd over 2f out* **100/1**
-000 **11** *6* **Lawyer To World**[7] 3863 4-8-13 41 ... (v) DaneO'Neill 9 — 32
(Mrs C A Dunnett) *hld up: rdn over 2f out: sn hung rt and wknd* **40/1**
525- **12** *3 1/4* **Sharmy (IRE)**[314] 5211 12-8-13 55 ... StephenDonohoe 4 — 27
(Ian Williams) *hld up: bhd fr 1/2-way* **16/1**
6/00 **13** *3/4* **Robbie Can Can**[6] 3901 9-8-5 45 ow1 ... MarkCoumbe(5) 5 — 23
(A W Carroll) *s.i.s: a wl bhd* **25/1**
P0 **14** *3 3/4* **Hungry For More**[38] 2885 4-9-0 0 ... RossAtkinson(7) 13 — 28
(M R Hoad) *hld up: bhd fr 1/2-way* **100/1**

2m 37.66s (3.76) **Going Correction** +0.225s/f (Good) — **14** Ran SP% **118.6**
Speed ratings (Par 103): **96,93,92,91,91 90,89,89,87,86 82,80,80,77**
CSF £13.27 TOTE £3.00: £1.40, £2.40, £2.30; EX 20.60 Trifecta £55.00 Pool: £214.07. 2.88 winning units..
Owner Paul Stamp **Bred** Kilfrush Stud Ltd **Trained** Woodingdean, E Sussex

FOCUS
A mixed bag in this claimer. The first two were prominent throughout and few got into it from the rear. The principals did not need to be at their best.
Robbie Can Can Official explanation: jockey said gelding never travelled

4124 LADBROKES.COM MOUNTSORREL MAIDEN STKS — 1m 1f 218y
5:00 (5:05) (Class 5) 3-4-Y-O — **£3,238** (£963; £481; £240) **Stalls** High

Form — RPR
-236 **1** **Changing Skies (IRE)**[28] 3153 3-8-9 100 ... JamieSpencer 12 — 94+
(B J Meehan) *mde all: pushed clr over 1f out: hung rt ins fnl f: heavily eased sn after* **8/11**[1]
45 **2** *4* **Kossack**[42] 2763 3-9-0 0 ... DaneO'Neill 2 — 85+
(L M Cumani) *hld up: swtchd rt over 3f out: swtchd lft and hdwy over 2f out: r.o ins fnl f: nvr nr to chal: can do much bttr* **12/1**
3 *3/4* **Red Kestrel (USA)** 3-9-0 0 ... KerrinMcEvoy 3 — 83
(Saeed Bin Suroor) *hld up: hdwy over 4f out: rdn to go remote 2nd over 1f out: styd on same pce* **12/1**
3 **4** *4 1/2* **Almonafis (IRE)**[14] 3654 3-9-0 0 ... RHills 8 — 74
(Sir Michael Stoute) *hld up in tch: rdn over 2f out: wknd fnl f* **11/2**[3]
2 **5** *5* **Skycap (IRE)**[14] 3654 3-9-0 0 ... LDettori 7 — 64
(Saeed Bin Suroor) *chsd ldrs: rdn over 2f out: wknd over 1f out* **7/2**[2]
00 **6** *2 1/2* **Solar Max (IRE)**[14] 3637 3-9-0 0 ... (b[1]) ChrisCatlin 6 — 59
(C R Egerton) *plld hrd: trckd wnr to 1/2-way: rdn and wknd over 2f out* **80/1**
06 **7** *3/4* **Amir Pasha (UAE)**[33] 3043 3-9-0 0 ... AdamKirby 1 — 58
(W R Swinburn) *mid-div: hdwy over 3f out: wknd over 2f out* **100/1**
0 **8** *4 1/2* **Angels Quest**[125] 885 3-8-5 0 ow1 ... MarkCoumbe(5) 4 — 45
(A W Carroll) *s.i.s: hld up: effrt and hmpd over 3f out: sn wknd* **150/1**
60 **9** *1 3/4* **Intercom**[14] 3654 3-9-0 0 ... TedDurcan 13 — 58+
(H R A Cecil) *s.i.s: sn prom: chsd wnr 1/2-way tl rdn over 2f out: wknd over 1f out* **33/1**

0 **10** ½ **Our Nations**[14] 3628 3-9-0 0 DNolan 5 44
(D Carroll) *chsd ldrs: rdn over 4f out: wknd over 3f out* **250/1**
11 *nk* **Brave Knave (IRE)** 3-8-11 0 JamesMillman(3) 9 43
(B De Haan) *hld up: rdn over 4f out: sn wknd* **150/1**
0 **12** 3 **Park Run**[13] 3694 3-8-2 0 StacyRenwick(7) 11 32
(A W Carroll) *hld up: hmpd wl over 3f out: sn wknd* **300/1**
2m 10.11s (2.21) **Going Correction** +0.225s/f (Good) **12** Ran SP% **118.1**
Speed ratings (Par 103): **100,96,96,92,88 86,86,82,81,80 80,77**
CSF £12.21 TOTE £1.90: £1.10, £2.60, £2.10; EX 14.50 Trifecta £143.80 Pool: £423.65. 2.18 winning units..
Owner Sangster Family **Bred** Swettenham Stud **Trained** Manton, Wilts
■ Stewards' Enquiry : Dane O'Neill two-day ban: careless riding (Aug 1,3)

FOCUS
A decent maiden in which the easy winner was value for 7l. The runner-up is capable of better.

4125 LADBROKES.COM APPRENTICE H'CAP 5f 218y
5:30 (5:34) (Class 5) (0-70,68) 3-Y-0+ **£3,885** (£1,156; £577; £288) **Stalls** Low

Form RPR
0160 **1** **Boldinor**[15] 3608 5-9-2 **54** KylieManser 14 67
(M R Bosley) *hmpd sn after s by loose horse: sn prom: rdn to ld over 1f out: r.o* **10/1**
0553 **2** 2 **Harrison's Flyer (IRE)**[7] 3872 7-9-5 **57** (p) MCGeran 11 64
(J M Bradley) *hmpd sn after s: hld up: hdwy over 2f out: rdn and hmpd ins fnl f: r.o* **12/1**
0620 **3** *nk* **Never Without Me**[7] 3868 8-9-9 **61** ShaneCreighton 17 67
(J F Coupland) *chsd ldrs: rdn and ev ch over 1f out: styd on same pce ins fnl f* **20/1**
4-06 **4** ½ **Hurricane Harriet**[53] 2427 3-8-12 **55** JPHamblett 9 58
(R M H Cowell) *led: rdn and hung lft over 2f out: hdd over 1f out: styng on same pce whn hung lft ins fnl f* **22/1**
0221 **5** 1½ **Mandarin Spirit (IRE)**[2] 4051 8-10-1 **67** 6ex WilliamCarson 3 66
(G C H Chung) *trckd ldrs: rdn over 2f out: styd on same pce appr fnl f* **3/1**[1]
6145 **6** *nk* **Cap St Jean (IRE)**[14] 3648 4-9-8 **63** (p) SoniaEaton(3) 6 61
(R Hollinshead) *s.s: bhd: styd on fnl f: nvr nrr* **14/1**
0403 **7** ¾ **Norcroft**[15] 3615 6-8-12 **50** DonnaCaldwell 2 46
(Mrs C A Dunnett) *sn outpcd: rdn and hung rt over 1f out: styd on ins fnl f: nvr nrr* **12/1**
-000 **8** ½ **Regal Dream (IRE)**[5] 3951 6-8-12 **50** PatrickDonaghy 10 44
(J W Unett) *chsd ldrs: rdn over 2f out: wknd fnl f* **28/1**
0523 **9** *nk* **All You Need (IRE)**[9] 3825 4-9-5 **60** (v) JamieKyne(3) 7 53
(R Hollinshead) *hld up: rdn over 2f out: styd on fnl f: nrst fin* **6/1**[2]
0002 **10** *nk* **Gross Prophet**[3] 4030 3-9-8 **68** RossAtkinson(3) 1 59
(Tom Dascombe) *prom: rdn over 2f out: wknd over 1f out* **6/1**[2]
003 **11** ¾ **Dubai To Barnsley**[15] 3600 3-8-4 **50** BillyCray(3) 8 39
(Garry Moss) *chsd ldrs: rdn over 2f out: wknd fnl f* **25/1**
006 **12** 1¼ **Bateleur**[2] 4051 4-9-9 **61** MatthewDavies 12 47
(M R Channon) *hmpd sn after s: hld up: hdwy over 1f out: wknd ins fnl f* **8/1**[3]
0000 **13** 6 **Tadlil**[15] 3608 6-9-2 **54** (v) MarkCoumbe 15 21
(J M Bradley) *sn outpcd: hdwy u.p over 2f out: wknd wl over 1f out* **40/1**
5000 **14** 2½ **Temtation (IRE)**[21] 3422 4-8-8 **46** oh1 SimonPearce 13 5
(J A Pickering) *hmpd sn after s: mid-div: rdn 1/2-way: wknd over 2f out* **50/1**
000 **15** ½ **Hundonette**[35] 2981 3-8-11 **54** HarryPoulton 18 10
(R M H Cowell) *s.i.s: hdwy over 3f out: wknd over 2f out: eased fnl f* **33/1**
2-00 **16** 6 **Bonny's Babe**[99] 1271 3-8-7 **50** (b1) StacyRenwick 4 —
(G D Blake) *a bhd: detached fr 1/2-way* **66/1**
5605 **U** **Gone'N'Dunnett (IRE)**[16] 3575 9-8-9 **47** (v) AmyBaker 16 —
(Mrs C A Dunnett) *uns rdr sn after s* **25/1**
1m 13.65s (0.65) **Going Correction** +0.10s/f (Good)
WFA 3 from 4yo+ 5lb **17** Ran SP% **124.9**
Speed ratings (Par 103): **99,96,95,95,93 92,91,91,90,90 89,87,79,76,75 67,—**
toteswinger: 1&2 £43.00, 1&3 £29.60, 2&3 £56.70. CSF £112.62 CT £2380.65 TOTE £15.10: £2.20, £3.00, £4.40, £4.50; EX 126.10 TRIFECTA Not won. Place 6: £269.14, Place 5: £113.34..
Owner Ron Collins **Bred** Ron Collins **Trained** Lockeridge, Wilts

FOCUS
An ordinary handicap. The form, rated around the placed horses, has a sound look to it.
T/Plt: £1,033.70 to a £1 stake. Pool: £58,835.99. 41.55 winning tickets. T/Qpdt: £24.90 to a £1 stake. Pool: £3,638.10. 108.10 winning tickets. CR

3739 SANDOWN (R-H)
Thursday, July 17

OFFICIAL GOING: Good to firm (round 9.1, sprint 8.7)
Rail realignment added 10yards to advertised distances on the rRound course.
Wind: Virtually nil Weather: overcast

4126 CONSERO HOMES SUPPORTING THE CHILDREN'S TRUST E B F MEDIAN AUCTION MAIDEN STKS 5f 6y
6:10 (6:13) (Class 4) 2-Y-0 **£4,986** (£1,483; £741; £370) **Stalls** High

Form RPR
1 **Ginobili (IRE)** 2-9-3 0 RyanMoore 10 81+
(R Hannon) *w'like: athletic: lw: s.i.s: bhd and pushed along: swtchd lft and hdwy 2f out: str run to ld wl ins fnl f: won gng away* **3/1**[1]
50 **2** 1½ **You've Been Mowed**[46] 2638 2-8-12 0 TPQueally 3 69
(D K Ivory) *lw: sn led: clr after 1f: rdn over 1f out: hdd and nt pce of wnr last 100yds* **5/1**[3]
3 ¾ **Brief Encounter (IRE)** 2-9-3 0 LPKeniry 6 71
(A M Balding) *w'like: str: bit bkwd: s.i.s: rn green and bustled along early: hdwy 3f out: chsd ldrs and rdn over 1f out: kpt on fnl f* **7/2**[2]
4 1¼ **Frognal (IRE)** 2-8-10 0 KMay(7) 4 67
(B J Meehan) *cmpt: s.i.s: hld up in tch: hdwy to chse ldrs 1/2-way: pushed along and rn green over 1f out: edgd rt and one pce fnl f* **7/1**
55 **5** 2 **Sharav**[64] 2098 2-9-3 0 EddieAhern 8 60+
(Eve Johnson Houghton) *leggy: chsd ldr: rdn and hung lft wl over 1f out: lost 2nd ins fnl f: wkng whn n.m.r wl ins fnl f* **7/2**[2]
6 7 **Piccolo Mondo** 2-9-3 0 IanMongan 7 34
(P Winkworth) *w'like: tall: chsd ldrs tl 1/2-way: sn rdn: wknd 2f out: sn bhd* **14/1**
7 12 **Miss Pusey Street** 2-8-12 0 MartinDwyer 1 —
(J Gallagher) *leggy: s.i.s: racd wd: hdwy to chse ldrs after 2f: wknd qckly 2f out: t.o* **22/1**
0 **8** 4 **Celtic Commitment**[10] 3798 2-9-3 0 RichardHughes 2 —
(R Hannon) *w'like: bit bkwd: broke wl: chsd ldrs for 2f: sn struggling and bhd: t.o fnl f* **9/1**
61.78 secs (0.18) **Going Correction** +0.075s/f (Good) **8** Ran SP% **119.6**
Speed ratings (Par 96): **101,98,97,95,92 81,61,55**
toteswinger: 1&2 £4.40, 1&3 £1.90, 2&3 £12.60. CSF £19.40 TOTE £3.50: £1.60, £2.30, £1.80; EX 17.40.
Owner Kemal Kurt **Bred** Victor Stud Bloodstock Ltd **Trained** East Everleigh, Wilts

FOCUS
Ordinary maiden form.

NOTEBOOK
Ginobili(IRE), a half-brother to five winners at up to a mile, was sent off favourite on his debut and did it nicely enough, coming with a good run down the centre of the track to get up inside the last. He will be suited by another furlong but will likely remain over the minimum trip for the time being. (op 9-4 tchd 2-1)
You've Been Mowed, with the benefit of two previous starts under her belt, showed good early speed to lead on the far rail. Her performance suggests the form is nothing special, and nurseries look the way to go with her now. (op 8-1)
Brief Encounter(IRE), whose dam was a 6f winner at two and is bred to be effective over this distance, looked in need of the run beforehand. He shaped encouragingly in the circumstances and should know more next time. (op 5-1 tchd 7-1)
Frognal(IRE), who is closely related to 6f juvenile winner Borthwick Girl, was too green to be seen at his best on his debut, but he should improve for the experience. (op 11-2 tchd 9-2)
Sharav went well for a long way but did not see it out. He does not appear to be progressing, but at least nurseries are now an option. (op 11-2)
Piccolo Mondo, who was retained for just £1,100 as a yearling, is a half-brother to 6f winner Beverley Beau. (op 20-1 tchd 25-1)
Miss Pusey Street Official explanation: vet said filly sustained a cut to its right-hind leg

4127 HITCHCOCK & KING AND ATKINS & CO. H'CAP 5f 6y
6:40 (6:43) (Class 4) (0-80,80) 3-Y-0 **£5,828** (£1,734; £866; £432) **Stalls** High

Form RPR
140- **1** **Speed Song**[324] 4923 3-9-8 **79** RyanMoore 2 91
(W J Haggas) *s.i.s: hld up bhd: swtchd lft and hdwy over 1f out: str run to ld last 100yds: r.o strly* **7/2**[1]
4162 **2** 1¼ **Requisite**[6] 3909 3-9-9 **80** GeorgeBaker 6 87
(I A Wood) *lw: hld up in tch: hdwy to chse ldrs 2f out: rdn to ld ent fnl f: hdd and no ex last 100yds* **7/2**[1]
1420 **3** 2¼ **Maggie Kate**[21] 3405 3-8-10 **67** RobertHavlin 5 66
(R Ingram) *led: hrd pressed and rdn 2f out: hdd ent fnl f: nt pce of ldng pair last 100yds* **16/1**
21-3 **4** ½ **Mistress Cooper**[33] 3026 3-8-11 **68** RichardHughes 8 65+
(W J Musson) *hld up towards rr: hdwy 2f out: chsng ldrs whn short of room briefly jst ins fnl f: kpt on same pce after* **7/2**[1]
0420 **5** ½ **Magical Speedfit (IRE)**[2] 4051 3-9-4 **75** TPO'Shea 10 70+
(G G Margarson) *stdd after s: hld up bhd: effrt whn nt clr run and swtchd lft over 1f out: plugged on fnl f but nvr pce to rch ldrs* **8/1**[3]
-031 **6** 1¼ **First Trim (IRE)**[27] 3224 3-9-0 **78** KMay(7) 7 69
(B J Meehan) *chsd ldrs: rdn wl over 1f out: wknd ent fnl f* **13/2**[2]
1000 **7** 3 **Ten Down**[20] 3462 3-9-0 **78** RosieJessop(7) 3 58
(Miss Gay Kelleway) *t.k.h: hld up in tch on outer: effrt and rdn wl over 1f out: wknd over 1f out* **33/1**
-600 **8** ¾ **Perfect Flight**[38] 2883 3-9-6 **77** EddieAhern 4 54+
(M Blanshard) *in tch: rdn 1/2-way: wkng whn squeezed for room over 1f out: no ch fnl f* **12/1**
651- **9** 2¼ **Really Really Wish**[292] 5815 3-9-4 **75** LPKeniry 1 44
(J R Best) *chsd ldr: ev ch and rdn 2f out: wknd qckly and hung rt over 1f out: wl bhd fnl f* **8/1**[3]
61.69 secs (0.09) **Going Correction** +0.075s/f (Good) **9** Ran SP% **118.7**
Speed ratings (Par 102): **102,100,96,95,94 92,88,86,83**
toteswinger: 1&2 £4.10, 1&3 £24.50, 2&3 £15.70. CSF £15.71 CT £175.86 TOTE £5.30: £2.00, £1.60, £4.40; EX 20.20.
Owner Lael Stable **Bred** Lael Stables **Trained** Newmarket, Suffolk

FOCUS
A fair sprint handicap that has been rated positively through the runner-up and third.

4128 DEVINE HOMES SUPPORTING THE CHILDREN'S TRUST H'CAP 1m 14y
7:15 (7:17) (Class 4) (0-80,80) 3-Y-0 **£5,828** (£1,734; £866; £432) **Stalls** High

Form RPR
331 **1** **Light From Mars**[24] 3312 3-9-9 **80** GeorgeBaker 8 88
(B R Millman) *lw: s.i.s: hld up in tch: hdwy over 2f out: rdn to ld over 1f out: styd on gamely u.p fnl f* **8/1**[3]
-506 **2** ¾ **Thunder Gorge (USA)**[17] 3563 3-8-11 **68** LPKeniry 5 74
(Mouse Hamilton-Fairley) *wnt rt s: chsd ldr: rdn and ev ch fr 2f out: kpt on same pce u.p fnl f* **25/1**
-300 **3** ¾ **The Which Doctor**[43] 2714 3-9-8 **79** TPQueally 7 83+
(J Noseda) *lw: t.k.h: hld up in midfield: hdwy over 2f out: nt clr run and swtchd lft jst over 1f out: r.o ins fnl f: wnt 3rd nr fin: nt rch ldng pair* **4/1**[1]
6046 **4** *hd* **Harry Gee**[17] 3561 3-9-2 **73** (b) RobertHavlin 9 77
(G Wragg) *t.k.h: in tch: rdn over 2f out: ev ch wl over 1f out: edgd rt and unable qckn fnl f* **8/1**[3]
-021 **5** *hd* **Sacrilege**[12] 3725 3-9-6 **77** MartinDwyer 3 80+
(D R C Elsworth) *lw: s.i.s: t.k.h: hld up in rr: effrt and nt clr run over 1f out: grad edging rt to find clr run after: styd on wl last 100yds: nt rch ldrs* **11/2**[2]
5-20 **6** 1¾ **King Columbo (IRE)**[12] 3745 3-9-6 **80** JerryO'Dwyer(3) 2 79
(Miss J Feilden) *in tch on outer: rdn and unable qck 2f out: kpt on same pce after* **10/1**
0-02 **7** 2½ **Storm Sir (USA)**[13] 3694 3-9-7 **78** (t) RichardHughes 4 72
(B J Meehan) *hld up in rr: effrt on inner over 1f out: no imp and wl hld whn nt clr run last 50yds* **10/1**
5461 **8** ¾ **King Kenny**[21] 3402 3-9-7 **78** JohnEgan 10 73+
(S Parr) *t.k.h: hld up in tch: hdwy on inner over 2f out: led over 1f out: sn hdd: btn whn hmpd wl ins fnl f: heavily eased after* **8/1**[3]
0404 **9** 1 **Seventh Hill**[21] 3407 3-8-10 **67** JamesDoyle 12 57
(M Blanshard) *led: rdn and hdd over 1f out: wknd ent fnl f: btn whn short of room ins fnl f* **16/1**
0-01 **10** 6 **Serious Choice (IRE)**[35] 2982 3-9-0 **71** RyanMoore 6 47
(J R Boyle) *bmpd s: a bhd: rdn over 3f out: n.d* **4/1**[1]
0 **11** 15 **Majority (IRE)**[5] 3969 3-9-4 **75** EddieAhern 11 16
(B J Meehan) *hld up in midfield: rdn and wknd qckly 2f out: eased fnl f: t.o* **33/1**
1m 42.38s (-0.92) **Going Correction** -0.075s/f (Good) **11** Ran SP% **119.6**
Speed ratings (Par 102): **101,100,99,99,99 97,94,94,93,87 72**
toteswinger: 1&2 £62.20, 1&3 £4.50, 2&3 £112.60. CSF £190.98 CT £924.89 TOTE £10.90: £2.40, £7.60, £2.20; EX 289.40.
Owner R K Arrowsmith **Bred** Harts Farm And Stud **Trained** Kentisbeare, Devon

FOCUS
A competitive handicap on paper, but the pace was not that strong and they finished in a bunch. The form looks fairly sound rated around the runner-up, however.

4129 CHILDREN'S TRUST CLAIMING STKS — 1m 14y
7:45 (7:49) (Class 5) 3-Y-O+ — **£3,885** (£1,156; £577; £288) **Stalls** High

Form — RPR

5651 **1** **Arctic Desert**[9] 3822 8-9-0 61 ....(t) RichardHughes 4 — 61
(Miss Gay Kelleway) *mde all: set stdy gallop: rdn and qcknd over 2f out: hrd rdn fnl f: hld on: all out* **7/2**[3]

0506 **2** *shd* **Optimus (USA)**[13] 3685 6-9-4 75 .... TQuinn 3 — 64
(B G Powell) *b: hld up in tch: hdwy and rdn over 2f out: chsd wnr over 1f out: r.o u.p: clsng grad last 100yds: jst hld* **11/4**[1]

1000 **3** *1 1/2* **Mick Is Back**[12] 3732 4-9-2 58 ....(vt) EddieAhern 6 — 59
(G G Margarson) *t.k.h: chsd ldrs: rdn jst over 2f out: chsd wnr 2f out tl over 1f out: unable qckn fnl f* **6/1**

0100 **4** *3/4* **Bartercard (USA)**[14] 3648 7-9-2 70 .... TPQueally 7 — 57
(Stef Liddiard) *t.k.h: hld up in last pair: rdn and effrt ent fnl 2f: kpt on same pce fnl f* **9/2**

-000 **5** *2* **Namid Reprobate (IRE)**[14] 3646 5-9-12 70 ....(b) RyanMoore 5 — 63
(P F I Cole) *racd in last pair: plld out and rdn jst over 2f out: no imp fr over 1f out* **3/1**[2]

0040 **6** *6* **Bollywood (IRE)**[55] 2352 5-8-10 42 .... MarcHalford(3) 2 — 36
(J J Bridger) *t.k.h: chsd ldr tl 2f out: wknd over 1f out* **20/1**

1m 46.96s (3.66) **Going Correction** -0.075s/f (Good)
WFA 3 from 4yo+ 8lb — **6** Ran SP% **111.1**
Speed ratings (Par 103): **78,77,76,75,73 67**
toteswinger: 1&2 £1.40, 1&3 £4.10, 2&3 £1.30. CSF £13.22 TOTE £3.80: £2.00, £2.10; EX 10.70.
Owner A MacLennan Gay Kelleway **Bred** Whatton Manor Stud **Trained** Exning, Suffolk
■ Stewards' Enquiry : T Quinn caution: used whip with excessive frequency

FOCUS
They went no pace here and the result was a sprint for the line. The form looks very dubious with the third the best guide.

4130 DRIVERS JONAS H'CAP — 1m 2f 7y
8:20 (8:20) (Class 4) (0-85,85) 3-Y-O — **£7,447** (£2,216; £1,107; £553) **Stalls** High

Form — RPR

4-14 **1** **Slip**[24] 3325 3-8-10 72 .... MartinDwyer 9 — 79+
(M P Tregoning) *lw: hld up in tch: hdwy to chse ldrs 4f out: rdn over 2f out: swvd bdly lft ent fnl f: straightened and r.o strly after to ld last 100yds* **11/4**[1]

6-55 **2** *3/4* **Ascot Lime**[36] 2954 3-8-11 73 .... RyanMoore 5 — 78+
(Sir Michael Stoute) *lw: t.k.h: chsd ldrs: rdn over 2f out: chsd ldr 2f out: drvn to ld over 1f out: hdd and unable qckn last 100yds* **3/1**[2]

-145 **3** *1* **Killcara Boy**[22] 3380 3-9-2 78 .... DaneO'Neill 7 — 81
(H Candy) *hld up in tch in rr: hdwy on outer over 2f out: styng on and chsng ldrs whn bmpd ent fnl f: kpt on last 100yds to go 3rd nr fin* **12/1**

015 **4** *hd* **Mcconnell (USA)**[34] 2996 3-9-3 79 .... GeorgeBaker 1 — 82
(G L Moore) *stdd after s: hld up bhd: pushed along 3f out: hdwy on inner 2f out: styd on u.p fnl f: nt rch ldrs* **16/1**

0331 **5** *1* **Palmerin**[12] 3745 3-9-2 78 .... RichardHughes 11 — 79
(R Hannon) *chsd ldr tl led and stdd gallop over 7f out: rdn and qcknd over 2f out: hdd over 1f out: one pce ins fnl f* **7/2**[3]

-316 **6** *2* **Black Jacari (IRE)**[33] 3048 3-9-9 85 .... EddieAhern 8 — 82
(A King) *lw: t.k.h: hld up in rr: hdwy 3f out: hanging rt fr 2f out: nt qckning whn sltly hmpd 1f out: n.d after* **7/1**

-646 **7** *nk* **La Columbina**[23] 3351 3-9-2 78 .... JimmyFortune 10 — 74
(R Hannon) *hld up in tch in rr: rdn and effrt on inner over 2f out: no imp fnl f* **16/1**

0201 **8** *6* **Addwaitya**[27] 3206 3-8-13 75 .... IanMongan 6 — 59
(C F Wall) *led tl over 7f out: chsd ldr after tl 2f out: wknd qckly over 1f out* **12/1**

1-13 **9** *11* **Avertis**[21] 3407 3-9-4 80 .... OscarUrbina 3 — 42
(M Botti) *prom tl rdn 3f out: wknd qckly 2f out: eased fnl f: t.o* **8/1**

2m 8.86s (-1.64) **Going Correction** -0.075s/f (Good) — **9** Ran SP% **124.6**
Speed ratings (Par 102): **103,102,101,101,100 99,98,94,85**
toteswinger: 1&2 £2.00, 1&3 £4.70, 2&3 £12.50. CSF £12.30 CT £89.72 TOTE £4.10: £1.70, £1.60, £3.50; EX 9.30.
Owner Mrs H Thomson Jones **Bred** Mrs H T Jones **Trained** Lambourn, Berks

FOCUS
A decent little handicap for the grade and, although the fourth appears to limit the level, the first two look progressive types.

4131 VARIETY CLUB DAY ON 30TH AUGUST H'CAP — 1m 2f 7y
8:50 (8:50) (Class 4) (0-80,80) 4-Y-O+ — **£5,828** (£1,734; £866; £432) **Stalls** High

Form — RPR

355 **1** **Presvis**[14] 3628 4-8-8 72 .... MJMurphy(7) 4 — 94+
(L M Cumani) *lw: stdd s: t.k.h: hld up in tch: hdwy over 2f out: led over 1f out: sn pushed clr: r.o strly* **3/1**[1]

4403 **2** *9* **Blacktoft (USA)**[28] 3181 5-9-2 73 ....(e) J-PGuillambert 9 — 77
(S C Williams) *led: rdn over 2f out: hdd over 1f out: no ch w wnr after but hld on wl for 2nd* **12/1**

-055 **3** *1/2* **Know The Law**[10] 3802 4-9-5 76 ....(b) MartinDwyer 3 — 79
(D R C Elsworth) *t.k.h: hld up in last trio: hdwy on outer over 2f out: kpt on to go 3rd ins fnl f: nvr nr wnr* **8/1**

1/10 **4** *1 3/4* **Benfleet Boy**[15] 3612 4-9-8 79 .... GeorgeBaker 7 — 79
(B G Powell) *chsd ldr tl over 6f out: chsd ldr again wl over 2f out tl wl over 1f out: kpt on same pce u.p fr over 1f out* **16/1**

0354 **5** *nk* **Mustajed**[14] 3649 7-9-6 80 .... JamesMillman(3) 10 — 79
(B R Millman) *hld up in midfield: rdn 3f out: plugged on same pce last 2f* **7/1**

6-03 **6** *nk* **Just Two Numbers**[34] 3003 4-9-7 78 .... JimmyFortune 5 — 76
(W Jarvis) *t.k.h: chsd ldr over 6f out tl over 4f out: drvn and one pce last 2f* **9/2**[2]

20-2 **7** *2 1/4* **Beverly Hill Billy**[17] 3561 4-9-9 80 .... RichardHughes 6 — 74
(A King) *lw: rrd s: t.k.h: hld up in midfield: rdn and hung rt 2f out: n.d* **6/1**[3]

0304 **8** *1* **Good Effect (USA)**[17] 3561 4-8-11 68 .... DaneO'Neill 11 — 60
(C P Morlock) *hld up in midfield: rdn 3f out: wl outpcd last 2f* **12/1**

5002 **9** *2* **Folio (IRE)**[10] 3800 8-9-6 77 .... TPO'Shea 8 — 65
(W J Musson) *hld up bhd: n.d* **11/1**

0 **10** *6* **Right Stuff (FR)**[42] 2762 5-8-12 69 .... RyanMoore 2 — 45
(G L Moore) *chsd ldrs: wnt 2nd over 4f out tl wl over 2f out: sn wknd* **12/1**

1-00 **11** *16* **Abydos**[25] 3294 4-9-4 75 .... TPQueally 1 — 19
(A P Stringer) *hld up bhd: lost tch over 2f out: t.o* **33/1**

2m 8.49s (-2.01) **Going Correction** -0.075s/f (Good) — **11** Ran SP% **121.3**
Speed ratings (Par 105): **105,97,97,96,95 95,93,92,91,86 73**
toteswinger: 1&2 £2.80, 1&3 £17.80, 2&3 £21.80. CSF £42.49 CT £271.14 TOTE £3.80: £1.90, £4.10, £2.50; EX 44.90 Place 6 £30.60, Place 5 £18.89.
Owner L Marinopoulos **Bred** Mrs M Campbell-Andenaes **Trained** Newmarket, Suffolk
■ Michael Murphy's first winner.

FOCUS
An ordinary handicap, turned into a procession by a handicap debutant that had been let in very lightly indeed. The second and third give a good guide to the level.
Just Two Numbers Official explanation: jockey said gelding was unsuited by the good to firm ground
T/Plt: £26.20 to a £1 stake. Pool: £57,615.95. 1,601.87 winning tickets. T/Qpdt: £13.00 to a £1 stake. Pool: £5,120.34. 290.64 winning tickets. SP

4137 - 4141a (Foreign Racing) - See Raceform Interactive

4113 HAMILTON (R-H)
Friday, July 18

OFFICIAL GOING: Good (good to soft in places) changing to good to soft after race 6 (9.00)
Rail realignment around the loop reduced advertised distances on the round course by about 25yards.
Wind: Light, across Weather: Overcast

4142 COLVILLE PARK COUNTRY CLUB APPRENTICE SERIES H'CAP (ROUND 3) — 1m 1f 36y
6:25 (6:25) (Class 6) (0-65,58) 4-Y-O+ — **£2,388** (£705; £352) **Stalls** High

Form — RPR

0-50 **1** **Sarraaf (IRE)**[37] 2940 12-9-0 48 .... PatrickDonaghy 9 — 58
(Miss L A Perratt) *hld up: hdwy and squeezed through over 1f out: led ins fnl f: comf* **14/1**

00-5 **2** *1 1/4* **Camolin (IRE)**[26] 3299 5-9-6 54 ....(b) EJMcNamara 4 — 61
(Michael McElhone, Ire) *led: rdn 3f out: hdd ins fnl f: kpt on same pce* **9/4**[1]

2-40 **3** *nk* **Thunderwing (IRE)**[55] 1824 6-9-5 58 .... NSLawes(5) 3 — 64
(James Moffatt) *hld up: effrt over 2f out: hdwy and hung rt over 1f out: ch ins fnl f: kpt on* **10/1**

4 *2 1/2* **Orange Orchid (IRE)**[752] 2963 9-8-11 45 .... SFoley 10 — 46
(James A Browne, Ire) *prom: rdn and edgd lft over 1f out: kpt on same pce* **18/1**

0055 **5** *2 1/4* **Rotuma (IRE)**[10] 3814 9-8-6 45 ....(b) JohnCavanagh(5) 7 — 41
(M Dods) *bhd: rdn after 4f: no imp tl hdwy over 1f out: nrst fin* **4/1**[3]

0241 **6** *3 1/4* **Papa's Princess**[12] 3755 4-9-8 56 6ex .... GaryBartley 6 — 45
(J S Goldie) *cl up tl rdn and wknd over 1f out* **7/2**[2]

5506 **7** *2 3/4* **Carefree**[18] 3552 4-8-12 46 ....(b) DeclanCannon 11 — 29
(Mrs R A Carr) *dwlt: hld up: drvn over 3f out: swtchd over 1f out: n.d* **12/1**

6-00 **8** *1 1/2* **Whittinghamvillage**[21] 3450 7-8-12 49 ....(b[1]) BMcHugh(3) 2 — 28
(Mrs H O Graham) *cl up tl rdn and wknd 2f out* **25/1**

42-0 **9** *1 1/4* **Always Best**[28] 3204 4-8-11 48 ....(p) LanceBetts(3) 5 — 25
(R Allan) *midfield: drvn over 3f out: wknd 2f out* **11/1**

06-0 **10** *1* **Royal Citadel (IRE)**[4] 4018 5-8-9 48 .... PaulPickard(5) 1 — 22
(Mrs L B Normile) *prom: drvn after 4f: wknd 3f out* **50/1**

/000 **11** *8* **Dance In Style**[40] 2866 7-8-6 45 .... GarryWhillans(5) 8 — 2
(A Crook) *midfield: rdn over 3f out: wknd over 2f out* **33/1**

2m 1.27s (1.57) **Going Correction** +0.20s/f (Good) — **11** Ran SP% **118.8**
Speed ratings (Par 101): **101,99,99,97,95 92,90,88,87,86 79**
toteswinger: 1&2 £10.40, 1&3 £29.80, 2&3 £5.90. CSF £45.54 CT £346.20 TOTE £19.00: £3.70, £1.10, £2.80; EX 62.90.
Owner Gordon McDowall **Bred** Joseph O'Brien **Trained** Carluke, S Lanarks
■ Stewards' Enquiry : S Foley two-day ban: used whip with excessive frequency (Aug 1,3)

FOCUS
A low-grade handicap but a sound pace throughout. Straightforward form.

4143 JOHN SMITH'S EXTRA SMOOTH NURSERY — 6f 5y
6:55 (6:55) (Class 4) 2-Y-O — **£6,476** (£1,927; £963; £481) **Stalls** Low

Form — RPR

233 **1** **Carnaby Haggerston (IRE)**[13] 3707 2-9-1 77 .... NCallan 1 — 80
(K A Ryan) *pressed ldr: led over 1f out: rdn and edgd rt: drvn out* **11/4**[2]

5121 **2** *1* **Alphabeth**[6] 3961 2-8-4 66 6ex .... TPO'Shea 4 — 66
(M R Channon) *in tch: effrt and hdwy over 1f out: wnt 2nd cl home: no ch w wnr* **7/4**[1]

253 **3** *shd* **Taazur**[22] 3400 2-8-13 75 .... JoeFanning 5 — 75
(M Johnston) *cl up: effrt 2f out: kpt on same pce fnl f* **15/2**

6122 **4** *2 3/4* **Madame Jourdain (IRE)**[10] 3809 2-8-2 64 .... JimmyQuinn 6 — 55
(N Wilson) *t.k.h: led to over 1f out: kpt on same pce fnl f* **11/2**[3]

0331 **5** *4* **Kheylide (IRE)**[9] 3846 2-9-2 78 6ex .... RobertHavlin 7 — 57
(Miss V Haigh) *hld up in tch: hdwy on outside over 2f out: rdn and wknd appr fnl f* **7/1**

4150 **6** *5* **Calley Ho**[13] 3706 2-8-7 69 .... PaulFessey 2 — 33+
(Mrs L Stubbs) *hld up in tch: rdn over 2f out: sn wknd* **16/1**

1m 14.36s (2.16) **Going Correction** +0.20s/f (Good) — **6** Ran SP% **108.6**
Speed ratings (Par 96): **93,91,91,87,82 75**
toteswinger: 1&2 £1.30, 1&3 £2.60, 2&3 £3.50. CSF £7.41 CT £25.26 TOTE £3.40: £2.50, £1.40; EX 9.20.
Owner Mr & Mrs Duncan Davidson **Bred** Mrs J A Dene **Trained** Hambleton, N Yorks

FOCUS
Not the most competitive of nurseries but one in which the pace was sound. Straightforward form.

NOTEBOOK
Carnaby Haggerston(IRE) ◆ proved suited by the step up to 6f and turned in his best effort on this nursery debut. There was plenty to like about this performance and he appears as the type to win more races this term. (op 7-2)
Alphabeth is a reliable sort who gave it her best shot under her 6lb penalty and she looks a decent guide to the worth of this form. She will be worth a try over 7f and should continue to give it her best shot. (tchd 15-8 tchd 2-1 in places)
Taazur, apart from a well beaten run in soft ground, is a consistent sort who ran creditably and is another that gives this form a solid look. He is likely to be placed to best advantage. (op 5-1)
Madame Jourdain(IRE) is not the most straightforward as she tends to race with the choke out and tends to hang, but she was not disgraced. While vulnerable to the more progressive sorts in this grade, she should continue to run creditably. (op 8-1)
Kheylide(IRE), who turned in an improved effort when successful on Polytrack on his previous start, did not get home after travelling strongly over this longer trip in this rain-softened ground under his penalty. He will be worth another chance over 5f on turf. (op 11-2)

Calley Ho, a fortunate winner over this course and distance last month, has failed to build on that since and was well beaten on this nursery debut. Quicker ground may be more to his liking. Official explanation: jockey said gelding was unsuited by the good (good to soft places) ground (op 20-1)

4144 NO NONSENSE (S) STKS — 5f 4y

7:25 (7:25) (Class 6) 3-Y-0+ — **£2,266** (£674; £337; £168) **Stalls** Centre

Form — RPR

6201 **1** **Guest Connections**[1] 4114 5-9-6 68.....(v) AdrianTNicholls 2 — 62
(D Nicholls) *trckd ldrs: effrt over 1f out: led ins fnl f: kpt on strly* **1/4**[1]

5340 **2** *1* **Obe One**[1] 4118 8-9-0 45..... JoeFanning 3 — 52
(A Berry) *hld up: hdwy and swtchd rt over 1f out: chsd wnr ins fnl f: r.o* **9/2**[2]

0604 **3** *2 1/2* **Ducal Regancy Red**[42] 2802 4-9-1 39..... DanielTudhope 5 — 44
(C J Teague) *led to ins fnl f: kpt on same pce* **16/1**[3]

6005 **4** *1/2* **Howards Prince**[11] 3784 5-8-9 37..... GaryBartley(5) 4 — 41
(D A Nolan) *t.k.h: trckd ldrs: effrt over 1f out: sn no ex* **28/1**

0000 **5** *hd* **Mutayam**[11] 3787 8-9-0 45.....(tp) JimmyQuinn 6 — 40
(D A Nolan) *cl up: effrt and ev ch over 1f out to ins fnl f: wknd* **20/1**

61.71 secs (1.71) **Going Correction** +0.20s/f (Good)
WFA 3 from 4yo+ 4lb — **5 Ran SP% 112.3**
Speed ratings (Par 101): **94,92,88,87,87**
toteswinger: 1&2 £2.00. CSF £1.89 TOTE £1.30: £1.10, £1.70; EX 1.90.The winner was bought in for £6,500.
Owner Hall Farm Racing & D Nicholls **Bred** The Lavington Stud **Trained** Sessay, N Yorks

FOCUS
A most uncompetitive race - even for a seller. The pace was just fair and those behind are flattered by their proximity to the winner, who did not need to get close to the form he showed over course and distance the previous day.

4145 JOHN SMITH'S SCOTTISH STEWARDS' CUP (H'CAP) — 6f 5y

8:00 (8:03) (Class 2) (0-105,103) 3-Y-0+ — **£21,808** (£6,531; £3,265; £1,634; £815; £409) **Stalls** Centre

Form — RPR

0544 **1** **Knot In Wood (IRE)**[13] 3722 6-9-4 98..... JamieMoriarty(3) 4 — 110
(R A Fahey) *in tch: effrt 2f out: led ins fnl f: edgd rt and hld on wl towards fin* **7/2**[1]

1456 **2** *nse* **Baby Strange**[6] 3973 4-9-2 93..... DarrenWilliams 12 — 105
(D Shaw) *hld up in midfield: smooth hdwy over 1f out: ev ch and rdn ins fnl f: rdr dropped whip last 50yds: kpt on: jst failed* **12/1**[3]

2021 **3** *2 1/4* **Pawan (IRE)**[15] 3647 8-8-8 90.....(b) AnnStokell(5) 8 — 95
(Miss A Stokell) *prom gng wl: effrt and ev ch ent fnl f: kpt on same pce* **16/1**

0010 **4** *3/4* **Barney McGrew (IRE)**[21] 3451 5-9-3 94..... DanielTudhope 16 — 97+
(M Dods) *hld up: rdn and hdwy over 1f out: kpt on: nrst fin* **22/1**

1120 **5** *1 1/4* **Valery Borzov (IRE)**[20] 3489 4-9-3 94.....(v) AdrianTNicholls 3 — 93
(D Nicholls) *t.k.h: cl up: rdn and ev ch over 1f out: no ex ins fnl f* **7/1**[2]

5005 **6** *1/2* **Maze (IRE)**[20] 3491 3-8-11 93..... RoystonFfrench 2 — 90
(B Smart) *led tl hdd and no ex ins fnl f* **14/1**

5236 **7** *1/2* **Stevie Gee (IRE)**[20] 3491 4-8-12 89..... FergalLynch 15 — 84
(G A Swinbank) *hld up: effrt on outside over 2f out: no imp over 1f out* **12/1**[3]

0610 **8** *1* **Ajigolo**[15] 3647 5-9-2 93..... TPO'Shea 13 — 85
(M R Channon) *hld up: rdn and effrt 2f out: nvr able to chal* **22/1**

3241 **9** *hd* **Everymanforhimself (IRE)**[24] 3336 4-9-1 92..... NCallan 6 — 84
(K A Ryan) *chsd ldrs tl rdn and wknd over 1f out* **7/2**[1]

145 **10** *hd* **Rising Shadow (IRE)**[13] 3722 7-9-6 97..... JimmyQuinn 9 — 88
(N Wilson) *dwlt: bhd and sn drvn along: nvr on terms* **25/1**

-000 **11** *1/2* **Sunrise Safari (IRE)**[27] 3248 5-9-0 98.....(p) BMcHugh(7) 5 — 87
(R A Fahey) *sn rdn in rr: n.d* **20/1**

120- **12** *2 1/4* **Protector (SAF)**[298] 7-9-9 100..... RobertHavlin 1 — 82
(A G Foster) *prom tl rdn and wknd fr 2f out* **25/1**

0001 **13** *hd* **Zomerlust**[6] 3973 6-9-0 91 6ex..... SebSanders 14 — 72+
(J J Quinn) *hld up: effrt on outside over 2f out: hmpd and wknd over 1f out* **12/1**[3]

0460 **14** *1 1/4* **Capricorn Run (USA)**[7] 3921 5-9-5 103.....(v) EJMcNamara(7) 11 — 80
(A J McCabe) *hld up: rdn over 2f out: nvr on terms* **20/1**

1031 **15** *2* **Tawzeea (IRE)**[16] 3601 3-8-4 86..... JoeFanning 10 — 57
(M Johnston) *prom tl rdn and wknd over 1f out* **14/1**

1m 11.96s (-0.24) **Going Correction** +0.20s/f (Good)
WFA 3 from 4yo+ 5lb — **15 Ran SP% 125.1**
Speed ratings (Par 109): **109,108,105,104,103 102,101,100,100,100 99,96,96,94,91**
toteswinger: 1&2 £9.80, 1&3 £15.40, 2&3 £48.80. CSF £43.77 CT £622.94 TOTE £3.70: £2.00, £3.90, £5.30; EX 60.70.
Owner Rhodes, Kenyon & Gill **Bred** Rathbarry Stud **Trained** Musley Bank, N Yorks

FOCUS
A competitive handicap in which the field raced on the stands side. The pace was sound and this form should prove reliable.

NOTEBOOK
Knot In Wood(IRE), the winner of this race last year, has run cracking races in some of the top handicaps since and he did just enough to notch his first win since. He is ideally suited by a strongly run 6f with a bit of give in the ground and he should continue to give a good account in this type of event. (op 3-1 tchd 4-1 in places)
Baby Strange ◆ got a bit bogged down in heavy ground at York the previous weekend but turned in a career best on ground that was on the soft side of good. He was arguably unlucky as his rider dropped his whip in the closing stages but he did more than enough to suggest a decent handicap can be found. (op 14-1)
Pawan(IRE), 7lb higher than when successful at Warwick, travelled strongly for much of the way and ran at least as well. He is at the top of his game at present and should continue to give a good account. (op 20-1 tchd 25-1)
Barney McGrew(IRE) ◆ would have been better suited by a sounder surface so he ran creditably in the circumstances, especially as he was drawn widest of all. He will be one to look out for in similar company when getting his ground. (op 20-1)
Valery Borzov(IRE), ridden with a bit more restraint than at Newcastle, was far from disgraced. He has so much foot that he may be most effective over the minimum trip and will be worth another chance. (op 11-2)
Maze(IRE) had the run of the race next to the stands' rail and ran creditably. However he still looks plenty high enough in the handicap and may well remain vulnerable to the more progressive or better handicapped sorts from this mark. (op 16-1)
Stevie Gee(IRE), who finished just behind Maze at Newcastle, may be a bit better than the bare form as he attempted to make ground on the outside from his high draw. He looks worth another try over 7f. (op 14-1)
Everymanforhimself(IRE) could not have looked in any better shape but he did not get home in the rain-soaked ground. The return to a faster surface will be in his favour and he has to be worth another chance in this type of event. (op 11-2)
Zomerlust did not get the run of the race under his penalty from his wide draw and this is probably best forgiven. He seems well suited by testing conditions but his overall record suggests he is not one to be taking too short a price about. (tchd 11-1 tchd 14-1 in places)

4146 JOHN SMITH'S STAYERS H'CAP — 1m 5f 9y

8:30 (8:30) (Class 4) (0-85,85) 3-Y-0+ — **£7,447** (£2,216; £1,107; £553) **Stalls** High

Form — RPR

2100 **1** **Always Bold (IRE)**[58] 2310 3-8-9 79..... JoeFanning 3 — 93
(M Johnston) *chsd ldrs: led 3f out: styd on strly* **8/1**

0252 **2** *4* **Gordonsville**[11] 3785 5-9-4 75..... DanielTudhope 5 — 83
(J S Goldie) *hld up: stdy hdwy 4f out: chsng wnr whn rdn and hung rt over 1f out: nt run on* **3/1**[1]

1641 **3** *15* **Nero West (FR)**[11] 3785 7-9-3 74 6ex.....(b) PaulFessey 4 — 60
(Miss L A Perratt) *led after 3f to 3f out: sn outpcd* **4/1**[3]

2-40 **4** *2* **Sin City**[23] 3368 5-9-1 75..... JamieMoriarty(3) 1 — 58
(R A Fahey) *prom: drvn over 3f out: sn wknd* **3/1**[1]

0320 **5** *26* **Red Wine**[20] 3480 9-9-0 78..... EJMcNamara(7) 6 — 22
(A J McCabe) *hld up: stdy hdwy 4f out: wknd 3f out* **9/1**

-324 **6** *73* **Dawn Sky**[21] 3461 4-10-0 85.....(b) SebSanders 2 — —
(D R Lanigan) *led 3f: cl up tl wknd fr 4f out: virtually p.u* **10/3**[2]

2m 52.53s (-1.37) **Going Correction** +0.20s/f (Good)
WFA 3 from 4yo+ 13lb — **6 Ran SP% 114.2**
Speed ratings (Par 105): **112,109,100,99,83 38**
toteswinger: 1&2 £3.40, 1&3 £14.10, 2&3 £1.70. CSF £32.75 TOTE £10.40: £4.00, £1.50; EX 33.00.
Owner Always Trying Partnership V **Bred** R N Auld **Trained** Middleham Moor, N Yorks

FOCUS
A fair handicap in which the pace was sound throughout. The form looks solid and the winner is the type to progress further.
Dawn Sky Official explanation: jockey said gelding lost its action but returned sound

4147 JOHN SMITH'S EXTRA COLD H'CAP — 1m 3f 16y

9:00 (9:00) (Class 6) (0-65,60) 3-Y-0 — **£2,266** (£674; £337; £168) **Stalls** High

Form — RPR

5511 **1** **Aleatricis**[4] 4019 3-8-13 52..... SebSanders 3 — 69+
(Sir Mark Prescott) *mde all: hung rt and drew clr fr 2f out* **1/8**[1]

0010 **2** *5* **Hoar Frost**[17] 3580 3-8-11 50..... TPO'Shea 6 — 52
(M R Channon) *cl up: effrt and chsd wnr over 1f out: no imp* **28/1**

2563 **3** *1 3/4* **Livvy Inn (USA)**[17] 3580 3-9-3 56..... RoystonFfrench 2 — 55
(Miss Lucinda V Russell) *chsd wnr: drvn over 3f out: no ex over 1f out* **10/1**[2]

2304 **4** *7* **Love Empire (USA)**[18] 3566 3-9-7 60.....(b) JoeFanning 5 — 46
(M Johnston) *bhd: hdwy over 3f out: wknd over 2f out* **12/1**[3]

005 **5** *10* **Notnowrosie (IRE)**[37] 2941 3-8-10 52..... PJMcDonald(3) 4 — 20
(A G Foster) *t.k.h: cl up tl hung rt and wknd fr over 3f out* **33/1**

2m 28.03s (2.43) **Going Correction** +0.20s/f (Good) — **5 Ran SP% 112.1**
Speed ratings (Par 98): **99,95,94,89,81**
toteswinger: 1&2 £5.50. CSF £6.99 TOTE £1.10: £1.10, £4.00; EX 5.40.
Owner The Green Door Partnership **Bred** Miss K Rausing **Trained** Newmarket, Suffolk

FOCUS
A one-sided event in which the well-in market leader won with plenty in hand, rated value for 8l. The pace was just fair.

4148 JOHN SMITH'S H'CAP (A QUALIFIER FOR THE RBS SCOTTISH TROPHY HANDICAP SERIES FINAL) — 1m 1f 36y

9:30 (9:30) (Class 5) (0-70,67) 3-Y-0+ — **£3,238** (£963; £481; £240) **Stalls** High

Form — RPR

3114 **1** **Wind Shuffle (GER)**[12] 3758 5-10-0 67..... DanielTudhope 8 — 77
(J S Goldie) *trckd ldrs: led over 2f out: sn hrd pressed: kpt on wl fnl f* **2/1**[1]

-064 **2** *1* **Prince Noel**[12] 3755 4-9-2 62..... BMcHugh(7) 2 — 70
(N Wilson) *prom: effrt over 2f out: ev ch and edgd rt over 1f out: no ex wl ins fnl f* **9/2**[3]

0064 **3** *2* **Regent's Secret (USA)**[5] 3579 8-9-9 62.....(p) FergalLynch 3 — 66+
(J S Goldie) *hld up: hdwy 2f out: kpt on fnl f: nt rch first two* **7/2**[2]

-255 **4** *1 1/2* **Bold Indian (IRE)**[12] 3755 4-9-6 62..... JamieMoriarty(3) 1 — 63
(Miss L A Perratt) *prom: effrt 3f out: no ex fnl f* **7/1**

0300 **5** *10* **Ducal Regancy Duke**[16] 3599 4-9-4 57..... RoystonFfrench 5 — 37
(C J Teague) *cl up tl rdn and wknd fr 2f out* **33/1**

5230 **6** *2 1/2* **Anthemion (IRE)**[4] 4018 11-8-9 48..... PaulFessey 7 — 22
(Mrs J C McGregor) *led to over 2f out: sn btn* **7/1**

4625 **7** *8* **Bocciani (GER)**[11] 3781 3-9-5 67.....(b) JoeFanning 4 — 25
(M Johnston) *dwlt: hld up in tch: rdn and hung rt over 3f out: sn btn* **8/1**

2m 2.31s (2.61) **Going Correction** +0.375s/f (Good)
WFA 3 from 4yo+ 9lb — **7 Ran SP% 112.8**
Speed ratings (Par 103): **103,102,100,99,90 87,80**
toteswinger: 1&2 £2.25, 1&3 £8.00, 2&3 £5.40. CSF £10.95 CT £28.41 TOTE £2.80: £2.20, £3.10; EX 11.60 Place 6 £11.77, Place 5 £5.28.
Owner Mrs S E Bruce **Bred** Gestut Elsetal **Trained** Uplawmoor, E Renfrews

FOCUS
An ordinary handicap in which the pace was fair. The winner probably didn't need to improve on his latest form in a better race.
T/Plt: £13.30 to a £1 stake. Pool: £48,157.26. 2,635.72 winning tickets. T/Qpdt: £6.20 to a £1 stake. Pool: £3,370.62. 397.49 winning tickets. RY

3913 NEWBURY (L-H)

Friday, July 18

OFFICIAL GOING: Good (good to firm in places; 7.9)
Wind: Moderate ahead

4149 HILLWOOD STUD E B F MAIDEN FILLIES' STKS — 6f 8y

1:30 (1:34) (Class 4) 2-Y-0 — **£5,828** (£1,734; £866; £432) **Stalls** Centre

Form — RPR

0 **1** **Ballyalla**[7] 3913 2-9-0 0..... RichardHughes 18 — 81+
(R Hannon) *s.i.s: sn trcking ldrs: impr travelling smoothly 2f out: drvn to ld 1f out: hld on wl whn chal thrght fnl f* **6/1**[3]

0 **2** *1/2* **Perfect Pride (USA)**[15] 3632 2-9-0 0..... AdamKirby 7 — 80+
(C G Cox) *lw: chsd ldrs: upsides ins fnl 2f: str chal u.p fnl f but a jst hld* **16/1**

3 *2 1/4* **Slant (IRE)** 2-9-0 0..... StephenCarson 8 — 73+
(Eve Johnson Houghton) *tall: w'like: mid-div: hdwy and swtchd lft over 1f out: styd on wl fnl f but nt pce to rch ldng duo* **40/1**

4 *1/2* **Demeanour (USA)** 2-9-0 0..... SebSanders 1 — 71+
(E A L Dunlop) *w'like: s.i.s: in rr: edgd to stands' side and hdwy ins fnl 2f: styd on wl fnl f: gng on cl home* **16/1**

4 **5** 1 1/4 **Solitary**[24] 3348 2-9-0 0 DaneO'Neill 15 68
(H Candy) *chsd ldrs tl slt advantage jst ins fnl 2f: hdd 1f: wknd ins fnl f* **9/2**[2]

6 3/4 **Peninsula Girl (IRE)** 2-9-0 0 EdwardCreighton 11 65
(M R Channon) *w'like: leggy: chsd ldrs: rdn 2f out: wknd fnl f* **13/2**

3 **7** 3/4 **Sharpener (IRE)**[7] 3923 2-9-0 0 RyanMoore 17 63+
(R Hannon) *sn slt advantage: hdd jst ins fnl 2f: wknd fnl f* **5/2**[1]

6 **8** shd **Order Order**[14] 3674 2-9-0 0 PaulDoe 16 63+
(H J L Dunlop) *chsd ldrs: shkn up 2f out: one pce whn n.m.r and edgd lft ins fnl f* **25/1**

0 **9** 1/2 **Costa Lotta**[34] 3032 2-9-0 0 TQuinn 4 61
(E A L Dunlop) *in tch: sme prog on outside 2f out: nt rch ldrs and sn wknd* **66/1**

10 1 1/4 **Suakin Dancer (IRE)** 2-8-11 0 TravisBlock(3) 14 57
(H Morrison) *leggy: s.i.s: in rr tl styd on fr over 1f out: nvr in contention* **40/1**

11 1 1/2 **Miss Tango Hotel** 2-9-0 0 JimmyFortune 10 53
(J H M Gosden) *w'like: cl cpld: on toes: chsd ldrs: rdn over 2f out: n.d after* **12/1**

6 **12** nk **Super Midge**[15] 3625 2-9-0 0 WilliamBuick 3 52
(B J Meehan) *in tch: rdn along 1/2-way: sn btn* **11/1**

13 1 1/2 **Brooksby** 2-9-0 0 EddieAhern 5 48
(R Hannon) *w'like: scope: rangy: slowly away: in rr tl sme prog fnl f* **50/1**

14 2 3/4 **Crown Affair (IRE)** 2-9-0 0 JamesDoyle 13 39
(J W Hills) *lengthy: lw: sn chsng ldrs: wknd fr 2f out* **50/1**

00 **15** 1 **Prima Fonteyn**[23] 3373 2-9-0 0 SamHitchcott 2 36
(M R Channon) *chsd ldrs over 3f* **100/1**

0 **16** nk **Lily Waters**[38] 2903 2-9-0 0 LiamJones 12 35
(W M Brisbourne) *early spd* **66/1**

17 shd **Intrepid Lady (IRE)** 2-9-0 0 DarryllHolland 9 35
(M R Channon) *w'like: dull in coat: a towards rr* **25/1**

0 **18** 3 **Fly Butterfly**[15] 3632 2-9-0 0 AlanMunro 6 26
(B J Meehan) *sn outpcd* **50/1**

1m 14.92s (1.92) **Going Correction** +0.175s/f (Good) **18 Ran SP% 124.6**
Speed ratings (Par 93): **94,93,90,89,88 87,86,85,85,83 81,81,79,75,74 73,73,69**
toteswinger: 1&2 £29.60, 1&3 £110.50, 2&3 £174.70. CSF £92.90 TOTE £8.10: £2.90, £6.10, £15.50; EX 165.70.

Owner Denis J Barry **Bred** Lostford Manor Stud **Trained** East Everleigh, Wilts

FOCUS
A big-field fillies' maiden in which almost half the field were making their racecourse debuts.

NOTEBOOK
Ballyalla, dropped in trip from her debut and on better ground, missed the break but soon recovered to track her stablemate. She went on over a furlong out but had to work hard to get the advantage over the runner-up. Alhough her Moyglare Stud Stakes entry may be optimistic, especially as this trip seemed to suit her better than 7f, she has a fair bit of scope and there could be more to come. (op 8-1)
Perfect Pride(USA), who had looked in need of her debut here at the beginning of the month, had to be ridden to get into contention but battled on well to give the winner a good fight. There are races to be won with her. (tchd 14-1)
Slant(IRE) ◆, the first foal of an unraced mare and bred to appreciate trips of around 1m in time, tracked the leaders and, ridden a quarter of a mile out, ran on well in the final furlong. This was a promising debut.
Demeanour(USA) ◆, a half-sister to Gaspar Van Wittel and Sugar Ray with plenty of stamina on her dam's side, looked as if the outing would bring her on but ran well from off the pace, doing her best work at the finish. (tchd 14-1)
Solitary, who showed promise on her debut over course and distance last month, disputed the lead with the favourite for much of the way but was brushed aside when the principals committed. This was a little disappointing but maybe she did too much too soon. (op 6-1 tchd 13-2)
Peninsula Girl(IRE), a 150,000gns first foal of a 1m2f winner from the family of Teggiano, was backed on this debut and revealed plenty of promise, showing up until fading in the final furlong. (op 16-1)
Sharpener(IRE), like her stable companion, the winner, was making a quick reappearance following her promising debut. She disputed the running but was soon in trouble when challenged and faded in a way which suggested that she may not have fully recovered from that initial appearance or wants dropping back to 5f.. (op 13-8)
Order Order showed up well on this second outing but was short of room in the closing stages and possibly could have finished closer had her rider given her a harder race. She looks one for handicaps after one more outing.
Brooksby Official explanation: jockey said, regarding running and riding, that his orders were to jump out, get a positive position, and finish as near as possible, adding that the filly was slowly away, ran very green, hung left, and did not get the hang of racing until the final 2f.

4150 HIGHCLERE THOROUGHBRED RACING MAIDEN STKS (DIV I) 7f (S)
2:00 (2:06) (Class 4) 2-Y-O **£5,342** (£1,589; £794; £396) **Stalls** Centre

Form RPR

3 **1** **Whispering Angel**[9] 3853 2-9-3 0 AlanMunro 1 84+
(B J Meehan) *trckd ldrs: led 2f out: in command 1f out: readily* **13/8**[1]

2 2 3/4 **Broad Cairn** 2-9-3 0 JimmyFortune 3 77+
(R Charlton) *unf: bit bkwd: s.i.s: in tch 1/2-way: drvn and styd on to chse wnr ins fnl f but a readily hld* **20/1**

2 **3** shd **Dreamwalk (IRE)**[19] 3519 2-9-3 0 SebSanders 8 77
(R M Beckett) *str; sn slt ld: rdn and hdd 2f out: one pce and lost 2nd ins fnl f but kpt on cl home* **6/1**[3]

4 1 1/4 **Bagber** 2-9-3 0 JamesDoyle 5 74
(H J L Dunlop) *w'like: in tch: rdn and outpcd 2f out: styd on again ins fnl f: nt trble ldrs* **100/1**

6 **5** 3/4 **Howard**[20] 3495 2-9-3 0 EddieAhern 7 72+
(J L Dunlop) *t.k.h: in tch: one pce and pushed along over 2f out: styd on again fnl f* **14/1**

22 **6** 1 **Noble Jack (IRE)**[36] 2972 2-9-3 0 RichardHughes 12 70+
(R Hannon) *hdwy over 3f out: outpcd and drvn 2f out: styd on appr fnl f: no imp and sn one pce* **11/4**[2]

7 1 **Hambledon Hill** 2-9-3 0 RyanMoore 10 67
(R Hannon) *athletic: bhd: rdn along 1/2-way: sme prog fnl f but nvr in contention* **25/1**

6 **8** nk **Mister Dee Bee (IRE)**[23] 3372 2-9-3 0 MichaelHills 2 66
(B W Hills) *t.k.h: chsd ldrs: chal 3f out tl over 2f out: wknd appr fnl f* **50/1**

3 **9** 3/4 **Perfect Citizen (USA)**[35] 3001 2-9-3 0 AdamKirby 11 64+
(W R Swinburn) *in rr: swtchd rt and hdwy whn n.m.r appr fnl f: nvr in contention* **9/1**

10 2 **Kayfiar (USA)** 2-9-3 0 TQuinn 9 59
(P F I Cole) *w'like: scope: s.i.s: green and pushed along: mod prog over 1f out: nvr in contention and wknd ins fnl f* **40/1**

6 **11** 9 **King's Counsel (IRE)**[27] 3277 2-9-3 0 RobertWinston 4 37
(B Smart) *w'like: str: pressed ldrs: chal 3f out tl wknd qckly over 2f out: eased whn no ch* **40/1**

12 1/2 **Davids Matador** 2-9-3 0 StephenCarson 13 36
(Eve Johnson Houghton) *str: slowly away: in tch 4f* **33/1**

13 12 **Royal Arthur** 2-9-3 0 PaulDoe 6 6
(L A Dace) *leggy: bit bkwd: slowly away: hrd rdn 1/2-way and no rspnse* **100/1**

1m 27.09s (1.39) **Going Correction** +0.175s/f (Good) **13 Ran SP% 116.1**
Speed ratings (Par 96): **99,95,95,94,93 92,91,90,89,87 77,76,63**
toteswinger: 1&2 £13.30, 1&3 £3.30, 2&3 £18.10. CSF £41.37 TOTE £2.70: £1.40, £5.10, £2.00; EX 43.80.

Owner Brimacombe, McNally, Rickman & Sangster **Bred** Grundy Bloodstock S L R **Trained** Manton, Wilts

FOCUS
A decent-looking maiden, run 1.14secs faster than the second division.

NOTEBOOK
Whispering Angel ◆, who ran well on his debut at the Newmarket July meeting, was always travelling on this occasion and, when asked to assert, did so without fuss and never looked like being reeled in. He should go on again from this. (op 11-8 tchd 6-5)
Broad Cairn ◆, a half-brother to three winners including Fretwork from the family of Right Approach, was backed in from 50/1 on this debut and showed plenty of promise. He tracked the pace before coming through to chase home the winner. He looked as if he will benefit from the experience and can win a similar race before long. (op 50-1)
Dreamwalk(IRE), who ran well on his debut at Salisbury, put up another solid effort. He raced up with the pace but got a little tapped for toe by the winner before keeping on again. He may benefit from a longer trip on this evidence. (tchd 7-1)
Bagber the rank outsider of the field, looked likely to need the outing so in the circumstances did well and showed plenty of promise.
Howard, a half-brother to the stayer Samuel, had shown ability on his debut and did so again. A step up in trip and handicaps are likely to be needed before we see the best of him. (op 12-1)
Noble Jack(IRE) runner-up in two previous starts, was below form over this longer trip. The distance may not have been in his favour but he does at least qualify for nurseries now. (tchd 5-2 and 10-3)
Hambledon Hill, a son of the King's Stand winner Dominica, clearly does not possess his mother's pace but was noted staying on quite nicely at the end and should come on for the experience. (op 33-1 tchd 40-1)
Mister Dee Bee(IRE) showed plenty of early pace on this second outing but was quite keen and paid the penalty in the last furlong. He has plenty of pace in his pedigree and may be suited by a drop in distance. (op 66-1)
Perfect Citizen(USA), third on his debut, was held up off the pace then failed to get a run at a vital stage. He can be given a chance to prove he is better than this.
Kayfiar(USA), half-brother to five winners in the USA, missed the break and ran green but did show signs of ability without ever really getting involved. (tchd 33-1)
Davids Matador Official explanation: jockey said colt had a breathing problem

4151 HIGHCLERE THOROUGHBRED RACING MAIDEN STKS (DIV II) 7f (S)
2:35 (2:41) (Class 4) 2-Y-O **£5,342** (£1,589; £794; £396) **Stalls** Centre

Form RPR

1 **Patrician's Glory (USA)** 2-9-3 0 JohnEgan 7 80+
(Jane Chapple-Hyam) *w'like: in tch: hdwy over 1f out: drvn and str run fnl f to collar ldr fnl strides* **25/1**

2 **2** nk **Imaam**[20] 3495 2-9-3 0 RHills 10 79+
(J L Dunlop) *lw: trckd ldrs: qcknd to ld over 1f out: styd on whn drvn fnl f: ct fnl strides* **1/1**[1]

3 1 1/4 **Arabian Flame (IRE)** 2-9-3 0 DarryllHolland 2 76
(M R Channon) *w'like: scope: chsd ldrs: drvn to chal fr ins fnl 2f: outpcd ins fnl f* **11/2**[2]

4 3/4 **Millway Beach (IRE)** 2-9-3 0 DaneO'Neill 12 74+
(Pat Eddery) *w'like: lengthy: s.i.s: in rr: drvn and hdwy whn hmpd ins fnl 2f: swtchd rt and styd on wl fnl f: gng on cl home* **33/1**

5 1 **Greensward** 2-9-3 0 EddieAhern 9 72+
(B J Meehan) *s.i.s: in rr tl hdwy 3f out: chsd ldrs 2f out: one pce fnl f* **25/1**

6 1 1/2 **Hydrant** 2-9-3 0 AlanMunro 8 68
(P W Chapple-Hyam) *gd sort: bit bkwd: chsd ldrs: drvn along ins fnl 3f and one pce: kpt on again fnl f* **14/1**

7 1 1/4 **Dalradian (IRE)** 2-9-3 0 PaulDoe 4 65
(W J Knight) *w'like: unruly stalls: t.k.h and chsd ldrs: slt ld 2f out: hdd over 1f out and sn wknd* **11/1**

8 1/2 **Felday** 2-9-3 0 RyanMoore 13 63+
(H Morrison) *athletic: swtg: s.i.s: in rr and green: pushed along over 3f out: kpt on fnl f but nvr in contention* **18/1**

0 **9** nse **Chiberta King**[14] 3682 2-9-3 0 WilliamBuick 11 63
(A M Balding) *chsd ldrs: rdn and outpcd 3f out: styd on again fnl f* **20/1**

6 **10** 1 **Spring Secret**[29] 3164 2-9-3 0 CatherineGannon 3 61
(B Palling) *leggy: on toes: led: rdn 3f out: hdd 2f out and sn wknd* **100/1**

11 1 1/2 **Old Street** 2-9-3 0 JimmyFortune 6 57
(R Charlton) *w'like: scope: bit bkwd: s.i.s: in rr: hdwy to chse ldrs 3f out: wknd over 1f out* **8/1**[3]

0 **12** nk **Storm Mist (IRE)**[14] 3682 2-9-3 0 KerrinMcEvoy 1 56
(P F I Cole) *pressed ldrs: upsides fr 3f out tl wknd ins fnl 2f* **50/1**

13 1 1/4 **Lethal Glaze (IRE)** 2-9-3 0 RichardHughes 5 53
(R Hannon) *str: athletic: s.i.s: brief effrt 1/2-way: sn bhd* **14/1**

1m 28.23s (2.53) **Going Correction** +0.175s/f (Good) **13 Ran SP% 121.8**
Speed ratings (Par 96): **92,91,90,89,88 86,85,84,84,83 81,81,79**
toteswinger: 1&2 £8.80, 1&3 £25.40, 2&3 £2.00. CSF £49.21 TOTE £30.50: £4.80, £1.40, £1.90; EX 64.80.

Owner Mrs Fitri Hay **Bred** And Mrs Robert David Randal **Trained** Lambourn, Berks

FOCUS
Another fair-looking maiden in which the majority were making their debuts. They were generally a good-looking bunch, but it was run 1.14secs slower than the first division.

NOTEBOOK
Patrician's Glory(USA), a chunky colt, who was held up and given plenty of cover, made good headway when asked and gained the lead inside the final furlong. He cost 200,000gns at the breeze-ups and clearly has a fair amount of ability, although connections had no specific plans for him at this stage. (op 20-1)
Imaam, who ran so well on his debut against a horse who was subsequently placed at Group 2 level, was prominent from the start. However, he was quite keen early and, although he did get to the front going into the last furlong, he had nothing in reserve to hold off the winner's late surge. He should have no trouble winning his maiden but may need to settle better. (op 11-10 tchd 6-5 and 5-4 in places)
Arabian Flame(IRE) ◆, who was quite excitable in the parade ring, tracked the leaders before moving up to challenge on the outside a quarter of a mile from home. He showed ahead briefly before the favourite went on, from which point he had no more to offer. This was a promising effort considering he saw so much daylight and he will know more next time. (op 9-2)
Millway Beach(IRE) missed the break on this debut but got the hang of things in the closing stages and stayed on well. He will know a lot more next time.
Greensward ◆, the first foal of the July Cup winner Frizzante and therefore related to several high-class sprinters, was another to make a promising debut, keeping on nicely under sympathetic handling. The kindness should be repaid before long. (op 33-1)

Hydrant, a 125,000gns half-brother to Inglenook from a family of middle-distance performers, looked as if the run would do him good and stayed on steadily in the final furlong. He will appreciate further in time. (op 16-1 tchd 20-1)

Dalradian(IRE), whose six siblings have all won, was restless in the stalls but travelled well up with the pace until weakening in the closing stages. He looks likely to improve if learning to settle better. (op 20-1)

Old Street, a half-brother to several middle-distance performers from the family of Wemyss Bight, showed ability despite being ponderous from the gate before dropping away in the closing stages. (op 16-1)

Lethal Glaze(IRE) Official explanation: jockey said colt hung badly left-handed

4152 JAMES COWPER FILLIES' H'CAP — 1m 2f 6y

3:05 (3:09) (Class 4) (0-80,79) 3-Y-0+ — **£4,857** (£1,445; £722; £360) **Stalls** Low

Form — RPR

-021 **1** — **Cosmea**[18] 3562 3-8-7 **71** — TravisBlock(3) 6 — 82+
(A King) *lw: towards rr tl stdy hdwy fr 4f out: led 2f out: rdn and hld on wl thrght fnl f* — **4/1**[2]

-655 **2** *nk* **Spell Caster**[21] 3459 3-9-1 **76** — GeorgeBaker 9 — 86+
(R M Beckett) *lw: t.k.h: in tch: hdwy and nt clr run over 2f out: swtchd rt and hdwy wl over 1f out: chsd wnr ins fnl f and clsng nr line but a hld* — **4/1**[2]

-316 **3** *4 1/2* **Hepburn Bell (IRE)**[46] 2665 3-9-1 **76** — KerrinMcEvoy 8 — 77+
(J R Fanshawe) *in rr and drvn along fr 4f out: stl plenty to do 2f out tl r.o u.p fnl f: fin wl* — **11/4**[1]

-552 **4** *1/2* **Saleima (IRE)**[20] 3479 3-9-0 **75** — DarryllHolland 7 — 75
(P W Chapple-Hyam) *sn led: rdn and hdd 2f out: wknd fnl f* — **8/1**[3]

63-0 **5** *1/2* **Snowy Indian**[33] 3057 3-8-11 **72** — RyanMoore 5 — 71
(Sir Michael Stoute) *in rr: rdn and hdwy on outside fr 2f out: nvr gng pce to be competitive* — **20/1**

-566 **6** *3/4* **Star Of Gibraltar**[20] 3500 3-9-0 **75** — EddieAhern 4 — 73
(J L Dunlop) *lw: mid-div: rdn over 3f out: kpt on fnl 2f but nvr in contention* — **10/1**

-304 **7** *9* **Rowan River**[25] 3322 4-9-5 **70** — RichardKingscote 1 — 50
(Tom Dascombe) *chsd ldrs: rdn over 3f out: wknd 2f out* — **10/1**

2314 **8** *1* **Friends Hope**[22] 3403 7-9-7 **79** — ManavNem(7) 11 — 57
(P A Blockley) *sn chsng ldrs: rdn 3f out: wknd qckly* — **20/1**

4034 **9** *2 1/2* **Lush (IRE)**[16] 3611 3-9-0 **75** — RichardHughes 10 — 48
(R Hannon) *in rr: rdn and sme prog 3f out: nvr in contention and sn wknd* — **14/1**

-002 **10** *2 1/4* **Broughtons Flight (IRE)**[14] 3667 3-8-4 **65** ow1 — JohnEgan 2 — 45+
(W J Musson) *in rr: hdwy 4f out: chsd ldrs 3f out: wknd 2f out: eased whn btn ins fnl f* — **20/1**

1-00 **11** *35* **Malibu Girl (USA)**[24] 3351 3-9-0 **75** — JimmyFortune 12 — —
(E A L Dunlop) *chsd ldrs tl over 2f out: eased and virtually p.u fnl f* — **20/1**

2m 7.41s (-1.39) **Going Correction** +0.05s/f (Good)
WFA 3 from 4yo+ 10lb — 11 Ran SP% **121.7**
Speed ratings (Par 102): **107,106,103,102,102 101,94,93,91,89 61**
toteswinger: 1&2 £5.70, 1&3 £3.50, 2&3 £3.70. CSF £19.79 CT £49.50 TOTE £5.20: £1.80, £2.00, £1.80; EX 21.60 Trifecta £85.00 Pool: £333.39. 2.90 winning units..
Owner Four Mile Racing **Bred** T R Lock **Trained** Barbury Castle, Wilts

FOCUS
A fair fillies' handicap run at a sound gallop in which the first two came clear. The winner is rated up 8lb, and the runner-up 3lb, but the form has not been rated as positively as it might have been.

Lush(IRE) Official explanation: jockey said filly had no more to give
Broughtons Flight(IRE) Official explanation: jockey said filly lost its action
Malibu Girl(USA) Official explanation: jockey said filly stopped quickly

4153 JUPITER UNIT TRUST MANAGERS CONDITIONS STKS — 7f (S)

3:40 (3:40) (Class 3) 3-Y-0

£7,477 (£2,239; £1,119; £560; £279; £140) **Stalls** Centre

Form — RPR

54-3 **1** — **Easy Target (FR)**[49] 2580 3-8-9 **100** — JimCrowley 2 — 102
(B Smart) *chsd ldrs: hrd drvn fr over 1f out to ld fnl 50yds: all out* — **10/1**[3]

16-1 **2** *3/4* **Atlantic Sport (USA)**[15] 3635 3-9-1 **108** — RichardHughes 1 — 106
(M R Channon) *lw: hld up in tch: smooth hdwy to trck ldrs: over 1f out: hrd rdn and one pce jst ins fnl f: rallied u.p but a hld* — **4/6**[1]

0114 **3** *shd* **Candle Sahara (IRE)**[7] 3907 3-8-5 **77** ow1 — EdwardCreighton 3 — 96?
(M R Channon) *lw: chsd ldrs: led over 1f out: hdd and no ex fnl 50yds* — **40/1**

-320 **4** *1 1/2* **Fateh Field (USA)**[29] 3155 3-8-9 **104** — KerrinMcEvoy 6 — 96+
(Saeed Bin Suroor) *lw: racd stands' side and in tch: c lft to join main gp 3f out: kpt on fnl f but no imp on ldrs nr fin* — **11/4**[2]

300 **5** *1* **Berbice (IRE)**[7] 3905 3-8-9 **97** — (t) RyanMoore 5 — 93
(R Hannon) *in rr: rdn 2f out: kpt on fnl f but nvr in contention* — **25/1**

-504 **6** *3 1/4* **Edge Of Light**[7] 3905 3-8-4 **97** — CatherineGannon 4 — 79
(B Palling) *led in centre crse: rdn over 2f out: hdd & wknd over 1f out* — **25/1**

-130 **7** *3 3/4* **Cobo Bay**[41] 2825 3-8-9 **100** — DarryllHolland 7 — 74
(K A Ryan) *lw: racd stands' side and upsides: c towards centre 3f out: wknd 2f out* — **10/1**[3]

-036 **8** *5* **Street Devil (USA)**[25] 3312 3-8-9 **75** — RichardKingscote 8 — 61
(P A Blockley) *chsd ldrs on stands' side: c towards centre 3f out and sn wknd* — **100/1**

1m 25.26s (-0.44) **Going Correction** +0.175s/f (Good) — 8 Ran SP% **116.0**
Speed ratings (Par 104): **109,108,108,106,105 101,97,91**
toteswinger: 1&2 £1.90, 1&3 £10.10, 2&3 £4.90. CSF £17.31 TOTE £11.40: £1.90, £1.10, £7.20; EX 23.10.
Owner Prime Equestrian **Bred** David Brown **Trained** Hambleton, N Yorks

FOCUS
A good little conditions stakes in which they split into two groups and those in the centre dominated. The pace was only ordinary and the form is muddling, with the third seeming to excel. Her stablemate in second has been rated only a length off his reappearance form.

NOTEBOOK
Easy Target(FR), who finished behind Fateh Field on his return in May, had been off for seven weeks since and this was a much better effort, as he travelled well and found plenty off the bridle to get the better of the favourite. He looks worth another try in Pattern company, with the City Of York stakes at the Ebor meeting a reasonable target. (op 12-1)

Atlantic Sport(USA), who impressed when winning a similar event over course and distance earlier in the month, was a hot favourite and looked like justifying the support when cruising in the wake of the leaders at the quarter-mile pole. However, when asked for his effort the response was disappointing and he was eventually run out of it by the winner. He may well have bounced and can be given a chance to atone, as he had looked a good prospect previously. (tchd 8-13, 8-11 and 4-5 in places)

Candle Sahara(IRE) had a great deal to find with most of her rivals and was only running to ensure a decent gallop for her stable companion, the favourite. However, she appeared to run well above herself and, apart from raising doubts over the form, has also probably blown her handicap mark.

Fateh Field(USA), who finished ahead of the winner at York in May, was 2lb worse off but was not helped by being in the group nearest the stands' side and did not get going until the race was over. (op 4-1 tchd 9-2 in a place)

Berbice(IRE) has not really gone on as looked likely when third in the Mill Reef here last September and also seems to have regressed since a couple of fair efforts in the spring. He was another not helped by racing nearer to the stands' rail. (op 18-1)

Cobo Bay Official explanation: jockey said colt was unsuited by the good (good to firm places) ground

4154 TKP SURFACING JOHN CHAPPELL MEMORIAL H'CAP — 5f 34y

4:10 (4:12) (Class 5) (0-70,70) 3-Y-0+ — **£2,590** (£770; £385; £192) **Stalls** Centre

Form — RPR

012 **1** — **Kelamon**[4] 4025 4-9-4 **69** — BillyCray(7) 5 — 81
(M D I Usher) *rrd stalls: towards rr but in tch: hdwy appr fnl f: drvn and str run fnl f to ld fnl 50yds* — **15/8**[1]

5146 **2** *nk* **Equuleus Pictor**[24] 3352 4-9-3 **66** — JackDean(5) 11 — 77
(J L Spearing) *lw: w ldrs tl led 1/2-way: rdn sn after: kpt on ins fnl f tl hdd and one pce fnl 50yds* — **7/1**[3]

563 **3** *1* **Hart Of Gold**[29] 3169 4-9-8 **66** — GeorgeBaker 6 — 73
(R A Harris) *lw: chsd ldrs: rdn 1/2-way: kpt on ins fnl f but nvr gng pce to chal* — **15/2**

0005 **4** *3/4* **Kempsey**[6] 3966 6-8-3 **50** — (b) MarcHalford(3) 7 — 55
(J J Bridger) *rdn to chse ldrs sn after s: styd front rnk and kpt on same pce ins fnl f* — **33/1**

0550 **5** *nk* **Pic Up Sticks**[1] 4103 9-9-8 **66** — RyanMoore 9 — 70
(B G Powell) *b: s.i.s: in rr but in tch: hdwy over 1f out: kpt on fnl f but nvr gng pce to be competitive* — **8/1**

406 **6** *2 1/4* **Desert Opal**[4] 4025 8-9-8 **66** — (b) LiamJones 2 — 62
(C R Dore) *chsd ldrs: rdn 1/2-way: wknd fnl f* — **16/1**

2350 **7** *1 1/2* **Kyllachy Storm**[25] 3316 4-8-9 **53** — EdwardCreighton 8 — 43
(R J Hodges) *in tch: rdn 1/2-way: one pce whn n.m.r over 1f out: n.d after* — **9/1**

1-10 **8** *1 1/4* **Joss Stick**[80] 1707 3-9-8 **70** — (p) JimmyFortune 1 — 56
(P J Makin) *chsd ldrs: rdn 1/2-way: wknd appr fnl f* — **25/1**

-002 **9** *nk* **Russian Symphony (USA)**[51] 2501 7-9-10 **68** — (b) RichardHughes 10 — 53
(C R Egerton) *chsd ldrs 3f* — **6/1**[2]

0050 **10** *1/2* **Hobson**[23] 3363 3-9-5 **67** — (b) StephenCarson 12 — 50
(Eve Johnson Houghton) *chsd ldrs 1/2-way: wknd over 1f out* — **25/1**

-405 **11** *1 1/2* **Smokin Beau**[44] 2710 11-9-11 **69** — JimCrowley 4 — 46
(N P Littmoden) *led to 1/2-way: grad wknd* — **20/1**

61.78 secs (0.38) **Going Correction** +0.175s/f (Good)
WFA 3 from 4yo+ 4lb — 11 Ran SP% **115.7**
Speed ratings (Par 103): **103,102,100,99,99 95,93,91,90,89 87**
toteswinger: 1&2 £4.00, 1&3 £4.80, 2&3 £11.10. CSF £13.78 CT £82.14 TOTE £2.70: £1.20, £2.70, £2.90; EX 17.20.
Owner Mr & Mrs Richard Hames And Friends **Bred** R And Mrs Hames **Trained** Upper Lambourn, Berks

FOCUS
A modest handicap but solid form and a progressive winner.

4155 WINTERTHUR LIFE APPRENTICE H'CAP — 1m 3f 5y

4:40 (4:40) (Class 5) (0-75,81) 4-Y-0+ — **£2,590** (£770; £385; £192) **Stalls** Low

Form — RPR

2 **1** — **Blakfrankisch (IRE)**[15] 3631 5-9-5 **70** — RossAtkinson 8 — 76
(Tom Dascombe) *hld up in rr: drvn and hdwy 3f out: hung lft u.p over 2f out: chsng ldr whn hung lft again 1f out: led sn after: drvn out* — **6/5**[1]

-300 **2** *1 1/2* **Touch Of Style (IRE)**[18] 3561 4-8-13 **67** — (p) RosieJessop(3) 6 — 70
(J R Boyle) *led: rdn over 2f out: hld on tl hdd and no ex ins fnl f* — **14/1**

4000 **3** *3/4* **Hatch A Plan (IRE)**[24] 3347 7-8-2 **56** — PNolan(3) 3 — 58
(Mouse Hamilton-Fairley) *s.i.s: chsd ldrs: rdn 3f out: styd on same pce fnl 2f* — **14/1**

3335 **4** *1* **Barbirolli**[7] 3912 6-8-2 **56** oh3 — DebraEngland(3) 5 — 56
(W M Brisbourne) *in tch: hdwy 3f out: styd on fnl 2f but nvr in contention* — **8/1**[3]

1404 **5** *1 1/2* **Bienheureux**[7] 3900 7-8-3 **61** — (t) AntiocoMurgia(7) 1 — 58
(Miss Gay Kelleway) *b: t.k.h in rr: sme prog on outside fr 2f out: nvr in contention* — **9/1**

5331 **6** *2 1/2* **Aegean Prince**[11] 3802 4-9-11 **81** 6ex — CharlesEddery(5) 7 — 74
(R Hannon) *s.i.s: hld up in rr: hdwy on ins 3f out: nvr gng pce to chal and wknd appr fnl f* — **5/2**[2]

3300 **7** *13* **Play Up Pompey**[82] 1643 6-8-5 **56** oh9 — BillyCray 4 — 25
(J J Bridger) *chsd ldrs: rdn 3f out: wknd over 2f out* — **33/1**

-000 **8** *nse* **Dr McFab**[24] 3347 4-8-8 **62** — AmyScott(3) 2 — 31
(Miss Tor Sturgis) *chsd ldrs tl wknd over 2f out* — **33/1**

2m 22.91s (1.71) **Going Correction** +0.05s/f (Good) — 8 Ran SP% **114.4**
Speed ratings (Par 103): **95,93,93,92,91 89,80,80**
toteswinger: 1&2 £5.00, 1&3 £4.40, 2&3 £16.60. CSF £20.64 CT £157.17 TOTE £1.90: £1.20, £3.20, £3.40; EX 26.80 Place 6: £20.46, Place 5: £3.08..
Owner Mrs A G Kavanagh **Bred** Rozelle Bloodstock **Trained** Lambourn, Berks

FOCUS
A modest apprentice race run at an ordinary gallop. Weak form, the winner 8lb off his more solid previous effort.
T/Plt: £74.30 to a £1 stake. Pool: £60,362.14. 592.60 winning tickets. T/Qpdt: £2.70 to a £1 stake. Pool: £5,256.98. 1,399.05 winning tickets. ST

3919 NEWMARKET (R-H)

Friday, July 18

OFFICIAL GOING: Good to firm (good in places; 8.4)
Wind: Light across Weather: Overcast turning showery prior to Race 4 (7.15)

4156 TALK NIGHTCLUB AND BECKS VIER H'CAP — 1m 2f

5:45 (5:49) (Class 5) (0-70,70) 3-Y-0+ — **£3,885** (£1,156; £577; £288) **Stalls** Centre

Form — RPR

5-02 **1** — **Papradon**[17] 3588 4-9-1 **57** — (v) LPKeniry 1 — 69
(J R Best) *hld up: hdwy over 3f out: rdn to ld and hung rt fr over 1f out: styd on* — **16/1**

-050 **2** *1 1/4* **Silent Applause**[15] 3655 5-9-5 **61** — KShea 17 — 70
(Dr J D Scargill) *hld up in tch: rdn over 1f out: chsd wnr ins fnl f: styd on* — **14/1**

1026 **3** *3/4* **Given A Choice (IRE)**[15] 3649 6-10-0 **70** — (p) RichardHughes 15 — 78
(J Pearce) *hld up: hdwy 2f out: sn rdn: styd on* — **16/1**

5062 **4** *1 3/4* **Trenchant**[8] 3873 3-9-1 **67** — JamieSpencer 10 — 71
(J R Fanshawe) *hld up: hdwy u.p over 1f out: nt rch ldrs* — **9/2**[1]

4233 **5** *hd* **Jackie Kiely**[73] 1904 7-9-7 **63**...........(t) NeilPollard 20 67
(R Brotherton) *hld up: rdn over 1f out: styd on ins fnl f: nt trble ldrs* **16/1**

2250 **6** *1 1/4* **Winning Show**[50] 2533 4-9-4 **60**........... AdamKirby 3 61
(C Gordon) *hld up: hdwy over 3f out: rdn over 1f out: no ex ins fnl f* **25/1**

6231 **7** *1* **Lunar River (FR)**[4] 4031 5-9-10 **66** 6ex...........(t) DaneO'Neill 16 65
(David Pinder) *s.i.s: sn mid-div: hdwy over 2f out: rdn over 1f out: styd on same pce fnl f* **9/1**

540 **8** *1* **Samahir (USA)**[10] 3814 4-8-6 **51**........... KirstyMilczarek(3) 12 48
(T T Clement) *s.i.s: hld up: hmpd over 8f out: hdwy over 2f out: rdn over 1f out: no ex fnl f* **20/1**

6440 **9** *nse* **Barry Island**[37] 2949 9-8-9 **51**........... RyanMoore 9 48
(D R C Elsworth) *hld up: rdn over 1f out: nvr trbld ldrs* **11/1**

0000 **10** *2 1/4* **Louisiade (IRE)**[17] 3591 7-8-9 **51**........... NickyMackay 14 44
(M C Chapman) *prom: rdn and hung lft over 1f out: sn wknd* **33/1**

-103 **11** *2* **Smirfy's Silver**[34] 3029 4-9-11 **67**........... TQuinn 18 56
(E S McMahon) *trckd ldrs: plld hrd: led over 3f out: rdn: hdd and hmpd over 1f out: wknd ins fnl f* **8/1**[3]

1640 **12** *1 3/4* **Resplendent Ace (IRE)**[38] 2921 4-9-7 **63**........... MichaelHills 4 48
(P Howling) *prom: rdn over 2f out: wknd over 1f out* **12/1**

6315 **13** *nk* **Prime Number (IRE)**[21] 3449 6-9-11 **67**........... J-PGuillambert 19 51
(J Akehurst) *led: hdd over 8f out: chsd ldrs: rdn over 2f out: wknd over 1f out* **8/1**[3]

0-43 **14** *4 1/2* **Princess Gee**[25] 3333 3-9-1 **67**........... ShaneKelly 6 42
(B J McMath) *chsd ldrs: rdn over 3f out: wknd 2f out* **20/1**

3-50 **15** *1 1/2* **Encores**[9] 3836 4-9-11 **67**........... KerrinMcEvoy 5 39
(M G Quinlan) *mid-div: rdn over 3f out: wknd 2f out* **25/1**

3020 **16** *1 1/2* **Maximus Aurelius (IRE)**[22] 3393 3-9-4 **70**........... JimmyFortune 13 39
(J Jay) *led over 8f out: hdd over 3f out: rdn and wknd over 1f out* **18/1**

0501 **F** **Dragon Slayer (IRE)**[6] 3965 6-9-6 **69**........... AshleyMorgan(7) 11 —
(John A Harris) *mid-div whn n.m.r, clipped heels and fell over 8f out* **7/1**[2]

2m 5.17s (-0.33) **Going Correction** +0.025s/f (Good) **17** Ran SP% **128.7**
WFA 3 from 4yo+ 10lb
Speed ratings (Par 103): **102,101,100,99,98 97,97,96,96,94 92,91,91,87,86 85,—**
toteswinger: 1&2 £72.60, 1&3 £74.50, 2&3 £57.70. CSF £218.47 CT £3658.06 TOTE £26.60: £5.00, £4.40, £4.00, £1.70; EX 802.80.
Owner Donna Rooks & Pam Rooks **Bred** B Whitehouse **Trained** Hucking, Kent

FOCUS
They went a good gallop here and the form looks sound enough.
Samahir(USA) Official explanation: jockey said filly sustained a cut on its near-fore caused by faller

4157 ROUTE NIGHTCLUB AND ANTICA MAIDEN FILLIES' STKS 7f
6:15 (6:20) (Class 4) 2-Y-O **£5,180** (£1,541; £770; £384) **Stalls** Low

Form RPR

1 **Rainbow View (USA)** 2-9-0 0........... JimmyFortune 8 90+
(J H M Gosden) *hld up in tch: led over 1f out: sn edgd lft: shkn up and r.o strly* **11/2**[1]

2 *6* **High Heeled (IRE)** 2-9-0 0........... MichaelHills 10 75+
(B W Hills) *s.s: shkn up over 1f out: r.o: no ch w wnr: improve* **10/1**

40 **3** *hd* **Snoqualmie Girl (IRE)**[15] 3632 2-9-0 0........... TQuinn 13 75
(D R C Elsworth) *hld up: pushed along 1/2-way: hdwy 2f out: styd on: no ch w wnr* **16/1**

4 *1* **Night Lily (IRE)** 2-9-0 0........... LPKeniry 12 72
(J Jay) *racd alone towards centre: prom: led 3f out: rdn and hdd over 1f out: no ex fnl f* **33/1**

5 *2 1/4* **Fallen In Love** 2-9-0 0........... KerrinMcEvoy 5 66+
(J L Dunlop) *hld up: hdwy over 1f out: sn hung lft and wknd* **7/1**[2]

6 *1 1/4* **Caravan Of Dreams (IRE)** 2-9-0 0........... DaneO'Neill 9 63
(M A Jarvis) *prom: rdn over 1f out: wknd fnl f* **9/1**

7 *3/4* **Careless Whisper** 2-9-0 0........... ShaneKelly 3 61
(J W Hills) *chsd ldrs: rdn and ev ch wl over 1f out: sn edgd lft and wknd* **16/1**

4 **8** *1* **Nashmiah (IRE)**[16] 3610 2-9-0 0........... KShea 2 59
(C E Brittain) *chsd ldrs: rdn over 2 out: hung lft and wknd over 1f out* **9/1**

9 *3/4* **Mitra Jaan (IRE)** 2-9-0 0........... AdamKirby 14 57
(W R Swinburn) *s.i.s: hld up: effrt and nt clr run over 1f out: sn hung lft and wknd* **14/1**

52 **10** *4* **Going Time (USA)**[43] 2746 2-9-0 0........... RyanMoore 4 47
(M Johnston) *led 4f: wknd fnl f* **11/2**[1]

0 **11** *nk* **Missou Maiden**[15] 3651 2-9-0 0........... RHills 6 46
(M H Tompkins) *hld up: effrt over 2f out: wknd over 1f out* **33/1**

12 *1* **Impressionist Art (USA)** 2-9-0 0........... AlanMunro 11 44+
(B J Meehan) *hld up in tch: shkn up over 2f out: wknd over 1f out* **8/1**[3]

13 *2 1/4* **Silk Cotton (USA)** 2-9-0 0........... RichardHughes 17 38
(E A L Dunlop) *hld up: rdn over 2f out: sn wknd* **16/1**

14 *nse* **Fleur De Lis** 2-9-0 0........... JamieSpencer 18 38
(M L W Bell) *hld up: rdn over 2f out: sn hung lft and wknd* **8/1**[3]

00 **15** *2 1/2* **Hosanna**[21] 3456 2-9-0 0........... NickyMackay 1 32
(B J Meehan) *chsd ldrs tl wknd wl over 1f out* **28/1**

1m 26.16s (0.46) **Going Correction** +0.025s/f (Good) **15** Ran SP% **128.2**
Speed ratings (Par 93): **98,91,90,89,87 85,84,83,82,78 78,76,74,74,71**
toteswinger: 1&2 £16.80, 1&3 £29.30, 2&3 £55.20. CSF £62.66 TOTE £6.80: £2.70, £4.10, £7.20; EX 85.90.
Owner George Strawbridge **Bred** Augustin Stable **Trained** Newmarket, Suffolk

FOCUS
A fair maiden on paper and it produced an impressive winner. Whether the form works out remains to be seen but Rainbow View could not have won any easier.

NOTEBOOK
Rainbow View(USA) ◆, a May foal, is a half-sister to Winter View, a 1m winner in France, out of a Del Mar Oaks winner, who is from the family of Raven's Pass. She picked up in really good style from over a furlong out and stretched out to win impressively, with a nice gap back to the runner-up, and she looks sure to appreciate a longer trip in time. In the shorter term, though, she will have to be of interest if turned out for races like the Prestige Stakes or Sweet Solera. (op 5-1 tchd 7-1)
High Heeled(IRE), who cost 110,000euros, is out of a mare who won over 1m winner at two in France and was later a high-class triple winner in the US. She had no chance with the impressive winner but shaped encouragingly nonetheless, staying on nicely once angled out for her run. She should improve for the experience. (tchd 11-1)
Snoqualmie Girl(IRE) was disappointing at Newbury last time, but this extra furlong promised to suit her as she has plenty of stamina in her pedigree. She was under pressure some way out but kept finding and saw her race out well. Nurseries are now an option for her. (op 12-1)
Night Lily(IRE) is by Night Shift out of a mare who placed over sprint distances at three so it was a little surprising to see her make her debut over as far as this, but she ran well, showing up prominently, and apart from the rest up the centre of the track, for most of the way. This was an encouraging debut.
Fallen In Love, whose dam won in Listed company and was placed at Group level at a mile, is by Galileo and will not be seen at her best until next year, but she came in for some support on her debut and ran with credit. She should come on for the experience. (op 12-1)
Caravan Of Dreams(IRE), a half-sister to high-class 1m4f-2m performer Royal And Regal, showed up well for a long way and is another who should come on for the run. She should get further in time, too. (op 10-1 tchd 11-1)
Careless Whisper, a half-sister to 7f winner Fuschia and 1m4f winner Flash Of Colour, is by Singspiel and would not be expected to show too much this term over this sort of trip. Middle distances will be her gig next year. (op 20-1)
Nashmiah(IRE) did not really build on her debut effort at Kempton. (op 12-1)
Going Time(USA) did not get home over this longer trip, but nurseries are now open to her. (tchd 9-2)
Impressionist Art(USA) is a half-sister to Secret Garden, a useful dual 7f-1m winner, and to juvenile winners Texas Hill and Lady Aquitaine. She looks the type to do better with this run under her belt. (tchd 9-1)

4158 DIAGEO GB H'CAP 7f
6:45 (6:51) (Class 4) (0-85,86) 3-Y-O **£6,476** (£1,927; £963; £481) **Stalls** Low

Form RPR

-221 **1** **Carniolan**[7] 3897 3-9-10 **86** 6ex........... AdamKirby 10 99+
(W R Swinburn) *hld up: hdwy and nt clr run over 1f out: swtchd rt ins fnl f: sn rdn: str burst to ld post* **8/11**[1]

1033 **2** *hd* **Brassini**[13] 3744 3-9-9 **85**........... AlanMunro 14 92
(B R Millman) *wnt rt s: sn chsng ldr: led over 2f out: rdn over 1f out: styd on gamely: hdd post* **10/1**

1430 **3** *1/2* **Solar Spirit (IRE)**[13] 3723 3-9-4 **80**........... RobertWinston 12 86
(G A Swinbank) *chsd ldrs: rdn and ev ch fr over 1f out: edgd lft: unable qck nr fin* **12/1**

4000 **4** *1/2* **Arctic Cape**[15] 3627 3-9-1 **77**........... RHills 3 81
(M Johnston) *led: hdd over 2f out: rdn and ev ch whn hung lft fr over 1f out: no ex towards fin* **16/1**

2163 **5** *1/2* **San Jose City (IRE)**[14] 3696 3-9-4 **80**........... JimmyFortune 15 83
(D Carroll) *hmpd s: sn prom: rdn and ev ch ins fnl f: styd on same pce towards fin* **12/1**

2000 **6** *1/2* **Talk Of Saafend (IRE)**[34] 3031 3-9-2 **78**........... RichardHughes 2 80
(R Hannon) *hld up: plld hrd: hdwy 2f out: nt clr run over 1f out: sn rdn: no ex ins fnl f* **20/1**

6-31 **7** *6* **Danish Art (IRE)**[20] 3499 3-9-0 **76**........... KerrinMcEvoy 6 61
(J A R Toller) *hld up: shkn up over 2f out: wknd over 1f out* **8/1**[3]

-005 **8** *hd* **Naval Review (USA)**[7] 3915 3-8-11 **73**...........(v[1]) RyanMoore 1 58
(Sir Michael Stoute) *chsd ldrs: rdn over 1f out: wknd fnl f* **7/1**[2]

1m 25.85s (0.15) **Going Correction** +0.025s/f (Good) **8** Ran SP% **116.6**
Speed ratings (Par 102): **100,99,99,98,98 97,90,90**
toteswinger: 1&2 £3.20, 1&3 £4.70, 2&3 £5.80. CSF £9.48 CT £52.94 TOTE £1.70: £1.10, £2.40, £3.20; EX 9.10.
Owner Exors Of The Late Mrs P W Harris **Bred** Jeremy Gompertz **Trained** Aldbury, Herts

FOCUS
Not a bad handicap, but the early pace was ordinary and that resulted in a sprint finish. The overall form may not be solid but the improving winner appeared to score despite everything.

4159 BUDWEISER CONDITIONS STKS 5f
7:15 (7:15) (Class 3) 3-Y-O+
£8,723 (£2,612; £1,306; £653; £326; £163) **Stalls** Low

Form RPR

20-6 **1** **Peace Offering (IRE)**[13] 3739 8-9-1 105........... TedDurcan 1 95
(D Nicholls) *sn led: rdn 1f out: r.o wl* **4/1**[2]

232- **2** *2 1/2* **Cute Ass (IRE)**[279] 6167 3-8-0 105........... AndrewElliott 7 75
(K R Burke) *sn chsng wnr: rdn over 1f out: styd on same pce* **11/2**[3]

2-05 **3** *nk* **Sakhee's Song (IRE)**[21] 3460 4-8-9 97........... TQuinn 4 79
(D R C Elsworth) *hld up in tch: plld hrd: rdn over 1f out: styd on same pce* **16/1**

5006 **4** *3/4* **Matsunosuke**[6] 3943 6-8-9 99........... KerrinMcEvoy 2 76
(A B Coogan) *chsd ldrs: rdn over 1f out: no ex ins fnl f* **9/1**

2206 **5** *2 1/4* **Thoughtsofstardom**[22] 3405 5-8-2 65........... TobyAtkinson(7) 5 68
(P S McEntee) *s.i.s: hld up: effrt over 1f out: wknd ins fnl f* **66/1**

5553 **6** *3* **Hoh Mike (IRE)**[13] 3739 4-9-1 112...........(v[1]) JamieSpencer 3 63
(M L W Bell) *s.s: hld up: rdn 2f out: sn hung lft: nt run on* **8/11**[1]

2066 **7** *nk* **Shatter Resistant (IRE)**[12] 3765 3-8-5 53...........(e) SaleemGolam 8 55
(M D Squance) *prom: rdn and wknd over 1f out* **100/1**

58.67 secs (-0.43) **Going Correction** +0.025s/f (Good)
WFA 3 from 4yo+ 4lb **7** Ran SP% **111.7**
Speed ratings (Par 107): **104,100,99,98,94 89,89**
toteswinger: 1&2 £2.50, 1&3 £6.70, 2&3 £7.00. CSF £24.66 TOTE £5.50: £2.20, £1.70; EX 25.80.
Owner Lady O'Reilly **Bred** Chevington Stud **Trained** Sessay, N Yorks

FOCUS
They only went an ordinary early gallop in this conditions race and the form is anchored by the modest fifth.

NOTEBOOK
Peace Offering(IRE), all the better for his return at Sandown 13 days earlier, looked to have every chance of reversing form with Hoh Mike, but with the favourite throwing in a stinker he did not even have to run to his Sandown form to score very easily. In front early, he made almost all the running, and presumably he will return to Pattern company now. (op 7-2 tchd 10-3)
Cute Ass(IRE), runner-up to Captain Gerrard in the Cornwallis Stakes on her final start at two, was making a belated seasonal reappearance. She put up a creditable effort against race-fit rivals and could be interesting in Listed company against her own sex. (op 5-1 tchd 6-1)
Sakhee's Song(IRE), dropping back in trip, did not settle early, but she came home quite well and was not disgraced against some higher-rated rivals. (op 20-1)
Matsunosuke remains difficult to place off his current mark. (op 8-1)
Thoughtsofstardom is just a modest handicapper and had no chance in this grade. He was not beaten far, though, which restricts the level of the form. (tchd 100-1)
Hoh Mike(IRE) was the one to beat on the ratings, and he had a visor on for the first time in an attempt no doubt to sharpen him up leaving the stalls. The headgear did not have the desired affect, though, and he was very slowly away. Looking less than enthusiastic once switched to be brought with his challenge, he has one or two question marks over him now. Official explanation: trainer said colt would not face the visor (op 5-6 tchd 10-11, Evens in places)

4160 WAVERLEY TBS H'CAP 1m 2f
7:50 (7:52) (Class 3) (0-95,95) 3-Y-O
£8,723 (£2,612; £1,306; £653; £326; £163) **Stalls** Low

Form RPR

-540 **1** **Upton Grey (IRE)**[19] 3535 3-9-0 **86**........... JimmyFortune 9 94
(J H M Gosden) *chsd ldr tl led over 7f out: rdn over 1f out: styd on gamely* **17/2**

2304 **2** 1 1/4 **Love Galore (IRE)**[8] 3877 3-9-4 90 RHills 5 96
(M Johnston) *hld up: hdwy u.p over 1f out: edgd lft: no imp ins fnl f* **2/1**[1]

2132 **3** 3/4 **Glorious Gift (IRE)**[25] 3325 3-9-1 87 AlanMunro 2 91
(P W Chapple-Hyam) *a.p: rdn over 1f out: styd on same pce ins fnl f* **6/1**[2]

2411 **4** nk **Prince Kalamoun (IRE)**[15] 3641 3-9-1 87 RobertWinston 7 90
(G A Swinbank) *hld up: switched lft and hdwy 2f out: sn rdn: styd on same pce ins fnl f* **7/1**[3]

3133 **5** 6 **Mexican Venture**[35] 3002 3-8-11 83 J-PGuillambert 4 74
(W Jarvis) *hld up: hdwy u.p over 1f out: edgd lft and wknd ins fnl f* **11/1**

1-10 **6** 1 3/4 **Strategic Mission (IRE)**[29] 3157 3-9-9 95 TQuinn 1 83
(P F I Cole) *chsd ldrs: rdn 2f out: wknd fnl f* **8/1**

15-4 **7** nse **Fool's Wildcat (USA)**[97] 1333 3-9-7 93 RichardHughes 11 81
(B J Meehan) *led: hdd over 7f out: remained handy: rdn over 2f out: wknd over 1f out* **20/1**

301 **8** 10 **Albarouche**[30] 3133 3-8-8 80 (b) PhilipRobinson 10 48
(M A Jarvis) *chsd ldrs: rdn over 2f out: wknd over 1f out* **14/1**

6-1 **9** 4 1/2 **Angel Rock (IRE)**[15] 3654 3-8-9 81 JohnEgan 12 40
(M Botti) *hld up: plld hrd: rdn over 2f out: sn hung lft and wknd* **8/1**

2m 5.22s (-0.28) **Going Correction** +0.025s/f (Good) **9 Ran SP% 112.6**
Speed ratings (Par 104): **102,101,100,100,95 93,93,85,82**
toteswinger: 1&2 £6.40, 1&3 £14.20, 2&3 £3.30. CSF £24.25 CT £97.87 TOTE £11.50: £2.80, £1.20, £2.10; EX 38.40.
Owner H R H Princess Haya Of Jordan **Bred** Hascombe And Valiant Studs **Trained** Newmarket, Suffolk
■ Qui Moi was withdrawn after refusing to enter the stalls.

FOCUS
A fair handicap, but it was run at a steady early gallop and was very much a tactical affair. The form may not be totally reliable.

NOTEBOOK
Upton Grey(IRE), who ran in the Irish Derby last time out, had the race run to suit as he was able to take them along for most of the way at no more than an ordinary gallop. When challenged he had enough in reserve to kick and hold off his rivals up the hill, but whether he would confirm the form with one or two in behind in a stronger-run race is open to doubt. (op 12-1)
Love Galore(IRE), who ran well to finish fourth in a valuable handicap over this trip at the July meeting, confirmed the good impression he left there with another solid performance. He was staying on well at the finish and a stronger pace would probably have suited him better. (op 5-2 tchd 11-4 in places)
Glorious Gift(IRE), stepping up two furlongs in distance, did not have his stamina fully tested in this steadily run affair, but he ran another solid race. (op 8-1 tchd 9-1)
Prince Kalamoun(IRE), chasing a hat-trick off a 7lb higher mark, would have been suited by a stronger pace as he is a confirmed hold-up performer. He finished well clear of the rest, however. (tchd 6-1)
Mexican Venture, stepping up in trip and grade, did not see it out and will no doubt be dropped back in distance next time. (op 14-1 tchd 16-1)
Strategic Mission(IRE) will probably be happier when he can get his toe in again. (tchd 15-2)
Angel Rock(IRE) failed to settle and gave himself little chance as a result. Official explanation: jockey said colt ran too free (op 7-1)

4161 VK MOJITO MAIDEN STKS 1m
8:20 (8:24) (Class 4) 3-Y-0 **£5,180** (£1,541; £770; £384) **Stalls Low**

Form RPR

1 **Summerstrand (IRE)** 3-8-12 0 PhilipRobinson 9 80
(M A Jarvis) *s.i.s: hld up: hdwy over 2f out: rdn over 1f out: r.o to ld nr fin* **25/1**

- **2** shd **Duncan** 3-9-3 0 EddieAhern 3 85+
(J L Dunlop) *hld up: nt clr run and swtchd rt 2f out: hdwy over 1f out: sn rdn: r.o* **14/1**

3 nk **Aflaam (IRE)** 3-9-3 0 RHills 15 84
(J H M Gosden) *hld up: hdwy over 3f out: rdn to ld and edgd lft over 1f out: hdd nr fin* **6/1**[2]

2 **4** 3 1/4 **Alsace Lorraine (IRE)**[37] 2955 3-8-12 0 JamieSpencer 14 72
(J R Fanshawe) *hld up in tch: rdn and ev ch over 2f out: styd on same pce appr fnl f* **6/1**[2]

45 **5** nk **Kidlat**[28] 3227 3-9-3 0 DaneO'Neill 10 76
(L M Cumani) *led: hdd over 5f out: rdn and ev ch over 1f out: wknd ins fnl f* **10/1**[3]

6 3 3/4 **Eleonora (FR)** 3-8-9 0 GilmarPereira(3) 1 62
(W J Haggas) *s.i.s: hld up: pushed along over 2f out: styd on ins fnl f: nvr nrr* **50/1**

7 shd **Black Coffee** 3-9-3 0 JohnEgan 6 67
(W J Musson) *s.s: hld up: pushed along over 2f out: rdn and edgd lft over 1f out: nt trble ldrs* **40/1**

2502 **8** shd **Sheer Bluff (IRE)**[8] 3870 3-9-3 72 TQuinn 13 67
(D R C Elsworth) *chsd ldr tl led over 5f out: hdd over 1f out: wknd ins fnl f* **20/1**

4 **9** shd **Blow Hole (USA)**[90] 1490 3-9-3 0 ShaneKelly 4 67+
(J Noseda) *hld up in tch: nt clr run over 2f out: sn rdn: wknd fnl f* **10/1**[3]

4 **10** 2 1/2 **Chatanoogachoochoo**[30] 3130 3-8-12 0 RobertWinston 5 56
(G A Swinbank) *plld hrd and prom: rdn and wknd over 1f out* **33/1**

4 **11** 10 **Royal Destination (IRE)**[67] 2056 3-9-3 0 RyanMoore 8 38
(J Noseda) *chsd ldrs: rdn over 3f out: wknd over 2f out* **5/6**[1]

12 nk **External Force (IRE)** 3-9-3 0 OscarUrbina 11 37
(S A Callaghan) *s.s: hld up: effrt over 2f out: sn hung lft and wknd* **50/1**

0-00 **13** 11 **Midnight Oasis**[11] 3790 3-8-12 45 (t) SaleemGolam 2 7
(Rae Guest) *s.i.s: hld up: n.m.r 1/2-way: wknd over 2f out* **66/1**

14 10 **River Naiad** 3-8-9 (v[1]) KirstyMilczarek(3) 16 —
(J A R Toller) *prom: lost pl over 5f out: bhd fr 1/2-way* **40/1**

1m 39.7s (-0.30) **Going Correction** +0.025s/f (Good) **14 Ran SP% 129.8**
Speed ratings (Par 102): **102,101,101,98,98 94,94,94,94,91 81,81,70,60**
toteswinger: 1&2 £59.80, 1&3 £20.60, 2&3 £14.20. CSF £342.33 TOTE £34.10: £5.40, £4.30, £2.50; EX 637.60.French Art was withdrawn. Price at time of withdrawal 5/1. Rule 4 applies to all bets struck prior to withdrawal. New market formed.
Owner Sheikh Ahmed Al Maktoum **Bred** Darley **Trained** Newmarket, Suffolk
■ French Art (5/1) was withdrawn because of unsuitable ground. R4 applies. New market formed.

FOCUS
Probably a fair maiden for the time of year. Sound enough form, though weakened by the poor run from the favourite.
Royal Destination(IRE) Official explanation: trainer had no explanation for the poor form shown

4162 YOUNG & PURE BEAUTY H'CAP 1m
8:50 (8:53) (Class 5) (0-75,75) 4-Y-0+ **£3,885** (£1,156; £577; £288) **Stalls Low**

Form RPR

1462 **1** **Oat Cuisine**[8] 3866 4-8-13 70 MCGeran(5) 17 80
(M L W Bell) *racd stands' side: a.p: rdn to ld and hung lft fr over 1f out: styd on* **11/1**

6523 **2** hd **Bobski (IRE)**[46] 2658 6-9-6 72 AdamKirby 14 82
(Miss Gay Kelleway) *racd stands' side: hld up: hdwy over 2f out: rdn and hung lft fr over 1f out: styd on* **16/1**

6460 **3** 2 1/2 **Effigy**[7] 3914 4-8-12 64 DaneO'Neill 20 68
(H Candy) *racd stands' side: chsd ldrs: rdn over 2f out: styd on* **16/1**

-602 **4** 3/4 **Palmetto Point**[21] 3457 4-9-0 69 (tp) TravisBlock(3) 18 71
(H Morrison) *racd stands' side: prom: rdn over 2f out: hung lft fnl f: styd on same pce* **16/1**

0045 **5** 1/2 **The Graig**[18] 3569 4-8-4 56 oh9 WilliamBuick 19 57
(J R Holt) *racd stands' side: chsd ldrs: rdn and ev ch over 1f out: edgd lft: styd on same pce* **66/1**

2-04 **6** 1/2 **Jawaab (IRE)**[55] 2406 4-9-4 70 RyanMoore 16 70
(M A Buckley) *racd stands' side: hld up: hdwy over 2f out: rdn and hung lft fnl f: styd on* **17/2**

-222 **7** 1/2 **Haasem (USA)**[31] 3116 5-9-4 70 DarryllHolland 8 69
(J R Jenkins) *racd stands' side: s.i.s: hld up: hdwy over 1f out: sn rdn: nt rch ldrs* **14/1**

6000 **8** 1 **Rain Stops Play (IRE)**[6] 3964 6-8-10 62 ShaneKelly 10 58
(M Quinn) *racd stands' side: overall ldr: rdn and hdd over 1f out: wknd ins fnl f* **25/1**

5654 **9** 3 3/4 **Star Strider**[24] 3345 4-8-9 61 JohnEgan 15 49
(Miss Gay Kelleway) *racd stands' side: hld up: hmpd 1/2-way: effrt over 1f out: n.d* **33/1**

5112 **10** hd **Paraguay (USA)**[7] 3915 5-9-7 73 JamieSpencer 5 60
(Miss V Haigh) *racd stands' side: hld up: hrd rdn over 1f out: nvr in contention* **3/1**[1]

6431 **11** shd **Sonny Parkin**[21] 3457 6-9-9 75 (v) RichardHughes 3 62
(J Pearce) *racd far side: hld up: swtchd rt and hdwy over 1f out: wknd fnl f* **8/1**[3]

-000 **12** 6 **Networker**[16] 3612 5-8-8 67 DavidProbert(7) 1 40
(P J McBride) *racd far side: chsd ldr: rdn over 2f out: wknd over 1f out* **20/1**

54-0 **13** 1 **Spanish Don**[21] 3457 10-9-1 70 MarcHalford(3) 9 41
(D R C Elsworth) *swtchd to r far side: sn chsng ldrs: wknd over 1f out* **25/1**

600 **14** 1 1/2 **Overrule (USA)**[15] 3646 4-9-8 74 EddieAhern 2 41
(B Ellison) *racd far side: chsd ldrs: rdn over 2f out: wkng whn hung rt over 1f out* **5/1**[2]

500- **15** 6 **Barkass (UAE)**[251] 6753 4-9-5 71 J-PGuillambert 6 25
(B Ellison) *racd far side: led far side: rdn over 2f out: wknd over 1f out* **33/1**

1200 **16** 2 3/4 **Josr's Magic (IRE)**[7] 3914 4-8-4 56 LiamJones 11 3
(H J Collingridge) *racd stands' side: chsd ldrs: rdn over 2f out: wknd over 1f out* **50/1**

3400 **17** 15 **Kindlelight Blue (IRE)**[6] 3947 4-9-8 74 TedDurcan 7 —
(N P Littmoden) *racd far side: a bhd* **50/1**

5006 **18** 3 **Banjo Patterson**[22] 3422 6-8-10 62 (b) AlanMunro 4 —
(M G Quinlan) *racd far side: hld up: wknd 2f out* **50/1**

0534 **19** 4 **Aggravation**[21] 3457 6-9-4 70 JimmyFortune 12 —
(D R C Elsworth) *racd stands' side: hld up: hmpd 1/2-way: a in rr: eased over 1f out* **9/1**

1m 39.11s (-0.89) **Going Correction** +0.025s/f (Good) **19 Ran SP% 131.7**
Speed ratings (Par 103): **105,104,102,101,101 100,100,99,95,95 95,89,88,86,80 77,62,59,55**
toteswinger: 1&2 £50.50, 1&3 £53.90, 2&3 £56.70. CSF £170.71 CT £2851.66 TOTE £11.70: £2.20, £2.60, £4.60, £4.50; EX 184.70 Place 6 £379.84, Place 5 £128.21.
Owner Mrs G Rowland-Clark **Bred** Glebe Stud & J F Dean **Trained** Newmarket, Suffolk

FOCUS
The field split into two groups and the first ten home came from the stands'-side bunch, although the first two both hung over towards the far side. The fifth limits the form.
Star Strider Official explanation: jockey said gelding ran too free
T/Plt: £850.60 to a £1 stake. Pool: £60,747.42. 52.13 winning tickets. T/Qpdt: £43.60 to a £1 stake. Pool: £4,846.87. 82.20 winning tickets. CR

3959 NOTTINGHAM (L-H)
Friday, July 18

OFFICIAL GOING: Good (good to soft in places; 7.1)
After 7mm rain the ground was reckoned 'dead in the home straight, softer than that on the round course'. Dolling out added circa 8yards to round course.
Wind: light, half against Weather: changeable, light showers

4163 SUBSCRIBE TO RACING UK H'CAP 6f 15y
2:15 (2:17) (Class 5) (0-70,70) 3-Y-O **£3,238** (£963; £481; £240) **Stalls High**

Form RPR

0402 **1** **Bonne**[12] 3753 3-8-6 55 HayleyTurner 2 68
(M L W Bell) *racd w one other far side: led that side over 2f out: r.o wl* **4/1**[2]

05-6 **2** 2 1/4 **Cape Rock**[36] 2976 3-9-5 68 PhilipRobinson 13 74
(C A Horgan) *hld up: hdwy over 2f out: styd on wl fnl f: tk 2nd nr line* **15/2**

1652 **3** nk **Moonage Daydream (IRE)**[6] 3960 3-9-1 64 (b) DavidAllan 15 69
(T D Easterby) *chsd ldrs: led and hung lft stands' side over 1f out: kpt on same pce* **3/1**[1]

6055 **4** 3 1/2 **Bohobe (IRE)**[13] 3727 3-9-0 63 TPQueally 16 57
(J G Given) *prom: outpcd over 2f out: kpt on fnl f* **10/1**

3305 **5** 1/2 **Devinius (IRE)**[14] 3672 3-8-11 60 JamieSpencer 14 52+
(G A Swinbank) *hld up in rr: hdwy centre 2f out: nt clr run and swtchd rt 1f out: kpt on wl* **11/2**[3]

6204 **6** 1/2 **Andrasta**[12] 3753 3-7-9 51 oh3 DavidProbert(7) 7 42
(A Berry) *chsd ldrs: led stands' side 2f out: sn hdd: one pce* **14/1**

500 **7** 3/4 **Seductive Witch**[25] 3332 3-8-8 57 PatrickMathers 10 45
(J Balding) *s.i.s: kpt on fnl 2f: nvr nr ldrs* **25/1**

54-6 **8** 1 1/2 **Nickel Silver**[13] 3712 3-9-7 70 TomEaves 11 53
(B Smart) *trckd ldrs: t.k.h: kpt on same pce fnl 2f* **14/1**

0-40 **9** 1 1/2 **Ramblin Bob**[28] 3224 3-8-8 57 ow1 StephenDonohoe 4 36
(W J Musson) *detached in last: kpt on fnl 2f: nvr on terms* **25/1**

0-00 **10** hd **Hawk Eyed Lady (IRE)**[25] 3314 3-9-4 67 (b[1]) ShaneKelly 1 45
(J A Osborne) *led w one other far side tl over 2f out: sn wknd* **33/1**

4030 **11** 1/2 **Diademas (USA)**[12] 3765 3-8-7 59 ow1 RussellKennemore(3) 9 35
(M J Gingell) *in rr: hdwy over 2f out: wknd fnl f* **33/1**

0000 **12** 3/4 **Wooden King (IRE)**[35] 2991 3-8-4 56 oh1 ow5 KevinGhunowa(3) 5 30
(P D Evans) *chsd ldrs: wknd 2f out* **20/1**

050- **13** 1/2 **Athboy Auction**[219] 7117 3-8-10 59 PatCosgrave 6 31
(H J Collingridge) *w ldrs: led stands' side after 2f tl 2f out: wknd* **18/1**

6-60 **14** 6 **Tobar Suil Lady (IRE)**[76] 1819 3-9-4 67 PaulMulrennan 3 20
(K A Ryan) *mid-div on outer: hung lft and lost pl 2f out* **25/1**

0-00 **15** *23* **The Real Guru**[14] 3696 3-9-5 **68** .... ChrisCatlin 17 —
(Miss Tor Sturgis) *led stands' side tl 4f out: wknd qckly and sn bhd: t.o* **50/1**

1m 15.73s (0.63) **Going Correction** +0.125s/f (Good) **15** Ran SP% **124.0**
Speed ratings (Par 100): **100,97,96,91,91 90,89,87,85,85 84,83,83,75,44**
toteswinger: 1&2 £11.30, 1&3 £2.10, 2&3 £6.30. CSF £31.97 CT £107.88 TOTE £4.40: £1.20, £3.90, £1.80; EX 40.10.

Owner Raymond Tooth **Bred** Jeremy Green And Sons **Trained** Newmarket, Suffolk

FOCUS
Only the winner and one other elected to race on the far side, and it is unclear whether there was an advantage there. The form is probably worth taking at face value.

4164 EUROPEAN BREEDERS' FUND MAIDEN STKS 6f 15y
2:45 (2:48) (Class 5) 2-Y-O **£3,885** (£1,156; £577; £288) **Stalls** High

Form RPR

3 **1** **Zuzu (IRE)**[15] 3625 2-8-12 0 .... PhilipRobinson 4 80+
(M A Jarvis) *mde all far side: styd on strly: readily: 1st of 7 that gp* **7/4[2]**

2 **2** *1 1/2* **Master Rooney (IRE)**[37] 2937 2-9-3 0 .... TedDurcan 5 83+
(B Smart) *t.k.h: racd far side: trckd ldrs: wnt 2nd that gp over 3f out: eased whn no imp on wnr ins fnl f: 2nd of 7 that gp* **6/4[1]**

0 **3** *3* **Cook's Endeavour (USA)**[64] 2134 2-9-3 0 .... RichardMullen 10 72+
(K A Ryan) *racd stands' side: chsd ldrs: led that gp ins fnl f: no ch w 1st 2 on other side* **9/1[3]**

5 **4** *1/2* **Mabait**[22] 3392 2-9-3 0 .... JamieSpencer 8 70
(L M Cumani) *t.k.h: swtchd lft after 100yds: racd far side: hdwy over 2f out: kpt on same pce: 3rd of 7 that gp* **20/1**

5 *1* **Definightly** 2-9-3 0 .... ChrisCatlin 12 67+
(R Charlton) *dwlt: racd stands' side: hdwy over 2f out: edgd lft over 1f out: kpt on* **28/1**

5 **6** *1 1/4* **Waahej**[36] 2972 2-9-3 0 .... MartinDwyer 13 63
(J L Dunlop) *racd stands' side: chsd ldrs: kpt on same pce appr fnl f* **11/1**

7 *hd* **Spinners End (IRE)** 2-9-3 0 .... FergusSweeney 9 63
(K R Burke) *racd stands' side: chsd ldr: kpt on same pce fnl f* **16/1**

05 **8** *shd* **Mattamia (IRE)**[35] 2999 2-9-0 0 .... JamesMillman(3) 11 62
(B R Millman) *led stands' side tl ins fnl f: no ex* **12/1**

0 **9** *6* **Prom**[6] 3959 2-8-9 0 .... MarkLawson(3) 6 39
(M Brittain) *swtchd lft to r far side after 1f: chsd ldrs: wknd 2f out: 4th of 7 that gp* **50/1**

00 **10** *2* **Join Up**[16] 3603 2-9-3 0 .... SaleemGolam 3 38
(W R Swinburn) *dwlt: racd far side: sn chsng ldrs: wknd 2f out: 5th of 7 that gp* **50/1**

0 **11** *16* **Yaldas Girl (USA)**[92] 1419 2-8-12 0 .... MohammedSaeed 2 —
(J R Best) *racd far side: chsd ldrs: lost pl over 2f out: sn bhd: 6th of 7 that gp* **50/1**

12 *9* **Liliaceae** 2-8-12 0 .... PatrickMathers 1 —
(D Shaw) *racd far side: in rr: bhd fnl 2: last of 7 that gp* **66/1**

1m 16.04s (0.94) **Going Correction** +0.125s/f (Good) **12** Ran SP% **123.9**
Speed ratings (Par 94): **98,96,92,91,90 88,88,87,79,77 55,43**
toteswinger: 1&2 £1.80, 1&3 £3.70, 2&3 £13.80. CSF £4.71 TOTE £3.00: £1.30, £1.10, £3.50; EX 4.70.

Owner Stephen Dartnell **Bred** Bryan Ryan **Trained** Newmarket, Suffolk

FOCUS
Six went to the far side including the first two home. The winner should improve again, the runner-up needs to learn to settle.

NOTEBOOK
Zuzu(IRE) had clearly learnt plenty first time. She dominated her wing and scored in most decisive fashion. A nice type, she will improve again. (tchd 6-4 and 15-8)

Master Rooney(IRE), quite a big, well-made type, was far too keen. He went in pursuit but was always going to come off second best and his rider accepted it inside the last. He will have to learn to settle if he is to progress. (op 13-8 tchd 2-1)

Cook's Endeavour(USA), a rangy individual, improved a good deal on his debut effort two months earlier. He was first home on the stands' side and will improve again. (op 20-1)

Mabait, a close-coupled, bonny colt, took a keen hold. He kept on in his own time and, happier on turf, will need another outing before he qualifies for a nursery mark. (tchd 25-1)

Definightly, quite an attractive newcomer, missed the break and then edged towards the centre. This should have taught him a fair bit. (op 25-1)

Waahej, who stands over a fair amount of ground, improved on his debut effort. (tchd 10-1)

4165 RACINGUK.TV (S) STKS 1m 2f 50y
3:20 (3:22) (Class 6) 3-Y-O **£2,388** (£705; £352) **Stalls** Low

Form RPR

0-01 **1** **Ambrose Princess (IRE)**[16] 3605 3-8-6 **54** .... KevinGhunowa(3) 4 54
(R A Harris) *trckd ldrs: t.k.h: drvn over 3f out: sn outpcd: styd on wl fnl f: led nr fin* **11/1**

3302 **2** *nk* **One Called Alice**[10] 3817 3-8-9 **54** .... HayleyTurner 7 53
(A W Carroll) *hld up: hdwy to trck ldrs over 4f out: chal 3f out: no ex towards fin* **4/1[3]**

3001 **3** *1/2* **Colorado Springs**[9] 3844 3-8-9 **57** .... (b) AdrianMcCarthy 5 52
(W Jarvis) *trckd ldrs: led and hung lft 3f out: hdd towards fin* **2/1[1]**

0560 **4** *1 3/4* **Linby (IRE)**[8] 3886 3-8-9 **61** .... TonyCulhane 2 49
(N Tinkler) *hld up towards rr: hdwy on outer over 3f out: hung lft over 1f out: one pce* **7/2[2]**

0005 **5** *2 1/4* **Charlie Be (IRE)**[23] 3359 3-8-2 **43** .... DavidProbert(7) 3 44
(Mrs P N Dutfield) *t.k.h in mid-div: effrt over 3f out: kpt on same pce* **14/1**

0-00 **6** *nk* **Peer Pressure**[60] 2255 3-8-5 **53** ow1 .... MarkCoumbe(5) 8 44
(B R Johnson) *s.i.s: hld up in last: sme hdwy over 2f out: nvr rchd ldrs* **12/1**

6014 **7** *1 1/2* **Carry On Cleo**[5] 3996 3-8-9 **57** .... (v) StephenDonohoe 1 40
(A Berry) *in rr: drvn 3f out: nvr a threat* **8/1**

-433 **8** *1 1/2* **Last Angel (IRE)**[120] 950 3-8-4 **46** .... SimonWhitworth 6 32
(M Wigham) *led: qcknd 4f out: hdd 3f out: wknd over 1f out* **14/1**

2m 18.18s (5.68) **Going Correction** +0.375s/f (Good) **8** Ran SP% **116.0**
Speed ratings (Par 98): **92,91,91,89,88 87,86,85**
toteswinger: 1&2 £4.50, 1&3 £7.10, 2&3 £4.10. CSF £55.41 TOTE £12.50: £3.40, £1.40, £1.30; EX 29.20.There was no bid for the winner.

Owner Brian Hicks **Bred** Tally-Ho Stud **Trained** Earlswood, Monmouths

■ Stewards' Enquiry : Adrian McCarthy three-day ban: used whip with excessive frequency (Aug 1,3-4)

FOCUS
A poor race even by selling-race standards and not that much to choose between the entire field in the end. The form is rtaed through the third and fifth.

4166 VISITNOTTINGHAM.COM MAIDEN FILLIES' STKS 1m 2f 50y
3:50 (3:53) (Class 5) 3-Y-O **£3,238** (£963; £481; £240) **Stalls** Low

Form RPR

4-2 **1** **Montbretia**[91] 1440 3-9-0 0 .... TedDurcan 5 79+
(H R A Cecil) *prom: chalng whn hit over hd by rival rdr's whip over a f out: styd on to ld fnl 150yds* **8/13[1]**

0-3 **2** *3/4* **Time Control**[20] 3479 3-9-0 0 .... JamieSpencer 12 77+
(L M Cumani) *trckd ldr: led 3f out tl ins fnl f: no ex* **4/1[2]**

5 **3** *3 1/2* **Cheeky Download (IRE)**[81] 1684 3-9-0 0 .... TPQueally 16 70
(E A L Dunlop) *led: hdd 3f out: styd on same pce appr fnl f* **33/1**

04 **4** *1 1/4* **Finney Hill**[9] 3854 3-9-0 0 .... FergusSweeney 7 68
(H Candy) *chsd ldrs: one pce fnl 2f* **15/2[3]**

5 *1* **Lura (USA)** 3-9-0 0 .... DO'Donohoe 4 67+
(Saeed Bin Suroor) *s.i.s: hdwy 6f out: effrt on inner over 3f out: wandered one pce fnl 2f* **16/1**

0 **6** *1 1/2* **Miss Pelling (IRE)**[33] 3061 3-9-0 0 .... MartinDwyer 14 63+
(B J Meehan) *mid-div: drvn 4f out: styd on fnl f* **33/1**

0 **7** *1 1/4* **Dream Of Olwyn (IRE)**[15] 3628 3-9-0 0 .... PatCosgrave 10 60
(J G Given) *s.i.s: t.k.h: hdwy over 3f out: one pce* **66/1**

4 **8** *3 1/4* **London Bid (USA)**[10] 3810 3-9-0 0 .... PatDobbs 9 54
(Sir Michael Stoute) *prom: effrt on outer over 4f out: edgd lft over 2f out: sn btn* **20/1**

5 **9** *3 3/4* **Whipma Whopma Gate (IRE)**[61] 2221 3-9-0 0 .... DNolan 8 46
(D Carroll) *s.i.s: nvr a factor* **50/1**

0 **10** *shd* **Lady Special (IRE)**[57] 2328 3-9-0 0 .... PhilipRobinson 15 46
(C G Cox) *chsd ldrs: outpcd fnl 2f* **66/1**

0 **11** *1 3/4* **Unawatuna**[20] 3479 3-9-0 0 .... TomEaves 1 42
(Mrs K Walton) *s.i.s: a in rr* **200/1**

6 **12** *3/4* **Can Can Dancer**[20] 3479 3-8-10 0 ow1 .... ShaneCreighton(5) 13 42
(J G Given) *chsd ldrs: lost pl over 4f out* **80/1**

46 **13** *9* **Mignonette (IRE)**[79] 1721 3-9-0 0 .... RichardMullen 2 23
(E A L Dunlop) *s.i.s: drvn over 4f out: sn bhd* **40/1**

0 **14** *37* **Sweet Destiny**[10] 3810 3-9-0 0 .... PaulMulrennan 6 —
(M H Tompkins) *rr-div: lost pl over 3f out: sn bhd: t.o* **100/1**

2m 15.19s (2.69) **Going Correction** +0.375s/f (Good) **14** Ran SP% **120.3**
Speed ratings (Par 97): **104,103,100,99,98 97,96,94,91,90 89,88,81,52**
toteswinger: 1&2 £2.40, 1&3 £8.30, 2&3 £10.70. CSF £2.83 TOTE £1.70: £1.10, £1.50, £4.20; EX 4.10.

Owner K Abdulla **Bred** Juddmonte Farms Ltd **Trained** Newmarket, Suffolk

FOCUS
An uncompetitive contest despite some well-bred maidens being on show, with the market going 16/1 bar three. The winner did not to need to run up to previous form to score with the placed horses both improvers.

4167 RACING UK ON CHANNEL 432 H'CAP 1m 75y
4:20 (4:21) (Class 4) (0-85,86) 3-Y-O+
£6,231 (£1,866; £933; £467; £233; £117) **Stalls** Centre

Form RPR

4044 **1** **Opus Maximus (IRE)**[13] 3744 3-9-0 **75** .... GregFairley 2 84
(M Johnston) *trckd ldrs: hung lft and led over 2f out: edgd rt and styd on wl ins fnl f* **7/2[3]**

0152 **2** *3/4* **Ink Spot**[7] 3928 3-9-6 **81** .... (v) JamieSpencer 5 88
(M L W Bell) *hld up in rr: hdwy on ins 4f out: hrd rdn over 1f out: keeping on whn checked nr line* **9/4[1]**

-323 **3** *1* **Hannicean**[21] 3457 4-9-4 **71** .... PhilipRobinson 4 78
(M A Jarvis) *chsd ldrs: effrt over 2f out: hung lft: styd on same pce ins fnl f* **5/2[2]**

5305 **4** *2 1/4* **Hartshead**[13] 3716 9-9-9 **76** .... TedDurcan 1 78
(G A Swinbank) *trckd ldrs: effrt over 2f out: kpt on same pce* **8/1**

0310 **5** *1 1/4* **Royal Storm (IRE)**[1] 4121 9-9-5 **75** .... JamesMillman(3) 9 74
(B R Millman) *led: drvn over 2f out: sn hdd: wknd fnl f* **8/1**

1431 **6** *8* **Riley Boys (IRE)**[13] 3711 7-9-10 **77** .... TPQueally 3 58
(J G Given) *in rr: drvn over 5f out: hdwy over 2f out: wknd and eased fnl f* **17/2**

14-0 **7** *41* **Italian Romance**[184] 185 5-9-3 **70** .... ShaneKelly 7 —
(J W Unett) *hld up in rr: effrt over 3f out: sn lost pl: t.o* **28/1**

1m 47.89s (2.49) **Going Correction** +0.375s/f (Good)
WFA 3 from 4yo+ 8lb **7** Ran SP% **117.8**
Speed ratings (Par 105): **102,101,100,98,96 88,47**
toteswinger: 1&2 £2.50, 1&3 £3.10, 2&3 £1.80. CSF £12.42 CT £22.84 TOTE £4.70: £3.40, £1.10; EX 10.70.

Owner Jim McGrath And Reg Griffin **Bred** Mrs Anne Marie Burns **Trained** Middleham Moor, N Yorks

FOCUS
A fair handicap run at a sound gallop and the form is best rated through the third.

4168 THE BEST RACECOURSES ON TURFTV H'CAP 1m 75y
4:50 (4:50) (Class 6) (0-60,59) 3-Y-O+ **£2,047** (£604; £302) **Stalls** Centre

Form RPR

00-2 **1** **Sarah Park (IRE)**[25] 3314 3-9-2 **59** .... MartinDwyer 11 69
(B J Meehan) *chsd ldrs: effrt over 2f out: led over 2f out: hld on towards fin* **4/1[2]**

2332 **2** *1 1/4* **Brouhaha**[9] 3839 4-9-6 **55** .... TedDurcan 17 67+
(B J McMath) *hld up in rr: hdwy and nt clr run over 2f out tl swtchd ins over 1f out: styd on wl ins fnl f: nt rch wnr* **7/2[1]**

0-60 **3** *nk* **Barataria**[17] 3593 6-9-5 **54** .... TPQueally 13 62
(R Bastiman) *s.i.s: hld up in rr: hdwy and n.m.r over 2f out: kpt on same pce fnl f* **12/1**

0300 **4** *3/4* **Apache Nation (IRE)**[12] 3755 5-9-5 **57** .... NeilBrown(3) 14 63
(M Dods) *mid-div: effrt 3f out: styd on same pce fnl f* **6/1[3]**

0001 **5** *1 1/4* **Kimono My House**[10] 3816 4-9-3 **52** 6ex .... PatCosgrave 6 55
(J G Given) *chsd ldrs: wnt 2nd 2f out: sn almost upsides: wknd ins fnl f* **10/1**

0326 **6** *2* **Just Oscar (GER)**[6] 3951 4-9-4 **53** .... RichardMullen 10 52
(W M Brisbourne) *in tch: t.k.h: drvn 3f out: one pce* **7/1**

4242 **7** *2 1/2* **Wizby**[16] 3604 5-9-4 **53** .... StephenDonohoe 3 46
(Ms Deborah J Evans) *s.s: sn mid-div: effrt 4f out: nvr trbld ldrs* **11/1**

-500 **8** *1 1/2* **Betteras Bertie**[10] 3814 5-9-2 **54** .... (v[1]) MarkLawson(3) 5 44
(M Brittain) *s.i.s: drvn over 4f out: nvr a factor* **18/1**

0001 **9** *1* **Alucica**[9] 3839 5-9-6 **55** 6ex .... (v) PatrickMathers 9 42
(D Shaw) *t.k.h in rr: effrt over 3f out: nvr a factor* **20/1**

4000 **10** *4* **Coup D'Etat**[16] 3607 6-9-4 **58**......................(b) HaddenFrost(5) 2 36
(R A Harris) *led: t.k.h: hdd over 2f out: wknd over 1f out* **12/1**
0000 **11** *1 3/4* **Osteopathic Care (IRE)**[27] 3279 4-9-1 **50**..........(p) DeanMcKeown 15 24
(Miss Tracy Waggott) *chsd ldrs: wknd 2f out* **40/1**
3150 **P** **Haroldini (IRE)**[31] 3108 6-8-12 **50**......................(p) TolleyDean(3) 7 —
(J Balding) *tk fierce grip towards rr: lost pl over 3f out: sn bhd and p.u: sddle slipped* **20/1**

1m 49.0s (3.60) **Going Correction** +0.375s/f (Good)
WFA 3 from 4yo+ 8lb **12** Ran SP% **119.0**
Speed ratings (Par 101): **97,95,95,94,93 91,88,87,86,82 80,—**
toteswinger: 1&2 £4.00, 1&3 £11.10, 2&3 £10.70. CSF £17.96 CT £156.96 TOTE £4.50: £1.90, £1.90, £4.90; EX 17.70 Place 6: £5.38, Place 5: £3.46..
Owner Mrs J & D E Cash **Bred** George S O'Malley **Trained** Manton, Wilts

FOCUS
A moderate handicap but solid form with the winner building on her reappearance and the third and fourth setting the level.
Betteras Bertie Official explanation: trainer said gelding failed to face first time visor
Coup D'Etat Official explanation: jockey said gelding ran too free
Haroldini(IRE) Official explanation: jockey said saddle slipped
T/Plt: £4.60 to a £1 stake. Pool: £46,800.27. 7,407.28 winning tickets. T/Qpdt: £3.70 to a £1 stake. Pool: £2,522.38. 494.09 winning tickets. WG

3809 PONTEFRACT (L-H)
Friday, July 18

OFFICIAL GOING: Good (7.2)
Wind: Virtually nil

4169 COUNTRYWIDE FREIGHT MAIDEN AUCTION STKS — 6f
6:35 (6:36) (Class 4) 2-Y-O **£4,533** (£1,348; £674; £336) **Stalls** Low

Form RPR
5 **1** **Diggeratt (USA)**[13] 3734 2-8-6 0 ow2...................... TonyHamilton 2 70
(R A Fahey) *trckd ldrs: effrt and swtchd rt over 1f out: sn rdn and styd on ins fnl f to ld nr line* **9/2**[3]
4 **2** *nk* **Identity**[11] 3792 2-8-4 0...................... ChrisCatlin 1 67
(E J O'Neill) *cl up on inner: led over 2f out: rdn and hdd over 1f out: rallied ins fnl f to ld fnl 100yds: drvn and hdd nr line* **9/1**
3 **3** *hd* **Annapolis**[15] 3651 2-8-13 0...................... GregFairley 8 75
(M Johnston) *led to over 2f out: rdn to ld again over 1f out: drvn ins fnl f: hdd and no ex fnl 100yds* **11/4**[1]
4 *3 1/2* **Big Apple Boy (IRE)** 2-8-6 0...................... AhmedAjtebi(5) 11 63+
(Jedd O'Keeffe) *trckd ldrs: hdwy on outer 2f out: rdn and ch wl over 1f out: sn drvn and nt qckn ent fnl f* **18/1**
4 **5** *4* **Doric Echo**[38] 2909 2-8-13 0...................... TomEaves 6 53+
(B Smart) *chsd ldrs: rdn along wl over 1f out: sn one pce* **11/2**
6 *3 3/4* **Abbey Steps (IRE)** 2-8-11 0...................... DavidAllan 7 39+
(T D Easterby) *dwlt and rr: swtchd rt and hdwy wl over 1f out: styd on ins fnl f: nrst fin* **14/1**
7 *3/4* **Home Before Dark** 2-8-8 0...................... MichaelJStainton(3) 14 37
(R M Whitaker) *in rr tl hdwy wl over 1f out: styd on ins fnl f: nrst fin* **33/1**
52 **8** *nk* **Cavendish Road (IRE)**[22] 3408 2-8-11 0...................... DO'Donohoe 9 36
(W R Muir) *chsd ldrs: rdn along 2f out: grad wknd* **10/3**[2]
9 *2* **Bluebaru** 2-8-9 0...................... HayleyTurner 4 28
(Mark Campion) *dwlt: a towards rr* **33/1**
10 *1* **Cyflymder (IRE)** 2-9-2 0...................... DaleGibson 13 32
(J G Given) *midfield: rdn along 1/2-way: sn outpcd and bhd* **25/1**
11 *1* **Venetian Lady** 2-8-3 0...................... AndrewMullen(3) 3 19
(Mrs A Duffield) *s.i.s: a in rr* **33/1**
00 **12** *6* **Pennine Rose**[11] 3792 2-8-4 0...................... PaulQuinn 10 —
(A Berry) *chsd ldrs: rdn along over 2f out and sn wknd* **100/1**
60 **13** *6* **Gems Star**[17] 3590 2-8-9 0...................... PaulMulrennan 12 —
(J J Quinn) *a towards rr* **50/1**
40 **14** *7* **Flog It**[42] 2783 2-8-6 0...................... DuranFentiman(3) 5 —
(T D Easterby) *a towards rr* **40/1**

1m 19.12s (2.22) **Going Correction** +0.225s/f (Good) **14** Ran SP% **123.3**
Speed ratings (Par 96): **94,93,93,88,83 78,77,76,74,72 71,63,55,46**
toteswinger: 1&2 £2.40, 1&3 £2.30, 2&3 £3.80. CSF £43.49 TOTE £5.50: £1.70, £3.10, £1.40; EX 28.50.
Owner J A Rattigan **Bred** Hobby Horse Farm Inc **Trained** Musley Bank, N Yorks
■ Stewards' Enquiry : Tony Hamilton one-day ban: careless riding (Aug 1)

FOCUS
Just a modest maiden, and they finished well strung out behind the first three.

NOTEBOOK
Diggeratt(USA) stepped up on her debut effort at Nottingham against her own sex to get the best of a three-way battle in the closing stages, despite Hamilton putting up 2lb overweight. She will stay at least another furlong and should hold her own in nurseries. (op 10-3)
Identity came on from her debut fourth against her own sex at Ripon last week and after showing great resolution to fight off the favourite was a tad unlucky to get mugged on the line. There are surely races to be won with her. (op 17-2 tchd 8-1)
Annapolis, who had run an eyecatching race behind a pair from big Newmarket yards at Yarmouth on debut, pressed on up front from the off but the weight concession just told in the closing stages. He will win races, but perhaps not at the level one might have hoped. (op 9-2)
Big Apple Boy(IRE), a rangy sort who looked as though he would come on for the race, was prominent for a long way and only got tired in the last furlong. He should improve. (op 22-1)
Doric Echo got a bit hot beforehand and refused to settle in the early stages, ultimately not being able to improve on his Redcar debut effort. (op 6-1 tchd 13-2)
Abbey Steps(IRE), a son of Choisir, kept on well to record a promising debut. The yard's juveniles invariably come on a lot for their first outing. (op 25-1 tchd 28-1)
Cavendish Road(IRE) failed to give his running. (tchd 4-1)
Gems Star Official explanation: jockey said colt hung right

4170 TOTESPORT.COM FILLIES' H'CAP — 1m 4f 8y
7:05 (7:05) (Class 5) (0-75,75) 3-Y-0+ **£3,885** (£1,156; £577; £288) **Stalls** Low

Form RPR
0351 **1** **Tcherina (IRE)**[15] 3624 6-9-11 **73**...................... DuranFentiman(3) 2 80
(T D Easterby) *trckd ldng pair: hdwy 2f out: rdn to chal over 1f out: drvn and styd on ins fnl f to ld fnl 75yds* **15/2**
6231 **2** *3/4* **Prelude**[7] 3912 7-9-12 **71** 6ex...................... DavidAllan 6 77
(W M Brisbourne) *led: rdn along over 2f out: drvn ent fnl f: hdd and no ex fnl 75yds* **15/2**
0056 **3** *9* **Snow Dancer (IRE)**[15] 3624 4-9-1 **60**..........(p) TonyHamilton 3 51
(H A McWilliams) *hld up in rr: hdwy on inner 3f out: chsd ldng pair wl over 1f out: sn rdn and no imp ent fnl f* **10/1**
4-34 **4** *2 1/2* **Ceka Dancer (IRE)**[9] 3841 3-9-0 **71**...................... ChrisCatlin 7 58
(E J O'Neill) *hld up in rr: hdwy on inner 2f out: sn rdn and kpt on appr fnl f: nvr a factor* **16/1**
6-32 **5** *9* **Flam**[13] 3729 3-9-3 **74**...................... PaulMulrennan 4 47
(J R Fanshawe) *hld up: in tch: hdwy to chse ldrs over 4f out: rdn along wl over 2f out: sn drvn and wknd* **3/1**[1]
0005 **6** *7* **Golden Dagger (IRE)**[9] 3832 4-9-3 **65**..........(p) NeilBrown(3) 5 27
(K A Ryan) *in tch: rdn along 3f out: sn wknd* **10/1**
4102 **7** *2 1/2* **Ever Rigg**[9] 3841 3-9-4 **75**...................... TomEaves 8 33
(E A L Dunlop) *hld up in tch: hdwy 4f out: rdn along 3f out: drvn 2f out and sn btn* **9/2**[2]
003 **8** *1 1/4* **Pure Song**[24] 3350 3-9-3 **74**...................... TPQueally 1 30
(J L Dunlop) *trckd ldrs: effrt over 4f out: rdn along over 3f out: sn wknd* **13/2**[3]
5-41 **9** *11* **Sweet Sara**[15] 3644 3-8-12 **74**...................... AhmedAjtebi(5) 9 12
(C E Brittain) *trckd ldr: hdwy and cl up 4f out: rdn along over 2f out: sn drvn and wknd* **9/1**

2m 42.08s (1.28) **Going Correction** +0.225s/f (Good)
WFA 3 from 4yo+ 12lb **9** Ran SP% **114.1**
Speed ratings (Par 100): **104,103,97,95,89 85,83,82,75**
toteswinger: 1&2 £3.40, 1&3 £14.70, 2&3 £24.20. CSF £61.55 CT £564.53 TOTE £9.90: £2.80, £2.50, £2.40; EX 31.30.
Owner Mr & Mrs W J Williams **Bred** Ken Carroll **Trained** Great Habton, N Yorks
■ Stewards' Enquiry : David Allan one-day ban: used whip with excessive frequency (Aug 1)
Duran Fentiman one-day ban: used whip with excessive frequency (Aug 1)

FOCUS
A fair fillies' handicap, the two at the top of the weights battling out the finish and pulling miles clear of the remainder, who finished strung out all over West Yorkshire. Unexposed three-year-olds filled the first three places in the market, yet none got to within twenty lengths of the front pair at the line. The form is rated through the winner to last year's best.
Ever Rigg Official explanation: trainer said filly was unsuited by the good ground
Sweet Sara Official explanation: jockey said filly hung right-handed and lost its action home straight

4171 ANTONIA DEUTERS H'CAP — 5f
7:35 (7:35) (Class 3) (0-90,89) 3-Y-0+
£9,346 (£2,799; £1,399; £700; £349; £175) **Stalls** Low

Form RPR
-003 **1** **Efistorm**[6] 3945 7-9-5 **83**...................... HayleyTurner 5 93
(C R Dore) *hld up towards rr: hdwy on inner 2f out: nt clr run and swtchd rt over 1f out: sn rdn and qckndl to chal ent fnl f: styd on to ld fnl 100yds* **6/1**[2]
6360 **2** *nk* **Hotham**[6] 3973 5-8-11 **75**...................... ChrisCatlin 3 84
(N Wilson) *chsd ldrs: swtchd rt and hdwy wl over 1f out: rdn ent fnl f and sn ev ch: drvn and nt qckn nr fin* **9/1**
5265 **3** *1* **Mr Wolf**[10] 3812 7-8-7 **71**..........(p) GregFairley 12 76
(D W Barker) *sn led: rdn wl over 1f out: drvn ins fnl f: hdd and no ex fnl 100yds* **5/1**[1]
-565 **4** *nk* **Avertuoso**[37] 2938 4-9-1 **79**..........(v) TomEaves 9 83
(B Smart) *prom: effrt to chse ldr wl over 1f out: rdn to chal ent fnl f and ev ch tl drvn and no ex last 100yds* **16/1**
0140 **5** *1 1/2* **Namir (IRE)**[13] 3708 6-8-7 **74**..........(vt) DuranFentiman(3) 1 73
(D Shaw) *trckd ldrs on inner: swtchd rt and hdwy wl over 1f out: rdn ent fnl f: kpt on same pce* **9/1**
0004 **6** *3/4* **Bond City (IRE)**[7] 3931 6-9-7 **88**..........(p) NeilBrown(3) 4 84
(G R Oldroyd) *chsd ldrs: rdn and hung bdly rt wl over 1f out: sn drvn and one pce appr fnl f* **9/1**
0140 **7** *nk* **Dickie Le Davoir**[5] 3998 4-8-13 **82** 6ex.......... MarkCoumbe(5) 10 77
(John A Harris) *s.i.s and bhd: gd hdwy on inner wl over 1f out: rdn and n.m.r ent fnl f: swtchd rt and styd on wl towards fin* **20/1**
0560 **8** *1/2* **Dig Deep (IRE)**[13] 3708 6-9-3 **81**...................... PaulMulrennan 2 74
(J J Quinn) *chzased ldrs on inner: rdn along 2f out: sn outpcd: styd on again u.p ins fnl f* **12/1**
2000 **9** *2 1/4* **Green Park (IRE)**[21] 3451 5-9-7 **85**..........(b[1]) TonyHamilton 13 70
(R A Fahey) *hld up towards rr: effrt on outer and sme hdwy wl over 1f out: sn rdn and no imp* **14/1**
0104 **10** *2 1/2* **Elhamri**[25] 3320 4-9-6 **89**...................... HaddenFrost(5) 6 65
(S Kirk) *hld up towards rr: hdwy wl over 1f out: sn rdn and kpt on ins fnl f: n.d* **9/1**
0333 **11** *1/2* **Mambo Spirit (IRE)**[13] 3708 4-9-3 **81**...................... TPQueally 15 55
(J G Given) *cl up: rdn along wl over 1f out: drvn and wknd appr fnl f* **8/1**[3]
60-3 **12** *1 3/4* **Topflightcoolracer**[5] 3998 4-9-2 **80**...................... DO'Donohoe 14 48
(Mrs G S Rees) *chsd ldrs: rdn along 1/2-way: wknd over 2f out* **18/1**
3015 **13** *3/4* **The Nifty Fox**[13] 3708 4-9-4 **82**...................... DavidAllan 7 47
(T D Easterby) *midfield: effrt 2f out: sn rdn and wknd* **14/1**
-000 **14** *1 3/4* **Divine Spirit**[13] 3708 7-9-2 **80**...................... DaleGibson 8 39
(M Dods) *a towards rr* **25/1**
6002 **15** *1* **The History Man (IRE)**[12] 3759 5-7-13 **70** oh6....(be) AdeleRothery(7) 11 25
(M Mullineaux) *chsd ldrs: rdn along 2f out: sn wknd* **20/1**

63.77 secs (0.47) **Going Correction** +0.225s/f (Good) **15** Ran SP% **127.6**
Speed ratings (Par 107): **105,104,102,102,100 98,98,97,93,89 89,86,85,82,80**
toteswinger: 1&2 £10.20, 1&3 £2.60, 2&3 £3.50. CSF £60.82 CT £307.03 TOTE £7.50: £2.80, £2.70, £2.20; EX 75.30.
Owner Sean J Murphy **Bred** E Duggan And D Churchman **Trained** West Pinchbeck, Lincs
■ Stewards' Enquiry : Chris Catlin six-day ban: used whip with excessive force, excessive frequency and in the wrong place (Aug 1-6)

FOCUS
Useful sprinters lined up for a decent prize. The winner ran well behind a most progressive sort at Ascot last weekend and confirmed that promise here, rated back to his best. Solid form.

NOTEBOOK
Efistorm came from towards the back to lead close home despite not enjoying the clearest of passages. All his best form has been with cut in the ground and if he can be found a suitable opportunity when juice is there he would have a great chance of following up this win. (op 15-2)
Hotham came back to the form of his York third in June to the progressive three-year-old Harrison George where he just lost out in a finish of heads. He is none too consistent but is sure to win a race sooner than later. (op 10-1 tchd 11-1)
Mr Wolf was bounced out from a draw near the outside and tacked across to lead against the rail. He only gave best inside the last half-furlong and is undoubtedly well-handicapped at present. (op 7-1)
Avertuoso is running consistently and respectably without quite looking like winning. He needs to come down a few pounds in order to facilitate that. (op 18-1 tchd 20-1)
Namir(IRE), a three-time course-and-distance winner, ran a solid race, but has never won off a mark this high in his life. (op 15-2 tchd 10-1)
Elhamri Official explanation: jockey said gelding never travelled

Mambo Spirit(IRE) had to do plenty of running to lay up close to the pace from his wide draw and tired quickly in the final furlong. (op 15-2 tchd 7-1)

4172 COLSTROPE CUP H'CAP — 1m 4y

8:10 (8:10) (Class 5) (0-70,69) 3-Y-O+ — **£3,885** (£1,156; £577; £288) **Stalls** Low

Form				RPR
2250	**1**		**Ours (IRE)**[23] 3366 5-9-5 **60** ....(p) StephenDonohoe 9 (John A Harris) *t.k.h: hld up in rr: hdwy into midfield 1/2-way: effrt and swtchd rt wl over 1f out: rdn and hung lft ins fnl f: styd on strly to ld nr fin* **10/1**	71
1362	**2**	*nk*	**Turn Me On (IRE)**[9] 3834 5-9-5 **65** .... KellyHarrison(5) 5 (T D Walford) *hld up in tch on inner: hdwy 3f out: swtchd rt and effrt to ld over 1f out: sn rdn and hung lft: drvn ins fnl f: hdd nr fin* **3/1**[1]	75
4100	**3**	*3*	**Society Music (IRE)**[12] 3758 6-9-11 **69** ....(p) NeilBrown(3) 2 (M Dods) *trckd ldrs on inner: nt clr run and swtchd rt over 1f out: rdn and styng on whn hmpd ins fnl f: kpt on* **12/1**	72
5030	**4**	*½*	**Ming Vase**[18] 3551 6-8-9 **50** oh4 .... TonyCulhane 13 (P T Midgley) *chsd ldrs: rdn along 2f out: drvn over 1f out: kpt on same pce ins fnl f* **40/1**	52
-540	**5**	*2 ½*	**Superior Star**[3] 4048 5-9-10 **65** ....(b) PatCosgrave 3 (N Wilson) *hld up towards rr: hdwy on inner whn nt clr run and swtchd rt over 1f out: sn rdn and styd on ins fnl f: nrst fin* **16/1**	61+
-006	**6**	*nk*	**Zain (IRE)**[6] 3964 4-8-11 **52** ....(t) TPQueally 14 (J G Given) *trckd ldr: hdwy to ld wl over 2f out: rdn wl over 1f out: sn hdd and drvn: wknd ins fnl f* **10/1**	48
3633	**7**	*½*	**Inside Story (IRE)**[15] 3643 6-9-11 **66** ....(b) DaleGibson 7 (M W Easterby) *chsd ldrs: rdn along wl over 2f out: drvn over 1f out: kpt on same pce* **12/1**	60
3205	**8**	*2*	**Society Venue**[18] 3551 3-9-6 **69** .... TonyHamilton 15 (Jedd O'Keeffe) *chsd ldng pair: hdwy and cl up over 2f out: rdn and ev ch wl over 1f out: sn drvn and wknd ent fnl f* **14/1**	59
5200	**9**	*1*	**Titinius (IRE)**[28] 3226 8-9-7 **62** ....(p) PaulMulrennan 8 (Micky Hammond) *nvr bttr than midfield* **25/1**	49
6414	**10**	*nk*	**Pianoforte (USA)**[18] 3557 6-9-7 **62** ....(b) DavidAllan 11 (E J Alston) *hld up towards rr: hdwy on outer over 2f out: sn rdn and btn wl over 1f out* **8/1**[3]	49
3060	**11**	*¾*	**Latif (USA)**[35] 2572 7-8-8 **52** .... RussellKennemore(3) 4 (Paul Green) *s.i.s: a in rr* **20/1**	37
451	**12**	*4 ½*	**Aussie Blue (IRE)**[18] 3557 4-9-5 **63** .... MichaelJStainton(3) 12 (R M Whitaker) *a towards rr* **4/1**[2]	38
010	**13**	*4*	**Gee Ceffyl Bach**[28] 3229 4-8-9 **55** .... MarkCoumbe(5) 10 (R C Guest) *a in rr* **20/1**	20
-200	**14**	*1 ¼*	**Forzarzi (IRE)**[13] 3713 4-9-0 **55** .... DO'Donohoe 6 (H A McWilliams) *chsd ldrs: rdn along 1/2-way: wknd wl over 2f out* **20/1**	18
560	**15**	*6*	**Tump Mac**[16] 3600 4-9-6 **64** .... MarkLawson(3) 1 (N Bycroft) *led: rdn along 3f out: hdd over 2f out and sn wknd* **33/1**	13

1m 48.08s (2.18) **Going Correction** +0.225s/f (Good)
WFA 3 from 4yo+ 8lb **15 Ran SP% 125.7**
Speed ratings (Par 103): **98,97,94,94,91 91,90,88,87,87 86,82,78,77,71**
toteswinger: 1&2 £16.70, 1&3 £0.00, 2&3 £5.30. CSF £37.68 CT £393.16 TOTE £13.20: £4.30, £1.60, £3.50; EX 48.80.
Owner D A Spencer **Bred** David John Brown **Trained** Eastwell, Leics
■ Stewards' Enquiry : Neil Brown two-day ban: careless riding (Aug 1,3)

FOCUS
A moderate handicap run at a steady pace. With mostly fully exposed sorts contesting the form is nothing special, rated through the third.
Latif(USA) Official explanation: jockey said gelding missed the break

4173 FRONTLINE BATHROOMS MAIDEN H'CAP — 1m 2f 6y

8:40 (8:42) (Class 5) (0-70,69) 3-Y-O+ — **£3,885** (£1,156; £577; £288) **Stalls** Low

Form				RPR
6050	**1**		**Cheers For Thea (IRE)**[46] 2659 3-8-11 **52** .... DavidAllan 3 (T D Easterby) *trckd ldrs: hdwy 3f out: chsd ldr 2f out: rdn to ld over 1f out: drvn ins fnl f and kpt on gamely* **40/1**	60
-304	**2**	*1 ¼*	**Pondapie (IRE)**[29] 3174 3-9-13 **68** .... TomEaves 4 (R M Whitaker) *dwlt and rr: hdwy over 4f out: rdn wl over 1f out: styd on to chse wnr ins fnl f: sn drvn and nt rch wnr* **8/1**	73
4400	**3**	*½*	**Right You Are (IRE)**[93] 1408 8-9-0 **48** .... RussellKennemore(3) 17 (Paul Green) *hld up in rr: hdwy 3f out: swtchd outside and rdn wl over 1f out: styd on ins fnl f: nrst fin* **50/1**	52
034	**4**	*3 ¾*	**Capstan**[15] 3654 3-10-0 **69** .... PatCosgrave 11 (L M Cumani) *hld up: hdwy over 4f out: rdn to chse ldrs 2f out: sn drvn and one pce* **3/1**[2]	66
005	**5**	*2 ¼*	**Into The Light**[15] 3629 3-9-12 **67** .... StephenDonohoe 12 (E S McMahon) *hld up in rr: hdwy 3f out: rdn along 2f out: sn no imp* **6/1**[3]	59
5205	**6**	*6*	**Bramcote Lorne**[28] 3226 5-9-0 **50** ....(p) MarkCoumbe(5) 1 (R C Guest) *led: rdn along and hdd over 3f out: drvn 2f out and grad wknd* **10/1**	30
0452	**7**	*1*	**Danamight (IRE)**[25] 3322 3-9-8 **63** .... TPQueally 7 (J L Dunlop) *trckd ldr: hdwy to ld over 3f out: rdn 2f out: hdd over 1f out and sn wknd* **5/2**[1]	41
5424	**8**	*19*	**Jemima's Art**[17] 3580 3-8-5 **46** ....(b) DaleGibson 9 (M W Easterby) *a towards rr* **6/1**[3]	—
0400	**9**	*9*	**Dr Light (IRE)**[17] 3588 4-9-6 **51** .... LeeEnstone 5 (M A Peill) *trckd ldrs: hdwy 4f out: rdn along over 2f out and wknd qckly* **12/1**	—
00-5	**10**	*1 ¾*	**Corking (IRE)**[44] 2716 3-9-12 **67** .... PaulMulrennan 14 (Eve Johnson Houghton) *trckd ldrs: rdn along 4f out and sn wknd* **12/1**	—
63-5	**11**	*4 ½*	**Run Free**[196] 42 4-9-12 **57** .... DNolan 15 (N Wilson) *in tch: rdn along 4f out: sn wknd* **20/1**	—

2m 18.04s (4.34) **Going Correction** +0.225s/f (Good)
WFA 3 from 4yo+ 10lb **11 Ran SP% 126.9**
Speed ratings (Par 103): **91,90,89,86,84 80,79,64,56,55 51**
toteswinger: 1&2 £0.00, 1&3 £0.00, 2&3 £52.70. CSF £353.49 CT £15099.93 TOTE £60.30: £10.90, £4.40, £11.90; EX 623.30.Northgate Maisie was withdrawn. Price at time of withdrawal 66/1. Rule 4 does not apply.
Owner Ron George **Bred** Crone Stud Farms Ltd **Trained** Great Habton, N Yorks

FOCUS
A moderate maiden handicap, but with a lot of unexposed potential improvers in the line-up, the race should throw up a number of future winners, albeit in minor grade. The form might be a bit better than average for the grade.
Cheers For Thea(IRE) Official explanation: trainer said, regarding apparent improvement in form, that the filly had been given time away from the racecourse and plenty of work at home following the previous bad run at Carlisle.
Danamight(IRE) Official explanation: jockey said filly ran too keen
Dr Light(IRE) Official explanation: jockey said gelding lost its action

4174 BOLLIN H'CAP — 6f

9:10 (9:10) (Class 5) (0-75,75) 3-Y-O+ — **£3,885** (£1,156; £577; £288) **Stalls** Low

Form				RPR
4046	**1**		**Royal Challenge**[14] 3665 7-8-9 **61** .... NeilBrown(3) 14 (I W McInnes) *in rr: swtchd outside and hdwy wl over 1f out: rdn ent fnl f: styd on strly to ld nr fin* **11/1**	72
5355	**2**	*½*	**Poppy's Rose**[8] 3883 4-9-0 **63** ....(p) PatrickMathers 3 (I W McInnes) *trckd ldrs on inner: effrt and nt clr run over 1f out: swtchd rt and rdn 1f out: led ins fnl f: drvn: hdd and no ex towards fin* **11/1**	72
0310	**3**	*1 ½*	**Bid For Gold**[21] 3454 4-9-2 **65** .... TonyHamilton 16 (Jedd O'Keeffe) *cl up: rdn 2f out and ev ch tl drvn ent fnl f and no ex last 100yds* **7/1**[2]	69
6600	**4**	*1 ¾*	**H Harrison (IRE)**[15] 3646 8-9-3 **73** .... ClGillies(7) 9 (I W McInnes) *sn led: rdn along 2f out: drvn over 1f out: hdd ins fnl f: wknd* **25/1**	72
0045	**5**	*nk*	**Cheery Cat (USA)**[17] 3591 4-8-9 **61** ....(p) MarkLawson(3) 12 (D W Barker) *chsd ldrs: rdn along 2f out: drvn over 1f out: kpt on same pce u.p ins fnl f* **8/1**[3]	59
-100	**6**	*2*	**We'Re Delighted**[27] 3263 3-9-3 **71** .... PaulMulrennan 6 (T D Walford) *hld up: hdwy 2f out: rdn wl over 1f out and kpt on same pce* **16/1**	62
3-42	**7**	*nse*	**Royal Composer (IRE)**[14] 3665 5-8-11 **60** ....(b) DavidAllan 10 (T D Easterby) *chsd ldrs: rdn along wl over 1f out: drvn and wknd appr fnl f* **6/1**[1]	51
1020	**8**	*nse*	**Avontuur (FR)**[10] 3825 6-8-13 **62** ....(b) DaleGibson 4 (Mrs R A Carr) *dwlt and rr: hdwy and rdn along 2f out: styd on u.p ins fnl f: nrst fin* **12/1**	53
4016	**9**	*1 ¾*	**Maison Dieu**[17] 3582 5-8-9 **58** .... PatCosgrave 2 (E J Alston) *hld up: hdwy 2f out: rdn to chse ldrs over 1f out: drvn and wknd ent fnl f* **9/1**	43
1303	**10**	*5*	**Support Fund (IRE)**[8] 3892 4-9-9 **75** .... PatrickHills(3) 15 (Eve Johnson Houghton) *nvr nr ldrs* **8/1**[3]	44
0-00	**11**	*nk*	**Multitude (IRE)**[17] 3591 4-8-7 **56** oh4 ....(b) TomEaves 5 (T D Easterby) *chsd ldrs: rdn along over 2f out: sn wknd* **33/1**	24
0002	**12**	*1 ¾*	**Winthorpe (IRE)**[13] 3708 8-8-12 **68** .... JamieKyne(7) 13 (J J Quinn) *chsd ldrs on outer: rdn along over 2f out and sn wknd* **7/1**[2]	31
-006	**13**	*2 ¼*	**Pearl Dealer (IRE)**[15] 3626 3-8-8 **69** .... SimonPearce(7) 7 (N J Vaughan) *in tch: rdn along over 2f out and sn wknd* **10/1**	25
33-0	**14**	*32*	**Mudhish (IRE)**[25] 3324 3-9-0 **73** ....(b) AhmedAjtebi(5) 1 (C E Brittain) *towards rr on inner whn stmbld bdly and lost action over 2f out: sn eased and bhd* **10/1**	—

1m 18.33s (1.43) **Going Correction** +0.225s/f (Good)
WFA 3 from 4yo+ 5lb **14 Ran SP% 126.7**
Speed ratings (Par 103): **99,98,96,94,93 90,90,90,88,81 81,79,76,33**
toteswinger: 1&2 £13.30, 1&3 £54.00, 2&3 £23.60. CSF £133.44 CT £952.49 TOTE £17.10: £5.80, £2.50, £2.30; EX 72.70 Place 6 £1,990.76, Place 5 £1,145.76.
Owner Truck Export **Bred** Capt A L Smith-Maxwell **Trained** Catwick, E Yorks
■ Stewards' Enquiry : Patrick Mathers one-day ban: used whip with excessive force (Aug 1)

FOCUS
Mainly moderate sorts on show in this sprint handicap. They tend to win in their turn over this trip at this level and it would be unwise to read the form literally. A 1-2 for trainer Ian McInnes, the winner close to his winter form.
T/Jkpt: Not won. T/Plt: £1,891.00 to a £1 stake. Pool: £73,232.11. 28.27 winning tickets. T/Qpdt: £1,989.80 to a £1 stake. Pool: £4,571.17. 1.70 winning tickets. JR

3996 HAYDOCK (L-H)

Saturday, July 19

OFFICIAL GOING: Heavy (6.4)
Rail realignment added 21yards to advertised distances on the round course.
Wind: Fresh, against. Weather: Overcast

4175 BETFRED NURSERY — 5f

6:40 (6:41) (Class 5) 2-Y-O — **£3,238** (£963; £481; £240) **Stalls** Centre

Form				RPR
3014	**1**		**La Brigitte**[15] 3663 2-8-11 **73** .... TolleyDean(3) 5 (A J McCabe) *trckd ldng pair: hdwy and cl up 2f out: rdn to ld and hung lft over 1f out: drvn ins fnl f and carried hd high: kpt on* **4/1**	79
21	**2**	*1 ¾*	**Sunset Crest**[28] 3259 2-9-4 **80** .... AndrewMullen(3) 6 (Mrs A Duffield) *sn rdn along and in tch: hdwy 2f out: styd on u.p ins fnl f: tk 2nd nr line* **11/4**[1]	80
532	**3**	*hd*	**Titus Andronicus (IRE)**[7] 3949 2-8-11 **70** .... NCallan 8 (K A Ryan) *led: jnd and pushed along 2f out: sn rdn and hdd over 1f out: drvn and one pce ins fnl f* **7/2**[3]	69
460	**4**	*6*	**Rio Cobolo (IRE)**[18] 3590 2-8-0 **59** .... DaleGibson 4 (Paul Green) *prom: rdn along over 2f out: sn drvn and wknd* **14/1**	36
0045	**5**	*5*	**Wigan Pier**[12] 3788 2-7-12 **57** oh1 .... CatherineGannon 1 (T D Easterby) *hld up in rr: hdwy to chse ldrs over 2f out: sn rdn and btn* **9/1**	16
1212	**6**	*2 ¼*	**Alphabeth**[1] 4143 2-8-6 **70** .... MCGeran(5) 7 (M R Channon) *hmpd sn after s: a in rr* **3/1**[2]	21

66.54 secs (6.04) **Going Correction** +1.00s/f (Soft) **6 Ran SP% 110.6**
Speed ratings (Par 94): **91,88,87,78,70 66**
toteswinger: 1&2 £2.60, 1&3 £3.70, 2&3 £2.30. CSF £14.87 CT £38.41 TOTE £5.60: £3.00, £2.50; EX 15.80.
Owner Paul J Dixon **Bred** M And Mrs V L Ritchie **Trained** Babworth, Notts
■ Stewards' Enquiry : N Callan one-day ban: careless riding (Aug 6)

FOCUS
The conditions were very testing. The winner reproduced her Southwell form and the third remains interesting for nurseries.

NOTEBOOK
La Brigitte gained her previous win on the deep Fibresand surface at Southwell so it was no surprise that she coped so well with the heavy conditions here. She carries her head high but that is in no way reflective of a lack of resolution with this daughter of Tobougg, who is speedy and tough. (op 7-1)
Sunset Crest, a course-and-distance winner in maiden company last month, was all out to lay up in the first half of the race before keeping on gamely to snatch second under her big weight. She can improve again over an extra furlong. (op 10-3 tchd 5-2)
Titus Andronicus(IRE) had shown up well in maiden company so didn't have any secrets from the Handicapper when it came to assessing him for nurseries. He made a decent enough fist of attempting to make all, and should find one of these when there is more emphasis on speed. (op 5-2)

Alphabeth was running for the fourth time in nine days, having been second less than 24 hours previously at Hamilton. She had coped with a similar gap between races last week when successful at Nottingham the day after running at Chester, so it is entirely plausible that underfoot conditions were primarily responsible for this poor effort. (op 11-4)

4176 J.J. MCLAUGHLIN E B F MAIDEN STKS 6f

7:10 (7:10) (Class 5) 2-Y-O **£3,885** (£1,156; £577; £288) **Stalls** Centre

Form RPR

1 **Playfellow (IRE)** 2-9-3 0 PhilipRobinson 5 89+
(M A Jarvis) *hld up in tch: hdwy over 2f out: rdn to chal over 1f out: styd on to ld ins fnl f: r.o wl* **4/1**[2]

2 1 ¾ **Prime Mood (IRE)** 2-9-3 0 TomEaves 9 84+
(B Smart) *dwlt and squeezed out s: swtchd rt and sn trcking ldrs: hdwy to ld wl over 1f out: sn rdn: drvn and hdd ins fnl f: kpt on same pce* **14/1**

20 3 5 **Becausewecan (USA)**28 [3254] 2-9-3 0 JoeFanning 4 69
(M Johnston) *trckd ldrs: hdwy and ev ch over 2f out: sn rdn and wknd over 1f out* **11/2**

00 4 4 ½ **Silent Hero**21 [3495] 2-9-3 0 EddieAhern 10 55
(M A Jarvis) *in midfield and pushed along 1/2-way: rdn along 2f out: styd on appr last: nrst fin* **22/1**

5 3 ½ **Shanavaz** 2-8-12 0 DaleGibson 1 40
(Mrs G S Rees) *in rr: rdn along and hdwy over 2f out: styd on u.p appr fnl f* **50/1**

5 6 1 ½ **Shifting Gold (IRE)**45 [2730] 2-9-3 0 NCallan 8 41
(K A Ryan) *in midfield: rdn along 1/2-way: n.d* **33/1**

3 7 1 ½ **Queen Sally (IRE)**28 [3259] 2-8-9 0 TolleyDean(3) 6 31
(J L Spearing) *led: rdn along 1/2-way: hdd over 2f out and sn wknd* **9/2**[3]

24 8 2 ¼ **Red Rosanna**14 [3734] 2-8-9 0 RussellKennemore(3) 12 24
(R Hollinshead) *chsd ldrs: hdwy 1/2-way: led over 2f out: sn rdn and hdd over 1f out: wknd qckly* **12/1**

0 9 1 ¼ **Ivor Novello (IRE)**34 [3055] 2-9-3 0 RobertWinston 7 25
(G A Swinbank) *cl up: rdn along 1/2-way: sn wknd* **25/1**

2 10 7 **Whisky Jack**12 [3798] 2-9-3 0 DO'Donohoe 11 4
(W R Muir) *prom: pushed along 1/2-way: sn rdn and wknd over 2f out* **5/2**[1]

0 11 13 **Jul's Lad (IRE)**15 [3669] 2-9-3 0 LiamJones 3 —
(Paul Green) *racd alone on far rail: outpcd and bhd fr 1/2-way* **8/1**

1m 20.5s (6.50) **Going Correction** +1.00s/f (Soft) 11 Ran SP% **120.7**
Speed ratings (Par 94): **96,93,87,81,76 74,72,69,67,58 41**
toteswinger: 1&2 £13.70, 1&3 £2.50, 2&3 £18.60. CSF £57.36 TOTE £4.80: £2.20, £3.60, £1.80; EX 62.00.
Owner Sheikh Ahmed Al Maktoum **Bred** Darley **Trained** Newmarket, Suffolk

FOCUS
They finished strung out like washing in this juvenile maiden. Given the underfoot conditions, it is best to forgive some of those who appeared to run badly, while the two debutants who were the first home look to have promising futures.

NOTEBOOK
Playfellow(IRE) ◆, an 80,000gns son of Kheleyf, made a most striking debut, stringing his rivals out all over Merseyside without Robinson ever getting serious with him. He looks a powerful sort, and ploughed his way through the testing conditions to continue the rich vein of form enjoyed by both his trainer and jockey this year. He looks a decent prospect and is well worth a crack at Listed level at least. (op 5-2 tchd 9-2 in places)
Prime Mood(IRE) ◆'s pedigree is all about speed and if he hadn't bumped into another smart prospect here he would have run out a most convincing debut winner. The son of Choisir coped well with the heavy conditions and saw out the trip well, despite not having quite the firepower of the winner. He is nailed on to win a maiden. (op 16-1 tchd 12-1)
Becausewecan(USA) had run well in soft ground on debut at and came back to that sort of form on similar going here after flopping on a fast surface at Ayr last time. He is no great shakes but can go well in nurseries. (op 7-1)
Silent Hero, a stable companion of the winner, had only beaten one home in two starts but the second of those was in a hot maiden at Newmarket, where he had shown up for a fair way. That race was over 7f, and the way he stayed on here suggests he deserves another chance over that trip, particularly now that he is qualified for nurseries. (op 33-1)
Queen Sally(IRE) who shaped well over the minimum trip here on debut, showed plenty of dash before getting tired in the ground. She is a late foal who probably still has a lot of strengthening to do. (op 4-1 tchd 5-1)
Red Rosanna had run well in a couple of fast-ground 5f maidens, but after leading two furlongs out and looking sure to play some kind of part in the finish she stopped as if shot in the final furlong. A return to the minimum, or at the very least to a sound surface, would see her do well now that she is qualified for nurseries. (op 16-1)
Whisky Jack, favourite to go one better than on his promising debut at Windsor, ran fast for four furlongs but became unbalanced for pressure and looked all at sea on the heavy ground. Official explanation: trainer had no explanation for the poor form shown (op 3-1 tchd 10-3)

4177 STANLEYBET SPORTS CONDITIONS STKS 7f 30y

7:40 (7:40) (Class 3) 3-Y-O+ **£11,333** (£3,372; £1,685; £841) **Stalls** Low

Form RPR

2044 1 **Welsh Emperor (IRE)**7 [3946] 9-9-7 110 TonyCulhane 3 108
(T P Tate) *set stdy pce: qcknd 4f out: rdn along 3f out: clr wl over 1f out: drvn and kpt on ins fnl f* **10/11**[1]

3-40 2 1 ¾ **We'll Come**31 [3122] 4-9-1 93 (b) PhilipRobinson 1 97
(M A Jarvis) *t.k.h: hld up: hdwy 3f out: chsd wnr wl over 1f out: rdn wl ins fnl f and no imp* **5/2**[2]

440- 3 6 **Trinity College (USA)**353 [4058] 4-9-7 0 KShea 5 87
(M F De Kock, South Africa) *trckd wnr: effrt over 3f out: rdn along over 2f out: drvn and wknd wl over 1f out* **7/2**[3]

-141 4 7 **Barons Spy (IRE)**22 [3435] 7-8-12 88 RussellKennemore(3) 2 63
(R J Price) *hld up: hdwy over 3f out: sn rdn along and wknd over 2f out* **10/1**

1m 38.41s (8.21) **Going Correction** +0.875s/f (Soft) 4 Ran SP% **112.3**
Speed ratings (Par 107): **88,86,79,71**
toteswinger: 1&2 £4.20. CSF £3.66 TOTE £1.60; EX 2.80.
Owner Mrs Sylvia Clegg **Bred** Times Of Wigan Ltd **Trained** Tadcaster, N Yorks
■ Tony Culhane's first winner since his recent comeback from 16 months out through injury and suspension.

FOCUS
The winner did no more than he was entitled to as he was favoured by the weights and had his ideal conditions.

NOTEBOOK
Welsh Emperor(IRE) has always been a bit of a 'tool' when the divots are flying and he gave short shrift to some rivals that he was basically in a different class to, although in these conditions even he was getting a little leg weary close home. He is set to go down his tried and trusted route of Hungerford Stakes at Newbury at August, providing there is some juice in the ground, followed by his main aim of the Prix de la Foret at the Arc meeting. (tchd 8-11 and evens in places)
We'll Come has only the one win, a Yarmouth maiden, on the credit side of his ledger, but he ran like a horse fully deserving of his official rating of 93 here in chasing home a proven Group-race performer on ground that he revels in. The son of Elnadim appears to go on any going, and back in Handicap company must surely go close to adding to that single success off his current mark. (tchd 3-1)
Trinity College(USA) was a useful performer for Aidan O'Brien, but with his penalty faced a tough task here on his first start for Mike de Kock, even on going that he was proven on. (op 5-1 tchd 11-2)
Barons Spy(IRE) has been in great form of late, but was a little outclassed here and ran as well as could be expected. Official explanation: trainer's rep said gelding was unsuited by the heavy ground (op 9-1)

4178 INSPIRED GAMING GROUP H'CAP 1m 6f

8:10 (8:10) (Class 4) (0-85,84) 4-Y-O+ **£5,504** (£1,637; £818; £408) **Stalls** Low

Form RPR

4323 1 **Bollin Felix**9 [3884] 4-9-1 76 (b) DavidAllan 9 92+
(T D Easterby) *trckd ldng pair: hdwy 4f out: led over 3f out: sn rdn clr: drvn and styd on wl appr fnl f* **5/2**[1]

0004 2 5 **Sphinx (FR)**10 [3832] 10-9-5 80 (b) RobertWinston 3 86
(E W Tuer) *hld up in rr: hdwy 4f out: rdn along over 2f out and sn chsng wnr: drvn over 1f out and no imp fnl f* **11/1**

0324 3 10 **Factotum**34 [3058] 4-9-9 84 JoeFanning 7 76
(L M Cumani) *chsd ldr: rdn along over 3f out: sn drvn and plugged on at one pce* **3/1**[2]

6333 4 1 ¾ **Stringsofmyheart**8 [3900] 4-9-2 77 TPO'Shea 8 67
(Miss Gay Kelleway) *led: rdn along 4f out: hdd over 3f out: sn drvn and grad wknd* **12/1**

-000 5 2 ¾ **Mikao (IRE)**8 [3925] 7-9-6 81 (b[1]) PaulMulrennan 2 67
(M H Tompkins) *trckd ldrs: effrt 4f out: rdn along 3f out and sn wknd* **22/1**

1/03 6 ½ **Burnt Oak (UAE)**23 [3414] 6-8-11 72 DeanMcKeown 5 57
(C W Fairhurst) *hld up: effrt and sme hdwy over 4f out: sn rdn along and wknd* **14/1**

5313 7 1 ½ **Cleaver**24 [3375] 7-9-5 80 NCallan 4 63
(Lady Herries) *hld up: a towards rr: rdn along and bhd fr over 3f out* **4/1**[3]

14 8 1 ½ **Cotton Eyed Joe (IRE)**24 [3368] 7-9-2 80 PJMcDonald(3) 6 61
(G A Swinbank) *in tch: rdn along 4f out: sn wknd* **9/2**

3m 14.49s (10.19) **Going Correction** +0.875s/f (Soft) 8 Ran SP% **118.8**
Speed ratings (Par 105): **105,102,96,95,93 93,92,91**
toteswinger: 1&2 £5.30, 1&3 £4.50, 2&3 £7.50. CSF £32.45 CT £87.93 TOTE £4.00: £1.30, £2.50, £1.70; EX 34.80.
Owner Sir Neil Westbrook **Bred** Sir Neil & Exors Of Late Lady Westbrook **Trained** Great Habton, N Yorks

FOCUS
Once again, conditions saw to it that the horses came home at intervals more reminiscent of a novice chase in this useful stayers' heat for older horses. The winner is rated value for 8l, the form rated through the runner-up.
Cleaver Official explanation: trainer said gelding was unsuited by the heavy ground

4179 MAVIS GALE CANCER RESEARCH UK H'CAP 1m 2f 120y

8:40 (8:40) (Class 5) (0-75,74) 3-Y-O **£3,238** (£963; £481; £240) **Stalls** High

Form RPR

344 1 **Times Vital (IRE)**16 [3628] 3-9-2 69 DeanMcKeown 6 81
(E J O'Neill) *stdd s: hld up in rr: hdwy on outer over 3f out: rdn to ld and hung lft over 2f out: sn clr: drvn out* **9/1**

5000 2 5 **Air Chief**10 [3836] 3-9-4 71 NCallan 10 73
(H J L Dunlop) *hld up: hdwy 3f out: rdn to chse wnr wl over 1f out: drvn ent fnl f and no imp* **7/2**[2]

004 3 3 ¼ **Dr Brass**30 [3161] 3-9-6 73 EddieAhern 2 69
(H J L Dunlop) *hld up: hdwy over 3f out: rdn to chse ldrs over 2f: sn drvn and one pce* **10/3**[1]

6003 4 8 **Doon Haymer (IRE)**5 [4017] 3-9-5 72 (v) TomEaves 3 53
(Miss L A Perratt) *cl up: led after 2f: rdn along over 3f out: drvn and hdd over 2f out: sn wknd* **7/2**[2]

0542 5 6 **Feisty Royale**7 [3957] 3-9-6 73 JoeFanning 5 42
(M Johnston) *trckd ldrs: hdwy to chse ldr 1/2-way: rdn along over 3f out: drvn and wknd wl over 2f out* **7/2**[2]

-300 6 8 **Topflightrebellion**47 [2659] 3-8-7 60 DaleGibson 4 14
(Mrs G S Rees) *led 2f: prom tl rdn along 1/2-way and sn wknd* **33/1**

5002 7 14 **Hawk Flight (IRE)**10 [3845] 3-9-1 68 (b[1]) DO'Donohoe 1 —
(W R Muir) *dwlt and wnt lft s: sn chsng ldrs on inner: rdn along 4f out: sn drvn and wknd* **6/1**[3]

2m 24.02s (7.32) **Going Correction** +0.875s/f (Soft) 7 Ran SP% **117.0**
Speed ratings (Par 100): **108,104,102,96,91 86,75**
toteswinger: 1&2 £13.30, 1&3 £15.10, 2&3 £3.40. CSF £41.85 CT £129.15 TOTE £11.00: £2.40, £3.00; EX 45.40.
Owner G A Lucas **Bred** Miss Louise Fitzgerald **Trained** Averham Park, Notts

FOCUS
Just a fair handicap for three-year-olds, and yet again they came home at intervals. Big improvement from the winner, up 12lb on his early-season form.

4180 JOAN COLLINS CANCER RESEARCH UK H'CAP 1m 30y

9:10 (9:10) (Class 5) (0-70,70) 3-Y-O **£3,238** (£963; £481; £240) **Stalls** Low

Form RPR

0221 1 **Natural Rhythm (IRE)**7 [3958] 3-8-5 55 (b) MichaelJStainton(3) 11 64
(Mrs R A Carr) *mde all: jnd and rdn 2f out: drvn over 1f out and styd on gamely ins fnl f* **7/1**

6541 2 3 ¼ **Tamasou (IRE)**12 [3790] 3-9-6 67 DaleGibson 3 69
(Garry Moss) *trckd ldrs: hdwy on inner 3f out: rdn 2f out: chsd wnr and styd on ins fnl f: tk 2nd nr fin* **8/1**

-224 3 1 **Stand In Flames**19 [3563] 3-9-3 64 NCallan 9 64
(Pat Eddery) *trckd wnr: effrt 3f out: rdn and ev ch 2f out: sn drvn and kpt on same pce: lost 2nd nr fin* **7/2**[1]

233 4 ½ **Hippolytus**16 [3628] 3-9-6 70 JamieMoriarty(3) 4 69+
(J J Quinn) *hld up in rr: hdwy 3f out: swtchd rt and rdn wl over 1f out: styd on u.p ins fnl f: nrst fin* **5/1**[3]

0552 5 ¾ **Earlsmedic**13 [3757] 3-9-4 65 EddieAhern 2 62+
(S C Williams) *trckd ldrs: effrt over 3f out and sn rdn: drvn 2f out and kpt on u.p ins fnl f: nrst fin* **4/1**[2]

0452 6 6 **Reve Vert (FR)**7 [3964] 3-8-4 51 oh1 CatherineGannon 7 36
(A W Carroll) *chsd ldng pair: rdn along 3f out: drvn over 2f out and grad wknd* **20/1**

0605 7 2 ¼ **Poulaine Bleue**11 [3816] 3-8-4 51 oh6 TPO'Shea 1 31
(M L W Bell) *in midfield: effrt and sme hdwy over 3f out: sn rdn and btn over 2f out* **25/1**

323 **8** ½ **Grit (IRE)**[4] 4044 3-9-2 **63** .... TonyCulhane 12 42
(M R Channon) *chsd ldrs: rdn along over 3f out: sn drvn and wknd over 2f out* **7/1**

4061 **9** 13 **Princess Rhianna (IRE)**[4] 4044 3-9-0 **61** 6ex .... LiamJones 5 13
(Mrs G S Rees) *hld up: a towards rr* **6/1**

000- **10** 28 **Riorun (IRE)**[283] 6099 3-8-8 **55** .... PaulMulrennan 6 —
(Ian Williams) *a towards rr* **66/1**

1m 51.8s (8.00) **Going Correction** +0.875s/f (Soft) **10** Ran SP% **119.4**
Speed ratings (Par 100): **95,91,90,90,89 83,81,80,67,39**
toteswinger: 1&2 £10.20, 1&3 £3.30, 2&3 £10.50. CSF £61.94 CT £236.93 TOTE £8.80: £2.50, £2.90, £1.90; EX 89.40 Place 6 £158.22, Place 5 £71.04..
Owner Michael Hill **Bred** Mark Commins **Trained** Stillington, N Yorks

FOCUS
The winner continued his good run of form and is getting back to something like his latter 2yo level. The form might not be entirely solid given the bad ground but has been rated at face value.
Princess Rhianna(IRE) Official explanation: jockey said filly was unsuited by the heavy ground
T/Plt: £373.50 to a £1 stake. Pool: £71,584.18. 139.90 winning tickets. T/Qpdt: £37.70 to a £1 stake. Pool: £5,058.29. 99.10 winning tickets. JR

4085 LINGFIELD (L-H)

Saturday, July 19

OFFICIAL GOING: Turf course - good to firm (8.6); all-weather - standard
Once again the stands' rail was a big advantage on the turf course.
Wind: Fresh, across Weather: bright but breezy

4181 OXTED CLAIMING STKS — 1m (P)

5:50 (5:51) (Class 6) 3-5-Y-O **£1,978** (£584; £292) **Stalls** High

Form RPR

604 **1** nk **Rankayo Hitam (USA)**[31] 3138 3-9-5 77 .... (b[1]) JohnEgan 3 72
(P F I Cole) *led: rdn and wnt clr 2f out: 3 l clr 1f out: kpt on tl hdd nr fin: fin 2nd, nk: awrdd r* **6/4**[1]

0036 **2** 2½ **Autograph Hunter**[12] 3789 4-9-1 46 .... LPKeniry 9 54
(Peter Grayson) *t.k.h: in tch: rdn and effrt over 2f out: disp 2nd 2f out: sn hung lft and one pce: fin 3rd, nk & 2½l: plcd 2nd* **16/1**

1230 **3** shd **Teasing**[26] 3317 4-9-6 74 .... JimmyQuinn 10 59
(J Pearce) *stdd s: hld up in midfield: snatched up and lost pl bnd 5f out: hdwy 3f out: rdn ent fnl 2f: sn swtchd rt: kpt on but nt pce to rch ldrs: fin 4th: plcd 3rd* **9/2**[3]

3106 **4** 2½ **Sistos Fascination**[16] 3648 3-8-2 63 .... AndreaAtzeni(7) 11 50
(M Botti) *rrd s and v.s.a: t.k.h: sn in tch in midfield: rdn and no imp fr over 2f out: fin 5th: plcd 4th* **12/1**

-000 **5** 1½ **Lady Lorins**[10] 3844 4-8-9 41 .... PaulEddery 8 39
(Andrew Turnell) *t.k.h: chsd ldr tl ent fnl 2f: sn outpcd: fin 6th: plcd 5th* **33/1**

0006 **6** 1½ **Tagula Sands (IRE)**[15] 3675 4-9-0 33 .... RichardSmith 5 40
(J C Fox) *stdd after s: hld up bhd: rdn and hdwy over 2f out: nvr pce to rch ldrs: fin 7th: plcd 6th* **66/1**

4025 **7** 5 **What's For Tea**[50] 2559 3-8-9 62 .... ChrisCatlin 2 32
(P Butler) *towards rr: rdn and effrt on outer over 2f out: nvr trbld ldrs: fin 8th: plcd 7th* **10/1**

0000 **8** nk **Ile Royale**[25] 3345 3-8-4 49 ow1 .... (e[1]) SimonWhitworth 7 26
(B R Johnson) *v.s.a: t.k.h: hld up in rr: effrt on outer 3f out: bhd last 2f: fin 9th: plcd 8th* **33/1**

5005 **9** 5 **Babieca (USA)**[84] 1626 4-8-8 48 .... GihanArnolda(7) 6 18
(A B Haynes) *sn shuffled along: chsd ldrs tl 5f out: bhd last 3f: fin 10th: plcd 9th* **33/1**

0400 **D** **Hilbre Court (USA)**[8] 3911 3-9-5 82 .... WilliamBuick 1 72
(B J Meehan) *chsd ldrs: rdn 3f out: chsd clr ldr 2f out: drvn and r.o fnl f to ld nr fin: fin 1st, nk; disq: jockey failed to draw correct weight* **5/2**[2]

1m 40.29s (2.09) **Going Correction** +0.125s/f (Slow)
WFA 3 from 4yo+ 8lb **10** Ran SP% **119.7**
Speed ratings (Par 101): **93,91,91,88,87 85,80,80,75,94**
toteswinger: 1&2 Not won. 1&3 £2.80, 2&3 £26.40. CSF £29.01 TOTE £2.90: £1.20, £5.10, £1.80; EX 33.40.
Owner Mrs Fitri Hay **Bred** Phil Booker **Trained** Whatcombe, Oxon
■ Stewards' Enquiry : William Buick three-day ban: weighed-in light (Aug 3-5)

FOCUS
A reasonable claimer but the early pace was just steady and the form is messy and far from solid.
Autograph Hunter Official explanation: jockey said gelding hung right

4182 SANDHAWS HILL (S) STKS — 1m 2f (P)

6:20 (6:22) (Class 6) 3-Y-O+ **£1,978** (£584; £292) **Stalls** Low

Form RPR

6566 **1** **Tabulate**[42] 2832 5-9-6 44 .... JimmyQuinn 12 63
(P Howling) *hld up wl bhd: stdy hdwy over 3f out: trckd ldrs gng wl over 1f out: sn drew clr: readily* **14/1**

3255 **2** 5 **Split The Wind (USA)**[18] 3572 4-8-8 50 ow1 .... HarryPoulton(7) 10 48+
(Miss Sheena West) *led for 1f: chsd ldrs after: rdn over 2f out: kpt on to go 2nd ins fnl f: no ch w wnr* **12/1**

0000 **3** 1¼ **Golden Brown (IRE)**[7] 3963 4-9-5 48 .... ChrisCatlin 14 50
(David Pinder) *racd in midfield: hdwy to chse ldrs over 2f out: sn rdn: plugged on u.p to go 3rd ins fnl f: no ch w wnr* **11/1**

0060 **4** 2¼ **Film Queen (IRE)**[28] 3265 4-9-0 45 .... IanMongan 4 40
(Mrs L J Mongan) *in tch: rdn to chse ldrs over 2f out: kpt on same pce u.p fnl f* **20/1**

3005 **5** 1¾ **Media Stars**[13] 3763 3-8-9 68 .... (b) ShaneKelly 7 42
(J A Osborne) *s.i.s: bhd tl hdwy to ld 5f out: rdn 3f out: hdd 1f out: wknd qckly fnl f* **7/1**[2]

5405 **6** nk **Green Pirate**[11] 3822 6-9-11 50 .... (v) LPKeniry 6 47
(C R Dore) *hld up in rr: rdn 4f out: plugged on u.p fnl f: n.d* **12/1**

40 **7** shd **Classy Affair**[16] 3654 4-9-0 0 .... PaulDoe 2 36+
(D Morris) *a towards rr: sme hdwy last 2f: nvr trbld ldrs* **40/1**

646 **8** 1¾ **Has To Be Abacus (IRE)**[28] 3264 3-8-6 50 .... KevinGhunowa(3) 8 37
(A B Haynes) *chsd ldrs: rdn over 3f out: chsd ldr over 2f out: ev ch 2f out: wknd qckly ent fnl f* **7/1**[2]

0140 **9** shd **Samuel Charles**[11] 3822 10-9-11 65 .... (b) JohnEgan 9 43
(C R Dore) *pushed up to ld after 1f: hdd 5f out: chsd ldr after tl over 2f out: wknd qckly over 1f out* **5/1**[1]

-000 **10** shd **Tous Les Deux**[7] 3956 5-9-5 56 .... AdamKirby 11 37
(Peter Grayson) *hld up bhd: gd hdwy on outer over 3f out: chal wd and ev ch bnd 2f out: wknd qckly ent fnl f* **5/1**[1]

0300 **11** 1 **Trivia (IRE)**[10] 3842 4-8-7 58 .... RossAtkinson(7) 13 30
(Ms J S Doyle) *stdd s: hld up in rr: nvr a factor* **16/1**

0-46 **12** 8 **Tenement (IRE)**[28] 3265 4-9-5 47 .... SimonWhitworth 1 19
(Jamie Poulton) *racd in midfield: rdn and effrt 3f out: sn struggling and bhd last 2f* **8/1**[3]

2400 **13** 4½ **Site Sentry (IRE)**[14] 3711 5-9-5 55 .... FrankieMcDonald 3 10
(M F Harris) *chsd ldrs for 2f: steadily lost pl: wl bhd last 3f: t.o* **10/1**

5500 **14** 3½ **Tewin Green**[10] 3841 3-8-4 60 .... (v[1]) WilliamBuick 5 —
(M Botti) *chsd ldrs: rdn over 4f out: wknd over 3f out: eased fr over 1f out: t.o* **14/1**

2m 7.50s (0.90) **Going Correction** +0.125s/f (Slow)
WFA 3 from 4yo+ 10lb **14** Ran SP% **128.7**
Speed ratings (Par 101): **101,97,96,94,92 92,92,91,91,90 90,83,80,77**
toteswinger: 1&2 £47.20, 1&3 £31.40, 2&3 £47.20. CSF £183.97 TOTE £18.70: £5.50, £2.90, £4.50; EX 369.40.There was no bid for the winner. Tous Les Deux was claimed by G. L. Moore for £6,000.
Owner Richard Berenson **Bred** Millsec Limited **Trained** Newmarket, Suffolk

FOCUS
A standard seller with the winner rated back to her best. The winning time was 2.10 seconds slower than the following 56-75 fillies' handicap.
Samuel Charles Official explanation: jockey said gelding had no more to give
Site Sentry(IRE) Official explanation: jockey said horse never travelled

4183 COPTHORNE FILLIES' H'CAP — 1m 2f (P)

6:50 (6:50) (Class 5) (0-75,73) 3-Y-O+ **£2,590** (£770; £385; £192) **Stalls** Low

Form RPR

-263 **1** **Finmore Queen (USA)**[15] 3672 3-9-3 **72** .... AdamKirby 8 86
(J R Fanshawe) *in tch: chsd ldr over 3f out: drvn 2f out: styd on wl to ld ins fnl f: won gng away* **3/1**[2]

-403 **2** 2½ **Marraasi (USA)**[15] 3679 3-8-12 **67** .... MartinDwyer 5 76
(M P Tregoning) *chsd ldr: led 4f out: clr 2f out: sn rdn: hdd ins fnl f: no ex* **11/2**

-426 **3** 4½ **Adorabella (IRE)**[10] 3843 5-9-4 **63** .... DarryllHolland 6 63
(A King) *bhd: rdn and swtchd rt wl over 2f out: poor 7th 2f out: r.o wl fnl f: snatched 3rd on line: nvr trbld ldrs* **11/2**

1215 **4** nse **Millie's Rock (IRE)**[10] 3843 3-8-12 **67** .... TedDurcan 1 67
(M J Wallace) *s.i.s: hld up in rr: hdwy 4f out: chsd ldng pair and rdn jst over 2f out: btn ent fnl f: lost 3rd on line* **11/4**[1]

13-0 **5** 2¾ **Princess India (IRE)**[63] 2196 3-9-3 **72** .... StephenCarson 2 66
(P Winkworth) *chsd ldrs: rdn over 3f out: outpcd over 2f out: no ch last 2f* **12/1**

1-04 **6** 3½ **Bauhaus Bourbon (USA)**[14] 3737 3-9-3 **72** .... (t) ChrisCatlin 9 59
(P F I Cole) *chsd ldrs: rdn 3f out: 4th and struggling 2f out: sn wl btn* **11/1**

6-00 **7** 3¼ **Bluebell Ridge (IRE)**[34] 3065 3-8-1 **56** .... WilliamBuick 7 37
(D W P Arbuthnot) *hld up in last trio: rdn 5f out: lost tch 3f out: wl bhd after* **25/1**

2432 **8** 16 **Our Kes (IRE)**[24] 3361 6-10-0 **73** .... IanMongan 4 22
(P Howling) *led tl 4f out: sn dropped out: t.o last 2f* **5/1**[3]

2m 5.40s (-1.20) **Going Correction** +0.125s/f (Slow)
WFA 3 from 5yo+ 10lb **8** Ran SP% **119.0**
Speed ratings (Par 100): **109,107,103,103,101 98,95,82**
toteswinger: 1&2 £4.30, 1&3 £8.20, 2&3 £6.60. CSF £20.89 CT £88.15 TOTE £4.20: £1.80, £2.40, £2.10; EX 26.60.
Owner Mrs C C Regalado-Gonzalez **Bred** Mr & Mrs Hugh G King **Trained** Newmarket, Suffolk

FOCUS
A modest fillies' handicap and very little strength in depth. They went a strong pace and the winning time was 2.10 seconds quicker than the previous seller, so the form has been treated fairly positively.

4184 EUROPEAN BREEDERS' FUND MAIDEN STKS — 7f

7:20 (7:23) (Class 5) 2-Y-O **£3,561** (£1,059; £529; £264) **Stalls** High

Form RPR

2 **1** **Kentish Dream**[9] 3879 2-9-3 0 .... DaneO'Neill 14 83+
(S A Callaghan) *mde all on stands' rail: rdn wl over 1f out: kpt on wl fnl f* **11/8**[1]

0 **2** ¾ **Oil Man (IRE)**[24] 3372 2-9-3 0 .... StephenCarson 9 81+
(P Winkworth) *chsd wnr thrght: rdn and tried to chal over 1f out: kpt on same pce fnl f* **50/1**

3 ¾ **On Our Way** 2-9-3 0 .... TedDurcan 16 79+
(H R A Cecil) *s.i.s: hld up towards rr on stands' rail: hdwy over 2f out: chsng ldrs whn rn green and hung lft ent fnl f: wnt 3rd ins fnl f: gng on wl at fin: nt rch ldng pair* **4/1**[3]

4 1¾ **Perception (IRE)** 2-8-12 0 .... SteveDrowne 6 70+
(R Charlton) *s.i.s: steadily crossed to stands' rail: hld up wl bhd: stdy hdwy on stands' rail 2f out: chsd ldng trio ins fnl f: gng on at fin: nt rch ldrs* **33/1**

2 **5** 3½ **Mythical Blue (IRE)**[26] 3309 2-9-3 0 .... SaleemGolam 2 66
(S C Williams) *chsd ldrs: wnt 3rd 3f out: rdn wl over 1f out: wknd jst ins fnl f* **16/1**

6 1¼ **Admiral Sandhoe (USA)** 2-9-3 0 .... JimCrowley 11 63
(Mrs A J Perrett) *dwlt: t.k.h: in tch in midfield: rdn and edgd lft over 2f out: outpcd 2f out: keeping on same pce whn swtchd rt ins fnl f* **20/1**

3 **7** nk **Reaction**[21] 3495 2-9-3 0 .... DarryllHolland 10 62
(M R Channon) *dwlt: sn pushed up to chse ldrs: stdd and in midfield after 2f: swtchd lft and rdn over 2f out: no prog after* **7/2**[2]

5 **8** ½ **Isabella Romee (IRE)**[49] 2614 2-8-12 0 .... JohnEgan 4 56
(Jane Chapple-Hyam) *wnt lft s: sn chsng ldrs: rdn over 2f out: wkng whn edgd lft jst ins fnl f* **14/1**

0 **9** 1 **Red Reef**[31] 3135 2-8-12 0 .... JimmyQuinn 7 54
(D J Coakley) *s.i.s: t.k.h: racd in midfield: struggling over 2f out: wl btn last 2f* **50/1**

4 **10** ½ **Perfect Shot (IRE)**[20] 3519 2-9-3 0 .... IanMongan 13 57
(J L Dunlop) *dwlt: t.k.h: hld up towards rr: rdn and hung lft 2f out: sn outpcd: keeping on same pce whn swtchd lft ins fnl f: nvr trbld ldrs* **11/1**

0 **11** shd **Taste The Wine (IRE)**[64] 2150 2-9-3 0 .... LPKeniry 5 57
(J R Best) *bmpd s: t.k.h in midfield: rdn and hung lft over 2f out: sn bhd* **33/1**

00 **12** 1¾ **Ain't Talkin'**[36] 3001 2-9-3 0 .... PaulDoe 17 53
(M J Attwater) *in tch in midfield: hung lft and wknd 2f out* **100/1**

13 1 **Mfi'Ve** 2-9-0 0 .... JamesMillman(3) 8 50
(B R Millman) *chsd ldrs: rdn wl over 2f out: wknd qckly wl over 1f out* **50/1**

0 **14** 6 **Crystallize**[20] 3519 2-9-3 0 .... ChrisCatlin 12 35
(A B Haynes) *a struggling in rr* **66/1**

The Form Book, Raceform Ltd, Compton, RG20 6NL

15 ½ **Kersivay** 2-9-3 0 AdamKirby 1 34
(W R Swinburn) *s.i.s: a bhd* **28/1**

1m 24.23s (0.93) **Going Correction** +0.075s/f (Good) **15** Ran SP% **127.7**
Speed ratings (Par 94): **97,96,95,93,89 87,87,86,85,85 85,83,81,75,74**
toteswinger: 1&2 £59.00, 1&3 £4.00, 2&3 Not won. CSF £116.57 TOTE £2.10: £1.40, £9.50, £1.80; EX 79.00.
Owner Gallagher Equine Ltd **Bred** Sunny Days Ltd **Trained** Newmarket, Suffolk

FOCUS
Just a fair juvenile maiden. A high draw was an advantage and not many got involved from off the pace.

NOTEBOOK
Kentish Dream confirmed the promise he showed when second on his debut in a 6f novice event on easy ground at the Newmarket July meeting, but he was only workmanlike. He could have been expected to win in better style, particularly as he had the benefit of the often-favoured stands' rail, but he is held in high regard and his trainer thinks he will be better back over 6f on a softer surface. (op 5-4 tchd Evens)
Oil Man(IRE) showed little on his debut over this trip on the Kempton Polytrack, but this was a lot better. He showed good speed to race handy, but still looked a little green and could improve again.
On Our Way ◆, a 55,000gns son of Oasis Dream, out of a three-year-old winner in France at around 1m, fared best of those to race off the pace and this was a pleasing debut. He should be up to winning a similar event next time. (tchd 6-1)
Perception(IRE), a 70,000euros daughter of Hawk Wing, half-sister to Pineda, a dual winner at around 1m2f in Germany, was very easy to back beforehand but she showed plenty of ability, easily faring best of the fillies. A low draw was no help, but she was keeping on nicely at the finish and should know more next time.
Mythical Blue(IRE), a £20,000 purchase, was an expensive failure on his debut for Paul Blockley in a 5f seller at Chepstow, as he was backed into 8/15 but found one too good and was claimed by Stuart Williams for just £6,000. This was a respectable effort, especially considering he was poorly drawn, and he can do better again when dropped back in trip.
Admiral Sandhoe(USA), a $65,000 son of Diesis, half-brother to triple 1m-1m1f winner Fahlawi, and multiple 7f-1m scorer Machinate, made a respectable debut and could do better when handicapped.
Reaction could not build on the promise he showed when third in a fair maiden on his debut on the Newmarket July course, but he was stuck out wide, which was not the place to be, and he might be worth another chance. (op 7-1 tchd 3-1)
Kersivay Official explanation: jockey said colt ran green

4185 EASTBOURNE NURSERY 6f
7:50 (7:52) (Class 5) 2-Y-O £3,238 (£963; £481; £240) Stalls High

Form RPR
301 1 **Khor Dubai (IRE)**[16] 3651 2-9-8 **84** KerrinMcEvoy 4 90+
(Saeed Bin Suroor) *stdd s: hld up in rr: edgd out off stands' rail and hdwy 2f out: gng wl and nt clr run ent fnl f: swtchd lft ins fnl f: qcknd wl to ld last 50yds: readily* **11/8**[1]
654 2 1 **Black N Brew (USA)**[28] 3267 2-8-5 **67** ow1 PaulFitzsimons 2 66
(J R Best) *stdd s: hld up bhd: rdn and hdwy on outer over 2f out: edgd rt but r.o to ld jst ins fnl f: hdd and nt pce of wnr last 50yds* **7/1**[3]
315 3 ½ **Dubai's Gazal**[23] 3412 2-9-3 **79** DarryllHolland 8 77
(M R Channon) *chsd ldrs: ev ch and squeezed for room ent fnl f: sn swtchd lft: kpt on* **3/1**[2]
0020 4 ½ **Elusive Ronnie (IRE)**[23] 3392 2-7-12 **60** oh1 (p) JimmyQuinn 6 56
(R A Teal) *led narrowly: rdn wl over 1f out: hdd jst ins fnl f: one pce last 100yds* **28/1**
036 5 2¼ **Scrapper Smith (IRE)**[30] 3178 2-8-6 **68** LPKeniry 9 57
(E F Vaughan) *pressed ldr on stands' rail: rdn and ev ch 2f out: wknd ent fnl f* **10/1**
603 6 4½ **Herring Senior (IRE)**[28] 3254 2-8-9 **71** ChrisCatlin 7 47
(P F I Cole) *bhd: rdn and no prog 2f out: wl hld whn hung lft ins fnl f* **8/1**
560 7 hd **Call Me Courageous (IRE)**[9] 3888 2-8-4 **66** JohnEgan 1 41
(A B Haynes) *sn rdn along and struggling to go pce: wl btn and eased fnl f* **20/1**
540 8 nse **Dalepak Flyer (IRE)**[12] 3798 2-8-1 **63** (b[1]) PaulEddery 5 38
(G D Blake) *chsd ldrs: rdn over 2f out: wknd wl over 1f out* **16/1**
664 9 ¾ **The Saucy Snipe**[35] 3019 2-7-13 **61** FrankieMcDonald 3 34
(P Winkworth) *stmbld sn after s: a struggling in rr* **16/1**

1m 11.54s (0.34) **Going Correction** +0.075s/f (Good) **9** Ran SP% **119.8**
Speed ratings (Par 94): **100,98,98,97,94 88,88,88,87**
toteswinger: 1&2 £2.20, 1&3 £1.40, 2&3 £2.60. CSF £12.45 CT £27.00 TOTE £2.00: £1.10, £2.30, £1.40; EX 15.10.
Owner Godolphin **Bred** K And Mrs Cullen **Trained** Newmarket, Suffolk
■ Stewards' Enquiry : Paul Fitzsimons two-day ban: careless riding (Aug 3,4)

FOCUS
An ordinary nursery run at a good pace and the winner looks to have improved. The 'official' ratings shown next to each horse are estimated and for information purposes only.

NOTEBOOK
Khor Dubai(IRE) ◆ was unimpressive when winning his maiden at odds of 4/9 at Yarmouth last time, but he produced his best effort yet to defy top weight and follow up on this switch to handicap company. This was an ordinary race, but he was actually quite impressive as, having been stopped in his run when going for a gap around a furlong out, he recovered his momentum and quickened when in the clear with only a couple of hundred yards left to run. He looks ready for a step up in class. (op 5-4 tchd 6-4)
Black N Brew(USA), dropped in trip on his nursery debut, ran a good race in second carrying 1lb overweight. He is flattered to get so close to the very useful winner, as that one was denied a clear run, but it is worth noting that he himself was stuck out wide for most of the way, which is rarely the place to be on the Lingfield turf course. He should win a similar race. (op 13-2 tchd 5-1)
Dubai's Gazal, back on better ground and trying nursery company for the first time, ran a respectable race off what looked a stiff mark. However, she did not convince with her head carriage when short of room on a couple of occasions. (op 9-2)
Elusive Ronnie(IRE), 1lb out of the handicap, took them along at a good pace and kept on surprisingly well. The first-time cheekpieces seemed to help. (op 33-1 tchd 40-1 and 25-1)
Scrapper Smith(IRE) was well held stepped back up in trip on his nursery debut. (tchd 11-1)
The Saucy Snipe Official explanation: jockey said filly jumped the crossing

4186 FOREST ROW H'CAP 6f
8:20 (8:22) (Class 6) (0-65,65) 3-Y-O+ £2,047 (£604; £302) Stalls High

Form RPR
0221 1 **Patavium Prince (IRE)**[13] 3761 5-9-10 **63** DaneO'Neill 17 73
(Miss Jo Crowley) *racd on stands' rail: prom: chsd ldr 2f out: sn led: r.o wl* **4/1**[1]
0-05 2 2 **Jonny Ebeneezer**[9] 3868 9-9-2 **62** (b) RobbieEgan(7) 13 66
(D Flood) *t.k.h: prom: chsd wnr over 1f out: unable qckn fnl f* **7/1**[3]
0326 3 nse **Corlough Mountain**[7] 3966 4-9-10 **63** (p) ChrisCatlin 1 66+
(P Butler) *racd in midfield on outer: rdn wl over 2f out: hdwy u.p over 1f out: disp 2nd ins fnl f: one pce* **16/1**
2006 4 ¾ **Rhapsilian**[26] 3316 4-8-12 **58** KMay(7) 18 59
(J A Geake) *t.k.h: hld up in tch tl hit stands' rail and lost pl 1/2-way: hdwy 2f out: swtchd lft 1f out: kpt on same pce after* **14/1**
3305 5 ½ **Duke Of Milan (IRE)**[4] 4064 5-9-0 **53** DarryllHolland 11 52+
(G C Bravery) *stdd s: t.k.h: hld up in rr: hdwy 2f out: swtchd lft and rdn 1f out: no imp after* **7/1**[3]
4-02 6 ¾ **Castano**[7] 3966 4-9-4 **60** JamesMillman(3) 14 57
(B R Millman) *towards rr: rdn 1/2-way: hdwy u.p and edgd rt over 1f out: r.o but nt pce to rch ldrs* **6/1**[2]
-053 7 hd **Summer Recluse (USA)**[17] 3608 9-9-4 **57** (t) SteveDrowne 16 53
(J M Bradley) *bhd: rdn 2f out: kpt on u.p fnl f: nvr able to chal* **10/1**
5404 8 2½ **Hucking Hill (IRE)**[24] 3374 4-9-3 **56** (b) TedDurcan 15 44
(J R Best) *t.k.h: hld up: bhd: rdn 2f out: nt clr run over 1f out: passed btn horses fnl f: n.d* **8/1**
0003 9 2¼ **Edge End**[10] 3847 4-8-9 **55** (p) BillyCray(7) 2 36
(R A Farrant) *chsd ldrs: rdn over 2f out: wknd ent fnl f* **25/1**
3000 10 nk **Cracking Nick (IRE)**[21] 3506 3-9-7 **65** (t) AdamKirby 3 44
(W R Swinburn) *led: rdn over 2f out: hdd wl over 1f out: wknd qckly ent fnl f* **16/1**
2120 11 1¼ **Danetime Lord (IRE)**[105] 1211 5-9-3 **63** (p) DavidProbert(7) 7 39
(J R Gask) *wnt lft s: racd in midfield: effrt to chse ldrs over 2f out: wknd qckly u.p wl over 1f out* **7/1**[3]
500 12 nk **Multahab**[57] 2351 9-9-12 **65** (t) JimmyQuinn 10 40
(M Wigham) *t.k.h: in tch: rdn over 2f out: wkng whn hmpd over 1f out: no ch after* **16/1**
0030 13 6 **Loyal Royal (IRE)**[2] 4103 5-9-11 **64** PaulFitzsimons 5 20
(J M Bradley) *bmpd s: chsd ldrs after 1f: rdn over 2f out: sn btn* **20/1**
00-0 14 2¼ **Calabaza**[7] 3945 6-9-10 **63** (p) PaulDoe 8 12
(M J Attwater) *t.k.h: chsd ldr tl 2f out: wkng qckly whn hmpd over 1f out: wl bhd fnl f* **33/1**

1m 11.37s (0.17) **Going Correction** +0.075s/f (Good)
WFA 3 from 4yo+ 5lb **14** Ran SP% **127.9**
Speed ratings (Par 101): **101,98,98,97,96 95,95,92,89,88 86,86,78,75**
toteswinger: 1&2 £6.80, 1&3 £14.70, 2&3 £25.50. CSF £32.42 CT £437.07 TOTE £5.40: £2.50, £2.70, £4.60; EX 27.20 Place 6 £124.43, Place 5 £75.77..
Owner Mrs Liz Nelson **Bred** J P Hardiman **Trained** Whitcombe, Dorset

FOCUS
A modest sprint handicap in which a high draw was a big advantage. The winner is getting back to his three-year-old form.
Hucking Hill(IRE) Official explanation: jockey said gelding was denied a clear run
T/Plt: £194.70 to a £1 stake. Pool: £54,630.95. 204.80 winning tickets. T/Qpdt: £8.70 to a £1 stake. Pool: £4,711.49. 397.40 winning tickets. SP

4149 NEWBURY (L-H)
Saturday, July 19

OFFICIAL GOING: Good (good to firm in places; 7.8)
Wind: Moderate, ahead

4187 TRAILFINDERS CONDITIONS STKS 7f (S)
1:50 (1:51) (Class 3) 2-Y-O
£7,477 (£2,239; £1,119; £560; £279; £140) Stalls Centre

Form RPR
1 1 **Doctor Crane (USA)**[21] 3476 2-8-13 0 RobertHavlin 5 93
(J H M Gosden) *leggy: sn led: hdd and rdn wl over 1f out: rallied u.p ins fnl f to ld fnl 75yds* **9/1**
01 2 1 **Oratory (IRE)**[20] 3519 2-8-13 0 RichardHughes 7 91+
(R Hannon) *w'like: scope: lw: trckd ldrs: travelling wl whn n.m.r 2f out: rdn and no immediate rspnse appr fnl f: styd on wl u.p ins fnl f: tk 2nd cl home but a hld by wnr* **15/8**[2]
216 3 hd **Awinnersgame (IRE)**[32] 3103 2-8-13 0 RyanMoore 2 90
(J Noseda) *hld up in rr: gd hdwy over 2f out to ld wl over 1f out: hdd and no ex fnl 75yds: wknd nr fin* **7/4**[1]
1 4 5 **Firebet (IRE)**[24] 3364 2-8-13 0 RoystonFfrench 3 78
(Mrs A Duffield) *w'like: scope: lw: t.k.h: chsd ldrs: rdn 2f out: wknd over 1f out* **13/2**[3]
124 5 2 **Polish Pride**[7] 3978 2-8-9 0 ow1 DarryllHolland 4 69
(M Brittain) *pressed ldrs: upside fr over 4f out tl 2f out: wknd qckly* **16/1**
450 6 5 **Flying Lady (IRE)**[15] 3674 2-8-5 0 TPO'Shea 6 52
(M R Channon) *in rr: sme prog 3f out: nvr in contention and sn wknd* **14/1**
7 19 **Kaiser Willie (IRE)** 2-8-4 0 DJMoran(3) 1 7
(B W Duke) *w'like: chsd ldrs to 1/2-way: wknd qckly* **20/1**

1m 28.58s (2.88) **Going Correction** +0.30s/f (Good) **7** Ran SP% **111.8**
Speed ratings (Par 98): **95,93,93,87,85 79,58**
toteswinger: 1&2 £3.10, 1&3 £3.40, 2&3 £1.20. CSF £25.17 TOTE £9.00: £3.40, £1.80; EX 20.20.
Owner Ms Rachel D S Hood **Bred** Weldon R Johnson Jr **Trained** Newmarket, Suffolk

FOCUS
A decent race featuring five previous winners. The first three came nicely clear.

NOTEBOOK
Doctor Crane(USA) did not achieve much in terms of form when successful on his debut at Doncaster, but he stepped up on that to win in this stronger company. In the lead from an early stage, he really responded to pressure and was always holding the runner-up, who had travelled sweetly, in the closing stages. He will get 1m without any problem. (op 8-1 tchd 15-2)
Oratory(IRE), who was the stable's selected representative from three entries, travelled well and looked very much the likeliest winner two furlongs out, but he got himself slightly boxed in and his challenge was delayed. Once in the clear he stayed on well, but to be fair the winner always looked to be holding him close home. It would be a mistake to suppose that he was an unlucky loser. (op 13-8 tchd 2-1)
Awinnersgame(IRE), sixth in the Coventry last time out, set the standard but, having had every chance when going to the front, he seemed to find this extra furlong just finding him out. (op 15-8 tchd 6-4)
Firebet(IRE), winner of a soft-ground Carlisle maiden on his debut, still looked a bit green and, having raced keenly early, he got tired in the final furlong. (op 15-2)
Polish Pride, stepping up in trip from 5f and taking on better opposition, is bred to stay, but she did not race like it. (tchd 20-1)
Flying Lady(IRE), who finished fifth in the Chesham on her second start but could only finish in mid-division back in maiden company last time out, never got competitive and is not progressing. (tchd 12-1)

Kaiser Willie(IRE), who faced a stiff task on his debut, is out of a mare who is a half-sister to those high-class middle-distance performers Amfortas and Legend Maker. (op 33-1)

4188 UPLANDS RACING HACKWOOD STKS (GROUP 3) 6f 8y

2:20 (2:21) (Class 1) 3-Y-O+

£36,900 (£13,988; £7,000; £3,490; £1,748; £877) **Stalls** Centre

Form					RPR
-200	1		**Intrepid Jack**[14] 3739 6-9-3 104	GeorgeBaker 8	115
			(H Morrison) *hld up towards rr but in tch: hdwy 2f out: led jst ins fnl f: styd on strly*	**12/1**	
-111	2	2	**Corrybrough**[35] 3041 3-8-12 110	RyanMoore 4	108
			(H Candy) *lw: in tch: gd hdwy 2f out: drvn to chal 1f out: kpt on but nt pce of wnr nr fin: jst hld on for 2nd*	**6/4**[1]	
0010	3	shd	**Balthazaar's Gift (IRE)**[28] 3247 5-9-3 110	DaneO'Neill 13	109+
			(L M Cumani) *hld up towards rr: nt clr run 2f out: swtchd lft over 1f out and rapid hdwy u.p ins fnl f: clsng on 2nd nr fin but nt rch wnr*	**15/2**[3]	
-505	4	½	**Strike The Deal (USA)**[31] 3119 3-8-12 108	SebSanders 11	106
			(J Noseda) *lw: chsd ldrs fr 1/2-way: styd on to chal 1f out: styd on same pce fnl 110yds*	**9/2**[2]	
2610	5	½	**Edge Closer**[28] 3248 4-9-3 112	RichardHughes 12	105
			(R Hannon) *lw: trckd ldrs: rdn to ld over 1f out: hdd jst ins fnl f: kpt on same pce*	**12/1**	
4000	6	2	**Excusez Moi (USA)**[21] 3504 6-9-3 97	LiamJones 7	99
			(C E Brittain) *towards rr: swtchd lft and hdwy fr 2f out: no imp on ldrs ins fnl f*	**50/1**	
3504	7	½	**Wi Dud**[14] 3739 4-9-3 103	NCallan 10	97
			(K A Ryan) *in tch: rdn and effrt to chse ldrs 2f out: wknd ins fnl f*	**12/1**	
6620	8	5	**Hoh Hoh Hoh**[7] 3948 6-9-3 104	MartinDwyer 6	81
			(R J Price) *chsd ldr tl led ins fnl 3f: hdd over 1f out and sn btn*	**25/1**	
6500	9	½	**Final Verse**[31] 3122 5-9-3 95	JohnEgan 2	80
			(Jane Chapple-Hyam) *chsd ldrs over 3f*	**50/1**	
3250	10	½	**Dark Missile**[28] 3247 5-9-0 100	WilliamBuick 3	75
			(A M Balding) *chsd ldrs: rdn and effrt 2f out: nvr gng pce to chal: wknd over 1f out: eased whn no ch cl home*	**12/1**	
6032	11	hd	**Beckermet (IRE)**[7] 3946 6-9-3 108	ChrisCatlin 1	78
			(R F Fisher) *lw: led 3f: sn bhd*	**10/1**	
-000	12	2	**Rowe Park**[14] 3739 5-9-7 105	LPKeniry 5	75
			(Mrs L C Jewell) *on toes: in tch over 3f*	**40/1**	

1m 12.83s (-0.17) **Going Correction** +0.30s/f (Good)
WFA 3 from 4yo+ 5lb **12** Ran SP% **120.0**
Speed ratings (Par 113): **113,110,110,109,108 106,105,98,97 97,94**
toteswinger: 1&2 £7.90, 1&3 £15.20, 2&3 £4.00. CSF £30.05 TOTE £14.20: £3.10, £1.30, £2.70; EX 43.20 Trifecta £181.80 Pool: £1,081.44 - 4.40 winning units..
Owner Michael T Lynch **Bred** Fonthill Stud **Trained** East Ilsley, Berks

FOCUS

A race in which three-year-olds have a good record, and they provided the first two in the betting, but they were both eclipsed by Intrepid Jack, who finally delivered the victory he has often threatened. With doubts about the strength of the form, he has been rated to his best level in handicaps.

NOTEBOOK

Intrepid Jack appreciated the return to 6f and sprang a bit of a shock. He has always had the ability but has very rarely delivered, but he won this race convincingly in the end. Whether he can build on this remains to be seen, but his trainer intends upping him in class now and, providing the ground is not on the soft side, sending him for the Prix Maurice de Gheest.

Corrybrough, a highly progressive sprinter this term and a winner in Listed company last time, was taking another step up in grade and returning to 6f for the first time since winning his maiden, but he was still heavily favoured in the market. He ran well on ground which would have been quicker than ideal, but his trainer later suggested that the tactics employed were the main reason he was beaten. He suggested that in future the colt would return to being held up well off the pace, especially over this distance. (op 11-8 tchd 5-4 and 13-8 in places)

Balthazaar's Gift(IRE), who finished in midfield in the Golden Jubilee last time out, has bizarrely recorded each of his five career wins on good to soft ground, including this race when it was run at Ascot last year. Finishing with his usual late effort, he only narrowly failed to take second from Corrybrough. (op 8-1 tchd 7-1)

Strike The Deal(USA), who was a smart juvenile sprinter last term, winning the Richmond and finishing second in the Mill Reef and Middle Park, was expected to appreciate the drop back to 6f having not got home in the Guineas but shown more in the Jersey last time. He was a well-backed second favourite and came to have every chance up the stands' rail, but just did not see it out that strongly. This has to go down as a slightly disappointing effort. (op 5-1 tchd 11-2)

Edge Closer, who finished last under top weight in the Wokingham last time out, ran much better here, quickening up well approaching the furlong marker but then flattening out inside the last. (op 14-1)

Excusez Moi(USA), who has not been at his best on turf this year, had a tough task in this grade. He never got in a blow but ran a bit better than of late. (op 66-1)

Wi Dud finds this trip stretching his stamina. (op 16-1 tchd 11-1)

Hoh Hoh Hoh remains a difficult horse to place.

4189 BATHWICK TYRES EBF FILLIES' STKS (H'CAP) 1m (S)

2:50 (2:53) (Class 2) (0-100,98) 3-Y-O+

£12,462 (£2,799; £2,799; £934; £466; £234) **Stalls** Centre

Form					RPR
2121	1		**Lindelaan (USA)**[19] 3560 3-9-7 93	(v) RyanMoore 7	98
			(Sir Michael Stoute) *hld up in rr: hdwy 2f out: drvn and squeezed through to ld ins fnl f: hld on all out*	**7/2**[2]	
-320	2	shd	**Fragrancy (IRE)**[31] 3120 4-10-0 92	NCallan 8	99
			(M A Jarvis) *lw pressed ldr fr 4f out: stl chalng 1f out: kpt on wl u.p ins fnl f: no ex last strides*	**7/1**[3]	
5060	2	dht	**Eva's Request (IRE)**[31] 3124 3-9-12 98	DarryllHolland 4	103
			(M R Channon) *hld up in rr: clsng but stl last 2f out: str run u.p ins fnl f: fin strly: jst failed*	**14/1**	
610	4	½	**La Coveta (IRE)**[5] 4022 3-8-8 80	(b[1]) WilliamBuick 2	84
			(B J Meehan) *plld hrd: led: rdn over 2f out: kpt narrow advantage tl hdd and hung lft ins fnl f: rallied u.p and coming bk last strides*	**20/1**	
0110	5	1	**Farley Star**[14] 3740 4-9-12 90	RichardHughes 10	94
			(R Charlton) *lw: in tch: hdwy 2f out: sn shkn up and outpcd: kpt on again ins fnl f: gng on cl home*	**9/1**	
1121	6	½	**Maghya (IRE)**[21] 3500 3-9-4 90	RHills 9	91
			(W J Haggas) *lw: t.k.h early: trckd ldrs 5f out: sltly outpcd over 1f out: kpt on again cl home*	**3/1**[1]	
-214	7	2	**Princess Taylor**[21] 3500 4-9-5 83	(t) TedDurcan 6	81
			(M Botti) *chsd ldrs: pushed along over 2f out: styd on same pce*	**10/1**	
1-4	8	shd	**Fantasy Princess (USA)**[16] 3636 3-8-6 78	HayleyTurner 3	74
			(G A Butler) *t.k.h: chsd ldrs: rdn ins fnl 3f: wknd appr fnl f*	**11/1**	
0-03	9	nk	**Falcolnry (IRE)**[35] 3039 3-8-11 83	DaneO'Neill 5	78
			(J R Fanshawe) *in rr: rdn and sme prog over 2f out: nvr gng pce to be competitive*	**12/1**	
2413	10	1 ¾	**Aphrodisia**[21] 3500 4-8-4 75	DavidProbert[(7)] 1	68
			(S C Williams) *towards rr but in tch: sme prog 3f out but nvr gng pce to be competitive*	**8/1**	

1m 42.04s (2.34) **Going Correction** +0.30s/f (Good)
WFA 3 from 4yo 8lb **10** Ran SP% **117.4**
Speed ratings (Par 96): **100,99,99,99,98 97,95,95,95,93**PL: Fragrancy £2.20, Eva's Request £3.30; EX: L-F £14.10, L-ER £30.80; CSF: L-F £14.30, L-ER £26.03; TRICAST: L-F-ER £153.95, L-ER-F £164.81. toteswinger: 1&2 (F) £4.40, 1&2 (ER) £10.70, 2&3 £16.10. TOTE £3.90: £1.80 TRIFECTA 427 Owner.

FOCUS

The early pace was far from hectic and that resulted in something of a sprint for the line. The form is not that solid.

NOTEBOOK

Lindelaan(USA), 8lb higher for her Windsor success, challenged between horses and was all out at the finish. In another few yards she may have only been third, but she is the type who needs delivering late and it is perfectly possible that she is capable of progressing even further. (tchd 3-1 and 4-1 in a place)

Eva's Request(IRE), who has been running in better races than this earlier this season, was taking on lesser rivals and she almost came from last to first in what was something of a tactical affair. She was in front a yard or two after the line. (op 16-1 tchd 11-1)

Fragrancy(IRE), who stays 1m2f, was not really suited by the way this race was run. She was keeping on well at the finish and was only narrowly denied, but a stronger pace will help her in future. (op 16-1 tchd 11-1)

La Coveta(IRE), blinkered for the first time, used up energy early pulling for her head and, although she briefly quickened from the front, she hung under pressure and the first three saw it out better. (op 22-1)

Farley Star was outpaced when the leaders quickened things up but she was keeping on at the finish, just being pushed out, and a stronger pace would no doubt have suited her. (op 10-1 tchd 8-1)

Maghya(IRE), a progressive type running off a 7lb higher mark, had every chance and was a bit disappointing. However, this was not a truly run race and she should not be too harshly judged. (op 7-2 tchd 4-1)

4190 WEATHERBYS SUPER SPRINT STKS 5f 34y

3:25 (3:27) (Class 2) 2-Y-O

£79,548 (£29,750; £14,490; £6,328; £2,898; £1,498) **Stalls** Centre

Form					RPR
31	1		**Jargelle (IRE)**[14] 3735 2-8-6 0	LiamJones 13	99
			(W J Haggas) *mde virtually all: hrd drvn fr 2f out: hld on all out*	**20/1**	
61	2	shd	**Infamous Angel**[35] 3019 2-7-13 0	JimmyQuinn 11	92
			(R Hannon) *chsd ldrs: styd on strly u.p ins fnl f: fin wl: jst failed*	**16/1**	
11	3	nse	**Senor Mirasol**[43] 2775 2-8-8 0	NCallan 6	100
			(K A Ryan) *leggy: chsd ldrs: rdn and styd on strly u.p fnl f: fin wl: jst failed*	**12/1**	
1110	4	¾	**Bahamian Babe**[31] 3123 2-8-3 0	HayleyTurner 22	93
			(M L W Bell) *lw: chsd ldrs: rdn: swtchd rt to rail and styd on strly ins fnl f: no ex cl home*	**15/2**[3]	
1222	5	½	**Caranbola**[16] 3625 2-7-12 0	WilliamBuick 20	86
			(M Brittain) *outpcd and sn rdn: styd on strly fnl f: edgd lft cl home and fin wl*	**5/1**[2]	
2120	6	½	**Harwalla (IRE)**[32] 3103 2-8-12 0	RHills 9	98
			(M Johnston) *chsd ldrs: rdn 2f out: kpt on same pce u.p fnl 110yds*	**33/1**	
3112	7	hd	**Penny's Gift**[29] 3192 2-8-0 0	MartinDwyer 15	90+
			(R Hannon) *lw: bhd: nt clr run 2f out and 1f out: swtchd lft fnl f and rapid hdwy: fining wl whn bmpd cl home*	**3/1**[1]	
01	8	hd	**Pure Poetry (IRE)**[15] 3669 2-9-1 0	RichardHughes 4	100
			(R Hannon) *towards rr: rdn and hdwy over 1f out: styd on ins fnl f but nt rch ldrs*	**16/1**	
3214	9	hd	**Raggle Taggle (IRE)**[15] 3681 2-8-1 0	NelsonDeSouza 7	85
			(R M Beckett) *sn chsng ldrs: kpt on u.p fnl 2f but no imp ins fnl f: pushed lft cl home*	**33/1**	
421	10	½	**Spring Tale (USA)**[34] 3067 2-8-4 0	NGMcCullagh 5	86+
			(M J Wallace) *pressed ldrs: rdn 1/2-way: wknd ins fnl f: btn whn hmpd cl home*	**25/1**	
1103	11	1	**Moss Likely (IRE)**[15] 3681 2-8-2 0	TPO'Shea 10	81
			(M R Channon) *swtg: mid-div: styd on u.p fr over 1f out but nt trble ldrs*	**18/1**	
4241	12	nk	**Doughnut**[8] 3908 2-8-5 0	ChrisCatlin 23	83
			(R Hannon) *pressed wnr stands' side tl over 1f out: wknd ins fnl f*	**16/1**	
5211	13	½	**Mullglen**[7] 3978 2-8-5 0 ow1	JohnEgan 8	81+
			(T D Easterby) *lw: chsd ldrs: wkng whn hmpd jst ins fnl f*	**16/1**	
3412	14	½	**Finnegan McCool**[15] 3677 2-9-1 0	GeorgeBaker 19	89
			(R M Beckett) *towards rr whn nt clr run ins fnl 2f: kpt on ins fnl f: nvr gng pce to rch ldrs*	**33/1**	
4213	15	nse	**Favourite Girl (IRE)**[15] 3663 2-8-2 0	DuranFentiman 12	76
			(T D Easterby) *lw: in rr: stmbld 2f out: swtchd lft and hdwy over 1f out: kpt on ins fnl f: nt rch ldrs*	**25/1**	
1010	16	nk	**Asaint Needs Brass (USA)**[32] 3105 2-8-9 0	SebSanders 21	82
			(R M Beckett) *chsd ldrs: rdn: edgd rt and wknd jst ins fnl f*	**40/1**	
032	17	½	**Pocket's Pick (IRE)**[21] 3485 2-8-12 0	RyanMoore 18	83
			(G L Moore) *lw: in rr: nt clr run 2f out: sme prog ins fnl f*	**33/1**	
3321	18	nk	**The Magic Of Rio**[14] 3734 2-8-2 0	RoystonFfrench 14	72
			(W J Haggas) *spd 3f*	**50/1**	
2321	19	1	**Souter's Sister (IRE)**[25] 3341 2-7-13 0	DavidKinsella 3	65
			(R Hannon) *racd far side w one opponent: outpcd fr 1/2-way*	**40/1**	
5236	20	½	**Riflessione**[53] 2473 2-8-6 0	(p) LPKeniry 2	70
			(J S Moore) *chsd ldrs to 1/2-way*	**100/1**	
210	21	2	**Rebecca De Winter**[31] 3123 2-8-3 0	RichardSmith 17	60
			(R Hannon) *chsd ldrs tl wknd 1f out*	**12/1**	
1100	22	2 ½	**Shampagne**[16] 3634 2-9-1 0	TedDurcan 1	63
			(P F I Cole) *swtg: racd far side: w one other opponent: outpcd fr 1/2-way*	**40/1**	
361	23	2 ¾	**Love You Louis**[44] 2759 2-8-4 0	DO'Donohoe 16	42+
			(J R Jenkins) *towards rr: no ch whn hmpd over 1f out*	**40/1**	

62.12 secs (0.72) **Going Correction** +0.30s/f (Good) **23** Ran SP% **134.5**
Speed ratings (Par 100): **106,105,105,104,103 102,102,102,102,101 99,99,98,97,97 96,96,95,94,93 90,86,81**
toteswinger: 1&2 £22.20, 1&3 £42.90, 2&3 £34.70. CSF £301.74 TOTE £29.10: £7.50, £5.60, £4.20; EX 512.10 Trifecta £3163.70 Pool: £10,260.78 - 2.40 winning units..
Owner B Smith,A Duke,J Netherthorpe,G Goddard **Bred** Mrs A Robinson **Trained** Newmarket, Suffolk

■ Stewards' Enquiry : N Callan three-day ban: careless riding (Aug 3-5)

FOCUS
The usual big field of juveniles of varying ability for this valuable sales race. All but two of the runners came towards the stands' side. This was a decent renewal in terms of recent years but the form is clearly limited with nine covered by just over two lengths.

NOTEBOOK
Jargelle(IRE) once again showed plenty of early speed, got to the stands'-side rail and made every yard of the running. Things got tight close home but she just held on and landed a valuable prize for her owners, who paid 28,000gns for her. The St Hugh's Stakes back here could be her next target, although the Molecomb is being considered as an alternative.
Infamous Angel, who did best of the Hannon sextet, kept on really well and was only just denied. She could have done with even quicker ground and, having only cost 9,000gns, now looks something of a bargain.
Senor Mirasol, unbeaten in his previous two starts, was never far away and kept on stoutly in the closing stages. This was a good effort considering he was drawn in a single-figure stall but the action developed towards the stands' side.
Bahamian Babe finished down the field in the Queen Mary last time but this was a lower quality event and she bounced back to her best, although she did have the advantage of the stands'-side rail. (op 7-1 tchd 13-2)
Caranbola struggled to go the early pace but she was putting in good work at the finish. A return to 6f will suit her. (op 8-1)
Harwalla(IRE), down the field in the Coventry Stakes last time out, returned to his best and ran a sound race, challenging more towards the outside of the bunch.
Penny's Gift, runner-up in the Albany Stakes last time, looked to hold sound claims and would have finished much closer had she enjoyed a clearer passage. She finished strongly and should be rated as having placed. (op 7-2 tchd 4-1)
Pure Poetry(IRE), who started off over 7f and won over 6f last time, found the drop back to the minimum trip too much of a test of speed.
Raggle Taggle(IRE), one of the more exposed runners in the line-up, ran a sound enough race.
Spring Tale(USA), runner-up in a Listed race at Cork last time, did not have a problem with the drop back to 5f as she showed plenty of speed.
Moss Likely(IRE) has the pedigree to stay further than this and she will be suited by stepping up to 6f. (op 20-1)
Doughnut was up there for a long way but did not see her race out. A sharper 5f probably suits her best. (op 18-1)
Finnegan McCool was attempting to stay on next to the stands' rail when hampered by a rival crossing in front of him. He kept on afterwards and shaped better than his finishing position suggests.
Favourite Girl(IRE) was hampered and stumbled two furlongs out, but for which she would have finished closer.
Pocket's Pick(IRE) never got a run of any sort and his finishing position is a poor reflection of how good he is.

4191 PUBS CALL 08703518834 FOR RACING UK H'CAP — 1m 2f 6y
3:55 (3:57) (Class 3) (0-95,95) 3-Y-0+
£7,477 (£2,239; £1,119; £560; £279; £140) **Stalls** Low

Form — RPR
4241 **1** **Hunting Country**[14] 3736 3-8-4 **81** .... GregFairley 8 96+
(M Johnston) *lw: chsd ldrs: qcknd to ld appr fnl 2f: sn clr: easily* **9/2**[1]
2320 **2** *4* **Pinch Of Salt (IRE)**[28] 3249 5-9-8 **89** .... MartinDwyer 7 96
(A M Balding) *towards rr: hdwy over 3f out: styd on u.p to chse wnr fnl f but nvr any ch: jst hld on to 2nd* **16/1**
2053 **3** *shd* **Rosbay (IRE)**[21] 3493 4-9-0 **84** .... DuranFentiman(3) 9 91
(T D Easterby) *chsd ldrs: rdn and lost position over 2f out: styd on again fnl f to cl on 2nd but nvr any ch w easy wnr* **16/1**
-005 **4** *hd* **Humungous (IRE)**[15] 3684 5-10-0 **95** ....(b) ChrisCatlin 10 101+
(C R Egerton) *in rr: n.m.r whn rival p.u 3f out: swtchd to outside and rapid hdwy appr fnl f: fin wl and clsng on ldrs nr fin* **11/1**
3-10 **5** *1* **Crete (IRE)**[8] 3929 6-9-8 **89** .... RichardHughes 1 93
(W J Haggas) *lw: chsd ldrs: rdn 3f out: kpt on same pce fnl 2f* **5/1**[2]
04-1 **6** *nk* **Sam Lord**[12] 3800 4-9-2 **83** .... DaneO'Neill 13 90+
(A King) *in rr: hdwy and nt clr run 2f out: improving again whn hmpd 1f out and n.m.r ins fnl f: r.o cl home but nt rcvr* **12/1**
0-0 **7** *½* **Strategic Mount**[28] 3249 5-9-13 **94** .... NCallan 5 97
(P F I Cole) *chsd ldrs: rdn 3f out: wknd fnl f* **16/1**
111/ **8** *¾* **Corran Ard (IRE)**[83] 5494 7-9-7 **88** .... StephenDonohoe 14 89
(Evan Williams) *in rr: pushed along and hdwy fr 3f out: nvr gng pce to rch ldrs: one pce fr over 1f out* **25/1**
0120 **9** *½* **Speedy Sam**[35] 3046 5-9-6 **87** .... FergusSweeney 12 87
(K R Burke) *led tl hdd appr fnl 2f: sn btn* **16/1**
40-0 **10** *¾* **William's Way**[17] 3613 6-9-2 **83** .... TedDurcan 2 82
(I A Wood) *in rr: sme prog over 2f out but nvr in contention* **50/1**
1254 **11** *1 ¼* **Jeer (IRE)**[15] 3684 4-9-3 **91** .... DavidProbert(7) 4 91+
(E A L Dunlop) *chsd ldrs: rdn over 2f out and sn edgd lft: wknd over 1f out* **8/1**[3]
212 **12** *½* **Just Lille (IRE)**[16] 3627 5-9-9 **90** ....(p) RoystonFfrench 16 85
(Mrs A Duffield) *chsd ldr to 3f out: sn wknd* **8/1**[3]
30-0 **13** *½* **Royal Jet**[21] 3505 6-9-9 **90** .... DarryllHolland 3 84
(M R Channon) *in rr: sme hdwy u.p on ins whn hmpd 2f out: sn wknd* **25/1**
36-5 **14** *2 ¾* **Officer**[24] 3382 4-9-2 **83** ....(bt) RyanMoore 11 72
(G L Moore) *chsd ldrs to 3f out: wknd fr 2f out* **16/1**
1330 **15** *9* **Rationale (IRE)**[21] 3490 5-9-3 **84** .... GeorgeBaker 6 55
(S C Williams) *bhd most of way* **9/1**
555 **P** **Bid For Glory**[23] 3398 4-9-7 **88** ....(v) SebSanders 15 —
(H J Collingridge) *lw: in tch whn p.u 3f out: dismntd* **16/1**

2m 5.74s (-3.06) **Going Correction** -0.125s/f (Firm)
WFA 3 from 4yo+ 10lb — **16 Ran SP% 128.0**
Speed ratings (Par 107): **107,103,103,103,102 102,102,101,101,100 99,99,98,96,89** —
toteswinger: 1&2 £23.90, 1&3 £27.00, 2&3 £79.70. CSF £79.83 CT £1101.50 TOTE £5.70: £1.70, £3.70, £3.80, £3.60; EX 114.00.
Owner Sheikh Hamdan Bin Mohammed Al Maktoum **Bred** Floors Farming & London Thoroughbred Services Ltd **Trained** Middleham Moor, N Yorks
■ Stewards' Enquiry : Duran Fentiman two-day ban: careless riding (Aug 3,4)

FOCUS
A good, competitive handicap but few unexposed sorts and it was won by one the exceptions. Solid form.

NOTEBOOK
Hunting Country, raised 5lb for winning at Nottingham on his handicap debut, was the only three-year-old in the field, and in a field largely consisting of exposed older horses, he was the one with the most improvement in him. He quickened up well to go clear and ran on to win decisively. Clearly progressing fast, he has the potential to take a decent handicap at one of the upcoming festival meetings. (op 11-2 tchd 6-1)
Pinch Of Salt(IRE), dropped 5lb since his last start, came out of the pack to win the separate race for second. He has still to win a race on turf. (op 25-1)
Rosbay(IRE) ran another solid race but the Handicapper knows all about him and remains just in charge.
Humungous(IRE), who had blinkers on for the first time this season, came from off the pace to get involved in the photo for the places. He has dropped 5lb since the beginning of the year and this was a fair effort. (op 12-1)
Crete(IRE) had an excuse or two last time but had every chance here after travelling well into contention. He was just one-paced in the closing stages. (tchd 11-2 in places)
Sam Lord did not get much luck in running as he tried to find a way through from over two furlongs out. He shaped a bit better than his finishing position suggests. (op 16-1)
Strategic Mount has done all his winning over 1m4f plus.
Jeer(IRE) Official explanation: jockey said gelding was denied a clear run
Royal Jet got no run as he was trying for a way through and he was not punished in a lost cause. Official explanation: jockey said gelding was denied a clear run
Rationale(IRE) Official explanation: jockey said gelding had no more to give
Bid For Glory Official explanation: jockey said saddle slipped

4192 DAVID WILSON HOMES STEVENTON STKS (LISTED RACE) — 1m 2f 6y
4:30 (4:30) (Class 1) 3-Y-0+
£24,978 (£9,468; £4,738; £2,362; £1,183; £594) **Stalls** Low

Form — RPR
3-40 **1** **Passage Of Time**[51] 2543 4-8-12 115 .... TedDurcan 7 111
(H R A Cecil) *chsd ldrs: rdn to ld over 1f out: hld on wl u.p whn strly chal thrght fnl f* **10/1**
-115 **2** *nk* **Bankable (IRE)**[31] 3122 4-9-6 113 .... DaneO'Neill 4 119
(L M Cumani) *lw: in tch: hdwy on outside fr 3f out: trckd wnr 1f out: drvn to chal ins fnl f but no ex fnl 100yds and a jst hld* **5/4**[1]
016- **3** *3 ¾* **Hearthstead Maison (IRE)**[300] 5671 4-9-9 112 .... GregFairley 13 114
(M Johnston) *lw: led after 2f: rdn 3f out: hdd over 1f out: sn outpcd by ldng duo* **16/1**
100 **4** *1 ¼* **Happy Boy (BRZ)**[28] 3246 5-9-9 0 .... MartinDwyer 9 112
(Saeed Bin Suroor) *lw: led 2f: rdn 3f out: wknd appr fnl f* **20/1**
6-40 **5** *2* **Selinka**[31] 3120 4-8-12 104 .... RichardHughes 11 97
(R Hannon) *in rr: sme hdwy whn bmpd appr fnl 2f: styd on fr over 1f out but nvr in contention* **40/1**
6-16 **6** *1 ¾* **Spanish Moon (USA)**[28] 3246 4-9-6 108 .... RyanMoore 12 101
(Sir Michael Stoute) *in rr: rdn 3f out: sme prog fnl 2f but nvr nr ldrs* **5/1**[2]
-004 **7** *½* **Levera**[9] 3885 5-9-3 95 .... HayleyTurner 2 97
(A King) *chsd ldrs: rdn 3f out: wknd over 2f out* **66/1**
-311 **8** *½* **Wise Dennis**[142] 743 6-9-6 110 .... DarrenWilliams 1 99
(A P Jarvis) *towards rr most of way* **16/1**
-134 **9** *¾* **Al Shemali**[43] 2797 4-9-3 108 ....(t) RHills 10 95
(Saeed Bin Suroor) *chsd ldrs tl wknd over 2f out* **6/1**[3]
045 **10** *2 ¾* **Halicarnassus (IRE)**[29] 3195 4-9-9 108 ....(v) DarryllHolland 6 95
(M R Channon) *in rr: effrt 3f out: nvr in contention and sn bhd* **10/1**
-125 **11** *1 ½* **Moyenne Corniche**[41] 2875 3-8-9 105 ow2 .... SebSanders 8 88
(G Wragg) *chsd ldrs: rdn 3f out: sn btn* **14/1**

2m 7.35s (-1.45) **Going Correction** -0.125s/f (Firm)
WFA 3 from 4yo+ 10lb — **11 Ran SP% 120.7**
Speed ratings (Par 111): **100,99,96,95,94 92,92,91,91,89 87**
toteswinger: 1&2 £5.30, 1&3 £30.30, 2&3 £8.20. CSF £23.15 TOTE £10.50: £2.90, £1.10, £5.40; EX 23.00.
Owner K Abdulla **Bred** Juddmonte Farms Ltd **Trained** Newmarket, Suffolk
■ Stewards' Enquiry : Dane O'Neill one-day ban: careless riding (Aug 4)

FOCUS
A strong Listed contest, with the third and fourth already winners in a higher grade. The third looks the best guide to the form. The early pace was not too strong, though, and the final time was 1.61sec slower than the handicap which preceded it.

NOTEBOOK
Passage Of Time was disappointing in her first two starts this season and had something to prove here. Given a nice break since the Brigadier Gerard, this was much more like it as she travelled well chasing the pace and picked up in good style when asked to quicken inside the final two furlongs. She found more when strongly challenged by Bankable in the closing stages and looks to be very much back to her best. The Nassau is now the plan, and while that will be much tougher, it should not be forgotten that she is a Group 1 winner and was twice placed at the top level last term, so the talent is there. Races like the Yorkshire Oaks, Prix Vermeille and Prix de l'Opera could also be on her agenda later in the season. (op 8-1)
Bankable(IRE), beaten by the draw in the Hunt Cup, carried a 3lb penalty for his Listed win at Goodwood in May. Stepping up two furlongs in distance, he tracked Passage Of Time through before being switched out with his run inside the final quarter mile. He was staying on really strongly in the closing stages and made a real race of it, but the filly just kept pulling out that bit extra. He was nicely clear of the rest and when all is said and done he has run a big race giving 8lb to a Group 1 calibre rival. (op 6-4 tchd 13-8 in places)
Hearthstead Maison(IRE) enjoyed the run of the race, being allowed an easy time of it up front for a long way, but he lacked the pace of the first two in the finish. This was still a fine effort, though, as he was carrying a 6lb penalty for winning an Irish Group 3 last term and was also returning from a ten-month absence. (op 20-1)
Happy Boy(BRZ) has yet to replicate anything like the level of form he displayed when successful on his debut in Dubai back in January, although of course that race was on dirt and he has not had the chance to race on that surface since. Nevertheless, this was his best effort for Godolphin so far. (tchd 16-1)
Selinka ran close to her best form in fourth and got the trip well enough, albeit off a steady enough early gallop. (op 33-1)
Spanish Moon(USA) was suited by coming from the back off a strong pace when winning in this grade back in May, and the steady early gallop here did not suit him. That Ascot race was not the strongest Listed contest ever run, and he has perhaps been overrated as a result of the manner of his victory there. (op 4-1)
Levera had the lowest mark in the field coming into the race and was not disgraced in the circumstances.
Wise Dennis was having his first outing since completing a double at the Dubai Carnival back in February. He has never won beyond a mile and was entitled to need this. (op 11-1)
Al Shemali, who carried the owner's first colours, dropped away quite tamely, although his rider did proffer an excuse later. Official explanation: jockey said colt had been struck into (op 15-2 tchd 8-1)

4193 GET RACING UK IN YOUR PUB: 08703518834 H'CAP — 2m
5:00 (5:00) (Class 4) (0-80,77) 4-Y-0+ **£5,180** (£1,541; £770; £384) **Stalls** High

Form — RPR
6214 **1** **Alnwick**[15] 3685 4-9-0 **70** .... DaneO'Neill 10 78
(P D Cundell) *trckd ldrs: rdn to ld appr fnl f: hld on wl u.p* **6/1**[2]
16-4 **2** *nk* **Callisto Moon**[16] 3650 4-8-12 **68** .... StephenDonohoe 5 75
(Ian Williams) *lw: towards rr: hdwy over 2f out: drvn to chal over 1f out: styd pressing wnr ins fnl f: no ex cl home* **12/1**
623 **3** *nk* **Cavendish**[10] 3832 4-9-0 **70** ....(b) RichardHughes 11 77
(J M P Eustace) *sn led: hdd 1/2-way: styd prom tl outpcd 2f out: rallied u.p fnl f: gng on cl home* **13/2**[3]
2234 **4** *1 ¾* **Right Option (IRE)**[17] 3613 4-8-12 **68** .... GregFairley 1 73
(J L Flint) *chsd ldrs: rdn over 2f out: kpt on same pce fnl f* **14/1**

5 **5** 1/2 **Carmond (GER)**[300] 4-9-5 **75** RyanMoore 2 79
(B G Powell) *in rr: rdn over 2f out: styd on fr over 1f out: kpt on ins fnl f but nt rch ldrs* **16/1**

-246 **6** 1 1/2 **Compton Falcon**[66] 2100 4-8-6 **62** HayleyTurner 4 65
(G A Butler) *in rr: rdn over 3f out: styd on fr 2f out: no imp on ldrs ins fnl f* **14/1**

-041 **7** 1/2 **Kasban**[28] 3276 4-9-7 **77** SebSanders 8 79
(Jane Chapple-Hyam) *lw: chsd ldrs: led 4f out: rdn fr 3f out: hdd & wknd appr fnl f* **15/8**[1]

0066 **8** 2 1/2 **Calculating (IRE)**[7] 3942 4-9-0 **77** DavidProbert(7) 6 76
(M D I Usher) *in rr: hdwy on outside fr 3f out: no imp on ldrs: wknd 2f out* **8/1**

5023 **9** nk **Mister Completely (IRE)**[3] 4087 7-7-10 **59** oh5 ow1(v) SophieDoyle(7) 3 58
(Ms J S Doyle) *pressed ldrs: led 1/2-way: hdd 4f out: sn rdn: wknd fr 2f out* **14/1**

/453 **10** 5 **Markington**[15] 3673 5-8-8 **64** (p) VinceSlattery 9 57
(P Bowen) *in tch: rdn over 3f out: sn btn* **10/1**

01-5 **11** 3/4 **Dark Energy**[9] 3884 4-8-9 **70** (t) JackDean(5) 12 62
(M J Scudamore) *nvr bttr then mid-div: no ch fr 3f out* **12/1**

3m 34.63s (-2.27) **Going Correction** -0.125s/f (Firm) **11** Ran SP% **123.9**
Speed ratings (Par 105): **100,99,99,98,98 97,97,96,96,93 93**
toteswinger: 1&2 £17.20, 1&3 £6.00, 2&3 £9.50. CSF £80.13 CT £495.57 TOTE £7.10: £2.40, £4.20, £2.10; EX 95.00 Place 6 £369.77, Place 5 £155.38.
Owner Entre Nous and P D Cundell **Bred** Roden House Stud **Trained** Compton, Berks

FOCUS
A truly run race over 2m and a good test of stamina. The form is ordinary but should work out.
T/Jkpt: Not won. T/Plt: £248.70 to a £1 stake. Pool: £135,546.66. 397.80 winning tickets. T/Qpdt: £82.00 to a £1 stake. Pool: £6,234.50. 56.20 winning tickets. ST

4156 NEWMARKET (R-H)
Saturday, July 19

OFFICIAL GOING: Good to firm (8.4)
Wind: Fresh, behind. Weather: Cloudy with sunny spells

4194 LETTERGOLD MAIDEN STKS (DIV I) 7f
1:30 (1:34) (Class 4) 3-Y-O **£4,695** (£1,397; £698; £348) **Stalls** High

Form RPR

224 **1** **Liberation Spirit (USA)**[36] 2994 3-9-3 84 ShaneKelly 8 77+
(J Noseda) *mde all: rdn and hung lft over 1f out: styd on* **5/4**[1]

0-66 **2** 1 1/2 **Warden Fizz**[21] 3502 3-9-3 53 TQuinn 4 73
(D R C Elsworth) *sn pushed along and prom: rdn to chse wnr fnl f: styd on* **66/1**

0-4 **3** nk **Jennie Jerome (IRE)**[59] 2307 3-8-5 0 MJMurphy(7) 10 67+
(L M Cumani) *chsd ldrs: shkn up over 1f out: styd on* **9/2**[3]

3- **4** 3 **Orchestrion**[313] 5281 3-8-12 0 KerrinMcEvoy 7 59
(G A Swinbank) *chsd ldrs: rdn and hung lft over 1f out: no ex fnl f* **9/1**

004 **5** 1 1/4 **Seven Royals (IRE)**[8] 3916 3-9-3 63 RichardKingscote 5 61
(Miss A M Newton-Smith) *chsd ldrs: rdn over 1f out: wknd ins fnl f* **33/1**

- **6** 1/2 **Apotheosis** 3-9-3 0 AdamKirby 3 60+
(W R Swinburn) *s.i.s and rn green in rr: rdn over 2f out: styd on: nt trble ldrs* **14/1**

7 2 3/4 **Sharki** 3-8-12 0 JimmyFortune 9 47+
(J H M Gosden) *dwlt: outpcd: styd on ins fnl f: nrst fin* **4/1**[2]

2-45 **8** 7 **Andaman Sunset**[95] 1379 3-9-3 77 AlanMunro 6 33
(G Wragg) *hld up: rdn 1/2-way: wknd over 2f out* **13/2**[3]

05 **9** 1 3/4 **Global Glory (IRE)**[22] 3445 3-9-3 0 OscarUrbina 2 29
(J A R Toller) *sn pushed along in rr: reminders 4f out: wknd over 2f out* **100/1**

00- **10** 3/4 **Golden Horus (USA)**[224] 7070 3-9-0 0 JerryO'Dwyer(3) 12 27
(P J O'Gorman) *chsd ldrs: rdn over 2f out: wknd over 1f out* **80/1**

0-0 **11** hd **Rahaan (USA)**[26] 3318 3-8-7 0 AhmedAjtebi(5) 1 21
(C E Brittain) *chsd ldrs: rdn 1/2-way: hung lft and wknd 2f out* **40/1**

1m 24.76s (-0.94) **Going Correction** -0.225s/f (Firm) **11** Ran SP% **113.5**
Speed ratings (Par 102): **96,94,93,90,89 88,85,77,75,74 74**
toteswinger: 1&2 £20.60, 1&3 £2.90, 2&3 £86.30. CSF £126.61 TOTE £2.20: £1.10, £8.90, £2.20; EX 120.20.
Owner Saeed Suhail **Bred** Farfellow Farms Ltd **Trained** Newmarket, Suffolk

FOCUS
An ordinary maiden in which the winner ran well his official mark in victory. The form is held down by the runner-up but otherwise makes plenty of sense.
Sharki Official explanation: jockey said, regarding running and riding, his orders were to jump out and finish as close as he could without knocking the filly about, adding that after missing the break he did not want to rush into the race and get unbalanced, they gradually got into the race but stay on one paced; trainer expressed himself as satisfied but did have slight concerns by the good to firm ground, and intends to run over a mile on better ground; vet said filly was found to be short and sore in front.

4195 LETTERGOLD MAIDEN STKS (DIV II) 7f
2:00 (2:00) (Class 4) 3-Y-O **£4,695** (£1,397; £698; £348) **Stalls** High

Form RPR

3 **1** **Lake Windermere (IRE)**[22] 3452 3-8-12 0 JimmyFortune 5 71+
(J H M Gosden) *b: mde virtually all: rdn and hung rt over 1f out: styd on* **1/2**[1]

4 **2** 2 1/4 **Spotty Muldoon (IRE)**[117] 997 3-9-3 0 RichardKingscote 9 70
(R M Beckett) *chsd ldrs: rdn and ev ch over 1f out: unable qckn ins fnl f* **6/1**[2]

04 **3** 4 1/2 **Harryana To**[23] 3419 3-8-12 0 AlanMunro 6 52
(B J McMath) *chsd wnr tl rdn over 2f out: wknd ins fnl f* **50/1**

00 **4** 1 1/4 **Island Treasure**[26] 3326 3-9-3 0 SteveDrowne 11 54+
(H Morrison) *hld up: hdwy 2f out: sn rdn: wknd ins fnl f* **16/1**

5 hd **Flight Of Fashion (IRE)** 3-8-12 0 ShaneKelly 4 48
(Dr J D Scargill) *hld up in tch: plld hrd: rdn over 1f out: hung lft and wknd fnl f* **20/1**

63-6 **6** 2 3/4 **Cotton Reel**[75] 1855 3-9-3 75 PatDobbs 3 46
(P F I Cole) *hld up in tch: rdn over 1f out: wknd fnl f* **8/1**[3]

7 nk **Truly Divine** 3-9-3 0 KerrinMcEvoy 1 45+
(E A L Dunlop) *chsd ldrs: rdn over 1f out: sn wknd* **9/1**

00- **8** 9 **Jolie Fleur**[327] 4875 3-8-9 0 KirstyMilczarek(3) 7 16
(D E Cantillon) *hmpd s: sn prom: rdn and wknd over 2f out* **80/1**

0 **9** 5 **Gun For Sale (USA)**[39] 2918 3-9-3 0 TPQueally 10 7
(P J Makin) *hld up: hdwy over 2f out: rdn: hung lft and wknd over 1f out* **25/1**

1m 24.84s (-0.86) **Going Correction** -0.225s/f (Firm) **9** Ran SP% **119.7**
Speed ratings (Par 102): **95,92,87,85,85 82,82,71,66**
toteswinger: 1&2 £1.30, 1&3 £10.30, 2&3 £23.90. CSF £4.06 TOTE £1.50: £1.02, £1.80, £7.80; EX 4.30.
Owner H R H Princess Haya Of Jordan **Bred** Castleton Group **Trained** Newmarket, Suffolk

FOCUS
An uncompetitive second division of this maiden and the first two came clear. The time was slower than the first division and the form weaker. The winner probably did not need to improve on her debut form.

4196 PLANTATION STUD STKS (REGISTERED AS THE APHRODITE STAKES) (LISTED RACE) (F&M) 1m 4f
2:35 (2:37) (Class 1) 3-Y-O+
£24,978 (£9,468; £4,738; £2,362; £1,183; £594) **Stalls** Centre

Form RPR

-133 **1** **Dar Re Mi**[20] 3543 3-8-4 105 RichardMullen 7 106
(J H M Gosden) *a.p: rdn to ld ins fnl f: r.o* **5/2**[1]

-114 **2** 3/4 **Folk Opera (IRE)**[14] 3720 4-9-5 107 KerrinMcEvoy 11 108
(Saeed Bin Suroor) *led: rdn over 1f out: hdd ins fnl f: r.o* **5/2**[1]

214 **3** hd **Icon Project (USA)**[30] 3153 3-8-5 97 ow1 AlanMunro 8 106
(B J Meehan) *trckd ldr: plld hrd: rdn and ev ch fr over 1f out: r.o* **4/1**[2]

-312 **4** 4 1/2 **Arthur's Girl**[30] 3153 3-8-6 102 ow2 SteveDrowne 12 100
(G Wragg) *chsd ldrs: rdn over 2f out: swtchd lft over 1f out: wknd ins fnl f* **9/2**[3]

1023 **5** 2 1/4 **Dancing Abbie (USA)**[34] 3076 3-8-4 92 SaleemGolam 5 94
(M L W Bell) *hld up: rdn over 3f out: hdwy 2f out: wknd ins fnl f* **25/1**

-034 **6** 3/4 **Presbyterian Nun (IRE)**[34] 3076 3-8-4 90 RichardKingscote 6 93
(J L Dunlop) *hld up: plld hrd: hdwy u.p 2f out: wknd fnl f* **25/1**

2 **7** 3 3/4 **Ragdollianna**[24] 3362 4-9-2 0 EdwardCreighton 4 87?
(Norma Twomey) *prom: rdn over 2f out: wknd fnl f* **100/1**

4511 **8** 1 3/4 **Ronaldsay**[33] 3088 4-9-5 102 JimmyFortune 10 87
(R Hannon) *s.i.s: hld up: rdn over 2f out: wknd over 1f out* **8/1**

6-0 **9** 3 3/4 **Generous Jem**[77] 1812 5-9-2 81 AdamKirby 13 78
(G G Margarson) *hld up: rdn and wknd over 2f out* **50/1**

3250 **10** 1/2 **Try Me (UAE)**[34] 3076 3-8-4 96 AhmedAjtebi 1 77
(C E Brittain) *chsd ldrs: rdn over 3f out: wknd over 1f out* **50/1**

2m 27.52s (-5.38) **Going Correction** -0.225s/f (Firm)
WFA 3 from 4yo+ 12lb **10** Ran SP% **119.0**
Speed ratings (Par 111): **108,107,107,104,102 102,99,98,96,95**
toteswinger: 1&2 £1.80, 1&3 £2.70, 2&3 £4.10. CSF £8.60 TOTE £3.50: £1.30, £1.60, £1.70; EX 10.00 Trifecta £52.00 Pool: £857.36 - 12.20 winning units..
Owner Lord Lloyd-Webber **Bred** Watership Down Stud **Trained** Newmarket, Suffolk

FOCUS
A decent renewal of this Listed race and those at the head of the market dominated. The form seems to make sense. The pace was ordinary and they raced up the stands' rail in the straight.

NOTEBOOK
Dar Re Mi, who had been placed in the Musidora and touched off in the Prix de Malleret since beating Icon Project in her maiden at Sandown, got good cover early and made her challenge from the quarter-mile pole, before asserting in the final furlong. She will go to Deauville next month for either the Prix de Pomone or Prix Minerve. (op 11-4 tchd 9-4)
Folk Opera(IRE), who is well suited by fast ground, set the pace but was being pressed by the eventual third from the three-furlong marker and, despite running on, could not hold off the winner up the final climb. She is a reliable sort who should win more races at this level. (op 10-3 tchd 7-2)
Icon Project(USA), who had finished seven lengths behind today's winner on her debut in a Sandown maiden, put up her best effort when fourth in the Ribblesdale. She finished much closer to Dar Re Mi, having been in the firing line from some way out, and is clearly still progressing. Connections will be pleased she has secured black type, but she looks more than capable of winning a race at this level. (op 9-2)
Arthur's Girl, who finished ahead of the third when runner-up in the Ribblesdale, was easy to back and was unable to make any impression in the closing stages. It may be that she is most effective over 1m2f or on an easier surface. (op 4-1 tchd 5-1 and 11-2 in a place)
Dancing Abbie(USA), third in the italian Oaks on her previous outing, is possibly more effective on an easier surface or Polytrack but appeared to run close to her official rating and will not be easy to place. (op 22-1)
Ronaldsay, who did well to take a relatively weak Listed race last time, missed the break and never figured. She seems best around 1m2f with some cut in the ground. (op 15-2)
Generous Jem Official explanation: jockey said mare hung left

4197 ADNAMS EAST GREEN H'CAP 1m
3:05 (3:09) (Class 2) (0-100,99) 3-Y-O
£12,462 (£3,732; £1,866; £934; £466; £234) **Stalls** High

Form RPR

3211 **1** **Always A Rock (IRE)**[50] 2575 3-8-9 **85** J-PGuillambert 2 92
(M Johnston) *led: hdd 2f out: rdn and hung lft over 1f out: rallied to ld ins fnl f: r.o* **6/1**[3]

321 **2** nk **Decameron (USA)**[35] 3051 3-9-0 **90** KerrinMcEvoy 8 97
(Sir Michael Stoute) *chsd ldrs: led 2f out: rdn and hung lft 1f out: sn hdd: styd on* **5/2**[1]

-624 **3** 3/4 **Kal Barg**[29] 3222 3-9-4 **94** PhilipRobinson 1 99
(M A Jarvis) *s.i.s: sn chsng ldrs: rdn over 1f out: styd on same pce ins fnl f* **10/3**[2]

2000 **4** 3/4 **Fathsta (IRE)**[8] 3919 3-9-2 **92** PatDobbs 9 95+
(S Kirk) *hld up: hdwy over 1f out: rdn and edgd lft ins fnl f: r.o* **14/1**

4-1 **5** 1 1/4 **Regal Best (IRE)**[36] 2994 3-8-10 **86** JimCrowley 3 86
(Mrs A J Perrett) *s.i.s: sn prom: rdn and nt clr run over 1f out: no ex ins fnl f* **15/2**

-250 **6** 2 1/2 **Meeriss (IRE)**[49] 2610 3-9-9 **99** AlanMunro 4 94
(M R Channon) *chsd ldr: rdn over 2f out: wknd fnl f* **22/1**

0-21 **7** 5 **Resurge (IRE)**[56] 2413 3-8-9 **85** ShaneKelly 5 68
(J Noseda) *hld up: rdn and hung rt over 1f out: sn wknd* **10/3**[2]

5-60 **8** shd **Tanweer (USA)**[35] 3046 3-8-9 **92** JPHamblett(7) 6 75
(Sir Michael Stoute) *hld up: rdn: hung rt and wknd over 1f out* **20/1**

1m 36.75s (-3.25) **Going Correction** -0.225s/f (Firm) **8** Ran SP% **116.6**
Speed ratings (Par 106): **107,106,105,105,103 101,96,96**
toteswinger: 1&2 £1.30, 1&3 £6.50, 2&3 £3.50. CSF £21.88 CT £59.28 TOTE £4.80: £1.30, £1.50, £1.70; EX 12.20 Trifecta £59.20 Pool: £392.65 - 4.90 winning units..
Owner Always Trying Partnership IV **Bred** Ascagnano S P A **Trained** Middleham Moor, N Yorks
■ City Of The Kings withdrawn; Rule 4 applies, deduction 15p in the £ from board prices prior to withdrawal.

The Form Book, Raceform Ltd, Compton, RG20 6NL

FOCUS
A decent three-year-old handicap in which the field raced up the centre of the track and the pace was ordinary. The winner confirmed his Musselburgh mark with the second up 8lb and the third close to his mark.

NOTEBOOK
Always A Rock(IRE) ◆, who started off on the All-Weather early in the year, has progressed with racing and is now unbeaten in two starts on turf. He again showed real battling qualities, sticking his head out and refusing to let the favourite past. He is on a roll and looks one to follow. (old market op 8-1 new market op 6-1)
Decameron(USA) was always close up and looked like winning when delivering his challenge but the winner proved just too determined. He lost little in defeat and remains on an upward curve. (old market tchd 10-3 new market tchd 11-4)
Kal Barg bounced back from his disappointing effort over 7f here last month under a positive ride on this step up in trip. He soon recovered from missing the break and seemed to get this longer trip, and comes out the best horse at the weights having had to give weight to those who finished in front of him. (new market op 7-2)
Fathsta(IRE), who had been very consistent and progressive until putting up a moderate effort at the July Festival here, bounced back with another decent effort from off the pace. Considering at the end of last turf season he was rated 70 and he has now risen to 92, during which time he has won five and been runner-up in another five of his 17 races, he is a credit to all concerned. (old market op 14-1 new market op 10-1)
Regal Best(IRE) missed the break but got a good lead into the race, and although he did not have much room he was unable to pick up when meeting the rising ground. He may not have appreciated the fast going and, as this was only his third outing, he can be given another chance. (old market op 8-1 tchd 9-1 new market tchd 7-1)
Resurge(IRE), who beat a subsequent winner when taking his maiden on fast ground on the Rowley Mile in May, produced a very lacklustre effort, hanging and dropping away tamely. (old market op 4-1 new market op 4-1 tchd 3-1)

4198 INVESCO PERPETUAL E B F FILLIES' H'CAP 6f
3:35 (3:35) (Class 3) (0-95,95) 3-Y-O+
£9,346 (£2,799; £1,399; £700; £349; £175) Stalls High

Form				RPR
0043	1		**Carcinetto (IRE)**[4] 4058 6-8-8 **82** RichardEvans(5) 8	91
			(P D Evans) *w ldr tl led 2f out: sn rdn: r.o* **10/1**	
0040	2	1 1/4	**Ripples Maid**[8] 3927 5-9-7 **90** SteveDrowne 9	95
			(J A Geake) *hld up: rdn and hdwy over 1f out: edgd lft ins fnl f: r.o* **7/1**	
10	3	3/4	**Temple Of Thebes (IRE)**[10] 3850 3-9-0 **88** KerrinMcEvoy 10	90
			(E A L Dunlop) *edgd rt s: chsd ldrs: rdn and ev ch over 1f out: styd on same pce ins fnl f* **2/1**[1]	
5-10	4	1 1/4	**Perfect Treasure (IRE)**[29] 3222 5-8-10 **79** AlanMunro 5	78
			(J A R Toller) *s.i.s: hld up: hdwy and hung lft over 1f out: sn rdn: styd on same pce insiide fnl f* **12/1**	
05-0	5	1	**Vital Statistics**[8] 3927 4-9-7 **90** TQuinn 11	85
			(D R C Elsworth) *s.i.s and hmpd s: hld up: outpcd over 1f out: styd on towards fin* **13/2**[3]	
6316	6	1/2	**Mango Music**[9] 3883 5-9-4 **87** TPQueally 3	81
			(M Quinn) *led 4f: sn rdn: wknd ins fnl f* **10/1**	
6113	7	1 1/4	**Angus Newz**[7] 3948 5-9-12 **95** ShaneKelly 1	85
			(M Quinn) *chsd ldrs: rdn and edgd lft over 1f out: wknd ins fnl f* **4/1**[2]	
4534	8	2 3/4	**Tia Mia**[22] 3460 3-9-0 **88** OscarUrbina 4	68
			(M Botti) *prom: rdn and edgd lft over 1f out: wknd fnl f* **8/1**	

1m 10.51s (-1.99) **Going Correction** -0.225s/f (Firm)
WFA 3 from 4yo+ 5lb 8 Ran SP% **116.2**
Speed ratings (Par 104): **104,102,101,99,98 97,96,92**
toteswinger: 1&2 £27.20, 1&3 £5.80, 2&3 £8.40. CSF £78.41 CT £197.98 TOTE £15.20: £2.50, £2.20, £1.60; EX 139.40 TRIFECTA Not won..
Owner Mrs Sally Edwards **Bred** M A Doyle **Trained** Pandy, Monmouths

FOCUS
A decent fillies' sprint run 1.36secs faster than the following juvenile maiden. The form is rated through the first two.

NOTEBOOK
Carcinetto(IRE), who had not won on turf for two years, had however scored six times on Polytrack since and been placed in Listed company on that surface. She took advantage of having dropped from a mark of 87 since the beginning of May and battled on well to score. She will not find it easy to win off her revised mark but should continue to run her race. (op 14-1)
Ripples Maid, who is usually at her best with some cut in the ground, has won on fast though and ran better than of late, taking advantage of a declining mark and a drop in grade. (op 8-1)
Temple Of Thebes(IRE), who is lightly raced and generally progressive, was encountering the fastest ground she has yet faced but ran her race without being able to get the better of the battle-hardened mares that finished ahead of her. (op 9-4 tchd 11-4)
Perfect Treasure(IRE) did not run badly considering she missed the break but her best form has all been at Brighton. (op 14-1)
Vital Statistics has never quite been able to build on the promise of her juvenile season despite running well in Listed company. Another who has slipped down the ratings, she is 18lb lower than at the start of last season and this staying-on effort having met trouble at the start suggest she may have another win in her. (op 6-1)
Mango Music has been in good form this season but, unlike several of her rivals, has been climbing the handicap and faded after making the running. (op 9-1)
Angus Newz, came into this in good form, her recent wins including one over course and distance, but she had the visor left off and this was a relatively tame effort. The Handicapper may also have her in his grip once again. (op 7-2 tchd 9-2)

4199 JULY COURSE MAIDEN STKS 6f
4:10 (4:11) (Class 4) 2-Y-O
£5,180 (£1,541; £770; £384) Stalls High

Form				RPR
2	1		**Rileyskeepingfaith**[8] 3895 2-9-3 0 EdwardCreighton 1	89
			(M R Channon) *chsd ldr: led over 1f out: r.o u.p* **7/2**[2]	
3	2	hd	**Crackdown (IRE)**[38] 2951 2-9-3 0 J-PGuillambert 3	88
			(M Johnston) *led: rdn and hdd over 1f out: r.o* **3/1**[1]	
	3	3 3/4	**Run For The Hills** 2-9-3 0 JimmyFortune 6	77+
			(J H M Gosden) *trckd ldrs: rdn over 1f out: styd on same pce* **7/2**[2]	
	4	1	**Elnawin** 2-9-3 0 PatDobbs 2	74
			(R Hannon) *s.s: hdwy over 4f out: rdn over 1f out: no ex whn rdr dropped reins wl ins fnl f* **14/1**	
	5	2	**Ayrus (USA)** 2-9-3 0 AlanMunro 10	68
			(B J Meehan) *mid-div: outpcd 2f out: styd on ins fnl f* **20/1**	
	6	1 1/4	**Ajjaadd (USA)** 2-9-3 0 KerrinMcEvoy 13	64
			(Saeed Bin Suroor) *s.s: hld up: hung lft over 1f out: styd on ins fnl f: nvr nrr* **9/2**[3]	
5	7	3	**Helpmeronda**[8] 3923 2-8-12 0 OscarUrbina 5	50
			(S A Callaghan) *hld up: effrt over 1f out: n.d* **16/1**	
	8	nk	**Medlock** 2-9-3 0 ShaneKelly 11	54
			(J Noseda) *hld up: nt clr run over 1f out: nvr trbld ldrs* **12/1**	
	9	3/4	**Lady Angelica** 2-8-12 0 SteveDrowne 8	47
			(Dr J D Scargill) *prom: lost pl over 2f out: wknd over 1f out* **50/1**	
	10	3/4	**Almazar** 2-9-3 0 RichardMullen 7	50
			(J L Dunlop) *mid-div: rdn: hung rt and wknd over 1f out* **20/1**	
0	11	nk	**Jacobite Prince (IRE)**[16] 3651 2-9-3 0 SaleemGolam 4	49
			(M H Tompkins) *s.i.s: sn prom: rdn and wknd over 1f out* **40/1**	
	12	1/2	**Against The Rules** 2-9-0 0 KirstyMilczarek(3) 14	47
			(P Howling) *hld up: a in rr* **40/1**	
	13	16	**Clodazone (IRE)** 2-8-9 0 JerryO'Dwyer(3) 15	—
			(M G Quinlan) *hld up: a in rr: rdn and wknd over 2f out* **50/1**	

1m 11.87s (-0.63) **Going Correction** -0.225s/f (Firm) 13 Ran SP% **126.2**
Speed ratings (Par 96): **95,94,89,88,85 84,80,79,78,77 77,76,55**
toteswinger: 1&2 £3.40, 1&3 £3.20, 2&3 £4.90. CSF £14.32 TOTE £4.40: £1.90, £1.80, £1.90; EX 10.30.
Owner Jolly Roger Racing **Bred** M Barrett **Trained** West Ilsley, Berks

FOCUS
A fair maiden run 1.36secs slower than the preceding fillies' handicap and dominated by those with previous experience. The first two finished clear.

NOTEBOOK
Rileyskeepingfaith, who missed the break and ran green on his debut at Ascot, had clearly learnt from that and, always close to the pace, took the advantage over a furlong out but had to pull out all the stops to hold on. He is likely to get a little further in time. (tchd 3-1 and 4-1)
Crackdown(IRE) ◆, who made a decent debut at Nottingham, set the pace but looked well beaten when the winner took over. However, he responded well to pressure and was gaining on his rival near the finish. He can win before long on this evidence. (op 5-1)
Run For The Hills ◆, a half-brother to four winners at between 6f and 1m4f, ran with credit for his in-form stable. Backed beforehand, he kept on steadily without being given an unduly hard race and should benefit from the experience. (op 6-1)
Elnawin, related to three winners at between 5-7f, missed the break but was soon racing close to the pace and held on until fading up the hill. He should know more next time and looks another to keep an eye on. (op 9-1)
Ayrus(USA), who cost the same, $200,000, when sold at the breeze-ups as he had as a yearling, was noted running on at the finish having been held up off the pace. The yard's juveniles often benefit from a run and the same should be the case with this one. (tchd 22-1)
Ajjaadd(USA), a half-brother to among others Baaridd out of the speedy Millstream, missed the break and never really got involved. The yard's juveniles have been needing their first runs and hopefully he will come on for this. (op 7-2)

4200 NEWMARKETRACECOURSES.CO.UK H'CAP 1m 6f 175y
4:45 (4:47) (Class 4) (0-85,85) 4-Y-O+
£6,476 (£1,927; £963; £481) Stalls Centre

Form				RPR
-252	1		**Daylami Dreams**[28] 3276 4-8-12 **74** SteveDrowne 10	84
			(T P Tate) *chsd ldrs: rdn to ld ins fnl f: r.o* **4/1**[2]	
2445	2	1/2	**Alonso De Guzman (IRE)**[17] 3613 4-8-5 **67** ow1 KerrinMcEvoy 3	76
			(J R Boyle) *trckd ldr: racd keenly: led 2f out: rdn and hdd ins fnl f: r.o* **11/1**	
1242	3	3 3/4	**Fregate Island (IRE)**[29] 3209 5-9-5 **81** TQuinn 7	85
			(A G Newcombe) *prom: rdn and hung lft over 2f out: styd on same pce fnl f* **11/4**[1]	
0300	4	1 1/4	**Invasian (IRE)**[28] 3250 7-9-7 **83** AlanMunro 2	86
			(P W D'Arcy) *led: rdn and hdd 2f out: sn hung lft: no ex fnl f* **13/2**	
410	5	hd	**Bell Island**[12] 3802 4-9-4 **80** RichardKingscote 4	82
			(Lady Herries) *hld up: hdwy over 5f out: rdn over 1f out: no ex* **14/1**	
1-00	6	3	**Inchpast**[49] 2628 7-9-0 **76** (b) SaleemGolam 8	74
			(M H Tompkins) *hld up: hdwy u.p over 2f out: wknd fnl f* **12/1**	
0-00	7	44	**Tusculum (IRE)**[16] 3630 5-8-13 **75** (p) TPQueally 1	16
			(A P Stringer) *hld up: rdn over 3f out: sn wknd* **6/1**	
663	8	2 1/4	**Cyborg**[42] 2847 4-9-3 **79** JimmyFortune 9	17
			(D R C Elsworth) *hld up: effrt over 3f out: sn hung lft and wknd* **5/1**[3]	
31/	9	20	**City Well**[869] 573 5-9-0 **76** J-PGuillambert 6	—
			(M Johnston) *s.i.s: hld up: sme hdwy 6f out: sn lost pl: wknd 4f out* **12/1**	

3m 4.30s (-7.00) **Going Correction** -0.225s/f (Firm) 9 Ran SP% **121.3**
Speed ratings (Par 105): **109,108,106,106,105 104,80,79,69**
toteswinger: 1&2 £6.50, 1&3 £2.80, 2&3 £10.00. CSF £49.76 CT £143.96 TOTE £5.30: £1.80, £3.20, £1.50; EX 51.50.
Owner Mrs Fitri Hay **Bred** Elsdon Farms **Trained** Tadcaster, N Yorks

FOCUS
A fair staying handicap run at a sound gallop. The field raced up the centre in the straight. The form looks sound enough, rated through the third.
Tusculum(IRE) Official explanation: trainer had no explanation for the poor form shown
Cyborg Official explanation: trainer said gelding was unsuited by the good to firm ground
City Well Official explanation: jockey said gelding lost its action

4201 TURFTV H'CAP 5f
5:15 (5:16) (Class 3) (0-95,94) 3-Y-O+
£9,066 (£2,697; £1,348; £673) Stalls High

Form				RPR
0-10	1		**Sohraab**[15] 3680 4-9-9 **93** TravisBlock(3) 5	104
			(H Morrison) *a.p: rdn over 1f out: r.o to ld nr fin* **11/2**[3]	
5230	2	nk	**Ocean Blaze**[42] 2828 4-8-13 **80** AlanMunro 1	90
			(B R Millman) *led: rdn over 1f out: edgd rt ins fnl f: hdd nr fin* **12/1**	
-006	3	1/2	**Tony The Tap**[15] 3680 7-8-12 **79** RichardMullen 8	87
			(W R Muir) *sn pushed along in rr: swtchd lft and hdwy over 1f out: r.o* **16/1**	
3111	4	3/4	**Misaro (GER)**[2] 4103 7-9-4 **90** 6ex (b) HaddenFrost(5) 2	95
			(R A Harris) *b. hind: chsd ldr: rdn over 1f out: styd on* **7/2**[1]	
0-13	5	shd	**Osiris Way**[15] 3680 6-9-4 **85** JimCrowley 6	90
			(P R Chamings) *chsd ldrs: rdn over 1f out: nt clr run ins fnl f: styd on* **9/2**[2]	
5606	6	nk	**Golden Dixie (USA)**[8] 3898 9-9-4 **85** RichardKingscote 10	89+
			(R A Harris) *hld up: gng wl and nt clr run fr 1/2-way tl r.o wl ins fnl f: nvr able to chal* **14/1**	
51	7	1/2	**Blue Tomato**[38] 2938 7-9-7 **88** AdrianTNicholls 7	90
			(D Nicholls) *s.i.s: hdwy 1/2-way: rdn over 1f out: sn ev ch: no ex wl ins fnl f* **9/1**	
3306	8	1/2	**Lord Of The Reins (IRE)**[9] 3881 4-8-13 **80** TQuinn 13	80
			(J G Given) *hld up: hdwy over 1f out: no ex wl ins fnl f* **12/1**	
30-6	9	1	**Pearly Wey**[42] 2831 5-9-13 **94** TPQueally 3	91
			(C G Cox) *s.i.s: sn prom: rdn over 1f out: wknd ins fnl f* **15/2**	
2400	10	2 1/4	**Northern Empire (IRE)**[22] 3451 5-9-10 **91** JimmyFortune 11	80
			(K A Ryan) *hld up: effrt over 1f out: carried hd high and eased ins fnl f* **12/1**	
0000	11	hd	**Bazroy (IRE)**[7] 3973 4-8-13 **85** RichardEvans(5) 12	73
			(P D Evans) *sn outpcd* **28/1**	
5000	12	3/4	**Canadian Danehill (IRE)**[9] 3881 6-9-9 **90** (p) J-PGuillambert 4	75
			(R M H Cowell) *chsd ldrs: rdn over 1f out: wkng whn n.m.r sn after* **20/1**	

5200 **13** *3/4* **Vhujon (IRE)**[8] 3905 3-9-8 **93** TGMcLaughlin 9 65
(P D Evans) *s.s: outpcd* **33/1**

57.43 secs (-1.67) **Going Correction** -0.225s/f (Firm)
WFA 3 from 4yo+ 4lb **13** Ran SP% **124.3**
Speed ratings (Par 107): **104,103,102,101,101 100,100,99,97,94 93,92,86**
toteswinger: 1&2 £23.60, 1&3 £29.00, 2&3 £46.30. CSF £71.46 CT £1053.02 TOTE £7.40: £2.30, £4.20, £3.90; EX 104.50 Place 6 £5.00, Place 5 £2.89.
Owner Pangfield Racing **Bred** T J Billington **Trained** East Ilsley, Berks

FOCUS
A competitive sprint handicap run at a good gallop helped by a tail wind. Solid form.

NOTEBOOK
Sohraab, who is a most consistent performer, was suited by the strong pace and came through on the climb to the line to just catch the long-time leader. He will probably be aimed at one of the big handicaps at Goodwood or York, but has run well on both his starts on this track so is one to be with if returning here. (op 13-2 tchd 7-1)
Ocean Blaze, who is well suited by a sharp 5f and a sound surface, made the running and battled on bravely despite drifting towards the stands' side and was unlucky to be caught close home. Given a return to an easier track she can gain compensation, and somewhere like Goodwood, where she has won before, could present her with a suitable opportunity. (op 14-1 tchd 16-1)
Tony The Tap, who is a regular in this race, having been touched off last season, wins rarely, his only success on turf being nearly four years ago, and is best suited by an easier surface. Nevertheless this good effort, following on from his decent effort at Sandown, where he finished just ahead of today's winner, suggests he is finding some form again.
Misaro(GER), who has been in terrific form of late, was bidding for his fourth win in a row and fifth in his last six outings. However, he has risen 19lb in the handicap as a result and, despite running his race, the penalty for his most recent success seems to have found him out. (op 4-1)
Osiris Way, who has a good record on turf, having won half of his six previous races and been placed in two others, finished ahead of today's winner and third at Sandown last time and so this was a little below par. Fully effective at 6f, possibly the tail wind meant it was not a stiff enough test for him at this trip. (op 5-1)
Golden Dixie(USA) has been in the grip of the Handicapper since scoring in August last year, but his mark has slipped quickly of late and he is now 6lb below his last winning rating. He travelled well just behind the pace but could not get a clear run to deliver a challenge. A stiff five or 6f suits and he looks capable of winning off this mark. Official explanation: jockey said gelding was denied a clear run (op 12-1 tchd 16-1)
Blue Tomato has won over a sharp five but the majority of his recent wins have been over 6f and he was not helped by missing the break here. He will no doubt be one of his trainer's team for Goodwood at the end of the month. (op 10-1 tchd 15-2)
Pearly Wey ◆, who won the Stewards' Cup consolation race last season, looks to have been laid out for the real thing this time. Best at 6f, he missed the break on this first attempt at the bare 5f but was soon in contention only to drop away late on. This should put him spot-on for Goodwood. (op 8-1 tchd 9-1 in places)
Northern Empire(IRE) Official explanation: trainer's rep said gelding was unsuited by the good to firm ground
T/Plt: £6.90 to a £1 stake. Pool: £91,677.08. 9,666.14 winning tickets. T/Qpdt: £4.20 to a £1 stake. Pool: £4,553.35. 790.60 winning tickets. CR

3791 RIPON (R-H)
Saturday, July 19

OFFICIAL GOING: Good
Wind: Fresh, half behind Weather: Cloudy, bright

4202 E B F DOBSONS GASKETS MAIDEN FILLIES' STKS 5f
2:30 (2:32) (Class 4) 2-Y-O **£5,180** (£1,541; £770; £384) **Stalls** Low

Form RPR
4 **1** **Sirenuse (IRE)**[18] 3590 2-9-0 0 TomEaves 6 77
(B Smart) *w ldrs: rdn to ld ins fnl f: hld on wl* **10/3**[3]
02 **2** *nk* **Minotaurious (IRE)**[17] 3598 2-9-0 0 AndrewElliott 2 76
(K R Burke) *led to ins fnl f: kpt on u.p* **5/2**[2]
02 **3** *hd* **Ishe Mac**[31] 3140 2-8-11 0 MarkLawson(3) 8 75
(N Bycroft) *in tch: drvn along 1/2-way: kpt on ins fnl f* **18/1**
20 **4** *1* **Salsa Star (USA)**[29] 3192 2-8-11 0 JamieMoriarty(3) 4 72
(R A Fahey) *prom: effrt whn edgd rt and n.m.r appr fnl f: kpt on ins fnl f* **9/4**[1]
5 **5** *2 1/4* **Soviet Rhythm**[9] 3865 2-8-11 0 PJMcDonald(3) 12 64
(G M Moore) *bhd and outpcd tl hdwy over 1f out: kpt on: nrst fin* **12/1**
00 **6** *nk* **Dark Velvet (IRE)**[7] 3949 2-8-11 0 MichaelJStainton(3) 7 63
(E J Alston) *in tch: drvn 1/2-way: no imp fr 2f out* **80/1**
45 **7** *1/2* **Impressible**[17] 3598 2-9-0 0 MickyFenton 10 61
(E J Alston) *racd wd in midfield: drvn along 1/2-way: one pce fr over 1f out* **33/1**
8 *nk* **Inthawain** 2-9-0 0 SamHitchcott 9 60+
(M R Channon) *bhd and outpcd: sme hdwy over 1f out: n.d* **22/1**
9 *3* **Monaco Mistress (IRE)** 2-9-0 0 LeeEnstone 1 49
(P C Haslam) *dwlt: bhd: shortlived effrt 1/2-way: sn btn* **40/1**
10 *shd* **Midnight Fantasy** 2-9-0 0 EddieAhern 11 48
(Rae Guest) *s.i.s: a bhd* **25/1**
0 **11** *3* **Smelly Cat**[7] 3976 2-9-0 0 DavidAllan 3 38
(T D Easterby) *w ldrs tl wknd fr 2f out* **20/1**
36 **12** *hd* **Peter's Gift (IRE)**[22] 3437 2-9-0 0 FergalLynch 13 37
(K A Ryan) *racd wd in midfield: rdn and wknd fr 2f out* **14/1**

61.45 secs (0.75) **Going Correction** +0.125s/f (Good) **12** Ran SP% **121.6**
Speed ratings (Par 93): **99,98,98,96,93 92,91,91,86,86 81,81**
toteswinger: 1&2 £2.40, 1&3 £24.90, 2&3 £12.70. CSF £11.45 TOTE £4.90: £2.00, £1.50, £4.70; EX 11.30 Trifecta £170.10 Part won. Pool: £229.95 - 0.79 winning units..
Owner M Barber **Bred** David Jamison Bloodstock And G Roddick **Trained** Hambleton, N Yorks

FOCUS
Just a fair event in which the pace was sound and the field raced stands' side. The form looks reasonably good rated around the fifth and seventh.

NOTEBOOK
Sirenuse(IRE), who shaped well, despite hanging, on her debut at Haydock, turned in an improved effort over this shorter trip with a brush-pricker fitted this time. She is open to further progress and is the type to win more races. (op 5-1)
Minotaurious(IRE) has improved with every outing and turned in her best effort yet, despite getting the run of the race next to the stands' rail. She is more than capable of picking up a similar event in the coming weeks. (op 4-1 tchd 9-4)
Ishe Mac bettered the form of her previous start over this course and distance and left the impression that the return to 6f would be in her favour. While vulnerable to the more progressive sorts in this grade, she is capable of picking up a modest event this term. (op 20-1 tchd 16-1)
Salsa Star(USA) ◆, who was far from disgraced in the Albany at Royal Ascot, failed to build on that form after meeting trouble at a crucial stage. She lacked the foot to take the gaps when they first appeared and will be suited by the return to 6f. She remains capable of winning races. (op 2-1 tchd 5-2)
Soviet Rhythm ◆, from a stable that has been on the mark with its juveniles in recent times, probably ran to a similar level of form as on her debut. She will be suited by the step up to 6f+ and is one to keep an eye on when handicapped. (op 8-1)
Dark Velvet(IRE) has improved at a modest level with every outing and left the impression this time that a much stiffer test of stamina would have been in her favour. She may do better in ordinary nursery company.

4203 BIRCHALL CATERING SUPPLIES (S) STKS 6f
3:00 (3:01) (Class 6) 2-Y-O **£2,590** (£770; £385; £192) **Stalls** Low

Form RPR
0540 **1** **Shadow Bay (IRE)**[15] 3677 2-8-11 0 SamHitchcott 15 72+
(M R Channon) *mde all far side: clr that gp 2f out: kpt on strly fnl f* **4/1**[2]
2 **2** *1 1/4* **Dean Iarracht (IRE)**[14] 3726 2-8-11 0 EddieAhern 7 68+
(John R Upson) *cl up stands' side: led and sn clr that gp 2f out: kpt on wl fnl f: nt rch far side wnr: 1st of 10 in gp* **7/1**
06 **3** *9* **Dougie Peel**[13] 3754 2-8-11 0 (b1) RobertWinston 12 41
(K A Ryan) *chsd wnr far side: rdn and one pce fr 2f out: 2nd of 6 in gp* **6/1**
2300 **4** *2 3/4* **Heaven Or Hell (IRE)**[2] 4119 2-9-2 0 PatCosgrave 3 38
(P D Evans) *cl up stands' side: drvn over 2f out: sn one pce: 2nd of 10 in gp* **11/4**[1]
00 **5** *1 1/4* **Royal Premium**[31] 3125 2-8-8 0 JamieMoriarty(3) 13 29
(H A McWilliams) *prom far side: drvn and hung lft 1/2-way: sn one pce: 3rd of 6 in gp* **50/1**
500 **6** *1 1/2* **The Canny Dove (USA)**[18] 3590 2-8-8 0 NeilBrown(3) 14 25+
(T D Barron) *rrd in stalls and lost grnd s: bhd far side: drvn 1/2-way no imp: 4th of 6 in gp* **9/1**
03U **7** *1/2* **Just Five (IRE)**[14] 3706 2-8-11 0 TomEaves 5 23
(M Dods) *dwlt: bhd stands' side tl hdwy over 1f out: n.d: 3rd of 10 in gp* **5/1**[3]
004 **8** *1 1/4* **Ernies Keep**[10] 3830 2-8-8 0 DominicFox(3) 16 20
(W Storey) *in tch far side tl outpcd fr over 2f out: 5th of 6 in gp* **50/1**
560 **9** *hd* **Quadrifolio**[29] 3225 2-8-11 0 (v1) KimTinkler 6 19
(N Tinkler) *towards rr stands' side: effrt on outside of that gp over 2f out: n.d: 4th of 10 in gp* **50/1**
06 **10** *hd* **Dispol Kintie (IRE)**[12] 3792 2-8-6 0 PaulFessey 2 13
(P T Midgley) *towards rr stands' side: drvn over 2f out: nt pce to chal: 5th of 10 in gp* **20/1**
000 **11** *3* **Holst (IRE)**[14] 3706 2-8-11 0 (b) DavidAllan 10 9
(T D Easterby) *bhd and rdn along stands' side: nvr on terms: 6th of 10 in gp* **25/1**
40 **12** *4 1/2* **Incy Wincy**[15] 3670 2-8-11 0 MickyFenton 1 —
(J M Bradley) *midfield stands' side: n.m.r over 2f out: sn btn: 7th of 10 in gp* **50/1**
0000 **13** *2 1/4* **Sharp Discovery**[70] 2011 2-8-1 0 KellyHarrison(5) 17 —
(J M Bradley) *bhd and sn outpcd far side: nvr on terms: last of 6 in gp* **33/1**
0600 **14** *shd* **Transformation (IRE)**[10] 3830 2-8-6 0 DeanMcKeown 9 —
(J R Weymes) *led stands' side to 2f out: sn wknd: 8th of 10 in gp* **66/1**
60 **15** *nk* **Keen Rabbit**[32] 3106 2-8-6 0 TonyHamilton 4 —
(Micky Hammond) *midfield stands' side: drvn 1/2-way: sn wknd: 9th of 10 in gp* **66/1**
66 **16** *14* **Charly's Rose**[29] 3225 2-8-8 0 ow2 (b1) PaulMulrennan 8 —
(P C Haslam) *chsd stands' side ldrs tl wknd over 2f out: last of 10 in gp* **20/1**

1m 14.72s (1.72) **Going Correction** +0.125s/f (Good) **16** Ran SP% **127.3**
Speed ratings (Par 92): **93,91,79,75,74 72,71,69,69,69 65,59,56,56,55 36**
toteswinger: 1&2 £5.60, 1&3 £32.40, 2&3 £25.90. CSF £30.80 TOTE £3.80: £1.90, £2.90, £2.80; EX 43.40 Trifecta £105.00 Part won. Pool: £142.01 - 0.40 winning units..The winner was bought in for £9,500. Dean Iarracht was claimed by M. J. K. Dods for £6,000.
Owner The Abercrombie Partnership **Bred** Thomas Cahalan & Sophie Hayley **Trained** West Ilsley, Berks

FOCUS
A low-grade event and a fair gallop but winner and second pulled well clear of their respective groups and the form looks solid and well above average for the grade. There seemed little in the draw.

NOTEBOOK
Shadow Bay(IRE), who had turned in his best effort at this course in April, proved well suited by the drop in grade and he turned in his best effort yet. His record is one of inconsistency so he would not be one to go in head down for next time. (op 7-2 tchd 9-2)
Dean Iarracht(IRE), with the tongue strap and blinkers left off, was held by the winner on the opposite side of the track but turned in an improved effort to pull clear of his group. He was claimed by Michael Dods, should stay 7f and is capable of winning a race. (op 15-2)
Dougie Peel, with the blinkers fitted, was not disgraced. He is in good hands and, although he may not be entirely straightforward, he left the impression that he would be worth a try over 7f. (op 11-2 tchd 13-2)
Heaven Or Hell(IRE), back in selling company, was below his very best attempting to concede weight all round. He is exposed as a moderate and inconsistent performer and is not really one to take too short a price about. (tchd 3-1)
Royal Premium, dropped in grade, turned in his best effort yet but looked less than an easy ride in the process. The step up to 7f could suit but he is going to have to show a fair bit more before he is a solid betting proposition. (op 40-1)
The Canny Dove(USA) was again well beaten after losing ground at the start. He is in good hands but does not look one to place too much faith in at present. (tchd 11-1)

4204 SKYBET SUPPORTING THE YORKSHIRE RACING FESTIVAL H'CAP 1m 1f 170y
3:30 (3:33) (Class 4) (0-85,84) 3-Y-O- **£6,938** (£2,076; £1,038; £519; £258) **Stalls** High

Form RPR
6-60 **1** **Nine Stories (IRE)**[21] 3494 3-9-0 **80** RobertWinston 12 89
(J Howard Johnson) *trckd ldrs: effrt over 1f out: led ins fnl f: rdn out* **12/1**
0604 **2** *3/4* **Ella Woodcock (IRE)**[7] 3947 4-9-8 **78** (p) EddieAhern 1 86
(E J Alston) *hld up: rdn and hdwy on ins over 2f out: chsd wnr wl ins fnl f: r.o* **10/1**
-236 **3** *1 1/4* **Elk Trail (IRE)**[18] 3592 3-8-10 **76** MickyFenton 6 81
(T P Tate) *led to 3f out: rallied and led over 1f out: hdd ins fnl f: one pce* **14/1**
6604 **4** *2* **Vicious Warrior**[9] 3864 9-9-6 **76** DeanMcKeown 7 77
(R M Whitaker) *t.k.h: cl up: led 3f to over 1f out: no ex ins fnl f* **12/1**
0042 **5** *1/2* **Hurlingham**[12] 3795 4-8-10 **69** (b1) JamieMoriarty(3) 10 69
(M W Easterby) *hld up: effrt whn nt clr run briefly over 2f out: effrt over 1f out: sn no imp* **13/2**
0454 **6** *nk* **Collateral Damage (IRE)**[16] 3627 5-9-12 **82** (bt1) DavidAllan 2 81
(T D Easterby) *cl up: effrt and ev ch over 2f out: no ex fnl f* **5/1**[2]
4204 **7** *1/2* **Giant Love (USA)**[10] 3855 3-8-13 **79** JoeFanning 3 77
(M Johnston) *prom: lost pl over 3f out: kpt on fnl f: no imp* **4/1**[1]

The Form Book, Raceform Ltd, Compton, RG20 6NL

0313 **8** *hd* **Wigwam Willie (IRE)**[13] 3758 6-10-0 **84**..................(p) PaulMulrennan 11 82
(K A Ryan) *sn in midfield: lost pl over 2f out: n.d after* **6/1**[3]

056- **9** *1 1/2* **Luna Landing**[139] 6357 5-9-9 **79**.............................. AndrewElliott 8 74
(Jedd O'Keeffe) *hld up: effrt on outside over 2f out: sn btn* **20/1**

4005 **10** *1/2* **Moheebb (IRE)**[7] 3972 4-8-11 **70**....................(b) MichaelJStainton(3) 5 63
(Mrs R A Carr) *hld up: effrt and cl up 3f out: rdn and wknd 2f out* **12/1**

2m 5.32s (-0.08) **Going Correction** +0.125s/f (Good)
WFA 3 from 4yo+ 10lb **10** Ran SP% **107.9**
Speed ratings (Par 105): **105,104,103,101,101 101,100,100,99,99**
toteswinger: 1&2 £24.10, 1&3 £25.20, 2&3 £9.90. CSF £99.80 CT £1068.59 TOTE £16.10: £4.00, £3.10, £4.20; EX 142.20 TRIFECTA Not won..

Owner Transcend Bloodstock LLP **Bred** Stefano Stivali **Trained** Billy Row, Co Durham
■ Demolition was withdrawn (9/2, refused to enter the stalls). R4 applies, deduct 15p in the £.

FOCUS
A fair handicap run at just an ordinary gallop. The third sets the standard.

4205 RIPON BELL-RINGER H'CAP 1m 4f 10y
4:00 (4:03) (Class 2) (0-100,92) 3-Y-O
£11,215 (£3,358; £1,679; £840; £419; £210) **Stalls** High

Form RPR

3212 **1** **Laterly (IRE)**[14] 3719 3-9-7 **92**.............................. MickyFenton 4 102
(T P Tate) *mde all: hrd pressed fr 2f out: styd on gamely fnl f* **10/3**[2]

21-3 **2** *3/4* **Detonator (IRE)**[27] 3294 3-9-5 **90**.............................. JoeFanning 5 99
(M Johnston) *chsd ldrs: effrt and disp ld over 1f out to ins fnl f: kpt on same pce nr fin* **9/2**

4402 **3** *1 3/4* **Celt**[22] 3459 3-8-9 **80**.............................. PatCosgrave 3 86
(L M Cumani) *hld up: hdwy on ins over 2f out: chsng ldrs and swtchd lft over 1f out: one pce ins fnl f* **5/2**[1]

-101 **4** *15* **Jabal Tariq**[30] 3174 3-9-3 **88**.............................. MichaelHills 6 70
(B W Hills) *cl up: ev ch 3f out tl wknd over 1f out* **4/1**[3]

1002 **5** *4* **The Oil Magnate**[9] 3864 3-8-9 **80**.............................. TonyHamilton 2 56
(M Dods) *hld up in tch: drvn 3f out: btn over 1f out* **12/1**

1341 **6** *3 1/2* **Downhiller (IRE)**[16] 3633 3-9-4 **89**.............................. EddieAhern 1 59
(J L Dunlop) *in tch: drvn and outpcd over 3f out: sn n.d* **9/2**

2m 37.21s (0.51) **Going Correction** +0.125s/f (Good) **6** Ran SP% **115.7**
Speed ratings (Par 106): **103,102,101,91,88 86**
toteswinger: 1&2 £3.50, 1&3 £3.40, 2&3 £3.20. CSF £19.17 TOTE £5.30: £2.40, £2.50; EX 19.60.

Owner Mrs Sylvia Clegg **Bred** Gestut Fahrhof Stiftung **Trained** Tadcaster, N Yorks

FOCUS
A decent contest and one in which the pace was fair. The winner is a progressive sort who is sure to win more races with the placed horses close to their marks.

NOTEBOOK
Laterly(IRE) ◆ is a progressive sort who had the run of the race but showed a splendid attitude to notch his third win. He acts on fast and soft ground, should stay further than 1m4f and is a grand sort who is the sort to improve further. (op 4-1)

Detonator(IRE) ◆ is an improving individual who lost little in defeat upped in trip against a more experienced rival who is also a progressive sort. He is very much the type to progress again and is sure to win races this term. (op 3-1 tchd 11-4)

Celt, 3lb higher than at Newmarket, has yet to win a race but was far from disgraced in a race where the leaders did not come back. He is well worth a try over 1m6f and it will be surprising if he cannot win a race this season. (op 11-4 tchd 3-1)

Jabal Tariq, up 7lb in the weights, had won his two previous starts at this course but proved disappointing, especially as he had the run of the race. The return to 1m2f may be more to his liking and he is not one to write off just yet. (op 9-2)

The Oil Magnate, flattered by his proximity to facile winner Boz at Doncaster on his previous start, was well beaten for the third time in handicaps. He has something to prove at present. (op 14-1)

Downhiller(IRE), who turned in a career best at Newbury on his previous start, looked in good shape but proved a disappointment from this 5lb higher mark. He was beaten a long way out but is worth another chance. Official explanation: jockey said colt was unsuited by the good ground (op 6-1 tchd 13-2)

4206 GO RACING IN YORKSHIRE SUMMER FESTIVAL H'CAP 1m
4:35 (4:37) (Class 4) (0-85,85) 3-Y-O- **£6,938** (£2,076; £1,038; £519; £258) **Stalls** High

Form RPR

3134 **1** **Hula Ballew**[24] 3366 8-9-3 **77**.............................. NeilBrown(3) 11 86
(M Dods) *trckd ldrs: rdn to ld over 1f out: kpt on strly fnl f* **5/1**[2]

5031 **2** *2 1/4* **Rainbow Mirage (IRE)**[9] 3887 4-9-12 **83**.............................. FergalLynch 10 87+
(E S McMahon) *hld up: nt clr run over 2f out: hdwy over 1f out: chsd wnr ins fnl f: r.o* **9/4**[1]

4303 **3** *2 1/4* **My Paris**[30] 3173 7-10-0 **85**.............................. TonyHamilton 4 84
(Ollie Pears) *pressed ldr: led over 3f tl over 1f out: kpt on same pce fnl f* **10/1**

0051 **4** *nk* **Blue Spinnaker (IRE)**[7] 3972 9-9-5 **83**.............................. BradleyRoper(7) 3 81+
(M W Easterby) *dwlt: bhd: effrt whn n.m.r over 2f out: swtchd rt and hdwy over 1f out: n.m.r ins fnl f: kpt on fin* **9/1**

3645 **5** *3/4* **Bere Davis (FR)**[7] 3969 3-8-11 **76**..................(b[1]) PatCosgrave 1 70
(P D Evans) *t.k.h: cl up: effrt and ev ch over 1f out: sn no ex* **20/1**

2305 **6** *1 3/4* **Nevada Desert (IRE)**[15] 3664 8-9-5 **76**.............................. PaulMulrennan 9 68
(R M Whitaker) *hld up: n.m.r fr 3f to over 1f out: nvr rchd ldrs* **17/2**[3]

-062 **7** *2* **Almoutaz (USA)**[18] 3592 3-9-4 **83**.............................. MichaelHills 5 69
(B W Hills) *hld up in tch: effrt over 2f out: edgd rt and no ex over 1f out* **5/1**[2]

5503 **8** *2* **Charlie Tipple**[24] 3366 4-9-4 **75**..................(p) TomEaves 7 58
(T D Easterby) *towards rr: drvn and outpcd over 3f out: n.d after* **17/2**[3]

1-06 **9** *5* **Flight To Quality**[8] 3899 3-8-11 **76**.............................. JoeFanning 2 46
(M Johnston) *sn niggled in rr: short-lived effrt over 2f out: sn wknd* **14/1**

10-0 **10** *2* **Apollo Shark (IRE)**[35] 3048 3-9-2 **81**.............................. RobertWinston 8 46
(J Howard Johnson) *in tch tl wknd over 3f out* **22/1**

5-2 **11** *9* **Celtic Strand (IRE)**[51] 2539 3-8-11 **76**.............................. MickyFenton 6 20
(T P Tate) *led to over 3f out: wknd fr 2f out* **10/1**

1m 42.47s (1.07) **Going Correction** +0.125s/f (Good)
WFA 3 from 4yo+ 8lb **11** Ran SP% **129.1**
Speed ratings (Par 105): **99,96,94,94,93 91,89,87,82,80 71**
toteswinger: 1&2 £5.40, 1&3 £13.00, 2&3 £7.20. CSF £18.42 CT £119.97 TOTE £7.40: £2.60, £1.40, £3.70; EX 24.10 Trifecta £232.90 Part won. Pool: £314.80 - 0.70 winning units..

Owner Mrs J W Hutchinson & Mrs P A Knox **Bred** T K & Mrs P A Knox **Trained** Denton, Co Durham

FOCUS
Mainly exposed performers in this reasonable handicap. The pace was sound and the runner-up is rated to his latest mark.

4207 GORACING.CO.UK MAIDEN H'CAP 6f
5:05 (5:07) (Class 5) (0-70,69) 3-Y-O+ **£3,885** (£1,156; £577; £288) **Stalls** Low

Form RPR

5-22 **1** **Frisbee**[11] 3818 4-9-7 **59**.............................. RobertWinston 10 78
(C J Teague) *trckd stands' side ldrs: led that gp 2f out: rdn and r.o strly fnl f* **15/2**[3]

-600 **2** *2* **Tyrannosaurus Rex (IRE)**[93] 1416 4-8-11 **52**.............................. PJMcDonald(3) 3 65
(D Shaw) *prom stands' side: effrt and chsd wnr over 1f out: kpt on fnl f: nt rch wnr: 2nd of 12 in gp* **14/1**

5003 **3** *7* **Miss Taboo (IRE)**[14] 3712 4-8-11 **52**.............................. JamieMoriarty(3) 12 43
(P T Midgley) *dwlt: bhd stands' side: hdwy over 1f out: r.o: no ch w first two: 3rd of 12 in gp* **16/1**

-054 **4** *nse* **Lake Sabina**[32] 3111 3-9-7 **69**.............................. PatrickDonaghy(5) 7 58
(E S McMahon) *prom: effrt over 2f out: one pce over 1f out: 4th of 12 in gp* **4/1**[1]

66-6 **5** *shd* **Invincible Rose (IRE)**[158] 534 3-8-2 **45**.............................. TWilliams 6 34
(M Brittain) *bhd stands' side tl hdwy over 1f out: nrst fin: 5th of 12 in gp* **50/1**

-003 **6** *2 3/4* **Uace Mac**[7] 3977 4-9-3 **55**.............................. DavidAllan 1 36
(N Bycroft) *cl up stands' side: ev ch tl no ex over 1f out: 6th of 12 in gp* **14/1**

0005 **7** *1/2* **Lady Fas (IRE)**[15] 3695 5-8-0 **45**.............................. StacyRenwick(7) 19 25
(A W Carroll) *bmpd s: bhd far side: hdwy on outside over 2f out: led that gp towards fin: no ch w stands' side: 1st of 8 in gp* **18/1**

0050 **8** *3/4* **Kool Katie**[33] 3081 3-9-0 **57**.............................. TonyHamilton 15 33
(Mrs G S Rees) *prom far side: effrt over 2f out: one pce fnl f: 2nd of 8 in gp* **20/1**

3000 **9** *hd* **Flying Sommelier (USA)**[12] 3790 3-8-12 **58**.............................. NeilBrown(3) 17 34
(T D Barron) *led far side: rdn over 2f out: nt pce of stands' side and hdd that gp towards fin: 3rd of 8 in gp* **16/1**

0000 **10** *3/4* **Naledi**[12] 3796 4-8-0 **45**.............................. JamieKyne(7) 4 19
(J R Norton) *towards rr stands' side: drvn 1/2-way: n.d: 7th of 12 in gp* **33/1**

0566 **11** *1 1/2* **Curio**[38] 2928 3-8-6 **49**..................(p) DeanMcKeown 13 17
(R M Whitaker) *in tch far side: drvn over 2f out: one pce over 1f out: 4th of 8 in gp* **16/1**

-204 **12** *nse* **Tugalu (IRE)**[29] 3231 3-9-4 **68**..................(p) ClGillies(7) 2 36
(K A Ryan) *led stands' side to 2f out: sn wknd: 8th of 12 in gp* **6/1**[2]

06-0 **13** *2 3/4* **Bettys Touch**[51] 2549 3-8-9 **52**.............................. TonyCulhane 20 12
(W J Musson) *hld up far side: pushed along 2f out: nvr rchd ldrs: 5th of 8 in gp* **16/1**

0000 **14** *1/2* **Wooden King (IRE)**[1] 4163 3-8-9 **52** ow2.............................. PatCosgrave 16 10
(P D Evans) *cl up far side tl wknd over 1f out: 6th of 8 in gp* **16/1**

0000 **15** *2 1/4* **Best Suited**[31] 3139 3-8-5 **48**..................(p) PaulFessey 5 —
(J J Quinn) *bhd stands' side: drvn 1/2-way: nvr on terms: 9th of 12 in gp* **25/1**

4642 **16** *5* **Buzbury Rings**[16] 3638 4-9-3 **55**.............................. FergalLynch 11 —
(R E Barr) *midfield on outside of stands' side gp: rdn 1/2-way: sn btn: 10th of 12 in gp* **15/2**[3]

-506 **17** *1* **Noche De Reyes**[7] 3958 3-8-8 **51** ow2.............................. MickyFenton 8 —
(E J Alston) *bhd and pushed along stands' side: hung rt 1/2-way: nvr on terms: 11th of 12 in gp* **40/1**

4650 **18** *1* **This Ones For Eddy**[42] 2823 3-9-7 **64**.............................. LeeEnstone 14 —
(S Parr) *cl up far side tl wknd over 2f out: 7th of 8 in gp* **16/1**

0004 **19** *3/4* **Saafend Geezer**[7] 3953 3-8-7 **50**..................(v) PaulMulrennan 9 —
(A Berry) *dwlt: a bhd stands' side: last of 12 in gp* **25/1**

4000 **20** *7* **Mujada**[3] 4076 3-8-5 **48**..................(b[1]) JoeFanning 18 —
(M Brittain) *wnt bdly rt s: sn wl bhd far side: last of 8 in gp* **20/1**

1m 15.3s (2.30) **Going Correction** +0.125s/f (Good)
WFA 3 from 4yo+ 5lb **20** Ran SP% **136.3**
Speed ratings (Par 103): **89,86,77,76,76 73,72,71,71,70 68,68,64,63,60 54,52,51,50,41**
toteswinger: 1&2 £19.30, 1&3 £18.20, 2&3 £41.60. CSF £109.47 CT £1730.06 TOTE £6.60: £1.70, £3.40, £3.50, £2.10; EX 187.00 TRIFECTA Not won. Place 6 £303.43, Place 5 £171.96.

Owner G T Carlton **Bred** Burton Agnes Stud Co Ltd **Trained** Station Town, Co Durham
■ Stewards' Enquiry : T Williams caution: careless riding

FOCUS
A modest handicap in which the larger stands' side group held a large advantage over the far-side bunch. The runner-up has form that suggests this could rate higher though there is little solid behind.

This Ones For Eddy Official explanation: jockey said gelding lost a front shoe
T/Plt: £599.40 to a £1 stake. Pool: £59,580.16. 72.56 winning tickets. T/Qpdt: £173.70 to a £1 stake. Pool: £3,474.09. 14.80 winning tickets. RY

4208 - 4211a (Foreign Racing) - See Raceform Interactive

3774
MAISONS-LAFFITTE (R-H)
Saturday, July 19

OFFICIAL GOING: Good

4212a PRIX MESSIDOR (GROUP 3) (STRAIGHT COURSE) 1m (S)
3:15 (3:15) 3-Y-O+ **£29,412** (£11,765; £8,824; £5,882; £2,941)

RPR

1 **Racinger (FR)**[135] 818 5-9-1 .... DBonilla 4 115
(F Head, France) *mde virtually all: set stdy pce: qcknd 2 1/2f out: rdn over 1f out: rdn out* **89/10**

2 *1 1/2* **Spirito Del Vento (FR)**[32] 3100 5-9-5 .... OPeslier 6 116
(J-M Beguigne, France) *hld up in 7th: rdn 2f out: hdwy towards centre to go 2nd over 1f out: styd on but a hld* **28/10**[2]

3 *2* **Chopastair (FR)**[56] 7-9-1 .... J-BEyquem 9 107
(T Lemer, France) *racd in 2nd to over 1f out: kpt on at one pce* **21/1**

4 *3/4* **Toque De Queda**[28] 4-8-11 .... TThulliez 8 101
(M Delzangles, France) *midfield: styd on at same pce fnl 1 1/2f* **19/1**

5 *1/2* **Indian Daffodil (IRE)**[25] 3356 3-8-11 .... C-PLemaire 5 108
(J-C Rouget, France) *trckd wnr in 3rd: one pce fnl 2f* **43/10**[3]

6 *1* **Crossharbour**[35] 3053 4-9-5 .... SPasquier 3 106
(A Fabre, France) *hld up in 5th: effrt over 1 1/2f out: nt qckn* **19/10**[1]

7 *snk* **Alamanni (USA)**[27] 4-8-11 .... ASanna 7 97
(E Borromeo, Italy) *hld up in last: hrd rdn on outside 2f out: kpt on at same pce* **20/1**

8 *3/4* **Light Green (BRZ)**[112] 1088 4-8-10 .... CSoumillon 2 95
(A De Royer-Dupre, France) *a in rr* **84/10**

9 10 **Salsalavie (FR)**[29] 3244 3-8-7 .... TJarnet 1 77
(P Demercastel, France) *prom early: sn restrained in midfield: outpcd fnl 2f* **41/1**

1m 35.7s (-6.60) **Going Correction** -0.50s/f (Hard)
WFA 3 from 4yo+ 8lb **9** Ran SP% **117.1**
Speed ratings: **113,111,109,108,108 107,107,106,96**
PARI-MUTUEL: WIN 9.90; PL 2.60, 1.60, 4.20; DF 15.60.
Owner Hamdan Al Maktoum **Bred** Mrs Renee Geffroy **Trained** France

NOTEBOOK
Racinger(FR), at the head of affairs from the start, injected pace at the furlong marker and sprinted clear to win with something in hand. This was an excellent performance as the five-year-old had not been out since racing at Nad al Sheba in March. He has now fully justified the price he fetched in last year's Arc sale. He can only come on from this race and connections are now looking at the Jacques Le Marois at Deauville.
Spirito Del Vento(FR) appears to show his best on right-handed tracks and never looked like catching the winner on this occasion. As usual he was held up in the early stages and even looked a little caught for speed when things were quickened at the furlong marker. He then stayed on one-paced. A rest is now on the cards and he will be prepared to win another Daniel Wildenstein in early October.
Chopastair(FR) was well up with the winner for much of the race and battled on in the final stages to hold third position. He is not really up to this quality of race.
Toque De Queda, who raced just behind the leaders, was virtually always in the same position and one-paced during the final furlong.

3638 REDCAR (L-H)
Sunday, July 20

OFFICIAL GOING: Good (good to firm in places; 8.7)
Wind: Fresh, half-against. Weather: overcast

4213 EUROPEAN BREEDERS' FUND MAIDEN STKS (DIV I) 7f
1:50 (1:54) (Class 5) 2-Y-O **£3,399** (£1,011; £505; £252) **Stalls** Centre

Form RPR
1 **Courageous (IRE)** 2-9-3 0 .... TedDurcan 4 76+
(B Smart) *hmpd s: hld up towards rr: gd hdwy over 2f out: rdn ent fnl f: styd on to ld nr line* **15/8**[1]
03 2 *shd* **Thunderball**[22] 3476 2-9-3 0 .... WilliamBuick 1 75
(A J McCabe) *wnt rt s: sn prom: chal 2f out and sn rdn: stmbld over 1f out: drvn to ld and edgd rt last 100yds: hdd nr line* **4/1**[3]
3 *3 1/2* **Justonefortheroad** 2-9-3 0 .... FergalLynch 5 67+
(N J Vaughan) *wnt lft s: trckd ldrs: smooth hdwy to ld 2f out: rdn ent fnl f: hdd: drvn and hld whn hmpd last 100yds* **5/2**[2]
4 *2 1/2* **Graycliffe (IRE)** 2-9-3 0 .... PatCosgrave 8 60
(D J G Murray Smith) *cl up: led 1/2-way: rdn along and hdd 2f out: sn drvn and wknd* **40/1**
5 *2 1/4* **Quanah Parker (IRE)** 2-9-0 0 .... MichaelJStainton[(3)] 2 54+
(R M Whitaker) *sltly hmpd s: sn trcking ldrs: rdn over 2f out and kpt on same pce* **16/1**
6 *nk* **Magic Haze** 2-9-3 0 .... AndrewElliott 6 54+
(Miss S E Hall) *in tch: hdwy to chse ldrs 2f out: sn rdn and no imp* **50/1**
0 7 *2 3/4* **Classic Contours (USA)**[34] 3078 2-9-3 0 .... RobertWinston 12 47
(G A Swinbank) *cl up: rdn along over 2f out and grad wknd* **12/1**
40 8 *3* **Pilot Light**[9] 3926 2-9-3 0 .... DavidAllan 9 39
(T D Easterby) *rdn along in rr 1/2-way: nvr a factor* **20/1**
0 9 *1 1/2* **Franali (IRE)**[18] 3597 2-8-12 0 .... TonyHamilton 3 31
(R F Fisher) *wnt lft s: a towards rr* **66/1**
0 10 *1 1/4* **Fizzy Friend**[74] 1907 2-8-12 0 .... DarryllHolland 10 27
(J R Weymes) *a towards rr* **50/1**
11 *1 3/4* **Berriedale** 2-8-12 0 .... RoystonFfrench 7 23
(Mrs A Duffield) *a towards rr* **25/1**
0 12 *5* **El Guevara (IRE)**[33] 3107 2-9-3 0 .... NCallan 11 16
(K A Ryan) *led to 1/2-way: sn rdn along and wknd* **25/1**

1m 28.75s (4.25) **Going Correction** +0.275s/f (Good) **12** Ran SP% **117.2**
Speed ratings (Par 94): **86,85,81,79,76 76,72,69,67,66 64,58**
toteswinger: 1&2 £2.10, 1&3 £2.60, 2&3 £2.50. CSF £8.70 TOTE £2.70: £1.20, £1.60, £1.50; EX 8.80.
Owner H E Sheikh Rashid Bin Mohammed **Bred** Yeomanstown Lodge Stud **Trained** Hambleton, N Yorks
■ Stewards' Enquiry : William Buick two-day ban: used whip with excessive frequency down shoulder in forehand position (Aug 7,8)

FOCUS
An ordinary maiden best rated around the runner-up. It was the slower of the two divisions by 1.28sec.

NOTEBOOK
Courageous(IRE), who cost 230,000euros, is out of a mare who won twice over 7f at three. The subject of good reports, he was sent off favourite on this debut and got the job done, albeit narrowly, from a more experienced rival. The bare form is nothing to get carried away with, but he looks bound to improve. (op 9-4 tchd 3-1)
Thunderball, third to Doctor Crane, who won a fair race at Newbury on Saturday, at Doncaster last time out, set a standard to aim at and ran well in defeat. Whether he improved greatly on his Doncaster effort is open to question, though. (op 7-2 tchd 3-1)
Justonefortheroad, whose dam was a sprint winner at two in France, was well supported. He travelled well to the front and looked likely to be tough to beat, but was weakening when hampered inside the last. He would have finished closer without that interference and he should not be long in winning in similar company. (op 7-2 tchd 6-4)
Graycliffe(IRE), whose dam is a sister to Tycoon Todd, a prolific winner in the US, showed up well for a long way and should benefit from the outing. (op 33-1)
Quanah Parker(IRE), a half-brother to eight winners including Lochbuie, a high-class multiple middle-distance winner, is out of a mare who won over 1m6f, but his sire Namid is an influence for speed. (op 10-1 tchd 9-1)
Magic Haze, a half-sister to Meeting Of Minds, a winner over a mile, is a May foal and is likely to do better in time. (op 66-1)
Pilot Light is now eligible to run in nurseries. (op 22-1 tchd 25-1)

4214 EUROPEAN BREEDERS' FUND MAIDEN STKS (DIV II) 7f
2:20 (2:20) (Class 5) 2-Y-O **£3,399** (£1,011; £505; £252) **Stalls** Centre

Form RPR
0 1 **Quatermain**[29] 3245 2-9-3 0 .... TomEaves 5 76+
(B Smart) *hmpd s: sn trcking ldrs: t.k.h: led jst ins fnl f: hld on wl* **20/1**
5 2 *nk* **Mannlichen**[31] 3164 2-9-3 0 .... JoeFanning 8 75
(M Johnston) *dwlt: sn w ldrs: led over 2f out tl jst ins fnl f: kpt on wl* **14/1**
3 *nk* **Henderson Park** 2-9-0 0 .... PJMcDonald[(3)] 11 75
(A G Foster) *chsd ldrs: kpt on wl ins fnl f* **80/1**
4 4 *1 1/4* **Stirling Castle**[20] 3568 2-9-3 0 .... TedDurcan 2 71
(M J Wallace) *sn outpcd and in rr: hdwy 2f out: styd on steadily ins fnl f* **7/1**[3]
5 *1 1/4* **Heading East (IRE)** 2-9-3 0 .... NCallan 7 68
(K A Ryan) *trckd ldrs: effrt over 1f out: kpt on same pce* **16/1**
632 6 *nk* **Tropical Blue**[18] 3597 2-9-3 0 .... PaulMulrennan 6 68
(Jennie Candlish) *chsd ldrs: one pce appr fnl f* **10/1**
6 7 *2 1/2* **Shaker Style (USA)**[35] 3055 2-9-3 0 .... JimmyQuinn 4 61
(J D Bethell) *hmpd s: hld up: nt clr run and swtchd lft over 1f out: wknd jst ins fnl f* **16/1**
33 8 *1 3/4* **Custard Cream Kid (IRE)**[45] 2746 2-9-3 0 .... PaulHanagan 1 57
(R A Fahey) *in rr: hdwy over 2f out: hung lft and wknd 1f out* **11/2**[2]
623 9 *4 1/2* **Mohanad (IRE)**[21] 3519 2-9-3 0 .... DarryllHolland 9 46
(M R Channon) *led: rdn 3f out: hdd over 2f out: wkng whn faltered appr fnl f* **5/6**[1]
00 10 *4 1/2* **Dark Moment**[24] 3411 2-9-3 0 .... DaleGibson 3 34
(A Dickman) *wnt rt s: sn chsng ldrs on outer: hung lft and lost pl over 1f out* **40/1**

1m 27.47s (2.97) **Going Correction** +0.275s/f (Good) **10** Ran SP% **118.4**
Speed ratings (Par 94): **94,93,93,91,90 90,87,85,80,74**
toteswinger: 1&2 £19.20, 1&3 £61.50, 2&3 £77.50. CSF £271.73 TOTE £22.40: £3.40, £2.90, £13.40; EX 398.30.
Owner Prime Equestrian **Bred** Gestut Friedrichsruh **Trained** Hambleton, N Yorks

FOCUS
A fair maiden and the faster of the two divisions by 1.28sec.

NOTEBOOK
Quatermain, thought good enough to start off in the Chesham, where he finished down the field, had clearly come on for that experience and found this company less daunting. He stayed on really well and, being by Peintre Celebre, will have little trouble getting a mile this season. (op 12-1)
Mannlichen, whose dam was a dual middle-distance winner at three, improved on his debut effort, showing up well from early on and battling on well to the line. He is clearly going the right way and should not be long in going one better. (op 10-1)
Henderson Park, whose dam won over 7f at two and is a half-sister to high-class hurdler Blazing Bailey, kept on well in the closing stages to make the frame, belying his long odds. He looks one for nurseries later in the season. (op 66-1)
Stirling Castle struggled to go the early gallop but stayed on well to be nearest at the finish. He will be suited by a mile as well. (op 8-1 tchd 13-2)
Heading East(IRE), a half-brother to Kafuu, a winner over 6f at two and later over 7f, and Naughty Frida, who also won over 6f at two and has since scored over 1m, cost 130,000gns at the breeze-ups and shaped encouragingly on his debut. (op 10-1)
Mohanad(IRE), beaten at long odds-on last time, again cost his supporters dearly, running his worst race to date. He looks one to leave alone at present. Official explanation: trainer had no explanation for the poor form shown (op 10-11)

4215 ALAN BURGESS MEMORIAL H'CAP 1m 1f
2:50 (2:51) (Class 6) (0-60,60) 3-Y-O+ **£2,266** (£674; £337; £168) **Stalls** Low

Form RPR
5042 1 **Lauro**[34] 3077 8-9-0 58 .... DawnRankin[(7)] 4 68
(Miss J A Camacho) *trckd ldrs: hdwy over 2f out: rdn over 1f out: swtchd ins ent fnl f: styd on u.p to ld last 50yds* **6/1**[3]
4006 2 *nk* **Evelith Regent (IRE)**[20] 3550 5-9-9 60 .... RobertWinston 5 69
(G A Swinbank) *led: qcknd over 3f out: rdn 2f out: drvn ins fnl f: hdd and no ex last 50yds* **6/1**[3]
0146 3 *2* **Boy Dancer (IRE)**[20] 3557 5-9-2 56 .... JamieMoriarty[(3)] 2 61
(J J Quinn) *trckd ldrs on inner: swtchd rt and hdwy over 2f out: sn rdn and styd on u.p ins fnl f: nrst fin* **5/1**[2]
563 4 *3/4* **Malinsa Blue (IRE)**[17] 3644 6-9-5 56 ....(p) J-PGuillambert 12 59
(B Ellison) *trckd ldng pair: hdwy to chse ldr over 3f out: rdn 2f out: drvn over 1f out: kpt on same pce ins fnl f* **13/2**
6463 5 *3* **Valdan (IRE)**[14] 3755 4-9-6 57 ....(t) AdrianTNicholls 9 54
(M A Barnes) *hld up in rr: swtchd outside and smooth hdwy over 3f out: chsd ldrs 2f out: rdn and one pce appr fnl f* **8/1**
4041 6 *nk* **Libre**[9] 3903 8-9-8 59 .... TomEaves 11 55
(F Jordan) *trckd ldrs: hdwy 3f out: rdn 2f out: drvn and one pce appr fnl f* **4/1**[1]
10P6 7 *1 1/4* **Jarvo**[5] 4066 7-9-6 57 ....(v) PatrickMathers 7 50
(I W McInnes) *t.k.h: hld up towards rr: effrt over 3f out: sn rdn and no imp fnl 2f* **25/1**
0606 8 *1 3/4* **Farne Island**[19] 3579 5-9-1 52 .... PaulMulrennan 14 41
(Micky Hammond) *hld up in rr: sme hdwy 3f out: sn rdn along and nvr a factor* **22/1**
0403 9 *1 3/4* **Roman History (IRE)**[30] 3230 5-9-6 57 ....(p) SilvestreDeSousa 3 43
(Miss Tracy Waggott) *cl up: rdn along over 3f out and sn wknd* **10/1**
2304 10 *3/4* **Penel (IRE)**[16] 3662 7-9-4 55 ....(p) MickyFenton 6 39
(P T Midgley) *hld up: effrt and sme hdwy 4f out: sn rdn along and nvr a factor* **12/1**
0000 11 *2* **Social Rhythm**[25] 3366 4-9-1 55 .... PJMcDonald[(3)] 15 35
(A C Whillans) *a in rr* **25/1**

1m 55.13s (2.13) **Going Correction** +0.175s/f (Good) **11** Ran SP% **118.5**
Speed ratings (Par 101): **97,96,94,94,91 91,90,88,87,86 84**
toteswinger: 1&2 £8.30, 1&3 £5.40, 2&3 £9.90. CSF £41.14 CT £166.88 TOTE £5.80: £2.50, £2.30, £1.90; EX 49.90.
Owner Miss Julie Camacho **Bred** Mrs S Camacho **Trained** Norton, N Yorks

FOCUS
A moderate affair run at an ordinary gallop, and it proved difficult to make up ground from off the pace.

4216 SKYBET SUPPORTING THE YORKSHIRE RACING FESTIVAL H'CAP 5f
3:20 (3:22) (Class 5) (0-70,70) 3-Y-O **£2,914** (£867; £433; £216) **Stalls** Centre

Form RPR
0040 1 **Braille**[10] 3868 3-9-2 65 .... PaulMulrennan 8 71
(T D Walford) *a.p: effrt to ld wl over 1f out and sn rdn: drvn ins fnl f and kpt on wl* **10/1**
4260 2 *1* **Grudge**[12] 3811 3-9-0 63 .... RobertWinston 10 65+
(D W Barker) *dwlt and in rr: hdwy 2f out: sn rdn and styd on strly ins fnl f: nrst fin* **8/1**[3]
2226 3 *hd* **Kyzer Chief**[18] 3600 3-9-2 65 .... RoystonFfrench 11 66
(R E Barr) *in tch: rdn along 1/2-way: hdwy u.p over 1f out: styd on strly ins fnl f* **9/1**
250 4 *hd* **Cheshire Rose**[7] 4000 3-8-9 65 .... DeanHeslop[(7)] 6 66
(T D Barron) *a.p: effrt 2f out: sn rdn and ev ch tl drvn ins fnl f and no ex last 100yds* **14/1**
3610 5 *nk* **Bishopbriggs (USA)**[12] 3819 3-9-7 70 .... LeeEnstone 3 69
(S Parr) *chsd ldrs: hdwy over 2f out: sn rdn and ev ch tl drvn and nt qckn ins fnl f* **11/1**

-050 **6** 1 ½ **Mystickhill (IRE)**[16] 3686 3-8-7 **59** ..... TolleyDean(3) 7 53
(J Balding) *towards rr: hdwy 2f out: sn rdn and styd on ins fnl f: nrst fin* **14/1**

010 **7** 1 ¼ **Royal Grace**[29] 3260 3-8-11 **60** ..... DavidAllan 1 50
(T D Easterby) *towards rr: hdwy 2f out: rdn to chse ldrs over 1f out: sn drvn and no imp ins fnl f* **9/1**

0621 **8** 2 ¼ **Foreign Rhythm (IRE)**[8] 3955 3-8-11 **60** .....(v) KimTinkler 16 40
(N Tinkler) *towards rr: rdn along 2f out: sn no imp* **9/1**

0600 **9** hd **Abitofafath (IRE)**[16] 3686 3-8-5 **54** .....(b) DeanMcKeown 4 33
(J G Given) *led: rdn along over 2f out: drvn and hdd wl over 1f out: wknd* **40/1**

-001 **10** ½ **Choisette**[16] 3665 3-9-5 **68** ..... TomEaves 13 45
(B Smart) *chsd ldrs: rdn along over 2f out: sn drvn and wknd* **7/2**[1]

0000 **11** 4 **Lovely Lilling**[15] 3712 3-8-2 **51** oh6 ..... PaulFessey 2 14
(P T Midgley) *a towards rr* **100/1**

5-50 **12** 3 ¼ **Do As I Say**[15] 3712 3-9-2 **65** ..... TedDurcan 9 16
(T D Easterby) *dwlt: sn rdn along and a in rr* **20/1**

3032 **13** 1 **Handsinthemist (IRE)**[21] 3526 3-8-4 **53** .....(p) FrankieMcDonald 15 —
(P T Midgley) *in tch on outer: rdn along 1/2-way and sn wknd* **7/1**[2]

1400 **14** hd **Orange Square (IRE)**[6] 4013 3-8-7 **56** ..... TonyHamilton 14 3
(D W Barker) *in tch on outer: rdn along 1/2-way and sn wknd* **25/1**

-255 **15** 4 ½ **Linnet Park**[43] 2823 3-8-8 **57** .....(b[1]) PatCosgrave 5 —
(J G Given) *prom: rdn along over 2f out and sn wknd* **12/1**

59.88 secs (1.28) **Going Correction** +0.275s/f (Good) **15** Ran SP% **126.3**
Speed ratings (Par 100): **100,98,98,97,97 94,92,88,88,87 80,75,74,73,66**
toteswinger: 1&2 £11.90, 1&3 £11.70, 2&3 £9.90. CSF £88.83 CT £768.97 TOTE £13.00: £4.30, £3.10, £3.20; EX 85.80.
Owner Mrs R J Mitchell **Bred** Beechgrove Stud Farm Ltd **Trained** Sheriff Hutton, N Yorks
■ Stewards' Enquiry : Dean Heslop caution: used whip down shoulder in forehand position

FOCUS
An ordinary sprint handicap run at a good gallop.
Handsinthemist(IRE) Official explanation: trainer said filly was found to be in season

4217 WEDDINGS AT REDCAR CLAIMING STKS 1m 2f

3:50 (3:52) (Class 6) 3-Y-O+ **£2,388** (£705; £352) **Stalls** Low

Form RPR

4-31 **1** **Tufton**[59] 2335 5-9-12 78 ..... StephenDonohoe 4 71
(Ian Williams) *bmpd s: hld up in tch: effrt 4f out: chal over 1f out: styd on to ld ins fnl f* **9/4**[1]

4311 **2** ½ **Little Jimbob**[8] 3954 7-9-9 73 ..... PaulHanagan 3 67
(R A Fahey) *led: hdd and no ex ins fnl f* **5/2**[2]

4260 **3** ½ **Seyaadi**[8] 3957 6-9-6 60 .....(p) DeanMcKeown 1 63
(Miss Tracy Waggott) *hld up in rr: stdy hdwy over 2f out: styd on wl ins fnl f* **20/1**

6000 **4** 1 **Bright Sun (IRE)**[16] 3666 7-9-3 52 .....(p) KimTinkler 8 58
(N Tinkler) *sn chsng ldrs: kpt on same pce fnl f* **33/1**

00-0 **5** 4 ½ **Diktatorial**[48] 2658 6-9-6 72 ..... RobertWinston 2 52
(J Howard Johnson) *hld up in rr: hdwy 3f out: hmpd and swtchd rt ins fnl f: nvr on terms* **12/1**

0342 **6** ½ **Rowan Lodge (IRE)**[30] 3230 6-9-0 62 .....(b) JamieMoriarty(3) 13 48
(Ollie Pears) *trckd ldrs: t.k.h: rdn over 2f out: edgd lft and wknd appr fnl f* **7/1**

2340 **7** nse **Nabir (FR)**[60] 654 8-9-0 50 .....(p) TomEaves 7 45
(P D Niven) *chsd ldrs: drvn 4f out: one pce* **33/1**

-400 **8** 3 ¼ **Miss Havisham (IRE)**[58] 2364 4-8-10 42 ..... DarryllHolland 9 34
(J R Weymes) *in rr: sme hdwy over 3f out: nvr on terms* **28/1**

0060 **9** 3 ¼ **College Land Boy**[18] 3602 4-9-2 45 ..... PaulMulrennan 12 34
(A Kirtley) *swtchd lft after s: sn mid-div: lost pl over 2f out* **66/1**

-050 **10** 8 **Miss Percy**[39] 2940 4-8-10 45 .....(p) PatrickMathers 6 12
(I W McInnes) *wnt lft s: t.k.h in rr: drvn over 4f out: sn wknd* **80/1**

52-5 **11** 4 **Torrens (IRE)**[22] 3474 6-9-6 74 ..... RichardEvans(5) 11 19
(Ollie Pears) *trckd ldrs: effrt over 3f out: edgd rt and lost pl over 2f out* **5/1**[3]

0200 **12** 16 **Lewis Lloyd (IRE)**[14] 3755 5-8-10 52 ..... BMcHugh(7) 10 —
(R E Barr) *s.v.s: hdwy into midfield over 4f out: sn lost pl: bhd and eased ins fnl f* **28/1**

2m 8.16s (1.06) **Going Correction** +0.175s/f (Good) **12** Ran SP% **116.5**
Speed ratings (Par 101): **102,101,101,100,96 96,96,93,91,84 81,68**
toteswinger: 1&2 £3.10, 1&3 £13.00, 2&3 £10.30. CSF £7.17 TOTE £3.30: £1.50, £1.40, £5.90; EX 8.60.Tufton was claimed by R. A. Fahey for £16,000.
Owner Dr Marwan Koukash **Bred** Gainsborough Stud Management Ltd **Trained** Portway, Worcs
■ Stewards' Enquiry : Jamie Moriarty two-day ban: careless riding (Aug 3,4)

FOCUS
A fair claimer.
Torrens(IRE) Official explanation: jockey said gelding had a breathing problem

4218 K D FLAVELL 50TH ANNIVERSARY H'CAP 6f

4:20 (4:21) (Class 4) (0-85,85) 3-Y-O+ **£4,857** (£1,445; £722; £360) **Stalls** Centre

Form RPR

0060 **1** **Wyatt Earp (IRE)**[12] 3812 7-9-6 **75** .....(b) PaulHanagan 3 88
(R A Fahey) *trckd ldrs: swtchd rt and hdwy 2f out: rdn to ld 1f out: styd on wl fnl f* **11/2**[3]

2363 **2** 2 **Alexander Huricane (IRE)**[16] 3668 4-9-2 **71** .....(p) NCallan 8 78
(K A Ryan) *sn led: rdn 2f out: drvn and hdd 1f out: kpt on u.p ins fnl f* **9/2**[2]

0404 **3** hd **First Order**[19] 3594 7-9-9 **78** .....(v) TomEaves 7 84
(Miss L A Perratt) *trckd ldrs: effrt to chal 2f out: sn rdn and ev ch tl drvn and nt qckn wl ins fnl f* **16/1**

2300 **4** ½ **Glasshoughton**[12] 3812 5-9-11 **80** ..... PaulMulrennan 6 84
(M Dods) *t.k.h: hld up towards rr: hdwy 2f out: rdn over 1f out: styd on wl fnl f: nrst fin* **16/1**

0660 **5** ¾ **Cornus**[17] 3626 6-9-6 **75** .....(be) PatCosgrave 9 77
(A J McCabe) *chsd ldrs: rdn wl over 1f out: kpt on same pce u.p ins fnl f* **10/1**

5012 **6** 4 **Steel City Boy (IRE)**[3] 4117 5-8-5 **65** ..... AnnStokell(5) 12 54
(Miss A Stokell) *swtchd lft after 1f and sn prom: rdn along 2f out: grad wknd* **10/1**

1631 **7** 2 **Baybshambles (IRE)**[19] 3594 4-8-13 **68** ..... RoystonFfrench 5 51
(R E Barr) *in tch: effrt to chse ldrs wl over 1f out: sn rdn and btn* **6/1**

6006 **8** 1 **Ingleby Arch (USA)**[12] 3812 5-9-12 **81** ..... PaulFessey 10 61
(T D Barron) *racd wd: prom tl rdn along 1/2-way and sn wknd* **9/1**

0421 **9** 1 **Prince Hamlet (IRE)**[43] 2842 3-9-11 **85** .....(b) TedDurcan 1 61
(B Smart) *trckd ldrs: effrt over 2f out: sn rdn and btn: eased fnl f* **7/2**[1]

-005 **10** 3 ¼ **Elkhorn**[19] 3581 6-9-3 **72** .....(b) TonyHamilton 4 38
(Miss J A Camacho) *dwlt: a in rr* **11/1**

1500 **11** 4 ½ **Pacific Pride**[26] 3336 5-9-9 **78** ..... RobertWinston 11 30
(J J Quinn) *hmpd and swtchd lft shortly after s: chsd ldrs: rdn along 1/2-way and sn wknd* **16/1**

1m 12.59s (0.79) **Going Correction** +0.275s/f (Good)
WFA 3 from 4yo+ 5lb **11** Ran SP% **124.2**
Speed ratings (Par 105): **105,102,102,101,100 95,92,91,89,85 79**
toteswinger: 1&2 £3.80, 1&3 £24.90, 2&3 £10.40. CSF £32.38 CT £393.90 TOTE £7.20: £2.40, £1.40, £5.20; EX 31.90 Trifecta £425.30 Part won..
Owner Los Bandidos Racing **Bred** J W Parker And Keith Wills **Trained** Musley Bank, N Yorks
■ Stewards' Enquiry : Paul Fessey three-day ban: careless riding (Aug 3-5)

FOCUS
A competitive handicap and a return to form for the well-handicapped Wyatt Earp.
Baybshambles(IRE) Official explanation: jockey said gelding had no more to give
Prince Hamlet(IRE) Official explanation: trainer said colt was unsuited by the 6f trip

4219 SURPRISE SURPRISE IT'S TERRY CARLINE'S 60TH H'CAP 1m

4:50 (4:51) (Class 5) (0-75,75) 3-Y-O+ **£2,914** (£867; £433; £216) **Stalls** Centre

Form RPR

0202 **1** **Efidium**[17] 3643 10-8-7 **62** ..... FrederikTylicki(7) 17 69
(N Bycroft) *hld up towards rr: stdy hdwy over 2f out: hrd rdn and styd on wl fnl f: led last stride* **14/1**

3020 **2** shd **Wovoka (IRE)**[7] 4001 5-9-11 **73** ..... FergalLynch 15 80
(D W Barker) *hmpd s: hld up gng wl in midfield: stdy hdwy 2f out: shkn up to ld jst ins fnl f: hdd post* **16/1**

0-06 **3** 1 ½ **Kaymich Perfecto**[30] 3229 8-8-5 **56** oh4 ..... MichaelJStainton(3) 19 59
(R M Whitaker) *in rr: hdwy over 2f out: kpt on same pce ins fnl f* **50/1**

1564 **4** hd **Island Music (IRE)**[15] 3717 3-8-12 **68** ..... PaulHanagan 1 69
(J J Quinn) *in rr: hdwy over 2f out: styd on wl ins fnl f* **16/1**

5434 **5** ½ **Dispol Isle (IRE)**[10] 3892 6-9-4 **69** ..... NeilBrown(3) 11 71
(T D Barron) *trckd ldrs: effrt over 2f out: edgd lft and kpt on same pce* **12/1**

5443 **6** ¾ **Darfour**[23] 3453 4-8-10 **63** ..... GaryBartley(5) 14 63
(J S Goldie) *hmpd s: effrt 3f out: n.m.r over 1f out: styd on ins fnl f* **10/1**

4411 **7** 1 ¾ **Supercast (IRE)**[19] 3579 5-9-13 **75** ..... NCallan 13 71
(N J Vaughan) *stmbld s: sn w ldrs: led over 3f out: hdd & wknd jst ins fnl f* **15/2**[2]

5540 **8** hd **Stoic Leader (IRE)**[18] 3599 8-9-9 **71** ..... RoystonFfrench 3 67
(R F Fisher) *mid-div: effrt over 2f out: kpt on: nvr rchd ldrs* **20/1**

0304 **9** 1 **Shosolosa (IRE)**[8] 3964 6-8-1 **56** oh3 ..... StacyRenwick(7) 12 49
(R C Guest) *hld up and bhd: styd on fnl 2f: nvr nr ldrs* **28/1**

-505 **10** 1 ¼ **Packers Hill (IRE)**[15] 3736 4-9-5 **67** ..... RobertWinston 5 57
(G A Swinbank) *hld up in midfield: hdwy over 3f out: hung lft and wknd fnl f* **10/1**

4122 **11** 3 **It's A Dream (FR)**[15] 3738 5-9-6 **68** .....(t) PaulMulrennan 8 51
(M W Easterby) *trckd ldrs: rdn over 2f out: lost pl over 1f out* **2/1**[1]

-010 **12** 2 ¼ **Umverti**[15] 3717 3-8-3 **59** ..... PaulFessey 4 35
(N Bycroft) *chsd ldrs: lost pl 2f out* **40/1**

-404 **13** 1 ¼ **Green Diamond**[24] 3402 3-9-2 **72** ..... JoeFanning 9 45
(M Johnston) *mid-div: drvn 4f out: n.d* **9/1**[3]

05/5 **14** ¾ **Out Of India**[8] 3964 6-8-6 **57** oh1 ow1 ..... PJMcDonald(3) 6 31
(P T Dalton) *led tl over 3f out: lost pl over 1f out* **40/1**

166- **15** nk **Surprise Pension (IRE)**[340] 4491 4-8-1 **56** oh1 ..... JamieKyne(7) 7 29
(J J Quinn) *prom: drvn 3f out: sn lost pl* **33/1**

000- **16** 1 **Mister Maq**[299] 5698 5-8-5 **56** oh11 .....(b) AndrewMullen(3) 18 27
(A Crook) *a in rr* **100/1**

00-0 **17** 6 **Ignition**[19] 3593 6-8-8 **56** oh5 ..... TomEaves 10 13
(A Kirtley) *chsd ldrs: lost pl over 3f out* **80/1**

0020 **18** 14 **Lap Of Honour (IRE)**[18] 3599 4-9-13 **75** ..... JimmyQuinn 2 —
(Jennie Candlish) *chsd ldrs on wd outside: drvn 3f out: sn lost pl: bhd whn eased ins fnl f* **25/1**

1m 39.7s (1.70) **Going Correction** +0.275s/f (Good)
WFA 3 from 4yo+ 8lb **18** Ran SP% **123.5**
Speed ratings (Par 103): **102,101,100,100,99 98,97,97,96,94 91,89,88,87,87 86,80,66**
toteswinger: 1&2 £31.90, 1&3 £84.10, 2&3 £91.10. CSF £203.26 CT £5397.92 TOTE £21.60: £3.10, £3.30, £10.30, £2.70; EX 185.60 Place 6 £475.39, Place 5 £425.11.
Owner Hambleton Racing Partnership **Bred** T Umpleby **Trained** Brandsby, N Yorks
■ Stewards' Enquiry : Frederik Tylicki three-day ban: used whip with excessive frequency (Aug 3-5)

FOCUS
A modest handicap.
It's A Dream(FR) Official explanation: jockey said gelding ran flat

4220 THE COMMITMENTS ARE HERE 23RD AUGUST APPRENTICE H'CAP 1m 6f 19y

5:20 (5:20) (Class 5) (0-70,69) 4-Y-O+ **£2,590** (£770; £385; £192) **Stalls** Low

Form RPR

4352 **1** **Let It Be**[10] 3863 7-8-7 **59** ..... FrederikTylicki(7) 1 71
(K G Reveley) *trckd ldrs: effrt on ins: nt clr run and swtchd rt over 2f out: styd on to ld jst ins fnl f: r.o* **10/3**[1]

3562 **2** 1 ¾ **Urban Warrior**[17] 3650 4-9-2 **64** ..... HaddenFrost(3) 3 74
(Ian Williams) *led 1f: chsd ldrs: led over 3f out: hdd ins fnl f: no ex* **10/1**

506 **3** 6 **Collette's Choice**[15] 3729 5-9-5 **64** .....(p) JamieMoriarty 12 66
(R A Fahey) *hld up in midfield: stdy hdwy over 2f out: kpt on to take 3rd ins fnl f* **8/1**

4320 **4** 1 ¾ **Jane Of Arc (FR)**[14] 3756 4-8-2 **50** .....(p) KellyHarrison(3) 16 49
(J S Goldie) *chsd ldrs: led over 3f out: hdd over 2f out: one pce* **18/1**

-003 **5** nk **Apsara**[17] 3642 7-8-0 **50** oh5 ..... PatrickDonaghy(5) 14 49
(G M Moore) *led after 1f: hdd over 3f out: edgd rt over 1f out: one pce* **20/1**

0-21 **6** hd **Mister Pete (IRE)**[15] 3718 5-8-8 **53** ..... NeilBrown 7 51
(W Storey) *hld up in rr: smooth hdwy on outer over 3f out: rdn over 2f out: one pce* **7/1**[3]

/000 **7** 1 ¾ **Lodgician (IRE)**[10] 3863 6-8-2 **50** oh3 ..... NicolPolli(3) 4 46
(K G Reveley) *hld up in rr: hdwy 3f out: nvr rchd ldrs* **33/1**

5354 **8** nk **Rocknest Island (IRE)**[34] 3083 5-8-8 **53** .....(p) AndrewMullen 8 49
(P D Niven) *hld up in rr: hdwy 7f out: sn chsng ldrs: wkng whn hmpd 1f out: eased* **18/1**

-041 **9** nse **Abstract Folly (IRE)**[17] 3642 6-9-9 **68** ..... WilliamBuick 5 64
(J D Bethell) *hld up in rr: drvn 6f out: hdwy on outside over 2f out: nvr nr ldrs* **9/2**[2]

03-0 **10** 1 ¼ **Hurricane Thomas (IRE)**[15] 3711 4-9-5 **69** ..... BMcHugh(5) 6 63
(R E Barr) *mid-div: hdwy 3f out: wknd 1f out* **33/1**

0-00 **11** 1 ¾ **Riodan (IRE)**[5] 4046 6-9-0 **59** ..... DuranFentiman 11 50
(L A Mullaney) *in rr: effrt on outer over 2f out: nvr nr ldrs* **40/1**

-063 **12** 1 ½ **Bollin Freddie**[18] 3602 4-8-5 **50** oh5 ..... TolleyDean 2 39
(A J Lockwood) *trckd ldrs: wknd over 2f out* **25/1**

0405 **13** 1 1/4 **Don Jose (USA)**[8] 3950 5-8-0 **50** oh5....................(e) StacyRenwick(5) 15 37
(N J Vaughan) *s.s: hdwy on outer 7f out: drvn over 4f out: sn btn* **40/1**

04-2 **14** 1 **Kerry's Blade (IRE)**[34] 2914 6-7-12 **50**....................(p) JamieKyne(7) 10 36
(Micky Hammond) *trckd ldrs: hrd rdn and hung lft over 3f out: sn btn* **22/1**

2530 **15** 14 **Blue Jet (USA)**[35] 3059 4-8-9 **54**....................(p) MichaelJStainton 9 20
(R M Whitaker) *hld up in rr: hdwy on outer 6f out: wknd over 2f out: bhd and eased ins fnl f* **15/2**

3m 6.08s (1.38) **Going Correction** +0.175s/f (Good) **15 Ran SP% 120.0**
Speed ratings (Par 103): **103,102,98,97,97 97,96,96,96,95 94,93,92,92,84**
toteswinger: 1&2 £8.70, 1&3 £7.40, 2&3 £17.50. CSF £33.37 CT £250.17 TOTE £3.60: £2.40, £3.80, £1.90; EX 52.10 Place 6 £475.39, Place 5 £425.11.
Owner A Frame **Bred** Sir Eric Parker **Trained** Lingdale, Redcar & Cleveland
■ Stewards' Enquiry : Patrick Donaghy two-day ban: careless riding (Aug 3,4)

FOCUS
A modest staying handicap.
T/Jkpt: Not won. T/Plt: £1,689.70 to a £1 stake. Pool: £69,559.23. 30.05 winning tickets. T/Qpdt: £41.60 to a £1 stake. Pool: £5,398.30. 95.90 winning tickets. JR

4221 - 4222a (Foreign Racing) - See Raceform Interactive

4132 FAIRYHOUSE (R-H)
Sunday, July 20

OFFICIAL GOING: Good

4223a BELGRAVE STKS (LISTED RACE) 6f
3:35 (3:36) 3-Y-0+ **£23,933** (£7,022; £3,345; £1,139)

RPR

1 **Dimenticata (IRE)**[18] 3619 4-9-3 100....................(b) CDHayes 12 105
(Kevin Prendergast, Ire) *trckd ldrs: 3rd 1/2-way: 4th 2f out: hdwy in 3rd 1f out: styd on to ld last 100yds: strly pressed: kpt on wl* **14/1**

2 hd **Sharleez (IRE)**[22] 3510 3-8-12 103.................... MJKinane 8 104
(John M Oxx, Ire) *mid-div: 7th 1/2-way: hdwy into 5th 2f out: rdn over 1f out: kpt on wl to chal last 100yds: no ex cl home* **6/1**

3 1 1/2 **Elletelle (IRE)**[21] 3533 3-8-12 102.................... KLatham 7 99
(G M Lyons, Ire) *dwlt and towards rr: hdwy into 8th 1 1/2f out: kpt on wl fnl f* **12/1**

4 1 **Flash McGahon (IRE)**[7] 4004 4-9-6 97....................(b) NGMcCullagh 9 100
(John M Oxx, Ire) *chsd ldrs: 4th 1/2-way: hdwy into 3rd 2f out: impr to ld 1 1/2f out: rdn over 1f out: hdd last 100yds and no ex: kpt on same pce* **25/1**

5 1 3/4 **Lipocco**[29] 3248 4-9-6 .... DPMcDonogh 11 95
(R M Beckett) *led: disp after 2f: led again 2f out: rdn and hdd 1 1/2f out: no ex over 1f out and wknd* **9/4**[1]

6 1/2 **Le Cadre Noir (IRE)**[7] 4004 4-9-11 107.................... PJSmullen 4 98
(D K Weld, Ire) *chsd ldrs: 6th 1/2-way: rdn into 3rd 1 1/2f out: no ex in 5th 1f out: kpt on same pce* **7/2**[2]

7 1 1/4 **Contest (IRE)**[21] 3533 4-9-9 106.................... JAHefferman 3 93
(David Wachman, Ire) *towards rr: sme hdwy into 9th over 1f out: kpt on one pce* **12/1**

8 hd **Bruges (IRE)**[76] 1879 3-9-4 107.................... WJSupple 10 91
(David P Myerscough, Ire) *in rr of mid-div: in rr ent st: rdn into 7th 2f out: 9th and no ex 1 1/2f out: kpt on one pce* **12/1**

9 4 **Fourpenny Lane**[67] 2111 3-8-12 98.................... PShanahan 2 73
(Ms Joanna Morgan, Ire) *in rr of mid-div: rdn and no imp over 2f out* **20/1**

10 2 **Rock Moss (IRE)**[21] 3532 3-9-1 108.................... KJManning 1 70
(J S Bolger, Ire) *a towards rr* **11/2**[3]

11 3 1/2 **Oasis Davis**[8] 3991 3-9-1 83.................... CO'Donoghue 6 59
(David Marnane, Ire) *chsd ldrs: 5th 1/2-way: rdn and wknd ent st* **33/1**

12 shd **An Tadh (IRE)**[21] 3532 5-9-6 98....................(b) EJMcNamara 5 60
(G M Lyons, Ire) *sn chsd ldrs: led and disp after 2f: hdd 2f out: sn no ex and wknd* **33/1**

1m 13.66s (1.16)
WFA 3 from 4yo+ 5lb **12 Ran SP% 126.9**
CSF £98.62 TOTE £18.30: £4.50, £1.80, £2.70; DF 94.40.
Owner Lady O'Reilly **Bred** Mrs John McEnery **Trained** Friarstown, Co Kildare

FOCUS
Ordinary Listed form rated through the fourth.

NOTEBOOK
Dimenticata(IRE), dropping to 6f for only the third time in a 21-race career, put up a gutsy effort under a well-crafted ride, asserting in the last half-furlong after being handily placed throughout. (op 16/1)
Sharleez(IRE) had her limitations exposed when tried in smart company earlier in the year, but a good win in a handicap at the Curragh provided a launch-pad for a spirited effort here that suggests she can pick up a race at this level, possibly over 7f.
Elletelle(IRE), last year's Queen Mary winner, made an encouraging return to something like her best on her third run of the season. She was a slow starter and had a fair bit to do two furlongs out before keeping on to good effect. (op 14/1)
Lipocco, a well-supported favourite to enhance an excellent record for British raiders in major Irish sprints, never looked particularly happy leading or disputing and had little to offer when the heat was turned on. Two handicap wins represent a fairly modest return for a horse of his ability. (op 9/4 tchd 2/1)

4224 - 4231a (Foreign Racing) - See Raceform Interactive

2655 DUSSELDORF (R-H)
Sunday, July 20

OFFICIAL GOING: Soft

4232a WWW.GERMANTOTE.DE-DEUTSCHLAND PREIS (GROUP 1) 1m 4f
4:00 (4:16) 3-Y-0+ **£66,176** (£25,735; £12,500; £6,250; £3,309)

RPR

1 **Adlerflug (GER)**[21] 3540 4-9-6 .... FJohansson 7 123
(J Hirschberger, Germany) *led after 1f: drvn and hung lft over 1f out: edgd lft ins fnl f: wnt steadily clr: drvn out* **21/10**[2]

2 7 **Quijano (GER)**[35] 3075 6-9-6 .... AStarke 2 113
(P Schiergen, Germany) *racd in cl 3rd to st: one pce fnl 1 1/2f* **7/5**[1]

3 6 **It's Gino (GER)**[21] 3540 5-9-6 .... KerrinMcEvoy 8 104
(P Vovcenko, Germany) *trckd wnr: 2nd st: rdn and btn wl over 1f out* **21/10**[2]

4 6 **Little Fighter (GER)**[35] 3074 3-8-6 .... J-PCarvalho 3 94
(H Blume, Germany) *first to show: racd in 5th: reminders 4f out: last and rdn st: plodded on to take 4th cl home* **77/10**[3]

5 1/2 **Prince Flori (GER)**[21] 3540 5-9-6 .... HGrewe 5 95
(S Smrczek, Germany) *hld up: last but cl up at 1/2-way: hdwy and 4th st: sn one pce* **104/10**

6 16 **Anton Chekhov**[21] 3540 4-9-6 .... ADeVries 6 73
(W Hickst, Germany) *racd in 4th: 5th st: t.o fr wl over 1f out* **138/10**

2m 37.58s (8.04)
WFA 3 from 4yo+ 12lb **6 Ran SP% 133.2**
(including ten euro stakes): WIN 31; PL 16, 13; SF 63.
Owner Gestut Schlenderhan **Bred** Gestut Schlenderhan **Trained** Germany

NOTEBOOK
Adlerflug(GER) revels in the mud and he ran away with this Group 1 contest, making every yard for a wide-margin success. He is likely to take in the Grosser Preis von Baden next, providing the ground is suitable, and the Arc remains a possibility if Paris has a wet autumn.
Quijano(GER), although a winner in heavy ground in Italy last time, found these very testing conditions too much, and very much favoured his main market rival.

2347 FRANKFURT (L-H)
Sunday, July 20

OFFICIAL GOING: Soft

4233a GROSSE HESSEN MEILE-FREPORT AG POKAL (GROUP 3) 1m
4:15 (4:21) 3-Y-0+ **£23,529** (£7,353; £3,676; £2,206)

RPR

1 **Abbashiva (GER)**[35] 3-8-6 .... NRichter 5 108
(P Rau, Germany) *pressed ldr tl led appr fnl f: drvn out* **43/10**

2 1 **Forthe Millionkiss (GER)**[22] 3517 4-9-2 .... THellier 6 108
(U Ostmann, Germany) *led tl appr fnl f: kpt on same pce* **56/10**

3 1/2 **Sehrezad (IRE)**[22] 3515 3-8-8 .... JiriPalik 3 107
(Andreas Lowe, Germany) *a cl up: 3rd st: chal wl over 1f out: drvn and ev ch 1f out: kpt on one pce* **38/10**[3]

4 nk **Willingly (GER)**[22] 3515 9-9-2 .... WMongil 4 106
(M Trybuhl, Germany) *cl 4th st: rdn and outpcd over 1f out: kpt on wl u.p fnl 100yds* **19/1**

5 1 3/4 **Rosenreihe (IRE)**[28] 3306 3-8-1 .... FilipMinarik 7 95
(P Schiergen, Germany) *5th to st: brought to outside: one pce fr wl over 1f out* **27/10**[2]

6 3 **Flashing Colour (GER)**[18] 3623 4-8-12 .... ShaneKelly 2 92
(J Hirschberger, Germany) *wl in tch to st: hrd rdn wl over 1f out: one pce* **19/10**[1]

7 3 1/2 **Antonym (USA)**[91] 4-8-12 .... AHelfenbein 1 84
(Mario Hofer, Germany) *in tch to st: sn btn* **86/10**

1m 36.43s (96.43)
WFA 3 from 4yo+ 8lb **7 Ran SP% 131.8**
WIN 53; PL 17, 18, 15; SF 536.
Owner Stall Schuoler-Gonzalez **Bred** Frau Nathalie & Bruno Schuoler **Trained** Germany

4234 - (Foreign Racing) - See Raceform Interactive

3995 BELMONT PARK (L-H)
Saturday, July 19

OFFICIAL GOING: Fast

4235a COACHING CLUB AMERICAN OAKS (GRADE 1) (FILLIES) (DIRT) 1m 2f (D)
10:15 (10:16) 3-Y-0 **£90,452** (£30,151; £15,075; £7,538; £4,523)

RPR

1 **Music Note (USA)**[21] 3-8-9 .... JJCastellano 5 122
(Saeed Bin Suroor) **7/20**[1]

2 11 **Little Belle (USA)**[78] 3-8-9 .... RMaragh 2 102
(Saeed Bin Suroor) **7/20**[1]

3 6 3/4 **Flaming Slew (USA)** 3-8-9 .... ECoa 4 90
(Niall M O'Callaghan, U.S.A) **205/10**

4 1 **Acoma (USA)**[49] 3-8-9 .... JRLeparoux 1 88
(David M Carroll, U.S.A) **23/10**[2]

5 2 1/2 **Never Retreat (USA)**[21] 3-8-9 .... MLuzzi 3 84
(Kiaran McLaughlin, U.S.A) **91/10**[3]

2m 1.66s (1.04) **5 Ran SP% 193.0**
PARI-MUTUEL (including $2 stakes): (Musical Note & Little Belle coupled in all pools) WIN 2.70; PL 2.10; SF (1-2 with Flaming Slew) 25.20.
Owner Godolphin Racing Inc **Bred** Gainsborough Farm Llc **Trained** Newmarket, Suffolk

NOTEBOOK
Music Note(USA) produced the best performance by a filly in America this year, swiftly pulling clear of the rest down the straight and recording a fast time in the process. Her next target is the Alabama Stakes at Saratoga.

4013 AYR (L-H)
Monday, July 21

OFFICIAL GOING: Good (7.8)
Wind: Breezy, half against Weather: Sunny, cloudy later

4236 BUD AND JOE PIERONI MEMORIAL H'CAP 6f
2:30 (2:31) (Class 5) (0-70,70) 3-Y-0 **£3,885** (£1,156; £577; £288) **Stalls** Low

Form RPR

2132 **1** **Leonid Glow**[16] 3717 3-9-4 **70**.................... PJMcDonald(3) 8 81+
(M Dods) *taken early to post: sn pushed along in rr: swtchd rt: hdwy and led over 1f out: edgd lft ins fnl f: sn clr* **15/8**[1]

-023 **2** 3 3/4 **Ubenkor (IRE)**[9] 3955 3-9-2 **65**.................... TomEaves 3 64
(B Smart) *dwlt: keen in tch: effrt whn nt clr run over 1f out: kpt on to take 2nd cl home: no ch w wnr* **11/2**[3]

6040 **3** 1/2 **Irving Place**[16] 3723 3-9-2 **65**.................... PaulHanagan 5 62
(R A Fahey) *prom: effrt and ev ch over 1f out: one pce ins fnl f: lost 2nd cl home* **7/2**[2]

5025 **4** 3 1/4 **Gainshare**[12] 3833 3-9-0 **66**.................... NeilBrown(3) 1 53
(T D Barron) *mde most to over 1f out: sn no ex* **6/1**

6340 **5** 3/4 **Fulford**[49] 2660 3-8-12 **61**.................... TWilliams 4 46
(M Brittain) *chsd ldrs: effrt and ev ch over 1f out: wknd ins fnl f* **14/1**

5600 **6** 1/2 **Miss Sunshine**[4] 4107 3-7-11 **51** oh6....................(v[1]) KellyHarrison(5) 2 34
(J S Goldie) *trckd ldrs tl rdn and wknd appr fnl f* **25/1**

0040 **7** *1* **Saafend Geezer**[2] 4207 3-8-2 **51** oh1.........................(v) RoystonFfrench 6 31
(A Berry) *reminders sn after s: a outpcd* **33/1**

-555 **8** *hd* **Bahamian Ballad**[31] 3202 3-8-7 **56**.................................... PaulFessey 7 35
(J D Bethell) *cl up tl rdn and wknd over 1f out* **10/1**

1m 11.52s (-2.08) **Going Correction** -0.275s/f (Firm) **8** Ran SP% **109.2**
Speed ratings (Par 100): **102,97,96,92,91 90,89,88**
toteswinger: 1&2 £1.70, 1&3 £3.40, 2&3 £3.10. CSF £11.24 CT £28.98 TOTE £2.70: £1.10, £1.90, £1.40; EX 7.50.
Owner M J K Dods **Bred** Mrs G C Stanley **Trained** Denton, Co Durham

FOCUS

A modest handicap but one in which the pace was sound throughout. The winner did it nicely but there were doubts over most of the opposition.

4237 EUROPEAN BREEDERS' FUND MAIDEN STKS 6f

3:00 (3:01) (Class 4) 2-Y-O **£5,180** (£1,541; £770; £384) **Stalls** Low

Form RPR

1 **Weatherstaff (USA)** 2-9-3 0.. GregFairley 4 86+
(M Johnston) *w ldrs: led over 2f out: edgd rt and hrd pressed over 1f out: hld on gamely* **3/1**[2]

2 **2** *nk* **Fitz Flyer (IRE)**[17] 3663 2-9-3 0.................................. RoystonFfrench 2 85
(D H Brown) *prom: effrt and disp ld over 1f out: kpt on: hld cl home* **5/4**[1]

3 *4 1/2* **Jobe (USA)** 2-9-3 0.. NCallan 5 72+
(K A Ryan) *wnt rt s: t.k.h: cl up: hung bdly rt over 2f out: sn one pce* **7/2**[3]

33 **4** *2 1/4* **Parisian Pyramid (IRE)**[17] 3670 2-9-3 0.................... AdrianTNicholls 3 65
(D Nicholls) *led to over 2f out: sn rdn and outpcd* **11/1**

5 *7* **New Tricks** 2-9-3 0.. TomEaves 1 44
(Miss L A Perratt) *bhd and outpcd: nvr rchd ldrs* **16/1**

6 *1* **Bun Penny** 2-8-12 0.. DanielTudhope 6 36
(G M Moore) *weht rt s: in tch: rdn over 2f out: sn btn* **16/1**

1m 11.94s (-1.66) **Going Correction** -0.275s/f (Firm) **6** Ran SP% **111.8**
Speed ratings (Par 96): **100,99,93,90,81 79**
toteswinger: 1&2 £1.70, 1&3 £1.70, 2&3 £1.50. CSF £7.10 TOTE £4.60: £2.30, £1.10; EX 7.50.
Owner Sheikh Hamdan Bin Mohammed Al Maktoum **Bred** Robert E Sangster **Trained** Middleham Moor, N Yorks

■ Stewards' Enquiry : Greg Fairley caution: careless riding

FOCUS

A couple of fair sorts on looks and a strong maiden for the track. The pace was sound and the first two pulled clear of the wayward Jobe.

NOTEBOOK

Weatherstaff(USA) ◆, who cost $150,000 and is out of a 7f-1m1f winner, was noisy and colty in the paddock but he is a fair sort with plenty of scope and he showed a decent attitude to beat a more experienced rival on this racecourse debut. He will be suited by 7f and is the type to win more races. (op 10-3 tchd 7-2 and 4-1 in places)

Fitz Flyer(IRE) ◆, who shaped with plenty of promise on his debut, fared at least as well against a rival that could turn out to be smart. He will stay 7f and should have no problems picking up an ordinary maiden at the very least. (op 15-8 tchd 2-1 in places)

Jobe(USA), a rig but a good sort who cost $410,000 and is related to sprint winners in the US, looked in tremendous condition. However he got noticeably edgy as his rider mounted and went very freely to post. He showed ability but looked less than straightforward and, although he is well worth another chance, he is going to have to settle much better if he is to progress. (op 9-4)

Parisian Pyramid(IRE), who had the run of the race, was not disgraced in the face of a stiff task and he will be seen to better effect in less competitive maiden company or when stepping into nurseries. He should stay 7f. (tchd 10-1)

New Tricks, a 30,000gns half-brother to a useful winner in Canada around 1m, was easy to back and was well beaten on this racecourse debut. He is the type to fare better in due course. (tchd 25-1 in a place)

Bun Penny, a half-sister to a juvenile 5f winner, is from a yard that has had a winning newcomer in recent times but this one did not show enough on this racecourse debut to suggest she is of much immediate interest. (op 20-1)

4238 GILES INSURANCE PREMIER H'CAP 1m 5f 13y

3:30 (3:30) (Class 5) (0-70,66) 4-Y-O+ **£3,885** (£1,156; £577; £288) **Stalls** Low

Form RPR

4- **1** **Signalman**[103] 4-8-2 **47**.. RoystonFfrench 3 57
(P Monteith) *trckd ldrs: rdn to ld wl over 1f out: drvn out* **16/1**

1510 **2** *2 3/4* **Kyber**[15] 3756 7-8-8 **58**.. GaryBartley(5) 4 64
(J S Goldie) *prom: effrt and edgd lft 2f out: chsd wnr appr fnl f: kpt on: no imp* **15/2**[3]

/-36 **3** *2 1/2* **Inch High**[15] 3756 10-7-11 **47** oh1.............................(p) KellyHarrison(5) 1 49
(J S Goldie) *t.k.h: led to over 1f out: sn no ex* **12/1**

/660 **4** *1/2* **Nelson Vettori**[33] 3131 4-8-5 **50**.................................. PaulFessey 6 52
(Miss L A Perratt) *hld up ins: rdn over 2f out: kpt on fnl f: n.d* **33/1**

-621 **5** *1 1/2* **Fistral**[19] 3602 4-8-5 **50**.. PaulHanagan 8 49
(P D Niven) *sn prom: drvn over 3f out: one pce fnl 2f* **2/1**[2]

6-55 **6** *1 1/4* **Zed Candy (FR)**[139] 789 5-8-7 **57**.............................. PatrickDonaghy(5) 7 54
(J T Stimpson) *hld up: hdwy and prom 3f out: no ex over 1f out* **12/1**

-200 **7** *4* **Rudry World (IRE)**[18] 3630 5-9-7 **66**............................ EddieAhern 2 57
(M Mullineaux) *missed break: hld up: shortlived effrt on outside 2f out: sn btn* **8/1**

3123 **8** *1/2* **Forrest Flyer (IRE)**[15] 3756 4-8-10 **55**.........................(v[1]) TomEaves 5 46
(Miss L A Perratt) *t.k.h: trckd ldr tl rdn and wknd over 2f out* **15/8**[1]

2m 50.89s (-5.71) **Going Correction** -0.40s/f (Firm) **8** Ran SP% **115.2**
Speed ratings (Par 103): **101,99,97,97,96 95,93,93**
toteswinger: 1&2 £8.70, 1&3 £15.20, 2&3 £18.50. CSF £129.61 CT £1499.34 TOTE £14.00: £3.00, £1.70, £2.30; EX 104.30.
Owner P Monteith **Bred** Aston House Stud **Trained** Rosewell, Midlothian

FOCUS

A low-grade handicap in which the pace was just fair. The form seems to make sense, rated around the runner-up.

Forrest Flyer(IRE) Official explanation: jockey said gelding ran too free

4239 GILES INSURANCE CORPORATE H'CAP 6f

4:00 (4:00) (Class 4) (0-80,80) 3-Y-O+ **£6,476** (£1,927; £963; £481) **Stalls** Low

Form RPR

4001 **1** **Methaaly (IRE)**[7] 4030 5-9-0 **68** 6ex..........................(be) EddieAhern 8 83
(M Mullineaux) *prom: hdwy to ld over 1f out: rdn out* **20/1**

4520 **2** *2 1/4* **Yorkshire Blue**[15] 3757 9-8-8 **67**................................ GaryBartley(5) 7 75
(J S Goldie) *bhd: drvn and outpcd 2f out: gd hdwy fnl f: wnt 2nd cl home: no ch w wnr* **16/1**

2530 **3** *nk* **Rainbow Fox**[24] 3454 4-8-11 **65**................................ PaulHanagan 9 72
(R A Fahey) *midfield: drvn over 2f out: kpt on fnl f: nrst fin* **11/2**[2]

3040 **4** *nk* **Angaric (IRE)**[30] 3281 5-9-1 **69**................................ TomEaves 12 75
(B Smart) *led to over 1f out: kpt on same pce fnl f* **12/1**

4060 **5** *1/2* **Curtail (IRE)**[23] 3489 5-9-6 **79**................................ PatrickDonaghy(5) 4 83
(Miss L A Perratt) *in tch: effrt over 2f out: one pce fnl f* **22/1**

1632 **6** *hd* **Dorn Dancer (IRE)**[7] 4016 6-9-2 **73**............................ NeilBrown(3) 11 77
(D W Barker) *bhd: hdwy on outside over 1f out: nvr rchd ldrs* **5/1**[1]

0031 **7** *1* **Sandwith**[14] 3787 5-9-3 **74**.. PJMcDonald(3) 2 75
(R Johnson) *cl up tl rdn and no ex appr fnl f* **9/1**

2221 **8** *1 1/4* **Rothesay Dancer**[7] 4016 5-9-0 **73** 6ex......................... KellyHarrison(5) 1 70
(J S Goldie) *t.k.h: in tch tl wknd over 1f out* **11/1**

3623 **9** *nse* **River Thames**[20] 3594 5-9-12 **80**................................ NCallan 5 76
(K A Ryan) *hld up: drvn over 2f out: nvr on terms* **6/1**[3]

5133 **10** *hd* **John Keats**[13] 3812 5-9-12 **80**................................ DanielTudhope 3 76+
(J S Goldie) *bhd on ins: rdn whn no room fr over 1f out: nt rcvr* **7/1**

2324 **11** *1/2* **Circuit Dancer (IRE)**[23] 3477 8-9-1 **69**........................ AdrianTNicholls 10 63
(D Nicholls) *dwlt: sn cl up: rdn and wknd over 1f out* **7/1**

0044 **12** *1/2* **Paris Bell**[11] 3890 6-9-0 **68**.. DavidAllan 6 61
(T D Easterby) *dwlt: bhd: rdn over 2f out: nvr a factor* **12/1**

1m 11.77s (-1.83) **Going Correction** -0.275s/f (Firm) **12** Ran SP% **120.0**
Speed ratings (Par 105): **101,98,97,97,96 96,94,93,93,92 92,91**
toteswinger: 1&2 £68.00, 1&3 £26.40, 2&3 £19.70. CSF £310.64 CT £2011.66 TOTE £23.80: £5.70, £4.90, £2.50; EX 442.20.
Owner The Bellflower Methaaly Partnership **Bred** Scuderia Golden Horse S R L **Trained** Alpraham, Cheshire

FOCUS

A fair handicap run at a decent gallop throughout. The form is rated through the runner-up and there is a slight doubt over it with the winner seemingly taking his form to a new high.

John Keats Official explanation: jockey said gelding was denied a clear run

4240 GILES INSURANCE STKS (HERITAGE H'CAP) 5f

4:30 (4:31) (Class 2) 3-Y-O+ **£25,904** (£7,708; £3,852; £1,924) **Stalls** Low

Form RPR

1114 **1** **Look Busy (IRE)**[10] 3927 3-8-13 **100**............................ SladeO'Hara(5) 7 110
(A Berry) *bhd: hdwy over 1f out: squeezed through and str run to ld towards fin* **10/1**

3300 **2** *1/2* **Fullandby (IRE)**[30] 3248 6-9-10 **102**............................ GregFairley 4 111
(T J Etherington) *hld up: hdwy over 1f out: ev ch wl ins fnl f: jst hld* **12/1**

2332 **3** *hd* **Inxile (IRE)**[37] 3041 3-9-7 **103**................................ AdrianTNicholls 9 110
(D Nicholls) *pressed ldr: rdn to ld over 1f out: hdd and no ex towards fin* **6/1**[1]

4120 **4** *3/4* **Princess Ellis**[23] 3472 4-8-7 **85**................................ PatrickMathers 8 91
(E J Alston) *led to over 1f out: rallied and ev ch ins fnl f: fdd towards fin* **12/1**

3200 **5** *3/4* **River Falcon**[24] 3451 8-9-0 **92**................................ DanielTudhope 10 95+
(J S Goldie) *bhd: hdwy and swtchd rt over 1f out: kpt on strly fnl f: nrst fin* **14/1**

-402 **6** *1 1/2* **Aegean Dancer**[58] 2390 6-9-4 **96**................................ TomEaves 1 93
(B Smart) *midfield: effrt over 1f out: sn one pce* **16/1**

0343 **7** *hd* **How's She Cuttin' (IRE)**[8] 4004 5-8-1 **84**..........(v) PatrickDonaghy(5) 11 81
(T D Barron) *in tch: drvn over 2f out: one pce over 1f out* **10/1**

6610 **8** *1/2* **Bo McGinty (IRE)**[16] 3708 7-8-5 **83**............................(b) PaulHanagan 3 78
(R A Fahey) *in tch: hung bdly rt fr over 1f out: no imp fnl f* **25/1**

6020 **9** *hd* **High Curragh**[13] 3812 5-8-7 **85**................................(p) PaulFessey 5 79
(K A Ryan) *midfield: drvn and outpcd over 2f out: n.d fnl f* **33/1**

0000 **10** *nse* **Green Park (IRE)**[3] 4171 5-8-5 **86** ow1..................(b) PJMcDonald(3) 15 80
(R A Fahey) *hld up: pushed along over 2f out: nvr able to chal* **25/1**

200 **11** *hd* **Fantasy Explorer**[38] 3009 5-8-5 **83**............................ RoystonFfrench 14 76
(J J Quinn) *t.k.h: hld up: rdn over 2f out: sn n.d* **9/1**

1023 **12** *1* **Swift Princess (IRE)**[9] 3973 4-8-6 **84**........................(v) AndrewElliott 13 74
(K R Burke) *hld up towards rr: drvn over 2f out: btn over 1f out* **14/1**

1111 **13** *2* **Whiskey Junction**[20] 3587 4-8-10 **88**............................ LPKeniry 6 71
(A M Balding) *hld up in midfield: rdn 2f out: sn btn* **17/2**[3]

1021 **14** *shd* **Hamish McGonagall**[10] 3909 3-9-0 **96**............................ DavidAllan 12 77
(T D Easterby) *cl up tl rdn and wknd over 1f out* **13/2**[2]

0150 **15** *nse* **The Nifty Fox**[3] 4171 4-8-1 **82**................................ DuranFentiman(3) 17 64
(T D Easterby) *hld up: rdn on outside over 2f out: btn over 1f out* **33/1**

0-51 **16** *1/2* **Kay Two (IRE)**[11] 3881 6-8-9 **87**................................(p) NCallan 16 67
(R J Price) *midfield on outside: rdn and wknd fr 2f out* **10/1**

57.87 secs (-2.23) **Going Correction** -0.275s/f (Firm)
WFA 3 from 4yo+ 4lb **16** Ran SP% **123.6**
Speed ratings (Par 109): **106,105,104,103,102 100,99,98,98,98 98,96,93,93,93 92**
toteswinger: 1&2 £32.00, 1&3 £13.00, 2&3 £17.50. CSF £121.55 CT £793.99 TOTE £11.10: £3.20, £3.80, £1.50, £3.60; EX 172.50.
Owner A Underwood **Bred** Tom And Hazel Russell **Trained** Cockerham, Lancs

FOCUS

A good-quality handicap run at a decent gallop throughout. The winner produced another personal best and the form should prove reliable.

NOTEBOOK

Look Busy(IRE) has done nothing but improve in the last 12 months and she turned in a career best effort returned to handicap company. While she stays 6f, a strongly run race over this trip are her requirements and she is more than capable of winning at Listed (again) or in minor Group company granted a suitable test.

Fullandby(IRE) ◆, who ran better than his finishing position suggests in the Wokingham, returned to something like his best. While he is effective over 6f, his optimum trip may be the extended 5f and he will be one to keep an eye on if bidding to follow up last year's victory in the Portland at Doncaster in September. (op 14-1)

Inxile(IRE) ◆, a lightly raced sort, has quickly made up into a smart performer and he fared the best of those to race up with the pace on this handicap debut. He is in very good hands and is capable of winning a decent race when the emphasis is on speed. (op 11-2)

Princess Ellis is a pure speedball and showed her latest running from a moderate draw to be all wrong with another solid effort. She will always be seen to best effect when allowed to dominate at courses that place an emphasis on speed. (tchd 13-1 in a place)

River Falcon is a useful sprinter whose finishing effort caught the eye. He is more than capable of winning from this sort of mark when the mood takes but a record of only one win since May 2005 means he would not be one to place maximum faith in. (op 16-1)

Aegean Dancer was far from disgraced but, as a consistent sort, he gets little respite from the handicapper and he has little margin for error on turf from a mark 14lb higher than his last grass win.

Bo McGinty(IRE) Official explanation: jockey said gelding hung right-handed throughout

Hamish McGonagall looked in good shape, despite being on his toes throughout the preliminaries, but he proved a disappointment after enjoying the run of the race. He has been a progressive sort, though, and is worth another chance. (op 6-1)

4241 WATERAID LADIES NIGHT 9TH AUGUST H'CAP 1m

5:00 (5:01) (Class 6) (0-65,64) 3-Y-O **£3,043** (£905; £452; £226) **Stalls** Low

Form RPR

006 **1** **Whaston (IRE)**[16] 3737 3-8-9 **52**................................(v) NCallan 2 58
(J D Bethell) *in tch: effrt 2f out: led ins fnl f: edgd lft: hld on wl* **7/1**[3]

00 **2** *nk* **Red Skipper (IRE)**[15] 3753 3-8-10 **53**............................ DavidAllan 5 58
(N Wilson) *chsd ldrs: effrt over 1f out: ev ch ins fnl f: kpt on: hld nr fin* **8/1**

3003 **3** 2 1/4 **Bourse (IRE)**[14] 3790 3-9-4 **64**........................ PJMcDonald(3) 10 64
(R Johnson) *hld up: hdwy over 1f out: kpt on fnl f: nrst fin* **7/4**[1]
0405 **4** *nk* **Miss Understanding**[4] 4115 3-8-2 **45**........................(b[1]) AndrewElliott 9 44
(J R Weymes) *cl up: led over 2f out to ins fnl f: no ex* **16/1**
3003 **5** 3 1/2 **Champagne Lawn (USA)**[9] 3958 3-8-7 **53**........................(v) NeilBrown(3) 4 44
(T D Barron) *hld up in tch: effrt over 2f out: edgd lft over 1f out: nvr able to chal* **12/1**
0506 **6** 2 **Scanno (IRE)**[10] 3907 3-8-7 **50**........................ EddieAhern 7 37
(M Mullineaux) *bhd tl sme late hdwy: nvr on terms* **33/1**
0056 **7** *nk* **Piverina (IRE)**[13] 3816 3-8-5 **48**........................ RoystonFfrench 6 34
(Miss J A Camacho) *hld up: rdn 3f out: sn n.d* **7/1**[3]
0452 **8** 2 1/2 **Casino Night**[9] 3958 3-9-1 **58**........................(p) PaulHanagan 8 38
(J R Weymes) *led to over 2f out: sn wknd* **4/1**[2]
0-60 **9** *nk* **Howards Hope**[4] 4115 3-9-3 **60**........................(b) TomEaves 3 40
(Miss L A Perratt) *hld up: drvn over 2f out: sn btn* **20/1**
0-20 **10** 1 1/4 **Varinia (IRE)**[37] 3030 3-8-5 **48**........................ TWilliams 1 25
(M Brittain) *unruly in preliminaries: trckd ldrs tl wknd over 2f out* **25/1**

1m 40.74s (-3.06) **Going Correction** -0.40s/f (Firm) **10** Ran SP% **117.6**
Speed ratings (Par 98): **99,98,96,96,92 90,90,87,87,86**
toteswinger: 1&2 £12.80, 1&3 £6.60, 2&3 £4.90. CSF £60.66 CT £144.55 TOTE £8.90: £2.20, £2.90, £1.50; EX 69.60.
Owner Clarendon Thoroughbred Racing **Bred** Herbertstown Stud Ltd **Trained** Middleham Moor, N Yorks
■ Stewards' Enquiry : David Allan one-day ban: used whip with excessive frequency (Aug 4)

FOCUS
A modest handicap in which the pace was just fair. The winner is rated to his AW winter form.

4242 RACINGUK.TV H'CAP 5f
5:30 (5:30) (Class 6) (0-65,60) 3-Y-O
£2,492 (£746; £373; £186; £93; £46) **Stalls Low**

Form RPR
0353 **1** **Embra (IRE)**[24] 3441 3-9-5 **58**........................ GregFairley 7 65
(T J Etherington) *prom: rdn over 2f out: led ins fnl f: kpt on strly* **6/1**[2]
0011 **2** 1 **Jaconet (USA)**[15] 3753 3-9-7 **60**........................(b) PaulFessey 5 63
(T D Barron) *led to ins fnl f: kpt on u.p* **2/1**[1]
2046 **3** 1 1/2 **Andrasta**[3] 4163 3-8-9 **48**........................ RoystonFfrench 3 46
(A Berry) *bhd and sn pushed along: hdwy over 1f out: nrst fin* **8/1**
0300 **4** *nk* **Dalarossie**[62] 2287 3-9-7 **60**........................ DavidAllan 4 57
(E J Alston) *pressed ldr: ev ch over 1f out: no ex ins fnl f* **16/1**
0001 **5** 1 1/4 **Lujiana**[4] 4107 3-8-8 **54**........................ MatthewLawson(7) 2 46
(M Brittain) *bhd and sn outpcd: hdwy over 1f out: nrst fin* **2/1**[1]
-060 **6** 1 1/4 **Fantasy Fighter (IRE)**[15] 3753 3-8-6 **45**........................(v[1]) PaulHanagan 8 33
(J J Quinn) *wnt rt s: bhd and sn pushed along: no imp fnl 2f* **15/2**[3]
0002 **7** 3 1/4 **Swift Acclaim (IRE)**[25] 3395 3-8-12 **51**........................ AndrewElliott 1 27
(K R Burke) *chsd ldrs tl rdn and wknd 2f out* **12/1**

59.90 secs (-0.20) **Going Correction** -0.275s/f (Firm) **7** Ran SP% **117.4**
Speed ratings (Par 98): **90,88,86,85,83 81,76**
toteswinger: 1&2 £3.80, 1&3 £8.80, 2&3 £4.00. CSF £19.26 CT £98.64 TOTE £5.50: £3.40, £1.10; EX 19.60 Place 6: £137.77 Place 5: £112.19 .
Owner The Carpe Diem Partnership **Bred** Michael Kavanagh **Trained** Norton, N Yorks

FOCUS
A strong pace but a moderate winning time for the type of contest. The winner is up 7lb with the runner-up close to his latest form.
T/Plt: £748.80 to a £1 stake. Pool: £68,733.01. 67.00 winning tickets. T/Qpdt: £165.00 to a £1 stake. Pool: £3,792.30. 17.00 winning tickets. RY

4043 BEVERLEY (R-H)
Monday, July 21

OFFICIAL GOING: Good to firm (good in places)
Wind: Moderate, half behind Weather: Dry and sunny

4243 SKY BET SUPPORTING THE YORKSHIRE RACING FESTIVAL CLAIMING STKS 5f
6:30 (6:30) (Class 5) 2-Y-O
£2,729 (£806; £403) **Stalls High**

Form RPR
5231 **1** **Metroland**[16] 3714 2-9-0 0........................ JoeFanning 9 75
(M Johnston) *t.k.h: trckd ldrs: pushed along 2f out: sn swtchd lft and rdn to chal: drvn to ld ins fnl f: kpt on* **4/6**[1]
6126 **2** 1 **Smalljohn**[9] 3978 2-9-5 0........................ DNolan 2 76
(D Carroll) *cl up: led after 2f: rdn over 1f out: drvn and hdd ins fnl f: kpt on* **7/2**[2]
0 **3** 1 3/4 **Blackwater Fort (USA)**[33] 3140 2-8-10 0........................ RobertWinston 1 61
(T D Barron) *awkward s: sn cl up on outer: pushed along whn bmpd 2f out: rdn and ev ch tl drvn and one pce ins fnl f* **50/1**
065 **4** 4 **Compton Ford**[21] 3547 2-9-2 0........................ PaulMulrennan 5 53
(M Dods) *stdd s: plld hrd and hld up in rr: hdwy 2f out: rdn over 1f out and sn one pce* **28/1**
0552 **5** 2 **Readily**[20] 3570 2-8-11 0........................ SebSanders 6 41
(J G Portman) *led 2f: cl up tl rdn along 2f out and sn wknd* **5/1**[3]
3064 **6** 7 **Dispol Mulofky (IRE)**[13] 3815 2-8-4 0........................(p) NickyMackay 4 8
(P T Midgley) *chsd ldrs whn n.m.r after 1f: sn rdn along and a in rr* **16/1**

63.68 secs (0.18) **Going Correction** -0.05s/f (Good) **6** Ran SP% **110.2**
Speed ratings (Par 94): **96,94,91,85,82 70**
toteswinger: 1&2 £1.30, 1&3 £8.20, 2&3 £44.80 CSF £3.12 TOTE £1.60: £1.20, £1.80; EX 3.70.The winner was claimed by P C Haslam for £15,000. Blackwater Fort was claimed by J Gallagher for £6,000.
Owner J Shack **Bred** West Dereham Abbey Stud **Trained** Middleham Moor, N Yorks
■ Stewards' Enquiry : D Nolan two-day ban: used whip with excessive frequency (Aug 4,5)
Joe Fanning one-day ban: careless riding (Aug 4)

FOCUS
An uncompetitive heat but the form is solid. The winner is a fair sort for the grade.

NOTEBOOK
Metroland, winner of a modest Carlisle maiden earlier in the month, was a strong favourite in this grade and she was expected to dominate throughout. Things did not quite go to plan, but having got in the clear she was always just doing enough. She may have more to offer in nurseries. (tchd 8-13 and 8-11)
Smalljohn, a winner in selling company earlier in the season, was always struggling to go the speed when dropped back down to 5f in a fair nursery at York last time, but this drop in grade helped and he went down fighting. A return to 6f should help and he can find another small race at this sort of level. (op 10-3 tchd 4-1)
Blackwater Fort(USA), well down the field in a maiden at Ripon, fared much better on this drop in grade and showed plenty of speed. Two more-experienced rivals proved too strong in the end, but there is a small race in him on this evidence. (op 25-1)
Compton Ford was ridden with more restraint than usual on this drop in grade, but it did not seem to work and, having failed to settle, he could make no further progress inside the final furlong. (op 18-1)
Readily beaten at odds of 4/7 in this grade last time, is not that big, and, having shown early speed, she dropped right out. This was a step in the wrong direction and she looks one to avoid. (op 13-2 tchd 7-1)
Dispol Mulofky(IRE) Official explanation: trainer said filly was found to be in season

4244 ROLLITS SOLICITORS AND PETER STOCKILL LTD H'CAP 1m 1f 207y
7:00 (7:00) (Class 5) (0-75,72) 3-Y-O+ **£3,238** (£963; £481; £240) **Stalls High**

Form RPR
3300 **1** **Jafra (IRE)**[11] 3886 3-8-2 **56**........................(p) PaulQuinn 9 68
(R M Whitaker) *dwlt and bhd: pushed along and hdwy over 2f out: rdn to chse ldrs ent fnl f: swtchd lft and styd on strly to ld fnl 100yds* **20/1**
2401 **2** 2 1/4 **Highland Love**[24] 3436 3-8-11 **65**........................ TonyHamilton 1 72
(Jedd O'Keeffe) *trckd ldrs: hdwy to ld wl over 2f out: sn jnd and rdn wl over 1f out: drvn ent fnl f: hdd and no ex last 100yds* **11/2**[3]
2026 **3** 2 1/4 **King Of Rhythm (IRE)**[16] 3711 5-10-0 **72**........................ DNolan 3 75
(D Carroll) *hld up: hdwy over 3f out: effrt to chal 2f out: sn rdn and ev ch tl drvn and wknd ins fnl f* **15/2**
-311 **4** 2 3/4 **Eijaaz (IRE)**[40] 2957 7-9-2 **60**........................ SebSanders 8 57
(G A Harker) *hld up: hdwy 3f out: rdn to chse ldrs over 1f out: sn drvn and no imp* **11/2**[3]
3426 **5** 6 **Princess Cocoa (IRE)**[24] 3433 5-9-6 **71**........................ FrederikTylicki(7) 10 56
(R A Fahey) *chsd ldrs: rdn along over 2f out: sn drvn and wknd wl over 1f out* **3/1**[1]
5055 **6** 1 3/4 **Ahlawy (IRE)**[38] 3006 5-9-11 **69**........................ PaulMulrennan 6 51
(M W Easterby) *hld up towards rr: hdwy 3f out: rdn 2f out: drvn over 1f out and nvr nr ldrs* **9/2**[2]
2600 **7** 3 1/2 **Sudden Impulse**[18] 3624 7-9-9 **70**........................ JamieMoriarty(3) 7 45
(A D Brown) *hld up towards rr: effrt and sme hdwy on outer over 2f out: sn rdn and nvr a factor* **16/1**
65 **8** 1 1/2 **Monfils Monfils (USA)**[9] 3965 6-9-12 **70**........................(be) WilliamBuick 5 42
(A J McCabe) *led: rdn along over 3f out: hdd over 2f out and sn wknd* **20/1**
0100 **9** 1 **Always Certain (USA)**[11] 3886 3-8-12 **66**........................ JoeFanning 2 36
(M Johnston) *prom to 1/2-way: sn lost pl and bhd fnl 3f* **10/1**
2100 **10** 89 **Maneki Neko (IRE)**[24] 3440 6-9-11 **69**........................ RobertWinston 4 —
(E W Tuer) *in tch: hdwy to chse ldng pair over 3f out: rdn over 2f out: sn wknd and eased over 1f out* **14/1**

2m 6.80s (-0.20) **Going Correction** +0.075s/f (Good)
WFA 3 from 5yo+ 10lb **10** Ran SP% **116.9**
Speed ratings (Par 103): **103,101,99,97,92 91,88,87,86,62**
toteswinger: 1&2 £20.60, 1&3 £61.20, 2&3 £10.80 CSF £126.68 CT £908.02 TOTE £28.40: £6.30, £2.30, £2.40; EX 233.70.
Owner G B Bedford **Bred** J Webb **Trained** Scarcroft, W Yorks

FOCUS
A moderate handicap run at a strong gallop. The winner is rated up 7lb but the form seems sound.
Ahlawy(IRE) Official explanation: jockey said gelding ran flat
Maneki Neko(IRE) Official explanation: jockey said gelding hung left-handed throughout

4245 NATWEST AGRICULTURAL TEAM H'CAP 7f 100y
7:30 (7:31) (Class 5) (0-75,72) 3-Y-O+ **£4,533** (£1,348; £674; £336) **Stalls High**

Form RPR
4345 **1** **Dispol Isle (IRE)**[1] 4219 6-9-11 **69**........................ JoeFanning 11 77+
(T D Barron) *hld up towards rr: nt clr run over 3f out and again over 2f out and sn last: swtchd outside and hdwy wl over 1f out: rdn and styd on strly ins fnl f to ld fnl 75yds* **11/1**
0104 **2** 1 **Handsome Falcon**[24] 3453 4-9-5 **70**........................ FrederikTylicki(7) 5 76
(R A Fahey) *in tch: hdwy to chse ldrs over 3f out: rdn to ld wl over 1f out: drvn ins fnl f: hdd and no ex fnl 75yds* **4/1**[1]
1440 **3** 2 **Shotley Mac**[10] 3928 4-9-6 **67**........................(b) JamieMoriarty(3) 2 68
(N Bycroft) *midfield: hdwy 3f out: rdn to chse ldrs over 1f out: drvn: edgd rt and one pce ins fnl f* **8/1**[3]
0004 **4** *nk* **Baltimore Jack (IRE)**[12] 3834 4-9-2 **60**........................(b) PaulMulrennan 3 60
(M W Easterby) *prom: rdn along over 2f out: drvn wl over 1f out and kpt on same pce appr fnl f* **20/1**
043 **5** 1 1/4 **Admiralcollingwood**[6] 4043 3-8-2 **53** oh3........................ NickyMackay 9 47
(T P Tate) *hld up: gd hdwy on outer over 2f out: rdn to chse ldrs over 1f out: sn drvn and wknd ent fnl f* **25/1**
1331 **6** 1 **Micky Mac (IRE)**[12] 3834 4-9-3 **61**........................ TonyHamilton 6 55
(T D Walford) *prom: hdwy to ld wl over 2f out: rdn and hdd wl over 1f out: sn drvn and wknd ent fnl f* **4/1**[1]
0002 **7** *nk* **Nuit Sombre (IRE)**[19] 3599 8-10-0 **72**........................(p) SebSanders 1 65
(G A Harker) *stdd s and hld up in rr: hdwy over 2f out: rdn and styng on whn n.m.r ins fnl f: swtchd rt and no imp* **11/1**
0404 **8** 5 **Nok Twice (IRE)**[72] 2007 7-9-8 **66**........................(e[1]) DNolan 4 47
(D Carroll) *dwlt: hld up towards rr: effrt and smer hdwy on outer over 2f out: sn rdn and n.d* **12/1**
0061 **9** 1 1/2 **Mister Jingles**[27] 3339 5-9-0 **61**........................ MichaelJStainton(3) 8 38
(R M Whitaker) *chsd ldrs: rdn over 3f out: drvn over 2f out and sn wknd* **9/2**[2]
-056 **10** 6 **Viva Volta**[24] 3443 5-9-12 **70**........................ RobertWinston 7 32
(T D Easterby) *chsd ldrs: rdn along over 3f out and sn wknd* **10/1**
2123 **11** 1 1/2 **Elusive Warrior (USA)**[13] 3819 5-9-9 **67**........................(p) WilliamBuick 10 25
(A J McCabe) *sn led: rdn along 3f: sn hdd & wknd* **14/1**

1m 33.64s (-0.16) **Going Correction** +0.075s/f (Good)
WFA 3 from 4yo+ 7lb **11** Ran SP% **118.0**
Speed ratings (Par 103): **103,101,99,97 96,96,90,88,82 80**
toteswinger: 1&2 £16.10, 1&3 £13.70, 2&3 £12.60. CSF £54.88 CT £388.86 TOTE £12.50: £3.90, £2.10, £2.70; EX 68.00.
Owner W B Imison **Bred** Mrs I A Balding **Trained** Maunby, N Yorks

FOCUS
They went a decent gallop for this relatively moderate handicap. Sound form rated through the second and fourth, with the winner rated back to her best.
Micky Mac(IRE) Official explanation: jockey said gelding ran too free early

4246 OLD GRAVEL PITS ALLERTHORPE H'CAP 5f
8:00 (8:02) (Class 5) (0-75,75) 3-Y-O+ **£3,238** (£963; £481; £240) **Stalls High**

Form RPR
0021 **1** **Rasaman (IRE)**[9] 3956 4-9-9 **73**........................(tp) JoeFanning 8 85
(K A Ryan) *cl up: led 2f out: rdn over 1f out: drvn and kpt on wl fnl f* **5/1**[2]
000 **2** 1 1/2 **Steelcut**[11] 3868 4-9-3 **74**........................ FrederikTylicki(7) 4 81
(R A Fahey) *chsd ldrs: hdwy 2f out: rdn to chal over 1f out and ev ch tl drvn and nt qckn wl ins fnl f* **8/1**

0064 **3** 2½ **Malapropism**[9] 3945 8-9-11 **75**.......... TonyCulhane 6 73
(M R Channon) *led: rdn along 1/2-way: hdd 2f out: sn drvn and one pce ent fnl f* **7/1**[3]

3602 **4** ½ **Hotham**[3] 4171 5-9-4 **73**.......... AshleyHamblett(5) 1 69+
(N Wilson) *towards rr: hdwy 2f out: sn rdn and kpt on ins fnl f: nrst fin* **3/1**[1]

3246 **5** ½ **Just Joey**[7] 4016 4-8-12 **65**..........(b) JamieMoriarty(3) 10 59
(J R Weymes) *dwlt and in rr: hdwy wl over 1f out: swtchd lft and rdn ent fnl f: kpt on: nrst fin* **18/1**

0302 **6** ½ **Soto**[6] 4047 5-8-12 **62**..........(b[1]) PaulMulrennan 5 55
(M W Easterby) *s.i.s and rr: hdwy wl over 1f out: sn rdn and kpt on ins fnl f: nrst fin* **10/1**

4064 **7** *shd* **Charles Parnell (IRE)**[11] 3868 5-9-10 **74**.......... FergalLynch 2 68+
(M Dods) *hld up and bhd: hdwy over 1f out: styng on ins fnl f* **12/1**

0004 **8** *shd* **Welcome Approach**[7] 4013 5-8-6 **56** oh4.......... WilliamBuick 9 48
(J R Weymes) *in tch: rdn along 2f out: sn no imp* **12/1**

0020 **9** *nk* **Winthorpe (IRE)**[3] 4174 8-8-11 **68**.......... JamieKyne(7) 11 59
(J J Quinn) *chsd ldrs: rdn along 2f out: sn wknd* **12/1**

0035 **10** ½ **Sands Crooner (IRE)**[6] 4047 5-8-12 **62**..........(v) SebSanders 3 51
(J G Given) *in tch: hdwy to chse ldrs 2f out: sn rdn and wknd appr fnl f* **11/1**

14-0 **11** *10* **Making Music**[11] 3868 5-8-13 **63**..........(b) RobertWinston 7 16
(T D Easterby) *cl up: rdn along over 2f out and sn wknd* **8/1**

366/ **12** *2* **Fitzwarren**[951] 6570 7-8-3 **56** oh11.......... AndrewMullen(3) 12 2
(A D Brown) *chsd ldrs on inner: rdn along over 2f out and sn wknd* **66/1**

63.12 secs (-0.38) **Going Correction** -0.05s/f (Good) **12** Ran SP% **123.6**
Speed ratings (Par 103): **101,98,94,93,93 92,92,91,91,90 74,71**
toteswinger: 1&2 £17.10, 1&3 £3.80, 2&3 £9.60. CSF £47.01 CT £289.45 TOTE £4.80: £2.20, £3.00, £2.50; EX 51.90.
Owner Royston Vasey **Bred** Rasana Partnership **Trained** Hambleton, N Yorks
■ Stewards' Enquiry : Jamie Moriarty one-day ban: careless riding (Aug 5)

FOCUS
A modest sprint won by the red-hot Rasaman who is getting back to something like his 3yo form..
Soto Official explanation: jockey said gelding fly-leapt to the start
Charles Parnell(IRE) Official explanation: jockey said gelding was denied a clear run

4247 SAILORS FAMILIES SOCIETY MAIDEN H'CAP 2m 35y
8:30 (8:31) (Class 6) (0-65,62) 3-Y-0 **£2,590** (£770; £385; £192) **Stalls High**

Form RPR

-064 **1** **Jackday (IRE)**[5] 4077 3-9-0 **55**.......... FergalLynch 7 61
(T D Easterby) *hld up towards rr: stdy hdwy 4f out: swtchd rt wl over 2f out: rdn over 1f out: styd on to ld fnl 100yds: drvn: edgd lft and kpt on* **10/1**

0460 **2** 1½ **Brave Boogie**[38] 2997 3-9-0 **55**..........(b[1]) MickyFenton 1 59
(H J L Dunlop) *cl up: rdn along over 2f out: drvn and led briefly 1f out: hdd jst ins fnl f and kpt on same pce* **20/1**

-230 **3** *hd* **Bouggler**[39] 2985 3-9-2 **57**.......... PAspell 15 61
(Miss J A Camacho) *hld up in tch: hdwy over 3f out: rdn wl over 1f out: styd on to ld jst ins fnl f: drvn and hdd last 100yds: hld whn hmpd and lost 2nd nr line* **12/1**

6520 **4** 1½ **Capal Dubh Alainn (IRE)**[17] 3671 3-9-6 **61**..........(t) WilliamBuick 16 63
(T J Pitt) *in tch on inner: hdwy 3f out: rdn to chse ldrs wl over 1f out: drvn and n.m.r ins fnl f: swtchd rt and kpt on same pce* **11/1**

-036 **5** *1* **Astrodome**[14] 3781 3-9-0 **55**.......... SebSanders 17 56
(Sir Mark Prescott) *trckd ldrs: effrt and hdwy 3f out: rdn 2f out: drvn over 1f out and kpt on same pce* **4/1**[2]

-040 **6** *nse* **Harrison's Star**[17] 3671 3-8-2 **46**..........(p) AndrewMullen(3) 9 47
(G M Moore) *hld up: hdwy on outer 3f out: rdn to chse ldrs 2f out: sn drvn and kpt on same pce appr fnl f* **50/1**

0-04 **7** *1* **Banquet (IRE)**[17] 3666 3-9-1 **56**.......... TonyHamilton 14 56
(T D Walford) *in tch: hdwy over 3f out: rdn along 2f out: sn drvn and kpt on same pce* **3/1**[1]

0044 **8** ¾ **Sparkling Montjeu (IRE)**[14] 3781 3-9-1 **56**..........(p) J-PGuillambert 3 55
(J W Hills) *led: rdn along over 2f out: drvn: hdd and hung rt 1f out: sn wknd* **25/1**

60-4 **9** *2* **Terrasini (FR)**[40] 2941 3-9-5 **60**.......... RobertWinston 10 59+
(J Howard Johnson) *prom: rdn along and sltly outpcd 3f out: styng on on inner whn hmpd appr fnl f: nt rcvr* **20/1**

005 **10** 3¾ **Rye Rocket**[45] 2779 3-7-11 **45**.......... DeclanCannon(7) 12 37
(K R Burke) *towards rr: sme hdwy over 3f out: sn rdn along and nvr a factor* **50/1**

-036 **11** *nk* **Sonny Sam (IRE)**[39] 2985 3-9-3 **58**.......... PaulMulrennan 2 50
(M H Tompkins) *hld up: stdy hdwy 4f out: rdn to chse ldrs 2f out: sn drvn and wknd appr fnl f* **6/1**[3]

5-50 **12** ½ **General Tufto**[28] 3327 3-9-7 **62**.......... DNolan 5 53
(C Smith) *a towards rr* **40/1**

5500 **13** 2½ **Eddie Dowling**[17] 3671 3-9-6 **61**.......... TonyCulhane 11 49
(M R Channon) *a in rr* **16/1**

0056 **14** ½ **Rivington Pike (IRE)**[5] 4077 3-8-12 **56**.......... JamieMoriarty(3) 13 43
(J J Quinn) *a towards rr* **16/1**

0-05 **15** *18* **Rutba**[17] 3671 3-8-9 **50**.......... DaleGibson 8 16
(M P Tregoning) *a in rr* **10/1**

-053 **16** *6* **Bobal Girl**[23] 3483 3-9-2 **57**.......... JoeFanning 4 16
(E F Vaughan) *prom: effrt 4f out: rdn along 3f out and sn wknd* **20/1**

0000 **17** *79* **Ten Hour Lunch**[109] 1163 3-8-4 **45**.......... NickyMackay 6 —
(S Lycett) *in tch: hdwy to chse ldrs 1/2-way: rdn along 6f out: sn lost pl: bhd and virtually p.u 3f out* **14/1**

3m 42.91s (3.11) **Going Correction** +0.075s/f (Good) **17** Ran SP% **136.4**
Speed ratings (Par 98): **95,94,94,93,92 92,92,92,91,89 88,88,87,87,78 75,60**
toteswinger: 1&2 £63.10, 1&3 £29.50, 2&3 £85.20. CSF £212.70 CT £2476.37 TOTE £11.70: £2.70, £6.70, £3.60, £2.30; EX 460.60.
Owner Mrs Jean P Connew **Bred** Mrs H D McCalmont **Trained** Great Habton, N Yorks
■ Stewards' Enquiry : Fergal Lynch one-day ban: careless riding (Aug 4)
William Buick one-day ban: careless riding (Aug 9)

FOCUS
A moderate staying contest, but Jackday is the type to progress further. The third is the best guide to the form.

4248 ANDREW LAMBETH TRI-GENESIS H'CAP 1m 100y
9:00 (9:00) (Class 5) (0-75,73) 3-Y-0+ **£2,914** (£867; £433; £216) **Stalls High**

Form RPR

0004 **1** **Moonlight Man**[16] 3725 7-10-0 **73**..........(t) SebSanders 3 81
(C R Dore) *set stdy pce: qcknd over 3f out: rdn and qcknd over 1f out: drvn and edgd lft ins fnl f: styd on wl* **13/2**

1003 **2** 1¼ **Society Music (IRE)**[3] 4172 6-9-9 **68**..........(p) FergalLynch 5 73
(M Dods) *plld hrd: hld up in rr: hdwy on inner 2f out: rdn over 1f out: ev ch whn n.m.r and swtchd rt ins fnl f: kpt on* **3/1**[2]

0642 **3** *hd* **Prince Noel**[3] 4148 4-8-13 **63**.......... AshleyHamblett(5) 7 68
(N Wilson) *trckd ldng pair gng wl: smooth hdwy 2f out: rdn to chal over 1f out: drvn and nt qckn ins fnl f* **2/1**[1]

4-03 **4** 1½ **Manuka Bee**[18] 3640 3-8-0 **60**.......... JamieKyne(7) 1 59
(J Howard Johnson) *t.k.h: chsd ldrs: pushed along and sltly outpcd 3f out: styd on u.p appr fnl f: nrst fin* **14/1**

0004 **5** 2¼ **Always Brave**[7] 4015 3-9-2 **69**.......... JoeFanning 4 63
(M Johnston) *t.k.h: hld up: effrt 3f out: sn rdn along and wknd over 2f out* **4/1**[3]

1-3 **6** *2* **San Silvestro (IRE)**[12] 3831 3-8-13 **69**.......... AndrewMullen(3) 2 58
(Mrs A Duffield) *t.k.h: hdwy to chse wnr after 1f: rdn along over 2f out and sn btn* **11/2**

1m 49.64s (2.04) **Going Correction** +0.075s/f (Good)
WFA 3 from 4yo+ 8lb **6** Ran SP% **113.7**
Speed ratings (Par 103): **92,90,90,89,86 84**
toteswinger: 1&2 £3.50, 1&3 £1.90, 2&3 £1.10. CSF £26.65 TOTE £8.30: £2.70, £2.20; EX 33.30 Place 6: £253.65, Place 5: £224.56..
Owner Liam Breslin **Bred** P T Tellwright **Trained** West Pinchbeck, Lincs

FOCUS
A moderate winning time. The winner enjoyed an easy lead and showed a return to form, but this was a very irdinary race.
T/Plt: £517.00 to a £1 stake. Pool: £63,393.57. 89.50 winning tickets. T/Qpdt: £76.70 to a £1 stake. Pool: £4,759.58. 45.90 winning tickets. JR

4020 WINDSOR (R-H)
Monday, July 21

OFFICIAL GOING: Good to firm (8.0)
A treble for Richard Hannon, who had another two runners beaten a nose.
Wind: Half behind, moderate becoming almost nil Weather: Sunny, warm

4249 GET ON WITH WILLIAM HILL 0800 44 40 40 MAIDEN STKS 1m 2f 7y
6:20 (6:22) (Class 5) 3-4-Y-0 **£2,729** (£806; £403) **Stalls Centre**

Form RPR

05 **1** **Spider Silk**[18] 3654 3-9-3 0.......... AlanMunro 14 78
(W Jarvis) *t.k.h: cl up bhd ldrs: effrt and carried hd high fr over 2f out: styd on wl fnl f to ld last stride* **25/1**

2023 **2** *nse* **Special Reserve (IRE)**[10] 3915 3-9-3 77.......... RichardHughes 12 77
(R Hannon) *trckd ldr: cruising 3f out: led 2f out: hrd rdn fnl f: hdd last stride* **2/1**[2]

3 ¾ **Madam President** 3-8-12 0.......... AdamKirby 10 71+
(W R Swinburn) *hld up in midfield: stdy prog to chse ldng pair over 1f out: rdn and r.o fnl f: nvr quite able to chal* **16/1**

4 *hd* **Sibi Saba (USA)** 3-8-12 0.......... KerrinMcEvoy 13 71+
(Saeed Bin Suroor) *dwlt: hld up in midfield: effrt over 2f out: nt qckn over 1f out: r.o again fnl f: gaining at fin* **9/1**

20-4 **5** 1¼ **Thought Is Free**[52] 2566 3-8-12 85.......... JohnEgan 4 68
(P F I Cole) *hld up in tch: prog 3f out: drvn to chal over 1f out: nt qckn ent fnl f: wknd fnl 100yds* **8/1**[3]

00 **6** 4½ **Look To This Day**[11] 3894 3-8-12 0.......... SteveDrowne 3 59
(R Charlton) *hld up in midfield: outpcd by ldrs over 2f out: pushed along and kpt on one pce* **20/1**

0 **7** 3½ **Missellieebee**[77] 1854 3-8-12 0.......... MichaelHills 6 52
(J W Hills) *mostly trckd ldng pair to over 2f out: steadily fdd* **100/1**

8 1½ **No Wonga** 3-8-12 0.......... RichardEvans(5) 11 54+
(P D Evans) *hld up in last trio: sme prog over 2f out: reminder over 1f out: no ch but kpt on steadily* **66/1**

00 **9** ¾ **Park Run**[4] 4124 3-8-5 0.......... StacyRenwick(7) 5 48
(A W Carroll) *dwlt: hld up wl in rr: effrt on outer 3f out: wknd 2f out* **150/1**

0- **10** 1½ **Aston Boy**[341] 4508 3-9-3 0.......... JamesDoyle 8 50
(M Blanshard) *a wl in rr: reminders and no prog 4f out: n.d* **100/1**

6- **11** *7* **Institute**[269] 6468 3-9-3 0.......... RyanMoore 2 36+
(Sir Michael Stoute) *dwlt but sn led: rdn 3f out: hdd and btn 2f out: eased* **11/10**[1]

500- **12** 1¼ **Ryan's Rock**[225] 7084 3-9-3 47.......... RobertHavlin 9 33
(T D McCarthy) *awkward gng to post and into stalls: t.k.h: trckd ldrs: rdn 3f out: wknd over 2f out* **100/1**

00 **13** 4½ **Alright Chuck**[13] 3810 4-9-13 0.......... ChrisCatlin 7 24
(P W Hiatt) *dwlt: a in last trio: lost tch over 2f out* **150/1**

2m 9.45s (0.75) **Going Correction** 0.0s/f (Good)
WFA 3 from 4yo 10lb **13** Ran SP% **122.3**
Speed ratings (Par 103): **97,96,96,96,95 91,88,87,87,85 80,79,75**
toteswinger: 1&2 £14.10, 1&3 £75.80, 2&3 £9.40 CSF £76.40 TOTE £28.30: £5.30, £1.30, £3.30; EX 114.70.
Owner John Kelsey-Fry **Bred** John Kelsey-Fry **Trained** Newmarket, Suffolk
■ Stewards' Enquiry : Richard Hughes two-day ban: careless riding (Aug 4-5)
John Egan Fine: £140, failed to report filly moving scratchily closing stages.

FOCUS
A slow pace but a fair heat considering most of them are into the second half of their three-year-old year and still maidens. The first five home put daylight between themselves and the remainder and are the ones to concentrate on for the future. The form might not prove entirely solid.
Thought Is Free Official explanation: jockey said filly moved scratchily closing stages
Institute Official explanation: vet said colt returned with cut on hind leg

4250 GET A BONUS AT WILLIAMHILLCASINO.COM (S) STKS 1m 3f 135y
6:50 (6:50) (Class 6) 3-Y-0+ **£2,047** (£604; £302) **Stalls Centre**

Form RPR

3-2 **1** **Check Up (IRE)**[12] 3844 7-9-4 0.......... KevinGhunowa(3) 4 61
(J L Flint) *t.k.h: trckd ldrs: led over 2f out: drvn clr over 1f out: in full command fnl f* **11/4**[1]

-500 **2** 2½ **Bundle Up**[7] 4026 5-9-2 54..........(t) PaulDoe 10 51
(Mrs L J Mongan) *hld up in midfield: hmpd bnd over 6f out: effrt 3f out: rdn and styd on fr over 1f out to take 2nd last stride* **7/1**

0504 **3** *hd* **Converti**[7] 4023 4-9-2 45.......... JamieJones(5) 7 56
(H J Manners) *hld up in midfield: prog 3f out: hrd rdn to chse wnr over 1f out: no imp: lost 2nd last stride* **9/1**

4535 **4** *1* **Missie Baileys**[23] 3482 6-9-2 51..........(p) IanMongan 2 49
(Mrs L J Mongan) *hld up in midfield: clsd on ldrs 3f out: sn drvn: no imp fr over 1f out* **3/1**[2]

4020 **5** ½ **Miss Porcia**[37] 3025 7-9-2 43.......... TPO'Shea 8 48
(P A Blockley) *cl up: chsd wnr over 2f out to over 1f out: one pce* **11/2**[3]

6 *hd* **Pairumani Pat (IRE)** 3-8-9 0.......... RobertHavlin 1 53
(J Pearce) *s.s: hld up in rr: drvn 2f out: styd on fr over 1f out: keeping on whn nt clr run ins fnl f* **20/1**

500 **7** ¾ **Nil Bleu (USA)**[8] 3588 4-9-7 52 ....(b[1]) GeorgeBaker 3 52
(Noel T Chance) *hld up wl in rr: stdy prog over 3f out: chsd ldrs 2f out: one pce and no imp after* **9/1**

P-00 **8** 5 **Panadin (IRE)**[6] 4054 6-9-7 38 ....(p) TQuinn 9 43
(Mrs L C Jewell) *led after 3f to over 2f out: sn btn* **66/1**

0503 **9** 10 **Persian Fox (IRE)**[40] 2932 4-9-7 47 ....(p) VinceSlattery 11 26
(A G Juckes) *s.s: plld hrd: hld up in last trio: snatched up bnd over 6f out: wknd 3f out: t.o* **16/1**

0500 **10** 3 ¾ **The Slider**[148] 691 4-9-2 40 ....(p) RichardThomas 6 15
(Mrs L C Jewell) *led 3f: chsd ldr to 3f out: wknd: t.o* **40/1**

-630 **11** 3 ½ **Leprechaun's Gold (IRE)**[7] 4023 4-9-7 46 .... ChrisCatlin 12 14
(B J Llewellyn) *cl up: awkward bnd over 6f out and lost pl: struggling in rr 3f out: t.o* **14/1**

2m 29.93s (0.43) **Going Correction** 0.0s/f (Good)
WFA 3 from 4yo+ 12lb 11 Ran SP% **120.8**
Speed ratings (Par 101): **98,96,96,95,95 95,94,91,84,82 79**
toteswinger: 1&2 £3.30, 1&3 £7.70, 2&3 £8.40. CSF £22.94 TOTE £3.80: £1.40, £2.70, £2.70; EX 26.70.The winner was bought in for £8,000. Bundle Up was claimed by P D Evans for £5,000.
Owner Andrew Leyshon **Bred** Martin Brennan **Trained** Kenfig Hill, Bridgend

FOCUS
A poor heat, even by selling standards, and Milton Johns must have been on fine form to get the bidding up to £8,000 at the subsequent auction. The winner ran to his latest form.

4251 EUROPEAN BREEDERS' FUND MAIDEN FILLIES' STKS 6f
7:20 (7:22) (Class 4) 2-Y-O **£5,569** (£1,242; £1,242; £413) **Stalls** High

Form RPR

1 **Mamlakati (IRE)** 2-9-0 0 .... RichardHughes 6 74+
(R Hannon) *t.k.h: hld up in midfield: prog on outer fr 2f out to press ldrs 1f out: rdn to ld fnl 100yds: readily* **9/1**

2 ¾ **Poyle Meg** 2-9-0 0 .... JamesDoyle 1 70
(R M Beckett) *sn prom on outer fr low draw: effrt 2f out: upsides ent fnl f: one pce fnl 100yds* **25/1**

2 dht **Victoria Sponge (IRE)** 2-9-0 0 .... RyanMoore 11 70
(R Hannon) *trckd ldrs: swtchd to nr side rail and effrt 2f out: led jst over 1f out: hdd and one pce fnl 100yds* **8/1**

32 **4** ½ **Sills Vincero**[16] 3734 2-9-0 0 .... AlanMunro 8 68
(P W Chapple-Hyam) *pressed ldr: chal 2f out: upsides ent fnl f: no ex fnl 100yds* **4/1**[2]

5 5 **Zelloof (IRE)** 2-9-0 0 .... KerrinMcEvoy 5 53
(Saeed Bin Suroor) *trckd ldrs: shkn up and outpcd 2f out: no imp on ldrs fnl f* **11/4**[1]

0 **6** 1 ¾ **Jewelled Reef (IRE)**[28] 3323 2-9-0 0 .... StephenCarson 2 48+
(Eve Johnson Houghton) *trckd ldrs on outer: cl up 2f out: fdd jst over 1f out* **20/1**

0 **7** 1 **Fleur De'Lion (IRE)**[10] 3913 2-9-0 0 .... MartinDwyer 7 45
(S Kirk) *hld up: outpcd in 12th after 2f: pushed along and prog fr 2f out: nvr rchd ldrs* **40/1**

4 **8** ¾ **Cocktail Party (IRE)**[72] 2011 2-9-0 0 .... MichaelHills 12 43+
(J W Hills) *led to jst over 1f out: wknd rapidly* **6/1**[3]

9 1 **Kaikoura** 2-9-0 0 .... PaulEddery 16 40
(G D Blake) *in tch in midfield: outpcd fr over 2f out: no ch after* **25/1**

10 nse **Turkish Lokum** 2-8-11 0 .... LukeMorris(3) 15 40+
(J M P Eustace) *in tch at rr of main gp: hmpd jst over 2f out: no ch after* **25/1**

11 hd **Turn To Dreams** 2-8-9 0 .... RichardEvans(5) 9 39+
(P D Evans) *dwlt: hld up wl off the pce: kpt on steadily fnl 2f and gng wl: nvr nr ldrs* **50/1**

12 hd **Wanted (GER)** 2-8-11 0 .... JamesMillman(3) 10 38
(B R Millman) *rn green and sn wl bhd: styd on fnl 2f: no ch* **33/1**

13 6 **It's A Game (USA)** 2-9-0 0 .... RobertHavlin 4 20
(J H M Gosden) *s.s: a wl detached in rr* **14/1**

14 1 ½ **Pansy Potter** 2-9-0 0 .... JamieSpencer 14 16
(B J Meehan) *trckd ldrs tl wknd rapidly over 2f out* **10/1**

15 3 ½ **Louise Bonne (USA)** 2-9-0 0 .... PhilipRobinson 3 5
(C G Cox) *in tch on outer: reminder 1/2-way: wknd over 2f out* **16/1**

16 4 **Spring Green** 2-9-0 0 .... SteveDrowne 13 —
(H Morrison) *s.s: rn green and a bhd* **20/1**

1m 13.39s (0.39) **Going Correction** -0.125s/f (Firm) 16 Ran SP% **132.1**
Speed ratings (Par 93): **92,91,91,90,83 81,80,79,77,77 77,77,69,67,62 57**
PL: Mamlakati £3.30, Poyle Meg £9.10, Victoria Sponge £2.60. toteswinger: M&PM £95.70, M&VS £6.70, PM&VS £73.60. Exacta with PM £197.60, CSF £115.59. Exacta with VS £32.40, CSF not won. TOTE £12.30.
Owner Malih L Al Basti **Bred** Raymond P Doyle **Trained** East Everleigh, Wilts

FOCUS
A slightly above-average fillies' maiden, typical of the course. The fourth and sixth are the best guides to the form. There are a few to take from this who look to have bright futures in reasonable grade.

NOTEBOOK
Mamlakati(IRE) ◆ continued the phenomenal run being enjoyed by the Hannon juggernaut with their juveniles. Her price shot up from 37,000euros as a yearling to 150,000gns at this year's Tattersalls Breeze-up sale and someone clearly knew what they were doing as she looks a filly with a good future. (op 8-1 tchd 10-1)
Poyle Meg ◆ a daughter of Dansili, did well to go close from an unpromising low draw. While her dam was a middle-distance winner, she was a half-sister to Lowther Stakes winner Jemima, and it looks as though this filly has inherited more of the family's speed than stamina, as indeed did her half-sister Another True Story, a dual 5f juvenile winner for Hannon in 2006. (op 12-1)
Victoria Sponge(IRE) ◆, stablemate of the winner and nibbled at in the market, knew her job on debut as so many from her yard appear to do, and led briefly at the furlong pole before just getting a bit tired close home. She is sure to be placed to advantage soon. (op 12-1)
Sills Vincero had been placed in a couple of 5f maidens and while she again ran her race, the extra furlong didn't appear to bring about any improvement. (op 7-2)
Zelloof(IRE) ◆ out of a Moyglare Stud Stakes winner and by the leading first-season sire, was given a tender introduction having been withdrawn after getting worked up before her intended debut at the Newmarket July meeting. Keeping on nicely under a hand ride, she is sure to do better. (op 7-2)
Cocktail Party(IRE), very heavily supported in the market, burst out and led until a furlong out, where once challenged she edged left and quickly ran up the white flag. A switch to the minimum is surely in order. (op 16-1)
Turn To Dreams Official explanation: jockey said filly ran green

4252 EVOLUTION SECURITIES H'CAP 6f
7:50 (7:53) (Class 4) (0-85,85) 3-Y-O **£5,828** (£1,734; £866; £432) **Stalls** High

Form RPR

3215 **1** **Superduper**[24] 3462 3-8-13 77 .... RichardHughes 9 85
(R Hannon) *pressed ldr: led jst over 2f out: kicked 2 l clr over 1f out: drvn out* **15/2**[3]

0051 **2** 1 **Masada (IRE)**[17] 3696 3-9-7 85 .... JamieSpencer 7 90
(B J Meehan) *dwlt: hld up in last pair: gd prog on wd outside fr 2f out: hrd rdn to chse wnr fnl f: no real imp fnl 100yds* **8/1**

0024 **3** ½ **Ivory Silk**[16] 3727 3-8-6 70 .... ChrisCatlin 3 73
(D K Ivory) *pushed along in midfield bef 1/2-way: prog over 2f out: disp 2nd over 1f out: kpt on same pce* **20/1**

-000 **4** ½ **Harlech Castle**[30] 3270 3-9-0 78 ....(b) KerrinMcEvoy 2 80
(P F I Cole) *hld up towards rr of main gp: prog but nt clrest of runs fr 2f out: styd on fnl f: nrst fin* **10/1**

1022 **5** ½ **Dunn'o (IRE)**[16] 3723 3-9-5 83 .... PhilipRobinson 6 83
(C G Cox) *awkward s: w ldrs: nt qckn wl over 1f out: disp 2nd after tl one pce fnl f* **7/2**[1]

6-30 **6** 1 ¼ **King's Wonder**[79] 1806 3-9-0 78 .... MartinDwyer 5 74
(W R Muir) *dwlt: hld up in last pair: effrt on outer 2f out: hanging but styd on fr over 1f out* **8/1**

03-5 **7** 1 **Zippi Jazzman (USA)**[88] 1584 3-8-13 77 .... JamesDoyle 13 70
(R M Beckett) *led to jst over 2f out: hanging bdly lft and sn btn* **9/1**

0435 **8** 2 **Tadalavil**[14] 3782 3-8-8 72 .... TPO'Shea 11 59
(M R Channon) *mostly in midfield: u.p over 2f out: no imp over 1f out: fdd* **20/1**

-101 **9** ¾ **Vigano (IRE)**[20] 3571 3-8-10 74 .... JimCrowley 10 58
(S Kirk) *nvr beyond midfield: rdn 1/2-way: no imp* **20/1**

3461 **10** 3 **Lodi (IRE)**[28] 3324 3-9-2 80 ....(t) IanMongan 4 55
(J Akehurst) *late to post: chsd ldrs: u.p sn after 1/2-way: steadily fdd fnl 2f* **6/1**[2]

405 **11** 3 ¾ **Miss Mujanna**[51] 2622 3-8-8 72 ....(p) TQuinn 12 35
(J Akehurst) *dwlt: sn rdn against nr side rail: nvr on terms w ldrs* **14/1**

0366 **12** 1 **Fifty (IRE)**[10] 3918 3-8-10 74 .... RyanMoore 8 34
(R Hannon) *mostly outpcd against nr side rail: nvr a factor* **12/1**

005 **13** 40 **Pha Mai Blue**[20] 3587 3-9-0 78 ....(v[1]) AlanMunro 1 —
(W J Knight) *chsd ldrs: u.p whn lost action 2f out: virtually p.u after* **33/1**

1m 11.74s (-1.26) **Going Correction** -0.125s/f (Firm) 13 Ran SP% **121.2**
Speed ratings (Par 102): **103,101,101,100,99 98,96,94,93,89 84,82,29**
toteswinger: 1&2 £5.50, 1&3 £42.30, 2&3 £86.30. CSF £63.53 CT £1211.46 TOTE £6.50: £2.10, £2.80, £6.60; EX 51.30.
Owner David & Jennifer Sieff & Bloomsbury Stud **Bred** Bloomsbury Stud & The Hon Sir David Sieff **Trained** East Everleigh, Wilts
■ Stewards' Enquiry : Jamie Spencer caution: used whip with excessive frequency

FOCUS
A competitive little sprint handicap, ultimately dominated by fillies, in which the bulk of the field came down the centre of the track after the intersection and a couple that stuck closer to the stands' rail ended up well beaten. Ordinary form for the grade but the front pair are on the up.
Masada(IRE) Official explanation: jockey said filly was unruly in stalls
Zippi Jazzman(USA) Official explanation: jockey said colt hung left
Pha Mai Blue Official explanation: jockey said colt lost its action

4253 GET YOUR CHIPS AT WILLIAMHILLPOKER.COM FILLIES' H'CAP 1m 67y
8:20 (8:20) (Class 5) (0-75,73) 3-Y-O **£3,070** (£906; £453) **Stalls** High

Form RPR

-000 **1** **Rescue Me**[10] 3918 3-8-8 63 .... PatrickHills(3) 10 71+
(R Hannon) *s.i.s: hld up in last trio: stdy prog on outer fr over 3f out: sustained effrt to ld ins fnl f: hld on wl* **14/1**

0-22 **2** nk **Rhadegunda**[9] 3977 3-9-3 69 .... JimmyFortune 1 77
(J H M Gosden) *sn trckd ldr: rdn to ld wl over 1f out: edgd lft u.p and hdd ins fnl f: kpt on* **2/1**[1]

-541 **3** 2 ½ **Oriental Girl**[28] 3314 3-8-11 63 ....(p) DavidKinsella 2 65
(J A Geake) *led: kicked on over 3f out: edgd lft and hdd wl over 1f out: nt qckn* **13/2**[3]

51 **4** nk **Zulu Princess (IRE)**[10] 3906 3-8-9 64 .... LukeMorris(3) 4 65
(J S Moore) *hld up in tch: rdn and nt qckn over 2f out: styd on fr over 1f out: unable to chal* **9/1**

5-41 **5** ½ **Shanzu**[23] 3507 3-9-7 73 .... RyanMoore 5 73
(H Candy) *chsd ldng pair: hanging lft and nt qckn 2f out: one pce after* **4/1**[2]

002 **6** ½ **Liberally (IRE)**[18] 3629 3-9-3 69 .... RichardHughes 3 68
(B J Meehan) *trckd ldrs: rdn and nt qckn over 2f out: one pce after* **8/1**

244- **7** 2 **Freedom Song**[247] 6855 3-9-6 72 .... SteveDrowne 9 69+
(R Charlton) *hld up in last pair: pushed along 3f out: sme prog and shkn up briefly 1f out: nvr any ch: eased nr fin* **16/1**

0205 **8** 1 ¼ **Miss Phoebe (IRE)**[11] 3874 3-8-11 63 .... MartinDwyer 8 55
(S Kirk) *hld up in midfield: pushed along and no prog 3f out: rdn and no hdwy over 1f out* **20/1**

0060 **9** 3 ½ **Elizabeth's Quest**[35] 3086 3-7-9 54 oh5 .... StacyRenwick(7) 11 37
(A W Carroll) *hld up in last: nvr a factor* **50/1**

4-04 **10** 1 ½ **Paradise Island (IRE)**[28] 3318 3-8-13 65 .... JamieSpencer 6 45
(E A L Dunlop) *plld hrd early: hld up bhd ldrs: rdn over 2f out: wknd wl over 1f out* **8/1**

6440 **11** 3 ¾ **Ambrix (IRE)**[126] 918 3-8-8 60 .... EdwardCreighton 7 33
(M R Channon) *dwlt: a in rr: struggling over 2f out: wknd* **33/1**

1m 45.28s (0.58) **Going Correction** 0.0s/f (Good) 11 Ran SP% **121.1**
Speed ratings (Par 97): **97,96,94,93,93 92,90,89,86,84 81**
toteswinger: 1&2 £9.90, 1&3 £9.00, 2&3 £3.30. CSF £42.86 CT £217.04 TOTE £16.90: £3.40, £1.30, £2.40; EX 54.60.
Owner P D Merritt **Bred** Raimon Bloodstock **Trained** East Everleigh, Wilts

FOCUS
A moderate fillies' handicap in which the pace was ordinary. The runners stayed fairly close to the stands' rail immediately after the intersection, but gradually migrated across the track and ended up closer to the far rail. The winner probably did well to win this though, as the other two fillies that finished in the frame held the first two positions for most of the contest. The form seems to make a fair bit of sense.
Paradise Island(IRE) Official explanation: jockey said filly lost its action

4254 OAKLEY COURT HOTEL H'CAP 1m 2f 7y
8:50 (8:50) (Class 5) (0-70,69) 3-Y-O+ **£2,729** (£806; £403) **Stalls** Centre

Form RPR

0320 **1** **Latin Scholar (IRE)**[26] 3384 3-9-3 68 .... FergusSweeney 4 79
(A King) *t.k.h: trckd clr ldng pair: wl ahd of rest 4f out: rdn to cl 2f out: led 1f out: edgd lft: jst hld on* **6/1**[3]

3322 **2** nse **King Supreme (IRE)**[37] 3022 3-9-3 68 ....(b) RichardHughes 11 79
(R Hannon) *stdd s: sn prom in chsng pack: plenty to do in 4th over 3f out: styd on to cl grad 2f out: r.o wl fnl f: needed one more stride* **7/2**[2]

4121 **3** 1 **Western Roots**[22] 3518 7-9-1 61 .... DavidProbert(5) 12 70
(A M Balding) *bowled along in front and sn had field stretched out: clr w 2 rivals 4f out: hdd and no ex 1f out* **11/4**[1]

4403 **4** 2 1/2 **Penang Cinta**[17] 3676 5-9-6 **66**.....(p) RichardEvans(5) 10 70
(P D Evans) *hld up in last pair and way off the pce: stdy prog fr 3f out: rdn and stdy on wl fnl f: too much to do* **8/1**

4021 **5** 4 **Coral Shores**[21] 3551 3-8-12 **63**.....(v) JimCrowley 14 59
(P W Hiatt) *chsd clr ldr to 2f out: wknd* **11/1**

431 **6** 1 1/2 **Bridgewater Boys**[23] 3482 7-10-0 **69**.....(b) RyanMoore 1 62
(G L Moore) *hld up wl in rr and way off the pce: sme prog on outer 3f out: no hdwy or imp fnl 2f* **8/1**

6066 **7** 1 3/4 **Muffett's Dream**[10] 3914 4-8-9 **50** oh4..... FrankieMcDonald 3 39
(J J Bridger) *chsd clr ldng trio 1/2-way: rdn and no imp 4f out: sn btn* **40/1**

0-02 **8** 3/4 **Everyman**[10] 3901 4-8-4 **50**..... MarkCoumbe(5) 5 38
(A W Carroll) *hld up wl in rr and way off the pce: limited prog u.p over 2f out: n.d* **25/1**

3300 **9** 5 **Ray Diamond**[22] 3524 3-7-13 **50**.....(p) DavidKinsella 8 28
(M Madgwick) *a wl bhd in last trio: struggling u.p over 4f out* **66/1**

6503 **10** hd **Eureka Moment**[17] 3667 3-9-3 **68**..... JimmyFortune 7 46
(E A L Dunlop) *hld up towards rr and way off the pce: rdn and v modest prog 3f out: sn wknd* **10/1**

6123 **11** 1 3/4 **Laish Ya Hajar (IRE)**[14] 3780 4-9-10 **65**..... ChrisCatlin 6 39
(P R Webber) *t.k.h: chsd clr ldng trio to 1/2-way: lost pl and struggling over 3f out* **12/1**

400- **12** 3 1/4 **Mystic Storm**[297] 5769 5-9-11 **66**..... TQuinn 2 34
(B G Powell) *hld up wl in rr and way off the pce: struggling over 3f out* **20/1**

0450 **13** 2 1/2 **Zabeel House**[43] 2870 5-9-1 **56**.....(p) AlanMunro 9 19
(John A Harris) *plld hrd: hld up and sn way off the pce in rr: nvr a factor* **25/1**

2m 6.32s (-2.38) **Going Correction** 0.0s/f (Good)
WFA 3 from 4yo+ 10lb **13** Ran SP% **126.9**
Speed ratings (Par 103): **109,108,108,106,102 101,100,99,95,95 94,91,89**
toteswinger: 1&2 £2.50, 1&3 £7.10, 2&3 £3.40. CSF £27.58 CT £74.65 TOTE £6.20: £2.00, £2.00, £1.70; EX 32.90 Place 6: £260.19, Place 5: £91.80..
Owner Four Mile Racing **Bred** David Brickley **Trained** Barbury Castle, Wilts

FOCUS
An ordinary handicap, but one run at a very rapid pace thanks to the favourite Western Roots and the winning time was smart, 3.13 seconds faster than the earlier maiden over the same trip. Very few ever managed to get into it. The form looks very solid.
Eureka Moment Official explanation: jockey said filly hung both ways
T/Jkpt: Not won. T/Plt: £171.10 to a £1 stake. Pool: £95,511.29. 407.45 winning tickets. T/Qpdt: £40.40 to a £1 stake. Pool: £6,637.26. 121.50 winning tickets. JN

4062 YARMOUTH (L-H)
Monday, July 21

OFFICIAL GOING: Good to firm (good in places)
Wind: Fresh half-behind Weather: Overcast

4255 FIRSTBET.COM 0800 230 0800 TELEBETTING £25 MATCHED BET MEDIAN AUCTION MAIDEN STKS — 1m 1f
2:15 (2:15) (Class 6) 3-4-Y-O £2,201 (£655; £327; £163) Stalls Low

Form RPR

4- **1** **Last Three Minutes (IRE)**[279] 6248 3-9-3 0..... TPQueally 3 89+
(E A L Dunlop) *trckd ldr: shkn up to ld over 1f out: r.o wl* **5/2**[1]

3443 **2** 6 **Seventh Cavalry (IRE)**[11] 3894 3-9-3 78.....(v1) TedDurcan 5 76
(H R A Cecil) *led: rdn and hdd over 1f out: styd on same pce: eased nr fin* **5/2**[1]

304 **3** 5 **Rio Guru (IRE)**[9] 3977 3-8-12 85..... DarryllHolland 4 60
(M R Channon) *chsd ldrs: rdn over 3f out: hung lft and wknd over 1f out* **5/1**[3]

4 1 **Mazaris (IRE)** 3-9-3 0..... PatCosgrave 7 63+
(L M Cumani) *hld up: shkn up 1/2-way: outpcd fnl 3f* **11/1**

5 5 **Lion Gate (USA)** 3-9-3 0..... JimmyFortune 1 52+
(J H M Gosden) *dwlt: hld up: shkn up over 3f out: sn wknd* **3/1**[2]

50 **6** 1 1/4 **Circadian Rhythm**[14] 3801 3-8-12 0..... SaleemGolam 2 44
(S C Williams) *hld up: rdn over 3f out: sn wknd* **80/1**

6 **7** 8 **Major Promise**[13] 3813 3-9-0 0..... LukeMorris(3) 6 31
(G G Margarson) *hld up: rdn over 4f out: sn wknd* **14/1**

1m 54.88s (-0.92) **Going Correction** 0.0s/f (Good) **7** Ran SP% **115.0**
Speed ratings (Par 101): **104,98,94,93,88 87,80**
toteswinger: 1&2 £2.00, 1&3 £2.50, 2&3 £3.70 CSF £9.13 TOTE £3.30: £2.40, £1.80; EX 9.20.
Owner The Right Angle Club **Bred** Apache Stud Pty Ltd **Trained** Newmarket, Suffolk

FOCUS
An uncompetitive maiden run at what looked a fair pace, and they finished strung out. The form is rated through the runner-up with the third disappointing but the winner capable of better.
Rio Guru(IRE) Official explanation: jockey said filly hung left

4256 LINDLEY CATERING MEDIAN AUCTION MAIDEN STKS — 7f 3y
2:45 (2:48) (Class 6) 2-Y-O £2,201 (£655; £327; £163) Stalls High

Form RPR

0 **1** **Dazinski**[23] 3495 2-9-3 0..... RichardMullen 6 73
(M H Tompkins) *hld up: hdwy over 1f out: rdn to ld ins fnl f: r.o* **3/1**[1]

2 nk **Captainrisk (IRE)** 2-9-0 0..... KirstyMilczarek(3) 10 72
(M Botti) *a.p: led over 2f out: rdn and hdd ins fnl f: r.o* **9/1**

40 **3** 1/2 **Temperence Hall (USA)**[24] 3444 2-9-3 0..... HayleyTurner 2 71
(J R Best) *chsd ldr: rdn over 1f out: ev ch ins fnl f: styd on* **9/2**[2]

4 1/2 **Noble Dictator** 2-9-3 0..... RichardKingscote 3 70
(E F Vaughan) *free to post: hld up: hdwy over 1f out: rdn ins fnl f: unable qck nr fin* **14/1**

5 7 **Teeky** 2-8-12 0..... JimmyFortune 11 50+
(J H M Gosden) *s.i.s: sn chsng ldrs: rdn over 2f out: wknd over 1f out* **3/1**[1]

6 3/4 **Baileys Red** 2-9-3 0..... TPQueally 14 50+
(J G Given) *s.i.s: hdwy 1/2-way: rdn whn stmbld 2f out: sn wknd* **10/1**

0 **7** 1/2 **Transfered (IRE)**[80] 1778 2-8-12 0..... TedDurcan 9 44
(M G Quinlan) *led: rdn and hdd over 2f out: wknd fnl f* **40/1**

5 **8** 1/2 **Ray Of Joy**[28] 3323 2-8-12 0..... StephenDonohoe 4 43
(J R Jenkins) *chsd ldrs: rdn over 2f out: sn wknd* **6/1**[3]

0 **9** 1 1/4 **Shape Shifter (USA)**[38] 3001 2-9-3 0..... MohammedSaeed 7 45
(J R Best) *free to post: chsd ldrs: rdn over 2f out: wknd over 1f out* **22/1**

10 3/4 **Rebounding** 2-8-12 0..... SaleemGolam 5 38+
(S C Williams) *hld up: rdn over 2f out: n.d* **33/1**

11 1/2 **Call It On (IRE)** 2-9-3 0..... JimmyQuinn 12 42
(M H Tompkins) *s.s: outpcd* **16/1**

12 hd **Count On Guest** 2-9-3 0..... AdrianMcCarthy 15 41
(G G Margarson) *hld up: rdn 1/2-way: wknd over 2f out* **28/1**

0 **13** 2 3/4 **Come On Toby**[7] 4024 2-9-3 0..... DO'Donohoe 13 34
(E A L Dunlop) *s.i.s: hld up: pushed along 1/2-way: wknd over 2f out* **25/1**

1m 26.7s (0.10) **Going Correction** -0.225s/f (Firm) **13** Ran SP% **131.1**
Speed ratings (Par 92): **90,89,89,88,80 79,79,78,77,76 75,75,72**
toteswinger: 1&2 £11.60, 1&3 £5.10, 2&3 £14.70. CSF £33.26 TOTE £4.30: £2.00, £4.00, £3.70; EX 44.70 Trifecta £99.20 Part won. Pool: £134.15 - 0.50 winning units..
Owner Mrs Beryl Lockey **Bred** Darley **Trained** Newmarket, Suffolk
■ Light Dubai was withdrawn (5/1, unruly going to post.) R4 applies, deduct 15p in the £. New market formed.

FOCUS
Probably just an ordinary juvenile maiden in which the first four finished clear. The winner improved by 10lb.

NOTEBOOK
Dazinski built on the promise he showed when seventh in a fair maiden at Newmarket on his debut, putting his experience to good use to get the better of a newcomer in a close finish. He looks capable of progressing in nurseries. (old market op 7-1, new market op 7-2)
Captainrisk(IRE), a 15,000gns son of Captain Rio, first foal of a 7f three-year-old winner, made a bold bid on his racecourse debut and was just held after edging right under pressure late on. He will know more next time and could win a similar race. (old market op 12-1)
Temperence Hall(USA) did not put up much of a show at Folkestone last time, but he had previously shown plenty of ability when fourth on his debut at Lingfield and he confirmed that initial promise with a respectable effort. He will have more options now he is eligible for nurseries. (old market op 9-1)
Noble Dictator, a son of Diktat, was a handful in the paddock and was free to post. He showed ability in the race itself, but his challenge just flattened out late on and it will have to be hoped he grows up a bit. (old market op 16-1 tchd 20-1)
Teeky, a daughter of Daylami, half-sister to among others high-class multiple 7f-1m winner Sleeping Indian, out of a smart 1m2f winner at three, showed up well for a long way and fared best of the fillies, but she finished up beaten a fair distance. This was slightly disappointing, but she might do better with a bit more give underfoot. (old market tchd 4-1, new market op 11-4)

4257 NORFOLK NELSON MUSEUM (S) STKS — 6f 3y
3:15 (3:17) (Class 6) 2-Y-O £1,942 (£578; £288; £144) Stalls High

Form RPR

0 **1** **River Dee (IRE)**[18] 3651 2-8-12 0..... JimmyQuinn 5 62+
(Miss Amy Weaver) *hld up: hdwy over 2f out: led and edgd rt over 1f out: shkn up and r.o* **1/2**[1]

50 **2** 5 **Kapowee**[9] 3959 2-8-7 0..... AdrianMcCarthy 6 39
(W J Musson) *chsd ldr: rdn and hung lft fr over 1f out: no ex fnl f* **5/1**[2]

004 **3** 2 1/2 **Benetti (IRE)**[20] 3570 2-8-12 0..... SamHitchcott 3 37
(M R Channon) *chsd ldrs: rdn over 2f out: styd on same pce appr fnl f* **6/1**[3]

0665 **4** hd **Dispol Toba**[12] 3830 2-8-7 0..... FrankieMcDonald 4 31
(P T Midgley) *led: rdn and hdd whn hmpd over 1f out: sn wknd* **10/1**

000 **5** 7 **Hunch**[13] 3815 2-8-7 0..... DavidProbert(5) 1 15
(Garry Moss) *s.i.s: hld up: rdn over 2f out: sn wknd* **20/1**

1m 14.23s (-0.17) **Going Correction** -0.225s/f (Firm) **5** Ran SP% **111.5**
Speed ratings (Par 92): **92,85,82,81,72**
toteswinger: 1&2 £3.30. CSF £3.53 TOTE £1.50: £1.10, £1.60; EX 3.40.The winner was bought in for 15,000gns.
Owner River Racing **Bred** Miss Anne Ormsby **Trained** Newmarket, Suffolk
■ A first winner from her third runner for Amy Weaver, who is Britain's youngest trainer.

FOCUS
An uncompetitive juvenile seller, but solid form and the winner can do better.

NOTEBOOK
River Dee(IRE) showed ability when down the field in a course-and-distance maiden on his debut and is probably better than this grade. He proved far too good for some very moderate rivals and could be one for a nursery off a light weight. He was bought in for 15,000gns. (op 8-11 after early 5-6)
Kapowee probably ran into an above-average type for the level, but she was still beaten a fair way. (tchd 6-1)
Benetti(IRE) looks very moderate. (op 7-2 tchd 7-1)

4258 GREAT YARMOUTH MERCURY H'CAP — 6f 3y
3:45 (3:46) (Class 5) (0-75,74) 3-Y-O+ £2,719 (£809; £404; £202) Stalls High

Form RPR

-552 **1** **Quaroma**[11] 3883 3-9-10 **72**..... FrankieMcDonald 7 84+
(Jane Chapple-Hyam) *hld up in tch: led over 1f out: rdn and edgd lft fnl f: r.o* **7/2**[2]

4516 **2** 1 3/4 **Beat The Bell**[13] 3811 3-9-4 **69**..... DominicFox(3) 8 75
(A Bailey) *led: rdn and hdd over 1f out: styd on same pce ins fnl f* **8/1**

6162 **3** 2 1/4 **Capone (IRE)**[12] 3833 3-9-11 **73**..... DaleGibson 6 72
(Garry Moss) *hmpd and stmbld sn after s: hld up: hdwy over 1f out: nt rch ldrs* **7/1**[3]

605U **4** 2 1/4 **Gone'N'Dunnett (IRE)**[4] 4125 9-8-2 **50** oh3.....(v) DavidProbert(5) 4 43
(Mrs C A Dunnett) *chsd ldrs: rdn over 2f out: wknd ins fnl f* **10/1**

4-04 **5** 3/4 **Kenton Street**[23] 3502 3-9-6 **68**..... JimmyFortune 2 57
(J A R Toller) *prom: rdn over 1f out: wknd ins fnl f* **14/1**

6143 **6** 1 3/4 **Rockfield Lodge (IRE)**[12] 3838 3-9-12 **74**..... NeilPollard 1 64+
(M E Rimmer) *hld up: hmpd over 1f out: n.d* **10/1**

00 **7** shd **Mugeba**[14] 3789 7-8-4 **52**.....(t) NicolPolli(5) 5 36
(Miss Gay Kelleway) *trckd ldrs: plld hrd: rdn and edgd lft over 1f out: wknd fnl f* **20/1**

1324 **8** 3/4 **Punching**[10] 3898 4-9-11 **68**..... HayleyTurner 3 50
(Miss Gay Kelleway) *hld up: plld hrd: rdn over 2f out: edgd rt over 1f out: wknd fnl f* **7/4**[1]

1m 11.97s (-2.43) **Going Correction** -0.225s/f (Firm)
WFA 3 from 4yo+ 5lb **8** Ran SP% **111.8**
Speed ratings (Par 103): **107,104,101,98,97 95,95,94**
toteswinger: 1&2 £6.20, 1&3 £2.30, 2&3 £5.70. CSF £29.86 CT £159.09 TOTE £3.60: £1.80, £2.10, £1.90; EX 36.60 Trifecta £320.90 Pool: £559.41 - 1.29 winning units..
Owner Elite Sports Organisation **Bred** Lady Fairhaven **Trained** Lambourn, Berks

FOCUS
A modest sprint handicap in which the time compared favourably with the other two straight races despite the early pace not looking strong. Sound form, with the winner up 5lb.
Rockfield Lodge(IRE) Official explanation: jockey said gelding was denied a clear run

4259 CAPE INDUSTRIAL FILLIES' H'CAP — 1m 3f 101y
4:15 (4:15) (Class 6) (0-65,65) 3-Y-O+ £1,942 (£578; £288; £144) Stalls Low

Form RPR

004 **1** **Star Grazer**[18] 3655 3-8-4 **57**..... JackMitchell(5) 8 65
(C F Wall) *sn chsng ldr: led over 3f out: pressed 1f: rdn and r.o wl* **9/1**

4061 **2** 1 3/4 **Granary Girl**[24] 3448 6-9-3 **54**.............................. LiamJones 4 59
(J Pearce) *hld up in tch: pushed along 4f out: rdn to chal 1f out: styd on same pce ins fnl f* **16/1**

4046 **3** *nse* **Blandys Wood**[12] 3845 3-8-12 **60**.............................. SamHitchcott 9 65
(M R Channon) *hld up: hdwy over 2f out: rdn over 1f out: r.o* **40/1**

065 **4** 2 1/4 **Citron Presse (USA)**[14] 3801 3-9-0 **62**.............................. JimmyFortune 10 63
(J H M Gosden) *chsd ldrs: rdn over 2f out: hung lft fr over 1f out: styd on same pce fnl f* **7/1**[3]

4-00 **5** 2 1/2 **Sendefaa (IRE)**[44] 2833 3-8-6 **57**.............................. KirstyMilczarek[(3)] 7 54
(M Botti) *sn led: hdd over 3f out: rdn over 2f out: wknd fnl f* **17/2**

2001 **6** 2 1/2 **Jemiliah**[22] 3524 3-8-4 **59**.............................. RossAtkinson[(7)] 12 52
(B G Powell) *hld up: rdn over 3f out: styd on ins fnl f: nvr nrr* **16/1**

4000 **7** 1 **Pretty Demanding (IRE)**[19] 3606 4-10-0 **65**.............................. TedDurcan 2 56
(M G Quinlan) *hld up: hdwy 1/2-way: rdn over 2f out: wknd fnl f* **7/2**[1]

3500 **8** 1 1/2 **Sforzando**[18] 3624 7-9-2 **60**.............................. (p) KristinStubbs[(7)] 5 49
(Mrs L Stubbs) *hld up: effrt over 3f out: wknd over 2f out* **20/1**

656 **9** 1 1/2 **Fleurs De Censier**[37] 3035 3-8-7 **55**.............................. RichardMullen 11 41
(D M Simcock) *hld up: rdn over 4f out: wknd over 2f out* **40/1**

-004 **10** *nk* **Rabeera**[16] 3729 3-8-8 **61**.............................. (v) DavidProbert[(5)] 3 47
(A M Balding) *chsd ldrs: rdn over 3f out: wknd over 1f out* **13/2**[2]

2m 32.01s (3.31) **Going Correction** 0.0s/f (Good)
WFA 3 from 4yo+ 11lb **10** Ran SP% **90.0**
Speed ratings (Par 98): **87,85,85,84,82 80,79,78,77,77**
toteswinger: 1&2 £15.30, 1&3 £25.90, 2&3 £31.10. CSF £80.28 CT £2233.06 TOTE £8.90: £2.10, £3.00, £4.90; EX 61.00 Trifecta £440.10 Part won. Pool: £594.80 - 0.40 winning units..
Owner Racingeight Partners **Bred** R Haim **Trained** Newmarket, Suffolk
■ Naughty Thoughts was withdrawn on vet's advice (11/4F). Deduct 25p in the £ under Rule 4.

FOCUS
A modest fillies' handicap. The runner-up is the best guide to the form with the winner rated up 4lb.

4260 INDAL/WRTL & AMEY H'CAP — 1m 2f 21y
4:45 (4:45) (Class 6) (0-65,64) 3-Y-O — **£1,942** (£578; £288; £144) **Stalls** Low

Form / RPR

2200 **1** **Director's Chair**[19] 3614 3-9-2 **62**.............................. RussellKennemore[(3)] 4 69
(Miss J Feilden) *led after 1f: pushed clr 4f out: rdn over 1f out: styd on u.p* **7/1**

-006 **2** 1 3/4 **Carmela Maria**[53] 2549 3-9-1 **58**.............................. TedDurcan 12 62
(C F Wall) *chsd ldrs: rdn over 3f out: sn outpcd: rallied fnl f: r.o* **9/2**[3]

-506 **3** 1 1/2 **Azure Mist**[34] 3117 3-9-3 **60**.............................. JimmyQuinn 3 61
(M H Tompkins) *plld hrd: led 1f: remained handy: chsd wnr 4f out: rdn over 1f out: styd on same pce fnl f* **10/1**

000- **4** 3 3/4 **China Pink**[344] 4422 3-8-7 **50**.............................. DO'Donohoe 5 43+
(Sir Mark Prescott) *hld up in tch: n.m.r over 8f out: rdn over 4f out: sn outpcd: styd on fnl f* **10/1**

4050 **5** 3/4 **Princess Raya**[23] 3483 3-9-1 **58**.............................. (t) NeilPollard 10 50
(M E Rimmer) *hld up: rdn over 3f out: hung lft over 1f out: styd on: nt trble ldrs* **50/1**

-652 **6** 1/2 **Pretty Officer (USA)**[14] 3780 3-8-9 **52**.............................. RichardMullen 9 43
(Rae Guest) *hld up: rdn over 3f out: sn outpcd: n.d after* **3/1**[1]

0-05 **7** 5 **Shraayef**[23] 3479 3-9-2 **64**.............................. AhmedAjtebi[(5)] 7 45
(M Botti) *sn chsng wnr: rdn over 4f out: wknd over 2f out* **10/1**

00-6 **8** 1 1/4 **Halsion Challenge**[14] 3780 3-8-9 **52**.............................. HayleyTurner 6 30
(J R Best) *hld up: sme hdwy over 1f out: wknd fnl f* **20/1**

0530 **9** 7 **Polychrome**[65] 2208 3-8-9 **55**.............................. KirstyMilczarek[(3)] 8 19
(John Berry) *hld up: a in rr* **16/1**

0505 **10** 21 **Sarah's First**[41] 2915 3-8-10 **53**.............................. TPQueally 11 —
(E A L Dunlop) *hld up in tch: lost pl over 5f out: sn bhd* **4/1**[2]

0600 **11** 17 **Lavender And Lace**[24] 3459 3-8-0 **50**.............................. (p) RossAtkinson[(7)] 1 —
(T Keddy) *hld up: rdn over 4f out: wknd and eased fnl 2f* **20/1**

2m 10.8s (0.30) **Going Correction** 0.0s/f (Good) **11** Ran SP% **120.3**
Speed ratings (Par 98): **98,96,95,92,91 91,87,86,80,64 50**
toteswinger: 1&2 £8.70, 1&3 £13.20, 2&3 £10.50. CSF £38.59 CT £322.70 TOTE £11.30: £2.60, £2.60, £2.90; EX 55.20 TRIFECTA Not won..
Owner Ocean Trailers Ltd **Bred** D R Tucker **Trained** Exning, Suffolk

FOCUS
A modest handicap in which it paid to race prominently. The winner was given too much rope in front and nothing could get involved from behind, so the form is not too solid. The winning time was 0.14 seconds slower than 46-60 older-horse handicap. The winner was one of just two male horses in the field.
Pretty Officer(USA) Official explanation: jockey said filly slipped on bend
Lavender And Lace Official explanation: trainer said filly lost its action on bend

4261 LORD NELSON APPRENTICE RIDERS' H'CAP — 1m 2f 21y
5:15 (5:15) (Class 6) (0-60,53) 4-Y-O+ — **£1,942** (£578; £288; £144) **Stalls** Low

Form / RPR

-040 **1** **Itsy Bitsy**[104] 1262 6-8-6 **45**.............................. (p) DebraEngland[(5)] 10 51
(W J Musson) *s.i.s: sn prom: chsd ldr over 6f out: led over 2f out: shkn up over 1f out: edgd lft: styd on* **40/1**

-006 **2** 1 **Thornaby Green**[13] 3814 7-9-2 **53**.............................. DeanHeslop[(3)] 1 57
(T D Barron) *sn led: rdn and hdd over 2f out: ev ch over 1f out: styd on same pce ins fnl f* **10/1**

0403 **3** *shd* **King Of Connacht**[10] 3914 5-9-4 **52**.............................. (p) WilliamCarson 3 56
(M Wellings) *a.p: rdn over 1f out: styd on same pce ins fnl f* **4/1**[1]

0-05 **4** *hd* **Colton**[18] 3655 5-9-0 **51**.............................. BMcHugh[(3)] 9 54
(J M P Eustace) *s.i.s: hld up: hdwy over 2f out: rdn and edgd rt over 1f out: styd on same pce ins fnl f* **6/1**

040 **5** 4 **Meohmy**[26] 3361 5-8-11 **45**.............................. MCGeran 7 40
(M R Channon) *hld up: hdwy 2f out: sn rdn: wknd ins fnl f* **16/1**

-000 **6** 3/4 **Barley Moon**[26] 3371 4-8-4 **45**.............................. AntiocoMurgia[(7)] 5 39
(T Keddy) *prom: outpcd 3f out: styd on ins fnl f* **66/1**

0-40 **7** 1 1/4 **Revolving World (IRE)**[41] 2914 5-8-8 **47** ow1.............................. (t) MJMurphy[(5)] 4 38
(L R James) *s.s: hld up: hdwy over 3f out: sn rdn: wknd over 1f out* **14/1**

00-0 **8** 3 **Sierra Rose**[12] 3839 4-8-11 **52**.............................. AndreaAtzeni[(7)] 2 37
(P J McBride) *prom: rdn over 3f out: wknd over 1f out* **22/1**

2506 **9** 3 1/4 **Convivial Spirit**[15] 3764 4-9-0 **53**.............................. (t) JPFeatherstone[(5)] 8 32
(E F Vaughan) *racd keenly: trckd ldr tl over 6f out: wknd over 2f out* **12/1**

1506 **10** *hd* **Chapter (IRE)**[18] 3657 6-8-11 **45**.............................. (p) KylieManser 6 24
(Mrs A L M King) *s.s: a in rr* **5/1**[3]

2420 **11** 2 3/4 **Mid Valley**[24] 3448 5-9-1 **52**.............................. BillyCray[(3)] 11 25
(J R Jenkins) *dwlt: hld up: effrt over 3f out: a in rr* **7/1**

0-04 **12** 14 **Monsieur Dumas (IRE)**[31] 3201 4-9-2 **50**.............................. RobbieEgan 12 —
(R Bastiman) *hld up: plld hrd: bhd fr 1/2-way* **9/2**[2]

2m 10.66s (0.16) **Going Correction** 0.0s/f (Good) **12** Ran SP% **119.2**
Speed ratings (Par 101): **99,98,98,97,94 94,93,90,88,88 85,74**
toteswinger: 1&2 £47.00, 1&3 £13.60, 2&3 £10.50. CSF £398.95 CT £1977.99 TOTE £37.20: £7.60, £3.50, £1.70; EX 755.80 Trifecta £260.80 Pool of £352.53 - 1.00 winning units. Place 6: £124.82 Place 5: £81.05 .
Owner W J Musson **Bred** C P Ranson **Trained** Newmarket, Suffolk

FOCUS
A very moderate handicap restricted to apprentices who had not ridden more than 25 winners. The winning time was 0.14 seconds quicker than the previous 46-65 handicap. Once again the principals raced prominently. The form has been rated around the third and fourth and looks dubious with the winner wrong at the weights.
Chapter(IRE) Official explanation: jockey said gelding was slowly away
T/Plt: £370.00 to a £1 stake. Pool: £55,357.28. 109.20 winning tickets. T/Qpdt: £69.20 to a £1 stake. Pool: £3,722.00. 39.80 winning tickets. CR

4056 GREAT LEIGHS (A.W) (L-H)
Tuesday, July 22

OFFICIAL GOING: Standard
Speed was holding up well at this meeting with four winners making all or making most. It is probably best to forgive hold-up horses for getting beaten.
Wind: virtually nil Weather: bright, partly cloudy

4267 FORD END APPRENTICE H'CAP — 1m 2f (P)
6:20 (6:21) (Class 6) (0-65,65) 4-Y-O+ — **£2,590** (£770; £385; £192) **Stalls** Low

Form / RPR

0003 **1** **Ruwain**[19] 3657 4-7-12 **46** oh1.............................. AndreaAtzeni[(7)] 1 56
(P J McBride) *mde all: rdn wl over 1f out: kpt on wl and forged clr last 100yds* **16/1**

2205 **2** 2 1/2 **Kings Topic (USA)**[31] 3265 8-8-12 **58**.............................. (b) PNolan[(5)] 4 63
(A B Haynes) *s.i.s: sn niggled along: hdwy and rdn 4f out: chsd ldng pair over 2f out: kpt on to chse wnr towards fin: nvr pce to chal wnr* **9/1**[3]

/202 **3** 1 **Kangrina**[19] 3657 6-9-2 **62**.............................. FrederikTylicki[(5)] 5 65
(George Baker) *chsd wnr: rdn and tried to chal fr over 1f out: wknd ins fnl f: lost 2nd towards fin* **11/4**[1]

1606 **4** 3 1/2 **Noah Jameel**[41] 2949 6-8-11 **52**.............................. JamieJones 10 48
(A G Newcombe) *bhd: rdn and n.m.r 3f out: chsd ldng trio and edgd lft 1f out: neve rable to chal* **7/2**[2]

0-00 **5** 4 1/2 **Fantasy Crusader**[7] 4053 9-8-5 **49**.............................. JPHamblett[(3)] 3 36
(R M H Cowell) *stdd after s: hld up in midfield: rdn and nt qckn 3f out: hld hd high and no imp fr wl over 1f out* **16/1**

500 **6** 1 1/2 **Kylkenny**[22] 3551 13-9-3 **65**.............................. (t) RyanClark[(7)] 7 49
(H Morrison) *in tch on outer: pushed along wl over 3f out: no ch last 2f* **16/1**

0050 **7** 2 3/4 **Oasis Sun (IRE)**[13] 3843 5-8-11 **55**.............................. (b) JemmaMarshall[(3)] 2 34
(J R Best) *hld up in midfield: rdn and nt qckn 3f out: wl hld last 2f* **20/1**

6500 **8** 4 **Lordswood (IRE)**[47] 2755 4-8-5 **49**.............................. RossAtkinson[(3)] 6 20
(J R Best) *hld up in last trio: dropped to last and rdn 3f out: no ch after* **10/1**

60-5 **9** 5 **Zalkani (IRE)**[8] 4026 8-8-9 **53**.............................. SimonPearce[(3)] 8 14
(J Pearce) *a bhd: no ch fr wl over 2f out: t.o* **10/1**

2024 **P** **Alfie Tupper (IRE)**[138] 811 5-9-4 **62**.............................. HarryPoulton[(3)] 11 —
(J R Boyle) *sddle slipped and p.u sn after s* **11/4**[1]

2m 9.70s (1.10) **Going Correction** +0.175s/f (Slow) **10** Ran SP% **126.1**
Speed ratings (Par 101): **102,100,99,96,92 91,89,86,82,—**
toteswinger: 1&2 £10.70, 1&3 £18.70, 2&3 £5.40. CSF £163.88 CT £530.07 TOTE £21.70: £4.00, £3.20, £1.70; EX 191.40.
Owner P J McBride **Bred** W J Musson **Trained** Newmarket, Suffolk
■ A first winner on his 13th ride for 17-year-old Italian Andrea Atzeni.

FOCUS
A modest apprentice handicap weakened further by the early exit of joint-favourite Alfie Tupper. It was also a race in which it was crucial to race handily and very few ever got into it. The winner was up 12lb with the next two close to form.
Zalkani(IRE) Official explanation: jockey said gelding was never travelling
Alfie Tupper(IRE) Official explanation: jockey said gelding's saddle slipped

4268 CHIPPING ONGAR H'CAP — 1m (P)
6:50 (6:50) (Class 5) (0-70,70) 3-Y-O+ — **£3,238** (£963; £481; £240) **Stalls** Low

Form / RPR

0406 **1** **Mount Hermon (IRE)**[10] 3970 4-9-11 **70**.............................. (b) TravisBlock[(3)] 10 83
(H Morrison) *hld up in midfield: hdwy 4f out: rdn and effrt over 2f out: chal and hung lft ent fnl f: sn led: drew clr last 100yds: comf* **7/2**[2]

2660 **2** 3 3/4 **Zorn**[13] 3842 9-8-6 **51** oh6.............................. KirstyMilczarek[(3)] 13 55
(P Howling) *led and sn crossed over to rail: rdn over 3f out: hrd pressed 2f out: edgd rt and hdd 1f out: sn outpcd by wnr: plugged on* **16/1**

0310 **3** 1 **Wahoo Sam (USA)**[25] 3431 8-9-5 **66**.............................. RichardEvans[(5)] 4 68
(P D Evans) *chsd ldrs: rdn and tried to chal wl over 1f out: kpt on same pce fnl f* **10/1**

0443 **4** *nk* **Gazboolou**[6] 4081 4-9-12 **68**.............................. SebSanders 9 69
(David Pinder) *chsd ldrs: wnt 2nd 4f out: rdn to chal 2f out: kpt on same pce whn squeezed for room and snatched up ent fnl f: no ch after* **3/1**[1]

6520 **5** 3 **Happy As Larry (USA)**[34] 3132 6-9-11 **70**.............................. (t) LukeMorris[(3)] 12 64
(J S Moore) *stmbld bdly: nrly uns rdr s and lost grnd s: in tch in rr after 2f: effrt 3f out: rdn and kpt on same pce last 2f* **8/1**

5545 **6** 1 3/4 **Landucci**[28] 3345 7-9-11 **70**.............................. (p) PatrickHills[(3)] 3 60
(J W Hills) *short of room sn after s: hld up in rr: hdwy on outer over 3f out: chsd ldrs and rdn 2f out: wknd jst over 1f out* **10/1**

0022 **7** 2 3/4 **Ardent Prince**[8] 4031 5-8-6 **51** oh2.............................. TolleyDean[(3)] 8 35
(A J McCabe) *t.k.h: chsd ldr tl 4f out: rdn over 2f out: wknd wl over 1f out* **5/1**[3]

51-2 **8** 5 **Pop Music (IRE)**[187] 196 5-9-10 **66**.............................. (p) JamesDoyle 2 39
(Ms J S Doyle) *hld up towards rr: rdn and unable to qckn 3f out: no ch after* **9/1**

0004 **9** 2 3/4 **Just A Dancer (IRE)**[12] 3893 3-9-1 **65**.............................. MichaelHills 5 29
(B W Hills) *in tch: rdn and lost pl over 3f out: no ch last 2f* **14/1**

0000 **10** *hd* **Baba Ghanoush**[60] 2355 6-8-9 **51** oh6.............................. DavidKinsella 11 17
(M J Attwater) *t.k.h: hld up towards rr: rdn and struggling 3f out: n.d after* **40/1**

60-0 **11** 1 1/4 **Rocheport**[17] 3738 3-8-7 **57**.............................. OscarUrbina 6 18
(G C H Chung) *in midfield whn short of room after 1f: rdn and struggling 3f out: wl btn last 2f* **22/1**

-606 **P** **Torquemada (IRE)**[33] 3165 7-9-7 **63**.............................. NCallan 1 —
(M J Attwater) *t.k.h: hld up towards rr: lost tch wl over 2f out: eased 2f out: p.u 1f out* **16/1**

1m 42.05s (2.15) **Going Correction** +0.175s/f (Slow)
WFA 3 from 4yo+ 8lb **12** Ran SP% **128.4**
Speed ratings (Par 103): **96,92,91,90,87 86,83,78,75,75 74,—**
toteswinger: 1&2 £20.30, 1&3 £13.90, 2&3 £46.30. CSF £64.51 CT £549.88 TOTE £4.80: £2.30, £3.90, £3.80; EX 192.80.

Owner Wood Street Syndicate III **Bred** Illumnatus Investments And Elite Bloodst **Trained** East Ilsley, Berks
■ Stewards' Enquiry : Kirsty Milczarek one-day ban: careless riding (Aug 5)
FOCUS
Just a fair handicap and the early gallop was by no means strong. Again the principals were never far off the pace and with the front-running second racing from 8lb wrong this form is not that solid.
Happy As Larry(USA) ◆ Official explanation: jockey said gelding charged the gates prior to the off.
Pop Music(IRE) Official explanation: jockey said gelding hung badly left
Torquemada(IRE) Official explanation: jockey said gelding had a breathing problem

4269 COUNTY H'CAP — 1m (P)
7:20 (7:21) (Class 3) (0-90,95) 3-Y-0+ **£7,771** (£2,312; £1,155; £577) **Stalls** Low

Form — RPR
1111 **1** **Master Of Arts (USA)**[6] 4089 3-9-12 **95** 6ex.................... SebSanders 1 104+
(Sir Mark Prescott) *s.i.s: in tch: bustled along 4f out: rdn to chse ldr over 2f out: led over 1f out: wl in command fnl 100yds* **2/5**[1]
060 **2** *2* **Prince Of Thebes (IRE)**[11] 3899 7-9-2 **80**.............. KirstyMilczarek(3) 6 83
(M J Attwater) *t.k.h: hld up in tch: rdn 3f out: chsd wnr jst ins fnl f: no imp* **20/1**[3]
000- **3** *1 3/4* **Killena Boy (IRE)**[284] 6143 6-9-3 **85**.................... JPHamblett(7) 3 84
(W Jarvis) *t.k.h: hld up in tch: effrt and c wd bnd 2f out: styd on to go 3rd ins fnl f: nvr trbld wnr* **22/1**
-251 **4** *3 1/4* **Kafuu (IRE)**[19] 3646 4-10-0 **89**..............................(p) NCallan 2 81
(S A Callaghan) *sn led: qcknd 4f out: rdn and hdd over 1f out: wknd fnl f* **3/1**[2]
6660 **5** *nse* **Neardown Beauty (IRE)**[125] 929 5-9-10 **88**.............. TolleyDean(3) 5 79
(A J McCabe) *hld up in last pl: hdwy over 3f out: chsd ldng pair and drvn over 2f out: wknd wl over 1f out* **25/1**
1560 **6** *7* **Tilapia (IRE)**[11] 3896 4-9-12 **87**.................... JohnEgan 7 62
(Miss Gay Kelleway) *t.k.h: prom tl stdd to rr after 2f: rdn and struggling wl over 2f out: wl btn last 2f* **25/1**
3-06 **7** *7* **Kinnego Bay (IRE)**[31] 3275 3-8-3 **72**.................... TPO'Shea 4 29
(B W Hills) *t.k.h: chsd ldr: rdn 4f out: lost pl wl over 1f out: wl bhd last 2f* **25/1**

1m 41.95s (2.05) **Going Correction** +0.175s/f (Slow)
WFA 3 from 4yo+ 8lb — **7** Ran SP% **117.1**
Speed ratings (Par 107): **96,94,92,89,88 81,74**
toteswinger: 1&2 £4.20, 1&3 £6.00, 2&3 £11.80. CSF £14.48 TOTE £1.40: £1.10, £3.50; EX 8.20.
Owner Eclipse Thoroughbreds-Osborne House III **Bred** Cyril Humphris **Trained** Newmarket, Suffolk
FOCUS
A very uncompetitive handicap and the pace was modest, but it was still won by a rapidly progressive gelding who will be bordering on Listed class soon.
NOTEBOOK
Master Of Arts(USA), bidding for a six-timer, was under a penalty for his recent victory in a Lingfield classified event, so was 13lb higher than for his last win in a proper handicap. Those that took short odds about him may have been nervous on the home bend as he was being niggled along, but he picked up really well in the straight and was always in command despite hanging over to the inside rail. There is no telling how much further he can go and he will be a better horse in a more strongly run race. He needs an easy surface and the Cambridgeshire could be just his sort of contest. (op 4-7 tchd 4-6 and 8-13 in a place)
Prince Of Thebes(IRE), whose only previous try on sand in a 42-race career was well over two years ago, kept the favourite company for much of the way but could not go with him on the home bend. He plodded on to finish a clear second best, but it is debatable how much he actually achieved. He is on a career-low mark now though, and he showed enough here to suggest he might find an opportunity on this surface. (op 14-1)
Killena Boy(IRE), who was running poorly when last seen, ran on past beaten horses late on but again it is hard to gauge how much he achieved. He is sliding down the weights though, and he should at least be fitter for this first run in nine months. (op 25-1)
Kafuu(IRE), raised 7lb for his Warwick victory, had the run of the race out in front and given the advantage enjoyed by pace-setters at his meeting it was disappointing to see him drop out. Perhaps this trip is beyond him. (tchd 4-1)
Neardown Beauty(IRE) was without the cheekpieces on this return from a four-month break and a mid-race move amounted to little. She still looks too high in the weights at present. (op 20-1)

4270 WALTHAM ABBEY MAIDEN AUCTION STKS — 5f (P)
7:50 (7:51) (Class 5) 2-Y-0 **£3,561** (£1,059; £529; £264) **Stalls** Low

Form — RPR
23 **1** **Evelyn May (IRE)**[19] 3632 2-8-6 0.................... MichaelHills 4 79+
(B W Hills) *mde virtually all: pushed clr over 1f out: nt extended* **2/5**[1]
2 *5* **Dakota Hills** 2-9-1 0.................... LPKeniry 3 63+
(J R Best) *in tch in midfield: rdn 2f out sn no ch w wnr: kpt on u.p to go modest 2nd ins fnl f* **8/1**[3]
50 **3** *1 1/2* **Handcuff**[8] 4027 2-9-1 0.................... ShaneKelly 7 58
(J A Osborne) *chsd wnr after 1f: rdn over 2f out: sn wl outpcd by wnr: lost 2nd ins fnl f* **25/1**
0 **4** *1 1/4* **Jubilee Juggins (IRE)**[13] 3848 2-8-12 0.............. KirstyMilczarek(3) 1 54
(N P Littmoden) *hld up in rr: rdn and effrt wl over 1f out: kpt on but nvr nr wnr* **33/1**
402 **5** *2 1/2* **Kitty Allen**[21] 3584 2-8-6 0.................... JohnEgan 5 36
(M Botti) *hld up in rr: effrt and wating to hang lft 2f out: nvr a danger* **5/1**[2]
0 **6** *hd* **Elsie Jo (IRE)**[25] 3456 2-8-8 0.................... NickyMackay 6 37
(M Wigham) *wnt lft s: rn green in rr: no ch last 2f* **14/1**
00 **7** *nk* **Rebelwithoutacause (IRE)**[12] 3888 2-9-3 0.............. DO'Donohoe 2 45
(George Baker) *led: sn hdd: chsd ldrs after tl wknd wl over 1f out* **33/1**

61.79 secs (1.59) **Going Correction** +0.175s/f (Slow) — **7** Ran SP% **115.6**
Speed ratings (Par 94): **102,94,91,89,85 85,84**
toteswinger: 1&2 £2.50, 1&3 £3.30, 2&3 £3.00. CSF £4.50 TOTE £1.20: £1.20, £3.50; EX 3.60.
Owner Mrs B W Hills **Bred** Mrs S Dutfield **Trained** Lambourn, Berks
FOCUS
A one-horse race from some way out and the others may as well have not bothered. She was value for much more than the winning margin. The winning time was very decent, 0.06 seconds faster than the later three-year-old handicap.
NOTEBOOK
Evelyn May(IRE) ◆ only had to reproduce her turf form to win this, but it was still hard not to be taken by the way she pulverised her rivals over the last furlong or so. Her pedigree is all speed and, with this likely to have boosted her confidence, she can go on to win rather better races than this. (op 4-9 tchd 4-7 and 8-13 in a place)
Dakota Hills, a 20,000gns half-brother to 7f juvenile winner Little Eskimo, stayed on to win the separate race for second and will not always come across one so smart. There is plenty of stamina on the dam's side of his pedigree, so he may appreciate a bit further. (op 10-1 tchd 13-2)
Handcuff raced handily for a long way, but once the favourite engaged the afterburner he was left choking on Polytrack. This was a small improvement on his first two starts, but he will still need to find much more if he is to win a race. (tchd 33-1)
Jubilee Juggins(IRE), beaten a long way on his Lingfield debut, was down a furlong and could never summon the pace to land a blow, but his breeding suggests that he needs a good deal further than this. (op 25-1)
Kitty Allen was the most experienced in the field, but she still looked green and did not look entirely happy on this surface. (op 4-1 tchd 7-2)
Elsie Jo(IRE), who showed nothing on her Newmarket debut, still looked as green as grass early and was badly hampered by Kitty Allen after a furlong. There was no way back from there, but she is a half-sister to four winners so may have a bit more to offer later on. (op 16-1)
Rebelwithoutacause(IRE), beaten out of sight in his first two outings on turf, was up there early but even a pace bias could not stop him from being well and truly stuffed once again. (op 50-1)

4271 SHALFORD CLAIMING STKS — 6f (P)
8:20 (8:22) (Class 6) 3-Y-O **£2,590** (£770; £385; £192) **Stalls** Low

Form — RPR
5003 **1** **Bazguy**[7] 4056 3-8-11 70....................(b) JohnEgan 7 73
(P D Evans) *mde all: grad crossed to rail: rdn clr over 1f out easily* **15/8**[1]
-002 **2** *4* **Wreningham**[7] 4056 3-8-11 63.................... EddieAhern 2 60
(T Keddy) *in tch: rdn and effrt 3f out: chsd wnr over 1f out: no imp* **9/4**[2]
50-5 **3** *4* **Jennifer's Dream (IRE)**[47] 2747 3-8-11 75.................... NCallan 1 47
(K A Ryan) *dwlt: sn chsng wnr: rdn wl over 1f out: lost 2nd over 1f out: fdd fnl f* **7/2**[3]
5504 **4** *1 1/4* **Cheeky Chilli**[7] 4043 3-8-4 60.................... DO'Donohoe 8 36
(A J McCabe) *sn rdn along: outpcd and swtchd lft 3f out: no ch last 2f* **8/1**
0000 **5** *1* **Santa Clara**[18] 3686 3-7-8 50.................... AmyBaker(7) 5 30
(P Leech) *a w last pair: wl bhd fr 1/2-way* **33/1**
0020 **6** *1/2* **Ma Mirage (IRE)**[17] 3727 3-7-11 45....................(v[1]) LukeMorris(3) 3 27
(S C Williams) *s.i.s: a bhd: no ch fr 1/2-way* **33/1**
0066 **P** **Rough Rock (IRE)**[15] 3782 3-9-2 63....................(b) MickyFenton 6 —
(Miss Gay Kelleway) *chsd ldrs: rdn over 3f out: struggling whn eased and p.u 2f out* **18/1**

1m 14.44s (0.74) **Going Correction** +0.175s/f (Slow) — **7** Ran SP% **110.0**
Speed ratings (Par 98): **102,96,91,89,88 87,—**
toteswinger: 1&2 £1.10, 1&3 £1.10, 2&3 £2.00. CSF £5.85 TOTE £3.30: £1.50, £1.80; EX 5.60.
Owner B McCabe & K J Mercer **Bred** Usk Valley Stud **Trained** Pandy, Monmouths
■ Just Sort It was withdrawn (14/1, unruly in stalls). R4 applies, deduct 5p in the £.
FOCUS
A moderate claimer and again early pace was crucial. They finished very well spread out and there is little to get excited about amongst the also-rans. The winner is rated back to his winter form.
Santa Clara Official explanation: jockey said filly was kicked on the head in stalls
Rough Rock(IRE) Official explanation: jockey said gelding had a breathing problem

4272 CHURCH END H'CAP — 5f (P)
8:50 (8:50) (Class 5) (0-70,73) 3-Y-O **£3,238** (£963; £481; £120; £120) **Stalls** Low

Form — RPR
3026 **1** **Mac Dalia**[5] 4107 3-8-13 **60**....................(p) SebSanders 2 68
(A J McCabe) *mde all: rdn wl over 1f out: styd on strly* **8/1**[3]
3111 **2** *2 1/4* **Hurricane Hen**[8] 4028 3-9-7 **73** 6ex.................... RichardEvans(5) 1 73
(P D Evans) *chsd wnr: swtchd rt over 1f out: kpt on but nt pce to chal wnr* **2/1**[1]
4254 **3** *4 1/2* **Wynberg (IRE)**[34] 3136 3-9-7 **68**....................(p) NCallan 3 52
(S A Callaghan) *stdd s: hld up in tch: hdwy 1/2-way: chsng ldrs and bmpd over 1f out: onpcd after* **5/2**[2]
4051 **4** *hd* **Enodoc**[16] 3765 3-9-5 **66**....................(t) DO'Donohoe 6 49
(W R Muir) *chsd ldrs: disp 2nd and rdn 2f out: outpcd fnl f* **12/1**
-303 **4** *dht* **Town And Gown**[25] 3447 3-9-1 **62**....................(e[1]) SaleemGolam 4 45
(S C Williams) *rring in stalls: t.k.h: trckd ldrs: rdn over 1f out: fnd little and outpcd fnl f* **12/1**
0660 **6** *hd* **Shatter Resistant (IRE)**[4] 4159 3-8-6 **53**....................(p) JohnEgan 9 35
(M D Squance) *chsd ldrs: effrt and edging lft wl over 1f out: one pce fnl f* **12/1**
03-3 **7** *1 1/2* **Glenveagh (IRE)**[10] 3953 3-8-5 **52**.................... TPO'Shea 7 29
(K A Ryan) *sn struggling in rr* **8/1**[3]
205 **8** *2 3/4* **Filemot**[25] 3447 3-8-12 **62**.................... KirstyMilczarek(3) 5 29
(John Berry) *t.k.h: chsd ldrs tl 1/2-way: lost pl and c v wd 2f out: wl btn after* **14/1**
0005 **9** *1/2* **The Magic Blanket (IRE)**[21] 3585 3-8-10 **57**....................(t) MickyFenton 8 22
(Stef Liddiard) *rring in stalls: bhd: hmpd over 2f out: no prog fr 2f out: eased towards fin* **25/1**

60.85 secs (0.65) **Going Correction** +0.175s/f (Slow) — **9** Ran SP% **117.7**
Speed ratings (Par 100): **101,97,90,89,89 89,87,82,81**
toteswinger: 1&2 £3.30, 1&3 £7.90, 2&3 £2.20. CSF £24.89 CT £53.26 TOTE £13.40: £3.40, £1.40, £1.30; EX 32.20 Place 6: £16.15 Place 5: £5.95 .
Owner Paul J Dixon & Brian Morton **Bred** Chippenham Lodge Stud **Trained** Babworth, Notts
■ Stewards' Enquiry : Richard Evans two-day ban: careless riding (Aug 5-6)
FOCUS
A moderate sprint handicap and the winning time was slightly slower than the earlier two-year-old maiden. The pace bias again had a big say in the outcome and so did the draw, with the first three horses starting from the three lowest stalls. Not form to be too positive about, the front-running winner rated back to her winter form.
Filemot Official explanation: jockey said filly was unsuited by the track
T/Plt: £33.20 to a £1 stake. Pool: £55,391.74. 1,216.61 winning tickets. T/Qpdt: £2.80 to a £1 stake. Pool: £4,686.44. 1,237.25 winning tickets. SP

3966 SALISBURY (R-H)
Tuesday, July 22

OFFICIAL GOING: Good to firm (9.2)
Wind: virtually nil Weather: overcast, muggy

4273 VC BET H'CAP — 5f
2:30 (2:34) (Class 6) (0-65,62) 3-Y-O+ **£2,914** (£867; £433; £216) **Stalls** High

Form — RPR
640- **1** **Drumming Party (USA)**[313] 5349 6-9-4 **55**....................(t) LPKeniry 12 63+
(A M Balding) *trckd ldrs: swtchd lft over 2f out: shkn up to ld ins fnl f: edgd rt but r.o strly: readily* **11/2**[3]
6-00 **2** *1 1/4* **Damhsoir (IRE)**[45] 2836 4-8-8 **45**.................... SteveDrowne 7 48
(H S Howe) *s.i.s: towards rr: hdwy over 2f out: rdn whn swtchd lft ent fnl f: r.o: snatched 2nd fnl strides* **20/1**
0600 **3** *hd* **Bluebok**[5] 4106 7-9-8 **62**....................(bt) KevinGhunowa(3) 11 64
(J M Bradley) *led: rdn and hrd pressed fr 2f out: hdd ins fnl f: no ex: lost 2nd fnl strides* **16/1**
4000 **4** *1 1/4* **Pajada**[25] 3445 4-8-8 **45**....................(v) HayleyTurner 4 43
(M D I Usher) *hmpd leaving stalls: bhd: pushed along wl over 2f out: hdwy wl over 1f out: r.o: nvr able to get on terms* **66/1**

233 **5** *1 1/4* **Matterofact (IRE)**[45] 2836 5-9-5 **56**............ TGMcLaughlin 1 49
(M S Saunders) *hld up: hdwy 3f out: sn rdn: styd on fnl f: nvr trbld ldrs* **7/1**
1222 **6** *hd* **Black Moma (IRE)**[45] 2836 4-9-11 **62**............ RichardHughes 9 55
(A B Haynes) *prom: rdn and ev ch fr 2f out: fdd ins fnl f* **4/1**[1]
5000 **7** *2 1/4* **Ishibee (IRE)**[52] 2622 4-8-8 **48**............(p) MarcHalford(3) 3 32
(J J Bridger) *towards rr: sme late prog: nvr a factor* **33/1**
06 **8** *1/2* **Jucebabe**[5] 4106 5-9-4 **55**............(p) LiamJones 5 38
(J L Spearing) *wnt lft s: a towards rr* **15/2**
2314 **9** *3/4* **Arfinnit (IRE)**[15] 3783 7-9-1 **55**............(p) KirstyMilczarek(3) 10 35
(Mrs A L M King) *chsd ldrs: rdn over 2f out: wknd over 1f out* **9/2**[2]
0-64 **10** *1/2* **Miss Poppy**[25] 3447 3-9-7 **62**............ JimCrowley 8 40
(P R Chamings) *mid-div: rdn over 2f out: wknd over 1f out* **10/1**
0154 **11** *1* **Who's Winning (IRE)**[5] 4102 7-9-9 **60**............(b) TQuinn 2 35
(B G Powell) *chsd ldrs: rdn wl over 2f out: sn wknd* **7/1**
5060 **12** *3 1/4* **Half A Tsar (IRE)**[15] 3779 4-8-8 **45**............ AlanDaly 6 8
(Mark Gillard) *mid-div tl wknd over 2f out* **18/1**

61.63 secs (0.83) **Going Correction** +0.05s/f (Good)
WFA 3 from 4yo+ 4lb **12** Ran SP% **119.8**
Speed ratings (Par 101): **95,93,92,90,88 88,84,83,82,81 80,75**
toteswinger: 1&2 £20.60, 1&3 £20.40, 2&3 £64.40. CSF £113.45 CT £1688.97 TOTE £6.70: £2.10, £7.20, £4.70; EX 150.60.
Owner Mrs P Hastings **Bred** Robert N Clay, Et Al **Trained** Kingsclere, Hants

FOCUS
An ordinary handicap run in a modest winning time. Very ordinary form the winner rated to last year's first-time-out level.

4274 EMMA ARBERY MEMORIAL MAIDEN STKS 6f
3:00 (3:10) (Class 4) 2-Y-O **£4,533** (£1,348; £674; £336) **Stalls** High

Form RPR
30 **1** **Square Eddie (CAN)**[35] 3103 2-9-3 0............ SteveDrowne 6 83+
(J R Best) *trckd ldrs: led 2f out: edgd rt but r.o wl fnl f: comf* **6/4**[1]
03 **2** *3 1/4* **Jeremiah (IRE)**[13] 3848 2-9-3 0............ JamesDoyle 1 72
(J G Portman) *sn led: rdn and hdd 2f out: kpt on but nt pce of wnr* **25/1**
3 *2* **Galpin Junior (USA)** 2-9-3 0............ TedDurcan 3 66+
(B J Meehan) *s.i.s: bhd: hdwy over 2f out: wandered and rn green ent fnl f: r.o* **14/1**
5 **4** *3/4* **Retro (IRE)**[8] 4024 2-9-3 0............ RichardHughes 11 64
(R Hannon) *wnt bdly lft at s: in tch: hdwy 3f out: effrt 2f out: kpt on same pce* **11/4**[2]
5 *nk* **Papa Meilland** 2-9-3 0............ StephenCarson 5 63+
(Eve Johnson Houghton) *mid-div: rdn over 2f out: kpt on fnl f* **33/1**
0 **6** *hd* **Sister Clement (IRE)**[49] 2691 2-8-12 0............ RobertHavlin 12 58+
(C R Egerton) *mid-div: hdwy 3f out: rdn 2f out: kpt on same pce* **80/1**
0 **7** *2 1/2* **Red Robert**[15] 3798 2-9-3 0............ IanMongan 10 55
(J L Dunlop) *trckd ldrs: rdn and ev ch 2f out: wknd fnl f* **66/1**
6 **8** *1 1/4* **Louie's Lad**[36] 3092 2-9-3 0............ PatDobbs 9 51
(J A Geake) *prom: rdn over 2f out: fdd ent fnl f* **50/1**
9 *2 1/2* **Dark Desert** 2-9-3 0............ FergusSweeney 15 44
(A G Newcombe) *s.i.s: a towards rr* **66/1**
0 **10** *2 1/2* **Hellbender (IRE)**[52] 2601 2-9-3 0............ AdamKirby 14 36
(S Kirk) *chsd ldrs: effrt 2f out: wknd over 1f out* **10/1**[3]
11 *1* **Scarlets** 2-8-12 0............ TQuinn 7 28
(P D Evans) *a towards rr* **33/1**
0 **12** *2 3/4* **Short Cut**[61] 2338 2-9-3 0............ LPKeniry 4 25
(S Kirk) *plld hrd: mid-div: rdn over 2f out: wknd over 1f out* **100/1**
6 **13** *12* **Tasman Gold**[55] 2502 2-9-3 0............ WilliamBuick 8 —
(A M Balding) *chsd ldrs tl wknd over 2f out* **12/1**
14 *6* **Arrogance** 2-9-3 0............ GeorgeBaker 13 —
(G L Moore) *s.i.s: a bhd* **20/1**

1m 15.61s (0.81) **Going Correction** +0.05s/f (Good) **14** Ran SP% **111.8**
Speed ratings (Par 96): **96,91,89,88,87 87,84,82,79,75 74,70,54,46**
toteswinger: 1&2 £7.50, 1&3 £5.50, 2&3 £11.80. CSF £43.05 TOTE £2.20: £1.30, £4.20, £3.20; EX 38.10.
Owner D Gorton **Bred** Kinghaven Farms Limited **Trained** Hucking, Kent
■ Auld Arty (6/1, uns rdr bef s) & Luvmedo (100/1, uns rdr & galloped loose) were withdrawn. Deduct 10p in the £ under Rule 4.

FOCUS
A fair maiden and it proved a good opportunity for Square Eddie to get off the mark having been highly tried in his previous two starts. The form makes plenty of sense in behind.

NOTEBOOK
Square Eddie(CAN), who ran well on his debut in a conditions event at Windsor and did not disgrace himself when finishing in midfield in the Coventry Stakes next time after pulling hard (came back with sore shins), had much less to do in this company and duly won with a degree of ease. He ran on strongly at the finish and deserves another crack at a better race, but apparently he will not be overraced this term. (op 2-1)
Jeremiah(IRE), who is improving with every run, finished third behind the John Best-trained Deposer at Lingfield last time, and he again found a rival from that stable too strong here. Handicaps are now an option for him and he could well find an opening in that sphere. (op 33-1)
Galpin Junior(USA), whose price rose from $120,000 as a yearling to $280,000 as a two-year-old, is a half-brother to After The Beep, a smart, multiple dirt sprint winner. He ran a promising race on his debut, running on well for third despite being green, and he looks sure to improve a bundle for this outing. (op 12-1)
Retro(IRE), a brother to Aahgowangowan, a prolific winning sprinter, Stolt, a multiple 5f winner, and Super Genius, a dual 5f winner at two in Italy, did not improve greatly on his debut effort, finding only the one pace in the closing stages. (op 9-4 tchd 10-3)
Papa Meilland, whose dam was placed over 7f and 1m and is a half-sister to Notnowcato and Heaven Knows, is bred to get further than this and shaped encouragingly in the circumstances. (op 66-1)
Sister Clement(IRE), who cost 180,000gns, is a half-sister to Corsario, a smart 6f winner at two in France, and to Bentong, a multiple 6f-7f winner. She finished tailed off on her debut but this was far more promising and she looks one for nurseries after one more run. (op 66-1)
Scarlets Official explanation: jockey said filly lost its action
Tasman Gold Official explanation: jockey said colt had a breathing problem
Arrogance Official explanation: jockey said gelding ran green

4275 MATTHEW CLARK H'CAP 1m 4f
3:35 (3:35) (Class 6) (0-60,62) 3-Y-O+ **£2,914** (£867; £433; £216) **Stalls** High

Form RPR
600- **1** **The Composer**[145] 6500 6-9-4 **53**............ SteveDrowne 4 60
(M Blanshard) *cl up: rdn over 3f out: kpt on u.p fr over 1f out: led fnl 75yds: drvn out* **25/1**
1524 **2** *3/4* **Compton Charlie**[28] 3347 4-9-4 **58**............ JackDean(5) 6 64
(J G Portman) *in tch: rdn and hdwy over 2f out: led and hung lft over 1f out: hdd fnl 75yds: kpt on but no ex* **14/1**
3436 **3** *nse* **Amwell Brave**[14] 3820 7-8-12 **47**............ LiamJones 3 53
(J R Jenkins) *hld up towards rr: rdn and stdy hdwy over 2f out: swtchd lft over 1f out: fin strly: snatched 3rd fnl stride* **10/1**
-521 **4** *shd* **Faith And Reason (USA)**[7] 4054 5-9-13 **62** 6ex............(v) TPQueally 11 68
(A P Stringer) *travelled wl and sn mid-div: hdwy over 2f out: sn rdn: styd on fnl f: nvr quite able to mount chal* **11/8**[1]
-006 **5** *nk* **Ocean Avenue (IRE)**[20] 3614 9-9-9 **58**............(p) TQuinn 7 63
(C A Horgan) *trckd ldr: led over 2f out: rdn and hdd whn carried sltly lft over 1f out: kpt on but no ex* **8/1**[3]
0-35 **6** *1/2* **Daring Racer (GER)**[19] 3631 5-9-10 **59**............ IanMongan 13 63
(Mrs L J Mongan) *trckd ldrs: rdn over 3f out: chal over 1f out: kpt on same pce fnl f* **14/1**
036 **7** *1 1/4* **Musango**[35] 788 5-9-6 **55**............(tp) PaulDoe 10 57
(Tim Vaughan) *mid-div: rdn over 3f out: stdy prog over 2f out: styd on fnl f: n.m.r towards fin* **33/1**
0503 **8** *1 1/2* **Icannshift (IRE)**[25] 3448 8-9-4 **53**............ FrankieMcDonald 12 53
(T M Jones) *led: rdn and hdd over 2f out: wknd fnl f* **16/1**
40-1 **9** *2 1/4* **Soviet Sceptre (IRE)**[20] 3606 7-9-9 **58**............(tp) FergusSweeney 9 54
(Tim Vaughan) *slowly away: bhd: sme prog and rdn over 2f out: no further imp fnl f* **6/1**[2]
00-0 **10** *3* **Ganymede**[28] 3137 7-9-1 **50**............ AlanDaly 14 42
(Mark Gillard) *mainly towards rr* **40/1**
2633 **11** *4 1/2* **Megalala (IRE)**[46] 2799 7-9-5 **57**............ MarcHalford(3) 5 41
(J J Bridger) *mid-div: hung lft fr 5f out: rdn over 3f out: wknd over 1f out* **16/1**
/002 **12** *2 3/4* **Irish Ballad**[7] 4055 6-8-12 **47**............(t) WilliamBuick 1 27
(S Dow) *mid-div: rdn over 3f out: wknd 2f out* **8/1**[3]
1506 **13** *5* **Ledgerwood**[41] 2932 3-8-7 **57**............ EmmettStack(3) 8 29
(A J Chamberlain) *a bhd* **100/1**

2m 37.63s (-0.37) **Going Correction** +0.05s/f (Good)
WFA 3 from 4yo+ 12lb **13** Ran SP% **123.0**
Speed ratings (Par 101): **103,102,102,102,102 101,101,100,98,96 93,91,88**
toteswinger: 1&2 £55.90, 1&3 £26.60, 2&3 £23.70. CSF £342.66 CT £3727.47 TOTE £36.70: £8.00, £3.10, £2.80; EX 434.10.
Owner A D Jones **Bred** D A And Mrs Hicks **Trained** Upper Lambourn, Berks

FOCUS
A moderate handicap and, with very little separating the first six home, the form looks ordinary. The winner was close to last year's form.
Soviet Sceptre(IRE) Official explanation: jockey said gelding missed the break
Irish Ballad Official explanation: jockey said gelding lost a shoe

4276 GLENSIDE MANOR HEALTHCARE SERVICES LTD H'CAP 1m 1f 198y
4:05 (4:06) (Class 4) (0-85,85) 3-Y-O+ **£5,180** (£1,541; £770; £384) **Stalls** High

Form RPR
6406 **1** **Higgy's Boy (IRE)**[8] 4021 3-8-9 **76**............ RichardHughes 6 83+
(R Hannon) *trckd ldrs: rdn over 2f out: swtchd lft over 1f out: led fnl 100yds: r.o* **7/2**[1]
1355 **2** *3/4* **Basra (IRE)**[18] 3676 5-9-11 **82**............ AdamKirby 4 90+
(Miss Jo Crowley) *hld up: prog and travelling wl bhd wall of horses fr over 2f out: nt clr run and swtchd lft ent fnl f: r.o wl: nt rch wnr* **6/1**[3]
6040 **3** *1/2* **Man Of Gwent (UAE)**[13] 3836 4-9-3 **74**............(b^1) TQuinn 10 79
(P D Evans) *chsd ldr: led 2f out: sn rdn: edgd rt and hdd fnl 100yds: lost 2nd nr fin* **11/1**
4406 **4** *1 1/4* **Resonate (IRE)**[38] 3045 10-9-2 **73**............ FergusSweeney 2 75
(A G Newcombe) *hld up bhd: rdn over 2f out: styd on ins fnl f: wnt 4th fnl strides* **14/1**
0056 **5** *shd* **Proper (IRE)**[18] 3676 4-9-1 **72**............ WilliamBuick 1 74
(C J Mann) *hld up: sme hdwy over 3f out: outpcd over 2f out: swtchd rt over 1f out: styd on again fnl f* **16/1**
0043 **6** *hd* **Wester Ross (IRE)**[23] 3518 4-8-9 **66**............ HayleyTurner 7 67
(J M P Eustace) *in tch: rdn over 2f out: kpt on fnl f but nt pce to chal* **8/1**
-025 **7** *1 1/2* **Flying Applause**[20] 3607 3-8-4 **71**............ SimonWhitworth 8 71+
(A King) *sat down leaving stalls: bhd: rcvrd steadily into mid-div over 5f out: rdn 3f out: one pce fnl f* **7/1**
-053 **8** *1/2* **Del Mar Sunset**[17] 3736 9-9-4 **75**............ LiamJones 5 78+
(W J Haggas) *t.k.h in rr: hdwy on rails over 2f out: sn rdn: chalng for cl 3rd whn squeezed up wl ins fnl f: nt rcvr* **4/1**[2]
204/ **9** *nk* **Kinrande (IRE)**[739] 3497 6-10-0 **85**............ RichardSmith 9 88+
(P J Makin) *led: qcknd pce jst ins 3f out: sn rdn: hdd narrowly 2f out: rallied gamely: disputing cl 3rd whn squeezed up wl ins fnl f: nt rcvr* **14/1**
6605 **10** *2* **Full Victory (IRE)**[12] 3887 6-9-4 **75**............ SteveDrowne 3 68
(R A Farrant) *racd keenly: trckd ldrs: rdn over 2f out: btn whn short of room ins fnl f* **10/1**

2m 12.0s (2.10) **Going Correction** +0.05s/f (Good)
WFA 3 from 4yo+ 10lb **10** Ran SP% **116.8**
Speed ratings (Par 105): **93,92,92,91,90 90,89,89,88,87**
toteswinger: 1&2 £4.50, 1&3 £9.40, 2&3 £16.10. CSF £24.62 CT £210.20 TOTE £3.20: £1.80, £1.90, £4.10; EX 25.70.
Owner I Higginson **Bred** M Henochsberg **Trained** East Everleigh, Wilts
■ Stewards' Enquiry : T Quinn three-day ban: careless riding (Aug 5-7)

FOCUS
An ordinary handicap for the grade and the winning time was moderate. The winner had seemed exposed and the next two are rated to this year's turf form.
Flying Applause Official explanation: jockey said gelding sat down as stalls opened
Full Victory(IRE) Official explanation: jockey said gelding ran too free

4277 ASHBRITTLE STUD MAIDEN FILLIES' STKS 6f 212y
4:40 (4:42) (Class 4) 3-Y-O+ **£4,533** (£1,348; £674; £336) **Stalls** High

Form RPR
2-63 **1** **Provence**[40] 2966 3-8-12 **74**............ TQuinn 6 73
(B W Hills) *mid-div: hdwy 3f out: led wl over 1f out: sn hrd rdn: all out* **9/2**[3]
3-3 **2** *nk* **Mille Feuille (IRE)**[18] 3694 3-8-12 0............ TPQueally 8 72
(R M Beckett) *t.k.h in mid-div: rdn over 2f out: swtchd lft over 1f out: r.o strly: wnt 2nd nr fin: nt rch wnr* **11/2**
0 **3** *1/2* **Poyle Dee Dee**[27] 3379 3-8-12 0............ AdamKirby 1 71
(R M Beckett) *chsd ldrs: rdn to ld 2f out: narrowly hdd wl over 1f out: kpt on: lost 2nd nr fin* **33/1**
2 **4** *2 1/4* **Emirates Lady (USA)**[29] 3318 3-8-12 0............ TedDurcan 7 65
(Saeed Bin Suroor) *chsd ldrs: rdn over 2f out: kpt on same pce fnl f* **3/1**[2]
5 *3* **Ethaara** 3-8-12 0............ RHills 2 57+
(W J Haggas) *hld up: hdwy over 3f out: rdn over 2f out: hung lft over 1f out: no further imp* **5/2**[1]
-006 **6** *1* **Acquifer**[37] 3064 3-8-12 **68**............ IanMongan 15 54
(J L Dunlop) *trckd ldrs: effrt 2f out: one pce fnl f* **12/1**

7 nk **Make Amends (IRE)** 3-8-12 0 SteveDrowne 13 53
(R J Hodges) *sltly hmpd s: towards rr: styd on but edgd rt fnl f: nvr trbld ldrs* **100/1**

0 8 1 1/2 **Lady Brora**33 3161 3-8-12 0 WilliamBuick 14 53+
(A M Balding) *hld up: snatched up on rails over 4f out: sme late prog: n.d* **16/1**

00 9 nse **Russian Empress (USA)**29 3318 3-8-12 0 PatDobbs 4 49+
(Sir Michael Stoute) *nvr bttr than mid-div* **14/1**

10 1 **Kappalyn (IRE)** 3-8-12 0 RichardHughes 3 46+
(R Hannon) *t.k.h and nvr bttr than mid-div* **25/1**

0-4 11 8 **Alto Singer (IRE)**15 3801 3-8-9 0 JamesMillman(3) 11 25
(B R Millman) *w ldr: rdn and ev ch jst over 2f out: wknd over 1f out* **20/1**

12 2 **Aegean Pride** 3-8-10 0 ow3 HaddenFrost(5) 9 22
(R Hannon) *s.i.s: a bhd* **28/1**

13 shd **Rose Of Torridge** 3-8-12 0 FergusSweeney 10 19
(A G Newcombe) *s.i.s: a bhd* **100/1**

0030 14 1 3/4 **Milldown Bay**27 3381 3-8-12 65 RobertHavlin 12 14
(B R Millman) *wnt rt s: led tl over 2f out: sn wknd* **50/1**

15 12 **Redefine** 3-8-12 0 AmirQuinn 5 —
(Mrs A L M King) *s.i.s: a outpcd in rr* **100/1**

1m 28.49s (-0.51) **Going Correction** +0.05s/f (Good) **15 Ran SP% 127.3**
Speed ratings (Par 102): **104,103,103,100,97 95,95,93,93,92 83,81,81,79,65**
toteswinger: 1&2 £5.10, 1&3 £43.70, 2&3 £37.80 CSF £29.33 TOTE £6.30: £1.90, £2.20, £9.80; EX 27.10.
Owner D J Deer **Bred** D J And Mrs Deer **Trained** Lambourn, Berks

FOCUS
An ordinary fillies' maiden. The winner and fourth have been rated to form at face value, with apparent improvement from the Beckett pair in second and third.
Milldown Bay Official explanation: jockey said filly hung right-handed

4278 COUNTRY LEISURE (GRP) LTD H'CAP 1m
5:10 (5:12) (Class 6) (0-60,60) 3-Y-O £2,914 (£867; £433; £216) Stalls High

Form RPR

0110 1 **Lancaster Lad (IRE)**7 4053 3-9-2 58 (p) SteveDrowne 13 63
(A B Haynes) *in mid-div: hdwy and nt clr run over 2f out: led over 1f out: kpt on: rdn out* **8/1**2

2054 2 nk **Mganga**5 4115 3-8-8 57 MatthewDavies(7) 7 61
(M R Channon) *hld up towards rr: hdwy over 2f out: swtchd rt over 1f out: sn rdn to chse wnr: kpt on* **4/1**1

20 3 1/2 **Duty Doctor**11 3918 3-9-4 60 RichardHughes 4 63
(S Kirk) *hld up bhd: rdn and hdwy fr 2f out: swtchd rt over 1f out: r.o fnl f* **4/1**1

5600 4 1 1/2 **Annes Rocket (IRE)**22 3564 3-9-4 60 PatDobbs 5 59
(J C Fox) *s.i.s: hld up bhd: gd hdwy on rails over 2f out: rdn to chal over 1f out: edgd lft and no ex fnl f* **14/1**

00-0 5 1 3/4 **Follow The Band**11 3916 3-8-10 57 HaddenFrost(5) 2 52
(R Hannon) *prom: led over 2f out: sn rdn: hdd over 1f out: sn hung lft: no ex* **28/1**

0000 6 3/4 **Squire Boldwood (IRE)**12 3873 3-9-3 59 (b) TQuinn 15 53
(D R C Elsworth) *chsd ldrs: rdn over 2f out: kpt on same pce fnl f* **20/1**

-000 7 1/2 **Bathwick Man**23 3524 3-8-11 56 (v1) KevinGhunowa(3) 8 49
(D E Pipe) *chsd ldrs: effrt 3f out: one pce fnl 2f* **18/1**

0003 8 nse **Mrs Jefferson (IRE)**20 3604 3-8-9 56 JackDean(5) 11 48
(J G Portman) *a in mid-div* **9/1**3

-000 9 3/4 **Turfani (IRE)**29 3322 3-9-1 57 AmirQuinn 1 48
(W J Knight) *hld up: hdwy over 3f out: sn rdn for effrt: wknd jst over 1f out* **8/1**2

60-4 10 1 **Janet's Delight**64 2260 3-9-0 56 PaulDoe 3 44
(S Curran) *bmpd over 4f out: a towards rr* **10/1**

0-00 11 8 **Headache**39 2994 3-8-13 55 (t) TPQueally 12 25
(B W Duke) *chsd ldrs: nt clr run 3f out: wknd over 1f out* **12/1**

5000 12 1 1/4 **Talamahana**18 3678 3-8-13 55 (b) TGMcLaughlin 9 22
(A B Haynes) *prom: rdn over 3f out: wknd over 1f out* **40/1**

0-00 13 hd **Bad Moon Rising**18 3678 3-8-13 55 IanMongan 14 22
(J Akehurst) *led for 2f: styd pressing ldrs tl wknd over 1f out* **33/1**

6600 14 8 **Oxbridge**6 4083 3-8-13 55 AdamKirby 10 3
(J M Bradley) *in mid-div tl 2f out* **20/1**

-030 15 3 1/2 **Reel Man**46 2805 3-8-13 55 JimCrowley 6 —
(D K Ivory) *chsd ldrs: led after 2f: rdn and hdd over 2f out: sn wknd* **16/1**

1m 44.26s (0.76) **Going Correction** +0.05s/f (Good) **15 Ran SP% 125.2**
Speed ratings (Par 98): **98,97,97,95,93 93,92,92,91,90 82,81,81,73,69**
toteswinger: 1&2 £7.60, 1&3 £6.70, 2&3 £4.70. CSF £38.60 CT £157.01 TOTE £8.30: £2.70, £2.10, £2.10; EX 32.90 Place 6: £752.22 Place 5: £164.39.
Owner Mrs S M Maine **Bred** Tom Foley **Trained** Limpley Stoke, Bath
■ Stewards' Enquiry : Kevin Ghunowa caution: used whip with whip arm above shoulder height

FOCUS
A moderate but competitive handicap. Limited form, with the winner up 7lb and the next two close to their marks.
Squire Boldwood(IRE) Official explanation: jockey said gelding was denied a clear run
T/Jkpt: Not won. T/Plt: £1,765.60 to a £1 stake. Pool: £85,138.57. 35.20 winning tickets. T/Qpdt: £85.80 to a £1 stake. Pool: £5,107.59. 44.05 winning tickets. TM

4255 YARMOUTH (L-H)
Tuesday, July 22

OFFICIAL GOING: Good to firm (8.4)
Wind: Light across Weather: Overcast

4279 EUROPEAN BREEDERS' FUND MAIDEN STKS 5f 43y
2:15 (2:15) (Class 5) 2-Y-O £3,784 (£1,132; £566; £283) Stalls High

Form RPR

2 1 **Global City (IRE)**17 3707 2-9-3 0 (t) KerrinMcEvoy 2 80+
(Saeed Bin Suroor) *mde all: shkn up and edgd lft over 1f out: r.o strly* **1/3**1

43 2 4 1/2 **Green Poppy**26 3417 2-8-12 0 SebSanders 1 59
(Eve Johnson Houghton) *chsd wnr: effrt over 1f out: sn outpcd* **9/1**3

2 3 1 3/4 **Joe Caster**110 1168 2-9-3 0 RyanMoore 4 58
(J M P Eustace) *s.i.s: hld up: effrt 1/2-way: no imp appr fnl f* **4/1**2

00 4 1 3/4 **Usual Suspects**29 3315 2-8-12 0 PatrickMathers 3 46
(Peter Grayson) *prom: racd keenly: outpcd fnl 2f* **50/1**

62.83 secs (0.63) **Going Correction** +0.025s/f (Good) **4 Ran SP% 107.0**
Speed ratings (Par 94): **95,87,85,82**
toteswinger: 1&2 £3.50. CSF £3.91 TOTE £1.30; EX 3.50.
Owner Godolphin **Bred** Mrs Monica Hackett **Trained** Newmarket, Suffolk

FOCUS
A modest race in terms of overall strength but the winner built on his debut win and is a nice type.

NOTEBOOK
Global City(IRE), a keen type, had to be taken to the start early. He improved on his debut effort for this better ground and made all for a comfortable success. This is his trip for now and he is capable of better. (op 2-5 tchd 4-9)
Green Poppy tried to challenge the favourite going to the furlong pole but he was basically too good for her. She can now switch to nurseries. (op 10-1 tchd 11-1)
Joe Caster has had niggly problems seen since his debut second to subsequent impressive Coventry winner Art Connoisseur on soft ground at Leicester in early April (subsequent selling winners third and fourth). After a slow start, he moved into third place at halfway but was never in a position from which to challenge. This ground was too fast for him. Official explanation: jockey said colt slipped leaving stalls (op 10-3 tchd 3-1)
Usual Suspects has shown a very modest level of ability in her three outings to date. (op 40-1)

4280 LINDLEY CATERING (S) STKS 1m 2f 21y
2:45 (2:49) (Class 6) 3-Y-O £1,942 (£578; £288; £144) Stalls Low

Form RPR

0 1 **Bella Medici**14 3813 3-8-7 0 JimmyQuinn 2 54+
(M H Tompkins) *s.i.s: hld up: pushed along over 3f out: hdwy over 2f out: led over 1f out: shkn up and r.o wl* **12/1**

4403 2 4 1/2 **Yakama (IRE)**10 3963 3-8-12 50 (b) DMylonas 5 51+
(G Prodromou) *dwlt: hld up: nt clr run over 2f out: swtchd rt and hdwy over 1f out: styd on to go 2nd ins fnl f: no ch w wnr* **10/1**

04 3 2 3/4 **Wouldn'Titbenice**13 3844 3-8-7 0 ChrisCatlin 6 40
(V Smith) *hld up: plld hrd: hdwy over 3f out: rdn and ev ch over 1f out: no ex ins fnl f* **5/2**1

056 4 1 1/4 **Ask Nicely**18 3688 3-8-7 62 DO'Donohoe 3 37
(W R Muir) *trckd ldrs: plld hrd: chsd ldr over 3f out: rdn over 2f out: wknd fnl f: nt clr run towards fin* **3/1**2

0160 5 shd **Landikhaya (IRE)**6 4086 3-9-4 57 (p) SebSanders 8 48
(D K Ivory) *chsd ldr tl led over 4f out: rdn and hdd over 1f out: wknd ins fnl f* **7/2**3

0-00 6 1/2 **Latimer House (IRE)**40 2984 3-8-2 44 DavidProbert(5) 1 36
(Dr J D Scargill) *hld up: hdwy over 4f out: rdn over 1f out: wknd ins fnl f* **33/1**

0-04 7 25 **Lenouska (IRE)**17 3730 3-8-7 50 JamieSpencer 4 —
(J W Hills) *chsd ldrs: rdn and wknd over 2f out* **7/1**

4330 8 97 **Last Angel (IRE)**4 4165 3-8-7 46 KerrinMcEvoy 7 —
(M Wigham) *unruly in stalls: s.i.s: sn rcvrd to ld: hdd over 4f out: sn wknd: eased fnl 2f* **10/1**

2m 10.87s (0.37) **Going Correction** +0.025s/f (Good) **8 Ran SP% 117.1**
Speed ratings (Par 98): **99,95,93,92,92 91,71,—**
toteswinger: 1&2 £49.30, 1&3 £6.50, 2&3 £5.10. CSF £125.64 TOTE £13.60: £2.90, £3.00, £1.60; EX 128.00 TRIFECTA Not won.. The winner was bought in for 10,000 guineas. Wouldn'titbenice was claimed by M. Harris for £5000.
Owner S M Hall **Bred** Pollards Stables **Trained** Newmarket, Suffolk
■ Stewards' Enquiry : Chris Catlin caution: careless riding

FOCUS
A moderate seller. The winner is rated up a stone with the runner-up a sound guide but the next two are on the downgrade.
Lenouska(IRE) Official explanation: jockey said filly stumbled 2f out
Last Angel(IRE) Official explanation: jockey said filly had a breathing problem

4281 FIRSTBET.COM ONLINE SPORTSBOOK £50 IN FREE BETS H'CAP 1m 3f 101y
3:15 (3:21) (Class 6) (0-65,65) 3-Y-O £1,942 (£578; £288; £144) Stalls Low

Form RPR

5111 1 **Aleatricis**4 4147 3-9-0 58 6ex SebSanders 7 72+
(Sir Mark Prescott) *mde all: rdn over 1f out: styd on u.p* **4/5**1

0025 2 2 1/4 **Golden Bishop**22 3555 3-9-4 62 JamieSpencer 2 72+
(M L W Bell) *a.p: rdn to chse wnr fnl f: edgd rt and no imp wl ins fnl f* **10/3**2

000 3 1 1/2 **Catholic Hill (USA)**36 3094 3-8-6 50 MartinDwyer 4 58
(B J Meehan) *hld up in tch: plld hrd: chsd wnr over 2f out tl rdn over 1f out: no ex fnl f* **33/1**

2450 4 8 **Graylyn Ruby (FR)**18 3671 3-9-4 62 NCallan 9 57
(J Jay) *chsd ldr tl rdn 3f out: sn hung rt: wknd 2f out* **11/1**

5056 5 3 **Ministerofinterior**22 3566 3-9-3 61 (b1) AlanMunro 10 51
(C F Wall) *chsd ldrs: rdn over 3f out: wknd over 2f out* **18/1**

044 6 6 **Day Trip (IRE)**21 3573 3-9-7 65 RyanMoore 5 45
(B J Meehan) *hld up: rdn over 3f out: sn hung lft and wknd* **17/2**3

4553 7 24 **Scientific**54 2552 3-8-9 53 (b) SaleemGolam 8 —
(G Prodromou) *s.i.s: hld up: rdn and wknd over 3f out* **20/1**

0000 8 4 1/2 **Tank Commander**18 3671 3-8-12 56 (b1) DO'Donohoe 3 —
(W R Muir) *hld up: rdn and wknd over 3f out* **40/1**

2m 26.82s (-1.88) **Going Correction** +0.025s/f (Good) **8 Ran SP% 112.9**
Speed ratings (Par 98): **107,105,104,98,96 91,74,71**
toteswinger: 1&2 £1.50, 1&3 £12.90, 2&3 £16.30. CSF £3.36 CT £40.88 TOTE £1.80: £1.10, £1.20, £6.70; EX 3.80 Trifecta £80.00 Pool: £80.00 - 5.67 winning units..
Owner The Green Door Partnership **Bred** Miss K Rausing **Trained** Newmarket, Suffolk
■ Stewards' Enquiry : Martin Dwyer caution: careless riding

FOCUS
A decent winning time for a race like this. The well in winner made all and not many got into the race with the first three clear. The form has been rated on the positive side.

4282 STANLEY THREADWELL MEMORIAL FILLIES' H'CAP 1m 3y
3:50 (3:51) (Class 5) (0-70,67) 3-Y-O+ £2,719 (£809; £404; £202) Stalls High

Form RPR

2030 1 **Al Rayanah**73 2003 5-8-12 49 (p) SaleemGolam 6 57
(G Prodromou) *s.i.s: hld up: hdwy u.p over 1f out: edgd rt and r.o to ld nr fin* **20/1**

-516 2 nk **Navene (IRE)**24 3481 4-9-11 62 AlanMunro 1 69
(C F Wall) *trckd ldr: plld hrd: led wl over 1f out: rdn and edgd rt ins fnl f: hdd nr fin* **13/2**

0213 3 2 1/4 **Luck Will Come (IRE)**12 3866 4-9-9 65 JackMitchell(5) 9 67
(H J Collingridge) *chsd ldrs: rdn over 2f out: ev ch over 1f out: styd on same pce fnl f* **11/2**2

0506 4 3/4 **Khazina (USA)**27 3381 3-9-6 65 NCallan 3 63
(C E Brittain) *hld up: swtchd lft and hdwy over 1f out: sn rdn and ev ch: no ex wl ins fnl f* **14/1**

0305 5 1/2 **Tuscan Treaty**44 2863 8-8-4 46 oh1 (t) AhmedAjtebi(5) 5 45
(R W Price) *s.i.s: sn prom: rdn over 1f out: styd on same pce fnl f* **33/1**

-133 6 nk **Imperial Lucky (IRE)**13 3834 5-9-6 57 PatCosgrave 10 56
(M J Wallace) *hld up: rdn over 1f out: hung rt and r.o towards fin* **6/1**3

400 7 3 1/4 **Samahir (USA)**4 4156 4-8-13 50 SebSanders 2 41
(T T Clement) *led: rdn and hdd wl over 1f out: wknd ins fnl f* **6/1**3

660 8 3/4 **Alzaroof (USA)**20 3611 3-9-8 67 MartinDwyer 7 54
(E A L Dunlop) *trckd ldrs: rdn and ev ch wl over 1f out: wknd fnl f* **12/1**

0632 **9** 2 ¼ **Striving (IRE)**[22] 3552 3-9-3 **62**...........(v) RyanMoore 4 44
(Sir Michael Stoute) *hld up: rdn over 3f out: wknd over 1f out* **9/4**[1]

0466 **10** ½ **Life's A Whirl**[7] 4065 6-8-11 **48**...........(p) ChrisCatlin 8 31
(Mrs C A Dunnett) *chsd ldrs: rdn over 3f out: wknd over 2f out* **12/1**

1m 40.7s (0.10) **Going Correction** +0.025s/f (Good)
WFA 3 from 4yo+ 8lb **10** Ran SP% **117.8**
Speed ratings (Par 100): **100,99,97,96,96 95,92,91,89,89**
toteswinger: 1&2 £21.50, 1&3 £24.40, 2&3 £6.90. CSF £145.97 CT £842.53 TOTE £21.40: £4.50, £3.10, £1.80; EX 210.30 TRIFECTA Not won..
Owner Faisal Al-Nassar **Bred** R P Kernohan **Trained** East Harling, Norfolk

FOCUS
An ordinary fillies' handicap with the winner rated to her winter sand form.
Striving(IRE) Official explanation: trainer's rep had no explanation for the poor form shown

4283 GREAT YARMOUTH GLASS MAIDEN STKS 7f 3y
4:20 (4:21) (Class 5) 3-4-Y-O **£2,719** (£809; £404; £202) **Stalls** High

Form RPR

0-05 **1** **Mut'Ab (USA)**[87] 1632 3-9-3 94...........(b[1]) RyanMoore 2 87
(C E Brittain) *trckd ldr tl led over 1f out: led over 1f out: drvn out* **1/4**[1]

2 4 ½ **Classic Lass** 3-8-12 0........... ChrisCatlin 3 73
(Rae Guest) *s.i.s: sn prom: rdn to chse wnr over 1f out: eased whn btn wl ins fnl f* **14/1**[3]

-303 **3** 18 **Robert Burns (IRE)**[19] 3629 3-9-3 73...........(t) PaulEddery 1 26
(Miss D Mountain) *led: edgd lft over 4f out: rdn: hdd and hung lft over 1f out: sn wknd* **4/1**[2]

4 9 **Pas De Roland** 3-8-10 0........... StevenCorrigan(7) 4 2
(S W Hall) *s.s: hdwy over 5f out: wknd 3f out* **50/1**

1m 27.04s (0.44) **Going Correction** +0.025s/f (Good) **4** Ran SP% **108.6**
Speed ratings (Par 103): **98,92,72,62**
toteswinger: 1&2 £3.90. CSF £4.94 TOTE £1.20; EX 3.90.
Owner Saeed Manana **Bred** Darley **Trained** Newmarket, Suffolk

FOCUS
An uncompetitive maiden with the winner facing what looked a simple task. It is difficult to actually know what he achieved but he has been rated close to form.

4284 NORFOLK CHAMBER OF COMMERCE H'CAP 7f 3y
4:55 (4:55) (Class 5) (0-75,75) 3-Y-O+ **£2,590** (£770; £385; £192) **Stalls** High

Form RPR

1122 **1** **Oh So Saucy**[19] 3653 4-9-9 **72**........... JackMitchell(5) 13 85
(C F Wall) *hld up in tch: swtchd lft over 1f out: rdn to ld wl ins fnl f* **7/2**[2]

01-6 **2** nk **Parisian Gift (IRE)**[66] 2189 3-9-10 **75**........... RichardKingscote 4 84
(Tom Dascombe) *w ldr tl led 2f out: sn rdn: hdd wl ins fnl f* **5/1**[3]

343 **3** 1 ¾ **Gulch's Rose (USA)**[16] 3762 3-8-12 **63**........... RyanMoore 11 67+
(J Noseda) *hld up: last 2f out: nt clr run, swtchd lft and hdwy over 1f out: sn rdn: stayed on same pce towards fin* **8/1**

2121 **4** ½ **Isphahan**[27] 3383 5-9-7 **70**........... DavidProbert(5) 6 76
(A M Balding) *chsd ldrs: rdn over 1f out: edgd rt and styd on same pce ins fnl f* **10/3**[1]

-542 **5** 3 **Oi Vay Joe (IRE)**[73] 1996 4-9-7 **65**........... AlanMunro 7 63
(W Jarvis) *chsd ldrs: rdn over 2f out: wkng whn nt clr run ins fnl f* **10/1**

2026 **6** 2 **Fiefdom (IRE)**[18] 3664 6-9-12 **70**...........(p) PaulMulrennan 12 62
(I W McInnes) *hld up: rdn over 2f out: btn whn hmpd ins fnl f* **12/1**

0-05 **7** ½ **Marvin Gardens**[7] 4052 5-8-4 **53** oh8........... KellyHarrison(5) 8 44
(P S McEntee) *led: rdn and hdd 2f out: wknd fnl f* **66/1**

0125 **8** 1 ¼ **Forced Upon Us**[20] 3615 4-8-6 **53** oh1...........(b) DominicFox(3) 3 41
(P J McBride) *hld up: hdwy over 2f out: sn rdn: wknd fnl f* **16/1**

0031 **9** nse **Registrar**[19] 3653 6-8-12 **56**...........(p) PatCosgrave 1 44
(Mrs C A Dunnett) *s.s: hld up: plld hrd: wknd wl over 1f out* **10/1**

0600 **10** nk **Empire Dancer (IRE)**[38] 3034 5-8-9 **53**........... PatrickMathers 5 40
(I W McInnes) *prom: rdn over 2f out: wknd wl over 1f out* **33/1**

-000 **11** 3 ½ **Sorrel Point**[13] 3842 5-8-9 **53** oh4........... JimmyQuinn 2 30
(H J Collingridge) *s.i.s: hld up: rdn and wknd wl over 1f out* **40/1**

0300 **12** 1 **Atheer Dubai (IRE)**[25] 3442 3-9-7 **72**...........(b) MartinDwyer 10 44
(C E Brittain) *chsd ldrs: rdn over 2f out: wknd wl over 1f out* **18/1**

1m 26.04s (-0.56) **Going Correction** +0.025s/f (Good)
WFA 3 from 4yo+ 7lb **12** Ran SP% **117.0**
Speed ratings (Par 103): **104,103,101,101,97 95,94,93,93,92 88,87**
toteswinger: 1&2 £5.10, 1&3 £5.80, 2&3 £9.40. CSF £20.87 CT £133.09 TOTE £4.30: £1.80, £2.40, £2.60; EX 25.80 Trifecta £186.90 Pool: £303.17 - 1.20 winning units..
Owner The Eight Of Diamonds **Bred** Mrs C J Walker **Trained** Newmarket, Suffolk
■ Stewards' Enquiry : Dominic Fox caution: used whip down the shoulder in the forehand position

FOCUS
A decent pace and fair form for the grade with the winner continuing to progress. The next two were unexposed and the fourth came here in good form.
Fiefdom(IRE) Official explanation: jockey said gelding hung right

4285 EASTERN EVENING NEWS H'CAP 5f 43y
5:25 (5:27) (Class 6) (0-60,60) 4-Y-O+ **£2,047** (£604; £302) **Stalls** High

Form RPR

0000 **1** **Taboor (IRE)**[7] 4064 10-8-8 **50**........... AlanMunro 12 58
(R M H Cowell) *dwlt: hld up: hdwy over 1f out: r.o u.p to ld wl ins fnl f* **22/1**

0450 **2** 1 **Rann Na Cille (IRE)**[5] 4107 4-8-10 **52**........... MickyFenton 3 56
(P T Midgley) *led: hdd over 3f out: led 2f out: sn rdn and edgd rt: hdd wl ins fnl f* **12/1**

-420 **3** 3 **Smirfys Gold (IRE)**[28] 3340 4-8-10 **52**........... StephenDonohoe 14 46
(E S McMahon) *chsd ldrs: outpcd 2f out: styd on u.p ins fnl f* **3/1**[1]

0-36 **4** hd **Puskas (IRE)**[61] 2330 5-8-7 **52** ow2...........(b) RussellKennemore(3) 8 45
(J M Bradley) *sn pushed along in rr: swtchd rt over 3f out: hdwy u.p over 1f out: styd on same pce ins fnl f* **16/1**

000- **5** shd **Smiddy Hill**[308] 5507 6-8-8 **50** ow2........... PatCosgrave 11 43
(R Bastiman) *chsd ldrs: rdn and edgd lft over 1f out: styd on same pce ins fnl f* **16/1**

5610 **6** ¾ **Town House**[17] 3724 6-8-4 **53**........... BillyCray(7) 2 43
(B P J Baugh) *chsd ldrs: rdn over 1f out: one pce fnl f* **12/1**

00-6 **7** 1 ½ **Kindallachan**[21] 3585 5-8-12 **54**........... JimmyQuinn 15 38
(G C Bravery) *hld up: nt clr run 2f out: styd on ins fnl f: nvr nrr* **25/1**

0304 **8** ½ **Charlotte Grey**[7] 4064 4-8-2 **47**........... DominicFox(3) 13 30
(P J McBride) *prom: outpcd 1/2-way: n.d after* **5/1**[2]

5362 **9** shd **Niteowl Lad (IRE)**[18] 3668 6-9-3 **59**...........(p) PaulMulrennan 5 41
(J Balding) *chsd ldrs: rdn and edgd rt over 1f out: wknd ins fnl f* **6/1**[3]

6600 **10** 2 ½ **Peopleton Brook**[5] 4106 6-8-3 **50**...........(b) DavidProbert(5) 7 23
(J M Bradley) *sn pushed along and prom: outpcd 1/2-way: rallied over 1f out: wknd fnl f* **14/1**

0502 **11** nk **Violet's Pride**[10] 3953 4-8-6 **48**........... KimTinkler 6 20
(N Tinkler) *s.s: sn pushed along in rr: hdwy u.p over 1f out: wknd ins fnl f* **20/1**

0100 **12** 2 **Lithaam (IRE)**[5] 4106 4-8-13 **60**...........(p) JackMitchell(5) 9 25
(J M Bradley) *prom: rdn and wknd over 1f out* **25/1**

6046 **13** 1 **Bold Minstrel (IRE)**[7] 4064 6-9-3 **59**........... ChrisCatlin 4 20
(M Quinn) *chsd ldrs: rdn whn hmpd 2f out: sn wknd* **17/2**

0-05 **14** nk **Calypso King**[46] 2802 5-8-6 **48**........... PatrickMathers 10 8
(Peter Grayson) *chsd ldrs: led over 3f out: rdn and hdd 2f out: wkng whn hmpd sn after* **8/1**

4600 **15** 2 ¾ **Macademy Royal (USA)**[70] 2075 5-8-0 **47**...........(t) KellyHarrison(5) 16 —
(P S McEntee) *sn outpcd* **33/1**

62.99 secs (0.79) **Going Correction** +0.025s/f (Good) **15** Ran SP% **131.1**
Speed ratings (Par 101): **94,92,87,87,87 85,83,82,82,78 78,74,73,72,68**
toteswinger: 1&2 £65.00, 1&3 £27.00, 2&3 £10.00. CSF £270.44 CT £1063.61 TOTE £30.20: £6.40, £4.10, £1.70; EX 403.00 Trifecta £422.80 Part won. Pool: £ 571.42 - 0.60 winning units. Place 6: £37.55 Place 5: £27.20 .
Owner T W Morley **Bred** Rathasker Stud **Trained** Six Mile Bottom, Cambs

FOCUS
A moderate winning time for this low-grade handicap. The winner is rated to something like his winter sand form.
Niteowl Lad(IRE) Official explanation: jockey said gelding got upset in stalls
Macademy Royal(USA) Official explanation: trainer said gelding bled from the nose
T/Plt: £41.90 to a £1 stake. Pool: £55,960.47. 973.73 winning tickets. T/Qpdt: £7.10 to a £1 stake. Pool: £3,901.28. 406.30 winning tickets. CR

4286 - 4288a (Foreign Racing) - See Raceform Interactive

4072 CATTERICK (L-H)
Wednesday, July 23

OFFICIAL GOING: Good to firm (firm in places; 9.4)
Wind: Light, half behind Weather: Dry and warm

4289 YORKSHIRE RADIO MAIDEN STKS 5f 212y
2:20 (2:22) (Class 5) 2-Y-O **£2,590** (£770; £385; £192) **Stalls** Low

Form RPR

1 **Aldermoor (USA)** 2-9-3 0........... DanielTudhope 5 85+
(S C Williams) *stdd s: hld up in rr: gd hdwy 2f out: chal on bit on outer over 1f out: shkn up to ld ins fnl f: comf* **6/1**

4 **2** 1 **Starry Sky**[7] 4080 2-8-12 0........... SebSanders 9 71
(Sir Mark Prescott) *trckd ldrs: hdwy over 2f out: rdn to ld 1f out: sn drvn and hdd ins fnl f: kpt on same pce* **6/4**[1]

0 **3** 1 ¼ **Come And Go (UAE)**[28] 3364 2-9-3 0........... PaulMulrennan 8 72
(G A Swinbank) *chsd ldrs: hdwy 2f out: rdn and n.m.r over 1f out: sn ev ch tl drvn and styd on same pce ins fnl f* **20/1**

35 **4** 2 **Go Go Green (IRE)**[67] 2186 2-9-3 0........... DarrenWilliams 10 66
(S Parr) *led 2f: cl up tl rdn to ld again over 2f out: drvn and hdd 1f out: wknd ins fnl f* **8/1**

0 **5** 2 ¼ **Sampower Rose (IRE)**[18] 3707 2-8-12 0........... DNolan 12 55
(D Carroll) *in rr and rdn along 1/2-way: hdwy 2f out: styd on u.p ins fnl f: nrst fin* **100/1**

6 hd **Proclaim** 2-9-3 0........... GregFairley 4 59
(M Johnston) *midfield: pushed along 1/2-way: rdn over 2f out: no imp appr fnl f* **5/1**[3]

7 2 **Agent Stone (IRE)** 2-9-3 0........... AdrianTNicholls 6 53+
(D Nicholls) *s.i.s and bhd tl sme late hdwy* **12/1**

63 **8** shd **Exceedingly Good (IRE)**[26] 3437 2-8-12 0........... TedDurcan 1 48
(B Smart) *free to s: cl up on inner tl led after 2f: rdn and hdd over 2f out: sn wknd* **9/2**[2]

46 **9** 1 ¾ **Artesium**[23] 3568 2-9-3 0...........(t) PatCosgrave 2 47
(D J G Murray Smith) *midfield: rdn along over 2f out: sn drvn and wknd* **50/1**

10 5 **Poaka Beck (IRE)** 2-9-0 0........... JamieMoriarty(3) 7 32
(R F Fisher) *in tch: rdn along over 2f out: sn wknd* **28/1**

1m 12.99s (-0.61) **Going Correction** -0.15s/f (Firm) **10** Ran SP% **119.1**
Speed ratings (Par 94): **98,96,95,92,89 89,86,86,83,77**
toteswinger: 1&2 £4.30, 1&3 £22.30, 2&3 £8.70. CSF £15.38 TOTE £7.10: £1.70, £1.40, £3.20; EX 18.90.
Owner Phil & Frances Kendall **Bred** Gulf Coast Farms LLC **Trained** Newmarket, Suffolk

FOCUS
A modest maiden, but the gambled-on Aldermoor won comfortably and can be rated a couple of lengths better than the bare result. The runner-up is assessed as running to his mark.

NOTEBOOK
Aldermoor(USA), a 95,000gns two-year-old whose dam was a high-class performer in Brazil, comes from a yard hardly renowned for their success with juveniles, but they know how to land a gamble and the fact he was backed into 6/1 from an opening 25/1 suggested a big run was expected. Held up early, he made stylish headway and was travelling all over the favourite from a furlong out. He won with more in hand than the official margin suggests and looks to have a bright future. (op 25-1)
Starry Sky, a promising fourth over 7f at Kempton on her debut last week, was far from certain to be helped by the drop in trip, but she was always likely to have improved on that and ran well in defeat. She was no match for the cosy winner, but will be helped by a return to further and definitely has a future. (op 13-8 tchd 7-4 and 15-8 in a place)
Come And Go(UAE), who showed up well to a point on last month's debut at Carlisle (soft ground) fared better on this faster surface and stuck on under pressure in third, but never really looked like winning. He will require further than this in time and could be the type to do well in nurseries. (op 25-1 tchd 28-1)
Go Go Green(IRE) has been off since May and was trying 6f for the first time. He showed plenty of speed, but was readily passed and could find no more inside the final furlong. He ought to stay this trip, but may be best kept to 5f for the time being and may be more of a nursery type. (op 11-1 tchd 15-2)
Sampower Rose(IRE) improved markedly on her debut effort and was noted making some good late progress. She will be qualified for a handicap mark following one more run and should fare better in that sphere. (op 80-1)
Proclaim, a half-brother to the useful Dhaular Dhar, comes from a yard who have had a couple of debut winners recently, but this one looked in need of the experience and was always struggling for pace. He should improve. (op 4-1)
Agent Stone(IRE), whose dam was a 6f winner, was going on at the end of his race and should learn from this. (op 11-1 tchd 10-1)

Exceedingly Good(IRE) was the disappointment of the race. She had previously improved to finish third at Doncaster, but was free to post beforehand and may have spent up her energy a bit too soon. She is qualified for a handicap mark now and probably deserves another chance. (op 3-1 tchd 11-4)

4290 SUBSCRIBE ONLINE @ RACINGUK.TV (S) STKS 7f
2:50 (2:50) (Class 6) 2-Y-0 **£2,047** (£604; £302) **Stalls** Low

Form RPR
063 **1** **Dougie Peel**[4] 4203 2-8-11 0 ....(p) FergalLynch 1 60
(K A Ryan) *chsd ldrs: rdn and hdwy to ld wl over 1f out: drvn and edgd lft ins fnl f: hld on* **11/2**[2]
0522 **2** *nk* **Debbys Boy**[18] 3706 2-8-11 0 ....(b) MickyFenton 8 59
(Miss Gay Kelleway) *led: rdn 2f out: hdd and drvn wl over 1f out: rallied u.p ins fnl f and ev ch tl n.m.r and no ex towards fin* **5/6**[1]
03U0 **3** *6* **Just Five (IRE)**[4] 4203 2-8-11 0 .... TomEaves 6 44
(M Dods) *prom: rdn along and outpcd wl over 2f out: styd on u.p ins fnl f* **7/1**[3]
005 **4** *1 3/4* **Royal Premium**[4] 4203 2-8-11 0 ....(p) DavidAllan 2 40
(H A McWilliams) *in tch: pushed along and hdwy 1/2-way: rdn to chse ldrs 2f ut: sn drvn and wknd* **40/1**
0044 **5** *3 1/2* **Kosama**[8] 4063 2-8-6 0 .... EdwardCreighton 5 26
(M R Channon) *dwlt and in rr: rdn along and sme hdwy over 2f out: nvr a factor* **10/1**
000 **6** *9* **Senora Verde**[19] 3689 2-8-6 0 .... TonyCulhane 7 —
(P T Midgley) *cl up: pushed along and hung bdly rt home turn: sn rdn and wknd* **50/1**
0 **7** *1 3/4* **Red Eric**[13] 3888 2-8-11 0 .... SebSanders 4 —
(W M Brisbourne) *dwlt and a in rr* **7/1**[3]
00 **8** *3/4* **Without Equal**[16] 3792 2-8-6 0 .... PaulHanagan 3 —
(A Dickman) *dwlt and a in rr* **28/1**

1m 27.4s (0.40) **Going Correction** -0.15s/f (Firm) **8** Ran SP% **111.9**
Speed ratings (Par 92): **91,90,83,81,77 67,65,64**
toteswinger: 1&2 £2.00, 1&3 £4.60, 2&3 £2.50. CSF £10.01 TOTE £6.60: £1.10, £1.10, £2.00; EX 11.40.The winner was bought in for 5,000gns. Debbys Boy was claimed by Mrs J Holder for £6,000.
Owner Roger Peel **Bred** Brook Stud Bloodstock Ltd **Trained** Hambleton, N Yorks

FOCUS
Two came clear in what was a modest seller overall.

NOTEBOOK
Dougie Peel, a well-beaten third in this company at Redcar just four days earlier (first-time blinkers) was trying the cheekpieces this time and he found enough improvement to score, battling on well under pressure. He is probably not any better than this grade. (tchd 7-1)
Debbys Boy has shown improved form since wearing blinkers and having found one too good in selling/claiming company at Yarmouth and Beverley the last twice, he again just came up short. This was a gallant effort though and he deserves to find a small race. (op Evens tchd 8-11 and 11-10 in a place)
Just Five(IRE) ran one of his better races, but was well beaten by the front pair and needs to pull out more if he is to win, even at this sort of level. (tchd 8-1)
Royal Premium showed his first sign of ability in the first-time cheekpieces, but was never really travelling and will struggle to win unless improving again. (op 33-1)
Kosama, fourth in a selling nursery at Yarmouth recently, was soon in trouble and could have been expected to fare much better. (op 8-1)
Senora Verde Official explanation: trainer said filly hung left-handed throughout

4291 SKY BET SUPPORTING THE YORKSHIRE RACING FESTIVAL H'CAP 5f
3:20 (3:20) (Class 4) (0-85,85) 3-Y-0+ **£4,857** (£1,445; £722; £360) **Stalls** Low

Form RPR
-404 **1** **Hypnosis**[18] 3708 5-9-0 74 .... TonyHamilton 6 85
(D W Barker) *cl up: rdn to ld 1 1/2f out: drvn ins fnl f: edgd lft and kpt on towards fin* **6/1**[3]
0420 **2** *1* **Nomoreblondes**[13] 3868 4-8-6 66 ....(p) FrankieMcDonald 8 73
(P T Midgley) *cl up on outer: rdn along over 1f out: drvn ent fnl f and kpt on towards fin* **8/1**
1204 **3** *nse* **Princess Ellis**[2] 4240 4-9-11 85 .... DavidAllan 3 92
(E J Alston) *chsd ldrs: rdn 2f out: swtchd lft and drvn ins fnl f: n.m.r and no ex nr fin* **13/8**[1]
0643 **4** *2 1/2* **Malapropism**[2] 4246 8-9-1 75 .... TonyCulhane 7 73
(M R Channon) *dwlt and sn rdn along in rr: hdwy on inner 2f out: drvn over 1f out and sn one pce* **4/1**[2]
0406 **5** *shd* **Windjammer**[16] 3787 4-8-6 66 oh1 ....(b) PaulHanagan 11 63
(T D Easterby) *chsd ldrs: rdn along wl over 1f out: sn one pce* **16/1**
1-00 **6** *1/2* **Northern Bolt**[68] 2171 3-9-3 81 .... AdrianTNicholls 9 77
(D Nicholls) *dwlt: sn rdn along in rr: sme hdwy appr fnl f: nvr a factor* **16/1**
0000 **7** *1 1/2* **Classic Encounter (IRE)**[22] 3594 5-9-0 79 .... AhmedAjtebi(5) 4 69
(D M Simcock) *led: rdn along 1/2-way: hdd 1 1/2f out and sn wknd* **14/1**
600 **F** **Deserted Dane (USA)**[28] 3370 4-9-0 74 .... TomEaves 2 —
(G A Swinbank) *rrd and fell as stalls opened: dead* **6/1**[3]

58.63 secs (-1.17) **Going Correction** -0.20s/f (Firm)
WFA 3 from 4yo+ 4lb **8** Ran SP% **116.2**
Speed ratings (Par 105): **101,99,99,95,95 94,91,—**
toteswinger: 1&2 £7.10, 1&3 £2.70, 2&3 £2.40. CSF £53.41 CT £114.24 TOTE £6.20: £1.90, £2.50, £1.10; EX 52.30.
Owner R W Snowden **Bred** Mrs V E Hughes **Trained** Scorton, N Yorks

FOCUS
This modest handicap was run at a decent gallop.

4292 15TH AUGUST IS ALPHA 103.2 LADIES NIGHT NURSERY 7f
3:50 (3:50) (Class 5) 2-Y-0 **£2,590** (£770; £385; £192) **Stalls** Low

Form RPR
003 **1** **Pride Of Kings**[29] 3334 2-8-11 68 .... GregFairley 6 74+
(M Johnston) *cl up: rdn to ld over 2f out: drvn and hdd ins fnl f: rallied to ld nr line* **6/1**[3]
6321 **2** *nse* **Rapid Release (CAN)**[17] 3760 2-9-7 78 .... SebSanders 8 84+
(Sir Mark Prescott) *prom: hdwy 2f out: rdn to chal over 1f out: drvn to ld briefly ins fnl f: hdd and nt qckn nr line* **6/4**[1]
1554 **3** *5* **Scenic Pass**[7] 4079 2-8-7 64 .... EdwardCreighton 9 56
(M R Channon) *hld up: hdwy 1/2-way: rdn to chse ldng pair wl over 1f out: sn drvn and one pce* **9/2**[2]
323 **4** *3 1/4* **Musical Maze**[13] 3869 2-8-5 65 .... DuranFentiman(3) 4 49
(W M Brisbourne) *dwlt and in rr tl rdn and styd on appr fnl f: nrst fin* **12/1**
6323 **5** *3/4* **Jimwil (IRE)**[17] 3754 2-9-5 76 .... TomEaves 7 58
(M Dods) *trckd ldrs: pushed along 3f out: rdn over 2f out and sn btn* **6/1**[3]
4400 **6** *nk* **Another Luke (IRE)**[7] 4079 2-8-6 63 .... RoystonFfrench 5 44
(T J Etherington) *chsd ldrs: rdn along over 2f out: sn drvn and wknd* **20/1**
464 **7** *4 1/2* **Tito Gobbi**[43] 2910 2-7-12 55 oh1 .... DaleGibson 3 24
(P C Haslam) *led: rdn along and hdd over 2f out: sn wknd* **14/1**
556 **8** *6* **Old Father Zieten**[15] 3821 2-8-11 68 ....(b[1]) RichardKingscote 1 20
(Tom Dascombe) *s.i.s: a in rr* **9/1**

1m 26.35s (-0.65) **Going Correction** -0.15s/f (Firm) **8** Ran SP% **115.9**
Speed ratings (Par 94): **97,96,91,87,86 86,81,74**
toteswinger: 1&2 £2.60, 1&3 £5.50, 2&3 £3.30. CSF £15.67 CT £44.85 TOTE £6.70: £2.30, £1.40, £1.40; EX 12.40.
Owner Jaber Abdullah **Bred** Floors Farming And Dominic Burke **Trained** Middleham Moor, N Yorks

FOCUS
The front pair came clear in what was a fair nursery overall. The form of the first two looks strong for the grade. The 'official' ratings are estimated and are intended as a guide.

NOTEBOOK
Pride Of Kings left his first two efforts behind (beat one home) when finishing third at Beverley last time and he looked a likely improver for this switch to handicaps. Soon near the speed, he took it up over two out, but looked beaten when narrowly passed by the winner as they raced inside the final furlong. However, he picked up again once Fairley put his whip down and just edged it in a bobbing finish. This win suggest he will improve again for the step up to 1m and he may well have more to offer. (op 7-1 tchd 8-1)
Rapid Release(CAN) improved for the step up to 7f when winning a modest firm-ground maiden at Brighton last time and looked the one to beat, despite shouldering top weight. He came to challenge and looked the likely winner a furlong out, but Pride Of Kings battled back and he was just run out of it. Clear of the remainder, he is clearly going the right way, but things are not going to get any easier for him, as he will almost certainly go up a few pounds for this. (tchd 15-8 and 7-4 in a place)
Scenic Pass has shown improved form since going handicapping and she stuck on in third, but could not match the front pair. She is a consistent sort, likely to be capable of better. (op 5-1)
Musical Maze had shown enough in maidens to suggest she will find a minor race in this sphere and she stuck on well having been outpaced early, going on nicely close home.
Jimwil(IRE) failed to improve for the extra furlong and was beaten soon after two out. He has a bit to prove now off this mark. (op 7-1 tchd 11-2)
Old Father Zieten was never going following a slow start and the first-time blinkers evidently had little effect on this handicap debut. (op 8-1 tchd 15-2)

4293 BOOK ON-LINE @ CATTERICKBRIDGE.CO.UK H'CAP 5f 212y
4:20 (4:20) (Class 6) (0-60,60) 3-Y-0+ **£2,104** (£626; £312; £156) **Stalls** Low

Form RPR
5001 **1** **Johnston's Glory (IRE)**[11] 3953 4-9-1 54 ....(p) DavidAllan 12 63
(E J Alston) *stdd s and hld up: hdwy 2f out: rdn and edgd lft ent fnl f: kpt on to ld fnl 100yds* **16/1**
2600 **2** *3/4* **Darcy's Pride (IRE)**[19] 3665 4-9-6 59 .... FergalLynch 1 66
(D W Barker) *chsd ldrs on inner: hdwy 2f out: rdn and qckn to ld ent fnl f: sn drvn: hdd and no ex fnl 100yds* **11/1**
4444 **3** *1 1/4* **Rainbow Bay**[7] 4073 5-8-13 55 ....(p) NeilBrown(3) 5 58
(Miss Tracy Waggott) *hld up: hdwy 2f out and sn rdn: styd on ins fnl f: nrst fin* **8/1**[3]
0400 **4** *1/2* **Ryedane (IRE)**[8] 4047 6-8-13 55 ....(b) DuranFentiman(3) 6 56
(T D Easterby) *plld hrd: chsd ldrs: rdn and ev ch wl over 1f out: drvn and kpt on same pce ins fnl f* **10/1**
2503 **5** *1 3/4* **Quicks The Word**[18] 3713 8-9-4 57 .... GregFairley 7 52
(T A K Cuthbert) *prom: hdwy over 2f out: rdn to ld 1 1/2f out: drvn and hdd ent fnl f: wknd* **8/1**[3]
0044 **6** *nk* **Baltimore Jack (IRE)**[2] 4245 4-9-7 60 ....(b) PaulMulrennan 3 54
(M W Easterby) *led: rdn along over 2f out: hdd wl over 1f out and grad wknd* **11/2**[2]
2033 **7** *1* **Jun Fan (USA)**[6] 4107 6-8-9 55 .... LanceBetts(7) 11 46
(B Ellison) *chsd ldrs: hdwy on outer and cl up 2f out: ev ch tl rdn and wknd appr fnl f* **11/2**[2]
3030 **8** *1/2* **Dark Champion**[8] 4047 8-9-6 59 ....(v) PaulHanagan 8 49
(R E Barr) *in tch: rdn along over 2f out and sn no imp* **14/1**
0416 **9** *1 1/4* **Conjecture**[8] 4047 6-9-4 57 .... PatCosgrave 10 43
(R Bastiman) *stmbld bdly s: a in rr* **9/1**
0060 **10** *3 1/4* **Spirit Of Coniston**[8] 4047 5-9-0 53 ....(p) MickyFenton 2 28
(P T Midgley) *cl up: rdn over 2f out and sn wknd* **20/1**
0512 **11** *12* **Messiah Garvey**[7] 4073 4-9-5 58 .... AdrianTNicholls 9 —
(D Nicholls) *midfield: c wd st and hdwy to chse ldrs 2f out: sn rdn and wknd* **7/2**[1]

1m 12.44s (-1.16) **Going Correction** -0.15s/f (Firm) **11** Ran SP% **119.9**
Speed ratings (Par 101): **101,100,98,97,95 94,93,92,91,86 70**
toteswinger: 1&2 £49.30, 1&3 £26.90, 2&3 £22.00. CSF £184.09 CT £1551.63 TOTE £27.20: £4.40, £4.60, £2.90; EX 210.60.
Owner The Good Shepherds **Bred** Gerard Keane **Trained** Longton, Lancs
■ Stewards' Enquiry : Paul Mulrennan one-day ban: careless riding (Aug 6)

FOCUS
A low-grade sprint full of exposed sorts. Modest form, rated through the second and third.
Conjecture Official explanation: jockey said gelding slipped on leaving stalls
Messiah Garvey Official explanation: jockey said gelding hung left-handed

4294 GO RACING AT DONCASTER TOMORROW NIGHT CLAIMING STKS 5f
4:50 (4:50) (Class 6) 3-Y-0+ **£2,217** (£654; £327) **Stalls** Low

Form RPR
4214 **1** **Whinhill House**[17] 3759 8-9-1 65 ....(v) TonyHamilton 5 72
(D W Barker) *led to 1/2-way: cl up: rdn to ld wl over 1f out: drvn and hdd ins fnl f: rallied to ld nr line* **3/1**[2]
5310 **2** *nse* **Raccoon (IRE)**[8] 4064 8-8-11 66 .... PJMcDonald(3) 8 71
(Mrs R A Carr) *cl up: effrt 2f out: rdn over 1f out: led ins fnl f: edgd lft and hdd nr fin* **7/2**[3]
0303 **3** *2 3/4* **Whozart (IRE)**[7] 4073 5-9-0 48 .... DanielTudhope 6 61
(A Dickman) *chsd ldrs: swtchd lft and hdwy over 1f out: sn rdn and styd on ins fnl f: nrst fin* **15/2**
0032 **4** *1/2* **Harry Up**[6] 4114 7-9-0 77 ....(b) FrederikTylicki(7) 15 66
(K A Ryan) *cl up on wd outside: led 1/2-way: rdn 2f out: drvn and hdd over 1f out: wknd ins fnl f* **11/4**[1]
3505 **5** *3* **Mr Rooney (IRE)**[23] 3559 5-8-4 53 .... AdeleRothery(7) 14 45
(D Nicholls) *chsd ldrs: rdn wl over 1f out: sn edgd lft and one pce* **13/2**
0006 **6** *2 1/2* **Strensall**[17] 3759 11-9-2 54 .... PaulHanagan 4 41
(R E Barr) *chsd ldrs: rdn 2f out: sn one pce* **11/1**
00-0 **7** *5* **Amanda's Lad (IRE)**[7] 4073 8-8-6 49 .... RussellKennemore(3) 1 16
(M C Chapman) *chsd ldrs on inner: rdn along 1/2-way and sn wknd* **40/1**
0-00 **8** *3/4* **Minimum Fuss (IRE)**[18] 3733 4-7-13 38 .... NicolPolli(5) 7 9
(M C Chapman) *dwlt: a in rr* **100/1**
0600 **9** *14* **Mill Creek**[22] 3582 3-8-3 40 ow1 .... AndrewElliott 3 —
(Jedd O'Keeffe) *a in rr* **40/1**

0000 10 9 **On The Map**[51] 2658 4-8-4 45..............................(b) AdrianTNicholls 13 —
(Joss Saville) *a in rr* **40/1**

58.21 secs (-1.59) **Going Correction** -0.20s/f (Firm)
WFA 3 from 4yo+ 4lb **10** Ran SP% **115.6**
Speed ratings (Par 101): **104,103,99,98,93 89,81,80,58,43**
toteswinger: 1&2 £3.50, 1&3 £5.10, 2&3 £6.00. CSF £13.60 TOTE £4.00: £1.50, £1.80, £2.20; EX 16.20.Mr Rooney was claimed by E Nisbet for £5,000.
Owner Destiny Racing Club **Bred** W R And Mrs Arblaster **Trained** Scorton, N Yorks

FOCUS
A reasonable claimer run at a strong pace. The front pair are rated to form.

4295 WILLIE CARSON - PINKER'S POND APPRENTICE H'CAP 1m 3f 214y
5:20 (5:20) (Class 6) (0-65,65) 3-Y-0+ **£2,217** (£654; £327) **Stalls** Low

Form RPR

3543 1 **Dan Tucker**[15] 3814 4-10-0 **65**.............................. AndreaAtzeni 1 72
(N Tinkler) *trckd ldrs: hdwy over 2f out: str run to ld 1f out: rdn out* **5/2**[1]

560 2 2 **Saluscraggie**[8] 4048 6-9-9 **60**.............................. AntiocoMurgia 6 64
(R E Barr) *hld up in rr: hdwy 3f out: rdn wl over 1f out: styd on ins fnl f: nrst fin* **9/1**

2610 3 2 **Thorny Mandate**[20] 3650 6-9-5 **56**.............................. RyanClark 4 57
(W M Brisbourne) *hld up in rr: hdwy 2f out: sn rdn and hung lft over 1f out: kpt on ins fnl f: nrst fin* **11/4**[2]

0304 4 ½ **Hugs Destiny (IRE)**[5] 3756 7-8-13 **50**..............................(t) AnthonyBetts 2 50
(M A Barnes) *trckd ldrs: hdwy to chse ldr after 4f: effrt 3f out: rdn to ld over 2f out: hdd 1f out: wknd ins fnl f* **5/2**[1]

-006 5 5 **Marieschi (USA)**[33] 3204 4-9-2 **53**.............................. StevenCorrigan 5 45
(R F Fisher) *sn led: rdn along 3f out: hdd over 2f out and sn wknd* **20/1**

10/0 6 14 **Jungle Lion**[15] 3820 10-8-10 **47** oh2..............................(t) GemmaElford 7 16
(P A Kirby) *chsd ldng pair: rdn along over 3f out: sn wknd* **40/1**

-000 7 24 **Falimar**[64] 2286 4-8-10 **47** oh2.............................. MartinGuest 8 —
(C W Fairhurst) *prom: rdn along 4f out: sn wknd* **40/1**

3050 S **Ben Bacchus (IRE)**[91] 1562 6-8-10 **47** oh2.............................. HollyHall 3 —
(P W Hiatt) *hld up in rr: slipped up bnd after 4f* **8/1**[3]

2m 36.45s (-2.45) **Going Correction** -0.15s/f (Firm) **8** Ran SP% **114.6**
Speed ratings (Par 101): **102,100,99,99,95 86,70,—**
toteswinger: 1&2 £4.60, 1&3 £2.10, 2&3 £6.50. CSF £24.98 CT £64.15 TOTE £3.50: £1.10, £2.50, £1.80; EX 23.20 Place 6: £56.22, Place 5: £29.57..
Owner Leeds Plywood And Doors Ltd **Bred** N And Mrs N Nugent **Trained** Langton, N Yorks

FOCUS
A very modest race, where the second and third had plenty to do from off the pace. The front pair ran to form. It was confined to apprentices who had not ridden a winner prior to July 20, and the successful jockey Andrea Azteni had only got off the mark the previous day.
T/Plt: £53.70 to a £1 stake. Pool: £50,594.12. 686.85 winning tickets. T/Qpdt: £32.00 to a £1 stake. Pool: £3,093.20. 71.50 winning tickets. JR

4119 LEICESTER (R-H)
Wednesday, July 23

OFFICIAL GOING: Good to firm (good in places; 8.4)
Wind: Almost nil Weather: Overcast, but humid

4296 MIDLAND HR MAIDEN AUCTION STKS 7f 9y
6:15 (6:16) (Class 5) 2-Y-O **£3,885** (£1,156; £577; £288) **Stalls** Centre

Form RPR

32 1 **Wilbury Star (IRE)**[17] 3760 2-8-12 0.............................. PatDobbs 9 78+
(R Hannon) *chsd ldr tl led over 2f out: sn edgd lft: rdn and hung lft ins fnl f: r.o: eased nr fin* **9/4**[1]

34 2 1¼ **Young Dottie**[24] 3522 2-8-3 0.............................. CatherineGannon 6 64
(P M Phelan) *led: hdd over 2f out: sn rdn: styd on* **6/1**[2]

3 ½ **Splinter Cell (USA)** 2-8-12 0.............................. JamieSpencer 13 72
(M Botti) *s.i.s: sn chsng ldrs: rdn over 2f out: hung lft over 1f out: styd on* **10/1**

4 ¾ **Bad Baron (IRE)** 2-8-6 0.............................. LukeMorris(3) 8 67
(Eve Johnson Houghton) *s.i.s: hld up: stmbld over 4f out: nt clr run over 2f out: hdwy over 1f out: rdn and hung lft ins fnl f: nt rch ldrs* **25/1**

5 ½ **Viking Awake (IRE)** 2-8-10 0.............................. RichardKingscote 7 67+
(J W Unett) *s.i.s: hld up: hdwy 1/2-way: rdn over 1f out: styd on* **40/1**

0 6 3½ **Welcome Applause (IRE)**[27] 3411 2-8-3 0.............................. DominicFox(3) 3 54
(M G Quinlan) *prom: rdn over 2f out: wknd fnl f* **8/1**

7 ¾ **Iron Out (USA)** 2-8-13 0.............................. JimCrowley 1 59
(R Hollinshead) *hld up: rdn over 2f out: styd on ins fnl f: nvr nrr* **33/1**

00 8 hd **Kyle Of Bute**[19] 3682 2-9-0 0.............................. MartinDwyer 14 59
(J L Dunlop) *hld up in tch: rdn over 1f out: wknd fnl f* **33/1**

9 2¾ **La Diosa (IRE)** 2-8-8 0.............................. KerrinMcEvoy 5 47
(W J Haggas) *sn pushed along in rr: effrt over 2f out: wknd over 1f out* **12/1**

10 ¾ **Hesketh (IRE)** 2-9-3 0.............................. SebSanders 2 54
(R M Beckett) *prom: reminder over 2f out: wknd over 1f out: will improve* **15/2**[3]

05 11 1¼ **Positive Opinion**[19] 3674 2-8-4 0.............................. HayleyTurner 11 38
(B R Millman) *trckd ldrs: racd keenly: rdn over 2f out: wknd over 1f out* **8/1**

50 12 shd **Charismatic Charli (IRE)**[33] 3219 2-8-10 0.......... StephenDonohoe 12 43
(P W D'Arcy) *mid-div: rdn over 2f out: sn wknd* **20/1**

13 9 **Abner** 2-8-11 0.............................. JoeFanning 10 22
(W J Haggas) *chsd ldrs: lost pl over 4f out: wknd over 2f out* **14/1**

1m 26.57s (0.37) **Going Correction** -0.10s/f (Good) **13** Ran SP% **119.4**
Speed ratings (Par 94): **93,91,91,90,89 85,84,84,81,80 79,78,68**
CSF £13.81 TOTE £2.50: £1.20, £3.30, £3.70; EX 8.30.
Owner John Tobin, Ian Higginson & Fergus Carey **Bred** Rathasker Stud **Trained** East Everleigh, Wilts

FOCUS
An ordinary auction maiden, but interesting for the fact that more than half the runners were making their debuts. However, the market was dominated by two of the most experienced runners and they held the poll positions throughout. The first two set the level.

NOTEBOOK
Wilbury Star(IRE), who had been close up throughout, scored with a little in hand and seems to be progressing, despite being beaten in terrible weather conditions at Brighton last time, and should be able to make his mark in nurseries. (tchd 13-8 and 5-2)
Young Dottie hads some decent form to her name, finishing behind two subsequent Newmarket July festival winners on her second outing at Salisbury, after running third on her debut in a race in which the runner-up, fourth and fifth have all won since. She was a little keen in front which did not help her chance of staying this longer trip, but has enough ability to pick up a maiden, possibly back at 6f. (op 5-1 tchd 7-1)
Splinter Cell(USA), the first foal of a 1m4f winner and sister to the high-class Kirkwall, did best of the newcomers. He finished well and should know a lot better next time. (op 8-1)
Bad Baron(IRE), the first foal of a multiple winner in the USA from the family of Valiramix and Condessa, is not that big, but ran on well after missing the break and stumbling mid-race. (op 33-1)
Viking Awake(IRE), bred to be better with time and over further, will have given connections encouragement. (op 50-1)
Hesketh(IRE), a 72,000euros half-brother to five winners including Only If I Laugh, was well supported and moved into contention soon after halfway, but when his chance had gone he was allowed to come home in his own time. (op 8-1)
Abner Official explanation: jockey said colt never travelled

4297 PICK EVERARD NURSERY 5f 218y
6:45 (6:46) (Class 4) 2-Y-O **£3,885** (£1,156; £577; £288) **Stalls** Low

Form RPR

3410 1 **Burning Flute**[36] 3105 2-9-5 **78**.............................. JamieSpencer 6 87+
(B J Meehan) *s.i.s: hld up: hdwy over 2f out: sn hung lft: hrd rdn to ld over 1f out: clr ins fnl f: eased nr fin* **5/6**[1]

4043 2 3½ **Amber Sunset**[18] 3734 2-8-3 **65**.............................. LukeMorris(3) 4 63
(J Jay) *plld hrd: trckd ldr 2f: remained handy: hrd rdn over 1f out: chsd wnr ins fnl f: no imp* **4/1**[2]

2150 3 1¾ **Red Cell (IRE)**[15] 3809 2-8-5 **64**..............................(b[1]) DeanMcKeown 3 56
(E J O'Neill) *led: rdn: wandered and hdd over 1f out: wknd ins fnl f* **10/1**[3]

0315 4 1 **Common Diva**[20] 3625 2-9-4 **80**.............................. TolleyDean(3) 5 69
(A J McCabe) *chsd ldrs: rdn 1/2-way: wknd ins fnl f* **4/1**[2]

060 5 3 **Samba Queen (IRE)**[20] 3645 2-7-5 **57** oh6.............. CharlesEddery(7) 1 37
(J L Spearing) *s.s: plld hrd: hdwy to chse ldr 4f out: rdn over 2f out: hmpd and wknd sn after* **11/1**

1m 12.93s (-0.07) **Going Correction** -0.10s/f (Good) **5** Ran SP% **112.0**
Speed ratings (Par 96): **96,91,89,87,83**
CSF £4.64 TOTE £1.80: £1.50, £2.80; EX 4.40.
Owner Clipper Logistics **Bred** Wood Hall Stud Limited **Trained** Manton, Wilts

FOCUS
A small field for this nursery and not much strength in depth. The form has been rated through the runner-up. The 'official' ratings are estimated and shown for guidance only.

NOTEBOOK
Burning Flute made all to get off the mark at Bath on his third start, but had been hampered when unplaced in the Windsor Castle at Royal Ascot since. Back to a more suitable grade, he was held up early this time, but came through to score easily. He looks progressive in this grade and also has an entry in the DBS Sales race at York. (op 6-4 tchd 13-8)
Amber Sunset, who ran better over 5f at Nottingham having appeared not to be getting home over this trip previously, was also held up but merely ran on past beaten horses. She may be better ridden more positively back at the minimum trip. (op 11-2)
Red Cell(IRE) was very keen in the first-time blinkers and went off at a rate of knots. However, he faltered and wandered as the winner closed on him just over a furlong out and was soon done with. (op 13-2 tchd 11-1)
Common Diva, who made all when winning her maiden over this trip at Pontefract, was kept to the centre of the track and raced separately from the rest, but she never really got involved. (op 11-4 tchd 5-2)
Samba Queen(IRE), racing from 6lb out of the handicap, was walked to the start and then missed the break, but she got into contention after a couple of furlongs before the effort took its toll. She does not look the easiest ride. Official explanation: jockey said filly was slowly away (op 17-2)

4298 EVERARD FOUNDATION (S) STKS 1m 60y
7:20 (7:22) (Class 6) 3-Y-O **£1,942** (£578; £288; £144) **Stalls** High

Form RPR

6600 1 **The Hoofer (IRE)**[17] 3764 3-8-6 47..............................(b) MartinDwyer 13 52
(J L Dunlop) *hld up in tch: rdn over 2f out: sn hung rt: styd on u.p to ld wl ins fnl f* **5/1**[2]

5320 2 1 **Red Rouge**[8] 4048 3-8-6 56.............................. SimonWhitworth 8 50
(G J Smith) *hld up: hdwy over 3f out: swtchd lft 2f out: sn led: rdn and hdd wl ins fnl f* **11/2**[3]

-006 3 2½ **Gainsborough's Art (IRE)**[26] 3458 3-8-11 59.............. SebSanders 6 49
(D R C Elsworth) *hld up in tch: rdn and ev ch over 1f out: edgd rt: no ex ins fnl f* **7/2**[1]

0 4 2¼ **Atteme Bomb**[19] 3692 3-8-6 0.............................. HayleyTurner 5 39
(S Curran) *hld up: hdwy over 3f out: nt clr run and swtchd lft over 1f out: styd on* **40/1**

0006 5 1¾ **Bewdley**[28] 3359 3-8-6 45.............................. CatherineGannon 11 35
(Mrs K Waldron) *led: rdn and hdd over 1f out: wknd ins fnl f* **20/1**

40-0 6 1 **Demure Princess**[10] 2549 3-8-2 52 ow1.............................. JackDean(5) 3 33
(W G M Turner) *mid-div: rdn 1/2-way: hung rt and styd on ins fnl f: n.d* **12/1**

0006 7 1¼ **Bagenalstown (IRE)**[8] 4043 3-8-11 30..............................(p) RichardKingscote 7 35+
(M Wellings) *chsd ldrs: rdn and lost pl whn hmpd 2f out: n.d after* **40/1**

0000 8 ¾ **Infinite Patience**[8] 4052 3-8-3 55..............................(p) LukeMorris(3) 1 28
(J S Moore) *s.s and reluctant in rr: rdn over 3f out: hung rt over 1f out: nvr nrr* **13/2**

000 9 1 **Jakam (IRE)**[16] 3791 3-8-11 43..............................(b[1]) DeanMcKeown 4 31
(E J O'Neill) *trckd ldrs: racd keenly: rdn over 2f out: hmpd wl over 1f out: sn hung rt: wknd fnl f* **8/1**

3605 10 1¼ **Cherished Song**[21] 3605 3-8-3 46.............................. DominicFox(3) 12 23
(M G Quinlan) *s.i.s: hld up: rdn over 2f out: n.d* **12/1**

0-0 11 22 **Lady Amy**[15] 3818 3-8-6 0.............................. JoeFanning 9 —+
(Miss Amy Weaver) *chsd ldr: pushed along over 2f out: hmpd and wknd sn after* **50/1**

00- 12 8 **Here And How**[308] 5527 3-8-6 0.............................. SaleemGolam 14 —
(M H Tompkins) *chsd ldrs: rdn over 2f out: wknd over 1f out* **14/1**

050- 13 31 **Gaitskell**[207] 7272 3-8-11 60.............................. JimCrowley 2 —
(Miss J S Davis) *hld up: bhd fr 1/2-way* **25/1**

1m 44.69s (-0.41) **Going Correction** -0.10s/f (Good) **13** Ran SP% **116.2**
Speed ratings (Par 98): **98,97,94,92,90 89,88,87,86,85 63,55,24**
CSF £29.83 TOTE £5.80: £1.70, £2.90, £1.60; EX 37.90.There was no bid for the winner.
Owner J L Dunlop **Bred** Hesmonds Stud Ltd **Trained** Arundel, W Sussex
■ Stewards' Enquiry : Simon Whitworth two-day ban: careless riding (Aug 6,7)

FOCUS
A big field for this seller but very few had a major chance judged on official ratings. The winner is up 7lb on his recent poor handicap form. The poor seventh helps set the level.
Bagenalstown(IRE) Official explanation: jockey said gelding hung left
Lady Amy Official explanation: jockey said filly suffered interference in running
Gaitskell Official explanation: jockey said colt had a breathing problem

4299 NEXT PLC H'CAP 1m 3f 183y
7:50 (7:50) (Class 4) (0-80,79) 4-Y-O+ **£4,857** (£1,445; £722; £360) **Stalls** High

Form RPR

/020 1 **Channel Crossing**[23] 3550 6-8-6 **64**.............................. JoeFanning 5 72
(S Wynne) *mde all: shkn up over 2f out: rdn ins fnl f: styd on wl* **16/1**

6446 **2** 1½ **Alfie Noakes**[12] [3917] 6-8-13 **71** .... JimCrowley 7 77
(Mrs A J Perrett) *chsd wnr: rdn over 2f out: styd on* **11/4**[2]

4616 **3** ¾ **Opera Writer (IRE)**[12] [3900] 5-8-2 **60** oh3 .... (p) HayleyTurner 3 65
(R Hollinshead) *chsd ldrs: rdn over 2f out: styd on* **6/1**[3]

3-40 **4** ¾ **Crystal Prince**[62] [2335] 4-9-0 **72** .... (p) SamHitchcott 6 76
(C E Longsdon) *hld up: hdwy over 3f out: rdn over 2f out: hung rt and no ex ins fnl f* **14/1**

-500 **5** 1½ **Dzesmin (POL)**[46] [2830] 6-9-7 **79** .... (p) JohnEgan 2 80
(R C Guest) *hld up: hdwy u.p over 2f out: nt clr run ins fnl f: nvr able to chal* **5/2**[1]

2006 **6** 1 **Cruise Director**[20] [3630] 8-9-1 **73** .... StephenDonohoe 4 73
(Ian Williams) *chsd ldrs: rdn over 3f out: styd on same pce appr fnl f* **10/1**

-000 **7** 11 **John Dillon (IRE)**[18] [3711] 4-8-1 **64** .... (b) PatrickDonaghy(5) 9 46
(P C Haslam) *s.i.s: hld up: rdn over 2f out: sn wknd* **9/1**

-500 **8** 8 **Clueless**[6] [4111] 6-9-3 **75** .... (be) NeilPollard 1 44
(A J McCabe) *s.s: hld up: a in rr: wknd and eased 2f out* **8/1**

1-00 **9** 6 **Eva Soneva So Fast (IRE)**[7] [3375] 6-9-2 **74** .... VinceSlattery 8 34
(G F Bridgwater) *hld up: wknd 3f out* **20/1**

2m 32.6s (-1.30) **Going Correction** -0.10s/f (Good) **9 Ran SP% 117.0**
Speed ratings (Par 105): **100,99,98,98,97 96,89,83,79**
CSF £60.82 CT £305.62 TOTE £32.20: £6.40, £1.10, £1.70; EX 101.90.
Owner Miss Gillian Milner **Bred** M H Dixon **Trained** Whitchurch, Shropshire

FOCUS
A fair handicap but mainly featuring runners who have been out of form or are on the downgrade. The winner seemed to confirm his much improved run two starts back, with the third probably the best guide.

4300 E B F / C & G CONSTRUCTION SOLUTIONS FILLIES' H'CAP 7f 9y
8:25 (8:26) (Class 4) (0-80,80) 3-Y-O **£6,938** (£2,076; £1,038; £519; £258) **Stalls** Centre

Form RPR

2321 **1** **Desert Chill (USA)**[17] [3762] 3-9-7 **80** .... KerrinMcEvoy 1 87
(Saeed Bin Suroor) *chsd ldrs: rdn over 2f out: r.o to ld post* **9/2**[2]

0203 **2** nk **The Jostler**[20] [3636] 3-9-5 **78** .... MichaelHills 2 84
(B W Hills) *hld up: rdn over 2f out: hdwy over 1f out: r.o u.p to ld wl ins fnl f: hdd post* **9/1**

51-5 **3** 1½ **Coachhouse Lady (USA)**[67] [2190] 3-9-5 **78** .... FergalLynch 3 80
(K A Ryan) *led: rdn and hung rt fr over 2f out: clr over 1f out: hdd wl ins fnl f* **18/1**

1- **4** 1 **Delta Diva (USA)**[350] [4273] 3-9-1 **74** .... JamieSpencer 5 73+
(P F I Cole) *hld up: rdn over 1f out: hung rt and r.o ins fnl f: nrst fin* **8/1**

6-60 **5** ½ **Brasingaman Hifive**[32] [3263] 3-9-1 **74** .... DaleGibson 10 72
(Mrs G S Rees) *s.i.s: hld up: racd keenly: rdn over 2f out: hdwy over 1f out: styd on* **16/1**

5-61 **6** hd **Lekita**[25] [3502] 3-9-2 **75** .... SaleemGolam 9 72
(W R Swinburn) *chsd ldrs: rdn over 1f out: styd on* **8/1**

0321 **7** 1¾ **Loveinanelevator**[18] [3731] 3-8-11 **70** .... HayleyTurner 6 63
(M L W Bell) *hmpd s: hld up: rdn over 2f out: styd on ins fnl f: nvr nrr* **7/1**[3]

021- **8** nse **Ballora (FR)**[301] [5727] 3-9-3 **76** .... LPKeniry 8 69
(S Kirk) *hld up: effrt over 2f out: n.d* **12/1**

0262 **9** 4 **La Chicaluna**[12] [3907] 3-9-6 **79** .... JimCrowley 11 61
(J G Given) *chsd ldrs: rdn over 2f out: wknd fnl f* **14/1**

0015 **10** 2½ **Elysee Palace (IRE)**[18] [3744] 3-9-7 **80** .... PhilipRobinson 12 55
(M A Jarvis) *prom: rdn over 2f out: wknd fnl f* **3/1**[1]

4-30 **11** 15 **Wusuul**[14] [3854] 3-9-1 **74** .... SebSanders 7 8
(C E Brittain) *wnt lft s: hld up: rdn over 2f out: sn wknd and eased* **16/1**

-005 **12** 2½ **Alseraaj (USA)**[42] [2956] 3-8-13 **72** .... StephenDonohoe 14 —
(Ian Williams) *hld up: wknd over 2f out* **33/1**

366- **13** ½ **Sayedati Elhasna (IRE)**[263] [6648] 3-8-12 **71** .... MartinDwyer 4 —
(J L Dunlop) *hld up: hdwy over 3f out: wknd over 2f out* **20/1**

1m 24.93s (-1.27) **Going Correction** -0.10s/f (Good) **13 Ran SP% 127.0**
Speed ratings (Par 99): **103,102,100,99,99 99,97,96,92,89 72,69,68**
CSF £48.12 CT £517.40 TOTE £4.80: £2.10, £4.10, £7.00; EX 47.70.
Owner Godolphin **Bred** Darley **Trained** Newmarket, Suffolk

FOCUS
Another big field for this fillies' handicap and quite a competitive race with only 10lb covering them. Solid form, the first two both progressing.
Loveinanelevator Official explanation: jockey said filly suffered interference leaving stalls

4301 LEICESTERSHIRE & RUTLAND CRIMEBEAT MAIDEN STKS 5f 218y
8:55 (8:55) (Class 5) 3-Y-O+ **£3,238** (£963; £481; £240) **Stalls** Low

Form RPR

6033 **1** **Internationaldebut (IRE)**[6] [4121] 3-9-3 78 .... JohnEgan 8 77
(S Parr) *trckd ldrs: led 2f out: rdn clr fr over 1f out* **6/4**[1]

0- **2** 3 **Prince Afram**[327] [5003] 3-9-3 0 .... SebSanders 3 67+
(R M Beckett) *a.p: rdn over 2f out: chsd wnr fnl f: no imp* **8/1**

0504 **3** 3¼ **Ma Vie En Rose (IRE)**[13] [3867] 3-8-12 56 .... (t) LPKeniry 12 50
(A M Balding) *led: hdd 2f out: sn rdn: wknd fnl f* **8/1**

4 1 **Baby Rock** 3-9-3 0 .... MartinDwyer 4 52+
(C F Wall) *hld up: hdwy over 2f out: rdn over 1f out: wknd fnl f* **11/2**[3]

0466 **5** ¾ **Flying Seasons**[21] [3605] 3-9-3 50 .... TGMcLaughlin 2 49
(B R Millman) *s.i.s: sn pushed along: hdwy u.p over 1f out: nrst fin* **40/1**

64 **6** ¾ **Holly Cleugh**[46] [2824] 3-8-12 0 .... HayleyTurner 10 42
(J R Fanshawe) *prom: rdn over 1f out: wknd fnl f* **5/1**[2]

3 **7** 1¾ **Crataegus**[15] [3818] 3-9-3 0 .... FrankieMcDonald 1 41
(H Candy) *prom: rdn 1/2-way: wknd wl over 1f out* **16/1**

0-0 **8** hd **Too Hot To Handle (IRE)**[14] [3847] 3-8-9 0 .... LukeMorris(3) 7 36
(J M P Eustace) *s.s: hld up: n.d* **25/1**

050 **9** 4 **The Young Fella**[12] [3916] 3-9-3 0 .... JamieSpencer 6 28
(S A Callaghan) *chsd ldr: rdn over 2f out: wkng whn hung rt fnl f* **16/1**

10 ¾ **Bedloe's Island (IRE)** 3-9-3 0 .... DeanMcKeown 5 26
(R C Guest) *s.s: hld up: a in rr* **25/1**

5 **11** 3¼ **Ellalucianna**[15] [3818] 3-8-9 0 .... MichaelJStainton(3) 11 10
(M Wigham) *chsd ldrs: rdn over 3f out: sn lost pl* **50/1**

0000 **12** 5 **Marysedge**[21] [3605] 3-8-12 39 .... NeilPollard 9 —
(R Brotherton) *s.i.s and hmpd s: hdwy over 4f out: wknd 2f out* **200/1**

1m 12.3s (-0.70) **Going Correction** -0.10s/f (Good) **12 Ran SP% 118.6**
Speed ratings (Par 103): **100,96,91,89,88 87,85,85,79,78 74,67**
CSF £13.61 TOTE £2.80: £1.40, £2.40, £3.00; EX 17.30 Place 6 £36.16, Place 5 £21.25.
Owner W McKay, J Barton **Bred** Ennistown Stud **Trained** Bawtry, S Yorks

FOCUS
A very ordinary sprint maiden for three-year-olds but the form appears sound enough, if pretty weak.
Bedloe's Island(IRE) Official explanation: jockey said gelding ran too freely
T/Jkpt: £60,839.90 to a £1 stake. Pool: £685,520.19. 8.00 winning tickets. T/Plt: £14.90 to a £1 stake. Pool: £77,451.78. 3,792.70 winning tickets. T/Qpdt: £10.60 to a £1 stake. Pool: £4,268.19. 295.20 winning tickets. CR

4181 LINGFIELD (L-H)
Wednesday, July 23

OFFICIAL GOING: Standard
Wind: nil Weather: warm and muggy

4302 ASHDOWN FOREST MAIDEN STKS 1m 4f (P)
2:00 (2:01) (Class 5) 3-Y-O+ **£2,590** (£770; £385; £192) **Stalls** Low

Form RPR

2432 **1** **Coin Of The Realm (IRE)**[16] [3802] 3-9-1 0 .... RyanMoore 13 78+
(E A L Dunlop) *t.k.h: hld up in tch: hdwy over 3f out: led 2f out: styd on u.p fnl f* **9/4**[2]

6 **2** 1¼ **Fortune City (UAE)**[13] [3894] 3-9-1 0 .... RichardMullen 6 76+
(Saeed Bin Suroor) *t.k.h: in tch: rdn to chse wnr and hung lft over 1f out: nt qckn fnl f* **5/1**[3]

32 **3** 1¼ **Dazzling Light (UAE)**[20] [3637] 3-8-10 0 .... SteveDrowne 3 69+
(R Charlton) *hld up in midfield: hdwy over 3f out: nt clr run and swtchd rt over 2f out: hanging lft and nt qckn over 1f out: styd on u.p fnl f: nt rch ldng pair* **11/8**[1]

4 **4** 4½ **Darksideofthemoon (IRE)**[20] [3637] 6-9-13 0 .... PaulDoe 4 67
(N J Gifford) *s.i.s: hld up in midfield: hdwy over 3f out: chsd ldrs and rdn over 2f out: outpcd fnl f* **16/1**

0 **5** 7 **Oops Another Act**[35] [3133] 3-8-10 0 .... AdamKirby 7 51+
(W R Swinburn) *led for 1f: chsd ldrs after tl wnt 2nd 5f out: led over 3f out: rdn and hdd 2f out: wknd over 1f out* **10/1**

60 **6** 9 **Bathwick Minstrel**[13] [3894] 3-8-10 0 .... TPQueally 5 36
(A B Haynes) *hld up towards rr: hdwy into midfield 5f out: rdn and wl outpcd over 2f out* **100/1**

0 **7** nk **La Rochette**[29] [3350] 3-8-10 0 .... AlanMunro 12 36
(P W Chapple-Hyam) *racd in midfield: rdn and struggling over 2f out: wl btn fnl 2f* **25/1**

8 1¼ **Sleepy Mountain**[24] 4-9-6 0 .... KMay(7) 10 39
(A Middleton) *s.i.s: hld up bhd: rdn over 3f out: sn lost tch:* **100/1**

9 3 **King's Colour** 3-9-1 0 .... SamHitchcott 11 34
(B R Johnson) *wnt rt s and v.s.a: hdwy 8f out: chsd ldrs 7f out tl wknd qckly over 3f out: t.o* **80/1**

00 **10** 11 **Kavatcha (FR)**[13] [3894] 5-9-10 0 .... TravisBlock(3) 9 17
(Miss Tor Sturgis) *s.i.s: bhd: rdn over 4f out: sn lost tch: t.o* **66/1**

11 ¾ **Blameitontheboogie** 3-9-1 0 .... JamesDoyle 8 15
(M Blanshard) *rn green: bhd: lost tch over 3f out: t.o* **40/1**

00 **12** nk **Tuxedo**[15] [3813] 3-9-1 0 .... LPKeniry 1 15
(P W Hiatt) *s.i.s: led after 1f tl over 3f out: wknd qckly over 2f out: t.o* **100/1**

00 **13** 31 **Renege The Joker**[20] [3654] 5-9-6 0 .... (t) JPFeatherstone(7) 2 —
(S Regan) *chsd ldr after 1f tl 5f out: wknd qckly 4f out: t.o* **100/1**

2m 33.65s (0.65) **Going Correction** +0.175s/f (Slow)
WFA 3 from 4yo+ 12lb **13 Ran SP% 117.5**
Speed ratings (Par 103): **104,103,102,99,94 88,88,87,85,78 77,77,56**
toteswinger: 1&2 £2.60, 1&3 £2.10, 2&3 £2.30. CSF £13.39 TOTE £3.20: £1.40, £1.70, £1.10; EX 12.90 Trifecta £31.90 Pool: £356.97. 8.26 winning units..
Owner Rick Barnes **Bred** Grangecon Stud **Trained** Newmarket, Suffolk
■ Stewards' Enquiry : J P Featherstone caution: used whip when out of contention

FOCUS
A burst water main had resulted in an area of false ground on the turf course and as result the first two races were switched to this slightly longer 1m4f trip on the Polytrack. There was not much strength in this, but the first two in the betting had shown fair form and the Godolphin representative was supported on the exchanges in the morning. The pace was fairly steady and the form is fairly shaky as a result with the three market leaders, who finished clear of the rest, all capable of better than the bare form.
Blameitontheboogie Official explanation: jockey said gelding ran green

4303 FORMOST FABRICATION H'CAP 1m 4f (P)
2:30 (2:30) (Class 5) (0-75,75) 3-Y-O **£2,590** (£770; £385; £192) **Stalls** Low

Form RPR

301 **1** **Dance The Star (USA)**[24] [3530] 3-9-7 **75** .... RichardMullen 2 88+
(D M Simcock) *hld up in tch: hdwy 3f out: rdn to ld over 1f out: edgd lft but sn clr: easily* **9/2**[3]

2353 **2** 4 **Brexca (IRE)**[18] [3737] 3-9-6 **74** .... (v) AdamKirby 7 78
(C G Cox) *hld up in tch: hdwy over 3f out: rdn to dispute 2nd over 2f out: hung lft over 1f out: nt pce of wnr fnl f* **6/1**

1054 **3** 2¾ **Flash Of Colour**[22] [3586] 3-9-4 **72** .... (v[1]) JimCrowley 5 72
(Mrs A J Perrett) *w ldr tl led 4f out: rdn over 2f out: hdd over 1f out: sn no ch w wnr: lost 2nd ins fnl f* **7/2**[1]

1-03 **4** ½ **Wing Play (IRE)**[27] [3421] 3-9-2 **73** .... TravisBlock(3) 3 72
(H Morrison) *trckd ldrs: rdn to dispute 2nd over 2f out: hung lft over 1f out: nt pce of wnr fnl f* **4/1**[2]

020- **5** 14 **Suite Francaise**[342] [4524] 3-8-5 **59** .... J-PGuillambert 6 35
(Sir Mark Prescott) *dwlt: t.k.h sn trcking ldrs: rdn and qckly lost pl over 3f out: wl btn after* **8/1**

0-02 **6** 6 **Trawlerman (IRE)**[24] [3530] 3-9-3 **71** .... AlanMunro 1 38
(M H Tompkins) *slowly into stide: t.k.h: hld up in tch: rdn and lost tch qckly over 3f out: t.o* **9/1**

10 **7** 6 **Eventide**[20] [3624] 3-9-2 **70** .... PaulDoe 4 27
(W J Knight) *led tl rdn and hdd 4f out: sn dropped and wl bhd: t.o* **11/2**

2m 32.04s (-0.96) **Going Correction** +0.175s/f (Slow) **7 Ran SP% 111.2**
Speed ratings (Par 100): **110,107,105,105,95 91,87**
toteswinger: 1&2 £4.50, 1&3 £4.40, 2&3 £3.30. CSF £29.33 CT £100.35 TOTE £4.90: £2.40, £3.90; EX 18.30 Trifecta £96.80 Pool: £234.32. 1.79 winning units..
Owner Sultan Ali **Bred** B M Kelley And B P Walden **Trained** Newmarket, Suffolk

FOCUS
A reasonable event. Most of the runners had shown some competitive recent form. The early pace was only modest, but the winning time was decent, 1.61 seconds faster than the earlier maiden. The winner put in a really likeable performance and is rated value for 6l. Sound form.
Eventide Official explanation: jockey said filly stopped quickly

4304 EUROPEAN BREEDERS' FUND MEDIAN AUCTION MAIDEN STKS (DIV I) 7f (P)
3:00 (3:02) (Class 5) 2-Y-O **£3,076** (£915; £457; £228) **Stalls** Low

Form RPR

1 **High Alert** 2-9-3 0 .... (b[1]) RyanMoore 8 77+
(J Noseda) *hld up in midfield on outer: hdwy over 2f out: shkn up to ld ins fnl f: r.o strly* **7/2**[1]

	2	2	**Fullback (IRE)** 2-9-3 0 .... LPKeniry 3	72
			(J S Moore) *chsd ldrs: wnt 2nd over 2f out: ev ch u.p over 1f out: kpt on but nt pce of wnr fnl f* **16/1**	
6	3	3	**Penton Hook**[53] 2601 2-9-3 0 .... StephenCarson 1	64
			(P Winkworth) *led: hdd and nt handle bnd jst over 2f out: one pce fr over 1f out* **7/2**[1]	
0	4	nk	**Tae Kwon Do (USA)**[8] 4062 2-9-3 0 .... TPQueally 5	63
			(E A L Dunlop) *in tch: hdwy to ld jst over 2f out: hdd ins fnl f: wknd fnl 100yds* **9/2**[2]	
	5	½	**Master Fong (IRE)** 2-9-3 0 .... MichaelHills 11	62+
			(B W Hills) *v.s.a: bhd and pushed along: styd on wl fnl f: nvr trbld ldrs* **6/1**[3]	
00	6	2¾	**Starlight Wish**[14] 3848 2-9-3 0 .... FergusSweeney 9	62+
			(E F Vaughan) *hld up in rr: rdn 3f out: nt clr run and sltly hmpd jst over 2f out: kpt on u.p over 1f out: nt pce to threaten ldrs* **25/1**	
06	7	1½	**Milly Rose**[27] 3408 2-8-12 0 .... JamesDoyle 6	46
			(M Blanshard) *hld up in midfield: rdn and effrt whn n.m.r jst over 2f out: no prog after* **12/1**	
	8	3½	**Marcus Crassus (IRE)** 2-9-3 0 .... IanMongan 10	43
			(H J L Dunlop) *a bhd: n.d* **14/1**	
	9	nk	**Dark Ranger** 2-9-3 0 .... RobertHavlin 4	42
			(M J Wallace) *s.i.s: sn pushed up to chse ldrs: rdn 3f out: wknd 2f out* **16/1**	
0	10	1½	**Coral Point (IRE)**[15] 3821 2-9-3 0 .... RichardHughes 2	38
			(S Kirk) *chsd ldr tl over 2f out: wknd u.p over 1f out* **14/1**	
	11	9	**Lastbustowoodstock (IRE)** 2-9-3 0 .... ShaneKelly 7	16
			(J A Osborne) *towards rr: rdn and wknd over 3f out: wl bhd and wd bnd 2f out* **14/1**	

1m 26.86s (2.06) **Going Correction** +0.175s/f (Slow) **11** Ran SP% **120.2**
Speed ratings (Par 94): **95,92,89,88,88 85,83,79,79,77 67**
toteswinger: 1&2 £15.80, 1&3 £3.90, 2&3 £16.00. CSF £64.11 TOTE £4.10: £1.90, £5.70, £1.40; EX 72.60 TRIFECTA Not won..
Owner Mrs Susan Roy and Mountgrange Stud **Bred** Cyril Humphris **Trained** Newmarket, Suffolk

FOCUS
An ordinary maiden, rated through the third. The market gave no strong clue about the outcome. The early pace looked fair but it slackened in mid-race.

NOTEBOOK
High Alert, a 120,000gns half-brother to a winner over jumps, is out of a half-sister to a couple of winners at up to 1m2f on the Flat. The application of blinkers for his debut was a possible explanation for his weakness in the market, but there was no sign of any quirks here. He was always moving fairly well under a confident ride and quickened well to assert in the closing stages. (op 9-4)
Fullback(IRE), a half-brother to Orpen Fire, changed hands cheaply as a yearling and at the breeze-ups in April, but he exceeded market expectations and ran a promising race on his debut. He did well to quicken off the steady pace, looked the possible winner at the furlong pole and eventually finished clear of the third. (op 12-1)
Penton Hook set the standard on form and had the run of the race, but displayed a slightly high head carriage and looked a bit reluctant when pressure was applied. Official explanation: jockey said gelding hung wide on final bend (op 5-1 tchd 11-2)
Tae Kwon Do(USA) showed no sign of the pre-race shenanigans he demonstrated at Yarmouth on his debut and he put in a reasonably promising effort here. He possibly hit the front too early in the straight but did well to keep going. He could step up again under more patient tactics next time. (op 7-1 tchd 15-2)
Master Fong(IRE) ◆, a 35,000gns yearling out of a fairly useful miler in France, was the one to really catch the eye. Looking very green, he was forced to race wide from a difficult draw but stayed on in really pleasing fashion. He should benefit from this experience. (op 7-1 tchd 5-1)
Starlight Wish Official explanation: jockey said colt was denied a clear run on final bend

4305 EUROPEAN BREEDERS' FUND MEDIAN AUCTION MAIDEN STKS (DIV II) 7f (P)
3:30 (3:31) (Class 5) 2-Y-O **£3,076** (£915; £457; £228) **Stalls** Low

Form				RPR
0	1		**Red Humour (IRE)**[33] 3219 2-9-3 0 .... MichaelHills 7	75
			(B W Hills) *pressed ldr: led narrowly 2f out: forged clr fnl 100yds* **8/1**[3]	
	2	1¾	**Equipe De Nuit** 2-9-3 0 .... RichardHughes 1	71
			(P W D'Arcy) *led narrowly tl rdn and hdd 2f out: ev ch tl no ex fnl 100yds* **20/1**	
032	3	2	**Zebrano**[26] 3444 2-9-3 0 .... AlanMunro 8	66
			(Miss E C Lavelle) *a chsng ldng pair: rdn and unable qck 2f out: one pce after* **8/15**[1]	
0	4	1¼	**Reel Ale**[32] 3267 2-9-3 0 .... StephenCarson 10	63
			(P Winkworth) *hld up bhd on outer: ridded over 2 fout: plugged on steadily fnl f: nvr trbld ldrs* **33/1**	
	5	nk	**Mr Udagawa** 2-9-3 0 .... GeorgeBaker 5	62
			(R M Beckett) *s.i.s: hld up bhd: rdn over 2f out: btn whn swtchd lft over 1f out: kpt on same pce* **8/1**[3]	
202	6	3	**Johnny Rook (GER)**[8] 4050 2-9-3 0 .... RyanMoore 4	54
			(E A L Dunlop) *in tch: rdn over 2f out: wknd 2f out* **5/1**[2]	
0	7	2¾	**Fantastic Fred (IRE)**[9] 4027 2-9-3 0 .... ShaneKelly 6	47
			(J A Osborne) *in tch: rdn over 2f out: wl hld whn edgd rt over 1f out* **40/1**	
	8	1	**Ivory's Icon (IRE)** 2-9-0 0 .... TravisBlock(3) 3	45
			(Miss Jo Crowley) *v.s.a: rn green and wl bhd: sme late hdwy* **66/1**	

1m 26.67s (1.87) **Going Correction** +0.175s/f (Slow) **8** Ran SP% **115.8**
Speed ratings (Par 94): **96,94,91,90,89 86,83,82**
toteswinger: 1&2 £8.20, 1&3 £2.10, 2&3 £3.70. CSF £134.03 TOTE £11.10: £2.30, £3.80, £1.02; EX 86.40 Trifecta £242.30 Part won. Pool: £327.47. 0.40 winning units..
Owner R J Arculi & B W Hills **Bred** Country Breeders **Trained** Lambourn, Berks

FOCUS
This looked stronger on paper than the first division of the maiden, but the two main contenders were very disappointing which casts major doubt over the value of the form. The first two dominated throughout.

NOTEBOOK
Red Humour(IRE) ◆ had not shown much on his debut, but won this with a bit in hand under a positive ride. Nothing got into the race from behind so the form looks suspect, but he should be capable of further progress and does seem to have a good attitude. (op 9-1 tchd 10-1)
Equipe De Nuit was probably suited by racing near the pace on his debut but looked fairly professional and battled on well in the closing stages. (op 22-1 tchd 25-1)
Zebrano had strong form claims and was the subject of a massive gamble. He was well positioned for a long way, but looked short of pace when asked for his effort and eventually finished well held, with no excuse as far as trip and surface are concerned. (op 10-11 tchd evens in a place)
Reel Ale improved from his debut effort on the turf here and may be one for modest handicaps over further in due course.
Mr Udagawa, a 28,000gns half-brother to Ciccone, looked very inexperienced and found a few traffic problems, but he stayed on steadily and showed signs of ability on his debut run. Official explanation: jockey said colt suffered interference in running (op 5-1)
Johnny Rook(GER), the other runner with solid form credentials, was struggling before the trip became an issue and eventually faded in the closing stages. Official explanation: jockey said colt never travelled (op 7-2 tchd 6-1)
Ivory's Icon(IRE) Official explanation: jockey said gelding missed the break

4306 FOREST ROW H'CAP 7f (P)
4:00 (4:02) (Class 5) (0-70,70) 3-Y-O+ **£2,590** (£770; £385; £192) **Stalls** Low

Form				RPR
0006	1		**Hazytoo**[20] 3653 4-9-13 **65** .... (p) RyanMoore 5	74
			(S A Callaghan) *mde all: hrd pressed and drvn wl over 1f out: styd on wl to assert fnl 100yds* **9/2**[1]	
6000	2	1	**Adantino**[28] 3374 9-9-11 **66** .... (b) JamesMillman(3) 8	72
			(B R Millman) *hld up towards rr: hdwy over 1f out: r.o strly fnl f: wnt 2nd nr fin: nt rch wnr* **9/1**[3]	
2500	3	hd	**Seneschal**[6] 4104 7-9-13 **65** .... RichardHughes 7	71
			(A B Haynes) *chsd wnr thrght: upsides wnr and drvn wl over 1f out: no ex fnl 100yds: lost 2nd nr fin* **14/1**	
0246	4	hd	**Joy And Pain**[21] 3615 7-9-10 **62** .... (p) IanMongan 12	67
			(M J Attwater) *in tch: hdwy to trck ldng pair jst over 2f out: rdn and nt qckn ent fnl f: one pce after* **12/1**	
560	5	¾	**Goose Green (IRE)**[28] 3383 4-9-3 **55** .... SteveDrowne 11	58
			(R J Hodges) *in tch in midfield: rdn and nt qckn 2f out: styd on u.p ins fnl f: nt rch ldrs* **10/1**	
-425	6	nse	**The City Kid (IRE)**[15] 3826 5-9-9 **61** .... PaulEddery 9	64
			(G D Blake) *chsd ldrs: rdn ent fnl f: unable qck u.p: eased whn btn nr fin* **12/1**	
0004	7	½	**Wadnagin (IRE)**[9] 4030 4-9-2 **54** .... AdamKirby 3	56+
			(I A Wood) *hld up bhd: hdwy over 1f out: r.o wl fnl f: nvr able to chal* **12/1**	
-536	8	1¼	**Nikki Bea (IRE)**[159] 571 5-9-3 **55** .... PaulDoe 14	53
			(Jamie Poulton) *dropped in after s: wl bhd: r.o wl fnl f: nvr able to chal* **16/1**	
2066	9	nse	**Blackmalkin (USA)**[55] 2547 4-9-9 **61** .... ShaneKelly 13	59
			(M Quinn) *hld up towards rr: hdwy on outer wl over 2f out: chsd ldrs and drvn ent fnl 2f: wknd ent fnl f* **16/1**	
3031	10	hd	**Benedetto**[13] 3893 3-9-11 **70** .... (p) TPQueally 6	68
			(Mrs A J Perrett) *in tch in midfield: n.m.r and jostled over 3f out: effrt on inner over 1f out: wknd fnl 100yds* **15/2**[2]	
4244	11	1½	**Top Draw (USA)**[25] 3487 3-9-6 **70** .... MCGeran(5) 2	64
			(M L W Bell) *t.k.h: chsd ldrs: rdn 2f out: fdd fnl f* **9/1**[3]	
003	12	1	**Lopinot (IRE)**[17] 3764 5-9-12 **64** .... (v[1]) GeorgeBaker 4	55
			(M R Bosley) *s.i.s: sn rcvrd and in tch: rdn jst over 2f out: wknd over 1f out* **15/2**[2]	
55-4	13	5	**Hucking Harkness**[46] 2823 3-9-3 **62** .... LPKeniry 1	39
			(J R Best) *in tch in midfield: rdn and struggling over 2f out: no ch after* **16/1**	
0060	14	2¾	**Pietersen (IRE)**[83] 1752 4-9-3 **60** .... NataliaGemelova(5) 10	30
			(J E Long) *v.s.a: a last* **20/1**	

1m 25.85s (1.05) **Going Correction** +0.175s/f (Slow)
WFA 3 from 4yo+ 7lb **14** Ran SP% **123.0**
Speed ratings (Par 103): **101,99,99,99,98 98,97,96,96,96 94,93,87,84**
toteswinger: 1&2 £13.20, 1&3 £15.10, 2&3 £34.80. CSF £44.63 CT £540.58 TOTE £5.90: £2.20, £3.70, £4.70; EX 50.20 TRIFECTA Not won..
Owner T Mohan,M Walsh & Allan McNamee **Bred** Mrs Liza Judd **Trained** Newmarket, Suffolk

FOCUS
The usual suspects in a race that could easily have been transported from the mid-winter programme. The disappointment was that the unexposed three-year-olds failed to figure. It paid to race prominenetly and the third and fourth are the best guide to the form.
Nikki Bea(IRE) Official explanation: jockey said mare resented the kickback
Blackmalkin(USA) Official explanation: vet said filly bled from the nose
Top Draw(USA) Official explanation: jockey said filly had no more to give
Pietersen(IRE) Official explanation: jockey said gelding missed the break

4307 BROADSTONE AMBLE H'CAP 6f (P)
4:30 (4:31) (Class 5) (0-70,70) 3-Y-O+ **£2,590** (£770; £385; £192) **Stalls** Low

Form				RPR
3143	1		**Chjimes (IRE)**[9] 4030 4-9-12 **70** .... LPKeniry 5	81
			(C R Dore) *in tch: trckd ldrs 2f out: rdn to chal ent fnl f: led ins fnl f: styd on strly* **9/2**[1]	
0052	2	1¼	**Vintage (IRE)**[22] 3587 4-9-12 **70** .... IanMongan 12	77
			(J Akehurst) *chsd ldrs on outer: rdn jst over 2f out: hrd drvn over 1f out: snatched 2nd on line: nt pce to rch wnr* **5/1**[2]	
0006	3	nse	**Bollin Franny**[42] 2933 4-8-2 **51** oh3 .... NataliaGemelova(5) 9	58
			(J E Long) *stmbld s: sn handy: chsd ldr over 3f out: rdn over 2f out: led over 1f out: hdd and nt pce of wnr ins fnl f: lost 2nd on line* **20/1**	
0000	4	1½	**Bobby Rose**[11] 3966 5-9-2 **60** .... (b) RobertHavlin 8	62
			(D K Ivory) *dwlt: t.k.h and sn in tch: nt clr run 2f out tl jst over 1f out: nt qckn u.p fnl df* **12/1**	
4040	5	nk	**Hucking Hill (IRE)**[4] 4186 4-9-5 **63** .... (b) GeorgeBaker 3	64
			(J R Best) *stdd after s: bhd: hdwy on inner wl over 1f out: r.o wl fnl f: nt rch ldrs* **7/1**	
3250	6	½	**Mambazo**[21] 3615 6-8-11 **60** .... (e) AshleyHamblett(5) 10	59
			(S C Williams) *taken down early: t.k.h: hld up towards rr: drvn wl over 1f out: kpt on ins fnl f: nvr trbld ldrs* **14/1**	
6125	7	2½	**Ever Cheerful**[92] 1534 7-9-9 **67** .... (p) SteveDrowne 11	58
			(A B Haynes) *dwlt: chsd ldrs: rdn and struggling over 2f out: no ch w ldrs after* **10/1**	
0030	8	nse	**Edge End**[4] 4186 4-8-11 **55** .... (p) PaulDoe 4	46
			(R A Farrant) *a towards rr: rdn 1/2-way: n.d after* **12/1**	
6005	9	1	**Quality Street**[30] 3316 6-9-1 **59** .... (p) RichardThomas 7	47
			(P Butler) *sn led: rdn over 2f out: hdd over 1f out: edgd lft and fdd fnl f* **6/1**	
0311	10	1½	**Regal Royale**[13] 3872 5-9-3 **61** .... (v) AdamKirby 2	63+
			(Peter Grayson) *stmbld s: sn drvn along: hdwy u.p into midfield 1/2-way: keeping on but looked hld whn nt clr run and snatched up ins fnl f: eased after* **11/2**[3]	
0-50	11	1¼	**Hucking Harmony (IRE)**[26] 3447 3-7-12 **52** .... DavidProbert(5) 1	31
			(J R Best) *a bhd: no ch fr 1/2-way* **33/1**	
3-40	12	7	**Sempre Libera (IRE)**[19] 3672 3-8-9 **58** .... AlanMunro 6	15
			(R T Phillips) *chsd ldr tl over 3f out: sn wknd* **33/1**	

1m 12.9s (1.00) **Going Correction** +0.175s/f (Slow)
WFA 3 from 4yo+ 5lb **12** Ran SP% **118.8**
Speed ratings (Par 103): **100,98,98,96,95 95,91,91,90,88 86,77**
toteswinger: 1&2 £4.60, 1&3 £34.00, 2&3 £38.10. CSF £26.00 CT £413.66 TOTE £5.60: £2.20, £2.10, £8.60; EX 21.60 TRIFECTA Not won..
Owner Sean J Murphy **Bred** Morgan O'Flaherty **Trained** West Pinchbeck, Lincs
■ Stewards' Enquiry : Richard Thomas two-day ban: careless riding (August 6-7)

FOCUS
A reasonable handicap. The runners that raced just behind the pace dominated the finish and few got into it from behind. Pretty straightforward form.
Regal Royale Official explanation: jockey said gelding suffered interference in running

4308 HINDLEAP WALK FILLIES' H'CAP 5f (P)
5:00 (5:04) (Class 6) (0-65,62) 3-Y-0+ **£2,047** (£604; £302) **Stalls** High

Form RPR
0324 1 **City For Conquest (IRE)**6 4107 5-8-10 **45** TPQueally 1 54
(John A Harris) *chsd ldrs: rdn 2f out: chsd ldr over 1f out: edgd rt: led jst ins fnl f: styd on wl* **4/1**1
0362 2 ¾ **Miss Firefly**17 3765 3-9-3 **61** MCGeran(5) 8 66
(R J Hodges) *in tch: rdn over 1f out: chsd wnr ins fnl f: one pce fnl 100yds* **4/1**1
3006 3 2 ¼ **Lady Bahia (IRE)**46 2836 7-9-11 **60** (b) GeorgeBaker 6 58
(Peter Grayson) *hld up bhd: rdn and gd hdwy on inner 2f out: disputd 2nd jst ins fnl fiurlong: no ex fnl 100yds* **7/1**2
2265 4 ½ **Stoneacre Chris (USA)**114 1120 3-8-13 **52** LPKeniry 2 47
(Peter Grayson) *led: rdn 2f out: hdd jst ins fnl f: fdd fnl 100yds* **14/1**
3034 5 nk **Town And Gown**1 4272 3-9-9 **62** (e) AlanMunro 7 56
(S C Williams) *hld up bhd: rdn 2f out: kpt on fnl f: nvr trbld ldrs* **4/1**1
33 6 1 ¾ **Our Kally**30 3332 3-8-3 **47** DavidProbert(5) 9 35
(M D I Usher) *hld up in midfield: rdn and struggling over 2f out: n.d after* **9/1**
006 7 2 **Summer Rose**13 3867 3-8-6 **45** (p) RichardMullen 3 26
(R M H Cowell) *s.i.s: hdwy into midfield after 1f: outpcd 2f out: n.d after* **33/1**
0533 8 3 ¾ **Kalligal**24 3526 3-9-9 **62** SteveDrowne 10 29
(R Ingram) *walked to s: bhd on outer: n.d* **8/1**3
1365 9 ½ **Stoneacre Sarah**21 3609 3-9-7 **60** AdamKirby 4 25
(Peter Grayson) *sn chsng ldr tl over 1f out: sn wknd* **8/1**3
60.24 secs (1.44) **Going Correction** +0.175s/f (Slow)
WFA 3 from 5yo+ 4lb **9** Ran SP% **114.3**
Speed ratings (Par 98): **95,93,90,89,88 86,82,76,76**
toteswinger: 1&2 £4.70, 1&3 £7.80, 2&3 £6.80. CSF £19.09 CT £107.96 TOTE £5.00: £1.60, £1.80, £2.40; EX 23.40 Trifecta £87.00 Pool: £799.20. 6.79 winning units. Place 6: £43.66, Place 5: £39.55..
Owner M F Schofield **Bred** Ballyhane Stud **Trained** Eastwell, Leics
FOCUS
Selling form to the fore says it all about the standard shown here, but it was run at a rattling pace with the pacesetting Stoneacre Chris and Stoneacre Sarah dropping right away for their efforts. Weak form, rated through the runner-up.
T/Plt: £102.80 to a £1 stake. Pool: £47,575.00. 337.60 winning tickets. T/Qpdt: £12.60 to a £1 stake. Pool: £3,162.60. 185.30 winning tickets. SP

4126 SANDOWN (R-H)
Wednesday, July 23

OFFICIAL GOING: Good to firm (8.7)
Wind: Almost nil Weather: Fine, warm

4309 ISLAND BARN APPRENTICE H'CAP 1m 2f 7y
6:05 (6:05) (Class 5) (0-75,73) 4-Y-0+ **£3,238** (£963; £481; £240) **Stalls** High

Form RPR
0122 1 **Wee Charlie Castle (IRE)**11 3965 5-8-7 **61** WilliamCarson(5) 3 72
(G C H Chung) *lw: hld up in midfield: stdy prog on outer fr over 2f out: hanging but swept into ld jst over 1f out: sn clr: rdn out* **4/1**1
5-00 2 3 ¼ **Stargazer Jim (FR)**12 3896 6-9-10 **73** (v) KirstyMilczarek 1 78
(W J Haggas) *hld up in last pair: rdn and prog fr jst over 2f out: wnt rt jst ins fnl f: tk 2nd last 150yds and clsd on wnr: no ch of chalng* **11/2**2
3150 3 5 **Prime Number (IRE)**5 4156 6-9-4 **67** TravisBlock 10 64+
(J Akehurst) *led: drvn and hdd jst over 3f out: sn outpcd: wl btn whn hmpd jst ins fnl f: kpt on again to snatch 3rd on line* **11/2**2
0135 4 nk **Artreju (GER)**16 3800 5-9-5 **71** JamieJones(3) 9 65
(G L Moore) *trckd ldng pair and sn clr of rest: wnt 2nd over 2f out: led briefly over 1f out: sn btn: wknd fnl f* **8/1**
100 5 shd **Vinces**12 3896 4-9-5 **68** WilliamBuick 6 62
(T D McCarthy) *chsd clr ldrs: no imp u.p over 2f out: plugged on fnl f* **12/1**
6220 6 1 ¾ **Zach's Harmoney (USA)**24 3518 4-9-2 **65** MarcHalford 8 55
(P W Hiatt) *pressed ldr: led jst over 3f out: drvn and hdd over 1f out: wknd* **16/1**
1303 7 1 ½ **Hucking Heat (IRE)**11 3965 4-8-5 **59** (p) SoniaEaton(5) 7 46
(R Hollinshead) *chsd clr ldrs: no imp over 2f out: wl btn whn sltly hmpd jst ins fnl f* **16/1**
4032 8 ½ **Blacktoft (USA)**6 4131 5-9-7 **73** (e) JackMitchell(3) 4 59
(S C Williams) *stdd s and s.i.s: hld up in last pair: hanging bdly and reluctant u.p over 2f out: no ch* **11/2**2
5052 9 3 ¾ **Davenport (IRE)**15 3824 6-9-8 **71** (p) JamesMillman 5 50
(B R Millman) *a wl in rr: struggling sn after 1/2-way* **14/1**
4042 10 5 **Follow The Colours (IRE)**24 3518 5-9-0 **63** PatrickHills 2 32
(J W Hills) *lw: nvr beyond midfield: nvr on terms: wknd 2f out* **13/2**3
2m 8.54s (-1.96) **Going Correction** -0.075s/f (Good) **10** Ran SP% **116.7**
Speed ratings (Par 103): **104,101,97,97,97 95,94,94,91,87**
CSF £25.63 CT £121.94 TOTE £3.40: £1.50, £2.60, £2.80; EX 25.70.
Owner The Maybe This Time Partnership **Bred** Bryan Ryan **Trained** Newmarket, Suffolk
■ Stewards' Enquiry : Patrick Hills two-day ban: struck gelding 4 times in fnl f, last 2 in annoyance (Aug 7-8)
Kirsty Milczarek three-day ban: careless riding (Aug 6-8)
FOCUS
A routine apprentice handicap in which cases could be made for several runners. However, there were a couple of confirmed front-runners in the line-up, plus others that like to race prominently, and that was always likely to suit the hold-up horses, two of whom occupied the first two places at the finish. Ordinary form for the grade, but pretty solid.
Davenport(IRE) Official explanation: jockey said gelding was unsuited by the good to firm ground

4310 WEY H'CAP 1m 14y
6:35 (6:36) (Class 4) (0-80,77) 3-Y-0+ **£5,180** (£1,541; £770; £384) **Stalls** High

Form RPR
3122 1 **Willow Dancer (IRE)**28 3376 4-9-11 **75** (p) AdamKirby 5 89+
(W R Swinburn) *lw: trckd ldr: shkn up to ld 2f out: clr 1f out: readily and eased nr fin* **2/1**1
5062 2 2 **Thunder Gorge (USA)**6 4128 3-8-10 **68** RyanMoore 2 73
(Mouse Hamilton-Fairley) *lw: led: rdn and hdd 2f out: sn no ch w wnr: hld on for 2nd* **3/1**2
-440 3 ¾ **Jo'Burg (USA)**12 3915 4-9-11 **75** TPQueally 7 80
(Mrs A J Perrett) *s.s: rcvrd to trck ldng pair: rdn and fnd nil over 2f out: wl btn after: kpt on again ins fnl f* **8/1**3
5012 4 shd **Yathreb (USA)**21 3607 3-9-5 **77** (b) RHills 1 80+
(J L Dunlop) *lw: scratchy to post: dwlt: hld up in last: asked for effrt over 2f out but hanging and no prog: eventually r.o fnl f: nrst fin* **3/1**2
6000 5 2 ¾ **Sofia's Star**28 3376 3-9-0 **72** StephenCarson 6 69
(P Winkworth) *t.k.h: hld up in tch: shkn up and nt qckn over 2f out: no imp on ldrs after* **12/1**
-030 6 1 ½ **Cape Of Luck (IRE)**14 3840 5-9-12 **76** (p) IanMongan 3 71
(P M Phelan) *t.k.h: hld up in tch: rdn and nt qckn over 2f out: no imp after: wknd ins fnl f* **10/1**
1m 43.54s (0.24) **Going Correction** -0.075s/f (Good)
WFA 3 from 4yo+ 8lb **6** Ran SP% **111.2**
Speed ratings (Par 105): **95,93,92,92,89 87**
CSF £8.05 TOTE £2.60: £1.60, £2.20; EX 8.60.
Owner Mrs G Godfrey & Mrs A Horner **Bred** Exors Of The Late R E Sangster **Trained** Aldbury, Herts
FOCUS
A small field, and only three with recent form. The form looks questionable, the runner-up perhaps the best guide, but the winner stepped forward again.

4311 EUROPEAN BREEDERS' FUND MAIDEN STKS 7f 16y
7:10 (7:13) (Class 4) 2-Y-0 **£5,180** (£1,541; £770; £384) **Stalls** High

Form RPR
1 **Cry Of Freedom (USA)** 2-9-3 0 DarryllHolland 5 81+
(M Johnston) *w'like: trckd ldr after 2f: chal 2f out: narrow ld 1f out: asserting whn edgd rt last 100yds* **7/1**3
6 2 3 ½ **Combat Zone (IRE)**14 3853 2-9-3 0 LDettori 1 76+
(Saeed Bin Suroor) *lw: led after 1f: shkn up whn pressed 2f out: narrowly hdd 1f out: hld whn intimidated last 75yds* **8/13**1
3 2 **Aathaar** 2-9-3 0 RHills 3 67+
(Sir Michael Stoute) *w'like: scope: led 1f: chsd ldrs after: shkn up in 4th over 2f out: styd on to take 3rd fnl f: nvr able to chal* **12/1**
6 4 3 **Granski (IRE)**11 3968 2-9-3 0 RichardHughes 4 60
(R Hannon) *plld hrd early: hld up in tch: chsd ldng pair over 2f out: lost grnd on them over 1f out: wknd fnl f* **13/2**2
5 ¾ **Sabi Star** 2-9-3 0 RobertHavlin 2 58+
(J H M Gosden) *w'like: scope: bit bkwd: dwlt: hld up in last pair: sme prog 2f out: kpt on but no threat* **10/1**
5 6 3 **Rio Del Oro (USA)**11 3939 2-9-3 0 RyanMoore 7 50
(R Hannon) *swtg: hld up in last pair: detached in last over 2f out: kpt on fnl f* **12/1**
0 7 1 ¾ **Dubai Crest**11 3968 2-9-3 0 TPQueally 6 46+
(Mrs A J Perrett) *hld up: prog to trck ldrs 1/2-way: shkn up over 2f out: sn wknd* **25/1**
8 ½ **Peter Grimes (IRE)** 2-9-3 0 IanMongan 8 45
(H J L Dunlop) *in tch: shkn up over 2f out: steadily wknd* **40/1**
1m 29.75s (0.25) **Going Correction** -0.075s/f (Good) **8** Ran SP% **118.5**
Speed ratings (Par 96): **95,91,88,85,84 81,79,78**
CSF £12.17 TOTE £8.90: £2.20, £1.10, £2.30; EX 13.60.
Owner Sheikh Hamdan Bin Mohammed Al Maktoum **Bred** Clovelly Farms **Trained** Middleham Moor, N Yorks
FOCUS
The betting was overwhelmingly dominated by Godolphin's recent close Newmarket sixth Combat Zone, but he was beaten on merit by Cry Of Freedom, one of four newcomers in the race. The winner did it well but the margin flatters him a little.
NOTEBOOK
Cry Of Freedom(USA) knew his job, like most from the Mark Johnston stable, and the trainer said afterwards that he had done everything asked of him at home. He added that while this son of Street Cry is not all that big, he has a good long stride and rides like a big horse. He will get 1m without any trouble. (op 15-2)
Combat Zone(IRE) could have no excuse, as he soon had the lead despite his wide draw. However, he really had to knuckle down when the winner ranged alongside, and he was headed at the furlong pole. In fairness he was still battling away and little more than half a length down when Cry Of Freedom edged right and crossed him inside the last half furlong, causing him to hit the rail, possibly having been intimidated by his rival's whip. He can be rated as having been beaten a length or so, rather than two, and is sure to win a similar race, but he probably isn't a star. (op 8-11)
Aathaar got a bit outpaced about two furlongs from home, but he was keeping on at the finish. He was allowed to go off a big price, so improvement is obviously on the cards. (op 8-1)
Granski(IRE), who had the benefit of a previous race, was really keen early on, and that told in the closing stages. (op 7-1 tchd 8-1)
Sabi Star, whose dam Balisada won the Coronation Stakes, was never in contention after being held up in rear. He should learn plenty from this. (op 14-1)
Rio Del Oro(USA) was difficult to load, but having looked as if he might finish tailed-off, he passed a couple of rivals late on. (op 11-1 tchd 14-1 in a place)
Dubai Crest Official explanation: jockey said colt hung left throughout

4312 THAMES H'CAP 7f 16y
7:40 (7:42) (Class 3) (0-90,90) 3-Y-0 **£7,771** (£2,312; £1,155; £577) **Stalls** High

Form RPR
0332 1 **Brassini**5 4158 3-9-2 **85** AlanMunro 1 93
(B R Millman) *trckd ldr: rdn 2f out: sustained effrt fr over 1f out to ld last 100yds: gamely* **6/1**2
-400 2 ¾ **Zakhaaref**25 3475 3-9-4 **87** RHills 5 93
(M Johnston) *led: shkn up 2f out: kpt on wl fr over 1f out: worn down last 100yds* **11/1**
11 3 1 ¾ **Main Aim**18 3744 3-9-7 **90** RyanMoore 7 91
(Sir Michael Stoute) *lw: hld up in 6th: stdy prog on outer fr over 2f out: clsd on ldng pair 1f out: sn rdn and nt qckn* **4/7**1
-653 4 1 **Noble Citizen (USA)**32 3270 3-8-12 **81** RichardMullen 4 80
(D M Simcock) *trckd ldng pair: rdn 2f out: stl cl up jst over 1f out: one pce after* **7/1**3
2260 5 3 ½ **Smokey Rye**7 4082 3-8-8 **77** FergusSweeney 6 66
(G L Moore) *hld up in 5th: rdn over 2f out: outpcd wl over 1f out: n.d after* **33/1**
6020 6 ½ **Sophie's Girl**14 3850 3-9-7 **90** JimmyQuinn 2 78
(C A Dwyer) *hld up in 4th: rdn 2f out: wknd over 1f out* **33/1**
5-56 7 10 **Pegasus Again (USA)**98 1402 3-9-7 **90** LDettori 3 51
(T G Mills) *dwlt: hld up: a last: rdn and lost tch wl over 2f out* **11/1**
1m 28.23s (-1.27) **Going Correction** -0.075s/f (Good) **7** Ran SP% **113.0**
Speed ratings (Par 104): **104,103,101,100,96 95,84**
CSF £64.73 TOTE £6.10: £1.80, £4.40; EX 74.20.
Owner The Links Partnership **Bred** B N And Mrs Toye **Trained** Kentisbeare, Devon

FOCUS
A decent little handicap, even if hot favourite Main Aim could not win. That said, Brassini had the beating of him strictly on their meeting here earlier in the month.

NOTEBOOK
Brassini, still 8lb higher than when winning at Lingfield earlier in the season, seems to have improved for the step up to 7f the last twice and was just touched off at Newmarket last week. Able to race off the same mark here, he looked the one most likely to benefit if the favourite ran below expectations and that is exactly what happened. Always well positioned, he wore down Zakhaaref inside the final half-furlong and managed to reverse earlier course form with Main Aim. He is progressing well and, although things will be harder from now on, this consistent sort is likely to continue to pay his way. (op 8-1)

Zakhaaref has basically been a disappointment this season, but his stable is going better now and he made a bold attempt to lead throughout. He has slipped to a fair mark now and may soon be back winning. (op 14-1 tchd 16-1)

Main Aim is seemingly held in quite high regard by his trainer, but had made hard enough work of winning his two starts this season (unraced at two). He was clearly expected to laugh in the face of his 5lb rise, but having got within striking distance, there was no finishing kick forthcoming and he could find no extra. His half-brothers stayed further than this and perhaps he is worth a try at 1m now, as for both his previous wins at this trip he left it late to get on top. (op 1-2)

Noble Citizen(USA) ran more encouragingly at Newmarket last time (off this mark) and again gave the impression he will be capable of winning once slipping back to a mark in the 70s. (op 8-1)

Smokey Rye was always likely to struggle against these and she was never going like a winner. It was better than her last effort, but she is unlikely to be winning off her current rating.

Sophie's Girl has not built on last month's Newmarket second and found this 7f trip too far. (op 25-1)

Pegasus Again(USA), returning from a break and running in his first handicap, was always last and it was disconcerting to see him finish so far adrift. He has it all to prove following this. (op 9-1)

4313 ESHER GREEN H'CAP — 5f 6y
8:15 (8:16) (Class 5) (0-75,75) 4-Y-0+ — **£4,533** (£1,348; £674; £336) **Stalls** High

Form — RPR

2220 **1** **Rocker**[22] 3585 4-8-10 **62** ....(b) RyanMoore 9 — 73
(G L Moore) *trckd ldng pair and racd against far rail: tk gap lft by runner-up 1f out and squeezed through: led ins fnl f: drvn out* **4/1**[1]

1040 **2** ¾ **Judge 'n Jury**[28] 3363 4-9-7 **73** ....(t) RichardHughes 2 — 81
(R A Harris) *lw: trckd ldng pair gng wl: swtchd lft jst over 1f out: effrt and pressed wnr last 100yds: jst hld* **7/1**

4-41 **3** ½ **Make My Dream**[9] 4025 5-9-2 **68** 6ex .... TPO'Shea 5 — 74
(J Gallagher) *lw: hld up in rr: rdn 2f out: prog jst over 1f out: r.o wl to take 3rd nr fin: nt rch ldng pair* **5/1**[2]

-122 **4** 1 **Realt Na Mara (IRE)**[153] 636 5-9-8 **74** .... SteveDrowne 1 — 77+
(H Morrison) *chsd ldng quartet: outpcd fr 1/2-way: styd on again fnl f: nvr able to chal* **6/1**[3]

0006 **5** nk **Cape Royal**[11] 3945 8-9-6 **75** ....(bt) KevinGhunowa(3) 10 — 77
(J M Bradley) *lw: w ldr: led 2f out: drvn and hdd ins fnl f: fdd nr fin* **8/1**

621- **6** ½ **Tubby Isaacs**[247] 6877 4-8-10 **62** .... TPQueally 8 — 62+
(P J Makin) *s.s: wl off the pce in last trio: swtchd to outer and effrt over 1f out: styd on: nrst fin* **8/1**

0466 **7** hd **Billy Red**[25] 3486 4-8-6 **58** ....(b) LiamJones 4 — 57
(J R Jenkins) *hld up towards rr: rdn and sme prog over 1f out: nt qckn and no imp ins fnl f* **16/1**

1666 **8** nk **Drifting Gold**[39] 3024 4-9-7 **73** ....(b) AdamKirby 3 — 71
(C G Cox) *mde most to 2f out: stl pressing ent fnl f: wknd last 100yds* **25/1**

2065 **9** nk **Thoughtsofstardom**[5] 4159 5-8-8 **65** .... KellyHarrison(5) 7 — 62
(P S McEntee) *dwlt: wl off the pce in last trio: rdn over 2f out: styd on fnl f: nrst fin* **10/1**

3046 **10** ½ **Tiger Trail (GER)**[14] 3847 4-8-8 **60** ....(p) DarryllHolland 11 — 55
(Mrs N Smith) *nvr bttr than midfield against rail: outpcd 1/2-way: kpt on fnl f: n.d* **10/1**

1460 **11** 2½ **Dualagi**[9] 4025 4-8-13 **65** .... FergusSweeney 6 — 51
(M R Bosley) *s.i.s: a in last trio: detached in last over 1f out* **14/1**

60.10 secs (-1.50) **Going Correction** -0.225s/f (Firm) — **11** Ran SP% **120.3**
Speed ratings (Par 103): **103,101,101,99,98 98,97,97,96,96 92**
CSF £32.69 CT £148.37 TOTE £5.00: £1.90, £2.80, £1.70; EX 35.60.
Owner Sir Eric Parker **Bred** Sir Eric Parker **Trained** Woodingdean, E Sussex

FOCUS
A decent sprint handicap and solid form, with the winner pretty much back to his best.

4314 MOLE H'CAP — 1m 6f
8:45 (8:45) (Class 4) (0-85,85) 4-Y-0+ — **£6,476** (£1,927; £963; £481) **Stalls** High

Form — RPR

6641 **1** **Rajeh (IRE)**[25] 3480 5-9-9 **85** .... LiamJones 8 — 92
(J L Spearing) *t.k.h: trckd ldng pair: wnt 2nd wl over 2f out: drvn to ld narrowly over 1f out: a jst prevailing in gd battle fnl f* **3/1**[1]

6-42 **2** nk **Callisto Moon**[4] 4193 4-8-6 **68** ....(p) RichardMullen 6 — 75
(Ian Williams) *trckd ldr: led after 5f: drvn and hdd over 1f out: battled on wl fnl f: jst hld nr fin* **7/2**[2]

5031 **3** 1¼ **Hawridge King**[24] 3523 6-9-1 **80** .... JamesMillman(3) 5 — 85
(W S Kittow) *lw: hld up in cl tch: rdn to chse ldng pair over 2f out: kpt on wl enough but nvr quite able to chal* **4/1**[3]

-006 **4** 4 **Inchpast**[4] 4200 7-9-0 **76** ....(b) JimmyQuinn 1 — 76
(M H Tompkins) *hld up in tch: rdn over 2f out: nt qckn and no imp fnl 2f* **17/2**

1213 **5** 2¾ **Trachonitis (IRE)**[24] 3523 4-9-5 **81** .... DarryllHolland 2 — 77
(J R Jenkins) *hld up in 6th: rdn over 2f out: no imp wl over 1f out: wknd ins fnl f* **4/1**[3]

04-0 **6** 1¾ **Simba Sun (IRE)**[19] 3685 4-8-13 **75** .... RichardHughes 4 — 68
(A King) *s.s: hld up in detached last: shkn up over 2f out: no real prog* **12/1**

3551 **7** ½ **Salute (IRE)**[21] 3613 9-8-13 **75** .... RobertHavlin 7 — 68
(P G Murphy) *led 5f: pressed ldr tl wl over 2f out: steadily wknd u.p* **8/1**

3m 6.08s (-0.52) **Going Correction** -0.075s/f (Good) — **7** Ran SP% **116.6**
Speed ratings (Par 105): **98,97,97,94,93 92,91**
CSF £14.24 CT £42.05 TOTE £3.60: £2.10, £1.50; EX 15.70 Place 6 £30.40, Place 5 £18.90.
Owner Miss C Ive **Bred** Mrs C S Acham **Trained** Kinnersley, Worcs

FOCUS
A fair staying handicap run at a steady pace, and ordinary form.

T/Plt: £89.20 to a £1 stake. Pool: £62,051.01. 507.58 winning tickets. T/Qpdt: £30.30 to a £1 stake. Pool: £5,541.15. 135.20 winning tickets. JN

4315 - 4319a (Foreign Racing) - See Raceform Interactive

VICHY
Wednesday, July 23

OFFICIAL GOING: Soft

4320a GRAND PRIX DE VICHY-AUVERGNE (GROUP 3) — 1m 2f
8:45 (8:55) 3-Y-0+ — **£29,412** (£11,765; £8,824; £5,882; £2,941)

RPR

1 **Hapsburg (FR)**[55] 2553 4-8-13 .... IMendizabal 1 — 108
(E Libaud, France) *hld up in 7th to st: swtchd rt and hdwy 2f out: led over 1f out: drvn out* **249/10**

2 snk **Kocab**[22] 3595 6-9-2 .... SPasquier 2 — 111
(A Fabre, France) *4th st: stdy hdwy fnl 2f: pushed along and ev ch last 100yds: unable qck cl home* **11/10**[1]

3 1 **Boris De Deauville (IRE)**[39] 3053 5-9-2 .... TThulliez 7 — 109
(S Wattel, France) *hld up: 6th st: hdwy 1 1/2f out: styd on fnl 150yds but no threat to first two* **37/10**[3]

4 1½ **Daly Daly (FR)**[22] 3595 4-8-13 .... WMongil 8 — 103
(R Laplanche, France) *led: c to middle ent st: edgd rt 2f out: hdd and edgd rt over 1f out: kpt on one pce* **12/1**

5 nse **Diyakalanie (FR)**[32] 3291 4-8-13 .... MAndrouin 5 — 103
(J Boisnard, France) *sn trcking ldr: 2nd st: rdn wl over 1f out: kpt on one pce u.p* **16/1**

6 ¾ **Aspectus (IRE)**[108] 1240 5-9-2 .... JVictoire 6 — 104
(A Fabre, France) *a cl up: 3rd st: chal and hung rt 2f out: carried rt by ldr 1 1/2f out: wknd* **15/1**

6 dht **Willywell (FR)**[22] 3595 6-9-2 .... FBlondel 3 — 104
(J-P Gauvin, France) *hld up in rr: last st: nvr a factor* **31/1**

8 5 **La Boum (GER)**[55] 2553 5-8-13 .... CSoumillon 4 — 92
(Robert Collet, France) *5th st: effrt 2f out: carried rt wl over 1f out: rdn and btn appr fnl f: eased* **7/2**[2]

2m 5.45s (-3.15) — **8** Ran SP% **117.9**
PARI-MUTUEL (including one euro stakes): WIN 25.90; PL 2.30, 1.20,1.30; SF 23.30.
Owner J Luck **Bred** Mickael M Kelly **Trained** France

NOTEBOOK
Hapsburg(FR) has come to hand at exactly the right time. She had put in an impressive piece of work before this Group race but still started at 25/1. Held up in the early stages, she surged impressively up the far rail from one out and collared the even favourite close home. If all goes well, she will now be aimed at the Group 2 Prix Jean Romanet at Deauville next month.
Kocab was given every possible chance in mid division for much of the race. He quickened well from the furlong marker, but could not hold off the winner inside the final furlong. This consistent performer has never won a group race and his chance may come on the Prix Gontaut-Biron at Deauville.
Boris De Deauville(IRE), a soft ground specialist, this horse put up a decent effort. Settled in sixth place, he ran a little free early on and did not have the best of runs in the straight. Nevertheless he finished well and he always gives his best.
Daly Daly(FR) tried to make every yard of the running. She fended off all challengers at the furlong marker but failed to continue her defence later in the race. Nevertheless she battled on well to hold fourth place.

4101 BATH (L-H)
Thursday, July 24

OFFICIAL GOING: Firm (10.5)
Wind: Fresh behind Weather: Sunny periods

4321 JOHN SMITH'S MEDIAN AUCTION MAIDEN STKS — 5f 161y
2:20 (2:21) (Class 6) 2-Y-0 — **£2,266** (£674; £337; £168) **Stalls** Centre

Form — RPR

22 **1** **Qalahari (IRE)**[30] 3348 2-8-12 0 .... TPO'Shea 8 — 93+
(D J Coakley) *w ldr: led on bit over 3f out: clr 2f out: v easily* **8/13**[1]

0 **2** 12 **Handful Of Magic**[15] 3837 2-8-12 0 .... RichardKingscote 1 — 50
(Tom Dascombe) *s.i.s: sn chsng ldrs: rdn and wnt 2nd 1f out: no ch w wnr* **14/1**

3 1¾ **Five Star Junior (USA)** 2-9-3 0 .... OscarUrbina 10 — 49
(S A Callaghan) *a.p: rdn to chse wnr over 2f out to 1f out: no ex* **9/2**[2]

00 **4** 2¾ **Goodenough Magic**[29] 3378 2-8-12 0 .... AlanDaly 2 — 35
(Andrew Turnell) *led: hdd over 3f out: rdn 2f out: wknd 1f out* **66/1**

5 nse **Silky Way (GR)** 2-8-12 0 .... FergusSweeney 12 — 35
(P R Chamings) *s.s: bhd tl hdwy 2f out: edgd lft jst over 1f out: no further prog* **25/1**

36 **6** 1¼ **Tillers Satisfied (IRE)**[28] 3417 2-8-9 0 .... RussellKennemore(3) 13 — 31
(R Hollinshead) *prom tl rdn and wknd jst over 1f out* **12/1**[3]

00 **7** 8 **Zaftil (IRE)**[29] 3358 2-8-9 0 .... KirstyMilczarek(3) 15 — 4
(H S Howe) *hld up in mid-div: sme hdwy over 2f out: wknd over 1f out* **66/1**

8 3 **Killyea** 2-8-9 0 .... KevinGhunowa(3) 5 — —
(R A Harris) *mid-div: rdn 4f out: bhd fnl 3f* **40/1**

0 **9** 1½ **Spiritual Bond**[29] 3358 2-8-12 0 .... TGMcLaughlin 7 — —
(R A Harris) *sn outpcd* **100/1**

000 **10** shd **Lucky Bid**[20] 3670 2-9-0 0 .... TolleyDean(3) 9 — —
(J M Bradley) *prom: rdn 3f out: sn wknd* **100/1**

0000 **11** 12 **Sharp Discovery**[5] 4203 2-8-12 0 .... CatherineGannon 11 — —
(J M Bradley) *outpcd: a in rr* **100/1**

68.70 secs (-2.50) **Going Correction** -0.45s/f (Firm) 2y crse rec — **11** Ran SP% **106.7**
Speed ratings (Par 92): **98,82,79,76,75 74,63,59,57,57 41**
toteswinger: 1&2 £2.80, 1&3 £1.30, 2&3 £6.20. CSF £8.06 TOTE £1.50: £1.02, £2.80, £1.30; EX 7.80 Trifecta £22.60 Pool: £93.86. 3.06 winning units..
Owner West Ilsley Racing **Bred** M Fahy **Trained** West Ilsley, Berks

FOCUS
A very modest maiden but won in as easy a fashion as any race will be this summer and the winner looks ready for a step up in class.

NOTEBOOK
Qalahari(IRE), who was nailed in the shadow of the post here on debut before again filling the runner-up berth behind a nice prospect when favourite at Newbury, blew these rivals away in effortless fashion. Albeit that they weren't much behind her, the daughter of Bahri simply could not have beaten them any more impressively and is probably worthy of a shot at a conditions race at the very least. (op 5-6 tchd Evens in places)
Handful Of Magic improved nicely for her debut effort on the Polytrack at Kempton where she was too green to show much of her ability. She will be of interest in nurseries after one more qualifying run. (op 20-1)

Five Star Junior(USA), a $140,000 purchase whose family have flourished mostly on dirt in the US, showed good pace and was not at all knocked about, indeed, his pilot must have only just made sufficient effort to avoid incurring the wrath of the Stewards. He is sure to improve for this. (op 13-2)
Goodenough Magic had shown absolutely nothing on her two previous starts so this effort was something of a revelation. She is now qualified for nurseries
Silky Way(GR), a debutante daughter of Harmonic Way, started slowly but made some progress towards the leaders of the peloton before getting tired close home. She should do better. (op 18-1)
Tillers Satisfied(IRE) is modest but certainly not short on speed and with her likely to get a lowly mark now that she is qualified for nurseries, could be of interest over one of the faster 5f courses. (op 11-1 tchd 14-1)
Killyea Official explanation: jockey said filly was unsuited by the firm ground
Spiritual Bond Official explanation: trainer said filly was unsuited by the firm ground

4322 CREST NICHOLSON (S) STKS — 1m 2f 46y
2:55 (2:56) (Class 6) 4-Y-0+ — **£1,942** (£578; £288; £144) **Stalls** Low

Form — RPR
2222 **1** **Hester Brook (IRE)**[10] 4023 4-8-12 50................(p) TGMcLaughlin 5 52
(J G M O'Shea) *s.i.s: sn hld up in tch: hdwy over 2f out: rdn to ld over 1f out: drvn out* **5/2**[1]
4 **2** *1 1/4* **Orange Orchid (IRE)**[6] 4142 9-8-12 0.................. EdwardCreighton 9 49
(James A Browne, Ire) *chsd ldrs: rdn over 3f out: styd on to take 2nd cl home* **8/1**
222 **3** *3/4* **Fairly Honest**[9] 4054 4-9-3 51.................................. SaleemGolam 11 53
(P W Hiatt) *chsd ldr: led 6f out: rdn and hdd wl over 1f out: styd on same pce ins fnl f* **9/2**[3]
3505 **4** *3/4* **Personify**[22] 3604 6-9-3 47..................................(p) RichardKingscote 3 51
(R A Harris) *hld up and bhd: plld to outside out over 2f out: rdn and hdwy wl over 1f out: styd on same pce fnl f* **4/1**[2]
003 **5** *3/4* **Danish Monarch**[15] 3844 7-9-3 52.................................. FergusSweeney 2 50
(David Pinder) *a.p: wnt 2nd over 3f out: rdn to ld wl over 1f out: sn hdd: no ex ins fnl f* **6/1**
0200 **6** *2 1/2* **Beckenham's Secret**[21] 3657 4-9-3 46.................... CatherineGannon 4 45
(A W Carroll) *hld up towards rr: hdwy on outside over 2f out: sn rdn: wknd ins fnl f* **12/1**
00-5 **7** *3 1/2* **Escobar (POL)**[143] 776 7-9-3 42.................................. FrankieMcDonald 6 38
(Mrs P Townsley) *hld up in mid-div: rdn over 2f out: no rspnse* **20/1**
3600 **8** *1/2* **Shaheer (IRE)**[105] 1282 6-9-0 44...............................(v) JerryO'Dwyer(3) 8 37
(J Gallagher) *s.i.s: sn prom: rdn over 3f out: wknd over 2f out* **14/1**
0/6- **9** *1* **Pips Assertive Way**[16] 5606 7-8-9 41.......................... EmmettStack(3) 12 30
(A W Carroll) *led: hdd 6f out: chsd ldr tl rdn over 3f out: wknd over 2f out* **33/1**
5046 **10** *15* **Far Seeking**[117] 1083 4-9-3 40.......................................(t) VinceSlattery 7 5
(A G Juckes) *t.k.h in mid-div: rdn over 3f out: sn struggling* **33/1**
00-0 **11** *1/2* **Come On Nellie (IRE)**[19] 3733 4-8-12 41.................... DavidKinsella 1 —
(J G M O'Shea) *hld up in rr: rdn 3f out: edgd lft 2f out: eased whn no ch over 1f out* **50/1**
000- **12** *4* **Pretty Posey**[367] 3794 4-8-7 33.................................. GabrielHannon(5) 13 —
(J G M O'Shea) *rel to r: a in rr* **40/1**

2m 8.53s (-2.47) **Going Correction** -0.30s/f (Firm) **12** Ran SP% **121.6**
Speed ratings (Par 101): **97,96,95,94,94 92,89,89,88,76 75,72**
toteswinger: 1&2 £5.10, 1&3 £3.70, 2&3 £6.00. CSF £22.86 TOTE £3.20: £1.40, £3.10, £2.00; EX 21.00 Trifecta £210.60 Pool: £310.34. 1.09 winning units..The winner was bought in for 6,000gns.
Owner W R Baddiley **Bred** Keen To Please Syndicate **Trained** Elton, Gloucs

FOCUS
This was a desperate affair, even by selling standards, and it saw the winner break her duck at the 22nd time of asking. She sets the level.
Personify Official explanation: jockey said gelding jumped awkwardly from stalls

4323 E B F / DAVID CHARLES 1968 NOVICE STKS — 5f 11y
3:30 (3:30) (Class 4) 2-Y-0 — **£4,857** (£1,445; £722) **Stalls** Centre

Form — RPR
01 **1** **Amour Propre**[28] 3417 2-9-2 0.................................. FergusSweeney 2 100+
(H Candy) *mde all: rdn ins fnl f: r.o wl* **5/2**[2]
145 **2** *3/4* **Lucky Leigh**[15] 3851 2-8-9 0.................................. EdwardCreighton 3 90+
(M R Channon) *sn chsng wnr: rdn 1f out: no imp* **2/5**[1]
6125 **3** *11* **Gone Hunting**[69] 2154 2-8-9 0.................................. JackDean(5) 1 64+
(W G M Turner) *sn last: pushed along over 3f out: rdn and struggling wl over 1f out: eased ins fnl f* **16/1**[3]

59.50 secs (-3.00) **Going Correction** -0.45s/f (Firm) 2y crse rec **3** Ran SP% **105.9**
Speed ratings (Par 96): **106,104,87**
CSF £4.01 TOTE £2.80; EX 3.60.
Owner Simon Broke And Partners **Bred** Mrs Sheila Oakes **Trained** Kingston Warren, Oxon

FOCUS
A juvenile course record time, faster than both the later all-aged claimer and the three-year-old handicap, marks this winner down as a smart colt who is well worth a crack at Pattern company.

NOTEBOOK
Amour Propre, who broke the course record at Warwick when making all there on his last start, 'did the clock' here as well, and took the scalp of a filly with proven Group-race form to boot. The son of Paris House is from a family that has included Cape Merino, Cape Of Good Hope, Artie, Kingscross, and Henry Candy's current smart three-year-old, Corrybrough. He looks a decent sprinting prospect. (op 3-1)
Lucky Leigh who has kept Group Two company (far from disgraced on either occasion) on both starts since a bright winning debut at Redcar, probably didn't quite run up to the best of that form here, but it is also quite likely that she ran into a much above-average colt. She is not to be given up on by any means, despite this short-priced defeat. (tchd 4-11 and 4-9)
Gone Hunting's run at Thirsk in April cannot be taken literally and he was outclassed here. (op 11-1)

4324 GEWEFA PRECISION TOOLHOLDING CLAIMING STKS — 5f 11y
4:05 (4:05) (Class 6) 3-Y-0+ — **£2,266** (£674; £337; £168) **Stalls** Centre

Form — RPR
3243 **1** **Desperate Dan**[7] 4102 7-9-7 70..................................(b) TGMcLaughlin 12 66
(A B Haynes) *mid-div: pushed along and hdwy over 2f out: rdn fnl f: r.o to ld towards fin* **11/4**[1]
0562 **2** *1* **Music Box Express**[27] 3446 4-8-6 52..................(t) MatthewDavies(7) 9 54
(George Baker) *w ldr: led 3f out: rdn over 1f out: hdd towards fin* **7/2**[2]
5235 **3** *1/2* **Night Prospector**[7] 4102 8-8-12 54..........................(p) HaddenFrost(5) 1 56
(R A Harris) *hld up in tch on ins: swtchd rt over 1f out: rdn and r.o same pce fnl f* **8/1**
0000 **4** *1* **Indian Lady (IRE)**[24] 3559 5-8-3 40..................(b) KirstyMilczarek(3) 14 42
(Mrs A L M King) *hld up in rr: hdwy on wd outside over 1f out: kpt on ins fnl f: nvr able to chal* **25/1**
0406 **5** *1 1/4* **Jal Music**[17] 3779 3-8-8 60.................................. KevinGhunowa(3) 5 46
(R A Harris) *chsd ldrs: rdn wl over 1f out: no ex ins fnl f* **14/1**
3002 **6** *3/4* **Towy Boy (IRE)**[7] 4102 3-9-5 60..................................(t) GregFairley 4 51
(I A Wood) *hld up in tch: no hdwy fnl 2f* **4/1**[3]
0300 **7** *1/2* **Makabul**[12] 3966 5-9-2 63.................................. JamesMillman(3) 13 46+
(B R Millman) *hld up and bhd: nt clr run on ins: swtchd rt jst over 1f out: kpt on ins fnl f: nvr nrr* **8/1**
0046 **8** *nse* **Spic 'n Span**[10] 4028 3-8-13 62..................(b) RichardKingscote 3 43+
(R A Harris) *hld up in mid-div: nt clr run on ins jst over 1f out: nvr trbld ldrs* **14/1**
400- **9** *1/2* **Heavens Walk**[330] 4944 7-9-13 65.................................. FergusSweeney 6 52
(P J Makin) *stdd s: hld up towards rr: hdwy over 1f out: no further prog* **10/1**
-000 **10** *2* **Mr Forthright**[19] 3724 4-9-4 45..................................(v[1]) TolleyDean(3) 15 38
(J M Bradley) *a bhd* **28/1**
0-30 **11** *3 1/2* **Rose De Rita**[24] 3565 3-8-1 33.................................. DominicFox(3) 8 13
(L P Grassick) *led 2f: rdn and wknd over 1f out* **100/1**
6000 **12** *1 1/2* **Vlasta Weiner**[30] 3346 8-8-12 33..................(b) RussellKennemore(3) 7 14
(J M Bradley) *chsd ldrs: rdn over 2f out: wknd wl over 1f out* **66/1**
6006 **13** *5* **Signor Panettiere**[17] 3783 7-9-7 45.................................. OscarUrbina 2 2
(A D Brown) *w ldrs tl rdn and wknd over 1f out: eased ins fnl f* **40/1**
0400 **14** *8* **Framington**[22] 3605 3-8-11 41.................................. EdwardCreighton 11 —
(M R Channon) *sn bhd: eased whn no ch fnl f* **40/1**

60.37 secs (-2.13) **Going Correction** -0.45s/f (Firm)
WFA 3 from 4yo+ 4lb **14** Ran SP% **128.2**
Speed ratings (Par 101): **99,97,96,95,93 91,91,90,90,86 81,78,70,58**
toteswinger: 1&2 £3.50, 1&3 £6.30, 2&3 £7.90. CSF £12.45 TOTE £3.70: £1.50, £2.00, £2.80; EX 17.40 Trifecta £84.40 Pool: £362.75. 3.18 winning units..Music Box Express was subject to a friendly claim of £4,000.
Owner Joe McCarthy **Bred** Sheikh Amin Dahlawi **Trained** Limpley Stoke, Bath

FOCUS
A motley mix of has-beens and never-will-bes contested this claimer and the form is best rated through the runner-up to his latest handicap mark.
Jal Music Official explanation: jockey said gelding hung both ways
Towy Boy(IRE) Official explanation: jockey said colt never travelled
Spic 'n Span Official explanation: jockey said gelding was denied a clear run

4325 JOE WYNNE MEMORIAL H'CAP — 5f 11y
4:40 (4:40) (Class 5) (0-70,70) 3-Y-0 — **£2,719** (£809; £404; £202) **Stalls** Centre

Form — RPR
3622 **1** **Miss Firefly**[1] 4308 3-8-9 61.................................. KirstyMilczarek(3) 3 63
(R J Hodges) *w ldrs: hrd rdn to ld wl ins fnl f: r.o* **5/2**[1]
0454 **2** *nk* **Barraland**[16] 3811 3-9-7 70.................................. EdwardCreighton 7 71
(M R Channon) *led: hrd rdn over 1f out: hdd wl ins fnl f: r.o* **6/1**
-100 **3** *1 3/4* **Joss Stick**[6] 4154 3-9-7 70..................................(p) FergusSweeney 1 65
(P J Makin) *hld up in mid-div on ins: kpt on u.p to take 3rd cl home* **12/1**
0013 **4** *nk* **Pennyspider (IRE)**[7] 4106 3-8-11 60.................................. TGMcLaughlin 2 54
(M S Saunders) *w ldr: hrd rdn wl over 1f out: no ex ins fnl f* **3/1**[2]
54 **5** *nk* **Our Acquaintance**[11] 4000 3-9-6 69..................(b) RichardSmith 8 61
(W R Muir) *hld up: hdwy over 2f out: ev ch over 1f out: rdn and one pce ins fnl f* **11/2**[3]
0514 **6** *nk* **Enodoc**[2] 4272 3-9-0 66..................................(t) JerryO'Dwyer(3) 6 57
(W R Muir) *hld up: rdn and no hdwy fnl 2f* **6/1**
3-10 **7** *1 1/4* **Lambrini Lace (IRE)**[20] 3668 3-8-11 63.................................. TolleyDean(3) 5 50
(Mrs L Williamson) *hld up: pushed along over 2f out: rdn over 1f out: nvr trbld ldrs* **14/1**
1560 **8** *2* **Swindon Town Flyer (IRE)**[23] 3575 3-9-4 67..........(b) DavidKinsella 4 47
(A B Haynes) *a bhd* **28/1**

60.22 secs (-2.28) **Going Correction** -0.45s/f (Firm) **8** Ran SP% **115.3**
Speed ratings (Par 100): **100,99,96,96,95 95,93,90**
toteswinger: 1&2 £3.70, 1&3 £7.10, 2&3 £9.30. CSF £18.20 CT £151.01 TOTE £3.20: £1.30, £2.10, £3.30; EX 18.60 Trifecta £428.30 Part won. Pool: £578.88. 0.99 winning units..
Owner D Charlesworth **Bred** Jeremy Gompertz **Trained** Charlton Mackrell, Somerset
■ Stewards' Enquiry : T G McLaughlin caution: used whip with excessive frequency.

FOCUS
The fourth sprint on a six-race card, and a moderate affair it was. They clocked what looked a decent time but on a day when course records were flying around it was nothing out of the ordinary. The winner is rated to his recent mark with the runner-up running his best race since March, but the proximity of the fifth and sixth raises doubts about the form.

4326 DIGIBET.CO.UK FILLIES' H'CAP — 1m 2f 46y
5:10 (5:11) (Class 5) (0-70,67) 3-Y-0 — **£2,719** (£809; £404; £202) **Stalls** Low

Form — RPR
1132 **1** **Amicable Terms**[8] 4086 3-9-2 62.................................. GregFairley 9 79+
(Rae Guest) *hld up in mid-div: hdwy 4f out: led on bit over 2f out: rdn over 1f out: eased cl home* **11/8**[1]
3463 **2** *2 1/4* **Solo River**[9] 4054 3-8-9 55.................................. RichardSmith 3 62
(P J Makin) *a.p: chal over 2f out: rdn over 1f out: one pce: jst hld on for 2nd* **10/1**
245 **3** *shd* **Beautiful Lady (IRE)**[22] 3611 3-9-4 67.................................. JerryO'Dwyer(3) 4 74
(P F I Cole) *hld up in rr: rdn and hdwy over 2f out: kpt on ins fnl f: jst failed to take 2nd* **17/2**
5655 **4** *3* **Orbital Orchid**[9] 4054 3-8-9 55..................................(v) FergusSweeney 7 56
(W S Kittow) *hld up towards rr: c wd st: rdn wl over 2f out: hdwy over 1f out: no further prog fnl f* **7/1**[3]
6-50 **5** *3 1/2* **Ever Dreaming (USA)**[15] 3841 3-9-1 61.................................. EdwardCreighton 10 55
(A M Balding) *hld up towards rr: rdn and hdwy over 2f out: wknd ins fnl f* **6/1**[2]
0-00 **6** *5* **Xaravella (IRE)**[44] 2922 3-8-4 50.................................. DavidKinsella 5 34
(J G M O'Shea) *sn led: hdd over 2f out: sn rdn: wknd wl over 1f out* **40/1**
-011 **7** *1 1/4* **Ambrose Princess (IRE)**[6] 4165 3-8-11 60 6ex.... KevinGhunowa(3) 11 41+
(R A Harris) *prom: hmpd and lost pl over 8f out: rdn 3f out: no ch whn edgd lft jst over 1f out* **9/1**
0-60 **8** *8* **Imperial Decree**[60] 2429 3-9-4 64.................................. TGMcLaughlin 2 29
(John Berry) *hld up towards rr: pushed along 3f out: sn struggling* **14/1**
-006 **9** *4 1/2* **Poppy Dean (IRE)**[18] 3763 3-8-1 52 ow2.................................. JackDean(5) 12 8
(J G Portman) *sn w ldrs: ev ch over 2f out: sn rdn and wknd* **20/1**
0225 **10** *8* **Hurstpierpoint (IRE)**[48] 2801 3-8-6 55.................................. KirstyMilczarek(3) 8 —
(M G Rimell) *led early: hld up in mid-div: pushed along over 2f out: sn lost pl* **16/1**
-000 **11** *41* **Medici Gold**[9] 4054 3-8-4 50.................................. CatherineGannon 1 —
(B G Powell) *s.i.s: sn rcvrd: prom tl wknd 4f out: eased whn no ch fnl 2f* **66/1**

00-0 **12** 1 3/4 **Les Allues (IRE)**[29] 3359 3-7-9 48 oh3 AmyBaker(7) 6 —
(H S Howe) *t.k.h: prom: sddle slipped and lost pl over 5f out: rn wd 3f out* **100/1**

2m 7.54s (-3.46) **Going Correction** -0.30s/f (Firm) 12 Ran SP% **120.7**
Speed ratings (Par 97): **101,99,99,96,93 89,88,82,78,72 39,38**
toteswinger: 1&2 £4.10, 1&3 £6.00, 2&3 £8.50. CSF £16.35 CT £93.08 TOTE £2.10: £1.10, £2.90, £3.00; EX 16.10 Trifecta £69.20 Pool: £528.48. 5.65 winning units. Place 6: £22.63, Place 5: £23.78..
Owner Sentinel Bloodstock **Bred** Brook Stud Bloodstock Ltd **Trained** Newmarket, Suffolk

FOCUS
More modest fare, but another impressive winner on the card who was value for double the official margin. They finished well strung out and the form looks solid rated around those in the frame behind the winner.
Ambrose Princess(IRE) Official explanation: jockey said filly hampered after the start
Les Allues(IRE) Official explanation: jockey said saddle slipped
T/Plt: £26.60 to a £1 stake. Pool: £43,495.24. 1,192.29 winning tickets. T/Qpdt: £17.10 to a £1 stake. Pool: £1,906.10. 82.30 winning tickets. KH

4107 DONCASTER (L-H)
Thursday, July 24

OFFICIAL GOING: Good to firm
Rail realignment added 13yards to advertised distances on round course.
Wind: Blustery, half-across Weather: Fine and dry

4327 DONNY MOD GODS SEPTEMBER 2008 H'CAP 6f
6:20 (6:21) (Class 5) (0-70,67) 4-Y-0+ **£3,412** (£1,007; £504) **Stalls** High

Form RPR
2646 **1** **Steel Blue**[11] 3998 8-9-0 60 (p) PaulMulrennan 15 74
(R M Whitaker) *trckd ldrs: hdwy 2f out: rdn to ld appr fnl f: styd on strly* **9/2**[2]
0131 **2** 2 1/4 **No Grouse**[10] 4018 8-9-7 67 6ex DavidAllan 14 73
(E J Alston) *chsd ldrs: hdwy 2f out: rdn over 1f out: styd on ins fnl f: nrst fin* **8/1**
0416 **3** 3/4 **Danzili Bay**[35] 3169 6-8-11 64 StacyRenwick(7) 8 68
(A W Carroll) *cl up on outer: effrt 2f out: sn rdn and ev ch tl kpt on same pce ent fnl f* **14/1**
6050 **4** 3/4 **Grimes Faith**[9] 4047 5-9-5 65 (b) DarryllHolland 11 67
(K A Ryan) *cl up: rdn 2f out: led briefly over 1f out: sn hdd & wknd ins fnl f* **33/1**
0461 **5** nk **Royal Challenge**[6] 4174 7-9-4 67 6ex NeilBrown(3) 2 68
(I W McInnes) *in midfield: hdwy 2f out: sn rdn and kpt on ins fnl f: nrst fin* **7/1**[3]
3626 **6** 1 1/4 **Wiltshire (IRE)**[21] 3638 6-8-9 55 (v) MickyFenton 10 52
(P T Midgley) *dwlt: hdwy over 2f out: sn rdn and kpt on appr fnl f: nt rch ldrs* **18/1**
0034 **7** 3/4 **Greek Secret**[21] 3638 5-8-6 52 AndrewElliott 12 46
(J O'Reilly) *chsd ldrs: rdn along and outpcd over 2f out: kpt on u.p ins fnl f* **16/1**
4003 **8** nk **Woqoodd**[7] 4118 4-8-13 59 (b[1]) PaulHanagan 1 52
(R A Fahey) *in midfield: effrt on outer wl over 2f out: sn rdn and no imp* **12/1**
2000 **9** nse **Kunte Kinteh**[22] 3599 4-9-0 60 AdrianTNicholls 4 53
(D Nicholls) *s.i.s: a towards rr* **16/1**
/003 **10** 3/4 **Namu**[9] 4064 5-8-9 55 KerrinMcEvoy 7 46
(Miss T Spearing) *chsd ldrs: rdn along wl over 2f out and grad wknd* **16/1**
5202 **11** 1/2 **Yorkshire Blue**[3] 4239 9-9-7 67 DanielTudhope 9 56
(J S Goldie) *a in rr* **10/3**[1]
0540 **12** 2 1/4 **Brigadore**[15] 3834 9-8-8 54 JoeFanning 5 36
(J G Given) *s.i.s: a in rr* **20/1**
0010 **13** shd **Avoncreek**[21] 3638 4-8-4 57 BillyCray(7) 6 39
(B P J Baugh) *a in rr* **40/1**
5041 **14** nk **Gleaming Spirit (IRE)**[9] 4064 4-9-6 66 6ex (v) DarrenWilliams 13 47
(A P Jarvis) *led: rdn 2f out: drvn and hdd over 1f out: wknd qckly* **12/1**

1m 10.23s (-3.37) **Going Correction** -0.45s/f (Firm) 14 Ran SP% **120.0**
Speed ratings (Par 103): **104,101,100,99,98 96,95,95,95,94 93,90,90,90**
toteswinger: 1&2 £10.00, 1&3 £43.20, 2&3 £43.20. CSF £39.52 CT £488.01 TOTE £5.80: £2.50, £3.50, £4.30; EX 55.20.
Owner Country Lane Partnership **Bred** R T And Mrs Watson **Trained** Scarcroft, W Yorks
■ Stewards' Enquiry : Micky Fenton caution: careless riding

FOCUS
A modest sprint in which a high draw proved an advantage. The form is rated through the winner.
Avoncreek Official explanation: jockey said gelding hung left

4328 MOSSPM.CO.UK MAIDEN AUCTION FILLIES' STKS 7f
6:50 (6:50) (Class 4) 2-Y-0 **£3,885** (£1,156; £577; £288) **Stalls** High

Form RPR
30 **1** **Daheeya**[54] 2618 2-8-4 0 TPO'Shea 7 75+
(M R Channon) *chsd ldr: lft in ld 1/2-way: rdn 2f out: styd on strly appr fnl f* **7/1**
04 **2** 3 **Our Day Will Come**[7] 4109 2-8-8 0 PatDobbs 6 71
(R Hannon) *trckd ldrs: gd hdwy to chse wnr 2f out: swtchd lft and rdn over 1f out: no imp ins fnl f* **5/2**[1]
4 **3** 2 **Surprise Party**[12] 3959 2-8-11 0 TomEaves 3 69
(C F Wall) *trckd ldrs: hdwy over 2f out: rdn over 1f out: kpt on same pce* **7/1**
6 **4** 2 **When Doves Cry**[20] 3669 2-8-7 0 ow1 MichaelHills 2 60+
(B W Hills) *in tch on outer tl lost pl and towards rr after 2f: pushed along and hdwy 3f out: sn rdn and kpt on appr fnl f: nvr nr ldrs* **3/1**[2]
0245 **5** 2 1/4 **Digit**[13] 3908 2-8-4 0 RoystonFfrench 9 51
(B Smart) *led tl hung bdly lft and hdd 1/2-way: hung rt across trck to far rail and grad wknd fnl 2f* **13/2**[3]
0 **6** 1/2 **Protiva**[22] 3610 2-8-7 0 NeilPollard 4 53
(A P Jarvis) *towards rr: pushed along over 2f out: sn rdn and kpt on ins fnl f: nvr a factor* **50/1**
00 **7** 1/2 **Bitza Baileys (IRE)**[42] 2979 2-8-7 0 JoeFanning 5 52
(J G Given) *chsd ldrs: rdn along over 2f out: sn wknd* **50/1**
8 3/4 **Punch Drunk** 2-8-6 0 PaulHanagan 8 49
(J G Given) *s.i.s and bhd: swtchd lft and rdn whn hung bdly lft over 2f out:* **33/1**
0 **9** 2 **Lovely Thought**[13] 3923 2-8-12 0 KerrinMcEvoy 1 50
(W J Haggas) *a towards rr* **7/1**
10 10 **High Society Girl (IRE)** 2-8-8 0 DavidAllan 10 21
(T D Easterby) *a towards rr* **33/1**
11 20 **Staceys Girl** 2-8-4 0 DO'Donohoe 11 —
(T P Tate) *sn outpcd and a bhd* **28/1**

1m 24.5s (-1.80) **Going Correction** -0.45s/f (Firm) 11 Ran SP% **117.7**
Speed ratings (Par 93): **92,88,86,84,81 80,80,79,77,65 42**
toteswinger: 1&2 £10.00, 1&3 £13.10, 2&3 £3.20. CSF £23.97 TOTE £8.70: £2.20, £1.30, £2.00; EX 30.40.
Owner Jaber Abdullah **Bred** Gainsborough Stud Management Ltd **Trained** West Ilsley, Berks

FOCUS
The winner was back to form in this ordinary maiden with the runner-up fitting in too.

NOTEBOOK
Daheeya, upped in trip, put a poor run on soft ground behind her and confirmed her debut promise. Showing just about in front at halfway as the leader began to veer across the course, she stayed on well against the stands' rail and nothing was able to get in a challenge. (op 12-1 tchd 6-1)
Our Day Will Come, who was dropped in leaving the stalls, went after the winner with two to run but was always being held. Nurseries are another option now and her in-form yard should soon find the right opportunity for her. (op 10-3 tchd 9-4)
Surprise Party shaped quite well on her debut over 6f on easy ground and improved for the experience, but after racing somewhat keenly early on she could never quite get to the leaders. (op 13-2 tchd 6-1 and 15-2)
When Doves Cry, upped in trip for this second start, was doing her best work at the finish and might require a bit further still. (op 5-2)
Digit has some ability, but has also hung to her left on four of her five starts. On this occasion, after making the running she went all the way across the course to end up racing alone next to the far rail. A little race, perhaps a seller over 6f, could come her way if she gets a left-hand rail to race against. Official explanation: jockey said filly hung left (op 8-1)
Protiva, on her turf debut, was slow to break. She made a bit of late progress and there could be better to come as she picks up experience. (op 28-1)
Punch Drunk Official explanation: jockey said filly hung left throughout

4329 SKY BET SUPPORTING YORKSHIRE RACING FESTIVAL H'CAP 6f
7:25 (7:25) (Class 4) (0-80,78) 3-Y-0 **£4,857** (£1,445; £722; £360) **Stalls** High

Form RPR
2020 **1** **Leading Edge (IRE)**[21] 3636 3-9-3 74 DarrylHolland 9 76
(M R Channon) *trckd ldng pair: swtchd lft and rdn wl over 1f out: qcknd to ld appr fnl f: drvn out* **5/1**[3]
0404 **2** 1/2 **Legendary Guest**[22] 3601 3-8-8 65 (p) TonyHamilton 3 65+
(D W Barker) *t.k.h: hld up in rr: swtchd rt and hdwy on inner 1/2f out: sn rdn and ev ch ent fnl f: kpt on* **14/1**
0220 **3** 1 **Dancing Maite**[7] 4121 3-8-10 67 DeanMcKeown 8 64+
(S R Bowring) *squeezed out s: hdwy 1/2-way: effrt and nt clr run 2f out: swtchd rt and rdn over 1f out: kpt on u.p ins fnl f* **18/1**
5411 **4** 1/2 **Novellen Lad (IRE)**[42] 2967 3-9-7 78 DavidAllan 7 74+
(E J Alston) *hld up: pushed along 1/2-way: rdn and nt clr run over 2f out: drvn to chse ldrs ent fnl f: one pce* **6/4**[1]
1146 **5** 1 1/4 **Dhhamaan (IRE)**[91] 1576 3-9-4 78 (b) MichaelJStainton(3) 5 70
(Mrs R A Carr) *set stdy pce: qcknd 3f out: rdn and edgd lft wl over 1f out: hdd appr fnl f and wknd* **28/1**
0-01 **6** 2 1/4 **Another Decree**[62] 2380 3-9-1 72 TomEaves 6 56
(M Dods) *trckd ldrs: effrt over 2f out: sn rdn and wknd appr fnl f* **10/1**
-000 **7** 1 **Brother Barry (USA)**[33] 3271 3-8-10 67 TPO'Shea 4 48
(P T Midgley) *chsd ldr: rdn along over 2f out: wknd over 1f out* **33/1**
0124 **8** 1/2 **Royal Acclamation (IRE)**[15] 3831 3-8-10 67 SilvestreDeSousa 1 47
(G A Harker) *hld up: a in rr* **11/1**
5413 **9** nk **Averoo**[20] 3678 3-8-10 67 (p) KerrinMcEvoy 2 46
(M D Squance) *in tch: rdn along 1/2-way: drvn 2f out and sn btn* **3/1**[2]

1m 11.56s (-2.04) **Going Correction** -0.45s/f (Firm) 9 Ran SP% **117.4**
Speed ratings (Par 102): **95,94,93,92,90 87,86,85,85**
toteswinger: 1&2 £17.50, 1&3 £22.60, 2&3 £46.80. CSF £72.76 CT £1172.73 TOTE £5.60: £1.70, £3.30, £4.40; EX 60.10.
Owner David Heath **Bred** Rathasker Stud **Trained** West Ilsley, Berks

FOCUS
The pace was only steady in this fair handicap and the form is messy.

4330 CROWNHOTEL-BAWTRY.COM CONDITIONS STKS 1m (S)
7:55 (7:56) (Class 3) 4-Y-0+ **£7,771** (£2,312; £1,155; £577) **Stalls** High

Form RPR
0300 **1** **Dream Lodge (IRE)**[36] 3122 4-8-9 92 (v) J-PGuillambert 4 103
(J G Given) *wnt bdly lft and reminders s: cl up tl led after 2f: hanging lft and rdn over 2f out: hrd drvn wl over 1f out: styd on strly* **20/1**
12-3 **2** 6 **Army Of Angels (IRE)**[12] 3946 6-8-9 107 (t) KerrinMcEvoy 1 89
(Saeed Bin Suroor) *hld up: hdwy 3f out and sn pushed along rdn to chse wnr 2f out: drvn and no imp appr fnl f* **5/6**[1]
0004 **3** 4 1/2 **Dubai's Touch**[19] 3740 4-8-12 100 RoystonFfrench 3 82
(M Johnston) *hmpd s: sn trcking ldng pair: rdn along over 2f out: sn drvn and one pce* **7/4**[2]
0-10 **4** 6 **Jack Junior (USA)**[19] 3740 4-8-12 98 (b[1]) JoeFanning 5 68
(B J Meehan) *led 2f: chsd wnr tl rdn along over 2f out and sn wknd* **7/1**[3]

1m 35.52s (-3.78) **Going Correction** -0.45s/f (Firm) course record 4 Ran SP% **108.2**
Speed ratings (Par 107): **100,94,89,83**
CSF £38.23 TOTE £14.20; EX 39.10.
Owner The G-Guck Group **Bred** C H Wacker Iii **Trained** Willoughton, Lincs

FOCUS
Dream Lodge made most to spring a surprise in this decent event but with the extended distances the form looks dubious.

NOTEBOOK
Dream Lodge(IRE), who was visored for only the second time, needed a couple of cracks after veering left leaving the stalls but soon settled down in the lead. Dictating the pace under a good ride, he gradually wound it up despite hanging and not helping Guillambert, and he was clear entering the final furlong with the race as good as won. (op 18-1 tchd 16-1)
Army Of Angels(IRE), back up to a mile for this second start of the campaign, was meeting the winner on 15lb better terms than in a handicap. Held up last of the four, he went after the leader a quarter of a mile out but was never able to reduce his advantage to any significant degree. This was disappointing. (op Evens tchd 4-5)
Dubai's Touch, who was inconvenienced by the winner when exiting the stalls, was not really suited by the way the race was run but still should have performed better than he did. (op 13-8 tchd 15-8)
Jack Junior(USA) ran a disappointing race in the first-time blinkers and was the first beaten. (op 13-2)

4331 HENDERSON GARAGE DOOR SUPERCENTRE H'CAP 1m 4f
8:30 (8:30) (Class 5) (0-75,70) 3-Y-0+ **£3,238** (£963; £481; £240) **Stalls** Low

Form RPR
0-01 **1** **Lilac Moon (GER)**[23] 3588 4-9-5 61 RichardKingscote 8 67
(N J Vaughan) *trckd ldr: hdwy to ld over 3f out: rdn along and hdd jst over 1f out: drvn to ld again ins fnl f: kpt on* **11/2**[3]

650 **2** *nk* **Monfils Monfils (USA)**[3] 4244 6-9-7 **70** FrederikTylicki(7) 5 76
(A J McCabe) *trckd ldrs: pushed along and sltly outpcd 3f out: swtchd lft and rdn 2f out: styd on ins fnl f* **18/1**

-303 **3** *hd* **Dar Es Salaam**[10] 4015 4-9-12 **68** DanielTudhope 6 74
(J S Goldie) *hld up in rr: hdwy on wd outside over 2f out: rdn wl over 1f out: drvn and styd on ins fnl f* **7/2**[2]

3114 **4** *1* **Eijaaz (IRE)**[3] 4244 7-9-4 **60** DO'Donohoe 2 64
(G A Harker) *hld up in rr: gd hdwy on inner 3f out: rdn to ld briefly over 1f out: drvn and hdd ins fnl f: wknd towards fin* **11/2**[3]

6515 **5** *3 1/4* **Fenners (USA)**[35] 3176 5-9-6 **62** DaleGibson 7 61
(M W Easterby) *hld up: hdwy over 3f out and sn rdn along: kpt on u.p fnl 2f* **7/1**

0006 **6** *3 1/4* **Shanafarahan (IRE)**[17] 3793 3-8-9 **63** ow3 MickyFenton 3 57
(T P Tate) *trckd ldng pair: effrt and cl up 4f out: rdn along over 3f out: wknd over 2f out* **18/1**

2226 **7** *15* **War Of The Roses (IRE)**[84] 1744 5-9-10 **66** J-PGuillambert 1 54+
(R Brotherton) *trckd ldrs: effrt over 3f out: rdn over 2f out: sn drvn and wknd over 1f out* **8/1**

-612 **8** *3 1/2* **Smarterthanuthink (USA)**[35] 3174 3-9-2 **70** (p) PaulHanagan 4 34
(R A Fahey) *led: rdn along and hdd over 3f out: drvn over 2f out and sn wknd* **9/4**[1]

2m 32.99s (-2.11) **Going Correction** -0.05s/f (Good)
WFA 3 from 4yo+ 12lb 8 Ran SP% **117.9**
Speed ratings (Par 103): **105,104,104,104,101 99,89,87**
toteswinger: 1&2 £23.20, 1&3 £9.40, 2&3 £13.60. CSF £97.04 CT £398.01 TOTE £6.00: £1.50, £4.20, £2.00; EX 530.70.
Owner A Black **Bred** Graf Und Grafin Von Stauffenberg **Trained** Hampton, Cheshire
FOCUS
A modest handicap in which the form looks messy and pretty limited.
War Of The Roses(IRE) Official explanation: jockey said gelding lost its action
Smarterthanuthink(USA) Official explanation: trainer's rep said colt lost a front shoe

4332 URBAN-I FIRST TIME BUYER H'CAP 1m 2f 60y
9:00 (9:00) (Class 5) (0-70,70) 3-Y-O **£3,238** (£963; £481; £240) **Stalls** Low

Form RPR
-230 **1** **Sinbad The Sailor**[29] 3384 3-9-6 **69** KerrinMcEvoy 6 75
(J W Hills) *in midfield: hdwy to trck ldrs over 4f out: effrt to chal wl over 1f out: rdn to ld ent fnl f: kpt on wl* **7/2**[2]

035 **2** *1/2* **Offshore Anna (IRE)**[17] 3796 3-9-1 **64** PaulHanagan 7 69+
(J J Quinn) *dwlt and towards rr: hdwy on inner 3f out: rdn along over 2f out: swtchd lft over 1f out: styd on strly ins fnl f* **12/1**

3053 **3** *1* **Hawk House**[14] 3886 3-9-0 **63** MichaelHills 10 66
(B W Hills) *trckd ldrs: hdwy 4f out: chal 2f out: sn rdn and ev ch tl drvn and nt qckn ins fnl f* **3/1**[1]

-001 **4** *1/2* **Stage Acclaim (IRE)**[15] 3845 3-9-4 **70** (p) JamesMillman(3) 9 72
(B R Millman) *led: rdn along over 2f out: drvn over 1f out: hdd ent fnl f and one pce towards fin* **7/1**

0304 **5** *1 1/4* **Defies Logic**[9] 4044 3-8-5 **54** JoeFanning 4 54+
(J G Given) *prom on inner: effrt 3f out: rdn along 2f out: swtchd rt and drvn ent fnl f: sn edgd lft and one pce* **16/1**

0342 **6** *1 1/4* **Grey Command (USA)**[7] 4112 3-9-2 **68** MarkLawson(3) 3 65+
(M Brittain) *hld up: hdwy over 2f out: rdn wl over 1f out: styng on whn n.m.r wl ins fnl f* **7/1**

-006 **7** *3 1/4* **Honeycott (IRE)**[21] 3644 3-8-2 **51** oh5 (v) PaulFessey 8 42
(J D Bethell) *towards rr tl styd on fnl 2f: n.d* **40/1**

1-00 **8** *2 1/2* **Loyal Knight (IRE)**[19] 3745 3-9-7 **70** RichardKingscote 5 56
(S Kirk) *trckd ldrs: hdwy 4f out: rdn along over 2f out and grad wknd* **10/1**

0012 **9** *2 1/4* **Hasty Lady**[7] 4115 3-8-13 **62** (p) DarryllHolland 1 43
(K A Ryan) *in tch on inner: effrt and hdwy over 3f out: rdn along over 2f out and sn btn* **6/1**[3]

0402 **10** *3 3/4* **Mouse White**[19] 3730 3-8-6 **55** FrankieMcDonald 2 29
(H Candy) *chsd ldrs: rdn along 4f out and sn wknd* **20/1**

1260 **11** *1 3/4* **Bury Treasure (IRE)**[9] 4061 3-9-4 **67** MickyFenton 12 37
(Miss Gay Kelleway) *a towards rr* **20/1**

5220 **12** *1 1/2* **John Potts**[124] 976 3-8-11 **60** DanielTudhope 11 27
(B P J Baugh) *t.k.h in midfield: hdwy on outer to chse ldrs over 3f out: sn rdn and wknd 2f out* **33/1**

2m 11.13s (-0.07) **Going Correction** -0.05s/f (Good) 12 Ran SP% **124.1**
Speed ratings (Par 100): **98,97,96,96,95 94,91,89,88,85 83,82**
toteswinger: 1&2 £13.30, 1&3 £3.00, 2&3 £4.70. CSF £45.31 CT £145.71 TOTE £5.30: £1.90, £4.30, £1.40; EX 58.20 Place 6: £2,687.71, Place 5: £925.86..
Owner Wauchope Cottam Sir S Dunning Mrs Caroe **Bred** Sir Eric Parker **Trained** Upper Lambourn, Berks
FOCUS
This ordinary handicap was run at a moderate pace. The form is rated around the winner and third.
Grey Command(USA) Official explanation: jockey said colt was unsuited by the good to firm ground
Bury Treasure(IRE) Official explanation: jockey said gelding hung left
T/Plt: £1,210.80 to a £1 stake. Pool: £53,742.58. 32.40 winning tickets. T/Qpdt: £275.50 to a £1 stake. Pool: £3,872.02. 10.40 winning tickets. JR

3869 FOLKESTONE (R-H)
Thursday, July 24

OFFICIAL GOING: Good to firm
Wind: Gentle, across Weather: warm and sunny

4333 BETTER APPRENTICE H'CAP 6f
6:00 (6:18) (Class 5) (0-70,68) 3-Y-O **£2,590** (£770; £385; £192) **Stalls** Low

Form RPR
5213 **1** **Arabian Art (USA)**[17] 3782 3-9-10 **68** DNolan 1 83
(H R A Cecil) *mde all: drew clr 1/2-way: v easily* **4/7**[1]

4600 **2** *15* **Dhahab (USA)**[20] 3665 3-8-8 **57** ow5 KylieManser(5) 3 24
(C E Brittain) *sn detached and outpcd in last: plugged on to go poor 2nd ins fnl f* **25/1**

0500 **3** *1 1/2* **Hobson**[6] 4154 3-9-2 **67** (b) DanielBlackett(7) 6 29
(Eve Johnson Houghton) *chsd wnr: outpcd over 2f out: no ch w wnr last 2f: lost 2nd ins fnl f* **12/1**

0550 **4** *2 3/4* **Nawaaff**[12] 3960 3-8-12 **63** RosieJessop(7) 2 16
(M R Channon) *awkward s: sn chsng ldrs: outpcd over 2f out: no ch w wnr last 2f* **3/1**[2]

66-0 **5** *5* **Celtic Charlie (FR)**[55] 2563 3-9-4 **62** PatrickHills 4 —
(P M Phelan) *chsd ldrs: rdn wl over 2f out: sn struggling* **13/2**[3]

1m 12.05s (-0.65) **Going Correction** 0.0s/f (Good) 5 Ran SP% **113.5**
Speed ratings (Par 100): **104,84,82,78,71**
toteswinger: 1&2 £10.90. CSF £17.18 TOTE £1.70: £1.20, £7.20; EX 16.10.
Owner Malih L Al Basti **Bred** Kidder, Cole & Robenalt **Trained** Newmarket, Suffolk
FOCUS
A modest handicap that looked a straightforward opportunity for Arabian Art and she could not have won easier, although the question is what did she beat.

4334 BETTERCASINO H'CAP 1m 4f
6:30 (6:45) (Class 6) (0-65,65) 3-Y-O **£2,047** (£604; £302) **Stalls** Low

Form RPR
1111 **1** **Aleatricis**[2] 4281 3-8-13 **64** 12ex RosieJessop(7) 2 75+
(Sir Mark Prescott) *dwlt: led after 1f: mde rest: clr w runner up over 2f out: rdn and a holding rival fr over 1f out* **4/6**[1]

0-03 **2** *1 1/4* **Pinnacle Point**[17] 3781 3-8-11 **55** StephenCarson 6 64
(G L Moore) *led for 1f: chsd wnr after: only danger to wnr over 2f out: rdn and hanging rt fr 2f out: one pce* **14/1**

-043 **3** *5* **All Lit Up**[24] 3566 3-8-7 **51** (b[1]) SimonWhitworth 10 52
(A King) *hld up in midfield: hmpd bnd after 3f: hdwy to chse ldng pair over 3f out: no imp after* **8/1**[3]

-633 **4** *8* **King Of Pentacles**[63] 2340 3-9-4 **62** (t) DNolan 5 50
(H Morrison) *chsd ldrs: rdn and outpcd 3f out: wl btn last 2f* **6/1**[2]

-000 **5** *1 3/4* **Empire Seeker (USA)**[34] 3206 3-8-13 **60** PatrickHills(3) 7 45
(J W Hills) *chsd ldrs: edgd rt bnd after 3f: rdn and outpcd 3f out: wl btn last 2f* **18/1**

00-0 **6** *1/2* **Miss Cruisecontrol**[15] 3843 3-7-10 **47** ow1 DanielBlackett(7) 8 32
(J R Best) *awkward and v.s.a: hld up towards rr: rdn over 3f out: sn wknd: no ch last 2f* **12/1**

4632 **7** *3 1/4* **Loveofmylife**[23] 3574 3-8-5 **56** ow2 KylieManser(7) 9 35
(R M Beckett) *hld up in midfield tl lost pl and bhd 7f out: wl bhd last 3f* **8/1**[3]

0000 **8** *11* **House Of Tudor**[8] 4086 3-8-13 **57** (p) RichardThomas 13 19
(David Pinder) *hld up in rr: rdn 5f out: wl bhd last 3f: t.o* **25/1**

000- **9** *1/2* **High Dee Jay (IRE)**[287] 6127 3-8-4 **55** ow3 PNolan(7) 11 16
(A King) *hld up bhd on outer: lost tch over 3f out: t.o* **16/1**

2m 37.77s (-3.13) **Going Correction** -0.275s/f (Firm) 9 Ran SP% **125.8**
Speed ratings (Par 98): **99,98,94,89,88 88,85,78,78**
toteswinger: 1&2 £4.60, 1&3 £6.10, 2&3 £27.30. CSF £14.51 CT £55.36 TOTE £1.90: £1.20, £3.10, £2.70; EX 18.40.
Owner The Green Door Partnership **Bred** Miss K Rausing **Trained** Newmarket, Suffolk
FOCUS
A moderate handicap that saw Aleatricis complete the five-timer with the third just a little off some pretty sound recent form.

4335 JEWSON H'CAP 1m 1f 149y
7:05 (7:20) (Class 4) (0-85,84) 3-Y-O **£4,857** (£1,445; £722; £360) **Stalls** Centre

Form RPR
6-61 **1** **Vineyard**[52] 2678 3-8-8 **71** LiamJones 5 77
(W J Haggas) *led for 1f: chsd ldr after: rdn to ld 2f out: styd on wl fnl f* **7/4**[2]

1046 **2** *1 3/4* **Master Spy**[19] 3745 3-9-7 **84** (b) RobertHavlin 1 86
(J H M Gosden) *bustled up to ld after 1f: rdn over 2f out: hdd 2f out: kpt on same pce u.p fnl f* **6/1**

0154 **3** *1/2* **Mcconnell (USA)**[7] 4130 3-9-2 **79** GeorgeBaker 4 80
(G L Moore) *hld up in bhd ldng pair: rdn and effrt 2f out: sn edging rt and nt qckn: kpt on same pce* **5/4**[1]

34 **4** *2 1/4* **Mission Control (IRE)**[20] 3676 3-8-5 **68** SaleemGolam 2 64
(J R Boyle) *hld up in tch in last: rdn and outpcd 3f out: n.d after* **5/1**[3]

2m 2.05s (-2.85) **Going Correction** -0.275s/f (Firm) 4 Ran SP% **111.8**
Speed ratings (Par 102): **100,98,98,96**
CSF £11.43 TOTE £2.30; EX 9.60.
Owner Highclere Thoroughbred Racing (VCI) **Bred** Petra Bloodstock Agency **Trained** Newmarket, Suffolk
FOCUS
A competitive heat, despite the small field, but the pace was just steady and Vineyard was always well placed to strike. The form looks ordinary.

4336 BETTERPOKER (S) STKS 6f
7:35 (7:51) (Class 6) 3-Y-O+ **£2,047** (£604; £302) **Stalls** Low

Form RPR
6243 **1** **High Reach**[7] 4118 8-9-6 56 RobertHavlin 1 62
(J G M O'Shea) *mde all on stands' rail: rdn and clr ent fnl f: styd on wl* **7/4**[1]

1501 **2** *1 1/4* **Mannello**[9] 4052 5-9-1 54 (b) RichardThomas 3 53
(Jim Best) *chsd ldrs: rdn to chse wnr wl over 1f out: kpt on fnl f but nvr able to chal* **2/1**[2]

0605 **3** *2 3/4* **Penrice Castle**[10] 4028 3-8-3 57 ow2 PatrickHills(3) 5 39
(R Hannon) *wnt rt s: hld up in tch: swtchd rt and rdn 2f out: chsd ldng pair ent fnl f: wknd last 100yds* **8/1**

6605 **4** *nk* **Heron (IRE)**[14] 3872 3-8-7 45 ow3 JackMitchell(5) 2 44
(M R Hoad) *s.i.s: hld up in tch: rdn and nt qckn jst over 2f out: kpt on again last 100yds: nvr nr wnr* **12/1**

000- **5** *2 1/2* **Romany Nights (IRE)**[232] 7033 8-8-7 64 (bt) KylieManser(7) 6 34
(Miss Gay Kelleway) *awkward leaving stalls and v.s.a: a bhd: sme modest late hdwy* **15/2**[3]

5035 **6** *1 1/4* **Midnite Blews (IRE)**[18] 3765 3-8-8 58 PNolan(7) 4 35
(A B Haynes) *wnt rt s: chsd wnr: rdn over 3f out: lost 2nd wl over 1f out: wknd qckly* **8/1**

0-00 **7** *hd* **Lady Maya**[39] 3065 3-8-4 48 (v) AlanDaly 7 24
(Dr J R J Naylor) *a bhd: rdn and struggling 1/2-way: n.d after* **33/1**

1m 12.46s (-0.24) **Going Correction** 0.0s/f (Good)
WFA 3 from 5yo+ 5lb 7 Ran SP% **114.3**
Speed ratings (Par 101): **101,99,95,95,91 90,90**
toteswinger: 1&2 £1.60, 1&3 £18.90, 2&3 £3.50. CSF £5.49 TOTE £3.00: £2.60, £1.80; EX 6.70.There was no bid for the winner.
Owner W R Baddiley **Bred** S R Hope **Trained** Elton, Gloucs
FOCUS
Low-grade stuff and High Reach dominated against the stands' rail. The proximity of the fourth suggest the form is high enough.

4337 EUROPEAN BREEDERS' FUND MAIDEN FILLIES' STKS 7f (S)
8:10 (8:25) (Class 5) 2-Y-O **£4,209** (£1,252; £625; £312) **Stalls** Low

Form RPR
04 **1** **Bobbie Soxer (IRE)**[27] 3456 2-9-0 0 TPQueally 2 76+
(J L Dunlop) *t.k.h: hld up in tch: travelling wl and nt clr run 2f out: squeezed through to ld 1f out: pushed clr: readily* **2/1**[1]

0 **2** *2 1/4* **Very Distinguished**[54] 2618 2-9-0 0 LiamJones 10 67+
(M G Quinlan) *hld up towards rr: hdwy jst over 2f out: chsd ldrs and carried sltly rt ent fnl f: kpt on to go 2nd towards fin: nt trble wnr* **10/1**

23 **3** ¾ **Raise All In (IRE)**[8] 4088 2-9-0 0 .... TQuinn 5 66
(R Hannon) *chsd ldrs: chsd ldr over 1f out: ev ch and edgd rt ent fnl f: nt pce of wnr after: lost 2nd towards fin* **7/2**[3]

4 ¾ **Caster Sugar (USA)** 2-9-0 0 .... PatCosgrave 12 64
(L M Cumani) *racd keenly: prom: chsd ldr over 3f out: ev ch 2f out tl 1f out: kpt on same pce fnl f* **20/1**

50 **5** *nse* **Lahaleeb (IRE)**[14] 3869 2-8-9 0 .... MCGeran(5) 9 64
(M R Channon) *s.i.s: bhd: swtchd rt and hdwy jst over 2f out: styng on and nt clr run over 1f out: sn swtchd rt again: flashed tail ins fnl f: kpt on* **25/1**

0 **6** *hd* **Dream Huntress**[21] 3632 2-8-11 0 .... PatrickHills(3) 4 63
(B J Meehan) *in tch in midfield: rdn and sltly outpcd over 2f out: swtchd rt over 1f out: kpt on fnl f: nt pce to rch ldrs* **14/1**

7 2 ¼ **Chalk Hill Blue** 2-9-0 0 .... StephenCarson 1 57+
(Eve Johnson Houghton) *s.i.s: detached in last tl 1/2-way: swtchd rt and hdwy over 2f out: kpt on same pce fr over 1f out* **33/1**

64 **8** ½ **Africa's Star (IRE)**[26] 3495 2-9-0 0 .... PhilipRobinson 6 56
(M A Jarvis) *led and crossed to stands' rail: t.k.h: rdn over 1f out: hdd 1f out: sn btn* **11/4**[2]

0 **9** 1 ¾ **Reel Hope**[20] 3674 2-9-0 0 .... RobertHavlin 8 52
(J R Best) *s.i.s: sn in tch: hdwy to press ldrs 2f out: sn rdn wknd ent fnl f* **66/1**

10 *1* **Charismatic Lady** 2-9-0 0 .... AdrianMcCarthy 3 49
(G G Margarson) *s.i.s: a towards rr: n.d* **50/1**

500 **11** *8* **Bounty Reef**[9] 4062 2-9-0 0 .... ShaneKelly 11 29
(P D Evans) *t.k.h: chsd ldr tl over 2f out: sn wknd: t.o* **12/1**

0000 **12** *20* **Herecomesbella**[22] 3610 2-8-9 0 .... JackMitchell(5) 13 —
(Stef Liddiard) *wnt rt s: sn prom: wknd rapidly over 2f out: t.o* **66/1**

1m 27.6s (0.30) **Going Correction** 0.0s/f (Good) **12 Ran SP% 122.2**
Speed ratings (Par 91): **98,95,94,93,93 93,90,90,88,87 78,55**
toteswinger: 1&2 £20.80, 1&3 £1.50, 2&3 £20.80. CSF £23.02 TOTE £3.30: £1.30, £3.50, £1.70; EX 28.00.
Owner Windflower Overseas Holdings Inc **Bred** Windflower Overseas Holdings Inc **Trained** Arundel, W Sussex

FOCUS
A fair maiden likely to produce its share of winners with the winner building on his debut and the runner-up showing improvement.

NOTEBOOK
Bobbie Soxer(IRE), whose trainer took this with a similar sort last year, had a good draw in stall two and she was hit hard in the betting, coming right into 2/1 from an opening 4/1. She was keen early and travelled strongly into contention but had to wait for a gap before picking up strongly once in the clear and came away to win well. She had finished fourth in a better race at Newmarket last time and it will be interesting to see what mark the Handicapper gives her. (op 4-1 tchd 9-2)
Very Distinguished showed up well to a point on her recent soft ground debut at Newbury and had clearly learned a good deal from that. The faster ground/extra furlong here suited well and she ran on late to grab second. This was a pleasing effort and she would have been closer had the draw been kinder. She should win an ordinary race. (op 11-1 tchd 12-1 and 9-1)
Raise All In(IRE), having her first try at 7f, was soon chasing the pace and she had every chance, but could not quicken and was run out of second close home. She is only modest, but can be found a race. (op 5-2)
Caster Sugar(USA) is bred to appreciate further this, her dam being a top-class middle-distance filly, and this has to go down as a pleasing first effort. The draw had not been kind to her, but she showed up well for a long way and should learn from the experience. (op 14-1)
Lahaleeb(IRE) has improved with each run and she looked unlucky not to challenge for third, getting a bit far back following a slow start and then not getting the gaps when needed. She is now qualified for nurseries and should find a race in that sphere. Official explanation: jockey said filly was denied a clear run
Dream Huntress improved a little on her debut effort and gave the impression she is ready for 1m. She will be qualified for handicaps following one more run and should fare better in that sphere. (op 20-1)
Chalk Hill Blue, who cost just 6,000gns, was slowly away and ran green early, but she seemed to get the message in the end and stuck on inside the final quarter mile. She should know more next time and will find easier opportunities. (op 40-1)
Africa's Star(IRE), fourth in a much better race at Newmarket last month, managed to get across to the stands' rail, but she raced a shade too freely and faded badly from a furlong out. She is obviously better than this and probably deserves another chance, as she will be qualified for nurseries now. (op 5-2 tchd 2-1 and 4-1)

4338 BETTER NOW OPEN AT SANDGATE ROAD H'CAP 7f (S)
8:40 (8:59) (Class 6) (0-65,65) 3-Y-O **£2,047** (£604; £302) **Stalls** Low

Form RPR

0240 **1** **Kannon**[20] 3678 3-8-10 **54** .... ShaneKelly 3 59+
(W J Knight) *s.i.s: hld up towards rr: hdwy over 2f out: nt clr run over 1f out: swtchd rt ent fnl f: r.o strly to ld last 75yds* **4/1**[2]

3300 **2** 1 ¼ **Micheals Boy (IRE)**[9] 4061 3-9-0 **58** ....(v[1]) PatCosgrave 6 60
(J R Boyle) *led and crossed to stands' rail: hrd pressed and rdn 2f out: kpt on wl tl hdd and no ex last 75yds* **25/1**

0-50 **3** *shd* **Valento**[41] 2991 3-9-7 **65** .... StephenCarson 10 67+
(Eve Johnson Houghton) *stdd s: bhd: last and rdn 1/2-way: hdwy u.p on outer over 2f out: chal jst ins fnl f: no ex last 100yds* **10/1**

5600 **4** 1 ¾ **Outside Edge (IRE)**[27] 3442 3-9-7 **65** ....(v) SaleemGolam 2 62
(W R Swinburn) *prom: chsd ldr 4f out: rdn and tried to chal 2f out: one pce fnl f* **9/2**[3]

5050 **5** *3* **Tea Cake (IRE)**[20] 3678 3-9-2 **60** ....(b[1]) PhilipRobinson 5 49
(H J L Dunlop) *stdd s: hld up in tch: smooth hdwy 3f out: chal and rdn jst over 1f out: fnd nil and sn btn* **9/2**[3]

5403 **6** ½ **Samurai Warrior**[28] 3406 3-9-2 **60** ....(be) TPQueally 9 48
(P J Makin) *t.k.h: prom on outer: rdn over 2f out: wknd ent fnl f* **7/2**[1]

4-54 **7** ½ **New Balls Please (IRE)**[22] 3605 3-8-7 **51** ....(p) LiamJones 11 37
(P M Phelan) *wnt rt s: hld up in midfield: hdwy over 2f out: keeping on same pce whn bmpd ent fnl f* **8/1**

-000 **8** ¾ **Midnight Oasis**[6] 4161 3-8-2 **46** oh1 ....(t) AdrianMcCarthy 1 30
(Rae Guest) *chsd ldrs: rdn over 2f out: wknd over 1f out* **40/1**

000 **9** 2 ¼ **Zeeran**[21] 3654 3-7-9 **46** oh1 ....(b[1]) RosieJessop(7) 4 24
(C E Brittain) *stdd s: t.k.h: hld up in rr: hdwy and jostled 3f out: no prog wl over 1f out* **16/1**

60-0 **10** *10* **Bathwick Icon (IRE)**[25] 3524 3-8-9 **53** .... RobertHavlin 8 4
(A B Haynes) *a towards rr: rdn and lost pl 1/2-way: t.o fnl f* **16/1**

000 **11** *30* **Ubiquitous**[26] 3484 3-8-6 **50** .... NickyMackay 7 —
(S Dow) *t.k.h: chsd ldr for 3f: wknd qckly: t.o last 2f* **33/1**

1m 27.5s (0.20) **Going Correction** 0.0s/f (Good) **11 Ran SP% 119.8**
Speed ratings (Par 98): **98,96,96,94,91 90,89,89,86,75 40**
toteswinger: 1&2 £29.90, 1&3 £6.60, 2&3 £38.90. CSF £103.99 CT £964.50 TOTE £5.50: £1.90, £5.20, £2.00; EX 116.20 Place 6: £41.63, Place 5: £26.96..
Owner Mrs W W Fleming **Bred** Stourbank Stud **Trained** Patching, W Sussex

FOCUS
A moderate handicap best rated through the runner-up.

T/Plt: £34.70 to a £1 stake. Pool: £43,200.19. 906.78 winning tickets. T/Qpdt: £18.50 to a £1 stake. Pool: £2,679.36. 106.85 winning tickets. SP

4078 KEMPTON (A.W) (R-H)
Thursday, July 24

OFFICIAL GOING: Standard
Wind: Moderate, behind.

4339 KEMPTON.CO.UK MEDIAN AUCTION MAIDEN FILLIES' STKS 7f (P)
6:10 (6:18) (Class 5) 2-Y-O **£3,885** (£1,156; £577; £288) **Stalls** High

Form RPR

1 **Floodlit** 2-9-0 0 .... RyanMoore 11 71+
(J H M Gosden) *bhd and sn drvn along: swtchd lft off rail 3f out: str run but plenty to do over 1f out: fin wl to ld last stride* **3/1**[1]

5 **2** *nse* **Tiger Goddess (IRE)**[48] 2783 2-9-0 0 .... TonyCulhane 14 71
(W J Haggas) *led: hrd drvn over 2f out: collared last strides* **4/1**[2]

4 **3** *1* **Prophetise (USA)**[20] 3674 2-9-0 0 .... JamesDoyle 9 68
(J W Hills) *chsd ldrs: rdn and outpcd 2f out: styd on ins fnl f* **11/2**

4 1 ¾ **Bishaara (IRE)** 2-9-0 0 .... RHills 7 64+
(J H M Gosden) *chsd ldrs: outpcd 3f out: styd on u.p appr fnl f* **9/2**[3]

6 **5** 1 ½ **Key To Love (IRE)**[15] 3837 2-9-0 0 .... IanMongan 4 60
(H J L Dunlop) *w ldr: rdn over 3f out: wknd over 1f out* **18/1**

6 **6** ½ **Bright Enough**[14] 3869 2-9-0 0 .... SebSanders 3 59
(E J O'Neill) *prom: outpcd over 2f out: styd on again fr over 1f out* **16/1**

0 **7** 1 ¾ **Manhattan Sunrise (USA)**[20] 3689 2-9-0 0 .... PaulEddery 13 54
(G D Blake) *chsd ldrs: rdn over 2f out: wknd fnl f* **33/1**

0 **8** *13* **Thewaytosanjose (IRE)**[20] 3674 2-9-0 0 .... SteveDrowne 6 22
(S Kirk) *in tch: rdn 4f out: racd wd: sn wknd* **40/1**

9 1 ¾ **Congenial** 2-9-0 0 .... JamieSpencer 10 18
(J R Fanshawe) *s.i.s: bhd and nvr in contention* **8/1**

10 *14* **Velox Vixen (IRE)** 2-9-0 0 .... FrancisNorton 1 —
(M Blanshard) *s.i.s: a in rr* **66/1**

11 *shd* **D'Nurse (IRE)** 2-9-0 0 .... RichardHughes 2 —
(R Hannon) *s.i.s: racd wd: prog over 3f out: sn btn* **14/1**

1m 29.27s (3.27) **Going Correction** +0.25s/f (Slow) **11 Ran SP% 114.4**
Speed ratings (Par 91): **91,90,89,87,86 85,83,68,66,50 50**
toteswinger: 1&2 £3.20, 1&3 £3.70, 2&3 £4.20. CSF £13.57 TOTE £3.80: £1.10, £1.70, £2.20; EX 17.60.Athania and Lady Oaksey were withdrawn. Prices at time of withdrawal were 14/1 and 33/1 respectively. Rule 4 applies to all bets. Deduct 5p in the pound.
Owner Cheveley Park Stud **Bred** Cheveley Park Stud Ltd **Trained** Newmarket, Suffolk

FOCUS
An ordinary maiden delayed by eight minutes when Lady Oaksey burst the stalls beforehand. The winning time was 1.31 seconds slower than the following nursery, and the form looks modest but a couple of these are entitled to improve.

NOTEBOOK
Floodlit, out of a winner over 1m1f from the family of Midnight Line, was all the rage in the market beforehand but her supporters must have been worried as she hardly went a yard early. However, once the penny had dropped and her stamina came into play, she stayed on down the wide outside to snatch the race right on the line. The form may not amount to much, but she is likely to come on a good deal for this and she will appreciate further. (op 5-1)
Tiger Goddess(IRE), who showed some promise on her Doncaster debut, tried to make every yard from the rails draw over this extra furlong and given the way she kept battling, she hardly deserved to have the race snatched from her right on the line. She has the ability to win a race like this. (op 7-2 tchd 11-4)
Prophetise(USA), fourth in a Salisbury maiden on her debut that has not worked out, was always up with the pace and kept on trying all the way to the line. She is bred to go on this surface, but her pedigree suggests this would be as far as she wants. Nurseries may be her sort of race after one more run. (tchd 6-1)
Bishaara(IRE), a half-sister to six winners including the top-class Muhtathir, took a similar route to the winner down the outside of the track over the last couple of furlongs. She did not see her race out to the same degree as her stable companion, but neither was she knocked about and she should come on a good deal for this. (op 5-1 tchd 13-2)
Key To Love(IRE) was given a more prominent ride than on her debut here, but she did not appear to see out the extra furlong. Official explanation: vet said filly lost a tooth (op 16-1 tchd 20-1)
Bright Enough showed a bit more than on her Folkestone debut, but although the form is probably still modest she looks to be crying out for further already. (op 20-1)
Congenial Official explanation: jockey said filly would not face kickback

4340 BOOK NOW ON 01372 470047 NURSERY 7f (P)
6:40 (6:46) (Class 4) 2-Y-O **£3,885** (£1,156; £577; £288) **Stalls** High

Form RPR

342 **1** **Night Of Fortune**[17] 3778 2-9-2 **70** .... SebSanders 7 77+
(Sir Mark Prescott) *mde all: pushed clr fnl 2f: readily* **9/4**[1]

023 **2** 2 ¼ **Hold The Bucks (USA)**[19] 3706 2-8-0 **57** .... LukeMorris(3) 9 58
(J S Moore) *chsd ldrs in 3rd: hrd drvn 4f out: styd on u.p fnl f to go 2nd nr fin* **16/1**

3310 **3** ½ **Daddy's Gift (IRE)**[13] 3924 2-9-7 **75** .... RichardHughes 11 75
(R Hannon) *sn chsd wnr: rdn over 2f out and lost 2nd nr fin* **7/2**[3]

0P42 **4** *5* **Misty Glade**[22] 3610 2-9-0 **68** .... RyanMoore 6 56
(B J Meehan) *chsd ldrs: rdn over 3f out: wknd 2f out* **11/1**

3302 **5** *5* **Gassal**[8] 4079 2-9-2 **70** .... RHills 8 45
(W J Haggas) *s.i.s: bhd: rdn and effrt over 2f out: nvr in contention after* **3/1**[2]

6303 **6** 1 ½ **Aegean Warning**[8] 4079 2-9-0 **68** .... JamieSpencer 4 39
(K A Ryan) *in tch: rdn over 3f out: sn btn* **7/1**

0005 **7** ½ **Forster Island**[14] 3888 2-8-4 **58** .... FrancisNorton 12 28
(M Blanshard) *in tch: rdn over 3f out: sn btn* **20/1**

003 **8** 1 ¼ **Lislin**[35] 3158 2-7-13 **53** oh4 ow1 .... JimmyQuinn 3 20
(S Kirk) *stdd s: drvn 1/2-way: sn btn* **33/1**

5056 **9** *5* **Noworneva**[20] 3677 2-7-5 **52** oh2 .... CharlesEddery(7) 10 7
(S Kirk) *stdd s: rdn 1/2-way: a bhd* **66/1**

000 **10** *5* **Flawless Diamond (IRE)**[34] 3207 2-7-12 **52** oh2 .... WilliamBuick 5 —
(J S Moore) *rdn 1/2-way: a bhd and no ch whn eased fnl f* **25/1**

1m 27.96s (1.96) **Going Correction** +0.25s/f (Slow) **10 Ran SP% 117.7**
Speed ratings (Par 96): **98,95,94,89,83 81,81,79,74,68**
toteswinger: 1&2 £7.80, 1&3 £2.900, 2&3 £14.80. CSF £39.22 CT £126.44 TOTE £3.40: £1.10, £4.20, £1.90; EX 31.10.
Owner P J McSwiney - Osborne House **Bred** Gainsborough Stud Management Ltd **Trained** Newmarket, Suffolk

FOCUS
They went a decent pace in this - the winning time was 1.31 seconds faster than the fillies' maiden - and very few ever got into it. The form looks very solid rated around the placed horses. The 'official' ratings shown next to each horse are estimated and for information purposes only.

The Form Book, Raceform Ltd, Compton, RG20 6NL

NOTEBOOK

Night Of Fortune ◆, who had shown ability in three outings on turf, was positively ridden right from the start on this switch to sand. Quickening again from the front passing the intersection, he never looked in any danger from that point and should continue to progress. (op 11-4 tchd 3-1 in a place)

Hold The Bucks(USA) was never too far off the pace, but he took a while to hit top stride when first asked, and by the time he did the favourite was already home. He should relish stepping up to a mile when juvenile races begin over that trip in the next couple of weeks. (op 12-1)

Daddy's Gift(IRE), winner of her only previous start on Polytrack, always had the favourite in her sights but try as she might she could never bridge the gap to him. (op 4-1)

Misty Glade benefited from racing prominently in a race dominated by those that raced handily, but she was comfortably shaken off and is still to prove that she truly gets this trip. (tchd 9-1)

Gassal, narrowly beaten in a similar event over course and distance eight days earlier, was given a totally contrasting ride here and never got into it, but neither did anything else that tried to come from off the pace. Official explanation: jockey said filly would not face kickback (op 7-2)

Aegean Warning, a couple of lengths behind Gassal here eight days ago, ran close to form with that rival but neither of them exactly boosted the previous week's contest. (tchd 13-2 and 15-2)

Lislin Official explanation: jockey said filly ran too free

4341 ENJOY GUINNESS NEXT WEDNESDAY H'CAP — 6f (P)

7:15 (7:16) (Class 4) (0-85,85) 3-Y-0+ £4,727 (£1,406; £702; £351) Stalls High

Form				RPR
4246	1		**Dvinsky (USA)**[9] 4058 7-9-4 77 .... (b) JimmyQuinn 11 — (P Howling) *slt ld tl drvn clr over 2f out: hld on: all out* 11/2[3]	87
2105	2	1 1/4	**Expensive Art (IRE)**[22] 3601 4-9-5 78 .... RyanMoore 5 — (S A Callaghan) *hld up in rr: stdy hdwy over 2f out: chsd wnr over 1f out: kpt on but a hld* 8/1	84
1642	3	3 3/4	**Rabbit Fighter (IRE)**[11] 3998 4-8-12 71 .... (v) AdamKirby 7 — (D Shaw) *chsd ldrs: disp 2nd u.p over 2f out: styd on same pce fnl f* 11/4[1]	65
1000	4	hd	**Halsion Chancer**[31] 3320 4-9-12 85 .... SteveDrowne 9 — (J R Best) *chsd ldrs: rdn to go 2nd briefly over 2f out: nvr any ch fr over 1f out* 12/1	78
1140	5	shd	**Honey Monster (IRE)**[15] 3850 3-9-5 83 .... (p) AlanMunro 6 — (A J McCabe) *chsd ldrs: rdn over 2f out: styd on same pce* 4/1[2]	76
0552	6	2 1/2	**Louphole**[9] 4051 6-8-13 72 .... SebSanders 2 — (P J Makin) *s.i.s: towards rr: rdn and effrt over 2f out: nvr rchd ldrs and wknd fnl f* 8/1	57
0100	7	3 1/4	**Applesnap (IRE)**[21] 3653 3-8-8 72 .... JohnEgan 3 — (Mrs C A Dunnett) *in tch: rdn 1/2-way: nvr in contention after* 25/1	47
5115	8	hd	**Seamus Shindig**[28] 3418 6-9-4 84 .... AmyScott(7) 1 — (H Candy) *a bhd* 10/1	58
-000	9	5	**Jebel Tara**[26] 3475 3-9-5 83 .... RichardMullen 4 — (C E Brittain) *bhd: hung rt hung rt and no ch fr 3f out* 25/1	41
1500	10	6	**Charles Darwin (IRE)**[13] 3898 5-9-7 80 .... (p) JamesDoyle 10 — (M Blanshard) *w wnr: rdn over 3f out: wknd qckly wl over 2f out* 20/1	19
3350	11	7	**Mogok Ruby**[77] 1928 4-9-7 80 .... RichardHughes 8 — (L Montague Hall) *stdd s: a in rr* 20/1	—

1m 13.38s (0.28) **Going Correction** +0.25s/f (Slow)
WFA 3 from 4yo+ 5lb 11 Ran SP% **118.3**
Speed ratings (Par 105): **108,106,101,101,100 97,93,93,86,79 74**
toteswinger: 1&2 £31.10, 1&3 £4.70, 2&3 £3.90. CSF £46.24 CT £149.21 TOTE £8.20: £2.20, £2.90, £1.20; EX 65.20.
Owner Richard Berenson **Bred** Eclipse Bloodstock & Tipperary Bloodstock **Trained** Newmarket, Suffolk

FOCUS

A decent handicap with plenty of pace and again the winner made all. The form looks decent despite the runner-up being a little tricky.

Charles Darwin(IRE) Official explanation: trainer said gelding lost a shoe

Mogok Ruby Official explanation: jockey said gelding never travelled

4342 IRISH NIGHT NEXT WEDNESDAY MAIDEN FILLIES' STKS — 1m 4f (P)

7:45 (7:47) (Class 4) 3-Y-0+ £4,727 (£1,406; £702; £351) Stalls Centre

Form				RPR
03-2	1		**Starfala**[20] 3688 3-8-12 77 .... RichardHughes 9 — (P F I Cole) *trckd ldr: drvn along 2f out: qcknd to ld fnl 100yds: readily* 3/1[1]	78
-302	2	1 1/4	**Amhooj**[22] 3611 3-8-12 77 .... RHills 13 — (M P Tregoning) *sn led: rdn and qcknd 2f out: hdd and outpcd fnl 100yds* 4/1[2]	76
05	3	1/2	**Winners Chant (IRE)**[20] 3688 3-8-12 0 .... RyanMoore 14 — (Sir Michael Stoute) *chsd ldrs: drvn to chal over 1f out: one pce ins fnl f* 16/1	75
023	4	4	**Lemonesse (USA)**[20] 3688 3-8-12 76 .... JimmyQuinn 8 — (H R A Cecil) *chsd ldrs early: rdn and outpcd in mid-div 5f out: styd on fr over 1f out* 5/1[3]	69+
24-4	5	1 1/4	**Full Marks**[50] 2717 3-8-12 78 .... (t) SebSanders 7 — (J Noseda) *in tch: chsd ldrs 1/2-way: rdn over 2f out: wknd fnl f* 3/1[1]	67
	6	5	**Mary Athena (FR)** 3-8-12 0 .... IanMongan 10 — (M G Quinlan) *bhd: rdn and rn green over 3f out: sn hung rt: styd on wl fr over 1f out* 66/1	59+
0	7	hd	**Water Violet**[68] 2191 3-8-12 0 .... JamieSpencer 12 — (J R Fanshawe) *chsd ldrs: rdn 3f out: wknd 2f out* 20/1	58
	8	nk	**Plaisterer** 3-8-12 0 .... AlanMunro 11 — (C F Wall) *in tch: rdn 3f out: wknd 2f out* 25/1	58
0-20	9	3/4	**National Day (IRE)**[147] 727 4-9-7 0 .... MarcHalford(3) 6 — (D R C Elsworth) *bhd: mod prog fnl 2f* 40/1	57
0	10	2	**Every Whisper (IRE)**[131] 903 3-8-12 0 .... JimCrowley 5 — (Mrs A J Perrett) *a towards rr* 10/1	54
	11	1/2	**Extreme Pleasure (IRE)** 3-8-12 0 .... PaulDoe 2 — (W J Knight) *a in rr* 33/1	53
4-4	12	3 1/4	**Sensible**[36] 3133 3-8-12 0 .... WilliamBuick 4 — (M J Wallace) *chsd ldrs tl wknd 2f out* 20/1	48
03-	13	4 1/2	**Bruki (IRE)**[225] 7114 3-8-12 0 .... (t) JohnEgan 3 — (M Botti) *in tch: rdn 5f out: wknd 4f out* 14/1	40
	14	15	**Dagua Briza (IRE)** 3-8-12 0 .... JamesDoyle 1 — (J W Mullins) *in rr: wd over 3f out: a bhd* 66/1	16

2m 38.69s (4.19) **Going Correction** +0.25s/f (Slow)
WFA 3 from 4yo 12lb 14 Ran SP% **130.0**
Speed ratings (Par 102): **96,95,94,92,91 88,87,87,87,85 85,83,80,70**
toteswinger: 1&2 £4.30, 1&3 £18.90, 2&3 £23.50. CSF £15.11 TOTE £4.00: £1.70, £2.30, £5.10; EX 17.90.
Owner Ben & Sir Martyn Arbib **Bred** Arbib Bloodstock Partnership **Trained** Whatcombe, Oxon

FOCUS

This fair fillies' maiden was nothing like as competitive as the numbers would suggest and the pace was also modest, but it still provided a cracking finish and the front three pulled clear of the others. This was another race where it was crucial to race handily and the principals were always close to the pace. The form makes sense rated around the first two.

4343 RUBBING HOUSE AT EPSOM DOWNS H'CAP — 1m 4f (P)

8:20 (8:21) (Class 5) (0-70,70) 4-Y-0+ £2,590 (£770; £385; £192) Stalls Centre

Form				RPR
6400	1		**Resplendent Ace (IRE)**[6] 4156 4-9-7 70 .... JimmyQuinn 4 — (P Howling) *in tch: drvn and hdwy 3f out: led ins fnl 2f: r.o strly* 4/1[2]	79
0253	2	2 1/2	**Mixing**[43] 2949 6-8-3 55 .... KirstyMilczarek(3) 8 — (M J Attwater) *chsd ldrs: rdn and outpcd 2f out: styd on again over 1f out: tk 2nd ins fnl f: nt pce of wnr* 9/1	59
3244	3	2 3/4	**Best Selection**[10] 4029 4-8-13 62 .... IanMongan 10 — (Mrs L J Mongan) *in rr: hdwy 3f out: styd on u.p to go 3rd ins fnl f* 16/1	61
0451	4	1	**Great View (IRE)**[13] 3901 9-8-13 62 .... (p) RyanMoore 1 — (Mrs A L M King) *in rr: rdn 4f out: hdwy on outside over 2f out: kpt on: nt rch ldrs* 7/2[1]	59
-000	5	1	**Silver Surprise**[30] 3347 4-7-11 51 oh6 .... DavidProbert(5) 9 — (J J Bridger) *chsd ldrs: rdn to chal 2f out: wknd fnl f* 100/1	46
4062	6	3 1/4	**Capistrano**[10] 4029 5-8-2 51 oh3 .... PaulEddery 6 — (G D Blake) *bhd: hdwy into mid-div: 1/2-way: styd on same pce fnl 2f* 16/1	39
0013	7	1/2	**Prince Charlemagne (IRE)**[23] 3583 5-8-13 62 .... (b) RichardHughes 12 — (R M Stronge) *hld up in mid-div: drvn and hdd to ld briefly 2f out: sn hdd and btn* 15/2[3]	49
5405	8	1 1/4	**Wild Fell Hall (IRE)**[17] 3785 5-9-7 70 .... (p) OscarUrbina 13 — (A D Brown) *sn led: rdn 3f out: hdd & wknd qckly 2f out* 22/1	55
066	9	12	**Jafaru**[9] 4067 4-9-2 65 .... HayleyTurner 3 — (G A Butler) *s.i.s: a in rr* 14/1	26
0006	10	3 3/4	**Birkspiel (GER)**[29] 3375 7-9-6 69 .... (t) SebSanders 11 — (S Dow) *chsd ldr: rdn 3f out: wknd sn after* 14/1	22
240	11	3 3/4	**The Wily Woodcock**[13] 3914 4-9-1 64 .... SteveDrowne 7 — (G Wragg) *in tch to 1/2-way* 15/2[3]	10
2254	12	3/4	**Alexander Guru**[8] 4078 4-9-1 64 .... JamesDoyle 5 — (M Blanshard) *chsd ldrs: rdn over 3f out: sn wknd* 8/1	8
05-0	13	64	**Montjeu's Melody (IRE)**[55] 2561 4-8-11 65 .... NataliaGemelova(5) 2 — (J E Long) *sn bhd: t.o fr 1/2-way* 25/1	—

2m 37.28s (2.78) **Going Correction** +0.25s/f (Slow) 13 Ran SP% **121.1**
Speed ratings (Par 103): **100,98,96,95,95 93,92,91,83,81 78,78,—**
toteswinger: 1&2 £7.50, 1&3 not won, 2&3 £31.30. CSF £40.02 CT £532.72 TOTE £6.60: £2.00, £2.90, £5.20; EX 53.70.
Owner Resplendent Racing Limited **Bred** Newlands House Stud **Trained** Newmarket, Suffolk

FOCUS

A much more end-to-end gallop than in the preceding maiden and the winning time was 1.41 seconds quicker, but still only about what would be expected for a race of its type. The proximity of the fifth from out of the handicap raises doubts about the form.

Birkspiel(GER) Official explanation: jockey said gelding had no more to give

Montjeu's Melody(IRE) Official explanation: trainer said filly returned lame

4344 U2 TRIBUTE BAND ZU2 NEXT WEDNESDAY H'CAP — 1m 3f (P)

8:50 (8:50) (Class 5) (0-75,81) 3-Y-0 £2,590 (£770; £385; £192) Stalls High

Form				RPR
0043	1		**Fair Gale**[16] 3824 3-9-4 72 .... RyanMoore 9 — (S Kirk) *led 1f: rdn 3f out: hdwy on ins to ld over 2f out: styd on strly* 9/2[2]	82
1030	2	2	**Mista Rossa**[24] 3555 3-8-11 68 .... TravisBlock(3) 2 — (H Morrison) *hld up in rr: plenty to do whn hdwy over 2f out: r.o strly to take 2nd fnl 100yds: nt rch wnr* 8/1	74+
553	3	1/2	**Hendersyde (USA)**[23] 3573 3-9-4 72 .... AdamKirby 7 — (W R Swinburn) *chsd ldr after 1f: rdn over 3f out: styd on wl 2f out: outpcd and lost 2nd fnl 100yds* 6/1[3]	77
-044	4	1 1/4	**Broken Moon**[15] 3843 3-9-2 70 .... JamieSpencer 11 — (J R Fanshawe) *bhd: rdn and and hdwy on outside but hung lft over 2f out: r.o fnl f but nvr in contention* 7/1	73+
52-2	5	1 3/4	**Vilna (USA)**[15] 3836 3-8-13 67 .... RichardHughes 8 — (S A Callaghan) *in tch: rdn and hdwy whn hung rt 2f out: kpt on wl: nt rch ldrs* 9/4[1]	67
4030	6	3 1/2	**Title Role**[31] 3327 3-9-7 75 .... JimmyQuinn 4 — (P F I Cole) *led after 1f: chsd ldrs: rdn 3f out: hdd over 2f out: wknd fnl f* 8/1	68
0304	7	4 1/2	**Classical Rhythm (IRE)**[14] 3886 3-8-13 67 .... AmirQuinn 10 — (J R Boyle) *chsd ldrs: rdn 4f out: wknd 2f out* 14/1	52
0620	8	11	**Heart Of Dubai (USA)**[21] 3641 3-9-1 69 .... (p) SebSanders 3 — (C E Brittain) *a bhd* 28/1	35
0105	9	3 3/4	**Ramprakash**[21] 3656 3-8-11 65 .... HayleyTurner 5 — (M L W Bell) *chsd ldrs tl wknd over 2f out* 25/1	24
404	10	15	**Tara's Garden**[15] 3845 3-8-8 62 .... FrancisNorton 1 — (M Blanshard) *a bhd* 33/1	—
2-30	11	19	**Cuban Rhythm (USA)**[42] 2973 3-9-1 69 .... SteveDrowne 6 — (R Charlton) *mid-div: rdn and btn 4f out* 16/1	—

2m 23.81s (1.91) **Going Correction** +0.25s/f (Slow) 11 Ran SP% **120.7**
Speed ratings (Par 100): **103,101,101,100,99 96,93,85,82,71 57**
toteswinger: 1&2 £5.40, 1&3 £6.10, 2&3 £9.70. CSF £40.77 CT £222.73 TOTE £8.10: £2.60, £2.40, £2.20; EX 65.80.
Owner Norman Ormiston **Bred** Hesmonds Stud Ltd **Trained** Upper Lambourn, Berks

FOCUS

An ordinary handicap, but they went a decent pace in this and the winning time was solid. This was also another race where those that raced handily were at an advantage. The third is the best guide to the form but the runner-up should rate higher.

4345 PANORAMIC BAR & RESTAURANT H'CAP — 7f (P)

9:20 (9:20) (Class 4) (0-85,85) 3-Y-0+ £4,727 (£1,406; £702; £351) Stalls High

Form				RPR
3-01	1		**Blue Sky Basin**[42] 2976 3-9-8 81 .... WilliamBuick 3 — (A M Balding) *mde all: qcknd over 2f out: sn drvn: readily* 6/4[1]	96+
5251	2	2 1/4	**Arabian Spirit**[13] 3904 3-9-11 84 .... RyanMoore 5 — (E A L Dunlop) *chsd ldrs: rdn to go 2nd 2f out: kpt on u.p but nt threaten wnr* 11/4[2]	93+
4621	3	3 3/4	**My Mentor (IRE)**[20] 3691 4-9-7 73 .... (b) SebSanders 6 — (Sir Mark Prescott) *sn chsd ldrs: rdn 3f out: styd on same pce fnl 2f* 9/2[3]	75
0000	4	2 1/4	**Last Of The Line**[33] 3266 3-9-0 73 .... (b) FrancisNorton 1 — (H J L Dunlop) *wnt lft s: hdwy fr 2f out but nvr in contention* 33/1	66
2406	5	hd	**Carmenero (GER)**[18] 3761 5-9-8 74 .... RichardHughes 7 — (W R Muir) *hld up: rdn and effrt 3f out: nvr in contention* 10/1	69

043- **6** ¾ **Quick Release (IRE)**[264] 6644 3-9-12 **85**........................ RichardMullen 4 75
(D M Simcock) *bhd: rdn and sme hdwy 3f out: but nt on terms fnl 2f* **22/1**

-002 **7** 4 **Street Star (USA)**[15] 3838 3-9-12 **85**........................ JamieSpencer 2 64
(J R Fanshawe) *chsd wnr after 2f: rdn 3f out: wknd qckly 2f out* **14/1**

050 **8** 7 **Mr Garston**[13] 3915 5-9-9 **75**........................ SteveDrowne 8 39
(J R Boyle) *chsd ldrs 4f* **10/1**

1m 26.61s (0.61) **Going Correction** +0.25s/f (Slow)
WFA 3 from 4yo+ 7lb **8** Ran SP% **117.0**
Speed ratings (Par 105): **106,103,99,96,96 95,90,82**
toteswinger: 1&2 £1.90, 1&3 £2.40, 2&3 £3.30. CSF £5.86 CT £14.59 TOTE £2.50: £1.60, £1.60, £2.00; EX 8.10 Place 6: £56.66, Place 5: £36.20..
Owner George Strawbridge **Bred** George Strawbridge **Trained** Kingsclere, Hants

FOCUS
This was a decent little handicap. The favourite made sure it was run at a strong pace and he became another winner to make all. The third was close to his Polytrack best.
T/Jkpt: Not won. T/Plt: £68.00 to a £1 stake. Pool: £52,508.09. 563.41 winning tickets. T/Qpdt: £39.00 to a £1 stake. Pool: £3,637.00. 68.86 winning tickets. ST

4309 SANDOWN (R-H)

Thursday, July 24

OFFICIAL GOING: Good to firm (firm in places; 9.2)
Wind: Light, behind Weather: Sunny, very warm

4346 INDEPENDENT AGE E B F MAIDEN STKS 5f 6y
2:10 (2:13) (Class 4) 2-Y-O **£5,180** (£1,541; £770; £384) **Stalls** High

Form RPR

1 **Triple Aspect (IRE)** 2-9-3 0........................ LiamJones 5 89+
(W J Haggas) *w.w in rr: swtchd to outer 2f out: prog to ld over 1f out: sn clr: pushed out: v comf* **12/1**

3 **2** 2 ¼ **Doctor Parkes**[13] 3895 2-9-3 0........................ LPKeniry 7 81
(E F Vaughan) *dwlt: hld up in rr: prog over 1f out to take 2nd jst ins fnl f: styd on wl but no ch w wnr* **13/8**[1]

346 **3** 2 ½ **Verlegen (IRE)**[41] 2999 2-8-12 0........................ PatDobbs 6 67
(R Hannon) *pressed ldng pair: rdn to chal over 1f out: sn outpcd* **10/1**

4 **4** 1 ¼ **Art Correspondent (IRE)**[10] 4020 2-9-3 0........................ RyanMoore 8 68
(G L Moore) *mostly chsd ldr: rdn to chal over 1f out: wknd fnl f* **7/4**[2]

02 **5** ¾ **Hawkspur (IRE)**[10] 4024 2-9-3 0........................ RichardHughes 3 65
(R Hannon) *led to over 1f out: wknd fnl f* **9/1**

6 ¾ **Master Lightfoot** 2-9-3 0........................ AdamKirby 1 62
(W R Swinburn) *wnt lft s: t.k.h early: hld up: struggling fnl 2f* **17/2**[3]

60.40 secs (-1.20) **Going Correction** -0.30s/f (Firm) **6** Ran SP% **111.8**
Speed ratings (Par 96): **97,93,89,87,86 85**
toteswinger: 1&2 £4.30, 1&3 £7.40, 2&3 £4.20. CSF £31.87 TOTE £14.90: £4.60, £1.50; EX 43.20.
Owner Mrs M Findlay **Bred** Noel O'Callaghan **Trained** Newmarket, Suffolk

FOCUS
An ordinary juvenile maiden, but a reasonably impressive winner and the form has to be given a chance.

NOTEBOOK
Triple Aspect(IRE), a £43,000 son of Danetime, brother to multiple 5f-7f winner Molcon and half-brother to successful sprinters Kathology and The Baroness, out of 6f juvenile winner, made a winning debut in good style. He made his move widest of all, but picked up smarty. He looks a useful prospect and, considering who he is owned by, it was a surprise he was allowed to go off at 12/1. He could now be aimed at the Roses Stakes at York. (op 10-1)
Doctor Parkes built on the form he showed on his debut over 6f at Ascot, but he found one too good. He looks capable of picking up a similar event. (op 2-1 tchd 9-4)
Verlegen(IRE) ran a respectable race, but she will probably be better off in nursery company. (op 8-1)
Art Correspondent(IRE) failed to really build on the form he showed when a beaten favourite on his debut at Windsor. (op 15-8 tchd 13-8)
Hawkspur(IRE) might be more of a nusery type and a flatter track may also suit better. (op 4-1)
Master Lightfoot, a 75,000gns son of Kyllachy half-brother to among others quite useful dual 5f juvenile winner Smooch, out of a dual 5f-7f winner, was well backed beforehand, but he never landed a blow after racing keenly. He will know more next time. Official explanation: jockey said colt ran green (op 20-1)

4347 UNIVERSAL BENEFICENT SOCIETY H'CAP 5f 6y
2:45 (2:46) (Class 4) (0-80,85) 3-Y-O **£5,504** (£1,637; £818; £408) **Stalls** High

Form RPR

0064 **1** **Bosun Breese**[20] 3696 3-9-3 **75**........................(t) RichardHughes 4 86
(P W D'Arcy) *racd wd: trckd ldr: led over 1f out: sn clr: shkn up and in n.d fnl f* **11/4**[2]

40-1 **2** 3 ¾ **Speed Song**[7] 4127 3-9-13 **85** 6ex........................ RyanMoore 1 83
(W J Haggas) *dwlt: hld up in last trio: nt clr run wl over 1f out: got through and r.o to take 2nd fnl 100yds: no ch w wnr* **6/5**[1]

0000 **3** 1 ¾ **Ten Down**[7] 4127 3-8-13 **78**........................ RosieJessop(7) 6 69
(Miss Gay Kelleway) *racd against rail: led to over 1f out: no ch w wnr after: lost 2nd fnl 100yds* **33/1**

5213 **4** 1 **Monsieur Reynard**[27] 3462 3-9-5 **77**........................ StephenDonohoe 5 65
(Ian Williams) *s.i.s: mostly in last trio: rdn 1/2-way: kpt on one pce* **5/1**[3]

-000 **5** ¾ **Regal Step**[13] 3909 3-9-3 **75**........................ LDettori 2 60
(R M H Cowell) *trckd ldrs: rdn 2f out: no prog and sn btn* **20/1**

-562 **6** shd **Weet A Surprise**[11] 4000 3-9-1 **73**........................ HayleyTurner 8 58
(R Hollinshead) *racd against rail: a in last trio: rdn 1/2-way: no prog* **14/1**

4205 **7** ¾ **Magical Speedfit (IRE)**[7] 4127 3-9-3 **75**........................ TPQueally 3 57
(G G Margarson) *chsd ldrs: rdn 1/2-way: struggling over 1f out* **11/1**

59.87 secs (-1.73) **Going Correction** -0.30s/f (Firm) **7** Ran SP% **111.5**
Speed ratings (Par 102): **101,95,92,90,89 89,88**
toteswinger: 1&2 £1.80, 1&3 £13.30, 2&3 £8.10. CSF £6.06 CT £74.33 TOTE £3.90: £2.20, £1.20; EX 6.30.Blue Jack was withdrawn. Price at time of withdrawal 4/1. Rule 4 applies to board prices prior to withdrawal only. Deduct 20p in the pound.
Owner Lodge Hyson Delnevo And Breese Racing **Bred** Lady Lonsdale **Trained** Newmarket, Suffolk
■ Stewards' Enquiry : Stephen Donohoe caution: careless riding

FOCUS
A fair three-year-old sprint handicap in which the runner-up was a little disappointing despite her penalty.

4348 KEEP ABLE STAR STKS (LISTED RACE) 7f 16y
3:20 (3:21) (Class 1) 2-Y-O
£17,031 (£6,456; £3,231; £1,611; £807; £405) **Stalls** High

Form RPR

31 **1** **Honest Quality (USA)**[54] 2627 2-8-12 0........................ TedDurcan 8 98
(H R A Cecil) *hld up in midfield: prog on outer over 2f out: led over 1f out and hung rt: hrd rdn and stl hanging fnl f: jst hld on* **6/4**[1]

4104 **2** hd **Beat Seven**[13] 3924 2-8-12 0........................ RyanMoore 2 98
(Miss Gay Kelleway) *veered bdly lft s: hld up in last pair: gd prog on outer over 2f out: chsd wnr jst over 1f out and edgd rt: str chal last 100yds: jst hld* **8/1**

31 **3** 4 ½ **Touching (IRE)**[15] 3837 2-8-12 0........................ RichardHughes 5 87
(R Hannon) *racd freely: led to over 1f out: steadily lost grnd on ldng pair fnl f* **7/1**

21 **4** 1 **Spanish Cygnet (USA)**[8] 4080 2-8-12 0........................ JimCrowley 3 85+
(Mrs A J Perrett) *trckd ldr: rdn to chal 2f out: already hld whn hmpd over 1f out: no prog fnl f* **10/1**

211 **5** ½ **Solo Attempt**[8] 4072 2-8-12 0........................ JohnEgan 6 83
(M Botti) *t.k.h: hld up bhd ldrs: rdn over 2f out: nt qckn and no prog* **12/1**

231 **6** nk **Maid For Music (IRE)**[20] 3674 2-8-12 0........................ RichardMullen 7 82
(E S McMahon) *trckd ldng pair: rdn over 2f out: nt qckn and lost pl wl over 1f out: n.d after* **9/2**[2]

62 **7** 2 ¼ **Shaws Diamond (USA)**[24] 3568 2-8-12 0........................ AdamKirby 4 76
(D Shaw) *stdd s: hld up in last trio: rdn and no imp over 2f out* **50/1**

51 **8** 5 **Isabella Grey**[21] 3625 2-8-12 0........................ FergalLynch 1 64
(K A Ryan) *carried lft s: mostly in last pair: rdn 3f out: wknd 2f out* **11/2**[3]

1m 28.25s (-1.25) **Going Correction** -0.20s/f (Firm) **8** Ran SP% **115.9**
Speed ratings (Par 102): **99,98,93,92,91 91,89,83**
toteswinger: 1&2 £3.90, 1&3 £3.20, 2&3 £9.10. CSF £14.81 TOTE £2.30: £1.40, £2.50, £2.10; EX 15.20.
Owner K Abdulla **Bred** Juddmonte Farms Inc **Trained** Newmarket, Suffolk
■ Stewards' Enquiry : Ted Durcan two-day ban: careless riding (Aug 7-8)

FOCUS
A weak fillies' Listed race in which the first pair finished clear and the form looks solid enough.

NOTEBOOK
Honest Quality(USA) was not sure to get this trip on breeding, but she improved on the form she showed when winning a decent 6f maiden at York with a game display. She hung right when coming under pressure in the straight, hampering a couple of her rivals in the process, but she stuck her neck out when strongly challenged by Beat Seven. She may now be dropped back to 6f for the Lowther Stakes, although she will have to be supplemented at a cost of £9,000. (tchd 11-8, 13-8 and 7-4 in places)
Beat Seven could only manage fourth off an estimated mark of 86 in a nursery on the Newmarket July course last time, but she improved on this switch back to better ground and was just held. She finished a long way clear of the remainder and is clearly very useful. (op 12-1)
Touching(IRE), who made all in a 6f maiden at Kempton on her previous start, ruined her chance by racing keenly in front and did well to hold on for third considering. (op 6-1)
Spanish Cygnet(USA), who landed a 7f maiden from the front on the Kempton Polytrack last time, was unable to dominate this time. She would have been slightly closer had she not been hampered over a furlong out, but she was not unlucky. (op 12-1)
Solo Attempt was worth a try at this level after winning a maiden and a minor novice event, but she did not help her chance by racing keenly and was well held. (tchd 14-1)
Maid For Music(IRE) produced quite a useful effort when winning her maiden over this trip at Salisbury, so this could be considered a little disappointing. (op 7-2 tchd 5-1)
Shaws Diamond(USA) will be better off back in maidens, although she does also now have the option of nurseries. (op 40-1)
Isabella Grey looked to have a great chance judged on the form she showed when getting up late on in a hot 6f novice event at Haydock on her previous start, but she ran no sort of race. The ground might have been quick enough, but even so she could have been expected to run better. (op 13-2)

4349 DAISY FANE MAIDEN STKS 1m 14y
3:55 (3:59) (Class 5) 3-4-Y-O **£3,885** (£1,156; £577; £288) **Stalls** High

Form RPR

22 **1** **Visions Of Johanna (USA)**[47] 2834 3-9-2 0........................ LDettori 12 82
(J Noseda) *led after 2f: mde rest: rdn 2f out: drew 2l clr ins fnl f: styd on* **11/8**[1]

- **2** ¾ **Taaresh (IRE)** 3-9-2 0........................ TedDurcan 6 80
(J L Dunlop) *dwlt: sn rcvrd to midfield: prog on inner over 2f out: plld out and styd on to chse wnr last 100yds: clsd but nvr quite able to chal* **14/1**

3 ¾ **Crackentorp** 3-9-2 0........................ GeorgeBaker 15 79
(G L Moore) *prom: chsd wnr over 2f out: chal over 1f out: one pce and hld ent fnl f: lost 2nd last 100yds* **25/1**

4 2 ¼ **Dollarsmile (USA)** 3-9-2 0........................ RyanMoore 14 73
(Sir Michael Stoute) *trckd ldrs: rdn and effrt 2f out: one pce and no imp on ldrs fr over 1f out* **5/1**[2]

5 2 **Mutawahej (USA)** 4-9-10 0........................ RHills 4 69
(J H M Gosden) *s.s: wl in rr early: sme prog 1/2-way: shkn up and kpt on fnl 2f: n.d* **8/1**[3]

3-66 **6** 3 ½ **Cotton Reel**[5] 4195 3-9-2 75........................ NelsonDeSouza 7 61
(P F I Cole) *plld hrd: prom: chsd wnr over 3f out to over 2f out: sn btn* **20/1**

5-0 **7** ½ **Qasayed (USA)**[42] 2971 3-8-11 0........................ LiamJones 9 55
(C E Brittain) *plld hrd: hld up bhd ldrs: cl enough over 2f out: sn outpcd and btn* **40/1**

-04 **8** nse **Encore Belle**[14] 3870 3-8-6 0........................ DavidProbert(5) 5 54
(Mouse Hamilton-Fairley) *hld up towards rr: pushed along over 2f out: styd on fnl f: nvr nr ldrs* **25/1**

5 **9** 2 ½ **Magpie (IRE)**[8] 4085 3-9-2 0........................ TQuinn 3 54
(B G Powell) *hld up in last quartet: pushed along and sme modest late prog: nvr nr ldrs* **33/1**

0 **10** ¾ **Rumline**[22] 3611 3-8-4 0........................ HollyHall(7) 2 47
(S A Callaghan) *s.s: mostly in last trio: shkn up and styd on fr over 1f out* **100/1**

11 ¾ **Mister Ross** 3-9-2 0........................ RichardHughes 10 50
(G L Moore) *led 2f: chsd wnr to over 3f out: wknd 2f out* **22/1**

05 **12** 2 ¼ **Miss Clarice (USA)**[29] 3379 3-8-11 0........................ AlanMunro 11 40
(B J Meehan) *t.k.h: hld up in rr of midfield: shkn up and modest prog 2f out: nvr on terms: eased nr fin* **14/1**

13 ½ **Serious Impact (USA)** 3-9-2 0........................ RobertHavlin 13 44
(J H M Gosden) *s.i.s: sn plld hrd and hld up in midfield: wknd 2f out* **10/1**

0-0 **14** 1 ¼ **Confide In Me**[21] 3628 4-9-10 0........................ HayleyTurner 1 41
(G A Butler) *s.s: a bhd* **50/1**

The Form Book, Raceform Ltd, Compton, RG20 6NL

3/ **15** *21* **Petroglyph**[631] 6297 4-9-10 0.. TPQueally 8 —
(P Bowen) *a in rr: wknd 3f out: t.o* **14/1**

1m 42.5s (-0.80) **Going Correction** -0.20s/f (Firm)
WFA 3 from 4yo 8lb **15 Ran SP% 124.1**
Speed ratings (Par 103): **96,95,94,92,90 86,86,86,83,82 82,79,79,78,57**
toteswinger: 1&2 £6.70, 1&3 £12.50, 2&3 £74.90. CSF £21.21 TOTE £2.40: £1.50, £3.10, £5.40; EX 26.10.
Owner Mountgrange Stud **Bred** David S Milch **Trained** Newmarket, Suffolk

FOCUS
Some big stables represented, but three-year-old plus maidens at this time of year don't tend to be too strong and the bare form is probably just fair with the winner the best guide. The pace was ordinary and it proved difficult to make up ground.
Cotton Reel Official explanation: jockey said gelding ran too free
Magpie(IRE) Official explanation: jockey said gelding ran too free

4350 FLORENCE NIGHTINGALE AID IN SICKNESS TRUST H'CAP 1m 2f 7y
4:30 (4:30) (Class 3) (0-90,88) 3-Y-O+ **£8,095** (£2,408; £1,203; £601) **Stalls** High

Form RPR
0341 **1** **Australia Day (IRE)**[24] 3561 5-9-7 **81**.................................. TedDurcan 5 99
(P R Webber) *mde all: shkn up over 2f out: styd on strly fnl 2f: in n.d over 1f out* **12/1**[3]

3551 **2** *2 ¾* **Presvis**[7] 4131 4-8-11 **78** 6ex.. MJMurphy[(7)] 1 91
(L M Cumani) *fluffed s and lost 8l: sn attached to rr of field: prog on inner to go 2nd over 2f out: rdn and no imp wnr over 1f out* **11/8**[2]

2411 **3** *10* **Hunting Country**[5] 4191 3-9-3 **87** 6ex...................................... LDettori 6 80
(M Johnston) *hld up in last pair: prog on outer to dispute 2nd over 2f out: sn shkn up and btn: wknd over 1f out* **11/10**[1]

6255 **4** *2* **Prince Sabaah (IRE)**[26] 3505 4-9-13 **87**...........................(p) RyanMoore 3 76
(R Hannon) *disp 2nd pl to over 2f out: wknd rapidly* **14/1**

0561 **5** *4 ½* **Colorado Blue (IRE)**[19] 3737 3-8-9 **79**...................(b) StephenDonohoe 4 59
(C E Longsdon) *disp 2nd pl to 3f out: hanging and wknd* **20/1**

2m 6.64s (-3.86) **Going Correction** -0.20s/f (Firm)
WFA 3 from 4yo+ 10lb **5 Ran SP% 108.8**
Speed ratings (Par 107): **107,104,96,95,91**
toteswinger: 1&2 £8.90. CSF £28.64 TOTE £11.20: £3.10, £1.30; EX 35.20.Hustle was withdrawn. Price at time of withdrawal 14/1. Rule 4 applies to board prices prior to withdrawal only. Deduct 5p in the pound.
Owner Samantha & Emma McQuiston Partnership **Bred** Kenilworth House Stud **Trained** Mollington, Oxon

FOCUS
This looked a straight match between Presvis and Hunting Country, who were both well ahead of the Handicapper under their respective penalties, but they were turned over by Australia Day, who had been allowed a soft lead. This looks good form, but it needs treating with a little caution.

NOTEBOOK
Australia Day(IRE) has often ruined his chance by racing too freely, but he won by eight lengths when ridden from the front on his first try over this trip at Windsor last time and, again able to dictate, he defied a 13lb higher mark in this tougher company. He was allowed to set just an ordinary pace, so is probably a little flattered, but this still rates as a very useful effort. He will be hammered for this considering the runner-up was racing off a mark 11lb lower than in future, and the pair were upwards of ten lengths clear, but he is clearly very useful when able to dominate on quick ground. His trainer said afterwards he may go back over hurdles at some point. (op 11-1 tchd 10-1)
Presvis won by nine lengths under this rider on his handicap over course and distance the previous week and he was 11lb well-in under his penalty, but this was tougher. He probably isn't straightforward, as he proved reluctant to canter to the start and then lost several lengths with a slow start. The steady gallop allowed him to make up the lost ground without too much fuss, but it was very much against him the respect that he is just a galloper. He was short of room when going for a gap against the rail about two furlongs out, but was in the clear for long enough if good enough. His new mark will make thing tougher, but he should still be competitive in strongly run races when in the right frame of mind. (op 5-4 tchd 6-5)
Hunting Country, bidding for a hat-trick, was 6lb well-in under the penalty he picked up for his clear-cut success in a decent Newbury handicap five days earlier, but he ran flat. Official explanation: jockey said colt was unsuited by the good to firm ground (op 5-4 tchd Evens)
Prince Sabaah(IRE) seems to be too high in the weights. (op 12-1 tchd 10-1)
Colorado Blue(IRE) was a winner at Nottingham on his final start for Roger Charlton, but this was tougher off a 5lb higher mark. His long-term future probably lies over hurdles. (op 28-1)

4351 GOLDEN LINK H'CAP 1m 6f
5:00 (5:01) (Class 3) (0-95,90) 3-Y-O **£9,714** (£2,890; £1,444; £721) **Stalls** High

Form RPR
3313 **1** **Victoria Montoya**[13] 3930 3-8-6 **75**.............................(p) FrancisNorton 7 84+
(A M Balding) *hld up bhd ldrs: rdn 3f out: prog u.p to go 2nd over 1f out: clsd fnl f: styd on wl to ld last 50yds* **5/1**[2]

1-32 **2** *½* **Detonator (IRE)**[5] 4205 3-9-7 **90**.. LDettori 2 98
(M Johnston) *trckd ldr: led wl over 2f out: sn 3 l clr and gng strly: rdn fnl f: worn down last 50yds* **11/8**[1]

2330 **3** *2 ¾* **The Betchworth Kid**[35] 3157 3-9-2 **85**................................ TPQueally 6 89+
(M L W Bell) *hld up in tch: lost pl 4f out: rdn and effrt over 2f out: styd on to take 3rd 1f out: unable to rch ldng pair* **5/1**[2]

01 **4** *3 ½* **Sevenna (FR)**[42] 2971 3-9-1 **84**.. TedDurcan 8 83
(H R A Cecil) *rel to r: sn in tch in last: effrt 4f out: outpcd over 2f out: plugged on* **9/1**

5061 **5** *2 ½* **Judgethemoment (USA)**[20] 3685 3-9-4 **87**............................ JohnEgan 1 83
(Jane Chapple-Hyam) *led: kicked on 4f out: hdd wl over 2f out: lost 2nd over 1f out and fdd* **17/2**[3]

5251 **6** *2 ¾* **Dalhaan (USA)**[32] 3297 3-9-5 **88**.................................... RyanMoore 3 80
(J L Dunlop) *hld up bhd ldrs: rdn 3f out: no rspnse and sn btn* **9/1**

2421 **7** *1 ½* **Dolly Penrose**[13] 3930 3-8-12 **81**................................ SamHitchcott 5 71
(M R Channon) *hld up in last pair: rdn and struggling 3f out* **9/1**

3m 3.80s (-2.80) **Going Correction** -0.20s/f (Firm) **7 Ran SP% 116.0**
Speed ratings (Par 104): **100,99,98,96,94 93,92**
toteswinger: 1&2 £2.10, 1&3 £4.50, 2&3 £2.80. CSF £12.70 CT £36.10 TOTE £6.00: £2.40, £1.40; EX 14.00 Place 6: £14.56, Place 5: £6.70..
Owner Kingsclere Racing CLub **Bred** Kingsclere Stud **Trained** Kingsclere, Hants

FOCUS
A good three-year-old staying handicap with the winner progressive and the runner-up to form.

NOTEBOOK
Victoria Montoya ◆ coped with the ground, the fastest she has encountered to date, and took well to the fitting of cheekpieces. She has plenty of size, so this galloping track suited, but she took an age to reel in the favourite and already looks in need of 2m. She may be given an entry in the Cesarewitch and gives the impression she will stay all day. Official explanation: trainer said, regarding apparent improvement in form, that the filly benefited from wearing first time cheek pieces. (op 13-2 tchd 7-1)
Detonator(IRE), upped to 1m6f for the first time, looked the winner when holding a clear lead inside the final two furlongs, but he was just reeled in. He didn't seem to do much wrong, but has a number of entries at Glorious Goodwood, a meeting his trainer likes to target. (op 5-4 tchd 7-4)
The Betchworth Kid, trying his furthest trip to date, ran a respectable race behind a couple of decent types for the grade. (op 15-2 tchd 8-1)
Sevenna(FR), a surprise Newbury maiden winner over 1m2f, started very awkwardly and was far from convincing with her attitude, but her connections apparently think she is still immature. (op 7-1 tchd 6-1)
Judgethemoment(USA), 2lb higher than when winning over course and distance on his previous start, had his chance from the front. Official explanation: jockey said colt hung left (op 8-1 tchd 9-1)
T/Plt: £29.10 to a £1 stake. Pool: £70,616.87. 1,768.02 winning tickets. T/Qpdt: £6.90 to a £1 stake. Pool: £4,334.70. 464.20 winning tickets. JN

4352 - (Foreign Racing) - See Raceform Interactive

4094 LEOPARDSTOWN (L-H)
Thursday, July 24

OFFICIAL GOING: Good to firm

4353a TYROS STKS (GROUP 3) 7f
6:25 (6:27) 2-Y-O **£33,507** (£9,830; £4,683; £1,595)

RPR
1 **Rip Van Winkle (IRE)**[27] 3463 2-9-1 .... JMurtagh 3 108+
(A P O'Brien, Ire) *hld up in rr: hdwy in 3rd 1 1/2f out: rdn into 2nd 1f out: qckdn to ld last 150yds: kpt on wl cl home: comf* **11/8**[2]

2 *1 ¼* **Cuis Ghaire (IRE)**[34] 3192 2-9-1 106.................................... KJManning 4 102
(J S Bolger, Ire) *chsd ldr in 2nd: impr to ld 1 1/2f out: rdn and hdd last 150yds: no ex: kpt on same pce* **8/11**[1]

3 *1 ½* **Vilasol (IRE)**[22] 3618 2-9-1 100.. DPMcDonogh 2 98
(Kevin Prendergast, Ire) *chsd ldrs in 3rd: rdn in 4th 1 1/2f out: 3rd 1f out: kpt on same pce fnl f* **14/1**[3]

4 *3 ½* **Lac A Dancer (IRE)**[8] 4095 2-8-12 90.................................... KLatham 1 87
(G M Lyons, Ire) *led: rdn and hdd 1 1/2f out: sn no ex and wknd over 1f out* **33/1**

1m 30.7s (0.40) **Going Correction** -0.025s/f (Good) **4 Ran SP% 109.6**
Speed ratings: **96,94,92,88**
CSF £2.76 TOTE £2.20; DF 3.30.
Owner Mrs John Magnier, M Tabor & D Smith **Bred** Roberto Brogi **Trained** Ballydoyle, Co Tipperary

NOTEBOOK
Rip Van Winkle(IRE) ◆, promoted to first having passed the post in second on his debut over this trip at the Curragh in June, took this step up in class in his stride and ultimately did the job in taking fashion. Having been ridden very patiently early on, he showed a nice turn of foot when asked to make up his ground in the home straight and it was clear nearing the final furlong he was the one to beat. He had plenty to spare on passing the post and looks a serious Classic contender for next season, with most bookmakers immediately promoting him towards the top of the 2000 Guineas ante-post betting. This son of Galileo promises to show even more when racing in a more truly-run affair and another step up in class now beckons, with the Group 2 Futurity Stakes back at the Curragh next month looking his sort of race. (op 11/8 tchd 5/4)
Cuis Ghaire(IRE), who landed the hat-trick when taking the Listed Albany Stakes at Royal Ascot last time, had her chance on this first attempt over the longer trip yet was firmly put in her place by the eventual winner at the business end. She may well have been better off forcing a stronger early pace and still lost little in defeat, rating the benchmark for this form. (op 4/5 tchd 9/10)

4356a MELD STKS (GROUP 3) 1m 2f
8:00 (8:00) 3-Y-O+ **£33,455** (£9,779; £4,632; £1,544)

RPR
1 **King Of Rome (IRE)**[18] 3773 3-8-11 106................................ JMurtagh 1 112
(A P O'Brien, Ire) *chsd ldr in 2nd: impr to chal 2f out: sn led: rdn and kpt on strly fnl f* **5/4**[1]

2 *2* **Lord Admiral (USA)**[74] 2026 7-9-12 112...........................(b) MJKinane 2 113
(Charles O'Brien, Ire) *racd 3rd: impr to 2nd 1 1/2f out: rdn and no imp 1f out: kpt on fnl f* **3/1**[3]

3 *2 ½* **Mustameet (USA)**[12] 3983 7-9-7 108................................ DPMcDonogh 4 103+
(Kevin Prendergast, Ire) *hld up in rr: rdn into 3rd 1 1/2f out: no ex over 1f out: kpt on same pce* **2/1**[2]

4 *12* **King Of Westphalia (USA)**[15] 3860 3-8-11 94.............. JAHeffernan 3 79
(A P O'Brien, Ire) *led: rdn and chal 2f out: sn hdd: no ex 1 1/2f out and sn wknd* **9/1**

2m 4.00s (-4.20) **Going Correction** -0.025s/f (Good)
WFA 3 from 7yo 10lb **4 Ran SP% 112.8**
Speed ratings: **115,113,111,101**
CSF £5.58 TOTE £2.00; DF 6.80.
Owner D Smith, Mrs J Magnier, M Tabor **Bred** The Amizette Partnership **Trained** Ballydoyle, Co Tipperary

NOTEBOOK
King Of Rome(IRE) opened his account for the year at the sixth time of asking on this drop back in trip and class, recording a career-best effort in the process. He tracked his pacemaking stable companion before taking it up around 2f out and then running on well to score readily enough. This should serve his confidence well and, while he is a little flattered as he had the run of the race, there are still more Group prizes to be won with him this term. (op 11/8 tchd 6/4)
Lord Admiral(USA) was unable to make a serious impression on the winner inside the final furlong, but still posted another commendable effort under top weight and looks well worth persevering with over this longer trip now. (op 100/30)
Mustameet(USA) is really happier over a sharper test than this and was below his recent level, but he was still not really suited by the way the race was run. (op 2/1 tchd 7/4)

4357 - 4358a (Foreign Racing) - See Raceform Interactive

3939 ASCOT (R-H)
Friday, July 25

OFFICIAL GOING: Good to firm
Wind: virtually nil Weather: warm

4359 JOHN GUEST MAIDEN FILLIES' STKS 6f
2:10 (2:12) (Class 3) 2-Y-O **£7,123** (£2,119; £1,059; £529) **Stalls** Centre

Form RPR
2 **1** **Good Again**[37] 3135 2-9-0 0.. HayleyTurner 3 79
(G A Butler) *w'like: chsd ldng pair: rdn and hung rt over 1f out: hrd rdn to chse ldr ins fnl f: r.o wl to ld nr fin* **7/2**[3]

2 **2** *nk* **Acquiesced (IRE)**[22] 3632 2-9-0 0.................................... RichardHughes 7 78
(R Hannon) *lw: led: rdn 2f out: edgd lft u.p fnl f: hdd nr fin* **11/8**[1]

0 **3** *1 ¾* **Sweet Possession (USA)**[21] 3674 2-9-0 0................ DarrenWilliams 2 73
(A P Jarvis) *dwlt: t.k.h: sn w ldr: ev ch and rdn 2f out: no ex last 100yds* **33/1**

4 5 **Wabi Sabi (IRE)** 2-9-0 0 .... WilliamBuick 1 58+
(B W Hills) *w'like: scope: bit bkwd: hld up in last: rdn and outpcd 1/2-way: no ch w ldrs after* **20/1**

5 *hd* **Kapsiliat (IRE)** 2-9-0 0 .... RyanMoore 4 57+
(J Noseda) *athletic: bit bkwd: t.k.h: hld up in last pair: rdn and outpcd 1/2-way: no ch w ldrs after* **9/4**[2]

6 *1 3/4* **No Nightmare (USA)** 2-9-0 0 .... (t) JohnEgan 6 52
(Jane Chapple-Hyam) *w'like: str: awkward leaving stalls and slowly away: sn trcking ldrs: rdn 2f out: sn wknd* **12/1**

1m 16.1s (1.70) **Going Correction** +0.075s/f (Good) **6** Ran SP% **110.5**
Speed ratings (Par 95): **91,90,88,81,81 79**
toteswinger: 1&2 £1.40, 1&3 £9.20, 2&3 £6.80. CSF £8.46 TOTE £4.60: £2.60, £1.30; EX 9.30.
Owner Future In Mind Partnership **Bred** L A Garfield **Trained** Newmarket, Suffolk

FOCUS
This has been a good maiden in recent years as three of the last five winners were subsequently successful in Group company - Carry On Katie, Silca's Sister and Albabilia. A very steady early pace means the form needs to be treated with some caution, but there were some nice types on show and the first three came clear with the runner-up rated to his debut mark for now. They raced down the middle early on before edging over towards the far rail in the closing stages.

NOTEBOOK
Good Again improved on the form she showed on her debut over 7f on the Kempton Polytrack on this drop in trip. She was never too far away from the steady early gallop, but she took a while to pick up once coming under pressure and only wore down the favourite near the line. There is a mix of speed and stamina in her pedigree, but a Cheveley Park entry suggests her connections believe her to have both plenty of pace and ability. (op 5-1)

Acquiesced(IRE), runner-up on her debut at Newbury, again found one too good. She had the run of the race, leading at just a steady pace, so there can be no excuses. (op 5-4 tchd 6-4)

Sweet Possession(USA) stepped up significantly on the form she showed on her debut over 7f at Salisbury. There has to be a chance she is flattered, as they went no pace early, but she clearly has ability.

Wabi Sabi(IRE) ◆, a 110,000euros daughter of Xaar and half-sister to 5f juvenile winner Durova, was too green to do herself justice. She struggled to get a position early and was never going to win having been last in a slowly run race, but she will know more next time.

Kapsiliat(IRE), a daughter of Cape Cross, half-sister to 1m three-year-old winner Kelowna, out of a very smart triple 7f-1m winner at two and three, has been given a Fillies' Mile entry, but she was well held on her racecourse debut. Her dam, Kootenay, had a preference for soft ground, so she could do better when there is some give underfoot. (op 2-1)

No Nightmare(USA), a 200,000gns daughter of Lion Heart and half-brother to useful juvenile sprinter Rabatash, and dual 6f winner Patternmaker, had a tongue-tie fitted for her debut. She recovered from a very slow start to chase the pace, and she travelled well to a point, but she weakened rather tamely late on. Entries in both the Lowther and the Fillies' Mile suggest she is considered capable of better. (op 11-1)

4360 JOHN GUEST E B F MAIDEN STKS 7f
2:45 (2:45) (Class 3) 2-Y-O £7,771 (£2,312; £1,155; £577) Stalls Centre

Form				RPR
4	1		**Derbaas (USA)**[16] 3853 2-9-3 0 .... JimmyFortune 5	89
			(E A L Dunlop) *led for 1f: chsd ldrs after: shkn up to ld narrowly wl over 1f out: hung lft and flashed tail fnl f: asserted last 50yds* **2/1**[1]	
	2	*3/4*	**Summers Target (USA)** 2-9-3 0 .... RyanMoore 7	87
			(B J Meehan) *unf: scope: bit bkwd: hld up bhd: hdwy over 2f out: rdn and ev ch fr wl over 1f out: hung lft ins fnl f: no ex last50yds* **10/1**	
3	3	*4*	**Sunny Future (IRE)**[25] 3568 2-9-3 0 .... WilliamBuick 6	77
			(M S Saunders) *w'like: t.k.h: chsd ldr: rdn to ld and hiung rt 2f out: sn hdd: outpcd by ldng pair fnl f* **16/1**	
	4	*1 3/4*	**Almiqdaad** 2-9-3 0 .... PhilipRobinson 3	73
			(M A Jarvis) *w'like: scope: bit bkwd: in tch in midfield: rdn 4f out: outpcd and dropped to rr 3f out: styd on again fr wl over 1f out: wnt 4th ins fnl f: gng on fin* **4/1**[3]	
	5	*3 1/4*	**Layer Cake** 2-9-3 0 .... EddieAhern 4	65
			(J W Hills) *w'like: leggy: awkward leaving stalls: hld up in tch: n.m.r over 2f out: rdn and rn green over 2f out: sn wknd* **33/1**	
	6	*5*	**Solar Graphite (IRE)** 2-9-3 0 .... SebSanders 9	52
			(J L Dunlop) *w'like: bit bkwd: s.i.s: a bhd: rdn and struggling fr 1/2-way* **14/1**	
	7	*9*	**Redding Colliery (USA)** 2-9-3 0 .... JohnEgan 8	30+
			(Jane Chapple-Hyam) *leggy: wnt rt at s: led: reminder 1/2-way: edgd rt and hdd 2f out: wkng whn n.m.r wl over 1f out: sn wl btn: eased ins fnl f* **11/4**[2]	
	8	*2 1/2*	**Tilos Gem (IRE)** 2-9-3 0 .... LDettori 2	23
			(M Johnston) *unf: a bhd: rdn and struggling 1/2-way: wl bhd last after* **9/1**	

1m 28.23s (0.23) **Going Correction** +0.075s/f (Good) **8** Ran SP% **114.6**
Speed ratings (Par 98): **101,100,95,93,89 84,73,71**
toteswinger: 1&2 £4.80, 1&3 £4.10, 2&3 £12.50. CSF £23.35 TOTE £2.90: £1.30, £3.60, £3.00; EX 28.10 Trifecta £120.30 Pool: £ 611.56 - 3.76 winning units..
Owner Hamdan Al Maktoum **Bred** Shadwell Farm LLC **Trained** Newmarket, Suffolk

FOCUS
This race was won last year by subsequent Royal Lodge winner City Leader, and Compton Admiral also won this before landing the 1999 Eclipse, but there have been some ordinary renewals as well. This looked a decent race, but they went steady early on and, although the level sees the winner and third as big improvers, it is worth treating the form positively for now. They raced up the middle of the track.

NOTEBOOK
Derbaas(USA) confirmed the promise he showed when fourth on his debut on soft ground on the July course, but he did not look straightforward, flashing his tail when hit with the whip and wandering around under pressure. He is entered in both the Champagne Stakes and the Royal Lodge, and is clearly pretty useful, but his resolution will be tested in better company. (op 13-8 tchd 6-4)

Summers Target(USA), an £88,000 son of Mr Greeley, first foal of dual winner on turf in the US, has no fancy entries, but this was a pleasing debut. He was just run out of it by a horse with experience, but he will know more next time and should difficult to beat in similar company. (op 25-1)

Sunny Future(IRE)'s debut third at Wolverhampton was a fair effort and he confirmed that promise with another decent showing. He could find a lesser maiden and will also be interesting when eligible for nurseries.

Almiqdaad, a son of Haafhd and half-brother to smart multiple 5f-7f winner Munaddam, out of a useful dual 7f-1m winner at two and three, who was also placed in the 1m4f Prix Vermeille, has been entered in the Champagne Stakes and the Royal Lodge. He seemed well fancied in the market, but ran green and looked in need of the experience. (tchd 7-2 and 9-2)

Layer Cake, a 26,000gns son of Monsieur Bond, half-brother to quite useful juvenile Genre, who was later a high-class miler in the US, travelled well for a long way but found little for pressure. He might have enough speed for 6f.

Redding Colliery(USA), a 310,000gns son of Mineshaft, half-brother to among others smart Joopy Doopy, a multiple dirt sprint winner at two and three in the US, out of a winner on turf at three in the States, is entered in both the Champagne Stakes and the Royal Lodge, but he failed to justify strong market support on this racecourse debut. This was disappointing, but he might be worth another chance, as he is clearly well regarded. Official explanation: jockey said colt had no more to give (op 3-1 tchd 10-3 in places)

4361 TRANSFORMERS AND RECTIFIERS E B F VALIANT STKS (LISTED RACE) (F&M) 1m (R)
3:20 (3:20) (Class 1) 3-Y-O+ £24,978 (£9,468; £4,738; £2,362; £1,183) Stalls High

Form				RPR
0150	1		**Baharah (USA)**[37] 3120 4-9-1 109 .... RichardHughes 6	109
			(G A Butler) *lw: hld up in last: plld out and hdwy 2f out: qcknd to ld over 1f out: edgd rt but r.o strly fnl f* **15/8**[1]	
0062	2	*1 1/2*	**Barshiba (IRE)**[13] 3940 4-9-1 110 .... TQuinn 3	105
			(D R C Elsworth) *chsd ldr: led over 2f out: rdn 2f out: hdd over 1f out: nt pce of wnr but battled on gamely to hold 2nd* **15/8**[1]	
2110	3	*hd*	**Kasumi**[16] 3852 5-9-5 102 .... TravisBlock 5	109
			(H Morrison) *lw: trckd ldng pair: rdn 3f out: plld out and jostled 2f out: kpt on same pce u.p fr over 1f out* **9/2**[2]	
-564	4	*3 1/4*	**Shaker (IRE)**[37] 3124 3-8-7 96 .... RobertHavlin 2	96
			(M L W Bell) *hld up in 4th pl: hdwy 3f out: jostled 2f out: wknd ent fnl f* **6/1**[3]	
3-24	5	*46*	**Candy Mountain**[48] 2820 4-9-1 79 .... SebSanders 4	—
			(L M Cumani) *led tl over 2f out: sn wknd: virtually p.u fnl f* **12/1**	

1m 39.55s (-1.25) **Going Correction** -0.175s/f (Firm)
WFA 3 from 4yo+ 8lb **5** Ran SP% **109.7**
Speed ratings (Par 111): **99,97,97,94,48**
toteswinger: 1&2 £2.90. CSF £5.46 TOTE £2.90: £1.70, £1.60; EX 3.80.
Owner Erik Penser **Bred** Darley **Trained** Newmarket, Suffolk

FOCUS
There were only five runners, but this was still a decent fillies & mares Listed contest. They went just an ordinary pace early on and the form is rated athrough the fourth, who also limits it to some extent.

NOTEBOOK
Baharah(USA)'s connections felt the race came too soon when she failed to beat a rival on the straight course here over this trip in the Group 2 Windsor Forest Stakes on her previous start but, freshened up after over a month off, she returned to form in good style. She was held up last, so the modest early pace can't have been ideal, but she quickly settled the race when switched out wide in the straight, showing a smart turn of foot. She has any number of options, both at home and abroad, but Gerard Butler's initial reaction was that the Group 1 Matron Stakes over 1m at Leopardstown may be her next target. (op 2-1 tchd 11-5 in a place)

Barshiba(IRE) ran well in second without matching the form she showed when runner-up over course and distance against colts in a Group 2 on her latest start. (op 7-4 tchd 2-1)

Kasumi had it all to do conceding upwards of 4lb all round, and her apprentice rider was unable to claim his 3lb allowance, but she ran a terrific race in defeat, clearly posting a career best. (op 11-2)

Shaker(IRE), the only three-year-old in the line up, found this tougher than the Sandringham Stakes in which she ran fourth at the Royal meeting.

Candy Mountain, rated only 79, was outclassed. (tchd 10-1)

4362 JOHN GUEST BROWN JACK STKS (H'CAP) 2m
3:55 (3:55) (Class 2) (0-100,100) 3-Y-O+ £12,952 (£3,854; £1,926; £962) Stalls High

Form				RPR
1121	1		**Wicked Daze (IRE)**[156] 630 5-9-3 92 .... SebSanders 5	99+
			(Sir Mark Prescott) *hld up in last trio: hdwy to chse ldng pair 5f out: rdn 3f out: led over 1f out: drvn and styd on wl* **2/1**[1]	
3-05	2	*1*	**Greenwich Meantime**[55] 2609 8-9-2 91 .... LDettori 2	96
			(R A Fahey) *lw: hld up in last pair: hdwy over 3f out: swtchd lft 2f out: hanging rt after: kpt on u.p to snatch 2nd on line: nt able to chal wnr* **4/1**[3]	
2-02	3	*nse*	**Colloquial**[55] 2609 7-9-7 96 .... (v) FergusSweeney 3	101
			(H Candy) *lw: chsd ldr: ev ch and rdn over 2f out: kpt on same pce fr over 1f out: lost 2nd on line* **3/1**[2]	
0-60	4	*4 1/2*	**Enjoy The Moment**[34] 3250 5-9-10 99 .... ShaneKelly 7	99
			(J A Osborne) *racd keenly: led stdy gallop: rdn wl over 2f out: hdd over 1f out: wknd fnl f* **15/2**	
12-6	5	*nk*	**Caracciola (GER)**[34] 3250 11-9-9 98 .... EddieAhern 6	97
			(N J Henderson) *t.k.h early: settled in bhd ldrs: rdn and effrt on inner over 2f out: gap clsd and nt clr run last 2f: no ch after* **5/1**	
00-0	6	*9*	**Vinando**[38] 3104 7-9-3 92 .... (bt) RyanMoore 4	80
			(C R Egerton) *in tch: rdn over 3f out: wknd over 1f out: wl btn and eased towards fin* **16/1**	
5-00	7	*51*	**Jadalee (IRE)**[34] 3249 5-9-11 100 .... RichardHughes 1	27
			(G A Butler) *taken down early: awkward leaving stalls: t.k.h: hld up in last: rdn and effrt 3f out: btn and eased last 2f* **16/1**	

3m 34.41s (1.81) **Going Correction** -0.175s/f (Firm) **7** Ran SP% **118.5**
Speed ratings (Par 109): **88,87,87,85,85 80,55**
toteswinger: 1&2 £2.50, 1&3 £1.80, 2&3 £2.50. CSF £11.00 TOTE £2.70: £1.90, £2.30; EX 9.90.
Owner Roger T Ferris **Bred** Bloomsbury Stud **Trained** Newmarket, Suffolk

■ Stewards' Enquiry : Shane Kelly one-day ban: careless riding (Aug 8)

FOCUS
A decent staying handicap, but the pace was just steady for much of the way and the form looks messy.

NOTEBOOK
Wicked Daze(IRE) had been off since February, but he had been progressing fast on the All-Weather when last seen, winning four of his five starts this year, and he continued where he left off with a determined success. He has picked up a 4lb penalty for the Ebor, in which he now has 8st 10lb and looks virtually certain to make the cut. Unsurprisingly, he is now vying for favouritism with Milne Graden at around 8-1.His trainer was apparently originally aiming him at the Northumberland Plate, and warns he will need a strong pace at York. The Cesarewitch will surely come into calculations later on. (op 15-8 tchd 7-4, 9-4 in a place)

Greenwich Meantime ran a decent race behind the improving winner, especially as he would have preferred a stronger end-to-end gallop. (op 9-2)

Colloquial could not confirm recent Haydock form with Greenwich Meantime, but he still ran well for his in-form yard. (op 10-3)

Enjoy The Moment stays all day and is often held up, but with no front runner in opposition he was forced to make his own running, which did not bring out the best in him. He is better than this. (op 9-1)

Caracciola(GER) looked to be travelling really strongly turning in, but he did not pick up immediately when asked to take a tight gap against the rail and the steady early pace was probably against him. He was continually short of room inside the final two furlongs, but it was basically a lack of tactical speed that found him out. Official explanation: jockey said gelding was denied a clear run (op 6-1 tchd 13-2)

4363 OCTOBER CLUB AND BRAINWAVE CHARITY H'CAP — 1m 2f

4:30 (4:32) (Class 2) (0-105,100) 3-Y-0+

£11,215 (£3,358; £1,679; £840; £419; £210) Stalls High

Form — RPR

-045 **1** **Buccellati**[20] 3721 4-10-0 **100**............(v) WilliamBuick 4 110+
(A M Balding) *hld up in last pl: plld out and hdwy over 2f out: qcknd to ld over 1f out: pushed clr fnl f* **2/1**[1]

1003 **2** 3 **William Blake**[14] 3896 3-8-6 **88**............ GregFairley 2 92
(M Johnston) *lw: chsd ldr: rdn to ld 2f out: hung lft over 1f out: sn hdd: no ch w wnr fnl f but kpt on gamely to hold 2nd* **5/1**[3]

133- **3** shd **King's Event (USA)**[272] 6499 4-8-13 **85**............ RyanMoore 3 89
(Sir Michael Stoute) *hld up in tch: rdn to chse ldng pair over 2f out: unable qck and swtchd lft over 1f out: rallied and kpt on fnl f: nrly snatched 2nd* **9/4**[2]

0411 **4** 3/4 **Press The Button (GER)**[21] 3676 5-8-12 **84**............ FergusSweeney 1 86
(J R Boyle) *led: jnd and rdn over 2f out: hdd 2f out: no ex u.p fnl f* **8/1**

6430 **5** 8 **Kayak (SAF)**[27] 3505 6-9-1 **87**............ RichardMullen 6 73
(D M Simcock) *hld up in last pair: rdn over 3f out: wknd over 1f out* **18/1**

0561 **6** 23 **Sahrati**[27] 3505 4-9-0 **91**............(b) AhmedAjtebi(5) 5 31
(C E Brittain) *lw: chsd ldrs: rdn 3f out: wknd 2f out: wl btn and eased fnl f* **11/2**

2m 5.61s (-4.19) **Going Correction** -0.175s/f (Firm)
WFA 3 from 4yo+ 10lb — **6 Ran SP% 112.5**
Speed ratings (Par 109): **109,106,106,105,99 81**
toteswinger: 1&2 £2.60, 1&3 £1.70, 2&3 £2.40. CSF £12.45 TOTE £3.30: £1.90, £2.80; EX 13.90.

Owner P C & Mrs J A McMahon **Bred** Burton Agnes Stud Co Ltd **Trained** Kingsclere, Hants

FOCUS
Only six runners, but they went a good pace and this was a decent handicap. However, there are doubts about the overall strength of the form.

NOTEBOOK
Buccellati has not had much luck in very hot handicaps on his last couple of starts, including when fifth over 1m4f on soft ground in the Old Newton Cup last time, but this was a little less competitive and everything fell into place. He will apparently skip the Ebor, as his trainer has even more enterprising plans for him. The Melbourne Cup, over a new distance, is still a possibility, and in the meantime he is likely to head either to Turkey for the Bosphorous Cup or to Woodbine for the Grade 1 Northern Dancer Stakes. He looks the type who could do very well abroad and is certainly with the right man for a globetrotting campaign. (op 9-4 tchd 5-2)

William Blake, the only three-year-old in the line up, was unable to dominate but he still ran well behind the smart winner. (op 9-2)

King's Event(USA), off the track for nine months with some niggly problems, made a satisfactory return and is entitled to improve for the run. (tchd 2-1 and 5-2)

Press The Button(GER) was bidding for a hat-trick off a mark 10lb higher than when starting his winning run at Folkestone, and 4lb higher than when following up at Salisbury, and he also didn't have the assistance of the 7lb claimer who had been on board for those two wins. He ran about as well as could have been expected. (op 7-1)

Kayak(SAF) has now been well beaten on his last two starts, but he shaped nicely on Polytrack on his first start in this country at Kempton and might be worth another try on that surface. (op 20-1)

Sahrati was only 4lb higher than when winning over 1m4f at Windsor on his previous start, but he ran no race this time. (op 6-1 tchd 13-2)

4364 EXCLUSIVE HOTELS H'CAP — 1m (S)

5:05 (5:05) (Class 4) (0-85,85) 3-Y-0+ £6,476 (£1,927; £963; £481) Stalls Centre

Form — RPR

4052 **1** **Red Somerset (USA)**[8] 4104 5-9-4 **80**............ MCGeran(5) 2 86
(R J Hodges) *lw: led tl 5f out: led again wl over 2f out: kpt on wl u.p last 2f* **5/2**[1]

3020 **2** 1 1/4 **Troubadour (IRE)**[21] 3684 7-9-7 **85**............(b) JPHamblett(7) 9 88
(W Jarvis) *t.k.h: hld up in tch: hdwy to chse wnr wl over 2f out: unable qckn u.p fnl f* **10/1**

10-5 **3** 1/2 **Danetime Panther (IRE)**[16] 3840 4-9-5 **76**............ RichardHughes 10 78
(P F I Cole) *stdd after s: t.k.h: hld up in rr: rdn and effrt over 2f out: kpt on and hung lft u.p fnl f: nt quite rch ldng pair* **15/2**

061 **4** 1/2 **Nightjar (USA)**[21] 3694 3-9-4 **83**............ LDettori 8 82
(M Johnston) *lw: in tch: rdn and unable qckn over 2f out: styd on u.p ent fnl f: edgd rt jst ins fnl f: kpt on but nt quite pce to rch ldrs* **7/2**[2]

006 **5** 4 1/2 **Cross The Line (IRE)**[23] 3612 6-8-13 **70**............(v[1]) DarrenWilliams 4 60
(A P Jarvis) *stdd after s: t.k.h: hld up in rr: rdn and nt qckn over 2f out: no ch w ldrs after* **11/1**

5-20 **6** 1 1/4 **Summer Dancer (IRE)**[30] 3367 4-9-7 **78**............ TQuinn 1 66
(D R C Elsworth) *taken down early: plld hrd: chsd ldr tl led and c to r alone towards stands' side 5f out: hdd over 2f out: sn btn: hung rt over 1f out* **13/2**[3]

5130 **7** 3 1/2 **Silver Blue (IRE)**[18] 3800 5-8-13 **70**............ JohnEgan 3 50
(W K Goldsworthy) *chsd ldrs: rdn 3f out: wknd over 2f out: eased whn wl btn fnl f* **7/1**

1140 **8** 13 **Daniel Thomas (IRE)**[21] 3664 6-9-6 **77**............ EddieAhern 5 27
(Mrs A L M King) *s.i.s: hld up in tch: rdn and hung rt over 2f out: eased fr wl over 1f out* **12/1**

1m 42.58s (1.98) **Going Correction** +0.075s/f (Good)
WFA 3 from 4yo+ 8lb — **8 Ran SP% 113.5**
Speed ratings (Par 105): **93,91,91,90,86 85,81,68**
toteswinger: 1&2 £6.20, 1&3 £5.90, 2&3 £11.90. CSF £27.93 CT £164.33 TOTE £3.40: £1.40, £2.90, £2.30; EX 30.30 Trifecta £563.10 Pool: £1141.58 - 1.50 winning units. Place 6: £14.70 Place 5: £9.09.

Owner R J Hodges **Bred** Haras D'Etreham **Trained** Charlton Mackrell, Somerset

FOCUS
A fair handicap but ordinary form for the course. They tended to race up the middle of the track.

Summer Dancer(IRE) Official explanation: jockey said gelding ran too free

Daniel Thomas(IRE) Official explanation: jockey said gelding lost its action

T/Jkpt: £3,090.80 to a £1 stake. Pool: £15,236.66. 3.50 winning tickets. T/Plt: £14.70 to a £1 stake. Pool: £93,873.45. 4,655.40 winning tickets. T/Qpdt: £8.70 to a £1 stake. Pool: £4,203.59. 355.60 winning tickets. SP

3901 CHEPSTOW (L-H)

Friday, July 25

OFFICIAL GOING: Good to firm (9.1)
Wind: Almost nil Weather: Fine

4365 PETESMITHCARSALES.CO.UK SOMETHING FOR EVERYONE AMATEUR RIDERS' H'CAP — 1m 4f 23y

6:20 (6:20) (Class 6) (0-65,63) 3-Y-0+ £2,186 (£677; £338; £169) Stalls Low

Form — RPR

000/ **1** **Mad Professor (IRE)**[248] 2131 5-10-5 **54**............(p) MrDColeman(7) 16 68
(Tim Vaughan) *hld up in mid-div: hdwy and hung lft over 3f out: led over 2f out: sn rdn and hung lft to far rail: styd on wl* **8/1**

2005 **2** 3 1/2 **Ryedale Ovation (IRE)**[16] 3836 5-11-7 **63**............ MissEJJones 17 71
(M Hill) *t.k.h in mid-div: hdwy over 5f out: wnt 2nd 2f out: sn ev ch: rdn and no ex fnl f* **9/1**

0453 **3** 1 1/4 **Under Fire (IRE)**[10] 4055 5-10-11 **58**............ MrMWall(5) 10 64
(A W Carroll) *led: rdn and hdd over 2f out: styd on same pce fnl f* **9/1**

/4-5 **4** shd **Tayman (IRE)**[9] 600 6-11-1 **62**............ MissZoeLilly(5) 12 68
(Carl Llewellyn) *chsd ldr: ev ch 3f out: rdn wl over 1f out: styd on same pce fnl f* **5/1**[1]

3633 **5** 4 1/2 **Postmaster**[16] 3839 6-9-10 **45**............ MissSSawyer(7) 11 44
(R Ingram) *hld up: sn towards rr: hdwy on wd outside over 2f out: sn rdn: nvr trbld ldrs* **8/1**

60-0 **6** 1/2 **Psychic Star**[23] 3604 5-10-11 **60**............ MrPJTolman(7) 15 58
(Mrs A M Thorpe) *hld up and bhd: rdn and hdwy over 2f out: no imp fnl f* **20/1**

500 **7** 2 3/4 **Hill Of Clare (IRE)**[8] 4123 6-10-0 **47**............ MrDFDevereux(5) 13 40
(G H Jones) *hld up and bhd: rdn over 2f out: n.d* **50/1**

6051 **8** hd **Trysting Grove (IRE)**[10] 4055 7-10-3 **52**............ MissIPickard(7) 6 45
(E G Bevan) *s.i.s: hld up and bhd: hdwy on ins over 4f out: no imp whn swtchd rt over 1f out* **11/2**[2]

300- **9** 1 1/4 **Great Man (FR)**[152] 1347 7-11-3 **59**............ MrWBiddick 9 50
(K M Prendergast) *hld up in tch: rdn and ev ch 3f out: wknd over 2f out* **16/1**

0210 **10** 1 1/2 **Bolckow**[29] 3399 5-10-12 **54**............ MrDRCook 7 43
(J T Stimpson) *prom: ev ch over 3f out: rdn and wknd over 2f out* **13/2**[3]

6000 **11** 3 **Opening Hand**[17] 2805 3-10-1 **55**............ MrLeeNewnes 3 39
(Evan Williams) *hld up in mid-div: reminder over 5f out: pushed along over 3f out: sn struggling* **12/1**

0/0- **12** 3/4 **Absolutelythebest (IRE)**[56] 5007 7-11-2 **63**............ MissSallyRandell(5) 14 46
(J G M O'Shea) *s.i.s: a bhd* **25/1**

0060 **13** 1 1/4 **King Of Diamonds**[11] 1207 7-9-10 **45**............ MissCHorsley(7) 4 26
(Norma Twomey) *s.i.s: sn hld up in mid-div: wknd 3f out* **40/1**

0/06 **14** shd **Spence Appeal (IRE)**[32] 3311 6-10-3 **50**............ MrIPopham(5) 8 31
(C Roberts) *prom tl rdn and wknd 3f out* **25/1**

0/ **15** 24 **Deo Gratias (POL)**[59] 3776 8-9-10 **45**............ MrSamPainting(7) 2 —
(Carl Llewellyn) *prom tl rdn and wknd 3f out* **20/1**

2m 39.31s (0.31) **Going Correction** -0.075s/f (Good)
WFA 3 from 5yo+ 12lb — **15 Ran SP% 122.8**
Speed ratings (Par 101): **95,92,91,91,88 88,86,86,85,84 82,82,81,81,65**
toteswinger: 1&2 £15.80, 1&3 £43.90, 2&3 £16.50. CSF £72.25 CT £675.74 TOTE £9.00: £3.10, £3.30, £3.10; EX 107.40.

Owner M Glastonbury **Bred** Jerry Murphy **Trained** Aberthin, Vale of Glamorgan

■ A winner on his first ride on the Flat for Dean Coleman.

FOCUS
A typically modest amateurs' contest and ordinary form rated around those in the frame behind the winner.

4366 BETINTERNET.COM CLAIMING STKS — 2m 49y

6:50 (6:50) (Class 6) 3-Y-0+ £2,266 (£674; £337; £168) Stalls Low

Form — RPR

534 **1** **Sonnengold (GER)**[14] 3901 7-9-6 49............ LPKeniry 12 59
(B J Llewellyn) *a.p: led on bit over 2f out: rdn over 1f out: styd on wl* **10/1**

-243 **2** 2 1/4 **Wotchalike (IRE)**[8] 4105 6-9-10 51............(p) PatDobbs 9 60
(Jim Best) *hld up in tch: rdn to chse wnr over 1f out: no imp* **9/2**[2]

240/ **3** 6 **Palace Walk (FR)**[12] 3035 6-9-9 52............ JimCrowley 5 52
(B G Powell) *led 1f: chsd ldr: led over 6f out: rdn and hdd over 2f out: wknd ins fnl f* **8/1**[3]

0000 **4** 2 1/4 **Poppy Gregg**[16] 3843 3-7-6 47............(b[1]) AmyBaker(7) 1 42+
(Dr J R J Naylor) *hld up and bhd: hdwy on outside 3f out: sn rdn: no real prog fnl f* **50/1**

0040 **5** 1 1/2 **Ronsard (IRE)**[49] 2776 6-9-8 44............ TGMcLaughlin 11 46
(P D Evans) *t.k.h towards rr: hdwy on ins over 3f out: rdn over 2f out: wknd over 1f out* **20/1**

542/ **6** nk **Arabian Moon (IRE)**[33] 4239 12-9-9 50............ NeilPollard 7 47+
(R Brotherton) *hld up in mid-div: rdn over 5f out: no real prog fnl 2f* **25/1**

6-03 **7** 3 3/4 **My Legal Eagle (IRE)**[14] 3901 14-9-4 45............ KevinGhunowa(3) 13 40
(E G Bevan) *hld up in tch: ev ch 3f out: rdn 2f out: wknd over 1f out* **18/1**

2000 **8** 1/2 **Queen Excalibur**[14] 3903 9-9-3 51............ RichardThomas 10 36
(C Roberts) *hld up in mid-div: hdwy over 3f out: rdn over 2f out: wknd over 1f out* **33/1**

24-1 **9** 4 1/2 **Tavalu (USA)**[36] 3160 6-10-0 65............(b) GeorgeBaker 3 41
(G L Moore) *prom: rdn over 4f out: wknd 3f out* **10/11**[1]

0 **10** 56 **Kosciusko**[31] 2988 7-9-5 0............ PaulFitzsimons 4 —
(J D Frost) *a bhd: t.o whn eased over 1f out* **33/1**

0-00 **11** 4 1/2 **Bold Josr**[11] 4023 4-9-5 0............ GabrielHannon(5) 15 —
(D J S Ffrench Davis) *s.s: a in rr: t.o whn eased over 1f out* **80/1**

4453 **12** 2 **Balais Folly (FR)**[11] 4026 3-8-6 50............(b) CatherineGannon 16 —
(B Palling) *t.k.h: led after 1f tl over 6f out: w ldr: rdn over 4f out: wknd qckly 3f out: eased 2f out: t.o* **16/1**

0- **13** 12 **Flexible Friend (IRE)**[50] 4620 4-10-0 63............(bt) VinceSlattery 2 —
(B J Llewellyn) *hld up in mid-div: rdn over 5f out: sn struggling: t.o* **16/1**

0- **14** 32 **Fine Edge**[88] 3366 7-9-4 0............(b[1]) WandersonD'Avila 6 —
(H E Haynes) *a in rr: t.o after 5f* **80/1**

3m 35.78s (-3.12) **Going Correction** -0.075s/f (Good)
WFA 3 from 4yo+ 17lb — **14 Ran SP% 126.7**
Speed ratings (Par 101): **104,102,99,98,98 97,95,95,93,65 63,62,56,40**
toteswinger: 1&2 £57.80, 1&3 £31.20, 2&3 £57.80. CSF £54.84 TOTE £15.20: £3.20, £1.60, £3.40; EX 75.10.Wotchalike was claimed by Mark Hughes for £6,000

Owner B J Llewellyn **Bred** J Schmidt **Trained** Fochriw, Caerphilly

■ Stewards' Enquiry : Wanderson D'Avila six-day ban: marked mare with whip (Aug 8-13)

FOCUS
A moderate staying claimer rated around the principals but not that solid.

Bold Josr Official explanation: jockey said gelding hung right-handed

4367 BEST ODDS GUARANTEED AT BETINTERNET.COM MAIDEN AUCTION STKS 6f 16y

7:20 (7:25) (Class 5) 2-Y-O £2,719 (£809; £404; £202) **Stalls High**

Form RPR

242 **1** **Stan's Cool Cat (IRE)**[39] 3085 2-8-11 0 ChrisCatlin 10 79
(P F I Cole) *trckd ldr on stands' rail: swtchd lft jst over 1f out: led ins fnl f: rdn out* **7/4**[1]

2222 **2** *1 1/4* **Hay Fever (IRE)**[15] 3888 2-8-9 0 JimCrowley 6 73
(Eve Johnson Houghton) *led on stands' rail: rdn and hdd ins fnl f: nt qckn* **7/4**[1]

032 **3** *3 1/2* **My Best Man**[15] 3889 2-8-9 0 TGMcLaughlin 3 63
(B R Millman) *t.k.h early: a.p: rdn over 1f out: wknd ins fnl f* **9/2**[2]

000 **4** *2 3/4* **Premier Demon (IRE)**[11] 4027 2-8-4 0 ow1 KirstyMilczarek(3) 1 53
(P D Evans) *w ldr over 2f: wknd over 1f out* **66/1**

50 **5** *shd* **Hum Cat (IRE)**[14] 3895 2-8-13 0 LPKeniry 5 58
(J S Moore) *prom: chsd ldr over 3f out tl wl over 1f out: wknd fnl f* **25/1**

6 *5* **Eager To Bow (IRE)** 2-9-2 0 GeorgeBaker 9 46
(P R Chamings) *dwlt: hld up and bhd: sme hdwy over 2f out: wknd over 1f out* **14/1**

7 *2 1/2* **Mr Flannegan** 2-8-9 0 FergusSweeney 7 32
(H Candy) *bhd: pushed along over 3f out: sn struggling* **10/1**[3]

8 *8* **Lady Meg (IRE)** 2-8-4 0 CatherineGannon 4 3
(B Palling) *bhd: hung lft over 3f out: lost tch over 2f out* **50/1**

1m 11.7s (-1.20) **Going Correction** -0.125s/f (Firm) 8 Ran SP% **114.0**

Speed ratings (Par 94): **103,101,96,93,92 86,82,72**

toteswinger: 1&2 £1.10, 1&3 £1.50, 2&3 £1.40. CSF £4.62 TOTE £2.50: £1.10, £1.30, £1.50; EX 5.00.

Owner Stan James Syndicate **Bred** Barronstown Stud **Trained** Whatcombe, Oxon

FOCUS

A decent contest for its type rated around the principals.

NOTEBOOK

Stan's Cool Cat(IRE) has some decent form to her name and only had to be kept up to her work to make sure of it. (op 5-4 tchd 2-1)

Hay Fever(IRE) did not find a drop back to 6f doing the trick and found one too good for the fifth time running. (op 9-4)

My Best Man raced freely early on back over an extra furlong and could not keep tabs on the two market leaders in the closing stages. (op 8-1 tchd 4-1)

Premier Demon(IRE) left her previous form behind although she was well held in the end. (tchd 80-1)

Hum Cat(IRE) does not appear to be progressing but is basically bred to require further. (op 33-1 tchd 20-1)

4368 PLAY LIVE CASINO AT BETINTERNET.COM E B F FILLIES' H'CAP 7f 16y

7:50 (7:51) (Class 5) (0-70,65) 3-Y-O+ £3,885 (£1,156; £577; £288) **Stalls High**

Form RPR

1540 **1** **Glencal**[15] 3892 4-9-11 **62** TravisBlock(3) 6 72
(H Morrison) *a.p: wnt 2nd over 3f out: rdn and chal over 1f out: led wl ins fnl f: r.o* **7/4**[1]

0-30 **2** *1/2* **Monda**[54] 2642 6-8-10 **51** AmyBaker(7) 2 60
(M Hill) *led: rdn over 1f out: hdd wl ins fnl f* **8/1**

-065 **3** *7* **Plumage**[21] 3679 3-9-5 **60** LPKeniry 8 47
(M Blanshard) *hld up: hdwy and wnt 3rd 3f out: rdn and no imp on ldng pair fnl 2f* **10/1**

0302 **4** *3 3/4* **Towy Girl (IRE)**[17] 3816 4-9-6 **57** KirstyMilczarek(3) 7 37
(A W Carroll) *dropped out s: t.k.h: hdwy over 3f out: wknd wl over 1f out* **7/2**[2]

0000 **5** *1 1/4* **Bidable**[30] 3383 4-9-2 **50** (t) CatherineGannon 10 27
(B Palling) *hld up in tch: rdn over 3f out: wkng whn edgd lft over 2f out* **12/1**

620- **6** *1/2* **Melt (IRE)**[268] 6578 3-9-5 **60** PatDobbs 3 32
(R Hannon) *hld up in mid-div: pushed along 3f out: rdn and wknd 2f out* **14/1**

-002 **7** *nk* **Secret Gem (IRE)**[15] 3893 3-9-5 **65** GabrielHannon(5) 5 36
(C G Cox) *prom tl rdn and wknd over 2f out* **17/2**

3-00 **8** *4* **Amyann (IRE)**[81] 1870 3-9-0 **55** ChrisCatlin 9 16
(J R Holt) *bhd fnl 4f* **40/1**

0-04 **9** *5* **Out Of Nothing**[86] 1729 5-10-0 **62** LiamTreadwell 4 12
(K M Prendergast) *hld up towards rr: struggling over 3f out* **15/2**[3]

0-00 **10** *5* **Oronsay**[21] 3678 3-8-6 **50** KevinGhunowa(3) 1 —
(B R Millman) *sn w ldr: wknd qckly over 3f out* **50/1**

1m 22.61s (-0.59) **Going Correction** -0.125s/f (Firm)

WFA 3 from 4yo+ 7lb 10 Ran SP% **119.8**

Speed ratings (Par 100): **98,97,89,85,83 83,82,78,72,66**

toteswinger: 1&2 £5.50, 1&3 £6.90, 2&3 £19.90. CSF £17.34 CT £117.83 TOTE £3.30: £1.40, £2.80, £2.50; EX 25.00.

Owner The Caledonian Racing Society **Bred** Fonthill Stud **Trained** East Ilsley, Berks

■ Stewards' Enquiry : Travis Block four-day ban: marked filly with whip (Aug 8-11)

FOCUS

A low-grade fillies' handicap which developed into a match in the final quarter of a mile. The first two are rated as slight improvers.

Secret Gem(IRE) Official explanation: jockey said filly lost its action

Oronsay Official explanation: jockey said filly ran too free

4369 CELEBRATING 10 YEARS AT BETINTERNET.COM H'CAP 7f 16y

8:20 (8:21) (Class 5) (0-75,74) 3-Y-O £3,238 (£963; £481; £240) **Stalls High**

Form RPR

0010 **1** **Monashee Rock (IRE)**[26] 3525 3-9-5 **72** TGMcLaughlin 3 76
(M Salaman) *stdd s: hld up in rr: pushed along and swtchd lft 2f out: hdwy over 1f out: hrd rdn to ld nr fin* **14/1**

603 **2** *hd* **Spin Again (IRE)**[9] 4083 3-9-3 **70** GeorgeBaker 8 73
(R M Beckett) *w ldr on stands' rail: swtchd lft over 2f out: rdn to ld ins fnl f: hdd nr fin* **13/8**[1]

-006 **3** *2* **Jay Gee Wigmo**[15] 3893 3-8-2 **55** oh10 FrancisNorton 4 53
(A W Carroll) *hld up in mid-div: rdn and hdwy wl over 1f out: kpt on to take 3rd cl home* **40/1**

-624 **4** *1 1/4* **Rondeau (GR)**[18] 3799 3-8-12 **65** LPKeniry 6 59
(P R Chamings) *led: rdn and hdd ins fnl f: fdd and lost 3rd cl home* **11/2**[3]

5043 **5** *1 1/2* **Just Jimmy (IRE)**[13] 3960 3-8-6 **59** CatherineGannon 7 49
(P D Evans) *chsd ldr: rdn over 2f out: wknd 1f out* **7/1**

1010 **6** *2 1/4* **Vigano (IRE)**[4] 4252 3-9-7 **74** JimCrowley 1 58
(S Kirk) *hld up and bhd: rdn and swtchd rt wl over 1f out: no hdwy* **8/1**

5046 **7** *1 1/2* **Ten Pole Tudor**[13] 3969 3-9-2 **72** KevinGhunowa(3) 2 52
(R A Harris) *hld up towards rr: last whn rdn wl over 1f out: no rspnse* **9/1**

0-41 **8** *3/4* **Rich Harvest (USA)**[42] 2988 3-8-5 **58** ChrisCatlin 5 36
(P D Evans) *w ldrs: rdn over 2f out: sn wknd* **7/2**[2]

1m 22.64s (-0.56) **Going Correction** -0.125s/f (Firm) 8 Ran SP% **118.4**

Speed ratings (Par 100): **98,97,95,94,92 89,88,87**

toteswinger: 1&2 £7.70, 1&3 £16.30, 2&3 £16.30. CSF £38.68 CT £950.97 TOTE £16.30: £3.40, £1.20, £6.90; EX 49.10.

Owner Mrs P G Lewin & D Grieve **Bred** M J Lewin And D Grieve **Trained** Baydon, Wilts

FOCUS

A very ordinary affair and the form looks pretty limited and not that solid.

4370 BETINTERNET.COM H'CAP 5f 16y

8:55 (8:55) (Class 5) (0-70,67) 3-Y-O+ £2,914 (£867; £433; £216) **Stalls High**

Form RPR

1232 **1** **Nusoor (IRE)**[10] 4064 5-9-4 **63** (v) KirstyMilczarek(3) 6 76
(Peter Grayson) *mde all: crossed to stands' rail over 3f out: rdn over 1f out: hld on wl* **4/1**[2]

1462 **2** *1/2* **Equuleus Pictor**[7] 4154 4-9-5 **66** JackDean(5) 1 77
(J L Spearing) *a.p: rdn and ev ch ins fnl f: r.o* **10/3**[1]

335 **3** *nse* **Matterofact (IRE)**[3] 4273 5-8-11 **56** TolleyDean(3) 3 67
(M S Saunders) *a.p: rdn over 1f out: ev ch ins fnl f: r.o* **11/1**

633 **4** *2 3/4* **Hart Of Gold**[7] 4154 4-9-10 **66** GeorgeBaker 11 67+
(R A Harris) *hld up and bhd: rdn wl over 1f out: swtchd lft and hdwy ins fnl f: r.o to take 4th nr post* **4/1**[2]

05-0 **5** *shd* **Back In The Red (IRE)**[31] 3352 4-9-6 **67** HaddenFrost(5) 10 68
(R A Harris) *hld up in mid-div: rdn over 2f out: hdwy over 1f out: rdn and kpt on same pce fnl f* **20/1**

6000 **6** *1/2* **Peopleton Brook**[3] 4285 6-8-8 **50** (p) ChrisCatlin 4 49
(J M Bradley) *chsd ldrs: swtchd lft to outside over 2f out: rdn fnl f: no ex towards fin* **28/1**

0100 **7** *3/4* **Metal Guru**[21] 3695 4-9-4 **63** (p) RussellKennemore(3) 5 59
(R Hollinshead) *towards rr: rdn over 2f out: hdwy 1f out: nvr trbld ldrs* **20/1**

6043 **8** *1/2* **The Little Fizzer (IRE)**[11] 4028 3-8-9 **55** FergusSweeney 2 49
(P D Evans) *prom tl wknd wl over 1f out* **20/1**

5532 **9** *hd* **Harrison's Flyer (IRE)**[8] 4125 7-8-9 **56** (p) MCGeran(5) 13 50+
(J M Bradley) *hld up in rr: sn hung lft: sme hdwy whn nt clr run wl ins fnl f: n.d* **9/1**[3]

0605 **10** *2 1/2* **Archilini**[8] 4106 3-8-11 **57** (p) JimCrowley 12 42
(M Sheppard) *a towards rr* **18/1**

00 **11** *3/4* **One Way Ticket**[10] 4051 8-8-13 **58** (b) KevinGhunowa(3) 8 40
(J M Bradley) *chsd ldrs tl wknd 2f out* **25/1**

0-10 **12** *3/4* **Danjet (IRE)**[16] 3842 5-9-4 **60** TGMcLaughlin 9 39
(P D Evans) *chsd ldrs: rdn over 2f out: wknd wl over 1f out* **9/1**[3]

00-0 **13** *6* **Talcen Gwyn (IRE)**[8] 4106 6-9-1 **57** (v) FrancisNorton 7 15
(M F Harris) *s.i.s: a in rr* **16/1**

58.20 secs (-1.10) **Going Correction** -0.125s/f (Firm)

WFA 3 from 4yo+ 4lb 13 Ran SP% **124.1**

Speed ratings (Par 103): **103,102,102,97,97 96,95,94,94,90 89,88,78**

toteswinger: 1&2 £2.10, 1&3 £35.30, 2&3 £67.90. CSF £16.87 CT £142.35 TOTE £4.80: £2.00, £1.70, £3.90; EX 19.40 Place 6 £ 89.06, Place 5 £ 15.32.

Owner R Teatum And Mrs S Grayson **Bred** Shadwell Estate Company Limited **Trained** Formby, Lancs

FOCUS

The three principals in this competitive low-key sprint handicap continue to perform well. The winner is rated to his best winter form.

Harrison's Flyer(IRE) Official explanation: jockey said gelding was denied a clear run

T/Plt: £95.60 to a £1 stake. Pool: £60,946.94. 465.06 winning tickets. T/Qpdt: £6.10 to a £1 stake. Pool: £5,609.18. 675.78 winning tickets. KH

4194 NEWMARKET (R-H)

Friday, July 25

OFFICIAL GOING: Good to firm (8.2)

Wind: Fresh against Weather: Cloudy with sunny spells

4371 BOLLINGER CHAMPAGNE CHALLENGE SERIES H'CAP (FOR GENTLEMAN AMATEUR RIDERS) 1m 2f

5:40 (5:42) (Class 5) (0-70,74) 3-Y-O+ £3,747 (£1,162; £580; £290) **Stalls High**

Form RPR

1230 **1** **Laish Ya Hajar (IRE)**[4] 4254 4-11-1 **65** MrPJones(7) 1 76
(P R Webber) *led after 1f: mde rest: clr 6f out: sddle sed to slip fr over 2f out: pushed along and hung lft fr over 1f out: styd on wl: uns rdr after post* **9/1**

0424 **2** *1 3/4* **Bavarica**[29] 3422 6-10-13 **61** MrRBirkett(5) 13 68
(Miss J Feilden) *a.p: rdn to chse wnr over 1f out: edgd lft: styd on* **7/1**[2]

3220 **3** *3/4* **Turner's Touch**[21] 3687 6-11-5 **67** (b) MrJoshuaMoore(5) 6 73
(G L Moore) *hld up: hdwy over 2f out: rdn fr over 1f out: edgd lft: nt run on* **10/1**

5214 **4** *8* **Faith And Reason (USA)**[3] 4275 5-11-5 **62** 6ex (b[1]) MrSWalker 4 52
(A P Stringer) *led 1f: racd keenly: chsd wnr tl rdn over 1f out: sn wknd* **1/1**[1]

-005 **5** *1/2* **Fantasy Crusader**[3] 4267 9-9-13 **49** MrIPMcBride(7) 10 38
(R M H Cowell) *s.s: wl bhd tl styd on fr over 1f out: nvr nrr* **20/1**

-000 **6** *2 3/4* **Le Corvee (IRE)**[12] 3606 6-11-5 **65** MrMJJSmith(3) 7 48
(A W Carroll) *mid-div: hdwy 1/2-way: rdn and wknd over 1f out* **17/2**[3]

0000 **7** *4* **Louisiade (IRE)**[7] 4156 7-10-1 **51** MrHSensoy(7) 11 26
(M C Chapman) *hld up: sn wl bhd: nvr nrr* **25/1**

00-0 **8** *hd* **Bournonville**[5] 2374 5-10-0 **48** oh3 MrSRees(5) 12 23
(M Wigham) *mid-div: hdwy over 5f out: rdn over 2f out: sn edgd lft and wknd* **66/1**

0000 **9** *1 1/2* **Kalasam**[40] 3054 4-11-1 **65** MrJakeGreenall(7) 5 37
(M W Easterby) *chsd ldrs: swtchd lft over 3f out: sn rdn: wknd over 1f out* **14/1**

5000 **10** *17* **Lordswood (IRE)**[3] 4267 4-9-13 **49** (v[1]) MrRTPierson(7) 9 —
(J R Best) *dwlt: sn wl bhd* **16/1**

6230 **11** *12* **Iceman George**[22] 3655 4-10-11 **59** (b) MrBMMorris(5) 2 —
(D Morris) *s.i.s: sn in mid-div: rdn and wknd over 3f out* **9/1**

2m 7.21s (1.71) **Going Correction** +0.075s/f (Good)

WFA 3 from 4yo+ 10lb 11 Ran SP% **124.8**

Speed ratings (Par 103): **96,94,94,87,87 85,81,81,80,66 57**

toteswinger: 1&2 £8.50, 1&3 £17.70, 2&3 £8.40. CSF £73.72 CT £661.45 TOTE £12.50: £2.90, £2.40, £2.10; EX 106.40.

Owner The Auctionair Racing Partnership **Bred** Gainsborough Stud Management Ltd **Trained** Mollington, Oxon

■ A first winner at the first attempt for amateur Peter Jones.

FOCUS
Three came clear in what was a moderate handicap and the form is ordinary rated through the runner-up. Much credit has to go the winning duo for overcoming a slipping saddle.

4372 NEWMARKETRACECOURSES.CO.UK MAIDEN STKS 1m 4f
6:10 (6:10) (Class 4) 3-Y-O £5,180 (£1,541; £770; £384) Stalls High

Form				RPR
0-32	1		**Woodcutter (IRE)**16 3854 3-9-3 85 JimmyFortune 1 (J H M Gosden) *a.p: edgd rt and led over 2f out: shkn up and r.o wl ins fnl f: eased towards fin* 1/1[1]	88
43	2	4 1/2	**King O'The Gypsies (IRE)**16 3854 3-9-3 0 SteveDrowne 7 (R Charlton) *chsd ldrs: rdn whn hmpd over 2f out: chsd wnr over 1f out: styd on same pce ins fnl f* 2/1[2]	81
0-4	3	4 1/2	**Houghton (IRE)**98 1446 3-9-3 0 RyanMoore 4 (Sir Michael Stoute) *hld up: pushed along over 3f out: hdwy over 2f out: rdn and wknd fnl f* 7/1[3]	74
0-50	4	6	**Dubai Samurai**56 2564 3-9-3 73 JamesDoyle 5 (J W Hills) *led after 1f: rdn and hdd over 2f out: wknd over 1f out* 18/1	64
63	5	2 1/4	**Optimus Maximus (IRE)**26 3530 3-9-3 0 (t) DarryllHolland 2 (P F I Cole) *chsd ldrs: rdn whn hmpd over 2f out: wknd over 1f out* 9/1	61
50	6	5	**Montevetro**102 1367 3-9-3 0 TonyCulhane 6 (R Hannon) *hld up: rdn 5f out: wknd over 3f out* 50/1	53
5	7	26	**Etta Place**25 3556 3-8-12 0 TPQueally 3 (P W Chapple-Hyam) *dwlt: hld up: rdn and wknd wl over 3f out: eased fnl f* 66/1	6

2m 30.3s (-2.60) **Going Correction** +0.075s/f (Good) 7 Ran SP% **114.5**
Speed ratings (Par 102): **111,108,105,101,99 96,78**
toteswinger: 1&2 £1.10, 1&3 £1.60, 2&3 £3.10. CSF £3.19 TOTE £2.10: £1.40, £1.80; EX 3.50.
Owner H R H Princess Haya Of Jordan **Bred** Airlie Stud **Trained** Newmarket, Suffolk

FOCUS
A useful maiden rated around the runner-up with the winner raised 4lb.
Etta Place Official explanation: trainer said filly suffered a breathing problem and appeared to be unsuited by the good to firm ground

4373 DRIVE VAUXHALL BURY ST EDMUNDS NURSERY 7f
6:40 (6:40) (Class 4) 2-Y-O £6,476 (£1,927; £963; £481) Stalls Low

Form				RPR
230	1		**Swingfire (USA)**9 4079 2-7-5 60 (p) AndreaAtzeni(7) 9 (R M H Cowell) *hld up: hdwy 2f out: rdn to ld 1f out: styd on* 16/1	62
2203	2	1/2	**Servoca (CAN)**21 3677 2-9-7 83 RyanMoore 7 (B W Hills) *chsd ldr: led over 1f out: sn rdn: edgd rt and hdd: styd on* 9/4[1]	84
0531	3	2	**Meydan Groove**20 3726 2-8-6 68 HayleyTurner 1 (P F I Cole) *chsd ldrs: rdn and ev ch over 1f out: styd on same pce ins fnl f* 6/1	64
2216	4	1 1/4	**The Dial House**9 4079 2-9-6 82 ShaneKelly 5 (J A Osborne) *a.p: rdn and ev ch over 1f out: no ex ins fnl f* 3/1[2]	75
01	5	1/2	**Fastnet Storm (IRE)**31 3334 2-9-0 76 TonyCulhane 4 (T P Tate) *led: rdn and hdd over 1f out: no ex ins fnl f* 7/2[3]	68
403	6	3/4	**One Cool Kitty**13 3959 2-8-5 70 DominicFox(3) 6 (M G Quinlan) *awkward leaving stalls: hld up: rdn over 2f out: no imp fnl f* 9/1	60
046	7	3/4	**Balladiene (IRE)**37 3135 2-8-6 68 NickyMackay 8 (M H Tompkins) *hld up: hdwy over 4f out: rdn over 2f out: sn lost pl* 25/1	56
050	8	21	**Indian Blade (IRE)**23 3603 2-7-5 60 oh1 CharlesEddery(7) 2 (M D I Usher) *mid-div: lost pl over 4f out: wkng whn hung lft fr over 2f out* 20/1	—

1m 26.82s (1.12) **Going Correction** +0.075s/f (Good) 8 Ran SP% **116.8**
Speed ratings (Par 96): **96,95,93,91,91 90,89,65**
toteswinger: 1&2 £10.20, 1&3 £16.30, 2&3 £2.60. CSF £53.47 CT £253.85 TOTE £23.60: £4.40, £1.30, £1.90; EX 78.40.
Owner Prestige Racing **Bred** Mike G Rutherford **Trained** Six Mile Bottom, Cambs

FOCUS
Just a fair nursery with the principals slightly up on pre-race figures. The 'official' ratings shown next to each horse are estimated and for information purposes only.

NOTEBOOK
Swingfire(USA) could make no impression off this mark on his recent nursery debut, two places behind The Dial House, but the first-time cheekpieces he was wearing here clearly made a difference and, having settled nicely off the pace, he came with a strong run to cut down the top weight. He was winning off a lowly mark here and it is likely he remains capable of better. (tchd 14-1)
Servoca(CAN) lacked the pace when only third on his recent nursery debut at Salisbury and showed improved form for this step up to 7f. He was run down late by the winner and is not going to find winning easy off this mark, but still has physical scope and may yet improve. (op 3-1)
Meydan Groove, easy winner of a seller at Leicester last time, had more on her plate here and was stepping back up in trip, but saw it out well enough and showed improved form. (op 13-2 tchd 9-2)
The Dial House had little go right for him when a beaten-favourite at Kempton last time, and was expected to go close off the same mark. However, having travelled up well two out, he was soon in trouble and could not pick up inside the final furlong. Perhaps a drop back to 6f in needed on this evidence. (op 11-4 tchd 10-3 tchd 7-2 in a place)
Fastnet Storm(IRE), narrow winner of a Beverley maiden, looked to be starting out his handicap career off just a fair mark and was a shade disappointing, emptying out rather quickly once headed. (tchd 5-1)

4374 EUROPEAN BREEDERS' FUND CONDITIONS STKS 6f
7:10 (7:10) (Class 3) 2-Y-O £9,066 (£2,697; £1,348; £673) Stalls Low

Form				RPR
010	1		**Pure Poetry (IRE)**6 4190 2-9-3 0 RyanMoore 3 (R Hannon) *mde all: rdn over 1f out: styd on wl* 11/8[1]	96
1	2	2 1/4	**Laahig**30 3365 2-9-3 0 ShaneKelly 4 (G A Butler) *hld up: hdwy to chse wnr fnl f: styd on* 10/1	89+
1	3	3	**Dove Mews**28 3456 2-9-0 0 HayleyTurner 1 (M L W Bell) *chsd ldrs: rdn over 2f out: hung lft over 1f out: edgd rt and wknd ins fnl f* 10/1	77
01	4	2 1/4	**Zaffaan**14 3895 2-9-5 0 JimmyFortune 2 (E A L Dunlop) *hld up in tch: rdn over 1f out: wknd and eased ins fnl f* 10/3[2]	76+
15	5	3	**Deadly Encounter (IRE)**48 2838 2-9-0 0 JamieMoriarty(3) 6 (R A Fahey) *chsd ldrs: rdn over 1f out: wknd fnl f* 11/1	65
1	6	1 1/4	**Chicago Cop (IRE)**56 2584 2-9-5 0 AdrianTNicholls 5 (D Nicholls) *trckd wnr: plld hrd: rdn over 1f out: sn wknd* 7/2[3]	63

1m 13.19s (0.69) **Going Correction** +0.075s/f (Good) 6 Ran SP% **113.9**
Speed ratings (Par 98): **98,95,91,88,84 82**
toteswinger: 1&2 £4.10, 1&3 £4.90, 2&3 £9.60. CSF £16.68 TOTE £2.50: £1.40, £3.20; EX 18.70.
Owner Mrs J Wood **Bred** R Collins And Jerry Kennedy **Trained** East Everleigh, Wilts

FOCUS
A decent little conditions race with the winner running close to his Super Sprint form.

NOTEBOOK
Pure Poetry(IRE), a Haydock maiden winner who found things happening too quickly in last weekend's Super Sprint (running on late for eighth) was making a quick reappearance, but that race had clearly not done him any harm and he appreciated the return to 6f. Soon in front, he was in complete control from a furlong out and it will be interesting to see where he goes next. (op 6-4)
Laahig, narrow winner of an ordinary Carlisle maiden, was up in trip here and had faster ground conditions to deal with, but he shaped better than expected and stayed on nicely in second, albeit he never looked like getting to the winner. He will stay further than this in time and remains capable of better. (op 8-1)
Dove Mews, a narrow course and distance winner on debut, was faced with stiffer opposition here, but she fared quite well back in third and will find easier opportunities. The way she travelled up before hanging suggests this ground would not have been in her favour and it is likely she remains capable of better. (op 11-1 tchd 12-1)
Zaffaan seemed to revel in the softening ground when bolting up at Ascot earlier in the month and there were doubts as to how he would cope with the faster surface here. He looked far from happy, giving the impression of a horse not letting himself down, and can be given another chance. Official explanation: trainer's rep said colt was unsuited by the good to firm ground (op 11-4 tchd 7-2)
Deadly Encounter(IRE) has not built on his impressive debut success and needs dropping in grade. (op 10-1 tchd 8-1)
Chicago Cop(IRE), a ready winner on debut at York back in May, was up in grade here an ruined his chance by pulling hard through the early stages. He dropped right out in the end and clearly needs to learn to settle. Official explanation: jockey said colt ran too free (op 6-1 tchd 7-1 in a place)

4375 NEWMARKET NIGHTS H'CAP 6f
7:40 (7:40) (Class 3) (0-90,89) 3-Y-O+ £9,066 (£2,697; £1,348; £673) Stalls Low

Form				RPR
3006	1		**The Game**29 3394 3-8-7 74 RichardKingscote 1 (Tom Dascombe) *chsd ldr: shkn up to ld over 1f out: edgd rt ins fnl f: readily* 12/1	86+
6605	2	1	**Cornus**5 4218 6-8-13 75 (be) JamesDoyle 2 (A J McCabe) *hld up: hdwy over 2f out: rdn over 1f out: r.o* 7/1	82
6-45	3	2	**King's Caprice**14 3905 7-9-12 88 (t) RyanMoore 4 (J A Geake) *led: rdn and hdd over 1f out: styd on same pce fnl f* 11/4[1]	89
4002	4	1 1/4	**Resplendent Alpha**34 3271 4-8-8 70 ShaneKelly 5 (P Howling) *hld up: plld hrd: rdn and hung lft over 1f out: nt rch ldrs* 6/1[3]	67
6000	5	nk	**Fantasy Believer**13 3973 10-9-1 77 DarryllHolland 3 (J J Quinn) *chsd ldrs: rdn over 1f out: no ex fnl f* 10/1	73
0100	6	nk	**Liberty Belle (IRE)**35 3224 3-8-4 71 HayleyTurner 9 (J R Best) *prom: rdn over 1f out: no ex fnl f* 20/1	65
010	7	nk	**Brunelleschi**14 3898 5-8-13 75 (b) TedDurcan 6 (P L Gilligan) *hld up: rdn over 2f out: n.d* 6/1[3]	69
-U00	8	2 3/4	**Lytton**16 3850 3-9-8 89 (b[1]) JimmyFortune 7 (W R Swinburn) *s.s: hld up: rdn over 1f out: eased fnl f* 15/2	76
0020	9	14	**Trojan Flight**27 3489 7-8-13 78 JamieMoriarty(3) 8 (R A Fahey) *hld up: rdn over 2f out: wknd over 1f out* 11/2[2]	18

1m 12.12s (-0.38) **Going Correction** +0.075s/f (Good)
WFA 3 from 4yo+ 5lb 9 Ran SP% **116.4**
Speed ratings (Par 107): **105,103,101,99,98 98,98,94,75**
toteswinger: 1&2 £19.80, 1&3 £17.50, 2&3 £6.80. CSF £93.68 CT £300.75 TOTE £17.60: £3.90, £2.60, £1.50; EX 159.80.
Owner M Khan X2 **Bred** Aston House Stud **Trained** Lambourn, Berks

FOCUS
Just a fair sprint handicap and doubts over the form with little solid recent form to go on.

NOTEBOOK
The Game, currently rated 6lb lower on turf, has beaten just two horses home on his last three starts, but he came right back to his best and won with a bit to spare on his first start for Tom Dascombe. He was 3lb lower here than when winning at Lingfield back in December, but may struggle to defy a rise. (op 11-1 tchd 10-1)
Cornus has worked his way back down to his last winning mark and, having run well off it last time, improved to take second in this slightly stronger contest. He seems to prefer some ease in the ground and may soon be back winning. (tchd 13-2 and 8-1)
King's Caprice has not won since October 2006, but he has slipped to a very favourable mark now and it was disappointing he could not put up more of a fight. It was still a fair effort though and he is certainly weighted to win again. (op 4-1)
Resplendent Alpha has never won a handicap, but he went close off a 2lb higher mark at the course recently and this was another reasonable effort, staying on too late. (op 11-2 tchd 5-1)
Fantasy Believer, well into the veteran stage of his career, continues to plummet in the weights and this was a little more encouraging. The old boy may still be capable of winning at the right level. Official explanation: trainer's rep said gelding was unsuited by the good to firm ground (op 8-1)
Liberty Belle(IRE), successful off a mark of 67 at Folkestone earlier in the season, has subsequently struggled off marks in the 70s and she ran about as well as could have been expected. (op 16-1)
Brunelleschi, a course and distance winner last month, subsequently flopped at Ascot and he was unable to confirm earlier form with Resplendent Alpha, again running below par.
Trojan Flight Official explanation: vet said gelding had bled from the nose

4376 TURFTV CONDITIONS STKS 1m 4f
8:10 (8:11) (Class 3) 3-Y-O+ £9,969 (£2,985; £1,492) Stalls High

Form				RPR
-23	1		**Eastern Anthem (IRE)**13 3975 4-9-1 109 (t) LDettori 4 (Saeed Bin Suroor) *mde virtually all: shkn up and hung rt over 1f out: styd on wl: eased nr fin* 8/15[1]	89+
2-52	2	10	**Munsef**76 1980 6-9-1 107 (b) JimmyFortune 1 (J L Dunlop) *chsd wnr: hung rt and chal over 1f out: sn hrd rdn and nt run on: eased wl ins fnl f* 6/4[2]	83
00-0	3	18	**Little Hotpotch**165 282 4-8-7 38 DominicFox(3) 5 (M J Gingell) *chsd ldrs tl rdn and wknd over 2f out* 66/1[3]	39

2m 34.12s (1.22) **Going Correction** +0.075s/f (Good) 3 Ran SP% **106.7**
Speed ratings (Par 107): **98,91,79**
CSF £1.61 TOTE £1.50; EX 1.50.
Owner Godolphin **Bred** Darley **Trained** Newmarket, Suffolk

FOCUS
A straight match on paper and Eastern Anthem proved the more willing.

NOTEBOOK
Eastern Anthem(IRE), who struggled to pick up in the heavy ground at York last time, had earlier run well on his seasonal reappearance at Goodwood (just losing out to Peppertree Lane in a Listed contest) and the better ground here seemed more to his liking. Soon in front, Munsef looked a big danger at one point, but he galloped on relentlessly and was well on top at the line. A slightly slower surface is believed to be preferable and he now has the Group 3 Geoffrey Freer at Newbury as a likely target. (op 4-6 tchd 8-11 in a place)

Munsef is capable of smart form on his day, but had not been seen since finishing second to Spanish Moon at Ascot in May. He came to have every chance, but looked far from enthusiastic under strong pressure and was eased off once his winning chance had gone. It is surely just a matter of time before he is retired. (op 5-4)

Little Hotpotch is rated just 38 and never stood any realistic chance.

4377 JULY COURSE H'CAP — 1m

8:45 (8:45) (Class 5) (0-75,73) 3-Y-0 — **£3,885** (£1,156; £577; £288) **Stalls** Low

Form — RPR

-160 **1** **Admiral Dundas (IRE)**[88] 1686 3-9-6 **70** ... J-PGuillambert 5 — 75
(W Jarvis) *a.p: rdn to ld over 1f out: r.o* — **12/1**

4015 **2** *1 1/4* **Priti Fabulous (IRE)**[14] 3918 3-9-9 **73** ... DarryllHolland 6 — 76+
(W J Haggas) *hld up: swtchd rt over 1f out: sn rdn: r.o wl ins fnl f: nt rch wnr* — **5/2**[2]

0040 **3** *nk* **Merrion Tiger (IRE)**[13] 3960 3-8-7 **57** ... AndrewElliott 3 — 59
(K R Burke) *chsd ldr: rdn over 1f out: styd on* — **14/1**

5020 **4** *3* **Sheer Bluff (IRE)**[7] 4161 3-9-8 **72** ... RichardKingscote 9 — 67
(D R C Elsworth) *led: rdn and hdd over 1f out: no ex ins fnl f* — **9/1**

0-21 **5** *1 3/4* **Sarah Park (IRE)**[7] 4168 3-9-1 **65** 6ex ... JimmyFortune 12 — 56
(B J Meehan) *chsd ldrs: rdn over 1f out: edgd lft: no ex ins fnl f* — **15/8**[1]

5-03 **6** *1* **Stormbeam (USA)**[26] 3525 3-9-1 **65** ... HayleyTurner 8 — 54
(G A Butler) *hld up: rdn and hung lft over 1f out: nt run on* — **9/2**[3]

0510 **7** *nk* **Redarsene**[9] 4083 3-9-3 **72** ... JamieJones(5) 11 — 60
(M G Quinlan) *stdd s: hld up: plld hrd: rdn over 1f out: nt run on* — **20/1**

0150 **8** *1/2* **Titfer (IRE)**[10] 4049 3-8-1 **54** ... LukeMorris(3) 7 — 41
(A W Carroll) *chsd ldrs: rdn over 3f out: wknd fnl f* — **25/1**

3033 **9** *8* **Robert Burns (IRE)**[3] 4283 3-9-9 **73** ...(t) PaulEddery 4 — 41
(Miss D Mountain) *s.i.s: hld up: rdn and hung lft fr over 2f out: wknd over 1f out* — **25/1**

1m 41.13s (1.13) **Going Correction** +0.075s/f (Good) — **9** Ran SP% **118.3**

Speed ratings (Par 100): **97,95,95,92,90 89,89,88,80**

toteswinger: 1&2 £8.10, 1&3 £30.40, 2&3 £8.10. CSF £42.35 CT £434.34 TOTE £16.90: £3.80, £1.60, £4.10; EX 73.50 Place 6 £ 42.28, Place 5 £ 7.42.

Owner Dr J Walker **Bred** John Hussey And Stephen Hillen **Trained** Newmarket, Suffolk

FOCUS

A modest handicap in which the fourth, to his turf mark, sets the standard.

T/Plt: £75.40 to a £1 stake. Pool: £46,721.04. 452.01 winning tickets. T/Qpdt: £11.70 to a £1 stake. Pool: £3,496.30. 219.50 winning tickets. CR

3589 THIRSK (L-H)

Friday, July 25

OFFICIAL GOING: Good to firm (firm in places; 10.1)

The ground was described as 'very fast but no jar whatsoever'.

Wind: moderate, half against Weather: fine, sunny and very warm

4378 SKY BET SUPPORTING THE YORKSHIRE RACING FESTIVAL MAIDEN STKS (DIV I) — 7f

1:30 (1:32) (Class 5) 3-Y-0+ — **£3,788** (£1,127; £563; £281) **Stalls** Low

Form — RPR

3 **1** **Stalking Shadow (USA)**[18] 3796 3-9-3 0 ... KerrinMcEvoy 2 — 86+
(Saeed Bin Suroor) *unruly at s: led: hung rt bnd over 3f out: sn clr: hung violently rt: fnl 2f: nvr in any danger* — **1/5**[1]

66 **2** *11* **Ceili Mor (IRE)**[13] 3977 3-8-12 0 ... JoeFanning 10 — 55+
(M Johnston) *chsd ldrs: wnt 2nd 3f out: styd on same pce* — **10/1**[2]

3 *nse* **Shakedown** 3-9-3 0 ... StephenDonohoe 8 — 56
(E S McMahon) *chsd ldrs: wnt mod 2nd over 1f out: one pce* — **11/1**[3]

4 *6* **Fell Pack** 4-9-7 0 ... JamieMoriarty(3) 5 — 40
(J J Quinn) *s.s: in rr: kpt on fnl 2f* — **25/1**

0-F2 **5** *1 1/4* **Flamestone**[20] 3733 4-9-5 **54** ... NataliaGemelova(5) 4 — 36
(A E Price) *chsd ldrs: wknd fnl 2f* — **33/1**

00 **6** *10* **Aspendale (IRE)**[20] 3712 3-9-3 0 ... DNolan 1 — 9
(D Carroll) *chsd ldrs: lost pl over 2f out* — **66/1**

7 *2* **Distant Rainbow (IRE)** 3-9-3 0 ... AdrianTNicholls 11 — —
(M Brittain) *dwlt: sn chsng ldrs on outside: rn v wd and lost pl bnd over 3f out* — **18/1**

6 **8** *hd* **Amy's Mercdes**[18] 3796 4-9-2 0 ... MarkLawson(3) 3 — —
(N Bycroft) *chsd ldrs: hung rt and lost pl 3f out* — **100/1**

9 *3 1/2* **Wrecker's Moon (IRE)** 3-8-9 0 ... PJMcDonald(3) 7 — —
(T J Etherington) *s.s: a bhd* — **33/1**

0 **10** *26* **Lighting Shadow**[7] 3338 3-9-3 0 ... JimmyQuinn 9 — —
(N Wilson) *swtchd lft after s: sn bhd: t.o* — **66/1**

1m 26.46s (-0.74) **Going Correction** +0.025s/f (Good)

WFA 3 from 4yo 7lb — **10** Ran SP% **119.7**

Speed ratings (Par 103): **105,92,92,85,84 72,70,70,66,36**

toteswinger: 1&2 £1.90, 1&3 £2.40, 2&3 £3.80. CSF £3.01 TOTE £1.10: £1.02, £1.60, £2.10; EX 1.20.

Owner Godolphin **Bred** Brushwood Stable **Trained** Newmarket, Suffolk

FOCUS

A poor maiden and a wayward but clear winner. The fifth is rated just 54, so the form behind is limited.

Amy's Mercdes Official explanation: jockey said filly hung right throughout

4379 SKY BET SUPPORTING THE YORKSHIRE RACING FESTIVAL MAIDEN STKS (DIV II) — 7f

2:00 (2:00) (Class 5) 3-Y-0+ — **£3,788** (£1,127; £563; £281) **Stalls** Low

Form — RPR

-524 **1** **Romantic Destiny**[28] 3452 3-8-12 **73** ... PaulMulrennan 7 — 61
(K A Ryan) *chsd ldrs: sharp reminders over 3f out: styd on to ld appr fnl f: hld on* — **11/8**[1]

46 **2** *1 1/4* **Hydrophonic**[32] 3333 3-8-5 0 ... BMcHugh(7) 2 — 58
(R A Fahey) *mid-div: hdwy over 2f out: hung rt and bmpd over 1f out: kpt on ins fnl f to take 2nd nr fin* — **7/1**[3]

3 *1/2* **Mr Burton**[30] 4-9-3 0 ... GarryWhillans(7) 9 — 64
(M Mullineaux) *s.i.s: hdwy on outside 2f out: edgd lft and bmpd over 1f out: styd on ins fnl f* — **200/1**

2- **4** *nk* **Somerset Falls (UAE)**[259] 6742 3-8-12 0 ... JoeFanning 6 — 56
(M Johnston) *chsd ldr: led over 2f out: hdd appr fnl f: no ex* — **7/4**[2]

50 **5** *5* **Nabeeda**[88] 1674 3-9-0 0 ... MarkLawson(3) 1 — 47
(M Brittain) *trckd ldrs: t.k.h: wknd 1f out* — **16/1**

0-0 **6** *1 1/2* **Uncle Harry**[23] 3600 3-9-3 0 ... PaulHanagan 3 — 43
(J J Quinn) *s.i.s: sn mid-div: hdwy over 2f out: wknd over 1f out* — **33/1**

0 **7** *2 1/2* **Mr Toshiwonka**[34] 3282 4-9-10 0 ... AdrianTNicholls 8 — 39
(D Nicholls) *led tl 4f out: chsd ldrs tl wknd fnl f* — **12/1**

05 **8** *20* **Anna Lane**[31] 3338 3-8-7 0 ... KellyHarrison(5) 5 — —
(W J H Ratcliffe) *in rr: faltered and lost pl over 5f out: bhd fnl 3f: virtually p.u* — **50/1**

9 *17* **Red Wind (IRE)** 3-9-3 0 ... PaulQuinn 10 — —
(N Wilson) *in rr: bhd fnl 2f: virtually p.u* — **25/1**

1m 27.29s (0.09) **Going Correction** +0.025s/f (Good)

WFA 3 from 4yo 7lb — **9** Ran SP% **113.8**

Speed ratings (Par 103): **100,98,98,97,91 90,87,64,45**

toteswinger: 1&2 £2.60, 1&3 £25.50, 2&3 £41.00. CSF £11.37 TOTE £2.40: £1.10, £1.50, £10.20; EX 12.40.

Owner T G & Mrs M E Holdcroft **Bred** Bearstone Stud **Trained** Hambleton, N Yorks

FOCUS

The highly-tried winner was not breaking her duck out of turn. Overall it was even weaker than the first division.

Nabeeda Official explanation: jockey said gelding was unsuited by the good to firm (firm in places) ground

4380 E B F SOLBERGE HALL MAIDEN FILLIES STKS — 7f

2:35 (2:36) (Class 4) 2-Y-0 — **£5,569** (£1,657; £828; £413) **Stalls** Low

Form — RPR

2 **1** **Vitoria (IRE)**[9] 4080 2-9-0 0 ... TedDurcan 4 — 82+
(M J Wallace) *trckd ldr: led and qcknd 2f out: rdn and styd on ins fnl f* — **6/5**[1]

2 *1/2* **Feeling Fab (FR)** 2-9-0 0 ... JoeFanning 1 — 81+
(M Johnston) *t.k.h: trckd ldrs: effrt and hung lft over 2f out: wnt 2nd over 1f out: kpt on wl ins fnl f* — **16/1**

54 **3** *2 3/4* **Dream In Waiting**[14] 3913 2-9-0 0 ... KerrinMcEvoy 3 — 74
(P F I Cole) *rr-div: effrt on outside 3f out: styd on to take 3rd ins fnl f* — **11/4**[2]

0 **4** *1 3/4* **Lock 'N' Load (IRE)**[33] 3292 2-9-0 0 ... TomEaves 6 — 70
(B Smart) *chsd ldrs: effrt over 2f out: kpt on same pce* — **16/1**

5 **5** *2 1/2* **Antigua Sunrise (IRE)**[13] 3976 2-9-0 0 ... PaulHanagan 5 — 63
(R A Fahey) *wnt lft s: in rr: kpt on fnl 2f: nvr a threat* — **7/1**

6 *1 1/4* **Hettie Hubble** 2-9-0 0 ... DavidAllan 2 — 60
(T D Easterby) *dwlt: effrt on ins over 2f out: hung rt: kpt on fnl f* — **66/1**

0 **7** *2* **Imperial Angel (IRE)**[31] 3334 2-9-0 0 ... DNolan 7 — 55
(D Carroll) *led tl 2f out: sn wknd* — **200/1**

3 **8** *3/4* **Mawjaat (IRE)**[48] 2835 2-9-0 0 ... JimmyQuinn 9 — 53
(J L Dunlop) *in rr: drvn over 3f out: nvr a factor* — **4/1**[3]

1m 27.97s (0.77) **Going Correction** +0.025s/f (Good) — **8** Ran SP% **118.4**

Speed ratings (Par 96): **96,95,92,90,87 86,83,82**

toteswinger: 1&2 £6.40, 1&3 £1.50, 2&3 £8.60. CSF £25.57 TOTE £2.00: £1.10, £3.20, £1.10; EX 26.50.

Owner H E Sheikh Rashid Bin Mohammed **Bred** Tom Deane **Trained** Newmarket, Suffolk

FOCUS

A fair two-year-old race which looks solid could be rated even higher. The winner looks a nice prospect and the runner-up will surely go one better sooner rather than later.

NOTEBOOK

Vitoria(IRE), a good-bodied filly, really took the eye beforehand. She went on and quickened the pace but in the end had to be kept right up to her work. (op 6-4 tchd 11-10 and 13-8 in a place)

Feeling Fab(FR), bred for stamina rather than speed, is a rangy, well-made filly but she has a pronounced knee action. She showed her inexperience but was buckling down at the end and at the line was just found wanting. She is sure to improve and win races. (op 10-1 tchd 20-1)

Dream In Waiting, a fluent mover, appreciated this quicker ground and stayed on in encouraging fashion. A mile nursery might be her cup of tea. (op 7-2 tchd 4-1)

Lock 'N' Load(IRE) appreciated the extra furlong and is still learning the ropes. (op 14-1 tchd 18-1)

Antigua Sunrise(IRE), still carrying condition, again put in her best work at the finish. She is not the finished article yet. (op 9-1 tchd 11-1)

Hettie Hubble, a very inexperienced newcomer, shaped by no means badly and can do a fair bit better given a little more time.

Imperial Angel(IRE), a moderate walker, took them along at just a steady pace and was readily swept aside. (op 100-1)

Mawjaat(IRE), who is only small, was in trouble turning for home and never threatened to enter the argument. (op 7-2 tchd 10-3)

4381 SILKS BRASSERIE (S) H'CAP — 1m

3:10 (3:11) (Class 6) (0-65,65) 3-Y-0 — **£2,978** (£886; £442; £221) **Stalls** Low

Form — RPR

3-40 **1** **Lujano**[17] 3825 3-9-0 **58** ... PaulMulrennan 12 — 65
(Ollie Pears) *led 1f: w ldrs: led 2f out: styd on wl ins fnl f* — **9/1**

0042 **2** *3* **Ace Of Spies (IRE)**[10] 4044 3-8-6 **50** ... JoeFanning 6 — 50
(M Johnston) *chsd ldrs: swtchd rt 2f out: styd on same pce fnl f: no imp* — **13/8**[1]

0-30 **3** *3/4* **Pintano**[16] 3831 3-9-7 **65** ...(b[1]) RobertWinston 5 — 63
(J Howard Johnson) *led after 1f tl 2f out: kpt on same pce* — **11/1**

0-05 **4** *hd* **Trojan Hero (IRE)**[25] 3549 3-8-2 **46** oh1 ... DaleGibson 16 — 44+
(A Dickman) *hld up in midfield: effrt over 2f out: styd on wl fnl f* — **28/1**

0024 **5** *nk* **Caught In Paradise (IRE)**[18] 3791 3-8-5 **49** ... SilvestreDeSousa 8 — 46
(D W Thompson) *chsd ldrs: outpcd over 2f out: kpt on fnl f* — **15/2**[3]

5600 **6** *3/4* **Zabougg**[10] 4049 3-8-10 **54** ... TomEaves 1 — 49
(D W Barker) *s.i.s: hdwy on ins over 2f out: kpt on fnl f* — **5/1**[2]

001 **7** *1* **One Night In May (IRE)**[20] 3715 3-8-0 **47** ow1 ... AndrewMullen(3) 13 — 40+
(M Dods) *s.i.s: in rr tl kpt on fnl 2f* — **8/1**

-000 **8** *1/2* **Carlton Mac**[10] 4043 3-7-9 **46** oh1 ...(b) JamieKyne(7) 2 — 38
(N Bycroft) *prom: rdn and outpcd over 3f out: nvr a factor* — **33/1**

-300 **9** *2 3/4* **Personal Choice**[10] 4044 3-8-7 **51** ow1 ... DavidAllan 3 — 36
(M Brittain) *mid-div: edgd rt over 1f out: nvr a factor* — **33/1**

0500 **10** *3 1/2* **Pentandra (IRE)**[17] 3816 3-8-8 **52** ... PaulHanagan 11 — 29
(J G Given) *chsd ldrs: lost pl over 2f out* — **14/1**

00-0 **11** *11* **Caribbean Cruiser**[50] 2747 3-8-2 **46** oh1 ... TWilliams 4 — —
(Bruce Hellier) *s.i.s: in rr: bhd fnl 3f* — **66/1**

0040 **12** *1/2* **Your Golf Travel**[10] 4043 3-7-13 **46** ... DuranFentiman(3) 10 — —
(J S Wainwright) *in rr: bhd fnl 3f* — **33/1**

0035 **13** *6* **Champagne Lawn (USA)**[4] 4241 3-8-9 **53** ...(v) PaulFessey 9 — —
(T D Barron) *mid-div: lost pl over 4f out: sn bhd* — **11/1**

1m 40.67s (0.57) **Going Correction** +0.025s/f (Good) — **13** Ran SP% **124.7**

Speed ratings (Par 98): **98,95,94,94,93 93,92,91,88,85 74,73,67**

toteswinger: 1&2 £4.80, 1&3 £10.10, 2&3 £3.70. CSF £24.10 CT £184.90 TOTE £12.40: £3.60, £1.30, £2.60; EX 42.30.The winner was bought in for 6,800gns.

Owner David Scott and Co (Pattern Makers) Ltd **Bred** D Scott **Trained** Norton, N Yorks

■ Stewards' Enquiry : Robert Winston one-day ban: careless riding (Aug 8)

FOCUS
An ordinary seller but a clear-cut and relatively unexposed winner and the third is rated to this year's form.

4382 STANLAND LAUNDRY H'CAP — 1m 4f
3:45 (3:45) (Class 4) (0-80,80) 3-Y-0 — **£5,569** (£1,657; £828; £413) **Stalls** Low

Form — RPR

4523 **1** — **Dramatic Solo**[28] 3459 3-8-7 **66**........(b[1]) AndrewElliott 6 — 76
(K R Burke) *swtchd lft and jnd ldr after 1f: drvn 4f out: led over 2f out: styd on wl fnl f* — **9/4**[1]

432 **2** *4* **Maha Dubai (USA)**[27] 3473 3-8-8 **67**........ JoeFanning 4 — 71
(M Johnston) *chsd ldrs: effrt over 3f out: wnt 2nd over 1f out: no imp* **7/2**[2]

0224 **3** *2 ¾* **Herrera (IRE)**[20] 3710 3-8-8 **67**........ PaulHanagan 5 — 66
(R A Fahey) *hld up in rr: hdwy on outer 6f out: drvn over 4f out: hung lft and one pce appr fnl f* — **5/1**[3]

0265 **4** *3 ½* **The Last Bottle (IRE)**[17] 3817 3-8-2 **64**........ DuranFentiman(3) 1 — 58
(W M Brisbourne) *led: qcknd over 4f out: hdd over 2f out: wknd fnl 150yds* — **16/1**

003 **5** *1 ¾* **Filun**[22] 3637 3-9-3 **76**........ PatCosgrave 2 — 67
(L M Cumani) *drvn to chse ldrs: effrt over 3f out: wknd jst ins fnl f* — **9/4**[1]

545- **6** *½* **Simone Martini (IRE)**[261] 6723 3-9-1 **74**........ PaulMulrennan 3 — 64
(R Charlton) *hld up towards rr: drvn over 4f out: outpcd over 2f out: no threat after* — **8/1**

2m 35.78s (-0.42) **Going Correction** +0.025s/f (Good) — **6** Ran SP% **117.4**
Speed ratings (Par 102): **102,99,97,95,94 93**
toteswinger: 1&2 £2.30, 1&3 £2.80, 2&3 £2.20. CSF £11.14 TOTE £3.40: £1.70, £1.70; EX 10.50.
Owner Malih L Al Basti **Bred** Matthews Breeding And Racing Ltd **Trained** Middleham Moor, N Yorks

FOCUS
A modest event but an improved effort from the seemingly exposed winner. the form is rated positively for now with runner-up exposed and the third setting the level.

4383 DEEPDALE SOLUTIONS NSPCC FILLIES' H'CAP — 6f
4:20 (4:20) (Class 5) (0-70,70) 3-Y-0+ — **£4,274** (£1,271; £635; £317) **Stalls** High

Form — RPR

4150 **1** — **Tilsworth Charlie**[23] 3608 5-9-0 **58**........(b) StephenDonohoe 5 — 71
(J R Jenkins) *hld up: stdy hdwy over 2f out: edgd rt and led over 1f out: sn clr: readily* — **16/1**

0050 **2** *2 ¼* **Lambency (IRE)**[8] 4118 5-8-10 **54**........ DanielTudhope 10 — 60
(J S Goldie) *hld up in rr: hdwy and swtchd outside over 2f out: chsng ldrs appr fnl f: kpt on same pce* — **7/2**[2]

2233 **3** *nk* **Strawberry Moon (IRE)**[34] 3280 3-9-4 **67**........ TomEaves 1 — 71
(B Smart) *chsd ldrs: kpt on same pce fnl f* — **9/2**[3]

0221 **4** *¾* **Pretty Bonnie**[21] 3695 3-8-6 **60**........ NataliaGemelova(5) 3 — 62
(A E Price) *w ldrs: edgd rt over 1f out: kpt on same pce* — **6/1**

3033 **5** *¾* **Katie Boo (IRE)**[8] 4117 6-9-7 **70**........ SladeO'Hara(5) 7 — 70
(A Berry) *mid-div: hdwy over 2f out: chsng ldrs whn n.m.r over 1f out: kpt on same pce* — **10/3**[1]

2102 **6** *shd* **Swallow Forest**[85] 1754 3-8-6 **55**........ PaulFessey 11 — 54
(T D Barron) *in rr: kpt on fnl 2f: nvr trbld ldrs* — **12/1**

6006 **7** *6* **Spinning Game**[13] 3952 4-8-7 **51** oh6........(b) AndrewElliott 6 — 32
(Mrs R A Carr) *led: hung bdly lft: hdd over 2f out: hdd sltly hmpd and lost pl over 1f out* — **50/1**

0000 **8** *¾* **Nabra**[41] 3026 4-8-0 **51** oh6........ MatthewLawson(7) 8 — 29
(M Brittain) *chsd ldrs: lost pl 2f out* — **66/1**

4532 **9** *¾* **Hansomis (IRE)**[11] 4018 4-8-11 **55**........ DaleGibson 2 — 31
(B Mactaggart) *chsd ldrs on outer: wknd 2f out* — **15/2**

0600 **10** *hd* **Mis Chicaf (IRE)**[36] 3172 7-8-0 **51** oh6........ PaulPickard(7) 9 — 26
(D Carroll) *in rr: hdwy on outer over 2f out: edgd lft and lost pl over 1f out* — **50/1**

0000 **11** *19* **Cow Girl (IRE)**[165] 521 4-8-7 **51** oh4........ PaulHanagan 4 — —
(Miss Gay Kelleway) *w ldrs: lost pl over 3f out: sn bhd and eased* — **10/1**

1m 13.11s (0.41) **Going Correction** +0.125s/f (Good)
WFA 3 from 4yo+ 5lb — **11** Ran SP% **117.6**
Speed ratings (Par 100): **102,99,98,97,96 96,88,87,86,86 60**
toteswinger: 1&2 £13.80, 1&3 £13.40, 2&3 £4.80. CSF £71.24 CT £309.03 TOTE £20.80: £5.10, £1.60, £1.90; EX 131.50.
Owner M Ng **Bred** Michael Ng **Trained** Royston, Herts

FOCUS
A low-grade fillies' sprint handicap but a most convincing winner. The form looks sound at this level with those in the frame behind the winner close to their marks.

4384 MAURICE CARRUTHERS MEDIAN AUCTION MAIDEN STKS — 5f
4:55 (4:57) (Class 5) 2-Y-0 — **£4,274** (£1,271; £635; £317) **Stalls** High

Form — RPR

223 **1** — **Secret Venue**[24] 3590 2-9-3 0........ TonyHamilton 5 — 71
(Jedd O'Keeffe) *chsd ldrs: swtchd ins over 1f out: led jst ins fnl f: all out* — **11/8**[1]

5 **2** *nk* **Sea Crest**[42] 3005 2-8-9 0........ MarkLawson(3) 9 — 65
(M Brittain) *led: hrd rdn and edgd lft over 1f out: hdd jst ins fnl f: kpt on wl towards fin* — **2/1**[2]

5 **3** *1 ½* **Capo Regime**[30] 3364 2-9-3 0........ SilvestreDeSousa 1 — 65+
(D Nicholls) *chsd ldrs: kpt on same pce fnl f* — **15/2**[3]

4 *1* **Sleepy Valley (IRE)** 2-8-12 0........ DanielTudhope 7 — 56+
(A Dickman) *dwlt: in rr: hdwy over 1f out: styng on at fin* — **50/1**

66 **5** *1 ¾* **Red Max (IRE)**[27] 3492 2-9-3 0........(b[1]) DavidAllan 4 — 55
(T D Easterby) *in tch: rdn over 2f out: kpt on: nvr a threat* — **12/1**

0 **6** *2 ¾* **Nimmy's Special**[62] 2388 2-8-12 0........ TomEaves 8 — 40
(B Smart) *sn outpcd and in rr: kpt on fnl f: nvr on terms* — **16/1**

34 **7** *2 ½* **Eden Park**[47] 2865 2-8-12 0........ PaulHanagan 6 — 31
(M Dods) *wnt rt s: chsd ldrs: edgd lft over 1f out: sn wknd* — **10/1**

8 *43* **Noble Artist** 2-9-3 0........ PaulMulrennan 2 — —
(D H Brown) *dwlt: sn wl detached in last: t.o fnl 2f* — **40/1**

60.37 secs (0.77) **Going Correction** +0.125s/f (Good) — **8** Ran SP% **114.3**
Speed ratings (Par 94): **98,97,95,93,90 86,82,13**
toteswinger: 1&2 £1.90, 1&3 £3.20, 2&3 £3.20. CSF £4.22 TOTE £2.20: £1.10, £1.30, £2.10; EX 4.70.
Owner Ken And Delia Shaw-KGS Consulting LLP **Bred** Sherwoods Transport Ltd **Trained** Middleham Moor, N Yorks

FOCUS
A modest maiden and the winner was fully entitled to take this. The form looks sound enough but fairly limited.

NOTEBOOK
Secret Venue, easily the most experienced in the line-up, in the end did just enough suited by the drop back to five. (op 6-4 tchd 6-5)

Sea Crest, on his toes beforehand and keen to post, took them along but moved off the running rail leaving the door open for the winner. To his credit he struck back hard under an untidy ride and he deserves to go one better. (op 15-8 tchd 9-4)
Capo Regime, who had the worst of the draw, was dropping back in trip and encountering much quicker ground. He stuck on in willing fashion and should improve again. (op 8-1)
Sleepy Valley(IRE), a late-May foal, is on the leg. After missing a beat at the start, she stayed on in most encouraging fashion late on. (op 40-1)
Red Max(IRE), in first-time blinkers, appreciated the return to quick ground but this trip is too short for him. At least this opens up the nursery route for him. (tchd 10-1)
Nimmy's Special, who made her debut two months earlier, stayed on in her own time and will relish a step up in distance. (op 14-1 tchd 12-1)

4385 PERTEMPS PEOPLE DEVELOPMENT "HANDS AND HEELS" APPRENTICE SERIES H'CAP — 5f
5:30 (5:33) (Class 5) (0-75,74) 3-Y-0+ — **£4,274** (£1,271; £635; £317) **Stalls** High

Form — RPR

2241 **1** — **Miss Daawe**[20] 3713 4-9-0 **66**........ AnthonyBetts(5) 14 — 74
(B Ellison) *in tch: hdwy stands' side 2f out: led ins fnl f: hld on towards fin* — **3/1**[1]

2000 **2** *nk* **Blessed Place**[8] 4106 8-9-1 **62**........(p) BillyCray 11 — 69
(D J S Ffrench Davis) *led tl over 1f out: kpt on wl towards fin* — **10/1**

0050 **3** *½* **Feelin Foxy**[15] 3883 4-9-9 **70**........ LanceBetts 8 — 75
(J G Given) *w ldr: led over 1f out tl ins fnl f: no ex nr fin* — **10/1**

00-0 **4** *4 ½* **Bahamian Duke**[205] 21 5-8-8 **55** oh5........ DeclanCannon 12 — 44
(K R Burke) *sn outpcd towards rr: kpt on fnl 2f: nvr rchd ldrs* — **33/1**

0252 **5** *1 ¼* **Colorus (IRE)**[15] 3868 5-9-4 **68**........ JamieKyne(3) 1 — 53
(W J H Ratcliffe) *chsd ldrs on outer: wknd over 1f out* — **11/2**[2]

0210 **6** *nk* **Ronnie Howe**[29] 3401 4-9-0 **64**........ JohnCavanagh(3) 13 — 47
(M Dods) *mid-div: one pce fnl 2f* — **7/1**[3]

0020 **7** *1 ¼* **The History Man (IRE)**[7] 4171 5-9-1 **65**........(b) GarryWhillans(3) 6 — 44
(M Mullineaux) *swtchd lft to r alone far side: nvr nr ldrs* — **20/1**

5010 **8** *3 ¼* **Toy Top (USA)**[25] 3546 5-9-2 **63**........(b) ClGillies 4 — 30
(M Dods) *chsd ldrs: lost pl over 1f out* — **25/1**

266 **9** *4* **Wicked Wilma (IRE)**[11] 4013 4-8-5 **55** oh3........ PaulPickard(3) 9 — 8+
(A Berry) *chsd ldrs: stmbld and lost pl after 1f* — **12/1**

2000 **10** *3 ½* **King Of Swords (IRE)**[31] 3336 4-9-13 **74**........ RyanMania 5 — 14
(N Tinkler) *chsd ldrs on outer: hung bdly lft over 2f out: sn lost pl* — **28/1**

5-02 **11** *3 ½* **Until When (USA)**[11] 4013 4-9-1 **65**........(v) SBushby(3) 2 — —
(B Smart) *rrd s: a bhd* — **12/1**

1-21 **12** *1* **By The Edge (IRE)**[182] 304 4-8-12 **62**........ AdamCarter(3) 7 — —
(T D Barron) *sn sn drvn along in rr* — **16/1**

59.84 secs (0.24) **Going Correction** +0.125s/f (Good) — **12** Ran SP% **107.3**
Speed ratings (Par 103): **103,102,101,94,92 92,90,84,78,72 67,65**
toteswinger: 1&2 £11.40, 1&3 £11.30, 2&3 £18.60. CSF £24.46 CT £171.62 TOTE £3.10: £1.30, £3.50, £3.60; EX 34.10 Place 6: £11.36 5: £10.92 .
Owner Mrs Andrea M Mallinson **Bred** N R C Trading Ltd **Trained** Norton, N Yorks
■ A first success for 20-year-old apprentice Anthony Betts whose brother rode the third.

FOCUS
A modest 'hands and heels' sprint handicap but sound form at this level rated through the placed horses.
King Of Swords(IRE) Official explanation: jockey said colt hung left-handed from halfway
T/Plt: £29.80 to a £1 stake. Pool: £41,685.60. 1,018.55 winning tickets. T/Qpdt: £15.20 to a £1 stake. Pool: £2,757.70. 134.10 winning tickets. WG

4026 WOLVERHAMPTON (A.W) (L-H)
Friday, July 25

OFFICIAL GOING: Standard
Wind: moderate, half behind Weather: hazy, sunshine

4386 FREE SPORTS BETS @ FREEBETS.CO.UK CLAIMING STKS — 1m 141y(P)
2:25 (2:27) (Class 6) 3-Y-0+ — **£2,388** (£705; £352) **Stalls** Low

Form — RPR

0236 **1** — **Le Chiffre (IRE)**[10] 4052 6-9-2 68........(p) J-PGuillambert 3 — 65
(John A Harris) *a.p: pushed along fr 1/2-way: plenty to do over 1f out: sustained run fnl f to ld nr fin* — **2/1**[1]

6103 **2** *nk* **Steig (IRE)**[22] 3648 5-9-6 62........ JamesDoyle 12 — 68
(Carl Llewellyn) *a.p: led over 4f out: clr over 1f out: kpt on u.p but hdd nr fin* — **11/2**

0225 **3** *1* **Casablanca Minx (IRE)**[11] 4031 5-8-11 55........(v) TGMcLaughlin 6 — 57
(P D Evans) *hld up towards rr: hdwy on outside 2f out: r.o fnl f: nvr nrr* — **5/1**[3]

3410 **4** *2 ½* **Dancing Deano (IRE)**[21] 3691 6-9-7 65........ RussellKennemore(3) 7 — 64
(R Hollinshead) *mid-div: rdn over 3f out: styd on but nt qckn fr over 1f out* — **7/1**

100 **5** *2* **Wogan's Sister**[25] 3569 3-9-0 55........ LiamJones 8 — 58
(I A Wood) *trckd ldr: rdn 3f out: wknd over 1f out* — **28/1**

6511 **6** *½* **Arctic Desert**[8] 4129 8-9-10 61........(t) ChrisCatlin 5 — 59
(Miss Gay Kelleway) *stdd s: in rr tl hdwy on outside over 3f out: rdn and one pce fr over 1f out* — **3/1**[2]

0004 **7** *hd* **Time To Regret**[24] 3593 8-9-2 55........(p) PatrickMathers 10 — 50
(I W McInnes) *led tl hdd over 4f out: chsd ldr tl wknd rapidly fnl f* — **20/1**

6006 **8** *7* **Hawa Khana (IRE)**[17] 3817 3-8-3 55........ KirstyMilczarek(3) 1 — 32
(N P Littmoden) *mid-div: rdn 3f out: wknd 2f out* — **25/1**

5046 **9** *8* **General Feeling (IRE)**[11] 4031 7-9-0 56........(p) PAspell 9 — 14
(S T Mason) *v.s.a: sn in tch on outside: rdn and wknd 3f out* — **20/1**

5-00 **10** *nk* **Petrosian**[8] 4121 4-9-11 62........ LeeVickers(3) 13 — 27
(W Clay) *hld up in rr: lost tch over 2f out* — **66/1**

1m 51.58s (1.08) **Going Correction** +0.175s/f (Slow)
WFA 3 from 4yo+ 9lb — **10** Ran SP% **121.2**
Speed ratings (Par 101): **102,101,100,98,96 96,96,90,82,82**
toteswinger: 1&2 £2.00, 1&3 £1.80, 2&3 £7.00. CSF £12.67 TOTE £2.70: £1.10, £2.10, £1.30; EX 16.50.Casablanca Minx was claimed by Gay Kelleway for £6000.
Owner Stan Wright Shaun Taylor **Bred** Agricola Del Parco **Trained** Eastwell, Leics
■ Stewards' Enquiry : Patrick Mathers caution: careless riding

FOCUS
An ordinary claimer in which the form is rated through the second and fifth. The winning time was 0.91 seconds slower than the later 56-75 handicap.

4387 FREE CASINO CHIPS @ FREEBETS.CO.UK FILLIES' (S) STKS — 7f 32y(P)
3:00 (3:01) (Class 6) 2-Y-0 — **£2,047** (£604; £302) **Stalls** High

Form — RPR

0000 **1** — **Nun Today (USA)**[10] 4063 2-8-9 0........(b[1]) LukeMorris(3) 10 — 60
(J S Moore) *trckd ldrs: led over 1f out: r.o wl* — **6/1**[3]

000 **2** 3/4 **Sienna Lake (IRE)**[35] 3207 2-8-10 0 ow3 HaddenFrost(5) 8 61
(S Kirk) *trckd ldrs: nt clr run and swtchd rt over 1f out: r.o to go 2nd ins fnl f* **7/1**

600 **3** 4 1/2 **August Days (IRE)**[30] 3378 2-8-12 0 JamesDoyle 4 47
(R M Beckett) *w ldr: rdn 2f out: nt qckn fnl f* **7/1**

024 **4** hd **Tarawa Atoll**[101] 1384 2-8-12 0 TPO'Shea 7 47
(M R Channon) *s.i.s: in rr: styd on ins fnl 2f: nvr nrr* **4/1**[1]

4 **5** 1 1/4 **Lavender Girl**[32] 3309 2-8-12 0 LiamJones 1 44
(P Winkworth) *mde most tl rdn and hdd over 1f out: fdd ins fnl f* **15/2**

0 **6** nse **Southoffrance (IRE)**[25] 3558 2-8-7 0 JackDean(5) 9 43
(W G M Turner) *in tch: rdn 4f out: wknd over 1f out* **9/2**[2]

5103 **7** 1 **Cherry Belle (IRE)**[10] 4063 2-9-4 0 (v) TGMcLaughlin 11 47
(P D Evans) *s.i.s: wl in rr tl sme hdwy fr over 1f out* **4/1**[1]

8 4 **Kabougg** 2-8-9 0 KevinGhunowa(3) 3 31
(P A Blockley) *a in rr* **8/1**

600 **9** 2 1/4 **Keen Rabbit**[6] 4203 2-8-12 0 RoystonFfrench 5 26
(Micky Hammond) *a bhd* **33/1**

4 **10** 77 **Red Myth**[67] 2239 2-8-12 0 J-PGuillambert 6 —
(Karen George) *s.i.s: lost tch over 3f out: t.o over 2f out* **28/1**

1m 32.96s (3.36) **Going Correction** +0.175s/f (Slow) **10 Ran SP% 126.7**
Speed ratings (Par 89): **87,86,81,80,79 79,78,73,71,—**
toteswinger: 1&2 £8.20, 1&3 £8.20, 2&3 £20.60. CSF £52.09 TOTE £6.20: £3.70, £4.10, £3.40; EX 65.70.There was no bid for the winner. Sienna Lake was claimed by R. Hannon for £6000.
Owner J S Moore **Bred** Tony Holmes And Walter Zent **Trained** Upper Lambourn, Berks

FOCUS
Confined to fillies. this was a poor race, even by selling standards. Not form to pay much attention to.

NOTEBOOK
Nun Today(USA) beat just two rivals in a selling nursery off an estimated handicap mark of 61 at Yarmouth on her previous start, but she produced an improved effort on this switch to Polytrack in first-time blinkers. (tchd 11-2)
Sienna Lake(IRE), upped in trip, switched to Polytrack and dropped in grade, ran her best race yet in second and was possibly a little unlucky. She travelled well into the straight, but was denied a clear run and had to switch right. Her rider also put up 3lb overweight. (op 9-1)
August Days(IRE), upped from 5f and dropped in grade, showed good speed but did not stay. (op 5-1 tchd 9-2)
Tarawa Atoll, upped two furlongs in trip, was never a danger after starting slowly. (op 9-2 tchd 7-2)
Lavender Girl's debut fourth in a 5f maiden at Chepstow did not amount to much. (op 8-1 tchd 9-1)
Cherry Belle(IRE) was well below form on her first start on Polytrack. Official explanation: jockey said filly would not face the kickback
Red Myth Official explanation: jockey said filly lost its action

4388 FREE POKER CHIPS @ FREEBETS.CO.UK MEDIAN AUCTION MAIDEN STKS 5f 216y(P)
3:35 (3:36) (Class 6) 3-4-Y-O **£2,729** (£806; £403) **Stalls** Low

Form RPR

3/5 **1** **Night Rocket (IRE)**[16] 3847 4-8-12 0 (t) DavidProbert(5) 5 66+
(A M Balding) *chsd ldrs: led over 1f out: r.o wl fnl f* **4/1**[2]

002 **2** nk **Diego Rivera**[14] 3916 3-9-3 70 RichardSmith 3 69+
(P J Makin) *in tch: rdn over 2f out: rdn to chse wnr fnl f and gaining cl home* **5/4**[1]

3 3 1/4 **Triumphant Welcome** 3-8-10 0 StacyRenwick(7) 7 59
(G F Bridgwater) *mid-div: styd on fr over 1f out to go 3rd ins fnl f* **40/1**

20-0 **4** hd **Lavande**[23] 3600 3-8-12 62 FergalLynch 8 53+
(M J Wallace) *towards rr: hdwy over 2f out: hdwy over 1f out: styd on: nvr nrr* **16/1**

2405 **5** 1 1/4 **Walragnek**[23] 3600 4-9-5 54 LukeMorris(3) 1 55
(J G M O'Shea) *led after 1f: rdn and hdd over 1f out: wknd ins fnl f* **10/1**

6-66 **6** nk **Ros Cuire (IRE)**[99] 1434 3-9-3 0 J-PGuillambert 4 53
(W A Murphy, Ire) *hld up: hdwy over 2f out: kpt on one pce fnl f* **9/1**[3]

00 **7** 7 **Professor Malone**[16] 3847 3-9-3 0 SamHitchcott 11 31
(J C Tuck) *mid-div: wknd over 1f out* **66/1**

3 **8** hd **Onebidkintymill (IRE)**[9] 4076 3-9-3 0 LiamJones 9 30
(M Mullineaux) *in tch on outside: rdn over 2f out: wknd over 1f out* **4/1**[2]

5 **9** 5 **Billy Cadiz**[18] 3786 3-9-3 0 ChrisCatlin 2 14
(E J O'Neill) *in tch early but bhd fr 1/2-way* **11/1**

0-4 **10** 1/2 **Ridley Didley (IRE)**[13] 3955 3-8-12 0 AshleyHamblett(5) 10 12+
(N Wilson) *led for 1f: prom tl wknd qckly over 1f out* **10/1**

0- **11** 2 1/2 **Be Superior**[258] 6755 3-8-9 0 TolleyDean(3) 12 —
(J Balding) *stdd s: a bhd* **66/1**

00 **12** 2 1/4 **Wendy Craig**[22] 3640 3-8-12 0 RoystonFfrench 13 —
(J Balding) *s.i.s: sn rdn: a bhd* **50/1**

1m 17.23s (2.23) **Going Correction** +0.175s/f (Slow) **12 Ran SP% 134.2**
WFA 3 from 4yo 5lb
Speed ratings (Par 101): **92,91,87,87,85 84,75,75,68,68 64,61**
toteswinger: 1&2 £2.10, 1&3 £77.40, 2&3 £18.10. CSF £10.67 TOTE £4.70: £2.00, £1.40, £16.50; EX 8.40.
Owner J C Smith **Bred** Littleton Stud **Trained** Kingsclere, Hants

FOCUS
A modest maiden. The form seems sound enough, rated through the second and fifth. The winning time was 1.03 seconds slower than the following nursery.
Ridley Didley(IRE) Official explanation: jockey said gelding ran too freely
Wendy Craig Official explanation: jockey said filly never travelled

4389 FREE BETS @ FREEBETS.CO.UK NURSERY 5f 216y(P)
4:10 (4:10) (Class 5) 2-Y-O **£2,914** (£867; £433; £216) **Stalls** Low

Form RPR

6160 **1** **Haven't A Clue**[14] 3924 2-8-13 75 (b[1]) J-PGuillambert 7 81+
(Sir Mark Prescott) *hld up in tch: pushed along 1/2-way: hung lft bef led 1f out: continued to edge lft but in command ins fnl f* **8/1**

41 **2** 2 1/2 **Time For Old Time**[24] 3570 2-7-12 60 oh1 CatherineGannon 4 59
(I A Wood) *s.i.s: in rr bef hdwy on ins to chse wnr fr 1f out* **16/1**

142 **3** 3 1/2 **Mister Green (FR)**[8] 4119 2-9-7 83 FergalLynch 1 74+
(M J Wallace) *in tch: rdn 2f out: chalng whn squeezed out appr fnl f: one pce after* **8/11**[1]

0030 **4** 2 **Mean Mr Mustard (IRE)**[17] 3809 2-7-7 60 oh5 (b[1]) DavidProbert(5) 5 42
(J A Osborne) *trckd ldr: led over 2f out: edgd rt bef hdd 1f out: wknd ins fnl f* **14/1**

4404 **5** 2 **Kingswinford (IRE)**[21] 3670 2-8-9 71 ow1 (v[1]) TGMcLaughlin 6 47
(P D Evans) *tracd ldr to over 2f out: wknd 1f out* **6/1**[3]

4461 **6** 1 3/4 **Transcentral**[14] 3910 2-8-8 70 TPO'Shea 3 41
(W M Brisbourne) *led tl hdd over 2f out: wknd fnl f* **3/1**[2]

1m 16.2s (1.20) **Going Correction** +0.175s/f (Slow) **6 Ran SP% 120.8**
Speed ratings (Par 94): **99,95,91,88,85 83**
toteswinger: 1&2 £8.10, 1&3 £2.80, 2&3 £3.30. CSF £115.15 TOTE £10.60: £2.90, £3.90; EX 69.40.
Owner Lady Fairhaven **Bred** Lady Fairhaven **Trained** Newmarket, Suffolk
■ Stewards' Enquiry : David Probert three-day ban: careless riding (Aug 8-9,12)

FOCUS
The 'official' ratings are estimated and are included as a guide. An ordinary nursery and the leaders went off too fast. Haven't A Clue won decisively in the end but it is hard to be sur of the level with the second having won a poor race and the hampered third below form. The winning time was 1.03 seconds quicker than the older-horse maiden.

NOTEBOOK
Haven't A Clue had not gone on since winning her maiden at Folkestone, when she benefited from a track bias, but she improved for first-time blinkers and the strong pace suited. She squeezed up Mister Green when making her move off the home bend, but was the winner on merit. (op 13-2)
Time For Old Time, a claiming winner at Brighton last time, was another to benefit from the strong pace and stayed on for second. She flashed her tail again, but seemed to try hard enough and should stay 7f. (op 14-1 tchd 18-1)
Mister Green(FR) won a maiden at Great Leighs on his only previous start on Polytrack and he looked to have an obvious chance judged on his recent second to Rosabee at Leicester, but he was below form. He was squeezed up by the eventual winner at the top of the straight, but was not unlucky. (op 4-5 tchd 5-6)
Mean Mr Mustard(IRE), fitted with blinkers for the first time, had it to do from 5lb out of the handicap and paid for chasing the strong pace. (op 12-1)
Kingswinford(IRE) did not improve for a first-time visor or a switch to Polytrack. (op 7-1 tchd 15-2)
Transcentral went off too quickly and could not defy an estimated 5lb rise for her recent Chester success. (op 4-1 tchd 9-2)

4390 FREE BETTING @ FREEBETS.CO.UK H'CAP 1m 141y(P)
4:45 (4:45) (Class 5) (0-75,74) 3-Y-O+ **£3,238** (£963; £481; £240) **Stalls** Low

Form RPR

11 **1** **Willie Ever**[17] 3826 4-9-5 65 J-PGuillambert 3 76
(B Ellison) *mid-div: hdwy to go 2nd over 2f out: rdn to ld towards fin* **5/4**[1]

1502 **2** 1/2 **Don Pietro**[12] 4001 5-9-7 67 (p) TPO'Shea 5 77
(P A Blockley) *sn trckd ldr: led over 3f out: rdn and kpt on but hdd towards fin* **6/1**[2]

5-1P **3** 1 3/4 **Trifti**[92] 1583 7-9-12 72 SimonWhitworth 8 78
(Miss Jo Crowley) *s.i.s: hdwy on ins over 3f out: styd on to go 3rd nr fin* **20/1**

5425 **4** nk **Merrymadcap (IRE)**[49] 2770 6-10-0 74 FrancisNorton 6 79
(M Blanshard) *a.p: rdn to go 3rd 2f out: no ex and lost that position nr fin* **9/1**

0060 **5** 3 3/4 **Fateful Attraction**[10] 4054 5-9-2 62 (b) LiamJones 1 59
(I A Wood) *in rr: sme hdwy over 1f out: n.d* **33/1**

5205 **6** 1 1/4 **Happy As Larry (USA)**[3] 4268 6-9-7 70 (t) LukeMorris(3) 12 64
(J S Moore) *nvr bttr than mid-div* **7/1**[3]

330 **7** 1 3/4 **Reveur**[13] 3951 5-8-6 55 oh6 KirstyMilczarek(3) 10 45
(M Mullineaux) *s.i.s: in rr: sme hdwy over 1f out: nvr on terms* **25/1**

5-40 **8** 1/2 **Royal Straight**[65] 2302 3-8-13 73 DavidProbert(5) 2 62+
(A M Balding) *towards rr and nvr on terms* **15/2**

6413 **9** 1 1/2 **April Fool**[30] 3360 4-9-3 63 (v) ChrisCatlin 4 48
(J A Geake) *prom on ins: rdn over 4f out: wknd rapidly over 3f out* **6/1**[2]

3250 **10** 1 **Jord (IRE)**[57] 2531 4-9-10 73 TolleyDean(3) 9 56
(A J McCabe) *led tl hdd over 3f out: wknd 2f out* **28/1**

0100 **11** 3 **Sun Catcher (IRE)**[23] 3612 5-9-11 74 (v[1]) RussellKennemore(3) 7 50
(P G Murphy) *trckd ldrs: rdn over 4f out: wknd over 2f out* **25/1**

0000 **12** 31 **Baaher (USA)**[35] 3211 4-9-6 66 FergalLynch 11 —
(T J Pitt) *v.s.a: a wl bhd: t.o* **50/1**

1m 50.67s (0.17) **Going Correction** +0.175s/f (Slow)
WFA 3 from 4yo+ 9lb **12 Ran SP% 128.1**
Speed ratings (Par 103): **106,105,104,103,100 99,97,97,95,95 92,64**
toteswinger: 1&2 £3.90, 1&3 £9.80, 2&3 £23.50. CSF £9.06 CT £118.26 TOTE £2.00: £1.40, £2.20, £6.60; EX 12.20.
Owner Black and White Diamond Partnership **Bred** G Russell **Trained** Norton, N Yorks
■ Stewards' Enquiry : Tolley Dean one-day ban: failed to keep straight stalls (Aug 25)

FOCUS
A modest handicap run at a decent pace. The winning time was 0.91 seconds quicker than the earlier claimer. The winner is progressive and this is solid form for the grade.
Baaher(USA) Official explanation: jockey said gelding lost its action

4391 FREEBETS.CO.UK APPRENTICE H'CAP 2m 119y(P)
5:20 (5:20) (Class 6) (0-65,64) 4-Y-O+ **£2,388** (£705; £352) **Stalls** Low

Form RPR

-040 **1** **Swords**[11] 4029 6-8-8 51 ow2 JamieJones(3) 5 59
(R E Peacock) *mid-div but a in tch: wnt 2nd 2f out: led 1f out: drvn out* **14/1**

-301 **2** 1/2 **Spanish Conquest**[17] 3820 4-9-5 64 RosieJessop(5) 4 71
(Sir Mark Prescott) *a.p: wnt 2nd 6f out: led over 2f out: rdn and hdd 1f out: no ex towards fin* **9/4**[1]

3003 **3** 3/4 **Chiff Chaff**[5] 3871 4-8-2 45 JackDean(3) 8 52
(C R Dore) *mid-div: hdwy over 2f out: styd on to go 3rd ins fnl f* **9/1**

5006 **4** 3/4 **Bobsleigh**[11] 4029 9-8-6 46 KirstyMilczarek 7 52
(H S Howe) *mid-div: hdwy over 3f out: hdwy over 1f out: styd on: nvr nrr* **16/1**

-315 **5** 3/4 **Moonshine Beach**[20] 3710 10-8-12 57 WilliamCarson(5) 9 62
(P W Hiatt) *trckd ldrs: led 1m out: hdd over 2f out: no ex ins fnl f* **6/1**[2]

-311 **6** 1 3/4 **Squirtle (IRE)**[11] 4029 5-9-2 56 6ex LukeMorris 3 59
(W M Brisbourne) *s.i.s: hld up: hdwy over 5f out: rdn over 3f out: one pce ins fnl 2f* **9/4**[1]

550 **7** 3 1/4 **Makai**[10] 4055 5-8-2 47 ow2 RossAtkinson(5) 10 46
(M R Hoad) *slowly away: in rr: mod hdwy ins fnl 3f* **25/1**

330 **8** 8 **King's Fable (USA)**[26] 3523 5-9-5 62 (p) HaddenFrost(3) 11 51
(Karen George) *stdd s: towards rr: hdwy 6f out: no prog ins fnl 4f* **7/1**[3]

/40- **9** 49 **Bold Trump**[84] 240 7-8-2 47 ow2 ThomasO'Brien(5) 2 —
(Mrs N S Evans) *led tl hdd 1m out: sn rdn and wknd: t.o* **50/1**

00-5 **10** 1 1/4 **Historic Place (USA)**[17] 3820 8-9-0 59 (p) HarryPoulton(5) 1 —
(J A Geake) *a bhd: t.o* **14/1**

64-0 **11** 2 3/4 **Rule For Ever**[17] 3820 6-9-3 62 PatrickDonaghy(5) 6 —
(I W McInnes) *trckd ldrs: wknd qckly over 5f out: t.o* **12/1**

3m 44.19s (2.39) **Going Correction** +0.175s/f (Slow) **11 Ran SP% 131.0**
Speed ratings (Par 101): **101,100,100,100,99 98,97,93,70,69 68**
toteswinger: 1&2 £12.60, 1&3 £23.70, 2&3 £5.00. CSF £50.94 CT £330.06 TOTE £17.50: £3.40, £1.60, £2.40; EX 98.00 Place 6: £552.86 Place 5: £339.09.
Owner J Babb **Bred** Mrs A Yearley **Trained** Kyre Park, Worcs

The Form Book, Raceform Ltd, Compton, RG20 6NL

■ Stewards' Enquiry : Jamie Jones one-day ban: used whip down shoulder in forehand position (Aug 8)

FOCUS
A moderate staying handicap restricted to apprentices. The winner was on a nice mark on his old form.

King's Fable(USA) Official explanation: jockey said gelding failed to pick up
Rule For Ever Official explanation: jockey said gelding had a breathing problem
T/Plt: £191.50 to a £1 stake. Pool: £48,379.83. 184.35 winning tickets. T/Qpdt: £49.00 to a £1 stake. Pool: £2,947.30. 44.50 winning tickets. JS

3972 YORK (L-H)
Friday, July 25

OFFICIAL GOING: Good to firm
Dolling out added 7yds to advertised distances of races of a mile and further.
Wind: Light across Weather: Dry and fine

4392 J. & S. SEDDON PAINTING APPRENTICE STKS (H'CAP) 1m 208y
6:00 (6:00) (Class 4) (0-85,84) 3-Y-O **£5,180** (£1,541; £770; £384) **Stalls** Low

Form RPR
1101 **1** **Gala Casino Star (IRE)**[20] 3709 3-9-4 **83**................ FrederikTylicki(5) 6 91
(R A Fahey) *trckd ldrs: hdwy 3f out: led over 2f out: rdn and hung lft over 1f out: clr ins fnl f* **2/1**[1]
1002 **2** *2 ¼* **American Art (IRE)**[20] 3745 3-9-10 **84**......................(t) DuranFentiman 2 87
(B W Hills) *trckd ldrs: pushed along 3f out: rdn 2f out: styng on whn n.m.r over 1f out and ins fnl f: styd on u.p to take 2nd nr fin* **9/2**[3]
2610 **3** *nse* **Premier Danseur (IRE)**[41] 3038 3-9-9 **83**.................. AndrewMullen 5 86
(M Johnston) *hld up in rr: swtchd outside and hdwy over 2f out: rdn wl over 1f out: kpt on ins fnl f* **10/3**[2]
4314 **4** *1 ¼* **Shaloo Diamond**[27] 3493 3-9-4 **78**........................ MichaelJStainton 8 78
(R M Whitaker) *hld up in rr: hdwy on outer over 3f out: rdn and ev ch 2f out: drvn and one pce appr fnl f* **9/2**[3]
6-64 **5** *½* **Destinys Dream (IRE)**[15] 3866 3-8-6 **71** ow1.............. GaryBartley(5) 1 70
(G W Barker) *cl up: led 1/2-way: rdn and hdd over 2f out: n.m.r and swtchd rt ent fnl f: sn drvn and no ex* **16/1**
4610 **6** *6* **King Kenny**[8] 4128 3-9-4 **78**.................................... DNolan 4 64
(S Parr) *hld up in rr: hdwy 3f out: rdn 2f out: sn drvn and no imp* **8/1**
2035 **7** *4* **Safebreaker**[20] 3709 3-8-9 **72**.............................. KellyHarrison(3) 7 49
(N Tinkler) *led to 1/2-way: rdn along over 3f out and sn wknd* **33/1**

1m 52.79s (0.79) **Going Correction** -0.125s/f (Firm) **7** Ran **SP% 112.7**
Speed ratings (Par 102): **91,89,88,87,87 82,78**
toteswinger: 1&2 £1.70, 1&3 £2.10, 2&3 £3.40. CSF £11.00 CT £27.34 TOTE £2.80: £1.90, £2.40; EX 8.30.
Owner The Friar Tuck Racing Club **Bred** Glashare House Stud **Trained** Musley Bank, N Yorks
■ Stewards' Enquiry : Frederik Tylicki caution: careless riding

FOCUS
This did not look a bad race, but one gets the impression that most of them are a touch high in the handicap. The winner continues to progress and this form is sound enough rated around those in the frame behind the winner. The winning time looked to be quite ordinary.

4393 IG SPORT STKS (H'CAP) 6f
6:30 (6:30) (Class 4) (0-80,79) 4-Y-O+ **£6,476** (£1,927; £963; £481) **Stalls** Low

Form RPR
0011 **1** **Methaaly (IRE)**[4] 4239 5-9-2 **74** 12ex.............................(be) AlanMunro 6 89
(M Mullineaux) *cl up: led after 2f: rdn and qcknd clr over 1f out: easily* **11/2**[2]
5000 **2** *4 ½* **Pacific Pride**[5] 4218 5-9-6 **78**......................................(p) RobertWinston 9 79
(J J Quinn) *led 2f: cl up: rdn and ev ch tl drvn and one pce appr fnl f* **16/1**
6206 **3** *nk* **Jake The Snake (IRE)**[14] 3905 7-9-5 **77**........................ SebSanders 1 77+
(A W Carroll) *hld up towards rr: swtchd rt over 2f out: sn rdn and styd on ins fnl f: nrst fin* **10/1**
6501 **4** *1 ½* **Scarlet Oak**[15] 3883 4-8-6 **64**....................................(p) JimmyQuinn 10 59+
(D J S Ffrench Davis) *hld up in rr: swtchd lft and hdwy 2f out: sn rdn and styd on ins fnl f: nrst fin* **10/1**
3552 **5** *2* **Poppy's Rose**[7] 4174 4-8-3 **61**...................................(p) PatrickMathers 2 49
(I W McInnes) *in tch: hdwy to chse ldrs over 2f out: sn rdn and hung bdly lft: one pce appr fnl f* **15/2**
-052 **6** *4 ½* **Jonny Ebeneezer**[6] 4186 9-7-13 **64** ow2..................(b) RobbieEgan(7) 11 38
(D Flood) *chsd ldrs: rdn along 2f out: sn wknd* **7/1**[3]
0050 **7** *nk* **Ice Planet**[30] 3370 7-8-13 **78**................................ AdeleRothery(7) 8 51
(D Nicholls) *in tch: effrt whn n.m.r over 2f out: sn rdn and no hdwy* **7/1**[3]
-420 **8** *3 ½* **Royal Composer (IRE)**[7] 4174 5-7-13 **60**..........(b) DuranFentiman(3) 12 22
(T D Easterby) *chsd ldrs: rdn along over 2f out: sn edgd lft and wknd* **16/1**
00-5 **9** *2 ¼* **Chookie Heiton (IRE)**[13] 3956 10-8-12 **70**.................. TomEaves 4 25
(Miss L A Perratt) *chsd ldng pair: rdn along over 2f out: grad wknd* **14/1**
-000 **10** *7* **Oranmore Castle (IRE)**[83] 1818 6-8-8 **66**.................. PaulHanagan 5 —
(R A Fahey) *awkward s: sn chsng ;ldrs: rdn along over 2f out and sn wknd* **9/1**
0003 **11** *2* **Trimlestown (IRE)**[14] 3928 5-8-10 **68**........................(tp) PaulMulrennan 7 —
(K A Ryan) *dwlt: a in rr* **4/1**[1]

1m 10.43s (-1.47) **Going Correction** -0.125s/f (Firm) **11** Ran **SP% 118.8**
Speed ratings (Par 105): **104,98,97,95,92 86,86,81,78,69 66**
toteswinger: 1&2 £33.90, 1&3 £9.70, 2&3 £11.80. CSF £90.70 CT £883.14 TOTE £5.50: £2.30, £6.00, £2.40; EX 126.10.
Owner The Bellflower Methaaly Partnership **Bred** Scuderia Golden Horse S R L **Trained** Alpraham, Cheshire
■ Stewards' Enquiry : Seb Sanders caution: careless riding

FOCUS
Methaaly destroyed his rivals from the front rank. The winning time was good, but the form cannot be taken too literally with the first two in those positions throughout.

Scarlet Oak ◆ Official explanation: jockey said filly was unsuited by the good to firm ground
Poppy's Rose Official explanation: jockey said filly hung left
Trimlestown(IRE) Official explanation: jockey said gelding never travelled

4394 SMITH BROTHERS MEDIAN AUCTION MAIDEN STKS 7f
7:00 (7:00) (Class 4) 2-Y-O **£6,476** (£1,927; £963; £481) **Stalls** Low

Form RPR
1 **Perpetually (IRE)** 2-9-3 0.. JoeFanning 3 80+
(M Johnston) *chsd ldrs: hdwy on inner over 2f out: rdn over 1f out: swtchd rt ins fnl f: styd on wl to ld last 50yds* **11/1**
02 **2** *nk* **Cosmic Sun**[24] 3590 2-8-10 0................................ FrederikTylicki(7) 5 79
(R A Fahey) *trckd ldrs: hdwy over 2f out: rdn to chal over 1f out: drvn and ev ch ins fnl f: edgd rt and no ex last 50yds* **5/1**[3]
0 **3** *¾* **Amethyst Dawn (IRE)**[8] 4109 2-8-12 0.............................. DavidAllan 6 72
(T D Easterby) *led: rdn along over 2f out: drvn over 1f out: hdd and no ex wl ins fnl f* **16/1**
3 **4** *1 ½* **Russian George (IRE)**[17] 3821 2-9-3 0............................ MickyFenton 2 74+
(T P Tate) *hld up in rr: hdwy over 2f out: sn rdn and styd on ins fnl f: nrst fin* **9/2**[2]
5 *1 ½* **Archie Rice (USA)** 2-9-3 0.. AlanMunro 11 70
(W Jarvis) *cl up: rdn 2f out and ev ch tl drvn and wknd appr fnl f* **7/1**
23 **6** *2 ¾* **Kyllachy Star**[29] 3411 2-9-3 0.. PaulHanagan 4 63
(R A Fahey) *t.k.h: chsd ldrs: rdn along over 2f out: wknd over 1f out* **3/1**[1]
4 **7** *4 ½* **Postman**[11] 4014 2-9-3 0.. TomEaves 8 52
(B Smart) *chsd ldrs on outer: rdn along over 2f out: grad wknd* **11/2**
43 **8** *6* **Mefraas (IRE)**[14] 3926 2-9-3 0...................................... SebSanders 10 37
(E A L Dunlop) *swtchd lft s and hld up: hdwy and in tch 3f out: sn rdn and btn 2f out* **13/2**
9 *7* **Feeling Stylish (IRE)** 2-8-12 0.. KimTinkler 1 14
(N Tinkler) *s.i.s: a in rr* **50/1**
10 *1 ¼* **Nayessence** 2-9-3 0.. PaulMulrennan 12 16
(M W Easterby) *wnt rt s: a in rr* **33/1**

1m 25.4s (0.10) **Going Correction** -0.125s/f (Firm) **10** Ran **SP% 120.2**
Speed ratings (Par 96): **94,93,92,91,89 86,81,74,66,64**
toteswinger: 1&2 £6.20, 1&3 £14.60, 2&3 £17.20. CSF £67.27 TOTE £9.90: £2.90, £1.90, £3.50; EX 69.10.
Owner Sheikh Hamdan Bin Mohammed Al Maktoum **Bred** Gainsborough Stud Management Ltd **Trained** Middleham Moor, N Yorks

FOCUS
A fair-looking maiden, which can produce a few winners this term. The form is rated through the runner-up and looks at least this good.

NOTEBOOK
Perpetually(IRE) did not travel as well as some in the early stages but he really found his stride late on to come home a comfortable winner. He will definitely stay further. (op 10-1)
Cosmic Sun stayed on well down the middle of the track to almost collect the prize. He remains progressive and can win something before the end of the season. (op 7-1 tchd 9-2)
Amethyst Dawn(IRE) ◆, who employed front-running tactics, lasted longer than she did on her debut. A drop in trip will not be against her and she looks more than capable of finding a race. (op 14-1)
Russian George(IRE) got outpaced as the tempo increased and was struggling to keep tabs on the leaders. However, he finished to good effect in the final furlong and is one to keep an eye on next time. (op 11-2 tchd 6-1)
Archie Rice(USA) looked a bit bigger than most of his rivals, so should have the scope for improvement. He did little wrong during the race, only tiring inside the final furlong after taking a bit of a grip early. The experience should have done him good and he can land an ordinary maiden. (op 11-2 tchd 8-1)
Kyllachy Star, stepping up in trip again, pulled much too hard and could not pick up when asked to. 6f will probably be the right distance for him. (op 4-1)
Postman chased the pace early but looked green under pressure. He was not given a hard time inside the final furlong, as he did not look completely sound. Official explanation: jockey said colt lost its action (op 9-2 tchd 6-1)

4395 EUROPEAN BREEDERS' FUND LYRIC STKS (LISTED RACE) (F&M) 1m 2f 88y
7:30 (7:32) (Class 1) 3-Y-O+
£22,708 (£8,608; £4,308; £2,148; £1,076; £540) **Stalls** Low

Form RPR
3250 **1** **Sweet Lilly**[20] 3720 4-9-4 102.............................. EdwardCreighton 2 106
(M R Channon) *hld up in rr: stdy hdwy on outer 3f out: rdn over 1f out: styd on wl to ld last 100yds* **6/1**
14-3 **2** *1 ¼* **Soft Morning**[15] 3885 4-9-7 105.................................. SebSanders 8 106
(Sir Mark Prescott) *cl up: led wl over 2f out: rdn wl over 1f out: drvn ins fnl f: hdd and no ex last 100yds* **4/1**[3]
-400 **3** *1 ¾* **Makaaseb (USA)**[20] 3742 3-8-8 95.............................. PhilipRobinson 6 100
(M A Jarvis) *trckd ldrs: hdwy 3f out: rdn to chse ldr 2f out: sn drvn and ch tl one pce ins fnl f* **8/1**
3211 **4** *3 ½* **Flying Clarets (IRE)**[13] 3974 5-9-4 113.............................. PaulHanagan 5 93
(R A Fahey) *led: rdn along 3f out: sn hdd: drvn 2f out and grad wknd* **2/1**[1]
1204 **5** *1 ½* **Sugar Mint (IRE)**[20] 3742 3-8-8 101.............................. AlanMunro 4 90
(B W Hills) *trckd ldng pair: hdwy 3f out: rdn and n.m.r over 2f out: hmpd over 1f out: sn btn* **5/2**[2]
21-0 **6** *5* **Miss Emma May (IRE)**[22] 3627 3-8-8 83..............(v) StephenDonohoe 3 80
(D R C Elsworth) *in tch: rdn along 3f out: sn wknd* **25/1**
30-0 **7** *27* **Treat**[46] 2890 4-9-4 97.. RobertWinston 1 26
(E A L Dunlop) *in tch: rdn along 3f out and sn wknd* **12/1**

2m 12.58s (0.08) **Going Correction** -0.125s/f (Firm)
WFA 3 from 4yo+ 10lb **7** Ran **SP% 118.8**
Speed ratings (Par 111): **94,93,91,88,87 83,62**
toteswinger: 1&2 £4.00, 1&3 £9.40, 2&3 £10.50. CSF £31.69 TOTE £7.30: £2.50, £2.30; EX 37.70.
Owner Jaber Abdullah **Bred** Red House Stud **Trained** West Ilsley, Berks

FOCUS
A good standard despite the small field. However, the winner's time was disappointing, considering the race had a confirmed front-runner in it, and Sugar Mint looked very unlucky not to be closer. The form is rated around the principals.

NOTEBOOK
Sweet Lilly, who was completely outclassed in Group 2 company last time, is not an easy horse to catch right, but everything fell in place for her in this and she showed a good turn-of-foot to win comfortably. Creighton gave this quirky filly a particularly good ride, but she is no good thing to repeat this sort of effort every time. (op 8-1)
Soft Morning, who made a fair seasonal debut behind Hala Bek last time, sat close to the leader and struck for home just over two furlongs out. She gave her all under pressure but could not hold off the winner in the final stages, giving away 3lb. One would expect her shrewd trainer to find another good opportunity before the end of the season for her. (op 9-2 tchd 3-1)
Makaaseb(USA), trying 1m2f for the first time, reversed form with Sugar Mint on their meeting at Sandown last time but was not quite good enough against the older generation. This trip may just stretch her stamina to the limit. (op 9-1 tchd 10-1)
Flying Clarets(IRE), who missed a week's cantering after nicking herself, dominated as usual but was unable to hold off her rivals this time in better company. All of her best form has come in easier ground. (op 7-4 tchd 9-4)
Sugar Mint(IRE) ◆ looked very unlucky in running and one could argue that she may have won had she not found trouble. The effort does confirm she has the ability to win at this sort of level at least. (op 7-2)

Treat finished last again and is not one to be interested in until showing much more zest. Official explanation: jockey said filly hung left throughout (tchd 16-1)

4396 SKY BET SUPPORTING THE YORKSHIRE RACING FESTIVAL CLAIMING STKS — 1m 4f

8:00 (8:00) (Class 4) 3-Y-0+ **£5,180** (£1,541; £770; £384) **Stalls** Centre

Form RPR

0130 **1** **Birkside**[14] 3929 5-9-12 86 .... DavidAllan 4 85
(D Carroll) *trckd ldng pair: hdwy on inner to ld wl over 2f out: sn rdn: drvn over 1f out: hld on gamely* **9/4**[2]

0166 **2** *nk* **Quince (IRE)**[20] 3736 5-9-11 78 .... (v) JimmyQuinn 1 84
(J Pearce) *hld up in tch: rdn along over 2f out: swtchd rt and drvn over 1f out: styd on strly ins fnl f* **11/1**

2445 **3** *1* **Peruvian Prince (USA)**[22] 3649 6-9-10 81 .... PaulHanagan 5 81
(R A Fahey) *hld up in tch: hdwy on outer over 2f out: rdn wl over 1f out: kpt on u.p and ch ins fnl f: no ex towards fin* **4/1**[3]

0002 **4** *1/2* **Philanthropy**[41] 3045 4-9-6 85 .... NeilBrown(3) 3 80
(K A Ryan) *stmbld s: sn cl up: effrt over 2f out and ev ch tl rdn and hung lft over 1f out and kpt on same pce* **5/4**[1]

0232 **5** *6* **Mister Fizzbomb (IRE)**[23] 3602 5-9-3 66 .... (v) SladeO'Hara(5) 6 69
(J S Wainwright) *led: rdn along 3f out: sn hdd & wknd* **10/1**

2m 39.47s (6.27) **Going Correction** -0.125s/f (Firm) **5** Ran SP% **112.6**
Speed ratings: **74,73,73,72,68**
toteswinger: 1&2 £16.00 CSF £23.98 TOTE £3.10: £1.70, £3.80; EX 25.20.
Owner J M Walsh & R Glynn **Bred** Pendley Farm **Trained** Sledmere, E Yorks
■ Stewards' Enquiry : Jimmy Quinn caution: used whip with excessive frequency
David Allan one-day ban: used whip with excessive frequency (Aug 8)

FOCUS
A decent-looking small field claimer but the early pace was poor, and the winning time was dreadful. The winner did not need to run to his previous marks with the runner-up setting the level for the form.

4397 CELEBRATING 25 YEARS OF MADEIRA UK STKS (H'CAP) — 5f 89y

8:30 (8:30) (Class 4) (0-80,78) 3-Y-0 **£6,152** (£1,830; £914; £456) **Stalls** Low

Form RPR

0112 **1** **Jaconet (USA)**[4] 4242 3-8-5 60 .... (b) PaulFessey 2 76
(T D Barron) *mde all: rdn and qckn clr wl over 1f out: styd on strly* **11/2**

330 **2** *4* **Captain Dunne (IRE)**[20] 3723 3-9-7 76 .... DavidAllan 6 78
(T D Easterby) *trckd ldrs: effrt to chse wnr over 2f out: drvn over 1f out and kpt on same pce* **3/1**[1]

2523 **3** *3 1/4* **Rio Sands**[12] 4000 3-9-0 72 .... MichaelJStainton(3) 8 62
(R M Whitaker) *hld up: hdwy 2f out: sn rdn and kpt on same pce* **5/1**

-051 **4** *2 1/2* **Know No Fear**[9] 4074 3-9-9 78 6ex .... RobertWinston 5 59
(J J Quinn) *chsd ldrs: rdn over 2f out: sn no imp* **9/2**[3]

4-60 **5** *nse* **Nickel Silver**[7] 4163 3-9-1 70 .... TomEaves 3 51
(B Smart) *chsd wnr: rdn along over 2f out: grad wknd* **16/1**

6210 **6** *1/2* **Foreign Rhythm (IRE)**[5] 4216 3-8-5 60 .... (v) KimTinkler 4 39
(N Tinkler) *a in rr* **25/1**

4321 **7** *3 3/4* **Splash The Cash**[8] 4118 3-8-8 66 6ex .... (p) NeilBrown(3) 1 31
(K A Ryan) *chsd ldrs: rdn along over 2f out: sn drvn and btn* **10/3**[2]

10 **8** *5* **Mayoman (IRE)**[28] 3455 3-9-4 73 .... SebSanders 7 20
(Paul Green) *s.i.s: a in rr* **10/1**

63.23 secs (-1.07) **Going Correction** -0.125s/f (Firm) **8** Ran SP% **117.1**
Speed ratings (Par 102): **103,96,91,87,87 86,80,72**
toteswinger: 1&2 £4.80, 1&3 £7.10, 2&3 £4.10 CSF £23.00 CT £89.24 TOTE £5.70: £1.90, £1.70, £1.90; EX 28.20 Place 6 £ 571.47, Place 5 £ 305.13.
Owner R G Toes **Bred** Team Block **Trained** Maunby, N Yorks

FOCUS
A modest sprint run at a sound gallop. The winner is in great heart and never saw another rival and the form is rated at face value.
T/Plt: £977.80 to a £1 stake. Pool: £65,504.11. 48.90 winning tickets. T/Qpdt: £84.70 to a £1 stake. Pool: £4,181.22. 36.50 winning tickets. JR

4398 - 4401a (Foreign Racing) - See Raceform Interactive

4359 ASCOT (R-H)

Saturday, July 26

OFFICIAL GOING: Good to firm
Wind: Virtually nil Weather: Warm, mainly sunny

4402 ANDREX WINKFIELD STKS (LISTED RACE) — 7f

2:00 (2:02) (Class 1) 2-Y-0 **£17,031** (£6,456; £3,231; £1,611; £807; £405) **Stalls** Centre

Form RPR

0211 **1** **Talking Hands**[14] 3941 2-9-2 0 .... JamieSpencer 5 96
(S Kirk) *stdd s: hld up in last: swtchd rt and hdwy over 1f out: r.o wl u.p last 100yds to ld nr fin* **9/2**[3]

6 **2** *nk* **The Legal Blonde (IRE)**[14] 3959 2-8-11 0 .... RichardKingscote 6 91
(Tom Dascombe) *w'like: scope: tall: lengthy: prom: rdn over 2f out: chsd ldr ent fnl 2f: ev ch u.p over 1f out: led last 100yds: hdd nr fin* **16/1**

16 **3** *1* **Prime Delivery (USA)**[16] 3876 2-9-2 0 .... NCallan 1 93
(R M H Cowell) *swtg: stdd after s: hld up in tch: swtchd lft and effrt 2f out: pressed ldrs ent fnl f: unable qckn last 100yds* **5/1**

11 **4** *1* **Wildcat Wizard (USA)**[29] 3439 2-9-2 0 .... RyanMoore 7 91
(P F I Cole) *lw: t.k.h: led and racd alone towards far side after 1f: rdn 2f out: edgd rt u.p: hdd last 100yds: fdd towards fin* **9/4**[2]

11 **5** *7* **Doctor Crane (USA)**[7] 4187 2-9-2 0 .... JimmyFortune 4 73+
(J H M Gosden) *lw: led for 1f: chsd ldr tl 2f out: wknd u.p over 1f out: eased whn btn ins fnl f* **15/8**[1]

4401 **6** *5* **Grand Honour (IRE)**[10] 4079 2-9-2 0 .... RobertWinston 2 61
(P Howling) *chsd ldrs: rdn 3f out: wknd 2f out* **20/1**

1m 29.43s (1.43) **Going Correction** +0.075s/f (Good) **6** Ran SP% **111.0**
Speed ratings (Par 102): **94,93,92,91,83 77**
toteswinger: 1&2 £9.90, 1&3 £3.40, 2&3 £9.20. CSF £61.94 TOTE £4.60: £2.10, £3.00; EX 59.00.
Owner Deauville Daze Partnership **Bred** Wood Hall Stud Limited **Trained** Upper Lambourn, Berks

FOCUS
A decent Listed race with the winner building on his solid win in a nursery here. The runner-up stepped forward considerably and the third confirmed his Newmarket form.

NOTEBOOK
Talking Hands, who got off the mark in a Wolverhampton maiden, followed up in a nursery here off an estimated mark of 81. Back up in trip and raised in grade, he was again held up by Spencer. After being taken to the outer of the bunch initially he was then switched back inside to deliver his challenge between horses, running on for pressure to get on top close home. On the upgrade, he handled this fast surface but his trainer thinks he will be happier with a bit of cut in the ground. (op 4-1)

The Legal Blonde(IRE) ◆, who showed promise in an ordinary 6f Nottingham maiden against her own sex on her debut, comes from a yard with a surprising amount of juvenile talent and ran a big race on this rise in grade. The lone filly in the line-up, she was always towards the fore and battled her way to a narrow lead with half a furlong to go but was just run out of it. She should soon get off the mark. (op 18-1 tchd 20-1)

Prime Delivery(USA), sixth in the Group 2 July Stakes, was facing a more realistic task here. Coming with his run on the stands' side of the bunch, he just about had every chance and was only forced to concede defeat deep inside the final furlong. The longer trip was not a problem and he confirmed that his Newmarket run does not flatter him. (op 11-2 tchd 9-2)

Wildcat Wizard(USA), unbeaten in two previous appearances, was keen as he had been at Doncaster and, showing in front overall, he raced apart from his rivals for the first half of the contest. Coming under pressure with a quarter of a mile to run, he only relinquished his lead in the last half-furlong. Official explanation: jockey said colt hung right (op 5-2 tchd 11-4)

Doctor Crane(USA) showed ahead in the main bunch for five furlongs but he did not find much when ridden and was eased when his chance had gone inside the last. This was not his running, and the race might have come too quickly following his Newbury win a week earlier. Official explanation: trainer had no explanation for the poor form shown (tchd 2-1 and 11-5 in a place)

Grand Honour(IRE), the most exposed in the field and a Kempton nursery winner last time, was found wanting in this company and was the first beaten.

4403 PRINCESS MARGARET INDEPENDENT NEWSPAPER STKS (GROUP 3) (FILLIES) — 6f

2:35 (2:39) (Class 1) 2-Y-0

£28,385 (£10,760; £5,385; £2,685; £1,345; £675) **Stalls** Centre

Form RPR

24 **1** **African Skies**[36] 3192 2-8-12 0 .... NCallan 4 100+
(K A Ryan) *lw: in tch: shkn up and hdwy over 2f out: rdn to ld wl over 1f out: styd on wl fnl f* **11/2**[2]

5111 **2** *1* **Rosabee (IRE)**[9] 4119 2-8-12 0 .... RobertWinston 15 97
(Miss V Haigh) *hld up in rr of far side gp: hdwy and rdn 2f out: styd on wl fnl f: wnt 2nd nr fin: nt pce to rch wnr* **10/1**

13 **3** *nk* **Excellerator (IRE)**[16] 3865 2-8-12 0 .... JamieSpencer 16 96
(George Baker) *swtg: led far side gp: chsd ldrs whn gps merged over 3f out: chsd wnr over 1f out: kpt on same pce u.p fnl f: lost 2nd nr fin* **14/1**

2252 **4** *1 1/2* **April Pride**[22] 3681 2-8-12 0 .... RichardHughes 1 92
(R Hannon) *swtg: stdd after s: t.k.h and hld up in rr: hdwy and rdn 2f out: kpt on u.p fnl f: nt pce to rch ldrs* **11/1**

41 **5** *3/4* **Rose Diamond (IRE)**[36] 3219 2-8-12 0 .... SteveDrowne 8 89
(R Charlton) *swtg: stdd after s: hld up bhd: rdn over 2f out: styd on u.p fr over 1f out: nt rch ldrs* **13/2**

616 **6** *1* **Ares Choix**[36] 3192 2-9-0 0 ow2 .... OPeslier 3 88
(P C Haslam) *chsd ldrs: led 3f out tl wl over 1f out: wknd ins fnl f* **22/1**

1030 **7** *2 1/4* **Moss Likely (IRE)**[7] 4190 2-8-12 0 .... EdwardCreighton 13 80
(M R Channon) *racd on far side: swtchd rt and effrt over 2f out: edgd lft and no imp u.p fnl f* **25/1**

1 **8** *1 1/2* **Kissing The Camera**[64] 2368 2-8-12 0 .... RyanMoore 14 75
(J Noseda) *racdc far side: ev ch over 2f out: wknd u.p over 1f out* **6/1**[3]

013 **9** *nk* **Danidh Dubai (IRE)**[36] 3192 2-8-12 0 .... ChrisCatlin 9 80+
(M R Channon) *lw: hld up towards rr: nt clr run and snatched up 3f out: forced way through and hdwy u.p 2f out: no hdwy last 100yds* **5/1**[1]

516 **10** *1 3/4* **Sea Of Leaves (USA)**[17] 3851 2-8-12 0 .... (t) JimmyFortune 17 69
(J H M Gosden) *in tch on far side: rdn over 2f out: wknd over 1f out* **10/1**

41 **11** *1 1/2* **Carina Nebula (USA)**[10] 4088 2-8-12 0 .... JimCrowley 5 64
(T G Mills) *lw: led tl 3f out: sn rdn: wknd u.p wl over 1f out* **40/1**

21 **12** *3 1/2* **Pyrrha**[32] 3348 2-8-12 0 .... MartinDwyer 10 63+
(C F Wall) *hld up wl in tch: shkn up and hmpd whn gps merged 3f out: bhd and hmpd again over 2f out: no ch after* **7/1**

14 **13** *hd* **Oasis Breeze**[23] 3634 2-8-12 0 .... PaulEddery 11 56+
(G D Blake) *swtg: in tch in midfield: rdn and hmpd whn gps merged wl over 2f out: no ch last 2f* **25/1**

44 **14** *2* **Peper Harow (IRE)**[28] 3496 2-8-12 0 .... WilliamBuick 6 47+
(M D I Usher) *prom: rdn 1/2-way: wkng whn hmpd wl over 2f out: wl bhd last 2f* **66/1**

15 **15** *1/2* **Royal Raider**[22] 3681 2-8-12 0 .... TGMcLaughlin 7 46+
(P D Evans) *in tch: rdn and edgd rt and bmpd 3f out: bhd whn hmpd again over 2f out: no ch after* **100/1**

0502 **16** *9* **Sweet Applause (IRE)**[19] 3792 2-8-12 0 .... DarrenWilliams 12 19
(A P Jarvis) *racd keenly on far side: prom tl wknd qckly jst over 2f out* **33/1**

1m 14.77s (0.37) **Going Correction** +0.075s/f (Good) **16** Ran SP% **125.3**
Speed ratings (Par 101): **100,98,98,96,95 93,90,88,88,86 84,79,79,76,75 63**
toteswinger: 1&2 £19.30, 1&3 £14.90, 2&3 £43.20. CSF £57.59 TOTE £6.70: £2.50, £3.70, £4.00; EX 88.20 TRIFECTA Not won..
Owner Cockerill Hillen & Graham **Bred** Mrs P Cockerill And Mr S Hillen **Trained** Hambleton, N Yorks
■ Stewards' Enquiry : Robert Winston two-day ban: used whip with excessive frequency (Aug 10,11)

FOCUS
The field split into two groups initially, with half a dozen racing on the far side, before the groups merged. This was a modest renewal of this Group 3, but the first two are both progressing well. It was a bit of a rough race and the fourth, along with the time, helps set the level.

NOTEBOOK
African Skies arrived here still a maiden but her Albany Stakes fourth over course and distance at the Royal meeting had shown her to be a very useful filly. Never too far from the pace, and blessed with a clearer passage than most, she came with her run on the stands' side of the field and did the job in good style. There is more to come from her, especially when stepped up to 7f or 1m, but she has work to do if she is to make an impact at a higher level. (op 6-1 tchd 13-2)

Rosabee(IRE) has been most progressive in recent weeks, completing a July hat-trick when defying a double penalty in a Leicester nursery. Racing towards the back in the group of six that raced on the far side through the early parts, she gradually edged over to her left and stayed on for pressure to take second close home, without troubling the winner. She ran a cracker on this sound surface but will not mind a return to easier underfoot conditions. (op 16-1)

Excellerator(IRE), her rookie trainer's first Group runner, was a close third to Rosabee at Doncaster last time but was not quite able to reverse that form on 3lb better terms. Showing in front in the far-side group, she edged left as the groups came together and battled on, only losing second spot close home. (op 16-1)

April Pride, who raced keenly at the back of the field towards the stands' side, was keeping on well in the final furlong. A consistent filly, she appreciated the return to this trip and might even be ready for a step up to 7f now. (op 12-1)

Rose Diamond(IRE) ◆ had five subsequent winners behind her when accounting for male opposition in a Newmarket maiden. Staying on takingly at the end on this rise in grade, she is capable of making her mark in this sort of company with further improvement likely. She should get another furlong or two as she is by stamina influence Daylami out of a mare who landed the Haydock Sprint Cup but stayed 7f well. (tchd 7-1 and 15-2 in places)

Ares Choix filled the same position in the Albany here last month and again finished behind African Skies and April Pride. She ran another good race, but her main asset seems to be pace and she again gave the impression that she would benefit from dropping back to 5f. (op 25-1 tchd 20-1)

Moss Likely(IRE), one of the most experienced runners in the line-up, stayed the extra furlong but just came up short in this higher grade. (op 22-1)
Kissing The Camera, not seen since her winning debut at Newmarket two months ago, was found out by this rise in grade but was not given too hard a time when held. (tchd 7-1)
Danidh Dubai(IRE) finished third in the Albany last time but could not maintain her superiority over the three fillies who finished just behind her then, including today's winner. She dropped to the rear of the field after being squeezed out at the halfway stage but did make up some ground before running out of steam in the last half-furlong. (op 6-1)
Sea Of Leaves(USA) had no apparent excuses but may be ready to tackle 7f now.
Pyrrha, who beat a subsequent winner when scoring at Newbury, was quite badly hampered with three furlongs to run. Her chance went altogether when she was again inconvenienced shortly afterwards. Official explanation: jockey said filly was denied a clear run (op 6-1 tchd 8-1 in places)
Oasis Breeze Official explanation: trainer said filly returned home with a very sore shin

4404 EMIRATES NBD CUP (HERITAGE H'CAP) 1m (S)

3:05 (3:12) (Class 2) 3-Y-O

£28,039 (£8,397; £4,198; £2,101; £1,048; £526) **Stalls** Centre

Form / RPR

12-0 **1** **Perfect Stride**[84] 1808 3-8-10 **89** .... RyanMoore 4 107+
(Sir Michael Stoute) *lw: hld up wl bhd: gd hdwy jst over 2f out: rdn to ld over 1f out: r.o strly and drew clr fnl f: readily* **4/1**[2]

-213 **2** *3* **Yaddree**[37] 3155 3-9-4 **97** .... PhilipRobinson 9 107
(M A Jarvis) *lw: led for 1f: chsd ldrs after: rdn to ld 2f out: hdd over 1f out: nt pce of wnr but kpt on fnl f* **5/2**[1]

1211 **3** *½* **Yamal (IRE)**[9] 4104 3-8-11 **90** .... JamieSpencer 1 101+
(M Johnston) *hld up bhd: effrt 2f out: swtchd lft over 1f out: r.o u.p fnl f: wnt 3rd nr fin: no ch w wnr* **7/1**

1550 **4** *1 ½* **Lazy Days**[16] 3877 3-8-10 **89** .... HayleyTurner 8 95
(D R C Elsworth) *lw: in tch in midfield: hdwy 3f out: ev ch and drvn jst over 2f out: kpt on same pce u.p fnl f* **15/2**

2-20 **5** *½* **Al Muheer (IRE)**[15] 3919 3-9-7 **100** .... NCallan 3 104
(C E Brittain) *hld up in midfield: hdwy to chse ldrs jst over 2f out: kpt on same pce fnl f* **28/1**

0004 **6** *3* **Fathsta (IRE)**[7] 4197 3-9-0 **93** ow2 .... OPeslier 7 90
(S Kirk) *hld up in midfield: effrt to chse ldrs 2f out: sn outpcd: wl hld fnl f* **12/1**

0004 **7** *5* **Arctic Cape**[8] 4158 3-7-7 **77** oh1 .... DavidProbert(5) 10 63
(M Johnston) *chsd ldrs: rdn 3f out: sn struggling: no ch fr wl over 1f out* **16/1**

2111 **8** *nse* **Always A Rock (IRE)**[7] 4197 3-8-9 **88** .... RoystonFfrench 12 74
(M Johnston) *chsd ldrs: led over 2f out: sn rdn: hdd 2f out: wknd qckly over 1f out* **6/1**[3]

-106 **9** *½* **Strategic Mission (IRE)**[8] 4160 3-9-0 **93** .... JimmyFortune 6 78
(P F I Cole) *a bhd: rdn and no rspnse 1/2-way* **20/1**

4-15 **10** *8* **Transfer**[28] 3475 3-8-4 **83** .... WilliamBuick 11 49
(A M Balding) *racd keenly: led after 1f: rdn over 3f out: hdd over 2f out: wknd qckly 2f out: no ch and eased ins fnl f* **16/1**

0-21 **11** *1 ¾* **Navajo Joe (IRE)**[49] 2834 3-8-9 **88** .... RichardHughes 5 50
(B J Meehan) *stdd after s: hdwy into midfield 1/2-way: rdn 3f out: sn struggling: wl btn fnl f* **14/1**

1m 39.24s (-1.36) **Going Correction** +0.075s/f (Good) **11** Ran **SP%** **121.5**
Speed ratings (Par 106): **109,106,105,104,103 100,95,95,94,86 85**
toteswinger: 1&2 £3.40, 1&3 £7.40, 2&3 £4.60. CSF £14.92 CT £71.18 TOTE £4.70: £2.20, £1.60, £2.40; EX 17.30 Trifecta £90.20 Pool: £2,170.29, 17.80 winning units.
Owner Saeed Suhail **Bred** Bloomsbury Stud **Trained** Newmarket, Suffolk

FOCUS
A strong three-year-old handicap won by the very well-treated Perfect Stride who will soon be back in Group company. The runner-up is very smart too and this form should work out well. A race to view positively overall.

NOTEBOOK
Perfect Stride ◆ has been given time since finishing 12th in the 2000 Guineas, for which he had been something of a talking horse earlier in the spring. Held up at the back, he improved going well on the stands' side of the group before coming away in fine style in the final furlong, proving much too good for this field. He will take a big hike for this and, capable of a good deal better, will surely be back in Group company before long. (op 3-1 tchd 9-2, 5-1 in places and 11-4 in places)
Yaddree ◆ was up another 2lb after his second in the Britannia here over course and distance. After striking the front with two furlongs to run he proved no match for the winner, but that was no disgrace at all. Not far off Group class himself, he should continue to perform with credit and could run in the Totesport Mile to Goodwood, in which his owner also has Laa Rayb. (op 7-2)
Yamal(IRE), dropped out on the stands' side of the group, then drifted towards the far side but the gap did not come for him and Spencer opted to switch him back towards the near flank. Eventually getting a run, he finished in good style but the lost momentum cost him. He has been commendably progressive and this was another fine run off a 6lb higher mark. (op 8-1)
Lazy Days ◆ raced closer to the pace than he had at Newmarket and was keeping on solidly at the end. He remains capable of bagging a big handicap and the return to 1m2f will not trouble him. (op 10-1)
Al Muheer(IRE), racing off a 3lb higher mark than when down the field at Newmarket, was far from disgraced under top weight. (op 33-1)
Fathsta(IRE), whose rider put up 2lb overweight, performed creditably enough but remains in the Handicapper's grip. This tough individual's season began in January and this was his 15th run of the campaign. (tchd 11-1)
Always A Rock(IRE) was another 3lb higher on this bid for the four-timer. Unable to adopt his usual front-running tactics, he did show ahead with more than two furlongs to run but he was soon headed and that was that. (op 7-1)

4405 TOTESPORT INTERNATIONAL STKS (HERITAGE H'CAP) 7f

3:40 (3:50) (Class 2) 3-Y-O+

£93,465 (£27,990; £13,995; £7,005; £3,495; £1,755) **Stalls** Centre

Form / RPR

U165 **1** **Laa Rayb (USA)**[36] 3197 4-9-7 **104** .... RoystonFfrench 27 116
(M Johnston) *sn niggled along in rr: gd hdwy over 2f out: forced way through 2f out: led ins fnl f: styd on wl* **18/1**

0120 **2** *1 ¼* **Dhaular Dhar (IRE)**[15] 3921 6-9-2 **99** .... DanielTudhope 3 108+
(J S Goldie) *lw: bhd: nt clr run over 2f out and again over 1f out: swtchd rt ent fnl f: r.o wl to go 2nd nr fin: nt rch wnr* **25/1**

0505 **3** *½* **Giganticus (USA)**[15] 3921 5-9-0 **97** .... MichaelHills 2 105
(B W Hills) *hld up in tch: hdwy and bmpd 2f out: rdn to ld over 1f out: hdd ins fnl f: one pce* **14/1**

0006 **4** *nk* **Excusez Moi (USA)**[7] 4188 6-9-0 **97** .... NCallan 7 104
(C E Brittain) *swtg: hld up bhd: gd hdwy over 2f out: ev ch ent fnl f: hung lft and nt qckn fnl f* **50/1**

0064 **5** *nk* **South Cape**[15] 3899 5-8-4 **87** .... TPO'Shea 19 93
(M R Channon) *lw: hld up towards rr: hdwy over 2f out: chsd ldrs ent fnl f: kpt on u.p* **33/1**

-101 **6** *nk* **Redford (IRE)**[28] 3491 3-8-9 **99** .... JamieSpencer 4 104
(M L W Bell) *lw: stdd s: hld up wl bhd: stl last over 2f out: rdn and hdwy 2f out: rn on but nvr able to rch ldrs* **13/2**[1]

2-30 **7** *shd* **Big Noise**[49] 2818 4-8-4 **87** .... RichardThomas 18 92+
(Dr J D Scargill) *hld up towards rr: hdwy and edgd rt fr 2f out: styd on wl fnl f: nt rch ldrs* **50/1**

-403 **8** *1* **Presumptive (IRE)**[36] 3222 8-8-6 **94** .... DavidProbert(5) 28 96
(R Charlton) *hld up wl in rr: hdwy on far side over 2f out: kpt on same pce fnl f* **33/1**

-024 **9** *shd* **Mastership (IRE)**[15] 3921 4-8-12 **95** .... RobertWinston 1 97+
(J J Quinn) *hld up bhd: rdn and effrt 2f out: keeping on whn n.m.r ins fnl f: nvr able to chal* **10/1**[3]

4101 **10** *¾* **Masai Moon**[36] 3222 4-8-9 **92** .... ChrisCatlin 16 92
(B R Millman) *chsd ldrs: rdn and ev ch over 2f out: wknd ent fnl f* **50/1**

0-50 **11** *½* **Dream Theme**[62] 2426 5-8-7 **90** .... SilvestreDeSousa 5 89
(D Nicholls) *in tch: rdn jst over 2f out: keeping on same pce whn hmpd jst ins fnl f: no ch after* **50/1**

0-30 **12** *hd* **Artimino**[15] 3921 4-9-3 **100** .... JMurtagh 8 98
(J R Fanshawe) *swtg: hld up in tch: effrt 2f out: hanging rt and nt qckning whn n.m.r jst ins fnl f: one pce after* **16/1**

0046 **13** *½* **Mujood**[17] 3840 5-8-7 **90** ....(b) WilliamBuick 21 87
(Eve Johnson Houghton) *swtg: hld up towards rr: hdwy 3f out: chsd ldng ldrs and drvn jst over 2f out: sn bmpd and one pce* **100/1**

2106 **14** *1 ½* **Gallantry**[11] 4060 6-7-9 **85** .... BillyCray(7) 24 78
(P Howling) *lw: hld up wl bhd: rdn 1/2-way: sme late hdwy: n.d* **66/1**

1-53 **15** *2* **King's Apostle (IRE)**[35] 3248 4-9-5 **102** .... LiamJones 13 89
(W J Haggas) *lw: in tch: pushed along 1/2-way: rdn and btn 2f out* **8/1**[2]

4310 **16** *½* **Zaahid (IRE)**[15] 3921 4-9-1 **98** .... PhilipRobinson 9 84
(B W Hills) *swtg: in tch: rdn 2f out: carried sltly rt over 1f out: wknd fnl f* **12/1**

25-1 **17** *shd* **Hitchens (IRE)**[28] 3504 3-9-3 **107** .... RyanMoore 29 93
(G L Moore) *hld up towards rr: hdwy over 2f out: rdn wl over 1f out: wknd fnl f* **10/1**[3]

-11 **18** *nse* **Musaalem (USA)**[41] 3056 4-8-11 **94** .... MartinDwyer 15 80
(W J Haggas) *hmpd s: t.k.h: hld up in tch: rdn over 2f out: wknd over 1f out* **13/2**[1]

-053 **19** *1 ¼* **Jedburgh**[36] 3197 7-8-6 **89** ....(b) HayleyTurner 23 71
(J L Dunlop) *stdd and swtchd lft after s: a bhd* **25/1**

1300 **20** *shd* **Slugger O'Toole**[15] 3919 3-8-0 **90** .... FrancisNorton 17 72
(B W Hills) *hld up in midfield: rdn over 2f out: keeping on same pce whn hmpd over 1f out: wl btn after* **33/1**

112 **21** *½* **Underworld**[35] 3251 3-8-5 **95** .... AdrianTNicholls 11 76
(M Johnston) *led tl 2f out: sn wknd* **25/1**

1100 **22** *shd* **Thebes**[17] 3850 3-7-12 **88** .... NickyMackay 6 68
(M Johnston) *chsd ldrs tl led 2f out: sn hung lft and hdd: wknd qckly* **33/1**

3236 **23** *¾* **Vainglory (USA)**[14] 3972 4-8-7 **90** .... RichardKingscote 20 68
(D M Simcock) *in tch: rdn 1/2-way: sn struggling* **50/1**

4600 **24** *2 ¾* **Capricorn Run (USA)**[8] 4145 5-9-6 **103** ....(p) JamesDoyle 10 74
(A J McCabe) *s.i.s: in tch in midfield: wknd 2f out* **66/1**

0100 **25** *36* **Plum Pudding (IRE)**[30] 3413 5-9-1 **98** ....(p) RichardHughes 12 —
(R Hannon) *chsd ldr tl over 2f out: wknd qckly: virtually p.u fnl f: t.o* **50/1**

1m 26.74s (-1.26) **Going Correction** +0.075s/f (Good)
WFA 3 from 4yo+ 7lb **25** Ran **SP%** **120.5**
Speed ratings (Par 109): **110,108,108,107,107 106,106,105,105,104 104,103,103,101,99 98,98,98,97,97 96,96,95,92,51**
toteswinger: 1&2 £112.00, 1&3 £78.40, 2&3 £22.80. CSF £353.57 CT £4768.64 TOTE £27.50: £7.20, £6.00, £3.40, £9.70; EX 525.70 Trifecta £9065.00 Pool: £12,250.12, 1 winning unit.
Owner Sheikh Ahmed Al Maktoum **Bred** Darley **Trained** Middleham Moor, N Yorks
■ Lovelace (6/1F) was withdrawn after giving trouble at the stalls. Deduct 10p in the £ under Rule 4.

FOCUS
A typically competitive renewal of this valuable handicap although weakened slightly by the late withdrawal of the favourite. Laa Rayb posted a minor Pattern-class effort, with improved efforts from both the second and third. The fourth ran much his best race on turf this year though and lends doubts over the reliability of the form.

NOTEBOOK
Laa Rayb(USA), who was fifth in the Buckingham Palace over course and distance at the Royal meeting, found himself carrying top weight after his stablemate, the favourite Lovelace, was withdrawn at the start. Not travelling particularly well in rear, he took a bit of a buffeting when bursting through but ran on strongly once clear to lead inside the last. He could go to Goodwood for the Totesport Mile, for which he picks up a 3lb penalty, although his owner reportedly does not like his horses running again within a fortnight. (op 25-1)
Dhaular Dhar(IRE), three places in front of Laa Rayb in the Buckingham Palace, was well held from this mark in the Bunbury Cup last time. Held up, he had to wait until the path in front of him was clear before running on well, and would have finished closer to the winner with a clear run. He could reoppose in the Totesport Mile.
Giganticus(USA) confirmed the impression he left at Newmarket that he is back to form. After racing on the stands' side of the pack, he took a bump from Thebes before nosing ahead and could not hold on inside the last. He was also fourth in this last year from an identical mark. (op 16-1)
Excusez Moi(USA), reverting to handicaps, is not the most consistent but he is smart on his day and this was his best effort of the turf season so far. He travelled well before edging to his left under pressure, perhaps feeling the fast ground.
South Cape, who was staying on well at the end, had been sixth in the Buckingham Palace and is clearly well suited by this course and distance. He should be capable of picking up a race from this sort of mark.
Redford(IRE), who was put up 6lb after his impressive Newcastle win, did best of the three-year-olds. Held up again, he was slightly impeded when beginning his effort on the stands' side of the pack and, although he was running on, he was never going to get to the principals. Easier ground probably suits him best. (op 7-1 tchd 8-1 in places)
Big Noise ◆ had been expensive to follow in recent starts but ran well at a big price. He would have been closer still had he not needed to switch right for a run in the final two furlongs and, still lightly raced, has a bit of improvement in him.
Presumptive(IRE) was keeping on late from the back of the field, but while this was a commendable run he still looks a little high in the weights.
Mastership(IRE) ◆ was in the process of keeping on when getting slightly squeezed up inside the last, after which his rider did not really persevere. His turn should come round, perhaps on slightly easier ground. (op 8-1)
Artimino again disappointed with his lack of response when the pressure was on. (tchd 18-1)
King's Apostle(IRE), a running-on third in the Wokingham, had shaped as if ready for another try over this trip but he was in trouble with a quarter of a mile still to run. (op 10-1 tchd 11-1 and 12-1 in places)
Zaahid(IRE) has now twice been found wanting from this mark after landing the Victoria Cup over course and distance from a 6lb lower rating. (op 14-1 tchd 16-1 in places)
Hitchens(IRE), raised 6lb after his Windsor win, could never really get into the hunt. He has yet to prove he stays this far. (op 12-1 tchd 14-1 in places)

Musaalem(USA) was 10lb higher and taking a big step up in grade on this bid for a hat-trick. Described as a character by his trainer, he was taken to post early. He was hampered leaving the stalls and his middle draw probably did not help either as he failed to make an impact. (tchd 7-1, 15-2 in places and 6-1 in places)
Jedburgh Official explanation: jockey said horse missed the break
Plum Pudding(IRE) Official explanation: jockey said gelding had no more to give

4406 KING GEORGE VI AND QUEEN ELIZABETH STKS (GROUP 1) 1m 4f
4:20 (4:25) (Class 1) 3-Y-0+

£482,545 (£182,920; £91,545; £45,645; £22,865; £11,475) **Stalls** High

Form RPR
-111 **1** **Duke Of Marmalade (IRE)**[38] 3121 4-9-7 0 JMurtagh 4 128
(A P O'Brien, Ire) *lw: hld up off pce in midfield: hdwy over 3f out: plld out over 2f out: qcknd to ld and edgd rt over 1f out: hdd ins fnl f: rallied gamely to ld again towards fin* **4/6**[1]
0-42 **2** ½ **Papal Bull**[16] 3878 5-9-7 121 OPeslier 8 127
(Sir Michael Stoute) *hld up in last pair: hmpd 9f out: plld out and qcknd 2f out: edgd rt over 1f out: rdn to chal ent fnl f: led ins fnl f: outbattled and hdd towards fin* **14/1**
-521 **3** 9 **Youmzain (IRE)**[27] 3542 5-9-7 125 RichardHughes 1 113+
(M R Channon) *v.s.a: hld up in rr: hdwy 5f out: rdn and nt clr run and swtchd lft 2f out: sn squeezed out and lost pl: rallied to go modest 3rd ins fnl f: no ch w ldng pair* **4/1**[2]
3-30 **4** 1 **Red Rock Canyon (IRE)**[38] 3121 4-9-7 0 CO'Donoghue 5 111
(A P O'Brien, Ire) *led: rdn 3f out: hdd over 1f out: sn outpcd but kpt on gamely* **125/1**
2-15 **5** 1 **Ask**[38] 3121 5-9-7 119 RyanMoore 3 110
(Sir Michael Stoute) *lw: hld up in midfield: effrt 3f out: rdn wl over 2f out: sltly hmpd and swtchd lft 2f out: sn outpcd: wl btn fnl f* **10/1**
3603 **6** 3½ **Petara Bay (IRE)**[16] 3878 4-9-7 105 JimCrowley 2 104
(T G Mills) *hld up in rr: rdn and effrt wl over 2f out: no prog and wl btn wl over 1f out* **66/1**
-061 **7** nk **Lucarno (USA)**[16] 3878 4-9-7 115 JimmyFortune 7 104
(J H M Gosden) *lw: t.k.h: chsd ldr: rdn wl over 2f out: wknd ins fnl 2f* **8/1**[3]
0131 **8** nk **Macarthur**[35] 3246 4-9-7 0 JAHeffernan 6 103
(A P O'Brien, Ire) *t.k.h: chsd ldng pair tl wl over 3f out: n.m.r and swtchd rt over 2f out: wknd u.p 2f out* **14/1**

2m 27.91s (-7.59) **Going Correction** -0.175s/f (Firm) 8 Ran SP% **115.8**
Speed ratings (Par 117): **118,117,111,111,110 108,107,107**
toteswinger: 1&2 £3.60, 1&3 £1.30, 2&3 £5.80. CSF £12.80 TOTE £1.70: £1.10, £2.60, £1.10; EX 13.60 Trifecta £36.10 Pool: £17,187.83, 363.97 winning units.
Owner Mrs John Magnier & M Tabor **Bred** Southern Bloodstock **Trained** Ballydoyle, Co Tipperary
■ Stewards' Enquiry : J Murtagh caution: careless riding.

FOCUS
A memorable finish and a worthy winner in Duke Of Marmalade, but it had the look of a below-par renewal and for the third consecutive year there were no three-year-olds in the line-up, although New Approach was reportedly an intended runner prior to injury. The first pair finished a long way clear and there are grounds for rating them both as improvers, but there are doubts over the strength of the form with pacemaker Red Rock Canyon holding on to fourth and Ask, Lucarno and Macarthur all underperforming.

NOTEBOOK
Duke Of Marmalade(IRE), competing in his tenth consecutive Group 1, maintained his unbeaten record for the year on this first try at 1m4f. A brilliant winner of the Prince of Wales's Stakes here at the Royal meeting, he was certainly not stopping at the end that day and connections were confident he would stay the extra quarter of a mile. Settled in around fifth and eased away from the rail before the home turn, he quickened up very smartly to lead but was quickly tackled by Papal Bull who went perhaps half a length up on him inside the last. Battling on, this big colt forced his head back in front near the finish. He is likely to step back in trip now, with the Juddmonte International and Irish Champion Stakes potential targets. (op 8-11 tchd 4-5 in places)
Papal Bull, held up at the back, was hampered against the rail after three furlongs. Still in a share of last place entering the straight, he then showed a fine turn of foot to sweep down the outside and challenge Duke Of Marmalade who had quickened to the front. He went about a neck up inside the last, but was outbattled by the favourite late on. He was probably in front too soon, but he finished nine lengths clear of the rest and this was a career-best performance from this quirky character. He is capable of landing a Group 1 if things go his way before he is retired to stud at the end of the year. (op 16-1)
Youmzain(IRE), runner-up to Dylan Thomas a year ago, was below par. Held up and rather keen after a slow start, he raced in touch alongside the winner from halfway. He had just come under pressure when he was hampered by Papal Bull well over a furlong out, costing him momentum, and although he rallied for a fairly remote third he was never a threat to the principals who had gone clear. His will be aimed at the Arc and he may have a prep run. (tchd 9-2 in places)
Red Rock Canyon(IRE) did a fine job as pacemaker for his winning stablemate and stuck on once headed for an unexpected and not inconsiderable fourth prize. This high-class maiden is further evidence of the remarkable strength in depth at Ballydoyle. (tchd 150-1)
Ask, chosen by Moore over Papal Bull, was back up to what looked his optimum trip. He was well placed in third spot turning into the straight, but was soon under pressure and he was well held after being slightly hampered at the two pole. This was not his form, with his jockey of the opinion that the ground was a bit quick for him. (op 11-1 tchd 12-1)
Petara Bay(IRE) has yet to win above Listed level and he faced a very stiff task. He was always at the back of the field but did pass a couple of rivals late on. (op 100-1)
Lucarno(USA) successfully gave away 5lb all round in the Princess of Wales's Stakes at Newmarket but he enjoyed a soft lead that day and could not confirm that form with Papal Bull or Petara Bay. Racing keenly behind the leader, he produced a disappointing response when let down in the straight and weakened steadily. (op 10-1)
Macarthur, the O'Brien second string, had split Youmzain and Papal Bull when third in the Coronation Cup prior to winning the Hardwicke Stakes over this course and distance. Keen through the early parts, he was close enough turning in but was slightly short of room over two furlongs out and was soon on the retreat. (op 12-1)

4407 LONGINES H'CAP (LADIES RACE) 7f
4:55 (4:59) (Class 3) (0-90,90) 3-Y-0+ **£8,744** (£2,711; £1,355; £677) **Stalls** Centre

Form RPR
2233 **1** **Golden Desert (IRE)**[15] 3898 4-10-4 83 MsKWalsh 12 94
(T G Mills) *racd in midfield: rdn and hdwy 2f out: drvn to ld 1f out: forged clr last 100yds* **6/1**[2]
352 **2** 2 **Secret Night**[23] 3636 5-9-5 75 (p) MissJFerguson(5) 15 81
(C G Cox) *lw: in tch: hdwy to chse ldrs over 2f out: ev ch over 1f out tl no ex last 100yds* **12/1**
4101 **3** ¾ **Bomber Command (USA)**[11] 4060 5-9-13 78 (v) MissEJJones 21 82
(J W Hills) *chsd ldrs: wnt 2nd 4f out: led over 3f out: hrd pressed and rdn 2f out: hdd 1f out: no ex u.p ins fnl f* **11/2**[1]
5202 **4** ½ **Hazzard County (USA)**[10] 4089 4-10-3 82 MissSBrotherton 8 85
(D M Simcock) *lw: in tch: effrt 3f out: edgd rt fr over 2f out: kpt on same pce ins fnl f* **12/1**
2050 **5** 2½ **Obezyana (USA)**[9] 4104 6-9-12 77 MrsMarieKing 20 73
(A Bailey) *chsd ldrs: wnt 2nd over 3f out: ev ch 2f out: wknd ins fnl f* **22/1**
1100 **6** 2½ **Daaweitza**[14] 3946 5-10-10 89 MissLEllison 1 78
(B Ellison) *bhd: rdn along 1/2-way: styd on last 2f: nvr a factor* **16/1**
5120 **7** nk **King's Bastion (IRE)**[36] 3197 4-10-1 85 MissFCumani(5) 10 73
(M L W Bell) *bhd: rdn 1/2-way: styd on last 2f: nvr nr ldrs* **14/1**
0451 **8** nk **Rambling Light**[27] 3529 4-9-9 74 (p) MissGDGracey-Davison 7 62
(A M Balding) *in tch: rdn and hmpd over 2f out: edgd rt and struggling after* **13/2**[3]
-106 **9** 2¼ **Tiger Dream**[42] 3039 3-9-13 85 MissARyan 16 66
(K A Ryan) *s.i.s: bhd: hdwy into midfield and rdn 1/2-way: nvr on terms* **14/1**
0600 **10** nk **Middlemarch (IRE)**[31] 3366 8-9-9 74 (v) MrsCBartley 2 55
(J S Goldie) *sn bhd and rdn: sme hdwy whn nt clr run over 1f out: nvr a factor* **16/1**
160 **11** ½ **Compton's Eleven**[36] 3222 7-10-7 86 MissEALalor 14 65
(M R Channon) *bhd: rdn and hld hd high fr 1/2-way: n.d* **25/1**
000 **12** 2¼ **Jilly Why (IRE)**[46] 2906 7-10-1 80 (b) MissADeniel 19 53
(Paul Green) *chsd ldrs: rdn over 3f out: wknd wl over 2f out* **33/1**
1040 **13** hd **Salient**[15] 3899 4-10-4 86 MissMSowerby(3) 4 59
(M J Attwater) *racd alone towards stands' side: nvr a factor* **33/1**
6046 **14** ½ **Kensington (IRE)**[9] 4104 7-9-7 72 MissEFolkes 5 43
(P D Evans) *chsd ldr tl 4f out: sn struggling: no ch whn swtchd rt over 1f out* **33/1**
-564 **15** hd **Paveroc**[142] 813 3-10-4 90 MrsMCowdrey 3 61
(Jane Chapple-Hyam) *a bhd: n.d* **16/1**
2455 **16** 1¼ **Nice To Know (FR)**[36] 3210 4-9-8 78 MissHayleyMoore(5) 11 45
(G L Moore) *stdd and swtchd lft after s: a bhd: hung rt last 2f: nvr a factor* **12/1**
0053 **17** 1½ **Blue Java**[14] 3966 7-9-0 70 oh1 MissVCartmel(5) 6 33
(H Morrison) *a bhd* **14/1**
6160 **18** 1¾ **Southandwest (IRE)**[15] 3898 4-10-9 88 (p) MrsSMoore 9 47
(J S Moore) *bhd: rdn over 4f out: nvr a factor* **28/1**
0431 **19** 1¼ **Carcinetto (IRE)**[7] 4198 6-10-3 87 MissAWallace(5) 17 42
(P D Evans) *s.i.s: a in rr* **20/1**
2312 **20** 16 **Ninefineirishmen (IRE)**[12] 4017 3-8-12 75 (b[1]) MissKellyBurke(5) 18 —
(K R Burke) *led at fast pce tl over 3f out: wkng qckly whn hmpd over 2f out: t.o* **20/1**

1m 28.26s (0.26) **Going Correction** +0.075s/f (Good)
WFA 3 from 4yo+ 7lb 20 Ran SP% **133.7**
Speed ratings (Par 107): **101,98,97,97,94 91,91,90,88,87 87,84,84,84,83 82,80,78,77,58**
toteswinger: 1&2 £17.60, 1&3 £4.50, 2&3 £6.10. CSF £72.73 CT £442.86 TOTE £6.50: £1.70, £2.40, £1.70, £4.00; EX 97.60 Trifecta £376.80 Pool: £1,940.45, 3.81 winning units.
Owner S Parker **Bred** Mervyn Stewkesbury **Trained** Headley, Surrey
■ Stewards' Enquiry : Ms K Walsh one-day ban: used whip with excessive frequency (Aug 14)

FOCUS
A big field for this ladies' event, but not many got into this from the rear and the first five were always prominent. The form is rated around the first two but this race rarely works out. The pace was strong.

NOTEBOOK
Golden Desert(IRE) has been running well in defeat in recent months and has been edging up the handicap as a result. With the assistance of one of the best riders in the race, he improved to lead at the furlong pole and was going away at the end. (op 9-1)
Secret Night ran another big race in the cheekpieces and only gave best to the winner in the final half-furlong. She deserves another victory on turf.
Bomber Command(USA), runner-up for this rider a year ago, came here off the back of a Great Leighs win over 1m. He was in front not long past halfway but could not repel the winner from the furlong pole. (op 13-2 tchd 7-1)
Hazzard County(USA) tends to run his best races on Polytrack but these look his ideal conditions on turf and he ran a good race under his experienced rider.
Obezyana(USA) was one of five battling for the lead in the latter stages but had no more to offer inside the last. He is rather inconsistent but is capable on his day. (op 25-1)
Daaweitza, racing off a career-high mark, did best of those to come from the rear after struggling to go the pace but was never really involved. (tchd 14-1 in places)
King's Bastion(IRE), still 7lb above his highest winning mark, was another putting in his best work when it was all over. (tchd 12-1 in places)
Rambling Light, put up just 2lb after his Windsor win, has never run at under a mile before and he was already being ridden when he ran into trouble around two out. (op 7-1 tchd 6-1 in places)
Middlemarch(IRE) won this a year ago when 3lb lower, but he has been out of sorts this term and never threatened a repeat.
Ninefineirishmen(IRE) set a fast pace in the first-time blinkers but did not last long once headed. (op 22-1)

4408 CANISBAY BLOODSTOCK H'CAP 6f
5:30 (5:32) (Class 4) (0-85,89) 3-Y-O **£7,123** (£2,119; £1,059; £529) **Stalls** Centre

Form RPR
0506 **1** **Silver Wind**[15] 3904 3-9-2 80 (v) RobertWinston 2 87
(P D Evans) *chsd overall ldr on stands' rail: hdwy to ld over 1f out: sn edgd lft: hld on wl fnl f: all out* **20/1**
-022 **2** hd **Sudden Impact (IRE)**[10] 4074 3-9-8 89 RussellKennemore(3) 9 96
(Paul Green) *awkward leaving stalls and slowly away: hdwy over 3f out: rdn wl over 1f out: r.o to chse wnr wl ins fnl f: hung lft and hld last strides* **12/1**
2411 **3** 1 **Autumn Blades (IRE)**[10] 4083 3-8-12 76 TQuinn 8 80
(J W Hills) *lw: t.k.h: hld up in rr: gd hdwy 2f out: chsd wnr 1f out: kpt on same pce last 100yds* **8/1**
0512 **4** 1½ **Rubirosa (IRE)**[44] 2967 3-9-7 85 DanielTudhope 4 84
(M Dods) *s.i.s: hld up bhd: hdwy over 2f out: chsd ldrs and rdn over 1f out: no ex last 100yds* **7/2**[2]
4043 **5** 2 **Fly Kiss**[28] 3487 3-8-9 73 NCallan 5 65
(C E Brittain) *prom: rdn and ev ch over 1f out: hung lft ent fnl f: fdd ins fnl f* **14/1**
0364 **6** 1½ **I Confess**[21] 3728 3-8-10 79 RichardEvans(5) 13 67
(P D Evans) *hld up in rr: rdn and effrt over 2f out: nvr threatened ldrs* **25/1**
0-41 **7** hd **Candela Bay (IRE)**[31] 3381 3-8-11 75 RyanMoore 3 62
(W J Haggas) *lw: stdd after s: t.k.h: hld up in tch: rdn over 2f out: wknd jst over 1f out* **15/8**[1]
0-04 **8** ½ **Sam's Cross (IRE)**[33] 3324 3-9-4 82 PaulEddery 10 67
(K R Burke) *led centre gp: rdn over 2f out: wknd u.p 1f out* **20/1**
1160 **9** ¾ **We Have A Dream**[13] 3999 3-9-5 83 MartinDwyer 1 66
(W R Muir) *led stands' side pair and overall: rdn and hdd over 1f out: sn wknd* **16/1**
1-34 **10** 4½ **Mistress Cooper**[9] 4127 3-8-2 66 HayleyTurner 7 35
(W J Musson) *prom: rdn over 2f out: wknd qckly over 1f out* **16/1**
4212 **11** ½ **Farthermost (IRE)**[28] 3506 3-9-1 79 PatDobbs 6 46
(R Hannon) *lw: prom: rdn 1/2-way: sn struggling: wl btn whn edgd lft ins fnl f* **5/1**[3]

1400 **12** 2 1/2 **Emperors Jade**[38] 3136 3-8-6 **70**.............................. RichardThomas 14 29
(A P Jarvis) *chsd ldrs: rdn over 2f out: sn struggling: wl btn whn eased ins fnl f* **50/1**

1m 14.55s (0.15) **Going Correction** +0.075s/f (Good) **12** Ran SP% **126.2**
Speed ratings (Par 102): **102,101,100,98,95 93,93,92,91,85 85,81**
toteswinger: 1&2 £58.10, 1&3 £29.90, 2&3 £10.50. CSF £246.06 CT £2134.76 TOTE £26.40: £5.00, £2.80, £2.50; EX 296.60 Trifecta £1632.50 Part won. Pool: £2,206.14, 0.79 winning units. Place 6 £488.67, Place 5 £82.46.
Owner Silver Wind Partnership **Bred** W H R John And Partners **Trained** Pandy, Monmouths

FOCUS
A fairly ordinary handicap in which the first two, who raced apart from each other, were pretty exposed. The winner was one of a pair to race on the stands' side which was certainly no disadvantage. The form is rated through the second and third.
I Confess Official explanation: jockey said gelding lost its action final 2f
Emperors Jade Official explanation: jockey said gelding had no more to give
T/Jkpt: Not won. T/Plt: £1,363.40 to a £1 stake. Pool: £191,293.45. 102.42 winning tickets. T/Qpdt: £40.00 to a £1 stake. Pool: £12,023.82. 222.20 winning tickets. SP

4302 LINGFIELD (L-H)
Saturday, July 26

OFFICIAL GOING: Firm (good to firm in places)
On this occasion, the draw seemed fairer than it often is on the straight course, with the stands' rail not appearing to be a huge material advantage for a change
Wind: Almost nil Weather: Fine, very warm

4409 WALK BEYOND THE PALE H'CAP — 1m 2f
5:50 (5:51) (Class 6) (0-65,70) 3-Y-0+ **£2,047** (£604; £302) **Stalls** Low

Form RPR
1321 **1** **Amicable Terms**[2] 4326 3-9-4 **70** 6ex........................ WilliamCarson(7) 10 84+
(Rae Guest) *trckd ldrs: prog to go 2nd 3f out: led jst ins fnl 2f: shkn up and sn clr: pushed out fnl f* **8/13**[1]

5033 **2** 1 3/4 **Gracechurch (IRE)**[41] 2770 5-9-8 **57**........................... FrancisNorton 3 64
(R J Hodges) *hld up in midfield: prog 3f out: rdn to chse ldng pair 2f out: kpt on fnl f to take 2nd nr fin: no ch w wnr* **4/1**[2]

2552 **3** nk **Split The Wind (USA)**[7] 4182 4-9-1 **50**..................... EdwardCreighton 8 56
(Miss Sheena West) *led: kicked 4 l clr 4f out: hdd 2f out: sn no ch w wnr: lost 2nd nr fin* **14/1**

0646 **4** nk **Sir Liam (USA)**[11] 4055 4-9-6 **55**.......................... IanMongan 6 60
(R A Teal) *t.k.h: hld up in rr: prog on inner over 2f out: drvn and styd on same pce fnl f* **15/2**[3]

5056 **5** 3 **Theatre Royal**[23] 3631 5-8-10 **45**............................ ChrisCatlin 5 44
(Mouse Hamilton-Fairley) *hld up in rr: prog 3f out: rdn and no rspnse 2f out* **14/1**

0-00 **6** 8 **Our Glenard**[32] 3344 9-8-10 **45**.................................. AlanDaly 2 28
(J E Long) *rousted along early: a towards rr: rdn and struggling over 2f out* **50/1**

0-60 **7** 5 **Halsion Challenge**[5] 4260 3-8-7 **52**........................ LPKeniry 9 25
(J R Best) *prom: chsd ldr over 4f out to 3f out: wknd* **33/1**

45-0 **8** 2 1/2 **Massams Lane**[58] 2550 4-9-4 **56**........................ TravisBlock(3) 4 24
(G C Bravery) *chsd ldr to over 4f out: wknd over 2f out* **16/1**

33-0 **9** 13 **Airman (IRE)**[9] 526 5-9-8 **62**........................... JamieJones(5) 7 4
(B P J Baugh) *rdn in last after 4f: t.o over 3f out* **33/1**

2m 8.65s (-1.85) **Going Correction** -0.175s/f (Firm)
WFA 3 from 4yo+ 10lb **9** Ran SP% **120.7**
Speed ratings (Par 101): **100,98,98,98,95 89,85,83,72**
toteswinger: 1&2 £1.10, 1&3 £3.50, 2&3 £5.20. CSF £3.51 CT £18.98 TOTE £1.70: £1.10, £1.50, £1.50; EX 3.30.
Owner Sentinel Bloodstock **Bred** Brook Stud Bloodstock Ltd **Trained** Newmarket, Suffolk

FOCUS
The in-form winner looked a cut above some moderate opponentsin this weak handicap and has been rated value for twice the margin. The pace was modest until the final half-mile.

4410 CHURCH HILL WALK H'CAP — 2m
6:20 (6:20) (Class 5) (0-70,65) 3-Y-0+ **£2,590** (£770; £385; £192) **Stalls** Low

Form RPR
6332 **1** **Greenwich Village**[24] 3606 5-10-0 **65**.......................... PaulDoe 1 71+
(W J Knight) *trckd ldr gng wl: led 3f out: sn kicked clr: rdn out fnl f* **7/4**[1]

-000 **2** 1 1/2 **Zia Zabel (IRE)**[26] 3562 3-8-9 **63**.......................... RobertHavlin 4 66
(J L Dunlop) *hld up in last pair: prog 3f out: rdn to chse ldng pair 2f out: kpt on to take 2nd narrowly fnl f: no real threat to wnr* **8/1**

5553 **3** nse **Is It Me (USA)**[23] 3650 5-9-12 **63**............................ ChrisCatlin 6 66
(A W Carroll) *led at decent pce: rdn and hdd 3f out: sn outpcd by wnr: lost 2nd ins fnl f but kpt on wl* **5/2**[2]

5000 **4** 8 **Eddie Dowling**[5] 4247 3-8-7 **61**...............................(v[1]) TPO'Shea 5 54
(M R Channon) *t.k.h: trckd ldng pair to over 5f out: rdn and wknd 3f out* **7/1**

0-40 **5** 3/4 **Lysander's Quest (IRE)**[52] 1052 10-8-9 **46** oh1............ DavidKinsella 3 39
(R Ingram) *hld up in last pair: rdn 3f out: sn struggling* **20/1**

4612 **6** 1/2 **Prince Of Medina**[162] 575 5-9-1 **52**.......................... LPKeniry 2 44
(J R Best) *cl up: trckd ldng pair over 5f out: shkn up and fnd nil over 2f out: sn wknd* **4/1**[3]

3m 33.52s (-1.28) **Going Correction** -0.175s/f (Firm)
WFA 3 from 5yo+ 17lb **6** Ran SP% **113.3**
Speed ratings (Par 103): **96,95,95,91,90 90**
toteswinger: 1&2 £9.70, 1&3 £2.00, 2&3 £21.00. CSF £16.59 TOTE £2.60: £1.60, £5.30; EX 17.80.
Owner Ecurie Franglaise **Bred** Cotswold Stud **Trained** Patching, W Sussex

FOCUS
A weak handicap, short on numbers too, but the pace was solid. It is doubtful if thw winner had to improve on his recent form.

4411 LIZ YARD 40TH BIRTHDAY MAIDEN AUCTION STKS — 5f
6:50 (6:50) (Class 6) 2-Y-0 **£2,388** (£705; £352) **Stalls** High

Form RPR
0 **1** **Lady Master**[21] 3734 2-8-5 0.............................. FrancisNorton 3 71
(H Candy) *mde virtually all and racd one off nr side rail: hrd pressed fr over 1f out: kpt on wl* **7/1**

4 **2** nk **Ruby Tallulah**[26] 3558 2-7-13 0....................... DavidProbert(5) 2 69
(N P Littmoden) *carried lft after 150yds: chsd ldrs: effrt on outer over 1f out: pressed wnr nr fin: jst hld* **13/2**[3]

502 **3** nk **You've Been Mowed**[9] 4126 2-8-4 0........................ ChrisCatlin 5 68
(D K Ivory) *awkward s: swtchd sharply lft after 150yds: sn w wnr: rdn and nt qckn over 1f out: kpt on but hld fnl f* **8/11**[1]

2 **4** 1 1/4 **Dakota Hills**[4] 4270 2-8-13 0..................................... LPKeniry 4 73
(J R Best) *racd against nr side rail: cl up: tried to chal fr over 1f out: nt qckn and hld ins fnl f* **10/3**[2]

00 **5** 10 **Franchesca's Gold**[14] 3959 2-8-7 0 ow1..................... RobertHavlin 1 31
(B R Millman) *dwlt: carried rt after 150yds: in tch to 1/2-way: sn wknd* **20/1**

58.03 secs (-0.17) **Going Correction** -0.175s/f (Firm) **5** Ran SP% **111.6**
Speed ratings (Par 92): **94,93,93,91,75**
CSF £47.00 TOTE £8.40: £2.50, £1.80; EX 45.80.
Owner Fighttheban Partnership VI **Bred** Mrs D Du Feu **Trained** Kingston Warren, Oxon
■ Stewards' Enquiry : Chris Catlin two-day ban: careless riding (Aug 9,10)

FOCUS
A routine maiden, lacking in numbers too, and three in close proximity at the end. Modest form.

NOTEBOOK
Lady Master looks well suited to making the running and, though only just holding on, should be able to use her natural speed again as long as she is kept to a realistic level. She will now switch to nuseries. (op 16-1)
Ruby Tallulah arrived late in the centre and was only just held off by the all-the-way winner. She should improve again, and looks capable of winning a maiden. (tchd 11-2)
You've Been Mowed let down her supporters, but was only beaten two necks in a tight finish. She is capable of winning a maiden, but looks made for sprint nurseries (op 4-5 tchd 5-6)
Dakota Hills kept persisting with an attempted challenge between the stands' rail and the winner, but he appeared to lack the experience to take it, and the proximity of the winning jockey's whip made sure of it entering the final furlong. However, he has shown ability in his first two races and cannot be dismissed yet at a modest level. (op 9-4 tchd 7-2)
Franchesca's Gold has shown little in maidens, and does not look likely to win one. (op 25-1)

4412 LUCY & TOM MITCHELL GETTING MARRIED TODAY MEDIAN AUCTION MAIDEN STKS — 7f
7:25 (7:25) (Class 6) 3-5-Y-0 **£2,388** (£705; £352) **Stalls** High

Form RPR
0-02 **1** **Station Place**[29] 3445 3-8-5 **48**.................................. PNolan(7) 7 55
(A B Haynes) *mde all: racd against nr side rail tl edgd lft fr over 2f out: hld on fnl f* **16/1**

42 **2** nk **Manchestermaverick (USA)**[10] 4076 3-9-0 0............. TravisBlock(3) 6 59
(H Morrison) *trckd ldrs: wnt 2nd 2f out: rdn to chal jst over 1f out: nt qckn and hld nr fin* **6/5**[1]

0 **3** 1 1/4 **Telephonist**[57] 2560 3-8-12 0.................................. LPKeniry 4 51
(Norma Twomey) *dwlt: sn swtchd to r against nr side rail and trckd ldrs: effrt 2f out: nt qckn over 1f out: kpt on* **33/1**

-636 **4** 3/4 **Sir Ike (IRE)**[26] 3564 3-9-3 **62**.............................. ChrisCatlin 1 54
(W S Kittow) *dwlt: sn chsd ldrs on outer: rdn over 2f out: one pce over 1f out* **9/4**[2]

00-0 **5** 3/4 **Golden Horus (USA)**[7] 4194 3-9-0 **53**...................... JerryO'Dwyer(3) 8 52
(P J O'Gorman) *dwlt: hld up towards rr: effrt over 2f out: hrd rdn to chse ldrs over 1f out: no imp after* **20/1**

0650 **6** 2 1/2 **Ma Ridge**[10] 4085 4-9-5 **47**.................................. DavidProbert(5) 5 48
(T D McCarthy) *chsd wnr: hung lft over 2f out: sn lost pl and btn* **25/1**

0 **7** shd **Triple Dream**[70] 2198 3-9-3 0.............................. RobertHavlin 3 45
(J L Dunlop) *dwlt: a towards rr and nvr gng that wl: struggling fnl 2f* **11/2**[3]

0/ **8** 7 **Pickled Again**[719] 4207 4-9-5 0.................................. IanMongan 9 24
(S Dow) *awkward s: sn detached in last: nvr a factor* **12/1**

0-04 **9** 1 **Bakers Boy**[29] 3445 4-9-5 **40**..............................(p) NataliaGemelova(5) 2 26
(J E Long) *sweating: hanging lft thrght: cl up on outer tl wknd 2f out* **33/1**

1m 23.03s (-0.27) **Going Correction** -0.175s/f (Firm)
WFA 3 from 4yo 7lb **9** Ran SP% **119.7**
Speed ratings (Par 101): **94,93,92,91,90 87,87,79,78**
toteswinger: 1&2 £2.10, 1&3 Not won, 2&3 Not won. CSF £36.04 TOTE £13.50: £2.90, £1.10, £6.30; EX 20.30.
Owner Dajam Ltd **Bred** M Burbidge **Trained** Limpley Stoke, Bath

FOCUS
A weak-looking maiden and less than solid form with the fifth and sixth close enough. The winner had the benefit of the rail and her big improvement is dubious.
Ma Ridge Official explanation: jockey said gelding hung left
Triple Dream Official explanation: jockey said gelding was unsuited by the firm (good to firm places) ground

4413 DEBBIE'S 50TH BIRTHDAY H'CAP — 7f
7:55 (7:55) (Class 5) (0-70,70) 3-Y-0 **£2,590** (£770; £385; £192) **Stalls** High

Form RPR
0310 **1** **Benedetto**[3] 4306 3-9-7 **70**.................................(p) JimCrowley 7 80
(Mrs A J Perrett) *stdd s: hld up: prog gng easily fr over 2f out: waited tl pounced to ld jst ins fnl f: pushed out* **11/2**[3]

-233 **2** 2 1/4 **El Fuser**[21] 3731 3-9-1 **67**.................................. TravisBlock(3) 8 71
(P J Makin) *prom: rdn over 2f out: kpt on to ld briefly 1f out: sn outpcd by wnr* **13/8**[1]

4503 **3** 1 **Complete Frontline (GER)**[21] 3717 3-8-6 **55**................. LiamJones 10 56
(K R Burke) *dwlt: plld hrd early: hld up and detached in last pair after 3f: no prog tl rattled home on nr side fnl f: snatched 3rd last strides* **5/1**[2]

3550 **4** 1/2 **Asian Lady**[29] 3442 3-9-2 **65**...............................(v[1]) ChrisCatlin 5 65
(R Charlton) *racd freely: led against nr side rail: edgd lft fr 2f out: hdd & wknd 1f out* **11/2**[3]

5004 **5** 3/4 **Bold Diva**[15] 3906 3-7-10 **52**.................................(v) StacyRenwick(7) 6 50
(A W Carroll) *mostly chsd ldr to 2f out: fdd fnl f* **20/1**

2411 **6** 1 3/4 **Lord Deevert**[10] 4090 3-8-13 **62**.............................. AlanDaly 1 55
(W G M Turner) *racd on wd outside early: w ldrs to 3f out: grad lost pl* **5/1**[2]

1101 **7** 2 1/4 **Lancaster Lad (IRE)**[4] 4278 3-9-1 **64** 6ex.................(p) RobertHavlin 2 51
(A B Haynes) *dwlt: wl in rr: prog on outer 3f out: no imp wl over 1f out: wknd* **7/1**

000- **8** 1 1/4 **Newcastle Sam**[319] 5313 3-7-11 **51** oh6..................... DavidProbert(5) 9 35
(J J Bridger) *a in last pair: detached after 3f: nvr a factor* **50/1**

5054 **9** 16 **Westwood Dawn**[11] 4056 3-7-13 **51** oh6.....................(p) LukeMorris(3) 4 —
(Mrs N Macauley) *t.k.h: prom 3f: sn lost pl: eased whn no ch: t.o* **33/1**

1m 22.04s (-1.26) **Going Correction** -0.175s/f (Firm) **9** Ran SP% **124.4**
Speed ratings (Par 100): **100,97,96,95,94 92,90,88,70**
toteswinger: 1&2 £7.30, 1&3 £6.70, 2&3 £4.10. CSF £15.89 CT £51.12 TOTE £8.60: £2.20, £1.10, £2.20; EX 19.00.
Owner Woodcote Stud Ltd **Bred** Woodcote Stud Ltd **Trained** Pulborough, W Sussex

FOCUS
A run-of-the-mill handicap and the form is not that solid with the third the best guide. The winner is rated up 9lb.

4414 WYCH CROSS H'CAP — 7f 140y
8:25 (8:28) (Class 6) (0-65,65) 3-Y-0+ — £2,047 (£604; £302) **Stalls Centre**

Form — RPR

0505 **1** **Grey Boy (GER)**[11] 4053 7-9-1 56 ... LukeMorris(3) 8 — 71
(A W Carroll) *wl in rr: shkn up and gd prog towards outer fr jst over 2f out: led 1f out: romped clr* — **7/2**[1]

0640 **2** 4 1/2 **Hollywood George**[36] 3201 4-8-13 51 ... (p) AdamKirby 16 — 55
(Miss M E Rowland) *racd against nr side rail: mde most: hdd and outpcd 1f out* — **14/1**

00-4 **3** 1/2 **Inquisitress**[17] 3839 4-8-10 48 ... JimCrowley 17 — 51
(J J Bridger) *racd against nr side rail: trckd ldrs gng wl: forced to switch sharply lft over 1f out: kpt on but unable to chal* — **6/1**[3]

0-20 **4** nk **Miracle Baby**[24] 3608 6-8-10 48 ... RobertHavlin 10 — 50
(J A Geake) *mostly pressed ldr and racd jst off nr side rail: chal 2f out: one pce* — **14/1**

66-0 **5** 3 1/2 **Kielty's Folly**[147] 769 4-8-8 51 ow4 ... JamieJones(5) 18 — 45
(B P J Baugh) *hld up and racd against nr side rail: effrt over 2f out: sn outpcd: wnt modest 5th 1f out: no imp* — **14/1**

0440 **6** 1/2 **Binnion Bay (IRE)**[36] 3208 7-8-9 50 ... (b) MarcHalford(3) 6 — 42+
(J J Bridger) *dwlt: wl in rr on outer and sn struggling: styd on fr over 1f out: no ch* — **14/1**

3600 **7** 1 1/2 **Recalcitrant**[11] 4053 5-8-8 51 ... DavidProbert(5) 4 — 40
(S Dow) *racd wd: nvr really on terms w ldrs: outpcd fr 2f out* — **11/1**

4444 **8** 1/2 **The Iron Giant (IRE)**[19] 3780 6-8-10 48 ... (b) AlanDaly 13 — 36
(Dr J R J Naylor) *taken down early: nvr beyond midfield: struggling in rr 3f out: modest late prog* — **16/1**

03-0 **9** 1/2 **Chalentina**[75] 2055 5-8-6 49 ... NataliaGemelova(5) 11 — 35
(J E Long) *prom in centre: wknd frinal 2f* — **20/1**

1055 **10** 1 3/4 **Contented (IRE)**[31] 3383 6-9-2 57 ... (p) JerryO'Dwyer(3) 9 — 39
(Mrs L C Jewell) *nvr beyond midfield: rdn and struggling in rr over 2f out* — **16/1**

1532 **11** 1/2 **Batchworth Blaise**[11] 4053 5-9-0 52 ... LiamJones 2 — 33
(E A Wheeler) *wl in rr: effrt on wd outside over 2f out: no real prog* — **7/1**

605 **12** 1 1/2 **Goose Green (IRE)**[3] 4306 4-9-0 55 ... TravisBlock(3) 7 — 32
(R J Hodges) *racd towards outer: chsd ldrs: u.p and losing pl over 2f out: sn no ch* — **11/2**[2]

3263 **13** 1 1/2 **Corlough Mountain**[7] 4186 4-9-11 63 ... (p) ChrisCatlin 1 — 37
(P Butler) *racd on outer: nvr really on terms w ldrs: struggling fnl 2f* — **8/1**

4240 **14** 1/2 **Only If I Laugh**[74] 2075 7-8-8 46 oh1 ... DavidKinsella 12 — 19
(M J Attwater) *chsd ldrs: wknd u.p over 2f out* — **14/1**

0200 **15** 5 **Falcon Flyer**[178] 356 4-8-8 46 ... LPKeniry 5 — 7
(J R Best) *t.k.h: restrained s: swtchd and hld up against nr side: a bhd* — **25/1**

0000 **16** 4 **Ile Royale**[7] 4181 3-8-4 50 ow3 ... (e) TPO'Shea 3 — —
(B R Johnson) *dwlt: t.k.h: sn w ldrs: wknd 3f out* — **40/1**

1m 29.62s (-2.68) **Going Correction** -0.175s/f (Firm)
WFA 3 from 4yo+ 8lb — **16 Ran SP% 140.0**
Speed ratings (Par 101): **106,101,101,100,97 96,95,94,94,92 91,90,88,88,83 79**
toteswinger: 1&2 £28.20, 1&3 £2.10, 2&3 £9.90. CSF £63.23 CT £327.35 TOTE £5.60: £1.70, £5.10, £2.70, £3.60; EX 78.70 Place 6 £86.60, Place 5 £71.52.
Owner Paul Downing **Bred** J Potempa **Trained** Cropthorne, Worcs

FOCUS
A poor handicap, nearly selling level, but the winner was better than this company in the past and came back to form with a bang off a generous mark. The second and fifth were favoured by racing closest to the rail.
Contented(IRE) Official explanation: jockey said gelding hung left
Ile Royale Official explanation: jockey said filly lost its action
T/Plt: £122.40 to a £1 stake. Pool: £53,752.15. 320.47 winning tickets. T/Qpdt: £46.00 to a £1 stake. Pool: £3,984.00. 64.00 winning tickets. JN

3488 NEWCASTLE (L-H)
Saturday, July 26

OFFICIAL GOING: Good to firm
Wind: Almost nil Weather: Hot, sunny

4415 PAVILLION PAYROLL SERVICES MAIDEN AUCTION STKS — 7f
2:20 (2:25) (Class 4) 2-Y-0 — £5,504 (£1,637; £818; £408) **Stalls Low**

Form — RPR

045 **1** **Richo**[57] 2584 2-8-8 0 ... PaulMulrennan 8 — 77
(D H Brown) *w far side ldrs: effrt 2f out: styd on to ld nr fin* — **16/1**

03 **2** hd **Tale Of Silver (IRE)**[22] 3669 2-8-5 0 ... PJMcDonald(3) 17 — 77+
(G A Swinbank) *chsd stands' side ldr: led that quintet over 1f out: kpt on strly: jst hld by far side wnr* — **13/2**[3]

02 **3** hd **Royal Executioner (USA)**[28] 3476 2-8-8 0 ... AlanMunro 2 — 76
(P W Chapple-Hyam) *mde most far side tl hdd nr fin: 2nd of 10 in gp* — **2/1**[1]

3 **4** 2 **Kudu Country (IRE)**[39] 3107 2-8-8 0 ... MickyFenton 16 — 71
(T P Tate) *led stands' side to over 1f out: kpt on same pce ins fnl f: 2nd of 5 in gp* — **7/1**

5 2 3/4 **Warrior One** 2-8-7 0 ... NeilBrown(3) 9 — 66+
(J Howard Johnson) *midfield far side: drvn over 2f out: kpt on fnl f: no imp: 3rd of 10 in gp* — **25/1**

53 **6** 1 1/2 **Tapis Wizard**[14] 3976 2-8-7 0 ... DaleGibson 5 — 59
(M W Easterby) *dwlt: bhd far side tl hdwy over 2f out: kpt on fnl f: no imp: 4th of 10 in gp* — **5/1**[2]

7 1 1/4 **Hawkeyethenoo (IRE)** 2-8-4 0 ... AndrewMullen(3) 6 — 56
(M W Easterby) *trckd far side ldrs tl rdn and no ex over 1f out: 5th of 10 in gp* — **66/1**

6 **8** 2 3/4 **Sharp Sovereign (USA)**[30] 3411 2-8-7 0 ... PaulFessey 3 — 49
(T D Barron) *towards rr far side tl kpt on fnl 2f: nvr nr ldrs: 6th of 10 in gp* — **14/1**

9 2 1/4 **Hartley** 2-8-9 0 ... DeanMcKeown 13 — 46
(J D Bethell) *chsd stands' side ldrs: hung lft thrght: wknd fr 2f out: 3rd of 5 in gp* — **33/1**

10 6 **K'Gari (USA)** 2-8-0 0 ... LanceBetts(7) 1 — 29
(B Ellison) *bhd and outpcd far side: nvr on terms: 7th of 10 in gp* — **40/1**

0 **11** 1 1/2 **Kladester (USA)**[39] 3107 2-8-8 0 ... TomEaves 11 — 26
(B Smart) *w far side ldrs tl wknd 2f out: 8th of 10 in gp* — **33/1**

4 **12** 4 **Castle Myth (USA)**[28] 3492 2-8-8 0 ... DO'Donohoe 4 — 16
(B Ellison) *hld up far side: drvn over 2f out: sn btn: 9th of 10 in gp* — **20/1**

0 **13** 5 **Paddyntrev Bakfavs (IRE)**[22] 3669 2-8-7 0 ... DuranFentiman(3) 10 — 6
(T D Easterby) *hld up outside of far side gp: rdn and wknd over 2f out: last of 10 in gp* — **66/1**

14 32 **Mister Bombastic (IRE)** 2-8-11 0 ... TonyHamilton 15 — —
(M Dods) *unruly bef s: missed break: a struggling stands' side: 4th of 5 in gp* — **11/1**

15 1/2 **Green Passion (USA)** 2-8-10 0 ... JoeFanning 14 — —
(M Johnston) *in tch stands' side tl wknd fr 3f out: t.o: last of 5 in gp* — **8/1**

1m 26.44s (-0.96) **Going Correction** -0.225s/f (Firm) — **15 Ran SP% 127.7**
Speed ratings (Par 96): **96,95,95,93,90 88,86,83,81,74 72,68,62,25,25**
toteswinger: 1&2 £22.60, 1&3 £13.90, 2&3 £5.10. CSF £116.62 TOTE £24.10: £5.90, £2.90, £1.60; EX 155.90.
Owner Ron Hull **Bred** Brian Yeardley Continental Ltd **Trained** Tickhill, S Yorks
■ Stewards' Enquiry : P J McDonald one-day ban: used whip with excessive frequency (Aug 9)

FOCUS
An ordinary maiden in which the pace was fair. There was no advantage in the draw.

NOTEBOOK
Richo, who has progressed steadily with every outing, appreciated the step up to 7f and turned in his best effort. He showed a good attitude and will be of interest in ordinary nursery company. (op 25-1)
Tale Of Silver(IRE) ◆ is a progressive sort who fared the best of those to race with the stands'-side group. He will have no problems with 1m, he is in good hands and is sure to win a similar event.
Royal Executioner(USA) looked to have fair prospects on his improved Doncaster run and he ran right up to his best. Although not one of the stable stars, he has the ability to pick up a similar event. (op 3-1)
Kudu Country(IRE), who shaped well in a race that threw up winners on his debut at Thirsk, turned in another creditable display. He will be suited by the step up to 1m and it will be a surprise if he does not win races in the North. (op 15-2)
Warrior One, a gelded half-brother to winners from middle distances, shaped with plenty of promise on this racecourse debut. A much stiffer test of stamina will suit and he is more than capable of winning a race in due course. (op 33-1)
Tapis Wizard, having his first run on fast ground, failed to reproduce the form of his improved York run. On this evidence he should have no problems with 1m but he may be ideally suited by easier ground. (tchd 9-2 and 6-1)
Hawkeyethenoo(IRE), a half-brother to 1m2f winner Soho Square, showed ability on this racecourse debut and is entitled to improve for the experience. He should do better once qualified for a handicap mark. (tchd 50-1)
Sharp Sovereign(USA) again showed ability without being knocked about and is the type to fare best once handicapped.

4416 I.T.P.S. CELLULAR SOLUTIONS H'CAP — 6f
2:50 (2:56) (Class 3) (0-90,87) 3-Y-0
£7,788 (£2,332; £1,166; £583; £291; £146) **Stalls Low**

Form — RPR

1136 **1** **Marvellous Value (IRE)**[21] 3723 3-9-7 87 ... TonyHamilton 4 — 97+
(M Dods) *trckd ldrs: effrt over 1f out: qckND to ld ins fnl f: r.o strly* — **13/2**

-040 **2** 1 1/2 **Guertino (IRE)**[18] 3812 3-9-6 86 ... TomEaves 3 — 91
(B Smart) *towards rr: outpcd 1/2-way: gd hdwy fnl f: tk 2nd cl home: nt rch wnr* — **9/1**

5211 **3** hd **Pavershooz**[17] 3833 3-9-2 82 ... DO'Donohoe 1 — 86+
(N Wilson) *led to ins fnl f: kpt on same pce* — **5/2**[1]

2444 **4** 1/2 **Sparton Duke (IRE)**[17] 3838 3-8-12 78 ... (p) AlanMunro 5 — 81
(K A Ryan) *s.i.s: sn wl bhd: gd hdwy over 1f out: nrst fin* — **8/1**

-002 **5** 1 1/4 **Cristal Clear (IRE)**[19] 3794 3-9-4 87 ... DuranFentiman(3) 6 — 86
(T D Easterby) *towards rr: drvn 1/2-way: hdwy over 1f out: nvr able to chal* — **18/1**

2205 **6** 1/2 **Baldemar**[21] 3723 3-9-6 86 ... DaleGibson 2 — 83
(K R Burke) *prom: outpcd 1/2-way: rallied fnl f: no imp* — **8/1**

345 **7** 2 **Irish Pearl (IRE)**[19] 3794 3-8-12 85 ... DeclanCannon(7) 7 — 76
(K R Burke) *w ldr tl no ex over 1f out* — **25/1**

5426 **8** 2 **Mister Hardy**[13] 3999 3-8-10 83 ... FrederikTylicki(7) 11 — 67
(R A Fahey) *swtchd to r alone stands' side over 4f out: nvr rchd far side ldrs* — **5/1**[3]

4404 **9** 4 **Mey Blossom**[19] 3794 3-9-6 86 ... JoeFanning 9 — 58
(R M Whitaker) *cl up tl rdn and wknd wl over 1f out* — **20/1**

4303 **10** nse **Solar Spirit (IRE)**[8] 4158 3-9-0 80 ... PaulMulrennan 10 — 51
(G A Swinbank) *t.k.h: prom tl wknd appr 2f out* — **4/1**[2]

1m 12.41s (-2.79) **Going Correction** -0.225s/f (Firm) — **10 Ran SP% 124.7**
Speed ratings (Par 104): **109,107,106,106,104 103,101,98,93,93**
toteswinger: 1&2 £16.90, 1&3 £5.00, 2&3 £19.10. CSF £68.28 CT £176.54 TOTE £8.80: £2.70, £3.80, £2.00; EX 86.50.
Owner A J Henderson **Bred** John Cullinan **Trained** Denton, Co Durham

FOCUS
A fair handicap run at a decent gallop and this form should prove reliable. The winner is fairly progressive and the form is rated through the fourth.

NOTEBOOK
Marvellous Value(IRE) ◆, who looked a bit better than the bare form of his previous start, turned in his best effort back on a sound surface. He won with a bit in hand and, as he has only had five starts, is more than capable of progressing again. (op 4-1 tchd 7-1)
Guertino(IRE), whose form has been patchy since his maiden win, ran at least as well as he has all season. He may be worth a try over a bit further but he has little margin for error from his current mark. (op 11-1)
Pavershooz, up 8lb for his Catterick success, is a progressive sort who ran well considering he forced a decent gallop throughout. He has the physical scope for further improvement and is capable of winning again. (op 7-2 tchd 4-1)
Sparton Duke(IRE) ran creditably in terms of form returned to turf, though it was disconcerting that he could not keep up with the early gallop. He is only lightly raced, though, and is worth another chance in this type of event. (op 12-1)
Cristal Clear(IRE), back on a sound surface, shaped as though she would be worth another try over 7f. However she may have to drop in the weights before she is able to regain the winning thread. (op 14-1 tchd 11-1)
Baldemar, who finished just in front of Marvellous Value in a race that suited prominent racers at Haydock, was not disgraced, shaping this time as though a stiffer test of stamina would suit. He has little room for manoeuvre from this mark, though. (op 10-1)
Mister Hardy, back on a sound surface, can be forgiven this run as he raced away from the main group. (op 6-1)

Solar Spirit(IRE) Official explanation: trainer's rep said gelding was unsuited by the good to firm ground

4417 BARCLAYS COMMERCIAL BEESWING H'CAP — 7f

3:25 (3:25) (Class 3) (0-95,95) 3-Y-O+

£9,969 (£2,985; £1,492; £747; £372; £187) **Stalls** Low

Form — RPR

0600 **1** **Sir Xaar (IRE)**[28] 3491 5-9-4 **85**.......................(v) TomEaves 12 94
(B Smart) *hld up in tch: qcknd to ld 1f out: edgd lft u.p: hld on wl* **8/1**

0035 **2** *nk* **Countdown**[15] 3928 6-8-13 **80**.......................(b) AlanMunro 9 88
(T D Easterby) *hld up: hdwy over 1f out: chsd wnr ins fnl f: r.o nr fin* **11/1**

6066 **3** *1 1/4* **Passion Fruit**[9] 4110 7-8-11 **78**.......................(p) DeanMcKeown 6 83+
(C W Fairhurst) *hld up: hdwy on far rail over 1f out: kpt on fnl f* **10/1**

0516 **4** *1/2* **City Of The Kings (IRE)**[16] 3877 3-9-2 **90**....................... DO'Donohoe 4 90+
(G A Harker) *towards rr: drvn 3f out: styd on wl fnl f: nrst fin* **6/1**[3]

5514 **5** *3/4* **Ezdeyaad (USA)**[29] 3443 4-8-10 **77**....................... TonyHamilton 5 78+
(G A Swinbank) *cl up: ev ch tl one pce fnl f* **9/2**[2]

4046 **6** *1* **Flipando (IRE)**[21] 3740 7-9-9 **93**....................... NeilBrown(3) 2 94+
(T D Barron) *trckd ldrs: effrt whn no room fnl f: nt rcvr* **3/1**[1]

3000 **7** *hd* **Something (IRE)**[14] 3943 6-9-4 **92**....................... AdeleRothery(7) 1 90
(D Nicholls) *t.k.h: led to 1f out: sn wknd* **16/1**

0-00 **8** *1/2* **Lone Wolfe**[28] 3491 4-9-7 **88**....................... FrankieMcDonald 11 85
(Jane Chapple-Hyam) *t.k.h: prom tl edgd lft and no ex over 1f out* **16/1**

-034 **9** *2 1/4* **Game Lad**[15] 3928 6-8-12 **82**....................... DuranFentiman(3) 10 73
(T D Easterby) *hld up: drvn over 2f out: n.d* **7/1**

-005 **10** *1 1/4* **Lucky Dance (BRZ)**[155] 673 6-10-0 **95**....................... MickyFenton 14 82
(A G Foster) *trckd ldrs tl rdn and wknd over 1f out* **22/1**

03LR **R** **Gunfighter (IRE)**[18] 3812 5-9-1 **85**....................... PJMcDonald(3) 7 —
(R Johnson) *ref to r* **12/1**

1m 24.76s (-2.64) **Going Correction** -0.225s/f (Firm)
WFA 3 from 4yo+ 7lb — 11 Ran SP% **122.3**
Speed ratings (Par 107): **106,105,104,103,102 101,101,100,98,96** —
toteswinger: 1&2 £30.50, 1&3 £10.80, 2&3 £14.40. CSF £96.53 CT £917.69 TOTE £9.30: £2.40, £3.00, £3.00; EX 86.30.
Owner Pinnacle Smart Partnership **Bred** Mick Quinn And Peter Jones **Trained** Hambleton, N Yorks

FOCUS
Several fair sorts but progressive or unexposed performers were thin on the ground. The pace was sound. The winner ran to a similar mark as when runner-up in this last year.

NOTEBOOK
Sir Xaar(IRE), who had not won since 2005 and is not the most consistent, was 7lb lower in the weights than when second in this race last year and he elected to put his best foot forward. His record suggests he would be no certainty to build on this next time. (tchd 7-1)
Countdown, in good form around this time last year, has not been totally reliable this time round but he ran right up to his best. Equally effective on softer ground, he is capable of picking up a race when things pan out ideally. (op 8-1)
Passion Fruit ◆, has edged down to a fair mark and showed clear signs of a return to form tried in the first-time cheekpieces. She goes on any ground and is one to keep a close eye on in similar company when it looks as though there will be a decent gallop on. (op 12-1)
City Of The Kings(IRE), having his first run for his new stable, turned in a creditable effort over a trip that is a bare minimum. The return to 1m and beyond will be in his favour and he is one to keep an eye on. (op 15-2 tchd 8-1)
Ezdeyaad(USA) may be a bit better than the bare form as he shaped the best of those that raced up with the pace. He will be suited by the return to 1m and is capable of winning from this mark. (op 5-1 tchd 11-2)
Flipando(IRE) was the hard luck story of the race as he was poised to challenge on the heels of the leaders when denied a run for much of the final furlong. Whether he would have won is open to debate but he would have finished a good deal closer and is well worth another chance, especially when returned to 1m. Official explanation: jockey said gelding was denied a clear run (op 4-1)
Something(IRE), who is slipping in the weights, ran his best race of the year returned to this longer trip, despite racing freely. He is likely to drop further for this and he will be of interest back over sprint distances. (op 14-1)
Lucky Dance(BRZ) Official explanation: jockey said horse hung right-handed final 2f

4418 PIMMS SUMMER CLASSIC H'CAP — 5f

3:55 (3:55) (Class 4) (0-85,85) 3-Y-O+

£7,165 (£2,145; £1,072; £537; £267; £134) **Stalls** Low

Form — RPR

4043 **1** **First Order**[6] 4218 7-9-1 **78**.......................(v) NeilBrown(3) 12 90
(Miss L A Perratt) *pressed ldr: rdn to ld ent fnl f: kpt on strly* **6/1**[3]

3060 **2** *1 1/4* **Lord Of The Reins (IRE)**[7] 4201 4-9-5 **79**....................... AlanMunro 11 86
(J G Given) *hld up in tch: hdwy over 1f out: chsd wnr ins fnl f: r.o* **8/1**

4230 **3** *shd* **The Bear**[16] 3868 5-8-7 **70**....................... PJMcDonald(3) 6 77
(R Johnson) *led to ent fnl f: kpt on same pce* **11/2**[2]

0310 **4** *1 1/4* **Sandwith**[5] 4239 5-8-9 **74**....................... PatrickDonaghy(5) 7 76
(R Johnson) *prom: effrt 2f out: nt qckn fnl f* **10/1**

3021 **5** *1 1/4* **He's A Humbug (IRE)**[21] 3708 4-9-4 **85**.......................(p) FrederikTylicki(7) 2 83
(K A Ryan) *prom: effrt over 2f out: kpt on fnl f: nvr able to chal* **2/1**[1]

0000 **6** *nk* **Divine Spirit**[8] 4171 7-9-1 **75**....................... DaleGibson 3 72
(M Dods) *trckd ldrs tl rdn and no ex over 1f out* **20/1**

0-04 **7** *2 1/4* **Thunder Bay**[15] 3909 3-9-4 **82**....................... TonyHamilton 10 70
(R A Fahey) *hld up: pushed along 2f out: nvr able to chal* **12/1**

0001 **8** *1 3/4* **Inspainagain (USA)**[15] 3931 4-8-8 **75**....................... DeanHeslop(7) 8 57
(T D Barron) *in tch tl rdn and outpcd fnl 2f* **14/1**

5654 **9** *3/4* **Avertuoso**[8] 4171 4-9-5 **79**.......................(v) TomEaves 9 58
(B Smart) *missed break: nvr on terms* **11/2**[2]

59.56 secs (-1.14) **Going Correction** -0.225s/f (Firm)
WFA 3 from 4yo+ 4lb — 9 Ran SP% **117.7**
Speed ratings (Par 105): **100,98,97,95,93 93,89,86,85**
toteswinger: 1&2 £4.10, 1&3 £9.00, 2&3 £10.10. CSF £54.10 CT £283.14 TOTE £8.90: £2.40, £2.60, £2.30; EX 32.40.
Owner Gordon McDowall **Bred** Mrs Hazel Conroy **Trained** Carluke, S Lanarks

FOCUS
A fair handicap in which the pace was sound. The form is pretty solid.
Avertuoso Official explanation: jockey said gelding reared as stalls opened and missed break

4419 THOMPKINS GROUP H'CAP — 1m 2f 32y

4:30 (4:31) (Class 4) (0-80,80) 3-Y-O+ **£7,447** (£2,216; £1,107; £553) **Stalls** Centre

Form — RPR

2016 **1** **Amanda Carter**[16] 3864 4-9-7 **78**....................... FrederikTylicki(7) 7 91
(R A Fahey) *trckd ldrs: rdn to ld appr fnl f: sn clr* **8/1**

6565 **2** *3 3/4* **Jamieson Gold (IRE)**[29] 3453 5-9-9 **73**....................... TonyHamilton 1 79
(Miss L A Perratt) *hld up in tch: effrt over 2f out: chsd wnr ins fnl f: r.o* **20/1**

1054 **3** *1 3/4* **Dechiper (IRE)**[18] 3814 6-8-10 **65**....................... PatrickDonaghy(5) 9 67
(R Johnson) *hld up: hdwy 2f out: r.o fnl f: nrst fin* **5/1**[2]

-225 **4** *1 1/2* **Inspector Clouseau (IRE)**[23] 3641 3-9-6 **80**....................... MickyFenton 8 79
(T P Tate) *led to appr fnl f: kpt on same pce* **13/2**

-322 **5** *1/2* **Nesno (USA)**[21] 3736 5-9-0 **64**.......................(v) AlanMunro 4 62
(J D Bethell) *t.k.h: cl up: led over 2f out to appr fnl f: sn outpcd* **7/1**

2603 **6** *1/2* **Seyaadi**[6] 4217 6-8-10 **60**.......................(p) DeanMcKeown 12 57
(Miss Tracy Waggott) *hld up: drvn over 2f out: rallied over 1f out: no imp* **20/1**

4212 **7** *1* **Keisha Kayleigh (IRE)**[9] 4111 5-9-3 **74**.......................(v) LanceBetts(7) 3 69
(B Ellison) *s.s: bhd tl kpt on fr 2f out: n.d* **11/2**[3]

061 **8** *3 3/4* **Zuwaar**[25] 3573 3-8-13 **73**.......................(t) PaulMulrennan 6 61
(P C Haslam) *midfield: rdn over 4f out: no imp fr 3f out* **10/1**

1322 **9** *10* **Annibale Caro**[12] 4015 6-9-6 **73**....................... NeilBrown(3) 10 41
(Grant Tuer) *t.k.h in midfield: effrt over 2f out: sn wknd* **10/3**[1]

-030 **10** *4 1/2* **Casa Catalina (IRE)**[29] 3433 3-9-6 **80**....................... JoeFanning 5 39
(M Johnston) *trckd ldrs tl wknd wl over 2f out* **10/1**

601 **11** *6* **Persian Peril**[13] 3996 4-9-10 **74**....................... TomEaves 11 21
(G A Swinbank) *midfield: drvn and wknd over 2f out* **16/1**

2m 9.71s (-2.19) **Going Correction** -0.05s/f (Good)
WFA 3 from 4yo+ 10lb — 11 Ran SP% **125.7**
Speed ratings (Par 105): **106,103,101,100,100 99,98,95,87,84 79**
toteswinger: 1&2 £31.60, 1&3 £11.70, 2&3 £44.60. CSF £165.79 CT £891.06 TOTE £10.40: £3.20, £3.90, £2.40; EX 145.90.
Owner Mrs Janis Macpherson **Bred** James G Thom **Trained** Musley Bank, N Yorks

FOCUS
An ordinary handicap in which the gallop was just fair. The winner showed her Haydock win two starts back was no fluke, and the runner-up is rated to his recent best.
Annibale Caro Official explanation: jockey said gelding ran flat

4420 SPRING OAK DEVELOPMENTS APPRENTICE H'CAP — 1m 2f 32y

5:05 (5:05) (Class 6) (0-60,53) 3-Y-O+ **£2,590** (£770; £385; £192) **Stalls** Centre

Form — RPR

0514 **1** **Malguru**[36] 3204 4-9-9 **48**.......................(p) FrederikTylicki 5 59
(A G Foster) *pressed ldr: led 3f out: sn drvn clr: styd on strly* **11/4**[2]

0062 **2** *4 1/2* **Thornaby Green**[5] 4261 7-10-0 **53**....................... DeanHeslop 1 55
(T D Barron) *led to 3f out: kpt on fnl 2f: nt rch wnr* **2/1**[1]

4603 **3** *1 1/4* **Zaplamation (IRE)**[12] 4019 3-8-10 **45**....................... BMcHugh 7 44
(D W Barker) *hld up in tch: effrt 3f out: kpt on same pce fnl f* **15/2**

050 **4** *1 1/4* **Martingrange Lass (IRE)**[84] 1795 3-9-1 **52**....................... KrishGundowry(2) 4 49
(S Parr) *hld up on ins: drvn 3f out: kpt on fnl f: nrst fin* **20/1**

0555 **5** *2* **Rotuma (IRE)**[8] 4142 9-9-5 **48**.......................(b) JohnCavanagh(4) 2 41
(M Dods) *prom: drvn 4f out: one pce over 1f out* **7/1**[3]

00-0 **6** *6* **Mister Maq**[6] 4219 5-9-4 **45**.......................(v[1]) NSLawes(2) 3 26
(A Crook) *t.k.h: prom tl rdn and wknd fr over 2f out* **12/1**

605/ **7** *2 1/4* **Galloway Mac**[178] 6154 8-9-8 **47**.......................(t) LanceBetts 6 23
(M A Barnes) *bhd: drvn 4f out: nvr on terms* **9/1**

0504 **8** *3 1/2* **Mozayada (USA)**[23] 3644 4-9-3 **46**....................... MatthewLawson(4) 8 15
(M Brittain) *hld up: rdn on outside over 3f out: btn 2f out* **12/1**

-653 **9** *12* **Volaticus (IRE)**[12] 4031 7-9-6 **47**.......................(b) JamesRogers(2) 10 —
(A D Brown) *in tch tl wknd fr 2f out* **10/1**

2m 11.23s (-0.67) **Going Correction** -0.05s/f (Good)
WFA 3 from 4yo+ 10lb — 9 Ran SP% **123.5**
Speed ratings (Par 101): **100,96,95,94,92 88,86,83,73**
toteswinger: 1&2 £1.60, 1&3 £5.90, 2&3 £6.60. CSF £9.41 CT £38.55 TOTE £4.00: £1.70, £1.30, £2.50; EX 8.70 Place 6 £327.80, Place 5 £176.07.
Owner Lothian Recycling Limited **Bred** Mrs M Walsh **Trained** Cousland, Midlothian
■ Stewards' Enquiry : B McHugh caution: used whip above shoulder height

FOCUS
A low-grade handicap in which the pace was just fair. The first two were right up with the pace throughout. The third is the best guide to the form.
T/Plt: £290.60 to a £1 stake. Pool: £72,620.08. 182.41 winning tickets. T/Qpdt: £86.90 to a £1 stake. Pool: £3,619.39. 30.80 winning tickets. RY

4371 NEWMARKET (R-H)

Saturday, July 26

OFFICIAL GOING: Good to firm (firm in places; 9.8)
Wind: Almost nil Weather: Cloudy but with plenty of sunshine

4421 S.C.B. LTD NSPCC EBF MAIDEN STKS — 7f

1:55 (1:56) (Class 4) 2-Y-O **£5,180** (£1,541; £770; £384) **Stalls** High

Form — RPR

1 **Parisian Art (IRE)** 2-9-3 0.......................(b[1]) TPQueally 8 80+
(J Noseda) *trckd ldr: led over 2f out: shkn up and r.o wl fnl f: j. mown path across winning line* **7/2**[2]

2 *5* **Too Tall** 2-9-3 0....................... GeorgeBaker 9 66
(L M Cumani) *chsd ldrs: rdn over 1f out: styd on same pce fnl f* **7/1**

3 *3/4* **Pergamon (IRE)** 2-9-3 0....................... RobertHavlin 1 64+
(J H M Gosden) *s.i.s: sn chsng ldrs: rdn and hung lft over 1f out: styd on same pce fnl f* **5/4**[1]

4 *2 1/4* **Hypnotist (UAE)** 2-9-3 0....................... RichardMullen 5 59
(C E Brittain) *s.s: hld up: hdwy over 2f out: rdn over 1f out: wknd fnl f* **17/2**

0 **5** *1 1/2* **Against The Rules**[7] 4199 2-9-0 0....................... KirstyMilczarek(3) 2 55
(P Howling) *s.i.s: sn chsng ldrs: rdn over 1f out: sn wknd* **20/1**

6 *nse* **By Precedence (USA)** 2-9-3 0....................... IanMongan 7 55
(H J L Dunlop) *s.s: hld up: rdn over 2f out: n.d* **6/1**[3]

40 **7** *3 1/4* **Terracotta Warrior**[22] 3669 2-9-0 0....................... LukeMorris(3) 3 47
(J Jay) *led: rdn and hdd over 2f out: wknd over 1f out* **40/1**

8 *3/4* **Sparkaway** 2-9-3 0....................... StephenDonohoe 6 45
(W J Musson) *hld up: wknd over 2f out* **33/1**

1m 27.13s (1.43) **Going Correction** -0.10s/f (Good) — 8 Ran SP% **114.1**
Speed ratings (Par 96): **87,81,80,77,76 76,72,71**
toteswinger: 1&2 £2.30, 1&3 £1.10, 2&3 £3.40. CSF £27.10 TOTE £3.70: £1.60, £1.50, £1.20; EX 20.10.
Owner Matthew Green **Bred** Lodge Park Stud **Trained** Newmarket, Suffolk

FOCUS
The winner was impressive but this was probably just an ordinary maiden by Newmarket standards. They went steady early on and raced up the centre of the track.

NOTEBOOK

Parisian Art(IRE), 135,000gns son of Clodovil, half-brother to Red Expresso, who was placed over 5f at two, is entered in both the Gimcrack and Champagne Stakes and made a winning debut in good style. He had blinkers fitted, which is a little unusual for a debutant, but his trainer won with a first-time out two-year-old at Lingfield earlier in the week who also had the headgear on. He was always well placed in a race run at a modest pace early on and picked up in decent style when asked to stretch, pulling well clear. He displayed a good attitude, but jumped the path across the winning line, so it seems the blinkers are on just to help keep him focused. It remains to be seen exactly when he beat, but he is clearly very talented and may now be aimed at the Acomb Stakes at York. (op 2-1 tchd 4-1)

Too Tall, a 145,000gns son of Medicean, first foal of an unplaced sister to top-class prolific winning miler Soviet Line, fared best of the rest. The steady pace did not suit and he never looked like mustering the speed to threaten the winner, but he kept on well enough. (op 13-2 tchd 11-2)

Pergamon(IRE), a 130,000gns son of Dalakhani, half-brother to eight winners, including high-class miler Pinfloron, out of a smart triple 1m winner at two and three, has a Royal Lodge entry, but he failed to justify a short price on his racecourse debut. Presumably he is thought capable of better. (op 15-8 tchd 2-1in a place)

Hypnotist(UAE), a son of Halling, brother to dual 6f-7f juvenile winner Gothenburg, out of a sister to Noverre, was originally registered in the care of Godolphin, but perhaps he didn't make the grade. He started slowly and looked a little green, but this was a satisfactory introduction. (op 9-1 tchd 8-1)

Against The Rules stepped up on the form he showed when beating only one rival in a 6f maiden here on his debut the previous week and should find his level once handicapped. (op 25-1)

By Precedence(USA), a 100,000gns son of Johannesburg, half-brother to among others useful Vestrey Lady, a multiple winner at around 5f-1m at two and three in the US, out of a sprint winner at three, was well backed on course, but he seemed too inexperienced to do himself justice. He was never seen with a chance after starting slowly, but will know more next time and has presumably been showing something at home. (op 12-1 tchd 5-1)

4422 TURFTV H'CAP 1m 2f

2:25 (2:26) (Class 3) (0-95,94) 3-Y-O+

£9,969 (£2,985; £1,492; £747; £372; £187) **Stalls** High

Form RPR

0-14 **1** **Ask The Butler**[42] 3045 4-9-9 **89** .... GeorgeBaker 9 103+
(L M Cumani) *hld up: hdwy u.p over 1f out: hit over hd by rival's whip sn after: led ins fnl f: r.o wl* **15/8**[1]

-254 **2** *2* **Bandama (IRE)**[15] 3896 5-9-9 **89** .... TPQueally 4 96
(Mrs A J Perrett) *a.p: rdn and ev ch fr over 1f out: no ex wl ins fnl f* **8/1**

2-10 **3** *hd* **Tazeez (USA)**[30] 3413 4-10-0 **94** .... RobertHavlin 5 101
(J H M Gosden) *led: rdn over 1f out: hung lft and hdd ins fnl f: styd on same pce* **13/2**[3]

4310 **4** *nk* **Sonny Parkin**[8] 4162 6-8-9 **75** oh1 ....(v) RichardMullen 3 81
(J Pearce) *s.s: hld up: rdn over 2f out: styd on ins fnl f: nt rch ldrs* **25/1**

0032 **5** *½* **Wind Star**[23] 3649 5-9-1 **81** .... ShaneKelly 7 86
(G A Swinbank) *hld up: hdwy 4f out: rdn and hung lft over 1f out: styd on* **8/1**

6-15 **6** *3 ½* **Envisage (IRE)**[15] 3929 4-9-12 **92** .... WJSupple 10 90
(Saeed Bin Suroor) *chsd ldrs: rdn over 2f out: wknd fnl f* **7/2**[2]

1200 **7** *hd* **Missioner (USA)**[16] 3877 3-8-8 **84** ....(b[1]) J-PGuillambert 2 82
(M Johnston) *trckd ldr: rdn and ev ch over 1f out: wknd ins fnl f* **13/2**[3]

0000 **8** *¾* **Capable Guest (IRE)**[14] 3974 6-9-13 **93** .... TonyCulhane 8 89
(M R Channon) *chsd ldrs: rdn and hung lft fr over 3f out: wknd over 1f out* **16/1**

5505 **9** *12* **Tender The Great (IRE)**[9] 4110 5-8-10 **76** .... SaleemGolam 6 48
(V Smith) *hld up: rdn over 2f out: wknd over 1f out* **33/1**

2m 4.42s (-1.08) **Going Correction** -0.10s/f (Good)
WFA 3 from 4yo+ 10lb **9** Ran **SP%** **118.6**
Speed ratings (Par 107): **100,98,98,98,97 94,94,94,84**
toteswinger: 1&2 £4.10, 1&3 £3.30, 2&3 £10.30. CSF £18.56 CT £84.03 TOTE £2.80: £1.60, £2.40, £2.60; EX 19.00 TRIFECTA Not won..
Owner R J Baines **Bred** Skymarc Farm Inc **Trained** Newmarket, Suffolk

FOCUS

An ordinary handicap for the grade and the early pace was just modest. The winner shaped better than the bare form in a slightly messy race and the second ran to his latest mark. The winning time was 1.38 seconds quicker than the closing three-year-old 56-75 apprentice handicap. They raced up the middle of the track in the straight.

NOTEBOOK

Ask The Butler was disappointing when a beaten favourite over 1m4f in a valuable lady amateur riders' race at York on his previous start, but he returned to winning form with a battling success. Having been continually short of room when trying to challenge inside the final three furlongs, he received a nasty whack across the face by a rival jockey's whip over a furlong out, but he still responded to pressure once in the clear, eventually pulling away. On this evidence he will appreciate a return to 1m4f and ought to stay even further. He will be well worth his place in the Ebor and a penalty will help his chances of making the cut. (op 5-2)

Bandama(IRE) has not won since June 2006 but this was a respectable effort behind the well-treated winner. (op 13-2)

Tazeez(USA), upped to his furthest trip to date, had no easy task conceding weight all round, but he posted a decent effort in defeat. (op 5-1 tchd 9-2)

Sonny Parkin has gained all his four wins to date over 1m, but this was a respectable effort. He was due to be dropped 1lb. (tchd 22-1)

Wind Star hung left under pressure and could not end a losing run stretching back to August 2006. (op 7-1 tchd 17-2)

Envisage(IRE) was well beaten on this drop in trip and return to better ground. (op 9-2)

4423 COOLUS AIR CONDITIONING H'CAP 1m

2:55 (2:55) (Class 3) (0-90,87) 3-Y-O

£9,969 (£2,985; £1,492; £747; £372; £187) **Stalls** High

Form RPR

31 **1** **Grande Annee (USA)**[50] 2786 3-8-11 **75** .... ShaneKelly 5 89
(J Noseda) *hld up: hdwy to ld over 1f out: shkn up and edgd lft ins fnl f: r.o wl* **8/1**

41-3 **2** *2 ¾* **Roaring Forte (IRE)**[15] 3897 3-9-4 **82** .... TonyCulhane 8 90+
(W J Haggas) *hld up: hdwy over 2f out: rdn and ev ch whn hung lft over 1f out: styd on same pce* **2/1**[1]

3232 **3** *1 ¾* **Ellemujie**[15] 3919 3-9-6 **87** .... PatrickHills[(3)] 4 91
(D K Ivory) *prom: lost pl 5f out: hdwy over 2f out: ev ch over 1f out: sn rdn: styd on same pce* **9/4**[2]

2040 **4** *1 ¾* **Giant Love (USA)**[7] 4204 3-8-13 **77** .... J-PGuillambert 1 77
(M Johnston) *led: rdn and hdd over 1f out: no ex* **5/1**[3]

6-05 **5** *3 ¼* **Shamayel**[23] 3646 3-9-3 **81** .... WJSupple 2 73
(B W Hills) *sn chsng ldr: rdn over 2f out: wknd over 1f out* **8/1**

-155 **6** *1 ¼* **Always Ready**[89] 1686 3-9-5 **83** ....(b) RichardMullen 7 73
(C E Brittain) *chsd ldrs: led wl over 1f out: sn rdn: hung lft and hdd: wknd fnl f* **12/1**

-020 **7** *3* **Storm Sir (USA)**[9] 4128 3-8-12 **76** ....(t) IanMongan 6 59
(B J Meehan) *prom: rdn over 3f out: wknd over 1f out* **22/1**

1m 37.46s (-2.54) **Going Correction** -0.10s/f (Good) **7** Ran **SP%** **115.0**
Speed ratings (Par 104): **108,105,103,101,98 97,94**
toteswinger: 1&2 £1.40, 1&3 £3.20, 2&3 £1.40. CSF £24.77 CT £48.64 TOTE £5.40: £2.50, £1.90; EX 14.80 Trifecta £33.10 Pool: £232.86, 5.20 winning units.
Owner Tom Ludt **Bred** Grapestock Llc **Trained** Newmarket, Suffolk

FOCUS

A decent three-year-old handicap, but the early pace was steady. They raced up the centre. The winner showed big improvement on her maiden win but the form looks sound.

NOTEBOOK

Grande Annee(USA) was unimpressive when winning an ordinary 7f maiden on easy ground at Doncaster last time, but she left that form behind with quite a taking effort in this much tougher company. Both the step up in trip and switch to better ground clearly suited and she is progressing into a very useful filly. (op 5-1)

Roaring Forte(IRE), who looked to blow up when third on his belated reappearance over 7f at Ascot, improved a little on that form but again failed to deliver what many people expect from him. The steady pace was not ideal and he hung when coming under pressure, suggesting he was feeling the quick ground. He has now been a beaten favourite on both his starts this year, but it is hard to believe he cannot exploit his current sort of mark at some point and he is worth sticking with. Easier ground or a return to Polytrack (he broke the juvenile course record at Lingfield last year) might help. (op 15-8 tchd 7-4 and 5-2 in places)

Ellemujie ran a blinder when a short-head second to Duntulm in a big-field handicap over course and distance on his previous start, but a 6lb rise made things tougher and this was also a much more tactical affair. (op 11-4 tchd 3-1)

Giant Love(USA) had conditions to suit, but he offered little and seemed to find the company a bit hot. He has become disappointing, but will find things easier in lesser handicaps. (op 13-2 tchd 15-2)

Shamayel continues out of form. (op 10-1 tchd 15-2)

4424 E B F CELIA MILLER FILLIES' STKS (HERITAGE H'CAP) 7f

3:30 (3:30) (Class 2) (0-105,95) 3-Y-O+ **£25,904** (£7,708; £3,852; £1,924) **Stalls** High

Form RPR

-026 **1** **Medicea Sidera**[36] 3210 4-9-2 **87** .... GeorgeBaker 4 96
(E F Vaughan) *mde all: rdn over 1f out: edgd rt ins fnl f: r.o u.p* **11/2**[2]

1230 **2** *½* **Meydan Princess (IRE)**[42] 3047 3-8-11 **89** .... ShaneKelly 3 94
(J Noseda) *s.s: hld up: hdwy over 1f out: rdn to chse wnr fnl f: r.o* **9/4**[1]

3140 **3** *2* **Oceana Blue**[17] 3849 3-7-7 **76** oh5 ....(t) NataliaGemelova[(5)] 8 75
(A M Balding) *s.i.s: hld up: rdn and hung lft 2f out: hdwy over 1f out: styd on* **11/1**

0-00 **4** *nk* **Lady Aquitaine (USA)**[21] 3742 3-9-3 **95** .... IanMongan 10 95+
(B J Meehan) *hld up in tch: plld hrd: nt clr run and lost pl 2f out: hdwy u.p over 1f out: edgd lft: styd on* **33/1**

002 **5** *1 ¼* **Musical Beat**[9] 4110 4-8-9 **80** .... J-PGuillambert 11 78
(Miss V Haigh) *hld up: hdwy over 2f out: rdn over 1f out: no ex ins fnl f* **6/1**[3]

0336 **6** *3 ¾* **Kay Es Jay (FR)**[30] 3420 3-9-0 **92** .... RobertHavlin 5 77
(B W Hills) *trckd ldrs: racd keenly: rdn over 1f out: wknd fnl f* **17/2**

-254 **7** *4* **Chantilly Tiffany**[47] 2890 4-9-7 **92** .... TPQueally 2 69
(E A L Dunlop) *prom: rdn over 1f out: wknd fnl f* **11/2**[2]

0-40 **8** *1 ¼* **Silca Chiave**[38] 3120 4-9-10 **95** .... TonyCulhane 6 69
(M R Channon) *chsd ldrs: rdn over 2f out: wknd over 1f out* **10/1**

0001 **9** *32* **Dubai Power**[10] 4082 3-8-6 **87** .... PatrickHills[(3)] 9 —
(C E Brittain) *chsd ldrs: rdn and wknd over 1f out: eased* **11/1**

1m 23.91s (-1.79) **Going Correction** -0.10s/f (Good)
WFA 3 from 4yo 7lb **9** Ran **SP%** **115.0**
Speed ratings (Par 96): **106,105,103,102,101 97,92,91,54**
toteswinger: 1&2 £2.80, 1&3 £31.50, 2&3 £8.00. CSF £18.19 CT £132.07 TOTE £6.60: £2.00, £1.40, £3.10; EX 18.80 Trifecta £247.10 Part won. Pool: £334.04, 0.20 winning units..
Owner M A Whelton **Bred** Broughton Bloodstock **Trained** Newmarket, Suffolk

FOCUS

A good fillies' handicap in which the winner set an even pace. They raced up the centre early on, but were spread across the track inside the final two furlongs. The form is sound enough, rated around the second.

NOTEBOOK

Medicea Sidera was struck into when below form at Goodwood on her previous start, but there were no excuses today and she produced a career best. She set a reasonable pace, but was not hassled up front and had enough left when strongly challenged by the favourite. Her form figures on the July course now read 6111. She might go for another fillies' handicap, but her connections want to get her some black type and may look for a suitable race abroad. (op 13-2)

Meydan Princess(IRE) missed the break as per usual, but she recovered to have her chance. Nicely clear of the remainder, this looked a career best and she remains one to keep on-side. (op 11-4 tchd 3-1)

Oceana Blue, just as on her latest start over course and distance, raced from 5lb out of the handicap. This was a good effort on ground that was probably plenty quick enough. (tchd 10-1 and 12-1)

Lady Aquitaine(USA), having her first start in a handicap having contested Group or Listed races in all five starts since winning her maiden, was too keen early on and did not get the clearest of runs at the business end. She has a really fluent action and gives the impression she is worth a try from the front, as she would be hard to pass if she dropped her head early. (op 20-1 tchd 18-1)

Musical Beat did not build on her recent second at Doncaster. (op 7-1 tchd 15-2)

Chantilly Tiffany proved a little disappointing on this drop in grade from Listed company. (op 13-2 tchd 5-1)

Dubai Power Official explanation: jockey said filly lost its action

4425 K.W.A. ARCHITECTS NSPCC MEDIAN AUCTION MAIDEN STKS 6f

4:05 (4:05) (Class 4) 2-Y-O **£4,533** (£1,348; £674; £336) **Stalls** High

Form RPR

0 **1** **Tidal Force (USA)**[12] 4024 2-9-3 0 .... NelsonDeSouza 2 78
(P F I Cole) *chsd ldr tl led over 1f out: edgd rt: rdn out* **9/1**[2]

33 **2** *1* **Annapolis**[8] 4169 2-9-3 0 .... J-PGuillambert 7 75
(M Johnston) *s.i.s: sn pushed along and prom: hrd rdn fr over 2f out: sn hung lft: styd on u.p* **1/3**[1]

00 **3** *shd* **Sicilian Pink**[23] 3632 2-8-12 0 .... RichardMullen 1 70
(J L Dunlop) *hld up: hdwy over 2f out: rdn over 1f out: styd on* **20/1**

4 *4 ½* **Chatterszaha** 2-8-12 0 .... TPQueally 6 56
(C Drew) *chsd ldrs: rdn and hung lft fr over 2f out: wknd fnl f* **33/1**

5 *2 ¾* **Mr Redford** 2-8-12 0 .... JackMitchell[(5)] 3 53
(N P Littmoden) *hld up: rdn 1/2-way: n.d* **20/1**

05 **6** *8* **Anjuna (USA)**[26] 3558 2-8-12 0 .... RobertHavlin 4 24
(J H M Gosden) *led: rdn and hdd over 1f out: wknd fnl f* **14/1**

03 **7** *29* **Mymateeric**[74] 2086 2-9-3 0 .... ShaneKelly 5 —
(J Pearce) *prom: rdn over 2f out: sn wknd* **11/1**[3]

1m 13.02s (0.52) **Going Correction** -0.10s/f (Good) **7** Ran **SP%** **112.5**
Speed ratings (Par 96): **92,90,90,84,80 70,31**
toteswinger: 1&2 £1.50, 1&3 £7.80, 2&3 £3.40. CSF £12.19 TOTE £8.50: £2.70, £1.10; EX 13.90.

The Form Book, Raceform Ltd, Compton, RG20 6NL

Owner Parrish Hill Partnerships **Bred** Parrish Hill Farm **Trained** Whatcombe, Oxon

FOCUS

A modest maiden and one would expect better at Newmarket. The winner was a big improver with the runner-up rated to form.

NOTEBOOK

Tidal Force(USA) did not enjoy the clearest of runs when mid-division on his debut in a fair Windsor maiden and he built on that effort to get off the mark at the second attempt. He proved much more willing than the runner-up, but this is modest form, so things will be tougher in nurseries. (op 7-1)

Annapolis never looked happy, missing the break and having to be niggled along early before ruining his chance by hanging left under pressure. He could not build on his first two efforts and might have found the ground too quick, but whatever, he has something to prove now. Official explanation: vet said colt stiffened up after race (op 8-15 and 4-7 in places)

Sicilian Pink had been well beaten on her first two starts so, although this was clearly an improved performance, her proximity adds weight to the belief that this is modest form. At least she is going the right way, however, and she now has the option of nurseries. (op 16-1 tchd 14-1)

Chatterszaha, a daughter of Zaha, half-brother to multiple 7f-1m4f winner Surdoue, made a satisfactory debut, but this was a modest heat. Official explanation: jockey said filly hung badly left

Mr Redford, a 29,000gns gelded son Dr Fong, half-brother to modest dual 1m-1m1f winner Ledgerwood, is probably more of a handicap prospect. (op 14-1 tchd 22-1)

Mymateeric Official explanation: trainer said gelding was unsuited by the good to firm (firm in places) ground

4426 BALLYGALLON STUD, IRELAND NSPCC H'CAP 1m 6f 175y

4:40 (4:43) (Class 4) (0-85,83) 3-Y-0+ **£6,476** (£1,927; £963; £481) **Stalls** High

Form				RPR
1001	**1**		**Always Bold (IRE)**[8] 4146 3-9-1 **83** J-PGuillambert 2 (M Johnston) *chsd ldr 5f: remained handy tl led over 3f out: rdn over 1f out: styd on wl* **1/1**[1]	93+
2221	**2**	*1 3/4*	**Spring Dream (IRE)**[16] 3884 5-9-9 **76** (b) ShaneKelly 6 (A King) *chsd ldrs: lost pl 8f out: hdwy over 2f out: rdn to chse wnr over 1f out: styd on same pce fnl f* **6/1**[3]	83
1250	**3**	*2*	**Brief Goodbye**[15] 3900 8-9-6 **73** RichardMullen 3 (John Berry) *stdd s: hld up: hdwy over 2f out: rdn over 1f out: no ex fnl f* **17/2**	78
0323	**4**	*2 3/4*	**Kiribati King (IRE)**[14] 3962 3-8-0 **68** CatherineGannon 4 (M R Channon) *hld up in tch: plld hrd: chsd ldr 10f out: wnt centre 5f out: rdn over 3f out: wknd fnl f* **9/2**[2]	70
6-00	**5**	*1*	**Generous Jem**[7] 4196 5-10-0 **81** AdrianMcCarthy 1 (G G Margarson) *hld up: hdwy 8f out: jnd wnr over 3f out: rdn and wknd over 1f out* **16/1**	82
3334	**P**		**Stringsofmyheart**[7] 4178 4-9-8 **75** GeorgeBaker 5 (Miss Gay Kelleway) *led: rdn and hdd over 3f out: wknd wl over 1f out: p.u and dismntd ins fnl f* **13/2**	—

3m 10.79s (-0.51) **Going Correction** -0.10s/f (Good)
WFA 3 from 4yo+ 15lb **6** Ran SP% **112.2**
Speed ratings (Par 105): **97,96,95,93,93** —
toteswinger: 1&2 £1.60, 1&3 £3.40, 2&3 £4.70. CSF £7.53 TOTE £2.00: £1.40, £1.90; EX 4.90.

Owner Always Trying Partnership V **Bred** R N Auld **Trained** Middleham Moor, N Yorks

■ Stewards' Enquiry : J-P Guillambert two-day ban: used whip with excessive force (Aug 9,10)

FOCUS

An ordinary staying handicap for the grade. The early pace was steady. Most of these stayed towards the near-side rail in the straight and that was where the main action took place. The winner was well in on his Hamilton form and ran to a similar level.

Stringsofmyheart Official explanation: trainer's rep said filly was unsuited by the good to firm (firm in places) ground

4427 BALLYGALLON STUD, IRELAND NSPCC APPRENTICE H'CAP 1m 2f

5:10 (5:12) (Class 5) (0-75,73) 3-Y-0 **£3,885** (£1,156; £577; £288) **Stalls** High

Form				RPR
1663	**1**		**Snowdrop Princess**[21] 3729 3-9-8 **71** (b[1]) KirstyMilczarek 7 (W J Haggas) *s.i.s: hld up: hdwy over 3f out: rdn to ld over 1f out: styd on u.p* **11/4**[1]	79
6025	**2**	*1 1/4*	**Red Icon**[21] 3729 3-9-7 **73** JackMitchell(3) 1 (R M Beckett) *prom: rdn over 2f out: chsd wnr fnl f: styd on same pce* **3/1**[2]	79
-360	**3**	*2*	**Dea Caelestis (FR)**[11] 4061 3-8-9 **65** CharlesEddery(7) 5 (H R A Cecil) *hld up: racd keenly: outpcd 4f out: edgd rt: running on whn nt clr run and swtchd lft ins fnl f: nt rch ldrs* **25/1**	67
6642	**4**	*nk*	**Sterope (FR)**[17] 3843 3-9-6 **69** DNolan 8 (H R A Cecil) *prom: chsd clr ldr 1/2-way: rdn over 2f out: styd on same pce fnl f* **5/1**[3]	70
1004	**5**	*3/4*	**Nikolaievich (IRE)**[10] 4086 3-9-0 **63** (b) PatrickHills 3 (P F I Cole) *led: clr 7f out: rdn and hdd over 1f out: no ex ins fnl f* **8/1**	63
3024	**6**	*3/4*	**Locum**[29] 3436 3-9-0 **66** NicolPolli(3) 10 (M H Tompkins) *hld up: hdwy over 2f out: sn rdn: styd on same pce fnl f* **5/1**[3]	64
1-60	**7**	*4*	**Brave Mave**[17] 3841 3-9-3 **71** JPHamblett(5) 2 (W Jarvis) *hld up: rdn over 3f out: wknd over 1f out* **14/1**	61
0-0F	**8**	*13*	**Wabbraan (USA)**[50] 2805 3-8-7 **63** ChrisHough(7) 9 (D M Simcock) *hld up: bhd fr 1/2-way* **40/1**	27
-003	**9**	*26*	**Fiume**[56] 2603 3-9-7 **70** LukeMorris 6 (G Prodromou) *chsd ldr tl rdn 1/2-way: wknd over 2f out: eased over 1f out* **11/1**	—

2m 5.80s (0.30) **Going Correction** -0.10s/f (Good) **9** Ran SP% **117.4**
Speed ratings (Par 100): **94,93,91,91,90 89,86,76,55**
toteswinger: 1&2 £2.70, 1&3 £11.20, 2&3 £17.00. CSF £11.40 CT £168.67 TOTE £4.30: £1.80, £1.60, £5.20; EX 13.70 Place 6 £5.91, Place 5 £5.61.

Owner Snowdrop Stud Co Limited **Bred** Snowdrop Stud Co Limited **Trained** Newmarket, Suffolk

FOCUS

A modest apprentice handicap. The winning time was 1.38 seconds slower than the earlier 76-95. The pace was strong after an early dawdle and they raced towards the near-side rail in the straight. The form looks sound.

Nikolaievich(IRE) Official explanation: jockey said gelding hung right

Fiume Official explanation: trainer's rep said colt was unsuited by the good to firm (firm in places) ground

T/Plt: £5.70 to a £1 stake. Pool: £72,988.58. 9,299.07 winning tickets. T/Qpdt: £3.80 to a £1 stake. Pool: £3,051.19. 581.34 winning tickets. CR

4273 SALISBURY (R-H)

Saturday, July 26

OFFICIAL GOING: Good to firm (good in places last 3f; 9.1)

The 6.05 and the 8.10 (flip start) were unofficially hand timed.

Wind: Nil Weather: Fine

4428 BUTLER WRIGHT TAX CONSULTANCY "CARNARVON" H'CAP (FOR GENTLEMEN AMATEUR RIDERS) 1m

6:05 (6:05) (Class 5) (0-75,70) 3-Y-0+ **£3,123** (£968; £484; £242) **Stalls** High

Form				RPR
6306	**1**		**Gallego**[13] 4001 6-10-3 **59** MrMPrice(7) 9 (R J Price) *hld up in rr: swtchd lft ins fnl 3f: rdn and hdwy 2f out: edgd rt fnl f: r.o to ld last strides* **10/1**	68
-626	**2**	*1/2*	**Sotik Star (IRE)**[15] 3915 5-11-7 **70** MrSWalker 7 (P J Makin) *a.p: led over 3f out: rdn 2f out: ct last strides* **5/2**[1]	78
0020	**3**	*3*	**Wrighty Almighty (IRE)**[10] 4081 6-10-13 **69** MrNdeBoinville(7) 1 (P R Chamings) *t.k.h: sn chsng ldr: ev ch 3f out: sn rdn: hung rt jst over 1f out: no ex* **12/1**	70
-000	**4**	*5*	**Vogarth**[21] 3733 4-9-9 **51** oh1 MrPMillman(7) 2 (B R Millman) *hld up and bhd: hdwy on outside over 2f out: rdn and wknd over 1f out* **33/1**	40
2143	**5**	*3/4*	**Dancing Storm**[15] 3903 5-10-12 **64** MrPCollington(3) 5 (W S Kittow) *hld up in mid-div: hdwy 3f out: rdn over 2f out: wknd over 1f out* **11/4**[2]	52
4000	**6**	*hd*	**King's Alchemist**[9] 4112 3-9-8 **51** oh1 (v) MrLeeNewnes 11 (M D I Usher) *hld up on ins in mid-div: rdn over 2f out: no hdwy* **12/1**	36
3603	**7**	*3*	**Wodhill Schnaps**[23] 3653 7-10-3 **57** (b) MrBMMorris(5) 8 (D Morris) *a bhd* **7/1**[3]	37
3266	**8**	*3 1/2*	**Just Oscar (GER)**[8] 4168 4-10-1 **53** ow1 MrBenBrisbourne(3) 4 (W M Brisbourne) *sn prom: rdn over 2f out: wknd wl over 1f out* **8/1**	25
0-00	**9**	*8*	**A One (IRE)**[11] 4052 9-9-9 **51** oh6 MrDRBass(7) 3 (H J Manners) *led: hdd over 3f out: sn wknd* **66/1**	5
3100	**10**	*1*	**Vanadium**[14] 3966 6-10-11 **65** MrJoshuaMoore(5) 6 (G L Moore) *hld up in mid-div: pushed along over 2f out: sn bhd* **9/1**	17

1m 43.0s (-0.50) **Going Correction** -0.05s/f (Good)
WFA 3 from 4yo+ 8lb **10** Ran SP% **117.8**
Speed ratings (Par 103): **100,99,96,91,90 90,87,84,76,75**
toteswinger: 1&2 £12.50, 1&3 £45.10, 2&3 £7.80. CSF £35.60 CT £322.15 TOTE £11.50: £3.00, £1.70, £3.20; EX 37.50.

Owner My Left Foot Racing Syndicate **Bred** Mrs C C Regalado-Gonzalez **Trained** Ullingswick, H'fords

■ A first win under rules for 19-year-old Marcus Price.

FOCUS

There was no hanging about in this moderate affair, the strong pace suiting the winner who is rated back to his best.

Wodhill Schnaps Official explanation: jockey said gelding hung right for first 2f

4429 ROBERT SCOTT CELEBRATION CLAIMING STKS 1m

6:35 (6:37) (Class 5) 3-4-Y-0 **£3,238** (£963; £481; £240) **Stalls** High

Form				RPR
0006	**1**		**Talk Of Saafend (IRE)**[8] 4158 3-8-7 76 RichardHughes 5 (R Hannon) *a.p: pushed along to ld over 1f out: rdn and r.o wl* **11/8**[1]	76+
4001	**2**	*3 3/4*	**Hilbre Court (USA)**[7] 4181 3-9-1 82 WilliamBuick 7 (B J Meehan) *hld up and bhd: rdn and hdwy over 1f out: tk 2nd wl ins fnl f: no ch w wnr* **5/1**[3]	75
4024	**3**	*1 1/2*	**Desiderio**[27] 3525 3-8-12 74 (b) HaddenFrost(5) 1 (R Hannon) *led: rdn whn edgd lft and hdd over 1f out: no ex ins fnl f* **5/2**[2]	73
0006	**4**	*2 1/4*	**Leptis Magna**[31] 3383 4-9-0 56 SebSanders 4 (D R C Elsworth) *hld up: hdwy and wnt 2nd over 3f out: rdn and ev ch whn hmpd over 1f out: wknd ins fnl f* **10/1**	59
1500	**5**	*1/2*	**Rockfield Tiger (IRE)**[9] 4104 3-8-10 76 (t) SteveDrowne 3 (J A Osborne) *prom: rdn over 1f out: wknd fnl f* **11/2**	60
0/06	**6**	*7*	**Follow The Buzz**[24] 3604 4-9-0 45 RichardKingscote 6 (M Wellings) *hld up in rr: effrt on outside over 2f out: sn rdn: wknd over 1f out* **50/1**	42
000	**7**	*20*	**Lekezia (IRE)**[22] 3694 3-8-5 52 SimonWhitworth 2 (J W Hills) *plld hrd: sn prom: chsd ldr over 5f out tl over 3f out: wknd over 2f out: eased fnl f* **50/1**	—

1m 42.99s (-0.51) **Going Correction** -0.05s/f (Good)
WFA 3 from 4yo 8lb **7** Ran SP% **115.7**
Speed ratings (Par 103): **100,96,94,92,92 85,65**
toteswinger: 1&2 £2.20, 1&3 £1.50, 2&3 £4.50. CSF £9.18 TOTE £2.40: £1.40, £2.40; EX 6.20.

Owner J B R Leisure Ltd **Bred** Michael Dalton **Trained** East Everleigh, Wilts

FOCUS

An ordinary claimer. The form is rated around the third and the poor sixth and the winner did not need to match this year's form.

4430 HIGHLAND PARK SINGLE MALT SCOTCH WHISKY MAIDEN STKS 6f

7:05 (7:06) (Class 4) 2-Y-0 **£3,885** (£1,156; £577; £288) **Stalls** High

Form				RPR
4	**1**		**Elnawin**[7] 4199 2-9-3 0 RichardHughes 5 (R Hannon) *a.p: wnt 2nd over 2f out: rdn to ld 1f out: rdn out* **1/2**[1]	85+
	2	*2 1/4*	**Outofoil (IRE)** 2-9-3 0 SebSanders 6 (R M Beckett) *led: rdn and hdd 1f out: nt qckn* **4/1**[2]	79
	3	*2 1/2*	**Champagne Fizz (IRE)** 2-8-12 0 SimonWhitworth 1 (Miss Jo Crowley) *wnt lft s: hld up and bhd: hdwy 2f out: sn rdn: one pce fnl f* **40/1**	66
06	**4**	*14*	**Who Art Thou (USA)**[13] 3997 2-9-0 0 KevinGhunowa(3) 4 (P A Blockley) *chsd ldr over 3f: sn wknd* **25/1**[3]	29
	5	*1 3/4*	**Trading Nation (USA)** 2-9-3 0 SteveDrowne 3 (R Charlton) *s.s: in rr: pushed along 2f out: sn struggling* **4/1**[2]	24

1m 15.09s (0.29) **Going Correction** -0.05s/f (Good) **5** Ran SP% **113.0**
Speed ratings (Par 96): **96,93,89,71,68**
toteswinger: 1&2 4.30. CSF £3.09 TOTE £1.40: £1.20, £1.60; EX 2.80.

Owner Noodles Racing **Bred** D R Tucker **Trained** East Everleigh, Wilts

FOCUS

This did not turn out to be that competitive, just as the betting suggested. The level of the form is a bit guessy but Elnawin certainly stepped forward from his debut form.

NOTEBOOK

Elnawin ◆ had shown plenty of promise at Newmarket last week and found what was required when asked to go and settle the issue. He can continue to progress. (tchd 4-9 and 8-15 tchd 4-7 in places)

Outofoil(IRE) ◆, a 32,000gns half-brother to 6f and 1m winner Simplify, was backed to turn over the favourite. Soon put in his place once tackled, there should be easier opportunities ahead. (op 7-1)

Champagne Fizz(IRE) is a half-sister to multiple All-Weather winner Sorbiesharry. She showed signs of ability and looks the type to do better over further in due course. (op 28-1)

4431 COLD SERVICE LTD MAIDEN STKS 6f
7:40 (7:40) (Class 5) 3-Y-O+ £3,885 (£1,156; £577; £288) Stalls High

Form / RPR

2 **1** **Palace Moon**[83] 1835 3-9-3 0 SteveDrowne 9 89+
(H Morrison) *hld up and bhd: swtchd lft and hdwy 2f out: led 1f out: pushed clr ins fnl f* 11/10[1]

-352 **2** 5 **Oarsman**[22] 3696 3-9-3 75 (b[1]) RichardHughes 1 73
(R Charlton) *led: racd wd over 2f: rdn and hdd 1f out: one pce* 2/1[2]

0 **3** 1 1/4 **Willridge**[18] 3823 3-9-3 0 RichardKingscote 7 69
(Tom Dascombe) *hld up in mid-div on ins: rdn and hdwy over 1f out: kpt on to take 3rd wl ins fnl f* 40/1

03 **4** 3/4 **Sydneysider**[15] 3916 3-9-3 0 StephenCarson 2 67
(Eve Johnson Houghton) *a.p: racd wd over 2f: rdn and wnt 2nd briefly wl over 1f out: one pce fnl f* 22/1

5-62 **5** 2 1/4 **Cape Rock**[8] 4163 3-9-3 70 TQuinn 5 60
(C A Horgan) *w ldr: rdn and wknd wl over 1f out* 8/1[3]

0506 **6** 2 3/4 **Miss Clonyn (IRE)**[17] 3838 3-8-12 70 RichardThomas 8 46
(Christian Wroe) *w ldrs on ins: rdn wl over 1f out: sn wknd* 33/1

5-22 **7** nk **Desert Pride**[17] 3847 3-9-3 70 SebSanders 4 50
(W S Kittow) *hld up in tch: rdn and wknd wl over 1f out* 8/1[3]

0- **8** 6 **Street Power (USA)**[230] 7084 3-9-3 0 StephenDonohoe 6 31
(J R Gask) *s.i.s: a in rr* 16/1

000 **9** hd **First Tracks (IRE)**[56] 2620 3-8-12 57 (b[1]) GabrielHannon[(5)] 3 30
(J W Hills) *racd wd over 2f: a bhd* 66/1

1m 14.39s (-0.41) **Going Correction** -0.05s/f (Good) 9 Ran SP% 120.3
Speed ratings (Par 103): **100,93,91,90,87 84,83,75,75**
toteswinger: 1&2 £1.02, 1&3 £19.70, 2&3 £27.70. CSF £3.49 TOTE £2.10: £1.20, £1.10, £11.20; EX 4.10.
Owner Miss B Swire **Bred** Miss B Swire **Trained** East Ilsley, Berks

FOCUS
The winner impressed in beating a 75-rated rival and looks smart, but what he achieved here is debatable with some of the more exposed types disappointing.
Cape Rock Official explanation: jockey said gelding lost its action in closing stages

4432 RACING UK H'CAP 1m 6f 21y
8:10 (8:10) (Class 5) (0-75,75) 3-Y-O+ £3,238 (£963; £481; £240) Stalls Far side

Form / RPR

0414 **1** **Mount Lavinia (IRE)**[22] 3671 3-8-5 64 ow2 RichardKingscote 4 81
(R M Beckett) *chsd ldr early: a.p: led 4f out: rdn and edgd rt whn false rail ended 2f out: clr ins fnl f: eased towards fin* 11/2[2]

5-31 **2** 4 1/2 **General Ting (IRE)**[14] 3962 3-8-10 69 SebSanders 10 80
(Sir Mark Prescott) *hld up towards rr: hdwy 4f out: chsd wnr over 2f out: rdn and edgd lft over 1f out: no imp* 4/6[1]

1625 **3** 2 1/4 **Colonel Flay**[15] 3900 4-9-7 71 JackMitchell[(5)] 7 79
(Mrs P N Dutfield) *hld up in 4th: hdwy whn n.m.r over 3f out: rdn and edgd rt whn false rail ended 2f out: wknd over 1f out* 20/1

6013 **4** 9 **Hadron Collider (FR)**[14] 3970 3-8-12 71 RichardHughes 5 66
(R Hannon) *hld up in rr: rdn and sme hdwy over 2f out: wknd over 1f out* 8/1[3]

6112 **5** 3 **Sea Admiral**[16] 3891 3-9-2 75 (b) SteveDrowne 2 66
(R Charlton) *sn chsng ldr: rdn and ev ch over 3f out: wknd over 2f out* 8/1[3]

-006 **6** 6 **Orphina (IRE)**[22] 3698 5-8-7 59 oh12 ow2 (t) KylieManser[(7)] 8 42
(B G Powell) *hld up in mid-div: pushed along over 3f out: bhd fnl 2f* 66/1

4454 **7** 7 **Vanquisher (IRE)**[14] 3950 4-9-5 64 (b[1]) StephenDonohoe 6 37
(Ian Williams) *led: hdd 4f out: sn wknd* 20/1

0213 **8** 9 **Double Spectre (IRE)**[32] 3347 6-10-0 73 StephenCarson 1 33
(Jean-Rene Auvray) *in rr: hung rt fr 4f out: sn struggling* 22/1

0320 **9** hd **They All Laughed**[16] 3884 5-9-13 72 TGMcLaughlin 9 32
(P W Hiatt) *hld up in rr: pushed along over 5f out: sn struggling* 16/1

3m 6.50s (-0.90) **Going Correction** -0.05s/f (Good)
WFA 3 from 4yo+ 14lb 9 Ran SP% 118.8
Speed ratings (Par 103): **100,97,96,91,89 85,81,76,76**
toteswinger: 1&2 £1.80, 1&3 £5.30, 2&3 £4.30. CSF £9.44 CT £72.42 TOTE £8.20: £1.70, £1.10, £4.60; EX 14.30.
Owner Thurloe Thoroughbreds XX **Bred** Knocklong House Stud **Trained** Whitsbury, Hants

FOCUS
There was no hanging about in what proved to be an uncompetitive staying handicap. The winner stepped forward and the form has been rated on the positive side with the first three clear.
Double Spectre(IRE) Official explanation: jockey said gelding hung right-handed

4433 HIGHLAND PARK SINGLE MALT SCOTCH WHISKY FILLIES' H'CAP 6f 212y
8:40 (8:41) (Class 4) (0-85,80) 3-Y-O+ £5,180 (£1,541; £770; £384) Stalls High

Form / RPR

2322 **1** **Victoria Reel**[14] 3971 3-9-5 77 RichardHughes 6 89
(R Hannon) *hld up in last: hdwy and swtchd lft over 1f out: led ins fnl f: drvn clr* 5/2[2]

3221 **2** 4 **Tableau Vivant (IRE)**[16] 3870 3-9-8 80 PatDobbs 3 83
(Sir Michael Stoute) *a.p: wnt 2nd over 2f out: rdn and ev ch 1f out: one pce* 9/4[1]

2-23 **3** 1/2 **Polar Annie**[14] 3944 3-9-3 75 TGMcLaughlin 5 77
(M S Saunders) *t.k.h: led: clr over 3f out: rdn over 1f out: hdd and no ex ins fnl f* 6/1

6104 **4** 1/2 **La Coveta (IRE)**[7] 4189 3-9-8 80 SteveDrowne 4 81
(B J Meehan) *chsd ldr tl over 2f out: sn rdn: one pce fnl f* 11/4[3]

3030 **5** 9 **Support Fund (IRE)**[8] 4174 4-9-9 74 StephenCarson 2 57
(Eve Johnson Houghton) *prom: rdn over 2f out: wknd over 1f out* 11/1

1m 27.69s (-1.31) **Going Correction** -0.05s/f (Good)
WFA 3 from 4yo 7lb 5 Ran SP% 108.6
Speed ratings (Par 102): **105,100,99,99,89**
toteswinger: 1&2 £4.00. CSF £8.27 TOTE £3.40: £1.40, £1.90; EX 5.20 Place 6 £6.02, Place 5 £2.53.
Owner The Queen **Bred** The Queen **Trained** East Everleigh, Wilts

FOCUS
Run at a decent pace, this did not look a great race for the grade. The winner looks to be getting her act together and is up 4lb, but the second is not really progressing and the third not obviously well treated.
T/Plt: £7.80 to a £1 stake. Pool: £51,914.59. 4,854.40 winning tickets. T/Qpdt: £2.50 to a £1 stake. Pool: £4,110.60. 1,198.20 winning tickets. KH

4392 YORK (L-H)
Saturday, July 26

OFFICIAL GOING: Good to firm (firm in places; 8.4)
Dolling out added 7yds to advertised distances of races of a mile and further.
Wind: Virtually nil Weather: Dry and sunny

4434 SKYPOKER.COM STKS (NURSERY H'CAP) 5f
2:10 (2:11) (Class 3) 2-Y-O £7,123 (£2,119; £1,059; £529) Stalls Low

Form / RPR

14 **1** **Anglezarke (IRE)**[23] 3625 2-9-6 82 DavidAllan 10 88+
(T D Easterby) *hld up towards rr: hdwy over 2f out: swtchd rt and rdn over 1f out: styd on to ld ins fnl f: kpt on strly* 7/1[3]

3251 **2** 1 1/2 **Faraway Sound (IRE)**[36] 3215 2-8-12 74 LeeEnstone 9 75
(P C Haslam) *trckd ldrs: hdwy 1/2-way and sn cl up: rdn to ld over 1f out: drvn and hdd ins fnl f: edgd lft and kpt on same pce* 10/1

5323 **3** 1/2 **Titus Andronicus (IRE)**[7] 4175 2-8-10 72 PaulHanagan 8 71
(K A Ryan) *led: rdn along 2f out: drvn and hdd over 1f out: edgd lft and one pce ins fnl f* 9/1

2532 **4** 1 1/4 **Mazzola**[15] 3902 2-9-7 83 SamHitchcott 2 77
(M R Channon) *cl up: rdn 2f out and ev ch tl drvn and wknd ins fnl f* 7/1[3]

4412 **5** 3 1/4 **Bahamian Ceilidh**[14] 3961 2-9-4 80 LDettori 11 63
(B R Millman) *chsd ldrs: rdn along 2f out: sn one pce* 4/1[2]

454 **6** 1 1/2 **Blow Your Mind**[26] 3547 2-8-11 73 KerrinMcEvoy 12 50
(Karen McLintock) *chsd ldrs on outer: rdn along 2f out: no imp appr fnl f* 20/1

0141 **7** 3/4 **La Brigitte**[7] 4175 2-9-1 80 TolleyDean[(3)] 5 55
(A J McCabe) *dwlt and in rr: pushed along and hdwy 2f out: rdn and styd on appr fnl f: nt rch ldrs* 10/1

4210 **8** nse **Spring Tale (USA)**[7] 4190 2-9-7 83 EddieAhern 1 57
(M J Wallace) *towards rr: rdn along 1/2-way: swtchd rt and drvn 2f out: nvr a factor* 3/1[1]

612 **9** shd **Simple Rhythm**[23] 3639 2-9-0 79 DominicFox[(3)] 4 53
(M G Quinlan) *cl up: rdn along 2f out: grad wknd* 14/1

315 **10** hd **Kheylide (IRE)**[8] 4143 2-9-2 78 SebSanders 7 51
(Miss V Haigh) *chsd ldrs: hanging lft and rdn along 1/2-way: sn wknd* 16/1

2605 **11** 3/4 **Woteva**[24] 3597 2-8-8 70 JimmyQuinn 6 41
(B Ellison) *dwlt: a in rr* 16/1

5420 **12** 6 **Dancing Wave**[12] 4024 2-7-5 60 oh1 JamieKyne[(7)] 3 9
(M C Chapman) *chsd ldrs: rdn along after 2f: sn lost pl and bhd fnl 2f* 33/1

58.40 secs (-0.90) **Going Correction** -0.05s/f (Good) 12 Ran SP% 124.3
Speed ratings (Par 98): **105,102,101,99,94 92,91,90,90,90 89,79**
toteswinger: 1&2 £20.70, 1&3 £13.60, 2&3 £26.70. CSF £79.11 CT £652.07 TOTE £9.20: £2.30, £3.30, £3.50; EX 90.60 Trifecta £284.40 Part won. Pool: £384.41, 0.80 winning units..
Owner David W Armstrong **Bred** Mount Coote Stud **Trained** Great Habton, N Yorks
■ Stewards' Enquiry : Sam Hitchcott one-day ban: using whip down the shoulder in the forehand position (August 9)

FOCUS
Some useful sorts on show in this nursery handicap, run in a very fast time. The form looks rock solid and the progressive winner won well. The 'official' ratings are estimated and are intended as a guide.

NOTEBOOK
Anglezarke(IRE) didn't get home when tried over 6f in a novice event at Haydock last time, but back at the minimum confirmed the promise of her winning debut at Ripon. She may now go for one of the valuable sales races. (op 6-1)
Faraway Sound(IRE) needed to be dropped to a claimer to get off the mark at Musselburgh last time but showed up well throughout on his handicap debut, keeping on despite jumping a path across the track over a furlong out. (op 11-1)
Titus Andronicus(IRE) showed plenty of pace and kept on well enough to suggest that he'll soon be winning. (op 10-1)
Mazzola ran his usual solid race but is fully exposed already and will remain vulnerable to improvers. (op 10-1)
Bahamian Ceilidh didn't help her chances by being fractionally tardy at the stalls and should be forgiven this effort. (tchd 9-2)
Spring Tale(USA) seemed to have no trouble laying up when dropped to 5f for last week's Super Sprint at Newbury but was never comfortable here. (op 9-2)

4435 SKYBET.COM E B F FILLIES' STKS (H'CAP) 1m 2f 88y
2:40 (2:40) (Class 3) (0-90,89) 3-Y-O+ £9,714 (£2,890; £1,444; £721) Stalls Low

Form / RPR

2-21 **1** **Crystal Capella**[58] 2536 3-8-9 80 KerrinMcEvoy 7 98
(Sir Michael Stoute) *trckd ldng pair: hdwy and cl up over 4f out: led over 2f out: rdn clr over 1f out: edgd rt ins fnl f and kpt on wl* 3/1[2]

0314 **2** 4 1/2 **Ornella**[11] 4055 4-8-10 71 JimmyQuinn 8 80
(H Morrison) *hld up in rr: hdwy 3f out: rdn to chse ldrs 2f out: drvn and kpt on ins fnl f to take 2nd towards fin* 12/1

1011 **3** 2 **Suzi's Decision**[21] 3729 3-9-4 89 JohnEgan 3 94
(P W D'Arcy) *hld up in tch: hdwy over 3f out: trckd ldrs over 2f out: sn rdn: drvn and one pce fr over 1f out* 5/2[1]

21 **4** 1 **Caprivi (IRE)**[28] 3479 3-8-11 82 LDettori 6 85
(J H M Gosden) *led: rdn along and qcknd over 3f out: hdd over 2f out: drvn and one pce fr over 1f out* 4/1[3]

31 **5** 4 **Boucheron**[18] 3813 3-9-1 86 PaulHanagan 10 81
(R A Fahey) *trckd ldr: effrt over 3f out: sn rdn along and wknd wl over 2f out* 9/2

3324 **6** 10 **Royal Fantasy (IRE)**[40] 3088 5-9-8 83 KimTinkler 2 58
(N Tinkler) *in tch: effrt on inner 4f out: sn rdn along and wknd 3f out* 14/1

0 **7** 32 **Really Ransom**[66] 2305 3-9-0 85 TedDurcan 1 —
(P C Haslam) *hld up: a in rr: outpcd and bhd fnl 3f* 20/1

2m 9.12s (-3.38) **Going Correction** -0.05s/f (Good)
WFA 3 from 4yo+ 10lb 7 Ran SP% 110.9
Speed ratings (Par 104): **111,107,105,105,101 93,68**
toteswinger: 1&2 £12.20, 1&3 £1.90, 2&3 £6.90. CSF £34.74 CT £96.41 TOTE £3.50: £2.20, £6.70; EX 37.90 Trifecta £87.40 Pool: £189.09, 1.60 winning units.
Owner Sir Evelyn De Rothschild **Bred** Southcourt Stud **Trained** Newmarket, Suffolk

FOCUS
A few lightly-raced fillies with any amount of improvement in them and the winner came out easily the best. The pace was good and the form looks very solid.

NOTEBOOK

Crystal Capella didn't have much to beat when winning her maiden at Newcastle last time but her previous runner-up effort when second in Scuffle's maiden at Leicester has turned out to be one of the hottest affairs of its type to be run this summer and she made light of an initial handicap mark of 80. A scopey filly, she goes well on fast ground and should continue to give a good account despite facing a hefty jack in the weights. (op 11-4)

Ornella ran on well but would be seen to even better effect granted a stronger pace to come off. (op 14-1)

Suzi's Decision has been mopping up in lesser grade this summer but could only keep on at the one pace against this better quality of opponent. (tchd 11-4)

Caprivi(IRE) was allowed her own way up front once again but proved to be very one-paced. (op 7-2)

Boucheron's win at Pontefract must have been a headache for the Handicapper to evaluate as she was visually impressive there but mainly at the expense of an underperforming odds-on favourite. The drop in trip and the fast ground wouldn't have helped here and she deserves another chance from this mark. (tchd 5-1)

Really Ransom Official explanation: jockey said filly was unsuited by the good to firm (firm in places) ground

4436 SKY BET YORK STKS (GROUP 2) — 1m 2f 88y

3:15 (3:15) (Class 1) 3-Y-0+

£56,770 (£21,520; £10,770; £5,370; £2,690; £1,350) **Stalls** Low

Form — RPR

3333 **1** **Pipedreamer**[21] 3741 4-9-2 117 .... SebSanders 11 115+
(J H M Gosden) *hld up in rr: stdy hdwy over 3f out: rdn to ld 2f out: drvn and edgd lft ent fnl f: styd on wl* **2/1**[1]

1314 **2** *1 ½* **Campanologist (USA)**[21] 3741 3-8-9 115 .... LDettori 1 115+
(Saeed Bin Suroor) *led 2f: cl up tl led again 3f out: rdn and hdd 2f out: drvn ent fnl f and kpt on same pce* **5/2**[3]

4310 **3** *nse* **Supaseus**[14] 3974 5-9-2 103 .... JohnEgan 9 112
(H Morrison) *cl up: led after 2f: rdn along and hdd 3f out: drvn 2f out: rallied wl u.p ins fnl f* **33/1**

450 **4** *¾* **Halicarnassus (IRE)**[7] 4192 4-9-2 107 .... SamHitchcott 4 111
(M R Channon) *hld up in rr: hdwy wl over 2f out: sn rdn: drvn over 1f out and kpt on u.p ins fnl f: nrst fin* **20/1**

0-10 **5** *½* **Tajaaweed (USA)**[49] 2829 3-8-6 112 .... RHills 3 110
(Sir Michael Stoute) *dwlt: sn trcking ldrs: effrt 3f out: rdn over 2f out and kpt on same pce* **9/4**[2]

16-3 **6** *½* **Hearthstead Maison (IRE)**[7] 4192 4-9-2 112 .... GregFairley 8 109
(M Johnston) *t.k.h: chsd ldng pair: rdn along 3f out: drvn 2f out and kpt on same pce* **14/1**

3131 **7** *20* **Blythe Knight (IRE)**[14] 3946 8-9-2 111 .... PatCosgrave 10 69
(J J Quinn) *chsd ldrs: rdn along 3f out and sn wknd* **16/1**

2m 8.28s (-4.22) **Going Correction** -0.05s/f (Good)
WFA 3 from 4yo+ 10lb — **7** Ran SP% **112.9**
Speed ratings (Par 115): **114,112,112,112,111 111,95**
toteswinger: 1&2 £1.10, 1&3 £18.30, 2&3 £19.00. CSF £7.13 TOTE £3.30: £1.80, £1.90; EX 7.20 Trifecta £215.00 Pool: £607.47, 2.09 winning units.
Owner Cheveley Park Stud **Bred** Cheveley Park Stud Ltd **Trained** Newmarket, Suffolk

FOCUS

This looked a cracking Group Two contest on paper, and two of those with the most solid pattern-race form filled the front two placings. The form is slightly questionable due to the presence of handicapper Supaseus in a close-up third, who appears to have run miles above himself, but the front pair went at it from a fair way out and had begun to idle.

NOTEBOOK

Pipedreamer has been threatening to win a good contest at pattern level since taking the Cambridgeshire from a mark of 102 last autumn. He has continued to progress since then, in terms of both his form and physically, and there is every reason to think that he will be genuinely competitive if he comes back here to contest to Group One Juddmonte International at the Ebor meeting. (tchd 9-4)

Campanologist(USA) was taken on for the lead by Supaseus, but seemed to run his race nonetheless. Competing with the winner on terms 3lb worse than the weight-for-age scale due to his penalty for winning the King Edward VII Stakes at Royal Ascot, there would be little between them in Group One company.

Supaseus cut out a lot of the running and though he was found wanting when the front pair quickened things up he was coming back at them relentlessly in the closing stages. That they were either idling, or tiring, having pressed on from early in the straight is indisputable, but either way, this was a career-best effort from a horse having his first run outside handicap company since his maiden days. (op 25-1)

Halicarnassus(IRE), back on the firm ground he acts best on, bounced back from a disappointing effort at Newbury last weekend. (op 25-1)

Tajaaweed(USA) who contested the Derby on his last outing after suffering an interrupted preparation, again failed to live up to the promise of his Dee Stakes success, the form of which has failed to work out at all well. He was unable to quicken with the principals and could prove difficult to place with his Group Three penalty. (op 11-4)

Hearthstead Maison(IRE) was keen in the early stages and that was probably more accountable for his flat effort than any 'bounce' factor coming into play on his second start in a week following ten months off the course. (op 12-1)

4437 SKY BET DASH (HERITAGE H'CAP) — 6f

3:45 (3:45) (Class 2) (0-105,103) 3-Y-0+

£31,155 (£9,330; £4,665; £2,335; £1,165; £585) **Stalls** Low

Form — RPR

5212 **1** **Lesson In Humility (IRE)**[30] 3420 3-8-12 **96** .... AndrewElliott 3 109
(K R Burke) *cl up on outer: led 1/2-way: rdn wl over 1f out: drvn and edgd rt ins fnl f: styd on strly* **12/1**

4-10 **2** *1 ¾* **Tombi (USA)**[35] 3248 4-9-9 **102** .... EddieAhern 13 110
(J Howard Johnson) *midfield: hdwy 2f out: rdn to chse wnr ins fnl f: sn drvn and kpt on same pce* **8/1**[3]

00-2 **3** *nk* **Express Wish**[62] 2426 4-8-12 **91** .... LDettori 11 102+
(J Noseda) *midfield: hdwy to trck ldrs over 2f out: nt clr run wl over 1f out: swtchd rt and rdn ins fnl f: styd on wl towards fin* **7/2**[1]

0031 **4** *½* **Efistorm**[8] 4171 7-8-8 **87** .... PatCosgrave 5 92
(C R Dore) *cl up: rdn along 2f out and ev ch: drvn and one pce ent fnl f* **16/1**

2360 **5** *shd* **Stevie Gee (IRE)**[8] 4145 4-8-9 **88** .... KerrinMcEvoy 4 93
(G A Swinbank) *trckd ldrs: smooth hdwy 2f out: rdn over 1f out: drvn ent fnl f and kpt on same pce* **12/1**

2005 **6** *nse* **River Falcon**[5] 4240 8-8-13 **92** .... TedDurcan 8 97+
(J S Goldie) *bhd: rdn along over 2f out: swtchd lft over 12f out: styd on strly ins fnl f: nrst fin* **17/2**

0213 **7** *1 ¾* **Pawan (IRE)**[8] 4145 8-8-6 **90** .... (b) AnnStokell(5) 14 89
(Miss A Stokell) *midfield: rdn along and hdwy whn n.m.r and swtchd lft over 1f out: styd on ins fnl f: nrst fin* **14/1**

2001 **8** *hd* **My Gacho (IRE)**[21] 3728 6-8-6 **85** .... (b) GregFairley 20 83
(M Johnston) *cl up on stands' rail: rdn along 2f out: sn drvn and grad wknd* **12/1**

0000 **9** *½* **Bazroy (IRE)**[7] 4201 4-8-5 **84** ow2 .... (b) JohnEgan 15 81
(P D Evans) *hld up: rdn and sme hdwy whn n.m.r over 1f out: nvr nr ldrs* **28/1**

-250 **10** *1 ¼* **Tamagin (USA)**[14] 3946 5-9-6 **99** .... FergalLynch 9 92
(K A Ryan) *led to 1/2-way: cl up tl rdn and wknd wl over 1f out* **13/2**[2]

10 **11** *hd* **Blue Tomato**[7] 4201 7-8-4 **88** .... MCGeran(5) 1 80
(D Nicholls) *stdd and swtchd rt s: hld up and a towards rr* **16/1**

3021 **12** *nse* **Phantom Whisper**[15] 3905 5-9-0 **96** .... JamesMillman(3) 7 88
(B R Millman) *a towards rr* **14/1**

0000 **13** *1* **Sunrise Safari (IRE)**[8] 4145 5-9-2 **95** .... (v) PaulHanagan 17 84
(R A Fahey) *a towards rr* **16/1**

6100 **14** *¾* **Ajigolo**[8] 4145 5-8-13 **92** .... SamHitchcott 19 78
(M R Channon) *nvr bttr than midfield* **25/1**

-566 **15** *2 ¾* **Malcheek (IRE)**[41] 3056 6-8-6 **85** .... DavidAllan 16 62
(T D Easterby) *cl up: rdn along over 2f out: sn drvn and wknd: eased fnl f* **14/1**

1m 10.12s (-1.78) **Going Correction** -0.05s/f (Good)
WFA 3 from 4yo+ 5lb — **15** Ran SP% **125.2**
Speed ratings (Par 109): **109,106,106,105,105 105,103,102,102,100 100,100,98,97,94**
toteswinger: 1&2 £16.80, 1&3 £10.30, 2&3 £5.30. CSF £108.24 CT £429.31 TOTE £15.30: £3.80, £2.90, £1.80; EX 107.30 Trifecta £220.80 Pool: £1104.48, 3.70 winning units..
Owner M Nelmes-Crocker **Bred** Kevin Quinn **Trained** Middleham Moor, N Yorks

FOCUS

A typically competitve high-grade sprint handicap won decisively by the only three-year-old in the field who was also the only representative of the fairer sex. She showed big improvement but there seemed no fluke and the form looks solid.

NOTEBOOK

Lesson In Humility(IRE) looks ready for a return to Listed company after beating a field of older horses from a perch of 96. She probably races a touch too generously to see out the 7f she was tried over last time, but sees this trip out well which is an asset in one who likes to race prominently. (op 14-1)

Tombi(USA), a course-and-distance winner on similar ground before flopping in the Wokingham, came back to his best form off a mark 10lb higher than his winning one. He won't always come up against a relatively unexposed type such as the winner in these handicaps. (tchd 15-2)

Express Wish, along with the winner by far the least exposed of these, was short of room approaching the two-furlong marker and shuffled back into the pack. Not seeing daylight until the winner had flown, he showed enough to suggest he can win off this mark. (op 9-2)

Efistorm confirmed that he is in fine fettle at the moment with another solid effort.

Stevie Gee(IRE) again ran well and shapes as though he has a decent handicap in him.

River Falcon got himself well behind but came with a wet sail when it was all too late. He has become hard to win with. (op 8-1)

Pawan(IRE) Official explanation: jockey said gelding missed the break

Tamagin(USA) went hard from the start, tactics which have paid rich dividends in the past, but he faded badly on this occasion. (tchd 6-1)

4438 SKYVEGAS.COM MAIDEN STKS — 6f

4:15 (4:17) (Class 3) 2-Y-0 — **£6,670** (£1,984; £991; £495) **Stalls** Low

Form — RPR

1 **Cruikadyke** 2-9-3 0 .... JohnEgan 4 82+
(P F I Cole) *chsd ldrs: hdwy 2f out and sn rdn: drvn and hung lft ent fnl f: kpt on u.p to ld nr line* **6/1**[3]

2 **2** *hd* **Captain Ellis (USA)**[22] 3669 2-9-3 0 .... FergusSweeney 2 81+
(K R Burke) *sed awkwardly: sn trcking ldrs: hdwy and cl up 1/2-way: shkn up to ld 2f out: rdn over 1f out: wandered ins fnl f: hdd and nt qckn nr fin* **1/2**[1]

002 **3** *1 ¼* **Olympic Dream**[13] 3997 2-9-3 0 .... PaulHanagan 3 77
(R A Fahey) *led: rdn along and hdd 2f out: drvn over 1f out: kpt on u.p ins fnl f* **5/1**[2]

03 **4** *6* **Rossett Rose (IRE)**[19] 3792 2-8-12 0 .... TWilliams 1 54
(M Brittain) *prom: rdn wl over 2f out and sn wknd* **16/1**

6 **5** *2 ¼* **Final Salute**[37] 3170 2-9-3 0 .... TedDurcan 6 53
(B Smart) *s.i.s: a bhd* **12/1**

1m 11.93s (0.03) **Going Correction** -0.05s/f (Good) — **5** Ran SP% **111.2**
Speed ratings (Par 98): **97,96,95,87,84**
toteswinger: 1&2 £3.60. CSF £9.76 TOTE £7.40: £2.30, £1.20; EX 10.50.
Owner JMH Lifestyle Ltd **Bred** Alan Gibson **Trained** Whatcombe, Oxon

FOCUS

A nice debut from Cruikadyke who should have improvement to come. The favourite is rated a length of his debut form.

NOTEBOOK

Cruikadyke, a debutant son of Kyllachy, was off the bridle soon after halfway and though he responded to pressure he still appeared a most unlikely winner a furlong out. Running on well despite tending to drift left, he was aided by the runner-up idling badly, but as most of the yard's juveniles come on for the run, he could well be a very useful prospect. (tchd 7-1)

Captain Ellis(USA) only needed to be shaken up to go a few lengths clear but seemed to falter inside the final furlong. Whether the big crowd flanking either side of the Knavesmire took his mind off the job or whether he is quirky and needs to be played as late as possible is not clear at this stage. (op 4-6 tchd 4-9)

Olympic Dream is coming along steadily and appears to go on any ground. The son of Kyllachy looks like the kind to make into a decent handicapper as a three-year-old. (op 4-1 tchd 6-1)

Rossett Rose(IRE)'s best form in three starts came in the mud at Ripon and the daughter of Rossini would be of interest if she gets those conditions now she is qualified for nurseries. (op 12-1 tchd 10-1)

Final Salute showed no more on this going than he had on soft ground at Ripon on debut and might not be up to much. (op 11-1)

4439 SKY BET SUPPORTING THE YORKSHIRE RACING FESTIVAL STKS (H'CAP) — 2m 2f

4:50 (4:50) (Class 3) (0-90,89) 4-Y-0+ — **£9,066** (£2,697; £1,348; £673) **Stalls** Low

Form — RPR

2012 **1** **Four Miracles**[28] 3480 4-8-13 **81** .... JimmyQuinn 3 88+
(M H Tompkins) *hld up in rr: hdwy 3f out: sn swtchd rt and rdn 2f out: drvn over 1f out: styd on u.p ent fnl f to ld last 75yds* **9/4**[1]

1061 **2** *nk* **Chocolate Caramel (USA)**[11] 4046 6-9-2 **84** .... PaulHanagan 6 89
(R A Fahey) *hld up in rr: hdwy over 3f out: effrt on outer 2f out and sn rdn: styd on to chal ent fnl f: sn drvn and ev ch tl no ex nr fin* **7/2**[2]

-000 **3** *½* **Inchnadamph**[28] 3490 8-9-3 **88** .... (t) JamieMoriarty(3) 5 92
(T J Fitzgerald) *hld up in tch: smooth hdwy over 4f out: effrt over 2f out: rdn to ld wl over 1f out: drvn ent fnl f: hdd and no ex last 75yds* **4/1**[3]

-000 **4** *4 ½* **Kasthari (IRE)**[14] 3975 9-9-7 **89** .... (v[1]) TedDurcan 7 89
(J D Bethell) *trckd ldng pair: hdwy to ld over 3f out: rdn and hdd wl over 1f out: drvn and wknd jst ins fnl f* **10/1**

0542 **5** 2 **Victory Quest (IRE)**[18] 3820 8-8-2 **70** oh1 ....(v) PaulFessey 4 67
(Mrs S Lamyman) *trckd ldrs: rdn along 4f out: drvn and one pce fnl 3f* **25/1**

1464 **6** 6 **Numero Due**[11] 4046 6-9-1 **83**...(v[1]) LDettori 2 74
(G M Moore) *led: rdn along 4f out: sn hdd and grad wknd* **9/2**

3-50 **7** 21 **Whispering Death**[28] 3490 6-9-5 **87**.................................(p) EddieAhern 1 55
(J Howard Johnson) *chsd ldrs: rdn along over 3f out and sn wknd* **7/1**

3m 58.94s (0.54) **Going Correction** -0.05s/f (Good) **7** Ran SP% **116.6**
Speed ratings (Par 107): **96,95,95,93,92 90,80**
toteswinger: 1&2 £2.40, 1&3 £3.10, 2&3 £4.30. CSF £10.73 TOTE £3.00: £1.90, £1.80; EX 6.00.
Owner Pat Swayne and Partners **Bred** A G Antoniades **Trained** Newmarket, Suffolk

FOCUS
No great pace to this staying handicap which developed into a bit of a sprint up the straight, and the form may not be the most reliable. That said it does make sense amongst the placed horses. The winner is rated better than the bare form.

NOTEBOOK
Four Miracles is progressive, and did well to win this because she pulled very hard in the early stages. She wasn't in the ideal position when the sprint began but, switched to the outside, she quickened up in good style to get up close home. She likes this ground, and will do better still off a stronger gallop. (tchd 11-4)
Chocolate Caramel(USA) was the first horse to come under pressure but he kept on most gamely and only gave best in the dying strides. (op 4-1 tchd 10-3)
Inchnadamph is a solid yardstick who loves this ground, and was far from disgraced, but would have been better suited by a stronger gallop to come off. (op 5-1)
Kasthari(IRE) is coming down the weights steadily but though he appears to be giving his all he is a shadow of his former self and even a visor couldn't halt his steady decline. (op 12-1)
Victory Quest(IRE) was predictably outclassed but far from disgraced. (op 20-1)
Numero Due was allowed a soft lead but couldn't quicken once the sprint started. Official explanation: jockey said gelding lost its action (op 6-1)

4440 SKYBINGO.COM STKS (H'CAP) 7f
5:20 (5:21) (Class 4) (0-80,80) 3-Y-0+ **£6,476** (£1,927; £963; £481) **Stalls** Low

Form RPR

2321 **1** **Esoterica (IRE)**[20] 3758 5-9-3 **73**..........................(b) GaryBartley(5) 2 86
(J S Goldie) *trckd ldrs on inner: swtchd rt and hdwy to ld over 1f out: sn rdn clr: kpt on wl* **4/1**[2]

3054 **2** 1 ¼ **Hartshead**[8] 4167 9-9-9 **74**..................................... KerrinMcEvoy 17 84+
(G A Swinbank) *hld up in rr: hdwy 2f out: rdn over 1f out: styd on ins fnl f: nt rch wnr* **15/2**[3]

0000 **3** 1 ¾ **Sedge (USA)**[12] 4030 8-8-9 **60**.................................(b) EddieAhern 16 65+
(P T Midgley) *hld up: hdwy on wd outside wl over 1f out: sn rdn and styd on ins fnl f: edgd lft and nrst fin* **33/1**

4312 **4** nk **Violent Velocity (IRE)**[14] 3972 5-9-7 **79**.......................... JamieKyne(7) 14 83
(J J Quinn) *chsd ldrs towards outer: rdn 2f out: drvn over 1f out: kpt on same pce* **7/2**[1]

0356 **5** 1 ¼ **Memphis Man**[12] 4030 5-9-2 **67**.................................. PatCosgrave 8 68
(P D Evans) *towards rr: hdwy 2f out: sn rdn: styd on u.p ins fnl f: nrst fin* **16/1**

0202 **6** nse **Wovoka (IRE)**[6] 4219 5-9-8 **73**.................................. FergalLynch 18 74+
(D W Barker) *stdd and swtchd lft s: hld up and bhd: hdwy on bit 2f out: shkn up ent fnl f: styd on wl: nrst fin* **8/1**

4102 **7** nk **Flores Sea (USA)**[36] 3203 4-9-5 **70**................................ PaulFessey 12 70
(T D Barron) *midfield: hdwy 2f out: sn rdn: styd on ins fnl f: nrst fin* **16/1**

0655 **8** 1 **Neon Blue**[23] 3643 7-8-10 **61**...(p) TedDurcan 9 58
(R M Whitaker) *chsd ldrs: rdn along 2f out: sn drvn and no imp appr fnl f* **8/1**

0560 **9** 1 ¾ **Viva Volta**[5] 4245 5-9-5 **70**...(b) DavidAllan 4 62
(T D Easterby) *led: rdn along over 2f out: drvn and hdd over 1f out: sn wknd* **12/1**

0126 **10** nk **Steel City Boy (IRE)**[6] 4218 5-8-9 **65**............................ AnnStokell(5) 3 57
(Miss A Stokell) *t.k.h: chsd ldrs: rdn wl over 1f out and sn wknd* **25/1**

-040 **11** 1 ¼ **Cat Whistle**[17] 3849 3-9-6 **78**...................................... PaulHanagan 11 63
(R A Fahey) *racd wd: cl up: rdn along over 2f out: wknd wl over 1f out* **12/1**

2021 **12** 4 **Efidium**[6] 4219 10-8-10 **68** 6ex.................................. GihanArnolda(7) 5 45
(N Bycroft) *midfield: rdn along 1/2-way: sn wknd* **14/1**

0235 **13** 2 **Yankee Storm**[17] 3838 3-8-13 **71**.................................. GregFairley 15 40
(M Johnston) *dwlt: swtchd lft s: a in rr* **16/1**

6044 **14** 4 **Obe Royal**[14] 3966 4-9-2 **67**...(b) JohnEgan 13 28
(P D Evans) *chsd ldrs: rdn along over 3f out: sn wknd* **16/1**

1m 23.78s (-1.52) **Going Correction** -0.05s/f (Good)
WFA 3 from 4yo+ 7lb **14** Ran SP% **128.6**
Speed ratings (Par 105): **106,104,102,102,100 100,100,99,97,96 95,90,88,84**
toteswinger: 1&2 £8.50, 1&3 £55.40, 2&3 £105.70. CSF £36.96 CT £935.61 TOTE £5.50: £2.10, £3.10, £16.80; EX 46.50 Place 6 £64.94, Place 5 £12.78.
Owner Mrs S E Bruce **Bred** A Lyons Bloodstock **Trained** Uplawmoor, E Renfrews
■ Stewards' Enquiry : Eddie Ahern one-day ban: used whip with excessive frequency (Aug 9)

FOCUS
Just a fair handicap but a very competitive one and sound form for the grade. The winner was drawn low, but four of the next five home came from the five outside stalls, implying that the winner deserves even more credit.
Obe Royal Official explanation: jockey said gelding lost its action
T/Plt: £48.40 to a £1 stake. Pool: £132,701.67. 1,999.75 winning tickets. T/Qpdt: £3.20 to a £1 stake. Pool: £6,240.49. 1,438.05 winning tickets. JR

4320 VICHY
Saturday, July 26

OFFICIAL GOING: Holding

4441a PRIX DES REVES D'OR JACQUES BOUCHARA (LISTED RACE) 5f
12:55 (12:54) 2-Y-0 **£20,221** (£8,088; £6,066; £4,044; £2,022)

RPR

1 **Matwan (FR)**[11] 2-8-11 .... MickaelForest 3 93
(C Boutin, France) **42/1**

2 ¾ **Little Dreams (FR)**[40] 2-9-0 .... FBlondel 5 93
(F Rossi, France) **11/2**[2]

3 1 **Mirageleve (FR)** 2-8-11 .... ASanglard 1 87
(Frau C Brandstatter, Germany) **109/1**

4 snk **Maggie Lou (IRE)**[16] 3865 2-8-11 .... IMendizabal 9 86+
(K A Ryan) *mid-div: hdwy over 1f out: hmpd ins fnl f: nrest at fin* **11/2**[2]

5 snk **Osty Eria (FR)**[21] 2-8-11 .... ARoussel 4 85
(C Diard, France) **73/10**[3]

6 ½ **Thorns Of Life (USA)**[21] 3749 2-8-11 .... SMaillot 2 84
(Robert Collet, France) **11/2**[2]

7 ½ **Pink Candie (FR)**[42] 3052 2-8-11 .... CSoumillon 8 82
(Y De Nicolay, France) **6/4**[1]

8 10 **Ciloster (ITY)** 2-9-0 .... GMarcelli 10 49
(R Betti, Italy) **12/1**

9 6 **Miguelight (FR)**[21] 2-9-0 ....(b) JVictoire 6 27
(Mme P Alexanian, France) **19/1**

10 hd **Rahan (FR)**[12] 2-9-0 .... DelphineSantiago 7 27
(G Bailly, France) **51/1**

60.20 secs (60.20) **10** Ran SP% **116.1**
PARI-MUTUEL (including one euro stakes): WIN 43.00; PL 8.80, 2.50,18.40; DF 86.90.
Owner G Pariente **Bred** M Jarlan **Trained** France

NOTEBOOK
Maggie Lou(IRE) did not have the best of runs in this Listed event and was promoted to fourth place. She was outpaced for much of this race, but did stay on towards the end and was hampered in the straight. Her jockey felt that the sudden change in the ground (to holding) definitely was against her chance and he felt also that she might appreciate a longer trip.

4442 - (Foreign Racing) - See Raceform Interactive

4402 ASCOT (R-H)
Sunday, July 27

OFFICIAL GOING: Good to firm
Wind: Virtually nil Weather: Warm and sunny

4443 SODEXO CLASSIFIED STKS 1m 2f
1:40 (1:40) (Class 2) 3-Y-0+
£12,462 (£3,732; £1,866; £934; £466; £234) **Stalls** High

Form RPR

0054 **1** **Humungous (IRE)**[8] 4191 5-9-7 **96**.................................(b) ChrisCatlin 4 104
(C R Egerton) *sn niggled along in last: rdn and str run on outer over 2f out: led over 1f out: r.o strly and drew clr last 100yds* **11/2**[3]

-221 **2** 2 **Kaateb (IRE)**[23] 3684 5-9-6 **94**...(v) RHills 3 99
(W J Haggas) *led for 1f: trckd ldrs after: nt clr run 3f out tl over 2f out: hdwy on rail 2f out: pressed wnr ent fnl f: edgd lft and one pce last 100yds* **11/10**[1]

-226 **3** ¾ **Midships (USA)**[50] 2825 3-8-10 **95**................................ JimCrowley 7 98
(Mrs A J Perrett) *chsd ldr after 1f: upsides ldr 7f out: led 3f out: sn rdn and hld hd high: hdd over 1f out: one pce fnl f* **11/4**[2]

4464 **4** 6 **Ballinteni**[29] 3503 6-9-6 **93**... SteveDrowne 6 86
(Miss Gay Kelleway) *hld up wl in tch: rdn 3f out: wknd over 1f out* **10/1**

3403 **5** 7 **Rayhani (USA)**[31] 3398 5-9-6 **92**.................................. MartinDwyer 1 72
(M P Tregoning) *s.i.s: hld up wl in tch: rdn 3f out: fnd little and btn 2f out: eased fnl f* **7/1**

000 **6** 21 **Free Tussy (ARG)**[31] 3398 4-9-4 **90**................................ GeorgeBaker 2 28
(G L Moore) *led after 1f: hdd 3f out: wknd over 2f out: wl btn and eased fnl f* **50/1**

2m 5.00s (-4.80) **Going Correction** -0.325s/f (Firm)
WFA 3 from 4yo+ 10lb **6** Ran SP% **113.2**
Speed ratings (Par 109): **106,104,103,99,93 76**
toteswinger: 1&2 £1.60, 1&3 £2.70, 2&3 £1.30. CSF £12.28 TOTE £6.70: £2.10, £1.20; EX 12.90.
Owner Exors of the Late Mrs E A Hankinson **Bred** Quay Bloodstock **Trained** Chaddleworth, Berks

FOCUS
A tight affair on the ratings, and it was run at a sound gallop.

NOTEBOOK
Humungous(IRE) got the good pace he needs despite the small field, and stayed on strongly down the outside for a clear-cut win. This was a tight affair on paper but the way the race was run suited him down to the ground. He will run at Goodwood next, in the heritage handicap over this trip on Tuesday, and possibly also the Totesport Mile, in which he was runner-up last year, on Friday. (op 5-1)
Kaateb(IRE), who won in a first-time visor at Sandown last time, looked the most progressive runner in the race and posted another sound effort. He had to wait for a clear run but got out early enough to have every chance, and the winner was just too strong for him. His rider blamed overwatering for the gelding's defeat. (op 5-6 tchd 6-5 in places)
Midships(USA), who was down in the paper as only running if the ground was suitable i.e. if there had been enough watering, was allowed to take his chance. He ran well enough but he may well come into his own in the autumn when the ground comes more in his favour. (op 9-2)
Ballinteni, who ran well from a poor draw in the Hunt Cup and was then far from disgraced in a Listed race at Windsor last time, has done his winning on good ground or softer. His trainer has said that he has had problems with his feet and is hard to keep sound so this ground was probably quick enough for him. (tchd 12-1)
Rayhani(USA), who is probably more effective over another two furlongs, found little under pressure and is difficult to place off his current mark. (op 8-1)

4444 CASINO AT THE EMPIRE STKS (HERITAGE H'CAP) 1m 4f
2:15 (2:16) (Class 2) (0-105,105) 3-Y-0+
£31,155 (£9,330; £4,665; £2,335; £1,165; £585) **Stalls** High

Form RPR

0-60 **1** **Pippa Greene**[22] 3721 4-8-11 **92**................................ ShaneKelly 6 102
(P F I Cole) *t.k.h: hld up in midfield: rdn over 2f out: swtchd lft over 1f out: str run on outer to ld last 100yds: r.o wl* **20/1**

0042 **2** 1 **Young Mick**[22] 3721 6-9-6 **101**...(v) TQuinn 9 111+
(G G Margarson) *hld up in midfield: hdwy and swtchd to rail wl over 2f out: denied clr run tl wl ins fnl f: r.o last 75yds to go 2nd last strides: nt threaten wnr* **11/2**[2]

-221 **3** hd **Luberon**[72] 2168 5-8-12 **93**... JoeFanning 8 101+
(M Johnston) *sn led: hrd pressed and drvn wl over 2f out: battled on gamely tl hdd last 100yds: lost 2nd last strides* **13/2**[3]

241- **4** ¾ **All The Good (IRE)**[301] 5830 5-9-5 **100**.......................... LDettori 16 107
(Saeed Bin Suroor) *t.k.h: chsd ldrs: effrt and n.m.r over 2f out: chsd ldr briefly jst ins fnl f: no ex towards fin* **13/2**[3]

0-00 **5** ½ **Royal Jet**[8] 4191 6-8-8 **89**... TonyCulhane 1 95
(M R Channon) *hld up in midfield: shkn up and unable qck over 2f out: rallied u.p fnl f: styng on wl at fin* **33/1**

53-0 **6** nk **Dansili Dancer**[72] 2168 6-9-6 **101**................................ IanMongan 17 107
(C G Cox) *t.k.h: chsd ldrs: rdn and pressed ldrs over 1f out: unable qck u.p ins fnl f* **18/1**

-000 **7** hd **Players Please (USA)**[36] 3249 4-8-12 **93**.......................... RHills 14 100+
(M Johnston) *hld up towards rr: hdwy on inner 2f out: running on whn nt clr run ins fnl f: r.o towards fin: nvr able to chal* **25/1**

-131 **8** 3/4 **Sugar Ray (IRE)**[36] 3249 4-9-10 **105**..............................(t) SebSanders 3 109
(Sir Michael Stoute) *sn chsng ldr: rdn to chal wl over 2f out: ev ch after tl ins fnl f: fdd last 100yds* **11/2**[2]

00/1 **9** 1/2 **Bureaucrat**[50] 2830 6-8-11 **92**.. MartinDwyer 13 95+
(P J Hobbs) *s.i.s: t.k.h and hld up in rr: reminder over 5f out: rdn over 2f out: r.o ins fnl f: nvr nr ldrs* **16/1**

1111 **10** nk **Hatton Flight**[16] 3900 4-8-7 **88**..............................(b) FrancisNorton 12 91
(A M Balding) *t.k.h: chsd ldrs: rdn and tried to chal over 2f out: kpt chsng ldrs tl btn ins fnl f: n.m.r towards fin* **11/1**

-203 **11** shd **Camps Bay (USA)**[22] 3721 4-9-3 **98**.................................... JimCrowley 4 101
(Mrs A J Perrett) *in tch: rdn 3f out: outpcd over 1f out: kpt on same pce* **5/1**[1]

6561 **12** 1/2 **Profit's Reality (IRE)**[16] 3925 6-9-0 **95**.............................. TPO'Shea 11 97
(P A Blockley) *t.k.h: hld up in rr: rdn and effrt jst over 2f out: nvr trbld ldrs* **33/1**

-502 **13** 2 1/4 **Ladies Best**[51] 2790 4-9-5 **100**...................................... JimmyFortune 15 98
(L M Cumani) *hld up in rr: n.d* **14/1**

0204 **14** 1/2 **Pevensey (IRE)**[22] 3721 6-8-13 **94**..............................(v[1]) SteveDrowne 5 92
(J J Quinn) *s.i.s: sn niggled along in rr on outer: rdn and no prog wl over 2f out* **14/1**

003 **15** 3 3/4 **John Terry (IRE)**[29] 3505 5-8-9 **90**.................................... TPQueally 7 82
(Mrs A J Perrett) *t.k.h: hld up in rr: rdn and no prog 2f out: eased ins fnl f* **20/1**

2m 28.7s (-6.80) **Going Correction** -0.325s/f (Firm) **15** Ran SP% **126.2**
Speed ratings (Par 109): **109,108,108,107,107 107,107,106,106,106 105,105,104,103,101**
toteswinger: 1&2 £51.90, 1&3 £52.50, 2&3 £5.00. CSF £124.70 CT £820.25 TOTE £27.90: £8.50, £1.90, £2.40; EX 234.10 Trifecta £236.40 Pool: £1,405.70 - 4.40 winning units..
Owner R A H Evans **Bred** David And Mrs Vicki Fleet **Trained** Whatcombe, Oxon

FOCUS

A good-quality handicap run at a decent gallop thanks to Luberon being taken on by Sugar Ray at the head of affairs.

NOTEBOOK

Pippa Greene, all the better for his return at Haydock earlier in the month, was just 2lb higher than when last successful. Suited by the decent gallop, he stayed on well down the outside to win his fourth race in a seven starts to date. It must be said, however, that had the eventual runner-up got a run he would probably not have won. He will go for the Ebor next, and should not have any trouble with the extra two furlongs, providing he settles. Official explanation: trainer had no explanation for the apparent improvement in form (op 25-1)

Young Mick, running off the same mark as when runner-up to handicap good thing Mad Rush at Haydock last time, had nowhere to go inside the final furlong as he was trapped on the rail behind the leader Luberon. A gap finally opened up in the closing stages and he burt through it, but the line came too soon. He looked an unlucky loser and it was no surprise to see him cut to a best price of 9-1 for the Ebor on the back of this. He looks sure to go well at York in a race in which he finished third in 2006 off a 1lb lower mark. (op 7-1)

Luberon ◆ was denied an easy time in front by Sugar Ray, who harried him, and the result was that they both went too fast and set it up for a finisher. That he was able to still finish third shows that he remains on a very winnable mark, and it would not be a surprise at all if he made amends in the 1m2f heritage handicap at Goodwood on Tuesday. (op 5-1)

All The Good(IRE), previously trained by Gerard Butler, was making a belated seasonal reappearance for his new stable. He had every chance but got tired in the closing stages and should be straighter next time. The Ebor could well be on the cards for him as well. (op 8-1)

Royal Jet, runner-up in this race off a 4lb lower mark two years ago, ran on well at the finish and shaped with more promise than in his previous two starts this term.

Dansili Dancer, off the track for a couple of months since his seasonal reappearance, had conditions to suit and ran a sound enough race. Whether he has enough in hand to win off his current three-figure mark remains in doubt, though. (op 20-1)

Players Please(USA), out the back in his previous three starts this season, was running on at the finish and shaped a lot better. He is still on a higher mark than when last successful, but could find improvement for a step up in distance - he is entered over 1m6f at Goodwood on Tuesday. (op 28-1 tchd 33-1)

Sugar Ray(IRE) made all in a tactical Duke of Edinburgh Handicap at the Royal meeting but was 10lb higher this time and, in trying to take on Luberon for the lead from a lower stall than his pacemaking rival, he only ruined his own chance. (op 13-2)

Bureaucrat was 4lb higher and taking on stronger opposition than when successful at Epsom on Derby day.

Hatton Flight, winner of five of his last six starts, was taking a significant rise in class and found it a bit too much of a step up. (op 10-1)

Camps Bay(USA), backed into favouritism, was only a short head behind Young Mick at Haydock but failed to repeat that form on this quicker ground. (op 8-1)

4445 CISCO HONG KONG SPRINT STKS (HERITAGE H'CAP) 5f

2:50 (2:51) (Class 2) 3-Y-0+

£43,617 (£13,062; £6,531; £3,269; £1,631; £819) **Stalls** Centre

Form RPR

6220 **1** **Toms Laughter**[16] 3898 4-8-3 **89** ow4................(b[1]) KevinGhunowa(3) 23 102
(R A Harris) *chsd ldrs on far side: rdn to ld over 1f out: in command whn hung lft nr fin* **50/1**

0242 **2** 1 1/2 **Strike Up The Band**[15] 3943 5-8-9 **92**.......................... AdrianTNicholls 27 100
(D Nicholls) *led on far side and overall: rdn 2f out: hdd over 1f out: kpt on but nt pce of wnr fnl f* **8/1**[1]

1223 **3** nk **Total Impact**[16] 3931 5-8-0 **83**.. DavidKinsella 28 90
(R A Fahey) *in midfield on far side: rdn and hdwy 2f out: styd on u.p fnl f: wnt 3rd nr fin* **16/1**

1232 **4** hd **Safari Mischief**[34] 3320 5-8-2 **88**.................................. LukeMorris(3) 25 94
(P Winkworth) *chsd ldrs on far side: rdn to chse ldng pair over 1f out: one pce fnl f: lost 3rd last strides* **20/1**

1310 **5** 1 1/4 **Orpsie Boy (IRE)**[29] 3504 5-8-10 **96**....................... KirstyMilczarek(3) 26 98+
(N P Littmoden) *racd in midfield on far side: rdn 2f out: kpt on fnl f: nt rch ldrs* **33/1**

1300 **6** 1 1/2 **Bertoliver**[15] 3948 4-8-12 **95**.. JimCrowley 14 91+
(D K Ivory) *racd in midfield on far side: effrt and hung rt wl over 1f out: no imp fnl f* **50/1**

0632 **7** 1/2 **Invincible Force (IRE)**[16] 3931 4-8-7 **90** ow1................(b) TPQueally 15 85
(Paul Green) *chsd overall ldr on far side tl ent fnl 2f: steadily wknd* **16/1**

-533 **8** nk **Siren's Gift**[15] 3943 4-8-12 **95**.. FrancisNorton 20 89
(A M Balding) *chsd ldrs on far side: rdn and effrt 2f out: kpt on same pce after* **10/1**[2]

1400 **9** 1/2 **Northern Fling**[36] 3248 4-9-4 **101**............................ SilvestreDeSousa 24 93+
(D Nicholls) *bhd on far side: hdwy u.p over 1f out: swtchd lft 1f out: edgd lft but kpt on after: n.d* **16/1**

5600 **10** shd **Dig Deep (IRE)**[9] 4171 6-7-7 **83**...................................... JamieKyne(7) 19 74
(J J Quinn) *bhd on far side: rdn 1/2-way: styd on fnl f: n.d* **16/1**

1040 **11** hd **Elhamri**[9] 4171 4-8-6 **89**... RichardKingscote 9 80+
(S Kirk) *dwlt: towards rr on far side: edgd rt but kpt on fnl f: nvr nr ldrs* **28/1**

4012 **12** 2 1/4 **Tabaret**[23] 3680 5-8-8 **91**...(p) DeanMcKeown 5 74
(R M Whitaker) *led centre gp but nvr bttr than midfield overall: rdn 2f out: kpt on but nvr a ch w far side: 1st of 6 in gp* **16/1**

4026 **13** 3/4 **Aegean Dancer**[6] 4240 6-8-13 **96**...................................... RichardMullen 3 76
(B Smart) *stdd s: t.k.h: hld up in centre gp: kpt on u.p fr over 1f out: no ch w far side: 2nd of 6 in gp* **25/1**

4060 **14** shd **Indian Trail**[36] 3248 8-9-3 **100**.....................................(v) JoeFanning 18 79
(D Nicholls) *chsd ldrs on far side: rdn 2f out: struggling whn n.m.r wl over 1f out: no ch after* **25/1**

-101 **15** 1/2 **Sohraab**[8] 4201 4-8-12 **98** 5ex.. TravisBlock(3) 8 76
(H Morrison) *racd in midfield on far side: rdn 2f out: nvr nr ldrs* **12/1**[3]

6100 **16** 1/2 **Bo McGinty (IRE)**[6] 4240 7-8-0 **83**..........................(b) FrankieMcDonald 7 59
(R A Fahey) *pressed ldr in centre gp: hung rt thrght and jnd far side gp 1/2-way: no ch w ldrs* **66/1**

2000 **17** nk **Fantasy Explorer**[6] 4240 5-8-0 **83**.................................. HayleyTurner 17 58
(J J Quinn) *racd in midfield on far side: rdn over 2f out: n.d* **25/1**

2-15 **18** 1/2 **Oldjoesaid**[15] 3948 4-9-10 **107**.. JimmyFortune 11 80
(H Candy) *racd on far side: hld up towards rr: n.d* **14/1**

00-0 **19** shd **The Tatling (IRE)**[33] 3336 11-8-0 **88** ow1.......................... MCGeran(5) 13 61
(J M Bradley) *s.i.s: a bhd on far side* **50/1**

4000 **20** hd **Northern Empire (IRE)**[8] 4201 5-8-8 **91**...........................(t) JohnEgan 16 63
(K A Ryan) *dwlt: sn chsng ldrs on far side: rdn 1/2-way: wknd wl over 1f out* **33/1**

6066 **21** 1/2 **Golden Dixie (USA)**[8] 4201 9-8-5 **88**.................................. LiamJones 1 58
(R A Harris) *racd in centre gp: nvr a factor: 3rd of 6 in gp* **20/1**

0106 **22** 1/2 **Fyodor (IRE)**[33] 3336 7-8-12 **95**..................................(v) TonyCulhane 10 63
(W J Haggas) *stdd s: hld up in rr on far side: n.d* **16/1**

2333 **23** 3/4 **Little Pete (IRE)**[16] 3909 3-8-1 **88**...................................... ChrisCatlin 4 54
(A M Balding) *racd in centre gp: dwlt: nvr a factor: 4th of 6 in gp* **22/1**

343 **24** 1 1/2 **Ebraam (USA)**[17] 3881 5-8-11 **94**...................................... JimmyQuinn 6 54
(P Howling) *s.i.s: a bhd in centre gp: 5th of 6 in gp* **20/1**

3506 **25** 3/4 **New Freedom (BRZ)**[22] 3722 7-9-7 **104**................................ TPO'Shea 2 62
(D R Lanigan) *a bhd in centre gp: 6th of 6 in gp* **33/1**

0064 **26** 2 3/4 **Matsunosuke**[9] 4159 6-9-2 **99**.. SebSanders 12 47
(A B Coogan) *bhd on far side: no ch whn eased fnl f: sddle slipped* **25/1**

59.48 secs (-1.02) **Going Correction** +0.025s/f (Good)
WFA 3 from 4yo+ 4lb **26** Ran SP% **123.5**
Speed ratings (Par 109): **109,106,106,105,103 101,100,100,99,99 98,95,94,93,93 92,91,91,90,90 89,88,87,85,84 79**
toteswinger: 1&2 £46.80, 1&3 £323.60, 2&3 £45.00. CSF £283.96 CT £2536.27 TOTE £55.80: £9.90, £1.90, £5.00, £4.60; EX 482.30 Trifecta £1304.70 Part won..
Owner Five To Follow **Bred** Mrs D J Hughes **Trained** Earlswood, Monmouths

FOCUS

An open sprint handicap on paper and a shock winner. The whole field migrated towards the far side and the race was dominated by the high numbers.

NOTEBOOK

Toms Laughter, dropped back in distance and fitted with blinkers for the first time, showed good speed from his favourable high draw and, racing close to the far-side rail, stayed on strongly to score decisively. In fact he was idling in the closing stages. His rider put up 4lb overweight, making the gelding's performance even more creditable, and he has the potential to improve further and could well contest Listed races by the end of the season. Official explanation: trainer said, regarding apparent improvement in form, that the gelding was better suited by the first-time blinkers and the way the race was run

Strike Up The Band, who has been running well in defeat recently, looked to have plenty in his favour drawn very high. He showed his usual early speed and had every chance, but the winner had him comfortably held at the finish. He has a modest strike-rate but does not do anything wrong. (tchd 15-2)

Total Impact, who was also favourably berthed, had conditions to suit and ran on late for third from off the pace. A big field seems to show him at his best as he needs cover.

Safari Mischief ran a sound race and looks the type to go well at Goodwood later in the week as he has run well in each of his previous four starts at the track.

Orpsie Boy(IRE) found this a bit too much of a test of speed. He is ideally served by 6f but he was drawn well and the strong pace suited him so he did not run too badly.

Bertoliver did best of those not drawn on the far side, but he did race at the head of affairs with the dominant group. His current mark makes things difficult for him. (op 40-1)

Invincible Force(IRE), whose rider put up 1lb overweight, was also drawn in the middle but he soon crossed over to race alongside Strike Up The Band. The early effort he put in probably cost him later on in the race.

Siren's Gift, who has only ever won two small-field events, was squeezed for room when weakening inside the last, but it made no real difference.

Northern Fling is weighted right up to his best at present.

Dig Deep(IRE), racing off the same mark as when successful over this course and distance last July, could never land a blow from off the pace. He has yet to really fire for his new yard.

Elhamri did best of those drawn in single figures and is entitled to be rated better than the bare form suggests. He remains on a fair mark.

Tabaret made the running up the centre of the track, which was not the place to be as the ground on the far side appeared to be appreciably quicker, and he ran better than his finishing position suggests. (op 20-1)

Aegean Dancer, second of those that raced mainly up the centre of the track, ran alright but does not look particularly well handicapped at present.

Bo McGinty(IRE) Official explanation: jockey said gelding hung right-handed throughout

Golden Dixie(USA), third in this race two years ago off a 3lb higher mark, had shaped as though returning to form at Newmarket last time. He found himself drawn on the wrong side this time, though, and could only finish third of the group that raced up the centre of the track.

Matsunosuke Official explanation: jockey said saddle slipped

4446 E B F OWEN BROWN CROCKER BULTEEL MAIDEN STKS (C&G) 6f

3:25 (3:27) (Class 4) 2-Y-0 **£6,476** (£1,927; £963; £481) **Stalls** Centre

Form RPR

1 **Albaher** 2-9-0 0.. MartinDwyer 2 80+
(J L Dunlop) *wnt rt s: in tch: hdwy to chal 2f out: edgd rt and led over 1f out: pushed out and styd on wl last 100yds* **9/2**

2 1 **Bawaardi (IRE)** 2-9-0 0.. RHills 3 77+
(J H M Gosden) *hmpd s: hld up in last: swtchd rt and hdwy 2f out: pressed wnr ent fnl f: no ex last 100yds* **11/4**[2]

3 2 1/4 **Marbled Cat (USA)** 2-9-0 0.. LDettori 6 70+
(M Johnston) *chsd ldrs: hdwy and ev ch jst over 2f out: led narrowly wl over 1f out: hdd over 1f out: wknd last 100yds* **5/2**[1]

4 1/2 **Euston Square** 2-9-0 0.. JimmyFortune 4 69+
(J H M Gosden) *chsd ldrs: ev ch and rdn jst over 2f out: wknd ins fnl f* **3/1**[3]

5 3 1/2 **Kings Ace (IRE)** 2-9-0 0.. DarrenWilliams 1 58
(A P Jarvis) *led: rdn and hdd wl over 1f out: wkng whn short of room sn after: wl btn fnl f* **16/1**

1m 16.73s (2.33) **Going Correction** +0.025s/f (Good) **5** Ran SP% **104.3**
Speed ratings (Par 96): **85,83,80,80,75**
toteswinger: 1&2 £6.20. CSF £15.15 TOTE £5.80: £2.30, £1.50; EX 14.10.
Owner Hamdan Al Maktoum **Bred** Cheveley Park Stud Ltd **Trained** Arundel, W Sussex

FOCUS
Questionable what the form of this maiden is worth as they went quite steady before sprinting.

NOTEBOOK
Albaher, who cost 150,000gns, is a half-brother to dual 5f juvenile winner Dance On, dual winning sprinter Hornpipe, and Sequential, a dual winner over middle distances, out of Lowther Stakes winner Dance Sequence. A Middle Park entry, he won in good style without being given a hard race, and as he comes from a stable whose juveniles are rarely wound up first time, there should be plenty of further improvement to come, especially when stepped up in trip. (op 5-1)
Bawaardi(IRE), whose price shot up from 14,000gns as a foal to 130,000gns as a yearling, is out of an unraced mare from the family of July Cup winner Continent. Held up last in a steadily run affair, he ran green when asked to pick up, but showed enough to suggest he can win his maiden. (tchd 5-2)
Marbled Cat(USA), whose dam was runner-up in the Queen Mary, was backed into favouritism. He was left behind as the Hamdan pair drew clear, but is entitled to come on for the experience. (op 3-1 tchd 7-2)
Euston Square, a half-brother to top-class sprinter Continent, who won the July Cup, was expected to need the run and that is how he ran. He should strip fitter next time. (op 11-4)
Kings Ace(IRE), whose dam won over 5f, showed early pace but was the first beaten. (tchd 14-1)

4447 HUAWEI MAIDEN FILLIES' STKS — 1m (S)
4:00 (4:01) (Class 4) 3-Y-O — £6,476 (£1,927; £963; £481) Stalls Centre

Form — RPR
3- **1** **Basque Beauty**[338] [4774] 3-9-0 0 .... RHills 7 — 92+
(W J Haggas) *hld up bhd: smooth hdwy over 3f out: chsd ldr cruising over 2f out: led over 1f out: rdn clr: v easily* — 6/5[1]
0250 **2** *6* **Queen's Speech (IRE)**[42] [3057] 3-9-0 74 .... (b[1]) RobertHavlin 4 — 78
(J H M Gosden) *led: pushed clr over 3f out: rdn 2f out: hdd over 1f out: no ch w wnr* — 14/1
2-43 **3** *4 1/2* **Siyabona (USA)**[19] [3810] 3-9-0 74 .... LDettori 1 — 68
(Saeed Bin Suroor) *hld up bhd: rdn and hdwy over 2f out: chsd ldng pair and hung rt 2f out: wl btn after* — 6/1[3]
6 **4** *2 1/2* **Orange River (IRE)**[45] [2973] 3-9-0 0 .... JimmyFortune 6 — 62+
(J H M Gosden) *s.i.s: hld up in rr: rdn and effrt wl over 2f out: wl outpcd 2f: wnt modest 4th ent fnl f* — 8/1
02 **5** *6* **Shadayid Khanum (IRE)**[33] [3342] 3-9-0 0 .... MartinDwyer 5 — 48
(M P Tregoning) *in tch in midfield: hdwy 3f out: chsd ldr briefly wl over 2f out: wknd 2f out: eased fnl f* — 12/1
6 *9* **Spring Season** 3-9-0 0 .... TPQueally 3 — 27
(H R A Cecil) *chsd ldrs: wnt 2nd over 3f out tl wl over 2f out: sn wknd: t.o and eased fnl f* — 3/1[2]
66- **7** *2 1/4* **Saratee**[299] [5881] 3-9-0 0 .... SebSanders 2 — 22
(C E Brittain) *chsd ldr tl over 3f out: wknd qckly over 2f out: t.o and eased fnl f* — 25/1

1m 41.06s (0.46) **Going Correction** +0.025s/f (Good) — **7 Ran SP% 114.1**
Speed ratings (Par 99): **98,92,87,85,79 70,67**
toteswinger: 1&2 £5.50, 1&3 £2.50, 2&3 £6.90. CSF £20.21 TOTE £2.20: £1.30, £5.70; EX 21.60.
Owner Mr & Mrs Neil Weekes **Bred** The Duke Of Devonshire **Trained** Newmarket, Suffolk

FOCUS
An ordinary maiden won in good style by the unexposed and well-regarded Basque Beauty, who looks capable of holding her own in better company.
Siyabona(USA) Official explanation: jockey said filly had a breathing problem

4448 CATHAY PACIFIC AIRWAYS H'CAP — 1m 4f
4:35 (4:36) (Class 4) (0-85,84) 3-Y-O — £6,476 (£1,927; £963; £481) Stalls High

Form — RPR
0313 **1** **Any Given Day (IRE)**[32] [3380] 3-8-13 **76** .... RichardMullen 2 — 85
(D M Simcock) *hld up in tch: hdwy 3f out: chsd ldr over 2f out: led over 1f out: edgd rt u.p: styd on wl* — 7/2[2]
1-10 **2** *1* **Sleepy Hollow**[66] [2342] 3-8-13 **76** .... SteveDrowne 1 — 83
(H Morrison) *s.i.s: hld up in rr: hdwy on outer over 2f out: edgd rt jst over 1f out: chsd wnr ins fnl f: no imp last 100yds* — 6/1
1040 **3** *1/2* **Yes Mr President (IRE)**[30] [3459] 3-9-1 **78** .... JoeFanning 3 — 84
(M Johnston) *chsd ldr: rdn 3f out: stl pressing ldrs and sltly hmpd jst over 1f out: kpt on same pce ins fnl f* — 9/1
0-21 **4** *1 1/4* **Craigstown**[28] [3521] 3-9-5 **82** .... LDettori 8 — 86
(Saeed Bin Suroor) *led: rdn wl over 2f out: drvn and hdd over 1f out: looked hld whn short of room and lost 2nd ins fnl f: wl hld after* — 2/1[1]
315 **5** *nse* **Deadly Silence (USA)**[43] [3048] 3-9-7 **84** .... ShaneKelly 5 — 88
(Dr J D Scargill) *t.k.h: hld up in tch: rdn and unable qck over 2f out: keeping on whn short of room and swtchd lft ent fnl f: plugged on but nvr pce to threaten ldrs* — 9/2[3]
0021 **6** *1 1/2* **Mahadee (IRE)**[11] [4086] 3-8-6 **69** .... (b) LiamJones 4 — 71
(C E Brittain) *t.k.h: hld up in rr: effrt and nt clr run on rail over 2f out: grad edgd out rt: kpt on but nvr pce to trble ldrs* — 10/1
0243 **7** *1/2* **Red Merlin (IRE)**[20] [3793] 3-8-9 **72** .... SebSanders 6 — 73
(C G Cox) *t.k.h: trckd ldrs: rdn ent fnl 2f: fnd little and sn btn* — 8/1

2m 31.33s (-4.17) **Going Correction** -0.325s/f (Firm) — **7 Ran SP% 118.2**
Speed ratings (Par 102): **100,99,99,98,98 97,96**
toteswinger: 1&2 £4.70, 1&3 £6.70, 2&3 £8.70. CSF £25.77 CT £176.69 TOTE £4.70: £2.60, £3.40; EX 29.10 Trifecta £580.80 Pool: £1,483.58 - 1.89 winning units. Place 6 £226.64, Place 5 £156.97..
Owner Malcolm Martin Partnership **Bred** Ralph And Helen O'Brien **Trained** Newmarket, Suffolk
■ Stewards' Enquiry : Richard Mullen one-day ban: careless riding (Aug 10)

FOCUS
Sound handicap form.
T/Jkpt: Not won. T/Plt: £104.20 to a £1 stake. Pool: £138,943.56. 973.14 winning tickets. T/Qpdt: £39.40 to a £1 stake. Pool: £6,945.88. 130.20 winning tickets. SP

3713 CARLISLE (R-H)
Sunday, July 27

OFFICIAL GOING: Firm
Wind: Almost nil Weather: Sunny

4449 NORTHERN RACING CLUB MAIDEN AUCTION STKS — 5f
1:55 (1:56) (Class 5) 2-Y-O — £2,590 (£770; £385; £192) Stalls High

Form — RPR
262 **1** **Sloop Johnb**[32] [3365] 2-8-12 0 .... PaulHanagan 7 — 74+
(R A Fahey) *t.k.h: mde all: hrd pressed fr over 1f out: hung lft ins fnl f: kpt on wl* — 2/7[1]
0 **2** *1/2* **Wotatomboy**[25] [3598] 2-8-7 0 .... MichaelJStainton(3) 5 — 68+
(R M Whitaker) *t.k.h: cl up: effrt and chal over 1f out: kpt on: hld nr fin* — 33/1
6 **3** *5* **Abbey Steps (IRE)**[9] [4169] 2-8-12 0 .... DavidAllan 6 — 52+
(T D Easterby) *in tch: rdn over 2f out: rallied over 1f out: nt rch first two* — 5/1[2]
06 **4** *5* **Jaslyn (IRE)**[36] [3259] 2-8-4 0 .... RoystonFfrench 2 — 25
(J R Weymes) *prom tl rdn and outpcd fr 2f out* — 16/1
200 **5** *3/4* **El Bobby (IRE)**[39] [3140] 2-8-9 0 .... (b[1]) PaulMulrennan 9 — 27
(J R Weymes) *in tch: drvn over 2f out: sn btn* — 14/1[3]
05 **6** *1 1/4* **Wee Bizzom**[10] [4113] 2-7-11 0 .... CharlotteKerton(7) 8 — 18
(A Berry) *sn chsng ldrs: hung lft and wknd fr 2f out* — 100/1

61.10 secs (0.30) **Going Correction** -0.175s/f (Firm) — **6 Ran SP% 110.9**
Speed ratings (Par 94): **90,89,81,73,72 70**
toteswinger: 1&2 £2.50, 1&3 £1.10, 2&3 £6.70. CSF £13.60 TOTE £1.20: £1.02, £8.80; EX 15.30.
Owner Jonathan Gill **Bred** Manor Farm Stud (rutland) **Trained** Musley Bank, N Yorks

FOCUS
An uncompetitive event in which the pace was just fair and the first two pulled clear in the closing stages. The winner can rate higher and the runner-up showed improved form.

NOTEBOOK
Sloop Johnb, who had previously run his best races in soft ground, did not have to improve too much to win an uncompetitive event on ground that looked plenty quick enough for him. He has plenty of physical scope and may be able to improve further granted an easier surface. (op 1-2)
Wotatomboy, soundly beaten after a tardy start on her debut, failed to settle but fared a good deal better against a rival that had shown fair form in maidens. She pulled clear of the remainder and is capable of winning races. (op 25-1 tchd 40-1)
Abbey Steps(IRE), who took the eye in the paddock as a workmanlike sort with scope, bettered the form of his racecourse debut and left the strong impression that the step up to 6f+ would be more to his liking. He is one to keep an eye on. (tchd 9-2 and 11-2)
Jaslyn(IRE), who had previously been well beaten in maidens, again underlined her vulnerability in this type of event. She will need to drop in grade or step into modest handicap company if she is to win a race. (op 14-1 tchd 12-1)
El Bobby(IRE), who has only one piece of worthwhile form to his name, was soundly beaten in the first-time blinkers and he is of little immediate interest. Official explanation: jockey said gelding would not face the first-time blinkers (op 8-1)
Wee Bizzom was again soundly beaten in the face of a stiff task and needs to drop considerably in grade. (op 66-1)

4450 CBS OUTDOOR H'CAP — 5f
2:30 (2:30) (Class 5) (0-70,70) 3-Y-O — £2,590 (£770; £385; £192) Stalls High

Form — RPR
4131 **1** **Mandalay King (IRE)**[15] [3952] 3-8-2 **56** .... PatrickDonaghy(5) 2 — 67
(Mrs Marjorie Fife) *hld up in tch: effrt and hdwy over 1f out: led ins fnl f: r.o* — 3/1[2]
0-20 **2** *1/2* **Ridge Wood Dani (IRE)**[30] [3455] 3-9-7 **70** .... DavidAllan 10 — 79
(E J Alston) *led tl hdd ins fnl f: kpt on same pce towards fin* — 9/4[1]
0463 **3** *1 3/4* **Andrasta**[6] [4242] 3-7-9 **51** oh3 .... CharlotteKerton(7) 3 — 54
(A Berry) *trckd ldrs: effrt and hung rt over 1f out: one pce ins fnl f* — 33/1
0403 **4** *1* **Irving Place**[6] [4236] 3-9-2 **65** .... (p) PaulHanagan 1 — 64
(R A Fahey) *racd on outside: outpcd after 2f: edgd rt and rallied over 1f out: nrst fin* — 6/1
5405 **5** *1 1/2* **Gelert (IRE)**[15] [3953] 3-8-2 **51** oh5 .... (b[1]) DaleGibson 8 — 45
(Peter Grayson) *prom: drvn 1/2-way: one pce over 1f out* — 50/1
6105 **6** *1/2* **Bishopbriggs (USA)**[7] [4216] 3-9-7 **70** .... PaulMulrennan 5 — 62
(S Parr) *pressed ldr: rdn over 2f out: edgd rt and wknd over 1f out* — 8/1
4042 **7** *1/2* **Legendary Guest**[3] [4329] 3-9-2 **65** .... (p) TonyHamilton 7 — 55
(D W Barker) *prom tl hung rt and wknd wl over 1f out* — 4/1[3]
5140 **8** *nk* **Mujahope**[15] [3960] 3-8-7 **56** .... (v) RoystonFfrench 6 — 45
(C J Teague) *dwlt: bhd and rdn 1/2-way: nvr rchd ldrs* — 25/1
4220 **9** *3/4* **Paddy Jack**[10] [4118] 3-8-8 **60** .... (p) NeilBrown(3) 4 — 46
(J R Weymes) *bhd: drvn over 2f out: nvr rchd ldrs* — 14/1

59.81 secs (-0.99) **Going Correction** -0.175s/f (Firm) — **9 Ran SP% 116.6**
Speed ratings (Par 100): **100,99,96,94,92 91,90,90,89**
toteswinger: 1&2 £2.60, 1&3 £35.10, 2&3 £5.60. CSF £10.13 CT £181.64 TOTE £3.60: £1.60, £1.50, £4.80; EX 11.70.
Owner Green Lane **Bred** Forenaghts Stud And Dermot Cantillon **Trained** Stillington, N Yorks

FOCUS
An ordinary sprint run at a decent gallop and this form should prove reliable. The winner is a progressive sort who won with more in hand than the winning margin suggests.
Bishopbriggs(USA) Official explanation: jockey said gelding hung right-handed throughout
Legendary Guest Official explanation: jockey said gelding hung right-handed throughout

4451 PES CLAIMING STKS — 7f 200y
3:05 (3:05) (Class 6) 3-Y-O+ — £2,047 (£604; £302) Stalls High

Form — RPR
3426 **1** **Rowan Lodge (IRE)**[7] [4217] 6-9-1 62 .... (b) PJMcDonald(3) 7 — 67
(Ollie Pears) *t.k.h in midfield: hdwy to ld over 1f out: hld on wl fnl f* — 8/1
2554 **2** *2 1/4* **Bold Indian (IRE)**[9] [4148] 4-9-2 60 .... NeilBrown(3) 5 — 63
(Miss L A Perratt) *hld up on outside: hdwy and edgd rt 2f out: kpt on fnl f: nt rch wnr* — 11/2[2]
031R **3** *hd* **Claret And Amber**[39] [3142] 6-9-4 74 .... PaulHanagan 1 — 61
(R A Fahey) *cl up: led over 3f out to over 1f out: kpt on same pce fnl f* — 1/1[1]
4040 **4** *hd* **Nok Twice (IRE)**[6] [4245] 7-9-5 66 .... PaulPickard(7) 13 — 69
(D Carroll) *hld up in tch: effrt and swtchd rt wl over 1f out: kpt on u.p fnl f* — 20/1
4140 **5** *nk* **Pianoforte (USA)**[9] [4172] 6-9-3 60 .... (p) DavidAllan 17 — 59+
(E J Alston) *hld up on ins: nt clr run over 2f out to over 1f out: r.o fnl f* 7/1[3]
3001 **6** *1* **Royal Applord**[12] [4043] 3-9-4 68 .... PaulMulrennan 4 — 64
(K A Ryan) *prom: effrt and ev ch over 1f out: one pce fnl f* — 10/1
4-64 **7** *2 3/4* **Riverhill (IRE)**[46] [2940] 5-9-5 47 .... RoystonFfrench 16 — 53
(J Howard Johnson) *in tch: effrt over 2f out: no ex over 1f out* — 25/1
0004 **8** *3 1/4* **Princely Ted (IRE)**[15] [3951] 7-9-4 50 .... LeeVickers(3) 8 — 47
(W Clay) *t.k.h: prom tl rdn and wknd fr 2f out* — 33/1
0-00 **9** *3 1/4* **Second Reef**[21] [3757] 6-9-4 44 .... DaleGibson 3 — 37
(T A K Cuthbert) *hld up: effrt on outside over 2f out: sn no imp* — 100/1
0-00 **10** *1 3/4* **Feeling (IRE)**[7] [3947] 4-8-9 56 .... SophieDoyle(7) 9 — 31
(W Clay) *s.i.s: hld up: rdn 3f out: n.d* — 66/1
1300 **11** *2 1/2* **Blue Empire (IRE)**[23] [3662] 7-9-3 62 .... (p) TonyHamilton 14 — 26
(Ollie Pears) *chsd ldrs tl wknd over 2f out* — 25/1
6000 **12** *1/2* **Telepathic (IRE)**[46] [2936] 8-8-11 43 .... SladeO'Hara(5) 10 — 24
(A Berry) *rrd s: a bhd* — 100/1
13 *8* **Pennybid (IRE)**[67] 6-9-5 0 .... PAspell 2 — 8
(C R Wilson) *racd wd in rr: wknd fr 3f out* — 100/1
00/0 **14** *10* **One Trick Pony**[20] [3784] 5-8-12 44 .... (p) AndrewMullen(3) 15 — —
(B Storey) *led to over 3f out: sn lost pl* — 100/1

0 15 32 **Idle Court**[15] 3955 3-8-6 0 .... TWilliams 11 —
(Bruce Hellier) *s.i.s: a bhd* **100/1**

1m 39.66s (-0.34) **Going Correction** -0.175s/f (Firm)
WFA 3 from 4yo+ 8lb **15** Ran SP% **119.9**
Speed ratings (Par 101): **94,91,91,91,91 90,87,84,80,79 76,76,68,58,26**
toteswinger: 1&2 £7.20, 1&3 £5.80, 2&3 £2.30. CSF £48.14 TOTE £10.30: £2.40, £2.40, £1.20; EX 49.80.
Owner K C West **Bred** M P B Bloodstock Ltd **Trained** Norton, N Yorks
■ Stewards' Enquiry : Sophie Doyle one-day ban: used whip when out of contention (tba)

FOCUS
The usual mixed bag for this run-of-the-mill claimer. The pace was sound and the form looks solid enough.
Royal Applord Official explanation: jockey said gelding was unsuited by the firm going

4452 BURGH BARONY PLATE (H'CAP) 2m 1f 52y
3:40 (3:40) (Class 4) (0-80,68) 4-Y-O+ **£4,857** (£1,445; £722; £360) **Stalls** High

Form RPR
3521 1 **Let It Be**[7] 4220 7-8-12 **59** .... PaulHanagan 7 65
(K G Reveley) *early ldr: pressed ldr: led over 3f out: hld on wl u.p fnl f* **11/10**[1]
0000 2 2 **Lodgician (IRE)**[7] 4220 6-7-13 **49** oh2 .... AndrewMullen(3) 5 53
(K G Reveley) *hld up in tch: hdwy to press wnr over 2f out: edgd rt and one pce ins fnl f* **9/1**
4235 3 6 **Thewhirlingdervish (IRE)**[12] 4046 10-9-7 **68** .... DavidAllan 4 64
(T D Easterby) *trckd ldrs: effrt 3f out: no ex over 1f out* **5/2**[2]
2453 4 9 **Danzatrice**[12] 4046 6-9-4 **68** .... PJMcDonald(3) 6 54
(C W Thornton) *hld up: hdwy over 3f out: wknd over 2f out* **7/2**[3]
0000 5 15 **Monte Pattino (USA)**[22] 3718 4-8-2 **54** oh4 ow5(vt) PatrickDonaghy(5) 2 22
(C J Teague) *dwlt: early reminders and sn led: hdd over 3f out: sn wknd* **100/1**

3m 47.57s (-5.43) **Going Correction** -0.175s/f (Firm) **5** Ran SP% **109.4**
Speed ratings (Par 105): **105,104,101,97,89**
toteswinger: 1&2 £19.50. CSF £11.47 TOTE £1.90: £1.20, £3.30; EX 8.80.
Owner A Frame **Bred** Sir Eric Parker **Trained** Lingdale, Redcar & Cleveland

FOCUS
An ordinary handicap in which the pace was fair and the winner did not need to run to recent form to score.

4453 SWIFTS H'CAP 6f 192y
4:15 (4:17) (Class 5) (0-75,73) 3-Y-O+ **£2,590** (£770; £385; £192) **Stalls** High

Form RPR
2604 1 **Grand Opera (IRE)**[24] 3643 5-9-12 **67** ....(b) PaulMulrennan 4 76
(J Howard Johnson) *hld up in tch: rdn over 2f out: rallied and led ins fnl f: styd on* **8/1**
1440 2 1 ¼ **The Salwick Flyer (IRE)**[50] 2846 5-9-3 **58** .... RoystonFfrench 6 64
(Miss L A Perratt) *w ldr: led over 2f out to ins fnl f: kpt on same pce* **9/1**
0001 3 1 ½ **Horatio Carter**[22] 3717 3-9-8 **73** .... NeilBrown(3) 10 72
(K A Ryan) *trckd ldrs: effrt over 2f out: one pce fnl f* **5/2**[1]
2113 4 3 ¼ **Zabeel Tower**[15] 3957 5-10-0 **69** ....(p) TonyHamilton 8 62
(R Allan) *led to over 2f out: outpcd fnl f* **11/2**[3]
0000 5 2 ½ **Pay Time**[18] 3834 9-8-7 **51** .... MichaelJStainton(3) 3 37
(R E Barr) *t.k.h: prom: edgd rt and wknd over 1f out* **10/1**
0455 6 1 ¼ **Cheery Cat (USA)**[9] 4174 4-9-2 **52** ....(p) PJMcDonald(3) 1 43
(D W Barker) *chsd ldrs tl wknd fr 2f out* **9/2**[2]
0500 7 1 ¼ **Orpen Bid (IRE)**[21] 3753 3-7-12 **53** oh5 ow3 .... SophieDoyle(7) 2 29
(A M Crow) *hld up: pushed along over 2f out: sn outpcd* **50/1**
045 8 ½ **First Swallow**[22] 3712 3-9-0 **62** .... PaulHanagan 9 37
(R A Fahey) *bhd: struggling over 3f out: nvr on terms* **7/1**
0200 9 ½ **Avontuur (FR)**[9] 4174 6-9-5 **60** ....(b) DaleGibson 7 37
(Mrs R A Carr) *taken early to post: missed break: a bhd* **10/1**

1m 24.85s (-2.25) **Going Correction** -0.175s/f (Firm)
WFA 3 from 4yo+ 7lb **9** Ran SP% **115.9**
Speed ratings (Par 103): **105,103,101,98,95 93,92,91,91**
toteswinger: 1&2 £13.20, 1&3 £6.30, 2&3 £6.40. CSF £77.49 CT £233.82 TOTE £10.70: £2.90, £3.40, £1.80; EX 84.60.
Owner Andrea & Graham Wylie **Bred** Ballyhane Stud **Trained** Billy Row, Co Durham

FOCUS
A run-of-the-mill handicap in which the pace was sound. The form looks solid with the first two to their marks.

4454 TURFTV MAIDEN STKS 6f 192y
4:50 (4:50) (Class 5) 3-Y-O+ **£2,590** (£770; £385; £192) **Stalls** High

Form RPR
0032 1 **Tartan Gigha (IRE)**[68] 2269 3-9-3 **80** .... RoystonFfrench 3 82
(M Johnston) *led: rdn and hung lft over 1f out: wnt bdly lft ins fnl f: r.o* **1/2**[1]
34- 2 3 ¼ **Beauchamp Wizard**[221] 7191 3-9-3 0 .... PaulMulrennan 4 73
(G A Butler) *t.k.h early: trckd ldrs: effrt and ev ch 2f out: kpt on u.p fnl f* **2/1**[2]
3 8 **Kama Night (IRE)** 3-9-3 0 .... TonyHamilton 1 51
(G A Swinbank) *dwlt: hld up in tch: outpcd over 3f out: rallied over 1f out: no imp* **12/1**[3]
-0 4 shd **Meinardus (IRE)**[157] 634 3-9-0 0 .... NeilBrown(3) 5 51
(T D Barron) *missed break: bhd tl hdwy 2f out: kpt on fnl f: nvr nr ldrs* **40/1**
0/00 5 6 **Frill A Minute**[36] 3260 4-9-0 15 .... SladeO'Hara(5) 7 30?
(Miss L C Siddall) *prom: drvn over 3f out: wknd 2f out* **250/1**
0600 6 13 **Senora Lenorah**[15] 3952 4-8-12 35 ....(t) PaulPickard(7) 6 —
(D A Nolan) *prom to 1/2-way: sn lost pl* **250/1**
00-0 7 27 **Ronnies Girl**[10] 4116 4-9-5 0 .... DavidAllan 2 —
(C J Teague) *chsd ldrs to 1/2-way: sn struggling* **250/1**

1m 26.4s (-0.70) **Going Correction** -0.175s/f (Firm)
WFA 3 from 4yo 7lb **7** Ran SP% **111.3**
Speed ratings (Par 103): **97,93,84,84,77 62,31**
toteswinger: 1&2 £1.10, 1&3 £1.70, 2&3 £1.50. CSF £1.63 TOTE £1.60: £1.10, £1.80; EX 2.20.
Owner Mrs I Bird **Bred** Gainsborough Stud Management Ltd **Trained** Middleham Moor, N Yorks

FOCUS
An uncompetitive event in which the two market leaders pulled clear of the rest in the straight. The pace was fair and the form makes sense rated around the front pair.

4455 STOBART FACTOR TALENT SEARCH H'CAP 1m 1f 61y
5:20 (5:20) (Class 5) (0-70,67) 3-Y-O **£2,590** (£770; £385; £192) **Stalls** High

Form RPR
0012 1 **Deep Winter**[26] 3578 3-9-7 **67** .... PaulHanagan 7 82+
(R A Fahey) *trckd ldrs: rdn over 2f out: led over 1f out: styd on strly to go clr fnl f* **11/8**[1]
0-06 2 4 ½ **Madison Heights (IRE)**[24] 3641 3-9-1 **61** .... TonyHamilton 2 63
(J Howard Johnson) *cl up: led over 2f out to over 1f out: kpt on: nt pce of wnr* **16/1**
00-0 3 1 ½ **Beauchamp Warrior**[89] 1696 3-9-2 **62** .... PaulMulrennan 9 61
(G A Butler) *hld up: hdwy over 2f out: kpt on fnl f: no imp* **25/1**
0002 4 ½ **Top Man Dan (IRE)**[12] 4049 3-8-11 **57** .... DavidAllan 1 55
(D Carroll) *hld up in tch: effrt and ev ch 2f out: one pce fnl f* **10/1**
3253 5 2 ¼ **Castlebury (IRE)**[10] 4115 3-9-2 **65** .... NeilBrown(3) 3 58
(G A Swinbank) *t.k.h: hld up in tch: effrt over 2f out: sn outpcd* **7/1**[3]
0033 6 9 **Bourse (IRE)**[6] 4241 3-9-1 **64** ....(p) PJMcDonald(3) 5 38
(R Johnson) *cl up: ev ch over 2f out: rdn and wknd wl over 1f out* **4/1**[2]
2211 7 nse **Natural Rhythm (IRE)**[8] 4180 3-8-12 **61** ....(b) MichaelJStainton(3) 8 35
(Mrs R A Carr) *t.k.h: led to over 2f out: sn wknd* **4/1**[2]

1m 57.16s (-0.44) **Going Correction** -0.175s/f (Firm) **7** Ran SP% **113.4**
Speed ratings (Par 100): **94,90,88,88,86 78,78**
toteswinger: 1&2 £10.10, 1&3 £5.70, 2&3 £13.00. CSF £25.78 CT £380.36 TOTE £2.00: £1.50, £8.60; EX 32.10 Place 6 £4.56, Place 5 £3.63..
Owner R A Fahey **Bred** Gainsborough Stud Management Ltd **Trained** Musley Bank, N Yorks

FOCUS
Not a strong handicap but the winner is a progressive sort who won with plenty in hand. The form is best rated around the fourth to his latest mark.
Natural Rhythm(IRE) Official explanation: jockey said colt was unsuited by the firm going
T/Plt: £6.50 to a £1 stake. Pool: £50,060.64. 5,569.35 winning tickets. T/Qpdt: £4.00 to a £1 stake. Pool: £2,723.39. 501.40 winning tickets. RY

4169 PONTEFRACT (L-H)
Sunday, July 27

OFFICIAL GOING: Good to firm (7.9)
12mm water had been put down over the two previous days but on a very hot day the ground was described as 'very firm'.
Wind: Almost nil Weather: Fine, sunny and very hot

4456 TOLENT CONSTRUCTION MAIDEN STKS 5f
2:05 (2:07) (Class 4) 2-Y-O **£5,180** (£1,541; £770; £384) **Stalls** Low

Form RPR
2 1 **Raedah (USA)**[32] 3378 2-8-12 0 .... PhilipRobinson 2 80
(M A Jarvis) *mde virtually all: rdn and hung rt fnl f: jst hld on* **1/5**[1]
2 nk **Magic Cat** 2-9-3 0 .... AndrewElliott 7 84
(K R Burke) *sn chsng ldrs on outside: wnt 2nd 1f out: styd on wl towards fin* **10/1**[2]
45 3 4 ½ **Doric Echo**[9] 4169 2-9-3 0 .... DO'Donohoe 4 68
(B Smart) *chsd ldrs: kpt on same pce fnl f* **12/1**[3]
5 4 2 ¼ **Chimbonda**[31] 3417 2-9-3 0 .... EddieAhern 3 60
(S Parr) *chsd ldrs: kpt on same pce appr fnl f* **14/1**
0040 5 nk **Port Ronan (USA)**[32] 3365 2-9-0 0 .... MarkLawson(3) 5 59
(J S Wainwright) *w ldrs: one pce appr fnl f* **33/1**
6 3 ½ **Pollish** 2-8-12 0 .... StephenDonohoe 1 41
(A Berry) *s.s: detached in last: kpt on fnl f* **50/1**
0 7 15 **Liliaceae**[9] 4164 2-8-9 0 .... DuranFentiman(3) 6 —
(D Shaw) *s.i.s: sme hdwy 2f out: sn lost pl and eased* **100/1**

64.21 secs (0.91) **Going Correction** -0.075s/f (Good) **7** Ran SP% **112.7**
Speed ratings (Par 96): **89,88,81,77,77 71,47**
toteswinger: 1&2 £1.20, 1&3 £1.30, 2&3 £4.20. CSF £2.98 TOTE £1.20: £1.02, £3.00; EX 2.40.
Owner Hamdan Al Maktoum **Bred** Shadwell Farm LLC **Trained** Newmarket, Suffolk
■ Stewards' Enquiry : Philip Robinson caution: used whip with excessive frequency

FOCUS
An ordinary maiden and the suspicion was that the winner was not at her best on the very firm ground. The form is rated around the third, fourth and fifth.

NOTEBOOK
Raedah(USA), a sturdily-made filly, was initially keen going to post. She hung off the fence possibly feeling the firm ground and in the end did just enough. (op 1-4 tchd 2-7 tchd 1-3 in a place)
Magic Cat, first foal of a useful sprinter, strode out well going to post. Drawn widest of all, he hit back strongly near the line giving odds-on supporters a real fright. He deserves to go one better. (op 12-1 tchd 9-1)
Doric Echo, very warm on a hot day, settled better but in the end was no match for the first two. (tchd 10-1)
Chimbonda improved on his debut effort but will need to find plenty more to get competitive. (op 12-1 tchd 16-1)
Port Ronan(USA), having his fifth start already, would surely be better off competing in low-grade nurseries. (op 25-1)
Pollish, very green to post, missed the break and was soon well behind. She gave connections a glimmer of hope passing one other in the final furlong. (op 33-1)

4457 YORKSHIRE SOCIETY H'CAP 1m 4f 8y
2:40 (2:40) (Class 5) (0-70,69) 3-Y-O+ **£3,885** (£1,156; £577; £288) **Stalls** Low

Form RPR
-143 1 **Master Nimbus**[16] 3912 8-8-12 **56** .... JamieMoriarty(3) 10 64
(J J Quinn) *trckd ldrs gng wl: led 1f out: drvn out* **9/2**[2]
6253 2 1 ½ **Sporting Gesture**[17] 3864 11-9-7 **69** .... NSLawes(7) 5 75
(M W Easterby) *trckd ldrs on inner: nt clr run over 2f out: styd on to take 2nd nr fin* **7/1**
56-3 3 ½ **Dimashq**[33] 3335 6-8-10 **51** oh6 .... MickyFenton 14 56
(P T Midgley) *led tl 1f out: kpt on same pce* **25/1**
1P01 4 3 ¼ **Caffari (GER)**[11] 4077 3-8-9 **62** .... AndrewElliott 1 62+
(K R Burke) *mid-div: n.m.r on inner over 2f out: styd on: nt rch ldrs* **11/4**[1]
54-1 5 8 **Chookie Hamilton**[27] 3550 4-9-4 **59** .... PaulFessey 4 46
(Miss L A Perratt) *hld up in rr: hdwy over 3f out: edgd rt over 1f out: sn wknd* **11/2**[3]
6-60 6 4 **Lady Killer Queen**[78] 2006 4-9-5 **60** ....(v[1]) EddieAhern 9 41
(D Carroll) *hdwy to chse ldrs after 3f: wknd 2f out* **22/1**
0060 7 hd **Campli (IRE)**[13] 4029 6-9-0 **55** .... DO'Donohoe 11 35
(Micky Hammond) *mid-div: hdwy 5f out: lost pl over 2f out* **25/1**
0003 8 2 **Templetuohy Max (IRE)**[11] 4077 3-7-9 **51** oh1....(v) DuranFentiman(3) 3 28
(J D Bethell) *t.k.h in rr: sme hdwy 3f out: nvr on terms* **20/1**
040- 9 hd **Mabel (IRE)**[72] 6330 5-9-3 **58** .... PatCosgrave 2 35
(J Mackie) *dwlt: in rr and sn drvn along: nvr a factor* **11/1**
6620 10 20 **Wulimaster (USA)**[12] 4048 5-8-9 **53** .... MarkLawson(3) 7 —
(D W Barker) *dwlt: hdwy on wd outside over 5f out: chal over 3f out: lost pl over 2f out: sn bhd and eased* **7/1**
052- 11 1 ¾ **Monet's Lady (IRE)**[426] 2096 4-8-3 **51** oh5 .... BMcHugh(7) 13 —
(R A Fahey) *trckd ldrs: rdn over 3f out: lost pl over 2f out: sn bhd* **20/1**

064 **12** *19* **Requia**[34] 3310 3-9-1 **68** FergusSweeney 6 —
(H Candy) *hld up in midfield: lost pl over 2f out: eased and sn bhd* **12/1**

2m 38.5s (-2.30) **Going Correction** -0.075s/f (Good)
WFA 3 from 4yo+ 12lb 12 Ran SP% **122.8**
Speed ratings (Par 103): **104,103,102,100,95 92,92,91,90,77 76,63**
toteswinger: 1&2 £6.30, 1&3 £14.00, 2&3 £60.50. CSF £34.15 CT £717.07 TOTE £5.50: £2.00, £2.40, £6.10; EX 30.70.
Owner J H Hewitt **Bred** A H Bennett **Trained** Settrington, N Yorks

FOCUS
A low-grade handicap but won in most convincing fashion by the in-form Master Nimbus. The runner-up is rated close to form and sets the standard.
Requia Official explanation: jockey said filly had no more to give

4458 GRAHAM ROCK MEMORIAL H'CAP 1m 2f 6y
3:15 (3:15) (Class 5) (0-70,67) 3-Y-0+ **£4,533** (£1,348; £674; £336) **Stalls** Low

Form RPR
1310 **1** **Holiday Cocktail**[13] 4015 6-9-13 **66** (p) LPKeniry 8 75
(J J Quinn) *trckd ldrs: effrt over 2f out: styd on to ld fnl 100yds* **7/1**
2212 **2** *1 3/4* **Sceilin (IRE)**[24] 3644 4-9-4 **57** (t) PatCosgrave 2 63
(J Mackie) *chsd ldrs: drvn 3f out: styd on wl to take 2nd wl ins fnl f* **7/2**[2]
2335 **3** *nk* **Jackie Kiely**[9] 4156 7-9-10 **63** (t) J-PGuillambert 14 68
(R Brotherton) *mid-div: effrt 3f out: edgd rt 1f out: styd on* **9/1**
2206 **4** *nk* **Zach's Harmoney (USA)**[4] 4309 4-9-12 **65** PhilipRobinson 3 69
(P W Hiatt) *led: qcknd over 2f out: hdd and no ex ins fnl f* **8/1**
5431 **5** *1/2* **Dan Tucker**[4] 4295 4-9-5 **65** AndreaAtzeni(7) 10 68+
(N Tinkler) *hld up in last: hdwy on ins 2f out: styd on wl ins fnl f: nt rch ldrs* **11/4**[1]
342 **6** *nk* **Princelywallywogan**[15] 3954 6-10-0 **67** StephenDonohoe 15 70
(John A Harris) *in rr: effrt on outer over 2f out: hung rt and kpt on fnl f* **6/1**[3]
5030 **7** *2 3/4* **Grethel (IRE)**[13] 4015 4-8-10 **56** BMcHugh(7) 6 53
(A Berry) *prom: drvn 3f out: one pce* **28/1**
54-0 **8** *3 3/4* **Royal Indulgence**[15] 3947 8-9-5 **61** MarcHalford(3) 11 51
(W M Brisbourne) *s.s: sme hdwy 6f out: wknd over 2f out* **20/1**
0304 **9** *nk* **Ming Vase**[9] 4172 6-8-9 **48** oh1 MickyFenton 7 37
(P T Midgley) *in rr: hdwy over 2f out: lost pl over 1f out* **25/1**
6034 **10** *2* **Boppys Pride**[179] 352 5-8-9 **48** oh1 EddieAhern 4 33
(P T Midgley) *chsd ldrs: lost pl over 1f out* **16/1**
3000 **11** *1 3/4* **Alberts Story (USA)**[19] 3814 4-8-9 **51** (b[1]) JamieMoriarty(3) 12 33
(R A Fahey) *chsd ldrs: rdn over 2f out: sn wknd* **25/1**
0100 **12** *1 3/4* **Moment Of Clarity**[19] 3814 6-9-3 **63** (p) StacyRenwick(7) 1 41
(R C Guest) *in rr-div: nvr a factor* **22/1**

2m 11.96s (-1.74) **Going Correction** -0.075s/f (Good)
WFA 3 from 4yo+ 10lb 12 Ran SP% **122.9**
Speed ratings (Par 103): **103,101,101,101,100 100,98,95,95,93 92,90**
toteswinger: 1&2 £3.10, 1&3 £16.60, 2&3 £8.90. CSF £30.51 CT £231.83 TOTE £8.60: £3.00, £2.00, £2.10; EX 42.40.
Owner Estio Racing **Bred** Mrs W H Gibson Fleming **Trained** Settrington, N Yorks

FOCUS
A low-grade handicap run at just a steady pace and rated through the fourth.
Princelywallywogan Official explanation: jockey said gelding hung right
Grethel(IRE) Official explanation: jockey said filly hung right

4459 POMFRET STKS (LISTED RACE) 1m 4y
3:50 (3:51) (Class 1) 3-Y-0+ **£25,546** (£9,684; £4,846; £2,416) **Stalls** Low

Form RPR
0232 **1** **Choose Your Moment**[10] 4122 3-8-7 **102** EddieAhern 6 108
(P C Haslam) *trckd ldr: effrt 3f out: styd on to ld post 100yds* **2/1**[1]
3001 **2** *3* **Dream Lodge (IRE)**[3] 4330 4-9-1 **92** (v) J-PGuillambert 7 103
(J G Given) *led: hrd rdn over 1f out: hdd and no ex ins fnl f* **2/1**[1]
4-31 **3** *3 1/4* **Easy Target (FR)**[9] 4153 3-8-7 **100** MickyFenton 4 94
(B Smart) *swvd rt s: t.k.h in 3rd: rdn 3f out: kpt on: nvr a threat* **9/2**[3]
5134 **4** *7* **Appalachian Trail (IRE)**[29] 3498 7-9-5 **110** (b) JamieMoriarty 8 83
(Miss L A Perratt) *s.s: hld up in last: effrt over 3f out: rdn over 2f out: nvr on terms: eased towards fin* **3/1**[2]

1m 43.01s (-2.89) **Going Correction** -0.075s/f (Good)
WFA 3 from 4yo+ 8lb 4 Ran SP% **109.8**
Speed ratings (Par 111): **111,108,104,97**
toteswinger: 1&2 £2.70. CSF £6.34 TOTE £3.20; EX 5.90.
Owner Mr & Mrs Duncan Davidson **Bred** Alpha Bloodstock Limited **Trained** Middleham Moor, N Yorks

FOCUS
A depleted field because of the very firm ground but a worthy winner. The runner-up is the best guide to the level.

NOTEBOOK
Choose Your Moment, who had the leader in his sights, gunned him down and scored in ready fashion. He richly deserved this. (op 5-2)
Dream Lodge(IRE), who scored in fast time at Doncaster three days earlier, made this a true test but he could never shake off the winner and was eventually put firmly in his place. (op 11-4)
Easy Target(FR), who dived right leaving the stalls, took a keen hold and this trip probably stretches him to the very limit. (op 4-1 tchd 7-2)
Appalachian Trail(IRE), who stood still when the traps opened, was never on terms and his rider eventually gave up. Official explanation: jockey said gelding was unsuited by the good to firm ground (op 2-1 tchd 10-3)

4460 SKYBET SUPPORTING THE YORKSHIRE RACING FESTIVAL H'CAP 6f
4:25 (4:25) (Class 3) (0-90,85) 3-Y-0+
£9,346 (£2,799; £1,399; £700; £349; £175) **Stalls** Low

Form RPR
5305 **1** **Bel Cantor**[15] 3973 5-8-13 **77** (p) KellyHarrison(5) 2 86
(W J H Ratcliffe) *mde all: qcknd 2f out: hld on towards fin* **12/1**
1110 **2** *nk* **Dressed To Dance (IRE)**[16] 3898 4-9-12 **85** (v) PatCosgrave 5 93
(P D Evans) *chsd ldrs: styd on wl to take 2nd ins fnl f: clsng at line* **13/2**[3]
5021 **3** *1 1/2* **Grazeon Gold Blend**[10] 4117 5-9-5 **78** MickyFenton 6 81
(J J Quinn) *chsd ldrs: kpt on same pce fnl f* **13/2**[3]
3403 **4** *3/4* **Signor Peltro**[16] 3905 5-9-12 **85** FergusSweeney 9 86
(H Candy) *hld up in rr: effrt over 2f out: styd on fnl f* **5/2**[1]
6004 **5** *shd* **H Harrison (IRE)**[9] 4174 8-8-13 **72** AndrewElliott 1 72
(I W McInnes) *w wnr: kpt on same pce fnl 2f* **12/1**
0601 **6** *1 3/4* **Wyatt Earp (IRE)**[7] 4218 7-9-5 **81** 6ex (b) JamieMoriarty(3) 8 76
(R A Fahey) *dwlt: swtchd lft after s: edgd rt 1f out: nvr nr ldrs* **7/2**[2]
1400 **7** *3/4* **Dickie Le Davoir**[9] 4171 4-9-3 **81** MarkCoumbe(5) 3 73
(John A Harris) *s.s: nvr a factor* **13/2**[3]
/0-0 **8** *nk* **Spirit Of France (IRE)**[16] 3928 6-9-10 **83** StephenDonohoe 4 74
(D Carroll) *in rr-div: nvr on terms* **25/1**
3410 **9** *3 1/2* **Flying Bantam (IRE)**[16] 3928 7-8-7 **73** BMcHugh(7) 7 53
(R A Fahey) *chsd ldrs: wknd over 1f out* **14/1**

1m 15.2s (-1.70) **Going Correction** -0.075s/f (Good) 9 Ran SP% **116.7**
Speed ratings (Par 107): **108,107,105,104,104 102,101,100,96**
toteswinger: 1&2 £10.60, 1&3 £13.90, 2&3 £5.70. CSF £88.40 CT £561.24 TOTE £17.20: £4.00, £2.20, £1.90; EX 105.20.
Owner W J H Ratcliffe **Bred** Henry And Mrs Rosemary Moszkowicz **Trained** Wensley, N Yorks

FOCUS
A competitive sprint handicap and the form looks rock solid rated through the runner-up.

NOTEBOOK
Bel Cantor repeated last year's win from an 8lb higher mark, dictating things and poaching sufficient lead coming off the home turn to see him home. (op 10-1 tchd 14-1)
Dressed To Dance(IRE), 6lb higher than her last win, loves fast ground and she was slowly but surely cutting down the winner's advantage all the way to the line. (op 6-1 tchd 5-1)
Grazeon Gold Blend, 6lb higher, ran right up to his very best. (tchd 11-2)
Signor Peltro, whose last win was in blinkers, stayed on from off the pace despite looking ill at ease on the very firm ground. (op 4-1)
H Harrison(IRE), having his 120th start, showed plenty of dash and is now 8lb below his last winning mark.
Wyatt Earp(IRE), under his penalty, had a wide draw and was not in the same mood as Redcar. (op 3-1)

4461 KEITH HAMMILL MEMORIAL MAIDEN STKS 1m 4y
5:00 (5:03) (Class 5) 3-4-Y-0 **£3,885** (£1,156; £577; £288) **Stalls** Low

Form RPR
030 **1** **Eton Fable (IRE)**[22] 3738 3-9-0 **63** JamieMoriarty(3) 13 72
(W J H Ratcliffe) *mde all: kpt on u.p fnl 2f: hld on towards fin* **14/1**
00 **2** *3/4* **Dream Of Olwyn (IRE)**[9] 4166 3-8-12 **0** PatCosgrave 8 65
(J G Given) *rrd s: t.k.h and sn trcking ldrs: wnt 2nd over 2f out: chal over 1f out: no ex towards fin* **12/1**
32 **3** *1 1/2* **Suede**[20] 3801 3-8-12 **0** PaulEddery 9 62
(Pat Eddery) *chsd ldrs: hung bdly rt and reminders over 4f out: wnt modest 3rd over 1f out: kpt on ins fnl f* **8/11**[1]
5 **4** *13* **Canyon Colours (USA)**[43] 3043 3-9-3 **0** EddieAhern 3 37
(G A Butler) *mid-div: hdwy over 3f out: tk modest 4th ins fnl f: nvr on terms* **7/2**[2]
0 **5** *2 1/2* **Thankfully (IRE)**[42] 3058 3-8-9 **0** MarcHalford(3) 12 26
(W M Brisbourne) *chsd ldrs: wknd over 1f out* **50/1**
0 **6** *nk* **Shaylee**[24] 3629 3-8-9 **0** DuranFentiman(3) 7 25
(T D Walford) *in rr: drvn over 3f out: nvr on terms* **33/1**
50 **7** *1* **Whipma Whopma Gate (IRE)**[9] 4166 3-8-12 **0** StephenDonohoe 10 23
(D Carroll) *towards rr: nvr on terms* **25/1**
0- **8** *2 1/4* **One Tou Many**[470] 1043 3-8-7 **0** KellyHarrison(5) 11 18
(C W Fairhurst) *sn bhd and drvn along* **28/1**
0 **9** *23* **Bandoran**[33] 3338 3-9-3 **0** FergusSweeney 5 —
(J R Holt) *trckd ldrs: t.k.h: lost pl over 2f out: sn bhd* **66/1**
00-0 **R** **Juce Of Hearts**[32] 3361 4-9-11 **43** MickyFenton 6 —
(John R Upson) *awkward to load: ref to r: tk no part* **50/1**
P **Redlynch** 3-9-3 **0** LeeEnstone 2 —
(S Parr) *s.s: sn p.u: lame* **7/1**[3]

1m 45.23s (-0.67) **Going Correction** -0.075s/f (Good)
WFA 3 from 4yo 8lb 11 Ran SP% **122.6**
Speed ratings (Par 103): **100,99,97,84,82 81,80,78,55,— —**
toteswinger: 1&2 £8.00, 1&3 £4.40, 2&3 £3.40. CSF £160.13 TOTE £17.70: £3.40, £2.60, £1.10; EX 154.80.
Owner The Gathering **Bred** Andrew Christy **Trained** Wensley, N Yorks
■ A first double for trainer Bill Ratcliffe.

FOCUS
The winner is rated just 63 and very few got into this very modest maiden. He sets the level along with the runner-up.
Redlynch Official explanation: trainer said gelding pulled up lame

4462 D & J ELECTRICAL SERVICES LTD H'CAP 5f
5:30 (5:40) (Class 5) (0-70,71) 3-Y-0+ **£3,885** (£1,156; £577; £288) **Stalls** Low

Form RPR
2226 **1** **Comptonspirit**[17] 3868 4-9-7 **66** J-PGuillambert 1 73
(B P J Baugh) *chsd ldrs: wnt 2nd over 1f out: styd on to ld last 75yds* **4/1**[2]
2653 **2** *1/2* **Mr Wolf**[9] 4171 7-9-12 **71** (p) GregFairley 5 76
(D W Barker) *led: hdd ins fnl f: no ex* **6/4**[1]
3241 **3** *hd* **City For Conquest (IRE)**[4] 4308 5-8-7 **52** 6ex ow1 FergusSweeney 4 56
(John A Harris) *mid-div: hdwy on outer over 1f out: styd on wl fnl 100yds* **10/1**
3402 **4** *1 1/4* **Obe One**[9] 4144 8-7-13 **51** oh6 AndreaAtzeni(7) 6 51+
(A Berry) *rrd s: hdwy 2f out: styd on wl ins fnl f: nt rch ldrs* **16/1**
0040 **5** *2 1/2* **Welcome Approach**[6] 4246 5-8-6 **51** AndrewElliott 12 42
(J R Weymes) *in rr-div: hdwy on outside over 1f out: nvr nr ldrs* **16/1**
-600 **6** *nk* **Yorke's Folly (USA)**[23] 3665 7-8-1 **51** oh6 (v) KellyHarrison(5) 9 41
(C W Fairhurst) *in rr: kpt on fnl 2f: nvr nr ldrs* **50/1**
2465 **7** *1/2* **Just Joey**[6] 4246 4-9-2 **64** (v[1]) JamieMoriarty(3) 7 52
(J R Weymes) *chsd ldrs: one pce fnl f* **16/1**
2525 **8** *3 1/4* **Colorus (IRE)**[2] 4385 5-9-2 **68** BMcHugh(7) 8 44
(W J H Ratcliffe) *chsd ldrs: wknd appr fnl f* **11/2**[3]
0002 **9** *hd* **Blessed Place**[2] 4385 8-8-6 **60** BillyCray(7) 11 35
(D J S Ffrench Davis) *w ldrs: lost pl 1f out* **8/1**
0060 **10** *2 1/2* **Safranine (IRE)**[13] 4016 11-8-6 **56** oh4 ow5 AnnStokell(5) 2 22
(Miss A Stokell) *sn outpcd and pushed along in rr: sme hdwy on ins 2f out: sn wknd* **66/1**
2000 **11** *1 3/4* **Jakeini (IRE)**[40] 3112 5-9-1 **60** (p) StephenDonohoe 3 20
(E S McMahon) *a in rr* **20/1**

62.71 secs (-0.59) **Going Correction** -0.075s/f (Good) 11 Ran SP% **121.4**
Speed ratings (Par 103): **101,100,99,97,93 93,92,87,87,83 80**
toteswinger: 1&2 £2.20, 1&3 £7.30, 2&3 £5.20. CSF £10.57 CT £58.10 TOTE £5.10: £1.70, £1.30, £2.80; EX 11.80 Place 6 £103.99, Place 5 £97.26..
Owner G B Hignett **Bred** Mrs F Wilson **Trained** Audley, Staffs

FOCUS
A modest sprint handicap but the form looks sound at this level with the winner to form.
T/Plt: £115.60 to a £1 stake. Pool: £62,666.14. 395.68 winning tickets. T/Qpdt: £31.90 to a £1 stake. Pool: £3,285.89. 76.10 winning tickets. WG

4002 CURRAGH (R-H)
Sunday, July 27

OFFICIAL GOING: Good to firm

4465a INDEPENDENT WATERFORD WEDGWOOD PHOENIX STKS (GROUP 1) (ENTIRE COLTS & FILLIES) 6f
3:00 (3:00) 2-Y-O **£137,205** (£42,352; £20,294; £7,058; £4,852)

RPR

1 **Mastercraftsman (IRE)**28 3534 2-9-1 .... JMurtagh 1 118+
(A P O'Brien, Ire) *trckd ldr in 2nd: rdn to ld over 1f out: styd on strly fnl f to pull clr: impressive* **4/1**3

2 4 1/2 **Art Connoisseur (IRE)**40 3103 2-9-1 .... JamieSpencer 6 104
(M L W Bell) *hld up in rr: hdwy to 3rd 1 1/2f out: rdn into 2nd 1f out: no imp on wnr fnl f* **1/1**1

3 1/2 **Bushranger (IRE)**14 4005 2-9-1 112 .... WMLordan 2 103
(David Wachman, Ire) *chsd ldrs: 4th 1/2-way: hdwy to 3rd 2f out: rdn in 4th 1 1/2f out: kpt on same pce to go 3rd ins fnl f* **2/1**2

4 3 1/2 **Sea Of Marmara (USA)**14 4005 2-9-1 98 .... JAHeffernan 5 92
(A P O'Brien, Ire) *sn led and clr after 1f: reduced advantage under 2f out: hdd and no ex over 1f out: sn wknd* **50/1**

5 3 **Alhaban (IRE)**28 3534 2-9-1 .... DPMcDonogh 4 83
(Kevin Prendergast, Ire) *chsd ldrs: 3rd 1/2-way: rdn in 4th 2f out: no ex and sn wknd* **12/1**

1m 13.3s (-1.20) **Going Correction** -0.075s/f (Good) **6 Ran SP% 113.0**
Speed ratings: **105,99,98,93,89**
CSF £8.78 TOTE £4.30: £1.70, £1.30; DF 4.90.
Owner Derrick Smith **Bred** Lynch Bages Ltd **Trained** Ballydoyle, Co Tipperary

NOTEBOOK
Mastercraftsman(IRE) ◆made it three wins from as many starts over course and distance with a seriously impressive display. He relished the decent early pace over a trip which now looks a bare minimum for him and this rates as the best display from a juvenile so far this season in either Britain or Ireland. With the promise of better now to come as he steps up in trip, he will no doubt now be kept to Group 1 company for the remainder of the year and it would be a surprise were he not to end his season in the Dewhurst at Newmarket in October. He could well take in the Railway Stakes at this venue over another furlong in September in the meantime and was immediately promoted to the top of the ante-post betting for next year's 2000 Guineas after this. He certainly has the scope to progress as a three-year-old. (op 7/2)
Art Connoisseur(IRE) had shown an electric turn of foot when coming from last to first in the Coventry last time and was very well supported to land the four-timer on this debut at the highest level. He was ridden out the back again and would have enjoyed the strong early pace, but his change of gear when asked for maximum effort was not so immediate and it was clear soon after the final furlong pole that he was going to have to settle for second place. He was some way below his Ascot form here and, while he clearly ran into a high-class performer in Mastercraftsman, he has to rate as a little disappointing. His trainer later blamed "over watering" for his below-par display and it may well be that this colt now prefers genuinely quick ground. However, it may also prove that he is a sprinter through and through, so his next outing really ought to reveal more as to whether he has already reached his peak. That outing may well come in the Gimcrack at York next month - a race renowned for producing future sprinting types. (op Evens tchd 11/10)
Bushranger(IRE), who took the Group 3 Anglesey Stakes over course and distance 11 days previously, was never a serious threat on this further step up in grade and was a well-held third at the finish. He could have found this coming a touch too soon, but it was interesting that he started second favourite here considering he races in the same ownership at the eventual winner and it is too soon to write him off at this sort of level just yet. It would not be surprising to see him renew rivalry with the runner-up in the Gimcrack at York next month. (op 9/4)

4467a IRISH STALLION FARMS EUROPEAN BREEDERS FUND SWEET MIMOSA STKS (LISTED RACE) (FILLIES) 6f
4:10 (4:10) 3-Y-O+ **£33,507** (£9,830; £4,683; £1,595)

RPR

1 **Elletelle (IRE)**7 4223 3-8-12 100 .... JMurtagh 9 100
(G M Lyons, Ire) *s.i.s: hdwy to 5th 1 1/2f out: 4th over 1f out: styd on to ld last 150yds: kpt on wl: jst hld on cl home* **7/2**2

2 shd **Aleagueoftheirown (IRE)**15 3982 4-9-3 98 ....(p) WMLordan 2 101
(David Wachman, Ire) *mid-div: 7th 1/2-way: short of room fr 1f out: r.o strly last 100yds: jst failed* **20/1**

3 3/4 **Akua'Ba (IRE)**10 4133 4-9-3 105 ....(tp) KJManning 7 99
(J S Bolger, Ire) *mid-div: hdwy to 5th 2f out: rdn to ld 1f out: hdd last 150yds: kpt on: no ex cl home* **13/2**3

4 hd **Age Of Chivalry (IRE)**25 3619 3-9-3 106 .... MJKinane 1 102
(John M Oxx, Ire) *chsd ldrs: 4th 1/2-way: rdn in 5th 1f out: kpt on fnl f* **5/2**1

5 nk **Miss Gorica (IRE)**10 4133 4-9-3 101 .... DPMcDonogh 3 97
(Ms Joanna Morgan, Ire) *chsd ldrs: 5th 1/2-way: rdn in 6th 1 1/2f out: kpt on fnl f* **8/1**

6 1/2 **Dimenticata (IRE)**7 4223 4-9-6 103 ....(b) CDHayes 11 99
(Kevin Prendergast, Ire) *chsd ldrs: 6th 1/2-way: hdwy to 4th 2f out: rdn to ld briefly over 1f out: 2nd and no ex 1f out: kpt on same pce fnl f* **7/1**

7 3/4 **Ghostmilk (IRE)**20 3804 4-9-3 85 .... JAHeffernan 10 94
(P D Deegan, Ire) *hld up towards rr: hdwy to 8th 1f out: kpt on same pce fnl f* **20/1**

8 3 1/2 **Wychwood Wanderer (IRE)**15 3981 5-9-3 81 ....(p) SFoley 5 83
(M Halford, Ire) *led: rdn and hdd over 1f out: sn no ex and wknd* **25/1**

9 2 **Salishan (IRE)**6 4264 6-9-3 54 .... RMBurke 4 77?
(Adrian McGuinness, Ire) *towards rr for most: nvr a factor* **100/1**

10 1 1/4 **Forthefirstime**25 3619 3-9-1 98 ....(b1) FMBerry 8 75
(John M Oxx, Ire) *mid-div: rdn in 8th 2f out: sn no ex and wknd* **16/1**

11 hd **Fancy Feathers (IRE)**3 4355 4-9-3 72 .... RPCleary 12 73
(David Marnane, Ire) *mid-div: rdn in 9th 2f out: sn no ex and wknd* **50/1**

12 3 1/2 **Toasted Special (USA)**38 3186 3-8-12 71 .... WJSupple 13 61
(W McCreery, Ire) *chsd ldrs: 3rd 1/2-way: rdn 2f out: sn no ex and wknd* **50/1**

13 1/2 **Manzila (FR)**16 3927 5-9-3 .... JamieSpencer 6 61
(D Nicholls) *chsd ldrs in 2nd: rdn and wknd 1 1/2f out* **7/1**

1m 12.23s (-2.27) **Going Correction** -0.075s/f (Good)
WFA 3 from 4yo+ 5lb **13 Ran SP% 124.4**
Speed ratings: **112,111,110,110,110 109,108,103,101,99 99,94,93**
CSF £81.46 TOTE £4.80: £1.70, £5.90, £2.40; DF 122.90.
Owner Jesse Club Syndicate **Bred** Timothy Gleeson & Ashley O'Lea **Trained** Dunsany, Co. Meath

NOTEBOOK
Elletelle(IRE) landed her first success since taking the Queen Mary last year and, just doing enough to repel the runner-up at the line, has been rated as running right up to that form here. She is indeed a bit better than the bare form as she missed the break and she now looks a sprinter all over, so there really should be more to come from her now. She needs to learn to hit the gates properly again, however, if she is to really progress back into Group company again. (op 4/1 tchd 100/30)
Aleagueoftheirown(IRE) ◆, racing in first-time cheekpieces, showed greatly-improved form on this drop back in distance and has to rate as unlucky as she endured a troubled passage at the crucial stage. Compensation should now await, however.
Akua'Ba(IRE) ran right up to the level of her win at Fairyhouse ten days previously and rates a solid benchmark for the form. (op 13/2 tchd 6/1)
Manzila(FR) dropped outy most tamely before the final furlong and something must have gone amiss. (op 8/1)

4466 - 4469a (Foreign Racing) - See Raceform Interactive

4012 MUNICH (L-H)
Sunday, July 27

OFFICIAL GOING: Good

4470a GROSSER DALLMAYR PREIS BAYERISCHES ZUCHTRENNEN (GROUP 1) 1m 2f
4:00 (4:14) 3-Y-O+ **£66,912** (£26,471; £13,235; £7,353)

RPR

1 **Linngari (IRE)**40 3100 6-9-6 .... RyanMoore 3 122
(Sir Michael Stoute) *hld up in 7th: hdwy down outside fr 2f out: led jst ins fnl f: drvn out* **7/1**

2 2 **Pressing (IRE)**15 3940 5-9-6 .... ASuborics 6 118
(M A Jarvis) *midfield: hdwy between rivals to ld under 2f out: hdd jst ins fnl f: one pce* **19/10**1

3 2 **Fair Breeze (GER)**59 2553 5-9-2 .... AHelfenbein 4 110
(Mario Hofer, Germany) *racd in 3rd: ev ch 2f out to over 1f out: one pce* **46/10**3

4 3 **Shrek (GER)**35 3306 4-9-6 .... EPedroza 7 108
(A Wohler, Germany) *midfield: styd on at one pce u.p fnl 2f* **132/10**

5 nk **Egerton (GER)**28 3540 7-9-6 .... TMundry 8 107
(P Rau, Germany) *racd in 2nd on outside: led briefly 2f out: wknd* **47/10**

6 1/2 **Santiago (GER)**29 3515 6-9-6 .... J-PCarvalho 2 106
(H Blume, Germany) *racd in 7th: nvr a factor* **112/10**

7 2 **Tempeltanzer (GER)** 6-9-6 .... GHind 5 102
(Frau Z Kubovicova, Slovakia) *racd in 4th: rdn over 2f out: sn wknd* **21/1**

8 5 **Wiesenpfad (FR)**35 3306 5-9-6 .... ADeVries 1 92
(W Hickst, Germany) *dropped out in last: a in rr* **32/10**2

9 11 **Axxos (GER)**43 3053 4-9-6 .... AStarke 9 70
(P Schiergen, Germany) *led to 2f out: wknd* **99/10**

2m 10.05s (1.08) **9 Ran SP% 135.2**
(including 10 Euro stake): WIN 80; PL 27, 15, 18; SF 253.
Owner R Plersch & P Walichnowski **Bred** His Highness The Aga Khan's Studs S C **Trained** Newmarket, Suffolk

NOTEBOOK
Linngari(IRE) ran out a ready winner on this second outing back for his original trainer and proved beyond doubt that he gets all of this longer trip now. He is now likely to head onto the Juddemonte International at York next month and, while he may find one or two too good there, he may still be open to some improvement over the trip.
Pressing(IRE) had every chance on this return to 10f and, while unable to cope with the improved winner, he eventually finished a clear second best. He rates the benchmark forn this form and does deserve to find an opening now.

4212 MAISONS-LAFFITTE (R-H)
Sunday, July 27

OFFICIAL GOING: Good

4472a PRIX ROBERT PAPIN (GROUP 2) (C&F) 5f 110y
2:45 (2:45) 2-Y-O **£54,485** (£21,029; £10,037; £6,691; £3,346)

RPR

1 **Lui Rei (ITY)**35 3308 2-9-2 .... DVargiu 4 111
(A Renzoni, Italy) *racd in 3rd: wnt 2nd 2f out: led ins fnl f: rdn out* **8/1**

2 1/2 **Percolator**21 3774 2-8-13 .... CSoumillon 3 106
(P F I Cole) *led tl hdd ins fnl f: one pce* **10/11**1

3 2 **Senor Mirasol**8 4190 2-9-2 .... FergalLynch 2 103
(K A Ryan) *racd in 2nd to 2f out: one pce* **7/1**3

4 shd **Enchanting Muse (USA)**52 2-8-13 .... C-PLemaire 6 99
(Robert Collet, France) *hld up towards rr: kpt on steadily fr over 1f out* **5/2**2

5 2 **Caparroso (FR)**21 3774 2-8-13 .... OPeslier 1 93
(T Lemer, France) *midfield on nr side: 4th over 1f out: one pce* **33/1**

6 6 **Kenz (FR)**21 3774 2-8-13 ....(b) OTrigodet 5 73
(C Baillet, France) *a towards rr: eased fnl f* **66/1**

7 3 **Higha (FR)**41 2-8-13 .... SPasquier 7 63
(P Demercastel, France) *a in rr: eased over 1f out* **10/1**

66.10 secs (-1.20) **Going Correction** -0.05s/f (Good) **7 Ran SP% 118.1**
Speed ratings: **106,105,102,102,99 91,87**
PARI-MUTUEL: WIN 10.20; PL 2.10M 1.20; SF 21.30.
Owner Scuderia Siba **Bred** Azienda Agricola Antezzate Srl **Trained** Italy

NOTEBOOK
Lui Rei(ITY), an Italian raider, won in good style and a little more easily than the official winning distance suggests. He tracked the favourite throughout before taking the lead running into the final furlong. He quickened well and dominated the final 50 yards. He looks likely to stay further and there are no real plans, although the Prix Morny at Deauville will certainly be taken into consideration.
Percolator, who broke the 5f track record here earlier in the month, was quickly into her stride and appeared to be going well one and a half out. She was then put under strong pressure and could not quicken as the race really warmed up. Connections felt the newly softened ground was not an advantage and it was her fourth trip to France in just three months, which is a lot to ask of a two-year-old. The extra half furlong might have caught her out and she may well line up for the Nunthorpe Stakes at York.

Senor Mirasol, who went down fighting in the Super Sprint the previous weekend, looked to have a double handful a furlong and a half out and then just stayed on one paced as the race came to a close. He fought well to hold third place by inches and will now be given a break, as this was just his second race in just eight days. The feeling is that he will stay further and the Middle Park Stakes at Newmarket is now being considered as a target.

Enchanting Muse(USA), who won in the style of a smart performer on debut, is still very green and found herself outpaced early on. She stayed on well though and was putting in her best work at the finish. She is bred to need further than this and remains a filly of much potential.

4473a PRIX EUGENE ADAM (GROUP 2) (RIGHT-HANDED) 1m 2f (S)

3:50 (3:52) 3-Y-O £167,647 (£64,706; £30,882; £20,588; £10,294)

RPR

1 **Twice Over**[40] 3102 3-9-2 TedDurcan 2 114
(H R A Cecil) *midfield: 6th st: hdwy towards ins to ld over 1 1/2f out: drvn out* **11/8**[1]

2 *3/4* **City Leader (IRE)**[37] 3193 3-9-2 RichardHughes 9 113
(B J Meehan) *hld up in last: hdwy down outside fr 2f out: 7th 1f out: styd on wl: tk 2nd cl home* **12/1**

3 *nk* **Chinchon (IRE)**[56] 2654 3-9-2 MBlancpain 7 112
(C Laffon-Parias, France) *hld up: 7th st: hdwy towards ins to dispute 2nd 1 1/2f out tl wnt 2nd 150yds out: lost 2nd cl home* **9/1**

4 *nk* **Ideal World (USA)**[20] 3806 3-9-2 SPasquier 4 111
(A Fabre, France) *in tch: 4th st: pushed along and sltly outpcd 2f out: styd on u.p fr over 1f ouy* **13/2**[3]

5 *3/4* **Collection (IRE)**[38] 3156 3-9-2 KerrinMcEvoy 3 110
(W J Haggas) *hld up: 9th stm hdwy on ins to dispute 2nd 1 1/2f out to 150yds out: one pce* **7/2**[2]

6 *1 1/2* **In Chambers**[33] 3356 3-9-2 CSoumillon 8 107
(M Delzangles, France) *cl up: 3rd st: effrt and one pce fr 2f out* **16/1**

7 *3/4* **Hello Morning (FR)**[38] 3191 3-9-2 AlexisBadel 1 105
(Mme C Head-Maarek, France) *led to over 1 1/2f out: one pce* **12/1**

8 *1/2* **Hopes And Fears (IRE)**[37] 3244 3-9-2 C-PLemaire 6 104
(J-C Rouget, France) *midfield: 5th st: rdn and one pce fnl 2f* **20/1**

9 *1* **Mundybash**[45] 3-9-2 TThulliez 5 102
(N Clement, France) *racd in 2nd: wknd over 1 1/2f out* **16/1**

10 *nse* **Lancetto (FR)**[49] 2880 3-9-2 OPeslier 10 102
(Mario Hofer, Germany) *8th st: a in rr* **33/1**

2m 7.80s (5.40) **Going Correction** +0.85s/f (Soft) **10 Ran SP% 122.5**

Speed ratings: **112,111,111,110,110 109,108,108,107,107**

PARI-MUTUEL: WIN 1.90 (coupled with Ideal World); PL 1.30, 2.20, 2.10;DF 9.50.

Owner K Abdulla **Bred** Juddmonte Farms Ltd **Trained** Newmarket, Suffolk

NOTEBOOK

Twice Over, who has been racing with the best all season, gained a deserved victory. He was given an excellent ride and tucked in just behind the leaders early before going to the head of affairs one and a half out. He looked like winning easily, but idled a bit in front and had to be shaken up in the last 50 yards. Certainly a colt on the upgrade, he is in both the Juddmonte International and Irish Champion Stakes and it would be no surprise if he was entered in the Guillaume d'Ornano at Deauville where he would carry a 2kg penalty. He is worth keeping an eye on for the rest of the season.

City Leader(IRE) put in an incredible late run in the straight. Dropped out in the early part of the race, he was still one of the backmarkers at the three furlong pole, but engaged top gear one and a half out and fairly flew the final stages and was closing on the winner with every stride. He is now really back on song and the intention is to step him back up to 1m4f.

Chinchon(IRE) was another to be held up for a late run and he started to make progress from the two furlong marker. He stayed on well, but could not quicken as well as the front pair. The colt's trainer was furious that the race had been changed from the straight to the turning track early in the month.

Ideal World(USA), always handy in the early stages, battled on well throughout the straight, and it was not a bad effort in this class of company for the first time. He looks likely to win a Group event before the end of the season and is certainly progressive.

Collection(IRE), an impressive winner at Royal Ascot, could have done without the rain. He still had plenty to do coming into the straight and made good progress up the far rail, but stayed on one paced inside the final furlong. Connections considered that the ground was not ideal and he can probably be rated a shade better than the bare form.

3815 SOUTHWELL (L-H)

Monday, July 28

OFFICIAL GOING: Standard

Wind: Almost nil Weather: Fine and sunny

4474 EUROPEAN BREEDERS' FUND MAIDEN STKS 5f (F)

2:15 (2:16) (Class 5) 2-Y-O £3,885 (£1,156; £577; £144; £144) **Stalls High**

Form RPR

236 **1** **Lesley's Choice**[26] 3603 2-9-3 0 NCallan 13 75+
(P A Blockley) *mde all: shkn up fnl f: sn clr* **13/8**[1]

06 **2** *5* **West Leake (IRE)**[14] 4024 2-9-3 0 MichaelHills 9 55
(B W Hills) *s.i.s: hdwy over 3f out: rdn 1/2-way: sn outpcd: r.o ins fnl f* **4/1**[2]

3 *1/2* **The Cuckoo** 2-9-3 0 EddieAhern 12 53
(M J Wallace) *chsd wnr: rdn 1/2-way: no ex fnl f* **4/1**[2]

35 **4** *hd* **Digger Derek (IRE)**[12] 4072 2-9-3 0 TonyHamilton 2 52
(R A Fahey) *mid-div: sn pushed along: outpcd over 3f out: hdwy u.p over 1f out: styd on* **9/1**[3]

6 **4** *dht* **Weet In Nerja**[14] 4027 2-9-3 0 HayleyTurner 7 52
(R Hollinshead) *mid-div: outpcd over 3f out: hdwy u.p over 1f out: styd on* **12/1**

06 **6** *nk* **Shadows Lengthen**[13] 4045 2-9-3 0 DaleGibson 8 51
(M W Easterby) *s.i.s: outpcd: hdwy u.p over 1f out: nvr trbld ldrs* **40/1**

6 **7** *nk* **Coniston Wood**[24] 3689 2-8-5 0 NSLawes(7) 3 45
(M W Easterby) *outpcd: hdwy u.p over 1f out:* **22/1**

05 **8** *1 1/4* **Royal Max (IRE)**[30] 3492 2-9-3 0 PaulHanagan 4 45
(R A Fahey) *prom: rdn and lost pl 3f out: n.d after* **11/1**

0 **9** *1 1/2* **Killyea**[4] 4321 2-8-9 0 KevinGhunowa(3) 10 35
(R A Harris) *chsd ldrs: rdn 1/2-way: wknd over 1f out* **100/1**

10 *7* **Valdemar** 2-9-3 0 SilvestreDeSousa 6 15
(A D Brown) *s.s: outpcd* **50/1**

0 **11** *1* **Minenotyours (IRE)**[30] 3485 2-9-3 0 TGMcLaughlin 11 11
(D E Cantillon) *mid-div: outpcd over 3f out: bhd fr 1/2-way* **50/1**

4 **12** *2* **Moomoo**[38] 3215 2-8-12 0 PaulMulrennan 5 —
(J R Weymes) *sn outpcd* **80/1**

0 **13** *15* **Under The Table**[47] 2924 2-8-9 0 DuranFentiman(3) 1 —
(Miss J E Foster) *s.i.s: outpcd* **200/1**

61.75 secs (2.05) **Going Correction** +0.275s/f (Slow) **13 Ran SP% 117.6**

Speed ratings (Par 94): **94,86,85,84,84 84,83,81,79,68 66,63,39**

toteswinger: 1&2 £2.50, 1&3 £3.80, 2&3 £6.80. CSF £7.40 TOTE £2.70: £1.50, £1.30, £2.40; EX 10.50.

Owner B C Allen **Bred** B C Allen **Trained** Lambourn, Berks

FOCUS

An uncompetitive and modest juvenile maiden.

NOTEBOOK

Lesley's Choice appreciated the drop back to 5f and, handling the Fibresand well at the first attempt, he comfortably got off the mark at the fourth time of asking. Although he had little to beat, this looked an improved effort and he should not be underestimated in nurseries. (op 15-8 tchd 6-4)

West Leake(IRE) promise to be suited by this drop in trip, but he was in trouble after missing the break. He might be worth another try at this distance on turf. (op 7-2 tchd 5-1)

The Cuckoo, a 24,000gns son of Invincible Spirit and brother to useful 5f-6f two and three-year-old winner Age Of Chivalry, out of a 1m winner, was the only one to lay up with the winner early, but he could not sustain his challenge. He will be sharper next time. (op 7-2 tchd 11-4)

Weet In Nerja is probably more of a nursery type. (op 12-1 tchd 17-2)

Digger Derek(IRE) was unsuited by this drop back from 7f and can do better over further in nurseries. (op 12-1 tchd 17-2)

Killyea Official explanation: jockey said filly hung left throughout

4475 FREE BETS @FREEBETS.CO.UK NURSERY 7f (F)

2:45 (2:45) (Class 5) 2-Y-O £2,729 (£806; £403) **Stalls** Low

Form RPR

1000 **1** **Shampagne**[9] 4190 2-9-10 **95** DTDaSilva(7) 1 100
(P F I Cole) *chsd ldr: rdn over 1f out: led ins fnl f: r.o* **17/2**[3]

3421 **2** *3/4* **Night Of Fortune**[4] 4340 2-8-12 **76** 6ex SebSanders 2 79
(Sir Mark Prescott) *sn led: rdn over 1f out: hdd and unable qck ins fnl f* **4/9**[1]

023 **3** *9* **Happy Anniversary (IRE)**[66] 2362 2-8-7 **71** EddieAhern 5 52
(Miss V Haigh) *prom: rdn 1/2-way: wknd 2f out: eased ins fnl f* **4/1**[2]

3004 **4** *9* **Heaven Or Hell (IRE)**[9] 4203 2-7-6 **63** oh4 ow1 AndreaAtzeni(7) 4 21
(P D Evans) *prom: plld hrd: lost pl 5f out: bhd fr 1/2-way* **20/1**

0500 **5** *4* **Indian Blade (IRE)**[3] 4373 2-7-7 **62** oh3 DavidProbert(5) 3 10
(M D I Usher) *hmpd s: sn pushed along and prom: n.m.r over 4f out: rdn and wknd 3f out* **33/1**

1m 30.38s (0.08) **Going Correction** +0.125s/f (Slow) **5 Ran SP% 107.5**

Speed ratings (Par 94): **104,103,92,82,78**

CSF £12.49 TOTE £7.20: £3.10, £1.10; EX 12.50.

Owner Sisters Syndicate **Bred** Stringston Farm **Trained** Whatcombe, Oxon

■ Stewards' Enquiry : Seb Sanders caution: used whip with excessive frequency

FOCUS

It's rare that a horse rated as high as Shampagne runs in a nursery at this sort of level, but two of his rivals were out of the handicap and this race lacked strength in depth. The front two look much better than this grade, though. The 'official' ratings are estimated and are intended as a guide.

NOTEBOOK

Shampagne was conceding a lot of weight, even after his rider's claim had be taken into account, but this was still easier than his recent assignments and he proved suited by both the step up in trip and switch to Fibresand. He is now 2-2 on sand having won his maiden at Kempton, but he is unlikely to be easy to place now. (tchd 8-1 and 9-1)

Night Of Fortune was a very short price to defy a 6lb penalty for his recent Kempton nursery success, but he found one too good, a very decent type for this sort of level. He had every chance from the front and there looked to be few excuses. (tchd 1-2)

Happy Anniversary(IRE), a Fillies' Mile entry, failed to improve for the step up to 7f. (op 9-2)

Heaven Or Hell(IRE), 5lb wrong, proved unsuited by the step up in trip. (op 16-1)

4476 GET YOUR FREE BETS @FREEBETS.CO.UK CLAIMING STKS 6f (F)

3:15 (3:16) (Class 6) 3-Y-O+ £1,978 (£584; £292) **Stalls** Low

Form RPR

1025 **1** **Varadouro (BRZ)**[13] 4058 6-9-12 78 AdrianTNicholls 9 84
(D Nicholls) *chsd ldrs: led 2f out: rdn and hdd ins fnl f: rallied to ld post* **6/5**[1]

3644 **2** *hd* **Swinbrook (USA)**[37] 3281 7-9-8 74 (v) PaulHanagan 6 79
(R A Fahey) *chsd ldrs: nt clr run over 2f out: shkn up to ld ins fnl f: sn rdn and hung rt: hdd post* **2/1**[2]

016 **3** *1 3/4* **Hamaasy**[77] 2050 7-8-11 59 KevinGhunowa(3) 12 66
(R A Harris) *s.i.s: hdwy over 2f out: rdn over 1f out: swtchd lft ins fnl f: styd on same pce* **20/1**

0000 **4** *8* **Apres Ski (IRE)**[12] 4073 5-8-8 47 ow1 NBazeley(7) 14 41
(J F Coupland) *chsd ldrs: rdn over 2f out: wknd fnl f* **100/1**

0401 **5** *3/4* **Majestical (IRE)**[21] 3779 6-8-13 58 (p) HaddenFrost(5) 10 42
(R A Harris) *sn outpcd: styd on ins fnl f: nvr nrr* **16/1**

0404 **6** *1 3/4* **Valhillen**[12] 4083 3-9-7 70 (p) HayleyTurner 8 44
(M D I Usher) *mid-div: sn pushed along: n.d* **12/1**[3]

1006 **7** *1 1/2* **Berrymead**[16] 3960 3-8-4 60 (b) DaleGibson 2 22
(M W Easterby) *sn pushed along in rr: hdwy over 3f out: no imp fnl 2f* **33/1**

0-00 **8** *1/2* **Benny The Bus**[12] 4073 6-8-10 53 (v) PaulMulrennan 5 22
(J R Weymes) *sn outpcd* **50/1**

0050 **9** *2 1/2* **Northern Boy (USA)**[20] 3826 5-9-8 56 (b[1]) SebSanders 13 26
(M W Easterby) *prom: jnd ldr over 4f out: rdn over 2f out: wknd over 1f out* **22/1**

0-00 **10** *1 1/4* **Amanda's Lad (IRE)**[5] 4294 8-8-3 47 AndreaAtzeni(7) 11 10
(M C Chapman) *hld up in tch: rdn over 3f out: sn wknd* **80/1**

00 **11** *1 3/4* **Phinerine**[34] 3340 5-8-11 50 (e) DuranFentiman(3) 3 8
(Miss J E Foster) *prom: rdn 1/2-way: wknd over 1f out* **100/1**

3253 **12** *1 3/4* **Pegasus Dancer (FR)**[171] 479 4-9-12 68 (p) NCallan 4 15
(K A Ryan) *mde most for 4f: sn rdn and wknd: eased fnl f* **16/1**

0125 **13** *1 1/4* **Copperbottomed (IRE)**[13] 4056 3-9-5 65 (e) VinceSlattery 7 9
(P G Murphy) *s.s: outpcd* **22/1**

1m 17.13s (0.63) **Going Correction** +0.125s/f (Slow) **13 Ran SP% 119.8**

WFA 3 from 4yo+ 5lb

Speed ratings (Par 101): **100,99,97,86,85 83,81,80,77,75 73,71,69**

toteswinger: 1&2 £1.30, 1&3 £7.60, 2&3 £7.50. CSF £3.19 TOTE £2.30: £1.30, £1.30, £3.00; EX 4.30.Varadouro was claimed by T. Dascombe for £12,000.

Owner Clarke & Harlow Partnership **Bred** Haras Valente **Trained** Sessay, N Yorks

FOCUS

A reasonable claimer but the front three were clear and close to their best.

The Form Book, Raceform Ltd, Compton, RG20 6NL

Majestical(IRE) Official explanation: jockey said gelding lost a shoe and returned sore

4477 FREE SPORTS BETS @FREEBETS.CO.UK H'CAP 1m 4f (F)

3:45 (3:45) (Class 6) (0-65,65) 3-Y-0+ £1,978 (£584; £292) Stalls Low

Form RPR

0401 1 **Swords**[3] 4391 6-8-3 47 oh1 AndreaAtzeni(7) 10 62+
(R E Peacock) *s.i.s: hld up: nt clr run over 4f out: hmpd over 3f out: hdwy u.p and hung lft over 1f out: led ins fnl f: styd on strly* **7/2**[2]

5006 2 6 **Parkview Love (USA)**[9] 3666 7-9-2 56 LeeVickers(3) 7 61
(J G Given) *hld up in tch: led over 4f out: rdn over 1f out: hdd and no ex ins fnl f* **22/1**

2100 3 hd **Bolckow**[3] 4365 5-8-12 54 PatrickDonaghy(5) 4 59
(J T Stimpson) *prom: rdn and ev ch fr over 2f out tl no ex ins fnl f* **14/1**

630- 4 2 1/4 **Diktatorship (IRE)**[60] 6835 5-8-10 47 oh2 HayleyTurner 3 48
(Jennie Candlish) *chsd ldrs: rdn over 3f out: wknd ins fnl f* **20/1**

2154 5 1/2 **Wizard Looking**[20] 3820 7-9-12 63 EddieAhern 1 64
(D E Cantillon) *hld up in tch: rdn over 3f out: wknd fnl f* **11/2**

0-00 6 5 **Iron Cross (IRE)**[30] 3483 3-8-8 57 ow2 SebSanders 12 50
(Sir Mark Prescott) *s.s: hld up: hdwy 1/2-way: rdn over 2f out: wknd over 1f out* **9/1**

6026 7 11 **Highland Homestead**[12] 4086 3-8-10 62 JamesMillman(3) 11 37
(B R Millman) *hld up: rdn 1/2-way: sme hdwy over 3f out: sn wknd* **5/1**[3]

3044 8 4 **Love Empire (USA)**[10] 4147 3-8-9 58 (b) JoeFanning 5 27
(M Johnston) *s.i.s: sn pushed along in rr: sme hdwy over 3f out: sn wknd* **11/1**

5115 9 32 **Black Falcon (IRE)**[11] 4123 8-10-0 65 NCallan 14 —
(John A Harris) *s.i.s: hld up: hdwy 1/2-way rdn over 3f out: sn wknd and eased* **10/3**[1]

/005 10 3 3/4 **High Command**[24] 3673 5-9-8 59 PaulMulrennan 8 —
(M W Easterby) *hld up: rdn over 4f out: sn wknd* **25/1**

-000 11 2 1/2 **Farsighted**[46] 2985 3-8-13 62 DaleGibson 6 —
(J M P Eustace) *chsd ldr tl rdn 1/2-way: wknd over 4f out* **66/1**

5056 12 2 **Coco L'Escargot**[66] 2354 4-8-10 47 oh2 (v[1]) PaulHanagan 13 —
(J R Jenkins) *sn led: rdn and hdd over 4f out: wknd over 3f out* **50/1**

00-4 13 19 **Dareios (GER)**[11] 4122 3-8-2 54 ow4 KevinGhunowa(3) 2 —
(G J Smith) *prom: lost pl 7f out: bhd fnl 5f* **33/1**

2m 42.6s (1.60) **Going Correction** +0.125s/f (Slow)
WFA 3 from 4yo+ 12lb 13 Ran SP% 121.7
Speed ratings (Par 101): **99,95,94,93,93 89,82,79,58,55 54,52,40**
toteswinger: 1&2 £19.50, 1&3 £12.70, 2&3 £41.40. CSF £88.05 CT £987.63 TOTE £4.20: £1.70, £5.60, £4.40; EX 91.40.
Owner J Babb **Bred** Mrs A Yearley **Trained** Kyre Park, Worcs
■ Stewards' Enquiry : Paul Hanagan one-day ban: failed to ride to draw (Aug 11)

FOCUS
A moderate handicap but the winner is back to his best and the third is the best guide for now.
Black Falcon(IRE) Official explanation: jockey said gelding hung badly left; vet said gelding returned lame
High Command Official explanation: jockey said gelding never travelled
Dareios(GER) Official explanation: jockey said gelding never travelled

4478 SUE AND ALAN WEDDING DAY H'CAP 6f (F)

4:15 (4:18) (Class 5) (0-75,74) 3-Y-0+ £2,729 (£806; £403) Stalls Low

Form RPR

4000 1 **Cool Sands (IRE)**[9] 3175 6-8-12 60 (v) J-PGuillambert 14 71
(J G Given) *chsd ldrs: rdn over 2f out: hung lft and led ins fnl f: jst hld on* **12/1**

5-55 2 nk **Dan Chillingworth (IRE)**[18] 3893 3-9-3 70 SebSanders 13 79+
(J R Fanshawe) *mid-div: sn pushed along: hdwy u.p over 1f out: r.o* **12/1**

4034 3 1 **Sheriff's Silk**[24] 3691 4-9-1 63 (b) PaulEddery 10 70
(G D Blake) *s.i.s: hdwy and hmpd 5f out: rdn over 3f out: styd on u.p* **10/1**

3240 4 nk **Punching**[7] 4258 4-9-8 70 NCallan 1 76
(Miss Gay Kelleway) *chsd ldrs: pushed along and led 2f out: rdn and hdd ins fnl f: styd on same pce* **5/1**[1]

0462 5 3 **Whitbarrow (IRE)**[13] 4058 9-9-9 74 (b) JamesMillman(3) 11 70
(B R Millman) *s.i.s: sn chsng ldrs: rdn and ev ch 2f out: wknd ins fnl f* **7/1**[3]

510 6 hd **Sir Boss (IRE)**[37] 3270 3-9-0 74 RosieJessop(7) 5 69+
(D E Cantillon) *sn pushed along in rr: hdwy over 1f out: n.d* **11/2**[2]

2466 7 1 3/4 **Prince Golan (IRE)**[23] 3725 4-8-13 66 JackMitchell(5) 12 56
(J W Unett) *sn pushed along in rr: styd on appr fnl f: nvr nrr* **10/1**

0-60 8 nk **Geoffdaw**[95] 1584 3-9-4 71 (p) EddieAhern 8 59+
(M J Wallace) *prom: hmpd and lost pl 5f out: n.d after* **12/1**

6002 9 shd **Tyrannosaurus Rex (IRE)**[9] 4207 4-8-7 55 PaulHanagan 6 44
(D Shaw) *led 1f: chsd ldrs: rdn over 2f out: wknd fnl f* **7/1**[3]

121 10 2 1/2 **Kelamon**[10] 4154 4-9-4 73 BillyCray(7) 9 54+
(M D I Usher) *prom: hmpd and lost pl 5f out: sn bhd* **11/2**[2]

2650 11 hd **Proud Killer**[55] 2692 5-8-12 60 (v) PaulMulrennan 2 40
(J R Jenkins) *led 5f out: rdn and hdd 2f out: wknd over 1f out* **22/1**

50-0 12 1 1/4 **Haajes**[18] 3868 4-9-7 69 (t) LeeEnstone 3 45
(S Parr) *s.i.s: a in rr* **22/1**

00-0 13 1 1/4 **Tarraburn (USA)**[13] 4051 4-8-10 65 AndreaAtzeni(7) 4 37
(G C H Chung) *hld up: hmpd 5f out: a in rr* **33/1**

400 14 19 **Compton Classic**[14] 4025 6-8-13 61 (p) RobertHavlin 7 —
(J R Boyle) *hld up: bhd fnl 4f* **40/1**

1m 17.34s (0.84) **Going Correction** +0.125s/f (Slow)
WFA 3 from 4yo+ 5lb 14 Ran SP% 127.8
Speed ratings (Par 103): **99,98,97,96,92 92,90,89,89,86 86,84,82,57**
toteswinger: 1&2 £29.70, 1&3 £42.50, 2&3 £15.90. CSF £151.50 CT £993.84 TOTE £20.20: £5.30, £3.00, £3.70; EX 293.70.
Owner Peter Swann **Bred** Rathasker Stud **Trained** Willoughton, Lincs
■ Stewards' Enquiry : J-P Guillambert three-day ban: careless riding (Aug 11-13)
Paul Eddery two-day ban: careless riding (Aug 11-12)

FOCUS
A modest but competitive sprint handicap and the form looks sound enough at face value.

4479 BETFAIR APPRENTICE TRAINING SERIES H'CAP 1m (F)

4:45 (4:48) (Class 6) (0-55,59) 3-Y-0+ £1,978 (£584; £292) Stalls Low

Form RPR

0015 1 **Kimono My House**[10] 4168 4-9-2 52 RosieJessop(3) 14 72
(J G Given) *sn chsng ldr: led over 2f out: hung lft over 1f out: rdn clr fnl f* **9/2**[3]

0000 2 10 **Mujma**[65] 2394 4-8-10 50 AnthonyBetts(7) 9 49
(S Parr) *sn led: rdn and hdd over 2f out: wknd fnl f* **18/1**

0301 3 6 **Al Rayanah**[6] 4282 5-9-12 59 6ex (p) JackDean 13 45
(G Prodromou) *s.i.s: sn pushed along in rr: hdwy u.p over 1f out: nvr nrr* **6/1**

0064 4 1 3/4 **Sir Bond (IRE)**[20] 3822 7-8-12 50 JohnCavanagh(5) 11 33
(G R Oldroyd) *s.i.s: in rr and pushed along: hdwy u.p over 1f out: nt rch ldrs* **4/1**[2]

0000 5 hd **Rain Stops Play (IRE)**[10] 4162 6-9-6 53 KMay 10 35
(M Quinn) *chsd ldrs tl rdn and wknd 3f out* **9/1**

3006 6 1/2 **Topflightrebellion**[9] 4179 3-8-7 55 (p) IanCraven(7) 7 34
(Mrs G S Rees) *mid-div: pushed along over 4f out: wknd over 3f out* **16/1**

0000 7 3/4 **Baylaw Star**[24] 3662 7-9-4 51 ClGillies 1 31
(I W McInnes) *prom: rdn over 4f out: wknd over 3f out* **33/1**

4056 8 3 **Green Pirate**[9] 4182 6-9-0 50 (p) BMcHugh(3) 5 23
(C R Dore) *s.i.s: outpcd* **14/1**

0222 9 12 **Tenancy (IRE)**[76] 2075 4-9-3 50 (e[1]) StacyRenwick 6 —
(R C Guest) *trckd ldrs: racd keenly: wknd 3f out* **8/1**

00/0 10 3/4 **Out Of This Way**[26] 3606 5-9-5 52 ThomasO'Brien 12 —
(Mrs N S Evans) *sn outpcd* **40/1**

500- 11 1/2 **Boogie Board**[384] 3406 4-9-1 53 JPFeatherstone(5) 2 —
(Garry Moss) *prom: rdn 1/2-way: wknd over 3f out* **66/1**

4/25 12 17 **Mystic Roll**[19] 3839 5-9-8 55 MCGeran 8 —
(Jane Chapple-Hyam) *sn pushed along in rr: bhd fr 1/2-way* **7/2**[1]

1m 44.2s (0.50) **Going Correction** +0.125s/f (Slow)
WFA 3 from 4yo+ 8lb 12 Ran SP% 120.5
Speed ratings (Par 101): **102,92,86,84,84 83,82,79,67,67 66,49**
toteswinger: 1&2 £30.30, 1&3 £5.80, 2&3 £27.20. CSF £82.96 CT £506.16 TOTE £5.60: £2.20, £4.60, £2.20; EX 153.20 Place 6: £135.92 Place 5: £115.14.
Owner Beadle Booth Bloodstock Limited **Bred** G And Mrs Middlebrook **Trained** Willoughton, Lincs

FOCUS
A moderate handicap restricted to apprentices who had not ridden more than the 20 winners. Very few got involved and the form cannot be take too seriously as it is unlikely to translate elsewhere.
Mystic Roll Official explanation: jockey said gelding never travelled
T/Jkpt: Not won. T/Plt: £48.40 to a £1 stake. Pool: £63,406.50. 954.58 winning tickets. T/Qpdt: £25.40 to a £1 stake. Pool: £3,689.30. 107.10 winning tickets. CR

4249 WINDSOR (R-H)

Monday, July 28

OFFICIAL GOING: Good to firm (8.0)
Wind: Almost nil Weather: Warm and muggy

4480 GET ON WITH WILLIAM HILL - 0800 44 40 40 MAIDEN STKS 6f

6:10 (6:13) (Class 4) 2-Y-0 £4,209 (£1,252; £625; £312) Stalls High

Form RPR

1 **Damien (IRE)** 2-9-3 0 MichaelHills 8 79+
(B W Hills) *in tch: led appr fnl f: drvn out* **13/2**[3]

56 2 1 1/4 **Barnezet (GR)**[35] 3323 2-8-12 0 RichardHughes 4 68
(R Hannon) *led tl hdd appr fnl f: nt pce of wnr ins fnl f* **7/1**

3 3/4 **Satwa Laird** 2-9-3 0 JimmyFortune 7 71+
(E A L Dunlop) *s.i.s: styd on fr over 1f out to go 3rd towards fin* **9/2**[2]

3 4 1/2 **Cawdor (IRE)**[21] 3798 2-9-3 0 FergusSweeney 11 69
(H Candy) *prom: rdn 2f out: nt qckn ins fnl f* **7/4**[1]

0 5 3 **Daily Double**[21] 3798 2-9-0 0 PatrickHills(3) 9 60
(R Hannon) *prom: rdn 2f out: one pce fr over 1f out* **7/1**

0 6 1/2 **Scarlets**[6] 4274 2-8-12 0 JohnEgan 14 54
(P D Evans) *nvr bttr than mid-div* **40/1**

5 7 2 **Good Buy Dubai (USA)**[35] 3315 2-9-3 0 LPKeniry 10 53
(J R Best) *in tch tl outpcd and wknd over 1f out* **14/1**

8 1 1/2 **Chifong** 2-8-12 0 IanMongan 15 43
(J Akehurst) *in rr: sme hdwy over 1f out: nvr on terms* **50/1**

0 9 1 1/2 **Alderbed**[49] 2893 2-9-3 0 StephenDonohoe 1 44
(George Baker) *nvr bttr than mid-div* **33/1**

60 10 1 **Louie's Lad**[6] 4274 2-9-3 0 ShaneKelly 5 41
(J A Geake) *mid-div on outside: wknd over 1f out* **40/1**

0 11 nk **Turn To Dreams**[7] 4251 2-8-12 0 NickyMackay 6 35
(P D Evans) *racd wd: effrt 2f out: sn btn* **50/1**

12 shd **Richardlionheart (USA)** 2-9-3 0 TPQueally 12 39
(B Gubby) *s.i.s: plld hrd: a bhd* **40/1**

13 6 **Strike Command (USA)** 2-9-3 0 SteveDrowne 3 21+
(R Charlton) *a bhd* **8/1**

14 6 **Itainteasybeingme** 2-9-3 0 JimCrowley 13 —
(J R Boyle) *a struggling in rr* **28/1**

1m 15.4s (2.40) **Going Correction** +0.125s/f (Good) 14 Ran SP% 128.3
Speed ratings (Par 96): **89,87,86,85,81 81,78,76,74,73 72,72,64,56**
toteswinger: 1&2 £7.30, 1&3 £9.50, 2&3 £11.50. CSF £52.68 TOTE £8.60: £2.60, £2.40, £2.00; EX 70.60.
Owner The Hon Mrs J M Corbett & C Wright **Bred** Dr Mariann And Richard Klay **Trained** Lambourn, Berks

FOCUS
A fair juvenile maiden, run at an average pace. The form is guessy but best rated around the third and fourth.

NOTEBOOK
Damien(IRE), whose pedigree suggests a mix of speed and stamina, got his career off to a perfect start with a ready effort. He knew his job and showed a likeable attitude when asked to put the race to bed, despite looking to find the ground plenty quick enough. His connections now intend to aim him at the valuable DBS Sales race at York's Ebor meeting and he looks potentially very useful. (tchd 7-1)
Barnezet(GR) got put in her place by the winner late on, but this was still her best effort to date in defeat. She is now eligible for nurseries. (op 11-2)
Satwa Laird ◆, a 150,000gns purchase bred to appreciate further in time, met some support in the betting ahead of this racecourse bow. He hampered his chance with a sluggish start, but was noted as doing some decent work late in the day and looks assured to improve nicely for the experience. He should go close next time. (op 11-2)
Cawdor(IRE), third on debut at the track last time, had his chance and posted an improved effort in defeat on this quicker ground. He is probably one to be more interested in when qualifying for a nursery mark after his next assignment. (op 15-8 tchd 2-1 and 6-4)

4481 GET A BONUS AT WILLIAMHILLCASINO.COM H'CAP 1m 2f 7y

6:40 (6:45) (Class 5) (0-75,74) 3-Y-0+ £3,070 (£906; £453) Stalls Low

Form RPR

0250 1 **Flying Applause**[6] 4276 3-9-7 71 FergusSweeney 10 82
(A King) *led: hdd briefly ent fnl f: rallied u.p to ld again ins fnl f: hld on* **7/2**[2]

2404 2 hd **Spanish Diva**[30] 3507 4-9-13 67 SteveDrowne 3 78
(S C Williams) *hld up: hdwy over 2f out: led briefly ent fnl f: kpt on: jst hld* **9/2**[3]

1004 3 5 **Bartercard (USA)**[11] 4129 7-9-13 67 MickyFenton 8 68
(Stef Liddiard) *in rr: hdwy over 1f out: nvr nrr* **33/1**

0010 4 ¾ **Obrigado (USA)**[16] 3970 8-10-0 **68**........(t) JimmyFortune 6 67
(G L Moore) *s.i.s: in rr: styd on fr over 1f out: nvr on terms* **11/2**

2454 5 1 ¼ **Indy Driver**[26] 3612 3-9-10 **74**........ GeorgeBaker 1 71
(J R Fanshawe) *t.k.h: in tch: rdn 2f out: sn btn* **11/4[1]**

4040 6 2 ¼ **Quaglino Way (GR)**[12] 4084 4-9-10 **64**........ JimCrowley 5 56
(P R Chamings) *in tch tl rdn and wknd over 1f out* **12/1**

0003 7 2 ¾ **Hatch A Plan (IRE)**[10] 4155 7-8-12 **55**........ TravisBlock(3) 4 42
(Mouse Hamilton-Fairley) *mid-div: rdn over 2f out: wknd over 1f out* **8/1**

4644 8 7 **Ba Dreamflight**[22] 3763 3-7-13 **49** oh2........(p) NickyMackay 7 22
(H Morrison) *trckd wnr to 2f out: sn wknd* **16/1**

-030 9 4 ½ **Muharjam**[11] 4112 3-9-3 **67**........(b) PaulDoe 2 31
(C E Brittain) *trckd ldrs: rdn and wknd over 2f out* **20/1**

2m 7.26s (-1.44) **Going Correction** +0.025s/f (Good)
WFA 3 from 4yo+ 10lb **9 Ran SP% 114.8**
Speed ratings (Par 103): **106,105,101,101,100 98,96,90,87**
toteswinger: 1&2 £5.40, 1&3 £115.40, 2&3 not won. CSF £19.57 CT £439.21 TOTE £4.70: £1.80, £1.50, £6.80; EX 19.90.
Owner Four Mile Racing **Bred** G H Beeby And Viscount Marchwood **Trained** Barbury Castle, Wilts

FOCUS
A modest handicap, run at a sound pace, which saw the first pair come clear. The runner-up looks the best guide to the form.
Indy Driver Official explanation: vet said colt returned lame

4482 GET YOUR CHIPS AT WILLIAMHILLPOKER.COM MAIDEN AUCTION STKS 5f 10y
7:10 (7:11) (Class 4) 2-Y-0 **£4,209** (£1,252; £625; £312) **Stalls** High

Form RPR

1 **Leadenhall Lass (IRE)** 2-8-5 0 ow1........ JohnEgan 5 75
(P M Phelan) *mde all: rdn out fnl f* **9/1**

2 1 **Louidor** 2-8-9 0........ FergusSweeney 1 75
(J R Boyle) *trckd ldrs: wnt 2nd 2f out: r.o but no imp ins fnl f* **14/1**

3 3 ¾ **Frank Street** 2-8-12 0........ StephenCarson 2 65
(Eve Johnson Houghton) *in tch tl rdn and one pce fr over 1f out* **6/1**

02 4 4 **Black Skirt**[16] 3967 2-8-4 0........ ChrisCatlin 7 42
(R Hannon) *trckd wnr to 2f out: wknd* **6/4[1]**

5 2 **Giverny (IRE)** 2-8-9 0........ ShaneKelly 4 40
(J Noseda) *slowly away: a bhd* **9/2[3]**

0 6 2 **Mount Ella**[91] 1680 2-8-8 0........ TPQueally 3 32+
(J A Osborne) *a bhd* **9/4[2]**

61.76 secs (1.46) **Going Correction** +0.125s/f (Good) **6 Ran SP% 119.9**
Speed ratings (Par 96): **93,91,85,79,75 72**
toteswinger: 1&2 £26.00, 1&3 £6.30, 2&3 £5.00. CSF £116.63 TOTE £13.20: £3.20, £3.70; EX 234.90.
Owner The Lime Street Syndicate **Bred** R N Auld **Trained** Epsom, Surrey

FOCUS
A modest juvenile maiden that was dominated by newcomers. The form is therefore not easy to rate with confidence.

NOTEBOOK
Leadenhall Lass(IRE), related to winners over further, pinged out of the gates and eventually made all to get off the mark at the first time of asking. She will get another furlong before all that long, but looks best at this trip for the short term and she clearly has a future. (op 10-1)
Louidor, a cheap purchase whose dam was a 1m winner in Germany, showed fair ability on this racecourse debut and finished a clear second best. He should come on nicely for the run. (op 12-1)
Frank Street, a half-brother to his stable's multiple 5-6f winner Judd Street, knew his job for this debut and left the impression he would improve with the experience now under his belt. Another furlong should suit him before too long. (tchd 7-1)
Black Skirt failed to raise her game for this drop to the minimum trip and ran a fair way below her previous level. She has something to prove after this, but is now at least qualified for a nursery mark. (op 7-4 tchd 2-1 in a places and 15-8 in places)
Giverny(IRE) Official explanation: jockey said filly ran green
Mount Ella, very well backed, was never in this and, despite her speedy pedigree, looked paceless. Official explanation: jockey said filly stumbled and lost its action closing stages (op 11-2)

4483 NIRVANA SPA 20TH ANNIVERSARY FILLIES' H'CAP 6f
7:40 (7:40) (Class 4) (0-80,80) 3-Y-0+ **£5,375** (£1,599; £799; £399) **Stalls** High

Form RPR

4560 1 **Linda Green**[21] 3797 7-8-9 **58** oh2........ ChrisCatlin 9 71
(M R Channon) *stdd s: hld up: rdn and sustained run fr over 1f out: to ld ins fnl f: sn clr* **12/1**

3-06 2 4 **Gentle Guru**[14] 4022 4-9-11 **74**........ SteveDrowne 6 74
(R T Phillips) *mid-div: rdn to ld over 1f out: hdd ins fnl f: nt pce of wnr* **10/1**

1-01 3 ¾ **River Bounty**[16] 3966 3-8-11 **65**........ NCallan 4 62+
(A P Jarvis) *chsd ldrs: rdn and nt qckn fr over 1f out* **8/1[3]**

0010 4 ½ **Sahaadi**[18] 3883 3-9-2 **70**........ JimmyFortune 3 65
(R Hannon) *s.i.s: in rr tl sme late hdwy* **14/1**

1-00 5 3 ½ **Our Piccadilly (IRE)**[19] 3838 3-9-8 **76**........ LPKeniry 2 60+
(W S Kittow) *chsd ldrs tl rdn and wknd over 1f out* **25/1**

2303 6 4 ½ **China Cherub**[13] 4051 5-9-10 **73**........(b) JohnEgan 8 44+
(S Dow) *led tl hdd & wknd qckly over 1f out* **9/2[2]**

4400 7 10 **Sweet Pickle**[14] 4016 7-10-0 **77**........(e) GeorgeBaker 1 16
(J R Boyle) *slowly away: a bhd and eaased fnl f* **14/1**

-221 8 9 **Orange Pip**[49] 2898 3-9-12 **80**........ RichardHughes 10 —+
(R Hannon) *w ldr tl rdn and wknd qckly 2f out* **8/11[1]**

1m 13.27s (0.27) **Going Correction** +0.125s/f (Good)
WFA 3 from 4yo+ 5lb **8 Ran SP% 121.2**
Speed ratings (Par 102): **103,97,96,96,91 85,72,60**
toteswinger: 1&2 £9.20, 1&3 £12.50, 2&3 £9.20. CSF £129.71 CT £1033.31 TOTE £8.60: £2.10, £2.70, £2.00; EX 71.10.
Owner John Livock **Bred** Colin Tinkler **Trained** West Ilsley, Berks
■ Stewards' Enquiry : L P Keniry three-day ban: used whip with excessive frequency (Aug 11-13)

FOCUS
A modest fillies' handicap, run at a generous early pace and the first two coame from well abck. The form could be rated higher but may be worth treating with a little caution.
China Cherub Official explanation: jockey said mare finished distressed
Sweet Pickle Official explanation: jockey said mare had no more to give

4484 ODL CAPITAL MAIDEN STKS 1m 67y
8:15 (8:15) (Class 5) 3-4-Y-0 **£2,729** (£806; £403) **Stalls** High

Form RPR

3433 1 **Border Owl (IRE)**[16] 3969 3-9-3 78........ RichardHughes 9 74+
(R Hannon) *broke wl: sn hdd: led again over 1f out: drvn clr* **8/11[1]**

666 2 4 ½ **Cheney Manor**[39] 3180 3-9-3 0........ MichaelHills 11 64
(B W Hills) *sn led: rdn and hdd over 1f out: nt pce of wnr* **8/1[3]**

5 3 1 **Unbiased (IRE)**[102] 1418 3-9-3 0........ JimmyFortune 2 62
(J L Dunlop) *chsd ldrs: rdn and one pce fr over 1f out* **5/2[2]**

00 4 2 **Angels Quest**[11] 4124 3-8-12 0........ JimCrowley 1 52
(A W Carroll) *in rr: styd on fr over 1f out: nvr nr to chal* **33/1**

00- 5 1 ½ **Our Lament**[315] 5470 3-9-3 0........ JamesDoyle 5 54
(J G Portman) *t.k.h: towards rr and nvr on terms* **33/1**

50 6 1 ¼ **Magpie (IRE)**[4] 4349 3-9-3 0........ TQuinn 10 51
(B G Powell) *stdd s: hld up: rdn over 2f out: nvr on terms* **12/1**

0 7 ¾ **No Wonga**[7] 4249 3-8-12 0........ RichardEvans(5) 4 49
(P D Evans) *a bhd* **16/1**

8 33 **Dancing Rhythm** 3-9-3 0........ TGMcLaughlin 8 —
(M S Saunders) *slowly away: a in rr and taking t.k.h: lost tch 3f out: t.o* **20/1**

0 9 3 ¼ **Dungleddy Star**[16] 3963 3-8-9 0........ KevinGhunowa(3) 6 —
(J M Bradley) *a bhd: lost tch 4f out: t.o* **66/1**

1m 45.22s (0.52) **Going Correction** +0.025s/f (Good)
WFA 3 from 4yo 8lb **9 Ran SP% 123.3**
Speed ratings (Par 103): **98,93,92,90,89 87,87,54,50**
toteswinger: 1&2 £1.70, 1&3 £1.60, 2&3 £4.40. CSF £8.40 TOTE £1.80: £1.20, £2.30, £1.10; EX 8.40.
Owner K T Ivory **Bred** Gainsborough Stud Management Ltd **Trained** East Everleigh, Wilts
■ Stewards' Enquiry : James Doyle caution: careless riding

FOCUS
A weak maiden, run at a fair pace. The winner won as he was entitled to with the second to his debut form and the race limited by the proximity of the fourth, fifth and sixth.

4485 SEVENTH HEAVEN EVENTS H'CAP 1m 3f 135y
8:45 (8:46) (Class 5) (0-70,67) 3-Y-0+ **£2,729** (£806; £403) **Stalls** Low

Form RPR

0544 1 **Isle Of Capri**[11] 4112 3-9-6 **66**........ RichardHughes 3 78
(R Hannon) *towards rr: rdn 3f out: hdwy 3f out: led 1f out: rdn clr* **4/1[1]**

-115 2 3 ¼ **Auntie Mame**[39] 3163 4-10-0 **62**........ TPO'Shea 8 68
(D J Coakley) *in tch: hdwy to chal appr fnl f: nt pce of wnr but kpt on* **7/1[3]**

0065 3 hd **Ocean Avenue (IRE)**[6] 4275 9-9-10 **58**........(p) TQuinn 7 64
(C A Horgan) *in rr: styd on fr over 1f out: nvr nrr* **13/2[2]**

0004 4 2 **The Grey One (IRE)**[24] 3698 5-8-8 **45**........(p) KevinGhunowa(3) 2 47
(J M Bradley) *stdd s: t.k.h: hdwy over 1f out: nvr nrr* **20/1**

5043 5 ¾ **Converti**[7] 4250 4-8-11 **50**........ JamieJones(5) 11 51
(H J Manners) *bhd: hdwy 2f out: styd on: nvr nrr* **20/1**

3360 6 6 **Bold Bobby Be (IRE)**[16] 3970 4-10-0 **62**........ JimmyFortune 1 53
(J L Dunlop) *in rr: hdwy over 2f out but nvr on terms* **13/2[2]**

-000 7 2 ¼ **Dancing Marabout (IRE)**[42] 3095 3-9-4 **64**........(b) ShaneKelly 5 51
(C R Egerton) *mid-div: effrt over 2f out: wknd over 1f out* **28/1**

0-14 8 1 ½ **Credential**[16] 3965 6-9-7 **55**........ StephenDonohoe 12 39
(John A Harris) *led tl hdd over 1f out: wknd qckly fnl f* **12/1**

0125 9 ¾ **Dancing Dik**[18] 3873 3-9-7 **67**........(p) JimCrowley 6 50
(Mrs A J Perrett) *trckd ldrs tl wknd over 2f out* **4/1[1]**

0660 10 ¾ **Muffett's Dream**[7] 4254 4-8-12 **46**........ FrankieMcDonald 4 28
(J J Bridger) *trckd ldr: rdn 3f out: sn wknd: eased ins fnl f* **40/1**

253 11 1 **Paddy Rielly (IRE)**[44] 3022 3-9-0 **60**........ TPQueally 10 40
(P D Evans) *bhd: effrt on outside over 2f out: sn btn* **4/1[1]**

2m 28.88s (-0.62) **Going Correction** +0.025s/f (Good)
WFA 3 from 4yo+ 12lb **11 Ran SP% 122.3**
Speed ratings (Par 103): **103,100,100,99,98 94,93,92,91,91 90**
toteswinger: 1&2 £10.40, 1&3 £12.80, 2&3 £11.00. CSF £32.39 CT £184.10 TOTE £4.30: £1.80, £3.30, £2.40; EX 41.20 Place 6: £1,438.43, Place 5: £639.51..
Owner The Queen **Bred** The Queen **Trained** East Everleigh, Wilts

FOCUS
A moderate handicap, run at a sound enough pace. The form is rated through the runner-up with the third and fourth just below their latest marks.
Credential Official explanation: jockey said horse ran too free
T/Plt: £12,891.00 to a £1 stake. Pool: £83,880.33. 4.75 winning tickets. T/Qpdt: £460.00 to a £1 stake. Pool: £6,029.77. 9.70 winning tickets. JS

4279 YARMOUTH (L-H)
Monday, July 28

OFFICIAL GOING: Good to firm
Wind: modest across Weather: warm but clouding over

4486 DIGIBET.COM FILLIES' MAIDEN AUCTION STKS 5f 43y
2:30 (2:30) (Class 6) 2-Y-0 **£2,137** (£635; £317; £158) **Stalls** High

Form RPR

2 1 **Leftontheshelf (IRE)**[23] 3735 2-8-6 0........ TolleyDean(3) 7 80+
(J L Spearing) *mde all: shkn up 2f out: hung lft over 1f out: r.o wl* **1/1[1]**

2420 2 1 ½ **Miss Hollybell**[41] 3105 2-8-6 0........ ChrisCatlin 2 71
(J Gallagher) *chsd wnr thrght: rdn and ev ch 2f out: edgd lft and kpt on same pce fnl f* **4/1[3]**

020 3 1 **Shiva Adiva**[58] 2618 2-8-4 0........ RichardKingscote 1 65
(Tom Dascombe) *chsd ldrs: rdn and tried to chal 2f out: edgd lft fr over 1f out: no ex last 100yds* **2/1[2]**

006 4 4 **Accomplishment (IRE)**[16] 3949 2-8-9 0........ DarrenWilliams 6 56
(A P Jarvis) *a chsng ldng trio: rdn and struggling 1/2-way: wl hld over 1f out* **100/1**

0 5 4 ½ **Lady Angelica**[9] 4199 2-8-4 0........ JimmyQuinn 4 35
(Dr J D Scargill) *a off the pce in midfield: rdn 1/2-way: no ch last 2f* **33/1**

6 ¾ **Princess Rebecca** 2-8-8 0........ TedDurcan 3 36
(E F Vaughan) *s.i.s: a struggling in last pair* **33/1**

7 1 ½ **Pedestrian (IRE)** 2-8-7 0........ LiamJones 5 30
(W J Haggas) *s.i.s: a struggling in last pair* **18/1**

61.87 secs (-0.33) **Going Correction** -0.075s/f (Good) **7 Ran SP% 115.5**
Speed ratings (Par 89): **99,96,95,88,81 80,77**
toteswinger: 1&2 £1.40, 1&3 £1.40, 2&3 £1.30. CSF £5.69 TOTE £1.90: £1.30, £2.10; EX 5.80.
Owner Miss C Ive **Bred** J F Tuthill **Trained** Kinnersley, Worcs

FOCUS
A decent heat for the grade, especially at this track. The market suggested that it was to all intents and purposes a three-horse contest, and this was borne out in the race itself as the leading trio pulled well clear and the form is rated around them.

NOTEBOOK
Leftontheshelf(IRE)'s debut second had been advertised by the winner going on to win the Super Sprint race at Newbury next time, and she made all for a decisive success despite tending to drift left in the closing stages, something her trainer put down to her feeling the firm ground. Indeed, she kept on well enough to suggest that she will be equally as effective at 6f, which will open up more options for her. (op 10-11 tchd 5-6)

Miss Hollybell was well backed on her first outing since running with great credit as a 100-1 outsider in the Windsor Castle Stakes at Royal Ascot, but had to settle for the runner-spot for the third time in five starts. There doesn't appear to be anything wrong with her attitude, she has just been finding one too good, and if she hung left under pressure it was because she was following the winner. (op 7-1 tchd 15-2)
Shiva Adiva's second start behind Sun Ship at Salisbury in a race that has thrown up a few winners stood out among her three previous efforts, but she went off at short enough price for what she'd done, possibly due to the overall good form of the yard's juveniles. She ran respectably but couldn't pick up with the front two, and followed them in tending to edge left in the closing stages. (op 85-40 tchd 10-3)
Accomplishment(IRE) showed up for a fair way, hinting at a modicum of ability. She could do better in time. (op 66-1)

4487 BEACH RADIO (S) STKS — 6f 3y
3:00 (3:01) (Class 6) 2-Y-O — **£1,942** (£578; £288) **Stalls** High

Form				RPR
0	1		**All Angel**[12] 4088 2-8-6 0 ... RichardKingscote 5 (M D Squance) *w ldr: shkn up to ld wl over 1f out: edgd lft but in command fnl f* **20/1**[3]	56
543	2	2½	**Royal Muwasim**[11] 4113 2-8-6 0 ... EdwardCreighton 6 (M R Channon) *nvr looked happy in last: rdn over2f out: drvn to chse wnr ent fnl f: no imp* **4/7**[1]	48
6335	3	4½	**Kheley (IRE)**[38] 3225 2-8-6 0 ... LiamJones 3 (W M Brisbourne) *led: rdn over 2f out: hdd wl over 1f out: wknd jst over 1f out* **7/4**[2]	35

1m 14.64s (0.24) **Going Correction** -0.075s/f (Good) — 3 Ran SP% **104.8**
Speed ratings (Par 92): **95,91,85**
.The winner was bought by M. Bringloe for 5,200gns. Royal Muwasim was claimed by Debbie Mountain for £5,000.\n\x\x
Owner Miss T J Fitzgerald **Bred** Kevin Daniel Crabb **Trained** Newmarket, Suffolk

FOCUS
A poor juvenile seller which cut up badly numbers-wise and best rated through the runner-up. The Channon-trained favourite is regressive as is the third home, and backers of the old 'outsider of three' maxim had a bumper pay-day.

NOTEBOOK
All Angel was tailed off on her debut on Lingfield's Polytrack 12 days ago and, although this was obviously a massive improvement and she has some ability, these opponents are going nowhere and it was something of a surprise that she was bought for 5,200gns at the auction. (op 9-1 tchd 8-1)
Royal Muwasim has gone steadily backwards in four starts to date and couldn't take advantage of a golden opportunity to break her maiden. Maybe the going was quick enough for her but she is one to have reservations about. (op 5-6 tchd 10-11 and evens in a place)
Kheley(IRE) probably finds this ground fast enough but she's had seven races now and it is looking increasingly unlikely that she is going to break her duck. (op 5-4)

4488 NATIONAL EXPRESS EAST ANGLIA MAIDEN AUCTION STKS — 7f 3y
3:30 (3:30) (Class 6) 2-Y-O — **£2,137** (£635; £317; £158) **Stalls** High

Form				RPR
254	1		**Fazbee (IRE)**[60] 2541 2-8-10 0 ... AlanMunro 2 (P W D'Arcy) *trckd ldrs: shkn up to ld narrowly over 1f out: hld hd high: rdn and forged ahd last 50yds* **1/3**[1]	75
33	2	1	**Blue Arctic**[34] 3348 2-8-7 0 ... LiamJones 7 (J M P Eustace) *t.k.h: pressed ldr: rdn and ev ch fr over 1f out tl hung rt and btn last 50yds* **10/3**[2]	69
0	3	3	**Rebounding**[7] 4256 2-8-7 0 ... RichardKingscote 6 (S C Williams) *hld up in tch: rdn over 1f out: chsd ldng pair ent fnl f: kpt on but nvr pce to chal* **33/1**	62
0	4	2¾	**Count On Guest**[7] 4256 2-9-1 0 ... AdrianMcCarthy 8 (G G Margarson) *t.k.h: led narrowly: rdn and hdd over 1f out: wknd jst over 1f out* **66/1**	63
	5	3	**Itsher** 2-8-7 0 ... SaleemGolam 4 (S C Williams) *v.s.a: hld up in rr: pushed along 3f out: nvr trbld ldrs* **22/1**	47
00	6	½	**Pokfulham (IRE)**[79] 1987 2-9-1 0 ... DarrenWilliams 1 (A P Jarvis) *t.k.h: chsd ldrs: rdn 3f out: wknd ent fnl 2f* **50/1**	54
	7	9	**My Choice** 2-8-9 0 ... TedDurcan 3 (A P Jarvis) *v.s.a: rn green and a detached in last* **20/1**[3]	25

1m 27.33s (0.73) **Going Correction** -0.075s/f (Good) — 7 Ran SP% **113.6**
Speed ratings (Par 92): **92,90,87,84,80 80,70**
toteswinger: 1&2 £1.20, 1&3 £4.10, 2&3 £5.10. CSF £1.54 TOTE £1.30: £1.10, £1.40; EX 1.60 Trifecta £17.60 Pool: £534.49 - 22.37 winning units..
Owner Mrs Dot Burlton **Bred** Stuart McPhee Bloodstock & Morton Bstock **Trained** Newmarket, Suffolk

FOCUS
No strength in depth to this maiden auction and the market made it a two-horse race beforehand. It proved to be a correct assumption and there is little to get excited about in the form as the winner was below her best in victory.

NOTEBOOK
Fazbee(IRE) had easily the best form of these, including in Listed company, and didn't have to run to anywhere near the best of her form to take this on her first start following a two-month break. She will need to step up if she is going to prove competitive in the Sweet Solera Stakes which connections put forward as her target. (op 4-11 tchd 2-5)
Blue Arctic has run to a fair level of form on all three starts now and gave the odds-on favourite quite a fright. She hasn't got any secrets from the Handicapper and won't be exactly thrown in if she goes into nurseries, while it wouldn't have to be the worst maiden in the world for her to break her duck in that company. (op 7-2 tchd 4-1 in a place)
Rebounding kept on nicely in the closing stages and looks as though she is being brought along with nurseries in mind.
Count On Guest showed up for a long way and may be of some interest off a lowly mark in nurseries after his next qualifying run. (op 50-1)
Itsher Official explanation: jockey said filly ran green
My Choice Official explanation: jockey said colt missed the break

4489 MARTIN FOULGER MEMORIAL H'CAP — 7f 3y
4:00 (4:01) (Class 4) (0-80,79) 3-Y-O+ **£4,667** (£1,397; £698; £349; £173) **Stalls** High

Form				RPR
0310	1		**Registrar**[6] 4284 6-8-9 **60** oh4 ... (p) SaleemGolam 6 (Mrs C A Dunnett) *hld up in tch: chsd clr ldr 2f out: sn rdn: kpt on relentlessly u.p fnl f to ld last strides* **9/1**	68
1436	2	hd	**Rockfield Lodge (IRE)**[7] 4258 3-9-2 **74** ... (b[1]) NeilPollard 8 (M E Rimmer) *awkward s: racd alone on stands rail and sn led and clr: 8l ld and rdn 2f out: hung lft over 1f out: stened and hung rt ins fnl f: hdd last strides* **11/1**	78
5232	3	1½	**Bobski (IRE)**[10] 4162 6-9-12 **77** ... (p) AlanMunro 4 (Miss Gay Kelleway) *stdd s: hld up in rr: sme hdwy 2f out: rdn and r.o fr over 1f out: nt rch ldrs* **5/2**[2]	80
20-0	4	½	**Daring Dream (GER)**[101] 1448 3-8-12 **70** ... DarrenWilliams 1 (A P Jarvis) *disp 2nd tl rdn to chse clr ldr 3f out tl 2f out: plugged on u.p fnl f: nvr able to chal* **12/1**	69
306	5	1½	**Hits Only Cash**[17] 3903 6-8-11 **62** ... (p) JimmyQuinn 3 (J Pearce) *stdd s: hld up in rr: rdn 3f out: kpt on wl fnl f: nvr threatened ldrs* **10/1**	60
0006	6	½	**Fitzroy Crossing (USA)**[14] 4017 3-9-5 **77** ... (b[1]) GregFairley 7 (M Johnston) *disp 2nd tl rdn over 3f out: lost pl u.p wl over 2f out: kpt on fnl f: nvr threatened ldrs* **5/1**[3]	70
0314	7	7	**Manchurian**[11] 4121 4-10-0 **79** ... (p) PatCosgrave 2 (M J Wallace) *stdd s: hld up in rr: effrt and edgd lft 3f out: no hdwy: no ch and eased ins fnl f* **2/1**[1]	56

1m 25.63s (-0.97) **Going Correction** -0.075s/f (Good)
WFA 3 from 4yo+ 7lb — 7 Ran SP% **113.7**
Speed ratings (Par 105): **102,101,100,99,97 97,89**
toteswinger: 1&2 £9.30, 1&3 £3.70, 2&3 £4.80. CSF £96.48 CT £320.94 TOTE £11.90: £3.40, £4.60; EX 110.10 Trifecta £191.60 Pool: £562.09 2.17 winning units..
Owner The Smart Syndicate **Bred** Cheveley Park Stud Ltd **Trained** Hingham, Norfolk
■ Stewards' Enquiry : Neil Pollard caution: used whip down shoulder in forehand position.

FOCUS
A fair handicap but with a couple of the more likely candidates failing to give their true running the form looks messy and dubious.
Manchurian Official explanation: jockey said gelding never travelled

4490 SHIRLEY GILL MEMORIAL H'CAP — 2m
4:30 (4:30) (Class 6) (0-65,55) 4-Y-O+ — **£2,072** (£616; £308; £153) **Stalls** Low

Form				RPR
0033	1		**Chiff Chaff**[3] 4391 4-8-9 **46** ... TolleyDean[(3)] 2 (C R Dore) *hld up in tch: effrt on chal 3f out: led 2f out: styd on u.p to assert last 100yds* **10/1**	53
65-1	2	1¼	**That Look**[18] 3863 5-9-7 **55** ... TedDurcan 9 (D E Cantillon) *chsd ldr tl led narrowly 4f out: sn rdn: hdd 2f out: ev ch after tl no ex last100yds* **8/11**[1]	61
4552	3	1¼	**Sand Repeal (IRE)**[18] 3871 6-9-4 **55** ... RussellKennemore[(3)] 8 (Miss J Feilden) *chsd ldng pair: swtchd ins and rdn to chal 4f out: ev ch after tl no ex u.str.p ins fnl f* **5/1**[2]	59
5-00	4	2¼	**Centenary (IRE)**[23] 3732 4-9-0 **48** ... (p) AlanMunro 7 (D E Cantillon) *hld up in midfield: rdn and nt qckn 3f out: wnt modest 4th over 1f out: kpt on fnl f: nt rch ldrs* **17/2**[3]	49
0-00	5	6	**Mighty Kitchener (USA)**[26] 3614 5-8-11 **45** ... JimmyQuinn 5 (P Howling) *hld up in midfield: rdn and effrt 3f out: sn no imp and wl btn* **25/1**	39
6560	6	3¾	**Muntami (IRE)**[20] 3820 7-9-6 **54** ... PatCosgrave 4 (John A Harris) *hld up in rr: rdn and no prog over 3f out* **14/1**	44
3000	7	2¼	**Title Deed (USA)**[20] 3820 4-9-7 **55** ... (v) DarrenWilliams 6 (A P Jarvis) *hld up in rr: drvn and no rspnse 3f out* **33/1**	42
0000	8	1¾	**Grafty Green (IRE)**[11] 4123 5-8-11 **45** ... LiamJones 3 (W M Brisbourne) *hld up in rr: nvr a factor* **50/1**	30
0-06	9	18	**Royal Tender (IRE)**[18] 3871 4-8-11 **45** ... (v[1]) SaleemGolam 1 (V Smith) *sn rdn along to ld: rdn and hdd 4f out: sn dropped out: t.o fnl f* **33/1**	8

3m 34.18s (-0.42) **Going Correction** -0.075s/f (Good) — 9 Ran SP% **112.5**
Speed ratings (Par 101): **98,97,96,95,92 90,89,88,79**
toteswinger: 1&2 £2.60, 1&3 £2.80, 2&3 £1.80. CSF £16.91 CT £42.41 TOTE £7.90: £2.70, £1.02, £1.40; EX 21.40 Trifecta £43.60 Pool: £567.95 - 9.63 winning units..
Owner J A Higson & Castles UK **Bred** Sir Thomas Pilkington **Trained** West Pinchbeck, Lincs
■ Stewards' Enquiry : Russell Kennemore five-day ban: used whip with excessive force (Aug 11-15)

FOCUS
A very poor staying handicap and, rated through the third, definitely form to forget.

4491 ROY & JOAN TANNER MEMORIAL LADY RIDERS' H'CAP — 1m 3y
5:00 (5:02) (Class 6) (0-65,65) 3-Y-O+ — **£1,998** (£619; £309; £154) **Stalls** High

Form				RPR
5152	1		**Sabre Light**[13] 4066 3-9-13 **65** ... (p) MissRLLockie[(7)] 11 (A Bailey) *hung lft thrght: chsd ldrs: wnt 2nd wl over 3f out: led over 1f out: kpt on fnl f* **11/2**[3]	69
05-5	2	1½	**Uhuru Peak**[23] 3732 7-9-12 **49** ... (bt) MissSBrotherton 5 (M W Easterby) *in tch: chsd wnr and swtchd rt ent fnl f: hung lft and nt qckn fnl f* **5/1**[2]	52
6004	3	1½	**Our Blessing (IRE)**[24] 3675 4-10-5 **61** ... MissKellyBurke[(5)] 9 (A P Jarvis) *led: edgd lft last 2f out: hdd over 1f out: one pce ins fnl f* **12/1**	60
000U	4	hd	**Dawn Wind**[17] 3906 3-9-0 **45** ... MissARyan 6 (I A Wood) *bhd: rdn wl over 3f out: styd on steadily last 2f: clsng on ldrs last 100yds: nvr able to chal* **25/1**	42
0-05	5	1½	**Piano Man**[52] 2795 6-9-8 **50** ... MissSarah-JaneDurman[(5)] 10 (J C Fox) *v.s.a: wl bhd: hdwy 3f out: kpt on but nvr threatened ldrs* **16/1**	45
0031	6	3½	**Ruwain**[6] 4267 4-9-5 **45** ... MissMSowerby[(3)] 8 (P J McBride) *chsd ldrs: lost pl 1/2-way: rdn and no rspnse wl over 2f out: no ch after* **2/1**[1]	32
0030	7	3¾	**Strike Force**[57] 2640 4-10-2 **58** ... MissALHutchinson[(5)] 3 (K F Clutterbuck) *a bhd: n.d* **14/1**	37
530-	8	6	**Almora Guru**[224] 7169 4-9-13 **50** ... MissEJJones 7 (W M Brisbourne) *stdd s: hld up in midfield: rdn and hung lft over 2f out: wl btn after* **22/1**	15
0/00	9	3½	**Naughty Girl (IRE)**[119] 1116 8-9-6 **48** ow3 ... MissABevan[(5)] 12 (John A Harris) *lost iron leaving stalls tl 5f out: w ldr tl over 3f out: wknd 3f out: wl bhd last 2f* **33/1**	5

1m 41.46s (0.86) **Going Correction** -0.075s/f (Good)
WFA 3 from 4yo+ 8lb — 9 Ran SP% **96.8**
Speed ratings (Par 101): **92,90,89,88,87 83,80,74,70**
toteswinger: 1&2 £3.90, 1&3 £5.80, 2&3 £7.10. CSF £21.66 CT £161.47 TOTE £5.00: £1.80, £1.40, £2.50; EX 19.90 Trifecta £105.90 Pool: £214.67 - 1.50 winning units. Place 6: £1179.40 Place 5: £741.91 .
Owner Phil Buchanan **Bred** D J And Mrs Deer **Trained** Newmarket, Suffolk

FOCUS
A typically modest handicap confined to lady riders and the form is weak and not solid.
T/Plt: £444.10 to a £1 stake. Pool: £63,222.18. 103.90 winning tickets. T/Qpdt: £12.80 to a £1 stake. Pool: £4,596.90. 264.60 winning tickets. SP

4492 - (Foreign Racing) - See Raceform Interactive

GALWAY (R-H)
Monday, July 28

OFFICIAL GOING: Good

4493a G.P.T. GALWAY (Q.R.) H'CAP — 2m
7:00 (7:00) (70-100,100) 4-Y-0+ **£47,867** (£14,044; £6,691; £2,279) **Stalls** Far side

RPR

1 **Majestic Concorde (IRE)**[13] 4069 5-10-12 87.....(b) MrRPMcNamara(3) 95
(D K Weld, Ire) *trckd ldrs: mainly 3rd: led on inner fr 3f out: rdn clr fr bef st: styd on wl* **7/1**[2]

2 4 **Power Of Future (GER)**[12] 4100 5-11-3 92........................ MrATDuff(3) 95
(Andrew Oliver, Ire) *chsd ldrs: 9th over 4f out: rdn to go mod 4th ent st: sn 2nd and no imp: kpt on* **25/1**

3 2 **Arc Bleu (GER)**[30] 3490 7-10-11 90........................ MrCPMcNally(7) 91
(A J Martin, Ire) *towards rr: hdwy over 3f out: rdn to go mod 6th early st: kpt on wout threatening* **10/1**[3]

4 3/4 **Fantoche (BRZ)**[15] 4003 6-10-6 85........................ MissKHarrington(7) 85
(Mrs John Harrington, Ire) *towards rr: hdwy over 3f out: rdn to go mod 5th early st: kpt on wout threatening* **25/1**

5 1 1/2 **Indian Pace (IRE)**[15] 4003 7-10-5 82........................ MrROHarding(5) 80+
(John E Kiely, Ire) *towards rr: hdwy appr st: kpt on wout threatening u.p* **14/1**

6 2 1/2 **Miss Fancy Pants**[15] 4003 4-11-1 87........................ MissNCarberry 83
(Noel Meade, Ire) *mid-div: 10th over 4f out: rdn appr st: sn no imp and kpt on same pce* **6/1**[1]

7 3/4 **Athlumney Lad (IRE)**[29] 3538 9-10-6 85........................(p) MrMJDoran(7) 80
(Noel Meade, Ire) *towards rr: 16th bef st: kpt on wl u.p wout threatening* **16/1**

8 1/2 **Queen Althea (IRE)**[16] 3989 4-10-4 81........................(p) MrEMullins(5) 75
(Noel Meade, Ire) *trckd ldr in 2nd: lost pl and no imp appr st* **16/1**

9 nk **Davorin (JPN)**[16] 3980 7-10-12 84........................(tp) MrKEPower 78
(M Halford, Ire) *trckd ldrs: 4th appr st: sn no imp u.p* **12/1**

10 shd **Jump For You (FR)**[64] 2434 6-11-9 100........................ MrBTO'Connell(5) 94
(H Rogers, Ire) *chsd ldrs: 8th over 4f out: rdn to go 3rd appr st: sn no ex* **50/1**

11 1 **Halla San**[30] 3490 6-11-3 96........................ MrBenHamilton(7) 89
(R A Fahey) *in rr of mid-div: no imp u.p and kpt on same pce fr 3f out* **12/1**

12 nk **P'Tit Fute (FR)**[78] 4013 7-10-13 85........................ MrDerekO'Connor 77
(F Flood, Ire) *in rr of mid-div: rdn fr under 4f out: sn no imp* **7/1**[2]

13 shd **Galistic (IRE)**[12] 4100 5-11-9 100........................ MMO'Connor(5) 92
(Patrick J Flynn, Ire) *chsd ldrs: 7th over 4f out: no imp u.p fr under 3f out* **12/1**

14 3/4 **Visit Wexford (IRE)**[15] 4003 7-10-1 78........................(b) MrCMotherway(5) 69
(John E Kiely, Ire) *towards rr early: clsr in 12th 1/2-way: 10th over 5f out: no imp u.p fr 3f out* **50/1**

15 hd **Serpentaria**[93] 5446 4-10-5 80........................ MrPWMullins(3) 71
(W P Mullins, Ire) *sn led: strly pressed and hdd 3f out: no ex st* **14/1**

16 1/2 **Ardalan (IRE)**[12] 4413 5-10-0 79........................ MrBO'Neill(7) 70
(Paul Nolan, Ire) *trckd ldrs: 6th over 4f out: wknd fr bef st* **16/1**

17 20 **Flashy Beau (IRE)**[16] 3980 8-10-7 82........................ MrMJO'Connor(3) 51
(A J Martin, Ire) *plld hrd in rr of mid-div: no ex u.p fr 3f out: eased fr bef st* **20/1**

18 1 **Ballet Boy (IRE)**[16] 3989 4-10-7 86........................ MrPaulJMcMahon(7) 54
(Charles O'Brien, Ire) *a bhd* **25/1**

19 1 **House Of Bourbon (IRE)**[17] 764 5-10-3 80...........(tp) MrCDSharkey(5) 46
(C F Swan, Ire) *mid-div: dropped away 6f out: rdn and no ex fr 4f out* **40/1**

20 22 **Mutadarrej (IRE)**[38] 3242 4-9-13 78........................ MrDMacAuley(7) 20
(Mrs Y Dunleavy, Ire) *prom: 5th over 4f out: sn wknd* **20/1**

3m 43.9s (-0.90) **20 Ran SP% 129.9**
CSF £184.88 CT £1784.08 TOTE £5.90: £2.30, £8.30, £3.30, £7.10; DF 355.10.
Owner Dr R Lambe **Bred** Martin Donovan **Trained** The Curragh, Co Kildare

NOTEBOOK
Halla San ran well below the level of his close second to today's third Arc Bleu in the Northumberland Plate and has to rate as somewhat disappointing. (op 10/1)

4494a G.P.T. CORK H'CAP — 7f
7:35 (7:35) (50-70,71) 3-Y-O **£7,621** (£1,775; £783; £452)

RPR

1 **Miranda's Girl (IRE)**[11] 4134 3-9-12 70........................(p) RPCleary 11 85
(Thomas Cleary, Ire) *trckd ldrs in 3rd: 2nd ent st: led u.p fr 1f out: styd on wl and sn clr: comf* **16/1**

2 4 **Drunken Sailor (IRE)**[36] 3299 3-9-12 70........................(tp) KJManning 12 74+
(Paul W Flynn, Ire) *chsd ldrs: clsr in 4th appr st: kpt on u.p wout troubling wnr into 2nd ins fnl f* **8/1**[3]

3 1 **Rebel Aclaim (IRE)**[12] 4093 3-9-2 67........................ BACurtis(7) 3 68
(P F Cashman, Ire) *led and disp: in front 1/2-way: strly pressed and hdd 1f out: sn no imp* **14/1**

4 2 1/2 **Separate Ways (IRE)**[12] 4093 3-9-8 66........................ JAHeffernan 13 60+
(Seamus G O'Donnell, Ire) *mid-div: 7th for much: kpt on wout threatening u.p st* **7/1**[2]

5 1 1/4 **Be Fantastic (IRE)**[26] 3617 3-9-11 69........................(p) KLatham 10 60
(G M Lyons, Ire) *led and disp: hdd 1/2-way: dropped to 3rd ent st: sn no imp u.p* **16/1**

6 nk **Jack Rio (IRE)**[7] 4265 3-9-11 69........................(p) WJSupple 14 59+
(Michael McElhone, Ire) *mid-div: 9th early: rdn to go 5th into st: sn no imp: kpt on same pce* **12/1**

7 1/2 **Archmani (USA)**[11] 4134 3-9-0 65........................(b) EJMcNamara(7) 15 53
(G M Lyons, Ire) *awkward leaving stalls and almost uns rdr: towards rr: rdn to go 7th early st: kpt on same pce* **25/1**

8 nk **Lecanvey**[324] 5216 3-9-5 66........................ JamieMoriarty(3) 7 54
(R A Fahey) *mid-div: reminders bef 1/2-way: no imp appr st: kpt on one pce* **7/2**[1]

9 5 **Gunavira (IRE)**[19] 3861 3-9-10 68........................(b) PJSmullen 5 42
(D K Weld, Ire) *dwlt: towards rr: no imp u.p and kpt on same pce fr bef st* **9/1**

10 3/4 **First In Command (IRE)**[5] 4315 3-9-10 71 5ex.............(t) PBBeggy(3) 9 43
(Daniel Mark Loughnane, Ire) *prom: t.k.h: 6th appr st: sn no imp u.p* **7/1**[2]

11 1 3/4 **Academic Accolade**[26] 3617 3-9-9 67........................(p) PShanahan 6 34
(Donal Kinsella, Ire) *in rr of mid-div: reminders early: rdn bef 1/2-way: sn no imp* **8/1**[3]

12 1 **The Pott Reidy (USA)**[7] 4265 3-9-5 68........................ PTownend(5) 1 32
(T J O'Mara, Ire) *dwlt: a towards rr* **20/1**

13 4 1/2 **Miss Aoife (IRE)**[12] 4093 3-9-8 66........................ WJLee 4 17
(C F Swan, Ire) *s.i.s: rdn to go 10th bef st: sn no imp* **20/1**

14 5 **Mister Bannon (USA)**[12] 4094 3-9-12 70........................(b[1]) DPMcDonogh 2 7
(Ms F M Crowley, Ire) *mid-div: 10th early: no ex appr st* **25/1**

15 1/2 **Magic Cloud**[47] 2960 3-9-9 67........................(bt[1]) FMBerry 8 3
(John Joseph Hanlon, Ire) *prom: rdn in 5th appr st: sn wknd* **14/1**

1m 29.22s (-2.38) **15 Ran SP% 129.5**
CSF £140.88 CT £1915.51 TOTE £25.50: £6.10, £2.30, £4.90; DF 140.90.
Owner John Cleary **Bred** Anthony Bryne **Trained** Athlone, Co Westmeath

NOTEBOOK
Separate Ways(IRE) Official explanation: jockey said gelding was denied clear run from before turn-in and would prefer a longer trip
Lecanvey, up in trip, was the subject of quite a gamble on this Irish debut, but he was never really going for his rider and it was clear before the final bend the support had gone astray. (op 4/1)

4010 CHANTILLY (R-H)
Monday, July 28

OFFICIAL GOING: Good

4496a PRIX LA MOSKOWA (LISTED RACE) — 1m 7f
3:20 (3:28) 4-Y-0+ **£19,118** (£7,647; £5,735; £3,824; £1,912)

RPR

1 **Limatus (GER)**[27] 3596 7-9-2........................ AStarke 3 106
(P Vovcenko, Germany)

2 hd **High Maintenance (FR)**[37] 3291 4-8-8........................ OPeslier 5 98
(A Fabre, France)

3 3 **Spanish Hidalgo (IRE)**[72] 2192 4-9-2........................ DBonilla 1 102
(J L Dunlop) *racd in 2nd bhd slow pce: 1 l down 2f out: sn rdn: one pce and lost 2nd 1f out: jst hld on for 3rd* **72/10**[2]

4 hd **Green Tango (FR)**[19] 5-8-11........................ RonanThomas 4 97
(P Van De Poele, France) **11/4**[1]

5 6 **Zadounevees (FR)**[27] 3596 5-8-11........................ DBoeuf 2 90
(W Gulcher, Germany)

3m 12.5s (-3.60) **5 Ran SP% 38.9**
PARI-MUTUEL: WIN 7.70; PL 2.50, 1.20; SF 20.30.
Owner Frau M Niebuhr **Bred** Frau M Niebuhr **Trained** Germany

NOTEBOOK
Spanish Hidalgo(IRE) shadowed the leader, who set a good gallop in front. When the pace quickened entering the straight he was caught a little flat footed and could not quicken in the style of the leader and eventual winner. He battled on slightly one-paced up the straight and was deprived of second by the fast-finishing High Maintenance. Connections reported that the going was too quick for him.

4243 BEVERLEY (R-H)
Tuesday, July 29

OFFICIAL GOING: Good to firm (firm in places; 10.2)
Wind: Fresh across Weather: Blutery and sunny

4497 E B F HOLDERNESS PONY CLUB MAIDEN STKS — 7f 100y
2:00 (2:02) (Class 5) 2-Y-O **£3,885** (£1,156; £577; £288) **Stalls** High

Form RPR

422 1 **Inheritor (IRE)**[13] 4072 2-9-3 0........................ PaulMulrennan 9 80
(B Smart) *led 2f: cl up on inner tl led again 3f out: rdn wl over 1f out: drvn ins fnl f and kpt on wl* **3/1**[1]

52 2 1 1/2 **Mannlichen**[9] 4214 2-9-3 0........................ J-PGuillambert 1 76
(M Johnston) *chsd ldrs on outer: effrt over 2f out and sn rdn along: drvn and hung rt ins fnl f: kpt on* **3/1**[1]

333 3 3/4 **Canwinn (IRE)**[17] 3968 2-9-3 0........................ TonyCulhane 3 75
(M R Channon) *prom: effrt over 2f out: sn rdn along and kpt on same pce appr fnl f* **7/2**[2]

5 4 2 1/4 **Heading East (IRE)**[9] 4214 2-9-3 0........................ FergalLynch 8 69+
(K A Ryan) *in tch: swtchd rt 3f out: swtchd lft and rdn to chse ldrs 2f out: styd on same pce u.p appr fnl f* **9/1**

5 5 1/2 **The Kyllachy Kid**[43] 3078 2-9-3 0........................ MickyFenton 7 68+
(T P Tate) *chsd ldrs whn hmpd and lost pl 3f out: kpt on appr fnl f* **9/1**

6 1 1/4 **Fantino** 2-9-3 0........................ PatCosgrave 4 65
(J Mackie) *outpcd and bhd after 2f: hdwy on outer 2f out: kpt on appr last: nt rch ldrs* **40/1**

4 7 1/2 **Blackstone Vegas**[18] 3926 2-9-3 0........................ RobertWinston 5 64+
(J Howard Johnson) *chsd ldrs: hung rt over 3f out: rdn along and wknd over 2f out* **11/2**[3]

25 8 9 **Mythical Blue (IRE)**[10] 4184 2-9-3 0........................ SaleemGolam 2 43
(S C Williams) *plld hrd: cl up tl led after 2f: rdn along and hdd 3f out: sn drvn and wknd 2f out* **25/1**

9 7 **Bollin Jimmy** 2-9-3 0........................ DavidAllan 6 27
(T D Easterby) *in rr: pushed along 3f out: rdn over 2f out: sn bhd and eased* **40/1**

1m 32.6s (-1.20) **Going Correction** -0.20s/f (Firm) **9 Ran SP% 116.3**
Speed ratings (Par 94): **98,96,95,92,92 90,90,80,72**
toteswinger: 1&2 £2.50, 1&3 £2.20, 2&3 £2.20. CSF £12.02 TOTE £4.50: £1.50, £1.50, £1.60; EX 13.90.
Owner Richard Page **Bred** Dominic O'Neill And Julie White **Trained** Hambleton, N Yorks

FOCUS
A pretty decent maiden for the course and with those with the best previous form filling the placings, the form should prove rock-solid.

NOTEBOOK
Inheritor(IRE) was proven over this trip and had the form in the book to be worthy of his position atop of the market. He was beating a fair pair of yardsticks here and should go on improving in nurseries. (tchd 11-4 and 10-3)
Mannlichen, who holds an entry in the Royal Lodge which now looks overly optimisitc, still looked green when asked to go and win his race. He should grow into a useful handicapper in time. (tchd 10-3 and 11-4 in a place)
Canwinn(IRE)'s early form in maidens was very promising but these are easier chances that he is passing up now and he is starting to look disappointing. (tchd 10-3)
Heading East(IRE) stayed on without threatening the principals. (tchd 8-1)
The Kyllachy Kid was already struggling when having to be snatched up off the home turn. He plugged on afterwards but the jury is out on him now. (op 10-1)

Fantino got well outpaced early on but that was forgivable on debut and he kept on nicely in the closing stages. He should learn from this. (op 50-1 tchd 80-1)

Blackstone Vegas was never really travelling and perhaps the ground was too firm for him. (op 7-1 tchd 15-2)

Mythical Blue(IRE) showed up well for a long way and it will be no surprise to see him drop back to sprinting now that he becomes eligible for a handicap mark.

4498 NATIONAL FESTIVAL CIRCUS (S) H'CAP — 1m 4f 16y

2:35 (2:35) (Class 6) (0-65,65) 3-Y-0 — £2,266 (£674; £337; £168) Stalls High

Form — RPR

5604 **1** **Linby (IRE)**[11] 4165 3-8-8 **52** .... TonyCulhane 6 — 57
(N Tinkler) *hld up in rr: hdwy over 2f out: rdn over 1f out: styd on ent fnl f to ld last 100yds* **6/1**

6250 **2** *2* **Bocciani (GER)**[11] 4148 3-9-7 **65** .... J-PGuillambert 7 — 67
(M Johnston) *trckd ldng pair: hdwy to ld wl over 2f out: sn rdn: drvn and edgd rt over 1f out and ent fnl f: hdd and no ex last 100yds* **7/2**[3]

0-04 **3** *1 1/2* **Lady Grantley**[15] 4019 3-8-2 **46** oh1 .... DaleGibson 5 — 45
(M W Easterby) *led: rdn along and hdd wl over 2f out: sn n.m.r: rallied wl u.p and ch ent fnl f: sn hrd drvn and one pce* **6/1**

033 **4** *1/2* **Bonny Bright Eyes**[13] 4075 3-7-12 **47** .... PatrickDonaghy(5) 3 — 46
(P C Haslam) *hld up: hdwy over 3f out: rdn to chal on wd outside wl over 2f out and ev ch tl drvn and wknd ins fnl f* **10/3**[2]

6460 **5** *2 1/4* **Howe's Jack (IRE)**[15] 4023 3-7-9 **46** oh1 .... (t) AndreaAtzeni(7) 4 — 41
(M C Chapman) *chsd ldrs: rdn along over 2f out: drvn wl over 1f out: grad wknd* **22/1**

-000 **6** *hd* **Syriana**[26] 3624 3-8-8 **55** .... DominicFox(3) 1 — 50
(A Bailey) *trckd ldr: effrt over 2f out: sn rdn and ev ch tl drvn and wknd appr fnl f* **16/1**

0002 **7** *7* **Bainisteoir**[15] 4026 3-8-9 **53** .... (b[1]) ChrisCatlin 2 — 36
(S Kirk) *trckd ldrs: hdwy 3f out: rdn to chal and ev ch tl drvn: edgd lft and wknd over 1f out* **11/4**[1]

2m 40.38s (-0.52) **Going Correction** -0.20s/f (Firm) **7 Ran SP% 110.8**
Speed ratings (Par 98): **93,91,90,90,88 88,84**
toteswinger: 1&2 £5.10, 1&3 £7.10, 2&3 £4.00. CSF £25.44 TOTE £7.40: £3.30, £2.30; EX 26.70.The winner was bought in for 5800gns. Bocciani was claimed by Anthony White for £6000.
Owner Derrick Bloy **Bred** Floors Farming **Trained** Langton, N Yorks
■ Stewards' Enquiry : J-P Guillambert caution: careless riding

FOCUS
A dire event in which the winner ran to his maiden form and the runner-up is rated up 4lb.

4499 BOOK ONLINE AT BEVERLEY-RACECOURSE.CO.UK MAIDEN AUCTION FILLIES' STKS — 5f

3:10 (3:13) (Class 5) 2-Y-0 — £2,590 (£770; £385; £192) Stalls High

Form — RPR

1 **Riotista (IRE)** 2-8-4 0 .... FrancisNorton 7 — 72+
(E J O'Neill) *hld up towards rr: gd hdwy 2f out: rdn to ld jst ins fnl f: rn green and wandered: hld on wl towards fin* **16/1**

2 *1/2* **Blades Princess** 2-8-7 0 .... FergalLynch 11 — 74+
(E S McMahon) *dwlt: sn pushed along and green in rr: swtchd lft and rdn wl over 1f out: str run ins fnl f: jst hld* **22/1**

2 **3** *1* **Positivity**[14] 4045 2-8-4 0 .... RoystonFfrench 5 — 67
(B Smart) *cl up: led 1/2-way: rdn wl over 1f out: drvn and hdd jst ins fnl f: sn hung lft and one pce* **5/2**[2]

52 **4** *4 1/2* **Sea Crest**[4] 4384 2-8-4 0 .... TWilliams 3 — 51
(M Brittain) *sn cl up: rdn 2f out and ev ch tl drvn and wknd appr fnl f* **9/2**[3]

00 **5** *nk* **Fashion Icon (USA)**[25] 3670 2-8-7 0 .... PaulFessey 10 — 53
(T D Barron) *chsd ldrs on inner: rdn along 2f out: kpt on same pce* **33/1**

324 **6** *1 1/2* **Sills Vincero**[8] 4251 2-8-7 0 .... ChrisCatlin 4 — 47
(P W Chapple-Hyam) *led to 1/2-way: sn rdn and cl up tl rdn and wknd over 1f out* **7/4**[1]

0 **7** *3/4* **Bubbly Baby**[49] 2909 2-8-7 0 ow3 .... DavidAllan 2 — 45
(T D Easterby) *wnt lft s: chsd ldrs on outer: rdn along 2f out: sn drvn and wknd* **50/1**

3445 **8** *1 3/4* **Rioja Ruby (IRE)**[47] 2965 2-8-7 0 .... AndrewElliott 8 — 38
(P C Haslam) *chsd ldrs: rdn along 2f out: sn drvn and wknd over 1f out* **25/1**

655 **9** *2 3/4* **Sale Or Return (IRE)**[14] 4045 2-8-1 0 .... (b) DuranFentiman(3) 1 — 25
(T D Easterby) *wnt lft s: sn cl up on outer: rdn along 2f out and sn wknd* **50/1**

5 **10** *hd* **Gee Gina**[24] 3707 2-8-7 0 .... MickyFenton 12 — 28
(P T Midgley) *a towards rr* **10/1**

00 **11** *6* **Peckforton**[17] 3949 2-8-7 0 .... DaleGibson 9 — 6
(D J G Murray Smith) *chsd ldrs: rdn along over 2f out: sn wknd* **100/1**

6 **12** *17* **Caledonia Princess**[43] 3085 2-8-4 0 .... TPO'Shea 6 — —
(P A Blockley) *s.i.s: a bhd: eased fnl 2f* **14/1**

63.20 secs (-0.30) **Going Correction** -0.20s/f (Firm) **12 Ran SP% 120.8**
Speed ratings (Par 91): **94,93,91,84,83 81,80,77,73,72 63,36**
toteswinger: 1&2 £36.50, 1&3 £10.70, 2&3 £17.70. CSF £325.86 TOTE £19.50: £3.30, £6.10, £1.40; EX 300.00.
Owner M Donovan **Bred** Martin Donovan **Trained** Averham Park, Notts

FOCUS
The two debutantes in the race came first and second, and considering they were representing yards which historically do well with juveniles, their juicy starting prices were surprising. They are both entitled to come on considerably for the race and must have more than their fair share of ability.

NOTEBOOK
Riotista(IRE) ◆, nibbled at in the market beforehand, made a winning debut. She seemed to know more about her job than the runner-up, for all that she got a touch unbalanced when her rider gave her a crack in the final furlong, and when he put his stick down she battled on well. The daughter of Captain Rio is one to follow. (op 33-1)

Blades Princess ◆ looked very green early on following a slow start, but once the penny dropped she really finished with a wet sail. She is bound to improve for this effort and a similar event would be almost a formality. (op 12-1)

Positivity took over the running at around halfway and only hoisted the white flag deep inside the final furlong. She appears to be making steady progress. (op 9-2)

Sea Crest showed up well for a long way but dropped out tamely and this might have come too soon after his good second at Thirsk four days ago. (op 10-3)

Fashion Icon(USA) had previously been well beaten in selling company so the fact that he could plug on for fifth puts the form of this race into perspective.

Sills Vincero was already beaten when hampered around a furlong out. Her stable is badly out of form at the moment. (tchd 13-8 and 2-1)

Caledonia Princess Official explanation: vet said filly returned lame

4500 WILFORD WATTS MEMORIAL H'CAP — 1m 100y

3:45 (3:46) (Class 4) (0-85,85) 3-Y-0+ — £5,180 (£1,541; £770; £384) Stalls High

Form — RPR

3056 **1** **Nevada Desert (IRE)**[10] 4206 8-9-1 **75** .... MichaelJStainton(3) 3 — 85
(R M Whitaker) *trckd ldrs: hdwy 3f out: chsd ldr 2f out: sn rdn and styd on wl ent fnl f to ld last 100yds* **9/2**[3]

0220 **2** *3/4* **Mesbaah (IRE)**[18] 3929 4-9-13 **84** .... (v) TonyHamilton 4 — 92
(R A Fahey) *led and sn clr: pushed along 2f out: rdn over 1f out: drvn ins fnl f: hdd and no ex last100yds* **10/3**[2]

510 **3** *3/4* **Never Ending Tale**[24] 3745 3-9-4 **83** .... AdrianMcCarthy 6 — 87
(W Jarvis) *hld up in tch: hdwy wl over 2f out: rdn wl over 1f out: kpt on ins fnl f: nrst fin* **14/1**

1610 **4** *shd* **Exit Smiling**[17] 3972 6-10-0 **85** .... MickyFenton 2 — 91
(P T Midgley) *hld up in rr: stdy hdwy on outer over 2f out: rdn over 1f out: styd on ins fnl f: nrst fin* **10/1**

1663 **5** *2 1/4* **Motafarred (IRE)**[18] 3899 6-9-4 **75** .... PaulHanagan 8 — 76
(Micky Hammond) *hld up in rr: hdwy over 2f out: sn rdn and kpt on ins fnl f: nt rch ldrs* **11/4**[1]

5425 **6** *shd* **Feisty Royale**[10] 4179 3-8-8 **73** .... J-PGuillambert 5 — 72
(M Johnston) *chsd ldrs: hdwy 3f out: rdn along over 2f out: drvn and one pce appr fnl f* **10/1**

4146 **7** *4 1/2* **Piper's Song (IRE)**[17] 3947 5-9-6 **77** .... (p) PatCosgrave 9 — 67
(D J G Murray Smith) *s.i.s: a in rr* **12/1**

0-20 **8** *14* **Stonehaugh (IRE)**[48] 2938 5-9-6 **77** .... (t) RobertWinston 7 — 35
(J Howard Johnson) *chsd clr ldr: rdn along 3f out: drvn 2f out and sn wknd* **14/1**

20 **9** *3/4* **Celtic Strand (IRE)**[10] 4206 3-8-11 **76** .... TonyCulhane 1 — 30
(T P Tate) *wnt lft s: sn chsng ldr: rdn along over 3f out and sn wknd* **16/1**

1m 44.56s (-3.04) **Going Correction** -0.20s/f (Firm)
WFA 3 from 4yo+ 8lb **9 Ran SP% 113.0**
Speed ratings (Par 105): **107,106,105,105,103 103,98,84,83**
toteswinger: 1&2 £3.60, 1&3 £12.00, 2&3 £11.70. CSF £19.42 CT £190.35 TOTE £6.10: £1.90, £1.60, £4.50; EX 16.80.
Owner J Barry Pemberton **Bred** Bryan Ryan **Trained** Scarcroft, W Yorks

FOCUS
Some useful types on show and the form has a solid look to it, rated around the first two.
Stonehaugh(IRE) Official explanation: jockey said gelding had a breathing problem; vet said gelding returned distressed

4501 WIFI EQUIPPED CONFERENCING H'CAP — 1m 4f 16y

4:20 (4:20) (Class 5) (0-70,70) 3-Y-0+ — £2,914 (£867; £433; £108; £108) Stalls High

Form — RPR

413 **1** **Trip The Light**[25] 3666 3-8-7 **57** .... (v) PaulHanagan 1 — 65
(R A Fahey) *trckd ldr: effrt 3f out: rdn over 2f out: drvn over 1f out: styd on u.p ins fnl f: led last 50yds* **2/1**[1]

2435 **2** *1 1/4* **Always Cruising (USA)**[18] 3911 3-9-6 **70** .... J-PGuillambert 3 — 76
(M Johnston) *chsd ldrs: rdn along wl over 2f out: drvn over 1f out: edgd rt ins fnl f: kpt on under severe press to take 2nd on line* **5/1**[3]

2325 **3** *nse* **Mister Fizzbomb (IRE)**[4] 4396 5-9-9 **66** .... (v) SladeO'Hara(5) 2 — 72
(J S Wainwright) *set stdy pce: qcknd 3f out: rdn 2f out: drvn over 1f out: hdd & wknd last 50yds* **8/1**

4061 **4** *1 1/4* **Fossgate**[25] 3666 7-9-6 **58** .... AndrewElliott 8 — 62
(J D Bethell) *trckd ldrs: effrt and hdwy 3f out: rdn along 2f out: n.m.r over 1f out: kpt on same pce* **5/1**[3]

6103 **4** *dht* **Thorny Mandate**[6] 4295 6-9-4 **56** .... FergalLynch 11 — 60
(W M Brisbourne) *hld up in rr: hdwy on outer 3f out: rdn along 2f out: drvn and kpt on ins fnl f: nrst fin* **9/2**[2]

3000 **6** *7* **Nelsons Column (IRE)**[13] 4075 5-9-10 **65** .... PJMcDonald(3) 4 — 58
(G M Moore) *trckd ldng pair: rdn along 3f out: sn drvn and wknd 2f out* **22/1**

040- **7** *8* **Terenzium (IRE)**[52] 5503 6-8-10 **48** oh1 .... (p) PaulMulrennan 6 — 28
(Micky Hammond) *in tch on inner: rdn along over 3f out andsn wknd* **14/1**

6500 **8** *9* **Firestorm (IRE)**[28] 3589 4-8-10 **48** oh3 .... (p) PaulFessey 7 — 14
(C W Fairhurst) *chsd ldrs: rdn along over 4f out and sn wknd* **80/1**

4003 **9** *18* **Right You Are (IRE)**[11] 4173 8-8-10 **51** .... RussellKennemore(3) 10 — —
(Paul Green) *hld up in rr: effrt and sme hdwy on outer over 3f out: sn rdn and wknd* **14/1**

2m 36.48s (-4.42) **Going Correction** -0.20s/f (Firm)
WFA 3 from 4yo+ 12lb **9 Ran SP% 114.9**
Speed ratings (Par 103): **106,105,105,104,104 99,94,88,76**
toteswinger: 1&2 £3.40, 1&3 £4.30, 2&3 £7.70. CSF £11.98 CT £64.93 TOTE £2.90: £1.10, £1.80, £2.30; EX 13.20.
Owner The Matthewman One Partnership **Bred** Darley **Trained** Musley Bank, N Yorks

FOCUS
A trappy handicap for moderate types, and the first five pulled miles clear. The only three-year-olds in the race finished first and second. Sound form with the first three running to their marks.

4502 GO RACING AT REDCAR TOMORROW H'CAP — 5f

4:55 (4:55) (Class 5) (0-75,80) 3-Y-0+ — £3,238 (£963; £481; £240) Stalls High

Form — RPR

3150 **1** **Timber Treasure (USA)**[26] 3626 4-9-10 **74** .... (b) FrancisNorton 1 — 85
(Paul Green) *trckd ldrs: hdwy wl over 1f out: rdn and qcknd to ld ins fnl f: kpt on wl* **10/3**[3]

0002 **2** *2 1/2* **Steelcut**[8] 4246 4-9-10 **74** .... PaulHanagan 4 — 76+
(R A Fahey) *stmbld s and bhd: rdn along and hdwy on outer wl over 1f out: drvn and kpt on ins fnl f: nt rch wnr* **6/4**[1]

6434 **3** *nk* **Malapropism**[6] 4291 8-9-11 **75** .... TonyCulhane 6 — 76
(M R Channon) *led: riddren 2f out: drvn and hdd ins fnl f: one pce* **3/1**[2]

6203 **4** *1/2* **Never Without Me**[12] 4125 8-8-10 **60** .... ChrisCatlin 5 — 59
(J F Coupland) *chsd ldng pair: rdn along wl over 1f out: kpt on same pce* **8/1**

4650 **5** *hd* **Just Joey**[2] 4462 4-8-11 **64** .... (v) NeilBrown(3) 3 — 62
(J R Weymes) *cl up: rdn and ch over 1f out: sn drvn and wknd ent fnl f* **9/1**

62.61 secs (-0.89) **Going Correction** -0.20s/f (Firm) **5 Ran SP% 109.2**
Speed ratings (Par 103): **99,95,94,93,93**
toteswinger: 1&2 £8.90. CSF £8.64 TOTE £4.20: £1.90, £1.50; EX 8.90.
Owner Gary Williams **Bred** London Thoroughbred Services & Derry Meeting Farm **Trained** Lydiate, Merseyside

FOCUS
An incredibly small turnout for a sprint handicap. The winner did it well and should stay competitive. The form is rated through the third.

4503 DOROTHY LAIRD MEMORIAL TROPHY (LADIES RACE) (H'CAP) 1m 1f 207y
5:30 (5:32) (Class 6) (0-65,65) 3-Y-0+ **£2,729** (£806; £403) **Stalls** High

Form RPR

6650 **1** **Don Pasquale**[62] 2513 6-9-5 **45**............................ MissMMullineaux(5) 9 55
(J T Stimpson) *hld up towards rr: stdy hdwy over 3f out: rdn wl over 1f out: str run to ld ins fnl f: styd on wl* **22/1**

2254 **2** *1* **Gala Sunday (USA)**[14] 4048 8-10-10 **59**.............(bt) MissSBrotherton 10 67
(M W Easterby) *a.p: hdwy to chse ldr over 2f out and sn rdn: drvn over 1f out and ev ch tl no ex wl ins fnl f* **5/1[2]**

0615 **3** *2* **Emperor's Well**[14] 4048 9-10-8 **57**............................ MissJCoward 7 61
(M W Easterby) *led: rdn along 2f out: hdd jst ins fnl f and kpt on same pce* **8/1**

45-0 **4** *½* **Amazing King (IRE)**[14] 4048 4-10-0 **54**............... MissSMStaveley(5) 16 57
(P A Kirby) *chsd ldr: rdn over 2f out: drvn and ev ch ent fnl f: kpt on same pce* **33/1**

4421 **5** *hd* **Gulf Coast**[14] 4048 3-10-6 **65**............................ KellyHarrison 17 68
(T D Walford) *trckd ldrs on inner: swtchd lft over 2f out: rdn and hung rt wl over 1f out: drvn and kpt on same pce ins fnl f* **9/4[1]**

0241 **6** *½* **Elite Land**[13] 4075 5-10-7 **56**............................ MissARyan 12 63+
(K A Ryan) *trckd ldrs: hdwy 3f out: effrt whn nt clr run and swtchd lft wl over 1f out: sn rdn and styng on whn n.m.r ins fnl f: stmbld, rdr lost irons and no ch after* **7/1**

3060 **7** *1 ¾* **Playtotheaudience**[36] 3329 5-10-1 **55**..................... MissNVorster(5) 11 53
(R A Fahey) *hld up towards rr: hdwy on inner over 2f out: rdn whn n.m.r over 1f out: sn one pce* **16/1**

3502 **8** *1 ¾* **Tizzy May (FR)**[14] 4048 8-10-8 **57**............................(v) MissLEllison 3 52
(B Ellison) *in tch: hdwy to chse ldrs 3f out: rdn over 2f out: grad wknd* **6/1[3]**

0-00 **9** *3 ½* **Weet Yer Tern (IRE)**[23] 1606 6-9-5 **45**..................... MissRKneller(5) 1 33
(W M Brisbourne) *s.i.s and bhd tl sme late hdwy* **50/1**

0-01 **10** *2* **Paparaazi (IRE)**[24] 3732 6-10-2 **56**........................(p) MissKSharp(5) 15 40
(I W McInnes) *s.i.s and rr: effrt and sme hdwy on wd outside 3f out: sn rdn and nvr a factor* **10/1**

0636 **11** *¾* **Scotty's Future (IRE)**[14] 4048 10-9-13 **48**..................... MrsCBartley 4 30
(A Berry) *towards rr: hdwy over 3f out: rdn wl over 2f out and sn btn* **20/1**

3046 **12** *5* **Weet For Ever (USA)**[79] 657 5-9-10 **45**..................... MissEJJones 14 17
(W M Brisbourne) *dwlt: a in rr* **28/1**

0000 **13** *4* **Mangano**[15] 4018 4-9-5 **45**............................ MissWGibson(5) 2 9
(A Berry) *towards rr: effrt and sme hdwy on outer 3f out: rdn over 2f out and sn wknd* **66/1**

/600 **14** *3 ½* **The Plainsman**[27] 3604 6-9-6 **46** ow1........... MissDawnBridgewater(5) 6 —
(P W Hiatt) *chsd ldrs on outer: rdn along over 3f out and sn wknd* **100/1**

-454 **15** *12* **Cecina Marina**[27] 3602 5-9-10 **45**............................ MissADeniel 8 —
(Mrs K Walton) *in tch: rdn along over 3f out and sn wknd* **22/1**

2m 6.14s (-0.86) **Going Correction** -0.20s/f (Firm)
WFA 3 from 4yo+ 10lb **15** Ran SP% **124.6**
Speed ratings (Par 101): **95,94,92,92,92 91,90,88,86,84 83,79,76,73,64**
toteswinger: 1&2 £26.20, 1&3 £39.90, 2&3 £9.00. CSF £124.84 CT £991.92 TOTE £22.40: £5.00, £2.50, £3.70; EX 431.90 Place 6: £62.01 Place 5: £47.30 .
Owner J T Stimpson **Bred** Chippenham Lodge Stud Ltd **Trained** Newcastle-Under-Lyme, Staffs
■ Stewards' Enquiry : Kelly Harrison caution: careless riding

FOCUS
The usual suspects for a race of this sort with six of these running in a similar race here a fortnight earlier. They are quite competitive and although the riders' abilities vary, the form tends to be fairly solid considering the level.
T/Plt: £79.40 to a £1 stake. Pool: £50,068.56. 459.78 winning tickets. T/Qpdt: £16.50 to a £1 stake. Pool: £3,791.08. 169.50 winning tickets. JR

3205 GOODWOOD (R-H)
Tuesday, July 29

OFFICIAL GOING: Good (good to firm in places; 8.8)
Dolling adding around 15yards to advertised distances on the round course.
Wind: Strong, half against Weather: Fine but cloudy

4504 BANK OF SCOTLAND INVESTMENT SERVICE STKS (HERITAGE H'CAP) 1m 1f 192y
2:15 (2:20) (Class 2) 4-Y-0+
£31,155 (£9,330; £4,665; £2,335; £1,165; £585) **Stalls** High

Form RPR

0002 **1** **Gulf Express (USA)**[25] 3684 4-8-12 **98**.............................(v) RyanMoore 3 110
(Sir Michael Stoute) *lw: hld up in last pair: trapped bhd wall of horses 3f out: eased to outer over 2f out: gd prog wl over 1f out: led 1f out: hung rt after but sn in command* **10/1**

4430 **2** *1 ¼* **Pinpoint (IRE)**[24] 3740 6-9-5 **105**............................ TedDurcan 2 114
(W R Swinburn) *hld up towards rr: prog on outer wl over 2f out: trying to mount a chal u.p whn hmpd ent fnl f: rallied to take 2nd last 100yds* **20/1**

1150 **3** *1* **Watamu (IRE)**[39] 3195 7-9-4 **104**.............................(v) EddieAhern 14 111
(P J Makin) *lw: quite keen: hld up in midfield: stdy prog over 2f out: led briefly jst over 1f out: outpcd fnl f* **25/1**

1002 **4** *2 ½* **Eradicate (IRE)**[17] 3974 4-9-6 **106**............................ GregFairley 10 108
(M Johnston) *trckd clr ldrs: prog to dispute ld 3f out: narrow advantage briefly over 1f out but hanging: wknd ins fnl f* **14/1**

-360 **5** *1 ½* **Monte Alto (IRE)**[17] 3974 4-8-13 **99**............................ JMurtagh 5 98+
(L M Cumani) *hld up in last quintet: trying to make prog on outer whn nt clr run over 2f out: hanging after but styd on wl fr over 1f out* **17/2**

11-3 **6** *hd* **Caravel (IRE)**[25] 3684 4-8-7 **93** ow2.................... SebSanders 17 92+
(Sir Mark Prescott) *lw: trckd ldng pair: u.p wl over 2f out but stl cl up: nt qckn over 1f out: outpcd fnl f* **13/2[2]**

-416 **7** *½* **Proponent (IRE)**[38] 3249 4-8-11 **97**............................ SteveDrowne 15 95+
(R Charlton) *lw: trckd ldng pair: led 3f out: sn joined: hdd and faded over 1f out* **11/2[1]**

1410 **8** *¾* **Championship Point (IRE)**[17] 3974 5-9-10 **110**........... DarryllHolland 4 106
(M R Channon) *hld up in last quintet: rdn over 3f out: sme prog 2f out: hung rt u.p over 1f out: nvr pce to rch ldrs* **12/1**

25-5 **9** *¾* **Kinsya**[19] 3885 5-8-9 **95**............................ JimmyQuinn 9 90
(M H Tompkins) *t.k.h: hld up in midfield: n.m.r 4f out: rdn and no real prog over 2f out: hanging and nt qckn in midfield over 1f out* **50/1**

2500 **10** *nk* **Illustrious Blue**[39] 3195 5-9-5 **105**............................ RichardKingscote 6 99
(W J Knight) *hld up in midfield: prog on outer 4f out to press ldrs 3f out: rdn over 2f out: losing pl whn hmpd 1f out* **12/1**

0541 **11** *hd* **Humungous (IRE)**[2] 4443 5-9-2 **102** 6ex.....................(b) JohnEgan 18 96+
(C R Egerton) *swtg: rrd s: sn pushed up to midfield: effrt whn snatched up jst over 2f out: swtchd ins and trying again whn chopped off 1f out* **14/1**

4- **12** *2 ¼* **Minkowski**[213] 5-8-7 **93**............................ ShaneKelly 1 82
(J Noseda) *swtg: hld up in last quintet: brief effrt on outer 3f out: sn no prog* **14/1**

1201 **13** *2 ¼* **Mr Aviator (USA)**[41] 3122 4-9-7 **107**............................ RichardHughes 13 92
(R Hannon) *lw: trckd clr ldrs: cl enough over 2f out: wknd and edgd rt jst over 1f out: eased* **12/1**

6-10 **14** *3* **Emirates Skyline (USA)**[39] 3195 5-9-9 **109**..................... LDettori 12 88
(Saeed Bin Suroor) *lw: trckd clr ldrs: rdn over 2f out: nt qckn and hld over 1f out: eased whn btn fnl f* **12/1**

20 **15** *1 ½* **Escape Route (USA)**[53] 2790 4-9-0 **100**...................(p) JimmyFortune 7 76
(J H M Gosden) *swtg: dwlt: a in last quintet: u.p and struggling wl over 2f out* **16/1**

0040 **16** *¾* **Levera**[10] 4192 5-8-13 **99**............................ FergusSweeney 11 73+
(A King) *mostly pressed ldr to 3f out: sn lost pl and wknd* **66/1**

2213 **17** *4 ½* **Luberon**[2] 4444 5-8-7 **93**............................ JoeFanning 8 58+
(M Johnston) *swtg: mde most to 3f out: wknd rapidly* **8/1[3]**

2m 6.09s (-1.91) **Going Correction** +0.15s/f (Good) **17** Ran SP% **128.2**
Speed ratings (Par 109): **113,112,111,109,108 107,107,106,106,106 105,104,102,99,98 98,94**
toteswinger: 1&2 £45.50, 1&3 £72.00, 2&3 £68.40. CSF £209.39 CT £4843.68 TOTE £13.70: £3.20, £5.60, £6.80, £3.70; EX 383.50 Trifecta £1775.90 Part won. Pool: £2399.99 - 0.10 winning units..
Owner Saeed Suhail **Bred** Gracefield And Brad Ray **Trained** Newmarket, Suffolk

FOCUS
A strong, competitive handicap in which they went a good gallop. The principals came from off the pace and the form looks solid for the grade with the winner up 4lb and the next three close to their marks.

NOTEBOOK
Gulf Express(USA), who ran well at Sandown last time in a race where the leader was able to dictate throughout, had the race run far more to suit here, with a good pace leading to those held up being brought into contention in the straight. He tended to hang right once hitting the front and did the eventual runner-up few favours, but the Stewards left the result unchanged. Given his style of running he will remain of more interest carrying a big weight in top handicap company than in Listed grade, where the pace is less likely to be strong. (op 12-1 tchd 14-1)
Pinpoint(IRE), who has struggled over the past year off marks in the mid to high 100s, was another who had the race very much run to suit. He came from off the pace as well but the winner hung across him inside the last, hampering his challenge, and he could not regain his momentum. He remains on a tough mark from which to win a handicap of this sort but clearly thrives off a strong pace. (op 25-1)
Watamu(IRE) pulled too hard at Ascot last time and was again keen in the early stages here, despite there being a good gallop on. Travelling well in behind horses early in the straight, he looked a possibility a furlong out before the winner appeared on the outside. He is clearly just as effective on turf as he is on Polytrack.
Eradicate(IRE), 4lb higher for his good effort at York in testing ground last time, did best of those who raced close to the pace. His current mark makes handicaps difficult, but he could be the type to steal a Listed race somewhere when guaranteed an easy lead.
Monte Alto(IRE) was another hold-up performer who benefited from the good early gallop, but he did not get the best of runs and hung right in the closing stages, failing to make any real progress once in the clear. (op 9-1 tchd 10-1)
Caravel(IRE), whose rider put up 2lb overweight, chased the strong pace and paid for that in the latter stages. He is better than the bare form suggests. (op 6-1)
Proponent(IRE) was expected to be more at home back in trip, but he too did too much too soon by chasing a strong early pace. (op 13-2)
Championship Point(IRE) defied top weight to win this race last year but he could not repeat the trick off a 1lb higher mark, despite having the race run to suit. It might be that he needs a little more give in the ground to be seen at his best. (tchd 10-1)
Kinsya was keen in the early part of the race, which did not help his chance, and then he hung right in the closing stages.
Illustrious Blue tried to challenge down the outside in the straight but could make no real progress. He has a good record here but is not in the best of form at present.
Humungous(IRE), making a quick reappearance, got squeezed up near the rail approaching the two-furlong marker and then had his path blocked again on the rail approaching the final furlong. He was not knocked about in a lost cause afterwards.
Minkowski, last seen being pulled up over hurdles in December, never threatened to get involved. (op 33-1)
Mr Aviator(USA) was only plugging on one-paced when finding his path blocked on the rail inside the last. Official explanation: jockey said colt slipped coming down hill (op 10-1)
Luberon, another making a quick reappearance, once again used up too much energy getting to the front and setting a strong gallop. (op 15-2 tchd 7-1)

4505 BETFAIR GORDON STKS (GROUP 3) 1m 4f
2:50 (2:53) (Class 1) 3-Y-0
£39,739 (£15,064; £7,539; £3,759; £1,883; £945) **Stalls** Low

Form RPR

-312 **1** **Conduit (IRE)**[39] 3193 3-9-0 112............................ RyanMoore 3 114
(Sir Michael Stoute) *lw: trckd ldng pair: pushed along to chal 3f out: disp ld 2f out: hanging u.p 1f out: asserted last 50yds* **1/2[1]**

-501 **2** *hd* **Donegal (USA)**[19] 3875 3-9-0 106............................ MartinDwyer 6 113
(A M Balding) *t.k.h early: pressed ldr: rdn to dispute ld 2f out: w wnr after tl jst outpcd last 50yds* **14/1**

3210 **3** *1 ½* **Hebridean (IRE)**[39] 3193 3-9-3 0............................ JMurtagh 4 114
(A P O'Brien, Ire) *trckd ldng pair: swtchd to inner to chal 2f out and nrly upsides: nt qckn over 1f out: hld fnl f* **5/1[2]**

2003 **4** *1 ¾* **Bouguereau**[19] 3875 3-9-0 111............................ AlanMunro 2 108+
(P W Chapple-Hyam) *led: drvn and worn down 2f out: jst getting the worst of it whn squeezed out over 1f out* **10/1[3]**

-002 **5** *8* **Scintillo**[69] 2303 3-9-0 109............................ RichardHughes 1 95
(R Hannon) *lw: hld up in last pair: shkn up 3f out: sn lost tch w ldrs and btn* **11/1**

-404 **6** *1* **Alan Devonshire**[19] 3880 3-9-0 100............................ EddieAhern 5 94
(M H Tompkins) *t.k.h early and racd awkwardly: hld up in last pair: fizzled out 3f out* **33/1**

2m 37.14s (-1.26) **Going Correction** +0.15s/f (Good) **6** Ran SP% **110.4**
Speed ratings (Par 110): **110,109,108,107,102 101**
toteswinger: 1&2 £2.80, 1&3 £1.10, 2&3 £3.70. CSF £8.68 TOTE £1.50: £1.10, £3.20; EX 8.20.
Owner Ballymacoll Stud **Bred** Ballymacoll Stud Farm Ltd **Trained** Newmarket, Suffolk

The Form Book, Raceform Ltd, Compton, RG20 6NL

FOCUS

A race that has produced three St Leger winners in the last ten years, Nedawi, Millenary and most recently Sixties Icon, as well as several other high-class performers such as Bandari and Maraahel. Conduit made hard work of winning, but was not seen at his best off the ordinary pace and remains one the likelier winners of the Doncaster event. Hebridean ran well under his 3lb penalty and can be rated on a par with the front pair.

NOTEBOOK

Conduit(IRE), unfortunate not to win the King Edward VII at Royal Ascot (unsuited by slow pace, winner stole race off front end), looked a strong St Leger candidate that day, despite his trainer's poor record in the race, and this was his chosen trial. Made more use of on this occasion, his rider felt the ground was not as fast as he likes it, but he showed a willing attitude and battled back to deny Donegal. This somewhat laboured effort was a shade disappointing, but he will be a different horse off a strong gallop and it would come as no surprise to see him returned to more restrained tactics next time. His St Leger price was unchanged in most places and he remains one of the likelier winners, for all that his yard have at least three other options. (op 4-7 tchd 8-13 in places)

Donegal(USA) ◆ has been highly tried since winning his maiden as a juvenile, struggling in the main, but he showed improved form when tackling soft ground at Newmarket last time, winning the Listed Bahrain Trophy, and progressed again to just miss out here. He looked the likeliest winner just inside the final furlong, but in the end was run out of it by the favourite. His trainer would have preferred even softer ground for him and this highly progressive three-year-old, who has been talked of as a potential hurdler, now has the Prix Kergorlay at Deauville as his next intended target. (op 11-1)

Hebridean(IRE), one of very few to disappoint for Ballydoyle at the Royal meeting (behind Conduit) had earlier been most progressive on a variety of ground and he came back to his best here. He faced a stiff task conceding 3lb to the favourite, but made a good fist of it and it was only in the final half furlong he backed out of it. There is another race in him at this level, but he has already been gelded and he too could make a fine hurdler. (tchd 4-1)

Bouguereau, who finished just worse than midfield in the Derby, was a shade disappointing when an even-money favourite at Newmarket last time, albeit not beaten far by Donegal, and he was made plenty of use of on this drop in trip. He ran well, already looking set for fourth when getting squeezed out, but this was evidently not enough of a test. His stable are hardly in the best of form at present and this maiden winner may need a drop in grade now. (tchd 12-1)

Scintillo was a Group 1 winner at the San Siro as a juvenile and came back to form when finishing second to City Leader in a 1m3f Listed event here last time, but he had been off since, having finished sore, and he offered little on this return. He was struggling over three out and dropped away tamely, leaving him with plenty to prove. (tchd 12-1)

Alan Devonshire seemed helped by the drop back to 1m when finishing fourth in a decent conditions event at Newmarket latest, but he was too keen here and failed to last home. He is not up to Group level. Official explanation: jockey said colt ran too free (op 40-1)

4506 BETFAIR CUP (REGISTERED AS THE LENNOX STKS) (GROUP 2) 7f

3:30 (3:31) (Class 1) 3-Y-O+

£87,993 (£33,356; £16,693; £8,323; £4,169; £2,092) **Stalls** High

Form	Pos	Dist	Horse / comment	Jockey	RPR
-110	**1**		**Paco Boy (IRE)**[79] 2032 3-8-9 110 (R Hannon) *trckd ldrs: effrt on outer 2f out: led 1f out and edgd rt: pushed out firmly ins fnl f* **7/1**[3]	RichardHughes 1	116
1024	**2**	*nk*	**Stimulation (IRE)**[41] 3119 3-8-9 110 (H Morrison) *lw: prom: trckd ldr 3f out: rdn to cl and inched ahd jst over 1f out: sn hdd: styd on but a hld* **14/1**	SteveDrowne 4	115
-201	**3**	*2 1/2*	**Dunelight (IRE)**[31] 3503 5-9-2 109 (C G Cox) *led at decent clip: hdd jst over 1f out: hanging and wknd ins fnl f but hld on for 3rd* **12/1**	(v) PhilipRobinson 5	111
-102	**4**	*hd*	**Il Warrd (IRE)**[41] 3119 3-8-9 109 (Saeed Bin Suroor) *lw: t.k.h: trckd ldr to 3f out: hanging and racd awkwardly after: nt qckn 2f out: kpt on again ins fnl f* **15/2**	LDettori 6	108
1422	**5**	*1 3/4*	**Infallible**[20] 3852 3-8-6 113 (J H M Gosden) *hld up towards rr: sme prog on outer over 2f out: shkn up and nt qckn over 1f out: n.d after: nt knocked abt* **5/4**[1]	RyanMoore 7	100
6-50	**6**	*1/2*	**Arabian Gleam**[42] 3100 4-9-6 114 (J Noseda) *lw: hld up in midfield on inner: bustled along 3f out: one pce and nvr any imp on ldrs* **8/1**	JMurtagh 9	109
-202	**7**	*2*	**Al Qasi (IRE)**[17] 3982 5-9-2 112 (P W Chapple-Hyam) *dwlt: hld up in midfield: rdn over 2f out: hanging and nt qckn: fdd over 1f out* **16/1**	TedDurcan 8	99
1312	**8**	*1/2*	**King Of Dixie (USA)**[31] 3498 4-9-2 109 (W J Knight) *a in last pair: rdn on wd outside 3f out and no prog* **13/2**[2]	SebSanders 2	98
6010	**9**	*3 3/4*	**Racer Forever (USA)**[18] 3921 5-9-2 108 (J H M Gosden) *t.k.h: hld up in rr: wknd 2f out* **25/1**	(b) JimmyFortune 3	88

1m 26.59s (-0.81) **Going Correction** +0.15s/f (Good)

WFA 3 from 4yo+ 7lb **9** Ran SP% **117.2**

Speed ratings (Par 115): **110,109,106,106,104 104,101,101,96**

toteswinger: 1&2 £11.80, 1&3 £17.80, 2&3 £28.30. CSF £99.97 TOTE £6.60: £1.60, £4.00, £3.20; EX 108.50 Trifecta £646.90 Pool: £1835.95 - 2.10 winning units..

Owner The Calvera Partnership No 2 **Bred** Mrs Joan Browne **Trained** East Everleigh, Wilts

FOCUS

The third is effective at this track, but his performance does limit the form somewhat in a race that was not run at a mad gallop. The winner's Greenham form has not worked out and this was a step up.

NOTEBOOK

Paco Boy(IRE), seventh in the French 2000 Guineas on his last start, found the drop in trip and grade in his favour. He quickened up well when asked to assert a furlong out and was always holding off Stimulation close home despite the fairly narrow margin. This distance seems to suit him well and the Prix de la Foret may offer him his best shot at Group 1 glory - he will certainly not be inconvenienced by the possible easier ground in France. The Celebration Mile, back here on 23 August is likely to be his next target, though. (op 15-2 tchd 8-1 in a place)

Stimulation(IRE), fourth in the Jersey Stakes last time, had every chance but the winner always just had his measure in the closing stages. He still finished clear of the rest, though, and deserves to break his Group-race duck. The Hungerford Stakes could provide him with that opportunity. (tchd 16-1)

Dunelight(IRE) was allowed his own way out in front, and while he set a solid gallop it was not too strong, as can be seen by the fact that after being crossed by the eventual runner-up inside the last he was able to regain his momentum and keep on for third. He goes well at this track and is a good guide to the level of the form. (op 11-1 tchd 14-1)

Il Warrd(IRE), who finished two places in front of Stimulation when runner-up in the Jersey, was unable to confirm that form as he appeared far from happy on the track, hanging right in the closing stages. (tchd 7-1 and 8-1)

Infallible was sent off a short-priced favourite on the back of her seconds in the Coronation Stakes and Falmouth Stakes, but she was taking on the colts for the first time and proved disappointing. She was brought to have every chance two furlongs out, but while the winner quickened she could only find the one pace. She was not beaten up in a lost cause and it could just be that this was one hard race too many for the time being. She is due to have a bit of a break now and could well be a different proposition in the autumn, when she could well come back in the Park Stakes at Doncaster. (op 11-8 after 6-4)

Arabian Gleam, who had to carry a penalty for his win in the Group 2 Park Stakes last autumn, was an unlucky-in-running fifth in this race last year, but he had no such excuse this time as he looked uncomfortable on the track and failed to run to his best.

Al Qasi(IRE), whose stable is not firing on all cylinders at the moment, was another who tended to hang in the closing stages. (tchd 20-1)

King Of Dixie(USA) reversed Newmarket form with Racer Forever, but that Group 3 race was a weak contest of its type and this company demanded even more. (op 7-1)

Racer Forever(USA) stole a Group 3 race at Newmarket last month but he is essentially difficult to place.

4507 BETFAIR MOLECOMB STKS (GROUP 3) 5f

4:05 (4:06) (Class 1) 2-Y-O

£34,062 (£12,912; £6,462; £3,222; £1,614; £810) **Stalls** Low

Form	Pos	Dist	Horse / comment	Jockey	RPR
12	**1**		**Finjaan**[61] 2541 2-9-0 0 (M P Tregoning) *lw: trckd ldng pair and racd towards outer: shkn up and clsd over 1f out: led last 150yds: hrd pressed fnl 75yds: pushed out and hld on* **5/1**[3]	RHills 6	108+
1	**2**	*hd*	**Bonnie Charlie**[106] 1363 2-9-0 0 (R Hannon) *w'like: lw: dwlt: settled in last trio and given time to rcvr: gd prog over 1f out: wnt 2nd last 100yds and threatened wnr: jst hld last strides* **8/1**	RichardHughes 8	108+
311	**3**	*1 1/4*	**Jargelle (IRE)**[10] 4190 2-8-11 0 (W J Haggas) *chsd ldr: clsd fr 2f out: drvn ahd narrowly 1f out: sn hdd and one pce* **7/1**	LiamJones 13	100
2211	**4**	*hd*	**Rievaulx World**[26] 3639 2-9-0 0 (K A Ryan) *lw: fast away: led against nr side rail and clr w two rivals: hdd 1f out: no ex* **9/2**[2]	NCallan 1	102
5112	**5**	*1 1/2*	**Spin Cycle (IRE)**[40] 3152 2-9-0 0 (B Smart) *lw: chsd ldrs but nt on terms: hanging fr 2f out: kpt on fnl f* **3/1**[1]	TedDurcan 2	97
3314	**6**	*nk*	**Flashmans Papers**[40] 3152 2-9-0 0 (J R Best) *lw: struggling to go the pce in rr: sme prog on outer over 1f out: n.d* **9/1**	SteveDrowne 15	96
310	**7**	*1/2*	**Thunderous Mood (USA)**[42] 3103 2-9-0 0 (P F I Cole) *chsd ldrs but nt on terms and sn off the bridle: no prog 2f out: nt hrd pushed whn all ch gone fnl f* **25/1**	JohnEgan 11	94
1240	**8**	*2 1/2*	**Effort**[19] 3876 2-9-0 0 (M Johnston) *dwlt and bmpd leaving stalls: a in rr and struggling to go the pce* **25/1**	JoeFanning 4	85+
21	**9**	*2 1/4*	**Global City (IRE)**[7] 4279 2-9-0 0 (Saeed Bin Suroor) *taken down early: awkward s: racd wdst of all and nvr beyond midfield: struggling fnl 2f* **12/1**	(t) LDettori 14	77
1110	**10**	*nk*	**Icesolator (IRE)**[42] 3103 2-9-0 0 (R Hannon) *lw: chsd ldrs but nvr on terms and sn off the bridle: struggling fr 1/2-way: wknd over 1f out* **14/1**	PatDobbs 9	76
	11	*6*	**Noverre To Hide (USA)** 2-9-0 0 (J R Best) *lengthy: a gng bdly in rr: couldn't handle the trck* **33/1**	LPKeniry 3	54+

57.88 secs (-0.52) **Going Correction** 0.0s/f (Good) **11** Ran SP% **118.5**

Speed ratings (Par 104): **104,103,101,101,98 98,97,93,90,89 80**

toteswinger: 1&2 £8.40, 1&3 £6.40, 2&3 £11.10. CSF £44.08 TOTE £6.40: £2.20, £2.50, £2.60; EX 57.40 Trifecta £279.60 Pool: £2187.99 - 5.79 winning units..

Owner Hamdan Al Maktoum **Bred** Shadwell Estate Company Limited **Trained** Lambourn, Berks

FOCUS

A strong renewal. They went a proper gallop thanks to speedball Rievaulx World and the form looks rock solid, despite Spin Cycle running below his Royal Ascot form. The time was only 0.35secs slower than the juvenile record set by Poet's Cove back in 1990.

NOTEBOOK

Finjaan, a tidy winner on debut before finding the ground too slow when second to Icesolator in the National Stakes at Sandown (received 5lb) had been given a nice break and looked a big player. Back on faster ground, he travelled up well on the tail of Jargelle and hit the front inside the final furlong. He looked likely to be caught as Bonnie Charlie swept through to challenge, but he picked up again once seeing the threat and just held on. This was a gutsy display from the son of Royal Applause, who is expected to improve for 6f, and the Middle Park looks a likely target. (op 4-1 tchd 11-2 and 6-1 in a place)

Bonnie Charlie, ready winner of an ordinary maiden at Windsor on debut (back in April) comes from a yard rich with two-year-old talent and he earned automatic respect, being their supposed number one. Still showing signs of inexperience following a slow start, he came with a sweeping challenge to close right in on the winner, but having got there, could find no extra. It could be argued he would have won had he not got behind early and this strong-looking colt can land a decent prize, with the St Leger Yearling Stakes at York in August looking a possible target. (op 9-1)

Jargelle(IRE), the only filly in the field following the non-runners, improved markedly on her maiden win to take the Super Sprint at Newbury the other day, and the form had received a couple of boosts with the third filling the same spot in the Group 2 Robert Papin and the eighth also scoring next time. She showed good early speed a couple of widths off the rail and stuck on well for pressure, but could not match the pace of the front pair. She may well get an extra furlong. (op 17-2 tchd 9-1 and 10-1 in a place)

Rievaulx World, up markedly in grade having bolted up off an estimated mark of 85 on his recent nursery debut, had the rails draw and again showed tons of early speed. However, fending off this stronger opposition proved far more difficult and he could find no extra from a furlong out. (tchd 5-1)

Spin Cycle(IRE), the one to beat on the evidence of his close second to South Central in the Norfolk at Royal Ascot, never looked entirely happy and failed to run up to his Ascot form, hanging from halfway and proving unable to quicken. His rider later reported he lost his action and he probably deserves another chance back on a more conventional track. Official explanation: jockey said colt lost its action (op 7-2)

Flashmans Papers, 100/1 winner of the Windsor Castle before finishing fourth in the Norfolk two days later, had bruised a foot the previous day and there was some doubt over him running. He was allowed to take his chance, but had the widest draw of all and was in trouble quite early. He could only make limited late headway and looks ready for a sixth furlong now. (op 15-2)

Thunderous Mood(USA), a York maiden winner who found himself out of his depth in the Coventry, was back down in trip here, but struggled to go the fast early gallop and was not unduly punished. He remains capable of better at a lower level. Official explanation: jockey said colot was unsuited by the good (good to firm places) ground

Effort once again did himself no favours with a sluggish start and he was never going the pace. (op 33-1)

Global City(IRE), easy winner of a modest Yarmouth maiden, was up markedly in grade here and never looked like playing a part, racing widest of all and being beaten at halfway. (tchd 11-1)

Icesolator(IRE) rattled up a hat-trick earlier in the season and beat Finjaan in the National Stakes, but the ground was soft that day and he was unable to run anywhere near to that level this time. He could be forgiven his Coventry effort over 6f as he got worked up beforehand, but this effort leaves him with a bit to prove. (op 20-1)

Noverre To Hide(USA), a 70,000gns half-brother to fair juvenile winner Hunt The Bottle, comes from a yard who have made quite a name for themselves with their juveniles over the past two seasons, but this was a very tough introduction and he looked all at sea on the undulations. He is rated on a par with Flashmans Papers at home and can be given another chance in lesser company. (op 25-1)

4508 DETICA SUMMER STKS (H'CAP) 1m 6f

4:40 (4:41) (Class 2) (0-105,105) 3-Y-0+

£15,577 (£4,665; £2,332; £1,167; £582; £292) **Stalls** High

Form RPR

2-34 **1** **Sanbuch**[17] 3942 4-10-0 **105**....................(b[1]) RyanMoore 7 115
(L M Cumani) *trckd ldrs: pushed along fr 4f out: effrt on outer over 2f out: urged along and led over 1f out: drvn out and hld on wl* **13/2**[3]

6-00 **2** ½ **Bauer (IRE)**[81] 1944 5-9-12 **103**.................... JMurtagh 1 112
(L M Cumani) *hld up bhd ldrs: sltly outpcd 5f out: plld wd and effrt over 2f out: clsd on ldrs over 1f out: pressed wnr last 100yds: a jst hld* **9/1**

6411 **3** 2 ¾ **Rajeh (IRE)**[6] 4314 5-9-0 **91** 6ex.................... LiamJones 4 97
(J L Spearing) *pressed ldr after 2f to 6f out: styd w ldrs: nrly upsides 2f out: one pce fr over 1f out* **20/1**

0000 **4** *nse* **Players Please (USA)**[2] 4444 4-9-2 **93**.................... JoeFanning 9 98
(M Johnston) *lw: trckd ldrs: poised to chal gng strly over 2f out: sn rdn: nt qckn over 1f out: one pce after* **10/1**

2513 **5** 1 ¾ **Formax (FR)**[39] 3209 6-9-0 **91**.................... PatDobbs 11 96+
(M P Tregoning) *stdd s: hld up wl in rr: coaxed along and sme prog fr 3f out: trying to cl whn nt clr run over 1f out: no ch after* **12/1**

11-1 **6** ¾ **Milne Graden**[87] 1799 4-9-7 **98**.................... TPQueally 12 100+
(J Noseda) *lw: stdd s: hld up and sn last: outpcd fr 5f out: no prog and looked uneasy tl styd on fnl 2f: nrst fin* **10/3**[1]

1301 **7** *hd* **Birkside**[4] 4396 5-9-1 **92** 6ex.................... DNolan 13 94
(D Carroll) *s.i.s: towards rr tl prog and wl plcd over 5f out: rdn 3f out: one pce and no hdwy after* **50/1**

-140 **8** *hd* **Double Banded (IRE)**[31] 3490 4-9-1 **92**.................... SebSanders 8 93+
(J L Dunlop) *settled in midfield: n.m.r after 2f: effrt and chsng ldrs over 2f out: crowded out and lost pls over 1f out: one pce fnl f* **14/1**

1-03 **9** 6 **Black Rock (IRE)**[18] 3929 4-9-5 **96**.................... PhilipRobinson 5 105+
(M A Jarvis) *lw: t.k.h early: w ldrs: drvn ahd jst over 2f out: hdd over 1f out: keeping on gamely u.p and nrly upsides whn broke down 100yds out and virtually p.u* **12/1**

-120 **10** ¾ **Record Breaker (IRE)**[24] 3721 4-9-4 **95**.................... GregFairley 6 87
(M Johnston) *mde most to 6f out: styd pressing ldr: upsides over 2f out: wknd jst over 1f out* **16/1**

4400 **11** 2 ¾ **Night Crescendo (USA)**[17] 3975 5-9-3 **94**.................... JimCrowley 2 82
(Mrs A J Perrett) *lw: a towards rr: struggling whn pce qcknd over 4f out: nvr a factor* **25/1**

1055 **12** 3 ¼ **Raincoat**[24] 3743 4-9-11 **102**....................(p) JimmyFortune 3 86
(J H M Gosden) *dwlt: a wl in rr: u.p and struggling 3f out* **10/1**

14-1 **13** 3 **Moon Quest (IRE)**[33] 3398 4-9-1 **92**.................... LDettori 14 71
(Saeed Bin Suroor) *t.k.h early: trckd ldrs: prog to ld 6f out and pressed on: hdd & wknd over 2f out: eased* **6/1**[2]

2300 **14** 8 **Tilt**[17] 3942 6-9-1 **92**....................(p) NCallan 10 60
(B Ellison) *swished tail s: t.k.h: hld up in rr: rdn and effrt over 3f out: sn no prog: wknd 2f out* **16/1**

3m 3.70s (0.10) **Going Correction** +0.15s/f (Good) **14** Ran SP% **123.3**

Speed ratings (Par 109): **105,104,103,103,102 101,101,101,98,97 94,94,92,87**

toteswinger: 1&2 £11.70, 1&3 £22.90, 2&3 £47.90. CSF £64.27 CT £1132.60 TOTE £7.50: £2.90, £3.20, £6.70; EX 64.10 Trifecta £350.40 Pool: £1799.48 - 3.80 winning units..

Owner Scuderia Rencati Srl **Bred** The Lavington Stud **Trained** Newmarket, Suffolk

FOCUS

Luca Cumani had won two of the last four runnings of this and he again dominated, this time registering a one-two. The pace was unsatisfactory and several horses can be rated better than the bare form. The race is sure to have some sort of bearing on the Ebor.

NOTEBOOK

Sanbuch, successful on his one previous try in a visor, had twice run well off slightly lower marks this season and the first-time blinkers improved him enough to defy a mark of 105. He got going too late over 2m at Ascot last time, but was ridden more prominently on this occasion and was always just holding on under a strong ride. His trainer's 2004 winner of this (Mephisto) went on to land the Ebor, but he will face a very tough task there under a penalty for this and it may be ebst to look elswhere. (tchd 6-1 and 7-1 in a place)

Bauer(IRE), a winner off 93 on his last start in handicap company, has been kept exclusively to Group 3 level since and this represented a drop in grade. Heavily supported beforehand, he was clearly expected to return to something like his best and he did just that, sticking on well close home to provide Cumani with a one-two. This effort has seen him promoted to the head of the Ebor market in many lists, but he will be vulnerable there to a lower-weighted rival. (op 20-1)

Rajeh(IRE), on a hat-trick following two wins at a lower level, was shouldering the 6lb penalty and ran a cracker back in third, being made plenty of use of and sticking on under pressure to just claim third. This represented another improved effort and this useful dual-purpose horse should continue to pay his way. (tchd 33-1 in a place)

Players Please(USA) is edging his way back to a decent mark and he ran more encouragingly when seventh, beaten three lengths, at Ascot two days earlier. He travelled very strongly just in behind the pace, but his rider was reluctant to commit him too soon, having not proved his stamina, but as it turned out he was unable to quicken once asked and could only keep on at the one pace. Connections will know more next time and he is another likely Ebor candidate. (op 8-1)

Formax(FR) has found some form since being stepped back up in trip, winning at this course two starts back before finishing third last time, and he travelled strongly, but found no room when it was required and crossed the line with some still left in the tank. He can be rated better than the bare form and remains capable of better. (op 14-1)

Milne Graden, unbeaten in three previous starts (all 1m2f) had not been seen since quickening up well to beat Formax here back in May, but there had been much talk surrounding him and it was no surprise to see him installed as favourite. Although he had looked certain to appreciate further when winning last time, he was taking a four-furlong hike in distance and found himself right at the back of the pack early on. He started to be ridden off the home bend and could only make limited late headway. A stronger pace would have suited and he should get that in the Ebor, but he has now been deposed as favourite. His stable has endured a tough spell and it is possible we will see a much improved effort next time. (op 11-4)

Birkside, narrow winner of a decent claimer at York the other day, was 11lb higher than when last winning a handicap with the penalty and ran surprisingly well. He was another well in rear early, but he moved well through the pack and in the end was unable to find any extra. This is as competitive as he likes it these day. (op 40-1)

Double Banded(IRE) has not quite gone on as expected this season, following a good win at Nottingham on his seasonal return, but he can be rated a shade better than the bare form here as he was squeezed out over a furlong from home. He did not find much after though, and was hardly powering home, giving the impression this mark is beyond him. (tchd 12-1)

Black Rock(IRE), who failed to stay in the Chester Cup, seemed to find the heavy ground against him at York last time, but he was in the process of running much better and was still in there fighting when breaking down half a furlong from the line. (op 16-1)

Record Breaker(IRE) came up well short off this mark last time and he was always likely to struggle in this more competitive contest. (op 20-1)

Night Crescendo(USA) never got into it and needs to come down further in the weights. (tchd 28-1)

Raincoat has a touch of class, but the first-time cheekpieces failed to make a difference and he was most disappointing. (op 14-1)

Moon Quest(IRE) looked a player, having won two of his three previous starts, but he was up markedly in trip here and failed to get home. (op 7-1)

Tilt never got into it and failed to run up to his best. (tchd 20-1)

4509 TATLER SUMMER SEASON STKS (H'CAP) 1m

5:15 (5:16) (Class 3) (0-90,90) 3-Y-0+ **£12,952** (£3,854; £1,926; £962) **Stalls** High

Form RPR

2113 **1** **Yamal (IRE)**[3] 4404 3-9-5 **90**.................... GregFairley 3 101+
(M Johnston) *lw: dwlt: dropped in fr wd draw to r on inner: prog fr rr 3f out: barged way through fr wl over 1f out and led jst ins fnl f: drvn out* **5/1**[2]

1-21 **2** *hd* **Swop (IRE)**[44] 3054 5-9-13 **90**.................... LDettori 10 102+
(L M Cumani) *lw: settled in midfield on outer: rdn over 2f out: gd prog to ld jst over 1f out and edgd rt: hdd jst ins fnl f: rallied wl nr fin: jst hld* **4/1**[1]

4311 **3** 1 ½ **The Fifth Member (IRE)**[20] 3840 4-9-2 **79**.................... NCallan 9 88
(J R Boyle) *awkward s but sn prom: drvn ahd over 1f out: sn hdd: no ex last 100yds* **20/1**

6004 **4** ¾ **Ivory Lace**[17] 3944 7-9-3 **80**.................... JimCrowley 14 87+
(S Woodman) *mostly in midfield: fnd way through towards outer over 1f out: drvn and r.o wl fnl f: nrst fin* **40/1**

1-10 **5** ¾ **Axiom**[26] 3627 4-9-10 **87**.................... SebSanders 5 93+
(L M Cumani) *lw: hld up wl in rr and racd wd: gd prog fr 2f out and wdst of all: edgd rt over 1f out: effrt nt quite sustained fnl f* **16/1**

-501 **6** ¾ **Mountain Pride (IRE)**[46] 3002 3-9-3 **88**.................... SteveDrowne 11 90
(J L Dunlop) *mostly in midfield: clsd 2f out: chsng ldrs and in tch jst over 1f out: hanging and nt qckn after* **16/1**

0602 **7** *nk* **Prince Of Thebes (IRE)**[7] 4269 7-9-0 **80**.................... KirstyMilczarek(3) 13 83
(M J Attwater) *a abt same pl: rdn and nt qckn over 1f out: one pce after* **28/1**

-416 **8** 1 **Kings Point (IRE)**[20] 3855 7-9-10 **87**.................... AdrianTNicholls 15 88
(D Nicholls) *trckd ldng pair: trapped bhd them on inner as they wknd fr 2f out and lost all ch: styd on fnl f* **20/1**

1440 **9** ¾ **Kavachi (IRE)**[24] 3740 5-9-12 **89**.................... RyanMoore 7 88
(G L Moore) *hld up wl in rr: effrt on outer over 2f out: nvr mustering enough pce to trble ldrs: kpt on* **15/2**[3]

4641 **10** *nk* **Habshan (USA)**[20] 3855 8-9-10 **87**.................... GeorgeBaker 18 85
(C F Wall) *dwlt: hld up wl in rr: eased off the rail and tried to make prog 2f out: hanging and n.d* **16/1**

15-1 **11** 1 **Red Birr (IRE)**[40] 3181 7-8-11 **79**.................... DavidProbert(5) 16 75
(P R Webber) *wl in rr: struggling over 2f out: modest late prog* **25/1**

3322 **12** 1 **Den's Gift (IRE)**[20] 3855 4-9-4 **81**....................(b) PhilipRobinson 8 75
(C G Cox) *led: drvn 2f out: hdd over 1f out: wkng whn bdly hmpd sn after* **16/1**

-025 **13** ¾ **Woodcote Place**[18] 3898 5-9-2 **79**.................... AlanMunro 20 71
(P R Chamings) *hld up on inner: trapped bhd rivals over 2f out: nvr fnd room and no ch* **12/1**

5-40 **14** 1 ¾ **Fool's Wildcat (USA)**[11] 4160 3-9-5 **90**....................(b) JimmyFortune 6 76
(B J Meehan) *prom: rdn and nt qckn whn bmpd over 1f out: no ch after* **50/1**

0003 **15** 3 ¼ **Prince Of Light (IRE)**[14] 4060 5-9-10 **87**.................... EddieAhern 4 68
(M Johnston) *trckd ldr: pushed along fr 1/2-way: losing pl whn hmpd over 1f out* **16/1**

5225 **16** 3 **The Snatcher (IRE)**[18] 3899 5-9-12 **89**.................... TedDurcan 17 63
(R Hannon) *trckd ldrs: n.m.r towards inner 2f out: sn lost pl and wknd* **16/1**

/21- **17** *nk* **Multakka (IRE)**[268] 6670 5-9-3 **80**.................... RHills 1 53
(M P Tregoning) *trckd ldrs: shkn up over 2f out: hanging and wknd tamely* **33/1**

1002 **18** 1 ¾ **Orchard Supreme**[34] 3382 5-9-11 **88**.................... RichardHughes 2 57
(R Hannon) *lw: hld up wl in rr: no prog over 2f out: no ch after* **14/1**

1330 **19** 6 **Cactus King**[25] 3684 5-9-4 **81**....................(p) IanMongan 19 36
(P M Phelan) *lw: nvr beyond midfield: u.p and struggling over 2f out: wknd* **50/1**

0530 **20** 7 **Very Wise**[20] 3840 6-9-8 **85**.................... JoeFanning 12 24
(W J Haggas) *hld up in rr on outer: no prog whn n.m.r briefly 2f out: sn eased* **16/1**

1m 39.14s (-0.76) **Going Correction** +0.15s/f (Good)

WFA 3 from 4yo+ 8lb **20** Ran SP% **130.1**

Speed ratings (Par 107): **109,108,107,106,105 105,104,103,103,102 101,100,99,98,94 91,91,89,83,76**

toteswinger: 1&2 £5.60, 1&3 £21.10, 2&3 £20.80. CSF £23.63 CT £398.28 TOTE £5.80: £2.10, £1.90, £4.90, £6.70; EX 26.50 Trifecta £1500.30 Part won. Pool: £2027.50 - 0.60 winning units..

Owner Sheikh Hamdan Bin Mohammed Al Maktoum **Bred** Gainsborough Stud Management Ltd **Trained** Middleham Moor, N Yorks

■ Stewards' Enquiry : Greg Fairley one-day ban: 1st incident, careless riding (Aug 12); three-day ban: 2nd incident, careless riding (Aug 13-15)

FOCUS

A good handicap run at a solid pace and, with the third rated to the best view of his three-year-old efforts, the form looks sound for the grade.

NOTEBOOK

Yamal(IRE), making a quick reappearance, was drawn in stall three but Fairley got him over to the rail and he saved ground in the first half of the race by racing on the fence. The impressive moment came when he was switched to overtake a line of three horses blocking his path on the inside two furlongs out, and he did it in a short space of time, staying on strongly once in the clear and holding the determined challenge of the favourite close home. A progressive three-year-old, he remains one to keep on side. (op 13-2)

Swop(IRE), 5lb higher than when successful at Doncaster and burdened with top weight here, came to have every chance down the outside and was simply beaten by a progressive youngster. He has clearly not been the easiest to train, but he has improved in each of his four starts to date and remains capable of better. He is likely to go to York next. (op 7-2 tchd 9-2)

The Fifth Member(IRE), 3lb higher back on turf, ran up to his best in defeat, sticking on well for pressure, and simply met a couple of progressive rivals from top yards. (op 25-1)

Ivory Lace, twice a winner over 7f here in the past, stayed on late down the outside to take fourth. She has dropped to a fair mark now and would not be one to dismiss in lesser company. (op 50-1)

Axiom, who could have done with softer ground, threatened briefly down the outside but was one-paced in the closing stages. He could be interesting in the autumn. (op 20-1)

Mountain Pride(IRE) did not get the clearest of runs but he also put his head in the air and did not look happy on the track either.

Prince Of Thebes(IRE), who has now gone 24 races since his last win, had every chance if good enough. Official explanation: jockey said gelding was hampered at start (op 33-1)

Kings Point(IRE) was stuck on the rail behind horses waiting for a run and apparently travelling well approaching the furlong marker, but he hardly picked up when switched into the clear. Official explanation: jockey said gelding was denied a clear run

Kavachi(IRE) had a strong pace to run off in the Hunt Cup but the balance of his form suggests he is better over further than a mile. (tchd 7-1 and 8-1)
Habshan(USA), stuck behind a wall of horses two furlongs out, plugged on once he got daylight but he never looked very happy on the track. (tchd 18-1)
Woodcote Place did not get the clearest of runs but he is the type who tends to almost look for it.

4510 MCKEEVER ST LAWRENCE BLOODSTOCK E B F MAIDEN STKS (C&G) 6f

5:50 (5:53) (Class 2) 2-Y-O £12,952 (£3,854; £1,926; £962) Stalls Low

Form RPR

4 **1** **Gyr (IRE)**[53] 2796 2-9-0 0 .... SebSanders 8 86+
(J L Dunlop) *lw: w'like: pressed ldr: drvn to chal over 1f out: narrow ld ins fnl f: styd on wl* **4/1[3]**

3 **2** *nk* **Run For The Hills**[10] 4199 2-9-0 0 .... JimmyFortune 10 85
(J H M Gosden) *w'like: scope: lw: mde most: hrd pressed over 1f out: narrowly hdd u.p ins fnl f: styd on* **3/1[2]**

4 **3** *nse* **Frognal (IRE)**[12] 4126 2-9-0 0 .... RyanMoore 11 85
(B J Meehan) *lw: t.k.h early: cl up: rdn to chal over 1f out: upsides fnl f: jst hld* **17/2**

2 **4** *2* **Magaling (IRE)**[26] 3651 2-9-0 0 .... LDettori 3 81+
(L M Cumani) *w'like: scope: rn green and hanging in midfield: reminders fr over 2f out: wnt 4 wl over 1f out: pushed along fnl f and lost no grnd on hrd rdn ldng trio* **2/1[1]**

04 **5** *4* **Al Mukaala (IRE)**[12] 4108 2-9-0 0 .... NCallan 4 67
(C E Brittain) *lw: trckd ldrs: shkn up over 2f out: outpcd fr over 1f out* **50/1**

6 *hd* **Count Paris (USA)** 2-9-0 0 .... RHills 12 66
(M Johnston) *leggy: chsd ldrs and racd on outer: prog and wl on terms over 2f out: wknd over 1f out* **16/1**

4 **7** *2 1/4* **Rocoppelia (USA)**[15] 4024 2-9-0 0 .... JimCrowley 1 60
(Mrs A J Perrett) *strong: lw: pushed along in rr bef 1/2-way: sn struggling* **20/1**

8 *1/2* **Ben's Dream (IRE)** 2-9-0 0 .... MartinDwyer 7 58
(A M Balding) *w'like: plld hrd early: hld up towards rr: nvr on terms w ldrs: no ch fnl 2f* **20/1**

9 *shd* **Desert Fever** 2-9-0 0 .... MichaelHills 13 58
(B W Hills) *w'like: lengthy: racd on outer: nvr on terms w ldrs: struggling over 2f out: fdd* **25/1**

0 **10** *shd* **Lethal Glaze (IRE)**[11] 4151 2-9-0 0 .... RichardHughes 5 58
(R Hannon) *stdd s: hld up in last pair: lost tch fnl 2f* **50/1**

0320 **11** *nse* **Pocket's Pick (IRE)**[10] 4190 2-9-0 0 .... GeorgeBaker 6 57
(G L Moore) *t.k.h: hld up in rr: wknd 2f out* **11/1**

1m 12.16s (-0.04) **Going Correction** 0.0s/f (Good) **11 Ran SP% 120.4**
Speed ratings (Par 100): **100,99,99,96,91 91,88,87,87,87 87**
toteswinger: 1&2 £2.90, 1&3 £6.00, 2&3 £5.00. CSF £15.79 TOTE £5.50: £1.70, £1.70, £2.50; EX 17.30 Trifecta £364.30 Pool: £1329.40 - 2.70 winning units. Place 6: £904.04 Place 5: £156.41.
Owner Prince A A Faisal **Bred** Nawara Stud Co Ltd **Trained** Arundel, W Sussex

FOCUS
A decent maiden that should produce winners. The time and the fifth help set the level.

NOTEBOOK
Gyr(IRE), a promising fourth over course and distance on debut, needed to have progressed to take this better race, but juveniles from the yard invariably do and he ran on strongly for pressure to just do enough. Subject to a more positive ride on this occasion, the son of Pivotal is going to appreciate an extra furlong before too long, but he holds many sales-race entries and it will be interesting to see where he turns up next. (op 6-1)
Run For The Hills, third in a fair Newmarket maiden on debut (fourth won next time) was soon in front, just ahead of Gyr, and kept finding for pressure, but was unable to hang on. He holds a couple of high-profile entries, but looks more a nursery type on this evidence. He should win his maiden. (op 10-3 tchd 7-2)
Frognal(IRE), slowly away and green before running on for fourth over an inadequate 5f on debut, knew more this time and raced just behind the speed. He was close enough if good enough from a furlong out, but found the line coming too soon. He should learn again and is the type to turn up in a valuable sales race later in the season. (op 10-1 tchd 11-1)
Magaling(IRE), just denied by a useful sort on debut (won nursery of 85 next time), still showed distinct signs of inexperience here and looked far from happy on the track. He plugged on having been outpaced, but on this evidence an extra furlong/more conventional track will help. (tchd 11-5 in a places and 9-4 in places)
Al Mukaala(IRE) ran well back in fifth and is now qualified for a mark. He has shown promise on all three starts and will appreciate a return to 7f on this showing.
Count Paris(USA), a son of Pivotal who is bred to need further, comes from a yard whose juveniles tend to benefit from a run and he shaped with enough promise to suggest he can win a maiden at two.
Rocoppelia(USA) was unable to improve on his debut effort at Windsor and may do better once handicapping. He will be qualified following another run. (op 25-1)
Ben's Dream(IRE), a £46,000 son of Kyllachy, comes from a yard that have introduced several first-time-out winners this season, but he got a bit lit up and refused to settle. He should know a bit more next time.
Desert Fever, a half-brother to high-class US miler Hawksley Hill, was soon struggling for speed and is going to need further.
Lethal Glaze(IRE) has not shown much in a couple of tries and is more of a nursery type.
Pocket's Pick(IRE), well down the field in the Super Sprint, had earlier posted a couple of fair efforts and should have done better. (op 8-1)
T/Jkpt: £50,581.50 to a £1 stake. Pool: £71,241.55. 0.50 winning tickets. T/Plt: £1,202.80 to a £1 stake. Pool: £250,707.66. 152.15 winning tickets. T/Qpdt: £196.90 to a £1 stake. Pool: £14,532.37. 54.60 winning tickets. JN

4492 GALWAY (R-H)

Tuesday, July 29

OFFICIAL GOING: Hurdle course - good; chase course - good to firm; flat course - yielding to soft

4511a TOTE JACKPOT H'CAP 2m

6:20 (6:20) (55-80,78) 3-Y-0+ £7,621 (£1,775; £783; £452) Stalls Far side

RPR

1 **My Valley (IRE)**[30] 3538 6-9-3 72 .... SMGorey(3) 2 79
(P A Fahy, Ire) *sn led: travelling wl over 4f out: rdn bef st: strly pressed 1f out: tired and kpt on gamely to assert fnl f* **10/1**

2 *2 1/2* **Mountain Snow (IRE)**[12] 4141 8-9-6 77 .... PTownend(5) 5 81
(W P Mullins, Ire) *mid-div: stdy hdwy into mod 3rd over 3f out: rdn to cl in 2nd bef st: chal 1f out: sn no imp* **11/2[3]**

3 *4* **Glamis Castle (USA)**[43] 4188 5-9-2 68 .... (t) WJLee 15 68
(C F Swan, Ire) *in rr of mid-div: clsr in 7th over 4f out: mod 5th over 3f out: sn no imp u.p: 4th and kpt on same pce fr bef st* **25/1**

4 *nk* **Darenjan (IRE)**[16] 4003 5-9-1 74 .... SFoley(7) 6 74
(John Joseph Hanlon, Ire) *in rr of mid-div: clsr in 8th over 4f out: no imp u.p fr over 3f out: 5th and kpt on same pce fr bef st* **16/1**

5 *8* **Savannah**[40] 3160 5-8-12 64 .... FFDaSilva 16 56
(Luke Comer, Ire) *towards rr: pushed along 1/2-way: wnt 8th bef st: kpt on wout threatening* **50/1**

6 *5 1/2* **Alamgiyr (IRE)**[37] 3305 5-9-7 73 .... DPMcDonogh 8 59
(Ms Joanna Morgan, Ire) *prom: 2nd and rdn over 4f out: dropped to 3rd and no imp fr bef st: sn no ex* **11/1**

7 *1/2* **Captain Hook**[17] 3980 4-8-3 62 .... (p) EJMcNamara(7) 10 48
(Daniel Mark Loughnane, Ire) *chsd ldrs: 6th and rdn over 4f out: no imp and kpt on same pce fr over 3f out* **20/1**

8 *3* **Mohtarres (USA)**[17] 3980 5-8-6 65 .... (p) DEMullins(7) 4 48
(D T Hughes, Ire) *chsd ldrs: 9th appr 1/2-way: rdn over 4f out: sn no imp* **16/1**

9 *12* **Mighty Moon**[75] 2135 5-9-7 76 .... JamieMoriarty(3) 18 47
(R A Fahey) *in rr of mid-div: rdn over 4f out: sn no imp: kpt on same pce* **9/2[1]**

10 *1 1/4* **Mr Bones (IRE)**[17] 3989 6-9-11 77 .... PJSmullen 14 46
(J G Coogan, Ire) *sn trckd ldr in 2nd: dropped to 4th and rdn over 4f out: mod 6th and no ex fr over 3f out* **12/1**

11 *4 1/2* **Eight Up (IRE)**[16] 4009 5-9-6 72 .... (p) WMLordan 1 37
(Michael David Murphy, Ire) *trckd ldrs: rdn in 3rd over 4f out: mod 5th over 3f out: dropped to 6th and wknd fr bef st* **33/1**

12 *shd* **Pretty Demanding (IRE)**[8] 4259 4-8-3 62 .... BACurtis(7) 17 27
(M G Quinlan) *mid-div best: no imp u.p fr over 4f out* **33/1**

13 *5* **Tangible**[32] 3464 6-9-3 69 .... MCHussey 7 29
(Liam McAteer, Ire) *mid-div: 10th appr 1/2-way: wknd 5f out* **33/1**

14 *15* **Flamingo Rainbow (GER)**[55] 2741 6-8-13 65 .... (p) PShanahan 11 10
(H Rogers, Ire) *a towards rr* **25/1**

15 *12* **Bluebyyou (IRE)**[311] 4033 7-9-12 78 .... (t) JAHeffernan 3 11
(T Hogan, Ire) *towards rr: no imp u.p fr over 4f out* **14/1**

16 *2* **Raise A Row (IRE)**[17] 3980 4-8-12 64 .... CO'Donoghue 13 —
(Edward P Harty, Ire) *chsd ldrs: 8th over 6f out: no imp u.p fr 4f out: eased bef st* **33/1**

17 *dist* **Raise The Goblet (IRE)**[16] 4003 4-9-10 76 .... CDHayes 12 —
(P Hughes, Ire) *chsd ldrs: lost pl and rdn under 6f out: sn wknd: eased bef st and t.o* **5/1[2]**

18 *nk* **Rainbow Dash (IRE)**[17] 3989 9-9-11 77 .... (p) KJManning 19 —
(T G McCourt, Ire) *prom: rdn in 5th fr 6f out: sn lost pl and wknd: eased bef st: t.o* **16/1**

19 *hd* **On The Other Hand (IRE)**[13] 4092 8-9-2 68 .... FMBerry 20 —
(C F Swan, Ire) *a bhd: eased bef st: t.o* **12/1**

20 *10* **Diamond Key (IRE)**[90] 6506 4-9-8 74 .... (b) MJKinane 9 —
(Eoin Doyle, Ire) *a bhd: rdn over 6f out: t.o* **25/1**

3m 42.8s (-2.00) **20 Ran SP% 137.4**
CSF £63.20 CT £1415.69 TOTE £11.20: £2.30, £1.70, £10.20, £4.80; DF 65.40.
Owner Ballyboggan Racing Syndicate **Bred** John Brophy **Trained** Leighlinbridge, Co Carlow
■ Stewards' Enquiry : P Townend four-day ban: excessive and unnecessary use of the whip (Aug 13-16)

NOTEBOOK
Mighty Moon had been kept for this event after winning comfortably over slightly further at York in May and met support in the betting ring. He turned in a laboured effort, however, and this was obviously not his true form. (op 7/2 tchd 5/1)
Pretty Demanding(IRE) ran a tame race from off the pace and is hard to predict these days.

4512a TOTE GALWAY MILE EUROPEAN BREEDERS FUND H'CAP (PREMIER HANDICAP) 1m 100y

7:00 (7:02) 3-Y-0+

£70,705 (£22,470; £10,705; £3,647; £2,470; £1,294)

RPR

1 **Celtic Dane (IRE)**[30] 3531 4-9-1 94 .... CDHayes 11 102
(Kevin Prendergast, Ire) *trckd ldrs: 6th bef 1/2-way: rdn to chal and ld under 2f out: clr fnl f: styd on wl* **7/1[2]**

2 *1 3/4* **She's Our Mark**[16] 4007 4-9-6 99 .... DMGrant 15 103
(Patrick J Flynn, Ire) *hmpd early and sn towards rr: rdn into 9th 2f out: hmpd early st: r.o wl into 2nd fnl f: nt rch wnr* **9/1**

3 *1 3/4* **Jalmira (IRE)**[16] 4007 7-10-0 107 .... WJLee 8 107
(C F Swan, Ire) *mid-div: hdwy in 7th 2f out: 4th ent st: sn rdn in 2nd: no imp and kpt on same pce ins fnl f* **20/1**

4 *shd* **Bolodenka (IRE)**[74] 5631 6-8-8 94 .... FrederikTylicki(7) 3 94
(R A Fahey) *in rr of mid-div: hdwy in 11th 2f out: 7th ent st: styd on to 3rd 1f out: kpt on same pce fnl f* **14/1**

5 *1/2* **Monteriggioni (IRE)**[13] 4098 6-9-3 99 .... PBBeggy(3) 14 98
(John Geoghegan, Ire) *hld up towards rr: rdn and hdwy ent st: kpt on wout threatening fnl f* **14/1**

6 *1* **Settigano (IRE)**[30] 3531 5-9-12 105 .... JAHeffernan 18 102
(Michael Joseph Fitzgerald, Ire) *chsd ldrs: rdn in 8th 2f out: short of room ent st: swtchd 1f out: kpt on wout threatening u.p* **6/1[1]**

7 *4 1/2* **Chevie (IRE)**[18] 3932 3-8-4 91 .... (p) WJSupple 12 78
(T Hogan, Ire) *mid-div and hmpd early: sn towards rr: hdwy in 12th 2f out: kpt on wout threatening u.p st* **20/1**

8 *3* **Incline (IRE)**[13] 4094 9-8-11 90 .... NGMcCullagh 7 71
(R McGlinchey, Ire) *trckd ldrs: rdn in 6th 2f out: sn no imp and kpt on same pce* **16/1**

9 *nk* **Alhabeeb (IRE)**[20] 3860 3-9-0 101 .... DPMcDonogh 2 81
(Kevin Prendergast, Ire) *cl up: 2nd for much: no ex u.p st* **8/1[3]**

10 *3/4* **Green Tobasco**[121] 1105 5-8-12 91 .... CO'Donoghue 16 70
(M J P O'Brien, Ire) *chsd ldrs: clsr in 5th 2f out: no imp u.p fr 1f out* **20/1**

11 *2* **No Strings (IRE)**[30] 3531 3-7-8 91 .... (bt) LFRoche(10) 10 65
(D K Weld, Ire) *prom: on terms under 3f out: 3rd and rdn ent st: sn no imp* **8/1[3]**

12 *2 1/2* **Benandonner (USA)**[17] 3974 5-9-3 99 .... JamieMoriarty(3) 17 69
(R A Fahey) *prom: 5th bef 1/2-way: lost pl and no ex fr over 2f out* **10/1**

13 *3* **Crooked Throw (IRE)**[17] 3983 9-9-7 105 .... DGHogan(5) 4 68
(C F Swan, Ire) *s.i.s and t.k.h towards rr: no imp u.p fr over 2f out* **25/1**

14 *nk* **Royal Astronomer (IRE)**[17] 3991 3-7-12 92 .... DEMullins(7) 6 54
(Lester Winters, Ire) *a towards rr* **14/1**

15 *2 1/2* **Majestic Times (IRE)**[18] 3932 8-8-12 91 .... MCHussey 1 48
(Liam McAteer, Ire) *mid-div: no ex u.p fr over 2f out* **33/1**

16 *13* **Ragged Staff (IRE)**[38] 3287 4-9-1 94 .... (p) FMBerry 5 24
(P A Fahy, Ire) *chsd ldrs: 7th bef 1/2-way: lost pl and wknd fr over 2f out* **12/1**

17 *7* **Impetious**[27] 3623 4-9-3 96 .... (b) RPCleary 9 11
(Eamon Tyrrell, Ire) *prom: 4th early: lost pl and wknd fr 3f out* **25/1**

18 *12* **Mojito Royale (IRE)**[33] 3425 4-10-0 107..........................(b[1]) PJSmullen 13 —
(Eoin Doyle, Ire) *sn led: hdd under 2f out: sn wknd and eased* **12/1**

1m 51.28s (1.08)
WFA 3 from 4yo+ 8lb **18** Ran SP% **134.3**
CSF £67.56 CT £1291.99 TOTE £9.30: £2.80, £2.00, £6.10, £4.50; DF 103.90.
Owner Gareth McCann **Bred** Don Collins **Trained** Friarstown, Co Kildare
■ Stewards' Enquiry : Frederik Tylicki two-day ban: careless riding (Aug 13-14)

NOTEBOOK
Celtic Dane(IRE), fifth last year, lasted home well after seizing the initiative early in the straight. (op 8/1 tchd 9/1)
Bolodenka(IRE) had won twice at a lesser level at this meeting in 2006 and had been a beaten favourite in this race last year. Having his first outing since falling on his hurdling bow in May, he posted a solid effort considering he lacked race-fitness and can be placed to get closer next time out. (op 12/1)
Benandonner(USA) had a decent draw and everything looked primed for a big run, but he dropped out tamely before the final turn and was a long way below his best. He has something to prove at present. (op 9/1 tchd 11/1)

4513a WWW.THETOTE.COM EUROPEAN BREEDERS FUND FILLIES MAIDEN 7f
7:35 (7:37) 2-Y-O **£9,573** (£2,808; £1,338; £455)

RPR
1 **Rare Ransom**[48] 2958 2-9-0 .... PJSmullen 12 89+
(D K Weld, Ire) *mde all: rdn clr fr 1f out: styd on wl: easily* **4/5**[1]
2 *7* **Mark Of An Angel (IRE)**[13] 4095 2-9-0 .... DPMcDonogh 1 69
(Kevin Prendergast, Ire) *chsd ldrs: 6th 1/2-way: clsr in 3rd bef st: mod 2nd and kpt on same pce u.p fnl f* **5/1**[2]
3 *1 ¾* **Lady Ruler (IRE)**[21] 3827 2-9-0 66.......................(t) RPCleary 6 65
(Thomas Cleary, Ire) *chsd ldrs: 5th 1/2-way: rdn in 6th 2f out: sn no imp: 4th 1f out: kpt on same pce* **16/1**
4 *shd* **Cluain Fhada (USA)** 2-9-0 .... KJManning 7 65
(J S Bolger, Ire) *trckd ldrs: 3rd 1/2-way: rdn in 5th 2f out: sn no imp: kpt on same pce st* **10/1**
5 *3* **Silver Abby (IRE)**[12] 4132 2-9-0 .... MCHussey 10 57
(Noel Lawlor, Ire) *trckd ldrs: 4th 1/2-way: rdn into 2nd 2f out: no imp over 1f out* **66/1**
6 *shd* **Lulu's Flight (IRE)** 2-8-7 .... JPFahy(7) 13 57
(J P Broderick, Ire) *dwlt: in rr of mid-div: 11th 2f out: sn no imp u.p: kpt on wl wout threatening fnl f* **50/1**
7 *1 ¾* **Lady Kent (IRE)**[54] 2765 2-8-7 .... JamesPSullivan(7) 4 53
(Timothy Doyle, Ire) *mid-div: rdn in 7th bef st: sn no imp* **50/1**
8 *hd* **Jays Secret (IRE)** 2-9-0 .... CDHayes 2 52
(H Rogers, Ire) *s.i.s: towards rr: rdn into 8th 2f out: sn no imp* **50/1**
9 *½* **Drombeg Dawn (IRE)** 2-8-7 .... EJMcNamara(7) 5 51
(A J McNamara, Ire) *s.i.s: a towards rr* **50/1**
10 *½* **Evening Sunset (GER)**[18] 3923 2-9-0 .... EdwardCreighton 9 50
(M R Channon) *trckd ldr in 2nd: rdn in 4th 2f out: sn wknd* **6/1**[3]
11 *11* **Indian Haze (IRE)** 2-9-0 .... JAHeffernan 3 22
(Daniel Mark Loughnane, Ire) *a towards rr* **40/1**
12 *3* **Dalpuiri (USA)**[86] 1843 2-8-7 .... RFKeogh(7) 11 15
(Charles Coakley, Ire) *s.i.s and a towards rr* **100/1**
13 *3* **Mrs Slocombe (IRE)**[20] 3856 2-9-0 .... FMBerry 8 7
(J C Hayden, Ire) *mid-div: rdn in 9th 2f out: sn wknd* **10/1**

1m 32.62s (1.02) **13** Ran SP% **123.3**
CSF £5.03 TOTE £1.90: £1.10, £1.50, £2.90; DF 4.80.
Owner Lady O'Reilly **Bred** Skymarc Farm & Castlemartin St **Trained** The Curragh, Co Kildare

NOTEBOOK
Evening Sunset(GER) had shown promise on her debut at Newmarket last month, but she looked to find this longer trip on the more demanding surface all too testing. (op 13/2)

4514a TOTE TELEBET 1850 238 669 H'CAP 7f
8:10 (8:12) (55-80,80) 4-Y-O+ **£7,621** (£1,775; £783; £452)

RPR
1 **Maundy Money**[14] 4070 5-10-0 80.............................. CO'Donoghue 13 95
(David Marnane, Ire) *a.p: 2nd bef st: chal and led under 1f out: sn drvn clr* **9/1**[3]
2 *3 ½* **Billy Dane (IRE)**[20] 3855 4-9-10 79.......................(p) JamieMoriarty(3) 9 84
(R A Fahey) *sn led: strly pressed and hdd ent st: no imp u.p and kpt on ins fnl f* **7/1**[2]
3 *½* **Six Of Hearts**[9] 4231 4-9-4 70...(p) FMBerry 10 74
(Cecil Ross, Ire) *in rr of mid-div: hdwy in 8th fr under 2f out: 5th ent st: 3rd and chal u.p 1f out: sn no imp and kpt on same pce* **6/1**[1]
4 *hd* **Maximo (GER)**[14] 4070 5-9-8 74.. KJManning 2 77
(T G McCourt, Ire) *chsd ldrs: rdn to chal and ld ent st: hdd and kpt on same pce fr under 1f out* **12/1**
5 *½* **Zhukhov (IRE)**[9] 4222 5-8-12 71................. AmyKathleenParsons(7) 16 73
(T G McCourt, Ire) *in rr of mid-div: hdwy to 5th bef st: kpt on same pce u.p fr 1f out* **7/1**[2]
6 *nk* **Headford View (IRE)**[18] 3934 4-9-3 69...........................(p) JAHeffernan 1 70
(James Halpin, Ire) *broke wl: sn chsd ldrs: 7th bef st: kpt on same pce u.p fr over 1f out* **14/1**
7 *1* **Luck Wud Have It (IRE)**[18] 3932 4-9-9 75............................ DMGrant 15 74
(Patrick J Flynn, Ire) *chsd ldrs: 6th bef st: sn no imp u.p* **10/1**
8 *¾* **Tenacious Greg (IRE)**[17] 3984 5-8-13 72............................ SFoley(7) 5 69
(A Kinsella, Ire) *trckd ldrs: mainly 3rd: no imp u.p fr bef st* **12/1**
9 *nk* **Glenmuir (IRE)**[27] 3616 5-8-12 71.................................... IJBrennan(7) 12 67
(Adrian McGuinness, Ire) *mid-div: 7th early: rdn in 6th over 1f out: sn no ex* **20/1**
10 *1* **Beach Bound (IRE)**[55] 2739 5-9-4 70...................................(b) PJSmullen 4 63
(D K Weld, Ire) *towards rr: rdn 3f out: no imp and kpt on same pce fr bef st* **6/1**[1]
11 *4* **Dont Tell Josie (IRE)**[9] 4222 4-9-6 72.................................. CDHayes 3 54
(Miss Maura McGuinness, Ire) *towards rr: no imp u.p fr over 2f out* **25/1**
12 *nk* **Roy's Delight (IRE)**[18] 3934 4-9-2 68...............................(t) PShanahan 14 49
(Edward P Harty, Ire) *towards rr: no imp u.p fr over 2f out* **20/1**
13 *5* **Five Two**[257] 5460 5-8-12 71.....................................(t) APThornton(7) 7 39
(Gavin Patrick Cromwell, Ire) *a towards rr* **25/1**
14 *3 ½* **Morotai Marauder (IRE)**[9] 4224 4-9-5 76.......................... PTownend(5) 11 35
(M J P O'Brien, Ire) *in rr of mid-div: rdn 1/2-way: sn no ex* **9/1**[3]
15 *10* **Upper Village**[10] 4208 4-9-3 69.. WMLordan 6 —
(John Halley, Ire) *t.k.h: disp ld sn after 2f: wknd fr over 2f out* **33/1**

1m 32.2s (0.60) **16** Ran SP% **124.9**
CSF £67.55 CT £421.55 TOTE £10.30: £3.40, £2.70, £1.90; DF 77.00.
Owner Push The Button Syndicate **Bred** Baydon House Stud **Trained** Bansha, Co Tipperary

NOTEBOOK
Billy Dane(IRE) turned in a very pleasing performance over a trip he would have found sharp enough. (op 7/1 tchd 8/1)
Valamareha(IRE) Official explanation: 60-day ban: uncompetitive performances

4515 - (Foreign Racing) - See Raceform Interactive

[4504] GOODWOOD (R-H)
Wednesday, July 30

OFFICIAL GOING: Good to firm (good in places) changing to good to firm after race 4 (4.05)
Dolling adding around 15yards to advertised distances on the round course.
Wind: Moderate, half-against (Races 1-3); Light, half-against (Races 4-7)
Weather: Glorious

4516 INVESCO PERPETUAL GOODWOOD STKS (H'CAP) 2m 5f
2:15 (2:16) (Class 2) (0-95,95) 3-Y-O+
£31,155 (£9,330; £4,665; £2,335; £1,165; £585) **Stalls** Far side

Form RPR
5000 1 **Baddam**[39] 3250 6-9-4 89.. JMurtagh 5 97
(Ian Williams) *lw: chsd clr ldrs: clsd 6f out: rdn wl over 3f out: forged ahd over 2f out: styd on wl* **12/1**
0064 2 *1* **Inchpast**[7] 4314 7-8-2 73...(b) JimmyQuinn 13 80
(M H Tompkins) *lw: t.k.h: trckd clr ldng pair: clsd 6f out: gng strly over 3f out: drvn and nt qckn over 2f out: styd on to chse wnr 1f out: a hld* **25/1**
0-63 3 *2* **Mith Hill**[20] 3891 7-8-2 73 ow1.. ChrisCatlin 7 78
(Ian Williams) *wl enough plcd in chsng gp: clsd 6f out: drvn over 3f out: styd on u.p fr over 2f out: tk 3rd nr fin* **25/1**
5/12 4 *¾* **Tomina**[20] 3884 8-7-11 73..................................... DavidProbert(5) 18 77+
(Miss E C Lavelle) *lw: trckd clr ldr and clr of rest: clsd 1/2-way: travelling wl 4f out: led over 3f out: hdd over 2f out: lost 2nd 1f out and 3rd nr post: rdr wout one rein fnl 2f* **17/2**
/611 5 *7* **Keelung (USA)**[18] 3950 7-8-7 78.. MickyFenton 4 75
(R Ford) *led and sn wl clr: c bk to nrest pursuer 1/2-way and to rest of field 6f out: hdd over 3f out: grad fdd* **18/1**
2521 6 *1* **Daylami Dreams**[11] 4200 4-8-7 78.. JohnEgan 8 74
(T P Tate) *wl plcd in chsng gp: tk clsr order 6f out: rdn and in tch 4f out: no imp over 2f out: wknd over 1f out* **15/2**[3]
122 7 *2 ¼* **Lady Dedlock**[14] 4087 4-8-0 71 ow1.................................. FrancisNorton 10 65+
(Jamie Poulton) *towards rr: tk clsr order 6f out: stl plenty to do 4f out: nt clr run and swtchd rt over 2f out: nvr on terms w ldrs* **10/1**
1211 8 *hd* **Directa's Digger (IRE)**[40] 3216 4-8-1 77 ow3..............(v) JackDean(5) 19 71
(M J Scudamore) *wl plcd in chsng gp: tk clsr order 6f out: rdn to chse ldrs 4f out: wknd 2f out* **16/1**
04-4 9 *hd* **Downing Street (IRE)**[20] 3884 7-8-6 77..............................(v) TPO'Shea 2 71+
(Jennie Candlish) *hld up in last pair: rdn over 4f out: no prog and nt gng wl: fnlly picked up 2f out: fin best of all* **16/1**
3012 10 *nk* **La Vecchia Scuola (IRE)**[18] 3942 4-9-3 88............... DanielTudhope 11 81
(J S Goldie) *lw: hld up in last quintet: sme prog over 4f out: no hdwy u.p in midfield over 2f out: fdd* **13/2**[2]
0410 11 *hd* **Abstract Folly (IRE)**[10] 4220 6-7-12 69 oh1.............. CatherineGannon 17 62
(J D Bethell) *swtg: hld up in last trio: sme prog into midfield 3f out: hrd rdn and no imp after: wknd over 1f out* **50/1**
0410 12 *4 ½* **Kasban**[11] 4193 4-8-6 77.. FrankieMcDonald 1 66
(Jane Chapple-Hyam) *warm: mostly in midfield: rdn 4f out: no prog: wknd 2f out* **28/1**
1131 13 *shd* **Silver Seeker (USA)**[39] 3279 8-7-12 69 oh5.................. WilliamBuick 20 58
(Miss P Robson) *hld up in last quintet: rdn over 4f out: no real prog: plugged on fnl f* **14/1**
030 14 *7* **John Terry (IRE)**[3] 4444 5-9-5 90.. JimCrowley 12 72
(Mrs A J Perrett) *t.k.h: hld up in last quintet: stl gng wl enough 4f out: sn no prog: wknd* **25/1**
-325 15 *6* **Som Tala**[43] 3104 5-9-10 95.. LDettori 14 71
(M R Channon) *lw: prom in chsng gp early: midfield by 1/2-way: rdn 4f out: no prog: hanging and wknd 2f out* **9/2**[1]
233 16 *2 ½* **Cavendish**[11] 4193 4-7-12 72...(b) LukeMorris(3) 3 45
(J M P Eustace) *chsd clr ldng pair: clsd 6f out: hrd rdn and stl cl up 3f out: wknd rapidly* **20/1**
5232 17 *hd* **Rose Bien**[27] 3642 6-7-9 69 oh5..(p) DominicFox(3) 16 42
(P J McBride) *hld up in midfield: prog to chse ldrs 6f out: rdn and stl in tch 4f out: wknd rapidly 3f out* **50/1**
50-0 18 *26* **Mudawin (IRE)**[32] 3490 7-9-4 89.. RyanMoore 15 36
(J S Goldie) *nvr on terms w ldrs: wknd 4f out: virtually p.u fnl 2f* **8/1**

4m 30.92s (-2.18) **Going Correction** 0.0s/f (Good) **18** Ran SP% **129.1**
Speed ratings (Par 109): **104,103,102,102,99 99,98,98,98,98 98,96,96,93,91 90,90,80**
toteswinger: 1&2 £72.30, 1&3 £86.60, 2&3 £124.90. CSF £298.56 CT £7204.56 TOTE £15.90: £3.60, £5.90, £6.80, £2.90; EX 385.40 Trifecta £1443.80 Part won..
Owner N Martin **Bred** Mrs V Rapkins **Trained** Portway, Worcs

FOCUS
A good staying handicap and they went a decent pace. As usual for this distance at Goodwood, they got under way with a flip start.

NOTEBOOK
Baddam had not been at his best since returning to the Flat after an unsuccessful spin over hurdles, but he had dropped to a good mark, only 2lb higher than when gaining his last success at Royal Ascot in 2006, and he bounced right back to form. The strong pace suited and, always well placed, he stayed on strongest of all. He stays all day, but there are limited opportunities for him. The Cesarewitch is the long-term aim. Official explanation: trainer said, regarding apparent improvement in form, that the last race came too soon for gelding following outing four days earlier (op 14-1)
Inchpast had never previously raced beyond 2m2f, but he saw his race out well. He travelled strongly into the straight, but his rider looked reluctant to get there too soon and the winner was probably the more resolute of the pair.
Mith Hill, a stablemate of the winner, is suited by extreme distances and this was a respectable effort carrying 1lb overweight.
Tomina had never run beyond 2m on the Flat, but he has won over 3m2f over hurdles. He was arguably travelling best of all when taking over entering the straight and, although passed with over two furlongs to run, he was still in with every chance when the buckle on his reins broke. His rider was unable to get serious throughout the final quarter mile as a result and it cost him third at the very least. He is worth another chance over an extreme distance, but may want holding on to for longer next time. Official explanation: jockey said buckle broke on reins ins 2f mark (op 10-1)
Keelung(USA), bidding for the hat-trick off a 7lb higher mark following a couple of wins from the front at around 2m, got a flyer when the tapes went up and was soon holding a clear lead, but this was the furthest trip he has raced over to date and he finished up well held. (op 16-1)
Daylami Dreams, 4lb higher than when winning over an extended 1m6f at Newmarket, failed to prove his stamina on his first run beyond 2m. (op 11-1)

Lady Dedlock, carrying 1lb overweight, was given a lot to do and could never quite get on terms. (op 9-1 tchd 11-1)

Downing Street(IRE) only got going when the race was all over. (tchd 20-1 in a place)

La Vecchia Scuola(IRE) won a 5f seller just last June, but she has come a long way since then, winning four times over hurdles and gaining another three Flat victories, the latest of which came over 1m6f. She was not at her best this time and, unproven beyond 2m on the level, a lack of stamina could be used as an excuse, but in fairness she never really looked like getting seriously involved. She has had plenty of racing in the past year or so. (op 7-1)

Som Tala was 7lb higher than when fifth in this race last year, but he should still have run better. Official explanation: jockey said gelding hung right-handed (op 6-1 tchd 13-2 in a place)

Mudawin(IRE) Official explanation: jockey said gelding was unsuited by the track

4517 VEUVE CLICQUOT VINTAGE STKS (GROUP 2) 7f

2:50 (2:51) (Class 1) 2-Y-O

£48,254 (£18,292; £9,154; £4,564; £2,286; £1,147) **Stalls** High

Form				RPR
15	**1**		**Orizaba (IRE)**[43] 3103 2-9-0 0 ... LDettori 7 (M R Channon) *hld up bhd ldrs: eased to outer over 2f out and sn prog: rdn to ld jst over 1f out: styd on wl* **11/4**[1]	112
313	**2**	*1 1/4*	**Lord Shanakill (USA)**[43] 3103 2-9-0 0 ... FergusSweeney 11 (K R Burke) *lw: t.k.h early: trckd ldrs: squeezed though between two ldrs to chal over 1f out: upsides ent fnl f: styd on* **9/2**[3]	109
22	**3**	*nk*	**Sayif (IRE)**[20] 3876 2-9-0 0 ... SebSanders 4 (P W Chapple-Hyam) *awkward s: plld hrd early and hld up in rr: plld wd over 2f out: prog to chal and w wnr jst over 1f out: fnd nil: jst hld on for 3rd* **4/1**[2]	108
41	**4**	*nse*	**Soul City (IRE)**[21] 3853 2-9-0 0 ... RyanMoore 9 (R Hannon) *lw: t.k.h: hld up in rr: rdn over 2f out: sme prog over 1f out: styd on strly ins fnl f* **16/1**	108+
3103	**5**	*shd*	**Shaweel**[19] 3920 2-9-0 0 ... GregFairley 3 (M Johnston) *trckd ldr: led 2f out: hdd jst over 1f out: kpt on fnl f* **11/1**	108
10	**6**	*2 1/4*	**Instalment**[43] 3103 2-9-0 0 ... RichardHughes 5 (R Hannon) *lw: dwlt and squeezed out s: t.k.h and hld up in last: rdn over 2f out: kpt on fr over 1f out: nvr rchd ldrs* **20/1**	102+
2311	**7**	*1 1/2*	**Firth Of Fifth (IRE)**[19] 3920 2-9-3 0 ... RichardKingscote 1 (Tom Dascombe) *sn led and set decent pce: hdd 2f out: grad wknd* **10/1**	102
	8	*1/2*	**Set Sail (IRE)**[73] 2222 2-9-0 0 ... JMurtagh 10 (A P O'Brien, Ire) *w'like: scope: pushed along early and chsd ldng pair: lost pl 2f out: hanging bdly and wknd* **11/1**	97
	9	*1 3/4*	**Ryehill Dreamer (IRE)**[28] 3618 2-9-0 0 ... WMLordan 2 (T Stack, Ire) *str: lw: a towards rr: u.p whn nudged over 2f out: wknd* **6/1**	93
110	**10**	*31*	**Baycat (IRE)**[41] 3152 2-9-0 0 ... JamesDoyle 8 (J G Portman) *on toes: chsd ldrs: rdn 3f out: bmpd over 2f out: wknd rapidly: t.o* **33/1**	15

1m 26.54s (-0.86) **Going Correction** 0.0s/f (Good) **10 Ran SP% 118.5**

Speed ratings (Par 106): **104,102,102,102,102 99,97,97,95,59**

toteswinger: 1&2 £3.30, 1&3 £3.30, 2&3 £3.80. CSF £15.26 TOTE £4.20: £1.40, £1.80, £2.00; EX 14.70 Trifecta £44.70 Pool: £1,324.66 - 21.89 winning tickets..

Owner Sheikh Hamdan Bin Mohammed Al Maktoum **Bred** W Powell-Harris **Trained** West Ilsley, Berks

■ Stewards' Enquiry : Seb Sanders one-day ban: careless riding (Aug 13)

FOCUS

This looked like just an average Vintage Stakes beforehand and the race itself did little to alter that thought, with the next four home after the winner finishing in a heap, despite the pace being strong from the start. The form is rated around the second and third and could prove a few pounds higher.

NOTEBOOK

Orizaba(IRE) was a nine-length maiden winner on his debut at Newbury but just found things happening a little too quickly when a beaten favourite in the Coventry. However, his Ascot run probably taught him plenty and he made no mistake this time, proving suited by the step up in trip. He will probably join Godolphin at some stage, but his current trainer is keen to hang on to him until the end of the year and mentioned the Dewhurst and Racing Post Trophy as possible targets. He should be suited by a step up to 1m in time. (op 7-2)

Lord Shanakill(USA) could not confirm Coventry form with Orizaba, but that one produced an improved effort and this was still a very decent run in defeat. He is likely to be continued with in Group company. (op 5-1 tchd 11-2)

Sayif(IRE), beaten a short-head in the July Stakes over 6f, ran well in third considering he was so keen early. He looked a real threat when switched wide with his effort inside the final two furlongs, but his challenge flattened out late on, with his earlier exertions probably just taking their toll. This effort is all the more creditable considering his stable has not been in much form lately. He will stay this trip just fine if he learns to settle, but will be just as effective back over 6f. (op 7-2)

Soul City(IRE) made all when winning a decent maiden at the July meeting, but he was reined back this time and raced keenly early, despite the pace being strong. He was doing all his best work at the finish and might have benefited from a more positive ride.

Shaweel reversed Newmarket form with Firth Of Fifth and seems to be improving. (op 12-1)

Instalment ran much better than when down the field in the Coventry on his previous start, but seemed to lack the pace of some of these and might want easier ground. (tchd 18-1)

Firth Of Fifth(IRE) had plenty to do carrying a 3lb penalty for his success in the Superlative Stakes at Newmarket and he was probably forced to go quicker than ideal in order to dominate. (op 9-1)

Set Sail(IRE) was due to be the mount of David McCabe until the same trainer's Westphalia was declared a non-runner. He probably improved on the bare form of his Gowran maiden success, but did not look up to this level at this stage of his career. (op 12-1)

Ryehill Dreamer(IRE) looked one of the more likely winners beforehand having won a Listed race at Leopardstown on his latest start, but he offered disappointingly little. He might have found the ground too quick. (op 7-1)

Baycat(IRE), upped in trip after being taken off his feet in the Norfolk, was again well beaten. He should appreciate a return to easy ground and also wants his sights lowering.

4518 BGC SUSSEX STKS (GROUP 1) 1m

3:30 (3:33) (Class 1) 3-Y-O+

£170,310 (£64,560; £32,310; £16,110; £8,070; £4,050) **Stalls** High

Form				RPR
-111	**1**		**Henrythenavigator (USA)**[43] 3102 3-8-13 0 ... JMurtagh 3 (A P O'Brien, Ire) *swtg: trckd ldrs: clsd to ld 2f out: qcknd and edgd rt over 1f out: strly pressed ins fnl f: rdn out and post a coming in time* **4/11**[1]	125
2422	**2**	*hd*	**Raven's Pass (USA)**[17] 4010 3-8-13 121 ... JimmyFortune 6 (J H M Gosden) *lw: hld up: 5th 1/2-way: effrt 2f out: chsd wnr over 1f out: hrd rdn and clsd thrght fnl f: nvr quite gng to get there* **4/1**[2]	124
-211	**3**	*3 1/4*	**Major Cadeaux**[60] 2607 4-9-7 114 ... RichardHughes 2 (R Hannon) *t.k.h: sn trckd ldr: led 3f out gng easily: hdd 2f out: sltly hmpd over 1f out and readily outpcd after* **14/1**[3]	118
11-0	**4**	*shd*	**Winker Watson**[17] 4010 3-8-13 114 ... RyanMoore 4 (P W Chapple-Hyam) *lw: stmbld s: hld up in last: prog on outer over 2f out: drvn and cl enough over 1f out: sn outpcd: fdd ins fnl f* **16/1**	116+
5-30	**5**	*6*	**Tariq**[43] 3100 4-9-7 115 ... SebSanders 5 (P W Chapple-Hyam) *lw: dwlt: rcvrd and rchd 3rd by 1/2-way: cl up on inner whn n.m.r briefly 2f out: wknd rapidly over 1f out* **20/1**	102
0-	**6**	*15*	**Windsor Palace (IRE)**[275] 6549 3-8-13 0 ... DavidMcCabe 1 (A P O'Brien, Ire) *led to 3f out: sn lost pl: wknd: t.o* **100/1**	68

1m 38.46s (-1.44) **Going Correction** 0.0s/f (Good)

WFA 3 from 4yo 8lb **6 Ran SP% 111.6**

Speed ratings (Par 117): **107,106,103,103,97 82**

toteswinger: 1&2 £1.10, 1&3 £2.40, 2&3 £1.70. CSF £2.13 TOTE £1.40: £1.10, £1.90; EX 2.30.

Owner Mrs John Magnier **Bred** Westrn Bloodstock **Trained** Ballydoyle, Co Tipperary

■ Stewards' Enquiry : J Murtagh two-day ban: careless riding (Aug 13-14)

FOCUS

Henrythenavigator v Raven's Pass Part III, and the result was the same as in the two previous instalments. The Ballydoyle axis were registering their 16th Group 1 success of what by even their standards has become an extraordinary season. The lack of top-class older milers is something of a disappointment at the moment, but Henrythenavigator can do no more than beat what is put in front of him, and that something is usually John Gosden's star inmate. It is hard to imagine Henrythenavigator getting beaten until he goes to the Breeders' Cup for the Classic, while it would be good if the connections of Raven's Pass could find him a race without Henrythenavigator in for a confidence-boosting victory before he too goes to California for the Mile.

NOTEBOOK

Henrythenavigator(USA) has proved himself to be the best miler in Europe this year of his or any generation and in doing so has now taken his unbeaten run in 2008 to four, all in Group 1 company. With the best of last year's three-year-olds now at stud, nothing has taken their chance to come through among the older milers, so the gloss on his reputation owes much to the runner-up, as without him there would have been very little to stretch him this year, apart from Derby winner New Approach, whose Guineas second over a trip plenty short enough for him becomes ever more creditable as this son of Kingmambo continues to pocket all of Europe's best prizes over 1m. This race proved to be no cake-walk, as his pacemaker first struggled to lead and then dropped out fully three furlongs from home. Henrythenavigator produced his usual telling turn of foot to take up the running soon after, but edged right across the third home, and had to knuckle down to repel the persistent challenge of the runner-up, though he always gave the impression that he wasn't going to be passed. He has an array of options before he aims to cap an illustrious career in the Breeders' Cup Classic over the extra quarter-mile on an artificial surface at Santa Anita. (op 2-5 tchd 4-9 in places)

Raven's Pass(USA) finished second for the third consecutive start, all in Group 1 events and twice behind Henrythenavigator. It is almost incredible that he has not won since his romp in the Solario Stakes at Sandown at the start of last September, but he has kept nothing but the best company and has run his race every time, though a couple of times, notably in the Guineas and the Prix Jean Prat, he has been held up plenty far enough off the pace, probably to his detriment. Ridden considerably closer to the gallop on this occasion, it is no coincidence that he got as close as he has ever done to the winner. His long-time objective is the Breeders' Cup Mile on turf at Santa Anita, where connections will no doubt be thankful not to see Henrythenavigator in the parade ring beforehand. (tchd 9-2)

Major Cadeaux is lightly raced for a four-year-old, and came here at the top of his game, having won in both Group 2 and Group 3 company on his last two starts. He has been found wanting on each previous attempt at the very highest echelon though, and it was the same story here. Keen enough early on when the presence of Ballydoyle's pacemaker alongside him probably wasn't helping, after taking up the running going well early in the straight he was hampered by the winner when that one surged by, and probably ultimately achieved no more form-wise than on his previous victories.

Winker Watson, who had looked so good as a juvenile before injury cruelly intervened, is never going to reach the heights once predicted for him, but after a somewhat inconclusive effort at Longchamp in the Jean Prat he ran much better here, travelling like the good horse that he undoubtedly is before stamina became an issue in the final furlong. There are good opportunities ahead in the late summer and autumn over 7f. (tchd 20-1)

Tariq, who won the Lennox Stakes at this meeting last year, made a promising reappearance in a sub-standard renewal of the Lockinge Stakes in May but has now not been competitive in two starts at the top level since. (op 16-1)

Windsor Palace(IRE) was in as a pacemaker on this seasonal return.

4519 SIR PETER O'SULLEVAN VOICE OF RACING STKS (HERITAGE H'CAP) 1m 4f

4:05 (4:09) (Class 2) (0-105,99) 3-Y-O

£52,963 (£15,861; £7,930; £3,969; £1,980; £994) **Stalls** Low

Form				RPR
3042	**1**		**Love Galore (IRE)**[12] 4160 3-9-1 93 ... JMurtagh 16 (M Johnston) *hld up wl in rr: stdy prog gng wl fr over 3f out stalking runner-up: produced to ld jst over 1f out: drvn and in command after* **8/1**	106
6162	**2**	*1 1/4*	**Savarain**[41] 3157 3-9-7 99 ... LDettori 8 (L M Cumani) *lw: trckd clr ldrs: stdy prog fr over 3f out: led jst over 2f out: wandering sltly and hdd jst over 1f out: kpt on wl but wl hld by wnr fnl f* **13/2**[2]	110
-601	**3**	*2 3/4*	**Howdigo**[16] 4021 3-8-2 80 ... HayleyTurner 14 (J R Best) *hld up in last trio: u.p over 3f out: prog over 2f out: nt clr run briefly over 1f out: wnt 3rd fnl f: no imp on ldng pair* **10/1**	87
0266	**4**	*2 1/4*	**Trenchtown (IRE)**[25] 3719 3-8-7 85 ... SteveDrowne 5 (R Charlton) *swtg: prom in chsng gp: effrt 3f out: kpt on same pce fnl 2f: no real threat to ldrs* **11/1**	88
0032	**5**	*2 1/2*	**William Blake**[5] 4363 3-8-10 88 ... GregFairley 4 (M Johnston) *one of 4 clr fr s: stl chalng over 2f out: fdd over 1f out* **16/1**	87+
3211	**6**	*nk*	**My Aunt Fanny**[19] 3911 3-8-9 87 ... LPKeniry 9 (A M Balding) *lw: hld up in midfield: effrt 3f out: readily outpcd fr over 2f out: hanging but kpt on fr over 1f out* **12/1**	86
141	**7**	*shd*	**Swinging Sixties (IRE)**[31] 3527 3-9-2 94 ... PhilipRobinson 1 (M A Jarvis) *led but harrassed fr the s: hdd jst over 2f out: steadily fdd* **9/1**	93+
-033	**8**	*2 1/4*	**Mystery Star (IRE)**[65] 2464 3-8-6 84 ... JimmyQuinn 2 (M H Tompkins) *dwlt: mostly in last trio: rdn 4f out: prog on inner and in tch over 2f out: wknd over 1f out* **33/1**	79
0411	**9**	*7*	**Goodwood Starlight (IRE)**[19] 3896 3-9-3 95 ... EddieAhern 7 (J L Dunlop) *edgy: scratchy to post: nvr beyond midfield: rdn on outer 3f out: sn btn: wknd* **7/1**[3]	79
-322	**10**	*hd*	**Detonator (IRE)**[6] 4351 3-9-1 93 ... JoeFanning 6 (M Johnston) *one of 4 clr fr s: wknd 2f out* **17/2**	77+
-131	**11**	*1*	**Colony (IRE)**[41] 3157 3-9-4 96 ... RyanMoore 13 (Sir Michael Stoute) *lw: scratchy to post: hld up in last trio: drvn and no rspnse over 3f out: eased whn no ch fnl 2f* **7/2**[1]	78
0011	**12**	*8*	**Always Bold (IRE)**[4] 4426 3-8-11 89 6ex ... MichaelHills 15 (M Johnston) *pressed ldr fr s: upsides over 2f out: wkng whn n.m.r over 1f out* **16/1**	58+

2-51 **13** *129* **North Parade**[61] [2573] 3-8-10 **88**....................................(t) WilliamBuick 3 —
(B J Meehan) *nvr beyond midfield: dropped to last 5f out and sn bhd: virtually p.u and allowed to walk in* **40/1**

2m 34.05s (-4.35) **Going Correction** 0.0s/f (Good) **13** Ran SP% **122.0**
Speed ratings (Par 106): **114,113,111,109,108 107,107,106,101,101 100,95,—**
toteswinger: 1&2 £11.10, 1&3 £25.80, 2&3 £18.20. CSF £60.54 CT £538.30 TOTE £10.80: £3.30, £2.90, £4.30; EX 73.60 Trifecta £1936.70 Part won..
Owner Crone Stud Farms Ltd **Bred** Razza Pallorsi **Trained** Middleham Moor, N Yorks
■ A new title for this race.

FOCUS
A heritage handicap with a rich tradition, for three-year-olds and chock-full of lightly-raced sorts, many stepping-up in trip, with vast potential for improvement. The first two home could well prove up to listed company before the year is out, and this race will undoubtedly throw up plenty of winners in the coming weeks.

NOTEBOOK
Love Galore(IRE), a son of Galileo, has done better the further he has gone and made his first try at 1m4f a winning one, Murtagh being the last to play his hand and his charge responding with a telling change of gear. What happened on the course was only half the story, however, as the colt suffered a deep cut to his left hind hoof on his way to the start which thankfully didn't appear to bother him during the race. He races in a net muzzle which has helped him to settle early on. (op 11-1)
Savarain travelled supremely well into the lead only to have his run trumped by a later, faster effort by the winner. Very lightly raced, his handicap mark is now sure to enter three figures which is unfortunate for an animal with just a maiden win to his name, and he wouldn't be out of place in listed company. (op 6-1)
Howdigo has improved greatly for the step up to middle distances, which is no surprise for a half-brother to Oaks runner-up Rising Cross. Raised only 3lb for a Windsor success in what looked a warm race for the grade, he is the sort who could win a couple of lesser handicaps than this from what is undoubtedly a handy perch in the weights. (op 16-1)
Trenchtown(IRE) seems to travel well enough in his races but isn't a very strong finisher. Perhaps he is just a few pounds too high in the handicap. (op 10-1)
William Blake was the last of the four to race on the suicidal early pace to weaken. He surely stays this trip and if ever he is allowed his own way in the lead he will surely go close, and he is undoubtedly well handicapped. (tchd 20-1)
My Aunt Fanny, held up to cope with a step up in trip, could only plug on at one pace and never got into the race at all. Only when she is put into a race at a stage where she has a realistic chance of winning will we find whether she stays or not. (op 16-1)
Swinging Sixties(IRE) set too strong a pace for his own good, as Robinson was intent on overcoming the disadvantage of his widest-out draw by bouncing out and tacking across to lead, but had three Johnston-trained animals snapping at his heels. (op 11-1 tchd 12-1)
Mystery Star(IRE), held up, moved onto the heels of the leading group into the straight but folded as though he was a non-stayer. (tchd 40-1)
Goodwood Starlight(IRE), who did not look that well in his coat beforehand, also moved poorly to post and ran very flat in the race itself. (op 13-2 tchd 6-1)
Colony(IRE), who moved poorly to the start, made no more than a token effort up the straight after being held up at the rear and this was definitely not his running. (tchd 10-3)
North Parade Official explanation: jockey said colt kicked out in stalls injuring hind leg

4520 WEATHERBYS BANK E B F FILLIES' STKS (H'CAP) 1m 1f
4:40 (4:48) (Class 2) (0-100,96) 3-Y-0+
£12,462 (£3,732; £1,866; £934; £466; £234) **Stalls** High

Form RPR

6552 **1** **Spell Caster**[12] [4152] 3-8-2 **79**.. WilliamBuick 6 89+
(R M Beckett) *lw: trckd ldng pair: cl up fr 2f out: swtchd to inner and got through 1f out: led last 100yds: r.o wl* **13/2**

1504 **2** *1 1/4* **Jazz Jam**[18] [3971] 3-9-2 **93**.. JimmyFortune 2 100
(P F I Cole) *lw: trckd ldrs: effrt 2f out: led ent fnl f: edgd rt and hdd 100yds out: outpcd* **16/1**

4-1 **3** *1* **Asfurah's Dream (IRE)**[40] [3205] 3-8-6 **83**...................... MartinDwyer 11 88
(M P Tregoning) *sn led: narrowly hdd jst over 2f out: kpt on and w ldr 1f out: one pce last 100yds* **9/1**

1105 **4** *hd* **Farley Star**[11] [4189] 4-9-8 **90**.. SteveDrowne 9 98+
(R Charlton) *hld up in last trio: stdy prog on inner fr 3f out: tried for gap 1f out but wnr got there first: rallied last 100yds and nrly snatched 3rd* **16/1**

216 **5** *3/4* **Ghaidaa (IRE)**[34] [3415] 3-9-0 **91**.. RHills 3 94
(M A Jarvis) *b.hind: t.k.h: hld up in midfield on outer: stdy prog 3f out: rdn to chal wl over 1f out: effrt petered out fnl f* **4/1**[1]

-054 **6** *1 1/4* **Free Offer**[33] [3433] 4-9-2 **84**.. EddieAhern 12 85+
(J L Dunlop) *t.k.h: hld up in midfield: trying to cl but nt clr run and hanging wl over 1f out: no imp whn in the clr fnl f* **14/1**

211- **7** *3/4* **Perfect Star**[305] [5794] 4-10-0 **96**.. AdamKirby 1 97+
(C G Cox) *pressed ldr: led narrowly jst over 2f out: hdd ent fnl f: cl 4th but hld whn hmpd and snatched up 100yds out* **12/1**

321 **8** *nk* **Lee Miller (IRE)**[30] [3556] 3-8-2 **79**.. ChrisCatlin 5 77
(L M Cumani) *lw: hld up: effrt on outer over 2f out: no prog u.p over 1f out: fdd* **6/1**[3]

3356 **9** *2 3/4* **Fongs Gazelle**[13] [4111] 4-8-10 **78**.. LDettori 13 77+
(M Johnston) *lw: trckd ldrs: covered up over 1f out and nowhere to go: hanging after and wknd ins fnl f* **8/1**

3-03 **10** *2 1/4* **Maramba (USA)**[18] [3971] 3-9-2 **93**.. RyanMoore 7 80
(Sir Michael Stoute) *lw: hld up in rr: rdn and struggling wl over 2f out: no prog* **12/1**

4130 **11** *4* **Aphrodisia**[11] [4189] 4-8-9 **77** oh3.. PhilipRobinson 4 56
(S C Williams) *s.s: a in rr: drvn and struggling 3f out* **33/1**

-110 **12** *3 1/4* **Algarade**[25] [3751] 4-9-4 **86**.. SebSanders 10 58
(Sir Mark Prescott) *hld up towards rr: rdn on outer 3f out: nt gng wl after: eased whn no ch fnl f* **9/2**[2]

1- **13** *36* **Maryqueenofscots (IRE)**[322] [5328] 3-8-4 **81**...................... HayleyTurner 8 —
(M L W Bell) *a in rr: wknd 3f out: t.o and eased* **33/1**

1m 54.56s (-1.74) **Going Correction** 0.0s/f (Good)
WFA 3 from 4yo 9lb **13** Ran SP% **126.6**
Speed ratings (Par 96): **107,105,105,104,104 103,102,102,99,97 94,91,59**
toteswinger: 1&2 £27.10, 1&3 £16.60, 2&3 £31.30. CSF £112.81 CT £983.81 TOTE £8.60: £2.70, £4.70, £3.20; EX 157.40 TRIFECTA Not won..
Owner D P Barrie & M J Rees **Bred** Peter E Clinton **Trained** Whitsbury, Hants
■ Stewards' Enquiry : William Buick two-day ban: careless riding (Aug 13-14)
Jimmy Fortune two-day ban: careless riding (Aug 13-14)

FOCUS
A competitive fillies' handicap, run at a fair pace. The form looks sound enough rated though the placed horses.

NOTEBOOK
Spell Caster, 3lb higher than when second at Newbury 12 days previously, showed herself to be an improving filly and went one better in gutsy fashion. She had endured a troubled passage on her previous start and that was again the case here, but she burst through on the inside when the gap appeared and rates value for a little further than the bare margin. A hike in the weights is inevitable, but her season just looks to be getting into gear now and further improvement cannot not ruled out. (op 8-1)
Jazz Jam posted her best effort of the current campaign, coming through to lead passing the final furlong marker, and enjoyed this return to a quicker surface. She is not easy to place successfully from her current mark, but this display would suggest she is well worth another try over a bit further now. (op 20-1)
Asfurah's Dream(IRE) had made all in a modest maiden over course and distance 40 days previously and set out to repeat the feat on this step into handicap company. She had pretty much the run of the race, but kept on willingly when the challengers mounted inside the final 2f and this rates a pleasing effort. (op 11-1)
Farley Star ◆ was ridden to get this longer distance and has to rate unlucky not have to filled a place. She went for the same gap the eventual winner grabbed on the rail approaching the final furlong and got hampered by that rival, losing a length or so in the process. The manner in which she ran on when in the clear would suggest she is still fairly handicapped at present and could find further improvement over this sort of distance.
Ghaidaa(IRE), a beaten favourite in Listed company last time, had to race wide from her low draw, but still emerged with her challenge at the 2f pole and can have no real excuses on this return to quicker ground. She is well regarded by her shrewd outfit and may well improve again for a step up in trip, but she still looks some way off Pattern class. (op 6-1 tchd 13-2 in places)
Free Offer took time to settle early on and then found some trouble nearing the final furlong, but she rather hung fire when put under maximum pressure. She is fairly handicapped and would enjoy a more prominent ride over this trip, but must learn to settle better if she is to progress further.
Perfect Star, who looked fit for this seasonal debut, got a positive ride from her outside stall and ran encouragingly under top weight. She would have been closer at the finish had she not been hampered by the runner-up late on and looks sure to come on a good deal for the run. (op 14-1)
Lee Miller(IRE), making her handicap debut, did not appear the most straightforward ride and has to rate as somewhat disappointing. (tchd 9-2)
Maramba(USA) had finished in front of Jazz Jam at Salisbury last time and was 2lb lower here, but she looked all at sea on the quicker ground. (op 8-1)
Aphrodisia Official explanation: jockey said filly missed the break
Algarade was dropping back in trip having been well beaten off in a German Listed event 25 days previously. She was in trouble soon after the turn for home and ultimately ran as though something went amiss. (op 7-1 tchd 4-1)
Maryqueenofscots(IRE) Official explanation: jockey said filly was unsuited by the track

4521 WINSTON'S WISH MAIDEN FILLIES' STKS 6f
5:15 (5:19) (Class 2) 2-Y-O **£12,952** (£3,854; £1,926; £962) **Stalls** Low

Form RPR

536 **1** **Gower Valentine**[38] [3292] 2-9-0 0.. AdrianTNicholls 3 80
(D Nicholls) *mde all: clr fnl f: drvn out* **14/1**

2 *2* **Intense** 2-9-0 0.. RHills 11 75+
(B W Hills) *w'like: bit bkwd: dwlt: off the pce towards rr: prog over 2f out: shkn up and styd on to take 2nd ins fnl f: unable to trble wnr* **10/1**

242 **3** *1* **Sterling Sound (USA)**[14] [4088] 2-9-0 0.. MartinDwyer 6 71
(M P Tregoning) *lw: racd freely and prom: chsd wnr after 2f: edgd rt and nt qckn over 1f out: lost 2nd ins fnl f* **9/2**[2]

4 *1 1/4* **Seradim** 2-9-0 0.. LDettori 15 68+
(P F I Cole) *w'like: scope: str: sn wl in rr: stdy prog on outer fr 1/2-way: shkn up and kpt on fr over 1f out: n.d* **14/1**

2 **5** *3/4* **Victoria Sponge (IRE)**[9] [4251] 2-9-0 0.. RichardHughes 14 65
(R Hannon) *w'like: scope: tall: chsd ldrs and racd on outer: effrt over 2f out: unable to mount a chal over 1f out: fdd ins fnl f* **9/4**[1]

3 **6** *2 1/4* **Slant (IRE)**[12] [4149] 2-9-0 0.. StephenCarson 4 58
(Eve Johnson Houghton) *chsd ldrs: hanging rt fr over 2f out: plugged on fr over 1f out but no ch* **8/1**

0 **7** *1/2* **Red Kyte**[18] [3959] 2-9-0 0.. JohnEgan 12 57+
(K A Ryan) *leggy: t.k.h early: chsd ldrs: outpcd fr jst over 2f out: shkn up and nvr on terms after* **20/1**

8 *3 1/4* **Save The Day** 2-9-0 0.. GregFairley 16 50+
(M Johnston) *leggy: dwlt: sn rdn in last pair and outpcd: modest late prog* **20/1**

5 **9** *nk* **Danzadil (IRE)**[35] [3378] 2-9-0 0.. SteveDrowne 10 46
(R A Teal) *dwlt: a off the pce in rr: pushed along and no prog 2f out* **25/1**

6 **10** *1 1/4* **Ruasgreyasme (USA)**[19] [3895] 2-9-0 0.. PatDobbs 1 42
(R Hannon) *rrd s: chsd wnr 2f: hanging and wknd over 1f out* **25/1**

0 **11** *6* **Harquahala (IRE)**[14] [4080] 2-9-0 0.. JoeFanning 5 24
(T G Mills) *chsd ldrs: in trble sn after 1/2-way: wknd* **33/1**

12 *13* **Equinine (IRE)** 2-9-0 0.. MichaelHills 8 —
(B W Hills) *w'like: scope: sn outpcd: a struggling in rr: t.o* **11/1**

13 *3* **Dane's World (IRE)** 2-9-0 0.. RyanMoore 13 —
(R Hannon) *w'like: attr: a in rr: virtually racing sideways fnl 2f: t.o* **7/1**[3]

1m 11.44s (-0.76) **Going Correction** -0.125s/f (Firm) **13** Ran SP% **123.5**
Speed ratings (Par 97): **100,97,96,94,93 90,89,85,84,83 75,57,53**
toteswinger: 1&2 £25.00, 1&3 £13.40, 2&3 £12.70. CSF £140.53 TOTE £18.00: £3.60, £3.90, £2.10; EX 238.50 Trifecta £510.50 Part won..
Owner David & Gwyn Joseph & Partner **Bred** Bearstone Stud **Trained** Sessay, N Yorks

FOCUS
A decent juvenile fillies' maiden and pretty strong form. The winner was a big improver and the form helps with the level.

NOTEBOOK
Gower Valentine had steadily progressed through each of her first three outings, but this was a greatly improved effort to get off the mark and she did the job readily from the front. She could have been called the winner from a fair way out, with the fast ground looking right up her street, and her previous experience was certainly a notable advantage. She would have to take all the beating if found a suitable opportunity under a penalty in a nursery before the Handicapper can have his say. (op 16-1)
Intense ◆, the first foal of a smart dual 1m3f-1m6f winner, hit a flat spot around halfway before keeping on with promise inside the final furlong. Her pedigree suggests she really wants a stiffer test and, granted the normal improvement for this debut experience, she ought to prove hard to beat when faced with another furlong. (op 12-1)
Sterling Sound(USA) again hampered her chance by racing too freely through the early stages. She has ability and this looks her trip at present, but a move into nurseries now looks her best option. She rates a sound benchmark for the form. (op 5-1 tchd 6-1)
Seradim ran distinctly green through the early parts and without cover, ultimately shaping as if this debut experience was needed. She was noted doing some decent late work, indeed her pedigree strongly suggests she will enjoy a stiffer test before that long, and she should prove a good deal sharper next time.
Victoria Sponge(IRE), second on debut at Windsor nine days previously, raced a little freely through the early parts and failed to build on her initial promise. She now has something to prove, but will be qualified for nurseries after her next outing. (tchd 5-2 tchd 11-4 in places)

Slant(IRE) performed some way below the level of her debut third at Newbury 12 days previously and tended to hang under pressure. She is another who will be eligible for nurseries after her next outing and she may enjoy a stiffer test in that sphere. Official explanation: jockey said filly was unsuited by the good to firm ground (op 11-1)

4522 KENNELS E B F CLASSIFIED STKS — 7f

5:50 (5:50) (Class 2) 3-Y-0+

£12,462 (£3,732; £1,866; £934; £466; £234) **Stalls** High

Form				RPR
0-22 **1** **Firestreak**[25] 3744 3-8-11 95 .... RichardHughes 9 99+
(R Hannon) *trckd ldng pair: clsd smoothly fr over 2f out: led over 1f out: rdn clr* **9/4**[2]

0460 **2** *1 1/2* **Mujood**[4] 4405 5-9-4 90 .... (b) StephenCarson 8 98
(Eve Johnson Houghton) *trckd ldr: clsd to ld jst over 2f out: hdd over 1f out: kpt on same pce* **12/1**

-402 **3** *nk* **We'll Come**[11] 4177 4-9-4 93 .... (b) PhilipRobinson 7 97
(M A Jarvis) *s.i.s: t.k.h: hld up in last: stl there 2f out: swtchd to inner and prog whn bmpd jst over 1f out: styd on and nrly ct runner-up* **7/2**[3]

2460 **4** *2 1/4* **Flawed Genius**[19] 3919 3-8-11 95 .... (vt) RyanMoore 6 88
(Sir Michael Stoute) *s.i.s: hld up in last pair: effrt on outer over 2f out: sn rdn and no rspnse* **2/1**[1]

3005 **5** *hd* **Berbice (IRE)**[12] 4153 3-8-11 94 .... (t) PatDobbs 2 88
(R Hannon) *t.k.h early: hld up in midfield: effrt over 2f out: edgd rt over 1f out: sn outpcd* **16/1**

3366 **6** *nk* **Kay Es Jay (FR)**[4] 4424 3-8-8 92 .... MichaelHills 5 84
(B W Hills) *s.i.s: t.k.h early: hld up towards rr: effrt over 2f out: keeping on one pce and wl hld whn carried rt jst over 1f out* **20/1**

3310 **7** *5* **Monkey Glas (IRE)**[109] 1334 4-9-4 93 .... (v) AndrewElliott 4 76
(K R Burke) *lw: led at gd pce: hdd jst over 2f out: wkng whn bmpd and hit rail jst over 1f out* **16/1**

0200 **8** *8* **Binanti**[15] 4060 8-9-4 90 .... FrancisNorton 3 55
(P R Chamings) *chsd ldng pair tl wknd rapidly over 2f out: t.o* **20/1**

1m 25.53s (-1.87) **Going Correction** 0.0s/f (Good)
WFA 3 from 4yo+ 7lb — **8** Ran SP% **115.3**
Speed ratings (Par 109): **110,108,107,105,105 104,99,89**
toteswinger: 1&2 £7.40, 1&3 £7.00, 2&3 £7.00. CSF £29.49 TOTE £2.90: £1.40, £2.60, £1.70; EX 36.30 Trifecta £184.60 Pool: £1,147.84 - 4.60 winning tickets. Place 6 £341.36, Place 5 £66.55.
Owner The Queen **Bred** The Queen **Trained** East Everleigh, Wilts

FOCUS
A typically tight classified event, run at a solid pace. Sound form.

NOTEBOOK
Firestreak, runner-up on his two previous outings this term, was racing from a 10lb higher mark then when he resumed this year and he ran out a much-deserved winner. He enjoyed the decent early pace, eventually scoring with something to spare, and should be high on confidence now. Another rise in the weights is now forthcoming, but he still has relatively few miles on the clock and could find further improvement when upped to 1m. (op 5-2 tchd 2-1)
Mujood was given a handy ride and, while being put in his place by the winner nearing the final furlong, stayed on to arguably post his best ever run in defeat. He would not want to be going up too much for this, however. (op 14-1)
We'll Come proved free through the early stages and endured a fairly rough passage through the race. He basically got going too late in the day and remains a frustrating yet talented performer. (op 10-3 tchd 4-1)
Flawed Genius, well backed for this drop in trip, found little when asked for maximum effort in the home straight and is in danger of becoming disappointing now. (op 9-4 tchd 5-2)
T/Jkpt: Not won. T/Plt: £976.60 to a £1 stake. Pool: £247,284.59. 184.84 winning tickets. T/Qpdt: £159.50 to a £1 stake. Pool: £13,304.70. 61.70 winning tickets. JN

4339 KEMPTON (A.W) (R-H)

Wednesday, July 30

OFFICIAL GOING: Standard
Wind: Nil

4523 THAMES MATERIALS MAIDEN STKS — 5f (P)

6:00 (6:00) (Class 4) 3-Y-0+

£4,727 (£1,406; £702; £351) **Stalls** High

Form				RPR
0-23 **1** **Silvanus (IRE)**[33] 3438 3-9-3 75 .... LiamJones 4 70+
(W J Haggas) *chsd ldrs: led wl over 1f out: sn clr: easily* **1/2**[1]

6- **2** *4* **Billberry**[275] 6540 3-9-0 .... LukeMorris(3) 6 56+
(S C Williams) *hld up in rr and outpcd 1/2-way: shkn up over 1f out and str run ins fnl f to take 2nd cl home but no ch w easy wnr* **16/1**

6606 **3** *1/2* **Shatter Resistant (IRE)**[8] 4272 3-9-3 53 .... (p) JimmyQuinn 1 54
(M D Squance) *chsd ldrs: wnt 2nd 1f out but no ch w wnr: outpcd into 3rd cl home* **8/1**[2]

30- **4** *3 3/4* **Captain Kir (IRE)**[346] 4629 3-8-12 0 .... DavidProbert(5) 2 41
(B De Haan) *pressed ldr tl led over 2f out: hdd wl over 1f out: wknd sn after* **14/1**

0040 **5** *1 3/4* **Jalons Bridewell**[26] 3686 3-9-3 61 .... (v) RobertHavlin 5 34
(M Quinn) *slt advantage tl over 2f out: sn btn* **10/1**

5600 **6** *4 1/2* **Hold That Call (USA)**[17] 3-9-0 44 .... EmmettStack(3) 10 18
(A J Chamberlain) *s.i.s: rdn 1/2-way: nvr in contention* **40/1**

7 *2* **Green Velvet** 3-8-9 0 .... TravisBlock(3) 3 6
(P J Makin) *s.i.s: in rr tl sme hdwy 1/2-way: sn dropped away* **9/1**[3]

R0 **8** *2 1/4* **Tot Hill**[26] 3688 5-9-2 0 .... SamHitchcott 8 —
(C N Kellett) *a in rr* **100/1**

5000 **9** *3 1/4* **Feeling Pretty**[53] 2823 3-8-12 30 .... (p) MickyFenton 9 —
(C Smith) *early spd* **100/1**

61.53 secs (1.03) **Going Correction** +0.25s/f (Slow)
WFA 3 from 4yo+ 4lb — **9** Ran SP% **113.8**
Speed ratings (Par 105): **101,94,93,87,85 77,74,71,65**
toteswinger: 1&2 £3.80, 1&3 £2.00, 2&3 £21.80. CSF £10.47 TOTE £1.40: £1.02, £3.20, £2.00; EX 10.60.
Owner Lee Man Yan **Bred** Barronstown Stud And Mrs T Stack **Trained** Newmarket, Suffolk

FOCUS
This is unlikely to be a race worth following in the long term because the winner had failed at very short odds in the past, while many of his rivals were either disappointing or not very good. The winner was 5lb off his best in a race rated through the third.
Feeling Pretty Official explanation: jockey said filly resented kickback and briefly lost its action

4524 DIGIBET CASINO H'CAP — 1m (P)

6:30 (6:33) (Class 6) (0-65,65) 3-Y-0

£2,047 (£604; £302) **Stalls** High

Form				RPR
0-01 **1** **Bluejain**[14] 4076 3-9-7 65 .... MickyFenton 12 79+
(Miss Gay Kelleway) *hld up in rr: stdy hdwy on outside over 2f out: qcknd to ld over 1f out: sn clr: easily* **8/1**

3600 **2** *5* **Feasible**[23] 3799 3-9-6 64 .... JamesDoyle 4 66
(J G Portman) *led: rdn over 2f out: hdd over 1f out: sn no ch w wnr but styd on wl for 2nd* **12/1**

1206 **3** *1* **Admirals Way**[15] 4061 3-8-11 60 .... MarkCoumbe(5) 13 60
(C N Kellett) *chsd ldrs: rdn and kpt on fnl 2f and clsng on inner nr fin but no ch w easy wnr* **8/1**

6500 **4** *1 3/4* **Timber Creek**[20] 3886 3-9-4 65 .... TravisBlock(3) 9 61
(H Candy) *chsd ldrs: rdn 3f out: styd on fr over 1f out but nvr in contention* **18/1**

6060 **5** *1/2* **Copperwood**[14] 4081 3-9-4 62 .... JimmyQuinn 10 57
(M Blanshard) *t.k.h early: chsd ldrs: rdn over 2f out: styd on same pce* **9/2**[1]

4-05 **6** *2 1/2* **Welsh Opera**[19] 3906 3-9-1 59 .... LPKeniry 11 48
(Mrs A J Perrett) *chsd ldrs: rdn 3f out: wknd fr 2f out* **14/1**

4400 **7** *4 1/2* **Where's Susie**[21] 3845 3-9-6 64 .... RobertHavlin 2 42
(D K Ivory) *in rr: rdn 3f out: mod prog u.p fnl 2f* **14/1**

0-06 **8** *6* **Todber**[14] 4090 3-9-0 58 .... SebSanders 14 23
(M P Tregoning) *pressed ldr 5f out: rdn 3f out: wknd qckly 2f out* **9/1**

6600 **9** *3/4* **Morocchius (USA)**[20] 3886 3-9-5 63 .... (p) SamHitchcott 7 26
(Miss J A Camacho) *in rr: rdn and effrt into mid-div 3f out: sn bhd again* **25/1**

-500 **10** *7* **Better In Heaven**[40] 3206 3-9-4 62 .... LiamJones 1 9
(H J L Dunlop) *sn rdn and a bhd* **20/1**

-050 **11** *1/2* **Coach And Four (USA)**[14] 4086 3-9-5 63 .... (p) GeorgeBaker 6 9
(S A Callaghan) *broke wl: stdd towards rr: rdn over 2f out and no rspnse* **5/1**[2]

0-64 **12** *1 1/2* **Bid To The Beat**[26] 3694 3-8-13 60 .... KirstyMilczarek(3) 8 2
(H J Collingridge) *in rr: brief effrt u.p into mid-div over 3f out: sn dropped away* **16/1**

0020 **13** *25* **Broughtons Flight (IRE)**[12] 4152 3-9-5 63 .... TedDurcan 5 —
(W J Musson) *sn bhd* **12/1**

44-0 **14** *4* **Blitzen (IRE)**[22] 3826 3-8-11 62 .... RossAtkinson(7) 3 —
(Tom Dascombe) *chsd ldrs 5f* **15/2**[3]

1m 40.89s (1.09) **Going Correction** +0.25s/f (Slow) — **14** Ran SP% **127.3**
Speed ratings (Par 98): **104,99,98,96,95 93,88,82,82,75 74,73,48,44**
toteswinger: 1&2 £23.20, 1&3 £19.70, 2&3 £34.40. CSF £106.61 CT £834.85 TOTE £5.80: £2.80, £5.10, £3.40; EX 122.10.
Owner Countrywide Classics Limited **Bred** David Sugars And Bob Parker **Trained** Exning, Suffolk
■ Stewards' Enquiry : Ross Atkinson two-day ban: careless riding (Aug 13-14)
George Baker one-day ban: careless riding (Aug 20)

FOCUS
This handicap contained a mix of modest but capable sorts and a few that promised to find a bit more for various reasons. The form looks solid overall and the winner is on the up.
Morocchius(USA) Official explanation: jockey said gelding suffered interference shortly after start
Bid To The Beat Official explanation: jockey said colt failed to handle the bend

4525 DIGIBET.COM NURSERY — 6f (P)

7:00 (7:02) (Class 4) 2-Y-0

£3,885 (£1,156; £577; £288) **Stalls** High

Form				RPR
14 **1** **Crystal Moments**[20] 3865 2-8-13 79 .... EddieAhern 6 83+
(E A L Dunlop) *trckd ldrs: drvn and qcknd over 1f out: styd on wl to ld cl home: readily* **15/8**[1]

1503 **2** *3/4* **Missile Dodger (USA)**[21] 3846 2-9-7 87 .... (v[1]) GeorgeBaker 12 87
(R M Beckett) *led: wnt sharply rt to ins rail 2f out: rdn and kpt on gamely whn strly chal fr over 1f out: ct cl home* **8/1**

51 **3** *1/2* **Night Seed (IRE)**[19] 3902 2-8-4 73 ow1 .... PatrickHills(3) 3 72
(R Hannon) *sn chsng ldr: chal u.p fr 2f out: outpcd fnl 100yds* **16/1**

6542 **4** *3/4* **Black N Brew (USA)**[11] 4185 2-8-3 69 .... JimmyQuinn 8 67+
(J R Best) *hmpd s: in rr: styd on wl appr fnl f: gng on cl home but nt rch ldng trio* **7/1**

032 **5** *3* **Today's The Day**[21] 3837 2-8-9 75 .... LiamJones 2 62
(M A Jarvis) *chsd ldrs 1/2-way: sn rdn and outpcd: kpt on again fnl f* **10/1**

521 **6** *nse* **Special Cuvee**[26] 3689 2-8-11 77 .... SebSanders 4 64
(Sir Mark Prescott) *chsd ldrs: rdn and outpcd 3f out: kpt on again fnl f* **7/2**[2]

005 **7** *3 1/4* **Claphands**[22] 3821 2-7-7 64 oh3 .... (p) DavidProbert(5) 9 41+
(A J McCabe) *bmpd s: in rr: hdwy on ins whn hmpd 2f out: n.d after* **16/1**

3044 **8** *1/2* **Premier Krug (IRE)**[27] 3639 2-7-5 64 oh4 .... (v[1]) AndreaAtzeni(7) 7 40
(P D Evans) *bmpd s: a towards rr* **33/1**

302 **9** *hd* **Court Approval (IRE)**[16] 4020 2-9-0 80 .... TedDurcan 11 55
(T G Mills) *wnt lft s: chsd ldrs: rdn and veered sharply rt to ins rail 2f out: sn wknd* **11/2**[3]

1m 14.83s (1.73) **Going Correction** +0.25s/f (Slow) — **9** Ran SP% **119.8**
Speed ratings (Par 96): **98,97,96,95,91 91,86,86,86**
toteswinger: 1&2 £5.50, 1&3 £17.90, 2&3 £50.00. CSF £18.82 CT £193.76 TOTE £3.30: £1.20, £3.10, £3.80; EX 25.90.
Owner Mohammed Jaber **Bred** Lady Jennifer Green And John Eyre **Trained** Newmarket, Suffolk

FOCUS
No more than a fair nursery and it proved difficult to make up ground, with each of the first three being up there from an early stage. The winner is progressing.

NOTEBOOK
Crystal Moments was expected to improve for this first try at 6f, having got done for toe behind a useful sort at Doncaster last time. Always well positioned, just in behind the speed, she did not respond immediately when asked for her effort, but it became clear from well over a furlong out her momentum was going to get her there and she got well on top close home. Both her parents won at middle-distances and on this showing the sooner she tackles 7f the better. (op 7-2 tchd 4-1)
Missile Dodger(USA) was thought well enough of to take his chance in the Windsor Castle at Royal Ascot and he ultimately proved disappointing at Lingfield last time on his nursery debut, finding little for pressure. He had been dropped 3lb though and proved more willing here in the first-time visor, finding off the front end and only getting run out of it late on. (op 17-2)
Night Seed(IRE) had won just a modest maiden at Chepstow last time and was up a furlong in trip for this nursery debut. She showed plenty of speed and appeared to be going best at just past halfway, but her stamina slowly gave out and she could find no extra. There is definitely a race in her off a mark in the low 70s, but it will be back at 5f. (op 14-1)
Black N Brew(USA) was the eyecatcher of the race, as having been slowest away and well in rear, he flew home inside the final quarter mile to claim a never-nearer fourth. He had finished second to the useful Khor Dubai on his recent nursery debut and clearly has a race in him off this sort of mark, with a return to 7f likely to help. Official explanation: jockey said colt suffered interference at the start (op 11-2 tchd 9-2)

Today's The Day placed in a couple of course-and-distance maidens, did best of the rest without suggesting she is ready to win off a mark of 75. (op 15-2)
Special Cuvee's Southwell maiden had worked out well, with the third winning a nursery at Newmarket over the weekend, but he was always struggling for speed here and gave a rather laboured effort. (tchd 3-1)

4526 DIGIBET H'CAP — 2m (P)
7:30 (7:30) (Class 5) (0-75,75) 4-Y-0+ — £2,590 (£770; £385; £192) Stalls High

Form				RPR
0123	1		**Cavallini (USA)**[43] 1933 6-9-2 70 ... GeorgeBaker 3	78
			(G L Moore) *in tch: hdwy 4f out: chsd ldr 3f out: str chal 2f out: led over 1f out: drvn out* **10/3**[1]	
064	2	2 ½	**Fiddlers Ford (IRE)**[35] 3377 7-8-2 56 oh2 ... JimmyQuinn 7	61
			(T Keddy) *chsd ldr: led appr fnl 4f: rdn 3f out: kpt on whn strly chal 2f out: hdd over 1f out: styd on same pce* **7/2**[2]	
2-46	3	2 ½	**Estate**[26] 3697 6-9-4 72 ... ChrisCatlin 8	74
			(E J O'Neill) *chsd ldrs: rdn and styd on same pce fr over 2f out* **4/1**[3]	
0230	4	hd	**Mister Completely (IRE)**[11] 4193 7-8-11 65 ...(v) JamesDoyle 4	67
			(Ms J S Doyle) *towards rr but in tch: rdn and styd on same pce fnl 2f* **8/1**	
634	5	22	**Just Intersky (USA)**[40] 3220 5-7-10 57 ... CharlesEddery(7) 1	32
			(V Smith) *a in rr* **16/1**	
5153	6	7	**The King And I (IRE)**[60] 2621 4-9-2 75 ...(b) DavidProbert(5) 2	42
			(Miss E C Lavelle) *hld up in rr: effrt over 4f out: sn wknd* **5/1**	
/1-4	7	3	**Master Wells (IRE)**[18] 3970 7-8-12 71 ow5 ... HaddenFrost(5) 5	34
			(J D Frost) *led: hdd over 4f out: sn wknd* **5/1**	

3m 35.64s (5.54) **Going Correction** +0.25s/f (Slow) — 7 Ran SP% **115.6**
Speed ratings (Par 103): **96,94,93,93,82 78,77**
toteswinger: 1&2 £2.40, 1&3 £1.50, 2&3 £23.90. CSF £15.67 CT £47.46 TOTE £3.60: £2.20, £2.50; EX 16.60.
Owner G L Moore **Bred** Newbiggin Ltd **Trained** Woodingdean, E Sussex

FOCUS
None of these could be ruled out with confidence, although most of them had something to prove one way or another. The early pace was only modest, which meant virtually everything had a chance leaving the back straight. The form is not too solid.
Mister Completely(IRE) Official explanation: jockey said gelding had bled from the nose
Just Intersky(USA) Official explanation: jockey said gelding ran too free
Master Wells(IRE) Official explanation: jockey said gelding had no more to give

4527 AZURE H'CAP — 1m 3f (P)
8:00 (8:01) (Class 5) (0-70,68) 3-Y-0 — £2,590 (£770; £385; £192) Stalls High

Form				RPR
2-25	1		**Vilna (USA)**[6] 4344 3-9-6 67 ...(v[1]) GeorgeBaker 6	75
			(S A Callaghan) *hld up in tch: stdy hdwy over 2f out: drvn to take slt ld 1f out: r.o strly* **4/1**[3]	
0302	2	1 ½	**Mista Rossa**[6] 4344 3-9-4 68 ... TravisBlock(3) 9	74+
			(H Morrison) *chsd ldrs: rdn 2f out: squeezed through on ins to chal 1f out: outpcd ins fnl f* **5/2**[2]	
0062	3	1 ½	**Carmela Maria**[9] 4260 3-8-11 58 ... TedDurcan 10	60
			(C F Wall) *led tl hdd 2f out: rallied to ld again sn after: hdd and n.m.r 1f out: sn no ch w ldng duo* **6/1**	
-265	4	½	**Politeia (USA)**[20] 3886 3-9-2 68 ... HaddenFrost(5) 5	70
			(R Hannon) *in rr: stl last and plenty to do over 2f out: str run on outside appr fnl f: fin wl but nvr gng pce to rch ldrs* **10/1**	
5-00	5	2 ¾	**Red Twist**[35] 3384 3-9-5 66 ... RobertHavlin 3	63
			(H Morrison) *in rr: rdn and hdwy fr 3f out: nvr gng pce to be competitive* **33/1**	
3000	6	1	**Ray Diamond**[9] 4254 3-8-3 50 ...(p) JimmyQuinn 2	45
			(M Madgwick) *s.i.s: sn rcvrd to chse ldrs: wnt 2nd over 3f out: led briefly 2f out and wknd qckly* **50/1**	
5-52	7	¾	**Berry Baby (IRE)**[36] 3351 3-9-2 63 ... EddieAhern 8	57+
			(G A Butler) *a towards rr* **15/8**[1]	
-000	8	1 ¾	**Appointment**[30] 3562 3-8-11 58 ...(b[1]) JamesDoyle 4	49
			(Mrs A J Perrett) *chsd ldrs: rdn 3f out: wknd fr 2f out* **40/1**	
000	9	4	**Testimonial**[37] 3326 3-9-4 65 ...(b[1]) SebSanders 1	49
			(E A L Dunlop) *s.i.s: in rr: sme prog over 3f out: nvr in contention* **25/1**	
00-0	10	5	**Promised Gold**[102] 1478 3-8-8 55 ... LPKeniry 7	31
			(J A Geake) *chsd ldrs to 3f out* **50/1**	

2m 24.53s (2.63) **Going Correction** +0.25s/f (Slow) — 10 Ran SP% **119.9**
Speed ratings (Par 100): **100,98,97,97,95 94,94,92,90,86**
toteswinger: 1&2 £2.10, 1&3 £2.50, 2&3 £2.10. CSF £14.37 CT £59.81 TOTE £5.20: £1.70, £1.40, £1.90; EX 16.70.
Owner Michael Tabor **Bred** Gerald O'Meara And Stanley Inman **Trained** Newmarket, Suffolk
■ Stewards' Enquiry : George Baker one-day ban: careless riding (Aug 13)

FOCUS
A modest handicap run at a steady pace producing a bit of a sprint finish. The form is rated through the runner-up.
Politeia(USA) Official explanation: jockey said filly never travelled early stages
Appointment Official explanation: jockey said filly had no more to give

4528 BYRNE GROUP H'CAP (LONDON MILE QUALIFIER) — 1m (P)
8:30 (8:33) (Class 3) (0-95,95) 3-Y-0+ — £7,477 (£2,239; £1,119; £560; £279; £140) Stalls High

Form				RPR
01-0	1		**Premio Loco (USA)**[66] 2426 4-9-11 92 ... GeorgeBaker 8	106
			(C F Wall) *trckd ldrs: smooth prog fr 2f out to take slt ld 1f out: sn drvn clr* **7/2**[2]	
12-	2	2 ½	**Rose Street (IRE)**[274] 6576 4-9-5 86 ... PhilipRobinson 12	94
			(M A Jarvis) *chsd ldrs: qcknd to chal 1f out: sn outpcd by wnr but kpt on wl for 2nd* **2/1**[1]	
0012	3	nk	**Hilbre Court (USA)**[4] 4429 3-8-7 82 ... EddieAhern 4	87
			(B J Meehan) *towards rr: rdn over 2f out and styd on: kpt on wl fnl f: gng on cl home* **16/1**	
1-10	4	1 ¾	**Russki (IRE)**[82] 1942 4-9-8 92 ... KirstyMilczarek(3) 7	95
			(D M Simcock) *drvn to ld after 1f: chal fr 4f out: rdn and asserted ins fnl 2f: hdd 1f out: sn btn* **11/2**[3]	
0604	5	7	**Buxton**[31] 3529 4-9-7 88 ...(t) RobertHavlin 14	75
			(R Ingram) *chsd ldrs: rdn over 2f out: wknd qckly fnl f* **18/1**	
6605	6	1	**Neardown Beauty (IRE)**[8] 4269 5-9-7 88 ...(p) JamesDoyle 11	73
			(A J McCabe) *s.i.s: bhd: mod prog fnl f* **33/1**	
0206	7	1	**Northern Spy (USA)**[54] 2790 4-9-1 82 ... PatDobbs 5	65
			(S Dow) *s.i.s: nvr bttr than mid-div* **8/1**	
0400	8	1 ½	**Samarinda (USA)**[42] 3122 5-10-0 95 ... MickyFenton 10	74
			(Mrs P Sly) *chsd ldr: upsides fr 4f out and stl chalng 2f out: wkng whn n.m.r 1f out: eased whn no ch* **25/1**	
0244	9	¾	**Alfresco**[17] 3363 4-9-11 92 ...(v) ChrisCatlin 2	69
			(I A Wood) *a towards rr* **16/1**	
13-6	10	4 ½	**Mount Hadley (USA)**[32] 3503 4-9-12 93 ... SebSanders 13	60
			(G A Butler) *nvr bttr than mid-div* **12/1**	
-200	11	1 ¼	**Evident Pride (USA)**[39] 3249 5-9-11 95 ... TravisBlock(3) 6	59
			(B R Johnson) *chsd ldrs: rdn over 3f out: sn btn* **8/1**	
-161	12	39	**Haydens Mark**[53] 1937 3-8-9 84 ... LiamJones 3	—
			(D G Bridgwater) *a in rr: t.o* **40/1**	

1m 39.62s (-0.18) **Going Correction** +0.25s/f (Slow)
WFA 3 from 4yo+ 8lb — 12 Ran SP% **127.1**
Speed ratings (Par 107): **110,107,107,105,98 97,96,94,94,89 88,49**
toteswinger: 1&2 £2.40, 1&3 £18.60, 2&3 £9.10. CSF £11.58 CT £108.10 TOTE £4.60: £2.00, £1.40, £5.20; EX 12.30.
Owner Bernard Westley **Bred** Kidder, Cole & Griggs **Trained** Newmarket, Suffolk

FOCUS
A competitive handicap for the grade, run at a solid pace. The form reads pretty well with the first two on the up and the next two close to their marks.

NOTEBOOK
Premio Loco(USA) ◆ was in exactly the right position to strike when the race got serious and eventually did the job in great style. He dispelled any concerns about staying the trip and looks and decent prospect for his very able trainer. (op 11-4)
Rose Street(IRE) ◆ is a fine-looking sort with plenty of size, so she could have reasonably been expected to need the run. She moved well turning into the straight and looked like winning until her effort flattened out a bit. She should progress from the run and, if getting to the track again this year, is one to be with. (tchd 9-4)
Hilbre Court(USA) was given some reminders halfway round the home bend and did well to finish where he did. After starting his career well, he had been beaten in a claimer last time, so this was an improved effort. (op 25-1)
Russki(IRE), well backed, set the gallop for a long way and kept on well. He is a bit too high in the handicap at the moment to have an obvious winning chance. (op 10-1)
Samarinda(USA) Official explanation: jockey said gelding was struck into
Evident Pride(USA) Official explanation: jockey said gelding hung left in straight
Haydens Mark Official explanation: jockey said gelding never travelled

4529 WEATHERBYS BLOODSTOCK INSURANCE APPRENTICE H'CAP (ROUND 8) — 1m (P)
9:00 (9:01) (Class 5) (0-70,70) 4-Y-0+ — £2,590 (£770; £385; £192) Stalls High

Form				RPR
0-43	1		**Inquisitress**[4] 4414 4-8-5 54 ... RossAtkinson(3) 10	66
			(J J Bridger) *trckd ldrs: led over 2f out: sn clr: pushed out* **5/1**[2]	
2253	2	3 ¼	**Juzilla (IRE)**[22] 3816 4-9-0 63 ... DavidProbert(3) 2	68
			(W R Swinburn) *chsd ldrs: kpt on to chse wnr fnl 2f but a wl hld* **6/1**[3]	
3103	3	7	**Wahoo Sam (USA)**[8] 4268 8-9-3 66 ... RichardEvans(3) 6	54
			(P D Evans) *led 2f: styd chsng ldrs: wknd over 1f out* **8/1**	
0110	4	hd	**Sularno**[26] 3691 4-9-3 70 ... RyanClark(7) 12	58
			(H Morrison) *w ldrs: slt advantage after 2f: hdd over 2f out and sn wknd* **9/1**	
6500	5	4	**He's Mine Too**[54] 2795 4-8-6 57 ... AndreaAtzeni(5) 4	36
			(D G Bridgwater) *chsd ldrs: rn wd and wknd 3f out* **16/1**	
6600	6	½	**Tuning Fork**[68] 2355 8-8-2 51 oh6 ... MCGeran(3) 7	29
			(M J Attwater) *chsd ldrs over 4f* **20/1**	
0000	7	15	**Baba Ghanoush**[8] 4268 6-8-5 51 oh6 ...(p) JackDean 1	—
			(M J Attwater) *a in rr* **66/1**	
5116	B		**Arctic Desert**[5] 4386 8-8-10 61 ...(t) RosieJessop(5) 11	—
			(Miss Gay Kelleway) *s.i.s: in tch whn b.d ins fnl 5f: dead* **6/1**[3]	
6630	B		**Imperium**[55] 2758 7-8-5 58 ...(p) LindseyWhite(7) 5	—
			(Jean-Rene Auvray) *in rr whn b.d ins fnl 5f* **20/1**	
0406	B		**Bollywood (IRE)**[13] 4129 5-8-2 51 oh6 ... BillyCray(3) 3	—
			(J J Bridger) *towards rr whn b.d ins fnl 5f* **40/1**	
0012	F		**Kaballero (GER)**[14] 4081 7-9-8 68 ... JamieJones 9	—
			(S Gollings) *trcking ldrs whn fell ins fnl 5f* **11/4**[1]	
3024	B		**Towy Girl (IRE)**[5] 4368 4-8-8 57 ... MarkCoumbe(3) 8	—
			(A W Carroll) *s.i.s: towards rr whn b.d ins fnl 5f: dead* **7/1**	

1m 41.65s (1.85) **Going Correction** +0.25s/f (Slow) — 12 Ran SP% **124.9**
Speed ratings (Par 103): **100,96,89,89,85 85,70,—,—,— —,—**
toteswinger: 1&2 £4.50, 1&3 £10.60, 2&3 £91.60. CSF £35.77 CT £248.91 TOTE £6.40: £1.80, £2.70, £2.50; EX 28.00 Place 6 £50.86, Place 5 £40.88.
Owner C Marshall T Wallace J J Bridger **Bred** A Saccomando **Trained** Liphook, Hants
■ Stewards' Enquiry : M C Geran seven-day ban: careless riding (Aug 13-19)
Ross Atkinson caution: careless riding

FOCUS
A highly eventful handicap, confined to apprentice riders. Two horses were killed in the pile-up and Jones and Coumbe were hospitalised. Modest form, rated through the first two.
T/Plt: £40.90 to a £1 stake. Pool: £45,673.83. 813.94 winning tickets. T/Qpdt: £14.40 to a £1 stake. Pool: £4,624.74. 236.80 winning tickets. ST

4296 LEICESTER (R-H)
Wednesday, July 30

OFFICIAL GOING: Good to firm (9.1)
Wind: Light, behind Weather: Fine and sunny

4530 E B F FENWICKS OF LEICESTER MAIDEN STKS — 5f 218y
6:15 (6:17) (Class 4) 2-Y-0 — £5,180 (£1,541; £770; £384) Stalls Low

Form				RPR
03	1		**Cook's Endeavour (USA)**[12] 4164 2-9-3 0 ... NCallan 2	80+
			(K A Ryan) *mde all: rdn over 1f out: jst hld on* **11/10**[1]	
0	2	hd	**Nasri**[16] 4024 2-9-3 0 ... TPQueally 1	79+
			(B J Meehan) *a.p: rdn to chse wnr over 1f out: r.o* **11/2**[3]	
	3	5	**Aladdin's Lamp (IRE)** 2-9-3 0 ... J-PGuillambert 7	64+
			(M Johnston) *chsd wnr: rdn over 2f out: no ex fnl f* **3/1**[2]	
54	4	nk	**Mabait**[12] 4164 2-8-10 0 ... MJMurphy(7) 3	64
			(L M Cumani) *chsd ldrs: rdn over 2f out: styd on same pce appr fnl f* **15/2**	
	5	3 ½	**Floor Show** 2-9-3 0 ... RichardMullen 6	53
			(E S McMahon) *mid-div: rn green and sn pushed along: n.d* **14/1**	
	6	7	**Ashwinder (IRE)** 2-8-12 0 ... GabrielHannon(5) 8	32
			(B J Meehan) *s.s: outpcd* **20/1**	
	7	18	**Tallulah's Secret** 2-8-12 0 ... TPO'Shea 10	—
			(J Gallagher) *s.s: outpcd* **50/1**	
	8	4 ½	**Piccolo Express** 2-9-3 0 ... NeilPollard 4	—
			(B P J Baugh) *s.s: outpcd: hung lft fr 1/2-way* **66/1**	
00	9	1	**Ruby's Song (IRE)**[49] 2951 2-8-9 0 ...(p) KevinGhunowa(3) 11	—
			(J M Bradley) *chsd ldrs tl rdn and wknd 1/2-way: sn hung lft* **100/1**	

1m 10.7s (-2.30) **Going Correction** -0.375s/f (Firm) — 9 Ran SP% **115.6**
Speed ratings (Par 96): **100,99,93,92,88 78,54,48,47**
toteswinger: 1&2 £1.40, 1&3 £1.10, 2&3 £1.90. CSF £7.56 TOTE £1.90: £1.10, £1.90, £1.40; EX 10.00.
Owner Graham Frankland **Bred** Charles Fipke **Trained** Hambleton, N Yorks

FOCUS
A fair maiden in which the first two came nicely clear of a fancied newcomer in third. The form could be alright.

NOTEBOOK
Cook's Endeavour(USA), first home on the wrong side at Nottingham last time, put his experience to good use, showing speed from the off and keeping on well to break his maiden tag. His future probably lies in the hands of the Handicapper and he will get further in time. (op 13-8)
Nasri, whose price rose from 48,000gns as a foal to 130,000gns as a yearling, did not show a great deal on his debut but his stable's juveniles invariably improve a deal for a run and he was well backed beforehand. Running on well at the finish, he pushed the favourite to pull out more close home, and on this evidence he should be up to winning his maiden, before tackling nursery company. (op 12-1 tchd 5-1)
Aladdin's Lamp(IRE), who cost 375,000gns, is the second foal of Prix Marcel Boussac third Luminata. Quite well fancied on this racecourse debut, he showed up well for a long way before tiring inside the last. He should come on a bundle for this and should have little trouble winning a similar race. Another furlong will not inconvenience him in time. (op 5-2 tchd 7-2)
Mabait, half a length behind Cook's Endeavour at Nottingham last time, had the stable apprentice on board this time and never looked like reversing the form. He has, however, now had the requisite three runs for a mark and will be of more interest in handicap company. (op 13-2)
Floor Show, a half-brother to four winners at up to a mile, ran green on his debut but showed enough to suggest he should benefit from this experience. (op 11-2 tchd 5-1 and 16-1)

4531 NOTTINGHAM AUTOPARK CLAIMING STKS — 7f 9y
6:45 (6:49) (Class 5) 3-Y-O — £3,238 (£963; £481; £240) Stalls Low

Form — RPR
4120 **1** **Party In The Park**[25] 3717 3-9-4 68 ... AndrewMullen(3) 9 — 68
(Miss J A Camacho) *chsd ldrs: rdn over 2f out: styd on to ld wl ins fnl f* **7/1**[3]
2345 **2** 1 **Bilboa**[18] 3963 3-8-11 55 ... (p) DarryllHolland 10 — 55
(B R Millman) *hld up: hdwy u.p and hung lft over 1f out: ev ch whn hung lft ins fnl f: nt run on* **11/4**[1]
6540 **3** ½ **Liberty Valance (IRE)**[14] 4090 3-9-3 70 ... (t) RichardKingscote 2 — 60
(S Kirk) *s.i.s: hld up: swtchd rt over 4f out: hdwy 1/2-way: led over 2f out: rdn and hdd wl ins fnl f* **8/1**
0000 **4** 2 **Jimmy Dean**[30] 3559 3-8-11 36 ... (tp) PaulFitzsimons 3 — 49
(M Wellings) *mid-div: lost pl over 4f out: rdn over 2f out: r.o ins fnl f: nt rch ldrs* **100/1**
5044 **5** 1¼ **Cheeky Chilli**[8] 4271 3-8-9 62 ow1 ... NCallan 4 — 43
(A J McCabe) *hld up: plld hrd: nt clr run 1/2-way: hdwy over 2f out: sn rdn: no ex fnl f* **11/1**
0-00 **6** 6 **Madam Carwell**[22] 3816 3-8-8 51 ... TPQueally 7 — 26
(J G Given) *chsd ldr tl led 1/2-way: rdn and hdd over 2f out: wknd over 1f out* **25/1**
0300 **7** nk **Hla Tun (USA)**[34] 3397 3-8-9 53 ... (p) SaleemGolam 11 — 26
(W R Swinburn) *chsd ldrs: rdn over 2f out: wknd over 1f out* **12/1**
4600 **8** 4 **Arrabiata**[44] 3086 3-8-10 43 ... J-PGuillambert 1 — 16
(C N Kellett) *hld up: hdwy over 4f out: sn rdn: wknd wl over 1f out: eased fnl f* **66/1**
9 ½ **Menfromallover (IRE)**[34] 3423 3-8-4 46 ow2 ... (vt[1]) TPO'Shea 5 — 9
(B N Pollock) *chsd ldrs: rdn 1/2-way: wknd 2f out* **33/1**
2- **10** 1½ **Moosley (IRE)**[222] 7217 3-8-13 0 ... PatCosgrave 6 — 14
(C A Dwyer) *chsd ldrs: pushed along 1/2-way: wknd over 2f out* **11/2**[2]
3202 **11** 2¾ **Red Rouge**[7] 4298 3-8-5 53 ... KevinGhunowa(3) 12 — 2
(G J Smith) *s.i.s: sn chsng ldrs: rdn 1/2-way: wknd over 2f out* **14/1**
6200 **12** nse **Twiglet (IRE)**[72] 2261 3-8-2 63 ... (v[1]) FrankieMcDonald 8 — —
(George Baker) *led to 1/2-way: sn rdn and wknd* **16/1**

1m 24.56s (-1.64) **Going Correction** -0.375s/f (Firm) — 12 Ran SP% 103.5
Speed ratings (Par 100): **94,92,92,90,88 81,81,76,76,74 71,71**
toteswinger: 1&2 £1.10, 1&3 £2.10, 2&3 £3.00. CSF £19.67 TOTE £6.40: £2.10, £1.10, £3.00; EX 28.30.The winner was subject to a friendly claim. Bilboa was claimed by J. M. Bradley for £7,000.
Owner Elite Racing Club **Bred** Lady Whent, Mrs B Burchett & R Hannon **Trained** Norton, N Yorks

FOCUS
An ordinary claimer with doubts over what most of these are capable of now, and in which the 36-rated fourth anchors the form.
Bilboa Official explanation: jockey said gelding hung both ways
Madam Carwell Official explanation: jockey said filly hung right
Red Rouge Official explanation: jockey said filly became unbalanced

4532 VICTORIA CENTRE NOTTINGHAM H'CAP — 1m 1f 218y
7:15 (7:16) (Class 4) (0-80,80) 3-Y-O+ £4,731 (£1,416; £708; £354; £176) Stalls High

Form — RPR
1300 **1** **Snowed Under**[25] 3711 7-9-8 74 ... DarryllHolland 8 — 86
(J D Bethell) *mde all: rdn 2f out: edgd lft ins fnl f: styd on gamely* **6/1**
0560 **2** nk **Soviet (IRE)**[16] 4018 3-7-13 61 ... NickyMackay 1 — 72
(M Johnston) *hld up in tch: chsd wnr fnl 2f: sn rdn: styd on* **14/1**
-320 **3** 6 **Drawn Gold**[18] 3947 4-8-11 66 ... RussellKennemore(3) 6 — 65
(R Hollinshead) *trckd wnr to 1/2-way: remained handy: rdn over 3f out: edgd lft over 1f out: wknd fnl f* **5/1**[3]
-325 **4** 1½ **Flam**[12] 4170 3-8-11 73 ... TPQueally 3 — 69
(J R Fanshawe) *prom: racd keenly: rdn over 2f out: wknd over 1f out* **11/2**
2363 **5** nse **Elk Trail (IRE)**[11] 4204 3-9-1 77 ... DNolan 4 — 73
(T P Tate) *prom: chsd wnr 1/2-way tl rdn over 2f out: wknd over 1f out* **9/2**[2]
3140 **6** 2¼ **Bull Market (IRE)**[13] 4111 5-9-10 76 ... PaulEddery 5 — 68
(Ian Williams) *s.s: hld up: rdn over 2f out: a in rr* **10/1**
-002 **7** ¾ **Stargazer Jim (FR)**[7] 4309 6-9-7 73 ... (v) NCallan 2 — 63
(W J Haggas) *hld up: sme hdwy over 2f out: rdn and wknd over 1f out* **9/4**[1]

2m 3.02s (-4.88) **Going Correction** -0.375s/f (Firm)
WFA 3 from 4yo+ 10lb — 7 Ran SP% 111.0
Speed ratings (Par 105): **104,103,98,97,97 95,95**
toteswinger: 1&2 £9.00, 1&3 £4.70, 2&3 £27.90. CSF £75.70 CT £433.40 TOTE £6.30: £2.90, £6.30; EX 78.70.
Owner Mrs G Fane **Bred** Mrs G Fane **Trained** Middleham Moor, N Yorks

FOCUS
A fair handicap in which the first two came well clear. The winner is rated back to his old best.
Snowed Under Official explanation: trainer said, regarding apparent improvement in form, that the gelding was better suited by the track
Flam Official explanation: jockey said bit slipped through filly's mouth
Stargazer Jim(FR) Official explanation: trainer said, regarding the poor form shown, that the gelding was unsuited by the inconsistent pace

4533 T.C. HARRISON GROUP H'CAP — 1m 60y
7:45 (7:46) (Class 5) (0-70,67) 3-Y-O — £3,238 (£963; £481; £240) Stalls High

Form — RPR
0-02 **1** **Certain Promise (USA)**[24] 3762 3-9-6 66 ... TPQueally 8 — 79+
(Sir Michael Stoute) *hld up in tch: gng wl over 2f out: led ins fnl f: shkn up and r.o wl: edgd lft towards fin* **7/2**[1]
000 **2** 3¼ **Stormin Heart (USA)**[14] 4076 3-8-4 50 ... RoystonFfrench 12 — 56+
(M Johnston) *chsd ldr: rdn over 2f out: ev ch ins fnl f: no ex* **22/1**
3054 **3** ¾ **Rich Kid (IRE)**[18] 3969 3-9-4 67 ... (p) KevinGhunowa(3) 9 — 71
(R A Harris) *chsd ldrs: rdn over 2f out: styd on same pce fnl f* **9/2**[2]
0-66 **4** 2¼ **Morestead (IRE)**[10] 1681 3-8-9 55 ... (v[1]) TQuinn 4 — 54
(B G Powell) *led: racd keenly: clr over 4f out: rdn over 1f out: hdd & wknd ins fnl f* **16/1**
0350 **5** ¾ **Looter (FR)**[24] 3763 3-8-12 58 ... (b) TPO'Shea 7 — 55
(J L Dunlop) *chsd ldrs: rdn over 3f out: wknd fnl f* **10/1**
0004 **6** shd **Semah Harold**[27] 3653 3-9-3 63 ... J-PGuillambert 11 — 60
(E S McMahon) *prom: rdn over 2f out: wknd fnl f* **9/2**[2]
0061 **7** nk **Whaston (IRE)**[9] 4241 3-8-12 58 6ex ... (v) NCallan 6 — 54
(J D Bethell) *hld up: rdn over 3f out: hung rt over 1f out: styd on ins fnl f: nvr nrr* **5/1**[3]
0600 **8** 5 **Elizabeth's Quest**[9] 4253 3-7-10 49 ... StacyRenwick(7) 10 — 34
(A W Carroll) *hld up: rdn over 3f out: hung lft and wknd over 2f out* **28/1**
6-00 **9** ½ **Bettys Touch**[11] 4207 3-8-3 49 ... AdrianMcCarthy 3 — 33
(W J Musson) *s.i.s: swtchd rt sn after s: hld up: hdwy over 2f out: rdn and wknd over 1f out* **33/1**
0410 **10** 2½ **Zaarmit (IRE)**[24] 3763 3-9-7 67 ... RichardMullen 2 — 45
(D M Simcock) *hld up: rdn and hung rt over 2f out: a in rr* **16/1**
00-0 **11** 2¼ **Riorun (IRE)**[11] 4180 3-8-6 52 ... PaulEddery 13 — 25
(Ian Williams) *hld up: rdn over 2f out: a in rr* **66/1**
100 **12** 17 **Tapas Lad (IRE)**[34] 3397 3-8-7 56 ... (v) RussellKennemore(3) 5 — —
(G J Smith) *hld up: a in rr: rn wd bnd 5f out: wknd over 3f out* **12/1**

1m 42.4s (-2.70) **Going Correction** -0.375s/f (Firm) — 12 Ran SP% 116.0
Speed ratings (Par 100): **98,94,94,91,91 90,90,85,85,82 80,63**
toteswinger: 1&2 £1.70, 1&3 £1.30, 2&3 £5.10. CSF £86.72 CT £354.39 TOTE £2.90: £1.30, £5.10, £1.70; EX 67.60.
Owner K Abdulla **Bred** Juddmonte Farms Inc **Trained** Newmarket, Suffolk

FOCUS
A modest handicap overal but the first two were both relatively unexposed.
Riorun(IRE) Official explanation: jockey said gelding hung to the right
Tapas Lad(IRE) Official explanation: jockey said colt ran too freely and hung left

4534 E B F WESTERMAN TRADITIONAL QUALITY HOMES MEDIAN AUCTION MAIDEN FILLIES' STKS — 5f 218y
8:15 (8:21) (Class 5) 2-Y-O — £3,885 (£1,156; £577; £288) Stalls Low

Form — RPR
6 **1** **Belle Des Airs (IRE)**[76] 2124 2-8-9 0 ... JackMitchell(5) 10 — 75+
(R M Beckett) *mde all: rdn over 1f out: r.o* **3/1**[2]
2 1½ **Kammaan** 2-9-0 0 ... NCallan 3 — 72+
(M A Jarvis) *hld up: hdwy and hung rt fr over 2f out: rdn to chse wnr over 1f out: r.o: eased towards fin* **10/3**[3]
0 **3** 6 **Superstitious Me (IRE)**[58] 2663 2-9-0 0 ... CatherineGannon 4 — 52
(B Palling) *chsd ldrs: rdn over 2f out: wknd fnl f* **25/1**
032 **4** 1 **Frame And Cover**[13] 4120 2-8-11 0 ... KevinGhunowa(3) 11 — 49
(R A Harris) *chsd wnr: rdn over 2f out: hung rt over 1f out: wknd fnl f* **16/1**
5 **5** ¾ **Bussell Along (IRE)**[14] 4088 2-9-0 0 ... TPQueally 8 — 46
(M L W Bell) *hld up: hdwy over 2f out: nt clr run over 1f out: sn wknd* **12/1**
0 **6** hd **Good Queen Best**[53] 2835 2-9-0 0 ... RichardMullen 6 — 46
(B De Haan) *prom: rdn over 2f out: wknd over 1f out* **50/1**
7 1½ **Eyes Like A Hawk (IRE)** 2-9-0 0 ... RichardKingscote 7 — 41
(Tom Dascombe) *s.s: bhd: hdwy over 1f out: wknd fnl f* **5/4**[1]
0 **8** 1¾ **Intrepid Lady (IRE)**[12] 4149 2-9-0 0 ... EdwardCreighton 2 — 36
(M R Channon) *in rr: hdwy over 4f out: rdn and wknd over 2f out* **28/1**
9 22 **Short N Swift** 2-9-0 0 ... PaulFitzsimons 9 — —
(M Wellings) *s.s: outpcd* **66/1**

1m 11.77s (-1.23) **Going Correction** -0.375s/f (Firm) — 9 Ran SP% 116.8
Speed ratings (Par 91): **93,91,83,81,80 80,78,76,46**
toteswinger: 1&2 £3.20, 1&3 £38.30, 2&3 £42.10. CSF £13.35 TOTE £4.40: £1.30, £1.40, £8.10; EX 13.60.
Owner Mrs M E Slade **Bred** Mrs M E Slade **Trained** Whitsbury, Hants

FOCUS
A modest juvenile fillies' maiden.

NOTEBOOK
Belle Des Airs(IRE) showed ability on her debut over 5f at Salisbury and she built on that effort with a decisive success. This was a modest race, but there could be more to come. (op 6-1 tchd 11-4)
Kammaan, a daughter of Diktat, first foal of a quite useful 7f winner on juvenile debut, made a satisfactory debut in a clear second. She is entitled to come on for this and easier ground might also suit better. (op 9-4)
Superstitious Me(IRE) found this less competitive than the course-and-distance maiden she contested first time up and she ran with credit. (op 33-1)
Frame And Cover had been beaten in selling company on her first three starts and she found this company a bit hot. (op 14-1)
Bussell Along(IRE) is probably more of a nursery type. (op 8-1)
Eyes Like A Hawk(IRE), a 9,000gns daughter of Diktat, half-sister to dual 1m1f-1m4f winner Elegant Hawk, out of a 1m2f winner, was backed almost as though defeat was out of the question on her racecourse debut, but she ran below expectations. She is another who might prefer easier ground and presumably she is thought capable of better. (op 13-8 tchd 7-4)
Intrepid Lady(IRE) Official explanation: jockey said filly had no more to give

4535 PALMERS GARDEN CENTRE H'CAP — 5f 218y
8:45 (8:48) (Class 5) (0-70,69) 3-Y-O+ — £3,238 (£963; £481; £240) Stalls Low

Form — RPR
-050 **1** **Just Spike**[126] 1029 5-8-7 48 ... CatherineGannon 1 — 63
(B P J Baugh) *chsd ldrs: led and edgd rt over 1f out: rdn out* **50/1**
5106 **2** 2¼ **Bold Argument (IRE)**[23] 3797 5-9-4 64 ... JackMitchell(5) 3 — 71
(Mrs P N Dutfield) *s.s: outpcd: hdwy u.p over 1f out: edgd rt: r.o: nt rch wnr* **4/1**[1]
5/50 **3** 2 **Out Of India**[10] 4219 6-8-11 55 ... PJMcDonald(3) 13 — 56
(P T Dalton) *chsd ldr: rdn and ev ch over 1f out: no ex ins fnl f* **33/1**
0000 **4** hd **Dakota Rain (IRE)**[25] 3713 6-9-11 66 ... (p) TPO'Shea 5 — 66
(Jennie Candlish) *led: rdn and hdd over 1f out: no ex ins fnl f* **12/1**
5-05 **5** nk **Back In The Red (IRE)**[5] 4370 4-9-9 67 ... KevinGhunowa(3) 6 — 66
(R A Harris) *chsd ldrs: rdn over 2f out: sn outpcd: styd on ins fnl f* **8/1**[2]

0050 **6** *shd* **Lady Fas (IRE)**[11] 4207 5-8-0 **48** oh3 StacyRenwick(7) 10 47
(A W Carroll) *hld up: rdn 1/2-way: swtchd rt and hdwy over 1f out: nvr nrr* **40/1**

5400 **7** *1/2* **Brigadore**[6] 4327 9-8-13 **54** TPQueally 9 51
(J G Given) *dwlt: hld up: rdn and nt clr run over 1f out: hmpd ins fnl f: nt trble ldrs* **9/1**[3]

0003 **8** *1* **Thabaat**[13] 4103 4-9-11 **66** (b) RichardKingscote 2 60
(J M Bradley) *chsd ldrs: rdn over 2f out: wknd fnl f* **14/1**

5320 **9** *1 1/4* **Harrison's Flyer (IRE)**[5] 4370 7-9-2 **57** (p) RoystonFfrench 4 47
(J M Bradley) *hld up in tch: rdn over 2f out: nt clr run over 1f out and ins fnl f: nt trble ldrs* **8/1**[2]

1601 **10** *2 1/4* **Boldinor**[13] 4125 5-9-0 **62** KylieManser(7) 14 45
(M R Bosley) *prom: rdn over 1f out: wknd ins fnl f* **8/1**[2]

-400 **11** *hd* **Ramblin Bob**[12] 4163 3-8-9 **55** NeilPollard 7 37
(W J Musson) *edgd rt s: hld up: rdn over 2f out: n.d* **40/1**

6334 **12** *1 1/2* **Hart Of Gold**[5] 4370 4-9-11 **66** AdrianMcCarthy 12 44
(R A Harris) *chsd ldrs: rdn over 2f out: wknd over 1f out* **8/1**[2]

6600 **13** *25* **Umpa Loompa (IRE)**[46] 3033 4-8-7 **48** oh2 (v) PaulEddery 8 —
(B J McMath) *hmpd s: sn pushed along in rr: bhd fr 1/2-way* **40/1**

0211 **F** **Lady Carollina**[18] 3960 3-9-9 **69** SaleemGolam 11 —
(Rae Guest) *mid-div: rdn over 2f out: wknd over 1f out: in rr whn fell ins fnl f* **4/1**[1]

1m 11.21s (-1.79) **Going Correction** -0.375s/f (Firm)
WFA 3 from 4yo+ 5lb **14** Ran SP% **121.0**
Speed ratings (Par 103): **96,93,90,90,89 89,88,87,85,82 82,80,47,—**
toteswinger: 1&2 £27.50, 1&3 Not won, 2&3 £58.30. CSF £239.40 CT £6913.02 TOTE £97.50: £12.80, £2.00, £11.30; EX 288.50 Place 6 £457.95, Place 5 £400.53.
Owner C R Watts **Bred** P D Moore **Trained** Audley, Staffs

FOCUS
A moderate sprint handicap. Unconvincing form, although the runner-up is a fairly solid guide, as both the winner and third seemed to show big improvement.
Thabaat Official explanation: jockey said gelding hung right
T/Plt: £180.70 to a £1 stake. Pool: £54,275.64. 219.20 winning tickets. T/Qpdt: £155.30 to a £1 stake. Pool: £4,682.46. 22.30 winning tickets. CR

4213 REDCAR (L-H)

Wednesday, July 30

OFFICIAL GOING: Good to firm (9.5)
Wind: Fresh, half-behind Weather: overcast, becoming fine and sunny but breezy

4536 EUROPEAN BREEDERS' FUND MEDIAN AUCTION MAIDEN STKS 6f

2:05 (2:07) (Class 6) 2-Y-O **£2,763** (£816; £408) **Stalls** Centre

Form RPR

0 **1** **Toledo Gold (IRE)**[17] 3997 2-9-3 0 DavidAllan 1 72
(E J Alston) *t.k.h: sn led: kpt on wl fnl f: hld on towards fin* **22/1**

2 *1/2* **Dr Jameson (IRE)** 2-9-3 0 PaulHanagan 10 71
(R A Fahey) *s.i.s: sn drvn along: hdwy over 2f out: wnt 2nd ins fnl f: kpt on wl* **6/1**

3 *4* **Beautiful Breeze (IRE)** 2-9-3 0 RoystonFfrench 2 59
(M Johnston) *led early: chsd ldrs: kpt on same pce fnl f* **9/2**[2]

6 **4** *1* **Winsome Hearts**[18] 3976 2-9-3 0 PaulMulrennan 9 56
(M W Easterby) *chsd ldrs: one pce appr fnl f* **7/1**

5 *2 1/4* **Senor Berti** 2-9-3 0 TomEaves 3 49+
(B Smart) *chsd ldrs: reminders and outpcd 3f out: edgd lft: kpt on fnl f* **11/4**[1]

6 *1 3/4* **Becky Blue (IRE)** 2-8-12 0 LeeEnstone 5 39
(P C Haslam) *chsd ldrs on outer: hung lft and one pce fnl 2f* **11/2**[3]

7 *3/4* **Steer** 2-8-10 0 AdamCarter(7) 8 41
(M Brittain) *w ldrs: edgd rt over 2f out: wknd over 1f out* **16/1**

0 **8** *5* **Future Gem**[15] 4045 2-8-12 0 DaleGibson 7 21
(A Dickman) *chsd ldrs: lost pl over 2f out* **100/1**

9 *7* **Stevies Song** 2-8-5 0 RobbieEgan(7) 6 —
(D Flood) *stmbld s: a wl bhd* **10/1**

0 **10** *12* **Dakota Two (IRE)**[18] 3976 2-8-12 0 (b1) TonyHamilton 4 —
(R A Fahey) *s.v.s: reminders after s: a wl bhd* **9/1**

1m 11.59s (-0.21) **Going Correction** -0.375s/f (Firm) **10** Ran SP% **117.3**
Speed ratings (Par 92): **86,85,80,78,75 73,72,65,56,40**
toteswinger: 1&2 £2.00, 1&3 £11.70, 2&3 £3.50. CSF £149.59 TOTE £35.20: £6.10, £2.10, £2.10; EX 179.60.
Owner J Stephenson **Bred** Rathbarry Stud **Trained** Longton, Lancs

FOCUS
A very ordinary maiden with little form going into the race. The first two pulled clear and the fourth looks the best guide to the level.

NOTEBOOK
Toledo Gold(IRE), well beaten on bad ground on his debut, was very coltish in the paddock. He soon pulled his way to the front and stuck to his task to hold on in determined fashion. He has plenty of size and scope and will improve again. (op 20-1 tchd 18-1)
Dr Jameson(IRE) ◆, a medium-sized newcomer, was quite keen to post. On the way back he took some organizing and, making significant inroads near the line, in the end made the winner pull out all the stops. Likely to be suited by a step up to seven, he should have little difficulty going one better. (op 5-1 tchd 4-1)
Beautiful Breeze(IRE), who is not that big, shaped nicely on his debut and will have learnt from it. (op 7-2)
Winsome Hearts, bred for stamina, was encountering much quicker ground. (op 9-2)
Senor Berti, a well-made newcomer who has plenty of size and scope, was very green to post. He dropped back at halfway but was picking up in encouraging fashion late on. This will have taught him plenty. (op 3-1 tchd 10-3 and 7-2 in a place)

4537 CELEBRATING DICK GLARVEY H'CAP 1m 2f

2:40 (2:40) (Class 5) (0-70,69) 3-Y-O+ **£2,590** (£770; £385; £192) **Stalls** Low

Form RPR

1463 **1** **Boy Dancer (IRE)**[10] 4215 5-8-12 **56** JamieMoriarty(3) 4 65
(J J Quinn) *trckd ldrs: led over 1f out: kpt on wl* **3/1**[1]

0446 **2** *1 1/4* **Baltimore Jack (IRE)**[7] 4293 4-9-5 **60** PaulMulrennan 5 66
(M W Easterby) *led tl over 1f out: kpt on same pce ins fnl f* **7/1**

5550 **3** *1 1/4* **Tour D'Amour (IRE)**[68] 2364 5-8-9 **50** oh4 (b) DavidAllan 3 54
(R Craggs) *hld up in midfield: effrt 4f out: styd on fnl f* **11/1**

3-36 **4** *2 1/4* **Waterloo Corner**[181] 368 6-9-4 **59** TomEaves 7 58
(R Craggs) *hld up in midfield: effrt 4f out: kpt on fnl f* **12/1**

1024 **5** *1/2* **Chin Wag (IRE)**[18] 3957 4-9-7 **62** (p) FergalLynch 9 60
(J S Goldie) *hld up in rr: hdwy 3f out: hung lft: kpt on: nvr rchd ldrs* **9/2**[3]

0004 **6** *3 1/2* **Bright Sun (IRE)**[10] 4217 7-8-11 **52** (p) KimTinkler 1 43
(N Tinkler) *t.k.h: sn trcking ldrs: rdn over 3f out: fdd fnl f* **11/2**

6400 **7** *nk* **King Of The Moors (USA)**[29] 3579 5-9-2 **60** NeilBrown(3) 6 50
(T D Barron) *chsd ldrs: wknd fnl f* **7/2**[2]

3-00 **8** *1 1/2* **Hurricane Thomas (IRE)**[10] 4220 4-9-7 **69** BMcHugh(7) 10 56
(R E Barr) *hld up in midfield: effrt on outside over 4f out: lost pl over 1f out* **14/1**

0-00 **9** *12* **Stones Of Venice (IRE)**[49] 2926 3-7-13 **50** oh1 PaulQuinn 2 13
(R M Whitaker) *s.i.s: a in rr: bhd fnl 3f* **33/1**

006 **10** *11* **I Feel Fine**[22] 3810 5-8-13 **54** PaulHanagan 8 —
(A Kirtley) *hld up in rr: bhd fnl 3f: virtually p.u* **66/1**

2m 5.84s (-1.26) **Going Correction** -0.15s/f (Firm)
WFA 3 from 4yo+ 10lb **10** Ran SP% **120.4**
Speed ratings (Par 103): **99,98,97,95,94 92,91,90,80,72**
toteswinger: 1&2 £4.80, 1&3 £9.20, 2&3 £15.00. CSF £25.58 CT £209.35 TOTE £3.90: £1.40, £2.00, £4.00; EX 25.60.
Owner A Turton & S Brown **Bred** Azienda Agricola Razza Emiliana **Trained** Settrington, N Yorks

FOCUS
A low-grade handicap run at a sound pace and in the end quite a convincing winner. The form has a messy look about it limited by the third, 4lb 'wrong'.
Chin Wag(IRE) Official explanation: jockey said gelding was unsuited by the good to firm ground

4538 REDCAR A COURSE FOR ALL REASONS RATING RELATED MAIDEN STKS 7f

3:20 (3:20) (Class 5) 3-Y-O+ **£2,590** (£770; £385; £192) **Stalls** Centre

Form RPR

-023 **1** **Deira Dubai**[20] 3870 3-8-12 70 PaulHanagan 3 67
(B W Hills) *wore net muzzle: t.k.h: w ldrs: led over 3f out: edgd lft and hld on fnl f* **4/1**[2]

4442 **2** *1* **Ancient Cross**[33] 3454 4-9-8 68 DaleGibson 1 71
(M W Easterby) *in rr: hdwy on outer over 2f out: wnt 2nd over 1f out: no ex ins fnl f* **6/4**[1]

6500 **3** *1/2* **This Ones For Eddy**[11] 4207 3-8-12 62 TolleyDean(3) 4 66
(S Parr) *in rr: effrt and edgd lft over 2f out: chsng ldrs over 1f out: kpt on same pce ins fnl f* **16/1**

-000 **4** *6* **Monte Cassino (IRE)**[15] 4044 3-9-1 47 DavidAllan 8 50
(J O'Reilly) *in rr: hdwy 3f out: one pce appr fnl f* **80/1**

0000 **5** *2* **Flying Sommelier (USA)**[11] 4207 3-9-1 55 PaulFessey 7 45
(T D Barron) *chsd ldrs: one pce fnl 2f* **33/1**

2222 **6** *2* **Great Knight (IRE)**[33] 3447 3-9-1 68 TonyCulhane 11 39
(W J Haggas) *stdd s: effrt and n.m.r over 2f out: wknd over 1f out* **9/2**[3]

-506 **7** *1/2* **Reel Buddy Blaze**[23] 3795 3-9-1 64 RoystonFfrench 9 38
(T P Tate) *led tl over 3f out: sn wl outpcd* **12/1**

0543 **8** *hd* **Emirate Isle**[23] 3795 4-9-8 65 RobertWinston 10 40
(C Grant) *chsd ldrs: lost pl over 1f out* **11/2**

00-5 **9** *3/4* **Sydneyroughdiamond**[18] 3952 6-9-3 41 SladeO'Hara(5) 2 38
(M Mullineaux) *chsd ldrs on outer: lost pl over 1f out* **100/1**

0-40 **10** *1/2* **Peltre**[14] 4076 3-8-12 48 TWilliams 6 31
(M Brittain) *chsd ldrs: lost pl 2f out* **80/1**

00-0 **11** *15* **Northgate Lodge (USA)**[149] 785 3-8-12 50 (b) MarkLawson(3) 5 —
(M Brittain) *t.k.h: sn trcking ldrs: lost pl over 2f out: sn bhd* **66/1**

1m 22.05s (-2.45) **Going Correction** -0.375s/f (Firm)
WFA 3 from 4yo+ 7lb **11** Ran SP% **115.0**
Speed ratings (Par 103): **99,97,97,90,88 85,85,85,84,83 66**
toteswinger: 1&2 £7.00, 1&3 £14.90, 2&3 £2.50. CSF £10.03 TOTE £4.70: £1.20, £1.10, £4.30; EX 15.20.
Owner Hamdan Al Maktoum **Bred** Shadwell Estate Co Ltd **Trained** Lambourn, Berks

FOCUS
A modest rating related maiden race and the winner was clear top on official figures.

4539 BODDINGTONS REDCAR STRAIGHT-MILE CHAMPIONSHIP STKS (QUALIFIER) (H'CAP) 1m

3:55 (3:55) (Class 4) (0-85,85) 3-Y-O **£4,857** (£1,445; £722; £360) **Stalls** Centre

Form RPR

03-1 **1** **Manhattan Dream (USA)**[34] 3419 3-8-10 **74** PaulHanagan 6 81
(B W Hills) *trckd ldrs: led and qcknd 3f out: hld on wl* **7/2**[2]

-040 **2** *1* **Midnight Muse (USA)**[19] 3919 3-9-1 **79** PaulFessey 4 84
(T D Barron) *trckd ldrs: effrt 3f out: kpt on ins fnl f* **8/1**

5540 **3** *nk* **Legislation**[17] 4010 3-9-4 **82** (b) DavidKinsella 7 86
(J H M Gosden) *led tl 3f out: hrd rdn and hung lft: kpt on same pce fnl f* **3/1**[1]

5310 **4** *3/4* **Kiwi Bay**[19] 3928 3-9-7 **85** TonyHamilton 3 87
(M Dods) *hld up in rr: effrt over 3f out: styd on fnl f: nvr able to chal* **13/2**

2525 **5** *1/2* **Astrodonna**[21] 3849 3-8-12 **76** PaulMulrennan 1 77
(M H Tompkins) *swtchd rt s: hld up: effrt over 3f out: hung lft and kpt on same pce appr fnl f* **5/1**[3]

2441 **6** *14* **King Fingal (IRE)**[29] 3592 3-8-12 **76** RobertWinston 2 45
(J J Quinn) *hld up: effrt over 3f out: sn rdn: lost pl and eased over 1f out* **3/1**[1]

1m 34.1s (-3.90) **Going Correction** -0.375s/f (Firm) **6** Ran SP% **113.3**
Speed ratings (Par 102): **104,103,102,101,101 87**
toteswinger: 1&2 £5.40, 1&3 £3.00, 2&3 £5.60. CSF £30.36 TOTE £3.40: £2.00, £4.30; EX 31.00.
Owner Lady Richard Wellesley **Bred** Vallee Des Reves Syndicate **Trained** Lambourn, Berks
■ Stewards' Enquiry : Paul Fessey caution: used whip with excessive frequency

FOCUS
A tight-knit handicap but the winner always looked in command and scored with a bit in hand. She should continue to progress.
Astrodonna Official explanation: jockey said filly was unsuited by the good to firm ground
King Fingal(IRE) Official explanation: trainerhad no explanation for the poor form shown

4540 WEDDINGS AT REDCAR H'CAP 1m

4:30 (4:32) (Class 6) (0-65,64) 3-Y-O+ **£2,266** (£674; £337; £168) **Stalls** Centre

Form RPR

4033 **1** **Silly Gilly (IRE)**[29] 3593 4-9-0 **51** TomEaves 13 61
(R E Barr) *chsd ldrs: styd on u.p to ld towards fin: all out* **14/1**

0220 **2** *shd* **Ardent Prince**[8] 4268 5-8-10 **50** TolleyDean(3) 14 60
(A J McCabe) *chsd ldrs: led 3f out: hdd last strides* **20/1**

-040 **3** *3/4* **Monsieur Dumas (IRE)**[9] 4261 4-8-13 **50** (p) DavidAllan 12 58
(R Bastiman) *chsd ldrs: ev ch ins fnl f: rdr dropped whip: struck on the nose by rival's whip and no ex towards fin* **20/1**

5060 **4** *2 1/2* **Carefree**[12] 4142 4-8-8 **45** SilvestreDeSousa 7 48
(Mrs R A Carr) *in rr: hdwy 2f out: styd on wl ins fnl f: nt rch ldrs* **33/1**

4436 **5** *nk* **Darfour**[10] 4219 4-9-7 **63** (p) GaryBartley(5) 2 65
(J S Goldie) *mid-div: hdwy on outer 2f out: kpt on: nvr trbld ldrs* **12/1**

5141 **6** *nk* **Malguru**[4] 4420 4-8-6 **50** ow2 (p) FrederikTylicki(7) 20 51
(A G Foster) *chsd ldrs stands' side: styd on same pce fnl 2f* **2/1**[1]

2056 **7** ½ **Misplaced Fortune**[13] 4112 3-9-2 **61** KimTinkler 15 59
(N Tinkler) *chsd ldrs: edgd lft and one pce appr fnl f* **20/1**
-404 **8** 2 **Astroangel**[15] 4053 4-9-4 **55** PaulMulrennan 19 50
(M H Tompkins) *dwlt and sn chsng ldrs: one pce fnl 2f* **14/1**
6060 **9** nk **Farne Island**[10] 4215 5-9-1 **52** TonyCulhane 3 47
(Micky Hammond) *in rr: edgd rt and styd on fnl 2f: nvr nr ldrs* **33/1**
1000 **10** nse **Staked A Claim (IRE)**[16] 4018 4-9-2 **53** DeanMcKeown 4 48
(T D Barron) *in rr: hdwy on ins 2f out: nvr nr ldrs* **16/1**
0035 **11** nk **Only A Grand**[27] 3640 4-8-12 **49** (b) TonyHamilton 9 43
(R Bastiman) *mid-div: edgd rt and kpt on fnl 2f* **22/1**
-063 **12** 12 **Kaymich Perfecto**[10] 4219 8-8-12 **52** MichaelJStainton(3) 10 18
(R M Whitaker) *s.i.s: in rr and drvn along: sme hdwy on outer over 2f out: lost pl over 1f out: eased* **4/1**[2]
6000 **13** 1¾ **Empire Dancer (IRE)**[8] 4284 5-9-2 **53** RoystonFfrench 5 15
(I W McInnes) *dwlt: nvr on terms* **40/1**
-000 **14** ½ **Whittinghamvillage**[12] 4142 7-8-5 **49** ow3 (bt) BMcHugh(7) 6 10
(Mrs H O Graham) *mid-div: lost pl over 2f out* **50/1**
6050 **15** 4½ **Miss Tilen**[124] 1051 3-8-0 **45** DaleGibson 18 —
(V Smith) *chsd ldrs stands' side: lost pl 3f out* **66/1**
-000 **16** 2 **Deadline (UAE)**[31] 2375 4-9-5 **59** JamieMoriarty(3) 1 5
(P T Midgley) *awkward s: reluctant and sn bhd* **25/1**
0062 **17** 2¾ **Evelith Regent (IRE)**[10] 4215 5-9-9 **60** RobertWinston 17 —
(G A Swinbank) *mid-div: drvn over 3f out: lost pl over 2f out* **8/1**[3]
3060 **18** 15 **Kabis Amigos**[30] 3567 6-9-9 **60** (vt[1]) PaulHanagan 8 —
(S T Mason) *led tl 3f out: sn lost pl and eased: t.o* **25/1**

1m 35.59s (-2.41) **Going Correction** -0.375s/f (Firm)
WFA 3 from 4yo+ 8lb **18** Ran SP% **129.5**
Speed ratings (Par 101): **97,96,96,93,93 93,92,90,90,90 89,77,76,75,71 69,66,51**
toteswinger: 1&2 £21.00, 1&3 £47.20, 2&3 £69.50. CSF £275.02 CT £5540.91 TOTE £13.00: £2.60, £4.60, £6.80, £10.40; EX 266.30.Yerevan was withdrawn. Price at the time of withdrawal was 25-1. Rule 4 does not apply.
Owner Malcolm O'Hair **Bred** Barronstown Stud **Trained** Seamer, N Yorks

FOCUS
A low-grade tight knit handicap, the first three clear at the line. It paid to race up with the pace.
Astroangel Official explanation: jockey said filly missed the break
Empire Dancer(IRE) Official explanation: jockey said gelding missed the break

4541 SUBSCRIBE TO RACING UK CLAIMING STKS 1m 2f
5:05 (5:05) (Class 6) 3-Y-0+ **£2,388** (£705; £352) **Stalls** Low

Form RPR
5513 **1** **Lucayan Dancer**[15] 4066 8-9-6 **70** AdeleRothery(7) 10 76
(D Nicholls) *trckd ldrs: rdn to ld 2f out: styd on strly ins fnl f: readily* **3/1**[2]
2-50 **2** 3½ **Torrens (IRE)**[10] 4217 6-9-8 **74** (t) TGMcLaughlin 5 64
(Ollie Pears) *hld up in rr: hdwy over 2f out: styd on to take 2nd ins fnl f: no ch w wnr* **15/2**[3]
0-40 **3** ½ **Garibaldi (GER)**[22] 3814 6-9-1 **49** (t) AshleyHamblett(5) 8 61
(N Wilson) *s.i.s: in rr: hdwy 3f out: kpt on wl* **22/1**
0-05 **4** 1¼ **Diktatorial**[10] 4217 6-9-8 **72** RobertWinston 2 61
(J Howard Johnson) *s.i.s: in rr: hdwy over 2f out: styd on fnl f* **8/1**
3112 **5** 1 **Little Jimbob**[10] 4217 7-9-11 **73** PaulHanagan 12 62
(R A Fahey) *led 2f: chsd ldrs: led over 2f out: sn hdd: wknd fnl f* **6/5**[1]
4030 **6** 1 **Roman History (IRE)**[10] 4215 5-9-5 **57** (p) SilvestreDeSousa 1 54
(Miss Tracy Waggott) *w ldr: led after 2f tl over 2f out: one pce* **16/1**
6303 **7** 1¼ **Skye But N Ben**[13] 4123 4-9-2 **47** (p) PaulFessey 7 48
(G A Harker) *dwlt: hld up in rr: effrt over 3f out: sn chsng ldrs: wknd appr fnl f* **11/1**
060- **8** ½ **Apache Point (IRE)**[282] 6380 11-9-4 **48** KimTinkler 4 49
(N Tinkler) *hld up in midfield: hdwy over 3f out: nvr a threat* **40/1**
0000 **9** 18 **Desert Rat (IRE)**[16] 4031 4-9-3 **45** (b) TonyCulhane 11 12
(Micky Hammond) *in rr: effrt on ins 4f out: lost pl over 1f out: eased and sn bhd* **50/1**
0000 **10** 28 **Paris Hall**[27] 3640 3-8-5 **40** PatrickMathers 3 —
(I W McInnes) *chsd ldrs: drvn 6f out: lost pl over 3f out: sn bhd: t.o* **100/1**

2m 4.64s (-2.46) **Going Correction** -0.15s/f (Firm)
WFA 3 from 4yo+ 10lb **10** Ran SP% **117.3**
Speed ratings (Par 101): **103,100,99,98,98 97,96,95,81,59**
toteswinger: 1&2 £5.60, 1&3 £12.30, 2&3 £27.30. CSF £25.26 TOTE £4.40: £1.80, £2.40, £4.60; EX 39.90.
Owner Racegoers Club Owners Group **Bred** The National Stud Owner Breeders Club Ltd **Trained** Sessay, N Yorks

FOCUS
A run-of-the-mill claimer with the winner back on song. The 49-rated third holds down the overall level of the form.

4542 THE COMMITMENTS ARE HERE 23RD AUGUST H'CAP 6f
5:40 (5:40) (Class 6) (0-65,64) 3-Y-0+ **£2,266** (£674; £337; £168) **Stalls** Centre

Form RPR
0011 **1** **Johnston's Glory (IRE)**[7] 4293 4-9-11 **60** 6ex (p) DavidAllan 9 71+
(E J Alston) *hld up in mid-div: hdwy on outer 2f out: r.o wl to ld ins fnl f* **6/1**[2]
4443 **2** 2 **Rainbow Bay**[7] 4293 5-8-12 **54** (v) FrederikTylicki(7) 3 59
(Miss Tracy Waggott) *led towards far side: hdd and no ex last 150yds* **5/1**[1]
0000 **3** ½ **Jellytot (USA)**[26] 3662 5-8-10 **45** TonyHamilton 2 49
(J O'Reilly) *mid-div: hdwy over 2f out: kpt on wl ins fnl f* **20/1**
3-00 **4** nk **Piccolo Diamante (USA)**[13] 4107 4-8-10 **45** (t) TonyCulhane 4 48
(S Parr) *hld up: hdwy on outer over 2f out: kpt on ins fnl f* **28/1**
0560 **5** 2 **Lady Benjamin**[34] 3416 3-9-9 **63** LeeEnstone 1 58
(P C Haslam) *chsd ldrs on outer: styd on same pce appr fnl f* **16/1**
0030 **6** nk **Woqoodd**[6] 4327 4-9-10 **59** (b) PaulHanagan 11 54+
(R A Fahey) *mid-div: styng on stands' side whn hung lft and bmpd 1f out: nt rch ldrs* **13/2**[3]
0004 **7** 1 **Littledodayno (IRE)**[137] 901 5-9-12 **61** TGMcLaughlin 17 53+
(M Wigham) *in rr: styng on whn hmpd 1f out: nvr nr ldrs* **14/1**
0-60 **8** ½ **Flaxton (UAE)**[74] 2208 3-8-13 **53** TWilliams 7 43
(M Brittain) *chsd ldrs: one pce whn edgd rt appr fnl f* **50/1**
3445 **9** nk **Jevington Star (IRE)**[15] 4043 3-8-0 **47** ow2 (p) LanceBetts(7) 16 36
(B Ellison) *mid-div: kpt on fnl 2f: nvr nr ldrs* **14/1**
501 **10** hd **Actabou**[39] 3280 3-9-7 **64** NeilBrown(3) 15 52
(M Dods) *chsd ldrs: kpt on same pce fnl 2f* **7/1**
4000 **11** ¾ **Myriola**[21] 3834 3-8-6 **46** PaulFessey 5 32
(S Gollings) *chsd ldrs on outer: one pce fnl 2f* **33/1**
0056 **12** ¾ **Fan Club**[21] 3834 4-8-7 **45** (b) MichaelJStainton(3) 6 29
(Mrs R A Carr) *s.i.s: nvr a factor* **18/1**
0200 **13** 1¼ **The Cube**[13] 4107 4-8-10 **45** (b) PaulMulrennan 8 25
(J Balding) *mid-div: hdwy 3f out: one pce whn hmpd 1f out* **16/1**
0033 **14** 3 **Miss Taboo (IRE)**[11] 4207 4-9-0 **52** JamieMoriarty(3) 14 23
(P T Midgley) *hld up: nvr bttr than mid-div* **16/1**
6420 **15** ½ **Buzbury Rings**[11] 4207 4-8-13 **55** BMcHugh(7) 18 24
(R E Barr) *mid-div: effrt over 2f out: nvr a factor* **12/1**
150P **16** nk **Haroldini (IRE)**[12] 4168 6-8-12 **50** (p) TolleyDean(3) 13 18
(J Balding) *in rr and sn drvn along* **20/1**
6000 **17** 3 **Mis Chicaf (IRE)**[5] 4383 7-8-13 **45** PaulPickard(7) 19 3
(D Carroll) *chsd ldrs: lost pl 2f out* **33/1**
0-00 **18** 3¼ **The Thrifty Bear**[44] 3080 5-8-10 **45** (p) DeanMcKeown 20 —
(C W Fairhurst) *racd alone stands' side: w ldrs: lost pl over 2f out* **33/1**
-000 **19** ¾ **Multitude (IRE)**[12] 4174 4-9-1 **50** (b) TomEaves 12 —
(T D Easterby) *in rr: reminders after 2f* **20/1**

69.69 secs (-2.11) **Going Correction** -0.375s/f (Firm)
WFA 3 from 4yo+ 5lb **19** Ran SP% **129.2**
Speed ratings (Par 101): **99,96,95,95,92 92,90,90,89,89 88,87,85,81,81 80,76,72,71**
toteswinger: 1&2 £5.60, 1&3 £48.80, 2&3 £50.20. CSF £33.35 CT £608.48 TOTE £4.60: £1.70, £2.20, £4.70, £6.60; EX 24.00 Place 6 £693.76, Place 5 £228.06.
Owner The Good Shepherds **Bred** Gerard Keane **Trained** Longton, Lancs

FOCUS
Another low-grade handicap rated through the runner-up and the winner continues on the upgrade. Those who raced towards the stands' side seemed at a disadvantage.
The Cube Official explanation: jockey said gelding was unsuited by the good to firm ground
Buzbury Rings Official explanation: jockey said gelding was unsuited by the good to firm ground
Multitude(IRE) Official explanation: jockey said gelding lost its action
T/Plt: £806.60 to a £1 stake. Pool: £37,903.60. 34.30 winning tickets. T/Qpdt: £190.50 to a £1 stake. Pool: £2,677.70. 10.40 winning tickets. WG

4516 GOODWOOD (R-H)
Thursday, July 31

OFFICIAL GOING: Good to firm
Dolling adding around 15yards to advertised distances on the round course.
Wind: Almost nil Weather: Cloudy,occasional drizzle, humid

4549 MOET HENNESSY FILLIES' STKS (REGISTERED AS THE LILLIE LANGTRY STAKES) (GROUP 3) 1m 6f
2:15 (2:15) (Class 1) 3-Y-0+
£39,739 (£15,064; £7,539; £3,759; £1,883; £945) **Stalls** Low

Form RPR
4132 **1** **Gravitation**[21] 3875 3-8-6 **100** AlanMunro 6 108
(W Jarvis) *trckd ldr: rdn and sustained chal fr 2f out: edgd clsr fnl f: led post* **9/2**[3]
1142 **2** shd **Folk Opera (IRE)**[12] 4196 4-9-6 **107** LDettori 7 108
(Saeed Bin Suroor) *led: hrd pressed 2f out: intimidated by wnr but kpt on wl fnl f: nailed on the post* **9/4**[1]
3104 **3** 3½ **Miracle Seeker**[32] 3543 3-8-6 **102** PhilipRobinson 3 103
(C G Cox) *lw: trckd ldng pair: cl enough over 2f out: sn outpcd: styd on same pce after* **6/1**
1132 **4** 3¾ **Susie May**[31] 3562 4-9-6 **70** GeorgeBaker 8 98
(G L Moore) *stdd s: hld up in 6th: outpcd fr 3f out: no ch after: kpt on* **40/1**
1463 **5** 1¼ **Queen Of Naples**[26] 3720 3-8-6 **103** (b) RichardMullen 2 96
(J H M Gosden) *lw: hld up in 4th: rdn to dispute 3rd wl over 2f out: wknd wl over 1f out* **10/1**
13-0 **6** 4 **Samira Gold (FR)**[26] 3720 4-9-6 **105** SebSanders 5 90
(L M Cumani) *lw: s.s: hld up in last: u.p and struggling 4f out: btn after* **15/2**
11-0 **7** 8 **Hi Calypso (IRE)**[40] 3246 4-9-11 **108** RyanMoore 4 84
(Sir Michael Stoute) *lw: dwlt: hld up in 5th: rdn 3f out: no prog: hanging and wknd 2f out* **3/1**[2]

3m 4.67s (1.07) **Going Correction** -0.025s/f (Good)
WFA 3 from 4yo 14lb **7** Ran SP% **111.5**
Speed ratings (Par 110): **95,94,92,90,90 87,83**
toteswinger: 1&2 £2.40, 1&3 £4.70, 2&3 £3.10. CSF £14.29 TOTE £5.20: £2.60, £1.90; EX 15.60 Trifecta £83.30 Pool: £1104.28 - 9.80 winning units..
Owner Gillian, Lady Howard De Walden **Bred** Plantation Stud **Trained** Newmarket, Suffolk

FOCUS
A race which, for a Group 3, has historically not taken much winning. In a steadily-run affair the first three home occupied the front three positions throughout and those held up couldn't get into the race at all, which makes the form questionable, as does the proximity of a 70-rated handicapper in fourth. A few promised to improve for a step-up trip on paper, but it was a proven stayer who gained the day.

NOTEBOOK
Gravitation is a thorough stayer and needed every yard of the 1m6f trip to get her head in front. A home-bred, Jarvis also trained the dam, and with the Plantation Stud long since sold it is nowadays something of rarity to see the famous apricot silks of the Howard de Walden family back in the winners enclosure. The Park Hill Stakes at Doncaster's St Leger meeting is the obvious next port of call for this daughter of Galileo, and if she improves as much from three to four as she did between two and three, there is no reason why she won't be competing in Cup races next year. (op 11-2)
Folk Opera(IRE) was granted a soft lead and Dettori steadied things up considerably to conserve his filly's stamina. She was in the best place when the sprint for home began, and just lost out after going at it hammer-and-tongs with the winner for fully two furlongs. She is consistent, and with small fields usually the order of the day in these fillies' pattern events, this won't be the last time she has the advantage of an uncontested lead. (tchd 5-2)
Miracle Seeker only previous encounter with fast going had resulted in her only win, the Lingfield Oaks Trial, but she was upped a quarter of a mile in trip here and didn't help her chances of seeing it out by taking a firm grip for much of the first half of the race. (op 8-1)
Susie May, who has been beaten in handicaps off marks in the high 60s recently, appeared to run considerably above herself, despite the fillies behind her obviously running below par. Travelling nicely until getting outpaced around 3f out, she boxed on bravely to be beaten less than eight lengths, a proximity that will ruin her handicap mark, but do plenty for her paddock value. She is in foal to Shirocco, so would probably only have time for one or two more races in any case. (op 50-1)
Queen Of Naples had looked sure to do even better over this trip when a staying-on third in the Lancashire Oaks, but on a faster surface she couldn't reproduce that form. For all her promise in pattern and listed company, her only win has come in a Wolverhampton maiden. (op 9-1 tchd 11-1)
Samira Gold(FR), up a quarter of a mile in trip, sweated up in the preliminaries and was beaten before stamina became an issue. Unraced at two, she was most progressive last year but has yet to prove that she has trained on. (op 7-1)

Hi Calypso(IRE) improved to win this race and the Park Hill last year, but she has been held back by problems with her feet in the interim and reportedly lost both front shoes here. She will have questions to answer if connections choose to pursue her racing career now. Official explanation: vet said filly lost both front shoes (op 11-4)

4550 AUDI STKS (REGISTERED AS THE KING GEORGE STAKES) (GROUP 3) 5f

2:50 (2:51) (Class 1) 3-Y-0+

£39,739 (£15,064; £7,539; £3,759; £1,883; £945) **Stalls** Low

Form RPR

-350 **1** **Enticing (IRE)**[44] 3101 4-8-11 104 JMurtagh 8 115
(W J Haggas) *lw: taken down early: stdd s: hld up in rr: a gng wl: swtchd to trck ldrs in centre 1/2-way: effrt over 1f out: led ins fnl f: decisively* **9/1**

1521 **2** *1* **Masta Plasta (IRE)**[18] 4004 5-9-0 111 AdrianTNicholls 12 114
(D Nicholls) *taken down early: sweating: trckd ldrs in centre: pressed overall ldr and carried rt fr 2f out: led jst ins fnl f: sn hdd and outpcd* **13/2**[2]

0-04 **3** *1 1/4* **Dandy Man (IRE)**[44] 3101 5-9-0 114 (t) LDettori 11 110
(Saeed Bin Suroor) *lw: racd centre: prom: hung rt to far side fr 1/2-way: overall ldr 2f out: hdd and nt qckn ins fnl f* **7/4**[1]

61-3 **4** *nk* **Starlit Sands**[16] 4059 3-8-7 111 SebSanders 13 105
(Sir Mark Prescott) *lw: overall ldr in centre to 2f out: sn outpcd: kpt on again ins fnl f* **10/1**

1100 **5** *1 1/4* **Fat Boy (IRE)**[20] 3922 3-8-10 112 RichardHughes 4 103
(P W Chapple-Hyam) *lw: chsd ldrs nr side: unable to mount a chal over 1f out: kpt on* **13/2**[2]

0000 **6** *nse* **Rowe Park**[12] 4188 5-9-5 102 LPKeniry 3 109
(Mrs L C Jewell) *sweating: blindfold off as stalls opened and dwlt: hld up in rr: rdn 2f out: styd on towards nr side fnl f: n.d* **66/1**

10-0 **7** *1* **Moorhouse Lad**[44] 3101 5-9-0 110 RyanMoore 2 101
(B Smart) *racd nr side: nt on terms wth ldrs: struggling 1/2-way: effrt over 1f out: hung rt ent fnl f and fdd* **8/1**[3]

1311 **8** *1 3/4* **Crimson Fern (IRE)**[19] 3943 4-8-11 94 TGMcLaughlin 1 91
(M S Saunders) *lw: racd nr side: nvr on terms w ldrs: struggling fr 1/2-way* **10/1**

32-2 **9** *shd* **Cute Ass (IRE)**[13] 4159 3-8-7 102 TedDurcan 10 90
(K R Burke) *chsd ldrs in centre: outpcd fr 2f out* **25/1**

-053 **10** *1 1/4* **Sakhee's Song (IRE)**[13] 4159 4-8-11 95 AlanMunro 5 86
(D R C Elsworth) *racd centre: nvr on terms w ldrs: lft bhd fr 2f out* **66/1**

2303 **11** *5* **Desert Lord**[32] 3533 8-9-0 106 (b) JamieSpencer 7 71
(K A Ryan) *early reminders to press overall ldr in centre: reluctant and wknd rapidly over 1f out* **17/2**

1000 **12** *3* **Morinqua (IRE)**[40] 3252 4-8-11 90 TPQueally 6 58
(J G Given) *chsd ldrs tl wknd 2f out* **66/1**

56.63 secs (-1.77) **Going Correction** -0.025s/f (Good)
WFA 3 from 4yo+ 4lb **12** Ran SP% **121.2**
Speed ratings (Par 113): **113,111,109,108,106 106,105,102,102,100 92,87**
toteswinger: 1&2 £15.20, 1&3 £5.40, 2&3 £3.50. CSF £66.95 TOTE £12.60: £3.10, £2.10, £1.30; EX 59.80 Trifecta £463.70 Pool: £4888.32 - 7.80 winning units..
Owner Lael Stable **Bred** Lael Stables **Trained** Newmarket, Suffolk

FOCUS
This can be counted as no more than a fair Group 3 sprint, as only Dandy Man among them is a familiar name in better company, and the winning time was only three-quarters of a second quicker than the later 71-90 handicap. High numbers proved advantaged, despite the stalls being placed stand's side, but this was more due to them getting towed along by the blisteringly quick Starlit Sands than any inherent bias across the course itself. The winner ran to a personal best.

NOTEBOOK
Enticing(IRE) won the Molecomb at two years and was second in this race last year on her only two previous visits to the course. Taken down early and amenable at stalls entry, which hasn't always been the case, Murtagh was content to sit well off the frenetic early gallop, and she came through the field travelling strongly, picking up to win in taking style. She is entered in the Flying Five race at the Curragh, and the firmer the ground the better for her. (op 12-1)
Masta Plasta(IRE) has come back to the form of his juvenile season, which saw him win the Norfolk when Royal Ascot was held at York. Although carried right across to the far rail by third home, this wouldn't have affected the result in any way. Connections are looking at a trip to Deauville for his next run and he should win a decent contest before the year is out. (op 5-1 tchd 7-1)
Dandy Man(IRE)'s only win in Group company came two years ago in the Palace House Stakes at Newmarket in the days when he was trained by Con Collins in Ireland. He passed up a glorious chance to add to that tally here as Starlit Sands gave him a terrific lead, but when Dettori gave him the office he hung right and found disappointingly little. He has had a plethora of excuses made for him over the years, and they have run out now. (op 9-4 tchd 5-2 in a place)
Starlit Sands made a belated reappearance at Great Leighs two weeks ago where she came a respectable third in a 6f conditions event that looked more like a listed heat. She has tremendous speed, as not many can lead Desert Lord up over the first 2f, and after looking like being swamped she kept on very well and was only just done for third. Ridden with a touch more conservatism, her metier could well be found over 6f. (op 12-1)
Fat Boy(IRE), back at the minimum, was unable to get into the race. He is hard to place to advantage given his stiff handicap mark. (op 8-1)
Rowe Park, disadvantaged by a 5lb Group 3 winner's penalty for his win in the World Trophy at Newbury last September, where Enticing was his closest pursuer, seems to be coming to hand in time for a crack at the same race this year.
Moorhouse Lad ran better than the bare from suggested, leading the stands'-side group and still with every chance entering the final furlong. Tying up, he was passed by two horses in the shadow of the post and is steadily coming to hand. Official explanation: jockey said gelding lost its action in closing stages (op 10-1)
Crimson Fern(IRE) was most inconvenienced by the draw and all things considered was not entirely disgraced. She has risen from a mark of 54 at the start of the year to 94 now and is probably still in form. (op 8-1)
Desert Lord didn't look happy, perhaps because he couldn't get to his usual role at the head of affairs. Official explanation: jockey said gelding lost both front shoes (op 10-1 tchd 8-1)

4551 ROYAL BANK OF SCOTLAND GOODWOOD CUP (GROUP 2) 2m

3:30 (3:30) (Class 1) 3-Y-0+

£56,770 (£21,520; £10,770; £5,370; £2,690; £1,350) **Stalls** Low

Form RPR

3-11 **1** **Yeats (IRE)**[42] 3154 7-9-12 0 JMurtagh 9 126+
(A P O'Brien, Ire) *swtg: trckd clr ldr: clsd over 3f out: led over 2f out: rdn clr over 1f out: galloped on relentlessly* **8/15**[1]

403 **2** *7* **Tungsten Strike (USA)**[26] 3743 7-9-7 105 (p) DarryllHolland 6 113
(Mrs A J Perrett) *led: clr after 6f: hdd over 2f out but stl wl ahd of rest: no ch w wnr but kpt on* **33/1**

-055 **3** *1 1/4* **Sagara (USA)**[21] 3878 4-9-7 110 TedDurcan 4 112
(Saeed Bin Suroor) *swtg: chsd clr ldng pair: outpcd and rdn over 4f out: n.d after: clsd grad on runner-up fnl f* **33/1**

-321 **4** *3 1/2* **Distinction (IRE)**[26] 3743 9-9-7 112 RyanMoore 10 107
(Sir Michael Stoute) *hld up in last: lot to do 5f out: prog on outer over 3f out: chal for modest 3rd over 1f out: wknd fnl f* **7/1**[3]

-236 **5** *5* **Regal Flush**[42] 3154 4-9-7 109 (v[1]) LDettori 1 101
(Saeed Bin Suroor) *swtg: hld up in 4th and off the pce: rdn over 4f out: chal for 3rd 3f out: wknd over 1f out* **12/1**

0-41 **6** *3 1/2* **Honolulu (IRE)**[40] 3250 4-9-7 0 RichardHughes 3 97
(A P O'Brien, Ire) *lw: hld up in 5th or 6th: pushed along over 5f out: no rspnse and wl btn over 3f out* **4/1**[2]

5-14 **7** *1/2* **Bulwark (IRE)**[40] 3250 6-9-7 102 (v) JimCrowley 7 97
(Ian Williams) *nvr bttr than 5th or 6th: dropped to last pair and struggling 5f out: nvr a factor after* **33/1**

-055 **8** *11* **Sergeant Cecil**[63] 2542 9-9-7 108 AlanMunro 11 83
(B R Millman) *settled in last pair: nvr a factor: wknd over 2f out* **33/1**

3m 25.75s (-7.45) **Going Correction** -0.025s/f (Good) **8** Ran SP% **117.2**
Speed ratings (Par 115): **117,113,112,111,108 106,106,101**
toteswinger: 1&2 £6.60, 1&3 £8.10, 2&3 £38.80. CSF £31.52 TOTE £1.40: £1.02, £8.10, £6.60; EX 30.20 Trifecta £306.60 Pool: £6090.81 - 14.70 winning units..
Owner Mrs John Magnier & Mrs David Nagle **Bred** Barrowsdale Stud & Orpendale **Trained** Ballydoyle, Co Tipperary
■ Stewards' Enquiry : J Murtagh £290 fine: used mobile phone

FOCUS
Another brilliant performance from Yeats, far and away the dominant force in staying races of the modern era, who showed disdain for his rivals under a 5lb penalty for his third Ascot Gold Cup win six weeks ago. He has been rated as having equalled his career best effort in the corresponding event in 2006.

NOTEBOOK
Yeats(IRE) had already cemented his reputation in legend after winning his third Gold Cup at Royal Ascot last time, and this wasn't so much a coronation as a victory parade, such was the manner of his superiority over his rivals here. With nothing hassling him in a clear second place, and Tungsten Strike offering him a target to aim at up the straight, the contemptuous manner that he pulled alongside and then drew clear of that rival will live long in the memory, and even forced Murtagh, who has seen most things in this game, into a shake of the head after he had looked around to see how far back the oppostion were deep inside the final furlong. He seems to be in as good as form as ever at the age of seven, and is to be enjoyed for as long as his racing career continues. (op 1-2 tchd 4-7 in places)
Tungsten Strike(USA) was allowed to bowl along in front at his own pace, and Yeats aside, the others really did sit too far off him, as although he isn't top class, he has proven Group form to his credit. None of the others were ever going to pass him, as once Yeats breezed by, he kept on admirably to the line, despite having been out on his own in front for so long. He could come back here for the March Stakes in three weeks.
Sagara(USA) had shown nothing in his previous races for Godolphin to suggest that he is anything like the same horse that finished third in the Arc for Jonathan Pease last autumn and this effort at least offered a little more encouragement, on ground would have been plenty fast for him. (op 25-1)
Distinction(IRE) still has the lumps and bumps over his neck which connections obviously don't think affects his ability to run quickly, and he came here on the back of a battling effort against Honolulu at Royal Ascot followed by a Listed victory at Sandown. While it was always going to be a different kettle of fish taking on Yeats, he was sat an awfully long way behind Tungsten Strike as the race panned out, and wasn't ultimately disgraced. (op 9-1)
Regal Flush was keen enough for the application of a first-time visor, especially for a horse not really proven over the trip. Dettori felt afterwards that he did not stay. (op 14-1)
Honolulu(IRE)'s Queen Alexandra Stakes form is not the most solid but for all that this was a bitterly disappointing effort, as he was one of the first horses beaten. (op 9-2)
Bulwark(IRE) is a hard horse to catch right at the best of times, and this year's Chester Cup winner was a little outclassed here anyway.
Sergeant Cecil has not been in much heart on the racecourse this year and the decision was taken after the race to retire him. To say that he has been a grand servant to connections would be the most crass understatement, and he goes out on his shield the winner of ten races, most notably the Group 1 Prix du Cadran in 2006, and over £800,000 in prize money. (tchd 40-1)

4552 MARJORIE AND BERNARD BENHAM EMERALD ANNIVERSARY STKS (HERITAGE H'CAP) 1m 1f 192y

4:05 (4:09) (Class 2) 3-Y-0

£62,310 (£18,660; £9,330; £4,670; £2,330; £1,170) **Stalls** High

Form RPR

2103 **1** **Indian Days**[21] 3877 3-8-6 **91** AlanMunro 12 101+
(J G Given) *lw: hld up in midfield: pushed along and prog on outer 3f out: pressed ldrs over 1f out: sustained effrt to ld last 50yds* **5/1**[2]

2311 **2** *nk* **Military Power**[47] 3048 3-8-3 **88** LiamJones 16 97
(J W Hills) *lw: a w ldrs: drvn ahd narrowly 2f out: kpt on wl whn pressed: hdd last 50yds* **4/1**[1]

5450 **3** *1* **Drill Sergeant**[27] 3684 3-8-8 **93** GregFairley 5 100
(M Johnston) *trckd ldrs: prog 3f out: drvn to chal 2f out: stl nrly upsides ins fnl f: no ex nr fin* **16/1**

1300 **4** *3/4* **Age Of Reason (UAE)**[21] 3877 3-9-1 **100** LDettori 15 106
(M Johnston) *led to 3f out: kpt battling away and stl pressing ldrs 1f out: no ex last 150yds* **16/1**

1212 **5** *1/2* **Steele Tango (USA)**[21] 3877 3-8-9 **94** TedDurcan 7 99
(R A Teal) *awkward s: hld up in midfield: shkn up 3f out: modest prog and reminders 2f out: styd on wl fnl f: nrst fin* **11/2**[3]

4200 **6** *nk* **Ramona Chase**[21] 3877 3-8-9 **94** RichardHughes 11 98
(S Kirk) *t.k.h: hld up in midfield: prog 3f out: rdn to chse ldrs 2f out: nt qckn over 1f out: styd on* **12/1**

5401 **7** *1 1/2* **Upton Grey (IRE)**[13] 4160 3-8-7 **92** RichardMullen 18 93
(J H M Gosden) *lw: prom: trying to chal on inner fr over 2f out: fdd fnl f* **12/1**

3-10 **8** *3/4* **Porthole (USA)**[32] 3527 3-8-3 **88** ChrisCatlin 6 87
(B W Hills) *dwlt: hld up in midfield: nt qckn and lft bhd by ldrs over 2f out: tried to cl fr over 1f out: nvr able to threaten* **25/1**

6000 **9** *1 1/4* **Latin Lad**[20] 3919 3-8-7 **92** FrancisNorton 13 89
(R Hannon) *t.k.h: hld up in rr: sme prog on inner fr 2f out: nt rch ldrs ins fnl f and effrt petered out* **50/1**

4113 **10** *3/4* **Hunting Country**[7] 4350 3-8-8 **93** JoeFanning 8 88
(M Johnston) *swtg: trckd ldr: led 3f out to 2f out: wknd rapidly ins fnl f* **14/1**

-100 **11** *1 1/4* **Dr Faustus (IRE)**[21] 3877 3-9-1 **100** RyanMoore 4 93
(Sir Michael Stoute) *hld up in last pair: rdn 3f out: no prog and wl btn 2f out: kpt on fnl f* **8/1**

-015 **12** *hd* **Dona Alba (IRE)**[21] 3877 3-8-6 **91** ow1 EddieAhern 9 84
(J L Dunlop) *hld up towards rr: outpcd fr over 2f out u.p: n.d after* **11/1**

13-3 **13** *nk* **Dauberval (IRE)**[35] 3396 3-8-5 **90** MartinDwyer 1 82
(S Kirk) *hld up in last pair: pushed along in last 3f out: shkn up over 1f out: kpt on: nvr nr ldrs* **40/1**

4540 **14** *2 1/4* **Siberian Tiger (IRE)**[42] 3155 3-8-13 **98**........................ DarryllHolland 2 85
(M R Channon) *hld up wl in rr: rdn and no prog 3f out: struggling after*
25/1

2144 **15** *17* **Khateeb (IRE)**[42] 3156 3-9-7 **106**...(t) RHills 10 59
(M A Jarvis) *hld up towards rr on outer: shkn up and no rspnse 3f out: eased whn no ch over 1f out: t.o*
8/1

2m 6.43s (-1.57) **Going Correction** -0.025s/f (Good) **15** Ran SP% **128.5**
Speed ratings (Par 106): **105,104,103,103,102 102,101,100,99,99 98,98,97,96,82**
toteswinger: 1&2 £6.00, 1&3 £26.10, 2&3 £23.00. CSF £26.05 CT £316.79 TOTE £6.20: £2.80, £2.30, £6.50; EX 32.30 Trifecta £824.00 Pool: £2449.87 - 2.20 winning units..
Owner D J Fish **Bred** Mrs C C Regalado-Gonzalez **Trained** Willoughton, Lincs

FOCUS
A very good three-year-old handicap, although the early pace was not as strong as one would have expected, which wouldn't have suited a few of these. Solid form, and plenty of positives to take out of the race.

NOTEBOOK
Indian Days ◆ stepped up on his recent third in a decent handicap at the July meeting, gamely defying a 3lb rise in the weights. This effort is all the more creditable considering he was held up off a modest gallop and the next four home all raced close up, so he is clearly progressing into a smart individual. He may be aimed the Cambridgeshire later in the season. (op 8-1)
Military Power came into this chasing the hat-trick, having finally begun to fulfil his potential since stepped up to this sort of trip, and he ran a blinder off a mark 5lb higher than when winning at York on his previous start. (op 5-1 tchd 11-2 in a place)
Drill Sergeant has not gone on as one might have expected since bolting up in a Newcastle maiden on his reappearance, but this was a highly creditable effort in defeat. He might be capable of even better back on easier ground. (op 8-1)
Age Of Reason(UAE) was allowed his own way at a rather modest gallop and as such can have no excuses. He does not look particularly well handicapped.
Steele Tango(USA), 4lb higher, could not confirm Newmarket form with Indian Days or Age Of Reason, but he did not have the race run to suit and is better than he showed. He was doing all his best work at the finish and would have appreciated a strong pace. Easier ground would probably have suited better as well. (op 15-2)
Ramona Chase ran better than of late, despite racing keenly, but he is not easy to win with. (op 14-1 tchd 16-1)
Upton Grey(IRE) was found out by a 6lb rise in the weights for his Newmarket success. (tchd 11-1)
Hunting Country ran flat at Sandown the previous week and this probably came too soon. (op 8-1)
Dr Faustus(IRE) was below form once again and has something to prove now. (op 10-1)
Khateeb(IRE), fourth in the Listed Hampton Court Stakes at Royal Ascot, had plenty on his plate conceding weight all round, but this was too bad to be true. Official explanation: jockey said colt failed to handle the hill (op 7-1)

4553 XL INSURANCE STKS (HERITAGE H'CAP) 7f
4:40 (4:44) (Class 2) (0-105,103) 3-Y-O

£24,924 (£7,464; £3,732; £1,868; £932; £468) **Stalls** High

Form RPR

-011 **1** **Blue Sky Basin**[7] 4345 3-8-5 **87** 6ex.................................. FrancisNorton 8 108+
(A M Balding) *lw: taken down early: mde all: drew clr fr 2f out: in n.d after: styd on wl*
11/1

43-1 **2** *3 1/4* **House**[47] 3031 3-8-4 **86**.. ChrisCatlin 16 98
(L M Cumani) *swtg: hld up in midfield on inner: prog fr 2f out to chse clr wnr over 1f out: r.o wl but nvr able to chal*
13/2[3]

6-13 **3** *2 1/4* **Relative Order**[20] 3919 3-8-5 **87**... LPKeniry 1 93+
(J R Best) *swtg: hld up wl in rr: last of main gp 2f out: sme prog over 1f out: swtchd lft ent fnl f: r.o wl: no ch w ldng pair*
20/1

2100 **4** *1* **Fervent Prince**[22] 3850 3-8-8 **90**....................................... SteveDrowne 4 93
(H Morrison) *lw: hld up in rr: no prog on outer over 2f out: styd on jst over 1f out: tk 4th nr fin*
25/1

0152 **5** *3/4* **Aye Aye Digby (IRE)**[41] 3222 3-8-8 **90**............................ RichardMullen 6 91
(H Candy) *swtg: cl up: rdn over 2f out: sn outpcd: disp modest 3rd 1f out: one pce*
20/1

0046 **6** *shd* **Fathsta (IRE)**[5] 4404 3-8-9 **91**.. JamieSpencer 18 92+
(S Kirk) *dwlt: tk fierce hold and hld up wl in rr: sme prog on inner fr 2f out: styd on: no ch*
8/1

6245 **7** *nk* **Royal Intruder**[22] 3850 3-8-8 **90**................................... RichardHughes 19 90
(R Hannon) *hld up in midfield: effrt over 2f out: no real prog over 1f out: kpt on fnl f*
10/1

2501 **8** *shd* **Adversity**[33] 3475 3-8-13 **95**.. RyanMoore 13 95
(Sir Michael Stoute) *hld up in midfield towards outer: effrt over 2f out: drvn to dispute modest 3rd 1f out: fdd*
3/1[1]

1002 **9** *nse* **Keep Discovering (IRE)**[20] 3897 3-8-7 **89**....................... GregFairley 20 89
(M Johnston) *lw: v keen and cl up on inner: stmbld after 3f: effrt to dispute 2nd 2f out: wknd ins fnl f*
16/1

-306 **10** *2 1/4* **King's Wonder**[10] 4252 3-7-12 **80** oh2............................... JimmyQuinn 12 73
(W R Muir) *pushed along early to go prom: sn t.k.h: outpcd 2f out: swtchd rt over 1f out and effrt: no hdwy after*
33/1

1103 **11** *3/4* **Tawaash (USA)**[22] 3850 3-9-2 **98**.. RHills 14 89
(M A Jarvis) *swtg: chsd wnr: no imp 2f out: wknd fr over 1f out* **6/1**[2]

0614 **12** *2 1/2* **Nightjar (USA)**[6] 4364 3-8-1 **83**.. LiamJones 11 68
(M Johnston) *lw: dwlt: a towards rr: struggling u.p over 2f out* **16/1**

-006 **13** *1 3/4* **Northern Bolt**[8] 4291 3-7-13 **81**................................ CatherineGannon 15 61
(D Nicholls) *chsd wnr tl wknd 2f out* **22/1**

0200 **14** *3 1/4* **Carleton**[22] 3850 3-8-8 **90**.. StephenDonohoe 17 61
(W J Musson) *dwlt: a wl in rr: no prog u.p over 2f out* **20/1**

1110 **15** *shd* **Always A Rock (IRE)**[5] 4404 3-8-6 **88**................................ JoeFanning 5 59
(M Johnston) *lw: racd wdst of all: u.p 3f out and gng nowhere: sn btn*
16/1

1110 **16** *2 3/4* **Summon Up Theblood (IRE)**[20] 3919 3-8-13 **95**....... DarryllHolland 10 58
(M R Channon) *swtg: chsd ldrs: u.p and struggling wl over 2f out: wknd*
25/1

-000 **17** *21* **Rettorical Lad**[62] 2563 3-7-13 **81** oh23 ow1..................... DavidKinsella 3 —
(Jamie Poulton) *a last: t.o sn after 1/2-way* **100/1**

1m 25.15s (-2.25) **Going Correction** -0.025s/f (Good) **17** Ran SP% **129.1**
Speed ratings (Par 106): **111,107,104,103,102 102,102,102,102,99 98,95,93,90,89 86,62**
toteswinger: 1&2 £12.50, 1&3 £28.70, 2&3 £25.80. CSF £75.79 CT £1510.10 TOTE £14.90: £3.20, £1.80, £4.60, £5.90; EX 74.60 TRIFECTA Not won..
Owner George Strawbridge **Bred** George Strawbridge **Trained** Kingsclere, Hants

FOCUS
Form to treat with a bit of caution perhaps, but this was a decent three-year-old handicap, and it was hard not to be impressed by Blue Sky Basin, even though he was allowed very much his own way on a day when racing prominently seemed a big advantage on the round track.

NOTEBOOK
Blue Sky Basin completed the hat-trick in great style, readily defying a penalty for his recent Kempton success, and both trainer and jockey think he could be better than a Handicapper. Having taken them along at a steady pace early, he quickened from the front and was never in the slightest danger. While he enjoyed a soft lead it was hard not to be impressed, and he ran to a mark that suggests he is already capable of holding his own in Listed company. (op 12-1)
House, who made a successful reappearance off a mark of 77 at Leicester on his first start since leaving Mick Channon, ran well in this tougher heat off a much higher mark. He seemed to lose about a length when shuffled back slightly entering the straight, and he was no match for the winner, but he kept on well for second. He should continue to progress. (op 5-1 tchd 9-2)
Relative Order ◆, dropped back from 1m, ran a massive race in defeat. Stall one was no help at all and, dropped in, he raced a long way off just a modest pace, leaving himself with no chance of threatening the winner. He was also denied a clear run for much of the straight, but stayed on strongly when finally switched into the clear inside the final furlong. He looks well up to winning off this sort of mark when things fall his way. (op 16-1)
Fervent Prince, back up in trip, was another to stay on from well back. He was forced to switch into the middle of the track to get a run, but kept on steadily once in the clear and should do even better off a stronger pace. (op 28-1 tchd 33-1)
Aye Aye Digby(IRE) ran respectably on ground quicker than ideal and appeals as one to be with when conditions are more suitable.
Fathsta(IRE), dropped back in trip, was too keen for his own good and did well to finish so close. A stronger pace would have suited better and, on this evidence, he will not mind a drop back to 6f. He was due to be dropped 1lb. (op 11-1)
Royal Intruder failed to prove his stamina on his first run beyond 6f. (op 12-1 tchd 14-1)
Adversity, 12lb higher than when bolting up at Chester, would not have appreciated the modest gallop, but he was still produced with a chance when it mattered and it was disappointing he could not finish closer. (op 7-2)
Keep Discovering(IRE) Official explanation: jockey said gelding ran too free
Tawaash(USA) was well placed turning in, but he dropped out and was some way below the form he showed when third over 6f at the July meeting on his previous start. (op 8-1)

4554 EUROPEAN BREEDERS' FUND NEW HAM MAIDEN FILLIES' STKS 7f
5:15 (5:16) (Class 2) 2-Y-O **£12,952** (£3,854; £1,926; £962) **Stalls** High

Form RPR

4 **1** **Pachattack (USA)**[48] 3001 2-9-0 0.. LDettori 11 84+
(G A Butler) *w'like: hld up in midfield on inner: prog over 2f out: led over 1f out: sn in command: styd on wl*
13/2

0 **2** *1 1/4* **Careless Whisper**[13] 4157 2-9-0 0..................................... EddieAhern 1 79+
(J W Hills) *leggy: scope: b.hind: dwlt: wl in rr: prog on inner over 2f out: styd on wl to take 2nd jst ins fnl f: nvr able to chal*
40/1

0 **3** *2 3/4* **Persian Memories (IRE)**[37] 3349 2-9-0 0........................ TPQueally 15 72+
(J L Dunlop) *cl up: effrt to chal 2f out: upsides over 1f out: outpcd fnl f*
66/1

6 **4** *1* **Bella Rowena**[61] 2614 2-9-0 0....................................... FrancisNorton 14 70
(A M Balding) *leggy: led: 2 l clr 1/2-way: hdd and outpcd over 1f out: brief rally ent fnl f: fdd*
66/1

36 **5** *shd* **Sanvean (IRE)**[20] 3920 2-9-0 0.. RyanMoore 7 69+
(M R Channon) *lw: trckd ldrs: tried to cl over 2f out: nvr pce to mount a chal: kpt on*
2/1[1]

2 **6** *1* **High Heeled (IRE)**[13] 4157 2-9-0 0.................................. MichaelHills 9 67
(B W Hills) *w'like: scope: v keen early: hld up and racd on outer: rdn over 2f out: prog over 1f out: styd on: nrst fin*
11/2[3]

7 *1 3/4* **Midday** 2-9-0 0.. TedDurcan 5 62+
(H R A Cecil) *unf: v awkward s: hld up in last pair: stl there over 2f out: shkn up and prog over 1f out: nrst fin*
10/1

44 **8** *1 1/2* **Russian Rave**[28] 3632 2-9-0 0.. JamesDoyle 2 59+
(J G Portman) *wl in rr on outer: rdn over 2f out: kpt on same pce fr over 1f out: n.d*
50/1

0 **9** *2* **Lake Kalamalka (IRE)**[20] 3913 2-9-0 0......................... RichardMullen 12 54
(J L Dunlop) *lw: dwlt: hld up wl in rr: effrt on inner over 2f out: no real prog: kpt on fnl f*
100/1

60 **10** *1/2* **Order Order**[13] 4149 2-9-0 0.. SebSanders 16 52+
(H J L Dunlop) *mostly chsd ldr to 2f out: sn wknd*
50/1

3 **11** *1 1/2* **Brief Candle**[15] 4080 2-9-0 0.. AlanMunro 10 49+
(W R Swinburn) *w'like: scope: tall: stmbld and nrly fell s: keen early and sn trckd ldrs: rdn and hanging 2f out: wknd*
4/1[2]

12 *nse* **Ja One (IRE)** 2-9-0 0.. RHills 6 49
(B W Hills) *dwlt: swishing tail in rr early: nvr a factor: wl btn over 2f out*
10/1

5 **13** *1* **Miss Sophisticat**[20] 3913 2-9-0 0...................................... PaulDoe 13 46
(W J Knight) *ldng trio to over 2f out: steadily wknd* **16/1**

4 **14** *6* **Princess Hannah**[36] 3378 2-9-0 0.............................. RichardHughes 8 31
(R Hannon) *cl up: hmpd after 2f: wknd rapidly 2f out* **9/1**

6 **15** *4 1/2* **Caravan Of Dreams (IRE)**[13] 4157 2-9-0 0........................ NCallan 4 20
(M A Jarvis) *a towards rr: wknd rapidly 2f out* **33/1**

1m 27.71s (0.31) **Going Correction** -0.025s/f (Good) **15** Ran SP% **129.4**
Speed ratings (Par 97): **97,95,92,91,91 90,88,86,84,83 81,81,80,73,68**
toteswinger: 1&2 £44.50, 1&3 £83.20, 2&3 £191.20. CSF £262.65 TOTE £9.10: £2.90, £7.70, £17.50; EX 570.10 Trifecta £627.90 Pool: £1187.98 - 1.40 winning units..
Owner M V Deegan **Bred** Dapple Broodmares 2004 **Trained** Newmarket, Suffolk

FOCUS
This looked a good maiden, but three of the first four home were rags and the bare form is probably not as strong as it promised to be.

NOTEBOOK
Pachattack(USA), the only filly in the field when fourth on her debut at Sandown, built on the promise of that effort to get off the mark with a clear-cut success, although she did look to carry her a head a touch awkwardly when first in front, still looking a little green. It remains to be seen how strong this form is, but she is well regarded and has the potential to be very useful if she can go the right way. Her trainer is apparently unsure about letting her take her chance in the Moyglare Stud Stakes and said the Fillies' Mile is her ultimate aim. (op 15-2)
Careless Whisper had the worst draw of all in stall one, but she still improved significantly on the form she showed when down the field on her debut at Newmarket. She is bred to be suited by middle-distances next year, so rates as a useful prospect. (op 50-1)
Persian Memories(IRE) ◆ showed little when beating just one home on her debut at Newbury, but this was much better. She still looked very green under pressure and can improve again.
Bella Rowena was allowed the run of the race in front, just as the stable's winner of the previous race had been, and she stepped up on the form she showed on her debut over 6f on the turf at Lingfield. She is probably flattered, but is going the right way. Official explanation: jockey said filly hung left-handed
Sanvean(IRE) ran nowhere near the form she showed when sixth in the Group 2 Superlative Stakes and was a major disappointment for the Channon team, who are having a rather in-and-out season. (op 9-4 tchd 15-8, 5-2 in places)
High Heeled(IRE) found herself poorly positioned throughout, racing well back and stuck out very wide. She can be given another chance to confirm debut promise. (tchd 6-1)
Midday, a daughter of Oasis Dream, out of a quite useful 1m3f winner, is entered in both the Fillies' Mile and the Cheveley Park. She looked in need of the experience and the steady pace was also against her, so better can be expected next time. (op 9-1 tchd 12-1)
Russian Rave found this company a bit hot and should find her level now she is qualified for nurseries.
Order Order did not run a bad race and she should be competitive in handicap company, with easier ground likely to suit better.
Brief Candle was a real eye-catcher on her debut at Kempton, but this run is best forgotten as she stumbled badly soon after leaving the stalls. (op 11-2 tchd 6-1)

Ja One(IRE) Official explanation: jockey said filly was slowly away
Princess Hannah did not confirm the ability she showed on her debut over 5f at Salisbury. Official explanation: jockey said filly lost its action (op 15-2)

4555 DE BOER STKS (H'CAP) 5f
5:50 (5:50) (Class 3) (0-90,91) 4-Y-0+ £12,952 (£3,854; £1,926; £962) Stalls Low

Form RPR

2233 1 **Total Impact**[4] 4445 5-8-8 82 FrederikTylicki(7) 9 95
(R A Fahey) *chsd nr side ldrs: rdn 2f out: prog over 1f out: styd on to take overall ld nr fin* 9/2[1]

-632 2 nk **Even Bolder**[21] 3872 5-8-3 70 LiamJones 3 82
(E A Wheeler) *chsd nr side ldrs and racd against rail: effrt u.p to ld overall jst ins fnl f: collared nr fin* 25/1

4401 3 1 **Mandurah (IRE)**[27] 3668 4-8-4 71 AdrianTNicholls 6 79
(D Nicholls) *w ldr nr side: upsides ent fnl f: no ex nr fin* 10/1

2201 4 nse **Toms Laughter**[4] 4445 4-9-7 91 6ex (b) KevinGhunowa(3) 8 99
(R A Harris) *lw: awkward s but led gp towards nr side tl ins fnl f: one pce nr fin* 6/1[2]

0063 5 shd **Tony The Tap**[12] 4201 7-8-13 80 RichardMullen 7 88
(W R Muir) *racd nr side: in rr: gd prog fnl f: gng on wl at fin* 25/1

2302 6 3/4 **Ocean Blaze**[12] 4201 4-9-1 82 AlanMunro 15 87+
(B R Millman) *swtg: overall ldr in centre and clr of rest: hdd and fdd ins fnl f* 9/1

0500 7 1/2 **Special Day**[34] 3451 4-9-3 84 MichaelHills 12 87
(B W Hills) *racd centre: outpcd: styd on fr over 1f out: nrst fin* 25/1

3035 8 nk **Johannes (IRE)**[28] 3647 5-8-11 78 ChrisCatlin 5 80
(E J O'Neill) *taken down early: chsd nr side ldrs: one pce fr over 1f out* 20/1

5145 9 nk **Bertie Southstreet**[17] 4025 5-8-3 70 (b) JimmyQuinn 19 71+
(J R Best) *lw: taken down early: chsd ldr on far side: styd on ins fnl f to hd him nr fin: nvr on terms* 14/1

0432 10 1/2 **Merlin's Dancer**[54] 2828 8-9-5 86 SebSanders 20 85+
(S Dow) *led quartet that racd far side: nrly on terms w overall ldrs to 1f out: fdd ins fnl f* 9/1

0406 11 1/2 **Blazing Heights**[19] 3956 5-8-6 73 HayleyTurner 14 71
(J S Goldie) *chsd ldrs in centre: effrt u.p 2f out: no imp fnl f* 25/1

2011 12 1/2 **Guest Connections**[13] 4144 5-8-3 70 (v) FrancisNorton 2 66
(D Nicholls) *t.k.h: hld up last of nr side gp: nvr on terms: modest late prog* 16/1

5005 13 nk **Magic Glade**[38] 3320 9-8-8 75 TGMcLaughlin 13 70
(Peter Grayson) *chsd clr ldr in centre: no imp u.p 2f out: fdd* 33/1

0046 14 nk **Bond City (IRE)**[13] 4171 6-9-5 86 (b[1]) LDettori 10 80
(G R Oldroyd) *racd centre: outpcd and nvr on terms w ldrs* 14/1

0010 15 2 **Diane's Choice**[16] 4051 5-7-9 69 oh1 (t) RosieJessop(7) 22 55
(Miss Gay Kelleway) *rrd at s: racd far side: nvr on terms* 20/1

0312 16 1 3/4 **Millfields Dreams**[20] 3905 9-8-8 75 (p) EddieAhern 4 55
(P Leech) *chsd nr side ldrs: wknd over 1f out* 50/1

0400 16 dht **Elhamri**[4] 4445 4-9-7 88 JamieSpencer 16 68
(S Kirk) *racd centre: nvr quite on terms w ldrs: hanging rt fr over 1f out: wknd* 7/1[3]

0302 18 nk **Digital**[19] 3945 11-8-11 78 (v) SamHitchcott 17 57
(M R Channon) *racd centre: bdly outpcd and wl bhd: nvr a factor* 25/1

3330 19 1/2 **Mambo Spirit (IRE)**[13] 4171 4-9-0 81 TPQueally 21 58
(J G Given) *lw: rrd at s: racd far side: a bhd* 20/1

0211 20 9 **Rasaman (IRE)**[10] 4246 4-8-12 79 6ex (tp) NCallan 1 24
(K A Ryan) *chsd nr side ldrs: u.p and struggling 2f out: wknd rapidly* 12/1

57.37 secs (-1.03) **Going Correction** -0.025s/f (Good) 20 Ran SP% **139.4**
Speed ratings (Par 107): **107,106,104,104,104 103,102,102,101,100 100,99,98,98,95 92,92,91,91,76**
toteswinger: 1&2 £184.30, 1&3 £20.80, 2&3 £146.50. CSF £132.70 CT £1144.51 TOTE £7.20: £2.50, £11.80, £2.60, £1.70; EX 481.20 TRIFECTA Not won..
Owner The Wakey Exiles **Bred** C A Cyzer **Trained** Musley Bank, N Yorks

FOCUS
A decent, competitive sprint handicap. The winning time was only 0.74 seconds slower than the earlier Group 3 won by Enticing. They split early, with nine racing near side and the remainder racing middle to far side. Those drawn low, the near-side group, seemed at a slight advantage.

NOTEBOOK
Total Impact has been in great form since returning to the turf this year and ran out a narrow winner, managing to reverse recent Ascot placings with Toms Laughter with the aid of a good 7-lb claimer. Following this personal best he will now be aimed at the Portland Handicap and the extra half furlong will be right up his street. (op 6-1)
Even Bolder was getting weight from most of the field but ran a cracker, just being pegged back close to the line.
Mandurah(IRE) had conditions in his favour and ran well off a mark 3lb higher than when winning an apprentice race at Haydock on his previous start. (op 9-1)
Toms Laughter was only 2lb higher than when winning a valuable sprint at Ascot four days earlier, having carried overweight that day, but he got warm beforehand and could not confirm form with Total Impact. Official explanation: jockey said gelding was unsuited by the good to firm ground (tchd 7-1 in places)
Tony The Tap was taken off his feet early but he finished well. His last two wins have come over 6f, so this was a respectable effort, but he does not have a very good strike rate.
Ocean Blaze was a winner over course and distance on her only previous try here and she ran well, faring best of those to race away from the near-side group. (op 10-1)
Special Day has dropped to a decent mark and this was a promising effort, faring second best of those to race away from the near-side group. (op 20-1)
Bertie Southstreet came out on top in the small group that raced far side.
Bond City(IRE) Official explanation: jockey said gelding lost its action
Elhamri could not build on a promising effort at Ascot four days easier. (op 10-1)
Mambo Spirit(IRE) Official explanation: jockey said gelding missed the break
T/Jkpt: Not won. T/Plt: £463.90 to a £1 stake. Pool: £251,694.14. 396.06 winning tickets. T/Qpdt: £157.10 to a £1 stake. Pool: £10,307.17. 48.55 winning tickets. JN

3784 MUSSELBURGH (R-H)
Thursday, July 31

OFFICIAL GOING: Good to firm (good in places)
Wind: Fresh, half against Weather: Overcast, raining

4556 WILKINSON & ASSOCIATES AMATEUR RIDERS' H'CAP 1m 5f
6:10 (6:12) (Class 6) (0-65,64) 4-Y-0+ £2,498 (£774; £387; £193) Stalls High

Form RPR

6-33 1 **Dimashq**[4] 4457 6-9-11 45 MissWGibson(5) 8 61
(P T Midgley) *prom: led over 3f out: sn clr: unchal* 15/2[3]

2416 2 5 **Elite Land**[2] 4503 5-10-13 56 MissARyan 9 64
(K A Ryan) *hld up in midfield: hdwy over 2f out: chsd wnr over 1f out: edgd rt: no imp* 10/3[2]

-052 3 3 1/4 **Sir Sandicliffe (IRE)**[20] 3912 4-10-12 58 MrBenBrisbourne(3) 11 61
(W M Brisbourne) *hld up: effrt and wd over 2f out: kpt on fnl f: nrst fin* 10/1

063 4 1/2 **Collette's Choice**[11] 4220 5-11-2 64 (p) MrBJToomey(5) 13 66
(R A Fahey) *hld up: effrt 3f out: kpt on fnl f: no imp* 17/2

5102 5 2 **Kyber**[10] 4238 7-11-1 58 MrsCBartley 7 57
(J S Goldie) *led 3f: cl up: led briefly over 3f out: no ex wl over 1f out* 10/1

4-1 6 1/2 **Signalman**[10] 4238 4-10-10 53 6ex MrSWalker 14 52
(P Monteith) *trckd ldrs: rdn 3f out: one pce fnl 2f* 5/2[1]

F035 7 3/4 **Dance Sauvage**[21] 3863 5-10-2 45 MrSDobson 1 43
(C W Thornton) *swtchd rt s: hld up: effrt over 2f out: nvr able to chal* 10/1

6333 8 3/4 **Court Of Appeal**[30] 3589 11-10-11 59 (tp) MrDaleSwift(5) 3 55
(B Ellison) *prom tl rdn and outpcd fr 2f out* 11/1

2-00 9 2 **Always Best**[13] 4142 4-10-0 46 (t) MissJCoward(3) 5 39
(R Allan) *midfield: drvn over 3f out: btn over 1f out* 40/1

1130 10 7 **Schinken Otto (IRE)**[111] 1296 7-10-7 53 MissNJefferson(3) 4 36
(J M Jefferson) *hdwy to ld after 3f: hdd over 3f out: sn btn* 40/1

-004 11 6 **Bond Casino**[31] 3550 4-9-12 46 MrDCottle(5) 12 20
(G R Oldroyd) *prom 4f: sn lost pl: n.d after* 25/1

4000 12 1 1/2 **Miss Havisham (IRE)**[11] 4217 4-9-10 46 ow1 MrBlakeStorrie(7) 6 18
(J R Weymes) *racd wd: in tch tl c v wd and wknd 4f out* 50/1

606- 13 1 1/2 **Phoenix Nights (IRE)**[68] 4410 8-9-11 45 MissBeverleyKendall(5) 10 14
(A Berry) *hld up: pushed over 3f out: nvr on terms* 100/1

2m 47.51s (-4.49) **Going Correction** -0.30s/f (Firm) course record 13 Ran SP% **121.2**
Speed ratings (Par 101): **101,97,95,95,94 94,93,93,91,87 83,83,82**
toteswinger: 1&2 £42.20, 1&3 £42.20, 2&3 £16.20 CSF £32.22 CT £260.43 TOTE £10.10: £2.40, £2.10, £2.70; EX 43.60.
Owner B Bruce **Bred** Darley **Trained** Westow, N Yorks
■ Stewards' Enquiry : Mr Blake Storrie two-day ban: used whip when out of contention (Aug 14-15)

FOCUS
A low-grade handicap in which the pace was soon fair.

4557 EUROPEAN BREEDERS' FUND MEDIAN AUCTION MAIDEN STKS 5f
6:40 (6:41) (Class 5) 2-Y-O £3,885 (£1,156; £577; £288) Stalls Low

Form RPR

556 1 **First Choice (IRE)**[29] 3598 2-8-12 0 (p) FergalLynch 1 67
(K A Ryan) *mde all: edgd rt appr fnl f: drvn and hld on wl* 8/1[2]

2 2 hd **Prime Mood (IRE)**[12] 4176 2-9-3 0 TomEaves 5 71+
(B Smart) *trckd ldrs: pushed along 1/2-way: effrt over 1f out: edgd rt and kpt on wl fnl f: jst hld* 1/7[1]

000 3 8 **Pennine Rose**[13] 4169 2-8-11 0 ow4 SladeO'Hara(5) 4 41
(A Berry) *cl up tl rdn and wknd appr fnl f* 80/1

3 4 32 **Forever's Girl**[23] 3815 2-8-12 0 SilvestreDeSousa 2 —+
(G R Oldroyd) *rdr failed to remove blindfold for 3.3 secs after s: t.o thrght* 12/1[3]

59.82 secs (-0.58) **Going Correction** -0.225s/f (Firm) 4 Ran SP% **107.5**
Speed ratings (Par 94): **95,94,81,30**
CSF £10.10 TOTE £9.90; EX 11.70.
Owner Countrywide Racing **Bred** Manister House Stud **Trained** Hambleton, N Yorks

FOCUS
An uncompetitive race and, with the short-priced favourite failing to match his debut form, this race took less winning than seemed likely beforehand.

NOTEBOOK
First Choice(IRE), fitted with first-time cheekpieces, did just enough to beat a rival who failed to run up to his debut form in this uncompetitive event. She showed bags of foot but her short term future lies at the door of the Handicapper. Official explanation: trainer's rep said, regarding apparent improvement in form, that the filly was better suited by the application of cheek pieces.
Prime Mood(IRE) looked to have a straightforward task judging on his debut run over 6f in heavy ground but he failed by a long chalk to reproduce that over this shorter trip on this much quicker going. The return to 6f will suit and he has to be worth another chance. (op 1-6)
Pennine Rose turned in her first piece of worthwhile form but this race looks a dubious one to take at face value and she is going to have to show a good deal more before she is of interest in this grade. (op 66-1)
Forever's Girl, who hinted at ability on her debut in a low-grade contest on Fibresand, was not given any chance to show what she could do on turf as her rider omitted to remove the blindfold once the stalls opened. Official explanation: jockey said, regarding running and riding, that having been distracted by the stalls rug worn by the filly, he failed to remove the blindfold in time and in doing so lost many lengths at the start. (op 10-1)

4558 SCOTBET.COM NURSERY 5f
7:15 (7:16) (Class 4) 2-Y-O £3,885 (£1,156; £577; £288) Stalls Low

Form RPR

401 1 **Visterre (IRE)**[31] 3547 2-9-4 74 TomEaves 7 79
(B Smart) *cl up on outside: effrt and ev ch over 1f out: led and edgd lft ins fnl f: kpt on wl* 9/1

423 2 nk **Majuba (USA)**[78] 2108 2-9-7 77 FergalLynch 1 81
(K A Ryan) *sn cl up: edgd rt and led over 1f out: hdd ins fnl f: carried lft nr fin: jst hld* 11/4[2]

2512 3 4 **Faraway Sound (IRE)**[5] 4434 2-9-4 74 LeeEnstone 5 64
(P C Haslam) *prom: effrt over 2f out: one pce over 1f out* 1/1[1]

5113 4 3 1/4 **Just The Lady**[24] 3788 2-8-10 66 TonyHamilton 2 44
(Ollie Pears) *led tl hung rt and hdd over 1f out: sn btn* 8/1[3]

6041 5 4 1/2 **Adozen Dreams**[24] 3788 2-8-11 67 SilvestreDeSousa 3 29
(G R Oldroyd) *sn drvn along in tch: struggling fr 1/2-way* 8/1[3]

0455 6 2 1/4 **Wigan Pier**[12] 4175 2-7-13 58 DuranFentiman(3) 6 12
(T D Easterby) *dwlt: a outpcd* 16/1

59.74 secs (-0.66) **Going Correction** -0.225s/f (Firm) 6 Ran SP% **114.8**
Speed ratings (Par 96): **96,95,89,83,76 73**
toteswinger: 1&2 £2.10, 1&3 £1.60, 2&3 £1.10. CSF £34.80 TOTE £6.90: £2.90, £1.60; EX 20.40.
Owner Prime Equestrian **Bred** Miss Eileen Farrelly **Trained** Hambleton, N Yorks
■ Stewards' Enquiry : Tom Eaves two-day ban: careless riding (Aug 14-15)

FOCUS
An ordinary nursery in which the pace was sound throughout.

NOTEBOOK
Visterre(IRE) ◆ looks a progressive type and she turned in her best effort to notch her second course and distance fast-ground win on this nursery debut. The return to 6f will not inconvenience and she is the type to win more races. (op 4-1)
Majuba(USA) is a consistent sort who seemed to give it his best shot on this nursery debut, despite being intimidated by the winner in the closing stages. He pulled clear of the remainder and he is sure to pick up a similar event. (op 4-1 tchd 9-2)

Faraway Sound(IRE), who showed improved form on his nursery debut at York, failed to match that at this sharper track. He looks exposed but left the impression that the return to 6f would be to his liking. (op 11-8 tchd 6-4 in a place)

Just The Lady has been a consistent sort but she was not at her best this time and she left the impression that the return to an easier surface may be in her favour. (tchd 9-1 in a place)

Adozen Dreams, in front of Just The Lady when winning an easy ground nursery over this course and distance on her previous start, was taken off her feet in this better company on quicker ground. Official explanation: jockey said filly ran flat

Wigan Pier once again was up against it from the outset after blowing the start but she did not show enough during the race to suggest she is of much short-term interest. (tchd 14-1)

4559 WILKINSON & ASSOCIATES (S) STKS — 1m

7:45 (7:45) (Class 6) 4-Y-0+ — **£1,942** (£578; £288; £144) **Stalls** High

Form — RPR

1211 **1** **Royal Dignitary (USA)**[28] 3643 8-9-3 83 — SilvestreDeSousa 9 — 78
(D Nicholls) *mde all: rdn over 1f out: kpt on strly* **4/7**[1]

0600 **2** 1 3/4 **Crocodile Bay (IRE)**[33] 3491 5-9-3 82 — TonyHamilton 1 — 74
(D W Barker) *w wnr tl rdn and kpt on same pce fnl f* **3/1**[2]

01-5 **3** 3 3/4 **Primo Way**[19] 3957 7-8-12 65 — TomEaves 4 — 61
(Miss L A Perratt) *hld up in tch: outpcd over 3f out: rallied over 1f out: nt rch ldrs* **7/1**[3]

0646 **4** 5 **Nufoudh (IRE)**[30] 3593 4-8-9 47 — NeilBrown(3) 6 — 49
(Miss Tracy Waggott) *plld hrd: chsd ldrs tl wknd wl over 1f out* **14/1**

005- **5** 3 1/2 **Height Of Esteem**[351] 4488 5-8-9 38 — DuranFentiman(3) 3 — 41
(W M Brisbourne) *hld up: outpcd 1/2-way: nvr on terms* **50/1**

-000 **6** 13 **Noble Edge**[28] 2578 5-8-12 36 — PaulFessey 2 — 11
(Karen McLintock) *trckd ldrs tl wknd fr 1/2-way* **66/1**

1m 39.65s (-1.55) **Going Correction** -0.30s/f (Firm) — **6** Ran SP% **111.3**
Speed ratings (Par 101): **95,93,89,84,81 68**
toteswinger: 1&2 £1.02, 1&3 £1.30, 2&3 £1.20 CSF £2.48 TOTE £1.70: £1.10, £1.30; EX 2.80.The winner was bought in for £22,000.
Owner Middleham Park Racing XXXVI **Bred** Bentley Smith, J Michael O'Farrell Jr , Joan Thor **Trained** Sessay, N Yorks

FOCUS
A couple of fair sorts for this grade and a truly run race in which the two market leaders had the race to themselves from some way out.

4560 SCOTBETPOKER.COM H'CAP — 7f 30y

8:20 (8:20) (Class 5) (0-75,73) 3-Y-0 — **£3,885** (£1,156; £577; £288) **Stalls** High

Form — RPR

-004 **1** **Mr Lu**[72] 2287 3-7-13 **54** oh1 — DuranFentiman(3) 3 — 63
(Miss L A Perratt) *pressed ldr: led over 1f out: edgd lft ins fnl f: kpt on wl* **20/1**

4542 **2** 2 3/4 **Willyn (IRE)**[17] 4019 3-8-2 **54** — (p) NickyMackay 5 — 56
(J S Goldie) *hld up in tch: effrt on outside over 2f out: chsd wnr ins fnl f: r.o: no imp* **4/1**[3]

2-26 **3** nk **Grand Value (USA)**[99] 1558 3-8-6 **58** — PaulFessey 2 — 59
(T D Barron) *led to over 1f out: kpt on same pce* **4/1**[3]

4061 **4** 1 1/2 **Infinity Bond**[24] 3786 3-8-12 **64** — SilvestreDeSousa 6 — 61
(G R Oldroyd) *prom: n.m.r over 3f out: effrt over 2f out: no ex fnl f* **11/4**[2]

05 **5** 7 **Thanxforthat (USA)**[31] 3557 3-8-6 **58** — TonyHamilton 4 — 36
(J J Quinn) *in tch tl rdn and wknd fr 2f out* **5/2**[1]

200 **6** 9 **Applaude**[22] 3854 3-9-7 **73** — PaulMulrennan 1 — 27
(G A Swinbank) *hld up: rdn over 3f out: sn wknd* **9/1**

1m 28.23s (-2.07) **Going Correction** -0.30s/f (Firm) — **6** Ran SP% **110.0**
Speed ratings (Par 100): **99,95,95,93,85 75**
toteswinger: 1&2 £7.70, 1&3 £10.40, 2&3 £1.90. CSF £92.16 TOTE £12.60: £5.90, £2.30; EX 37.80.
Owner The Greens Committee **Bred** Whitwell Bloodstock **Trained** Carluke, S Lanarks

FOCUS
A modest handicap in which the pace was just fair.
Applaude Official explanation: jockey said gelding never travelled

4561 SCOTBET INSTANT TELEPHONE BETTING - 08000 461061 H'CAP — 5f

8:50 (8:51) (Class 5) (0-70,66) 3-Y-0+ — **£3,885** (£1,156; £577; £288) **Stalls** Low

Form — RPR

5055 **1** **Mr Rooney (IRE)**[8] 4294 5-8-11 **57** ow4 — SladeO'Hara(5) 11 — 66
(A Berry) *pressed ldr: led over 1f out: rdn out fnl f* **11/1**

4202 **2** 1/2 **Nomoreblondes**[8] 4291 4-9-11 **66** — (p) PaulMulrennan 10 — 73
(P T Midgley) *led to over 1f out: kpt on ins fnl f* **4/1**[2]

00-5 **3** nk **Smiddy Hill**[9] 4285 6-8-2 **48** — KellyHarrison(5) 9 — 54
(R Bastiman) *trckd ldrs: effrt over 1f out: kpt on ins fnl f* **10/1**

3135 **4** nse **Howards Tipple**[14] 4114 4-9-3 **58** — (p) TomEaves 12 — 64
(Miss L A Perratt) *in tch: drvn and outpcd over 2f out: rallied fnl f: nrst fin* **6/1**

0405 **5** 1/2 **Welcome Approach**[4] 4462 5-8-10 **51** — SilvestreDeSousa 3 — 55
(J R Weymes) *towards rr: hdwy over 1f out: r.o fin* **5/1**[3]

-650 **6** 1/2 **Jojesse**[31] 3546 4-8-6 **47** oh2 — PaulQuinn 7 — 49
(G A Swinbank) *bhd tl hdwy and squeezed through over 1f out: kpt on: nrst fin* **13/2**

6006 **7** 4 1/2 **Miss Sunshine**[10] 4236 3-8-2 **47** oh2 — (v) NickyMackay 1 — 33
(J S Goldie) *bhd tl sme late hdwy: nvr rchd ldrs* **28/1**

0040 **8** 1/2 **Seafield Towers**[17] 4013 8-8-11 **57** ow5 — (p) GaryBartley(5) 13 — 41
(D A Nolan) *in tch on outside tl wknd over 1f out* **33/1**

6002 **9** nk **Darcy's Pride (IRE)**[8] 4293 4-9-4 **59** — FergalLynch 2 — 42
(D W Barker) *prom tl rdn and wknd fr 2f out* **3/1**[1]

04-0 **10** 1 3/4 **Throw The Dice**[27] 3668 6-8-7 **48** — (v) TonyHamilton 6 — 25
(A Berry) *trckd ldrs tl wknd wl over 1f out* **20/1**

0005 **11** hd **Mutayam**[13] 4144 8-8-3 **49** oh2 ow2 — (tp) PatrickDonaghy(5) 5 — 25
(D A Nolan) *dwlt: a bhd* **40/1**

59.16 secs (-1.24) **Going Correction** -0.225s/f (Firm)
WFA 3 from 4yo+ 4lb — **11** Ran SP% **120.3**
Speed ratings (Par 103): **100,99,98,98,97 97,89,89,88,85 85**
toteswinger: 1&2 £10.90, 1&3 £13.10, 2&3 £11.00. CSF £53.99 CT £468.69 TOTE £14.70: £3.70, £1.50, £2.80; EX 75.60 Place 6 £1,146.76, Place 5 £ 510.88..
Owner E Nisbet **Bred** Rathasker Stud **Trained** Cockerham, Lancs

FOCUS
A moderate handicap in which those held up were at a disadvantage. The form is straightforward rated through the runner-up.
Darcy's Pride(IRE) Official explanation: jockey said filly never travelled

T/Plt: £304.50 to a £1 stake. Pool: £48,561.46. 116.40 winning tickets. T/Qpdt: £15.40 to a £1 stake. Pool: £5,240.35. 251.70 winning tickets. RY

4163 NOTTINGHAM (L-H)

Thursday, July 31

OFFICIAL GOING: Good to firm (8.5)
There appeared to be a pace bias on the round course with all four races won by front-runners.
Wind: Virtually nil Weather: Overcast and showers

4562 EUROPEAN BREEDERS' FUND MAIDEN FILLIES' STKS — 6f 15y

2:05 (2:07) (Class 5) 2-Y-0 — **£3,885** (£1,156; £577; £288) **Stalls** High

Form — RPR

1 **Gamila (USA)** 2-9-0 0 — TQuinn 6 — 70+
(Saeed Bin Suroor) *s.i.s and bhd: stdy hdwy 1/2-way: rdn to ld 1f out: kpt on* **4/6**[1]

0 **2** 1 1/4 **Miss Scarlet**[26] 3714 2-9-0 0 — PaulHanagan 3 — 66+
(K A Ryan) *led: rdn along 2f out: drvn and hdd 1f out: kpt on u.p ins fnl f* **14/1**

3 2 1/2 **Chasing Amy** 2-9-0 0 — TPO'Shea 2 — 59+
(M G Quinlan) *trckd ldrs: hdwy to chse ldr over 2f out: rdn wl over 1f out and kpt on same pce* **8/1**[3]

4 3 1/4 **Location** 2-9-0 0 — ShaneKelly 4 — 49+
(Mrs A J Perrett) *trckd ldrs: rdn along wl over 1f out and sn wknd* **4/1**[2]

0 **5** 5 **Lady Dinsdale (IRE)**[28] 3651 2-9-0 0 — MickyFenton 7 — 34+
(T Keddy) *cl up: rdn along 1/2-way and sn wknd* **20/1**

0 **P** **Crown Affair (IRE)**[13] 4149 2-9-0 0 — J-PGuillambert 1 — —
(J W Hills) *sn lost action and p.u after 1f* **9/1**

1m 15.54s (0.44) **Going Correction** -0.15s/f (Firm) — **6** Ran SP% **112.5**
Speed ratings (Par 91): **91,89,86,81,75** —
toteswinger: 1&2 £2.70, 1&3 £1.70, 2&3 £5.00. CSF £11.84 TOTE £1.50: £1.10, £4.30; EX 9.60.
Owner Godolphin **Bred** Kilboy Estate, Inc **Trained** Newmarket, Suffolk

FOCUS
An ordinary fillies' juvenile maiden.

NOTEBOOK
Gamila(USA), whose dam was a useful dual 5-6f winner as a juvenile; was all the rage in the betting to get off the mark at the first time of asking and she duly obliged with a ready effort. She can be rated better than the bare margin as she fluffed the start and took time to get the hang of things, but she was well on clear at the finish. This experience should teach her plenty and it will be interesting to see where she is pitched in next. (op 11-8)
Miss Scarlet had shown next to nothing on her debut over 5f at Carlisle earlier this month, but this was a vastly-improved effort and she showed a much more professional attitude. Clear of the remainder in second, she can improve again from this. (op 9-1 tchd 8-1)
Chasing Amy, half-sister to her stable's former smart sprinter Dixie Belle, showed ability on this racecourse debut yet really shaped as though the run was needed. Better can be expected next time out. (op 9-2)
Location, a half-sister to Endless Summer, shaped well enough until tiring out of contention passing the final furlong marker. She is entitled to come on for the experience. (op 3-1 tchd 9-2)
Crown Affair(IRE) Official explanation: jockey said filly lost its action

4563 THE PADDOCKS CONFERENCE CENTRE @NOTTINGHAM RACECOURSE H'CAP — 5f 13y

2:40 (2:41) (Class 5) (0-75,75) 3-Y-0+ — **£3,238** (£963; £481; £240) **Stalls** High

Form — RPR

0065 **1** **Cape Royal**[8] 4313 8-9-11 **75** — (bt) PatCosgrave 10 — 84
(J M Bradley) *mde all: rdn over 1f out: kpt on wl* **12/1**

0503 **2** 1 **Feelin Foxy**[6] 4385 4-9-6 **70** — J-PGuillambert 6 — 75
(J G Given) *chsd ldrs: hdwy to chse wnr 1/2-way: rdn over 1f out: drvn ins fnl f and no imp towards fin* **4/1**[3]

0511 **3** 3/4 **Invincible Lad (IRE)**[17] 4013 4-9-3 **67** — DavidAllan 5 — 69
(E J Alston) *chsd ldrs: hdwy 2f out: swtchd lft and rdn over 1f out: drvn and one pce ins fnl f* **7/2**[2]

0323 **4** 5 **Cosmic Destiny (IRE)**[27] 3695 6-8-12 **69** — JPFeatherstone(7) 1 — 53
(E F Vaughan) *towards rr: hdwy on outer 1/2-way: sn rdn: styd on ins fnl f: nvr nr ldrs* **14/1**

3620 **5** 1 **Niteowl Lad (IRE)**[9] 4285 6-8-9 **59** — (p) RoystonFfrench 2 — 40
(J Balding) *midfield: effrt and sme hdwy 2f out: sn rdn and nvr nr ldrs* **10/1**

2321 **6** shd **Nusoor (IRE)**[6] 4370 5-9-3 **70** 6ex — (v) KirstyMilczarek(3) 9 — 50
(Peter Grayson) *chsd wnr: pushed along 1/2-way: sn rdn and btn wl over 1f out* **5/2**[1]

0064 **7** 1 3/4 **Don Pele (IRE)**[14] 4103 6-9-9 **73** — (p) PaulHanagan 3 — 47
(R A Harris) *chsd ldrs: rdn along 1/2-way: sn wknd* **8/1**

6003 **8** 1/2 **Bluebok**[9] 4273 7-8-9 **59** ow1 — (bt) ShaneKelly 7 — 31
(J M Bradley) *rrd s: a bhd* **8/1**

0000 **9** 3 3/4 **Groundhog Day**[14] 4107 4-8-6 **56** oh11 — (p) PatrickMathers 8 — 15
(J Balding) *s.i.s: a in rr* **100/1**

004- **10** 5 **Ingleby Star (IRE)**[233] 7106 3-9-0 **75** — DeanHeslop(7) 4 — 16
(T D Barron) *a in rr* **40/1**

59.29 secs (-1.41) **Going Correction** -0.15s/f (Firm)
WFA 3 from 4yo+ 4lb — **10** Ran SP% **119.9**
Speed ratings (Par 103): **105,103,102,94,92 92,89,88,82,74**
toteswinger: 1&2 £15.40, 1&3 £9.00, 2&3 £3.60. CSF £61.34 CT £216.20 TOTE £16.90: £3.20, £2.00, £1.60; EX 75.40.
Owner E A Hayward **Bred** D R Brotherton **Trained** Sedbury, Gloucs

FOCUS
A modest sprint handicap, but the form looks fair for the class with the first three coming clear and the placed horses to their recent marks.
Niteowl Lad(IRE) Official explanation: jockey said gelding had bled from the nose
Bluebok Official explanation: jockey said gelding reared in stalls and missed the break

4564 THE PADDOCKS WEDDING VENUE WITH A DIFFERENCE H'CAP — 2m 9y

3:20 (3:21) (Class 6) (0-60,60) 3-Y-0 — **£2,047** (£604; £302) **Stalls** Low

Form — RPR

-016 **1** **Casual Garcia**[30] 3574 3-9-0 **56** — (b) J-PGuillambert 9 — 70+
(Sir Mark Prescott) *mde all: rdn clr 3f out: styd on strly: eased nr fin* **7/1**[3]

0126 **2** 5 **Borrowdale**[16] 4054 3-9-2 **58** — ShaneKelly 15 — 64+
(J A Osborne) *hld up and bhd: stdy hdwy 5f out: rdn and gd prog on inner to chse wnr over 1f out: sn drvn and no imp* **10/1**

0102 **3** 2 1/2 **Hoar Frost**[13] 4147 3-8-8 **50** — TPO'Shea 13 — 53
(M R Channon) *hld up towards rr: hdwy over 4f out: rdn along over 2f out: styd on u.p ins fnl f to take 3rd nr line* **12/1**

0-00 **4** hd **Light Sea (IRE)**[88] 1840 3-9-2 **58** — TonyCulhane 1 — 61
(M R Channon) *chsd ldrs: rdn along over 3f out: drvn 2f out and plugged on same pce* **40/1**

-063 **5** *5* **Amwell House**[21] 3873 3-8-8 **50**........ AdrianMcCarthy 5 47
(J R Jenkins) *hld up towards rr: hdwy over 4f out: rdn along wl over 2f out: drvn wl over 1f out and plugged on same pce* **12/1**

0050 **6** *2* **Rye Rocket**[10] 4247 3-8-4 **46** oh1........ AndrewElliott 2 40
(K R Burke) *in tch on inner: rdn along 1/2-way: drvn along over 3f out: plugged on same pce fnl 2f* **22/1**

0433 **7** *5* **All Lit Up**[7] 4334 3-8-9 **51**........(b) SimonWhitworth 16 39
(A King) *hld up towards rr: hdwy on outer 5f out: rdn and edgd lft 3f out: sn drvn and no imp fnl 2f* **9/4**[1]

0006 **8** *1 3/4* **Kuriyama (IRE)**[53] 2868 3-8-10 **52**........ SaleemGolam 4 38
(M H Tompkins) *in tch: rdn along over 4f out: drvn 3f out and sn no imp* **25/1**

4331 **9** *1 1/4* **Lady Jinks**[17] 4023 3-8-4 **53**........ BillyCray(7) 12 38
(M D I Usher) *hld up a towards rr* **16/1**

0 **10** *2 3/4* **Harveys Spirit (IRE)**[87] 1855 3-9-1 **60**........ KirstyMilczarek(3) 3 41
(S Curran) *chsd wnr: rdn along 4f out: drvn over 2f out and sn wknd* **10/1**

1306 **11** *26* **Fantastic Lass**[27] 3671 3-9-1 **57**........ PaulHanagan 7 7
(R A Fahey) *hld up in tch: hdwy 4f out: rdn along 3f out: drvn over 2f out and sn btn* **9/2**[2]

06-0 **12** *5* **Alannah (IRE)**[114] 1251 3-8-4 **46** oh1........ PaulEddery 8 —
(Mrs P N Dutfield) *prom: rdn along over 4f out: wknd over 3f out* **40/1**

000 **13** *1 1/4* **Let Me Pass (USA)**[37] 3350 3-8-12 **54**........ FrankieMcDonald 6 —
(Jane Chapple-Hyam) *a bhd* **28/1**

5300 **14** *5* **Polychrome**[10] 4260 3-8-13 **55**........ PatCosgrave 11 —
(John Berry) *in midfield: effrt 4f out: sn rdn along and wkng whn n.m.r 3f out* **66/1**

0005 **15** *1 1/4* **Oberlin (USA)**[24] 3793 3-9-1 **57**........ MickyFenton 14 —
(T Keddy) *in tch on outer: rdn along 4f out: drvn 3f out and sn wknd* **16/1**

0505 **16** *75* **Princess Raya**[10] 4260 3-9-2 **58**........(t) NeilPollard 10 —
(M E Rimmer) *a in rr* **25/1**

3m 29.77s (-3.83) **Going Correction** -0.075s/f (Good) **16** Ran SP% **128.6**
Speed ratings (Par 98): **106,103,102,102,99 98,96,95,94,93 80,77,77,74,74 36**
toteswinger: 1&2 £14.20, 1&3 £17.90, 2&3 £31.80. CSF £74.27 CT £855.83 TOTE £8.80: £1.90, £2.80, £2.70, £6.70; EX 157.90.
Owner Ne'Er Do Wells Ii **Bred** Miss K Rausing **Trained** Newmarket, Suffolk

FOCUS
This moderate handicap represents a real stamina test for three-year-olds. The winner rates value for further.

4565 THE PADDOCKS CONFERENCE CENTRE AT 0870 8507635 H'CAP 1m 2f 50y
3:55 (3:55) (Class 4) (0-85,85) 3-Y-O+ **£6,476** (£1,927; £963; £481) **Stalls** Low

Form RPR

100 **1** **Tri Nations (UAE)**[27] 3676 3-9-2 **81**........ TQuinn 1 88
(J W Hills) *mde all: qckd 3f out: rdn and qcknd again over 1f out: styd on strly* **14/1**

0530 **2** *2 1/2* **Del Mar Sunset**[9] 4276 9-9-6 **75**........ TonyCulhane 4 77
(W J Haggas) *trckd ldrs: hdwy to chse wnr over 3f out: rdn along 2f out: drvn over 1f out and no imp ins fnl f* **13/2**[3]

0-20 **3** *nk* **Beverly Hill Billy**[14] 4131 4-9-9 **78**........ ShaneKelly 3 79
(A King) *t.k.h: hld up: hdwy over 3f out: rdn to chse ldng pair over 2f out: drvn and one pce appr fnl f* **8/1**

6042 **4** *2 1/4* **Ella Woodcock (IRE)**[12] 4204 4-9-11 **80**........(p) DavidAllan 6 77
(E J Alston) *hld up: hdwy 3f out: rdn to chse ldng pair 2f out: sn drvn and one pce* **5/2**[2]

501F **5** *3 1/4* **Dragon Slayer (IRE)**[13] 4156 6-9-4 **73**........ J-PGuillambert 5 63
(John A Harris) *hld up in tch: hdwy to chse ldng pair over 3f out: rdn along over 2f out: sn drvn and wknd wl over 1f out* **7/1**

05 **6** *17* **Rubacuori (BRZ)**[16] 4060 4-9-12 **83**........ PaulHanagan 7 37
(J M P Eustace) *chsd wnr: rdn along over 4f out: sn wknd* **25/1**

3215 **7** *3 1/2* **Full Speed (GER)**[26] 3719 3-9-6 **85**........ TPO'Shea 8 34
(G A Swinbank) *trckd ldrs on outer: pushed along over 4f out: sn rdn and btn over 3f out* **13/8**[1]

2m 11.22s (-1.28) **Going Correction** -0.075s/f (Good)
WFA 3 from 4yo+ 10lb **7** Ran SP% **114.1**
Speed ratings (Par 105): **102,100,99,97,95 81,78**
toteswinger: 1&2 £10.40, 1&3 £9.40, 2&3 £5.70. CSF £98.74 CT £783.72 TOTE £17.70: £4.90, £2.90; EX 101.60.
Owner Donald M Kerr **Bred** Darley **Trained** Upper Lambourn, Berks

FOCUS
A fair handicap in which the runner-up sets the level backed up by the third, but not the most solid.
Full Speed(GER) Official explanation: jockey said gelding had no more to give

4566 THEPADDOCKSNOTTINGHAM.CO.UK MEDIAN AUCTION MAIDEN STKS 1m 75y
4:30 (4:30) (Class 6) 3-4-Y-O **£3,070** (£906; £453) **Stalls** Centre

Form RPR

5224 **1** **Mr Hichens**[20] 3915 3-9-3 75........ TPO'Shea 7 77+
(B J Meehan) *mde all: pushed along 3f out: sn jnd and rdn: drvn wl over 1f out and styd on wl* **1/1**[1]

3- **2** *5* **Rahere (IRE)**[28] 2385 3-9-3 0........ RoystonFfrench 5 62
(M Johnston) *trckd ldrs: hdwy to chse wnr over 3f out: rdn to chal and ev ch 2f out: sn drvn: edgd lft and one pce* **15/2**

6-00 **3** *4* **Our Dolly**[27] 3694 3-8-12 49........ AndrewElliott 4 48
(Garry Moss) *chsd ldng pair: rdn along over 3f out: plugged on same pce fnl 2f* **100/1**

62 **4** *nk* **Quail Landing**[23] 3823 3-8-12 0........ MickyFenton 6 47+
(M P Tregoning) *hld up: hdwy on outer over 3f out: rdn along wl over 2f out: sn no imp* **5/1**[3]

03 **5** *5* **Veni Bidi Vici**[23] 3823 3-8-12 0........ TonyCulhane 1 36
(A M Balding) *towards rr: effrt 4f out: sn rdn along and nvr a factor* **20/1**

-662 **6** *5* **Warden Fizz**[12] 4194 3-9-3 74........ TQuinn 8 29
(D R C Elsworth) *cl up: rdn along over 3f out and sn wknd* **10/3**[2]

0 **7** *1 1/4* **Scorched (IRE)**[114] 1252 4-9-6 0........ PaulHanagan 2 21
(J R Fanshawe) *a in rr* **16/1**

1m 45.1s (-0.30) **Going Correction** -0.075s/f (Good)
WFA 3 from 4yo 8lb **7** Ran SP% **113.1**
Speed ratings (Par 101): **98,93,89,88,83 78,77**
toteswinger: 1&2 £2.50, 1&3 £12.90, 2&3 £26.00. CSF £9.34 TOTE £2.00: £1.20, £2.50; EX 7.60.
Owner Mrs J & D E Cash **Bred** C A Green **Trained** Manton, Wilts

FOCUS
A poor maiden, run at a solid pace. The winner had little to beat with the second favourite disappointing and the form is weakened by the proximity of the 49-rated third.
Rahere(IRE) Official explanation: jockey said colt slipped turning for home
Warden Fizz Official explanation: jockey said gelding lost its action in the straight

4567 THE PADDOCKS DAY DELEGATE £30 PER PERSON H'CAP 1m 75y
5:05 (5:05) (Class 5) (0-75,74) 3-Y-O+ **£3,238** (£963; £481; £240) **Stalls** Centre

Form RPR

0600 **1** **Very Well Red**[20] 3903 5-9-5 **65**........ DarrenWilliams 3 72
(P W Hiatt) *mde all: rdn along 3f out: drvn wl over 1f out: styd on strly ent fnl f* **20/1**

5340 **2** *1 1/2* **Aggravation**[13] 4162 6-9-9 **69**........ TQuinn 5 73
(D R C Elsworth) *hld up: hdwy on inner 3f out: rdn 2f out: swtchd rt and drvn to chse wnr over 1f out: kpt on* **7/1**

-600 **3** *3* **Kansas Gold**[31] 3569 5-8-11 **57**........(v[1]) TonyCulhane 8 54
(J Mackie) *chsd wnr: rdn and close up 3f out: drvn 2f out and grad wknd* **12/1**

1120 **4** *1 1/4* **Paraguay (USA)**[13] 4162 5-10-0 **74**........ PaulHanagan 6 68
(Miss V Haigh) *hld up: hdwy 3f out: rdn over 2f out: sn drvn and one pce* **3/1**[2]

0542 **5** *2 1/2* **Hartshead**[5] 4440 9-10-0 **74**........ DeanMcKeown 2 62
(G A Swinbank) *trckd ldrs: effrt over 3f out: sn rdn and btn* **9/4**[1]

1605 **6** *3* **Bold Cross (IRE)**[14] 4121 5-9-7 **67**........ PaulFitzsimons 4 48
(E G Bevan) *s.i.s: hld up in rr: hdwy on wd outside wl over 2f out: sn rdn and btn* **6/1**

6142 **7** *1* **Shabahar (IRE)**[16] 4065 4-9-12 **72**........ MickyFenton 7 51
(M J McGrath) *chsd ldng pair: rdn along over 3f out and sn wknd* **4/1**[3]

1m 47.32s (1.92) **Going Correction** -0.075s/f (Good) **7** Ran SP% **115.0**
Speed ratings (Par 103): **87,85,82,81,78 75,74**
toteswinger: 1&2 £9.90, 1&3 £11.90, 2&3 £9.90. CSF £149.78 CT £1765.20 TOTE £13.40: £5.10, £2.90; EX 89.50 Place 6: £2542.51 Place 5: £1710.82 .
Owner Phil Kelly **Bred** Butts Enterprises Limited **Trained** Hook Norton, Oxon

FOCUS
A modest handicap which saw another winner from the front. The runner-up helps to set the level but the form looks a bit suspect with the winner setting a slow pace.
Very Well Red Official explanation: trainer said, regarding apparent improvement in form, that the mare was better suited by the course
Hartshead Official explanation: jockey said gelding ran flat
T/Plt: £877.30 to a £1 stake. Pool: £34,434.91. 28.65 winning tickets. T/Qpdt: £106.10 to a £1 stake. Pool: £2,079.29. 14.50 winning tickets. JR

4346 SANDOWN (R-H)
Thursday, July 31

OFFICIAL GOING: Good to firm (good in places)
Rail realignment added circa 5yds to advertised distances on the round course.
Wind: Nil

4568 KIWI APPRENTICE H'CAP 1m 2f 7y
5:55 (5:57) (Class 5) (0-70,70) 4-Y-O+ **£3,238** (£963; £481; £240) **Stalls** High

Form RPR

024P **1** **Alfie Tupper (IRE)**[9] 4267 5-9-2 **62**........ JackMitchell 12 67
(J R Boyle) *t.k.h: chsd ldrs: wnt 2nd ins fnl 2f: hung lft to centre of crse and styd on u.p to ld last stride* **5/1**[2]

6002 **2** *shd* **Olimpo (FR)**[14] 4123 7-9-5 **65**........ JamesMillman 10 70
(B R Millman) *led: qcknd fr 3f out: styd on wl u.p fnl f: collared last stride* **5/1**[2]

4033 **3** *3/4* **King Of Connacht**[10] 4261 5-8-6 **52**........(p) MarcHalford 1 56
(M Wellings) *bhd: rdn and styd on fr 2f out: gng on u.p thrght fnl f but nvr quite gng pce to rch ldng duo* **6/1**[3]

0044 **4** *1 1/2* **The Grey One (IRE)**[3] 4485 5-8-2 **51** oh6........(p) MCGeran(3) 3 52
(J M Bradley) *t.k.h in rr: rdn and edgd rt ins fnl 2f: styd on u.p fnl f: nt rch ldrs* **14/1**

4263 **5** *1/2* **Adorabella (IRE)**[12] 4183 5-9-3 **63**........ TravisBlock 5 63+
(A King) *hld up in rr: nt clr run ins fnl 2f and again 1f out: str run on ins fnl f: styng on wl cl home* **4/1**[1]

5220 **6** *1 1/2* **Medieval Maiden**[31] 3562 5-8-2 **51** oh3........ RossAtkinson(3) 2 48+
(Mrs L J Mongan) *in rr tl styd on fr 2f out: kpt on wl fnl f but nvr in contention* **12/1**

30-6 **7** *3/4* **Yab Adee**[15] 4078 4-8-12 **63**........ KatiaScallan(5) 4 58
(M P Tregoning) *t.k.h: chsd ldrs: carried rt: n.m.r and lost position ins fnl 2f: kpt on again cl home* **14/1**

4000 **8** *3/4* **Sky Quest (IRE)**[30] 3583 10-8-11 **60**........(t) HarryPoulton(3) 8 54
(J R Boyle) *s.i.s: in rr tl styd on fnl 2f: nvr in contention* **25/1**

021- **9** *2 3/4* **Zelos (IRE)**[54] 6598 4-9-7 **70**........(bt) KylieManser(3) 9 58
(D G Bridgwater) *stmbld after 1f: styd chsng ldrs tl wknd over 1f out* **20/1**

2343 **10** *1 1/2* **High 'n Dry (IRE)**[47] 3036 4-9-2 **67**........(p) AndreaAtzeni(5) 6 52
(M A Allen) *t.k.h: chsd ldr tl wknd fr 2f out* **10/1**

0545 **11** *6* **Gold Prospect**[18] 3996 4-9-7 **70**........ JPHamblett(3) 7 43
(M L W Bell) *s.i.s: a towards rr* **8/1**

3000 **12** *hd* **Play Up Pompey**[13] 4155 6-8-0 **51** oh6........ CharlesEddery(5) 11 24
(J J Bridger) *s.i.s: sn mid-div: wknd fr 3f out* **50/1**

2m 10.02s (-0.48) **Going Correction** +0.125s/f (Good) **12** Ran SP% **119.4**
Speed ratings (Par 103): **106,105,105,104,103 102,101,101,99,97 93,92**
toteswinger: 1&2 £5.60, 1&3 £16.90, 2&3 £13.90 CSF £29.81 CT £156.22 TOTE £6.20: £2.30, £2.50, £2.20; EX 33.00.
Owner Epsom Equine Spa Partnership **Bred** Stone Ridge Farm **Trained** Epsom, Surrey

FOCUS
The pace was very steady and only a handful ever got involved. The form is not that solid and should be treated with caution.
The Grey One(IRE) Official explanation: jockey said gelding hung right

4569 WALLABY CLAIMING STKS 1m 14y
6:25 (6:29) (Class 5) 3-Y-O **£3,885** (£1,156; £577; £288) **Stalls** High

Form RPR

6001 **1** **The Hoofer (IRE)**[8] 4298 3-8-4 47........(b) MartinDwyer 2 56
(J L Dunlop) *trckd ldr off slow pce: led ins fnl 3f: pushed clr over 1f out: comf* **6/1**[3]

0015 **2** *1 3/4* **Coole Dodger (IRE)**[24] 3799 3-8-7 74........ GabrielHannon(5) 4 60
(M D I Usher) *disp 2nd: pushed along over 2f out: chsd wnr sn after and kpt on but no ch fr over 1f out* **5/6**[1]

-000 **3** *1 1/4* **Lilburn (IRE)**[21] 3886 3-9-2 64........ GeorgeBaker 1 61
(J R Fanshawe) *hld up in rr off slow pce: hdwy 3f out: drvn to go 3rd over 1f out: styd on same pce* **7/2**[2]

0054 **4** *3 1/4* **Bon Ton Roulet**[32] 3524 3-7-11 50........ CharlesEddery(7) 5 42
(R Hannon) *s.i.s: rr and plld hrd off slow pce: shkn up over 2f out: nvr in contention* **14/1**

6620 **5** *5* **Fly In Johnny (IRE)**[16] 4053 3-8-11 **58**..................(p) JimCrowley 3 37
(M R Hoad) *led at slow pce: hdd ins fnl 3f: sn btn* **16/1**

1m 45.36s (2.06) **Going Correction** +0.125s/f (Good) **5** Ran SP% **103.6**
Speed ratings (Par 100): **94,92,91,87,82**
toteswinger: 1&2 £1.70 CSF £10.14 TOTE £3.80: £1.60, £1.10; EX 7.20.Coole Dodger was claimed by Kristian Strangeway for £11,000. The Hoofer was claimed by I. A. Wood for £5,000.
Owner J L Dunlop **Bred** Hesmonds Stud Ltd **Trained** Arundel, W Sussex

FOCUS
An uncompetitive and slowly run claimer and the form is unconvincing.
Coole Dodger(IRE) Official explanation: jockey said colt hung badly right

4570 SPRINGBOK E B F MAIDEN STKS 7f 16y
7:00 (7:09) (Class 4) 2-Y-O **£5,180** (£1,541; £770; £384) **Stalls** High

Form RPR
302 **1** **Pegasus Lad (USA)**[19] 3939 2-9-3 0.................. JoeFanning 4 86+
(M Johnston) *mde all: forged clr fnl 2f: unchal* **11/4**[2]
0 **2** *3¾* **Beraimi (IRE)**[16] 4062 2-9-3 0.................. PhilipRobinson 3 75
(M A Jarvis) *chsd wnr thrght: rdn 3f out: no ch fnl 2f but styd on wl for clr 2nd* **25/1**
4 **3** *2* **Silver Print (USA)**[19] 3968 2-9-3 0.................. DarryllHolland 11 70
(W R Swinburn) *chsd ldrs and disputing 2nd thrght: one pce fnl 2f* **4/1**[3]
00 **4** *2* **Dubai Crest**[8] 4311 2-9-3 0.................. JamesDoyle 8 65+
(Mrs A J Perrett) *towards rr: rdn over 3f out: styd on fr over 1f out: gng on cl home but nvr any threat* **28/1**
5 *½* **Simplification** 2-8-9 0.................. PatrickHills(3) 12 58+
(R Hannon) *in rr: drvn along 3f out: styd on thrght fnl f but nvr any threat to ldrs* **50/1**
6 *1¼* **Marching Time** 2-9-3 0.................. RyanMoore 7 60
(Sir Michael Stoute) *sn disputing 3rd: rdn: effrt: green and hung rt over 2f out: nvr gng pce to rch wnr and wknd fnl f* **5/4**[1]
50 **7** *1* **River Captain (IRE)**[38] 3323 2-9-3 0.................. LPKeniry 14 58
(S Kirk) *wnt lft s: in rr: rdn over 3f out: styd on fr over 1f out but nvr a threat* **66/1**
00 **8** *½* **Captain Walcot**[32] 3519 2-9-3 0.................. PatDobbs 5 57
(R Hannon) *chsd ldrs: rdn over 3f out: wknd 2f out* **66/1**
9 *1½* **King's La Mont (IRE)** 2-9-3 0.................. JimCrowley 10 53
(Mrs A J Perrett) *a towards rr* **33/1**
10 *½* **Sehoy (USA)** 2-9-3 0.................. JimmyFortune 9 52
(J H M Gosden) *nvr in contention* **12/1**
00 **11** *3¾* **Daily Planet (IRE)**[28] 3645 2-8-12 0.................. GabrielHannon(5) 13 42
(B W Duke) *bmpd s: in rr: effrt u.p on ins over 3f out: sn wknd* **100/1**
12 *7* **Itlaaq** 2-9-3 0.................. MartinDwyer 1 25
(J L Dunlop) *slowly away: a bhd* **25/1**

1m 31.42s (1.92) **Going Correction** +0.125s/f (Good) **12** Ran SP% **118.8**
Speed ratings (Par 96): **94,89,87,85,84 83,82,81,79,79 74,66**
toteswinger: 1&2 £8.00, 1&3 £3.10, 2&3 £8.70. CSF £73.62 TOTE £3.90: £1.40, £4.50, £1.60; EX 42.90.
Owner A D Spence **Bred** Beechglen Farms Llc **Trained** Middleham Moor, N Yorks

FOCUS
There was very little change in the order in what was probably an ordinary maiden for the track.

NOTEBOOK
Pegasus Lad(USA), the most experienced member of the field, became warm in the preliminaries. Getting across from his low draw to lead, he dictated the pace and, maintaining the gallop, came away in the final two furlongs for a bloodless success. This wil have boosted his confidence and he is ready for a step back up in grade now. (op 5-2 tchd 3-1)
Beraimi(IRE) was all the better for his debut experience at Yarmouth. Chasing the winner for much of the way, though probably shaded for second by Silver Print for a time in the straight, he stayed on and should get another furlong. (op 16-1)
Silver Print(USA) shaped with promise on his debut at Salisbury and again ran well. Never far away, he did move into a narrow second briefly in the home straight but never looked like getting to the winner. (op 5-1 tchd 11-2)
Dubai Crest, who is in the same ownership as the winner, had shown only a very modest level of form in two previous 7f maidens. He did make late progress, doing best of those coming from off the pace, and is now qualified for nurseries. (op 50-1)
Simplification ◆ is the first foal of an unraced half-sister to the high-class pair Stagecraft and Mullins Bay, who were both best at around 1m2f, and to smart miler Hyabella. She made pleasing late progress on this debut and can probably improve to land an ordinary maiden, perhaps against her own sex over a mile. (op 33-1)
Marching Time is out of a mare who won over an extended 5f in France and who was a half-sister to the 2000 Guineas winner Zafonic and high-class miler Zamindar. Well enough placed in a race that nothing got into from the rear, he came under pressure in the straight and never picked up for his rider, looking green and inexperienced, and weakening out of the frame inside the final furlong. Juveniles from his stable often improve for their debut run and better can be expected next time, but this was certainly disappointing. (op 13-8 tchd 10-11 & 7-4 in a place)
Daily Planet(IRE) Official explanation: jockey said colt lost its action

4571 AUSTRALIA H'CAP 1m 14y
7:30 (7:38) (Class 4) (0-80,80) 3-Y-O **£7,123** (£2,119; £1,059; £529) **Stalls** High

Form RPR
3003 **1** **The Which Doctor**[14] 4128 3-9-8 **79**.................. ShaneKelly 2 89+
(J Noseda) *sn trcking ldr: rdn over 2f out: led over 1f out: hung rt to far rail ins fnl f: pushed out* **11/4**[2]
3540 **2** *1½* **Barliffey (IRE)**[14] 4104 3-8-13 **70**..................(v[1]) DarryllHolland 1 74
(D J Coakley) *in rr but in tch: rdn over 3f out: styd on u.p fr 2f out: swtchd lft 1f out and styd on to go 2nd ins fnl f: nt rch wnr* **16/1**
41 **3** *3½* **Cave Lion (USA)**[38] 3326 3-9-9 **80**.................. JimmyFortune 5 76
(J H M Gosden) *led: pushed along over 2f out: hdd 1f out: hld whn crossed ins fnl f: lost 2nd and wknd fnl 75yds* **7/4**[1]
1-0 **4** *½* **Mystery Sail (USA)**[71] 2302 3-9-9 **80**.................. JimCrowley 6 75
(Mrs A J Perrett) *in tch: wnt 3rd 4f out: rdn over 2f out: edgd rt u.p sn after: kpt on fnl f but nvr in contention* **4/1**[3]
-625 **5** *10* **E Major**[21] 3894 3-9-7 **78**.................. RyanMoore 3 50
(Sir Michael Stoute) *in rr but in tch: rdn 3f out: little rspnse* **7/1**
-140 **6** *16* **Animator**[80] 2045 3-9-1 **72**.................. JoeFanning 7 7
(P F I Cole) *plld hrd early: chsd ldrs over 4f: sn btn* **11/2**

1m 43.13s (-0.17) **Going Correction** +0.125s/f (Good) **6** Ran SP% **116.8**
Speed ratings (Par 102): **105,103,100,99,89 73**
toteswinger: 1&2 £16.40, 1&3 £1.02, 2&3 £10.80 CSF £42.38 CT £97.56 TOTE £3.90: £2.00, £4.90; EX 35.80.
Owner G C Stevens **Bred** Limestone And Tara Studs **Trained** Newmarket, Suffolk
■ Stewards' Enquiry : Shane Kelly one-day ban: careless riding (Aug 14)

FOCUS
A fair handicap and another steadily run race until the pace picked up around the bottom bend. The form makes some sense rated around the runner-up and fourth.
Barliffey(IRE) Official explanation: jockey said gelding hung both ways
Cave Lion(USA) Official explanation: jockey said colt hung left
Animator Official explanation: jockey said gelding hit rails turning in

4572 ACTIVEANTIPODEAN.COM FILLIES' H'CAP 1m 1f
8:05 (8:07) (Class 5) (0-75,73) 3-Y-O+ **£4,857** (£1,445; £722; £360) **Stalls** High

Form RPR
6631 **1** **Snowdrop Princess**[5] 4427 3-9-8 **71**..................(b) KirstyMilczarek(3) 2 82+
(W J Haggas) *hld up in tch: drvn and hdwy to ld 2f out: styd on strly thrght fnl f* **3/1**[1]
2133 **2** *2* **Luck Will Come (IRE)**[9] 4282 4-9-9 **65**.................. JackMitchell(5) 6 72+
(H J Collingridge) *hld up in rr: shkn up on outside over 2f out but stl plenty to do: hrd rdn and r.o to chse wnr 1f out: hung rt u.p ins fnl f: a hld* **8/1**[2]
0001 **3** *2¼* **Rescue Me**[10] 4253 3-9-6 **69** 6ex.................. PatrickHills(3) 5 71+
(R Hannon) *effrt on ins whn hmpd 4f out: styd on inner and kpt on u.p fnl 2f: tk 3rd fnl f but nvr a threat to ldng duo* **8/1**[2]
-605 **4** *3* **La Troupe (IRE)**[38] 3322 3-9-9 **69**.................. JimmyFortune 1 64
(J H M Gosden) *led over 6f out: rdn over 3f out: hdd 2f out: wknd over 1f out* **16/1**
-043 **5** *1¼* **Selsey**[33] 3507 3-9-10 **70**.................. RyanMoore 9 63
(Sir Michael Stoute) *in tch: hdwy to chse ldrs 4f out: nvr gng pce to chal: wknd over 1f out* **3/1**[1]
2310 **6** *1* **Lunar River (FR)**[13] 4156 5-9-13 **64**..................(t) SaleemGolam 10 54
(David Pinder) *chsd ldrs: rdn to chal over 2f out: wknd over 1f out* **12/1**
640 **7** *nk* **April's Daughter**[32] 3530 3-9-5 **65**.................. JimCrowley 11 55
(B R Millman) *sn led: hdd over 6f out: outpcd over 2f out: styd on same pce over 1f out* **25/1**
-415 **8** *1¾* **Shanzu**[10] 4253 3-9-13 **73**.................. MartinDwyer 12 59
(H Candy) *chsd ldrs: rdn 3f out: wknd 2f out* **12/1**
5002 **9** *1¾* **Sir Kyffin's Folly**[20] 3918 3-9-9 **69**.................. RobertHavlin 8 51
(J A Geake) *a in rr* **10/1**[3]
0055 **10** *1¾* **Quinzey's Best (IRE)**[22] 3845 3-8-11 **57**.................. PaulDoe 4 35
(W J Knight) *t.k.h: in rr: hdwy on outside over 3f out: nvr gng pce to be competitive and wknd over 2f out* **12/1**
000 **11** *2* **Bobster**[46] 3061 3-8-6 **52**.................. JohnEgan 7 26
(B R Millman) *a towards rr* **66/1**
0-23 **12** *2¾* **Rowan Dancer**[22] 3845 3-8-10 **56**.................. PatCosgrave 3 24
(J R Boyle) *a towards rr* **16/1**

1m 55.7s (-0.60) **Going Correction** +0.125s/f (Good)
WFA 3 from 4yo+ 9lb **12** Ran SP% **121.5**
Speed ratings (Par 100): **107,105,103,100,99 98,98,96,95,93 91,89**
toteswinger: 1&2 £5.80, 1&3 £3.40, 2&3 £7.10 CSF £28.36 CT £180.72 TOTE £3.20: £1.90, £2.40, £2.70; EX 27.50.
Owner Snowdrop Stud Co Limited **Bred** Snowdrop Stud Co Limited **Trained** Newmarket, Suffolk

FOCUS
An ordinary fillies' handicap but the form looks sound rated round the winner and third.

4573 NEW ZEALAND H'CAP 1m 6f
8:35 (8:38) (Class 4) (0-80,79) 3-Y-O **£7,123** (£2,119; £1,059; £529) **Stalls** Centre

Form RPR
-021 **1** **Askar Tau (FR)**[27] 3671 3-8-12 **68**.................. MartinDwyer 2 81+
(M P Tregoning) *trckd ldr: chal 3f out: led over 2f out: pushed clr fnl f: easily* **5/4**[1]
-132 **2** *2¾* **Riverscape (IRE)**[89] 1805 3-9-6 **76**.................. JimCrowley 5 81
(Mrs A J Perrett) *in rr: hdwy over 3f out: styd on u.p fnl 2f: tk 2nd nr fin but no ch w wnr* **12/1**
4563 **3** *nk* **Rock Peak (IRE)**[38] 3327 3-9-1 **71**..................(p) RobertHavlin 1 76
(H Morrison) *chsd ldrs: drvn to ld over 3f out: hdd over 2f out: outpcd by wnr over 1f out: lost 2nd nr fin* **16/1**
-053 **4** *2* **Silk Hall (UAE)**[48] 2997 3-8-8 **67**.................. KirstyMilczarek(3) 4 69+
(D W P Arbuthnot) *in rr: hdwy on outside over 2f out: hrd drvn and styd on fnl f: nvr gng pce to rch ldng trio* **14/1**
1065 **5** *2* **It's A Date**[17] 4021 3-9-3 **76**.................. TravisBlock(3) 9 75
(A King) *chsd ldrs: rdn 3f out: one pce fnl 2f* **15/2**[3]
0001 **6** *shd* **Benhego**[16] 4067 3-8-7 **63**.................. SaleemGolam 7 62+
(S C Williams) *in rr: rdn 3f out: sme modest prog fnl 2f* **7/1**[2]
5-01 **7** *2¼* **Tyrrells Wood (IRE)**[24] 3781 3-9-9 **79**.................. TedDurcan 10 75
(T G Mills) *in tch in mid-div: rdn over 3f out and nt raise pce to chal: sn btn* **16/1**
005 **8** *½* **Dixie Dean (USA)**[30] 3573 3-8-6 **62** oh2 ow2..................(v[1]) RyanMoore 12 57
(Sir Michael Stoute) *a towards rr* **16/1**
-346 **9** *1* **Blue Citadel (USA)**[19] 3962 3-9-6 **76**.................. JimmyFortune 6 70
(Mrs A J Perrett) *sn led: hdd over 3f out: wknd 2f out* **16/1**
412 **10** *1¾* **Cape Colony**[19] 3970 3-9-9 **79**.................. PatDobbs 8 70
(R Hannon) *chsd ldrs: rdn 3f out: wknd 2f out* **15/2**[3]

3m 12.49s (5.89) **Going Correction** +0.125s/f (Good) **10** Ran SP% **118.4**
Speed ratings (Par 102): **88,86,86,85,83 83,82,82,81,80**
toteswinger: 1&2 £11.80, 1&3 £12.50, 2&3 £12.10. CSF £18.39 CT £173.66 TOTE £2.40: £1.30, £3.10, £2.90; EX 26.50 Place 6 £56.71, Place 5 £29.52.
Owner Nurlan Bizakov **Bred** Gestut Zoppenbroich & Aerial Bloodstock **Trained** Lambourn, Berks

FOCUS
Another steadily run race but the winner is progressive with the placed horses setting the standard.
T/Plt: £59.50 to a £1 stake. Pool: £52,732.76. 646.44 winning tickets. T/Qpdt: £19.80 to a £1 stake. Pool: £5,887.17. 219.00 winning tickets. ST

4574 - 4575a (Foreign Racing) - See Raceform Interactive

4543 GALWAY (R-H)
Thursday, July 31
OFFICIAL GOING: Good changing to yielding after race 5 (4.25)

4576a ARTHUR GUINNESS H'CAP 1m 100y
5:35 (5:35) (60-90,89) 4-Y-O+ **£8,637** (£2,012; £887; £512)

RPR
1 **Maundy Money**[2] 4514 5-9-9 85 5ex.................. CO'Donoghue 7 95
(David Marnane, Ire) *chsd ldrs: 5th 1/2-way: rdn in 2nd ent st: kpt on to chal fnl f and led cl home* **11/2**[2]
2 *½* **Billy Dane (IRE)**[2] 4514 4-9-3 79..................(p) MCHussey 1 88
(R A Fahey) *led: rdn and chal fnl f: hdd cl home* **11/1**
3 *nk* **Shayrazan (IRE)**[15] 4098 7-9-5 81..................(t) DMGrant 2 89
(James Leavy, Ire) *trckd ldrs: hdwy to 4th 2f out: rdn in 3rd ent st: no ex and kpt on fnl f* **20/1**
4 *1* **Varsity**[18] 4009 5-9-8 84..................(t) WJLee 9 90+
(C F Swan, Ire) *s.i.s: hdwy to 10th ent st: 8th over 1f out: kpt on wl fnl f* **9/1**

5 2 ½ **Lonesome Maverick (IRE)**[18] 4009 4-8-13 75 .... PShanahan 16 75
(Donal Kinsella, Ire) *chsd ldrs: 4th 1/2-way: rdn into 3rd 2f out: no ex in 4th over 1f out: kpt on same pce* **8/1**[3]

6 ½ **Absolute Image (IRE)**[34] 3467 6-9-13 89 .... (b) PJSmullen 18 88
(D K Weld, Ire) *chsd ldrs: 2nd 1/2-way: rdn and dropped to 5th ent st: kpt on same pce fr over 1f out* **5/1**[1]

7 nk **Dul Ar An Ol (IRE)**[123] 1105 7-9-6 82 .... WMLordan 14 80
(Peter Henley, Ire) *mid-div: rdn in 9th ent st: no ex in 6th over 1f out: kpt on same pce* **12/1**

8 ½ **Belle's Ridge**[10] 4263 4-9-0 76 .... FMBerry 10 73
(Timothy Doyle, Ire) *towards rr: sme late hdwy st* **9/1**

9 ½ **Inwood (IRE)**[50] 2962 5-9-4 80 .... (bt) KLatham 3 76
(Paul Magnier, Ire) *towards rr: sme late hdwy st* **25/1**

10 3 **Braddock (IRE)**[11] 4222 5-8-4 66 .... RPCleary 6 55
(S Donohoe, Ire) *mid-div best: rdn and no imp fr 2f out* **50/1**

11 1 **Mull On The Run (IRE)**[15] 4098 4-9-4 80 .... MJKinane 12 67
(Michael McElhone, Ire) *sn towards rr: rdn and no imp over 2f out: kpt on one pce* **8/1**[3]

12 hd **Grisham**[16] 4070 10-9-0 76 .... KJManning 17 62
(Michael John Phillips, Ire) *chsd ldrs: rdn in 8th 2f out: sn no ex and wknd* **12/1**

13 1 ½ **Black Cat Crossing (USA)**[34] 3467 4-8-8 73 .... SMGorey(3) 8 56
(Michael Joseph Fitzgerald, Ire) *towards rr for most: nvr a factor* **25/1**

14 nk **Fit The Cove (IRE)**[34] 3467 8-9-8 84 .... (t) CDHayes 11 66
(H Rogers, Ire) *chsd ldrs: 3rd 1/2-way: rdn in 4th over 2f out: sn sltly hmpd: 8th and no ex ent st: sn wknd* **25/1**

15 hd **Shela House**[41] 3209 4-9-1 84 .... DEMullins(7) 13 66
(J H Culloty, Ire) *chsd ldrs: 8th 3f out: rdn in 7th ent st: sn no ex and wknd* **12/1**

16 1 ¼ **Skyscape**[16] 4070 6-8-9 71 .... (p) WJSupple 4 50
(Thomas Cooper, Ire) *mid-div best: rdn and wknd over 2f out* **25/1**

17 ½ **What's Up Doc (IRE)**[21] 3303 7-8-7 76 .... (p) EJMcNamara(7) 5 54
(D T Hughes, Ire) *chsd ldrs: 4th 3f out: rdn in 6th over 2f out: sn no ex and wknd* **25/1**

18 5 ½ **Funatfuntasia**[26] 3748 4-9-3 79 .... DPMcDonough 15 44
(Ms Joanna Morgan, Ire) *mid-div: rdn and wknd 2f out* **14/1**

1m 48.45s (-1.75) **18 Ran SP% 138.3**
CSF £67.29 CT £1198.20 TOTE £5.20: £1.70, £3.20, £5.50, £2.00; DF 43.10.
Owner Push The Button Syndicate **Bred** Baydon House Stud **Trained** Bansha, Co Tipperary

NOTEBOOK
Billy Dane(IRE), runner-up over 7f here two days earlier, again found Maundy Money too good despite being 5lb better off.

4321 BATH (L-H)
Friday, August 1

OFFICIAL GOING: Good, changing to good to soft after race 1 (6.05)
The ground eased after over 7mm of rain before the meeting and more during the first two races.
Wind: Light half against Weather: Heavy showers 6.05 and 6.35

4579 GAYMER CIDER COMPANY MAIDEN AUCTION STKS — 5f 161y
6:05 (6:09) (Class 5) 2-Y-O — £3,885 (£1,156; £577; £288) Stalls Centre

Form — RPR

6223 1 **Timeteam (IRE)**[21] 3902 2-8-9 0 .... LPKeniry 2 76+
(S Kirk) *mde all: clr whn rdn briefly ins fnl f: easily* **11/4**[2]

605 2 5 **Robin The Till**[52] 2903 2-8-11 0 .... PatDobbs 9 62
(R Hannon) *hld up in mid-div: hdwy on outside over 2f out: wnt 2nd and edgd lft jst over 1f out: sn rdn: no ch w wnr* **6/1**[3]

3 ½ **Edgeworth (IRE)** 2-8-9 0 .... TQuinn 4 58
(B G Powell) *hld up in mid-div: hdwy over 2f out: wnt 2nd briefly and edgd lft over 1f out: one pce fnl f* **33/1**

4 ½ **Rio Gael (IRE)** 2-8-10 0 ow1 .... TGMcLaughlin 7 57
(M S Saunders) *s.i.s: in rr: rdn 3f out: pushed along and hdwy over 1f out: one pce fnl f* **40/1**

0 5 3 **My Dixie Darling (USA)**[18] 4020 2-8-4 0 .... RichardSmith 10 41
(R Hannon) *in rr: rdn and hdwy over 1f out: no imp fnl f* **28/1**

0 6 1 ¼ **Inthawain**[13] 4202 2-8-6 0 .... SamHitchcott 3 39
(M R Channon) *prom: rdn to chse wnr over 2f out tl wknd over 1f out* **6/1**[3]

7 1 ½ **Lana's Charm** 2-8-4 0 .... SimonWhitworth 8 32
(P J Makin) *s.i.s: sn chsng ldrs: wknd over 2f out* **33/1**

8 nk **Belated Silver (IRE)** 2-8-8 0 .... MCGeran(5) 5 40+
(Tom Dascombe) *chsd ldrs: pushed along over 2f out: rdn and wknd wl over 1f out* **5/4**[1]

42 9 14 **Rockinit (IRE)**[28] 3693 2-8-3 0 .... EmmettStack(3) 1 —
(M R Channon) *w ldr tl wknd over 2f out: eased whn no ch fnl f* **11/1**

1m 13.2s (2.00) **Going Correction** +0.20s/f (Good) **9 Ran SP% 119.8**
Speed ratings (Par 94): **94,87,86,86,82 80,78,77,59**
toteswinger: 1&2 £24.30, 1&3 £7.50, 2&3 £24.30. CSF £19.73 TOTE £4.20: £1.50, £1.60, £5.80; EX 24.50.
Owner R Gander **Bred** R N Auld **Trained** Upper Lambourn, Berks

FOCUS
This minor affair was run in a heavy shower with the ground easing all the time.

NOTEBOOK
Timeteam(IRE) was hardly winning out of turn but his rider thought he would be suited by a return to the bare minimum trip despite the manner of this victory. (op 15-8)
Robin The Till yet again showed a tendency to hang left-handed and proved no match for the winner. (op 7-1 tchd 8-1)
Edgeworth(IRE), who only cost 8,500 euros, did best of the four newcomers and presumably ran above expectations given his starting price.
Rio Gael(IRE), a half-brother to a couple of smart performers at around a mile, showed some promise after a tardy start. (tchd 33-1 and 50-1)
My Dixie Darling(USA) fared better than on her Windsor debut although in the end she was beaten by a similar distance. (op 33-1 tchd 16-1)
Belated Silver(IRE), half-brother to mile winner Totally Focussed, failed to live up to being a well-backed favourite on his debut and may have been unsuited by the fact that the rain had started to get into the ground. (op 15-8 tchd 5-2)

4580 BLACKTHORN (S) STKS — 5f 161y
6:35 (6:38) (Class 5) 3-Y-O+ — £3,238 (£963; £481; £240) Stalls Centre

Form — RPR

2353 1 **Night Prospector**[8] 4324 8-8-11 53 .... (p) KevinGhunowa(3) 10 58
(R A Harris) *a.p: pushed along over 2f out: hrd rdn to ld wl ins fnl f: r.o* **7/2**[2]

6053 2 1 **Penrice Castle**[8] 4336 3-8-3 55 ow1 .... PatrickHills(3) 3 51
(R Hannon) *t.k.h: w ldr: led over 3f out: rdn over 1f out: hdd wl ins fnl f* **6/1**

0004 3 nse **Pajada**[10] 4273 4-8-2 35 .... (v) SeanPalmer(7) 4 49
(M D I Usher) *sn chsng ldrs: rdn over 1f out: kpt on towards fin: jst failed to take 2nd* **14/1**

0004 4 2 ¼ **Indian Lady (IRE)**[8] 4324 5-8-9 40 .... (b) SamHitchcott 6 42
(Mrs A L M King) *w ldrs: ev ch 2f out: sn rdn: no ex ins fnl f* **14/1**

0356 5 2 ¼ **Midnite Blews (IRE)**[8] 4336 3-8-8 58 .... PNolan(7) 13 44
(A B Haynes) *s.s: in rr: hdwy on outside 1f out: nvr trbld ldrs* **14/1**

3-00 6 1 ½ **Zeeuw (IRE)**[121] 1143 4-9-0 60 .... OscarUrbina 11 34
(D J Coakley) *hld up towards rr: rdn and hdwy over 1f out: no further prog* **14/1**

6050 7 nk **Archilini**[7] 4370 3-8-7 59 .... (p) TravisBlock(3) 2 33
(M Sheppard) *t.k.h: led: hdd over 3f out: rdn and wknd over 2f out: eased fnl f* **9/2**[3]

015 8 1 ¼ **Game Lady**[25] 3779 4-9-0 53 .... RichardMullen 9 29
(I A Wood) *a bhd* **10/3**[1]

0-06 9 3 ½ **Iamagrey (IRE)**[21] 3906 3-8-5 52 .... SimonWhitworth 8 12
(C J Down) *bhd fnl 3f: eased fnl f* **33/1**

0000 10 3 ¼ **Peruvian Style (IRE)**[15] 4102 7-9-0 40 .... (v) LPKeniry 5 6
(J M Bradley) *hld up in tch: wknd over 2f out* **16/1**

0-00 11 15 **Talcen Gwyn (IRE)**[7] 4370 6-9-0 55 .... (v) StephenCarson 7 —
(M F Harris) *a in rr: eased fnl f* **8/1**

1m 13.52s (2.32) **Going Correction** +0.20s/f (Good)
WFA 3 from 4yo+ 4lb **11 Ran SP% 124.4**
Speed ratings (Par 103): **92,90,90,87,84 82,82,80,75,71 51**
toteswinger: 1&2 £5.00, 1&3 £32.70, 2&3 £8.00. CSF £26.66 TOTE £5.10: £2.00, £1.80, £5.80; EX 20.30.There was no bid for the winner
Owner C.C.C.4.C. **Bred** Miss S N Ralphs **Trained** Earlswood, Monmouths

FOCUS
A pretty competitive sprint seller with the winner and fourth close to previous course form and the runner-up to his recent best.

4581 GAYMER'S ORIGINAL MEDIAN AUCTION MAIDEN STKS — 1m 3f 144y
7:10 (7:13) (Class 5) 3-5-Y-O — £3,335 (£992; £495; £247) Stalls Low

Form — RPR

20 1 **Ragdollianna**[13] 4196 4-9-5 0 .... LPKeniry 4 62
(Norma Twomey) *hld up: hdwy over 5f out: led over 1f out: drvn out* **2/1**[1]

3532 2 nk **Brexca (IRE)**[9] 4303 3-8-13 74 .... (v) RichardMullen 6 67
(C G Cox) *led 2f: chsd ldr: ev ch wl over 1f out: rdn fnl f: r.o towards fin* **2/1**[1]

0 3 ¾ **Street Crime**[22] 3894 3-8-13 0 .... PatDobbs 2 65
(A M Balding) *hld up: carried hd high and hdwy over 1f out: rdn and nt qckn ins fnl f* **9/1**[3]

60 4 1 ½ **Major Promise**[11] 4255 3-8-13 0 .... TQuinn 1 63
(G G Margarson) *led after 2f: rdn and hdd over 1f out: no ex ins fnl f* **18/1**

5 5 8 **Chioroscuro**[33] 3521 3-8-13 0 .... SteveDrowne 7 50
(J L Dunlop) *hld up: hung lft over 2f out: reminder wl over 1f out: sn btn: eased whn no ch ins fnl f* **9/4**[2]

2m 38.66s (8.06) **Going Correction** +0.275s/f (Good)
WFA 3 from 4yo 11lb **5 Ran SP% 112.7**
Speed ratings (Par 103): **84,83,83,82,76**
toteswinger: 1&2 £4.80 CSF £6.55 TOTE £2.90: £1.60, £1.60; EX 4.80.
Owner D M & Mrs M A Newland **Bred** Mrs M Newland **Trained** Rockley, Wilts

FOCUS
This slowly-run moderate maiden went to a bumper winner. Those in the frame behind the winner are the best guides to the level.

4582 GAYMER'S ORCHARD RESERVE H'CAP — 1m 2f 46y
7:40 (7:40) (Class 4) (0-80,80) 3-Y-O — £6,476 (£1,927; £963; £481) Stalls Low

Form — RPR

0431 1 **Fair Gale**[8] 4344 3-9-5 78 6ex .... LPKeniry 5 85
(S Kirk) *led: hdd wl over 2f out: sn led again: hrd rdn and wnt clr ins fnl f: r.o wl* **4/1**

5114 2 3 ¼ **Casilda (IRE)**[29] 3633 3-9-7 80 .... PaulDoe 1 80
(W J Knight) *chsd wnr tl over 6f out: rdn and sltly outpcd over 2f out: kpt on u.p to take 2nd wl ins fnl f: no ch w wnr* **5/2**[2]

2243 3 1 ½ **Barricado (FR)**[15] 4104 3-9-2 75 .... (v[1]) SteveDrowne 7 72
(R Charlton) *prom: wnt 2nd over 6f out: led briefly wl over 2f out: rdn and hung lft 1f out: lost 2nd wl ins fnl f* **7/4**[1]

-430 4 ½ **Clovis**[12] 3970 3-8-9 71 .... (b) PJMcDonald(3) 3 67
(N P Mulholland) *s.i.s: hld up in last: hdwy over 2f out: rdn over 1f out: wknd ins fnl f* **14/1**

0252 5 4 ½ **Red Icon**[6] 4427 3-9-0 73 .... (b[1]) JamesDoyle 6 60
(R M Beckett) *hld up: tk clsr order and wnt 3rd over 4f out: rdn and wknd over 1f out* **7/2**[3]

2m 19.36s (8.36) **Going Correction** +0.275s/f (Good) **5 Ran SP% 113.8**
Speed ratings (Par 102): **77,74,73,72,69**
toteswinger: 1&2 £14.70 CSF £14.80 TOTE £3.90: £1.60, £2.30; EX 14.70.
Owner Norman Ormiston **Bred** Hesmonds Stud Ltd **Trained** Upper Lambourn, Berks

FOCUS
A steadily-run little handicap but modest for the grade.

4583 GAYMER'S PEAR FILLIES' H'CAP — 1m 5y
8:15 (8:15) (Class 4) (0-80,77) 3-Y-O+ £6,308 (£1,888; £944; £472; £235) Stalls Low

Form — RPR

3054 1 **Cape Velvet (IRE)**[34] 3507 4-9-3 68 .... JamesDoyle 3 79
(H J L Dunlop) *mde all: rdn over 1f out: r.o wl: eased cl home* **5/1**[3]

3002 2 2 ½ **Bikini**[21] 3906 3-9-0 72 .... FergusSweeney 5 76
(H Candy) *w wnr: rdn over 1f out: one pce fnl f* **5/2**[1]

3-53 3 1 ½ **Shindy (FR)**[21] 3918 3-8-12 70 .... OscarUrbina 1 70
(J A R Toller) *hld up: hdwy and wnt 3rd 2f out: sn rdn: one pce fnl f* **7/1**

1023 4 1 **Mekong Melody (IRE)**[18] 4022 3-9-4 76 .... RichardMullen 4 74
(C G Cox) *hld up in rr: pushed along and outpcd 3f out: rdn over 1f out: kpt on same pce fnl f* **3/1**[2]

11 5 ½ **Flying Valentino**[32] 3552 4-9-9 77 .... PJMcDonald(3) 7 75
(G A Swinbank) *hld up in tch: rdn over 2f out: btn over 1f out* **5/2**[1]

1m 42.49s (1.69) **Going Correction** +0.275s/f (Good)
WFA 3 from 4yo 7lb **5 Ran SP% 111.3**
Speed ratings (Par 102): **102,99,98,97,96**
toteswinger: 1&2 £84.80 CSF £17.89 TOTE £7.80: £2.50, £1.60; EX 23.50.
Owner William Armitage **Bred** C Gavin **Trained** Lambourn, Berks

FOCUS
A competitive-looking little handicap with the winner back to her best and the runner-up to her latest mark.

4584 OLDE ENGLISH H'CAP 5f 11y
8:45 (8:49) (Class 5) (0-75,80) 3-Y-O **£4,209** (£1,252; £625; £312) **Stalls** Centre

Form RPR
61 **1** **Muftarres (IRE)**[41] 3282 3-9-5 **72**................................ MartinDwyer 8 79+
(Sir Michael Stoute) *bhd: hdwy over 2f out: rdn to ld wl ins fnl f: r.o* **11/8**[1]
0134 **2** *1* **Pennyspider (IRE)**[8] 4325 3-8-9 **62**................................ TGMcLaughlin 6 66
(M S Saunders) *led: rdn over 1f out: hdd wl ins fnl f: nt qckn* **15/2**
4640 **3** *1* **Apple Pie Order (IRE)**[20] 3960 3-8-10 **63**.................... SteveDrowne 1 63
(R J Hodges) *bhd: rdn and hdwy over 1f out: kpt on same pce ins fnl f* **11/2**[3]
4542 **4** *4 1/2* **Barraland**[8] 4325 3-9-3 **70**................................ EdwardCreighton 4 54
(M R Channon) *w ldr: rdn over 1f out: wknd ins fnl f* **10/3**[2]
-060 **5** *nk* **Sandy Par**[80] 2068 3-8-5 **58** oh1 ow3................................(p) PaulDoe 3 41
(J M Bradley) *prom: wnt 2nd briefly over 2f out: rdn and wknd over 1f out* **33/1**
0-00 **6** *6* **Man Appeal**[21] 3916 3-7-10 **56** oh10 ow1................................ KMay(7) 2 17
(B J Meehan) *prom tl wknd over 2f out* **33/1**

63.34 secs (0.84) **Going Correction** +0.20s/f (Good) **6 Ran SP% 98.2**
Speed ratings (Par 100): **101,99,97,90,90 80**
toteswinger: 1&2 £2.00, 1&3 £3.60, 2&3 £13.10. CSF £8.97 CT £23.12 TOTE £1.80: £1.50, £1.60; EX 6.20 Place 6 £ 78.04, Place 6 £ 31.63.
Owner Hamdan Al Maktoum **Bred** Shadwell Estate Company Limited **Trained** Newmarket, Suffolk

FOCUS
An ordinary sprint handicap in which the winner looks well treated and the placed horses are rated to form.
Barraland Official explanation: jockey said gelding was unsuited by the good to soft ground
T/Plt: £192.40 to a £1 stake. Pool: £44,887.05. 170.27 winning tickets. T/Qpdt: £18.60 to a £1 stake. Pool: £3,712.00. 147.60 winning tickets. KH

4549 GOODWOOD (R-H)
Friday, August 1

OFFICIAL GOING: Good to firm (9.1)
Wind: fresh half against Weather: overcast with brighter spells, breezy

4585 COUTTS GLORIOUS STKS (GROUP 3) 1m 4f
2:15 (2:15) (Class 1) 4-Y-0+
£39,739 (£15,064; £7,539; £3,759; £1,883; £945) **Stalls** Low

Form RPR
-210 **1** **Sixties Icon**[44] 3121 5-9-0 114................................ JMurtagh 7 116
(J Noseda) *lw: hld up in tch: hdwy over 4f out: rdn to ld and edgd rt over 1f out: styd on wl fnl f* **10/3**[1]
4-30 **2** *1* **Galactic Star**[61] 2653 5-9-0 112................................ RyanMoore 1 114+
(Sir Michael Stoute) *hld up in last trio: rdn and effrt over 2f out: plld out 2f out: edgd rt u.p: r.o wl to go 2nd nr fin: nvr gng to rch wnr* **7/2**[2]
5414 **3** *nk* **Lion Sands**[22] 3878 4-9-0 114................................ RichardHughes 5 114
(L M Cumani) *chsd ldrs: hdwy to chse ldng pair over 5f out: ev ch 3f out: rdn to ld over 2f out: hdd over 1f out: kpt on same pce fnl f* **15/2**
-100 **4** *nse* **Dansant**[64] 2543 4-9-0 104................................ EddieAhern 9 113+
(G A Butler) *t.k.h: hld up in midfield: hdwy and hanging rt fr wl over 1f out: n.m.r over 1f out: kpt on fnl f: nt pce to threaten wnr* **16/1**
1212 **5** *shd* **Tranquil Tiger**[34] 3497 4-9-0 115................................(b[1]) TedDurcan 11 113
(H R A Cecil) *lw: hld up in last trio: hdwy 3f out: rdn and edgd rt over 1f out: disp 2nd ins fnl f: no ex last 100yds* **7/2**[2]
-240 **6** *hd* **Dickens (GER)**[33] 3540 5-9-0 0................................ ASuborics 2 113+
(H Blume, Germany) *stdd s: hld up in last: stl last and bmpd 3f out: grad edgd out rt fr 2f out: r.o wl fnl f: nt rch ldrs* **50/1**
5566 **7** *1 1/2* **Stotsfold**[27] 3741 5-9-3 114................................ AlanMunro 8 114
(W R Swinburn) *lw: t.k.h: hld up in rr: effrt towards inner 3f out: kpt on but nvr pce to rch ldrs* **6/1**[3]
254- **8** *1 3/4* **Foxhaven**[277] 6538 6-9-0 104................................ JimCrowley 4 108
(P R Chamings) *chsd ldrs: wnt 2nd over 6f out: led narrowly 3f out: rdn and hdd over 2f out: wkng whn short of room ent fnl f* **50/1**
6-00 **9** *15* **Shahin (USA)**[41] 3246 5-9-0 104................................(b[1]) RHills 3 84
(M P Tregoning) *pushed up to ld after 1f: rdn and hdd 3f out: btn whn short of room and snatched up over 1f out: virtually p.u after* **33/1**
0300 **10** *3/4* **Diamond Quest (SAF)**[43] 3154 7-9-0 110................................ MartinDwyer 10 83
(A M Balding) *t.k.h: hld up in midfield: hdwy to chse ldrs 7f out: rdn over 3f out: wknd over 2f out: eased fnl f* **25/1**
330R **11** *1* **Carte Diamond (USA)**[27] 3721 7-9-0 104................................ J-PGuillambert 13 81
(B Ellison) *sn pushed up to ld for 1f: chsd ldrs after tl lost pl 5f out: bhd last 2f* **40/1**
41-6 **12** *2 1/2* **Crime Scene (IRE)**[148] 816 5-9-3 112................................ LDettori 6 80
(Saeed Bin Suroor) *chsd ldr after 1f tl over 6f out: wknd over 2f out: eased fnl f: t.o* **12/1**

2m 37.07s (-1.33) **Going Correction** +0.075s/f (Good) **12 Ran SP% 120.3**
Speed ratings (Par 113): **107,106,106,106,106 105,104,103,93,93 92,90**
toteswinger: 1&2 £2.90, 1&3 £5.90, 2&3 £6.00. CSF £14.76 TOTE £3.60: £1.80, £1.90, £2.30; EX 12.50 Trifecta £81.40 Pool: £1573.16 - 14.29 winning units..
Owner Mrs Susan Roy **Bred** Lordship Stud **Trained** Newmarket, Suffolk
■ This race has been promoted from Listed status.

FOCUS
Several runners might have defected because of not having the ease in the ground they wanted, but most stood their ground. There was not a strong gallop for the type of race, which may explain why there was something of a bunched finish. The form still looks just up to Group 3 level, with the placed horses having plenty of Listed wins under their belt

NOTEBOOK
Sixties Icon, whose participation was in doubt owing to the quickish ground, was a game winner, finding plenty for Murtagh under pressure, after edging to his right about a furlong from home. Despite a few problems, which included him having a wind operation, he remains a class act, who is competitive over a range of trips. Three from three at Goodwood after this victory, connections are eyeing the Breeders' Cup Turf for him as an end-of-season target. Official explanation: trainer's rep said, regarding apparent improvement in form, that their horses were under the weather at the time of the Ascot race (op 3-1 tchd 7-2 in places)
Galactic Star, who got a bit worked up in the stalls as Dickens took time to load alongside him, needed some pushing to really get going when pulled to the outside in the last two furlongs, but he was closing on the winner inside the final stages. He looks capable of winning at this level. (tchd 4-1)
Lion Sands had every chance and briefly got to the lead before the winner overpowered him. His rating must make him hard to place, so he will be forced to ply his trade at this sort of level. (op 8-1)
Dansant looked slightly unlucky not to go a bit closer, as he was short of room when the tempo increased, after coming up the inside rail. He hung to the right under pressure, making him difficult to steer, but still went close to getting up for second. A triple Listed winner on the AW, he has proved very versatile with regards to trip and ought to progress from his run, his first start since May. Official explanation: jockey said colt hung right-handed (op 25-1)
Tranquil Tiger, with blinkers on for the first time, travelled really well up the home straight but only plugged on at the one pace when placed under pressure. He looks a tricky ride and is not one to trust. (op 9-2 tchd 5-1 in a place)
Dickens(GER) was heavily restrained leaving the stalls after taking time to load, and sat towards the rear (which is his usual style of racing), off a slow-looking early pace. Eventually, after finding his way blocked down the inside, he was switched wide to make a challenge and kept on well when the race was all but over. Under a jockey who knew the course, he would have been challenging for at least third place, but it remains to be seen whether he comes back to Great Britain.
Stotsfold, who now has a BHA mark10lb higher than when third is this race last year, was not beaten far but was given a bit too much to do off the modest early gallop. He is better than he showed in this. (tchd 5-1)
Foxhaven ◆, without the visor he now usually wears, ran really well on his seasonal debut, only fading inside the final two furlongs after holding every chance. A Goodwood specialist, he is not quite up to this level, but can win again if building positively on this.
Shahin(USA), in first-time blinkers, led for much of the race but looked to be running around while weakening, and was then badly squeezed up against the inside rail. (tchd 40-1)
Crime Scene(IRE), having his first start since March, ran very poorly and will have everything to prove when seen again. (tchd 11-1)

4586 ROLF GROUP STEWARDS' SPRINT STKS (H'CAP) 6f
2:50 (2:53) (Class 2) 3-Y-0+
£18,693 (£5,598; £2,799; £1,401; £699; £351) **Stalls** Low

Form RPR
0-60 **1** **Pearly Wey**[13] 4201 5-9-10 **94**................................ PhilipRobinson 13 104
(C G Cox) *hld up in midfield: hdwy 1/2-way: rdn over 1f out: styd on wl to ld last stride* **10/1**
4562 **2** *nse* **Baby Strange**[14] 4145 4-9-9 **93**................................ MartinDwyer 21 103
(D Shaw) *swtg: in tch in midfield: rdn and hdwy 1/2-way: pressed ldrs ent fnl f: led last 100yds: hdd last stride* **8/1**[2]
2400 **3** *1* **Joseph Henry**[34] 3489 6-9-4 **88**................................ JimmyQuinn 10 95
(D Nicholls) *chsd ldrs: rdn 2f out: pressed ldrs ent fnl f: kpt on same pce last 100yds* **14/1**
-135 **4** *hd* **Osiris Way**[13] 4201 6-9-1 **85**................................ JimCrowley 20 91
(P R Chamings) *racd keenly: chsd ldr: rdn 2f out: led ent fnl f: hdd last 100yds: no ex* **11/1**
1000 **5** *nk* **Ajigolo**[6] 4437 5-9-9 **93**................................ TPO'Shea 19 98
(M R Channon) *bhd: rdn wl over 1f out: r.o strly fnl f: nt rch ldrs* **33/1**
1311 **6** *nk* **Harrison George (IRE)**[21] 3928 3-8-12 **86** 3ex................................ PaulHanagan 16 89
(R A Fahey) *lw: in tch in midfield: rdn 1/2-way: edging rt over 1f out: kpt on u.p: nt pce to threaten ldrs* **8/1**[2]
0036 **7** *1/2* **Gift Horse**[27] 3728 8-9-1 **85**................................(v) RichardHughes 18 87
(D Nicholls) *stdd s: hld up towards rr: hdwy 2f out: edgd lft u.p fnl f: kpt on but nvr rchd ldrs* **12/1**
0425 **8** *3/4* **Northern Dare (IRE)**[22] 3881 4-9-3 **87**................................ FrancisNorton 5 87
(D Nicholls) *towards rr: rdn 1/2-way: hdwy u.p over 1f out: plugged but nvr trbld ldrs* **10/1**
-500 **9** *1* **Dream Theme**[6] 4405 5-9-6 **90**................................ PaulDoe 2 87
(D Nicholls) *t.k.h: hld up in rr: rdn and effrt 2f out: sn hung rt: never trbld ldrs* **20/1**
1205 **10** *1/2* **Valery Borzov (IRE)**[14] 4145 4-9-10 **94**................................(v) AdrianTNicholls 12 89
(D Nicholls) *led: rdn over 1f out: hung rt and hdd ent fnl f: wknd* **9/1**[3]
0-23 **11** *2* **Express Wish**[6] 4437 4-9-7 **91**................................(v[1]) LDettori 7 80
(J Noseda) *lw: chsd ldrs: hung rt and struggling fr 2f out* **4/1**[1]
1206 **12** *3/4* **Obe Gold**[42] 3228 6-9-7 **91**................................(v) AlanMunro 8 77
(D Nicholls) *towards rr: rdn 1/2-way: keeping on same pce and wl hld whn hmpd ins fnl f* **20/1**
6442 **13** *1 3/4* **Swinbrook (USA)**[4] 4476 7-8-4 **74**................................(v) RoystonFfrench 3 55
(R A Fahey) *nvr bttr than midfield: rdn 2f out: sn wknd* **33/1**
2340 **14** *hd* **Sand Cat**[100] 1566 5-8-8 **78**................................(b) RyanMoore 4 58
(G L Moore) *a bhd: nvr a factor* **33/1**
0660 **15** *3 1/2* **Golden Dixie (USA)**[5] 4445 9-9-4 **88**................................ SteveDrowne 14 57
(R A Harris) *a towards rr: rdn and struggling fr 1/2-way* **25/1**
-605 **16** *3 1/2* **Flying Goose (IRE)**[27] 3728 4-8-5 **78**................................(b[1]) KevinGhunowa(3) 6 36
(R A Harris) *s.i.s: a bhd* **50/1**
4601 **17** *3* **Dubai Princess (IRE)**[41] 3273 3-9-9 **97**................................ ShaneKelly 11 44
(J A Osborne) *racd in midfield: rdn and struggling 1/2-way: wl btn and hung rt over 1f out* **16/1**
2201 **18** *4* **Rocker**[9] 4313 4-7-7 **68** 3ex oh2................................(b) NataliaGemelova(5) 17 3
(G L Moore) *stmbld s: racd keenly and sn w ldrs: wknd rapidly 1/2-way* **25/1**
3030 **U** **Pusey Street Lady**[20] 3973 4-9-7 **91**................................ TedDurcan 15 —
(J Gallagher) *rrd and uns rdr as stalls opened* **25/1**

1m 11.2s (-1.00) **Going Correction** +0.075s/f (Good)
WFA 3 from 4yo+ 4lb **19 Ran SP% 130.8**
Speed ratings (Par 109): **109,108,107,107,106 106,105,104,103,102 100,99,96,96,91 87,83,77,—**
toteswinger: 1&2 £25.30, 1&3 £24.60, 2&3 £25.70. CSF £81.35 CT £1186.40 TOTE £12.90: £3.30, £2.20, £3.80, £4.00; EX 114.20 Trifecta £680.40 Pool: £1839.04 - 2.00 winning units.
Owner Dennis Shaw **Bred** Leydens Farm Stud **Trained** Lambourn, Berks

FOCUS
There were two groups to begin with, but they gradually merged and the action was all concentrated towards the middle of the track. Nothing raced anywhere near either rail, but it could be significant that the first seven all raced from double-figure stalls. There was remarkably little incident for a race of this nature. This was a slight personal best from the winner, while the runner-up ran to his Hamilton form.

NOTEBOOK
Pearly Wey, the winner of this race last season, came with a persistent challenge down the centre of the course, which took him to the front virtually on the line. He was 4lb higher this time, but came here fresher than most and had his ideal ground. He will now be aimed at the Portland, in which he was third last year, and then the Ayr Gold Cup, in which he beat only one (that effort can be excused on account of the soft ground that day). (op 12-1)
Baby Strange came into the race well treated, as he is due to be raised 4lb for his excellent Hamilton second to Stewards' Cup sixth Knot In Wood. He did very little wrong and only got mugged on the line, so deserves to land a decent prize. He too heads for Doncaster and Ayr, and he might not run again before the Portland. (op 9-1 tchd 10-1 in places)
Joseph Henry, who was second in this 12 months ago and met Pearly Wey on 1lb better terms, ran to a very similar level, showing a lot of speed up the middle of the track. It was a good effort but he has not won since July 2006. (op 16-1)
Osiris Way, who has been in good form recently and was a few places in front of Pearly Way last time at Newmarket over 5f, had every chance but faded a little near the finish. Not over-raced for his age, he should have more to come. (op 12-1)

Ajigolo appeared to finish best of all but he had a bit too much to do from off the pace. The Handicapper is keeping him on a high-enough mark after his win back in May.
Harrison George(IRE) ◆, who beat his elders on his last two starts, stayed on really well and was gaining on the winner inside the final furlong. He is definitely worth another chance, as he had to come round a horse when making his challenge close to home. (tchd 17-2 and 9-1 in a place)
Gift Horse, a former Stewards' Cup winner, travelled really strongly before keeping on well at the finish, despite edging left under pressure. He has not won a race of any description since his big success at this course in 2005, but did signal a return to his best with this effort. (op 11-1)
Northern Dare(IRE) did best of those drawn in single figures. Second in last year's Ayr Silver Cup, one would imagine he will be heading back for another crack at that race.
Dream Theme has taken a while to come down the weights after leaving Barry Hills, but this effort suggests he is not far away from winning for new connections. (op 25-1)
Valery Borzov(IRE) showed plenty of good pace down the middle before not quite getting home. Official explanation: jockey said gelding hung right-handed (tchd 10-1 in a place)
Express Wish, wearing a first-time visor, weakened quickly after showing speed towards the stands' side, and was inclined to hang right. (op 6-1)
Golden Dixie(USA) Official explanation: jockey said gelding lost a front shoe
Dubai Princess(IRE) Official explanation: jockey said filly lost its action
Rocker was very keen towards the lead in the early stages, so failed to get home.
Pusey Street Lady reared in the stalls when they opened and then, after getting up, left her jockey standing in them.

4587 TOTESPORT MILE (HERITAGE H'CAP) (FORMERLY KNOWN AS THE GOLDEN MILE) 1m

3:30 (3:30) (Class 2) 3-Y-0+

£93,465 (£27,990; £13,995; £7,005; £3,495; £1,755) **Stalls** High

Form RPR

-015 **1** **Fifteen Love (USA)**[27] 3740 3-8-12 **100**....................(p) SteveDrowne 20 111
(R Charlton) *trckd ldrs: rdn ent 2f out: swtchd lft over 1f out: burst through to ld wl ins fnl f: hld on wl nr fin* **5/1**[2]

1223 **2** *hd* **Masaalek**[27] 3740 3-8-12 **100**.............................. RHills 19 110
(M P Tregoning) *dwlt: hld up in tch on inner: edgd out lft jst over 2f out: chsd ldrs ent fnl f: pressed wnr wl ins fnl f: hld nr fin* **4/1**[1]

0043 **3** *1* **Dubai's Touch**[8] 4330 4-9-5 **100**.................. RoystonFfrench 18 109
(M Johnston) *swtg: t.k.h: in tch: rdn 3f out: led jst over 1f out: hdd wl ins fnl f: hld whn n.m.r nr fin* **8/1**[3]

1541 **4** *1 ¾* **Cape Hawk (IRE)**[21] 3899 4-8-9 **90** 3ex.................. RichardHughes 17 95
(R Hannon) *led: rdn 3f out: hdd jst over 1f out: no ex u.p last 100yds* **8/1**[3]

106 **5** *nk* **Huzzah (IRE)**[21] 3919 3-8-11 **99**.................... MichaelHills 16 102
(B W Hills) *lw: chsd ldr: rdn and ev ch fr 3f out tl no ex last 100yds* **12/1**

5404 **6** *nk* **Vitznau (IRE)**[29] 3635 4-9-5 **100**.................. JimmyFortune 9 104+
(R Hannon) *hld up wl bhd: hdwy on rail over 2f out: swtchd lft and rt over 1f out: swtchd lft again ent fnl f: r.o but nvr able to chal* **25/1**

5000 **7** *1* **Illustrious Blue**[3] 4504 5-9-10 **105**..................(v) PaulDoe 14 106+
(W J Knight) *s.i.s: bhd: effrt u.p over 2f out: hdwy on inner wl over 1f out: no imp ins fnl f* **18/1**

0040 **8** *¾* **Fishforcompliments**[20] 3974 4-9-0 **95**.................. JimmyQuinn 13 95
(R A Fahey) *in tch: chsd ldrs over 3f out: rdn wl over 2f out: unable qck over 1f out* **25/1**

0466 **9** *¾* **Flipando (IRE)**[6] 4417 7-8-12 **93**.................. FrancisNorton 11 94+
(T D Barron) *hld up wl bhd: hdwy towards inner 2f out: keeping on whn nt clr run ins fnl f: nvr able to chal* **16/1**

2613 **10** *¾* **Regal Parade**[21] 3921 4-9-2 **97**.................. AdrianTNicholls 8 93
(D Nicholls) *stdd after s: hld up towrds rr: hdwy into midfield: 1/2-way: rdn over 2f out: keeping on same pce whn edgd rt ins fnl f* **16/1**

1200 **11** *1* **Extraterrestrial**[20] 3974 4-8-12 **93**..................(p) PaulHanagan 7 87
(R A Fahey) *lw: hld up bhd: rdn 3f out: kpt on fnl f: nvr trbld ldrs* **20/1**

01-1 **12** *1* **Military Cross**[37] 3382 5-9-6 **101**.................. SebSanders 5 93
(L M Cumani) *lw: s.i.s: swtchd rt after s: hdwy into midfield after 2f: rdn over 3f out: sn struggling and btn* **12/1**

6300 **13** *2 ½* **Royal Power (IRE)**[21] 3921 5-9-3 **98**.................. TPO'Shea 1 84
(D Nicholls) *stdd and dropped in after s: nvr trbld ldrs* **33/1**

4644 **14** *1 ¼* **Ballinteni**[5] 4443 6-8-12 **93**.................. C-PLemaire 10 76
(Miss Gay Kelleway) *lw: chsd ldrs early: steadily lost pl: towards rr and rdn over 2f out: no prog* **25/1**

1465 **15** *1 ¼* **Raptor (GER)**[20] 3982 5-9-5 **100**.................. FergusSweeney 4 80
(K R Burke) *lw: t.k.h: hld up in tch: hdwy to dispute ld wl over 3f out: wknd u.p ent fnl 2f* **66/1**

1202 **16** *2 ¾* **Dhaular Dhar (IRE)**[6] 4405 6-9-4 **99**.................. DanielTudhope 3 73
(J S Goldie) *lw: t.k.h: hld up in midfield on outer: rdn wl over 2f out: no rspnse and sn wl btn* **16/1**

-500 **17** *nk* **Pride Of Nation (IRE)**[44] 3122 6-9-9 **104**..................(t) EddieAhern 12 77
(J W Hills) *lw: in tch in midfield: rdn 3f out: wl btn whn hung rt wl over 1f out* **50/1**

1200 **18** *2 ¾* **Lang Shining (IRE)**[27] 3740 4-9-5 **100**.................. RyanMoore 6 67
(Sir Michael Stoute) *hld up in rr: rdn and no rspnse wl over 2f out* **12/1**

1m 38.15s (-1.75) **Going Correction** +0.075s/f (Good)
WFA 3 from 4yo+ 7lb **18** Ran SP% **127.6**
Speed ratings (Par 109): **111,110,109,108,107 107,106,105,104,104 103,102,99,98,97 94,94,91**
toteswinger: 1&2 £3.10, 1&3 £8.10, 2&3 £5.70. CSF £24.02 CT £145.49 TOTE £6.00: £1.70, £1.80, £2.00, £1.90; EX 14.40 Trifecta £55.90 Pool: £3956.69 - 52.29 winning units..
Owner K Abdulla **Bred** Juddmonte Farms Inc **Trained** Beckhampton, Wilts
■ The first three-year-old winner since Fly To The Stars in 1997, and he proved Group class.

FOCUS
A strong handicap run at a solid pace, which was again decided by the draw, as the first five home were from the five highest stalls. The form looks reliable (very few encountered much trouble in running) and a big positive is that the two that fought out the finish were progressive three-year-olds.

NOTEBOOK
Fifteen Love(USA), close behind Masaalek and Dubai's Touch when a good fifth at Sandown since his good win in the Britannia Handicap at Royal Ascot, added another major handicap prize. Settled just behind the leaders, he was produced with his effort inside the final furlong to win with something to spare. One would imagine that he will be stepped up to Group level next. (op 11-2 tchd 6-1 in places)
Masaalek looked all set to collect as Richard Hills went to send him past Dubai's Touch inside the final stages, but his rider may not have realised Fifteen Love was sneaking past the eventual third on the inside, and Masaalek was unable to cope with the strong finish of the Roger Charlton-trained colt. He has developed a good rivalry with the winner and, although held this time, one could easily see them clashing again in the near future, probably at a higher level than this. (op 5-1)
Dubai's Touch ◆, who won a Listed race at this meeting last year, goes really well on this track and added another good performance at the Sussex course. He showed admirable battling qualities, as after leading and being headed, he fought back to hold every chance. With confidence raised, he is one to be interested in next time.
Cape Hawk(IRE) has been in fine heart this season and ran right up to his best after leading for much of the race. He only just held on to fourth as his exertions in a soundly-run contest started to tell, but he should be capable of staying competitive in these sorts of races for a while. (tchd 9-1 in a place)
Huzzah(IRE) did very little wrong but did not quite get home. Tough though he is, one cannot help but think that the Handicapper has his measure after a successful early season. (op 16-1)
Vitznau(IRE) never really threatened to win and is on a stiff enough mark, but he did best of those drawn in single figures despite having to weave his way through the traffic.
Illustrious Blue, who ran moderately here on Tuesday, stayed on steadily without having the pace to challenge at this shorter trip. (op 20-1)
Fishforcompliments sat close to the pace on the outside of the pack but could not really quicken when asked to. It was not a bad effort and, if he builds on it, he can get his head in front again soon.
Flipando(IRE), who travelled well in an unpromising position, was short of room between rivals in the final furlong before staying on again. Although he has won off an official mark of 96, the handicapper needs to ease him a few pounds before he has an obvious winning chance in such competitive races. Official explanation: jockey said gelding was denied a clear run (op 14-1)
Military Cross had no chance of getting involved from such a poor draw, and this effort can be safely ignored.
Dhaular Dhar(IRE) did not have the run of the race from his low draw, but is probably most effective at seven furlongs. (tchd 14-1)
Lang Shining(IRE), who overshot the start and then looked most mulish when asked to rejoin the field, never got competitive from his low draw. He came under pressure quite early, and may not have handled the course. (tchd 11-1)

4588 SIR TRISTRAM RICKETTS MEMORIAL RICHMOND STKS (GROUP 2) (C&G) 6f

4:05 (4:05) (Class 1) 2-Y-0

£48,254 (£18,292; £9,154; £4,564; £2,286; £1,147) **Stalls** Low

Form RPR

1233 **1** **Prolific (IRE)**[22] 3876 2-9-0 0.................. RichardHughes 11 104
(R Hannon) *lw: w ldrs: rdn and ev ch over 1f out: led jst ins fnl f: hld on gamely last 50yds* **5/1**[2]

61 **2** *nk* **Gallagher**[30] 3603 2-9-0 0.................. JimmyFortune 7 103
(B J Meehan) *lw: hld up wl in tch: rdn jst over 1f out: checked briefly whn looking for a run ent fnl f: chal between horses ins fnl f: sn ev ch: wnt 2nd but hld by wnr nr fin* **7/2**[1]

4211 **3** *hd* **Reve De Soleil (FR)**[18] 4039 2-9-0 0.................. MartinDwyer 12 103
(E J O'Neill) *t.k.h: hld up in tch in midfield: hdwy jst over 2f out: ev ch jst ins fnl f: unable qck nr fin* **33/1**

6211 **4** *1* **Saxford**[29] 3634 2-9-0 0.................. ShaneKelly 6 100
(Mrs L Stubbs) *led: rdn and hung rt over 1f out: hdd jst ins fnl f: one pce* **8/1**

261 **5** *1* **Total Gallery (IRE)**[27] 3707 2-9-0 0.................. TedDurcan 4 97
(J S Moore) *lw: t.k.h: hld up in tch: hdwy jst over 2f out: rdn and edgd rt jst over 1f out: kpt on same pce* **6/1**[3]

21 **6** *nk* **Rileyskeepingfaith**[13] 4199 2-9-0 0.................. EdwardCreighton 10 96
(M R Channon) *hld up in midfield: swtchd rt and effrt over 1f out: no imp u.p fnl f* **15/2**

1 **7** *4 ½* **Waffle (IRE)**[97] 1616 2-9-0 0.................. JMurtagh 1 82
(J Noseda) *str: t.k.h: hld up in tch: rdn 2f out: wknd over 1f out* **8/1**

3011 **8** *hd* **Khor Dubai (IRE)**[13] 4185 2-9-0 0.................. LDettori 9 82
(Saeed Bin Suroor) *lw: stdd after s: hld up in tch in rr: swtchd lft and rdn wl over 1f out: sn struggling: wl hld fnl f* **6/1**[3]

152 **9** *1 ½* **Saucy Brown (IRE)**[29] 3634 2-9-0 0.................. RyanMoore 8 77
(R Hannon) *w ldr: rdn jst over 2f out: wknd over 1f out* **11/1**

1210 **10** *3 ¼* **Smokey Storm**[45] 3103 2-9-0 0.................. AlanMunro 3 67
(W Jarvis) *hld up in tch in rr: rdn over 2f out: sn struggling: wl btn last 2f* **25/1**

201 **11** *16* **Blown It (USA)**[18] 4027 2-9-0 0..................(b[1]) SteveDrowne 2 19
(J A Osborne) *a towards rr: rdn 1/2-way: sn wl btn: t.o* **50/1**

41 **P** **Desert Icon (IRE)**[25] 3798 2-9-0 0.................. SebSanders 5 —
(W J Knight) *s.i.s: p.u after 2f* **33/1**

1m 11.13s (-1.07) **Going Correction** +0.075s/f (Good) **12** Ran SP% **121.5**
Speed ratings (Par 106): **110,109,109,108,106 106,100,100,98,93 72,—**
toteswinger: 1&2 £5.00, 1&3 £33.50, 2&3 £35.30. CSF £22.73 TOTE £6.00: £2.10, £1.80, £7.80; EX 20.90 Trifecta £1150.60 Pool: £2176.94 - 1.40 winning units..
Owner Highclere Thoroughbred Racing (Stubbs) **Bred** David Jamison Bloodstock **Trained** East Everleigh, Wilts
■ Stewards' Enquiry : Jimmy Fortune one-day ban: used whip without giving horse time to respond (Aug 15)

FOCUS
A race that seems to be on the slide these days, and this latest renewal looked little better than Listed/Group 3 level.

NOTEBOOK
Prolific(IRE), a good third in the Norfolk, did not seem to get a stiff 6f on slow ground in the July Stakes at Newmarket, but the return to this faster surface was always likely to suit and he was seen to better affect on this track. Soon with the pace, he fought his way into the lead under a furlong out and was always just doing enough to hold the slightly unfortunate Gallagher. This is as far as he wants to go and, although he is clearly going the right way he might find one or two too good in stronger races such as the Gimcrack and Middle Park. (op 11-2 tchd 9-2)
Gallagher is evidently held in high regard and had left his debut running behind (beaten favourite behind this week's Vintage winner Orizaba) when bolting up in a modest Chepstow maiden. This was a big step up, but he was made favourite and probably should have won. Tucked in behind the pace, he was full of running racing into the final quarter mile, but was looking for a gap and, by the time he found one and hit top stride, the winner had enough momentum to hold him. He is clearly progressing and will head next for the Prix Morny. (tchd 4-1 and 10-3 in a place)
Reve De Soleil(FR), twice a winner at a lower level before finishing fifth in a 7f Listed race at Longchamp latest, looked to have plenty to find with the best of these, but he was helped by the drop in distance and ran a huge race in third. He briefly looked the winner when getting alongside Prolific, but in the end was just run out of it. He looks well up to winning at Listed level on this evidence and is an obvious type for the valuable Redcar Two-year-old Trophy later in the season.
Saxford has been a revelation since stepping up to 6f, his relentless galloping style bagging him back-to-back wins at Newcastle and Newbury (despite a slipped saddle latest) and he could not be ruled out. He took up his customary front-running role and did his best to repel the challengers, but tended to hang under pressure and was ultimately done for speed. This represented another step forward. (op 7-1)
Total Gallery(IRE), sixth in the Windsor Castle at Royal Ascot, had no trouble winning his maiden at Beverley latest and this step back up to 6f looked unlikely to present a problem. He looked a big threat two out, but could not quicken when asked for his effort and was not quite good enough. Another likely sort for the Redcar Two-year-old Trophy. (op 13-2 tchd 7-1)
Rileyskeepingfaith, backed beforehand, needed to step up markedly on his narrow Newmarket maiden win and he was simply not good enough. He briefly made a forward move, but could not quicken and probably needs an extra furlong now, his dam having won at up to 1m2f. (op 12-1)

Waffle(IRE), winner of a modest 5f maiden at Leicester back in April, had not been seen since and was forced to miss his engagement at Royal Ascot. His stable are back in top form now, but he was a big drifter beforehand and got no cover from his draw in stall 1. He was too keen to boot and can be given another chance back down in grade. (op 13-2)

Khor Dubai(IRE) had a lot more on his plate than when winning a nursery at Lingfield last time and it was no surprise to see him come up well short. (op 7-1 tchd 15-2 and 8-1 in a place)

Saucy Brown(IRE), second to Saxford at Newbury, had earlier been fifth in the Windsor Castle and should have finished closer than he did. He dropped right out, having shown good early speed, and this was not his form. (op 20-1)

Smokey Storm, winner of the Woodcote Stakes in June, was stuffed in the Coventry and this effort confirmed he is well short of Group 2 standard. (op 20-1)

Blown It(USA) comes from a yard who continue to struggle for form and he found this a lot tougher than his recent Wolverhampton maiden win. (tchd 40-1)

Desert Icon(IRE), a Windsor maiden winner, was pulled up after a couple of furlongs having gone lame. Official explanation: vet said colt pulled up lame behind

4589 RSA NURSERY 7f
4:40 (4:42) (Class 2) 2-Y-O **£12,952** (£3,854; £1,926; £962) **Stalls** High

Form RPR

51 **1** **Sohcahtoa (IRE)**[56] 2796 2-9-5 **83** RichardHughes 7 92+
(R Hannon) *lw: racd in midfield: swtchd lft 2f out: drvn hdwy over 1f out: r.o strly to ld last 50yds: in command nr fin* **10/3**[2]

604 **2** ½ **Northumberland**[37] 3372 2-8-2 **66** RoystonFfrench 15 73
(M Johnston) *lw: dwlt: sn pushed up to ld: rdn over 2f out: hrd drvn ins fnl f: hdd and no ex fnl 50yds* **16/1**

6321 **3** 1 **Jazacosta (USA)**[43] 3164 2-8-13 **77** JimCrowley 13 81
(Mrs A J Perrett) *trckd ldrs on rail: edgd out off rail over 2f out: rdn to chse ldr ent fnl 2f: kpt on same pce u.p: lost 2nd fnl 100yds* **9/2**[3]

4415 **4** 1 ¼ **Roly Boy**[20] 3941 2-9-2 **80** RyanMoore 8 81
(R Hannon) *lw: stdd after s: hld up in rr: hdwy towards inner over 2f out: looking to switch lft whn nt clr run ent fnl f: kpt on but nvr threatened ldrs* **8/1**

61 **5** shd **Swift Chap**[29] 3645 2-8-12 **76** AlanMunro 6 77
(B R Millman) *lw: in tch: rdn over 3f out: chsd ldrs 2f out: drvn and one pce ent fnl f* **16/1**

3103 **6** 1 ¼ **Daddy's Gift (IRE)**[8] 4340 2-8-11 **75** JimmyFortune 12 73
(R Hannon) *stmbld bdly leaving stalls: towards rr: hdwy on rail 3f out: no imp u.p fnl f* **12/1**

521 **7** 16 **Suruor (IRE)**[18] 4014 2-8-13 **77** RHills 5 35
(M Johnston) *wnt lft s: sn pressing ldrs: wnt 2nd 4f out tl 2f out: sn wknd* **9/1**

340 **8** 2 ½ **Imperial Skylight**[88] 1851 2-8-3 **67** TPO'Shea 9 19
(M R Channon) *hld up in rr: lost tch 3f out: t.o* **66/1**

3130 **9** 7 **Motor Home**[21] 3924 2-9-3 **81** MartinDwyer 4 15
(A M Balding) *bmpd s: sn in midfield: rdn 4f out: wknd wl over 2f out: t.o* **20/1**

513 **10** 3 ½ **Cornish Rose (IRE)**[21] 3910 2-8-10 **74** MichaelHills 1 —
(M H Tompkins) *racd wd: a struggling towards rr: lost tch 3f out: t.o* **40/1**

033 **11** nk **Fong's Alibi**[28] 3674 2-8-10 **74** RichardThomas 2 —
(J S Moore) *sn bustled along in rr: lost tch 3f out: t.o* **33/1**

3212 **12** 2 ¾ **Rapid Release (CAN)**[9] 4292 2-9-0 **78** SebSanders 10 —
(Sir Mark Prescott) *lw: chsd ldr tl 4f out: sn dropped out: t.o* **5/2**[1]

1m 27.0s (-0.40) **Going Correction** +0.075s/f (Good) 12 Ran SP% **122.0**

Speed ratings (Par 100): **105,104,103,101,101 100,82,79,71,67 66,63**

toteswinger: 1&2 £16.30, 1&3 £3.80, 2&3 £11.70. CSF £55.47 CT £253.69 TOTE £3.80: £1.90, £3.30, £1.90; EX 60.40 Trifecta £218.60 Pool: £1740.21 - 5.89 winning units..

Owner Mrs Sue Brendish **Bred** Knockainey Stud **Trained** East Everleigh, Wilts

■ Stewards' Enquiry : Jim Crowley one-day ban: used whip with excessive frequency (Aug 15)

FOCUS

A good, competitive nursery in which the front six pulled a long way clear. The race should produce winners.

NOTEBOOK

Sohcahtoa(IRE), winner of a 6f course maiden in June (from Richmond fifth Total Gallery) was always likely to improve for this extra furlong and he needed every yard of it. He looked on a good mark and, having taken a while to find top gear, charged down the front-running Northumberland close home. There are no specific plans, but he remains capable of better and should stay 1m. (op 5-2 tchd 7-2 in a place)

Northumberland showed fair form in two of his three maidens and had the best of the draw in stall 15. Driven to get the early lead, having been a bit tardy out the gate, he kept finding off the front end and looked to have them all beaten racing into the final furlong, but his stamina finally gave way and he was run down close home. This is as far as he wants to go on breeding and it would come as no surprise to see him end up being best at 6f. (op 10-1)

Jazacosta(USA), whose stable took this last year, won a 7f Leicester maiden last time and seemed fairly treated. He travelled strongly in the behind the runner-up and looked the likeliest winner two out, but could not quicken once switched. There was money for him beforehand and a similar race should come his way. (op 7-1)

Roly Boy disappointed on his nursery debut at Ascot, having earlier won a 7f maiden at Kempton, but the step back up in trip helped and he stayed on for fourth, having met some trouble. He can be rated a little better than the bare form. Official explanation: jockey said colt was denied a clear run (op 12-1 tchd 14-1 in a place)

Swift Chap, winner of a 7f Warwick maiden, was starting out handicap life off a stiff enough mark, but he performed well and only just lost out on fourth. He will find easier opportunities and perhaps slightly slower ground will help too. (op 20-1)

Daddy's Gift(IRE) bounced back from a disappointing run when third at Kempton last week, but she lost any chance here when stumbling badly coming out of the stalls. She did well to finish as close as she did and remains capable of winning off this mark, especially as she finished so far clear of the remainder. (op 14-1)

Suruor(IRE) made hard work of winning at Ayr last time and had earlier looked a non-stayer over this trip. He was up there early, but clearly had too much use made of him and failed to get home. (op 10-1)

Imperial Skylight, who showed modest form in three runs over sprint trips earlier in the season, has been gelded since last seen, but this was a tough return and he duly struggled.

Rapid Release(CAN) just lost out off this mark at Catterick the other day and held obvious claims, but he ran terribly and certainly failed to show his true form. He was reportedly never travelling and clearly had an issue with the track, so probably deserves another chance. Official explanation: jockey said colt never travelled (op 3-1)

4590 OAK TREE STKS (GROUP 3) (F&M) 7f
5:15 (5:16) (Class 1) 3-Y-O+

£39,739 (£15,064; £7,539; £3,759; £1,883; £945) **Stalls** High

Form RPR

20-2 **1** **Visit**[27] 3742 3-8-9 **108** RyanMoore 7 108
(Sir Michael Stoute) *hld up in midfield: hdwy over 2f out: wnt 2nd wl over 1f out: led over 1f out: hrd pressed ins fnl f: hld on gamely* **2/1**[1]

-031 **2** hd **Cheyenne Star (IRE)**[30] 3619 5-9-4 0 JMurtagh 3 112
(Ms F M Crowley, Ire) *lw: hld up off the pce in midfield: plld out and gd hdwy wl over 1f out: str chal ins fnl f: jst hld* **13/2**[3]

0235 **3** 2 ¼ **Shabiba (USA)**[27] 3742 3-8-9 **93** RHills 5 101
(M P Tregoning) *hld up wl bhd: hdwy ent 2f: rdn and styd on wl to go 3rd wl ins fnl f: nvr able to chal ldng pair* **25/1**

-211 **4** nk **Red Dune (IRE)**[23] 3849 3-8-9 **89** PhilipRobinson 16 100
(M A Jarvis) *led at gd gallop: rdn 2f out: hdd over 1f out: kpt on same pce and lost 2 pls fnl f* **4/1**[2]

3000 **5** 1 ¼ **Royal Confidence**[30] 3619 3-8-9 **105** MichaelHills 15 97
(B W Hills) *lw: chsd ldrs: looking to grab rail whn c off best in barging match w rival over 2f out: swtchd lft over 1f out: no imp after* **12/1**

-511 **6** 1 ½ **Clifton Dancer**[36] 3420 3-8-9 **97** RichardKingscote 10 93
(Tom Dascombe) *chsd ldr: rdn 3f out: lost 2nd wl over 1f out: wknd ent fnl f* **14/1**

3410 **7** ¾ **Nans Joy (IRE)**[44] 3120 4-9-1 **97** MartinDwyer 9 95+
(E J O'Neill) *s.i.s: bhd: edgd out lft over2f out: keeping on but no ch whn short of room ent fnl f: nvr nr ldrs* **33/1**

0-02 **8** 1 **Chantra (GER)**[38] 3357 4-9-1 0 AStarke 14 90
(P Rau, Germany) *stdd s: hld up wl bhd: rdn and effrt on outer over 2f out: kpt on but nvr able to chal* **20/1**

-605 **9** ½ **Nijoom Dubai**[61] 2651 3-8-9 **105** TPO'Shea 6 87
(M R Channon) *racd off the pce in midfield: rdn over 2f out: no imp* **20/1**

-500 **10** 3 ½ **Spinning Lucy (IRE)**[21] 3927 3-8-9 **98** SebSanders 13 77
(B W Hills) *swtg: chsd ldrs: rdn over 3f out: wknd over 2f out* **25/1**

1023 **11** ½ **Illusion**[27] 3742 3-8-9 **96** JimmyFortune 12 76
(J H M Gosden) *lw: hld up in tch: effrt on rail whn short of room and c off worst in barging match w a rival over 2f out: no ch after* **15/2**

5-05 **12** shd **Vital Statistics**[13] 4198 4-9-1 **88** EddieAhern 11 78
(D R C Elsworth) *swtg: racd in midfield: effrt on inner wl over 2f out: no hdwy and wl hld after* **50/1**

2-55 **13** 1 ¾ **Gipson Dessert (USA)**[21] 3938 3-8-9 0 C-PLemaire 2 71
(J-C Rouget, France) *s.i.s: a bhd* **25/1**

1220 **14** ½ **Many Colours**[44] 3120 4-9-1 **105** LDettori 1 72
(Saeed Bin Suroor) *lw: racd in midfield: rdn and struggling 3f out: hung rt and btn over 2f out* **14/1**

1m 26.02s (-1.38) **Going Correction** +0.075s/f (Good)

WFA 3 from 4yo+ 6lb 14 Ran SP% **125.4**

Speed ratings (Par 113): **110,109,107,106,105 103,102,101,101,97 96,96,94,93**

toteswinger: 1&2 £4.30, 1&3 £12.60, 2&3 £30.80. CSF £14.05 TOTE £3.00: £1.50, £2.20, £7.40; EX 12.30 Trifecta £395.60 Pool: £ 1973.05 - 3.69 winning units..

Owner K Abdulla **Bred** Juddmonte Farms Ltd **Trained** Newmarket, Suffolk

■ Stewards' Enquiry : Michael Hills five-day ban: careless riding (Aug 15-19)

FOCUS

A decent Group 3 contest which appeared to be run at a solid pace, although the time was nothing special. Fair form for the grade, and the winner still has the potential to go on to better things.

NOTEBOOK

Visit, a Group-class juvenile at up to 6f who made her belated reappearance at Sandown last month (finishing second in a Listed contest over 1m) was not expected to have any problems with this drop to 7f and she held strong claims. Restrained early on, she made a good move into contention racing to two out and, having hit the front, was always just holding the runner-up. She is now likely to step up in grade and there is no reason why she cannot continue to progress. (op 5-2 tchd 11-4 in places)

Cheyenne Star(IRE), winner of a Group 3 at Leopardstown last month, fared best of the older horses and was closing in on the winner with every stride at the line came, but she could not quite get there in time. She was conceding a 3lb penalty to the winner and is now likely to head for the Group 1 Matron Stakes back at Leopardstown. (tchd 7-1 in a place)

Shabiba(USA), not far behind the winner at Sandown last time, was back in trip here and came from an unpromising position to take third. She was doing all her best work late, having been quite a way back early on, and remains capable of winning at this sort of level.

Red Dune(IRE), cosy winner off a mark of 83 at Newmarket, had to do a bit more than Robinson would have liked to secure the lead and, as a result, was unable to find any extra late on. She stuck on well enough though and this represented another step forward, as she had plenty on at the weights. There is a Listed prize in her. (op 9-2 tchd 5-1 in a place)

Royal Confidence, well behind the runner-up at Leopardstown, has been unable to win this season, but she has run several good races in defeat and this was another example. She had to work her own gap and badly hampered Illusion in the process. It may take a return to Listed level for her to win again though.

Clifton Dancer is another progressive sort who, having beaten Shabiba at Newbury in May, led throughout for a Listed success at Warwick last time. There was more competition for the lead here though and she was forced to chase the early pace. She ran well, but could not race on and was ultimately not good enough. (tchd 16-1)

Nans Joy(IRE) continues to fall short at Group level and ran about as well as could have been expected.

Chantra(GER), narrowly denied in a Group 3 at Longchamp latest, had earlier finished behind Nans Joy and she ran as well as she was entitled to. (op 25-1 tchd 28-1)

Nijoom Dubai was again disappointing and it remains to be seen whether she has fully trained on. (op 25-1)

Illusion, under a length behind Visit at Sandown, lost any chance when coming off worse in a barging match with Royal Confidence. She can safely be given another chance. (op 10-1)

4591 TURF CLUB STKS (H'CAP) 5f
5:50 (5:51) (Class 3) (0-95,93) 3-Y-O

£12,462 (£3,732; £1,866; £934; £466; £234) **Stalls** Low

Form RPR

3546 **1** **Piscean (USA)**[25] 3794 3-8-3 **75** RoystonFfrench 6 82
(T Keddy) *stdd s: hld up in midfield: hdwy ent fnl 2f: sltly hmpd and swtchd lft 1f out: sn rdn: chal last 100yds: led on line* **17/2**

3330 **2** nse **Little Pete (IRE)**[5] 4445 3-9-2 **88** FrancisNorton 7 95
(A M Balding) *hld up in midfield: hdwy ent fnl 2f: chal jst ins fnl f: led last 100yds: hdd on line* **17/2**

0256 **3** 2 ¼ **Cake (IRE)**[21] 3909 3-9-6 **92** JimmyFortune 8 91
(R Hannon) *prom: chsd ldr 1/2-way: rdn to ld and edgd lft over 1f out: hdd last 100yds: nt pce of ldng pair after* **16/1**

-356 **4** nk **Rash Judgement**[50] 2967 3-9-1 **87** JMurtagh 9 85+
(W S Kittow) *rrd leaviing stalls and slowly away: bhd: hdwy and rdn 2f out: styd on u.p fnl f: nt rch ldrs* **6/1**[2]

3005 **5** ¾ **Fol Hollow (IRE)**[21] 3909 3-9-7 **93** SilvestreDeSousa 3 88
(D Nicholls) *w ldr tl led 3f out: hdd and edgd lft over 1f out: wknd last 100yds: btn and n.m.r last 50yds* **14/1**

3140 **6** 1 **Good Gorsoon (USA)**[23] 3850 3-9-5 **91** MichaelHills 12 82
(B W Hills) *stdd s: hld up towards rr: hdwy over 2f out: chsd ldrs and rdn jst over 1f out: no prog fnl f* **13/2**[3]

0316 **7** 2 **First Trim (IRE)**[15] 4127 3-8-6 **78** TPO'Shea 5 62
(B J Meehan) *lw: sn rdn along and outpcd in rr: sme late hdwy: n.d* **40/1**

014 **8** *1 1/4* **Light Hearted**[62] 2594 3-8-13 **85**................................ SebSanders 4 65
(J Noseda) *lw: racd in midfield: rdn and struggling 1/2-way: no ch after*
9/1

4250 **9** *3* **Cape Vale (IRE)**[23] 3850 3-9-0 **86**................................ AdrianTNicholls 11 55
(D Nicholls) *racd in midfield: rdn 3f out: wknd wl over 1f out* **7/2**[1]

0641 **10** *1 1/4* **Bosun Breese**[8] 4347 3-8-9 **81** 6ex................................(t) EddieAhern 10 45
(P W D'Arcy) *taken down early: in tch rdn and struggling 1/2-way: wl bhd fnl f: lame* **7/2**[1]

2113 **11** *1/2* **Wotashirtfull (IRE)**[25] 3794 3-8-8 **80**................................(p) PaulHanagan 2 43
(K A Ryan) *led for 2f: wknd u.p wl over 1f out* **14/1**

220 **12** *14* **Chartist**[41] 3273 3-9-3 **89**................................ RichardHughes 1 1
(R Hannon) *chsd ldrs: rdn 1/2-way: sn struggling: wl bhd over 1f out: eased: t.o* **12/1**

58.43 secs (0.03) **Going Correction** +0.075s/f (Good) **12** Ran SP% **132.5**
Speed ratings (Par 104): **102,101,98,97,96 95,91,89,85,83 82,59**
toteswinger: 1&2 £24.80, 1&3 £43.90, 2&3 £28.20. CSF £88.49 CT £1180.47 TOTE £14.70: £3.60, £3.20, £3.80; EX 142.60 Trifecta £1051.90 Pool: £2274.54 - 1.60 winning units. Place 6: £67.94 Place 5: £45.47 .
Owner Andrew Duffield **Bred** Connie And John Iacuone **Trained** Newmarket, Suffolk

FOCUS
A fair sprint handicap, run at a strong pace, which suited the winner. Fairly ordinary form by Goodwood standards, however.

NOTEBOOK
Piscean(USA) has run several good races in defeat this season and could be forgiven his most recent effort due to the heavy ground. Back down in trip, his only previous success had come at this course, and he overcame some slight interference to get up right on the line. This track clearly brings out the best in him and he may struggle to win off a higher mark elswhere. (op 20-1)
Little Pete(IRE) has had a good season, for all that he has won just once, and he bounced back from a below-par effort at Ascot the other day. He looked the winner when hitting the front late inside the final furlong, but Piscean came even later and nailed him. This was the sixth time he has finished either second or third this season. (op 11-1)
Cake(IRE) could make no impression from a high draw at Chester last time, but she had been dropped 3lb and was seen to much better effect this time. She showed plenty of pace and stuck on well under pressure, but in the end was unable to match the front pair. (op 14-1)
Rash Judgement has yet to win a handicap, but he has shown enough to suggest he can win a race off this sort of mark. Back in trip here, he did himself little good when rearing leaving the stalls and was soon behind. He made some eyecatching late headway though, suggesting he would have gone close with a bit more luck. (op 8-1 tchd 10-1 in a place)
Fol Hollow(IRE) is easing in the weights and it was no surprise to see improvement, showing plenty of speed before tiring inside the final furlong. He should be dropped again for this and will be winning again before too long. (op 16-1)
Good Gorsoon(USA) looked a contender back down in trip here, but he got warm beforehand and could never get into it. (op 7-1 tchd 15-2)
First Trim(IRE), 3lb higher than when winning at Newmarket in June, came up short off this mark last time and ran about as well as could have been expected here, getting going too late having been outpaced. (op 33-1)
Light Hearted, winner of a 6f Brighton maiden, finished fourth behind a useful sort at Doncaster last time, but she was always struggling for speed here and evidently needs a return to 6f. (op 8-1)
Cape Vale(IRE) has been shaping as though in need of further than 6f and it was a big surprise to see him dropping in trip. He was always going to struggle for speed and it was a surprise to see him so prominent in the betting. He can be given another chance back up in distance. Official explanation: trainer said colt was dehydrated (op 5-1)
Bosun Breese, shouldering a 6lb penalty for his recent Sandown romp (aided by a tongue tie) was well in under the penalty and looked a big player, but he was never really going and it emerged he had finished lame. Official explanation: trainer had no explanation for the poor form shown; vet said gelding returned lame behind (op 10-3 tchd 3-1)
Wotashirtfull(IRE) showed speed before dropping right out.
Chartist ran terribly and was reported to have lost his action. Official explanation: jockey said colt lost its action (op 11-1)
T/Jkpt: £33,996.00 to a £1 stake. Pool: £143,645.36. 3.00 winning tickets. T/Plt: £57.50 to a £1 stake. Pool: £292,055.38. 3,705.86 winning tickets. T/Qpdt: £10.40 to a £1 stake. Pool: £13,833.27. 976.70 winning tickets. SP

4175 HAYDOCK (L-H)
Friday, August 1

OFFICIAL GOING: Good to soft (good in places)
Dolling out added 21yards to advertised distances on the round course.
Wind: Moderate against Weather: Overcast

4592 KEVIN DARLEY APPRENTICE H'CAP — 1m 6f
6:10 (6:10) (Class 5) (0-70,70) 4-Y-0+ — £3,412 (£1,007; £504) Stalls Low

Form RPR

452 **1** **Alonso De Guzman (IRE)**[13] 4200 4-9-10 **70**................ MatthewBirch 3 80
(J R Boyle) *hld up in tch: hdwy 4f out: chal 2f out and sn led: edgd rt over 1f out: pushed clr ent fnl f: styd on* **9/4**[1]

23/0 **2** *8* **Depraux (IRE)**[22] 3884 5-9-1 **61**................ CraigPettigrew 8 60
(G M Moore) *in tch: rdn along and lost pl 1/2-way: sn bhd: hdwy on inner wl over 2f out: styd on strly appr last: tk 2nd nr line* **14/1**

6646 **3** *hd* **Apache Fort**[22] 3884 5-9-4 **64**................ AntiocoMurgia 5 63
(T Keddy) *hld up in rr: stdy hdwy 4f out: effrt to chse ldrs over 2f out: swtchd rt and rdn over 1f out: kpt on same pce ins fnl f* **6/1**

1-50 **4** *nk* **Dark Energy**[13] 4193 4-9-8 **68**................(t) MatthewCosham 1 66
(M J Scudamore) *hld up in rr: hdwy 1/2-way: wd st and effrt to chse clr ldr over 3f out: rdn wl over 2f out and ev ch tl one pce appr fnl f* **5/1**[3]

4050 **5** *1 1/2* **Don Jose (USA)**[12] 4220 5-8-5 **51** oh6................(be[1]) GemmaElford 7 47?
(N J Vaughan) *chsd clr ldr tl led after 6f and sn clr: rdn along over 3f out: jnd 2f out: sn hdd and grad wknd* **10/1**

1034 **6** *4* **Thorny Mandate**[3] 4501 6-8-10 **56**................ StevenCorrigan 2 46
(W M Brisbourne) *hld up towards rr: stdy hdwy 1/2-way: chsd ldrs 4f out: rdn along 3f out: wknd 2f out* **10/3**[2]

4351 **7** *9* **York Cliff**[18] 4026 10-8-11 **57**................ DanielBlackett 4 35
(W M Brisbourne) *hld up in rr: hdwy 1/2-way: chsd ldrs over 4f out: sn rdn along and wknd over 2f out* **8/1**

-000 **8** *18* **Petrosian**[7] 4386 4-9-0 **60**................ HollyHall 6 13
(W Clay) *set str pce and sn clr: hdd after 6f: chsd clr ldr tl rdn along and wknd 5f out: sn bhd* **50/1**

3m 9.50s (5.20) **Going Correction** +0.225s/f (Good) **8** Ran SP% **113.6**
Speed ratings (Par 103): **94,89,89,89,88 86,80,70**
toteswinger: 1&2 £3.40, 1&3 £3.00, 2&3 £9.10. CSF £35.06 CT £166.77 TOTE £2.50: £1.50, £3.00, £1.70; EX 28.10.
Owner M Khan X2 **Bred** G And Mrs Middlebrook **Trained** Epsom, Surrey

FOCUS
The first running of a race restricted to jockeys yet to ride a winner, and the inexperience of one or two of those taking part predictably showed. First Petrosian and then Don Jose cut out a suicidial gallop at the head of affairs, setting the race up for a finisher. The form is questionable but the winner is generally progressive.

4593 LAMBRINI MAIDEN AUCTION STKS — 6f
6:45 (6:46) (Class 5) 2-Y-0 — £3,238 (£963; £481; £240) Stalls Centre

Form RPR

2 **1** **Moonlight Affair (IRE)**[35] 3437 2-8-6 0................ FergalLynch 4 75
(E S McMahon) *trckd ldrs: effrt 2f out: n.m.r over 1f out: rdn to ld ent fnl f: kpt on wl* **5/2**[1]

2 *1 1/2* **Proud Times (USA)** 2-9-2 0................ NCallan 11 81
(G A Swinbank) *trckd ldrs: hdwy on outer over 2f out: rdn to ld briefly over 1f out: drvn and hdd ent fnl f: kpt on same pce* **14/1**

3 *3/4* **Hey Up Dad** 2-8-11 0................ TomEaves 12 73+
(M Dods) *s.i.s and bhd: j. path after 1f and rn green: hdwy 2f out: rdn and edgd lft over 1f out: styd on ins fnl f: nrst fin* **16/1**

52 **4** *2 1/2* **Bouggie Daize**[28] 3674 2-8-4 0................ NeilPollard 2 59
(C G Cox) *cl up: rdn to ld 2f out: drvn: edgd rt and hdd over 1f out: kpt on same pce u.p ent fnl f* **9/2**[3]

5 *hd* **Floods Of Tears** 2-8-1 0 ow2................ RobbieEgan[(7)] 5 62+
(D Flood) *v green to s: prom tl green and lost pl after 1f: sn rdn along in rr: hdwy wl over 1f out: kpt on u.p ins fnl f: nrst fin* **40/1**

6 *3/4* **Bob's Smithy** 2-9-2 0................ MickyFenton 6 68
(T P Tate) *s.i.s and bhd: hdwy over 2f out: rdn over 1f out and styd on wl fnl f: nrst fin* **20/1**

2 **7** *1/2* **Frontline Girl (IRE)**[20] 3976 2-8-8 0................ AndrewElliott 8 58
(K R Burke) *cl up: led 1/2-way: rdn along and hdd 2f out: grad wknd* **4/1**[2]

55 **8** *1* **Jobekani (IRE)**[44] 3125 2-8-11 0................ LiamJones 7 58
(Mrs L Williamson) *in tch: effrt over 2f out: sn rdn along and no imp* **20/1**

42 **9** *1/2* **Identity**[14] 4169 2-8-4 0................ GregFairley 10 50
(E J O'Neill) *cl up: effrt 1/2-way and ev ch tl rdn wl over 2f out and sn wknd* **5/1**

0 **10** *1/2* **Real Dandy**[19] 3997 2-9-2 0................ GeorgeBaker 13 60
(J G Given) *a towards rr* **12/1**

11 *7* **Lucy Brown** 2-8-10 0 ow4................ PaulMulrennan 9 33
(M W Easterby) *in tch: rdn along 1/2-way: sn wknd* **40/1**

0 **12** *18* **Nino Zachetti (IRE)**[27] 3714 2-8-8 0................ MichaelJStainton[(3)] 3 —
(E J Alston) *led to 1/2-way: rdn along over 2f out and sn wknd* **66/1**

13 *14* **Susurrayshaan** 2-8-11 0................ DaleGibson 1 —
(Mrs G S Rees) *a towards rr: rdn along and bhd fr 1/2-way* **50/1**

1m 16.09s (2.09) **Going Correction** +0.225s/f (Good) **13** Ran SP% **121.5**
Speed ratings (Par 94): **95,93,92,88,88 87,86,85,84,84 74,50,32**
toteswinger: 1&2 £8.00, 1&3 £13.10, 2&3 £8.10. CSF £38.87 TOTE £3.80: £1.80, £4.50, £4.10; EX 48.30.
Owner D J Allen S E Allen/ G A Weetman **Bred** Mull Enterprises Ltd **Trained** Lichfield, Staffs

FOCUS
Probably quite a decent affair for a race of its type. They seemed to go fast enough in the early stages, and the well-fancied Frontline Girl and Identity, who helped push the pace, were toiling in the final furlong as others kept on from the rear.

NOTEBOOK
Moonlight Affair(IRE) kept on well under pressure once hitting the front and looked as if she would not have been stopping after another furlong. The Doncaster maiden in which she finished second on her debut had not looked all that strong judged on the subsequent performances of some of the horses who finished behind her, but this success paid a compliment to the easy Barry Hills-trained winner Faraway Flower. (op 4-1)
Proud Times(USA) travelled particularly strongly but appeared to hold his head slightly high when pressure was applied, probably due to greenness. He was entitled to need the experience on his debut and showed so much speed that he is worth giving the benefit of the doubt.
Hey Up Dad has stamina all over his pedigree, but ran a race full of promise over what will clearly be an inadequate test. He jumped the path after a furlong and was chased along in rear in the early stages but picked his way through the pack throughout the second half of the race. He is interesting. (op 14-1)
Bouggie Daize, slightly hampered leaving the stalls, kept on well having been prominent early on and threw a decent marker down as to the value of the form. (op 3-1)
Floods Of Tears ◆ was arguably the most eyecatching of the lot as she ran green after a furlong and dropped right to the rear before making notable progress through her rivals in the final furlong and a half. It would be a surprise if she has not learnt something from his experience. (op 33-1)
Bob's Smithy was noted making steady late progress from the rear of the field having been slowly into stride. (tchd 25-1)

4594 TURN ON THE STYLE NURSERY — 6f
7:20 (7:22) (Class 4) 2-Y-0 — £5,504 (£1,637; £818; £408) Stalls Centre

Form RPR

0053 **1** **Lisburn (IRE)**[20] 3978 2-8-9 **71**................ TWilliams 7 72
(M Brittain) *a.p: rdn along 2f out: drvn ent fnl f: styd on u.p to ld on line* **12/1**

11 **2** *hd* **Fol Liam**[15] 4108 2-9-5 **81**................ StephenDonohoe 3 81
(Ian Williams) *sn outpcd and rdn along in rr: swtchd rt to stands' rails over 2f out: hdwy wl over 1f out: drvn and styd on ins fnl f to ld nr fin: hdd on line* **3/1**[2]

2331 **3** *shd* **Carnaby Haggerston (IRE)**[14] 4143 2-9-6 **82**................ NCallan 2 82
(K A Ryan) *cl up: led 2f out: sn rdn and edgd rt over 1f out: drvn ins fnl f: hdd and no ex towards fin* **9/4**[1]

0063 **4** *1* **Paymaster In Chief**[15] 4119 2-7-8 **63** ow2................ BillyCray[(7)] 8 60
(M D I Usher) *in tch: n.m.r and lost pl after 2f: sn in rr: rdn along and hdwy 2f out: drvn and edgd lft ins fnl f: styd on wl towards fin* **13/2**

1064 **5** *nk* **Klynch**[20] 3941 2-9-7 **83**................ PaulMulrennan 4 79
(B J Meehan) *chsd ldrs: rdn along and sltly outpcd 2f out: drvn and kpt on ins fnl f* **8/1**

666 **6** *nk* **That Boy Ronaldo**[34] 3470 2-7-5 **60** oh15................ CharlotteKerton[(7)] 5 55
(A Berry) *bmpd s: sn chsng ldrs: rdn along 2f out: edgd lft and kpt on u.p ins fnl f* **50/1**

10 **7** *nk* **Fathey (IRE)**[28] 3663 2-9-0 **79**................ JamieMoriarty[(3)] 1 73
(R A Fahey) *chsd ldrs on outer: rdn along over 3f out: drvn and sltly outpcd over 2f out: styd on u.p ins fnl f* **14/1**

2621 **8** *2 1/2* **Cutting Comments**[25] 3788 2-9-1 **77**................ TomEaves 6 64
(M Dods) *wnt lft s: led: rdn along 1/2-way: hdd 2f out and grad wknd* **9/2**[3]

663 **9** *2 3/4* **El Portet**[55] 2845 2-8-4 **66**................ AndrewElliott 10 44
(G M Moore) *chsd ldrs: rdn along and edgd lft over 2f out: sn drvn and wknd* **16/1**

0330 **10** 2 ½ **Carmanjoe**[20] 3978 2-8-2 **64**............ DaleGibson 9 35
(M W Easterby) *prom: rdn along 1/2-way: sn wknd* **25/1**

1m 16.57s (2.57) **Going Correction** +0.225s/f (Good) **10** Ran SP% **124.4**
Speed ratings (Par 96): **91,90,90,89,88 88,88,84,81,77**
toteswinger: 1&2 £17.30, 1&3 £16.60, 2&3 £2.50. CSF £51.36 CT £119.18 TOTE £15.10: £3.40, £1.50, £1.60; EX 74.00.
Owner Mel Brittain **Bred** Chevington Stud **Trained** Warthill, N Yorks

FOCUS
A competitive nursery and a blanket finish.

NOTEBOOK
Lisburn(IRE) scored for the first time since her debut when grabbing an unlikely-looking verdict in a three-way photo finish. Always prominent, she looked to have been put in her place at the furlong pole, but rallied in the dying strides to come between rivals and put her head in front right on the line. She was starting to look exposed having been put in her place in a couple of nurseries before this race, but the Handicapper had done his bit and she is nothing but tough. (op 16-1)
Fol Liam was niggled along for the first couple of furlongs but stayed on well once brought across to the stands'-side rail. Just as he had mastered Carnaby Haggerston he was himself mugged on the line. (tchd 7-2 tchgd 4-1 in a place)
Carnaby Haggerston(IRE) comes out of this contest with plenty of credit and his backers can probably count themselves a bit unlucky not to collect, as he went to the front very strongly with two furlongs to run and still looked by far the likeliest winner with 150 yards to run before he started to drift right having been in front for long enough. He could well make amends off a similar mark in another nursery next time out. (op 7-2)
Paymaster In Chief kept on reasonably well from the rear despite hanging left and looked as if another furlong might not go amiss. (op 8-1)
Klynch, the most experienced runner in the line-up, ran a solid race but looks vulnerable off his current mark. Official explanation: jockey said colt never travelled (op 6-1 tchd 11-2)
Fathey(IRE) did not run badly in a race that did not really pan out for him as the field edged across the track to the stands' side. (op 12-1)

4595 ARICABEAU RACING SYNDICATE H'CAP 6f
7:50 (7:51) (Class 4) (0-80,80) 3-Y-O **£5,504** (£1,637; £818; £408) **Stalls** Centre

Form RPR
4-40 **1** **Feeling Fresh (IRE)**[29] 3626 3-8-2 **61** oh1............ PaulQuinn 2 71
(Paul Green) *bhd and pushed along 1/2-way: swtchd rt and hdwy 2f out: rdn over 1f out: styd on strly ins fnl f to ld on line* **50/1**
-146 **2** *hd* **Mullein**[53] 2896 3-9-1 **74**............ GeorgeBaker 1 83
(R M Beckett) *hld up in tch: smooth hdwy on outer 2f out: rdn to ld over 1f out: drvn and edgd rt ins fnl f: hdd post* **8/1**
106 **3** *nk* **Hazelrigg (IRE)**[34] 3499 3-9-0 **73**............ PaulMulrennan 6 81
(T D Easterby) *hld up in tch: hdwy 2f out: rdn over 1f out: drvn and ev ch ins fnl f: no ex nr fin* **8/1**
1321 **4** ¾ **Leonid Glow**[11] 4236 3-9-0 **76** 6ex............ JamieMoriarty(3) 11 82
(M Dods) *towards rr: swtchd rt and rdn 2f out: styd on ent fnl f: nrst fin* **8/1**
4051 **5** 1 ¾ **Artsu**[19] 3999 3-9-5 **78**............ AndrewElliott 4 78+
(M L W Bell) *hld up in tch: hdwy 2f out: sn rdn and kpt on ins fnl f: nrst fin* **15/2**[3]
0441 **6** 2 **Supermassive Muse (IRE)**[19] 4000 3-9-7 **80**............(p) FergalLynch 9 74
(E S McMahon) *hmpd s and in rr: hdwy over 2f out: sn rdn and n.m.r over 1f out: kpt on ins fnl f: nrst fin* **12/1**
0004 **7** *hd* **Harlech Castle**[11] 4252 3-9-5 **78**............(b) NCallan 10 71
(P F I Cole) *wnt lft s: cl up: rdn along 2f out and ev ch tl drvn and wknd ent fnl f* **6/1**[2]
2131 **8** 1 ¼ **Arabian Art (USA)**[8] 4333 3-8-2 **68**............ CharlesEddery(7) 14 57
(H R A Cecil) *wnt lft s: sn cl up: rdn along 2f out and ev ch tl wknd and eased ent fnl f* **11/4**[1]
2134 **9** 1 **Monsieur Reynard**[8] 4347 3-9-4 **77**............ StephenDonohoe 3 63
(Ian Williams) *a towards rr* **20/1**
2-6 **10** 2 ½ **Royal Degree**[50] 2966 3-8-11 **70**............ TomEaves 5 48
(B Smart) *cl up: rdn along over 2f out: sn wknd* **20/1**
5300 **11** *nse* **Chinese Temple (IRE)**[24] 3811 3-9-0 **73**............ GregFairley 13 51
(M G Quinlan) *sltly hmpd s: sn prom: effrt over 2f out and sn rdn: wknd over 1f out* **25/1**
5162 **12** ¾ **Beat The Bell**[11] 4258 3-8-5 **71** ow2............ BMcHugh(7) 8 46
(A Bailey) *trckd ldrs: effrt over 2f out: sn rdn and wknd* **9/1**
0000 **13** 5 **Calmdownmate (IRE)**[34] 3475 3-9-6 **79**............(b) DarrenWilliams 7 38
(K R Burke) *led: rdn along over 2f out: drvn edgd rt and hdd over 1f out: wknd* **40/1**

1m 14.97s (0.97) **Going Correction** +0.225s/f (Good) **13** Ran SP% **121.5**
Speed ratings (Par 102): **102,101,101,100,98 95,95,93,92,88 88,87,81**
toteswinger: 1&2 £61.90, 1&3 £169.30, 2&3 £11.70. CSF £401.85 CT £3564.20 TOTE £43.80: £10.50, £3.00, £3.20; EX 518.40.
Owner Max Kay **Bred** J Mahon **Trained** Lydiate, Merseyside

FOCUS
A fair sprint handicap, and the form looks sound, but a surprise winner.
Feeling Fresh(IRE) Official explanation: trainer said, regarding apparent improvement in form, that the colt was better suited by the softer ground
Supermassive Muse(IRE) Official explanation: jockey said gelding was denied a clear run
Arabian Art(USA) Official explanation: jockey said filly was unsuited by the good to soft (good in places) ground

4596 HARVEY NICHOLS FILLIES' H'CAP 1m 2f 120y
8:25 (8:25) (Class 5) (0-75,75) 3-Y-O+ **£3,238** (£963; £481; £240) **Stalls** High

Form RPR
0300 **1** **Grethel (IRE)**[5] 4458 4-8-10 **56**............ StephenDonohoe 4 65
(A Berry) *hld up in tch: hdwy and swtchd lft 4f out: rdn to ld wl over 2f out: drvn clr ent fnl f: styd on wl* **16/1**
0563 **2** 2 ¾ **Snow Dancer (IRE)**[14] 4170 4-8-9 **58**............(p) JamieMoriarty(3) 1 62
(H A McWilliams) *hld up and bhd: hdwy and in tch 1/2-way: effrt over 2f out: rdn to chse wnr ent fnl f: sn drvn and no imp* **8/1**[3]
4345 **3** 4 ½ **Montrachet**[18] 4022 4-10-0 **74**............ MickyFenton 3 71
(M L W Bell) *led: rdn along 4f out: drvn 3f out: hdd over 2f out: sn wknd* **4/1**[2]
4215 **4** 2 ¾ **Black Dahlia**[38] 3351 3-8-12 **75**............ FrederikTylicki(7) 7 67
(A J McCabe) *trckd ldrs: hdwy on outer to chal 1/2-way: edgd lft 4f out: sn rdn and ev ch tl drvn 2f out and sn wknd* **2/1**[1]
2122 **5** 8 **Sceilin (IRE)**[5] 4458 4-8-11 **57**............(t) NCallan 6 35
(J Mackie) *cl up: pushed along and squeezed up 4f out: sn rdn and wknd qckly over 3f out* **2/1**[1]
563- **6** 2 ½ **Eternal Optimist (IRE)**[242] 7007 3-8-1 **57**............ DaleGibson 2 31
(Paul Green) *in tch: rdn along 1/2-way: wknd 4f out* **20/1**
0-00 **7** 1 ¾ **Ignition**[12] 4219 6-8-9 **55** oh4............(p) TomEaves 5 26
(A Kirtley) *t.k.h: chsd ldrs: rdn along 4f out: wknd 3f out* **40/1**

2m 17.95s (1.25) **Going Correction** +0.225s/f (Good)
WFA 3 from 4yo+ 10lb **7** Ran SP% **110.9**
Speed ratings (Par 100): **104,102,98,96,90 89,87**
toteswinger: 1&2 £8.30, 1&3 £23.40, 2&3 £3.90. CSF £124.83 TOTE £13.30: £4.90, £3.00; EX 74.60.
Owner Mrs Linda White **Bred** Liam Queally **Trained** Cockerham, Lancs

FOCUS
A weak fillies' handicap.
Montrachet Official explanation: jockey said filly hung left-handed up the straight
Sceilin(IRE) Official explanation: trainer had no explanation for the poor form shown

4597 ST HELENS H'CAP 1m 30y
8:55 (8:56) (Class 5) (0-70,69) 3-Y-O+ **£3,238** (£963; £481; £240) **Stalls** Low

Form RPR
6330 **1** **Inside Story (IRE)**[14] 4172 6-9-7 **64**............(b) DaleGibson 9 75
(M W Easterby) *midfield: hdwy 3f out: swtchd outside and rdn 2f out: styd on to ld ent fnl f: drvn clr* **13/2**
0556 **2** 2 ¾ **Polish Corridor**[18] 4015 9-8-10 **60**............ FrederikTylicki(7) 6 65
(M Dods) *chsd ldrs: hdwy 3f out: rdn 2f out: drvn to chse wnr ins fnl f: no imp* **10/3**[1]
-034 **3** 2 ½ **Orphan (IRE)**[18] 4018 6-8-11 **54**............ AndrewElliott 3 53
(G M Moore) *trckd ldrs: effrt 3f out: rdn 2f out: kpt on same pce u.p ins fnl f* **6/1**
5624 **4** ½ **Pitbull**[19] 4001 5-9-3 **60**............ LiamJones 7 58
(Mrs G S Rees) *s.i.s and bhd: stdy hdwy on inner over 3f out: rdn to ld 2f out: drvn and hdd ent fnl f: wknd* **11/2**[3]
34-0 **5** ½ **Beck**[35] 3431 4-8-9 **52**............ FergalLynch 2 49
(W M Brisbourne) *chsd ldrs on inner: hdwy 4f out: rdn to ld 3f out: drvn and hdd 2f out: grad wknd* **14/1**
0032 **6** 2 ½ **Society Music (IRE)**[11] 4248 6-9-11 **68**............(p) PaulMulrennan 12 59
(M Dods) *prom: effrt over 2f out and sn rdn along: drvn wl over 1f out and sn wknd* **5/1**[2]
010 **7** 2 ¼ **Ten To The Dozen**[15] 4121 5-9-6 **63**............ DarrenWilliams 14 49
(P W Hiatt) *stdd s and hld up in rr: hdwy 3f out: rdn to chse ldrs 2f out: sn drvn and wknd* **14/1**
/0-0 **8** 1 ¾ **Tender Moments**[55] 2841 4-9-10 **67**............ TomEaves 1 49
(B Smart) *hld up: a towards rr* **25/1**
3-50 **9** 4 ½ **Run Free**[14] 4173 4-8-7 **55**............ AshleyHamblett(5) 5 26
(N Wilson) *cl up: rdn along 4f out: sn drvn and wknd over 2f out* **16/1**
0455 **10** 2 ¾ **The Graig**[14] 4162 4-8-10 **53**............ StephenDonohoe 4 18
(J R Holt) *led: rdn along 4f out: drvn and jhdd 3f out: sn wknd* **8/1**

1m 46.83s (3.03) **Going Correction** +0.225s/f (Good) **10** Ran SP% **116.9**
Speed ratings (Par 103): **93,90,87,87,86 84,82,80,75,73**
toteswinger: 1&2 £6.00, 1&3 £4.70, 2&3 £5.10. CSF £28.53 CT £142.10 TOTE £7.70: £2.70, £1.80, £2.10; EX 34.50 Place 6 £1290.23, Place 5 £ 583.48.
Owner Mrs Jean Turpin **Bred** Arthur S Phelan **Trained** Sheriff Hutton, N Yorks

FOCUS
A modest if tight handicap full of hard-to-win-with types.
The Graig Official explanation: jockey said gelding hung right and shortened its stride final 2f
T/Plt: £865.90 to a £1 stake. Pool: £43,594.40. 36.75 winning tickets. T/Qpdt: £125.30 to a £1 stake. Pool: £4,352.48. 25.70 winning tickets. JR

4421 NEWMARKET (R-H)
Friday, August 1

OFFICIAL GOING: Good to firm (10.1)
Wind: Fresh across Weather: Showers

4598 EUROPEAN BREEDERS' FUND MAIDEN STKS 6f
5:55 (5:56) (Class 4) 2-Y-O **£5,180** (£1,541; £770; £384) **Stalls** Low

Form RPR
1 **War Native (IRE)** 2-9-3 0............ ShaneKelly 2 83+
(J Noseda) *trckd ldrs: racd keenly: edgd rt over 1f out: shkn up to ld ins fnl f: r.o wl* **8/11**[1]
5 **2** 2 ¼ **Spanish Baron (USA)**[18] 4027 2-9-3 0............(t) TedDurcan 5 73
(R M H Cowell) *sn led: rdn and hung rt over 1f out: hdd and unable qck ins fnl f: eased nr fin* **10/1**
3 2 ¾ **The Fonz** 2-9-3 0............ TPQueally 6 65+
(Sir Michael Stoute) *wnt rt s: sn prom: shkn up over 2f out: styd on same pce fnl f* **5/1**[3]
4 *hd* **Al Mugtareb (IRE)** 2-9-3 0............ DarryllHolland 1 64
(M Johnston) *chsd ldr: rdn and ev ch wl over 1f out: sn edgd rt and nt clr run: no ex fnl f* **7/2**[2]
5 2 ½ **Virginia's Choice** 2-8-12 0............ FrankieMcDonald 4 52
(Jane Chapple-Hyam) *s.s: hld up: rdn over 2f out: n.d* **25/1**
6 13 **Group Leader (IRE)** 2-9-3 0............ PatCosgrave 3 18
(J R Jenkins) *dwlt: sn pushed along in rr: rdn 1/2-way: wknd over 2f out* **33/1**

1m 14.04s (1.54) **Going Correction** +0.10s/f (Good) **6** Ran SP% **112.7**
Speed ratings (Par 96): **93,90,86,86,82 65**
toteswinger: 1&2 £3.20, 1&3 £1.80, 2&3 £4.80. CSF £9.45 TOTE £1.90: £1.50, £2.80; EX 8.80.
Owner Ballygallon Stud Limited **Bred** Ballygallon Stud Limited **Trained** Newmarket, Suffolk

FOCUS
They went a steady early pace in this maiden but the best horse won.

NOTEBOOK
War Native(IRE), whose dam was a high-class triple 1m-1m2f winner in France, was the subject of good reports beforehand and holds plenty of big-race entries, including the Group 1 National Stakes in Ireland. Keen tracking the leader, he travelled strongly and picked up when asked to go and win his race. He did it in good style and should be up to holding his own in decent company, although his trainer was reported as saying that he will not rush him this year. He ought not have any trouble getting 7f judged on his pedigree. (op 4-5 tchd 5-6 and 10-11 in a palce)
Spanish Baron(USA), the only runner in the race to have had the benefit of previous experience, soon got the front and was allowed to dictate a fairly sedate pace. He had no chance with the winner, who looked in a different league, but stayed on, despite hanging right, to hold onto his second place fairly comfortably. He looks more of a nursery type after one more run. (op 9-1 tchd 8-1)
The Fonz, a half-brother to four winners at up to 1m1f, holds no big race entries. He raced keenly early and was one-paced in the closing stages, but is entitled to improve for the run. (op 9-2)
Al Mugtareb(IRE), who cost 170,000euros, is out of a half-sister to Lil's Boy, a smart, multiple winner over 7f to 1m1f. Entered in the Mill Reef Stakes, he ran alright on this debut and is from a stable whose juveniles tend to improve for an outing. (op 4-1 tchd 5-1)

Virginia's Choice, the only filly in the field, is out of a half-sister to Night Sun, a smart triple 6f-1m winner in Germany. She never really got seriously involved on her debut. (tchd 22-1)

4599 NGK SPARK PLUGS FILLIES' H'CAP 1m 4f

6:25 (6:25) (Class 5) (0-70,65) 4-Y-O+ **£3,885** (£1,156; £577; £288) **Stalls** Centre

Form RPR

0612 **1** **Granary Girl**[11] [4259] 6-8-4 **53**.. SimonPearce[(7)] 1 54
(J Pearce) *hld up: hdwy over 2f out: rdn to ld over 1f out: edgd lft: styd on wl* **4/1**[3]

-060 **2** *4 ½* **Royal Tender (IRE)**[4] [4490] 4-8-4 **46** oh1......................(v) DavidKinsella 3 39
(V Smith) *reminders sn after s: chsd ldrs tl led 10f out: rdn over 2f out: hdd over 1f out: no ex ins fnl f* **22/1**

0560 **3** *nk* **Coco L'Escargot**[4] [4477] 4-8-4 **46** oh1..........................(v) NickyMackay 8 39
(J R Jenkins) *a.p: chsd ldr 8f out: rdn and ev ch over 1f out: no ex ins fnl f* **20/1**

013 **4** *hd* **Naughty Thoughts (IRE)**[32] [3562] 4-9-2 **65**.............. RossAtkinson[(7)] 5 58
(Tom Dascombe) *prom: racd keenly: rdn and ev ch over 1f out: no ex ins fnl f* **1/1**[1]

0401 **5** *13* **Itsy Bitsy**[11] [4261] 6-8-4 **46** oh1..(p) HayleyTurner 7 18
(W J Musson) *chsd ldrs: rdn over 3f out: wknd 2f out* **3/1**[2]

0-03 **6** *5* **Little Hotpotch**[7] [4376] 4-8-1 **46** oh1.............................. DominicFox[(3)] 6 10
(M J Gingell) *led: hdd 10f out: chsd ldrs tl lost pl 1/2-way: sn rdn: wknd over 3f out* **33/1**

0006 **7** *14* **Barley Moon**[11] [4261] 4-8-4 **46** oh1.............................. FrankieMcDonald 4 —
(T Keddy) *s.i.s: hld up: hdwy 1/2-way: rdn over 3f out: sn wknd: eased fnl f* **12/1**

2m 33.55s (0.65) **Going Correction** +0.10s/f (Good) 7 Ran SP% **114.7**
Speed ratings (Par 100): **101,98,97,97,89 85,76**
toteswinger: 1&2 £11.20, 1&3 £8.70, 2&3 £31.50. CSF £79.18 CT £1560.44 TOTE £3.90: £2.00, £6.80; EX 82.00.
Owner Mrs P O'Shea **Bred** Barry Minty **Trained** Newmarket, Suffolk
■ Stewards' Enquiry : Frankie McDonald one-day ban: used whip when out of contention (Aug 15)

FOCUS
A poor event for the July course and the weak form is underlined by the performances of the second and third.

4600 HOME OF RACING NOVICE STKS 7f

7:00 (7:01) (Class 4) 2-Y-O **£6,476** (£1,927; £963; £481) **Stalls** Low

Form RPR

2163 **1** **Awinnersgame (IRE)**[13] [4187] 2-9-5 0.............................. LDettori 4 94+
(J Noseda) *trckd ldrs: rdn to ld over 1f out: r.o wl* **6/5**[1]

0463 **2** *1 ¾* **Bad Beat**[21] [3924] 2-9-0 0.. TedDurcan 3 84
(V Smith) *hld up: hdwy over 1f out: sn rdn: styd on* **11/2**[3]

3 **3** *½* **Arabian Flame (IRE)**[14] [4151] 2-8-12 0.......................... DarryllHolland 5 81
(M R Channon) *led 6f out: qcknd over 2f out: shkn up and hdd over 1f out: rdn and no ex ins fnl f* **5/2**[2]

6 **4** *2* **Mirrored**[17] [4062] 2-8-12 0.. RyanMoore 1 76
(Sir Michael Stoute) *led early: hdd 6f out: chsd ldr: rdn over 1f out: no ex ins fnl f* **6/1**

5 *4 ½* **Andean Margin (IRE)** 2-8-9 0.. HayleyTurner 2 62?
(S A Callaghan) *hld up: rdn over 2f out: wknd over 1f out* **18/1**

1m 29.22s (3.52) **Going Correction** +0.10s/f (Good) 5 Ran SP% **109.0**
Speed ratings (Par 96): **83,81,80,78,73**
toteswinger: 1&2 £6.80 CSF £8.02 TOTE £2.20: £1.10, £2.60; EX 6.80.
Owner Saeed Suhail **Bred** J Joyce **Trained** Newmarket, Suffolk

FOCUS
No-one wanted to go on early and the pace was very steady as a result.

NOTEBOOK
Awinnersgame(IRE), who seemed to struggle a bit to get home over this trip at Newbury last time, would not have been inconvenienced by the lack of early pace, as that meant that there was a greater premium on a turn of speed, which is something he possesses. He did it easily enough, but was entitled to win this on his previous efforts, and the £300,000 sales race at Doncaster on September 11 over half a furlong shorter, which was mooted as possibly his next target, could be ideal for him. (op 5-4 tchd 11-8)
Bad Beat, the most experienced runner in the line-up, stayed on from off the pace without threatening the easy winner. He is in danger of becoming difficult to place. (op 13-2)
Arabian Flame(IRE), who ran with promise on his debut, took advantage of the fact that no-one wanted to make the pace and he got the run of things out in front. In the circumstances it was a bit disappointing that he was unable to hold onto second place. (tchd 9-4)
Mirrored, whose rider did not want to make the running, gladly accepted a lead off Arabian Flame early in the race. He was well placed for when the sprint began but did not pick up and was disappointing. (op 9-2)
Andean Margin(IRE), a 250,000gns purchase, is out of a mare who won over 6f at two. He holds entries in the Champagne Stakes and Royal Lodge Stakes but struggled to get involved against these more-experienced rivals on his debut. He should improve for the run. (op 25-1 tchd 14-1)

4601 GL EVENTS H'CAP 6f

7:30 (7:31) (Class 3) (0-90,88) 3-Y-O+ **£9,066** (£2,697; £1,348; £336; £336) **Stalls** Low

Form RPR

0024 **1** **Resplendent Alpha**[7] [4375] 4-8-7 **70**.............................. JimmyQuinn 4 79
(P Howling) *hld up: hdwy over 1f out: edgd lft ins fnl f: sn rdn to ld: r.o* **12/1**

0111 **2** *¾* **Methaaly (IRE)**[7] [4393] 5-9-0 **77** 12ex......................(be) DarryllHolland 7 84
(M Mullineaux) *chsd ldr: led 2f out: rdn and hdd ins fnl f: styd on* **9/4**[1]

0222 **3** *nk* **Dingaan (IRE)**[21] [3898] 5-9-5 **82**.. LDettori 10 88
(A M Balding) *hld up: hdwy u.p over 1f out: edgd lft: r.o* **7/2**[2]

1052 **4** *shd* **Expensive Art (IRE)**[8] [4341] 4-9-1 **78**.............................. HayleyTurner 2 84
(S A Callaghan) *broke wl: plld hrd: stdd and lost pl sn after s: hdwy over 2f out: rdn over 1f out: edgd rt: styd on* **14/1**

-615 **4** *dht* **Film Maker (IRE)**[56] [2793] 3-9-5 **86**.............................. RyanMoore 3 92
(B J Meehan) *chsd ldrs: rdn over 1f out: styd on* **11/2**[3]

0314 **6** *2* **Efistorm**[6] [4437] 7-9-10 **87**.. TedDurcan 6 86
(C R Dore) *hld up: rdn over 1f out: nt trble ldrs* **10/1**

3120 **7** *1 ¼* **Millfields Dreams**[1] [4555] 9-8-7 **75**..............................(p) JackMitchell[(5)] 5 70
(P Leech) *s.i.s: sn prom: rdn: n.m.r and lost pl over 1f out: hmpd sn after: styd on towards fin* **25/1**

1102 **8** *½* **Dressed To Dance (IRE)**[5] [4460] 4-9-8 **85**................(v) PatCosgrave 11 79
(P D Evans) *rrd s: hld up: rdn over 2f out: edgd lft and bmpd 1f out: n.d* **7/1**

3166 **9** *1 ¼* **Mango Music**[13] [4198] 5-9-8 **85**.. TPQueally 9 75
(M Quinn) *led 4f: sn rdn: hmpd and wknd ins fnl f* **20/1**

6104 **10** *½* **Zowington**[22] [3881] 6-9-7 **84**.. IanMongan 8 72
(C F Wall) *chsd ldrs: rdn over 1f out: sn wknd* **16/1**

1m 12.31s (-0.19) **Going Correction** +0.10s/f (Good)
WFA 3 from 4yo+ 4lb 10 Ran SP% **118.8**
Speed ratings (Par 107): **105,104,103,103,103 100,99,98,96,96**
toteswinger: 1&2 £8.30, 1&3 £10.30, 2&3 £1.90. CSF £40.01 CT £123.50 TOTE £18.40: £4.20, £1.30, £1.50; EX 63.40.
Owner Resplendent Racing Limited **Bred** Sunley Stud **Trained** Newmarket, Suffolk
■ Stewards' Enquiry : Jack Mitchell two-day ban: careless riding (Aug 15-16)

FOCUS
A decent handicap and there was a good pace on here. The majority of the principals came from behind and the form looks sound, with the third is the best guide.

NOTEBOOK
Resplendent Alpha has dropped a long way in the weights since the spring of last year when he was rated 98, but until now he had been unable to take advantage. He has been running well in defeat lately, though, and this race was very much run to suit his hold-up style. Whether he can build on this remains to be seen but hopefully it will have given him a confidence boost. (op 14-1)
Methaaly(IRE), chasing a four-timer and 8lb well in compared with future handicaps, looked to have plenty going for him, but he did too much too soon in a race run at a good gallop and, having hit the front with two furlongs to run, he was there to be shot at by the closers. This was a better effort by the gelding than the final result suggests. (op 2-1 tchd 5-2)
Dingaan(IRE), runner-up in his previous three starts, is a consistent sort but has only won once in his last 23 starts. He had the race run to suit and finished well, but he tended to edge left and was never quite getting there. (op 5-1)
Film Maker(IRE), the only three-year-old in the field, was dropping back to sprinting after finishing fifth of seven in a 7f Listed contest two months back. He was running on at the finish and is on a mark he should be able to win off. (op 15-2)
Expensive Art(IRE) did not settle that well in the early stages despite a good pace and, while she stayed on late, perhaps her early exertions just told on the climb to the line. (op 15-2)
Efistorm has recorded nine of his ten wins over 5f and this stiff 6f was probably not ideal for him.

4602 SIX WHITING STREET H'CAP 7f

8:05 (8:05) (Class 4) (0-85,85) 4-Y-O+ **£6,476** (£1,927; £963; £481) **Stalls** Low

Form RPR

-032 **1** **Rum Jungle**[15] [4121] 4-8-8 **70**.. FrankieMcDonald 3 86+
(H Candy) *chsd ldr tl led over 2f out: sn hung lft: rdn over 1f out: r.o* **7/2**[2]

1060 **2** *2* **Gallantry**[6] [4405] 6-9-9 **85**.. JimmyQuinn 6 91
(P Howling) *a.p: rdn over 1f out: styd on* **14/1**

1020 **3** *½* **Flores Sea (USA)**[6] [4440] 4-8-8 **70**.. RyanMoore 1 75
(T D Barron) *w ldrs but racd alone towards far side tl jnd main gp 1/2-way: rdn over 2f out: styd on same pce fnl f* **6/1**[3]

4-21 **4** *nk* **Irony (IRE)**[15] [4121] 9-9-2 **83**.. JackMitchell[(5)] 5 87
(A M Balding) *led over 4f: sn rdn: styd on same pce fnl f* **9/4**[1]

50-0 **5** *1* **Marajaa (IRE)**[23] [3855] 6-9-5 **81**.. AlanMunro 9 82
(W J Musson) *chsd ldrs: rdn over 1f out: no ex ins fnl f* **13/2**

0331 **6** *1 ½* **Harare**[20] [3951] 7-8-5 **70**..(v) RussellKennemore[(3)] 2 67
(R J Price) *hld up: rdn over 1f out: nvr trbld ldrs* **7/1**

025 **7** *2 ¾* **Musical Beat**[6] [4424] 4-9-4 **80**.. TPQueally 7 70
(Miss V Haigh) *s.i.s: hld up: hdwy 2f out: sn rdn: edgd lft and wknd over 1f out* **17/2**

66-0 **8** *2* **River Kirov (IRE)**[27] [3728] 5-8-6 **68**.............................. NickyMackay 8 52
(M Wigham) *trckd ldrs: edgd lft and wknd over 1f out* **33/1**

1m 25.26s (-0.44) **Going Correction** +0.10s/f (Good) 8 Ran SP% **113.2**
Speed ratings (Par 105): **106,103,103,102,101 99,96,94**
toteswinger: 1&2 £8.20, 1&3 £4.60, 2&3 £22.00. CSF £49.07 CT £285.30 TOTE £4.60: £1.30, £3.80, £2.10; EX 47.70.
Owner The Earl Cadogan **Bred** The Earl Cadogan **Trained** Kingston Warren, Oxon

FOCUS
A fair handicap run at an average pace. The form looks sound rated around the placed horses.
Harare Official explanation: trainer said gelding was unsuited by the good to firm ground

4603 RUSSELL MACEY MEMORIAL H'CAP 1m

8:35 (8:35) (Class 4) (0-80,78) 3-Y-O+ **£6,476** (£1,927; £963; £481) **Stalls** Low

Form RPR

1120 **1** **Carlitos Spirit (IRE)**[37] [3367] 4-9-13 **77**.............................. AlanMunro 8 87
(B R Millman) *racd stands' side: mde all: rdn over 1f out: styd on wl* **6/1**

5332 **2** *1 ¼* **Mumbleswerve (IRE)**[23] [3840] 4-9-12 **76**.................... J-PGuillambert 10 83
(W Jarvis) *racd stands' side: hld up in tch: rdn over 1f out: r.o towards fin: nt rch wnr: 2nd of 4 in gp* **7/2**[1]

2300 **3** *nk* **Last Sovereign**[23] [3840] 4-9-8 **72**........................(p) FrankieMcDonald 9 78
(Jane Chapple-Hyam) *racd stands' side: a.p: chsd wnr over 2f out: sn edgd rt: rdn and edgd lft over 1f out: styd on same pce ins fnl f: lost 2nd nr fin: 3rd of 4 in gp* **16/1**

3104 **4** *2 ¼* **Sonny Parkin**[6] [4422] 6-9-10 **74**......................................(v) PatCosgrave 3 75
(J Pearce) *racd far side: hld up: hdwy 2f out: led that side ins fnl f: no ch w stands' side: 1st of 6 in gp* **9/2**[3]

1204 **5** *hd* **Paraguay (USA)**[1] [4567] 5-9-5 **74**.............................. JackMitchell[(5)] 1 75
(Miss V Haigh) *racd far side: prom: chsd ldr over 2f out: led that side over 1f out: hdd and unable qckn ins fnl f: 2nd of 6 in gp* **6/1**

0000 **6** *4 ½* **Louisiade (IRE)**[7] [4371] 7-8-6 **59** oh12.............. RussellKennemore[(3)] 7 49
(M C Chapman) *racd stands' side: chsd wnr tl rdn over 2f out: wknd over 1f out: last of 4 in gp* **40/1**

0534 **7** *¾* **Murrin (IRE)**[23] [3836] 4-9-8 **72**....................................(b[1]) TedDurcan 5 61
(T G Mills) *led far side: tl rdn: hdd & wknd over 1f out: 3rd of 6 in gp* **11/1**

000 **8** *9* **Overrule (USA)**[14] [4162] 4-9-8 **72**.................................(t) RyanMoore 4 40
(B Ellison) *racd far side: hld up: rdn and wknd over 2f out: 4th of 6 in gp* **4/1**[2]

-206 **9** *1* **Summer Dancer (IRE)**[7] [4364] 4-10-0 **78**.............................. RobertHavlin 6 44
(D R C Elsworth) *racd far side: plld hrd: sn trcking ldrs: rdn and wknd 2f out: 5th of 6 in gp* **14/1**

5150 **10** *9* **Dancer's Legacy**[39] [3325] 3-9-6 **77**....................................(t) TPQueally 2 22
(E A L Dunlop) *racd far side: chsd ldr to over 2f out: sn rdn and wknd: last of 6 in gp* **14/1**

1m 39.91s (-0.09) **Going Correction** +0.10s/f (Good)
WFA 3 from 4yo+ 7lb 10 Ran SP% **119.0**
Speed ratings (Par 105): **104,102,102,100,100 95,94,85,84,75**
toteswinger: 1&2 £3.40, 1&3 £40.00, 2&3 £9.70. CSF £27.90 CT £274.49 TOTE £7.10: £2.50, £1.80, £5.20; EX 29.50 Place 6 £ 149.79, Place 5 £ 99.82.
Owner Karmaa Racing Limited **Bred** Tally-Ho Stud **Trained** Kentisbeare, Devon

FOCUS
They split into two here, and the smaller, four-horse group that raced on the stands'-side produced the first three home. The form is rated around the placed horses with those drawn on the far side capable of being rated higher.
T/Plt: £142.30 to a £1 stake. Pool: £42,089.19. 215.89 winning tickets. T/Qpdt: £17.40 to a £1 stake. Pool: £4,265.65. 180.40 winning tickets. CR

[4378]THIRSK (L-H)

Friday, August 1

OFFICIAL GOING: Good to soft (soft in places) changing to good to soft after race 4 (3.50)

After 15mm rain overnight on a drying day the ground was reckoned 'on the easy side in the back straight, mainly dead in the home straight'.

Wind: light 1/2 behind Weather: fine

4604 PICKERING CASTLE CLAIMING STKS — 7f

2:05 (2:06) (Class 4) 2-Y-O **£4,338** (£1,291; £645; £322) **Stalls** Low

Form RPR

1262 **1** **Smalljohn**[11] 4243 2-9-5 0 (v) DNolan 9 — 75
(D Carroll) *mde all: clr over 1f out: unchal* **4/1**[2]

1030 **2** *3 1/4* **Cherry Belle (IRE)**[7] 4387 2-8-5 0 (v) JohnEgan 7 — 53
(P D Evans) *in rr: hdwy over 3f out: styd on to take 2nd ins fnl f: no imp* **8/1**

0631 **3** *1 1/2* **Dougie Peel**[9] 4290 2-9-2 0 (p) FergalLynch 2 — 60
(K A Ryan) *chsd ldrs: wnt 2nd over 3f out: kpt on same pce fnl 2f* **4/1**[2]

00 **4** *2* **Hollow Green (IRE)**[30] 3603 2-8-5 0 CatherineGannon 4 — 44
(P D Evans) *in rr: hdwy on ins over 2f out: kpt on same pce* **33/1**

6030 **5** *7* **Nchike**[49] 3008 2-8-5 0 AdeleRothery(7) 5 — 34
(D Nicholls) *chsd ldrs: drvn over 2f out: wknd over 1f out* **16/1**

514 **6** *2* **Elaine's Folly**[31] 3576 2-8-10 0 JoeFanning 8 — 27
(P C Haslam) *mid-div: swtchd outside over 2f out: hung lft: wknd over 1f out* **7/1**[3]

00 **7** *3* **Prom**[14] 4164 2-8-7 0 TWilliams 1 — 16
(M Brittain) *s.i.s: hdwy over 3f out: wknd 2f out* **33/1**

044 **8** *3* **Conakry**[15] 4120 2-8-3 0 MatthewDavies(7) 3 — 12
(M R Channon) *a in rr* **12/1**

0 **9** *shd* **Irish Joe (USA)**[24] 3821 2-9-0 0 TomEaves 6 — 15
(T D Barron) *bhd: sme late hdwy* **16/1**

5543 **10** *5* **Scenic Pass**[9] 4292 2-8-7 0 TonyCulhane 12 — —
(M R Channon) *sn drvn along: chsd ldrs on outer: wknd over 2f out: eased* **11/4**[1]

060 **11** *3/4* **Dispol Kintie (IRE)**[13] 4203 2-8-8 0 ow2 PaulMulrennan 10 — —
(P T Midgley) *hung lft thrght: chsd ldrs: lost pl over 2f out* **66/1**

12 *43* **Scottish Colourist** 2-8-5 0 DaleGibson 11 — —
(M W Easterby) *s.s: sn wl bhd: t.o fnl 4f* **25/1**

1m 29.91s (2.71) **Going Correction** +0.30s/f (Good) 12 Ran SP% **121.0**
Speed ratings (Par 96): **96,92,90,88,80 78,74,71,71,65 64,15**
toteswinger: 1&2 £6.70, 1&3 £3.70, 2&3 £7.60. CSF £35.79 TOTE £5.90: £1.70, £3.10, £1.50; EX 41.00.Smalljohn was subject to a friendly claim.
Owner John Walsh & Reuben Glynn **Bred** W H R John And Partners **Trained** Sledmere, E Yorks

FOCUS

A modest claimer and the winner was always in total command. The third sets the standard.

NOTEBOOK

Smalljohn, who looked very lean, had this won some way from home.

Cherry Belle(IRE), happy to be back on turf, had just 2lb to find with the winner on nursery ratings but by the time she got going he was home and dry. (op 9-1 tchd 10-1)

Dougie Peel, who had a fair bit to find, had the cheekpieces retained. He went in pursuit of the winner but could never get anywhere near close enough to land a blow. (op 15-2 tchd 8-1)

Hollow Green(IRE), dropping in class, was the stable's second string. She showed her first worthwhile form and may be able to pick up a seller.

Nchike, last of 14 behind the winner at York, was on his toes beforehand and the extra furlong proved beyond him. (op 14-1)

Elaine's Folly, pulled wide to make her effort, wanted to do nothing but hang left. (tchd 11-2 and 15-2)

Prom Official explanation: jockey said filly failed to handle the bend

Scenic Pass, who had the same chance as the winner on official ratings, was drawn wide. He was driven along in pursuit but was on the retreat early in the home straight. This was his eighth start already. Official explanation: jockey said filly never travelled (op 5-2 tchd 9-4)

Dispol Kintie(IRE) Official explanation: jockey said filly hung left-handed throughout

4605 BYLAND ABBEY H'CAP — 7f

2:40 (2:40) (Class 5) (0-70,69) 3-Y-O+ **£4,338** (£1,291; £645; £322) **Stalls** Low

Form RPR

0502 **1** **Glenridding**[20] 3951 4-9-2 **65** RosieJessop(7) 3 — 79
(J G Given) *mde all: edgd rt over 2f out: sn clr: unchal* **15/2**[3]

-534 **2** *3* **Heureux (USA)**[15] 4117 5-9-9 **65** (b) PaulMulrennan 8 — 71
(J Howard Johnson) *in rr div: hdwy over 2f out: styd on to take 2nd ins fnl f* **8/1**

3622 **3** *1 1/4* **Turn Me On (IRE)**[14] 4172 5-9-8 **69** KellyHarrison(5) 2 — 72
(T D Walford) *chsd ldrs: wnt 2nd 2f out: kpt on same pce* **11/4**[1]

0060 **4** *1 3/4* **Pearl Dealer (IRE)**[14] 4174 3-9-4 **66** FergalLynch 7 — 62
(N J Vaughan) *s.i.s: in rr: hdwy over 2f out: on: nt rch ldrs* **16/1**

6302 **5** *3/4* **A Big Sky Brewing (USA)**[24] 3826 4-8-11 **60** (b) DeanHeslop(7) 14 — 56
(T D Barron) *in tch: rdn over 2f out: hung lft: kpt on same pce* **12/1**

1125 **6** *1/2* **Stellite**[32] 3548 8-9-8 **69** GaryBartley(5) 1 — 64
(J S Goldie) *hld up in midfield: effrt 3f out: nvr rchd ldrs* **7/1**[2]

0030 **7** *1/2* **Attacca**[25] 3789 7-8-8 **50** oh4 DeanMcKeown 4 — 43
(J R Weymes) *chsd ldrs: one pce fnl 2f* **40/1**

6000 **8** *4 1/2* **King Harson**[55] 2846 9-9-4 **60** JoeFanning 9 — 41
(J D Bethell) *w wnr: drvn over 3f out: wknd over 1f out* **8/1**

0060 **9** *2 1/2* **Bateleur**[15] 4125 4-9-3 **59** TonyCulhane 6 — 33
(M R Channon) *in rr div: drvn over 2f out: nvr a factor* **12/1**

0000 **10** *nk* **Mis Chicaf (IRE)**[2] 4542 7-8-3 **50** oh5 PatrickDonaghy(5) 5 — 23
(D Carroll) *towards rr: nvr a factor* **66/1**

0000 **11** *3* **Trees Of Green (USA)**[24] 3825 4-8-12 **54** NickyMackay 10 — 19
(M Wigham) *a towards rr* **28/1**

5303 **12** *1 3/4* **Rainbow Fox**[11] 4239 4-9-6 **65** JamieMoriarty(3) 12 — 26
(R A Fahey) *s.i.s: bhd and drvn over 4f out* **7/1**[2]

10/ **13** *1 1/2* **Keys Of Cyprus**[1045] 5413 6-9-3 **59** (t) TomEaves 13 — 16
(D Nicholls) *chsd ldrs on outer: hung lft and lost pl over 2f out* **16/1**

1m 28.37s (1.17) **Going Correction** +0.30s/f (Good)
WFA 3 from 4yo+ 6lb 13 Ran SP% **120.2**
Speed ratings (Par 103): **105,101,100,98,97 96,96,91,88,87 84,82,80**
toteswinger: 1&2 £6.70, 1&3 £3.70, 2&3 £7.60. CSF £66.04 CT £215.81 TOTE £10.50: £3.30, £3.40, £1.30; EX 82.50.
Owner Tremousser Partnership **Bred** Bolton Grange **Trained** Willoughton, Lincs

FOCUS

A low-grade handicap and another all-the-way winner. The form looks reliable rated through the placed horses.

4606 NATTRASS CONSTRUCTION MAIDEN STKS — 1m

3:15 (3:16) (Class 4) 3-Y-O+ **£5,634** (£1,676; £837; £418) **Stalls** Low

Form RPR

3 **1** **Aflaam (IRE)**[14] 4161 3-9-3 0 RobertHavlin 3 — 86+
(J H M Gosden) *sn trcking ldrs: wnt 2nd 4f out: pushed into ld 2f out: 3l ahd whn eased wl ins fnl f: faltered nr fin* **2/5**[1]

0-0 **2** *1/2* **Theonebox (USA)**[70] 2360 3-9-3 0 FergalLynch 6 — 78
(N J Vaughan) *hld up in rr: hdwy over 3f out: wnt 2nd 1f out: styd on wl towards fin* **40/1**

4432 **3** *7* **Seventh Cavalry (IRE)**[11] 4255 3-8-10 78 (v) CharlesEddery(7) 2 — 62
(H R A Cecil) *trckd ldr: sn taking fierce hold: led over 4f out: hdd 2f out: wknd appr fnl f* **7/1**[2]

4-00 **4** *2* **Beetuna (IRE)**[60] 2674 3-9-3 74 TomEaves 5 — 58
(B Smart) *in rr: effrt over 3f out: one pce fnl 2f* **28/1**

0- **5** *12* **Timocracy**[405] 2885 3-9-3 0 JoeFanning 4 — 30
(M Johnston) *chsd ldrs: lost pl over 4f out: sn bhd* **14/1**[3]

0-45 **6** *25* **Thought Is Free**[11] 4249 3-8-12 85 JohnEgan 1 — —
(P F I Cole) *chsd ldrs: lost pl over 2f out: bhd whn eased ins fnl f: t.o* **7/1**[2]

-00 **7** *19* **Missycomelightly**[58] 2735 5-9-2 0 JamieMoriarty(3) 7 — —
(W J H Ratcliffe) *drvn and reminders to ld: hung bdly rt and hdd over 4f out: sn lost pl and bhd: t.o* **200/1**

1m 42.36s (2.26) **Going Correction** +0.30s/f (Good)
WFA 3 from 5yo 7lb 7 Ran SP% **109.5**
Speed ratings (Par 105): **100,99,92,90,78 53,34**
toteswinger: 1&2 £8.00, 1&3 £7.50, 2&3 £15.20. CSF £23.44 TOTE £1.30: £1.30, £9.90; EX 27.10.
Owner Hamdan Al Maktoum **Bred** Shadwell Estate Company Limited **Trained** Newmarket, Suffolk

FOCUS

The winner was value for three lengths but with the three with official ratings disappointing this did not take much winning.

Thought Is Free Official explanation: jockey said filly moved poorly throughout

4607 MCCARTHY AND STONE FILLIES' H'CAP — 1m 4f

3:50 (3:50) (Class 5) (0-70,76) 3-Y-O **£4,338** (£1,291; £645; £322) **Stalls** Low

Form RPR

2453 **1** **Beautiful Lady (IRE)**[8] 4326 3-9-2 **65** JoeFanning 6 — 74
(P F I Cole) *in rr: rn wd bnd after 2f: hdwy on outer over 4f our: rdn over 2f out: styd on fnl f: led last stride* **4/1**[2]

3211 **2** *hd* **Amicable Terms**[6] 4409 3-9-6 **76** 12ex FrederikTylicki(7) 4 — 85+
(Rae Guest) *hld up in mid-div: hdwy 7f out: led over 2f out: sn rdn edgd rt 1f out: hdd post* **2/1**[1]

0352 **3** *3/4* **Offshore Anna (IRE)**[8] 4332 3-9-1 **64** PaulMulrennan 3 — 72
(J J Quinn) *in rr div: hdwy 3f out: styd on wl ins fnl f: no ex nr fin* **9/2**[3]

00-4 **4** *2 1/4* **China Pink**[11] 4260 3-8-2 **51** oh1 DaleGibson 10 — 55
(Sir Mark Prescott) *w ldr: led over 5f out tl over 2f out: one pce appr fnl f* **11/1**

0654 **5** *6* **Citron Presse (USA)**[11] 4259 3-8-13 **62** (p) RobertHavlin 5 — 57
(J H M Gosden) *chsd ldrs: wnt 2nd 4f out: wknd appr fnl f* **12/1**

354 **6** *nse* **Kimbolton**[34] 3484 3-8-8 **64** CharlesEddery(7) 11 — 59
(H R A Cecil) *in rr: outpcd over 3f out: kpt on fnl f* **14/1**

000 **7** *24* **Trinkila (USA)**[32] 3562 3-9-2 **65** TomEaves 2 — 21
(P F I Cole) *chsd ldrs: reminders 6f out: lost pl over 4f out: sn bhd* **12/1**

63-0 **8** *3 1/2* **Flop (IRE)**[51] 2956 3-8-12 **61** TWilliams 7 — 12
(M Brittain) *in rr: rdn 6f out: sn bhd* **50/1**

0-00 **9** *1 3/4* **Royal Tartan (USA)**[33] 3530 3-8-2 **51** oh6 CatherineGannon 9 — —
(G L Moore) *in rr: drvn over 4f out: nvr a factor* **50/1**

0233 **10** *hd* **Dream Esteem**[23] 3835 3-9-7 **70** DeanMcKeown 8 — 17
(E J O'Neill) *swtchd lft after s: in rr: lost pl over 3f out: sn bhd* **16/1**

504 **11** *18* **Martingrange Lass (IRE)**[6] 4420 3-8-4 **53** ow1 JohnEgan 1 — —
(S Parr) *led: hdd over 5f out: lost pl over 3f out: sn bhd: t.o* **20/1**

2m 39.96s (3.76) **Going Correction** +0.30s/f (Good) 11 Ran SP% **116.5**
Speed ratings (Par 97): **99,98,98,96,92 92,76,74,73,73 61**
toteswinger: 1&2 £3.00, 1&3 £3.90, 2&3 £3.50. CSF £12.01 CT £36.37 TOTE £5.60: £1.50, £1.60, £1.90; EX 13.30.
Owner H R H Sultan Ahmad Shah **Bred** Hrh Sultan Ahmad Shah **Trained** Whatcombe, Oxon

FOCUS

A fair fillies' handicap with the winner turning Bath form around with the runner-up who looked nailed-on when taking command. The third backs the form up and the race is rated positively.

4608 PETER BELL MEMORIAL H'CAP — 6f

4:25 (4:25) (Class 4) (0-85,85) 3-Y-O+ **£5,634** (£1,676; £837; £418) **Stalls** High

Form RPR

6461 **1** **Steel Blue**[8] 4327 8-8-7 **67** 6ex ow1 (p) PaulMulrennan 7 — 75
(R M Whitaker) *led: jnd ins fnl f: edgd lft and kpt on wl nr fin* **11/8**[1]

0000 **2** *3/4* **Bazroy (IRE)**[6] 4437 4-9-3 **82** (b) RichardEvans(5) 1 — 88
(P D Evans) *swtchd rt s: unbalanced in last over 2f out: hdwy to chal ins fnl f: no ex* **7/1**

6230 **3** *1 3/4* **River Thames**[11] 4239 5-8-13 **80** FrederikTylicki(7) 4 — 80
(K A Ryan) *trckd ldrs: effrt over 2f out: chal over 1f out: edgd lft and kpt on same pce ins fnl f* **9/4**[2]

1330 **4** *1 3/4* **John Keats**[11] 4239 5-9-6 **80** FergalLynch 3 — 75
(J S Goldie) *trckd ldrs: effrt over 2f out: edgd lft over 1f out: kpt on same pce* **9/2**[3]

0-00 **5** *3 1/2* **Apollo Shark (IRE)**[13] 4206 3-8-9 **76** JamieMoriarty(3) 2 — 60
(J Howard Johnson) *w wnr: drvn 3f out: edgd lft and wknd over 1f out* **14/1**

1m 12.07s (-0.63) **Going Correction** +0.025s/f (Good)
WFA 3 from 4yo+ 4lb 5 Ran SP% **110.2**
Speed ratings (Par 105): **105,104,101,99,94**
toteswinger: 1&2 £5.30. CSF £11.31 TOTE £2.10: £1.30, £2.10; EX 9.20.
Owner Country Lane Partnership **Bred** R T And Mrs Watson **Trained** Scarcroft, W Yorks

FOCUS

A moderate handicap and the winner only needed to run to his previous mark to score.

4609 HELMSLEY APPRENTICE H'CAP — 6f

5:00 (5:00) (Class 5) (0-70,69) 3-Y-O+ **£4,338** (£1,291; £645; £322) **Stalls** High

Form RPR

0200 **1** **The History Man (IRE)**[7] 4385 5-10-0 **65** (be) GarryWhillans 4 — 73
(M Mullineaux) *mde all: edgd lft fnl f: hld on towards fin* **14/1**

3026 **2** *nk* **Soto**[11] 4246 5-9-10 **64** (b) BradleyRoper(3) 10 — 71
(M W Easterby) *chsd ldrs: chal ins fnl f: no ex* **9/2**[2]

4021 **3** 1 1/2 **Bonne**14 4163 3-9-4 64 RyanClark(5) 9 65
(M L W Bell) *dwlt: hdwy and swtchd lft 2f out: styd on same pce ins fnl f* **15/8**1

0015 **4** hd **Lujiana**11 4242 3-9-4 62 MatthewLawson(3) 8 63
(M Brittain) *in rr: hdwy 2f out: styd on wl ins fnl f* **14/1**

0502 **5** 1 **Lambency (IRE)**7 4383 5-9-1 52 KrishGundowry 6 50
(J S Goldie) *hld up in rr: hdwy over 1f out: kpt on ins fnl f* **9/2**2

0560 **6** 1 1/4 **Fan Club**2 4542 4-8-9 46 oh1 (b) DebraEngland 1 40
(Mrs R A Carr) *taken to r alone far side: w ldrs: one pce appr fnl f* **33/1**

1026 **7** nk **Swallow Forest**7 4383 3-9-0 55 (b) AndreaAtzeni 2 48
(T D Barron) *chsd ldrs on outer: hung bdly lft 2f out and ended up racing on far side* **18/1**

0000 **8** 1 **My Kaiser Chief**21 3928 3-10-0 69 (t) NSLawes 7 59
(W J H Ratcliffe) *chsd ldrs: wknd over 1f out* **9/1**

4000 **9** nk **Brigadore**2 4535 9-9-3 54 JamieKyne 3 43
(J G Given) *dwlt: sn trcking ldrs on outer: wknd over 1f out* **8/1**3

3405 **10** 1 1/4 **Fulford**11 4236 3-9-3 61 AdamCarter(3) 5 46
(M Brittain) *mid-div: lost pl over 1f out* **33/1**

1m 13.35s (0.65) **Going Correction** +0.025s/f (Good)
WFA 3 from 4yo+ 4lb **10** Ran SP% **116.7**
Speed ratings (Par 103): **96,95,93,93,92 90,89,88,88,86**
toteswinger: 1&2 £14.30, 1&3 £7.70, 2&3 £4.70. CSF £76.11 CT £178.30 TOTE £16.10: £2.40, £2.60, £1.10; EX 115.80 Place 6: £12.00 Place 5: £4.47.
Owner D E Simpson & R Farrington-Kirkham **Bred** J Beckett **Trained** Alpraham, Cheshire
■ A first Flat winner for Garry Whillans who has two jump winners to his credit.

FOCUS
They ended up racing all over the track in this low-grade apprentice handicap. The race has been rated around the first two.
T/Plt: £8.90 to a £1 stake. Pool: £39,340.11. 3,207.87 winning tickets. T/Qpdt: £3.10 to a £1 stake. Pool: £2,474.88. 588.98 winning tickets. WG

4610 - 4612a (Foreign Racing) - See Raceform Interactive

4574 **GALWAY** (R-H)
Friday, August 1

OFFICIAL GOING: Yielding

4613a ARTHUR GUINNESS H'CAP 1m 100y
7:55 (7:55) (50-70,68) 3-Y-O £7,621 (£1,775; £783; £452)

RPR

1 **Metal Madness (IRE)**43 3183 3-9-0 65 DEMullins(7) 15 71
(M G Quinlan) *trckd ldrs: 7th 1/2-way: hdwy on inner to ld 2f out: jnd ent st: regained ld 1f out: styd on wl u.p* **6/1**3

2 1/2 **Golden Tokyo (IRE)**16 4093 3-9-7 65 (b1) WMLordan 1 70+
(T Stack, Ire) *towards rr: 9th and hdwy 2f out: 5th appr st: 3rd 1f out: sn chal: kpt on u.p* **12/1**

3 nk **Zulu Princess (IRE)**11 4253 3-9-5 63 MJKinane 16 67
(J S Moore) *mid-div: checked after 1f: 9th and hdwy 3f out: 4th under 2f out: disp ld ent st: hdd 1f out: kpt on* **3/1**1

4 2 1/2 **Dirtybirdie**18 4034 3-8-12 56 (p) DPMcDonogh 3 54+
(M Halford, Ire) *hld up towards rr: prog over 2f out: 9th whn swtchd to outer early st: kpt on* **7/1**

5 1 **Aliceaneileen (IRE)**13 4210 3-9-0 58 JAHeffernan 7 54
(Patrick J Flynn, Ire) *towards rr: hdwy over 2f out: 6th early st: kpt on* **14/1**

6 1 **Spanish Cross (IRE)**71 2343 3-9-9 67 PJSmullen 10 61
(D K Weld, Ire) *trckd ldrs: 5th on outer 1/2-way: 6th whn checked 2f out: kpt on same pce st* **9/2**2

7 nk **Dealmaker Frank (USA)**18 4036 3-9-3 66 (t) PTownend(5) 13 59
(Niall Moran, Ire) *chsd ldrs: 6th 1/2-way: prog over 3f out: 2nd 2f out: one pce st* **20/1**

8 8 **Em De Or (USA)**34 3508 3-9-2 60 (t) CDHayes 2 35
(H Rogers, Ire) *hld up: kpt on same pce fr under 3f out* **33/1**

9 4 1/2 **Too Rye Ay (IRE)**9 4315 3-9-2 60 CO'Donoghue 14 24
(Mrs A M O'Shea, Ire) *led: strly pressed 2 1/2f out: hdd 2f out: no ex st: eased ins fnl f* **33/1**

10 2 1/2 **Chesterton (IRE)**16 4093 3-9-1 59 MAPhillips 6 17
(John Joseph Murphy, Ire) *nvr a factor* **33/1**

11 shd **Morrigan (IRE)**15 4136 3-8-12 63 GFCarroll(7) 5 21
(Michael Fitzsimons, Ire) *chsd ldrs: mod 4th 1/2-way: no ex fr 2 1/2f out* **25/1**

12 4 1/2 **Mystic Mayfly (IRE)**30 3617 3-9-7 65 (p) DavidMcCabe 12 13
(Daniel Miley, Ire) *chsd ldrs: mod 3rd 1/2-way: rdn over 3f out: sn no ex* **20/1**

13 3 **More Time Tim (IRE)**46 3097 3-9-10 68 WJLee 9 9
(Timothy Doyle, Ire) *in rr of mid-div: no ex fr 2 1/2f out* **12/1**

14 1 **Yellow Thunder (IRE)**76 2191 3-9-0 58 MCHussey 8 —
(Luke Comer, Ire) *a bhd* **33/1**

15 2 1/2 **Kiltycross (IRE)**36 3428 3-9-1 59 RPCleary 11 —
(M Halford, Ire) *a towards rr* **25/1**

16 28 **Reine De Coeur (IRE)**13 4211 3-9-7 65 FMBerry 18 —
(David Marnane, Ire) *drvn along s: settled 2nd: wknd over 3f out: eased bef st: t.o* **11/1**

1m 53.79s (3.59) **18** Ran SP% **129.3**
CSF £72.12 CT £271.91 TOTE £4.80: £1.20, £3.00, £1.20, £1.60; DF 55.40.
Owner P Bohan **Bred** Patrick Bohan **Trained** Newmarket, Suffolk

NOTEBOOK
Metal Madness(IRE) got a great ride from his talented young rider and just did enough to record a second career win. He probably hit the front sooner than ideal as he began to idle, but he showed battling qualities once challenged for the lead inside the final furlong and clearly stays this trip very well. Relatively lightly raced, he should still have more to offer. (op 13/2)
Zulu Princess(IRE) came through with every chance on the final bend and, while eventually outbattled inside the final furlong, she ran right up to her recent best in defeat. (op 9/2)
Spanish Cross(IRE) Official explanation: jockey said filly was checked in the dip as a result of general bunching

4614 - (Foreign Racing) - See Raceform Interactive

4327 **DONCASTER** (L-H)
Saturday, August 2

OFFICIAL GOING: Good
Round course: the inside rail was moved out by 6m from the bottom of Rose Hill to the start of the straight, adding about 13 yards to distances.
Wind: Light half against Weather: Warm, sunny periods

4615 EVERYONE'S A WINNER WITH UNISON AND FRIZZELL H'CAP 5f
2:15 (2:15) (Class 5) (0-70,69) 3-Y-O £3,238 (£963; £481; £240) Stalls High

Form RPR

0100 **1** **Royal Grace**13 4216 3-8-11 59 EddieAhern 6 63
(T D Easterby) *cl up: effrt 2f out: rdn to ld ins fnl f: kpt on* **8/1**

0506 **2** 3/4 **Mystickhill (IRE)**13 4216 3-8-5 58 MCGeran(5) 3 60
(J Balding) *in tch on outer: gd hdwy 2f out: rdn to chal over 1f out and ev ch tl nt qckn wl ins fnl f* **16/1**

3300 **3** shd **Artistic License (IRE)**22 3918 3-9-0 69 MatthewDavies(7) 8 70
(M R Channon) *hld up in tch: hdwy 2f out: swtchd lft and rdn over 1f out: styd on ins fnl f* **28/1**

5550 **4** hd **Bahamian Ballad**12 4236 3-8-4 52 (v1) MartinDwyer 9 53
(J D Bethell) *trckd ldrs: effrt and n.m.r wl over 1f out: swtchd lft and rdn ent fnl f: drvn and no ex last 100yds* **12/1**

0000 **5** 1/2 **Mollyatti**36 3438 3-8-6 54 RichardMullen 14 53
(Miss V Haigh) *trckd ldrs: hdwy on stands' rail over 2f out: sn rdn and ev ch tl drvn and one pce ins fnl f* **18/1**

0030 **6** hd **Dubai To Barnsley**16 4125 3-8-2 50 oh2 NickyMackay 10 48
(Garry Moss) *led: rdn along 2f out: drvn and hdd jst ins fnl f: wknd* **20/1**

2203 **7** hd **Dancing Maite**9 4329 3-9-3 65 DeanMcKeown 13 62
(S R Bowring) *dwlt and towards rr: swtchd rt to stands' rail and hdwy 2f out: rdn and kpt on ins fnl f: nrst fin* **6/1**3

3602 **8** 2 **Admiral Bond (IRE)**16 4106 3-9-1 68 (v) SladeO'Hara(5) 11 58
(G R Oldroyd) *dwlt and towards rr: rdn along and hdwy 2f out: kpt on u.p appr fnl f: nrst fin* **11/2**2

2630 **9** nk **Tangerine Trees**36 3455 3-9-5 67 (p) RoystonFfrench 12 56
(B Smart) *towards rr tl sme late hdwy* **10/1**

0325 **10** nk **Peter's Storm (USA)**20 4000 3-9-7 69 (p) NCallan 7 57
(K A Ryan) *cl up: rdn along over 2f out: wkng whn n.m.r wl over 1f out* **7/2**1

50-0 **11** 3/4 **Athboy Auction**15 4163 3-8-8 56 SimonWhitworth 1 41
(H J Collingridge) *stdd and swtchd rt s: a in rr* **28/1**

0-00 **12** 1 1/2 **Tendulkar's Diva (IRE)**28 3712 3-7-9 50 oh5 CharlotteKerton(7) 2 30
(A Berry) *a towards rr* **66/1**

0254 **13** nse **Gainshare**12 4236 3-9-2 64 JimmyFortune 4 44
(T D Barron) *in tch: hdwy on outer to chse ldrs halfway: rdn 2f out and sn wknd* **11/2**2

000- **14** 2 1/4 **Ruby's Rainbow (IRE)**301 6023 3-8-2 50 oh5 PatrickMathers 5 22
(J Balding) *a towards rr* **100/1**

60.47 secs (-0.03) **Going Correction** -0.05s/f (Good) **14** Ran SP% **120.5**
Speed ratings (Par 100): **98,96,96,96,95 95,94,91,91,90 89,87,87,83**
toteswinger: 1&2 £101.00, 1&3 £68.70, 2&3 £101.00. CSF £122.87 CT £3400.69 TOTE £8.80: £3.10, £4.90, £6.40; EX 184.20 TRIFECTA Not won..
Owner David W Armstrong **Bred** The Aston House Stud **Trained** Great Habton, N Yorks

FOCUS
This looks like moderate form, even for this sort of level. They raced middle to stands' side. The form is rated around the fourth and sixth.
Peter's Storm(USA) Official explanation: trainer had no explanation for the poor form shown

4616 TRADE UNION UNISON & THOMPSONS LAWYERS MAIDEN AUCTION STKS 6f
2:50 (2:52) (Class 4) 2-Y-O £5,180 (£1,541; £770; £384) Stalls High

Form RPR

2 **1** **Diddums**19 4027 2-8-9 0 EddieAhern 9 76
(W J Haggas) *trckd ldrs on inner: swtchd lft and hdwy 2f out: rdn to chal over 1f out: styd on to ld jst ins fnl f: drvn out* **11/10**1

2 3/4 **Noverre To Go (IRE)** 2-9-2 0 RichardKingscote 4 81+
(Tom Dascombe) *cl up on outer: hdwy to ld 2f out: rdn and ducked violently lft over 1f out and sn hdd: rallied ins fnl f: styd on wl towards fin* **10/1**3

40 **3** 1/2 **Dr Smart (IRE)**42 3245 2-8-13 0 RoystonFfrench 8 76
(B Smart) *led: rdn along and hdd 2f out: drvn whn lft in ld again over 1f out: hdd jst ins fnl f and sn no ex* **9/4**2

0 **4** 3 **Cyflymder (IRE)**15 4169 2-9-2 0 JimmyFortune 5 70
(J G Given) *prom: rdn along over 2f out: grad wknd* **33/1**

5 4 1/2 **Royal Salsa (IRE)** 2-8-4 0 ow5 BMcHugh(7) 7 52
(R A Fahey) *s.i.s and bhd tl styd on fnl 2f: nrst fin* **22/1**

6 2 1/4 **Tricky Trev (USA)** 2-8-13 0 FergusSweeney 2 47
(S Curran) *hld up in tch: effrt to chse ldrs over 2f out: sn rdn and wknd wl over 1f out* **18/1**

0 **7** 1 1/2 **Are Can (USA)**35 3495 2-8-11 0 DeanMcKeown 3 41
(J S Wainwright) *chsd ldrs 1/2-way: sn rdn along and wknd over 2f out* **28/1**

6 **8** 3 1/4 **Give Us A Song (USA)**24 3848 2-8-9 0 SimonWhitworth 6 29
(J S Moore) *chsd ldrs: rdn along over 2f out and sn wknd* **14/1**

9 7 **Night Knight (IRE)** 2-8-13 0 MartinDwyer 1 12
(M L W Bell) *wnt lft s and s.i.s: a bhd* **11/1**

1m 13.64s (0.04) **Going Correction** -0.05s/f (Good) **9** Ran SP% **118.5**
Speed ratings (Par 96): **97,96,95,91,85 82,80,76,66**
toteswinger: 1&2 £3.30, 1&3 £1.20, 2&3 £5.00. CSF £13.95 TOTE £2.10: £1.20, £2.90, £1.30; EX 13.50 Trifecta £90.80 Pool: £490.02, 3.99 winning units.
Owner B Haggas **Bred** J B Haggas **Trained** Newmarket, Suffolk

FOCUS
No more than a fair maiden. They raced stands' side.

NOTEBOOK
Diddums built on the promise he showed when second in a fair maiden at Wolverhampton on his debut, although he may well have been beaten had the runner-up not run green. (op 6-4)
Noverre To Go(IRE) ◆, a 50,000gns son of Noverre, half-brother to five winners, including useful multiple 6f-7f winner Indian Steppes, out of a useful 1m2f performer, has been given an entry in the Group 2 Mill Reef Stakes. He was easy to back, but probably would have made a winning debut had he not ducked sharply left just over a furlong out. He re-gathered his momentum to stay on for second and should be hard to beat in similar company next time with the benefit of this experience. (op 5-1)
Dr Smart(IRE), fourth on his debut over course and distance before running down the field in the Chesham, seemed to have his chance and was clear of the remainder. He now has the option of nurseries. (op 3-1)

Cyflymder(IRE) was no match for three fair types, but this was still a big improvement on the form he showed on his debut at Pontefract. (tchd 28-1)
Royal Salsa(IRE), a 15,000gns daughter of Royal Applause, half-sister to 1m juvenile winner Cuban Missile, out of a 1m4f winner in France, carried 5lb overweight, with her rider only able to claim 2lb of his allowance, but this was a satisfactory introduction. She will know more next time. (op 14-1)

4617 UNISON BEYOND THE BARRIERS CONDITIONS STKS 6f
3:25 (3:25) (Class 3) 3-Y-O+
£9,346 (£2,799; £1,399; £700; £349; £175) **Stalls** High

Form RPR
204- **1** **Battle Paint (USA)**[419] 2499 4-8-13 108 .... JimmyFortune 5 100+
(J H M Gosden) *trckd ldrs: swtchd outside and gd hdwy over 2f out: rdn to ld wl over 1f out: edgd rt ent fnl f: styd on wl* **9/2**[3]
2130 **2** *1* **Pawan (IRE)**[7] 4437 8-8-8 90 .... (b) AnnStokell[(5)] 9 97
(Miss A Stokell) *trckd ldrs: effrt 2f out: sn rdn and kpt on wl u.p ins fnl f* **11/1**
2226 **3** *¾* **Tajdeef (USA)**[49] 3041 3-8-9 107 .... MartinDwyer 7 95
(B W Hills) *cl up: led 2f out: sn rdn and hdd wl over 1f out: sn drvn and one pce ins fnl f* **15/8**[1]
005- **4** *¾* **Somnus**[280] 6491 8-8-13 99 .... (t) FergusSweeney 1 92+
(J J Quinn) *dwlt and rr: hdwy over 2f out: swtchd rt and rdn wl over 1f out: kpt on strly ins fnl f* **12/1**
111- **5** *¾* **Floristry**[280] 6488 3-8-7 104 .... RichardMullen 6 88
(Saeed Bin Suroor) *in tch: hdwy over 2f out: sn rdn and kpt on same pce appr fnl f* **4/1**[2]
6000 **6** *2* **Capricorn Run (USA)**[7] 4405 5-9-7 100 .... (b[1]) DanielTudhope 2 91
(A J McCabe) *prom on outer: rdn along over 2f out: sn drvn and wknd* **16/1**
3020 **7** *1 ¼* **Hammadi (IRE)**[49] 3041 3-8-9 102 .... NCallan 4 79
(K A Ryan) *led: rdn along and hdd 2f out: grad wknd aqpproaching fnl f* **7/1**
0-00 **8** *7* **Spirit Of Sharjah (IRE)**[70] 2404 3-8-9 107 .... RobertWinston 3 57
(Miss J Feilden) *dwlt: a in rr* **14/1**
0000 **9** *8* **Loch Jipp (USA)**[42] 3252 3-8-4 84 .... (p) RoystonFfrench 8 26
(J S Wainwright) *prom: rdn along over 2f out and grad wknd* **50/1**

1m 12.2s (-1.40) **Going Correction** -0.05s/f (Good)
WFA 3 from 4yo+ 4lb **9 Ran SP% 116.0**
Speed ratings (Par 107): **107,105,104,103,102 100,98,89,78**
toteswinger: 1&2 £7.60, 1&3 £2.70, 2&3 £4.00. CSF £52.93 TOTE £6.40: £1.80, £2.00, £1.50; EX 70.50 Trifecta £176.80 Pool: £525.72, 2.20 winning units.
Owner Cheveley Park Stud **Bred** Joseph Allen **Trained** Newmarket, Suffolk

FOCUS
Not an easy race to assess, as the 90-rated Pawan looks to limit the form, but that one has a history of running above himself and this did look like a good conditions event. The winner did not need to match his best French form. They raced stands' side.

NOTEBOOK
Battle Paint(USA) ◆ was a very smart miler at three when trained in France, but he had been off the track for almost 14 months and has been switched to John Gosden. Dropped a couple of furlongs in trip for his return, he was never too far away and responded well to pressure when asked to pick up, although he did not do much once in front, possibly getting a little tired, and edged over to the stands' rail. His connections will surely be delighted and he looks worth his place back in Group company. (op 4-1 tchd 7-2)
Pawan(IRE) had it all to do at the weights - he was 18lb wrong with Battle Paint - but he has a history of running above himself and has been in great form this year. He was slightly short of room around a furlong out, but ran on well to the line. The Handicapper has no choice but to raise him for this and, for a horse who already has a poor strike-rate, he is not going to be easy to place to advantage. (op 12-1 tchd 10-1)
Tajdeef(USA), back up in trip and dropped down from Listed company, failed to justify favouritism and is not proving easy to win with this year. (op 9-4 tchd 11-4)
Somnus ◆, having his first start since leaving Tim Easterby after 280 days off, did not help his chance with a slow start and he raced in last for much of the way, but he finished in pleasing fashion. He could be one for a big handicap this season, maybe the Ayr Gold Cup. (op 14-1)
Floristry progressed to win a Listed race for Sir Michael Stoute last October, but she had been off since. This was a respectable effort on her debut for Godolphin and she can build on this. (op 3-1 tchd 11-4)
Capricorn Run(USA), swapping cheekpieces for blinkers, had it all to do conceding upwards of 8lb all round but he actually ran with credit, especially as he was a little short of room around two furlongs out.
Hammadi(IRE) looked to have the run of the race, but he found disappointingly little. (op 16-1)

4618 UNISON POSITIVELY PUBLIC STKS (H'CAP) 1m 2f 60y
4:00 (4:02) (Class 2) (0-100,95) 3-Y-O+
£12,462 (£3,732; £1,866; £934; £466; £234) **Stalls** Low

Form RPR
6-23 **1** **Nanton (USA)**[16] 4111 6-9-7 85 .... DanielTudhope 3 94
(J S Goldie) *hld up in rr: hdwy 3f out: n.m.r and swtchd lft 2f out: sn rdn: str run ent fnl f: led last 100yds and sn clr* **4/1**[2]
630 **2** *3* **Granston (IRE)**[16] 4111 7-9-6 84 .... RobertWinston 6 87
(J D Bethell) *trckd ldng pair: hdwy 4f out: chal over 2f out: rdn to ld wl over 1f out: hung lft ent fnl f: hdd and no ex last 100yds* **9/1**[3]
0000 **3** *¾* **Capable Guest (IRE)**[7] 4422 6-9-7 92 .... MatthewDavies[(7)] 5 94
(M R Channon) *hld up in rr: hdwy on outer wl over 2f out: rdn over 1f out: styd on ins fnl f* **16/1**
31 **4** *¾* **Checklow (USA)**[96] 1684 3-9-3 90 .... EddieAhern 4 90
(J Noseda) *hld up in tch: hdwy to trck ldrs 4f out and sn niggled along: rdn over 2f out: drvn over 1f out and sn one pce* **4/7**[1]
0620 **5** *2 ¾* **New Beginning (IRE)**[22] 3925 4-9-1 79 .... RichardMullen 1 74
(Mrs S Lamyman) *chsd ldrs on inner: rdn along 3f out: drvn 2f out and sn one pce* **18/1**
2200 **6** *½* **Jewelled Dagger (IRE)**[49] 3046 4-9-13 91 .... (b) NCallan 2 85
(Miss L A Perratt) *led: rdn along 3f out: drvn and hdd wl over 1f out: sn wknd* **16/1**
4453 **7** *1 ½* **Peruvian Prince (USA)**[8] 4396 6-9-2 80 .... RoystonFfrench 7 71
(R A Fahey) *chsd ldrs: rdn along over 3f out: sn drvn and wknd 2f out* **12/1**
2500 **8** *1 ¼* **Try Me (UAE)**[14] 4196 3-9-8 95 .... JimmyFortune 8 83
(C E Brittain) *chsd ldr: rdn along 3f out: drvn 2f out and sn wknd* **25/1**

2m 9.23s (-1.97) **Going Correction** +0.05s/f (Good)
WFA 3 from 4yo+ 9lb **8 Ran SP% 122.2**
Speed ratings (Par 109): **109,106,106,105,103 102,101,100**
toteswinger: 1&2 £3.80, 1&3 £12.90, 2&3 £17.00. CSF £42.26 CT £535.13 TOTE £5.20: £1.40, £2.70, £4.90; EX 47.50 Trifecta £491.30 Part won..
Owner J S Morrison **Bred** Samuel H And Mrs Rogers, Jr **Trained** Uplawmoor, E Renfrews
■ Stewards' Enquiry : Eddie Ahern caution: careless riding

FOCUS
A decent handicap, and sound form. The pace was good and the winning time was 1.07 seconds quicker than the later maiden.

NOTEBOOK
Nanton(USA) stepped up on his recent course-and-distance efforts with a clear-cut success, justifying a significant on-course market move. He looked to have plenty to do halfway up the straight, as he was still behind the favourite, who was struggling to pick up, but he found a decent turn of foot when in the clear to pull away from his field. His trainer felt he got to the front too soon last time, so he was waited with for longer this time and the new tactics worked a treat. He might be aimed at a Shergar Cup contest, but his connections also have a race at Haydock in mind. (op 6-1 tchd 13-2)
Granston(IRE) was only 2lb higher than when winning over course and distance in March and this was a respectable effort. (op 10-1 tchd 11-1)
Capable Guest(IRE) has struggled since winning the Zetland Gold Cup earlier in the season, but this was not a bad effort. (tchd 18-1)
Checklow(USA) created a good impression when beating the likes of fair handicappers Colorado Blue and Celt in a maiden at Windsor, and his trainer thinks quite a bit of him, hence entries in both the Great Voltigeur and the St Leger, but he ran below expectations on his return from thee months off, failing to justify a very short price. He's an out-and-out galloper, so a stronger pace would have suited better, and he gave the impression he was still a little green, as he ran around a bit under pressure. This was disappointing, but he can fulfil his potential when he matures, and a step up in trip is also likely to help, so he is not one to give up on just yet. (op 8-13 tchd 4-6 in places)
New Beginning(IRE) did not do enough to suggest he is about to win. (op 20-1)

4619 UNISON YOUR FRIEND AT WORK H'CAP 1m 4f
4:35 (4:35) (Class 4) (0-85,80) 3-Y-O
£6,476 (£1,927; £963; £481) **Stalls** Low

Form RPR
1453 **1** **Killcara Boy**[16] 4130 3-9-7 80 .... FergusSweeney 5 86
(H Candy) *trckd ldng pair: hdwy over 2f out: rdn to chse ldr over 1f out: drvn ins fnl f: styd on to ld nr line* **11/4**[2]
-321 **2** *nk* **Shady Gloom (IRE)**[45] 3130 3-9-6 79 .... NCallan 1 85
(K A Ryan) *trckd ldr: cl up 3f out: rdn to ld 2f out: drvn ent fnl f: hdd and no ex nr line* **5/1**[3]
0123 **3** *hd* **Mezzanisi (IRE)**[19] 4021 3-9-6 79 .... HayleyTurner 3 84
(M L W Bell) *hld up in rr: hdwy on outer 2f out: rdn over 1f out: drvn to chal ins fnl f: no ex fnr fin* **13/8**[1]
-531 **4** *2 ½* **Neve Lieve (IRE)**[24] 3843 3-8-11 70 .... MartinDwyer 4 71
(M Botti) *led: rdn along 3f out: hdd 2f out: sn drvn and one pce* **7/1**
-440 **5** *nk* **Trianon**[61] 2675 3-9-3 76 .... JimmyFortune 2 77
(R Charlton) *chsd ldrs: rdn along over 3f out: drvn over 2f out and sn one pce* **11/2**

2m 34.92s (-0.18) **Going Correction** +0.05s/f (Good) **5 Ran SP% 109.3**
Speed ratings (Par 102): **102,101,101,100,99**
toteswinger: 1&2 £4.00 CSF £15.81 TOTE £3.60: £1.70, £2.20; EX 15.70.
Owner Miss Julianna Byrne **Bred** Penfold Bloodstock Ltd **Trained** Kingston Warren, Oxon
■ Stewards' Enquiry : Fergus Sweeney two-day ban: used whip with excessive frequency (Aug 16-17)

FOCUS
This looked a fair handicap, but they went a modest pace and, having still been well bunched two out, the first three finished in a heap. Ordinary form for the grade.

4620 UNISON AND UIB THERE FOR YOU MAIDEN STKS 1m 2f 60y
5:10 (5:12) (Class 5) 3-4-Y-O
£3,238 (£963; £481; £240) **Stalls** Low

Form RPR
2-3 **1** **Sortita (GER)**[86] 1931 3-8-9 0 .... MartinDwyer 9 83+
(M A Jarvis) *sn led: pushed along over 2f out: rdn over 1f out: clr ent fnl f and styd on strly* **7/4**[1]
6 **2** *3 ¼* **Censored**[79] 2119 3-8-9 0 .... RobertWinston 1 76
(Sir Michael Stoute) *trckd ldrs: hdwy 3f out: rdn to chse wnr over 1f out: sn drvn and kpt on same pce* **14/1**
3 *¾* **Star Rocker** 3-9-0 0 .... JimmyFortune 5 80+
(J H M Gosden) *hld up towards rr: hdwy wl over 2f out: effrt whn n.m.r and swtchd lft over 1f out: kpt on ins fnl f: nrst fin* **5/1**
0-2 **4** *2 ¾* **Plavius (USA)**[17] 4085 3-9-0 0 .... RichardMullen 12 74
(Saeed Bin Suroor) *trckd ldrs: hdwy to chse wnr 4f out: rdn along wl over 2f out: drvn over 1f out and sn wknd* **4/1**[3]
0-0 **5** *3 ½* **Falcativ**[77] 2199 3-8-7 0 .... MJMurphy[(7)] 13 67+
(L M Cumani) *midfield: hdwy on outer 3f out: rdn along 2f out: no imp appr fnl f* **40/1**
6 *¾* **Culloden (UAE)** 3-9-0 0 .... NCallan 4 66
(J H M Gosden) *midfield: hdwy on inner 3f out: rdn 2f out and sn no imp* **20/1**
7 *1 ¼* **Blessing (USA)** 3-8-9 0 .... EddieAhern 11 58
(J Noseda) *midfield: hdwy on outer 3f out: rdn to chse ldrs 2f out: sn wknd* **9/4**[2]
00 **8** *1 ½* **Cwm Rhondda (USA)**[23] 3894 3-8-9 0 .... HayleyTurner 3 55
(P W Chapple-Hyam) *chsd ldrs: rdn along 3f out: drvn and n.m.r over 2f out and sn wknd* **66/1**
66 **9** *nse* **Lady Marguerite**[30] 3637 3-8-9 0 .... FergusSweeney 2 55
(M P Tregoning) *midfield: effrt 3f out: sn rdn along and wknd over 2f out* **50/1**
10 *3* **American Madness (USA)** 3-8-11 0 .... JerryO'Dwyer[(3)] 7 54
(M G Quinlan) *stdd s: hld up and a in rr* **50/1**
5 **11** *7* **Opera De Luna**[45] 3133 3-8-4 0 ow2 .... LeeTopliss[(7)] 8 37
(D Shaw) *towards rr: effrt on wd outside and sme hdwy 3f out: sn wknd* **80/1**
60 **12** *10* **Can Can Dancer**[15] 4166 3-8-9 0 .... RoystonFfrench 6 15
(J G Given) *chsd wnr: rdn along 4f out and sn wknd* **40/1**
13 *5* **Alltheclews** 3-8-7 0 .... MatthewDavies[(7)] 10 10
(B J McMath) *s.i.s: a bhd* **100/1**

2m 10.3s (-0.90) **Going Correction** +0.05s/f (Good) **13 Ran SP% 127.7**
Speed ratings (Par 103): **105,102,101,99,96 96,95,94,93,91 85,77,73**
toteswinger: 1&2 £8.00, 1&3 £3.20, 2&3 £7.10. CSF £30.25 TOTE £2.60: £1.40, £3.70, £2.10; EX 42.90 Trifecta £276.20 Pool: £593.57, 1.59 winning units Place 6 £189.04, Place 5 £22.34.
Owner Hamdan Al Maktoum **Bred** Gestut Karlshof **Trained** Newmarket, Suffolk

FOCUS
Plenty of big stables represented, but the winning time was 1.07 seconds slower than the earlier 81-100 handicap, suggesting the winner got away with setting ordinary fractions, and the bare form is probably just fair if pretty solid. Winners should come out of the race.
Star Rocker Official explanation: jockey said, regarding tender handling, that the colt had been hard ridden down the straight, had no more to give and achieved best possible placing.
Blessing(USA) Official explanation: vet said filly finished lame
T/Plt: £348.80 to a £1 stake. Pool: £64,065.17. 134.05 winning tickets. T/Qpdt: £18.00 to a £1 stake. Pool: £4,478.85. 183.20 winning tickets. JR

[4585]GOODWOOD (R-H)

Saturday, August 2

OFFICIAL GOING: Straight course - good; round course - good to firm

4mm of rain on top of well-watered ground meant that it rode much easier than the previous day.

Wind: Light to moderate, against Weather: Becoming bright after overcast start

4621 BLUESQUAREPOKER.COM STKS (H'CAP) 1m 3f

2:05 (2:10) (Class 3) (0-90,87) 3-Y-0

£12,462 (£3,732; £1,866; £934; £466; £234) **Stalls** Low

Form RPR

31-4 **1** **Southpaw Lad**[43] 3221 3-8-7 **73** AlanMunro 8 85+
(J R Best) *swtg: hld up in last trio: rdn over 4f out: last whn nt clr run 2f out: swtchd to outer: rapid prog over 1f out: led last 75yds and stormed clr* **25/1**

0211 **2** 1½ **Cosmea**[15] 4152 3-8-11 **77** JMurtagh 13 83
(A King) *settled midfield: rdn over 2f out: sme prog over 1f out: drvn and r.o fnl f to take 2nd nr fin: outpcd by wnr* **4/1**[1]

4303 **3** ¾ **Greylami (IRE)**[28] 3745 3-9-0 **80** MichaelHills 1 85
(T G Mills) *hld up in rr: stdy prog on outer fr 3f out gng easily: shkn up to ld over 1f out and looked sure to win: swamped last 75yds* **16/1**

3315 **4** 2½ **Palmerin**[16] 4130 3-8-12 **78** RichardHughes 11 78
(R Hannon) *lw: trckd ldrs: effrt and rdn to ld 2f out: hdd over 1f out: sn outpcd* **12/1**

2301 **5** ¾ **Sinbad The Sailor**[9] 4332 3-8-10 **76** TQuinn 16 75
(J W Hills) *cl up: effrt to dispute 2nd over 2f out: outpcd fr over 1f out* **20/1**

0-31 **6** 1 **Wikaala (USA)**[39] 3338 3-9-0 **80** RHills 10 77
(M P Tregoning) *lw: prom: led over 6f out: rdn and hdd 2f out: wknd fnl f* **11/1**[3]

3120 **7** shd **Woolfall Treasure**[44] 3157 3-9-7 **87** RyanMoore 3 84+
(G L Moore) *stdd s: hld up in last pair: pushed along over 3f out: nt clr run 2f out: limited prog towards inner over 1f out: plld out and styd on ins fnl f* **15/2**[2]

-510 **8** 1½ **Tomintoul Flyer**[23] 3877 3-9-6 **86** TedDurcan 2 80+
(H R A Cecil) *lw: hld up wl in rr: nt clr run over 2f out: sme prog over 1f out: drifted rt after: fdd fnl f* **12/1**

-313 **9** 3¼ **Stow**[50] 3004 3-8-9 **78** TravisBlock(3) 7 66
(H Morrison) *swtg: sn pushed up to ld: hdd over 6f out: chsd ldr to over 2f out: sn btn* **15/2**[2]

0121 **10** ½ **Deep Winter**[6] 4455 3-8-7 **73** 6ex PaulHanagan 9 61
(R A Fahey) *wl plcd bhd ldrs: u.p over 2f out: wknd over 1f out* **4/1**[1]

342 **11** 4½ **Cathedral Walk (USA)**[28] 3709 3-8-8 **74** AndrewElliott 15 53
(K R Burke) *prom on inner: losing pl whn n.m.r over 1f out* **50/1**

3124 **12** 1¼ **St Jean Cap Ferrat**[28] 3745 3-8-13 **79** SebSanders 6 56
(G Wragg) *hld up in midfield: no prog over 2f out: wknd and eased over 1f out* **12/1**

5551 **13** nk **Bencoolen (IRE)**[30] 3649 3-9-7 **87** (v[1]) SteveDrowne 14 64
(R Charlton) *mostly in midfield: effrt over 2f out: wkng whn short of room over 1f out* **16/1**

2m 26.66s (-1.64) **Going Correction** +0.125s/f (Good) **13** Ran SP% **117.3**
Speed ratings (Par 104): **110,108,108,106,106 105,105,104,101,101 98,97,96**
toteswinger: 1&2 £24.20, 1&3 £76.30, 2&3 £13.20. CSF £118.55 CT £1690.28 TOTE £30.10: £6.90, £2.00, £4.40; EX 179.30 Trifecta £1047.10 Part won..
Owner SN Racing II **Bred** S Nunn **Trained** Hucking, Kent

FOCUS

A competitive handicap, and the good gallop saw the first three coming from well off the pace. Although there were not that many progressive types in the field, the form looks sound enough.

NOTEBOOK

Southpaw Lad, last and with nowhere to go two furlongs out, was switched wide and brought with a storming late run down the outside. Unimpeded, he stayed on strongly to lead well inside the last, showing improved form for the three furlong step up in trip. On this evidence there should be even better to come, and he could run at York next.

Cosmea, chasing a hat-trick off a 6lb higher mark, had seen her Newbury form given a boost when Spell Caster won here on Wednesday. She came home well but the winner just always had her measure and it is possible that a trip to Bath the previous night, where she was a non-runner, did her no favours. (op 11-2 tchd 7-2)

Greylami(IRE), poorly drawn, came from behind with what looked like a winning effort from two furlongs out, but he was overhauled well inside the last by two who were finishing even better. On reflection he probably hit the front too soon, and there should be a similar race in him. (tchd 14-1)

Palmerin ran a solid race but the Handicapper may just have his measure now. (op 16-1)

Sinbad The Sailor, raised 7lb for his Doncaster win, was taking on tougher opposition this time. He kept on one-paced under pressure. (op 25-1)

Wikaala(USA), whose pedigree suggested he might improve quite a bit for the step up in distance, was quite weak in the market and, after racing prominently, he did not get home. Weakening as he did does not necessarily mean he will not stay this trip in time as the pace was probably just too strong for those who raced prominently to hold off the closers, but a drop back to 1m2f will probably help. (op 9-1 tchd 8-1)

Woolfall Treasure ran poorly at Royal Ascot last time, but this was more like it. He ran a fair race from a poor draw and shapes as though he needs 1m4f now. Longer term his new owner sees him as a bright hurdling prospect. (op 9-1 tchd 10-1)

Tomintoul Flyer, another who had a low draw to overcome, did not get the clearest of runs and is a bit better than the bare form suggests.

Stow had too much use made of him and did not get home. (op 8-1)

Deep Winter, up in trip chasing a four-timer, had a 6lb penalty to carry, and she was found out by the rise in class. (tchd 9-2 in a place)

4622 BLUE SQUARE PREMIER STKS (REGISTERED AS THE THOROUGHBRED STAKES) (LISTED RACE) 1m

2:40 (2:42) (Class 1) 3-Y-0

£28,385 (£10,760; £5,385; £2,685; £1,345; £675) **Stalls** High

Form RPR

0-43 **1** **River Proud (USA)**[83] 2032 3-9-0 **112** RichardHughes 5 115
(P F I Cole) *lw: t.k.h early: mde all: set stdy pce to 1/2-way: drew clr fr 2f out: readily* **5/2**[2]

-420 **2** 2½ **Alexandros**[46] 3102 3-9-0 **109** LDettori 9 109
(Saeed Bin Suroor) *lw: t.k.h early: hld up in 3rd: nt qckn 2f out: styd on to take 2nd last 150yds: no imp wnr* **9/2**[3]

6-12 **3** nk **Atlantic Sport (USA)**[15] 4153 3-9-0 **105** EdwardCreighton 3 108+
(M R Channon) *lw: t.k.h early: hld up in last pair: prog u.p over 2f out: disp 2nd 1f out: kpt on one pce* **12/1**

1250 **4** ¾ **Moyenne Corniche**[14] 4192 3-9-0 **105** AlanMunro 1 107
(G Wragg) *sweating: trckd wnr: outpcd fr 2f out: nt qckn and lost 2 pls fnl f* **25/1**

2161 **5** 1½ **Duntulm**[22] 3919 3-9-0 **100** DaneO'Neill 8 103+
(H Candy) *lw: hld up in rr: rdn and struggling whn nt clr run 2f out: swtchd and one pce after* **11/2**

2-01 **6** shd **Perfect Stride**[7] 4404 3-9-0 **89** RyanMoore 6 103+
(Sir Michael Stoute) *hld up in last: effrt on outer over 2f out: limited prog over 1f out: no hdwy and jst pushed along fnl f* **9/4**[1]

2506 **7** 3½ **Meeriss (IRE)**[14] 4197 3-9-0 **96** TPO'Shea 4 95
(M R Channon) *t.k.h early: trckd ldrs: wknd on inner over 1f out* **33/1**

-062 **8** 3 **Alfathaa**[23] 3880 3-9-0 **105** RHills 2 88
(W J Haggas) *t.k.h early: trckd ldrs: rdn over 2f out: wknd wl over 1f out* **14/1**

1m 38.29s (-1.61) **Going Correction** +0.125s/f (Good) **8** Ran SP% **114.1**
Speed ratings (Par 108): **113,110,110,109,107 107,104,101**
toteswinger: 1&2 £3.10, 1&3 £7.10, 2&3 £8.00. CSF £14.18 TOTE £3.60: £1.40, £1.60, £2.40; EX 14.20 Trifecta £102.80 Pool: £1,166.07, 8.39 winning units.
Owner Mrs Michael Spencer **Bred** Brereton C Jones And B Ned Jones **Trained** Whatcombe, Oxon

FOCUS

A good race for the grade with the first two both having form at a higher level. Sound form.

NOTEBOOK

River Proud(USA), an unlucky third in the French 2000 Guineas last time, gained a measure of recompense on this drop in grade. He gave no problem at the start this time, again fitted with a rug for stalls entry, and set off in front although it had not been the plan to lead. Kicking with two furlongs to run, he stayed on well and was never seriously threatened. He will get further and his trainer has in mind the Group 2 Prix Guillaume d'Ornano over 1m2f at Deauville later this month. (op 11-4 tchd 10-3)

Alexandros, down in grade after finishing seventh in the St James's Palace Stakes, was always prominent. He could not quicken up when the pace lifted but stayed on determinedly for second. He really needs a bit of cut and this ground suited him more than that at Ascot. (op 8-1)

Atlantic Sport(USA) was beaten at 4/6 last time but that was a decent run formwise. Having his first run over 1m, he made good progress from the rear to dispute second before his effort just flattened out a little in the last half-furlong. (op 9-1)

Moyenne Corniche, down in trip again, became warm in the preliminaries. He ran well, tracking the winner before fading gradually in the final furlong, but his yard remains out of form. (tchd 22-1)

Duntulm has won two decent handicaps at Newmarket this year, the latest off 93, but was found wanting on this rise in grade. He would have been perhaps a length closer had he not run into trouble about a quarter of a mile out. (op 7-1)

Perfect Stride was raised 11lb to a mark of 100 following his impressive win in an Ascot handicap the previous weekend, form franked at Goodwood by third home Yamal. In this hotter company he failed to really pick up from the rear and Moore did not persevere late on in a lost cause. The rain-eased ground was against him as was the quick reappearance, and he is worth another chance back on a sound surface. Official explanation: jockey said, regarding failing to ride out for 5th place, that the colt was unsuited by the good (good to firm in places) ground and became unbalanced in closing stages. (op 7-4 tchd 13-8)

Meeriss(IRE) won in this grade here last season but had the lowest BHA rating in this field and was not up to the task. (op 50-1)

Alfathaa, again a bit keen even with the blinkers left off, was well enough placed when the pace quickened but his response under pressure was disappointing. (tchd 12-1)

4623 BLUE SQUARE NASSAU STKS (GROUP 1) (F&M) 1m 1f 192y

3:15 (3:19) (Class 1) 3-Y-0+

£113,540 (£43,040; £21,540; £10,740; £5,380; £2,700) **Stalls** High

Form RPR

231 **1** **Halfway To Heaven (IRE)**[69] 2433 3-8-10 **0** JMurtagh 4 113
(A P O'Brien, Ire) *w'like: scope: tall: lw: led 1f: trckd ldr: effrt over 2f out: hd high but led narrowly over 1f out: drvn and styd on fnl f: hld on* **5/1**[2]

6151 **2** hd **Lush Lashes**[43] 3194 3-8-10 **0** KJManning 6 116+
(J S Bolger, Ire) *lw: t.k.h: hld up and sn midfield: pushed along and n.m.r 3f out: nt clr run and hanging 2f out: prog whn swtchd ins and nowhere to go 1f out: swtchd lft and fin strly: nt rch wnr* **1/1**[1]

-401 **3** hd **Passage Of Time**[14] 4192 4-9-5 **115** TedDurcan 3 112
(H R A Cecil) *trckd ldrs: rdn and effrt over 2f out: drvn and clsd grad on wnr fnl f but lost 2nd nr fin* **8/1**

1123 **4** nk **Heaven Sent**[24] 3852 5-9-5 **111** RyanMoore 8 111+
(Sir Michael Stoute) *lw: hld up in 7th: shkn up and effrt over 2f out: n.m.r and swtchd outside over 1f out: styd on wl fnl f but nvr able to chal* **15/2**

-105 **5** 1¼ **Muthabara (IRE)**[43] 3194 3-8-10 **109** RHills 1 109
(J L Dunlop) *led after 1f and set v stdy gallop: increased pce over 3f out: narrowly hdd over 1f out: pressed wnr tl no ex last 100yds* **7/1**[3]

4521 **6** ¾ **Classic Remark (IRE)**[37] 3415 3-8-10 **100** MickyFenton 7 107
(H J L Dunlop) *t.k.h: cl up: lost pl on inner 3f out: outpcd fr over 2f out: styd on again ins fnl f* **50/1**

4-32 **7** 2¼ **Soft Morning**[8] 4395 4-9-5 **105** SebSanders 9 103+
(Sir Mark Prescott) *hld up in last pair: struggling and detached in last 3f out: kpt on fnl f* **25/1**

0546 **8** 7 **Majestic Roi (USA)**[24] 3852 4-9-5 **112** EdwardCreighton 2 89
(M R Channon) *t.k.h: hld up in 6th: effrt 3f out: wknd rapidly wl over 1f out* **20/1**

2045 **9** 10 **Sugar Mint (IRE)**[8] 4395 3-8-10 **101** MichaelHills 10 69
(B W Hills) *swtg: dwlt: hld up in last pair: effrt on outer over 2f out: wknd v rapidly wl over 1f out* **66/1**

2m 9.73s (1.73) **Going Correction** +0.125s/f (Good)
WFA 3 from 4yo+ 9lb **9** Ran SP% **114.1**
Speed ratings (Par 117): **98,97,97,97,96 95,94,88,80**
toteswinger: 1&2 £1.60, 1&3 £6.80, 2&3 £2.90. CSF £9.95 TOTE £3.40: £1.10, £1.50, £2.30; EX 8.70 Trifecta £35.40 Pool: £8,853.94, 184.70 winning units.
Owner M Tabor, D Smith & Mrs John Magnier **Bred** T Stewart **Trained** Ballydoyle, Co Tipperary

■ A second successive Nassau for Aidan O'Brien, on the day it was announced that 2007 winner Peeping Fawn has been retired.

FOCUS

This was run at a very steady pace and is messy form. Halfway To Heaven is progressive and up 4lb on her Irish Guineas form, but the unlucky Lush Lashes has been rated a clear winner.

NOTEBOOK

Halfway To Heaven(IRE) gained her second Group 1 success following her narrow win in the Irish 1000 Guineas. By Pivotal out of the sprinter Cassandra Go, there was an obvious doubt about her stamina over this longer trip, but she got away with it under a fine ride in a steadily run race. The early leader, she then tracked Muthabara before taking a narrow lead with more than a furlong to run. Battling on despite showing a high head carriage, she held on in a tight finish. She is an admirable performer but was a lucky winner as Lush Lashes was the best horse in the race. (op 4-1 tchd 11-2 in a place)

The Form Book, Raceform Ltd, Compton, RG20 6NL

Lush Lashes ◆ should have won. Reverting to this trip after her fine victory in the Coronation Stakes at Ascot, she took a bit of a hold in about fifth or sixth in a tightly bunched field. When the pace quickened at around the three pole she failed to immediately pick up and then found herself rather trapped in by horses around her, hanging a little too. With nowhere to go Manning switched her to the rail, only to see the gap close as Halfway To Heaven edged in on Muthabara. Switched out again, she finished strongly, despite Manning dropping his reins close home, but the line just beat her. She is capable of making amends. (op 5-4 tchd 11-8 in places)

Passage Of Time, who resumed winning ways with a defeat of Bankable in a Newbury Listed contest, confirmed she is back to form with a solid effort. She lacked a real turn of foot at the end of this steadily run race, but was closing on the winner at the line, despite edging to her left, as Lush Lashes finished fast to divide the pair. (op 15-2 tchd 7-1 in a place)

Heaven Sent, third in the Falmouth Stakes last time, ran another big race at this level and was staying on well down the outside after being forced to switch. This was only her second run over this far and she saw it out well, albeit in a falsely run race. (op 7-1)

Muthabara(IRE) set a very modest pace and wound it up going to the final three furlongs. Just headed by the winner a furlong and a half out, she kept trying and was only run out of the frame in the last half-furlong. She will be better suited by a stiffer test at this trip. (op 8-1 tchd 9-1 in a place)

Classic Remark(IRE), the most inexperienced filly in the line-up, came here on the back of a Newcastle Listed win at 40/1. She ran well in this top company although the suspicion is that she may have been a little flattered to finish as close as she did. (op 66-1)

Soft Morning adopted very different tactics on this steep rise in grade and she could never make her presence felt.

Majestic Roi(USA), upped in trip, failed to settle at all off the very steady gallop and was baeten with two furlongs to run. (op 22-1 tchd 25-1 in a place)

Sugar Mint(IRE), who sweated up, was always towards the back of the field and is not up this level. (op 80-1 tchd 50-1)

4624 BLUESQUARE.COM STEWARDS' CUP (HERITAGE H'CAP) 6f

3:50 (3:53) (Class 2) 3-Y-0+

£62,310 (£18,660; £9,330; £4,670; £2,330; £1,170) **Stalls** Low

Form RPR

5000 **1** **Conquest (IRE)**[22] 3905 4-8-9 **95** DaneO'Neill 14 106
(W J Haggas) *racd centre: hld up: a gng wl: prog 2f out: rdn to ld ins fnl f: edgd lft: styd on wl* **40/1**

-530 **2** *hd* **King's Apostle (IRE)**[7] 4405 4-9-2 **102** LiamJones 3 113+
(W J Haggas) *lw: in rr of nr side gp: hanging bdly fr over 2f out: fnlly picked up jst over 1f out: r.o wl to take 2nd nr fin* **12/1**

1222 **3** *½* **Borderlescott**[21] 3948 6-9-10 **110** PatCosgrave 1 119
(R Bastiman) *overall ldr nr side: clr 2f out: hung rt jst over 1f out: hdd and nt qckn ins fnl f* **7/1**[2]

4000 **4** *2 ½* **Machinist (IRE)**[42] 3248 8-8-11 **97** SilvestreDeSousa 7 98
(D Nicholls) *lw: towards rr nr side: outpcd 2f out: styd on ins fnl f: no threat to ldng trio* **20/1**

0140 **5** *½* **Mac Gille Eoin**[21] 3943 4-9-0 **100** JimCrowley 8 99
(J Gallagher) *racd towards nr side: prom: nt qckn over 1f out: edgd lft but styd on fnl f* **20/1**

441 **6** *nk* **Knot In Wood (IRE)**[15] 4145 6-8-12 **101** 3ex JamieMoriarty(3) 17 99
(R A Fahey) *lw: disp ld in gp nr far side: overall ldr of far side jst over 1f out: nt on terms w nr side fnl f* **9/1**[3]

6050 **7** *½* **Off The Record**[22] 3922 4-8-12 **98** RichardHughes 28 95
(J G Given) *lw: s.s: wl off the pce far side: prog 2f out: styd on wl fnl f: nrst fin* **12/1**

4000 **8** *½* **Northern Fling**[6] 4445 4-8-12 **101** AndrewMullen(3) 23 96
(D Nicholls) *chsd far side ldrs: nt qckn over 1f out: kpt on ins fnl f* **25/1**

5330 **9** *¾* **Siren's Gift**[6] 4445 4-8-9 **95** FrancisNorton 4 88
(A M Balding) *lw: pressed overall ldr nr side to jst over 1f out: wknd* **25/1**

5501 **10** *½* **Buachaill Dona (IRE)**[36] 3451 5-9-3 **103** AdrianTNicholls 27 94
(D Nicholls) *lw: t.k.h early: pressed far side ldr: led gp briefly over 1f out: one pce fnl f* **14/1**

5-10 **11** *½* **Hitchens (IRE)**[7] 4405 3-9-3 **107** RyanMoore 5 97
(G L Moore) *dwlt: racd nr side: mostly in rr: outpcd fr 2f out: kpt on fnl f* **25/1**

3020 **12** *¾* **Prime Defender**[22] 3922 4-9-4 **104** MichaelHills 19 91
(B W Hills) *racd towards far side: hld up bhd ldng pair: effrt over 2f out: nt qckn over 1f out: plugged on* **11/2**[1]

6105 **13** *shd* **Edge Closer**[14] 4188 4-9-7 **112** HaddenFrost(5) 10 99
(R Hannon) *lw: w ldrs in centre: hanging rt fr over 2f out: fdd fr over 1f out* **33/1**

-350 **14** *½* **Ashdown Express (IRE)**[22] 3921 9-8-13 **99** PaulDoe 2 84
(W J Knight) *trckd ldrs nr side: outpcd fr 2f out: no hdwy after* **50/1**

0020 **15** *nse* **Beaver Patrol (IRE)**[35] 3504 6-9-4 **104** (v) RHills 6 89
(Eve Johnson Houghton) *lw: dwlt: chsd ldrs nr side: struggling 2f out: no prog after* **25/1**

3105 **16** *1 ½* **Orpsie Boy (IRE)**[6] 4445 5-8-7 **96** KirstyMilczarek(3) 20 76
(N P Littmoden) *hld up in gp towards far side: nvr on terms w ldrs: modest late prog* **25/1**

00-0 **17** *¾* **Patavellian (IRE)**[28] 3722 10-9-3 **103** (b) SteveDrowne 25 81
(R Charlton) *taken down early: led far side gp to over 1f out: wknd fnl f* **50/1**

3200 **18** *½* **Hinton Admiral**[22] 3921 4-8-6 **99** ow2 FrederikTylicki(7) 21 75
(R A Fahey) *taken down early: racd far side: nvr on terms w ldrs: struggling 2f out* **28/1**

0600 **19** *hd* **Indian Trail**[6] 4445 8-9-0 **100** (v) AlanMunro 9 76
(D Nicholls) *prom in centre: hanging bdly rt fr 1/2-way: wknd wl over 1f out* **50/1**

6460 **20** *nk* **Confuchias (IRE)**[21] 3982 4-9-5 **105** (p) AndrewElliott 18 80
(K R Burke) *sweating: disp ld in gp racing towards far side: wknd over 2f out* **66/1**

6200 **21** *1 ¾* **Hoh Hoh Hoh**[14] 4188 6-9-4 **104** SebSanders 22 73
(R J Price) *racd far side: pressed ldrs over 3f: wknd* **40/1**

0000 **22** *½* **Something (IRE)**[7] 4417 6-8-10 **96** JimmyQuinn 15 64
(D Nicholls) *racd centre: hld up: gng wl 1/2-way: effrt over 2f out: wknd tamely over 1f out* **14/1**

450 **23** *2 ¾* **Rising Shadow (IRE)**[15] 4145 7-8-6 **97** AshleyHamblett(5) 26 56
(N Wilson) *s.s: racd far side and wl off the pce: nvr a factor* **50/1**

0104 **24** *2 ¾* **Barney McGrew (IRE)**[15] 4145 5-8-8 **94** TedDurcan 16 44
(M Dods) *s.v.s: swtchd to r towards far side: nvr on terms: brief prog over 1f out: eased fnl f* **16/1**

1010 **25** *4* **Sohraab**[6] 4445 4-8-7 **96** 3ex TravisBlock(3) 13 33
(H Morrison) *wl on terms in centre: rdn hlfway: wknd over 2f out* **25/1**

20-0 **26** *3 ¼* **Protector (SAF)**[15] 4145 7-9-0 **100** PaulHanagan 11 27
(A G Foster) *taken down early: spd in centre to 1/2-way: wknd rapidly* **50/1**

1663 **L** **Bentong (IRE)**[28] 3722 5-9-2 **102** (t) TQuinn 24 —
(P F I Cole) *ref to r: tk no part* **14/1**

1m 11.91s (-0.29) **Going Correction** +0.125s/f (Good)

WFA 3 from 4yo+ 4lb **27** Ran SP% **134.3**

Speed ratings (Par 109): **106,105,105,101,101 100,100,99,98,97 97,96,95,95,95 93,92,91,91,90 88,87,84,80,75 70,—**

Toteswinger: 1&2 £202.60, 1&3 £130.40, 2&3 £19.40. CSF £407.62 CT £3816.41 TOTE £64.90: £10.50, £4.40, £1.90, £6.60; EX 987.00 Trifecta £28737.10 Part won..

Owner Highclere Thoroughbred Racing XXXVIII **Bred** Gerrardstown House Stud **Trained** Newmarket, Suffolk

■ A 1-2 for William Haggas in this hugely competitive handicap.

FOCUS

After initially forming four groups, then three, they were spread right across the course, but the pace was on the stands' side and it also looked as if the far side may have been overwatered. The first three finished clear, with the winner coming over from the centre to join the second and third on the stands' side. The form is rated through the third.

NOTEBOOK

Conquest(IRE) has been largely disappointing since his Gimcrack win two years ago and had been dropped 7lb since the start of this season. Racing off the pace down the centre of the track, he came with a good run to take up the running before edging over towards the stands' rail. He showed a high head carriage but did enough to hold off his stablemate close home.

King's Apostle(IRE), held up out the back on the near side, made good progress from the two pole despite hanging. He finished strongly but just failed to peg back his stablemate. This is his optimum trip, although he does stay 7f, and following his third in the Wokingham he does deserve to pick up a nice prize, although it may have to be in Listed company as he is going up in the handicap. (op 14-1)

Borderlescott, who won this race two years ago, was beaten a short head by Zidane last year and has accumulated a further six second places since. His connections having chosen stall 1 for him, he showed fine speed against the stands' fence but could not repel the Haggas pair inside the last. (op 9-1 tchd 13-2)

Machinist(IRE), as in the Wokingham, was doing his best work late, finishing well from the rear without threatening the three in front of him. (tchd 22-1)

Mac Gille Eoin, who sweated up, likes it at Goodwood and ran another good race, albeit on the favoured side of the track. It could be that the handicapper just has his measure now.

Knot In Wood(IRE) picked up a 3lb penalty for his win in the Scottish version of this race at Hamilton, taking him to a mark 3lb higher than when third last year. Showing fine speed, he ran a cracking race, doing best of those to race on the far side, where the ground seemed slower. (op 8-1 tchd 10-1 in places)

Off The Record, not disgraced in the July Cup last time, found himself a good way in rear down the far side but was finishing well closest to the rail. (op 16-1)

Northern Fling had also finished eighth in this year's Wokingham when a pound higher. (op 20-1)

Siren's Gift raced close behind Borderlescott near the stands' rail until weakening in the final furlong.

Buachaill Dona(IRE) ran a reasonable race back up in trip and on the wrong side of the track. (op 16-1)

Hitchens(IRE), back down in trip for this quick return, faced a stiff task for a three-year-old and was only really passing rivals when it was all over. (op 20-1)

Prime Defender was officially 9lb well in following his good seventh in the July Cup but could not take advantage. Connections blamed the easing in the ground. Official explanation: jockey said colt was unsuited by the good (good to firm in places) ground (op 6-1)

Beaver Patrol(IRE), racing off a career-high mark, 9lb higher than when fifth in this last year, was eased when beaten inside the final furlong.

Patavellian(IRE), who won this race back in 2003, showed up well for a long way down the far side. (op 40-1)

Rising Shadow(IRE) Official explanation: jockey said gelding lost a front shoe

4625 BLUE SQUARE E B F MAIDEN STKS (C&G) 7f

4:25 (4:28) (Class 2) 2-Y-0 **£12,952** (£3,854; £1,926; £962) **Stalls** High

Form RPR

1 **Jukebox Jury (IRE)** 2-9-0 0 JMurtagh 2 82+
(M Johnston) *w'like: scope: str: bit bkwd: towards rr: brought wd in st: green but prog over 2f out: str run fnl f: edgd rt but led nr fin* **14/1**

2 **2** *nk* **Full Toss**[21] 3968 2-9-0 0 RichardHughes 15 81
(R Hannon) *str: wnt lft at s: led: gng strly and 2 l clr wl over 1f out: hung lft fnl f: hdd nr fin* **4/1**[2]

0 **3** *1 ½* **Cloudy Start**[24] 3853 2-9-0 0 TedDurcan 8 80+
(H R A Cecil) *trckd ldrs: effrt over 2f out: disp 2nd over 1f out: styng on but hld in 3rd whn snatched up nr fin* **13/2**[3]

4 *2* **Asateer (IRE)** 2-9-0 0 RHills 14 73+
(B W Hills) *w'like: scope: tall: str: dwlt and hmpd sn after s: keen and sn prom: shkn up to dispute 2nd wl over 1f out: edgd lft and wknd fnl f* **25/1**

5 *3 ½* **Dialogue** 2-9-0 0 LDettori 11 64
(M Johnston) *w'like: scope: chsd ldrs: outpcd fr 2f out: one pce and n.d after* **15/2**

32 **6** *1 ½* **Highland Storm**[22] 3926 2-9-0 0 AlanMunro 6 60+
(J G Given) *leggy: scope: wl in rr and stl looked green: shkn up 3f out: styd on fr over 1f out: n.d* **14/1**

4 **7** *hd* **Holyrood**[24] 3853 2-9-0 0 RyanMoore 7 60
(Sir Michael Stoute) *lw: nvr beyond midfield: rdn 1/2-way: outpcd fr 2f out* **2/1**[1]

0 **8** *¾* **Appraisal**[29] 3682 2-9-0 0 TPO'Shea 4 58
(R Hannon) *hld up in midfield: carried wd bnd 4f out: hanging over 2f out: kpt on fr over 1f out* **66/1**

9 *2 ¼* **Capeability (IRE)** 2-9-0 0 EdwardCreighton 12 52
(M R Channon) *unf: scope: mostly chsd ldr to wl over 1f out: wknd* **16/1**

10 *nk* **Admirable Duque (IRE)** 2-9-0 0 TQuinn 5 51+
(D J S Ffrench Davis) *leggy: s.v.s: wl in rr: rdn 3f out: modest late prog* **66/1**

42 **11** *1 ½* **Tepmokea (IRE)**[38] 3364 2-9-0 0 AndrewElliott 1 48
(K R Burke) *wl in tch on outer tl wknd 2f out* **33/1**

4 **12** *½* **Millway Beach (IRE)**[15] 4151 2-9-0 0 DaneO'Neill 10 46
(Pat Eddery) *pressed ldrs tl wknd 2f out* **12/1**

13 *1 ½* **Khan Tengri (IRE)** 2-9-0 0 SteveDrowne 3 43
(M P Tregoning) *w'like: scope: s.v.s: a wl in rr* **50/1**

5 **14** *6* **Master Fong (IRE)**[10] 4304 2-9-0 0 MichaelHills 16 28
(B W Hills) *lw: a in rr: bhd fnl 2f* **33/1**

15 *2 ¾* **Monetary Fund (USA)** 2-9-0 0 JamieMoriarty 13 21
(G A Butler) *leggy: s.v.s: a wl bhd* **50/1**

00 **16** *6* **Saunton Sands**[80] 2098 2-9-0 0 PaulHanagan 9 6
(A G Newcombe) *plld hrd: hld up in tch: hung lft 4f out: wknd rapidly 3f out: t.o* **100/1**

1m 28.61s (1.21) **Going Correction** +0.125s/f (Good) **16** Ran SP% **123.0**

Speed ratings (Par 100): **98,97,95,93,89 87,87,86,84,83 82,81,79,73,69 63**

Toteswinger: 1&2 £13.10, 1&3 £15.90, 2&3 £5.70. CSF £66.95 TOTE £11.60: £2.80, £1.80, £2.70; EX 77.20 Trifecta £523.90 Pool: £1,203.75, 1.70 winning units.

Owner A D Spence **Bred** Paul Nataf **Trained** Middleham Moor, N Yorks

■ Stewards' Enquiry : Richard Hughes two-day ban: careless riding (Aug 16-17)

FOCUS
A decent looking maiden which included some well-bred types who hold big race entries. It should throw up a few winners.
NOTEBOOK
Jukebox Jury(IRE), who cost 270,000euros, is a half-brother to six winners including Belle Allure, a 1m1f Group 3 winner in France, Pierrot Solitaire, a prolific winner between 6f and 1m4f in Italy, and The Mask, a smart, multiple winner between 6f and 1m4f in France. He has entries in the Group 1 National Stakes and Group 2 Champagne and Royal Lodge Stakes, but was weak in the market beforehand. Towards the back of the field, he was angled out three furlongs out, carried his head a bit high and ran green, but stayed on really strongly to get up and lead close home. He looks sure to appreciate a step up to 1m later in the season and his pedigree suggests he will make a middle-distance colt next year. He looks a very useful prospect. (op 11-1 tchd 9-1)
Full Toss, who ran with promise on his debut at Salisbury, was well drawn and looked to have a bit going for him here. Allowed a fairly easy time of it in front, he poached a two-length advantage approaching the final furlong but hung left in the closing stages and was collared. (op 9-2)
Cloudy Start again sweated up beforehand, as he had on his debut at Newmarket, but it clearly does not hamper his performance, as he comprehensively reversed form with Holyrood and would have finished slightly closer had Full Toss not hung left and forced Durcan to snatch up close home. (tchd 7-1)
Asateer(IRE) ◆, whose sales price rose from 55,000gns as a foal to 220,000gns as a yearling, is a half-brother to Hostage, a winner over 7f at two and over 1m at three. A Champagne/Royal Lodge entry, he shaped with plenty of promise on his debut, travelling well behind the leader for a long way. He should come on for the experience and can win his maiden. Official explanation: jockey said colt hung left-handed (op 20-1 tchd 16-1)
Dialogue, a half-brother to seven winners including Zoning, who won at up to 1m and was fourth in the 2000 Guineas, holds a Royal Lodge entry. The rain-softened ground might not have been ideal for this son of Singspiel but he shaped with promise and should do better as he gains experience. (op 12-1)
Highland Storm had two runs under his belt coming here so had an edge in experience, but he still looked green and, although running on at the end, was never really in the hunt. Another furlong will suit him in nursery company. (op 20-1)
Holyrood, racing on quicker ground than on his debut at Newmarket when finishing ahead of Cloudy Start, could not confirm that form, but he may just not have taken to this place and can be given another chance on a more galloping track. (op 15-8 tchd 9-4 in places)
Appraisal, who showed a bit more than on his debut, looks more of a handicap type after one more run.
Capeability(IRE), who cost 175,000gns, is the first foal of a mare who is very closely related to Arc winner Carnegie. Entries in the National Stakes, Futurity and Royal Lodge suggest he is well regarded, and this debut experience should not be lost on him. (op 20-1 tchd 14-1)
Saunton Sands Official explanation: jockey said colt did not handle the first bend

4626 BLUESQUARE.COM NURSERY STKS (H'CAP) 6f
5:00 (5:00) (Class 2) 2-Y-O £12,952 (£3,854; £1,926; £962) **Stalls** Low

Form RPR
334 **1** **Parisian Pyramid (IRE)**[12] 4237 2-8-1 68 SilvestreDeSousa 7 84+
(D Nicholls) *str: wnt rt s: mde virtually all: edgd lft fr over 2f out: drew rt away fr over 1f out* **11/1**
2533 **2** *4 1/2* **Taazur**[15] 4143 2-8-10 77 RHills 10 79
(M Johnston) *chsd ldrs on outer: rdn over 2f out: prog fnl 2f to take 2nd ins fnl f: no ch w wnr* **12/1**
226 **3** *2 3/4* **Noble Jack (IRE)**[15] 4150 2-9-5 86 RyanMoore 5 79
(R Hannon) *hld up in tch: rdn over 2f out: sn outpcd: styd on u.p to take 3rd wl ins fnl f* **13/2**[3]
0413 **4** *2* **Tagula Breeze (IRE)**[25] 3809 2-8-10 80 (t) JamieMoriarty[(3)] 4 67
(I W McInnes) *w wnr to 1/2-way: rdn whn hmpd 2f out and lost 2nd: sn outpcd: kpt on fnl f* **20/1**
516 **5** *1/2* **Golden Rosie (IRE)**[16] 4119 2-8-12 79 MichaelHills 3 65+
(B W Hills) *w ldrs: wnt 2nd 2f out: hmpd over 1f out: sn wknd* **5/1**[2]
4120 **6** *2* **Finnegan McCool**[14] 4190 2-9-5 86 SebSanders 8 66
(R M Beckett) *sltly hmpd s: wl in rr: rdn over 2f out: sme prog over 1f out: sn lft bhd* **5/1**[2]
31 **7** *2 1/2* **Tishtar**[72] 2338 2-9-7 88 RichardHughes 6 60
(R Hannon) *lw: chsd ldrs: rdn over 2f out: lft wl bhd fr over 1f out* **2/1**[1]
236 **8** *1* **Kyllachy Star**[8] 4394 2-8-13 80 PaulHanagan 1 49+
(R A Fahey) *s.s: rcvrd and in tch after 2f: losing pl whn hmpd against rail over 2f out: bhd after* **12/1**
141 **9** *1* **Fault**[16] 4101 2-9-5 86 SteveDrowne 2 52
(R Charlton) *lw: hld up in rr: rdn over 2f out: sn wknd* **15/2**
3350 **10** *9* **In Transit (IRE)**[16] 4119 2-8-11 78 TPO'Shea 9 17
(M R Channon) *lw: nvr on terms: bhd fnl 2f* **16/1**

1m 12.24s (0.04) **Going Correction** +0.125s/f (Good) **10** Ran SP% **126.1**
Speed ratings (Par 100): **104,98,94,91,91 88,85,83,82,70**
Toteswinger: 1&2 £11.30 1&3 £15.20, 2&3 £12.80. CSF £145.54 CT £975.29 TOTE £12.10: £3.50, £3.30, £2.20; EX 92.70 Trifecta £852.50 Pool: £1,152.03, 1.00 winning units.
Owner D Nicholls **Bred** Illuminatus Investments **Trained** Sessay, N Yorks
■ Stewards' Enquiry : Silvestre De Sousa one-day ban: careless riding (Aug 16)
FOCUS
A fair nursery run in a very good time, only 0.33sec slower than the Stewards' Cup earlier on the card. The winner, who proved very well treated indeed, can hold his own in good sprint handicaps next year.
NOTEBOOK
Parisian Pyramid(IRE) ◆, representing the stable that had sent out the winner of this race the previous two years, got in off bottom weight following three ordinary efforts including a defeat in selling company. He showed that he was a very well-handicapped horse, though, displaying great speed from the off and pulling clear in the closing stages for wide-margin success in a time only 0.33sec slower than Conquest recorded in winning the Stewards' Cup earlier on the card. His trainer later said that he would not run again this season, which suggests that he wants to protect his mark (likely to be in the low to mid 80s following this) for the valuable big sprint handicaps next season. He is thought to need decent ground to be at his best. (op 9-1 tchd 12-1)
Taazur looks like a good guide to the level of the form as he has been very consistent in his career so far. He would have been a clear winner himself had Parisian Pyramid not been in the race.
Noble Jack(IRE), running in a handicap for the first time, ran on well in the closing stages having initially got outpaced approaching the two-furlong marker. He might prefer a stiffer track over this distance. (op 9-1)
Tagula Breeze(IRE), wearing a tongue tie for the first time, shared pacemaking duties with the eventual winner for a long way but was weakening when crossed by that rival.
Golden Rosie(IRE), dropped a few pounds since her handicap debut at Leicester, holds a Lowther entry so she had to be of interest off a mark of 79. She showed good early pace next to the rail and simply appeared to not get home, despite having won over this distance at Doncaster on her second start. (op 9-2)
Finnegan McCool, unlucky in running in the Weatherbys Super Sprint last time out, was one of the more experienced runners in the line-up. He failed to land a blow from off the pace. (op 6-1 tchd 13-2 in a places)
Tishtar, who holds a Middle Park entry, was representing a stable that had won this race three times in the past ten years and he was solidly backed beforehand. In the circumstances he was very disappointing. Official explanation: jockey said colt never travelled (op 3-1)
Kyllachy Star was going nowhere really when hampered on the rail.
Fault travelled well enough to halfway but found little under pressure. (tchd 7-1)

4627 BLUESQUARECASINO.COM APPRENTICE STKS (H'CAP) 1m 1f
5:35 (5:35) (Class 3) (0-90,86) 4-Y-O+ £12,952 (£3,854; £1,926; £962) **Stalls** High

Form RPR
0245 **1** **Count Ceprano (IRE)**[16] 4104 4-8-9 79 DavidProbert[(5)] 12 89+
(M D I Usher) *trckd ldrs: a gng wl: produced to ld ent fnl f and qckly drew clr* **7/1**
0600 **2** *3 3/4* **White Deer (USA)**[51] 2969 4-9-2 81 AndrewMullen 5 83
(D Nicholls) *hld up in last trio: prog on inner over 2f out: kpt on u.p to take 2nd ins fnl f: no ch w wnr* **10/1**
/104 **3** *1 1/4* **Benfleet Boy**[16] 4131 4-8-7 77 FrederikTylicki[(5)] 1 76
(B G Powell) *disp ld: rdn over 2f out: hdd and outpcd ent fnl f* **10/1**
1200 **4** *1 3/4* **Speedy Sam**[14] 4191 5-9-1 85 DeclanCannon[(5)] 10 80
(K R Burke) *disp ld: rdn over 2f out: hdd & wknd ent fnl f* **6/1**[2]
0-53 **5** *hd* **Danetime Panther (IRE)**[8] 4364 4-8-6 76 DTDaSilva[(5)] 2 71
(P F I Cole) *b. off fore: hld up bhd ldrs: swtchd sharply lft jst over 3f out: bmpd along and edgd lft fnl 2f: nt pce to trble ldrs* **7/1**
0330 **6** *1/2* **Lord Theo**[50] 3006 4-9-0 79 KirstyMilczarek 6 73+
(N P Littmoden) *dwlt: rousted along to go prom on outer: brought to nr side in st: on terms over 2f out: wknd over 1f out* **20/1**
3532 **7** *1/2* **Jagger**[38] 3375 8-9-7 86 (p) TolleyDean 7 79
(G A Butler) *sn wl in rr: struggling whn hmpd 3f out: n.d after* **7/1**
3560 **8** *1 3/4* **Fongs Gazelle**[3] 4520 4-8-13 78 PatrickHills 8 67
(M Johnston) *chsd ldrs: hrd rdn wl over 2f out: wknd over 1f out* **5/1**[1]
3036 **9** *1* **Zero Cool (USA)**[24] 3836 4-8-10 80 JemmaMarshall[(5)] 13 67
(G L Moore) *pressed ldrs tl wknd rapidly over 1f out* **12/1**
0000 **10** *1/2* **Fort Churchill (IRE)**[21] 3947 7-8-5 75 (bt) LanceBetts[(5)] 9 61+
(B Ellison) *hld up in last pair: v bdly hmpd 3f out: no ch after* **11/1**
1140 **11** *4 1/2* **Sunnyside Tom (IRE)**[21] 3972 4-8-12 77 JamieMoriarty 4 53
(R A Fahey) *t.k.h: hld up and racd wd: wknd over 2f out* **13/2**[3]

1m 57.55s (1.25) **Going Correction** +0.125s/f (Good) **11** Ran SP% **120.8**
Speed ratings (Par 107): **99,95,94,93,92 92,91,90,89,89 85**
Toteswinger: 1&2 £15.40, 1&3 £15.30, 2&3 £27.20. CSF £77.20 CT £722.41 TOTE £6.80: £2.20, £4.50, £3.40; EX 95.30 Place 6 £433.22, Place 5 £122.95.
Owner G A Summers **Bred** Pendley Farm **Trained** Upper Lambourn, Berks
■ Stewards' Enquiry : D T Da Silva five-day ban: careless riding (Aug 16-20)
FOCUS
An ordinary apprentice handicap, contested mainly by horses who have been struggling to win of late.
NOTEBOOK
Count Ceprano(IRE) had never run over a trip this far before but he is the type who is often running on at the finish over 7f and 1m, and the extra furlong suited him. He could be seen travelling best from some way out and, once the button was pressed, he quickened clear in good style. He is entered at Brighton on Wednesday, where he will be able to run without a penalty. (op 13-2 tchd 15-2 tchd 8-1 in a place)
White Deer(USA) also showed improved form on only his second try beyond 1m. He has slipped back to a good mark and it would not be a surprise if his first success for this stable is not far away. (tchd 12-1)
Benfleet Boy, despite being poorly drawn, was again up there throughout and battled on well to post another solid effort. (op 12-1)
Speedy Sam looked to have less to do in this company than in the races he has been contesting of late, but he was denied the uncontested lead he would have liked. (op 13-2 tchd 5-1)
Danetime Panther(IRE) kept on towards the centre of the track after being switched sharply left, causing interference to Jagger and Fort Churchill in the process, but could never get close enough to land a proper blow. (op 9-1 tchd 13-2)
Lord Theo was brought to the stands' side entering the straight, which, given the bias against those racing on the far side in the Stewards' Cup, was worth a try. His rider should be applauded for taking the chance, even though it did not come off. (op 16-1)
Jagger, as expected, struggled to go the pace on this drop back in distance. (op 13-2 tchd 6-1)
Fongs Gazelle, making a quick reappearance after finishing down the field in the fillies' handicap here on Wednesday, was disappointing in what was a weaker race. (op 9-2 tchd 11-2 in a place)
T/Jkpt: Not won. T/Plt: £489.30 to a £1 stake. Pool: £263,985.66. 393.78 winning tickets. T/Qpdt: £53.60 to a £1 stake. Pool: £14,709.95. 202.75 winning tickets. JN

4142 HAMILTON (R-H)
Saturday, August 2

OFFICIAL GOING: Good (good to firm in places)
Rail realignment around the loop reduced distances on the round course by circa 25yards.
Wind: Fresh, across Weather: Bright

4628 HAMILTON ACCIES IN THE SPL AUCTION NURSERY 6f 5y
6:35 (6:36) (Class 4) 2-Y-O £3,885 (£1,156; £577; £288) **Stalls** Low

Form RPR
5324 **1** **Mazzola**[7] 4434 2-9-7 82 TonyCulhane 5 82
(M R Channon) *mde all: qcknd 2f out: hld on wl u.p fnl f* **9/4**[2]
51 **2** *shd* **Diggeratt (USA)**[15] 4169 2-9-2 77 TonyHamilton 3 77
(R A Fahey) *trckd ldrs: effrt and edgd rt over 1f out: kpt on wl fnl f: jst hld* **7/2**[3]
41 **3** *2 1/2* **Lakeman (IRE)**[21] 3976 2-9-2 77 J-PGuillambert 2 69
(B Ellison) *trckd wnr: sn niggled along: effrt over 2f out: kpt on same pce fnl f* **15/8**[1]
2104 **4** *5* **Officer Mor (USA)**[22] 3910 2-9-0 75 DarrenWilliams 1 52
(K R Burke) *hld up in tch: effrt over 2f out: sn btn over 1f out* **12/1**
553 **5** *10* **Amorachy**[74] 2281 2-8-9 70 FergalLynch 4 17
(K A Ryan) *in tch: drvn and outpcd 1/2-way: sn btn* **15/2**
004 **6** *8* **Usual Suspects**[11] 4279 2-8-0 61 ow1 PatrickMathers 6 —
(Peter Grayson) *prom tl edgd rt and wknd fr 1/2-way* **20/1**

1m 12.51s (0.31) **Going Correction** -0.075s/f (Good) **6** Ran SP% **112.0**
Speed ratings (Par 96): **94,93,90,83,70 59**
toteswinger: 1&2 £1.30, 1&3 £1.10, 2&3 £2.30. CSF £10.48 TOTE £3.20: £1.50, £2.20; EX 12.60.
Owner M Channon **Bred** Mrs E C Dowling **Trained** West Ilsley, Berks
FOCUS
A fair little nursery in which first pair came clear in a bobbing finish.
NOTEBOOK
Mazzola, dropped 1lb after finishing fourth in a higher grade at York a week previously, relished the step back up a furlong and just had enough left in the tank at the finish to repel the fast-finishing runner-up. He had the run of the race, but this is his trip at present and he is a likeable juvenile. (op 5-1)
Diggeratt(USA) ◆ had got off the mark at Pontefract over this trip last time and confirmed herself an improving two-year-old with a very narrow defeat on this nursery bow. Clear of the remainder in second, she will not be long in finding compensation. (op 4-1)

Lakeman(IRE), narrowly off the mark on heavy ground at York last month, failed to raise his game on this nursery debut and probably found this different surface too lively. (op 5-4 tchd 2-1)
Officer Mor(USA) had looked at sea on soft ground last time out, but he never looked like troubling the principals on this return to a sounder surface and is in danger of going backwards. (op 9-1)

4629 CHAMPAGNE COCKTAILS AT HAMILTON PARK CLAIMING STKS 1m 65y
7:05 (7:06) (Class 6) 3-4-Y-O **£2,388** (£705; £352) **Stalls** High

Form RPR
424 1 **Five Wishes**[21] 3963 4-8-7 52 (be) PJMcDonald(3) 1 63
(M Dods) *hld up: hdwy and squeezed through to ld over 1f out: sn clr* **5/1**
0204 2 7 **Ghafeer (USA)**[30] 3640 4-9-1 60 (p) J-PGuillambert 4 52
(B Ellison) *chsd clr ldr: led briefly over 1f out: kpt on same pce fnl f* **4/1**[3]
5542 3 ¾ **Bold Indian (IRE)**[6] 4451 4-9-2 60 TomEaves 7 51
(Miss L A Perratt) *prom: smooth hdwy over 2f out: rdn over 1f out: fnd little* **7/4**[1]
5036 4 2 **Roundthetwist (IRE)**[18] 4049 3-8-13 60 DarrenWilliams 5 51
(K R Burke) *hld up in tch: effrt over 2f out: hung rt and blkd over 1f out: no ex* **15/2**
-600 5 1 **Polish Star**[19] 4015 4-8-13 44 (b[1]) TonyHamilton 6 41
(Miss L A Perratt) *sn led and clr: hdd over 1f out: sn btn* **25/1**
230 6 6 **Grit (IRE)**[14] 4180 3-9-2 62 TonyCulhane 2 37
(M R Channon) *hld up: drvn over 4f out: edgd rt and no imp fnl 2f* **7/2**[2]
0140 7 3 ½ **Carry On Cleo**[15] 4165 3-7-8 59 (v) JamieKyne(7) 3 14
(A Berry) *cl up tl rdn and wknd over 2f out* **16/1**

1m 46.24s (-2.16) **Going Correction** -0.175s/f (Firm)
WFA 3 from 4yo 7lb **7 Ran SP% 116.7**
Speed ratings (Par 101): **103,96,95,93,92 86,82**
toteswinger: 1&2 £6.00, 1&3 £2.20, 2&3 £2.50. CSF £26.08 TOTE £6.20: £3.00, £2.90; EX 32.90.
Owner Exors of the late Mark Swift **Bred** Alan A Wright **Trained** Denton, Co Durham
■ Stewards' Enquiry : P J McDonald two-day ban: careless riding (Aug 16-17)
Jamie Kyne one-day ban: careless riding (Aug 16)

FOCUS
A typically moderate claimer and difficult to be confident about the form. The winner looks back to his best.

4630 MACGREGOR FLOORING COMPANY H'CAP 1m 3f 16y
7:35 (7:37) (Class 6) (0-60,58) 3-Y-O+ **£2,266** (£674; £337; £168) **Stalls** High

Form RPR
0365 1 **Astrodome**[12] 4247 3-8-12 **54** (b[1]) J-PGuillambert 3 67
(Sir Mark Prescott) *mde all: stdy pce early: rdn and qcknd over 4f out: hrd pressed over 1f out: hld on gamely fnl f* **10/3**[2]
0000 2 1 ¼ **Ulysees (IRE)**[42] 3255 9-9-0 **46** (p) TomEaves 11 56
(Miss L A Perratt) *t.k.h: hld up: gd hdwy to chal over 1f out: no ex wl ins fnl f* **20/1**
3204 3 4 ½ **Jane Of Arc (FR)**[13] 4220 4-9-2 **48** (p) JoeFanning 10 50
(J S Goldie) *cl up: effrt 3f out: one pce fr 2f out* **4/1**[3]
0230 4 ½ **Grandad Bill (IRE)**[27] 3755 5-9-5 **51** FergalLynch 4 52
(J S Goldie) *bhd: pushed along 4f out: hdwy over 1f out: nrst fin* **5/1**
5632 5 3 ½ **Snow Dancer (IRE)**[1] 4596 4-9-7 **58** (p) PBradley(5) 2 53
(H A McWilliams) *hld up: outpcd 3f out: sme late hdwy: n.d* **15/2**
3354 6 3 ¼ **Barbirolli**[15] 4155 6-9-7 **53** DarrenWilliams 1 42
(W M Brisbourne) *hld up in tch: effrt 3f out: btn over 1f out* **10/1**
5633 7 ½ **Livvy Inn (USA)**[15] 4147 3-8-10 **55** NeilBrown(3) 6 43
(Miss Lucinda V Russell) *chsd ldrs: effrt over 2f out: wknd wl over 1f out* **3/1**[1]
6-00 8 1 **Royal Citadel (IRE)**[15] 4142 5-8-8 **45** KellyHarrison(5) 5 31
(Mrs L B Normile) *towards rr: drvn and outpcd 4f out: n.d after* **66/1**
/30- 9 8 **Border Tale**[66] 1532 8-9-1 **50** (v) PJMcDonald(3) 8 22
(James Moffatt) *in tch tl wknd over 3f out* **16/1**
3405 10 10 **Nayarna**[19] 4019 3-9-2 **58** (b[1]) TonyHamilton 9 12
(R A Fahey) *unruly leaving paddock: t.k.h: prom tl rdn and wknd over 3f out* **20/1**

2m 23.17s (-2.43) **Going Correction** -0.175s/f (Firm)
WFA 3 from 4yo+ 10lb **10 Ran SP% 122.5**
Speed ratings (Par 101): **101,100,96,96,93 91,91,90,84,77**
toteswinger: 1&2 £38.70, 1&3 £5.50, 2&3 £24.00. CSF £72.97 CT £285.06 TOTE £4.80: £2.10, £4.80, £1.90; EX 141.60.
Owner W E Sturt - Osborne House II **Bred** Miss K Rausing And Mrs S Rogers **Trained** Newmarket, Suffolk

FOCUS
A weak handicap, run at an uneven pace. The third and fourth help to set the level and the form looks solid.

4631 EUROPEAN BREEDERS' FUND FILLIES' H'CAP 5f 4y
8:05 (8:06) (Class 4) (0-85,85) 3-Y-O+ **£7,123** (£2,119; £1,059; £529) **Stalls** Centre

Form RPR
0335 1 **Katie Boo (IRE)**[8] 4383 6-8-8 **69** JoeFanning 8 80
(A Berry) *cl up: effrt over 1f out: led ins fnl f: rdn out* **7/2**[3]
4041 2 ¾ **Hypnosis**[10] 4291 5-9-2 **77** TonyHamilton 2 86
(D W Barker) *wnt rt s: sn pressing ldr: led over 2f out to ins fnl f: kpt on same pce* **11/4**[1]
2210 3 1 ¼ **Rothesay Dancer**[12] 4239 5-8-4 **70** KellyHarrison(5) 7 74
(J S Goldie) *hld up in tch: effrt over 1f out: swtchd rt ins fnl f: kpt on same pce* **10/3**[2]
1126 4 ½ **Wibbadune (IRE)**[22] 3931 4-8-13 **74** DarrenWilliams 6 76
(D Shaw) *prom: effrt 2f out: nt qckn fnl f* **11/2**
0201 5 4 ½ **Leading Edge (IRE)**[9] 4329 3-8-13 **77** TonyCulhane 9 62
(M R Channon) *prom tl rdn and wknd wl over 1f out* **5/1**
01-2 6 2 ½ **Blakeshall Diamond**[198] 199 3-8-7 **71** DeanMcKeown 1 47
(K G Wingrove) *led to over 2f out: sn rdn and btn* **16/1**
00-6 7 3 **Rocking**[42] 3256 3-8-8 **72** (b) TomEaves 10 37
(Miss L A Perratt) *racd wd: prom tl wknd fr 2f out* **20/1**
00-0 8 2 ¾ **Vondova**[21] 3952 6-8-4 **70** oh21 ow4 (t) PatrickDonaghy(5) 3 26
(D A Nolan) *dwlt: a bhd* **100/1**

59.02 secs (-0.98) **Going Correction** -0.075s/f (Good)
WFA 3 from 4yo+ 3lb **8 Ran SP% 115.7**
Speed ratings (Par 102): **104,102,100,100,92 88,84,79**
toteswinger: 1&2 £2.10, 1&3 £3.20, 2&3 £2.50. CSF £13.77 CT £34.41 TOTE £3.40: £1.30, £1.40, £1.70; EX 15.70.
Owner The Early Doors Partnership **Bred** Michael McGlynn **Trained** Cockerham, Lancs

FOCUS
Just a fair fillies' handicap for the class, run at a solid pace. The form looks sound rated through the placed horses.

4632 SCOTTISH RACING MAIDEN STKS 6f 5y
8:35 (8:36) (Class 5) 3-Y-O+ **£3,238** (£963; £481; £240) **Stalls** Centre

Form RPR
5525 1 **Earlsmedic**[14] 4180 3-9-3 64 (v[1]) J-PGuillambert 9 81
(S C Williams) *mde all: carried hd high but drew clr fr over 1f out: eased nr fin* **15/8**[1]
0423 2 6 **Forrest Star**[26] 3786 3-8-12 58 TomEaves 5 57
(Miss L A Perratt) *cl up: rdn over 2f out: one pce fr over 1f out* **3/1**[2]
3626 3 1 ¼ **Ride A White Swan**[16] 4118 3-9-3 65 DarrenWilliams 4 58
(D Shaw) *t.k.h: hld up in tch: effrt over 2f out: no imp over 1f out* **9/2**
2040 4 nk **Tugalu (IRE)**[14] 4207 3-9-0 65 (p) NeilBrown(3) 10 57
(K A Ryan) *t.k.h: hld up: hdwy on outside over 2f out: no imp over 1f out* **7/2**[3]
2000 5 hd **Forzarzi (IRE)**[15] 4172 4-9-2 53 PBradley(5) 7 56
(H A McWilliams) *towards rr: hdwy over 2f out: no ex over 1f out* **9/1**
0400 6 10 **Saafend Geezer**[12] 4236 3-8-12 45 SladeO'Hara(5) 8 24
(A Berry) *in tch: drvn over 2f out: sn btn* **25/1**
0000 7 7 **Sokoke**[21] 3953 7-9-2 32 (p) GaryBartley(5) 3 —
(D A Nolan) *cl up tl rdn over 2f out: sn wknd* **100/1**
500 8 ¾ **La Guancha**[26] 3784 3-8-12 33 (bt) PatrickMathers 2 —
(D A Nolan) *s.s: nvr on terms* **80/1**
00-0 9 32 **Wolf Pack**[43] 3200 6-9-2 33 (t) PatrickDonaghy(5) 1 —
(D A Nolan) *bhd and sn outpcd: nvr on terms* **100/1**

1m 11.45s (-0.75) **Going Correction** -0.075s/f (Good)
WFA 3 from 4yo+ 4lb **9 Ran SP% 117.2**
Speed ratings (Par 103): **102,94,92,91,91 78,69,68,25**
toteswinger: 1&2 £1.70, 1&3 £2.80, 2&3 £1.70. CSF £7.79 TOTE £3.20: £1.20, £1.50, £2.00; EX 8.50.
Owner Mad Man Plus One **Bred** W N Greig **Trained** Newmarket, Suffolk

FOCUS
A poor maiden, run at a fair pace. The easy winner rates value for further and the form can be rated through the runner-up.

4633 TENTS AND EVENTS H'CAP (A QUALIFIER FOR THE RBS SCOTTISH TROPHY HANDICAP SERIES FINAL) 1m 1f 36y
9:05 (9:05) (Class 5) (0-75,74) 3-Y-O+ **£3,238** (£963; £481; £240) **Stalls** High

Form RPR
1141 1 **Wind Shuffle (GER)**[15] 4148 5-9-6 **71** GaryBartley(5) 3 80
(J S Goldie) *mde all: stdy pce: qcknd 2f out: unchal* **3/1**[2]
634 2 1 ¼ **Malinsa Blue (IRE)**[13] 4215 6-8-10 **56** (p) J-PGuillambert 7 63
(B Ellison) *chsd wnr: effrt over 2f out: kpt on fnl f: nt pce of wnr* **17/2**
0643 3 hd **Regent's Secret (USA)**[3] 4148 8-9-1 **61** (p) FergalLynch 8 67+
(J S Goldie) *in tch: outpcd 3f out: rallied over 1f out: kpt on fin* **11/4**[1]
-501 4 1 ¼ **Sarraaf (IRE)**[15] 4142 12-8-4 **55** oh3 PatrickDonaghy(5) 5 59
(Miss L A Perratt) *hld up: hdwy 2f out: no imp fnl f* **10/1**
3230 5 1 ¾ **Hawkit (USA)**[21] 3957 7-9-7 **70** NeilBrown(3) 6 70
(P Monteith) *hld up on outside: effrt over 2f out: no imp over 1f out* **12/1**
0045 6 3 ¼ **Always Brave**[12] 4248 3-8-12 **66** JoeFanning 4 59
(M Johnston) *hld up in tch on outside: effrt over 2f out: hung rt and wknd wl over 1f out* **7/1**
4162 7 ½ **New Star (UAE)**[21] 3947 4-10-0 **74** TonyHamilton 10 66
(W M Brisbourne) *prom tl rdn and wknd over 2f out* **13/2**
0652 8 8 **Oeuf A La Neige**[16] 4118 8-8-9 **55** TomEaves 2 30
(Miss L A Perratt) *prom: effrt over 2f out: sn wknd* **6/1**[3]

1m 59.0s (-0.70) **Going Correction** -0.175s/f (Firm)
WFA 3 from 4yo+ 8lb **8 Ran SP% 119.1**
Speed ratings (Par 103): **96,94,94,93,92 89,88,81**
toteswinger: 1&2 £7.50, 1&3 £3.40, 2&3 £8.30. CSF £29.92 CT £78.98 TOTE £3.80: £1.70, £2.90, £1.60; EX 39.60 Place 6: £42.59 Place 5: £19.69 .
Owner Mrs S E Bruce **Bred** Gestut Elsetal **Trained** Uplawmoor, E Renfrews

FOCUS
A modest handicap which saw the in-form winner dictate from the front at at steady gallop. The form is rated at face value but should be treated with some caution.
Oeuf A La Neige Official explanation: jockey said gelding ran too free
T/Plt: £64.50 to a £1 stake. Pool: £59,957.50. 678.55 winning tickets. T/Qpdt: £6.10 to a £1 stake. Pool: £5,639.32. 680.20 winning tickets. RY

4409 LINGFIELD (L-H)
Saturday, August 2

OFFICIAL GOING: Good to firm

4634 ELITESPORTSORGANISATION.CO.UK MAIDEN STKS 5f (P)
5:50 (5:50) (Class 5) 2-Y-O **£3,561** (£1,059; £529; £264) **Stalls** High

Form RPR
0 1 **Olynard (IRE)**[19] 4024 2-9-3 0 GeorgeBaker 10 81+
(R M Beckett) *hld up in midfield on outer: hdwy to trck ldrs and edgd lft jst over 2f out: led gng wl ent fnl f: sn in command: eased nr fin* **3/1**[2]
0 2 1 **Cat Patrol**[56] 2835 2-8-12 0 JimmyQuinn 4 70
(H J L Dunlop) *sn pushed along: in tch: rdn wl over 1f out: styd on wl to chse wnr last 100yds: nvr pce to trble wnr* **25/1**
0 3 1 ¾ **Cheap Thrills**[92] 1762 2-8-12 0 ShaneKelly 2 64
(J A Osborne) *t.k.h: hld up in tch: edgd out off rail 1f out: wnt 3rd wl ins fnl f: kpt on: no ch w wnr* **16/1**
42 4 1 ¾ **Ruby Tallulah**[7] 4411 2-8-12 0 JimCrowley 1 65+
(N P Littmoden) *dwlt: hld up in rr: nt clr run jst over 2f out and again jst ins fnl f: r.o to go 4th last 50yds: nvr able to chal* **5/1**[3]
30 5 ¾ **Sharpener (IRE)**[15] 4149 2-8-12 0 FrancisNorton 6 55
(R Hannon) *w ldr tl led over 3f out: rdn wl over 1f out: hdd ent fnl f: edgd lft and wknd last 100yds* **11/8**[1]
04 6 nk **Jubilee Juggins (IRE)**[11] 4270 2-8-12 0 JackMitchell(5) 3 59
(N P Littmoden) *led narrowly tl over 3f out: chsd ldrs after: drvn and effrt on rail over 1f out: wknd last 100yds* **25/1**
3 7 ½ **The Cuckoo**[5] 4474 2-9-3 0 PatCosgrave 8 57
(M J Wallace) *prom: chsd ldr over 3f out: ev ch and rdn wl over 1f out: edgd rt and wknd qckly fnl f* **15/2**
40 8 ½ **Cocktail Party (IRE)**[12] 4251 2-8-12 0 JamesDoyle 5 50
(J W Hills) *hld up in tch: bdly hmpd and lost pl jst over 2f out: rn green and kpt on same pce after* **16/1**

9 *8* **Alexander Newstalk (IRE)** 2-8-12 0 OscarUrbina 9 22
(S A Callaghan) *sn outpcd and detached in last: nvr on terms* **20/1**

10 *3 1/2* **Badtanman** 2-9-3 0 SamHitchcott 7 14
(Peter Grayson) *s.i.s: in tch in rr tl rdn and struggling 1/2-way: wl bhd last 2f* **50/1**

59.44 secs (0.64) **Going Correction** +0.025s/f (Slow) **10** Ran SP% **121.7**
Speed ratings (Par 94): **95,93,90,87,86 86,85,84,71,66**
toteswinger: 1&2 £0.00, 1&3 £11.50, 2&3 £0.00. CSF £82.96 TOTE £4.10: £1.40, £4.50, £5.10; EX 98.20.

Owner R Roberts **Bred** Redmyre Bloodstock & John Cullinan **Trained** Whitsbury, Hants

■ Stewards' Enquiry : Shane Kelly caution: careless riding

FOCUS
An ordinary sprint maiden for juveniles which, for all that, should throw up a few winners. It was run at a strong gallop.

NOTEBOOK
Olynard(IRE), a half-brother to the smart sprinter Pivotal Flame, was sent off vying for favouritism on his Windsor debut where he ran too keen for his own good, and, settling much better this time, led travelling sweetly and soon settled matters once given the office. By the first-season sire Exceed And Excel, who is doing just that to his expectations having already been responsible for 13 winners, Olynard should continue to progress. (op 11-4 tchd 5-2)

Cat Patrol ◆ was a market springer over on the turf course over 6f when last of 12 here on debut, but the daughter of One Cool Cat showed a lot more this time, running on very well after a slow start. She can be found races. (op 33-1)

Cheap Thrills stayed on well from the rear and looks as though she is being brought along with nurseries in mind.

Ruby Tallulah ◆ was once again tardy at the start and, held up in rear, found her passage repeatedly blocked when she hit her stride in the last couple of furlongs. She is now qualified for handicaps and having strongly hinted at ability on all three starts so far, she is one to watch. (op 9-2 tchd 4-1 and 11-2)

Sharpener(IRE) was dropped to the minimum after showing good speed over 6f, but with the same result - folding tamely after leading at a good clip. She cannot be recommended for betting purposes while her finishing effort remains so weak. (op 15-8 tchd 2-1, 9-4 in a place)

4635 GAY KELLEWAY WINNING RACING SYNDICATE H'CAP — 1m 2f (P)

6:20 (6:20) (Class 6) (0-55,55) 3-Y-0+ **£2,047** (£604; £302) **Stalls** Low

Form — RPR

2 **1** **Action Impact (ARG)**[22] 3914 4-9-0 **50** RyanMoore 12 66+
(G L Moore) *t.k.h: trckd ldrs: rdn to chse clr ldr wl over 1f out: styd on u.p fnl f: hung lft and led towards fin* **4/6**[1]

5523 **2** *3/4* **Split The Wind (USA)**[7] 4409 4-8-8 **50** HarryPoulton[(7)] 8 59
(Miss Sheena West) *chsd ldr tl led 6f out: clr over 3f out: 4 l ld 2f out: rdn ent fnl f: tired and hdd towards fin* **16/1**

0500 **3** *2 1/4* **Shouldntbethere (IRE)**[32] 3583 4-8-13 **53** JackMitchell[(5)] 5 58
(Mrs P N Dutfield) *hld up in tch in rr: hdwy over 3f out: rdn ent fnl 2f: chsd ldng pair fnl f: kpt on but no imp* **50/1**

0000 **4** *1 1/2* **Play Up Pompey**[2] 4568 6-9-1 **50** MickyFenton 9 52
(J J Bridger) *dwlt: hld up in rr: rdn and hdwy on outer wl over 1f out: r.o fnl f but nvr pce to rch ldrs* **33/1**

1003 **5** *3/4* **Formidable Guest**[32] 3588 4-8-11 **53** SimonPearce[(7)] 2 53+
(J Pearce) *t.k.h: in tch: shuffled bk and dropped to rr over 3f out: hdwy u.p 2f out: kpt on but nvr gng to rch ldrs* **10/1**[3]

0365 **6** *1 1/4* **Trevian**[33] 3563 7-9-1 **50** SamHitchcott 11 48
(Tim Vaughan) *in tch: rdn 3f out: outpcd over 2f out: plugged on same pce u.p* **6/1**[2]

2253 **7** *1/2* **Casablanca Minx (IRE)**[8] 4386 5-8-12 **54** (b) KylieManser[(7)] 6 51
(Miss Gay Kelleway) *stdd s: hld up in rr: hdwy over 2f out: c wd wl over 1f out: styd on steadily fnl f: nvr trbld ldrs* **12/1**

00-0 **8** *hd* **Hallings Overture (USA)**[150] 795 9-9-0 **49** (p) JimCrowley 3 45
(C A Horgan) *t.k.h: hld up in rr: hdwy 3f out: n.m.r wl over 1f out: sn rdn: plugged on but nvr pce to threaten ldrs* **50/1**

0024 **9** *1* **Mix N Match**[32] 3588 4-9-3 **55** TravisBlock[(3)] 4 49
(R M Stronge) *taken down early: hld up in midfield: lost pl over 3f out: rdn and hdwy over 2f out: nvr trbld ldrs* **16/1**

4406 **10** *1/2* **Binnion Bay (IRE)**[7] 4414 7-9-2 **54** (b) MarcHalford[(3)] 13 47
(J J Bridger) *dwlt: reminder after s: t.k.h: hld up in tch: hdwy to chse ldr 3f out: rdn over 2f out: wknd over 1f out* **33/1**

000- **11** *nse* **Oakley Absolute**[31] 6801 6-9-6 **55** (b[1]) LPKeniry 14 48
(J C Fox) *chsd ldrs: wnt 2nd over 5f out: drvn over 3f out: lost 2nd 2f out: wknd qckly over 1f out* **100/1**

/250 **12** *1/2* **Mystic Roll**[5] 4479 5-9-6 **55** FrankieMcDonald 10 47
(Jane Chapple-Hyam) *hld up in tch: rdn over 2f out: wknd wl over 1f out* **25/1**

0635 **13** *3 1/2* **Soldiers Quest**[19] 4023 4-9-1 **50** AdamKirby 7 35
(Peter Grayson) *stdd s: hld up in rr: hdwy on outer 5f out: disp 2nd u.p 2f out: sn wknd* **22/1**

6602 **14** *31* **Zorn**[11] 4268 9-9-2 **51** ShaneKelly 1 —
(P Howling) *led tl 6f out: lost pl qckly 4f out: t.o and virtually p.u fr wl over 1f out* **20/1**

2m 6.83s (0.23) **Going Correction** +0.025s/f (Slow) **14** Ran SP% **126.6**
Speed ratings (Par 101): **100,99,97,96,95 94,94,94,93,93 93,92,89,65**
toteswinger: 1&2 £8.40, 1&3 £44.00, 2&3 £44.00. CSF £13.30 CT £364.09 TOTE £1.80: £1.20, £3.50, £9.90; EX 17.80.

Owner T Bowley & R Plersch **Bred** Santa Maria De Araras **Trained** Woodingdean, E Sussex

FOCUS
Some very modest types on show here but it was at least run at a good pace so the form, for what it's worth, should stand up. The winner was well in on his turf mark.

Zorn Official explanation: jockey said gelding lost its action

4636 ROWAN RACING PARTNERSHIPS MEDIAN AUCTION MAIDEN STKS — 7f 140y

6:50 (6:51) (Class 6) 2-Y-0 **£2,047** (£604; £302) **Stalls** Centre

Form — RPR

40 **1** **Nashmiah (IRE)**[15] 4157 2-8-12 0 LiamJones 8 79+
(C E Brittain) *in tch: swtchd lft: sn rdn to chse ldng pair: edgd lft jst ins fnl f: led and edgd rt last 100yds: won gng away* **14/1**

5 **2** *2* **Zelloof (IRE)**[12] 4251 2-8-12 0 LDettori 12 74+
(Saeed Bin Suroor) *led: grad got across to stands rail: hrd pressed and rdn over 1f out: hdd and nt pce of wnr last 100yds* **11/8**[1]

30 **3** *nse* **Reaction**[14] 4184 2-9-3 0 RyanMoore 4 79+
(M R Channon) *chsd ldr: upsides ldr 2f out: sn rdn: ev ch tl outpcd by wnr last 100yds* **7/2**[2]

04 **4** *8* **Tae Kwon Do (USA)**[10] 4304 2-9-3 0 SteveDrowne 1 60
(E A L Dunlop) *hld up in tch: effrt and edgd lft 2f out: sn outpcd and wl btn* **15/2**

0 **5** *1 1/2* **Sherman McCoy**[23] 3888 2-9-0 0 JamesMillman[(3)] 7 57
(B R Millman) *in tch in midfield: lost pl and reminder 4f out: wknd over 2f out: wl btn after* **33/1**

6 *2 1/4* **Mykingdomforahorse** 2-9-3 0 EdwardCreighton 5 51
(M R Channon) *hld up bhd: effrt and rn green wl over 2f out: nvr a factor* **20/1**

56 **7** *4* **Rio Del Oro (USA)**[10] 4311 2-9-3 0 DaneO'Neill 10 42
(R Hannon) *dwlt: bhd: sme hdwy 3f out: wl outpcd over 2f out: wl bhd fnl f* **9/2**[3]

8 *1/2* **Clear Hand** 2-9-3 0 TPO'Shea 13 41
(B R Millman) *chsd ldrs tl 1/2-way: sn lost pl and wl bhd* **33/1**

00 **9** *1 3/4* **Shape Shifter (USA)**[12] 4256 2-9-3 0 LPKeniry 3 37
(J R Best) *a bhd* **20/1**

10 *23* **Flamboyant Red (IRE)** 2-9-3 0 MickyFenton 2 —
(Miss Gay Kelleway) *awkward leaving stalls: rn v green and sn t.o* **20/1**

1m 31.27s (-1.03) **Going Correction** -0.075s/f (Good) **10** Ran SP% **121.1**
Speed ratings (Par 92): **102,100,99,91,90 88,84,83,81,58**
toteswinger: 1&2 £3.70, 1&3 £3.70, 2&3 £1.10 CSF £32.99 TOTE £19.80: £3.10, £1.40, £1.70; EX 41.90.

Owner Saeed Manana **Bred** Deerpark Stud **Trained** Newmarket, Suffolk

FOCUS
No strength in depth to this modest maiden, in which the first three pulled miles clear and there was little sign of any promise among the also-rans.

NOTEBOOK
Nashmiah(IRE) had no more than hinted at ability on two previous starts and might well have been expected to have had to wait until qualified for nurseries before being placed to best advantage, so it was a mild surprise to see this amount of improvement on her third start in maidens. Her immediate future depends on how the Handicapper reacts to this. (op 9-1)

Zelloof(IRE) who was made favourite for her racecourse bow at Windsor, bounced out smartly and got to the favoured stands' rail from a good draw. She didn't find a great deal for pressure though and had no answer to the winner's late surge. (op 6-4 tchd 13-8)

Reaction turned in a shocker here a fortnight ago after shaping with no little promise behind a couple of nice types on his debut start on the July course. This was much more like it, and the colt from the family of Al Bahathri is now eligible for a handicap mark. (op 11-4)

Tae Kwon Do(USA) finished well beaten after travelling well. The best of his three starts was also the only one on Polytrack, which is no surprise considering his American pedigree. (op 10-1)

Mykingdomforahorse Official explanation: jockey said colt ran green

Rio Del Oro(USA) came here on the back of contesting decent maidens at Ascot and Sandown but could never get into this much easier opportunity. (op 8-1)

4637 INSIDETRACK-RACING.CO.UK H'CAP — 7f

7:20 (7:21) (Class 5) (0-75,73) 3-Y-0 **£2,590** (£770; £385; £192) **Stalls** High

Form — RPR

032 **1** **Spin Again (IRE)**[8] 4369 3-9-6 **72** SebSanders 10 77
(R M Beckett) *mde all: grad crossed over to stands rail: rdn wl over 1f out: hung lft fnl f: hld on: all out* **6/5**[1]

-503 **2** *shd* **Valento**[9] 4338 3-8-13 **65** StephenCarson 2 70+
(Eve Johnson Houghton) *bhd on outer: shkn up 1/2-way: rdn and hdwy over 2f out: str chal wl ins fnl f: jst hld* **16/1**

004 **3** *1/2* **Island Treasure**[14] 4195 3-8-8 **60** SteveDrowne 4 64
(H Morrison) *in tch: rdn jst over 2f out: chsd wnr 1f out: ev ch last 100yds: unable qck and lost 2nd towards fin* **11/1**

6244 **4** *3/4* **Rondeau (GR)**[8] 4369 3-8-13 **65** LPKeniry 13 68+
(P R Chamings) *t.k.h: hld up in tch: rdn over 1f out: swtchd lft ent fnl f: chsng ldr and keeping on same pce whn squeezed out and snatched up nr fin* **5/1**[2]

2000 **5** *1 1/4* **Too Grand**[17] 4083 3-7-11 **54** oh4 DavidProbert[(5)] 8 52
(J J Bridger) *dwlt: sn bustled along: in tch: swtchd lft and rdn over 1f out: kpt on same pce ins fnl f* **20/1**

5064 **6** *1/2* **Khazina (USA)**[11] 4282 3-8-11 **63** (p) LiamJones 5 60
(C E Brittain) *in tch: rdn to chse wnr wl over 1f out tl ent fnl f: btn whn short of room and snatched up last 100yds* **14/1**

050- **7** *3* **Clear Daylight**[246] 6973 3-8-8 **60** MickyFenton 9 49
(J R Best) *chsd wnr tl wl over 1f out: wknd u.p jst over 1f out* **33/1**

4040 **8** *2* **Seventh Hill**[16] 4128 3-8-11 **63** JimmyQuinn 12 46
(M Blanshard) *in tch: rdn over 2f out: stuggling wl over 1f out: wl hld fnl f* **5/1**[2]

5-40 **9** *1/2* **Hucking Harkness**[10] 4306 3-8-7 **59** FrancisNorton 11 41
(J R Best) *t.k.h: chsd ldrs tl wknd 2f out: wl hld fnl f* **10/1**[3]

000 **10** *5* **Mick's Dancer**[28] 3717 3-8-10 **62** (b[1]) ShaneKelly 7 31
(W R Muir) *hld up on towards rr on outer: rdn over 2f out: fnd little and sn btn* **20/1**

1m 22.86s (-0.44) **Going Correction** -0.075s/f (Good) **10** Ran SP% **121.2**
Speed ratings (Par 100): **99,98,98,97,96 95,92,89,89,83**
toteswinger: 1&2 £1.30, 1&3 £4.00, 2&3 £6.60. CSF £24.67 CT £164.93 TOTE £2.20: £1.50, £2.90, £2.00; EX 21.30.

Owner Richard Morecombe **Bred** Barry Lyons **Trained** Whitsbury, Hants

■ Stewards' Enquiry : Seb Sanders three-day ban: careless riding (Aug 16-18)

FOCUS
A modest if competitive handicap, the form of which should work out reliably enough in the coming weeks.

4638 IRISHRACINGSHARES MAIDEN STKS — 6f

7:50 (7:51) (Class 5) 3-Y-0+ **£2,590** (£770; £385) **Stalls** High

Form — RPR

32 **1** **Without Prejudice (USA)**[51] 2966 3-9-3 0 ShaneKelly 1 62+
(J Noseda) *hld up trcking ldng ldr: cruised upsides ent fnl f: led wl ins fnl f: hrd hld* **1/8**[1]

5043 **2** *1/2* **Ma Vie En Rose (IRE)**[10] 4301 3-8-12 56 (t) LPKeniry 4 55
(A M Balding) *led: rdn over 1f out: hdd wl ins fnl f: no ch w wnr* **9/1**[2]

3 *10* **Flying Free** 3-9-3 0 AdamKirby 3 28
(J R Fanshawe) *awkward leaving stalls: t.k.h: hld up in last: rdn and easily outpcd jst over 1f out* **9/1**[2]

1m 11.8s (0.60) **Going Correction** -0.075s/f (Good) **3** Ran SP% **108.9**
Speed ratings (Par 103): **93,92,79**
CSF £2.04 TOTE £1.20; EX 1.50.

Owner Michael Tabor **Bred** Skymarc Farm And Castlemartin Stud **Trained** Newmarket, Suffolk

The Form Book, Raceform Ltd, Compton, RG20 6NL

FOCUS
With the Fanshawe newcomer obviously nothing out of the ordinary, this was the proverbial penalty kick for the winner. The time was slow and the runner-up is the obvious guide to the form, with the winner 17lb off his Haydock mark.

4639 HAVE A HUCKING HORSE WITH JOHNBESTRACING H'CAP 6f
8:20 (8:20) (Class 6) (0-65,64) 3-Y-0+ £2,047 (£604; £302) Stalls High

Form RPR
5200 1 **Exit Strategy (IRE)**[40] 3313 4-8-13 **53**................(b) KevinGhunowa(3) 13 62
(R A Harris) *racd against stands' rail: chsd ldrs: rdn over 1f out: ev ch ins fnl f: led last strides* 8/1[2]
3110 2 *hd* **Regal Royale**[10] 4307 5-9-10 **61**..............................(v) AdamKirby 2 70
(Peter Grayson) *led and grad crossed to stands rail: rdn 2f out: hung lft ins fnl f: hdd last strides* 8/1[2]
0030 3 *nse* **Namu**[9] 4327 5-9-2 **53**.............................. DaneO'Neill 3 61
(Miss T Spearing) *wnt rt s: stmbld after 1f: racd in midfield: hdwy u.p 2f out: pressed ldrs wl ins fnl f: nt quite get up* 14/1
0440 4 *1 1/4* **Trinculo (IRE)**[21] 3966 11-9-7 **63**..................(b) HaddenFrost(5) 4 68
(R A Harris) *bmpd sn after s: sn chsng ldr: ev ch u.p over 1f out: no ex last 100yds* 16/1
1062 5 *1* **Bold Argument (IRE)**[3] 4535 5-9-8 **64**.................. JackMitchell(5) 7 65+
(Mrs P N Dutfield) *s.i.s: bhd: rdn and hdwy on outer 2f out: styd on u.p fnl f: nvr getting to ldrs* 11/4[1]
3000 6 *hd* **Makabul**[9] 4324 5-9-4 **58**.............................. JamesMillman(3) 12 59
(B R Millman) *stdd s: hld up bhd: edgd out lft off rail and rdn 2f out: kpt on fnl f: nvr able to chal* 17/2[3]
0526 7 *nk* **Jonny Ebeneezer**[8] 4393 9-9-4 **62**..................(be) RobbieEgan(7) 1 62
(D Flood) *s.i.s: bhd: swtchd lft and hdwy wl over 1f out: plugged on but nvr able to chal* 17/2[3]
00-5 8 *1 1/2* **Romany Nights (IRE)**[9] 4336 8-9-0 **58**..................(bt) KylieManser(7) 14 53
(Miss Gay Kelleway) *racd in midfield: swtchd lft and drvn over 1f out: kpt on same pce fnl f* 10/1
000 9 *2* **Multahab**[14] 4186 9-9-11 **62**..............................(t) JimmyQuinn 6 51
(M Wigham) *chsd ldrs tl rdn and wknd qckly 1f out* 25/1
-000 10 *2 1/4* **Hawk Eyed Lady (IRE)**[15] 4163 3-9-7 **62**..................(b) ShaneKelly 8 43
(J A Osborne) *racd off the pce in midfield: rdn 2f out: no prog and wl btn fnl f* 20/1
2316 11 *1/2* **Musical Script (USA)**[141] 875 5-9-6 **60**..................(b) TravisBlock(3) 10 40
(Mouse Hamilton-Fairley) *chsd ldrs tl rdn and struggling over 2f out: wl btn fnl f* 10/1
2523 12 *3 1/4* **Cape Of Storms**[81] 2081 5-9-3 **54**..............................(b) NeilPollard 11 23
(R Brotherton) *racd in midfield tl lost pl u.p over 2f out: wl btn last 2f* 8/1[2]
0345 13 *2* **Town And Gown**[10] 4308 3-8-12 **60**.............................. WilliamCarson(7) 9 23
(S C Williams) *swtchd rt sn after s: a bhd* 16/1

1m 10.33s (-0.87) **Going Correction** -0.075s/f (Good)
WFA 3 from 4yo+ 4lb 13 Ran SP% **126.3**
Speed ratings (Par 101): **102,101,101,100,98 98,98,96,93,90 89,85,82**
toteswinger: 1&2 £17.70, 1&3 £9.50, 2&3 £0.00 CSF £74.89 CT £938.70 TOTE £10.70: £3.70, £3.00, £5.20; EX 123.60 Place 6: £54.19 Place 5: £10.59 .
Owner E A Poynter **Bred** Shortgrove Manor Stud **Trained** Earlswood, Monmouths

FOCUS
The usual suspects for a modest sprint handicap around the southern gaffs. Sound form for the grade.
Multahab Official explanation: jockey said gelding stumbled on the crossing
Cape Of Storms Official explanation: jockey said gelding was never travelling
T/Plt: £128.30 to a £1 stake. Pool: £45,146.78. 256.80 winning tickets. T/Qpdt: £7.50 to a £1 stake. Pool: £5,495.84. 541.59 winning tickets. SP

4598
NEWMARKET (JULY) (R-H)
Saturday, August 2

OFFICIAL GOING: Good to firm, changing to good after race 3 (3.30)
Wind: Light across Weather: Rain giving way to sunshine after race 2

4640 HSS HIRE FILLIES' NURSERY 6f
2:25 (2:26) (Class 2) 2-Y-0 £12,952 (£3,854; £1,926; £962) Stalls High

Form RPR
3210 1 **Souter's Sister (IRE)**[14] 4190 2-9-3 **79**.............................. PatDobbs 5 85
(R Hannon) *chsd ldrs: rdn over 1f out: r.o to ld post* 7/2[2]
0214 2 *nse* **Starlarks (IRE)**[21] 3967 2-9-4 **80**.............................. ShaneKelly 7 86
(W J Knight) *w ldr: led 1/2-way: rdn and hung lft over 1f out: hdd post* 11/2
1245 3 *1 3/4* **Polish Pride**[14] 4187 2-8-11 **73**.............................. PhilipRobinson 6 74
(M Brittain) *led: wnt towards centre over 4f out: hdd 1/2-way: rdn and edgd rt over 1f out: no ex ins fnl f* 4/1[3]
055 4 *1* **Abby Belle (IRE)**[30] 3632 2-8-4 **66**.............................. AdrianMcCarthy 2 64
(J G Portman) *hld up: rdn over 2f out: styd on ins fnl f: nt rch ldrs* 11/1
541 5 *1 1/2* **Wohaida (IRE)**[26] 3778 2-8-8 **70**.............................. DarryllHolland 4 63
(M R Channon) *trckd ldrs: racd keenly: wnt towards centre over 4f out: swtchd rt to join main bunch over 3f out: rdn and edgd lft over 1f out: no ex* 5/2[1]
3310 6 *1 1/2* **Barbee (IRE)**[35] 3496 2-9-7 **83**.............................. TPQueally 3 72
(E A L Dunlop) *s.i.s: hld up: rdn over 1f out: wknd fnl f* 5/1

1m 12.96s (0.46) **Going Correction** +0.075s/f (Good) 6 Ran SP% **111.2**
Speed ratings (Par 97): **99,98,96,95,93 91**
toteswinger: 1&2 £4.00, 1&3 £3.10, 2&3 £4.60. CSF £21.96 TOTE £4.40: £2.30, £3.30; EX 24.90.
Owner P D Merritt **Bred** John Cullinan **Trained** East Everleigh, Wilts

FOCUS
Just a fair nursery.

NOTEBOOK
Souter's Sister(IRE), winner of a moderate maiden at Brighton in June, struggled to make an impact in the Super Sprint last time, but she was starting out handicap life off a mark of 79 and looked in with a chance. She looked held racing into the final furlong, but sayed on strongly against the stands' rail and nailed Starlarks on the line. On this evidence an extra furlong is required and she may yet be capable of better still. (op 5-1)
Starlarks(IRE) had looked progressive until flopping at Salisbury last time (beating just one home at odds of 8/13) but she showed that running to be all wrong and looked all over the winner. However, Souter's Sister stayed on strongly and she was done right on the line. This faster ground clearly suited her better and on this evidence she could be worth a try back at 5f. (op 4-1 tchd 7-1)
Polish Pride failed to see out the 7f trip at Newbury last time and was seen to better effect here. The slight drop in grade also helped, but she has plenty of speed and may do better again dropped back to 5f. (op 7-1)
Abby Belle(IRE), an interesting contender on this nursery debut, showed steady progress in maidens and a mark of 66 seemed fair enough. However, she was never really travelling and could only stay on at the one pace. There is definitely a race in her, but it will probably be at 7f. (op 10-1 tchd 9-1)
Wohaida(IRE), off the mark at Brighton last time, from a subsequent winner, took a keen grip early and did not find a great deal for pressure. This was disappointing considering she looked to be on a fair enough mark. (op 9-4)
Barbee(IRE) has not gone on from her maiden win and showed disappointingly little here. (op 4-1)

4641 HSS TRAINING H'CAP 7f
2:55 (2:57) (Class 4) (0-85,85) 3-Y-0 £6,476 (£1,927; £963; £481) Stalls High

Form RPR
14 1 **Kalahari Gold (IRE)**[22] 3897 3-9-9 **85**.............................. LPKeniry 4 109+
(A M Balding) *s.i.s: hld up: hdwy over 2f out: hung rt and led over 1f out: rdn clr: eased wl ins fnl f* 5/1[3]
-510 2 *6* **Portodora (USA)**[42] 3272 3-9-2 **78**.............................. IanMongan 5 86
(H R A Cecil) *prom: rdn over 1f out: wknd ins fnl f* 12/1
0020 3 *1 1/4* **Gross Prophet**[16] 4125 3-8-2 **71** ow3.............................. RossAtkinson(7) 1 76
(Tom Dascombe) *chsd ldr: rdn over 2f out: wkng whn n.m.r over 1f out* 12/1
-300 4 *3/4* **Nezami (IRE)**[28] 3744 3-9-9 **85**.............................. DarryllHolland 2 88
(B J Meehan) *prom: rdn and ev ch over 1f out: sn hung rt: wknd ins fnl f* 12/1
2241 5 *1* **Liberation Spirit (USA)**[14] 4194 3-9-8 **84**.............................. TPQueally 6 84
(J Noseda) *prom: rdn 2f out: wknd over 1f out* 9/2[2]
36 6 *nk* **Non Sucre (USA)**[36] 3442 3-9-0 **76**..............................(b) GregFairley 8 75
(P A Blockley) *led: rdn and hdd over 1f out: wknd fnl f* 20/1
005 7 *3* **Writingonthewall (IRE)**[36] 3441 3-8-7 **69**.............................. PhilipRobinson 7 60
(M L W Bell) *s.i.s: hld up: effrt over 2f out: wknd over 1f out* 14/1
6-11 8 *6* **Harald Bluetooth (IRE)**[22] 3915 3-9-7 **83**.............................. JamieSpencer 9 81
(J R Fanshawe) *s.i.s: hld up: swtchd rt over 2f out: sn rdn: wknd and eased over 1f out* 11/10[1]

1m 24.46s (-1.24) **Going Correction** +0.075s/f (Good) 8 Ran SP% **117.0**
Speed ratings (Par 102): **110,103,101,100,99 99,95,89**
toteswinger: 1&2 £8.00, 1&3 £11.70, 2&3 £16.30. CSF £63.16 CT £686.44 TOTE £6.30: £1.80, £2.10, £2.80; EX 43.70 Trifecta £239.90 Part won..
Owner The Toucan Syndicate **Bred** Mick McGinn And James Waldron **Trained** Kingsclere, Hants

FOCUS
This was run in a downpour, but it did not affect Kalahari Gold, who won in the style of a smart performer. His task was eased by his two market rivals underperforming, but his figure could underrate him.
Harald Bluetooth(IRE) Official explanation: trainer had no explanation for the poor form shown

4642 HSS HIRE H'CAP 1m 2f
3:30 (3:32) (Class 3) (0-90,90) 3-Y-0+ £10,361 (£3,083; £1,540; £769) Stalls Centre

Form RPR
51-0 1 **Bee Sting**[105] 1473 4-9-6 **82**.............................. AdamKirby 1 93
(W R Swinburn) *hld up: pushed along over 4f out: hdwy over 2f out: rdn to ld and hung rt wl over 1f out: edgd lft 1f out: styd on* 9/1
-262 2 *2* **Redesignation (IRE)**[22] 3896 3-9-2 **87**.............................. PatDobbs 6 94
(R Hannon) *chsd ldr: rdn and ev ch wl over 1f out: edgd rt: styd on u.p* 2/1[1]
2500 3 *1/2* **Yarqus**[45] 3122 5-9-11 **87**.............................. DarryllHolland 4 93
(C E Brittain) *hld up: hdwy over 2f out: nt clr run and swtchd rt over 1f out: styd on u.p* 9/1
2542 4 *hd* **Bandama (IRE)**[7] 4422 5-9-13 **89**.............................. JamieSpencer 2 95
(Mrs A J Perrett) *broke wl: lost pl over 8f out: sn pushed along: hdwy u.p over 2f out: chsd wnr over 1f out: no ex wl ins fnl f* 4/1[3]
2540 5 *16* **Jeer (IRE)**[14] 4191 4-10-0 **90**.............................. TPQueally 8 64
(E A L Dunlop) *chsd ldrs: rdn over 2f out: edgd rt and wknd over 1f out* 8/1
1422 6 *8* **Trans Siberian**[37] 3398 4-9-11 **87**.............................. JohnEgan 7 45
(P F I Cole) *sn led: clr 8f out: hdd wl over 1f out: wkng whn hmpd sn after* 11/4[2]

2m 5.05s (-0.45) **Going Correction** +0.075s/f (Good)
WFA 3 from 4yo+ 9lb 6 Ran SP% **111.1**
Speed ratings (Par 107): **104,102,102,101,89 82**
Toteswinger: 1&2 £4.80 1&3 £9.20, 2&3 £4.20. CSF £26.89 CT £162.52 TOTE £9.70: £3.00, £1.70; EX 27.10 Trifecta £139.60 Pool: £245.40, 1.30 winning units.
Owner Exors Of The Late Mrs P W Harris **Bred** R And Mrs Watson And Mrs A J Ralli **Trained** Aldbury, Herts
■ Stewards' Enquiry : Darryll Holland one-day ban: careless riding (Aug 16)

FOCUS
A decent handicap run at a strong pace. The form looks sound.

NOTEBOOK
Bee Sting looked a useful prospect when winning his maiden just over a year ago at Chester, but he flopped in testing ground at Newbury on his reappearance in April and had not been seen since. The quicker ground was an unknown here, but the rain that fell helped and, having worked his way to the front, he stuck on strongly to keep the favourite at bay. This was only the fifth start of his career and there may well be more to come. (op 15-2)
Redesignation(IRE) has shown useful form in good handicaps and looked the one to beat against several more-exposed sorts. He had his chance, but Bee Sting stayed on too strongly and he had to settle for second. There is a race in him off this sort of mark. (tchd 9-4 in places)
Yarqus has not won in well over two years, yet remains 1lb higher than when last scoring. Without the tongue tie, he stayed on having briefly been blocked, but was never getting to the winner and was held for second. He should continue to pay his way. (op 10-1)
Bandama(IRE), behind Redesignation at Ascot, ran an improved race when finishing second to Ask The Butler over course and distance last week, but he was unable to build on that and it is likely he needs to be dropped a few more pounds before winning again. (tchd 9-2)
Jeer(IRE) has started to lose his form and this was a dire effort. He looks best left alone at present. (op 6-1)
Trans Siberian has been in good form, just losing out to Moon Quest off a 3lb lower mark at Great Leighs latest, and again looked set to run his race. He was soon in front and tried to stretch them out, but could not sustain the gallop and was already beaten when interfered with. This was not his true form. Official explanation: jockey said colt had no more to give (op 4-1)

4643 MARTIN HEYES MATT JE'MAR EUROPEAN BREEDERS' FUND MAIDEN FILLIES' STKS 7f
4:05 (4:07) (Class 4) 2-Y-0 £5,180 (£1,541; £770; £384) Stalls High

Form RPR
1 **Spy Eye (USA)** 2-8-9 0.............................. Louis-PhilippeBeuzelin(5) 1 74+
(Sir Michael Stoute) *chsd ldrs: led and edgd rt over 1f out: rdn out* 10/1
6 2 *1* **Peninsula Girl (IRE)**[15] 4149 2-9-0 0.............................. DarryllHolland 11 72
(M R Channon) *hld up in tch: rdn and ev ch ins fnl f: unable qck towards fin* 4/1[2]

	3	1 3/4	**Moneycantbuymelove (IRE)** 2-9-0 0 JamieSpencer 3 (M L W Bell) *hld up: hdwy over 1f out: r.o*	6/1[3]	67+
6	4	shd	**Eliza Griffith (IRE)**[60] 2691 2-9-0 0 PatDobbs 16 (R Hannon) *s.i.s: hld up: hdwy over 2f out: rdn over 1f out: r.o*	8/1	67
	5	shd	**Simple Solution (USA)** 2-9-0 0 AdamKirby 6 (B W Hills) *hld up: hdwy over 2f out: outpcd over 1f out: r.o ins fnl f*	16/1	67+
	6	1/2	**Al Tamooh (IRE)** 2-9-0 0 TPQueally 9 (J L Dunlop) *s.s: hld up: rdn 1/2-way: swtchd lft and hdwy over 1f out: nt trble ldrs*	8/1	65
06	7	nk	**Protiva**[9] 4328 2-9-0 0 LPKeniry 7 (A P Jarvis) *led: rdn and hdd over 1f out: no ex ins fnl f*	33/1	65
	8	1 1/2	**Breach Of Peace (USA)** 2-9-0 0 PhilipRobinson 4 (R Charlton) *dwlt: sn prom: rdn over 1f out: no ex ins fnl f*	11/1	61
	9	hd	**Dahama** 2-8-7 0 DebraEngland(7) 13 (C E Brittain) *s.i.s: hld up: hdwy over 1f out: nt clr run ins fnl f: nt rch ldrs*	33/1	60+
	10	1 3/4	**Sri Kandi** 2-9-0 0 JohnEgan 12 (P F I Cole) *chsd ldrs: rdn and ev ch wl over 1f out: wknd fnl f*	3/1[1]	56
	11	4 1/2	**Sutania** 2-9-0 0 GregFairley 15 (P F I Cole) *in rr whn rdn over 4f out: n.d*	33/1	45
	12	1 1/2	**Golden Games (IRE)** 2-9-0 0 StephenCarson 5 (J L Dunlop) *hld up: rdn over 2f out: sn wknd*	33/1	41
	13	1/2	**Guilin (IRE)** 2-9-0 0 NelsonDeSouza 10 (P F I Cole) *hld up in tch: racd keenly: rdn and wknd over 2f out*	16/1	40
0	14	1/2	**It's A Game (USA)**[12] 4251 2-9-0 0 RobertHavlin 8 (J H M Gosden) *chsd ldrs tl wknd over 1f out*	16/1	39
	15	3	**Wetherby Place (IRE)** 2-9-0 0 JosedeSouza 14 (R M Beckett) *chsd ldrs: rdn 2f out: wknd over 1f out*	22/1	31
0	16	24	**Silk Meadow (IRE)**[30] 3625 2-9-0 0 (b1) IanMongan 2 (B J Meehan) *chsd ldrs: rdn 5f out: wknd 1/2-way: eased over 1f out*	33/1	—

1m 26.8s (1.10) **Going Correction** +0.075s/f (Good) **16** Ran SP% **135.6**
Speed ratings (Par 93): **96,94,92,92,92 92,91,90,89,87 82,80,80,79,76 48**
Toteswinger: 1&2 £9.90, 1&3 £12.50, 2&3 £6.90. CSF £52.11 TOTE £11.40: £3.20, £2.30, £2.40; EX 85.20.
Owner Niarchos Family **Bred** Flaxman Holdings Ltd **Trained** Newmarket, Suffolk
■ A winner on his first ride in Britain for French-born, Barbados-based Louis-Philippe Beuzelin.

FOCUS
A fair fillies' maiden likely to produce its share of winners.

NOTEBOOK
Spy Eye(USA), whose dam developed into a high-class performer in the US, comes from a top yard who can ready one, but she holds no notable entries. A first ride in this country for her rider, who had previously ridden in the West Indies, she seemed to know her job well enough and, having hit the front a furlong out, just had to be ridden out to score. This was a highly satisfactory debut and there may well be more to come. (op 12-1 tchd 17-2)
Peninsula Girl(IRE), sixth over an inadequate 6f on her recent Newbury debut, was nibbled at beforehand and came to have every chance, but was always coming off second best. This was a step up and she has a standard maiden in her. (tchd 6-1)
Moneycantbuymelove(IRE), a 75,000gns daughter of Pivotal, is a half-sister to a couple of 1m winners and she made a pleasing debut back in third. It is likely she will learn from this initial experience and she is another for whom winning an ordinary maiden should not prove too difficult, assuming she makes normal progress. (op 13-2 tchd 15-2)
Eliza Griffith(IRE), who showed only moderate form when sixth at Folkestone on debut, was returning from a small break and was seen to much better effect over this extra furlong. She will be qualified for a handicap mark following one more run and should fare better in that sphere. (op 12-1)
Simple Solution(USA), an American-bred who holds a Group 1 Fillies' Mile entry, was a bit green early, but she made a promising forward move and kept on under considerate riding. This was a good start and she is another likely to win a maiden. (op 12-1)
Al Tamooh(IRE) ◆, a 260,000gns daughter of Dalakhani, comes from a highly successful family and it is unlikely the best of her will be seen until next season and beyond. She was outpaced and green from before halfway, but plugged on and will improve markedly for an extra furlong. She is in the Fillies' Mile, but will need to win well next time if she is to take up that engagement. Official explanation: jockey said filly hung left (op 7-1)
Protiva put her experience to use and set off in front, but struggled to hold off several unexposed, classier types. She is now qualified for a handicap mark and should find easier opportunities in that sphere. (op 40-1)
Breach Of Peace(USA), an American-bred daughter of Royal Academy, was not helped by a slow start, but showed enough before getting tired to suggest she has a future. (op 9-1 tchd 12-1)
Dahama, a 30,000gns daughter of Green Desert, comes from a yard whose juveniles usually need a run and she shaped well following a sluggish start, running on late having been denied a clear run. She should know more next time. Official explanation: jockey said filly was denied a clear run
Sri Kandi, a 100,000gns daughter of Pivotal, is a half-sister to the high-class two-year-old Pearl Of Love and it was easy to see why she was made favourite on this racecourse debut, especially as her yard can often ready one to win first time up. However, having come to challenge, she found little and dropped right out. There were positives to take from this, but it would have been nice to see her going on at the finish. (op 9-2)
Silk Meadow(IRE) Official explanation: jockey said filly never travelled

4644 HSS HIRE E B F CONDITIONS STKS 1m
4:40 (4:42) (Class 2) 4-Y-O+ **£12,462** (£3,732; £1,866; £934; £466) **Stalls** High

Form					RPR
-222	1		**Dijeerr (USA)**[156] 743 4-8-9 109 (v) JamieSpencer 5 (Saeed Bin Suroor) *racd stands' side: mde virtually all: rdn over 1f out: styd on*	11/8[1]	113
F-33	2	2 3/4	**Drumfire (IRE)**[94] 1716 4-8-9 104 GregFairley 1 (M Johnston) *racd far side: chsd ldr tl led that pair over 2f out: sn rdn and edgd rt: styd on: 1st of 2 that side*	3/1[3]	107
40-3	3	3/4	**Trinity College (USA)**[14] 4177 4-8-9 0 DarryllHolland 4 (M F De Kock, South Africa) *swtchd to r stands' side 7f out: chsd wnr: rdn and edgd lft over 1f out: styd on same pce: 2nd of 3 in gp*	11/2	105
3202	4	4	**Fragrancy (IRE)**[14] 4189 4-8-6 93 ow2 PhilipRobinson 2 (M A Jarvis) *racd far side: led that pair tl over 2f out: rdn and edgd rt over 1f out: wknd fnl f: last of 2 that side*	11/4[2]	93
5/	5	22	**Charming Escort**[672] 5665 4-8-9 0 HollyHall 3 (T T Clement) *dwlt: racd stands' side: sn chsng ldrs: rdn and wknd over 2f out: sn hung lft: last of 3 in gp*	100/1	45

1m 38.76s (-1.24) **Going Correction** +0.075s/f (Good) **5** Ran SP% **110.1**
Speed ratings (Par 109): **109,106,105,101,79**
Toteswinger: 1&2 £2.90 CSF £5.84 TOTE £2.20: £1.60, £1.90; EX 5.80.
Owner Godolphin **Bred** Monticule **Trained** Newmarket, Suffolk

FOCUS
A decent little conditions event, but with Drumfire and Fragrancy splitting off to race far side, the form has little value although it does make sense. The runner-up may well have won had he stayed on the better ground.

NOTEBOOK
Dijeerr(USA), bidding to break a run of five consecutive seconds, had not been seen since he was beaten narrowly at Nad Al Sheba in February, but was still made favourite with Spencer on board. Kept to the stands' side, that seemed to make all the difference and he never had a challenger, his only serious rival racing on the slower ground more towards the far side. He did not achieve a great deal here and would be one to take on in a better race. (op 13-8 tchd 7-4 in a place)
Drumfire(IRE), off since finishing third to Cesare at Ascot in April, was a Group 3 winner at two and he looked a big danger to the favourite. However, his rider decided to follow Philip Robinson towards the far side and the move did not pay off. He tried his best to get on terms with the winner, pulling clear of Fragrancy on his side, but was unable to do so. He would have gone close to winning had he raced on the same side as Dijeerr, but should gain compensation in a similar contest. (op 10-3 tchd 7-2)
Trinity College(USA), bogged down by heavy ground at Haydock last time, came out second best of those on the stands' side and seemed to appreciate the slightly better ground, but never looked like matching the winner. It is likely he will remain hard to place. (op 5-1 tchd 4-1)
Fragrancy(IRE) is a consistent handicapper and she took Drumfire along on the far side, but did not find a great deal for pressure and dropped away tamely. Her rider was putting up 2lb overweight, but that cannot be used as an excuse, and perhaps the rain led to her poor showing. (op 5-2 tchd 9-4 and 3-1 in a place)
Charming Escort, last of five on his only other start, back in 2006, was always likely to finish where he did.

4645 ROBIN GREENING WOODBUTCHER H'CAP 1m 4f
5:15 (5:17) (Class 4) (0-85,81) 4-Y-O+ **£6,476** (£1,927; £963; £481) **Stalls** Centre

Form					RPR
0000	1		**Ainama (IRE)**[22] 3925 4-9-0 72 NickyMackay 3 (M Wigham) *a.p: rdn to chse ldr over 1f out: styd on to ld wl ins fnl f*	20/1	84
3004	2	1/2	**Invasian (IRE)**[14] 4200 7-9-9 81 JohnEgan 2 (P W D'Arcy) *led: rdn and hung lft fr over 2f out: hdd wl ins fnl f*	3/1[1]	92
1043	3	3 1/2	**Aypeeyes (IRE)**[17] 4078 4-9-5 77 DarryllHolland 8 (A King) *a.p: rdn over 1f out: styd on same pce fnl f*	5/1[3]	82
3002	4	4 1/2	**Touch Of Style (IRE)**[15] 4155 4-8-2 67 (p) RosieJessop(7) 6 (J R Boyle) *chsd ldr: rdn and edgd rt over 1f out: wknd fnl f*	9/1	65
3316	5	2 3/4	**Aegean Prince**[15] 4155 4-9-9 81 PatDobbs 4 (R Hannon) *hld up: rdn over 3f out: nvr trbld ldrs*	8/1	75
3511	6	1/2	**Tcherina (IRE)**[15] 4170 6-9-3 78 DuranFentiman(3) 7 (T D Easterby) *s.i.s: sn prom: rdn over 3f out: wknd wl over 1f out*	6/1	71
-523	7	30	**Potentiale (IRE)**[50] 3010 4-9-1 73 JamieSpencer 5 (J W Hills) *hld up and bhd: shkn up 1/2-way: rdn over 4f out: wknd and eased 3f out*	7/2[2]	18
3456	8	1	**Zaif (IRE)**[22] 3896 5-9-2 74 PaulEddery 1 (Simon Earle) *hld up: rdn over 4f out: wknd over 3f*	10/1	17

2m 31.95s (-0.95) **Going Correction** +0.075s/f (Good) **8** Ran SP% **113.1**
Speed ratings (Par 105): **106,105,103,100,98 98,78,77**
Toteswinger: 1&2 £17.30, 1&3 £15.60, 2&3 £4.20. CSF £77.87 CT £355.36 TOTE £26.60: £4.80, £1.60, £2.30; EX 106.30.
Owner R Morecombe & D Morrison **Bred** Roundhill Stud And A Stroud **Trained** Newmarket, Suffolk

FOCUS
A fair handicap. The winner is rated back to form with the second running to his turf form.
Ainama(IRE) Official explanation: trainer said, regarding apparent improvement in form, that the gelding appreciated the good ground rather than the soft it ran on last time
Potentiale(IRE) Official explanation: trainer's rep said gelding was unsuited by the good ground
Zaif(IRE) Official explanation: trainer said gelding finished distressed

4646 NEWMARKET NIGHTS H'CAP 1m 4f
5:45 (5:50) (Class 5) (0-70,67) 3-Y-O **£3,885** (£1,156; £577; £288) **Stalls** Centre

Form					RPR
3365	1		**Sea Chorus**[33] 3562 3-9-9 67 (t) JamieSpencer 4 (M L W Bell) *racd wd for the first 4f: led main gp: chsd clr ldr 8f out: tk clsr order over 3f out: led over 1f out: sn rdn and hung lft: all out*	3/1[1]	76
345	2	shd	**Fairfield Flame (GER)**[18] 4067 3-9-9 67 (b) RobertHavlin 3 (D R C Elsworth) *racd wd for 4f: hld up: hdwy over 2f out: hmpd 1f out: swtchd rt and r.o wl: jst failed*	15/2	76+
6403	3	2 1/4	**Lady Sorcerer**[24] 3841 3-9-9 67 PatDobbs 5 (A P Jarvis) *racd wd for 4f: plld hrd and sn prom: rdn over 2f out: styd on*	8/1	72
040	4	nse	**Colleoni (IRE)**[75] 2259 3-8-8 52 JohnEgan 6 (G A Butler) *racd wd for 4f: hld up: hdwy over 2f out: rdn and hung lft over 1f out: styd on*	11/2[3]	57
1250	5	4	**Dancing Dik**[5] 4485 3-9-9 67 (v1) DarryllHolland 8 (Mrs A J Perrett) *racd alone for 4f: sn led: clr 9f out: rdn and hdd over 1f out: hmpd sn after: no ex*	7/1	66
0020	6	8	**Tantris (IRE)**[17] 4086 3-9-6 64 GregFairley 2 (J A Osborne) *racd wd for 4f: hld up: nt clr run fr over 4f out to over 3f out: rdn and wknd over 1f out*	9/1	50
-065	7	4 1/2	**Fearless Warrior**[21] 3962 3-9-2 60 TPQueally 1 (J L Dunlop) *racd wd for 4f: chsd ldrs: rdn over 2f out: wknd over 1f out: eased*	7/2[2]	39
01	8	1 1/4	**Bella Medici**[11] 4280 3-8-11 62 AshleyMorgan(7) 7 (M H Tompkins) *racd wd for 4f: chsd ldrs: rdn over 2f out: wknd wl over 1f out*	14/1	39

2m 34.83s (1.93) **Going Correction** +0.075s/f (Good) **8** Ran SP% **114.6**
Speed ratings (Par 100): **96,95,94,94,91 86,83,82**
Toteswinger: 1&2 £4.00, 1&3 £4.80, 2&3 £11.60. CSF £25.99 CT £162.46 TOTE £3.50: £1.50, £2.10, £2.90; EX 26.10 Place 6 £180.98, Place 5 £54.30.
Owner The Eclipse Partnership **Bred** Car Colston Hall Stud **Trained** Newmarket, Suffolk

FOCUS
An ordinary handicap lacking progressive sorts, but it should produce winners at a similar level.
T/Plt: £395.20 to a £1 stake. Pool: £87,804.15. 162.18 winning tickets. T/Qpdt: £30.90 to a £1 stake. Pool: £4,831.30. 115.59 winning tickets. CR

4604 THIRSK (L-H)
Saturday, August 2

OFFICIAL GOING: Good
Wind: moderate 1/2 behind Weather: changeable

4647 EUROPEAN BREEDERS' FUND MAIDEN STKS 5f
2:00 (2:01) (Class 4) 2-Y-O **£5,504** (£1,637; £818; £408) **Stalls** High

Form					RPR
54	1		**Lucky Art (USA)**[28] 3707 2-9-3 0 RobertWinston 10 (J Howard Johnson) *mde all: styd on wl u.p fnl f*	5/2[1]	85+
	2	2 1/4	**Enderby Spirit (GR)** 2-9-3 0 DavidAllan 7 (D Carroll) *chsd ldrs: wnt 2nd over 1f out: kpt on same pce ins fnl f*	11/4[2]	77+

The Form Book, Raceform Ltd, Compton, RG20 6NL

3 *1* **Dark Lane** 2-9-3 0 .... PaulFessey 4 73
(T D Barron) *chsd ldrs: outpcd 2f out: styd on wl ins fnl f* **33/1**

02 **4** *6* **Wotatomboy**[6] 4449 2-8-9 0 .... MichaelJStainton(3) 3 47
(R M Whitaker) *chsd ldrs: wknd appr fnl f* **5/1**[3]

3534 **5** *4* **Mesyaal**[16] 4101 2-9-3 0 .... TonyCulhane 5 37
(M R Channon) *mid-div: sn drvn along and hung lft: nvr nr ldrs* **13/2**

6 *2 ¼* **Charles Dickens (IRE)** 2-9-3 0 .... JoeFanning 9 29
(M Johnston) *sn outpcd: hung lft and sme hdwy over 2f out: wknd over 1f out* **5/1**[3]

0 **7** *3 ¼* **Mousy Mousy (IRE)**[98] 1627 2-8-12 0 .... PaulMulrennan 6 13
(T D Easterby) *s.i.s: nvr wnt pce* **33/1**

8 *¾* **Mayorstone (IRE)** 2-8-12 0 .... TomEaves 1 10
(B Smart) *swvd lft s: sn hanging lft: nvr on terms* **20/1**

00 **9** *2 ¼* **Davana**[39] 3334 2-8-7 0 .... KellyHarrison(5) 2 —
(W J H Ratcliffe) *sn outpcd and in rr* **100/1**

10 *2* **Spiritofthewest (IRE)** 2-9-3 0 .... LeeEnstone 8 —
(S Parr) *rrd s and v.s.a: a detached in last* **50/1**

58.61 secs (-0.99) **Going Correction** -0.225s/f (Firm) **10** Ran SP% **115.5**
Speed ratings (Par 96): **98,94,92,83,76 73,68,66,63,60**
toteswinger: 1&2 £3.00, 1&3 £23.30, 2&3 £31.30. CSF £9.03 TOTE £3.70: £1.20, £1.70, £6.00; EX 10.70.
Owner Matthew Green and J H Johnson **Bred** Gaines-Gentry Thoroughbreds **Trained** Billy Row, Co Durham
■

FOCUS
The winner grabbed the stands'-side rail and always looked in command. The three finished clear and the winner's Beverley third is the best guide.
NOTEBOOK
Lucky Art(USA), fourth in a strong maiden at Beverley, made every yard and in the end won going away. (op 3-1 tchd 10-3)
Enderby Spirit(GR), a rangy February foal, holds a Middle Park entry. He looked to be carrying tons of condition and after looking a real threat to the winner was definitely second best at the line. (op 10-3 tchd 7-2 in places)
Dark Lane, a January foal out of a speedy mare, is not that big but well put together. He didn't move well to post but after getting tapped for toe was putting in some solid late work. This will have taught him plenty.
Wotatomboy, keen to post, showed bags of toe but tired noticeably in the final furlong. (op 9-2 tchd 6-1)
Mesyaal, having his fifth start and with a provisional rating of 71, was always being run off his feet and he is not a 5f horse. (tchd 5-1)
Charles Dickens(IRE), first foal of a Cheveley Park winner, is small and lacks scope. He moved poorly to post and wanted to do nothing but hang left. (op 4-1)

4648 HERTEL NURSERY 5f
2:30 (2:31) (Class 3) 2-Y-O **£8,159** (£2,428; £1,213; £606) **Stalls** High

Form RPR

1106 **1** **Dispol Kylie (IRE)**[56] 2838 2-8-1 **74** .... PaulFessey 4 84
(P T Midgley) *mde all: edgd lft 1f out: styd on strly to forge clr* **7/1**[3]

41 **2** *3 ¾* **Sirenuse (IRE)**[14] 4202 2-8-6 **79** ow1 .... TomEaves 5 75
(B Smart) *t.k.h: trckd ldrs: plld wd to s chal over 1f out: sn rdn and kpt on same pce* **6/5**[1]

1104 **3** *2 ¼* **Bahamian Babe**[14] 4190 2-9-7 **94** .... HayleyTurner 3 82
(M L W Bell) *chsd wnr: effrt 2f out: kpt on same pce* **7/4**[2]

2126 **4** *nk* **Alphabeth**[14] 4175 2-7-12 **71** .... CatherineGannon 2 58
(M R Channon) *chsd ldrs on outer: hrd drvn over 2f out: one pce* **9/1**

140 **5** *1 ½* **Ykikamoocow**[16] 4119 2-7-12 **71** .... PaulQuinn 1 52
(G A Harker) *dwlt: sn outpcd and detached in rr: kpt on fnl f: nvr a factor* **14/1**

58.66 secs (-0.94) **Going Correction** -0.225s/f (Firm) **5** Ran SP% **111.0**
Speed ratings (Par 98): **98,92,88,87,85**
CSF £16.22 TOTE £8.30: £2.30, £1.40; EX 14.90.
Owner W B Imison **Bred** Century Farms **Trained** Westow, N Yorks
FOCUS
The winner showed a very good attitude.
NOTEBOOK
Dispol Kylie(IRE), given an eight-week break, needs some juice in the ground. She hit the traps running and in the end won going right away. She is a fine advert for her trainer. (op 13-2)
Sirenuse(IRE), taken quietly to post, took a fierce grip. She looked the likely winner when pulled off the fence to mount her challenge but the winner soon proved much too strong. (op 6-4)
Bahamian Babe, a stone and a half worse off with the winner compared to York, looked at her very best, but was asked to concede 16lb and more away all round and the task simply proved beyond her. (op 13-8 tchd 6-4)
Alphabeth, though handy, was always struggling to keep up. To her credit she kept going all the way to the line and a return to six will suit her. (op 11-1)
Ykikamoocow, on her toes beforehand, missed a beat at the start and could never go the pace. She needs six now. (op 10-1 tchd 9-1)

4649 EKOSGEN H'CAP 1m
3:05 (3:05) (Class 3) (0-90,87) 3-Y-0+ **£8,159** (£2,428; £1,213; £606) **Stalls** Low

Form RPR

2250 **1** **Observatory Star (IRE)**[21] 3972 5-9-2 **75** .... (p) DavidAllan 2 87
(T D Easterby) *chsd ldrs: led over 2f out: hld on wl towards fin* **11/2**[3]

2230 **2** *nk* **Just Bond (IRE)**[16] 4104 6-9-0 **76** .... PJMcDonald(3) 8 88
(G R Oldroyd) *t.k.h in rr: effrt on outside over 2f out: chal ins fnl f: no ex* **11/1**

111 **3** *½* **Osteopathic Remedy (IRE)**[38] 3367 4-9-12 **85** .... TomEaves 1 96
(M Dods) *sn trcking ldrs: effrt over 2f out: kpt on wl ins fnl f* **4/1**[1]

3211 **4** *3 ¼* **Esoterica (IRE)**[7] 4440 5-8-13 **77** .... (b) GaryBartley(5) 5 80
(J S Goldie) *hld up in rr: styd on fnl 2f: nt rch ldrs* **5/1**[2]

1341 **5** *½* **Hula Ballew**[14] 4206 8-9-7 **83** .... NeilBrown(3) 3 85
(M Dods) *mid-div: effrt over 2f out: kpt on: nvr trbld ldrs* **8/1**

0505 **6** *5* **Obezyana (USA)**[7] 4407 6-8-13 **75** .... DominicFox(3) 11 66
(A Bailey) *in rr: kpt on fnl 2f: nvr a factor* **16/1**

3033 **7** *¾* **My Paris**[14] 4206 7-9-10 **83** .... TonyHamilton 4 72
(Ollie Pears) *led after 1f: qcknd over 3f out: hdd over 2f out: wknd fnl f* **5/1**[2]

6200 **8** *2 ½* **Danehillsundance (IRE)**[42] 3261 4-10-0 **87** .... TonyCulhane 6 70
(S Parr) *s.i.s: a in rr* **10/1**

31 **9** *3 ¾* **Bustan (IRE)**[29] 3664 9-9-8 **81** .... JoeFanning 12 55
(G C Bravery) *mid-div: lost pl 2f out* **14/1**

0250 **10** *10* **Bold Marc (IRE)**[21] 3972 6-9-5 **78** .... LeeEnstone 10 29
(K R Burke) *led 1f: lost pl over 2f out: bhd whn eased ins fnl f* **12/1**

1465 **11** *12* **Dhhamaan (IRE)**[9] 4329 3-8-6 **75** .... (b) MichaelJStainton(3) 7 —
(Mrs R A Carr) *w ldrs: wknd over 2f out: bhd whn eased ins fnl f* **40/1**

1m 40.16s (0.06) **Going Correction** +0.20s/f (Good)
WFA 3 from 4yo+ 7lb **11** Ran SP% **119.9**
Speed ratings (Par 107): **107,106,106,102,102 97,96,94,90,80 68**
toteswinger: 1&2 £20.00, 1&3 £7.80, 2&3 £23.70. CSF £66.07 CT £276.77 TOTE £7.30: £2.20, £4.20, £2.20; EX 107.30.
Owner Mr And Mrs J D Cotton **Bred** C J Foy **Trained** Great Habton, N Yorks
FOCUS
Not a strong early pace but in the end the first three finished clear of two good yardsticks. A good race for the grade, and sound form whic h should be reliable.
NOTEBOOK
Observatory Star(IRE), as usual taken to post early, kicked for home at just the right time and in the end did just enough. (tchd 6-1)
Just Bond(IRE), whose seven career wins have been on the All-Weather, came there on the outer and looked sure to get there but in the end the winner proved just the more determined. (op 12-1 tchd 14-1)
Osteopathic Remedy(IRE), ideally drawn, is settling much better these days. Up 6lb, to his credit he kept going all the way to the line. He should continue to give a good account of himself. (op 11-2)
Esoterica(IRE), who usually runs well here, was 4lb higher and would have appreciated a strong early pace. (op 4-1)
Hula Ballew, seeking her fifth win on her 15th start here, was up another 6lb and found a career-high mark too much.
My Paris went on and kicked on once in line for home but he was soon readily swallowed up. That seventh career win is proving elusive. (op 13-2)

4650 BURN HALL HOTEL AT HUBY H'CAP 1m
3:40 (3:41) (Class 5) (0-75,74) 3-Y-0+ **£4,274** (£1,271; £635; £317) **Stalls** Low

Form RPR

03 **1** **Myfrenchconnection (IRE)**[33] 3557 4-8-13 **59** .... LeeEnstone 1 69
(P T Midgley) *trckd ldrs gng wl: led on bit 2f out: jnd ins fnl f: hrd rdn and kpt on gamely nr fin* **9/2**[1]

0263 **2** *hd* **King Of Rhythm (IRE)**[12] 4244 5-9-12 **72** .... DNolan 11 81
(D Carroll) *prom: effrt over 2f out: edgd lft and upsides ins fnl f: no ex nr fin* **8/1**

4403 **3** *3 ½* **Shotley Mac**[12] 4245 4-9-3 **66** .... (b) NeilBrown(3) 8 67
(N Bycroft) *led 1f: sn settled and in rr: hdwy on outside over 2f out: kpt on same pce fnl f* **6/1**[3]

5201 **4** *hd* **West End Lad**[21] 3964 5-9-3 **63** .... (b) TomEaves 5 64
(S R Bowring) *trckd ldrs: hrd rdn and hung lft over 1f out: kpt on same pce* **11/2**[2]

2300 **5** *2 ¼* **Champain Sands (IRE)**[31] 3599 9-9-2 **65** .... MichaelJStainton(3) 2 60
(E J Alston) *chsd ldrs: effrt over 2f out: one pce* **7/1**

46-0 **6** *1 ¼* **Pinewood Lulu**[49] 3031 3-8-10 **63** .... PAspell 6 54
(R C Guest) *s.i.s: kpt on fnl 2f: nvr nr ldrs* **50/1**

510 **7** *shd* **Aussie Blue (IRE)**[15] 4172 4-9-3 **63** .... DaleGibson 10 55
(R M Whitaker) *in rr: kpt on fnl 2f: nvr nr ldrs* **9/1**

1006 **8** *¾* **We'Re Delighted**[15] 4174 3-9-2 **69** .... PaulMulrennan 14 59
(T D Walford) *in rr on outer: drvn over 3f out: nvr a factor* **16/1**

3451 **9** *2 ½* **Dispol Isle (IRE)**[12] 4245 6-9-13 **73** .... PaulFessey 12 58
(T D Barron) *in rr-div: effrt on outer over 2f out: nvr nr ldrs* **7/1**

0200 **10** *6* **Lap Of Honour (IRE)**[13] 4219 4-10-0 **74** .... (b[1]) LiamTreadwell 3 45
(Jennie Candlish) *led after 1f: hdd 2f out: sn lost pl* **20/1**

5030 **11** *6* **Chicken George (IRE)**[33] 3563 4-9-1 **68** .... AdeleRothery(7) 7 25
(D Nicholls) *s.i.s: sn chsng ldrs: lost pl over 3f out: bhd whn eased ins fnl f* **8/1**

5405 **12** *6* **Superior Star**[15] 4172 5-9-4 **64** .... (b) PaulQuinn 4 7
(N Wilson) *s.i.s: drvn over 2f out: wknd 2f out: bhd and eased ins fnl f* **16/1**

1m 40.95s (0.85) **Going Correction** +0.20s/f (Good)
WFA 3 from 4yo+ 7lb **12** Ran SP% **123.6**
Speed ratings (Par 103): **103,102,99,99,96 95,95,94,92,86 80,74**
toteswinger: 1&2 £6.60, 1&3 £7.20, 2&3 £12.40. CSF £42.35 CT £228.25 TOTE £5.50: £2.10, £3.40, £2.70; EX 43.40.
Owner J F Wright **Bred** Mrs Stephanie Winters **Trained** Westow, N Yorks
■ Stewards' Enquiry : Lee Enstone three-day ban: used whip with excessive frequency and down the shoulder in forehand position (Aug 16 -18)
FOCUS
The first two finished clear and the form looks sound rated around them.

4651 WEATHERBYS BLOODSTOCK INSURANCE MAIDEN FILLIES' STKS 7f
4:15 (4:17) (Class 4) 3-Y-0+ **£5,569** (£1,657; £828; £413) **Stalls** Low

Form RPR

1 **Wallonia (IRE)**[76] 3-8-11 0 .... NeilBrown(3) 8 66
(K A Ryan) *in tch: drvn 3f out: edgd rt and styd on fnl f: led last 100yds* **16/1**

3-4 **2** *1* **Orchestrion**[14] 4194 3-9-0 0 .... PaulMulrennan 10 63
(G A Swinbank) *sn chsng ldr: no ex wl ins fnl f* **5/1**[3]

3 *½* **Straight Sets (IRE)** 4-9-1 0 .... MCGeran(5) 4 64
(M R Channon) *chsd ldrs: outpcd over 2f out: styd on wl ins fnl f* **15/2**

6334 **4** *½* **Theory**[22] 3918 3-9-0 71 .... (b) DavidKinsella 5 60
(J H M Gosden) *led: edgd rt: faltered and hdd fnl 100yds* **5/2**[2]

5 *2 ¾* **Gheed (IRE)** 3-9-0 0 .... (t) JoeFanning 2 53
(Saeed Bin Suroor) *s.i.s: hdwy to chse ldrs over 4f out: edgd lft and fdd fnl f* **9/4**[1]

0005 **6** *1 ½* **First Valentini**[68] 2463 4-8-13 38 .... JonathanHinch(7) 7 51?
(N Bycroft) *v unruly gng to s: mid-div: kpt on fnl 2f: nvr a threat* **100/1**

7 *6* **Emily's Secret** 3-9-0 0 .... DavidAllan 12 33
(G C Bravery) *in rr: nvr on terms* **16/1**

50 **8** *½* **Ellalucianna**[10] 4301 3-8-11 0 .... MichaelJStainton(3) 13 31
(M Wigham) *a towards rr* **80/1**

9 *3* **Melia (GR)** 3-9-0 0 .... TGMcLaughlin 6 23
(Jane Chapple-Hyam) *s.i.s: hdwy to chse ldrs over 4f out: wknd over 1f out* **16/1**

10 *5* **Kiss Me Hardy** 3-9-0 0 .... CatherineGannon 9 10
(J D Bethell) *s.s: drvn along and a bhd* **8/1**

11 *8* **High Shanamara** 3-9-0 0 .... PaulFessey 11 —
(P T Midgley) *a in rr: bhd fnl 2f* **66/1**

1m 28.87s (1.67) **Going Correction** +0.20s/f (Good)
WFA 3 from 4yo 6lb **11** Ran SP% **120.2**
Speed ratings (Par 102): **98,96,96,95,92 90,84,83,80,74 65**
toteswinger: 1&2 £13.10, 1&3 £25.00, 2&3 £5.20. CSF £96.42 TOTE £25.90: £4.50, £2.00, £1.80; EX 105.20.
Owner Mrs J Ryan **Bred** Kildaragh Stud **Trained** Hambleton, N Yorks

FOCUS
A modest maiden with the sixth rated just 38 and the form choice fourth below par.

4652 BOB AND MARIE MILBURN GOLDEN WEDDING ANNIVERSARY H'CAP — 2m
4:50 (4:50) (Class 5) (0-75,74) 4-Y-0+ **£4,274** (£1,271; £635; £317) **Stalls** Low

Form				RPR
5000	1		**Clear Reef**[30] 3630 4-9-7 **74** ... TGMcLaughlin 2 *(Jane Chapple-Hyam) hld up in last: effrt 3f out: wnt 2nd 2f out: hrd rdn and edgd rt: styd on to ld nr fin* **7/1**	83
3116	2	½	**Squirtle (IRE)**[8] 4391 5-7-13 **55** ... LukeMorris(3) 3 *(W M Brisbourne) hld up: hdwy to chse ldrs 7f out: drvn over 4f out: led over 2f out: hrd rdn and edgd lft 1f out: hdd towards fin* **10/3**[1]	63
/036	3	1 ½	**Burnt Oak (UAE)**[14] 4178 6-9-2 **69** ... DeanMcKeown 1 *(C W Fairhurst) hld up: n.m.r over 3f out: hdwy to chse ldrs appr fnl f: kpt on same pce* **10/1**	75
0164	4	4 ½	**Brave Bugsy (IRE)**[16] 4105 5-8-4 **57** ... DavidKinsella 6 *(A M Balding) hld up: hdwy to chse ldrs 9f out: wnt 2nd over 3f out: one pce fnl 2f* **7/2**[2]	58
4-35	5	5	**Industrial Star (IRE)**[35] 3480 7-9-0 **67** ...(p) DavidAllan 8 *(Micky Hammond) chsd ldr: led over 3f out: sn hdd: wknd over 1f out* **5/1**[3]	62
4355	6	1 ½	**Its Moon (IRE)**[14] 3624 4-8-12 **65** ... PaulMulrennan 5 *(T D Walford) trckd ldrs: pushed along 6f out: wknd 2f out* **7/1**	58
1/46	7	2 ¾	**Spring Breeze**[23] 3863 7-8-7 **60** ...(v) DaleGibson 7 *(M Dods) reminders after s: led: qcknd over 4f out: hdd over 3f out: lost pl over 2f out* **14/1**	50
1640	8	2 ¼	**Ritsi**[18] 4046 5-8-9 **62** ... PaulFessey 4 *(Grant Tuer) hld up in tch: drvn over 5f out: outpcd and lost pl over 3f out* **8/1**	49

3m 33.42s (0.02) **Going Correction** +0.20s/f (Good) **8 Ran SP% 113.8**
Speed ratings (Par 103): **107,106,106,103,101 100,99,98**
toteswinger: 1&2 £5.00, 1&3 £11.50, 2&3 £7.50. CSF £30.30 CT £233.18 TOTE £8.90: £2.90, £1.60, £2.10; EX 32.40.
Owner Chapple-Hyam Serrell Tegel Ward **Bred** Hesmonds Stud Ltd **Trained** Lambourn, Berks
■ Stewards' Enquiry : T G McLaughlin one-day ban: used whip with excessive frequency (Aug 16)

FOCUS
An ordinary stayers' handicap rated through the placed horses with the winner back to form.

4653 WHITBY H'CAP (LADIES' RACE) — 6f
5:25 (5:27) (Class 6) (0-55,55) 3-Y-0+ **£2,873** (£891; £445; £222) **Stalls** High

Form				RPR
4004	1		**Ryedane (IRE)**[10] 4293 6-10-4 **52** ...(b) MissJCoward(3) 11 *(T D Easterby) swtchd rt s and racd stands' side: sn chsng ldrs: styd on fnl f: led nr fin* **11/1**	66
2000	2	hd	**Ensign's Trick**[21] 3951 4-10-0 **50** ... MissRKneller(5) 18 *(W M Brisbourne) chsd ldrs: led over 1f out: hdd towards fin* **22/1**	63
4024	3	3	**Obe One**[6] 4462 8-9-10 **46** oh1 ... MissBeverleyKendall(5) 17 *(A Berry) mid-div: edgd lft snd styd on fnl 2f* **9/1**	49
6303	4	3 ½	**High Window (IRE)**[30] 3638 8-10-1 **46** oh1 ... MissSBrotherton 19 *(G P Kelly) prom: edgd lft and one pce fnl 2f: sddle slipped* **12/1**	38
0624	5	1	**Roman Quintet (IRE)**[29] 3665 8-10-5 **55** ...(b) MissABevan(5) 12 *(A J McCabe) clr ldr stands' side: hdd over 1f out: wknd towards fin* **6/1**[2]	44
0340	6	nk	**Greek Secret**[9] 4327 5-10-6 **51** ... MissADeniel 16 *(J O'Reilly) in rr: styd on fnl 2f: nt rch ldrs* **17/2**	39
6266	7	1 ¾	**Wiltshire (IRE)**[9] 4327 6-10-4 **54** ...(b) MissWGibson(5) 14 *(P T Midgley) prom: one pce fnl 2f* **16/1**	36
5025	8	hd	**Lambency (IRE)**[1] 4609 5-10-9 **54** ... MrsCBartley 20 *(J S Goldie) hld up stands' side: hdwy 2f out: nvr nr ldrs* **11/2**[1]	36
5/01	9	2	**Valverde (IRE)**[16] 4102 5-10-9 **54** ...(v) MissEJJones 9 *(George Baker) in rr: kpt on fnl 2f: nvr on terms* **7/1**[3]	29
0000	10	2 ¾	**Empire Dancer (IRE)**[3] 4540 5-10-0 **50** ...(p) MissKSharp(5) 1 *(I W McInnes) racd far side: chsd ldr: led that side 1f out: no ch w stands' side: 1st of 4 that gp* **33/1**	17
000	11	shd	**Jordi Roper (IRE)**[21] 3958 3-10-6 **55** ... MissARyan 10 *(S Parr) chsd ldrs: wknd over 1f out* **8/1**	21
500-	12	1 ¼	**Celeb Style (IRE)**[226] 7206 4-9-12 **46** ... MissNJefferson(3) 3 *(Paul Green) led 3 others on far side tl 1f out: wknd: 2nd of 4 that gp* **16/1**	8
3033	13	1	**Whozart (IRE)**[10] 4294 5-10-0 **50** ... MissMMullineaux(5) 8 *(A Dickman) swtchd rt s and racd towards stands' side: nvr bttr than mid-div* **10/1**	9
0-04	14	nk	**Bahamian Duke**[8] 4385 5-10-0 **50** ... MissKellyBurke(5) 2 *(K R Burke) racd far side: nvr nr ldrs* **14/1**	8
4000	15	5	**Cabourg (IRE)**[29] 3662 5-10-0 **50** ...(b) MissRBastiman(5) 13 *(R Bastiman) s.s: a bhd* **33/1**	—
4200	16	3 ¼	**Buzbury Rings**[3] 4542 4-10-3 **55** ...(p) MissVBarr(7) 4 *(R E Barr) racd far side: chsd ldr: wknd over 1f out: last of 4 that gp* **33/1**	—
-F25	17	3 ¾	**Flamestone**[8] 4378 4-9-12 **50** ... MissIPickard(7) 6 *(A E Price) swtchd rt after 1f and racd centre: in tch: lost pl 2f out* **40/1**	—
-000	18	hd	**Law Maker**[57] 2802 8-9-10 **46** ...(v) MissRLLockie(5) 7 *(A Bailey) swtchd rt s and racd stands' side: a in rr* **33/1**	—

1m 12.72s (0.02) **Going Correction** -0.225s/f (Firm)
WFA 3 from 4yo+ 4lb **18 Ran SP% 135.9**
Speed ratings (Par 101): **90,89,85,81,79 79,77,76,74,70 70,68,67,66,60 55,50,50**
toteswinger: 1&2 £71.60, 1&3 £30.70, 2&3 £74.30. CSF £256.23 CT £2318.20 TOTE £13.00: £2.80, £6.80, £2.20, £4.40; EX 333.60 Place 6 £82.58, Place 5 £46.41.
Owner Ryedale Partners No 5 **Bred** Tally-Ho Stud **Trained** Great Habton, N Yorks
■ Stewards' Enquiry : Miss K Sharp one-day ban: failed to ride to draw (Aug 16)

FOCUS
A low-grade lady riders' sprint handicap and strength from the saddle carried the day. It paid to race on the stands' side. The form is rated through the third.
High Window(IRE) Official explanation: jockey said saddle slipped
T/Plt: £314.50 to a £1 stake. Pool: £50,259.09. 116.64 winning tickets. T/Qpdt: £63.80 to a £1 stake. Pool: £3,511.79. 40.70 winning tickets. WG

4654 - (Foreign Racing) - See Raceform Interactive

4610 GALWAY (R-H)
Saturday, August 2

OFFICIAL GOING: Flat course, hurdle course - good, chase course- yielding

4655a CHEESTRINGS H'CAP — 2m
4:35 (4:36) (50-70,70) 4-Y-0+ **£7,621** (£1,775; £783; £452)

			RPR
1		**Hill Fairy**[16] 4141 6-8-12 59 ... MACleere(5) 2 *(J Morrison, Ire) a.p: 2nd 1/2-way: cl 4th under 3f out: sn rdn to chal: led 1f out: styd on u.p* **14/1**	65
2	1 ¾	**Sesenta (IRE)**[130] 6685 4-10-0 70 ... FMBerry 6 *(W P Mullins, Ire) in rr of mid-div on outer: 6th and hdwy 4f out: 4th 3f out: chal appr st: 2nd and kpt on ins fnl f* **20/1**	74
3	½	**Sagarich (FR)**[2] 4574 4-9-8 64 ... WJLee 1 *(C F Swan, Ire) slowly away and hld up in rr: hdwy into 8th 3f out: impr into 2nd on inner ent st: disp ld briefly 1f out: no ex cl home* **16/1**	67
4	shd	**Captain Hook**[4] 4511 4-9-6 62 ...(p) CDHayes 8 *(Daniel Mark Loughnane, Ire) towards rr: hdwy 2 1/2f out: 6th on outer ent st: 4th and kpt on ins fnl f* **16/1**	65
5	1 ¼	**Mohtarres (USA)**[4] 4511 5-9-9 65 ...(t) DPMcDonogh 5 *(D T Hughes, Ire) mid-div: 9th under 2f out: 6th 1f out: 5th and no imp last 100yds* **16/1**	67
6	1	**Monahullan Prince**[26] 2471 7-9-1 57 ...(t) RPCleary 20 *(Gerard Keane, Ire) dwlt: hld up: prog into 9th 2f out: kpt on ins fnl f* **14/1**	58
7	2 ½	**Call Me Max**[20] 1977 6-9-6 65 ...(p) CPGeoghegan(3) 9 *(Eoin Doyle, Ire) mid-div: 8th 1/2-way: rdn 2 1/2f out: kpt on same pce* **11/1**	63
8	¾	**Pretty Demanding (IRE)**[4] 4511 4-8-13 62 ... BACurtis(7) 17 *(M G Quinlan) led: strly pressed fr under 3f out: hdd 1f out: no ex* **25/1**	59
9	3	**Heights Of Golan**[11] 6564 4-9-4 60 ... WMLordan 14 *(T J O'Mara, Ire) towards rr: hdwy on outer 5f out: 3rd over 4f out: 2nd and chal 2f out: no ex ent st* **28/1**	53
10	1	**Flamenco Prince**[21] 3989 4-8-13 62 ...(b) DEMullins(7) 4 *(Patrick O Brady, Ire) hld up: rdn and one pce fr under 3f out* **20/1**	54
11	¾	**The Chip Chopman (IRE)**[21] 3980 6-9-1 62 ...(t) PTownend(5) 10 *(Seamus G O'Donnell, Ire) trckd ldrs in 6th: rdn and lost pl under 4f out: no ex bef st* **14/1**	53
12	2 ½	**Eritrea**[22] 3937 4-9-7 63 ... DMGrant 11 *(Patrick J Flynn, Ire) trckd ldrs: 7th 1/2-way: no ex fr under 3f out* **5/1**[1]	51
13	2 ½	**Cybersnow (USA)**[28] 2815 4-9-2 65 ...(t) MHarley(7) 12 *(Barry Potts, Ire) trckd ldrs in 5th: 4th travelling wl 3f out: wknd appr st* **20/1**	50
14	¾	**Diyla (IRE)**[20] 3622 5-9-2 58 ...(b) CO'Donoghue 3 *(M Flannery, Ire) hld up: no ex fr 4f out* **25/1**	42
15	19	**Laureldean (IRE)**[16] 4141 10-9-13 69 ... JAHeffernan 19 *(Michael Cunningham, Ire) mid-div: 9th 1/2-way: no ex fr over 3f out* **9/1**[3]	30
16	16	**Vampress (IRE)**[2112] 9-9-4 60 ... MCHussey 13 *(Liam McAteer, Ire) trckd ldrs in 4th: 5th 4f out: sn wknd* **33/1**	2
17	8	**Grand Corniche (IRE)**[22] 5398 5-9-6 62 ...(b) MJKinane 18 *(A J Martin, Ire) a bhd* **6/1**[2]	—
18	24	**Clarricien (IRE)**[23] 2415 4-9-12 68 ... KLatham 16 *(Patrick Griffin, Ire) prom: 3rd 6f out: wknd fr 4f out: t.o* **40/1**	—
P		**Karlu (GER)**[20] 1100 6-9-10 66 ...(p) NPMadden 15 *(John C McConnell, Ire) towards rr: p.u 5f out* **6/1**[2]	—

3m 39.4s (-5.40) **20 Ran SP% 132.0**
CSF £282.70 CT £4523.94 TOTE £14.00: £3.00, £5.80, £3.90, £4.00; DF 451.70.
Owner J Morrison **Bred** Gestut Goerlsdorf **Trained** Tallow, Co Waterford

NOTEBOOK
Hill Fairy Official explanation: trainer's rep said, regarding the improved form shown, mare may not be suited by Killarney, where her only two previous bad runs have been
Pretty Demanding(IRE) had been well beaten off over the course and distance four days previously, but she showed improved form under this much more aggressive ride.
Karlu(GER) Official explanation: jockey said gelding burst a blood vessel

4656 - (Foreign Racing) - See Raceform Interactive

3994 DEAUVILLE (R-H)
Saturday, August 2

OFFICIAL GOING: Turf course - soft; all-weather - standard

4657a PRIX DE PSYCHE (GROUP 3) (FILLIES) — 1m 2f
2:20 (2:24) 3-Y-O **£29,412** (£11,765; £8,824; £5,882; £2,941)

			RPR
1		**Top Toss (IRE)**[27] 3775 3-8-11 ... CSoumillon 1 *(Y De Nicolay, France) hld up in tch: 8th on ins st: drvn and hdwy over 1 1/2f out: qcknd to chal 100yds out: led on line: rdn out* **19/10**[1]	112
2	snk	**Changing Skies (IRE)**[16] 4124 3-8-11 ... DBonilla 10 *(B J Meehan) led: rdn and r.o 1 1/2f out: fnd more fnl f: hdd on line* **23/1**	111
3	nse	**Proviso**[27] 3775 3-8-11 ... SPasquier 8 *(A Fabre, France) hld up in tch: 5th st: hdwy on outside 2f out: rdn and wnt 2nd 1f out to 100yds out: styd on: jst missed 2nd* **27/10**[2]	111
4	½	**Albisola (IRE)**[62] 2651 3-8-11 ... C-PLemaire 2 *(Robert Collet, France) hld up: 10th st: pushed along in centre 2f out: rdn and fin wl fnl f: nrest at fin* **6/1**[3]	110
5	snk	**Lady Deauville (FR)**[62] 2651 3-8-11 ... DBoeuf 5 *(P A Blockley) mid-div: disputing 6th st: rdn and styd on in centre fr over 1f out: wnt 4th briefly cl home: styd on* **21/1**	110
6	1	**Goathemala (GER)**[29] 3705 3-8-11 ... AStarke 4 *(P Schiergen, Germany) mid-div: disputing 6th st: rdn 1 1/2f out: nvr able to chal* **22/1**	108
7	nk	**Caesarine (FR)**[27] 3775 3-8-11 ... MGuyon 7 *(A Fabre, France) prom: 2nd st: rdn 1 1/2f out: nvr able to chal* **31/1**	107
8	2 ½	**Prudenzia (IRE)**[62] 2650 3-8-11 ... TThulliez 9 *(P Bary, France) hld up: 9th st: nvr a factor* **28/1**	102
9	3	**Loutka (FR)**[50] 3018 3-8-11 ...(b) OPeslier 11 *(J-M Beguigne, France) s.i.s: rcvrd to r in mid-div: disputing 3rd st: sn pushed along: rdn and one pce fr over 1 1/2f out* **8/1**	96
10	snk	**Zina Blue (FR)**[43] 3-8-11 ... ACrastus 3 *(J De Rouale, France) prom: disputing 3rd st: drvn and u.p 1 1/2f out: sn one pce* **13/1**	96

11 **Myakoda (FR)**34 3543 3-8-11 .... IMendizabal 6 96
(Y De Nicolay, France) *hld up: last st: drvn 2f out: no imp* **30/1**

2m 9.80s (-0.40) **Going Correction** +0.225s/f (Good) **11** Ran SP% **116.9**
Speed ratings: **110,109,109,109,109 108,108,106,103,103 103**
PARI-MUTUEL: WIN 2.90; PL 1.30, 4.00, 1.50; DF 31.80.
Owner Ecurie Skymarc Farm **Bred** Skymarc Farm Inc **Trained** France
■ Stewards' Enquiry : C Soumillon €200 fine: whip abuse

NOTEBOOK
Top Toss(IRE) came with a sweeping late run to just get up on the line. This consistent filly was under pressure one and a half out and victory seemed out of the question, but she suddenly found top gear and won in the final few strides. Her only bad run in her career had come in the Prix de Diane and she has now won a pair of Group 3 races. Her main target is the Prix de L'Opera at Longchamp on October 5th.
Changing Skies(IRE) made a very brave effort to make all the running, as she broke well from her outside draw and was soon in command. She quickened things up in the straight and defeat looked out of the question at the furlong marker, but she did not quite hold on. She will probably be aimed at a Listed race at Longchamp.
Proviso has not quite lived up to expectations this season, but she was only beaten by under a neck on this occasion. Given every chance, she was beautifully poised to challenge at the furlong marker and ran on well. It would be no surprise if she lined up for the Prix de la Nonette later in the month but she is not the quickest and needs trips of 1m4f plus to be seen at her best.
Albisola(IRE) was given an awful lot to do. She was towards the tail of the field in the early part of the race and then was brought with a challenge up the centre of the track. This distance seems to suit her and she is a filly who likes to get her toe in.
Lady Deauville(FR), a soft-ground specialist, was beaten under a length and had to wait a little before being able to deliver her final challenge. She looked dangerous one and a half out but did not quite go through with her effort. She will run next where the ground is soft and possibly over a shorter distance.

3946 CHESTER (L-H)
Sunday, August 3

OFFICIAL GOING: Good (good to soft in places)
The false rail on the home bend added about 15yards per circuit to race distances.
Wind: Moderate, against Weather: Showers before racing

4658 JEWSON SUPPORTING BRITISH HEART FOUNDATION EBF MAIDEN STKS 7f 2y
2:20 (2:21) (Class 4) 2-Y-O **£5,180** (£1,541; £770; £384) **Stalls** Low

Form RPR
6 1 **Proclaim**11 4289 2-9-3 0 .... J-PGuillambert 2 76
(M Johnston) *mde all: rdn over 1f out: r.o ins fnl f: in command towards fin* **5/2**1
64 2 2 1/4 **Flintlock (IRE)**30 3682 2-9-3 0 .... (b) JimmyFortune 7 70
(J H M Gosden) *chsd wnr: chal 3f out: nt qckn 2f out: sn rdn: no imp fnl 75yds* **5/1**
0 3 1 3/4 **Game Roseanna**31 3625 2-8-12 0 .... LiamJones 3 61
(W M Brisbourne) *s.i.s: chsd front quartet: pushed along abt 8l off the pce 4f out: styd on ins fnl f: tk 3rd fnl 75yds: nt pce to chal ldrs* **20/1**
4 1 **Kristopher James (IRE)** 2-9-3 0 .... TGMcLaughlin 4 64
(W M Brisbourne) *s.i.s: midfield: pushed along 4f out: styd on ins fnl f: nt pce to rch ldrs* **20/1**
03 5 1 3/4 **Lady Salama**37 3432 2-8-12 0 .... AndrewElliott 5 54
(K R Burke) *w ldrs tl n.m.r over 5f out: rdn over 2f out: sn outpcd: wknd ins fnl f* **10/1**
0 6 1 1/4 **Citizenship**25 3853 2-9-3 0 .... JimCrowley 12 56+
(Pat Eddery) *sn pushed along towards rr: kpt on steadily ins fnl f: nvr able to trble ldrs* **3/1**2
56 7 4 **Shifting Gold (IRE)**15 4176 2-9-3 0 .... TedDurcan 11 46
(K A Ryan) *sn pushed along towards rr: nvr on terms* **18/1**
00 8 3 1/4 **Talsarnau (IRE)**47 3107 2-9-3 0 .... DanielTudhope 13 38
(W M Brisbourne) *sn rdn along: a bhd* **66/1**
U 9 5 **Lucky Dan (IRE)**59 2746 2-9-3 0 .... PaulMulrennan 6 25
(Paul Green) *w ldrs tl over 5f out: rdn 3f out: wknd 2f out* **7/2**3
0 10 96 **Redolini**65 2569 2-9-3 0 .... (b1) TPO'Shea 10 —
(W M Brisbourne) *s.s: a wl bhd and racd wd: t.o fnl 4f* **50/1**

1m 29.16s (2.66) **Going Correction** +0.225s/f (Good) **10** Ran SP% **119.8**
Speed ratings (Par 96): **93,90,88,87,85 83,79,75,69,—**
toteswinger: 1&2 £3.90, 1&3 £15.30, 2&3 £19.40 CSF £15.34 TOTE £3.60: £1.50, £2.00, £5.90; EX 15.10.
Owner Sheikh Hamdan Bin Mohammed Al Maktoum **Bred** Gainsborough Stud Management Ltd **Trained** Middleham Moor, N Yorks

FOCUS
A modest maiden run at a good pace.

NOTEBOOK
Proclaim, whose half-brother Dhaular Dhar has a great record around here, showed early speed to get to the front next to the rail, but it was a contested lead and he was not able to take it easy in that position. He went on to make every yard and looks a likely type for a nursery as the Handicapper is unlikely to hit him too hard. (op 3-1)
Flintlock(IRE) ran well considering he raced four wide early and was always giving ground away to the favourite. He kept on well up the straight and, having now had the requisite three runs for a mark, will be of interest in handicap company. (op 7-2)
Game Roseanna could not match the early pace of the four horses up front, but she was able to pick up the pieces when two of them cracked in the straight. She came through to take third and will be eligible for handicaps herself after one more run. (op 14-1 tchd 22-1)
Kristopher James(IRE), a cheap purchase, was never competitive but was another beneficiary of the strong pace and came through for a flattering fourth place. Nevertheless, he is entitled to improve for his debut outing. (tchd 16-1)
Lady Salama paid for trying to match the pace of the other leaders up front on ground that would be soft enough for her. A quicker surface will suit her in handicap company. (op 8-1)
Citizenship never got into it despite the strong pace. A more galloping track is going to suit him once handicapped. (op 10-3 tchd 7-2)
Lucky Dan(IRE) also paid for using up too much energy disputing the lead early. (op 7-1)

4659 CHESHIRE COUNTY COUNCIL FOSTER NURSERY 6f 18y
2:50 (2:51) (Class 4) 2-Y-O **£5,180** (£1,541; £770; £384) **Stalls** Low

Form RPR
221 1 **Red Baron Dancer**22 3949 2-9-3 77 .... PatCosgrave 1 83
(J R Boyle) *racd keenly: mde all: rdn over 1f out: kpt on wl towards fin* **5/6**1
240 2 1 1/4 **Aahaygirl (IRE)**44 3192 2-9-7 81 .... FergusSweeney 3 83
(K R Burke) *trckd ldrs: rdn over 1f out: wnt 2nd ins fnl f: styd on but a looked hld* **10/1**
01 3 3/4 **River Dee (IRE)**13 4257 2-8-7 67 .... JimmyQuinn 9 67
(Miss Amy Weaver) *s.s: bhd: nt clr run over 1f out: sn rdn: prog ent fnl f: swtchd wd of field fnl 100yds: fin wl* **9/1**3
025 4 1/2 **Hawkspur (IRE)**10 4346 2-8-11 71 .... JimCrowley 6 70
(R Hannon) *trckd ldrs: rdn over 2f out: nt qckn: styd on u.p ins fnl f: nt quite pce to chal ldrs* **11/2**2
450 5 nse **Impressible**15 4202 2-8-6 66 ow2 .... DavidAllan 5 64
(E J Alston) *w wnr tl rdn 1f out: no ex towards fin* **11/2**2
4045 6 3 1/2 **Kingswinford (IRE)**9 4389 2-8-8 68 .... TomEaves 8 56
(P D Evans) *in tch on outside: rdn and wknd 2f out* **10/1**
050 7 1 1/4 **Drachenfels**58 2783 2-8-0 60 .... (b1) PaulHanagan 2 44
(K A Ryan) *bmpd s: rdn along early: sn racd keenly and hld up: rdn over 2f out: nvr able to chal* **25/1**
040 8 nk **Lunar Romance**27 3792 2-7-5 58 oh7 .... JamieKyne(7) 4 41
(T J Pitt) *hld up: rdn over 2f out: sn outpcd* **33/1**

1m 15.99s (2.19) **Going Correction** +0.225s/f (Good) **8** Ran SP% **120.3**
Speed ratings (Par 96): **94,92,91,90,90 85,84,83**
toteswinger: 1&2 £2.50, 1&3 £3.40, 2&3 £8.80 CSF £11.59 CT £52.18 TOTE £1.90: £1.30, £1.90, £2.20; EX 8.30.
Owner M Khan X2 **Bred** P M Hicks **Trained** Epsom, Surrey

FOCUS
A fair nursery and sound enough form for the grade.

NOTEBOOK
Red Baron Dancer, a winner of his maiden over 5f here last month, was quickly away from the rail draw and got the all-important rail. He was very keen but it did not stop him winning comfortably, and presumably this sort of ground suits him as he has suffered from sore shins in the past. (op 6-5 tchd 5-4 inplaces)
Aahaygirl(IRE), highly tried on her last two starts, had a lot less to do in this company, and she bagged a good early position tracking the leader on the rail. She had every chance the way the race panned out but came up short. (op 5-1)
River Dee(IRE), winner of a Yarmouth seller last time, was named to run here. Drawn widest of all and out the back in the early stages, he finished his race off well to take third place, and rates better than the bare form suggests. (op 8-1)
Hawkspur(IRE), running in a handicap for the first time, was under pressure some way out but kept on quite well. He might be worth a try over 7f. (op 5-1 tchd 9-2)
Impressible, whose rider put up 2lb overweight, was challenging for the lead on the eventual winner's outside entering the straight, but she was one-paced from there. A drop back to 5f should help. (op 7-1)

4660 CHILDRENS ADVENTURE FARM QUEENSFERRY STKS (LISTED RACE) 6f 18y
3:25 (3:26) (Class 1) 3-Y-O+
£24,978 (£9,468; £4,738; £2,362; £1,183; £594) **Stalls** Low

Form RPR
-631 1 **Green Manalishi**22 3948 7-9-4 100 .... PaulHanagan 2 106
(K A Ryan) *broke wl: trckd ldrs: r.o to take 2nd over 1f out: rdn to ld ins fnl f: a doing enough to hold on wl cl home* **7/2**1
0316 2 1/2 **Damika (IRE)**23 3921 5-9-0 106 .... JimCrowley 6 101+
(R M Whitaker) *trckd ldrs: lost pl under 3f out: sn rdn: rallied over 1f out: r.o strly ins fnl f: gaining on wnr at fin* **7/2**1
050 3 nk **Reverence**29 3722 7-9-0 103 .... DavidAllan 13 100+
(E J Alston) *swtchd lft s: hld up off the pce: forced to wait for run fr over 2f out tl hdwy over 1f out: fin strly* **20/1**
6320 4 shd **Invincible Force (IRE)**7 4445 4-9-0 92 .... (b) PaulMulrennan 4 100
(Paul Green) *sn led: rdn over 1f out: hdd ins fnl f: hld fnl strides* **8/1**3
4310 5 1/2 **Carcinetto (IRE)**8 4407 6-8-9 87 .... StephenDonohoe 3 93
(P D Evans) *trckd ldrs: pushed along 2f out: rdn over 1f out: r.o ins fnl f: no imp fnl strides* **40/1**
1141 6 1 3/4 **Look Busy (IRE)**13 4240 3-8-9 100 .... PatCosgrave 12 91+
(A Berry) *hld up: hdwy over 1f out: r.o ins fnl f: unable to threaten ldrs towards fin* **8/1**3
1130 7 3 3/4 **Angus Newz**15 4198 5-8-9 93 .... (v) MickyFenton 8 75
(M Quinn) *bustled along early: pressed ldr after 1f tl rdn over 1f out: fdd ins fnl f* **14/1**
0410 8 1 1/2 **Brave Prospector**36 3488 3-8-10 105 .... (t) TPQueally 1 76+
(P W Chapple-Hyam) *missed break: sn n.m.r and hmpd: racd in midfield after: nt clr run over 2f out: rdn over 1f out: nvr able to chal* **9/2**2
-105 9 1 1/2 **Aahayson**77 2232 4-9-4 108 .... FergusSweeney 10 75
(K R Burke) *midfield: outpcd over 2f out* **14/1**
-203 10 1/2 **Burnwynd Boy**36 3488 3-8-10 105 .... TomEaves 11 69
(Miss L A Perratt) *towards rr: rdn over 1f out: nvr on terms* **25/1**
1622 11 hd **Requisite**17 4127 3-8-5 83 .... JimmyQuinn 14 64
(I A Wood) *missed break: a bhd* **66/1**
-305 12 1/2 **Eisteddfod**31 3635 7-9-4 105 .... NelsonDeSouza 9 71
(P F I Cole) *in tch on outside: rdn over 2f out: wknd over 1f out* **16/1**
13 1 **Que Piensa Cat (ARG)**485 4-8-9 105 .... TedDurcan 7 59
(Saeed Bin Suroor) *prom: pushed along over 2f out: wknd over 1f out: eased whn btn ins fnl f* **8/1**3

1m 13.9s (0.10) **Going Correction** +0.225s/f (Good)
WFA 3 from 4yo+ 4lb **13** Ran SP% **127.7**
Speed ratings (Par 111): **108,107,106,106,106 103,98,96,94,94 93,93,91**
toteswinger: 1&2 £3.60, 1&3 £17.80, 2&3 £23.80. CSF £15.75 TOTE £3.80: £1.70, £2.00, £6.00; EX 18.60.
Owner Mrs S McCarthy, J Brennan & J Smith **Bred** E Aldridge **Trained** Hambleton, N Yorks

FOCUS
A competitive Listed race in which as usual the draw played a huge part. The first three are rated below their best, with the fourth and fifth setting the standard and at the same time limiting the form.

NOTEBOOK
Green Manalishi, who won this race last year, had a good draw and, after breaking well, was able to take up a prominent early position tracking the leader on the rail. It took him a while to get on top of Invincible Force in the straight, but in truth everything fell perfectly this time and the closers were never quite going to get to him. (tchd 3-1)
Damika(IRE), dropping back a furlong in distance, ran on strongly in the closing stages but could never quite get to the winner, who very much enjoyed the run of the race. It was a sound effort. (op 4-1 tchd 9-2)
Reverence had a terrible draw and inevitably did not get much luck in running. He finished his race well, though, appreciating the bit of give in the ground, and clearly retains plenty of ability. (op 18-1)
Invincible Force(IRE) was one of the worst in at the weights, but he has winning form here and his early speed was always going to make him tough to catch from his low draw. He led to the last half furlong and made a good fist of it. (op 20-1)
Carcinetto(IRE) ran a good race at the weights, but she was well drawn and one should not get carried away.
Look Busy(IRE), who has been in great form this season over 5f, had more to do over this longer trip from her wide draw. She was far from disgraced. (tchd 10-1in places)

Angus Newz, who had the headgear back on this time, had too much use made of her early from her ordinary draw. (op 16-1)
Brave Prospector, whose stable is still not in great form, failed to capitalise on his plum draw as he missed the break. (tchd 6-1)
Que Piensa Cat(ARG) Official explanation: jockey had no explanation for the poor form shown

4661 HALLIWELL JONES BMW - MILE (H'CAP) 7f 122y
4:00 (4:00) (Class 3) (0-95,95) 3-Y-0+ **£10,037** (£2,986; £1,492; £745) **Stalls** Low

Form RPR
0024 **1** **The Kiddykid (IRE)**[31] 3646 8-9-1 **82**........................ TGMcLaughlin 11 91
(P D Evans) *mde all: rdn over 1f out: pressed ins fnl f: hld on gamely cl home* **12/1**
0645 **2** *hd* **South Cape**[8] 4405 5-8-12 **86**........................ MatthewDavies(7) 4 95
(M R Channon) *trckd ldrs: rdn over 1f out: wnt 2nd ins fnl f: sn pressed wnr: jst hld* **10/3**[1]
5056 **3** *¾* **Obezyana (USA)**[1] 4649 6-8-6 **76** oh1........................ DominicFox(3) 10 83
(A Bailey) *prom: rdn over 2f out: chalng and ev ch ins fnl f: r.o but a looked hld* **25/1**
3124 **4** *1 ¼* **Violent Velocity (IRE)**[8] 4440 5-8-5 **79**........................ JamieKyne(7) 3 83+
(J J Quinn) *hld up: nt clr run over 1f out: hdwy ent fnl f: r.o but nt rch front trio* **4/1**[2]
5323 **5** *½* **Guilded Warrior**[22] 3972 5-9-7 **88**........................ FergusSweeney 12 90
(W S Kittow) *trckd ldrs: wnt 2nd 3f out: rdn over 1f out: lost 2nd ins fnl f: no ex fnl 50yds* **7/1**[3]
4120 **6** *½* **Goodbye Mr Bond**[25] 3855 8-9-5 **86**........................ PatCosgrave 5 87
(E J Alston) *midfield: hdwy to chse ldrs over 1f out: styd on: one pce fnl 50yds* **7/1**[3]
4260 **7** *¾* **Mister Hardy**[8] 4416 3-8-8 **82**........................ PaulHanagan 1 80
(R A Fahey) *in tch: lost pl 4f out: styd on ins fnl f: nt pce to chal* **9/1**
115 **8** *nse* **Medici Pearl**[24] 3892 4-8-10 **77**........................ DavidAllan 14 76+
(T D Easterby) *dwlt: sn swtchd lft: in rr: rdn and swtchd rt over 1f out: styd on ins fnl f: nt pce to rch ldrs* **20/1**
1414 **9** *2 ¾* **Barons Spy (IRE)**[15] 4177 7-9-4 **88**........................ RussellKennemore(3) 6 80
(R J Price) *midfield: hdwy to chse ldrs 3f out: rdn over 1f out: wknd ins fnl f* **7/1**[3]
500- **10** *nk* **Roman Maze**[247] 6981 8-9-4 **85**........................ TedDurcan 9 76+
(W M Brisbourne) *hld up: rdn whn n.m.r and hmpd 1f out: nvr a threat* **20/1**
0043 **11** *1* **Danzig Fox**[23] 3907 3-8-2 **76** oh12........................(p) TWilliams 2 64
(M Mullineaux) *trckd ldrs: n.m.r over 5f out: rdn over 2f out: wknd fnl f* **28/1**
12 *2 ¼* **Turfshuffle (GER)**[96] 5-10-0 **95**........................ StephenDonohoe 13 78
(Ian Williams) *dwlt: a bhd* **40/1**
1006 **13** *3 ½* **Daaweitza**[8] 4407 5-9-6 **87**........................ TomEaves 7 62
(B Ellison) *midfield: lost pl 4f out: bhd fnl 2f* **12/1**

1m 34.19s (0.39) **Going Correction** +0.225s/f (Good)
WFA 3 from 4yo+ 7lb **13** Ran SP% **125.2**
Speed ratings (Par 107): **107,106,106,104,104 103,103,103,100,99 98,96,93**
toteswinger: 1&2 £12.30, 1&3 £46.00, 2&3 £24.10. CSF £50.91 CT £1062.30 TOTE £15.70: £3.80, £1.80, £6.90; EX 100.40 TRIFECTA Not won..
Owner Mrs Claire Massey **Bred** Knocklong House Stud **Trained** Pandy, Monmouths

FOCUS
A competitive event in which once again it paid to be up with the pace. Despite the first two running close to their marks the form is not totally solid.

NOTEBOOK
The Kiddykid(IRE), despite being poorly drawn, was keen to lead and successfully got over to to the rail to make the running. He goes well here and, despite setting a decent pace, had enough in reserve to hold off the late challenge of South Cape. (op 14-1)
South Cape, fifth in the totesport International Handicap last time, came wide into the straight and ran on well, but he could never quite catch the enterprisingly ridden winner. (op 7-2 tchd 3-1 & 4-1 in places)
Obezyana(USA), who was 1lb out of the handicap, was making a quick reappearance following an outing at Thirsk the previous afternoon. He got over from his double-figure draw to chase the leader and ran a solid race. (op 28-1)
Violent Velocity(IRE) picked up well and was staying on strongly at the finish. This track was not ideal for him. (op 11-2 tchd 6-1in places)
Guilded Warrior, who could have done with softer ground, was on the winner's outside entering the straight but was one-paced in the closing stages.
Goodbye Mr Bond needs a more galloping track to be seen at his best. (op 11-1 tchd 13-2)
Barons Spy(IRE) Official explanation: jockey said gelding ran flat
Roman Maze Official explanation: jockey said gelding was denied a clear run

4662 MACMILLAN CANCER SUPPORT H'CAP 1m 4f 66y
4:30 (4:30) (Class 4) (0-85,85) 3-Y-0+ **£5,828** (£1,734; £866; £432) **Stalls** Low

Form RPR
6221 **1** **Cheshire Prince**[22] 3947 4-9-2 **80**........................ DeanHeslop(7) 5 91
(W M Brisbourne) *trckd ldrs early: led after 3f: mde rest: rdn to qckn away over 1f out: r.o and in command after* **13/2**[3]
-356 **2** *2 ¾* **Spirit Of Adjisa (IRE)**[27] 3802 4-9-3 **74**........................(b) JimCrowley 1 80
(Pat Eddery) *s.s: sn in midfield: rdn and hdwy over 1f out: chsd wnr thrght fnl f but no real imp* **13/2**[3]
4034 **3** *2 ¼* **Penang Cinta**[13] 4254 5-8-9 **66** oh1........................(p) PatCosgrave 4 68
(P D Evans) *midfield: hdwy to chse ldrs 7f out: rdn 2f out: kpt on same pce fnl f* **7/1**
4321 **4** *1 ½* **Coin Of The Realm (IRE)**[11] 4302 3-9-3 **85**........................ TedDurcan 10 85
(E A L Dunlop) *midfield: hdwy over 3f out: chsd wnr briefly over 1f out: no ex ins fnl f* **6/1**[2]
0005 **5** *1 ¾* **Mikao (IRE)**[15] 4178 7-9-7 **78**........................(b) JimmyQuinn 2 75
(M H Tompkins) *midfield: rdn over 4f out: rapid prog over 3f out to take 2nd and press wnr: u.p 2f out: lost 2nd over 1f out: wknd ins fnl f* **8/1**
2312 **6** *2* **Prelude**[16] 4170 7-9-4 **75**........................ TGMcLaughlin 6 69
(W M Brisbourne) *chsd ldrs: rdn over 2f out: wknd over 1f out* **5/1**[1]
2062 **7** *½* **Command Marshal (FR)**[22] 3950 5-9-4 **78**........................ PatrickHills(3) 11 71
(M J Scudamore) *led for 3f: remained handy: rdn 3f out: losing pl whn n.m.r over 2f out: n.d after* **8/1**
0100 **8** *1 ½* **Bajan Parkes**[52] 2970 5-9-13 **84**........................ DavidAllan 9 74
(E J Alston) *hld up: rdn over 2f out: no imp* **20/1**
/35- **9** *¾* **Crow Wood**[506] 345 9-10-0 **85**........................ PaulHanagan 3 74
(J J Quinn) *cl up: lost pl 5f out: n.d after* **12/1**
020/ **10** *1* **Risk Runner (IRE)**[120] 5869 5-9-2 **76**........................(v) PJMcDonald(3) 8 64
(James Moffatt) *a bhd* **14/1**
1406 **11** *3* **Bull Market (IRE)**[4] 4532 5-9-5 **76**........................ StephenDonohoe 7 59
(Ian Williams) *a bhd* **12/1**

2m 39.43s (-0.47) **Going Correction** +0.225s/f (Good)
WFA 3 from 4yo+ 11lb **11** Ran SP% **119.2**
Speed ratings (Par 105): **110,108,106,105,104 103,102,101,101,100 98**
toteswinger: 1&2 £12.20, 1&3 £9.60, 2&3 £13.80. CSF £49.12 CT £309.82 TOTE £5.30: £2.10, £2.50, £2.70; EX 94.10.
Owner D C Rutter & H Clewlow **Bred** The National Stud **Trained** Great Ness, Shropshire

FOCUS
An ordinary handicap and another winner to make most of the running. The form makes sense at face value but this may not be the strongest of races despite the good gallop.
Crow Wood Official explanation: jockey said gelding hung right-handed throughout

4663 GILDS RECRUITMENT SOLUTIONS LTD H'CAP 1m 2f 75y
5:00 (5:00) (Class 5) (0-75,75) 3-Y-0 **£4,435** (£1,309; £655) **Stalls** High

Form RPR
3532 **1** **Bowder Stone (IRE)**[23] 3911 3-9-7 **75**........................ JimmyQuinn 3 86
(M H Tompkins) *chsd ldrs: led over 2f out: kicked clr over 1f out: r.o wl and in command after* **11/10**[1]
2651 **2** *3* **Riqaab (IRE)**[19] 4065 3-9-4 **72**........................ TedDurcan 8 77+
(E A L Dunlop) *hld up: swtchd rt and hdwy over 2f out: styd on fnl f: tk 2nd towards fin: no imp on wnr* **7/2**[2]
2654 **3** *nk* **The Last Bottle (IRE)**[9] 4382 3-8-7 **61**........................ TPO'Shea 6 65
(W M Brisbourne) *chsd ldr: led over 4f out: hdd over 2f out: sn u.p: outpcd by wnr over 1f out: styd on same pce fnl f: lost 2nd towards fin* **7/1**
4053 **4** *4 ½* **Joinedupwriting**[31] 3641 3-9-1 **69**........................ DeanMcKeown 4 64
(R M Whitaker) *midfield: hdwy to chse ldrs 4f out: rdn 2f out: wknd fnl f* **6/1**[3]
0034 **5** *3 ½* **Doon Haymer (IRE)**[15] 4179 3-9-4 **72**........................ TomEaves 5 60
(Miss L A Perratt) *hld up in rr: rdn over 3f out: nvr on terms* **13/2**
605- **6** *1 ¾* **Ras Laffan**[26] 6150 3-8-6 **60**........................ PaulHanagan 1 45
(D McCain Jnr) *led: rdn and hdd over 4f out: wknd 2f out* **25/1**
0050 **7** *½* **Alseraaj (USA)**[11] 4300 3-9-1 **69**........................ StephenDonohoe 2 53
(Ian Williams) *midfield: rdn over 2f out: sn btn* **20/1**

2m 13.54s (1.34) **Going Correction** +0.225s/f (Good) **7** Ran SP% **118.6**
Speed ratings (Par 100): **103,100,100,96,93 92,92**
toteswinger: 1&2 £1.40, 1&3 £3.00, 2&3 £4.60. CSF £5.52 CT £18.59 TOTE £2.20: £1.80, £2.30; EX 4.20 Place 6 £ 44.44, Place 5 £ 19.08.
Owner Mr & Mrs G Middlebrook **Bred** G And Mrs Middlebrook **Trained** Newmarket, Suffolk

FOCUS
Ordinary handicap form rated around the placed horses.
T/Plt: £44.70 to a £1 stake. Pool: £90,832.97. 1,481.84 winning tickets. T/Qpdt: £19.10 to a £1 stake. Pool: £6,094.96. 235.70 winning tickets. DO

4187 NEWBURY (L-H)
Sunday, August 3

OFFICIAL GOING: Good (good to firm in places)

4664 ACADEMY INSURANCE AMATEUR RIDERS' H'CAP 1m 2f 6y
1:40 (1:41) (Class 5) (0-70,72) 3-Y-0+ **£2,498** (£774; £387; £193) **Stalls** Low

Form RPR
1213 **1** **Western Roots**[13] 4254 7-10-8 **64**........................ MrNdeBoinville(7) 4 73+
(A M Balding) *in tch: hdwy on ins to ld over 4f out: rdn 2f out: hld on wl cl home* **2/1**[1]
3061 **2** *½* **Gallego**[8] 4428 6-10-9 **63**........................ MrMPrice(5) 3 71
(R J Price) *s.i.s: hld up in rr: swtchd to outside and stdy hdwy over 2f out: fin strly fnl f: nt rch wnr* **13/2**[2]
2041 **3** *4 ½* **Home**[82] 2080 3-10-3 **68**........................ MissLGray(7) 8 67
(C Gordon) *mid-div: lost position over 4f out: shkn up and r.o wl appr fnl f: gng on cl home* **16/1**
0043 **4** *hd* **Our Blessing (IRE)**[6] 4491 4-10-7 **61**........................ MissKellyBurke(5) 6 60
(A P Jarvis) *led tl hdd over 4f out: styd w wnr to 2f out: wknd appr fnl f* **9/1**
-055 **5** *2* **Piano Man**[6] 4491 6-9-11 **51** oh1........................ MissSarah-JaneDurman(5) 1 46
(J C Fox) *in rr: stl plenty to do whn c grad rt fr 2f out: kpt on wl fnl f but nvr in contention* **10/1**
0000 **6** *hd* **Title Deed (USA)**[6] 4490 4-10-1 **55**........................ MissLEBurke(5) 9 50
(A P Jarvis) *chsd ldrs: rdn 3f out: wknd fr 2f out* **10/1**
0000 **7** *hd* **It's Josr**[36] 3483 3-9-8 **55**........................(v[1]) MrPCollington(3) 11 49
(I A Wood) *in tch: rdn and styd on to chse ldrs 3f out: sn one pce* **14/1**
0205 **8** *½* **Miss Porcia**[13] 4250 7-9-9 **51** oh6........................ MissJGeeson(7) 2 44
(P A Blockley) *in tch: hdwy on ins to chse ldrs 3f out: no prog fnl 2f* **16/1**
400 **9** *2* **Classy Affair**[15] 4182 4-9-11 **51** oh3........................ MrBMMorris(5) 15 40
(D Morris) *s.i.s: in rr: hdwy and rdn 3f out: nvr rchd ldrs and one pce fnl 2f* **40/1**
-664 **10** *3 ¼* **Morestead (IRE)**[4] 4533 3-9-4 **55**........................ MrJeremiahMcGrath(7) 14 38
(B G Powell) *chsd ldrs: rdn over 3f out: btn 2f out* **18/1**
0040 **11** *5* **Princely Ted (IRE)**[7] 4451 7-9-11 **51** oh1........................ MrRBirkett(5) 13 24
(W Clay) *chsd ldrs tl wknd over 2f out* **20/1**
-000 **12** *2 ¾* **Snark (IRE)**[65] 2561 5-11-2 **65**........................ MrSWalker 12 32
(Simon Earle) *chsd ldrs 5f* **8/1**[3]
-450 **13** *nse* **Ground Patrol**[59] 2755 7-9-9 **51** oh3........................ MrRGHenderson(7) 7 18
(N R Mitchell) *slowly away: a in rr* **18/1**
-000 **14** *4 ½* **Feeling (IRE)**[7] 4451 4-10-2 **56**........................ MrJoshuaMoore(5) 10 14
(W Clay) *chsd ldrs to 3f out* **66/1**
0250 **15** *1* **What's For Tea**[15] 4181 3-9-2 **51**........................ MissZoeLilly(5) 5 7
(P Butler) *bhd fr 1/2-way* **20/1**

2m 9.97s (1.17) **Going Correction** 0.0s/f (Good)
WFA 3 from 4yo+ 9lb **15** Ran SP% **128.4**
Speed ratings (Par 103): **95,94,91,90,89 89,88,88,86,84 80,78,78,74,73**
toteswinger: 1&2 £3.30, 1&3 £6.10, 2&3 £10.10 CSF £14.40 CT £180.11 TOTE £3.00: £1.50, £2.20, £3.70; EX 8.40.
Owner I A Balding **Bred** Stratford Place Stud **Trained** Kingsclere, Hants
■ A first winner for Nicolai de Boinville.

FOCUS
A modest amateur riders' handicap and they went a steady pace early on but the form looks pretty sound rated around the fourth and fifth. The main action took place down the middle of the track in the straight.

4665 EUROPEAN BREEDERS' FUND MAIDEN STKS — 6f 8y
2:10 (2:13) (Class 4) 2-Y-O — £5,828 (£1,734; £866; £432) Stalls Centre

Form — RPR

1 **Marine Boy (IRE)** 2-9-3 0 .... RichardKingscote 5 — 100+
(Tom Dascombe) *led: c easily clr over 1f out and edgd lft ins fnl f: unchal* **9/4**[1]

2 7 **Glen Molly (IRE)** 2-8-12 0 .... MichaelHills 8 — 71+
(B W Hills) *sn chsng wnr: stl travelling ok 2f out: sn outpcd by wnr and no ch but kpt on wl for clr 2nd* **3/1**[2]

0 3 3 1/4 **D'Nurse (IRE)**[10] 4339 2-8-12 0 .... RyanMoore 7 — 61
(R Hannon) *chsd ldrs: rdn over 2f out: styd on same pce* **33/1**

5 4 2 3/4 **Kings Ace (IRE)**[7] 4446 2-9-3 0 .... DarrenWilliams 12 — 58
(A P Jarvis) *chsd ldrs: rdn 3f out: no ch fr over 2f out* **20/1**

5 3/4 **Fanditha (IRE)** 2-8-12 0 .... RichardHughes 15 — 51+
(R Hannon) *in rr tl drvn and styd on fr 2f out: kpt on ins fnl f but nvr anywhere nr ldrs* **9/1**

6 1 **Shooting Party (IRE)** 2-9-3 0 .... PatDobbs 10 — 53+
(R Hannon) *in rr: rdn 3f out: styd on fnl 2f out: nvr anywhere nr ldrs* **28/1**

7 3/4 **Rulesn'Regulations** 2-9-3 0 .... RichardMullen 6 — 51
(M Salaman) *chsd ldrs 4f* **25/1**

0 8 2 1/2 **Hesketh (IRE)**[11] 4296 2-9-3 0 .... SebSanders 14 — 43
(R M Beckett) *chsd ldrs: rdn 3f out: btn 2f out* **9/1**

9 1 3/4 **Navajo Nation (IRE)** 2-9-3 0 .... JamieSpencer 13 — 38+
(B J Meehan) *in rr tl sme hdwy fr over 1f out* **18/1**

10 3/4 **Pearl Of Manacor (IRE)** 2-9-3 0 .... EdwardCreighton 16 — 36
(M R Channon) *in rr: drvn and sme prog 1/2-way: no prog sn after* **6/1**[3]

0 11 nk **Xaaroon (IRE)**[23] 3923 2-8-12 0 .... FrancisNorton 4 — 30
(P J McBride) *chsd ldrs over 3f* **66/1**

12 1/2 **Cayman Sky** 2-8-12 0 .... HaddenFrost(5) 9 — 33
(R Hannon) *s.i.s: a in rr* **33/1**

13 1 3/4 **Blue Bogey (USA)** 2-9-3 0 .... SteveDrowne 1 — 28
(R Charlton) *in tch: rdn 1/2-way and sn bhd* **25/1**

00 14 1/2 **Hellbender (IRE)**[12] 4274 2-9-3 0 .... GeorgeBaker 11 — 26
(S Kirk) *rdn 3f out: a towards rr* **20/1**

15 23 **Naizak** 2-8-12 0 .... RHills 3 — —
(J L Dunlop) *s.i.s: a in rr* **16/1**

16 4 **Harry Raffle** 2-9-3 0 .... LPKeniry 2 — —
(S Kirk) *slowly away: a bhd* **66/1**

1m 13.14s (0.14) **Going Correction** +0.225s/f (Good) — **16** Ran SP% **130.7**
Speed ratings (Par 96): **108,98,94,90,89 88,87,84,81,80 80,79,77,76,45 40**
toteswinger: 1&2 £3.60, 1&3 £34.20, 2&3 £43.00 CSF £8.21 TOTE £3.10: £1.50, £2.00, £7.30; EX 12.10.
Owner A Black **Bred** Eugene McDermott **Trained** Lambourn, Berks

FOCUS
Probably not that strong a maiden, but Marine Boy was a very impressive winner. They raced up the middle of the track.

NOTEBOOK
Marine Boy(IRE) ◆, a £52,000 gelded son of One Cool Cat, and first foal of a 7f juvenile winner in France, is entered in both the Gimcrack and the Mill Reef, suggesting he is well regarded, and he was all the rage in the market. Soon in front, he was always travelling strongly and gradually drew clear, despite edging left, without his rider having to get stuck into him, indeed Kingscote had several looks round, letting his mount coast home inside the final furlong. He jinked slightly after the line, possibly seeing the chute back to the paddock, and got ride of his rider before running loose for a few minutes. It remains to be seen exactly what he beat, but there have been few, if any more impressive juvenile maiden winners in Britain this season and he will now be aimed at the Gimcrack Stakes at York. There are limited opportunities for two and three-year-old geldings in Group 1 company in this country, so his connections are considering Grade 1 options in the US. (op 11-4 tchd 2-1)
Glen Molly(IRE), a 110,000euros daughter of Danetime, out of a dual 1m-1m2f three-year-old winner, was no match for the smart winner, but this was still a pleasing debut. (op 5-1 tchd 6-1)
D'Nurse(IRE) failed to beat a rival on her debut over 7f on the Kempton Polytrack, but she stepped up significantly on that effort with a respectable, if well-beaten third.
Kings Ace(IRE) was well beaten on his debut at Ascot and he again failed to feature at the buisness end. He might be more of a nursery type. (op 22-1)
Fanditha(IRE), a 140,000euros daughter of Danehill Dancer, half-sister to among others quite useful multiple sprint winner Bohunk, looked in need of the experience and will know more next time. She might appreciate easier ground. (op 13-2)
Shooting Party(IRE), a 84,000gns son of Noverre, half-brother to among others useful Embossed, a 7f winner at two who was later a triple 1m1f-1m4f winner, looked the second string of her stable's three runners and seemed to need the run. (op 25-1 tchd 33-1)
Rulesn'Regulations, a son of Forzando, half-brother to 1m2f winner Venir Rouge, was backed at big odds in the morning and showed up well for a long way. (op 22-1)
Pearl Of Manacor(IRE), a 270,000euros son of Danehill Dancer, half-brother to dual 7f-1m winner High Court Drama, could not dominate his rivals in the same manner his namesake tends to, running below market expectations, but he will learn from this and could well gain that number one spot at some point. He is another who may also benefit from a slower surface. (op 7-1 tchd 8-1)

4666 GRUNDON RECYCLE NURSERY — 7f (S)
2:40 (2:44) (Class 4) 2-Y-O — £3,885 (£1,156; £577; £288) Stalls Centre

Form — RPR

505 1 **Lahaleeb (IRE)**[10] 4337 2-8-1 **72** ow4 .... MCGeran(5) 4 — 77+
(M R Channon) *hmpd s: in rr: rdn over 2f out: hdwy to ld 1f out: styd on strly* **17/2**

2311 2 2 **Lucky Redback (IRE)**[30] 3693 2-9-5 **85** .... RichardHughes 9 — 85
(R Hannon) *sn slt advantage: narrowly hdd over 2f out: stl upsides 1f out: chsd wnr ins fnl f but a wl hld* **7/2**[3]

0635 3 1 1/2 **Fasalee (IRE)**[18] 4079 2-8-1 **67** ow1 .... FrancisNorton 8 — 63
(A P Jarvis) *in rr: rdn and hdwy 2f out: swtchd lft and qcknd to chse ldrs 1f out: sn one pce* **16/1**

243 4 1 1/2 **Sparkling Crystal (IRE)**[17] 4109 2-8-5 **71** .... RHills 10 — 64
(B W Hills) *w ldrs tl slt advantage over 2f out: rdn and hdd 1f out: wknd ins fnl f* **9/4**[2]

4040 5 7 **Redhead (IRE)**[18] 4079 2-7-13 **65** oh1 ow1 .... DavidKinsella 3 — 40
(R Hannon) *wnt rt s: chsd ldrs: rdn to chal 2f out: wknd over 1f out* **20/1**

441 6 11 **Watergate (IRE)**[32] 3597 2-9-10 **90** .... SebSanders 7 — 38
(Sir Mark Prescott) *wnt lft s: pressed ldrs 4f: sn rdn: wknd 2f out* **6/4**[1]

0000 7 1 3/4 **Ba Globetrotter**[37] 3444 2-7-12 **64** oh9 .... CatherineGannon 5 — 7+
(M R Channon) *hmpd s: rr: stl bhd whn hmpd over 3f out and nvr any ch after* **66/1**

000 8 2 3/4 **Prima Fonteyn**[16] 4149 2-7-13 **65** oh18 ow1 .... FrankieMcDonald 2 — —
(M R Channon) *sn chsng ldrs: wknd 1/2-way* **66/1**

1m 27.81s (2.11) **Going Correction** +0.225s/f (Good) — **8** Ran SP% **117.1**
Speed ratings (Par 96): **96,93,92,90,82 69,67,64**
toteswinger: 1&2 £5.90, 1&3 £9.60, 2&3 £6.60 CSF £38.83 CT £477.19 TOTE £11.20: £2.00, £1.30, £2.70; EX 50.00.
Owner M Al-Qatami & K M Al-Mudhaf **Bred** Tom Twomey **Trained** West Ilsley, Berks

FOCUS
A fair nursery. They raced stands' side.

NOTEBOOK
Lahaleeb(IRE) ◆ caught the eye in three runs in maiden company over this trip at Folkestone and she duly posted an improved effort on her nursery bow, justifying a market move in the process. She was actually carrying 4lb overweight, with her apprentice rider only able to claim 1lb of his allowance, but she showed a decent turn of pace out widest of all and took this quite convincingly. She will only be 2lb higher if turned out under a penalty and will be hard to beat. Official explanation: trainer said, regarding the apparen improvement in form, that filly had been denied a clear run on its last two outings. (op 8-1 tchd 10-1)
Lucky Redback(IRE) was bidding for a hat-trick, but his recent Warwick success didn't amount to much. This was a respectable effort off a stiff enough mark. (tchd 10-3 and 4-1)
Fasalee(IRE), carrying 1lb overweight, confirmed recent Kempton form with Redhead, but he found one too good.
Sparkling Crystal(IRE) did not look too harshly treated for her nursery debut, but she is not progressing. She might appreciate a drop in trip and easier ground. (op 7-2)
Redhead(IRE), 2lb wrong, was produced with every chance, but she could not reverse recent Kempton form with Fasalee and gave the impression this trip stretched her.
Watergate(IRE) was impressive when winning a Catterick maiden on his previous start, but he beat little of note that day and looked harshly treated on his nursery debut. As it turned out, he failed to give his running and he is probably more of a three-year-old. Official explanation: trainer's rep had no explanation for the poor form shown (op 5-4 tchd 6-5)

4667 EUROPEAN BREEDERS' FUND CHALICE STKS (LISTED RACE) (F&M) — 1m 4f 5y
3:15 (3:16) (Class 1) 3-Y-O+
£24,978 (£9,468; £4,738; £2,362; £1,183; £594) Stalls Low

Form — RPR

0113 1 **Suzi's Decision**[8] 4435 3-8-5 **89** .... JohnEgan 4 — 102
(P W D'Arcy) *in rr: hdwy 3f out: led ins fnl 2f: hrd drvn fnl f: hld on wl* **15/2**

5110 2 3/4 **Ronaldsay**[15] 4196 4-9-5 **102** .... RichardHughes 7 — 104
(R Hannon) *hld up towards rr: hdwy 2f out: n.m.r over 1f out: sn squeezed through to chse wnr: kpt on but a jst hld* **9/1**

0346 3 1 1/2 **Presbyterian Nun (IRE)**[15] 4196 3-8-5 **93** .... RichardMullen 1 — 99
(J L Dunlop) *chsd ldrs: rdn and one pce 2f out: kpt on again u.p fnl f but nvr gng pce to press ldng duo* **25/1**

1-0U 4 nk **Les Fazzani (IRE)**[21] 4007 4-9-5 **103** .... RichardKingscote 11 — 101
(M J Wallace) *chsd ldrs: rdn and upsides 2f out: styd on same pce fnl f* **14/1**

2501 5 3/4 **Sweet Lilly**[9] 4395 4-9-5 **102** .... EdwardCreighton 10 — 100
(M R Channon) *hld up in rr: hdwy on outside to press ldrs 2f out: no ex ins fnl f* **15/2**

-515 6 2 1/4 **Elmaleeha**[45] 3153 3-8-5 **97** .... RHills 3 — 93
(J L Dunlop) *led: hdd over 2f out: outpcd sn after: kpt on again ins fnl f* **9/2**[3]

223- 7 nk **Silver Mitzva (IRE)**[251] 6953 4-9-2 **90** .... (b) RyanMoore 8 — 93
(M Botti) *chsd ldr: led over 2f out: hdd ins fnl 2f: wknd fnl f* **20/1**

-562 8 2 1/2 **Cosmodrome (USA)**[48] 3088 4-9-2 **101** .... SebSanders 5 — 89
(L M Cumani) *chsd ldrs: rdn 3f out: sn btn* **4/1**[2]

01 9 15 **Colourways (IRE)**[40] 3350 3-8-5 **83** .... FrancisNorton 9 — 65+
(Mrs A J Perrett) *towards rr: rdn and sme prog over 3f out: sn wknd* **14/1**

-152 10 2 **Gull Wing (IRE)**[22] 3975 4-9-5 **99** .... JamieSpencer 2 — 65+
(M L W Bell) *in tch: rdn 3f out: sn wknd: eased whn no ch fnl f* **3/1**[1]

2m 32.83s (-2.67) **Going Correction** 0.0s/f (Good)
WFA 3 from 4yo 11lb — **10** Ran SP% **118.7**
Speed ratings (Par 111): **108,107,106,106,105 104,104,102,92,91**
toteswinger: 1&2 £13.90, 1&3 £25.80, 2&3 £30.50 CSF £74.39 TOTE £10.90: £2.40, £2.80, £6.40; EX 93.00.
Owner Greenstead Hall Racing **Bred** David And Mrs Vicki Fleet **Trained** Newmarket, Suffolk

FOCUS
There was little between most of these and this was a weak fillies & mares' Listed contest but the form looks sound enough. The early pace was just ordinary and they raced middle to far side in the straight.

NOTEBOOK
Suzi's Decision has been progressing rapidly in handicaps this season and she improved again for this step back up to 1m4f, justifying market support. She was a winner over 1m2f on her only previous start at Newbury and this galloping course clearly suits, as she was able to sustain one continuous run throughout the final three furlongs. This was an ordinary race by Listed standards, but she is very tough and has now acquired the valuable black type. (op 11-1)
Ronaldsay found this easier than the Listed race she contested at Newmarket last time and ran well in second. She was denied a clear run inside the final two furlongs, but eventually had her chance and was not unlucky. (op 10-1)
Presbyterian Nun(IRE) could not confirm recent Newmarket form with Ronaldsay, but this was still a respectable effort. She raced more towards the far rail than the front two, which might not have been ideal. (op 33-1 tchd 22-1)
Les Fazzani(IRE), trying her furthest trip to date, ran well on ground possibly a little quicker than ideal. (op 18-1 tchd 12-1)
Sweet Lilly was below the form she showed when winning a 1m2f Listed race at York on her previous start and she did not appear to stay. (tchd 8-1)
Elmaleeha was well held after making her move more towards the far rail than most of these and she looks flattered by the bare result of her fifth in the Ribblesdale at Royal Ascot. (op 6-1)
Silver Mitzva(IRE) is entitled to come on for this first run in eight months.
Cosmodrome(USA) was nowhere near the form she showed when just beaten by Ronaldsay in a 1m2f Listed race at Warwick on her previous start. (op 11-4 tchd 5-1)
Colourways(IRE) was stepping up in class after winning a course-and-distance maiden, but she should still have run better. Official explanation: jockey said filly was hanging left in straight (op 16-1 tchd 18-1)
Gull Wing(IRE) was heavily eased in the straight and she wants much easier ground. Official explanation: jockey said filly was unsuited by the good (good to firm in places) ground (tchd 5-2)

4668 BLACKMORE BUILDING CONTRACTORS H'CAP — 5f 34y
3:50 (3:53) (Class 4) (0-85,83) 3-Y-O+ — £4,857 (£1,445; £722; £360) Stalls Centre

Form — RPR

2111 1 **Cheveton**[22] 3945 4-9-10 **83** .... RyanMoore 9 — 96
(R J Price) *chsd ldrs: drvn to ld jst ins fnl f: drvn out* **9/2**[1]

030 2 1 **Brandywell Boy (IRE)**[24] 3868 5-7-12 **64** oh1 .... BillyCray(7) 3 — 74
(D J S Ffrench Davis) *chsd ldrs: slt ld 1f out: sn hdd and nt pce of wnr: hld on wl for 2nd* **16/1**

0402 **3** *hd* **Judge 'n Jury**[11] 4313 4-9-1 **74**......(t) RichardHughes 11 83
(R A Harris) *hld up in rr: drvn and str run fnl f: fin wl to cl on 2nd but nt rch wnr* **5/1**[2]

0635 **4** *1/2* **Tony The Tap**[3] 4555 7-9-7 **80**...... RichardMullen 1 87
(W R Muir) *chsd ldrs: drvn to chal over 1f out: outpcd ins fnl f* **8/1**

0035 **5** *nk* **Hereford Boy**[22] 3945 4-9-5 **78**...... RobertHavlin 12 84
(D K Ivory) *in rr tl hdwy over 1f out: kpt on ins fnl f but nt rch ldrs* **25/1**

525 **6** *1 3/4* **Playful**[30] 3680 5-9-7 **80**...... SebSanders 10 80
(R M Beckett) *towards rr: rdn over 2f out: hdwy appr fnl f: one pce ins fnl f* **11/2**[3]

4343 **7** *3/4* **Malapropism**[5] 4502 8-9-1 **74**...... EdwardCreighton 5 71
(M R Channon) *pressed ldr: slt advantage u.p over 1f out: wknd ins fnl f* **16/1**

4022 **8** *3 3/4* **Bahamian Ballet**[17] 4103 6-9-0 **78**...... JackMitchell(5) 4 62
(E S McMahon) *chsd ldrs: rdn over 2f out: wknd over 1f out* **10/1**

0651 **9** *2 3/4* **Cape Royal**[3] 4563 8-9-6 **79** 6ex......(bt) JamieSpencer 6 53
(J M Bradley) *led tl hdd over 1f out: sn btn* **10/1**

51- **10** *3/4* **Lochstar**[430] 2173 4-9-7 **80**...... FrancisNorton 8 51
(A M Balding) *towards rr: hdwy over 2f out: nvr gng pce to rch ldrs and sn wknd* **7/1**

1100 **11** *9* **Godfrey Street**[143] 866 5-9-10 **83**......(b) LPKeniry 7 22
(A G Newcombe) *pressed ldrs to 1/2-way* **33/1**

63.03 secs (1.63) **Going Correction** +0.225s/f (Good)
WFA 3 from 4yo+ 3lb 11 Ran SP% **110.6**
Speed ratings (Par 105): **95,93,93,92,91 89,87,81,77,76 61**
toteswinger: 1&2 £17.80, 1&3 £3.80, 2&3 £16.70 CSF £68.67 CT £326.38 TOTE £4.70: £1.80, £5.10, £2.00; EX 131.30.
Owner Mrs K Oseman **Bred** Miss K Rausing **Trained** Ullingswick, H'fords

FOCUS
An ordinary sprint handicap for the grade but the winner continues on the upgrade and the form looks solid enough rated around the next three home. They raced up the middle of the track.
Cape Royal Official explanation: jockey said gelding got upset in the starting stalls

4669 BOYZONE ARE HERE 16TH AUGUST FILLIES' H'CAP 1m 2f 6y
4:20 (4:25) (Class 5) (0-75,75) 3-Y-O £2,590 (£770; £385; £192) **Stalls** Low

Form RPR

0-34 **1** **Miss Rochester (IRE)**[60] 2716 3-9-1 **69**...... RyanMoore 7 83+
(Sir Michael Stoute) *in tch: drvn and hdwy 2f out: led over 1f out: sn pushed clr* **9/4**[1]

0612 **2** *4* **Houri (IRE)**[38] 3421 3-9-5 **73**......(p) SebSanders 6 79
(R M Beckett) *chsd ldrs tl led appr fnl 2f: hdd over 1f out: sn no ch w wnr but kpt on for clr 2nd* **5/1**[2]

1-42 **3** *2 3/4* **Berrynarbor**[30] 3692 3-8-3 **57**...... FrancisNorton 2 57
(A G Newcombe) *towards rr: rdn over 3f out: hdwy 2f out: kpt on to chse ldng duo ins fnl f but nvr any ch* **20/1**

6-05 **4** *3/4* **Mistress Eva**[22] 3970 3-9-2 **70**...... StephenCarson 5 69
(P Winkworth) *in tch: rdn over 2f out: styd on fnl f but nvr in contention* **14/1**

2051 **5** *7* **Xtravaganza (IRE)**[24] 3874 3-8-12 **66**...... MichaelHills 8 51
(J W Hills) *towards rr: pushed along 3f out: no imp under mod prog ins fnl f* **16/1**

6460 **6** *1/2* **La Columbina**[17] 4130 3-9-7 **75**......(b1) RichardHughes 3 59
(R Hannon) *chsd ldrs: rdn 3f out: wknd over 1f out* **6/1**

0340 **7** *1 3/4* **Lush (IRE)**[16] 4152 3-9-6 **74**...... PatDobbs 9 54
(R Hannon) *bhd most of way* **14/1**

1-3 **8** *1* **Hallingdal (UAE)**[32] 3607 3-9-7 **75**...... JamesDoyle 1 53
(Ms J S Doyle) *s.i.s: hld up in rr: hdwy over 2f out: nt pce to rch ldrs and sn wknd* **9/1**

506 **9** *7* **Sacred Flame (USA)**[18] 4085 3-8-6 **60**...... JohnEgan 11 24
(B J Meehan) *chsd ldrs: rdn over 2f out: sn wknd* **16/1**

04- **10** *31* **Street Diva (USA)**[269] 6734 3-8-9 **66**...... KevinGhunowa(3) 10 —
(P A Blockley) *chsd ldrs to 3f out: sn wknd: t.o* **50/1**

013- **11** *3/4* **Heavenly Saint**[272] 6693 3-8-6 **63** ow2...... TolleyDean(3) 12 —
(R J Price) *a in rr: t.o* **40/1**

5023 **12** *3 1/2* **Italian Goddess**[24] 3874 3-8-9 **63**...... JamieSpencer 4 —
(M L W Bell) *led tl hdd over 3f out: wknd qckly: eased whn no ch fnl f: t.o* **11/2**[3]

2m 6.55s (-2.25) **Going Correction** 0.0s/f (Good) **12** Ran SP% **121.4**
Speed ratings (Par 97): **109,105,103,103,97 97,95,94,89,64 63,61**
toteswinger: 1&2 £4.40, 1&3 £12.20, 2&3 £13.20 CSF £12.96 CT £186.09 TOTE £2.70: £1.70, £2.20, £4.30; EX 17.00 Place 6 £ 209.61, Place 5 £ 112.96.
Owner Cheveley Park Stud **Bred** Sir E J Loder **Trained** Newmarket, Suffolk

FOCUS
A fair fillies' handicap and the winner is entitled to rate higher. They raced down the middle of the track in the straight.
Sacred Flame(USA) Official explanation: jockey said filly had no more to give
Street Diva(USA) Official explanation: jockey said filly ran too free
Italian Goddess Official explanation: jockey said filly ran too free
T/Jkpt: Not won. T/Plt: £196.90 to a £1 stake. Pool: £86,641.62. 321.09 winning tickets. T/Qpdt: £49.00 to a £1 stake. Pool: £4,786.57. 72.20 winning tickets. ST

4657 DEAUVILLE (R-H)
Sunday, August 3

OFFICIAL GOING: Turf course - good to soft; all-weather - standard

4673a PRIX DE CABOURG - JOCKEY-CLUB DE TURQUIE (GROUP 3) (STRAIGHT COURSE) 6f
1:10 (1:09) 2-Y-O £29,412 (£11,765; £8,824; £5,882; £2,941)

RPR

1 **Silver Frost (IRE)**[55] 2-8-11 ...... OPeslier 3 104
(Y De Nicolay, France) *trckd ldr in centre gp: styd on u.p fnl f to ld fnl 50yds* **11/2**[3]

2 *nk* **Abbeyside**[29] 3749 2-8-11 ...... CSoumillon 5 103
(P F I Cole) *overall ldr of centre gp: hrd rdn 1f out: hdd and no ex fnl 50yds* **1/1**[1]

3 *2* **Madda's Force (ITY)**[48] 2-8-8 ...... PConvertino 2 94
(R Betti, Italy) *trckd solitary rival on stands' rail: rdn and edgd rt fnl 1 1/2f: wnt 3rd over 1f out: styd on* **8/1**

4 *2* **Bargouzine (USA)**[28] 3774 2-8-8 ...... SPasquier 1 88
(A Fabre, France) *a in rr in centre gp: tk 4th cl home* **8/1**

5 *1/2* **Enchanting Muse (USA)**[7] 4472 2-8-8 ...... C-PLemaire 4 87
(Robert Collet, France) *led two-horse gp on stands' rail: wknd over 1f out: lost 4th cl home* **11/4**[2]

1m 11.2s **Going Correction** -0.075s/f (Good) **5** Ran SP% **114.3**
Speed ratings: **97,96,93,91,90**
PARI MUTUEL (including 1 Euro Stake): WIN 5.60; PL 1.80, 1.40;SF 12.90.
Owner J D Cotton **Bred** Skymarc Farm **Trained** France

NOTEBOOK
Silver Frost(IRE), who was always well placed behind the leader up the centre of the track, came with his challenge at the furlong marker and took over the lead shortly before the post. He is a promising juvenile and his trainer now has ambitions for this colt as he is to be aimed at the Prix Morny at this track on August 24. He appears to go well with cut in the ground.
Abbeyside, a strapping individual, tried to make all the running up the centre of the track and still appeared to be going well at the two furlong marker, but was run out of it in the final 50 yards. Connections felt that the soft ground was not to his liking and he may well be raced over a longer distance next time out. He is still a little on the green side but he is a decent colt in the making.
Madda's Force(ITY) was raced on the stands' side, just behind the leader of this group. She hugged the rail and ran on really well from the furlong marker but could not catch the front pair in the centre of the track.
Bargouzine(USA) raced with the winner and runner-up throughout the race, but was a beaten force by the furlong marker.
Enchanting Muse(USA), a close-up fourth in the last week's Robert Papin, failed to build on that and may have found the race coming too soon.

4674a PRIX ROTHSCHILD (EX PRIX D'ASTARTE) (GROUP 1) (F&M) 1m
2:15 (2:24) 3-Y-O+ £105,037 (£42,022; £21,011; £10,496; £5,257)

RPR

1 **Goldikova (IRE)**[28] 3775 3-8-8 ow1...... OPeslier 5 123
(F Head, France) *cl up in 3rd: led travelling strly 1 1/2f out: rdn over 1f out: hung rt u.p fnl f: hld on wl* **4/1**[3]

2 *1/2* **Darjina (FR)**[47] 3100 4-9-0 ...... CSoumillon 7 122
(A De Royer-Dupre, France) *hld up towards rr: hdwy to go 3rd over 1 1/2f out: rdn to go 2nd 1f out: edgd lft to rch stands' rail: r.o but a hld* **11/4**[2]

3 *2* **Natagora (FR)**[63] 2654 3-8-7 ...... C-PLemaire 8 116
(P Bary, France) *set fast pce to 1 1/2f out: one pce* **7/4**[1]

4 *3* **Nahoodh (IRE)**[25] 3852 3-8-7 ...... LDettori 3 110
(M Johnston) *dropped out in rr: hdwy on stands' side to go 3rd 2f out: rdn and lost 3rd over 1 1/2f out: outpcd fnl 1 1/2f* **9/2**

5 *1 1/2* **Sabana Perdida (IRE)**[46] 3120 5-9-0 ...... TJarnet 6 107
(A De Royer-Dupre, France) *racd in 4th 4 l off front three: clsd gap bef 1/2-way: one pce fr over 2f out* **10/1**

6 *1/2* **Barshiba (IRE)**[9] 4361 4-9-0 ...... TQuinn 1 106
(D R C Elsworth) *racd in 5th: pushed along bef 1/2-way: 3rd under 4f out tl outpcd fnl 2f* **33/1**

7 *20* **Briseida**[25] 3852 3-8-7 ...... MartinDwyer 2 59
(P Schiergen, Germany) *in rr: sme hdwy in centre over 3f out: rdn and btn over 2f out* **40/1**

8 *2* **Raymi Coya (CAN)**[44] 3194 3-8-7 ...... SPasquier 4 54
(M Botti) *a towards rr: rdn and btn over 2 1/2f out* **66/1**

9 *dist* **Spring Touch (USA)**[20] 3-8-7 ...... DBonilla 9 —
(F Head, France) *sn pushed along and unable to get to ld: racd in 2nd tl wknd bef 1/2-way: t.o fnl 3f* **200/1**

1m 37.5s (-3.50) **Going Correction** -0.075s/f (Good)
WFA 3 from 4yo+ 7lb **9** Ran SP% **117.7**
Speed ratings: **114,113,111,108,107 106,86,84,—**
PARI-MUTUEL: WIN 3.60 (coupled with Spring Touch);PL 1.20, 1.20, 1.10; DF 6.90.
Owner Wertheimer Et Frere **Bred** Wertheimer Et Frere **Trained** France
■ Stewards' Enquiry : C Soumillon €400 fine: whip abuse

FOCUS
A cracking contest, formerly known as the Prix d'Astarte, with top fillies filling the first four places.

NOTEBOOK
Goldikova(IRE) has gone from strength-to-strength all season and thoroughly deserved this Group 1 victory, having already been placed in two Group 1 events before an easy win at Maisons-Laffitte. Always travelling strongly in third place up the centre of the track, she took the lead running into the final furlong and, responding well to pressure, she seemed to win a little easier than the official distance suggests. She certainly appreciated the cut in the ground and there may still be some more good races in her. She is likely to miss the Jacques Le Marois and head for the Prix du Moulin de Longchamp.
Darjina(FR) is a very brave filly who always gives her best, and although conditions were not in her favour she still ran her heart out. She started her run near the stands' rail from one and a half out and kept up the good work until the bitter end. Considering the conditions it was an excellent effort and she will now go back to Longchamp and try and win her third Group 1 race at the track in the Moulin, where she is likely to renew rivalry with the winner.
Natagora(FR) looked well and impressed on the way to the start. Very smartly away, she immediately took control of the race but was a little eager in the early stages. She still looked to have plenty in hand two out but was in trouble by the furlong marker and just stayed on one paced. Her jockey felt the soft ground was not to her liking but her only two major defeats have come at this track and she will now go off to Longchamp for the Prix du Moulin, where she will probably take on the first two here once again.
Nahoodh(IRE), who was well behind early on, began to make a forward move from one and a half out but could not go through with her effort. Dettori felt that this race might have come a little soon after her victory in the Falmouth at Newmarket.
Sabana Perdida(IRE), winner of the Windsor Forest, does not like soft ground and she failed to run up to her best.
Barshiba(IRE), an unlucky fourth in this a year ago, looked dangerous two and a half furlongs out on the stands' rail but was struggling soon afterr. She will now be given a rest until the Sun Chariot Stakes at Newmarket at the beginning of October and she will be retired to stud at the end of the season.
Raymi Coya(CAN) had it all to do against these and she made no show. Already a beaten force at the two furlong marker, the only one she beat was the pacemaker.

4232 DUSSELDORF (R-H)
Sunday, August 3

OFFICIAL GOING: Good

4675a PREIS DER DIANA (GERMAN OAKS) (GROUP 1) (FILLIES) 1m 3f
4:10 (4:22) 3-Y-O £169,118 (£66,176; £33,088; £18,382; £7,353)

RPR

1 **Rosenreihe (IRE)**[14] 4233 3-9-2 ...... AStarke 13 107
(P Schiergen, Germany) *hld up in rr: midfield st: sn swtchd outside: styd on strly to ld fnl strides* **114/10**

2 nk **Lady Marian (GER)**[30] 3705 3-9-2 .... DBoeuf 4 106
(W Baltromei, Germany) *a.p: uneasy negotiating both bnds: led over 1f out: hdd fnl strides* **78/10**

3 1 1/4 **Baila Me (GER)**[49] 3073 3-9-2 .... DVargiu 9 104
(W Baltromei, Germany) *in tch: styd on wl fr over 1f out: tk 3rd cl home* **59/10**

4 3/4 **Tres Rapide (IRE)**[84] 2031 3-9-2 .... JVictoire 14 103
(H-A Pantall, France) *prom on outside: 2nd st: led 2f out to over 1f out: one pce* **103/10**

5 nk **Peace Royale (GER)**[32] 3623 3-9-2 .... EPedroza 6 103
(A Wohler, Germany) *5th st: nt clr run towards ins 1 1/2f out: one pce* **32/10**[1]

6 1 1/4 **Dawn Dew (GER)**[106] 3-9-2 .... FilipMinarik 7 100
(P Schiergen, Germany) *6th st: one pce fnl 2f* **31/1**

7 nk **Auentime (GER)**[30] 3705 3-9-2 .... THellier 2 100
(U Ostmann, Germany) *a in midfield* **23/1**

8 1/2 **Porta Westfalica (IRE)** 3-9-2 .... DarryllHolland 11 99
(W Hickst, Germany) *led after 3f tl hdd 2f out: one pce* **38/1**

9 3/4 **Umirage (GER)**[30] 3705 3-9-2 .... ASuborics 3 98
(H Blume, Germany) *s.i.s: nvr a factor* **57/10**[3]

10 2 **Larella (GER)**[49] 3073 3-9-2 .... NRichter 18 94
(P Rau, Germany) *rn wd on first bnd: nvr a factor* **66/1**

11 1/2 **Azalee (GER)** 3-9-2 .... ShaneKelly 16 94
(J Hirschberger, Germany) *rrd up s: in rr tl sme late hdwy* **131/10**

12 1/2 **Bella Amica (GER)**[73] 3-9-2 .... AGoritz 19 93
(Frau Marion Rotering, Germany) *in tch: 4th st: sn wknd* **40/1**

13 shd **Salve Germania (IRE)**[30] 3705 3-9-2 .... MJKinane 8 93
(W Hickst, Germany) *midfield: sltly hmpd 2f out: nt rcvr* **52/10**[2]

14 4 **Affair (FR)** 3-9-2 .... TMundry 5 86
(P Rau, Germany) *led early: hdd after 3f: remained cl up tl wknd over 2f out* **37/1**

15 5 **Themelie Island (IRE)**[32] 3623 3-9-2 .... ADeVries 12 77
(A Trybuhl, Germany) *a in rr* **27/1**

16 1 1/4 **Ianapourna (GER)** 3-9-2 .... FJohansson 1 75
(J Hirschberger, Germany) *a bhd* **129/10**

2m 19.32s (139.32) **16** Ran SP% **131.9**
(including 10 Euro stake): WIN 124; PL 33, 26, 28; SF 806.
Owner Gestut Wittekindshof **Bred** Gestut Wittekindshof **Trained** Germany

KLAMPENBORG
Sunday, August 3

OFFICIAL GOING: Good to firm

4676a SCANDINAVIAN OPEN CHAMPIONSHIP (GROUP 3) 1m 4f
2:55 (2:55) 3-Y-O+ £29,557 (£9,852; £4,926; £2,956; £1,970)

RPR

1 **Chinese Mandarin (USA)**[683] 5488 5-9-2 .... NCordrey 9 94
(E Van Doorn, Sweden) *rn in snatches: towards rr: pushed along after 3f: hdwy 3f out: str run to ld wl ins fnl f* **67/10**[3]

2 3/4 **Peas And Carrots (DEN)**[35] 3541 5-9-4 .... MSantos 13 95
(L Reuterskiold Jr, Sweden) *racd in 8th on outside: hdwy 3f out: led 1f out: hdd and no ex wl ins fnl f* **9/10**[1]

3 1/2 **Dan Tucket**[281] 6486 3-8-5 .... AlanMunro 3 92
(B Olsen, Denmark) *midfield: hdwy 3f out: led 2f out: hdd 1f out: one pce* **69/10**

4 1 **Django (SWE)**[35] 3541 5-9-2 .... MLarsen 12 90
(Caroline Stromberg, Sweden) *racd in 4th: led 3f out to 2f out: one pce* **98/10**

5 2 **Alnitak (USA)**[31] 7-9-2 ....(b) KAndersen 2 87
(B Olsen, Denmark) *a in midfield: nvr threatened ldrs* **33/1**

6 1 1/2 **Hot Fudge (SWE)**[294] 5-8-11 .... MRodriguez 8 80
(L Reuterskiold Jr, Sweden) *trckd ldrs: rdn and one pce fr over 2f out* **22/1**

7 nk **Jagodin (IRE)**[33] 3596 8-9-2 .... P-AGraberg 5 84
(L Reuterskiold Jr, Sweden) *midfield: outpcd 1/2-way: n.d after* **26/1**

8 1 1/2 **Bongo Bello (DEN)**[295] 7-9-2 .... AnnNielsen 7 82
(T Christensen, Denmark) *last to st: modest late hdwy* **41/1**

9 1 **Mick Jerome (IRE)**[31] 7-9-2 .... LSantos 6 80
(Rune Haugen, Norway) *nvr a factor* **68/1**

10 1/2 **Alpacco (IRE)**[31] 6-9-2 .... ManuelMartinez 10 80
(L Kelp, Denmark) *cl up pulling hrd early: rdn and wknd over 2f out* **66/10**[2]

11 12 **Eko Arabian Night (DEN)**[35] 3541 6-9-2 .... LVillaroel 15 60
(Anja Runoe, Denmark) *prom tl wknd 1/2-way* **49/1**

12 1 1/2 **Lumen (FR)**[29] 3751 6-8-11 ....(b) EspenSki 1 53
(O Larsen, Sweden) *4th early: led after 5f tl 3f out: wknd qckly* **15/1**

13 6 **Pecoiquen (CHI)**[77] 2233 7-9-2 ....(b) DinaDanekilde 4 48
(F Castro, Sweden) *plld hrd early: led 5f: wknd* **61/1**

2m 26.0s (146.00)
WFA 3 from 4yo+ 11lb **13** Ran SP% **125.4**
(including 1Dkr stake): WIN 7.67; Pl 1.89, 1.22, 1.71; SF 31.45.
Owner Stall Amiska **Bred** High Creek Farm **Trained** Sweden

MONMOUTH PARK (L-H)
Sunday, August 3

OFFICIAL GOING: Fast

4678a HASKELL INVITATIONAL (GRADE 1) (DIRT) 1m 1f
11:14 (11:17) 3-Y-O
£301,508 (£100,503; £50,251; £30,151; £15,075; £2,512)

RPR

1 **Big Brown (USA)**[57] 2858 3-8-10 .... KDesormeaux 4 121
(Richard Dutrow Jr, U.S.A) **1/5**[1]

2 1 3/4 **Coal Play (USA)**[183] 3-8-6 .... JBravo 6 113
(Nicholas Zito, U.S.A) **202/10**

3 4 1/4 **Cool Coal Man (USA)**[92] 1820 3-8-6 .... ECastro 2 104
(Nicholas Zito, U.S.A) **13/2**[2]

4 2 1/2 **Alaazo (USA)** 3-8-6 .... JLezcano 3 99
(William Mott, U.S.A) **331/10**

5 10 1/4 **Nistle's Crunch (USA)**[43] 3-8-6 .... ETrujillo 5 77
(Kenneth McPeek, U.S.A) **201/10**

6 20 **Atoned (USA)**[22] 3-8-6 ....(b) EPrado 7 35
(Todd Pletcher, U.S.A) **84/10**[3]

7 3 **Magical Forest (USA)**[21] 3-8-6 ....(b) JChavez 1 29
(Joseph DeMola, U.S.A) **196/10**

1m 48.31s (108.31) **7** Ran SP% **124.5**
PARI-MUTUEL (including $2 stake): WIN 2.40; PL (1-2) 2.10, 8.00;SHOW (1-2-3) 2.10, 4.20, 2.80; SF 25.20.
Owner IEAH Stables & P Pompa Jr **Bred** Monticule **Trained** USA

NOTEBOOK

Big Brown(USA), whose defeat in the Belmont was, by photographic evidence, put down to a shoe coming loose early in the race, nevertheless had something to prove here. The leader set a good pace and, turning into the straight, he was under pressure and looked in trouble, but he battled on well and got on top inside the final half furlong. This was not an impressive success like his wins in the Kentucky Derby or the Preakness, but he did show that he can win by battling this time, and as this was his first outing for almost two months he might well come on for it. The Breeders' Cup Classic remains the long-term objective this season.

4449 CARLISLE (R-H)
Monday, August 4

OFFICIAL GOING: Good (good to soft in places on straight course; 7.8)
After 10mm overnight rain the ground was reckoned 'very tacky'.
Wind: Moderate, half-against Weather: fine and sunny

4679 LLOYD MINI LADY AMATEUR RIDERS' H'CAP 7f 200y
6:15 (6:16) (Class 5) (0-70,65) 3-Y-O+ £2,498 (£774; £387; £193) Stalls High

Form RPR

5430 1 **Emirate Isle**[5] 4538 4-10-10 **65** ....(p) MissARyan 3 73
(C Grant) *trckd ldrs: wnt 2nd over 1f out: kpt on to ld last 50yds* **10/1**

6153 2 nk **Emperor's Well**[6] 4503 9-9-13 **57** ....(b) MissJCoward(3) 12 64
(M W Easterby) *led: rdn over 2f out: hdd wl ins fnl f* **11/4**[1]

0003 3 1 1/4 **Sedge (USA)**[9] 4440 8-10-0 **60** ....(p) MissWGibson(5) 4 64
(P T Midgley) *in rr: hdwy over 2f out: hung rt: styd on fnl f* **12/1**

3004 4 nk **Apache Nation (IRE)**[17] 4168 5-10-2 **57** .... MissADeniel 5 61
(M Dods) *mid-div: hdwy over 2f out: kpt on fnl f* **8/1**

6360 5 1/2 **Scotty's Future (IRE)**[6] 4503 10-9-7 **48** .... MrsCBartley 10 51
(A Berry) *in rr: styd on fnl 2f: nt rch ldrs* **18/1**

4635 6 3/4 **Valdan (IRE)**[15] 4215 4-9-10 **56** ....(t) MissAngelaBarnes(5) 11 57
(M A Barnes) *mid-div: hmpd bnd over 5f out: hdwy over 2f out: one pce appr fnl f* **10/1**

0600 7 5 **Playtotheaudience**[6] 4503 5-9-7 **55** .... MissNVorster(7) 6 44
(R A Fahey) *in rr: sme hdwy over 2f out: nvr on terms* **10/1**

-500 8 nse **Susiedil (IRE)**[44] 3281 7-8-12 **46** oh1 ....(p) MissStephanieBowey(7) 1 35
(S T Mason) *unruly gng to s: racd v wd: swtchd rt after 1f: sn chsng ldrs: wknd 2f out* **100/1**

2220 9 1 1/2 **March Mate**[26] 3834 4-10-0 **55** ....(p) MissLEllison 2 41
(B Ellison) *t.k.h: trckd ldrs: lost pl over 1f out* **9/2**[2]

5-52 10 2 1/2 **Uhuru Peak**[7] 4491 7-9-8 **49** ....(bt) MissSBrotherton 8 29
(M W Easterby) *chsd ldrs: hmpd bnd and swtchd outside after 2f: effrt on wd outside over 2f out: hung rt and sn wknd* **11/2**[3]

-000 11 2 **Second Reef**[8] 4451 6-9-0 **46** oh1 .... MissHCuthbert(5) 7 21
(T A K Cuthbert) *sn bhd* **80/1**

014- 12 5 **Kirstys Lad**[234] 7146 6-10-0 **60** .... MissMMullineaux(5) 14 24
(M Mullineaux) *chsd ldrs: lost pl over 1f out* **20/1**

4/00 13 5 **Woody Valentine (USA)**[51] 2568 7-10-2 **62** .... MissECSayer(5) 9 14
(Mrs Dianne Sayer) *s.s: sme hdwy over 3f out: hung rt and lost pl 2f out* **50/1**

6000 14 1 **Busy Man (IRE)**[23] 3964 9-9-13 **54** oh1 ow8.... MissCharmaineO'Neill 13 4
(R C Guest) *s.s: a bhd* **100/1**

1m 43.22s (3.22) **Going Correction** +0.35s/f (Good) **14** Ran SP% **121.5**
Speed ratings (Par 103): **97,96,95,95,94 93,88,88,87,84 82,77,72,71**
toteswinger: 1&2 £11.80, 1&3 £28.60, 2&3 £12.10. CSF £37.23 CT £356.46 TOTE £13.40: £4.00, £1.10, £4.80; EX 45.70.
Owner John Wade **Bred** J Wade **Trained** Newton Bewley, Co Durham
■ Stewards' Enquiry : Miss J Coward two-day ban: used whip with excessive frequency (Aug 20, 23)
Miss A Ryan two-day ban: careless riding (Aug 20, 23)

FOCUS

A modest lady amateur riders' handicap but the form looks sound rated through the runner-up, third and fourth.

4680 EDINBURGH WOOLLEN MILL CLAIMING STKS 1m 1f 61y
6:45 (6:45) (Class 6) 3-Y-O £2,047 (£604; £302) Stalls High

Form RPR

2306 1 **Grit (IRE)**[2] 4629 3-9-1 62 .... TonyCulhane 1 61
(M R Channon) *sn w ldr: led over 3f out: hung rt: all out* **8/1**[2]

06 2 nk **Shaylee**[8] 4461 3-8-9 .... SilvestreDeSousa 6 55
(T D Walford) *in rr: rdn over 3f out: hdwy 2f out: styd on wl fnl f: jst hld* **50/1**

0560 3 1 3/4 **Piverina (IRE)**[14] 4241 3-8-8 46 .... TomEaves 9 50
(Miss J A Camacho) *trckd ldrs: styd on same pce fnl f* **14/1**[3]

1400 4 1 **Carry On Cleo**[2] 4629 3-8-2 59 ....(v) FrancisNorton 8 42
(A Berry) *led tl over 3f out: one pce fnl 2f* **8/1**[2]

-645 5 2 3/4 **Destinys Dream (IRE)**[10] 4392 3-8-11 69 .... TonyHamilton 7 45
(D W Barker) *hld up: hdwy to go 2nd over 2f out: rdn and swvd bdly lft over 1f out* **8/11**[1]

-600 6 4 **Howards Hope**[14] 4241 3-8-5 56 ....(b) RoystonFfrench 4 31
(Miss L A Perratt) *in tch on outer: rdn 3f out: hung rt and sn wknd* **25/1**

435 7 3/4 **Admiralcollingwood**[14] 4245 3-8-5 52 .... DominicFox(3) 3 32
(T P Tate) *dwlt: in rr: sme hdwy and hung lft 2f out: nvr on terms* **16/1**

0245 8 8 **Caught In Paradise (IRE)**[10] 4381 3-8-10 49 .... DeanMcKeown 2 17
(D W Thompson) *chsd ldrs: rdn over 3f out: wknd over 2f out* **33/1**

0010 9 10 **One Night In May (IRE)**[10] 4381 3-8-5 46 .... PaulHanagan 5 —
(M Dods) *in rr: drvn over 4f out: c wd and lost pl over 2f out: bhd whn eased ins fnl f* **8/1**[2]

2m 0.31s (2.71) **Going Correction** +0.35s/f (Good) **9** Ran SP% **112.5**
Speed ratings (Par 98): **101,100,99,98,95 92,91,84,75**
toteswinger: 1&2 £27.10, 1&3 £8.90, 2&3 £17.10. CSF £329.74 TOTE £7.60: £1.90, £8.20, £3.10; EX 181.50.
Owner M Channon **Bred** M G Masterson **Trained** West Ilsley, Berks

■ Stewards' Enquiry : Silvestre De Sousa three-day ban: used whip with excessive frequency (Aug 18-20)

FOCUS
A weak claimer rated through the third's handicap form this time.

4681 BEADLE & HILL MAIDEN AUCTION STKS — 5f
7:15 (7:24) (Class 5) 2-Y-O — £2,590 (£770; £385; £192) Stalls High

Form — RPR

3 **1** — **Zelos Girl (IRE)**[21] 4020 2-8-7 0 .... SaleemGolam 6 — 72+
(Rae Guest) *trckd ldr: shkn up to ld over 1f out: pushed out* — **4/9**[1]

564 **2** 1 3/4 **Fitzolini**[30] 3714 2-8-9 64 .... (p) SilvestreDeSousa 4 — 68
(A D Brown) *led tl over 1f out: kpt on same pce* — **14/1**[3]

04 **3** nk **Lucky Numbers (IRE)**[23] 3949 2-8-7 0 .... RussellKennemore(3) 5 — 68
(Paul Green) *tk fierce hold: sn trcking ldrs: kpt on same pce fnl f* — **7/2**[2]

0 **4** 5 **Lemon Dash**[23] 3949 2-8-4 0 .... PaulHanagan 1 — 44
(J J Quinn) *w ldrs: wknd over 1f out* — **33/1**

5 2 **Kellies Rocket (IRE)** 2-8-8 0 .... FrancisNorton 3 — 41
(G A Swinbank) *s.s: hdwy over 2f out: wknd appr fnl f* — **16/1**

6 7 **Liberty Lodge (IRE)** 2-8-11 0 .... TomEaves 2 — 19
(G A Swinbank) *hld up: effrt on outer over 2f out: lost pl appr fnl f* — **16/1**

63.08 secs (2.28) **Going Correction** +0.35s/f (Good) — **6** Ran SP% **112.8**
Speed ratings (Par 94): **95,92,91,83,80 69**
toteswinger: 1&2 £2.10, 1&3 £1.10, 2&3 £5.00. CSF £8.69 TOTE £1.50: £1.20, £3.30; EX 6.10.
Owner Beadle, Booth, Davies & Jennings **Bred** Corduff Stud And J Corcoran **Trained** Newmarket, Suffolk

FOCUS
A weak maiden but the long odds-on winner made quite hard work of it. She basically matched her debut form.

NOTEBOOK
Zelos Girl(IRE) had the leader covered and looked poised for a comfortable success, but in the end her rider had to leave little to chance. (op 1-2 tchd 4-7 in places)
Fitzolini, with the cheekpieces retained on his sixth outing, took them along and to his credit did not go down without a fight. (op 12-1 tchd 16-1)
Lucky Numbers(IRE), who had two handlers, was reluctant to go to post. He pulled very hard and threw his head about and in the circumstances kept on surprisingly well. He is clearly not straightforward. (op 11-2)
Lemon Dash finished roughly the same distance behind the third as she had done at Chester three weeks earlier. (op 16-1)
Kellies Rocket(IRE), a May foal, is quite an excitable filly and hopefully this will have helped settle her down. (op 12-1 tchd 10-1)
Liberty Lodge(IRE), speedily-bred, had two handlers in the paddock and continually swished his tail. In the end he dropped right away. (op 12-1 tchd 10-1)

4682 EDINBURGH WOOLLEN MILL H'CAP — 6f 192y
7:45 (7:52) (Class 4) (0-85,85) 3-Y-O — £4,857 (£1,445; £722; £360) Stalls High

Form — RPR

0013 **1** — **Horatio Carter**[8] 4453 3-8-9 73 .... (p) RoystonFfrench 8 — 83
(K A Ryan) *mde all: clr over 1f out: edgd rt: drvn rt out* — **6/1**[3]

0024 **2** 2 1/4 **Kashimin (IRE)**[22] 3999 3-8-13 80 .... PJMcDonald(3) 10 — 84
(G A Swinbank) *trckd ldrs: tk fierce grip: kpt on fnl f: no real imp* — **8/1**

4131 **3** 3/4 **Dream Express (IRE)**[26] 3831 3-8-9 76 .... NeilBrown(3) 1 — 78
(M Dods) *swtchd rt after s: hld up in rr: hdwy over 2f out: styd on wl fnl f* — **11/2**[2]

6455 **4** 1/2 **Bere Davis (FR)**[16] 4206 3-8-9 73 .... (v[1]) DeanMcKeown 2 — 74
(P D Evans) *chsd ldrs on outer: one pce appr fnl f* — **8/1**

1500 **5** 1 3/4 **Jonny Lesters Hair (IRE)**[47] 3141 3-8-5 69 .... PaulHanagan 4 — 65
(T D Easterby) *mid-div: hdwy over 2f out: kpt on same pce* — **14/1**

4210 **6** 3/4 **Prince Hamlet (IRE)**[15] 4218 3-9-7 85 .... (b) TomEaves 3 — 79
(B Smart) *dwlt: in rr: rdn and hdwy 3f out: kpt on same pce appr fnl f* — **9/1**

1635 **7** 2 1/4 **San Jose City (IRE)**[17] 4158 3-9-1 79 .... StephenDonohoe 9 — 67
(D Carroll) *mid-div: effrt 3f out: nvr trbld ldrs* — **15/2**

-300 **8** 1 1/4 **Montaquila**[30] 3723 3-9-2 80 .... (t) PaulMulrennan 6 — 65
(J Howard Johnson) *t.k.h in rr: hdwy over 2f out: nvr nr ldrs* — **12/1**

-150 **9** 8 **Transfer**[9] 4404 3-9-2 80 .... FrancisNorton 5 — 43
(A M Balding) *mid-div: drvn over 3f out: lost pl over 2f out: sn bhd* — **4/1**[1]

3120 **10** 7 **Ninefineirishmen (IRE)**[9] 4407 3-8-11 75 .... (p) DarrenWilliams 7 — 36
(K R Burke) *chsd ldrs: wknd over 1f out* — **20/1**

1305 **11** 3 **Blindspin**[34] 3592 3-8-13 77 .... TonyHamilton 11 — 29
(M Dods) *trckd ldrs: wknd over 1f out: eased ins fnl f* — **16/1**

1-50 **12** 7 **River Ardeche**[35] 3557 3-8-11 75 .... TonyCulhane 12 — 9
(P C Haslam) *hld up in rr: sme hdwy on ins over 2f out: wknd and eased over 1f out* — **25/1**

1m 29.04s (1.94) **Going Correction** +0.35s/f (Good) — **12** Ran SP% **122.5**
Speed ratings (Par 102): **102,99,98,98,96 95,92,91,82,80 77,69**
toteswinger: 1&2 £10.40, 1&3 £8.00, 2&3 £8.50. CSF £55.42 CT £290.47 TOTE £5.90: £2.50, £2.60, £2.30; EX 39.90.
Owner T Alderson **Bred** Mrs T Brudenell **Trained** Hambleton, N Yorks

FOCUS
The winner was repeating his course-and-distance win two outings ago. The form has a solid look about it with the next four home pretty close to their pre-race marks.
Transfer Official explanation: jockey said gelding was never travelling
Ninefineirishmen(IRE) Official explanation: jockey said gelding hung left in straight
River Ardeche Official explanation: jockey said gelding hung badly right throughout

4683 CHAMPAGNE LANSON H'CAP — 6f 192y
8:15 (8:25) (Class 6) (0-60,58) 3-Y-O+ — £2,047 (£604; £302) Stalls High

Form — RPR

6000 **1** — **Distant Pleasure**[29] 3755 4-8-11 50 .... NeilBrown(3) 3 — 65
(M Dods) *hld up in rr: hdwy over 2f out: styd on wl to ld last 75yds* — **12/1**

321- **2** 3 1/2 **Dendor**[305] 5935 4-9-6 56 .... TonyHamilton 15 — 62
(D W Barker) *t.k.h: led: hdd and no ex ins fnl f* — **10/1**

4402 **3** nk **The Salwick Flyer (IRE)**[8] 4453 5-9-8 58 .... RoystonFfrench 4 — 63
(Miss L A Perratt) *chsd ldrs: chal over 2f out: styd on same pce ins fnl f* — **11/4**[1]

055 **4** 3/4 **Charlie Allnut**[21] 4018 3-9-1 57 .... (b[1]) DarrenWilliams 14 — 58
(K R Burke) *chsd ldrs: kpt on same pce fnl f* — **11/2**[3]

2463 **5** 1 1/4 **Vesuvio**[21] 4018 4-9-2 52 .... LeeEnstone 9 — 52
(C W Thornton) *s.i.s: hdwy over 2f out: kpt on one pce appr fnl f* — **15/2**

-000 **6** 1 3/4 **Resolute Defender (IRE)**[18] 4118 3-8-10 52 .... PaulMulrennan 8 — 45
(J Howard Johnson) *mid-div: drvn over 3f out: kpt on: nvr a threat* — **33/1**

6643 **7** shd **Tanforan**[23] 3951 6-9-5 55 .... TonyCulhane 2 — 50
(B P J Baugh) *in rr: kpt on fnl 2f: nvr nr ldrs* — **5/1**[2]

-500 **8** 3/4 **Smart Pick**[23] 3951 5-8-11 47 .... TomEaves 10 — 40
(Mrs L Williamson) *mid-div: kpt on fnl 2f: nvr trbld ldrs* — **50/1**

2220 **9** shd **Tenancy (IRE)**[7] 4479 4-9-0 50 .... (e) PAspell 13 — 42
(R C Guest) *s.i.s: hung rt and kpt on fnl 2f: nvr on terms* — **16/1**

0-00 **10** 2 1/2 **Linden's Lady**[26] 3834 8-8-9 45 .... (v) DeanMcKeown 11 — 31
(J R Weymes) *chsd ldrs: wknd over 1f out* — **50/1**

5450 **11** 2 3/4 **Spy Gun (USA)**[52] 2988 8-8-6 45 .... (p) RussellKennemore(3) 12 — 23
(T Wall) *chsd ldrs: lost pl over 1f out* — **50/1**

6464 **12** 1/2 **Nufoudh (IRE)**[4] 4559 4-8-11 47 .... SaleemGolam 5 — 24
(Miss Tracy Waggott) *prom: rdn over 3f out: lost pl over 1f out* — **9/1**

0000 **13** 2 3/4 **Kirkby's Treasure**[63] 2658 10-9-8 58 .... StephenDonohoe 6 — 27
(A Berry) *s.i.s: hdwy on ins over 2f out: wknd jst ins fnl f* — **20/1**

505- **14** 13 **Catherines Cafe (IRE)**[275] 6638 5-8-11 50 .... AndrewMullen(3) 1 — —
(A C Whillans) *in rr: bhd fnl 2f* — **20/1**

1m 29.51s (2.41) **Going Correction** +0.35s/f (Good)
WFA 3 from 4yo+ 6lb — **14** Ran SP% **121.5**
Speed ratings (Par 101): **100,96,95,94,93 91,91,90,90,87 84,83,80,65**
toteswinger: 1&2 £62.90, 1&3 £17.40, 2&3 £10.30. CSF £119.14 CT £438.49 TOTE £17.60: £4.20, £2.70, £1.70; EX 232.30.
Owner Pontefract Racecourse Racing Syndicate **Bred** Mrs M T Dawson **Trained** Denton, Co Durham
■ Stewards' Enquiry : Neil Brown caution: used whip with excessive frequency

FOCUS
A low-grade handicap with the winner bouncing back. The form looks reliable rated through the next three home.
Distant Pleasure Official explanation: trainer had no explanation for the improved form shown
Tenancy(IRE) Official explanation: jockey said, regarding the running and riding, his orders were to hold gelding up to get the trip and achieve the best possible placing, but it missed break due to blindfold being stuck, got further beind that ideal, and then stayed on through beaten horses

4684 COORS GROLSCH H'CAP — 5f 153y
8:45 (8:54) (Class 6) (0-60,66) 3-Y-O — £2,047 (£604; £302) Stalls High

Form — RPR

3-30 **1** — **Glenveagh (IRE)**[13] 4272 3-8-7 49 .... (p) RoystonFfrench 17 — 60
(K A Ryan) *mde virtually all: hld on wl towards fin* — **12/1**

1311 **2** nk **Mandalay King (IRE)**[8] 4450 3-9-1 62 6ex .... KellyHarrison(5) 6 — 72
(Mrs Marjorie Fife) *trckd ldrs: chal over 1f out: no ex wl ins fnl f* — **2/1**[1]

-410 **3** 1 3/4 **Rich Harvest (USA)**[10] 4369 3-9-0 56 .... StephenDonohoe 8 — 60
(P D Evans) *chsd ldrs: styd on same pce fnl f* — **16/1**

-401 **4** 3/4 **Feeling Fresh (IRE)**[3] 4595 3-9-7 66 6ex .... RussellKennemore(3) 16 — 68
(Paul Green) *s.i.s: hdwy over 2f out: kpt on same pce fnl f* — **9/2**[2]

3064 **5** 6 **Flight Plan**[30] 3733 3-9-2 58 .... PaulHanagan 9 — 40
(R A Fahey) *s.i.s: hung rt and kpt on fnl 2f: nvr nr ldrs* — **8/1**[3]

3006 **6** 5 **Kyllis**[26] 3831 3-9-0 56 .... TomEaves 14 — 21
(B Smart) *in rr div: hdwy on ins over 2f out: wknd appr fnl f* — **20/1**

000 **7** 1/2 **Ourbelle**[23] 3953 3-8-1 46 oh1 .... DominicFox(3) 11 — 10
(Miss Tracy Waggott) *hmpd s: outpcd in rr: edgd rt and kpt on fnl f* — **100/1**

114 **8** hd **Ursus**[26] 3833 3-9-1 57 .... SilvestreDeSousa 2 — 20
(C R Wilson) *s.i.s: hdwy on outer over 2f out: nvr nr ldrs* — **8/1**[3]

5504 **9** 5 **Nawaaff**[11] 4333 3-9-4 60 .... TonyCulhane 4 — 6
(M R Channon) *chsd ldrs on outer: hung rt and lost pl over 1f out: eased ins fnl f* — **11/1**

0500 **10** 4 **Kool Katie**[16] 4207 3-8-13 55 .... TonyHamilton 5 — —
(Mrs G S Rees) *w ldrs: hung rt and lost pl over 1f out* — **25/1**

6000 **11** 3 **Azzaamm**[20] 4056 3-8-5 47 .... (tp) SaleemGolam 13 — —
(C A Dwyer) *mid-div: effrt on ins over 2f out: sn wknd* — **80/1**

0004 **12** 1 1/4 **Young Ivanhoe**[28] 3779 3-9-1 57 .... (b) FrancisNorton 3 — —
(C A Dwyer) *chsd ldrs on outer: lost pl 2f out* — **22/1**

3400 **13** 3/4 **Note Perfect**[31] 3686 3-8-4 46 .... (b) DaleGibson 1 — —
(M W Easterby) *chsd ldrs on outside: wknd over 2f out* — **25/1**

0350 **14** 1/2 **Recent Times**[45] 3231 3-9-3 59 .... PaulMulrennan 12 — —
(T D Easterby) *w ldrs: wknd 2f out* — **22/1**

0606 **15** 3 **Fantasy Fighter (IRE)**[14] 4242 3-8-4 46 oh1 .... (v) AndrewElliott 7 — —
(J J Quinn) *virtually ref to r: a detached in last* — **33/1**

1m 12.88s (72.88) — **15** Ran SP% **122.0**
toteswinger: 1&2 £6.20, 1&3 £74.00, 2&3 £40.90. CSF £33.10 CT £421.06 TOTE £15.90: £4.20, £1.80, £5.80; EX 41.80 Place 6 £207.75,Place 5 £88.02..
Owner J Duddy,L Duddy,P Mcbride,E Duffy **Bred** Wardstown Stud Ltd **Trained** Hambleton, N Yorks

FOCUS
Another low-grade handicap, run over 40 yards less than the advertised distance due to a bad patch of ground. Another all-the-way winner and the form looks sound at this level.
T/Plt: £112.70 to a £1 stake. Pool: £63,494.87. 410.98 winning tickets. T/Qpdt: £5.50 to a £1 stake. Pool: £5,070.08. 671.70 winning tickets. WG

4202 RIPON (R-H)
Monday, August 4

OFFICIAL GOING: Good
Wind: Virtually nil Weather: Sunny periods

4685 E B F BBC RADIO YORK 103.7FM & 104.3FM NOVICE STKS — 6f
2:15 (2:15) (Class 5) 2-Y-O — £4,209 (£1,252; £625; £312) Stalls Low

Form — RPR

1 — **Summer Fete (IRE)** 2-8-3 0 .... RoystonFfrench 3 — 80+
(B Smart) *trckd ldng pair: hdwy on inner whn nt clr run and rn green 1/2-way: swtchd rt and rdn over 1f out: styd on strly to ld ins fnl f: sn clr* — **10/1**

1 **2** 2 1/2 **Aldermoor (USA)**[12] 4289 2-9-5 0 .... DanielTudhope 4 — 88
(S C Williams) *stdd s and hld up: smooth hdwy 2f out: led 1f out and sn rdn: hdd and one pce ins fnl f* — **6/4**[1]

166 **3** nk **Cerito**[32] 3634 2-9-2 92 .... DarryllHolland 1 — 84
(M R Channon) *led: edgd lft 1/2-way: rdn 2f out: drvn and hdd ent fnl f: sn hung rt and one pce* — **4/1**[3]

21 **4** 3 **Kentish Dream**[16] 4184 2-9-5 87 .... ShaneKelly 2 — 78
(S A Callaghan) *cl up: effrt 2f out: sn rdn and ev ch tl drvn: n.m.r and wknd ent fnl f* — **13/8**[2]

1m 13.83s (0.83) **Going Correction** +0.075s/f (Good) — **4** Ran SP% **107.2**
Speed ratings (Par 94): **97,93,93,89**
CSF £24.93 TOTE £7.20; EX 13.40.
Owner H E Sheikh Rashid Bin Mohammed **Bred** Darley **Trained** Hambleton, N Yorks
■ Stewards' Enquiry : Darryll Holland one-day ban: careless riding (Aug 18)

FOCUS
Only four runners, but this looked a reasonable novice event. They raced near side early, but drifted towards the middle late on. The winner took advantage of a sizeable weight concession, with the form rated through the other three.

NOTEBOOK

Summer Fete(IRE) ◆, a daughter of Pivotal, first foal of a 1m juvenile winner who was later smart over 1m1f in the UAE, was easy to back, but she made a winning debut in good style and her trainer revealed he thinks quite a bit of her. She raced in last early and showed distinct signs of greenness, but once switched right, away from the near-side rail, she picked up really well. She will apparently not have many more races this season and she ought to make a very nice three-year-old, particularly on easy ground. (op 9-1 tchd 15-2)

Aldermoor(USA) created a good impression when a cosy winner of a Catterick maiden on his debut, but he got to the front much sooner this time and was quickly pegged back. He probably ran into a nice type and might be capable of even better if held on to for longer next time. (op 15-8)

Cerito looked really good when bolting up on his debut at Bath, but he has struggled in better company since and does not seem to be progressing. To be fair, he might be happier back over 5f on quick ground. (op 5-2)

Kentish Dream's trainer said he felt this one would be best suited by 6f on an easy surface after he won a quick-ground 7f maiden at Lingfield, so this has to be considered a rather disappointing effort. (op 2-1)

4686 DENNEY O'HARA (S) H'CAP — 5f

2:45 (2:46) (Class 6) (0-65,62) 3-Y-O — **£2,590** (£770; £385; £192) **Stalls** Low

Form — RPR

3004 **1** — **Dalarossie**[14] 4242 3-9-5 **60** ... ShaneKelly 12 — 67
(E J Alston) *led far side gp and cl up: rdn and overall ldr wl over 1f out: clr whn edgd lft ins fnl f: kpt on fin 1st in gp* **12/1**

4055 **2** *1 3/4* **Gelert (IRE)**[8] 4450 3-8-5 **46** ...(b) PatrickMathers 14 — 47
(Peter Grayson) *chsd wnr far side: rdn along 2f out: drvn and kpt on ins fnl f: 2nd in gp* **20/1**

5660 **3** *1/2* **Curio**[16] 4207 3-8-4 **45** ...(p) PaulQuinn 15 — 44
(R M Whitaker) *hld up far side: hdwy 2f out: sn rdn and styd on wl fnl f: 3rd in gp* **12/1**

4633 **4** *2 1/4* **Andrasta**[8] 4450 3-8-8 **49** ... PaulHanagan 5 — 40+
(A Berry) *cl up stands' side: rdn and ev ch 2f out: drvn and one pce appr fnl f: 1st in gp* **7/2**[2]

5035 **5** *1* **Foxy Jane**[32] 3638 3-8-12 **53** ... TWilliams 6 — 40+
(M Brittain) *dwlt and towards rr stands' side tl styd on appr fnl f: nrst fin: 2nd in gp* **12/1**

2550 **6** *shd* **Linnet Park**[15] 4216 3-8-11 **52** ... J-PGuillambert 4 — 39+
(J G Given) *cl up stands' side: rdn to ld that gp and overall ldr briefly 2f out: sn drvn and hdd: kpt on same pce: 3rd in gp* **8/1**[3]

0454 **7** *1/2* **Imperial Djay (IRE)**[19] 4076 3-9-7 **62** ...(v) StephenDonohoe 13 — 47
(D Carroll) *chsd ldng pair far side: rdn along 2f out: wknd wl over 1f out: 3rd in gp* **10/1**

5000 **7** *dht* **Cool Fashion (IRE)**[21] 4028 3-8-5 **46** ...(b) RoystonFfrench 3 — 31+
(Ollie Pears) *dwlt: in tch stands' side: rdn along 2f out: sn one pce: 3rd in gp* **28/1**

6000 **9** *nk* **Mill Creek**[12] 4294 3-8-4 **45** ... AndrewElliott 2 — 29
(Jedd O'Keeffe) *cl up stands' side: rdn along 1/2-way: grad wknd: 5th in gp* **66/1**

6000 **10** *3/4* **Abitofafath (IRE)**[15] 4216 3-8-10 **51** ...(b) DeanMcKeown 9 — 32
(J G Given) *cl up stands' side: rdn along over 2f out and sn wknd: 6th in gp* **33/1**

4000 **11** *3/4* **Orange Square (IRE)**[15] 4216 3-8-10 **51** ...(p) TonyHamilton 1 — 30
(D W Barker) *overall ldr stands' side: rdn along 1/2-way: hdd 2f out and sn wknd: 7th in gp* **25/1**

0-00 **12** *6* **Whispering Desert**[63] 2660 3-9-4 **59** ... FrankieMcDonald 11 — 16
(P T Midgley) *in tch stands' side: rdn along 1/2-way: sn wknd: 11th in gp* **28/1**

0020 **13** *7* **Swift Acclaim (IRE)**[14] 4242 3-7-12 **46** ...(v) DeclanCannon(7) 8 — —
(K R Burke) *in tch stands' side: rdn along 1/2-way: sn wknd: 9th in gp* **12/1**

1004 **14** *2 1/4* **Arkando (IRE)**[149] 835 3-8-9 **50** ...(b) DarrenWilliams 10 — —
(K R Burke) *s.i.s: a in rr stands' side: 10th in gp* **50/1**

3232 **15** *10* **Fast Feet**[21] 4028 3-9-5 **60** ...(p) JamieSpencer 7 — —
(K A Ryan) *cl up stands' side: rdn along 1/2-way: sn wknd and eased* **3/1**[1]

60.60 secs (-0.10) **Going Correction** +0.075s/f (Good) — **15** Ran SP% **120.1**

Speed ratings (Par 98): **103,100,99,95,94 94,93,93,92,91 90,80,69,65,49**

toteswinger: 1&2 £55.80, 1&3 £41.10, 2&3 £58.60. CSF £235.01 CT £1764.43 TOTE £14.70: £4.20, £5.20, £4.60; EX 378.90 TRIFECTA Not won. ..There was no bid for the winner.

Owner Liam & Tony Ferguson **Bred** Liam & Tony Ferguson **Trained** Longton, Lancs

FOCUS

Moderate form, as one would expect in a selling handicap, and there was clearly a draw/pace bias, so the form needs treating with real caution. Only four raced far side (remainder middle to near side), but they dominated, filling the first three placings. It is hard to rate the bare form any more positively.

Foxy Jane Official explanation: trainer said filly was unsuited by the soft ground and the track

Fast Feet Official explanation: jockey said gelding boiled over prior to race

4687 ARMSTRONG MEMORIAL H'CAP — 6f

3:15 (3:18) (Class 3) (0-95,95) 3-Y-O+

£9,346 (£2,799; £1,399; £700; £349; £175) **Stalls** Low

Form — RPR

0460 **1** — **Bond City (IRE)**[4] 4555 6-8-13 **86** ... PJMcDonald(3) 10 — 97
(G R Oldroyd) *prom far side: effrt 2f out: rdn over 1f out: styd on to ld and overall ldr wl ins fnl f: 1st in gp* **14/1**

4410 **2** *3/4* **Harbour Blues**[20] 4058 3-8-10 **84** ...(t) CatherineGannon 5 — 92
(A W Carroll) *cl up stands' side: led and overall ldr over 2f out and sn rdn: drvn over 1f out: hdd and no ex wl ins fnl f: fin 1st in gp* **20/1**

0213 **3** *3/4* **Grazeon Gold Blend**[8] 4460 5-8-8 **78** ... PaulMulrennan 1 — 85
(J J Quinn) *overall ldr stands' side: pushed along and hdd over 2f out: sn rdn and ev ch tl drvn and no ex ins fnl f 2nd in gp* **12/1**

1210 **4** *1 3/4* **Great Charm (IRE)**[26] 3850 3-9-1 **89** ... JamieSpencer 9 — 89
(M L W Bell) *led far side gp and cl up: rdn along 2f out: drvn over 1f out: wknd ins fnl f 2nd in gp* **2/1**[1]

0502 **5** *1 1/2* **Prior Warning**[25] 3881 4-9-6 **95** ...(t) MCGeran(5) 4 — 91
(Miss D Mountain) *chsd ldng pair stands' side: effrt 2f out: sn rdn and ch over 1f out: kpt on same pce: 3rd in gp* **8/1**[3]

0014 **6** *hd* **Geojimali**[22] 3998 6-9-0 **84** ... DanielTudhope 8 — 80+
(J S Goldie) *s.i.s and rr far side tl hdwy wl over 1f out: sn rdn and kpt on ins fnl f: 3rd in gp* **8/1**[3]

0005 **7** *1/2* **Fantasy Believer**[10] 4375 10-8-6 **76** oh1 ... PaulHanagan 2 — 70
(J J Quinn) *chsd ldrs stands' side: hdwy 2f out: sn rdn and kpt on same pce appr fnl f: 4th in gp* **16/1**

5660 **8** *1 1/4* **Malcheek (IRE)**[9] 4437 6-8-12 **82** ... TomEaves 11 — 72
(T D Easterby) *chsd ldrs far side: rdn along 2f out: sn no imp: 4th in gp* **9/1**

0005 **9** *hd* **Ajigolo**[3] 4586 5-9-7 **91** ... DarryllHolland 6 — 80
(M R Channon) *chsd ldrs far side: rdn along over 2f out and sn wknd: 5th in gp* **11/2**[2]

5000 **10** *6* **Final Verse**[16] 4188 5-9-9 **93** ... JohnEgan 3 — 63
(Jane Chapple-Hyam) *swtchd to far side after 1f: prom tl rdn along 2f out and sn wknd - 6th in gp* **10/1**

1m 12.86s (-0.14) **Going Correction** +0.075s/f (Good)

WFA 3 from 4yo+ 4lb — **10** Ran SP% **115.0**

Speed ratings (Par 107): **103,102,101,98,96 96,95,94,93,85**

toteswinger: 1&2 £42.30, 1&3 £22.40, 2&3 £26.00. CSF £243.44 CT £3022.58 TOTE £15.30: £3.90, £5.90, £2.60; EX 300.80 Trifecta £492.10 Part won. Pool: £665.09 - 0.10 winning units..

Owner R C Bond **Bred** David Ryan **Trained** Brawby, N Yorks

■ Ingleby Arch (11/1) was withdrawn after breaking out of the stalls. Deduct 5p in the £ under rule 4.

■

FOCUS

In the preceding 5f seller those on the far side were at a huge advantage but, over this extra furlong, in a smaller field, there seemed to be no bias. The winner again raced far side, but the next two raced near side. This looked a fair sprint handicap and the winner took advantage of a good mark, rated to this year's form.

NOTEBOOK

Bond City(IRE) was 13lb lower than when last successful in 2006 and, with the headgear left off and stepped back up in trip, he returned to form to end a 26-race losing run. This should have helped his confidence and he is likely to stick to 6f for the time being, but he has never followed up a success.

Harbour Blues ran much better than at Great Leighs on his previous start, faring best of those on the stands' side. (op 18-1 tchd 33-1)

Grazeon Gold Blend again looked to run right up to form, coming out second best on the near side. (op 9-1)

Great Charm(IRE) did not run badly, but he was unable to justify a very short price and probably wants even easier ground. (op 7-2)

Prior Warning could not quite match the form he showed when second at Newmarket on his previous start, but this was still a respectable effort. (op 7-1 tchd 6-1)

Geojimali Official explanation: jockey said gelding missed the break

Ajigolo failed to give his running and was rather disappointing. (tchd 6-1)

Final Verse Official explanation: jockey said gelding lost its action

4688 WEATHERBYS BLOODSTOCK INSURANCE H'CAP — 1m 1f 170y

3:45 (3:46) (Class 4) (0-85,84) 3-Y-O+ **£4,731** (£1,416; £708; £354; £176) **Stalls** High

Form — RPR

5422 **1** — **Demolition**[47] 3143 4-9-2 **77** ... AshleyHamblett(5) 1 — 84
(N Wilson) *chsd ldr: hdwy over 2f out: rdn to chal over 1f out: led ent fnl f: sn drvn and kpt on* **9/2**[2]

0424 **2** *1/2* **Ella Woodcock (IRE)**[4] 4565 4-9-10 **80** ... ShaneKelly 2 — 86
(E J Alston) *trckd ldrs: hdwy over 2f out: rdn to chal over 1f out: drvn and ev ch ins fnl f: no ex towards fin* **4/1**[1]

1210 **3** *1 1/4* **Buddy Holly**[30] 3745 3-9-2 **81** ... PatDobbs 4 — 84+
(Pat Eddery) *trckd ldrs on inner: hdwy wl over 2f out: effrt and nt clr run over 1f out: swtchd lft and rdn ent fnl f: styd on to take 3rd nr line* **4/1**[1]

0020 **4** *1/2* **Nuit Sombre (IRE)**[14] 4245 8-9-2 **72** ...(p) SilvestreDeSousa 9 — 74
(G A Harker) *led: rdn along 2f out: drvn over 1f out: hdd & wknd ent fnl f* **10/1**

-060 **5** *1 1/2* **Flight To Quality**[16] 4206 3-8-7 **72** ... GregFairley 3 — 71
(M Johnston) *chsd ldrs: rdn along over 2f out: drvn wl over 1f out and kpt on same pce* **14/1**

3001 **6** *1/2* **Jafra (IRE)**[14] 4244 3-8-0 **65** oh1 ...(p) PaulQuinn 7 — 63
(R M Whitaker) *hld up towards rr: effrt on inner over 2f out and sn rdn along: styd on u.p appr fnl f: nrst fin* **9/1**

1505 **7** *2* **Veiled Applause**[43] 3294 5-9-7 **84** ... JamieKyne(7) 6 — 78
(J J Quinn) *dwlt: hld up in rr: hdwy on outer 3f out: rdn to chse ldrs wl over 1f out: sn drvn and wknd ent fnl f* **5/1**[3]

0020 **8** *1* **Folio (IRE)**[18] 4131 8-9-7 **77** ... StephenDonohoe 5 — 69
(W J Musson) *hld up towards rr: effrt and sme hdwy 2f out: sn rdn and btn over 1f out* **12/1**

530- **9** *11* **Go Tech**[275] 6185 8-9-9 **79** ... PaulMulrennan 8 — 48
(T D Easterby) *prom: hdwy to chse ldr 1/2-way: rdn along wl over 2f out and sn wknd* **20/1**

2m 4.69s (-0.71) **Going Correction** +0.075s/f (Good)

WFA 3 from 4yo+ 9lb — **9** Ran SP% **113.1**

Speed ratings (Par 105): **105,104,103,103,102 101,100,99,90**

toteswinger: 1&2 £2.50, 1&3 £4.70, 2&3 £4.00. CSF £22.32 CT £76.40 TOTE £3.80: £1.70, £1.60, £1.60; EX 18.50 Trifecta £73.10 Pool: 658.15 - 6.66 winning units..

Owner M Wormald **Bred** P D And Mrs Player **Trained** Flaxton, N Yorks

FOCUS

A fair handicap run at an ordinary pace. The form is rated through the second and third.

4689 BLACK SHEEP BREWERY MAIDEN STKS — 1m 4f 10y

4:15 (4:17) (Class 5) 3-Y-O+ — **£2,914** (£867; £433; £216) **Stalls** High

Form — RPR

452 **1** — **Kossack**[18] 4124 3-9-3 85 ... JamieSpencer 3 — 82+
(L M Cumani) *hld up in tch: hdwy over 4f out: rdn to ld over 2f out: hung rt wl over 1f out: rdn out* **2/5**[1]

4 **2** *6* **Sibi Saba (USA)**[14] 4249 3-8-12 0 ... TedDurcan 10 — 69+
(Saeed Bin Suroor) *prom: hdwy to chse ldr 4f out: sn led: rdn along and hdd over 2f out: n.m.r wl over 1f out: sn one pce* **6/1**[2]

00- **3** *3 1/2* **Babilu**[311] 5770 3-8-11 0 ow2 ... LeeVickers(3) 1 — 61
(J G Given) *hld up towards rr: stdy hdwy on outer 3f out: rdn to chse ldrs wl over 1f out: kpt on ins fnl f: nrst fin* **200/1**

34 **4** *3* **Almonafis (IRE)**[18] 4124 3-9-3 0 ...(v[1]) PatDobbs 8 — 59
(Sir Michael Stoute) *t.k.h: chsd ldrs: hdwy over 3f out: rdn and ev ch over 2f out: sn drvn and wknd wl over 1f out* **6/1**[2]

0-2 **5** *1/2* **Bollin Greta**[55] 2912 3-8-12 0 ... PaulHanagan 7 — 53
(T D Easterby) *t.k.h: hld up in tch: hdwy to chse ldrs wl over 2f out: sn rdn along: edgd rt and kpt on same pce* **16/1**[3]

6 *shd* **Poppy Day**[92] 5-9-2 0 ... NSLawes(7) 9 — 53
(M W Easterby) *s.i.s and bhd: hdwy over 2f out: rdn and styd on appr fnl f: nrst fin* **200/1**

00 **7** *5* **Unawatuna**[17] 4166 3-8-12 0 ... GregFairley 12 — 45
(Mrs K Walton) *a towards rr* **200/1**

0 **8** *1/2* **Baileys Benchmark**[162] 694 3-8-12 0 ... J-PGuillambert 14 — 49+
(J G Given) *towards rr: rdn along 4f out: nvr a factor* **66/1**

04 **9** *2* **Doctor Delta**[61] 2735 3-9-3 0 ... TWilliams 5 — 46
(M Brittain) *in tch on inner: rdn along over 3f out and grad wknd* **100/1**

00 **10** *1 1/4* **Our Nations**[18] 4124 3-9-3 0 StephenDonohoe 2 44
(D Carroll) *a towards rr* **250/1**

4 **11** *10* **Fell Pack**[10] 4378 4-10-0 0 PaulMulrennan 6 28
(J J Quinn) *in tch: effrt on outer over 3f out: sn rdn along and wknd over 2f out* **80/1**

3005 **12** *14* **Ducal Regancy Duke**[17] 4148 4-10-0 50 DanielTudhope 4 6
(C J Teague) *led after 2f: rdn along and hdd over 3f out: sn wknd* **200/1**

0 **13** *1 3/4* **Sherbet Lemon**[66] 2573 3-8-12 0 TomEaves 11 —
(Miss J A Camacho) *a in rr* **80/1**

00 **14** *36* **Lighting Shadow**[10] 4378 3-8-12 0 (b[1]) AshleyHamblett(5) 13 —
(N Wilson) *led 2f: prom tl rdn along and wknd 4f out* **300/1**

2m 39.46s (2.76) **Going Correction** +0.075s/f (Good)
WFA 3 from 4yo+ 11lb **14** Ran SP% **113.6**
Speed ratings (Par 103): **93,89,86,84,84 84,80,80,79,78 71,62,61,37**
toteswinger: 1&2 £2.60, 1&3 £23.50, 2&3 £54.50. CSF £3.00 TOTE £1.40: £1.10, £1.50, £19.70; EX 3.30 Trifecta £406.60 Pool: £ 989.04 - 1.80 winning units..
Owner Fittocks Stud & Mrs John Magnier **Bred** Fittocks Stud **Trained** Newmarket, Suffolk

FOCUS
A weak, uncompetitive maiden. They went steady early and the winning time was 3.30 seconds slower than the following 51-70 handicap. The comfortable winner did not have a great deal to beat and the third holds the form down.
Baileys Benchmark Official explanation: jockey said filly ran green
Fell Pack Official explanation: jockey said gelding hung left-handed throughout

4690 CHILDREN'S DAY H'CAP 1m 4f 10y
4:45 (4:47) (Class 5) (0-70,70) 3-Y-O+ **£2,914** (£867; £433; £216) **Stalls** High

Form RPR

0614 **1** **Fossgate**[6] 4501 7-9-2 58 DarryllHolland 7 74
(J D Bethell) *trckd ldr: hdwy to ld over 2f out: rdn 2f out and sn wl clr: rdn out* **4/1**[3]

0062 **2** *11* **Parkview Love (USA)**[7] 4477 7-8-11 56 LeeVickers(3) 2 54
(J G Given) *hld up in tch: hdwy 4f out: rdn to chse ldng apir wl over 2f out: drvn and kpt on to take 2nd ent fnl f: no ch w wnr* **9/1**

1431 **3** *2* **Master Nimbus**[8] 4457 8-9-6 62 6ex PaulHanagan 4 57
(J J Quinn) *led: rdn along 4f out: hdd over 3f out: drvn and one pce fnl 2f* **9/4**[1]

4514 **4** *2 1/2* **Great View (IRE)**[11] 4343 9-9-7 70 (p) KylieManser(7) 1 61
(Mrs A L M King) *t.k.h: hld up towards rr: effrt and sme hdwy 4f out: rdn along 3f out and n.d* **14/1**

4315 **5** *4 1/2* **Dan Tucker**[8] 4458 4-9-6 69 AndreaAtzeni(7) 3 53
(N Tinkler) *hld up towards rr: hdwy on outer over 3f out: rdn over 2f out: sn drvn and wknd* **7/2**[2]

466 **6** *3/4* **Amical Risks (FR)**[69] 2483 4-8-13 55 StephenDonohoe 8 38
(W J Musson) *s.i.s: a bhd* **8/1**

0343 **7** *35* **Orphan (IRE)**[3] 4597 6-8-9 54 PJMcDonald(3) 5 —
(G M Moore) *chsd ldng pair: rdn along over 2f out: sn wknd and bhd whn eased over 1f out* **8/1**

2m 36.16s (-0.54) **Going Correction** +0.075s/f (Good)
WFA 3 from 4yo+ 11lb **7** Ran SP% **111.9**
Speed ratings (Par 103): **104,96,95,93,90 90,66**
toteswinger: 1&2 £5.60, 1&3 £3.00, 2&3 £4.30. CSF £36.75 CT £97.33 TOTE £4.20: £2.40, £3.80; EX 26.20 Trifecta £90.00 Pool: £760.26 - 6.25 winning units. Place 6: £15857.50 Place 5: £1119.20.
Owner Mrs James Bethell **Bred** Mrs P A Clark **Trained** Middleham Moor, N Yorks

FOCUS
A modest handicap and, despite the pace appearing to be quite strong, very few got involved. The winning time was 3.30 seconds quicker than the previous maiden. Fossgate won by a wide margin and is rated pretty much back to his best.
Orphan(IRE) Official explanation: jockey said gelding failed to stay the one and a half miles
T/Plt: £2,347.70 to a £1 stake. Pool: £73,325.95. 22.80 winning tickets. T/Qpdt: £25.00 to a £1 stake. Pool: £6,567.19. 194.30 winning tickets. JR

4480 WINDSOR (R-H)
Monday, August 4

OFFICIAL GOING: Good to soft (good in places; 7.2)
Wind: Moderate, behind Weather: Fine but cloudy

4691 BOLLINGER CHAMPAGNE CHALLENGE SERIES H'CAP (FOR GENTLEMAN AMATEUR RIDERS) 1m 3f 135y
6:00 (6:01) (Class 5) (0-75,75) 3-Y-O+ **£2,637** (£811; £405) **Stalls** Low

Form RPR

5523 **1** **Sand Repeal (IRE)**[7] 4490 6-9-11 56 oh1 MrRBirkett(5) 7 65
(Miss J Feilden) *trckd ldr: led over 3f out and kicked on: rdn and jnd wl over 1f out: kpt on wl* **13/2**

4042 **2** *3/4* **Spanish Diva**[7] 4481 4-10-13 67 MrSWalker 8 75
(S C Williams) *hld up in midfield: prog to go 3rd over 4f out: wnt 2nd over 2f out and sn chalng wnr: hanging lft and fnd nil fr over 1f out* **7/4**[1]

000 **3** *6* **A One (IRE)**[9] 4428 9-9-9 56 oh11 MrECookson(7) 6 54
(H J Manners) *led: clr w wnr 4f out: hdd over 3f out: lost 2nd over 2f out: jst hld on for 3rd* **80/1**

0435 **4** *1/2* **Converti**[7] 4485 4-9-9 56 oh6 MrDRBass(7) 1 53
(H J Manners) *hld up in rr: rdn over 4f out: sme prog u.p fr 3f out: nvr rchd ldrs* **20/1**

2506 **5** *1/2* **Wyeth**[32] 3650 4-10-1 60 (b[1]) MrJoshuaMoore(5) 5 56
(G L Moore) *trckd ldrs: rdn over 4f out: sn outpcd: one pce and no imp u.p after* **11/2**[3]

0/4- **6** *1 1/4* **Neutrino**[138] 4333 6-10-10 67 (p) MrMJJSmith(3) 4 61
(D G Bridgwater) *hld up towards rr: rdn and struggling over 4f out: modest late prog under individualistic handling* **40/1**

-026 **7** *hd* **Trawlerman (IRE)**[12] 4303 3-10-4 74 ow3 MrJAkehurst(5) 12 68
(M H Tompkins) *hld up: prog to go 4th 1/2-way: outpcd over 4f out: struggling after: plugged on* **16/1**

0660 **8** *3/4* **Calculating (IRE)**[16] 4193 4-11-7 75 MrLeeNewnes 2 67
(M D I Usher) *towards rr: rdn and lost tch 5f out: plugged on but nvr on terms* **7/2**[2]

2203 **9** *3* **Turner's Touch**[10] 4371 6-10-9 68 (b) SamHanson(5) 11 55
(G L Moore) *hld up wl in rr: sme prog over 4f out: rdn and no rspnse 3f out: no ch after* **10/1**

25-0 **10** *16* **Sharmy (IRE)**[18] 4123 12-9-9 56 oh4 MrJRavenall(7) 10 16
(Ian Williams) *in tch tl wknd over 4f out: t.o* **33/1**

122- **11** *6* **Boot 'n Toot**[15] 5422 7-11-1 69 MrSDobson 13 19
(M Sheppard) *hld up in rr: lost tch 1/2-way: sn wl bhd: t.o* **14/1**

-000 **12** *4 1/2* **Amanda's Lad (IRE)**[7] 4476 8-9-11 58 oh11 ow2 MrHSensoy(7) 3 —
(M C Chapman) *plld hrd: prom 4f: wd bnd over 6f out and sn lost pl bdly: t.o 4f out* **100/1**

0/0 **13** *1/2* **Deo Gratias (POL)**[10] 4365 8-9-9 56 oh11 (p) MrSamPainting(7) 9 —
(Carl Llewellyn) *hld up: a bhd: t.o 4f out* **66/1**

2m 34.79s (5.29) **Going Correction** +0.20s/f (Good)
WFA 3 from 4yo+ 11lb **13** Ran SP% **122.8**
Speed ratings (Par 103): **90,89,85,85,84 84,83,83,81,70 66,63,63**
toteswinger: 1&2 £3.50, 1&3 £68.30, 2&3 Not won. CSF £18.09 CT £883.74 TOTE £9.20: £2.60, £1.10, £20.40; EX 23.60.
Owner The Sultans of Speed **Bred** Don Commins **Trained** Exning, Suffolk

FOCUS
A typically moderate contest for amateur riders and the form is highly contentious with the third, officially rated 35, running from 21lb wrong. The winner ran to this year's turf form.

4692 E B F THEATRE ROYAL WINDSOR "SEE HOW THEY RUN" MAIDEN FILLIES' STKS 6f
6:30 (6:34) (Class 4) 2-Y-O **£5,569** (£1,657; £828; £413) **Stalls** High

Form RPR

22 **1** **Acquiesced (IRE)**[10] 4359 2-9-0 0 RyanMoore 8 77
(R Hannon) *w ldr: led over 3f out: rdn over 2f out: narrow ld fnl f and drifted to far side: jst hld on* **4/11**[1]

0 **2** *nse* **Dubai Legend**[19] 4080 2-9-0 0 MartinDwyer 7 77
(D M Simcock) *trckd ldrs: effrt over 2f out: chsd wnr wl over 1f out: drifted to far rail: upsides fnl f: jst pipped* **20/1**

3 *3 1/4* **Lady Rusty (IRE)** 2-9-0 0 JimCrowley 11 70+
(P Winkworth) *chsd ldrs but sn pushed along: outpcd over 2f out: picked up over 1f out: r.o to take 3rd last 50yds* **20/1**

4 *1/2* **Port De La Ponche** 2-9-0 0 NelsonDeSouza 6 66+
(P F I Cole) *w ldrs: pressed wnr over 2f out: one pce over 1f out* **16/1**[3]

6 **5** *1/2* **Ageebah**[19] 4088 2-9-0 0 EddieAhern 4 64
(C E Brittain) *w ldrs: taken to far side 1/2-way: on terms 2f out: grad fdd* **16/1**[3]

00 **6** *1 1/2* **Heartsease**[25] 3869 2-9-0 0 PatCosgrave 12 60
(J G Portman) *led to over 3f out: outpcd 2f out: steadily fdd* **33/1**

00 **7** *4* **Costa Lotta**[17] 4149 2-9-0 0 TQuinn 2 48
(E A L Dunlop) *w ldrs: taken to far side 1/2-way: wknd wl over 1f out* **33/1**

8 *3/4* **Lady Lu** 2-9-0 0 TedDurcan 16 45
(P F I Cole) *dwlt: sn midfield: pushed along and outpcd 2f out: fdd fnl f* **16/1**[3]

0 **9** *3 1/4* **Queens Forester**[41] 3348 2-8-7 0 DTDaSilva(7) 9 36
(P F I Cole) *rn green in rr: nvr on terms w ldrs* **100/1**

5 **10** *shd* **Giverny (IRE)**[7] 4482 2-9-0 0 ShaneKelly 14 35
(J Noseda) *dwlt: rcvrd and wl in tch in midfield: outpcd over 2f out: wknd over 1f out* **12/1**[2]

00 **11** *1 3/4* **Lily Waters**[17] 4149 2-9-0 0 LiamJones 3 30
(W M Brisbourne) *s.s: a towards rr: outpcd over 2f out* **100/1**

12 *3/4* **Laraffelle (GR)** 2-9-0 0 JimmyFortune 10 28
(E A L Dunlop) *spd over 2f: sn lost pl: grad wknd* **25/1**

13 *1 1/4* **Santoriney (IRE)** 2-8-7 0 RobbieEgan(7) 5 24
(D Flood) *rn green and reminders in rr after 1f: nvr a factor* **80/1**

14 *2 1/2* **Autumn Morning (IRE)** 2-9-0 0 StephenCarson 1 17
(Eve Johnson Houghton) *s.s: hld up in last: hanging bdly lft 2f out: a bhd* **50/1**

06 **15** *6* **Sister Clement (IRE)**[13] 4274 2-9-0 0 JamieSpencer 13 —
(C R Egerton) *dwlt: rcvrd and in tch after 2f: wknd rapidly 2f out* **20/1**

1m 15.02s (2.02) **Going Correction** +0.20s/f (Good) **15** Ran SP% **127.8**
Speed ratings (Par 93): **94,93,89,88,88 86,80,79,75,75 73,72,70,67,59**
toteswinger: 1&2 £3.90, 1&3 £4.00, 2&3 £41.80. CSF £15.05 TOTE £1.30: £1.10, £4.00, £4.30; EX 12.90.
Owner Mrs J Wood **Bred** Thurso Limited **Trained** East Everleigh, Wilts

FOCUS
This course often stages some very warm maiden events and this could go down as no more than an average contest, although that is not to say that there isn't plenty of promise amongst the fillies who took part. The winner is rated to form.

NOTEBOOK
Acquiesced(IRE) was heavily backed despite opening up at odds-on, but only managed to gain the day by the narrowest of margins. She didn't run up to the bare form of her previous runner-up efforts but connections feel that she made have been idling after having been in front for much of the way. (op 8-13 tchd 4-6 in places)
Dubai Legend ◆ had debuted in a warm little maiden for the course at Kempton last month and gave those who had taken the prohibitive odds about the winner the fright of their lives by going inches away from running her down. The daughter of Cadeaux Genereux is sure to win races. (op 25-1)
Lady Rusty(IRE) ◆'s yard do quietly well with their juveniles, and at this course in particular, and this daughter of Verglas showed a lot of promise on debut by keeping on well to snatch a place after getting a little outpaced 2f out. She should know more next time. (op 25-1)
Port De La Ponche knew her job and was always up in the vanguard. She kept on well enough without being able to go with the front pair and should do better as she strengthens up. (op 28-1 tchd 33-1)
Ageebah showed signs of ability in what was a very good maiden for the track on the all-weather at Lingfield on her debut, and after showing up with every chance two furlongs out confirmed that impression here. She is one to bear in mind when qualified for nurseries. (op 20-1)
Heartsease cut out the early running before fading. Tried over a different trip on each of her three starts, she is now eligible for a handicap mark and it will be interesting to see over what distance connections choose to run her over next.
Autumn Morning(IRE) Official explanation: jockey said filly hung badly left-handed throughout; vet said filly had a sore in right corner of mouth

4693 ANGELA CHIGNALL BIRTHDAY H'CAP 5f 10y
7:00 (7:02) (Class 5) (0-75,79) 3-Y-O+ **£2,934** (£866; £433) **Stalls** High

Form RPR

353 **1** **Matterofact (IRE)**[10] 4370 5-8-5 59 TolleyDean(3) 4 72
(M S Saunders) *cl up: led 2f out: hrd pressed fr over 1f out: kpt on wl nr fin* **15/2**

-413 **2** *hd* **Make My Dream**[12] 4313 5-9-3 68 TPO'Shea 3 80
(J Gallagher) *settled in rr: rdn and prog fr 1/2-way: clsd on ldng pair 1f out: kpt on fnl f: jst hld* **6/1**[3]

4622 **3** *nse* **Equuleus Pictor**[10] 4370 4-8-13 69 JackDean(5) 5 81
(J L Spearing) *trckd ldrs: effrt to chal 2f out: w wnr over 1f out: nt qckn nr fin* **2/1**[1]

6510 **4** *5* **Cape Royal**[1] 4668 8-10-0 79 6ex (bt) PatCosgrave 15 73+
(J M Bradley) *blindfold removed as stalls opened and nt that wl away: chsd ldrs: styd alone towards nr side after 2f: lft bhd sn after: modest 4th ins fnl f* **6/1**[3]

2060 **5** *1 ¾* **Jayanjay**[21] 4025 9-8-5 **56** oh3..............................(v) MartinDwyer 12 44
(B R Johnson) *chsd ldrs: lft bhd fr 2f out: no ch after: sddle slipped* **16/1**
0043 **6** *3 ½* **Woodcote (IRE)**[21] 4025 6-9-9 **74**..............................(tp) JimCrowley 14 49
(P R Chamings) *led to 1/2-way: wknd rapidly over 1f out* **5/1**[2]
0000 **7** *4 ½* **Classic Encounter (IRE)**[12] 4291 5-9-10 **75**.............. FergusSweeney 6 34
(D M Simcock) *taken down early: w ldr: led 1/2-way to 2f out: wknd rapidly over 1f out* **16/1**
4062 **8** *hd* **Twosheetstothewind**[107] 1476 4-8-12 **63**.............................. LPKeniry 9 21
(C R Dore) *dwlt: in tch in rr to 1/2-way: sn wknd* **16/1**
1000 **9** *½* **Bertbrand**[21] 4030 3-8-11 **72**..............................(b) RobbieEgan(7) 8 28
(D Flood) *chsd ldrs: rdn 1/2-way: sn wknd* **28/1**
1-34 **10** *nk* **A Wish For You**[190] 324 3-9-4 **72**.............................. RichardKingscote 2 27
(D K Ivory) *a in rr: in tch to 1/2-way: sn wknd and bhd* **28/1**

60.56 secs (0.26) **Going Correction** +0.20s/f (Good)
WFA 3 from 4yo+ 3lb **10** Ran SP% **114.9**
Speed ratings (Par 103): **105,104,104,96,93 88,81,80,79,79**
toteswinger: 1&2 £7.60, 1&3 £7.80, 2&3 £3.20. CSF £51.21 CT £121.87 TOTE £10.20: £2.90, £1.80, £1.30; EX 58.40.
Owner Prempro Racing **Bred** Tony Gleeson **Trained** Green Ore, Somerset

FOCUS
Some fair sorts on show at the top end of the weights but essentially this was a moderate handicap, and the protagonists tend to win in their turn. The first three finished clear but seemed favoured by racing on the far rail. The winner is rated back to last year's best with the second up 6lb.
Jayanjay Official explanation: jockey said saddle slipped

4694 TALKSPORT 1089/1053 AM H'CAP — 1m 67y
7:30 (7:31) (Class 4) (0-85,85) 3-Y-0+ **£5,698** (£1,695; £847; £423) **Stalls** High

Form RPR
126 **1** **Born Tobouggie (GER)**[72] 2412 3-9-7 **83**.............................. TedDurcan 4 95
(H R A Cecil) *hld up in last pair: first over to far side in st and grabbed rail: prog 2f out: rdn to ld ent fnl f: r.o wl* **6/1**
1221 **2** *1 ¼* **Willow Dancer (IRE)**[12] 4310 4-9-13 **82**..............................(p) AdamKirby 12 92
(W R Swinburn) *sweating: trckd ldng pair: led wl over 2f out: hanging lft wl over 1f out: hdd ent fnl f: styd on same pce* **7/2**[2]
031 **3** *3* **Fountains Abbey (USA)**[28] 3801 3-9-4 **80**.............................. RyanMoore 1 82
(Sir Michael Stoute) *trckd ldr: upsides 3f out: nt qckn 2f out: one pce fr over 1f out* **3/1**[1]
1 **4** *nse* **Summerstrand (IRE)**[17] 4161 3-9-5 **81**.............................. PhilipRobinson 9 86+
(M A Jarvis) *dwlt: t.k.h: hld up in midfield: rdn and nt qckn over 2f out: effrt over 1f out: sn outpcd: kpt on* **4/1**[3]
4215 **5** *nk* **Formation (USA)**[24] 3896 3-9-9 **85**.............................. JamieSpencer 8 86
(E A L Dunlop) *hld up in last: rdn and prog over 2f out: chsd ldrs and in tch over 1f out: fnd nil and sn btn* **7/1**
3644 **6** *2 ½* **Phluke**[25] 3887 7-10-0 **83**.............................. StephenCarson 5 80
(Eve Johnson Houghton) *led at mod pce: hdd and nt qckn wl over 2f out: breif rally wl over 1f out: wknd fnl f* **16/1**
0406 **7** *2 ¾* **Master Pegasus**[102] 1585 5-9-8 **77**.............................. PatCosgrave 10 67
(J R Boyle) *trckd ldng trio: rdn and lost pl over 2f out: wknd* **33/1**
0521 **8** *2 ¼* **Run For Ede'S**[21] 4022 4-8-12 **67**..............................(p) IanMongan 11 52
(P M Phelan) *t.k.h: hld up towards rr: prog over 3f out: rdn over 2f out: sn wknd* **17/2**

1m 47.37s (2.67) **Going Correction** +0.20s/f (Good)
WFA 3 from 4yo+ 7lb **8** Ran SP% **113.4**
Speed ratings (Par 105): **94,92,89,89,89 86,84,81**
toteswinger: 1&2 £4.70, 1&3 £10.30, 2&3 £2.50. CSF £26.79 CT £75.27 TOTE £7.00: £2.30, £1.60, £1.80; EX 24.60.
Owner The Sticky Wicket Syndicate **Bred** Graf Und Grafin Von Stauffenberg **Trained** Newmarket, Suffolk

FOCUS
A very useful handicap and with the first four home consisting of three lighty-raced fillies possessing bags of potential for improvement and a consistent sort in the runner-up berth, the form looks pretty solid. On the downside the pace was only steady and the winner was probably helped by being first to the far rail.

4695 BODY FIRM HEALTH AND BEAUTY MAIDEN STKS — 1m 2f 7y
8:00 (8:03) (Class 5) 3-4-Y-0 **£2,729** (£806; £403) **Stalls** Low

Form RPR
2- **1** **Island Vista**[332] 5202 3-8-12 0.............................. PhilipRobinson 13 77+
(M A Jarvis) *trckd ldng trio: rdn over 2f out: wnt 3rd over 1f out: sustained effrt fnl f to ld last 50yds* **9/2**[3]
-2 **2** *½* **Duncan**[17] 4161 3-9-3 0.............................. EddieAhern 10 81+
(J L Dunlop) *pressed ldr: chal fr over 2f out: fnlly led jst over 1f out: hdd and nt qckn last 50yds* **5/4**[1]
3 *½* **Wellington Square** 3-9-3 0.............................. SteveDrowne 2 80+
(H Morrison) *hld up wl in rr and wl off the pce: prog fr 3f out but stl plenty to do: hanging lft fr over 1f out but fin strly* **40/1**
5-33 **4** *½* **Moville (IRE)**[45] 3223 3-9-3 79.............................. MichaelHills 7 79
(B W Hills) *led: hrd pressed over 2f out: hdd jst over 1f out: one pce ins fnl f* **16/1**
52 **5** *7* **Crusoe's Return**[49] 3094 3-9-3 0.............................. JamieSpencer 5 65
(L M Cumani) *mostly in 7th pl and nt on terms w ldrs: pushed along and effrt over 3f out: sme prog over 2f out: no imp over 1f out: wknd fnl f* **3/1**[2]
3 **6** *2 ¼* **Madam President**[14] 4249 3-8-12 0.............................. AdamKirby 6 56+
(W R Swinburn) *trckd ldng pair: nrly upsides 3f out: fdd fr 2f out: eased* **10/1**
7 *1 ½* **Inquest** 3-9-3 0.............................. JimCrowley 1 58+
(Mrs A J Perrett) *dwlt: hld up wl in rr and wl off the pce: nudged along and styd on takingly fr over 2f out: nvr nr ldrs* **50/1**
50 **8** *1 ¼* **Etta Place**[10] 4372 3-8-12 0.............................. IanMongan 11 50
(P W Chapple-Hyam) *chsd ldng quartet: shkn up 3f out: wknd fnl 2f* **66/1**
6 **9** *½* **Eleonora (FR)**[17] 4161 3-8-12 0.............................. MartinDwyer 8 49
(W J Haggas) *chsd ldng quartet: pushed along fr 3f out: wknd fnl 2f* **20/1**
00 **10** *2* **Civitas Filius (USA)**[25] 3894 3-9-3 0.............................. FergusSweeney 14 50
(D M Simcock) *off the pce in rr gp: rchd midfield u.p 3f out: sn struggling* **40/1**
0 **11** *3 ¾* **Coliseum**[32] 3654 3-9-3 0.............................. RyanMoore 15 43
(Sir Michael Stoute) *mostly in 8th pl and nt on terms w ldng gp: shkn up 4f out: no imp: fdd fnl 2f* **16/1**
5 **12** *10* **Lion Gate (USA)**[14] 4255 3-9-3 0..............................(t) JimmyFortune 9 23
(J H M Gosden) *s.s: a towards rr: nvr a factor* **20/1**
13 *nse* **Hard To Resist (IRE)** 3-9-3 0.............................. TedDurcan 3 22
(P R Webber) *dwlt: last to 1/2-way: a wl bhd* **40/1**
00 **14** *1 ¾* **Rumline**[11] 4349 3-8-5 0.............................. HollyHall(7) 4 14
(S A Callaghan) *hld up wl in rr: sme prog into midfield 4f out and gng wl enough: shuffled along and steadily lost pl* **100/1**
60 **15** *11* **Iraschko**[25] 3894 3-8-9 0.............................. TolleyDean(3) 16 —
(J L Spearing) *a towards rr: u.p and struggling over 4f out: t.o* **100/1**
0 **16** *16* **Blameitontheboogie**[12] 4302 3-9-3 0.............................. JamesDoyle 12 —
(M Blanshard) *towards rr: reluctant fr 5f out: t.o* **125/1**

2m 10.09s (1.39) **Going Correction** +0.20s/f (Good) **16** Ran SP% **131.5**
Speed ratings (Par 103): **102,101,101,100,95 93,92,91,90,89 86,78,78,76,67 55**
toteswinger: 1&2 £3.00, 1&3 £61.30, 2&3 £44.30. CSF £10.68 TOTE £6.20: £1.90, £1.30, £10.10; EX 18.70.
Owner Helena Springfield Ltd **Bred** Meon Valley Stud **Trained** Newmarket, Suffolk
■ Stewards' Enquiry : Holly Hall caution: prematurely eased unplaced horse

FOCUS
A maiden full of interest featuring a number of well-bred sorts, the possessors of untold potential. The first four finished clear but the fourth does limit the form a little.
Madam President Official explanation: jockey said filly hung left

4696 FRENCH BROTHERS BOATS TO WINDSOR RACECOURSE H'CAP — 6f
8:30 (8:30) (Class 5) (0-75,73) 3-Y-0+ **£2,934** (£866; £433) **Stalls** High

Form RPR
5601 **1** **Linda Green**[7] 4483 7-9-3 **62** 6ex.............................. EdwardCreighton 3 69
(M R Channon) *hld up last: effrt 2f out: squeezed through ins fnl f and r.o to ld last strides* **3/1**[1]
2211 **2** *nk* **Patavium Prince (IRE)**[16] 4186 5-9-7 **69**.............................. TravisBlock(3) 4 75
(Miss Jo Crowley) *sn pressed ldr: chal fr over 2f out: narrow ld jst over 1f out: hdd last strides* **3/1**[1]
-100 **3** *½* **Danjet (IRE)**[10] 4370 5-9-0 **59**.............................. JamesDoyle 8 63
(P D Evans) *t.k.h: pressed ldrs: rdn to chal fr 2f out: nrly upsides fnl f: nt qckn nr fin* **16/1**
4201 **4** *nse* **Sovereignty (JPN)**[19] 4084 6-9-7 **66**.............................. RichardKingscote 9 73+
(D K Ivory) *taken down early: hld up: effrt 2f out: nt clr run over 1f out and swtchd sharply rt: r.o last 150yds: gaining at fin* **9/2**[2]
0-60 **5** *2* **Dresden Doll (USA)**[19] 4090 3-9-10 **73**.............................. JamieSpencer 6 70
(M L W Bell) *mde most to jst over 1f out: wknd ins fnl f* **7/1**[3]
5260 **6** *1* **Jonny Ebeneezer**[2] 4639 9-9-3 **62**..............................(b) SteveDrowne 2 57
(D Flood) *taken down early: hld up in tch: effrt towards far rail over 2f out: chal over 1f out: cl up but hld whn hmpd ins fnl f: wknd* **9/2**[2]
1000 **7** *1 ¾* **Applesnap (IRE)**[11] 4341 3-9-9 **72**.............................. PatCosgrave 5 60
(Mrs C A Dunnett) *w ldrs to over 1f out: wknd fnl f* **20/1**
2100 **8** *18* **Fools Gold**[26] 3838 3-9-4 **67**.............................. PaulEddery 7 —
(G D Blake) *chsd ldrs: u.p 1/2-way: wknd over 2f out: t.o* **16/1**

1m 14.79s (1.79) **Going Correction** +0.20s/f (Good)
WFA 3 from 5yo+ 4lb **8** Ran SP% **115.4**
Speed ratings (Par 103): **96,95,94,94,92 90,88,64**
toteswinger: 1&2 £1.30, 1&3 £9.10, 2&3 £16.30. CSF £12.01 CT £121.48 TOTE £4.00: £1.70, £1.40, £3.10; EX 10.20 Place 6 £9.16, Place 5 £4.71. .
Owner John Livock **Bred** Colin Tinkler **Trained** West Ilsley, Berks

FOCUS
Just a modest bunch went to post for this sprint handicap, the winner following up her recent course-and-distance success after enduring a long losing run. The pace was strong and they again headed for the far rail.
Dresden Doll(USA) Official explanation: starter said filly lost a hind shoe
T/Jkpt: Part won. £28,289.70 to a £1 stake. Pool: £39,844.68. 0.50 winning tickets. T/Plt: £6.90 to a £1 stake. Pool: £101,151.39. 10,640.98 winning tickets. T/Qpdt: £4.50 to a £1 stake. Pool: £5,890.05. 952.05 winning tickets. JN

4289 CATTERICK (L-H)
Tuesday, August 5

OFFICIAL GOING: Good to firm (good in places; 9.3)
Wind: Virtually nil Weather: Overcast and light rain

4697 GO RACING AT PONTEFRACT TOMORROW MAIDEN STKS — 7f
2:30 (2:32) (Class 5) 2-Y-0 **£2,590** (£770; £385; £192) **Stalls** Low

Form RPR
6 **1** **Sultans Way (IRE)**[25] 3926 2-9-3 0.............................. PaulHanagan 9 70
(P F I Cole) *cl up: rdn 2f out: led wl over 1f out: kpt on ins fnl f comf* **10/3**[2]
00 **2** *1* **Classic Contours (USA)**[16] 4213 2-9-3 0.............................. TomEaves 4 67
(G A Swinbank) *chsd ldrs: rdn along over 2f out: rdn and hdwy over 1f out: styd on wl fnl f* **50/1**
2 **3** *hd* **Feeling Fab (FR)**[11] 4380 2-8-12 0.............................. GregFairley 3 62
(M Johnston) *t.k.h: sn led: rdn along over 2f out: hdd wl over 1f out: swtchd rt and drvn: hung rt and one pce ins fnl f* **4/11**[1]
4 *1* **Diesis Of Cloyne (USA)** 2-8-12 0.............................. DarrenWilliams 2 59+
(K R Burke) *dwlt: green and sn pushed along in rr: hdwy and rn green 2f out: styd on ins fnl f: nrst fin* **25/1**[3]
4 **5** *8* **Montmartre (USA)**[40] 3400 2-9-3 0.............................. PaulMulrennan 5 44
(K A Ryan) *chsd ldrs: rdn along over 2f out: sn wknd* **33/1**
00 **6** *1 ½* **Imperial Angel (IRE)**[11] 4380 2-8-12 0.............................. DavidAllan 1 35
(D Carroll) *chsd ldng pair on inner: rdn along 1/2-way: wknd 2f out* **50/1**

1m 29.06s (2.06) **Going Correction** +0.175s/f (Good) **6** Ran SP% **107.1**
Speed ratings (Par 94): **95,93,93,92,83 81**
toteswinger: 1&2 £6.70 1&3 £1.10, 2&3 £4.40. CSF £88.07 TOTE £3.10: £1.30, £18.70; EX 99.30.
Owner H R H Sultan Ahmad Shah **Bred** Airlie Stud **Trained** Whatcombe, Oxon

FOCUS
A fair juvenile maiden run at a sound pace. The first four came clear. The winner stepped up but the favourite was well below par.

NOTEBOOK
Sultans Way(IRE), sixth on his debut at York 25 days previously, rewarded market support with a ready display to score over this extra furlong. This much quicker surface also played more to his strengths and he is clearly going the right way, so it will be interesting to see where he heads next. (op 9-2)
Classic Contours(USA) belied his odds of 50-1 and ran by far his best race to date. He saw out the trip an awful lot better than had been the case at Redcar last time, if anything looking better the further he went, and now qualifies for a nursery mark. (tchd 66-1)
Feeling Fab(FR) set the standard on her debut second at Thirsk 11 days previously, but she spoilt her chance by refusing to settle on the early lead and could offer no more when challenged by the eventual winner. This was disappointing and she may not be the most straightforward, but it is still too soon to write her off. (op 1-3 tchd 3-10 and 4-9 in a place)

Diesis Of Cloyne(USA), the first foal of a very well related dam who was herself unplaced in the US, posted a pleasing debut effort and left the impression she would learn a great deal for the experience. She got the trip without much fuss having raced too green through the early parts and should prove a lot sharper next time. (op 16-1)

4698 BEST UK RACECOURSES ON TURFTV (S) STKS — 1m 7f 177y
3:00 (3:02) (Class 6) 3-5-Y-0 — £2,047 (£604; £302) Stalls Low

Form — RPR

1 **Spiders Star**[19] 5-9-4 0 ow1 .... MHNaughton 5 — 47
(Miss Kate Milligan) *in tch: hdwy on outer over 4f out: effrt over 2f out: rdn to ld over 1f out: kpt on* — 80/1

6 2 ½ **Pairumani Pat (IRE)**[15] 4250 3-8-7 0 .... JimmyQuinn 4 — 50+
(J Pearce) *hld up in rr: effrt over 4f out and sn rdn along: hdwy wl over 1f out: swtchd rt and str run ent fnl f: kpt on* — 11/4[1]

0006 3 nk **Nelsons Column (IRE)**[7] 4501 5-9-5 65 .... PJMcDonald(3) 8 — 50
(G M Moore) *a.p: effrt 4f out: led over 2f out: sn rdn and hdd over 1f out: drvn ent fnl f and kpt on same pce* — 4/1[2]

3000 4 3 ¼ **Matinee Idol**[32] 3687 5-9-3 40 .... (b) PaulHanagan 2 — 41
(Mrs S Lamyman) *chsd ldrs: rdn along 3f out: drvn 2f out and kpt on same pce* — 17/2

-500 5 2 ¼ **General Tufto**[15] 4247 3-8-7 59 .... TomEaves 7 — 43
(C Smith) *hld up: hdwy 4f out: rdn along over 2f out: sn drvn and no imp* — 4/1[2]

0000 6 11 **Miss Havisham (IRE)**[5] 4556 4-9-3 38 .... DeanMcKeown 6 — 25
(J R Weymes) *hld up and bhd: hdwy 3f out: effrt on outer 2f out: sn rdn: hung lft and btn* — 8/1

-043 7 3 ½ **Lady Grantley**[7] 4498 3-8-2 45 .... (b[1]) DaleGibson 1 — 21
(M W Easterby) *led and sn clr: rdn along over 3f out: hdd 2f out and sn wknd* — 11/2[3]

00 8 21 **Evianne**[19] 4123 4-9-3 0 .... DarrenWilliams 9 — —
(P W Hiatt) *trckd ldrs: hdwy 5f out: rdn along over 3f out: sn drvn and wknd over 2f out* — 16/1

9 61 **Key To Caius (IRE)**[19] 5-9-8 0 .... PaulMulrennan 3 — —
(R F Fisher) *dwlt: plld hrd and hdwy to chse ldr after 4f: rdn along over 4f out and sn wknd* — 22/1

3m 37.27s (5.27) **Going Correction** +0.175s/f (Good)
WFA 3 from 4yo+ 15lb — 9 Ran SP% **115.2**
Speed ratings (Par 101): **93,92,92,90,89 84,82,72,41**
toteswinger: 1&2 £24.50, 1&3 £39.80, 2&3 £3.60. CSF £291.91 TOTE £72.30: £16.70, £1.70, £1.10; EX 212.40.There was no bid for the winner.
Owner Miss Kate Milligan **Bred** Acrum Lodge Stud **Trained** Middleham Moor, N Yorks
■ The first winner on the Flat since his amateur days for Mick Naughton.

FOCUS
A dire affair. The first three came clear and the fourth rates the best guide to the form.

4699 BOOK TICKETS ON-LINE AT CATTERICKBRIDGE.CO.UK H'CAP — 1m 5f 175y
3:30 (3:30) (Class 4) (0-85,80) 3-Y-0+ — £4,857 (£1,445; £722; £360) Stalls Low

Form — RPR

3236 1 **Casual Affair**[59] 2822 5-9-6 72 .... JimmyQuinn 1 — 79
(J D Bethell) *trckd ldr: pushed along 3f out: rdn to chal wl over 1f out: led ent fnl f and kpt on wl* — 5/2[1]

-310 2 2 **Altitude**[22] 4021 3-9-0 79 .... (b[1]) SebSanders 5 — 83
(Sir Mark Prescott) *led: pushed along and qcknd 4f out: rdn and edgd rt 2f out: drvn: edgd lft and hit rail ent fnl f: sn hdd and one pce* — 7/2[3]

6502 3 ¾ **Monfils Monfils (USA)**[12] 4331 6-9-6 72 .... DanielTudhope 4 — 75
(A J McCabe) *hld up in rr: hdwy over 2f out: swtchd lft and rdn over 1f out: kpt on ins fnl f* — 7/1

-005 4 2 ¾ **Generous Jem**[10] 4426 5-9-10 79 .... NeilBrown(3) 2 — 78
(G G Margarson) *trckd ldng pair: effrt over 3f out: rdn and ch wl over 1f out: sn edgd lft and wknd appr fnl f* — 10/3[2]

0325 5 3 **Wind Star**[10] 4422 5-10-0 80 .... (b[1]) ShaneKelly 3 — 75
(G A Swinbank) *t.k.h: hld up in tch: hdwy 3f out: rdn to chse ldrs 2f out: sn drvn and wknd over 1f out* — 10/3[2]

3m 4.07s (0.47) **Going Correction** +0.175s/f (Good)
WFA 3 from 5yo+ 13lb — 5 Ran SP% **109.5**
Speed ratings (Par 105): **105,103,103,101,100**
CSF £11.24 TOTE £3.20: £1.40, £1.90; EX 9.70.
Owner Peter J Mitchell **Bred** Ian Neville Marks **Trained** Middleham Moor, N Yorks

FOCUS
Just a modest handicap for the class. The third sets the level.
Generous Jem Official explanation: jockey said mare was never travelling

4700 NEXT FRIDAY'S ALPHA 103.2 LADIES NIGHT H'CAP — 5f 212y
4:00 (4:00) (Class 5) (0-75,74) 3-Y-0+ — £2,590 (£770; £385; £192) Stalls Low

Form — RPR

0006 1 **Lucayos**[35] 3587 5-9-11 74 .... DarrenWilliams 8 — 83
(K R Burke) *trckd ldr: effrt 2f out: rdn to ld over 1f out: edgd lft ins fnl f: kpt on* — 15/2

1312 2 ½ **No Grouse**[12] 4327 8-9-4 67 .... DavidAllan 9 — 74
(E J Alston) *midfield: hdwy 2f out: swtchd rt and rdn over 1f out: fin strly* — 4/1[1]

3104 3 nse **Sandwith**[10] 4418 5-9-6 74 .... PatrickDonaghy(5) 5 — 81
(R Johnson) *in tch: effrt 2f out: sn rdn and styd on strly ins fnl f: nrst fin* — 11/1

4501 4 ½ **Lethal**[20] 4073 5-9-7 70 .... PaulHanagan 7 — 76
(R A Fahey) *led: rdn 2f out: hdd over 1f out: drvn and one pce ins fnl f* 7/1

4556 5 1 **Cheery Cat (USA)**[9] 4453 4-8-11 60 .... (p) TonyHamilton 1 — 62
(D W Barker) *chsd ldng pair: rdn along 2f out: drvn over 1f out: sn one pce* — 11/2[3]

4432 6 1 **Rainbow Bay**[6] 4542 5-8-3 55 oh1 .... (v) DuranFentiman(3) 4 — 54
(Miss Tracy Waggott) *midfield: effrt 2f out: sn rdn and kpt on ins fnl f: nrst fin* — 5/1[2]

1260 7 1 **Steel City Boy (IRE)**[10] 4440 5-8-10 64 .... AnnStokell(5) 6 — 60
(Miss A Stokell) *chsd ldrs: rdn along 2f out: wknd appr fnl f* — 9/1

0420 8 2 ½ **Legendary Guest**[9] 4450 3-8-13 66 .... (v) TomEaves 3 — 54
(D W Barker) *in tch on inner: rdn along 2f out: sn btn* — 16/1

1240 9 3 **Royal Acclamation (IRE)**[12] 4329 3-8-13 66 .... SilvestreDeSousa 10 — 44
(G A Harker) *hld up: a towards rr* — 9/1

66/0 10 hd **Fitzwarren**[15] 4246 7-8-7 55 oh10 .... AndrewMullen(3) 2 — 33
(A D Brown) *s.i.s: a in rr* — 80/1

136- 11 2 ¼ **Angle Of Attack (IRE)**[263] 6834 3-9-5 72 .... AndrewElliott 11 — 43
(A D Brown) *a towards rr* — 40/1

1m 14.01s (0.41) **Going Correction** +0.175s/f (Good)
WFA 3 from 4yo+ 4lb — 11 Ran SP% **114.2**
Speed ratings (Par 103): **104,103,103,102,101 99,98,95,91,91 88**
toteswinger: 1&2 £7.60, 1&3 £20.80, 2&3 £8.50. CSF £36.39 CT £329.82 TOTE £8.00: £2.80, £1.40, £3.70; EX 40.50.
Owner Alex Sweeting **Bred** P Sweeting **Trained** Middleham Moor, N Yorks

FOCUS
A fair sprint for the class. The form looks sound rated through the third to a personal best.
Royal Acclamation(IRE) Official explanation: jockey said gelding had no more to give

4701 TELEPHONE 01748 810165 TO BOOK CORPORATE HOSPITALITY CLAIMING STKS — 1m 3f 214y
4:30 (4:30) (Class 6) 3-Y-0+ — £2,388 (£705; £352) Stalls High

Form — RPR

5131 1 **Lucayan Dancer**[6] 4541 8-9-5 70 .... AdeleRothery(7) 3 — 76
(D Nicholls) *trckd ldrs: smooth hdwy to ld 2f out: rdn ins fnl f and kpt on wl* — 9/4[1]

2502 2 3 ¼ **Bocciani (GER)**[7] 4498 3-8-9 65 .... FergalLynch 7 — 65
(A Berry) *trckd ldr: effrt and cl up 4f out: rdn and ev ch 2f out: drvn and outpcd over 1f out: kpt on u.p ins fnl f: tk 2nd nr fin* — 14/1

6000 3 1 ½ **Sudden Impulse**[15] 4244 7-9-4 66 .... SilvestreDeSousa 2 — 61
(A D Brown) *hld up in tch on inner: hdwy 4f out: rdn over 2f out: chsd wnr over 1f out: drvn and wknd ins fnl f: lost 2nd nr fin* — 5/1[3]

4 10 **Kings Maiden (IRE)**[71] 5-8-13 0 .... PJMcDonald(3) 1 — 43
(James Moffatt) *s.i.s and bhd tl styd on fnl 2f: n.d* — 66/1

0 5 ½ **Getrah**[39] 3450 4-9-8 62 .... (p) JimmyQuinn 5 — 48
(C Grant) *hld up in tch: effrt 3f out: rdn along over 2f out and sn no imp* — 8/1

-502 6 ¾ **Torrens (IRE)**[6] 4541 6-9-6 70 .... (t) TGMcLaughlin 9 — 45
(Ollie Pears) *hld up in tch: effrt 3f out: rdn to chse ldrs 2f out: sn wknd* — 3/1[2]

2404 7 2 ¼ **Tidy (IRE)**[20] 4075 8-9-1 50 .... (v) PaulHanagan 10 — 36
(Micky Hammond) *hld up towards rr: effrt 4f out: sn rdn along and nvr a factor* — 25/1

5000 8 2 ¾ **Clueless**[13] 4299 6-9-12 71 .... (p) SebSanders 8 — 43
(A J McCabe) *cl up- on outer: reminders 4f out: rdn along wl over 2f out: sn btn* — 5/1[3]

0000 9 2 ¾ **Lord Laing (USA)**[22] 4029 5-9-9 42 .... MickyFenton 4 — 35
(H J Collingridge) *led: rdn along 4f out: drvn and hdd 2f out: sn wknd* — 20/1

6 10 55 **Cabin Gate (IRE)**[29] 3786 5-8-12 0 .... PatrickDonaghy(5) 12 — —
(R Johnson) *a in rr* — 125/1

2m 38.91s (0.01) **Going Correction** +0.175s/f (Good)
WFA 3 from 4yo+ 11lb — 10 Ran SP% **117.8**
Speed ratings (Par 101): **106,103,102,96,95 95,93,92,90,53**
.Lucayan Dancer was subject to a friendly claim. \n\x\x
Owner Racegoers Club Owners Group **Bred** The National Stud Owner Breeders Club Ltd **Trained** Sessay, N Yorks

FOCUS
Three came clear in what was a fair claimer overall, contested by some disappointing types. The runner-up is the guide to the form.

4702 BOOK NOW FOR SATURDAY 20TH SEPTEMBER H'CAP — 7f
5:00 (5:02) (Class 6) (0-65,65) 3-Y-0 — £2,388 (£705; £352) Stalls Low

Form — RPR

0232 1 **Ubenkor (IRE)**[15] 4236 3-9-7 65 .... TomEaves 10 — 73
(B Smart) *dwlt and towards rr: gd hdwy 2f out: rdn over 1f out: drvn ins fnl f and styd on wl to ld nr fin* — 9/2[2]

5000 2 nk **Afton View (IRE)**[19] 4107 3-8-8 52 .... (p) TonyCulhane 11 — 59
(S Parr) *cl up: led 3f out: rdn wl over 1f out: edgd lft ins fnl f: hdd and no ex nr fin* — 12/1

3236 3 3 **Johnny Friendly**[19] 4115 3-9-5 63 .... AndrewElliott 6 — 62
(K R Burke) *cl up on inner: led after 2f: hdd 3f out and sn rdn along: drvn over 1f out and kpt on same pce* — 4/1[1]

-600 4 ½ **Tobar Suil Lady (IRE)**[18] 4163 3-9-2 63 .... NeilBrown(3) 2 — 61
(K A Ryan) *hld up towards rr: gd hdwy 2f out: rdn to chse ldrs over 1f out: drvn and kpt on same pce ins fnl f* — 14/1

3360 5 ½ **Bertie Vista**[40] 3416 3-9-1 62 .... DuranFentiman(3) 5 — 58
(T D Easterby) *midfield: hdwy 2f out: sn rdn and kpt on same pce appr fnl f* — 25/1

-000 6 1 **Amyann (IRE)**[11] 4368 3-8-6 50 .... GregFairley 9 — 44
(J R Holt) *midfield: rdn along over 2f out: sn no imp* — 66/1

0554 7 1 ¾ **Bohobe (IRE)**[18] 4163 3-9-4 62 .... SebSanders 1 — 51
(J G Given) *chsd ldrs on inner: rdn over 2f out: drvn over 1f out and sn wknd* — 11/2

002 8 ¾ **Red Skipper (IRE)**[15] 4241 3-8-13 57 .... DavidAllan 7 — 44
(N Wilson) *nvr nr ldrs* — 11/2

6060 9 3 ¼ **Fantasy Fighter (IRE)**[1] 4684 3-8-2 46 oh1 .... (v) PaulHanagan 3 — 24
(J J Quinn) *dwlt and sn rdn along: a in rr* — 20/1

0004 10 1 **Monte Cassino (IRE)**[6] 4538 3-8-4 48 ow1 .... JoeFanning 8 — 23
(J O'Reilly) *t.k.h: led 2f: rdn along 3f out and sn wknd* — 16/1

4332 11 7 **Just Sam (IRE)**[21] 4043 3-8-9 53 .... TonyHamilton 4 — 9
(D W Barker) *chsd ldrs: rdn along 3f out: sn drvn and btn 2f out* — 5/1[3]

1m 29.19s (2.19) **Going Correction** +0.175s/f (Good) — 11 Ran SP% **116.0**
Speed ratings (Par 98): **94,93,90,89,89 87,85,85,81,80 72**
toteswinger: 1&2 £15.20, 1&3 £4.20, 2&3 £13.00. CSF £55.22 CT £238.51 TOTE £6.00: £2.20, £3.00, £2.00; EX 79.90.
Owner Prime Equestrian **Bred** Petra Bloodstock Agency Ltd **Trained** Hambleton, N Yorks

FOCUS
A moderate handicap rated through the runner-up.

4703 GORACING.CO.UK H'CAP — 5f
5:30 (5:31) (Class 6) (0-60,60) 3-Y-0+ — £2,388 (£705; £352) Stalls Low

Form — RPR

0050 1 **Guto**[21] 4047 5-8-8 52 .... KellyHarrison(5) 11 — 64
(W J H Ratcliffe) *chsd ldrs: hdwy 2f out: swtchd lft and rdn over 1f out: drvn to ld and edgd lft ins fnl f: kpt on* — 11/1

6055 2 ¾ **Fast Freddie**[19] 4107 4-9-4 57 .... (b) TonyCulhane 9 — 67
(S Parr) *led and sn clr: rdn wl over 1f out: drvn and hdd ins fnl f: no ex towards fin* — 9/1

0350 3 1 ½ **Sands Crooner (IRE)**[15] 4246 5-9-7 60 .... (v) SebSanders 13 — 64
(J G Given) *chsd ldrs: hdwy whn bmpd over 1f out: rdn and styng on whn sltly hmpd ins fnl f: kpt on same pce* — 6/1[3]

2660 4 ½ **Wicked Wilma (IRE)**[11] 4385 4-8-12 51 .... FergalLynch 2 — 54+
(A Berry) *stdd and swtchd rt s: bhd tl hdwy wl over 1f out: swtchd lft and rdn ent fnl f: fin strly* — 17/2

0-00 5 ½ **Northern Chorus (IRE)**[32] 3665 5-8-13 52 .... (v) DeanMcKeown 10 — 53
(J O'Reilly) *chsd ldr: rdn along 2f out: drvn over 1f out: wkng whn sltly hmpd ins fnl f* — 16/1

2400 **6** *1 ½* **Tanley**[44] [3298] 3-8-6 **55**...............................(p) NBazeley(7) 3 50
(J F Coupland) *racd alone far side and prom: swtchd rt to join main gp 2f out: sn rdn and kpt on same pce appr fnl f* **33/1**
0330 **7** *1 ¾* **Jun Fan (USA)**[13] [4293] 6-8-9 **55**....................... LanceBetts(7) 14 44
(B Ellison) *chsd ldrs: rdn along 2f out: sn drvn and no imp* **7/1**
5020 **8** *1* **Violet's Pride**[14] [4285] 4-8-7 **46** oh1..................... KimTinkler 5 31
(N Tinkler) *chsd ldrs: rdn 2f out: drvn and wknd appr fnl f* **33/1**
0001 **9** *½* **Taboor (IRE)**[14] [4285] 10-8-7 **53**....................... AndreaAtzeni(7) 12 37
(R M H Cowell) *dwlt: a towards rr* **17/2**
0300 **10** *¾* **Dark Champion**[13] [4293] 8-9-3 **56**..........................(v) TomEaves 8 37
(R E Barr) *chsd ldrs: rdn along 1/2-way: sn wknd* **10/1**
0343 **11** *13* **Mormeatmic**[22] [4013] 5-8-13 **52**....................... PaulMulrennan 7 —
(M W Easterby) *chsd ldrs: rdn along 1/2-way: sn wknd* **11/2**[2]
4203 **12** *2 ¼* **Smirfys Gold (IRE)**[14] [4285] 4-8-12 **51**...............(v) StephenDonohoe 4 —
(E S McMahon) *chsd ldrs: rdn along over 2f out and grad wknd* **5/1**[1]

60.46 secs (0.66) **Going Correction** +0.175s/f (Good)
WFA 3 from 4yo+ 3lb **12** Ran SP% **119.1**
Speed ratings (Par 101): **101,99,97,96,95 93,90,89,88,87 66,62**
toteswinger: 1&2 £33.10, 1&3 £18.40, 2&3 £14.90. CSF £106.90 CT £654.84 TOTE £16.90: £4.20, £3.70, £2.20; EX 141.70 Place 6: £91.64 Place 5: £17.83.
Owner W J H Ratcliffe **Bred** H B Hughes **Trained** Wensley, N Yorks

FOCUS
A competitive little sprint rated around the fairly consistent third and fourth.
Guto Official explanation: trainer had no explanation for the apparent improvement in form
T/Plt: £261.20 to a £1 stake. Pool: £66,565.38. 186.03 winning tickets. T/Qpdt: £10.40 to a £1 stake. Pool: £7,235.70. 512.30 winning tickets. JR

4365

CHEPSTOW (L-H)

Tuesday, August 5

OFFICIAL GOING: Soft changing to heavy after race 5 (4.15pm)
Wind: Almost nil Weather: Raining after 2.15

4704 DIGIBET.CO.UK H'CAP 1m 4f 23y
2:15 (2:15) (Class 6) (0-60,60) 3-Y-0+ **£2,266** (£674; £337; £168) **Stalls** Low

Form RPR
145- **1** **Flying Grey (IRE)**[20] [3274] 4-9-2 **54**....................(t) TravisBlock(3) 16 63
(Tim Vaughan) *hld up in mid-div: hdwy to ld 3f out: sn rdn: r.o wl* **8/1**
3-21 **2** *1 ¼* **Check Up (IRE)**[15] [4250] 7-9-4 **56**....................... KevinGhunowa(3) 17 62
(J L Flint) *hld up in tch: ev ch 3f out: rdn 2f out: swtchd rt 1f out: kpt on* **7/1**
0-10 **3** *¾* **Soviet Sceptre (IRE)**[14] [4275] 7-9-8 **57**..................(tp) FergusSweeney 15 62
(Tim Vaughan) *s.i.s: hld up and bhd: hdwy over 2f out: rdn wl over 1f out: kpt on ins fnl f* **13/2**[3]
0510 **4** *4 ½* **Trysting Grove (IRE)**[11] [4365] 7-8-12 **54**....................... AshleyMorgan(7) 9 52
(E G Bevan) *s.s: hld up in rr: hdwy on outside 3f out: rdn over 1f out: wknd wl ins fnl f* **12/1**
0305 **5** *¾* **Artzola (IRE)**[52] [3025] 8-9-1 **50**....................... PaulEddery 10 47
(C A Horgan) *s.i.s: hld up and bhd: styd on fr over 1f out: nvr nrr* **20/1**
/0P- **6** *1* **Very Green (FR)**[258] [6902] 6-9-4 **60**....................... KylieManser(7) 11 55
(Mrs A L M King) *s.i.s: hld up towards rr: hdwy over 3f out: wknd ins fnl f* **66/1**
-032 **7** *¾* **Pinnacle Point**[12] [4334] 3-9-0 **60**....................... GeorgeBaker 1 54
(G L Moore) *t.k.h: hld up in tch: lost pl over 4f out: n.d after* **5/1**[1]
056- **8** *4 ½* **Bathwick Breeze**[20] [5710] 4-9-0 **54**....................(p) HaddenFrost(5) 12 41
(D E Pipe) *led: hdd 3f out: rdn and wknd 2f out* **11/2**[2]
1665 **9** *¾* **Dansilver**[20] [3179] 4-9-7 **56**....................(p) VinceSlattery 7 41
(D J Wintle) *hld up in mid-div: rdn and wknd over 1f out* **25/1**
2102 **10** *nk* **Faraday (IRE)**[31] [3732] 5-9-4 **53**....................... JamieSpencer 14 38
(N P Mulholland) *hld up towards rr: hdwy over 3f out: wknd and eased ins fnl f* **9/1**
4600 **11** *3 ½* **Beech Games**[20] [3321] 4-9-1 **50**....................... AdamKirby 3 29
(F Jordan) *hld up in tch: rdn and wknd over 2f out* **18/1**
00-1 **12** *shd* **The Composer**[14] [4275] 6-9-6 **55**....................... SteveDrowne 2 34
(M Blanshard) *prom: rdn over 4f out: wknd over 3f out* **13/2**[3]
0046 **13** *1 ¼* **Pearl (IRE)**[89] [1933] 4-9-11 **60**....................... LiamJones 8 37
(I A Wood) *sn chsng ldr: rdn and ev ch 3f out: wknd over 2f out* **33/1**

2m 47.64s (8.64) **Going Correction** +0.75s/f (Yiel)
WFA 3 from 4yo+ 11lb **13** Ran SP% **118.3**
Speed ratings (Par 101): **101,100,99,96,96 95,95,92,91,91 88,88,88**
toteswinger: 1&2 £19.10 1&3 £13.80, 2&3 £14.50. CSF £60.04 CT £391.03 TOTE £9.50: £3.50, £3.00, £2.10; EX 78.70 TRIFECTA Not won..
Owner Paul Morgan **Bred** Swordlestown Stud **Trained** Aberthin, Vale of Glamorgan

FOCUS
Persistent heavy rain throughout the day meant that the going was changed to soft before racing began, although the times of the races suggest something even more testing. This handicap was no better than a seller and the form is not considered reliable, although the third looks the best guide.

4705 WEST COAST MARKETS MEDIAN AUCTION MAIDEN FILLIES' STKS 5f 16y
2:45 (2:46) (Class 5) 2-Y-0 **£2,719** (£809; £404; £202) **Stalls** High

Form RPR
06 **1** **It's Toast (IRE)**[25] [3913] 2-9-0 0....................... GeorgeBaker 11 70+
(R M Beckett) *bhd: hdwy whn edgd lft wl over 1f out: sn rdn and edgd rt: r.o wl to ld wl ins fnl f* **5/6**[1]
65 **2** *1* **Key To Love (IRE)**[12] [4339] 2-9-0 0....................... JamesDoyle 4 63
(H J L Dunlop) *led: edgd lft and rdn 1f out: hdd and nt qckn wl ins fnl f* **6/1**[3]
64 **3** *2 ¾* **Imaginary Diva**[29] [3778] 2-9-0 0....................... DaneO'Neill 6 54
(G G Margarson) *hld up towards rr: hdwy 2f out: rdn over 1f out: no ex wl ins fnl f* **20/1**
00 **4** *½* **Turn To Dreams**[8] [4480] 2-9-0 0....................... JohnEgan 2 52
(P D Evans) *w ldr: rdn over 1f out: wknd wl ins fnl f* **14/1**
00 **5** *2 ¼* **Lady Norlela**[20] [4080] 2-9-0 0....................... PatDobbs 9 44
(R Hannon) *prom tl wknd over 1f out* **28/1**
6 **6** *4 ½* **Place The Duchess**[52] [3032] 2-9-0 0....................... FrancisNorton 3 27
(D W P Arbuthnot) *hung lft thrght: hld up in tch: wknd ins fnl f* **7/1**
2306 **7** *2 ½* **Amosite**[31] [3734] 2-9-0 78....................(v) LiamJones 10 18
(J R Jenkins) *hld up towards rr: nt clr run on stands' rail 2f out: swtchd lft over 1f out: sn rdn: no rspnse* **7/1**
8 *3* **Abacus House (IRE)** 2-8-9 0....................... JackDean(5) 7 8
(W G M Turner) *s.s: outpcd* **22/1**
00 **9** *14* **Silver Salsa**[22] [4020] 2-9-0 0....................... AdrianMcCarthy 8 —
(J R Jenkins) *t.k.h: prom tl wknd over 2f out* **66/1**

63.47 secs (4.17) **Going Correction** +0.525s/f (Yiel) **9** Ran SP% **117.4**
Speed ratings (Par 91): **87,85,81,80,76 69,65,60,38**
toteswinger: 1&2 £2.20, 1&3 £8.50, 2&3 £6.50. CSF £6.03 TOTE £1.70: £1.02, £1.80, £4.30; EX 5.20 Trifecta £38.60 Pool: £364.62 - 6.99 winning units..
Owner The Sunday Club **Bred** Stone Ridge Farm **Trained** Whitsbury, Hants

FOCUS
An ordinary fillies maiden and, while there were most certainly no superstars on show, the winner won a shade comfortably, value an extra length.

NOTEBOOK
It's Toast(IRE) looked to be floundering out the back at halfway but it was probably something of a shock to her trying the minimum trip for the first time and once she found her stride she came through and did it nicely. Her future depends on how the Handicapper reacts to this. (op 5-4 tchd 11-8 in a place)
Key To Love(IRE) had not shown much in two Polytrack maidens over further but she is obviously not short of speed and could be of interest now that her trip is established and she is eligible for handicaps. (op 13-2 tchd 7-1 and 11-2)
Imaginary Diva has now hinted at ability on all three starts and should find herself on a handy perch in nurseries. (op 12-1)
Turn To Dreams had shown next to nothing on two previous starts but the penny must have started to drop with her and she showed a lot of dash here. Now eligible for a handicap mark, her improvement is coming at the right time. (op 22-1)
Amosite is becoming very exposed and had never encountered these sort of conditions before. She was slightly short of room at one point but was beaten at the time and is one to have reservations about. Official explanation: jockey said filly did not face the visor (op 3-1 tchd 6-1)

4706 JENKINSONS CATERERS NURSERY 6f 16y
3:15 (3:17) (Class 5) 2-Y-O **£2,914** (£867; £433; £216) **Stalls** High

Form RPR
3504 **1** **Magical Illusion**[24] [3961] 2-8-5 **64** ow2....................... JohnEgan 8 65
(P D Evans) *n.m.r s: bhd: rdn and hdwy over 2f out: led ins fnl f: r.o* **16/1**
010 **2** *¾* **Anacaona (IRE)**[32] [3670] 2-8-0 **59**....................... DavidKinsella 10 58
(R Hannon) *bhd: hdwy to ld 3f out: rdn over 1f out: hdd ins fnl f: kpt on* **16/1**
1451 **3** *½* **Soul Sista (IRE)**[24] [3967] 2-9-7 **80**....................... AdamKirby 2 77
(J L Spearing) *a.p: rdn over 2f out: edgd rt over 1f out: sn ev ch: nt qckn ins fnl f* **5/2**[2]
0634 **4** *1* **Paymaster In Chief**[4] [4594] 2-7-11 **61**....................... DavidProbert(5) 9 55
(M D I Usher) *hld up in tch: rdn over 2f out: kpt on same pce fnl f* **15/8**[1]
0004 **5** *5* **Premier Demon (IRE)**[11] [4367] 2-7-11 **59** oh2 ow2........ LukeMorris(3) 6 38
(P D Evans) *hld up in tch: lost pl over 3f out: swtchd lft 2f out: hrd rdn and rallied over 1f out: wknd ins fnl f* **33/1**
504 **6** *4* **Abhainn (IRE)**[22] [4027] 2-9-1 **74**....................... CatherineGannon 1 41
(B Palling) *w ldr: rdn and wknd over 1f out* **12/1**
P424 **7** *2 ¾* **Misty Glade**[12] [4340] 2-8-8 **67** ow1....................(b[1]) JamieSpencer 7 26
(B J Meehan) *wnt sltly rt s: t.k.h: a towards rr* **7/1**[3]
0044 **8** *4* **Song Of Praise**[19] [4119] 2-8-3 **62**....................... FrancisNorton 5 9
(M Blanshard) *t.k.h: prom tl wknd over 1f out* **8/1**
061 **9** *1 ¼* **Cashed Up**[21] [4050] 2-8-12 **71**....................... StephenCarson 11 14
(P Winkworth) *led on stands' rail: hdd 3f out: sn wknd* **18/1**

1m 16.61s (3.71) **Going Correction** +0.525s/f (Yiel) **9** Ran SP% **114.6**
Speed ratings (Par 94): **96,95,94,93,86 81,77,72,70**
toteswinger: 1&2 £14.20, 1&3 £8.60, 2&3 £10.40. CSF £239.25 CT £861.46 TOTE £16.20: £4.10, £4.10, £1.30; EX 211.00 TRIFECTA Not won..
Owner Bathfield Stud **Bred** B F Gray **Trained** Pandy, Monmouths

FOCUS
A couple of fair sorts at the top of the weights but this was a nursery contested by mostly moderate animals and the form looks ordinary. The runner-up and third set the level.

NOTEBOOK
Magical Illusion, in common with many of Tobougg's progeny, appeared to relish conditions and came through with a strong run to land the spoils despite Egan putting up 2lb overweight. Her yard is having another great season with their juveniles. (op 18-1 tchd 20-1)
Anacaona(IRE), a winner in selling company, looked the likely winner when racing into the lead before the two-furlong pole, and although she carries her head a little high she does not do much wrong. 6f in this ground probably streches her a little. (op 12-1 tchd 11-1)
Soul Sista(IRE) won at Salisbury when there was juice in the ground but this was a different kettle of fish and it was a lot to ask of a two-year-old filly to lump such a big weight in these conditions. She was far from disgraced. (op 2-1 tchd 7-4 and 11-4 in a place)
Paymaster In Chief, the well-supported favourite, was making the frame for the third time in three nursery starts and just looks as though he may be keeping something for himself at the business end of his races. (op 5-2)
Misty Glade was awkward at the gates and took too strong a hold early on in first-time blinkers to give herself a chance in these conditions. Official explanation: jockey said filly had run too freely in the blinkers (op 9-1 tchd 10-1)

4707 JENKINSONS CATERERS 1ST CHOICE FOR HOSPITALITY (S) STKS 1m 14y
3:45 (3:49) (Class 6) 3-Y-0+ **£1,942** (£578; £288; £144) **Stalls** Low

Form RPR
5050 **1** **Royal Island (IRE)**[29] [3800] 6-9-5 77....................... JamieSpencer 17 74
(M G Quinlan) *hld up and bhd: smooth prog over 2f out: led over 1f out: rdn clr ins fnl f: comf* **4/5**[1]
004 **2** *8* **The Gaikwar (IRE)**[34] [3604] 9-9-0 49....................(b) HaddenFrost(5) 6 57
(R A Harris) *hld up in mid-div: rdn and hdwy over 2f out: wnt 2nd jst over 1f out: no ch w wnr* **14/1**
5054 **3** *1 ½* **Personify**[12] [4322] 6-9-2 52....................(b) KevinGhunowa(3) 3 54
(R A Harris) *hld up in tch: led over 2f out tl over 1f out: sn rdn: one pce* **14/1**
050 **4** *2* **Goose Green (IRE)**[10] [4414] 4-9-5 53....................... SteveDrowne 2 50
(R J Hodges) *hld up towards rr: hdwy over 2f out: rdn over 1f out: one pce* **10/1**[3]
0600 **5** *2* **Compulsion**[21] [4052] 5-9-0 44....................... PaulEddery 1 41
(Pat Eddery) *hld up in rr: hdwy over 2f out: rdn over 1f out: no further prog* **33/1**
0000 **6** *6* **Coup D'Etat**[18] [4168] 6-9-5 55....................(b) LiamJones 9 33
(R A Harris) *prom: led 4f out tl over 2f out: rdn and wknd over 1f out* **16/1**
04 **7** *1 ½* **Atteme Bomb**[13] [4298] 3-8-7 0....................... JamesDoyle 4 25
(S Curran) *prom: n.m.r 2f out: sn wknd* **20/1**
2620 **8** *4 ½* **Apache Dawn**[75] [2329] 4-9-5 67....................(b) GeorgeBaker 11 20
(G L Moore) *hld up in tch: wknd 2f out* **4/1**[2]
0055 **9** *8* **Charlie Be (IRE)**[18] [4165] 3-8-7 46....................... JackMitchell(5) 5 4
(Mrs P N Dutfield) *plld hrd early: sn towards rr* **33/1**
5030 **10** *3 ¾* **Poppy Red**[21] [4052] 3-8-7 47....................... PaulFitzsimons 10 —
(Miss J R Tooth) *s.i.s: hld up in tch: rdn 3f out: sn wknd* **66/1**

6000 **11** 1 1/2 **Heroic Lad**[37] 3524 3-8-5 50 PNolan(7) 13 —
(A B Haynes) *prom 4f* **100/1**

00 **12** 1/2 **Dungleddy Star**[8] 4484 3-8-2 0 DavidProbert(5) 16 —
(J M Bradley) *a in rr* **125/1**

00-0 **13** 43 **Foxy Diplomat**[34] 3604 4-8-12 45 WilliamCarson(7) 8 —
(R Dickin) *led 4f: sn wknd: eased whn no ch over 1f out* **66/1**

1m 42.94s (6.74) **Going Correction** +0.975s/f (Soft)
WFA 3 from 4yo+ 7lb **13** Ran SP% **119.3**
Speed ratings (Par 101): **105,97,95,93,91 85,84,79,71,67 66,65,22**
toteswinger: 1&2 £4.60, 1&3 £5.80, 2&3 £10.70. CSF £13.74 TOTE £1.90: £1.10, £2.50, £4.10; EX 16.40 Trifecta £23.50 Pool: £991.97 - 31.21 winning units..The winner was bought in for 7000gns.
Owner M T Neville **Bred** Mrs Bill O'Neill **Trained** Newmarket, Suffolk

FOCUS
A shocker of a seller, and on all known form Royal Island was entitled to win as he liked, which he duly did. It has been rated around the placed horses.
Apache Dawn Official explanation: jockey said gelding had no more to give
Foxy Diplomat Official explanation: jockey said gelding had run too freely

4708 JENKINSONS CATERERS 1ST CHOICE FOR CONFERENCES FILLIES' H'CAP 1m 14y
4:15 (4:19) (Class 5) (0-75,73) 3-Y-0+ **£3,238** (£963; £481; £240) **Stalls** Low

Form RPR

4630 **1** **Addiena**[25] 3903 4-9-11 **63** CatherineGannon 2 69
(B Palling) *half-rrd leaving stalls: t.k.h early in rr: rdn over 2f out: hdwy over 1f out: r.o u.p to ld wl ins fnl f* **12/1**

542 **2** nk **Ainia**[29] 3796 3-10-0 **73** RichardMullen 11 77
(D M Simcock) *hld up and bhd: hdwy whn n.m.r wl over 2f out: sn rdn: ev ch wl ins fnl f: kpt on* **5/2**[1]

4000 **3** 1/2 **Red Current**[37] 3518 4-9-3 **58** KevinGhunowa(3) 7 62
(R A Harris) *hld up in tch: led wl over 2f out: sn rdn: hdd and nt qckn wl ins fnl f* **20/1**

0002 **4** 1 1/4 **Ken's Girl**[26] 3892 4-9-9 **64** JamesMillman(3) 4 65
(W S Kittow) *led over 1f: a.p: one pce fnl f* **11/2**[3]

0-60 **5** 2 1/4 **Siryena**[29] 3799 3-8-2 **52** (t) DavidProbert(5) 8 48
(B I Case) *prom: rdn wl over 2f out: btn over 1f out* **40/1**

040 **6** 3/4 **Tara's Garden**[12] 4344 3-9-1 **60** FrancisNorton 6 54
(M Blanshard) *hld up in tch: rdn over 2f out: wknd wl ins fnl f* **13/2**

-303 **7** 20 **Poppets Sweetlove**[66] 2622 4-9-11 **63** SteveDrowne 5 16
(A B Haynes) *hld up and bhd: hdwy over 3f out: wknd over 1f out: eased ins fnl f* **11/4**[2]

050 **8** 19 **Miss Clarice (USA)**[12] 4349 3-9-3 **62** JamieSpencer 3 —
(B J Meehan) *s.s: a wl in rr: t.o* **12/1**

003 **9** 5 **Ci Vediamo (IRE)**[51] 3061 3-9-0 **66** RichardFelton(7) 1 —
(R M Beckett) *wnt bdly lft and rdr lost iron briefly s: led over 6f out: clr over 4f out: hdd wl over 2f out: wknd qckly: t.o* **10/1**

1m 45.46s (9.26) **Going Correction** +0.975s/f (Soft)
WFA 3 from 4yo 7lb **9** Ran SP% **115.6**
Speed ratings (Par 100): **92,91,91,89,87 86,66,47,42**
toteswinger: 1&2 £7.80, 1&3 £19.10, 2&3 £9.80. CSF £42.30 CT £615.76 TOTE £15.70: £3.30, £1.40, £3.80; EX 54.10 Trifecta £403.20 Part won. Pool: £544.99 -0.89 winning units..
Owner Wayne Devine **Bred** Newsells Park Stud Limited **Trained** Tredodridge, Vale Of Glamorgan

FOCUS
A modest handicap for fillies with the finish more reminiscent of a 3m chase around Towcester, with the winner hardly holding a claim to be the best filly at the weights the way the race was run.
Addiena Official explanation: trainer said, regarding the improved form shown, filly had benefited from a change in tactics, by being hled up
Miss Clarice(USA) Official explanation: jockey said filly had been unsuited by the soft ground

4709 JENKINSONS CATERERS MAIDEN STKS 7f 16y
4:45 (4:48) (Class 5) 3-Y-0+ **£2,719** (£809; £404; £202) **Stalls** Low

Form RPR

0 **1** **Make Amends (IRE)**[14] 4277 3-8-12 0 SteveDrowne 8 69
(R J Hodges) *prom: t.k.h: stdd over 4f out: lost pl over 4f out: hdwy over 2f out: led over 1f out: r.o wl* **9/2**[2]

0-2 **2** 2 1/4 **Prince Afram**[13] 4301 3-9-3 0 GeorgeBaker 5 68
(R M Beckett) *hld up in tch: ev ch wl over 1f out: sn rdn: nt qckn fnl f* **6/4**[1]

30 **3** 3 3/4 **Crataegus**[13] 4301 3-9-3 0 DaneO'Neill 1 59
(H Candy) *a.p: led 4f out: rdn over 2f out: hdd over 1f out: wknd ins fnl f* **11/1**

00 **4** 2 1/2 **No Wonga**[8] 4484 3-9-3 0 JamesDoyle 9 52
(P D Evans) *s.s: in rr tl rdn and hdwy over 1f out: nvr trbld ldrs* **20/1**

0 **5** 1 3/4 **Kappalyn (IRE)**[14] 4277 3-8-12 0 PatDobbs 10 43
(R Hannon) *t.k.h: prom: ev ch 2f out: rdn and wknd over 1f out* **5/1**[3]

0 **6** 7 **Rose Of Torridge**[14] 4277 3-8-12 0 FergusSweeney 2 26
(A G Newcombe) *dwlt and wnt lft: short-lived effrt on far side over 2f out* **50/1**

7 1 1/4 **Ink Stone (IRE)** 3-9-3 0 JohnEgan 3 27
(Jane Chapple-Hyam) *s.s: bhd tl hdwy over 3f out: rdn and wknd over 2f out* **6/1**

03 **8** 1 1/2 **Bluebird Chariot**[39] 3445 5-9-6 0 KevinGhunowa(3) 4 24
(J M Bradley) *wnt lft s: led: hdd 4f out: wknd 3f out* **40/1**

3/0 **9** 34 **Petroglyph**[12] 4349 4-9-9 0 JamieSpencer 6 —
(P Bowen) *s.s and wnt lft: t.k.h: sn mid-div: hdwy to join ldr 4f out: wknd over 2f out* **14/1**

1m 31.82s (8.62) **Going Correction** +1.25s/f (Soft)
WFA 3 from 4yo+ 6lb **9** Ran SP% **113.3**
Speed ratings (Par 103): **100,97,93,90,88 80,78,77,38**
toteswinger: 1&2 £3.20, 1&3 £8.50, 2&3 £3.80. CSF £11.19 TOTE £6.20: £1.80, £1.20, £2.60; EX 13.20 Trifecta £75.90 Pool: £542.63 - 5.29 winning units..
Owner Miss R Dobson **Bred** Moyglare Stud Farm Ltd **Trained** Charlton Mackrell, Somerset

FOCUS
The ground was offically changed to heavy before this race and by now the desperate conditions were taking their toll with half of them beaten before halfway. The winner looks ground dependent and the form as a whole is shaky. It has been rated through the runner-up.

4710 JENKINSONS CATERERS 1ST CHOICE FOR HOSPITALITY H'CAP (LADIES RACE) 1m 14y
5:15 (5:17) (Class 5) (0-70,70) 3-Y-0+ **£2,623** (£813; £406; £203) **Stalls** Low

Form RPR

0260 **1** **Barathea Dreams (IRE)**[21] 4048 7-10-0 **61** MrsSMoore 5 71
(J S Moore) *stdd s: hld up in rr: rdn and hdwy over 2f out: led jst over 1f out: r.o wl* **5/1**[1]

0416 **2** 2 **Libre**[16] 4215 8-9-12 **59** MissEJJones 6 65
(F Jordan) *hung lft thrght: chsd ldrs: wnt 2nd 3f out: ev ch over 1f out: nt qckn fnl f* **6/1**[2]

5560 **3** 1 3/4 **Outer Hebrides**[34] 3604 7-9-5 **52** (v) MissSBrotherton 1 54
(J M Bradley) *hld up in mid-div: hdwy over 3f out: one pce fnl f* **11/1**

5022 **4** 3/4 **Don Pietro**[11] 4390 5-10-2 **70** (b[1]) MissCBoxall(7) 4 71
(P A Blockley) *t.k.h: w ldr: led over 6f out tl jst over 1f out: no ex ins fnl f* **6/1**[2]

3030 **5** nk **Hucking Heat (IRE)**[13] 4309 4-9-4 **56** (p) MissRKneller(5) 3 56
(R Hollinshead) *in rr: hdwy over 1f out: kpt on same pce fnl f* **9/1**

-026 **6** shd **Castano**[17] 4186 4-9-13 **60** MissGDGracey-Davison 7 60
(B R Millman) *hld up and bhd: hdwy over 1f out: one pce fnl f* **9/1**

003 **7** hd **Mick Is Back**[19] 4129 4-9-4 **58** (vt) MissKMargarson(7) 10 57
(G G Margarson) *chsd ldrs: lost pl 5f out: hdwy over 2f out: one pce fnl f out* **9/1**

5600 **8** 6 **Indian Edge**[25] 3903 7-10-0 **61** MissLEllison 11 48
(B Palling) *prom tl wknd wl over 1f out: fin lame* **13/2**[3]

0-06 **9** 1/2 **Psychic Star**[11] 4365 5-9-5 **57** MissJodieHughes(5) 8 43
(Mrs A M Thorpe) *reminders after s: prom: rdn over 3f out: wknd over 2f out* **25/1**

1500 **10** 2 1/2 **Titfer (IRE)**[11] 4377 3-8-12 **52** MissARyan 9 33
(A W Carroll) *hld up in mid-div: rdn and struggling 4f out* **20/1**

2064 **11** 20 **Zach's Harmoney (USA)**[9] 4458 4-10-2 **63** MrsMarieKing 2 2
(P W Hiatt) *led over 1f: wknd over 3f out: t.o* **8/1**

1m 45.46s (9.26) **Going Correction** +1.25s/f (Soft)
WFA 3 from 4yo+ 7lb **11** Ran SP% **116.6**
Speed ratings (Par 103): **103,101,99,98,98 98,97,91,91,88 68**
toteswinger: 1&2 £5.70, 1&3 £14.40, 2&3 £12.10. CSF £33.97 CT £323.14 TOTE £6.50: £2.30, £1.70, £3.70; EX 25.20 Trifecta £160.60 Pool: £434.09 - 2.00 winning units. Place 6: £55.73 Place 5: £14.02 .
Owner J S Moore **Bred** Shadwell Estate Company Limited **Trained** Upper Lambourn, Berks

FOCUS
A moderate handicap for lady riders. Three of the more able pilots partnered the first three home so outside this type of race the form could prove to be misleading. It has been rated through the runner-up and third to earlier course and distance form.
Mick Is Back Official explanation: jockey said, regarding the running and riding, her orders had been to jump out handy, adding that gelding hung left throughout, and that she herself did not feel well as race progressed and so she was unable to ride out gelding more vigorously
Indian Edge Official explanation: jockey said gelding finished lame
Zach's Harmoney(USA) Official explanation: jockey said gelding had been unsuited by the soft ground
T/Jkpt: Not won. T/Plt: £42.80 to a £1 stake. Pool: £85,215.83. 1,451.84 winning tickets. T/Qpdt: £5.00 to a £1 stake. Pool: £7,334.90. 1,068.50 winning tickets. KH

4711 - 4714a (Foreign Racing) - See Raceform Interactive

3302 GOWRAN PARK (R-H)
Tuesday, August 5

OFFICIAL GOING: Good to yielding

4715a PAULSTOWN H'CAP 1m
7:35 (7:37) (45-65,70) 3-Y-O **£4,318** (£1,006; £443; £256)

RPR

1 **King's Road**[22] 4037 3-9-9 62 FMBerry 14 71+
(John Joseph Murphy, Ire) *chsd ldrs: 3rd 3f out: rdn fr 2f out: led ins fnl f: kpt on wl* **8/1**[3]

2 1 3/4 **Rue De Cabestan (IRE)**[24] 3992 3-8-9 48 JAHeffernan 4 53
(T G McCourt, Ire) *chsd ldrs: rdn in 4th 2f out: kpt on wl fnl f* **14/1**

3 nk **Metal Madness (IRE)**[4] 4613 3-9-10 70 5ex DEMullins(7) 5 74
(M G Quinlan) *mid-div: prog on outer into 5th over 2f out: kpt on fnl f* **9/4**[1]

4 3/4 **Turk (IRE)**[28] 3828 3-9-4 64 (p) EJMcNamara(7) 2 67
(G M Lyons, Ire) *chsd ldrs: led 2f out: sn rdn: hdd ins fnl f: sn no ex* **9/2**[2]

5 1 1/4 **Just Like Ivy (CAN)**[81] 2179 3-9-7 60 (p) DPMcDonogh 16 59
(Patrick Martin, Ire) *chsd ldrs: rdn in 5th 2f out: kpt on same pce* **20/1**

6 3/4 **Lord Rathvinden (IRE)**[9] 4469 3-9-7 60 PShanahan 6 57
(Tracey Collins, Ire) *mid-div: kpt on same pce st* **8/1**[3]

7 hd **Step Dancing**[9] 4469 3-8-13 59 SFoley(7) 11 56
(Mrs Prunella Dobbs, Ire) *in rr of mid-div: no imp fr 2f out* **20/1**

8 hd **Verumontanum (IRE)**[20] 4093 3-9-6 59 MCHussey 3 55
(Henry De Bromhead, Ire) *chsd ldrs: rdn in 7th 2f out: sn no ex* **12/1**

9 1 3/4 **Jack's A Guest (IRE)**[14] 4286 3-7-13 45 (b[1]) GFCarroll(7) 12 37
(Miss Jane Thomas, Ire) *led: rdn and hdd 2f out: sn wknd* **33/1**

10 nk **Who Needs A Hand (IRE)**[19] 4135 3-8-10 49 DMGrant 15 41
(Patrick J Flynn, Ire) *nvr bttr than mid-div* **20/1**

11 1/2 **Solo Performer (IRE)**[14] 4286 3-8-9 51 PBBeggy(3) 7 42
(H Rogers, Ire) *a towards rr* **20/1**

12 1/2 **Digital Dish (IRE)**[28] 3828 3-9-1 54 RPCleary 9 43
(Eamon Tyrrell, Ire) *nvr a factor* **14/1**

13 nk **Lady Marquet (IRE)**[14] 4286 3-7-13 45 (b[1]) JPFahy(7) 1 34
(Jarlath P Fahey, Ire) *a bhd* **20/1**

14 7 **Marceau (IRE)**[32] 3702 3-8-5 54 MariaQuinlan(10) 13 27
(Patrick J Flynn, Ire) *nvr a factor* **16/1**

15 1/2 **Kingsdalemillenium (IRE)**[24] 3985 3-9-9 62 WJSupple 10 34
(W M Roper, Ire) *trckd ldrs: wknd st* **16/1**

16 1 1/2 **Vica Pota (IRE)**[96] 1758 3-9-10 63 CDHayes 8 31
(H Rogers, Ire) *a bhd* **20/1**

1m 43.76s (2.26) **16** Ran SP% **135.5**
CSF £114.45 CT £360.95 TOTE £10.40: £3.00, £13.80, £1.20, £1.20; DF 234.80.
Owner Mrs John J Murphy **Bred** Mrs M Rogers **Trained** Upton, Co. Cork
■ Stewards' Enquiry : E J McNamara one-day ban: careless riding (Aug 19)

NOTEBOOK
Metal Madness(IRE), 5lb higher than when winning at Galway, ran another fine race in defeat and clearly has no problem with soft ground. (op 9/4 tchd 2/1)

4716 - 4718a (Foreign Racing) - See Raceform Interactive

4673 DEAUVILLE (R-H)
Tuesday, August 5

OFFICIAL GOING: Turf course - soft; all-weather - standard

4719a PRIX DE TOURGEVILLE (LISTED RACE) (C&G) (ROUND COURSE) 1m (R)
2:20 (2:24) 3-Y-O **£20,221** (£8,088; £6,066; £4,044; £2,022)

RPR

1 **Calming Influence (IRE)**[48] 3119 3-9-2 LDettori 10 109
(Saeed Bin Suroor) *hld up towards rr on outside: 5th st: hrd rdn 1 1/2f out: led ins fnl f: edgd rt u.p: drvn out* **26/10**[1]

2 ½ **Royal God (USA)**^{58} [2875] 3-9-2 .... OPeslier 5 108
(F Head, France)
3 snk **World Ruler**^{42} [3356] 3-8-12 .... SPasquier 7 104
(A Fabre, France)
4 ½ **Bermuda Rye (IRE)**^{43} 3-8-12 .... CSoumillon 2 103
(M Delzangles, France)
5 nk **Raspoutine (USA)**^{34} 3-8-12 .... ACrastus 9 102
(E Lellouche, France)
6 1½ **Violon Sacre (USA)**^{31} [3750] 3-8-12 .... C-PLemaire 4 99
(J-C Rouget, France)
7 ½ **Putney Bridge (USA)**^{31} [3750] 3-8-12 .... TThulliez 3 98
(Mme C Head-Maarek, France)
8 hd **Kitaj**^{46} 3-8-12 .... IMendizabal 4 97
(J-C Rouget, France)
9 nk **Salut L'Africain (FR)**^{25} [3938] 3-9-2 .... DBoeuf 6 100
(Robert Collet, France)

1m 44.2s (3.20) **9** Ran SP% **27.8**
PARI-MUTUEL: WIN 3.60; PL 1.70, 3.00, 3.60; DF 24.20.
Owner Godolphin **Bred** Mrs Helen Lyons **Trained** Newmarket, Suffolk

NOTEBOOK
Calming Influence(IRE), held up off the pace in seventh position for much of the race, took time to find top gear in the straight before producing a run up the centre of the track. He accelerated well at the furlong marker and was always doing enough to hold the runner-up. This softer ground seemed to suit and he remains capable of better.

4050 **BRIGHTON** (L-H)
Wednesday, August 6
OFFICIAL GOING: Good to firm (good in places)
Wind: Slight, against

4720 E B F KING'S HEAD AT BURGESS HILL MAIDEN STKS 6f 209y
2:30 (2:30) (Class 5) 2-Y-O **£3,784** (£1,132; £566; £283; £141) **Stalls** Low

Form RPR
42 1 **Starry Sky**^{14} [4289] 2-8-12 0 .... SebSanders 3 70
(Sir Mark Prescott) *awkward leaving stalls: led for 1f: trckd ldr: led jst ins fnl f: r.o wl* **8/11**^{1}
02 2 1¾ **Saharan Royal**^{34} [3645] 2-8-7 0 .... DavidProbert$^{(5)}$ 2 65
(M Salaman) *led after 1f: rdn and hdd jst ins fnl f: nt qckn* **7/2**^{2}
0 3 nk **Kersivay**^{18} [4184] 2-9-3 0 .... AdamKirby 1 70
(W R Swinburn) *s.i.s: hld up: rdn and hdwy 2f out: kpt on fnl f* **25/1**
50 4 1½ **Helpmeronda**^{18} [4199] 2-8-12 0 .... AlanMunro 5 61
(S A Callaghan) *in rr: drvn 1/2-way: swtchd rt over 1f out: r.o ins fnl f* **15/2**
6 5 1½ **Admiral Sandhoe (USA)**^{18} [4184] 2-9-3 0 .... JimCrowley 4 62
(Mrs A J Perrett) *t.k.h: hld up in tch: rdn over 2f out: kpt on one pce fnl f* **6/1**^{3}
00 6 1¾ **Red Reef**^{18} [4184] 2-8-12 0 .... TPO'Shea 7 52
(D J Coakley) *a in rr* **40/1**
56 7 2¼ **Teneo Vestri**^{41} [3412] 2-9-3 0 .... DaneO'Neill 6 51
(A B Haynes) *chsd ldrs: rdn 1/2-way: wknd over 1f out* **80/1**

1m 22.95s (-0.15) **Going Correction** -0.075s/f (Good) **7** Ran SP% **113.7**
Speed ratings (Par 94): **97,95,94,92,91 89,86**
toteswinger: 1&2 £1.50, 1&3 £6.40, 2&3 £9.40. CSF £3.47 TOTE £1.70: £1.10, £1.90; EX 3.70 Trifecta £33.00 Pool: £447.65. 10.02 winning units..
Owner Dr Catherine Wills **Bred** St Clare Hall Stud **Trained** Newmarket, Suffolk

FOCUS
A modest maiden, but one that should produce winners. The winner sets the level of the form.

NOTEBOOK
Starry Sky, who bumped into a useful sort at Catterick last time, was back up to 7f and set a good standard. Weak at the head of the market, she was never far from the lead and, having come under pressure, kept finding to get on top inside the final furlong. Although by top sprinter Oasis Dream, her dam was a middle-distance winner and 1m should be within her range this season. There may be more to come from her in nurseries. (op 4-6 tchd 8-13 and 4-5 tchd 10-11 in places)
Saharan Royal improved on her debut effort when finishing second at Warwick last time and she took another step forward here. She held a narrow advantage over the winner until a furlong out, but was always just coming off worse. Holding on for second, she is clearly going the right way and has the option of nurseries now. (op 5-1 tchd 11-2)
Kersivay, far too inexperienced to overcome a poor draw on his debut at Lingfield, had clearly learned a bit from that and ran a much improved race. He travelled well early and stuck on to just miss out on second, showing enough to suggest a similarly modest maiden should come his way. (op 40-1)
Helpmeronda, who got a bit behind early, made some late gains and is now eligible for a handicap mark. She will stay further than this and should find a small race. (op 9-2)
Admiral Sandhoe(USA), several places ahead of Kersivay on his debut, was a bit keen early on and then found himself unable to quicken. His stable have hardly had a vintage season, but he probably deserves another chance. (op 9-1)

4721 JACK SANDHU PUB CO H'CAP 1m 1f 209y
3:00 (3:00) (Class 5) (0-70,71) 3-Y-O+ **£3,154** (£944; £472; £236; £117) **Stalls** High

Form RPR
0332 1 **Gracechurch (IRE)**^{11} [4409] 5-9-4 57 .... SteveDrowne 8 59
(R J Hodges) *hld up in rr: hdwy on outside over 2f out: rdn and sustained run to ld ins fnl f* **5/1**^{3}
0533 2 1 **Hawk House**^{13} [4332] 3-9-3 65 .... MichaelHills 5 65
(B W Hills) *led tl hdd 7f out: styd prom: rdn over 1f out: r.o and wnt 2nd nr fin* **11/4**^{2}
0016 3 nk **Jemiliah**^{16} [4259] 3-8-11 59 .... SebSanders 2 58
(B G Powell) *prom on ins: led 7f out tl rdn and hdd ins fnl f: lost 2nd nr fin* **10/1**
0055 4 ¾ **Fantasy Crusader**^{12} [4371] 9-8-9 48 oh2 .... DaneO'Neill 7 46
(R M H Cowell) *t.k.h: sn prom: rdn over 2f out: fdd wl ins fnl f* **20/1**
0422 5 shd **Spanish Diva**^{2} [4691] 4-9-7 67 .... WilliamCarson$^{(7)}$ 4 65
(S C Williams) *hld up in rr: hdwy on outside over 2f out: hung lft appr fnl f: styd on ins fnl f* **5/2**^{1}
6000 6 1¼ **Recalcitrant**^{11} [4414] 5-8-10 49 .... JamesDoyle 6 44
(S Dow) *s.i.s: hld up in tch: rdn 2f out: wknd over 1f out* **10/1**
1521 7 3½ **Sabre Light**^{9} [4491] 3-9-6 71 6ex .... (p) DominicFox$^{(3)}$ 9 59
(A Bailey) *hld up: rdn over 3f out: wknd over 1f out* **12/1**
00-0 8 ½ **Fleur De Montjeu (IRE)**^{60} [2833] 3-8-7 55 .... SaleemGolam 1 42
(W R Swinburn) *hld up: rdn over 3f out: wknd over 1f out* **33/1**
5235 P **Nightspot**^{26} [3914] 7-9-13 66 .... StephenCarson 3 —
(Eve Johnson Houghton) *t.k.h: prom tl qckly lost pl over 5f out: p.u over 3f out: dismntd* **13/2**

2m 4.80s (1.20) **Going Correction** -0.075s/f (Good)
WFA 3 from 4yo+ 9lb **9** Ran SP% **118.8**
Speed ratings (Par 103): **92,91,90,90,90 89,86,86,—**
toteswinger: 1&2 £1.80, 1&3 £7.10, 2&3 £8.20. CSF £19.77 CT £135.12 TOTE £4.00: £1.70, £1.50, £2.30; EX 13.80 Trifecta £125.70 Pool: £543.99. 3.20 winning units..
Owner Mrs S G Clapp **Bred** Major K R Thompson **Trained** Charlton Mackrell, Somerset

FOCUS
Nobody wanted to lead and they crawled through the early stages in what was a race full of disappointing sorts. Weak form, and it is doubtful whether the winner had to improve on his latest form.

4722 DRINK IN BRIGHTON (S) H'CAP 1m 3f 196y
3:30 (3:32) (Class 6) (0-55,55) 3-Y-O+ **£1,942** (£578; £288; £144) **Stalls** High

Form RPR
5002 1 **Bundle Up**^{16} [4250] 5-8-13 47 .... RichardHughes 2 53
(P D Evans) *s.i.s: sn in tch: swtchd rt over 1f out: rdn and r.o to ld ins fnl f* **3/1**^{1}
0110 2 1 **Ambrose Princess (IRE)**^{13} [4326] 3-8-7 55 .... KevinGhunowa$^{(3)}$ 4 59
(R A Harris) *in tch tl lost pl 5f out: swtchd rt over 2f out: r.o u.p to go 2nd nr fin* **14/1**
-030 3 shd **My Legal Eagle (IRE)**^{12} [4366] 14-8-8 45 .... LukeMorris$^{(3)}$ 9 49
(E G Bevan) *hld up: hdwy 5f out: rdn and r.o fnl f: nvr nrr* **11/1**
6464 4 ½ **Sir Liam (USA)**^{11} [4409] 4-9-6 54 .... IanMongan 5 58
(R A Teal) *hld up in rr: hdwy 7f out: wnt 2nd 2f out: led briefly ins fnl f: no ex* **9/2**^{2}
5354 5 ½ **Missie Baileys**^{16} [4250] 6-9-1 49 .... (p) LPKeniry 1 52
(Mrs L J Mongan) *a.p: rdn to ld over 2f out: hdd and fdd ins fnl f* **11/1**
0605 6 nk **Fateful Attraction**^{12} [4390] 5-8-11 45 .... (t) PaulDoe 3 47
(I A Wood) *mid-div: rdn to chse ldrs over 1f out: wknd ins fnl f: sddle slipped* **16/1**
3310 7 2¼ **Lady Jinks**^{6} [4564] 3-8-2 54 .... BillyCray$^{(7)}$ 12 53
(M D I Usher) *in tch: rdn 4f out: wknd fnl f* **12/1**
0564 8 9 **Ask Nicely**^{15} [4280] 3-8-9 54 .... SebSanders 11 38
(W R Muir) *s.i.s: hdwy 3f out: one pce ins fnl 2f* **8/1**^{3}
6000 9 3½ **Shaheer (IRE)**^{13} [4322] 6-8-11 45 .... (v) JimCrowley 14 24
(J Gallagher) *sn prom: wknd wl over 1f out* **33/1**
-006 10 1½ **Peer Pressure**^{19} [4165] 3-8-3 48 .... (v^{1}) JimmyQuinn 16 24
(B R Johnson) *mid-div: chsd ldrs 2f out: wknd qckly appr fnl f* **33/1**
0020 11 16 **Bainisteoir**^{8} [4498] 3-8-7 52 .... RichardKingscote 8 —
(S Kirk) *hld up in rr: a bhd* **12/1**
605- 12 2½ **Rock Me (IRE)**^{232} [7176] 3-7-9 45 .... (p) DavidProbert$^{(5)}$ 13 —
(S A Callaghan) *a bhd* **11/1**
035 13 12 **Danish Monarch**^{13} [4322] 7-9-4 52 .... FergusSweeney 6 —
(David Pinder) *led tl hdd over 2f: wknd qckly* **14/1**
0006 14 8 **Syriana**^{8} [4498] 3-8-7 55 .... (v^{1}) DominicFox$^{(3)}$ 15 —
(A Bailey) *sn trckd ldr: lost pl over 5f out: sn bhd* **40/1**

2m 31.31s (-1.39) **Going Correction** -0.075s/f (Good)
WFA 3 from 4yo+ 11lb **14** Ran SP% **122.2**
Speed ratings (Par 101): **101,100,100,100,99 99,98,92,89,88 78,76,68,63**
toteswinger: 1&2 £6.80, 1&3 £8.00, 2&3 £19.70. CSF £47.40 CT £423.58 TOTE £3.30: £1.60, £3.70, £4.90; EX 49.10 Trifecta £157.60 Part won. Pool: £213.05. 0.40 winning units..The winner was bought in for £8,000. Sir Liam was claimed by Mustafa Khan for £6,000.
Owner M D Jones **Bred** Bloomsbury Stud **Trained** Pandy, Monmouths

FOCUS
This handicap looked a shade better than its lowly selling status. It appeared to be run at a good pace and the form is sound.
Fateful Attraction Official explanation: jockey said saddle slipped
Danish Monarch Official explanation: jockey said gelding felt jarred up

4723 JOHN SMITH'S BRIGHTON MILE CHALLENGE TROPHY (H'CAP) 7f 214y
4:00 (4:02) (Class 4) (0-80,80) 3-Y-O+
£15,480 (£4,640; £2,322; £1,157; £580; £292) **Stalls** Low

Form RPR
1310 1 **Choreography**^{34} [3653] 5-9-6 76 .... (p) PaulDoe 6 86
(Jim Best) *a.p: chal ldr fr over 1f out: led 1f out: hld on* **12/1**
0041 2 nk **Moonlight Man**^{16} [4248] 7-9-7 77 .... (t) SebSanders 8 86
(C R Dore) *led tl rdn and hdd narrowly 1f out: kpt on to line* **20/1**
5050 3 1½ **Tender The Great (IRE)**^{11} [4422] 5-9-1 71 .... RichardKingscote 11 77
(V Smith) *a.p: rdn over 1f out: kpt on to go 3rd ins fnl f* **16/1**
2451 4 shd **Count Ceprano (IRE)**^{4} [4627] 4-9-4 79 .... DavidProbert$^{(5)}$ 14 84+
(M D I Usher) *towards rr: rdn 2f out: rdn and r.o fnl f: nvr enarer* **9/2**^{1}
6045 5 1¼ **Buxton**^{7} [4528] 4-9-5 75 .... (t) RobertHavlin 3 77
(R Ingram) *mid-div: rdn over 2f out: kpt on fnl f* **18/1**
2323 6 ½ **Bobski (IRE)**^{9} [4489] 6-9-7 77 .... (p) RichardHughes 2 78
(Miss Gay Kelleway) *prom: rdn over 1f out: one pce fnl f* **7/1**^{3}
6-50 7 shd **Officer**^{18} [4191] 4-9-9 79 .... (bt) GeorgeBaker 10 80
(G L Moore) *trckd ldr tl wknd over 1f out* **14/1**
0044 8 nk **Ivory Lace**^{8} [4509] 7-9-10 80 .... JimCrowley 16 80+
(S Woodman) *mid-div: rdn 4f out: no hdwy fnl 2f* **13/2**^{2}
4061 9 shd **Mount Hermon (IRE)**^{15} [4268] 4-9-4 77 .... (b) TravisBlock$^{(3)}$ 4 77
(H Morrison) *trckd ldrs tl wknd ins fnl f* **17/2**
0305 10 nk **Support Fund (IRE)**^{11} [4433] 4-9-2 72 .... StephenCarson 12 71+
(Eve Johnson Houghton) *in rr: making sme hdwy whn hmpd ent fnl f* **40/1**
0010 11 ½ **Eastern Emperor**^{20} [4121] 4-9-4 74 .... (p) AdamKirby 15 72
(W R Swinburn) *hld up: hdwy but hung lft fr over 2f out: short of room ins fnl f* **16/1**
0250 12 ½ **Woodcote Place**^{8} [4509] 5-9-9 79 .... DaneO'Neill 9 76
(P R Chamings) *in tch: rdn 2f out: wknd 1f out* **7/1**^{3}
3306 13 ¾ **Lord Theo**^{4} [4627] 4-9-9 79 .... JamesDoyle 13 74+
(N P Littmoden) *hld up: effrt over 2f out: wknd over 1f out* **25/1**
0521 14 2 **Millfield (IRE)**^{21} [4081] 5-9-4 74 .... LPKeniry 5 65+
(P R Chamings) *squeezed out s: t.k.h: making sme hdwy whn hmpd ins fnl f* **12/1**
-104 15 nk **Perfect Treasure (IRE)**^{18} [4198] 5-9-8 78 .... AlanMunro 1 68
(J A R Toller) *mid-div on ins: rdn over 2f out: sn btn* **14/1**
6050 16 ¾ **Full Victory (IRE)**^{15} [4276] 6-9-4 74 .... SteveDrowne 7 62+
(R A Farrant) *in rr: effrt whn hmpd over 1f out: nt rcvr* **20/1**

1m 33.51s (-2.49) **Going Correction** -0.075s/f (Good) **16** Ran SP% **128.6**
Speed ratings (Par 105): **109,108,107,107,105 105,105,104,104,104 104,103,102,100,100 99**
toteswinger: 1&2 £43.20, 1&3 £72.70, 2&3 £98.70. CSF £246.77 CT £3857.01 TOTE £17.20: £3.80, £4.80, £4.80, £1.60; EX 209.80 TRIFECTA Not won..
Owner Bill Wallace **Bred** Cheveley Park Stud Ltd **Trained** Lewes, E Sussex

FOCUS
A sound line-up for a good prize, slightly spoilt by a steady early pace and the first three were always prominent. The winner improved for his new yard; both Choreography and Moonlight Man came down the inside rail, and had the race between them inside the final furlong.
Count Ceprano(IRE) Official explanation: vet said gelding had been struck into behind
Eastern Emperor Official explanation: jockey said gelding hung left
Woodcote Place Official explanation: jockey said gelding had been denied a clear run
Lord Theo Official explanation: jockey said gelding reared in the stalls and missed the break
Millfield(IRE) Official explanation: jockey said gelding was denied a clear run

4724 SOUTH EAST LEISURE GROUP H'CAP — 7f 214y
4:30 (4:30) (Class 5) (0-70,70) 3-Y-O **£2,838** (£849; £424; £212; £105) **Stalls** Low

Form RPR
4111 **1** **Ogre (USA)**[35] 3604 3-9-5 **68** .... TGMcLaughlin 4 73
(P D Evans) *hld up: hdwy 2f out: rdn to ld 1f out: drvn out* **3/1**[1]
5003 **2** 1 3/4 **This Ones For Eddy**[7] 4538 3-8-13 **62** .... AlanMunro 1 63
(S Parr) *hld up: hdwy 2f out: ev ch whn hung rt ent fnl f: kpt on ins fnl f* **10/3**[2]
0622 **3** nk **Thunder Gorge (USA)**[14] 4310 3-9-6 **69** .... LPKeniry 6 69
(Mouse Hamilton-Fairley) *led tl rdn and hdd 1f out: lost 2nd ins fnl f* **3/1**[1]
3134 **4** 2 1/4 **Jollyhockeysticks**[21] 4082 3-9-2 **65** .... TPO'Shea 3 60
(M R Channon) *trckd ldrs: edgd lft over 1f out: fdd ins fnl f* **7/2**[3]
-300 **5** 3 1/4 **Wusuul**[14] 4300 3-9-7 **70** .... SebSanders 5 58
(C E Brittain) *chsd ldr fr 1/2-way tl rdn and wknd appr fnl f* **14/1**
1010 **6** 1 **Lancaster Lad (IRE)**[11] 4413 3-8-13 **62** ....(p) SteveDrowne 7 47
(A B Haynes) *s.i.s: hld up: rdn 2f out: edgd lft and wknd 1f out* **8/1**
0P0- **7** 20 **Valentine Blue**[273] 6714 3-8-3 **55** ....(t) KevinGhunowa(3) 2 —
(A B Haynes) *t.k.h: trckd ldr to 1/2-way: sn wknd* **40/1**
1m 36.81s (0.81) **Going Correction** -0.075s/f (Good) **7 Ran SP% 115.5**
Speed ratings (Par 100): **92,90,89,87,84 83,63**
toteswinger: 1&2 £2.80, 1&3 £3.10, 2&3 £2.00. CSF £13.63 TOTE £4.20: £2.10, £1.90; EX 16.80.
Owner Diamond Racing Ltd **Bred** Gulf Coast Farms LLC **Trained** Pandy, Monmouths
FOCUS
This was notable for a new tactic, usually employed on softer ground, in that the field shunned the inside rail and, having spun midtrack, ended up all over the place and nearer the stands' side, although the ready winner Ogre stuck straightest and truest midtrack in the final two furlongs. The pace was not strong either and the form is ordinary.
Valentine Blue Official explanation: jockey said gelding had been unbalanced

4725 HARDINGS BAR AND CATERING SERVICES H'CAP — 5f 213y
5:00 (5:02) (Class 6) (0-55,55) 3-Y-O **£2,590** (£770; £385; £192) **Stalls** Low

Form RPR
0-00 **1** **Cryptonite Diamond (USA)**[41] 3395 3-8-11 **52** ....(t) AdamKirby 14 62
(W R Swinburn) *hld up in rr: rdn and hdwy 1f out: r.o to ld ins fnl f* **9/1**
0430 **2** 3/4 **The Little Fizzer (IRE)**[12] 4370 3-8-11 **52** .... TGMcLaughlin 12 60
(P D Evans) *mid-div: rdn over 1f out: styd on and ev ch ins fnl f: nt qckn cl home* **4/1**[2]
0460 **3** 1/2 **Spic 'n Span**[13] 4324 3-8-11 **55** ....(b) KevinGhunowa(3) 9 61
(R A Harris) *trckd ldrs: rdn over 1f out: led briefly u.p ins fnl f: no ex* **13/2**[3]
0520 **4** 2 1/2 **Bye Baby Bunting**[22] 4052 3-8-5 **46** oh1 .... JimmyQuinn 2 45
(B R Johnson) *s.i.s: towards rr: hdwy on ins 2f out: one pce fnl f* **13/2**[3]
-540 **5** 1/2 **New Balls Please (IRE)**[13] 4338 3-8-9 **50** ....(b) IanMongan 1 47
(P M Phelan) *led tl wknd and hdd ins fnl f* **10/1**
3450 **6** 1 1/2 **Run From Nun**[41] 3395 3-8-5 **46** .... TPO'Shea 4 39
(John Berry) *t.k.h: in tch: rdn 2f out: wknd fnl f* **33/1**
0000 **7** 1 1/2 **Talamahana**[15] 4278 3-8-11 **52** ....(b) SteveDrowne 10 40
(A B Haynes) *in rr: rdn 1/2-way: nvr on terms* **33/1**
060 **8** 1 **Cherries On Top (IRE)**[57] 2918 3-8-5 **46** oh1 .... PaulDoe 6 31
(I A Wood) *slowly away: in rr and nvr on terms* **16/1**
030 **9** 1/2 **Rossini Byline (IRE)**[50] 3118 3-8-10 **51** .... SebSanders 13 35
(J L Spearing) *c to ins fr wd draw sn after s: rdn 2f out: a bhd* **11/1**
0206 **10** 1 3/4 **Ma Mirage (IRE)**[15] 4271 3-8-5 **46** oh1 ....(v) SaleemGolam 7 24
(S C Williams) *in tch tl wknd over 1f out* **33/1**
-540 **11** 1 1/2 **Tittle**[20] 4107 3-9-0 **55** .... DaneO'Neill 5 29+
(H Candy) *trckd ldr tl wknd over 1f out: eased ins fnl f* **7/2**[1]
0050 **12** 1/2 **The Magic Blanket (IRE)**[15] 4272 3-8-11 **52** ....(t) JamesDoyle 8 24+
(Stef Liddiard) *prom tl wknd over 1f out: eased ins fnl f* **14/1**
6054 **13** 15 **Heron (IRE)**[13] 4336 3-8-2 **46** oh1 .... DominicFox(3) 11 —
(M R Hoad) *a bhd* **16/1**
68.99 secs (-1.21) **Going Correction** -0.075s/f (Good) **13 Ran SP% 123.6**
Speed ratings (Par 98): **105,104,103,100,99 97,95,94,93,91 89,88,68**
toteswinger: 1&2 £10.80, 1&3 £16.90, 2&3 £7.90. CSF £45.77 CT £255.42 TOTE £12.70: £3.90, £1.70, £2.80; EX 56.00 Trifecta £456.60 Pool: £617.09. 1.00 winning units. Place 6: £67.54, Place 5: £55.80..
Owner The Code Breakers **Bred** George Brunachini & Bona Terra Farm **Trained** Aldbury, Herts
FOCUS
A poor handicap, rated around the third to last month's course-and-distance effort and sound enough for the grade.
Cryptonite Diamond(USA) Official explanation: trainer's rep said, regarding the apparent improvement in form, she is a smart filly who always tries hard and everything went right on this occasion
Cherries On Top(IRE) Official explanation: jockey said gelding had missed the break
The Magic Blanket(IRE) Official explanation: jockey said gelding had no more to give
Heron(IRE) Official explanation: jockey said gelding had been struck into
T/Plt: £98.40 to a £1 stake. Pool: £70,336.42. 521.55 winning tickets. T/Qpdt: £39.10 to a £1 stake. Pool: £4,063.00. 76.80 winning tickets. JS

4523 KEMPTON (A.W) (R-H)
Wednesday, August 6

OFFICIAL GOING: Standard
Wind: Almost Nil Weather: Fine, humid

4726 WEATHERBYS BANK APPRENTICE H'CAP (ROUND 9) — 1m 3f (P)
6:20 (6:20) (Class 4) (0-85,85) 4-Y-O+ **£4,727** (£1,406; £702; £351) **Stalls** High

Form RPR
206- **1** **Shimoni**[185] 7055 4-9-0 **78** .... JemmaMarshall(3) 1 85
(G L Moore) *trckd ldng pair to 4f out: outpcd 3f out: rdn and grad clsd fr 2f out: wnt 2nd 1f out: kpt on to ld last 75yds* **20/1**
2522 **2** 1 1/4 **Show Winner**[21] 4078 5-9-2 **80** .... DavidProbert(3) 9 85
(A M Balding) *disp ld to over 3f out: sn rdn and nt qckn: clsd grad u.p fr 2f out: kpt on* **6/4**[1]
0101 **3** 3/4 **Safari Sundowner (IRE)**[21] 4078 4-9-7 **85** .... WilliamCarson(3) 8 89+
(P Winkworth) *lw: trckd ldrs: rdn and swift prog to ld over 3f out: drvn 3 l clr over 2f out: tired over 1f out: collared last 75yds* **11/4**[2]
1503 **4** 5 **Prime Number (IRE)**[14] 4309 6-9-3 **81** .... MCGeran(3) 5 76
(J Akehurst) *disp ld to over 3f out: nt qckn u.p sn after: wknd over 1f out* **11/1**
1354 **5** 1 1/2 **Motarjm (USA)**[52] 2076 4-9-9 **84** ....(t) JackMitchell 7 76
(H J Collingridge) *s.i.s: in tch in rr: outpcd 3f out: effrt 2f out: sn no prog* **7/1**[3]
4001 **6** 6 **Resplendent Ace (IRE)**[13] 4343 4-8-10 **76** .... MrJPFeatherstone(5) 2 57
(P Howling) *hld up: racd v wd bnd over 4f out: sn lost tch: struggling fnl 3f* **8/1**
1315 **7** 1 1/4 **Wind Flow**[74] 2414 4-8-8 **72** .... JPHamblett(3) 4 51
(C A Dwyer) *hld up: racd wd bnd over 4f out: sn lost tch: struggling fnl 3f* **10/1**
4560 **8** 25 **Lisathedaddy**[32] 3729 6-9-6 **84** .... KylieManser(3) 6 18
(B G Powell) *v rel to r and lft 25 l: a t.o* **16/1**
2m 21.11s (-0.79) **Going Correction** +0.05s/f (Slow) **8 Ran SP% 118.3**
Speed ratings (Par 105): **104,103,102,98,97 93,92,74**
toteswinger: 1&2 £11.70, 1&3 £23.00, 2&3 £2.40. CSF £52.50 CT £117.45 TOTE £27.20: £5.10, £1.30, £1.10; EX 69.00.
Owner The Welldiggers Partnership **Bred** Lakin Bloodstock And H And W Thornton **Trained** Woodingdean, E Sussex
FOCUS
Quite a decent race for its type although the time was only modest. The winner is rated to her 3yo best.
Lisathedaddy Official explanation: jockey said mare was reluctant to race

4727 KEMPTON FOR WEDDINGS H'CAP — 1m (P)
6:50 (6:52) (Class 6) (0-65,65) 3-Y-O+ **£2,047** (£604; £302) **Stalls** High

Form RPR
02 **1** **Anthill**[21] 4084 4-9-8 **59** .... GeorgeBaker 9 70
(I A Wood) *trckd ldr: led 2f out: kicked 2 l clr over 1f out: in command after: rdn out* **4/1**[1]
-046 **2** 1 **Bauhaus Bourbon (USA)**[18] 4183 3-9-7 **65** .... RichardHughes 4 73
(P F I Cole) *trckd ldrs: rdn to go 2nd over 1f out: tried to cl on wnr and clr of rest but a hld fnl f* **7/1**[3]
5004 **3** 3 3/4 **Timber Creek**[7] 4524 3-9-7 **65** .... FergusSweeney 7 64+
(H Candy) *hld up in rr of main gp: gng wl but ldrs kicking on over 2f out: prog wl over 1f out: r.o to take 3rd last 150yds: no ch of catching ldng pair* **10/1**
0424 **4** 1 3/4 **Grizedale (IRE)**[21] 4084 9-9-1 **57** ....(tp) DavidProbert(5) 6 53
(M J Attwater) *t.k.h early: hld up in midfield: nt qckn over 2f out: sme prog u.p on outer over 1f out: one pce fnl f* **7/1**[3]
-040 **5** nk **Paradise Island (IRE)**[16] 4253 3-9-7 **65** .... JimmyFortune 11 60
(E A L Dunlop) *lw: trckd ldng pair to 2f out: nt qckn: one pce after* **12/1**
0510 **6** 4 1/2 **Parthenope**[28] 3839 5-9-4 **55** .... RobertHavlin 1 40
(J A Geake) *trckd ldrs and racd wd: outpcd fr over 2f out: n.d after* **25/1**
-040 **7** hd **Yes Eighteen (IRE)**[79] 2261 3-9-7 **65** .... MichaelHills 14 49
(J W Hills) *pushed up into midfield on inner: nt qckn over 2f out: shkn up and no prog over 1f out* **20/1**
02 **8** nk **Lady Amberlini**[56] 2946 3-8-13 **60** .... LukeMorris(3) 2 43
(P D Evans) *b.hind: settled in rr of main gp: rdn 3f out: no real prog* **16/1**
05/ **9** 1 **Mohawk Star (IRE)**[116] 6762 7-9-7 **58** ....(b) MartinDwyer 12 40
(I A Wood) *slowest away and rousted along early: detached in last trio and nvr gng wl: kpt on fnl f* **20/1**
2361 **10** nk **Le Chiffre (IRE)**[12] 4386 6-10-0 **65** ....(p) StephenDonohoe 13 46
(John A Harris) *led to 2f out: stl 3rd ent fnl f: wknd rapidly* **5/1**[2]
50-6 **11** 3/4 **Pride Of Northcare (IRE)**[29] 3826 4-9-6 **57** .... AdamKirby 5 36
(D Shaw) *hld up in last trio and detached: rdn and struggling 3f out* **16/1**
4045 **12** 10 **Milanollo**[44] 3314 3-9-4 **62** .... HayleyTurner 8 17
(M L W Bell) *lw: nvr beyond midfield: wknd over 2f out: t.o* **9/1**
1-20 **13** 11 **Pop Music (IRE)**[15] 4268 5-10-0 **65** .... JamesDoyle 10 —
(Ms J S Doyle) *a in last trio and detached: t.o* **14/1**
1m 40.28s (0.48) **Going Correction** +0.05s/f (Slow)
WFA 3 from 4yo+ 7lb **13 Ran SP% 120.3**
Speed ratings (Par 101): **99,98,94,92,92 87,87,87,86,85 85,75,64**
toteswinger: 1&2 £7.50, 1&3 £5.00, 2&3 £21.50. CSF £30.59 CT £267.40 TOTE £3.80: £1.90, £3.00, £3.90; EX 33.30.
Owner C S Tateson **Bred** Mrs A Ruggles **Trained** Upper Lambourn, Berks
FOCUS
A pretty dire contest offering a good opportunity for the winner to break her maiden after some good placed efforts. The form wouldn't be the most reliable however and the winning time was the slowest of the three races run over the trip on the card.

4728 DIGIBET MEDIAN AUCTION MAIDEN STKS — 7f (P)
7:20 (7:22) (Class 5) 2-Y-O **£2,590** (£770; £385; £192) **Stalls** High

Form RPR
30 **1** **Perfect Citizen (USA)**[19] 4150 2-9-3 0 .... AdamKirby 14 79+
(W R Swinburn) *lw: reluctant to enter stalls: mde virtually all: wandering but styd on wl fnl 2f: pushed out* **15/8**[1]
63 **2** 2 1/4 **Andhaar**[22] 4062 2-9-3 0 .... RHills 7 73
(E A L Dunlop) *lw: prom: chsd wnr 2f out: shkn up over 1f out: clr of rest but no imp fnl f* **11/4**[2]
3 6 **Do Be Brave (IRE)** 2-9-3 0 .... OscarUrbina 5 58
(G D Blake) *leggy: sn wl off the pce in rr: pushed along and prog fr over 2f out: styd on to take 3rd last 100yds* **33/1**
4 3/4 **Mayta Capac (USA)** 2-9-3 0 .... AlanMunro 12 57
(E F Vaughan) *w'like: scope: dwlt: sn in tch in midfield: effrt but outpcd over 2f out: shkn up and styd on to press for 3rd ins fnl f* **20/1**
05 **5** 2 **Daily Double**[9] 4480 2-9-3 0 .... RichardHughes 2 52
(R Hannon) *str: chsd wnr to 2f out: hanging and green after: wknd and lost 3rd fnl f* **8/1**
6 2 1/4 **Got Flash (FR)** 2-9-3 0 .... DaneO'Neill 9 46
(E J O'Neill) *unf: nvr beyond midfield: outpcd fr 3f out: n.d after* **16/1**
4 **7** 1 **Mr Snowballs**[30] 3798 2-9-3 0 .... FergusSweeney 13 43
(R A Farrant) *prom: disp 3rd 3f out but rdn: fdd fnl 2f* **14/1**
8 1/2 **Parc Des Princes (USA)** 2-9-3 0 .... LPKeniry 11 42
(A M Balding) *leggy: b.bkwd: dwlt: sn chsd ldrs: rdn 3f out: grad wknd* **6/1**[3]
9 1/2 **Sandor** 2-9-3 0 .... SebSanders 8 41
(P J Makin) *str: b.bkwd: s.s: rushed up on outer to rch midfield after 3f: wknd over 2f out* **12/1**
10 2 3/4 **Foxtrot Charlie** 2-9-3 0 .... StephenCarson 1 34
(P Winkworth) *w'like: str: dwlt: bdly outpcd and sn t.o in last: sme prog fnl 2f: nrst fin* **20/1**

0 **11** *hd* **My Choice**[9] 4488 2-9-3 0 ShaneKelly 10 34
(A P Jarvis) *w'like: chsd ldrs early: losing pl and struggling bef 1/2-way* **66/1**

12 *11* **Dubai Storming** 2-9-3 0 (b[1]) TPQueally 4 —
(E A L Dunlop) *w'like: scope: b'bkwd: dwlt: hld up in 11th: struggling sn after 1/2-way: t.o* **20/1**

13 *12* **Dicksons Delight (USA)** 2-9-3 0 MartinDwyer 3 —
(D K Ivory) *unf: scope: dwlt: sn t.o* **50/1**

14 *1 1/4* **Ditzy Diva** 2-8-12 0 HayleyTurner 6 —
(Jean-Rene Auvray) *a bhd: t.o fnl 3f* **66/1**

1m 26.73s (0.73) **Going Correction** +0.05s/f (Slow) **14** Ran SP% **129.3**
Speed ratings (Par 94): **97,94,87,86,84 81,80,80,79,76 76,63,49,48**
toteswinger: 1&2 £2.70, 1&3 £25.30, 2&3 £7.50. CSF £6.80 TOTE £2.20: £1.20, £1.80, £9.60; EX 8.00.
Owner Clark, Cunnane, Godfrey & Rice **Bred** Brereton C Jones **Trained** Aldbury, Herts

FOCUS
Not much strength in depth to this maiden despite the numbers but the front two, who dominated, look decent prospects.

NOTEBOOK
Perfect Citizen(USA) had shaped with great promise on his Sandown debut and things didn't really go his way at Newbury next time, so this was a good chance to get his career back on an upward curve. Bounced out of the stalls from a good draw against the inside rail, he made almost every yard, and won well despite tending to wander around in the closing stages. (op 11-4)
Andhaar had finished behind the winner when both made their debut at Sandown and finished exactly the same distance behind him here. He beat the rest senseless though and ought to go well enough in nurseries. (op 5-2 tchd 3-1)
Do Be Brave(IRE) came from a mile back to take a modest third under tender handling. He can only improve on this introduction. (op 50-1 tchd 25-1)
Mayta Capac(USA), a son of Thunder Gulch, made a pleasing debut, running on well after getting outpaced two furlongs out. He should do better. (op 16-1)
Daily Double still looks green but is in the right hands to exploit his ability to the maximum in his juvenile year. Official explanation: jockey said colt hung right

4729 DIGIBET.COM NURSERY 6f (P)
7:50 (7:52) (Class 4) 2-Y-O **£3,885** (£1,156; £577; £288) **Stalls** High

Form RPR

0645 **1** **Klynch**[5] 4594 2-9-3 **83** (b[1]) JimmyFortune 7 85
(B J Meehan) *s.i.s: t.k.h and sn trckd ldng pair: effrt on inner 2f out: drvn ahd ins fnl f: styd on wl* **15/2**

5424 **2** *1 1/2* **Black N Brew (USA)**[7] 4525 2-8-3 **69** JimmyQuinn 2 67
(J R Best) *s.i.s: settled in 6th: rdn over 2f out: styd on u.p fnl 2f: snatched 2nd last strides* **7/2**[2]

5032 **3** *hd* **Missile Dodger (USA)**[7] 4525 2-9-7 **87** SebSanders 8 84
(R M Beckett) *lw: led: kicked on over 2f out: worn down ins fnl f: lost 2nd last strides* **7/2**[2]

01 **4** *1/2* **Red Humour (IRE)**[14] 4305 2-9-0 **80** MichaelHills 6 75
(B W Hills) *swtg: trckd ldr: rdn 2f out: nt qckn over 1f out: one pce fnl f* **5/2**[1]

1343 **5** *1/2* **River Rye (IRE)**[25] 3961 2-8-12 **78** RichardHughes 1 72
(R Hannon) *reluctant to enter stalls: keen and hld up in last pair: shkn up and outpcd 2f out: kpt on fr over 1f out: nt pce to rch ldrs* **12/1**

000 **6** *1/2* **Join Up**[19] 4164 2-7-7 **64** oh8 DavidProbert[(5)] 4 56+
(W R Swinburn) *trckd ldng quartet: outpcd 2f out: urged along and styd on again fnl f* **40/1**

3630 **7** *1 3/4* **Duke Of Aquitaine (USA)**[26] 3924 2-8-6 **72** ow1 ShaneKelly 3 59
(P F I Cole) *mostly in last pair: rdn and fnd nil over 2f out: btn after* **7/1**

552 **8** *1 1/4* **Azwa**[25] 3959 2-8-4 **70** MartinDwyer 5 53
(E A L Dunlop) *trckd ldrs: rdn over 2f out: no imp over 1f out: wknd rapidly fnl f* **9/2**[3]

1m 14.29s (1.19) **Going Correction** +0.05s/f (Slow) **8** Ran SP% **125.6**
Speed ratings (Par 96): **94,92,91,91,90 89,87,85**
toteswinger: 1&2 £8.80, 1&3 £6.90, 2&3 £2.40. CSF £37.47 CT £114.17 TOTE £9.70: £2.60, £1.30, £1.60; EX 43.30.
Owner L P R Partnership **Bred** J C S Wilson Bloodstock **Trained** Manton, Wilts

FOCUS
Some fair sorts on show in this nursery. Solid form.

NOTEBOOK
Klynch made it two-from-two on Polytrack, producing a good turn of foot to mow down his rivals inside the final furlong. The first-time blinkers seemed to make a difference and the son of Kyllachy could well build on this. (op 10-1)
Black N Brew(USA) finished strongly and is surely worth another try at 7f. (op 10-3 tchd 3-1)
Missile Dodger(USA) had the run of things up front from the best draw, but having tried to steal the contest when kicking on two furlongs out found himself worn down in the closing stages. (op 10-3)
Red Humour(IRE) won a weak auction maiden over 7f at Lingfield when the odds-on favourite flopped but that didn't put off his supporters who ploughed into him at all rates down to favouritism. He is a decent type physically but still looks a bit green. (op 13-2 tchd 7-1)
River Rye(IRE) never saw much daylight up the straight and is likely to prove better than this. (op 11-1 tchd 10-1)
Azwa found herself stuck out wide throughout with no cover and faded tamely at the business end. Official explanation: trainer had no explanation for the poor form shown (op 11-4)

4730 DIGIBET CASINO MAIDEN STKS 1m (P)
8:20 (8:25) (Class 5) 3-Y-O+ **£2,590** (£770; £385; £192) **Stalls** High

Form RPR

2 **1** **Once A Gulch (USA)**[85] 2079 3-9-3 0 SebSanders 3 89+
(J Noseda) *w'like: scope: hld up in rr of main gp: gd prog on outer 3f out: led wl over 1f out: sn wl in command: styd on wl* **9/2**[2]

2 *2 1/2* **Mawatheeq (USA)** 3-9-3 0 RHills 9 83+
(M P Tregoning) *neat: w ldr: led wl over 2f out to wl over 1f out: outpcd by wnr but styd on wl enough* **7/1**[3]

3 *3* **Pivka** 3-8-12 0 JimmyFortune 2 71+
(Sir Michael Stoute) *w'like: scope: b.bkwd: hld up in rr of main gp: swtchd fr inner to outer over 2f out: prog after: pushed along and styd on wl to take 3rd fnl f* **20/1**

40 **4** *2 3/4* **Blow Hole (USA)**[19] 4161 3-9-3 0 ShaneKelly 13 70
(J Noseda) *trckd ldng pair: gng wl 3f out: outpcd and nudged along 2f out: kpt on steadily* **14/1**

5 *1* **Gaelic Dancer (IRE)** 3-9-3 0 TPQueally 1 68
(J G Given) *w'like: pressed ldrs and racd wd: lost pl 5f out: rdn and effrt to go prom again 3f out: outpcd fnl 2f* **66/1**

6 *2 1/4* **Act Of Diplomacy (USA)** 3-9-3 0 LDettori 11 63+
(Saeed Bin Suroor) *scope: s.i.s: sn in midfield: pushed along 1/2-way: outpcd and struggling over 2f out: n.d after* **8/15**[1]

7 *5* **Mayfair's Future** 3-9-3 0 StephenDonohoe 6 51
(J R Jenkins) *neat: trckd ldrs: cl up over 2f out: hanging and lost pl qckly wl over 1f out* **80/1**

04 **8** *3 3/4* **Cape Roberto (IRE)**[21] 4085 3-9-3 0 RobertHavlin 7 42
(Jamie Poulton) *hld up towards rr: prog to trck ldrs over 2f out: wknd over 1f out* **66/1**

9 *1* **Hammer** 3-9-3 0 RichardHughes 14 40
(M P Tregoning) *leggy: led to wl over 2f out: wknd and eased* **25/1**

10 *5* **Walhalla (IRE)** 3-9-3 0 MartinDwyer 8 29
(M P Tregoning) *w'like: b.bkwd: sn pushed along in last pair: nvr a factor* **33/1**

11 *nse* **Summer Loving (IRE)** 4-9-5 0 LPKeniry 10 24
(Mrs L C Jewell) *leggy: chsd ldrs tl wknd rapidly over 2f out* **66/1**

36 **12** *2 1/4* **Seasonal Cross**[145] 885 3-8-12 0 HayleyTurner 12 18
(S Dow) *sn last: a bhd* **50/1**

1m 39.82s (0.02) **Going Correction** +0.05s/f (Slow)
WFA 3 from 4yo 7lb **12** Ran SP% **121.8**
Speed ratings (Par 103): **101,98,95,92,91 89,84,80,79,74 74,72**
toteswinger: 1&2 £4.20, 1&3 £19.70, 2&3 £9.10. CSF £32.44 TOTE £5.20: £1.40, £1.70, £3.10; EX 27.50.
Owner Hesmonds Stud **Bred** Langsem Farm **Trained** Newmarket, Suffolk

FOCUS
Plenty of well-bred newcomers on show here but the horse with the best previous form came home a convincing winner. There are doubts ove the form, with the favourite below expectations, but a few winners should come out of this maiden.

4731 LONDON MILE H'CAP (LONDON MILE QUALIFIER) 1m (P)
8:50 (8:54) (Class 4) (0-85,84) 3-Y-O **£4,727** (£1,406; £702; £351) **Stalls** High

Form RPR

4322 **1** **Golden Penny**[30] 3799 3-8-7 **73** TravisBlock[(3)] 13 80
(H Morrison) *trckd ldng pair: effrt to chal over 1f out: led ent fnl f: drvn out and hld on* **11/1**

1-50 **2** *nk* **Rochefort (IRE)**[27] 3877 3-9-5 **82** JimmyFortune 7 88
(J H M Gosden) *lw: trckd ldrs: rdn and effrt over 2f out: prog to chal fnl f and edgd lft: jst hld nr fin* **3/1**[1]

0123 **3** *3/4* **Hilbre Court (USA)**[7] 4528 3-9-0 **77** AlanMunro 8 82+
(B J Meehan) *lw: hld up in rr: nt clr run briefly wl over 2f out: prog wl over 1f out: styd on wl to take 3rd last strides* **4/1**[2]

0-41 **4** *shd* **Ebn Malk (IRE)**[64] 2700 3-8-13 **76** PhilipRobinson 2 80
(M A Jarvis) *trckd ldrs and racd on outer: effrt over 2f out: edgd lft over 1f out: cl up fnl f: nt qckn* **9/2**[3]

0645 **5** *1/2* **King Hafhafah**[26] 3907 3-9-5 **82** GeorgeBaker 12 85
(I A Wood) *sn led: rdn over 2f out: edgd lft over 1f out: hdd & wknd ent fnl f* **20/1**

-616 **6** *1* **Lekita**[14] 4300 3-8-12 **75** AdamKirby 9 76+
(W R Swinburn) *settled in rr: sme prog 2f out: rdn and styd on same pce fr over 1f out: nvr nr enough to chal* **14/1**

-600 **7** *3* **Afram Blue**[55] 2974 3-8-13 **76** (t) RichardKingscote 4 70
(W J Knight) *racd v wd in midfield: lost grnd bnd over 3f out: nvr on terms after: plugged on* **40/1**

2323 **8** *1/2* **Ocean Legend (IRE)**[28] 3840 3-8-13 **76** MartinDwyer 3 69
(Miss J Feilden) *chsd ldr to 2f out: wknd rapidly fnl f* **6/1**

0-50 **9** *1/2* **Dry Speedfit (IRE)**[32] 3723 3-9-3 **80** DaneO'Neill 5 72
(G G Margarson) *a in rr: u.p and no prog over 2f out* **50/1**

0062 **10** *1 1/2* **Meydan Dubai (IRE)**[26] 3899 3-9-7 **84** (v) MohammedSaeed 6 72
(J R Best) *lw: racd wd and hld up in midfield: effrt over 2f out: urged along and sn no prog: wknd over 1f out* **12/1**

3160 **11** *4* **Sir Billy Nick**[82] 2161 3-8-10 **73** (v[1]) TPQueally 11 52
(J Noseda) *lw: nvr gng that wl in rr: struggling fr 3f out* **13/2**

130 **12** *4 1/2* **Avertis**[20] 4130 3-9-3 **80** (v[1]) SebSanders 10 49
(M Botti) *hld up in midfield on inner: reminders wl over 2f out: no prog sn after: eased whn no ch fnl f* **16/1**

1m 39.21s (-0.59) **Going Correction** +0.05s/f (Slow) **12** Ran SP% **128.5**
Speed ratings (Par 102): **104,103,102,102,102 101,98,97,97,95 91,87**
toteswinger: 1&2 £10.00, 1&3 £6.70, 2&3 £11.50. CSF £47.18 CT £168.67 TOTE £14.20: £3.70, £1.70, £1.50; EX 73.70.
Owner Mrs B Oppenheimer **Bred** Mrs B D Oppenheimer **Trained** East Ilsley, Berks

FOCUS
A competitive three-year-old handicap for the class and the quickest of the three races over the trip, although the pace seemed only ordinary and it seemed an advantage to race prominently. The form is rated through the fifth.
King Hafhafah Official explanation: jockey said gelding hung both ways
Sir Billy Nick Official explanation: jockey said colt was never travelling

4732 MIX BUSINESS WITH PLEASURE H'CAP 1m 3f (P)
9:20 (9:22) (Class 5) (0-75,74) 3-Y-O **£2,590** (£770; £385; £192) **Stalls** High

Form RPR

2006 **1** **Bushy Dell (IRE)**[28] 3841 3-8-6 **66** AmyBaker[(7)] 2 73
(Miss J Feilden) *sn trckd ldr: led over 2f out: sn pushed clr: styd on strly* **16/1**

-251 **2** *3* **Vilna (USA)**[7] 4527 3-9-6 **73** 6ex (v) GeorgeBaker 5 74
(S A Callaghan) *hld up in last pair: nt clr run over 2f out: squeezed through 2f out: drvn to chse wnr ins fnl f: limited rspnse and nvr clsd* **10/11**[1]

-000 **3** *2* **Harting Hill**[22] 4061 3-8-3 **56** ow1 MartinDwyer 8 54
(M P Tregoning) *t.k.h: prom: chsd wnr jst over 2f out: no imp: lost 2nd ins fnl f* **7/1**[3]

3225 **4** *1/2* **Shy**[28] 3841 3-9-6 **73** StephenCarson 7 70
(P Winkworth) *hld up in midfield: effrt on inner over 2f out: no imp over 1f out: kpt on same pce* **9/2**[2]

-420 **5** *6* **Wise Hawk**[41] 3407 3-9-7 **74** JimmyFortune 6 60
(C J Down) *trckd ldrs: rdn and nt qckn over 2f out: steadily outpcd after w hd high* **16/1**

-000 **6** *3 1/2* **Loyal Knight (IRE)**[13] 4332 3-8-13 **66** SebSanders 1 46
(S Kirk) *hld up towards rr: rdn and no prog over 2f out: sn btn* **11/1**

1301 **7** *3/4* **Novestar (IRE)**[29] 3824 3-9-1 **71** KevinGhunowa[(3)] 3 49
(G J Smith) *led to over 2f out: sn wknd* **8/1**

U5-5 **8** *9* **Greek Theatre (USA)**[200] 225 3-9-0 **67** (e) JamesDoyle 4 29
(Mrs A J Perrett) *v awkward s: hld up in last: tk fierce hold and wnt 3rd 4f out: wknd rapidly over 2f out* **25/1**

2m 21.01s (-0.89) **Going Correction** +0.05s/f (Slow) **8** Ran SP% **118.1**
Speed ratings (Par 100): **105,102,101,101,96 94,93,87**
toteswinger: 1&2 £6.70, 1&3 £17.00, 2&3 £2.00. CSF £32.32 CT £124.98 TOTE £22.10: £4.10, £1.10, £2.10; EX 37.50 Place 6 £ 50.30, Place 5 £ 35.43.
Owner R J Creese **Bred** Don Commins **Trained** Exning, Suffolk

FOCUS
A modest handicap run at an ordinary pace. The winner rates full value for the winning margin and is back to her best, but the form is on the weak side.
Novestar(IRE) Official explanation: jockey said colt had no more to give
T/Plt: £19.20 to a £1 stake. Pool: £57,224.68. 2,167.84 winning tickets. T/Qpdt: £6.30 to a £1 stake. Pool: £4,200.27. 485.90 winning tickets. JN

4415 NEWCASTLE (L-H)
Wednesday, August 6

OFFICIAL GOING: Soft
After 10mm rain the ground was described as 'very soft, heavy in places'.
Wind: light, half against Weather: rain before racing then overcast but dry

4733 OWACOUSTIC CEILINGS NURSERY — 7f
2:20 (2:22) (Class 5) 2-Y-O — **£3,784** (£1,132; £566; £283; £141) **Stalls Low**

Form — RPR
5051 **1** **Lahaleeb (IRE)**[3] 4666 2-9-1 **74** 6ex .... SamHitchcott 3 — 90+
(M R Channon) *trckd ldrs: swtchd rt 2f out: led over 1f out: sn clr: easily* **9/2**[1]
01 **2** 7 **Quatermain**[17] 4214 2-9-7 **80** .... TomEaves 8 — 79
(B Smart) *hld up in rr: hdwy over 2f out: wnt 2nd 1f out: no ch w wnr* **9/1**
032 **3** 1 **Thunderball**[17] 4213 2-9-3 **76** .... DanielTudhope 5 — 72
(A J McCabe) *trckd ldrs: effrt 2f out: wnt 3rd 1f out: kpt on same pce* **8/1**
536 **4** 8 **Tapis Wizard**[11] 4415 2-8-12 **74** .... AndrewMullen(3) 10 — 50
(M W Easterby) *s.s: swtchd rt and racd alone stands' side: hdwy to chse ldrs over 2f out: kpt on same pce* **5/1**[2]
3036 **5** 1 ¾ **Aegean Warning**[13] 4340 2-8-6 **65** .... (b[1]) FrancisNorton 11 — 37
(K A Ryan) *chsd ldrs: edgd lft and wknd 1f out* **16/1**
000 **6** 9 **Dark Moment**[17] 4214 2-8-8 **67** .... DaleGibson 13 — 16
(A Dickman) *in rr: nvr on terms* **40/1**
2621 **7** ¾ **Smalljohn**[5] 4604 2-9-6 **79** 6ex .... (v) DNolan 1 — 26
(D Carroll) *led tl over 1f out: wkng whn sltly hmpd 1f out* **8/1**
6630 **8** nk **El Portet**[5] 4594 2-8-7 **66** .... (p) RoystonFfrench 12 — 13
(G M Moore) *in rr: rdn 3f out: nvr on terms* **25/1**
500 **9** 3 ¼ **Monsieur Jourdain (IRE)**[22] 4045 2-7-12 **60** .... DuranFentiman(3) 2 — —
(T D Easterby) *in rr: sn drvn along: bhd fnl 3f* **8/1**
134 **10** 7 **Toby Tyler**[74] 2392 2-8-12 **74** .... JamieMoriarty(3) 7 — —
(P T Midgley) *sn trcking ldrs: wknd 2f out* **13/2**[3]
330 **11** 10 **Custard Cream Kid (IRE)**[17] 4214 2-8-10 **69** .... PaulHanagan 6 — —
(R A Fahey) *hld up in rr: rdn 3f out: sn wknd* **12/1**
443 **12** 7 **Little Tokyo (USA)**[21] 4072 2-8-7 **66** .... PaulFessey 9 — —
(J Howard Johnson) *w ldrs: lost pl over 3f out: bhd whn eased ins fnl f* **16/1**

1m 30.35s (2.95) **Going Correction** +0.275s/f (Good) — **12 Ran SP% 117.3**
Speed ratings (Par 94): **94,86,84,75,73 63,62,62,58,50 39,31**
toteswinger: 1&2 £5.90, 1&3 £8.40, 2&3 £5.90. CSF £44.38 CT £317.33 TOTE £4.40: £2.10, £2.80, £3.20; EX 21.80.
Owner M Al-Qatami & K M Al-Mudhaf **Bred** Tom Twomey **Trained** West Ilsley, Berks

FOCUS
The far side rail was the place to be and they came home well strung out. Further improvement from the winner and the placed horses deserve credit.

NOTEBOOK
Lahaleeb(IRE), turned out quickly under her penalty, started on terms this time. Pulled two horses wide for a run, she had this won in a matter of strides. The penny seems to have finally dropped. (op 10-3 tchd 3-1)
Quatermain, anchored off the pace, stayed on to chase home the winner but it was a hopelessly one-sided contest. (op 11-2)
Thunderball, never far away, could only stay on in his own time and probably appreciates much less soft ground than he encountered here. (op 10-1)
Tapis Wizard missed the break, possibly by design so he could switch to race alone on the stands' side. In the end he was well adrift of the first three on the other wing. (op 9-1)
Aegean Warning, in first-time blinkers, had no more to give when rolling off a straight line coming to the final furlong. (op 14-1)
Smalljohn Official explanation: jockey said gelding lost action

4734 ARMSTRONG WORLD INDUSTRIES MEDIAN AUCTION MAIDEN STKS — 6f
2:50 (2:51) (Class 6) 2-Y-O — **£2,590** (£770; £385; £192) **Stalls Low**

Form — RPR
3 **1** **Needwood Lad**[57] 2909 2-9-3 0 .... PaulHanagan 5 — 76+
(R A Fahey) *trckd ldrs: led appr fnl f: styd on strly* **7/4**[1]
0 **2** 2 ½ **Brazilian Art**[58] 2893 2-9-3 0 .... GregFairley 15 — 68+
(P W Chapple-Hyam) *swtchd lft after s: in rr: rdn and hdwy 2f out: styd on strly to take 2nd nr fin* **9/2**[2]
03 **3** ¾ **Cash In The Attic**[22] 4050 2-8-12 0 .... SamHitchcott 1 — 60
(M R Channon) *led tl appr fnl f: no ex* **11/1**
533 **4** 1 **Desert Falls**[22] 4045 2-9-3 70 .... DeanMcKeown 10 — 62
(R M Whitaker) *t.k.h: hdwy over 2f out: hung lft: kpt on ins fnl f* **13/2**[3]
5 2 ¼ **Liberty Diamond** 2-8-9 0 .... AndrewMullen(3) 4 — 51+
(K R Burke) *chsd ldrs: wkng whn sltly hmpd 1f out* **33/1**
6 ¾ **Kheleyf's Silver (IRE)** 2-8-12 0 .... TomEaves 7 — 48+
(B Smart) *in rr: hdwy over 2f out: nt clr run 1f out: kpt on wl* **8/1**
0054 **7** 1 ¾ **Royal Premium**[14] 4290 2-9-0 41 ow2 .... (p) PBradley(5) 14 — 50
(H A McWilliams) *racd wd: w ldr: edgd lft over 4f out: wkng whn edgd lft 1f out* **200/1**
8 3 ½ **Bubses Boy** 2-9-3 0 .... RoystonFfrench 13 — 38
(M L W Bell) *in rr snd sn drvn along* **16/1**
0 **9** 1 **Miss Gibboa (IRE)**[72] 2462 2-8-12 0 .... J-PGuillambert 6 — 30
(G A Swinbank) *chsd ldrs: lost pl over 1f out* **11/1**
6 **10** 5 **Magic Haze**[17] 4213 2-9-3 0 .... DanielTudhope 2 — 20
(Miss S E Hall) *chsd ldrs: wknd 2f out* **20/1**
11 7 **Following Wind** 2-8-12 0 .... FrancisNorton 16 — —
(K A Ryan) *swvd rt s: bhd and drvn along* **20/1**
00 **12** 1 ½ **Look For Value**[68] 2584 2-8-12 0 .... KimTinkler 11 — —
(N Tinkler) *s.i.s: swtchd lft after s: a towards rr* **80/1**
00 **13** 1 **Fizzy Friend**[17] 4213 2-8-9 0 .... JamieMoriarty(3) 8 — —
(J R Weymes) *mid-div: lost pl over 2f out* **100/1**

1m 17.35s (2.15) **Going Correction** +0.275s/f (Good) — **13 Ran SP% 116.7**
Speed ratings (Par 92): **96,92,91,90,87 86,84,79,78,71 62,60,58**
toteswinger: 1&2 £3.10, 1&3 £2.10, 2&3 £15.80. CSF £8.13 TOTE £2.60: £1.40, £1.70, £2.30; EX 11.60.
Owner Beechgrove Stud & David Bourne **Bred** Helshaw Grange Stud Ltd **Trained** Musley Bank, N Yorks

FOCUS
The winner is going the right away, and a much improved and highly creditable effort from the badly drawn runner-up.

NOTEBOOK
Needwood Lad, still carrying plenty of condition, knew his job this time and scored in most convincing fashion. Nurseries now beckon. (op 13-8 tchd 11-8)
Brazilian Art, who has plenty of size about him, spread a plate when well beaten on his debut. Racing wide, he made up a considerable amount of ground to snatch second spot near the finish. Seven furlongs will suit him much better. (op 13-2)
Cash In The Attic, who is not that big, took them along but had come to the end of her tether near the line. She should certainly win a claimer. (op 9-1)
Desert Falls, stepping up in trip, seemed to resent the hold-up tactics. (op 8-1)
Liberty Diamond, who looked in need of this first outing, was beating the retreat when tightened up coming to the final furlong.
Kheleyf's Silver(IRE), a half-sister to Masta Plasta, cost 230,000 euros. A well-made filly, she was quite excitable beforehand but finished in pleasing fashion after having to be checked coming to the final furlong. Hopefully this will have set her out on the right path. (op 7-1 tchd 13-2 and 9-1)

4735 CPD DISTRIBUTION PLC H'CAP — 2m 19y
3:20 (3:20) (Class 5) (0-70,67) 3-Y-O+ — **£3,154** (£944; £472; £236; £117) **Stalls Low**

Form — RPR
2303 **1** **Bouggler**[16] 4247 3-8-4 **58** .... RoystonFfrench 6 — 63
(Miss J A Camacho) *led after 1f: qcknd over 4f out: hld on wl* **5/2**[1]
0543 **2** ¾ **Dechiper (IRE)**[11] 4419 6-9-7 **65** .... PatrickDonaghy(5) 3 — 69
(R Johnson) *hld up in last: hdwy 2f out: wnt 2nd 1f out: kpt on same pce towards fin* **7/1**
3004 **3** 3 **Trance (IRE)**[60] 2844 8-9-0 **60** .... DeanHeslop(7) 9 — 60
(T D Barron) *drvn along and reluctant early: rn in snatches: hdwy to chse ldrs 7f out: styd on ins fnl f to take 3rd nr fin* **8/1**
0641 **4** hd **Jackday (IRE)**[16] 4247 3-8-2 **59** .... DuranFentiman(3) 4 — 59
(T D Easterby) *led 1f: chsd ldrs: drvn over 3f out: one pce fnl 2f* **11/4**[2]
0211 **5** shd **Bijou Dan**[31] 3756 7-9-8 **61** .... GregFairley 5 — 61+
(G M Moore) *trckd wnr: chal 2f out: fdd ins fnl f* **3/1**[3]
6604 **6** 7 **Nelson Vettori**[16] 4238 4-8-13 **52** oh4 .... TomEaves 7 — 44
(Miss L A Perratt) *chsd ldrs: drvn over 3f out: wknd over 1f out* **11/1**
05/0 **7** 17 **Galloway Mac**[11] 4420 8-8-6 **52** oh6 .... (t) LanceBetts(7) 8 — 23
(M A Barnes) *chsd ldrs: drvn over 4f out: edgd rt and lost pl 3f out: sn bhd* **28/1**

3m 45.88s (9.68) **Going Correction** +0.45s/f (Yiel)
WFA 3 from 4yo+ 15lb — **7 Ran SP% 115.6**
Speed ratings (Par 103): **93,92,91,91,90 87,78**
toteswinger: 1&2 £4.70, 1&3 £4.90, 2&3 £14.30. CSF £20.96 CT £122.29 TOTE £3.90: £2.20, £2.20; EX 22.60.
Owner Axom (III) **Bred** David Brown, Slatch Farm Stud & G B Turnbull Ltd **Trained** Norton, N Yorks

FOCUS
A low-grade stayers' handicap run at just a steady pace. Straightforward form, rated through the runner-up.

4736 CLASSIC EXCEL 25TH ANNIVERSARY H'CAP — 7f
3:50 (3:50) (Class 5) (0-75,75) 3-Y-O+ — **£3,154** (£944; £472; £236; £117) **Stalls Low**

Form — RPR
3632 **1** **Alexander Huricane (IRE)**[17] 4218 4-9-10 **72** .... FrancisNorton 7 — 81
(K A Ryan) *trckd ldrs: led appr fnl f: hld on wl* **4/1**[1]
0640 **2** ¾ **Charles Parnell (IRE)**[16] 4246 5-9-9 **74** .... JamieMoriarty(3) 5 — 81
(M Dods) *dwlt: hld up: hdwy over 3f out: styd on to take 2nd towards fin* **10/1**
3103 **3** 1 ¼ **Bid For Gold**[19] 4174 4-9-3 **65** .... J-PGuillambert 3 — 69
(Jedd O'Keeffe) *chsd clr ldr: led over 2f out: hdd appr fnl f: no ex* **11/2**[2]
6520 **4** hd **Oeuf A La Neige**[4] 4633 8-8-8 **56** oh1 .... RoystonFfrench 4 — 59
(Miss L A Perratt) *chsd ldrs: styd on same pce appr fnl f* **10/1**
0404 **5** 2 ¾ **Angaric (IRE)**[16] 4239 5-9-6 **68** .... TomEaves 9 — 64
(B Smart) *t.k.h in rr: effrt over 2f out: nvr rchd ldrs* **6/1**[3]
4635 **6** ½ **Vesuvio**[2] 4683 4-8-5 **56** oh4 .... AndrewMullen(3) 10 — 51
(C W Thornton) *hmpd s: in rr: hdwy over 2f out: nvr nr ldrs* **7/1**
6326 **7** 4 **Dorn Dancer (IRE)**[16] 4239 6-9-10 **75** .... NeilBrown(3) 1 — 59
(D W Barker) *hld up in last: lost pl over 3f out: hdwy outer 2f out: nvr on terms* **12/1**
6550 **8** 4 ½ **Neon Blue**[11] 4440 7-8-11 **59** .... (p) DeanMcKeown 2 — 32
(R M Whitaker) *chsd ldrs: sn drvn along: lost pl over 1f out* **12/1**
2316 **9** 2 ¾ **Optical Illusion (USA)**[20] 4117 4-8-12 **60** .... PaulHanagan 12 — 26
(R A Fahey) *rrd s: t.k.h in rr: hdwy and nt clr run over 2f out: lost pl over 1f out* **4/1**[1]
0600 **10** 7 **Kabis Amigos**[7] 4540 6-8-12 **60** .... (vt) PAspell 6 — 7
(S T Mason) *led and sn clr: hdd over 2f out: sn lost pl* **66/1**

1m 30.62s (3.22) **Going Correction** +0.275s/f (Good) — **10 Ran SP% 117.2**
Speed ratings (Par 103): **92,91,89,89,86 85,81,76,72,64**
toteswinger: 1&2 £11.00, 1&3 £3.10, 2&3 £10.90. CSF £45.44 CT £222.75 TOTE £4.20: £2.10, £3.30, £3.10; EX 49.80.
Owner N O'Callaghan, R Fagan & R O'Callaghan **Bred** Mrs M Fox **Trained** Hambleton, N Yorks

FOCUS
A competitive handicap run at a good pace, and sound form. The first two are better known as sprinters.
Optical Illusion(USA) Official explanation: jockey said gelding was unsuited by the soft going

4737 SHEFFIELD INSULATIONS RATING RELATED MAIDEN STKS — 1m 1f 9y
4:20 (4:21) (Class 5) 3-Y-O+ — **£3,154** (£944; £472; £236; £117) **Stalls Low**

Form — RPR
-344 **1** **Ceka Dancer (IRE)**[19] 4170 3-8-12 68 .... RoystonFfrench 1 — 72
(E J O'Neill) *mde all: sn clr: kpt on u.p fnl f: jst lasted* **9/2**[3]
3426 **2** ½ **Grey Command (USA)**[13] 4332 3-8-12 69 .... MarkLawson(3) 3 — 74
(M Brittain) *in rr: drvn over 4f out: wnt 2nd 1f out: hung lft: kpt on towards fin* **9/2**[3]
2334 **3** ¾ **Hippolytus**[18] 4180 3-8-12 69 .... JamieMoriarty(3) 2 — 72
(J J Quinn) *chsd wnr: effrt 3f out: styd on same pce fnl f* **9/4**[1]
462 **4** 2 ¾ **Hydrophonic**[12] 4379 3-8-12 68 .... PaulHanagan 6 — 63
(R A Fahey) *chsd ldrs: one pce fnl 2f* **8/1**
2522 **5** 4 **Calcutta Cup (UAE)**[40] 3450 5-9-9 62 .... J-PGuillambert 4 — 58
(Karen McLintock) *hld up: effrt 2f out: wknd 1f out* **11/4**[2]
-653 **6** 16 **Talon (IRE)**[79] 2247 3-9-1 52 .... FrancisNorton 7 — 22
(G A Swinbank) *trckd ldrs: effrt over 3f out: wknd 2f out* **12/1**

2m 1.15s (3.05) **Going Correction** +0.45s/f (Yiel)
WFA 3 from 5yo 8lb — **6 Ran SP% 112.6**
Speed ratings (Par 103): **104,103,102,100,96 82**
toteswinger: 1&2 £3.90, 1&3 £4.40, 2&3 £2.70. CSF £24.65 TOTE £7.30: £2.20, £3.00; EX 23.80.
Owner D Brennan **Bred** Robert De Vere Hunt **Trained** Averham Park, Notts

FOCUS
The winner was allowed to set up a long lead and her rider deserves full marks. Overall it was a very modest rating-related maiden race with the winner rated to form.

4738 USG APPRENTICE H'CAP 1m 2f 32y
4:50 (4:50) (Class 6) (0-65,63) 3-Y-O **£2,590** (£770; £385; £192) **Stalls** Low

Form RPR
4240 **1** **Jemima's Art**[19] 4173 3-8-3 **45**..............................(b) LanceBetts(3) 4 57
(M W Easterby) *hld up: hdwy 6f out: led over 1f out: rdn wl clr* **14/1**
0501 **2** *8* **Cheers For Thea (IRE)**[19] 4173 3-9-3 **59**.............................. BMcHugh(3) 1 55
(T D Easterby) *in rr: drvn over 4f out: hdwy over 2f out: styd on to take 2nd ins fnl f* **10/1**
6033 **3** *2 1/4* **Zaplamation (IRE)**[11] 4420 3-8-1 **45**.............................. JamieKyne(5) 8 37
(D W Barker) *t.k.h: trckd ldrs: kpt on same pce fnl 2f* **6/1**
-034 **4** *1 1/2* **Manuka Bee**[16] 4248 3-9-5 **58**.............................. ClGillies 5 47
(J Howard Johnson) *chsd ldrs: drvn over 3f out: kpt on to take modest 3rd over 1f out* **11/2**[3]
3045 **5** *1/2* **Defies Logic**[13] 4332 3-8-11 **53**.............................. RosieJessop(3) 9 41
(J G Given) *led: hdd over 1f out: wknd jst ins fnl f* **7/2**[1]
05 **6** *2 3/4* **Kargan (IRE)**[62] 2750 3-9-10 **63**.............................. PatrickDonaghy 7 45
(R Johnson) *s.s: hdwy over 4f out: wknd 1f out* **9/2**[2]
0024 **7** *1/2* **Top Man Dan (IRE)**[10] 4455 3-8-13 **57**.............................. PaulPickard(5) 2 38
(D Carroll) *chsd ldrs: wknd 2f out* **15/2**
000 **8** *1 1/4* **Snake Catcher**[30] 3796 3-8-3 **45**.............................. DeanHeslop(3) 3 24
(M W Easterby) *t.k.h in rr: hdwy over 4f out: wknd 2f out* **50/1**
0422 **9** *nk* **Ace Of Spies (IRE)**[12] 4381 3-8-6 **52**.............................. CraigPettigrew(7) 6 30
(M Johnston) *chsd ldrs: lost pl over 1f out* **11/2**[3]

2m 16.86s (4.96) **Going Correction** +0.45s/f (Yiel) **9 Ran SP% 114.9**
Speed ratings (Par 98): **98,91,89,88,88 86,85,84,84**
toteswinger: 1&2 £23.50, 1&3 £13.70, 2&3 £7.70. CSF £143.93 CT £935.13 TOTE £19.20: £4.00, £2.50, £2.30; EX 181.50 Place 6: £308.87, Place 5: £126.33..
Owner Matthew Green **Bred** Milton Park Stud Partnership **Trained** Sheriff Hutton, N Yorks
■ Stewards' Enquiry : Lance Betts two-day ban: used whip when clearly winning (Aug 20,23)

FOCUS
A low-grade apprentice handicap and the further she went the further the winner came clear. She turned round Pontefract form with the runner-up but it is hard to gauge how much she improved with nothing else giving their running.
Jemima's Art Official explanation: trainer was unable to explain the improved form
T/Plt: £189.30 to a £1 stake. Pool: £60,485.69. 233.15 winning tickets. T/Qpdt: £66.90 to a £1 stake. Pool: £3,310.90. 36.60 winning tickets. WG

4456 PONTEFRACT (L-H)
Wednesday, August 6

OFFICIAL GOING: Good (good to firm in places; 7.1)
Wind: Virtually nil Weather: Warm and overcast - showers

4739 BOLLINGER CHAMPAGNE CHALLENGE SERIES H'CAP (FOR GENTLEMAN AMATEUR RIDERS) 1m 2f 6y
2:10 (2:10) (Class 5) (0-75,75) 3-Y-O+ **£3,747** (£1,162; £580; £290) **Stalls** Low

Form RPR
3101 **1** **Holiday Cocktail**[10] 4458 6-11-4 **72** 6ex.............................. MrSWalker 10 81
(J J Quinn) *trckd ldrs: effrt 3f out: rdn along 2f out: styd on to chal whn edgd lft over 1f out: led ent fnl f: drvn out* **4/1**[1]
04 **2** *2* **Night Orbit**[26] 3914 4-10-9 **66**.............................. MrPCollington(3) 2 71
(Miss J Feilden) *a.p: hdwy to ld over 2f out and sn rdn: drvn over 1f out: hdd ent fnl f: kpt on same pce* **5/1**[2]
3353 **3** *1 1/4* **Jackie Kiely**[10] 4458 7-10-4 **63**..............................(t) MrBJToomey(5) 1 66
(R Brotherton) *hld up in rr: hdwy 4f out: rdn along 2f out: drvn and styd on wl fnl f: nrst fin* **5/1**[2]
4242 **4** *3/4* **Bavarica**[12] 4371 6-10-4 **63**.............................. MrRBirkett(5) 7 64
(Miss J Feilden) *t.k.h: prom: effrt to chal over 2f out: sn rdn and ev ch tl drvn and wknd ent fnl f* **5/1**[2]
0000 **5** *4* **Fort Churchill (IRE)**[4] 4627 7-11-2 **75**..............................(bt) MrDaleSwift(5) 4 68
(B Ellison) *hld up towards rr: hdwy 1/2-way: effrt and ch 3f out: rdn 2f out: sn hung lft and wknd* **8/1**[3]
1354 **6** *9* **Artreju (GER)**[14] 4309 5-10-10 **69**.............................. MrJoshuaMoore(5) 3 44
(G L Moore) *hld up in rr: stdy hdwy on inner 4f out: rdn to chse ldrs 2f out: sn drvn and wknd over 1f out* **4/1**[1]
-300 **7** *nse* **Littleton Telchar (USA)**[21] 4081 8-10-8 **69**..............................(p) MrIPMcBride(7) 5 44
(S W Hall) *t.k.h: trckd ldrs on inner: rdn along over 3f out and sn wknd* **20/1**
2300 **8** *8* **Iceman George**[12] 4371 4-9-11 **56**..............................(b) MrBMMorris(5) 6 15
(D Morris) *trckd ldrs: effrt over 3f out: sn rdn and wknd* **14/1**
06-0 **9** *20* **Phoenix Nights (IRE)**[6] 4556 8-10-1 **62** oh11 ow6 MrThomasHogg(7) 8 —
(A Berry) *towards rr: sme hdwy on outer over 4f out: sn rdn and wknd* **100/1**
-000 **10** *3/4* **Cheviot Red**[56] 2946 3-9-5 **61** oh1 ow5.............................. MrJWaggott(7) 9 —
(Miss Tracy Waggott) *racd wd: led: rdn along 3f out: sn hdd & wknd* **66/1**

2m 18.05s (4.35) **Going Correction** +0.225s/f (Good)
WFA 3 from 4yo+ 9lb **10 Ran SP% 115.0**
Speed ratings (Par 103): **91,89,88,87,84 77,77,70,54,54**
toteswinger: 1&2 £5.50, 1&3 £2.80, 2&3 £7.50. CSF £23.39 CT £101.27 TOTE £3.40: £1.70, £1.80, £2.00; EX 25.10.
Owner Estio Racing **Bred** Mrs W H Gibson Fleming **Trained** Settrington, N Yorks

FOCUS
A modest handicap, confined to amateur riders. The form looks straightforward with the runner-up rated to his best and a new career high from the winner.
Iceman George Official explanation: trainer said gelding was struck into during the race

4740 RONNIE SENIOR 80TH BIRTHDAY MAIDEN STKS 6f
2:40 (2:42) (Class 4) 2-Y-O **£5,180** (£1,541; £770; £384) **Stalls** Low

Form RPR
0 **1** **Alexander Gulch (USA)**[33] 3663 2-9-3 0.............................. DarryllHolland 8 83
(K A Ryan) *j. awkwardly: sn led: rdn along wl over 1f out: drvn ins fnl f and styd on wl* **16/1**
0023 **2** *2* **Olympic Dream**[11] 4438 2-9-3 82.............................. TonyHamilton 7 77
(R A Fahey) *wnt rt s: a cl up: effrt 2f out: rdn over 1f out and ev ch tl drvn and one pce ins fnl f* **7/2**[2]
0 **3** *5* **Agent Stone (IRE)**[14] 4289 2-9-3 0..............................(t) AdrianTNicholls 5 62
(D Nicholls) *sn chsng ldrs: rdn along and hdwy 2f out: drvn over 1f out and kpt on same pce* **13/2**[3]
630 **4** *1* **Ay Tay Tate (IRE)**[50] 3107 2-9-3 0.............................. FergalLynch 3 59
(I W McInnes) *towards rr: hdwy over 2f out: sn rdn and styd on appr fnl f* **7/1**
5 *2* **Veroon (IRE)** 2-9-0 0.............................. LeeVickers(3) 10 53
(J G Given) *hmpd s: sn in tch: hdwy to chse ldrs over 2f out: sn rdn and one pce* **40/1**
05 **6** *4 1/2* **Sampower Rose (IRE)**[14] 4289 2-8-12 0.............................. TonyCulhane 9 35
(D Carroll) *sltly hmpd s: sn chsng ldng pair: rdn along over 2f out: drvn wl over 1f out and grad wknd* **12/1**
7 *1 3/4* **Zelos Diktator** 2-9-3 0.............................. PatCosgrave 12 34
(J G Given) *in tch: rdn along over 2f out: sn no imp* **33/1**
8 *1/2* **Demand** 2-8-12 0.............................. LiamJones 1 28
(W J Haggas) *s.i.s: rr whn hmpd 2f out* **3/1**[1]
06 **9** *hd* **Sweet Virginia (USA)**[49] 3125 2-8-5 0.............................. DeclanCannon(7) 6 27
(K R Burke) *towards rr: hdwy on inner and in tch 3f out: sn rdn and wknd 2f out* **100/1**
10 *1* **Moorhouse Lass (IRE)** 2-8-12 0.............................. DavidAllan 2 24
(D Carroll) *a towards rr* **16/1**
11 *1/2* **Rising Kheleyf (IRE)** 2-9-3 0.............................. TedDurcan 4 28
(G A Swinbank) *a towards rr* **9/1**
12 *19* **Age Of Magic (USA)** 2-8-12 0.............................. JoeFanning 11 —
(M Johnston) *hmpd s: t.k.h and sn in tch: pushed along over 2f out and sn wknd* **13/2**[3]

1m 18.85s (1.95) **Going Correction** +0.225s/f (Good) **12 Ran SP% 122.2**
Speed ratings (Par 96): **96,93,86,85,82 76,74,73,73,72 71,46**
toteswinger: 1&2 £9.00, 1&3 £14.80, 2&3 £4.10. CSF £73.19 TOTE £14.60: £3.00, £1.30, £2.50; EX 75.80.
Owner Noel O'Callaghan **Bred** Two Sisters' Farm Inc **Trained** Hambleton, N Yorks

FOCUS
A modest juvenile maiden, but the form looks sound enough with the first pair coming clear and the runner-up a fairly reliable guide.

NOTEBOOK
Alexander Gulch(USA), seventh of eight on his debut in novice company at Beverley 33 days previously, was still a bit awkward from the stalls but broke a lot better than had been the case last time. He eventually came home to score in gutsy fashion, relishing this extra furlong, and looks a useful prospect. However, this 100,000gns breeze-up purchase was awash with sweat and is clearly still a little headstrong, so probably needs to mature before reaching his peak. (tchd 14-1 and 20-1)
Olympic Dream was always on the pace and gave his all in defeat, but eventually failed to see out the race as well as the winner. He deserves to find a race, and the best of him has probably still to be seen, but he is better off trying to find a maiden on one of the smaller tracks as an official mark of 82 looks to flatter him at present. (op 7-4)
Agent Stone(IRE) showed the benefit of his debut experience a fortnight previously and the addition of a first-time tongue tie. He never seriously threatened, but is going the right way and should find his feet when entering the nursery arena. (op 9-1 tchd 11-2)
Ay Tay Tate(IRE), who lost his action at Thirsk 50 days previously, showed that run to be all wrong and kept on steadily from off the pace without ever threatening. He has ability and will not mind a return to 7f now. (op 11-1)
Veroon(IRE), who has plenty of speed in his pedigree, fared best of the newcomers and can be rated a little better than the bare form as he was not done any favours at the start from his wide draw. (op 66-1)
Sampower Rose(IRE) Official explanation: jockey said filly moved poorly throughout
Demand is the first foal of a useful 1m winner at three and proved popular in the betting ring ahead of this racecourse bow. She never figured after running too green through the early parts, however, and got hampered on the final bend when trying to make up ground. The way in which she eventually finished her race would suggest she is worth another chance when racing on a more conventional track. (op 7-2 tchd 4-1)
Rising Kheleyf(IRE) Official explanation: jockey said gelding hung left in straight

4741 STYLE BAR & BAR LIQUID PONTEFRACT H'CAP 1m 4y
3:10 (3:10) (Class 5) (0-75,75) 3-Y-O **£3,885** (£1,156; £577; £288) **Stalls** Low

Form RPR
1601 **1** **Admiral Dundas (IRE)**[12] 4377 3-9-7 **75**.............................. JoeFanning 4 85+
(W Jarvis) *trckd ldrs: swtchd outside and effrt wl over 1f out: sn rdn and styd on ent fnl f to ld fnl 50yds* **13/2**[3]
0301 **2** *1/2* **Thumbs Up**[22] 4061 3-9-3 **71**.............................. JamieSpencer 3 79+
(L M Cumani) *t.k.h: hld up towards rr: stdy hdwy 1/2-way: rdn wl over 1f out: drvn and styd on to ld briefly wl ins fnl f: hdd and no ex fnl 50yds* **7/4**[1]
301 **3** *1 1/4* **Eton Fable (IRE)**[10] 4461 3-9-1 **69** 6ex.............................. FergalLynch 6 74
(W J H Ratcliffe) *cl up: rdn to ld wl over 1f out: drvn and hdd wl ins fnl f: kpt on* **12/1**
0431 **4** *1 3/4* **Penchesco (IRE)**[30] 3799 3-9-6 **74**.............................. PaulEddery 7 75
(Pat Eddery) *led: rdn along 2f out: drvn and hdd wl over 1f out: wknd ins fnl f* **9/2**[2]
244 **5** *hd* **Valferno (IRE)**[30] 3796 3-9-2 **70**.............................. MickyFenton 5 71
(Mrs P Sly) *prom: rdn along over 2f out and sn edgd rt: drvn over 1f out: kpt on same pce* **20/1**
0232 **6** *2 1/4* **Welcome Return (IRE)**[33] 3672 3-8-12 **66**..............................(b) DavidAllan 1 61
(T D Easterby) *towards rr: hdwy on inner over 2f out: sn rdn and no imp appr fnl f* **13/2**[3]
5644 **7** *2 1/4* **Island Music (IRE)**[17] 4219 3-9-0 **68**.............................. PatCosgrave 10 58
(J J Quinn) *chsd ldrs: rdn along 2f out: sn drvn and grad wknd* **9/1**
6006 **8** *3/4* **Zabougg**[12] 4381 3-7-9 **56** oh4..............................(p) AdeleRothery(7) 12 44
(D W Barker) *towards rr: rdn along and sme hdwy 2f out: nvr a factor* **40/1**
-360 **9** *3 1/4* **The Twelve Steps**[64] 2705 3-9-2 **73**.............................. PJMcDonald(3) 2 53
(G A Swinbank) *chsd ldrs: rdn along 2f out: sn drvn and wknd* **9/1**
0-00 **10** *29* **Geordie Girl**[65] 2670 3-8-8 **62**.............................. PatrickMathers 8 —
(R C Guest) *a towards rr* **66/1**
045 **11** *69* **Mill Beattie**[21] 4076 3-8-3 **57**.............................. AdrianTNicholls 11 —
(G M Moore) *a in rr: lost pl and bhd whn virtually p.u wl over 1f out* **33/1**

1m 47.27s (1.37) **Going Correction** +0.225s/f (Good) **11 Ran SP% 120.5**
Speed ratings (Par 100): **102,101,100,98,98 96,93,93,89,60 —**
toteswinger: 1&2 £2.50, 1&3 £14.40, 2&3 £7.90. CSF £18.20 CT £140.09 TOTE £8.40: £2.60, £1.20, £3.10; EX 27.10.
Owner Dr J Walker **Bred** John Hussey And Stephen Hillen **Trained** Newmarket, Suffolk

FOCUS
A modest three-year-old handicap and although the first two are capable of better the form has not been rated too positively. The winning time was 0.57 seconds slower than the later 61-80 handicap for six-year-olds and upwards.
Geordie Girl Official explanation: vet said filly finished distressed

Mill Beattie Official explanation: jockey said filly was never travelling

4742 BIG FELLAS & SILKS NIGHTCLUB PONTEFRACT H'CAP 1m 4f 8y

3:40 (3:44) (Class 3) (0-90,90) 3-Y-0+

£9,346 (£2,799; £1,399; £700; £349; £175) **Stalls** Low

Form RPR

-044 **1** **Night Hour (IRE)**[26] 3929 6-10-0 **90**.................... TedDurcan 9 99
(Saeed Bin Suroor) *trckd ldrs: hdwy over 3f out: led over 2f out: rdn wl over 1f out: drvn and hdd wl ins fnl f: rallied to ld again on line* **9/2**[2]

3010 **2** *shd* **Birkside**[8] 4508 5-9-9 **85**.................... DavidAllan 8 94
(D Carroll) *hld up: stdy hdwy over 2f out: rdn to chal 1f out: drvn to ld wl ins fnl f: hdd on line* **9/1**

0533 **3** *1* **Rosbay (IRE)**[18] 4191 4-9-9 **85**.................... MickyFenton 7 92
(T D Easterby) *hld up: gd hdwy 3f out: rdn to chse ldrs wl over 1f out: styd on u.p ins fnl f: nrst fin* **17/2**

56-0 **4** *1 1/4* **Luna Landing**[18] 4204 5-9-1 **77**.................... DarrylIHolland 11 82
(Jedd O'Keeffe) *hld up in rr: swtchd outside and gd hdwy wl over 1f out: drvn and styd on ins fnl f: nrst fin* **25/1**

140 **5** *1 1/4* **Cotton Eyed Joe (IRE)**[18] 4178 7-9-0 **79**.................... PJMcDonald(3) 15 82
(G A Swinbank) *prom: effrt 3f out: sn rdn and ev ch tl drvn and wknd over 1f out* **16/1**

3205 **6** *1 1/2* **Red Wine**[19] 4146 9-8-7 **76**.................... StacyRenwick(7) 6 77
(A J McCabe) *hld up towards rr: hdwy on outer 3f out: rdn 2f out: kpt on appr fnl f: nrst fin* **33/1**

1006 **7** *2* **Maslak (IRE)**[26] 3929 4-9-9 **85**.................... DarrenWilliams 3 82
(P W Hiatt) *trckd ldrs: rdn along over 2f out: drvn wl over 1f out and sn one pce* **25/1**

422 **8** *hd* **Motarid (USA)**[29] 3813 3-8-5 **78**.................... SilvestreDeSousa 2 75+
(T D Walford) *trckd ldrs on inner: hdwy whn nt clr run and lost pl over 2f out: styd on appr fnl f* **17/2**

020- **9** *3/4* **Leslingtaylor (IRE)**[125] 6169 6-8-13 **75**.................... PatCosgrave 13 71
(J J Quinn) *hld up in rr: effrt 3f out: nvr nr ldrs* **14/1**

13-2 **10** *1 1/2* **Riguez Dancer**[120] 1020 4-8-11 **73**.................... LeeEnstone 4 66
(P C Haslam) *in tch: rdn along over 4f out: sn lost pl and bhd* **16/1**

3545 **11** *3* **Mustajed**[20] 4131 7-8-13 **78**.................... JamesMillman(3) 12 67
(B R Millman) *in tch: swtchd outside and hdwy 3f out: rdn along 2f out and sn btn* **20/1**

2554 **12** *2 1/4* **Prince Sabaah (IRE)**[13] 4350 4-9-10 **86**....................(p) PatDobbs 10 71
(R Hannon) *cl up: led briefly 3f out: sn rdn and hdd: wknd fnl 2f* **14/1**

-005 **13** *1 1/2* **Royal Jet**[10] 4444 6-9-13 **89**.................... TonyCulhane 5 72
(M R Channon) *hld up: effrt and sme hdwy over 2f out: sn rdn and nvr a factor* **8/1**[3]

1001 **14** *14* **Boz**[27] 3864 4-9-12 **88**....................(v) JamieSpencer 14 48
(L M Cumani) *hld up: swtchd rt and hdwy over 3f out: rdn to chse ldrs 2f out: sn drvn and btn: eased over 1f out* **4/1**[1]

6105 **15** *17* **Step This Way (USA)**[26] 3930 3-8-13 **86**.................... JoeFanning 1 19
(M Johnston) *led: rdn along 4f out: hdd & wknd 3f out* **20/1**

2m 40.16s (-0.64) **Going Correction** +0.225s/f (Good)
WFA 3 from 4yo+ 11lb **15** Ran SP% **125.6**
Speed ratings (Par 107): **111,110,110,109,108 107,106,106,105,104 102,101,100,90,79**
toteswinger: 1&2 £12.90, 1&3 £10.00, 2&3 £20.00. CSF £42.95 CT £346.08 TOTE £5.90: £2.60, £3.40, £3.50; EX 57.50.
Owner Godolphin **Bred** C H Wacker Iii **Trained** Newmarket, Suffolk
■ Stewards' Enquiry : Ted Durcan one-day ban: used whip without giving horse time to respond (Aug 20)

FOCUS
A decent handicap rated around the runner-up, who has been given a rating equal to his previous best, which came on Polytrack. Solid form.

NOTEBOOK
Night Hour(IRE) ruined his chance by hanging badly left on heavy ground at York on his previous start but, back on a better surface, he ran straight this time and showed a good attitude to just prevail. This rates as a career-best effort on RPRs. (op 7-1)
Birkside has won an extraordinary number of races for a horse of his ability and this was very nearly another. He still seems to be improving. (op 12-1)
Rosbay(IRE) ran a good race, but he has not won for over a year and the Handicapper seemingly remains in charge. He was doing all his best work at the finish and might be worth a try over further. (op 9-1)
Luna Landing is another without a win for over a year, but this was a reasonable effort. Official explanation: jockey said gelding missed break (op 20-1)
Cotton Eyed Joe(IRE) ran better than when failing to beat a rival at Haydock on his previous start. (tchd 14-1)
Riguez Dancer Official explanation: jockey said gelding was denied a clear run
Mustajed Official explanation: jockey said gelding had no more to give
Boz, raised 9lb for his recent Doncaster success, failed to run his race in a second-time visor. Official explanation: jockey said colt was unsuited by the good (good to firm in places) ground (op 7-2 tchd 9-2)

4743 CHAPLINS CLUB H'CAP 5f

4:10 (4:15) (Class 5) (0-75,75) 3-Y-0+ **£3,885** (£1,156; £577; £288) **Stalls** Low

Form RPR

0231 **1** **Commander Wish**[22] 4047 5-9-0 **63**....................(p) LiamJones 8 75
(Lucinda Featherstone) *bmpd s and rdn along in rr 1/2-way: gd hdwy on outer wl over 1f out: str run ins fnl f: led nr fin* **9/1**

1405 **2** *3/4* **Namir (IRE)**[19] 4171 6-9-10 **73**....................(vt) TedDurcan 11 82
(D Shaw) *sltly hmpd s: hld up in midfield: gd hdwy on outer over 1f out: rdn and styd on to ld fnl 100yds: drvn and hdd nr fin* **9/2**[1]

2344 **3** *1/2* **Kings College Boy**[20] 4114 8-8-8 **64**....................(b) FrederikTylicki(7) 2 71
(R A Fahey) *led: rdn along 2f out: drvn over 1f out: hdd and no ex fnl 100yds* **6/1**[3]

2001 **4** *nk* **The History Man (IRE)**[5] 4609 5-8-9 **65**............(be) GarryWhillans(7) 14 71
(M Mullineaux) *chsd ldrs: rdn along wl over 1f out: drvn and kpt on same pce ins fnl f* **11/1**

0006 **5** *nk* **Divine Spirit**[11] 4418 7-9-10 **73**.................... DarrylIHolland 16 78
(M Dods) *bhd: swtchd outside and gd hdwy over 1f out: rdn and styd on ins fnl f: nrst fin* **14/1**

0110 **6** *1* **Guest Connections**[6] 4555 5-9-7 **70**....................(v) SilvestreDeSousa 4 71
(D Nicholls) *chsd ldrs: rdn along whn n.m.r over 1f out: kpt on u.p ins fnl f* **6/1**[3]

6532 **7** *3/4* **Mr Wolf**[10] 4462 7-9-8 **71**....................(p) FergalLynch 15 70
(D W Barker) *cl up: rdn 2f out: drvn over 1f out and grad wknd* **11/2**[2]

00 **8** *1/2* **Garstang**[23] 4025 5-8-13 **62**.................... PatrickMathers 10 59+
(Peter Grayson) *sltly hmpd s: in rr tl hdwy 2f out: sn rdn and n.m.r over 1f out: kpt on ins fnl f* **33/1**

-300 **9** *1 1/2* **Pickering**[29] 3812 4-9-4 **67**.................... MickyFenton 1 59
(E J Alston) *chsd ldrs: rdn wl over 1f out: wknd ent fnl f* **12/1**

4013 **10** *1 1/2* **Mandurah (IRE)**[6] 4555 4-9-8 **71**.................... AdrianTNicholls 17 57+
(D Nicholls) *stdd and swtchd lft s: hld up in rr: hdwy on inner whn n.m.r wl over 1f out: sn no imp* **15/2**

0000 **11** *1 3/4* **King Of Swords (IRE)**[12] 4385 4-9-7 **70**.................... TonyCulhane 3 50
(N Tinkler) *chsd ldrs: rdn along over 2f out: sn drvn and wknd* **40/1**

504 **12** *1* **New York Oscar (IRE)**[23] 4028 4-9-4 **67**....................(v) PatCosgrave 6 43
(A J McCabe) *chsd ldrs: rdn along 2f out: sn wknd* **40/1**

1030 **13** *3/4* **Castles In The Air**[20] 4121 3-9-9 **75**.................... PaulEddery 7 49
(Pat Eddery) *wnt rt s: chsd ldrs: rdn along over 2f out and sn wknd* **16/1**

4-00 **14** *nk* **Making Music**[16] 4246 5-8-13 **62**.................... DavidAllan 12 34
(T D Easterby) *nvr bttr than midfield* **20/1**

64.88 secs (1.58) **Going Correction** +0.225s/f (Good)
WFA 3 from 4yo+ 3lb **14** Ran SP% **125.1**
Speed ratings (Par 103): **96,94,94,93,93 91,90,89,87,84 81,80,79,78**
toteswinger: 1&2 £16.10, 1&3 £11.00, 2&3 £11.90. CSF £49.53 CT £278.82 TOTE £12.80: £3.10, £3.10, £2.50; EX 82.20.
Owner J Roundtree **Bred** P R Featherstone **Trained** Atlow, Derbyshire

FOCUS
A competitive sprint handicap run at a strong pace. Sound form, rated through the second and third.
Pickering Official explanation: vet said gelding lost a front shoe and finished lame
Mandurah(IRE) ◆ Official explanation: jockey said gelding was denied a clear run
King Of Swords(IRE) Official explanation: jockey said colt was denied a clear run
Making Music Official explanation: jockey said mare was denied a clear run

4744 MATTY BOWN VETERANS H'CAP 1m 4y

4:40 (4:41) (Class 4) (0-80,81) 6-Y-0+ **£5,180** (£1,541; £770; £384) **Stalls** Low

Form RPR

3036 **1** **Major Magpie (IRE)**[27] 3887 6-9-7 **78**.................... DarrylIHolland 7 87
(M Dods) *hld up: hdwy 2f out: swtchd outside over 1f out: sn rdn and styd on to ld wl ins fnl f: drvn out* **7/2**[1]

6635 **2** *1/2* **Motafarred (IRE)**[8] 4500 6-9-4 **75**.................... FergalLynch 3 83
(Micky Hammond) *trckd ldng pair: smooth hdwy on outer 2f out: in front and hung lft over 1f out and ent fnl f: sn drvn: hdd and nt qckn fnl 100yds* **11/2**[3]

3005 **3** *3* **Champain Sands (IRE)**[4] 4650 9-8-8 **65**.................... DavidAllan 8 71+
(E J Alston) *hld up in rr: gd hdwy 2f out: effrt and nt clr run over 1f out and jst ins fnl f: rdn and styd on wl towards fin* **9/1**

4510 **4** *1* **Dispol Isle (IRE)**[4] 4650 6-9-2 **73**.................... JoeFanning 2 72+
(T D Barron) *trckd ldrs: hdwy 2f out: nt clr run and swtchd rt over 1f out: sn rdn and kpt on same pce ins fnl f* **9/1**

0303 **5** *1 3/4* **Prince Samos (IRE)**[24] 4001 6-9-1 **72**.................... TedDurcan 5 67
(E S McMahon) *in tch: hdwy over 2f out: rdn wl over 1f out and sn no imp* **7/2**[1]

3105 **6** *1* **Royal Storm (IRE)**[19] 4167 9-8-13 **73**.................... JamesMillman(3) 4 65
(B R Millman) *led: rdn along and jnd 2f out: drvn whn n.m.r and hdd jst over 1f out: hmpd ent fnl f and wknd* **9/1**

0561 **7** *6* **Nevada Desert (IRE)**[8] 4500 8-9-7 **81** 6ex............ MichaelJStainton(3) 1 60
(R M Whitaker) *trckd ldr: hdwy on inner to chal 2f out: sn rdn and ev ch whn n.m.r over 1f out: wkng whn bdly hmpd jst ins fnl f* **5/1**[2]

5460 **8** *1 1/2* **Bahiano (IRE)**[44] 3319 7-9-9 **80**.................... LiamJones 6 55
(C E Brittain) *a towards rr* **9/1**

1m 46.7s (0.80) **Going Correction** +0.225s/f (Good) **8** Ran SP% **116.5**
Speed ratings: **105,104,101,100,98 97,91,90**
toteswinger: 1&2 £4.20, 1&3 £8.20, 2&3 £10.80. CSF £23.41 CT £161.43 TOTE £4.30: £1.80, £2.00, £2.70; EX 29.00.
Owner Mrs Patsy Monk **Bred** J Hutchinson **Trained** Denton, Co Durham
■ Stewards' Enquiry : Fergal Lynch four-day ban: careless riding (Aug 20 & 23-25)

FOCUS
A race for six-year-olds and upwards, so this was never going to be strong form, but the winning time was 0.57 seconds quicker than the earlier three-year-old 56-75 handicap. The winner is rated pretty much back to his best. They went a strong pace, which favoured the hold-up horses.
Champain Sands(IRE) Official explanation: jockey said gelding was denied a clear run

4745 KEN AND KATHLEEN GLANCY 80TH BIRTHDAY H'CAP 6f

5:10 (5:11) (Class 5) (0-75,75) 3-Y-0 **£3,885** (£1,156; £577; £288) **Stalls** Low

Form RPR

5-53 **1** **Elijah Pepper (USA)**[36] 3577 3-8-6 **60**.................... PaulFessey 2 67
(T D Barron) *trckd ldng pair: rdn to chse ldr wl over 1f out: drvn ent fnl f and styd on wl to ld nr fin* **17/2**

0505 **2** *nk* **Anosti**[21] 4083 3-9-5 **73**....................(p) FergalLynch 5 79
(K A Ryan) *led: rdn and qcknd clr wl over 1f out: drvn ins fnl f: edgd rt and hdd nr fin* **7/1**[3]

6106 **3** *3/4* **King Kenny**[12] 4392 3-9-7 **75**.................... DarrylIHolland 4 78
(S Parr) *hld up in rr: gd hdwy wl over 1f out: rdn to chse ldng pair whn hung rt jst ins fnl f: styng on whn hung bdly rt nr fin* **7/1**[3]

-600 **4** *2 1/4* **Geoffdaw**[9] 4478 3-9-3 **71**....................(p) TedDurcan 3 67
(M J Wallace) *trckd ldrs: hdwy 2f out: rdn and wandered ent fnl f: kpt on same pce* **14/1**

1623 **5** *2 1/2* **Capone (IRE)**[16] 4258 3-9-4 **72**.................... JoeFanning 10 60
(Garry Moss) *hld up towards rr: hdwy on outer wl over 1f out: sn rdn and one pce ins fnl f* **9/2**[2]

3010 **6** *2 3/4* **Koraleva Tectona (IRE)**[33] 3678 3-9-6 **74**.................... PaulEddery 8 53
(Pat Eddery) *hld up in rr: effrt over 2f out: sn rdn and nvr a factor* **7/2**[1]

6523 **7** *3/4* **Moonage Daydream (IRE)**[19] 4163 3-8-12 **66**............(b) DavidAllan 11 43
(T D Easterby) *chsd ldrs: rdn along wl over 1f out: wkng whn hmpd appr fnl f* **9/2**[2]

0550 **8** *2 3/4* **Rossini's Dancer**[32] 3717 3-8-3 **57**.................... DaleGibson 7 25
(R A Fahey) *chsd ldrs: rdn along over 2f out: sn wknd* **15/2**

0204 **9** *7* **Sheer Bluff (IRE)**[12] 4377 3-9-1 **69**.................... TonyCulhane 6 15
(D R C Elsworth) *chsd ldr: rdn along over 2f out and sn wknd* **8/1**

1m 17.71s (0.81) **Going Correction** +0.225s/f (Good) **9** Ran SP% **123.7**
Speed ratings (Par 100): **103,102,101,98,95 91,90,86,77**
toteswinger: 1&2 £18.70, 1&3 £11.90, 2&3 £11.10. CSF £71.28 CT £451.76 TOTE £8.40: £2.40, £2.70, £2.10; EX 93.80 Place 6: £102.56, Place 5: £126.33..
Owner Harrowgate Bloodstock Ltd **Bred** Liberation Farm & Oratis Thoroughbreds **Trained** Maunby, N Yorks
■ Stewards' Enquiry : Fergal Lynch one-day ban: used whip down shoulder in forehand position (Aug 26)

FOCUS
A modest sprint handicap but the form makes plenty of sense.
Koraleva Tectona(IRE) Official explanation: trainer said, regarding the poor form shown, filly was in season
T/Jkpt: Not won. T/Plt: £78.90 to a £1 stake. Pool: £68,792.52. 636.34 winning tickets. T/Qpdt: £28.20 to a £1 stake. Pool: £3,315.92. 86.88 winning tickets. JR

4486 **YARMOUTH** (L-H)

Wednesday, August 6

OFFICIAL GOING: Good (7.5)

Wind: Light, half-against Weather: Overcast

4746 GEORGE DARLING MEMORIAL APPRENTICE H'CAP 7f 3y

5:35 (5:35) (Class 5) (0-70,65) 4-Y-0+ £2,590 (£770; £385; £192) Stalls High

Form RPR

0-50 1 **Romany Nights (IRE)**[4] 4639 8-8-10 58..........(bt) AntiocoMurgia(7) 8 70
(Miss Gay Kelleway) *chsd ldr 6f out: led over 2f out: pushed clr fr over 1f out* **6/1**[3]

2143 2 4½ **Bentley**[29] 3826 4-9-2 62.......... MJMurphy(5) 4 62
(J G Given) *chsd ldrs: lost pl over 4f out: hdwy u.p over 1f out: no imp fnl f* **7/2**[2]

00 3 *hd* **Mugeba**[16] 4258 7-8-9 50..........(t) AshleyMorgan 3 49
(Miss Gay Kelleway) *hld up: hdwy u.p over 1f out: styd on same pce fnl f* **9/1**

100 4 6 **Gee Ceffyl Bach**[19] 4172 4-8-6 52..........(b[1]) CharlesEddery(5) 7 35
(R C Guest) *s.s: hdwy 1/2-way: rdn and wknd over 1f out* **10/1**

0-50 5 2¾ **Sydneyroughdiamond**[7] 4538 6-8-2 46 oh1.......... RichardRowe(3) 2 22
(M Mullineaux) *hung lft thrght: led 1f: chsd ldrs: rdn and lost pl over 3f out: wknd over 2f out* **33/1**

3101 6 *nk* **Registrar**[9] 4489 6-9-4 62 6ex..........(p) KrishGundowry(3) 1 37
(Mrs C A Dunnett) *prom: rdn over 2f out: edgd rt and wknd over 1f out* **3/1**[1]

5002 7 2 **Fun In The Sun**[22] 4052 4-8-8 52.......... PNolan(3) 5 22
(A B Haynes) *chsd ldrs: rdn over 2f out: wknd over 1f out* **6/1**[3]

0600 8 11 **Bateleur**[5] 4605 4-8-13 59..........(v) NatashaEaton(5) 9 —
(M R Channon) *led 6f out: hdd over 2f out: sn rdn and wknd* **6/1**[3]

1m 29.31s (2.71) **Going Correction** +0.075s/f (Good) 8 Ran SP% **112.1**

Speed ratings (Par 103): **87,81,81,74,71 71,69,56**

toteswinger: 1&2 £6.00, 1&3 £6.90, 2&3 £11.10. CSF £26.18 CT £187.01 TOTE £8.60: £2.00, £1.40, £2.60; EX 17.60.

Owner Miss Gay Kelleway **Bred** The Lloyd Farm Stud **Trained** Exning, Suffolk

■ The first winner for Italian apprentice Antioco Murgia.

FOCUS

They went a decent gallop for what was a moderate handicap. The pace was steady and this was only modest form.

4747 NORFOLK NELSON MUSEUM MAIDEN AUCTION STKS 7f 3y

6:05 (6:14) (Class 6) 2-Y-0 £2,331 (£693; £346; £173) Stalls High

Form RPR

26 1 **Calahonda**[56] 2944 2-8-4 0.......... JohnEgan 3 72+
(P W D'Arcy) *racd centre: a.p: rdn to ld overall over 1f out: edgd rt: r.o wl: eased towards fin* **9/2**[3]

2 4 **Never Lose** 2-8-1 0.......... Louis-PhilippeBeuzelin(5) 8 64
(C E Brittain) *chsd ldrs: led centre gp 4f out: rdn and hdd over 1f out: no ex ins fnl f* **7/1**

3 ¾ **Omokoroa (IRE)** 2-8-11 0.......... RichardMullen 1 67+
(M H Tompkins) *racd centre: dwlt: hld up: hdwy over 1f out: styd on* **20/1**

0U 4 *nk* **Chantilly Dancer (IRE)**[28] 3848 2-8-3 0 ow1.......... JackDean(5) 5 63
(M J Wallace) *racd centre: prom: lost pl 5f out: hdwy over 1f out: styd on* **50/1**

02 5 *hd* **Handful Of Magic**[13] 4321 2-8-3 0.......... AdrianMcCarthy 12 58
(Tom Dascombe) *racd alone stands' side: w ldrs tl led overall 4f out: rdn and hdd over 1f out: no ex ins fnl f* **8/1**

4 6 4½ **Noble Dictator**[16] 4256 2-8-8 0.......... TolleyDean(3) 11 55
(E F Vaughan) *unruly to post: racd centre: hld up in tch: racd keenly: rdn and hung lft over 2f out: nt run on* **7/2**[2]

6 7 ½ **Oscar Silk**[43] 3348 2-8-7 0.......... EdwardCreighton 9 49
(M R Channon) *racd centre: s.i.s: hdwy over 5f out: rdn and wknd over 1f out* **15/8**[1]

0 8 ½ **Dark Ranger**[14] 4304 2-8-10 0.......... EddieAhern 10 51
(M J Wallace) *overall ldr centre 3f: rdn and wknd over 1f out* **20/1**

0 9 16 **Fawaz**[33] 3689 2-8-9 0.......... DMylonas 7 10
(Mrs C A Dunnett) *racd centre: chsd ldrs: rdn and hung lft over 2f out: sn wknd and hung rt* **40/1**

0 10 6 **Pedestrian (IRE)**[9] 4486 2-8-3 0.......... GilmarPereira(3) 2 —
(W J Haggas) *racd centre: chsd ldrs: rdn and wknd 2f out* **25/1**

1m 28.7s (2.10) **Going Correction** +0.075s/f (Good) 10 Ran SP% **116.6**

Speed ratings (Par 92): **91,86,85,85,85 79,79,78,60,53**

toteswinger: 1&2 £11.10, 1&3 £22.20, 2&3 £27.80. CSF £32.93 TOTE £4.90: £2.20, £2.80, £4.80; EX 47.00.

Owner Gongolphin & Racing **Bred** Eurostrait Ltd **Trained** Newmarket, Suffolk

FOCUS

Modest form in all probability, the fifth helping with the level. The winner is rated up 5lb on her debut form.

NOTEBOOK

Calahonda, who failed to build on her debut effort when only sixth at Kempton last time, had been given a short break and was up a furlong in trip. She came through over a furlong out and quickly came clear, winning with plenty in hand. There should be more to come from her on this evidence and it will be interesting to see what mark she gets for nurseries. (op 4-1 tchd 10-3)

Never LoseR, a 10,000gns daughter of Diktat who holds entries in the Lowther Stakes and Fillies' Mile, comes from a yard whose juveniles often need a run and as a result this has to go down as a highly satisfactory debut. The experience should not be lost on her and she can probably win a modest maiden. (op 8-1)

Omokoroa(IRE) cost just 11,000gns and comes from a modest family. He did not shape without promise back in third, but will need to improve if he is to win a maiden. (op 14-1)

Chantilly Dancer(IRE), who unseated her rider having reared coming out of the stalls at Lingfield last time, stuck on right he way to the line and should have a future in handicaps. (op 40-1)

Handful Of Magic is now qualified for an official mark and she is another who should find life easier in that sphere. (op 6-1 tchd 11-2 and 9-1)

Noble Dictator had to be walked to the start and is clearly not straightforward. He failed to build on his debut effort and is evidently not one to have too much faith in. (op 10-3 tchd 4-1)

Oscar Silk, a promising sixth on debut at Newbury, was strongly supported at the head of the market, but she was a bit tardy coming out of the stalls and never really travelled. Perhaps this slower ground was not to her liking, despite being bred to enjoy it, and she probably deserves another chance. (op 10-3)

4748 PKF (UK) LLP (S) H'CAP 1m 3y

6:35 (6:42) (Class 6) (0-65,63) 4-Y-0+ £1,942 (£578; £288; £144) Stalls High

Form RPR

0064 1 **Leptis Magna**[11] 4429 4-8-11 56.......... MarcHalford(3) 11 66
(D R C Elsworth) *s.i.s and hmpd s: hdwy and hmpd 3f out: shkn up to ld over 1f out: rdn out* **4/1**[1]

50-0 2 ¾ **Singleb (IRE)**[23] 4026 4-9-4 60.......... EddieAhern 5 68
(George Baker) *led: hdd over 4f out: edgd rt over 2f out: rdn and ev ch over 1f out: styd on same pce ins fnl f* **10/1**

326 3 1¼ **Ugenius**[29] 3822 4-8-8 50.......... DMylonas 12 55
(G Prodromou) *wnt lft s: hld up: hdwy over 2f out: rdn to ld over 1f out: sn hdd: no ex ins fnl f* **12/1**

1400 4 *shd* **Samuel Charles**[18] 4182 10-9-7 63..........(b) JohnEgan 15 68
(C R Dore) *chsd ldrs: led over 3f out: rdn and hdd over 1f out: styd on same pce insde fnl f* **10/1**

0-00 5 12 **Sierra Rose**[16] 4261 4-7-12 47.......... AndreaAtzeni(7) 7 24
(P J McBride) *prom: edgd rt 3f out: sn rdn: wknd over 1f out* **14/1**

-000 6 2½ **Royal Choir**[70] 2513 4-7-12 45.......... Louis-PhilippeBeuzelin(5) 14 17
(C E Brittain) *chsd ldrs: rdn and edgd lft over 2f out: wknd over 1f out* **25/1**

0440 7 6 **Crafty Fox**[23] 4026 5-8-3 45..........(v) FrankieMcDonald 9 3
(John A Harris) *chsd ldrs: rdn over 3f out: n.m.r and wknd sn after* **18/1**

/000 8 1 **Naughty Girl (IRE)**[9] 4491 8-7-11 46 ow1.......... SophieDoyle(7) 4 —
(John A Harris) *hld up: hdwy over 3f out: rdn and wknd over 1f out* **33/1**

4260 9 2½ **Million Percent**[21] 4084 9-9-4 60.......... CatherineGannon 13 10
(C R Dore) *hld up: hdwy 1/2-way: rdn and wknd over 2f out* **7/1**[2]

006 10 *hd* **Dushstorm (IRE)**[23] 4026 7-8-11 56..........(p) TolleyDean(3) 1 5
(C R Dore) *chsd ldrs: rdn 1/2-way: wknd over 2f out* **8/1**[3]

054/ 11 *hd* **Adalar (IRE)**[827] 1395 8-8-3 45..........(vt) NickyMackay 8 —
(B N Pollock) *chsd ldrs: rdn 1/2-way: wkng whn n.m.r over 3f out* **33/1**

0350 12 1½ **Only A Grand**[7] 4540 4-8-7 49..........(b) RichardMullen 2 —
(R Bastiman) *prom: rdn over 2f out: wknd over 1f out* **7/1**[2]

0002 13 3 **The London Gang**[102] 1636 5-8-3 45..........(b) AndrewElliott 6 —
(W M Brisbourne) *hld up: rdn and wknd over 2f out* **12/1**

00-0 14 ¾ **Sir Mikeale**[42] 3371 5-8-3 45.......... AdrianMcCarthy 10 —
(J Pearce) *hld up: effrt over 2f out: sn wknd* **50/1**

0000 15 22 **Lordswood (IRE)**[12] 4371 4-7-12 47 ow2..........(v) RossAtkinson(7) 16 —
(J R Best) *stdd s: hld up: plld hrd: hdwy over 5f out: led over 4f out: hdd & wknd over 3f out* **12/1**

1m 41.95s (1.35) **Going Correction** +0.075s/f (Good) 15 Ran SP% **121.0**

Speed ratings (Par 101): **96,95,94,93,81 79,73,72,69,69 69,68,65,64,42**

toteswinger: 1&2 £11.50, 1&3 £8.00, 2&3 £60.20. CSF £42.05 CT £461.56 TOTE £5.20: £2.40, £4.00, £4.20; EX 38.90.The winner was bought in for 4,600 guineas

Owner Charles Green **Bred** Mrs M Gutkin **Trained** Newmarket, Suffolk

FOCUS

An ordinary seller with nearly half the field out of the weights, but the first four, who finished clear, were among the top six in the weights. The winner was up 7lb on this year's form after a big slide in the weights.

The London Gang Official explanation: jockey said gelding was never travelling

4749 BANHAM POULTRY H'CAP 6f 3y

7:05 (7:10) (Class 5) (0-70,70) 3-Y-0+ £2,719 (£809; £404; £202) Stalls High

Form RPR

3103 1 **Mafaheem**[69] 2547 6-9-11 67..........(b) RichardMullen 8 77
(A B Haynes) *hld up in tch: rdn over 1f out: led ins fnl f: r.o wl* **7/1**[3]

4030 2 ¾ **Norcroft**[20] 4125 6-8-6 48.......... JohnEgan 4 56
(Mrs C A Dunnett) *hld up: swtchd lft and hdwy over 2f out: rdn over 1f out: sn ev ch: styd on* **7/2**[1]

0501 3 *shd* **Just Spike**[7] 4535 5-8-12 54 6ex.......... CatherineGannon 9 62
(B P J Baugh) *sn w ldr: rdn and ev ch whn edgd lft over 1f out: kpt on* **4/1**[2]

3045 4 2¼ **Angel Voices (IRE)**[23] 4013 5-9-8 64.......... AndrewElliott 7 64
(K R Burke) *sn led: rdn over 1f out: hdd and no ex ins fnl f* **15/2**

6011 5 1½ **Linda Green**[2] 4696 7-9-5 68 12ex.......... MatthewDavies(7) 1 64
(M R Channon) *s.i.s: hld up: hdwy over 1f out: no ex ins fnl f* **4/1**[2]

3040 6 2½ **Charlotte Grey**[15] 4285 4-7-13 48 oh2.......... AndreaAtzeni(7) 5 36
(P J McBride) *racd keenly: w ldrs: lost pl over 2f out: rdn and swtchd lft over 1f out: wknd fnl f* **8/1**

05U4 7 ½ **Gone'N'Dunnett (IRE)**[16] 4258 9-8-6 48 oh1..........(v) DMylonas 2 34
(Mrs C A Dunnett) *chsd ldrs: rdn over 1f out: wknd ins fnl f* **16/1**

1006 8 *nk* **Liberty Belle (IRE)**[12] 4375 3-9-10 70.......... EddieAhern 3 55
(J R Best) *plld hrd: led early: stdd to trck ldrs: rdn 2f out: wknd fnl f* **17/2**

1m 14.3s (-0.10) **Going Correction** +0.075s/f (Good)

WFA 3 from 4yo+ 4lb 8 Ran SP% **114.0**

Speed ratings (Par 103): **103,102,101,98,96 93,92,92**

toteswinger: 1&2 £11.30, 1&3 £15.30, 2&3 £5.50. CSF £31.51 CT £112.36 TOTE £8.30: £2.70, £1.90, £1.60; EX 39.30.

Owner W Clifford **Bred** J H And J M Wall **Trained** Limpley Stoke, Bath

FOCUS

A modest sprint handicap and ordinary form rated around the first three.

4750 BEACH RADIO CLAIMING STKS 1m 2f 21y

7:35 (7:37) (Class 6) 3-Y-0 £2,072 (£616; £308; £153) Stalls Low

Form RPR

005 1 **Wogan's Sister**[12] 4386 3-8-10 55.......... CatherineGannon 10 61
(I A Wood) *mde all: rdn over 1f out: styd on* **20/1**

-005 2 ½ **Sendefaa (IRE)**[16] 4259 3-7-13 53..........(b[1]) AndreaAtzeni(7) 7 56
(M Botti) *trckd wnr: racd keenly: rdn over 1f out: styd on* **6/1**

-0F0 3 *nse* **Wabbraan (USA)**[11] 4427 3-8-9 56.......... RichardMullen 5 59
(D M Simcock) *s.i.s: sn in mid-div: outpcd over 3f out: hdwy u.p over 1f out: edgd lft: r.o* **16/1**

3361 4 2½ **Maddy**[32] 3730 3-8-4 58..........(p) FrankieMcDonald 3 49
(George Baker) *chsd ldrs: rdn over 2f out: styd on same pce fnl f* **11/4**[1]

0013 5 1¾ **Colorado Springs**[19] 4165 3-8-8 54..........(b) AdrianMcCarthy 8 49
(W Jarvis) *trckd ldrs: rdn over 1f out: edgd lft: no ex fnl f* **4/1**[2]

0350 6 2 **Safebreaker**[12] 4392 3-9-1 69..........(p) JohnEgan 1 52
(N Tinkler) *hld up: hdwy over 2f out: rdn whn nt clr run 1f out: wknd ins fnl f* **5/1**[3]

0023 7 1¼ **Royal Soverin**[23] 4023 3-8-11 52..........(v) EddieAhern 9 46
(M J Wallace) *prom: rdn over 2f out: wknd over 1f out* **15/2**

4032 **8** 7 **Yakama (IRE)**[15] 4280 3-8-11 55..........(b) DMylonas 4 32
(G Prodromou) *s.i.s: hld up: rdn over 2f out: sn wknd* **8/1**

4050 **9** 2 **Fortunes Maid (IRE)**[23] 4023 3-8-3 41..........(v[1]) NickyMackay 2 20
(M H Tompkins) *hld up: rdn over 3f out: wknd over 2f out* **33/1**

U0-0 **10** 1 **Amouretta**[88] 2015 3-8-5 45..........(v) MarcHalford(3) 6 23
(T T Clement) *s.i.s: reminders sn after s: a in rr: rdn and wknd 3f out* **66/1**

2m 10.68s (0.18) **Going Correction** +0.075s/f (Good) **10** Ran SP% **115.6**

Speed ratings (Par 98): **102,101,101,99,98 96,95,89,88,87**

toteswinger: 1&2 £22.90, 1&3 £38.80, 2&3 £13.20. CSF £132.64 TOTE £24.30: £4.90, £2.30, £4.00; EX 83.00.The winner was claimed by D Elsworth for £12,000. Sendefaa was claimed by Michael Gates for £8,000

Owner Neardown Stables **Bred** Mrs J A Gawthorpe **Trained** Upper Lambourn, Berks

FOCUS

A weak claimer run at a steady early pace. The winner and third were the only two not to wear headgear and the form is rated around the placed horses.

4751 PRODUCEDINNORFOLK.COM H'CAP — 1m 6f 17y

8:05 (8:05) (Class 5) (0-75,75) 3-Y-0+ **£2,719** (£606; £606; £202) **Stalls** High

Form RPR

0211 **1** **Askar Tau (FR)**[6] 4573 3-9-0 74 6ex.......... RichardMullen 7 85+
(M P Tregoning) *racd keenly: sn trcking ldrs: led over 11f out: shkn up over 1f out: r.o strly: eased wl ins fnl f* **4/11**[1]

0660 **2** 1 3/4 **Irish Quest (IRE)**[35] 3613 4-9-7 75.......... MartinGuest(7) 6 81
(M A Jarvis) *sn led: hdd over 11f out: chsd ldrs: rdn over 2f out: styd on same pce fnl f* **12/1**[3]

3062 **2** dht **Sphere (IRE)**[34] 3624 3-8-11 71.......... EddieAhern 5 77
(J R Fanshawe) *trckd ldrs: wnt 2nd 8f out: rdn over 1f out: styd on same pce fnl f* **11/2**[2]

0263 **4** 4 **Given A Choice (IRE)**[19] 4156 6-9-5 73..........(p) SimonPearce(7) 2 73
(J Pearce) *hld up: hdwy over 5f out: lost pl over 2f out: wknd over 1f out* **20/1**

0134 **5** 4 1/2 **Naughty Thoughts (IRE)**[5] 4599 4-8-11 65.......... RossAtkinson(7) 4 59
(Tom Dascombe) *s.s: hld up: hdwy over 4f out: rdn over 2f out: sn wknd* **12/1**[3]

0-00 **6** 2 1/2 **Peas 'n Beans (IRE)**[107] 776 5-8-4 58 oh13..........(t) AndreaAtzeni(7) 3 49?
(T Keddy) *hld up in tch: racd keenly: rdn over 2f out: wknd wl over 1f out* **80/1**

3m 20.52s (12.92) **Going Correction** +0.075s/f (Good)

WFA 3 from 4yo+ 13lb **6** Ran SP% **110.1**

Speed ratings (Par 103): **66,65,65,62,60 58**

2nd PL IQ 2.00, S 0.80; Ex AT-IQ 3.10, AT-S 1.10; CSF AT-IQ 2.84, AT-S 1.32; toteswinger: AT-S £1.10, AT-IQ £3.10; Place 6 £ 217.77, Place 5 £ 91.16 TOTE £1.30: £1.30.

Owner Nurlan Bizakov **Bred** Gestut Zoppenbroich & Aerial Bloodstock **Trained** Lambourn, Berks

FOCUS

A reasonable handicap for the grade, but they went no pace early, resulting in a very moderate winning time. The winner would have won by about 4l if pushed out and is capable of better with the placed horses setting the level.

T/Plt: £772.90 to a £1 stake. Pool: £47,539.79. 44.90 winning tickets. T/Qpdt: £30.00 to a £1 stake. Pool: £5,144.06. 126.50 winning tickets. CR

4752 - 4761a (Foreign Racing) - See Raceform Interactive

4579 BATH (L-H)

Thursday, August 7

OFFICIAL GOING: Good to soft (good in places; 7.4)

Wind: Brisk, behind Weather: Partial cloud

4762 GROSVENOR CASINOS BRISTOL MEMBERSHIP IS FREE APPRENTICE H'CAP — 1m 3f 144y

5:55 (5:56) (Class 5) (0-75,73) 3-Y-0 **£2,719** (£809; £404; £202) **Stalls** Low

Form RPR

303 **1** **Deer Daylami (IRE)**[21] 4116 3-9-10 73.......... MatthewDavies 5 78
(M R Channon) *mde all: rdn over 2f out: styd on strly fr over 1f out* **11/4**[2]

20-5 **2** 1 1/2 **Suite Francaise**[15] 4303 3-8-6 58.......... RosieJessop(3) 2 61
(Sir Mark Prescott) *t.k.h early: chsd wnr thrght: rdn and no imp fnl 2f* **9/1**

4552 **3** 3/4 **Dubai Petal (IRE)**[26] 3962 3-9-4 70.......... AshleyMorgan(3) 1 71+
(J S Moore) *disputing cl 3rd whn bmpd and lost pl over 4f out: effrt: bmpd and slipped again sn after and lost pl: styd on u.p fr over 1f out and clsng on ldng duo ins fnl f but a hld* **15/8**[1]

344 **4** 7 **Mission Control (IRE)**[14] 4335 3-8-13 67.......... AndreaAtzeni(5) 3 57
(J R Boyle) *disputing cl 3rd whn bmpd over 4f out: n.m.r sn after: sn rdn: wknd fr 3f out* **9/2**

6424 **5** 33 **Sterope (FR)**[12] 4427 3-9-5 68..........(v[1]) JPHamblett 4 5
(H R A Cecil) *slowly away: in rr tl hdwy to dispute cl 3rd and edgd lft over 4f out: rdn sn after and wknd 3f out: virtually p.u fnl f* **7/2**[3]

2m 33.66s (3.06) **Going Correction** +0.325s/f (Good) **5** Ran SP% **111.9**

Speed ratings (Par 100): **102,101,100,95,73**

CSF £24.75 TOTE £3.80: £2.40, £2.70; EX 16.60.

Owner Jaber Abdullah **Bred** Mrs Jane Bailey **Trained** West Ilsley, Berks

■ Stewards' Enquiry : J P Hamblett three-day ban: careless riding (August 23-25)

FOCUS

A fair bunch contested what turned out to be a strange handicap for apprentices, as the runners occupied virtually the same positions throughout, making the form somewhat suspect.

Dubai Petal(IRE) Official explanation: jockey said filly slipped on bend

4763 GROSVENOR CASINOS TRY OUR EXPERIENCE PACKAGES MAIDEN AUCTION FILLIES' STKS — 5f 161y

6:25 (6:25) (Class 6) 2-Y-0 **£2,266** (£674; £337; £168) **Stalls** Centre

Form RPR

5 **1** **Rioliina (IRE)**[44] 3348 2-8-8 0.......... AdrianMcCarthy 5 82+
(J G Portman) *disp ld tl slt advantage fr 4f out: drvn and qcknd clr appr fnl f: v easily* **3/1**[2]

2 7 **Wake Me Now (IRE)** 2-8-8 0.......... JamesDoyle 1 59+
(R M Beckett) *towards rr whn bmpd over 4f out: swtchd rt to outside over 2f out: styd on to take 2nd ins fnl f and hld that position but nvr any ch w v easy wnr* **3/1**[2]

3 nk **Via Mia** 2-8-12 0.......... PatDobbs 2 62
(P F I Cole) *bmpd over 4f out whn towards rr: sn rcvrd to chse ldrs: wnt 2nd 2f out: no imp and outpcd into 3rd ins fnl f* **2/1**[1]

4 3 1/2 **Yanza** 2-8-8 0.......... DavidKinsella 4 50+
(J R Gask) *s.i.s: in rr tl hdwy and hmpd over 2f out: sn lost pl: styd on again fnl f but nvr in contention* **14/1**

5 1/2 **Phoenix Enforcer** 2-8-8 0.......... LPKeniry 8 45
(George Baker) *chsd ldrs: rdn and outpcd 2f out* **8/1**[3]

0 **6** 1 1/4 **Bold Ring**[44] 3348 2-8-6 0.......... EdwardCreighton 7 39
(D W P Arbuthnot) *s.i.s: sn rdn and nvr gng pce to be competitive* **8/1**[3]

7 7 **Erris Lady** 2-8-6 0.......... CatherineGannon 6 15
(Mrs L Williamson) *slt ld tl hdd 4f out: wknd over 2f out* **25/1**

1m 12.97s (1.77) **Going Correction** +0.325s/f (Good) **7** Ran SP% **116.1**

Speed ratings (Par 89): **101,91,91,86,85 84,74**

toteswinger: 1&2 £3.50, 1&3 £2.10, 2&3 £1.10. CSF £12.86 TOTE £4.00: £1.50, £2.30; EX 13.50.

Owner A S B Portman **Bred** Catridge Farm Stud Ltd **Trained** Compton, Berks

FOCUS

With five newcomers taking on a pair with just one run apiece, the form of this maiden for fillies was always going to be questionable, and with the winner going in by seven lengths it is unlikely that any of those behind her are going to set the world alight.

NOTEBOOK

Rioliina(IRE), a half-sister to the yard's triple-winning juvenile Cheap Street, showed enough on her debut at Newbury despite running very green to suggest that it would take a decent performance from one of the newcomers to lower her colours here, and in the event she ran out a facile winner. With so many unknown quantities in the race this form is hard to assess and it will be interesting to see how the Handicapper reacts. (new market new market op 2-1 tchd 15-8 and 7-2)

Wake Me Now(IRE) was squeezed out against the rail early on and shuffled back to last as a consequence. Pulled out and showing good speed to hold every chance on the outside two furlongs out, she had done her running and was no match for the winner. She should improve but looks modest. Official explanation: jockey said filly was hampered at the start (new market new market op 9-2)

Via Mia was hammered in the market beforehand to make a winning start but was no match for the winner. She should know more about the game next time but looks ordinary. (new market new market op 4-1)

Yanza was murdered at around the two-furlong marker but to her credit kept on again, albeit at a respectful distance behind. She is entitled to come on for this. (new market new market op 16-1 tchd 12-1)

Bold Ring Official explanation: jockey said filly ran green

4764 GROSVENOR CASINO BRISTOL FREE BET FOR JOINING (S) STKS — 5f 11y

7:00 (7:01) (Class 6) 2-Y-0 **£1,942** (£578; £288; £144) **Stalls** Centre

Form RPR

3235 **1** **Like For Like (IRE)**[26] 3949 2-8-11 68.......... PatDobbs 6 58+
(R Hannon) *reluctant to go to s: bmpd s: in rr but in tch whn hdwy and hmpd 2f out: hdwy again 1f out and styd on wl to dispute 2nd ins fnl f: led fnl 50yds: hld on wl* **6/5**[1]

00 **2** 1/2 **Intrepid Lady (IRE)**[8] 4534 2-8-11 0.......... EdwardCreighton 3 56
(M R Channon) *chsd ldrs tl n.m.r and outpcd 2f out: styd on wl to dispute 2nd ins fnl f and led briefly 100yds out: hdd and no ex fnl 50yds* **8/1**

6003 **3** 1 3/4 **August Days (IRE)**[13] 4387 2-8-11 52.......... JamesDoyle 5 50
(R M Beckett) *w ldr tl led 3f out: rdn and styd on fr 2f out: hdd fnl 100yds: sn btn* **11/2**[3]

0324 **4** 2 1/2 **Frame And Cover**[8] 4534 2-8-8 52..........(p) KevinGhunowa(3) 8 41
(R A Harris) *chsd ldrs: rdn and hung lft 2f out: wknd fnl f* **7/2**[2]

0 **5** 3/4 **Jimwasright (IRE)**[36] 3603 2-8-11 0.......... RichardEvans(5) 1 43
(P D Evans) *chsd ldrs: rdn over 2f out: wknd over 1f out* **8/1**

6 2 1/4 **Cwmni** 2-8-11 0.......... CatherineGannon 2 30
(B Palling) *a outpcd* **16/1**

2605 **7** 3 3/4 **Makaluna**[21] 4120 2-8-11 44.......... JackDean(5) 7 22+
(W G M Turner) *slt ld tl hdd 3f out: edgd rt 2f out and bmpd: sn wknd* **14/1**

0564 **8** 7 **Tyler**[28] 3889 2-9-2 42..........(v[1]) TGMcLaughlin 4 —
(W M Brisbourne) *a bhd* **33/1**

64.79 secs (2.29) **Going Correction** +0.325s/f (Good) **8** Ran SP% **120.8**

Speed ratings (Par 92): **94,93,90,86,85 81,75,64**

toteswinger: 1&2 £2.00, 1&3 £1.40, 2&3 £3.00. CSF £13.01 TOTE £2.00: £1.10, £3.10, £1.60; EX 12.70.The winner was sold to Richard Prince for £6,500. Intrepid Lady was claimed by J. C. Tuck for £6,000.

Owner S French R Morecombe J perryman **Bred** W Maxwell Ervine **Trained** East Everleigh, Wilts

■ Stewards' Enquiry : Kevin Ghunowa two-day ban: careless riding (Aug 23-24)

FOCUS

A typically modest seller and, despite the fact that she is not progressive, the winner was entitled to break her duck against this grade of opponent. The fourth helps set the level.

NOTEBOOK

Like For Like(IRE) had not been progressing in maiden company and in this sort of field the daughter of leading first-season sire Kheleyf didn't have to improve any to gain her first win. She was sold for £6,500 at the subsequent auction. (op Evens tchd 5-6)

Intrepid Lady(IRE) was dropped down to the basement grade for the first time and turned around Leicester form with the fourth home without being a match for the winner. She won't always have a 68-rated animal to contend with in these events and should be winning one sooner rather than later. (op 14-1)

August Days(IRE), back to a trip over which she had shown some promise on her first couple of starts, had got to the front and missed the scrimmaging that occurred just behind her two furlongs out, but wasn't good enough to take advantage. (tchd 6-1)

Frame And Cover showed some early speed in first-time cheekpieces but is becoming exposed as very modest. (op 4-1)

Jimwasright(IRE) was nibbled at in the market beforehand but never showed anything like enough for supporters to think the gamble might be justified, and probably showed no more than when finishing mid-division in a better race on his debut. (op 14-1)

Cwmni Official explanation: jockey said filly hung left-handed

4765 GROSVENOR PRIZE DRAW NIGHT FRIDAY 8TH AUGUST CLAIMING STKS — 5f 161y

7:30 (7:30) (Class 6) 3-Y-0+ **£2,072** (£616; £308; £153) **Stalls** Centre

Form RPR

0016 **1** **Kyle (IRE)**[58] 2923 4-9-4 79.......... HaddenFrost(5) 7 81
(R Hannon) *in rr tl smooth hdwy to chal 2f out: led sn after: rdn and narrowly hdd ins fnl f: rallied u.p to ld again last stride* **7/4**[1]

40-1 **2** nse **Drumming Party (USA)**[16] 4273 6-9-0 60..........(t) LPKeniry 1 72
(A M Balding) *trckd ldrs: stl on bit 2f out: chal 1f out: rdn to take slt ld ins fnl f: hdd last stride* **9/2**[3]

0031 **3** 4 1/2 **Bazguy**[16] 4271 3-9-0 65..........(b) JamesDoyle 3 60
(P D Evans) *in rr but in tch: bmpd 2f out: styd on to take wl hld 3rd fnl f* **11/1**

3531 **4** 1 3/4 **Night Prospector**[6] 4580 8-8-11 55..........(p) KevinGhunowa(3) 5 50
(R A Harris) *chsd ldrs: bmpd and u.p 2f out: wknd fnl f* **7/1**

3-50 **5** 1 3/4 **Zippi Jazzman (USA)**[17] 4252 3-8-11 75.......... DavidProbert(5) 8 49
(R M Beckett) *outpcd most of way* **7/2**[2]

2431 **6** 8 **High Reach**[14] 4336 8-9-2 58..........(p) TGMcLaughlin 4 16
(J G M O'Shea) *w ldr tl led over 3f out: hdd ins fnl 2f: sn wknd* **14/1**

The Form Book, Raceform Ltd, Compton, RG20 6NL

5622 **7** 2 ½ **Music Box Express**[14] 4324 4-8-5 52...(tp) MatthewDavies(7) 2 —
(George Baker) *sn drvn to take slt ld: hdd over 3f out: wknd qckly 2f out* **10/1**

1m 13.25s (2.05) **Going Correction** +0.325s/f (Good)
WFA 3 from 4yo+ 4lb **7** Ran SP% **113.4**
Speed ratings (Par 101): **99,98,92,90,88 77,74**The winner was claimed by R. A. Harris for £15,000. Drumming Party was claimed by Mustafa Khan for £6,000..The winner was claimed by R. A. Harris for £15,000. Drumming Party was claimed by Mustafa Khan for £6,000.
Owner Noodles Racing **Bred** John Cullinan **Trained** East Everleigh, Wilts

FOCUS
Mainly modest sorts contesting this claimer, run in a slower time than the earlier juvenile heat over the trip. The winner was entitled to land the spoils on official ratings but the form is muddling with the runner-up the best guide.

4766 GROSVENOR CASINO GREAT NIGHT OUT EXPERIENCE H'CAP 1m 5y
8:05 (8:05) (Class 5) (0-75,74) 3-Y-O **£2,914** (£867; £433; £216) **Stalls** Low

Form RPR
5413 **1** **Oriental Girl**[17] 4253 3-8-10 **63**...(p) DavidKinsella 2 67
(J A Geake) *hld up in rr: hdwy 3f out: hrd drvn fr 2f out: chsd ldr 1f out: styd on u.p to ld last stride* **3/1**[2]

0243 **2** *shd* **Desiderio**[12] 4429 3-9-7 **74**...(b) PatDobbs 4 78
(R Hannon) *led: hrd rdn whn chal fr 2f out: kpt on u.p fnl f: ct last stride* **9/2**

4304 **3** 1 ½ **Clovis**[6] 4582 3-8-13 **71**...(b) HaddenFrost(5) 1 71
(N P Mulholland) *in rr tl hdwy fr 3f out to chal ins fnl 2f: styd on same pce ins fnl f* **11/2**

0014 **4** ½ **Stage Acclaim (IRE)**[14] 4332 3-9-1 **71**...(p) JamesMillman(3) 3 70
(B R Millman) *chsd ldr: rdn to chal ins fnl 2f: outpcd ins fnl f* **10/3**[3]

-215 **5** *shd* **Sarah Park (IRE)**[13] 4377 3-8-11 **64**... LPKeniry 5 63
(B J Meehan) *chsd ldrs: drvn to chal ins fnl 2f: outpcd fnl f* **11/4**[1]

0045 **6** 5 **Bold Diva**[12] 4413 3-7-9 **55** oh5...(v) StacyRenwick(7) 6 42
(A W Carroll) *a in rr* **16/1**

1m 43.94s (3.14) **Going Correction** +0.325s/f (Good) **6** Ran SP% **114.2**
Speed ratings (Par 100): **97,96,95,94,94 89**
toteswinger: 1&2 £4.70, 1&3 £8.40, 2&3 £1.40. CSF £17.10 TOTE £3.40: £1.70, £2.90; EX 18.80.
Owner Kimpton Down Partnership **Bred** Aston Mullins Stud And D J Erwin **Trained** Kimpton, Hants

FOCUS
A tight little handicap in which tactics were always likely to play a big part in the outcome. The form is a bit muddling with the first two the best guides.

4767 E.B.F./GROSVENOR CASINO £4,000 JACKPOT SLOT MACHINES FILLIES' H'CAP 5f 11y
8:35 (8:36) (Class 5) (0-75,72) 3-Y-O+ **£3,561** (£1,059; £529; £264) **Stalls** Centre

Form RPR
2214 **1** **Pretty Bonnie**[13] 4383 3-8-7 **60**... NataliaGemelova(5) 1 74
(A E Price) *pressed ldr tl drvn to ld wl over 1f out: edgd rt u.p fnl f: all out* **12/1**

0100 **2** 1 ½ **Diane's Choice**[7] 4555 5-9-6 **68**... KevinGhunowa(3) 5 77
(Miss Gay Kelleway) *chsd ldrs: chal over 1f out: rdn and styd on to chse wnr ins fnl f but a hld* **7/1**

3/51 **3** 1 ½ **Night Rocket (IRE)**[13] 4388 4-9-2 **66**...(t) DavidProbert(5) 8 70+
(A M Balding) *s.i.s: bhd: hdwy over 2f out: styd on ins fnl f: gng on cl home* **10/3**[1]

1342 **4** *hd* **Pennyspider (IRE)**[6] 4584 3-9-0 **62**... TGMcLaughlin 7 65
(M S Saunders) *pressed ldrs: chal 2f out: wknd ins fnl f* **5/1**[3]

0115 **5** *hd* **Linda Green**[1] 4749 7-9-2 **68** 12ex... MatthewDavies(7) 6 70
(M R Channon) *in rr: drvn and hdwy fr 2f out: no imp on ldrs ins fnl f* **5/1**[3]

6015 **6** 1 **Diminuto**[21] 4103 4-8-10 **62**... BillyCray(7) 10 61
(M D I Usher) *in rr and sn drvn along: kpt on fnl 2f but nvr gng pce to chal* **16/1**

2645 **7** *hd* **The Jailer**[29] 3842 5-9-0 **59**... VinceSlattery 3 57
(J G M O'Shea) *in tch: rdn 1/2-way: nvr gng pce to get into contention* **10/1**

5626 **8** 1 ¼ **Weet A Surprise**[14] 4347 3-9-10 **72**... LPKeniry 9 65
(R Hollinshead) *in tch and rdn 1/2-way: wknd over 1f out* **12/1**

1003 **9** ¾ **Danjet (IRE)**[3] 4696 5-9-0 **59**... JamesDoyle 4 50
(P D Evans) *chsd ldrs over 3f* **9/2**[2]

-100 **10** 3 ½ **Lambrini Lace (IRE)**[14] 4325 3-8-13 **61**... EdwardCreighton 2 39
(Mrs L Williamson) *led tl hdd & wknd wl over 1f out* **22/1**

63.93 secs (1.43) **Going Correction** +0.325s/f (Good)
WFA 3 from 4yo+ 3lb **10** Ran SP% **121.8**
Speed ratings (Par 100): **101,98,96,95,95 93,93,91,90,84**
toteswinger: 1&2 £13.20, 1&3 £33.80, 2&3 Not won. CSF £97.53 CT £359.72 TOTE £17.30: £3.40, £2.10, £1.70; EX 70.80 Place 6: £73.76, Place 5: £26.31..
Owner N Field **Bred** P And Mrs A G Venner & Alpha Bloodstock Ltd **Trained** Leominster, H'fords
■ Stewards' Enquiry : Kevin Ghunowa two-day ban: (August 23-24)

FOCUS
A trappy, modest sprint handicap for fillies won by an improving three-year-old. the runner-up sets the level.
T/Plt: £67.20 to a £1 stake. Pool: £43,275.94. 469.80 winning tickets. T/Qpdt: £11.50 to a £1 stake. Pool: £3,571.60. 229.80 winning tickets. ST

4720 BRIGHTON (L-H)
Thursday, August 7

OFFICIAL GOING: Good (good to firm in places)
Wind: Moderate, against

4768 TOTEPLACEPOT NURSERY 5f 59y
2:30 (2:31) (Class 5) 2-Y-O **£2,964** (£887; £443; £221; £110) **Stalls** Low

Form RPR
3210 **1** **The Magic Of Rio**[19] 4190 2-9-3 **79**... LiamJones 5 79
(W J Haggas) *in tch: strly rdn fr 2f out: r.o to ld jst ins fnl f: drvn out* **5/1**[2]

6302 **2** ½ **Kate The Great**[29] 3846 2-9-1 **77**... DaneO'Neill 7 75
(M J Wallace) *mid-div: rdn and hdwy on outside 1f out: r.o wl to take 2nd ins fnl f* **13/2**

1503 **3** 1 ½ **Red Cell (IRE)**[15] 4297 2-8-2 **64** ow1...(b) ChrisCatlin 2 57
(E J O'Neill) *led: rdn and hdd jst ins fnl f: one pce* **8/1**

4106 **4** ½ **Skruton (IRE)**[28] 3865 2-8-13 **75**... TPO'Shea 8 66
(M G Quinlan) *bmpd s: racd on outside: styd on fnl f: nvr nrr* **12/1**

3200 **5** *hd* **Pocket's Pick (IRE)**[9] 4510 2-9-7 **83**... GeorgeBaker 4 73
(G L Moore) *chsd ldrs: rdn 2f out: rn wd into st: one pce fnl f* **7/2**[1]

3463 **6** 1 ¼ **Verlegen (IRE)**[14] 4346 2-8-10 **72**... RichardHughes 11 58
(R Hannon) *in rr: effrt over 1f out: nt pce to chal* **11/2**[3]

306 **7** ½ **Satwa Boy**[31] 3798 2-7-11 **62**... LukeMorris(3) 6 48+
(E A L Dunlop) *mid-div: hung lft over 1f out: swtchd rt: one pce fnl f* **12/1**

0304 **8** 1 ¾ **Mean Mr Mustard (IRE)**[13] 4389 2-7-7 **60** oh5...(b) DavidProbert(5) 3 38
(J A Osborne) *chsd ldrs tl rdn and wknd over 1f out* **10/1**

4241 **9** *shd* **Sub Prime (IRE)**[59] 2882 2-7-10 **63**... Louis-PhilippeBeuzelin(5) 1 40
(J A Osborne) *trckd ldrs: rdn and wknd appr fnl f* **14/1**

3623 **10** 2 ½ **Sonhador**[21] 4101 2-8-10 **72**... JimCrowley 9 40
(P Winkworth) *taken to ins rail fr outside draw: rdn and hung lft over 1f out: sn btn* **8/1**

63.10 secs (0.80) **Going Correction** +0.05s/f (Good) **10** Ran SP% **121.0**
Speed ratings (Par 94): **95,94,91,91,90 88,87,85,84,80**
toteswinger: 1&2 £9.10, 1&3 £13.60, 2&3 £7.50. CSF £39.10 CT £267.94 TOTE £7.30: £1.80, £2.20, £3.30; EX 28.70 Trifecta £273.20 Part won. Pool: £369.25. 0.70 winning units..
Owner M Scotney/ D Asplin/ A Symonds **Bred** R F And S D Knipe **Trained** Newmarket, Suffolk

FOCUS
A fairly competitive nursery rated around the first two.

NOTEBOOK
The Magic Of Rio, down the field in the Weatherbys Super Sprint last time, found this company far less taxing and got her career back on track. She was always holding on at the finish and looks quietly progressive. (tchd 9-2, 11-2 in places)

Kate The Great, runner-up in a similar event at Lingfield on her previous start, was 2lb higher and ran a solid race without ever quite looking like she would catch the winner. She can expect another slight rise for this and it is possible that the Handicapper will remain in charge for the time being. (op 6-1 tchd 15-2)

Red Cell(IRE), down in class compared with his last two outings, had to carry 1lb overweight. He settled better in front this time but again found a couple too good at the finish. (op 10-1)

Skruton(IRE), who did not enjoy the best of trips, looks to be crying out for a return to 6f, the distance over which she won her maiden back in May. (op 10-1)

Pocket's Pick(IRE) finished last in a decent maiden at Goodwood last time but he had finished one place in front of The Magic Of Rio in the Weatherbys Super Sprint. He did not really handle this track. Official explanation: jockey said colt did not handle the bend (op 4-1 tchd 9-2)

Verlegen(IRE), running in a handicap for the first time, never got competitive. 6f on a more galloping track should suit her. (op 7-1)

4769 TOTESWINGER MAIDEN AUCTION STKS 6f 209y
3:00 (3:01) (Class 5) 2-Y-O **£2,964** (£887; £443; £221; £110) **Stalls** Low

Form RPR
520 **1** **Cavendish Road (IRE)**[20] 4169 2-8-12 76... RichardHughes 4 73
(W R Muir) *led to 1/2-way: led again 2f out: rdn and kpt on wl u.p fnl f* **2/1**[1]

032 **2** ½ **Hameildaeme**[32] 3754 2-8-5 68... SaleemGolam 5 65
(S C Williams) *in tch: rdn 2f out: kpt on to press wnr fnl f: no ex cl home* **10/3**[3]

6 **3** 2 **Spit And Polish**[39] 3519 2-8-13 0... TPQueally 1 68
(J L Dunlop) *hld up: swtchd rt and c wd into st: hdwy over 2f out: nt qckn fnl f* **8/1**

4 **4** *hd* **Bad Baron (IRE)**[15] 4296 2-8-10 0... StephenCarson 2 64
(Eve Johnson Houghton) *s.i.s: t.k.h: j. path over 2f out: hung lft appr fnl f: one pce after* **9/4**[2]

0 **5** 2 ¾ **Lyonesse**[24] 4024 2-8-5 0... ChrisCatlin 7 52
(R Hannon) *w wnr: led 1/2-way: hdd 2f out: sn wknd* **8/1**

06 **6** 6 **Persian Tomcat (IRE)**[87] 2054 2-8-9 0... RussellKennemore(3) 6 43
(Miss J Feilden) *in tch to over 2f out: sn wknd* **20/1**

1m 25.21s (2.11) **Going Correction** +0.05s/f (Good) **6** Ran SP% **114.2**
Speed ratings (Par 94): **89,88,86,85,82 75**
toteswinger: 1&2 £1.80, 1&3 £3.70, 2&3 £4.00. CSF £9.32 TOTE £2.90: £1.50, £2.30; EX 9.70.
Owner C L A Edginton **Bred** Garry Chong **Trained** Lambourn, Berks

FOCUS
Ordinary maiden form with the time slow, but the winner is rated to form.

NOTEBOOK
Cavendish Road(IRE) looked the one to beat on his Leicester second and, showing up well throughout, was always just holding off his pursuers. The extra furlong seemed to suit him and, with nurseries in mind, he should not go up in the handicap for this. (tchd 5-2)

Hameildaeme has improved with each start and with each step up in distance, as her pedigree might suggest. She put up a strong challenge but was always just being held at the finish. (op 3-1 tchd 5-2)

Spit And Polish, whose dam was a sprint winner at two in France, looked to have every chance on the outside but ran green and could not go through with his effort. (tchd 9-1)

Bad Baron(IRE) did not do a lot right. He was slowly away, keen in the early stages and jumped the path approaching the two-furlong marker. He also hung under pressure. This track clearly did not suit him, and in the circumstances he did not do too badly. He should be seen in a better light back on a more conventional course. (op 5-2 tchd 11-4, 3-1 in a place)

Lyonesse, a half-sister to Cavewarrior, a 6f winner at two, showed speed but did not get home. (op 9-1)

4770 NEW SOMERFIELD BRIGHTON NORTH STREET FILLIES' H'CAP 6f 209y
3:30 (3:31) (Class 5) (0-70,67) 3-Y-O+ **£3,154** (£944; £472; £236; £117) **Stalls** Low

Form RPR
2000 **1** **Palais Polaire**[30] 3816 6-8-8 **48** oh1...(p) RobertHavlin 8 57
(J A Geake) *trckd ldr: led over 2f out: pushed out fnl f* **16/1**

2401 **2** 1 ¾ **Kannon**[14] 4338 3-8-11 **57**... RichardHughes 1 59
(W J Knight) *in tch: rdn over 2f out: kpt on to go 2nd ins fnl f* **9/4**[1]

040 **3** 1 ¼ **Coup De Torchon (FR)**[45] 3333 3-8-9 **55**... ShaneKelly 7 54
(J A Osborne) *led tl hdd over 2f out: one pce and lost 2nd ins fnl f* **12/1**[3]

5401 **4** *nk* **Glencal**[13] 4368 4-9-10 **67**... TravisBlock(3) 5 67
(H Morrison) *in tch: rdn 2f out: nt qckn fr over 1f out* **9/4**[1]

1336 **5** 1 ½ **Imperial Lucky (IRE)**[16] 4282 5-9-2 **56**...(p) DaneO'Neill 4 52
(M J Wallace) *in tch: rdn 2f out: sn wknd* **11/4**[2]

5-00 **6** 1 ½ **Qasayed (USA)**[14] 4349 3-9-0 **60**... LiamJones 2 50
(C E Brittain) *slowly away: hld up: t.k.h: rdn over 2f out: wknd fnl f* **12/1**[3]

-001 **7** 6 **Bahamian Princess**[100] 1709 3-9-2 **65**... RussellKennemore(3) 6 39
(R Hollinshead) *slowly away: t.k.h: a bhd* **16/1**

1m 23.27s (0.17) **Going Correction** +0.05s/f (Good)
WFA 3 from 4yo+ 6lb **7** Ran SP% **115.4**
Speed ratings (Par 100): **101,99,97,97,95 93,86**
toteswinger: 1&2 £6.90, 1&3 £23.50, 2&3 £4.60. CSF £53.17 CT £464.28 TOTE £25.60: £9.20, £1.90; EX 77.60 Trifecta £252.80 Pool: £478.43. 1.40 winning units..
Owner Miss B Swire **Bred** Miss B Swire **Trained** Kimpton, Hants

FOCUS
They went an ordinary pace in this weak fillies' handicap and the form does not look entirely reliable.

4771 TOTESPORT.COM BRIGHTON CHALLENGE CUP (H'CAP) 1m 3f 196y
4:00 (4:04) (Class 4) (0-80,80) 3-Y-0+
£13,622 (£4,083; £2,043; £1,018; £510; £257) **Stalls** High

Form RPR
3222 **1** **King Supreme (IRE)**[17] 4254 3-8-6 **73**.....................(b) TPO'Shea 2 84
(R Hannon) *mid-div: hdwy over 2f out: led 1f out: drvn out* **7/1**[3]
2212 **2** *1* **Spring Dream (IRE)**[12] 4426 5-9-8 **78**.....................(b) RichardHughes 11 87
(A King) *a in tch: led 2f out: hung lft and hdd 1f out: kpt on ins fnl f* **13/2**[2]
5302 **3** *1 1/4* **Del Mar Sunset**[7] 4565 9-9-4 **74**..................................... LiamJones 8 81
(W J Haggas) *in rr: hdwy on outside over 3f out: styd on to go 3rd ins fnl f* **10/1**
4306 **4** *1/2* **Haarth Sovereign (IRE)**[27] 3925 4-9-8 **78**.................. AdamKirby 12 84
(W R Swinburn) *mid-div: hdwy over 3f out: ev ch over 1f out: no ex ins fnl f* **7/1**[3]
42-0 **5** *nk* **Heathyards Pride**[28] 3864 8-9-2 **75**.................... RussellKennemore(3) 9 81
(R Hollinshead) *slowly away: in rr: swtchd rt and hdwy on outside 3f out: edgd lft and one pce fnl f* **16/1**
3300 **6** *3* **Rationale (IRE)**[19] 4191 5-9-10 **80**............................ JimCrowley 15 81
(S C Williams) *v.s.a: in rr tl hdwy on outside 3f out: kpt on one pce ins fnl 2f* **14/1**
0054 **7** *nk* **Generous Jem**[2] 4699 5-9-6 **79**............................ LukeMorris(3) 10 79
(G G Margarson) *towards rr: nt clr run fr over 2f out: edgd lft over 1f out: no further hdwy* **20/1**
1221 **8** *1* **Wee Charlie Castle (IRE)**[15] 4309 5-8-5 **68**........... WilliamCarson(7) 4 67+
(G C H Chung) *towards rr: rdn and hmpd over 1f out: no hdwy after* **9/1**
6463 **9** *1/2* **Apache Fort**[6] 4592 5-8-8 **64**.. PaulDoe 14 62
(T Keddy) *trckd ldr: led over 3f out: rdn and hdd 2f out: wknd appr fnl f* **20/1**
014 **10** *6* **Mon Plaisir (USA)**[41] 3459 3-8-8 **75**............................ TPQueally 3 63
(J L Dunlop) *trckd ldrs: rdn 2f out: wknd appr fnl f* **5/1**[1]
0565 **11** *shd* **Proper (IRE)**[16] 4276 4-8-12 **71**.................................. TravisBlock(3) 1 59+
(C J Mann) *hld up: rdn whn nt clr run over 1f out: swtchd rt: nt rcvr* **22/1**
6100 **12** *1 3/4* **Transvestite (IRE)**[35] 3650 6-8-12 **73**................... GabrielHannon(5) 13 58
(J W Hills) *trckd ldrs: rdn 3f out: wknd 2f out* **22/1**
2215 **13** *3 1/4* **Bassinet (USA)**[27] 3925 4-9-6 **76**.................................... ShaneKelly 6 56+
(J A R Toller) *in tch tl lost pl over 3f out* **9/1**
2130 **14** *5* **Double Spectre (IRE)**[12] 4432 6-9-1 **71**........................ DaneO'Neill 5 43
(Jean-Rene Auvray) *t.k.h: in tch: rdn over 2f out: sn wknd* **33/1**
2104 **15** *51* **Dove Cottage (IRE)**[31] 3802 6-9-5 **75**......................... FergusSweeney 16 —
(W S Kittow) *led tl lost action and hdd over 3f out: sn bhd: virtually p.u* **10/1**

2m 31.44s (-1.26) **Going Correction** +0.05s/f (Good)
WFA 3 from 4yo+ 11lb **15** Ran SP% **126.9**
Speed ratings (Par 105): **106,105,104,104,103 101,101,101,100,96 96,95,93,90,56**
toteswinger: 1&2 £6.70, 1&3 £13.60, 2&3 £10.50. CSF £50.26 CT £472.82 TOTE £8.60: £2.90, £2.20, £4.00; EX 49.30 Trifecta £398.00 Pool: £640.16. 1.19 winning units..
Owner Brian C Oakley **Bred** Miss Joan Murphy **Trained** East Everleigh, Wilts

FOCUS
A competitive handicap and fair form that looks sound judging by the way the first five came clear.
Haarth Sovereign(IRE) Official explanation: jockey said gelding hung left in the home straight
Double Spectre(IRE) Official explanation: jockey said gelding had no more to give
Dove Cottage(IRE) Official explanation: jockey said gelding lost its action

4772 TOTESPORT 0800 221 221 H'CAP 7f 214y
4:30 (4:35) (Class 6) (0-60,60) 3-Y-0+ **£2,396** (£712; £356; £177) **Stalls** Low

Form RPR
0030 **1** **Lopinot (IRE)**[15] 4306 5-9-3 **54**........................(p) FergusSweeney 1 61
(M R Bosley) *mde virtually all: rdn over 2f out: fdd towards fin* **9/1**
3055 **2** *1/2* **Tuscan Treaty**[16] 4282 8-8-6 **46** oh1..................(t) LukeMorris(3) 11 52
(R W Price) *s.i.s: hdwy to chse ldrs over 2f out: kpt on to go 2nd ins fnl f* **20/1**
6540 **3** *1/2* **Star Strider**[20] 4162 4-9-6 **60**.................................... TravisBlock(3) 9 65
(Miss Gay Kelleway) *s.i.s: hdwy 3f out: swtchd rt to outside over 2f out: kpt on u.p: nvr nrr* **8/1**
0346 **4** *3/4* **Moves Goodenough**[23] 4053 5-9-7 **58**........................(b) AlanDaly 12 61
(Andrew Turnell) *t.k.h in mid-div: hdwy over 2f out: chsd wnr tl no ex ins fnl f* **4/1**[2]
20-6 **5** *1 1/2* **Melt (IRE)**[13] 4368 3-8-13 **57**.. TPO'Shea 2 57
(R Hannon) *trckd ldrs: rdn on ins 2f out: wknd fnl f* **12/1**
0321 **6** *3* **Prince Valentine**[23] 4053 7-9-2 **53**........................(p) GeorgeBaker 5 46
(G L Moore) *t.k.h in mid-div: effrt over 1f out: wknd fnl f* **10/3**[1]
0500 **7** *1 1/2* **Darley Star**[40] 3483 3-8-10 **54**..................................... LiamJones 13 43
(C E Brittain) *trckd ldrs tl wknd over 1f out* **16/1**
630B **8** *2 3/4* **Imperium**[8] 4529 7-9-7 **58**.......................................(p) DaneO'Neill 15 41
(Jean-Rene Auvray) *s.i.s: hld up: hdwy over 2f out: wknd over 1f out* **10/1**
5320 **9** *2 1/4* **Batchworth Blaise**[12] 4414 5-8-12 **52**................. RussellKennemore(3) 6 30
(E A Wheeler) *hld up: hdwy over 2f out: wknd over 1f out* **13/2**[3]
0011 **10** *2 3/4* **The Hoofer (IRE)**[7] 4569 3-8-11 **60** 6ex.....(b) Louis-PhilippeBeuzelin(5) 8 32
(I A Wood) *trckd wnr tl wknd over 1f out* **9/1**
5000 **11** *6* **The Slider**[17] 4250 4-8-7 **49** oh1 ow3..................(p) GabrielHannon(5) 7 7
(Mrs L C Jewell) *mid-div tl lost pl 1/2-way* **50/1**
0-05 **12** *2 3/4* **Follow The Band**[16] 4278 3-8-10 **54**............................ RichardSmith 14 5
(R Hannon) *mid-div tl wknd over 3f out* **28/1**

1m 36.12s (0.12) **Going Correction** +0.05s/f (Good)
WFA 3 from 4yo+ 7lb **12** Ran SP% **120.4**
Speed ratings (Par 101): **101,100,100,99,97 94,93,90,88,85 79,76**
toteswinger: 1&2 £29.80, 1&3 £14.50, 2&3 £30.00. CSF £179.25 CT £1526.67 TOTE £11.70: £3.20, £6.60, £3.20; EX 194.30 Trifecta £284.70 Part won. Pool: £384.77. 0.20 winning units..
Owner Mrs Jean M O'Connor **Bred** G And Mrs Middlebrook **Trained** Lockeridge, Wilts

FOCUS
They went steady early in this moderate handicap and the winner was always best placed. The form does not look the most reliable.
Moves Goodenough Official explanation: vet said gelding had been struck into behind

4773 TOTEEXACTA BRIGHTON H'CAP 5f 213y
5:00 (5:00) (Class 5) (0-75,75) 3-Y-0 **£2,964** (£887; £443; £221; £110) **Stalls** Low

Form RPR
5114 **1** **Filligree (IRE)**[47] 3280 3-9-0 **75**........................ WilliamCarson(7) 3 87
(Rae Guest) *in tch: hdwy over 2f out: rdn to ld over 1f out: kpt up to work fnl f* **2/1**[1]
3003 **2** *1/2* **Artistic License (IRE)**[5] 4615 3-9-1 **69**..................... SamHitchcott 7 79
(M R Channon) *wnt lft s: in tch: rdn and hdwy 2f out: chal fnl f and kpt on u.p* **7/1**
0435 **3** *3* **Fly Kiss**[12] 4408 3-9-4 **72**... LiamJones 1 73
(C E Brittain) *in tch on ins: rdn and ev ch over 1f out: fdd ins fnl f* **5/1**[3]
4535 **4** *3 3/4* **Easy Wonder (GER)**[31] 3783 3-7-11 **56**....(p) Louis-PhilippeBeuzelin(5) 5 45
(I A Wood) *wnt rt s: in rr: passed btn horses fnl f* **10/1**
5146 **5** *2 1/4* **Enodoc**[14] 4325 3-8-11 **65**...(t) TPO'Shea 4 47
(W R Muir) *trckd ldrs: rdn and wknd over 1f out* **9/1**
4362 **6** *1/2* **Rockfield Lodge (IRE)**[10] 4489 3-9-2 **73**........(b) RussellKennemore(3) 6 53
(M E Rimmer) *bmpd s: sn trckd ldrs: led over 2f out: hdd & wknd qckly over 1f out* **7/2**[2]
0460 **7** *4 1/2* **Connor's Choice**[22] 4083 3-9-0 **68**................................... AlanDaly 2 34
(Andrew Turnell) *led tl hdd over 2f out: wknd over 1f out* **7/1**

1m 10.03s (-0.17) **Going Correction** +0.05s/f (Good) **7** Ran SP% **116.3**
Speed ratings (Par 100): **103,102,98,93,90 89,83**
toteswinger: 1&2 £3.30, 1&3 £2.90, 2&3 £5.00. CSF £17.29 TOTE £2.80: £1.50, £3.10; EX 14.10 Place 6: £330.80, Place 5: £125.38..
Owner The Filligree Partnership **Bred** T Hirschfeld **Trained** Newmarket, Suffolk

FOCUS
The first two drew clear in this modest affair but there are doubts over the form.
Rockfield Lodge(IRE) Official explanation: jockey said gelding suffered interference at the start and did not come down the hill
T/Plt: £542.40 to a £1 stake. Pool: £55,810.40. 75.10 winning tickets. T/Qpdt: £450.80 to a £1 stake. Pool: £3,229.30. 5.30 winning tickets. JS

4333 FOLKESTONE (R-H)
Thursday, August 7

OFFICIAL GOING: Good to firm
Wind: Medium across Weather: Sunny

4774 TOTESPORTCASINO.COM FILLIES' H'CAP 1m 1f 149y
5:35 (5:37) (Class 6) (0-65,59) 3-Y-0+ **£2,047** (£604; £302) **Stalls** Centre

Form RPR
5232 **1** **Split The Wind (USA)**[5] 4635 4-9-3 **50**.................... HarryPoulton(7) 11 53
(Miss Sheena West) *mde virtually all: rdn 2f out: edgd lft u.p: hld on: all out* **2/1**[1]
0405 **2** *nk* **Meohmy**[17] 4261 3-9-0 **45**.. MCGeran(5) 7 48+
(M R Channon) *hld up in midfield: nt clr run and lost pl over 2f out: rdn and swtchd lft 2f out: r.o strly fnl f: nt quite rch wnr* **11/1**
4060 **3** *nk* **Blur**[48] 3206 3-8-13 **48**.. RobertHavlin 13 50
(R Hannon) *chsd wnr tl 3f out: lost pl u.p 2f out: rallied fnl f: styd on to go 3rd nr fin* **9/1**
-000 **4** *nk* **Lady Petrus**[64] 2719 3-9-4 **53**.. IanMongan 1 54
(H J L Dunlop) *in tch: rdn and unable qckn 3f out: hdwy u.p and swtchd rt ent fnl f: styd on: nt rch ldrs* **12/1**
00-2 **5** *1* **Wicked Lady (UAE)**[28] 3874 5-10-0 **54**............................. DMylonas 6 53
(B J McMath) *hld up in midfield: hdwy on outer over 3f out: chsd ldrs and rdn 2f out: sn hung bdly lft: nt rcvr* **12/1**
0000 **6** *shd* **Rosy Dawn**[29] 3844 3-8-10 **45**...............................(v) FrankieMcDonald 8 44
(J J Bridger) *chsd ldng pair: wnt 2nd 3f out tl 2f out: chsd wnr again u.p jst ins fnl f: one pce and lost 4 pls fnl 100yds* **50/1**
343 **7** *nk* **Shenandoah Girl**[29] 3843 5-9-7 **54**...........................(b) KylieManser(7) 3 53
(Miss Gay Kelleway) *s.i.s: hld up bhd: stdy hdwy on outer 6f out: chsd wnr 2f out: rdn and edgd lft over 1f out: wknd jst ins fnl f* **7/2**[2]
0000 **8** *1 1/2* **Ubiquitous**[14] 4338 3-8-12 **47**.. SaleemGolam 14 43
(S Dow) *t.k.h: hld up in tch: rdn over 2f out: nt clr run over 1f out: swtchd lft ent fnl f: kpt on but nvr pce to rch ldrs* **33/1**
6000 **9** *6* **Lavender And Lace**[17] 4260 3-9-1 **50**..................(tp) NelsonDeSouza 9 34
(T Keddy) *t.k.h: chsd ldrs: rdn over 2f out: wknd wl over 1f out* **40/1**
0000 **10** *3/4* **Jelly Mo**[23] 4054 3-9-5 **54**.. SebSanders 12 36
(J W Hills) *in tch: nt clr run briefly 3f out: rdn over 2f out: wknd over 1f out* **13/2**[3]
-000 **11** *6* **Bluebell Ridge (IRE)**[19] 4183 3-8-13 **48**..........................(b[1]) ChrisCatlin 5 18
(D W P Arbuthnot) *t.k.h: hld up in midfield tl dropped to rr 7f out: struggling over 3f out: no ch after* **25/1**
2000 **12** *3 3/4* **Falcon Flyer**[12] 4414 4-9-5 **45**.................................. MohammedSaeed 4 8
(J R Best) *t.k.h: hld up in rr: struggling over 3f out: no ch after* **20/1**

2m 5.32s (0.42) **Going Correction** -0.325s/f (Firm)
WFA 3 from 4yo+ 9lb **12** Ran SP% **118.6**
Speed ratings (Par 98): **85,84,84,84,83 83,83,81,77,76 71,68**
toteswinger: 1&2 £8.00, 1&3 £6.10, 2&3 £17.00. CSF £24.07 CT £167.74 TOTE £3.00: £1.40, £3.70, £3.00; EX 30.50.
Owner Graham Flight **Bred** Malcolm Kelly **Trained** Falmer, E Sussex

FOCUS
A moderate fillies' handicap in which they went an ordinary pace and spread out across the track in the straight and something of a blanket finish. The form is rated negatively with the winner not having to run to her most recent marks to score.
Wicked Lady(UAE) Official explanation: jockey said mare hung badly left

4775 BRAEMARPENSIONRELEASE.CO.UK H'CAP 1m 7f 92y
6:05 (6:07) (Class 5) (0-70,67) 3-Y-0+ **£2,590** (£770; £385; £192) **Stalls** Low

Form RPR
0161 **1** **Casual Garcia**[7] 4564 3-8-9 **62** 6ex.................................(b) SebSanders 5 80+
(Sir Mark Prescott) *mde all: pushed along and drew clr wl over 2f out: unchal* **5/6**[1]
-356 **2** *9* **Daring Racer (GER)**[16] 4275 5-9-5 **58**............................... IanMongan 8 64
(Mrs L J Mongan) *chsd ldng pair tl wnt 2nd 6f out: rdn over 3f out: sn outpcd by wnr: hung bdly lft fr over 1f out* **7/1**[3]
153 **3** *5* **Lapina (IRE)**[34] 3697 4-9-9 **62**.................................(p) StephenCarson 2 62
(Pat Eddery) *hld up in rr: sme hdwy on outer 4f: sn outpcd and no ch w ldrs: wnt modest 3rd ent fnl f* **7/1**[3]
1650 **4** *2* **Synonymy**[50] 3137 5-9-3 **56**..(b) ChrisCatlin 1 53
(M Blanshard) *in tch: chsd ldng trio and rdn over 4f out: sn lost tch* **16/1**
1411 **5** *1 3/4* **Trigger's Friend**[21] 4105 4-9-0 **56**................................ TolleyDean(3) 4 51
(Jamie Poulton) *chsd wnr: reminders after 3f: rdn 8f out: lost 2nd 6f out: wknd u.p over 3f* **7/2**[2]
405 **6** *11* **Lysander's Quest (IRE)**[12] 4410 10-8-12 **51** oh6........... RobertHavlin 3 31
(R Ingram) *racd in midfield: rdn and over 6f out: wknd 4f out: t.o* **33/1**
6126 **7** *4* **Prince Of Medina**[12] 4410 5-8-12 **51** oh2.............. MohammedSaeed 6 26
(J R Best) *stdd s: hld up in rr: lost tch over 4f out: t.o* **14/1**

 The Form Book, Raceform Ltd, Compton, RG20 6NL

4-40 **8** *13* **Bulberry Hill**[165] 695 7-8-12 51 oh6..........................(t) NelsonDeSouza 9 9
(R W Price) *t.k.h: hld up in midfield: lost pl 4f out: t.o fnl 3f* **33/1**
3m 24.16s (-5.54) **Going Correction** -0.325s/f (Firm)
WFA 3 from 4yo+ 14lb **8** Ran SP% **120.2**
Speed ratings (Par 103): **101,96,93,92,91 85,83,76**
toteswinger: 1&2 £4.50, 1&3 £1.90, 2&3 £2.10. CSF £8.23 CT £26.87 TOTE £1.80: £1.10, £2.00, £2.10; EX 8.60.
Owner Ne'Er Do Wells Ii **Bred** Miss K Rausing **Trained** Newmarket, Suffolk

FOCUS
A moderate staying handicap but run at a good pace and the winner ran his rivals ragged. The runner-up is the best guide to the level withy the third to her latest mark.
Trigger's Friend Official explanation: jockey said filly found the ground too fast

4776 OVER 100 GAMES AT TOTESPORTCASINO.COM MEDIAN AUCTION MAIDEN STKS 7f (S)
6:40 (6:42) (Class 6) 2-Y-O **£2,266** (£674; £337; £168) **Stalls** Low

Form RPR
02 **1** **Oil Man (IRE)**[19] 4184 2-9-3 0.. JimCrowley 10 87+
(P Winkworth) *prom: rdn to ld over 1f out: edgd lft but sn rdn clr: eased towards fin* **10/11**[1]
66 **2** *7* **Bright Enough**[14] 4339 2-8-12 0.. ChrisCatlin 8 62
(E J O'Neill) *t.k.h: pressed ldr: chsd wnr and rdn over 1f out: no ch w wnr fnl f: kpt on to hold 2nd pl* **13/2**[3]
3 *1 1/4* **Spinning Waters** 2-9-3 0.. StephenCarson 1 63
(Eve Johnson Houghton) *sn bhd and bustled along: rdn 4f out: styd on fnl f: snatched 3rd fnl strides: nvr nr ldrs* **33/1**
4 *shd* **Doncosaque (IRE)** 2-9-3 0.. IanMongan 9 63+
(H R A Cecil) *sn bhd: shkn up and hdwy 3f out: rn green and hung lft over 1f out: kpt on to go 4th on line: n.d* **5/1**[2]
5 **5** *nse* **Itsher**[10] 4488 2-8-12 0.. NelsonDeSouza 7 58
(S C Williams) *chsd ldrs: hdwy over 2f out: chsd ldng pair and hung lft over 1f out: no ch w wnr fnl f: lost 2 pls nr fin* **40/1**
6036 **6** *3 1/2* **Herring Senior (IRE)**[19] 4185 2-9-3 68.. ShaneKelly 2 54
(P F I Cole) *led tl over 1f out: sn btn: wknd fnl f* **8/1**
7 *1/2* **Primo Dilettante** 2-9-3 0.. AmirQuinn 4 53
(W J Knight) *chsd ldrs: rdn 1/2-way: wknd wl over 1f out* **25/1**
50 **8** *4* **Good Buy Dubai (USA)**[10] 4480 2-9-3 0.. SebSanders 11 43
(J R Best) *swtchd lft and dropped in after s: a bhd* **10/1**
5 **9** *14* **Premier Superstar**[28] 3869 2-8-12 0.. SaleemGolam 6 3
(M H Tompkins) *racd in midfield: rdn and struggling 1/2-way: no ch fnl 2f: t.o* **12/1**
1m 26.21s (-1.09) **Going Correction** -0.175s/f (Firm) **9** Ran SP% **119.5**
Speed ratings (Par 92): **99,91,89,89,89 85,84,80,64**
toteswinger: 1&2 £7.70, 1&3 £19.80, 2&3 not won. CSF £7.62 TOTE £1.80: £1.10, £2.80, £8.30; EX 9.60.
Owner David Holden **Bred** Diana Webley **Trained** Chiddingfold, Surrey

FOCUS
An ordinary median auction maiden run 0.35secs slower than the following three-year-old handicap and the field came up the stands' rail. The winner scored easily and the time is probably the best guide to the level.

NOTEBOOK
Oil Man(IRE), despite having an outside draw, was soon well placed and, although coming off the bridle at the quarter-mile pole, came right away and eventually won eased down. He is clearly progressive but this will not help his handicap mark. (op 6-4)
Bright Enough raced up with the winner, but did not settle that well and could only plug on at one pace once the winner set sail for home. She is eligible for a handicap mark now and it should be low enough to help her be competitive in nurseries. (op 8-1 tchd 10-1)
Spinning Waters, related to several winners and out of a staying half-sister to Tenby, did just best of the newcomers, staying on up the rail to snatch third under a considerate ride. He is likely to make his mark in handicaps next season. (tchd 25-1)
Doncosaque(IRE), the first foal of a 7f winner from a middle-distance family, was green on this debut and will know more next time. Official explanation: jockey said colt hung left (op 9-2 tchd 11-2)
Itsher, who missed the break on her debut, ran better this time and chased the leading group throughout. She appeared to get tired in the last furlong and was run out of the places by the two newcomers. (op 33-1)
Herring Senior(IRE) had previous experience and the benefit of the stands' rail, but after making the running dropped away in the final furlong. He may not have stayed the longer trip. (op 7-1)

4777 PLAY ROULETTE AT TOTESPORTCASINO.COM H'CAP 7f (S)
7:10 (7:12) (Class 5) (0-70,69) 3-Y-O **£2,590** (£770; £385; £192) **Stalls** Low

Form RPR
-060 **1** **Kinnego Bay (IRE)**[16] 4269 3-9-3 65.. ChrisCatlin 2 73
(B W Hills) *racd against stands' rail: trckd ldrs: rdn to ld over 1f out: styd on wl fnl f* **8/1**
5032 **2** *1 3/4* **Valento**[5] 4637 3-9-3 65.. StephenCarson 5 68
(Eve Johnson Houghton) *bhd: reminder after 2f: rdn and hdwy 1/2-way: drvn to chse wnr ent fnl f: no imp after* **9/4**[2]
4526 **3** *4* **Reve Vert (FR)**[19] 4180 3-7-13 50 oh1.. LukeMorris(3) 4 42
(A W Carroll) *t.k.h: in tch: lost pl and rdn jst over 2f out: plugged on u.p to go 3rd wl ins fnl f: no ch w ldng pair* **7/1**[3]
-400 **4** *1 1/2* **Hucking Harkness**[5] 4637 3-8-11 59.. JimCrowley 8 47
(J R Best) *stdd after s: hld up in rr: hdwy over 3f out: chsd ldrs and rdn wl over 1f out: wknd fnl f* **16/1**
0005 **5** *nk* **Too Grand**[5] 4637 3-8-2 50.. FrankieMcDonald 1 37
(J J Bridger) *towards rr: rdn over 3f out: grad edgd out rt over and hdwy 1f out: keeping on whn nt clr run and swtchd rt ins fnl f: nvr trbld ldrs* **20/1**
6002 **6** *nk* **Dhahab (USA)**[14] 4333 3-8-4 52.. PaulDoe 6 39
(C E Brittain) *chsd ldr tl led 4f out: rdn ent fnl 2f: hdd over 1f out: wknd u.p fnl f* **20/1**
2332 **7** *3 1/2* **El Fuser**[12] 4413 3-9-5 67.. SebSanders 3 44
(P J Makin) *hld up in midfield: hdwy 3f out: pressed ldrs and rdn 2f out: wknd qckly jst over 1f out* **2/1**[1]
0050 **8** *1/2* **Ike Quebec (FR)**[22] 4083 3-9-7 69..........................(v[1]) PatCosgrave 9 45
(J R Boyle) *chsd ldrs: wnt 2nd over 3f out tl 2f out: sn wknd* **20/1**
-550 **9** *14* **Charmel's Lad**[39] 3525 3-8-13 61.. SaleemGolam 10 —
(W R Swinburn) *racd alone in centre: in tch: hung lft 4f out: rdn and wknd over 2f out: t.o* **16/1**
-666 **10** *2 3/4* **Cotton Reel**[14] 4349 3-9-4 66.. NelsonDeSouza 7 —
(P F I Cole) *racd freely: led tl over 4f out: wknd qckly: t.o fnl 2f* **14/1**
1m 25.86s (-1.44) **Going Correction** -0.175s/f (Firm) **10** Ran SP% **120.4**
Speed ratings (Par 100): **101,99,94,92,92 92,88,87,71,68**
toteswinger: 1&2 £11.00, 1&3 £9.40, 2&3 £8.50. CSF £26.46 CT £131.92 TOTE £11.00: £2.80, £1.40, £2.60; EX 44.80.
Owner John C Grant & R J Arculli **Bred** Mrs Josephine Hughes **Trained** Lambourn, Berks

FOCUS
A modest handicap run only fractionally faster than the preceding juvenile contest. The runner-up is rated to previous course form.

4778 PLAY BLACKJACK AT TOTESPORTCASINO.COM MAIDEN STKS 6f
7:45 (7:46) (Class 5) 2-Y-O **£2,590** (£770; £385; £192) **Stalls** Low

Form RPR
3 **1** **Galpin Junior (USA)**[16] 4274 2-9-3 0.. SebSanders 2 84+
(B J Meehan) *racd on stands' rail: w ldrs tl led 3f out: pushed along over 1f out: r.o wl and in command fnl f* **8/15**[1]
6 **2** *2* **Secret Society**[71] 2507 2-9-3 0.. IanMongan 3 78+
(M L W Bell) *hld up in tch: swtchd rt and effrt to chse wnr ent fnl f: r.o but nvr pce to chal wnr* **13/2**[2]
3 *6* **Dannios** 2-9-3 0.. PatCosgrave 1 57
(L M Cumani) *s.i.s: bhd: pushed along over 3f out: sme hdwy whn rn green and lost action over 1f out: kpt on fnl f: wnt 3rd nr fin: nvr nr ldrs* **12/1**
40 **4** *nk* **Rocoppelia (USA)**[9] 4510 2-9-3 0.. JimCrowley 7 56
(Mrs A J Perrett) *towards rr: rdn over 2f out: no prog tl plugged on u.p fnl f: wnt 4th nr fin: nvr trbld ldrs* **7/1**[3]
0 **5** *3/4* **Itainteasybeingme**[10] 4480 2-8-10 0.. HarryPoulton(7) 4 54
(J R Boyle) *pressed ldr: chsd wnr wl over 2f out tl ent fnl f: sn wl btn: lost 2 pls nr fin* **50/1**
04 **6** *hd* **Reel Ale**[15] 4305 2-9-3 0.. StephenCarson 9 53
(P Winkworth) *t.k.h: led tl 3f out: chsd ldrs after tl wknd u.p over 1f out* **20/1**
7 *1 1/2* **Rebel City** 2-9-3 0.. ShaneKelly 6 49
(M J McGrath) *s.i.s: t.k.h: hld up towards rr: hdwy 1/2-way: rdn wl over 1f out: sn wknd* **25/1**
0 **8** *5* **Orangeleg**[40] 3485 2-9-3 0.. SaleemGolam 8 34
(S C Williams) *in tch: rdn 1/2-way: sn struggling: no ch fr wl over 1f out* **66/1**
9 *6* **Nala (USA)** 2-8-12 0.. MohammedSaeed 10 11
(J R Best) *wnt rt s: a bhd: hung lft over 2f out: t.o* **28/1**
3 **10** *2 3/4* **Five Star Junior (USA)**[14] 4321 2-9-3 0.. ChrisCatlin 5 8
(S A Callaghan) *a bhd: lost tch 1/2-way: t.o* **12/1**
1m 11.98s (-0.72) **Going Correction** -0.175s/f (Firm) **10** Ran SP% **122.0**
Speed ratings (Par 94): **97,94,86,85,84 84,82,76,68,64**
toteswinger: 1&2 £2.10, 1&3 £2.60, 2&3 £5.80. CSF £4.48 TOTE £1.40: £1.10, £2.10, £3.50; EX 6.10.
Owner Roldvale Limited **Bred** Meadow Oaks Farm Llc **Trained** Manton, Wilts

FOCUS
An ordinary maiden run 0.41secs slower than the closing all-aged handicap. The fourth and sixth help set the level.

NOTEBOOK
Galpin Junior(USA) who had shaped well when badly in need of the experience at Salisbury on his debut, and he justified strong support in style. He got the rail and was right up with the pace throughout then started to assert at halfway, and with entries in the Middle Park and the Dewhurst he is likely to be stepped up in grade before long. (op 8-11)
Secret Society, who had miseed the break and disappointed when starting at odds-on for his debut, ran much better here, chasing the winner home and drawing clear of the rest. He should be able to win a similar race. (op 5-1)
Dannios did best of the newcomers. He was not well enough away to take advantage of his rail draw, and was very green in the early stages, but he got the message in the end and stayed on from an unpromising position to snatch a moderate third. (op 16-1 tchd 10-1)
Rocoppelia(USA), having his third run, has shown a measure of ability and may be able to fare better in handicaps. (op 13-2 tchd 8-1)
Itainteasybeingme, who finished a tailed-off last on his debut, ran much better but was ultimately well held. (op 66-1 tchd 40-1)
Reel Ale Official explanation: jockey said colt ran too free
Nala(USA), who has a speedy dirt pedigree, wandered about and was always behind on her debut. (op 22-1)
Five Star Junior(USA), carrying the second colours of the winner's owner but another relatively expensive breeze-ups buy at $140,000, was coltish in the preliminaries and was always out the back. His debut run suggested he has ability but he now has questions to answer. (op 11-1 tchd 9-1)

4779 PLAY VIDEO POKER AT TOTESPORTCASINO.COM FILLIES' H'CAP 6f
8:15 (8:15) (Class 5) (0-70,67) 3-Y-O+ **£2,590** (£770; £385; £192) **Stalls** Low

Form RPR
1240 **1** **Overwing (IRE)**[28] 3883 5-9-11 67.. ShaneKelly 7 77
(R M H Cowell) *mde all: sn crossed over to stands' rail: rdn and hung rt fnl f: styd on wl* **3/1**[2]
-640 **2** *1 3/4* **Miss Poppy**[16] 4273 3-8-13 59.. NelsonDeSouza 1 62
(P R Chamings) *chsd ldrs: rdn over 2f out: hung rt fnl f: chsd wnr fnl 100yds: no imp* **8/1**
00 **3** *1 1/2* **Gower Belle**[33] 3727 3-9-0 60.. SebSanders 2 59
(W R Muir) *chsd wnr: rdn 2f out: kpt on same pce u.p: lost 2nd fnl 100yds* **7/1**
003 **4** *1 3/4* **Mugeba**[1] 4746 7-8-8 50..........................(t) ChrisCatlin 4 44
(Miss Gay Kelleway) *hld up bhd: rdn and effrt on outer jst over 2f out: no imp fnl f* **7/2**[3]
1501 **5** *3 1/4* **Tilsworth Charlie**[13] 4383 5-9-9 65..........................(b) JimCrowley 3 47
(J R Jenkins) *wnt lft s: hld up in rr: rdn and effrt jst over 2f out: sn no imp: wl btn fnl f* **5/2**[1]
0506 **6** *2 3/4* **Lady Fas (IRE)**[8] 4535 5-8-3 48 oh3.. LukeMorris(3) 6 21
(A W Carroll) *in tch in midfield: rdn over 2f out: drvn and btn wl over 1f out* **15/2**
0000 **7** *2 3/4* **Ishibee (IRE)**[16] 4273 4-8-6 48 oh3..........................(p) FrankieMcDonald 5 12
(J J Bridger) *towards rr: rdn and hdwy 3f out: drvn and wknd ent fnl f: wl btn whn eased towards fin* **20/1**
1m 11.57s (-1.13) **Going Correction** -0.175s/f (Firm)
WFA 3 from 4yo+ 4lb **7** Ran SP% **115.9**
Speed ratings (Par 100): **100,97,95,93,88 84,81**
toteswinger: 1&2 £4.00, 1&3 £3.30, 2&3 £5.10. CSF £27.47 TOTE £4.40: £2.40, £2.40; EX 29.70 Place 6: £22.72, Place 5: £11.63..
Owner Keith Robinson & Ian Robinson **Bred** Noel Finegan And Noel Cogan **Trained** Six Mile Bottom, Cambs

FOCUS
A modest fillies' handicap run just 0.41secs faster than the preceding juvenile contest. The form looks relatively weak with the winner the best guide and the placed horses out of form prior to this.
T/Plt: £63.20 to a £1 stake. Pool: £38,223.50. 441.21 winning tickets. T/Qpdt: £23.30 to a £1 stake. Pool: £3,178.70. 100.70 winning tickets. SP

4592 HAYDOCK (L-H)

Thursday, August 7

OFFICIAL GOING: Soft (6.9)

8mm overnight rain resulted in 'very soft ground, even more testing in places'. Rail realignment added 25yards to advertised distances on round course.

Wind: Light, half against Weather: fine

4780 PAUL SCULTHORPE TESTIMONIAL MAIDEN AUCTION STKS — 1m 30y

2:10 (2:13) (Class 5) 2-Y-O — £3,238 (£963; £481; £240) Stalls Low

Form — RPR

3 **1** **Splinter Cell (USA)**[15] 4296 2-8-11 0 ....(t) JamieSpencer 9 — 82+
(M Botti) *trckd ldrs: led over 2f out: rdn and styd on strly fnl f* — **3/1**[1]

2 3 ½ **Union Island (IRE)** 2-9-2 0 .... NCallan 14 — 80+
(K A Ryan) *trckd ldrs: effrt over 3f out: chal over 1f out: kpt on same pce* — **9/2**[2]

3 2 **Ubi Ace** 2-8-8 0 .... DuranFentiman(3) 11 — 70
(T D Walford) *s.i.s: hdwy on ins over 3f out: styd on same pce fnl 2f* **100/1**

34 **4** 1 **Russian George (IRE)**[13] 4394 2-8-11 0 .... MickyFenton 3 — 68
(T P Tate) *led tl over 2f out: edgd rt over 1f out: one pce* — **3/1**[1]

5 **5** ½ **Viking Awake (IRE)**[15] 4296 2-8-11 0 .... RichardKingscote 1 — 67
(J W Unett) *trckd ldrs: kpt on same pce fnl 2f* — **6/1**[3]

0 **6** ½ **Huxaar**[53] 3055 2-8-9 0 .... TomEaves 8 — 64
(Mrs L Stubbs) *in tch: rdn 4f out: one pce fnl 2f* — **33/1**

7 ½ **What A Day** 2-8-9 0 .... TonyHamilton 2 — 63
(J J Quinn) *in tch: one pce fnl 2f* — **16/1**

05 **8** 3 ¾ **Victorian Tycoon (IRE)**[44] 3334 2-8-9 0 .... FrancisNorton 10 — 56+
(E J O'Neill) *chsd ldrs: rdn over 3f out: wknd over 1f out* — **28/1**

9 hd **Flashgun (USA)** 2-8-13 0 .... AlanMunro 5 — 58+
(M G Quinlan) *mid-div: t.k.h: effrt over 3f out: wknd over 1f out* — **10/1**

10 4 ½ **Shady Lady (IRE)** 2-8-6 0 .... GregFairley 12 — 41+
(M Johnston) *s.i.s: sn drvn along: bhd fnl 3f* — **16/1**

11 7 **Tombov (FR)** 2-8-9 0 .... EddieAhern 6 — 29
(A King) *unruly in paddock: s.s: in rr: bhd fnl 3f* — **10/1**

12 5 **Herawati** 2-8-9 0 .... DavidAllan 4 — 18
(T D Easterby) *in rr: reminders over 4f out: sn bhd* — **40/1**

0 **13** 19 **High Society Girl (IRE)**[14] 4328 2-8-6 0 .... PaulHanagan 7 — —
(T D Easterby) *in tch: lost pl over 3f out: bhd whn eased fnl f* — **40/1**

1m 49.48s (5.68) **Going Correction** +0.575s/f (Yiel) — **13** Ran SP% **124.7**

Speed ratings (Par 94): **94,90,88,87,87 86,86,82,82,77 70,65,46**

toteswinger: 1&2 £6.30, 1&3 £39.70, 2&3 £100.90. CSF £16.49 TOTE £3.50: £1.60, £2.00, £24.10; EX 23.10.

Owner E Bulgheroni **Bred** Old Carhue Stud **Trained** Newmarket, Suffolk

FOCUS

An ordinary maiden, but they went a good pace and this proved quite a test for these juveniles. They raced up the middle of the track and the first two look decent prospects.

NOTEBOOK

Splinter Cell(USA) ◆, fitted with a tongue-tie this time, confirmed the promise he showed when third on his debut over 7f at Leicester, proving well suited by the step up in trip and handling the soft ground well. He travelled strongly, but had to battle to see off Union Island and gradually drew clear once his stamina kicked in. He looks a decent staying juvenile. (tchd 10-3 and 7-2 in places)

Union Island(IRE) ◆, a 70,000euros son of Rock Of Gibraltar, half-brother to 1m winners Golden Island, Gandor and Oakley Heffert, as well as dual 1m2f winner Golden Grimshaw, has been entered in the Champagne Stakes, the Royal Lodge and the Dewhurst. He threw down a big challenge to Splinter Cell inside the final quarter mile, but was eventually just outstayed. This was a pleasing debut and his big-race entries suggest he is expected to develop into a very useful type. (op 7-1 tchd 15-2 in places)

Ubi Ace, a 14,000gns gelded son of First Trump, half-brother to five winners, including multiple 5f-1m winner Flying Hen, belied his massive odds with a pleasing debut. He looks a thorough stayer.

Russian George(IRE) kept on for pressure once headed and will have more options now he is qualified for a handicap mark. (op 7-2 tchd 4-1)

Viking Awake(IRE) again showed ability, but he is probably more of a handicap type. (op 9-1 tchd 10-1)

Victorian Tycoon(IRE) ◆ showed up for a long way but was found out by a lack of stamina. He will be one to watch in handicaps if dropping in trip. (tchd 25-1)

4781 E B F JAMES EDWARDS LANDROVER NOVICE FILLIES' STKS — 6f

2:40 (2:41) (Class 4) 2-Y-O — £6,476 (£1,927; £963; £481) Stalls Centre

Form — RPR

2225 **1** **Carانbola**[19] 4190 2-9-0 91 .... AlanMunro 1 — 89
(M Brittain) *w ldrs: led 1f out: hld on gamely towards fin* — **9/4**[2]

31 **2** hd **Sneak Preview**[26] 3959 2-9-3 0 .... RichardMullen 2 — 91
(E S McMahon) *trckd ldrs: effrt 2f out: styd on to chal ins fnl f: no ex nr fin* — **15/8**[1]

1 **3** 1 **First City**[31] 3792 2-9-0 0 .... StephenDonohoe 5 — 85
(D M Simcock) *trckd ldrs: effrt 3f out: styd on same pce ins fnl f* — **9/1**

152 **4** 2 ½ **Madame Trop Vite (IRE)**[27] 3908 2-9-3 85 .... NCallan 3 — 81
(K A Ryan) *w ldr: t.k.h: led over 1f out: sn hdd: edgd rt and wknd ins fnl f* — **11/2**

1 **5** 3 ½ **Rafiqa (IRE)**[28] 3882 2-9-0 0 .... EddieAhern 4 — 73+
(C F Wall) *led tl hdd over 1f out: wkng whn hmpd and eased ins fnl f* **4/1**[3]

1m 16.16s (2.16) **Going Correction** +0.40s/f (Good) — **5** Ran SP% **110.9**

Speed ratings (Par 93): **101,100,99,96,91**

CSF £6.95 TOTE £3.00: £1.50, £1.30; EX 5.00.

Owner Mel Brittain **Bred** T E Pocock **Trained** Warthill, N Yorks

■ Stewards' Enquiry : N Callan two-day ban: careless riding (Aug 23-24)

FOCUS

A good little contest. The winning time was 0.22 seconds quicker than the following three-year-old 51-70 handicap. They raced stands' side.

NOTEBOOK

Caranbola looked a little unlucky not to finish closer in the Super Sprint on her previous start, but she made no mistake this time, gamely seeing off Sneak Preview's strong challenge. She has already been placed in Listed company and can gain some more black type if returned to that level. She may be aimed at the Roses Stakes at York's Ebor meeting and the Redcar Two-Year-Old Trophy. (tchd 5-2)

Sneak Preview won really well at Nottingham on her previous start, and Lowther and Cheveley Park entries suggest she is well regarded, but she just found the concession of 3lb to Caranbola too much. This was a very useful effort in defeat. (op 2-1 tchd 9-4)

First City, a winner on her debut over this trip on heavy ground at Ripon, was badly outpaced when the race got serious and was last a furlong out, but she finished strongly for third. She looks ready for a step up in trip. (op 8-1 tchd 7-1)

Madame Trop Vite(IRE) ran like a non stayer on this step back up in trip. (op 6-1)

Rafiqa(IRE) did not build on the form she showed when winning on her debut at 25/1 at Nottingham. (op 9-2)

4782 DAVID SPENCER LTD H'CAP — 6f

3:10 (3:10) (Class 5) (0-70,70) 3-Y-O — £3,238 (£963; £481; £240) Stalls Centre

Form — RPR

6533 **1** **Whiteoak Lady (IRE)**[28] 3893 3-9-0 68 .... JackDean(5) 1 — 76
(J L Spearing) *w ldr: styd on to ld towards fin* — **11/1**

4350 **2** hd **Tadalavil**[17] 4252 3-9-6 69 .... TonyCulhane 7 — 76
(M R Channon) *led: hrd rdn over 1f out: hdd towards fin* — **7/1**[3]

2333 **3** 2 ½ **Strawberry Moon (IRE)**[13] 4383 3-9-4 67 .... TomEaves 2 — 66
(B Smart) *s.i.s: hdwy on wd outside over 2f out: kpt on same pce* — **5/1**[2]

0213 **4** 1 **Bonne**[6] 4609 3-9-1 64 .... JamieSpencer 6 — 60
(M L W Bell) *s.i.s: hdwy stands' stand over 2f out: chsng ldrs over 1f out: hrd rdn and little rspnse* — **5/2**[1]

0022 **5** 2 ¾ **Diego Rivera**[13] 4388 3-9-7 70 .... NCallan 4 — 57
(P J Makin) *chsd ldrs: outpcd over 2f out: kpt on same pce* — **8/1**

1530 **6** 1 **Big Slick (IRE)**[32] 3753 3-8-10 59 .... TWilliams 8 — 43
(M Brittain) *chsd ldrs stands' side: lost pl 2f out: styd on wl ins fnl f* — **28/1**

0505 **7** nk **Hunt The Bottle (IRE)**[35] 3626 3-9-3 66 .... PaulHanagan 3 — 49
(B W Hills) *towards rr: kpt on fnl 2f: nvr a threat* — **5/1**[2]

2106 **8** nk **Foreign Rhythm (IRE)**[13] 4397 3-8-6 55 .... (v) KimTinkler 9 — 37
(N Tinkler) *chsd ldrs stands' side: edgd lft and lost pl over 1f out* — **20/1**

6621 **9** 2 ¼ **To Bubbles**[30] 3818 3-8-11 63 .... NeilBrown(3) 10 — 38
(T D Barron) *w ldrs stands' side: hung lft: lost pl over 1f out* — **11/1**

6000 **10** 3 ¾ **Straight (IRE)**[26] 3960 3-8-6 55 .... AlanMunro 5 — 18
(M Brittain) *chsd ldrs: lost pl over 2f out* — **28/1**

1m 16.38s (2.38) **Going Correction** +0.40s/f (Good) — **10** Ran SP% **113.8**

Speed ratings (Par 100): **100,99,96,95,91 90,89,89,86,81**

toteswinger: 1&2 £6.30, 1&3 £39.70, 2&3 £100.90. CSF £81.47 CT £444.70 TOTE £13.90: £3.70, £2.20, £1.70; EX 111.30.

Owner Leonard Kinsella **Bred** Thomas J Reid **Trained** Kinnersley, Worcs

■ Stewards' Enquiry : Neil Brown one-day ban: failing to ride to draw (Aug 23)

FOCUS

A modest but competitive sprint handicap in which the first two dominated throughout. The winning time was 0.22 seconds slower than the previous novice event for juvenile fillies and the form does not look reliable. They raced middle to stands' side.

Straight(IRE) Official explanation: trainer said the colt was found to be lame on returning home

4783 NETFLIGHTS.COM H'CAP — 1m 30y

3:40 (3:42) (Class 3) (0-95,91) 3-Y-O — £9,714 (£2,890; £1,444; £721) Stalls Low

Form — RPR

1323 **1** **Mangham (IRE)**[27] 3911 3-8-10 80 .... PaulMulrennan 7 — 88
(D H Brown) *mde all: styd on gamely* — **6/1**[3]

-200 **2** 1 **Unbreak My Heart (IRE)**[27] 3919 3-9-7 91 .... SteveDrowne 10 — 97+
(R Charlton) *mid-div: hdwy over 3f out: upsides and wandered fr over 1f out: no ex nr fin* — **14/1**

442 **3** nk **Reel Buddy Star**[28] 3887 3-8-3 73 .... FrancisNorton 9 — 78
(G M Moore) *w wnr: t.k.h: styd on same pce ins fnl f* — **12/1**

4114 **4** hd **Stevie Thunder**[27] 3919 3-9-5 89 .... NCallan 4 — 94
(G A Swinbank) *trckd ldrs: t.k.h: effrt over 2f out: styd on same pce ins fnl f* — **5/2**[1]

2140 **5** 1 ¼ **Albaqaa**[27] 3919 3-9-0 84 .... PaulHanagan 1 — 86
(R A Fahey) *trckd ldrs: effrt over 2f out: styd on same pce* — **8/1**

2211 **6** 4 **Topazes**[26] 3969 3-9-5 89 .... JamieSpencer 2 — 81+
(M L W Bell) *swtchd rt s: hdwy and edgd lft over 2f out: wknd over 2f out* — **6/1**[3]

4410 **7** 1 **Mukhber**[27] 3919 3-9-3 87 .... MartinDwyer 11 — 77
(J H M Gosden) *trckd ldrs: rdn over 2f out: lost pl over 2f out* — **5/1**[2]

0461 **8** 3 **Boy Blue**[24] 4017 3-9-0 84 .... TonyHamilton 3 — 67
(D W Barker) *in rr-div: effrt over 3f out: nvr on terms* — **16/1**

05 **9** 4 ½ **Irish Mayhem (USA)**[45] 3325 3-9-0 84 .... (b) AlanMunro 5 — 57
(B J Meehan) *sn bhd: detached 4f out* — **14/1**

-210 **10** 2 **Timetable**[27] 3919 3-8-12 82 .... (v[1]) EddieAhern 6 — 50
(H R A Cecil) *trckd ldrs: t.k.h: hrd rdn over 3f out: carried hd high and hung rt: nt keen: lost pl 2f out* — **11/1**

1m 47.83s (4.03) **Going Correction** +0.575s/f (Yiel) — **10** Ran SP% **120.2**

Speed ratings (Par 104): **102,101,100,100,99 95,94,91,86,84**

toteswinger: 1&2 £15.90, 1&3 £13.00, 2&3 £19.10. CSF £88.86 CT £709.56 TOTE £8.10: £2.40, £3.40, £4.20; EX 101.40.

Owner Ron Hull **Bred** Dr Dean Harron **Trained** Tickhill, S Yorks

■ Stewards' Enquiry : Steve Drowne caution: used whip with excessive frequency

FOCUS

A decent handicap that looks pretty solid rated around the third and fourth. They raced up the middle of the track in the straight.

NOTEBOOK

Mangham(IRE) benefited from a positive ride on this drop in trip and stayed on strongly. He beat quite a useful field and is versatile with regards to trip and ground. (op 10-1)

Unbreak My Heart(IRE) is well suited by soft ground and he ran a big race under top weight, improving on his recent efforts. (tchd 11-1)

Reel Buddy Star, getting plenty of weight all round, was always well placed and kept on to the line.

Stevie Thunder had conditions to suit, but he is plenty high enough in the weights now and found a few too good. (op 4-1 tchd 9-2 in places)

Albaqaa could not muster the pace of some of his rivals in the straight and gave the impression he will benefit from a step back up in trip. (op 7-1)

Topazes was bidding for his sixth win of the year off a mark 7lb higher than when successful at Salisbury on his previous start, and 31lb higher than when first successful. He was below form this time and his recent bust spell must have caught up with him. Official explanation: trainer had no explanation for the poor form shown (op 7-2)

Mukhber won his maiden on soft ground, so conditions should not have posed him any problems, but he was well beaten. (op 13-2 tchd 7-1)

Irish Mayhem(USA) Official explanation: jockey said colt lost its action

4784 PAUL SCULTHORPE TESTIMONIAL RACEDAY H'CAP — 1m 6f

4:10 (4:11) (Class 3) (0-95,94) 3-Y-O — £9,714 (£2,890; £1,444; £721) Stalls Low

Form — RPR

2103 **1** **Daraahem (IRE)**[33] 3719 3-9-6 93 .... MartinDwyer 8 — 99
(B W Hills) *trckd ldrs: drvn over 3f out: edgd rt and led jst ins fnl f: readily* — **11/1**

21 **2** 2 ¼ **Meshtri (IRE)**[103] 1615 3-9-1 88 .... PhilipRobinson 7 — 91
(M A Jarvis) *stdd s: hdwy to chse ldrs over 6f out: edgd rt and styd on same pce fnl f* — **9/1**

14 **3** shd **Allied Powers (IRE)**[33] 3719 3-9-4 91 .... JamieSpencer 2 — 94
(M L W Bell) *hld up in rr: stdy hdwy over 3f out: led and edgd rt over 1f out: hdd and no ex jst ins fnl f* — **11/2**[3]

421 **4** *shd* **Manyriverstocross (IRE)**[45] 3310 3-8-13 **86**................ EddieAhern 10 89+
(A King) *t.k.h: trckd ldr: n.m.r and swtchd lft over 2f out: swtchd lft ins fnl f: styd on* **9/1**

014 **5** *1/2* **Sevenna (FR)**[14] 4351 3-8-10 **83**.................................... RichardMullen 4 85
(H R A Cecil) *hld up: effrt over 3f out: sn outpcd: styd on fnl 2f* **11/1**

-321 **6** *1* **Woodcutter (IRE)**[13] 4372 3-9-0 **87**................................ JimmyFortune 6 88+
(J H M Gosden) *hld up: hdwy to trck ldrs 7f out: led on outer over 2f out: hdd and hmpd over 1f out: sn wknd* **2/1**[1]

-161 **7** *2 1/4* **Inventor (IRE)**[33] 3719 3-9-7 **94**.. AlanMunro 1 91
(B J Meehan) *in rr: drvn 6f out: hdwy and upsides on inner over 2f out: wknd fnl f* **7/2**[2]

315 **8** *1/2* **Boucheron**[12] 4435 3-8-13 **86**.. PaulHanagan 5 83
(R A Fahey) *led tl over 2f out: wknd 1f out* **14/1**

2124 **9** *14* **Criterion**[40] 3471 3-8-8 **81**.. StephenDonohoe 9 58
(Ian Williams) *prom: drvn over 4f out: sn lost pl and bhd* **33/1**

4-32 **10** *25* **Merchant Of Dubai**[34] 3673 3-8-2 **75**................................ PaulFessey 3 17
(G A Swinbank) *prom: lost pl 6f out: sn bhd: t.o* **20/1**

3m 10.79s (6.49) **Going Correction** +0.575s/f (Yiel) **10** Ran SP% **122.0**
Speed ratings (Par 104): **104,102,102,102,102 101,100,100,92,77**
toteswinger: 1&2 £17.60, 1&3 £15.20, 2&3 £12.30. CSF £110.66 CT £615.81 TOTE £15.20: £3.60, £2.50, £2.00; EX 108.10.

Owner Hamdan Al Maktoum **Bred** Shadwell Estate Company Limited **Trained** Lambourn, Berks

FOCUS
A very good three-year-old staying handicap and although the form looks a bit muddling but appears sound enough rated around the winner and third. They raced stands' side.

NOTEBOOK
Daraahem(IRE), who is entered in the St Leger, improved for the step up to 1m6f and ran out a clear-cut winner, reversing recent course form with Inventor. He could make up into a Pattern-class horse at some stage, but in the meantime the Melrose Handicap at York will surely come under consideration if the ground is suitable. (op 10-1)

Meshtri(IRE), off the mark in an extended 1m3f maiden at Haydock on his previous start, built on that effort over this longer trip but probably ran into a pretty decent animal. He should continue to progress. (op 5-1 tchd 9-2)

Allied Powers(IRE) would not have minded the conditions and he ran a good race stepped up to his furthest trip to date. (op 13-2 tchd 7-1)

Manyriverstocross(IRE) would have found this a lot tougher than the 1m4f Chepstow maiden on his previous start, but he ran well, keeping on strongly after being switched left with his challenge. He seemed to stay the trip, the furthest he has tried to date, and is progressing. (op 12-1)

Sevenna(FR) had no easy task against some talented colts, but she ran with real credit and seems to be going the right way. (op 16-1 tchd 9-1)

Woodcutter(IRE) looked good when winning his maiden over 1m4f on quick ground at Newmarket last time, but he was not in the same form this time and may have been unsuited by the testing ground. Official explanation: jockey said colt was unsuited by the soft ground (op 11-4)

Inventor(IRE) had today's winner and third behind when successful over 1m4f here on good ground on his previous start, but he failed to run his race this time and was another who looked unsuited by the ground. (op 5-1 tchd 11-2)

Criterion Official explanation: jockey said gelding was unsuited by the soft ground

4785 PAUL SCULTHORPE H'CAP — 1m 2f 120y

4:40 (4:41) (Class 5) (0-70,69) 3-Y-0+ **£3,238** (£963; £481; £240) **Stalls** High

Form RPR

0425 **1** **Hurlingham**[19] 4204 4-10-0 **69**.. PaulMulrennan 16 82
(M W Easterby) *hld up in rr: hdwy to go 2nd over 2f out: carried hd high and led over 1f out: drvn out* **10/1**

505 **2** *2 1/4* **Mae Cigan (FR)**[27] 3917 5-9-11 **66**................................ SteveDrowne 9 74
(M Blanshard) *hld up in rr: hdwy on wd outside over 3f out: styd on to take 2nd ins fnl f: no real imp* **4/1**[1]

3060 **3** *1 3/4* **Three Strings (USA)**[30] 3814 5-9-0 **55**................................(p) TomEaves 6 60
(P D Niven) *trckd ldrs: hung lft and styd on same pce appr fnl f* **14/1**

2110 **4** *1 1/2* **High Five Society**[115] 1371 4-9-1 **56**................................(bt) MickyFenton 15 58
(S R Bowring) *led tl hdd over 1f out: one pce* **16/1**

1030 **5** *4 1/2* **Smirfy's Silver**[20] 4156 4-9-11 **66**.. AlanMunro 5 60
(E S McMahon) *chsd ldrs: wknd appr fnl f* **8/1**[3]

4540 **6** *1 3/4* **Vanquisher (IRE)**[12] 4432 4-9-7 **62**........................(p) StephenDonohoe 10 52
(Ian Williams) *mid-div: sn drvn along: sme hdwy over 3f out: nvr rchd ldrs* **11/1**

2014 **7** *1* **West End Lad**[5] 4650 5-9-8 **63**..(b) DeanMcKeown 2 51
(S R Bowring) *unruly s: trckd ldrs: one pce fnl 2f* **9/1**

3001 **8** *nse* **Grethel (IRE)**[6] 4596 4-9-2 **62** 6ex.. SladeO'Hara(5) 4 50
(A Berry) *mid-div: hdwy over 3f out: nvr trbld ldrs* **8/1**[3]

0333 **9** *16* **King Of Connacht**[7] 4568 5-8-13 **54**................................(p) MartinDwyer 1 12
(M Wellings) *in rr: sme hdwy over 3f out: lost pl over 1f out* **5/1**[2]

6423 **10** *2 3/4* **Prince Noel**[17] 4248 4-9-4 **64**.. AshleyHamblett(5) 7 17
(N Wilson) *hld up in rr: effrt over 3f out: wknd 2f out* **9/1**

F000 **11** *3 1/4* **Jontobel**[21] 4112 3-8-2 **53** oh5 ow3.. PaulFessey 13 —
(Jedd O'Keeffe) *racd in last: drvn 4f out: nvr on terms* **100/1**

0052 **12** *1* **Ryedale Ovation (IRE)**[13] 4365 5-9-9 **64**........................ PaulHanagan 8 9
(M Hill) *in rr: effrt over 2f out: hung rt and sn wknd* **8/1**[3]

00 **13** *21* **Mean Machine (IRE)**[21] 4105 6-8-2 **50** oh5............(b) RobbieEgan(7) 14 —
(D Flood) *chsd ldrs: wknd over 3f out: sn bhd: t.o* **50/1**

2m 21.89s (5.19) **Going Correction** +0.575s/f (Yiel)
WFA 3 from 4yo+ 10lb **13** Ran SP% **122.9**
Speed ratings (Par 103): **104,102,101,100,96 95,94,94,83,81 78,77,62**
toteswinger: 1&2 £6.30, 1&3 £39.70, 2&3 £100.90. CSF £51.15 CT £581.71 TOTE £15.20: £3.40, £1.90, £5.10; EX 51.60 Place 6: £428.51, Place 5: £192.40..

Owner A G Black **Bred** Aston Mullins Stud **Trained** Sheriff Hutton, N Yorks

FOCUS
A modest handicap but straighforward form rated around the placed horses. They raced towards the stands' side in the straight.

Ryedale Ovation(IRE) Official explanation: jockey said gelding hung right-handed throughout

T/Jkpt: Not won. T/Plt: £850.30 to a £1 stake. Pool: £77,240.46. 66.31 winning tickets. T/Qpdt: £188.10 to a £1 stake. Pool: £4,092.50. 16.10 winning tickets. WG

4568 SANDOWN (R-H)

Thursday, August 7

OFFICIAL GOING: Sprint course - good (good to soft in places); round course - good to soft (good in places)
Rail realignment added circa 10yards to advertised distances on round course
Wind: Moderate, across (Races 3 & 4); Remainder - Light, against Weather: Mostly fine - overcast race 3 and shower during race 4

4786 HARINO.COM VIRTUAL RACING, REAL EXCITEMENT MAIDEN FILLIES' STKS — 5f 6y

5:45 (5:50) (Class 4) 2-Y-O **£3,885** (£1,156; £577; £288) **Stalls** High

Form RPR

1 **Cut The Cackle (IRE)** 2-9-0 0.. DarryllHolland 9 80+
(P Winkworth) *trckd ldrs: chsd ldr wl over 1f out: shkn up and clsd sn after: led last 100yds: readily* **8/1**

440 **2** *1* **Peper Harow (IRE)**[12] 4403 2-9-0 84................................ PaulEddery 4 76
(M D I Usher) *led at mod pce: kicked on 2f out: hdd and outpcd last 100yds* **6/1**[3]

2 **3** *1 1/2* **Poyle Meg**[17] 4251 2-9-0 0.. TPQueally 6 71+
(R M Beckett) *hld up in last pair: outpcd 2f out: effrt sn after and c wd: styd on fnl f: no ch to chal* **11/10**[1]

4 *1 3/4* **Florentia** 2-9-0 0.. J-PGuillambert 5 65+
(Sir Mark Prescott) *s.i.s: hld up in last pair: prog to dispute modest 3rd 1f out: pushed along and kpt on steadily* **16/1**

562 **5** *3/4* **Barnezet (GR)**[10] 4480 2-9-0 0.. MichaelHills 8 62
(R Hannon) *hld up: effrt 2f out: sn hung lft and threw away ch: one pce fnl f* **11/4**[2]

6 *1 1/4* **Fortune In Faith (USA)** 2-9-0 0.. AdamKirby 1 58
(C G Cox) *chsd ldr to wl over 1f out: fdd* **16/1**

7 *2 1/2* **Smokey Ryder** 2-8-7 0.. JemmaMarshall(7) 2 49
(G L Moore) *wl in tch: wkng whn stmbld bdly over 1f out* **50/1**

64.02 secs (2.42) **Going Correction** +0.225s/f (Good) **7** Ran SP% **113.4**
Speed ratings (Par 93): **89,87,85,82,81 79,75**
toteswinger: 1&2 £5.90, 1&3 £3.40, 2&3 £1.50. CSF £53.25 TOTE £8.20: £2.30, £2.20; EX 49.80.

Owner P Winkworth **Bred** Mountarmstrong Stud **Trained** Chiddingfold, Surrey

FOCUS
An ordinary maiden run at just a modest pace and best rated around the placed horses.

NOTEBOOK
Cut The Cackle(IRE) is a sister to useful 6f winner Film Maker. She needed cajoling along up the inside rail, running a shade green, but the further they went the better she looked and, having switched out to challenge the leader approaching the final furlong, she asserted close home to win with something spare. She is clearly above average and connections are keen to step her up in class and get some black type as the intention is to sell her at the end of the season. (op 12-1 tchd 7-1)

Peper Harow(IRE), down in grade, was having her first run over the minimum trip. She made good use of her experience and set a modest pace, but could not hold off the winner late on. She should be able to win a maiden. (op 4-1)

Poyle Meg, runner-up on her debut at Windsor, where she raced prominently, is better than this as she wasn't suited by being held up in a steadily run race. She stayed on at the end but she was too far back and she could never land a blow. Official explanation: jockey said filly was slow into stride (op 6-4)

Florentia is a half-sister to eight winners including the smart Flying Officer, who raced for the Prescott yard, but none of them won first time out. She shaped with some encouragement on her debut, keeping on quite nicely in the closing stages having looked very green in rear through the first half of the race. She should improve plenty for this. (op 10-1)

Barnezet(GR), back down in trip and held up this time, hung across the track when the pressure was on and threw away what chance she still had. Official explanation: jockey said filly hung left (op 3-1 tchd 7-2)

Fortune In Faith(USA) is a half-sister to five winners in the USA notably the top-class 5f-1m performer Vivid Angel. She showed pace on this debut but faded through the final furlong. (op 14-1 tchd 12-1)

4787 GROUP CLEAN H'CAP — 5f 6y

6:15 (6:19) (Class 4) (0-80,80) 3-Y-O **£4,533** (£1,348; £674; £336) **Stalls** High

Form RPR

-202 **1** **Ridge Wood Dani (IRE)**[11] 4450 3-8-13 **70**................ RichardHughes 4 78
(E J Alston) *trckd ldng pair: wnt 2nd over 1f out: led ent fnl f: hrd rdn and jst hld on* **3/1**[2]

1442 **2** *nse* **Blue Jack**[40] 3499 3-9-4 **75**.. AdamKirby 2 83
(W R Muir) *wnt lft s and s.i.s: hld up in last pair: prog over 1f out: drvn to chse wnr wl ins fnl f: clsd nr fin: jst failed* **9/2**[3]

22-1 **3** *1 1/2* **Barbary Boy (FR)**[33] 3712 3-9-4 **75**................................ TPQueally 3 78
(M L W Bell) *hld up in abt 5th: effrt on outer over 1f out: drvn and kpt on to take 3rd last strides* **9/2**[3]

4111 **4** *hd* **Le Toreador**[30] 3811 3-9-2 **80**................................(t) FrederikTylicki(7) 7 82
(K A Ryan) *led: hdd ent fnl f: one pce* **9/4**[1]

5560 **5** *nk* **Extreme North (USA)**[48] 3217 3-8-4 **61** oh4................ MatthewHenry 5 62
(Miss V Haigh) *cl up: edgd lft and nt qckn u.p over 1f out: styd on ins fnl f* **33/1**

2211 **6** *3 3/4* **Heaven**[21] 4106 3-9-8 **79**.. DarryllHolland 1 67
(P J Makin) *pushed along in last after 2f: nvr gng pce to trble ldrs: plugged on fnl f* **13/2**

0003 **7** *2 3/4* **Ten Down**[14] 4347 3-9-4 **75**.. JohnEgan 8 53
(Miss Gay Kelleway) *pressed ldr tl wknd over 1f out* **16/1**

62.41 secs (0.81) **Going Correction** +0.225s/f (Good) **7** Ran SP% **114.3**
Speed ratings (Par 102): **102,101,99,99,98 92,88**
toteswinger: 1&2 £3.50, 1&3 £4.50, 2&3 £4.90. CSF £16.86 CT £58.81 TOTE £4.10: £2.30, £2.80; EX 18.40.

Owner Con Harrington **Bred** Con Harrington **Trained** Longton, Lancs

FOCUS
A competitive handicap run at a sound pace and the form makes sense with the first four close to their marks.

Le Toreador Official explanation: trainer said gelding was unsuited by the good (good to soft in places) ground

Heaven Official explanation: trainer said filly was unsuited by the good (good to soft in places) ground

4788 LONDON FOCUS 15 YEARS MAIDEN STKS 1m 14y
6:50 (6:52) (Class 4) 2-Y-O £4,533 (£1,348; £674; £336) Stalls High

Form				RPR
3	1		**On Our Way**[19] 4184 2-9-3 0 ... TPQueally 3 (H R A Cecil) *trckd ldr after 3f: led 3f out: immediately pressed: shkn up and asserted 2f out: styd on strly* **2/1**[1]	83+
5	2	3 1/2	**Atabaas Allure (FR)**[21] 4109 2-8-12 0 ... J-PGuillambert 8 (M Johnston) *led to 3f out: sn outpcd: kpt on to take 2nd again wl over 1f out: no imp on wnr* **7/2**[3]	70+
0	3	1 3/4	**Khan Tengri (IRE)**[5] 4625 2-9-3 0 ... DaneO'Neill 9 (M P Tregoning) *trckd ldrs: shkn up over 2f out: stl green but kpt on steadily: no imp on ldng pair* **25/1**	71
0	4	1/2	**Hambledon Hill**[20] 4150 2-9-3 0 ... MichaelHills 1 (R Hannon) *dwlt: hld up towards rr: prog on outer over 2f out: shkn up and one pce fr over 1f out* **8/1**	70
	5	3 1/2	**Harlestone Snake** 2-9-3 0 ... FergusSweeney 2 (J L Dunlop) *s.s: mostly in last pair: rdn 3f out: nvr on terms: modest prog fnl 2f* **33/1**	62+
23	6	1 3/4	**Dreamwalk (IRE)**[20] 4150 2-9-3 0 ... GeorgeBaker 6 (R M Beckett) *trckd ldr 3f: steadily wknd over 2f out* **9/4**[2]	59
	7	1 1/4	**Blue Dynasty (USA)** 2-9-3 0 ... DarryllHolland 5 (Mrs A J Perrett) *dwlt: pushed along early in last pair: detached in last 3f out: modest late prog* **10/1**	56+
03	8	shd	**Arushore (IRE)**[35] 3645 2-9-3 0 ... RichardHughes 7 (R Hannon) *trckd ldrs: prog to join wnr 3f out: btn off over 2f out: wknd rapidly over 1f out* **16/1**	56
0	9	1/2	**Corredor Sun (USA)**[43] 3372 2-9-3 0 ... AdamKirby 4 (Carl Llewellyn) *in tch towards rr: shkn up over 2f out: sn struggling: wknd fnl f* **66/1**	54

1m 48.64s (5.34) **Going Correction** +0.35s/f (Good) **9** Ran SP% **120.7**
Speed ratings (Par 96): **87,83,81,81,77 76,74,74,74**
toteswinger: 1&2 £2.00, 1&3 £13.60, 2&3 £29.20. CSF £9.81 TOTE £3.00: £1.40, £2.00, £3.90; EX 9.20.
Owner J R May **Bred** Whatton Manor Stud **Trained** Newmarket, Suffolk

FOCUS
Probably just an ordinary maiden and the gallop wasn't at all strong, so not form to get excited about. There should be more to come from the winner.

NOTEBOOK
On Our Way, who shaped with promise at Lingfield over 7f on his debut, had no problem with the rise in trip and easier ground. He travelled strongly close to the pace before taking over and saw out the trip strongly. He is improving, and connections think there is plenty more to come as he's such a big horse. (op Evens)
Atabaas Allure(FR) set a steady gallop but she was very one-paced when things quickened. She did rally for second but her big-race entries look pretty fanciful on this evidence. (op 6-1)
Khan Tengri(IRE) stayed on steadily once switched out and he took a step forward on his debut, where he blew the start. There should be further improvement in him.
Hambledon Hill improved on what he had shown on his debut but, although keeping on down the outer in the straight, he could never really land a blow. (op 10-1 tchd 15-2)
Harlestone Snake got going very late from the back, following a slow start. Out of an unraced half-sister to decent stayer Harlestone Brook, he will need further so this was an encouraging first run in the circumstances. (op 50-1 tchd 25-1)
Dreamwalk(IRE) had shown fair form in 7f maidens on his first two starts but this was disappointing. Official explanation: trainer said colt was unsuited by the good to soft (good in places) ground (op 11-4, tchd 3-1 in places)
Arushore(IRE) challenged with around three furlongs to run but the effort quickly petered out. He did not stay the trip on this stiff track. (op 20-1)

4789 INKERMAN LONDON H'CAP 1m 14y
7:20 (7:27) (Class 5) (0-75,75) 3-Y-0+ £3,885 (£1,156; £577; £288) Stalls High

Form				RPR
1214	1		**Isphahan**[16] 4284 5-9-10 70 ... DarryllHolland 8 (A M Balding) *trckd ldr: led main gp towards nr side in st but hanging bdly rt and ended up in middle: overall ldr 3f out: straightened out and r.o wl fnl f* **3/1**[1]	85
4603	2	1 3/4	**Effigy**[20] 4162 4-9-4 64 ... DaneO'Neill 4 (H Candy) *hld up in rr: rdn and prog over 2f out: styd on wl to take 2nd last 150yds: no real imp on wnr* **4/1**[3]	75
6024	3	2 1/4	**Palmetto Point**[20] 4162 4-9-6 69 ...(tp) TravisBlock(3) 12 (H Morrison) *led: styd alone far side ent st: hdd 3f out: drifted across to middle and stl in 2nd 2f out: one pce over 1f out* **13/2**	74
0101	4	3 1/2	**Monashee Rock (IRE)**[13] 4369 3-9-8 75 ... GeorgeBaker 2 (M Salaman) *stdd s: hld up in last: rdn 3f out: plugged on fr over 2f out: nvr pce to trble ldrs* **10/1**	69
6262	5	3/4	**Sotik Star (IRE)**[12] 4428 5-9-12 72 ... RyanMoore 10 (P J Makin) *t.k.h: hld up bhd ldrs: hanging rt u.p over 2f out: sn btn: struggled home* **7/2**[2]	68
0043	6	1	**Bartercard (USA)**[10] 4481 7-9-7 67 ... JohnEgan 6 (Stef Liddiard) *hld up in last pair: rdn 3f out: kpt on fnl 2f: n.d* **16/1**	60
054/	7	1	**Cover Drive (USA)**[160] 5-9-10 70 ... SamHitchcott 3 (Christian Wroe) *racd wd: chsd ldrs: rdn and no rspnse 3f out: sn btn* **50/1**	61
1420	8	nse	**Onenightinlisbon (IRE)**[24] 4022 4-9-12 72 ... FergusSweeney 11 (J R Boyle) *t.k.h: prom: rdn over 2f out: wknd qckly over 1f out* **14/1**	63
0054	9	3/4	**Golden Prospect**[33] 3738 4-9-6 66 ... MichaelHills 9 (J W Hills) *trckd ldrs: effrt and disp 2nd on nr side gp 2f out: wknd rapidly jst over 1f out* **8/1**	55
2600	10	3	**Jill Dawson (IRE)**[22] 4081 5-8-12 58 ... J-PGuillambert 5 (John Berry) *mostly in midfield on outer: rdn 3f out: wknd wl over 1f out* **16/1**	40

1m 45.36s (2.06) **Going Correction** +0.35s/f (Good)
WFA 3 from 4yo+ 7lb **10** Ran SP% **121.1**
Speed ratings (Par 103): **103,101,99,95,94 93,92,92,91,88**
toteswinger: 1&2 £4.90, 1&3 £4.80, 2&3 £7.00. CSF £15.77 CT £76.57 TOTE £4.40: £1.90, £1.90, £2.60; EX 24.00.
Owner Mohamad Rafique **Bred** J H Wall **Trained** Kingsclere, Hants

FOCUS
Leader Palmetto Point stayed on the far side once into the straight but the remainder made for the stands' fence, although winner Ispahan hung into the centre of the track. Not many got into the action on the rain-affected ground but the form looks sound.

Sotik Star(IRE) Official explanation: jockey said gelding hung right

4790 ARE YOU COVERED? H'CAP 1m 2f 7y
7:55 (8:00) (Class 3) (0-90,87) 3-Y-O £7,771 (£2,312; £1,155; £577) Stalls High

Form				RPR
-552	1		**Ascot Lime**[21] 4130 3-8-11 77 ... RyanMoore 10 (Sir Michael Stoute) *sn pushed up to go prom: rdn over 2f out: effrt to ld wl over 1f out: narrowly hdd ent fnl f: battled bk wl to ld last strides* **11/4**[1]	89+
-210	2	hd	**Conquisto**[66] 2665 3-9-3 83 ... AdamKirby 8 (C G Cox) *hld up in rr: stdy prog gng wl fr over 2f out: rdn to ld narrowly ent fnl f: styd on: hdd last strides* **8/1**	95+
21	3	3 1/4	**Tanto Faz (IRE)**[35] 3628 3-9-5 85 ... LiamJones 5 (W J Haggas) *plld hrd: hld up in midfield: prog in centre w hd high over 2f out: chsd ldng pair jst over 1f out: kpt on but easily outpcd* **7/2**[2]	90+
-130	4	3	**Burn The Breeze (IRE)**[56] 2975 3-9-4 84 ... TPQueally 1 (H R A Cecil) *t.k.h: hld up bhd ldrs: n.m.r briefly over 2f out: plugged on one pce over 1f out* **12/1**	83
5225	5	3/4	**Eqbaal**[29] 3854 3-9-3 83 ...(b[1]) J-PGuillambert 7 (J L Dunlop) *hld up last early: prog into midfield 1/2-way: nt qckn 2f out: n.d after* **16/1**	81
0022	6	1 1/4	**American Art (IRE)**[13] 4392 3-9-4 84 ...(t) MichaelHills 12 (B W Hills) *mde most to 2f out: nt qckn and sn btn* **7/1**	79
3311	7	1/2	**Light From Mars**[21] 4128 3-9-4 84 ... DarryllHolland 11 (B R Millman) *t.k.h: hld up in rr: rdn 3f out: sme prog but hanging rt and wdst of all 2f out: sn no hdwy and btn* **6/1**[3]	78
0405	8	1/2	**Drum Major (IRE)**[33] 3745 3-8-8 74 ... FergusSweeney 2 (G L Moore) *hld up in rr: struggling in last pair over 2f out: no ch after* **25/1**	67
0330	9	1/2	**Mystery Star (IRE)**[8] 4519 3-9-4 84 ... GeorgeBaker 9 (M H Tompkins) *hld up in last: u.p and limited prog over 2f out: n.d after* **13/2**	76
421	10	1/2	**Qui Moi (CAN)**[64] 2717 3-9-5 85 ... DaneO'Neill 6 (J R Fanshawe) *tk quite t.k.h early: pressed ldr: led briefly 2f out: wknd rapidly over 1f out* **16/1**	76
-560	11	13	**Pegasus Again (USA)**[15] 4312 3-9-7 87 ... JohnEgan 3 (T G Mills) *settled in midfield: rdn 3f out: wknd rapidly 2f out: t.o* **33/1**	52

2m 12.61s (2.11) **Going Correction** +0.35s/f (Good) **11** Ran SP% **126.4**
Speed ratings (Par 104): **105,104,102,99,99 98,97,97,97,96 86**
toteswinger: 1&2 £12.10, 1&3 £2.80, 2&3 £14.30. CSF £27.87 CT £83.98 TOTE £4.80: £2.00, £2.90, £2.00; EX 39.10.
Owner R Ahamad & P Scott **Bred** P And C Scott & Exors Of The Late N Ahamad **Trained** Newmarket, Suffolk

FOCUS
This looked quite a hot handicap beforehand but they finished quite well strung out in the end and many didn't really see out the trip, perhaps because of deteriorating conditions but the form looks reasonable rated through the third. The whole field came over to the stands' rail in the home straight.

NOTEBOOK
Ascot Lime ◆ went up 4lb after his defeat over course and distance by last-race runner-up Slip last month. Taking a narrow lead going to the final furlong but soon joined, he stuck his neck out willingly close home to get off the mark and continue his steady upward curve. He saw out this trip strongly and there could be more to come, with his attitude a real plus. (op 7-2)
Conquisto, who was held off this mark when last seen two months ago, travelled well and looked full of running approaching the final furlong. He picked up when shaken up to draw clear with the winner, but just missed out in a fine finish. (op 11-1 tchd 14-1)
Tanto Faz(IRE) was the least exposed horse in the field having taken a Haydock maiden on the second of his two starts. He was very keen off the slow early pace, but kept on down the middle of the track in the straight without troubling the first two. He should have more to offer (op 3-1)
Burn The Breeze(IRE), dropped in grade and another to take a hold, travelled quite well for a long way but was one-paced in the final two furlongs. (tchd 14-1)
Eqbaal was not really helped by the first-time blinkers, and was unable to quicken up near the stands' rail after stumbling slightly over two furlongs out. He appears to be on a high enough mark. (tchd 20-1)
Light From Mars, 4lb higher for this hat-trick bid, had an extra two furlongs and softer conditions to contend with. Things did not go his way during the race and he can do better than this. (op 7-1 tchd 9-2)
Pegasus Again(USA) Official explanation: jockey said colt became upset in the stalls

4791 BETNOW INSTANT TEXT BETTING H'CAP 1m 2f 7y
8:25 (8:30) (Class 4) (0-80,80) 3-Y-O+ £5,180 (£1,541; £770; £384) Stalls High

Form				RPR
003	1		**Novikov**[29] 3836 4-9-9 80 ...(tp) Louis-PhilippeBeuzelin(5) 4 (J H M Gosden) *led: rdn 2l clr over 1f out: narrowly hdd ins fnl f: sn rallied and led again nr fin* **10/1**	90
-141	2	hd	**Slip**[21] 4130 3-9-5 80 ... RichardHughes 2 (M P Tregoning) *trckd ldng pair: rdn to go 2nd over 2f out: no imp tl clsd 1f out: led narrowly ins fnl f and edgd rt: hdd nr fin* **15/8**[1]	90+
5421	3	1 3/4	**La Sarrazine (FR)**[31] 3796 3-9-3 78 ... DaneO'Neill 6 (J R Fanshawe) *trckd ldng trio: gng wl 3f out: rdn and nt qckn 2f out: chsd ldng pair over 1f out: no real imp* **11/4**[2]	84
0553	4	1 1/2	**Know The Law**[21] 4131 4-9-10 76 ...(b) RyanMoore 10 (D R C Elsworth) *stdd s: hld up in last pair: brought to r against nr side rail in st and prog over 2f out: chsd ldrs over 1f out: kpt on same pce* **8/1**	79
300	5	2 1/4	**Silver Blue (IRE)**[13] 4364 5-9-2 68 ... GeorgeBaker 5 (W K Goldsworthy) *hld up in 6th: rdn and prog to chse ldrs over 1f out: no imp after: fdd ins fnl f* **18/1**	67
0660	6	3 1/4	**Nur Tau (IRE)**[43] 3368 4-9-8 77 ... TravisBlock(3) 1 (H Morrison) *chsd wnr but on and off the bridle: lost 2nd over 2f out: wknd over 1f out* **8/1**	69
24P1	7	3	**Alfie Tupper (IRE)**[7] 4568 5-8-6 63 ow1 ... JackMitchell(5) 7 (J R Boyle) *t.k.h: hld up in 5th: rdn and nt qckn over 2f out: floundering after* **11/2**[3]	49
1030	8	15	**Ross Moor**[22] 4078 6-9-1 67 ... FergusSweeney 3 (Mike Murphy) *s.s: a in last pair: rdn and struggling over 2f out: t.o* **20/1**	23
030/	9	6	**Spear Thistle**[223] 6107 6-9-7 73 ... AdamKirby 9 (Mrs N Smith) *hld up in 7th: rdn and no prog over 2f out: wknd: t.o* **40/1**	17

2m 13.04s (2.54) **Going Correction** +0.35s/f (Good)
WFA 3 from 4yo+ 9lb **9** Ran SP% **120.6**
Speed ratings (Par 105): **103,102,101,100,98 95,93,81,76**
toteswinger: 1&2 £4.80, 1&3 £7.70, 2&3 £1.30. CSF £30.50 CT £69.75 TOTE £13.40: £2.80, £1.50, £1.60; EX 37.70 Place 6: £98.66, Place 5: £9.97..
Owner George Strawbridge **Bred** The Duke Of Devonshire **Trained** Newmarket, Suffolk

FOCUS
The winner set a seemingly modest gallop, bringing the field over to the stands' side in the straight. The form is rated through the third and fourth to their marks.
Alfie Tupper(IRE) Official explanation: trainer said gelding was unsuited by the good to soft (good in places) ground

The Form Book, Raceform Ltd, Compton, RG20 6NL

T/Plt: £78.90 to a £1 stake. Pool: £64,831.92. 599.69 winning tickets. T/Qpdt: £4.80 to a £1 stake. Pool: £6,425.10. 982.00 winning tickets. JN

4746 **YARMOUTH** (L-H)

Thursday, August 7

OFFICIAL GOING: Good changing to good to soft after race 1 (2.20)

Wind: Light across Weather: Cloudy with sunny spells

4792 EUROPEAN BREEDERS' FUND MAIDEN STKS — 6f 3y

2:20 (2:24) (Class 5) 2-Y-O £3,784 (£1,132; £566; £283; £141) Stalls High

Form RPR

20 1 **Aakef (IRE)**[51] 3105 2-9-3 0 RHills 8 79+
(M A Jarvis) *led 1f: trckd ldr tl led over 1f out: edgd rt: rdn out* 6/4[1]

4 2 ½ **Hajoum (IRE)**[26] 3976 2-9-3 0 LDettori 3 74
(Saeed Bin Suroor) *trckd ldrs: chsd wnr over 1f out: sn rdn: r.o* 7/2[3]

3 nk **Bounty Box** 2-8-7 0 JackMitchell(5) 2 68
(C F Wall) *hld up in tch: shkn up over 1f out: r.o* 33/1

4 1¼ **Nizhoni Dancer** 2-8-12 0 HayleyTurner 6 64
(C F Wall) *hld up: hdwy 1/2-way: sn rdn: r.o* 50/1

5 1½ **Intikama (IRE)** 2-8-12 0 JimmyQuinn 5 63+
(M H Tompkins) *s.s: hld up: rdn over 2f out: nt clr run 1f out: r.o: nt rch ldrs* 100/1

06 6 ½ **Welcome Applause (IRE)**[15] 4296 2-8-9 0 JerryO'Dwyer(3) 1 58
(M G Quinlan) *hld up: shkn up over 1f out: nvr nr to chal* 40/1

7 2¼ **Leahurst (IRE)** 2-9-3 0 RyanMoore 7 57
(J Noseda) *s.i.s: sn prom: rdn over 2f out: wknd fnl f* 2/1[2]

3 8 nk **Eagles Call (USA)**[79] 2275 2-9-3 0 JoeFanning 4 56
(P W Chapple-Hyam) *chsd wnr tl led 5f out: rdn and hdd over 1f out: wknd ins fnl f* 11/1

9 7 **Burma Rock (IRE)** 2-9-3 0 PatCosgrave 9 35
(L M Cumani) *sn pushed along in rr: wknd over 1f out* 33/1

1m 15.25s (0.85) **Going Correction** +0.05s/f (Good) 9 Ran SP% 115.2

Speed ratings (Par 94): **96,95,94,93,91 90,87,87,77**

toteswinger: 1&2 £1.80, 1&3 £8.10, 2&3 £14.20. CSF £6.92 TOTE £2.50: £1.10, £1.10, £6.40; EX 8.20.

Owner Hamdan Al Maktoum **Bred** Grangecon Stud **Trained** Newmarket, Suffolk

■ Stewards' Enquiry : Jack Mitchell two-day ban: careless riding (August 23-24)

FOCUS

A fair maiden for the grade with the runner-up confirming the good impression from his debut.

NOTEBOOK

Aakef(IRE) had run as though something went amiss when down the field in the Windsor Castle Stakes (poor run blamed on being sandwiched by two fillies in the stalls) on his previous outing, but he showed his true colours on this step up to 6f and broke his duck at the third attempt. He has both speed and stamina in his pedigree, a sound surface looks important to his cause, and he holds a host of big-race entries. (op 9-4)

Hajoum(IRE) stepped up on debut fourth at York 26 days previously and made the winner work all the way to the line, but was always being held by that rival. He holds a Group 2 Mill Reef entry so is presumably well thought-of and can soon be placed to go one better in this sort of class. (op 5-2)

Bounty Box ◆ is a half-sister to her yard's 6f juvenile winner Vive Les Rouges and her dam was a multiple winner over 7-9f. Allowed to go off at a big price for this racecourse bow, she exceeded market expectations with a very promising effort and looks sure to take some beating next time out.

Nizhoni Dancer, whose dam was a very useful 1m-12f winner, emulated her stable companion Bounty Box by belying her big odds and running a debut race full of promise. She kept on nicely without being given too hard a time against the rail inside the final 2f and should come on nicely for the experience. Another furlong will also likely suit her before that long. (tchd 66-1)

Intikama(IRE) is a half-sister to a 12f winner, so it was little surprise to see her staying on at the finish after taking time to get organised. She can build on this as she gains further experience and as she steps up in distance.

Leahurst(IRE), a 95,000gns half-brother to Dunelight, came to the track with a reputation and holds multiple big-race entries. He overcame a sluggish start and moved well enough until feeling the pinch approaching 2f out and then tamely dropping out. No doubt he is thought capable of a great deal better than this, so while he has something to prove already, his next outing should reveal more as to his talents. (tchd 13-8, 9-4 in places)

4793 BET365 BEST ODDS GUARANTEED ON EVERY RACE MAIDEN H'CAP — 6f 3y

2:50 (2:52) (Class 6) (0-65,63) 3-Y-O+ £2,072 (£616; £308; £153) Stalls High

Form RPR

-064 1 **Hurricane Harriet**[21] 4125 3-9-1 53 OscarUrbina 11 70+
(R M H Cowell) *chsd ldrs: led over 1f out: rdn out* 6/1[2]

0026 2 2½ **Towy Boy (IRE)**[14] 4324 3-9-11 63 (t) PatrickMathers 5 70
(I A Wood) *a.p: rdn and ev ch over 1f out: edgd rt: styd on same pce ins fnl f* 14/1

3235 3 3 **Peas In A Pod**[42] 3395 3-8-11 54 JackMitchell(5) 10 51
(J R Fanshawe) *chsd ldrs: rdn over 1f out: styd on same pce fnl f* 7/2[1]

000 4 nk **Dalla Finestra**[41] 3452 3-9-0 52 HayleyTurner 15 48
(C F Wall) *chsd ldrs: rdn over 1f out: no ex fnl f* 8/1

0000 5 2¾ **Cow Girl (IRE)**[13] 4383 4-8-9 46 ow1 JerryO'Dwyer(3) 14 34+
(Miss Gay Kelleway) *s.i.s: hld up: hdwy u.p over 1f out: nt trble ldrs* 25/1

-004 6 1 **Inwaan (IRE)**[41] 3446 5-9-4 52 (tp) RHills 2 36
(P R Webber) *hld up: hdwy 1/2-way: rdn and edgd rt over 1f out: no ex* 13/2[3]

2060 7 3¾ **Ma Mirage (IRE)**[1] 4725 3-8-7 45 (v) NickyMackay 13 17
(S C Williams) *mid-div: rdn and hung lft over 2f out: wknd over 1f out* 33/1

0000 8 1½ **Creative (IRE)**[28] 3886 3-9-4 56 (b[1]) JimmyQuinn 6 24
(M H Tompkins) *led and sn clr: wknd and hdd over 1f out* 10/1

0-04 9 2½ **Lavande**[13] 4388 3-9-8 60 LDettori 8 20
(M J Wallace) *hld up: wknd 2f out* 14/1

6063 10 7 **Shatter Resistant (IRE)**[8] 4523 3-8-12 50 (tp) JoeFanning 12 —
(M D Squance) *rn wout declared tongue strap: hld up: effrt over 2f out: sn wknd* 12/1

5002 11 1¼ **Al Gillani (IRE)**[22] 4090 3-9-5 57 PatCosgrave 9 —
(J R Boyle) *chsd ldrs: eased over 1f out* 6/1[2]

-500 12 7 **Hucking Harmony (IRE)**[15] 4307 3-8-7 48 MarcHalford(3) 3 —
(J R Best) *hld up: plld hrd: wknd 3f out* 33/1

043 13 1¾ **Harryana To**[19] 4195 3-9-6 58 NeilPollard 1 —
(B J McMath) *mid-div: sn pushed along: wknd 1/2-way* 16/1

6-35 14 ¾ **O'Casey (IRE)**[169] 623 3-8-8 46 AndrewElliott 7 —
(J G M O'Shea) *chsd ldrs: rdn 1/2-way: sn wknd* 66/1

0-6 15 5 **Terandeil**[50] 3139 4-8-11 45 AdrianTNicholls 4 —
(J G M O'Shea) *s.i.s: hld up: eased wl over 1f out* 100/1

1m 14.33s (-0.07) **Going Correction** +0.05s/f (Good)

WFA 3 from 4yo+ 4lb 15 Ran SP% 123.4

Speed ratings (Par 101): **102,98,94,94,90 89,84,82,78,69 67,58,56,55,48**

toteswinger: 1&2 £14.00, 1&3 £5.50, 2&3 £17.40. CSF £85.84 CT £354.27 TOTE £7.50: £2.40, £4.60, £1.80; EX 100.40.

Owner Mr & Mrs R Foulkes & Mrs Eugenie Abel Smith **Bred** Mrs K E Collie **Trained** Six Mile Bottom, Cambs

FOCUS

A typically weak maiden handicap, run at a fair pace. The form is set by the placed horses.

Al Gillani(IRE) Official explanation: jockey said gelding stumbled leaving the stalls and moved badly thereafter

Hucking Harmony(IRE) Official explanation: trainer said filly was unsuited by the good to soft ground

Terandeil Official explanation: jockey said filly hung badly left

4794 GREAT YARMOUTH MERCURY (S) STKS — 1m 3y

3:20 (3:20) (Class 6) 3-Y-O £1,942 (£578; £288; £144) Stalls High

Form RPR

6045 1 **Redsensor**[33] 3730 3-9-3 59 PatCosgrave 3 57
(M Quinn) *chsd ldr: rdn to ld over 2f out: styd on wl to go clr ins fnl f* 5/2[1]

300 2 4 **Last Angel (IRE)**[16] 4280 3-8-12 43 (t) JimmyQuinn 8 43
(M Wigham) *hld up in tch: swtchd lft over 3f out: rdn over 1f out: edgd rt and no ex ins fnl f* 10/1

6050 3 1¼ **Cherished Song**[15] 4298 3-8-9 44 JerryO'Dwyer(3) 6 40
(M G Quinlan) *hld up: hdwy over 1f out: sn rdn: no ex fnl f* 9/1

-003 4 1¼ **Our Dolly**[7] 4566 3-8-12 49 JoeFanning 7 37
(Garry Moss) *sn pushed along in rr: effrt and nt clr run wl over 1f out: sn rdn: no imp fnl f* 10/3[3]

06 5 3 **Mensadil**[26] 3953 3-8-10 0 KristinStubbs(7) 4 35
(Mrs L Stubbs) *led: rdn and hdd over 2f out: edgd rt over 1f out: wknd fnl f* 25/1

02 6 2 **Never Sold Out (IRE)**[36] 3605 3-9-3 54 (b[1]) AndrewElliott 2 31
(J G M O'Shea) *hld up in tch: rdn and edgd rt over 1f out: wknd fnl f* 3/1[2]

0500 7 3½ **Miss Tilen**[8] 4540 3-8-5 45 CharlesEddery(7) 5 18
(V Smith) *prom: rdn over 3f out: wknd wl over 1f out* 10/1

5000 8 3 **Cobbold Point**[29] 3844 3-8-10 39 StevenCorrigan(7) 1 16
(S W Hall) *chsd ldrs: rdn over 3f out: wknd 2f out* 40/1

1m 42.03s (1.43) **Going Correction** +0.05s/f (Good) 8 Ran SP% 111.1

Speed ratings (Par 98): **94,90,88,87,84 82,79,76**

toteswinger: 1&2 £5.90, 1&3 £7.60, 2&3 £16.80. CSF £26.64 TOTE £3.00: £1.10, £2.80, £2.70; EX 27.80.There was no bid for the winner.

Owner Brian Morton **Bred** Waney Racing Group Inc **Trained** Newmarket, Suffolk

FOCUS

A very weak affair which provided a straightforward opportunity for the winner who did not need to run up to this year's form to score.

4795 PARKLANDS LEISURE HOLIDAY CARAVANS FILLIES' H'CAP — 1m 3y

3:50 (3:50) (Class 5) (0-75,72) 3-Y-O £2,590 (£770; £385; £192) Stalls High

Form RPR

-021 1 **Certain Promise (USA)**[8] 4533 3-9-9 72 6ex RyanMoore 2 81+
(Sir Michael Stoute) *trckd ldrs: led over 1f out: shkn up and r.o* 4/6[1]

-600 2 ¾ **Brave Mave**[12] 4427 3-9-4 67 (b[1]) JoeFanning 6 71
(W Jarvis) *led: rdn and hdd over 1f out: styd on* 14/1

3210 3 1¼ **Loveinanelevator**[15] 4300 3-9-7 70 HayleyTurner 4 71
(M L W Bell) *hld up: hdwy over 2f out: rdn ins fnl f: no ex towards fin* 9/2[2]

-003 4 3 **Suzi Spends (IRE)**[23] 4061 3-9-2 70 JackMitchell(5) 8 64+
(H J Collingridge) *hld up: hmpd over 6f out: hdwy over 1f out: rdn and hung lft ins fnl f: wknd towards fin* 6/1[3]

060 5 4 **Sleeping**[71] 2509 3-8-11 60 JimmyQuinn 7 45
(M H Tompkins) *hld up: a in rr: rdn and wknd over 1f out* 50/1

10 6 1 **Nice Matin (USA)**[22] 4082 3-9-7 70 OscarUrbina 5 53
(J A R Toller) *hld up in tch: plld hrd: swtchd rt over 6f out: rdn over 1f out: sn wknd* 16/1

3204 7 6 **Bookiebasher Babe (IRE)**[79] 2288 3-9-4 67 AdrianTNicholls 1 36
(M Quinn) *w ldr tl rdn over 2f out: wknd over 1f out* 12/1

1m 41.25s (0.65) **Going Correction** +0.05s/f (Good) 7 Ran SP% 114.7

Speed ratings (Par 97): **98,97,96,93,89 88,82**

toteswinger: 1&2 £3.80, 1&3 £1.70, 2&3 £6.00. CSF £12.33 CT £27.44 TOTE £1.60: £1.30, £3.60; EX 11.10.

Owner K Abdulla **Bred** Juddmonte Farms Inc **Trained** Newmarket, Suffolk

FOCUS

A modest handicap. The form is rated through the third but looks pretty shaky.

4796 FDS - LOOKING AFTER YOUR FRANCHISING NEEDS H'CAP — 1m 3f 101y

4:20 (4:22) (Class 6) (0-65,65) 3-Y-O £1,942 (£578; £288; £144) Stalls Low

Form RPR

0-44 1 **China Pink**[6] 4607 3-8-6 50 JoeFanning 6 57+
(Sir Mark Prescott) *mde all: rdn clr 2f out: edgd rt ins fnl f: styd on* 3/1[2]

010 2 ¾ **Bella Medici**[5] 4646 3-9-4 62 JimmyQuinn 7 68
(M H Tompkins) *s.i.s: hld up: hdwy u.p over 1f out: r.o* 16/1

03-0 3 nk **Bruki (IRE)**[14] 4342 3-8-13 60 (t) JerryO'Dwyer(3) 3 65
(M Botti) *hld up: hdwy over 4f out: sn rdn: styd on u.p* 25/1

0252 4 2 **Golden Bishop**[16] 4281 3-9-7 65 HayleyTurner 1 67
(M L W Bell) *hld up: hdwy over 4f out: rdn to chse wnr over 1f out: styd on same pce ins fnl f* 2/1[1]

0050 5 1¼ **Dixie Dean (USA)**[7] 4573 3-9-0 58 (v) RyanMoore 5 58
(Sir Michael Stoute) *chsd ldrs: rdn and edgd lft over 2f out: no ex fnl f* 9/1

3603 6 1¼ **Dea Caelestis (FR)**[12] 4427 3-9-0 65 CharlesEddery(7) 9 62
(H R A Cecil) *hld up: rdn and hung lft over 1f out: nt trble ldrs* 10/1

-000 7 3½ **Bunty Malenoir**[29] 3841 3-7-10 47 AmyBaker(7) 4 38
(Mrs C A Dunnett) *chsd ldrs: rdn over 2f out: wknd over 1f out* 80/1

506 8 13 **Circadian Rhythm**[17] 4255 3-8-10 54 NickyMackay 11 22
(S C Williams) *chsd wnr tl rdn 2f out: wknd over 1f out: eased fnl f* 40/1

4060 9 9 **In Toto**[28] 3893 3-8-11 55 OscarUrbina 10 6
(M Wigham) *hld up: rdn: hung lft and wknd over 2f out* 15/2

-061 10 2¾ **Rampant Ronnie (USA)**[34] 3692 3-9-4 62 LDettori 8 8
(P W D'Arcy) *prom: rdn and edgd lft over 4f out: wknd over 2f out* 11/2[3]

050 11 16 **Global Glory (IRE)**[19] 4194 3-8-3 47 oh1 ow1 (v[1]) AdrianTNicholls 2 —
(J A R Toller) *s.i.s: hld up: rr: bhd fr 1/2-way: eased fnl 2f* 20/1

2m 29.51s (0.81) **Going Correction** +0.05s/f (Good) 11 Ran SP% 122.7

Speed ratings (Par 98): **99,98,98,96,95 94,92,82,76,74 62**

toteswinger: 1&2 £9.50, 1&3 £15.00, 2&3 £29.20. CSF £50.32 CT £1048.78 TOTE £3.70: £1.80, £4.00, £5.40; EX 63.60.

Owner Faisal Salman **Bred** Genesis Green Stud Ltd **Trained** Newmarket, Suffolk

FOCUS
A moderate handicap for three-year-olds. The form looks fair with the first three pulling clear.
Rampant Ronnie(USA) Official explanation: trainer said gelding was unsuited by the good to soft ground

4797 INJURED JOCKEYS FUND H'CAP — 1m 1f
4:50 (4:54) (Class 6) (0-65,63) 3-Y-O+ — £1,942 (£578; £288; £144) Stalls Low

Form				RPR
0151	1		**Kimono My House**[10] 4479 4-9-3 52 ... LDettori 4	63
			(J G Given) *a.p: rdn to ld ins fnl f: r.o: eased nr fin* 7/2[1]	
5063	2	1 1/4	**Azure Mist**[17] 4260 3-9-3 60 ... JimmyQuinn 8	68
			(M H Tompkins) *chsd ldrs: led over 2f out: rdn over 1f out: hdd and unable qckn ins fnl f* 14/1	
046	3	3 1/2	**Ghufa (IRE)**[35] 3628 4-10-0 63 ... RHills 6	63
			(E A L Dunlop) *hld up: hdwy over 3f out: rdn and edgd lft over 1f out: styd on same pce fnl f* 8/1	
3322	4	3 1/2	**Brouhaha**[20] 4168 4-9-9 58 ... NeilPollard 11	51
			(B J McMath) *hld up: hdwy u.p 2f out: wknd ins fnl f* 4/1[2]	
-050	5	2 1/4	**Shraayef**[17] 4260 3-8-11 59 ... JackMitchell(5) 5	47
			(M Botti) *hld up: hdwy over 2f out: sn rdn: n.d* 50/1	
3013	6	1 1/2	**Al Rayanah**[10] 4479 5-9-4 53 ... (p) HayleyTurner 9	37
			(G Prodromou) *s.i.s: hld up: hdwy u.p 2f out: nvr trbld ldrs* 16/1	
0625	7	1 1/4	**Anduril**[23] 4065 7-8-12 50 ... (p) LeeVickers(3) 10	32
			(I W McInnes) *hld up: effrt over 2f out: n.d* 40/1	
25-3	8	1 1/2	**Viable**[26] 3964 6-9-9 58 ... AdrianTNicholls 1	36
			(Mrs P Sly) *w ldr: rdn and ev ch over 2f out: wknd over 1f out* 10/1	
0000	9	3/4	**Hundonette**[21] 4125 3-8-7 50 ... OscarUrbina 2	27
			(R M H Cowell) *chsd ldrs: rdn over 2f out: wknd over 1f out* 50/1	
2221	10	1 1/2	**Hester Brook (IRE)**[14] 4322 4-9-3 52 ... (p) AndrewElliott 13	25
			(J G M O'Shea) *sn led: rdn and hdd over 2f out: wknd over 1f out* 18/1	
0P60	11	1 1/4	**Jarvo**[18] 4215 7-9-6 55 ... (b) PatrickMathers 3	26
			(I W McInnes) *prom: rdn over 3f out: wknd over 1f out* 33/1	
0002	12	4	**Stormin Heart (USA)**[8] 4533 3-8-7 50 ... JoeFanning 7	12
			(M Johnston) *mid-div: rdn: hung lft and wknd 3f out* 7/1[3]	
0020	13	9	**The London Gang**[1] 4748 5-8-7 45 ... (b) MarcHalford(3) 14	—
			(W M Brisbourne) *s.i.s: hld up: rdn and wknd over 2f out* 50/1	

1m 56.41s (0.61) **Going Correction** +0.05s/f (Good)
WFA 3 from 4yo+ 8lb — **13** Ran SP% **104.0**
Speed ratings (Par 101): **99,97,94,91,89 88,87,85,85,83 82,79,71**
toteswinger: 1&2 £9.20, 1&3 £13.00. CSF £39.72 CT £261.01 TOTE £3.20: £1.70, £3.30, £2.10; EX 46.30 Place 6: £52.98, Place 5: £32.65..
Owner Beadle Booth Bloodstock Limited **Bred** G And Mrs Middlebrook **Trained** Willoughton, Lincs

FOCUS
A weak handicap, run at a fair pace. The in-form winner is value for further and the form is rated through the runner-up.
Viable Official explanation: jockey said gelding hung right throughout
T/Plt: £97.70 to a £1 stake. Pool: £54,178.77. 404.55 winning tickets. T/Qpdt: £28.70 to a £1 stake. Pool: £3,004.00. 77.45 winning tickets. CR

4798 - (Foreign Racing) - See Raceform Interactive

4759 SLIGO (R-H)
Thursday, August 7

OFFICIAL GOING: Yielding

4799a DERRINSTOWN STUD APPRENTICE H'CAP — 1m 4f
5:40 (5:40) (50-70,72) 4-Y-O+ — £5,588 (£1,302; £574; £331) Stalls Far side

			RPR
1		**Pretty Demanding (IRE)**[5] 4655 4-9-4 60 ... SMGorey 8	66
		(M G Quinlan) *chsd ldrs: hdwy to 2nd 1/2-way: led 5f out: rdn and chal 2f out: hdd ent st: no ex and kpt on same pce* 8/1	
2	1	**Roll Over Rover (IRE)**[21] 4138 4-8-6 52 ... EJMcNamara(4)	56+
		(Noel Meade, Ire) *chsd ldrs early: mid-div bef 1/2-way: 6th 4f out: rdn into 4th 3f out: sn no imp ldrs: kpt on one pce to mod 3rd ins fnl f* 9/4[1]	
3	2	**Her Courtesy (IRE)**[24] 4033 4-9-2 60 ... MACleere(2)	61
		(Jarlath P Fahey, Ire) *disp early: sn chsd ldrs: 4th 1/2-way: impr to 2nd 4f out: rdn in 3rd and no ex over 2f out: kpt on same pce* 20/1	
4	nk	**Tin Town Boy (IRE)**[7] 4574 7-9-9 72 ... (t) SMMcGuinness(7)	73
		(H Rogers, Ire) *hld up towards rr: hdwy fr 4f out: 6th 3f out: 5th ent st and no ex: kpt on same pce* 5/1[2]	
5	4	**Ashby (IRE)**[7] 4574 5-9-5 63 ... (b) APCawley(2)	57
		(Niall Moran, Ire) *hld up: hdwy to 7th 4f out: sn rdn: styd on to mod 6th bef st: kpt on one pce* 7/1	
6	nk	**Amarula Ridge (IRE)**[36] 3616 7-9-1 61 ... (p) JamesPSullivan(4)	55
		(Niall Madden, Ire) *hld up: hdwy to 8th 4f out: sn rdn: kpt on same pce* 16/1	
7	15	**Barnabas (IRE)**[48] 1100 4-9-7 63 ... DGHogan	33
		(C P Donoghue, Ire) *towards rr for most: sme hdwy to 9th 4f out: rdn and kpt on one pce* 20/1	
8	1/2	**Singh Street (IRE)**[220] 5927 9-8-4 50 ... (tp) MJLane(4)	19
		(Donal Hassett, Ire) *chsd ldrs: 5th 1/2-way: rdn and no ex 3f out: wknd bef st* 16/1	
9	12	**Inis Ceithleann (IRE)**[259] 5926 4-9-0 60 ... KarenKenny(4)	10
		(Peter Casey, Ire) *chsd ldrs: 7th 1/2-way: rdn and wknd 4f out* 12/1	
10	1/2	**Dr Knock (IRE)**[95] 5579 10-10-0 70 ... CPGeoghegan	19
		(Michael McElhone, Ire) *sn led: hdd after 3f and chsd ldrs: 3rd 1/2-way: rdn in 4th 5f out: sn no ex and wknd* 13/2[3]	
11	dist	**Savoury Gem (IRE)**[381] 3809 4-8-9 55 ... (t) SMLevey(4)	—
		(P D Deegan, Ire) *chsd ldrs: led after 3f: hdd 5f out: rdn and wknd 4f out: t.o* 20/1	
12	2	**Dobravany (IRE)**[27] 3936 4-9-1 57 ... (b) PBBeggy	—
		(Adrian McGuinness, Ire) *a towards rr: trailing fr over 3f out: t.o* 12/1	
D		**Muskatsturm (GER)**[44] 3354 9-9-8 68 ... MHarley(4)	87+
		(Shaun Harley, Ire) *chsd ldrs: 6th 1/2-way: hdwy to 3rd 4f out: 2nd 3f out: impr to chal 2f out: led ent st: clr fnl f: easily* 8/1	

2m 54.4s (-10.90) — **13** Ran SP% **136.9**
CSF £79.25 CT £198.23 TOTE £9.80: £3.40, £2.90, £1.70; DF 376.50.
Owner Liam Mulryan & M C Fahy **Bred** Moyglare Stud Farm Ltd **Trained** Newmarket, Suffolk

4228 TIPPERARY (L-H)
Thursday, August 7

OFFICIAL GOING: Soft (heavy in places on flat course)

4804a COOLMORE HURRICANE RUN STKS (LISTED RACE) — 7f 100y
7:05 (7:06) 2-Y-O — £26,327 (£7,724; £3,680; £1,253)

			RPR
1		**Westphalia (IRE)**[25] 4005 2-9-1 106 ... JMurtagh 2	107+
		(A P O'Brien, Ire) *hld up in last: prog travelling wl into 3rd 1 1/2f out: led ins fnl f: styd on strly: easily* 1/1[1]	
2	3	**Sawtooth Mountain (USA)**[36] 3618 2-9-1 98 ... JAHeffernan 5	97
		(A P O'Brien, Ire) *led: rdn and hdd under 2f out: no ex and dropped to 3rd fnl f* 14/1	
3	2	**Driving Snow**[25] 4002 2-9-1 97 ... CDHayes 1	92
		(Kevin Prendergast, Ire) *racd in 4th: 3rd ent st: rdn and kpt on same pce fr 2f out* 5/1[3]	
4	1 1/2	**Marina Of Venice (IRE)**[41] 3465 2-8-12 ... KJManning 6	86
		(J S Bolger, Ire) *trckd ldr in 2nd: rdn to ld under 2f out: hdd under 1f out: no imp and dropped to 4th ins fnl f* 7/4[2]	
5	9	**Aerach (USA)** 2-8-12 ... DJMoran 3	65
		(J S Bolger, Ire) *chsd ldrs in 3rd and racd green early: rdn and dropped to 4th 3f out: sn no imp* 40/1	
R		**High Queen (IRE)**[11] 4468 2-8-12 ... WJLee 4	—
		(T Stack, Ire) *lft stalls and ref to r* 20/1	

1m 39.77s (99.77) — **6** Ran SP% **116.9**
CSF £17.69 TOTE £1.50: £1.30, £3.80; DF 7.70.
Owner Michael Tabor **Bred** Lynch Bages Ltd & Samac Ltd **Trained** Ballydoyle, Co Tipperary

NOTEBOOK
Westphalia(IRE) relished this step up a longer trip and eventually ran out an easy winner. Given time to find his stride early on, he picked off each of his rivals in the home straight without really having to come out of third gear, and looked right at home on the softer surface. This was also the first time he has raced around a bend and it suited his style. He basically ourclassed his rivals here and he does show a tendency to carry his head high when put under pressure, but this was his best effort to date all the same. (op 10/11 tchd 11/10)
Sawtooth Mountain(USA) set the race up from the front for his winning stable companion and performed very close to his official mark in defeat. on ground he probably found too easy for his own liking. (op 12/1)
Driving Snow had won a decent-looking maiden at the Curragh on his previous outing, but he was found out on this softer surface. He still ran close enough to his debut form with the runner-up, however, and the best of him has probably still to be seen. (op 11/2 tchd 6/1)
Marina Of Venice(IRE) had looked good when winning her maiden at the Curragh, but that form has not worked out so far and she was a spent force at the final furlong marker on this step up in class. (op 2/1)

4805 - (Foreign Racing) - See Raceform Interactive

4768 BRIGHTON (L-H)
Friday, August 8

OFFICIAL GOING: Good (good to firm in places; 7.7)
Wind: Moderate, across Weather: Cloudy

4806 TOTEPLACEPOT MAIDEN H'CAP — 6f 209y
2:30 (2:33) (Class 6) (0-65,62) 3-Y-O+ — £2,396 (£712; £356; £177) Stalls Low

Form				RPR
0605	1		**Spent**[32] 3780 3-9-9 58 ... ChrisCatlin 4	64
			(Mouse Hamilton-Fairley) *mid-div on outside: rdn over 2f out: edgd alone towards stands' rail over 1f out: styd on wl to ld fnl strides* 5/1[2]	
600-	2	1/2	**Royal Sovereign (IRE)**[340] 5081 3-9-9 58 ... OscarUrbina 7	63
			(G C H Chung) *t.k.h: in tch: led and hrd rdn 2f out: kpt on wl: ct fnl strides* 33/1	
4040	3	3/4	**Astroangel**[9] 4540 4-9-5 55 ... AshleyMorgan(7) 9	60
			(M H Tompkins) *lost 7l s: bhd tl rdn and hdwy fr 2f out: drvn to chal 1f out: nt qckn nr fin* 9/2[1]	
03	4	nk	**Duty Doctor**[17] 4278 3-9-8 62 ... HaddenFrost(5) 13	64
			(S Kirk) *chsd ldrs: hrd rdn 2f out: kpt on to chal fnl f: nt qckn nr fin* 9/2[1]	
0005	5	shd	**Cow Girl (IRE)**[1] 4793 4-8-13 45 ... JerryO'Dwyer(3) 2	49
			(Miss Gay Kelleway) *s.i.s: bhd tl rdn and hdwy fr 2f out: pressed ldrs ins fnl f: kpt on* 6/1[3]	
0-00	6	2 3/4	**Come On Nellie (IRE)**[15] 4322 4-9-2 45 ... TGMcLaughlin 12	41
			(J G M O'Shea) *towards rr and sn pushed along: edgd lft and styd on fnl f: nvr nrr* 40/1	
4400	7	2 1/4	**Ambrix (IRE)**[18] 4253 3-9-7 56 ... SamHitchcott 1	44
			(M R Channon) *t.k.h in rr of midfield: effrt and in tch 2f out: no ex over 1f out* 20/1	
0043	8	3/4	**Pajada**[7] 4580 4-8-9 45 ... (v) SeanPalmer(7) 11	33
			(M D I Usher) *prom tl edgd lft and wknd over 1f out* 12/1	
0000	9	nk	**Little Cee (IRE)**[43] 3395 3-8-12 50 ... MarcHalford(3) 3	36
			(D R C Elsworth) *in rr of midfield: hrd rdn 3f out: n.d after* 14/1	
0-00	10	2 1/2	**Ducal Pip Squeak**[31] 3825 4-9-4 54 ... GihanArnolda(7) 8	35
			(A B Haynes) *hld up in midfield: effrt whn n.m.r and bmpd over 2f out: sn lost pl* 20/1	
3002	11	hd	**Micheals Boy (IRE)**[15] 4338 3-9-9 58 ... (v) FergusSweeney 10	36
			(J R Boyle) *chsd ldr: led briefly over 2f out: wknd over 1f out* 7/1	
3006	12	8	**Bahamian Blue (IRE)**[24] 4056 3-8-11 49 ... (b) RussellKennemore(3) 6	6
			(P G Murphy) *led tl over 2f out: sn wknd* 18/1	
-050	13	20	**Marvin Gardens**[17] 4284 5-8-13 45 ... TolleyDean(3) 5	—
			(P S McEntee) *prom: hrd rdn 3f out: sn wknd: bhd whn eased fnl f* 11/1	

1m 24.11s (1.01) **Going Correction** -0.025s/f (Good)
WFA 3 from 4yo+ 6lb — **13** Ran SP% **122.7**
Speed ratings (Par 101): **93,92,91,91,91 87,85,84,84,81 81,71,49**
toteswinger: 1&2 £38.20, 1&3 £9.20, 2&3 £35.00. CSF £172.59 CT £811.79 TOTE £6.50: £2.00, £8.00, £2.20; EX 188.50 TRIFECTA Not won..
Owner Hamilton-Fairley Racing **Bred** Downland Bloodstock **Trained** Bramshill, Hants

FOCUS
A weak maiden handicap that seems sound but limited if rated around the third and fourth. The winner ended up on the stands' rail, but only because he edged there in the last furlong and a half. However, that set a pattern that became established later in the afternoon.

The Form Book, Raceform Ltd, Compton, RG20 6NL

Bahamian Blue(IRE) Official explanation: jockey said gelding hung both ways

4807 FOR A QUALITY BETTING EXPERIENCE CHOOSE BETTER CLAIMING STKS 7f 214y

3:00 (3:00) (Class 6) 3-Y-O+ £2,072 (£616; £308; £153) Stalls Low

Form RPR

1032 **1** **Steig (IRE)**[14] 4386 5-9-0 70 JamesDoyle 13 63
(Carl Llewellyn) *trckd ldr: led over 4f out and led field to stands' side: rdn and styd on fnl 2f: a in control* **11/8**[1]

0000 **2** *1 ¼* **Rockjumper**[24] 4056 3-8-3 45 EmmettStack(3) 6 57+
(H Morrison) *prom: losing pl whn bdly squeezed over 2f out: rallied wl u.p fr over 1f out: wnt 2nd on line* **50/1**

2530 **3** *hd* **Casablanca Minx (IRE)**[6] 4635 5-8-4 54(b) Louis-PhilippeBeuzelin(5) 12 55
(Miss Gay Kelleway) *dwlt: hld up in midfield: effrt and swtchd lft wl over 1f out: edgd lft and chsd wnr fnl f: kpt on same pce: lost 2nd on line* **12/1**

0100 **4** *1 ¼* **Ten To The Dozen**[7] 4597 5-9-0 63 ChrisCatlin 8 57
(P W Hiatt) *chsd ldrs: rdn 3f out: no ex fnl f* **13/2**[3]

0030 **5** *hd* **Takitwo**[44] 3383 5-8-11 54 DaneO'Neill 3 53
(P D Cundell) *hld up in rr: shkn up and hdwy towards centre 2f out: styd on same pce: no imp* **9/2**[2]

3505 **6** *4* **Looter (FR)**[9] 4533 3-8-4 58 RichardKingscote 9 42
(J L Dunlop) *chsd ldrs: rdn 4f out: wknd over 1f out* **7/1**

0543 **7** *1 ½* **Personify**[3] 4707 6-8-9 52 (b) KevinGhunowa(3) 11 42
(R A Harris) *in rr of mid-div: rdn and edgd lft 2f out: nt pce to chal* **9/1**

-000 **8** *1* **Lady Maya**[15] 4336 3-7-6 41 (v) AndreaAtzeni(7) 7 31
(Dr J R J Naylor) *towards rr: mod effrt towards centre 2f out: unable to chal* **50/1**

2300 **9** *12* **Arturius (IRE)**[94] 1898 6-9-2 60 (b[1]) TGMcLaughlin 4 16
(R A Harris) *dwlt: plld hrd: sn rushed up and prom: wknd over 2f out* **25/1**

-066 **10** *6* **Illusionary**[35] 3692 3-8-5 40 AdrianMcCarthy 2 —
(J G Portman) *led tl over 4f out: hrd rdn and wknd over 2f out* **80/1**

0500 **11** *7* **Goodwood Spirit**[56] 2988 6-8-9 45 (v) TolleyDean(3) 10 —
(J M Bradley) *bhd: drvn along 3f out: no rspnse* **50/1**

1m 35.97s (-0.03) **Going Correction** -0.025s/f (Good)
WFA 3 from 4yo+ 7lb 11 Ran SP% **114.8**
Speed ratings (Par 101): **99,97,97,96,96 92,90,89,77,71 64**
toteswinger: 1&2 £17.10, 1&3 £14.70, 2&3 £14.70. CSF £102.23 TOTE £2.10: £1.10, £12.00, £3.20; EX 94.20 Trifecta £315.40 Part won. Pool: £426.27. 0.79 winning units..
Owner Something In The City 2 **Bred** Elisabeth And Neil Draper **Trained** Upper Lambourn, Berks
■ Stewards' Enquiry : Louis-Philippe Beuzelin one-day ban: careless riding (Aug 23)

FOCUS
A routine claimer, but the winner had 12lb to spare over his rivals and was always in charge. The form makes sense rated around the third to fifth. The runners all came to the stands' side of the course in the straight.

4808 AJC UK (S) STKS 5f 213y

3:30 (3:30) (Class 6) 3-Y-O+ £1,942 (£578; £288; £144) Stalls Low

Form RPR

1540 **1** **Who's Winning (IRE)**[17] 4273 7-9-7 57 (t) GeorgeBaker 6 64
(B G Powell) *racd in 5th: c towards stands' side st: effrt over 2f out: r.o u.p to ld jst ins fnl f: in control nr fin* **4/1**[1]

-632 **2** *½* **Razzano (IRE)**[87] 2069 4-8-4 50 AndreaAtzeni(7) 8 52
(A M Hales) *mid-div: hdwy on stands' rail 2f out: pressed wnr ins fnl f: kpt on: hld nr fin* **5/1**[3]

3603 **3** *2* **Cleveland**[32] 3779 6-9-4 50 RussellKennemore(3) 1 56
(R Hollinshead) *led at gd pce: c towards stands' side st: hrd rdn and hdd jst ins fnl f: one pce* **10/1**

0060 **4** *2* **Nordic Light (USA)**[24] 4052 4-8-13 55 (b) TolleyDean(3) 2 44
(J M Bradley) *prom: led far side pair over 2f out: hrd rdn and wknd 1f out* **25/1**

0015 **5** *shd* **Klarity**[23] 4073 3-8-9 50 (e) JerryO'Dwyer(3) 12 43
(J Pearce) *plld hrd early: towards rr: c towards stands' side st: rdn over 2f out: styd on u.p: nt rch ldrs* **14/1**

5012 **6** *1 ¼* **Mannello**[15] 4336 5-9-2 53 (b) RichardThomas 11 40
(Jim Best) *chsd ldrs: styd centre st: hrd rdn 2f out: wknd over 1f out* **9/2**[2]

-006 **7** *1* **Zeeuw (IRE)**[7] 4580 4-9-2 60 OscarUrbina 4 37
(D J Coakley) *mid-div: c towards stands' side st: rdn over 2f out: no imp* **16/1**

0500 **8** *nk* **Archilini**[7] 4580 3-8-12 57 (p) ChrisCatlin 5 35
(M Sheppard) *plld hrd early: bhd: styd centre st: rdn over 2f out: n.d* **16/1**

4015 **9** *1* **Majestical (IRE)**[11] 4476 6-9-4 58 (p) KevinGhunowa(3) 7 38
(R A Harris) *racd in 6th: c towards stands' side st: rdn over 2f out: edgd lft: sn wknd* **5/1**[3]

0006 **10** *1 ¼* **Coup D'Etat**[3] 4707 6-8-11 55 (b) HaddenFrost(5) 10 29
(R A Harris) *prom: led far side pair 3f out tl over 2f out: hrd rdn and: wknd wl over 1f out* **7/1**

0000 **11** *2* **Peruvian Style (IRE)**[7] 4580 7-9-2 40 (p) DaneO'Neill 9 22
(J M Bradley) *c towards stands' side st: rdn 3f out: a bhd* **33/1**

1m 10.73s (0.53) **Going Correction** -0.025s/f (Good)
WFA 3 from 4yo+ 4lb 11 Ran SP% **118.3**
Speed ratings (Par 101): **95,94,91,88,87 87,85,85,84,82 79**
toteswinger: 1&2 £6.70, 1&3 £8.50, 2&3 £6.30. CSF £23.98 TOTE £4.20: £1.60, £2.20, £3.30; EX 27.90 Trifecta £162.30 Pool: £351.00. 1.60 winning units..There was no bid for the winner.
Owner Tony Head and Caroline Andrus **Bred** Colin Kennedy **Trained** Upper Lambourn, Berks

FOCUS
A competitive seller, with the winner setting a respectable standard for the grade backed up by the second. Only two runners stayed on the far rail, with two more remaining in the middle; the others all came towards the stands' rail

4809 TOTESWINGER BRIGHTON ROCKET H'CAP 5f 213y

4:00 (4:01) (Class 4) (0-80,79) 3-Y-O+

£6,231 (£1,866; £933; £467; £233; £117) Stalls Low

Form RPR

0021 **1** **Billion Dollar Kid**[24] 4056 3-9-7 79 (t) KevinGhunowa(3) 7 89
(R A Harris) *chsd ldr: rdn 2f out: drvn to ld fnl 75yds* **11/2**[3]

4132 **2** *¾* **Peter Island (FR)**[29] 3890 5-9-9 74 (v) ChrisCatlin 9 82
(J Gallagher) *led at gd gallop and claimed stands' rail: kpt on wl fnl 2f: hdd and jst outpcd fnl 75yds* **7/2**[1]

3234 **3** *½* **Cosmic Destiny (IRE)**[8] 4563 6-9-4 69 GeorgeBaker 2 76
(E F Vaughan) *t.k.h in midfield: smooth hdwy 2f out: pressed ldrs over 1f out: hrd rdn and nt qckn ins fnl f* **9/1**

5526 **4** *3 ½* **Louphole**[15] 4341 6-9-4 69 FergusSweeney 4 65
(P J Makin) *stdd s: bhd: hdwy 2f out: no further prog over 1f out* **9/2**[2]

650 **5** *¾* **Thoughtsofstardom**[16] 4313 5-8-11 62 JamesDoyle 3 55
(P S McEntee) *chsd ldrs: shkn up fnl 2f: no ex 1f out* **11/1**

6050 **6** *hd* **Flying Goose (IRE)**[7] 4586 4-9-11 76 TGMcLaughlin 1 69
(R A Harris) *s.s: rdn 3f out: wl bhd tl sme hdwy over 1f out: hrd rdn: nt rch ldrs* **12/1**

2215 **7** *¾* **Mandarin Spirit (IRE)**[22] 4125 8-9-0 65 OscarUrbina 8 55
(G C H Chung) *half-rrd s: hld up in rr of midfield: drvn along over 2f out: nt pce to chal* **11/2**[3]

2404 **8** *hd* **Punching**[11] 4478 4-9-2 67 (v[1]) DaneO'Neill 6 57
(Miss Gay Kelleway) *hld up in tch: rdn over 2f out: wknd over 1f out* **11/2**[3]

3-00 **9** *8* **Mudhish (IRE)**[21] 4174 3-8-13 73 (b) Louis-PhilippeBeuzelin(5) 5 36
(C E Brittain) *mid-div: outpcd 3f out: drvn along and n.d after* **20/1**

0-00 **10** *7* **Calabaza**[20] 4186 6-8-6 60 (p) TolleyDean(3) 10 2
(M J Attwater) *prom: rdn over 2f out: sn wknd* **33/1**

69.20 secs (-1.00) **Going Correction** -0.025s/f (Good)
WFA 3 from 4yo+ 4lb 10 Ran SP% **120.3**
Speed ratings (Par 105): **105,104,103,98,97 97,96,96,85,76**
toteswinger: 1&2 £2.30, 1&3 £7.30, 2&3 £5.10. CSF £25.96 CT £178.77 TOTE £6.20: £2.30, £1.60, £3.50; EX 28.70 Trifecta £285.90 Part won. Pool: £386.42. 0.59 winning units..
Owner Mrs J Bloomfield **Bred** Catridge Farm Stud And Mrs J Hall **Trained** Earlswood, Monmouths

FOCUS
A fair race for the track, run at a good pace and the form looks pretty solid rated around the placed horses. The runners all came towards the stands' rail.

Calabaza Official explanation: trainer said gelding had bled from the nose

4810 SPEARMINT RHINO ROUGE BRIGHTON H'CAP 1m 1f 209y

4:30 (4:32) (Class 6) (0-60,60) 3-Y-O £2,331 (£693; £346; £173) Stalls High

Form RPR

4632 **1** **Solo River**[15] 4326 3-8-13 55 ChrisCatlin 8 67
(P J Makin) *prom: effrt over 2f out: edgd lft fr over 1f out: led ins fnl f: drvn out* **10/3**[1]

6-60 **2** *1* **Bosamcliff (IRE)**[41] 3483 3-9-0 56 DaneO'Neill 3 66
(A B Haynes) *chsd ldrs: led wl over 1f out tl ins fnl f: carried lft: kpt on u.p* **16/1**

6526 **3** *5* **Pretty Officer (USA)**[18] 4260 3-8-3 52 WilliamCarson(7) 12 52
(Rae Guest) *in tch: effrt over 2f out: one pce appr fnl f* **10/3**[1]

0-00 **4** *½* **Crimsonwing (IRE)**[24] 4053 3-9-0 56 OscarUrbina 5 55
(A M Hales) *mid-div: effrt over 2f out: styd on slowly u.p: nt pce to chal* **11/1**

0-00 **5** *1 ¾* **Epsom Salts**[23] 4086 3-8-11 53 IanMongan 11 49
(P M Phelan) *dwlt: sn in midfield: rdn over 2f out: no imp* **14/1**

0-04 **6** *1* **Artistic Light**[35] 3667 3-9-1 57 GeorgeBaker 2 51
(W R Muir) *hld up in tch: rdn to chse ldrs 2f out: no ex over 1f out* **8/1**[3]

000 **7** *nk* **Owain James**[31] 3264 3-7-11 46 oh1 (b[1]) SophieDoyle(7) 9 39
(M Salaman) *plld hrd early: bhd: rdn 3f out: sme late hdwy* **50/1**

0542 **8** *1 ¼* **Mganga**[17] 4278 3-8-13 60 MCGeran(5) 6 50
(M R Channon) *bhd: rdn over 3f out: nvr trbld ldrs* **11/2**[2]

4003 **9** *¾* **Space Pirate**[24] 4049 3-8-8 53 (v) JerryO'Dwyer(3) 1 42
(J Pearce) *dwlt: sn pressing ldr: led over 3f out tl wl over 1f out: sn wknd* **10/1**

0530 **10** *¾* **Bobal Girl**[18] 4247 3-8-13 55 (b[1]) RichardKingscote 7 42
(E F Vaughan) *a bhd: drvn along 3f out: nvr a factor* **14/1**

-006 **11** *nk* **Xaravella (IRE)**[15] 4326 3-8-3 48 ow1 KevinGhunowa(3) 10 35
(J G M O'Shea) *bhd: modest effrt on outside 4f out: n.d* **25/1**

0000 **12** *6* **Harlequinn Danseur (IRE)**[39] 3555 3-8-4 46 oh1(b) AdrianMcCarthy 14 21
(G L Moore) *plld hrd early: mid-div: rdn along 5f out: bhd fnl 3f* **14/1**

0000 **13** *1 ½* **Jordi Roper (IRE)**[6] 4653 3-8-10 55 (p) TolleyDean(3) 13 27
(S Parr) *led tl over 3f out: wknd over 2f out* **20/1**

0-60 **14** *21* **Dhaka Dazzle**[173] 597 3-8-6 48 (t) FrankieMcDonald 4 —
(M F Harris) *sn towards rr: rdn 6f out: no ch fnl 3f* **66/1**

2m 4.43s (0.83) **Going Correction** -0.025s/f (Good) **14 Ran SP% 128.0**
Speed ratings (Par 98): **95,94,90,89,88 87,87,86,85,85 84,80,78,62**
toteswinger: 1&2 £14.60, 1&3 £3.70, 2&3 £19.30. CSF £64.83 CT £202.33 TOTE £3.30: £1.70, £6.60, £1.90; EX 69.20 Trifecta £252.90 Part won. Pool: £341.80. 0.61 winning units..
Owner Ten Of Hearts II **Bred** D J And Mrs Deer **Trained** Ogbourne Maisey, Wilts

FOCUS
A desperate race best rated around the third and fourth. With the exception of the first two, none of the runners emerged with much credit. The runners all came towards the stands' rail.

Space Pirate Official explanation: jockey said colt had run too free

4811 DANCO H'CAP 1m 3f 196y

5:00 (5:03) (Class 6) (0-65,64) 3-Y-O+ £2,331 (£693; £346; £173) Stalls High

Form RPR

0320 **1** **Soundbyte**[25] 4026 3-8-7 54 ow1 FergusSweeney 13 66+
(J Gallagher) *t.k.h towards rr: stdy hdwy whn hmpd over 3f out: swtchd lft and briefly nt clr run over 2f out: styd on to ld fnl 30yds* **20/1**

30-0 **2** *½* **She's So Pretty (IRE)**[103] 1643 4-9-6 56 (b[1]) GeorgeBaker 6 65
(G L Moore) *hld up in tch gng strly: led over 4f out and claimed stands' rail: hrd rdn fnl f: kpt on: hdd fnl 30yds* **9/2**[2]

6363 **3** *½* **Dusk**[23] 4086 3-9-2 63 (b) DaneO'Neill 5 71
(J L Dunlop) *dwlt: hld up in rr: hdwy 4f out: drvn to chal ins fnl 2f: nt qckn fnl 50yds* **5/2**[1]

4045 **4** *3 ¼* **Bienheureux**[21] 4155 7-9-4 61 (t) KylieManser(7) 12 64
(Miss Gay Kelleway) *hld up towards rr: stdy hdwy over 3f out: wnt 3rd 2f out: one pce appr fnl f* **10/1**

3031 **5** *nk* **Looks The Business (IRE)**[4] 3321 7-8-13 56 (tp) WilliamCarson(7) 7 59
(W G M Turner) *mid-div: hdwy to chse ldrs 4f out: one pce fnl 2f* **10/1**

4 **6** *16* **Moonshine Creek**[28] 3912 6-9-6 56 ChrisCatlin 2 33
(P W Hiatt) *dwlt: sn in midfield: hdwy over 4f out: wknd 2f out* **8/1**

00/6 **7** *3 ½* **Jomelamin**[22] 4105 6-8-9 45 (t) SamHitchcott 1 17
(M Sheppard) *hld up and bhd: reminders over 6f out: gd hdwy 5f out: wknd over 2f out* **20/1**

0-06 **8** *26* **Muraco**[59] 2914 4-9-11 64 JerryO'Dwyer(3) 3 —
(A M Hales) *led tl over 4f out: outpcd and starting to lose pl whn n.m.r 3f out: eased* **25/1**

500 **9** *8* **Makai**[14] 4391 5-8-9 45 (b) RichardKingscote 14 —
(M R Hoad) *in tch: rdn to chse ldrs 4f out: wknd over 3f out: bhd and eased fnl 2f* **20/1**

0206 **10** *15* **Classic Hall (IRE)**[30] 3844 5-8-9 45 (p) JamesDoyle 8 —
(J Akehurst) *w ldrs tl wknd qckly over 5f out: bhd and eased fnl 2f* **25/1**

0020 **11** *2* **Irish Ballad**[17] 4275 6-9-0 50 (t) IanMongan 9 —
(S Dow) *chsd ldrs: rdn and wknd over 3f out: bhd and eased fnl 2f* **13/2**[3]

00/1 **12** *15* **Cordage (IRE)**[55] 3025 6-9-0 50 FrankieMcDonald 4 —
(M F Harris) *prom tl wknd qckly 5f out: wl bhd and eased fnl 2f* **10/1**

-460 **13** *9* **Tenement (IRE)**[20] 4182 4-8-6 **45**.................................. TolleyDean(3) 10 —
(Jamie Poulton) *sn towards rr: drvn along 6f out: sn no ch: eased fnl 2f* **20/1**

2m 33.41s (0.71) **Going Correction** -0.025s/f (Good)
WFA 3 from 4yo+ 11lb **13** Ran SP% **125.2**
Speed ratings (Par 101): **96,95,95,93,92 82,79,62,57,47 45,35,29**
toteswinger: 1&2 £24.60, 1&3 £14.00, 2&3 £3.90. CSF £103.39 CT £314.62 TOTE £24.60: £5.50, £2.00, £1.70; EX 215.10 TRIFECTA Not won..
Owner Oliver Parsons **Bred** Mrs R J Gallagher **Trained** Moreton-in-Marsh, Gloucs

FOCUS
Modest stuff with the runnerup rated to last year's form. After the first five, the field were strung out like three-mile chasers. The pace was modest until halfway, and the runners all came towards the stands' rail off the final turn.
Muraco Official explanation: jockey said gelding had no more to give

4812 TOTEEXACTA H'CAP — 5f 59y
5:30 (5:31) (Class 6) (0-60,61) 3-Y-0+ **£2,331** (£693; £346; £173) **Stalls** Low

Form RPR
0605 **1** **Jayanjay**[4] 4693 9-9-0 **53**.................................. RichardSmith 5 62
(B R Johnson) *prom: led over 1f out: maintained narrow ld thrght fnl f: all out* **5/1**[3]
4346 **2** *shd* **Azygous**[50] 3159 5-9-7 **60**..........................(p) DaneO'Neill 1 69
(J Akehurst) *led at gd pce tl over 1f out: rallied gamely: jst pipped* **11/4**[1]
5314 **3** *1 ¼* **Night Prospector**[1] 4765 8-9-5 **61** 6ex..........................(p) KevinGhunowa(3) 8 66
(R A Harris) *chsd ldrs: hrd rdn fnl 2f: kpt on: a hld by first 2* **5/1**[3]
3200 **4** *1* **Harrison's Flyer (IRE)**[9] 4535 7-8-13 **57**..........................(p) MCGeran(5) 2 58
(J M Bradley) *towards rr: hrd rdn over 1f out: styd on fnl f* **4/1**[2]
060 **5** *shd* **Jucebabe**[17] 4273 5-8-10 **52**..........................(p) TolleyDean(3) 7 53
(J L Spearing) *in tch: effrt over 2f out: one pce appr fnl f* **7/1**
0044 **6** *½* **Indian Lady (IRE)**[7] 4580 5-8-7 **46** oh1..........................(b) SamHitchcott 3 45
(Mrs A L M King) *bhd: rdn and hdwy 2f out: no ex fnl f* **15/2**
1000 **7** *¾* **Lithaam (IRE)**[17] 4285 4-9-1 **54**..........................(p) ChrisCatlin 4 50
(J M Bradley) *prom tl wknd over 1f out* **16/1**
5000 **8** *3* **Rosie Cross (IRE)**[158] 774 4-8-6 **52**.................. DanielBlackett(7) 9 37
(Eve Johnson Houghton) *wnt rt s: in rr: hdwy on outside and in tch after 2f: wknd wl over 1f out* **16/1**
4055 **9** *3 ¾* **Walragnek**[14] 4388 4-9-1 **54**.................................. TGMcLaughlin 6 26
(J G M O'Shea) *bhd: rdn 3f out: nvr wnt pce* **12/1**

61.41 secs (-0.89) **Going Correction** -0.025s/f (Good)
WFA 3 from 4yo+ 3lb **9** Ran SP% **123.7**
Speed ratings (Par 101): **106,105,103,102,102 101,100,95,89**
toteswinger: 1&2 £4.90, 1&3 £4.30, 2&3 £3.50. CSF £20.69 CT £76.15 TOTE £7.00: £2.30, £1.50, £1.40; EX 25.20 Trifecta £154.80 Pool: £395.38. 1.89 winning units. Place 6: £32.15, Place 5: £13.81..
Owner Peter Crate **Bred** P D Crate **Trained** Ashtead, Surrey
■ Stewards' Enquiry : Richard Smith one-day ban: excessive use of the whip (Aug 23)

FOCUS
Modest in terms of handicap ratings, but these proven spinters are useful at their level with the runner-up setting the standard. The runners all came towards the stands' rail.
T/Jkpt: Not won. T/Plt: £95.90 to a £1 stake. Pool: £81,452.70. 619.74 winning tickets. T/Qpdt: £10.60 to a £1 stake. Pool: £4,616.80. 319.50 winning tickets. LM

4780 HAYDOCK (L-H)
Friday, August 8

OFFICIAL GOING: Good to soft (soft in places) (6.8)
Rail realignment added 25yards to advertised distances on round course.
Wind: Light against Weather: Warm with sunny periods

4813 STEVE DONOHUE APPRENTICE H'CAP — 1m 30y
6:05 (6:05) (Class 5) (0-70,71) 4-Y-0+ **£3,238** (£963; £481; £240) **Stalls** Low

Form RPR
6430 **1** **Tanforan**[4] 4683 6-8-5 **55**.................................. BillyCray(5) 7 65
(B P J Baugh) *hld up in midfield: hdwy 1/2-way: swtchd rt and rdn to chse ldrs 2f out: drvn ent fnl f: styd on to ld nr fin* **11/1**
5021 **2** *nk* **Glenridding**[7] 4605 4-9-7 **71** 6ex.................................. RosieJessop(5) 11 80
(J G Given) *led: rdn 2f out: kpt on u.p ins fnl f tl hdd and no ex nr fin* **3/1**[1]
6244 **3** *½* **Pitbull**[7] 4597 5-8-10 **60**..........................(p) FrederikTylicki(5) 8 68
(Mrs G S Rees) *hld up towards rr: stdy hdwy 1/2-way: hdwy to chse ldng pair over 2f out: drvn to chal wl over 1f out and ev ch tl no ex last 50yds* **7/2**[2]
-040 **4** *2 ½* **Gracie's Gift (IRE)**[66] 2706 6-8-7 **52**.................................. JamieMoriarty 3 54
(A G Newcombe) *hld up in rr: hdwy 3f out: rdn 2f out: styd on ins fnl f: nrst fin* **9/1**
0326 **5** *3* **Society Music (IRE)**[7] 4597 6-9-10 **69**..........................(p) NeilBrown 10 64
(M Dods) *towards rr: hdwy on outer 3f out: rdn over 2f out: styd on ins fnl f: nrst fin* **17/2**
0200 **6** *hd* **Joshua's Gold (IRE)**[33] 3755 7-8-10 **62**..........................(v) PaulPickard(7) 6 57
(D Carroll) *trckd ldr: hdwy 4f out: rdn along wl over 2f out: drvn and wknd wl over 1f out* **16/1**
1400 **7** *nk* **Terminate (GER)**[59] 2908 6-8-11 **59**.................................. JackMitchell(3) 2 53
(Ian Williams) *hld up in rr: hdwy 3f out: swtchd to wd outside and rdn to chse ldrs 2f out: sn drvn and kpt on same pce* **12/1**
0025 **8** *4* **Fern House (IRE)**[22] 4118 6-8-5 **50** oh1.................................. AndrewMullen 4 35
(Bruce Hellier) *s.i.s: a towards rr* **22/1**
-302 **9** *1 ½* **Monda**[14] 4368 6-8-5 **55**.................................. AmyBaker(5) 5 37
(M Hill) *trckd ldrs: hdwy on outer 3f out: rdn along over 2f out: grad wknd* **8/1**[3]
605- **10** *1* **United Nations**[232] 7200 7-9-3 **65**.................................. AshleyHamblett(3) 13 44
(N Wilson) *stdd s and hld up in rr: hdwy over 3f out: rdn along wl over 2f out and sn btn* **25/1**
0340 **11** *13* **Boppys Pride**[12] 4458 5-8-5 **50** oh3.................................. DuranFentiman 9 —
(P T Midgley) *chsd ldng pair: rdn along 3f out and sn wknd* **22/1**
-510 **12** *8* **Derricks Dotty**[27] 3951 4-8-13 **63**..........................(vt) SimonPearce(5) 1 —
(N J Vaughan) *chsd ldng pair: rdn along on inner over 3f out and sn wknd* **14/1**

1m 47.77s (3.97) **Going Correction** +0.425s/f (Yiel) **12** Ran SP% **120.0**
Speed ratings (Par 103): **97,96,96,93,90 90,90,86,84,83 70,62**
toteswinger: 1&2 £6.60, 1&3 £4.60, 2&3 £2.00. CSF £43.40 CT £145.09 TOTE £12.30: £3.40, £1.50, £1.70; EX 78.90.
Owner F Gillespie **Bred** Bearstone Stud **Trained** Audley, Staffs
■ Stewards' Enquiry : Paul Pickard two-day ban: excessive use of the whip (Aug 23 & tbn)
Billy Cray one-day ban: excessive use of the whip (Aug 23)
Frederik Tylicki two-day ban: excessive use of the whip (Aug 23-24)

FOCUS
A modest handicap, confined to apprentice riders, run at a sound pace. The form looks fair and solid enough with the first three coming clear.

4814 LAMBRINI CLAIMING STKS — 1m 2f 120y
6:35 (6:35) (Class 5) 3-4-Y-0 **£3,238** (£963; £481; £240) **Stalls** High

Form RPR
6010 **1** **Persian Peril**[13] 4419 4-9-12 72.................................. TomEaves 5 76
(G A Swinbank) *hld up in rr: smooth hdwy over 3f out: led over 2f out and sn rdn: drvn over 1f out: styd on u.p fnl f* **3/1**[3]
5022 **2** *3* **Bocciani (GER)**[3] 4701 3-8-8 65.................................. PaulHanagan 3 62
(A Berry) *prom: effrt 3f out: rdn to chal 2f out and ev ch: hit in face by opponent's whip wl over 1f out: sn drvn: hung lft and one pce* **11/4**[2]
0000 **3** *12* **Petrosian**[7] 4592 4-8-8 55.................................. CharlotteKerton(7) 1 37
(W Clay) *cl up: rdn to ld briefly 3f out: sn hdd and outpcd fnl 2f* **20/1**
0504 **4** *9* **Harvest Joy (IRE)**[24] 4065 4-9-1 67..........................(b) NCallan 4 19
(J Gallagher) *led: rdn along and hdd 3f out: sn wknd* **2/1**[1]
0500 **5** *12* **Alseraaj (USA)**[5] 4663 3-8-7 69..........................(t) StephenDonohoe 2 —
(Ian Williams) *trckd ldrs: smooth hdwy to chal over 3f out: sn rdn and wknd qckly over 2f out* **4/1**

2m 21.41s (4.71) **Going Correction** +0.425s/f (Yiel)
WFA 3 from 4yo 10lb **5** Ran SP% **109.8**
Speed ratings (Par 103): **99,96,88,81,72**
CSF £11.46 TOTE £3.90: £1.80, £1.40; EX 9.60.
Owner Mrs J Porter **Bred** Mrs P Lewis **Trained** Melsonby, N Yorks

FOCUS
A modest little claimer which saw the first pair come clear and not a race to rate too positively.

4815 EBF HAYDOCK PARK PONY CLUB MAIDEN STKS — 6f
7:05 (7:06) (Class 5) 2-Y-0 **£3,885** (£1,156; £577; £288) **Stalls** Centre

Form RPR
03 **1** **Come And Go (UAE)**[16] 4289 2-9-3 0.................................. NCallan 9 80
(G A Swinbank) *cl up: led 1/2-way: rdn wl over 1f out: drvn ins fnl f and styd on gamely* **8/1**[3]
2032 **2** *nk* **Servoca (CAN)**[14] 4373 2-9-3 88.................................. PaulHanagan 2 79
(B W Hills) *trckd ldrs: hdwy 1/2-way: effrt to chal wl over 1f out: sn rdn and ev ch tl drvn and no ex wl ins fnl f* **4/5**[1]
00 **3** *4 ½* **Gilbertian**[44] 3358 2-8-12 0.................................. JackMitchell(5) 10 66
(R M Beckett) *racd wd: rdn along towards rr 1/2-way: hdwy 2f out: kpt on wl u.p ins fnl f: nrst fin* **33/1**
4 *1 ½* **Dark Echoes** 2-9-3 0.................................. TonyHamilton 6 61
(Jedd O'Keeffe) *prom: rdn along and outpcd 1/2-way: styd on ins fnl f* **25/1**
00 **5** *½* **Real Dandy**[7] 4593 2-9-3 0.................................. MartinDwyer 7 60
(J G Given) *chsd ldrs: rdn along wl over 2f out: kpt on same pce* **25/1**
3 **6** *nk* **Justonefortheroad**[19] 4213 2-9-3 0.................................. GregFairley 3 59
(N J Vaughan) *led: hdd 1/2-way and sn rdn along: drvn and edgd lft over 1f out: sn wknd* **11/4**[2]
7 *2* **Lyric Art (USA)** 2-8-12 0.................................. TomEaves 1 48
(B Smart) *towards rr on outer: rdn along 1/2-way: n.d* **10/1**
5 **8** *3* **Shanavaz**[20] 4176 2-8-12 0.................................. DaleGibson 8 39
(Mrs G S Rees) *dwlt: chsd ldrs: rdn along 1/2-way and sn wknd* **33/1**
0 **9** *1 ¾* **Dark Desert**[17] 4274 2-9-0 0.................................. JamieMoriarty(3) 5 38
(A G Newcombe) *a towards rr* **50/1**
10 *6* **Our Angel** 2-8-9 0.................................. DuranFentiman(3) 4 15
(Ms N M Hugo) *s.i.s: a in rr* **50/1**

1m 16.41s (2.41) **Going Correction** +0.275s/f (Good) **10** Ran SP% **119.9**
Speed ratings (Par 94): **94,93,87,85,84 84,81,77,75,67**
toteswinger: 1&2 £1.40, 1&3 £46.40, 2&3 £11.60. CSF £14.70 TOTE £10.90: £2.50, £1.10, £10.80; EX 19.30.
Owner B Valentine **Bred** Darley **Trained** Melsonby, N Yorks
■ Stewards' Enquiry : Paul Hanagan caution: used whip with excessive frequency
N Callan one-day ban: used whip with exessive frequency (Aug 25)

FOCUS
A modest maiden, run at a fair pace. The first pair came nicely clear and the form is rated through the runner-up.

NOTEBOOK
Come And Go(UAE) confirmed himself a progressive juvenile and got off the mark at the third attempt with a gutsy effort. The form of his previous third at Catterick is starting to work out and he had no trouble with a return to softer ground. His future lies with the Handicapper, but he should really continue to improve as he matures and another furlong will suit in due course. (tchd 9-1)
Servoca(CAN) set the standard on his previous efforts and looked to have been found a suitable opportunity to shed his maiden tag. He held every chance on this easier ground and only just lost out, but was really worried out of it by the winner late on. He was a clear second best and has a small maiden within his grasp, but a mark of 88 probably flatters him. (op 8-11 tchd 4-6 and 10-11 in places)
Gilbertian showed his most encouraging form to date on this softer surface and did more than enough to suggest he will appreciate another furlong. He also now has the option of nurseries.
Dark Echoes is a half-brother to this season's promising sprinter Corrybrough among others and he posted a pleasing debut effort, but on this evidence looks to want a stiffer test than his siblings. He should come on a good deal for the experience. (tchd 20-1)
Justonefortheroad was not surprisingly given a positive ride on this drop back a furlong, but the easier ground found him out and he eventually disappointed. He will be qualifies for a nurseries after his next assignment and is not to be written off yet has he really looks to need a stiffer test. (op 7-2 tchd 5-2)

4816 COUNTRYWIDE FREIGHT NURSERY — 6f
7:35 (7:39) (Class 4) (0-80,77) 2-Y-0 **£5,504** (£1,637; £818; £408) **Stalls** Centre

Form RPR
2453 **1** **Polish Pride**[6] 4640 2-9-0 **73**.................................. MarkLawson(3) 3 87
(M Brittain) *prom: hdwy 1/2-way: led over 2f out: sn rdn and hung lft over 1f out: drvn clr fnl f* **15/8**[1]
416 **2** *6* **Sweet Smile (IRE)**[38] 3576 2-9-4 **74**.................................. NCallan 6 70
(K A Ryan) *cl up: rdn along over 2f out: drvn over 1f out: kpt on same pce ent fnl f* **7/1**
6210 **3** *2* **Cutting Comments**[7] 4594 2-9-7 **77**.................................. TomEaves 5 67
(M Dods) *chsd ldrs: hdwy on outer over 2f out: rdn wl over 1f out: kpt on same pce* **4/1**[3]
034 **4** *½* **Rossett Rose (IRE)**[13] 4438 2-9-2 **72**.................................. TWilliams 1 61
(M Brittain) *led: rdn along 1/2-way: hdd over 2f out and grad wknd* **12/1**
4265 **5** *7* **Raimond Ridge (IRE)**[38] 3576 2-8-11 **67**.................................. TonyCulhane 2 35
(M R Channon) *trckd ldrs: effrt over 2f out: sn rdn: wandered and outpcd* **9/2**

The Form Book, Raceform Ltd, Compton, RG20 6NL

2311 **6** 3/4 **Metroland**[18] 4243 2-9-1 **71** StephenDonohoe 4 36
(P C Haslam) *t.k.h: trckd ldrs: pushed along after 2f: sn lost pl and bhd fr over 2f out* **7/2**[2]

1m 16.22s (2.22) **Going Correction** +0.275s/f (Good) **6 Ran SP% 115.4**
Speed ratings (Par 96): **96,88,85,84,75 74**
toteswinger: 1&2 £3.80, 1&3 £2.50, 2&3 £4.10. CSF £16.24 TOTE £2.70: £1.40, £2.40; EX 14.90.
Owner Mel Brittain **Bred** Darley **Trained** Warthill, N Yorks

FOCUS
A modest nursery and the form looks solid with the winner value for the winning margin.

NOTEBOOK
Polish Pride ◆ maintained the decent form of her stable's juveniles and recorded her second success with a most decisive display. She relished racing with more cover this time and on the softer surface, rating full value for the winning margin. While she beat largely out-of-form rivals here, she will be high on confidence now and ought to take some beating if turning out under a penalty. (op 3-1)
Sweet Smile(IRE) ran with a lot more encouragement on this return from a 38-day break, but was still made to look decidedly one paced by the winner. He needs some respite in the weights. (op 11-2)
Cutting Comments could offer no more from the final furlong marker, but still ran a bit better than had been the case over course and distance a week previously. He is another who looks too high in the weights. (op 9-2 tchd 5-1)
Rossett Rose(IRE) eventually set the race up from the front for her winning stable companion and looks to have begun life in this sphere on a stiff mark. (tchd 8-1)
Metroland was bidding for a hat-trick and making her nursery debut for new connections, but she spoilt her chances by running too freely early on. (op 3-1)

4817 MTB GROUP H'CAP — 1m 6f
8:05 (8:05) (Class 5) (0-70,70) 4-Y-O+ **£3,238** (£963; £481; £240) **Stalls Low**

Form RPR
-556 **1** **Zed Candy (FR)**[18] 4238 5-8-1 **55** PatrickDonaghy[(5)] 5 64
(J T Stimpson) *hld up in rr: stdy hdwy 4f out: rdn to ld 2f out: hung lft over 1f out: sn drvn and kpt on* **12/1**
4521 **2** 3/4 **Alonso De Guzman (IRE)**[7] 4592 4-9-0 **70** HarryPoulton[(7)] 2 77
(J R Boyle) *prom: trckd clr ldr 6f out: cl up gng wl 4f out: effrt over 2f out: sn rdn and sltly outpcd: drvn and rallied ins fnl f: kpt on towards fin* **4/7**[1]
3/02 **3** 1 3/4 **Depraux (IRE)**[7] 4592 5-8-9 **61** PJMcDonald[(3)] 4 66
(G M Moore) *chsd clr ldr: hdwy over 4f out: rdn to ld 3f out: drvn and hdd 2f out: styng on u.p whn sltly hmpd ent fnl f: no ex* **9/1**[3]
510/ **4** 8 **Santando**[289] 6075 8-8-6 **55** (p) PaulHanagan 6 49
(P Bowen) *hld up in rr: stdy hdwy over 4f out: rdn along 3f out: ch over 2f out: sn drvn and btn* **11/1**
50-0 **5** 1 1/2 **Boxhall (IRE)**[22] 3010 6-8-6 **55** PaulQuinn 1 47
(N Wilson) *led and sn clr: rdn along 4f out: hdd 3f out: sn drvn and wknd wl over 1f out* **14/1**
62- **6** 5 **Raffish**[353] 4544 6-8-11 **67** (p) JPHamblett[(7)] 3 52
(M J Scudamore) *hld up in tch: hdwy and cl up 4f out: rdn along wl over 2f out and sn btn* **5/1**[2]

3m 8.80s (4.50) **Going Correction** +0.425s/f (Yiel) **6 Ran SP% 113.0**
Speed ratings (Par 103): **104,103,102,98,97 94**
toteswinger: 1&2 £2.60, 1&3 £4.90, 2&3 £1.10. CSF £19.97 TOTE £14.10: £3.30, £1.10; EX 24.80.
Owner J T S (International) Ltd **Bred** Haras De Saint Pair Du Mont **Trained** Newcastle-Under-Lyme, Staffs

FOCUS
A moderate staying handicap although the pace was fair. The form is rated through the third

4818 HARVEY NICHOLS H'CAP — 1m 30y
8:35 (8:36) (Class 4) (0-80,80) 3-Y-O **£5,504** (£1,637; £818; £408) **Stalls Low**

Form RPR
605 **1** **Brasingaman Hifive**[16] 4300 3-9-0 **73** DaleGibson 4 79
(Mrs G S Rees) *hld up in tch: hdwy 3f out: rdn 2f out: styd on to ld 1f out: drvn ins fnl f and hld on wl* **20/1**
0-64 **2** 3/4 **Holden Eagle**[36] 3629 3-8-12 **71** StephenDonohoe 7 75
(A G Newcombe) *hld up in rr: hdwy on wd outside over 2f out: rdn over 1f out: drvn and styd on ins fnl f* **9/1**
0402 **3** 1/2 **Midnight Muse (USA)**[9] 4539 3-9-6 **79** PaulFessey 1 82
(T D Barron) *cl up on inner: effrt 3f out: sn rdn and ev ch tl drvn and one pce wl ins fnl f* **7/1**[3]
-450 **4** hd **Resounding Glory (USA)**[25] 4017 3-9-3 **76** PaulHanagan 5 79
(R A Fahey) *hld up in rr: effrt 3f out and sn rdn along: drvn over 1f out: styd on u.p ins fnl f: nrst fin* **16/1**
01 **5** hd **Amber Queen (IRE)**[27] 3977 3-9-7 **80** MartinDwyer 2 82
(B W Hills) *t.k.h: led: pushed along 3f out: rdn and hdd over 2f out: sn drvn and ev ch tl wandered and wknd ent fnl f* **4/6**[1]
3115 **6** 3 **Willkandoo (USA)**[40] 3525 3-8-12 **71** NCallan 6 66
(K A Ryan) *cl up: hdwy to ld wl over 2f out and sn rdn: drvn over 1f out: hdd & wknd qckly appr fnl f* **5/1**[2]

1m 48.37s (4.57) **Going Correction** +0.425s/f (Yiel) **6 Ran SP% 109.8**
Speed ratings (Par 102): **94,93,92,92,92 89**
toteswinger: 1&2 £8.20, 1&3 £28.80, 2&3 £6.00. CSF £164.93 TOTE £25.80: £7.30, £2.30; EX 140.50 Place 6 £231.67, Place 5 £150.23..
Owner R Morgan **Bred** Mrs Heather Morgan **Trained** Sollom, Lancs

FOCUS
A fair three-year-old handicap. The early pace was only modest and it resulted in a bunched finish, so the form is muddling and should be treated with a little caution.
T/Plt: £183.60 to a £1 stake. Pool: £53,459.06. 212.50 winning tickets. T/Qpdt: £101.60 to a £1 stake. Pool: £4,630.44. 33.70 winning tickets. JR

[4634]LINGFIELD (L-H)
Friday, August 8

OFFICIAL GOING: Turf - good (good to firm in places); aw - standard
Wind: Light, against Weather: Overcast with drizzle

4819 SURREY MIRROR H'CAP — 1m 2f
2:10 (2:12) (Class 6) (0-65,68) 3-Y-O+ **£2,047** (£604; £302) **Stalls Low**

Form RPR
6600 **1** **Muffett's Dream**[11] 4485 4-8-9 **46** oh1 MickyFenton 12 52
(J J Bridger) *mde all: kicked on 3f out: styd on steadily fnl 2f: unchal* **50/1**
0554 **2** 1 1/2 **Fantasy Crusader**[2] 4721 9-8-9 **46** JimmyQuinn 1 49
(R M H Cowell) *disp 2nd pl thrght: rdn 3f out: no imp wnr: kpt on ins fnl f* **10/1**
0060 **3** nk **Rehabilitation**[24] 4061 3-9-5 **65** (p) AdamKirby 5 67
(W R Swinburn) *disp 2nd pl thrght: rdn over 2f out: no imp wnr after: kpt on* **7/1**[3]
4254 **4** nk **Merrymadcap (IRE)**[14] 4390 6-9-12 **63** SteveDrowne 2 65
(M Blanshard) *trckd ldrs: rdn and prog to dispute 2nd wl over 1f out: no imp wnr: no ex ins fnl f* **7/1**[3]
21 **5** 2 **Action Impact (ARG)**[6] 4635 4-10-2 **68** 6ex RyanMoore 6 65
(G L Moore) *trckd ldrs: rdn and nt qckn over 2f out: nvr on terms after: plugged on* **2/1**[1]
4520 **6** 1 **Danamight (IRE)**[21] 4173 3-9-3 **63** RichardMullen 3 59
(J L Dunlop) *dwlt: t.k.h: hld up in last pair: rdn 3f out: sme prog u.p 2f out: nvr on terms* **8/1**
0-05 **7** 1 **Cormorant Wharf (IRE)**[70] 2561 8-10-0 **65** JimCrowley 9 59
(T E Powell) *dwlt: t.k.h: hld up in rr: effrt on wd outside over 2f out: one pce and no imp* **14/1**
-500 **8** 11 **Power Player**[55] 3035 4-10-0 **65** TPO'Shea 14 37
(D J Coakley) *hld up in rr: lost tch downhill over 3f out: last and detached over 2f out: t.o* **40/1**
-021 **9** 5 **Papradon**[21] 4156 4-9-13 **64** (v) LPKeniry 4 26
(J R Best) *t.k.h: hld up in midfield: no prog 3f out: wknd 2f out: eased: t.o* **3/1**[2]

2m 12.83s (2.33) **Going Correction** +0.175s/f (Good)
WFA 3 from 4yo+ 9lb **9 Ran SP% 114.6**
Speed ratings (Par 101): **97,95,95,95,93 92,92,83,79**
toteswinger: 1&2 £16.70, 1&3 £36.00, 2&3 £11.40. CSF £479.14 CT £3914.78 TOTE £43.90: £8.30, £3.00, £2.50; EX 330.80.
Owner Mr & Mrs K Finch **Bred** Berry Racing **Trained** Liphook, Hants

FOCUS
A modest handicap and the pace looked steady, and the first three were in the first four virtually throughout.
Muffett's Dream Official explanation: trainer said, regarding the improved form shown, there had been a change of tactics in that the filly had made the running and stayed on well

4820 EAST GRINSTEAD COURIER AND OBSERVER H'CAP — 1m 3f 106y
2:40 (2:41) (Class 5) (0-70,69) 3-Y-O+ **£2,590** (£770; £385; £192) **Stalls High**

Form RPR
0022 **1** **Olimpo (FR)**[8] 4568 7-9-9 **65** JamesMillman[(3)] 7 80
(B R Millman) *mde all: drew clr 3f out: styd on wl fnl 2f: unchal* **5/1**[3]
6250 **2** 4 1/2 **Cupid's Glory**[44] 3376 6-10-0 **67** RyanMoore 10 74+
(G L Moore) *t.k.h: hld up in last pair and wl off the pce: rapid prog over 2f out: wnt 2nd 1f out and hanging lft: styd on: far too much to do* **3/1**[1]
0444 **3** 3 1/4 **The Grey One (IRE)**[8] 4568 5-8-9 **48** oh3 (p) LPKeniry 3 49
(J M Bradley) *t.k.h: hld up in midfield: rdn and prog 3f out: chsd wnr 2f out to 1f out: one pce* **11/1**
2506 **4** 7 **Winning Show**[21] 4156 4-9-6 **59** AdamKirby 9 49
(C Gordon) *stdd s: hld up in last trio: stl wl in rr 3f out: prog over 2f out: plugged on one pce over 1f out* **13/2**
00-0 **5** 1/2 **Mystic Storm**[18] 4254 5-9-11 **64** (t) SebSanders 2 53
(B G Powell) *hld up in midfield: rdn and outpcd 3f out: no ch after* **16/1**
0060 **6** hd **Barley Moon**[7] 4599 4-8-9 **48** oh3 (b[1]) JimmyQuinn 6 36
(T Keddy) *t.k.h: prom: rdn 3f out: steadily wknd fnl 2f* **66/1**
3040 **7** 2 **Good Effect (USA)**[27] 4131 4-9-11 **64** (p) SteveDrowne 4 49
(C P Morlock) *wl in rr: last and losing tch over 4f out: no ch after* **14/1**
0653 **8** 3 **Ocean Avenue (IRE)**[11] 4485 9-9-5 **58** (p) DarryllHolland 11 38
(C A Horgan) *chsd wnr after 2f to 2f out: wknd rapidly* **7/2**[2]
-504 **9** 14 **Dubai Samurai**[14] 4372 3-9-6 **69** MichaelHills 8 25
(J W Hills) *trckd ldrs tl wknd 3f out: t.o* **15/2**
0005 **10** 6 **Silver Surprise**[15] 4343 4-8-9 **48** oh3 MickyFenton 5 —
(J J Bridger) *chsd wnr 2f: wknd over 4f out: t.o* **50/1**

2m 32.37s (0.87) **Going Correction** +0.175s/f (Good)
WFA 3 from 4yo+ 10lb **10 Ran SP% 113.3**
Speed ratings (Par 103): **103,99,97,92,91 91,90,88,77,73**
toteswinger: 1&2 £4.00, 1&3 £6.60, 2&3 £7.20. CSF £19.72 CT £155.25 TOTE £5.90: £1.70, £1.50, £3.10; EX 22.70.
Owner Pot Black Racing **Bred** Ewar Stud Farm **Trained** Kentisbeare, Devon

FOCUS
A very modest race, where the winner was allowed an easy lead. The form is not reliable.
Cupid's Glory Official explanation: jockey said gelding hung left in the straight
Ocean Avenue(IRE) Official explanation: jockey said gelding failed to handle the final bend
Silver Surprise Official explanation: jockey said filly was unsuited by the track

4821 HENRY STREETER MAIDEN STKS — 1m 6f
3:10 (3:10) (Class 5) 3-Y-O+ **£2,590** (£770; £385; £192) **Stalls High**

Form RPR
44 **1** **Darksideofthemoon (IRE)**[16] 4302 6-9-13 0 PaulDoe 11 75
(N J Gifford) *pressed ldr: rdn to take narrow ld 2f out: maintained it tl asserted nr fin* **20/1**
62 **2** 1/2 **Fortune City (UAE)**[16] 4302 3-9-0 0 LDettori 13 74
(Saeed Bin Suroor) *mde most: jinked bnd after 2f: drvn and narrowly hdd 2f out: upsides after but reluctant to overtake: hld nr fin* **4/1**[2]
2 **3** shd **Wild Rhubarb**[29] 3894 3-8-9 0 SebSanders 6 69
(C G Cox) *trckd ldrs: wnt 3rd 5f out: outpcd 3f out: no imp on ldng pair tl styd on fr over 1f out: gaining at fin* **4/1**[2]
-534 **4** 1 **Mushtaaq (USA)**[27] 3962 3-9-0 76 (b) RHills 3 72
(M A Jarvis) *trckd ldng pair: outpcd and lost pl 4f out: sn u.p: kpt on again over 1f out* **7/2**[1]
0-30 **5** 3/4 **Basanti (USA)**[51] 3133 3-8-9 72 MichaelHills 2 66
(B W Hills) *trckd ldrs: wl outpcd over 3f out: no imp tl kpt on fr over 1f out: gaining grad at fin* **12/1**
3460 **6** 6 **Blue Citadel (USA)**[8] 4573 3-9-0 76 JimCrowley 10 63
(Mrs A J Perrett) *settled in midfield: outpcd over 3f out: plugged on u.p: no ch* **8/1**[3]
0 **7** shd **Sleepy Mountain**[16] 4302 4-9-6 0 KMay[(7)] 1 63?
(A Middleton) *hld up towards rr: rdn and outpcd fr 3f out: n.d after* **100/1**
8 2 **Lagavulin (IRE)**[52] 4-9-13 0 RichardHughes 9 60
(Miss E C Lavelle) *dwlt: hld up in last quartet: sme prog 4f out: pushed along and kpt on steadily fnl 3f: nvr nr ldrs* **20/1**
0234 **9** 10 **Lemonesse (USA)**[15] 4342 3-8-9 75 JimmyQuinn 4 41
(H R A Cecil) *trckd ldrs: rdn and lost pl 4f out: sn wknd and bhd* **4/1**[2]
10 4 **Lyster (IRE)**[21] 9-9-8 0 RichardEvans[(5)] 8 40
(P D Evans) *s.s: a in rr: lost tch over 4f out: wl bhd after* **40/1**
11 shd **Nomadic Warrior** 3-9-0 0 LPKeniry 7 40
(J R Best) *dwlt: a towards rr: lost tch u.p over 4f out: bhd after* **66/1**
0 **12** 1/2 **Dagua Briza (IRE)**[15] 4342 3-8-9 0 MickyFenton 12 35
(J W Mullins) *a in rr: lost tch 5f out: wl bhd after* **100/1**

030/ **13** *45* **Lookouthereicome**[1099] 4123 7-9-8 33..........(p) AdamKirby 5 —
(T T Clement) *s.s: a in rr: wknd 5f out: t.o* **100/1**

3m 12.15s (2.15) **Going Correction** +0.175s/f (Good)
WFA 3 from 4yo+ 13lb **13** Ran SP% **117.5**
Speed ratings (Par 103): **100,99,99,99,98 95,95,94,88,86 85,85,59**
toteswinger: 1&2 £9.90, 1&3 £8.80, 2&3 £4.50. CSF £94.43 TOTE £15.80: £2.60, £1.80, £1.80; EX 112.80.
Owner David Dunsdon **Bred** Sean Gannon **Trained** Findon, W Sussex

FOCUS
A bunch finish and a shock winner here, so there is a doubt over the form but no obvious fluke about it. The winning time was nothing to get excited about.
Lemonesse(USA) Official explanation: jockey said filly had no more to give

4822 THISISSURREYTODAY.CO.UK NOVICE STKS 5f (P)
3:40 (3:41) (Class 5) 2-Y-O **£3,885** (£1,156; £577; £288) **Stalls** High

Form RPR

1 **1** **Masamah (IRE)**[86] 2108 2-9-5 0.......... RHills 4 97+
(E A L Dunlop) *mde all: shkn up and styd on wl fr over 1f out: unchal* **5/2**[1]

1 **2** *2* **Art Preview (USA)**[46] 3315 2-9-5 0.......... RyanMoore 5 89+
(G L Moore) *t.k.h: hld up bhd ldrs: effrt 2f out: kpt on fnl f to snatch 2nd last stride* **5/2**[1]

231 **3** *shd* **Evelyn May (IRE)**[17] 4270 2-8-11 78.......... MichaelHills 6 81
(B W Hills) *chsd wnr after 1f: rdn and no imp over 1f out: lost 2nd last stride* **4/1**[3]

2615 **4** *1 1/2* **Agente Parmigiano (IRE)**[40] 3522 2-9-0 92.......... LDettori 1 79
(G A Butler) *chsd wnr 1f out: in tch after: rdn 2f out: one pce after* **7/2**[2]

1253 **5** *1 1/4* **Gone Hunting**[15] 4323 2-8-9 84.......... JackDean(5) 2 74
(W G M Turner) *hld up and sn last: rdn 2f out: one pce and no real prog* **25/1**

6 *9* **Big Stormy (USA)** 2-8-9 0.......... SebSanders 3 37
(C E Brittain) *s.s: t.k.h and rcvrd into 3rd after 2f: wknd 2f out and wd bnd sn after* **14/1**

59.15 secs (0.35) **Going Correction** +0.05s/f (Slow) **6** Ran SP% **109.9**
Speed ratings (Par 94): **99,95,95,93,91 76**
toteswinger: 1&2 £1.90, 1&3 £2.40, 2&3 £2.10. CSF £8.53 TOTE £3.20: £1.70, £1.60; EX 7.50.
Owner Hamdan Al Maktoum **Bred** Stanley Estate & Stud Co & Mount Coote Stud **Trained** Newmarket, Suffolk

FOCUS
A decent little novice, and Masamah confirmed himself a smart prospect when following up his York win with a convincing all-the-way win. The form looks strong.

NOTEBOOK
Masamah(IRE), not seen since his York win in May and without the blinkers he wore, made all for a comprehensive success. He had hung badly left at York, but when he was checked out afterwards, something (a rib injury) was found that could have caused him to edge so badly across the course. Given plenty of time since that debut success, he had too much pace for his five rivals and looks a colt of some potential. He holds a Middle Park entry and looks an ideal candidate for the race, even allowing for the fact that the owner also has the very speedy Finjaan. (op 2-1 tchd 15-8 and 3-1)
Art Preview(USA), who won nicely on his debut over the course and distance in late June, could never get to grips with the winner and only took second in the last strides. He remains a decent prospect. (op 11-4 tchd 2-1)
Evelyn May(IRE), the only filly in the race, was soon chasing the winner but was easily held by him when push came to shove. She had started favourite on all of her three previous starts, and had shown a good level of ability, so helps to give the result a solid look. (op 7-2)
Agente Parmigiano(IRE) ran badly last time over 6f and again failed to get involved against some decent-looking opposition. He does not seem well treated (for handicap purposes) on his previous form. (tchd 4-1)
Gone Hunting was far from disgraced in what was a hot contest. He stayed on quite nicely inside the final furlong to finish on the heels of the principals. (op 33-1)
Big Stormy(USA) did not get away too quickly but soon recovered and got into midfield. He held that position until the home bend, but was quickly outpaced as his classy rivals stretched clear. (op 20-1)

4823 ALAN HOGG'S 60TH @ THE BRICKLAYERS CHIPSTEAD FILLIES' (S) STKS 6f (P)
4:10 (4:10) (Class 6) 2-Y-O **£1,978** (£584; £292) **Stalls** Low

Form RPR

0000 **1** **Flawless Diamond (IRE)**[15] 4340 2-8-12 49..........(b[1]) LPKeniry 6 57
(J S Moore) *trckd ldr: led over 2f out: drvn clr over 1f out: all out nr fin* **33/1**

16 **2** *1/2* **Missus Christie**[22] 4108 2-9-3 58.......... SebSanders 9 60
(Ian Williams) *chsd ldrs: rdn 1/2-way: effrt on outer over 1f out: wnt 2nd ins fnl f: clsng on wnr at fin* **7/1**[3]

051 **3** *2* **Silent Treatment (IRE)**[31] 3815 2-9-3 58..........(t) RyanMoore 7 54
(Miss Gay Kelleway) *chsd ldng pair: rdn over 2f out: wnt 2nd briefly jst ins fnl f: kpt on same pce* **7/1**[3]

030 **4** *1 1/2* **Lislin**[15] 4340 2-8-12 48.......... PatDobbs 5 45
(S Kirk) *chsd ldrs and in tch: rdn over 2f out: kpt on same pce fr over 1f out: n.d* **11/1**

60 **5** *4* **Ruasgreyasme (USA)**[9] 4521 2-8-12 0.......... RichardHughes 2 33+
(R Hannon) *led to over 2f out: hrd rdn and steadily wknd* **6/4**[1]

050 **6** *1/2* **Positive Opinion**[16] 4296 2-8-12 60.......... DarryllHolland 11 31
(B R Millman) *outpcd and sn drvn: nvr a factor: kpt on fr over 1f out* **11/2**[2]

45 **7** *3/4* **Lavender Girl**[14] 4387 2-8-12 0.......... JimCrowley 8 29
(P Winkworth) *chsd ldrs: rdn bef 1/2-way: struggling and outpcd 2f out* **12/1**

8 *1* **Abitofaboost (IRE)** 2-8-12 0.......... AdamKirby 10 26
(Peter Grayson) *dwlt: outpcd and wl bhd: nvr a factor* **50/1**

0 **9** *3/4* **Elusive Intentions (IRE)**[60] 2893 2-8-12 0.......... GMosse 12 24
(P D Evans) *sn outpcd and wl bhd: nvr a factor* **8/1**

0016 **10** *1 3/4* **Missy Que (IRE)**[24] 4063 2-9-3 55..........(b) PaulDoe 1 23
(W R Muir) *chsd ldrs: rdn 1/2-way: wknd 2f out* **16/1**

11 *7* **Ravine Rose** 2-8-12 0..........(t) TPO'Shea 3 —
(B I Case) *s.s: sn t.o* **66/1**

00 **12** *1 1/4* **Miss Belle Eve**[91] 1955 2-8-9 0..........(p) LukeMorris(3) 4 —
(T M Jones) *dwlt: outpcd and a bhd: t.o* **50/1**

1m 13.53s (1.63) **Going Correction** +0.05s/f (Slow) **12** Ran SP% **121.8**
Speed ratings (Par 89): **91,90,87,85,80 79,78,77,76,74 64,63**
toteswinger: 1&2 £30.40, 1&3 £38.70, 2&3 £3.50. CSF £254.07 TOTE £45.60: £10.80, £2.40, £3.00; EX 489.00.There was no bid for the winner. Ruasgreyasme was claimed by W R Muir for £6,000.
Owner Owen Mullen & John Griffin **Bred** R Coffey **Trained** Upper Lambourn, Berks

FOCUS
Three of the field were already winners, and few of them had run in this grade before so the form looks sound enough. However, the winner had shown little previously, and about half the field were done for by the home bend, so it would be unwise to go overboard about the strength

NOTEBOOK
Flawless Diamond(IRE) had never finished closer than seventh, including off a low mark in a nursery, but the trainer had always thought that she had plenty of ability. Dropped in class and equipped with blinkers for the first time, she showed much more pace than before and did just enough to hold on.
Missus Christie, a claiming winner on her debut, finished strongly from an unpromising position to grab second place. This is definitely her level, as she disappointed in better company last time. (op 4-1)
Silent Treatment(IRE), having her first start for this stable after being purchased out of a seller last time, was never far away but could not pick up when asked to really quicken. (op 6-1 tchd 11-2)
Lislin, dropped into a seller for the first time, was not disgraced but she will need to be found a very weak race to get off the mark. Official explanation: jockey said filly hung badly left 165yds out (op 10-1)
Ruasgreyasme(USA) got away really well but faded badly once joined. She will definitely benefit from a drop in trip. (op 15-8 tchd 2-1 in places)
Positive Opinion, dropped down to selling company for the first time, could not go the early gallop but kept on at the one pace in the final stages to finish within hailing distance of the winner. Official explanation: jockey said filly did not face the kickback (op 15-2 tchd 8-1)
Lavender Girl is a leggy sort who may need more time. (op 33-1)
Abitofaboost(IRE) is bred to be quick but she broke slowly and got badly outpaced. Official explanation: jockey said filly missed the break (op 40-1)

4824 "MAKING LOCAL MATTER" MORE H'CAP 6f (P)
4:40 (4:41) (Class 6) (0-60,60) 3-Y-O+ **£2,047** (£604; £302) **Stalls** Low

Form RPR

21-6 **1** **Tubby Isaacs**[16] 4313 4-9-8 60.......... SebSanders 1 71+
(P J Makin) *dwlt: hld up in midfield and off the pce: effrt 2f out: hrd rdn on inner and r.o fnl f to ld fnl 75yds* **2/1**[1]

0400 **2** *3/4* **Our Fugitive (IRE)**[27] 3966 6-9-7 59..........(p) AdamKirby 6 68
(C Gordon) *led: drvn and narrowly hdd over 2f out: pressed ldr after: upsides ins fnl f: outpcd nr fin* **7/1**[3]

0063 **3** *1/2* **Bollin Franny**[16] 4307 4-8-8 51.......... NataliaGemelova(5) 12 58
(J E Long) *pressed ldr: rdn to ld narrowly over 2f out: hdd and outpcd fnl 75yds* **10/1**

0004 **4** *1/2* **Bobby Rose**[16] 4307 5-9-7 59..........(b) RobertHavlin 5 64
(D K Ivory) *t.k.h: trckd ldng pair: cl enough 1f out: hrd rdn and fnd little* **6/1**[2]

0660 **5** *shd* **Blackmalkin (USA)**[16] 4306 4-9-8 60.......... TPO'Shea 7 65+
(M Quinn) *pushed along in last pair early: gd prog jst over 1f out: shuffled along and styd on wl fnl f* **10/1**

0050 **6** *1/2* **Quality Street**[16] 4307 6-9-5 57..........(p) JimCrowley 9 60+
(P Butler) *settled off the pce towards rr: effrt 2f out: kpt on fr over 1f out but nvr able to chal* **8/1**

3000 **7** *3/4* **Zazous**[85] 2128 7-9-0 52.......... J-PGuillambert 4 53
(J J Bridger) *sn rdn in midfield: struggling fr 1/2-way: kpt on but no threat* **14/1**

2506 **8** *1 1/2* **Mambazo**[16] 4307 6-9-4 59..........(e) LukeMorris(3) 8 55
(S C Williams) *chsd ldrs: u.p and struggling 1/2-way: nvr on terms* **14/1**

466 **9** *2 3/4* **Night Premiere (IRE)**[81] 2260 3-9-0 56.......... PatDobbs 3 43
(R Hannon) *chsd ldrs: rdn 1/2-way: lost pl and btn over 1f out* **14/1**

0363 **10** *17* **Autograph Hunter**[20] 4181 4-9-1 53.......... LPKeniry 11 —
(Peter Grayson) *dwlt: rdn in last after 2f: nvr a factor: t.o* **14/1**

1m 11.93s (0.03) **Going Correction** +0.05s/f (Slow)
WFA 3 from 4yo+ 4lb **10** Ran SP% **116.1**
Speed ratings (Par 101): **101,100,99,98,98 97,96,94,91,68**
toteswinger: 1&2 £5.70, 1&3 £6.50, 2&3 £13.60. CSF £15.85 CT £116.36 TOTE £2.40: £1.50, £2.30, £2.90; EX 23.60.
Owner John Khan & Arnold Bros **Bred** J W Ford **Trained** Ogbourne Maisey, Wilts

FOCUS
Probably a decent race of its type for the grade with the third and fourth close to form. The winner was unexposed and should be capable of a bit better, but his rivals regularly operate in this sort of class, so the form looks reliable.
Zazous Official explanation: jockey said gelding was denied a clear run in the closing stages
Mambazo Official explanation: jockey said gelding hung right throughout

4825 BLINDLEY HEATH FILLIES' H'CAP 7f (P)
5:10 (5:14) (Class 6) (0-65,65) 3-Y-O+ **£2,047** (£604; £302) **Stalls** Low

Form RPR

2000 **1** **Convallaria (FR)**[48] 3265 5-9-3 52..........(b[1]) RobertHavlin 5 62
(G Wragg) *hld up in 5th: gng strly over 2f out: effrt over 1f out: shkn up to ld fnl 75yds: decisively* **12/1**

0653 **2** *3/4* **Plumage**[14] 4368 3-9-3 58.......... LPKeniry 2 64
(M Blanshard) *trckd ldrs: effrt on inner over 1f out: pressed ldr ent fnl f: outpcd fnl 75yds* **16/1**

4012 **3** *hd* **Kannon**[1] 4770 3-8-13 57.......... LukeMorris(3) 11 62
(W J Knight) *trckd ldng pair: effrt to ld 1f out: hdd and outpcd fnl 75yds* **3/1**[1]

-010 **4** *1/2* **Pragmatist**[44] 3383 4-9-13 62.......... JimCrowley 8 68+
(P Winkworth) *shkn up in midfield after 3f: no prog tl styd on wl fr over 1f out: nrst fin* **7/2**[2]

-204 **5** *2* **Miracle Baby**[13] 4414 6-8-6 48.......... KMay(7) 4 49
(J A Geake) *led: drvn and hdd 1f out: fdd* **8/1**

6600 **6** *2 3/4* **Alzaroof (USA)**[17] 4282 3-9-10 65.......... NeilPollard 7 56
(E A L Dunlop) *pressed ldr to wl over 1f out: wknd fnl f* **16/1**

0603 **7** *shd* **Djalalabad (FR)**[30] 3842 4-9-3 52..........(t) CatherineGannon 14 45
(Mrs C A Dunnett) *settled in rr: effrt on outer 3f out: sn rdn: no imp fnl 2f* **14/1**

5360 **8** *hd* **Nikki Bea (IRE)**[16] 4306 5-9-5 54.......... PaulDoe 10 46
(Jamie Poulton) *chsd ldrs: rdn wl over 2f out: fdd over 1f out* **8/1**

020 **9** *hd* **Lady Amberlini**[2] 4727 3-9-5 60.......... GMosse 6 50
(P D Evans) *hld up towards rr: rdn and no real prog 2f out* **7/1**[3]

3-00 **10** *2 1/4* **Chalentina**[13] 4414 5-8-7 47.......... NataliaGemelova(5) 9 33
(J E Long) *hld up in rr: struggling fr 3f out* **33/1**

504- **11** *1/2* **Grand Symphony**[225] 6573 4-9-11 60..........(t) TPO'Shea 12 44
(B I Case) *hld up in last pair: nvr a factor* **40/1**

0-60 **12** *1 1/4* **Kindallachan**[17] 4285 5-9-5 54.......... AdamKirby 3 35
(G C Bravery) *uns rdr and on way to post: chsd ldrs: u.p 1/2-way: wknd wl over 1f out* **14/1**

0400 **13** *2 1/2* **Mythical Charm**[49] 3208 9-8-11 46..........(t) J-PGuillambert 13 20
(J J Bridger) *stdd s: t.k.h: hld up in last pair: nt clr run over 2f out: no prog* **14/1**

-400 **14** *7* **Sempre Libera (IRE)**[16] 4307 3-8-9 **50**.................... PatDobbs 1 3
(R T Phillips) *hld up on inner towards rr: no prog over 2f out: wknd: t.o* **33/1**

1m 25.0s (0.20) **Going Correction** +0.05s/f (Slow)
WFA 3 from 4yo+ 6lb **14** Ran SP% **129.7**
Speed ratings (Par 98): **100,99,98,98,96 92,92,92,92,89 89,87,84,76**
toteswinger: 1&2 £31.90, 1&3 £17.40, 2&3 £9.30. CSF £202.45 CT £760.85 TOTE £16.70: £5.40, £4.40, £1.80; EX 356.00 Place 6: £198.09, Place 5: £34.07..
Owner Mrs Claude Lilley **Bred** Jan Krzywicki **Trained** Newmarket, Suffolk

FOCUS
A moderate mares; race and most of them were exposed. The race was won by a long-standing maiden, who wore headgear for the first time, so the form, rated through the third, would not look particularly reliable out of this type of contest.
T/Plt: £276.50 to a £1 stake. Pool: £53,857.13. 142.14 winning tickets. T/Qpdt: £5.90 to a £1 stake. Pool: £4,108.30. 508.10 winning tickets. JN

4640 **NEWMARKET (JULY)** (R-H)

Friday, August 8

OFFICIAL GOING: Good to soft (7.7)
Wind: Light, half-behind Weather: Cloudy with sunny spells

4826 HIGH STREET CAFE MAIDEN STKS 7f
5:50 (5:53) (Class 4) 2-Y-O **£5,180** (£1,541; £770; £384) **Stalls** Low

Form RPR
1 **Wingwalker** 2-9-3 0.................... TPQueally 2 88+
(H R A Cecil) *trckd ldrs: racd keenly: led 2f out: sn edgd rt and hdd: rallied to ld ins fnl f: drvn out* **9/4**[1]
2 *1* **Delegator** 2-9-3 0.................... JimmyFortune 6 83+
(B J Meehan) *dwlt: sn prom: led over 1f out: sn rdn: hdd and unable qckn ins fnl f* **6/1**[2]
3 *1* **Midnight Cruiser (IRE)** 2-8-12 0.................... GabrielHannon(5) 9 80+
(R Hannon) *s.i.s: sn pushed along in rr: hdwy over 1f out: styd on* **14/1**
4 *1 1/2* **Invincible Heart (GR)** 2-9-3 0.................... JohnEgan 10 76
(Jane Chapple-Hyam) *chsd ldrs: rdn over 1f out: no ex ins fnl f* **25/1**
5 *1/2* **Mishrif (USA)** 2-9-3 0.................... AlanMunro 12 75+
(P W Chapple-Hyam) *s.i.s and hmpd s: sn prom: outpcd 1/2-way: hdwy over 1f out: styd on* **12/1**
6 *1 1/4* **Gordy Bee (USA)** 2-9-3 0.................... PaulEddery 1 72
(G D Blake) *hld up: hdwy over 2f out: sn rdn: no ex ins fnl f* **66/1**
7 *1 3/4* **Adios Juan** 2-9-3 0.................... SaleemGolam 11 68
(S C Williams) *led: rdn and hdd 2f out: sn edgd rt: wknd fnl f* **33/1**
8 *2 1/2* **King Of Wands** 2-9-3 0.................... EddieAhern 19 61+
(J L Dunlop) *sn pushed along in rr: styd on ins fnl f: nvr nrr* **9/1**
9 *1* **Forte Dei Marmi** 2-9-3 0.................... PatCosgrave 16 59
(L M Cumani) *hld up in tch: rdn over 2f out: nt clr run and wknd over 1f out* **33/1**
10 *2 3/4* **Aqwaal (IRE)** 2-9-3 0.................... PaulMulrennan 8 52
(E A L Dunlop) *prom: rdn 1/2-way: wknd wl over 1f out* **16/1**
11 *1 1/4* **Sequillo** 2-9-3 0.................... DavidKinsella 3 49
(R Hannon) *hld up: hdwy over 2f out: edgd lft and wknd over 1f out* **11/1**
12 *shd* **Highland River** 2-9-3 0.................... TQuinn 17 49
(D R C Elsworth) *hld up: plld hrd: rdn over 2f out: n.d* **20/1**
13 *hd* **Murhee (USA)** 2-9-3 0.................... RichardMullen 4 48
(D R Lanigan) *hld up in tch: rdn over 2f out: edgd lft and wknd over 1f out* **8/1**[3]
14 *nk* **Print (IRE)** 2-9-3 0.................... EdwardCreighton 13 47
(M R Channon) *trckd ldrs: plld hrd: rdn and wknd over 1f out* **16/1**
15 *4 1/2* **Strongarm** 2-9-3 0.................... DarrenWilliams 7 36
(A Bailey) *trckd ldr: plld hrd: rdn and wknd over 1f out* **25/1**
16 *2 1/2* **Mezzoforte (IRE)** 2-9-3 0.................... SteveDrowne 14 30
(J S Moore) *hld up: wknd over 2f out* **40/1**
17 *1/2* **Duar Mapel (USA)** 2-9-3 0.................... HayleyTurner 18 29
(G D Blake) *s.i.s: rn green and a outpcd* **66/1**

1m 28.21s (2.51) **Going Correction** +0.45s/f (Yiel) **17** Ran SP% **124.4**
Speed ratings (Par 96): **103,101,100,99,98 97,95,92,91,87 86,86,86,85,80 77,77**
toteswinger: 1&2 £2.60, 1&3 £13.10, 2&3 £32.90. CSF £13.07 TOTE £3.50: £1.80, £2.60, £4.00; EX 18.60.
Owner K Abdulla **Bred** Juddmonte Farms Ltd **Trained** Newmarket, Suffolk

FOCUS
Rain the previous day and in the morning had eased the ground to good to soft. Despite this being a race for newcomers it looked a decent contest with the time being nearly half a second faster than the quickest of the other two juvenile races over the trip. The form has been rated positively.

NOTEBOOK
Wingwalker ◆, related to several good winners at 7f-1m in France, was sent off a well-backed favourite despite the fact that his trainer's juveniles have not been as forward as in previous seasons. He was unable to get much cover from his low draw, and as a result tended to take a hold, but travelled well until looking in trouble when taken on by the runner-up. He responded nicely up the hill to settle the issue and looks sure to progress, and couple be taking up one of his big-race entries before the end of the season if going the right way. (op 2-1 tchd 5-2 and 3-1 in palces)
Delegator ◆, by the same sire as the winner, is out of a half-sister to the top-class performers Tomba and Holding Court, both of whom raced for this colt's owner. Settled just off the pace, he was produced to lead going in to the dip and looked ready to draw away, but hitting the rising ground he appeared to see the crowd, edge right and prop, losing his momentum in so doing. He responded once the winner went by but could not recover the lost ground. He can be forgiven this on account of greenness and this Dewhurst entry looks sure to pick up a maiden before going on to better things. (tchd 13-2)
Midnight Cruiser(IRE) ◆, a 65,000gns half-brother to five winners, mainly at middle distances, was another to perform with credit. Having missed the break, he was in the rear until making good headway over a furlong out and, although he never reached the first two, he ran on nicely under a sympathetic ride. He should be capable of repaying the kindness before long. (op 12-1)
Invincible Heart(GR), a speedily-bred first foal of a 5f winner, showed up from the start and kept going without being able to find an extra gear up the hill. It may be that the ease in the ground stretched his stamina on this first outing.
Mishrif(USA), a 150,000gns two-year-old related to some speedy types on both dirt and turf in the USA, got into trouble early but was noted keeping quite nicely at the finish. He looks likely to benefit from the experience and will be helped by a faster surface. (op 11-1 tchd 10-1)
Gordy Bee(USA), a half-brother to six winners including a couple of multiple scorers in the USA, made far less money at the breeze-ups than when sold as a yearling. He did show a fair amount of ability though, finishing not far behind the placed horses, and can be expected to benefit from the experience. (op 100-1)
Adios Juan, the second foal of a mile juvenile winner, jumped off in front and set the pace until taken on by the principals. He did not drop away totally and could be capable of emulating his dam at a lower level.
King Of Wands, a Derby and Royal Lodge entry and first foal of a daughter of the useful Maid For The Hills, could not go the early pace but was noted doing some good work in the closing stages. He will appreciate longer trips in time and will probably come into his own next season. (op 12-1 tchd 14-1)
Murhee(USA), another with some fancy entries, comes from a decent American family. He showed up early but dropped out in the final quarter-mile. he is another who may prefer a sounder surface. (op 10-1 tchd 12-1)

4827 ECENI PRODUCTIONS (S) STKS 7f
6:20 (6:25) (Class 4) 2-Y-O **£3,885** (£1,156; £577; £288) **Stalls** Low

Form RPR
0002 **1** **Sienna Lake (IRE)**[14] 4387 2-8-8 62.................... RyanMoore 7 64+
(R Hannon) *hld up: hdwy over 1f out: rdn to ld ins fnl f: r.o wl* **10/3**[2]
006 **2** *2 1/4* **Pokfulham (IRE)**[11] 4488 2-8-13 0....................(v[1]) DarrenWilliams 5 63
(A P Jarvis) *led: rdn over 1f out: hdd and unable qckn ins fnl f* **33/1**
6 **3** *3 1/4* **Ashwinder (IRE)**[9] 4530 2-8-8 0.................... GabrielHannon(5) 1 55
(B J Meehan) *chsd ldrs: rdn over 1f out: wknd ins fnl f* **12/1**
6 **4** *hd* **Heaven Knows When (IRE)**[37] 3610 2-8-8 0.................... MichaelHills 14 50
(B W Hills) *s.i.s: racd alone towards stands' side: hung lft thrght: hdwy u.p and swished tail fr over 2f out: nt trble ldrs* **11/1**
555 **5** *1 1/4* **Miss Moloney (IRE)**[35] 3689 2-8-8 54.................... JimmyQuinn 9 47
(Mrs S Lamyman) *prom: chsd ldr 3f out tl rdn over 1f out: wknd fnl f* **12/1**
00 **6** *1 1/4* **Strikemaster (IRE)**[31] 3821 2-8-13 0.................... EddieAhern 4 49
(J W Hills) *s.i.s: hld up: rdn over 2f out: n.d* **16/1**
0000 **7** *3/4* **Barcode**[23] 4079 2-8-8 54.................... SteveDrowne 2 42
(R Hannon) *prom: rdn over 2f out: wknd over 1f out* **10/1**
0043 **8** *1 1/4* **Benetti (IRE)**[18] 4257 2-8-6 47.................... MatthewDavies(7) 6 44
(M R Channon) *hld up: rdn over 2f out: n.d* **25/1**
0000 **9** *3/4* **Ba Globetrotter**[5] 4666 2-8-13 55.................... EdwardCreighton 12 42
(M R Channon) *mid-div: hdwy u.p 3f out: wknd over 1f out* **40/1**
01 **10** *1 3/4* **All Angel**[11] 4487 2-8-13 0.................... HayleyTurner 13 37
(Miss Amy Weaver) *prom: rdn 1/2-way: wknd over 1f out* **9/1**[3]
502 **11** *3 1/4* **Kapowee**[18] 4257 2-8-8 48.................... AlanMunro 10 24
(W J Musson) *chsd ldrs: rdn over 2f out: sn wknd* **16/1**
05 **12** *11* **Against The Rules**[13] 4421 2-8-13 0.................... JimmyFortune 8 2
(P Howling) *hld up: rdn 1/2-way: wknd over 2f out: eased* **9/4**[1]
655 **13** *1/2* **Buddy Marvellous (IRE)**[27] 3967 2-8-13 61.................... RichardHughes 11 —
(R Hannon) *s.i.s: hld up: rdn 1/2-way: wknd and eased 2f out* **9/1**[3]

1m 28.7s (3.00) **Going Correction** +0.45s/f (Yiel) **13** Ran SP% **127.6**
Speed ratings (Par 96): **100,97,93,93,92 90,89,88,87,85 81,69,68**
toteswinger: 1&2 £69.30, 1&3 £23.30, 2&3 £82.70. CSF £122.45 TOTE £4.70: £1.80, £13.30, £4.90; EX 150.10.The winner was bought in for £12,500.
Owner Knockainey Stud Limited **Bred** Davin Investments Ltd **Trained** East Everleigh, Wilts

FOCUS
Not a bad seller and run faster than the following nursery over the same trip. The form is above average for the grade.

NOTEBOOK
Sienna Lake(IRE), who had changed yards since finishing a slightly unlucky runner-up in a Polytrack seller for Sylvester Kirk, was held up off the pace but came through to run down the long-time leader and in the end score cosily. There was quite a bit of interest in her at the subsequent auction but she was retained by connections and could be up to winning in nursery company. (op 4-1 tchd 9-2)
Pokfulham(IRE), dropping in grade and with the visor applied after showing little in three maidens, set off in front and looked as though he had stolen it coming out of the dip, but the winner ran on too strongly for him. Nevertheless, he was clear of the rest and can score at this level if the blinkers have the same effect next time. (op 25-1)
Ashwinder(IRE), quickly dropped to this level having been outpaced ina 6f maiden on his debut, did not fare badly having seen plenty of daylight throughout. (op 20-1)
Heaven Knows When(IRE), who was quite keen on her debut on Polytrack, was kept away from the rest of the field nearer the stands' side and tended to hang. She stayed on in the closing stages without looking the easiest of rides but, if the key can be found, she can win at this level. (op 14-1 tchd 16-1)
Miss Moloney(IRE), stepping up in trip and dropping in grade, showed up throughout but had nothing in reserve for the final climb.
All Angel, the only previous winner in the line-up, having taken a three-runner seller for Michael Squance, never really looked likely to get involved in the finish on this softer ground. (op 8-1 tchd 15-2)
Against The Rules, who was sent off a well-backed favourite, was dropping in class having showed ability in his previous outing over course and distance. It may be that the softer going did not suit, although considering he is by Diktat that would be somewhat surprising. Official explanation: trainer said, regarding the poor form shown, gelding was unsuited by the good to soft ground (op 2-1 tchd 5-2 and 11-4 in places)

4828 LUCID THINKING NURSERY 7f
6:50 (6:53) (Class 4) 2-Y-O **£5,180** (£1,541; £770; £384) **Stalls** Low

Form RPR
466 **1** **Battle Of Hastings**[34] 3707 2-8-2 **67**.................... HayleyTurner 11 68
(M L W Bell) *hld up: rdn over 1f out: r.o to ld ins fnl f: drvn out* **7/1**
561 **2** *3/4* **Kings Troop**[29] 3888 2-9-6 **85**.................... TPQueally 6 84
(H R A Cecil) *trckd ldrs: racd keenly: rdn and ev ch fr over 1f out: styd on* **5/2**[1]
004 **3** *nse* **Super Fourteen**[35] 3693 2-7-12 **63** oh2.................... DavidKinsella 12 62
(R Hannon) *racd alone tl jnd main gp 4f out: chsd ldrs: rdn to ld over 1f out: edgd lft: hdd ins fnl f: styd on* **20/1**
004 **4** *1/2* **Silent Hero**[20] 4176 2-7-13 **64** ow1.................... JimmyQuinn 8 62+
(M A Jarvis) *s.i.s: hld up: rdn and hung lft over 2f out: nt clr run ent fnl f: swtchd rt and r.o wl towards fin* **6/1**[3]
410 **5** *1 1/4* **Imperial Guest**[48] 3245 2-9-7 **86**.................... EddieAhern 3 81
(G G Margarson) *hld up: rdn over 1f out: r.o ins fnl f: no ex towards fin* **8/1**
5313 **6** *2 3/4* **Meydan Groove**[14] 4373 2-8-5 **70**.................... JoeFanning 4 58
(P F I Cole) *chsd ldr: rdn and ev ch over 1f out: wknd ins fnl f* **11/2**[2]
321 **7** *3/4* **Wilbury Star (IRE)**[16] 4296 2-9-4 **83**.................... RyanMoore 7 69
(R Hannon) *set stdy pce: qcknd over 2f out: rdn and hdd over 1f out: hung lft and wknd ins fnl f* **5/2**[1]
000 **8** *7* **Clerical (USA)**[36] 3651 2-7-12 **63** oh12.................... NickyMackay 1 31
(M J Gingell) *chsd ldrs: rdn over 2f out: wknd over 1f out* **50/1**

1m 29.5s (3.80) **Going Correction** +0.45s/f (Yiel) **8** Ran SP% **117.1**
Speed ratings (Par 96): **96,95,95,94,93 89,89,81**
toteswinger: 1&2 £6.60, 1&3 £33.90, 2&3 £9.30. CSF £25.56 CT £345.08 TOTE £10.50: £2.50, £1.40, £5.00; EX 33.50.
Owner R A Green **Bred** Myriad Communications & New England Stud **Trained** Newmarket, Suffolk

FOCUS
A fair nursery but the field was reduced by a third due to withdrawals and the time was a fair bit slower than the other races over the trip. The form is probably not that strong although the winner could do better.

NOTEBOOK

Battle Of Hastings, making his handicap debut having been short of pace over shorter trips on faster ground, was held up before coming through the pack to lead inside the last and was doing his best work at the finish. The longer trip and easier ground seemed to help and, although he will go up in the weights for this, he starts from a modest mark. (op 11-1)

Kings Troop, who encountered similar conditions when winning his maiden, was quite keen to get on with things under restraint and, although staying on, he could not hold off the winner to whom he was conceding 18lb. He can score in similar company if settling better. (tchd 11-4)

Super Fourteen, encountering soft ground for the first time on this handicap debut, was racing from 2lb out of the handicap and raced wide of his rivals in the early stages. He hit the front coming out of the dip and kept going once headed, so there may be a small race in him if able to build on this.

Silent Hero, stepping back up in trip on this handicap debut, missed the break and was settled at the back. He did not get the best of runs when asked to make his effort but was keeping on well in the closing stages to finish on the heels of the principals. (op 9-1 tchd 10-1)

Imperial Guest, who was conceding weight all round, was settled at the rear and never got involved. The race was probably not run to suit but he may be happier on a slightly faster surface. (op 11-2)

Meydan Groove, who ran well in a course and distance nursery following her success in a seller at Leicester, again performed with credit and will prefer a return to a faster surface. (tchd 13-2)

Wilbury Star(IRE), who won quite nicely over this trip at Leicester last time, set off in front but struggled at the business end and may have been found out by the easy ground. Official explanation: jockey said colt hung left in the final 2f. (tchd 9-4 and 11-4 in places)

4829 DAVIDCROFT.CO.UK H'CAP — 1m 2f

7:20 (7:22) (Class 5) (0-75,75) 3-Y-O+ — **£3,885** (£1,156; £577; £288) **Stalls** Centre

Form — RPR

0566 **1** **Krugerrand (USA)**[60] 2895 9-9-5 **66**....... RyanMoore 10 — 73+
(W J Musson) *hld up: swtchd lft and hdwy over 1f out: rdn to ld post* **7/1**[2]

0600 **2** *nse* **Balnagore**[28] 3914 4-9-3 **64**....... JimmyFortune 14 — 71
(J L Dunlop) *led: rdn over 1f out: hdd post* **11/1**

345 **3** *1 ¼* **Just Intersky (USA)**[9] 4526 5-8-3 **57**....... (p) CharlesEddery[(7)] 5 — 62
(V Smith) *dwlt: hld up: hdwy and swtchd far side over 3f out: swtchd bk to join main gp 2f out: rdn and ev ch over 1f out: styd on same pce towards fin* **33/1**

5602 **4** *nk* **Soviet (IRE)**[9] 4532 3-8-5 **61**....... JoeFanning 9 — 65
(M Johnston) *chsd ldrs: rdn over 1f out: styd on* **3/1**[1]

1044 **5** *¾* **Sonny Parkin**[7] 4603 6-10-0 **75**....... (v) PatCosgrave 7 — 78+
(J Pearce) *plld hrd and prom: stdd and lost pl over 8f out: rdn over 1f out: styd on ins fnl f* **9/1**[3]

3233 **6** *½* **Hannicean**[21] 4167 4-9-10 **71**....... PhilipRobinson 6 — 73
(M A Jarvis) *s.s: hld up: plld hrd: hdwy over 7f out: swtchd to far side over 3f out: rdn and hung rt over 1f out: no ex ins fnl f* **3/1**[1]

0-04 **7** *¾* **Daring Dream (GER)**[11] 4489 3-9-0 **70**....... DarrenWilliams 4 — 70
(A P Jarvis) *plld hrd and prom: rdn over 2f out: styng on same pce whn sddle slipped towards fin* **25/1**

5062 **8** *1* **Optimus (USA)**[22] 4129 6-9-12 **73**....... TQuinn 2 — 71
(B G Powell) *hld up: plld hrd: swtchd lft and hdwy over 1f out: wknd ins fnl f* **16/1**

6015 **9** *½* **Jebel Ali (IRE)**[23] 4081 5-9-6 **67**....... (v) SebSanders 1 — 64
(B Gubby) *hld up in tch: rdn over 1f out: wknd ins fnl f* **16/1**

-005 **10** *1* **Forget It**[78] 2327 3-8-11 **67**....... RichardHughes 8 — 62
(R Hannon) *chsd ldr: rdn over 2f out: wkng whn n.m.r 1f out* **7/1**[2]

2m 12.86s (7.36) **Going Correction** +0.45s/f (Yiel)
WFA 3 from 4yo+ 9lb — **10** Ran SP% **111.9**
Speed ratings (Par 103): **88,87,86,86,86 85,85,84,83,83**
toteswinger: 1&2 £17.00, 1&3 £28.80, 2&3 £35.50. CSF £70.33 CT £1747.76 TOTE £9.10: £2.60, £3.10, £7.90; EX 92.30.
Owner The Square Table II **Bred** T Farmer **Trained** Newmarket, Suffolk

FOCUS

A modest handicap for the track in which the pace was very steady and the time was 2secs slower than the following conditions stakes. The form looks somewhat shaky with the runner-up the best guide.

Balnagore Official explanation: jockey said colt lost an iron
Soviet(IRE) Official explanation: vet said colt finished lame in his near fore
Hannicean Official explanation: jockey said gelding hung right

4830 KIDS COMPANY CONDITIONS STKS — 1m 2f

7:50 (7:50) (Class 3) 3-Y-O — **£8,723** (£2,612; £1,306; £653; £326) **Stalls** Centre

Form — RPR

31 **1** **Meydan City (USA)**[30] 3854 3-9-0 **90**....... LDettori 1 — 106+
(Saeed Bin Suroor) *dwlt: sn prom: trckd ldr over 7f out: led on bit over 2f out: shkn up over 1f out: rdn clr and edgd lft fnl f* **4/5**[1]

5400 **2** *3 ½* **Siberian Tiger (IRE)**[8] 4552 3-9-0 **98**....... EdwardCreighton 2 — 99
(M R Channon) *set stdy pce: qcknd 3f out: sn rdn and hdd: hung lft fr over 1f out: no ex fnl f* **5/1**[3]

5-15 **3** *10* **By Command**[90] 1992 3-9-0 **99**....... SebSanders 3 — 79
(J L Dunlop) *hld up: plld hrd: rdn over 2f out: wknd over 1f out* **5/2**[2]

5640 **4** *shd* **Paveroc**[13] 4407 3-9-0 **88**....... JohnEgan 6 — 79
(Jane Chapple-Hyam) *plld hrd: trckd ldr to over 7f out: remained handy: rdn 3f out: wknd over 1f out* **12/1**

0300 **5** *53* **Diademas (USA)**[21] 4163 3-8-7 **56**....... AndreaAtzeni[(7)] 5 — —
(M J Gingell) *hld up: plld hrd: rdn: hung lft and wknd 3f out* **100/1**

2m 10.86s (5.36) **Going Correction** +0.45s/f (Yiel) — **5** Ran SP% **109.5**
Speed ratings (Par 104): **96,93,85,85,42**
toteswinger: 1&2 £3.40 CSF £5.29 TOTE £1.70: £1.10, £1.70; EX 4.80.
Owner Godolphin **Bred** Jayeff 'B' Stables **Trained** Newmarket, Suffolk

FOCUS

An ordinary conditions stakes run 2secs faster than preceding handicap. The form is muddling although the winner may be underrated.

NOTEBOOK

Meydan City(USA), who is saddled with an enormous price-tag, had beaten a subsequent winner when taking his maiden over course and distance and followed up here despite having a bit to find with his main rivals on official ratings. He travelled well throughout and, once taking the advantage, came away to win cosily. He looks capable of further progress and it will not be long before he is taking his chance in Pattern company; the question is how will he handle a faster surface. (op 11-10 tchd 6-5 after early 5-4)

Siberian Tiger(IRE), who has been struggling for form of late, made the running on only this second encounter with softer ground and ran creditably, although he was no match for the winner. (op 11-2 tchd 9-2)

By Command, who scooted up on his only previous run on rain-softened ground, was held up but when asked for an effort the response was limited. (op 13-8 tchd 11-4 in places)

Paveroc, another whose sole win was on easy ground, has gone backwards since his juvenile days and was another to produce a lacklustre performance. (op 14-1 tchd 10-1)

4831 JET AIRWAYS (INDIA) H'CAP — 6f

8:20 (8:20) (Class 4) (0-85,83) 3-Y-O+ — **£6,476** (£1,927; £963; £481) **Stalls** Low

Form — RPR

1150 **1** **Seamus Shindig**[15] 4341 6-9-4 **83**....... AmyScott[(7)] 5 — 91
(H Candy) *mde all: pushed along over 1f out: jst hld on* **10/1**

62/1 **2** *nse* **Amicus Meus (IRE)**[42] 3438 4-8-10 **71**....... DominicFox[(3)] 3 — 79
(A Bailey) *hld up in tch: rdn over 2f out: r.o wl: jst failed* **5/1**[2]

6052 **3** *½* **Cornus**[14] 4375 6-9-5 **77**....... (be) JamesDoyle 12 — 83
(A J McCabe) *s.i.s: hld up: hdwy over 1f out: r.o* **15/2**

3004 **4** *½* **Glasshoughton**[19] 4218 5-9-8 **80**....... PaulMulrennan 9 — 85
(M Dods) *hld up: rdn over 1f out: r.o wl ins fnl f* **7/1**[3]

153 **5** *nk* **Baunagain (IRE)**[60] 2883 3-9-6 **82**....... PatCosgrave 7 — 85
(M J Wallace) *trckd ldrs: hrd rdn ins fnl f: no ex towards fin* **12/1**

0241 **6** *1 ½* **Resplendent Alpha**[7] 4601 4-9-3 **75** 6ex....... JimmyQuinn 6 — 78+
(P Howling) *s.i.s: sn hld up in tch: racd keenly: nt clr run and lost pl over 2f out: r.o ins fnl f* **9/2**[1]

3036 **7** *1 ½* **China Cherub**[11] 4483 5-9-1 **73**....... (b) RyanMoore 14 — 67
(S Dow) *chsd ldrs: rdn over 1f out: styd on same pce* **8/1**

0002 **8** *½* **Bazroy (IRE)**[7] 4608 4-9-9 **81**....... (b) JohnEgan 11 — 74
(P D Evans) *chsd ldrs: rdn over 1f out: wknd ins fnl f* **7/1**[3]

5000 **9** *½* **Charles Darwin (IRE)**[15] 4341 5-9-8 **80**....... SteveDrowne 8 — 71
(M Blanshard) *hld up in tch: rdn over 1f out: wknd ins fnl f* **20/1**

62-0 **10** *1 ¼* **Mansii**[31] 3812 3-9-1 **77**....... LiamJones 1 — 63
(P J McBride) *hld up: pushed along 3f out: sme hdwy over 1f out: wknd ins fnl f* **33/1**

100 **11** *2* **Brunelleschi**[14] 4375 5-9-2 **74**....... (b) AlanMunro 13 — 55
(P L Gilligan) *s.i.s: hld up: rdn: edgd rt and wknd over 1f out* **11/1**

12 *15* **Ell Mona (IRE)**[53] 3-9-7 **83**....... SebSanders 2 — 15
(R W Price) *chsd ldrs: rdn over 2f out: wknd over 1f out* **14/1**

04-4 **13** *hd* **Piece Of My Heart**[87] 2077 3-8-13 **75**....... (bt[1]) SaleemGolam 4 — 6
(R W Price) *chsd ldrs tl rdn and wknd over 2f out* **33/1**

1m 14.34s (1.84) **Going Correction** +0.45s/f (Yiel)
WFA 3 from 4yo+ 4lb — **13** Ran SP% **125.2**
Speed ratings (Par 105): **105,104,104,103,103 101,99,98,97,96 93,73,73**
toteswinger: 1&2 £23.30, 1&3 £18.30, 2&3 £5.90 CSF £61.10 CT £421.80 TOTE £12.70: £3.60, £2.50, £2.90; EX 95.20 Place 6 £342.36, Place 5 £164.61..
Owner Henry Candy **Bred** R S A Urquhart **Trained** Kingston Warren, Oxon

FOCUS

A fair sprint handicap that produced a blanket finish but the form looks believable rated around the first three.

Bazroy(IRE) Official explanation: jockey said gelding lost its action
T/Plt: £534.20 to a £1 stake. Pool: £67,038.39. 91.60 winning tickets. T/Qpdt: £91.20 to a £1 stake. Pool: £5,351.50. 43.40 winning tickets. CR

3932 CORK (R-H)

Friday, August 8

OFFICIAL GOING: Good to yielding

4833a LADBROKES GIVE THANKS STKS (GROUP 3) (F&M) — 1m 4f

6:10 (6:12) 3-Y-O+ — **£47,867** (£14,044; £6,691; £2,279)

RPR

1 **Unsung Heroine (IRE)**[22] 4137 3-8-10....... WMLordan 14 — 106+
(T Stack, Ire) *mid-div: pushed along in 7th 4f out: prog into 4th 2 1/2f out: 2nd 1 1/2f out: led under 1f out: styd on wl* **11/2**[3]

2 *2* **Hasanka (IRE)**[41] 3513 4-9-7 **106**....... MJKinane 1 — 103
(John M Oxx, Ire) *prom: led fr 4f out: rdn clr 2 1/2f out: strly pressed over 1f out: hdd under 1f out: kpt on same pce* **8/1**

3 *2* **Arkadina (IRE)**[32] 3805 4-9-7 **98**....... DPMcDonogh 15 — 100
(David Wachman, Ire) *trckd ldrs: 4th 4f out: rdn in mod 2nd 2 1/2f out: no ex over 1f out* **14/1**

4 *1 ¾* **Ezima (IRE)**[34] 3720 4-9-7 **109**....... KJManning 11 — 97
(J S Bolger, Ire) *trckd ldrs: 5th 4f out: sn rdn: mod 3rd 2 1/2f out: no ex over 1f out* **7/2**[2]

5 *hd* **Hold Me Love Me (IRE)**[23] 4100 3-8-10 **93**....... WJSupple 9 — 97
(A P O'Brien, Ire) *led: hdd 4f out: sn no imp: kpt on same pce fr 2f out* **33/1**

6 *1 ¼* **Honoria (IRE)**[14] 4399 3-8-10 **100**....... JAHeffernan 13 — 95
(A P O'Brien, Ire) *trckd ldrs: 6th 4f out: sn rdn and no imp* **8/1**

7 *¾* **Love To Dance (IRE)**[22] 4137 3-8-10 **85**....... MichellePayne 4 — 93
(A P O'Brien, Ire) *towards rr on inner: no imp fr 3f out* **50/1**

8 *2 ½* **Sweet Sixteen (IRE)**[23] 4100 3-8-10 **80**....... SMLevey 16 — 89?
(A P O'Brien, Ire) *trckd ldrs: 6th and stmbld 5f out: lost pl: no imp fr 4f out* **40/1**

9 *1* **Juniper Berry (IRE)**[23] 4091 3-8-10 **83**....... CDHayes 10 — 88?
(John Joseph Murphy, Ire) *mid-div: 8th 4f out: no imp st* **50/1**

10 *4* **Nick's Nikita (IRE)**[41] 3513 5-9-7 **103**....... RPCleary 6 — 81
(M Halford, Ire) *mid-div: no imp fr 4f out* **12/1**

11 *hd* **Glitter Baby (IRE)**[7] 4611 5-9-7 **88**....... MCHussey 2 — 81
(P F Cashman, Ire) *in rr of mid-div: no imp fr 4f out* **20/1**

12 *4* **Chinese White (IRE)**[26] 4006 3-8-10 **110**....... (t) PJSmullen 12 — 75
(D K Weld, Ire) *trckd ldrs: 3rd 4f out: rdn fr 3f out: sn wknd: eased fnl f* **9/4**[1]

13 *9* **Sail (IRE)**[41] 3511 3-8-10 **105**....... CO'Donoghue 7 — 60
(A P O'Brien, Ire) *s.i.s and a towards rr* **14/1**

14 *2 ½* **Gentle On My Mind (IRE)**[26] 4006 3-8-10....... WJLee 5 — 56
(A P O'Brien, Ire) *mid-div: no imp fr 4f out* **33/1**

15 *3 ½* **Always Beautiful (USA)**[23] 4100 3-8-10 **97**....... FMBerry 3 — 51
(David Wachman, Ire) *towards rr: wknd fr 4f out: eased ins fnl f* **25/1**

16 *10* **Perihelion (IRE)**[11] 4495 3-8-10 **88**....... DavidMcCabe 8 — 35
(A P O'Brien, Ire) *a towards rr: eased fr 2f out* **40/1**

2m 35.28s (-12.62)
WFA 3 from 4yo+ 11lb — **16** Ran SP% **134.9**
CSF £50.90 TOTE £5.90: £1.20, £2.20, £5.00, £1.50; DF 122.50.
Owner Adahessonsplusone Syndicate **Bred** Grange Stud **Trained** Golden, Co Tipperary

NOTEBOOK

Unsung Heroine(IRE) had run out a workmanlike winner on her debut at Fairyhouse, but that form has since taken a big boost with the runner-up, Shreyas, going onto win by eleven lengths next time out. She followed up in taking fashion on this big step up in class, looking better the further she went over this longer trip, and is clearly a filly with aspirations of better things to come. This experience will teach her plenty again and she is now being considered for the St Leger at Doncaster. (op 11/2 tchd 6/1)

Hasanka(IRE) performed right up to her best on this return to the shorter trip, finishing a clear second best, and helps to set the standard of this form. (op 7/1)

Arkadina(IRE) turned in a slightly improved effort on this step up from Listed company and is another who helps to set this level. (op 12/1)

Ezima(IRE) took time to find her full stride on ground she would have found plenty easy enough. (op 9/2)

Sweet Sixteen(IRE) Official explanation: jockey said filly slipped on bend out of back straight

Chinese White(IRE) has to rate as very disappointing and she was beaten before the 2f pole. Her rider was not long in accpeting the situation and perhaps this came a little too soon after her fourth in the Irish Oaks last month, but she still has it all to prove now. Official explanation: jockey said filly made a noise and stopped quickly (op 9/4 tchd 5/2)

4834 - 4839a (Foreign Racing) - See Raceform Interactive

4443

ASCOT (R-H)

Saturday, August 9

OFFICIAL GOING: Good changing to good to soft after race 2 (1.45)

Wind: Modest, half against Weather: Rain

4840 BARCLAYS SHERGAR CUP DASH STKS (H'CAP) 5f

1:10 (1:12) (Class 2) (0-105,100) 3-Y-0+

£17,278 (£6,081; £2,805; £2,200; £1,944; £1,426) **Stalls** Low

Form					RPR
2422	1		**Strike Up The Band**[13] 4445 5-9-3 **94** ... YTake 7		106
			(D Nicholls) *stmbld s: sn led: rdn over 1f out: styd on wl to forge ahd fnl 100yds*	**3/1**[1]	
-365	2	1 1/4	**Fathom Five (IRE)**[43] 3451 4-9-5 **96** ... HKaratas 10		104
			(B Smart) *racd keenly: chsd wnr: ev ch and rdn over 1f out: unable qckn ins fnl f*	**8/1**[3]	
5004	3	3/4	**Evens And Odds (IRE)**[28] 3943 4-9-6 **97** ...(bt) LDettori 4		102
			(K A Ryan) *chsd ldrs: rdn 2f out: kpt on fnl f: nvr pce to chal ldrs*	**14/1**	
2500	4	hd	**Dark Missile**[21] 4188 5-9-7 **98** ...(t) KJManning 9		102
			(A M Balding) *awkward s: sn chsng ldrs: rdn and chal over 1f out: one pce fnl f*	**3/1**[1]	
3110	5	hd	**Crimson Fern (IRE)**[9] 4550 4-9-3 **94** ... HayleyTurner 5		97+
			(M S Saunders) *stdd s: swtchd lft and hld up bhd on rail: nt clr run and swtchd rt over 1f out: kpt on u.p fnl f: nt rch ldrs*	**5/1**[2]	
1405	6	1/2	**Mac Gille Eoin**[7] 4624 4-9-8 **99** ... RBaze 8		101
			(J Gallagher) *chsd ldrs: rdn and hung lft over 1f out: kpt on same pce u.p fnl f*	**14/1**	
5060	7	6	**New Freedom (BRZ)**[13] 4445 7-9-9 **100** ... SebSanders 3		80
			(D R Lanigan) *awkward s: hung rt thrght: a in rr: rdn over 2f out: no prog: eased whn no ch ins fnl f*	**16/1**	
0005	8	2	**The Trader (IRE)**[28] 3943 10-9-4 **95** ...(b) JRicardo 2		68
			(M Blanshard) *s.i.s: bhd: carried rt over 3f out: effrt ent fnl 2f: wknd over 1f: eased ins fnl f*	**25/1**	
-301	9	5	**Stoneacre Lad (IRE)**[66] 2712 5-9-9 **100** ...(b) MDemuro 6		55
			(Peter Grayson) *racd in midfield: rdn over 2f out: wknd over 1f out*	**14/1**	
663L	R		**Bentong (IRE)**[7] 4624 5-9-9 **100** ...(bt[1]) JamieSpencer 1		—
			(P F I Cole) *ref to r: tk no part*	**10/1**	

61.19 secs (0.69) **Going Correction** +0.375s/f (Good) **10** Ran SP% **116.6**

Speed ratings (Par 109): **109,107,105,105,105 104,94,91,83,—**

toteswinger: 1&2 £8.50, 1&3 £16.80, 2&3 £8.60. CSF £27.85 CT £299.14 TOTE £3.90: £1.60, £2.80, £3.00; EX 37.80 Trifecta £361.60 Pool: £1,202.19 - 2.46 winning units..

Owner Barker Moser Nicholls Power & Short **Bred** Miss A J Rawding And P M Crane **Trained** Sessay, N Yorks

■ Stewards' Enquiry : R Baze four-day ban: used whip with excessive frequency and without giving horse time to respond (Aug 23-26)

FOCUS

A decent sprint, run at a solid pace. The field came towards the stands' side and the form looks straightforward and makes sense.

NOTEBOOK

Strike Up The Band, runner-up at the track the last twice, recovered from an awkward start to grab the early lead and, soon making his way towards the stands' rail, eventually came home to score in decisive fashion. This success was much deserved and he is clearly right at the very top of his game at present, so he may well be able to build on this first success since 2006 despite another weight rise. (op 7-2)

Fathom Five(IRE) was never going to get the winner and did not really help himself by running freely early on, but still performed right up to his previous best in defeat. He looks handicapped about right, but deserves some reward for his consistency. (op 15-2)

Evens And Odds(IRE) followed the eventual winner up the rail and, racing on 6lb better terms, finished closer to that rival than had been the case over course and distance in July. He is still 3lb higher than his last winning mark. (op 12-1)

Dark Missile, well backed and racing in a first-time tongue tie, overcame an awkward start and was soon up with the pace. She eventually had her chance, but simply looked to find this drop in trip too sharp. No doubt she is well handicapped at present - being only 2lb higher than when winning the Wokingham last season - and a return to 6f should really see her get closer again in handicap company now. (op 6-1)

Crimson Fern(IRE) fared best of those to come from off the pace and can be rated a bit better than the bare form as she met a troubled passage approaching the final furlong. This progressive filly enjoyed the return to a handicap and does not look weighted out of winning just yet. (op 7-2)

Mac Gille Eoin, dropped 1lb for finishing fifth in the Stewards' Cup a week previously, looked to find this drop to the minimum too sharp and was beaten soon after the final furlong marker. This was still another creditable effort.

Bentong(IRE) had planted himself in the stalls in the Stewards' Cup last week and was equipped with first-time blinkers for this first-ever run over the minimum. He repeated the feat, however, refusing to budge when the gates flew back, and is obviously one to avoid at all costs at present. (op 12-1)

4841 TITANIC QUARTER SHERGAR CUP DISTAFF (H'CAP) (F&M) 7f

1:45 (1:47) (Class 2) (0-100,95) 4-Y-0+

£17,230 (£6,034; £2,758; £2,152; £1,897; £1,379) **Stalls** Low

Form					RPR
4100	1		**Nans Joy (IRE)**[8] 4590 4-10-0 **95** ... YTake 6		105
			(E J O'Neill) *s.i.s: hld up bhd: gd hdwy on outer wl over 1f out: led ins fnl f: r.o wl*	**7/1**	
2540	2	1 1/2	**Chantilly Tiffany**[14] 4424 4-9-9 **90** ... GMosse 10		96
			(E A L Dunlop) *hld up towards rr: hdwy over 2f out: chal over 1f out: led ent fnl f: hdd and no ex ins fnl f*	**13/2**[3]	
5314	3	1	**Froissee**[77] 2389 4-9-1 **82** ... RichardHughes 5		85
			(S A Callaghan) *wnt rt s: hld up in tch: rdn over 2f out: ev ch over 1f out: unable qckn fnl f*	**11/2**[2]	
101	4	1	**Summer Gold (IRE)**[30] 3866 4-9-1 **82** ... SebSanders 8		82
			(E J Alston) *chsd ldr: rdn to ld 2f out: hdd 1f out: wknd ins fnl f*	**9/2**[1]	
-050	5	shd	**Vital Statistics**[8] 4590 4-9-4 **85** ... LDettori 2		85+
			(D R C Elsworth) *s.i.s: t.k.h: hld up bhd: nt clr run and swtchd rt wl over 1f out: r.o fnl f: nvr rchd ldrs*	**15/2**	
0440	6	1 1/2	**Ivory Lace**[3] 4723 7-8-13 **80** ... HKaratas 4		76+
			(S Woodman) *hld up towards rr: effrt whn hmpd wl over 1f out: kpt on u.p fnl f: nvr trbld ldrs*	**14/1**	
5305	7	hd	**Steam Cuisine**[42] 3500 4-9-11 **92** ... JRicardo 3		87+
			(M G Quinlan) *t.k.h: hld up wl in tch: nt clr run over 2f out: swtchd rt and nt clr run wl over 1f out: swtchd lft sn after: no imp fnl f*	**8/1**	
3105	8	8	**Carcinetto (IRE)**[6] 4660 6-9-6 **87** ... MDemuro 9		61
			(P D Evans) *chsd ldrs: rdn and edgd lft over 2f out: struggling whn jostled wl over 1f out: no ch after*	**9/1**	
1020	9	1 1/4	**Dressed To Dance (IRE)**[8] 4601 4-9-6 **87** ... KJManning 1		57
			(P D Evans) *chsd ldrs: rdn 1/2-way: wknd 2f out*	**10/1**	
0530	10	3/4	**Sakhee's Song (IRE)**[9] 4550 4-9-12 **93** ... HayleyTurner 7		61
			(D R C Elsworth) *racd freely: led tl rdn and hdd 2f out: sn wknd*	**16/1**	

1m 29.12s (1.12) **Going Correction** +0.375s/f (Good) **10** Ran SP% **113.9**

Speed ratings (Par 109): **108,106,105,104,103 102,101,92,91,90**

toteswinger: 1&2 £30.20, 1&3 £9.40, 2&3 £20.80. CSF £50.71 CT £274.90 TOTE £8.30: £2.20, £3.10, £1.90; EX 105.90 Trifecta £391.50 Pool: £1,105.89 - 2.09 winning units..

Owner Frank Cosgrove **Bred** Mrs Brid Cosgrove **Trained** Averham Park, Notts

FOCUS

A competitive renewal of the Distaff. It produced a worthy winner and the form is rated through the placed horses.

NOTEBOOK

Nans Joy(IRE), despite making another sluggish start, found this drop out of Group company ideal and, confidently ridden, eventually scored decisively under top weight. She would have enjoyed the decent early pace and this effort confirms her as better than just a handicapper, so no doubt connections will go in search of some more black type now. (op 8-1)

Chantilly Tiffany emerged from off the pace going as well as any passing the 2f pole and took it up entering the final furlong, but eventually had no answer to the winner's late challenge. This was her best run for a while and she could just build on this when returning to another furlong. (op 10-1)

Froissee came from off the pace with every chance nearing the final furlong, but she eventually found just the same pace when put under maximum pressure. This rates a pleasing return from her 77-day break. (op 4-1)

Summer Gold(IRE) was bidding for her third win from just four outings this term and was not surprisingly ridden positively, but she simply found this trip too sharp in the end. She should not be discounted from this sort of mark when returning to a suitably stiffer test. (op 11-2)

Vital Statistics made a tardy start and then took time to settle under early restraint. She was making up her ground prior to meeting some trouble in between the final two furlongs and, a little better than the bare form, this was certainly a more encouraging effort. She now looks to have found her level. (op 12-1)

Ivory Lace would have been closer at the finish had she not been hampered approaching the final furlong and this was not a bad effort from her. (op 11-1)

4842 PORTHAULT SHERGAR CUP SPRINT (H'CAP) 6f

2:20 (2:22) (Class 2) (0-100,100) 3-Y-0

£17,230 (£6,034; £2,758; £2,152; £1,897; £1,379) **Stalls** Low

Form					RPR
3411	1		**Shifting Star (IRE)**[29] 3898 3-9-6 **92** ... GMosse 6		101
			(W R Swinburn) *hld up in tch: swtchd lft and hdwy over 1f out: rdn and qcknd to ld 1f out: r.o strly: readily*	**7/2**[1]	
-205	2	1 1/4	**Al Muheer (IRE)**[14] 4404 3-9-12 **98** ... RBaze 8		103
			(C E Brittain) *pressed ldr thrght: rdn over 1f out: kpt on but nt pce of wnr ins fnl f*	**14/1**	
002	3	1	**Kaldoun Kingdom (IRE)**[28] 3973 3-9-5 **91** ... SebSanders 2		93
			(R A Fahey) *t.k.h: hld up in tch: swtchd rt and hdwy jst over 2f out: chsd ldrs ent fnl f: kpt on same pce u.p*	**6/1**[3]	
0231	4	nk	**Spanish Bounty**[31] 3850 3-9-10 **96** ... HKaratas 7		97
			(J G Portman) *led: rdn and hdd 1f out: fdd and lost 2 pls wl ins fnl f*	**8/1**	
2052	5	2	**Spitfire**[31] 3850 3-9-12 **98** ... LDettori 1		93
			(J R Jenkins) *hld up in tch: rdn and hdwy on stands rail 2f out: ev ch ent fnl f: hung rt and wknd ins fnl f*	**9/2**[2]	
3302	6	3/4	**Little Pete (IRE)**[8] 4591 3-9-6 **92** ... JamieSpencer 9		84
			(A M Balding) *s.i.s: swtchd lft and hld up bhd: edgd out rt and effrt over 2f out: hung lft u.p: nvr nr ldrs*	**15/2**	
0222	7	3 1/2	**Sudden Impact (IRE)**[14] 4408 3-9-6 **92** ... YTake 5		73
			(Paul Green) *prom tl wknd qckly 1/2-way: wl bhd fnl 2f*	**8/1**	
0055	8	5	**Berbice (IRE)**[10] 4522 3-9-6 **92** ...(t) RichardHughes 4		57
			(R Hannon) *v.s.a: nvr a factor*	**8/1**	
2000	9	5	**Carleton**[9] 4553 3-9-3 **89** ... KJManning 10		38
			(W J Musson) *chsd ldrs: rdn wl over 2f out: wknd wl over 1f out*	**12/1**	

1m 15.39s (0.99) **Going Correction** +0.375s/f (Good) **9** Ran SP% **114.1**

Speed ratings (Par 106): **108,106,105,104,101 100,96,89,82**

toteswinger: 1&2 £12.10, 1&3 £4.40, 2&3 £25.60. CSF £52.84 CT £285.86 TOTE £4.60: £1.70, £4.90, £2.20; EX 66.00 Trifecta £713.30 Pool: £1,166.48 - 1.21 winning units..

Owner Night Shadow Syndicate **Bred** Hardys Of Kilkeel Ltd **Trained** Aldbury, Herts

FOCUS

A decent sprint handicap, run at a strong pace. The progressive winner rates value for a little further and the form is rated around the runner-up and fourth, backed up by the third.

NOTEBOOK

Shifting Star(IRE) ◆ maintained his progression and bagged the hat-trick from another 4lb higher mark. There was plenty to like about the manner in which he moved through the race and then settled the issue, ultimately doing the job with something to spare. His connections will now surely be eyeing a big handicap prize with him now and further improvement is hard to rule out. (op 4-1)

Al Muheer(IRE) showed speed on this drop in trip, but ultimately looked to find the trip a little too sharp. This was a solid effort in defeat and a return to 7f could just see him go one better now. (tchd 16-1)

Kaldoun Kingdom(IRE) ◆ did not help his chances by running freely under restraint, but he still came through to post another solid effort in defeat and rates a fair benchmark for the form. He would have liked the easing ground and could be placed to strike in the coming weeks. (op 5-1)

Spanish Bounty, raised 6lb for resuming winning ways at Newbury a month previously, displayed his customary early dash and ran right up to form. He just looks held by the Handicapper now. (op 15-2)

Spitfirewas 3lb better off with Spanish Bounty on their Newbury form a month ago and he looked a player entering the final furlong, only for his effort to flatten out at the business end. He ideally wants a sharper test over this trip. (op 5-1)

Little Pete(IRE), 4lb higher, made a tardy start and failed to land a blow from off the pace on this first outing over 6f. (op 8-1 tchd 7-1)

4843 CARVILL SHERGAR CUP STAYERS (H'CAP) 2m

2:55 (2:58) (Class 2) (0-100,100) 4-Y-0+

£17,230 (£6,034; £2,758; £2,152; £1,897; £1,379) **Stalls** High

Form				RPR
5150	1		**Gee Dee Nen**[28] 3942 5-9-4 **90** .... HayleyTurner 7 (M H Tompkins) *hld up wl off the pce in midfield: hdwy 4f out: hmpd 2f out: styd on u.p to chse ldr ins fnl f: led last strides* **5/1**[2]	98+
5233	2	*hd*	**Bogside Theatre (IRE)**[28] 3942 4-9-5 **91** .... GMosse 9 (G M Moore) *led and sn clr: rdn 2f out: 4l clr 1f out: hdd last strides* **10/3**[1]	99
3600	3	*2*	**Grande Caiman (IRE)**[29] 3925 4-9-2 **88** .... (p) MDemuro 2 (R Hannon) *chsd clr ldng pair: lost pl 6f out: poor 8th and rdn 3f out: hdwy and swtchd lft jst over 2f out: r.o wl to go 3rd nr fin: nt rch ldrs* **33/1**	94
2-65	4	*nk*	**Caracciola (GER)**[15] 4362 11-9-12 **98** .... JamieSpencer 3 (N J Henderson) *chsd clr ldng pair: rdn and swtchd sharply lft and hmpd wnr 2f out: kpt on u.p but nt pce to rch ldrs* **15/2**	103
0120	5	*1*	**La Vecchia Scuola (IRE)**[10] 4516 4-9-2 **88** .... KJManning 6 (J S Goldie) *chsd clr ldr but clr of remainder: rdn 3f out: no imp: lost 3 pls ins fnl f* **11/2**[3]	92
0-10	6	*11*	**Desert Sea (IRE)**[42] 3490 5-9-6 **92** .... JRicardo 10 (D W P Arbuthnot) *racd wl off the pce in midfield: hdwy over 3f out: rdn and btn over 2f out* **16/1**	83
-150	7	*1 1/4*	**Highland Legacy**[42] 3490 4-9-9 **95** .... SebSanders 8 (M L W Bell) *racd off the pce in midfield: hdwy to chse ldng pair over 4f out: keeping on same pce whn sltly hmpd 2f out: sn wknd* **7/1**	84
-052	8	*nse*	**Greenwich Meantime**[15] 4362 8-9-6 **92** .... RBaze 5 (R A Fahey) *t.k.h: hld up in rr: nvr a factor* **16/1**	81
0-00	9	*36*	**Mudawin (IRE)**[10] 4516 7-9-2 **88** .... YTake 1 (J S Goldie) *hld up wl bhd in last: t.o and virtually p.u fnl f* **14/1**	34
-604	10	*4 1/2*	**Enjoy The Moment**[15] 4362 5-9-11 **97** .... RichardHughes 4 (J A Osborne) *hld up wl bhd: gd hdwy 5f out: chsd ldrs and rdn 3f out: btn 2f out: virtually p.u fnl f* **11/2**[3]	38

3m 35.22s (2.62) **Going Correction** +0.225s/f (Good) **10 Ran SP% 116.2**
Speed ratings (Par 109): **102,101,100,100,100 94,94,94,76,73**
toteswinger: 1&2 £5.60, 1&3 £72.60, 2&3 £64.60. CSF £21.93 CT £497.16 TOTE £7.30: £2.60, £1.80, £12.80; EX 28.90 TRIFECTA Not won..
Owner David P Noblett **Bred** Kingwood Bloodstock **Trained** Newmarket, Suffolk
■ Stewards' Enquiry : Jamie Spencer one-day ban: careless riding (Aug 23)

FOCUS
A competitive staying handicap, run at a decent gallop. The first pair finished clear and the form looks pretty straightforward with the next three home all close to their marks.

NOTEBOOK
Gee Dee Nen relished being held up again off a decent gallop and, under a well-timed ride, just did enough to collar the long-time leader near the line. Reversing his Northumberland Plate and course-and-distance form with that rival, he rates value for better than the bare margin as he got hampered 2f out, and he enjoyed this rain-softened ground. He is evidently in top form at present and a 4lb penalty now takes his weight in the Ebor to 8st 8lb, but the 2m trip there is probably a little too sharp for him. (op 9-1 tchd 9-2)
Bogside Theatre(IRE), in front of the winner in the Northumberland Plate and over course and distance on her last two outings, was racing from another 2lb higher mark. She had his own way out in front, setting off at a decent clip, and looked to have done enough when shaking off his fellow pacesetters at the final furlong pole. Her stride began to shorten in the final 100 yards, however, and she was agonisingly collared at the line. She richly deserves to find compensation, but is clearly weighted to her best now and may go up again for this. (op 4-1 tchd 3-1)
Grande Caiman(IRE) looked held at the top of the home straight, but he responded positively to maximum pressure and was eventually doing all of his best work towards the finish. This was his first run beyond 12f and he clearly stays very well, so has more options now. (op 25-1)
Caracciola(GER), a runner-up in this event last term from an 11lb lower mark, showed himself to be as good as ever with a sound effort in defeat. He is being lined up for another crack at the Cesarewitch in October. (op 6-1)
La Vecchia Scuola(IRE), back down in trip, had finished in front of the first pair over course and distance on her penultimate outing. She ran another sound race in defeat, still bang there between the final two furlongs, but her effort eventually flattened out when it really mattered. She obviously takes her racing very well, but may just appreciate a little break now. (op 15-2 tchd 8-1)
Highland Legacy would have enjoyed the rain-softened ground and he looked a player when moving up before the final bend, but his effort proved short-lived. This was another disappointing performance.

4844 MICHAEL PAGE INTERNATIONAL SHERGAR CUP CHALLENGE (H'CAP) 1m 4f

3:30 (3:33) (Class 2) (0-100,101) 4-Y-0+

£17,230 (£6,034; £2,758; £2,152; £1,897; £1,379) **Stalls** High

Form				RPR
0-00	1		**Strategic Mount**[21] 4191 5-9-6 **94** .... MDemuro 3 (P F I Cole) *hld up in rr: hdwy on outer 4f out: rdn over 2f out: chsd ldr jst over 1f out: led ins fnl f: r.o wl* **16/1**	103
1200	2	*1*	**Record Breaker (IRE)**[11] 4508 4-9-6 **94** .... RichardHughes 5 (M Johnston) *chsd ldr tl led over 5f out: rdn 3l clr wl over 2f out: hdd and no ex ins fnl f* **7/1**	102
5135	3	*1 3/4*	**Formax (FR)**[11] 4508 6-9-3 **91** .... HayleyTurner 9 (M P Tregoning) *t.k.h: hld up bhd: rdn and effrt wl over 2f out: swtchd rt 2f out: kpt on u.p fnl f* **9/2**[2]	96
12-0	4	*1 1/4*	**Filios (IRE)**[191] 381 4-9-9 **97** .... JamieSpencer 7 (Saeed Bin Suroor) *hld up in midfield: hdwy and rdn wl over 2f out: swtchd lft over 1f out: chsd ldr briefly jst over 1f out: one pce fnl f* **5/1**[3]	100
5616	5	*4*	**Sahrati**[15] 4363 4-9-2 **90** .... (b) LDettori 2 (C E Brittain) *in tch in midfield: hdwy to chse ldrs over 3f out: rdn wl over 2f out: keeping on same pce whn sltly hmpd over 1f out: wknd fnl f* **10/1**	87
-042	6	*2*	**Candle**[29] 3925 5-9-6 **94** .... JRicardo 10 (H Candy) *chsd ldrs: wknd ent fnl 2f* **6/1**	87
5610	7	*1/2*	**Profit's Reality (IRE)**[13] 4444 6-9-6 **94** .... SebSanders 1 (P A Blockley) *chsd ldrs: wnt 2nd over 5f out: rdn 3f out: wkng whn hmpd over 1f out: wl btn after* **8/1**	87
0110	8	*2 1/4*	**Polish Power (GER)**[27] 4003 8-9-4 **92** .... GMosse 4 (J S Moore) *hld up bhd: effrt wl over 2f out: no hdwy* **14/1**	81
41-4	9	*nk*	**All The Good (IRE)**[13] 4444 5-9-13 **101** .... HKaratas 8 (Saeed Bin Suroor) *hld up bhd: effrt and rdn wl over 2f out: no hdwy* **4/1**[1]	90
0000	10	*101*	**Coeur De Lionne (IRE)**[49] 3249 4-9-4 **92** .... (p) RBaze 6 (E A L Dunlop) *racd freely: led tl over 5f out: sn dropped out: t.o and virtually p.u fr over 2f out* **25/1**	—

2m 35.36s (-0.14) **Going Correction** +0.225s/f (Good) **10 Ran SP% 118.2**
Speed ratings (Par 109): **109,108,107,106,103 102,102,100,100,—**
toteswinger: 1&2 £25.50, 1&3 £18.30, 2&3 £10.00. CSF £125.24 CT £598.81 TOTE £17.70: £4.10, £3.10, £2.10; EX 138.80 TRIFECTA Not won..
Owner Ben & Sir Martyn Arbib **Bred** Arbib Bloodstock Partnership **Trained** Whatcombe, Oxon

FOCUS
A decent handicap, run at a solid pace. The form is straightforward rated through the third.

NOTEBOOK
Strategic Mount was racing from his last winning mark, which came in this event on faster ground last term, and he bounced back to his best with a ready display to repeat the feat. This return to 1m4f is really what he wanted and he obviously handles easier ground better now, although it would have been riding quicker in the home straight where he was asked for his effort. (op 11-1 tchd 18-1)
Record Breaker(IRE) returned to form under a positive ride, looking the one to beat for most of the home straight, and only got picked off by the winner late on. This was a much-improved effort, but he remains 6lb higher than his last win. (op 10-1 tchd 13-2)
Formax(FR) took time to settle under early restraint and was eventually doing all of his best work too late in the day on this drop back in trip. He is running consistently at present, but is not that easy to catch right. (op 5-1 tchd 11-2)
Filios(IRE) showed up nicely from off the pace on this first outing for 191 days and should really come on a deal for the run. He has presumably had his problems since joining Godolphin, but should be placed to get closer next time out. (op 8-1)
Candle, 6lb higher than when behind Profit's Reality at Newmarket last time, finished in front of that rival yet still ran well below her previous level. (op 9-2)
All The Good(IRE) was never in the hunt from off the pace and failed to build on the promise of his seasonal bow in better company a fortnight previously. There is a chance this came too soon. (op 3-1)

4845 LES AMBASSADEURS CLUB SHERGAR CUP MILE (H'CAP) 1m (R)

4:05 (4:11) (Class 2) (0-100,100) 4-Y-0+

£17,230 (£6,034; £2,758; £2,152; £1,897; £1,379) **Stalls** High

Form				RPR
11-0	1		**Perfect Star**[10] 4520 4-9-8 **95** .... GMosse 4 (C G Cox) *hld up in last trio: wanting to hang rt and n.m.r fr over 2f out tl swtchd lft over 1f out: str run to ld ins fnl f: in command towards fin* **4/1**[3]	105+
-422	2	*1*	**Ace Of Hearts**[35] 3740 9-9-8 **95** .... RBaze 7 (C F Wall) *t.k.h: chsd ldrs: rdn 3f out: led ent fnl f: hdd and no ex ins fnl f* **8/1**	102
-256	3	*1*	**Kay Gee Be (IRE)**[44] 3398 4-9-7 **94** .... YTake 5 (M J Wallace) *hld up in tch: effrt on outer over 2f out: chsd ldrs and rdn ent fnl f: kpt on* **16/1**	99
13-1	4	*nk*	**Gold Sovereign (IRE)**[60] 2913 4-9-12 **99** .... RichardHughes 3 (Saeed Bin Suroor) *in tch: swtchd rt and hdwy ent fnl f: one pce u.p fnl f* **7/2**[2]	103
-610	5	*3 1/2*	**Scartozz**[44] 3413 6-9-11 **98** .... (bt) HKaratas 9 (M Botti) *pressed ldr: led over 2f out: sn rdn: hdd ent fnl f: wknd ins fnl f* **20/1**	94
5-50	6	*1*	**Kinsya**[11] 4504 5-9-6 **93** .... HayleyTurner 2 (M H Tompkins) *stdd and swtchd rt after s: sn chsng ldrs on inner: rdn and fnd little 2f out: plugged on same pce after* **8/1**	87
	7	*1 1/4*	**Tamimi's History**[107] 4143 4-9-10 **97** .... KJManning 8 (P D Evans) *hld up in tch in rr: rdn jst over 2f out: wknd over 1f out* **14/1**	88
0400	8	*6*	**Fishforcompliments**[8] 4587 4-9-6 **93** .... JRicardo 10 (R A Fahey) *led at stdy gallop: hdd over 2f out: wkng whn hmpd over 1f out: wl btn and eased fnl f* **12/1**	70
5414	9	*2 1/4*	**Cape Hawk (IRE)**[8] 4587 4-9-5 **92** .... LDettori 1 (R Hannon) *hld up bhd: rdn and effrt 3f out: no prog* **10/3**[1]	64

1m 44.33s (3.53) **Going Correction** +0.225s/f (Good) **10 Ran SP% 112.5**
Speed ratings (Par 109): **91,90,89,88,85 84,82,76,74**
toteswinger: 1&2 £3.60, 1&3 £13.90, 2&3 £48.60. CSF £33.40 CT £397.43 TOTE £4.20: £1.40, £2.10, £3.30; EX 29.80 Trifecta £178.20 Pool: £1,683.59 - 6.99 winning units. Place 6 £184.55, Place 5 £73.90.Vanderlin was withdrawn. Price at time of withdrawal 14/1. Rule 4 applies to all bets. Deduct 5p in the pound.
Owner Dr Bridget Drew & E E Dedman **Bred** Mrs A M Jenkins And E D Kessly **Trained** Lambourn, Berks

FOCUS
Another decent handicap, but the early pace was only modest. The winner did well to come from off the pace and recorded a career-best, while the runner-up helps to give the form a sound enough look.

NOTEBOOK
Perfect Star, who shaped pleasingly on her comeback at Goodwood ten days previously, showed the clear benefit of that run and returned to the sort of form that saw her win a Listed handicap over course and distance on her final outing last term. She was ridden with a lot more patience than is usually the case and did well to come from off the modest early pace, so should rate a little better than the bare form. It will not be at all surprising to see her go in search of more black type now and there could be more to come. (tchd 7-2 and 9-2)
Ace Of Hearts, runner-up in this event last season, paid inside the final furlong for running freely on the modest early pace and again managed to find one too good. He has now finished second on his last three outings, there is no doubting he is great form at present, and he ran right up to his recent level here so rates the benchmark for the form. While the Handicapper knows all about this nine-year-old, he has won from a 1lb higher mark in the past, and certainly deserves to go one better again.
Kay Gee Be(IRE) was dropping back in trip for this first run on turf since June last year and he posted a much better effort in defeat. He is another who would have ideally enjoyed a stronger early pace. (op 12-1)
Gold Sovereign(IRE) had been raised 9lb for his seasonal-debut win at Redcar 60 days previously and, while he creditably in defeat, this was a little below his previous form. Despite his sire's progeny having shown a liking for soft ground it may be that he is really happiest on a quicker surface. (op 4-1 tchd 9-2)
Scartozz had the tongue tie back on and showed his latest run at Newcastle to be all wrong with a fair effort from the front, but probably needs a sharper test over this trip. (tchd 16-1)
Cape Hawk(IRE) never looked a threat from off the pace and ultimately performed a long way below his recent level. He may be in need of a break now. (op 3-1 tchd 4-1)
T/Plt: £417.60 to a £1 stake. Pool: £132,631.62. 231.80 winning tickets. T/Qpdt: £84.90 to a £1 stake. Pool: £6,953.08. 60.60 winning tickets. SP

4236 AYR (L-H)

Saturday, August 9

OFFICIAL GOING: Good to soft (soft in places)

Wind: Slight, across Weather: Overcast

4846 BETFAIR APPRENTICE TRAINING SERIES H'CAP 6f

5:50 (5:51) (Class 5) (0-70,66) 3-Y-0+ **£3,885** (£1,156; £577; £288) **Stalls** High

Form				RPR
-400	1		**Almost Married (IRE)**[26] 4013 4-9-7 **55** .... PatrickDonaghy 5 (J S Goldie) *chsd ldrs: rdn over 2f out: led over 1f out: kpt on wl: rdn out* **14/1**	65

2002 **2** 1 **Imperial Sword**28 3952 5-9-10 **58**....................(b) DeanHeslop 8 65+
(T D Barron) *s.i.s: sn outpcd in rr: stdy prog fr 3f out: nt clr run and swtchd lft 2f out: styd on to go 2nd ins fnl f* **4/1**1

5000 **3** ½ **Argentine (IRE)**34 3080 4-9-7 **55**.................... SimonPearce 10 60
(L Lungo) *mid-div: rdn and hdwy over 2f out: chsd wnr ent fnl f: no ex and lost 2nd towards fin* **8/1**

0400 **4** 3¾ **Seafield Towers**9 4561 8-8-13 **52**.................... MatthewLawson(5) 7 45
(D A Nolan) *mid-div: rdn over 2f out: kpt on but nt pce to mount chal* **25/1**

5 3¾ **Absa Lutte (IRE)**42 3508 5-9-10 **61**.................... BMcHugh(3) 3 42
(Jarlath P Fahey, Ire) *s.i.s: sn mid-div: rdn over 2f out: no imp* **8/1**

0054 **6** nk **Howards Prince**22 4144 5-8-6 **45**.................... PaulPickard(5) 9 25
(D A Nolan) *t.k.h: prom: rdn and ev ch 2f out: wknd ent fnl f* **80/1**

7 1¼ **Rocketball (IRE)**21 4208 3-10-0 **66**.................... PTownend 12 42
(Patrick Morris, Ire) *prom: rdn to ld over 2f out: hdd over 1f out: sn wknd* **9/2**2

0504 **8** 1 **Grimes Faith**16 4327 5-9-9 **62**....................(b) JamieKyne(5) 2 35
(K A Ryan) *hld up towards rr: sme prog u.p over 2f out: wknd over 1f out* **10/1**

0551 **9** 1¼ **Mr Rooney (IRE)**9 4561 5-9-9 **60**.................... RyanMania(3) 1 29
(A Berry) *chsd ldrs: rdn over 2f out: wknd over 1f out* **12/1**

000 **10** nse **Tom Tower (IRE)**26 4018 4-9-2 **53**.................... LanceBetts(3) 11 22
(A C Whillans) *led: rdn 3f out: hdd over 2f out: grad fdd* **25/1**

0002 **11** nk **Ensign's Trick**7 4653 4-9-5 **53**.................... DeclanCannon 6 21
(W M Brisbourne) *awkward leaving stalls: mid-div: rdn 3f out: sn wknd* **7/1**3

1354 **12** ¾ **Howards Tipple**9 4561 4-9-3 **58**....................(p) SFeeney(7) 4 24
(Miss L A Perratt) *a towards rr* **7/1**3

1m 13.37s (-0.23) **Going Correction** +0.05s/f (Good)
WFA 3 from 4yo+ 4lb **12** Ran SP% **117.8**
Speed ratings (Par 103): **103,101,101,96,91 90,88,87,85,85 85,84**
toteswinger: 1&2 £13.50, 1&3 £32.50, 2&3 £10.40. CSF £67.84 CT £498.68 TOTE £11.80: £3.00, £1.60, £3.70; EX 108.50.
Owner Murphy - Colvin **Bred** Swettenham Stud **Trained** Uplawmoor, E Renfrews
■ Stewards' Enquiry : P Townend caution: excessive use of the whip

FOCUS
Bog-standard handicap form but the form looks sound rated around the placed horses.
Mr Rooney(IRE) Official explanation: jockey said gelding lost a shoe and hung right
Ensign's Trick Official explanation: trainer had no explanation for the poor form shown

4847 WATERAID EBF MAIDEN STKS 6f
6:20 (6:21) (Class 5) 2-Y-O **£4,015** (£1,194; £597; £298) **Stalls High**

Form RPR

3 **1** **Jobe (USA)**19 4237 2-9-3 0.................... NCallan 7 88+
(K A Ryan) *mde all: shkn up and qcknd clr wl over 1f out: readily* **10/11**1

5 **2** 7 **Quanah Parker (IRE)**20 4213 2-9-3 0.................... DeanMcKeown 2 67
(R M Whitaker) *chsd ldrs: rdn to go 2nd over 2f out: kpt on but no ch w wnr* **11/1**3

3 **3** 3 **Aladdin's Lamp (IRE)**10 4530 2-9-3 0.................... RoystonFfrench 5 58
(M Johnston) *chsd wnr: rdn over 2f out: kpt on same pce* **15/8**2

4 1¾ **Salgrev (IRE)**24 4096 2-8-5 0.................... EJMcNamara(7) 1 48
(Irene J Monaghan, Ire) *in tch: rdn over 2f out: kpt on same pce* **25/1**

5 ½ **Lady Dunhill (IRE)** 2-8-12 0.................... DanielTudhope 8 46+
(J S Goldie) *towards rr: rdn 3f out: sme prog over 1f out: no further imp fnl f* **20/1**

40 **6** 1¼ **Igneous**26 4027 2-9-3 0.................... DaleGibson 6 48
(K R Burke) *sn pushed along: a towards rr* **33/1**

00 **7** shd **Franali (IRE)**20 4213 2-8-12 0.................... GrahamGibbons 9 42
(R F Fisher) *chsd ldrs: rdn over 2f out: wknd ent fnl f* **66/1**

8 2½ **Jatman** 2-9-3 0.................... DO'Donohoe 3 40
(Mrs L Stubbs) *a outpcd in rr* **14/1**

9 20 **Thatwasthepension (IRE)** 2-9-0 0.................... NeilBrown(3) 4 —
(B Storey) *a towards rr* **40/1**

1m 12.95s (-0.65) **Going Correction** +0.05s/f (Good) **9** Ran SP% **117.6**
Speed ratings (Par 94): **106,96,92,90,89 88,87,84,57**
toteswinger: 1&2 £3.00, 1&3 £1.20, 2&3 £2.90. CSF £12.06 TOTE £1.90: £1.10, £1.80, £1.30; EX 13.20.
Owner J Duddy L Duddy A Bailey B McDonald **Bred** David Garvin **Trained** Hambleton, N Yorks

FOCUS
A fair maiden won very easily by the only Group-race entry in the field. The placed horses help set the level.

NOTEBOOK
Jobe(USA) ◆ shaped well in a better race than this on his debut here last month and, settling better this time and, with the rail to help throughout, came home an easy winner. His rider later claimed that he could have won by a double-figure margin had he wanted to. He holds entries in the Gimcrack and Middle Park Stakes and looks a promising colt. (op 11-10)
Quanah Parker(IRE) is by a sire whose progeny usually appreciate some cut, and he ran a solid race in the face of what turned out to be an impossible task. (tchd 12-1)
Aladdin's Lamp(IRE) found Cook's Endeavour five lengths too good at Leicester on his debut and once again he came up against a rival from the Ryan stable that was just too good. (op 11-8)
Salgrev(IRE), who had shown little in her first three starts in Ireland, kept on one-paced on this drop in distance, and is arguably the guide to the level of the form. (op 20-1 tchd 28-1)
Lady Dunhill(IRE) is bred to want a good deal further than this in time. (op 25-1)

4848 BIWATER SERVICES H'CAP 1m 7f
6:50 (6:50) (Class 6) (0-65,69) 4-Y-O+ **£2,590** (£770; £385; £192) **Stalls Low**

Form RPR

56/ **1** **Spring Charm (IRE)**6 3829 6-8-6 **57**....................(p) EJMcNamara(7) 10 65
(Irene J Monaghan, Ire) *jinked rt s: mid-div: hdwy over 3f out: rdn over 2f out: chal ent fnl f: led fnl stride: drvn out* **16/1**

4-16 **2** shd **Signalman**9 4556 4-8-8 **52**.................... RoystonFfrench 2 60
(P Monteith) *trckd ldrs: led over 4f out: rdn and hrd pressed ent fnl f: battled on gamely: hdd fnl stride* **6/1**3

0523 **3** hd **Sir Sandicliffe (IRE)**9 4556 4-8-6 **57**.................... DeanHeslop(7) 15 65
(W M Brisbourne) *restrained s: towards rr: hdwy 4f out: rdn over 2f out: ev ch ent fnl f: sn edgd lft: no ex towards fin* **9/1**

321- **4** 3 **Balakar (IRE)**18 5586 12-9-0 **63**....................(p) PTownend(5) 17 67
(J J Lambe, Ire) *mid-div: struggling 5f out: styd on fnl 2f: nvr trbld ldrs* **5/1**1

3540 **5** 3 **Rocknest Island (IRE)**20 4220 5-8-7 **51**....................(v) DO'Donohoe 11 51
(P D Niven) *bmpd leaving stalls: sn pushed along to chse ldrs: rdn 3f out: one pce fnl 2f* **16/1**

0043 **6** 13 **Trance (IRE)**3 4735 8-8-13 **60**....................(p) NeilBrown(3) 1 43
(T D Barron) *s.i.s: sn rousted along and detached: n.d* **11/2**2

310/ **7** nse **Shankly Bond (IRE)**328 108 6-9-0 **65**.................... BMcHugh(7) 9 48
(Mrs L B Normile) *hld up towards rr: rdn and hdwy 3f out: one pce fnl 2f* **33/1**

- **8** nse **Hawksbury Heights**253 3966 6-8-8 **52**.................... DeanMcKeown 8 35
(J J Lambe, Ire) *mid-div tl lost pl and dropped to rr 5f out: nvr bk on terms* **18/1**

00-3 **9** 20 **Florentino**35 3718 4-8-1 **48**.................... AndrewMullen(3) 3 5
(C W Thornton) *a towards rr* **7/1**

4533 **10** 1¼ **Muncaster Castle (IRE)**40 3550 4-8-0 **51** ow2.................... LanceBetts(7) 12 7
(R F Fisher) *trckd ldrs: rdn 4f out: wknd over 2f out* **14/1**

055- **11** 4½ **Toshi (USA)**260 4933 6-9-4 **69** ow5.................... RyanMania(7) 5 19
(P Monteith) *hld up towards rr: hdwy 5f out: rdn 3f out: wknd 2f out* **20/1**

1230 **12** 3½ **Forrest Flyer (IRE)**19 4238 4-8-5 **54**.................... PatrickDonaghy(5) 14 —
(Miss L A Perratt) *led tl over 4f out: sn rdn: wknd 2f out* **6/1**3

/050 **13** 22 **Bramantino (IRE)**34 3756 8-7-13 **48** oh1 ow2.................... KellyHarrison(5) 7 —
(T A K Cuthbert) *chsd ldrs: rdn over 4f out: wknd 3f out* **20/1**

52-0 **14** 57 **Monet's Lady (IRE)**13 4457 4-8-2 **46**.................... DaleGibson 13 —
(R A Fahey) *a towards rr: virtually p.u over 3f out* **20/1**

3m 24.97s (4.57) **Going Correction** +0.35s/f (Good) **14** Ran SP% **124.0**
Speed ratings (Par 101): **101,100,100,99,97 90,90,90,79,79 76,75,63,32**
toteswinger: 1&2 £12.30, 1&3 £24.40, 2&3 £14.10. CSF £106.81 CT £945.05 TOTE £21.50: £5.40, £2.40, £3.10; EX 187.90.
Owner S Monaghan **Bred** Cliveden Stud Ltd **Trained** Navan, Co. Meath
■ Stewards' Enquiry : Dean Heslop one-day ban: careless riding (Aug 23)

FOCUS
A competitive, if moderate, staying handicap which resulted in a thrilling finish. The form is modest rated around the third and fourth.
Forrest Flyer(IRE) Official explanation: jockey said saddle slipped

4849 WATERAID CLAIMING STKS 7f 50y
7:20 (7:21) (Class 5) 3-Y-O+ **£3,238** (£963; £481; £240) **Stalls Low**

Form RPR

60-1 **1** **Sea Salt**100 1752 5-8-5 69.................... BMcHugh(7) 1 52+
(R A Fahey) *trckd ldr: led 2f out: sn rdn: kpt on: drvn out* **1/1**1

0245 **2** ¾ **Chin Wag (IRE)**10 4537 4-9-2 61....................(p) DanielTudhope 4 54
(J S Goldie) *in tch: rdn 2f out: chsd wnr ent fnl f: kpt on hld towards fin* **9/2**2

5204 **3** 1½ **Oeuf A La Neige**3 4736 8-8-13 55.................... RoystonFfrench 2 47
(Miss L A Perratt) *hld up: hdwy 3f out: chal 2f out: kpt on but no ex ins fnl f* **5/1**3

5500 **4** shd **Neon Blue**3 4736 7-9-0 59....................(b) DeanMcKeown 6 48+
(R M Whitaker) *s.i.s: towards rr: rdn and hdwy fr 2f out: kpt on wl fnl f: nt rch ldrs* **12/1**

000 **5** nk **Geordie Dancer (IRE)**65 2751 6-8-8 42 ow2.................... SladeO'Hara(5) 3 46
(A Berry) *led: rdn and hdd 2f out: kpt on but no ex fnl f* **50/1**

00-0 **6** 7 **Ugly Betty**49 3262 3-8-4 35.................... AndrewMullen(3) 9 25
(Bruce Hellier) *chsd ldrs: rdn whn hung lft over 2f out: wknd over 1f out* **100/1**

4220 **7** 8 **Westport**23 4117 5-9-7 74.................... DO'Donohoe 7 14
(K A Ryan) *hld up: rdn and nt qckn over 2f out: eased whn btn* **9/2**2

03-0 **8** ½ **Astronomical Odds (USA)**34 3759 5-8-11 0........(p) GrahamGibbons 8 2
(J J Lambe, Ire) *t.k.h: in tch: rdn over 2f out: sn btn: eased fnl f* **18/1**

1m 35.54s (2.14) **Going Correction** +0.35s/f (Good)
WFA 3 from 4yo+ 6lb **8** Ran SP% **118.9**
Speed ratings (Par 103): **101,100,98,98,97 89,80,80**
toteswinger: 1&2 £1.80, 1&3 £2.20, 2&3 £3.10. CSF £6.27 TOTE £2.20: £1.10, £1.60, £1.80; EX 6.20.Sea Salt was claimed by Paul J. Dixon for £6,000.
Owner J H Tattersall **Bred** D R Tucker **Trained** Musley Bank, N Yorks

FOCUS
A modest claimer but fairly solid, although the promixity of the fifth raises doubts over the form.
Westport Official explanation: jockey said gelding was never travelling

4850 WATERAID H'CAP 1m 2f
7:50 (7:51) (Class 5) (0-70,70) 3-Y-O+ **£3,561** (£1,059; £529; £264) **Stalls Low**

Form RPR

2304 **1** **Grandad Bill (IRE)**7 4630 5-8-4 **51** oh2.................... KellyHarrison(5) 3 64
(J S Goldie) *a.p: led over 2f out: rdn clr over 1f out: comf* **7/2**2

4-15 **2** 4½ **Chookie Hamilton**13 4457 4-9-2 **58**.................... RoystonFfrench 1 62
(Miss L A Perratt) *awkward leaving stalls: bhd: hdwy over 2f out: sn rdn: styd on fnl f: snatched 2nd fnl stride* **11/1**

4631 **3** nse **Boy Dancer (IRE)**10 4537 5-9-5 **61**.................... GrahamGibbons 10 65
(J J Quinn) *in tch: hdwy over 3f out: rdn to chse wnr over 2f out: kpt on but a hld: lost 2nd fnl stride* **8/1**

-000 **4** shd **Royal Citadel (IRE)**7 4630 5-8-2 **51** oh6....................(v) JamieKyne(7) 5 55
(Mrs L B Normile) *trckd ldrs: rdn over 4f out: nt pce to chal but kpt on ins fnl f* **40/1**

4/0- **5** 1¼ **English City (IRE)**57 3815 5-8-11 **53**.................... DO'Donohoe 9 56+
(Mrs L B Normile) *s.i.s: towards rr: rdn over 2f out: hdwy over 1f out: styd on fnl f* **10/1**

-403 **6** 3 **Thunderwing (IRE)**22 4142 6-8-9 **58**.................... NSLawes(7) 6 53
(James Moffatt) *in tch: rdn over 2f out: kpt on same pce* **9/1**

4050 **7** ¾ **Superior Star**7 4650 5-9-4 **60**....................(b) DanielTudhope 2 54
(N Wilson) *in tch: rdn to chal for 2nd 2f out: wknd ins fnl f* **15/2**3

2305 **8** ½ **Hawkit (USA)**7 4633 7-9-9 **68**.................... NeilBrown(3) 4 61
(P Monteith) *hld up: rdn and hdwy over 2f out: wknd ent fnl f* **2/1**1

0500 **9** 23 **Rascasse**23 4115 3-8-1 **55** ow2.................... AndrewMullen(3) 8 2
(Bruce Hellier) *trckd ldrs: rdn over 4f out: wknd over 2f out* **50/1**

0161 **10** 7 **Shy Glance (USA)**26 4015 6-9-7 **70**.................... RyanMania(7) 7 3
(P Monteith) *led: 3 l clr after 2f: rdn and hdd over 2f out: wknd over 1f out: eased whn btn* **15/2**3

2m 14.84s (2.84) **Going Correction** +0.35s/f (Good)
WFA 3 from 4yo+ 9lb **10** Ran SP% **122.0**
Speed ratings (Par 103): **102,98,98,98,97 94,94,93,75,69**
toteswinger: 1&2 £10.90, 1&3 £4.80, 2&3 £15.40. CSF £44.11 CT £297.60 TOTE £5.30: £1.70, £2.40, £2.50; EX 45.90.
Owner Tough Construction Ltd **Bred** M Hosokawa **Trained** Uplawmoor, E Renfrews

FOCUS
They went a decent pace here and the form looks sound for the grade through the placed horses, although the form is limited by the proximity of the fifth from out of the weights.
Shy Glance(USA) Official explanation: trainer had no explanation for the poor form shown

4851 LADIES DAY 19 SEPTEMBER H'CAP 1m
8:20 (8:21) (Class 6) (0-65,64) 3-Y-O+ **£2,729** (£806; £403) **Stalls Low**

Form RPR

5005 **1** **Wednesdays Boy (IRE)**26 4015 5-8-13 **49**....................(p) DO'Donohoe 6 58+
(P D Niven) *hld up: hdwy 2f out: rdn over 1f out: styd on strly to ld fnl 50yds: won gng away* **13/2**

2416 **2** 1 **Papa's Princess**[22] 4142 4-9-6 **56** DanielTudhope 7 62
(J S Goldie) *mid-div: hdwy over 3f out: rdn to chal over 2f out: ev ch ins fnl f: no ex fnl 50yds* **9/2**[2]

5000 **3** nk **Orpen Bid (IRE)**[13] 4453 3-7-13 **47** ow2 KellyHarrison(5) 10 51
(A M Crow) *trckd ldrs: tk narrow advantage over 2f out: sn rdn and hrd pressed: no ex whn hdd fnl 50yds* **40/1**

60 **4** 2 1/4 **Mystical Ayr (IRE)**[39] 3579 6-9-7 **57** RoystonFfrench 2 57
(Miss L A Perratt) *trckd ldrs: rdn to chal over 2f out: ch ent fnl f: no ex* **6/1**[3]

0044 **5** 1/2 **Apache Nation (IRE)**[5] 4679 5-9-4 **57** NeilBrown(3) 5 56
(M Dods) *mid-div: rdn 3f out: kpt on same pce fnl 2f* **15/8**[1]

4365 **6** 3 1/4 **Darfour**[10] 4540 4-9-6 **61** (p) GaryBartley(5) 9 52
(J S Goldie) *led: rdn and hdd over 2f out: sn one pce* **9/1**

0000 **7** 3/4 **Mangano**[11] 4503 4-8-8 **49** ow4 SladeO'Hara(5) 4 38
(A Berry) *towards rr: rdn and hdwy over 2f out: wknd fnl f* **16/1**

1-53 **8** 2 **Primo Way**[9] 4559 7-9-9 **64** (p) PatrickDonaghy(5) 1 49
(Miss L A Perratt) *hld up: rdn over 2f out: nt pce to chal* **11/1**

5320 **9** 9 **Hansomis (IRE)**[15] 4383 4-9-5 **55** DaleGibson 11 19
(B Mactaggart) *prom: rdn 3f out: wknd 2f out* **14/1**

3 **10** shd **Rebecca's Pride (IRE)**[28] 3952 5-8-9 **45** (v[1]) DeanMcKeown 8 9
(John C McConnell, Ire) *s.i.s: towards rr: effrt over 2f out: sn wknd* **16/1**

1m 45.47s (1.67) **Going Correction** +0.35s/f (Good)
WFA 3 from 4yo+ 7lb **10** Ran SP% **119.8**
Speed ratings (Par 101): **105,104,103,101,100 97,96,94,85,85**
toteswinger: 1&2 £6.00, 1&3 £127.20, 2&3 £30.80. CSF £36.93 CT £1102.33 TOTE £8.70: £2.80, £1.40, £13.40; EX 29.90.
Owner The Wednesday Club **Bred** Sean Collins **Trained** Barton-le-Street, N Yorks

FOCUS
An ordinary handicap, but it was run at a sound gallop and the winner came from last to first to score. The form looks pretty sound despite the proximity of the third.

4852 MACDONALDS SOLICITORS H'CAP 5f
8:50 (8:50) (Class 6) (0-65,64) 3-Y-O **£2,590** (£770; £385; £192) **Stalls** High

Form RPR

2504 **1** **Cheshire Rose**[20] 4216 3-9-0 **64** DeanHeslop(7) 7 69
(T D Barron) *mde all: kpt on gamely: rdn out* **4/1**[2]

2654 **2** 1 3/4 **Stoneacre Chris (USA)**[17] 4308 3-8-2 **50** KellyHarrison(5) 6 49
(Peter Grayson) *hld up bhd ldrs: nt clr run and swtchd lft over 1f out: sn rdn: r.o: snatched 2nd towards fin* **8/1**

0230 **3** 1/2 **Killer Class**[27] 4000 3-9-2 **64** GaryBartley(5) 3 61+
(J S Goldie) *hld up bhd ldrs: rdn and hdwy over 1f out: kpt on fnl f* **4/1**[2]

015 **4** hd **Select Committee**[32] 3811 3-9-3 **60** (v) GrahamGibbons 4 56
(J J Quinn) *prom: rdn over 2f out: kpt on same pce fnl f* **11/4**[1]

016 **5** 1 1/4 **Stoneacre Pat (IRE)**[38] 3609 3-8-8 **56** PatrickDonaghy(5) 5 48
(Peter Grayson) *chsd ldrs: effrt over 2f out: kpt on same pce fnl f* **16/1**

6334 **6** 6 **Andrasta**[5] 4686 3-8-6 **49** DO'Donohoe 1 19
(A Berry) *prom: rdn over 2f out: wknd ent fnl f* **9/2**[3]

2200 **7** 6 **Paddy Jack**[13] 4450 3-9-1 **58** (p) RoystonFfrench 8 6+
(J R Weymes) *in tch tl short of room and snatched up over 3f out: nt rcvr and no ch after* **6/1**

00 **U** **La Guancha**[7] 4632 3-7-9 **45** (tp) MatthewLawson(7) 2 —
(D A Nolan) *fly leapt and uns rdr leaving stalls* **66/1**

60.54 secs (0.44) **Going Correction** +0.05s/f (Good) **8** Ran SP% **117.6**
Speed ratings (Par 98): **98,95,94,94,92 82,72,—**
toteswinger: 1&2 £7.10, 1&3 £3.40, 2&3 £9.60. CSF £36.75 CT £138.32 TOTE £5.60: £1.70, £3.30, £1.60; EX 31.80 Place 6 £140.93, Place 5 £47.41.
Owner D C Rutter P J Huntbach **Bred** Northcombe Stud **Trained** Maunby, N Yorks
■ Stewards' Enquiry : Kelly Harrison three-day ban: careless riding (Aug 23-25)

FOCUS
A moderate sprint handicap in which the all-the-way winner is rated to form.
T/Plt: £69.80 to a £1 stake. Pool: £47,930.00. 500.59 winning tickets. T/Qpdt: £40.60 to a £1 stake. Pool: £4,860.00. 88.40 winning tickets. TM

4813 HAYDOCK (L-H)
Saturday, August 9

OFFICIAL GOING: Heavy
A wet day led to conditions becoming very testing. The realignment of the bend on the home turn meant that distances were increased by 30 yards.
Wind: Light across Weather: Raining until after 3.40

4853 RACING UK H'CAP 1m 30y
1:25 (1:28) (Class 2) (0-100,96) 3-Y-O+ **£16,190** (£4,817; £2,407; £1,202) **Stalls** Low

Form RPR

32 **1** **Zero Tolerance (IRE)**[41] 3531 8-9-1 **85** NeilBrown(3) 2 101+
(T D Barron) *hld up in mid-div: hdwy 4f out: led on bit over 1f out: shkn up and wnt clr ins fnl f: easily* **11/4**[1]

3113 **2** 4 **The Fifth Member (IRE)**[11] 4509 4-9-0 **81** PatCosgrave 4 85
(J R Boyle) *t.k.h: a.p: led 3f out: sn rdn: hdd over 1f out: kpt on same pce u.p fnl f: no ch w wnr* **6/1**[3]

11-4 **3** 1/2 **Webbow (IRE)**[49] 3278 6-9-8 **89** DavidAllan 10 92
(T D Easterby) *s.i.s: sn swtchd lft: hld up in rr: rdn and hdwy wl over 1f out: wnt 2nd briefly ins fnl f: one pce* **10/1**

2000 **4** 2 **Extraterrestrial**[8] 4587 4-9-11 **92** (p) PaulHanagan 9 90
(R A Fahey) *hld up in mid-div: hdwy over 3f out: swtchd lft 2f out: rdn over 1f out: one pce* **14/1**

0312 **5** 3 1/4 **Rainbow Mirage (IRE)**[21] 4206 4-9-3 **84** GrahamGibbons 11 75
(E S McMahon) *a.p: rdn 2f out: sn hung lft: wknd ins fnl f* **12/1**

4023 **6** 1/2 **We'll Come**[10] 4522 4-9-12 **93** (p) NCallan 5 82
(M A Jarvis) *t.k.h: prom: ev ch over 2f out: rdn and wknd over 1f out* **10/1**

3212 **7** 6 **Decameron (USA)**[21] 4197 3-9-4 **92** RyanMoore 7 68
(Sir Michael Stoute) *hld up in rr: c to stands' rail over 4f out: rdn over 2f out: nvr nr ldrs* **9/2**[2]

1131 **8** 3 3/4 **Yamal (IRE)**[11] 4509 3-9-8 **96** GregFairley 8 63
(M Johnston) *t.k.h: prom: ev ch over 2f out: sn rdn: wknd over 1f out* **7/1**

0002 **9** 1 1/4 **The Osteopath (IRE)**[42] 3491 5-9-4 **85** TonyCulhane 3 49
(M Dods) *hld up towards rr: c to stands' rail over 3f out: hdwy over 2f out: rdn and wknd wl over 1f out* **11/1**

0150 **10** 5 **Bahar Shumaal (IRE)**[35] 3740 6-9-7 **88** MartinDwyer 6 41
(C E Brittain) *led: hdd 3f out: sn rdn and wknd* **33/1**

0 **11** 1 1/2 **Turfshuffle (GER)**[6] 4661 5-10-0 **95** StephenDonohoe 1 44
(Ian Williams) *hld up towards rr: rdn over 3f out: sn struggling* **66/1**

1m 48.47s (4.67) **Going Correction** +0.80s/f (Soft)
WFA 3 from 4yo+ 7lb **11** Ran SP% **116.9**
Speed ratings (Par 109): **108,104,103,101,98 97,91,88,86,81 80**
toteswinger: 1&2 £4.60, 1&3 £8.20, 2&3 £17.10. CSF £18.90 CT £147.24 TOTE £3.40: £1.50, £2.50, £3.20; EX 19.40 Trifecta £214.40 Pool: £405.74 - 1.40 winning units..
Owner The Hornsey Warriors Racing Syndicate **Bred** Cliveden Stud Ltd **Trained** Maunby, N Yorks

FOCUS
A decent handicap with several failing to get home after running freely in the rain-softened ground. The placed horses are rated close to their soft-ground form.

NOTEBOOK
Zero Tolerance(IRE), raised 3lb, made amends for his narrow defeat at the Curragh in no uncertain manner and is now unbeaten on three visits to Haydock. He loves the mud and where he goes next is ground dependent. (op 7-2)
The Fifth Member(IRE), already a winner in heavy ground, remains in good form but proved no match for the winner after going up 2lb for his fine effort at Glorious Goodwood. (op 7-1 tchd 11-2)
Webbow(IRE) is another who is running particularly well at the moment. He did not mind the testing conditions and just lost out in the separate battle for second. (op 9-1)
Extraterrestrial, a winner on a similar surface when trained in Ireland, had been quite highly tried in top handicaps since his unlucky second at the Chester May meeting. (tchd 12-1)
Rainbow Mirage(IRE) was up in class on ground that was probably more demanding than is ideal for him. (op 16-1)
We'll Come probably struggles to get a mile on ground as bad as this. (op 8-1)
Decameron(USA) was unsuited by the ground according to his rider. Official explanation: jockey said colt was unsuited by the heavy ground (op 5-1 tchd 6-1)
Yamal(IRE), raised 6lb, paid the penalty for racing too freely in rain-soaked ground. (op 6-1)

4854 CORAL.CO.UK H'CAP 6f
2:00 (2:01) (Class 3) (0-95,92) 3-Y-O+ **£12,952** (£3,854; £1,926; £962) **Stalls** Centre

Form RPR

2050 **1** **Valery Borzov (IRE)**[8] 4586 4-9-11 **92** FrancisNorton 8 107
(D Nicholls) *chsd ldrs: rdn over 1f out: led wl ins fnl f: r.o* **8/1**[3]

3051 **2** 3/4 **Bel Cantor**[13] 4460 5-8-6 **80** (p) AndreaAtzeni(7) 2 93
(W J H Ratcliffe) *led: rdn wl over 1f out: hdd wl ins fnl f: kpt on* **8/1**[3]

-406 **3** 2 3/4 **Burning Incense (IRE)**[42] 3489 5-9-6 **87** RyanMoore 13 91+
(M Dods) *s.i.s: hld up towards rr: rdn and hdwy wl over 1f out: kpt on same pce fnl f* **11/2**[1]

4003 **4** 1/2 **Joseph Henry**[8] 4586 6-9-1 **89** AdeleRothery(7) 3 92
(D Nicholls) *hld up in mid-div: hdwy over 2f out: rdn and hung lft wl over 1f out: no ex ins fnl f* **12/1**

6024 **5** 2 3/4 **Hotham**[19] 4246 5-8-6 **78** AshleyHamblett(5) 16 72
(N Wilson) *hld up in mid-div: hdwy over 3f out: rdn wl over 1f out: btn whn rdr lost whip ins fnl f* **20/1**

1000 **6** 2 1/4 **Bonnie Prince Blue**[27] 3998 5-9-0 **81** (b) MartinDwyer 11 68
(B W Hills) *wnt sltly rt s: towards rr: sn pushed along: rdn over 3f out: hdwy over 2f out: edgd lft over 1f out: no further prog* **25/1**

0-30 **7** hd **Topflightcoolracer**[22] 4171 4-8-13 **80** TedDurcan 6 66
(Mrs G S Rees) *hld up in mid-div: pushed along 3f out: sn lost pl: sme prog fnl f: n.d* **22/1**

6016 **8** 1 1/4 **Wyatt Earp (IRE)**[13] 4460 7-9-1 **82** (b) PaulHanagan 12 64
(R A Fahey) *outpcd: sme late prog: nvr nrr* **12/1**

4102 **9** 3/4 **Harbour Blues**[5] 4687 3-8-13 **84** (t) CatherineGannon 15 64
(A W Carroll) *chsd ldr to 2f out: hung lft and wknd over 1f out* **10/1**

0200 **10** 1/2 **High Curragh**[19] 4240 5-9-2 **83** (p) NCallan 7 61
(K A Ryan) *prom: rdn over 2f out: wknd over 1f out* **14/1**

0515 **11** 3/4 **Artsu**[8] 4595 3-8-6 **77** GregFairley 5 53
(M L W Bell) *t.k.h: chsd ldrs: rdn over 2f out: wknd over 1f out* **6/1**[2]

160 **12** 1 1/2 **Cape**[68] 2680 5-9-11 **92** TonyCulhane 9 63
(P Howling) *s.i.s: a bhd* **18/1**

1600 **13** 1 **Compton's Eleven**[14] 4407 7-8-10 **84** MatthewDavies(7) 4 52
(M R Channon) *chsd ldrs 3f* **28/1**

1340 **14** 3/4 **Monsieur Reynard**[8] 4595 3-8-6 **77** ow1 (p) StephenDonohoe 10 42
(Ian Williams) *t.k.h: hdwy into mid-div 3f out: wknd 2f out* **25/1**

010 **15** 7 **Zomerlust**[22] 4145 6-9-9 **90** GrahamGibbons 1 33
(J J Quinn) *s.i.s whn rdr late to remove blindfold: outpcd* **6/1**[2]

000 **16** nse **Steenberg (IRE)**[32] 3812 9-8-12 **79** JimmyQuinn 14 22
(M H Tompkins) *s.i.s: a in rr* **25/1**

1m 16.06s (2.06) **Going Correction** +0.675s/f (Yiel)
WFA 3 from 4yo+ 4lb **16** Ran SP% **126.7**
Speed ratings (Par 107): **113,112,108,107,104 101,100,99,98,97 96,94,93,92,82 82**
toteswinger: 1&2 £18.10, 1&3 £16.10, 2&3 £12.40. CSF £66.18 CT £409.86 TOTE £10.10: £3.20, £2.60, £1.70, £2.30; EX 91.30 Trifecta £314.70 Part won. Pool: £425.30 - 0.10 winning units..
Owner D Kilburn/I Hewitson/D Nicholls **Bred** Vincent Harrington **Trained** Sessay, N Yorks
■ Stewards' Enquiry : Andrea Atzeni one-day ban: failed to keep straight from stalls (Aug 23)
Catherine Gannon one-day ban: failed to keep straight from stalls (Aug 23)

FOCUS
The heavy going took its toll on this big field in what was a decent wide-open sprint handicap. The runner-up is rated to his best but probably not form to take too literally.

NOTEBOOK
Valery Borzov(IRE) settled better without the visor and that enabled him to see it out well enough in the heavy ground. (op 10-1)
Bel Cantor, up 3lb, again tried to make all and deserves full marks for a very game effort. (op 11-1)
Burning Incense(IRE) again ran well but could never get to grips with the first two. He has slipped back to the same mark as his last win almost two years ago. (op 5-1 tchd 6-1 in places)
Joseph Henry, a winner on similar ground as juvenile, turned in another solid performance despite hanging under his inexperienced rider. (op 11-1)
Hotham needs better ground than this to be effective over 6f and was making no impression when his rider dropped his stick.
Bonnie Prince Blue was never travelling particularly well and could not make his presence felt.
Zomerlust Official explanation: trainer had no explanation for the poor form shown

4855 TOTESWINGER ROSE OF LANCASTER STKS (GROUP 3) 1m 2f 120y
2:35 (2:35) (Class 1) 3-Y-O+
£42,577 (£16,140; £8,077; £4,027; £2,017; £1,012) **Stalls** High

Form RPR

4020 **1** **Multidimensional (IRE)**[35] 3741 5-9-3 118 TedDurcan 6 114
(H R A Cecil) *chsd ldr: led over 2f out: rdn and wandered fr over 1f out: drvn out* **2/1**[1]

0 **2** 1 1/4 **Bahia Breeze**[27] 4007 6-9-0 100 MartinDwyer 3 109
(Rae Guest) *hld up: hdwy over 3f out: rdn and ev ch wl over 1f out: nt qckn ins fnl f* **25/1**

The Form Book, Raceform Ltd, Compton, RG20 6NL

-166 **3** 4 1/2 **Spanish Moon (USA)**[21] 4192 4-9-3 108 RyanMoore 2 103
(Sir Michael Stoute) *hld up and bhd: pushed along 4f out: hdwy over 2f out: edgd rt over 1f out: wknd ins fnl f* **5/1**

2114 **4** nk **Flying Clarets (IRE)**[15] 4395 5-9-0 112 PaulHanagan 1 100
(R A Fahey) *led: rdn and hdd over 2f out: wknd fnl f* **7/2**[3]

4100 **5** 6 **Championship Point (IRE)**[11] 4504 5-9-7 110 TonyCulhane 7 95
(M R Channon) *hld up in tch: rdn and wknd over 1f out* **20/1**

-161 **6** 1 1/2 **Smokey Oakey (IRE)**[72] 2543 4-9-7 111 JimmyQuinn 4 93
(M H Tompkins) *dropped out s: hld up in rr: hdwy over 3f out: rdn and wknd over 2f out* **11/4**[2]

2000 **7** 2 1/4 **Hattan (IRE)**[52] 3121 6-9-7 113 NCallan 5 88
(C E Brittain) *hld up and bhd: rdn 2f out: no rspnse* **16/1**

2m 22.92s (6.22) **Going Correction** +0.80s/f (Soft) 7 Ran SP% **113.4**
Speed ratings (Par 113): **109,108,104,104,100 99,97**
toteswinger: 1&2 £10.20, 1&3 £2.70, 2&3 £14.00. CSF £49.91 TOTE £2.90: £1.60, £8.20; EX 54.10.

Owner Niarchos Family **Bred** The Niarchos Family **Trained** Newmarket, Suffolk

■ Stewards' Enquiry : Ryan Moore one-day ban: careless riding (Aug 23)

FOCUS
The fact they went a good clip early, considering the conditions, may have led to the time being 1.16 seconds slower than the following handicap. The runner-up is rated to the best of last year's form.

NOTEBOOK
Multidimensional(IRE), who found the ground too firm in the Eclipse, was considered to have conditions heavier than he prefers because it blunted his acceleration. Inclined to run around after striking the front, he was always finding enough after eventually being straightened by the stands' rail. It may be that the Juddmonte International at York comes too soon for him after these exertions. (op 9-4 tchd 5-2 in places)

Bahia Breeze ran a cracker and this was easily her best effort since she was just touched off over this trip in the Group 2 Prix Jean Romanet at Deauville on soft ground nearly a year ago.

Spanish Moon(USA) had no encountered this sort of ground since winning his only race at two. He appeared ill at ease in the conditions and it was only Moore's perseverance that saw him gain third prize. (tchd 6-1)

Flying Clarets(IRE) eventually paid the penalty for taking the field along at a decent gallop for the prevailing ground. (op 5-1)

Championship Point(IRE), on ground softer than he prefers, had a tough task under a penalty for his Group 3 win at Chester in May when he defeated the winner by nearly four lengths. (op 14-1)

Smokey Oakey(IRE) did not have the ground as an excuse and may have simply had an off day on his first outing since landing the Brigadier Gerard at Sandown towards the end of May. (op 5-2)

4856 TOTESCOOP6 STKS (HERITAGE H'CAP) 1m 2f 120y
3:10 (3:10) (Class 2) (0-105,105) 3-Y-0+
£49,848 (£14,928; £7,464; £3,736; £1,864; £936) **Stalls** High

Form RPR

1300 **1** **Perks (IRE)**[29] 3919 3-8-0 91 JimmyQuinn 3 109
(J L Dunlop) *hld up in rr: hdwy over 3f out: led jst over 1f out: rdn clr ins fnl f* **4/1**[2]

4503 **2** 6 **Drill Sergeant**[9] 4552 3-8-5 96 GregFairley 4 103
(M Johnston) *led: racd alone on far rail in home st: rdn and hdd jst over 1f out: sn btn* **13/2**

2211 **3** 3 1/4 **Cheshire Prince**[6] 4662 4-8-2 86 6ex LukeMorris(3) 14 87
(W M Brisbourne) *a.p: chsd ldr over 3f out tl edgd lft wl over 1f out: one pce* **16/1**

3130 **4** 3 **Wigwam Willie (IRE)**[21] 4204 6-8-2 83 (p) CatherineGannon 12 78
(K A Ryan) *s.i.s: hld up and bhd: rdn and hdwy over 3f out: edgd lft to far rail fr 2f out: no imp* **20/1**

1103 **5** 1 3/4 **Ezdiyaad (IRE)**[28] 3974 4-9-8 103 MartinDwyer 1 95
(M P Tregoning) *prom tl rdn and wknd over 2f out* **9/2**[3]

0003 **6** 2 1/2 **Capable Guest (IRE)**[7] 4618 6-8-3 91 MatthewDavies(7) 9 78
(M R Channon) *hld up in tch: rdn over 3f out: wknd over 2f out* **20/1**

0050 **7** 10 **Lucky Dance (BRZ)**[14] 4417 6-8-11 92 FrancisNorton 2 60
(A G Foster) *awkward leaving stalls: hld up and bhd: rdn over 2f out: no rspnse* **50/1**

3004 **8** 6 **Age Of Reason (UAE)**[9] 4552 3-8-11 102 AndrewElliott 11 59
(M Johnston) *racd wd: hld up in mid-div: swtchd lft to far rail over 3f out: sn struggling* **20/1**

4006 **9** 1/2 **Charlie Tokyo (IRE)**[28] 3974 5-8-11 92 (v) PaulHanagan 7 48
(R A Fahey) *hld up in mid-div: wknd over 3f out* **14/1**

33-3 **10** 1 1/4 **King's Event (USA)**[15] 4363 4-8-7 88 ow3 RyanMoore 10 41
(Sir Michael Stoute) *hld up in mid-div: rdn and wknd over 2f out* **11/4**[1]

6523 **11** 18 **Suits Me**[37] 3627 5-8-5 86 RoystonFfrench 8 —
(T P Tate) *w ldr tl over 4f out: lost 2nd over 3f out: wknd over 2f out: eased over 1f out* **12/1**

-405 **12** 1 1/2 **Greek Envoy**[28] 3975 4-9-3 98 TonyCulhane 13 14
(T P Tate) *hld up in rr: rdn over 2f out: sn struggling* **16/1**

2m 21.76s (5.06) **Going Correction** +0.80s/f (Soft)
WFA 3 from 4yo+ 10lb 12 Ran SP% **120.6**
Speed ratings (Par 109): **113,108,106,104,102 101,93,89,89,88 75,73**
toteswinger: 1&2 £6.40, 1&3 £18.80, 2&3 £13.40. CSF £29.13 CT £384.11 TOTE £5.30: £2.10, £2.50, £4.00; EX 29.60 Trifecta £581.70 Part won. Pool: £786.20 - 0.10 winning units..

Owner Benny Andersson **Bred** Chess Racing Ab **Trained** Arundel, W Sussex

FOCUS
This good handicap did not turn out to be as competitive as expected and that was probably down to the ground. The form is best rated through the solid runner-up.

NOTEBOOK
Perks(IRE) ◆ relished the step-up in distance with ground conditions in his favour. He can continue on the upgrade and his rider is hoping that he will be aimed at the Cambridgeshire. (tchd 9-2 and 5-1 in places)

Drill Sergeant was back on soft ground having gone up 3lb following his solid effort at Goodwood. (op 7-1 tchd 8-1)

Cheshire Prince was making a quick reappearance under a penalty after his back-to-back wins at Chester. He was far from disgraced on ground that was probably too soft for him. (op 14-1)

Wigwam Willie(IRE) did not have the ground as an excuse but this was a step-up in grade. (tchd 18-1)

Ezdiyaad(IRE), is another who likes these conditions but he had been raised 3lb and it could be that the Handicapper has taken his measure. (op 11-2 tchd 6-1 in places)

Capable Guest(IRE) was back to the same mark as when winning the Zetland Gold Cup in May but got found out by the rain-softened going. (op 28-1)

King's Event(USA) was unsuited by the heavy ground according to Moore who put up 3lb overweight. Official explanation: trainer's rep said colt was unsuited by the heavy ground (tchd 5-2 and 3-1 tchd 7-2 in places)

4857 RACING UK £12.99 A MONTH NURSERY 5f
3:40 (3:44) (Class 2) 2-Y-0
£12,952 (£3,854; £1,926; £962) **Stalls** Centre

Form RPR

2130 **1** **Favourite Girl (IRE)**[21] 4190 2-8-9 78 DavidAllan 11 82
(T D Easterby) *a.p: rdn over 1f out: r.o to ld towards fin* **6/1**

61 **2** 1/2 **Suzie Quw**[23] 4113 2-8-6 75 AndrewElliott 6 77
(K R Burke) *chsd ldr: rdn to ld wl over 1f out: hdd towards fin: jst hld on for 2nd* **7/2**[1]

530 **3** shd **Coleorton Choice**[39] 3590 2-7-13 68 JimmyQuinn 8 70+
(K A Ryan) *towards rr: hrd rdn and swtchd rt 1f out: str run u.p and hung lft ins fnl f: jst failed to take 2nd* **20/1**

241 **4** 1 1/4 **Red Rossini (IRE)**[26] 4020 2-8-11 80 RyanMoore 12 77
(R Hannon) *hld up in mid-div: rdn and hdwy over 1f out: hung lft ins fnl f: hld whn carried lft towards fin* **9/2**[2]

10 **5** 1/2 **Waffle (IRE)**[8] 4588 2-9-7 90 TedDurcan 7 85
(J Noseda) *hld up in tch: rdn and ev ch over 1f out: no ex ins fnl f* **5/1**[3]

2361 **6** 7 **Lesley's Choice**[12] 4474 2-8-9 78 NCallan 5 48
(P A Blockley) *led: rdn and hdd wl over 1f out: wknd ins fnl f* **8/1**

6666 **7** 1 1/2 **That Boy Ronaldo**[8] 4594 2-7-5 67 oh10 CharlotteKerton(7) 9 32
(A Berry) *s.i.s: rdn over 2f out: hung lft over 1f out: nvr nr ldrs* **50/1**

150 **8** hd **Kheylide (IRE)**[14] 4434 2-8-2 74 LukeMorris(3) 1 38
(Miss V Haigh) *hld up in mid-div: rdn and hung lft wl over 1f out: sn struggling* **33/1**

13 **9** 2 1/4 **Mister Laurel**[23] 4108 2-9-1 84 PaulHanagan 2 40
(R A Fahey) *hld up in tch: lost pl over 2f out: sn toiling* **13/2**

155 **10** 1 **Deadly Encounter (IRE)**[15] 4374 2-9-4 87 RoystonFfrench 4 39
(R A Fahey) *dwlt: outpcd* **20/1**

63.90 secs (3.40) **Going Correction** +0.675s/f (Yiel) 10 Ran SP% **110.2**
Speed ratings (Par 100): **99,98,98,96,95 84,81,81,77,76**
toteswinger: 1&2 £5.20, 1&3 £19.80, 2&3 £14.90. CSF £23.44 CT £337.28 TOTE £5.90: £1.80, £1.80, £3.90; EX 26.00.

Owner Peter C Bourke **Bred** Limestone And Tara Studs **Trained** Great Habton, N Yorks

■ Stewards' Enquiry : Jimmy Quinn caution: careless riding

FOCUS
A well-contested, decent sprint nursery with the form rated through the runner-up backed up by the third.

NOTEBOOK
Favourite Girl(IRE) handled the ground well and the fact that she had already scored over a furlong further stood her in good stead in this ground. Her owner wants to go for the Lowther at York which will be a much hotter contest. (op 5-1)

Suzie Quw ◆, a well-backed favourite, lost little in defeat after her win over the stiff 5f at Hamilton. She can remain competitive off this sort of mark. (op 13-2)

Coleorton Choice is proving to be far from straightforward and would have finished second had he not come off a straight line. (op 28-1)

Red Rossini(IRE) ran a fair race having never previously encountered ground worse than good. (tchd 4-1)

Waffle(IRE), highly tried last time, was not disgraced under his big weight in this heavy ground. (op 4-1 tchd 6-1)

Lesley's Choice did not find the demanding conditions suiting his style of running. (op 11-1)

Deadly Encounter(IRE) Official explanation: jockey said colt missed the break

4858 DUKE OF LANCASTER'S OWN YEOMANRY H'CAP 6f
4:15 (4:17) (Class 5) (0-70,73) 4-Y-0+
£4,857 (£1,445; £722; £360) **Stalls** Centre

Form RPR

3565 **1** **Memphis Man**[14] 4440 5-8-12 66 RichardEvans(5) 6 81
(P D Evans) *hld up in mid-div: hdwy 3f out: led 2f out: rdn over 1f out: r.o wl* **7/2**[1]

6056 **2** 3 3/4 **Morse (IRE)**[24] 4084 7-8-10 59 (p) TedDurcan 3 62
(J A Osborne) *a.p: rdn and ev ch 2f out: kpt on one pce fnl f* **16/1**

3351 **3** nk **Katie Boo (IRE)**[7] 4631 6-9-10 73 FrancisNorton 12 75
(A Berry) *hld up in mid-div: hdwy 3f out: rdn over 1f out: kpt on same pce fnl f* **9/2**[2]

2413 **4** 1 1/2 **City For Conquest (IRE)**[13] 4462 5-8-3 52 AndrewElliott 13 49
(John A Harris) *hld up: hdwy over 2f out: rdn and edgd lft 1f out: one pce* **16/1**

0030 **5** 1 **Trimlestown (IRE)**[15] 4393 5-9-3 66 (tp) DavidAllan 8 60
(K A Ryan) *s.i.s: sn chsng ldrs: rdn 2f out: fdd wl ins fnl f* **6/1**[3]

0205 **6** 1/2 **Gilded Cove**[82] 2263 8-8-10 62 RussellKennemore(3) 1 54
(R Hollinshead) *sn outpcd: rdn and hdwy over 1f out: no further prog fnl f* **25/1**

0445 **7** 3 1/2 **Orotund**[54] 3079 4-8-2 51 oh3 PaulHanagan 10 32
(T D Easterby) *chsd ldr: led 3f out to 2f out: rdn and wknd over 1f out* **8/1**

0134 **8** 1 1/2 **Ingleby Princess**[26] 4016 4-9-3 66 RyanMoore 11 42
(T D Barron) *a in rr* **7/1**

0014 **9** shd **The History Man (IRE)**[3] 4743 5-8-11 67 (be) GarryWhillans(7) 2 43
(M Mullineaux) *led: hdd 3f out: rdn over 2f out: wknd wl over 1f out* **6/1**[3]

4660 **10** nse **Prince Golan (IRE)**[12] 4478 4-9-1 64 MartinDwyer 7 40
(J W Unett) *in rr: rdn and hung lft over 2f out: sn toiling* **9/1**

1m 17.46s (3.46) **Going Correction** +0.675s/f (Yiel) 10 Ran SP% **118.2**
Speed ratings (Par 103): **103,98,97,95,94 93,88,86,86,86**
toteswinger: 1&2 £15.20, 1&3 £4.10, 2&3 £15.50. CSF £62.67 CT £265.97 TOTE £5.30: £1.90, £5.20, £1.20; EX 131.50.

Owner M D Jones **Bred** R T And Mrs Watson **Trained** Pandy, Monmouths

FOCUS
An ordinary handicap rated through the winner to last year's best and backed up by the second.

4859 BEST HORSE RACING SKY CHANNEL 432 H'CAP 1m 6f
4:45 (4:45) (Class 5) (0-70,70) 3-Y-0
£4,857 (£1,445; £722; £360) **Stalls** Low

Form RPR

3234 **1** **Kiribati King (IRE)**[14] 4426 3-9-4 67 TonyCulhane 3 75
(M R Channon) *hld up in mid-div: hdwy 6f out: led 4f out: rdn 3f out: hung lft to far rail 2f out: drvn out* **8/1**[3]

0001 **2** 1 1/4 **Okafranca (IRE)**[30] 3873 3-8-8 62 JackMitchell(5) 12 68
(W R Muir) *sn led: hdd 10f out: led over 5f out to 4f out: rdn over 2f out: styd on to take 2nd wl ins fnl f: nt trble wnr* **12/1**

604 **3** 3 **Lisbon Lion (IRE)**[42] 3473 3-8-7 59 LukeMorris(3) 4 61
(N J Vaughan) *hld up in rr: hdwy 5f out: rdn and ev ch wl over 1f out: hung lft ent fnl f: one pce* **28/1**

0066 **4** 1 1/4 **No Rules**[57] 2997 3-8-7 56 JimmyQuinn 10 56
(M H Tompkins) *hld up in tch: rdn over 3f out: one pce fnl 2f* **10/1**

4300 **5** 1/2 **Kalokairi (IRE)**[37] 3624 3-8-12 **61** ...... TedDurcan 5 61
(J L Dunlop) *hld up in tch: rdn over 3f out: swtchd rt 2f out: fdd ins fnl f* **11/1**

-345 **6** 1 1/2 **Dubai's Wonder (IRE)**[71] 2573 3-9-7 **70** ...... GregFairley 1 68
(B W Hills) *led early: prom: rdn over 2f out: wknd over 2f out* **12/1**

5-22 **7** 12 **Next Of Kin (IRE)**[24] 4077 3-9-5 **68** ...... FrancisNorton 11 49
(G A Swinbank) *hld up in mid-div: hdwy on outside 5f out: rdn 4f out: wknd over 2f out* **5/1**[2]

506 **8** 4 1/2 **Montevetro**[15] 4372 3-8-6 **55** ...... DavidKinsella 6 29
(R Hannon) *hld up in rr: rdn 4f out: sn struggling* **33/1**

654 **9** 8 **Circus Clown (IRE)**[23] 4116 3-8-8 **57** ...... DavidAllan 9 20
(Miss L A Perratt) *hld up in rr: struggling fnl 4f* **20/1**

2243 **10** 38 **Herrera (IRE)**[15] 4382 3-9-2 **65** ...... PaulHanagan 7 —
(R A Fahey) *hld up towards rr: rdn 5f out: lost tch 4f out: t.o* **9/1**

3050 **11** 6 **Tamrai Dancer**[44] 3393 3-8-7 **56** ...... JamesDoyle 8 —
(R M Beckett) *prom tl wknd 4f out: t.o* **20/1**

4531 **12** 2 **Beautiful Lady (IRE)**[8] 4607 3-9-7 **70** ...... RyanMoore 13 —
(P F I Cole) *a towards rr: lost tch 3f out: t.o* **2/1**[1]

-006 **13** 107 **Iron Cross (IRE)**[12] 4477 3-8-5 **54** ...... MartinDwyer 14 —
(Sir Mark Prescott) *s.s and sn rdn along: sn prom: led 10f out: rdn and hdd over 5f out: sn wknd: t.o fnl 3f* **12/1**

3m 15.44s (11.14) **Going Correction** +0.80s/f (Soft) **13** Ran SP% **127.5**
Speed ratings (Par 100): **100,99,97,96,96 95,88,86,81,60 56,55,—**
toteswinger: 1&2 £25.50, 1&3 £36.10, 2&3 £66.70. CSF £102.05 CT £2604.47 TOTE £9.90: £2.20, £4.40, £10.20; EX 130.70 Place 6 £84.75, Place 5 £48.08.
Owner Box 41 **Bred** Noel Finnegan **Trained** West Ilsley, Berks

FOCUS
This predictably turned into a slog for these moderate young stayers and the first two are quite exposed.
Beautiful Lady(IRE) Official explanation: jockey said filly was unsuited by the heavy ground
T/Plt: £82.20 to a £1 stake. Pool: £108,941.46. 967.18 winning tickets. T/Qpdt: £37.70 to a £1 stake. Pool: £4,762.56. 93.45 winning tickets. KH

4819 LINGFIELD (L-H)
Saturday, August 9

OFFICIAL GOING: Aw course - standard; turf course - soft
Contrary to the normal pattern here, the middle of the track looked the best place to be on the straight (turf) course
Wind: Strong, behind Weather: Damp

4860 LEANGEFELD MEDIAN AUCTION MAIDEN STKS — 1m 2f (P)
5:40 (5:43) (Class 6) 3-4-Y-O — £2,266 (£674; £337; £168) Stalls Low

Form RPR

3 **1** **Crackentorp**[16] 4349 3-9-3 0 ...... GeorgeBaker 6 87+
(G L Moore) *hld up in 4th: prog to trck ldr over 2f out: led over 1f out: rdn wl clr* **11/10**[1]

3043 **2** 3 1/4 **Rio Guru (IRE)**[19] 4255 3-8-12 80 ...... EdwardCreighton 10 73
(M R Channon) *hld up in last pair: prog 2f out: styd on wl to take 2nd last 100yds: no ch w wnr* **11/2**[3]

6662 **3** 2 1/2 **Cheney Manor**[12] 4484 3-9-3 69 ...... FergusSweeney 8 73
(B W Hills) *mde most at stdy pce: hdd over 1f out: immediately wl outpcd* **12/1**

2 **4** 6 **Miss Carlotta**[42] 3484 3-8-12 0 ...... RobertHavlin 4 56
(M P Tregoning) *trckd ldng pair: rdn over 2f out: fnd nil: wknd fnl f* **2/1**[2]

0 **5** 1 **Plaisterer**[16] 4342 3-8-9 0 ow2 ...... GabrielHannon(5) 2 56
(C F Wall) *hld up in 5th: rdn and outpcd over 2f out: no ch after* **16/1**

6 4 **Candy Rose** 3-8-12 0 ...... StephenCarson 7 46
(M P Tregoning) *s.s: rn green in last: brief effrt on outer over 3f out: sn wknd* **25/1**

0/0 **7** 1 1/2 **Pickled Again**[14] 4412 4-9-7 0 ...... IanMongan 11 43
(S Dow) *hld up in 6th: outpcd and rdn over 2f out: wknd over 1f out* **50/1**

0 **8** 7 **Redefine**[18] 4277 3-8-12 0 ...... PaulEddery 12 29
(Mrs A L M King) *trckd ldr: rdn to chal over 3f out: wknd rapidly over 2f out* **50/1**

2m 9.01s (2.41) **Going Correction** +0.025s/f (Slow)
WFA 3 from 4yo 9lb **8** Ran SP% **117.7**
Speed ratings (Par 101): **91,88,86,81,80 77,76,70**
toteswinger: 1&2 £2.10, 1&3 £3.20, 2&3 £7.90. CSF £8.17 TOTE £2.30: £1.10, £1.80, £2.80; EX 7.80.
Owner Mrs Charles Cyzer **Bred** C A Cyzer **Trained** Woodingdean, E Sussex

FOCUS
A modest gallop until the tempo increased 3f from home. The form looks weak although the winner scored nicely.

4861 CHALYBEATE SPRING MAIDEN STKS — 1m (P)
6:10 (6:14) (Class 5) 2-Y-O — £2,590 (£770; £385; £192) Stalls High

Form RPR

44 **1** **Stirling Castle**[20] 4214 2-9-3 0 ...... PatCosgrave 8 81+
(M J Wallace) *trckd ldr: led over 2f out: pressed 1f out: styd on stoutly* **3/1**[2]

2 **2** 1 1/2 **Fullback (IRE)**[17] 4304 2-9-3 0 ...... LPKeniry 7 78+
(J S Moore) *trckd ldrs: prog to chse wnr wl over 1f out: swtchd ins to chal: flashed tail and nt qckn* **11/2**[3]

3 8 **Officer In Command (USA)** 2-9-3 0 ...... SimonWhitworth 10 61+
(J S Moore) *dwlt: last 1st 2f: stl wl in rr over 2f out: prog on inner after: styd on to take 3rd nr fin* **25/1**

0 **4** 1 **Hassadin**[49] 3267 2-9-3 0 ...... GeorgeBaker 12 58
(A B Haynes) *trckd ldrs: rdn over 3f out: sn lost pl and wl outpcd: plugged on fnl f* **50/1**

5 hd **Sergeant Pink (IRE)** 2-9-3 0 ...... FergusSweeney 1 57
(S Gollings) *dwlt: sn in midfield but rn green: pushed along fr 1/2-way: wl outpcd over 2f out: kpt on again fnl f* **40/1**

6 hd **Sumani (FR)** 2-9-3 0 ...... IanMongan 3 57
(S Dow) *in tch: in midfield: rdn and struggling 3f out: sn outpcd: plugged on* **66/1**

53 **7** 1 **Churchills Victory (IRE)**[44] 3408 2-9-3 0 ...... AlanMunro 6 55
(W Jarvis) *trckd ldrs: cl up in 4th over 2f out: sn wl outpcd: wknd fnl f* **11/2**[3]

8 1 **Orsippus (USA)** 2-9-3 0 ...... EdwardCreighton 5 53
(M R Channon) *chsd ldrs on outer: lost pl sn after 1/2-way: wl outpcd over 2f out: no ch after* **25/1**

22 **9** 2 3/4 **Seminole (IRE)**[36] 3682 2-9-3 0 ......(b) RobertHavlin 11 47
(J H M Gosden) *led: rdn and hdd over 2f out: immediately gave up: lost several pls fnl f* **5/4**[1]

10 3 3/4 **D'Artagnans Dream** 2-9-3 0 ...... PaulEddery 9 38
(G D Blake) *detached in last pair after 3f: bhd rest of way* **66/1**

04 **11** 4 1/2 **Kaada**[37] 3645 2-8-12 0 ...... AdamKirby 2 23
(C E Brittain) *dwlt: rn in snatches: struggling in rr 3f out: sn bhd* **33/1**

12 11 **My Les** 2-8-12 0 ...... SteveDrowne 4 —
(J R Best) *dwlt: detached in last pair after 3f: t.o* **25/1**

1m 38.47s (0.27) **Going Correction** +0.025s/f (Slow) **12** Ran SP% **122.1**
Speed ratings (Par 94): **99,97,89,88,88 88,87,86,83,79 75,64**
toteswinger: 1&2 £3.70, 1&3 £21.90, 2&3 £23.20. CSF £18.93 TOTE £4.40: £1.30, £2.10, £8.20; EX 17.30.
Owner H E Sheikh Rashid Bin Mohammed **Bred** Whatton Manor Stud **Trained** Newmarket, Suffolk

FOCUS
A fair race and solid-enough form, although with the disappointing favourite fading rapidly off the turn, the first two looked a cut above the others.

NOTEBOOK
Stirling Castle battled well to hold the challenge of the runner-up, with the pair of them finishing clear. There is no doubt that he stays 1m well, and he looks progressive as well as having a good attitude. (op 11-2)
Fullback(IRE) briefly threatened nearing the furlong pole, but was unable to get past the winner. However, she got the trip alright and has shown enough in both runs to win a routine maiden. (op 4-1 tchd 6-1)
Officer In Command(USA) is bred to be quick, but his speed was not exploited on this debut and he just stayed on to reach third place at the finish. He may do better ridden closer to the pace, and can improve on this first effort.
Hassadin ran a bit better than on his debut, but essentially looks a modest handicapper in the making. (op 40-1)
Sergeant Pink(IRE), who is from a successful family, made a fair debut. He should step up on this as he gains experience, but needs to find a lot more to win. (tchd 50-1)
Sumani(FR) made an ordinary sort of debut and, while likely to benefit a bit, ran as if he will need a bit farther.
Churchills Victory(IRE) is now qualified for handicaps, and that looks his scene, though it appears as if 6f and 7f may suit him better at present. (op 15-2 tchd 9-1)
Orsippus(USA) Official explanation: jockey said colt ran very green
Seminole(IRE) has been blinkered worryingly early in his career, and the way he capitulated once headed suggests he will not be on many lists of horses to follow at the moment. Though he may be better at shorter trips, and could well appreciate a return to turf, the overriding impression is that he is starting to look disappointing. Official explanation: jockey said colt stopped very quickly (op 11-10 tchd 11-8, 6-4 in places)
Kaada Official explanation: jockey said filly was never travelling

4862 TALKSPORT RADIO H'CAP — 7f (P)
6:40 (6:43) (Class 5) (0-70,69) 3-Y-O+ — £2,590 (£770; £385; £192) Stalls Low

Form RPR

2224 **1** **Dawson Creek (IRE)**[129] 1152 4-9-3 **59** ...... GeorgeBaker 3 71
(B Gubby) *trckd ldrs: prog wl over 1f out: plenty to do but styd on strly fnl f to ld last strides* **7/2**[1]

0045 **2** 1/2 **H Harrison (IRE)**[13] 4460 8-8-12 **57** ...... PatrickHills(3) 4 68
(I W McInnes) *trckd ldng pair: rdn over 2f out: prog to ld jst over 1f out and sn 2l clr: collared last strides* **7/1**[2]

5100 **3** 3 **Shot To Fame (USA)**[33] 3797 9-9-8 **69** ......(t) HaddenFrost(5) 11 72
(S Kirk) *trckd ldng pair: rdn and sltly outpcd over 2f out: kpt on again to take 3rd nr fin* **8/1**[3]

1033 **4** 1/2 **Wahoo Sam (USA)**[10] 4529 8-9-9 **65** ...... FergusSweeney 7 67
(P D Evans) *w ldr at gd pce: led over 2f out and drvn: hdd jst over 1f out: wknd nr fin* **9/1**

202- **5** 3 1/4 **Rydal (USA)**[285] 6531 7-9-12 **68** ...... SimonWhitworth 6 61+
(Miss Jo Crowley) *hld up in rr: n.m.r wl over 1f out: shkn up and styd on steadily fnl f: nrst fin* **16/1**

1250 **6** hd **Ever Cheerful**[17] 4307 7-9-11 **67** ......(p) SteveDrowne 10 59
(A B Haynes) *mde most at gd pce to over 2f out: wknd fnl f* **11/1**

0040 **7** nk **Wadnagin (IRE)**[17] 4306 4-8-10 **52** ...... AdamKirby 5 43
(I A Wood) *hld up in rear: rdn on inner over 2f out: no prog tl kpt on fnl f* **8/1**[3]

4600 **8** nse **Cinnamon Hill**[42] 3506 4-9-10 **66** ......(p) StephenCarson 1 57
(Eve Johnson Houghton) *hld up in rr: pushed along 4f out: no prog 2f out: kpt on fnl f* **25/1**

0600 **9** hd **Smokin Joe**[45] 3376 7-9-13 **69** ......(b) LPKeniry 2 60+
(J R Best) *dwlt: hld up towards rr: gng wl enough 3f out: nt clr run wl over 1f out: kpt on fnl f* **25/1**

-340 **10** 1 1/2 **Shaded Edge**[45] 3383 4-9-2 **58** ...... AlanMunro 14 45
(D W P Arbuthnot) *a in rr: rdn and struggling 3f out* **8/1**[3]

004- **11** 1 **Comrade Cotton**[289] 6455 4-8-11 **60** ...... DannyDunnachie(7) 12 44
(J Ryan) *s.s: rcvrd into midfield on outer after 2f: prog into 5th 3f out: wd and wknd bnd 2f out* **40/1**

4060 **12** 2 1/4 **Bookish**[30] 3874 3-9-1 **66** ......(p) KirstyMilczarek(3) 8 44
(Jamie Poulton) *nvr beyond midfield: urged along 1/2-way: wl in rr and no ch whn hmpd jst ins fnl f* **25/1**

2464 **13** 3 1/2 **Joy And Pain**[17] 4306 7-9-6 **62** ......(p) IanMongan 13 30
(M J Attwater) *mostly in midfield: struggling u.p 3f out: wknd and eased over 1f out* **7/1**[2]

-050 **14** 7 **Pasta Prayer**[95] 1897 3-8-11 **59** ...... PatCosgrave 9 9
(S A Callaghan) *hld up in last: bhd fr 1/2-way* **33/1**

1m 24.41s (-0.39) **Going Correction** +0.025s/f (Slow)
WFA 3 from 4yo+ 6lb **14** Ran SP% **121.7**
Speed ratings (Par 103): **103,102,99,98,94 94,94,94,93,92 91,88,84,76**
toteswinger: 1&2 £5.40, 1&3 £11.20, 2&3 £20.10. CSF £25.47 CT £193.39 TOTE £4.10: £1.40, £2.00, £4.40; EX 23.00.
Owner Brian Gubby **Bred** Eastersnow Stud **Trained** Bagshot, Surrey
■ Stewards' Enquiry : Hadden Frost two-day ban: careless riding (Aug 23-24)

FOCUS
A moderate race, but run at a decent gallop. The winner is generally progressive and the form looks sound enough.
Wadnagin(IRE) Official explanation: jockey said filly hung right up the straight and suffered interference in running

4863 PETER BOWDITCH 70TH BIRTHDAY H'CAP — 7f 140y
7:10 (7:14) (Class 6) (0-65,72) 3-Y-O+ — £2,047 (£604; £302) Stalls Centre

Form RPR

2243 **1** **Stand In Flames**[21] 4180 3-9-4 **64** ...... ShaneKelly 2 83
(Pat Eddery) *only one to r in centre thrght: overall ldr after 3f: wl clr over 2f out: unchal* **9/2**[2]

5162 **2** *8* **Navene (IRE)**[18] 4282 4-9-12 **65**........ AlanMunro 12 66
(C F Wall) *hld up bhd ldrs: effrt and taken to centre over 2f out: wnt 2nd 1f out: kpt on but no ch w wnr* **7/2**[1]

506 **3** *3 1/4* **Dr Synn**[31] 3839 7-8-13 **55**........ KirstyMilczarek(3) 5 48
(M J Attwater) *hld up towards rr: taken to centre and effrt 3f out: plugged on to take 3rd ins fnl f* **12/1**

5003 **4** *1 1/4* **Seneschal**[17] 4306 7-9-12 **65**........ GeorgeBaker 13 55
(A B Haynes) *trckd ldr of main gp: led gp wl over 1f out but no ch w wnr: fdd fnl f* **13/2**

4040 **5** *1 3/4* **Jessica Wigmo**[24] 4084 5-8-8 **47**........ FergusSweeney 11 33
(A W Carroll) *hld up in rr: prog 3f out: chsd ldrs 2f out but no ch w wnr: fdd fnl f* **12/1**

5425 **6** *3* **Oi Vay Joe (IRE)**[18] 4284 4-9-12 **65**........(b) LPKeniry 10 44
(W Jarvis) *dwlt: t.k.h and hld up in rr: sme prog 2f out: nvr on terms and n.d after* **7/1**

6402 **7** *1 1/4* **Hollywood George**[14] 4414 4-8-13 **52**........(p) AdamKirby 8 28
(Miss M E Rowland) *led nr side gp: overall ldr 3f: hung lft over 2f out and no ch w wnr: wknd over 1f out* **6/1**[3]

0020 **8** *1 3/4* **Secret Gem (IRE)**[15] 4368 3-9-0 **65**........ GabrielHannon(5) 7 36
(C G Cox) *prom tl wknd wl over 2f out* **16/1**

0605 **9** *3* **Copperwood**[10] 4524 3-8-13 **59**........(b[1]) SteveDrowne 1 22
(M Blanshard) *chsd wnr in centre 2f: taken to r w main gp after: no ch whn taken bk to centre over 2f out* **8/1**

0600 **10** *10* **Pietersen (IRE)**[17] 4306 4-8-13 **57**........ NataliaGemelova(5) 3 —
(J E Long) *rel to r and nvr gng wl: a bhd: t.o* **33/1**

0030 **11** *47* **Cheonmado (USA)**[122] 1266 4-9-1 **54**........(p) EdwardCreighton 4 —
(J R Gask) *nvr gng wl: bhd fr 1/2-way: virtually p.u fnl 2f* **25/1**

1m 31.82s (-0.48) **Going Correction** 0.0s/f (Good)
WFA 3 from 4yo+ 7lb **11** Ran SP% **119.7**
Speed ratings (Par 101): **102,94,90,89,87 84,83,81,78,68 21**
toteswinger: 1&2 £4.00, 1&3 £14.70, 2&3 £13.20. CSF £21.03 CT £183.50 TOTE £4.80: £1.70, £1.90, £5.10; EX 19.80.
Owner Chris Hardy **Bred** Chris E Hardy **Trained** Nether Winchendon, Bucks

FOCUS
Normally the stands' rail is the best place on the Lingfield straight course, but the winner of this moderate handicap bolted up in the middle of the course. The winner is rated in line with recent form but not a race to take too literally.
Hollywood George Official explanation: trainer said colt was unsuited to the soft going
Cheonmado(USA) Official explanation: jockey said gelding had a breathing problem

4864 SPECIALIST LIABILITY SERVICES H'CAP 6f
7:40 (7:42) (Class 4) (0-85,84) 3-Y-0 **£4,604** (£1,378; £689; £344; £171) **Stalls** High

Form RPR

6000 **1** **Perfect Flight**[23] 4127 3-8-8 **74**........ KirstyMilczarek(3) 9 81
(M Blanshard) *t.k.h: hld up in tch: jnd ldrs 2f out: led jst over 1f out: hanging lft but asserted last 75yds* **14/1**

5061 **2** *3/4* **Silver Wind**[14] 4408 3-9-7 **84**........(v) PatCosgrave 7 89
(P D Evans) *trckd ldrs: drvn to chal over 1f out: nt qckn ent fnl f: kpt on to take 2nd nr fin* **5/1**[2]

4610 **3** *hd* **Lodi (IRE)**[19] 4252 3-9-3 **80**........(t) IanMongan 10 84
(J Akehurst) *t.k.h: pressed ldr: led briefly over 1f out: hld by wnr ins fnl f: lost 2nd last strides* **6/1**[3]

6220 **4** *1/2* **Requisite**[6] 4660 3-9-6 **83**........ GeorgeBaker 1 85
(I A Wood) *hld up in tch: prog over 2f out: chal over 1f out: sn rdn and fnd little: hld ins fnl f* **7/2**[1]

366 **5** *4 1/2* **Non Sucre (USA)**[7] 4641 3-8-11 **74**........ ShaneKelly 6 62
(P A Blockley) *led to over 1f out: wknd fnl f* **5/1**[2]

1600 **6** *1/2* **We Have A Dream**[14] 4408 3-9-5 **82**........ LiamJones 3 68
(W R Muir) *trckd ldrs: rdn over 2f out: wknd jst over 1f out* **14/1**

4320 **7** *3/4* **Prime Factor**[37] 3626 3-8-10 **73**........ AlanMunro 2 57
(B W Hills) *dwlt: struggling in last after 2f: nvr on terms after* **5/1**[2]

2015 **8** *shd* **Leading Edge (IRE)**[7] 4631 3-9-0 **77**........ EdwardCreighton 4 61
(M R Channon) *trckd ldrs: rdn 1/2-way: wknd wl over 1f out* **12/1**

3060 **9** *3* **C'Mon You Irons (IRE)**[57] 2998 3-9-3 **80**........ SteveDrowne 5 54
(M R Hoad) *in tch tl wknd u.p over 2f out* **8/1**

1m 10.82s (-0.38) **Going Correction** 0.0s/f (Good) **9** Ran SP% **118.6**
Speed ratings (Par 102): **102,101,100,100,94 93,92,92,88**
toteswinger: 1&2 £15.90, 1&3 £8.20, 2&3 £7.80. CSF £84.68 CT £382.85 TOTE £18.50: £4.70, £2.30, £2.20; EX 137.80.
Owner John Drew **Bred** Biddestone Stud **Trained** Upper Lambourn, Berks

FOCUS
A decent race for the money, comprising a competitive field and a four-horse finish. They all raced in the centre of the track and the third and fourth were close to their form.

4865 ST PETER'S CROSS H'CAP 6f
8:10 (8:10) (Class 5) (0-75,73) 3-Y-0+ **£2,590** (£770; £385; £192) **Stalls** High

Form RPR

1102 **1** **Regal Royale**[7] 4639 5-8-12 **63**........(v) KirstyMilczarek(3) 3 74
(Peter Grayson) *mde all: hung lft fnl f but hld on wl* **3/1**[1]

2440 **2** *3/4* **Alfresco**[10] 4528 4-9-8 **70**........(v) GeorgeBaker 1 79
(I A Wood) *trckd wnr: poised to chal 2f out: rdn and fnd nil jst over 1f out: hld whn carried lft fnl f* **6/1**

2064 **3** *1 1/2* **Cativo Cavallino**[25] 4058 5-9-5 **72**........ NataliaGemelova(5) 4 76
(J E Long) *chsd ldng pair: rdn 2f out: one pce fr over 1f out* **13/2**

6004 **4** *shd* **Outside Edge (IRE)**[16] 4338 3-8-12 **64**........(vt) AdamKirby 2 67
(W R Swinburn) *chsd ldng pair: hrd rdn fnl 2f: one pce fr over 1f out* **11/1**

664 **5** *1 1/4* **Starlight Gazer**[29] 3904 5-9-5 **72**........(t) HaddenFrost(5) 9 72
(J A Geake) *hld up and sn off the pce: hanging lft fr 1/2-way: sme prog 2f out: no imp fnl f* **5/1**[3]

1224 **6** *13* **Realt Na Mara (IRE)**[17] 4313 5-9-11 **73**........ SteveDrowne 7 31
(H Morrison) *hld up: sn off the pce: no prog 1/2-way: wl btn fnl 2f: t.o* **9/2**[2]

2630 **7** *2 1/2* **Corlough Mountain**[14] 4414 4-9-1 **63**........(p) ShaneKelly 8 13
(P Butler) *hld up: sn off the pce: nvr a factor: t.o* **7/1**

6403 **8** *7* **Apple Pie Order (IRE)**[8] 4584 3-8-10 **62**........ AlanMunro 6 —
(R J Hodges) *awkward s: hld up and sn off the pce: no ch whn eased fnl 2f: t.o* **11/1**

1m 11.05s (-0.15) **Going Correction** 0.0s/f (Good)
WFA 3 from 4yo+ 4lb **8** Ran SP% **116.6**
Speed ratings (Par 103): **101,100,98,97,96 78,75,66**
toteswinger: 1&2 £6.30, 1&3 £3.60, 2&3 £3.70. CSF £21.79 CT £109.38 TOTE £3.10: £1.80, £2.30, £3.00; EX 16.90 Place 6 £69.48, Place 5 £46.16.
Owner S Kamis And Mrs S Grayson **Bred** Cheveley Park Stud Ltd **Trained** Formby, Lancs
■ Stewards' Enquiry : Kirsty Milczarek 16-day ban (inc 14 days totted up; four days deferred): careless riding (Aug 31-Sep 11)

FOCUS
A moderate to fair contest for the track, but few seemed to handle the rain-softened ground and it was a two-horse race in the final furlong and a half. They raced middle to stands' side, with the first two both in the centre and they set the level for the form.
Corlough Mountain Official explanation: trainer said gelding was unsuited by the soft ground
Apple Pie Order(IRE) Official explanation: jockey said filly lost her action and was eased
T/Plt: £147.30 to a £1 stake. Pool: £51,639.00. 255.83 winning tickets. T/Qpdt: £23.30 to a £1 stake. Pool: £5,176.00. 165.70 winning tickets. JN

4826
NEWMARKET (JULY) (R-H)
Saturday, August 9

OFFICIAL GOING: Good to soft changing to soft after race 3 (3.15)
Wind: Fresh, across Weather: Raining

4866 SKY BET FOR ALL YOUR FOOTBALL BETTING H'CAP 2m 24y
2:10 (2:10) (Class 3) (0-90,85) 3-Y-0+ **£10,361** (£3,083; £1,540; £769) **Stalls** Centre

Form RPR

220 **1** **Lady Dedlock**[10] 4516 4-8-13 **70**........ RobertHavlin 10 81
(Jamie Poulton) *a.p: led over 3f out: sn rdn: hung lft fr over 1f out: styd on* **8/1**

4210 **2** *3 1/4* **Dolly Penrose**[16] 4351 3-8-8 **80**........ EdwardCreighton 6 87
(M R Channon) *hld up: hdwy over 5f out: ev ch over 2f out: sn rdn and hung lft: no ex fnl f* **11/2**

3231 **3** *2 1/4* **Bollin Felix**[21] 4178 4-10-0 **85**........(b) AlanMunro 7 89
(T D Easterby) *sn led: hdd 14f out: chsd ldrs: rdn over 3f out: styd on same pce appr fnl f* **9/2**[2]

1-25 **4** *shd* **Whenever**[28] 3942 4-9-12 **83**........ JohnEgan 8 87
(R T Phillips) *hld up: hdwy over 3f out: sn rdn and edgd lft: styd on same pce appr fnl f* **2/1**[1]

0001 **5** *3 1/2* **Clear Reef**[7] 4652 4-9-1 **77**........(p) Louis-PhilippeBeuzelin(5) 9 77
(Jane Chapple-Hyam) *s.i.s: hld up: hdwy over 2f out: rdn and edgd lft over 1f out: wknd fnl f* **9/1**

3031 **6** *6* **Swingkeel (IRE)**[24] 4087 3-8-8 **80**........ RichardMullen 3 72
(J L Dunlop) *stmbld s: chsd ldrs: rdn over 3f out: hung lft and wknd over 1f out* **5/1**[3]

5-40 **7** *60* **Velvet Heights (IRE)**[56] 3044 6-9-11 **82**........ TPQueally 2 —
(J L Dunlop) *led 14f out: rdn and hdd over 3f out: sn edgd rt and wknd* **14/1**

0620 **P** **Command Marshal (FR)**[6] 4662 5-9-2 **76**........ PatrickHills(3) 4 —
(M J Scudamore) *rdr lost iron sn after s: hung lft and p.u sn after* **20/1**

3m 32.1s (5.10) **Going Correction** +0.525s/f (Yiel)
WFA 3 from 4yo+ 15lb **8** Ran SP% **116.1**
Speed ratings (Par 107): **108,106,105,105,103 100,70,—**
toteswinger: 1&2 £11.80, 1&3 £7.10, 2&3 £6.20. CSF £52.05 CT £224.38 TOTE £9.00: £2.90, £2.20, £1.70; EX 54.60 Trifecta £269.60 Part won. Pool: £364.36 - 0.90 winning units..
Owner Oceana racing **Bred** C A Cyzer **Trained** Lewes, E Sussex
■ Stewards' Enquiry : Robert Havlin caution: excessive use of the whip

FOCUS
A fair handicap with the top weight 5lb below the race ceiling and after the early leader was pulled up with tack problems the pace was steady until halfway. The time was reasonable in the conditions and the form is best assessed around the placed horses.

NOTEBOOK
Lady Dedlock, who stays really well and has been generally progressive this season, was also proven on soft ground and, always travelling well, she ran on two strongly for the other mare in the race. She is the type connections might aim at the Cesarewitch as she is sure to go up a fair amount for this. (op 11-1 tchd 12-1)
Dolly Penrose, whose win was gained on heavy ground, was stepping up in distance but travelled really well into the race. She was outstayed by the other mare in the final furlong or so, but she deserves credit and looks capable of picking up more races on easy ground this autumn. (op 9-1)
Bollin Felix, another proven on the ground, was quite keen at the steady early pace and, although close enough three furlongs out, could not pick up when ridden. (op 6-1)
Whenever, a progressive sort who handles cut in the ground, was sent off favourite. He was held up off the pace but, after making headway from the half-mile pole, he had no more to give from the two-furlong marker. Possibly he did not get home in this ground. (op 15-8 tchd 7-4 tchd 9-4 in places)
Clear Reef, who was held up at the back, made good headway towards the far side of the track at one point only for his effort to flatten out on the climb to the line. (op 12-1 tchd 17-2)
Swingkeel(IRE), who had beaten the winner on much faster ground last time, was 6lb worse off. He tracked the leaders from the start and had every chance over 2f out but was another one to drop away in the last quarter-mile. Official explanation: trainer's rep said gelding was unsuited by the good to soft ground (op 10-3 tchd 3-1)
Velvet Heights(IRE) Official explanation: jockey said horse stopped quickly and hung right

4867 CHAMPIONSHIP KICK OFF WITH SKY BET H'CAP 1m 2f
2:40 (2:42) (Class 2) (0-100,97) 3-Y-0+ **£12,952** (£3,854; £1,926; £962) **Stalls** Centre

Form RPR

-103 **1** **Tazeez (USA)**[14] 4422 4-9-11 **94**........ RHills 8 107
(J H M Gosden) *mde all: rdn over 1f out: jst hld on* **8/1**

2125 **2** *hd* **Steele Tango (USA)**[9] 4552 3-9-3 **95**........ GeorgeBaker 5 108
(R A Teal) *a.p: chsd wnr over 2f out: rdn over 1f out: styd on* **2/1**[1]

1-30 **3** *7* **Samsons Son**[29] 3896 4-9-2 **85**........ LPKeniry 7 84
(J R Best) *chsd ldrs: rdn over 2f out: edgd lft over 1f out: wknd fnl f* **16/1**

1060 **4** *2 1/2* **Tiger Dream**[14] 4407 3-8-5 **83**........ JohnEgan 9 77
(K A Ryan) *hld up: hdwy over 3f out: swtchd lft over 2f out: rdn and edgd rt over 1f out: wknd fnl f* **12/1**

4564 **5** *3 1/2* **Prince Forever (IRE)**[28] 3974 4-10-0 **97**........ PhilipRobinson 4 84
(M A Jarvis) *hld up: plld hrd: hdwy over 3f out: rdn and wknd over 1f out* **13/2**[3]

0202 **6** *1/2* **Eglevski (IRE)**[64] 2784 4-9-2 **85**........ DaneO'Neill 11 71
(J L Dunlop) *hmpd s: trckd ldr tl rdn over 2f out: wknd over 1f out* **8/1**

61 **7** *1/2* **Voice Coach (IRE)**[56] 3043 3-8-11 **89**........ TPQueally 3 74
(Sir Michael Stoute) *hld up: hung lft fr 1/2-way: n.d* **11/2**[2]

55P **8** *7* **Bid For Glory**[21] 4191 4-9-5 **88**........(v) DarrylHolland 10 59
(H J Collingridge) *wnt rt s: chsd ldrs tl wknd 2f out* **16/1**

600- **9** *15* **Ofaraby**[301] 6172 8-9-2 **92**........ MartinGuest(7) 6 33
(M A Jarvis) *hld up: wknd over 3f out* **40/1**

30-6 **10** *10* **Greek Well (IRE)**[184] 477 5-9-11 **94**........(v) RichardMullen 2 15
(Saeed Bin Suroor) *hld up: plld hrd: rdn and wknd over 2f out: eased fnl f* **15/2**

2m 8.45s (2.95) **Going Correction** +0.525s/f (Yiel)
WFA 3 from 4yo+ 9lb **10** Ran SP% **117.9**
Speed ratings (Par 109): **109,108,103,101,98 98,97,92,80,72**
toteswinger: 1&2 £3.20, 1&3 £16.30, 2&3 £8.20. CSF £24.62 CT £258.85 TOTE £8.80: £3.00, £1.20, £3.20; EX 27.50 Trifecta £327.30 Part won. Pool: £442.30 - 0.20 winning units..
Owner Hamdan Al Maktoum **Bred** Clovelly Farms **Trained** Newmarket, Suffolk

FOCUS
A decent handicap run at a sound gallop in the conditions and the first two came clear. They are rated as improvers but could rate higher.

NOTEBOOK
Tazeez(USA) had run creditably in two outings since winning his maiden, but was allowed an uncontested early lead and that made the difference. He looked set to score by a fair margin but started to tire up the hill and only just lasted home. He is still unexposed and could make an even better five-year-old. (tchd 15-2 tchd 17-2 in a place)
Steele Tango(USA), who has been consistent and progressive this year, was proven on both track and ground and it was no surprise that he started favourite. He went in pursuit of the winner from the quarter-mile pole and was gaining all the way to the line. He was clear of the rest and deserves to pick up another race. (op 5-2 tchd 15-8)
Samsons Son, who kept the runner-up company for much of the race, could not go with that rival but did keep on steadily in the closing stages. He has won over 1m4f and may appreciate a return to that trip. (op 20-1 tchd 14-1)
Tiger Dream, stepping up in trip and encountering soft ground for the first time, drifted over to the far rail 3f out but kept on steadily to provide positive answers as to whether he would handle the unknowns. (op 20-1)
Prince Forever(IRE), who was quite keen under restraint, made a brief effort in the last half-mile without ever getting into contention. Official explanation: trainer said colt was unsuited by the good to soft ground (op 6-1 tchd 7-1)
Eglevski(IRE), who goes well on soft ground, showed up for much of the way but dropped out tamely in the last quarter-mile. (op 11-1)
Voice Coach(IRE) who is very inexperienced but did make his debut on easy ground, was held up out the back and could never get into a challenging position. Official explanation: trainer's rep said colt was unsuited by the good to soft ground (op 3-1)
Greek Well(IRE) Official explanation: trainer's rep said gelding was unsuited by the good to soft ground

4868 SKYBET.COM SWEET SOLERA STKS (GROUP 3) (FILLIES) 7f
3:15 (3:15) (Class 1) 2-Y-O
£28,385 (£10,760; £5,385; £2,685; £1,345; £675) Stalls High

Form RPR
1 **1** **Rainbow View (USA)**[22] 4157 2-8-12 0 ... JimmyFortune 9 111+
(J H M Gosden) *s.i.s: hld up: swtchd rt over 2f out: hdwy to ld over 1f out: edgd lft: shkn up and r.o wl: impressive* **6/4**[1]
021 **2** 6 **Misdaqeya**[52] 3135 2-8-12 85 ... RHills 12 93
(B W Hills) *chsd ldr tl led 2f out: rdn and hdd over 1f out: sn outpcd* **8/1**[3]
61 **3** hd **Minor Vamp (IRE)**[29] 3913 2-8-12 83 ... DaneO'Neill 2 93
(R Hannon) *hld up: hdwy 2f out: rdn over 1f out: styd on same pce fnl f* **10/1**
401 **4** 1 1/4 **Nashmiah (IRE)**[7] 4636 2-8-12 0 ... LiamJones 13 89
(C E Brittain) *s.i.s: sn pushed along in rr: hdwy over 2f out: rdn and hung lft over 1f out: styd on same pce* **33/1**
10 **5** 1/2 **Kissing The Camera**[14] 4403 2-8-12 84 ... ShaneKelly 14 88+
(J Noseda) *trckd ldrs: rdn and hmpd over 1f out: no ex* **16/1**
62 **6** 3/4 **The Legal Blonde (IRE)**[14] 4402 2-8-12 0 ... RichardKingscote 6 86
(Tom Dascombe) *led: rdn and hdd 2f out: wknd fnl f* **11/1**
2 **7** 1 1/2 **Yorksters Girl (IRE)**[25] 4062 2-8-12 0 ... AlanMunro 10 83
(M G Quinlan) *hld up: hdwy 1/2-way: rdn and wknd over 1f out* **16/1**
1042 **8** 3 **Beat Seven**[16] 4348 2-8-12 96 ... SteveDrowne 4 75
(Miss Gay Kelleway) *hld up: rdn over 2f out: sn wknd* **7/1**[2]
1 **9** 1/2 **Ballantrae (IRE)**[30] 3869 2-8-12 0 ... JimCrowley 3 74
(M L W Bell) *chsd ldrs: rdn over 2f out: wknd over 1f out* **10/1**
365 **10** 1/2 **Sanvean (IRE)**[9] 4554 2-8-12 0 ... DarryllHolland 7 73
(M R Channon) *s.i.s: hld up: a in rr: eased and edgd lft over 1f out* **16/1**
03 **11** 3 **Sweet Possession (USA)**[15] 4359 2-8-12 0 ... DarrenWilliams 5 65
(A P Jarvis) *hld up: racd kenly: hdwy 1/2-way: rdn over 2f out: wknd over 1f out* **66/1**
2541 **12** 3 1/4 **Fazbee (IRE)**[12] 4488 2-8-12 88 ... PhilipRobinson 1 57
(P W D'Arcy) *s.i.s: sn prom: rdn and wknd over 1f out* **16/1**
513 **13** 4 1/2 **Ahla Wasahl**[31] 3851 2-8-12 98 ... RichardMullen 11 46
(D M Simcock) *prom: rdn 1/2-way: wknd 2f out: eased fnl f* **16/1**

1m 27.8s (2.10) **Going Correction** +0.525s/f (Yiel) 13 Ran SP% 124.0
Speed ratings (Par 101): **109,102,101,100,99 99,97,93,93,92 89,85,80**
toteswinger: 1&2 £4.30, 1&3 £3.60, 2&3 £9.40. CSF £14.13 TOTE £2.40: £1.30, £3.20, £2.10; EX 14.80 Trifecta £231.30 Part won. Pool: £312.60 - 0.60 winning units..
Owner George Strawbridge **Bred** Augustin Stable **Trained** Newmarket, Suffolk

FOCUS
A fair renewal of this Group 3 but producing an impressive winner in an exceptional time for the age and grade being 0.55secs faster than the following Class 2 handicap for older horses. She looks a Group 1 filly in the making with the placed horses decent yardsticks. The ground description was changed to soft after this race.

NOTEBOOK
Rainbow View(USA) ◆, who had bolted up on her debut over course and distance, repeated the feat against this much better company. She was held up at the back before cruising into contention and, once asked for her effort, swept into the lead and was clear in a matter of strides. She looks a Group 1 filly in the making and it is no surprise that she was quoted as short as 5/1 favourite for the 1000 Guineas. She will go for the May Hill at Doncaster next. (op 2-1)
Misdaqeya, who was returning from a break, had been progressive when last seen having beaten three subsequent winners when scoring at Kempton. She ran well but was absolutely no match for the winner, although she should be able to win at Listed level. (op 9-1)
Minor Vamp(IRE), who won her maiden on similar ground, was held up at the back with the winner and came through on the other flank. She stayed on steadily to earn black type and is another who can win in Listed company given some cut in the ground. (op 11-1)
Nashmiah(IRE), who finished well behind the winner here last month, also had form that tied in with the runner-up. She got closer to Rainbow View, having looked in trouble soon after halfway but then staying on as if a mile plus will suit before too long.
Kissing The Camera, who narrowly beat today's runner-up on her debut, seemed to run her race and the very different ground may have been responsible.
The Legal Blonde(IRE), who finished runner-up on her previous outing in an Ascot Listed race in which all the other runners were previous winners, set the pace but could not pick up on the ground. She put up another creditable effort and should be winning before long. (op 9-1 tchd 12-1)
Beat Seven came into this with some solid form including on easy ground, but this may have been softer than she would have liked. (tchd 8-1)
Ahla Wasahl Official explanation: trainer said filly was unsuited by the good to soft ground

4869 SOCCER SATURDAY SUPER 6 H'CAP 7f
3:50 (3:50) (Class 2) (0-105,103) 3-Y-O+
£24,924 (£7,464; £3,732; £1,868; £932; £468) Stalls High

Form RPR
141 **1** **Kalahari Gold (IRE)**[7] 4641 3-9-1 97 ... LPKeniry 11 109+
(A M Balding) *hld up in tch: led over 1f out: rdn out* **7/2**[1]
1302 **2** 1 1/4 **Pawan (IRE)**[7] 4617 8-8-9 90 ... (b) AnnStokell(5) 4 97
(Miss A Stokell) *a.p: rdn over 1f out: r.o* **16/1**
211 **3** hd **Little White Lie (IRE)**[29] 3921 4-9-13 103 ... DarryllHolland 7 109
(J R Jenkins) *chsd ldr: rdn and ev ch over 1f out: edgd lft: styd on same pce ins fnl f* **4/1**[2]
-300 **4** hd **Big Noise**[14] 4405 4-8-11 87 ... RichardThomas 2 93
(Dr J D Scargill) *hld up: swtchd rt and hdwy over 1f out: sn rdn and hung rt: r.o towards fin* **8/1**
4046 **5** 2 **Vitznau (IRE)**[8] 4587 4-9-9 99 ... JimmyFortune 12 100
(R Hannon) *hld up: hdwy and hmpd over 1f out: sn rdn: nt run on* **4/1**[2]
300 **6** 1 1/2 **Cobo Bay**[22] 4153 3-9-4 100 ... (p) PatDobbs 15 94
(K A Ryan) *chsd ldrs: rdn over 1f out: no ex* **16/1**
1010 **7** 3/4 **Masai Moon**[14] 4405 4-8-13 92 ... JamesMillman(3) 1 86
(B R Millman) *chsd ldrs: rdn and ev ch over 1f out: wknd ins fnl f* **16/1**
0000 **8** 1 **Obe Brave**[28] 3973 5-8-8 84 ... ShaneKelly 8 76
(R A Fahey) *led: rdn and hdd over 1f out: wknd ins fnl f* **25/1**
0S00 **9** 2 1/4 **Tathkaar**[31] 3849 3-8-3 85 ... LiamJones 9 69
(C E Brittain) *prom: rdn over 2f out: wknd over 1f out* **33/1**
6452 **10** 3/4 **South Cape**[6] 4661 5-8-10 86 ... DaneO'Neill 14 70
(M R Channon) *hld up: rdn over 2f out: wknd over 1f out* **6/1**[3]
3-40 **11** 2 1/2 **Nacho Libre**[64] 2793 3-9-3 99 ... MichaelHills 13 74
(B W Hills) *hld up: racd keenly: rdn and wknd over 2f out* **14/1**

1m 28.35s (2.65) **Going Correction** +0.525s/f (Yiel)
WFA 3 from 4yo+ 6lb 11 Ran SP% 118.7
Speed ratings (Par 109): **105,103,103,103,100 99,98,97,94,93 90**
toteswinger: 1&2 £19.60, 1&3 £4.20, 2&3 £22.10. CSF £62.04 CT £237.10 TOTE £4.60: £1.80, £3.60, £1.80; EX 77.00 Trifecta £706.90 Pool: £38,979.53 - 40.80 winning units..
Owner The Toucan Syndicate **Bred** Mick McGinn And James Waldron **Trained** Kingsclere, Hants

FOCUS
A good handicap but the time was unexceptional, being 0.55secs slower than the preceding Group 3 juvenile contest. The third is rated to his Bunbury Cup form with the winner progressive.

NOTEBOOK
Kalahari Gold(IRE) ◆ is a really progressive performer and defied a 12lb rise for his course and distance win the previous week. Always going well, he scored in most decisive fashion and had no problems with the softer surface. He looks the sort who can pick up more valuable handicaps at this trip, but he is now bordering on Listed class so connections may have to look for opportunities at that level. (op 4-1)
Pawan(IRE) is a consistent performer at 5f-6f but, despite winning over this trip in the distant past, had not totally convinced that it suits. However, he does like soft ground and has now been runner-up on his last six starts under such conditions. He deserves to win a big prize and his consistency and durability is a credit to connections. (tchd 18-1)
Little White Lie(IRE) has done really well for current connections and put up another creditable performance off a 5lb higher mark than for his Bunbury Cup success. He will not find things easy in the short term, but he does handle soft ground and also stays a mile, which increases his options. (op 7-2 tchd 9-2 in a place)
Big Noise, who won on soft ground last season, has done most of his recent racing on a faster surface. He ran well despite hanging and backed up his recent good effort in the Totesport International Handicap. He looks to have a decent handicap in him. (op 11-2)
Vitznau(IRE) goes well on soft ground and would probably have finished a little closer but for being hampered by the fourth. He has dropped a little in the weights and is another to consider for good handicaps over this trip from now until the end of the season. (op 5-1)
Cobo Bay, wearing cheekpieces for the first time and back on his favourite surface, showed up well for a long way. He does, however, look as though he needs a little help from the Handicapper now. (tchd 20-1)
Masai Moon does handle these conditions but has looked most effective on a faster surface of late. He saw quite a lot of daylight and faded out of contention on the rise to the line.
Tathkaar Official explanation: trainer said filly was unsuited by the soft ground
South Cape finished ahead of today's fourth and seventh in the Totesport International and should have run better, but he has never shown his best form on ground this soft. (op 15-2)

4870 WYCK HALL STUD MAIDEN FILLIES' STKS 7f
4:25 (4:28) (Class 4) 2-Y-O £5,180 (£1,541; £770; £384) Stalls High

Form RPR
403 **1** **Snoqualmie Girl (IRE)**[22] 4157 2-9-0 77 ... TQuinn 14 87+
(D R C Elsworth) *hld up: hdwy over 2f out: rdn over 1f out: styd on to ld wl ins fnl f* **9/2**[2]
2 1 1/4 **Bouvardia** 2-9-0 0 ... TPQueally 13 84+
(H R A Cecil) *chsd ldrs: led over 1f out: hdd wl ins fnl f* **7/2**[1]
4 **3** 3 1/2 **Night Lily (IRE)**[22] 4157 2-9-0 0 ... RichardKingscote 17 75
(J Jay) *led: rdn and hung lft over 2f out: hdd over 1f out: wknd ins fnl f* **8/1**[3]
4 3 1/4 **Fen Spirit (IRE)** 2-9-0 0 ... JimmyFortune 9 67+
(J H M Gosden) *chsd ldrs: shkn up over 1f out: wknd ins fnl f* **8/1**[3]
5 shd **Purple Sage (IRE)** 2-9-0 0 ... MichaelHills 11 67+
(B W Hills) *s.i.s: hld up: swtchd lft over 2f out: styd on fr over 1f out: nt trbld ldrs* **14/1**
64 **6** 2 3/4 **Eliza Griffith (IRE)**[7] 4643 2-9-0 0 ... PatDobbs 6 60
(R Hannon) *chsd ldrs: rdn over 1f out: sn wknd* **9/1**
7 nse **The Miniver Rose (IRE)** 2-9-0 0 ... DarryllHolland 8 60
(R Hannon) *prom: rdn 1/2-way: wknd wl over 1f out* **20/1**
8 1/2 **Sairaam (IRE)** 2-9-0 0 ... PaulDoe 16 59+
(J L Dunlop) *s.s: in rr: hdwy over 1f out: nvr trbld ldrs* **33/1**
53 **9** 1 3/4 **Mutually Mine (USA)**[48] 3292 2-9-0 0 ... MickyFenton 10 54
(Mrs P Sly) *chsd ldrs tl rdn: hung lft and wknd over 1f out* **14/1**
00 **10** 1 **Missou Maiden**[22] 4157 2-9-0 0 ... RichardThomas 18 52
(M H Tompkins) *prom: lost pl over 4f out: sme hdwy over 1f out: sn hung lft and wknd* **66/1**
0 **11** shd **Sapphire Rose**[43] 3456 2-9-0 0 ... JimCrowley 4 51
(J G Portman) *hld up: a in rr* **25/1**
12 1 **Hoboob (USA)** 2-9-0 0 ... RHills 19 49
(J L Dunlop) *s.i.s: hdwy 1/2-way: rdn and wknd over 1f out* **9/1**
13 1 **Free Falling** 2-9-0 0 ... DaneO'Neill 7 46
(L M Cumani) *prom: shkn up and wknd over 2f out* **14/1**
14 1 1/4 **Implication** 2-9-0 0 ... ShaneKelly 2 43
(E A L Dunlop) *s.s: a in rr: rdn and wknd over 2f out* **14/1**
56 **15** 1 3/4 **Betws Y Coed (IRE)**[61] 2887 2-8-11 0 ... DominicFox(3) 12 39
(A Bailey) *s.i.s: hld up: a in rr: wknd over 2f out* **66/1**
16 nk **Aula** 2-9-0 0 ... NeilPollard 1 38
(E A L Dunlop) *s.s: bhd: effrt over 2f out: sn hung rt and wknd* **50/1**
0 **17** 16 **Konka (USA)**[85] 2150 2-9-0 0 ... LiamJones 3 —
(E F Vaughan) *mid-div: rdn 1/2-way: wknd over 2f out* **66/1**

1m 28.76s (3.06) **Going Correction** +0.525s/f (Yiel) 17 Ran SP% 127.3
Speed ratings (Par 93): **103,101,97,93,93 90,90,89,87,86 86,85,84,83,81 80,62**
toteswinger: 1&2 £4.60, 1&3 £6.10, 2&3 £8.70. CSF £20.23 TOTE £6.00: £2.20, £1.90, £3.50; EX 23.30.
Owner J C Smith **Bred** Littleton Stud **Trained** Newmarket, Suffolk

FOCUS
A fair fillies' maiden run almost a second slower than the earlier Group 3 over the trip but still decent for the grade and the form looks solid enough

NOTEBOOK

Snoqualmie Girl(IRE) ◆, who finished third to the earlier Group 3 winner Rainbow View here in July, was well backed and duly scored cosily, giving that filly's form a boost in the process. She was held up and looked to have a fair bit to do in the dip if she was to catch the runner-up, but she hit full stride up the hill and swept past her rival. She looks to be progressing with racing and could add to her score on this evidence. (op 7-1)

Bouvardia ◆, a half-sister to the dual 6f winner Camacho out of a mare who also won twice at that trip, has a Cheveley Park Stakes entry. It was surprising, therefore, that she made her debut over 7f but when she strode to the front inside the final 2f she looked sure to score. However, she was run down by the winner once meeting the rising ground, but appeared to stay as she was drawing away from the rest. She should not be long in winning her maiden on this evidence. (op 10-3)

Night Lily(IRE), who finished a length behind today's winner here last time, set a decent gallop and had most of her rivals in trouble at the quarter-mile pole. It was no disgrace to be beaten by two such useful sorts and possibly she did not quite get home on the ground. She should be up to winning an ordinary maiden on what she has shown so far. (op 12-1)

Fen Spirit(IRE), who sold for less at the breeze-ups than as a yearling, is a half-sister to the useful Nine Stories and related to milers. She showed plenty of pace until fading out of contention in the closing stages and was not given a hard race once her chance had gone, so should show the benefit of the outing next time. (op 9-1)

Purple Sage(IRE), a 155,000euros daughter of Danehill Dancer out of a sister to Ballingarry and Aristotle, missed the break and was at the back for a long way, but was noted making decent late progress and is another who should be better for the experience. (op 11-1)

Eliza Griffith(IRE), who put up a fair effort in a similar maiden here the previous week, helps set the level for the form in what looked a better race. She now qualifies for handicaps and that is probably where she will make her mark. (op 11-2)

The Miniver Rose(IRE), who cost 100,000gns at the sales, showed some early pace and more can be expected in time. (tchd 22-1)

4871 SUNLEY MAIDEN STKS — 1m 4f

4:55 (4:58) (Class 4) 3-Y-0+ — **£5,180** (£1,541; £770; £384) **Stalls** Centre

Form				RPR
4	**1**		**Interchange (IRE)**[30] 3894 3-8-10 0 .... JimCrowley 4 (J R Fanshawe) *a.p: chsd ldr over 3f out: rdn to ld over 1f out: styd on wl* **5/1**[3]	77+
04	**2**	*1 3/4*	**Lough Diver (IRE)**[32] 3813 3-9-1 0 .... SaleemGolam 12 (M H Tompkins) *hld up: hdwy over 2f out: rdn over 1f out: edgd lft: styd on wl* **16/1**	80+
0-32	**3**	*2 3/4*	**Time Control**[22] 4166 3-8-10 82 .... DaneO'Neill 6 (L M Cumani) *chsd ldrs tl led 4f out: rdn: edgd rt and hdd over 1f out: no ex ins fnl f* **13/8**[1]	70+
50	**4**	*4 1/2*	**Opera De Luna**[7] 4620 3-8-10 0 .... DarrenWilliams 13 (D Shaw) *hld up: hdwy u.p over 3f out: wknd over 1f out* **66/1**	63
	5	*1 3/4*	**Lazeyma** 3-8-10 0 .... PhilipRobinson 5 (M A Jarvis) *hld up: hdwy over 4f out: wknd over 1f out* **16/1**	60
54	**6**	*hd*	**Canyon Colours (USA)**[13] 4461 3-8-8 0 .... DebraEngland(7) 2 (G A Butler) *hld up: shkn up 3f out: nvr nr to chal* **50/1**	65
62	**7**	*9*	**Kritzia**[25] 4057 3-8-10 0 .... TPQueally 7 (H R A Cecil) *chsd ldrs: rdn over 4f out: wknd over 2f out* **12/1**	45
5	**8**	*5*	**Amaakin (USA)**[84] 2197 3-9-1 0 .... RichardMullen 3 (P W Chapple-Hyam) *hld up in tch: rdn over 3f out: sn wknd* **10/1**	42
32	**9**	*18*	**Solar Dance (USA)**[46] 3350 3-8-10 0 .... JimmyFortune 8 (J H M Gosden) *chsd ldr tl led over 5f out: hdd 4f out: rdn: edgd rt and wknd over 2f out* **5/2**[2]	9
0	**10**	*3 3/4*	**American Madness (USA)**[7] 4620 3-8-12 0 .... JerryO'Dwyer(3) 9 (M G Quinlan) *led over 6f: wknd over 3f out: eased over 1f out* **66/1**	8

2m 39.55s (6.65) **Going Correction** +0.525s/f (Yiel)
WFA 3 from 6yo 11lb — **10** Ran SP% **116.8**
Speed ratings (Par 105): **98,96,95,92,90 90,84,81,69,66**
toteswinger: 1&2 £12.40, 1&3 £3.20, 2&3 £8.60. CSF £80.04 TOTE £4.40: £1.80, £4.00, £1.40; EX 86.60.

Owner Lady Clague **Bred** Newberry Stud Company **Trained** Newmarket, Suffolk

FOCUS

A fair maiden in which the field ended up on the far rail in the straight. The pace was modest and there area few doubts about the form.

Solar Dance(USA) Official explanation: jockey said filly hung right and stopped very quickly

4872 HALF MOON MONTEGO BAY EBF FILLIES' H'CAP — 1m

5:25 (5:27) (Class 4) (0-80,79) 3-Y-0+ — **£5,828** (£1,734; £866; £432) **Stalls** High

Form				RPR
4022	**1**		**Trumpet Lily**[26] 4022 3-9-10 **79** .... JimCrowley 2 (J G Portman) *hld up: swtchd lft and hdwy 2f out: led 1f out: sn clr* **3/1**[2]	86
0061	**2**	*2 1/4*	**Talk Of Saafend (IRE)**[14] 4429 3-9-7 **76** .... DaneO'Neill 9 (R Hannon) *chsd ldrs: rdn to ld over 1f out: sn hung lft and hdd: styd on same pce* **7/2**[3]	78
1-40	**3**	*nk*	**Fantasy Princess (USA)**[21] 4189 3-9-8 **77** .... TPQueally 4 (G A Butler) *chsd ldrs: rdn over 1f out: styd on same pce* **6/1**	78
2212	**4**	*3/4*	**Tatbeeq (IRE)**[24] 4082 3-9-8 **77** .... RHills 3 (M A Jarvis) *w ldr: rdn and ev ch over 1f out: edgd lft and no ex ins fnl f* **2/1**[1]	77
0005	**5**	*2 1/4*	**Miss Bootylishes**[28] 3971 3-9-6 **78** .... JerryO'Dwyer(3) 10 (A B Haynes) *led: rdn and hdd over 1f out: wknd ins fnl f* **8/1**	72
66-0	**6**	*9*	**Sayedati Elhasna (IRE)**[17] 4300 3-9-0 **69** .... RichardMullen 7 (J L Dunlop) *s.i.s: hld up: rdn and wknd 2f out* **12/1**	43

1m 44.14s (4.14) **Going Correction** +0.525s/f (Yiel)
WFA 3 from 4yo 7lb — **6** Ran SP% **113.6**
Speed ratings (Par 102): **100,97,96,94 85**
toteswinger: 1&2 £2.30, 1&3 £2.40, 2&3 £3.00. CSF £14.14 CT £57.43 TOTE £3.50: £2.00, £2.40; EX 10.40 Place 6 £37.51, Place 5 £10.40.

Owner Mrs J Edwards-Heathcote **Bred** The Hon Mrs R Pease **Trained** Compton, Berks

FOCUS

A fair fillies' handicap decimated by five withdrawals. The form looks ordinary with the runner-up and fourth the best guides.

Talk Of Saafend(IRE) Official explanation: jockey said filly hung left

T/Jkpt: £40,987.20 to a £1 stake. Pool: £115,457.08. 2.00 winning tickets. T/Plt: £67.20 to a £1 stake. Pool: £109,970.55. 1,192.98 winning tickets. T/Qpdt: £7.60 to a £1 stake. Pool: £5,211.97. 502.40 winning tickets. CR

4536 REDCAR (L-H)

Saturday, August 9

OFFICIAL GOING: Good (good to soft in places)

Wind: Virtually nil Weather: Overcast and raining

4873 SUBSCRIBE TO RACING UK (S) STKS — 6f

1:50 (1:53) (Class 6) 2-Y-0 — **£2,047** (£604; £302) **Stalls** Centre

Form				RPR
5430	**1**		**Scenic Pass**[8] 4604 2-8-12 60 .... TPO'Shea 8 (M R Channon) *trckd ldrs: hdwy over 2f out: rdn to ld over 1f out: styd on* **9/4**[1]	63+
0305	**2**	*2 1/4*	**Nchike**[8] 4604 2-8-11 53 .... (v[1]) SilvestreDeSousa 10 (D Nicholls) *a.p: cl up 1/2-way: rdn wl over 1f out and ev ch tl drvn and one pce ins fnl f* **7/1**	54
0006	**3**	*4*	**Senora Verde**[17] 4290 2-8-6 38 .... PaulFessey 6 (P T Midgley) *led: rdn along over 2f out: drvn: edgd lft and hdd over 1f out: sn one pce* **33/1**	37
3300	**4**	*2 1/4*	**Carmanjoe**[8] 4594 2-8-11 58 .... PaulMulrennan 2 (M W Easterby) *in tch: hdwy over 2f out: sn rdn and no imp appr fnl f* **5/1**[3]	36
064	**5**	*1*	**Jaslyn (IRE)**[13] 4449 2-8-7 50 ow1 .... TomEaves 9 (J R Weymes) *towards rr: hdwy over 2f out: sn rdn and kpt on appr fnl f: nrst fin* **14/1**	29
5146	**6**	*6*	**Elaine's Folly**[8] 4604 2-8-12 56 .... JoeFanning 12 (P C Haslam) *prom: rdn along over 2f out and sn wknd* **10/3**[2]	16
4450	**7**	*2*	**Rioja Ruby (IRE)**[11] 4499 2-8-6 52 .... TonyHamilton 4 (P C Haslam) *in tch: rdn along 1/2-way: sn wknd* **8/1**	4
	8	*1 1/2*	**Our Bridget** 2-8-6 0 .... PaulQuinn 13 (C W Fairhurst) *in rr: rdn along 1/2-way: sme late hdwy* **25/1**	—
400	**9**	*2*	**Flog It**[22] 4169 2-8-11 41 .... (b[1]) LeeEnstone 1 (T D Easterby) *chsd ldrs on outer: rdn along over 2f out and sn wknd* **25/1**	—
5600	**10**	*nk*	**Quadrifolio**[21] 4203 2-8-11 33 .... (v) KimTinkler 3 (N Tinkler) *nvr nr ldrs* **50/1**	—
0	**11**	*1 3/4*	**Mosspaul**[126] 1220 2-8-6 0 .... DaleGibson 11 (A C Whillans) *midfield: rdn along 1/2-way: sn in rr* **33/1**	—
000	**12**	*1 1/4*	**Without Equal**[17] 4290 2-8-3 31 .... DuranFentiman(3) 7 (A Dickman) *s.i.s: a in rr* **66/1**	—
0040	**13**	*1 1/2*	**Ernies Keep**[21] 4203 2-8-11 38 .... TWilliams 5 (W Storey) *a towards rr* **50/1**	—
0	**14**	*1*	**Northern Shore (IRE)**[60] 2909 2-8-8 0 .... TolleyDean(3) 14 (J O'Reilly) *a in rr* **40/1**	—

1m 13.17s (1.37) **Going Correction** +0.10s/f (Good) — **14** Ran SP% **122.2**
Speed ratings (Par 92): **94,91,85,82,81 73,70,68,66,65 63,61,59,58**
toteswinger: 1&2 £5.60, 1&3 £26.10, 2&3 £26.10. CSF £17.49 TOTE £3.50: £1.50, £2.20, £19.80; EX 19.70.The winner was sold to Alan McWilliam for 8,000gns.

Owner M Channon **Bred** Norman Court Stud **Trained** West Ilsley, Berks

FOCUS

After morning rain the ground was changed to good, good to soft in places. There were mainly exposed sorts in this seller but the form looks solid with the first three close to their marks.

NOTEBOOK

Scenic Pass proved her running at Thirsk last week to be all wrong. She travelled much better this time, and was ridden clear on the final furlong. She is pretty exposed and, after being sold afterwards, she now joins Ed McMahon. (op 3-1 tchd 2-1)

Nchike, who finished in front of the winner at Thirsk, had a visor on for the first time here and probably ran close to form having shown up from the outset. (op 8-1 tchd 6-1)

Senora Verde, unplaced in her four previous starts, raced towards the far side and kept on though she was beaten more than six lengths. (op 50-1)

Carmanjoe ran a little better than in his recent starts, but was still well beaten and looks to be going the wrong way. (op 11-2 tchd 7-1)

Jaslyn(IRE) ran as though finding this trip inadequate, but still did not achieve much. (op 9-1)

Elaine's Folly ran poorly and has been very disappointing since winning a claimer over course and distance in June. (op 9-2)

4874 TRANSMORE VEHICLE HIRE LTD NURSERY — 6f

2:25 (2:27) (Class 3) 2-Y-0 — **£6,799** (£2,023; £1,011; £505) **Stalls** Centre

Form				RPR
1410	**1**		**La Brigitte**[14] 4434 2-9-2 **80** .... TolleyDean(3) 10 (A J McCabe) *cl up on outer: effrt over 2f out: led wl over 1f out: rdn and edgd lft ins fnl f: kpt on* **13/2**	84+
023	**2**	*1 1/2*	**Ishe Mac**[21] 4202 2-9-1 **76** .... SilvestreDeSousa 9 (N Bycroft) *trckd ldrs: pushed along and sltly outpcd over 2f out: sn rdn and hdwy to chse wnr ent fnl f: sn drvn and kpt on* **13/2**	76+
2U26	**3**	*3*	**Verinco**[32] 3809 2-9-5 **80** .... (b) TomEaves 3 (B Smart) *t.k.h: cl up: led after 2f: rdn along and hdd wl over 1f out: drvn and one pce appr fnl f* **17/2**	71
305	**4**	*1*	**Secret City (IRE)**[27] 3997 2-8-8 **69** ow2 .... (b[1]) PaulMulrennan 5 (R Bastiman) *t.k.h: in tch: hdwy to chse ldrs 1/2-way: rdn along over 2f out and kpt on same pce* **20/1**	57
203	**5**	*2 1/2*	**Becausewecan (USA)**[21] 4176 2-8-11 **72** .... JoeFanning 6 (M Johnston) *prom: rdn along 1/2-way: drvn over 2f out and grad wknd* **5/1**[3]	52
601	**6**	*nk*	**Oriental Rose**[23] 4108 2-9-1 **76** .... TPO'Shea 1 (G M Moore) *chsd ldrs: rdn along over 2f out and grad wknd* **8/1**	55
1052	**7**	*3 1/2*	**Fivefootnumberone (IRE)**[28] 3978 2-9-4 **82** .... JamieMoriarty(3) 7 (J J Quinn) *in tch: rdn along 1/2-way: sn drvn and btn 2f out* **7/2**[1]	51
0500	**8**	*4 1/2*	**Drachenfels**[6] 4659 2-7-13 **60** .... (p) PaulFessey 4 (K A Ryan) *bmpd s: sn rdn along and a in rr* **33/1**	15
2621	**9**	*3/4*	**Sloop Johnb**[13] 4449 2-9-3 **78** .... TonyHamilton 8 (R A Fahey) *s.i.s and in rr: effrt and sme hdwy whn n.m.r over 2f out: sn rdn and wknd* **4/1**[2]	31
005	**10**	*6*	**El Bobby (IRE)**[13] 4449 2-8-1 **65** .... (t) DuranFentiman(3) 2 (J R Weymes) *led 2f: prom tl rdn along 1/2-way and sn wknd* **50/1**	—

1m 12.68s (0.88) **Going Correction** +0.10s/f (Good) — **10** Ran SP% **116.9**
Speed ratings (Par 98): **98,96,92,90,87 86,82,76,75,67**
toteswinger: 1&2 £7.90, 1&3 £36.80, 2&3 £47.10. CSF £47.48 CT £372.79 TOTE £7.30: £2.70, £2.30, £3.10; EX 67.30 Trifecta £61.20 Part won. Pool: £82.78 - 0.60 winning units..

Owner Paul J Dixon **Bred** M And Mrs V L Ritchie **Trained** Babworth, Notts

FOCUS

This was faster than the seller and once again the principals came up the centre. The form looks solid enough rated through the runner-up.

NOTEBOOK

La Brigitte, for whom the rain came just in time, was winning for the third time, her two previous successes having come on heavy ground and on Southwell's Fibresand. Breaking better than she did at York on her previous start, she travelled well and, going on well over a furlong out, edged left and carried her head high as usual, but she ran on well. She is going the right way. Official explanation: trainer said, regarding the apparent improvement in form, filly jumped off quicker on this occasion and had been better suited by the give underfoot (op 12-1)

Ishe Mac came home quite well after getting outpaced soon after halfway and on this showing she can pick up a similar race, with a stiffer 6f likely to suit her. (op 5-1)

Verinco, keen early, had every chance but could not quicken in the final furlong. He seemed to stay the sixth furlong. (op 11-1)

Secret City(IRE) did not fare too badly in fourth considering she was keen early, though she never looked like winning. Official explanation: jockey said gelding ran too free in the early stages (op 16-1)

Becausewecan(USA) was never really going on this nursery debut and may need it softer. (op 9-2 tchd 11-2 in a place)

Fivefootnumberone(IRE) was beaten soon after halfway, running well below his best, and is yet to prove he stays this far. Official explanation: trainer had no explanation for the poor form shown (op 9-2)

Drachenfels, tried in cheekpieces instead of blinkers, was squeezed and lost ground early on. (tchd 40-1)

Sloop Johnb lost his chance with a slow break and he then met a bit of trouble. (op 9-2)

4875 £1MILLION TOTESCOOP6 H'CAP 7f

3:00 (3:00) (Class 4) (0-80,80) 3-Y-0+ **£4,857** (£1,445; £722; £360) **Stalls** Centre

Form RPR

3-01 **1** **Borasco (USA)**[44] 3416 3-9-3 **76** PaulFessey 8 89
(T D Barron) *mde all: rdn along and qcknd 2f out: kpt on strly fnl f* **6/1**[2]

3140 **2** 1 3/4 **Celtic Lynn (IRE)**[30] 3883 3-8-11 **70** TomEaves 12 78
(M Dods) *hld up in tch: smooth hdwy to trck ldrs 1/2-way: effrt to chse wnr over 1f out: edgd lft and rdn ent fnl f: kpt on: but no imp on wnr towards fin* **16/1**

1033 **3** 3 **Bid For Gold**[3] 4736 4-8-12 **65** TonyHamilton 2 67
(Jedd O'Keeffe) *chsd ldrs: rdn along wl over 2f out: drvn wl over 1f out: kpt on u.p ins fnl f* **13/2**[3]

2020 **4** nse **Yorkshire Blue**[16] 4327 9-8-9 **67** GaryBartley(5) 3 69+
(J S Goldie) *hmpd s: sn outpcd and wl bhd: hdwy over 2f out: rdn wl over 1f out: str run ent fnl f: nrst fin* **9/1**

1042 **5** 1/2 **Handsome Falcon**[19] 4245 4-8-12 **72** FrederikTylicki(7) 7 72
(R A Fahey) *prom: pushed along over 2f out: rdn wl over 1f out and kpt on same pce* **9/2**[1]

5600 **6** 1 **Viva Volta**[14] 4440 5-8-11 **67** JamieMoriarty(3) 9 65
(T D Easterby) *midfield: hdwy to chse ldrs 1/2-way: rdn along 2f out and sn one pce* **14/1**

3422 **7** hd **Follow The Flag (IRE)**[40] 3563 4-9-2 **72** TolleyDean(3) 1 69
(A J McCabe) *sn in tch: hdwy to chse ldrs 3f out: rdn along 2f out: sn drvn and no imp* **12/1**

0663 **8** 1 1/4 **Passion Fruit**[14] 4417 7-9-11 **78** (p) PaulMulrennan 10 72
(C W Fairhurst) *hld up towards rr: hdwy over 2f out: sn rdn and n.m.r over 1f out: sn no imp* **9/1**

0242 **9** 1/2 **Kashimin (IRE)**[5] 4682 3-9-7 **80** (b[1]) JoeFanning 4 70
(G A Swinbank) *hmpd s: sn in tch: hdwy on outer and ev ch over 2f out: sn rdn: edgd lft and wknd over 1f out* **6/1**[2]

1 **10** nk **Chosen Forever**[30] 3867 3-8-7 **66** SilvestreDeSousa 5 56
(G R Oldroyd) *wnt lft s: chsd ldrs: rdn along 1/2-way: sn drvn and wknd* **12/1**

0340 **11** 2 **Game Lad**[14] 4417 6-9-10 **80** DuranFentiman(3) 6 66
(T D Easterby) *towards rr: effrt and sme hdwy 3f out: sn rdn along and nvr a factor* **10/1**

-000 **12** 16 **Bespoke Boy**[93] 1925 3-9-4 **77** LeeEnstone 11 18
(P C Haslam) *cl up: rdn along 1/2-way sn lost pl and bhd* **50/1**

1m 25.95s (1.45) **Going Correction** +0.10s/f (Good)
WFA 3 from 4yo+ 6lb 12 Ran SP% **119.1**
Speed ratings (Par 105): **95,93,89,89,88 87,87,86,85,85 82,64**
toteswinger: 1&2 £30.60, 1&3 £10.00, 2&3 £45.10. CSF £98.50 CT £660.42 TOTE £6.10: £3.50, £4.40, £2.90; EX 125.10 Trifecta £159.10 Part won. Pool: £215.00 - 0.10 winning units..
Owner Patrick Toes & R G Toes **Bred** Kidder, Cole & J K & Linda Griggs **Trained** Maunby, N Yorks

FOCUS

No more than a fair gallop to this 7f handicap in which those who raced close to the pace seemed favoured in a race in which the field congregated towards the stands' side. The runner-up is the best guide with the progressive winner an improver.

Chosen Forever Official explanation: jockey said gelding hung right-handed throughout

4876 BODDINGTONS REDCAR STRAIGHT-MILE CHAMPIONSHIP H'CAP (QUALIFIER) 1m

3:35 (3:36) (Class 3) (0-90,89) 3-Y-0+ **£7,771** (£2,312; £1,155; £577) **Stalls** Centre

Form RPR

5030 **1** **Charlie Tipple**[21] 4206 4-8-12 **74** (p) PaulMulrennan 7 85
(T D Easterby) *a.p: pushed along 2f out: rdn over 1f out: drvn ins fnl f and styd on to ld fnl 50yds* **20/1**

6104 **2** 3/4 **Exit Smiling**[11] 4500 6-9-9 **85** LeeEnstone 4 94
(P T Midgley) *t.k.h: hdwy to ld after 2f: rdn along 2f out: drvn ent fnl f: hdd and no ex fnl 50yds* **20/1**

4-1 **3** 3 **Last Three Minutes (IRE)**[19] 4255 3-9-4 **87** TGMcLaughlin 1 88
(E A L Dunlop) *hld up in tch on outer: stdy hdwy 3f out: rdn to chse ldr wl over 1f out and ev ch tl drvn and one pce ent fnl f* **7/2**[1]

1244 **4** 1/2 **Violent Velocity (IRE)**[6] 4661 5-8-10 **79** FrederikTylicki(7) 3 80
(J J Quinn) *hld up: hdwy over 2f out: rdn to chse ldrs over 1f out: drvn and one pce ent fnl f* **5/1**[3]

4546 **5** 3/4 **Collateral Damage (IRE)**[21] 4204 5-9-2 **81** (t) DuranFentiman(3) 8 80
(T D Easterby) *in tch: rdn along and outpcd 3f out: swtchd outside and drvn over 1f out: styd on ins fnl f: nrst fin* **12/1**

/240 **6** 1/2 **Alqaahir (USA)**[36] 3664 6-8-13 **75** PAspell 6 73
(J S Wainwright) *hld up towards rr: gd hdwy 3f out: chsd ldrs wl over 1f out: sn drvn and one pce ent fnl f* **33/1**

3554 **7** 2 **Celtic Change (IRE)**[23] 4111 4-9-1 **77** (v) TomEaves 14 70
(M Dods) *trckd ldrs on stands' rail: effrt 3f out and sn rdn: drvn 2f out and sn one pce* **8/1**

1110 **8** 3/4 **El Dececy (USA)**[23] 4111 4-9-5 **88** KrishGundowry(7) 10 80
(S Parr) *led 2f: cl up: rdn over 2f out: sn drvn and grad wknd appr fnl f* **16/1**

0441 **9** 2 1/2 **Opus Maximus (IRE)**[22] 4167 3-8-11 **80** JoeFanning 9 65
(M Johnston) *prom: rdn along 3f out: drvn over 2f out and grad wknd* **15/2**

2110 **10** 3/4 **Spinning**[28] 3972 5-9-6 **82** (b) PaulFessey 2 66
(T D Barron) *stdd and swtchd rt to stands' rails s: hdwy and swtchd lft 3f out: sn rdn along and no imp* **12/1**

2026 **11** 1/2 **Wovoka (IRE)**[14] 4440 5-9-0 **76** TonyHamilton 13 59
(D W Barker) *hld up: effrt and hdwy whn hmpd 3f out: bhd after* **14/1**

1011 **12** 1 1/4 **Gala Casino Star (IRE)**[15] 4392 3-9-3 **89** JamieMoriarty(3) 5 68
(R A Fahey) *in tch: rdn along over 3f out: sn drvn and wknd wl over 2f out* **8/1**

000 **13** 3 3/4 **Middlemarch (IRE)**[14] 4407 8-8-8 **75** ow3 (p) GaryBartley(5) 11 47
(J S Goldie) *a in rr* **33/1**

2302 **14** 2 1/2 **Just Bond (IRE)**[7] 4649 6-9-3 **79** (p) SilvestreDeSousa 12 45
(G R Oldroyd) *chsd ldrs: rdn along over 3f out and sn wknd* **9/2**[2]

1m 39.66s (1.66) **Going Correction** +0.10s/f (Good)
WFA 3 from 4yo+ 7lb 14 Ran SP% **134.4**
Speed ratings (Par 107): **95,94,91,90,90 89,87,86,84,83 83,81,78,75**
toteswinger: 1&2 £43.40, 1&3 £71.10, 2&3 £12.70. CSF £395.36 CT £1794.82 TOTE £31.50: £5.80, £5.40, £2.30; EX 787.30 TRIFECTA Not won..
Owner Norman Jackson **Bred** Paul Wyatt Ranby Hall **Trained** Great Habton, N Yorks
■ Stewards' Enquiry : Silvestre De Sousa two-day ban: careless riding (Aug 23-24)

FOCUS

Quite a competitive handicap run at a fair gallop and once again the field edged over to race towards the stands' side. The form loks fairly ordinary for the grade, rated around the placed horses

NOTEBOOK

Charlie Tipple was hard driven over a furlong out, but ran on well to get on top inside the final furlong. He is suited by some give in the ground and, though his two previous wins were over 6f, he ran well when third over a mile at Carlisle back in June. However, he does not have the best of win records. (tchd 28-1)

Exit Smiling is high in the weights now and was also a touch keen early on, so overall he ran a fine race on ground that suited, for he was up with the pace throughout and kept on to finish clear of the remainder. (tchd 18-1)

Last Three Minutes(IRE) is a lightly raced sort who was far from disgraced on his handicap debut particularly as he was not ideally drawn in stall one. He showed up well just off the pace, but could not quicken inside the last 2f and, having won his maiden over 1m1f, he might be suited by a step back up in trip. (op 10-3 tchd 3-1)

Violent Velocity(IRE) has gained all his wins over shorter distances, but was not disgraced back up in trip. (op 8-1)

Collateral Damage(IRE) outpaced at halfway, kept on to finish fifth but does look better with a bit more give. (op 11-1)

Alqaahir(USA) racing stands' side, finished a creditable sixth on his second run in a handicap and still has few miles on the clock for a horse of his age. (op 50-1)

4877 REDCAR CONFERENCE CENTRE MEDIAN AUCTION MAIDEN STKS 7f

4:10 (4:15) (Class 5) 3-4-Y-0 **£2,590** (£770; £385; £192) **Stalls** Centre

Form RPR

0036 **1** **Uace Mac**[21] 4207 4-8-11 55 FrederikTylicki(7) 6 70
(N Bycroft) *mde all: rdn clr wl over 1f out: styd on strly* **13/2**[3]

00 **2** 4 1/2 **Mr Toshiwonka**[15] 4379 4-9-9 0 SilvestreDeSousa 1 63
(D Nicholls) *prom: rdn along over 2f out: chsd wnr ent fnl f: sn drvn and no imp* **8/1**

3605 **3** 1 1/4 **Bertie Vista**[4] 4702 3-9-0 62 DuranFentiman(3) 10 58
(T D Easterby) *trckd ldrs: hdwy and clsoe up 1/2-way: rdn and ev ch over 2f out: drvn wl over 1f out and kpt on same pce* **11/1**

53 **4** 2 1/4 **Unbiased (IRE)**[12] 4484 3-9-3 0 TPO'Shea 7 51
(J L Dunlop) *trckd ldrs: hdwy 3f out: cl up and rdn along over 2f out: sn drvn: edgd lft and btn wl over 1f out* **15/8**[1]

5 2 **Chosen One (IRE)** 3-9-3 0 TomEaves 3 46+
(B Smart) *hmpd s and bhd: hdwy 2f out: sn rdn and kpt on appr fnl f: nrst fin* **10/1**

-004 **6** 3/4 **Cranworth Blaze**[33] 3786 4-9-1 45 LeeVickers(3) 4 41
(T J Etherington) *in tch: hdwy over 2f out: sn rdn along and kpt on appr fnl f: nt rch ldrs* **50/1**

7 4 **Dolly Royal (IRE)** 3-8-12 0 PaulFessey 13 28
(K A Ryan) *in tch on outer: rdn along 1/2-way: sn wknd* **16/1**

8 shd **Cullybackey (IRE)** 3-8-12 0 PaulMulrennan 9 28
(G A Swinbank) *dwlt and towards rr: sme hdwy 3f out: sn rdn along and nvr a factor* **20/1**

042 **9** 1/2 **Billy Bowmore**[30] 3867 3-9-3 65 TonyHamilton 5 32
(M Dods) *chsd ldrs: rdn along 3f out and sn wknd* **3/1**[2]

0 **10** 4 **Carr On Fire (USA)**[95] 1894 3-9-3 0 JoeFanning 2 21
(G A Swinbank) *wnt rt s: a towards rr* **16/1**

0 **11** 6 **High Shanamara**[7] 4651 3-8-9 0 JamieMoriarty(3) 11 —
(P T Midgley) *in tch towards outer: rdn along 1/2-way: sn wknd* **100/1**

12 17 **Predictable (IRE)** 3-8-5 0 BradleyRoper(7) 12 —
(M W Easterby) *s.i.s: a in rr* **40/1**

0 **13** 1 **Distant Rainbow (IRE)**[15] 4378 3-9-0 0 MarkLawson(3) 14 —
(M Brittain) *in tch on outer: rdn along 1/2-way and sn wknd* **50/1**

1m 25.98s (1.48) **Going Correction** +0.10s/f (Good)
WFA 3 from 4yo 6lb 13 Ran SP% **125.5**
Speed ratings (Par 103): **95,89,88,85,83 82,78,78,77,72 66,46,45**
toteswinger: 1&2 £16.90, 1&3 £24.30, 2&3 £23.50. CSF £58.84 TOTE £8.20: £2.70, £4.10, £3.80; EX 124.80.
Owner N Bycroft **Bred** Mrs R W Gore-Andrews **Trained** Brandsby, N Yorks

FOCUS

This was a moderate maiden, especially with the winner rated just 55. The form looks unreliable with the first two improvers and the third and fourth not the most solid guides.

Uace Mac Official explanation: trainer said, regarding the apparent improvement in form, filly had been better suited by today's track in a race which she was able to dominate and was helped by the step up in trip and softer ground

Unbiased(IRE) Official explanation: jockey said colt was unsuited by the good (good to soft in places) ground

Dolly Royal(IRE) Official explanation: jockey said filly had no more to give

4878 WEDDINGS AT REDCAR CLAIMING STKS 1m 1f

4:40 (4:41) (Class 6) 4-Y-0+ **£2,388** (£705; £352) **Stalls** Low

Form RPR

4261 **1** **Rowan Lodge (IRE)**[13] 4451 6-8-8 62 (b) JamieMoriarty(3) 6 69+
(Ollie Pears) *t.k.h: trckd ldrs: hdwy 3f out: nt clr run 2f out and again over 1f out: sn rdn and styd on ins fnl f to ld nr fin* **11/2**[3]

620 **2** nk **Evelith Regent (IRE)**[10] 4540 5-9-1 64 TomEaves 3 69
(G A Swinbank) *led: rdn along 3f out: drvn over 1f out: hdd and no ex nr line* **9/1**

31R3 **3** 1 1/4 **Claret And Amber**[13] 4451 6-8-7 73 TonyHamilton 4 58
(R A Fahey) *trckd ldrs: hdwy 3f out: rdn along 2f out: drvn over 1f out: kpt on same pce ins fnl f* **15/8**[1]

6006 **4** ¾ **Fever**[27] 3996 4-9-1 64 .... PaulMulrennan 8 65
(M W Easterby) *in tch: hdwy 3f out: rdn to chse ldrs 2f out: drvn over 1f out: kpt on same pce ins fnl f* **12/1**

6036 **5** 2 ¼ **Seyaadi**[14] 4419 6-8-8 59 ow4 .... (p) FrederikTylicki[(7)] 2 60
(Miss Tracy Waggott) *chsd ldng pair: rdn along on inner 3f out: drvn 2f out: sn one pce* **10/3**[2]

4140 **6** 1 ¾ **Mountain Pass (USA)**[23] 4104 6-8-11 60 .... (p) TWilliams 9 52
(B J Llewellyn) *hld up in rr: effrt and hdwy 3f out: rdn over 2f out and sn no imp* **11/1**

3040 **7** 1 ½ **Ming Vase**[13] 4458 6-8-7 47 .... PaulFessey 7 45
(P T Midgley) *chsd ldr: rdn along 3f out: drvn 2f out and sn wknd* **20/1**

100 **8** 2 ¼ **Aussie Blue (IRE)**[7] 4650 4-9-11 62 .... JoeFanning 10 58
(R M Whitaker) *hld up in rr: hdwy on outer 3f out: rdn to chse ldrs 2f out: wknd over 1f out* **8/1**

0 **9** 1 ¾ **Pennybid (IRE)**[13] 4451 6-8-11 0 .... PAspell 1 40
(C R Wilson) *towards rr: effrt and sme hdwy on inner 3f out: sn rdn and btn 2f out* **150/1**

1m 56.23s (3.23) **Going Correction** +0.325s/f (Good) **9** Ran SP% **115.8**
Speed ratings (Par 101): **98,97,96,95,93 92,91,89,87**
toteswinger: 1&2 £6.40, 1&3 £2.10, 2&3 £5.80. CSF £53.98 TOTE £5.80: £1.70, £2.70, £1.30; EX 32.80.Claret And Amber was claimed by K. Goldsworthy for £6,000. Seyaadi was claimed by J. J. Best for £8,000.
Owner K C West **Bred** M P B Bloodstock Ltd **Trained** Norton, N Yorks

FOCUS
Just an ordinary claimer and one run at an ordinary gallop. The favourite was again disappointing with the first two the best guides to the level.

4879 THE COMMITMENTS ARE HERE IN AUGUST H'CAP 1m 6f 19y
5:10 (5:11) (Class 6) (0-60,61) 3-Y-0+ **£2,266** (£674; £337; £168) **Stalls** Low

Form RPR

131 **1** **Trip The Light**[11] 4501 3-9-4 **61** .... (v) TonyHamilton 14 72
(R A Fahey) *trckd ldrs: hdwy 4f out: rdn along 3f out: drvn to chse ldr and edgd lft over 1f out: styd on u.p to ld ins fnl f* **15/8**[1]

0040 **2** 1 ¾ **Bond Casino**[9] 4556 4-9-1 **45** .... SilvestreDeSousa 3 54
(G R Oldroyd) *led: rdn along 3f out: drvn clr 2f out: hdd ins fnl f and no ex fnl 100yds* **16/1**

6200 **3** 11 **Wulimaster (USA)**[13] 4457 5-9-8 **52** .... PaulMulrennan 11 46
(D W Barker) *hld up in rr: stdy hdwy on inner 3f out: rdn to chse ldrs 2f out: sn drvn and kpt on same pce* **14/1**

32/6 **4** nk **Nevsky Bridge**[8] 3718 6-9-1 **45** .... TomEaves 12 38
(M Todhunter) *hld up towards rr: hdwy over 3f out: rdn and in tch 2f out: sn drvn and no imp* **20/1**

0000 **5** 1 ¾ **Leitmotif (USA)**[28] 3962 3-8-8 **51** .... (b[1]) TPO'Shea 6 42
(J L Dunlop) *trckd ldrs: hdwy over 4f out: chsd ldr 3f out and sn rdn: drvn 2f out and sn wknd* **11/1**

-004 **6** 3 **Centenary (IRE)**[12] 4490 4-9-2 **46** .... (p) JoeFanning 4 33
(D E Cantillon) *in tch: hdwy to chse ldrs over 4f out: rdn along 3f out: drvn over 2f out and sn btn* **5/1**[2]

330/ **7** 10 **Amjad**[77] 4105 11-9-3 **47** ow2 .... MHNaughton 7 20
(Miss Kate Milligan) *a towards rr* **50/1**

-304 **8** 1 ¼ **Jenny Soba**[30] 3863 5-8-8 **45** .... (v) MrJPFeatherstone[(7)] 2 16
(Lucinda Featherstone) *reminders sn after s: midfield: effrt and sme hdwy on inner 4f out: sn rdn and wknd* **9/1**

-040 **9** 5 **Banquet (IRE)**[19] 4247 3-8-9 **55** .... DuranFentiman[(3)] 10 19
(T D Walford) *in tch: pushed along over 5f out: rdn over 3f out and sn wknd* **5/1**[2]

0035 **10** 4 **Apsara**[20] 4220 7-9-1 **45** .... LeeEnstone 15 3
(G M Moore) *chsd ldr: reminders 1/2-way: rdn along over 4f out and sn wknd* **8/1**[3]

002- **11** 59 **Hill Cloud**[225] 7262 6-9-3 **47** .... TGMcLaughlin 8 —
(W M Brisbourne) *a towards rr* **25/1**

3m 8.56s (3.86) **Going Correction** +0.325s/f (Good)
WFA 3 from 4yo+ 13lb **11** Ran SP% **120.7**
Speed ratings (Par 101): **101,100,93,93,92 90,85,84,81,79 45**
toteswinger: 1&2 £9.60, 1&3 £7.90, 2&3 £23.90. CSF £37.14 CT £345.54 TOTE £2.20: £1.40, £5.00, £4.20; EX 44.50 Place 6 £527.78, Place 5 £257.52.
Owner The Matthewman One Partnership **Bred** Darley **Trained** Musley Bank, N Yorks

FOCUS
A staying handicap for horses rated 46-60 in which the pace was no more than ordinary, and the first two finished well clear of the rest. The form is weak and the runner-up is the best guide.
T/Plt: £4,608.30 to a £1 stake. Pool: £56,815.05. 9.00 winning tickets. T/Qpdt: £999.50 to a £1 stake. Pool: £3,511.87. 2.60 winning tickets. JR

[4719] DEAUVILLE (R-H)
Saturday, August 9

OFFICIAL GOING: Turf course - soft; all-weather - standard

4880a PRIX BEACHCOMBER HOTELS 'ROYAL PALM' (PRIX DE REUX) (LISTED RACE) 1m 4f 110y
2:45 (2:44) 3-Y-0+ **£19,118** (£7,647; £5,735; £3,824; £1,912)

RPR

1 **Magadino (FR)**[49] 3291 7-9-4 .... FBlondel 6 107
(Mme Brigitte Renk, Switzerland)

2 ¾ **Tempelstern (GER)**[92] 1944 4-9-7 .... (b) OPeslier 3 109
(H R A Cecil) *led: hrd rdn 1 1/2f out: hdd and no ex fnl 50yds* **56/10**[1]

3 2 ½ **Cristobal (USA)**[77] 4-9-4 .... C-PLemaire 7 102
(J-C Rouget, France)

4 2 **Quest For Honor**[34] 4-9-4 .... JVictoire 4 99
(A Fabre, France)

5 2 **Classic Swain (USA)**[39] 3-8-6 .... SPasquier 9 96
(A Fabre, France)

6 snk **Quartz Jem (IRE)**[31] 4-9-4 .... MGuyon 8 96
(Mme Pia Brandt, France)

7 1 **Zack Dream (FR)**[51] 3191 3-8-9 .... TJarnet 5 97
(M Delzangles, France)

8 hd **Candy Gift (ARG)**[96] 1888 5-9-4 .... JAuge 1 94
(A Fabre, France)

9 2 **Prairie Spirit (FR)**[34] 4-9-4 .... ACrastus 2 91
(E Lellouche, France)

2m 45.7s (-0.70)
WFA 3 from 4yo+ 11lb **9** Ran SP% **15.2**
PARI-MUTUEL: WIN 17.90; PL 4.00, 2.60, 2.30; DF 63.90.
Owner A Renk **Bred** Adolf Renk **Trained** Switzerland
■ Stewards' Enquiry : F Blondel €200 fine: whip abuse

NOTEBOOK
Tempelstern(GER) made a brave effort to make all the running in this Listed event. He came under pressure soon after entering the straight but still looked likely to win at the furlong marker. However, he finally went under to a horse who had the better acceleration inside the final furlong.

4881a PRIX MTPA 'OFFICE DE TOURISME DE L'ILE MAURICE' (PRIX DU CERCLE) (LISTED RACE) 5f
3:20 (3:19) 3-Y-0+ **£19,118** (£7,647; £5,735; £3,824; £1,912)

RPR

1 **Inxile (IRE)**[19] 4240 3-8-10 .... AdrianTNicholls 7 104
(D Nicholls) *pushed along in midfield early: hdwy to ld over 1 1/2f out: edgd lft u.p fnl f: drvn out* **103/10**[2]

2 ½ **Mood Music**[50] 3243 4-9-4 .... (b) MGuyon 8 108
(Mario Hofer, Germany)

3 shd **Best Joking (GER)** 3-8-7 .... JVictoire 6 99
(W Hefter, Germany)

4 2 **Sacho (GER)**[55] 10-9-4 .... AlexisBadel 12 100
(W Kujath, Germany)

5 ½ **Corrybrough**[21] 4188 3-9-1 .... OPeslier 2 98
(H Candy) *dropped out in rr: stl last whn angled to outside jst ins fnl f: fin wl: too much to do* **14/10**[1]

6 nk **Derison (USA)**[90] 2034 6-9-4 .... (b) TJarnet 13 98
(P Van De Poele, France)

7 1 **Sarissa (BRZ)**[133] 1089 5-8-10 .... C-PLemaire 10 86
(P Bary, France) **17/1**[3]

8 nk **Smarten Die (IRE)**[174] 603 5-9-0 .... J-PCarvalho 5 89
(Frau E Mader, Germany)

9 1 ½ **Etoile Nocturne (FR)**[27] 4011 4-8-10 .... DBoeuf 3 79
(W Baltromei, Germany)

10 hd **Garden City (FR)**[58] 3-8-8 ow1 .... CSoumillon 4 79
(Y De Nicolay, France)

0 **Dramatic Turn**[10] 4-8-10 .... SMartinMoriano 1 —
(Mme J Bidgood, France)

0 **Acotango (GER)**[344] 5028 3-8-10 .... MSuerland 11 —
(Frau E Mader, Germany)

0 **Zoriana (FR)**[263] 6888 3-8-7 .... SPasquier 9 —
(F Rohaut, France)

58.00 secs (0.50)
WFA 3 from 4yo+ 3lb **13** Ran SP% **56.1**
PARI-MUTUEL: WIN 11.30; PL 2.90, 6.20, 3.00; DF 93.50.
Owner Ian Hewitson **Bred** Denis And Mrs Teresa Bergin **Trained** Sessay, N Yorks

NOTEBOOK
Inxile(IRE), well placed behind the leaders early on, started his challenge a furlong and a half out and ran on gamely to the line, finally winning with just a little in hand. It was a well-deserved victory for this very consistent gelding, and he may well make his mark at Group level in the future.
Corrybrough lost his chance at the start as he was slowly out of the stalls. Well behind at the halfway stage, he had to move round several other runners before making his challenge. He finished well up the centre of the track but it was too late. This performance is best ignored, especially as he had beaten the winner on two previous occasions.

4882 - 4886a (Foreign Racing) - See Raceform Interactive

ARLINGTON (L-H)
Saturday, August 9

OFFICIAL GOING: Firm

4887a SECRETARIAT STKS (GRADE 1) (TURF) 1m 2f
9:12 (9:13) 3-Y-O
£119,397 (£39,799; £19,899; £9,950; £5,970; £3,980)

RPR

1 **Winchester (USA)**[41] 3535 3-8-7 .... (b) RRDouglas 2 118
(D K Weld, Ire) *held up in touch, switched outside 3f out, led well over 1f out, ridden clear, ran on strongly* **15/2**[3]

2 7 ¼ **Plan (USA)**[28] 3983 3-8-9 .... JMurtagh 3 106
(A P O'Brien, Ire) *not much room early, sttled disputing 5th, headway well over 1f out, stayed on but never near winner* **26/10**[2]

3 2 ½ **Tizdejavu (USA)**[28] 3-9-0 .... GKGomez 6 106
(Gregory Fox, U.S.A) *led to well over 1f out, one pace* **1/1**[1]

4 1 ¼ **Prime Realestate (USA)**[28] 3-8-7 .... JRLeparoux 1 96
(Wayne Catalano, U.S.A) **14/1**

5 nk **Strait Of Mewsina (IRE)**[77] 3-8-7 .... EBaird 4 95
(Larry Rivelli, U.S.A) **62/1**

6 ½ **Your Round (USA)**[21] 3-8-7 .... JRVelazquez 7 94
(M Hubley, U.S.A) **117/10**

7 2 ½ **Snoose Goose (USA)** 3-8-7 .... RAlbarado 5 89
(McLean Robertson, U.S.A) **22/1**

8 1 ¾ **Secret Getaway (USA)**[28] 3-8-11 .... (b) EmmaJayneWilson 9 90
(Michael Stidham, U.S.A) **102/10**

9 12 **Sr. Henry (USA)**[28] 3-8-7 .... ERazoJr 8 62
(Michael Stidham, U.S.A) **31/1**

2m 1.76s (0.12) **9** Ran SP% **122.1**
PARI-MUTUEL (including $2 stakes): WIN 17.00; PL (1-2) 7.60, 5.00;SHOW (1-2-3) 3.80, 2.80, 2.20; SF 62.00.
Owner Bertram R Firestone **Bred** Mr & Mrs B Firestone **Trained** The Curragh, Co Kildare

NOTEBOOK
Winchester(USA) had struggled a touch since beating subsequent Irish Oaks winner Moonstone in a 1m2f maiden at Leopardstown earlier in the season, but he proved suited by the return to this trip and took well to the fitting of blinkers. Always well placed, he took over going easily early in the straight and pulled well clear for an impressive success. He may now be aimed at the Breeders' Cup Turf.
Plan(USA) earned a shot at a race like this when beating older rivals in a 1m1f Group 3 at the Curragh on his previous start, but he still looked inexperienced and was well held in second. He came under pressure leaving the back straight, but kept responding and gave the impression he will progress again from this. Before this race IEAH Stables, owners of Big Brown, acquired controlling and managing interest in this horse, and he has since been switched to Rick Dutrow Junior. His new connections said he will be pointed at some "big races" on both fast turf and dirt, and the latter surface promises to bring out the best in this son of Storm Cat, who is out of Breeders' Cup Distaff winner Spain.

Tizdejavu(USA) is already a multiple Graded winner, but this was his toughest assignment yet. He got an easy lead, but found the European challengers too strong.

4888a BEVERLY D STKS (GRADE 1) (F&M) (TURF) 1m 1f 110y(T)

9:50 (9:53) 3-Y-0+

£223,869 (£74,623; £37,312; £18,656; £11,193; £7,462)

RPR

1 **Mauralakana (FR)**[49] 5-8-11 .... KDesormeaux 4 113
(Christophe Clement, U.S.A) *always close up, progress on outside over 2f out, quickened to lead inside final furlong, driven out* **24/10**[2]

2 1 1/4 **Communique (USA)**[28] 4-8-11 .... RRDouglas 8 110
(George R Arnold II, U.S.A) *raced in rear to over 2f out, brought wide and headway straight, finished well* **126/10**

3 3/4 **Toque De Queda**[21] 4212 4-8-11 .... JMurtagh 7 108
(M Delzangles, France) *held up in midfield to straight, brought wide & stayed on, nearest at finish* **54/1**

4 1/2 **Dreaming Of Anna (USA)**[56] 4-8-11 .... GKGomez 1 107
(Wayne Catalano, U.S.A) **34/10**[3]

5 hd **Precious Kitten (USA)**[75] 5-8-11 .... RBejarano 3 107
(Robert Frankel, U.S.A) **19/10**[1]

6 hd **Cicerole (FR)**[63] 2827 4-8-11 .... IMendizabal 9 107
(J-C Rouget, France) *held up in midfield, stayed on from over 1f out but never able to challenge* **73/10**

7 1 **Meribel (USA)**[34] 5-8-11 .... RAlbarado 6 104
(Helen Pitts, U.S.A) **36/1**

8 nse **Ciao (USA)**[28] 4-8-11 .... JRVelazquez 5 104
(Frank J Kirby, U.S.A) **56/1**

9 5 **Rosinka (IRE)**[28] 5-8-11 .... CVelasquez 2 94
(H Graham Motion, U.S.A) **88/10**

1m 55.18s (-0.29) **9 Ran SP% 122.5**
PARI-MUTUEL: WIN 6.80; PL (1-2) 4.00, 9.00; SHOW (1-2-3) 3.40, 6.00,13.00: SF 65.40.
Owner Robert Scarborough **Bred** Classic Breeding Sarl & M Hassan **Trained** USA

NOTEBOOK
Mauralakana(FR), purchased by Robert Scarborough as a broodmare prospect for $900,000 at the Keeneland 2007 November Breeding Stock Sale, has never been better and gained her fifth win from six starts this year. She has now earned an automatic starting berth in the Breeders' Cup Filly & Mare Turf. Her owner plans on sending her to Australia next year.

4889a ARLINGTON MILLION (GRADE 1) (TURF) 1m 2f

10:44 (10:45) 3-Y-0+

£298,492 (£99,497; £49,749; £24,874; £14,925; £9,950)

RPR

1 **Spirit One (FR)**[56] 3053 4-9-0 .... IMendizabal 3 122
(P Demercastel, France) *made all, quickened approaching straight, ran on gamely final furlong, driven out* **137/10**

2 3/4 **Archipenko (USA)**[28] 3940 4-9-0 ....(b) KShea 1 121
(M F De Kock, South Africa) *raced in 3rd on inside, switched to centre and ran on entering straight, soon went 2nd, not reach winner* **6/5**[1]

3 1 1/2 **Mount Nelson**[35] 3741 4-9-0 .... JMurtagh 6 118
(A P O'Brien, Ire) *raced in 2nd, driven approaching straight, soon lost place, no extra* **39/10**[3]

4 nk **Silverfoot (USA)**[36] 8-9-0 .... RRDouglas 7 117
(Dallas Stewart, U.S.A) *held up, 6th straight, ran on down outside final furlong, nearest at finish* **18/1**

5 1/2 **Einstein (BRZ)**[36] 6-9-0 .... RAlbarado 5 116
(Helen Pitts, U.S.A) *missed break and towards rear, 4th straight, soon driven along, no impression* **32/10**[2]

6 1/2 **Stream Cat (USA)**[28] 5-9-0 ....(b) JRLeparoux 2 115
(George R Arnold II, U.S.A) *held up, 5th straight, never in contention* **5/1**

7 7 3/4 **Cloudy's Knight (USA)**[36] 8-9-0 .... RZimmerman 4 100
(Frank J Kirby, U.S.A) *always in rear* **21/1**

2m 2.17s (0.53) **7 Ran SP% 123.0**
PARI-MUTUEL: WIN 29.40; PL (1-2) 10.20, 3.40; SHOW (1-2-3) 6.00, 2.60,4.00; SF 68.40.
Owner B Chehboub **Bred** K & B Chehboub **Trained** France

NOTEBOOK
Spirit One(FR), whose best form in France has been at Group 2 and 3 level, gained his first Group 1 win on his first encounter with fast ground. He made all the running and gamely held off the favourite and now connections will be aiming for the Breeders' Cup Turf, although he is as yet unproven at 1m4f.
Archipenko(USA), who was formerly with Aidan O'Brien and has improved a fair amount for his current trainer, has looked somewhat unlucky with connections berating Murtagh (on the O'Brien representative) for holding their horse in a pocket for much of the way. However, Murtagh did not do anything untoward and the Breeders' Cup Mile may offer their best chance for compensation, with a return to Hong Konjg likely to be on the cards at the end of the year.
Mount Nelson, a narrow winner of the Eclipse last time out, ran his race until dropping out of it late on. He could drop back to a mile for the Breeders' Cup Mile, but connections have other contenders for that race, and maybe the Champion Stakes offers a better option.

4530 LEICESTER (R-H)

Sunday, August 10

OFFICIAL GOING: Good (good to firm in places)
Wind: Fresh behind Weather: Sunshine and showers

4890 EBF BAGWORTH MAIDEN STKS 7f 9y

2:20 (2:22) (Class 4) 2-Y-O £5,046 (£1,510; £755; £377; £188) Stalls Low

Form RPR

4 1 **Poster (IRE)**[26] 4062 2-9-3 0 .... DaneO'Neill 11 82+
(L M Cumani) *s.i.s: hld up: hdwy over 2f out: led over 1f out: rdn out* **8/1**

2 1/2 **Kite Wood (IRE)** 2-9-3 0 .... PhilipRobinson 4 81+
(M A Jarvis) *chsd ldrs: rdn and ev ch over 1f out: r.o* **11/2**[3]

62 3 1 1/4 **Combat Zone (IRE)**[18] 4311 2-9-3 0 .... DarryllHolland 8 78
(Saeed Bin Suroor) *hld up in tch: racd keenly: rdn and ev ch over 1f out: unable qckn ins fnl f* **2/1**[1]

3 4 2 **Aathaar**[18] 4311 2-9-3 0 .... RHills 7 73+
(Sir Michael Stoute) *trckd ldr tl led over 2f out: rdn and hdd over 1f out: styd on same pce* **4/1**[2]

0 5 3 1/2 **Kayfiar (USA)**[23] 4150 2-9-3 0 .... GregFairley 5 64
(P F I Cole) *hld up: hdwy over 2f out: rdn and hung rt over 1f out: styd on same pce* **25/1**

0 6 1 3/4 **Makhaaleb (IRE)**[32] 3853 2-9-3 0 .... MichaelHills 10 60
(B W Hills) *hld up: rdn over 2f out: styd on appr fnl f: nvr trbld ldrs* **6/1**

7 1 3/4 **Squad** 2-9-3 0 .... JimCrowley 9 55
(Pat Eddery) *s.s: outpcd: styd on appr fnl f: nvr nrr* **16/1**

0 8 1 **Achromatic**[26] 4062 2-9-3 0 .... SaleemGolam 14 53
(W R Swinburn) *mid-div: rdn over 2f out: wknd over 1f out* **20/1**

0 9 1 3/4 **Medlock**[22] 4199 2-9-3 0 .... ShaneKelly 6 48
(J Noseda) *hld up: rdn and hung rt over 2f out: n.d* **18/1**

10 1/2 **Brad's Luck (IRE)** 2-9-3 0 .... FrancisNorton 15 47+
(M Blanshard) *s.i.s: rn green and outpcd: last 3f out: running on whn eased ins fnl f: improve* **66/1**

0 11 1 3/4 **Old Street**[23] 4151 2-9-3 0 .... SteveDrowne 3 43
(R Charlton) *s.i.s: sn outpcd* **33/1**

0 12 1 1/2 **Rock On Ciara (IRE)**[75] 2479 2-8-9 0 ow4 .... JWStevenson(7) 2 38
(D J Wintle) *chsd ldrs: rdn over 2f out: wknd fnl f* **200/1**

0 13 3/4 **Kidson (USA)**[29] 3968 2-9-3 0 .... MickyFenton 13 37
(George Baker) *mid-div: sn pushed along: lost pl 4f out: sn bhd* **200/1**

00 14 1 3/4 **Alderbed**[13] 4480 2-9-3 0 .... StephenDonohoe 1 33
(George Baker) *sn outpcd* **200/1**

00 15 3 1/4 **Endofmytether**[39] 3603 2-8-7 0 .... RichardEvans(5) 12 20
(P D Evans) *led over 4f: sn rdn and wknd* **150/1**

1m 25.14s (-1.06) **Going Correction** -0.275s/f (Firm) **15 Ran SP% 120.5**
Speed ratings (Par 96): **95,94,93,90,86 84,82,81,79,79 77,75,74,72,68**
toteswinger: 1&2 £8.10, 1&3 £4.60, 2&3 £5.30. CSF £49.61 TOTE £10.70: £3.00, £2.20, £1.50; EX 57.90.
Owner Scuderia Archi Romani **Bred** Sc Archi Romani **Trained** Newmarket, Suffolk

FOCUS
A fair juvenile maiden and the form is rated around the principals.

NOTEBOOK
Poster(IRE), despite making a sluggish start, responded positively for pressure nearing the final furlong and eventually just did enough to open his account at the second attempt. He showed a willing attitude here and evidently stays well, so it will be interesting to see how the Handicapper assesses this effort now. Despite the fact he is evidently progressive, however, he must learn to jump better from the gates. (op 10-1 tchd 15-2)
Kite Wood(IRE) ◆, a 270,000gns purchase who has been given big-race entries, knew his job and only just failed to make a winning debut. He was handy from the off and was brought to the stands' rail with his effort inside the final furlong, but just found the more experienced winner too wise at the business end. This rates a very pleasing start to his career and, while he will want further before long, he should soon be placed to get off the mark over this trip in the coming weeks. (op 7-2 tchd 10-3 and 6-1)
Combat Zone(IRE), who made the early running last time, paid late in the day for running freely under early restraint yet still posted another sound-enough effort in defeat. He confirmed Sandown form with the fourth and so rates the benchmark, plus now has the option of nurseries. (op 5-2 tchd 10-3)
Aathaar was beaten by the third on his debut at Sandown 18 days previously and so failed to obviously improve on that effort, but did little wrong in defeat. This rather confirms his limitations and he is now looking more of a future handicap prospect. (op 7-2 tchd 3-1)
Kayfiar(USA) showed a much more professional attitude than had been the case at Newbury on his debut 23 days previously and looks to be getting the hang of things now. He will probably make up into a better three-year-old, but will still look interesting after qualifying for a nursery mark following his next run. (op 50-1)
Makhaaleb(IRE) ran below the level of his Newmarket debut and again got going too late from off the pace. (op 13-2 tchd 11-2)
Squad, whose dam is an unraced half-sister to Zafonic, was never in the hunt after a slow start and he ran too green to do himself justice. However, he still showed some ability late on and has been given an entry in the Champagne Stakes, so should be capable of better now he has this initial experience under his belt. (op 25-1)
Medlock Official explanation: jockey said colt was unsuited by the good (good to firm in places) ground
Brad's Luck(IRE), a half-brother to his stable's very useful sprinter Charles Darwin, gave himself a lot to do with a tardy start and then looked clueless through the first half of the race. The penny began to drop from the 2f pole, however, and he left the impression he would come on a bundle from this debut experience. Official explanation: jockey said gelding was denied a clear run in the closing stages (op 100-1)
Endofmytether Official explanation: jockey said filly ran too freely

4891 RUTLAND (S) STKS 7f 9y

2:50 (2:54) (Class 5) 3-4-Y-O £2,590 (£770; £385; £192) Stalls Low

Form RPR

0-02 1 **Singleb (IRE)**[4] 4748 4-9-2 60 .... DaneO'Neill 3 61+
(George Baker) *chsd ldr: rdn to ld over 1f out: sn clr: eased wl ins fnl f* **11/4**[1]

0305 2 3 1/4 **Straight Face (IRE)**[25] 4084 4-9-7 50 .... MickyFenton 10 53
(Miss Gay Kelleway) *sn pushed along in rr: hdwy over 2f out: rdn to chse wnr fnl f: no imp* **11/1**

1456 3 3/4 **Cap St Jean (IRE)**[24] 4125 4-9-7 62 ....(p) DarryllHolland 5 51
(R Hollinshead) *stdd s: hld up: hung rt over 4f out: hdwy over 2f out: sn rdn: one pce fnl f* **3/1**[2]

6-00 4 2 **Road To Recovery**[10] 4053 4-8-10 45 ow1 ....(p) JWStevenson(7) 2 42
(D J Wintle) *prom: rdn over 2f out: edgd rt over 1f out: styd on same pce* **50/1**

-053 5 1/2 **Yerevan**[26] 4052 4-8-11 60 ....(t) LiamJones 8 34
(M Mullineaux) *led: racd keenly: rdn and hdd over 1f out: wknd ins fnl f* **13/2**[3]

0-53 6 6 **Jennifer's Dream (IRE)**[19] 4271 3-8-5 67 .... FrancisNorton 11 16
(K A Ryan) *dwlt: hld up: hdwy u.p over 1f out: n.d* **8/1**

4036 7 3 1/4 **Samurai Warrior**[17] 4338 3-8-10 58 ....(be) SteveDrowne 6 12
(P J Makin) *hld up: rdn 1/2-way: n.d* **15/2**

F250 8 1 1/4 **Flamestone**[8] 4653 4-8-11 46 ....(p) NataliaGemelova(5) 4 11
(A E Price) *chsd ldrs: rdn over 4f out: wknd wl over 1f out* **40/1**

0034 9 7 **Our Dolly**[3] 4794 3-7-12 54 .... AndreaAtzeni(7) 7 —
(Garry Moss) *mid-div: rdn over 4f out: wknd over 2f out* **16/1**

00-0 10 2 **Boogie Board**[13] 4479 4-8-11 51 .... ShaneKelly 9 —
(Garry Moss) *chsd ldrs: rdn 1/2-way: wknd over 2f out* **28/1**

00-0 11 2 1/4 **Here And How**[18] 4298 3-8-5 45 .... SaleemGolam 1 —
(M H Tompkins) *mid-div: hdwy 1/2-way: sn rdn: hung rt and wknd over 2f out* **50/1**

5030 12 12 **Persian Fox (IRE)**[20] 4250 4-9-2 46 ....(b1) StephenDonohoe 12 —
(A G Juckes) *plld hrd and prom: wknd over 2f out* **20/1**

1m 25.02s (-1.18) **Going Correction** -0.275s/f (Firm)
WFA 3 from 4yo 6lb **12 Ran SP% 116.7**
Speed ratings (Par 103): **95,91,90,88,87 80,77,75,67,65 62,49**
toteswinger: 1&2 £6.80, 1&3 £1.70, 2&3 £5.20. CSF £31.32 TOTE £3.90: £1.50, £2.30, £1.40; EX 35.70.The winner was bought in for 9,500gns.
Owner The Betfair Radioheads **Bred** Spratstown Stud Gm **Trained** Moreton Morrell, Warwicks

FOCUS
A typically weak seller. The winner is value for around double the winning margin.

Here And How Official explanation: jockey said filly hung right

4892 ROBINS AND DAY PEUGEOT BIPPER VAN H'CAP 1m 3f 183y
3:20 (3:20) (Class 5) (0-75,72) 4-Y-0+ **£4,533** (£1,348; £674; £336) **Stalls** High

Form RPR

5023 **1** **Monfils Monfils (USA)**[5] 4699 6-9-7 **72**.............................. ShaneKelly 2 83
(A J McCabe) *hld up: racd keenly: hdwy over 3f out: led over 1f out: sn rdn: styd on wl* **6/1**

0201 **2** *3 ¾* **Channel Crossing**[18] 4299 6-9-3 **68**.............................. LiamJones 4 73
(S Wynne) *led: rdn and hdd over 3f out: rallied and ev ch over 1f out: no ex ins fnl f* **6/1**

-002 **3** *8* **Etain (IRE)**[65] 2804 4-9-1 **66**.............................. SaleemGolam 5 58
(W R Swinburn) *chsd ldrs: rdn over 4f out: sn edgd rt: wknd over 2f out* **3/1**[2]

1610 **4** *¾* **Royal Premier (IRE)**[30] 3917 5-9-1 **69**..................(v) JerryO'Dwyer(3) 3 60
(H J Collingridge) *hld up: rdn over 3f out: a in rr* **8/1**

4462 **5** *½* **Alfie Noakes**[18] 4299 6-9-7 **72**..................(p) JimCrowley 1 62
(Mrs A J Perrett) *chsd ldr tl led over 3f out: rdn and hdd over 1f out: folded tamely* **11/4**[1]

3021 **6** *nk* **Pocketwood**[30] 3917 6-9-5 **70**.............................. DaneO'Neill 6 60
(Jean-Rene Auvray) *chsd ldrs: rdn over 4f out: sn wknd* **4/1**[3]

2m 33.88s (-0.02) **Going Correction** +0.075s/f (Good) **6** Ran SP% **111.3**
Speed ratings (Par 103): **103,100,95,94,94 94**
toteswinger: 1&2 £5.80, 1&3 £4.80, 2&3 £5.00. CSF £39.37 TOTE £7.80: £3.40, £3.10; EX 36.90.
Owner Brian Morton **Bred** Douglas McIntyre **Trained** Babworth, Notts

FOCUS
A modest handicap which saw the first pair finish clear.

4893 LEICESTER MERCURY FAMILY FUN DAY H'CAP 7f 9y
3:50 (3:51) (Class 2) (0-100,92) 3-Y-0
£11,215 (£3,358; £1,679; £840; £419; £210) **Stalls** Low

Form RPR

3004 **1** **Nezami (IRE)**[8] 4641 3-8-12 **83**.............................. DaneO'Neill 4 91
(B J Meehan) *hld up: stl last over 2f out: hdwy over 1f out: led ins fnl f: edgd rt: rdn out* **9/1**

4002 **2** *¾* **Zakhaaref**[18] 4312 3-9-5 **90**.............................. RHills 6 96
(M Johnston) *chsd ldrs: rdn to ld and edgd lft over 1f out: hdd ins fnl f: kpt on* **9/4**[1]

6534 **3** *3 ¼* **Noble Citizen (USA)**[18] 4312 3-8-10 **81**.................. StephenDonohoe 8 78
(D M Simcock) *prom: outpcd over 2f out: hdwy u.p over 1f out: no ex ins fnl f* **13/2**[3]

3104 **4** *nk* **Kiwi Bay**[11] 4539 3-8-13 **84**.............................. ShaneKelly 3 80
(M Dods) *hld up: rdn over 2f out: styd on ins fnl f: nt trble ldrs* **6/1**[2]

4113 **5** *4* **Autumn Blades (IRE)**[15] 4408 3-8-5 **76**.............................. LiamJones 7 62
(J W Hills) *hld up: hdwy over 1f out: wknd fnl f* **13/2**[3]

3120 **6** *hd* **Lindoro**[36] 3744 3-9-7 **92**.............................. SaleemGolam 2 77
(W R Swinburn) *hld up: hdwy 1/2-way: rdn and wknd over 1f out* **15/2**

2000 **7** *¾* **Vhujon (IRE)**[22] 4201 3-9-0 **90**.............................. RichardEvans(5) 9 73
(P D Evans) *plld hrd: led and sn clr: wnt far side 1/2-way: rdn and hdd over 1f out: wknd fnl f* **25/1**

1-53 **8** *6* **Coachhouse Lady (USA)**[18] 4300 3-8-8 **79**.............................. FrancisNorton 5 46
(K A Ryan) *chsd clr ldr to over 2f out: sn rdn and edgd rt: wknd over 1f out* **13/2**[3]

1m 23.21s (-2.99) **Going Correction** -0.275s/f (Firm) **8** Ran SP% **110.7**
Speed ratings (Par 106): **106,105,101,101,96 96,95,88**
toteswinger: 1&2 £6.40, 1&3 £9.10, 2&3 £6.40. CSF £27.72 CT £136.60 TOTE £10.30: £2.30, £1.50, £2.30; EX 43.30.
Owner Ed McCormack **Bred** Falah Ithnein **Trained** Manton, Wilts

FOCUS
No more than a fair handicap for the grade, run at a solid pace. The form makes sense.

NOTEBOOK
Nezami(IRE) took full advantage of a 3lb drop in the weights and scored under a well-judged ride. He displayed a neat turn of foot to get to the front from off the pace and, despite wanting to hang right late on, was always doing enough to repel the runner-up. It was a career-best effort and his season could just be about to really take off. (op 11-1)

Zakhaaref, 3lb higher, held every chance only to again find one too good. He can be rated a little better than the bare result as he chased the generous early pace, may just prefer a return to 1m now, and does deserve to find another opening. (tchd 5-2)

Noble Citizen(USA) hit a flat spot before running on again and had his chance. He ran close to his Newmarket form with the runner-up and just looks held by the Handicapper at present. (op 8-1)

Kiwi Bay would have been suited by racing off the decent early pace and and simply looks weighted to his best now. (op 5-1)

Autumn Blades(IRE) failed to raise his game on this step back up in trip and was well beaten off. A drop back down in grade now looks in order. (op 11-2 tchd 5-1)

4894 JOHN SMITH'S H'CAP 1m 1f 218y
4:20 (4:20) (Class 4) (0-85,85) 3-Y-0+ **£5,046** (£1,510; £755; £377; £188) **Stalls** High

Form RPR

1420 **1** **Mazaaya (USA)**[27] 4021 3-9-3 **83**.............................. RHills 9 91
(D R Lanigan) *mde virtually all: rdn over 1f out: styd on gamely* **7/1**

3403 **2** *1* **Marvo**[29] 3947 4-9-1 **72**.............................. MichaelHills 6 78
(M H Tompkins) *sn chsng wnr: rdn and ev ch ins fnl f: nt qckn nr fin* **10/1**

-245 **3** *2 ¼* **Candy Mountain**[16] 4361 4-9-8 **79**.............................. DaneO'Neill 10 81
(L M Cumani) *chsd ldrs: rdn over 2f out: styd on same pce ins fnl f* **9/2**[2]

-201 **4** *nk* **She's Our Lass (IRE)**[28] 4001 7-9-5 **76**.............................. DNolan 7 77+
(D Carroll) *hld up: hdwy over 2f out: rdn over 1f out: styd on same pce ins fnl f* **12/1**

0404 **5** *½* **Giant Love (USA)**[15] 4423 3-8-9 **75**.............................. GregFairley 3 75
(M Johnston) *prom: rdn over 3f out: sn outpcd: rallied fnl f* **4/1**[1]

0-1 **6** *1* **Who's This (IRE)**[25] 4085 4-10-0 **85**.............................. SaleemGolam 11 83
(W R Swinburn) *hld up in tch: racd keenly: rdn over 2f out: no ex fnl f* **10/1**

1662 **7** *½* **Quince (IRE)**[16] 4396 5-9-9 **80**..................(v) FrancisNorton 4 77+
(J Pearce) *hld up: hdwy and nt clr run over 1f out: nt rch ldrs* **8/1**

5606 **8** *½* **Tilapia (IRE)**[19] 4269 4-9-3 **81**.............................. KylieManser(7) 5 77
(Miss Gay Kelleway) *hld up: hdwy 2f out: nt trble ldrs* **33/1**

-530 **9** *2 ¼* **Sign Of The Cross**[32] 3836 4-9-9 **80**.............................. JimCrowley 8 71
(J R Fanshawe) *plld hrd and prom: rdn over 2f out: wknd over 1f out* **8/1**

6-00 **10** *¾* **Port Quin**[53] 3134 3-8-7 **73**.............................. SteveDrowne 1 63
(G Wragg) *hld up: a in rr* **33/1**

-203 **11** *1 ¾* **Beverly Hill Billy**[10] 4565 4-9-6 **77**.............................. ShaneKelly 2 63
(A King) *hld up: rdn over 2f out: a in rr* **13/2**[3]

2m 8.30s (0.40) **Going Correction** +0.075s/f (Good)
WFA 3 from 4yo+ 9lb **11** Ran SP% **118.0**
Speed ratings (Par 105): **101,100,98,98,97 96,96,96,94,93 92**
toteswinger: 1&2 £18.00, 1&3 £8.70, 2&3 £12.10. CSF £75.35 CT £349.99 TOTE £9.10: £2.90, £4.40, £1.90; EX 112.00.
Owner Saif Ali **Bred** Needham/betz Thoroughbreds & Carl Freeman **Trained** Newmarket, Suffolk

FOCUS
A fair handicap, run at an uneven pace. The form is rated through the placed horses.

4895 LEICESTERSHIRE AND RUTLAND LIFE H'CAP 1m 60y
4:50 (4:51) (Class 5) (0-75,75) 3-Y-0+ **£3,885** (£1,156; £577; £288) **Stalls** High

Form RPR

0450 **1** **Russian Epic**[30] 3928 4-9-13 **74**..................(t) PhilipRobinson 7 84
(M A Jarvis) *chsd ldrs: rdn and edgd rt over 1f out: r.o to ld post* **9/2**[1]

6056 **2** *nse* **Bold Cross (IRE)**[10] 4567 5-9-5 **66**.............................. PaulFitzsimons 3 75
(E G Bevan) *hld up: hdwy over 2f out: led 1f out: rdn and hdd post* **14/1**

0460 **3** *2 ¼* **Kensington (IRE)**[15] 4407 7-9-9 **70**.............................. JimCrowley 10 74
(P D Evans) *a.p: rdn over 2f out: n.m.r over 1f out: styd on same pce fnl f* **14/1**

6121 **4** *2 ½* **San Antonio**[34] 3795 8-9-13 **74**..................(b) MickyFenton 1 72
(Mrs P Sly) *led: clr 5f out: rdn and hdd 1f out: no ex* **7/1**

2501 **5** *hd* **Ours (IRE)**[23] 4172 5-9-4 **65**..................(p) SteveDrowne 8 63
(John A Harris) *hld up: hdwy over 3f out: nt clr run over 1f out: styd on* **6/1**[3]

5106 **6** *½* **Sir Boss (IRE)**[13] 4478 3-9-4 **72**.............................. LiamJones 12 69
(D E Cantillon) *hld up: rdn over 2f out: styd on ins fnl f* **9/1**

2220 **7** *2 ¼* **Haasem (USA)**[23] 4162 5-9-8 **69**.............................. StephenDonohoe 4 61
(J R Jenkins) *hld up: rdn over 3f out: nt clr run over 1f out: nvr trbld ldrs* **8/1**

-050 **8** *nk* **Baizically (IRE)**[24] 4104 5-9-12 **73**.............................. DaneO'Neill 2 64
(George Baker) *hld up: rdn over 2f out: n.d* **16/1**

2632 **9** *¾* **King Of Rhythm (IRE)**[8] 4650 5-10-0 **75**..................(p) DNolan 5 64
(D Carroll) *hld up: racd keenly: rdn over 2f out: wknd over 1f out* **11/2**[2]

0334 **10** *8* **Wahoo Sam (USA)**[1] 4862 8-8-13 **65**.............................. RichardEvans(5) 11 36
(P D Evans) *prom: racd keenly: rdn over 2f out: sn hung rt and wknd* **10/1**

6001 **11** *6* **Very Well Red**[10] 4567 5-9-7 **68**.............................. DarrenWilliams 6 25
(P W Hiatt) *chsd ldr tl rdn over 2f out: sn wknd* **16/1**

1m 43.72s (-1.38) **Going Correction** +0.075s/f (Good)
WFA 3 from 4yo+ 7lb **11** Ran SP% **115.7**
Speed ratings (Par 103): **109,108,106,104,104 103,101,100,100,92 86**
toteswinger: 1&2 £5.90, 1&3 £12.70, 2&3 £25.50. CSF £67.30 CT £831.92 TOTE £4.90: £2.20, £4.30, £3.90; EX 75.50 Place 6: £204.23, Place 5: £126.58..
Owner Magno-Pulse Ltd **Bred** Derek R Price **Trained** Newmarket, Suffolk

■ Stewards' Enquiry : Paul Fitzsimons one-day ban: used whip down shoulder in forehand position (Aug 24)
Philip Robinson caution: used whip without giving horse time to respond

FOCUS
A modest handicap, run at a good pace. The first pair came clear in a bobbing finish.
Ours(IRE) Official explanation: jockey said gelding lost its action
T/Plt: £258.10 to a £1 stake. Pool: £67,345.34. 190.47 winning tickets. T/Qpdt: £121.20 to a £1 stake. Pool: £4,258.70. 26.00 winning tickets. CR

4873 REDCAR (L-H)
Sunday, August 10

OFFICIAL GOING: Good to soft (good in places)
Wind: Strong behind Weather: Sunny periods - windy

4896 EUROPEAN BREEDERS' FUND MAIDEN FILLIES' STKS (DIV I) 7f
1:40 (1:41) (Class 5) 2-Y-0 **£3,561** (£1,059; £529; £264) **Stalls** Centre

Form RPR

4 **1** **Seradim**[11] 4521 2-9-0 0.............................. TomEaves 7 73+
(P F I Cole) *towards rr: pushed along wl over 2f out: swtchd lft and rdn 2f out: hdwy over 1f out: styd on strly ins fnl f to ld fnl 75yds* **2/1**[1]

2 *1* **Izzy Lou (IRE)** 2-9-0 0.............................. NCallan 1 71+
(K A Ryan) *trckd ldrs: hdwy to chal over 2f out: rdn to ld over 1f out: sn hung rt: drvn ins fnl f: hdd and no ex fnl 75yds* **8/1**

6 **3** *1 ¼* **Enhancing**[24] 4109 2-9-0 0.............................. PaulMulrennan 2 67
(A J McCabe) *sn cl up: effrt over 2f out: sn rdn and ev ch whn carried rt ent fnl f: sn drvn and one pce* **3/1**[2]

0 **4** *1 ½* **Silk Cotton (USA)**[23] 4157 2-9-0 0.............................. TPQueally 4 64
(E A L Dunlop) *hmpd s: towards rr: hdwy over 2f out: rdn over 1f out: kpt on ins fnl f: nrst fin* **25/1**

4 **5** *1 ½* **Caster Sugar (USA)**[17] 4337 2-9-0 0.............................. PatCosgrave 3 60
(L M Cumani) *trckd ldrs: rdn along 3f out: drvn 2f out and sn one pce* **9/2**[3]

0 **6** *nk* **Save The Day**[11] 4521 2-9-0 0.............................. JoeFanning 5 59
(M Johnston) *wnt rt s: sn cl up: led wl over 2f out: sn rdn and hdd over 1f out: n.m.r and swtchd lft ent fnl f: one pce* **17/2**

0 **7** *nk* **Ever Loved (USA)**[29] 3959 2-9-0 0.............................. DO'Donohoe 11 58
(Saeed Bin Suroor) *trckd ldrs: effrt over 2f out: sn rdn: edgd lft and wknd* **12/1**

8 *½* **Maybeme** 2-8-11 0.............................. NeilBrown(3) 6 57
(N Bycroft) *towards rr: rdn along over 2f out: sme late hdwy* **100/1**

6 **9** *4 ½* **Hettie Hubble**[16] 4380 2-9-0 0.............................. DavidAllan 10 46
(T D Easterby) *led: rdn along 1/2-way: hdd wl over 2f out and sn wknd* **14/1**

0 **10** *26* **Another Echo**[66] 2746 2-8-11 0.............................. DominicFox(3) 9 —
(W Storey) *chsd ldrs: rdn along appr 1/2-way and sn wknd* **66/1**

1m 28.83s (4.33) **Going Correction** +0.40s/f (Good) **10** Ran SP% **118.8**
Speed ratings (Par 91): **91,89,88,86,85 84,84,83,78,48**
toteswinger: 1&2 £4.80, 1&3 £2.20, 2&3 £6.20. CSF £19.46 TOTE £2.30: £1.20, £3.50, £1.10; EX 18.60.
Owner The Fairy Story Partnership **Bred** Deepwood Farm Stud **Trained** Whatcombe, Oxon

FOCUS
A fair fillies' maiden and the winning time was 0.24 seconds slower than the second division. The third is the best guide to the level.

NOTEBOOK
Seradim was an uneasy favourite, but she was able to build on the form she showed when fourth on her debut over 6f at Goodwood. A bit flighty in the paddock, she took a good hold early on before going through a flat spot at halfway, but then responded to some strong driving to get up well inside the last furlong and win going away. She certainly saw her race out well, but it's hard to predict how she will progress. (op 5-4 tchd 9-4)

Izzy Lou(IRE), a 90,000euros daughter of Spinning World, half-sister to high-class dual 6f-1m winner Missit, and 7f juvenile winner Night Sphere, showed plenty of ability, but she was also green and ruined her chance by drifting right under pressure. She will know more next time. (op 17-2 tchd 9-1)
Enhancing was well backed to improve on her Doncaster debut run, and though she couldn't be counted as an unlucky loser, the runner-up did her no favours by carrying her across the track towards the stands'-side rails. (op 7-1 tchd 15-2)
Silk Cotton(USA) progressed from her debut run and has the scope to improve further. (op 20-1)
Caster Sugar(USA) tracked the leaders, but could never get to them and didn't improve on her debut fourth at Folkestone. She is likely to be more of a handicap sort. (tchd 4-1 and 5-1)
Save The Day may do better when qualified for handicaps. (op 12-1)
Ever Loved(USA), down the field on her debut over 6f at Nottingham, again finished up well held.

4897 EUROPEAN BREEDERS' FUND MAIDEN FILLIES' STKS (DIV II) 7f
2:10 (2:12) (Class 5) 2-Y-O £3,561 (£1,059; £529; £264) Stalls Centre

Form RPR
0 **1** **Punch Drunk**[17] 4328 2-9-0 0 TPQueally 5 71+
(J G Given) *mde all: pushed along and edgd lft 2f out: rdn and clr whn hung lft over 1f out: kpt on strly* **22/1**
0 **2** 1 1/2 **Haulage Lady (IRE)**[45] 3411 2-9-0 0 DavidAllan 4 65
(Karen McLintock) *chsd wnr: pushed along: rn green and sltly outpcd over 2f out: sn rdn and styd on appr fnl f* **100/1**
4 **3** 5 **Demeanour (USA)**[23] 4149 2-9-0 0 MartinDwyer 11 53
(E A L Dunlop) *trckd ldrs: cl up 1/2-way: rdn along over 2f out: sn drvn and one pce* **1/2**[1]
34 **4** 1 3/4 **Forever's Girl**[10] 4557 2-8-11 0 PJMcDonald(3) 1 48
(G R Oldroyd) *prom: rdn along to chse wnr over 2f out: sn drvn: edgd lft and wknd wl over 1f out* **33/1**
5 2 **Madamlily (IRE)** 2-9-0 0 GrahamGibbons 8 43
(J J Quinn) *in rr: hdwy 2f out: styd on appr fnl f: nrst fin* **14/1**
6 5 **Kochanski (IRE)** 2-9-0 0 JoeFanning 10 31
(M Johnston) *chsd ldrs: rdn along wl over 2f out and sn wknd* **10/1**[3]
7 3 **Straits Of Hormuz (USA)** 2-9-0 0 RoystonFfrench 7 23
(E J O'Neill) *chsd ldrs: rdn along 3f out and sn wknd* **9/2**[2]
8 1/2 **Accumulation (UAE)** 2-9-0 0 PaulMulrennan 2 22
(M W Easterby) *towards rr: sme hdwy 3f out: rdn over 2f out and sn wknd* **50/1**
9 2 1/2 **Who's Shirl** 2-9-0 0 DeanMcKeown 6 16
(C W Fairhurst) *dwlt: a in rr* **100/1**
00 **10** 11 **Dakota Two (IRE)**[11] 4536 2-9-0 0 TonyHamilton 9 —
(R A Fahey) *a towards rr* **80/1**
1m 28.59s (4.09) **Going Correction** +0.40s/f (Good) **10** Ran SP% **113.1**
Speed ratings (Par 91): **92,90,84,82,80 74,71,70,67,55**
toteswinger: 1&2 £50.00, 1&3 £4.40, 2&3 £14.40. CSF £1169.49 TOTE £22.40: £4.70, £19.70, £1.02; EX 930.00.
Owner Lovely Bubbly Racing **Bred** Mrs Deborah O'Brien **Trained** Willoughton, Lincs

FOCUS
Hard to be sure of the level with a 100/1 shot in second and the odds-on favourite running below form, but the winning time was 0.24 seconds quicker than the first division. The form is guessy but looks modest.

NOTEBOOK
Punch Drunk showed little on her debut on quick ground at Doncaster, but she clearly learnt from that and was much better suited by these earlier conditions. She is either quirky or still very green, as she wandered around quite badly in the closing stages, but she clearly has plenty of ability. (tchd 25-1)
Haulage Lady(IRE), who didn't show a great deal on her debut over 6f, shaped much better this time, though like the winner she was green and raced with her head up. However, she stuck on well to pull well clear of the rest and overall turned in a creditable effort. (op 66-1)
Demeanour(USA) was off the bridle soon after halfway and was below the form she showed on her debut over 6f at Newbury. (tchd 2-5)
Forever's Girl, who was beaten in a seller on her debut and had no chance on her previous start when the blindfold came off too late, ran her best race yet stepped up two furlongs in trip. (op 20-1)
Madamlily(IRE), a 52,000gns daughter of Refuse To Bend, ran to just a moderate level on her racecourse deut, but she is entitled to come on a fair bit for this. (tchd 18-1)
Straits Of Hormuz(USA), a $150,000 daughter of War Chant, half-sister to 7f juvenile winner Delta Diva, out of a winner over 1m4f, was well supported on course but showed little. She probably wants better ground. (op 8-1)

4898 BUTTERWICK HOSPICE CHARITY DAY H'CAP 1m
2:40 (2:40) (Class 6) (0-60,60) 3-Y-O+ £2,388 (£705; £352) Stalls Centre

Form RPR
5000 **1** **Trans Sonic**[26] 4048 5-8-13 50 (v) DO'Donohoe 1 65
(A J Lockwood) *cl up centre: led after 1f: rdn clr wl over 1f out: styd on strly* **33/1**
1405 **2** 5 **Pianoforte (USA)**[14] 4451 6-9-8 59 (b) DavidAllan 5 63
(E J Alston) *sltly hmpd s and towards rr: hdwy 1/2-way: rdn along over 2f out: drvn to chse wnr over 1f out: no imp ins fnl f* **10/1**
6-05 **3** 2 1/2 **Kielty's Folly**[15] 4414 4-8-10 47 TonyCulhane 3 45
(B P J Baugh) *in tch: hdwy to chse ldrs 3f out: drvn to chse wnr over 2f out: kpt on same pce fr wl over 1f out* **16/1**
0331 **4** shd **Silly Gilly (IRE)**[11] 4540 4-9-4 55 TomEaves 16 53
(R E Barr) *hld up towards stands rail: hdwy 3f out: sn rdn along: styd on u.p fnl 2f* **8/1**
3040 **5** 2 1/2 **Penel (IRE)**[21] 4215 7-9-3 54 (p) LeeEnstone 8 46
(P T Midgley) *hmpd s and rr: hdwy 3f out: rdn 2f out: kpt on u.p: nt rch ldrs* **16/1**
4000 **6** 3/4 **King Of The Moors (USA)**[11] 4537 5-9-7 58 (p) PaulFessey 13 48
(T D Barron) *led 1f: cl up: rdn along 3f out: drvn 2f out and grad wknd* **8/1**
56F2 **7** 3 1/2 **Lizzie Wiggins**[34] 3791 3-9-1 59 PaulMulrennan 18 41
(Mrs Marjorie Fife) *midfield: effrt 3f out and sn rdn along: nvr a factor* **9/1**
5562 **8** 3/4 **Polish Corridor**[9] 4597 9-9-2 60 FrederikTylicki(7) 19 41
(M Dods) *in tch towards stands' rail: hdwy 3f out: rdn to chse ldrs 2f out: sn drvn and btn* **4/1**[1]
0403 **9** 3 1/4 **Monsieur Dumas (IRE)**[11] 4540 4-9-1 52 (v[1]) PatCosgrave 9 25
(R Bastiman) *wnt lft s: chsd ldrs: rdn along 3f out and sn wknd* **7/1**[3]
2146 **10** 2 1/2 **Little Firecracker**[136] 1034 3-9-2 60 RoystonFfrench 14 27
(Miss M E Rowland) *chsd ldrs: hdwy 3f out: rdn along over 2f out and grad wknd* **33/1**
-403 **11** 8 **Garibaldi (GER)**[11] 4541 6-8-13 55 (t) AshleyHamblett(5) 20 4
(N Wilson) *racd towards stands' rail: chsd ldrs: rdn along 1/2-way: sn wknd* **22/1**
3034 **12** 2 **High Window (IRE)**[8] 4653 8-8-4 48 oh1 ow2 BradleyRoper(7) 12 —
(G P Kelly) *a towards rr* **20/1**
-036 **13** 24 **Cadwell**[118] 1369 4-8-12 49 NCallan 4 —
(T J Pitt) *a towards rr* **28/1**
2202 **14** 7 **Ardent Prince**[11] 4540 5-8-13 53 TolleyDean(3) 15 —
(A J McCabe) *cl up: rdn along over 3f out and sn wknd* **11/2**[2]
1m 41.21s (3.21) **Going Correction** +0.40s/f (Good)
WFA 3 from 4yo+ 7lb **14** Ran SP% **119.4**
Speed ratings (Par 101): **99,94,91,91,88 88,84,83,80,78 70,68,44,37**
toteswinger: 1&2 £90.90, 1&3 £58.50, 2&3 £45.50. CSF £316.87 CT £3178.14 TOTE £33.90: £11.30, £3.30, £6.70; EX 184.20.
Owner Mrs Lynne Lumley **Bred** I A Balding **Trained** Brawby, N Yorks

FOCUS
A moderate, uncompetitive handicap.
Polish Corridor Official explanation: jockey said gelding was unsuited by the good to soft, good in places ground
High Window(IRE) Official explanation: jockey said gelding was unsuited by the good to soft, good in places ground
Ardent Prince Official explanation: jockey said gelding was unsuited by the good to soft, good in places ground

4899 REDCAR CRICKET CLUB (S) STKS 1m 2f
3:10 (3:10) (Class 6) 3-5-Y-O £2,047 (£604; £302) Stalls Low

Form RPR
4056 **1** **Sweet World**[27] 4023 4-9-6 50 NCallan 7 61
(B J Llewellyn) *mde all: rdn clr 2f out: styd on* **7/1**[3]
4540 **2** 6 **Cecina Marina**[12] 4503 5-8-10 42 KellyHarrison(5) 9 44
(Mrs K Walton) *trckd ldrs: hdwy 4f out: rdn to chse wnr 3f out: drvn and no imp fr wl over 1f out* **9/1**
1244 **3** 19 **Cherri Fosfate**[60] 2927 4-9-12 68 DavidAllan 12 17
(D Carroll) *trckd ldrs: hdwy to chse wnr 1/2-way: rdn along 4f out: drvn 3f out and sn btn* **4/6**[1]
2500 **4** 5 **Feeling Peckish (USA)**[56] 1814 4-9-3 40 (t) LeeVickers(3) 11 1
(M C Chapman) *chsd wnr to 1/2-way: sn rdn along and outpcd fnl 4f* **40/1**
60 **5** 24 **Cabin Gate (IRE)**[5] 4701 5-9-1 0 (e[1]) PatrickDonaghy(5) 2 —
(R Johnson) *trckd ldrs on inner: rdn along 4f out: sn wknd* **66/1**
05 **6** 19 **Getrah**[5] 4701 4-9-6 62 (b) TPQueally 5 —
(C Grant) *v.s.a and virtually ref to r: a t.o* **7/2**[2]
00 **P** **Lassie Goes West (IRE)**[39] 3605 3-8-7 30 ow1 TonyCulhane 6 —
(E J Creighton) *a bhd: t.o fnl 4f: p.u and dismntd ins fnl f* **50/1**
2m 11.36s (4.26) **Going Correction** +0.40s/f (Good)
WFA 3 from 4yo+ 9lb **7** Ran SP% **110.6**
Speed ratings (Par 101): **98,93,78,74,54 39,—**
toteswinger: 1&2 £5.60, 1&3 £2.10, 2&3 £2.50. CSF £58.96 TOTE £7.50: £2.30, £3.10; EX 64.30.The winner was bought in for 6,000gns.
Owner B J Llewellyn **Bred** Natton House Thoroughbreds **Trained** Fochriw, Caerphilly

FOCUS
A truly terrible horserace. The winning time was 1.64 seconds slower than the later 56-75 maiden handicap.
Lassie Goes West(IRE) Official explanation: trainer's rep said filly returned lame

4900 OPTIMUMRACING.CO.UK H'CAP 6f
3:40 (3:41) (Class 4) (0-85,85) 3-Y-O £4,857 (£1,445; £722; £360) Stalls Centre

Form RPR
5230 **1** **Moonage Daydream (IRE)**[4] 4745 3-7-13 66 (bt) DuranFentiman(3) 5 73
(T D Easterby) *led: rdn along and hdd over 1f out: drvn and edgd lft 1f out: styd on ins fnl f to ld nr fin* **8/1**
4444 **2** nk **Sparton Duke (IRE)**[15] 4416 3-9-0 78 (p) NCallan 12 84
(K A Ryan) *dwlt and hld up: hdwy 2f out: rdr dropped whip and swtchd lft and rdn over 1f out: led ins fnl f: sn edgd lft: hdd and no ex nr fin* **11/2**
3030 **3** nk **Solar Spirit (IRE)**[15] 4416 3-9-2 80 PaulMulrennan 3 85
(G A Swinbank) *cl up: rdn to ld and edgd rt over 1f out: drvn and hdd ins fnl f: no ex towards fin* **9/2**[2]
0400 **4** 2 1/2 **Cat Whistle**[15] 4440 3-8-11 75 TonyHamilton 10 72
(R A Fahey) *trckd ldrs: hdwy 2f out: rdn and ch whn hmpd 1f out: one pce after* **9/1**
2113 **5** 1 1/2 **Pavershooz**[15] 4416 3-9-5 83 DO'Donohoe 14 75+
(N Wilson) *in rr: rdn along and hdwy wl over 1f out: kpt on ins fnl f* **6/1**
4114 **6** 2 1/2 **Novellen Lad (IRE)**[17] 4329 3-9-0 78 DavidAllan 11 62
(E J Alston) *trckd ldrs: effrt 2f out: sn rdn and no imp* **5/1**[3]
0310 **7** 1/2 **Tawzeea (IRE)**[23] 4145 3-9-7 85 MartinDwyer 6 68
(M Johnston) *trckd ldrs: hdwy chal 2f out: sn rdn and ev ch whn hmpd 1f out: nt rcvr* **4/1**[1]
230 **8** 2 **Loose Caboose (IRE)**[41] 3554 3-8-10 74 (p) PatCosgrave 9 50
(A J McCabe) *cl up: rdn along and ev ch over 2f out: sn drvn and wknd* **16/1**
1-50 **9** 12 **Bright Falcon**[12] 2819 3-9-6 84 JohnEgan 4 22
(S Parr) *cl up: rdn along 1/2-way: sn wknd* **33/1**
2-12 **10** 11 **Only A Game (IRE)**[184] 489 3-9-1 79 RoystonFfrench 13 —
(Miss M E Rowland) *chsd ldrs: rdn along 1/2-way: sn wknd* **12/1**
1m 12.94s (1.14) **Going Correction** +0.40s/f (Good) **10** Ran SP% **122.1**
Speed ratings (Par 102): **108,107,107,103,101 98,97,95,79,64**
toteswinger: 1&2 £10.60, 1&3 £13.40, 2&3 £11.10. CSF £54.18 CT £232.98 TOTE £9.60: £3.00, £1.90, £2.20; EX 65.20.
Owner Rio Grande Partnership **Bred** Miss Nicola Kent **Trained** Great Habton, N Yorks
■ Stewards' Enquiry : Duran Fentiman caution: careless riding

FOCUS
A fair, competitive three-year-old handicap. The winning time was 0.85 seconds quicker than the later 46-60 handicap.
Only A Game(IRE) Official explanation: jockey said gelding lost its action

4901 REDCAR CONFERENCE CENTRE CLAIMING STKS 1m
4:10 (4:10) (Class 6) 3-4-Y-O £2,388 (£705; £352) Stalls Centre

Form RPR
4033 **1** **Shotley Mac**[8] 4650 4-9-6 65 (b) FrederikTylicki(7) 8 75
(N Bycroft) *mde virtually all: rdn clr wl over 1f out: styd on* **7/4**[1]
0045 **2** 5 **Nikolaievich (IRE)**[15] 4427 3-9-6 62 JoeFanning 11 63
(P F I Cole) *midfield: hdwy 3f out: rdn along 2f out: styd on u.p to chse wnr appr fnl f: sn no imp* **7/1**[3]
3 1 3/4 **Sorrento Moon (IRE)**[84] 2228 4-8-11 43 PJMcDonald(3) 9 46
(G M Moore) *towards rr: hdwy over 2f out: sn rdn: drvn and edgd lft ent fnl f: nrst fin* **12/1**
-200 **4** 1 3/4 **Fantasy Parkes**[59] 2968 4-8-7 72 (p) DavidAllan 7 35
(E J Alston) *cl up: rdn along over 2f out: sn drvn and wknd over 1f out* **9/4**[2]
6536 **5** 3/4 **Talon (IRE)**[4] 4737 3-8-13 52 (bt[1]) NeilBrown(3) 5 49
(G A Swinbank) *chsd ldrs: rdn along wl over 2f out and no hdwy* **12/1**
4006 **6** 6 **Saafend Geezer**[5] 4632 3-7-12 45 CharlotteKerton(7) 14 24
(A Berry) *towards rr: effrt and sme hdwy over 2f out: sn rdn: hung lft and nvr a factor* **40/1**

The Form Book, Raceform Ltd, Compton, RG20 6NL

0000 7 23 **So Sublime**[22] 3690 3-8-8 45 ..... TomEaves 4 —
(M C Chapman) *a in rr* **66/1**
00-0 8 1 **Spooky**[25] 4077 3-8-4 46 ..... DominicFox(3) 6 —
(W Storey) *chsd ldrs 3f: sn lost pl and bhd* **40/1**
9 6 **Ma Nadri** 3-8-5 0 ..... PaulFessey 2 —
(S T Mason) *a bhd* **50/1**
-500 10 57 **Encores**[23] 4156 4-9-5 63 ..... (b[1]) NCallan 16 —
(M G Quinlan) *racd alone towards stands' rail: prom: rdn along after 3f: sn wknd* **15/2**
U **Mandrake Miss** 4-8-9 0 ..... PAspell 10 —
(C R Wilson) *stmbld and uns rdr s* **66/1**

1m 40.59s (2.59) **Going Correction** +0.40s/f (Good)
WFA 3 from 4yo 7lb **11** Ran SP% **116.6**
Speed ratings (Par 101): **103,98,96,94,93 87,64,63,57,— —**
toteswinger: 1&2 £3.80, 1&3 £5.90, 2&3 £12.50. CSF £14.33 TOTE £2.80: £1.50, £1.80, £3.50; EX 13.30.Fantasy Parkes was claimed by K. Bishop for £5,000.
Owner J A Swinburne **Bred** N Bycroft **Trained** Brandsby, N Yorks

FOCUS
A moderate claimer. The winning time was 1.64 seconds slower than the later maiden.
So Sublime Official explanation: jockey said gelding hung right
Spooky Official explanation: jockey said gelding hung right
Encores Official explanation: jockey said gelding was never travelling

4902 WEDDINGS AT REDCAR MAIDEN H'CAP 1m 2f
4:40 (4:40) (Class 5) (0-75,72) 3-Y-O+ £2,590 (£770; £385; £192) Stalls Low

Form RPR
1 **Follow The Sun (IRE)**[20] 4264 4-8-9 **53** oh1 ..... TonyHamilton 1 62
(Ronald O'Leary, Ire) *trckd ldrs: hdwy on inner to ld over 3f out: rdn 2f out: drvn ent fnl f and styd on wl* **12/1**
340- 2 1 ¾ **White Moss (IRE)**[297] 6277 4-9-1 **59** ..... NCallan 3 64
(M H Tompkins) *trckd ldrs: hdwy on inner over 3f out: rdn to chse wnr 2f out: drvn to chal and ev ch ent fnl f: no ex* **9/2**[2]
3-05 3 4 **Snowy Indian**[23] 4152 3-9-2 **69** ..... RoystonFfrench 6 66
(Sir Michael Stoute) *trckd ldrs: effrt 4f out: sn rdn along and outpcd 3f out: drvn and kpt on same pce fnl 2f* **10/3**[1]
0066 4 3 **Shanafarahan (IRE)**[17] 4331 3-8-7 **60** ow1 ..... TonyCulhane 5 51
(T P Tate) *hld up in rr: hdwy 3f out: sn rdn and styd on same pce fnl 2f* **16/1**
0240 5 4 **Top Man Dan (IRE)**[4] 4738 3-8-6 **59** ow2 ..... (v[1]) DavidAllan 11 42
(D Carroll) *hld up towards rr: hdwy 3f out and sn rdn: drvn 2f out and nvr nr ldrs* **14/1**
0025 6 6 **Mystic Art (IRE)**[25] 4086 3-8-12 **65** ..... (b[1]) PaulMulrennan 10 36
(C R Egerton) *chsd ldr: rdn along 4f out: drvn wl over 2f out and sn wknd* **6/1**
22-0 7 3 ½ **Augustus John (IRE)**[24] 4111 5-10-0 **72** ..... JohnEgan 2 36
(S Parr) *led: rdn along 4f out: hdd over 3f out: sn drvn and wknd* **11/2**[3]
3606 8 1 ¾ **Bold Bobby Be (IRE)**[13] 4485 4-9-2 **60** ..... TPQueally 8 21
(J L Dunlop) *hld up in rr: hdwy on outer 3f out: rdn to chse ldrs over 2f out: sn drvn and wknd* **11/2**[3]
3042 9 51 **Pondapie (IRE)**[23] 4173 3-9-5 **72** ..... TomEaves 9 —
(R M Whitaker) *in tch: rdn along over 4f out and sn wknd* **8/1**

2m 9.72s (2.62) **Going Correction** +0.40s/f (Good)
WFA 3 from 4yo+ 9lb **9** Ran SP% **117.7**
Speed ratings (Par 103): **105,103,100,98,94 90,87,85,45**
toteswinger: 1&2 £10.40, 1&3 £8.30, 2&3 £5.00. CSF £66.50 CT £225.73 TOTE £14.30: £3.30, £1.50, £1.60; EX 99.10.
Owner Mrs Ronald O'Leary **Bred** Ronnie O'Leary **Trained** Killaloe, Co. Clare

FOCUS
A moderate race, but the winning time was still 1.64 seconds quicker than the earlier seller.
Follow The Sun(IRE) Official explanation: trainer said, regarding the apparent improvement in form, that gelding was better suited by a weaker race and softer ground

4903 THE COMMITMENTS ARE HERE IN AUGUST H'CAP 6f
5:10 (5:10) (Class 6) (0-60,58) 3-Y-O+ £2,388 (£705; £352) Stalls Centre

Form RPR
0060 1 **Woodsley House (IRE)**[60] 2936 6-9-7 **57** ..... TomEaves 15 67
(A G Foster) *dwlt and towards rr: hdwy over 2f out: rdn over 1f out: str run ent fnl f to ld nr fin* **16/1**
0243 2 ½ **Obe One**[8] 4653 8-8-8 **49** ow2 ..... SladeO'Hara(3) 3 57
(A Berry) *in tch: hdwy over 2f out: rdn to ld over 1f out: drvn ins fnl f: hdd and no ex nr fin* **8/1**
0004 3 1 ¼ **Apres Ski (IRE)**[13] 4476 5-8-7 **48** ow1 ..... AshleyHamblett(5) 7 52
(J F Coupland) *dwlt and towards rr: swtchd wd and gd hdwy 2f out: rdn to chse ldrs over 1f out: kpt on u.p ins fnl f* **22/1**
0002 4 1 ½ **Mujma**[13] 4479 4-9-0 **50** ..... JohnEgan 2 49
(S Parr) *prom: hdwy to ld 2f out: sn rdn and hdd over 1f out: drvn and wknd ins fnl f* **17/2**
0041 5 1 ¾ **Ryedane (IRE)**[8] 4653 6-9-3 **56** ..... (b) DuranFentiman(3) 12 50
(T D Easterby) *trckd ldrs: hdwy 1/2-way: chal 2f out: soon rdn and ev ch tl drvn and one pce appr fnl f* **6/1**[2]
0160 6 5 **Maison Dieu**[23] 4174 5-9-7 **57** ..... DavidAllan 1 35
(E J Alston) *cl up on outer: effrt over 2f out and ev ch tl rdn and wknd over 1f out* **4/1**[1]
0530 7 3 ½ **Summer Recluse (USA)**[22] 4186 9-9-6 **56** ..... (t) NCallan 11 22
(J M Bradley) *midfield: hdwy 2f out: sn rdn and no imp* **12/1**
0000 8 ½ **Tadlil**[24] 4125 6-8-11 **50** ..... (v) TolleyDean(3) 16 15
(J M Bradley) *in tch: rdn along over 2f out and sn btn* **33/1**
-364 9 1 **Puskas (IRE)**[19] 4285 5-8-11 **50** ..... (b) RussellKennemore(3) 10 12
(J M Bradley) *chsd ldrs: led over 3f out: rdn and hdd 2f out: sn drvn and wknd* **10/1**
055 10 nk **Double Carpet (IRE)**[98] 1827 5-9-7 **57** ..... PaulFessey 4 18
(G Woodward) *led over 2f: cl up tl rdn over 2f out and sn wknd* **7/1**[3]
0/05 11 1 ¼ **Bigalo's Banjo**[52] 3172 5-9-2 **52** ..... LeeEnstone 17 9
(L A Mullaney) *racd towards stands' rail: in tch: rdn along 1/2-way: sn wknd* **20/1**
-000 12 hd **Paint Stripper**[35] 3753 3-8-10 **53** ..... DominicFox(3) 14 9
(W Storey) *s.i.s: a bhd* **14/1**
0600 13 1 **Safranine (IRE)**[14] 4462 11-8-6 **47** ..... AnnStokell(5) 19 —
(Miss A Stokell) *racd towards stands' rail: in tch: rdn along 1/2-way: sn wknd* **40/1**
000 14 1 ½ **Inca Soldier (FR)**[83] 2251 5-9-8 **58** ..... DeanMcKeown 9 6
(R C Guest) *a in rr* **6/1**[2]

1m 13.79s (1.99) **Going Correction** +0.40s/f (Good)
WFA 3 from 4yo+ 4lb **14** Ran SP% **126.5**
Speed ratings (Par 101): **102,101,99,97,95 88,84,83,82,81 79,79,78,76**
toteswinger: 1&2 £33.80, 1&3 £72.20, 2&3 £27.90. CSF £140.13 CT £2936.77 TOTE £19.60: £6.40, £2.50, £7.90; EX 215.30 Place 6: £823.70, Place 5: £566.97..
Owner Mrs V L Davis **Bred** Roger G English **Trained** Cousland, Midlothian

FOCUS
A moderate sprint. The winning time was 0.85 seconds slower than the earlier 66-85 three-year-old handicap.
T/Jkpt: Not won. T/Plt: £600.30 to a £1 stake. Pool: £61,227.71. 74.45 winning tickets. T/Qpdt: £263.80 to a £1 stake. Pool: £3,957.66. 11.10 winning tickets. JR

4691 WINDSOR (R-H)
Sunday, August 10

OFFICIAL GOING: Good to soft (soft in places)
Wind: Brisk, behind Weather: Sunshine and showers, heavy after Race 5

4904 BRIAN WHITEHEAD 70TH YEAR CELEBRATION APPRENTICE H'CAP 5f 10y
2:30 (2:32) (Class 5) (0-75,72) 3-Y-O £2,729 (£806; £403) Stalls High

Form RPR
45 1 **Our Acquaintance**[17] 4325 3-8-12 **65** ..... (b) DavidProbert(5) 6 68+
(W R Muir) *t.k.h early: trckd ldrs: cruising over 1f out w rest u.p: shkn up to ld jst ins fnl f: sn wl in command* **9/4**[1]
36 2 1 ¼ **Our Kally**[18] 4308 3-8-0 **53** oh8 ..... BillyCray(5) 2 51
(M D I Usher) *last early: rdn over 2f out: prog to chal 1f out: edgd lft and styd on same pce* **16/1**
4046 3 nk **Valhillen**[13] 4476 3-9-8 **70** ..... (p) PatrickHills 1 67
(M D I Usher) *late to post: chsd ldrs: rdn 2f out and grabbed far side rail: clsd to chal 1f out: kpt on same pce* **13/2**
0510 4 1 ¾ **Mr Funshine**[27] 4025 3-8-9 **60** ..... JackMitchell(3) 7 51
(Mrs P N Dutfield) *w ldr: hrd rdn and upsides 1f out: fdd* **16/1**
5424 5 1 **Barraland**[9] 4584 3-9-5 **72** ..... MCGeran(5) 3 59
(M R Channon) *mde most: rdn 2f out: hdd and fdd jst ins fnl f* **7/1**
4203 6 hd **Maggie Kate**[24] 4127 3-9-4 **66** ..... KirstyMilczarek 4 52
(R Ingram) *chsd ldrs: tried to chal over 1f out: keeping on one pce and hld whn hmpd and snatched up 100yds out* **4/1**[3]
1300 7 1 **Brazilian Brush (IRE)**[27] 4025 3-9-8 **70** ..... (t) JamieMoriarty 5 53
(H Morrison) *pressed ldrs: lost pl sltly 1/2-way: tried to rally over 1f out: wknd ins fnl f* **7/2**[2]

61.23 secs (0.93) **Going Correction** +0.05s/f (Good) **7** Ran SP% **110.6**
Speed ratings (Par 100): **94,92,91,88,87 86,85**
toteswinger: 1&2 £6.70, 1&3 £4.00, 2&3 £15.60. CSF £36.21 TOTE £3.30: £1.90, £6.50; EX 47.10.
Owner Quaintance Partnership **Bred** S R Hope **Trained** Lambourn, Berks
■ Stewards' Enquiry : Billy Cray two-day ban: careless riding (Aug 24-25)

FOCUS
A moderate bunch fought out this handicap for apprentices and the form is not strong and is rated negatively. It seemed to be an advantage to come from the rear and perhaps those on the front end went a little too quickly in the conditions.
Maggie Kate Official explanation: jockey said filly suffered interference in running

4905 YORKSHIRE TEA TEATIME MAIDEN AUCTION STKS (DIV I) 6f
3:00 (3:00) (Class 5) 2-Y-O £2,388 (£705; £352) Stalls High

Form RPR
1 **Serious Attitude (IRE)** 2-8-0 0 ..... DavidProbert(5) 6 80+
(Rae Guest) *dwlt: hld up in rr: smoooth prog on outer over 2f out: led over 1f out: drew rt away fnl f* **9/2**[2]
0456 2 5 **Kingswinford (IRE)**[7] 4659 2-8-12 68 ..... TQuinn 4 72
(P D Evans) *pressed ldrs: led jst over 2f out: hdd and easily outpcd over 1f out* **8/1**
0 3 1 ¾ **Brooksby**[23] 4149 2-8-8 0 ..... RyanMoore 2 63+
(R Hannon) *dwlt: sn in midfield: effrt 2f out: styd on fnl f to take 3rd nr fin* **8/1**
3020 4 ¾ **Court Approval (IRE)**[11] 4525 2-9-1 78 ..... JamieSpencer 12 68
(T G Mills) *led 1f: styd pressing ldrs: upsides over 1f out: sn btn* **7/2**[1]
50 5 hd **Ray Of Joy**[20] 4256 2-8-5 0 ..... JimmyQuinn 7 57
(J R Jenkins) *chsd ldrs: rdn over 2f out: hanging lft over 1f out: kpt on ins fnl f* **16/1**
4 6 4 ½ **Importer (IRE)**[32] 3848 2-8-12 0 ..... JimmyFortune 3 50
(W R Muir) *mostly in midfield: outpcd 2f out: hrd rdn 1f out: hanging lft but plugged on fnl f* **15/2**
30 7 2 ¼ **Damassin**[47] 3348 2-8-6 0 ..... StephenCarson 11 38
(Eve Johnson Houghton) *chsd ldrs: in tch 2f out: wknd over 1f out* **6/1**[3]
0 8 1 ¾ **Mfi'Ve**[22] 4184 2-8-11 0 ..... TGMcLaughlin 8 37
(B R Millman) *nvr beyond midfield: rdn and struggling over 2f out: steadily wknd* **28/1**
00 9 hd **Fleur De'Lion (IRE)**[20] 4251 2-8-8 0 ..... LPKeniry 9 34
(S Kirk) *mostly in midfield: rdn over 2f out: wknd over 1f out* **25/1**
05 10 ¾ **Kayceebee**[27] 4020 2-8-11 0 ..... JamesDoyle 1 35
(R M Beckett) *wnt lft s: rcvrd to ld after 1f: hdd jst over 2f out: wknd rapidly* **14/1**
0 11 1 ½ **Bermondsey Bob (IRE)**[29] 3968 2-8-5 0 ..... JackDean(5) 5 29
(J L Spearing) *dwlt: sn struggling in rr: nvr a factor* **50/1**
12 14 **Maisie Mouse** 2-8-10 0 ..... AlanMunro 10 —
(S C Williams) *dwlt: a last and struggling: t.o* **16/1**

1m 13.4s (0.40) **Going Correction** +0.05s/f (Good) **12** Ran SP% **116.4**
Speed ratings (Par 94): **99,92,90,89,88 82,79,77,77,76 74,55**
toteswinger: 1&2 £10.20, 1&3 £8.50, 2&3 £12.30. CSF £38.89 TOTE £4.60: £1.40, £2.80, £3.10; EX 40.70 Trifecta £195.80 Part won. Pool: £264.60. 0.25 winning units..
Owner The Purple & Yellow Partnership 1 **Bred** Paddy Twomey **Trained** Newmarket, Suffolk

FOCUS
Those who had run had posted some uninspiring efforts so it was no surprise that this moderate maiden auction eventually went to one of the newcomers, landing something of a gamble in the process. The form looks solid enough.

NOTEBOOK
Serious Attitude(IRE) had obviously been working well on the Newmarket gallops and she was backed at all rates down to make a winning debut. Fairly slowly away, Probert seemed content to let her bowl along towards the rear, and when he allowed the filly her head she drew easily into contention before lengthening away impressively. She probably didn't beat much, but the manner of her victory stamps her out as one to watch in better company. (op 11-1)
Kingswinford(IRE) has been beaten in selling grade so his proximity does little for the form. (tchd 7-1)
Brooksby stayed on nicely enough and could do with an extra furlong or so. (op 10-1 tchd 15-2)
Court Approval(IRE) raced prominently throughout but couldn't find anything other than the one pace. (op 11-4)
Ray Of Joy is now eligible for a handicap mark and she should be seen to better effect in nurseries. (tchd 20-1)

Damassin was most disappointing as both her previous efforts entitled her to go very close in this company. It is highly likely that she needs a sound surface to show her best. (op 9-2)

4906 OSSIE AND HUTCH MEMORIAL H'CAP — 1m 2f 7y
3:30 (3:31) (Class 4) (0-85,84) 3-Y-O — £5,698 (£1,695; £847; £423) Stalls Low

Form — RPR

5210 **1** — **Soft Shoe Shuffle (IRE)**[36] 3742 3-9-6 **83**........................ AdamKirby 6 — 88+
(W R Swinburn) *hld up in 6th: stdy prog over 3f out: led over 2f out: rdn over 1f out: looked in command fnl f: jst hld on* — **11/4**[1]

4061 **2** *shd* **Higgy's Boy (IRE)**[19] 4276 3-9-3 **80**........................ RyanMoore 5 — 85
(R Hannon) *hld up in last: shkn up 3f out: prog u.p fr 2f out: styd on wl fnl f to cl on wnr: jst failed* — **9/1**

5321 **3** *1 1/4* **Bowder Stone (IRE)**[7] 4663 3-9-4 **81** 6ex........................ JimmyQuinn 2 — 84
(M H Tompkins) *t.k.h: trckd ldng pair: gng strly over 2f out: rdn to chal over 1f out: one pce ins fnl f* — **3/1**[2]

051 **4** *1/2* **Spider Silk**[20] 4249 3-8-8 **78**........................ JPHamblett(7) 8 — 80
(W Jarvis) *hld up in tch: rdn over 2f out: cl enough over 1f out: fnd nil and sn btn* — **16/1**

4311 **5** *2 1/2* **Fair Gale**[9] 4582 3-9-6 **83**........................ LPKeniry 4 — 80
(S Kirk) *led 2f: trckd ldr: rdn over 3f out: stl chalng over 2f out: wknd wl over 1f out* — **9/1**

544 **6** *3/4* **Mega Watt (IRE)**[27] 4021 3-9-0 **77**........................ AlanMunro 3 — 72
(W Jarvis) *dwlt: hld up in tch: rdn over 3f out: struggling over 2f out* — **3/1**[2]

154 **7** *nk* **House Of Lords (USA)**[78] 2412 3-9-1 **78**........................ JamieSpencer 9 — 72
(M L W Bell) *s.i.s: rcvrd and led after 2f: hdd over 2f out: hrd rdn and sn lost pl* — **6/1**[3]

2m 11.82s (3.12) **Going Correction** +0.375s/f (Good) — 7 Ran SP% **116.8**
Speed ratings (Par 102): **102,101,100,100,98 97,97**
toteswinger: 1&2 £4.50, 1&3 £2.70, 2&3 £5.80. CSF £28.68 CT £79.42 TOTE £3.10: £2.60, £3.10; EX 28.70 Trifecta £65.10 Pool: £221.74. 2.52 winning units..
Owner Exors Of The Late Mrs P W Harris **Bred** Pendley Farm **Trained** Aldbury, Herts

FOCUS
A useful handicap for three-year-olds. The winner was unraced at two and is proving highly progressive, and the third and fourth ran to their marks giving the form a solid look.

4907 YORKSHIRE TEA TEATIME MAIDEN AUCTION STKS (DIV II) — 6f
4:00 (4:03) (Class 5) 2-Y-O — £2,388 (£705; £352) Stalls High

Form — RPR

05 **1** — **Golden Destiny (IRE)**[32] 3848 2-8-0 0........................ DavidProbert(5) 12 — 69
(P J Makin) *w ldrs: disp ld wl over 1f out: narrowly hdd ins fnl f: kpt on wl: won on the nod* — **11/1**

00 **2** *nse* **Hi Shinko**[45] 3417 2-8-11 0........................ TGMcLaughlin 5 — 75
(B R Millman) *trckd ldrs: prog to dispute ld wl over 1f out: narrow ld ins fnl f: pipped on the post* — **50/1**

3 *3 1/4* **Safari Guide** 2-8-11 0........................ StephenCarson 6 — 65
(P Winkworth) *pushed along in midfield after 2f: effrt 2f out: styd on to take 3rd jst ins fnl f: no imp on ldng pair* — **16/1**

3 **4** *2 1/4* **Rumble Of Thunder (IRE)**[48] 3323 2-8-12 0........................ JimmyFortune 10 — 60
(D W P Arbuthnot) *w ldrs to 2f out: hrd rdn and wknd fnl f* — **10/3**[2]

00 **5** *3/4* **Buckers Beauty (IRE)**[37] 3669 2-8-4 0........................ CatherineGannon 3 — 49
(P D Evans) *free to post: chsd ldrs: outpcd fr 2f out: plugged on* — **33/1**

3 **6** *1* **Wing Home (IRE)**[92] 2011 2-8-11 0........................ RichardKingscote 7 — 53
(Tom Dascombe) *w ldrs: hanging lft fr 1/2-way: 3rd and btn over 1f out: wknd ins fnl f* — **6/4**[1]

7 *1* **Cabo Polonio (IRE)** 2-8-8 0........................ LPKeniry 4 — 47
(S Kirk) *uns rdr and bolted to post: pushed along in rr after 2f: nvr on terms: plugged on fr over 1f out* — **40/1**

2 **8** *3* **Louidor**[13] 4482 2-8-9 0........................ FergusSweeney 9 — 39
(J R Boyle) *mde most to wl over 1f out: sn wknd* — **4/1**[3]

9 *3 3/4* **Miss Tikitiboo (IRE)** 2-8-8 0 ow2........................ JamieSpencer 8 — 27
(E F Vaughan) *s.s: pushed along in rr after 2f: nvr on terms* — **11/1**

00 **10** *4 1/2* **Tobizzy**[31] 3869 2-8-8 0........................ TQuinn 11 — 14
(J R Jenkins) *nvr beyond midfield: in tch 2f out: sn wknd* — **33/1**

11 *20* **Igotim** 2-8-9 0........................ JimmyQuinn 1 — —
(J Gallagher) *s.v.s: a t.o* — **50/1**

1m 14.33s (1.33) **Going Correction** +0.05s/f (Good) — 11 Ran SP% **117.9**
Speed ratings (Par 94): **93,92,88,85,84 83,81,77,72,66 40**
toteswinger: 1&2 £46.00, 1&3 £16.80, 2&3 £55.10. CSF £464.61 TOTE £11.60: £2.20, £12.80, £3.30; EX 600.00 TRIFECTA Not won..
Owner H J W Davies P Spencer-Jones M H Holland **Bred** Yeomanstown Stud **Trained** Ogbourne Maisey, Wilts
■ Stewards' Enquiry : David Probert one-day ban: used whip with excessive frequency (Aug 24)

FOCUS
A maiden that was no stronger than the first division and with the three once-raced horses at the head of the market floundering on the going it was left to this year's apprentice find, David Probert, to drive his filly home on the nod and complete his first-ever treble. The form is weak and this is not a race to be with.

NOTEBOOK
Golden Destiny(IRE) had never got competitve on either of her two previous starts but the daughter of Captain Rio had shown signs of ability for all that and in a weakish race was able to translate her promise into a hard-fought victory. Her future lies in the hands of the Handicapper. (op 12-1 tchd 10-1)

Hi Shinko was a revelation in the soft ground as he improved by at least a couple of stone on either of his two previous starts. He can now go for nurseries but he will be rated on this effort and will hold no secret from the assessor. (tchd 40-1)

Safari Guide ran on in taking fashion after looking very green in the first half of the contest. The first foal of a sister to three winners, the Primo Valentino colt can win races for a yard that do well with their juveniles. (op 12-1 tchd 18-1)

Rumble Of Thunder(IRE) is bred to require further with time so despite going off as second favourite it was no surprise that he appeared to get outpaced at a vital stage over a sprint distance. (op 9-2 tchd 11-2)

Wing Home(IRE) was punted to continue the good run of Dascombe's juveniles but having his first start since his Warwick debut three months ago, the son of Hawk Wing looked far from comfortable on the soft going. (op 9-4)

Louidor made a very promising debut when runner-up here a fortnight ago, but after showing up early folded tamely in these starkly differing conditions. (op 9-4)

Igotim Official explanation: jockey said colt missed the break and ran green

4908 EBF SUNSEEKER CHARTERS CONDITIONS STKS — 6f
4:30 (4:33) (Class 3) 2-Y-O — £7,771 (£2,312; £1,155; £577) Stalls High

Form — RPR

1 **1** — **Desert Phantom (USA)**[28] 3997 2-8-12 0........................ JamieSpencer 1 — 91
(D M Simcock) *mde all: drvn and gained upper hand over 1f out: a holding on fnl f* — **9/4**[2]

216 **2** *1/2* **Rileyskeepingfaith**[9] 4588 2-8-12 **86**........................ EdwardCreighton 3 — 90+
(M R Channon) *bucked rdr off coming on to crse and galloped off to post: t.k.h early: hld up in tch: rdn 2f out: styd on to take 2nd ins fnl f and clsng on wnr fin* — **7/4**[1]

1 **3** *1* **Ginobili (IRE)**[24] 4126 2-8-12 0........................ RyanMoore 4 — 86
(R Hannon) *t.k.h early: pressed wnr: rdn and nt qckn over 1f out: fdd ins fnl f* — **4/1**[3]

61 **4** *2* **Zezao**[83] 2239 2-8-12 0........................ AlanMunro 6 — 80
(B J Meehan) *free to post: dwlt: t.k.h early and cl up: rdn over 2f out: edgd lft and nt qckn over 1f out: fdd* — **11/1**

4513 **5** *4* **Soul Sista (IRE)**[5] 4706 2-8-5 **80**........................(b[1]) JimmyQuinn 2 — 61
(J L Spearing) *t.k.h early: hld up in tch: wknd over 1f out* — **9/1**

1100 **6** *2 1/2* **Baycat (IRE)**[11] 4517 2-8-11 **101**........................ JackMitchell(5) 5 — 65
(J G Portman) *dwlt: a last: rdn and struggling over 2f out: wknd over 1f out* — **12/1**

1m 13.82s (0.82) **Going Correction** +0.05s/f (Good) — 6 Ran SP% **113.2**
Speed ratings (Par 98): **96,95,94,91,86 82**
toteswinger: 1&2 £1.70, 1&3 £2.30, 2&3 £2.60. CSF £6.72 TOTE £3.30: £1.80, £1.70; EX 6.90.
Owner Ahmad Al Shaikh **Bred** John R Penn & Frank Penn **Trained** Newmarket, Suffolk

FOCUS
A decent little conditions event, the form of which could stand up at a higher level. The runner-up to his maiden win sets the standard.

NOTEBOOK
Desert Phantom(USA) ◆ had coped with even worse underfoot conditions when well backed to make a winning start to his career at Haydock, and the strapping son of Arch made all under a confident ride from Spencer in the manner of a colt who can hold his own in better company. (op 10-3 tchd 7-2)

Rileyskeepingfaith, who had galloped loose to the start after depositing Creighton to the turf, never looked like getting to the winner and it was only in the last half-furlong that he seemed to really put his head down and consent to race, at which point he had to be switched around the winner which cost him any chance he may have had. He set the form standard coming into the race, with his sixth in the Richmond Stakes at Goodwood last time, and wouldn't be one to give up on, despite his obvious temperament. (op 11-8 tchd 15-8 and 2-1 in a place)

Ginobili(IRE) improved on the bare form of his debut win in a Sandown maiden auction, without ever looking like getting to grips with the winner. He shouldn't be long in finding more races. (tchd 9-2 in a place)

Zezao was keen both to post and in the early stages of the race and upped in trip gave himself little chance of lasting home in the conditions. (op 9-1 tchd 15-2)

Soul Sista(IRE) is a fair filly in her own grade but was a little outclassed here. (op 14-1)

Baycat(IRE) has not beaten a horse home in three starts since winning his first two races at Ascot and Newbury in fetching style. (tchd 14-1)

4909 DEREK DICKENS 60TH BIRTHDAY MAIDEN FILLIES' STKS — 1m 2f 7y
5:00 (5:04) (Class 5) 3-Y-O+ — £2,729 (£806; £403) Stalls Low

Form — RPR

23 **1** — **Inquisitive Look**[58] 2989 3-8-11 0........................ AlanMunro 7 — 82+
(P W Chapple-Hyam) *trckd ldrs: prog to ld over 3f out: pressed and rdn 2f out: kpt on wl u.p* — **11/4**[2]

-022 **2** *2 3/4* **Syvilla**[33] 3810 3-8-11 **82**........................ JimmyFortune 12 — 80+
(Rae Guest) *trckd ldrs: prog to chse wnr wl over 2f out: hrd rdn to chal 2f out: hld whn veered lft into rail u.p ins fnl f: eased* — **10/11**[1]

0 **3** *5* **Shayera**[111] 1525 3-8-11 0........................ RichardSmith 10 — 66
(B R Johnson) *dwlt: wl in rr: shkn up over 4f out: green but prog over 3f out: hung lft over 1f out: styd on to take 3rd 1f out: no ch w ldng pair* — **66/1**

3-56 **4** *3 1/4* **Hamalka (IRE)**[164] 727 3-8-11 **68**........................ TQuinn 8 — 60
(B W Hills) *free to post: prom: outpcd by ldng pair over 2f out: fdd and lost 3rd 1f out* — **16/1**[3]

05 **5** *9* **Oops Another Act**[18] 4302 3-8-11 0........................ AdamKirby 1 — 42
(W R Swinburn) *settled midfield: effrt to chse ldrs over 3f out: wknd 2f out* — **16/1**[3]

00 **6** *3 1/2* **Munlochy Bay**[37] 3688 4-9-6 0........................ FergusSweeney 4 — 35
(W S Kittow) *s.i.s: towards rr: rdn over 4f out: nvr on terms after: wl btn fnl 2f* — **80/1**

00 **7** *3 1/2* **Misselliebee**[20] 4249 3-8-8 0........................ PatrickHills(3) 15 — 28
(J W Hills) *pressed ldr to 4f out: wknd over 2f out* — **33/1**

6-0 **8** *shd* **Green Wonder (GER)**[57] 3035 3-8-11 0........................ LPKeniry 14 — 27
(D M Simcock) *hld up in midfield: shkn up 4f out: struggling 3f out: sn wl btn* — **50/1**

9 *1/2* **Euroceleb (IRE)** 3-8-11 0........................ EdwardCreighton 9 — 26
(H Morrison) *awkward s: racd v awkwardly in rr: green u.p and bhd fnl 3f* — **33/1**

00 **10** *nk* **Every Whisper (IRE)**[17] 4342 3-8-11 0........................ JamesDoyle 2 — 26
(Mrs A J Perrett) *led to over 3f out: wknd over 2f out* — **33/1**

11 *1/2* **Percyslavenderblue** 3-8-11 0........................ SamHitchcott 6 — 25
(J Gallagher) *s.s: wl in rr: prog 4f out into midfield: wknd wl over 2f out* — **66/1**

00 **12** *31* **Lady Special (IRE)**[23] 4166 3-8-11 0........................ IanMongan 13 — —
(C G Cox) *in tch in midfield: hrd rdn over 4f out: sn wknd: virtually p.u fnl f* — **50/1**

13 *55* **Melody Fair (IRE)** 3-8-11 0........................ RichardKingscote 3 — —
(W R Muir) *sn detached in last: t.o 4f out: virtually p.u fnl 2f* — **33/1**

2m 14.49s (5.79) **Going Correction** +0.375s/f (Good)
WFA 3 from 4yo 9lb — 13 Ran SP% **110.7**
Speed ratings (Par 100): **91,88,84,82,75 72,69,69,68,68 68,43,—**
toteswinger: 1&2 £1.40, 1&3 £39.50, 2&3 £18.50. CSF £4.22 TOTE £3.90: £1.30, £1.10, £18.70; EX 5.50 Trifecta £93.20 Part won. Pool: £126.00. 0.10 winning units..
Owner T Hyde & Mrs P Shanahan **Bred** Mrs A M Upsdell **Trained** Newmarket, Suffolk
■ Stewards' Enquiry : Alan Munro two-day ban: careless riding (Aug 24-25)

FOCUS
Absolutely no strength in depth to this maiden, and they came home at intervals more apposite to a 3m chase in bottomless ground in the depths of winter. The runner-up was eased and the winner is rated value for a length.

Melody Fair(IRE) Official explanation: jockey said filly had breathing problems

4910 COLIN-BROWN.CO.UK BIRTHDAY H'CAP — 1m 67y
5:30 (5:31) (Class 5) (0-70,69) 3-Y-O+ — £2,729 (£806; £403) Stalls High

Form — RPR

0203 **1** — **Gross Prophet**[8] 4641 3-9-13 **68**........................ RichardKingscote 4 — 82
(Tom Dascombe) *led 100yds: trckd ldr: c centre in st: led 2f out: edgd rt but sn clr* — **4/1**[2]

0013 **2** *5* **Rescue Me**[10] 4572 3-10-0 **69**........................ RyanMoore 1 — 71
(R Hannon) *hld up in last: prog over 3f out: drvn to take 2nd jst over 1f out: no imp on wnr* — **2/1**[1]

003 **3** *1* **A One (IRE)**[6] 4691 9-8-4 **45**........................ WilliamCarson(7) 8 — 46
(H J Manners) *led after 100yds: stretched field 1/2-way: hdd 2f out: sn btn but plugged on* — **8/1**

5460 **4** *6* **Art Market (CAN)**[57] 3036 5-10-0 **62**.......................... SimonWhitworth 9 49
(Miss Jo Crowley) *chsd ldrs: snatched up bnd 5f out: nvr on terms after: brief effrt over 2f out: wknd over 1f out* **12/1**

0400 **5** *3 1/4* **River N' Blues (IRE)**[25] 4090 3-9-0 **55**.......................... JimmyQuinn 5 33
(Dr J R J Naylor) *hld up in last pair: prog over 3f out: chsd ldrs 2f out but nt on terms: sn wknd* **25/1**

063 **6** *8* **Dr Synn**[1] 4863 7-9-4 **55**..........................(p) KirstyMilczarek(3) 2 15
(M J Attwater) *prog to trck ldrs 5f out: outpcd over 3f out: sn struggling* **5/1**[3]

66 **7** *12* **Welcome Releaf**[63] 2870 5-9-7 **58**.......................... LukeMorris(3) 3 —
(P Leech) *in tch in rr: struggling over 3f out: wknd over 2f out: t.o* **11/2**

2250 **8** *4* **Hurstpierpoint (IRE)**[17] 4326 3-8-7 **53**.......................... DavidProbert(5) 6 —
(M G Rimell) *t.k.h early: trckd ldrs: wknd over 3f out: t.o* **14/1**

1m 48.59s (3.89) **Going Correction** +0.375s/f (Good)
WFA 3 from 5yo+ 7lb **8** Ran SP% **114.7**
Speed ratings (Par 103): **95,90,89,83,79 71,59,55**
toteswinger: 1&2 £1.70, 1&3 £5.70, 2&3 £5.50. CSF £12.47 CT £60.07 TOTE £5.60: £2.00, £1.50, £2.00; EX 13.30 Trifecta £54.60 Pool: £708.74. 9.60 winning units. Place 6: £247.44, Place 5: £108.67..
Owner Alan Solomon **Bred** A David Solomon **Trained** Lambourn, Berks

FOCUS
A modest handicap and, just as in the previous race, they finished strung out like washing. The runner-up sets the standard.
Welcome Releaf Official explanation: trainer said gelding was unsuited by the good to soft ground
T/Plt: £924.90 to a £1 stake. Pool: £70,385.93. 55.55 winning tickets. T/Qpdt: £89.00 to a £1 stake. Pool: £5,225.56. 43.40 winning tickets. JN

3073 COLOGNE (R-H)
Sunday, August 10

OFFICIAL GOING: Soft

4911a AUTOHAUS JACOB FLEISCHAUER-CUP (LISTED RACE) 1m 7f
3:35 (3:48) 3-Y-0+ £9,559 (£2,941; £1,471; £735)

RPR

1 **Valdino (GER)** 3-8-6 .... J-PCarvalho 2 97
(U Ostmann, Germany) **4/1**[2]

2 *2* **Si Belle (IRE)**[59] 2985 3-8-2 .... NickyMackay 8 91
(Rae Guest) *disp 4th: wnt 3rd on ins st: outpcd over 2f out: r.o steadily fnl f* **19/2**

3 *1 1/4* **Ryan (IRE)**[28] 5-9-9 ....(b) RJuracek 6 96
(J Hanacek, Czech Republic) **46/10**[3]

4 *2* **Alleviate (IRE)**[49] 3307 4-9-2 .... THellier 4 87
(Sir Mark Prescott) *sn trcaking ldr: 2nd st: ev ch over 1f out: one pce* **15/2**

5 *shd* **Brisant (GER)**[27] 4041 6-9-7 .... ASuborics 3 92
(M Trybuhl, Germany) **6/4**[1]

6 *1/2* **Sapiranga (GER)**[49] 3307 4-9-0 .... AGoritz 9 84
(Frau Marion Rotering, Germany) **13/1**

7 *17* **Saraab (GER)**[399] 6-9-7 .... EFrank 7 71
(P Vovcenko, Germany) **38/1**

8 *86* **Medan (GER)**[14] 4-9-4 .... AStarke 1 —
(P Schiergen, Germany) **4/1**[2]

9 *22* **Schnipp Schnapp (FR)**[1378] 7-9-4 .... MichelleSwinnens 5 —
(M Swinnens, Belgium) **68/1**

3m 16.83s (196.83)
WFA 3 from 4yo+ 14lb **9** Ran SP% **130.3**
(including ten euro stakes): WIN 50; PL 14, 28, 18: SF 397.
Owner Frau H Endres **Bred** Gestut Auenquelle **Trained** Germany

NOTEBOOK
Alleviate(IRE) again came up just short in her bid for black type.

4912a OPPENHEIM FONDS TRUST SILBERNE PEITSCHE (GROUP 3) 6f 110y
4:10 (4:27) 3-Y-0+ £23,529 (£7,353; £3,676; £2,206)

RPR

1 **Abbadjinn (GER)**[36] 3752 4-9-5 .... TMundry 4 109
(P Rau, Germany) *a cl up: 3rd st: drvn to ld over 1 1/2f out: kpt on u.p* **14/10**[1]

2 *1 1/4* **Contat (GER)**[14] 5-9-5 .... RJuracek 10 105
(P Vovcenko, Germany) *led after 1 1/2f: hdd over 1 1/2f out: styd on same pce* **99/10**

3 *hd* **Shinko's Best (IRE)**[14] 7-9-5 .... THellier 7 105
(A Kleinkorres, Germany) *a in tch: 5th st: effrt on outside fr over 1f out: styd on one pce* **18/1**

4 *nk* **Prince Fasliyev**[43] 3517 4-9-5 .... MGuyon 2 104
(H-A Pantall, France) *hld up: 7th st: r.o fr over 1f out: nrest at fin* **132/10**

5 *3/4* **Lips Arrow (GER)**[14] 3-8-7 .... J-PCarvalho 1 94
(Andreas Lowe, Germany) *towards rr to st: styd on fnl f: nrest at fin* **96/10**[3]

6 *nse* **Key To Pleasure (GER)**[14] 8-9-5 .... ADeVries 3 101
(Mario Hofer, Germany) *last st: brought wdst: hdwy fr over 1f out: nrest at fin*

7 *1/2* **Iguazu Falls (USA)**[51] 3197 3-8-11 .... TedDurcan 6 96
(Saeed Bin Suroor) *hld up: hdwy and 6th st: outpcd over 2f out: disp 3rd over 1f out: one pce* **14/10**[1]

8 *1 3/4* **Florado (GER)**[14] 5-9-5 .... AGoritz 8 95
(T Potters, Australia) *trckd ldrs: 4th st: wknd over 1f out* **38/1**

9 *5* **Alaska River (GER)**[36] 3752 4-9-5 .... AStarke 9 80
(P Schiergen, Germany) *led 1 1/2f: 2nd st: sn wknd* **53/10**[2]

10 *nse* **Manipura (GER)**[50] 3-8-7 .... ASuborics 5 72
(A Wohler, Germany) *a towards rr* **136/10**

1m 19.71s (79.71)
WFA 3 from 4yo+ 4lb **10** Ran SP% **147.0**
WIN 24; PL 15, 34, 33; SF 287.
Owner Stall Schuoler-Gonzalez **Bred** Nathalie & Bruno Schuoler **Trained** Germany

NOTEBOOK
Iguazu Falls(USA), who ran poorly when sent off joint-favourite for the Buckingham Palace Stakes at Royal Ascot, again failed to trouble the judge on this return to Pattern company.

4913 - (Foreign Racing) - See Raceform Interactive

4880 DEAUVILLE (R-H)
Sunday, August 10

OFFICIAL GOING: Turf course - soft; all-weather - standard

4914a PRIX DE POMONE HARAS D'ETREHAM (GROUP 2) (F&M) 1m 4f 110y
2:45 (2:44) 3-Y-0+ £54,485 (£21,029; £10,037; £6,691; £3,346)

RPR

1 **Avanti Polonia (GER)**[27] 4041 4-9-4 .... DBonilla 5 110
(F Head, France) *hld up in last: shkn up 3f out: rdn and gd hdwy to chal ins fnl f: led 50yds out: comf* **124/10**

2 *1 1/2* **Turfrose (GER)**[84] 2238 4-9-4 .... SPasquier 4 108
(A Fabre, France) *hld up: 3rd 1/2-way: pushed along to chal 1 1/2f out: led 1f out: hdd 50yds out* **22/10**[2]

3 *2 1/2* **Believe Me (IRE)**[73] 2553 4-9-4 .... OPeslier 6 104
(J-M Beguigne, France) *in tch: 3rd 1/2-way: 4th st: drvn over 1 1/2f out: styd on fnl f: tk 3rd fnl strides* **47/10**

4 *snk* **Mrs Lindsay (USA)**[73] 2553 4-9-4 .... C-PLemaire 2 104
(F Rohaut, France) *led: pushed along st: pressed 1 1/2f out: hdd 1f out: sn rdn and no ex* **41/10**[3]

5 *1/2* **Anna Pavlova**[31] 3878 5-9-8 .... PaulHanagan 1 107
(R A Fahey) *in tch: 4th 1/2-way: 3rd st: pushed along to chse ldrs over 1 1/2f out: no ex fnl f* **2/1**[1]

6 *2* **Alix Road (FR)**[27] 5-9-4 .... AlexisBadel 3 100
(Mme M Bollack-Badel, France) *racd in 2nd: drvn 1 1/2f out: sn one pce* **11/1**

2m 47.1s (0.70) **Going Correction** +0.375s/f (Good) **6** Ran SP% **117.5**
Speed ratings: **112,111,109,109,109 107**
PARI-MUTUEL: WIN 13.40; PL 3.60, 1.80; SF 42.50.
Owner Mme I Von Schubert **Bred** Gestut Ebbesloh **Trained** France

NOTEBOOK
Avanti Polonia(GER) posted a much better effort than when disappointing at Longchamp on her previous start. On this occasion, waiting tactics were employed and she seemed to appreciate the change. Brought with a progressive run towards the stands' side, she quickened well in the final stages and won with plenty in hand. She is now likely to come back to Deauville for the Grand Prix at the end of the month.
Turfrose(GER), settled behind the leader, appeared to be going well within herself running down the back straight and quickened to take the lead halfway up the straight, but she had little left when tackled by the winner. She was not given a hard time when the writing was on the wall and this race was a preparation for the Prix Vermeille next month.
Believe Me(IRE) came with a late challenge on the stands' side and fought bravely, taking third place well inside the final furlong. She is a most consistent performer who deserves to win a Group race one day.
Mrs Lindsay(USA)'s connections decided that she should go from pillar to post on this occasion and she set a pretty fair gallop. She was still at the head of affairs coming into the straight but was in trouble a furlong and a half out and was agin below her best. The Prix Jean Romanet is now on the cards.
Anna Pavlova was nearly withdrawn before the race but she was finally allowed to take her chance on ground that was not as testing as she would have liked. This was not a bad effort considering she was conceding 4lb all round, but she was still below her best. If the ground is soft she could go for the Yorkshire Oaks, but there is also a chance that she will be retired from racing.

4915a PRIX MAURICE DE GHEEST (GROUP 1) (STRAIGHT) 6f 110y(S)
3:15 (3:18) 3-Y-0+
£105,037 (£42,022; £21,011; £10,496; £1,752; £1,752)

RPR

1 **Marchand D'Or (FR)**[30] 3922 5-9-2 .... DBonilla 14 123+
(F Head, France) *hld up trcking ldrs: pushed along 1 1/2f out: 3rd and chalng 1f out: rdn and r.o to ld 50yds out: styd on wl* **16/10**[1]

2 *3/4* **African Rose**[47] 3357 3-8-8 .... SPasquier 5 116
(Mme C Head-Maarek, France) *hld up in mid-div: pushed along over 2f out: r.o to chal 1 1/2f out: rdn to ld 1f out: r.o tl hdd 50yds out* **17/1**

3 *2 1/2* **Belliflore (FR)**[47] 3357 4-8-13 .... TJarnet 16 110
(Mlle S-V Tarrou, France) *towards rr on far side: hdwy 1 1/2f out: r.o wl through field fnl f: tk 3rd 100yds out* **65/1**

4 *3/4* **Utmost Respect**[43] 3488 4-9-2 .... PaulHanagan 6 111
(R A Fahey) *mid-div: pushed along 2f out: sltly short of room 1 1/2f out: fin wl fnl f* **58/1**

5 *1/2* **Diabolical (USA)**[30] 3922 5-9-2 .... LDettori 8 109
(Saeed Bin Suroor) *in tch on far side: hdwy to chal 2f out: ev ch appr fnl f: styd on tl no ex cl home* **12/1**

5 *dht* **Astronomer Royal (USA)**[30] 3922 4-9-2 .... CSoumillon 3 109
(A P O'Brien, Ire) *in tch on stands' rail: rdn over 1f out: styd on at one pce* **28/10**[2]

5 *dht* **US Ranger (USA)**[30] 3922 4-9-2 .... JMurtagh 12 109
(A P O'Brien, Ire) *prom: 4th 1/2-way: drvn to chal 2f out: rdn and in front rnk 1 1/2f out: no ex u.p ins fnl f* **28/10**[2]

8 *1 1/2* **Tiza (SAF)**[30] 3938 6-9-2 .... GMosse 1 105
(A De Royer-Dupre, France) *hld up: pushed along over 1 1/2f out: rdn and styd on fnl f but n.d* **20/1**

9 *snk* **Balthazaar's Gift (IRE)**[22] 4188 5-9-2 .... C-PLemaire 10 104
(L M Cumani) *in tch on far side: rdn over 1f out: kpt on same pce* **53/1**

10 *1* **Mariol (FR)**[30] 3938 5-9-2 .... SMaillot 2 101
(Robert Collet, France) *towards rr on stands' rail: rdn over 1 1/2f out: n.d* **21/1**

11 *4* **Jumbajukiba**[29] 3982 5-9-2 ....(b) JVictoire 11 90
(Mrs John Harrington, Ire) *led: drvn to hold pl 2f out: hdd over 1 1/2f out: one pce* **9/1**[3]

12 *3/4* **Only Answer**[30] 3938 4-8-13 .... OPeslier 13 84
(A Fabre, France) *cl 2nd: pushed along to ld over 1 1/2f out to 1f out: sn wknd* **21/1**

13 *5* **Intrepid Jack**[22] 4188 6-9-2 .... GeorgeBaker 7 73
(H Morrison) *mid-div: rdn 2f out: nvr in chalng position* **33/1**

14 *snk* **Garnica (FR)**[29] 3982 5-9-2 .... CDHayes 15 72
(D Nicholls) *prom on far side: 3rd 1/2-way: drvn 1 1/2f out: sn one pce* **41/1**

15 *2* **Vertigineux (FR)**[47] 3357 4-9-2 .... PSogorb 9 66
(Mme C Dufreche, France) *prom: cl 6th 1/2-way: u.p over 2f out: wknd* **28/1**

16 1 ½ **Assertive**[30] 3922 5-9-2 .... RichardHughes 4 62
(R Hannon) *towards rr on stands' side: effrt 2f out: no imp* **76/1**

1m 18.4s (1.20) **Going Correction** +0.60s/f (Yiel)
WFA 3 from 4yo+ 4lb 16 Ran SP% **143.3**
Speed ratings: **117,116,113,112,111 111,111,110,109,108 104,103,97,97,95 93**
PARI-MUTUEL: WIN 2.60; PL 1.50, 4.00, 9.20; DF 25.00.
Owner Mme J-L Giral **Bred** Mme C Giral **Trained** France
■ Marchand D'Or became the first horse to win the Prix Maurice de Gheest three times.

NOTEBOOK
Marchand D'Or(FR) was, as usual, taken to the start after one circuit of the paddock and loaded last into the stalls. Settled behind the main group up the centre of the track, a split came for him at the furlong marker and he ran on to take this race for the third year running. He has a rare mixture for a sprinter of both speed and stamina and the Betfred Haydock Sprint is probably his next race, where he will bid to improve on last year's second placing, and then the Prix de l'Abbaye may be on the agenda. The new Breeder's Cup turf sprint over this distance is also being considered.
African Rose's trainer felt she has blossomed at exactly the right moment and she produced a much-improved performance. Covered up in the early stages of the race, she burst into the lead at the furlong marker not far from the stands' rails and victory looked within her grasp until the classy winner came by. There are no exact plans for the moment but she will surely be kept to sprint distances in the future.
Bellifiore(FR) ran a fine race at a massive price. She had been towards the tail of the field in the early part of the race and then came with a run on the outside which took her past rivals, many of whom were not happy on the soft ground.
Utmost Respect, upped in grade after winning a Group 3 at Newcastle, had the ground in his favour and he ran well. Indeed, he could have finished even closer as he did not enjoy the best of runs, having nowhere to go a furlong and a half out.
Diabolical(USA) ran well on ground much softer than ideal. He may now be aimed at the Haydock Sprint Cup and and will be dangerous if getting quicker ground.
Astronomer Royal(USA) ran a reasonable race, but this soft ground was not for him. He will surely win a big one when getting quick conditions.
US Ranger(USA) may also want better ground, but he is proving most frustrating.
Balthazaar's Gift(IRE) ran on up the centre of the track in the final furlong but was never really seen with a chance.
Jumbajukiba struggled on this step up in class.
Intrepid Jack never made it into a position to take a hand in the finish and both the extended trip and the soft ground were against him.
Garnica(FR), fourth in this last year, was well up with the leading group in the early part of the race but was a beaten force one and a half out.
Assertive tried to make a challenge on the rail at the 300 metre mark but was beaten soon after.

4011 HANOVER (L-H)
Sunday, August 10

OFFICIAL GOING: Good

4916a GROSSER PREIS DER SPARKASSE HANNOVER (GROUP 2) 1m
3:55 (4:09) 3-Y-O+ £29,412 (£11,029; £4,412; £2,941)

RPR

1 **Forthe Millionkiss (GER)**[21] 4233 4-9-6 .... AHelfenbein 5 111
(Uwe Ostmann, Germany) *racd in 2nd to st: c over to stands' rails: rdn to ld 100yds out: r.o wl* **7/2**[3]

2 1 ¼ **Konig Concorde (GER)**[14] 3-8-11 .... WPanov 6 106
(C Sprengel, Germany) *hld up in rr: last but cl up st: hdwy to ld wl over 1f out: sn drvn: hdd 100yds out: one pce* **19/10**[2]

3 2 **Waky Love (GER)**[14] 4-9-2 .... JLermyte 4 100
(Frau Jutta Mayer, Germany) *disp 3rd: 4th st: kpt on one pce* **13/2**

4 ½ **Abbashiva (GER)**[21] 4233 3-8-11 .... NRichter 3 100
(P Rau, Germany) *disp 3rd: 3rd st: ev ch over 1f out: one pce* **4/5**[1]

5 2 ½ **Willingly (GER)**[21] 4233 9-9-6 .... FilipMinarik 2 97
(M Trybuhl, Germany) *led: sn 4 l clr: brought field over to stands' side: hdd & wknd wl over 1f out* **17/2**

1m 39.56s (99.56)
WFA 3 from 4yo+ 7lb 5 Ran SP% **136.1**
WIN 45; PL 17, 17; SF 133..
Owner Reinhard Ubber **Bred** R Ubber **Trained** Germany

2232 JAGERSRO (R-H)
Sunday, August 10

OFFICIAL GOING: Sloppy

4917a MARGARETA WETTERMARKS MINNESLOPNING (LISTED RACE) (F&M) (DIRT) 1m 143y(D)
1:25 (1:25) 3-Y-O+ £18,648 (£6,216; £3,108; £1,943; £1,166)

RPR

1 **Sourire**[32] 3849 3-8-13 .... FJohansson 1 95
(Sir Mark Prescott) *broke wl: settled in 3rd on rail: chal appr st: hung rt but led 100yds out: stvd on wl* **5/2**[1]

2 ½ **Auchroisk (SWE)**[273] 5-9-7 ....(b) CarlosLopez 7 94
(L Reuterskiold Jr, Sweden)

3 5 **Ellicat (SWE)**[24] 4-9-7 .... JacobJohansen 4 84
(E Van Doorn, Sweden)

4 ½ **Mummy's Lodge (IRE)** 4-9-7 ....(b) DPSanchez 5 83
(F Castro, Sweden)

5 1 ½ **Novasky (SWE)**[54] 6-9-7 .... ManuelMartinez 9 80
(T Gustafsson, Sweden)

6 9 **Sydney (DEN)** 3-8-13 .... LSantos 3 62
(Birgitte Nielsen, Sweden)

7 6 **Choco Express (DEN)**[707] 5-9-7 .... MLarsen 2 50
(O Larsen, Sweden)

8 5 **Tebheagnaneilan (SWE)**[301] 4-9-7 ....(b) MSantos 6 40
(L Reuterskiold Jr, Sweden)

1m 49.8s (109.80)
WFA 3 from 4yo+ 8lb 8 Ran SP% **28.6**
(Including SKr1 stake): WIN 3.49; PL 1.69, 4.89, 1.68; DF 71.84.
Owner Miss K Rausing **Bred** Miss K Rausing **Trained** Newmarket, Suffolk

NOTEBOOK
Sourire, who has an official mark of 89, had no trouble with the sloppy track, appreciated the longer trip and picked up valuable black type on her first foray abroad.

4918a SVENSKT DERBY 2008 (LISTED RACE) (DIRT) 1m 4f
3:45 (3:45) 3-Y-O

£82,751 (£38,065; £16,550; £11,585; £8,275; £4,965)

RPR

1 **Swing That Cat (USA)** 3-9-4 ....(b) ManuelMartinez 15 —
(F Reuterskiold, Sweden)

2 1 **Tertio Bloom (SWE)** 3-9-4 .... KAndersen 13 —
(F Reuterskiold, Sweden)

3 9 **Golden Metalimo (IRE)** 3-9-4 ....(b) DPSanchez 8 —
(F Castro, Sweden)

4 1 **Carpe Diem (DEN)** 3-9-4 .... MSantos 14 —
(L Reuterskiold Jr, Sweden)

5 8 **Superman (DEN)** 3-9-4 ....(b) NCordrey 12 —
(Hanne Bechmann)

6 4 **Artie Bucco (DEN)** 3-9-4 .... FJohansson 6 —
(Wido Neuroth, Norway)

7 hd **Itsagroom (SWE)** 3-9-4 .... LHammer-Hansen 5 —
(Vanja Sandrup, Sweden)

8 4 **Egon (USA)** 3-9-4 ....(b) EddieAhern 10 —
(F Reuterskiold, Sweden)

9 1 **Master Kid (DEN)** 3-9-4 .... JacobJohansen 7 —
(B Olsen, Denmark)

10 ½ **Hot Marta** 3-9-0 .... FDiaz 2 —
(L Reuterskiold Jr, Sweden)

11 ½ **Montgomery (SWE)** 3-9-4 .... EspenSki 1 —
(B Olsen, Denmark)

12 hd **Piaras (IRE)** 3-9-4 .... DinaDanekilde 3 —
(Vanja Sandrup, Sweden)

13 hd **Points Of View**[50] 3251 3-9-4 .... MLarsen 11 —
(Sir Mark Prescott) *broke wl and led or disp ld: u.p and checked in run 5f out: lost pl: eased in st* **64/10**[1]

14 7 **Common Sense (SWE)** 3-9-4 .... P-AGraberg 4 —
(B Bo, Sweden)

15 8 **Duriana (DEN)** 3-9-0 .... LisaMagnusson 9 —
(A McLaren)

2m 35.2s (155.20) 15 Ran SP% **13.5**
WIN 4.67; PL 2.04, 3.95, 3.14; DF 28.86.
Owner Mec-Comm Klippan A B & Fourfold H B **Bred** Mill Ridge Farm & Jamm & J Chandler & McGaughey **Trained** Sweden

NOTEBOOK
Points Of View, who has an official mark of 86, was stepping up from a mile for the first time and, being by Galileo, there was a decent chance it would suit him. However, after being up there from the start, he did not get home.

4647 THIRSK (L-H)
Monday, August 11

OFFICIAL GOING: Soft
The ground was described as 'genuine soft, heavy on the home turn'.
Wind: Almost nil Weather: overcast, light rain 1st 3 races

4919 OTTERINGTON SHORTHORN (S) H'CAP 1m
6:00 (6:00) (Class 6) (0-65,63) 3-Y-O+ £2,978 (£886; £442; £221) Stalls Low

Form RPR

0040 1 **Time To Regret**[17] 4386 8-9-6 55 ....(p) DanielTudhope 6 63
(I W McInnes) *in tch: hdwy to ld over 1f out: jst hld on* **16/1**

6064 2 nk **Noah Jameel**[20] 4267 6-9-0 52 .... JamieMoriarty[(3)] 7 59
(A G Newcombe) *in rr: hdwy on outer over 2f out: styd on wl fnl f: jst hld* **11/2**[2]

6250 3 hd **Anduril**[4] 4797 7-9-1 50 ....(b) PaulMulrennan 15 57
(I W McInnes) *chsd ldrs: kpt on fnl f: no ex fnl 75yds* **16/1**

2503 4 ½ **Zennerman (IRE)**[48] 3339 5-9-8 57 ....(b) DarryllHolland 4 62
(G A Swinbank) *in rr: hdwy on outside over 2f out: styd on wl fnl f* **7/2**[1]

4220 5 1 ¼ **Ace Of Spies (IRE)** 4738 3-8-10 52 .... GregFairley 5 54
(M Johnston) *mid-div: effrt on outer over 2f out: kpt on wl fnl f* **9/1**

0120 6 ½ **Hasty Lady**[18] 4332 3-9-6 62 .... NCallan 14 62
(K A Ryan) *chsd ldr: led over 2f out tl over 1f out: one pce* **14/1**

60-0 7 1 **Apache Point (IRE)**[12] 4541 11-8-13 48 .... KimTinkler 3 47
(N Tinkler) *in rr: styd on fnl 2f: nt rch ldrs* **16/1**

0-00 8 nk **Petite Mac**[26] 4073 8-8-8 50 ow2 .... FrederikTylicki[(7)] 13 48
(N Bycroft) *mid-div: hdwy over 2f out: kpt on same pce: nvr nr ldrs* **11/1**

0060 9 1 ¼ **Zabougg**[5] 4741 3-8-10 52 ....(p) TonyHamilton 1 47
(D W Barker) *s.i.s: drvn along on ins to chse ldrs over 5f out: one pce fnl 2f* **12/1**

5120 10 1 **Messiah Garvey**[19] 4293 4-9-2 58 .... AdeleRothery[(7)] 8 54
(D Nicholls) *tk fierce hold in midfield: kpt on fnl 2f: nvr rchd ldrs* **7/1**[3]

0000 11 9 **Mangano**[2] 4851 4-8-10 45 .... JoeFanning 10 18
(A Berry) *a towards rr* **14/1**

0644 12 3 ¾ **Sir Bond (IRE)**[14] 4479 7-8-12 50 .... PJMcDonald[(3)] 11 14
(G R Oldroyd) *s.i.s: a in rr* **16/1**

000- 13 ¾ **Sunley Sovereign**[332] 5386 4-8-10 48 .... MichaelJStainton[(3)] 2 10
(Mrs R A Carr) *sn chsng ldrs: lost pl over 1f out* **40/1**

0000 14 3 ¼ **Cabourg (IRE)**[9] 4653 5-8-11 46 .... DavidAllan 17 1
(R Bastiman) *led tl over 2f out: lost pl over 1f out* **33/1**

0000 15 8 **Mis Chicaf (IRE)**[10] 4605 7-8-10 45 .... DNolan 9 —
(D Carroll) *chsd ldrs: lost pl over 2f out: sn bhd* **80/1**

4004 16 1 ¼ **Samuel Charles**[5] 4748 10-10-0 63 ....(b) TPQueally 12 —
(C R Dore) *mid-div on outer: lost pl 3f out: sn bhd* **14/1**

1m 44.98s (4.88) **Going Correction** +0.65s/f (Yiel)
WFA 3 from 4yo+ 7lb 16 Ran SP% **126.3**
Speed ratings (Par 101): **101,100,100,100,98 98,97,96,95,94 85,81,81,77,69 68**
toteswinger: 1&2 £55.80, 1&3 £24.40, 2&3 £26.70. CSF £104.22 CT £1536.26 TOTE £23.40: £4.00, £2.10, £4.40, £1.40; EX 211.30.There was no bid for the winner.
Owner I D Woolfitt **Bred** Speedlith Group **Trained** Catwick, E Yorks

FOCUS
A run-of-the-mill selling handicap with little to choose between the first four at the line. Ordinary form for the grade, but sound.

4920 BEATRICE STEPHENSON MEMORIAL H'CAP 1m
6:30 (6:31) (Class 5) (0-75,73) 3-Y-O **£4,274** (£1,271; £635; £317) **Stalls** Low

Form RPR
3055 **1** **Devinius (IRE)**[24] 4163 3-8-5 **60**.............................. PJMcDonald(3) 10 66
(G A Swinbank) *hld up in last: stdy hdwy on outside over 2f out: led over 1f out: edgd lft: styd on wl* **7/1**
0360 **2** *2 1/4* **Street Devil (USA)**[24] 4153 3-9-6 **72**.............................. GregFairley 2 73
(P A Blockley) *trckd ldrs: t.k.h: chal over 1f out: edgd lft and kpt on same pce* **11/1**
2333 **3** *nk* **Montiboli (IRE)**[26] 4082 3-9-7 **73**.............................. NCallan 9 73+
(K A Ryan) *w ldrs: edgd rt and styd on same pce fnl f* **10/3**[1]
2063 **4** *1 3/4* **Admirals Way**[12] 4524 3-8-10 **62**.............................. DarryllHolland 5 58+
(C N Kellett) *trckd ldrs: tk fierce hold: n.m.r 2f out: edgd rt and kpt on same pce appr fnl f* **4/1**[3]
002 **5** *3 3/4* **Dream Of Olwyn (IRE)**[15] 4461 3-8-13 **65**.............................. TPQueally 6 53
(J G Given) *sn w ldrs: led 2f out: sn hdd: wkng whn n.m.r appr fnl f* **4/1**[3]
-401 **6** *3 3/4* **Lujano**[17] 4381 3-8-13 **65**.............................. PaulMulrennan 4 44
(Ollie Pears) *led tl 2f out: sn wknd* **7/2**[2]
4650 **7** *2 3/4* **Dhhamaan (IRE)**[9] 4649 3-9-3 **72**..............(b) MichaelJStainton(3) 3 45
(Mrs R A Carr) *t.k.h in rr: drvn over 3f out: wknd 2f out* **18/1**

1m 45.85s (5.75) **Going Correction** +0.65s/f (Yiel) **7** Ran SP% **111.4**
Speed ratings (Par 100): **97,94,94,92,88 85,82**
toteswinger: 1&2 £4.20, 1&3 £3.70, 2&3 £3.30. CSF £72.94 CT £295.12 TOTE £8.20: £3.40, £3.60; EX 87.00.
Owner The Jags Syndicate **Bred** P McAteer & Co **Trained** Melsonby, N Yorks

FOCUS
A very steady pace even in the conditions and an improved effort from the winner, but overall not strong form.

4921 MOUSEMAN OF KILBURN MAIDEN AUCTION STKS 7f
7:00 (7:01) (Class 5) 2-Y-O **£4,274** (£1,271; £635; £317) **Stalls** Low

Form RPR
03 **1** **Captain Imperial (IRE)**[32] 3888 2-8-12 0.............................. MickyFenton 1 73
(T P Tate) *sn led: rdn over 2f out: kpt on ins fnl f: all out* **13/8**[1]
2 *hd* **Bandanaman (IRE)** 2-9-1 0.............................. PaulMulrennan 7 76
(G A Swinbank) *mid-div: hdwy over 2f out: styd on to chal ins fnl f: no ex nr fin* **9/1**
3 *1 1/4* **Denton Diva** 2-8-4 0.............................. DaleGibson 8 63+
(M Dods) *drvn along to chse ldrs: styd on same pce whn n.m.r fnl f* **25/1**
4 *1* **Chilly Filly (IRE)** 2-8-7 0.............................. GregFairley 11 62+
(M Johnston) *mid-div: rn green and swvd rt fnl 2f: styd on wl ins fnl f: improve* **6/1**[3]
5 *nk* **Norwegian Dancer (UAE)** 2-8-12 0.............................. RichardMullen 13 66
(E S McMahon) *sn trcking ldrs on outer: chal 2f out: kpt on same pce* **9/2**[2]
6 *3 1/2* **Island Chief** 2-8-9 0.............................. NCallan 5 64+
(K A Ryan) *dwlt: bucked early on: wnt lft: hmpd and hopelessly lost pl after 1f: hdwy over 2f out: nvr nr ldrs* **8/1**
0 **7** *6* **Noble Heart (IRE)**[27] 4045 2-8-10 0.............................. PaulFessey 10 40
(T D Barron) *chsd ldrs: rdn and edgd rt 2f out: sn wknd* **40/1**
8 *1* **Yeoman Of England (IRE)** 2-8-12 0.............................. TomEaves 6 40
(B Smart) *dwlt: reminders after 1f: nvr on terms* **14/1**
00 **9** *3* **Aven Mac (IRE)**[35] 3792 2-8-4 0.............................. FrancisNorton 2 24
(N Bycroft) *mid-div: lost pl over 2f out* **100/1**
50 **10** *1 3/4* **Gee Gina**[13] 4499 2-8-1 0.............................. DuranFentiman(3) 3 20
(P T Midgley) *w ldrs: hung bdly rt over 3f out and ended up racing along stands' side: bhd fnl 2f* **40/1**
0 **11** *9* **Coniston Reload**[65] 2845 2-8-4 0 ow2.............................. BradleyRoper(7) 14 5
(M W Easterby) *mid-div: lost pl over 4f out: sn bhd* **50/1**
12 *34* **Kilsyth (IRE)** 2-8-7 0.............................. TonyCulhane 4 —
(S Parr) *dwlt: hmpd sn after s: sn detached in last: t.o 5f out: virtually p.u* **20/1**

1m 32.64s (5.44) **Going Correction** +0.65s/f (Yiel) **12** Ran SP% **118.2**
Speed ratings (Par 94): **94,93,92,91,90 86,80,78,75,73 63,24**
toteswinger: 1&2 £4.20, 1&3 £10.30, 2&3 £36.90. CSF £16.33 TOTE £2.50: £1.10, £2.60, £7.90; EX 20.90.
Owner T P Tate **Bred** Hugo Merry And Theo Waddington **Trained** Tadcaster, N Yorks

FOCUS
The winner set the standard, followed home by five newcomers each of whom has the potential to make their mark at a similar level.

NOTEBOOK
Captain Imperial(IRE) made very hard work of it but proved very game and in the end simply would not be denied. Presumably nurseries now beckon. (op 9-4)
Bandanaman(IRE), a medium-sized, likeable newcomer, came through to draw almost level but in the end just missed out. A son of Danehill Dancer from the dam line of Derby winner Dr Devious, he deserves to go one better. (op 10-1)
Denton Diva, a rangy filly, looked to be carrying condition and her inexperience showed beforehand. She was only keeping on in her own time when tightened up by the winner late on but she will improve a fair bit for the outing and the experience. (op 16-1)
Chilly Filly(IRE) ◆, on the leg and narrow, has a middle-distance pedigree. She was hopelessly green but to her credit was sticking on in good style at the end. This will have taught her plenty. (op 5-1 tchd 13-2)
Norwegian Dancer(UAE), who has size and scope, was edgy beforehand. He was lucky not to be taken wide turning in and after throwing down a strong challenge he was found lacking. He looks a stayer in the making. (op 5-1 tchd 6-1)
Island Chief missed a beat at the start and spent the first furlong trying to buck his rider out of the saddle before striking heels. He came from an impossible position and hopefully this initial outing will not be lost on him. Official explanation: jockey said colt bucked for first furlong (tchd 15-2)
Gee Gina Official explanation: jockey said filly hung right throughout

4922 BLACK SHEEP BREWERY H'CAP 5f
7:30 (7:31) (Class 4) (0-85,85) 3-Y-O **£5,569** (£1,657; £828; £413) **Stalls** High

Form RPR
302 **1** **Captain Dunne (IRE)**[17] 4397 3-8-12 **76**.............................. DavidAllan 6 89+
(T D Easterby) *mde all: pushed clr ins fnl f: eased towards fin* **7/2**[2]
2602 **2** *1 3/4* **Grudge**[22] 4216 3-8-2 **66** oh3.............................. FrancisNorton 3 71
(D W Barker) *chsd wnr on outer: t.k.h and hung lft: kpt on fnl 2f: no imp* **10/1**
1130 **3** *4* **Wotashirtfull (IRE)**[10] 4591 3-9-0 **78**..............(p) NCallan 2 69
(K A Ryan) *swvd lft s: sn chsng ldrs: outpcd fnl 2f* **9/2**[3]
5005 **4** *2* **Style Award**[26] 4074 3-8-10 **79**.............................. KellyHarrison(5) 5 62
(W J H Ratcliffe) *chsd ldrs: edgd rt over 2f out: wknd over 1f out* **15/2**
1121 **5** *nse* **Jaconet (USA)**[17] 4397 3-8-6 **70**..............................(b) PaulFessey 4 53
(T D Barron) *chsd ldrs: edgd rt over 2f out: wknd over 1f out* **7/2**[2]
4416 **6** *5* **Supermassive Muse (IRE)**[10] 4595 3-9-1 **79**..............(p) DarryllHolland 7 44
(E S McMahon) *sn outpcd and in rr: nvr a factor* **11/4**[1]
1-26 **7** *4* **Blakeshall Diamond**[9] 4631 3-8-6 **70**.............................. DeanMcKeown 9 21
(K G Wingrove) *in rr: effrt on inner whn hmpd over 2f out: swtchd lft: lost pl over 1f out* **33/1**

60.15 secs (0.55) **Going Correction** +0.175s/f (Good) **7** Ran SP% **113.1**
Speed ratings (Par 102): **102,99,92,89,89 81,75**
toteswinger: 1&2 £8.10, 1&3 £2.80, 2&3 £9.90. CSF £36.08 CT £158.10 TOTE £4.20: £2.70, £3.60; EX 42.80.
Owner Middleham Park Racing Xv **Bred** Ballybrennan Stud Ltd **Trained** Great Habton, N Yorks
■ Stewards' Enquiry : Kelly Harrison two-day ban: careless riding (Aug 26-27)
Paul Fessey one-day ban: careless riding (Aug 25)

FOCUS
The winner grabbed the favoured stands' side rail and dominated throughout, readily seeing off his sole serious challenger. He was value for four lengths. Only the first two showed their form.
Supermassive Muse(IRE) Official explanation: jockey said gelding was never travelling

4923 EBF DORINE ROBINSON MEMORIAL MEDIAN AUCTION MAIDEN STKS 5f
8:00 (8:05) (Class 5) 2-Y-O **£4,274** (£1,271; £635; £317) **Stalls** High

Form RPR
043 **1** **Lucky Numbers (IRE)**[7] 4681 2-9-3 0.............................. PaulMulrennan 11 72
(Paul Green) *hld up: swtchd outside 2f out: r.o to ld towards fin* **11/1**
33 **2** *nk* **Captain Scooby**[29] 3997 2-9-3 0.............................. DeanMcKeown 10 71
(R M Whitaker) *chsd ldrs: led ins fnl f: hdd nr fin* **9/2**[3]
32 **3** *shd* **Count Almaviva (USA)**[122] 1303 2-9-3 0.............................. NCallan 2 71
(K A Ryan) *swvd rt s: sn chsng ldrs: no ex wl ins fnl f* **6/1**
54 **4** *nk* **Chimbonda**[15] 4456 2-9-3 0.............................. TonyCulhane 6 69
(S Parr) *w ldrs: led over 1f out: hdd and no ex ins fnl f* **25/1**
3 **5** *1/2* **Dark Lane**[9] 4647 2-9-3 0.............................. PaulFessey 9 68
(T D Barron) *chsd ldrs: rdn 2f out: kpt on same pce fnl f* **5/2**[1]
33 **6** *3/4* **Noble Storm (USA)**[32] 3882 2-9-3 0.............................. DarryllHolland 8 69+
(E S McMahon) *trckd ldrs: t.k.h: n.m.r over 1f out: kpt on same pce appr fnl f* **11/4**[2]
55 **7** *1* **Soviet Rhythm**[23] 4202 2-8-12 0.............................. AndrewElliott 5 56
(G M Moore) *w ldrs on outer: led over 2f out: hdd over 1f out: wknd ins fnl f* **8/1**
8 *1/2* **Mr Freddy (IRE)** 2-9-0 0.............................. JamieMoriarty(3) 7 60
(R A Fahey) *s.i.s: kpt on fnl 2f: nvr trbld ldrs* **25/1**
00 **9** *2 1/2* **Mousy Mousy (IRE)**[9] 4647 2-8-12 0.............................. DavidAllan 13 46
(T D Easterby) *hld up towards rr: sme hdwy over 2f out: wkng whn n.m.r over 1f out* **28/1**
00 **10** *10* **Future Gem**[12] 4536 2-8-12 0.............................. DaleGibson 12 10
(A Dickman) *led tl hdd and lost pl over 2f out: sn bhd* **100/1**
11 *10* **Houdella** 2-8-12 0.............................. JoeFanning 4 —
(B P J Baugh) *s.s: wl bhd fnl 2f* **50/1**

62.33 secs (2.73) **Going Correction** +0.175s/f (Good) **11** Ran SP% **121.2**
Speed ratings (Par 94): **85,84,84,83,83 81,80,79,75,59 43**
toteswinger: 1&2 £15.40, 1&3 £16.60, 2&3 £6.80. CSF £59.36 TOTE £13.20: £3.20, £1.80, £1.80; EX 54.80.
Owner Men Behaving Badly Two **Bred** Rory O'Brien **Trained** Lydiate, Merseyside
■ Stewards' Enquiry : Paul FesseyR two-day ban: used whip with excessive frequency (Aug 26-27)

FOCUS
A moderate winning time. Modest form with the first half-dozen stacked up at the line.

NOTEBOOK
Lucky Numbers(IRE), who had to be walked riderless to post, settled better. Making his way to the wide outside, he grabbed the prize out of the fire near the line. (op 12-1 tchd 10-1)
Captain Scooby, happy to be back over the minimum trip, worked hard to take a narrow advantage inside the last only to miss out near the line. (op 7-1 tchd 4-1)
Count Almaviva(USA), absent for four months, was inclined to get warm beforehand. In the end he was just found wanting and this opens up the nursery route for him. (op 11-2 tchd 8-1)
Chimbonda, very warm beforehand, took a narrow advantage but missed out in the dash to the line. He too is now qualified for a nursery mark. (op 28-1 tchd 33-1)
Dark Lane, who really took the eye in the paddock, made very hard work of it. Under maximum pressure, he never looked like pulling it off. (tchd 9-4 and 11-4)
Noble Storm(USA) was again far too free and was making no real impression when finding himself short of room. Official explanation: jockey said colt was denied a clear run (tchd 5-2 and 3-1)
Soviet Rhythm showed bags of toe on the wide outside but in the end she did not last out. (tchd 11-1)
Mr Freddy(IRE), a well-made newcomer, showed ability, staying on steadily after a tardy start. (op 20-1 tchd 18-1)

4924 BUCK INN H'CAP 2m
8:30 (8:30) (Class 6) (0-65,65) 4-Y-0+ **£2,978** (£886; £442; £221) **Stalls** Low

Form RPR
1162 **1** **Squirtle (IRE)**[9] 4652 5-8-10 **57**.............................. LukeMorris(3) 11 65+
(W M Brisbourne) *hld up towards rr: gd hdwy over 3f out: led over 2f out: clr 1f out: v comf* **7/2**[1]
0106 **2** *3 3/4* **Sendali (FR)**[37] 3710 4-8-5 **49**.............................. JoeFanning 2 50
(J D Bethell) *hld up in rr: hdwy over 3f out: wnt 2nd 2f out: no ch w wnr* **9/2**[3]
-606 **3** *1* **Lady Killer Queen**[15] 4457 4-8-13 **57**..............................(v) DavidAllan 1 57
(D Carroll) *hld up in rr: hdwy 4f out: kpt on one pce fnl 2f* **8/1**
-216 **4** *hd* **Mister Pete (IRE)**[22] 4220 5-8-5 **52**.............................. DominicFox(3) 3 52
(W Storey) *hld up in mid-div: hdwy 2f out: styd on ins fnl f* **4/1**[2]
6400 **5** *1 1/2* **Ritsi**[9] 4652 5-9-2 **60**.............................. TomEaves 9 58
(Grant Tuer) *dwlt: rn wd bnd after 6f: hdwy to ld and qcknd over 5f out: hdd over 2f out: one pce* **15/2**
0331 **6** *12* **Chiff Chaff**[14] 4490 4-8-5 **49**.............................. LiamJones 12 33
(C R Dore) *trckd ldrs: t.k.h: wnt 2nd over 3f out: wknd 2f out* **6/1**
050S **7** *2* **Ben Bacchus (IRE)**[19] 4295 6-8-2 **46** oh1.............................. ChrisCatlin 7 27
(P W Hiatt) *trckd ldrs: t.k.h: wknd 2f out* **20/1**
5000 **8** *16* **Firestorm (IRE)**[13] 4501 4-8-2 **46** oh1.............................. PaulFessey 15 8
(C W Fairhurst) *rrd s: in rr: drvn 6f out: bhd fnl 4f* **50/1**
06-0 **9** *hd* **Cottam Grange**[48] 3335 8-7-9 **46** oh1.............................. JamieKyne(7) 5 8
(M W Easterby) *t.k.h in midfield: reminders over 6f out: hung rt and lost pl 3f out* **28/1**
-000 **10** *11* **Vice Admiral**[41] 3589 5-8-2 **46** oh1.............................. DaleGibson 10 —
(M W Easterby) *t.k.h: trckd ldrs: drvn 7f out: lost pl over 2f out* **16/1**
0050 **11** *hd* **Ducal Regancy Duke**[7] 4689 4-8-1 **50**.............................. KellyHarrison(5) 14 —
(C J Teague) *t.k.h: led after 3f: hdd over 5f out: lost pl over 2f out* **50/1**

0060 **12** *1 ½* **Compton Commander**[32] 3863 10-8-1 **48** oh1 ow2 AndrewMullen(3) 16 —
(E W Tuer) *t.k.h: set mod pce: led 3f: n.m.r bnd over 8f out: lost pl over 4f out: sn bhd* **25/1**

3m 47.11s (13.71) **Going Correction** +0.65s/f (Yiel) 12 Ran SP% **119.4**
Speed ratings (Par 101): **91,89,88,88,87 81,80,72,72,67 67,66**
toteswinger: 1&2 £4.30, 1&3 £9.40, 2&3 £16.40. CSF £18.20 CT £118.44 TOTE £4.60: £1.50, £2.70, £2.00; EX 23.10 Place 6: £1121.54, Place 5: £461.09..
Owner J Jones Racing Ltd **Bred** Ballygallon Stud Limited **Trained** Great Ness, Shropshire

FOCUS
A very steady gallop for this low-grade stayers' handicap until the final three-quarters of a mile, resulting in a moderate winning time for the grade. The bang in-form winner was value half-a-dozen lengths.
Chiff Chaff Official explanation: jockey said filly ran too free
T/Jkpt: Not won. T/Plt: £423.00 to a £1 stake. Pool: £67,531.30. 116.53 winning tickets. T/Qpdt: £26.50 to a £1 stake. Pool: £5,514.54. 153.90 winning tickets. WG

4904 WINDSOR (R-H)

Monday, August 11

OFFICIAL GOING: Good to soft (soft in places; 6.6)
Wind: Virtually nil

4925 GET ON WITH WILLIAM HILL - 0800 444040 FILLIES' AUCTION NURSERY 6f

5:50 (5:51) (Class 5) 2-Y-O £2,729 (£806; £403) **Stalls** High

Form RPR

23 **1** **Hip Hip Hooray**[39] 3652 2-7-12 **58** oh1 CatherineGannon 6 60
(L A Dace) *in tch: rdn and hung lft oevr 2f out: styd on but edgd lft again 1f out: led fnl 100yds: kpt on wl* **14/1**

513 **2** *¾* **Night Seed (IRE)**[12] 4525 2-9-0 **74** RichardHughes 8 74
(R Hannon) *in tch: hdwy to ld appr fnl f and sn hanging lft: rdn and hdd fnl 100yds: no ex* **9/4**[1]

10 **3** *2 ½* **Foxtrot Alpha (IRE)**[52] 3192 2-9-2 **76** StephenCarson 1 68
(P Winkworth) *chsd ldrs: ev ch and rdn over 1f out: one pce whn hmpd sn after* **11/2**[3]

606 **4** *¾* **Give (IRE)**[31] 3923 2-8-0 **60** DavidKinsella 3 54+
(R Hannon) *in tch: hdwy to chal ins fnl 2f: rdn and one pce whn hmpd 1f out and sn btn* **8/1**

400 **5** *¾* **Cocktail Party (IRE)**[9] 4634 2-7-12 **58** FrankieMcDonald 5 46
(J W Hills) *chsd ldr: rdn over 2f out: wkng whn hmpd 1f out* **8/1**

432 **6** *3 ¼* **Green Poppy**[20] 4279 2-8-11 **71** SebSanders 7 49
(Eve Johnson Houghton) *in tch: rdn over 2f out: wknd over 1f out* **11/2**[3]

342 **7** *1 ¼* **Young Dottie**[19] 4296 2-8-10 **70** JohnEgan 4 44
(P M Phelan) *led tl hdd & wknd appr fnl f* **7/2**[2]

1m 15.51s (2.51) **Going Correction** +0.40s/f (Good) 7 Ran SP% **112.6**
Speed ratings (Par 91): **99,98,94,93,92 88,86**
toteswinger: 1&2 £5.60, 1&3 £17.00, 2&3 £1.90. CSF £44.45 CT £198.93 TOTE £17.30: £5.10, £1.60; EX 26.70.
Owner M C S D Racing Partnership **Bred** Mrs R S Evans **Trained** Five Oaks, W Sussex
■ Stewards' Enquiry : Richard Hughes caution: careless riding

FOCUS
A modest fillies' nursery. The winning time was 0.61 seconds slower than the following maiden. They headed over to the far rail in the straight.

NOTEBOOK
Hip Hip Hooray, claimed out of Ed McMahon's yard after running third in a very good race by selling standards at Yarmouth on quick ground last time, proved suited by these easier conditions and made a winning debut for her new connections on this switch to nursery company. She will find things tougher off higher marks, but her rider, who looked strong in the finish, thinks there may be more to come over 7f. This ended an 18-month drought for her trainer. (op 11-1)
Night Seed(IRE) had the ground in her favour, but she was outstayed by the winner, who was getting 16lb. (tchd 7-4)
Foxtrot Alpha(IRE) didn't beat much when winning on her debut at Lingfield before being outclassed in the Albany Stakes. This was more realistic, but she looks too high in the weights. (op 7-1 tchd 8-1)
Give(IRE) was well held on her nursery debut and is not progressing. Official explanation: jockey said filly suffered interference (op 7-1)
Cocktail Party(IRE) looks pretty limited. Official explanation: jockey said filly was hampered (op 10-1)
Green Poppy was below form on her nursery debut and, being a daughter of Green Desert, she probably wants better ground. (op 5-1)
Young Dottie was well backed dropped a furlong in trip on her nursery debut, but she ran no sort of race. Official explanation: jockey said filly was unsuited by the ground (op 9-2 tchd 5-1 in a place)

4926 GET A BONUS AT WILLIAMHILLCASINO.COM MAIDEN STKS 6f

6:20 (6:21) (Class 4) 2-Y-O £4,209 (£1,252; £625; £312) **Stalls** High

Form RPR

1 **Exceptional Art** 2-9-3 0 SebSanders 2 92+
(P W Chapple-Hyam) *s.i.s: sn in tch: drvn and qcknd to ld over 1f out: forged clr ins fnl f: easily* **7/4**[1]

53 **2** *6* **Auld Arty (FR)**[51] 3274 2-9-3 0 PhilipRobinson 12 73+
(T G Mills) *towards rr: rdn and outpcd over 2f out: drvn and styd on fnl over 1f out: fin wl to go 2nd fnl 100yds but no ch w easy wnr* **11/4**[2]

50 **3** *2 ¼* **Danzadil (IRE)**[12] 4521 2-8-12 0 DaneO'Neill 10 60
(R A Teal) *in tch: rdn and styd on to chse ldrs over 1f out but nvr gng pce to chal and sn one pce* **7/1**

4 *1 ¼* **Bartica (IRE)** 2-9-3 0 RichardHughes 5 62
(R Hannon) *chsd ldrs tl led 2f out: sn pushed along and hdd over 1f out: wknd ins fnl f* **13/2**[3]

00 **5** *¾* **Spring Quartet**[32] 3882 2-9-3 0 ShaneKelly 9 59
(Pat Eddery) *chsd ldrs: rdn over 2f out: wknd fnl f* **40/1**

00 **6** *¾* **Lovely Thought**[18] 4328 2-8-12 0 EddieAhern 11 52
(W J Haggas) *s.i.s: in rr but in tch: hdwy on ins to trck ldrs 2f out: wknd ins fnl f* **12/1**

00 **7** *½* **Yaldas Girl (USA)**[24] 4164 2-8-12 0 JimCrowley 4 51
(J R Best) *led tl hdd 2f out: wknd over 1f out* **33/1**

0 **8** *2 ¼* **Strike Command (USA)**[14] 4480 2-9-3 0 SteveDrowne 1 49
(R Charlton) *chsd ldrs: rdn over 2f out: sn btn* **20/1**

00 **9** *1 ¼* **Brer Rabbit**[28] 4020 2-8-12 0 MichaelHills 7 40
(B W Hills) *chsd ldrs: rdn and btn 2f out* **11/1**

10 *13* **Going Going Gone** 2-9-3 0 RichardKingscote 6 6
(Tom Dascombe) *unruly in stalls: slowly away and sn rdn: a wl bhd* **12/1**

1m 14.9s (1.90) **Going Correction** +0.40s/f (Good) 10 Ran SP% **122.7**
Speed ratings (Par 96): **103,95,92,90,89 88,87,84,83,65**
toteswinger: 1&2 £3.20, 1&3 £1.50, 2&3 £4.40. CSF £6.78 TOTE £3.20: £1.30, £1.40, £2.20; EX 10.00.
Owner Matthew Green **Bred** Mascalls Stud **Trained** Newmarket, Suffolk

FOCUS
This maiden lacked strength in depth, but the winner was impressive. The winning time was 0.61 seconds quicker than the fillies' nursery. They raced far side in the straight.

NOTEBOOK
Exceptional Art, a 40,000gns son of Exceed And Excel, half-brother to among others useful 5f-6f juvenile winner Cape Fear, out of a 7f juvenile winner, is entered in the Champagne Stakes, the Mill Reef and the Royal Lodge. A well-backed favourite, he recovered from a slow start to keep tabs on the leaders and drew clear when asked to lengthen in the straight. He deserves to be stepped up in class now. (op 9-4 tchd 5-2 in places)
Auld Arty(FR) ran a solid race dropped a furlong in trip, but the winner looks above average. He will have more options now he has qualified for a handicap mark. (op 4-1)
Danzadil(IRE) seemed to handle the easy ground and this was her best effort yet. She is now qualified for a handicap mark. (op 11-1 tchd 13-2)
Bartica(IRE), a 35,000gns son of Tagula, out of a 7f winner, showed ability on his racecourse debut and should improve. (op 11-2 tchd 15-2)
Spring Quartet ran a little better with blinkers left off this time.

4927 GET YOUR CHIPS AT WILLIAMHILLPOKER.COM H'CAP 1m 67y

6:50 (6:50) (Class 4) (0-85,85) 3-Y-O+ £5,375 (£1,599; £799; £399) **Stalls** High

Form RPR

0521 **1** **Red Somerset (USA)**[17] 4364 5-9-9 **85** MCGeran(5) 5 93
(R J Hodges) *chsd ldrs tl rdn and outpcd over 2f out: styd on again u.p fr over 1f out: fin wl to ld fnl 50yds* **8/1**

0321 **2** *1* **Rum Jungle**[10] 4602 4-9-5 **76** DaneO'Neill 7 82+
(H Candy) *sn led: rdn and styd on gamely whn strly chal fr 3f out: stl narrow ld ins fnl f: hdd and no ex fnl 50yds* **9/4**[1]

0412 **3** *nse* **Moonlight Man**[5] 4723 7-9-6 **77** (t) SebSanders 6 83
(C R Dore) *chsd ldrs tl rdn and outpcd over 2f out: styd on again u.p over 1f out: kpt on ins fnl f: gng on cl home* **10/1**

0620 **4** *½* **Meydan Dubai (IRE)**[5] 4731 3-9-6 **84** (v) JimCrowley 9 88
(J R Best) *t.k.h early: chsd ldrs: chal over 2f out tl ins fnl f: no ex nr fin* **11/2**[3]

4512 **5** *1 ½* **Brave Hawk**[42] 3560 3-9-0 **78** (p) PhilipRobinson 1 78
(M A Jarvis) *chsd ldr and chal fr 3f out: stl upsides u.p ins fnl f: wknd fnl 50yds* **7/2**[2]

0500 **6** *2 ½* **Full Victory (IRE)**[5] 4723 6-9-3 **74** SteveDrowne 3 70
(R A Farrant) *in tch: rdn and sme prog 2f out: nvr gng pce to be competitive and wknd fnl f* **14/1**

202 **7** *½* **Lordship (IRE)**[31] 3903 4-8-9 **66** RichardHughes 4 61
(A W Carroll) *t.k.h in rr early: rdn and sme prog over 2f out: nvr in contention and sn wknd* **7/1**

0060 **8** *4* **Trafalgar Square**[52] 3197 6-9-6 **80** (p) KirstyMilczarek(3) 8 65
(M J Attwater) *in rr but in tch: sme prog u.p fr 3f out: nvr rchd ldrs and wknd sn after* **11/1**

0-00 **9** *3 ¾* **St Petersburg**[32] 3887 8-9-7 **78** AmirQuinn 10 55
(J R Boyle) *t.k.h early: a towards rr* **33/1**

1m 47.66s (2.96) **Going Correction** +0.50s/f (Yiel)
WFA 3 from 4yo+ 7lb 9 Ran SP% **119.0**
Speed ratings (Par 105): **105,104,103,103,101 99,98,94,91**
toteswinger: 1&2 £4.90, 1&3 £13.70, 2&3 £3.70. CSF £27.23 CT £188.94 TOTE £7.60: £2.20, £1.60, £2.50; EX 20.20.
Owner R J Hodges **Bred** Haras D'Etreham **Trained** Charlton Mackrell, Somerset
■ Stewards' Enquiry : M C Geran caution: used whip down shoulder in forehand position

FOCUS
A fair handicap, but they went steady for much of the way. They raced far side in the straight. The form is rated through the second and fourth.

4928 DUNNHUMBY ESSENTIAL CUSTOMER GENIUS H'CAP 6f

7:20 (7:20) (Class 3) (0-95,92) 3-Y-O+ £8,418 (£2,505; £1,251; £625) **Stalls** High

Form RPR

1462 **1** **Mullein**[10] 4595 3-8-6 **77** JamesDoyle 6 92
(R M Beckett) *hld up towards rr: hdwy 2f out: styd on wl to ld fnl 100yds: sn in command: readily* **7/1**

1354 **2** *2* **Osiris Way**[10] 4586 6-9-5 **86** JimCrowley 5 96
(P R Chamings) *chsd ldrs: rdn to ld appr fnl f: hdd and outpcd fnl 100yds* **5/1**[2]

1501 **3** *1 ¼* **Diriculous**[27] 4058 4-9-7 **88** JimmyFortune 11 94
(T G Mills) *towards rr: rdn and gd hdwy fr 2f out: styd on fnl f but nvr gng pce to trble ldng duo* **7/1**

1210 **4** *nse* **Kelamon**[14] 4478 4-7-13 **73** BillyCray(7) 10 79
(M D I Usher) *towards rr 1/2-way: rdn over 2f out: styd on wl fnl f but nvr gng pce to rch ldrs* **9/2**[1]

4315 **5** *1* **Idle Power (IRE)**[65] 2831 10-9-3 **84** AmirQuinn 3 87
(J R Boyle) *led: rdn over 2f out: hdd over 1f out: wknd ins fnl f* **10/1**

2433 **6** *1 ¼* **Orpenindeed (IRE)**[39] 3647 5-9-10 **91** (t) JohnEgan 1 92
(M Botti) *chsd ldrs rdn over 2f out: wknd ins fnl f and no ch whn n.m.r nr fin* **6/1**[3]

3146 **7** *nse* **Efistorm**[10] 4601 7-9-6 **87** PhilipRobinson 2 85
(C R Dore) *chsd ldrs: rdn over 2f out: wknd fnl f* **8/1**

0160 **8** *3* **Imperial Echo (USA)**[80] 2358 7-8-6 **73** JimmyQuinn 8 62
(P Howling) *rrd in stall: a towards rr* **16/1**

6000 **9** *½* **Dig Deep (IRE)**[15] 4445 6-8-12 **79** GrahamGibbons 9 66
(J J Quinn) *chsd ldrs 4f* **12/1**

00-0 **10** *hd* **El Bosque (IRE)**[121] 1334 4-9-8 **92** JamesMillman(3) 7 79
(B R Millman) *pressed ldr over 3f: sn wknd* **20/1**

0-16 **11** *3 ¾* **Little Edward**[39] 3647 10-9-11 **92** SteveDrowne 4 67
(R J Hodges) *chsd ldrs 1/2-way* **20/1**

1m 14.27s (1.27) **Going Correction** +0.40s/f (Good)
WFA 3 from 4yo+ 4lb 11 Ran SP% **117.4**
Speed ratings (Par 107): **107,104,102,102,101 99,99,95,94,94 89**
toteswinger: 1&2 £11.50, 1&3 £10.00, 2&3 £3.70. CSF £41.87 CT £257.28 TOTE £7.70: £2.70, £2.00, £2.70; EX 43.10.
Owner Landmark Racing Limited **Bred** C D S Bryce And Mrs M Bryce **Trained** Whitsbury, Hants

FOCUS
A decent sprint handicap for the grade. They again went far side in the straight. The first two are progressive with the winner rated up another 8lb.

NOTEBOOK
Mullein ◆ defied a 3lb rise in the weights for her recent close second at Haydock and produced a career best, taking this with something to spare. She can progress into a very useful filly when getting these sorts of conditions. (op 8-1 tchd 13-2)

Osiris Way handles easy ground and he continued his good run of form with a creditable second behind the improved winner. (op 9-2)
Diriculous promised to be suited by the ground, being a son of Diktat, but he was given a lot to do and also made his move more towards the middle of the track than most of these. (op 6-1 tchd 11-2)
Kelamon is a course specialist and he had the ground to suit, but he found the company a bit hot. (op 7-1)
Idle Power(IRE) did not seem to have many excuses. Official explanation: jockey said gelding had no more to give (op 11-1)
Orpenindeed(IRE) Official explanation: jockey said gelding was unsuited by the ground
Imperial Echo(USA) Official explanation: jockey said gelding missed the break

4929 TRINIDAD CARNIVAL MAIDEN STKS 1m 67y
7:50 (7:51) (Class 5) 3-Y-0+ **£2,729** (£806; £403) **Stalls** High

Form RPR
1 **Acclaimed (IRE)** 3-9-3 0 ShaneKelly 4 88+
(J Noseda) *trckd ldrs in 3rd: pushed along to ld appr fnl 2f: sn clr: comf* **9/2**[2]
2 **2** *7* **French Art**[39] 3628 3-9-3 84 SebSanders 13 71
(D R C Elsworth) *chsd ldr: led ins fnl 3f: hdd appr fnl 2f: sn no ch w wnr but styd on for clr 2nd* **2/5**[1]
0 **3** *3* **Mister Ross**[18] 4349 3-9-3 0 RichardHughes 8 64+
(G L Moore) *led tl hdd ins fnl 3f: styd to r alone stands' side and kpt on same pce fnl 2f* **33/1**
-6 **4** *1* **Apotheosis**[23] 4194 3-9-3 0 AdamKirby 6 62
(W R Swinburn) *in rr: rdn 3f out: styd on fnl 2f but nvr anywhere nr ldrs* **6/1**[3]
5 *shd* **Superior Duchess** 3-8-12 0 FrankieMcDonald 9 57
(Jane Chapple-Hyam) *s.i.s: in rr: hdwy 4f out: styd on same pce fnl 2f* **40/1**
0 **6** *2* **Black Coffee**[24] 4161 3-9-3 0 StephenDonohoe 2 57
(W J Musson) *in rr tl shkn up over 2f out: styd on wl fnl f but nvr remotely in contention* **12/1**
33 **7** *¾* **Saintly Gaze**[46] 3419 3-9-3 0 SaleemGolam 3 56
(W R Swinburn) *a towards rr* **16/1**
0 **8** *½* **Mayfair's Future**[5] 4730 3-9-3 0 PatDobbs 10 55
(J R Jenkins) *chsd ldrs: rdn 3f out: sn btn* **66/1**
0-0 **9** *5* **Aston Boy**[21] 4249 3-9-3 0 SteveDrowne 5 43
(M Blanshard) *a towards rr* **66/1**
10 *1 ½* **James Pollard (IRE)** 3-9-3 0 TQuinn 7 40
(D R C Elsworth) *s.i.s: a towards rr* **20/1**
00-0 **11** *26* **Ryan's Rock**[21] 4249 3-9-3 45 PatCosgrave 1 —
(T D McCarthy) *in tch 5f: wknd qckly* **100/1**

1m 47.69s (2.99) **Going Correction** +0.50s/f (Yiel)
WFA 3 from 4yo 7lb **11** Ran SP% **131.6**
Speed ratings (Par 103): **105,98,95,94,93 91,91,90,85,84 58**
toteswinger: 1&2 £1.70, 1&3 not won, 2&3 £9.00. CSF £7.32 TOTE £7.20: £1.50, £1.10, £7.00; EX 10.00.
Owner Cheveley Park Stud **Bred** Lodge Park Stud **Trained** Newmarket, Suffolk

FOCUS
A weakish and uncompetitive maiden, with only three ever getting involved. The winning time was only 0.03 seconds slower than the earlier 66-85 handicap won by the 85-rated Red Somerset. The majority of these raced down the middle of the track in the straight, but the third home raced against the stands' rail. The winner looks a useful prospect but there are doubts over what he actually achieved.
Mister Ross ◆ Official explanation: jockey said gelding hung right
Apotheosis Official explanation: jockey said colt ran too free

4930 FLY BMI TO INTIMATE HOTELS BARBADOS H'CAP 1m 3f 135y
8:20 (8:21) (Class 5) (0-70,70) 3-Y-0+ **£2,729** (£806; £403) **Stalls** Centre

Form RPR
00 **1** **Right Stuff (FR)**[25] 4131 5-9-9 **65** RichardHughes 6 78
(G L Moore) *hld up in rr: stdy hdwy over 3f out: chsd ldr over 1f out: drvn to ld fnl 75yds: hld on wl* **16/1**
4430 **2** *shd* **Celticello (IRE)**[32] 3884 6-9-9 **70** RichardEvans(5) 10 83
(P D Evans) *hld up in tch: smooth hdwy to ld 2f out: rdn over 1f out hdd fnl 75yds: rallied but a jst hld* **4/1**[2]
2056 **3** *7* **Bold Adventure**[27] 4046 4-9-9 **65** StephenDonohoe 7 66
(W J Musson) *in rr: rdn 3f out: styd on u.p fnl 2f to take wl-hld 3rd last strides* **8/1**
2532 **4** *hd* **Mixing**[18] 4343 6-8-11 **56** KirstyMilczarek(3) 8 57
(M J Attwater) *chsd ldrs: hrd rdn over 2f out: styd on same pce sn after* **8/1**
5242 **5** *2* **Compton Charlie**[20] 4275 4-9-2 **58** PatCosgrave 9 55
(J G Portman) *in tch: hrd to chse ldrs over 2f out: no imp and wknd fnl f* **11/4**[1]
0000 **6** *1 ½* **Robbmaa (FR)**[29] 3604 3-7-7 **51** DavidProbert(5) 2 46
(A W Carroll) *in tch: hdwy 3f out: chal over 2f out: wknd over 1f out* **50/1**
-200 **7** *nk* **National Day (IRE)**[18] 4342 4-9-1 **60** MarcHalford(3) 5 54
(D R C Elsworth) *chsd ldrs: rdn over 3f out: wknd 2f out* **20/1**
44 **8** *1 ¼* **Street Life (IRE)**[70] 2682 10-9-2 **58** NeilPollard 4 50
(W J Musson) *chsd ldrs: wnt 2nd 3f out: sn rdn: wknd 2f out* **9/1**
3-05 **9** *5* **Princess India (IRE)**[23] 4183 3-9-2 **69** JimCrowley 3 53
(P Winkworth) *w ldr tl led 5f out: rdn 3f out: hdd & wknd 2f out* **8/1**
0450 **10** *16* **Moon Mix (FR)**[31] 3925 5-9-11 **67** PatDobbs 12 23
(J R Jenkins) *bhd fnl 4f* **25/1**
243- **11** *3 ½* **War Anthem**[326] 5568 4-9-12 **68** AmirQuinn 11 18
(J R Boyle) *slt ld tl hdd narrowly 5f out: wknd qckly 3f out* **6/1**[3]

2m 35.32s (5.82) **Going Correction** +0.50s/f (Yiel)
WFA 3 from 4yo+ 11lb **11** Ran SP% **120.7**
Speed ratings (Par 103): **100,99,95,95,93 92,92,91,88,77 75**
toteswinger: 1&2 £14.40, 1&3 £21.00, 2&3 £11.00. CSF £79.75 CT £570.36 TOTE £17.40: £4.30, £1.90, £3.30; EX 110.40 Place 6: £58.91, Place 5: £22.52..
Owner The Ashden Partnership & Partners **Bred** N P Bloodstock Ltd **Trained** Woodingdean, E Sussex

FOCUS
A modest handicap in which the first two pulled well clear. They raced up the middle of the track. The winner is rated in line with last year's French form, with the runner-up showing his best form since he was a 3-y-o.
T/Plt: £28.00 to a £1 stake. Pool: £80,061.28. 2,087.01 winning tickets. T/Qpdt: £15.10 to a £1 stake. Pool: £6,151.00. 300.88 winning tickets. ST

4386 WOLVERHAMPTON (A.W) (L-H)
Monday, August 11

OFFICIAL GOING: Standard
Race times suggest that the Polytrack surface was riding very slow.
Wind: Moderate half behind Weather: Cloudy

4931 EUROPEAN BREEDERS' FUND MEDIAN AUCTION MAIDEN STKS 5f 216y(P)
2:30 (2:32) (Class 5) 2-Y-0 **£3,885** (£1,156; £577; £288) **Stalls** Low

Form RPR
455 **1** **Elegant Cad (CAN)**[36] 3774 2-9-3 0 SebSanders 3 77+
(J R Best) *w ldr: led over 3f out: rdn wl over 1f out: hdd wl ins fnl f: led last stride* **4/11**[1]
5 **2** *hd* **Layer Cake**[17] 4360 2-9-3 0 EddieAhern 1 76+
(J W Hills) *s.i.s: sn hld up in tch: rdn to chal on ins over 1f out: led wl ins fnl f: hdd last stride* **10/1**[3]
64 **3** *6* **Weet In Nerja**[14] 4474 2-9-3 0 HayleyTurner 4 58
(R Hollinshead) *led: hdd over 3f out: w ldr tl pushed along wl over 1f out: sn rdn and edgd lft: wknd ins fnl f* **25/1**
03 **4** *1 ½* **Superstitious Me (IRE)**[12] 4534 2-8-12 0 CatherineGannon 2 49
(B Palling) *s.i.s: t.k.h: sn in tch: pushed along over 2f out: rdn and wknd over 1f out* **40/1**
4 **5** *1 ¼* **Chatterszaha**[16] 4425 2-8-12 0 RobertHavlin 5 45+
(C Drew) *w ldrs to 2f out: wkng whn hung lft over 1f out* **25/1**
260 **6** *2* **Skid Solo (IRE)**[53] 3152 2-9-3 84 AlanMunro 7 44
(P W Chapple-Hyam) *hld up in tch: lost pl 3f out: bhd fnl 2f* **11/4**[2]
00 **7** *19* **Liliaceae**[15] 4456 2-8-12 0 TGMcLaughlin 6 —
(D Shaw) *s.i.s: a last: rdn and lost tch wl over 1f out* **100/1**

1m 18.95s (3.95) **Going Correction** +0.40s/f (Slow) **7** Ran SP% **120.2**
Speed ratings (Par 94): **89,88,80,78,77 74,49**
toteswinger: 1&2 £1.70, 1&3 £2.50, 2&3 £4.50. CSF £5.90 TOTE £1.50: £1.10, £2.80; EX 3.90.
Owner D Gorton **Bred** Ron Clarkson **Trained** Hucking, Kent

FOCUS
An uncompetitive maiden with a long odds-on favourite and the market going 10-1 bar two. There was nearly a major shock and the modest time suggests the form is ordinary.

NOTEBOOK
Elegant Cad(CAN), who has been plying his trade in Group company in his last two outings and not been disgraced in either, looked to face a straightforward task in this company despite the extra furlong and different surface. However, after having been ridden up with the pace throughout he had a real fight to hold off the runner-up and a few strides from the line it looked as though he would be beaten, but he forced his head back in front where it mattered. This was a bit disappointing and he will need to improve plenty on this if he is pitched back into Pattern company, but he shapes as though he will appreciate stepping up in trip again. (op 4-9)
Layer Cake appreciated dropping back a furlong from his debut and put in a spirited run up the inside rail to give the red-hot favourite a real fright. Whether the winner was at his best is debatable and the modest time puts a question mark against the form, but given how far he pulled clear of the rest he should be up to winning an ordinary maiden. (op 6-1 tchd 11-1)
Weet In Nerja showed up for a fair way, but he only possessed modest sand form coming into this and probably did not improve on that. Modest nurseries or a drop in class look required now. (tchd 28-1)
Superstitious Me(IRE), a remote third at Leicester last time, never figured on this switch to sand but is another that should now get a modest nursery mark. (op 25-1)
Chatterszaha did not look happy on this surface and hung badly in the home straight though she was already beaten at the time. This effort rather reinforces the view that the Newmarket maiden she finished fourth in on her debut was moderate.
Skid Solo(IRE), over five lengths behind Elegant Cad in the Norfolk, was nonetheless well backed against him here but he was one of the first beaten. He looks to be going the wrong way. (op 9-2 tchd 11-2)

4932 CLEANEVENT (S) STKS 1m 4f 50y(P)
3:00 (3:01) (Class 6) 3-Y-0+ **£1,978** (£584; £292) **Stalls** Low

Form RPR
053- **1** **Saameq (IRE)**[332] 5389 7-9-7 50 RoystonFfrench 12 61+
(D W Thompson) *t.k.h towards rr: smooth prog on outside 3f out: led on bit over 2f out: clr whn rdn over 1f out: eased cl home* **9/2**[2]
3510 **2** *4 ½* **York Cliff**[10] 4592 10-9-12 54 EddieAhern 8 58
(W M Brisbourne) *hld up in mid-div: hdwy over 3f out: nt clr run ent st: rdn over 1f out: wnt 2nd ins fnl f: no ch w wnr* **5/1**[3]
3 *½* **Allez Frank (GER)**[53] 7-9-12 0 FergusSweeney 9 57
(Mrs L J Young) *prom: pushed along and outpcd over 3f out: rdn over 2f out: rallied to chse wnr over 1f out tl ins fnl f: one pce* **8/1**
54/0 **4** *12* **Adalar (IRE)**[5] 4748 8-9-7 0 (t) VinceSlattery 2 33
(B N Pollock) *chsd ldr: rdn over 3f out: wknd over 2f out* **40/1**
1150 **5** *hd* **Black Falcon (IRE)**[14] 4477 8-9-12 64 SebSanders 6 38
(John A Harris) *a.p: wnt 2nd briefly wl over 1f out: wknd fnl f* **11/2**
-005 **6** *25* **Mighty Kitchener (USA)**[14] 4490 5-9-7 43 JimmyQuinn 1 —
(P Howling) *led: rdn and hdd over 2f out: wknd wl over 1f out: eased fnl f* **13/2**
60 **7** *6* **Musango**[20] 4275 5-9-7 53 (tp) PaulDoe 4 —
(Tim Vaughan) *hld up in mid-div: stdy hdwy 6f out: rdn over 2f out: sn wknd: eased whn no ch over 1f out* **5/2**[1]
0006 **8** *3 ¼* **Lady Lorins**[23] 4181 4-9-2 41 AlanDaly 7 —
(Andrew Turnell) *hld up in mid-div: pushed along 7f out: rdn over 5f out: struggling 4f out* **20/1**
0460 **9** *97* **Weet For Ever (USA)**[13] 4503 5-9-7 43 TGMcLaughlin 5 —
(W M Brisbourne) *t.k.h towards rr: rdn 4f out: sn struggling: t.o 2f out: virtually p.u* **18/1**
4500 **10** *18* **Mi Odds**[185] 481 12-9-2 39 KellyHarrison(5) 3 —
(Mrs N Macauley) *hld up in mid-div: pushed along 7f out: sn struggling: t.o fnl 5f: virtually p.u* **40/1**

2m 49.09s (7.99) **Going Correction** +0.40s/f (Slow)
WFA 3 from 4yo+ 11lb **10** Ran SP% **118.2**
Speed ratings (Par 101): **89,86,85,77,77 60,56,54,—,—**
toteswinger: 1&2 £5.00, 1&3 £3.90, 2&3 £7.10. CSF £27.19 TOTE £6.10: £1.90, £2.10, £2.40; EX 29.80 Trifecta £178.60 Pool: £424.93. 1.76 winning units..There was no bid for the winner. Allez Frank was claimed by T Exall for £6,000.
Owner Mrs L Irving **Bred** Shadwell Estate Company Limited **Trained** Bolam, Co Durham

FOCUS
A moderate seller, full of the usual suspects, and they went no pace early resulting in a very slow winning time. Despite that, the field finished spread out over Dunstall Park and there was only one horse in it from the home turn. The form is rated through the second, with the third in line with his jumps form.

Musango Official explanation: jockey said gelding had a breathing problem

4933 CLEAN WASTE SOLUTIONS NURSERY — 7f 32y(P)

3:30 (3:30) (Class 5) 2-Y-O — £3,238 (£963; £481; £240) Stalls High

Form — RPR

01 **1** **Rocket Rob (IRE)**[39] 3652 2-8-3 62 .... TPO'Shea 3 — 62
(S A Callaghan) *sltly bmpd s: t.k.h: prom: wnt 2nd over 4f out: rdn to ld over 1f out: jst hld on* **3/1[2]**

0006 **2** *nse* **Josiah Bartlett (IRE)**[33] 3846 2-8-1 60 .... LiamJones 4 — 61+
(J W Hills) *hld up and bhd: rdn and hdwy wl over 1f out: r.o towards fin: jst failed* **7/1**

0001 **3** *hd* **Nun Today (USA)**[17] 4387 2-7-13 61 ....(b) LukeMorris(3) 6 — 60
(J S Moore) *hld up in tch: rdn over 2f out: edgd lft u.str.p fr over 1f out: r.o towards fin* **11/2**

601 **4** *3* **Haven't A Clue**[17] 4389 2-9-12 85 ....(b) SebSanders 5 — 77
(Sir Mark Prescott) *led: rdn and hdd over 1f out: fdd towards fin* **2/1[1]**

0050 **5** *1 ¾* **Forster Island**[18] 4340 2-7-13 58 oh2 ow1 ....(b[1]) JimmyQuinn 2 — 46
(M Blanshard) *hmpd s: hld up in rr: rdn wl over 1f out: nvr trbld ldrs* **16/1**

466 **6** *8* **Mr Clearview**[58] 3019 2-7-12 57 oh2 .... AdrianMcCarthy 7 — 25
(B R Millman) *s.i.s: hld up and bhd: rdn over 3f out: struggling over 2f out* **22/1**

403 **7** *1 ¾* **Temperence Hall (USA)**[21] 4256 2-9-0 73 .... HayleyTurner 1 — 37
(J R Best) *wnt rt s: t.k.h: chsd ldr tl over 4f out: wknd over 2f out* **4/1[3]**

1m 33.34s (3.74) **Going Correction** +0.40s/f (Slow) — **7 Ran SP% 116.4**
Speed ratings (Par 94): **94,93,93,90,88 79,77**
toteswinger: 1&2 £4.70, 1&3 £3.40, 2&3 £6.30. CSF £24.79 TOTE £4.50: £2.20, £3.80; EX 28.80.
Owner Bill Hinge, J Searchfield & N Callaghan **Bred** Mrs Marita Rogers **Trained** Newmarket, Suffolk

■ Stewards' Enquiry : Luke Morris one-day ban: careless riding (Aug 25)

FOCUS
An ordinary nursery, but a cracking finish with little to separate the front three at the line.

NOTEBOOK
Rocket Rob(IRE), taking another step up in trip, was always up there and after taking over from the favourite he battled on really well to hold off his two main challengers. He is entitled to improve again and a least he has already started to pay back some of the 16,000gns it cost connections to retain him after winning a Yarmouth seller last time. (op 9-4)
Josiah Bartlett(IRE), unplaced in his four previous starts, appreciated the step up in trip and his strong challenge down the home straight only just failed. He should be able to win a race like this. (op 9-1 tchd 13-2)
Nun Today(USA), successful in first-time blinkers in a course-and-distance seller last time, looked as though she was going to pick up the front pair down the home straight despite racing wide around the home bend, but she rather ducked and dived rather than concentrating on going forward and was never quite doing enough. This looked an opportunity missed as her chance was there had she been inclined to take it. (op 13-2)
Haven't A Clue, successful in first-time blinkers over 6f here last time, was nonetheless ridden positively but as soon as the winner put pressure on her turning in she was in trouble. Her stamina for the trip remains unproven. (op 5-2)
Forster Island, blinkered for the first time and effectively 3lb wrong with the 1lb overweight, never figured but he was badly hampered by Temperence Hall after leaving the stalls which knocked him back to last, so it may be worth giving him another chance. (op 14-1)
Temperence Hall(USA), making his nursery debut, swerved violently away to his right leaving the stalls and then took a fierce hold, but it was not long before he was off the bridle and he found nothing. He has a few questions to answer now. (op 9-2 tchd 7-2)

4934 STAY AT THE WOLVERHAMPTON HOLIDAY INN H'CAP — 7f 32y(P)

4:00 (4:02) (Class 5) (0-70,70) 3-Y-O+ — £2,729 (£806; £403) Stalls High

Form — RPR

0110 **1** **Wisdom's Kiss**[41] 3591 4-9-10 68 ....(b) JimmyQuinn 4 — 84
(J D Bethell) *s.i.s: hld up and bhd: hdwy over 2f out: rdn to ld wl ins fnl f: r.o* **6/1[3]**

3025 **2** *¾* **A Big Sky Brewing (USA)**[10] 4605 4-8-13 60 ....(b) NeilBrown(3) 3 — 74
(T D Barron) *led: rdn 2f out: hdd and no ex wl ins fnl f* **5/1[2]**

4104 **3** *6* **Dancing Deano (IRE)**[17] 4386 6-9-7 65 .... FergusSweeney 6 — 63
(R Hollinshead) *hld up and bhd: hdwy whn hung rt bnd over 2f out: rdn over 1f out: kpt on to take 3rd cl home: no ch w ldng pair* **16/1**

4615 **4** *hd* **Royal Challenge**[18] 4327 7-9-2 65 .... GaryBartley(5) 8 — 62
(I W McInnes) *hld up and bhd: hdwy wl over 1f out: kpt on same pce u.p fnl f* **8/1**

0540 **5** *¾* **Golden Prospect**[4] 4789 4-9-5 66 ....(p) PatrickHills(3) 10 — 61
(J W Hills) *hld up in rr: rdn and kpt on fr over 1f out: n.d* **13/2**

1220 **6** *2* **It's A Dream (FR)**[22] 4219 5-9-10 68 ....(t) GrahamGibbons 2 — 58
(M W Easterby) *a.p: chsd ldr over 2f out: sn rdn: wknd fnl f* **3/1[1]**

35-5 **7** *hd* **Ochre Bay**[28] 4030 5-9-10 68 ....(p) StephenDonohoe 7 — 57
(R Hollinshead) *hld up in mid-div: hdwy over 3f out: rdn over 2f out: wknd over 1f out* **9/1**

500- **8** *7* **Dowlleh**[239] 7164 4-9-4 65 .... KirstyMilczarek(3) 12 — 36
(T T Clement) *hld up in rr: rdn and wknd over 3f out* **40/1**

4-30 **9** *2* **Mafasina (USA)**[28] 4016 3-9-6 70 .... RoystonFfrench 5 — 35
(B Smart) *prom tl rdn and wknd over 3f out* **16/1**

5230 **10** *½* **All You Need (IRE)**[25] 4125 4-9-2 60 .... HayleyTurner 1 — 24
(R Hollinshead) *s.i.s: hld up towards rr: hdwy on ins over 3f out: wknd wl over 1f out* **13/2**

0002 **11** *4 ½* **Adantino**[19] 4306 9-9-6 67 ....(b) JamesMillman(3) 11 — 19
(B R Millman) *hld up: sn impr into mid-div: lost pl over 3f out: in rr whn swtchd lft wl over 1f out* **11/1**

100 **12** *6* **Sion Hill (IRE)**[47] 3371 7-8-13 62 ....(p) KellyHarrison(5) 9 — —
(John A Harris) *sn chsng ldr: rdn and wknd over 2f out* **20/1**

1m 31.52s (1.92) **Going Correction** +0.40s/f (Slow)
WFA 3 from 4yo+ 6lb — **12 Ran SP% 131.0**
Speed ratings (Par 103): **105,104,97,97,96 93,93,85,83,82 77,70**
toteswinger: 1&2 £7.70, 1&3 £12.60, 2&3 £17.90. CSF £40.22 CT £484.77 TOTE £8.90: £2.40, £1.60, £5.30; EX 35.00 Trifecta £241.90 Part won. Pool: £620.50 - 0.39 winning units..
Owner Hornblower Racing **Bred** Snowdrop Stud Co Ltd **Trained** Middleham Moor, N Yorks

FOCUS
A fair handicap and the runner-up made sure it was run at a true pace. The front pair pulled well clear, very few ever got into it, and the form looks solid, rated through the third.

4935 CLEAN CONCIERGE H'CAP — 2m 119y(P)

4:30 (4:30) (Class 6) (0-65,64) 4-Y-O+ — £2,388 (£705; £352) Stalls Low

Form — RPR

31-0 **1** **Master At Arms**[40] 3606 5-9-2 62 .... JerryO'Dwyer(3) 12 — 79+
(Daniel Mark Loughnane, Ire) *stdd s: hld up in rr: gd hdwy on outside over 2f out: led wl over 1f out: styd on wl* **12/1**

4011 **2** *6* **Swords**[14] 4477 6-8-9 57 .... AshleyHamblett(5) 6 — 67+
(R E Peacock) *hld up towards rr: hdwy 3f out: rdn and edgd lft whn wnt 2nd 1f out: no imp* **3/1[1]**

5-12 **3** *3 ¾* **That Look**[14] 4490 5-8-6 56 .... RosieJessop(7) 11 — 61
(D E Cantillon) *chsd ldr tl over 6f out: outpcd over 3f out: swtchd rt over 1f out: styd on same pce u.p fnl f* **10/3[2]**

5253 **4** *1 ¾* **Merrymaker**[30] 3950 8-9-7 64 .... TGMcLaughlin 7 — 67
(W M Brisbourne) *s.i.s: hld up in rr: hdwy on outside over 4f out: rdn 3f out: wknd ins fnl f* **7/1**

2443 **4** *dht* **Best Selection**[18] 4343 4-9-3 60 .... IanMongan 4 — 63
(Mrs L J Mongan) *hld up and bhd: hdwy over 4f out: rdn wl over 1f out: wknd ins fnl f* **12/1**

6504 **6** *2 ¼* **Synonymy**[4] 4775 5-8-13 56 ....(b) JamesDoyle 8 — 57
(M Blanshard) *prom: wnt 2nd over 6f out: led over 4f out: rdn and hdd wl over 1f out: wknd fnl f* **4/1[3]**

35-0 **7** *¾* **Teorban (POL)**[71] 2643 9-8-12 55 .... StephenDonohoe 2 — 55
(Mrs N S Evans) *hld up towards rr: rdn and short-lived effrt on ins over 2f out* **33/1**

0-50 **8** *19* **Historic Place (USA)**[17] 4391 8-8-13 56 ....(p) RobertHavlin 10 — 33
(J A Geake) *hld up in mid-div: rdn and hdwy whn n.m.r wl over 3f out: sn wknd* **40/1**

9 *8* **Axinit (GER)**[183] 3886 8-9-6 63 ....(p) EdwardCreighton 3 — 30
(E J Creighton) *led: hdd over 4f out: wknd over 3f out* **25/1**

6044 **10** *5* **Archimboldo (USA)**[19] 3697 5-8-13 56 ....(b) AlanMunro 9 — 17
(T Wall) *s.i.s: hld up in mid-div: struggling over 3f out* **25/1**

3100 **11** *2 ½* **Arabian Sun**[25] 4105 4-8-8 54 ....(v) TolleyDean(3) 13 — 12
(M J Attwater) *hld up in tch: rdn 6f out: sn lost pl* **16/1**

00/1 **12** *78* **Mad Professor (IRE)**[17] 4365 5-9-4 61 ....(p) FergusSweeney 1 — —
(Tim Vaughan) *hld up in mid-div: rdn over 5f out: sn struggling: t.o* **9/1**

3m 47.66s (5.86) **Going Correction** +0.40s/f (Slow) — **12 Ran SP% 124.9**
Speed ratings (Par 101): **102,99,97,96,96 95,95,86,82,80 78,42**
toteswinger: 1&2 £10.50, 1&3 £11.00, 2&3 £3.20. CSF £49.03 CT £156.03 TOTE £22.00: £4.30, £1.60, £1.90; EX 76.80 TRIFECTA Not won..
Owner F Purcell **Bred** Fittocks Stud **Trained** Trim, Co Meath

FOCUS
A moderate handicap, but the pace was solid enough and this was a true test of stamina. The winner proved different class to the others and is rated up 8lb, with the runner-up to his recent form.

4936 CLEAN VU APPRENTICE H'CAP — 1m 1f 103y(P)

5:00 (5:01) (Class 6) (0-60,59) 4-Y-O+ — £2,388 (£705; £352) Stalls Low

Form — RPR

0306 **1** **Desert Hawk**[37] 3732 7-8-1 46 ....(b) MatthewLawson(5) 5 — 58
(W M Brisbourne) *hmpd s: towards rr: hdwy over 2f out: c wd st: rdn and edgd lft over 1f out: r.o to ld wl ins fnl f* **10/1**

6430 **2** *1 ¼* **Stark Contrast (USA)**[145] 941 4-8-12 59 .... SeanPalmer(7) 9 — 68
(M D I Usher) *hld up in mid-div: hdwy on outside 4f out: led over 2f out: rdn and hdd wl ins fnl f: nt qckn* **16/1**

000- **3** *2* **Summer Lodge**[284] 3705 5-8-13 58 .... MrJPFeatherstone(5) 7 — 63
(A J McCabe) *a.p: rdn and ev ch over 2f out: nt qckn ins fnl f* **8/1**

2000 **4** *2* **Josr's Magic (IRE)**[24] 4162 4-9-1 58 .... DebraEngland(3) 6 — 59
(H J Collingridge) *hld up in tch: rdn wl over 1f out: one pce fnl f* **17/2**

0030 **5** *shd* **Hatch A Plan (IRE)**[14] 4481 7-8-11 54 .... PNolan(3) 8 — 54
(Mouse Hamilton-Fairley) *hld up towards rr: hdwy over 3f out: rdn and one pce fnl f* **8/1**

-000 **6** *9* **Weet Yer Tern (IRE)**[13] 4503 6-8-4 47 .... KrishGundowry(3) 13 — 28
(W M Brisbourne) *stdd s: sn swtchd rt: hld up in rr: rdn over 2f out: kpt on fr over 1f out: nvr nr ldrs* **20/1**

00-0 **7** *1 ½* **Great Man (FR)**[17] 4365 7-9-2 56 .... AshleyMorgan 11 — 34
(K M Prendergast) *hld up in mid-div: pushed along over 2f out: rdn wl over 1f out: no rspnse* **8/1**

6501 **8** *7* **Don Pasquale**[13] 4503 6-8-11 51 .... SoniaEaton 4 — 15
(J T Stimpson) *hld up and bhd: no ch whn rdn and hung lft wl over 1f out* **7/1[3]**

0400 **9** *¾* **Princely Ted (IRE)**[8] 4664 7-8-1 46 ....(v) TobyAtkinson(5) 10 — 8
(W Clay) *sn chsng ldr: led over 3f out tl over 2f out: wknd wl over 1f out* **33/1**

066/ **10** *2 ¾* **Karramalu (IRE)**[18] 4358 7-9-4 58 .... BMcHugh 12 — 14
(Daniel Mark Loughnane, Ire) *hld up towards rr: rdn 4f out: sn struggling* **16/1**

0622 **11** *shd* **Thornaby Green**[16] 4420 7-9-1 55 .... RosieJessop 1 — 11
(T D Barron) *led: hdd over 3f out: sn rdn: wknd over 2f out* **10/3[1]**

2200 **12** *3 ¾* **Mighty Mover (IRE)**[71] 2640 6-8-13 56 .... AndreaAtzeni(3) 2 — 4
(B Palling) *prom: rdn over 4f out: wknd over 3f out* **7/2[2]**

60-0 **13** *½* **Alekhine (IRE)**[179] 559 7-8-9 56 .... AlexEdwards(7) 3 — 3
(J W Unett) *hld up in mid-div: rdn and wknd 2f out* **25/1**

2m 4.80s (3.10) **Going Correction** +0.40s/f (Slow) — **13 Ran SP% 134.1**
Speed ratings (Par 101): **102,100,99,97,97 89,87,81,81,78 78,75,74**
toteswinger: 1&2 £19.90, 1&3 £21.10, 2&3 £28.10. CSF £175.16 CT £1383.24 TOTE £11.90: £2.50, £5.70, £4.30; EX 192.70 TRIFECTA Not won. Place 6: £265.15, Place 5: £196.14.
Owner J Jones Racing Ltd **Bred** C J Mills **Trained** Great Ness, Shropshire

FOCUS
A low-grade apprentice handicap, but they went a decent enough pace and those responsible for doing so paid the penalty. Sound form.
T/Plt: £250.30 to a £1 stake. Pool: £55,396.47. 161.52 winning tickets. T/Qpdt: £128.30 to a £1 stake. Pool: £3,470.05. 20.00 winning tickets. KH

4860 LINGFIELD (L-H)

Tuesday, August 12

OFFICIAL GOING: Standard
Wind: strong, half behind Weather: overcast, showers

4941 100 AKER WOODS MEDIAN AUCTION MAIDEN STKS — 1m 4f (P)

2:30 (2:30) (Class 5) 3-5-Y-O — £2,590 (£770; £385; £192) Stalls Low

Form — RPR

3 **1** **Red Kestrel (USA)**[26] 4124 3-9-0 0 .... LDettori 6 — 93+
(Saeed Bin Suroor) *s.i.s: hld up in tch: chsd ldr 5f out: led 2f out: sn clr: easily* **8/13[1]**

252 **2** *7* **Buddhist Monk**[26] 4116 3-9-0 77 .... SebSanders 5 — 79+
(Sir Mark Prescott) *led: clr 8f out: rdn over 2f out: hdd 2f out: sn no ch w wnr: eased ins fnl f* **7/4[2]**

03 **3** *18* **Street Crime**[11] 4581 3-9-0 0 .... FrancisNorton 1 — 50+
(A M Balding) *hld up in last pair: wnt 3rd wl over 3f out: sn rdn and wl outpcd by ldrs* **16/1[3]**

06 **4** *13* **Futurity**[36] 3801 3-8-9 0 StephenCarson 2 24
(Eve Johnson Houghton) *chsd ldr tl 5f out: rdn and wknd wl over 3f out: t.o* **50/1**

5 *5* **Marsh Court**[145] 5-9-6 0 JamesDoyle 3 16
(J W Hills) *s.i.s: a last: rdn and lost tch 4f out: t.o* **66/1**

2m 30.15s (-2.85) **Going Correction** -0.10s/f (Stan)
WFA 3 from 5yo 11lb **5** Ran SP% **107.6**
Speed ratings (Par 103): **105,100,88,79,76**
toteswinger: 1&2 £2.50. CSF £1.78 TOTE £1.60: £1.10, £1.10; EX 2.10.
Owner Godolphin **Bred** Darley **Trained** Newmarket, Suffolk

FOCUS
This provided the favourite with a good opportunity to get off the mark and he duly scored with an easy success. There was no strength in depth but the first two set a decent standard and the winner looks potentially smart.

4942 OWL NURSERY 5f (P)
3:00 (3:01) (Class 5) 2-Y-O **£3,885** (£1,156; £577; £288) **Stalls** High

Form RPR

424 **1** **Ruby Tallulah**[10] 4634 2-8-2 **69** KirstyMilczarek[(3)] 8 73
(N P Littmoden) *racd in midfield: rdn over 2f out: hdwy ent fnl f: chsd ldr ins fnl f: r.o wl to ld towards fin* **4/1**[3]

5033 **2** *½* **Red Cell (IRE)**[5] 4768 2-8-1 **65** ow2 (b) ChrisCatlin 3 68
(E J O'Neill) *broke wl: led: rdn 2f out: hdd and no ex towards fin* **6/1**

2360 **3** *1 ¼* **Riflessione**[24] 4190 2-8-8 **75** (p) LukeMorris[(3)] 4 73
(J S Moore) *s.i.s: bhd: rdn over 2f out: styd on u.p fnl f: wnt 3rd last 100yds: nt pce to rch ldng pair* **11/2**

2210 **4** *¾* **Predict**[35] 3809 2-9-0 **78** SebSanders 7 73
(Sir Mark Prescott) *chsd ldr: ev ch and rdn 2f out: edgd lft over 1f out: wknd ins fnl f* **2/1**[1]

0000 **5** *1* **Agnes Love**[59] 3032 2-7-12 **62** oh17 NickyMackay 5 54
(J Akehurst) *chsd ldng pair: rdn and edgd lft over 1f out: wknd fnl f* **50/1**

046 **6** *nk* **Jubilee Juggins (IRE)**[10] 4634 2-8-1 **65** CatherineGannon 6 56
(N P Littmoden) *racd in last pair: rdn over 2f out: kpt on same pce and nvr able to chal* **25/1**

1410 **7** *½* **Fault**[10] 4626 2-9-8 **86** (t) SteveDrowne 1 75
(R Charlton) *dwlt: in tch: rdn over 2f out: no imp whn nt clr run over 1f out: kpt on same pce after* **10/3**[2]

58.46 secs (-0.34) **Going Correction** -0.10s/f (Stan) 2y crse rec **7** Ran SP% **111.9**
Speed ratings (Par 94): **98,97,95,94,92 91,91**
toteswinger: 1&2 £3.10, 1&3 £4.30, 2&3 £5.70. CSF £26.54 CT £129.14 TOTE £5.00: £2.50, £3.30; EX 25.70 Trifecta £177.60 Pool: £446.57 - 186 winning units..
Owner Mrs Vanessa Leaver **Bred** Larkwood Stud **Trained** Newmarket, Suffolk
■ Kirsty Milczarek rode out her claim with this 95th career win. She is only the fifth woman to do so in Britain.

FOCUS
A modest nursery, run at a solid pace. The runner-up sets the form.

NOTEBOOK
Ruby Tallulah opened her account at the fourth attempt on this nursery debut and provided her stable with a very welcome winner in the process. She tracked the early leaders into the home straight and, while taking a while to find her top gear, eventually mowed down rivals to get up. She has obviously begun in this sphere on a good mark and should find further improvement when faced with another furlong. (op 9-2)
Red Cell(IRE), third on his last two outings, was again sent out in front and held every chance. This was a brave effort in defeat and he is a sound benchmark for the form, but is clearly handicapped about right all the same. (op 11-2 tchd 13-2)
Riflessione, making his All-Weather debut, struggled to go the early pace after a sluggish start and basically got going all too late in the day. This drop in grade helped and, while he is not the most straightforward, he now looks more than ready to tackle a sixth furlong. Official explanation: jockey said colt was hampered at start (op 6-1)
Predict was rushed up to go with the early leader, but she was unable to sustain her effort like that rival and had no more to give from the final furlong pole. This was still a lot better from her, but she probably needs 6f now. (op 15-8 tchd 7-4 and 9-4 in a place)
Agnes Love, making her All-Weather and nursery bow after a two-month break, proved very one-paced yet still posted her best effort to date. She is worth trying over a stiffer test. (op 33-1)

4943 KANGA CLAIMING STKS 6f (P)
3:30 (3:30) (Class 6) 3-Y-O **£2,590** (£770; £385; £192) **Stalls** Low

Form RPR

-000 **1** **Deal Flipper**[26] 4102 3-8-0 60 FrankieMcDonald 3 62
(P Winkworth) *stdd s: hld up: swtchd rt and hdwy 3f out: chsd ldrs and wd bnd jst over 2f out: led over 1f out: clr fnl f: easily* **16/1**

505 **2** *5* **Zippi Jazzman (USA)**[5] 4765 3-9-5 75 (v[1]) GeorgeBaker 4 65
(R M Beckett) *chsd ldr: ev ch and rdn jst over 2f out: outpcd by wnr over 1f out: wnt 2nd ins fnl f* **6/4**[1]

0050 **3** *½* **Meridian Line (IRE)**[26] 4102 3-8-10 69 (b[1]) EddieAhern 1 54
(J G Portman) *sn led: rdn and flashed tail jst over 2f out: hdd over 1f out: no ch w wnr fnl f: lost 2nd ins fnl f* **6/1**[3]

5403 **4** *3 ¼* **Liberty Valance (IRE)**[13] 4531 3-9-1 67 (t) SebSanders 2 49
(S Kirk) *chsd ldrs: rdn and fnd nil over 1f out: wl btn fnl f* **13/8**[2]

35-0 **5** *4* **Sinead Of Aglish (IRE)**[29] 4028 3-8-1 65 ow1 ChrisCatlin 6 22
(Peter Grayson) *in tch: hdwy 3f out: rdn and outpcd jst over 2f out: wl btn over 1f out* **8/1**

6006 **6** *16* **Hold That Call (USA)**[13] 4523 3-8-8 44 EmmettStack[(3)] 5 —
(A J Chamberlain) *bhd and rdn over 4f out: sn lost tch: t.o* **66/1**

1m 11.27s (-0.63) **Going Correction** -0.10s/f (Stan) **6** Ran SP% **110.9**
Speed ratings (Par 98): **100,93,92,88,83 61**
toteswinger: 1&2 £5.60, 1&3 £9.20, 2&3 £1.80. CSF £39.80 TOTE £23.00: £7.50, £1.50; EX 61.90.Deal Flipper was subject to a friendly claim.
Owner Badger's Set **Bred** Darley **Trained** Chiddingfold, Surrey

FOCUS
A modest claimer, run at a sound pace. The winner is value for a bit further but this is not a race to be positive about.

4944 GOPHER H'CAP 6f (P)
4:00 (4:07) (Class 4) (0-85,85) 4-Y-O+ **£5,677** (£1,699; £849; £424; £211) **Stalls** Low

Form RPR

0524 **1** **Expensive Art (IRE)**[11] 4601 4-9-2 **80** HayleyTurner 8 88
(S A Callaghan) *awkward s and s.i.s: dropped in bhd: gd hdwy on inner jst over 2f out: drvn to ld ins fnl f: jst hld on* **11/2**[1]

0522 **2** *nse* **Vintage (IRE)**[20] 4307 4-8-6 **70** EddieAhern 12 78
(J Akehurst) *t.k.h: in tch: hdwy wl over 1f out: rdn over 1f out: ev ch wl ins fnl f: jst hld* **13/2**[2]

0150 **3** *½* **Cerebus**[76] 2504 6-9-0 **78** (bt) JamesDoyle 2 84
(A J McCabe) *led: rdn 2 l clr 2f out: hdd ins fnl f: no ex and edgd rt last 50yds* **33/1**

302 **4** *hd* **Brandywell Boy (IRE)**[9] 4668 5-7-11 **68** BillyCray[(7)] 5 74
(D J S Ffrench Davis) *chsd ldrs: rdn wl over 1f out: unable qck last 100yds* **10/1**

1505 **5** *1 ¼* **Buy On The Red**[28] 4051 7-8-12 **76** (p) ShaneKelly 3 78
(W R Muir) *chsd ldr: rdn over 2f out: wknd last 100yds* **16/1**

2461 **6** *½* **Dvinsky (USA)**[19] 4341 7-9-1 **82** (b) KirstyMilczarek[(3)] 10 82
(P Howling) *stdd after s: hld up bhd: hdwy ent fnl f: kpt on but nvr pce to rch ldrs* **8/1**

1431 **7** *1* **Chjimes (IRE)**[20] 4307 4-8-10 **74** SebSanders 11 71+
(C R Dore) *hld up bhd: hdwy on outer 3f out: no imp fr wl over 1f out* **7/1**[3]

0004 **8** *1 ¾* **Halsion Chancer**[19] 4341 4-9-7 **85** SteveDrowne 7 76
(J R Best) *hmpd after 1f: racd in midfield: rdn over 2f out: lost pl bnd 2f out: no imp after* **8/1**

6440 **9** *½* **Hammer Of The Gods (IRE)**[28] 4058 8-8-2 **69** (bt) LukeMorris[(3)] 9 59
(G C Bravery) *racd on outer: towards rr: rdn over 2f out: nvr threatened ldrs* **20/1**

-504 **10** *½* **Titan Triumph**[82] 2329 4-8-12 **76** (t) PaulDoe 1 64
(W J Knight) *s.i.s: sn in midfield: hdwy on iner 3f out: chsd ldrs and rdn jst ver 2f out: wknd fnl f* **7/1**[3]

1m 10.49s (-1.41) **Going Correction** -0.10s/f (Stan) course record **10** Ran SP% **98.6**
Speed ratings (Par 105): **105,104,104,102 101,100,98,97,96**
toteswinger: 1&2 £5.00, 1&3 £23.50, 2&3 £20.70. CSF £29.29 CT £660.79 TOTE £5.00: £1.80, £2.30, £7.60; EX 29.40 Trifecta £397.70 Part won. Pool: £537.51 - 0.10 winning units..
Owner Matthew Green **Bred** Stone Ridge Farm **Trained** Newmarket, Suffolk
■ Lochstar was withdrawn after rearing over when entering the stalls and running loose (5/1F, deduct 15p in the £ under rule 4).
■ Stewards' Enquiry : Hayley Turner one-day ban: used whip with excessive frequency (Sep 1)
Eddie Ahern two-day ban: careless riding (Aug 26-27)

FOCUS
A fair sprint for the class, run at a strong pace. The runner-up sets the level and the form looks solid.

4945 ROO FILLIES' H'CAP 1m 2f (P)
4:30 (4:32) (Class 4) (0-85,85) 4-Y-O+ **£5,677** (£1,699; £849; £424; £211) **Stalls** Low

Form RPR

1332 **1** **Luck Will Come (IRE)**[12] 4572 4-8-2 **66** ChrisCatlin 6 72
(H J Collingridge) *chsd ldr: rdn and qcknd to ld over 2f out: styd on u.p: a holding on* **11/4**[2]

3142 **2** *nk* **Ornella**[17] 4435 4-8-8 **72** SteveDrowne 4 77
(H Morrison) *t.k.h: chsd ldng pair: sltly outpcd wl over 2f out: rdn and hdwy over 1f out: chsd wnr ent fnl f: styd on but nvr quite getting to wnr* **6/4**[1]

2424 **3** *¾* **Bavarica**[6] 4739 6-7-11 **66** oh3 AmyBaker[(5)] 5 70
(Miss J Feilden) *s.i.s: t.k.h: n.m.r and lost pl over 2f out: sn swtchd rt: styd on fnl f: nvr getting to wnr* **13/2**[3]

6056 **4** *3 ¾* **Neardown Beauty (IRE)**[13] 4528 5-9-7 **85** (p) JamesDoyle 2 81
(A J McCabe) *s.i.s: hld up in last pair: hdwy on outer 3f out: ev ch over 2f out: wknd ent fnl f* **13/2**[3]

5600 **5** *1* **Lisathedaddy**[6] 4726 6-9-6 **84** GeorgeBaker 3 78
(B G Powell) *v.s.a: bhd: rdn over 2f out: nvr trbld ldrs* **10/1**

6-35 **6** *1 ¾* **Lady Friend**[104] 1730 6-8-13 **77** EddieAhern 1 68
(J W Hills) *led: stdd gallop after 2f: rdn and hdd over 2f out: wknd over 1f out* **10/1**

2m 9.72s (3.12) **Going Correction** -0.10s/f (Stan) **6** Ran SP% **111.5**
Speed ratings (Par 102): **83,82,82,79,78 76**
toteswinger: 1&2 £1.80, 1&3 £2.90, 2&3 £2.60. CSF £7.19 TOTE £3.50: £2.00, £1.40; EX 8.50.
Owner Greenstead Hall Racing **Bred** Mull Enterprises Ltd **Trained** Exning, Suffolk

FOCUS
A modest fillies' handicap, run at a modest early pace. The form still looks fair with the first three coming clear.

4946 TIGGER H'CAP 1m (P)
5:00 (5:01) (Class 5) (0-70,70) 3-Y-O+ **£3,238** (£963; £481; £240) **Stalls** High

Form RPR

5340 **1** **Murrin (IRE)**[11] 4603 4-9-9 **70** JackMitchell[(3)] 10 81
(T G Mills) *wl bhd: stl plenty to do and swtchd rt over 1f out: str run on outer to ld ins fnl f: sn in command* **9/2**[3]

4040 **2** *1 ¼* **Green Diamond**[23] 4219 3-9-6 **69** DarryllHolland 11 76
(M Johnston) *chsd ldr: rdn to ld 2f out: edgd rt u.p ent fnl f: hdd and nt pce of wnr ins fnl f* **7/1**

4434 **3** *1* **Gazboolou**[21] 4268 4-9-11 **67** FergusSweeney 9 73
(David Pinder) *chsd ldrs: rdn to go wl over 1f out: carried rt ent fnl f: kpt on one pce fnl f* **7/1**

4256 **4** *½* **The City Kid (IRE)**[20] 4306 5-9-4 **60** OscarUrbina 7 65
(G D Blake) *hld up towards rr on outer: hdwy wl over 1f out: sltly hmpd and swtchd rt ent fnl f: styd on last 100yds: nvr able to chal* **10/1**

3430 **5** *½* **High 'n Dry (IRE)**[12] 4568 4-9-3 **66** (p) AndreaAtzeni[(7)] 6 70+
(M A Allen) *hld up towards rr: swtchd rt and hdwy 3f out: chsd ldrs and carried rt ent fnl f: no ex ins fnl f* **12/1**

0203 **6** *¾* **Wrighty Almighty (IRE)**[17] 4428 6-9-12 **68** JimCrowley 8 70
(P R Chamings) *stdd s: t.k.h: hld up towards rr: hdwy over 2f out: kpt on same pce u.p fnl f* **12/1**

5060 **7** *nk* **King After**[59] 3037 6-8-12 **54** (v) SebSanders 3 55
(J R Best) *t.k.h: hld up in midfield: hdwy jst over 2f out: no imp fnl f* **16/1**

3402 **8** *nk* **Aggravation**[12] 4567 6-9-13 **69** TQuinn 1 70
(D R C Elsworth) *t.k.h: hld up bhd: hdwy 2f out: weaved through over 1f out: plugged on fnl f: nvr trbld ldrs* **7/2**[1]

0061 **9** *3 ¾* **Hazytoo**[20] 4306 4-9-12 **68** GeorgeBaker 5 60
(S A Callaghan) *t.k.h: hld up in midfield: hdwy over 2f out: chsd ldrs and rdn over 1f out: wknd qckly 1f out* **4/1**[2]

0020 **10** *2 ¾* **Garden Party**[27] 4081 4-9-13 **69** (p) FrankieMcDonald 2 55
(Jane Chapple-Hyam) *racd in midfield on inner: rdn and lost pl 3f out: no ch last 2f* **16/1**

400 **11** *4* **The Wily Woodcock**[19] 4343 4-9-6 **62** SteveDrowne 4 38
(G Wragg) *chsd ldrs: rdn and struggling over 2f out: no ch last 2f* **16/1**

-000 **12** *4 ½* **Minnis Bay (CAN)**[37] 3761 4-9-9 **65** EddieAhern 12 31
(E F Vaughan) *led: rdn and hdd 2f out: sn wknd: eased ins fnl f* **25/1**

1m 37.41s (-0.79) **Going Correction** -0.10s/f (Stan)
WFA 3 from 4yo+ 7lb **12** Ran SP% **131.4**
Speed ratings (Par 103): **99,97,96,96,95 95,94,94,90,87 83,79**
toteswinger: 1&2 £10.70, 1&3 £7.90, 2&3 £10.90. CSF £40.59 CT £195.50 TOTE £6.30: £2.40, £2.70, £2.70; EX 51.40 TRIFECTA Not won..
Owner Craig Faulkner **Bred** E Campion **Trained** Headley, Surrey

FOCUS
A fair handicap for the class, run at a sound pace. Sound form, the winner rated back to his best.
T/Plt: £131.60 to a £1 stake. Pool: £94,378.90. 523.23 winning tickets. T/Qpdt: £37.00 to a £1 stake. Pool: £6,410.82. 128.20 winning tickets. SP

4556 MUSSELBURGH (R-H)

Tuesday, August 12

OFFICIAL GOING: Soft

Wind: Virtually nil Weather: Raining

4947 SCOTTISH RACING APPRENTICE H'CAP — 1m 6f

6:10 (6:10) (Class 6) (0-65,58) 4-Y-O+ £2,590 (£770; £385; £192) Stalls Low

Form | | | | RPR
1025 **1** **Kyber**[12] 4556 7-9-7 **58** .... GaryBartley[(3)] 2 66
(J S Goldie) *trckd ldrs: smooth hdwy over 3f out: cl up 2f out: shkn up to ld over 1f out: rdn ent fnl f and styd on strly* **15/2**[3]
650- **2** 2 3/4 **Rightful Ruler**[23] 6802 6-8-12 **49** .... AshleyHamblett[(3)] 1 53
(N Wilson) *led: rdn along over 2f out: drvn and hdd over 1f out: rallied and ch tl no ex wl ins fnl f* **9/4**[2]
-000 **3** hd **Always Best**[12] 4556 4-8-6 **45** .... LanceBetts[(5)] 5 49
(R Allan) *trckd ldrs: hdwy 3f out: rdn along 2f out: sn drvn and kpt on same pce ins fnl f* **8/1**
0400 **4** 1 **Stravonian**[38] 3718 8-8-4 **45** .... PaulPickard[(7)] 6 47
(D A Nolan) *hld up in rr: hdwy wl over 2f out: sn rdn and kpt on appr fnl f: nrst fin* **16/1**
-331 **5** 9 **Dimashq**[12] 4556 6-9-4 **52** .... JamieMoriarty 8 42
(P T Midgley) *trckd ldr: n.m.r on inner bnd over 4f out: effrt 3f out and sn rdn: drvn on inner over 2f out and sn wknd* **6/5**[1]
6035 **6** 4 1/2 **Asrar**[43] 3545 6-8-11 **45** .... AndrewMullen 3 29
(Miss Lucinda V Russell) *a towards rr* **25/1**
000/ **7** 8 **Merryvale Man**[79] 303 11-8-6 **45** .... PatrickDonaghy[(5)] 4 17
(Miss Kariana Key) *trckd ldrs: hdwy to chse ldr 5f out: rdn along 3f out and sn wknd* **20/1**
0005 **8** 42 **Monte Pattino (USA)**[16] 4452 4-8-11 **45** ....(vt) DuranFentiman 7 —
(C J Teague) *a towards rr: wl bhd fnl 3f* **66/1**

3m 12.69s (7.39) **Going Correction** +0.575s/f (Yiel) 8 Ran SP% **115.1**
Speed ratings (Par 101): **101,99,99,98,93 91,86,62**
toteswinger: 1&2 £1.70, 1&3 £6.70, 2&3 £2.20. CSF £24.56 CT £140.65 TOTE £5.70: £2.00, £1.50, £1.80; EX 20.30.
Owner Great Northern Partnership **Bred** P B Holmes **Trained** Uplawmoor, E Renfrews

FOCUS
A low-grade race with half the field wrong at the weights. The third and fourth, a regressive sort and a long-standing maiden, give the form a weak look.
Dimashq Official explanation: jockey said mare was unsuited by the soft ground

4948 FIRST TRANSPENNINE EXPRESS NURSERY — 5f

6:40 (6:41) (Class 5) 2-Y-O £3,885 (£1,156; £577; £288) Stalls Low

Form | | | | RPR
0004 **1** **Dispol Grand (IRE)**[36] 3788 2-8-0 **61** ow2 .... PaulFessey 3 65
(P T Midgley) *cl up: rdn to ld 2f out: drvn ent fnl f: edgd rt and kpt on wl towards fin* **13/2**[3]
4232 **2** 1/2 **Majuba (USA)**[12] 4558 2-9-1 **79** .... NeilBrown[(3)] 6 81
(K A Ryan) *wnt rt s: cl up on outer: effrt 2f out: drvn and edgd rt ent fnl f: ev ch tl no ex last 100yds* **5/2**[2]
1061 **3** 3 **Dispol Kylie (IRE)**[10] 4648 2-9-7 **85** .... JamieMoriarty[(3)] 1 76
(P T Midgley) *led: rdn along 1/2-way: hdd 2f out: drvn and wknd appr fnl f* **1/1**[1]
056 **4** 1 3/4 **Wee Bizzom**[16] 4449 2-7-5 **59** oh14 .... CharlotteKerton[(7)] 2 44
(A Berry) *in rr tl styd on fnl 2f: nrst fin* **80/1**
4546 **5** 2 **Blow Your Mind**[17] 4434 2-8-9 **70** .... PaulHanagan 4 48
(Karen McLintock) *cl up: rdn along after 2f: sn lost pl and bhd* **7/1**
2053 **6** 1 1/2 **Jethro Bodine (IRE)**[34] 3830 2-7-5 **59** oh8 .... JamieKyne[(7)] 5 31
(W J H Ratcliffe) *sltly hmpd s: a in rr* **20/1**

62.93 secs (2.53) **Going Correction** +0.475s/f (Yiel) 6 Ran SP% **110.4**
Speed ratings (Par 94): **98,97,92,89,86 84**
toteswinger: 1&2 £2.70, 1&3 £1.90, 2&3 £1.20. CSF £22.29 TOTE £9.00: £3.40, £1.40; EX 21.50.
Owner W B Imison **Bred** Martyn J McEnery **Trained** Westow, N Yorks

FOCUS
A fair nursery. The winner is the best guide to the strength of the race, as the runner-up looks a bit over-rated on his bare form. The fourth also appeared to run a personal best, which may devalue the form.

NOTEBOOK
Dispol Grand(IRE) ◆, whose jockey was putting up 2lb overweight, was always up with the pace and kept on in determined style to win with something to spare. He may have just come to himself, as he had not been finishing his races off in the past, and could nick a similar event next time. (op 9-1)
Majuba(USA) showed a lot of pace down the centre of the course but could not resist the late thrust of the winner. He does not look ungenuine, as a string of placed efforts may make him appear, but the Handicapper has made his life hard. (op 7-4)
Dispol Kylie(IRE) had every chance down the stands'-side rail but started to weaken inside the two-furlong marker. Carrying the first colours of her owner, who also had the winner of the race, it is probably fair to say that the Handicapper has her measure, as she does handle easy ground. (op 11-8 tchd 6-4)
Wee Bizzom, running from well out of the handicap, was completely outpaced in the early stages but did make some eyecatching late ground. (op 66-1)

4949 KWIK-FIT GROUP H'CAP — 1m

7:10 (7:10) (Class 6) (0-65,64) 4-Y-O+ £2,590 (£770; £385; £192) Stalls High

Form | | | | RPR
0006 **1** **King Of The Moors (USA)**[2] 4898 5-9-1 **58** ....(p) PaulFessey 1 70
(T D Barron) *racd wd: led 2f: cl up tl rdn to ld again wl over 1f out: drvn ent fnl f and styd on strly* **11/2**[3]
604 **2** 3 3/4 **Mystical Ayr (IRE)**[3] 4851 6-8-11 **57** .... JamieMoriarty[(3)] 3 61+
(Miss L A Perratt) *midfield: pushed along over 4f out: rdn to chse ldrs 3f out: swtchd lft: drvn and styng on whn hmpd over 1f out: swtchd rt and styd on ins fnl f: tk 2nd nr line* **5/2**[1]
0000 **3** nk **Kirkby's Treasure**[8] 4683 10-9-1 **58** .... TonyCulhane 6 61
(A Berry) *hld up towards rr: stdy hdwy over 2f out: rdn over 1f out: drvn to chse wnr ent fnl f: one pce* **9/1**
2006 **4** 3 **Joshua's Gold (IRE)**[4] 4813 7-9-5 **62** ....(v) DavidAllan 9 58
(D Carroll) *trckd ldrs: hdwy 3f out: rdn to chse wnr wl over 1f out and ev ch tl drvn and wknd ent fnl f* **7/1**
1300 **5** 3/4 **King Of Legend (IRE)**[53] 3201 4-8-5 **51** ow1 .... PJMcDonald[(3)] 5 45
(A G Foster) *prom: hdwy to ld 3f out: rdn over 2f out: hdd wl over 1f out: sn drvn: hung lft and wknd* **13/2**
2041 **6** 1 3/4 **Grand Diamond (IRE)**[36] 3789 4-9-7 **64** ....(p) DanielTudhope 7 54
(J S Goldie) *trckd ldrs gng wl: hdwy 3f out: rdn over 2f out and ev ch tl wknd wl over 1f out* **9/2**[2]
-000 **7** 1 1/2 **Linden's Lady**[8] 4683 8-8-0 **46** ow1 ....(v) AndrewMullen[(3)] 8 33
(J R Weymes) *dwlt: hld up towards rr: stdy hdwy 3f out: rdn to chse ldrs 2f out: no imp appr fnl f* **12/1**
6005 **8** 13 **Polish Star**[10] 4629 4-8-4 **47** ....(v[1]) PaulHanagan 2 4
(Miss L A Perratt) *cl up: led after 2f: rdn along and hdd 3f out: sn drvn and wknd 2f out* **18/1**
000- **9** 25 **Centreboard (USA)**[286] 6582 4-8-7 **50** .... TonyHamilton 4 —
(Mrs L Williamson) *a in rr* **50/1**

1m 46.43s (5.23) **Going Correction** +0.575s/f (Yiel) 9 Ran SP% **112.9**
Speed ratings (Par 101): **96,92,91,88,88 86,84,71,46**
toteswinger: 1&2 £2.60, 1&3 £14.00, 2&3 £7.10. CSF £19.13 CT £120.47 TOTE £6.20: £2.30, £1.10, £2.30; EX 21.30.
Owner G Fawcett **Bred** Frank Brown, Hedberg Hall & K Hernandez **Trained** Maunby, N Yorks

FOCUS
A very moderate race, full of horses that rarely win or do not handle soft ground. The winner is rated close to this year's form.
King Of The Moors(USA) Official explanation: trainer had no explanation for the improved form shown
Grand Diamond(IRE) Official explanation: jockey said gelding was unsuited by the soft ground

4950 SUBSCRIBE TO RACING UK (S) STKS — 5f

7:40 (7:44) (Class 6) 3-Y-O+ £1,942 (£578; £288; £144) Stalls Low

Form | | | | RPR
2351 **1** **Highland Warrior**[36] 3784 9-9-5 70 .... MickyFenton 12 66
(P T Midgley) *midfield on outer: hdwy over 2f out: rdn to ld jst ins fnl f: edgd lft and kpt on towards fin* **11/8**[1]
0223 **2** 1/2 **Fire Up The Band**[26] 4114 9-9-5 64 .... TonyCulhane 11 64
(A Berry) *cl up: led 1/2-way: rdn over 1f out: hdd jst ins fnl f: drvn and rallying whn n.m.r towards fin* **3/1**[2]
0205 **3** 1 1/2 **Princess Charlmane (IRE)**[43] 3546 5-8-9 43 ....(t) DavidAllan 5 48
(C J Teague) *chsd ldrs: swtchd rt and rdn over 1f out: kpt on u.p ins fnl f* **12/1**
2530 **4** 4 **Pegasus Dancer (FR)**[15] 4476 4-9-0 65 ....(b) PaulMulrennan 4 39
(K A Ryan) *led: rdn along and hdd 1/2-way: sn drvn and one pce fr wl over 1f out* **7/1**[3]
4004 **5** 1 **Seafield Towers**[3] 4846 8-8-9 52 .... PatrickDonaghy[(5)] 6 35
(D A Nolan) *wnt rt s and rr tl hdwy wl over 1f out: rdn and kpt on ins fnl f: nrst fin* **22/1**
04-0 **6** 2 **Ingleby Star (IRE)**[12] 4563 3-8-11 70 .... PaulFessey 3 28
(T D Barron) *chsd ldrs: rdn along over 2f out and grad wknd* **12/1**
03 **7** 1 1/4 **Alfie Lee (IRE)**[53] 3212 11-8-7 48 ....(tp) PaulPickard[(7)] 9 24
(D A Nolan) *a towards rr* **50/1**
0000 **8** 1/2 **Oranmore Castle (IRE)**[18] 4393 6-9-0 62 .... PaulHanagan 10 22
(R A Fahey) *rrd s: midfield: rdn along over 2f out and n.d* **8/1**
0060 **9** 1/2 **Percy Douglas**[29] 4013 8-8-9 38 ....(p) AnnStokell[(5)] 8 20
(Miss A Stokell) *bmpd s: a towards rr* **40/1**
6043 **10** 3 1/4 **Ducal Regancy Red**[25] 4144 4-9-0 39 .... DanielTudhope 7 8
(C J Teague) *sltly hmpd s: a towards rr* **25/1**
-000 **11** 1 1/4 **Mister Marmaduke**[31] 3952 7-8-11 30 ow2 .... GaryBartley[(5)] 2 6
(D A Nolan) *s.i.s: a towards rr* **200/1**
0-00 **12** 3 3/4 **Ronnies Girl**[16] 4454 4-8-6 1 .... DuranFentiman[(3)] 1 —
(C J Teague) *s.i.s: a in rr* **200/1**

63.08 secs (2.68) **Going Correction** +0.475s/f (Yiel)
WFA 3 from 4yo+ 3lb 12 Ran SP% **119.7**
Speed ratings (Par 101): **97,96,93,87,85 82,80,79,79,73 71,65**
toteswinger: 1&2 £1.60, 1&3 £5.90, 2&3 £7.00. CSF £5.10 TOTE £2.50: £1.30, £1.10, £3.30; EX 6.00.There was no bid for the winner.
Owner Frank & Annette Brady **Bred** Rowcliffe Stud **Trained** Westow, N Yorks

FOCUS
A very modest seller. Two 'classy' horses dominated the finish and the form seems sound enough.

4951 RACING UK FOCUSED ON RACING H'CAP — 7f 30y

8:10 (8:11) (Class 5) (0-75,79) 3-Y-O+ £3,885 (£1,156; £577; £288) Stalls High

Form | | | | RPR
1134 **1** **Zabeel Tower**[16] 4453 5-9-10 **69** ....(p) TonyHamilton 3 79+
(R Allan) *trckd ldng pair: gd hdwy over 2f out: rdn to ld appr fnl f: styd on* **3/1**[1]
0131 **2** 1 **Horatio Carter**[8] 4682 3-9-11 **79** 6ex .... NeilBrown[(3)] 6 84+
(K A Ryan) *led and sn clr: rdn along over 2f out: drvn and hdd over 1f out: kpt on u.p ins fnl f* **10/3**[2]
0203 **3** hd **Flores Sea (USA)**[11] 4602 4-9-10 **69** ....(p) PaulFessey 5 75
(T D Barron) *chsd clr ldr: rdn over 2f out: drvn over 1f out: kpt on u.p ins fnl f* **4/1**
4100 **4** 3 1/2 **Flying Bantam (IRE)**[16] 4460 7-9-13 **72** .... PaulHanagan 2 69
(R A Fahey) *in rr: effrt 3f out and sn rdn along: kpt on u.p fr wl over 1f out: nrst fin* **9/1**
3500 **5** 1 3/4 **Botham (USA)**[26] 4117 4-8-3 **53** oh1 .... PatrickDonaghy[(5)] 8 45
(J S Goldie) *dwlt: towards rr: hdwy wl over 2f out: sn rdn and no imp fr wl over 1f out* **11/1**
2000 **6** nk **Avontuur (FR)**[16] 4453 6-8-13 **58** ....(b) DaleGibson 1 49
(Mrs R A Carr) *s.i.s: bhd tl sme late hdwy* **18/1**
1063 **7** nk **King Kenny**[6] 4745 3-9-10 **75** .... TonyCulhane 4 65
(S Parr) *in tch: effrt over 3f out: sn rdn along and no imp fnl 2f* **7/2**[3]
0300 **8** 8 **Attacca**[11] 4605 7-8-5 **53** oh7 ....(p) AndrewMullen[(3)] 7 22
(J R Weymes) *chadsed ldrs: rdn along over 3f out: sn drvn and wknd* **16/1**

1m 34.5s (4.20) **Going Correction** +0.575s/f (Yiel)
WFA 3 from 4yo+ 6lb 8 Ran SP% **119.8**
Speed ratings (Par 103): **99,97,97,93,91 91,90,81**
toteswinger: 1&2 £4.30, 1&3 £1.80, 2&3 £4.60. CSF £14.02 CT £41.05 TOTE £4.50: £1.50, £1.70, £1.40; EX 16.80.
Owner R. H. I. Ltd **Bred** Gainsborough Stud Management Ltd **Trained** Duns, Scottish Borders

FOCUS
A modest race run at a decent tempo. The form should work out but the winner, while progressing, should struggle under a penalty or when reassessed by the Handicapper.

4952 GLORIOUS 12TH H'CAP — 7f 30y

8:40 (8:41) (Class 6) (0-65,64) 3-Y-O £2,590 (£770; £385; £192) Stalls High

Form | | | | RPR
0020 **1** **Red Skipper (IRE)**[7] 4702 3-8-9 **57** .... AshleyHamblett[(5)] 3 66
(N Wilson) *towards rr: hdwy wl over 2f out: rdn to chse ldrs whn nt clr run over 1f out: sn swtchd rt and styd on to ld wl ins fnl f: drvn clr* **11/2**

5422 **2** 3 ½ **Willyn (IRE)**[12] 4560 3-8-11 **54**....................(p) DanielTudhope 5 53
(J S Goldie) *trckd ldrs on outer: gd hdwy over 3f out: rdn to ld wl over 1f out: drvn ins fnl f: hdd and one pce ins fnl f* **7/2**[2]

0002 **3** 1 ½ **Afton View (IRE)**[7] 4702 3-8-9 **52**....................(p) TonyHamilton 2 47
(S Parr) *sn led: rdn along 3f out: hdd wl over 1f out: drvn and rallied to have ev ch ent fnl f: sn one pce* **10/3**[1]

0336 **4** 2 **Bourse (IRE)**[16] 4455 3-9-4 **64**.................... PJMcDonald[(3)] 6 54
(R Johnson) *hld up towards rr: hdwy 3f out: rdn to chse ldrs wl over 1f out: sn drvn and kpt on same pce* **8/1**

-066 **5** 3 ¼ **La Fortalesa (IRE)**[47] 3416 3-9-6 **63**....................(p) PaulMulrennan 12 44
(K A Ryan) *s.i.s: sn pushed along on inner to ld after 2f: rdn along and hdd 3f out: drvn and grad wknd fnl 2f* **7/1**

-316 **6** 2 ½ **Rio L'Oren (IRE)**[62] 2946 3-9-7 **64**.................... PaulFessey 9 38
(N J Vaughan) *chsd ldng pair: rdn along 3f out: drvn 2f out and sn wknd* **8/1**

0032 **7** ½ **This Ones For Eddy**[6] 4724 3-9-7 **64**.................... TonyCulhane 10 37
(S Parr) *midfield: pushed along and lost pl after 2f: bhd after* **5/1**[3]

5066 **8** 1 **Scanno (IRE)**[22] 4241 3-8-1 **47**....................(be[1]) DuranFentiman[(3)] 1 17
(M Mullineaux) *a in rr* **33/1**

00 **9** 5 **Distant Rock**[53] 3213 3-9-6 **63**.................... DavidAllan 11 20
(D Carroll) *chsd ldrs: rdn along 3f out: sn drvn and wknd over 2f out* **14/1**

1m 35.31s (5.01) **Going Correction** +0.575s/f (Yiel) **9** Ran SP% **121.7**
Speed ratings (Par 98): **94,90,88,86,82 79,78,77,72**
toteswinger: 1&2 £6.50, 1&3 £9.10, 2&3 £3.60. CSF £26.58 CT £76.49 TOTE £7.00: £1.90, £1.70, £1.80; EX 33.70.
Owner The Sandburn Racing Partnership **Bred** Keith Moran **Trained** Flaxton, N Yorks
■ Stewards' Enquiry : Daniel Tudhope one-day ban: used whip down the shoulder in the forehand position (Aug 26)

FOCUS
An open but weak affair won in good style by Red Skipper who appreciated the ground. The pace looked sound.
Red Skipper(IRE) Official explanation: trainer said, regarding the improved form shown, that the gelding was better suited by today's soft ground
T/Plt: £20.50 to a £1 stake. Pool: £67,873.60. 2,406.76 winning tickets. T/Qpdt: £4.80 to a £1 stake. Pool: £4,809.92. 731.90 winning tickets. JR

4562 NOTTINGHAM (L-H)
Tuesday, August 12

OFFICIAL GOING: Soft
Wind: Fresh against Weather: Cloudy with sunny spells

4953 JOHN SMITH'S PLEASLEY MINERS WELFARE APPRENTICE H'CAP 1m 2f 50y
5:55 (5:56) (Class 5) (0-75,73) 4-Y-0+ **£2,914** (£867; £433; £216) **Stalls** Low

Form RPR

500- **1** **Clear Sailing**[374] 4184 5-9-10 **73**.................... FrederikTylicki 6 82
(George Baker) *mde all: rdn clr over 2f out: styd on wl* **7/4**[1]

3604 **2** 2 ¾ **Master Mahogany**[44] 3518 7-9-0 **63**.................... MCGeran 1 67
(R J Hodges) *chsd clr ldrs: wnt 2nd over 2f out: sn rdn: no ex ins fnl f* **5/1**[3]

01F5 **3** 8 **Dragon Slayer (IRE)**[12] 4565 6-9-5 **71**.................... AshleyMorgan[(3)] 5 59
(John A Harris) *s.i.s: sn chsng clr ldrs: effrt over 3f out: no imp whn hung lft over 1f out* **4/1**[2]

2634 **4** ¾ **Given A Choice (IRE)**[6] 4751 6-9-10 **73**....................(p) SimonPearce 4 59
(J Pearce) *sn outpcd and bhd: nvr nrr* **9/1**

0024 **5** 4 **Touch Of Style (IRE)**[10] 4645 4-9-3 **66**....................(p) HarryPoulton 3 44
(J R Boyle) *chsd wnr tl rdn and wknd over 2f out* **4/1**[2]

2210 **6** 95 **Hester Brook (IRE)**[5] 4797 4-8-5 **54** oh2....................(v[1]) WilliamCarson 2 —
(J G M O'Shea) *rel to r: a t.o* **12/1**

2m 11.17s (-1.33) **Going Correction** +0.05s/f (Good) **6** Ran SP% **110.7**
Speed ratings (Par 103): **107,104,98,97,94 18**
toteswinger: 1&2 £4.20, 1&3 £2.50, 2&3 £4.20. CSF £10.50 TOTE £2.60: £1.10, £3.00; EX 10.10.
Owner Michael H Watt **Bred** Juddmonte Farms Ltd **Trained** Moreton Morrell, Warwicks

FOCUS
An uncompetitive handicap restricted to apprentices who had not ridden more than 25 winners. They went a good pace. The winner was back to something like his 3yo form and could build on this.

4954 E.B.F./JOHN SMITH'S EXTRA COLD NOVICE STKS 1m 75y
6:25 (6:25) (Class 5) 2-Y-O **£3,885** (£1,156; £577) **Stalls** Centre

Form RPR

3333 **1** **Canwinn (IRE)**[14] 4497 2-8-12 79.................... EdwardCreighton 2 83
(M R Channon) *hld up in tch: shkn up to ld ins fnl f: edgd lft: r.o* **6/1**[3]

3 **2** 1 ¼ **Pergamon (IRE)**[17] 4421 2-8-12 0.................... JimmyFortune 4 80
(J H M Gosden) *led: rdn and hdd 2f out: stl ev ch ins fnl f: unable qck towards fin* **5/2**[2]

32 **3** 1 ¼ **Crackdown (IRE)**[24] 4199 2-8-12 0.................... JoeFanning 3 78
(M Johnston) *trckd ldr: led 2f out: sn rdn: hdd and no ex ins fnl f* **8/15**[1]

1m 47.99s (2.59) **Going Correction** +0.05s/f (Good) **3** Ran SP% **108.1**
Speed ratings (Par 94): **89,87,86**
CSF £17.13 TOTE £7.00; EX 16.80.
Owner Sheikh Ahmed Al Maktoum **Bred** Oak Lodge Stud **Trained** West Ilsley, Berks

FOCUS
A disappointing turnout for this novice event and it remains to be seen what the form is worth. The winner only had to run to his previous best

NOTEBOOK
Canwinn(IRE) was the first off the bridle, but he kept responding to pressure and is clearly a strong stayer, despite his pedigree suggesting otherwise. This was his first success at the fifth attempt and the easy ground suited. (op 7-1)
Pergamon(IRE) ran better than when a beaten favourite on his debut over 7f on quick ground at Newmarket, but it was still a little disappointing that he was beaten by the outsider of the three. (op 7-4 tchd 11-4)
Crackdown(IRE) had shown plenty of ability in two runs over 6f on quick ground, but this was disappointing. He was taking a significant step up in trip, but is by the same sire as today's winner and there is also plenty of stamina on his dam's side. (op 4-5 tchd 5-6 in places)

4955 JOHN SMITH'S PREMIER CLUB H'CAP 1m 6f 15y
6:55 (6:55) (Class 3) (0-90,88) 3-Y-0+ **£7,771** (£2,312; £1,155; £577) **Stalls** Low

Form RPR

3303 **1** **The Betchworth Kid**[19] 4351 3-9-0 **85**.................... JamieSpencer 1 94
(M L W Bell) *hld up: hdwy over 3f out: hrd rdn and edgd lft over 1f out: styd on u.p to ld ins fnl f: eased nr fin* **3/1**[2]

-020 **2** 2 **Yossi (IRE)**[33] 3884 4-9-5 **77**....................(b) JimmyQuinn 2 83
(M H Tompkins) *led 6f: chsd ldr tl led again 4f out: rdn over 1f out: hdd and no ex ins fnl f* **8/1**[3]

2311 **3** nk **Tasheba**[39] 3697 3-9-0 **85**.................... AlanMunro 9 91
(P W Chapple-Hyam) *chsd ldrs: pushed along 5f out: rdn over 2f out: bmpd over 1f out: styd on same pce fnl f* **4/7**[1]

5510 **4** 1 **Salute (IRE)**[20] 4314 9-9-1 **73**.................... RobertHavlin 3 77
(P G Murphy) *chsd ldr tl led 8f out: hdd 4f out: rdn over 2f out: styd on same pce fnl f* **33/1**

2110 **5** 8 **Directa's Digger (IRE)**[13] 4516 4-8-10 **73**....................(v) JackDean[(5)] 5 66
(M J Scudamore) *prom: rdn over 2f out: sn wknd* **16/1**

3m 6.77s (-0.53) **Going Correction** +0.05s/f (Good)
WFA 3 from 4yo+ 13lb **5** Ran SP% **108.6**
Speed ratings (Par 107): **103,101,101,101,96**
toteswinger: 1&2 £5.50. CSF £23.59 TOTE £5.30: £1.30, £3.00; EX 20.50.
Owner W H Ponsonby **Bred** R P Williams **Trained** Newmarket, Suffolk
■ Stewards' Enquiry : Jamie Spencer caution: careless riding; two-day ban: used whip with excessive force (Aug 26-27)

FOCUS
A weak staying handicap for the grade, run at an ordinary pace. The form is sound enough.

NOTEBOOK
The Betchworth Kid handled the soft ground and built on the form he showed when third on his first run over this trip in a better race at Sandown. He may struggle to follow up. (tchd 10-3)
Yossi(IRE) had the blinkers back on, but he was well held in second. He is just 1-17. (op 6-1 tchd 11-2)
Tasheba came into this chasing the hat-trick, but he was a very short price considering he was unproven on ground this soft and he could not defy a 7lb rise for his recent Warwick victory. (op 10-11 tchd 8-15 and evens in places)
Salute(IRE) is not the easiest to predict and he was well held in fourth. (op 18-1 tchd 16-1)
Directa's Digger(IRE) Official explanation: jockey said colt ran flat

4956 JOHN SMITH'S SMOOTH NURSERY 6f 15y
7:25 (7:26) (Class 5) (0-75,74) 2-Y-O **£3,238** (£963; £481; £240) **Stalls** High

Form RPR

5401 **1** **Shadow Bay (IRE)**[24] 4203 2-9-1 **68**.................... RichardKingscote 7 75+
(Tom Dascombe) *prom: rdn over 3f out: led over 1f out: hung lft: r.o u.p* **9/4**[1]

0233 **2** 1 ¾ **Happy Anniversary (IRE)**[15] 4475 2-9-5 **72**.................... EdwardCreighton 5 74+
(Miss V Haigh) *sn pushed along in rr: swtchd rt and hdwy over 1f out: chsd wnr and hung lft ins fnl f: r.o* **11/2**[3]

0531 **3** 2 ¼ **Lisburn (IRE)**[11] 4594 2-9-7 **74**.................... TWilliams 10 69
(M Brittain) *edgd rt s: sn led: rdn and hdd over 1f out: no ex ins fnl f* **6/1**

056 **4** 7 **Anjuna (USA)**[17] 4425 2-7-11 **55**.................... Louis-PhilippeBeuzelin[(5)] 3 29
(J H M Gosden) *sn prom: edgd lft thrght: rdn and wknd over 2f out* **12/1**

003 **5** hd **Gemini Jive (IRE)**[38] 3735 2-8-12 **65**.................... AlanMunro 11 38
(M G Quinlan) *s.i.s and hmpd s: hdwy 4f out: rdn and edgd lft over 2f out: wknd over 1f out* **12/1**

444 **6** ½ **Abu Derby (IRE)**[38] 3735 2-8-13 **66**.................... TPQueally 6 38
(J G Given) *chsd ldrs: rdn over 2f out: wkng whn hmpd over 1f out* **12/1**

501 **7** shd **Time Loup**[26] 4120 2-8-4 **62**.................... WilliamCarson[(5)] 13 34
(S R Bowring) *sn chsng ldr: rdn and ev ch over 2f out: hung lft and wknd over 1f out* **18/1**

550 **8** 1 **Jobekani (IRE)**[11] 4593 2-8-11 **67**.................... TolleyDean[(3)] 9 36
(Mrs L Williamson) *s.i.s: hld up: stmbld 5f out: hdwy over 2f out: sn rdn and wknd* **25/1**

0030 **9** 2 **Calypso Prince**[27] 4079 2-8-2 **60**....................(v) MCGeran[(5)] 14 23
(M D I Usher) *broke wl: sn lost pl: bhd fr 1/2-way* **33/1**

062 **10** 1 ½ **West Leake (IRE)**[15] 4474 2-8-9 **62**.................... MichaelHills 1 20
(B W Hills) *prom: rdn and wknd over 1f out* **4/1**[2]

1m 16.51s (1.41) **Going Correction** +0.175s/f (Good) **10** Ran SP% **115.6**
Speed ratings (Par 94): **97,94,91,82,82 81,81,79,77,75**
toteswinger: 1&2 £3.60, 1&3 £2.40, 2&3 £4.90. CSF £14.45 CT £65.16 TOTE £3.10: £1.50, £2.40, £2.10; EX 21.20.
Owner ONEWAY Partners **Bred** Thomas Cahalan & Sophie Hayley **Trained** Lambourn, Berks

FOCUS
A modest nursery in which the front three finished well clear. They raced towards the near-side rail. Improvement from the winner in his new yard and the form looks sound.

NOTEBOOK
Shadow Bay(IRE), bought out of Mick Channon's yard after winning a seller at Ripon on his previous start, produced an improved effort to follow up in convincing fashion, although he was inclined to edge left. He was well suited by the ground and will be one to respect when getting these sorts of conditions. (op 3-1)
Happy Anniversary(IRE) failed to prove her stamina for 7f on the Fibresand at Southwell last time, but she was doing all her best work at the finish on this drop in trip. However, she did not help her chance by hanging right. (op 9-1)
Lisburn(IRE) had conditions to suit, but she was found out by a 3lb rise for her recent Haydock success. (op 5-1 tchd 13-2)
Anjuna(USA) did not improve for the switch to soft ground on her nursery debut. (op 8-1 tchd 14-1)
Gemini Jive(IRE) did not improve as one might have expected for the switch to soft ground on her nursery debut, although she was hampered soon after the start. (op 8-1)
Jobekani(IRE) Official explanation: jockey said colt stumbled in early stages
West Leake(IRE), making his nursery debut, went out like a light when asked for his effort and it may have been more than just the soft ground that was bothering him. (op 11-2 tchd 7-2)

4957 JOHN SMITH'S EXTRA SMOOTH CONDITIONS STKS 5f 13y
7:55 (7:55) (Class 3) 3-Y-0+
£7,477 (£2,239; £1,119; £560; £279; £140) **Stalls** High

Form RPR

0-61 **1** **Peace Offering (IRE)**[25] 4159 8-9-6 108.................... AdrianTNicholls 5 115
(D Nicholls) *mde virtually all: rdn over 1f out: r.o wl* **13/2**

1-21 **2** 2 ½ **Chief Editor**[111] 1571 4-8-11 98.................... JamieSpencer 4 97
(M J Wallace) *hld up and bhd: hdwy over 1f out: sn rdn: hung lft ins fnl f: styd on same pce* **11/4**[2]

112 **3** shd **Befortyfour**[52] 3273 3-8-12 107.................... PhilipRobinson 8 101
(M A Jarvis) *hung lft thrght: chsd ldrs: rdn over 1f out: styd on same pce fnl f* **2/1**[1]

0006 **4** 1 ½ **Rowe Park**[12] 4550 5-9-0 104.................... DaneO'Neill 6 94
(Mrs L C Jewell) *chsd ldrs: rdn over 2f out: no ex fnl f* **9/2**[3]

3204 **5** 1 ¼ **Invincible Force (IRE)**[9] 4660 4-8-11 89....................(b) TPQueally 9 87
(Paul Green) *dwlt: hdwy 2f out: rdn and hung lft over 1f out: nt trble ldrs* **6/1**

6000 **6** 2 ½ **The Jobber (IRE)**[33] 3881 7-8-11 88.................... TedDurcan 7 78
(M Blanshard) *hld up: rdn and wknd over 1f out* **25/1**

-000 7 ¾ **The Lord**[68] 2760 8-8-11 80....(t) AlanDaly 2 75
(W G M Turner) *chsd ldrs: rdn over 2f out: wknd over 1f out* **40/1**

60.09 secs (-0.61) **Going Correction** +0.175s/f (Good)
WFA 3 from 4yo+ 3lb **7** Ran SP% **112.1**
Speed ratings (Par 107): **111,107,106,104,102 98,97**
toteswinger: 1&2 £1.40, 1&3 £1.70, 2&3 £1.10. CSF £23.71 TOTE £6.10: £3.50, £1.80; EX 13.10.
Owner Lady O'Reilly **Bred** Chevington Stud **Trained** Sessay, N Yorks

FOCUS
A good conditions race. They raced up the middle of the track. The winner was close to his best and is probably the best guide to the form.

NOTEBOOK
Peace Offering(IRE) was able to set just a sensible pace and ran on strongly to the line to follow up his recent Newmarket success, again confirming he goes on any ground. In this sort of form he will be well worth his place back in Group company. (op 11-2 tchd 5-1)
Chief Editor had the ground in his favour, but he still hung left under pressure and never looked like catching Peace Offering, who got a soft lead. (op 15-8)
Befortyfour is an improving type, but he failed to justify strong market support. He hung to his left and may have found the ground a little too soft. (op 11-4)
Rowe Park was below the pick of his form and probably wants quicker ground. (op 13-2 tchd 7-1)
Invincible Force(IRE) had plenty to find at the weights and ran about as well as could have been expected. Official explanation: jockey said gelding missed the break (op 15-2)

4958 JOHN SMITH'S NO NONSENSE RACING H'CAP 5f 13y
8:25 (8:25) (Class 5) (0-70,69) 3-Y-O+ **£3,238** (£963; £481; £240) **Stalls** High

Form RPR
6223 1 **Equuleus Pictor**[8] 4693 4-9-5 **69**.... JackDean(5) 4 82+
(J L Spearing) *mde virtually all: edgd lft ins fnl f: rdn out* **9/4**[1]
3531 2 1 ½ **Matterofact (IRE)**[8] 4693 5-9-3 **65** 6ex.... TolleyDean(3) 11 73
(M S Saunders) *s.i.s: hdwy 1/2-way: rdn over 1f out: styd on* **10/1**
050 3 ½ **Tender Process (IRE)**[35] 3819 5-9-0 **59**....(b[1]) GrahamGibbons 3 65
(E S McMahon) *s.i.s: outpcd: r.o ins fnl f: nt rch ldrs* **14/1**
-055 4 ¾ **Back In The Red (IRE)**[13] 4535 4-9-3 **65**.... KevinGhunowa(3) 12 69
(R A Harris) *outpcd: hung lft over 1f out: r.o wl ins fnl f: nrst fin* **11/1**
2261 5 nse **Comptonspirit**[16] 4462 4-9-9 **68**.... TPQueally 10 71
(B P J Baugh) *sn pushed along in rr: hdwy u.p over 1f out: hung lft: styd on same pce ins fnl f* **9/1**
2226 6 hd **Black Moma (IRE)**[21] 4273 4-9-2 **61**.... JamieSpencer 6 64
(A B Haynes) *broke wl: stdd and lost pl sn after s: hdwy u.p over 1f out: no ex ins fnl f* **7/1**[3]
0-00 7 shd **Haajes**[15] 4478 4-9-6 **65**....(t) DaneO'Neill 1 67
(S Parr) *sn outpcd: r.o u.p ins fnl f: nvr nrr* **10/1**
4316 8 ½ **High Reach**[5] 4765 8-8-13 **58**.... RobertHavlin 2 58
(J G M O'Shea) *chsd wnr: rdn over 1f out: wknd ins fnl f* **22/1**
3424 9 2 ½ **Pennyspider (IRE)**[5] 4767 3-9-0 **62**.... TGMcLaughlin 7 52+
(M S Saunders) *chsd ldrs: rdn 1/2-way: wkng whn hmpd ins fnl f* **14/1**
3600 10 1 ¼ **Spoof Master (IRE)**[29] 4025 4-9-6 **65**.... PhilipRobinson 9 52
(C R Dore) *s.i.s and stmbld s: sn chsng ldrs: lost pl 1/2-way: sn bhd* **5/1**[2]
0060 11 7 **Signor Panettiere**[19] 4324 7-8-5 **50** oh5....(bt[1]) SilvestreDeSousa 8 12
(A D Brown) *s.i.s: sn chsng ldrs: rdn 1/2-way: sn wknd* **66/1**

61.11 secs (0.41) **Going Correction** +0.175s/f (Good)
WFA 3 from 4yo+ 3lb **11** Ran SP% **115.6**
Speed ratings (Par 103): **103,100,99,98,98 98,98,97,93,91 80**
toteswinger: 1&2 £2.20, 1&3 £10.40, 2&3 £33.20. CSF £25.31 CT £261.53 TOTE £3.30: £1.50, £4.10, £5.60; EX 16.40 Place 6: £386.82 Place 5: £196.12 .
Owner Masonaires **Bred** A J And Mrs L Brazier **Trained** Kinnersley, Worcs

FOCUS
A modest sprint handicap in which they tended to race up the middle of the track. Solid form for the grade.
Back In The Red(IRE) Official explanation: jockey said gelding became unbalanced
T/Plt: £175.90 to a £1 stake. Pool: £63,153.21. 261.95 winning tickets. T/Qpdt: £16.00 to a £1 stake. Pool: £5,024.54. 231.75 winning tickets. CR

4913 DEAUVILLE (R-H)
Tuesday, August 12

OFFICIAL GOING: Turf course - soft; all-weather - standard

4959a PRIX MICHEL HOUYVET (LISTED RACE) 1m 7f
1:20 (1:24) 3-Y-O **£20,221** (£8,088; £6,066; £4,044; £2,022)

RPR
1 **Watar (IRE)**[54] 3191 3-8-11.... DBonilla 2 107
(F Head, France) **1/1**[1]
2 ½ **Americain (USA)**[29] 4042 3-8-11.... OPeslier 5 106
(A Fabre, France)
3 ¾ **Mount Helicon**[54] 3191 3-8-11.... MGuyon 8 106
(A Fabre, France)
4 ¾ **Enroller (IRE)**[33] 3875 3-8-11.... MartinDwyer 7 105
(W R Muir) *led: pushed along st: hdd 1 1/2f out: r.o tl no ex fnl 100yds* **27/1**
5 2 ½ **Tsar De Russie (IRE)**[30] 3-8-11....(b) ACrastus 1 102
(E Lellouche, France) **5/1**[2]
6 ¾ **Pompeyano (IRE)**[45] 3516 3-8-11.... MBlancpain 4 101
(C Laffon-Parias, France)
7 1 **Blue Bresil (FR)**[53] 3244 3-8-11.... WMongil 6 100
(L Larrigade, France) **12/1**[3]
8 2 **Weald**[54] 3191 3-8-11.... SPasquier 3 97
(P Bary, France)
9 dist **Major Wing (IRE)**[28] 3-8-11.... DBoeuf 9 —
(W Menuet, France)

3m 18.6s (-0.50) **9** Ran SP% **77.9**
PARI-MUTUEL: WIN 2.00; PL 1.20, 2.10, 2.70; DF 8.10.
Owner Hamdan Al Maktoum **Bred** Haras Du Mezeray **Trained** France

NOTEBOOK
Enroller(IRE), quickly at the head of affairs, bowled along in front and accelerated well on the turn into the straight. He battled well throughout the final furlong but could not go with the winner. He stayed on a little one-paced but was not disgraced to finish fourth beaten a total of two lengths. This was an above-average Listed race and his trainer hinted that he could go for the St Leger at Doncaster.

4497 BEVERLEY (R-H)
Wednesday, August 13

OFFICIAL GOING: Good to soft
The ground was described as 'soft, tacky, like a gluepot'.
Wind: Moderate, half against, becoming fresh Weather: fine and sunny becoming overcast and cool

4960 EBF "FEMALE" MAIDEN STKS 7f 100y
2:10 (2:12) (Class 4) 2-Y-O **£5,018** (£1,493; £746; £372) **Stalls** High

Form RPR
3 1 **Beautiful Breeze (IRE)**[14] 4536 2-9-3 0.... RoystonFfrench 11 76+
(M Johnston) *mde virtually all: kpt on wl fnl f: hld on towards fin* **15/2**[3]
022 2 nk **Cosmic Sun**[19] 4394 2-9-3 85.... PaulHanagan 8 76
(R A Fahey) *towards rr: hdwy over 4f out: effrt over 3f out: hung rt and styd on ins fnl f: jst hld* **11/10**[1]
55 3 ¾ **The Kyllachy Kid**[15] 4497 2-9-3 0.... RobertWinston 2 74
(T P Tate) *sn chsng ldrs: chal appr fnl f: no ex wl ins fnl f* **5/1**[2]
00 4 2 ½ **Jacobite Prince (IRE)**[25] 4199 2-9-3 0.... JimmyQuinn 3 68
(M H Tompkins) *in rr: hdwy over 3f out: chsng ldrs over 1f out: one pce* **33/1**
03 5 6 **Agent Stone (IRE)**[7] 4740 2-9-3 0....(t) AdrianTNicholls 13 54
(D Nicholls) *chsd ldrs: lost pl over 1f out* **17/2**
64 6 2 ¾ **Winsome Hearts**[14] 4536 2-9-3 0.... DaleGibson 1 48
(M W Easterby) *sn bhd: sme hdwy over 2f out: nvr on terms* **33/1**
7 2 **Ysing Yi** 2-9-3 0.... NCallan 12 43
(K A Ryan) *w wnr: wknd over 1f out* **12/1**
8 ½ **Addison De Witt** 2-9-3 0.... TonyHamilton 7 42
(Micky Hammond) *slowly away: a bhd* **66/1**
40 9 ½ **Blackstone Vegas**[15] 4497 2-9-0 0.... JamieMoriarty(3) 5 41
(J Howard Johnson) *in rr-div: sme hdwy over 2f out: sn wknd* **10/1**
0 10 18 **Susurrayshaan**[12] 4593 2-8-10 0.... IanCraven(7) 4 —
(Mrs G S Rees) *chsd ldrs: edgd lft and wknd 2f out: sn bhd* **100/1**

1m 36.31s (2.51) **Going Correction** +0.30s/f (Good) **10** Ran SP% **111.7**
Speed ratings (Par 96): **97,96,95,92,86 82,80,80,79,58**
toteswinger: 1&2 £2.00, 1&3 £3.70, 2&3 £2.60. CSF £14.68 TOTE £6.10: £1.60, £1.10, £2.10; EX 12.30.
Owner Crone Stud Farms Ltd **Bred** Patrick M Ryan **Trained** Middleham Moor, N Yorks
■ Ask Dan was withdrawn (11/1, refused to enter stalls). R4 applies, deduct 5p in the £.
■ Stewards' Enquiry : Paul Hanagan one-day ban: used whip with excessive frequency (Aug 27)

FOCUS
A fair maiden with the runner-up provisionally officially rated 85. It was quite a severe test in the conditions.

NOTEBOOK
Beautiful Breeze(IRE), who had a favourable draw, still looked very inexperienced but showed a battling spirit to get there in the end with not an ounce to spare. (op 8-1 tchd 7-1)
Cosmic Sun made his effort on the outer coming off the home turn. He did not prove an easy ride but, galvanized, was cutting back the winner at the line. (op 11-8)
The Kyllachy Kid, drawn wide, threw down the gauntlet coming to the final furlong but had no more to give in the closing stages. Less-testing ground would be in his favour. (op 13-2)
Jacobite Prince(IRE), stepping up in trip on his third start, showed much-improved form but this will have blown a possibly lenient nursery mark out of the water. (op 40-1)
Agent Stone(IRE), having his third outing, seemed to find this extended trip on this uphill finish stretching him to breaking point. (op 8-1 tchd 9-1)
Winsome Hearts, a length behind the winner at Redcar, showed his inexperience beforehand. This sets him up for a nursery campaign.

4961 JOURNAL CLAIMING STKS 7f 100y
2:40 (2:41) (Class 5) 3-Y-O+ **£2,590** (£770; £385; £192) **Stalls** High

Form RPR
3610 1 **Le Chiffre (IRE)**[7] 4727 6-9-2 65....(p) NCallan 13 64
(John A Harris) *chsd ldrs: drvn over 3f out: plld outside over 1f out: hung rt and styd on to ld fnl 100yds* **4/1**[1]
0404 2 ¾ **Nok Twice (IRE)**[17] 4451 7-9-12 65.... DNolan 9 72
(D Carroll) *hld up in mid-div: hdwy on ins to ld 1f out: hdd and no ex ins fnl f* **8/1**
3605 3 4 **Scotty's Future (IRE)**[9] 4679 10-8-13 46.... SladeO'Hara(5) 15 54
(A Berry) *s.s: sn detached in last: hdwy and plld outside 2f out: styd on wl fnl f* **15/2**
-200 4 shd **Stonehaugh (IRE)**[15] 4500 5-9-8 75....(t) RobertWinston 1 58+
(J Howard Johnson) *led 1f: chsd ldr: wknd fnl f: lost 3rd line* **7/1**[3]
0003 5 2 **Jellytot (USA)**[14] 4542 5-9-3 44.... TonyHamilton 3 48
(J O'Reilly) *in rr: hdwy over 3f out: kpt on fnl 2f: nvr rchd ldrs* **12/1**
0056 6 hd **First Valentini**[11] 4651 4-8-7 45.... PaulFessey 14 37
(N Bycroft) *led after 1f: hdd 1f out: sn wknd* **20/1**
4235 7 nse **Wiseman's Diamond (USA)**[36] 3819 3-8-10 65 ow1 GrahamGibbons 2 46
(G P Kelly) *chsd ldrs: fdd over 1f out* **8/1**
6 8 hd **Poppy Day**[9] 4689 5-8-4 0.... NSLawes(7) 7 41
(M W Easterby) *s.i.s: sme hdwy on outside over 2f out: nvr a factor* **14/1**
0000 9 ¾ **Baylaw Star**[16] 4479 7-8-11 48.... AndrewMullen(3) 5 42
(I W McInnes) *chsd ldrs: sn drvn along: one pce fnl 2f* **16/1**
2000 10 nk **Desert Hunter (IRE)**[43] 3582 5-9-6 44.... JimmyQuinn 12 47
(Micky Hammond) *in rr: kpt on fnl 2f: nvr on terms* **16/1**
0405 11 ½ **Penel (IRE)**[3] 4898 7-9-2 54....(p) LeeEnstone 16 42
(P T Midgley) *s.i.s: in rr: sme hdwy whn nt clr run over 1f out: nvr on terms* **9/2**[2]
0460 12 1 **General Feeling (IRE)**[19] 4386 7-9-0 48.... PAspell 10 37
(S T Mason) *s.i.s: nvr on terms* **25/1**
0000 13 20 **Shaftesbury Avenue (USA)**[103] 1776 5-9-4 48....(bt) DeanMcKeown 6 —
(J O'Reilly) *prom: hung rt and lost pl 3f out: sn bhd: t.o* **25/1**
05-5 14 2 ½ **Height Of Esteem**[13] 4559 5-8-13 46.... DuranFentiman(3) 8 —
(W M Brisbourne) *prom: lost pl 3f out: sn bhd: t.o* **25/1**

1m 35.16s (1.36) **Going Correction** +0.30s/f (Good)
WFA 3 from 4yo+ 6lb **14** Ran SP% **127.1**
Speed ratings (Par 103): **104,103,98,98,96 95,95,95,94,94 93,92,69,67**
toteswinger: 1&2 £7.20, 1&3 £14.00, 2&3 £15.00. CSF £36.20 TOTE £5.60: £2.40, £2.50, £2.60; EX 48.90.Le Chiffre was subject to a friendly claim of £5,000. Wiseman's Diamond was claimed by P T Midgley for £7,000.
Owner Stan Wright Shaun Taylor **Bred** Agricola Del Parco **Trained** Eastwell, Leics
■ Stewards' Enquiry : N Callan That's 18 winners on grass, and a total of 26 in all, so things have gone well. His owners, Stan Wright and Shaun Taylor, are good supporters, and they've had a good year as well. - John Harris, jockey

FOCUS
An ordinary claimer and the winner probably ran to his pre-race mark. The form looks fairly sound at this level.

4962 RAWFIELD H'CAP — 5f
3:15 (3:15) (Class 4) (0-85,85) 3-Y-O+ **£5,180** (£1,541; £770; £384) **Stalls** High

Form — RPR

0065 **1** **Divine Spirit**[7] 4743 7-8-12 **73** .... RoystonFfrench 9 — 84+
(M Dods) *stmbld s: sn mid-div: styd on to ld ins fnl f* **5/1**[1]

0000 **2** *1* **Green Park (IRE)**[23] 4240 5-9-7 **82** .... (b) PaulHanagan 3 — 89
(R A Fahey) *in rr-div: hdwy over 2f out: edgd rt jst ins fnl f: styd on fnl f* **9/1**

2540 **3** *shd* **Gallery Girl (IRE)**[75] 2583 5-9-2 **77** .... FergalLynch 12 — 84
(T D Easterby) *chsd ldr: led appr fnl f: hdd and no ex ins fnl f* **14/1**

0-00 **4** *2 1/4* **The Tatling (IRE)**[17] 4445 11-9-10 **85** .... PaulFitzsimons 5 — 84
(J M Bradley) *in rr: hdwy 2f out: kpt on fnl f* **25/1**

0002 **5** *1/2* **Pacific Pride**[19] 4393 5-9-3 **78** .... GrahamGibbons 11 — 75
(J J Quinn) *chsd ldrs: sn drvn along: kpt on same pce appr fnl f* **11/1**

450 **6** *shd* **Irish Pearl (IRE)**[18] 4416 3-9-5 **83** .... AndrewElliott 6 — 79+
(K R Burke) *in rr: hdwy and nt clr run over 1f out: kpt on wl ins fnl f* **20/1**

6423 **7** *nse* **Rabbit Fighter (IRE)**[20] 4341 4-8-12 **73** .... (v) DarrenWilliams 10 — 69+
(D Shaw) *hld up towards rr: hdwy on ins over 2f out: nt clr run over 1f out and jst ins fnl f: nvr rchd ldrs* **8/1**[3]

-444 **8** *2* **Foxy Music**[32] 3948 4-9-7 **82** .... DeanMcKeown 8 — 71
(E J Alston) *led tl over 1f out: sn wknd* **8/1**[3]

6540 **9** *1/2* **Avertuoso**[18] 4418 4-9-4 **79** .... (v) RobertWinston 1 — 66
(B Smart) *dwlt: hld up on outside in rr: effrt 2f out: hung rt: nvr on terms* **20/1**

4052 **10** *1 1/2* **Namir (IRE)**[7] 4743 6-8-9 **73** .... (vt) DuranFentiman(3) 13 — 55
(D Shaw) *chsd ldrs: wkng whn n.m.r jst ins fnl f* **5/1**[1]

0215 **11** *2 1/2* **He's A Humbug (IRE)**[18] 4418 4-9-10 **85** .... (p) NCallan 7 — 58
(K A Ryan) *chsd ldrs: hung rt 2f out: wknd and eased jst ins fnl f* **6/1**[2]

1000 **12** *2 1/4* **Bo McGinty (IRE)**[17] 4445 7-9-3 **81** .... (b) JamieMoriarty(3) 14 — 46
(R A Fahey) *in rr: hung rt over 1f out: nvr on terms* **12/1**

0 **13** *23* **Porto Santana (IRE)**[147] 942 3-8-13 **77** .... AdrianTNicholls 2 — —
(D Nicholls) *in rr-div on outer: hung bdly lft and eased over 1f out* **33/1**

64.32 secs (0.82) **Going Correction** +0.30s/f (Good)
WFA 3 from 4yo+ 3lb **13** Ran SP% **118.8**
Speed ratings (Par 105): **105,103,103,99,98 98,98,95,94,92 88,84,47**
toteswinger: 1&2 £14.00, 1&3 £15.70, 2&3 £29.70. CSF £46.68 CT £620.30 TOTE £5.20: £2.10, £3.70, £3.60; EX 62.80.
Owner The Newcastle Racing Club **Bred** S R Hope And D Erwin Bloodstock **Trained** Denton, Co Durham
■ Stewards' Enquiry : Paul Hanagan one-day ban: careless riding (Aug 28)

FOCUS
A tight sprint handicap with near the far rail the place to be. The well treated winner did very well after losing his footing exiting the stalls. The form is rated through the third.
Avertuoso Official explanation: jockey said gelding was slow away
Namir(IRE) Official explanation: jockey said gelding ran flat
Bo McGinty(IRE) Official explanation: jockey said gelding hung right
Porto Santana(IRE) Official explanation: jockey said gelding moved poorly throughout and hung left

4963 WBX.COM H'CAP — 2m 35y
3:45 (3:45) (Class 4) (0-85,80) 3-Y-O+ **£5,180** (£1,541; £770; £384) **Stalls** High

Form — RPR

5211 **1** **Let It Be**[17] 4452 7-8-12 **64** .... PaulHanagan 3 — 72
(K G Reveley) *sn trcking ldrs: wnt 2nd after 5f: led 3f out: hld on gamely* **9/2**[2]

-463 **2** *3/4* **Estate**[14] 4526 6-9-4 **70** .... RoystonFfrench 7 — 77
(E J O'Neill) *chsd ldrs: drvn over 3f out: wnt handy 2nd 2f out: no ex ins fnl f* **15/8**[1]

4534 **3** *3 1/2* **Danzatrice**[17] 4452 6-8-12 **67** .... DuranFentiman(3) 5 — 70
(C W Thornton) *hld up in rr: hdwy on outside over 2f out: styd on same pce* **8/1**

0042 **4** *3/4* **Sphinx (FR)**[25] 4178 10-10-0 **80** .... (b) RobertWinston 1 — 82
(E W Tuer) *hld up in rr: effrt 3f out: one pce* **11/2**[3]

0100 **5** *3 1/2* **Rock 'N' Roller (FR)**[32] 3950 4-9-8 **74** .... NCallan 4 — 72
(W R Muir) *trckd ldrs: rdn over 2f out: fdd over 1f out* **8/1**

0000 **6** *5* **Clueless**[8] 4701 6-9-5 **71** .... (be) NeilPollard 2 — 63
(A J McCabe) *led: drvn over 4f out: hdd 3f out: lost pl over 1f out* **14/1**

0510 **7** *shd* **Mister Arjay (USA)**[29] 4046 8-9-8 **74** .... TonyHamilton 9 — 66
(B Ellison) *chsd ldr: wknd 2f out* **13/2**

350- **8** *29* **Wait For The Light**[161] 6357 4-9-9 **75** .... (p) JimmyQuinn 8 — 32
(Mrs S Leech) *hld up in midfield: drvn over 4f out: lost pl over 3f out: sn bhd* **33/1**

3m 46.18s (6.38) **Going Correction** +0.30s/f (Good) **8** Ran SP% **113.5**
Speed ratings (Par 105): **96,95,93,93,91 89,89,74**
toteswinger: 1&2 £3.10, 1&3 £4.10, 2&3 £6.80. CSF £13.15 CT £63.74 TOTE £3.90: £1.50, £1.10, £2.30; EX 12.80.
Owner A Frame **Bred** Sir Eric Parker **Trained** Lingdale, Redcar & Cleveland
■ Stewards' Enquiry : Paul Hanagan I thought the ground might beat her, but she's so tough and genuine. We were going to get her in foal, but I'm glad we didn't. She's never won three in a season before. - Keith Reveley, trainer

FOCUS
A modest stayers' handicap run at just a steady pace. The first two were in the firing line throughout and the winner is rated back to her best old form.
Rock 'N' Roller(FR) Official explanation: trainer said gelding did not handle the track

4964 EAST RIDING MAIL H'CAP — 1m 1f 207y
4:20 (4:20) (Class 5) (0-70,69) 3-Y-O **£3,076** (£915; £457; £228) **Stalls** High

Form — RPR

4012 **1** **Highland Love**[23] 4244 3-9-6 **68** .... TonyHamilton 8 — 72
(Jedd O'Keeffe) *led 3f: wnt 2nd over 3f out: styd on to ld ins fnl f: jst hld on* **9/4**[1]

4322 **2** *shd* **Maha Dubai (USA)**[19] 4382 3-9-5 **67** .... RoystonFfrench 2 — 71
(M Johnston) *chsd ldrs: drvn 5f out: styd on to chal jst ins fnl f: jst failed* **5/1**[3]

0215 **3** *nk* **Coral Shores**[23] 4254 3-9-0 **62** .... (v) DarrenWilliams 7 — 65
(P W Hiatt) *trckd ldrs: led over 5f out tl ins fnl f: no ex nr fin* **9/1**

2401 **4** *1/2* **Jemima's Art**[7] 4738 3-7-13 **50** oh5 .... (b) DuranFentiman(3) 5 — 52
(M W Easterby) *hld up in rr: hdwy 5f out: styd on to chal jst ins fnl f: kpt on same pce* **3/1**[2]

0066 **5** *6* **Topflightrebellion**[16] 4479 3-8-2 **50** .... AndrewElliott 11 — 40
(Mrs G S Rees) *in rr and sn drvn along: sme hdwy on outer over 2f out: edgd rt and nvr nr ldrs* **33/1**

0-06 **6** *14* **Uncle Harry**[19] 4379 3-8-4 **52** .... PaulHanagan 3 — 14
(J J Quinn) *hld up in rr: drvn over 3f out: nvr on terms* **16/1**

50-0 **7** *hd* **Clear Daylight**[11] 4637 3-8-10 **58** ow1 .... GrahamGibbons 10 — 20
(J R Best) *drvn along in rr: bhd fnl 3f* **6/1**

5060 **8** *3* **Reel Buddy Blaze**[14] 4538 3-8-12 **60** .... RobertWinston 12 — 16
(T P Tate) *chsd ldrs: outpcd over 3f out: lost pl over 2f out* **14/1**

2110 **9** *22* **Natural Rhythm (IRE)**[17] 4455 3-8-10 **61** .... (b) MichaelJStainton(3) 6 — —
(Mrs R A Carr) *t.k.h: trckd ldrs: led after 3f: hdd over 5f out: wknd 3f out* **9/1**

2m 9.63s (2.63) **Going Correction** +0.30s/f (Good) **9** Ran SP% **122.2**
Speed ratings (Par 100): **101,100,100,100,95 84,84,81,64**
toteswinger: 1&2 2.90, 1&3 £4.70, 2&3 £7.90. CSF £14.92 CT £89.25 TOTE £3.40: £1.50, £1.60, £3.00; EX 10.40.
Owner Ken And Delia Shaw-KGS Consulting LLP **Bred** Farmers Hill Stud **Trained** Middleham Moor, N Yorks
■ Stewards' Enquiry : Tony Hamilton He's a big strong horse, so I hope he'll improve a bit more yet. - Jedd O'Keeff, jockey

FOCUS
A modest handicap run at a very steady pace with four in line just inside the last. The first three finished clear and the form is rated around the fourth.

4965 MAIL NEWS AND MEDIA MAIDEN AUCTION STKS — 5f
4:50 (4:51) (Class 5) 2-Y-O **£3,561** (£1,059; £529; £264) **Stalls** High

Form — RPR

1 **Roof Fiddle (USA)** 2-8-6 0 .... PaulHanagan 6 — 81+
(Kevin Prendergast, Ire) *dwlt: in rr: hdwy u.p over 1f out: styd on strly to ld fnl 75yds: drew clr* **15/8**[1]

240 **2** *2 3/4* **Red Rosanna**[25] 4176 2-8-4 67 .... PaulQuinn 10 — 69
(R Hollinshead) *led tl 3f out: led over 1f out: hdd and no ex ins fnl f* **4/1**[2]

324 **3** *nse* **Sir Geoffrey (IRE)**[48] 3392 2-8-7 78 .... AndrewElliott 9 — 72
(A J McCabe) *w ldr: led 3f out: hdd over 1f out: hung lft: styd on towards fin* **15/8**[1]

00 **4** *1* **Bubbly Baby**[15] 4499 2-7-11 0 .... DuranFentiman(3) 1 — 61
(T D Easterby) *mid-div: hdwy 2f out: styd on same pce ins fnl f* **14/1**

02 **5** *6* **Iorek Byrnison**[36] 3815 2-8-7 0 .... AdrianTNicholls 8 — 47
(D Nicholls) *chsd ldrs: wknd over 1f out* **12/1**

005 **6** *3 1/2* **Fashion Icon (USA)**[15] 4499 2-8-2 68 .... PaulFessey 4 — 29
(T D Barron) *outpcd and lost pl after 1f* **9/1**[3]

6 **7** *2* **Pollish**[17] 4456 2-7-7 0 .... CharlotteKerton(7) 5 — 20
(A Berry) *gave problems in stalls: dwlt: sn outpcd and in rr* **40/1**

0 **8** *3/4* **Kilsyth (IRE)**[2] 4921 2-8-1 0 .... KrishGundowry(7) 2 — 25
(S Parr) *sn wl outpcd and bhd* **66/1**

65.14 secs (1.64) **Going Correction** +0.30s/f (Good) **8** Ran SP% **117.9**
Speed ratings (Par 94): **98,93,93,91,82 76,73,72**
toteswinger: 1&2 2.50, 1&3 £2.00, 2&3 £2.30. CSF £10.22 TOTE £3.10: £1.30, £1.80, £1.30; EX 11.50.
Owner Norman Ormiston **Bred** Hunter Valley Farm **Trained** Friarstown, Co Kildare

FOCUS
The leaders went off very quick in the conditions and the first and fourth came from off the pace.

NOTEBOOK
Roof Fiddle(USA), a medium-sized, well-made newcomer, came here because she is not EBF qualified and opportunities in Ireland are thin on the ground for her. After a tardy start she responded gamely to pressure and burst through to show ahead and go clear. (op 7-4 tchd 9-4 and 5-2 in places)
Red Rosanna, very edgy beforehand, appreciated the return to turf and had the plum far-side rails draw. She regained the lead but had no answer when the winner swept past her inside the last. (tchd 5-1)
Sir Geoffrey(IRE), whose three previous starts were on the Polytrack, was taken to post ahead of the rest. Dropping back in trip, he went on coming to the halfway mark but he wandered when headed. He was coming back at the line but his provisional nursery mark of 78 looks plenty high enough. (op 2-1 tchd 7-4)
Bubbly Baby, worst drawn, couldn't match the furious pace. She stuck on in her own time from halfway and will be suited by six in nursery company. (op 20-1 tchd 9-1)
Iorek Byrnison, runner-up in a Fibresand seller, looked to be carrying plenty of condition on his first outing for five weeks. (op 8-1)
Fashion Icon(USA), beaten in selling company before her fifth in maiden company here two weeks ago, was given a rating of 68 after that which looks far too high. (op 16-1)

4966 FINDAPROPERTY H'CAP — 1m 4f 16y
5:20 (5:21) (Class 6) (0-65,65) 3-Y-O+ **£2,266** (£674; £337; £168) **Stalls** High

Form — RPR

502 **1** **Red Fama**[98] 1913 4-9-4 **51** .... JimmyQuinn 4 — 59
(N Bycroft) *hld up in mid-divsision: hdwy 5f out: stydn on to ld ins fnl f* **8/1**

3-00 **2** *1 1/4* **Edas**[32] 3947 6-9-13 **60** .... GrahamGibbons 7 — 66
(J J Quinn) *trckd ldrs: t.k.h: led appr fnl f: hdd and no ex ins fnl f* **7/1**[3]

3044 **3** *nk* **Sabancaya**[44] 3562 3-9-0 **58** .... AdrianTNicholls 1 — 64
(Mrs P Sly) *w ldr: led over 2f out: hdd and no ex ins fnl f* **17/2**

6141 **4** *2 1/2* **Fossgate**[9] 4690 7-10-3 **64** 6ex .... NCallan 9 — 66
(J D Bethell) *hld up in midfield: drvn over 3f out: sn chsng ldrs: hung rt and one pce over 1f out* **85/40**[1]

3030 **5** *6* **Skye But N Ben**[14] 4541 4-9-0 **47** .... (p) RoystonFfrench 12 — 39
(G A Harker) *trckd ldrs: wknd over 1f out* **20/1**

0630 **6** *shd* **Bollin Freddie**[24] 4220 4-8-9 **45** .... AndrewMullen(3) 2 — 37
(A J Lockwood) *t.k.h: hdwy to trck ldrs after 3f: outpcd over 3f out: no ch after* **20/1**

4215 **7** *3/4* **Gulf Coast**[15] 4503 3-9-7 **65** .... PaulHanagan 11 — 56
(T D Walford) *led tl over 2f out: wknd 1f out* **9/4**[2]

00-0 **8** *7* **Fuel Cell (IRE)**[14] 193 7-8-12 **45** .... TonyHamilton 6 — 25
(I W McInnes) *in rr: drvn over 4f out: nvr on terms* **14/1**

5155 **9** *5* **Fenners (USA)**[20] 4331 5-9-7 **61** .... NSLawes(7) 10 — 33
(M W Easterby) *in rr: drvn over 4f out: nvr on terms* **11/1**

4040 **10** *nk* **Tidy (IRE)**[8] 4701 8-9-3 **50** .... (v) RobertWinston 3 — 21
(Micky Hammond) *swtchd rt after s: hld up in rr: nvr on terms* **20/1**

2m 45.29s (4.39) **Going Correction** +0.30s/f (Good)
WFA 3 from 4yo+ 11lb **10** Ran SP% **126.2**
Speed ratings (Par 101): **97,96,95,94,90 90,89,85,81,81**
toteswinger: 1&2 13.90, 1&3 £12.70, 2&3 £14.00. CSF £66.11 CT £492.61 TOTE £12.80: £2.80, £2.80, £3.00; EX 120.80 Place 6: £12.34, Place 5: £10.29..
Owner B F Rayner **Bred** N Bycroft **Trained** Brandsby, N Yorks

FOCUS
A low-grade handicap run at a very steady pace. Pretty ordinary form, rated around the placed horses.
T/Jkpt: Not won. T/Plt: £21.60 to a £1 stake. Pool: £59,409.37. 1,999.90 winning tickets. T/Qpdt: £10.40 to a £1 stake. Pool: £3,491.36. 248.15 winning tickets. WG

4628 HAMILTON (R-H)

Wednesday, August 13

OFFICIAL GOING: Soft

Wind: Virtually nil Weather: Overcast and rain

4967 PERTEMPS PEOPLE DEVELOPMENT "HANDS AND HEELS" APPRENTICE H'CAP (ROUND 4: APPRENTICE RIDER SERIES) 6f 5y

5:50 (5:50) (Class 6) (0-65,65) 3-Y-O+ £2,266 (£674; £337; £168) Stalls Centre

Form RPR

0454 1 **Angel Voices (IRE)**[7] 4749 5-9-13 **64**.........................(p) DeclanCannon 7 73
(K R Burke) *mde virtually all: rdn wl over 1f out: kpt on wl fnl f* **7/1**

0262 2 1 1/4 **Soto**[12] 4609 5-9-9 **65**.........................(b) BradleyRoper(5) 3 70
(M W Easterby) *towards rr: hdwy whn hmpd 1/2-way: rdn wl over 1f out: styd on ins fnl f: nt rch wnr* **7/2**[2]

2043 3 1/2 **Oeuf A La Neige**[4] 4849 8-9-4 **55**......................... LanceBetts 2 58
(Miss L A Perratt) *towards rr: hdwy 2f out: rdn over 1f out: kpt on ins fnl f* **3/1**[1]

0546 4 3 **Howards Prince**[4] 4846 5-8-4 **46** oh1......................... PaulPickard(5) 1 40
(D A Nolan) *towards rr on outside: hdwy and hung rt 1/2-way: rdn to chse wnr wl over 1f out: wknd ins fnl f* **66/1**

0003 5 3 1/2 **Orpen Bid (IRE)**[4] 4851 3-7-12 **46** oh1......................... GemmaElford(7) 4 29
(A M Crow) *wnt rt s: towards rr: swtchd to far rail wl over 2f out: styd on appr fnl f: nrst fin* **11/1**

604 6 6 **Mrs Bun**[39] 3712 3-8-7 **51**......................... BMcHugh(3) 5 14
(K A Ryan) *sltly hmpd s: sn rdn along in rr and a outpcd* **7/2**[2]

0-00 7 1 1/4 **Vondova**[11] 4631 6-8-9 **46** oh1......................... DeanHeslop 6 5
(D A Nolan) *a towards rr* **66/1**

0024 8 3 3/4 **Mujma**[3] 4903 4-8-13 **50**.........................(p) KylieManser 11 —
(S Parr) *cl up: rdn along 2f out and sn wknd* **11/2**[3]

0060 9 1 3/4 **Spinning Game**[19] 4383 4-8-9 **46** oh1.........................(b) AdeleRothery 9 —
(Mrs R A Carr) *prom: rdn along 1/2-way: sn wknd* **22/1**

1m 16.94s (4.74) **Going Correction** +0.475s/f (Yiel)

WFA 3 from 4yo+ 4lb **9** Ran SP% **113.0**

Speed ratings (Par 101): **87,85,84,80,76 68,66,61,59**

toteswinger: 1&2 £5.00, 1&3 £3.90, 2&3 £2.60. CSF £30.66 CT £88.71 TOTE £9.20: £1.80, £2.00, £1.30; EX 35.40.

Owner Mrs Elaine M Burke **Bred** W Haggas And W Jarvis **Trained** Middleham Moor, N Yorks

FOCUS

An ordinary handicap for apprentices in which it proved quite difficult to challenge from off the pace, setting the tone for the evening. The winning time was moderate, even allowing for the conditions. Sound and straightforward form.

Mrs Bun Official explanation: jockey said filly was never travelling

4968 EUROPEAN BREEDERS' FUND NOVICE STKS 1m 65y

6:20 (6:22) (Class 4) 2-Y-O £5,180 (£1,541; £770; £384) Stalls High

Form RPR

5 1 **Warrior One**[18] 4415 2-8-9 0......................... NeilBrown(3) 2 83+
(J Howard Johnson) *set stdy pce: qcknd 3f out: rdn 2f out: styd on strly ins fnl f* **9/2**[3]

1 2 1 3/4 **High Alert**[21] 4304 2-9-2 0.........................(b) TPQueally 6 79
(J Noseda) *trckd ldng pair: smooth hdwy over 2f out: rdn over 1f out: drvn ent fnl f and kpt on same pce* **11/10**[1]

1 3 2 3/4 **Rising Prospect**[33] 3926 2-9-2 0......................... PJMcDonald(3) 1 76
(G M Moore) *trckd wnr: effrt over 2f out: rdn wl over 1f out: sn hung lft and one pce* **7/2**[2]

4 8 **Battle Royal (IRE)** 2-8-8 0......................... TomEaves 7 47
(B Smart) *v.s.a: sn in tch: hdwy on outer and cl up 3f out: rdn over 2f out and sn wknd* **8/1**

52 5 4 1/2 **Tiger Goddess (IRE)**[20] 4339 2-8-7 0......................... TonyCulhane 4 36
(W J Haggas) *in tch: pushed along bef 1/2-way: rdn over 3f out and sn btn* **8/1**

0 6 6 **K'Gari (USA)**[18] 4415 2-8-5 0......................... LanceBetts(7) 5 28
(B Ellison) *sn outpcd and bhd fr 1/2-way* **66/1**

1m 57.27s (8.87) **Going Correction** +0.625s/f (Yiel) **6** Ran SP% **111.7**

Speed ratings (Par 96): **80,78,75,67,63 57**

toteswinger: 1&2 £1.90, 1&3 £2.80, 2&3 £1.60. CSF £9.83 TOTE £6.80: £2.20, £1.70; EX 11.10.

Owner J Howard Johnson **Bred** Ermyn Lodge Stud Limited **Trained** Billy Row, Co Durham

FOCUS

An extended mile on soft ground proved quite a test for these two-year-olds and stamina came to the fore. The winning time was moderate.

NOTEBOOK

Warrior One had run with promise on his debut and this son of Act One promised to be well suited by the test of stamina that this extra furlong on soft ground presented. In front from the start, he was allowed to bowl along at his own pace and, on a day when it proved difficult to make up ground, he was in the box seat throughout. Stamina is clearly his strong suit. (op 15-2)

High Alert, sent off a hot favourite on the back of his debut win on the Polytrack, had very different conditions to deal with this time but was representing a stable with a record of seven winners from its nine runners at the track since 2004. He came to have every chance two furlongs out but the winner, who has a stouter pedigree, just kept pulling out more in these testing conditions. (op 5-6 tchd 6-5 in places)

Rising Prospect had won in heavy ground on his debut so had fewer question marks next to his name than most. However, he had a 7lb penalty to carry as a result, and in the end that found him out. (op 9-2)

Battle Royal(IRE), who cost 200,000gns, is a half-brother to eight winners, including Grey Swallow, a champion Irish two-year-old and later winner of the Irish Derby. Very slowly away, he soon made up the lost ground, but it all proved a bit much for him against more experienced rivals in the latter stages. He will be all the better for the run and quicker ground will probably suit. (op 11-1)

Tiger Goddess(IRE) was up in grade and not sure to appreciate this test of stamina. She was well held in the end but is at least now eligible for a mark. (op 13-2)

4969 FRESH'N'LO CLAIMING STKS 1m 65y

6:55 (6:55) (Class 6) 3-Y-O+ £2,388 (£705; £352) Stalls High

Form RPR

241 1 **Five Wishes**[11] 4629 4-8-13 65.........................(be) PJMcDonald(3) 7 67
(M Dods) *in tch on inner: pushed along 3f out: swtchd lft 2f out and sn rdn: drvn to chse wnr ent fnl f: styd on to ld nr line* **5/1**[3]

-530 2 1/2 **Primo Way**[4] 4851 7-8-13 64.........................(b) TomEaves 4 63
(Miss L A Perratt) *trckd ldr: led over 5f out: rdn clr 2f out: drvn ins fnl f: hdd and no ex nr fin* **6/1**

3301 3 4 **Inside Story (IRE)**[12] 4597 6-9-5 70.........................(b) DaleGibson 5 60
(M W Easterby) *hld up in rr: pushed along over 3f out: rdn wl over 2f out: styd on u.p ins fnl f* **11/10**[1]

0016 4 nk **Royal Applord**[17] 4451 3-9-6 68......................... PaulMulrennan 3 66
(K A Ryan) *led to over 5f out: cl up: rdn along 3f out: sn drvn and grad wknd* **18/1**

2452 5 5 **Chin Wag (IRE)**[4] 4849 4-9-3 61.........................(p) DanielTudhope 2 46
(J S Goldie) *trckd ldng pair: hdwy to chse wnr 2f out: sn rdn and wknd wl over 1f out* **7/2**[2]

5014 6 8 **Sarraaf (IRE)**[11] 4633 12-8-5 53......................... PatrickDonaghy(5) 1 20
(Miss L A Perratt) *hld up: hdwy to chse ldrs over 3f out: rdn wl over 2f out and sn btn* **14/1**

0-00 7 42 **Wolf Pack**[11] 4632 6-8-3 31......................... PaulPickard(7) 6 —
(D A Nolan) *outpcd and bhd fr 1/2-way* **250/1**

1m 55.45s (7.05) **Going Correction** +0.625s/f (Yiel)

WFA 3 from 4yo+ 7lb **7** Ran SP% **113.1**

Speed ratings (Par 101): **89,88,84,84,79 71,29**

toteswinger: 1&2 £2.70, 1&3 £2.40, 2&3 £1.80. CSF £33.65 TOTE £6.00: £2.20, £3.10; EX 35.10.

Owner Exors of the late Mark Swift **Bred** Alan A Wright **Trained** Denton, Co Durham

■ Stewards' Enquiry : P J McDonald one-day ban: careless riding (Aug 27)

FOCUS

A weakish claimer with the favourite below par, in which once again it was an advantage to be on the front end. The winning time was moderate for the type of race.

4970 EBF CAPTAIN J.C. STEWART FILLIES' H'CAP 1m 65y

7:25 (7:26) (Class 3) (0-95,90) 3-Y-O+ £11,009 (£3,275; £1,637; £817) Stalls High

Form RPR

0003 1 **Insaaf**[35] 3849 3-9-3 **87**.........................(v) TonyCulhane 4 96+
(W J Haggas) *sn led: rdn and qcknd over 2f out: clr wl over 1f out: drvn out* **4/1**[2]

-242 2 3 **Badalona**[32] 3944 3-8-10 **83**......................... PJMcDonald(3) 2 84
(M L W Bell) *trckd ldrs: hdwy 3f out: effrt to chse wnr 2f out and sn rdn: drvn ent fnl f and sn no imp* **5/1**[3]

3201 3 7 **Nutkin**[32] 3944 4-9-5 **82**......................... JamieSpencer 7 68
(J R Fanshawe) *hld up towards rr: pushed along 4f out: effrt and hdwy 3f out: sn rdn: edgd lft and btn wl over 1f out* **11/10**[1]

1413 4 6 **Magic Echo**[48] 3403 4-9-12 **89**......................... TomEaves 3 61
(M Dods) *hld up: sme hdwy over 3f out: sn rdn and no imp* **16/1**

3415 5 5 **Hula Ballew**[11] 4649 8-9-2 **82**......................... NeilBrown(3) 5 43
(M Dods) *trckd wnr: rdn along 3f out: drvn 2f out and sn wknd* **7/1**

2120 6 2 **Keisha Kayleigh (IRE)**[18] 4419 5-8-11 **74**.........................(v) TPQueally 1 30
(B Ellison) *s.i.s: a in rr* **9/1**

1m 52.53s (4.13) **Going Correction** +0.625s/f (Yiel)

WFA 3 from 4yo+ 7lb **6** Ran SP% **112.7**

Speed ratings (Par 104): **104,101,94,88,83 81**

toteswinger: 1&2 £1.60, 1&3 £2.70, 2&3 £1.10. CSF £23.86 TOTE £5.20: £2.10, £2.90; EX 17.20.

Owner Hamdan Al Maktoum **Bred** Lostford Manor Stud **Trained** Newmarket, Suffolk

FOCUS

Some decent prizemoney on offer for this feature race resulted in a competitive handicap. The winner had a firaly easy time of it up front and is rated up 3lb, with the runner-up to form.

NOTEBOOK

Insaaf, who gained her sole previous success on soft ground, has been running reasonably on faster going but the return to an easier surface worked the oracle. She was given a positive ride and proved she stayed this longer trip by drawing clear in the last furlong and a half. She should be capable of winning again when she gets her favoured conditions. (op 3-1)

Badalona is a pretty consistent sort but her win also came on soft ground. She chased the winner all the way up the straight but could not reduce the gap and probably offers the best guide to the level. She deserves to pick up another race. (op 6-1 tchd 7-1)

Nutkin, who beat today's runner-up at Ascot last time, was 5lb worse off but was never travelling and Spencer was niggling at her a long way from home. She just ran on at one pace and is clearly better than this. (op 11-8 tchd 13-8 in a place)

Magic Echo, who ran as well as could be expected in a conditions race here last time, stays further than this and seems better ridden more prominently. (op 12-1)

Hula Ballew tried to keep tabs on the winner but dropped away in the last quarter-mile and looks to be in the Handicapper's grip now. (op 8-1)

4971 VARIETY CLUB H'CAP 5f 4y

7:55 (7:56) (Class 5) (0-75,73) 3-Y-O+ £3,238 (£963; £481; £240) Stalls Centre

Form RPR

36-0 1 **Angle Of Attack (IRE)**[8] 4700 3-9-6 **72**......................... SilvestreDeSousa 4 83+
(A D Brown) *mde all: rdn over 1f out: drvn and edgd lft ins fnl f: styd on gamely* **22/1**

3513 2 1 3/4 **Katie Boo (IRE)**[4] 4858 6-9-10 **73**......................... JoeFanning 7 79
(A Berry) *cl up on outer: effrt 2f out and sn rdn: drvn and ev ch ins fnl f: nt qckn last 100yds* **9/2**[2]

4060 3 nk **Blazing Heights**[13] 4555 5-9-3 **71**......................... GaryBartley(5) 1 76
(J S Goldie) *trckd ldrs on stands' rail: hdwy 2f out: rdn ent fnl f: kpt on u.p towards fin* **5/1**[3]

2600 4 1/2 **Steel City Boy (IRE)**[8] 4700 5-8-10 **64**......................... AnnStokell(5) 2 67
(Miss A Stokell) *chsd ldrs: rdn along wl over 1f out: kpt on same pce u.p ins fnl f* **5/1**[3]

2103 5 nk **Rothesay Dancer**[11] 4631 5-9-2 **70**......................... KellyHarrison(5) 5 72
(J S Goldie) *trckd ldrs: hdwy 2f out: rdn and ev ch ent fnl f: sn drvn and one pce* **11/2**

2411 6 2 **Miss Daawe**[19] 4385 4-8-12 **68**......................... LanceBetts(7) 6 63
(B Ellison) *cl up: effrt wl over 1f out: sn rdn and wknd ent fnl f* **3/1**[1]

3540 7 1 1/2 **Howards Tipple**[4] 4846 4-8-9 **58**.........................(p) TomEaves 8 47
(Miss L A Perratt) *hld up in tch: effrt 2f out: sn rdn and no hdwy* **11/2**

0050 8 5 **Mutayam**[13] 4561 8-8-7 **59** oh9 ow5.........................(tp) PJMcDonald(3) 3 30
(D A Nolan) *dwlt: a in rr* **100/1**

61.94 secs (1.94) **Going Correction** +0.475s/f (Yiel)

WFA 3 from 4yo+ 3lb **8** Ran SP% **112.6**

Speed ratings (Par 103): **103,100,99,98,98 95,92,84**

toteswinger: 1&2 £3.90, 1&3 £25.10, 2&3 £1.90. CSF £114.29 CT £585.87 TOTE £30.90: £6.20, £1.80, £1.60; EX 156.80.

Owner Bill McEvoy **Bred** Travel Spot Girl Partnership **Trained** Pickering, York

FOCUS

An ordinary sprint handicap in which the field raced centre to stands' side. Again the winner made all, so may have been advantaged, but the form of the placed horses looks pretty solid.

Angle Of Attack(IRE) Official explanation: trainer had no explanation for the improved form shown.

The Form Book, Raceform Ltd, Compton, RG20 6NL

Miss Daawe Official explanation: trainer said filly was unsuited by the soft ground

4972 OFFICER AND A GENTLEMAN H'CAP 1m 4f 17y
8:25 (8:25) (Class 5) (0-70,70) 3-Y-O+ £3,238 (£963; £481; £240) Stalls High

Form RPR
3651 1 **Astrodome**[11] 4630 3-8-7 60......(b) PaulMulrennan 5 74
(Sir Mark Prescott) *t.k.h: mde virtually all: rdn wl over 2f out: drvn over 1f out: kpt on gamely u.p ins fnl f* 7/4[1]
63-0 2 1 3/4 **Los Nadis (GER)**[143] 981 4-9-7 70...... RyanMania(7) 7 81
(P Monteith) *hld up in midfield: stdy hdwy 4f out: rdn to chse wnr wl over 1f out: drvn and ev ch ins fnl f: no ex last 100yds* 11/2[3]
2000 3 3 1/4 **Rudry World (IRE)**[23] 4238 5-9-2 65...... GarryWhillans(7) 10 71
(M Mullineaux) *hld up towards rr: hdwy and pushed along 5f out: swtchd wd and rdn 3f out: drvn and kpt on same pce fnl 2f* 4/1[2]
-152 4 2 3/4 **Chookie Hamilton**[4] 4850 4-8-13 58...... PJMcDonald(3) 9 59
(Miss L A Perratt) *chsd ldrs: rdn along over 4f out: drvn 3f out and plugged on same pce* 4/1[2]
2/00 5 8 **Herakles (GER)**[38] 3756 7-9-8 64...... JoeFanning 6 53
(M Mullineaux) *dwlt and towards rr: rapid hdwy to chse ldng pair 1/2-way: rdn along 4f out and grad wknd* 16/1
3050 6 2 **Hawkit (USA)**[4] 4850 7-9-9 68...... NeilBrown(3) 3 53
(P Monteith) *chsd ldng pair: hdwy to chse wnr 5f out: rdn over 2f out: sn drvn and grad wknd* 8/1
2500 7 78 **Kirkie (USA)**[50] 3339 3-8-12 65......(t) TonyCulhane 2 —
(S Parr) *a in rr: wl bhd fr 1/2-way* 16/1
8 92 **White Ross (IRE)**[332] 5457 3-7-5 51 oh3...... JamieKyne(7) 8 —
(Neill McCluskey, Ire) *t.k.h: cl up to 1/2-way: sn lost pl and bhd fnl 4f* 25/1

2m 48.75s (10.15) **Going Correction** +0.625s/f (Yiel)
WFA 3 from 4yo+ 11lb 8 Ran SP% 118.5
Speed ratings (Par 103): **91,89,87,85,80 79,27,—**
toteswinger: 1&2 £5.60, 1&3 £2.60, 2&3 £3.10. CSF £12.44 CT £34.88 TOTE £2.60: £1.30, £1.50, £1.60; EX 14.10 Place 6 £112.92, Place 5 £68.28..
Owner W E Sturt - Osborne House II **Bred** Miss K Rausing And Mrs S Rogers **Trained** Newmarket, Suffolk
■ Stewards' Enquiry : Garry Whillans two-day ban: used whip with excessive frequency (Aug 27-28)
Paul Mulrennan four-day ban: used whip with excessive frequency (Aug 27-30)

FOCUS
A modest handicap and the time was moderate, even for the conditions. The form is rated through the second and third and there is probably more to come from the winner.
T/Plt: £67.20 to a £1 stake. Pool: £49,439.34. 536.89 winning tickets. T/Qpdt: £26.40 to a £1 stake. Pool: £4,282.26. 119.95 winning tickets. JR

4428 SALISBURY (R-H)
Wednesday, August 13

OFFICIAL GOING: Good to soft changing to good to soft (soft in places) after race 4 (3.35) changing to soft after race 5 (4.05)
Wind: Brisk ahead

4973 EBF/CARMEN WINES MAIDEN STKS (DIV I) 6f
2:00 (2:03) (Class 4) 2-Y-O £4,371 (£1,300; £650; £324) Stalls High

Form RPR
40 1 **Princess Hannah**[13] 4554 2-8-12 0...... RichardHughes 7 70
(R Hannon) *lw: w ldrs tl drvn ahd ins fnl 2f: hld on wl cl home* 5/2[2]
2 1/2 **Cavera (USA)** 2-8-12 0...... FrancisNorton 6 71+
(A M Balding) *unf: scope: on toes: s.i.s: in rr but in tch: hdwy 2f out: squeezed between horses over 1f out and chsd wnr ins fnl f: fin strly but a jst hld* 9/2[3]
3 1 3/4 **Zero Money (IRE)** 2-9-3 0...... SteveDrowne 4 68+
(R Charlton) *w'like: str: scope: t.k.h: in tch: pushed along over 2f out: styd on to chse ldng duo fnl f but nvr gng pce to be competitive* 13/8[1]
0 4 nk **Mr Flannegan**[19] 4367 2-9-3 0...... DaneO'Neill 3 67
(H Candy) *w'like: chsd ldrs: rdn and one pce fnl 2f* 14/1
0 5 1 **Davids Matador**[26] 4150 2-9-3 0...... StephenCarson 8 64
(Eve Johnson Houghton) *in tch: drvn to chse ldrs over 2f out: one pce fnl f* 12/1
6 3 **Jarrah Bay** 2-8-12 0...... TGMcLaughlin 1 50
(J G M O'Shea) *lean: leggy: a towards rr* 40/1
7 1 1/4 **Banda Sea (IRE)** 2-9-3 0...... FergusSweeney 9 52
(P J Makin) *w'like: scope: bit bkwd: on toes: slt advantage: rdn 3f out: hdd ins fnl 2f: sn wknd* 14/1
8 2 3/4 **Baby Josr** 2-9-3 0...... DMylonas 10 43
(I A Wood) *w'like: bit bkwd: s.i.s: sn chsng ldrs: wknd over 1f out* 33/1

1m 18.97s (4.17) **Going Correction** +0.325s/f (Good) 8 Ran SP% 111.3
Speed ratings (Par 96): **85,84,82,81,80 76,74,70**
toteswinger: 1&2 £2.30, 1&3 £1.50, 2&3 £2.10. CSF £13.40 TOTE £3.20: £1.40, £1.80, £1.10; EX 11.60.
Owner A P Patey **Bred** Gainsborough Stud Management Ltd **Trained** East Everleigh, Wilts

FOCUS
An ordinary maiden run 1.57secs slower than the second division. The field raced down the stands' rail and the going was changed to good to soft all round after this race.

NOTEBOOK
Princess Hannah, who showed promise on her debut over 5f here, had since dropped out after suffering trouble in running when tried over 7f at Goodwood. Handling the rain-softened ground well, she made the best of her previous experience by getting to the rail and, establishing a clear advantage over a furlong out, ran on to hold the strong-finishing second. She should prove competitive in nurseries now. (op 9-4 tchd 11-4)
Cavera(USA) ◆, an American-bred filly out of a multiple sprint winner on dirt, missed the break on this debut and did not get the clearest of runs when making her move, but stayed on well and was closing down the winner at the line. She should not be long in going one better. (op 7-2 tchd 10-3)
Zero Money(IRE), a 180,000gns half-brother to five winners, was quite keen on this debut then ran green when asked for his effort before staying on well in the closing stages. He should come on a lot for the outing and should be capable of winning races, possibly over slightly further. (op 15-8 tchd 2-1)
Mr Flannegan, a chunky gelding, improved considerably on his debut on fast ground at the end of last month and showed up until fading in the final furlong. He will qualify for handicaps after another run and should make his mark in that sphere. (op 20-1)
Davids Matador, a nice type who reportedly had a breathing problem following his debut over 7f, raced towards the centre of the track and ran well enough on this drop in trip until fading late on. (op 16-1)

4974 EBF/CARMEN WINES MAIDEN STKS (DIV II) 6f
2:30 (2:37) (Class 4) 2-Y-O £4,371 (£1,300; £650; £324) Stalls High

Form RPR
2 1 **Outofoil (IRE)**[18] 4430 2-9-3 0...... RyanMoore 4 79
(R M Beckett) *lw: chsd ldrs: drvn along 2f out: hdwy on ins to chal fnl f: kpt on u.p to ld cl home* 7/4[1]
3 2 hd **Frank Street**[16] 4482 2-9-3 0...... StephenCarson 7 78
(Eve Johnson Houghton) *str: lengthy: lw: pressed ldr tl slt advantage over 1f out: hrd drvn fnl f: hdd cl home* 20/1
65 3 1/2 **Admiral Sandhoe (USA)**[7] 4720 2-9-3 0...... JimCrowley 9 77
(Mrs A J Perrett) *lw: s.i.s: towards rr: hdwy over 1f out: drvn and styd on ins fnl f: fin wl and gng on cl home* 18/1
2462 4 1 3/4 **Heliodor (USA)**[32] 3941 2-9-3 80...... RichardHughes 8 72
(R Hannon) *chsd ldrs: rdn and effrt over 1f out: no imp ins fnl f and sn btn* 3/1[2]
56 5 2 3/4 **Waahej**[26] 4164 2-9-3 0...... RHills 1 63
(J L Dunlop) *lw: slt ld tl rdn: hung rt and hdd over 1f out: sn btn* 6/1
0 6 3/4 **Dalradian (IRE)**[26] 4151 2-9-3 0...... PaulDoe 10 61
(W J Knight) *lw: pressed ldrs: rdn 3f out: wknd over 1f out* 7/2[3]
7 2 3/4 **Rest By The River** 2-8-12 0...... FergusSweeney 5 48
(A G Newcombe) *w'like: str: chsd ldrs: rdn 2f out: wknd over 1f out* 66/1
0 8 hd **Blue Bogey (USA)**[10] 4665 2-9-3 0...... RichardKingscote 6 52
(R Charlton) *lw: in tch: rdn over 2f out and sn dropped away* 33/1
9 3 1/2 **Countess Zara (IRE)** 2-8-12 0...... FrancisNorton 3 37
(A M Balding) *w'like: bit bkwd: green: veered rt s: rdn and green: a bhd* 14/1
10 1 **Day In Dubai** 2-8-7 0...... DavidProbert(5) 2 34
(J J Bridger) *leggy: green and a in rr* 66/1

1m 17.4s (2.60) **Going Correction** +0.325s/f (Good) 10 Ran SP% 120.5
Speed ratings (Par 96): **95,94,94,91,88 87,83,83,78,77**
toteswinger: 1&2 £6.10, 1&3 £7.70, 2&3 £17.90. CSF £44.71 TOTE £2.80: £1.20, £5.30, £5.00; EX 33.50.
Owner I J Heseltine **Bred** Barouche Stud Ireland Ltd **Trained** Whitsbury, Hants

FOCUS
This second division was run 1.47secs faster than the first and they again came to the stands' rail, as they did in all the subsequent races.

NOTEBOOK
Outofoil(IRE), who showed plenty of promise on his debut over course and distance but on much faster ground, was well supported and justified that with a narrow success. He got a good split up the rail to get to the front and that made the difference between victory and defeat. He should be able to build on this in nurseries. (op 11-4 tchd 13-8)
Frank Street ◆, who showed promise on his debut, was sent off at surprisingly long odds and ran really well, making the winner fight all the way to the line. Effective on fast and easy ground, this half-brother to the same connections' Judd Street should not be long in getting off the mark. (op 33-1)
Admiral Sandhoe(USA), who had shown signs of ability in two tries over 7f on fast ground, was doing his best work late on and now qualifies for a handicap mark. (op 16-1 tchd 20-1)
Heliodor(USA), the most experienced runner in the line-up and with form on easy ground, travelled well enough but found less than looked likely under pressure. His current rating of 80 looks to flatter him and it may be that he needs some sort of headgear to help him produce his optimum performance. (op 9-4 tchd 10-3)
Waahej, another who has shown a modest level of ability in two previous starts, was supported in the market and, getting the rail early, showed up until tiring in the last furlong. He should get a reasonable handicap mark now. (op 10-1)
Dalradian(IRE) was well fancied to build on the promise of his debut over an extra furlong at Newbury, but again raced keenly and ran out of steam in the closing stages. He will have to learn to settle better if he is to fulfil his potential. (op 3-1)
Rest By The River, a speedily-bred filly, was green in the paddock but showed good early pace on the outside of her field before fading and may be able to make her mark at an ordinary level. (op 100-1)
Countess Zara(IRE) Official explanation: jockey said filly hung badly right-handed

4975 JAMES & SONS NURSERY 6f 212y
3:00 (3:04) (Class 5) 2-Y-O £3,238 (£963; £481; £240) Stalls High

Form RPR
500 1 **River Captain (IRE)**[13] 4570 2-8-10 63...... RichardKingscote 6 70
(S Kirk) *chsd ldrs: chal 2f out: led over 1f out: drvn and styd on strly fnl f* 10/1
013 2 2 1/4 **River Dee (IRE)**[10] 4659 2-9-0 67...... HayleyTurner 2 68
(Miss Amy Weaver) *in tch: pushed along and hdwy 2f out: hrd drvn over 1f out: styd on wl fnl f but nvr gng pce to rch wnr* 4/1[1]
042 3 1 3/4 **Our Day Will Come**[20] 4328 2-9-7 74...... RichardHughes 9 71
(R Hannon) *stdd s and hld up in rr: hdwy fr 2f out: swtchd rt and styd on u.p fnl f but nvr gng pce to get nr wnr* 9/2[2]
0254 4 1 1/2 **Hawkspur (IRE)**[10] 4659 2-9-4 71...... RyanMoore 1 68+
(R Hannon) *in rr: hdwy on ins whn hmpd ins fnl 2f: rdn 2f out: styd on fnl f but nvr in contention* 9/2[2]
0204 5 2 3/4 **Elusive Ronnie (IRE)**[25] 4185 2-8-1 59......(p) DavidProbert(5) 11 45
(R A Teal) *w ldr: rdn to take slt ld ins fnl 2f: hdd over 1f out and sn btn* 11/1
555 6 nk **Sharav**[27] 4126 2-8-12 65...... StephenCarson 12 50
(Eve Johnson Houghton) *in rr and off pce early: hdwy over 2f out: swtchd rt over 1f out and styd on fnl f but nvr in contention* 8/1
5345 7 3 **Mesyaal**[11] 4647 2-9-4 71...... SamHitchcott 5 49
(M R Channon) *chsd ldrs: rdn fr 3f out: wknd ins fnl 2f* 14/1
003 8 1 3/4 **Sicilian Pink**[18] 4425 2-9-1 68...... RichardMullen 8 41
(J L Dunlop) *lw: in rr: pushed along over 2f out and no rspnse* 7/1[3]
0043 9 1/2 **Rich Red (IRE)**[32] 3941 2-8-12 65...... PatDobbs 7 37
(R Hannon) *sn towards rr: rdn and edgd lft to rail ins fnl 3f: nvr in contention* 10/1
600 10 4 1/2 **Louie's Lad**[16] 4480 2-8-4 57...... MartinDwyer 4 18
(J A Geake) *sn led: hdd ins fnl 2f and sn hung rt: wknd qckly* 25/1
000 11 2 1/4 **Zaftil (IRE)**[20] 4321 2-7-12 51 oh6...... CatherineGannon 13 6
(H S Howe) *chsd ldrs over 4f* 66/1

1m 32.11s (3.11) **Going Correction** +0.325s/f (Good) 11 Ran SP% 118.5
Speed ratings (Par 94): **95,92,90,88,85 85,81,79,79,74 71**
toteswinger: 1&2 £8.90, 1&3 £11.10, 2&3 £4.60. CSF £50.19 CT £214.09 TOTE £11.70: £3.00, £1.80, £1.90; EX 45.50.
Owner S J McCay **Bred** Sean Finnegan **Trained** Upper Lambourn, Berks

FOCUS
A modest nursery but run 0.3secs faster than the later apprentice handicap.

NOTEBOOK

River Captain(IRE), who had been well beaten in two outings since showing promise on his debut on Polytrack, put up a much-improved effort on this handicap debut. As a son of Captain Rio the softer ground may well have been a factor, but he is likely to go up a fair bit for this effort and will have to improve to follow up. Official explanation: trainer said, regarding the improved form shown, that colt was better suited by the soft ground (op 12-1)

River Dee(IRE), who won a fast-ground seller at Yarmouth before improving on that in a Chester nursery, put up another decent effort and seems to appreciate some cut in the ground. (op 9-2)

Our Day Will Come, who had been in the frame in two Doncaster maidens over 7f, was held up on this drop in trip and looked to be going well at one point. However, she was denied a run up the rail as the runner-up drifted and, after being switched, could not make any further impression. (op 4-1 tchd 7-2)

Hawkspur(IRE) was held up a fair way off the pace, but was starting to make progress when not getting the clearest of runs before staying on quite nicely in the closing stages. He looked as if this extra furlong was in his favour and can be given another chance. (op 11-2 tchd 6-1)

Elusive Ronnie(IRE) has shown ability in plating company and in a nursery on fast ground, and appeared to handle this softer surface, although the extra furlong may have found him out. (tchd 10-1 and 12-1)

Sharav, who had been fifth on all three starts over 5f, was stepping up 2f on this handicap debut. He went right out of the stalls and was at the back of the field after switching to the stands' rail, but then had switch out to the middle of the track to get a run. He kept on quite well from off the pace and this half-brother to Bygone Days, who was suited by cut in the ground, is not one to give up on yet. (op 11-1 tchd 12-1)

Sicilian Pink, a half-sister to Scarlet Runner who ran well on fast ground last time, was never in contention on this handicap debut and may not have handled the ground. (op 6-1 tchd 11-2)

Louie's Lad Official explanation: jockey said gelding ran too free

4976 GOLDRING SECURITY SERVICES PEMBROKE CUP (H'CAP) 1m

3:35 (3:38) (Class 4) (0-85,85) 3-Y-O **£5,180** (£1,541; £770; £384) **Stalls** High

Form				RPR
31	**1**		**Stalking Shadow (USA)**[19] 4378 3-9-2 **80** ... LDettori 8 (Saeed Bin Suroor) *lw: t.k.h early: trckd ldrs: shkn up 2f out: qcknd over 1f out and led ins fnl f: pushed out and a holding runner-up cl home* **15/8**[1]	91+
531	**2**	*nk*	**Acrostic**[63] 2955 3-9-6 **84** ... DaneO'Neill 2 (L M Cumani) *lw: trckd ldr: led jst ins fnl 2f: sn rdn: hdd ins fnl f: kpt on cl home but a hld* **3/1**[3]	94+
21-0	**3**	*4 1/2*	**Ballora (FR)**[21] 4300 3-8-12 **76** ... RyanMoore 1 (S Kirk) *chsd ldrs: nvr gng pce to be competitive and one pce fnl 2f* **5/2**[2]	76
3060	**4**	*2*	**King's Wonder**[13] 4553 3-8-12 **76** ... RichardMullen 6 (W R Muir) *in rr: rdn and no prog fnl 2f* **11/2**	71
2630	**5**	*3 1/2*	**Ben Ami**[48] 3393 3-8-8 **72** ... JohnEgan 3 (Miss J R Gibney) *slt ld tl drvn 3l clr 3f out: hdd jst ins fnl 2f and sn wknd* **10/1**	59

1m 47.57s (4.07) **Going Correction** +0.475s/f (Yiel) **5** Ran SP% **112.8**

Speed ratings (Par 102): **98,97,93,91,87**

toteswinger: 1&2 £4.30. CSF £8.05 TOTE £2.10: £1.40, £2.00; EX 5.30.

Owner Godolphin **Bred** Brushwood Stable **Trained** Newmarket, Suffolk

FOCUS

A race affected by three non-runners on account of the ground and the field once again came down the stands' side. The pace was nothing special, but the front pair pulled clear and are clearly above average. although it is not easy to pin down exactly what they achieved.

4977 EUROPEAN BREEDERS' FUND UPAVON FILLIES' STKS (LISTED RACE) 1m 1f 198y

4:05 (4:10) (Class 1) 3-Y-O+

£28,385 (£10,760; £5,385; £2,685; £1,345; £675) **Stalls** High

Form				RPR
3045	**1**		**Lady Deauville (FR)**[11] 4657 3-8-5 **106** ... FrancisNorton 2 (P A Blockley) *chsd ldrs: led jst ins fnl 2f: styd on wl u.p ins fnl f* **4/1**[3]	104
5015	**2**	*1*	**Sweet Lilly**[10] 4667 4-9-4 **105** ... EdwardCreighton 13 (M R Channon) *in rr: hdwy on outside fr 2f out: drvn and kpt on fnl f to take 2nd nr fin but no imp on wnr* **14/1**	106
-260	**3**	*hd*	**Cape Amber (IRE)**[55] 3153 3-8-5 **104** ... AlanMunro 1 (P W Chapple-Hyam) *plld hrd and led after 2f: hdd jst ins fnl 2f: styd on again ins fnl f* **7/2**[2]	102
-405	**4**	*nse*	**Selinka**[25] 4192 4-9-0 **103** ... RichardHughes 4 (R Hannon) *in rr but in tch: hdwy 3f out: styd on fnl f but nvr gng pce to chal* **8/1**	102
23-	**5**	*2*	**In The Light**[30] 4-9-0 **0** ... RyanMoore 12 (A Fabre, France) *w'like: str: lw: sn trcking ldrs: rdn 3f out: styd on same pce fr over 1f out* **3/1**[1]	98
2130	**6**	*1/2*	**Wood Chorus**[34] 3875 3-8-5 **97** ... HayleyTurner 3 (M L W Bell) *led 2f: styd chsng ldrs tl wknd over 1f out* **25/1**	97
3-1	**7**	*1/2*	**Basque Beauty**[17] 4447 3-8-5 **90** ... RHills 7 (W J Haggas) *lw: in rr but in tch: rdn and effrt over 2f out: nvr gng pce to be competitive and sn btn* **5/1**	96
5620	**8**	*shd*	**Cosmodrome (USA)**[10] 4667 4-9-0 **101** ... DaneO'Neill 9 (L M Cumani) *in rr tl rdn and effrt over 2f out: nvr in contention and sn wknd* **9/1**	95

2m 12.6s (2.70) **Going Correction** +0.475s/f (Yiel)

WFA 3 from 4yo 9lb **8** Ran SP% **115.5**

Speed ratings (Par 108): **108,107,107,107,105 105,104,104**

toteswinger: 1&2 7.50, 1&3 £4.50, 2&3 £10.40. CSF £57.41 TOTE £4.90: £1.80, £2.90, £1.90; EX 57.20.

Owner P J Hughes Developments Ltd **Bred** Aerial Bloodstock Et Al **Trained** Lambourn, Berks

FOCUS

An ordinary Listed race, not competitive as it might have been with four non-runners due to the ground and another (66/1 shot Folly Lodge) withdrawn at the start. The pace set by the keen Cape Amber was solid enough in the conditions and again the runners came over to the stands' rail on reaching the home straight. Even though a little over a length separated the eight runners passing the furlong pole, the time was about what you would expect. The form is rated through the placed fillies.

NOTEBOOK

Lady Deauville(FR), for whom the easing of the ground was a godsend, has been plying her trade at Group level lately but she had been successful in her last two outings in Listed company. She could be seen travelling much the best just behind the leaders from a long way out and kept on finding enough when asked. She is likely to bid for a quick follow-up in a similar event at Bath where once again her chances will be ground-dependent. (op 9-2)

Sweet Lilly, back over a more suitable trip, was switched right off out the back and stayed on very strongly once manoeuvred to make her effort down the centre of the track, but the winner had gone beyond recall. She has won with cut in the ground, but the very best of her form has come on a faster surface. (op 11-1)

Cape Amber(IRE), like the winner stepping down from Group company, not for the first time took quite a hold out in front and it is testament to her class that she hung in there for as long as she did. This was her first try with ease in the ground and there is no real evidence that she did not handle it. (op 9-2)

Selinka, unplaced in her two previous tries over this trip, plugged on over the last couple of furlongs and looked like finishing second until collared on either side in the last 50 yards. Stamina did not seem to be an issue here and she was probably just not quite good enough on the day. (op 17-2)

In The Light, her trainer's first runner at the track, has just missed out on a few occasions at this level in her native land. She had her chance, but had nothing more to offer over the last furlong or so. (tchd 7-2)

Wood Chorus again found herself out of her depth and her apparently decent effort in a similar event at Newcastle in June has left her with very few options. (op 28-1 tchd 33-1)

Basque Beauty, rated just 90 and trying a longer trip in only her third start, started short enough in the market and that must have been on potential rather than on proven ability. As it turned out she never looked like winning and she may be better off in handicap company. Official explanation: jockey said filly was unsuited by the soft ground (tchd 9-2)

4978 CHAMPAGNE JOSEPH PERRIER H'CAP 1m 1f 198y

4:40 (4:40) (Class 5) (0-70,70) 3-Y-O+ **£3,238** (£963; £481; £240) **Stalls** High

Form				RPR
140-	**1**		**Tuanku (IRE)**[303] 6233 3-9-7 **68** ... FergusSweeney 6 (A King) *in tch: stdy hdwy to trck ldrs 3f out: led 2f out: rdn and hld on wl fnl f* **4/1**[1]	76
0400	**2**	*nk*	**Seventh Hill**[11] 4637 3-8-13 **60** ... FrancisNorton 12 (M Blanshard) *hld up in rr: stdy hdwy fr over 2f out: styd on strly thrght fnl f but a jst hld* **15/2**	67
6554	**3**	*1 1/2*	**Orbital Orchid**[20] 4326 3-8-5 **52** ... (v) SimonWhitworth 2 (W S Kittow) *towards rr tl hdwy 4f out: drvn and kpt on fnl 2f but nvr gng pce to press ldrs* **11/1**	56
6440	**4**	*1 3/4*	**Ba Dreamflight**[16] 4481 3-8-0 **47** ... NickyMackay 4 (H Morrison) *pressed ldr: chal over 4f out tl narrow ld ins fnl 3f: hdd 2f out: wknd ins fnl f* **9/1**	48
0260	**5**	*2*	**Highland Homestead**[16] 4477 3-8-13 **60** ... (b[1]) TGMcLaughlin 11 (B R Millman) *chsd ldrs tl rdn and outpcd over 3f out: styd on again appr fnl f but nvr a threat* **8/1**	57
10-6	**6**	*5*	**Garrulous (UAE)**[189] 450 5-9-12 **64** ... JimCrowley 13 (G L Moore) *led: rdn and narrowly hdd ins fnl 3f: wknd fr 2f out* **6/1**[3]	51
	7	*1 1/4*	**Querido (GER)**[115] 4-10-0 **66** ... VinceSlattery 1 (M Bradstock) *w'like: in rr: hdwy to chse ldrs 4f out: sn rdn: wknd over 2f out* **5/1**[2]	50
0000	**8**	*1 1/4*	**Havanavich**[35] 3845 3-8-10 **57** ... CatherineGannon 10 (S Kirk) *a towards rr* **10/1**	39
00-0	**9**	*3/4*	**Newcastle Sam**[18] 4413 3-7-7 **47** oh2 ... BillyCray[(7)] 8 (J J Bridger) *a towards rr* **50/1**	27
3043	**10**	*3 1/4*	**Clovis**[6] 4766 3-9-2 **68** ... (b) HaddenFrost[(5)] 9 (N P Mulholland) *towards rr tl hdwy 5f out: chsd ldrs 4f out to 3f out: wknd 2f out* **7/1**	42

2m 15.22s (5.32) **Going Correction** +0.60s/f (Yiel)

WFA 3 from 4yo+ 9lb **10** Ran SP% **115.7**

Speed ratings (Par 103): **102,101,100,99,97 93,92,91,90,88**

toteswinger: 1&2 9.00, 1&3 £10.00, 2&3 £16.40. CSF £33.84 CT £305.69 TOTE £5.50: £2.40, £2.70, £2.50; EX 37.50.

Owner C.G.A Racing Partnership 3 **Bred** Stone Ridge Farm **Trained** Barbury Castle, Wilts

■ Stewards' Enquiry : Fergus Sweeney two-day ban: used whip with excessive frequency (Aug 27-28)

FOCUS

Just a fair pace for this handicap and the winning time was about what you would expect for the grade despite being 2.62 seconds slower than the fillies' Listed event. However, with the four horses behind the winner all maidens it remains to be seen what the form adds up to, although it reads sound enough. Again the runners came down the stands' rail on reaching the straight.

4979 AXMINSTER CARPETS APPRENTICE H'CAP (WHIPS SHALL BE CARRIED BUT NOT USED) 6f 212y

5:10 (5:11) (Class 5) (0-70,70) 3-Y-O+ **£3,238** (£963; £481; £240) **Stalls** High

Form				RPR
0266	**1**		**Castano**[8] 4710 4-8-13 **60** ... (p) MJMurphy[(5)] 12 (B R Millman) *in tch: hdwy 4f out: led ins fnl 2f: drvn and hung rt sn after: kpt on wl* **9/2**[2]	71
5603	**2**	*3 1/4*	**Outer Hebrides**[8] 4710 7-8-10 **52** ... (v) BillyCray 11 (J M Bradley) *chsd ldrs: led over 3f out: hdd ins fnl 2f: kpt on same pce ins fnl f* **5/1**[3]	54
0305	**3**	*1 1/4*	**Takitwo**[5] 4807 5-8-7 **54** ... TobyAtkinson[(5)] 4 (P D Cundell) *in rr: hdwy fr 2f out: kpt on ins fnl f but nvr gng pce to trble ldng duo* **8/1**	53
000	**4**	*3 3/4*	**Flying Flute**[64] 2918 3-8-7 **60** ... AmyScott[(5)] 9 (H Candy) *in rr: drvn over 2f out: hdwy over 1f out: kpt on ins fnl f but n.d* **9/1**	49
0530	**5**	*1 1/4*	**Blue Java**[18] 4407 7-9-7 **68** ... RyanClark[(5)] 8 (H Morrison) *in tch: drvn along 3f out: one pce fnl 2f* **9/2**[2]	53
-040	**6**	*1 3/4*	**Out Of Nothing**[19] 4368 5-9-4 **60** ... WilliamCarson 10 (K M Prendergast) *in rr: pushed along 3f out: mod prog fnl f* **15/2**	40
0000	**7**	*1 1/4*	**Ishibee (IRE)**[6] 4779 4-8-9 **51** oh6 ... (p) MatthewDavies 6 (J J Bridger) *chsd ldrs* **33/1**	28
6006	**8**	*16*	**Tuning Fork**[14] 4529 8-8-4 **51** oh6 ... (p) AndreaAtzeni[(5)] 7 (M J Attwater) *led tl hdd & wknd over 3f out* **20/1**	—
2320	**9**	*8*	**Magroom**[49] 3360 4-10-0 **70** ... JemmaMarshall 3 (R J Hodges) *chsd ldrs over 4f* **4/1**[1]	—
-000	**10**	*3/4*	**The Real Guru**[26] 4163 3-9-0 **62** ... JPHamblett 1 (Miss Tor Sturgis) *a towards rr* **40/1**	—
0-0	**11**	*6*	**Pretty Selma**[65] 2881 4-8-6 **51** oh5 ... (t) AshleyMorgan[(3)] 2 (Mark Gillard) *in tch to 1/2-way* **50/1**	—

1m 32.41s (3.41) **Going Correction** +0.60s/f (Yiel)

WFA 3 from 4yo+ 6lb **11** Ran SP% **118.0**

Speed ratings (Par 103): **104,100,98,94,93 91,89,71,62,61 54**

toteswinger: 1&2 6.10, 1&3 £7.10, 2&3 £9.00. CSF £26.44 CT £179.72 TOTE £4.90: £1.90, £2.10, £2.20; EX 24.30 Place 6: £29.06, Place 5: £25.52..

Owner H G Gooding & Mrs A A Gooding **Bred** Mrs V J Bjerke & Mrs E K Tope-Ottesen **Trained** Kentisbeare, Devon

FOCUS

A modest handicap in which these apprentices were allowed to carry whips but not use them unless for safety reasons. Unlike in the previous races, these riders made more use of the full width of the track and the winner stayed closest to the far side where the ground had not been churned up. The pace was solid enough and they finished very well spread out, with few getting into it. The winner is rated back to his best.

Magroom Official explanation: jockey said gelding was unsuited by the soft ground

T/Plt: £42.10 to a £1 stake. Pool: £53,397.15. 923.95 winning tickets. T/Qpdt: £17.80 to a £1 stake. Pool: £3,127.06. 129.80 winning tickets. ST

4786 SANDOWN (R-H)

Wednesday, August 13

OFFICIAL GOING: Sprint coure - soft (good to soft in places; 7.1); round course - good to soft (soft in places; 7.4)

Wind: Moderate, against Weather: Mostly overcast with showers

4980 M J MILWARD PRINTING MAIDEN STKS 5f 6y

5:35 (5:36) (Class 5) 2-Y-O £3,885 (£1,156; £577; £288) **Stalls** High

Form RPR

1 **Sharp Bullet (IRE)** 2-9-3 0 AdamKirby 12 78+
(W R Swinburn) *hld up in midfield on inner: smooth prog over 1f out: got through to ld ins fnl f: sn clr: v comf* **11/2**

0 **2** 2 **Always There (IRE)**[41] 3632 2-8-12 0 RyanMoore 10 66
(R Hannon) *prom: chsd ldr 2f out: squeezed through on inner to ld jst over 1f out: hdd and easily outpcd ins fnl f* **10/3**[2]

25 **3** ½ **Victoria Sponge (IRE)**[14] 4521 2-8-12 0 RichardHughes 6 64
(R Hannon) *trckd ldrs: effrt over 1f out: rdn and kpt on same pce fnl f: nvr able to chal* **11/4**[1]

4 shd **Albaseet (IRE)** 2-9-3 0 MartinDwyer 7 69+
(M P Tregoning) *settled in midfield: eased to outer and prog over 1f out: styd on steadily fnl f: nrst fin* **14/1**

033 **5** 1 **Cash In The Attic**[7] 4734 2-8-12 0 ChrisCatlin 9 60
(M R Channon) *led to jst over 1f out: fdd last 100yds* **10/1**

6 3 ¼ **Overbright (IRE)** 2-9-3 0 RobertHavlin 13 53
(G L Moore) *nvr beyond midfield: plugged on fnl f: nvr on terms* **20/1**

0 **7** shd **Noverre To Hide (USA)**[15] 4507 2-9-3 0 TedDurcan 3 53
(J R Best) *chsd ldr to 2f out: sn lost pl u.p: wknd ins fnl f* **7/2**[3]

6 **8** ¾ **Piccolo Mondo**[27] 4126 2-9-3 0 StephenCarson 1 50
(P Winkworth) *hld up in midfield on outer: shkn up over 1f out: fdd* **28/1**

00 **9** 1 ¼ **Short Cut**[22] 4274 2-9-3 0 RichardKingscote 2 46
(S Kirk) *wnt lft s: a in rr: lft bhd fr over 1f out* **66/1**

0 **10** 2 **Alexander Newstalk (IRE)**[11] 4634 2-8-5 0 HollyHall(7) 5 34
(S A Callaghan) *mostly in last pair: struggling fr 1/2-way* **66/1**

11 1 ¼ **Ruby Best** 2-8-9 0 KevinGhunowa(3) 4 29
(D K Ivory) *s.i.s: sn struggling and rdn in rr: nvr a factor* **40/1**

12 ½ **Lujeanie** 2-9-0 0 TravisBlock(3) 8 32
(D K Ivory) *s.v.s: a struggling in last pair* **33/1**

65.65 secs (4.05) **Going Correction** +0.675s/f (Yiel) **12** Ran SP% **119.7**

Speed ratings (Par 94): **94,90,90,89,88 83,82,81,79,76 74,73**

toteswinger: 1&2 £4.80, 1&3 £5.10, 2&3 £5.60. CSF £23.03 TOTE £7.20: £2.90, £1.50, £1.50; EX 26.50.

Owner Exors Of The Late Mrs P W Harris **Bred** Gerrardstown House Stud **Trained** Aldbury, Herts

FOCUS

A modest juvenile maiden, run at a sound pace. The third sets the level.

NOTEBOOK

Sharp Bullet(IRE), a 105,000euros first foal of a smart dual 5-6f juvenile winner, maintained the good form of his yard and ran out a comfortable debut winner. He travelled kindly in midfield for the first half of the race and it was clear nearing the final furlong he was the one to beat with a clear run. One the gap opened he soon put the race to bed, showing a liking for the soft ground, and looks a colt with pretensions to better things. (op 5-1 tchd 6-1)

Always There(IRE) met support in the betting ring and showed improved form on the softer ground, but was no match for the debutant winner. She may appreciate the return to another furlong now and will be qualified for nurseries after her next run. (op 13-2 tchd 3-1)

Victoria Sponge(IRE) was always on the pace and had her chance, but she was unable to raise her game when it really mattered. She ran close to her previous level on the softer surface and now has the option of nurseries, where she may appreciate another furlong. (op 5-2 tchd 9-4 and 3-1)

Albaseet(IRE) is a 52,000gns, already gelded half-brother to winners from 6f-1m5f. He caught the eye doing his best work towards the finish and left the impression he would come on nicely for the experience. (tchd 12-1)

Noverre To Hide(USA) had been pitched in at the deep end on his debut, finishing last in the Molecomb, but he proved disappointing on this drop into maiden company and ran right up to his initial form. Perhaps he failed to act on the softer ground. (tchd 4-1 and 9-2 in a place)

4981 MEDIATORS @ LAMBBUILDING.CO.UK H'CAP 5f 6y

6:05 (6:06) (Class 4) (0-80,79) 4-Y-O+ £5,828 (£1,734; £866; £432) **Stalls** High

Form RPR

4023 **1** **Judge 'n Jury**[10] 4668 4-9-1 **74** (t) KevinGhunowa(3) 9 87
(R A Harris) *trckd ldr: led jst over 1f out: sn in command: rdn out* **10/3**[1]

-062 **2** 1 ½ **Gentle Guru**[16] 4483 4-9-3 **73** RichardHughes 11 81
(R T Phillips) *trckd ldng pair: effrt to chse wnr ins fnl f: styd on but nvr able to chal* **7/2**[2]

2311 **3** 1 ¾ **Commander Wish**[7] 4743 5-8-13 **69** 6ex (p) LiamJones 7 71+
(Lucinda Featherstone) *sn outpcd: rdn in abt 6th after 2f: prog over 1f out: kpt on wl to take 3rd nr fin* **6/1**

1450 **4** ¾ **Bertie Southstreet**[13] 4555 5-8-13 **69** (b) TedDurcan 2 68
(J R Best) *chsd ldng trio to 1/2-way: rdn to cl on them 1f out: nt qckn and no imp fnl f* **7/1**

5104 **5** nk **Cape Royal**[9] 4693 8-9-9 **79** (bt) LDettori 10 77
(J M Bradley) *led at str pce to jst over 1f out: grad wknd* **5/1**[3]

3020 **6** ¾ **Digital**[13] 4555 11-9-6 **76** ChrisCatlin 8 71
(M R Channon) *sn wl outpcd in last: no prog tl styd on fr over 1f out: fin wl* **12/1**

3160 **7** shd **Musical Script (USA)**[11] 4639 5-7-13 **60** oh3 (b) DavidProbert(5) 4 55
(Mouse Hamilton-Fairley) *t.k.h early: hld up in last trio: rdn 2f out: sme prog and swtchd to inner over 1f out: nt qckn sn after* **28/1**

3400 **8** 3 ¼ **Sand Cat**[12] 4586 5-9-5 **75** (b) RyanMoore 1 58
(G L Moore) *a wl in rr: struggling bef 1/2-way* **20/1**

0140 **9** 1 ¾ **The History Man (IRE)**[4] 4858 5-8-11 **67** (be) RichardMullen 3 44
(M Mullineaux) *chsd ldng trio to 1/2-way: sn lost pl u.p* **10/1**

64.24 secs (2.64) **Going Correction** +0.675s/f (Yiel) **9** Ran SP% **113.7**

Speed ratings (Par 105): **105,102,99,98,98 96,96,91,88**

toteswinger: 1&2 £5.70, 1&3 £4.20, 2&3 £2.30. CSF £14.90 CT £65.76 TOTE £4.10: £1.60, £1.40, £1.90; EX 11.20.

Owner Mrs Ruth M Serrell **Bred** C A Cyzer **Trained** Earlswood, Monmouths

FOCUS

A fair sprint for the class, run at a decent early pace. Fairly solid form, the winner rated in line with his Newbury form which has been franked since.

4982 LAMB BUILDING FAMILY TEAM MEDIAN AUCTION MAIDEN STKS 7f 16y

6:35 (6:38) (Class 4) 2-Y-O £4,533 (£1,348; £674; £336) **Stalls** High

Form RPR

5 **1** **Papa Meilland**[22] 4274 2-9-3 0 StephenCarson 10 74+
(Eve Johnson Houghton) *led 1f: trckd ldr: rdn to ld again over 1f out: kpt on wl* **5/1**[3]

64 **2** 1 ½ **Granski (IRE)**[21] 4311 2-9-3 0 RichardHughes 7 70
(R Hannon) *led after 1f: rdn 2f out: hdd over 1f out: one pce fnl f* **7/2**[2]

0 **3** nk **Lucky Score (IRE)**[106] 1693 2-8-7 0 DavidProbert(5) 8 65
(Mouse Hamilton-Fairley) *trckd ldrs: shkn up 2f out: kpt on one pce: unable to chal* **25/1**

2 **4** ½ **Too Tall**[18] 4421 2-9-3 0 DaneO'Neill 1 68+
(L M Cumani) *trckd ldrs on outer: hrd rdn 2f out: one pce and nvr able to chal* **13/8**[1]

0 **5** ¾ **Itlaaq**[13] 4570 2-9-3 0 MartinDwyer 3 66+
(J L Dunlop) *hld up in last trio: shkn up and no prog over 2f out: pushed along and styd on steadily fnl f: nrst fin* **25/1**

0 **6** 3 **Survivor's Song**[89] 2146 2-9-3 0 RobertHavlin 6 59
(D K Ivory) *trckd ldrs: rdn and no imp 2f out: wknd fnl f* **16/1**

000 **7** 8 **Four Green Fields (IRE)**[56] 3135 2-8-7 40 GabrielHannon(5) 9 34
(B W Duke) *a in rr: struggling over 2f out: sn bhd* **100/1**

8 10 **King Of Defence** 2-9-3 0 PhilipRobinson 4 14
(M A Jarvis) *slowly away: a in last pair: wknd over 2f out: t.o* **8/1**

1m 33.77s (4.27) **Going Correction** +0.35s/f (Good) **8** Ran SP% **102.7**

Speed ratings (Par 96): **89,87,86,86,85 82,72,61**

toteswinger: 1&2 £3.60, 1&3 £20.80, 2&3 £25.30. CSF £17.86 TOTE £5.10: £1.50, £1.40, £5.00; EX 17.20.

Owner Mrs P Robeson **Bred** Southcourt Stud **Trained** Blewbury, Oxon

■ Leulahleulahlay was withdrawn on vet's advice (7/1, deduct 10p in the £ under Rule 4).

FOCUS

A modest juvenile maiden, run at an average pace. It was a moderate winning time for the class of contest.

NOTEBOOK

Papa Meilland showed the real benefit of his debut experience at Salisbury 22 days previously and scored under a positive ride. He relished every yard of this extra furlong, appreciated the easier ground, and is evidently progressive. It will be interesting to see how the Handicapper now assesses this. (op 6-1 tchd 13-2)

Granski(IRE), the subject of market support, settled a lot better for being allowed his head early on and recorded his best effort to date on this switch to a softer surface. His future now lies with the Handicapper. (op 11-2 tchd 3-1)

Lucky Score(IRE) stepped up markedly on the level of her Bath debut back in April and the step up to this trip clearly helped her cause. She needs one more run to qualify for a mark. (op 33-1)

Too Tall looked the one to beat on the form of his debut second at Newmarket 18 days previously, but he was in trouble at the 2f pole on this much softer ground and lacked the pace to land a telling blow. (op 15-8 tchd 6-4)

Itlaaq stayed on without seriously threatening and looks sure to come on again for the experience. (op 16-1)

4983 XL INSURANCE H'CAP 7f 16y

7:10 (7:11) (Class 3) (0-90,90) 3-Y-O £7,771 (£2,312; £866; £866) **Stalls** High

Form RPR

0225 **1** **Dunn'o (IRE)**[23] 4252 3-9-2 **83** PhilipRobinson 3 88
(C G Cox) *led: racd against nr side rail in st: narrowly hdd over 1f out: sn led again: fought on wl fnl f* **6/1**[3]

5600 **2** ¾ **Jeninsky (USA)**[35] 3850 3-9-2 **83** RichardHughes 7 86
(P J McBride) *wl in tch: effrt over 2f out: clsd grad to chal fnl f: jst hld last 75yds* **11/1**

3321 **3** nk **Brassini**[21] 4312 3-9-9 **90** AlanMunro 2 92
(B R Millman) *sn pressed ldr: rdn to chal 2f out: narrow ld over 1f out: sn hdd: kpt on but hld last 75yds* **6/1**[3]

2512 **3** dht **Arabian Spirit**[20] 4345 3-9-4 **85** RyanMoore 6 87+
(E A L Dunlop) *hld up in detached last: shkn up over 2f out: prog on outer over 1f out: styd on thrght fnl f but nvr gng to get there: too much to do* **9/4**[1]

2256 **5** ½ **Wigram's Turn (USA)**[35] 3850 3-9-0 **86** (v) DavidProbert(5) 4 87
(A M Balding) *trckd ldrs: rdn and cl up fr 2f out: nt qckn ent fnl f: kpt on* **4/1**[2]

0464 **6** nse **Harry Gee**[27] 4128 3-8-6 **73** (b) SteveDrowne 1 74+
(G Wragg) *hld up in tch: effrt over 2f out: cl enough but nt qckn u.p over 1f out: kpt on* **8/1**

-101 **7** 1 ¾ **Divine Power**[33] 3918 3-8-13 **80** AdamKirby 8 76
(R M Beckett) *hld up in 7th: effrt over 2f out: clsd over 1f out: no ex and lost grnd ins fnl f* **8/1**

-000 **8** 27 **Westwood**[51] 3324 3-8-13 **80** TedDurcan 5 3
(D Haydn Jones) *v free to post: t.k.h: trckd ldng pair tl wknd rapidly over 2f out: t.o* **25/1**

1m 31.18s (1.68) **Going Correction** +0.35s/f (Good) **8** Ran SP% **113.7**

Speed ratings (Par 104): **104,103,102,102,102 102,100,69**

toteswinger: 1&2 £24.00, 1&3 (D/AS) £1.30, (D/AS) £1.00, 2&3 (J/B) £6.10, (J/AS) £4.00. CSF £67.52 TOTE £7.10: £2.10, £2.90; EX 63.40 Place: Brassini £1.00, Arabian Spirit £0.70; Tricast Dunn'o/Jeninsky/Brassini £206.96, Dunn'o/Jeninsky/Arabian Spirit £96.18..

Owner Dennis Shaw **Bred** R Hodgins **Trained** Lambourn, Berks

FOCUS

A useful standard of handicap for three-year-olds where it appeared to be an advantage to race on or close to the pace as the hold-up horses struggled to make up ground. The form is ordinary for the grade, with the winner to form.

NOTEBOOK

Dunn'o(IRE) made his first start beyond sprint distances a winning one under a typically astute front-running ride from Robinson. Proven in the ground, he was ridden positively, as though he was definitely going to get the trip, and the confidence paid off as he was able to grab the favoured stands'-side running rail up the straight. Looking sure to be swamped entering the final furlong, Robinson had kept something up his sleeve and he battled back to land the spoils. He can be found more opportunities now it is clear that this is his trip. (tchd 11-2)

Jeninsky(USA) has faced some stiff tasks this year and seemed to come back to her best on ground she was proven on. (op 14-1)

Arabian Spirit found himself a lot further back than ideal on a night where conditions made it difficult to quicken up from the rear. To his credit, he made up a lot more ground than seemed possible at one point and even held a chance a furlong out before his exertions took their toll and his run petered out in the final 50 yards. (op 3-1)

Brassini ran a solid race but the 5lb jack in the weights he suffered for a course-and-distance win three weeks ago has probably handicapped him out of things for a while. (op 3-1)

Wigram's Turn(USA) held every chance but 7f on this going stretches his stamina to the limit. (op 9-2)

Harry Gee is running respectably without threatening to win and the yard hasn't really hit form at any point this year. (op 13-2 tchd 6-1)

4984 LAMB BUILDING CIVIL AND PUBLIC TEAMS H'CAP — 1m 2f 7y
7:40 (7:42) (Class 4) (0-80,79) 3-Y-O — **£6,476** (£1,927; £963; £481) **Stalls** High

Form				RPR
-036	**1**		**Kingdom Of Fife**[33] 3911 3-9-0 **70** .... RyanMoore 2	79+
			(Sir Michael Stoute) *trckd ldrs: shkn up over 2f out: prog to ld last 150yds: flashed tail but stvd on stoutly* **14/1**	
3010	**2**	*1*	**Albarouche**[26] 4160 3-9-8 **78** ....(tp) PhilipRobinson 6	85
			(M A Jarvis) *prom: led briefly 2f out: chsd ldr after: upsides ent fnl f: kpt on same pce after* **16/1**	
014	**3**	*nk*	**Closertobelieving**[37] 3800 3-9-8 **78** .... TQuinn 8	84+
			(D R C Elsworth) *settled in rr: urged along over 3f out: prog on outer over 2f out: cl enough jst over 1f out: one pce ins fnl f* **11/4**[1]	
3154	**4**	*2*	**Palmerin**[11] 4621 3-9-8 **78** .... RichardHughes 9	80
			(R Hannon) *hld up in midfield: stdy prog to ld wl over 1f out: hdd & wknd last 150yds* **4/1**[3]	
611	**5**	*2 3/4*	**Vineyard**[20] 4335 3-9-5 **75** .... LiamJones 1	72
			(W J Haggas) *racd freely: led to 2f out: wknd fnl f* **7/2**[2]	
001-	**6**	*2*	**Desert Thistle (IRE)**[309] 6079 3-9-6 **76** .... SteveDrowne 5	69
			(H J L Dunlop) *wl in rr: nt gng wl over 3f out: struggling after and nvr on terms* **20/1**	
2136	**7**	*3/4*	**Top Ticket (IRE)**[46] 3471 3-9-9 **79** .... RichardMullen 3	70
			(D M Simcock) *chsd ldr to over 2f out: steadily wknd* **8/1**	
0035	**8**	*1/2*	**Filun**[19] 4382 3-9-5 **75** .... DaneO'Neill 4	65
			(L M Cumani) *s.i.s: hld up in rr: effrt over 2f out: in tch over 1f out: sn wknd* **8/1**	
-034	**9**	*2*	**Wing Play (IRE)**[21] 4303 3-8-12 **71** .... TravisBlock(3) 7	57
			(H Morrison) *t.k.h early and hld up in last pair: rdn and fnd nil over 2f out* **9/1**	

2m 14.63s (4.13) **Going Correction** +0.35s/f (Good) **9** Ran SP% **118.4**
Speed ratings (Par 102): **97,96,95,94,92 90,89,89,87**
toteswinger: 1&2 £32.10, 1&3 £6.40, 2&3 £12.40. CSF £217.28 CT £804.22 TOTE £12.40: £2.50, £4.50, £1.80; EX 111.40.
Owner The Queen **Bred** The Queen **Trained** Newmarket, Suffolk

FOCUS
A useful bunch of three-year-olds contested this handicap, and a couple of the least exposed finished first and second. The fourth looks the best guide.

4985 LAMB BUILDING CRIMINAL QCS & BARRISTERS H'CAP — 1m 6f
8:10 (8:12) (Class 4) (0-80,80) 3-Y-O — **£6,476** (£1,927; £963; £481) **Stalls** High

Form				RPR
5533	**1**		**Hendersyde (USA)**[20] 4344 3-9-2 **73** ....(t) AdamKirby 3	82+
			(W R Swinburn) *hld up in rr gp off the pce: stdy prog over 2f out: drvn and r.o to ld ins fnl f: styd on* **8/1**	
0534	**2**	*3/4*	**Silk Hall (UAE)**[13] 4573 3-8-10 **67** .... DaneO'Neill 8	75
			(D W P Arbuthnot) *rring as stalls opened and slowly away: last tl prog over 5f out: gd hdwy over 2f out to ld 1f out: sn hdd: jst hld fnl 100yds* **8/1**	
4103	**3**	*4*	**Murcar**[40] 3671 3-8-12 **69** .... PhilipRobinson 10	71
			(C G Cox) *pressed ldrs: rdn over 3f out: styd chsng and disp 2nd over 1f out: wknd ins fnl f* **7/2**[1]	
1322	**4**	*1 1/4*	**Riverscape (IRE)**[13] 4573 3-9-6 **77** .... JimCrowley 5	78
			(Mrs A J Perrett) *pressed ldr: led wl over 2f out: 2 l clr wl over 1f out: wknd and hdd 1f out* **9/2**[2]	
-010	**5**	*3 3/4*	**Tyrrells Wood (IRE)**[13] 4573 3-9-7 **78** .... TedDurcan 1	73
			(T G Mills) *pressed ldrs: lost pl: and hanging rt fr wl over 2f out: n.d over 1f out* **12/1**	
2-06	**6**	*2 1/2*	**Black Rain**[72] 2675 3-9-9 **80** ....(v[1]) LiamJones 6	72
			(P J McBride) *t.k.h mostly: cl up: suddenly shkn up over 3f out: nt qckn over 2f out: wknd over 1f out* **14/1**	
030	**7**	*1 1/2*	**Byblos**[88] 2197 3-9-5 **76** .... AlanMunro 11	66
			(B J Meehan) *hld up in rr and off the pce: nt gng wl fr 6f out: struggling wl over 2f out on outside* **9/1**	
5633	**8**	*1/2*	**Rock Peak (IRE)**[13] 4573 3-9-1 **72** .... RobertHavlin 9	61
			(H Morrison) *led at decent pce: hdd wl over 2f out: steadily wknd* **11/2**[3]	
0-54	**9**	*3*	**Dedicate**[72] 2669 3-9-1 **72** .... SteveDrowne 7	57
			(R Charlton) *hld up in rr gp off the pce: tried to cl on ldrs over 2f out: sn no prog and btn: wknd over 1f out* **12/1**	
053	**10**	*1*	**Winners Chant (IRE)**[20] 4342 3-9-5 **76** ....(v[1]) RyanMoore 2	60
			(Sir Michael Stoute) *a wl in rr: struggling 3f out: sn no ch in last* **8/1**	

3m 7.94s (1.34) **Going Correction** +0.35s/f (Good) **10** Ran SP% **121.2**
Speed ratings (Par 102): **110,109,107,106,104 103,102,101,100,99**
toteswinger: 1&2 £16.70, 1&3 £6.10, 2&3 £7.10. CSF £73.25 CT £270.08 TOTE £10.60: £2.20, £2.80, £2.10; EX 74.90 Place 6 £31.86, Place 5 £21.32. .
Owner Exors Of The Late Mrs P W Harris **Bred** Iron County Farms Inc **Trained** Aldbury, Herts

FOCUS
The Swinburn yard is in terrific form, and his Giant's Causeway colt got off the mark with a strong staying performance, clocking a decent winning time for the type of contest considering the conditions. Sound form.
T/Plt: £106.40 to a £1 stake. Pool: £62,363.30. 427.53 winning tickets. T/Qpdt: £31.80 to a £1 stake. Pool: £5,411.58. 125.70 winning tickets. JN

4792 YARMOUTH (L-H)
Wednesday, August 13

OFFICIAL GOING: Soft
Wind: Fairly strong, half against Weather: bright spells with heavy showers

4986 BEACH RADIO (S) STKS — 5f 43y
2:20 (2:26) (Class 6) 2-Y-O — **£1,942** (£578; £288; £144) **Stalls** High

Form				RPR
513	**1**		**Silent Treatment (IRE)**[5] 4823 2-8-13 58 ....(t) DarryllHolland 1	62
			(Miss Gay Kelleway) *uns rdr leaving paddock and led to s: mde all: sn crossed to stands' rail: idled and jnd ins fnl f: fnd ex and asserted fnl 100yds* **2/1**[1]	
5	**2**	*1 1/4*	**Pressed For Time (IRE)**[55] 3178 2-8-7 0 .... EddieAhern 5	52
			(E J Creighton) *in tch: chsd wnr 1/2-way: rdn over 1f out: ev ch ins fnl f: nt pce of wnr fnl 100yds* **11/4**[2]	
	3	*2 1/4*	**Bid To Dance** 2-8-7 0 .... JamesDoyle 6	43
			(K A Morgan) *s.i.s: sn pushed along in rr: hdwy to chse ldng pair over 1f out: kpt on but nvr pce to chal* **33/1**	
53	**4**	*5*	**Chicken Momo**[54] 3215 2-8-12 0 .... PatCosgrave 4	30
			(K R Burke) *chsd ldr tl short of room after 1f: chsd ldng pair after tl rdn wl over 1f out: sn wknd* **9/2**	
0605	**5**	*1/2*	**Samba Queen (IRE)**[21] 4297 2-8-8 51 ow1 .... MickyFenton 2	25
			(J L Spearing) *taken down early: s.i.s: chsd ldr after 1f tl 1/2-way: sn wknd* **7/2**[3]	
05	**6**	*1 3/4*	**Jack Jicaro**[54] 3199 2-8-9 0 .... TolleyDean(3) 3	22
			(Mrs L Williamson) *s.i.s: a bhd: rdn and struggling bdly fr 1/2-way* **17/2**	

65.46 secs (3.26) **Going Correction** +0.35s/f (Good) **6** Ran SP% **113.9**
Speed ratings (Par 92): **87,85,81,73,72 69**
toteswinger: 1&2 £1.90, 1&3 £7.50, 2&3 £14.50. CSF £7.98 TOTE £2.70: £1.10, £2.60; EX 10.60.There was no bid for the winner.
Owner Countrywide Classics Limited **Bred** Gerard And Yvonne Kennedy **Trained** Exning, Suffolk

FOCUS
A weak juvenile seller. The form is set by the runner-up.

NOTEBOOK
Silent Treatment(IRE) got off the mark at the second attempt for her current connections, scoring a first win on turf, and did the job with a little left up her sleeve. She played up before the start and evidently has her share of temperament, but she clearly enjoys it out in front and looks well up to further success in this sort of class. (op 3-1)
Pressed For Time(IRE) came through to press the winner as that rival began to idle inside the final furlong, but was always being readily held at the business end. The drop in grade helped and she ran right up to her previous level on this easier surface. (op 4-1 tchd 9-2 and 5-2)
Bid To Dance, a cheaply-bought first foal of a 5f winner at three, ran too green to do herself full justice on this racecourse bow. She is clearly only moderate, but will learn for the experience. (op 11-1)
Chicken Momo was racing on the softest ground he had encountered to date and he was found out. (op 7-2 tchd 3-1 and 5-1)
Samba Queen(IRE), whose yard won this event last year, proved most disappointing on this first outing in selling company and looks to have temperament issues. (op 3-1 tchd 5-2)

4987 NORFOLK NELSON MUSEUM MAIDEN FILLIES' STKS — 6f 3y
2:50 (2:56) (Class 5) 3-Y-O — **£2,719** (£809; £404; £202) **Stalls** High

Form				RPR
-04	**1**		**Siren Party**[55] 3177 3-9-0 0 .... ShaneKelly 2	70
			(L M Cumani) *hld up in tch: hdwy 2f out: chsd ldr ent fnl f: led ins fnl f: edgd rt but styd on wl fnl 100yds* **10/1**	
0243	**2**	*3/4*	**Ivory Silk**[23] 4252 3-9-0 70 .... OscarUrbina 7	68
			(D K Ivory) *hld up in midfield: rdn over 2f out: hdwy over 1f out: chal ins fnl f: fnd nil and btn fnl 100yds* **9/2**[2]	
	3	*1/2*	**Onemoreandstay** 3-8-11 0 .... LukeMorris(3) 4	66
			(R W Price) *s.i.s: off the pce in midfield: hdwy u.p over 1f out: styd on wl fnl f: nt rch ldng pair* **80/1**	
P-30	**4**	*3/4*	**Laureldean Dream (USA)**[32] 3977 3-9-0 0 ....(t) AdrianMcCarthy 1	64
			(P W Chapple-Hyam) *hld up wl in tch: jnd ldr travelling wl 2f out: led over 1f out: rdn ent fnl f: hdd ins fnl f: no ex fnl 100yds* **25/1**	
0544	**5**	*3/4*	**Lake Sabina**[25] 4207 3-9-0 68 .... DarryllHolland 6	62
			(E S McMahon) *hld up in tch: swtchd rt and rdn 2f out: kpt on same pce u.p fnl f* **11/2**[3]	
20	**6**	*4*	**Safaseef (IRE)**[53] 3282 3-9-0 0 .... JamesDoyle 3	49
			(K A Morgan) *prom in centre: led overall over 2f out: rdn 2f out: hdd over 1f out: wknd fnl f* **25/1**	
05	**7**	*nk*	**Mischief Lady**[67] 2834 3-9-0 0 .... EddieAhern 8	48
			(E A L Dunlop) *wnt rt s: racd in midfield: hdwy and rdn 2f out: no prog fr over 1f out* **8/1**	
	8	*4 1/2*	**Prescription** 3-9-0 0 .... DO'Donohoe 11	33+
			(Sir Mark Prescott) *s.i.s and hmpd s: sn bustled along and rn green in rr: carried lft 2f out: modest late hdwy: nvr on terms* **5/2**[1]	
0000	**9**	*1 3/4*	**Myriola**[14] 4542 3-9-0 46 .... MickyFenton 13	28
			(S Gollings) *racd alone on stands' rail: led overall tl over 2f out: wknd u.p wl over 1f out* **66/1**	
-60	**10**	*1 1/4*	**Dancing Belle**[33] 3916 3-8-11 0 .... KirstyMilczarek(3) 10	24
			(J A R Toller) *a towards rr: n.d* **25/1**	
	11	*hd*	**Tomatina** 3-9-0 0 .... IanMongan 9	23
			(C F Wall) *s.i.s and hmpd s: a wl bhd* **33/1**	
	12	*7*	**May Parkin (IRE)** 3-9-0 0 .... PatCosgrave 12	1
			(Eamon Tyrrell, Ire) *in tch: rdn over 2f out: wkng whn hmpd 2f out: wl bhd after: t.o* **11/2**[3]	
	13	*6*	**Xandra (IRE)** 3-8-9 0 .... JackMitchell(5) 5	—
			(C F Wall) *led in centre and chsd overall ldr tl over 2f out: wkng qckly whn hmpd 2f out: t.o fnl f* **20/1**	

1m 16.14s (1.74) **Going Correction** +0.35s/f (Good) **13** Ran SP% **119.7**
Speed ratings (Par 97): **102,101,100,99,98 93,92,86,84,82 82,73,65**
toteswinger: 1&2 £5.80, 1&3 £68.10, 2&3 £59.20. CSF £50.98 TOTE £11.90: £2.80, £1.60, £22.70; EX 48.30 TRIFECTA Not won..
Owner Equibreed S.R.L. **Bred** Equibreed S R L **Trained** Newmarket, Suffolk

FOCUS
A modest fillies' maiden, run at an average pace. The first five were closely covered at the finish.
Xandra(IRE) Official explanation: trainer said filly was unsuited by the soft ground

4988 LOWESTOFT JOURNAL FILLIES' H'CAP — 6f 3y
3:25 (3:27) (Class 5) (0-70,74) 3-Y-O — **£2,590** (£770; £385; £192) **Stalls** High

Form				RPR
0641	**1**		**Hurricane Harriet**[6] 4793 3-8-11 **59** 6ex .... OscarUrbina 4	74+
			(R M H Cowell) *a travelling wl: hld up wl in tch: led over 1f out: in command whn swvd lft ins fnl f: comf* **15/8**[1]	
0032	**2**	*1 1/4*	**Artistic License (IRE)**[6] 4773 3-9-7 **69** .... TPO'Shea 3	80
			(M R Channon) *s.i.s: bhd and pushed along early: hdwy 1/2-way: rdn 2f out: chsd wnr ins fnl f: swtchd rt and one pce fnl 100yds* **15/2**[3]	
0-00	**3**	*2 1/4*	**Athboy Auction**[11] 4615 3-8-2 **53** .... KirstyMilczarek(3) 8	57
			(H J Collingridge) *hld up in tch: outpcd over 2f out: rdn and swtchd rt over 1f out: styd on to go 3rd nr fin: no ch w ldng pair* **16/1**	
5331	**4**	*1/2*	**Whiteoak Lady (IRE)**[6] 4782 3-9-7 **74** 6ex .... JackDean(5) 5	76
			(J L Spearing) *chsd ldr: led wl over 1f out: sn rdn and hdd: lost 2nd ins fnl f: wknd fnl 100yds* **9/2**[2]	
-340	**5**	*2 1/4*	**Mistress Cooper**[18] 4408 3-9-2 **64** .... StephenDonohoe 6	59
			(W J Musson) *s.i.s: bhd: hdwy and rdn 2f out: chsd ldrs over 1f out: wknd fnl f* **12/1**	
2244	**6**	*1*	**Regal Veil**[43] 3571 3-7-13 **50** oh2 .... LukeMorris(3) 2	42
			(R W Price) *in tch: effrt and rdn over 2f out: hung lft 2f out: sn struggling* **12/1**	
0005	**7**	*shd*	**Mollyatti**[11] 4615 3-8-5 **53** .... MatthewHenry 9	44
			(Miss V Haigh) *prom: rdn 2f out: wknd fnl f* **12/1**	
0040	**8**	*7*	**Just A Dancer (IRE)**[22] 4268 3-9-0 **62** .... MichaelHills 7	31
			(B W Hills) *led tl wl over 1f out: wknd qckly u.p over 1f out: t.o* **17/2**	

The Form Book, Raceform Ltd, Compton, RG20 6NL

5540 **9** 3 1/4 **Bohobe (IRE)**[8] 4702 3-9-0 **62**...(b[1]) PatCosgrave 1 21
(J G Given) *prom: drvn over 2f out: sn struggling: wl bhd fnl f: t.o* **10/1**
1m 16.66s (2.26) **Going Correction** +0.35s/f (Good) **9** Ran SP% **113.3**
Speed ratings (Par 97): **98,96,93,92,89 88,88,78,74**
toteswinger: 1&2 1.70, 1&3 £16.30, 2&3 £23.70. CSF £15.94 CT £171.09 TOTE £3.00: £1.10, £2.30, £5.60; EX 11.00 Trifecta £118.70 Pool: £413.88, 2.58 winning units.
Owner Mr & Mrs R Foulkes & Mrs Eugenie Abel Smith **Bred** Mrs K E Collie **Trained** Six Mile Bottom, Cambs
FOCUS
A modest fillies' handicap. The form looks solid enough rated through the placed horses.

4989 GREAT YARMOUTH TOURISM H'CAP 7f 3y
3:55 (3:58) (Class 5) (0-75,75) 3-Y-0+ **£2,590** (£770; £385; £192) **Stalls** High

Form RPR
-253 **1** **Viscountess (IRE)**[85] 2282 3-8-11 **64**... DarryllHolland 7 76
(M Johnston) *mde all: rdn wl over 1f out: clr ent fnl f: styd on wl* **12/1**
501 **2** 1 1/2 **Myanmar (IRE)**[33] 3916 3-9-8 **75**... ShaneKelly 9 83+
(J Noseda) *stdd after s: hld up in last: swtchd lft over 3f out: shkn up over 1f out: chsd wnr ins fnl f: nvr getting to wnr* **8/13**[1]
-552 **3** 3/4 **Dan Chillingworth (IRE)**[16] 4478 3-9-5 **72**... EddieAhern 1 78+
(J R Fanshawe) *hld up bhd: hdwy 3f out: sn rdn and unable qck: plugged on fnl f: nvr pce to threaten wnr* **6/1**[3]
503 **4** 2 1/2 **Resplendent Nova**[63] 2947 6-9-12 **73**... PatCosgrave 8 74
(P Howling) *chsd ldrs: wnt 2nd wl over 2f out: sn rdn and nt pce of wnner: lost 2 pls ins fnl f* **4/1**[2]
6626 **5** 9 **Warden Fizz**[13] 4566 3-9-4 **74**... MarcHalford(3) 2 49
(D R C Elsworth) *in tch in rr: rdn 1/2-way: wknd over 2f out: wl bhd fr 1f out* **20/1**
-000 **6** nk **Mudhish (IRE)**[5] 4809 3-9-6 **73**...(b) TPO'Shea 4 47
(C E Brittain) *t.k.h: chsd wnr tl over 2f out: sn rdn and struggling: wl bhd fr over 1f out* **40/1**
1m 29.32s (2.72) **Going Correction** +0.35s/f (Good)
WFA 3 from 4yo+ 6lb **6** Ran SP% **111.1**
Speed ratings (Par 103): **98,96,95,92,82 81**
toteswinger: 1&2 2.50, 1&3 £2.90, 2&3 £1.70. CSF £19.81 CT £49.85 TOTE £8.30: £2.50, £1.10; EX 23.20 Trifecta £63.30 Pool: £526.87, 6.15 winning units.
Owner Sheikh Hamdan Bin Mohammed Al Maktoum **Bred** Darley **Trained** Middleham Moor, N Yorks
FOCUS
A fair handicap which saw the winner nick the race from the front. The form has been rated through the fourth but could have been underrated.

4990 EASTERN DAILY PRESS CLAIMING STKS 1m 2f 21y
4:30 (4:31) (Class 6) 3-Y-0 **£1,942** (£578; £288; £144) **Stalls** Low

Form RPR
3614 **1** **Maddy**[7] 4750 3-7-12 58...(p) FrankieMcDonald 2 54
(George Baker) *taken down early: chsd ldng pair: wnt 2nd 4f out: led over 3f out: clr and rdn wl over 1f out: kpt on* **10/11**[1]
5406 **2** 5 **Flash Of Fire (USA)**[34] 3873 3-8-4 51...(b[1]) LukeMorris(3) 1 53
(J M P Eustace) *hld up in midfield: hdwy over 4f out: chsd wnr 3f out: rdn over 2f out: one pce after* **4/1**[2]
3061 **3** 1 1/4 **Grit (IRE)**[9] 4680 3-9-7 60... TPO'Shea 7 64
(M R Channon) *racd in midfield: rdn and hdwy over 3f out: chsd ldng pair wl over 2f out: no imp* **7/1**[3]
05-0 **4** 3 1/2 **Rock Me (IRE)**[7] 4722 3-7-12 45...(p) Louis-PhilippeBeuzelin(5) 8 39
(S A Callaghan) *sn bustled up to chse ldr: rdn: reluctant and lost pl 4f out: no ch after* **16/1**
3506 **5** 7 **Safebreaker**[7] 4750 3-9-1 69... DO'Donohoe 4 37+
(N Tinkler) *hld up in rr: rdn and brief effrt 3f out: sn wl btn: eased fnl f* **8/1**
0005 **6** 6 **Santa Clara**[22] 4271 3-7-7 47...(p) AmyBaker(5) 3 8+
(P Leech) *racd freely: led: clr 5f out: hdd over 3f out: sn wknd* **16/1**
-006 **7** 9 **Latimer House (IRE)**[22] 4280 3-8-4 43... RichardThomas 6 —
(Dr J D Scargill) *hld up in rr: rdn and lost tch over 3f out: t.o* **28/1**
0060 **8** 38 **Bagenalstown (IRE)**[21] 4298 3-8-6 42...(p) TolleyDean(3) 5 —
(M Wellings) *s.i.s: a last: lost tch 4f out: virtually p.u last 2f: t.o* **50/1**
2m 13.13s (2.63) **Going Correction** +0.35s/f (Good) **8** Ran SP% **113.2**
Speed ratings (Par 98): **103,99,98,95,89 84,77,47**
toteswinger: 1&2 1.80, 1&3 £2.30, 2&3 £3.80. CSF £4.53 TOTE £1.80: £1.10, £1.30, £1.50; EX 5.00 Trifecta £31.50 Pool: £660.30, 15.51 winning units.Maddy was claimed by Graham Smith for £4,000.
Owner Collings, Powner, Sword & Partners **Bred** P K Gardner **Trained** Moreton Morrell, Warwicks
FOCUS
A bad claimer for three-year-olds and they came home at intervals. The winner did not need to match her early-season form.
Latimer House(IRE) Official explanation: jockey said filly was never travelling
Bagenalstown(IRE) Official explanation: trainer said gelding was unsuited by the soft ground

4991 GREAT YARMOUTH IN BLOOM H'CAP 1m 1f
5:00 (5:02) (Class 6) (0-65,65) 3-Y-0+ **£1,942** (£578; £288; £144) **Stalls** Low

Form RPR
0051 **1** **Wogan's Sister**[7] 4750 3-8-13 **61** 6ex... MarcHalford(3) 7 75
(D R C Elsworth) *mde all: shkn up and drew wl clr 2f out: unchal* **4/1**[2]
-036 **2** 5 **Stormbeam (USA)**[19] 4377 3-9-5 **64**...(t) ShaneKelly 6 67
(G A Butler) *trckd ldrs: swtchd rt over 2f out: chsd wnr jst over 2f out: sn no ch w wnr: hld on for 2nd pl* **6/1**
0436 **3** 1 1/4 **Bartercard (USA)**[6] 4789 7-10-0 **65**... MickyFenton 1 65
(Stef Liddiard) *stdd s: t.k.h: hld up in rr: rdn and effrt 3f out: wnt 3rd ins fnl f: nvr nr wnr* **10/1**
0456 **4** 1/2 **Always Brave**[11] 4633 3-9-5 **64**... DarryllHolland 8 63
(M Johnston) *chsd ldrs: rdn over 3f out: kpt on same pce u.p fnl 2f* **10/3**[1]
0-12 **5** 1 **Fantasy Ride**[200] 320 6-9-13 **64**... PatCosgrave 10 61
(J Pearce) *s.i.s: rdn and effrt 4f out: plugged on same pce fnl 3f* **5/1**[3]
0300 **6** nse **Nordic Commander (IRE)**[34] 3886 3-9-3 **62**... EddieAhern 4 59
(E A L Dunlop) *hld up in midfield: rdn and effrt on inner wl over 2f out: no prog* **11/2**
605 **7** 1/2 **Trireme (IRE)**[51] 3312 4-9-3 **54**... JamesDoyle 5 50
(K A Morgan) *hld up bhd: rdn and effrt 3f out: no prog* **16/1**
00U4 **8** 3 1/4 **Dawn Wind**[16] 4491 3-8-2 **47** oh1 ow1...(v) TPO'Shea 2 36
(I A Wood) *stdd s: hld up in last: nvr a factor* **16/1**
0000 **9** nse **Bunty Malenoir**[6] 4796 3-7-11 **47**... AmyBaker(5) 9 35
(Mrs C A Dunnett) *chsd wnr tl jst over 2f out: steadily wknd* **22/1**
1m 58.78s (2.98) **Going Correction** +0.35s/f (Good)
WFA 3 from 4yo+ 8lb **9** Ran SP% **114.6**
Speed ratings (Par 101): **100,95,94,94,93 93,92,89,89**
toteswinger: 1&2 5.40, 1&3 £10.80, 2&3 £8.70. CSF £28.01 CT £223.95 TOTE £5.30: £1.60, £2.30, £3.20; EX 33.60 Trifecta £181.40 Pool: £355.52, 1.45 winning units.
Owner D R C Elsworth **Bred** Mrs J A Gawthorpe **Trained** Newmarket, Suffolk

FOCUS
A moderate handicap won in good style by a recent course winner who had been claimed for £12,000 after that effort and was having her first outing for a new yard here. The form has been rated at face value with the winner up a stone.

4992 HAPPY 65TH BIRTHDAY TO RICKY HARWOOD H'CAP 1m 3f 101y
5:30 (5:31) (Class 5) (0-70,70) 3-Y-0 **£2,590** (£770; £385; £192) **Stalls** Low

Form RPR
5314 **1** **Neve Lieve (IRE)**[11] 4619 3-9-7 **70**...(b[1]) DarryllHolland 3 78
(M Botti) *mde all: jnd and rdn 3f out: forged ahd over 1f out: styd on dourly* **7/2**[2]
0041 **2** 3 **Star Grazer**[23] 4259 3-8-8 **62**... JackMitchell(5) 6 65
(C F Wall) *chsd wnr: hdwy and upsides 3f out: rdn over 2f out: btn ent fnl f* **7/2**[2]
000- **3** 1 1/2 **Limelight (USA)**[383] 3916 3-8-3 **52**... DO'Donohoe 5 53
(Sir Mark Prescott) *in tch in midfield: rdn 5f out: plugged on to go 3rd wl ins fnl f: nvr pce to chal ldng pair* **7/1**[3]
6-00 **4** 1/2 **Toballa**[55] 3161 3-7-13 **51** oh5... LukeMorris(3) 2 51
(H J Collingridge) *trckd ldng pair: rdn 3f out: kpt on same pce u.p last 2f: lost 3rd wl ins fnl f* **16/1**
0624 **5** 1 1/4 **Trenchant**[26] 4156 3-9-4 **67**... EddieAhern 8 65
(J R Fanshawe) *hld up in last pair: rdn and hld hd awkwardly 4f out: wanting to hang and one pce after* **13/8**[1]
560 **6** 25 **Rockellio (IRE)**[50] 3351 3-8-13 **62**... MichaelHills 7 20
(B W Hills) *hld up in last pair: dropped to last over 6f out: lost tch 3f out: t.o* **8/1**
2m 33.24s (4.54) **Going Correction** +0.35s/f (Good) **6** Ran SP% **112.0**
Speed ratings (Par 100): **97,94,93,93,92 74**
toteswinger: 1&2 1.70, 1&3 £3.50, 2&3 £2.80. CSF £15.95 CT £78.33 TOTE £4.90: £2.80, £1.90; EX 13.80 Trifecta £46.40 Pool: £367.65, 5.86 winning units. Place 6: £39.83, Place 5: £27.00..
Owner The Great Partnership **Bred** Darley **Trained** Newmarket, Suffolk
FOCUS
A moderate handicap for three-year-olds dominated by fillies, in which it paid to race on or close to the pace, as the hold-up performers never got competitive. The winner is rated up 3lb.
Trenchant Official explanation: trainer's rep had no explanation for the poor form shown
T/Plt: £42.50 to a £1 stake. Pool: £51,835.03. 889.66 winning tickets. T/Qpdt: £8.80 to a £1 stake. Pool: £3,662.94. 308.00 winning tickets. SP

4993 - 5002a (Foreign Racing) - See Raceform Interactive

4960 BEVERLEY (R-H)
Thursday, August 14

OFFICIAL GOING: Soft
Wind: Light, half against Weather: Dry and sunny periods

5003 GEO HOULTON (S) H'CAP 1m 4f 16y
2:10 (2:10) (Class 6) (0-60,58) 3-Y-0+ **£2,266** (£674; £337; £168) **Stalls** High

Form RPR
430 **1** **Shenandoah Girl**[7] 4774 5-9-2 **54**...(p) KylieManser(7) 5 62
(Miss Gay Kelleway) *s.i.s: hld up in rr: smooth hdwy over 4f out: trckd ldrs 2f out: led appr fnl f: comf* **6/1**
3330 **2** 1 1/2 **Court Of Appeal**[14] 4556 11-9-5 **57**...(tp) LanceBetts(7) 8 63
(B Ellison) *trckd ldrs: hdwy over 3f out: led over 2f out and sn rdn: drvn and hdd appr fnl f: one pce* **3/1**[1]
1505 **3** 2 3/4 **Black Falcon (IRE)**[3] 4932 8-9-6 **51**... NCallan 6 53
(John A Harris) *hld up in tch: hdwy over 3f out: chal wl over 1f out: sn rdn and ev ch tl drvn and one pce ent fnl f* **4/1**[2]
0650 **4** 1 3/4 **Qaasi (USA)**[44] 3589 6-9-1 **49**... MarkLawson(3) 2 48
(M Brittain) *cl up: effrt 3f out and sn rdn along: drvn and wknd over 1f out* **12/1**
0-06 **5** 2 3/4 **Miss Cruisecontrol**[21] 4334 3-8-0 **45**... DuranFentiman(3) 11 39
(J R Best) *hld up towards rr: hdwy 3f out: rdn 2f out: styd on appr fnl f: nrst fin* **12/1**
05/0 **6** 1/2 **Mohawk Star (IRE)**[8] 4727 7-9-13 **58**... TonyHamilton 9 52
(I A Wood) *hld up in rr: hdwy over 3f out: sn rdn and no imp* **16/1**
3405 **7** hd **Parchment (IRE)**[41] 3666 6-9-2 **47**...(b) PaulHanagan 3 40
(A J Lockwood) *in rr: effrt whn n.m.r over 3f out: rdn and hdwy 2f out: drvn over 1f out and nvr nr ldrs* **11/2**[3]
0046 **8** 2 1/4 **Bright Sun (IRE)**[15] 4537 7-9-7 **52**... KimTinkler 4 42
(N Tinkler) *plld hrd: cl up: rdn along 3f out: wknd over 2f out* **16/1**
0006 **9** 1/2 **Ellies Faith**[51] 3335 4-9-0 **45**... AndrewElliott 7 34
(L R James) *led: rdn along 3f out: sn hdd and grad wknd* **33/1**
3044 **10** 30 **Floodlight Fantasy**[17] 3606 5-9-4 **56**...(b) BMcHugh(7) 10 —
(Dr R D P Newland) *trckd ldrs on inner: rdn along over 4f out and sn wknd* **8/1**
4000 **11** 36 **George Henson (IRE)**[67] 2867 4-9-0 **45**... DaleGibson 12 —
(Garry Moss) *midfield: rdn along over 3f out and sn wknd* **66/1**
2m 51.8s (10.90) **Going Correction** +0.725s/f (Yiel)
WFA 3 from 4yo+ 11lb **11** Ran SP% **117.4**
Speed ratings (Par 101): **92,91,89,88,86 85,85,84,83,63 39**
toteswinger: 1&2 £10.70, 1&3 £5.40, 2&3 £7.60. CSF £24.22 CT £81.78 TOTE £6.00: £2.00, £1.40, £1.90; EX 22.50.There was no bid for the winner.
Owner Gay Kelleway Tim Lightbowne **Bred** Julian Czerpak And Robert Cole **Trained** Exning, Suffolk
FOCUS
A wet morning and ground officially described as soft was riding pretty testing. Unsurprisingly, the runners in this selling handicap came wide in the straight, a traditional route when the mud is flying on this course. Ordinary form for the grade, and it was run in a moderate time, even for a seller.
Parchment(IRE) Official explanation: jockey said gelding was unsuited by the soft ground
George Henson(IRE) Official explanation: jockey said gelding lost its action

5004 EBF PRESTIGE RECRUITMENT MAIDEN FILLIES' STKS 5f
2:40 (2:42) (Class 4) 2-Y-0 **£5,018** (£1,493; £746; £372) **Stalls** High

Form RPR
00 **1** **Red Kyte**[15] 4521 2-9-0 0... NCallan 15 78+
(K A Ryan) *mde all: rdn and edgd lft over 1f out: kpt on wl* **4/1**[3]
4 **2** 1 1/2 **Florentia**[7] 4786 2-9-0 0... PaulMulrennan 9 73+
(Sir Mark Prescott) *chsd ldrs: pushed along 1/2-way: rdn and hdwy wl over 1f out: chsd wnr ins fnl f: kpt on same pce* **2/1**[1]
3 1 3/4 **Le Reve Royal** 2-8-11 0... PJMcDonald(3) 3 66
(G R Oldroyd) *sn outpcd and bhd: hdwy 2f out: rdn and styd on strly ent fnl f: nrst fin* **28/1**
0 **4** 1 **Monaco Mistress (IRE)**[26] 4202 2-9-0 0... LeeEnstone 11 63
(P C Haslam) *prom: rdn along to chse wnr wl over 1f out: sn drvn and one pce ent fnl f* **16/1**

4505 **5** 1 **Impressible**[11] 4659 2-9-0 64 .... DavidAllan 10 59
(E J Alston) *prom: rdn along 2f out: drvn and wknd appr fnl f* **11/4**[2]
55 **6** nk **Bussell Along (IRE)**[15] 4534 2-9-0 0 .... AndrewElliott 1 58+
(M L W Bell) *midfield: hdwy 2f out: swtchd lft over 1f out: kpt on ins fnl f: nrst fin* **25/1**
024 **7** ½ **Wotatomboy**[12] 4647 2-8-11 73 .... MichaelJStainton(3) 8 56
(R M Whitaker) *prom: rdn along 2f out: grad wknd* **8/1**
05 **8** 3 **Val De Flores**[46] 3528 2-9-0 0 .... DeanMcKeown 12 45
(E F Vaughan) *chsd ldrs: rdn along 2f out: grad wknd* **12/1**
9 ½ **Petella** 2-9-0 0 .... DanielTudhope 5 44
(C W Thornton) *sn outpcd and a in rr* **50/1**
10 2¾ **Valentine Bay** 2-8-7 0 .... DeanHeslop(7) 16 34
(M Mullineaux) *s.i.s: a bhd* **20/1**

67.89 secs (4.39) **Going Correction** +0.725s/f (Yiel) **10** Ran SP% **118.7**
Speed ratings (Par 93): **93,90,87,86,84 84,83,78,77,73**
toteswinger: 1&2 £2.10, 1&3 £25.50, 2&3 £21.40. CSF £12.13 TOTE £4.80: £1.90, £1.10, £3.90; EX 11.60.
Owner Malih L Al Basti **Bred** Peter Hodgson And Star Pointe Limited **Trained** Hambleton, N Yorks

FOCUS
Just an ordinary maiden for fillies but one worth keeping on video as a few winners should come out of it nonetheless.

NOTEBOOK
Red Kyte, dropped in trip, made all, in doing so proving her ability to handle testing ground. Draw one from the far side, she ended up racing against the stands' rail. She should go on from here. (op 3-1)
Florentia confirmed the ability she showed on her debut only to run into a superior rival. She remains a promising filly, who should not be long in winning. (op 11-4)
Le Reve Royal took a long time to grasp what was required on her debut, but she made stealthy progress from well over a furlong out to be nearest at the finish down the centre of the course. This experience will surely not have been wasted on her. (op 22-1 tchd 20-1)
Monaco Mistress(IRE) improved on her debut performance to hold every chance a furlong out. (op 25-1)
Impressible, in conditions that her half-brother Reverence would have relished, threatened to pose a serious threat at one point but could never raise her game sufficiently to pose a major challenge. (op 5-1)
Bussell Along(IRE) did some good work late on and was far from discredited. (op 22-1 tchd 20-1)

5005 MOTORS.CO.UK H'CAP 1m 1f 207y
3:15 (3:15) (Class 3) (0-90,89) 3-Y-0+ **£7,641** (£2,273; £1,136; £567) **Stalls** High

Form RPR
6-50 **1** **Kings Quay**[131] 962 6-9-6 81 ....(t) GrahamGibbons 6 88
(J J Quinn) *hld up in rr: pushed along over 2f out: hdwy over 1f out: rdn to chal ent fnl f: drvn and styd on wl to ld fnl 75yds* **14/1**
6044 **2** 1 **Vicious Warrior**[26] 4204 9-9-0 75 .... DeanMcKeown 9 80
(R M Whitaker) *led: rdn along over 2f out: drvn over 1f out: hdd and no ex last 75yds* **6/1**[3]
0014 **3** 1¾ **Kingsdale Orion (IRE)**[33] 3972 4-9-5 87 .... LanceBetts(7) 7 89
(B Ellison) *hld up in rr: hdwy on inner 3f out: rdn to chal wl over 1f out and ev ch tl drvn and no ex wl ins fnl f* **10/3**[2]
6352 **4** 2 **Motafarred (IRE)**[8] 4744 6-8-13 74 .... PaulMulrennan 2 72
(Micky Hammond) *trckd ldr: hdwy to chal over 2f out: sn rdn and ev ch tl drvn and wknd over 1f out* **7/1**
-311 **5** 2¾ **Tufton**[25] 4217 5-9-3 78 .... PaulHanagan 4 70
(R A Fahey) *hld up in rr: hdwy over 3f out: rdn to chse ldng pair wl over 1f out: wknd ent fnl f* **9/1**
0325 **6** 42 **William Blake**[15] 4519 3-9-4 88 .... JoeFanning 1 —
(M Johnston) *chsd ldr: rdn along over 2f out: drvn and wknd wl over 1f out: eased* **5/4**[1]

2m 12.34s (5.34) **Going Correction** +0.725s/f (Yiel)
WFA 3 from 4yo+ 9lb **6** Ran SP% **111.0**
Speed ratings (Par 107): **107,106,104,103,101 67**
toteswinger: 1&2 £17.10, 1&3 £13.40, 2&3 £2.60. CSF £88.76 CT £337.09 TOTE £18.40: £7.80, £2.70; EX 49.50.
Owner Mrs Marie Taylor **Bred** Newsells Park Stud Limited **Trained** Settrington, N Yorks

FOCUS
Some useful handicappers on show but the only three-year-old in the race, sent off as hot favourite, didn't run his race at all. The form is rated around the third.

NOTEBOOK
Kings Quay, coming back from a break of more than four months, was patiently ridden. Produced to challenge wide of the stands' rail, where the field came in the straight, he was always finding enough to prevail inside the last. He is clearly in good heart and this comeback victory should have set him up nicely to continue his successful dual-purpose career. (tchd 16-1)
Vicious Warrior, a proven mudlark, set out to expose any weaknesses in his rivals by setting a searching gallop in the conditions, only to be worried out of it by the winner late on. This was a creditable display from the old-timer. (op 13-2)
Kingsdale Orion(IRE), proven on soft ground, had every chance but upped two furlongs in trip did not get home as well as the principals. (op 7-2 tchd 5-2)
Motafarred(IRE) held every chance two furlongs out but this trip stretches him, especially in these conditions. (op 13-2 tchd 11-2)
William Blake, the hot favourite, ran as though amiss. Official explanation: jockey said colt was unsuited by the soft ground (op 11-8 tchd 6-4)

5006 SPORTHULL.CO.UK NURSERY 7f 100y
3:50 (3:51) (Class 5) (0-75,75) 2-Y-0 **£2,752** (£818; £409; £204) **Stalls** High

Form RPR
3234 **1** **Musical Maze**[22] 4292 2-8-4 61 .... DuranFentiman(3) 4 64
(W M Brisbourne) *mde most: rdn along 2f out: drvn ent fnl f: styd on gamely* **6/1**
354 **2** 1 **Digger Derek (IRE)**[17] 4474 2-8-8 62 .... PaulHanagan 3 63
(R A Fahey) *t.k.h: chsd ldrs: hdwy 2f out: rdn and nt clr run ent fnl f: sn swtchd rt: drvn and ev ch tl nt qckn nr fin* **3/1**[1]
4211 **3** 3¾ **Rose Of Coma (IRE)**[30] 4063 2-8-3 57 .... AdrianMcCarthy 9 49
(Miss Gay Kelleway) *sltly hmpd s: sn chsng ldng pair: rdn over 2f out: drvn over 1f out: kpt on same pce u.p fnl f* **10/1**
1036 **4** hd **Dispol Diva**[40] 3706 2-8-2 56 ....(v[1]) PaulFessey 12 47
(P T Midgley) *in rr: rdn along 1/2-way: hdwy 2f out: drvn and styng on whn sltly hmpd ent fnl f: kpt on: nrst fin* **16/1**
015 **5** shd **Fastnet Storm (IRE)**[20] 4373 2-9-7 75 .... TonyCulhane 5 66
(T P Tate) *midfield: hdwy to chse ldrs over 2f out and sn rdn: swtchd rt and drvn over 1f out: kpt on same pce ins fnl f* **9/2**[3]
6050 **6** 1 **Woteva**[19] 4434 2-8-6 67 .... LanceBetts(7) 1 56
(B Ellison) *hld up: hdwy on outer 1/2-way: rdn over 2f out: sn drvn and no imp appr fnl f* **12/1**
606 **7** ½ **Astroleo**[42] 3645 2-7-12 52 oh1 .... NickyMackay 11 40
(M H Tompkins) *in tch on inner: hdwy over 2f out: sn rdn and no imp appr fnl f* **11/1**
1505 **8** 1½ **Kneesy Earsy Nosey**[40] 3706 2-7-12 52 oh2 .... KimTinkler 6 36
(N Tinkler) *in rr tl sme late hdwy* **28/1**
0232 **9** 8 **Hold The Bucks (USA)**[21] 4340 2-8-2 59 .... LukeMorris(3) 10 24
(J S Moore) *wnt lft s: t.k.h: cl up: rdn along 2f out: drvn and wkng whn hmpd ent fnl f* **4/1**[2]
520 **10** 1¼ **Going Time (USA)**[27] 4157 2-8-13 67 .... JoeFanning 2 29
(M Johnston) *hld up towards rr: hdwy 3f out: rdn to chse ldrs wl over 1f out: sn drvn and btn* **12/1**

1m 38.75s (4.95) **Going Correction** +0.725s/f (Yiel) **10** Ran SP% **119.6**
Speed ratings (Par 94): **100,98,94,94,94 93,92,90,81,80**
toteswinger: 1&2 £6.10, 1&3 £8.90, 2&3 £5.70. CSF £25.02 CT £182.01 TOTE £10.00: £2.20, £1.90, £2.70; EX 30.20.
Owner The Nelson Pigs Might Fly Racing Club **Bred** Juddmonte Farms Ltd **Trained** Great Ness, Shropshire
■ Stewards' Enquiry : Paul Hanagan one-day ban: careless riding (Aug 29)

FOCUS
Some of the juveniles contesting this nursery clearly had plenty of improvement in them after the regulation number of starts in maiden company so despite the official ratings implying that it was only a fair race of its type the form could well prove solid, particularly as they clocked a decent time for the grade.

NOTEBOOK
Musical Maze clearly coped well with this slower ground and improved for the step-up in trip. Strongly pressed late on by the runner-up, she stuck to her task in good style and can build on this. (op 8-1 tchd 17-2)
Digger Derek(IRE) showed improved form on this handicap debut, being forced to wait for a gap to open over a furlong out before picking up well for pressure to finish clear of the remainder. (op 5-1)
Rose Of Coma(IRE), a dual winner in selling company, ran with credit upped in grade. (op 11-2)
Dispol Diva, visored for the first time, ran better than of late. (op 20-1 tchd 12-1)
Fastnet Storm(IRE) could never get in a challenging position after having to be switched off the stands' rail when tight for room over a furlong out. (op 5-1 tchd 11-2)
Hold The Bucks(USA) faded sharply after making the running. (op 9-2)

5007 HULL CITY, TIGERS 50K CHALLENGE FILLIES' H'CAP 5f
4:25 (4:26) (Class 5) (0-70,68) 3-Y-0+ **£2,914** (£867; £433; £216) **Stalls** High

Form RPR
210 **1** **By The Edge (IRE)**[20] 4385 4-8-12 60 .... DeanHeslop(7) 12 72+
(T D Barron) *prom on outer: smooth hdwy 2f out: led over 1f out: rdn ins fnl f and kpt on* **10/1**
2141 **2** ¾ **Pretty Bonnie**[7] 4767 3-9-3 66 6ex .... NataliaGemelova(5) 9 74
(A E Price) *cl up: rdn to chal 2f out and ev ch tl drvn and one pce ins fnl f* **3/1**[1]
4134 **3** 1½ **City For Conquest (IRE)**[5] 4858 5-8-11 52 .... AndrewElliott 10 56
(John A Harris) *prom: rdn along 2f out and sltly outpcd: styd on u.p ins fnl f* **7/2**[2]
/503 **4** ½ **Out Of India**[15] 4535 6-8-9 53 .... PJMcDonald(3) 11 55
(P T Dalton) *trckd ldrs: smooth hdwy 1/2-way: effrt wl over 1f out: sn swtchd rt and rdn: kpt on same pce* **6/1**[3]
0010 **5** ½ **Choisette**[25] 4216 3-9-5 68 .... GaryBartley(5) 7 67
(B Smart) *led: rdn along 2f out: hdd over 1f out: sn drvn and wknd ins fnl f* **7/1**
0406 **6** ¾ **Charlotte Grey**[8] 4749 4-8-5 46 .... JoeFanning 2 43
(P J McBride) *chsd ldr: rdn along 2f out: sn drvn and wknd over 1f out* **10/1**
0330 **7** 1½ **Miss Taboo (IRE)**[15] 4542 4-8-8 49 .... PaulFessey 3 41
(P T Midgley) *in tch: hdwy on outer 1/2-way: sn rdn along and n.d* **17/2**
0154 **8** 1¼ **Lujiana**[13] 4609 3-8-10 61 .... MatthewLawson(7) 6 47
(M Brittain) *chsd ldrs: rdn along 2f out: sn btn* **8/1**
0000 **9** 10 **Groundhog Day**[14] 4563 4-8-5 46 oh1 ....(p) DaleGibson 4 —
(J Balding) *s.i.s: a in rr* **40/1**

66.82 secs (3.32) **Going Correction** +0.725s/f (Yiel)
WFA 3 from 4yo+ 3lb **9** Ran SP% **116.3**
Speed ratings (Par 100): **102,100,98,97,96 95,93,91,75**
toteswinger: 1&2 £5.80, 1&3 £6.00, 2&3 £3.30. CSF £40.46 CT £128.95 TOTE £13.10: £3.10, £1.30, £1.50; EX 45.80.
Owner J Starbuck **Bred** A M Burke **Trained** Maunby, N Yorks

FOCUS
Not much strength in depth to this fillies' handicap but the second has been in grand heart of late so the form has a solid look to it.
Miss Taboo(IRE) Official explanation: jockey said filly hung right-handed

5008 HARD HAT GALLOPS H'CAP (FOR AMATEUR RIDERS) 1m 100y
5:00 (5:08) (Class 6) (0-65,69) 3-Y-0+ **£2,186** (£677; £338; £169) **Stalls** High

Form RPR
-520 **1** **Uhuru Peak**[10] 4679 7-10-6 50 ....(bt) MissSBrotherton 4 59
(M W Easterby) *chsd ldrs: hdwy 3f out: led over 2f out: rdn clr over 1f out: kpt on wl fnl f* **22/1**
0641 **2** 1½ **Leptis Magna**[8] 4748 4-11-4 62 6ex .... MrSWalker 3 68
(D R C Elsworth) *stdd s: hld up in rr: stdy hdwy 4f out: trckd ldrs over 2f out: rdn to chse wnr ent fnl f: sn drvn and no imp* **7/2**[2]
5500 **3** 1 **Rossini's Dancer**[8] 4745 3-9-13 57 .... MrBenHamilton(7) 8 60
(R A Fahey) *trckd ldrs: hdwy 3f out: rdn 2f out: edgd rt and kpt on u.p fnl f* **9/1**
6000 **4** 2½ **Playtotheaudience**[10] 4679 5-10-4 53 ....(p) MrsVFahey(5) 2 51
(R A Fahey) *cl up: led after 1f: pushed along and hdd over 3f out: rdn and chsd wnr 2f out: kpt on same pce u.p fnl f* **14/1**
0612 **5** 1 **Gallego**[11] 4664 6-11-0 63 .... MrMPrice(5) 17 59
(R J Price) *bhd: hdwy 3f out: rdn 2f out: styd on u.p appr fnl f: nrst fin* **9/1**
-010 **6** ¾ **Paparaazi (IRE)**[16] 4503 6-10-7 56 ....(p) MissKSharp(5) 10 50
(I W McInnes) *s.i.s and towards rr: hdwy over 3f out: rdn over 2f out: styd on u.p: nrst fin* **20/1**
4301 **7** ½ **Emirate Isle**[10] 4679 4-11-11 69 6ex ....(p) MissARyan 6 62
(C Grant) *chsd ldrs: hdwy 3f out: rdn 2f out: drvn and wknd appr fnl f* **9/1**
14-0 **8** shd **Kirstys Lad**[10] 4679 6-10-11 60 .... MissMMullineaux(5) 7 53
(M Mullineaux) *chsd ldrs: rdn along 3f out: kpt on same pce fnl 2f* **33/1**
5020 **9** 1¼ **Tizzy May (FR)**[16] 4503 8-10-8 57 ....(v) MrDaleSwift(5) 15 47
(B Ellison) *chsd ldrs: rdn along 3f out: drvn and n.m.r 2f out: sn one pce* **8/1**[3]
0555 **10** ¾ **Piano Man**[11] 4664 6-9-13 48 .... MissSarah-JaneDurman(5) 11 36
(J C Fox) *a towards rr* **18/1**
0046 **11** nk **Semah Harold**[15] 4533 3-10-4 62 ....(b[1]) MissEGeorge(5) 12 48
(E S McMahon) *in tch: hdwy on outer to chse ldrs 3f out: sn rdn and grad wknd fnl 2f* **33/1**
4400 **12** 5 **Barry Island**[27] 4156 9-9-13 50 .... MissGAndrews(7) 13 26
(D R C Elsworth) *a towards rr* **18/1**

1532 **13** ¾ **Emperor's Well**[10] 4679 9-10-10 **57**..........................(b) MissJCoward(3) 5 31
(M W Easterby) *led 1f: cl up tl led again over 3f out: rdn over 2f out and sn wknd* **5/2**[1]

1m 54.81s (7.21) **Going Correction** +0.725s/f (Yiel)
WFA 3 from 4yo+ 7lb **13** Ran SP% **124.1**
Speed ratings (Par 101): **92,90,89,87,86 85,84,84,83,82 82,77,76**
toteswinger: 1&2 £22.30, 1&3 £30.10, 2&3 £11.20. CSF £97.96 CT £776.45 TOTE £31.00: £6.60, £1.80, £3.80; EX 174.10 Place 6 £223.39, Place 5 £155.77.
Owner K Hodgson & Mrs J Hodgson **Bred** M W Easterby And K Hodgson **Trained** Sheriff Hutton, N Yorks
■ Fort Amhurst (14/1) was withdrawn (bolted to post and rider Mr Jake Greenall injured.) R4 applies, deduct 5p in the £.

FOCUS
Some moderate, exposed, inconsistent animals contested this handicap for amateur riders. Ordinary form, the winner rated back to his best.
Emperor's Well Official explanation: trainer had no explanation for the poor form shown
T/Jkpt: Not won. T/Plt: £326.00 to a £1 stake. Pool: £53,620.69. 120.05 winning tickets. T/Qpdt: £78.50 to a £1 stake. Pool: £3,618.59. 34.10 winning tickets. JR

4704 CHEPSTOW (L-H)
Thursday, August 14
5009 Meeting Abandoned - Waterlogged

4267 GREAT LEIGHS (A.W) (L-H)
Thursday, August 14
OFFICIAL GOING: Standard
Wind: Virtually nil Weather: Bright, showers possible

5015 CAVENDISH H'CAP 5f (P)
5:30 (5:32) (Class 6) (0-65,65) 3-Y-O **£2,266** (£674; £337; £168) **Stalls** Low

Form RPR
1465 **1** **Enodoc**[7] 4773 3-9-2 **65**..........................(t) DavidProbert(5) 3 69
(W R Muir) *chsd ldr: rdn to ld over 1f out: styd on wl* **5/1**[2]
0540 **2** ¾ **Westwood Dawn**[19] 4413 3-8-4 **48** oh1 ow2..........(v) DMylonas 5 49
(Mrs N Macauley) *t.k.h: hld up wl in tch: rdn and effrt over 1f out: kpt on to go 2nd wl ins fnl f* **33/1**
5506 **3** ½ **Linnet Park**[10] 4686 3-8-1 **52**.......................... RosieJessop(7) 2 52
(J G Given) *led: rdn wl over 1f out: hdd over 1f out: kpt on one pce fnl f* **12/1**
0060 **4** 3 ¾ **Summer Rose**[22] 4308 3-7-9 **46** oh1..........(p) AndreaAtzeni(7) 4 32
(R M H Cowell) *dwlt: sn bustled along on inner: in tch rdn and effrt 2f out: wnt modest 4th ins fnl f: nvr trbld ldrs* **25/1**
0630 **5** ½ **Shatter Resistant (IRE)**[7] 4793 3-8-9 **53**..........(p) JohnEgan 7 37
(M D Squance) *s.i.s: a in rr: rdn 1/2-way: nvr trbld ldrs* **17/2**
0404 **6** ½ **Tugalu (IRE)**[12] 4632 3-9-4 **62**..........(b[1]) FergalLynch 8 44
(K A Ryan) *chsd ldng pair: rdn 2f out: hung lft and wknd over 1f out* **4/1**[1]
0000 **7** 2 **Cracking Nick (IRE)**[26] 4186 3-9-4 **62**..........(t[1]) AdamKirby 14 37
(W R Swinburn) *chsd ldrs: rdn and struggling 1/2-way: no ch w ldrs last 2f* **4/1**[1]
0040 **8** nk **Young Ivanhoe**[10] 4684 3-8-13 **57**.......................... JimmyQuinn 6 31
(C A Dwyer) *a in rr: rdn over 3f out: no ch whn edgd rt ent fnl f* **11/1**
0200 **9** ½ **Swift Acclaim (IRE)**[10] 4686 3-8-7 **51**.......................... HayleyTurner 12 23
(K R Burke) *s.i.s: a bhd* **12/1**
0505 **10** 1 ½ **Tea Cake (IRE)**[21] 4338 3-9-1 **59**..........(b) ChrisCatlin 10 26
(H J L Dunlop) *a bhd: no ch whn nt clr run ent fnl f* **13/2**[3]
000 **11** ½ **Seductive Witch**[27] 4163 3-8-11 **55**.......................... PaulDoe 13 20
(J Balding) *in tch in midfield: rdn 1/2-way: sn struggling: no ch w ldrs last 2f* **7/1**

61.23 secs (1.03) **Going Correction** +0.25s/f (Slow) **11** Ran SP% **123.5**
Speed ratings (Par 98): **101,99,99,93,92 91,88,87,86,84 83**
toteswinger: 1&2 Not won, 1&3 Not won, 2&3 Not won. CSF £161.52 CT £1337.00 TOTE £6.90: £2.90, £8.40, £5.00; EX 404.80.
Owner Mrs D Edginton **Bred** Fonthill Stud **Trained** Lambourn, Berks

FOCUS
A moderate sprint handicap in which winning form was very thin on the ground. The draw played its part with the first four home coming from the five inside stalls. The front three pulled well clear of the others, but the form looks weak.
Cracking Nick(IRE) Official explanation: jockey said gelding hung left in the straight

5016 BROXTED NOVICE STKS 6f (P)
6:00 (6:01) (Class 4) 2-Y-O **£3,885** (£1,156; £577; £288) **Stalls** Low

Form RPR
2 **1** **Celtic Spur (IRE)**[50] 3372 2-8-7 0.......................... DavidProbert(5) 4 84+
(A M Balding) *trckd ldr: pushed into ld ent fnl f: idled and edgd lft fnl f: pushed out* **15/8**[1]
014 **2** 1 **Zaffaan**[20] 4374 2-9-5 92.......................... RHills 3 88
(E A L Dunlop) *sn led: rdn wl over 1f out: hdd ent fnl f: kpt on but a hld* **5/2**[2]
2421 **3** 6 **Stan's Cool Cat (IRE)**[20] 4367 2-8-11 86.......................... ChrisCatlin 1 62
(P F I Cole) *in tch: rdn 3f out: outpcd by ldng pair over 1f out: no ch fnl f* **5/2**[2]
4 2 **Rare Art** 2-8-9 0.......................... HayleyTurner 2 54+
(S A Callaghan) *hld in wl in tch: rdn and outpcd by ldng pair over 1f out: no ch fnl f* **5/1**[3]

1m 15.3s (1.60) **Going Correction** +0.25s/f (Slow) **4** Ran SP% **108.6**
Speed ratings (Par 96): **99,97,89,87**
CSF £6.77 TOTE £2.20; EX 10.50.
Owner Mick and Janice Mariscotti **Bred** John O'Connor **Trained** Kingsclere, Hants

FOCUS
A small field, but despite that the pace was a solid one and it was noticeable that the quartet came away from the inside rail entering the home straight. Also the market got this race spot-on and the front pair came well clear of the other two.

NOTEBOOK
Celtic Spur(IRE) ◆, down a furlong from his Kempton debut, was well backed and raced much more handily this time. Once picking off the pacesetter, he tended to hang and idle in front but he had the race won by then. He still does not look the finished article and there is probably plenty more to come from him. (op 5-2)
Zaffaan was given a positive ride on this sand debut and, although he eventually found the well-backed and unexposed winner too good for him, it may be best to measure this performance by the distance he pulled clear of the other two. (tchd 2-1)
Stan's Cool Cat(IRE), another making her sand debut, was firmly put in her place by the front pair from a long way out. She was the most experienced in the field and she may be better suited by fast ground on turf. (op 9-4)
Rare Art, a 92,000gns colt, faced a stiff task on this debut and there was not a great deal of market confidence behind him either. He was never out of last place, but although he is by a top-class sprinter his dam is a half-sister to seven winners including the prolific winning stayer On Call, so it may be that he needs a bit more time and experience. (op 7-2)

5017 CRESSING H'CAP 1m 6f (P)
6:30 (6:30) (Class 4) (0-80,80) 3-Y-O+ **£4,857** (£1,445; £722; £360) **Stalls** Low

Form RPR
3321 **1** **Greenwich Village**[19] 4410 5-9-2 **68**.......................... PaulDoe 8 77
(W J Knight) *chsd ldng pair tl wnt 2nd 10f out: rdn and clr w ldr 3f out: led fnl 100yds: forged clr* **5/1**[3]
-312 **2** 2 ¼ **General Ting (IRE)**[19] 4432 3-8-7 **72** ow1.......................... SebSanders 4 78
(Sir Mark Prescott) *sn led: rdn and clr w wnr 3f out: hdd fnl 100yds: sn btn* **6/4**[1]
1005 **3** 2 ¼ **Vinces**[22] 4309 4-8-11 **66**.......................... KirstyMilczarek(3) 6 69
(T D McCarthy) *t.k.h: hld up in rr: hdwy 5f out: chsd clr ldng pair over 2f out: plugged on steadily u.p fnl f: nt trble ldng pair* **25/1**
100 **4** ½ **Eventide**[22] 4303 3-7-12 **68**.......................... DavidProbert(5) 7 70
(W J Knight) *hld up towards rr: hdwy 5f out: wnt modest 4th over 2f out: kpt on steadily u.p: nvr trbld ldrs* **25/1**
015- **5** 7 **Turban Heights (IRE)**[303] 6249 4-9-10 **76**.......................... ChrisCatlin 3 68
(E J O'Neill) *v.s.a: bhd: rdn 6f out: past btn horses fr 3f out: nvr on terms* **16/1**
4105 **6** 20 **Bell Island**[26] 4200 4-9-12 **78**.......................... RichardKingscote 1 42
(Lady Herries) *chsd ldr tl 10f out: rdn over 5f out: wknd wl over 3f out: eased fr over 1f out: t.o* **14/1**
512 **7** 4 **Vilna (USA)**[8] 4732 3-8-8 **73**..........(v) HayleyTurner 5 32
(S A Callaghan) *hld up bhd: rdn and effrt 4f out: no prog: t.o* **3/1**[2]
2135 **8** 6 **Trachonitis (IRE)**[22] 4314 4-10-0 **80**.......................... JohnEgan 10 30
(J R Jenkins) *racd off the pce in midfield: hdwy to chse ldng pair 4f out: sn rdn: wknd 3f out: eased fnl f: t.o* **8/1**
3150 **9** 20 **Wind Flow**[8] 4726 4-9-6 **72**.......................... JimmyQuinn 2 —
(C A Dwyer) *chsd ldrs: rdn 6f out: wknd over 4f out: t.o and eased last 2f* **16/1**
-000 **10** 23 **Eva Soneva So Fast (IRE)**[22] 4299 6-10-0 **80**.......... VinceSlattery 9 —
(G F Bridgwater) *towards rr: rdn over 7f out: lost tch over 5f out: wl t.o last 3f* **50/1**

3m 5.95s (2.75) **Going Correction** +0.25s/f (Slow)
WFA 3 from 4yo+ 13lb **10** Ran SP% **120.9**
Speed ratings (Par 105): **102,100,99,99,95 83,81,78,66,53**
toteswinger: 1&2 £5.00, 1&3 £27.00, 2&3 £27.00. CSF £13.17 CT £178.49 TOTE £7.80: £1.40, £1.30, £5.00; EX 16.80.
Owner Ecurie Franglaise **Bred** Cotswold Stud **Trained** Patching, W Sussex

FOCUS
Not the most competitive of handicaps, but the pace was solid enough and very few ever got into it as the front pair dominated throughout. They are progressive and could have been rated higher.
Bell Island Official explanation: jockey said gelding had no more to give

5018 BOREHAM H'CAP 1m (P)
7:00 (7:01) (Class 4) (0-80,80) 3-Y-O+ **£4,857** (£1,445; £722; £360) **Stalls** Low

Form RPR
6-10 **1** **Angel Rock (IRE)**[27] 4160 3-9-4 **79**.......................... JohnEgan 3 86
(M Botti) *hld up in tch: rdn over 2f out: chsd ldng pair 2f out: kpt on gamely u.p to ld fnl stride* **12/1**
0610 **2** shd **Mount Hermon (IRE)**[8] 4723 4-9-6 **77**..........(b) TravisBlock(3) 9 85
(H Morrison) *hld up in tch: hdwy over 3f out: ev ch wl over 1f out: carried rt 1f out: led narrowly ins fnl f: hdd fnl stride* **5/1**[2]
4123 **3** nse **Moonlight Man**[3] 4927 7-9-9 **77**..........(t) LPKeniry 6 85
(C R Dore) *chsd ldr tl led 4f out: rdn and hung rt 1f out: hdd ins fnl f: unable qck nr fin* **7/1**
6020 **4** 3 ¾ **Prince Of Thebes (IRE)**[16] 4509 7-9-9 **80**.......... KirstyMilczarek(3) 2 79
(M J Attwater) *hld up in tch in rr: rdn over 2f out: chsd ldng trio ent fnl f: kpt on but nvr able to chal* **7/1**
-005 **5** 1 ¾ **Heroes**[36] 3855 4-9-12 **80**.......................... GeorgeBaker 1 75
(C F Wall) *trckd ldrs: lost pl and rdn 3f out: kpt on u.p fr over 1f out but no ch w ldrs* **4/1**[1]
1 **6** 1 ½ **Paint The Town Red**[56] 3161 3-9-1 **76**.......................... DarryllHolland 7 67
(H J Collingridge) *in tch towards rr: rdn and struggling wl over 3f out: kpt on u.p fr over 1f out: nvr pce to trble ldrs* **4/1**[1]
6213 **7** 4 **My Mentor (IRE)**[21] 4345 4-9-5 **73**..........(b) SebSanders 8 56
(Sir Mark Prescott) *chsd ldrs: rdn 3f out: wknd jst over 2f out: wl btn fnl f* **11/2**[3]
-623 **8** 3 ¼ **Lawyers Choice**[152] 910 4-9-11 **79**.......................... PatDobbs 5 54
(Pat Eddery) *hld up in rr: rdn 4f out: no imp and wl btn after* **14/1**
4320 **9** 3 **Our Kes (IRE)**[26] 4183 6-9-5 **73**.......................... IanMongan 10 41
(P Howling) *stdd after s: hld up in last: rdn and brief effrt on outer 3f out: wl btn last 2f* **33/1**
1332 **10** 1 ¼ **My Mirasol**[141] 1032 4-8-10 **64**.......................... ChrisCatlin 4 29
(D E Cantillon) *led tl 4f out: rdn and wknd over 3f out: wl bhd last 2f* **25/1**

1m 41.16s (1.26) **Going Correction** +0.25s/f (Slow)
WFA 3 from 4yo+ 7lb **10** Ran SP% **118.2**
Speed ratings (Par 105): **103,102,102,99,97 95,91,88,85,84**
toteswinger: 1&2 £28.30, 1&3 Not won, 2&3 £28.30. CSF £72.02 CT £471.80 TOTE £20.00: £4.30, £2.40, £2.70; EX 148.70.
Owner Tenuta Dorna Di Montaltuzzo SRL **Bred** Ascagnano S P A **Trained** Newmarket, Suffolk
■ Stewards' Enquiry : L P Keniry two-day ban: careless riding (Aug 28-29)

FOCUS
A competitive little handicap and a thrilling finish with nothing separating the front three at the line. The third is a solid guide to the form.
Heroes Official explanation: jockey said gelding was denied a clear run

5019 GEOFF VAUGHAN 50TH BIRTHDAY CELEBRATION FILLIES' H'CAP 1m (P)
7:30 (7:32) (Class 5) (0-75,74) 3-Y-O **£2,590** (£578; £578; £192) **Stalls** Low

Form RPR
0034 **1** **Suzi Spends (IRE)**[7] 4795 3-9-3 **70**.......................... JohnEgan 6 76
(H J Collingridge) *hld up in tch: rdn and hdwy wl over 1f out: ev ch 1f out: led fnl 100yds: r.o wl* **9/2**[2]
0000 **2** 1 **Turfani (IRE)**[23] 4278 3-7-11 **55**.......................... DavidProbert(5) 11 59
(W J Knight) *hld up in tch on outer: rdn and hdwy ent fnl f: r.o wl fnl 100yds: nt rch wnr* **25/1**
-056 **2** dht **Welsh Opera**[15] 4524 3-8-3 **56**.......................... JimmyQuinn 3 60
(Mrs A J Perrett) *t.k.h: chsd ldr tl 5f out: rdn effrt on inner 2f out: led 1f out: hdd and no ex fnl 100yds* **12/1**

-114 **4** ¾ **Charlevoix (IRE)**[35] 3874 3-9-5 **72** .... GeorgeBaker 8 74
(C F Wall) *in tch: hdwy over 2f out: ev ch 2f out: kpt on one pce u.p fnl f* **2/1**[1]

5524 **5** 1 **Saleima (IRE)**[27] 4152 3-9-6 **73** .... SebSanders 5 76+
(P W Chapple-Hyam) *hld up in tch: rdn and keeping on whn nt clr run and snatched up ins fnl f: nvr able to chal* **9/2**[2]

2502 **6** 1 **Queen's Speech (IRE)**[18] 4447 3-9-7 **74** ....(b) RobertHavlin 7 72
(J H M Gosden) *chsd ldrs: wnt 2nd 5f out: led 3f out: rdn 2f out: hdd 1f out: sn edgd rt: wknd fnl 100yds* **6/1**[3]

3-00 **7** 3½ **La Famiglia**[50] 3379 3-8-7 **60** .... ChrisCatlin 4 50
(H Candy) *t.k.h: led tl 3f out: sn rdn and edging rt: wknd over 1f out* **20/1**

0-00 **8** 2½ **Aura**[78] 2500 3-8-2 **55** .... HayleyTurner 1 39
(M L W Bell) *t.k.h: hld up in tch on inner: lost pl over 3f out: n.d after* **25/1**

323 **9** hd **Suede**[18] 4461 3-9-3 **70** .... TedDurcan 9 53
(Pat Eddery) *dwlt: dropped in bhd: rdn 4f out: n.d* **6/1**[3]

1m 42.41s (2.51) **Going Correction** +0.25s/f (Slow) **9** Ran SP% **118.4**
Speed ratings (Par 97): **97,96,96,95,94 93,89,87,87**PL: Suzi Spends £1.80, Welsh Opera £4.10, Turfani £7.80; EX: SS-WO £36.80, SS-T £75.70; CSF: SS-WO £27.93, SS-T £56.31; TRICAST: SS-WO-T £606.55, SS-T-WO £632.71; toteswinger: 1&2 (Welsh Opera) £22.80, 1&2 (Turfani) £48.00, 2&3 £21.80. TOTE £7.90: £0.0027, £Owner, £Greenstead Hall Racing, £BredG Callanan Trained Trifecta £Exning, Suffolk.

FOCUS

Just a fair fillies' handicap and the pace was ordinary, resulting in a winning time 1.25 seconds slower than the preceding handicap. Sound form overall.

5020 LITTLE BADDOW H'CAP — 1m 2f (P)

8:00 (8:01) (Class 6) (0-50,50) 3-Y-O+ **£1,942** (£578; £288; £144) **Stalls** Low

Form RPR

0-00 **1** **Hallings Overture (USA)**[12] 4635 9-8-12 **48** ....(p) RichardKingscote 8 61
(C A Horgan) *t.k.h: hld up bhd: smooth hdwy 3f out: rdn over 1f out: led 1f out: sn clr: comf* **28/1**

000- **2** 3¼ **King Canute (IRE)**[432] 2456 4-8-12 **48** .... TedDurcan 10 55
(Mrs S Leech) *t.k.h: hld up towards rr: hdwy and jostled 3f out: sn rdn: styd on u.p fr over 1f out: wnt 2nd fnl 100yds: no ch w wnr* **5/2**[1]

4443 **3** 1 **The Grey One (IRE)**[6] 4820 5-8-13 **49** ....(p) PatCosgrave 7 54
(J M Bradley) *t.k.h: chsd ldrs: hdwy over 3f out: ev ch u.p over 1f out: nt pce of wnr fnl f: lost 2nd fnl 100yds* **9/1**[3]

-253 **4** 1½ **Magic Amigo**[116] 1505 7-8-5 **46** ....(b) DavidProbert[(5)] 6 48
(J R Jenkins) *chsd ldr: rdn to ld wl over 1f out: hdd 1f out: one pce after* **9/1**[3]

3061 **5** nk **Desert Hawk**[3] 4936 7-8-10 **46** ....(b) EddieAhern 13 47
(W M Brisbourne) *hld up towards rr: rdn and effrt on outer 3f out: styd on steadily fr over 1f out: nvr trbld ldrs* **5/2**[1]

0006 **6** 1¼ **Recalcitrant**[8] 4721 5-8-13 **49** .... SebSanders 2 47
(S Dow) *chsd ldrs: rdn over 3f out: ev ch u.p over 1f out: wknd fnl f* **14/1**

30/4 **7** 1½ **Shropshirelass**[31] 1207 5-8-13 **49** .... LPKeniry 4 44
(Norma Twomey) *in tch: rdn 4f out: plugged on same pce u.p last 2f* **16/1**

316 **8** 3 **Ruwain**[17] 4491 4-8-7 **50** .... AndreaAtzeni[(7)] 5 39
(P J McBride) *led tl rdn and hdd wl over 1f out: sn wknd* **8/1**[2]

0200 **9** 2½ **Bainisteoir**[8] 4722 3-8-5 **50** .... JimmyQuinn 12 34
(S Kirk) *hld up in midfield: hdwy 4f out: sn rdn: wknd over 2f out* **25/1**

6335 **10** 2¾ **Postmaster**[20] 4365 6-9-0 **50** .... RobertHavlin 16 29
(R Ingram) *hld up bhd: rdn and effrt on outer over 3f out: no prog* **12/1**

00-0 **11** ¾ **Womaniser (IRE)**[125] 1311 4-8-10 **46** .... J-PGuillambert 9 23
(T Keddy) *s.i.s: sn swtchd lft: a bhd* **50/1**

6-26 **12** 3¾ **Kilmeena Magic**[50] 415 6-8-11 **47** .... PatDobbs 11 17
(J C Fox) *hld up in last pair: nvr a factor* **28/1**

0003 **13** 10 **Golden Brown (IRE)**[26] 4182 4-8-12 **48** .... ChrisCatlin 15 —
(David Pinder) *hld up in midfield: rdn 4f out: sn wknd: t.o and eased over 1f out* **18/1**

-030 **14** 20 **Bold Phoenix (IRE)**[78] 2513 7-8-11 **47** ....(b) HayleyTurner 1 —
(Miss Amy Weaver) *hld up in midfield: rdn and wknd 4f out: t.o and eased over 1f out* **20/1**

0320 **15** 10 **Yakama (IRE)**[8] 4750 3-8-5 **50** ....(b) DMylonas 14 —
(G Prodromou) *dwlt: t.k.h: sn chsng ldrs: wkng qckly whn jostled 3f out: t.o fr wl over 1f out* **28/1**

4000 **16** 5 **Classy Affair**[11] 4664 4-8-12 **48** .... JohnEgan 3 —
(D Morris) *hld up in rr: lost tch wl over 3f out: eased fr wl over 1f out: t.o* **20/1**

2m 10.26s (1.66) **Going Correction** +0.25s/f (Slow)
WFA 3 from 4yo+ 9lb **16** Ran SP% **139.4**
Speed ratings (Par 101): **103,100,99,98,98 97,95,93,91,89 88,85,77,61,53 49**
toteswinger: 1&2 £44.90, 1&3 £49.40, 2&3 £16.40. CSF £103.80 CT £759.76 TOTE £27.40: £4.80, £1.30, £2.00, £3.20; EX 287.00 Place 6 £577.30, Place 5 £129.81.
Owner Mrs B Sumner **Bred** Spectrum Bloodstock S A And Partners **Trained** Uffcott, Wilts

FOCUS

A moderate but competitive handicap. The early pace was ordinary and several pulled as a result, though the final time was reasonable enough. The form is rated around the third.

Bold Phoenix(IRE) Official explanation: trainer said gelding had a breathing problem

Classy Affair Official explanation: trainer said filly had a breathing problem

T/Plt: £1,086.20 to a £1 stake. Pool: £50,591.37. 34.00 winning tickets. T/Qpdt: £42.20 to a £1 stake. Pool: £6,141.39. 107.60 winning tickets. SP

4973 SALISBURY (R-H)

Thursday, August 14

OFFICIAL GOING: Good to soft (soft in places)

Wind: Virtually nil Weather: Sunny

5021 COORS BREWERS MAIDEN AUCTION STKS (DIV I) — 6f 212y

2:00 (2:06) (Class 5) 2-Y-O **£2,914** (£867; £433; £216) **Stalls** High

Form RPR

1 **Such Optimism** 2-8-8 0 ow2 .... SebSanders 2 87+
(R M Beckett) *leggy: lw: s.i.s: bhd on stands' side: gd prog fr over 3f out: led over 2f out: sn clr: r.o wl: readily* **11/1**

33 **2** 5 **Sunny Future (IRE)**[20] 4360 2-8-13 0 .... TGMcLaughlin 13 78
(M S Saunders) *lw: trckd ldrs on far side tl swtchd to centre 3f out: rdn and ev ch over 2f out: kpt on but nt pce of ready wnr* **4/1**[2]

60 **3** 1½ **Mister Dee Bee (IRE)**[27] 4150 2-8-13 0 .... MichaelHills 1 74+
(B W Hills) *lw: chsd ldrs on stands' side: outpcd and edgd rt over 2f out: wnt 3rd ent fnl f: styd on* **8/1**[3]

6 **4** 3¾ **Mykingdomforahorse**[12] 4636 2-8-9 0 .... EdwardCreighton 12 61
(M R Channon) *towards rr on far side: swtchd to centre 3f out: sn rdn: styd on same pce fnl 2f: nvr trbld ldrs* **20/1**

5 ½ **Perfect Friend** 2-8-4 0 .... MartinDwyer 10 54
(S Kirk) *w'like: hld up on far side: swtchd to centre and hdwy 3f out: sn rdn: one pce fr over 1f out* **25/1**

2305 **6** nk **I Am The Best**[35] 3876 2-9-2 95 .... RoystonFfrench 3 66
(D M Simcock) *lw: stmbld bdly leaving stalls: sn chsng ldrs on stands' side: ev ch over 2f out: sn rdn: wknd ent fnl f* **4/6**[1]

0 **7** 5 **Harry Raffle**[11] 4665 2-8-11 0 .... DaneO'Neill 6 48
(S Kirk) *a towards rr on stands' side* **100/1**

6 **8** 1½ **Tax Dodger (IRE)**[35] 3882 2-8-6 0 .... TolleyDean[(3)] 5 42
(J L Spearing) *prom on stands' side: led 3f out: sn rdn and hdd: wknd jst over 1f out* **66/1**

6 **9** ¾ **Solar Graphite (IRE)**[20] 4360 2-9-2 0 .... EddieAhern 9 48
(J L Dunlop) *racd on far side tl 3f out: a towards rr* **16/1**

0 **10** 4 **Marcus Crassus (IRE)**[22] 4304 2-8-11 0 .... RichardMullen 11 33
(H J L Dunlop) *lw: led far side gp tl 3f out: styd on far side and racd alone: sn btn* **40/1**

005 **11** 1½ **Free To Choose (IRE)**[41] 3693 2-8-11 49 .... DarrenWilliams 8 29
(A P Jarvis) *led stands' side gp tl 3f out: grad fdd* **100/1**

1m 30.42s (1.42) **Going Correction** +0.175s/f (Good) **11** Ran SP% **119.8**
Speed ratings (Par 94): **98,92,90,86,85 85,79,77,77,72 70**
toteswinger: 1&2 £4.50, 1&3 £8.30, 2&3 £4.10. CSF £53.43 TOTE £13.60: £2.90, £1.30, £2.90; EX 51.30.
Owner G C Myddelton **Bred** Mystic Meg Limited **Trained** Whitsbury, Hants
■ Gearbox (12/1, vet's advice) and Efficiency (100/1, ref to ent stalls) were withdrawn. Deduct 5p in the £ under R4.

FOCUS

Initially six raced on the stands' side and five stayed on the inside rail, but the course had been narrowed by the stands' rail being pushed out up to 6m following the previous day's action and the two groups merged halfway through the race.

NOTEBOOK

Such Optimism is an attractive sister to 1m2f winner Astrolibra. Green to post but professional through the race, she was always travelling well near the stands' rail and moved easily clear when shown the front. This trip looked a minimum requirement on breeding, so the signs are positive that she can go on to better things. (old market tchd 14-1 new market op 12-1)

Sunny Future(IRE), who got warm at the start, started in the inside-rail group but effectively ended mid-track as he finished a clear second after showing decent pace on this very different ground. He is now qualified for nurseries. (old market op 4-1 tchd 5-1)

Mister Dee Bee(IRE) was staying on stoutly on this third run, but the effort was made to look better by others floundering around him. He is still strengthening up and is interesting for a nursery. (old market op 14-1 tchd 16-1 new market op 9-1)

Mykingdomforahorse does not have that much scope and was ridden along to go the steady early pace, but made modest late gains. A half-brother to smart Irish performer Ghimaar, he is bred to get considerably further. (old market op 33-1 new market op 25-1)

Perfect Friend is a half-sister to prolific 6-7f winner Benllech, who was formerly trained by Kirk. She was green and looked uneasy on the ground, and was held together when well beaten inside the last two furlongs. (old market op 16-1)

I Am The Best, fifth in the Group 2 July Stakes last time, was clearly below form. He was down on his nose leaving the stalls and, although recovering to have his chance, he found nothing off the bridle and was beaten way before the extra furlong became an issue. Official explanation: trainer said colt was unsuited by the ground (old market op 5-6 new market tchd 10-11 in a place)

5022 COORS BREWERS MAIDEN AUCTION STKS (DIV II) — 6f 212y

2:30 (2:36) (Class 5) 2-Y-O **£2,914** (£867; £433; £216) **Stalls** High

Form RPR

0 **1** **Athania (IRE)**[36] 3837 2-8-4 0 .... RichardThomas 11 70
(A P Jarvis) *awkward leaving stalls: mde all: 4 l clr over 3f out: rdn over 2f out: kpt on gamely* **8/1**

6 **2** ¾ **Blazing Buck**[54] 3267 2-8-11 0 .... DaneO'Neill 5 75
(H J L Dunlop) *trckd ldrs: wnt 2nd 4f out: rdn over 2f out: styd on and clsng on wnr at fin but a hld* **5/1**[3]

0 **3** 2 **Peter Grimes (IRE)**[22] 4311 2-8-11 0 .... FrancisNorton 13 70
(H J L Dunlop) *trckd wnr tl 4f out: rdn over 2f out: kpt on same pce* **16/1**

00 **4** ½ **Lethal Glaze (IRE)**[16] 4510 2-8-13 0 .... RichardHughes 4 71
(R Hannon) *mid-div: rdn 3f out: styd on steadily: nvr pce to chal* **7/2**[2]

5 5 **Googoobarabajagal (IRE)** 2-8-11 0 .... RichardKingscote 2 56
(W S Kittow) *w'like: rn green: towards rr: rdn over 3f out: prog whn hung lft over 1f out: no further imp* **12/1**

6 1¼ **Devil To Pay** 2-9-2 0 .... TedDurcan 7 58+
(J L Dunlop) *w'like: scope: lw: s.i.s: towards rr: hdwy over 3f out: sn rdn: one pce fnl 2f* **6/1**

7 3 **Hypnotic Gaze (IRE)** 2-8-13 0 .... RichardMullen 1 48
(C G Cox) *w'like: lw: nvr bttr than mid-div* **7/1**

0 **8** ¾ **Eightdaysaweek**[41] 3674 2-8-8 0 .... JamieSpencer 3 41+
(S Kirk) *hmpd leaving stalls: a in rr* **4/1**[2]

0 **9** 10 **Julie Mill (IRE)**[37] 3821 2-8-4 0 .... DavidKinsella 10 12
(P G Murphy) *leggy: s.i.s: hmpd 2f out: a towards rr* **100/1**

0 **10** 1¾ **Autumn Morning (IRE)**[10] 4692 2-8-6 0 .... StephenCarson 6 10
(Eve Johnson Houghton) *mid-div: rdn 3f out: drifted lft fr over 2f out and wknd* **25/1**

00 **11** 6 **Coral Point (IRE)**[22] 4304 2-8-9 0 .... MartinDwyer 12 —
(S Kirk) *mid-div: rdn over 3f out: sn wknd* **28/1**

0 **12** 9 **Jasper Cliff**[66] 2893 2-8-5 0 ow1 .... JackDean[(5)] 9 —
(Mark Gillard) *w'like: trckd ldrs: rdn over 3f out: sn btn* **100/1**

1m 30.37s (1.37) **Going Correction** +0.175s/f (Good) **12** Ran SP% **119.6**
Speed ratings (Par 94): **99,98,95,95,89 88,84,83,72,70 63,53**
toteswinger: 1&2 £6.30, 1&3 £24.10, 2&3 £12.90. CSF £47.30 TOTE £8.20: £3.10, £2.10, £5.40; EX 29.70.
Owner Mrs Ann Jarvis **Bred** Mrs Anne Marie Burns **Trained** Twyford, Bucks

FOCUS

They all grouped up the inside rail this time but with the winner recording a very similar time to the first winner, the course did not seem to have a favoured side.

NOTEBOOK

Athania(IRE), well beaten after a slow start on her debut at Kempton, refused to go in the stalls on a return visit. She made all and, despite wanting to hang left such that she ended well off the inside rail, she showed too much pace for her rivals. She has the pace to drop back to 6f and looks a nursery type. (op 9-2 tchd 9-1)

Blazing Buck, given plenty of time since his June debut, looks open to further improvement as he was still green under pressure. After being readily held going to the final furlong, he was staying on to good effect in the final 100yds to suggest a mile will suit. (op 7-1 tchd 9-2)

Peter Grimes(IRE), a stablemate of the runner-up, showed more than on his debut at Sandown last month and kept on to take third place.

Lethal Glaze(IRE), down in class but back up in trip, was a little slow to break. He lacked the pace to really make an impact but was doing good work late on this step back up in trip and is a likely sort for a nursery now. (op 11-4 tchd 4-1)

Googoobarabajagal(IRE), a commentator's worst nightmare, is out of a 1m winner from a family of sprinters. After showing his inexperience, he was staying on well without threatening the first four who finished clear. Official explanation: jockey said colt was slowly away (tchd 14-1)

Devil To Pay is out of an unraced half-sister to high-class juvenile Strategic Prince and the very useful middle-distance stayer Yorkshire. Ending up virtually racing alone nearest the inside rail in the final two furlongs, he was not knocked about in a lost cause but still shaped with promise on this debut. (op 8-1 tchd 9-1)

Hypnotic Gaze(IRE), whose dam won over 5f, was readily left behind in the last two furlongs but is another who can build on the bare form. (tchd 13-2 and 10-1)

Eightdaysaweek, whose dam is an unraced half-sister to Champion Hurdle winner Sublimity, could never get into it after being hampered exiting the stalls. She is going to need further in time. (op 6-1)

Autumn Morning(IRE) Official explanation: jockey said filly hung badly left

5023 MARY WORT MEMORIAL MAIDEN STKS — 6f 212y

3:05 (3:08) (Class 5) 3-4-Y-0 — £3,885 (£1,156; £577; £288) Stalls High

Form — RPR

03 **1** **Willridge**[19] 4431 3-9-3 0 ... RichardKingscote 1 — 72
(Tom Dascombe) *edgy: mde all: rdn 3l clr over 2f out: kpt on: drvn out* **7/1**[3]

2 *1 1/4* **Surprise Package (FR)** 3-9-3 0 ... EddieAhern 3 — 69+
(H J L Dunlop) *tall: lengthy: scope: s.i.s: towards rr: swtchd lft and hdwy over 2f out: rdn over 1f out: r.o to go 2nd ins fnl f: nt rch wnr* **11/2**[2]

0 **3** *1/2* **Aegean Pride**[23] 4277 3-8-12 0 ... RyanMoore 6 — 62
(R Hannon) *lw: mid-div: rdn over 3f out: hdwy over 2f out: r.o fnl f* **25/1**

03 **4** *3* **Poyle Dee Dee**[23] 4277 3-8-12 0 ... SebSanders 8 — 54
(R M Beckett) *lw: trckd ldrs: effrt over 2f out: kpt on same pce fnl f* **4/6**[1]

5 *6* **Uncle Fred** 3-9-3 0 ... NelsonDeSouza 11 — 43
(P R Chamings) *w'like: trckd ldrs: rdn over 2f out: one pce whn swtchd lft over 1f out* **16/1**

6 *3/4* **Tampopo (IRE)** 3-8-10 0 ... BillyCray(7) 4 — 41
(D J S Ffrench Davis) *w'like: mid-div: pumped along fr 5f out: wandered u.p fr over 2f out: no imp* **50/1**

7 *1/2* **Casela Park (IRE)** 3-9-3 0 ... JamieSpencer 7 — 40
(S Kirk) *w'like: str: restrained s: tk v t.k.h in rr: swtchd lft and sme hdwy 3f out: sn rdn: one pce fnl 2f* **16/1**

05 **8** *1 1/4* **Kappalyn (IRE)**[9] 4709 3-8-12 0 ... RichardHughes 9 — 31
(R Hannon) *on toes: chsd wnr: rdn over 2f out: wknd over 1f out* **14/1**

-000 **9** *2 1/4* **Oronsay**[20] 4368 3-8-12 45 ... (t) TGMcLaughlin 2 — 25
(B R Millman) *hung rt over 2f out: a towards rr* **100/1**

0 **10** *7* **Dancing Rhythm**[17] 4484 3-8-10 0 ... JakePayne(7) 10 — 11
(M S Saunders) *chsd ldrs tl wknd over 2f out* **100/1**

11 *5* **Faintly Hopeful** 3-9-3 0 ... DaneO'Neill 5 — —
(R A Teal) *w'like: str: s.i.s: a bhd* **25/1**

1m 30.22s (1.22) **Going Correction** +0.175s/f (Good) — 11 Ran SP% 117.9

Speed ratings (Par 103): **100,98,98,94,87 86,86,84,82,74 68**

toteswinger: 1&2 £4.30, 1&3 £14.20, 2&3 £16.50. CSF £43.89 TOTE £8.10: £1.80, £1.50, £4.00; EX 32.80.

Owner Mayden Stud **Bred** Mayden Stud, J A And D S Dewhurst **Trained** Lambourn, Berks

FOCUS

They again stayed against the inside rail before fanning out in the final two furlongs in what looked a weak maiden which did not take much winning.

Casela Park(IRE) Official explanation: jockey said gelding ran too free

5024 E B F / TENON RECOVERY FILLIES' H'CAP — 1m 4f

3:40 (3:41) (Class 4) (0-80,78) 3-Y-0+ — £7,447 (£2,216; £1,107; £553) Stalls High

Form — RPR

5666 **1** **Star Of Gibraltar**[27] 4152 3-8-12 73 ... DaneO'Neill 5 — 81
(J L Dunlop) *hld up: hdwy over 3f out: rdn to chal over 2f out: led wl over 1f out: hld on: drvn out* **16/1**

3651 **2** *nk* **Sea Chorus**[12] 4646 3-8-10 71 ... (t) JamieSpencer 6 — 79
(M L W Bell) *in tch: hdwy 3f out: rdn and hung in bhd rival 2f out: styd on to go 2nd ins fnl f: fin strly: jst failed* **8/1**[3]

3541 **3** *3 1/2* **Moon Sister (IRE)**[35] 3894 3-9-3 78 ... AlanMunro 3 — 80
(W Jarvis) *trckd ldrs: wnt 2nd after 6f: led over 2f out: rdn and hdd wl over 1f out: no ex fnl f* **8/1**[3]

06-1 **4** *3/4* **Shimoni**[8] 4726 4-9-7 78 ... JemmaMarshall(7) 8 — 79
(G L Moore) *lw: trckd ldr for 6f: cl 3rd: rdn over 3f out: edgd lft fr 2f out: kpt on same pce fnl f* **14/1**

3163 **5** *1/2* **Hepburn Bell (IRE)**[27] 4152 3-9-0 75 ... EddieAhern 2 — 75
(J R Fanshawe) *lw: hld up: swtchd rt and sme prog u.p over 2f out: kpt on same pce fnl f* **11/2**[2]

-341 **6** *12* **Miss Rochester (IRE)**[11] 4669 3-9-0 75 6ex ... RyanMoore 1 — 56
(Sir Michael Stoute) *lw: hld up: niggled along fr over 5f out: rdn and no imp fr over 2f out: eased whn btn* **4/6**[1]

6001 **7** *3* **Muffett's Dream**[6] 4819 4-8-6 59 6ex oh8 ... MarcHalford(3) 4 — 35
(J J Bridger) *led tl over 2f out: sn rdn and wknd* **50/1**

2m 38.82s (0.82) **Going Correction** +0.175s/f (Good)

WFA 3 from 4yo 11lb — 7 Ran SP% 112.1

Speed ratings (Par 102): **104,103,101,100,100 92,90**

toteswinger: 1&2 £8.20, 1&3 £8.80, 2&3 £3.30. CSF £127.52 CT £1101.87 TOTE £18.50: £5.90, £2.50; EX 86.40.

Owner Normandie Stud Ltd **Bred** Normandie Stud Ltd **Trained** Arundel, W Sussex

FOCUS

Probably a moderate race for the class, and dubious form with the odds-on favourite not running her race. Improvement from the winner and second.

Miss Rochester(IRE) Official explanation: trainer had no explanation for the poor form shown

5025 TOTESWINGER SOVEREIGN STKS (GROUP 3) (C&G) — 1m

4:15 (4:15) (Class 1) 3-Y-0+

£36,900 (£13,988; £7,000; £3,490; £1,748; £877) Stalls High

Form — RPR

5152 **1** **Ordnance Row**[47] 3503 5-9-0 106 ... RyanMoore 3 — 116
(R Hannon) *trckd ldrs: niggled along over 3f out: hrd rdn to chal wl over 1f out: drifted rt and led jst ins fnl f: dug deep to assert nr fin: drvn out* **5/1**[3]

1651 **2** *3/4* **Laa Rayb (USA)**[19] 4405 4-9-0 109 ... RoystonFfrench 11 — 114
(M Johnston) *swtg: disp ld: rdn over 2f out: narrowly hdd jst ins fnl f: battled on: hld towards fin* **17/2**

4112 **3** *2 1/4* **Redolent (IRE)**[52] 3306 3-8-7 107 ... (p) RichardHughes 2 — 108
(R Hannon) *disp ld tl rdn and hdd over 1f out: kpt on but no ex* **4/1**[2]

1016 **4** *nk* **Redford (IRE)**[19] 4405 3-8-7 99 ... JamieSpencer 8 — 107
(M L W Bell) *lw: hld up: hdwy 2f out: sn rdn: kpt on fnl f* **11/4**[1]

-211 **5** *hd* **Third Set (IRE)**[168] 745 5-9-0 112 ... LDettori 9 — 108
(Saeed Bin Suroor) *lw: in tch: rdn over 2f out: kpt on fnl f: nt pce to chal* **11/4**[1]

3-40 **6** *3* **Caldra (IRE)**[75] 2600 4-9-0 103 ... AlanMunro 1 — 101
(S Kirk) *racd keenly: sn trcking ldr: rdn 3f out: one pce fnl 2f* **25/1**

3110 **7** *shd* **Wise Dennis**[26] 4192 6-9-0 110 ... DarrenWilliams 10 — 101
(A P Jarvis) *hld up: rdn 3f out: effrt 2f out: one pce after* **14/1**

135- **8** *9* **Mount Pleasure (USA)**[224] 3-8-7 102 ... RichardThomas 7 — 79
(Christian Wroe) *in tch: rdn over 3f out: wknd over 1f out* **50/1**

1m 44.24s (0.74) **Going Correction** +0.35s/f (Good)

WFA 3 from 4yo+ 7lb — 8 Ran SP% 113.0

Speed ratings (Par 113): **110,109,107,106,106 103,103,94**

toteswinger: 1&2 £6.60, 1&3 £3.90, 2&3 £5.60. CSF £45.19 TOTE £6.70: £2.10, £2.00, £1.60; EX 37.70 Trifecta £158.10 Pool: £512.95 - 2.40 winning units..

Owner Mrs P Good **Bred** Mrs P Good **Trained** East Everleigh, Wilts

FOCUS

Just a reasonable renewal of this Group 3, run at a fairly steady pace. Ordnance Row produced a personal best, with Laa Rayb a length off his Ascot form and the next pair close to form.

NOTEBOOK

Ordnance Row, runner-up in this event twelve months ago, is a consistent individual who thoroughly deserved this first Group-race success. Never far behind the leaders, he led inside the last and stuck his neck out courageously to the line. (tchd 11-2)

Laa Rayb(USA), successful in the valuable Totesport International Handicap over 7f at Ascot last time, ran a fine race on this rise in grade and there was no disgrace in going down to such a tough opponent as the winner. He can make his mark in this sort of company. (op 7-1 tchd 9-1)

Redolent(IRE), a stablemate of the winner who was second in this grade in Germany last time, had ground conditions in his favour and ran well, but could not muster a renewed effort once headed. (tchd 9-2 in a place)

Redford(IRE), stepping out of handicap company, had the ground to suit, but he was held up in a steadily run race and could never get in a blow despite staying on for pressure. He is set to drop back in trip again now. (op 7-2 tchd 4-1 in a place)

Third Set(IRE), in good form in Dubai earlier in the year, was disappointing on this first start since February, not really picking up when brought under pressure. He is entitled to come on for the outing. Official explanation: jockey said gelding was unsuited by the ground (tchd 9-4 tchd 3-1 in places)

Caldra(IRE), who did not look right in his coat, showed decent pace on this return from a break, but had raced keenly and that ultimately took its toll. (op 20-1 tchd 18-1)

Wise Dennis tried to get into the race from the rear but could not build on his comeback run last month. (tchd 16-1)

5026 WILTSHIRE LIFE FILLIES' H'CAP — 6f

4:50 (4:51) (Class 5) (0-70,69) 3-Y-0+ — £3,238 (£963; £481; £240) Stalls High

Form — RPR

/513 **1** **Night Rocket (IRE)**[7] 4767 4-9-11 66 ... (t) FrancisNorton 11 — 76+
(A M Balding) *lw; a.p: rdn over 2f out: led over 1f out: kpt on: drvn out* **5/2**[1]

4600 **2** *1/2* **Dualagi**[22] 4313 4-9-7 62 ... DaneO'Neill 5 — 70
(M R Bosley) *t.k.h: hld up: swtchd rt and hdwy u.p fr 2f out: r.o fnl f: wnt 2nd nr fin* **11/1**

-013 **3** *1/2* **River Bounty**[17] 4483 3-9-6 65 ... DarrenWilliams 2 — 70
(A P Jarvis) *led main gp on far side: rdn and edgd lft 2f out: hdd over 1f out: kpt on but no ex whn lost 2nd nr fin* **3/1**[2]

6402 **4** *6* **Miss Poppy**[7] 4779 3-9-0 59 ... NelsonDeSouza 3 — 45
(P R Chamings) *chsd ldrs: rdn over 2f out: sn one pce* **6/1**[3]

0156 **5** *3/4* **Diminuto**[7] 4767 4-9-4 62 ... PatrickHills(3) 10 — 47
(M D I Usher) *prom: rdn over 2f out: wknd ent fnl f* **16/1**

0-40 **6** *7* **Alto Singer (IRE)**[23] 4277 3-9-4 63 ... AlanMunro 6 — 24
(B R Millman) *chsd ldrs: rdn 3f out: sn btn* **14/1**

000 **7** *9* **Bountiful Bay**[42] 3629 3-8-9 54 ... RichardHughes 1 — —
(B J Meehan) *lw: racd alone on stands' side: prom: rdn over 2f out: wknd over 1f out: eased whn btn* **12/1**

1m 17.67s (2.87) **Going Correction** +0.525s/f (Yiel)

WFA 3 from 4yo+ 4lb — 7 Ran SP% 96.4

Speed ratings (Par 100): **101,100,99,91,90 81,69**

toteswinger: 1&2 £5.20, 1&3 £2.10, 2&3 £6.50. CSF £20.56 CT £44.13 TOTE £2.60: £1.30, £4.20; EX 21.10.

Owner J C Smith **Bred** Littleton Stud **Trained** Kingsclere, Hants

■ Namu was withdrawn (4/1, unruly in the stalls). Deduct 20p in the £ under R4.

FOCUS

Not much winning form on offer which hinted at the low grade of this contest. The form is rated through the placed fillies with the winner up 7lb.

5027 PAT BOAKES MEMORIAL H'CAP — 1m 6f 21y

5:20 (5:21) (Class 5) (0-70,70) 3-Y-0+ — £3,238 (£963; £481; £240) Stalls Far side

Form — RPR

4033 **1** **Lady Sorcerer**[12] 4646 3-9-1 67 ... DarrenWilliams 6 — 74
(A P Jarvis) *hld up towards rr: rdn and hdwy over 2f out: chal ent fnl f: styd on u.str.p to ld fnl strides* **17/2**

0-02 **2** *shd* **Act Three**[34] 3917 4-9-12 65 ... DaneO'Neill 3 — 72
(Mouse Hamilton-Fairley) *mid-div: hdwy over 3f out: sn rdn to chal: tk narrow advantage ent fnl f: kpt on u.str.p: hdd fnl strides* **5/1**[2]

0134 **3** *1 1/2* **Hadron Collider (FR)**[19] 4432 3-9-3 69 ... RichardHughes 4 — 74
(R Hannon) *mid-div: rdn 3f out: no imp tl styd on fr over 1f out: fin strly to snatch 3rd nr fin* **13/2**[3]

0213 **4** *1* **Kokkokila**[34] 3917 4-9-8 61 ... JamieSpencer 2 — 65
(Lady Herries) *trckd ldrs: tk narrow advantage over 3f out: sn rdn and hrd pressed: hdd ent fnl f: no ex* **5/1**[2]

5622 **5** *shd* **Urban Warrior**[25] 4220 4-9-12 65 ... RichardMullen 5 — 68
(Ian Williams) *trckd ldrs: rdn 3f out: chal over 1f out: styd on same pce* **5/1**[2]

0050 **6** *3/4* **Silver Surprise**[6] 4820 4-8-8 50 oh5 ... MarcHalford(3) 11 — 52
(J J Bridger) *hld up towards rr: rdn and hdwy over 2f out: swtchd to far side rail and styd on fnl f* **66/1**

7 *3/4* **Cold Mountain (IRE)**[26] 4875 6-8-11 50 oh5 ... FrancisNorton 10 — 51+
(J W Mullins) *trckd ldrs: rdn 3f out: effrt 2f out: one pce after* **4/1**[1]

6320 **8** *1 1/4* **Loveofmylife**[21] 4334 3-7-9 52 ... Louis-PhilippeBeuzelin(5) 9 — 52
(R M Beckett) *trckd ldrs: rdn 3f out: one pce fnl 2f* **12/1**

0250 **9** *1 1/4* **Bob's Your Uncle**[43] 3606 5-9-2 55 ... AlanMunro 8 — 53
(J G Portman) *t.k.h in mid-div: rdn 3f out: wknd 2f out* **11/1**

0064 **10** *2 1/2* **Bobsleigh**[20] 4391 9-8-11 50 oh5 ... CatherineGannon 1 — 44
(H S Howe) *led tl over 3f out: sn rdn and btn* **16/1**

0066 **11** *7* **Orphina (IRE)**[19] 4432 5-8-8 50 oh5 ... (t) PatrickHills(3) 7 — 35
(B G Powell) *hld up towards rr: rdn and sme prog over 2f out: wknd over 1f out* **25/1**

3m 14.49s (7.09) **Going Correction** +0.525s/f (Yiel)

WFA 3 from 4yo+ 13lb — 11 Ran SP% 121.1

Speed ratings (Par 103): **100,99,99,98,98 98,97,96,96,94 90**

toteswinger: 1&2 £10.20, 1&3 £9.00, 2&3 £6.50. CSF £52.27 CT £302.33 TOTE £12.70: £2.60, £2.40, £3.00; EX 53.30 Place 6 £1,943.29, Place 5 £703.93.

Owner The Aston Partnership **Bred** David J Brown And Mrs J Berry **Trained** Twyford, Bucks

FOCUS
A flip start was used. A moderate contest run at a muddling pace which did not put the emphasis on stamina. The form is rated through the second and third with the sixth a slight doubt.
T/Plt: £768.90 to a £1 stake. Pool: £49,929.53. 47.40 winning tickets. T/Qpdt: £151.40 to a £1 stake. Pool: £4,624.07. 22.60 winning tickets. TM

4980 SANDOWN (R-H)
Thursday, August 14

OFFICIAL GOING: Good to soft
Wind: Light, across Weather: Fine but cloudy

5028 GENTLEMEN'S DAY ON 8TH NOVEMBER H'CAP 5f 6y
2:20 (2:20) (Class 5) (0-75,75) 3-Y-O **£4,533** (£1,348; £674; £336) **Stalls** High

Form RPR
502 1 **Tadalavil**[7] 4782 3-9-3 **69** DarryllHolland 7 77
(M R Channon) *racd against far rail: pressed ldr: led wl over 1f out: rdn clr fnl f* **6/4**[1]
1620 2 2 ¾ **Beat The Bell**[13] 4595 3-8-13 **70** DavidProbert(5) 5 68+
(A Bailey) *n.m.r after 1f and lost pl: swtchd to outer 1/2-way: rdn and styd on fnl f to take 2nd nr fin* **8/1**[3]
5330 3 ½ **Kalligal**[22] 4308 3-8-13 **65** RobertHavlin 4 61
(R Ingram) *led to wl over 1f out: no ch w wnr ent fnl f: lost 2nd nr fin* **20/1**
0463 4 ½ **Valhillen**[4] 4904 3-9-4 **70** (p) HayleyTurner 1 65
(M D I Usher) *outpcd and sn rdn in last: no prog tl styd on against far rail ins fnl f* **10/1**
2-13 5 ½ **Barbary Boy (FR)**[7] 4787 3-9-2 **75** JPHamblett(7) 6 68
(M L W Bell) *in tch: chsd ldng pair 1/2-way: bmpd along and no imp over 1f out: lost 2 pls nr fin* **85/40**[2]
-005 6 1 **Our Piccadilly (IRE)**[17] 4483 3-9-6 **72** FergusSweeney 3 61
(W S Kittow) *chsd ldng pair to 1/2-way: steadily fdd over 1f out* **10/1**
5605 7 ½ **Extreme North (USA)**[7] 4787 3-8-5 **57** MatthewHenry 2 44
(Miss V Haigh) *racd on outer: sn lost pl: struggling in rr over 1f out* **12/1**
62.06 secs (0.46) **Going Correction** +0.10s/f (Good) 7 Ran SP% **113.7**
Speed ratings (Par 100): **100,95,94,94,93 91,90**
toteswinger: 1&2 £3.50, 1&3 £6.90, 2&3 £15.50. CSF £14.27 TOTE £2.50: £1.30, £3.60; EX 12.50.
Owner A R Parrish **Bred** Theakston Stud **Trained** West Ilsley, Berks

FOCUS
Just a modest sprint handicap with recent winning form among the septet thin on the ground. The winning time was 1.56 seconds outside Racing Post standard, which reinforced the view that the ground was on the slow side. The winner, who had the advantage of the rail, is rated to his recent best.

5029 EUROPEAN BREEDERS' FUND MAIDEN STKS 1m 14y
2:50 (2:51) (Class 4) 2-Y-O **£5,180** (£1,541; £770; £384) **Stalls** High

Form RPR
1 **Too Much Trouble** 2-9-3 0 DarryllHolland 3 76+
(M R Channon) *dwlt: chsd ldng pair after 3f but nt gng that wl: wnt 2nd wl over 1f out: drvn to ld jst ins fnl f: styd on wl* **15/8**[1]
50 2 1 ¼ **Miss Sophisticat**[14] 4554 2-8-12 0 PaulDoe 1 68
(W J Knight) *led at decent pce: rdn over 2f out: hdd and one pce jst ins fnl f* **9/4**[2]
3 1 ¾ **Zafisio (IRE)** 2-9-3 0 TPO'Shea 4 69+
(P A Blockley) *sn last: shkn up 3f out: green after and stmbld 2f out: styd on fnl f: nrst fin* **9/2**[3]
0 4 6 **Blue Dynasty (USA)**[7] 4788 2-9-3 0 JimCrowley 5 56
(Mrs A J Perrett) *chsd ldng pair 3f: rdn and struggling 3f out: sn btn* **5/1**
5 3 ½ **Kaloni (IRE)** 2-8-12 0 MickyFenton 2 43
(Mrs P Sly) *dwlt: sn chsd ldr: wknd rapidly wl over 1f out* **9/1**
1m 46.78s (3.48) **Going Correction** +0.275s/f (Good) 5 Ran SP% **110.4**
Speed ratings (Par 96): **93,91,90,84,80**
CSF £6.41 TOTE £2.20: £1.60, £1.50; EX 4.90.
Owner Jaber Abdullah **Bred** Fittocks Stud **Trained** West Ilsley, Berks

FOCUS
Quite a test for two-year-olds in the conditions and it was no surprise that the field cut up badly from the initial five-day entry. Still, it will probably turn out to be an above-average contest.

NOTEBOOK
Too Much Trouble, a debutant son of Barathea, has a Derby entry. He obviously knew his job, stayed every yard of the trip, and showed a pleasing attitude to overcome the runner-up and become the yard's 29th juvenile winner this term. (op 7-4 tchd 13-8 and 2-1 in a place)
Miss Sophisticat had proved that she handles cut in the ground when a promising fifth at Newbury on her debut and made a brave fist of attempting to make every yard of the running. She appeared to have everything in trouble when tacking across to the favoured stands' rail in the straight, but a combination of the 1m trip, soft ground and the Sandown hill eventually found her out. (op 2-1)
Zafisio(IRE) shaped with a good deal of promise. Settled at the back, he looked very green when asked for an effort, and seemed to spook slightly at the point where the stands' rail runs out and the hedge begins, losing his footing in the process. Once over that stumble, he kept on well as the penny appeared to drop and he should come on significantly for the experience. It is highly likely that connections will keep him to this sort of ground as he showed a pronounced knee action. (op 7-1)
Blue Dynasty(USA), another Derby entry, was the first horse beaten despite holding the advantage of previous racecourse experience. (tchd 6-1)
Kaloni(IRE), the bottom line of whose pedigree shows that she is a great-granddaughter of Mick Easterby's 1977 1,000 Guineas winner Mrs McArdy, raced prominently for a long way before getting tired in the ground. She will do better with time. (op 10-1)

5030 MONEYCORP CURRENCY CANTER H'CAP 7f 16y
3:25 (3:25) (Class 3) (0-90,89) 3-Y-O+ **£9,714** (£2,890; £1,444; £721) **Stalls** High

Form RPR
0020 1 **Keep Discovering (IRE)**[14] 4553 3-9-7 **89** DarryllHolland 7 98
(M Johnston) *trckd ldr: drvn to ld ent fnl f: sn in command: styd on wl* **9/2**[3]
4034 2 1 ¼ **Signor Peltro**[18] 4460 5-9-8 **84** FergusSweeney 8 91+
(H Candy) *hld up in 7th: urged along and prog fr 2f out: styd on to take 2nd nr fin: nvr able to chal* **7/2**[1]
2223 3 ½ **Dingaan (IRE)**[13] 4601 5-9-6 **82** LPKeniry 5 88
(A M Balding) *trckd ldng pair: cajoled along fr 2f out: fnd v little and readily hld* **7/2**[1]
0400 4 ¾ **Salient**[19] 4407 4-9-5 **84** KirstyMilczarek(3) 9 88
(M J Attwater) *led: rdn 2f out: hdd and no ex ent fnl f* **5/1**
3322 5 1 ¾ **Mumbleswerve (IRE)**[13] 4603 4-9-1 **77** J-PGuillambert 3 76
(W Jarvis) *t.k.h early: hld up in 4th: rdn over 2f out: hung lft over 1f out: cl enough ent fnl f: wknd* **4/1**[2]
1600 6 ¾ **Southandwest (IRE)**[19] 4407 4-9-10 **86** TPO'Shea 1 83
(J S Moore) *dwlt: hld up in 6th: rdn over 2f out: nt qckn and no prog whn hmpd over 1f out: no ch after* **20/1**
2000 7 7 **Binanti**[15] 4522 8-9-12 **88** GeorgeBaker 6 66
(P R Chamings) *settled in 5th: wknd tamely 2f out: sn bhd* **8/1**
000/ 8 21 **Esenin**[1884] 1867 9-8-11 **80** oh24 ow11 JWStevenson(7) 4 2
(Mrs Tracey Barfoot-Saunt) *a last: lost tch 3f out: t.o* **200/1**
1m 31.89s (2.39) **Going Correction** +0.275s/f (Good)
WFA 3 from 4yo+ 6lb 8 Ran SP% **115.7**
Speed ratings (Par 107): **97,95,95,94,92 91,83,59**
toteswinger: 1&2 £4.40, 1&3 £4.50, 2&3 £3.00. CSF £20.92 CT £61.07 TOTE £4.90: £1.90, £1.30, £1.50; EX 20.40.
Owner Sheikh Hamdan Bin Mohammed Al Maktoum **Bred** Kilfrush Stud **Trained** Middleham Moor, N Yorks

FOCUS
Quite an open handicap and the majority were still in with a chance over a furlong out. The early pace was decent as Salient and the keen-going Keep Discovering vied for the lead. The form is rated through the third and the winner is progressive.

NOTEBOOK
Keep Discovering(IRE), the only three-year-old in the line-up, had shown in the past he handles easy ground and this mile winner, who had been too keen last time and was ridden more positively on this occasion, put his proven stamina to good use to give Holland a treble. He should not go up too much for this and can find further opportunities this autumn. (op 11-2 tchd 6-1)
Signor Peltro, a course and distance winner and another with form on the ground, was 1lb lower than when last successful. Returning to 7f having run over 6f for most of the season, he came from the rear to finish on the heels of the winner and, although he is yet to score at this trip, looks capable of doing so now he is more mature. (op 3-1)
Dingaan(IRE) was never far away from the pace and is a pretty consistent sort but he does not find that much off the bridle, so is one for the Placepot rather than win purposes. (op 3-1)
Salient, who is now 2lb below his last winning mark, took the field along, but the attentions of the winner meant he did not get a soft lead and he could not respond when the challenges were delivered. (op 13-2)
Mumbleswerve(IRE), who had been narrowly beaten off slightly lower marks on his previous three starts, got a good tow into the race but wandered when asked for his effort. (op 9-2 tchd 7-2)
Southandwest(IRE) has yet to prove he is as effective on this ground as he is on a sound surface or Polytrack. He had the cheekpieces left off this time and might have finished closer had he not been stopped in his run by Mumbleswerve approaching the final furlong. (op 16-1)
Binanti is struggling for form and never got involved. (op 14-1)

5031 DI GOLDSMITH'S 60TH BIRTHDAY CELEBRATION MAIDEN FILLIES' STKS 1m 14y
4:00 (4:02) (Class 5) 3-Y-O+ **£3,885** (£1,156; £577; £288) **Stalls** High

Form RPR
62 1 **Censored**[12] 4620 3-8-12 0 RobertWinston 5 81
(Sir Michael Stoute) *trckd ldng pair: wnt 2nd over 2f out: shkn up to ld wl over 1f out: styd on wl and drew rt away* **4/6**[1]
60 2 9 **Greyfriarsblessing (IRE)**[99] 1918 3-8-12 0 DarryllHolland 6 59
(M Johnston) *last after 3f: rdn and virtually t.o 3f out: styd on wl fr over 1f out: snatched 2nd on post* **16/1**
24 3 hd **Emirates Lady (USA)**[23] 4277 3-8-12 0 TPQueally 4 59
(Saeed Bin Suroor) *led: rdn and hdd wl over 1f out: floundering and wknd rapidly fnl f: lost 2nd on post* **11/4**[2]
5 4 3 **Flight Of Fashion (IRE)**[26] 4195 3-8-12 0 JimCrowley 1 52
(Dr J D Scargill) *dwlt: wnt 4th after 3f: rdn and lost tch w ldrs over 2f out: wknd* **20/1**
5 13 **Sea Swell (USA)** 3-8-12 0 MickyFenton 3 22
(G A Butler) *t.k.h early: chsd ldr to over 2f out: wkng whn jinked and lost action sn after: t.o* **7/1**[3]
1m 46.06s (2.76) **Going Correction** +0.275s/f (Good) 5 Ran SP% **109.8**
Speed ratings (Par 100): **97,88,87,84,71**
toteswinger: 1&2 £10.50. CSF £12.51 TOTE £1.70: £1.10, £3.20; EX 9.40.
Owner Cheveley Park Stud **Bred** Cheveley Park Stud Ltd **Trained** Newmarket, Suffolk

FOCUS
A fillies' maiden for three-year-olds, run at an average pace. It is not easy to know what Censored achieved with her market rival disappointing, and it is hard to rate this too positively despite the winning margin.

5032 WILD WEST SALOON CHRISTMAS PARTY NIGHTS H'CAP 1m 14y
4:35 (4:36) (Class 4) (0-80,81) 3-Y-O **£6,476** (£1,927; £963; £481) **Stalls** High

Form RPR
-414 1 **Ebn Malk (IRE)**[8] 4731 3-9-6 **76** PhilipRobinson 5 88+
(M A Jarvis) *trckd ldr: rdn to ld over 1f out: hung lft fnl f: styd on* **6/4**[1]
434 2 1 ¾ **Arts Guild (USA)**[54] 3275 3-9-5 **75** StephenDonohoe 2 83
(W J Musson) *t.k.h early: hld up in 4th: effrt over 2f out: rdn and nt qckn over 1f out: styd on to take 2nd ins fnl f: nvr able to chal* **5/1**
2010 3 3 **Addwaitya**[28] 4130 3-8-11 **72** JackMitchell(5) 6 73
(C F Wall) *led: edgd rt 2f out: hdd over 1f out: wknd fnl f* **4/1**[2]
1-30 4 hd **Hallingdal (UAE)**[11] 4669 3-9-5 **75** JamesDoyle 3 76
(Ms J S Doyle) *t.k.h early: hld up in 5th: rdn and no imp on ldrs over 2f out: plugged on fnl f* **8/1**
061- 5 1 ½ **Rosy Alexander**[381] 4028 3-9-5 **75** TPQueally 1 72
(S A Callaghan) *t.k.h early: hld up in last: rdn and nt qckn over 2f out: n.d after* **16/1**
-011 6 4 ½ **Bluejain**[15] 4524 3-9-4 **74** MickyFenton 7 61
(Miss Gay Kelleway) *awkward s: trckd ldng pair to 3f out: lost pl qckly and btn after* **9/2**[3]
1m 45.97s (2.67) **Going Correction** +0.275s/f (Good) 6 Ran SP% **111.8**
Speed ratings (Par 102): **97,95,92,92,90 86**
toteswinger: 1&2 £1.70, 1&3 £2.20, 2&3 £3.30. CSF £9.31 TOTE £2.20: £1.60, £2.30; EX 7.60.
Owner Sheikh Ahmed Al Maktoum **Bred** Tony Doyle **Trained** Newmarket, Suffolk

FOCUS
A fair little handicap. Improvement from the winner and sound form amongst the first three.
Bluejain Official explanation: trainer's representative said colt was unsuited by the track

5033 VARIETY CLUB 50TH ANNIVERSARY H'CAP 1m 1f
5:10 (5:10) (Class 4) (0-85,85) 3-Y-O+ **£7,123** (£2,119; £1,059; £529) **Stalls** High

Form RPR
3140 1 **Curzon Prince (IRE)**[49] 3398 4-9-8 **84** JackMitchell(5) 1 98
(C F Wall) *hld up in midfield: prog over 2f out: led wl over 1f out: sn rdn clr* **6/1**[2]
6140 2 6 **Nightjar (USA)**[14] 4553 3-9-3 **82** J-PGuillambert 4 83
(M Johnston) *trckd ldr: rdn to chal 2f out: one pce fr over 1f out: jst hld on for 2nd* **13/2**[3]
5-10 3 nse **Red Birr (IRE)**[16] 4509 7-9-8 **79** PhilipRobinson 3 80
(P R Webber) *hld up in 6th: rdn and struggling 3f out: prog u.p 2f out: styd on dourly to take 3rd last stride* **10/1**

-535 **4** *shd* **Danetime Panther (IRE)**[12] 4627 4-9-4 **75** MickyFenton 9 76
(P F I Cole) *led: drvn and pressed 2f out: hdd wl over 1f out: one pce u.p* **13/2**[3]

0031 **5** *1 3/4* **The Which Doctor**[14] 4571 3-9-6 **85** TPQueally 2 82
(J Noseda) *trckd ldng pair: rdn over 2f out: chal wl over 1f out: sn outpcd: wknd ins fnl f* **6/4**[1]

2306 **6** *nk* **Baylini**[59] 3088 4-9-7 **85** SophieDoyle(7) 7 81
(Ms J S Doyle) *stdd s: hld up in 7th: sme prog over 2f out: urged along and no hdwy over 1f out* **12/1**

1-06 **7** *1/2* **Lunar Promise (IRE)**[138] 1072 6-9-0 **71** StephenDonohoe 6 66
(Ian Williams) *s.s: hld up in last: lost tch 3f out: styd on fnl f: gaining at fin* **11/1**

4060 **8** *3 1/4* **Master Pegasus**[10] 4694 5-9-6 **77** PatCosgrave 5 66
(J R Boyle) *trckd ldng trio: rdn and wknd over 2f out* **14/1**

1m 56.84s (0.54) **Going Correction** +0.275s/f (Good)
WFA 3 from 4yo+ 8lb **8 Ran SP% 112.7**
Speed ratings (Par 105): **108,102,102,102,100 100,100,97**
toteswinger: 1&2 £6.60, 1&3 £6.80, 2&3 £9.20. CSF £43.02 CT £380.22 TOTE £7.00: £2.10, £1.90, £2.30; EX 49.70 Place 6 £16.92, Place 5 £9.08.
Owner H N Alsabah **Bred** Scuderia San Pancrazio **Trained** Newmarket, Suffolk

FOCUS
A fair handicap run at an ordinary pace. The runners shunned the inside rail down the back and came down the centre of the track into the home straight. The winner is rated up 7lb but had seemed exposed prior to this.
Lunar Promise(IRE) Official explanation: jockey said gelding missed the break and ran too free
T/Plt: £34.60 to a £1 stake. Pool: £47,138.72. 992.38 winning tickets. T/Qpdt: £12.20 to a £1 stake. Pool: £3,444.09. 207.70 winning tickets. JN

5034 - 5037a (Foreign Racing) - See Raceform Interactive

4959 DEAUVILLE (R-H)
Thursday, August 14

OFFICIAL GOING: Turf course - good to soft; all-weather - standard

5038a PRIX DE LIEUREY - SHADWELL (LISTED RACE) (FILLIES) (ROUND COURSE) 1m (R)
1:20 (1:23) 3-Y-O **£20,221** (£8,088; £6,066; £4,044; £2,022)

RPR

1 **Sefroua (USA)**[33] 3994 3-8-12 IMendizabal 7 101
(J-C Rouget, France)

2 *hd* **Trip To Glory (FR)**[109] 1664 3-9-2 C-PLemaire 9 105
(J-C Rouget, France)

3 *3/4* **Quarayed (USA)**[49] 3430 3-8-12 FBlondel 8 99
(J-C Rouget, France)

4 *1 1/2* **Rainbow Crossing**[18] 4471 3-8-12 TThulliez 5 96
(F Rohaut, France)

5 *2* **Lessing (FR)**[33] 3994 3-9-2 OPeslier 4 95
(R Gibson, France)

6 *1/2* **Time To Beat (GER)**[16] 3-8-12 DBoeuf 3 90
(W Baltromei, Germany)

7 *1 1/2* **Desert Chill (USA)**[22] 4300 3-8-12 CSoumillon 6 86
(Saeed Bin Suroor) *led: 3 l clr 1/2-way: pushed along and r.o st: rdn 1f out: hdd 150yds out: wknd* **23/10**[1]

8 *5* **Thanks Again (IRE)**[33] 3994 3-8-12 ACrastus 2 75
(J De Roualle, France)

1m 44.9s (3.90) **Going Correction** +0.475s/f (Yiel) **8 Ran SP% 30.3**
Speed ratings: **99,98,98,96,94 94,92,87**
PARI-MUTUEL: WIN 4.40; PL 1.70, 2.10, 3.80; DF 9.40.
Owner N Radwan **Bred** Pacelco S A **Trained** Pau, France
■ Stewards' Enquiry : I Mendizabal two-day ban: careless riding

NOTEBOOK
Desert Chill(USA) went straight into the lead and appeared to be going well around the final turn but found nothing under pressure and gradually dropped out of contention.

5039a PRIX MINERVE - SHADWELL (GROUP 3) (FILLIES) 1m 4f 110y
3:20 (3:24) 3-Y-O **£29,412** (£11,765; £8,824; £5,882; £2,941)

RPR

1 **Dar Re Mi**[26] 4196 3-8-9 OPeslier 8 109+
(J H M Gosden) *racd in 2nd: chalng ent st: led over 1f out: pushed along and r.o fnl f: comf* **26/10**[1]

2 *1 1/2* **Shemima**[31] 4040 3-8-9 CSoumillon 5 106
(A De Royer-Dupre, France) *in tch: disputing 4th st: drvn and r.o over 1f out: styd on fnl f to take 2nd cl home* **29/10**[2]

3 *3/4* **Alpine Rose (FR)**[37] 3-8-9 IMendizabal 7 105
(J-C Rouget, France) *in tch: cl 3rd st: ev ch over 1f out: lost 2nd cl home* **29/10**[2]

4 *1* **Tangaspeed (FR)**[25] 4234 3-8-9 TJarnet 1 104
(R Laplanche, France) *last but in tch: drvn and styd on fr over 1f out: wnt 4th cl home: nvr nrr* **12/1**

5 *1/2* **Astrologie (FR)**[31] 4040 3-8-9 SPasquier 3 103
(A Fabre, France) *a in tch: disputing 4th st: drvn to press ldrs appr fnl f: rdn and no ex fnl 100yds* **31/10**[3]

6 *1/2* **Cosmic Fire (FR)**[10] 3-8-9 C-PLemaire 6 102
(D Sepulchre, France) *hld up: pushed along in cl 6th st: rdn 1 1/2f out: outpcd* **88/10**

7 *3/4* **Kareemah (IRE)**[29] 3-8-9 TGillet 2 101
(J E Hammond, France) *led to over 1f out: one pce* **37/10**

2m 50.2s (3.80) **Going Correction** +0.475s/f (Yiel) **7 Ran SP% 142.6**
Speed ratings: **107,106,105,105,104 104,103**
PARI-MUTUEL: WIN 3.60; PL 1.50, 2.00, 2.80; DF 10.50.
Owner Lord Lloyd-Webber **Bred** Watership Down Stud **Trained** Newmarket, Suffolk

NOTEBOOK
Dar Re Mi, a rapidly improving filly, put up an impressive performance. Handy throughout, she was not asked to challenge for the lead until a furlong and a half out and she never looked like being beaten once at the head of affairs. A beautifully bred and fine-looking individual, she is now going to take on the best as the Prix Vermeille is her next target. She has already proved that she stays the distance and she acts on any ground. She might give Zarkava more to do than the formbook suggests in the Vermeille.
Shemima was not given a hard race at all once the writing was on the wall. Brought with a run up the stands' side, she was just pushed out in the final stages and was comfortably held in second place. A Listed race is now on the cards for this filly, and her main autumn target will be the Prix de Royallieu in early October.
Alpine Rose(FR) put up a fair effort considering she was being jumped up considerably in class. She tried to challenge for the lead at the two-furlong marker but then just stayed on one-paced. She still looks on the upgrade.
Tangaspeed(FR) was given a waiting race and did not produce her effort until well into the straight. She ran on but never looked like catching the first three.

4697 CATTERICK (L-H)
Friday, August 15

OFFICIAL GOING: Good to soft (good in places; 7.9)
After a drying day the ground was described as 'tacy, like glue in places'.
Wind: almost nil Weather: fine becoming overcast, light rain race 4

5040 INTERNATIONAL RACECOURSE MANAGEMENT AMATEUR RIDERS' H'CAP 1m 3f 214y
5:45 (5:45) (Class 5) (0-75,76) 3-Y-O+ **£2,498** (£774; £387; £193) **Stalls** High

Form RPR

4162 **1** **Elite Land**[15] 4556 5-10-6 **57** MissARyan 9 66
(K A Ryan) *trckd ldrs: led 2f out: styd on wl* **3/1**[1]

0000 **2** *1 1/4* **Kalasam**[21] 4371 4-10-8 **64** ow3 MrOGreenall(5) 4 71
(M W Easterby) *hld up in midfield: stdy hdwy on ins over 2f out: wnt 2nd over 1f out: kpt on same pce* **28/1**

1011 **3** *3 1/2* **Holiday Cocktail**[9] 4739 6-11-11 **76** 6ex (p) MrSWalker 7 77
(J J Quinn) *trckd ldrs: effrt over 3f out: kpt on same pce appr fnl f* **15/2**

3044 **4** *2 1/4* **Hugs Destiny (IRE)**[23] 4295 7-9-11 **53** oh5 (t) MissAngelaBarnes(5) 3 51
(M A Barnes) *led 1f: w ldr: fdd appr fnl f* **14/1**

0-64 **5** *shd* **Graceful Descent (FR)**[35] 3930 3-10-7 **74** MrsVFahey(5) 6 72
(R A Fahey) *hld up in rr: hdwy over 2f out: nvr rchd ldrs* **13/2**[3]

1000 **6** *5* **Maneki Neko (IRE)**[25] 4244 6-11-4 **69** MissLHorner 10 59
(E W Tuer) *hld up in rr: hdwy over 2f out: sn chsng ldrs: wknd over 1f out* **20/1**

0413 **7** *hd* **Home**[12] 4664 3-9-13 **68** MissLGray(7) 2 57
(C Gordon) *swvd lft s: led after 1f tl 2f out: sn wknd* **8/1**

4032 **8** *4 1/2* **Marvo**[5] 4894 4-11-2 **72** MrJAkehurst(5) 1 54
(M H Tompkins) *trckd ldrs: plld to outside over 2f out: hung lft and wknd over 1f out* **10/3**[2]

5602 **9** *3* **Saluscraggie**[23] 4295 6-10-2 **60** MissVBarr(7) 5 37
(R E Barr) *t.k.h in rr: drvn over 3f out: nvr on terms* **9/1**

5102 **10** *2 1/2* **York Cliff**[4] 4932 10-10-4 **58** ow4 MrBenBrisbourne(3) 8 31
(W M Brisbourne) *in rr-div: reminders over 6f out: lost pl over 3f out: bhd whn eased ins fnl f* **16/1**

2m 42.98s (4.08) **Going Correction** +0.40s/f (Good)
WFA 3 from 4yo+ 11lb **10 Ran SP% 115.0**
Speed ratings (Par 103): **102,101,98,97,97 93,93,90,88,87**
toteswinger: 1&2 £11.50, 1&3 £3.20, 2&3 £42.10. CSF £85.97 CT £579.64 TOTE £4.00: £1.70, £8.60, £2.60; EX 122.40.
Owner Mrs J Ryan **Bred** T Umpleby **Trained** Hambleton, N Yorks
■ Stewards' Enquiry : Miss Angela Barnes two-day ban: used whip with excessive frequency (Aug 29, Sep 1)

FOCUS
A weak handicap for amateurs and slightly dubious form with the runner-up having shown nothing previously this year and the second favourite disappointing.

5041 K.W. LINFOOT PLC (S) STKS 7f
6:15 (6:17) (Class 6) 2-Y-O **£2,047** (£604; £302) **Stalls** Low

Form RPR

6313 **1** **Dougie Peel**[14] 4604 2-8-11 61 (p) FergalLynch 6 67
(K A Ryan) *chsd ldng pair: drvn 4f out: styd on to ld 1f out: drvn out* **9/4**[1]

6300 **2** *3 1/2* **El Portet**[9] 4733 2-8-8 63 PJMcDonald(3) 8 58
(G M Moore) *s.i.s: reminders after 1f: hdwy over 2f out: styd on to take 2nd ins fnl f* **8/1**

2455 **3** *1 3/4* **Digit**[22] 4328 2-8-6 71 RoystonFfrench 2 49
(B Smart) *led tl hdd 1f out: sn fdd* **11/4**[2]

004 **4** *3/4* **Hollow Green (IRE)**[14] 4604 2-8-6 54 CatherineGannon 4 47
(P D Evans) *prom: kpt on fnl 2f: nt rch ldrs* **18/1**

0000 **5** *1* **Ba Globetrotter**[7] 4827 2-8-11 55 EdwardCreighton 12 50
(M R Channon) *in tch: kpt on fnl 2f: nvr rchd ldrs* **33/1**

0302 **6** *shd* **Cherry Belle (IRE)**[14] 4604 2-7-13 55 (v) JamieKyne(7) 13 44
(P D Evans) *s.i.s: in rr: kpt on fnl 2f: nvr nr ldrs* **15/2**

30 **7** *1/2* **Loched Up**[38] 3821 2-8-11 0 (v[1]) PaulHanagan 1 48
(P A Blockley) *mid-div: drvn 4f out: kpt on fnl 2f: nvr nr ldrs* **16/1**

3052 **8** *1/2* **Nchike**[6] 4873 2-8-11 53 (v) AdrianTNicholls 5 47
(D Nicholls) *chsd ldr: wknd appr fnl f* **7/1**[3]

00 **9** *27* **Red Eric**[23] 4290 2-8-11 0 PaulQuinn 11 —
(W M Brisbourne) *prom: lost pl over 3f out: sn bhd: t.o* **100/1**

0 **10** *1/2* **One Cool Quest (IRE)**[60] 3092 2-8-4 0 ManavNem(7) 3 —
(P A Blockley) *in rr: lost pl over 4f out: sn bhd: t.o* **28/1**

11 *3/4* **Any Luck (IRE)** 2-8-11 0 PatrickMathers 10 —
(I W McInnes) *s.v.s: a wl detached in rr: t.o* **66/1**

1m 29.37s (2.37) **Going Correction** +0.40s/f (Good) **11 Ran SP% 112.8**
Speed ratings (Par 92): **102,98,96,95,94 93,93,92,61,61 60**
toteswinger: 1&2 £5.70, 1&3 £1.80, 2&3 £8.20. CSF £19.52 TOTE £3.50: £1.70, £3.30, £1.10; EX 26.20.The winner was bought in for 5,500gns.
Owner Roger Peel **Bred** Brook Stud Bloodstock Ltd **Trained** Hambleton, N Yorks

FOCUS
A very decent winning time for a juvenile seller, 0.13 seconds faster than the later handicap for older horses. An improved effort from the winner, useful at this low level.

NOTEBOOK
Dougie Peel made it two course-and-distance wins in three starts. He made hard work of it but ran out a decisive winner in the end. (op 10-3 tchd 7-2 in a place)
El Portet made a tardy start and was soon feeling his rider's whip. He stayed on once in line for home to snatch second spot and will be suited by a step up to a mile. (op 10-1)
Digit, suited by this left-handed track, took them along but in the end did not see it out anywhere near as well as the winner. (op 7-2)
Hollow Green(IRE), two lengths behind the winner when they were third and fourth in a claimer at Thirsk, looks fully exposed now. (op 12-1)
Ba Globetrotter, never far away, kept on without ever threatening to enter the argument. (op 40-1)

Cherry Belle(IRE), who made a tardy start, tended to duck and dive. She is certainly being made to earn her crust. (op 6-1 tchd 8-1)

5042 CEMEX MATERIALS (NORTH EAST) MAIDEN STKS — 1m 3f 214y
6:45 (6:45) (Class 5) 3-Y-O+ £2,590 (£770; £385; £192) Stalls High

Form				RPR
	1		**Another Moment**[12] 4-9-10 0 ... PJMcDonald(3) 8	78+
			(G A Swinbank) *trckd ldrs: drvn over 4f out: sn outpcd: styd on to ld over 1f out: hld on towards fin* 7/2[3]
23-0	2	hd	**City Stable (IRE)**[111] 1618 3-9-2 77 ... RobertWinston 10	77+
			(Sir Michael Stoute) *trckd ldr: led over 2f out: hdd over 1f out: rallied ins fnl f: no ex towards fin* 11/4[2]
00	3	6	**River Danube**[77] 2573 5-9-10 0 ... JamieMoriarty(3) 14	68
			(T J Fitzgerald) *prom: rdn and outpcd over 3f out: kpt on to take modest 3rd ins fnl f* 100/1
323	4	1 ¼	**Dazzling Light (UAE)**[23] 4302 3-8-11 75 ... PaulMulrennan 4	61
			(R Charlton) *trckd ldrs: effrt over 3f out: one pce fnl 2f* 11/8[1]
232	5	3 ½	**Hollins**[37] 3835 4-9-13 74 ... PaulHanagan 9	60
			(Micky Hammond) *led: hdd over 2f out: wknd over 1f out* 11/1
	6	¾	**Nakoma (IRE)**[24] 6-9-1 0 ... LanceBetts(7) 5	54
			(B Ellison) *s.i.s: hdwy over 5f out: kpt on fnl 2f: nvr nr ldrs* 20/1
6	7	1 ¼	**Mary Athena (FR)**[22] 4342 3-8-11 0 ... TonyHamilton 13	52
			(M G Quinlan) *in rr: sme hdwy 6f out: lost pl over 2f out* 33/1
	8	1 ¼	**Nodform William**[266] 6-9-13 0 ... PAspell 11	55
			(Karen McLintock) *in rr: sme hdwy over 5f out: lost pl over 3f out* 80/1
0	9	1 ½	**Bertie Boo**[69] 2847 3-9-2 0 ... RoystonFfrench 6	52
			(B Smart) *prom: reminders 5f out: sn lost pl* 50/1
	10	33	**Oscar Wild**[79] 6-9-13 0 ... PatrickMathers 12	—
			(James Moffatt) *trckd ldrs: t.k.h: rn wd bnd over 8f out: lost pl over 3f out: bhd whn eased ins fnl f: t.o* 100/1
0	11	3 ½	**Key To Caius (IRE)**[10] 4698 5-9-13 0 ... DougieCostello 3	—
			(R F Fisher) *hld up in rr: hmpd on bnd over 7f out: sme hdwy over 4f out: sn lost pl and bhd: t.o* 300/1
4	12	6	**Kings Maiden (IRE)**[10] 4701 5-9-8 0 ... FergalLynch 7	—
			(James Moffatt) *s.s: a bhd: t.o 4f out* 40/1
0030	13	8	**Fiume**[20] 4427 3-9-2 68 ... EdwardCreighton 1	—
			(G Prodromou) *in tch: lost pl over 7f out: sn bhd: t.o 4f out* 33/1

2m 42.75s (3.85) **Going Correction** +0.40s/f (Good)
WFA 3 from 4yo+ 11lb **13** Ran SP% **117.9**
Speed ratings (Par 103): **103,102,98,98,95 95,94,93,92,70 68,64,58**
toteswinger: 1&2 £3.00, 1&3 £26.00, 2&3 £28.80. CSF £12.65 TOTE £3.70: £1.60, £1.10, £17.90; EX 12.00.
Owner Elsa Crankshaw & G Allan Ii **Bred** Shadwell Estate Company Limited **Trained** Melsonby, N Yorks

FOCUS
The first two pulled clear but this was ordinary maiden form overall with the third a surprise improver and the fourth disappointing.

5043 SAVILLS IN YORKSHIRE NURSERY — 5f 212y
7:15 (7:15) (Class 4) 2-Y-O £3,885 (£1,156; £577; £288) Stalls Low

Form				RPR
642	1		**Fitzolini**[11] 4681 2-8-6 64 ... (p) SilvestreDeSousa 6	70
			(A D Brown) *mde all: styd on strly to draw clr fnl f: v readily* 7/2
000	2	4 ½	**Real Diamond**[31] 4045 2-7-5 56 oh6 ... JamieKyne(7) 1	49
			(A Dickman) *trckd wnr: t.k.h: chal over 2f out: kpt on same pce* 12/1
630	3	nk	**Exceedingly Good (IRE)**[23] 4289 2-8-13 71 ... PaulMulrennan 5	63
			(B Smart) *hld up and swtchd lft after s: hdwy on ins over 2f out: sn rdn: one pce fnl f* 10/3[3]
1264	4	nk	**Alphabeth**[13] 4648 2-8-11 69 ... EdwardCreighton 2	60
			(M R Channon) *chsd ldrs: chal over 2f out: sn rdn: kpt on same pce* 11/4[2]
332	5	7	**Annapolis**[20] 4425 2-9-7 79 ... JoeFanning 3	49
			(M Johnston) *sn drvn along: lost pl over 4f out: eased ins fnl f* 9/4[1]

1m 16.69s (3.09) **Going Correction** +0.40s/f (Good) **5** Ran SP% **110.4**
Speed ratings (Par 96): **95,89,88,88,78**
toteswinger: 1&2 £23.70 CSF £36.88 TOTE £4.10: £1.80, £2.70; EX 32.60.
Owner Mrs Susan Johnson **Bred** Mrs S Johnson **Trained** Pickering, York

FOCUS
A modest nursery but an improved effort from the seemingly exposed winner.

NOTEBOOK
Fitzolini is not that big but all heart. His rider picked up his stick but merely waved it a couple of times inside the last. He soon drew clear and was not winning out of turn. (tchd 3-1)
Real Diamond, 6lb out of the handicap, refused to settle yet kept going all the way to the line. (op 14-1 tchd 16-1)
Exceedingly Good(IRE), dropped in and switched to the rails, moved up once in line for home but in the end, like the rest, found the winner much too strong. (op 4-1 tchd 9-2)
Alphabeth, averaging a race a week, looked a big danger when moving upsides once in line for home but in the end had no excuse. (op 3-1 tchd 7-2)
Annapolis was soon being driven along and, never happy on the false ground, lost touch down the hill and in the end completed in his own time. Official explanation: jockey said colt never travelled (op 15-8 tchd 13-8)

5044 SIMON BAILES PEUGEOT BIPPER CLAIMING STKS — 5f
7:45 (7:45) (Class 6) 3-Y-O+ £2,388 (£705; £352) Stalls Low

Form				RPR
1106	1		**Guest Connections**[9] 4743 5-9-7 68 ... (v) AdrianTNicholls 7	69+
			(D Nicholls) *sn outpcd: reminders over 3f out: hdwy and nt clr run over 1f out: hrd rdn and styd on to ld post* 5/2[2]
0-00	2	shd	**Head To Head (IRE)**[34] 3953 4-8-4 44 ... JamesRogers(7) 1	56
			(A D Brown) *in rr: hdwy and swtchd to outside over 1f out: led ins fnl f: hdd last stride* 80/1
5250	3	¾	**Colorus (IRE)**[19] 4462 5-9-1 67 ... JamieMoriarty(3) 4	60+
			(W J H Ratcliffe) *led tl hdd and no ex ins fnl f* 5/1[3]
0330	4	3 ¾	**Whozart (IRE)**[13] 4653 5-9-0 48 ... PaulHanagan 5	43
			(A Dickman) *prom: kpt on fnl f* 17/2
2232	5	½	**Fire Up The Band**[3] 4950 9-9-3 64 ... FergalLynch 2	44
			(A Berry) *stmbld s: hdwy over 2f out: nvr rchd ldrs* 15/8[1]
-000	6	1	**She's Our Beauty (IRE)**[40] 3759 5-8-2 40 ... (v) DuranFentiman(3) 9	28
			(S T Mason) *w ldrs: kpt on same pce fnl f* 22/1
666	7	3	**Firenza Bond**[30] 4074 3-9-2 73 ... PJMcDonald(3) 8	35
			(G R Oldroyd) *mid-div: hdwy to chse ldrs over 1f out: sn fdd* 15/2
4-00	8	1	**Throw The Dice**[15] 4561 6-8-9 43 ... (v) SladeO'Hara(5) 3	23
			(A Berry) *trckd ldrs: rdn and lost pl over 2f out* 16/1
0-00	9	5	**Champagne Sue**[44] 3600 4-8-7 30 ow1 ... TonyHamilton 6	—
			(D W Barker) *w ldrs: lost pl over 1f out* 66/1

61.71 secs (1.91) **Going Correction** +0.40s/f (Good)
WFA 3 from 4yo+ 3lb **9** Ran SP% **115.3**
Speed ratings (Par 101): **100,99,98,92,91 90,85,83,75**
toteswinger: 1&2 £31.90, 1&3 £1.30, 2&3 £45.00. CSF £187.55 TOTE £3.30: £1.10, £10.30, £1.80; EX 225.30.
Owner Hall Farm Racing & D Nicholls **Bred** The Lavington Stud **Trained** Sessay, N Yorks

FOCUS
The form of this claimer looks a bit dubious with the runner-up showing big improvement. He has been rated to last year's sand form, which puts the rest 10lb or more off.
Whozart(IRE) Official explanation: jockey said gelding hung both ways
Fire Up The Band Official explanation: jockey said gelding stumbled leaving stalls

5045 TENNANTS FINE ART AUCTIONEERS H'CAP — 7f
8:15 (8:15) (Class 6) (0-60,60) 3-Y-O+ £2,388 (£705; £352) Stalls Low

Form				RPR
10/0	1		**Keys Of Cyprus**[14] 4605 6-9-3 55 ... AdrianTNicholls 8	75
			(D Nicholls) *in rr-div: hdwy over 2f out: styd on wl to ld 1f out: sn clr: readily* 20/1
0055	2	3 ¾	**Megalo Maniac**[37] 3834 5-8-8 46 oh1 ... (p) TonyHamilton 11	56
			(R A Fahey) *chsd ldrs: led over 1f out: sn hdd and no ex* 9/1
0252	3	2	**A Big Sky Brewing (USA)**[4] 4934 4-9-5 60 ... (b) NeilBrown(3) 3	65
			(T D Barron) *chsd ldrs: styd on fnl f to take 3rd nr line* 3/1[1]
0000	4	nk	**King Harson**[14] 4605 9-9-5 57 ... RobertWinston 2	61
			(J D Bethell) *led early: led 4f out tl over 1f out: kpt on same pce* 11/2[3]
4301	5	½	**Tanforan**[7] 4813 6-9-3 55 ... DavidAllan 13	57
			(B P J Baugh) *in rr and sn drvn along: styd on fnl 2f: nt rch ldrs* 9/2[2]
5000	6	¾	**Smart Pick**[11] 4683 5-8-6 47 ... (v[1]) AndrewMullen(3) 5	47
			(Mrs L Williamson) *s.s: bhd tl kpt on fnl 2f: nt rch ldrs* 33/1
0000	7	1 ¼	**Creative (IRE)**[8] 4793 3-8-12 56 ... (b) JoeFanning 14	51
			(M H Tompkins) *chsd ldrs: lost pl over 1f out* 20/1
4640	8	2 ½	**Nufoudh (IRE)**[11] 4683 4-8-11 52 ... JamieMoriarty(3) 12	42
			(Miss Tracy Waggott) *sn led: hdd 4f out: wknd appr fnl f* 25/1
5605	9	¾	**Lady Benjamin**[16] 4542 3-8-11 60 ... (v[1]) PatrickDonaghy(5) 15	46
			(P C Haslam) *sn chsng ldrs: drvn over 3f out: lost pl over 1f out* 16/1
4103	10	5	**Rich Harvest (USA)**[11] 4684 3-8-9 56 ... PJMcDonald(3) 1	29
			(P D Evans) *mid-div: effrt over 2f out: sn lost pl* 11/2[3]
3263	11	nk	**Ugenius**[9] 4748 4-8-12 50 ... DMylonas 10	24
			(G Prodromou) *in rr: effrt on outer over 2f out: sn btn* 16/1
0000	12	1	**Wooden King (IRE)**[27] 4207 3-8-3 47 ... CatherineGannon 9	16
			(P D Evans) *in rr: effrt on outer 3f out: sn btn* 33/1
0000	13	1	**Linden's Lady**[3] 4949 8-8-8 46 oh1 ... (v) PaulMulrennan 7	15
			(J R Weymes) *in tch: t.k.h: effrt on outer over 2f out: sn btn* 28/1
000-	14	3 ¾	**Victory Spirit**[151] 5778 4-9-1 53 ... (p) RoystonFfrench 4	11
			(Ollie Pears) *t.k.h in rr: bhd fnl 3f* 50/1

1m 29.5s (2.50) **Going Correction** +0.40s/f (Good)
WFA 3 from 4yo+ 6lb **14** Ran SP% **120.4**
Speed ratings (Par 101): **101,96,94,94,93 92,91,88,87,81 81,80,79,74**
toteswinger: 1&2 £19.40, 1&3 £14.50, 2&3 £6.10. CSF £178.40 CT £721.02 TOTE £25.90: £5.00, £3.00, £1.90; EX 232.00 Place 6 £ 210.35, Place 5 £ 89.76.
Owner The Beasley Gees **Bred** Juddmonte Farms **Trained** Sessay, N Yorks

FOCUS
A moderate handicap with a lightly raced winner. The form looks sound.
T/Plt: £163.70 to a £1 stake. Pool: £45,437.22. 202.61 winning tickets. T/Qpdt: £57.10 to a £1 stake. Pool: £3,153.00. 40.80 winning tickets. WG

4726 KEMPTON (A.W) (R-H)
Friday, August 15

OFFICIAL GOING: Standard
Wind: Light, across Weather: Fine, warm

5046 BOOK NOW FOR BANK HOLIDAY H'CAP — 5f (P)
5:55 (5:55) (Class 5) (0-75,74) 3-Y-O+ £2,590 (£770; £385; £192) Stalls High

Form				RPR
0436	1		**Woodcote (IRE)**[11] 4693 6-9-10 74 ... (vt[1]) GeorgeBaker 8	88
			(P R Chamings) *mde all: drew 2 l clr over 1f out: shkn up and kpt on wl: unchal* 11/2[2]
0020	2	2 ¾	**Russian Symphony (USA)**[28] 4154 7-9-9 73 ... (b) RyanMoore 6	77
			(C R Egerton) *a chsng wnr: nt qckn wl over 1f out: vain pursuit after* 15/2[3]
51-0	3	1 ¼	**Really Really Wish**[29] 4127 3-9-5 72 ... MartinDwyer 12	71
			(J R Best) *t.k.h early: cl up on inner but hanging: chsd ldng pair 2f out: nt qckn and readily hld fr over 1f out* 8/1
024	4	nk	**Brandywell Boy (IRE)**[3] 4944 5-8-11 68 ... BillyCray(7) 5	67+
			(D J S Ffrench Davis) *hld up: sn in last pair and detached: urged along and stl in last pair jst over 1f out: styd on wl fnl f* 3/1[1]
066	5	½	**Desert Opal**[28] 4154 8-8-13 63 ... (b) LiamJones 2	60
			(C R Dore) *forced to r v wd fr low draw: chsd ldrs: lost pl completely bnd 2f out: styd on again fnl f* 12/1
2543	6	2	**Wynberg (IRE)**[24] 4272 3-8-6 66 ... HollyHall(7) 7	55
			(S A Callaghan) *sn chsd ldrs: nt qckn in 4th over 1f out: shuffled along and lost 2 pls ins fnl f* 14/1
1003	7	¾	**Joss Stick**[22] 4325 3-9-3 70 ... (p) FergusSweeney 4	56
			(P J Makin) *t.k.h early: squeezed out after 1f: no bttr than midfield after: outpcd fr over 1f out* 12/1
43-3	8	nk	**Fabuleux Cherie**[44] 3609 3-9-1 68 ... RichardMullen 10	53
			(W R Muir) *t.k.h early: squeezed out after 1f: prog on inner over 1f out: sn no hdwy: wknd ins fnl f* 8/1
030	9	¾	**Bluebok**[15] 4563 7-8-12 62 ... (bt) ChrisCatlin 11	45
			(J M Bradley) *sn detached in last pair: nvr a factor* 11/1
0410	10	1	**Gleaming Spirit (IRE)**[22] 4327 4-9-1 65 ... DarrenWilliams 3	44
			(A P Jarvis) *forced to r wd fr low draw: chsd ldrs: lost grnd bnd 2f out: sn lost pl and wknd* 12/1
1264	11	1 ½	**Wibbadune (IRE)**[13] 4631 4-9-10 74 ... JamesDoyle 9	48
			(D Shaw) *awkward s: nvr bttr than midfield: struggling over 1f out: wknd* 9/1

60.35 secs (-0.15) **Going Correction** +0.025s/f (Slow)
WFA 3 from 4yo+ 3lb **11** Ran SP% **122.4**
Speed ratings (Par 103): **102,97,95,95,94 91,89,89,88,86 84**
toteswinger: 1&2 £8.40, 1&3 £8.50, 2&3 £3.50. CSF £48.60 CT £343.49 TOTE £6.90: £1.80, £2.60, £3.30; EX 46.70.
Owner Patrick Chamings Sprint Club **Bred** Liscannor Stud Ltd **Trained** Baughurst, Hants

FOCUS
An ordinary sprint handicap rated around the runner-up to his recent best and the third to last year's maiden win.

Wibbadune(IRE) Official explanation: jockey said filly hung left

5047 PANORAMIC BAR & RESTAURANT MAIDEN STKS 1m 2f (P)
6:25 (6:27) (Class 4) 3-Y-O **£4,727** (£1,406; £702; £351) **Stalls** High

Form RPR

3 **1** **King Olav (UAE)**[71] 2763 3-9-3 0 PhilipRobinson 3 82+
(M A Jarvis) *trckd ldng pair: urged along to go 2nd over 1f out: carried hd to one side and looked awkward: forced ahd last 100yds: sn clr* **10/11**[1]

0-02 **2** *2 ¼* **Aboriginie (USA)**[43] 3656 3-9-3 78 NCallan 5 77
(J H M Gosden) *led: stdd pce after 4f: tried to kick on 2f out: hdd and outpcd last 100yds* **9/2**[2]

3 *2 ¼* **Winter Miss (USA)** 3-8-12 0 RichardHughes 9 68
(J Noseda) *trckd ldng trio: disp 2nd wl over 1f out: pushed along and one pce after: bttr for experience* **12/1**

0 **4** *1 ½* **Hammer**[9] 4730 3-9-3 0 PatDobbs 2 70
(M P Tregoning) *hld up in 6th: shkn up over 2f out: kpt on one pce fr over 1f out: n.d* **8/1**

06-0 **5** *2* **Eseej (USA)**[119] 1453 3-9-3 68 DarrenWilliams 7 66
(P W Hiatt) *mostly in 5th: rdn 2f out: hanging and fnd nil over 1f out: wl btn after* **66/1**

6255 **6** *nse* **E Major**[15] 4571 3-9-3 75 RyanMoore 8 65
(Sir Michael Stoute) *reminder sn after s: chsd ldr to over 1f out: wknd tamely* **6/1**[3]

7 *6* **Resentful Angel** 3-8-12 0 PaulEddery 4 48
(Pat Eddery) *reluctant to enter stalls and nt too keen to leave them: detached in last: shkn up and green 3f out: nvr on terms* **33/1**

8 *20* **Thoas (GR)** 3-9-3 0 TGMcLaughlin 6 13
(Jane Chapple-Hyam) *dwlt: rn green in 7th: wknd over 2f out: t.o* **40/1**

2m 7.72s (-0.28) **Going Correction** +0.025s/f (Slow) 8 Ran SP% **110.5**
Speed ratings (Par 102): **102,100,98,97,95 95,90,74**
toteswinger: 1&2 £1.10, 1&3 £4.60, 2&3 £7.40. CSF £4.71 TOTE £1.60: £1.10, £1.50, £3.40; EX 3.70.
Owner Sheikh Ahmed Al Maktoum **Bred** Darley **Trained** Newmarket, Suffolk
■ Vallani was withdrawn (9/1, unruly in stalls). Deduct 10p in the £ under rule 4.

FOCUS
An average maiden in which the winner did not need to improve to win. The runner-up sets the standard of the form.
Eseej(USA) Official explanation: jockey said gelding hung right
Resentful Angel Official explanation: jockey said filly ran very green

5048 EUROPEAN BREEDERS' FUND MAIDEN FILLIES' STKS 7f (P)
6:55 (6:58) (Class 4) 2-Y-O **£4,533** (£1,348; £674; £336) **Stalls** High

Form RPR

52 **1** **Key Signature**[35] 3913 2-9-0 0 ShaneKelly 11 77+
(Pat Eddery) *hld up in midfield: lost pl sltly after 2f: prog on outer over 2f out: rdn and r.o to ld last 150yds: sn in command* **11/8**[1]

2 *1 ¼* **Three Moons (IRE)** 2-9-0 0 RichardHughes 1 74
(H J L Dunlop) *dwlt: rcvrd wl on outer and sn pressed ldr: shkn up to ld narrowly over 1f out: hdd and outpcd last 150yds* **33/1**

43 **3** *2 ½* **Prophetise (USA)**[22] 4339 2-9-0 0 JamesDoyle 8 68
(J W Hills) *led: hrd pressed over 2f out: narrowly hdd over 1f out: fdd ins fnl f* **6/1**[3]

4 *1 ¼* **Money Money Money** 2-9-0 0 LiamJones 13 65
(P Winkworth) *mostly in midfield: effrt over 2f out: wl outpcd over 1f out: kpt on fnl f* **20/1**

5 *hd* **Mayaalah** 2-9-0 0 MartinDwyer 10 67+
(J H M Gosden) *dwlt: green and bdly outpcd in last pair: latched on to bk of field 1/2-way: stl only 10th 1f out: r.o fnl f: nrst fin* **8/1**

6 *½* **Spinning Belle (IRE)** 2-8-11 0 PatrickHills[(3)] 3 63
(J W Hills) *cl up on inner: disp 3rd over 2f out: stl wl there over 1f out: fdd fnl f* **50/1**

7 *1* **Molly The Witch (IRE)** 2-9-0 0 PatDobbs 7 60
(M P Tregoning) *rn green in midfield: prog over 2f out: chsng ldrs and looked possible threat over 1f out: wknd rapidly ins fnl f* **20/1**

8 *¾* **Qelaan (USA)** 2-9-0 0 RichardMullen 4 58
(M P Tregoning) *in tch in midfield: n.m.r briefly over 2f out: effrt over 1f out: plugged on one pce* **12/1**

9 *nk* **Damini (USA)** 2-9-0 0 RyanMoore 12 58+
(Sir Michael Stoute) *chsd ldrs: rdn after 3f: kpt pl on inner to over 2f out: steadily wknd* **7/2**[2]

10 *2* **Choral Festival** 2-9-0 0 J-PGuillambert 2 53
(Sir Mark Prescott) *prom: disp 3rd over 2f out: sn lost pl: eased fnl f* **25/1**

11 *3 ¼* **Romantic Interlude (IRE)** 2-9-0 0 DarrenWilliams 5 45
(A P Jarvis) *s.v.s and lft 10 l: nvr rcvrd* **66/1**

5 **12** *68* **Virginia's Choice**[14] 4598 2-9-0 0 TGMcLaughlin 6 —
(Jane Chapple-Hyam) *dwlt: v green in rr: hung bdly lft bnd 3f out: t.o after: virtually p.u* **33/1**

1m 27.73s (1.73) **Going Correction** +0.025s/f (Slow) 12 Ran SP% **120.1**
Speed ratings (Par 93): **91,89,86,85,85 84,83,82,82,79 76,—**
toteswinger: 1&2 £27.10, 1&3 £2.00, 2&3 £59.90. CSF £67.80 TOTE £2.30: £1.10, £8.00, £2.20; EX 94.30.
Owner F C T Wilson **Bred** Bolton Grange **Trained** Nether Winchendon, Bucks

FOCUS
A fair maiden with the winner stepping up a little on her previous form, but the second favourite was disappointing.

NOTEBOOK
Key Signature looked to have a fair amount to do in the straight but she put this to bed with a decisive run. Her second in a Newbury maiden set the standard and there was a lot to like about the turn of foot she found when Shane Kelly gave her the office. (op 2-1 tchd 5-4)
Three Moons(IRE), a half-sister to quite useful 5f juvenile winner Black Velvet, showed promise on her debut and was in front over a furlong out. She is bred to make a two-year-old, although her trainer's youngsters have yet to deliver this year.
Prophetise(USA) had it to do with Key Signature on the book, but she displayed slight improvement from her previous starts. She now qualifies for a handicap mark. (op 8-1 tchd 11-2)
Money Money Money did well to trouble the judge taking into account her stout pedigree.
Mayaalah, whose dam was unraced but is closely related to 1000 Guineas winner Lahan, was too green to do herself justice on her debut, but she ran on in the closing stages and can do much better with this experience under her belt. (op 13-2 tchd 11-2)
Damini(USA) did not appear to know what was required and was being pushed along throughout. She is considered much better than this effort indicates. (op 10-3 tchd 3-1)
Romantic Interlude(IRE) Official explanation: jockey said filly missed the break

Virginia's Choice Official explanation: jockey said filly had steering problems

5049 KEMPTON.CO.UK MEDIAN AUCTION MAIDEN STKS 7f (P)
7:25 (7:26) (Class 6) 3-5-Y-O **£2,047** (£604; £302) **Stalls** High

Form RPR

34-2 **1** **Beauchamp Wizard**[19] 4454 3-9-3 73 RichardHughes 2 77
(G A Butler) *hld up in 5th: plenty to do whn effrt 2f out: prog over 1f out: r.o fnl f: drvn ahd nr fin* **2/1**[2]

3-32 **2** *hd* **Mille Feuille (IRE)**[24] 4277 3-8-12 73 JamesDoyle 1 71
(R M Beckett) *hld up in last: pushed along over 4f out: prog over 2f out: tk time to find stride but fin wl to take 2nd and cl on wnr* **11/8**[1]

0-0 **3** *nk* **Spate River**[95] 2056 3-9-3 0 GeorgeBaker 8 76
(C F Wall) *led: kicked clr over 2f out: drvn over 1f out: collared nr fin and lost 2nd last strides* **20/1**

2 **4** *4* **Crafty Dealer (IRE)**[184] 543 3-9-3 0 RyanMoore 6 65
(J W Hills) *hld up in 6th: effrt whn nt clr run jst over 2f out to wl over 1f out: pushed along and kpt on steadily after: no ch w ldrs* **5/1**[3]

2-00 **5** *shd* **Mansii**[7] 4831 3-9-3 77 LiamJones 9 65
(P J McBride) *prom: chsd ldr wl over 2f out to over 1f out: styd cl up tl wknd ins fnl f* **9/1**

0022 **6** *14* **Wreningham**[24] 4271 3-9-3 68 NCallan 5 27
(T Keddy) *prom: disp 2nd wl over 2f out: sn wknd: t.o* **12/1**

0-0 **7** *7* **Amber Bamber**[51] 3379 3-8-12 0 AdamKirby 4 —
(D Haydn Jones) *pressed ldr tl wknd rapidly wl over 2f out: t.o* **100/1**

00 **8** *8* **Super Al**[113] 1581 3-9-3 0 NickyMackay 3 —
(M Wigham) *hld up in last pair: pushed along 1/2-way: sn struggling: t.o* **80/1**

1m 26.16s (0.16) **Going Correction** +0.025s/f (Slow)
WFA 3 from 4yo 6lb 8 Ran SP% **116.8**
Speed ratings (Par 101): **100,99,99,94,94 78,70,61**
toteswinger: 1&2 £1.30, 1&3 £11.30, 2&3 £9.60. CSF £5.20 TOTE £2.70: £1.40, £1.10, £5.20; EX 6.40.
Owner Erik Penser **Bred** E Penser **Trained** Newmarket, Suffolk

FOCUS
The most exciting race of the night, and the finish was dominated by the two rivals in the market beforehand. The form is only modest, with the winner the best guide.
Super Al Official explanation: jockey said gelding never travelled

5050 MIX BUSINESS WITH PLEASURE CLAIMING STKS 6f (P)
7:55 (7:55) (Class 6) 3-5-Y-O **£2,047** (£604; £302) **Stalls** High

Form RPR

0313 **1** **Bazguy**[8] 4765 3-8-10 70 (b) RyanMoore 6 73
(P D Evans) *led to over 4f out: led again over 2f out: drvn and hld on wl fnl f* **7/2**[2]

1010 **2** *¾* **Came Back (IRE)**[31] 4059 5-9-9 94 NCallan 5 81
(K A Ryan) *t.k.h early: trckd ldrs: wnt 2nd wl over 1f out: hrd rdn and nt qckn fnl f* **1/2**[1]

0434 **3** *½* **Our Blessing (IRE)**[12] 4664 4-9-5 60 DarrenWilliams 10 75
(A P Jarvis) *trckd ldng pair: nt qckn 2f out: kpt on to press for 2nd nr fin* **14/1**[3]

0550 **4** *1 ¾* **Bertie Swift**[41] 3733 4-8-11 55 (v[1]) TPO'Shea 3 61
(J Gallagher) *dwlt and hmpd s: wl detached in last: prog 2f out: clsd on ldrs over 1f out: one pce fnl f* **40/1**

4304 **5** *1* **Blue Zenith (IRE)**[30] 4090 3-8-1 61 LukeMorris[(3)] 4 54
(J S Moore) *towards rr: rdn and struggling over 2f out: no imp on ldrs after* **25/1**

6605 **6** *1* **Blackmalkin (USA)**[7] 4824 4-8-10 60 MartinDwyer 1 54
(M Quinn) *s.i.s: towards rr: effrt and sme prog 2f out: no imp 1f out: wknd* **14/1**[3]

0-00 **7** *13* **Daddy Cool**[31] 4064 4-8-10 63 JackDean[(5)] 2 17
(W G M Turner) *wnt rt s: pressed wnr: led over 4f out to over 2f out: wknd rapidly wl over 1f out: t.o* **50/1**

1m 12.87s (-0.23) **Going Correction** +0.025s/f (Slow)
WFA 3 from 4yo+ 4lb 7 Ran SP% **110.5**
Speed ratings (Par 101): **102,101,100,98,96 95,78**
toteswinger: 1&2 £1.10, 1&3 £2.20, 2&3 £2.20. CSF £5.19 TOTE £4.70: £1.80, £1.30; EX 6.70.
Owner B McCabe & K J Mercer **Bred** Usk Valley Stud **Trained** Pandy, Monmouths

FOCUS
The form book effectively went out of the window in this claimer as the runner-up was very well in with the winner on official ratings. Nothing else had a realistic chance at the weights and the third possibly holds down the form.

5051 KEMPTON FOR OUTDOOR EVENTS H'CAP 1m (P)
8:25 (8:26) (Class 3) (0-95,95) 3-Y-0+
£7,477 (£2,239; £1,119; £560; £279; £140) **Stalls** High

Form RPR

-104 **1** **Russki (IRE)**[16] 4528 4-9-9 **90** (b) RichardMullen 8 101
(D M Simcock) *taken down early: pushed up to ld: mde all: stretched field over 2f out: 4 l clr over 1f out: all out* **6/1**[3]

3550 **2** *nk* **Murfreesboro**[62] 3045 5-9-2 **83** AdamKirby 7 93
(D Shaw) *dwlt: hld up in rr: plld out and stdy prog 2f out: wnt 2nd jst ins fnl f: drvn and clsd on wnr fin: too much to do* **20/1**

5040 **3** *3* **Titan Triumph**[3] 4944 4-8-6 **76** (t) LukeMorris[(3)] 9 79
(W J Knight) *t.k.h early: hld up bhd ldrs: rdn 3f out: effrt on inner 2f out but outpcd: kpt on to take 3rd nr fin* **12/1**

221 **4** *nk* **Visions Of Johanna (USA)**[22] 4349 3-8-10 **84** RichardHughes 3 85
(J Noseda) *sn chsd wnr: outpcd over 2f out: no imp over 1f out: lost 2nd jst ins fnl f: one pce* **5/1**[2]

5040 **5** *½* **Beauchamp Viceroy**[50] 3398 4-9-10 **91** LiamJones 5 92
(G A Butler) *t.k.h early: hld up in rr: rdn on outer and fnd nil over 2f out: styd on ins fnl f: nrst fin* **10/1**

1013 **6** *½* **Bomber Command (USA)**[20] 4407 5-9-10 **94** (v) PatrickHills[(3)] 2 94
(J W Hills) *trckd ldrs: drvn and outpcd over 2f out: disp 2nd over 1f out: wknd last 100yds* **8/1**

00-3 **7** *¾* **Killena Boy (IRE)**[24] 4269 6-9-4 **85** RyanMoore 11 83
(W Jarvis) *a in midfield: shkn up and outpcd over 2f out: no imp after* **9/2**[1]

-214 **8** *nk* **Irony (IRE)**[14] 4602 9-8-11 **83** DavidProbert[(5)] 10 81
(A M Balding) *sn in 3rd: outpcd over 2f out: steadily fdd* **7/1**

2000 **9** *½* **Missioner (USA)**[20] 4422 3-8-9 **83** (b) J-PGuillambert 6 79
(M Johnston) *t.k.h early: hld up towards rr: outpcd over 2f out: n.d after* **7/1**

2060 **10** *½* **Northern Spy (USA)**[16] 4528 4-9-0 **81** PatDobbs 1 76
(S Dow) *t.k.h early: hld up wl in rr: outpcd over 2f out: nvr a factor after* **8/1**

0/1- **11** *6* **Xtra Torrential (USA)**[567] 255 6-10-0 **95**.................. FergusSweeney 4 77
(D M Simcock) *taken down early: hld up in last: pushed along and no prog over 2f out: t.o* **25/1**

1m 38.19s (-1.61) **Going Correction** +0.025s/f (Slow)
WFA 3 from 4yo+ 7lb **11** Ran SP% **121.7**
Speed ratings (Par 107): **109,108,105,105,104 104,103,103,102,102 96**
toteswinger: 1&2 £16.00, 1&3 £11.70, 2&3 £64.60. CSF £122.71 CT £1413.32 TOTE £4.40: £1.70, £8.80, £4.40; EX 161.90.
Owner DXB Bloodstock Ltd **Bred** Mark Commins **Trained** Newmarket, Suffolk

FOCUS
A useful bunch on show in this decent handicap, and the winner became the third all-the-way scorer on the card. He is rated up 5lb.

NOTEBOOK
Russki(IRE) had dropped in the weights and was re-equipped with blinkers and, although tying up in the final 100 yards, was always holding Murfreesboro. (tchd 8-1)
Murfreesboro put in an encouraging first effort for his new trainer in a class drop, and can go on from this. (op 25-1 tchd 28-1)
Titan Triumph was suited by the strong pace and was able to raise his game as his stamina came into play. (op 14-1)
Visions Of Johanna(USA) was unable to repeat the forcing tactics employed for his Sandown win. (op 4-1 tchd 7-2)
Bomber Command(USA) threatened but then weakened under pressure off an elevated mark. (op 6-1)
Killena Boy(IRE) never really got into the race. (op 5-1 tchd 11-2)

5052 SUNRISE RADIO H'CAP 7f (P)
8:55 (8:56) (Class 4) (0-80,77) 3-Y-O **£4,727** (£1,406; £702; £351) **Stalls** High

Form RPR
1043 **1** **Minus Fifteen (IRE)**[33] 3999 3-9-5 **75**....................................... NCallan 3 84
(K A Ryan) *s.i.s: sn rcvrd to dispute 2nd: hrd rdn and nt qckn over 2f out: clsd suddenly to ld jst ins fnl f: kpt on wl* **11/2**[3]
-212 **2** *1 1/2* **Greystoke Prince**[30] 4083 3-9-3 **73**.................................... AdamKirby 1 78
(W R Swinburn) *led: rdn 3 l clr 2f out: looked wnr but mown down jst ins fnl f* **6/4**[1]
0604 **3** *1 1/4* **King's Wonder**[2] 4976 3-9-6 **76**....................................... MartinDwyer 9 78
(W R Muir) *plld hrd: hld up in rr: prog 2f out but outpcd: wnt 3rd 1f out: nt qckn after* **7/2**[2]
2605 **4** *1 1/2* **Smokey Rye**[23] 4312 3-9-4 **74**...............................(p) GeorgeBaker 2 72
(G L Moore) *s.i.s: sn trckd ldrs: rdn and outpcd over 2f out: kpt on one pce after* **10/1**
2620 **5** *nk* **La Chicaluna**[23] 4300 3-9-0 **77**.................................. RosieJessop(7) 6 74
(J G Given) *hld up in midfield: rdn and outpcd over 2f out: one pce and no imp after* **10/1**
0004 **6** *nse* **Last Of The Line**[22] 4345 3-9-1 **71**...............................(v1) JamesDoyle 7 68
(H J L Dunlop) *t.k.h: hld up in rr: swtchd to inner and prog 2f out: one pce and no hdwy fnl f* **16/1**
1600 **7** *10* **Sir Billy Nick**[9] 4731 3-9-3 **73**..................................... RichardHughes 5 43
(J Noseda) *hld up in rr: rdn 3f out: sn struggling: t.o* **10/1**
1500 **8** *1 3/4* **Dancer's Legacy**[14] 4603 3-9-5 **75**..........................(vt1) TGMcLaughlin 4 40
(E A L Dunlop) *disp 2nd: rdn and outpcd over 2f out: wknd rapidly over 1f out: t.o* **20/1**
000 **9** *22* **Emperors Jade**[20] 4408 3-9-0 **70**.................................... DarrenWilliams 8 —
(A P Jarvis) *v restless in stalls: rrd bdly s: a last: eased whn no ch 2f out: t.o* **28/1**

1m 26.31s (0.31) **Going Correction** +0.025s/f (Slow) **9** Ran SP% **119.0**
Speed ratings (Par 102): **99,97,95,94,93 93,82,80,55**
toteswinger: 1&2 £3.80, 1&3 £4.80, 2&3 £2.90. CSF £14.60 CT £34.16 TOTE £8.00: £3.00, £1.80, £1.10; EX 18.90 Place 6 £ 27.77, Place 5 £ 8.24.
Owner Clipper Logistics **Bred** Denis McDonnell **Trained** Hambleton, N Yorks

FOCUS
A fair handicap in which the winner was back to his previous sand form.
T/Plt: £68.50 to a £1 stake. Pool: £44,682.44. 475.91 winning tickets. T/Qpdt: £12.90 to a £1 stake. Pool: £4,123.10. 235.65 winning tickets. JN

4664 NEWBURY (L-H)
Friday, August 15

OFFICIAL GOING: Good to soft (soft in places; 6.3)
Wind: Virtually nil

5053 EUROPEAN BREEDERS' FUND MAIDEN STKS 6f 8y
1:20 (1:25) (Class 4) 2-Y-O **£5,828** (£1,734; £866; £432) **Stalls** High

Form RPR
02 **1** **Nasri**[16] 4530 2-9-0 0... SebSanders 6 83+
(B J Meehan) *str: lw: mde all: drvn and hld on wl thrght fnl f* **2/1**[1]
5 **2** *1/2* **Definightly**[28] 4164 2-9-0 0... ChrisCatlin 8 82+
(R Charlton) *unf: chsd ldrs: wnt 2nd and rdn 2f out: styd on u.p to cl on wnr fnl 100yds but a hld* **5/1**[3]
0 **3** *5* **Pearl Of Manacor (IRE)**[12] 4665 2-9-0 0........................... TPO'Shea 2 67
(M R Channon) *chsd ldrs: drvn along fr 1/2-way: styd on same pce fnl 2f* **11/2**
4 *1 1/4* **Park Lane** 2-9-0 0.. DaneO'Neill 4 63+
(B W Hills) *w'like: leggy: s.i.s: sn in tch: outpcd over 2f out: styd on again fnl f* **33/1**
5 *1 1/4* **Absent Pleasure (USA)** 2-9-0 0.. NCallan 1 59+
(B J Meehan) *unf: s.i.s: sn chsng ldrs: one pce fnl 2f* **16/1**
6 *1* **History Lesson** 2-9-0 0... RichardHughes 9 56+
(R Hannon) *str: tch: effrt 3f out: nvr nr ldrs and wknd over 1f out* **14/1**
6 **7** *shd* **Count Paris (USA)**[17] 4510 2-9-0 0................................ DarryllHolland 7 56
(M Johnston) *lw: chsd ldr 4f: sn wknd* **11/4**[2]
8 *3/4* **Decision** 2-9-0 0.. PhilipRobinson 3 53
(C G Cox) *unf: s.i.s: rdn over 3f out and a towards rr* **12/1**
9 *nk* **Dustry (IRE)** 2-9-0 0... RyanMoore 5 53
(R Hannon) *w'like: scope: bit bkwd: s.i.s: a towards rr* **20/1**

1m 15.6s (2.60) **Going Correction** +0.50s/f (Yiel) **9** Ran SP% **120.0**
Speed ratings (Par 96): **102,101,94,93,91 90,89,88,88**
toteswinger: 1&2 £3.20, 1&3 £3.70, 2&3 £3.50. CSF £13.08 TOTE £3.10: £1.60, £2.00, £2.10; EX 14.10.
Owner Saleh Al Homaizi & Imad Al Sagar **Bred** Lady Hardy **Trained** Manton, Wilts

FOCUS
Probably not the most competitive of Newbury maidens with five of the nine runners starting at 12-1 or longer, but the front two came right away from the others and the time was identical to the later 70-85 handicap for three-year-olds, suggesting the pair are well above average.

NOTEBOOK
Nasri ◆, on the softest surface he has faced so far, bossed this field from the start and knuckled down really well when challenged. He is improving with every run and the fact that he coped so well with the ground bodes well for the weeks to come. He now looks ready for something a bit better. (op 6-4)
Definightly ◆, who showed promise despite running green on his Nottingham debut, had about a length to find with the favourite on a line through Nasri's Leicester conqueror Cook's Endeavour. He still looked a little green under pressure as he hung out towards the centre of the track late on but was still the only one able to go with the winner and never stopped trying. Normal improvement should see him winning a race like this before too long. (op 6-1 tchd 13-2)
Pearl Of Manacor(IRE), as on his debut here, attracted significant market support but although he had every chance, he could do nothing to stop the front pair running right away from him. This was still improvement of sorts, but he shapes as though another furlong would not come amiss. (op 14-1 tchd 5-1)
Park Lane ◆, a 55,000gns half-brother to 7f winner Azeema, looked very much in need of this introduction but stayed on past beaten rivals in the closing stages without being given at all a hard time. He should come on a fair bit for this. (op 20-1)
Absent Pleasure(USA) ◆, a 35,000gns two-year-old whose dam is closely related to the smart Savethisdanceforme, was a stable-companion of the winner but did not go off unbacked despite his big price. He was travelling as well as anything entering the last quarter-mile and looked sure to be placed at least, but then the petrol ran out and he was galloping on the spot in the last furlong. He should come on plenty for this and showed enough here to suggest he will be winning races. (op 18-1 tchd 25-1)
Count Paris(USA) did not progress from his Goodwood debut as might have been expected and, despite racing handily early, was just about the first beaten. He has questions to answer now. (op 10-3)

5054 STUART MICHAEL ASSOCIATES H'CAP 1m 5f 61y
1:50 (1:50) (Class 3) (0-90,90) 3-Y-O+ **£7,771** (£2,312; £1,155; £577) **Stalls** Low

Form RPR
4-20 **1** **Tropical Strait (IRE)**[72] 2711 5-9-13 **89**........................... SebSanders 7 100+
(D W P Arbuthnot) *lw: trckd ldrs: led over 2f out: sn pushed clr: styd on strly* **10/1**
1200 **2** *3* **Woolfall Treasure**[13] 4621 3-8-12 **86**.............................(p) RyanMoore 5 92
(G L Moore) *in rr but in tch: hdwy 4f out: styd on to chse wnr fnl f but a wl hld* **9/4**[2]
5320 **3** *nk* **Jagger**[13] 4627 8-9-9 **85**.. DarrylHolland 10 91
(G A Butler) *sn chsng ldr: led appr fnl 4f: hdd over 2f out: no ch w wnr over 1f out: and outpcd for 2nd ins fnl f* **14/1**
214 **4** *1 1/4* **Manyriverstocross (IRE)**[8] 4784 3-8-7 **86**.................. DavidProbert(5) 1 90
(A King) *lw: led: narrowly hdd over 4f out: styd w ldr to 2f out: sn one pce* **13/8**[1]
2040 **5** *5* **Akarem**[34] 3942 7-10-0 **90**.. FergusSweeney 4 86
(K R Burke) *chsd ldrs: rdn over 3f out: wknd 2f out* **10/1**
11/0 **6** *1/2* **Corran Ard (IRE)**[27] 4191 7-9-11 **87**.............................. StephenDonohoe 2 82
(Evan Williams) *s.i.s: bhd: shkn up and one pce fr over 2f out* **20/1**
-510 **7** *21* **North Parade**[16] 4519 3-9-0 **88**......................................(t) NCallan 6 52
(B J Meehan) *in tch: rdn over 3f out: sn btn* **25/1**
5 **8** *20* **Carmond (GER)**[27] 4193 4-8-13 **75**..................................... TQuinn 8 9
(B G Powell) *chsd ldrs tl rdn and wknd 4f out* **16/1**
6003 **9** *3 1/2* **Grande Caiman (IRE)**[6] 4843 4-9-12 **88**...................(p) RichardHughes 3 17
(R Hannon) *lw: stdd s: hld up: rdn 4f out: no rspnse: eased whn no ch fnl 2f* **9/1**[3]

2m 54.44s (2.44) **Going Correction** +0.125s/f (Good)
WFA 3 from 4yo+ 12lb **9** Ran SP% **118.2**
Speed ratings (Par 107): **97,95,94,94,91 90,77,65,63**
toteswinger: 1&2 £7.00, 1&3 £16.80, 2&3 £10.20. CSF £33.65 CT £327.70 TOTE £13.90: £3.00, £1.10, £3.80; EX 66.70.
Owner Francis Ward and Anthony Ward **Bred** George Ward **Trained** Compton, Berks

FOCUS
This looked a decent handicap beforehand, but it was spoilt by an early dawdle and it was not the test of stamina it would otherwise have been. Therefore the form should be treated with a bit of caution, although it does read sound enough.

NOTEBOOK
Tropical Strait(IRE), back over a more suitable trip, would not necessarily have been suited by the slow early pace but the longer distance more than compensated for that. He travelled particularly well behind the leaders and once unleashed there was only ever going to be one winner. He is set to turn out again in the Ebor under a 4lb penalty, and he has won when reappearing after eight days in the past, so there is a chance that he could cope with the quick return. (tchd 12-1)
Woolfall Treasure, trying his longest trip to date and in first-time cheekpieces, stayed on well from off the pace to just win the separate race for second but had no chance with the winner. The slow early pace meant that his stamina was not proved conclusively, but this was still an encouraging step towards a hurdling career for his new and very lucky owner Harry Findlay. (op 5-2)
Jagger, back over a more suitable trip, was sent for home down the middle of the track starting up the home straight but could never stamp his authority on the race. He kept plodding on to maintain a place in the frame, but despite looking very well handicapped these days on his best form, is still to convince that he is anything like the horse he once was. (op 16-1)
Manyriverstocross(IRE) very much had his own way out in front and set a very modest early tempo. His rider did not seem bothered when Jagger headed him as he was still travelling better than that rival, but when the winner cruised alongside it was a different matter and although he tried to respond it became a very unequal struggle. He may have been better off setting a more searching pace as does not look blessed with much in the way of a change of pace, but he is still relatively unexposed. (op 15-8 tchd 2-1)
Akarem had every chance, but was well and truly put in his place over the last couple of furlongs. He has not won on the Flat for over two years and although well handicapped on the form he was showing then, he is not as good now and despite his decent effort in the Northumberland Plate he is looking held off this sort of mark these days. (tchd 11-1)
Corran Ard(IRE), a winning hurdler but racing over his longest trip on the Flat by some way, was held up to get it and the modest early tempo would have helped him in that respect, but even so he found very little once off the bridle. This second start on the level after finishing lame on his chasing debut at Ludlow in April should help put him right for a return to jumping, however, if that is the intention (op 16-1)
Carmond(GER) Official explanation: jockey said gelding hung right-handed in home straight
Grande Caiman(IRE) Official explanation: jockey said colt ran flat

5055 BATHWICK TYRES ST HUGH'S STKS (LISTED RACE) (FILLIES) 5f 34y
2:20 (2:21) (Class 1) 2-Y-O
£17,031 (£6,456; £3,231; £1,611; £807; £405) **Stalls** High

Form RPR
1524 **1** **Madame Trop Vite (IRE)**[8] 4781 2-8-12 85........................ NCallan 3 103
(K A Ryan) *mde all: rdn and edgd rt to stands' rail fnl f: unchal* **20/1**
3310 **2** *2 3/4* **Kerrys Requiem (IRE)**[37] 3851 2-9-1 92............................ TPO'Shea 1 96
(M R Channon) *lw: towards rr and sn pushed along: hdwy on rail whn nt clr run and swtchd lft over 1f out: styd on wl to take 2nd ins fnl f but no ch w wnr* **20/1**

1 **3** 1 ½ **Riotista (IRE)**[17] 4499 2-8-12 0........ ChrisCatlin 2 88
(E J O'Neill) *str: cmpt: sn disputing 2nd: rdn 2f out: styd on same pce u.p fnl f* **14/1**
321 **4** 1 **Shyrl**[44] 3598 2-8-12 101........ SebSanders 4 84
(S A Callaghan) *sn disputing 2nd and chsd wnr 1/2-way: no imp sn after and wknd ins fnl f* **8/11**[1]
2330 **5** 2 ¼ **Aspen Darlin (IRE)**[56] 3192 2-8-12 92........ RyanMoore 5 76
(A Bailey) *lw: chsd ldrs: rdn 1/2-way: wknd over 1f out* **7/1**[3]
02 **6** 2 ½ **Cat Patrol**[13] 4634 2-8-12 0........ JimmyQuinn 6 67
(H J L Dunlop) *outpcd: rdn 1/2-way: mod prog fnl f* **33/1**
5132 **7** shd **Night Seed (IRE)**[4] 4925 2-8-12 74........ RichardHughes 9 67
(R Hannon) *lw: chsd ldrs over 3f* **14/1**
452 **8** 8 **Lucky Leigh**[22] 4323 2-8-12 100........ SamHitchcott 7 38
(M R Channon) *spd to 1/2-way* **9/2**[2]

63.70 secs (2.30) **Going Correction** +0.50s/f (Yiel) **8 Ran SP% 114.4**
Speed ratings (Par 99): **101,96,94,92,89 85,84,72**
toteswinger: 1&2 £20.70, 1&3 £15.80, 2&3 £13.20. CSF £324.55 TOTE £20.40: £5.10, £5.40, £4.00; EX 253.00.
Owner Mrs T Marnane **Bred** Mark & Pippa Hackett **Trained** Hambleton, N Yorks

FOCUS
Not a race with a rich tradition recently and with two 20-1 shots and a 14-1 shot filling the frame, the form of this year's renewal is open to question. The time was solid though and the winner did it very nicely with no fluke about it.

NOTEBOOK
Madame Trop Vite(IRE), back down to the minimum trip, had shown enough on an easy surface before to suggest this ground was not going to be a problem. Sent straight into the lead, she ran this lot into the ground and was in no danger from some way out despite hanging right over to the stands' rail. This was impressive and whether she can buck the trend of recent winners of this race and make her mark in better company remains to be seen, but this will still have enhanced her value somewhat. (op 16-1)
Kerrys Requiem(IRE), down in grade after finishing seventh in the Cherry Hinton, got into all sorts of trouble when launched with her effort, but even though she would have finished a lot closer with a clear run it is hard to say she would have given the winner much more to think about otherwise given the margin between them. A return to further looks needed. (op 12-1)
Riotista(IRE), the form of whose winning debut at Beverley has yet to be really boosted, was far from disgraced in this much stronger company and she kept on well having been up there all the way. She still has room for improvement, but she is not going to be easy to place from now on. (op 11-1 tchd 10-1)
Shyrl, back up in grade after her confidence-boosting maiden win, had every chance but she folded rather disappointingly and the easier ground may have been the problem. She still has questions to answer though. (op 10-11 tchd 4-6 and evens in places)
Aspen Darlin(IRE), who scored on soft ground on her debut, was racing for the first time since finishing eighth in the Albany at Royal Ascot. She capitulated rather tamely after showing early pace and although she might have just needed it, better might still have been expected. (op 9-1 tchd 10-1)
Lucky Leigh, just behind Shyrl in the Queen Mary and beaten at long odds-on in a three-runner event at Bath last time, was bitterly disappointing and even though this different ground may have been the reason, she still has a lot to prove now. (op 4-1)

5056 CHRISTOPHER SMITH ASSOCIATES H'CAP 6f 8y
2:55 (2:55) (Class 4) (0-80,85) 3-Y-O £4,857 (£1,445; £722; £360) Stalls High

Form RPR
-233 **1** **Polar Annie**[20] 4433 3-9-1 74........ TGMcLaughlin 3 83
(M S Saunders) *w ldrs tl slt advantage fr 1/2-way: styd on wl u.p fnl f* **8/1**[3]
-625 **2** ¾ **Cape Rock**[20] 4431 3-8-11 70........ TQuinn 1 77+
(C A Horgan) *in rr: rdn over 2f out: styng on whn nt clr run and swtchd rt 1f out: fiinished strly to take 2nd cl home but no imp on wnr* **9/1**
611 **3** hd **Muftarres (IRE)**[14] 4584 3-9-3 76........ MartinDwyer 9 82
(Sir Michael Stoute) *lw: in rr: hdwy over 2f out: disp 2nd over 1f out tl chsd wnr ins fnl f: no imp and outpcd into 3rd cl home* **5/1**[2]
-003 **4** ¾ **Errigal Lad**[41] 3723 3-9-4 77........ NCallan 8 81
(K A Ryan) *lw: led to 1/2-way: styd disputing cl 2nd to 1f out: outpcd fnl 50yds* **4/1**[1]
0211 **5** 1 **Billion Dollar Kid**[7] 4809 3-9-9 85 6ex........(t) KevinGhunowa(3) 5 86
(R A Harris) *chsd ldrs: disp 2nd fr 3f out tl outpcd ins fnl f* **17/2**
0106 **6** 1 ¼ **Vigano (IRE)**[21] 4369 3-9-0 73........ RyanMoore 2 70
(S Kirk) *hdwy to chse ldrs 1/2-way: rdn over 2f out: no ex ins fnl f* **16/1**
3646 **7** 6 **I Confess**[20] 4408 3-8-13 77........ RichardEvans(5) 6 55
(P D Evans) *in tch: rdn 1/2-way: no ch fnl 2f* **8/1**[3]
3160 **8** 1 ½ **First Trim (IRE)**[14] 4591 3-9-4 77........ TPO'Shea 4 50
(B J Meehan) *chsd ldrs tl wknd 2f out* **28/1**
6103 **9** nk **Lodi (IRE)**[6] 4864 3-9-7 80........(t) IanMongan 10 52
(J Akehurst) *chsd ldrs tl wknd and bmpd 1f out* **8/1**[3]
5021 **10** hd **Tadalavil**[1] 5028 3-9-2 75 6ex........ SamHitchcott 7 46
(M R Channon) *chsd ldrs 4f* **4/1**[1]

1m 15.6s (2.60) **Going Correction** +0.50s/f (Yiel) **10 Ran SP% 119.9**
Speed ratings (Par 102): **102,101,100,99,98 96,88,86,86,86**
toteswinger: 1&2 £11.40, 1&3 £6.80, 2&3 £8.20. CSF £80.00 CT £411.38 TOTE £9.60: £2.50, £2.90, £1.90; EX 94.40.
Owner Lockstone Business Services Ltd **Bred** Cobhall Court Stud **Trained** Green Ore, Somerset
■ Stewards' Enquiry : T G McLaughlin one-day ban: used whip with excessive frequency (Aug 29)
T Quinn caution: careless riding

FOCUS
A competitive little sprint and though the time was identical to the earlier two-year-old maiden it was still acceptable for the type of race. They finished in a beat of a heap though and one or two took rather wayward passages, so the form may be a little suspect. It has been rated through the placed horses.

5057 MALONE ROOFING MAIDEN FILLIES' STKS 7f (S)
3:30 (3:31) (Class 5) 3-Y-O+ £3,238 (£963; £481; £240) Stalls High

Form RPR
3 **1** **Straight Sets (IRE)**[13] 4651 4-9-4 0........ SamHitchcott 1 74
(M R Channon) *w'like: scope: pressed ldrs: rdn over 2f out: led over 1f out: styd on wl u.p* **7/2**[2]
2 1 **Party Frock** 3-8-12 0........ RyanMoore 2 69
(J H M Gosden) *tall; w'like: scope: lw: hld up in rr but in tch: gd hdwy over 1f out and hrd drvn to chse wnr ins fnl f: kpt on but a jst hld* **6/4**[1]
0-4 **3** ¾ **Perfect Silence**[51] 3379 3-8-12 0........ AdamKirby 7 67
(C G Cox) *lw: narrow ld tl hdd over 1f out: rallied ins fnl f but a hld* **7/2**[2]
4 1 ½ **Lyceana** 3-8-12 0........ PhilipRobinson 4 63+
(M A Jarvis) *unf: bit bkwd; in tch tl outpcd over 2f out: shkn up and kpt on again fnl f but nvr in contention* **6/1**[3]
40- **5** 5 **Kinlochard**[382] 4016 3-8-9 0........ LukeMorris(3) 6 49
(Eve Johnson Houghton) *chsd ldrs tl wknd 2f out* **33/1**
6 1 ¾ **Turfwolke (GER)** 3-8-12 0........ TQuinn 3 45
(J W Hills) *w'like: edgy: w ldrs: rdn 3f out: wknd ins fnl 2f* **14/1**
7 45 **Blush Tone**[78] 3-8-12 85........ NCallan 5 —
(C J Down) *plld hrd early: chsd ldrs tl wknd qckly 2f out: t.o* **20/1**

1m 30.09s (4.39) **Going Correction** +0.50s/f (Yiel)
WFA 3 from 4yo 6lb **7 Ran SP% 113.1**
Speed ratings (Par 100): **94,92,92,90,84 82,31**
toteswinger: 1&2 £1.90, 1&3 £2.30, 2&3 £1.90. CSF £8.95 TOTE £4.10: £1.50, £1.60; EX 10.00.
Owner Billy Parish **Bred** Mount Coote Stud **Trained** West Ilsley, Berks

FOCUS
A moderate event as older-horse maidens from this time of year onwards tend to be. The early pace was also modest and it developed into something of a sprint. The front four came right away and the form looks ordinary, though a couple are entitled to improve. The winner was up 8lb on her debut form.

5058 PETER BRETT ASSOCIATES H'CAP 1m 3f 5y
4:05 (4:05) (Class 5) (0-70,70) 3-Y-O+ £2,590 (£770; £385; £192) Stalls Low

Form RPR
6330 **1** **Megalala (IRE)**[24] 4275 7-8-12 54........ MarcHalford(3) 6 62
(J J Bridger) *led tl hdd 2f out: rallied gamely u.p to ld again cl home* **16/1**
0-02 **2** nk **She's So Pretty (IRE)**[7] 4811 4-9-3 56........(b) RyanMoore 2 63
(G L Moore) *lw: hld up towards rr: hdwy fr 3f out: str run u.p to chal fnl 100yds: no ex cl home* **9/2**[3]
2430 **3** shd **Red Merlin (IRE)**[19] 4448 3-9-7 70........(b[1]) AdamKirby 5 77
(C G Cox) *trckd ldrs: t.k.h: led gng wl 2f out: hrd rdn fnl f: hdd and no ex cl home* **7/2**[1]
0436 **4** 1 **Wester Ross (IRE)**[24] 4276 4-9-10 66........ LukeMorris(3) 9 71
(J M P Eustace) *chsd ldrs: rdn over 2f out: styd on same pce fnl f* **8/1**
5104 **5** 2 ¼ **Trysting Grove (IRE)**[10] 4704 7-8-8 54........ AshleyMorgan(7) 8 55
(E G Bevan) *slowly away: rr: hdwy on outside over 2f out: kpt on u.p but nvr gng pce to rch ldrs* **16/1**
5052 **6** 1 ½ **Mae Cigan (FR)**[8] 4785 5-9-13 66........ NCallan 4 65
(M Blanshard) *in tch: hdwy 4f out: trckd ldrs over 2f out: sn rdn: wknd fnl f* **4/1**[2]
-212 **7** 2 ½ **Check Up (IRE)**[10] 4704 7-9-0 56........ KevinGhunowa(3) 3 50
(J L Flint) *chsd ldrs: rdn 3f out: wknd fr 2f out* **11/2**
105/ **8** 8 **Tagula Blue (IRE)**[32] 2104 8-10-0 67........ StephenDonohoe 1 47
(Ian Williams) *a towards rr: no ch fnl 2f* **12/1**
2260 **9** 2 **War Of The Roses (IRE)**[22] 4331 5-9-12 65........ J-PGuillambert 10 41
(R Brotherton) *in rr: sme prog over 2f out: sn rdn: wknd qckly* **20/1**
0515 **10** 3 **Xtravaganza (IRE)**[12] 4669 3-9-3 66........ TQuinn 7 37
(J W Hills) *chsd ldr: chal fr 4f out tl over 2f out: wknd rapidly* **11/1**

2m 23.66s (2.46) **Going Correction** +0.125s/f (Good)
WFA 3 from 4yo+ 10lb **10 Ran SP% 119.5**
Speed ratings (Par 103): **96,95,95,94,93 92,90,84,83,80**
toteswinger: 1&2 £20.30, 1&3 £17.20, 2&3 £6.00. CSF £88.79 CT £319.07 TOTE £22.00: £4.80, £2.00, £1.80; EX 92.40 Trifecta £345.90 Part won. Pool: £467.44. 0.20 winning units..
Owner Tommy Ware **Bred** Joseph Gallagher **Trained** Liphook, Hants

FOCUS
They went an ordinary pace in this moderate handicap and it paid to be up there with the gallop. Modest form, but sound for the grade.
Check Up(IRE) Official explanation: jockey said gelding suffered interference in running
War Of The Roses(IRE) Official explanation: jockey said gelding lost its action

5059 JACK COLLING POLAR JEST APPRENTICE H'CAP 1m 1f
4:35 (4:36) (Class 5) (0-70,70) 4-Y-O+ £2,590 (£770; £385; £192) Stalls Low

Form RPR
2544 **1** **Merrymadcap (IRE)**[7] 4819 6-9-3 63........ JackDean 4 73
(M Blanshard) *in tch: trckd ldrs over 2f out: rdn and kpt on fnl f to ld fnl 100yds* **4/1**[2]
0003 **2** nk **Red Current**[10] 4708 4-8-12 58........ HaddenFrost 7 68
(R A Harris) *chsd ldr tl led ins fnl 3f: rdn over 1f out: hdd and no ex fnl 100yds* **17/2**
4302 **3** 3 ½ **Celticello (IRE)**[4] 4930 6-9-7 70........ RichardEvans(3) 5 72
(P D Evans) *in rr: pushed along and hdwy over 2f out: kpt on fnl f but nt rch ldrs* **6/4**[1]
3106 **4** 1 ½ **Lunar River (FR)**[15] 4572 5-8-13 62........(t) DavidProbert(3) 8 61
(David Pinder) *in tch: rdn to chse ldrs over 2f out: styd on same pce* **11/2**[3]
0350 **5** nk **Danish Monarch**[9] 4722 7-8-6 52........ AshleyHamblett 6 50
(David Pinder) *led tl hdd ins fnl 3f: wknd over 1f out* **14/1**
4000 **6** 4 **Mythical Charm**[7] 4825 9-8-2 51 oh5........(t) JemmaMarshall(3) 10 41
(J J Bridger) *towards rr: rdn over 2f out: sme prog fnl f* **20/1**
00-0 **7** 2 ½ **Vehari**[75] 2642 5-8-0 51 oh1........ RichardRowe(5) 2 35
(Ian Williams) *a towards rr* **50/1**
00-0 **8** nk **Corrib (IRE)**[217] 128 5-8-12 61........ AlanRutter(3) 1 44
(B Palling) *chsd ldrs: rdn over 2f out: sn wknd* **14/1**
0000 **9** 11 **Ruffie (IRE)**[37] 3842 5-8-2 51 oh6........ AmyBaker(3) 3 10
(Miss J Feilden) *chsd over 5f* **28/1**
0603 **10** 8 **Blue Charm**[85] 2329 4-9-5 70........ MatthewBirch(5) 9 12
(S Kirk) *chsd ldr to 3f out: sn btn* **12/1**

1m 55.92s (0.42) **Going Correction** +0.125s/f (Good) **10 Ran SP% 117.1**
Speed ratings (Par 103): **103,102,99,98,98 94,92,91,82,75**
toteswinger: 1&2 £4.40, 1&3 £2.90, 2&3 £5.20. CSF £37.21 CT £72.79 TOTE £5.00: £1.70, £2.20, £1.20; EX 27.00 Place 6: £391.67, Place 5: £249.12..
Owner Mrs N L Young **Bred** Wickfield Farm Partnership **Trained** Upper Lambourn, Berks
■ Stewards' Enquiry : Hadden Frost three-day ban: used whip with excessive frequency (Aug 29-31)

FOCUS
A moderate handicap featuring exposed performers. Ordinary form for the grade, with the favourite below par.
T/Plt: £1,302.50 to a £1 stake. Pool: £67,270.77. 37.70 winning tickets. T/Qpdt: £148.30 to a £1 stake. Pool: £5,280.90. 26.35 winning tickets. ST

4733 NEWCASTLE (L-H)
Friday, August 15
5060 Meeting Abandoned - Waterlogged

4866

NEWMARKET (JULY) (R-H)

Friday, August 15

OFFICIAL GOING: Good (8.2)

Wind: virtually nil Weather: bright

5066 STABLECARE MEDIAN AUCTION MAIDEN STKS 7f

5:30 (5:31) (Class 4) 2-Y-O £4,533 (£1,348; £674; £336) Stalls High

Form RPR

1 **Ashram (IRE)** 2-9-3 0 ... EddieAhern 8 87+
(J W Hills) *s.i.s: wl bhd: hdwy 2f out: modest 5th over 1f out: hung lft, hld hd high and flashed tail after: str run ins fnl f to ld last 50yds* **10/1**

2 **2** 1 1/2 **Equipe De Nuit**[23] 4305 2-9-3 0 ... JohnEgan 12 83
(P W D'Arcy) *led: clr after 1f: rdn wl over 1f out: edgd lft but battled on gamely tl hdd and no ex last 50yds* **5/1**[2]

5 **3** 2 **Syrinx (IRE)**[72] 2713 2-8-12 0 ... ShaneKelly 14 73
(J Noseda) *hld up in midfield: hdwy 1/2-way: modest 3rd and rdn jst over 2f out: hung lft after: kpt on fnl f* **16/1**

4 **4** 3/4 **Asateer (IRE)**[13] 4625 2-9-3 0 ... RHills 5 76
(B W Hills) *stdd s: t.k.h: hld up in midfield: hdwy 4f out: chsd clr ldr 1/2-way: rdn and hung lft fr over 1f out: plugged on steadily but nvr getting to clr ldr: lost 2 pls wl ins fnl f* **1/1**[1]

5 1 **Stevie Junior** 2-9-3 0 ... AlanMunro 10 74+
(P W Chapple-Hyam) *hld up towards rr: hdwy over 2f out: modest 4th wl over 1f out: kpt on steadily fnl f: nvr nr enough to chal* **8/1**[3]

30 **6** 2 1/4 **Mawjaat (IRE)**[21] 4380 2-8-12 0 ... DaneO'Neill 3 63+
(J L Dunlop) *towrads rr: rdn over 2f out: kpt on steadily fnl f: nvr nr ldrs* **16/1**

5 **7** 5 **Mr Redford**[20] 4425 2-9-3 0 ... SteveDrowne 15 56
(N P Littmoden) *s.i.s: hld up in rr: hdwy 3f out: no prog and edgd lft over 1f out* **22/1**

0 **8** 1 1/4 **Sparkaway**[20] 4421 2-8-10 0 ... DebraEngland(7) 7 53
(W J Musson) *hld up in rr: sme modest hdwy 2f out: nvr trbld ldrs* **100/1**

00 **9** 2 3/4 **Thewaytosanjose (IRE)**[22] 4339 2-8-12 0 ... RichardKingscote 6 41
(S Kirk) *a bhd: nvr a factor* **100/1**

0 **10** 6 **Flamboyant Red (IRE)**[13] 4636 2-8-10 0 ... KylieManser(7) 2 31
(Miss Gay Kelleway) *chsd ldr tl 1/2-way: grad wknd* **100/1**

0 **11** 1/2 **Chadwell Spring (IRE)**[36] 3869 2-8-12 0 ... SaleemGolam 11 25+
(Miss J Feilden) *hld up in midfield: rdn and struggling 3f out: no ch whn hmpd 2f out* **50/1**

4200 **12** 3 1/2 **Dancing Wave**[20] 4434 2-8-10 55 ow1 ... LeeVickers(3) 13 17
(M C Chapman) *chsd ldrs tl 1/2-way: sn wknd: t.o* **100/1**

13 1/2 **Red Horse (IRE)** 2-9-3 0 ... DarryllHolland 4 20
(M L W Bell) *chsd ldrs tl 1/2-way: sn wknd: t.o* **14/1**

14 5 **Persian Buddy** 2-8-10 0 ... HarryPoulton(7) 1 7
(Jamie Poulton) *v.s.a: a struggling in rr: t.o* **66/1**

15 4 1/2 **Expensive Dinner** 2-8-12 0 ... LPKeniry 9 —
(E F Vaughan) *in tch: rdn and struggling wl over 2f out: t.o* **33/1**

1m 26.58s (0.88) **Going Correction** +0.075s/f (Good) 15 Ran SP% **120.0**

Speed ratings (Par 96): **97,95,93,92,91 88,82,81,78,71 70,66,66,60,55**

toteswinger: 1&2 £5.70, 1&3 £27.70, 2&3 £10.70. CSF £57.17 TOTE £11.20: £3.20, £2.20, £4.40; EX 56.80.

Owner Mountgrange Stud **Bred** Waterford Hall Stud **Trained** Upper Lambourn, Berks

FOCUS

This looked like a very much above-average maiden for one of its type, limited by its nature to the progeny of relatively "unfashionable" sires. The runner-up set a very strong pace and only the winner was good enough to come from well off the gallop.

NOTEBOOK

Ashram(IRE), from the first crop of Irish 2,000 Guineas winner Indian Haven and a half-brother to the smart Blackat Blackitten, came from well back with a searing late run despite hanging so badly left that the head-on replays showed him to be running in a manner resembling the movements of a crab. Also flashing his tail violently, he obviously has his share of temperament but if connections can manage that side of him, the Dewhurst entry obviously has a future. (tchd 9-1)

Equipe De Nuit was well supported in some offices throughout the day and though the form-book shows that he didn't improve on the runner-up spot he filled at Lingfield on debut that only tells half the story. Bounced out of the stalls by Egan and setting a fierce gallop, it was only in the closing stages that he gave best to the winner's storming run after gamely battling off the challenges of the third and fourth home. Despite being from the first crop of French Derby winner Sulamani, he surely looks more likely to break his maiden over sprint distances. (op 9-2)

Syrinx(IRE) was held up but nothing like as far back off the scorching pace as the winner was, and she improved considerably on her debut effort. She shouldn't be long in winning a maiden, particularly if confined to her own sex. (op 8-1)

Asateer(IRE) had shaped well enough on his debut over the same trip at Goodwood in a better class maiden than this, and this has to go down as a rather disappointing effort, although in his defence he raced plenty close enough to the break-neck early pace. Official explanation: jockey said colt hung left (op 11-8 tchd 6-4 in a place)

Stevie Junior, a debutant from a yard which appears to be emerging from something of a mid-season slump, kept on nicely and there are races to be won with this son of Monsieur Bond. (op 7-1 tchd 6-1)

Mawjaat(IRE) disappointed at Thirsk last time but here again showed something of the promise of her debut run, and this well-bred daughter of Sakhee, who has been held up at the back on all three starts, is now eligible to run in handicaps where she would be most intersting. (op 14-1)

Chadwell Spring(IRE) Official explanation: jockey said filly was denied a clear run

5067 NGK SPARK PLUGS H'CAP 6f

6:00 (6:01) (Class 4) (0-85,84) 3-Y-O+ £6,476 (£1,927; £963; £481) Stalls High

Form RPR

5251 **1** **Earlsmedic**[13] 4632 3-8-7 70 ... (v) SaleemGolam 12 88
(S C Williams) *swtchd rt onto stands' rail s: mde all: rdn clr ent fnl f: r.o strly* **5/1**[2]

3304 **2** 4 **John Keats**[14] 4608 5-9-5 78 ... DanielTudhope 11 83
(J S Goldie) *in tch in midfield: rdn wl over 1f out: styd on to chse wnr ins fnl f: r.o but no ch w wnr* **14/1**

0360 **3** nse **Gift Horse**[14] 4586 8-9-11 84 ... (p) DaneO'Neill 4 89+
(D Nicholls) *stdd after s: hld up in midfield: nt clr run over 1f out tl ins fnl f: r.o wl last 100yds: nrly snatched 2nd but no ch w wnr* **9/1**

2/12 **4** 3/4 **Amicus Meus (IRE)**[7] 4831 4-8-9 71 ... DominicFox(3) 13 74+
(A Bailey) *swtchd lft s: hld up in midfield: rdn 2f out: n.m.r over 1f out: swtchd rt jst ins fnl f: kpt on but nvr able to chal* **7/2**[1]

535 **5** nk **Baunagain (IRE)**[7] 4831 3-9-5 82 ... PatCosgrave 9 84
(M J Wallace) *in tch: n.m.r wl over 1f out: swtchd lft and effrt over 1f out: disp 2nd ent fnl f: one pce last 100yds* **16/1**

0523 **6** 1/2 **Cornus**[7] 4831 6-9-4 77 ... (be) LDettori 10 77
(A J McCabe) *t.k.h: hld up wl in tch in midfield: rdn jst over 2f out: kpt on same pce fnl f* **7/1**[3]

1000 **7** nk **Brunelleschi**[7] 4831 5-9-1 74 ... (b) EddieAhern 1 73
(P L Gilligan) *stdd after s: hld up in midfield: nt clr run 2f out tl swtchd lft ent fnl f: sn rdn: kpt on same pce* **25/1**

0044 **8** nk **Glasshoughton**[7] 4831 5-9-7 80 ... DarryllHolland 6 78
(M Dods) *chsd wnr: rdn 2f out: wknd jst ins fnl f* **8/1**

2416 **9** hd **Resplendent Alpha**[7] 4831 4-9-0 73 ... JimmyQuinn 7 70
(P Howling) *t.k.h: hld up in rr: rdn and effrt wl over 1f out: nvr able to chal* **10/1**

0-10 **10** 1 **Restless Genius (IRE)**[103] 1837 3-9-2 79 ... (t) LPKeniry 5 73
(A M Balding) *t.k.h: chsd ldrs: rdn wl over 1f out: wknd fnl f* **20/1**

0050 **11** 3/4 **Fantasy Believer**[11] 4687 10-9-2 75 ... SteveDrowne 2 67
(J J Quinn) *stdd after s: hld up in rr: rdn and swtchd sharply lft over 1f out: nvr able to chal* **20/1**

4611 **12** 1/2 **Steel Blue**[14] 4608 8-8-12 71 ... (p) AlanMunro 3 61
(R M Whitaker) *t.k.h: prom: rdn 2f out: wknd fnl f* **10/1**

0455 **13** 1 **Buxton**[9] 4723 4-9-2 75 ... (t) RobertHavlin 8 62
(R Ingram) *chsd ldrs: rdn 2f out: wknd u.p over 1f out* **14/1**

1m 11.74s (-0.76) **Going Correction** +0.075s/f (Good)

WFA 3 from 4yo+ 4lb 13 Ran SP% **124.4**

Speed ratings (Par 105): **108,102,102,101,101 100,100,99,99,98 97,96,95**

toteswinger: 1&2 £25.30, 1&3 £8.00, 2&3 £19.40. CSF £76.75 CT £650.40 TOTE £7.50: £3.10, £4.50, £3.10; EX 130.60.

Owner Mad Man Plus One **Bred** W N Greig **Trained** Newmarket, Suffolk

FOCUS

These sprinters tend to beat one another in their turn and they all finished in a bit of a blanket behind the easy winner, who quickened nicely from the front going into the dip and streaked away up the rising ground. The form has been rated at face value and the winner is much improved.

5068 HAPPY FIRST BIRTHDAY BETFAIRCLUB ROA EBF MAIDEN STKS 1m

6:35 (6:35) (Class 4) 2-Y-O £5,180 (£1,541; £770; £384) Stalls High

Form RPR

4 **1** **Almiqdaad**[21] 4360 2-9-3 0 ... RHills 10 87
(M A Jarvis) *chsd ldrs: wnt 2nd wl over 2f out: rdn to ld 1f out: hung lft ins fnl f: r.o wl* **2/1**[1]

2 1 **Cityscape** 2-9-3 0 ... SteveDrowne 7 85+
(R Charlton) *s.i.s: hld up bhd: hdwy over 3f out: chsd ldng trio ent fnl f: styng on whn swtchd sharply rt last 100yds: r.o wl to grab 2nd nr fin* **16/1**

3 nk **Espiritu (FR)** 2-9-3 0 ... SebSanders 3 84
(J Noseda) *in tch: rdn and effrt 2f out: hanging lft but ev ch jst ins fnl f: chsd wnr wl ins fnl f: kpt on same pce: lost 2nd nr fin* **3/1**[2]

5 **4** hd **Dialogue**[13] 4625 2-9-3 0 ... LDettori 5 84+
(M Johnston) *led: rdn and qcknd over 2f out: hdd 1f out: lost 2nd and no ex last 100yds* **7/2**[3]

5 6 **Free Thinker** 2-9-3 0 ... JohnEgan 11 71
(P W D'Arcy) *hld up in tch: shkn up 3f out: rdn 2f out: edgd lft and outpcd by ldrs over 1f out: kpt on* **25/1**

0 **6** 3/4 **Adios Juan**[7] 4826 2-9-3 0 ... SaleemGolam 6 69
(S C Williams) *hld up towards rr: rdn ent fnl 2f: sn outpcd: no ch fnl f* **16/1**

7 2 **Super Flight** 2-9-3 0 ... AlanMunro 1 64
(P W Chapple-Hyam) *chsd ldrs: rdn wl over 2f out: wknd 2f out* **20/1**

6 **8** nk **State General (IRE)**[55] 3274 2-9-3 0 ... JimmyQuinn 2 64
(Miss J Feilden) *chsd ldr tl wl over 2f out: sn rdn: wknd 2f out* **50/1**

9 nse **Thief** 2-9-3 0 ... DaneO'Neill 4 64
(L M Cumani) *stdd s: hld up in rr: rdn and lost tch over 2f out* **12/1**

10 nk **Excelsior Academy** 2-9-3 0 ... EddieAhern 8 63
(B J Meehan) *s.i.s: bhd: rdn over 2f out: sn lost tch* **25/1**

11 10 **Satwa Gold (USA)** 2-9-3 0 ... TedDurcan 9 41
(E A L Dunlop) *a bhd: lost tch over 2f out* **25/1**

1m 41.66s (1.66) **Going Correction** +0.075s/f (Good) 11 Ran SP% **118.3**

Speed ratings (Par 96): **94,93,92,92,86 85,83,83,83,83 73**

toteswinger: 1&2 £12.50, 1&3 £2.10, 2&3 £7.00. CSF £34.32 TOTE £3.10: £1.70, £4.30, £1.90; EX 35.50.

Owner Hamdan Al Maktoum **Bred** Shadwell Estate Company Limited **Trained** Newmarket, Suffolk

FOCUS

A maiden that has been won by some fair animals in recent years, including Motivator in 2004. This renewal should produce its share of winners, too.

NOTEBOOK

Almiqdaad, green on his debut, had clearly learnt plenty from that and put his experience to good use to get off the mark at the second attempt. He appreciated the extra furlong and stiff finish and clearly there are no stamina issues. He could be aimed at a race like the Royal Lodge or Racing Post Trophy at the backend. (op 15-8 tchd 7-4)

Cityscape is a half-brother to Scuffle, a triple 1m winner at three, out of a mare who won her first four races, including two at Listed level, all over 7f. Slowly away, he ran pretty green on his debut but put in some good late work once switched, and on this evidence he will not be long in going one better. He holds no big-race entries at the moment, however. (op 14-1)

Espiritu(FR), whose price rose from 140,000euros as a yearling to 490,000gns as a two-year-old, is a half-brother to Bodeguita, a winner at two in France over an extended 7f. He holds entries in the Champagne, Royal Lodge and Racing Post Trophy, and was popular in the market beforehand. He made things difficult for his rider by carrying his head awkwardly and then hanging left inside the last, but that was probably just greenness and he is entitled to improve for the run. (op 7-2)

Dialogue, racing on easier ground than at Goodwood, may not have been ideally suited by it as he is by Singspiel, but he ran a sound race and certainly improved on his debut effort. Official explanation: trainer's rep said colt had a breathing problem (op 9-2 tchd 5-1)

Free Thinker, whose dam was unraced but is a half-sister to Middle Park winner Mon Tresor, did best of the rest. His pedigree suggests that the best of him will not be seen until he steps up to middle distances next year. (op 16-1)

Adios Juan again shaped well enough against tough opposition. He will make his mark in handicap company in time. (op 14-1)

5069 PORTLAND PLACE PROPERTIES H'CAP 1m

7:05 (7:06) (Class 5) (0-75,75) 3-Y-O+ £3,885 (£1,156; £577; £288) Stalls High

Form RPR

3003 **1** **Last Sovereign**[14] 4603 4-9-11 72 ... (p) LDettori 14 81
(Jane Chapple-Hyam) *hld up in midfield: edgd out lft and hdwy over 2f out: chsd ldr wl over 1f out: rdn to ld over 1f out: styd on wl u.p last 100yds* **9/2**[1]

0040 **2** 1 **Arctic Cape**[20] 4404 3-9-7 75 ... RHills 7 81
(M Johnston) *hld up towards rr: hdwy and rdn over 1f out: chsd wnr wl ins fnl f: edgd lft and no imp towards fin* **5/1**[2]

0043 **3** hd **Timber Creek**[9] 4727 3-8-9 63 ... DaneO'Neill 8 68
(H Candy) *hld up in midfield: hdwy 2f out: rdn to chse wnr ent fnl f: unable qck u.p: lost 2nd wl ins fnl f* **14/1**

0445 **4** *hd* **Sonny Parkin**[7] 4829 6-10-0 **75**....................(v) PatCosgrave 11 81
(J Pearce) *stdd s: hld up in rr: smooth hdwy over 2f out: chsng ldrs and shkn up ent fnl f: rdn and fnd little last 100yds* **5/1**[2]

0/0 **5** *1 1/2* **Pugilist**[29] 4104 6-9-11 **72**.................... JohnEgan 4 75
(B J Meehan) *chsd ldrs: swtchd lft after 2f: rdn over 1f out: wknd last 100yds* **20/1**

3050 **6** *1 1/4* **Support Fund (IRE)**[9] 4723 4-9-11 **72**.................... StephenCraven 9 72
(Eve Johnson Houghton) *hld up towards rr: hdwy 2f out: chsd ldrs u.p over 1f out: wknd ins fnl f* **12/1**

0620 **7** *4* **Optimus (USA)**[7] 4829 6-9-12 **73**.................... SebSanders 5 63
(B G Powell) *s.i.s: bhd: reminder 3f out: hdwy and drvn 2f out: wknd jst over 1f out* **20/1**

0005 **8** *1 1/2* **Rain Stops Play (IRE)**[18] 4479 6-8-9 **56** oh1.................... TPQueally 1 43
(M Quinn) *sn led: grad crossed to stands' rail: rdn 2f out: hung lft and hdd over 1f out: wknd* **12/1**

4024 **9** *1/2* **Idesia (IRE)**[30] 4081 4-9-7 **68**.................... DarryllHolland 6 54
(W R Swinburn) *chsd ldrs: rdn over 2f out: struggling whn n.m.r over 1f out: sn wl btn* **15/2**[3]

3224 **10** *1 3/4* **Brouhaha**[8] 4797 4-8-11 **58**.................... TedDurcan 13 40
(B J McMath) *a bhd: rdn wl over 2f out: wl btn last 2f* **15/2**[3]

2560 **11** *3* **Surwaki (USA)**[42] 3691 6-9-6 **67**.................... EddieAhern 2 42
(R M H Cowell) *chsd ldr: rdn over 2f out: lost 2nd wl over 1f out: wkng whn hmpd over 1f out: wl btn after* **16/1**

555- **12** *1 3/4* **Govenor Eliott (IRE)**[304] 6246 3-9-1 **69**.................... AlanMunro 3 39
(M Johnston) *chsd ldrs: rdn over 2f out: wknd: wl bhd fr over 1f out* **14/1**

1m 39.82s (-0.18) **Going Correction** +0.075s/f (Good)
WFA 3 from 4yo+ 7lb **12** Ran SP% **119.2**
Speed ratings (Par 103): **103,102,101,101,100 98,94,93,92,91 88,86**
toteswinger: 1&2 £1.60, 1&3 £11.20, 2&3 £14.20. CSF £26.56 CT £293.13 TOTE £3.60: £1.70, £2.30, £4.10; EX 16.00.
Owner Howard Spooner **Bred** Gestut Hof Ittlingen & Cheveley Park Stud Ltd **Trained** Lambourn, Berks

FOCUS
A very trappy handicap with no recent winning form on offer amongst the protagonists. The form is pretty solid but fairly ordinary.

5070 YOUNG & PURE BEAUTY CONDITIONS STKS 1m 2f
7:35 (7:36) (Class 2) 3-Y-O+
£12,462 (£3,732; £1,866; £934; £466; £234) **Stalls** Centre

Form RPR

-332 **1** **Drumfire (IRE)**[13] 4644 4-9-1 104.................... DarryllHolland 1 111
(M Johnston) *t.k.h: trckd ldrs: wnt 2nd jst over 2f out: led over 1f out: r.o wl fnl f* **7/1**

/40- **2** *1 1/2* **Blue Monday**[272] 7-9-1 0.................... SteveDrowne 9 108
(R Charlton) *hld up in tch: edgd out rt and hdwy jst over 2f out: chsd wnr ent fnl f: one pce last 100yds* **3/1**[2]

1440 **3** *1 1/4* **Khateeb (IRE)**[15] 4552 3-8-9 106....................(t) RHills 2 109
(M A Jarvis) *t.k.h: hld up in midfield: hdwy over 2f out: chsd ldng pair ent fnl f: no imp after* **15/2**

/411 **4** *1* **With Interest**[169] 739 5-9-1 109.................... LDettori 11 104
(Saeed Bin Suroor) *hld up in midfield: hdwy over 2f out: swtchd rt 2f out: sn rdn: chsd ldrs 1f out: one pce* **5/2**[1]

00 **5** *3* **Escape Route (USA)**[17] 4504 4-9-1 98....................(p) RobertHavlin 3 98
(J H M Gosden) *chsd ldr tl led 6f out: rdn 2f out: hdd over 1f out: wknd fnl f* **12/1**

-320 **6** *4* **Imperial Star (IRE)**[162] 816 5-9-1 110.................... TedDurcan 6 90
(Saeed Bin Suroor) *stdd after s: hld up in last trio: hdwy over 3f out: rdn ent fnl 2f: no prog after* **13/2**[3]

10-0 **7** *1/2* **Hotel Du Cap**[111] 1619 5-9-4 103.................... AlanMunro 4 92
(G Wragg) *t.k.h: in tch: rdn over 3f out: wknd 2f out* **22/1**

0000 **8** *3/4* **Illustrious Blue**[14] 4587 5-9-1 103....................(v) PaulDoe 8 87
(W J Knight) *t.k.h: hld up in midfield: rdn 3f out: wknd 2f out* **8/1**

9 *1/2* **Wild Desert (FR)**[54] 3-8-9 0.................... StephenDonohoe 7 89?
(Ian Williams) *led: racd alone towards nr side fr 8f out: hdd 6f out: rdn and wknd over 2f out* **50/1**

6640 **10** *41* **Only Hope**[80] 1726 4-8-10 41.................... TobyAtkinson 5 —
(P S McEntee) *a in last pair: lost tch 4f out: t.o* **150/1**

-036 **11** *3 1/2* **Little Hotpotch**[14] 4599 4-8-10 38.................... AndreaAtzeni 10 —
(M J Gingell) *a in last pair: lost tch 4f out: t.o* **200/1**

2m 4.19s (-1.31) **Going Correction** +0.075s/f (Good)
WFA 3 from 4yo+ 9lb **11** Ran SP% **117.4**
Speed ratings (Par 109): **108,106,105,105,102 99,99,98,98,65 62**
toteswinger: 1&2 £6.50, 1&3 £7.50, 2&3 £5.70. CSF £27.97 TOTE £6.70: £1.90, £1.80, £2.30; EX 40.00.
Owner Kennet Valley Thoroughbreds Iv **Bred** Epona Bloodstock Ltd **Trained** Middleham Moor, N Yorks

■ Stewards' Enquiry : Paul Doe caution: used whip down shoulder in forehand position
Andrea Atzeni three-day ban: used whip when out of contention (Aug 29-31)

FOCUS
A trappy conditions event as though there was undoubtedly plenty of talent on show, most of the contenders had plenty of question marks hanging over them, not least from a fitness angle. The form has been rated around the winner and third.

NOTEBOOK
Drumfire(IRE) was beaten in a hotch-potch of a race here two weeks ago, but like so many of his yard's representatives is a tough horse to pass when he gets to the front and, though the dangers seemed to be queueing behind him at one point, he was a decisive enough victor in the end. He has obviously had his training problems, but merits another crack at pattern company now. (op 5-1)
Blue Monday was running for the first time since the Spring Carnival in Melbourne last November, when he'd finished a terrific seventh in the Melbourne Cup for David Hayes. Now back with Roger Charlton, this looked like a pipe-opener over an inadequate trip and in the circumstances he ran an encouraging race, travelling like the best horse for a long way but lacking an extra gear at the finish. (op 4-1 tchd 9-2)
Khateeb(IRE) failed to act on the gradients around Goodwood last time but had previously run fourth in the Hampton Court Stakes at Royal Ascot on only his fourth racecourse appearance. Taking on older horses for the first time, he travelled like a good horse, and shouldn't be long in adding to his solitary victory in a Polytrack maiden. (op 11-1 tchd 10-1 in a place)
With Interest travelled well through the race on his hat-trick bid, but found little off the bridle on his first start for almost six months, while those two wins in Dubai came in handicap company. (tchd 9-4 tchd 11-4 in places)
Escape Route(USA) was poorly in at the weights with all the leading contenders and ran about as well as his official rating entitled him to. (tchd 10-1 and 14-1)
Imperial Star(IRE), like his stablemate, was running for the first time since the Dubai Carnival, but will have to come on significantly for this run if he is going to win again as he is too high in the weights to go handicapping. (tchd 6-1 and 8-1)

5071 WALKER TRANSPORT SERVICES FILLIES' H'CAP 7f
8:05 (8:05) (Class 3) (0-95,95) 3-Y-O+ **£9,066** (£2,697; £1,348; £673) **Stalls** High

Form RPR

2032 **1** **The Jostler**[23] 4300 3-8-7 **82**.................... RHills 2 91
(B W Hills) *hld up in tch: swtchd lft and hdwy wl over 1f out: r.o strly to ld last 100yds* **12/1**

2212 **2** *1* **Tableau Vivant (IRE)**[20] 4433 3-8-0 **80**........ Louis-PhilippeBeuzelin[(5)] 6 86
(Sir Michael Stoute) *chsd ldrs: rdn to ld over 1f out: hdd and no ex last 100yds* **7/1**[3]

1 **3** *1 1/4* **Laddies Poker Two (IRE)**[207] 244 3-9-2 **91**.................... TPQueally 13 94+
(J Noseda) *stdd s: t.k.h: hld up bhd: smooth hdwy 2f out: ev ch ent fnl f: sn rdn and fnd little: wnt 3rd last strides* **11/2**[2]

-004 **4** *shd* **Lady Aquitaine (USA)**[20] 4424 3-9-5 **94**.................... SebSanders 8 96
(B J Meehan) *led narrowly: rdn 2f out: hdd over 1f out: kpt on same pce u.p fnl f* **16/1**

1403 **5** *1/2* **Oceana Blue**[20] 4424 3-8-1 **76**....................(t) FrancisNorton 4 77
(A M Balding) *trckd ldrs: rdn and effrt wl over 1f out: unable qck u.p fnl f* **8/1**

2224 **6** *3* **Just Like A Woman**[29] 4110 3-8-4 **79**.................... HayleyTurner 10 72
(M L W Bell) *hld up wl in tch: rdn and unable qck ent fnl 2f: no imp after* **10/3**[1]

0503 **7** *3/4* **Tender The Great (IRE)**[9] 4723 5-8-7 **76** oh5....... RichardKingscote 11 69
(V Smith) *stdd s: t.k.h: hld up in tch: rdn and unable qck 2f out: wl hld fnl f* **16/1**

-400 **8** *1 1/2* **Silca Chiave**[20] 4424 4-9-7 **90**.................... DarryllHolland 7 79
(M R Channon) *stdd s: hld up in tch in rr: edgd lft and brief effrt wl over 1f out: no ch fnl f* **20/1**

233 **9** *1* **Cha Cha Cha**[29] 4110 4-8-13 **82**.................... TedDurcan 9 68
(K A Ryan) *dropped in after s: hld up towards rr: rdn 2f out: no prog: wl hld fnl f* **7/1**[3]

2600 **10** *hd* **Olympic City (BRZ)**[162] 814 5-9-12 **95**.................... KShea 5 81
(M F De Kock, South Africa) *pressed ldr tl 2f out: wknd u.p over 1f out* **14/1**

060 **11** *3* **Gone Fast (USA)**[37] 3849 3-8-9 **84**.................... DaneO'Neill 12 59
(D M Simcock) *hld up in tch in rr: rdn 3f out: no hdwy* **25/1**

-030 **12** *nk* **Falcolnry (IRE)**[27] 4189 3-8-7 **82**.................... EddieAhern 14 57
(J R Fanshawe) *s.i.s: hld up bhd: rdn and no hdwy wl over 2f out* **9/1**

312 **13** *17* **Naughty Frida (IRE)**[56] 3210 3-8-8 **83**.................... JohnEgan 15 12
(M Botti) *tk keeen hold: hld up in tch: rdn and wknd qckly over 2f out: t.o* **9/1**

1m 25.36s (-0.34) **Going Correction** +0.075s/f (Good)
WFA 3 from 4yo+ 6lb **13** Ran SP% **129.3**
Speed ratings (Par 104): **104,102,101,101,100 97,96,94,93,93 89,89,70**
toteswinger: 1&2 £21.00, 1&3 £24.80, 2&3 £18.70. CSF £101.42 CT £552.79 TOTE £14.10: £3.30, £3.40, £2.80; EX 148.80 Place 6 £ 208.63, Place 5 £ 61.64.
Owner Burton Agnes Bloodstock **Bred** Burton Agnes Stud Co Ltd **Trained** Lambourn, Berks

FOCUS
This was a very useful handicap, with many of the contenders coming into the race with consistently good recent form to their names. It was run in a slightly quicker time than the opening maiden and three-year-olds dominated. The form makes sense with the winner up 9lb.

NOTEBOOK
The Jostler has been rising in the handicap without winning this year but under a well-timed ride from Hills gained due reward for her consistency. She is a real specialist at this trip and seems to go better on a straight course. (tchd 11-1)
Tableau Vivant(IRE), a lightly raced daughter of Pivotal, went to Folkestone to win her maiden and consequently started off in handicaps off a decent mark. She has now been runner-up on both starts in the grade, and it should only be a matter of time before she goes one better. (op 8-1 tchd 10-1)
Laddies Poker Two(IRE) ◆, a grey daughter of Choisir, didn't see the racecourse at two, making a winning debut over this distance on Polytrack back in January, but has obviously had further problems as this was her first outing since. This was a very stiff mark to overcome on only her second start, and the way she travelled throughout the race marks her down as a very useful sort, even though lack of a recent spin told close home. If connections can manage her obvious fragility, she can be found lots of winning opportunities. (op 7-2 tchd 11-4)
Lady Aquitaine(USA) ran well in the very top two-year-old company last year and while she hasn't progressed well enough to still be competing in pattern/listed company, she is prohibitively handicapped as a result, and this was a brave effort.
Oceana Blue is consistent but quite exposed now and she needs to find improvement from somewhere to overcome her mark. (tchd 9-1 in a place)
Just Like A Woman has crept up the handicap without adding to her solitary success in a Catterick maiden last back-end. (op 5-1 tchd 11-2)
Cha Cha Cha Official explanation: jockey said filly had no more to give
T/Jkpt: Not won. T/Plt: £426.80 to a £1 stake. Pool: £66,302.67. 113.40 winning tickets. T/Qpdt: £21.00 to a £1 stake. Pool: £5,884.50. 206.60 winning tickets. SP

4953 NOTTINGHAM (L-H)
Friday, August 15

OFFICIAL GOING: Good (7.4)
Wind: Light against Weather: Sunny

5072 PADDOCKS CONFERENCE CENTRE @NOTTINGHAM RACECOURSE MAIDEN STKS 6f 15y
2:00 (2:00) (Class 5) 2-Y-O **£3,238** (£963; £481; £240) **Stalls** High

Form RPR

3 **1** **Satwa Laird**[18] 4480 2-9-3 0.................... TedDurcan 7 82+
(E A L Dunlop) *trckd ldrs: led over 1f out: shkn up and r.o wl: eased nr fin* **1/1**[1]

43 **2** *4 1/2* **Lookafternumberone (IRE)**[72] 2730 2-9-3 0.................... TPQueally 3 66
(J G Given) *prom: chsd ldr 1/2-way: led 2f out: sn rdn and hdd: no ex fnl f* **11/2**[2]

3 *3/4* **Sensacion Sensual** 2-8-12 0.................... PatCosgrave 4 58+
(J G Given) *s.s: bhd: hdwy over 1f out: sn rdn and hung lft: styd on same pce fnl f* **28/1**

0 **4** *3 1/2* **Feeling Stylish (IRE)**[21] 4394 2-8-12 0.................... KimTinkler 9 48
(N Tinkler) *racd keenly: trckd ldr to 1/2-way: sn rdn: hung lft and wknd over 1f out* **80/1**

5 *hd* **Scottish Affair** 2-9-3 0.................... NeilPollard 5 52
(E A L Dunlop) *hld up: rdn over 1f out: n.d* **14/1**

200 **6** *1/2* **Black Attack (IRE)**[45] 3590 2-9-3 72.................... PaulQuinn 6 51
(Paul Green) *trckd ldrs: racd keenly: rdn over 1f out: sn wknd* **13/2**[3]

60 **7** *nk* **Coniston Wood**[18] [4474] 2-8-12 0 .... PaulMulrennan 10 45
(M W Easterby) *led 4f: sn rdn and edgd lft: wknd fnl f* **22/1**
8 *1* **Roar Of Applause** 2-9-3 0 .... EddieAhern 8 47
(B J Meehan) *s.s: a in rr* **8/1**
4 **9** *½* **Svindal (IRE)**[100] [1907] 2-9-3 0 .... FergalLynch 2 45
(K A Ryan) *prom: rdn 1/2-way: wknd over 1f out* **11/1**
1m 15.93s (0.83) **Going Correction** -0.025s/f (Good) **9** Ran SP% **113.9**
Speed ratings (Par 94): **93,87,86,81,81 80,80,78,78**
toteswinger: 1&2 £2.50, 1&3 £6.10, 2&3 £9.80. CSF £6.39 TOTE £1.90: £1.60, £1.10, £7.10; EX 4.70.
Owner The Lamprell Partnership **Bred** The Policy Setters **Trained** Newmarket, Suffolk

FOCUS
An uncompetitive maiden, won readily by Satwa Laird who has more to offer. The placed horses set the standard.

NOTEBOOK
Satwa Laird, who had shaped well on his debut last time, found the expected improvement from his first effort to see off this bunch with the minimum of fuss. He should certainly be able to hold his own in better company. (op 5-6 tchd 4-5)
Lookafternumberone(IRE), not beaten far on soft ground at Ripon last time, was no match for the winner but ran well enough to suggest he can his win something, possibly a nursery for which he is now eligible. (tchd 5-1 and 6-1)
Sensacion Sensual was a little inexperienced on her debut, but the penny was dropping for her late on as she ran on well for pressure. She showed obvious signs of greenness and will undoubtedly be better for the run. (op 33-1)
Feeling Stylish(IRE) showed more than she did when well beaten at York on her debut, but was inclined to hang left and could not sustain her challenge late on. Official explanation: jockey said filly hung left throughout (op 66-1)
Black Attack(IRE) had been very disappointing on fast ground on his last two starts, and again failed to build on the promise of his debut second at Ripon in June. (op 7-1 tchd 15-2)
Coniston Wood Official explanation: jockey said filly hung left
Svindal(IRE) Official explanation: jockey said gelding hung left

5073 KELLY MASON WALKER 30TH BIRTHDAY FILLIES' H'CAP 6f 15y
2:35 (2:36) (Class 4) (0-80,78) 3-Y-0+ **£5,180** (£1,541; £770; £384) **Stalls** High

Form RPR
5521 **1** **Quaroma**[25] [4258] 3-9-7 78 .... JohnEgan 2 96
(Jane Chapple-Hyam) *chsd ldr tl led 2f out: rdn clr fnl f: eased nr fin* **5/2**[1]
4416 **2** *4 ½* **Badweia (USA)**[37] [3849] 3-9-6 77 .... TedDurcan 6 81
(J L Dunlop) *chsd ldrs: rdn over 2f out: sn edgd lft: wnt 2nd ins fnl f: no ch w wnr* **5/2**[1]
2401 **3** *¾* **Overwing (IRE)**[8] [4779] 5-9-6 73 6ex .... EddieAhern 4 75
(R M H Cowell) *hmpd s: sn led: rdn and hdd 2f out: edgd lft: styd on same pce fnl f* **12/1**
1050 **4** *¾* **Savannah Poppy (IRE)**[63] [3000] 3-9-4 75 .... HayleyTurner 3 74
(M L W Bell) *s.i.s and hmpd s: heled up: plld hrd: hdwy and nt clr run ins fnl f: hung rt: nt rch ldrs* **15/2**[3]
5015 **5** *2 ½* **Tilsworth Charlie**[8] [4779] 5-8-12 65 .... (b) AdrianMcCarthy 5 56
(J R Jenkins) *wnt lft s: chsd ldrs: rdn over 1f out: wknd fnl f* **25/1**
5014 **6** *hd* **Scarlet Oak**[21] [4393] 4-8-11 64 .... (p) JoeFanning 1 55
(D J S Ffrench Davis) *hld up: hdwy to chse wnr over 1f out: sn rdn: wknd ins fnl f* **10/3**[2]
00 **7** *3 ¼* **Jilly Why (IRE)**[20] [4407] 7-9-11 78 .... (b) PaulMulrennan 7 58
(Paul Green) *chsd ldrs: rdn over 2f out: wknd over 1f out* **16/1**
1m 14.47s (-0.63) **Going Correction** -0.025s/f (Good)
WFA 3 from 4yo+ 4lb **7** Ran SP% **109.4**
Speed ratings (Par 102): **103,97,96,95,91 91,87**
toteswinger: 1&2 £2.00, 1&3 £2.80, 2&3 £3.90. CSF £8.02 TOTE £2.80: £1.90, £1.80; EX 8.80.
Owner Elite Sports Organisation **Bred** Lady Fairhaven **Trained** Lambourn, Berks

FOCUS
A fair-looking fillies' sprint run at a sensible pace. The first two are progressive.

5074 PADDOCKS CONFERENCE CENTRE 0870 8507635 H'CAP 5f 13y
3:10 (3:11) (Class 6) (0-55,58) 3-Y-0+ **£2,047** (£604; £302) **Stalls** High

Form RPR
0020 **1** **Tyrannosaurus Rex (IRE)**[18] [4478] 4-9-2 55 .... FrancisNorton 2 66
(D Shaw) *racd far side: chsd ldrs: led that gp over 1f out: rdn clr* **5/1**[2]
0000 **2** *2* **Mr Forthright**[22] [4324] 4-8-8 47 oh1 ow1 .... (b[1]) TedDurcan 4 51
(J M Bradley) *racd far side: hld up: hdwy over 1f out: chsd wnr ins fnl f: r.o: 2nd of 7 in gp* **50/1**
0000 **3** *1 ¾* **Lithaam (IRE)**[7] [4812] 4-8-12 54 .... (p) TravisBlock(3) 9 52
(J M Bradley) *racd stands' side: chsd ldr: rdn and hung lft fr over 1f out: led that gp ins fnl f: styd on: 1st of 8 in gp* **16/1**
6220 **4** *nk* **Music Box Express**[8] [4765] 4-8-6 52 .... (t) MatthewDavies(7) 11 48
(George Baker) *led stands' side: rdn and hung lft fr over 1f out: hdd and unable qck ins fnl f: 2nd of 8 in gp* **7/1**[3]
0050 **5** *1 ¾* **Mollyatti**[2] [4988] 3-8-11 53 .... MatthewHenry 3 42
(Miss V Haigh) *racd far side: hld up: hdwy over 1f out: nt rch ldrs: 3rd of 7 in gp* **16/1**
6106 **6** *1* **Town House**[24] [4285] 6-8-13 52 .... HayleyTurner 8 39
(B P J Baugh) *overall ldr far side tl hdd over 1f out: no ex: 4th of 7 in gp* **14/1**
0200 **7** *1* **Violet's Pride**[10] [4703] 4-8-7 46 oh1 .... KimTinkler 16 29+
(N Tinkler) *racd stands' side: chsd ldrs: rdn and hung lft fnl 2f: styd on same pce: sddle slipped: 3rd of 8 in gp* **14/1**
0500 **8** *1 ¾* **Northern Boy (USA)**[18] [4476] 5-9-2 55 .... TPQueally 5 32
(M W Easterby) *racd far side: hld up: hdwy 1/2-way: sn rdn and hung rt: wknd over 1f out: 5th of 7 in gp* **14/1**
0501 **9** *¾* **Guto**[10] [4703] 5-9-0 58 6ex .... KellyHarrison(5) 6 32
(W J H Ratcliffe) *racd far side: chsd ldr: rdn 1/2-way: edgd rt over 1f out: sn wknd: 6th of 7 in gp* **4/1**[1]
0605 **10** *1 ¾* **Sandy Par**[14] [4584] 3-8-4 49 .... (p) KirstyMilczarek(3) 12 16
(J M Bradley) *racd stands' side: chsd ldrs: rdn 1/2-way: wkng whn carried lft 2f out: 4th of 8 in gp* **40/1**
040 **11** *1 ¼* **Monte Major (IRE)**[31] [4047] 7-8-10 49 .... (v) TonyCulhane 14 12+
(D Shaw) *racd stands' side: hld up: hmpd 2f out: eased: 5th of 8 in gp* **9/1**
0306 **12** *½* **Dubai To Barnsley**[13] [4615] 3-8-6 48 .... NickyMackay 7 8
(Garry Moss) *racd far side: chsd ldrs: rdn 1/2-way: wknd over 1f out: eased: last of 7 in gp* **11/1**
0605 **13** *2 ¼* **Jucebabe**[7] [4812] 5-8-10 52 .... (p) TolleyDean(3) 13 5
(J L Spearing) *racd stands' side: s.i.s: sn pushed along in rr: wknd 1/2-way: 6th of 8 in gp* **9/1**
604 **14** *1 ¾* **Sosostris Pitch (FR)**[38] [3818] 3-8-13 55 .... (bt) PaulMulrennan 10 —
(P C Haslam) *racd stands' side: dwlt: hld up: a in rr: 7th of 8 in gp* **18/1**
0360 **15** *13* **Jastaanhi**[27] [917] 3-8-13 55 .... VinceSlattery 15 —
(B N Pollock) *racd stands' side: chsd ldrs to 1/2-way: last of 8 in gp* **66/1**
60.36 secs (-0.34) **Going Correction** -0.025s/f (Good)
WFA 3 from 4yo+ 3lb **15** Ran SP% **120.4**
Speed ratings (Par 101): **101,97,95,94,91 90,88,85,84,81 79,78,75,72,51**
toteswinger: 1&2 £36.90, 1&3 £26.70, 2&3 £77.70. CSF £242.92 CT £3797.61 TOTE £7.10: £3.00, £8.90, £7.90; EX 258.50.
Owner Market Avenue Racing Club Ltd **Bred** Limestone And Tara Studs **Trained** Danethorpe, Notts

FOCUS
A low-grade sprint, where the far-side had a definite advantage. The form has been rated through the winner.
Violet's Pride Official explanation: jockey said saddle slipped
Guto Official explanation: jockey said gelding hung right
Monte Major(IRE) Official explanation: jockey said gelding suffered interference in running

5075 RACING UK ON CHANNEL 432 FILLIES' H'CAP 1m 2f 50y
3:45 (3:45) (Class 4) (0-85,82) 3-Y-0 **£6,476** (£1,927; £963; £481) **Stalls** Low

Form RPR
-401 **1** **Quirina**[42] [3672] 3-9-7 82 .... TedDurcan 1 89+
(J H M Gosden) *chsd ldr 2f: remained handy: rdn to chse ldr over 1f out: r.o u.p to ld wl ins fnl f* **7/2**[3]
2154 **2** *1* **Black Dahlia**[14] [4596] 3-8-12 73 .... PatCosgrave 3 78
(A J McCabe) *led: shkn up over 1f out: hrd rdn and hdd wl ins fnl f* **9/2**
6311 **3** *3* **Snowdrop Princess**[15] [4572] 3-8-12 76 .... (b) KirstyMilczarek(3) 6 75
(W J Haggas) *s.i.s: hld up: plld hrd: hdwy over 2f out: rdn over 1f out: styd on same pce* **2/1**[1]
2112 **4** *1 ¼* **Amicable Terms**[14] [4607] 3-9-0 80 .... WilliamCarson(5) 2 77
(Rae Guest) *chsd ldr 8f out: rdn over 1f out: no ex ins fnl f* **3/1**[2]
1-0 **5** *5* **Maryqueenofscots (IRE)**[16] [4520] 3-9-4 79 .... HayleyTurner 7 67
(M L W Bell) *dwlt: hld up: rdn over 3f out: n.d* **20/1**
00 **6** *13* **Really Ransom**[20] [4435] 3-9-7 82 .... (b) PaulMulrennan 5 45
(P C Haslam) *hld up in tch: plld hrd: rdn and wknd 3f out* **25/1**
2m 10.32s (-2.18) **Going Correction** -0.225s/f (Firm) **6** Ran SP% **107.3**
Speed ratings (Par 99): **99,98,95,94,90 80**
toteswinger: 1&2 £3.20, 1&3 £2.30, 2&3 £2.40. CSF £17.51 TOTE £4.10: £2.10, £2.30; EX 19.70.
Owner Dr Ornella Carlini Cozzi **Bred** Dr Ornella Cozzi Carlini **Trained** Newmarket, Suffolk
■ Stewards' Enquiry : Kirsty Milczarek two-day ban: careless riding (Aug 29-30)

FOCUS
A decent fillies' handicap but the form is a bit muddling with the runner-up granted an easy lead. The winner is progressing nicely and can win again.
Really Ransom Official explanation: jockey said filly had no more to give

5076 THEPADDOCKSNOTTINGHAM.CO.UK MAIDEN STKS 1m 75y
4:15 (4:16) (Class 5) 3-Y-0 **£3,238** (£963; £481; £240) **Stalls** Centre

Form RPR
1 **Summer's Lease** 3-8-12 0 .... HayleyTurner 6 82
(M L W Bell) *s.s: hld up: hdwy over 2f out: rdn to ld wl ins fnl f* **16/1**
042 **2** *1 ½* **Mohathab (IRE)**[56] [3205] 3-9-3 83 .... SebSanders 3 84
(J H M Gosden) *chsd ldrs: led over 1f out: rdn and hdd wl ins fnl f* **10/11**[1]
35- **3** *3 ¼* **Pragmatism**[293] [6493] 3-9-3 0 .... JoeFanning 2 77
(M Johnston) *led 1f: chsd ldr tl led over 2f out: rdn and hdd over 1f out: no ex* **6/1**[3]
3 **4** *2 ¼* **Pivka**[9] [4730] 3-8-12 0 .... TedDurcan 7 66
(Sir Michael Stoute) *hld up: plld hrd: hdwy u.p over 2f out: wknd fnl f* **9/4**[2]
5 **5** *2 ¼* **Gaelic Dancer (IRE)**[9] [4730] 3-9-3 0 .... TPQueally 1 66
(J G Given) *led after 1f: hdd over 2f out: sn rdn: wknd fnl f* **12/1**
6 *5* **Yetholm (USA)** 3-9-0 0 .... TravisBlock(3) 8 55
(J R Fanshawe) *rn green in rr: sn pushed along: hung lft and wknd 2f out* **28/1**
00 **7** *1 ¼* **La Rochette**[23] [4302] 3-8-12 0 .... AdrianMcCarthy 3 47
(P W Chapple-Hyam) *chsd ldrs: rdn over 3f out: wknd over 2f out* **50/1**
8 *5* **Curly Brown** 3-9-3 0 .... MickyFenton 4 40
(A Bailey) *s.s: hld up: rdn over 3f out: sn wknd* **100/1**
1m 44.29s (-1.11) **Going Correction** -0.225s/f (Firm) **8** Ran SP% **117.4**
Speed ratings (Par 100): **96,94,91,89,86 81,80,75**
toteswinger: 1&2 £5.10, 1&3 £8.10, 2&3 £2.40. CSF £32.16 TOTE £18.90: £3.10, £1.10, £1.90; EX 44.90.
Owner Mrs C R Philipson & Mrs H G Lascelles **Bred** Mrs C R Philipson & Mrs H G Lascelles **Trained** Newmarket, Suffolk

FOCUS
An ordinary maiden overall although the runner-up set a fair standard for the time of year and is rated to form.

5077 RACINGUK.TV H'CAP 1m 6f 15y
4:45 (4:45) (Class 6) (0-60,60) 3-Y-0 **£1,942** (£578; £288; £144) **Stalls** Low

Form RPR
0-63 **1** **Hawk Mountain (UAE)**[46] [3555] 3-8-9 51 .... GrahamGibbons 2 70+
(J J Quinn) *hld up in tch: rdn to ld wl over 1f out: styd on strly: eased wl ins fnl f* **3/1**[2]
-065 **2** *7* **Miss Cruisecontrol**[1] [5003] 3-8-2 49 oh1 ow3 .... KellyHarrison(5) 8 52
(J R Best) *s.i.s: hld up: hdwy over 2f out: rdn over 1f out: sn hung lft: styd on same pce* **16/1**
3-03 **3** *nk* **Bruki (IRE)**[8] [4796] 3-9-1 60 .... (bt[1]) JerryO'Dwyer(3) 6 63
(M Botti) *hld up: hmpd 3f out: hdwy u.p and hung lft over 1f out: nt trble ldrs* **10/1**
6200 **4** *¾* **Miss Mactango**[42] [3671] 3-8-5 50 .... KirstyMilczarek(3) 9 52
(W M Brisbourne) *prom: outpcd over 5f out: hdwy u.p over 2f out: rdr dropped whip over 1f out: hung lft and no ex fnl f* **25/1**
0030 **5** *1* **Miss Serena**[30] [4077] 3-9-1 57 .... MickyFenton 7 57
(Mrs P Sly) *hld up: hdwy u.p over 2f out: no ex fnl f* **14/1**
5420 **6** *shd* **Smetana**[42] [3671] 3-8-9 54 .... TravisBlock(3) 3 54
(H Morrison) *prom: rdn over 2f out: no ex fnl f* **6/1**[3]
0635 **7** *3 ¾* **Amwell House**[15] [4564] 3-8-6 48 .... AdrianMcCarthy 10 43
(J R Jenkins) *hld up: hdwy 3f out: sn rdn: wknd wl over 1f out* **14/1**
0026 **8** *2* **Kijivu**[27] [3562] 3-8-1 50 .... SophieDoyle(7) 4 42
(A J Lidderdale) *chsd ldr: rdn over 3f out: wknd wl over 1f out* **16/1**
-441 **9** *6* **China Pink**[8] [4796] 3-9-1 57 6ex .... (b[1]) SebSanders 12 41
(Sir Mark Prescott) *trckd ldrs: racd keenly: led 6f out: rdn and hdd wl over 1f out: sn wknd* **5/2**[1]
-004 **10** *24* **Light Sea (IRE)**[15] [4564] 3-9-2 58 .... TonyCulhane 1 8
(M R Channon) *led 8f: rdn and wknd over 2f out* **12/1**
0000 **11** *23* **Tank Commander**[24] [4281] 3-8-8 50 .... HayleyTurner 5 —
(W R Muir) *prom: rdn over 3f out: sn wknd* **33/1**
0000 **12** *nse* **Snake Catcher**[9] [4738] 3-8-1 46 oh1 .... AndrewMullen(3) 13 —
(M W Easterby) *hld up: rdn over 6f out: bhd fnl 4f* **66/1**

 The Form Book, Raceform Ltd, Compton, RG20 6NL

5050 **13** *36* **Princess Raya**[15] 4564 3-8-10 52....................(bt[1]) NeilPollard 11 —
(M E Rimmer) *mid-div: lost pl 6f out: bhd fnl 4f* **40/1**

3m 2.23s (-5.07) **Going Correction** -0.225s/f (Firm) **13** Ran SP% **120.5**
Speed ratings (Par 98): **105,101,100,100,99 99,97,96,93,79 66,66,45**
toteswinger: 1&2 £17.50, 1&3 £6.40, 2&3 £29.30. CSF £49.59 CT £440.01 TOTE £5.50: £1.80, £6.90, £2.70; EX 103.80 Place 6: £103.15, Place 5: £72.42..
Owner P Morrison & N Luck **Bred** Darley **Trained** Settrington, N Yorks
■ Stewards' Enquiry : Graham Gibbons one-day ban: careless riding (Aug 29)

FOCUS
A weak handicap that produced an easy winner in the improved Hawk Mountain. The form does look moderate, however.
T/Plt: £99.50 to a £1 stake. Pool: £50,385.06. 369.42 winning tickets. T/Qpdt: £67.80 to a £1 stake. Pool: £4,292.00. 46.80 winning tickets. CR

5078 - 5085a (Foreign Racing) - See Raceform Interactive

4941 LINGFIELD (L-H)
Saturday, August 16

OFFICIAL GOING: Turf course - good to soft (good in places; 7.0); all-weather - standard
Wind: Moderate, behind

5086 FOREST ROW CLAIMING STKS 1m (P)
5:30 (5:30) (Class 6) 3-Y-O £1,978 (£584; £292) **Stalls** High

Form RPR
4606 **1** **La Columbina**[13] 4669 3-8-11 73....................(v[1]) HaddenFrost(5) 9 70
(R Hannon) *hld up: hdwy on outside over 3f out: led jst ins fnl f: sn clr: easily* **2/1**[1]
0030 **2** *4 1/2* **Mrs Jefferson (IRE)**[25] 4278 3-8-8 60.................... PatCosgrave 10 52
(J G Portman) *a.p on outside: led ent fnl f: sn hdd: nt pce of wnr* **10/1**
-400 **3** *nk* **Royal Straight**[22] 4390 3-9-1 68.................... LPKeniry 1 58+
(A M Balding) *s.i.s: racd on ins: short of room over 3f out: swtchd rt wl over 1f out: r.o to take 3rd ins fnl f* **4/1**[3]
0-00 **4** *1 3/4* **Ryan's Rock**[5] 4929 3-8-6 45.................... TolleyDean(3) 5 48
(T D McCarthy) *trckd ldr: led over 3f out: rdn and hdd ent fnl f: wknd* **50/1**
6000 **5** *1/2* **Afram Blue**[10] 4731 3-9-7 73....................(t) PaulDoe 11 59
(W J Knight) *in rr: hdwy on outside over 3f out but nvr pce to chal after* **3/1**[2]
5056 **6** *1 1/4* **Looter (FR)**[8] 4807 3-8-7 51....................(v[1]) StephenCarson 6 42
(J L Dunlop) *led after 1f: hdd over 3f out: chsd ldr tl wknd appr fnl f* **17/2**
7 *3/4* **Diktat Tempo** 3-8-12 0....................(p) RichardThomas 12 45
(I A Wood) *a towards rr* **40/1**
0000 **8** *1 3/4* **Bobster**[16] 4572 3-8-4 48.................... NickyMackay 2 33
(B R Millman) *prom tl rdn and wknd over 1f out* **50/1**
2500 **9** *1* **What's For Tea**[13] 4664 3-9-2 60....................(p) IanMongan 7 43
(P Butler) *chsd ldrs: rdn 3f out: wknd 2f out* **16/1**
03 **10** *3* **Telephonist**[21] 4412 3-8-12 0.................... ShaneKelly 4 32
(Norma Twomey) *led for 1f: wknd 2f out* **16/1**
0-60 **11** *1* **Starfinch**[31] 4083 3-8-3 44.................... MarcHalford(3) 8 24
(J J Bridger) *a in rr* **33/1**
0400 **12** *6* **Yes Eighteen (IRE)**[10] 4727 3-9-7 62....................(p) ChrisCatlin 3 25
(J W Hills) *towards rr: rdn over 3f out: sn lost tch* **16/1**

1m 37.92s (-0.28) **Going Correction** -0.075s/f (Stan) **12** Ran SP% **124.9**
Speed ratings (Par 98): **98,93,93,91,90 89,88,87,86,83 82,76**
toteswinger: 1&2 £23.40, 1&3 £1.70, 2&3 £5.80. CSF £24.98 TOTE £3.60: £2.00, £3.40, £1.80; EX 29.40.Royal Straight was claimed by B. Pollock for £9,000.
Owner Raymond Tooth **Bred** P And Mrs A G Venner **Trained** East Everleigh, Wilts

FOCUS
Mostly moderate sorts on show in this claimer and the winner had the best chance on official ratings. The bare form is limited.

5087 COWDEN H'CAP 1m 2f (P)
6:00 (6:02) (Class 6) (0-62,62) 3-Y-O+ £2,047 (£604; £302) **Stalls** Low

Form RPR
215 **1** **Action Impact (ARG)**[8] 4819 4-9-5 57.................... GeorgeBaker 11 71+
(G L Moore) *in tch on outside: gd hdwy on outside into 2nd over 2f out: led ins fnl f: rdn clr* **9/4**[1]
5054 **2** *3* **Magic Warrior**[41] 3764 8-9-7 58.................... LPKeniry 6 66
(J C Fox) *towards rr: hdwy 3f out: r.o to go 2nd ins fnl f* **20/1**
5661 **3** *1/2* **Tabulate**[28] 4182 5-9-8 59.................... IanMongan 8 68+
(P Howling) *mid-div on ins: nt clr run over 3f out: hdwy and rdn over 1f out: r.o to go 3rd ins fnl f: nvr nrr* **16/1**
04 **4** *hd* **Old Romney**[67] 2908 4-9-7 58.................... NickyMackay 5 64
(M Wigham) *led tl rdn and hdd ins fnl f: no ex towards fin* **11/4**[2]
2052 **5** *nse* **Kings Topic (USA)**[25] 4267 8-9-7 58....................(p) PatCosgrave 12 64
(A B Haynes) *trckd ldr tl rdn and wknd ent fnl f* **8/1**[3]
030 **6** *1 3/4* **Garafena**[27] 3631 5-9-5 61.................... HaddenFrost(5) 10 64
(B G Powell) *prom on outside: no hdwy ins fnl 2f* **33/1**
0130 **7** *1 1/4* **Prince Charlemagne (IRE)**[23] 4343 5-9-7 61..........(b) TravisBlock(3) 9 61
(R M Stronge) *in rr: rdn over 2f out: nvr on terms* **12/1**
1050 **8** *3/4* **Ramprakash**[23] 4344 3-9-0 62.................... MarcHalford(3) 4 61
(M L W Bell) *chsd ldrs: rdn over 2f out: no hdwy after* **25/1**
0035 **9** *shd* **Formidable Guest**[14] 4635 4-9-2 53.................... ChrisCatlin 14 51
(J Pearce) *mid-div on ins tl effrt over 2f out: sn btn* **12/1**
4000 **10** *5* **The Flying Cowboy (IRE)**[61] 3089 4-9-9 60.......... FrankieMcDonald 13 48
(Jane Chapple-Hyam) *a in rr* **40/1**
662 **11** *8* **Ceili Mor (IRE)**[22] 4378 3-8-13 58.................... GregFairley 7 30
(M Johnston) *in tch: rdn 1/2-way: sn btn* **11/1**
5000 **12** *4 1/2* **Better In Heaven**[17] 4524 3-8-13 58....................(b[1]) MickyFenton 1 21
(H J L Dunlop) *slowly away: a bhd* **33/1**
0-03 **13** *1 1/2* **Beauchamp Warrior**[20] 4455 3-9-2 61.................... ShaneKelly 3 21
(G A Butler) *trckd ldrs tl rdn and wknd 2f out: eased fnl f* **16/1**
000- **14** *17* **Spartan Dance**[388] 3848 4-9-3 54.................... DavidKinsella 2 —
(J A Geake) *stdd s: t.k.h: rdn 4f out: sn struggling in rr* **66/1**

2m 5.51s (-1.09) **Going Correction** -0.075s/f (Stan)
WFA 3 from 4yo+ 8lb **14** Ran SP% **122.5**
Speed ratings (Par 101): **101,98,98,98,98 96,95,95,94,90 84,80,79,66**
toteswinger: 1&2 £12.40, 1&3 £49.70, 2&3 £49.70. CSF £57.56 CT £615.10 TOTE £3.50: £1.80, £5.20, £4.60; EX 69.60.
Owner T Bowley **Bred** Santa Maria De Araras **Trained** Woodingdean, E Sussex

FOCUS
A modest handicap won in good style by a horse who is probably still acclimatising to this country and likely has more improvement in him.

5088 BEN MILLS H'CAP 7f 140y
6:30 (6:32) (Class 6) (0-65,74) 3-Y-O+ £2,047 (£604; £302) **Stalls** Centre

Form RPR
2431 **1** **Stand In Flames**[7] 4863 3-10-2 74.................... ShaneKelly 3 84
(Pat Eddery) *sn trckd ldr: led over 2f out: 3 l clr ent fnl f: stride shortened and jst hld on* **5/2**[2]
065 **2** *nk* **Hits Only Cash**[19] 4489 6-9-8 60....................(p) ChrisCatlin 7 70
(J Pearce) *in rr: reminders 1/2-way: swtchd lft over 1f out: str run to press wnr towards fin* **14/1**
2661 **3** *2 1/4* **Castano**[3] 4979 4-9-4 59....................(p) JamesMillman(3) 12 63
(B R Millman) *in tch: chsd wnr 2f out tl one pce towards fin* **9/4**[1]
21 **4** *nse* **Anthill**[10] 4727 4-9-13 65.................... GeorgeBaker 5 69
(I A Wood) *t.k.h: nvr far away: rdn over 1f out: one pce after* **9/2**[3]
501 **5** *2 1/2* **Romany Nights (IRE)**[10] 4746 8-9-6 65..........(bt) AntiocoMurgia(7) 13 63
(Miss Gay Kelleway) *hld up: hdwy over 2f out: kpt on but nvr nr to chal* **14/1**
646 **6** *1 1/2* **Khazina (USA)**[14] 4637 3-9-4 62....................(b[1]) AlanMunro 1 55
(C E Brittain) *prom on outside: rdn over 1f out: wknd fnl f* **14/1**
0000 **7** *1/2* **Zazous**[8] 4824 7-8-9 50.................... MarcHalford(3) 14 43
(J J Bridger) *towards rr: effrt 2f out: one pce after* **25/1**
0020 **8** *1 3/4* **Charlie Bear**[163] 693 7-8-9 50.................... KevinGhunowa(3) 2 39
(Miss Z C Davison) *chsd ldrs: rdn over 2f out: wknd appr fnl f* **33/1**
0550 **9** *2 3/4* **Contented (IRE)**[21] 4414 6-9-3 55....................(p) FrankieMcDonald 4 37
(Mrs L C Jewell) *hld up in tch: rdn and wknd 2f out* **22/1**
2200 **10** *6* **Tenancy (IRE)**[12] 4683 4-8-12 50....................(e) GregFairley 11 17
(R C Guest) *led to over 2f out: wknd qckly* **20/1**
6004 **11** *6* **Annes Rocket (IRE)**[25] 4278 3-9-1 59.................... PatDobbs 10 10
(J C Fox) *a bhd* **20/1**
4244 **12** *6* **Grizedale (IRE)**[10] 4727 9-9-0 55....................(t) TolleyDean(3) 6 —
(M J Attwater) *a bhd* **16/1**

1m 31.82s (-0.48) **Going Correction** +0.025s/f (Good)
WFA 3 from 4yo+ 6lb **12** Ran SP% **124.1**
Speed ratings (Par 101): **103,102,100,100,97 96,95,94,91,85 79,73**
toteswinger: 1&2 £11.10, 1&3 £2.20, 2&3 £8.50. CSF £35.94 CT £95.13 TOTE £4.30: £1.80, £2.50, £1.50; EX 39.40.
Owner Chris Hardy **Bred** Chris E Hardy **Trained** Nether Winchendon, Bucks

FOCUS
A decent handicap for the grade and the winner was continuing a fine run of form that has seen her mark rise from one of 60 to 74 this year. Her next rise could be a stopper though.
Tenancy(IRE) Official explanation: jockey said gelding ran too free
Annes Rocket(IRE) Official explanation: jockey said colt moved poorly behind

5089 INTRODUCING MRS CLAIR MCGARRY MAIDEN STKS 6f
7:00 (7:00) (Class 5) 2-Y-O £2,590 (£770; £385; £192) **Stalls** High

Form RPR
52 **1** **Spanish Baron (USA)**[15] 4598 2-9-3 0....................(t) EddieAhern 3 77+
(R M H Cowell) *s.i.s but led after 1f: rdn and kpt on gamely ins fnl f* **1/1**[1]
06 **2** *hd* **Norfolk Broads (IRE)**[64] 3005 2-8-12 0.................... GregFairley 1 71+
(M Johnston) *wnt 2nd after 1f: rdn over 2f out: kpt on to press wnr thrght fnl f* **6/1**[3]
3 *4* **Montmorency (IRE)** 2-9-3 0.................... ChrisCatlin 2 64+
(Saeed Bin Suroor) *w.w in 3rd: shkn up to chal over 1f out: fnd nil and wknd ins fnl f* **6/4**[2]
05 **4** *6* **Itainteasybeingme**[9] 4778 2-8-10 0.................... HarryPoulton(7) 4 46
(J R Boyle) *led for 1f: rdn and lost tch 2f out* **20/1**

1m 12.16s (0.96) **Going Correction** +0.025s/f (Good) **4** Ran SP% **109.0**
Speed ratings (Par 94): **94,93,88,80**
CSF £7.16 TOTE £2.00; EX 6.40.
Owner Atlantic Thoroughbreds **Bred** Fran Stolich **Trained** Six Mile Bottom, Cambs
■ Stewards' Enquiry : Eddie Ahern one-day ban: used whip with excessive frequency (Aug 30)

FOCUS
A three-runner race to all intents and purposes and the market got it right with the favourites flip-flopping beforehand.

NOTEBOOK
Spanish Baron(USA) chased home a hot-pot at Newmarket last time and recovered from a tardy start here to make most of the running. His future is in nurseries and much will depend on how the Handicapper reacts to this. (op 11-8)
Norfolk Broads(IRE) made the winner fight hard. She was returning from a break and is qualified for a handicap mark after this improved effort. (op 9-2)
Montmorency(IRE), a 210,000gns breeze-up purchase, was the first of the three principals beaten and even accounting for the fact that this year's crop of Godolphin's juveniles have been in need of their first runs, on this evidence the son of Pivotal will have difficulty in living up to his price tag. (tchd 15-8)
Itainteasybeingme was predictably outclassed. (op 12-1)

5090 DARREN & JADE WEDDING CELEBRATION (S) STKS 6f
7:30 (7:30) (Class 6) 3-Y-O+ £2,047 (£604; £302) **Stalls** High

Form RPR
150 **1** **Game Lady**[15] 4580 4-9-1 51.................... CatherineGannon 6 61
(I A Wood) *a.p: led 1/2-way: drvn clr fnl f* **11/1**
2001 **2** *1 1/4* **Exit Strategy (IRE)**[14] 4639 4-9-3 56....................(b) KevinGhunowa(3) 1 62
(R A Harris) *wnt lft s but sn in tch: chsd wnr 2f out: no imp fnl f* **7/2**[2]
5066 **3** *1/2* **Lady Fas (IRE)**[9] 4779 5-8-3 44.................... StacyRenwick(7) 8 50
(A W Carroll) *hld up: hdwy over 1f out: wnt 3rd ins fnl f* **25/1**
0006 **4** *1 3/4* **Makabul**[14] 4639 5-8-13 58 ow1.................... JamesMillman(3) 7 51
(B R Millman) *hld up: rdn and kpt on one pce fr over 1f out* **5/2**[1]
0150 **5** *1 3/4* **Majestical (IRE)**[8] 4808 6-9-1 55....................(p) HaddenFrost(5) 9 49
(R A Harris) *towards rr: no hdwy ins fnl 2f* **15/2**
6-00 **6** *nk* **River Kirov (IRE)**[15] 4602 5-9-1 66.................... NickyMackay 4 43
(M Wigham) *s.i.s: hrd rdn over 2f out: one pce after* **7/1**[3]
0004 **7** *2 1/4* **Vogarth**[21] 4428 4-9-1 48.................... AlanMunro 2 36
(B R Millman) *chsd ldrs tl wknd over 1f out* **8/1**
0006 **8** *hd* **Mudhish (IRE)**[3] 4989 3-8-12 68.................... PaulDoe 5 35
(C E Brittain) *led to 1/2-way: wknd ins fnl 2f* **7/1**[3]
0430 **9** *hd* **Pajada**[8] 4806 4-8-3 45....................(v) SeanPalmer(7) 3 30
(M D I Usher) *prom tl wknd over 2f out* **20/1**

1m 11.94s (0.74) **Going Correction** +0.025s/f (Good)
WFA 3 from 4yo+ 3lb **9** Ran SP% **115.6**
Speed ratings (Par 101): **96,94,93,91,89 88,85,85,85**
toteswinger: 1&2 £18.50, 1&3 £17.40, 2&3 £29.70. CSF £49.49 TOTE £8.40: £2.30, £2.00, £5.90; EX 63.10.There was no bid for the winner.
Owner C S Tateson **Bred** The Hon Mrs E J Wills **Trained** Upper Lambourn, Berks

FOCUS
An ordinary seller and sound form for the grade rated through the first two.
Majestical(IRE) Official explanation: jockey said gelding never travelled

5091 **TRI-LEO H'CAP** **6f**
8:00 (8:00) (Class 5) (0-70,72) 4-Y-0+ **£2,590** (£770; £385; £192) **Stalls** High

Form RPR
2112 **1** **Patavium Prince (IRE)**[12] 4696 5-9-4 **70**.......... TravisBlock(3) 9 81+
(Miss Jo Crowley) *hld up: hdwy whn short of room over 1f out: swtchd lft and squeezed though to ld cl home* **4/1**[2]
4402 **2** ¾ **Alfresco**[7] 4865 4-9-4 **72**..........(v) DavidProbert(5) 5 78
(I A Wood) *led tl hdd over 1f out: rallied and regained 2nd cl home* **7/2**[1]
2-00 **3** ½ **Efisio Princess**[63] 3042 5-8-7 **56**.......... RichardThomas 1 60
(J E Long) *trckd ldr: led over 1f out: rdn: hdd and lost 2nd towards fin* **12/1**
5120 **4** *nk* **Doubtful Sound (USA)**[53] 3352 4-9-0 **66**..........(b) KevinGhunowa(3) 4 69
(R A Harris) *s.i.s: sn in tch: rdn 1/2-way: one pce fnl f* **8/1**
0562 **5** *shd* **Morse (IRE)**[7] 4858 7-8-10 **59**..........(p) AlanMunro 6 62
(J A Osborne) *chsd ldrs: rdn 2f out: no hdwy after* **5/1**
1031 **6** ½ **Mafaheem**[10] 4749 6-9-7 **70**..........(b) RobertHavlin 2 72
(A B Haynes) *hld up: hdwy on outside over 2f out: wknd ins fnl f* **9/2**[3]
4404 **7** *hd* **Trinculo (IRE)**[14] 4639 11-8-11 **65** ow2..........(b) HaddenFrost(5) 7 66
(R A Harris) *hld up: a bhd* **15/2**
4163 **8** 4 ½ **Danzili Bay**[23] 4327 6-8-8 **64**.......... StacyRenwick(7) 3 50
(A W Carroll) *chsd ldrs on outside tl rdn and wknd 2f out* **10/1**
000- **9** 3 ¼ **Shavoulin (USA)**[255] 7033 4-8-6 **55**.......... EdwardCreighton 10 31
(Christian Wroe) *a struggling in rr* **33/1**

1m 12.05s (0.85) **Going Correction** +0.025s/f (Good) **9** Ran SP% **119.7**
Speed ratings (Par 103): **95,94,93,92,92 92,91,85,81**
toteswinger: 1&2 £7.80, 1&3 £10.10, 2&3 £9.40. CSF £19.21 CT £158.65 TOTE £5.00: £1.90, £1.70, £3.50; EX 13.60 Place 6 £53.24, Place 5 £31.57.
Owner Mrs Liz Nelson **Bred** J P Hardiman **Trained** Whitcombe, Dorset
■ Stewards' Enquiry : David Probert two-day ban: used whip with excessive frequency (Aug 30-31)

FOCUS
Another moderate bunch of handicappers on show and the form, which is ordinary, wouldn't be the most reliable.
T/Plt: £30.40 to a £1 stake. Pool: £46,990.88. 1,125.14 winning tickets. T/Qpdt: £8.20 to a £1 stake. Pool: £4,764.97. 425.09 winning tickets. JS

5053 NEWBURY (L-H)
Saturday, August 16

OFFICIAL GOING: Good to soft
Wind: Brisk ahead

5092 **BATHWICK TYRES LADIES DERBY H'CAP (FOR LADY AMATEUR RIDERS)** **1m 4f 5y**
1:35 (1:36) (Class 4) (0-80,78) 3-Y-0+ **£13,741** (£4,261; £2,129; £1,064) **Stalls** Low

Form RPR
0433 **1** **Aypeeyes (IRE)**[14] 4645 4-10-9 **77**..........(v[1]) MissSBrotherton 13 86
(A King) *in rr tl gd hdwy over 3f out: led 2f out: drvn out fnl f* **10/1**
1536 **2** 1 ½ **The King And I (IRE)**[17] 4526 4-10-1 **74**..........(b) MissCAllen(5) 2 81
(Miss E C Lavelle) *hld up in rr: stdy hdwy on bit over 2f out: chsd wnr gng wl 1f out: rdn and nt run on ins fnl f* **25/1**
40-2 **3** ½ **Guardian Of Truth (IRE)**[169] 758 4-10-0 **73**(p) MissHayleyMoore(5) 15 79
(G L Moore) *edgy: chsd ldrs: rdn to ld 3f out: narrowly hdd 2f out: one pce ins fnl f* **16/1**
32-1 **4** 1 ¼ **Oldrik (GER)**[36] 3914 5-9-12 **71**..........(p) MissKHobbs(5) 10 75
(P J Hobbs) *towards rr: hdwy 4f out: drvn to chse ldrs over 2f out: styd on same pce ins fnl f* **7/1**[3]
0231 **5** ½ **Monfils Monfils (USA)**[6] 4892 6-10-10 **78** 6ex.......... MissARyan 11 81
(A J McCabe) *mid-div: hdwy 3f out: chsd ldrs 2f out: styd on one pce* **10/1**
0-00 **6** *hd* **William's Way**[28] 4191 6-10-10 **78**.......... MrsSMoore 14 81
(I A Wood) *lw: slowly away: bhd: hdwy over 2f out: kpt on fnl f but nvr in contention* **25/1**
-035 **7** *hd* **Venir Rouge**[64] 2990 4-10-5 **73**.......... MrsRDobbin 9 75
(M Salaman) *chsd ldrs: rdn along 3f out: one pce fnl 2f* **18/1**
5450 **8** ¾ **Mustajed**[10] 4742 7-10-9 **77**.......... MissGDGracey-Davison 4 78
(B R Millman) *sn chsng ldrs: rdn and styd on same pce fr over 2f out* **22/1**
5600 **9** *hd* **Fongs Gazelle**[14] 4627 4-10-7 **75**.......... MissADeniel 7 76
(M Johnston) *sn chsng ldr: rdn 3f out: wknd fnl f* **18/1**
3-20 **10** *nk* **Riguez Dancer**[10] 4742 4-10-0 **71**.......... MissJCoward(3) 1 71
(P C Haslam) *sn led: hdd 3f out: styd pressing ldrs tl wknd fnl f* **12/1**
2056 **11** *1* **Red Wine**[10] 4742 9-10-3 **76**.......... MissABevan(5) 5 75
(A J McCabe) *slowly away: sn in mid-div: rdn 3f out: wknd over 1f out* **11/1**
2503 **12** *nk* **Brief Goodbye**[21] 4426 8-9-13 **72**.......... MissFCumani(5) 8 70
(John Berry) *chsd ldrs: rdn 3f out: wknd ins fnl 2f* **14/1**
0101 **13** *nk* **Persian Peril**[8] 4814 4-10-6 **74**.......... MrsCBartley 12 72
(G A Swinbank) *in rr: rdn and hdwy to chse ldrs over 2f out: wknd over 1f out* **16/1**
3023 **14** ¾ **Celticello (IRE)**[1] 5059 6-10-2 **70**.......... MissEFolkes 3 67
(P D Evans) *b.hind: hld up towards rr: hdwy 3f out: rdn to chse ldrs over 2f: sn wknd* **13/2**[2]
21 **15** 1 ½ **Blakfrankisch (IRE)**[29] 4155 5-10-4 **75**.......... MissMSowerby(3) 16 69
(Tom Dascombe) *lw: in tch: qcknd to chal 5f out to 3f out: wknd qckly 2f out* **9/2**[1]
1000 **16** *12* **Transvestite (IRE)**[9] 4771 6-10-4 **72**..........(v) MissEJJones 6 47
(J W Hills) *plld hrd: chsd ldrs: n.m.r on bnd over 5f out: wknd 3f out* **33/1**

2m 39.51s (4.01) **Going Correction** -0.10s/f (Good) **16** Ran SP% **122.2**
Speed ratings (Par 105): **82,81,80,79,79 79,79,78,78,78 77,77,77,76,75 67**
toteswinger: 1&2 £55.60, 1&3 £36.90, 2&3 £57.40. CSF £248.48 CT £3941.66 TOTE £13.30: £2.80, £5.30, £4.90, £2.20; EX 326.60.
Owner D A Wallace **Bred** John Malone **Trained** Barbury Castle, Wilts

FOCUS
A modest contest for lady riders and, having gone steady early, the race developed into a bit of a sprint up the straight. The winning time was pedestrian. Ordinary form, rated through the second and third.

5093 **USK VALLEY STUD STKS (REGISTERED AS THE WASHINGTON SINGER STAKES) (LISTED RACE)** **7f (S)**
2:10 (2:10) (Class 1) 2-Y-O
£17,031 (£6,456; £3,231; £1,611; £807; £405) **Stalls** Centre

Form RPR
1 **1** **Cry Of Freedom (USA)**[24] 4311 2-9-0 0.......... LDettori 3 100+
(M Johnston) *lw: mde all: shkn up over 1f out: forged clr ins fnl f: unchal* **15/8**[2]
2 2 ¼ **Mustaqer (IRE)** 2-8-11 0.......... MartinDwyer 1 91+
(B W Hills) *gd sort: rangy: lw: chsd ldrs: tk narrow 2nd ins fnl 2f: styd on wl u.p fnl f but no ch w unchal wnr* **11/1**
1 **3** 1 ¾ **Jazz Police**[56] 3274 2-9-0 0.......... RyanMoore 6 90
(R Hannon) *chsd ldrs: rdn and effrt 2f out: nvr gng pce to rch wnr and one pce ins fnl f* **5/1**[3]
31 **4** 1 ¼ **Whispering Angel**[29] 4150 2-9-0 0.......... AlanMunro 5 87
(B J Meehan) *lw: t.k.h: chsd wnr tl rdn and green 2f out: sn no ex* **7/4**[1]
1 **5** 1 ½ **Courageous (IRE)**[27] 4213 2-9-0 0.......... TedDurcan 4 83
(B Smart) *w'like: str: scope: plld hrd 1st 3f: towards rr tl rdn and no imp over 2f out* **9/1**
6 *1* **Akhenaten** 2-8-11 0.......... TonyCulhane 2 78
(M R Channon) *tall: lengthy: scope: t.k.h in rr: rdn and hdwy to chse ldrs 3f out: no imp 2f out and sn bhd* **16/1**

1m 27.67s (1.97) **Going Correction** +0.20s/f (Good) **6** Ran SP% **112.0**
Speed ratings (Par 102): **96,93,91,90,88 87**
toteswinger: 1&2 £3.50, 1&3 £2.50, 2&3 £5.00. CSF £21.49 TOTE £2.70: £1.60, £4.10; EX 20.20.
Owner Sheikh Hamdan Bin Mohammed Al Maktoum **Bred** Clovelly Farms **Trained** Middleham Moor, N Yorks

FOCUS
A race that has produced some Classic winners in the past, including Haafhd and Lammtarra. This looked a fair renewal on paper but the winner was gifted an uncontested lead.

NOTEBOOK
Cry Of Freedom(USA), who won well at Sandown on his debut, was soon into the lead and, in all truth, given a very easy time of it in front. He did, however, quicken up well inside the final two furlongs and won very comfortably in the end. A Dewhurst and Racing Post Trophy entry, he should have little trouble staying a mile if connections decide to up him in trip. (tchd 2-1 tchd 11-5 in a place)
Mustaqer(IRE) ◆, whose dam was a very smart triple winner, including twice over 1m2f in Listed company at three, is by Dalakhani and therefore bred to get middle distances next season. He briefly threw down a challenge inside the final two furlongs and, while comfortably seen off by the more experienced winner, he kept on well and shaped with distinct promise. A maiden should be a formality on the way to better things. (op 14-1)
Jazz Police, a winner at Newmarket on his debut, was keen in the early stages and could not pick up when the winner quickened. He stayed on one-paced. (op 11-2)
Whispering Angel, who won his maiden over the course and distance last time out, was another who raced keenly early, and he carried his head a bit high in the closing stages. Perhaps it was just greenness, but this was his third run and his grandsire is Woodman. (op 2-1 tchd 9-4 in places)
Courageous(IRE) had a lot more to do than when narrowly successful in a minor Redcar maiden on his debut, but he cost a lot and is well entered up so his connections clearly hold him in some regard. He gave himself little chance by failing to settle off the ordinary pace, and can do better in a stronger-run race, and probably on quicker ground. (op 6-1 tchd 10-1)
Akhenaten, who cost 60,000gns, is out of a mare who placed over 1m at three in France. He took quite a hold in the early stages and weakened inside the last, but this was a stiff introduction and he is bred to do better as he is stepped up in distance. (op 25-1)

5094 **CGA GEOFFREY FREER STKS (GROUP 3)** **1m 5f 61y**
2:40 (2:41) (Class 1) 3-Y-0+
£36,900 (£13,988; £7,000; £3,490; £1,748; £877) **Stalls** Low

Form RPR
2101 **1** **Sixties Icon**[15] 4585 5-9-5 114.......... JMurtagh 9 117+
(J Noseda) *lw: s.i.s: hld up in rr: hdwy 3f out: chsd ldr ins fnl f: styd on gamely u.p to ld last stride* **2/1**[1]
302 **2** *shd* **Tempelstern (GER)**[7] 4880 4-9-3 111..........(b) TedDurcan 1 115
(H R A Cecil) *chsd ldr to 6f out and styd wl there: drvn to take narrow ld 2f out: hrd rdn fnl f: ct last stride* **16/1**
5012 **3** *2* **Donegal (USA)**[18] 4505 3-8-6 111.......... MartinDwyer 10 112
(A M Balding) *chsd ldrs: narrow 2nd 6f out: drvn to take slt advantage 3f out: narrowly hdd 2f out: styd on same pce u.p ins fnl f* **7/2**[2]
4-52 **4** *2* **Sell Out**[51] 3415 4-9-0 98.......... SteveDrowne 5 106
(G Wragg) *chsd ldrs: rdn and kpt on fnl 2f but nvr gng pce to be competitive* **33/1**
2-12 **5** ½ **Geordieland (FR)**[58] 3154 7-9-7 117.......... ShaneKelly 8 112
(J A Osborne) *hld up: hdwy on ins over 2f out: styd on same pce fnl f* **7/1**[3]
231 **6** *2* **Eastern Anthem (IRE)**[22] 4376 4-9-3 109..........(t) LDettori 7 105
(Saeed Bin Suroor) *edgy: s.i.s: hld up in rr: hdwy 6f out: drvn to chse ldrs over 2f out: sn no imp: wknd over 1f out* **8/1**
0426 **7** ¾ **Balkan Knight**[42] 3743 8-9-3 110.......... TQuinn 3 104
(D R C Elsworth) *b.hind: lw: chsd ldrs: pushed along fr 6f out: styd on to chse ldrs over 2f out but nvr in contention: sn btn* **25/1**
4143 **8** *4* **Lion Sands**[15] 4585 4-9-3 112.......... RyanMoore 11 98
(L M Cumani) *hld up in rr: drvn along and no prog 3f out* **9/1**
43/0 **9** 2 ¾ **Self Defense**[35] 3942 11-9-3 92.......... AlanMunro 6 94
(Miss E C Lavelle) *chsd ldrs: rdn over 3f out: wknd 2f out* **80/1**
133 **10** *4* **Peppertree Lane (IRE)**[31] 4100 5-9-3 108.......... JimmyFortune 2 88
(M Johnston) *led tl narrowly hdd 3f out: styd pressing ldrs tl wknd fr 2f out* **7/1**[3]

2m 51.55s (-0.45) **Going Correction** -0.10s/f (Good)
WFA 3 from 4yo+ 11lb **10** Ran SP% **115.6**
Speed ratings (Par 113): **97,96,95,94,94 92,92,90,88,85**
toteswinger: 1&2 £6.50, 1&3 £2.50, 2&3 £8.30. CSF £36.58 TOTE £2.90: £1.40, £3.10, £1.70; EX 31.10 Trifecta £345.30 Pool: £1,260.02 - 2.70 w/u..
Owner Mrs Susan Roy **Bred** Lordship Stud **Trained** Newmarket, Suffolk

FOCUS
A competitive renewal apparently run at a sound pace, but it was run in a very slow winning time for a Group 3. Sixties Icon is a class act at this level and is rated to this year's form. The fourth holds the form down somewhat but overall this is decent form for the grade.

NOTEBOOK

Sixties Icon, who was ridden very patiently, needed every yard of the trip to get on top, but as we know he is not short of speed, and it must be simply a combination of being given a bit too much to do and perhaps not being quite as effective on an easy surface as he is on quick ground that led to him making such hard work of it. His end-of-season target is the Breeders' Cup Marathon, a new race to be run over 1m4f on the cushion track at Santa Anita, where he may well avoid the top European middle-distance challengers as a result of them being aimed at the Turf. (op 3-1 tchd 15-8 and 10-3 in a place)

Tempelstern(GER) loves some dig in the ground, but he also likes to dominate and he was denied his favoured front-running role by Peppertree Lane. He took it up inside the final two furlongs, though, and although he hung left to the far-side rail, he stayed on well and was only just denied right on the line. This was probably a career-best effort from him, and he is clearly up to winning a Group race when conditions are suitable. (op 10-1)

Donegal(USA), not beaten far by Conduit at Goodwood last time, was the only three-year-old in the field and he received at least 11lb from the older males. Another who appreciates soft ground, he ran a sound race in third, finishing clear of the rest, and his connections pointed to the Prix Lutece over 1m7f at Longchamp as his next target. (op 4-1)

Sell Out had plenty to find with the principals at the ratings but she is another who runs her best races with plenty of cut in the ground, and the step up in trip seemed to suit her. This was clearly a career-best effort.

Geordieland(FR), running for the first time since finishing runner-up in the Gold Cup two months ago, had to give weight all round as a result of winning the Yorkshire Cup earlier in the season. Ridden patiently as usual, he could not make up the ground on these pacier types like he can over further, but it was still a sound effort. (op 6-1)

Eastern Anthem(IRE), up in trip and grade, did not see it out well enough. He will be suited by a return to 1m4f and Listed company. (op 13-2)

Balkan Knight, who stays further than this, was keeping on at the finish without ever threatening to land a blow.

Lion Sands had every chance on the ratings but he proved disappointing and probably just found the ground too soft. Official explanation: jockey said colt never travelled (op 17-2 tchd 10-1)

Peppertree Lane(IRE) may have done too much in front as he weakened quickly from two furlongs out. (op 13-2)

5095 CGA HUNGERFORD STKS (GROUP 2) 7f (S)

3:15 (3:16) (Class 1) 3-Y-0+

£56,770 (£21,520; £10,770; £5,370; £2,690; £1,350) **Stalls** Centre

Form				RPR
1101	1		**Paco Boy (IRE)**[18] 4506 3-9-0 110 ... RyanMoore 4 *(R Hannon) hld up in tch: qcknd fr 2f out to ld over 1f out: c clr ins fnl f: easily* **6/5**[1]	121+
2020	2	4 1/2	**Al Qasi (IRE)**[18] 4506 5-9-3 112 ... JimmyFortune 2 *(P W Chapple-Hyam) chsd ldrs tl rdn to ld 2f out: hdd over 1f out: sn no ch w wnr but hld on wl for 2nd* **15/2**[3]	108
0200	3	1/2	**Beaver Patrol (IRE)**[14] 4624 6-9-3 104 ...(v) StephenCarson 6 *(Eve Johnson Houghton) chsd ldrs: rdn 3f out: styd on u.p to hold 3rd ins fnl f but nvr any ch w easy wnr* **25/1**	107
-506	4	hd	**Arabian Gleam**[18] 4506 4-9-5 114 ... JMurtagh 7 *(J Noseda) lw: chsd ldrs: rdn and styd on u.p fnl 2f but nvr gng pce to be competitive* **8/1**	108
1024	5	6	**Il Warrd (IRE)**[18] 4506 3-8-12 109 ... TedDurcan 8 *(Saeed Bin Suroor) awkward stalls and slow into stride: sn rcvrd to chse ldrs: rdn 3f out: wknd over 1f out* **9/1**	88
0441	6	4	**Welsh Emperor (IRE)**[28] 4177 9-9-3 108 ... TonyCulhane 3 *(T P Tate) led to 2f out: wknd qckly over 1f out* **17/2**	79
4202	7	2	**Alexandros**[14] 4622 3-8-12 109 ... LDettori 10 *(Saeed Bin Suroor) hld up in tch: rdn and effrt over 2f out: nvr gng pce to rch ldrs and sn wknd* **4/1**[2]	72
0064	8	3/4	**Excusez Moi (USA)**[21] 4405 6-9-3 99 ... MartinDwyer 1 *(C E Brittain) edgy: towards rr early: rdn and clsd up 3f out: wknd fr 2f out* **25/1**	72
0306	9	nk	**Aeroplane**[32] 4059 5-9-3 97 ...(p) DaneO'Neill 9 *(S A Callaghan) bhd most of way* **33/1**	71

1m 24.35s (-1.35) **Going Correction** +0.20s/f (Good)

WFA 3 from 4yo+ 5lb **9** Ran SP% **119.5**

Speed ratings (Par 115): **115,109,109,109,102 97,95,94,94**

toteswinger: 1&2 £3.30, 1&3 £8.00, 2&3 £20.70. CSF £11.31 TOTE £2.10: £1.20, £2.20, £3.50; EX 10.90 Trifecta £200.40 Pool: £1,137.87 - 4.20 winning units..

Owner The Calvera Partnership No 2 **Bred** Mrs Joan Browne **Trained** East Everleigh, Wilts

FOCUS

A soundly run Group 2 race and another fine performance from Paco Boy, who looks well up to taking on the best over this trip. The place to be appeared to be up the centre of the track and the form is probably not up to the grade of contest.

NOTEBOOK

Paco Boy(IRE), whose only defeat since his debut came when not getting the run of things in the French Guineas, continues on an upward curve and demonstrated a fine turn of foot to take this Group 2 contest. He likes some cut in the ground and this is his ideal trip, and as a result his best chance of Group 1 glory will come in the Prix de la Foret. (op 11-8 tchd 11-10 and 6-4 in places)

Al Qasi(IRE), seventh behind Paco Boy at Goodwood last time, shaped better here with the ground to suit, but he was still left for dead when the winner quickened past him. (op 8-1 tchd 10-1)

Beaver Patrol(IRE), who normally competes in the top 6f handicaps, excelled himself on this step up in class and trip, on ground which one would have thought was easier than ideal. He will presumably pay for it with a hike in the weights, however, and his best chance of winning in future will be in a small conditions race. (op 33-1)

Arabian Gleam, sixth behind Paco Boy at Goodwood, never really threatened to reverse the form, although it is possible that the ground was on the slow side for him. (op 7-1)

Il Warrd(IRE), fourth to Paco Boy in the Lennox Stakes, was one of three who stayed more towards the stands' side. He was away from the pacesetter Welsh Emperor, so can be excused this to some extent. (op 10-1 tchd 11-1)

Welsh Emperor(IRE), winner of this race in 2006 and runner-up last year, could have done with even softer ground. He took them along at a decent clip but dropped out tamely in the closing stages and just has not been at his very best this term. (op 15-2)

Alexandros, second to River Proud in a Listed race over 1m at Goodwood last time, should have been suited by the softer ground. He proved disappointing, albeit having raced more towards the stands' side and away from the pacemaker Welsh Emperor. (op 9-2 tchd 5-1 and 11-2 in a place)

Excusez Moi(USA) would have been better employed running in the Great St Wilfrid at Ripon off the same mark which he won off two years ago rather than taking on this class of opposition.

5096 CGA LADIES DAY H'CAP 7f (S)

3:50 (3:50) (Class 2) (0-100,95) 3-Y-0+

£11,215 (£3,358; £1,679; £840; £419; £210) **Stalls** Centre

Form				RPR
1120	1		**Underworld**[21] 4405 3-9-7 95 ... LDettori 7 *(M Johnston) lw; hld up in rr but in tch: rdn and hdwy to chal over 1f out and styd pressing ldr under asserted fnl 50yds* **4/1**[2]	101
2250	2	1/2	**The Snatcher (IRE)**[18] 4509 5-9-4 87 ... RyanMoore 9 *(R Hannon) lw: chsd ldrs: rdn to ld wl over 1f out: kpt slt advantage u.p tl hdd and no ex fnl 50yds* **9/1**	93
1200	3	shd	**King's Bastion (IRE)**[21] 4407 4-9-1 84 ... JamieSpencer 4 *(M L W Bell) lw; hld up in rr: rdn and hdwy appr fnl f: str run u.p ins fnl f: edgd lft cl home but fin wl* **8/1**	90
1525	4	3/4	**Aye Aye Digby (IRE)**[16] 4553 3-9-2 90 ... DaneO'Neill 2 *(H Candy) lw: chsd ldrs: rdn over 2f out: effrt over 1f out but nvr quite gng pce to chal: kpt on ins fnl f* **7/2**[1]	92
0210	5	3/4	**Phantom Whisper**[21] 4437 5-9-9 95 ... JamesMillman[(3)] 6 *(B R Millman) lw: chsd ldrs: rdn and outpcd 3f out: styd on and squeezed through 1f out: gng on cl home* **12/1**	97
4602	6	1/2	**Mujood**[17] 4522 5-9-8 91 ...(v) StephenCarson 5 *(Eve Johnson Houghton) chsd ldrs: rdn over 3f out: styd on same pce fr over 1f out* **14/1**	92
3050	7	3/4	**Steam Cuisine**[7] 4841 4-9-7 90 ... TedDurcan 10 *(M G Quinlan) s.i.s: in rr: rdn over 2f out: hdwy over 1f out: styng on whn hmpd ins fnl f: nvr a threat after* **6/1**[3]	89
6000	8	nk	**Compton's Eleven**[7] 4854 7-9-0 83 ... EdwardCreighton 11 *(M R Channon) s.i.s: hld up towards rr but in tch: rdn and effrt 2f out: nvr quite gng pce to rch ldrs and one pce appr fnl f* **25/1**	81
-453	9	1	**King's Caprice**[22] 4375 7-9-4 87 ...(t) SteveDrowne 8 *(J A Geake) plld hrd: led and sn clr: wknd and hdd wl over 1f out* **10/1**	82
0612	10	1/2	**Silver Wind**[7] 4864 3-8-11 85 ...(v) TQuinn 3 *(P D Evans) chsd ldrs: rdn 1/2-way: wknd appr fnl f* **8/1**	77
0020	11	1	**Bazroy (IRE)**[8] 4831 4-8-9 83 ...(b) RichardEvans[(5)] 1 *(P D Evans) b: a outpcd* **16/1**	74

1m 26.13s (0.43) **Going Correction** +0.20s/f (Good)

WFA 3 from 4yo+ 5lb **11** Ran SP% **121.9**

Speed ratings (Par 109): **105,104,104,103,102 102,101,100,99,99 97**

toteswinger: 1&2 £7.20, 1&3 £7.00, 2&3 £17.90. CSF £41.75 CT £288.04 TOTE £3.80: £1.90, £2.80, £2.50; EX 53.20 Trifecta £503.60 Pool: £952.86 - 1.40 w/u..

Owner Sheikh Hamdan Bin Mohammed Al Maktoum **Bred** St Clare Hall Stud **Trained** Middleham Moor, N Yorks

FOCUS

Not a strong race for the grade, but it was run at a fair pace thanks to King's Caprice. They finished in something of a heap, though. The form is sound enough.

NOTEBOOK

Underworld, who showed pace but was ultimately well beaten in the totesport International last time out, was well backed and showed his Ascot running to be all wrong. The least exposed runner in the field, this was only his fifth start and there is probably more to come from him. (op 6-1)

The Snatcher(IRE), who still looks high enough in the handicap, ran well and gave the winner a real race. However, any rise for this will mean he remains vulnerable in this sort of grade. (tchd 8-1 and 10-1)

King's Bastion(IRE) had conditions to suit and returned to form having run below par on fast ground in his last two starts. (op 7-1 tchd 13-2)

Aye Aye Digby(IRE), another who looks held off his current mark, threatened down the outside but ultimately found only the one pace. (op 6-1 tchd 10-3)

Phantom Whisper got the extra furlong well enough but he is yet another now struggling against a high handicap mark. (op 9-1)

Mujood, who had the visor back on, chased the trailblazing leader for much of the race but was swamped as soon as he got to his tail. (op 12-1)

Steam Cuisine was squeezed up when staying on inside the last, but for which she would have finished a little closer. (op 7-1 tchd 5-1)

King's Caprice went off at a very fast pace and gave himself little chance of getting home. (op 8-1 tchd 14-1)

5097 EUROPEAN BREEDERS' FUND MAIDEN FILLIES' STKS 6f 8y

4:25 (4:27) (Class 4) 2-Y-0

£5,828 (£1,734; £866; £432) **Stalls** Centre

Form				RPR
2	1		**Glen Molly (IRE)**[13] 4665 2-9-0 0 ... TedDurcan 12 *(B W Hills) in tch: drvn and qcknd to ld 1f out: styd on wl thrght fnl f* **5/4**[1]	77+
525	2	1/2	**Forward Feline (IRE)**[37] 3882 2-9-0 78 ... CatherineGannon 4 *(B Palling) chsd ldrs: led appr fnl 2f: styd pressing wnr ins fnl f but a jst hld* **20/1**	75
	3	1 3/4	**Suba (USA)** 2-9-0 0 ... LDettori 8 *(Saeed Bin Suroor) w'like: attr: lw: in tch: drvn and hdwy fr 2f out: kpt on wl fnl f but nvr quite gng pce of ldng duo* **9/2**[2]	70+
00	4	hd	**Piste**[52] 3378 2-9-0 0 ... MartinDwyer 13 *(B J Meehan) w'like: str; bit bkwd: t.k.h: led: hdd and rdn appr fnl 2f: kpt on ins fnl f* **33/1**	69
	5	1 1/4	**La Adelita (IRE)** 2-9-0 0 ... JamieSpencer 11 *(M L W Bell) w'like: str: in tch: outpcd 1/2-way: rdn and hdwy fr 2f out: styd on fnl f but nvr gng pce to be competitive* **12/1**[3]	65+
5	6	1	**Fanditha (IRE)**[13] 4665 2-9-0 0 ... RyanMoore 5 *(R Hannon) lw: in rr: pushed along over 2f out: kpt on fr over 1f out and gng on cl home: nvr gng pce to be competitive* **9/2**[2]	62+
	7	1/2	**Shamwari Lodge (IRE)** 2-9-0 0 ... RichardSmith 6 *(R Hannon) in rr: hdwy over 1f out: styd on ins fnl f but nvr in contention* **50/1**	61+
50	8	shd	**Isabella Romee (IRE)**[28] 4184 2-8-9 0 ... RichardEvans[(5)] 9 *(Jane Chapple-Hyam) broke wl: pushed along and one pce 1/2-way: kpt on again fnl f* **28/1**	61+
0	9	shd	**Suakin Dancer (IRE)**[29] 4149 2-9-0 0 ... JimmyFortune 14 *(H Morrison) leggy: chsd ldrs: rdn over 2f out: wknd fnl f* **25/1**	60
	10	3	**Lilly Blue (IRE)** 2-9-0 0 ... EdwardCreighton 2 *(M R Channon) w'like: in rr: hdwy to get in tch whn rdn 3f out: wknd over 1f out* **12/1**[3]	51
	11	3/4	**Silver Games (IRE)** 2-9-0 0 ... TonyCulhane 3 *(M R Channon) w'like: tall: in tch: rdn 1/2-way: wknd over 1f out* **12/1**[3]	49
0	12	2 3/4	**Pansy Potter**[26] 4251 2-9-0 0 ...(b[1]) AlanMunro 16 *(B J Meehan) lengthy: chsd ldrs: rdn over 2f out: sn wknd* **25/1**	41
	13	2	**Happy And Glorious (IRE)** 2-9-0 0 ... DaneO'Neill 10 *(J W Hills) w'like: athletic: outpcd most of way* **25/1**	35
	14	nk	**Top Town Girl** 2-9-0 0 ... JamesDoyle 15 *(R M Beckett) unf: chsd ldrs 4f* **20/1**	34
06	15	10	**Scarlets**[19] 4480 2-9-0 0 ... TQuinn 1 *(P D Evans) in tch over 3f* **40/1**	4

1m 14.54s (1.54) **Going Correction** +0.20s/f (Good) **15** Ran SP% **135.7**

Speed ratings (Par 93): **97,96,94,93,92 90,90,89,89,85 84,81,78,78,64**

toteswinger: 1&2 £9.50, 1&3 £3.70, 2&3 £22.70. CSF £39.48 TOTE £2.30: £1.30, £4.90, £2.30; EX 34.80.

Owner John C Grant **Bred** Noel O'Callaghan **Trained** Lambourn, Berks

FOCUS

Just an ordinary maiden for the track if one rates it around the exposed runner-up.

NOTEBOOK

Glen Molly(IRE) paid Marine Boy a compliment as he beat her seven lengths over this course and distance on her debut. She ran green when hitting the front and there looks to be more to come from her (op 5-2 tchd 6-5 and 11-4 in a place)

Forward Feline(IRE), proven with cut in the ground and with an official mark of 78 following four previous starts, is the benchmark for the form. She was drawn low but ended up challenging up the stands' rail.

Suba(USA), who is closely related to top-class two-year-old and Irish 2000 Guineas winner Dubawi, shaped well enough on her debut and, being by Seeking The Gold, another furlong and quicker ground should suit. (op 10-3)

Piste has improved with every start and is now eligible for a mark. She is a half-sister to 1m juvenile winner Alfathaa, and one would expect this daughter of Falbrav to appreciate a longer trip in nursery company. (op 40-1)

La Adelita(IRE), who cost 140,000gns, is a half-sister to Easy Target, a dual 6f winner at two. She might do better over 7f on this evidence. (tchd 14-1)

Fanditha(IRE) kept on out wide and again shaped as though she will be suited by further than her pedigree suggests. (tchd 5-1)

Shamwari Lodge(IRE), whose dam was unplaced over sprint distances but is a half-sister to top-class sprinter Pipalong, was green and did not get the best of runs. She shaped better than her finishing position suggests.

Scarlets Official explanation: jockey said filly had no more to give

5098 MIRAGE SIGNS H'CAP — 1m 2f 6y
5:00 (5:00) (Class 4) (0-85,84) 3-Y-O — **£4,857** (£1,445; £722; £360) **Stalls** Low

Form				RPR
-214	1		**Craigstown**[20] [4448] 3-9-6 **83** ... LDettori 6 (Saeed Bin Suroor) *trckd ldr: nudged along 2f out: rdn to ld jst ins fnl f: readily* **4/1**[2]	94+
6-45	2	2 ½	**Totem Flower (IRE)**[89] [2261] 3-8-5 **68** ... MartinDwyer 2 (R Charlton) *led: rdn over 2f out: kpt narrow advantage tl hdd jst insde fnl f: kpt on same pce* **16/1**	74
250	3	5	**Ballochroy (IRE)**[101] [1919] 3-9-6 **83** ... JamieSpencer 4 (B W Hills) *lw; in rr: rdn and hdwy whn n.m.r 2f out: styd on for modest 3rd fnl f* **8/1**	79
2103	4	1 ¼	**Buddy Holly**[12] [4688] 3-9-4 **81** ... TedDurcan 3 (Pat Eddery) *chsd ldrs: rdn and wl there whn veered bdly rt to stands' rail 1f out and no ch after* **3/1**[1]	75
4331	5	2 ½	**Border Owl (IRE)**[19] [4484] 3-9-3 **80** ... RyanMoore 8 (R Hannon) *lw; in rr: rdn and hdwy 3f out: wknd fnl f* **11/2**[3]	69
5050	6	shd	**No To Trident**[40] [3800] 3-8-10 **78** ... RichardEvans(5) 7 (P D Evans) *rdn 3f out: a towards rr* **14/1**	66
3166	7	¾	**Black Jacari (IRE)**[30] [4130] 3-9-7 **84** ... DaneO'Neill 1 (A King) *lw: chsd ldrs: rdn 3f out: wknd over 1f out* **3/1**[1]	71
45-6	8	3 ¼	**Simone Martini (IRE)**[22] [4382] 3-8-8 **71** ... (t) SteveDrowne 5 (R Charlton) *lw: in rr: lost tch fnl 3f* **9/1**	51

2m 7.28s (-1.52) **Going Correction** -0.10s/f (Good) — **8** Ran SP% **119.0**

Speed ratings (Par 102): **102,100,96,95,93 92,92,89**

toteswinger: 1&2 £12.20, 1&3 £5.50, 2&3 £12.40. CSF £66.19 CT £497.08 TOTE £4.50: £1.60, £5.20, £2.50; EX 72.30 Place 6 £ 85.40, Place 5 £ 22.06.

Owner Godolphin **Bred** Peter Player **Trained** Newmarket, Suffolk

FOCUS

A fair handicap for the grade but only two mattered from two furlongs out. The winner is progressive and the runner-up is a surprising improver, but the form has been rated at face value.

Buddy Holly Official explanation: jockey said gelding hung right-handed

Border Owl(IRE) Official explanation: jockey said gelding hung right-handed

T/Jkpt: £3,222.80 to a £1 stake. Pool: £47,661.86. 10.50 winning tickets. T/Plt: £75.60 to a £1 stake. Pool: £111,709.44. 1,078.29 winning tickets. T/Qpdt: £7.00 to a £1 stake. Pool: £7,024.77. 738.48 winning tickets. ST

5066
NEWMARKET (JULY) (R-H)
Saturday, August 16

OFFICIAL GOING: Good (good to firm in places)

Wind: medium, half against Weather: bright, fluffy clouds

5099 LLOYDS TSB INSURANCE E B F MAIDEN STKS — 6f
1:50 (1:52) (Class 4) 2-Y-O — **£5,180** (£1,541; £770; £384) **Stalls** High

Form				RPR
5	1		**Greensward**[29] [4151] 2-9-3 0 ... EddieAhern 2 (B J Meehan) *in tch: rdn to chse ldr over 1f out styd on u.p fnl f to ld nr fin* **1/1**[1]	78+
0	2	nk	**Miss Tango Hotel**[29] [4149] 2-8-12 0 ... DavidKinsella 4 (J H M Gosden) *led at stdy pce: rdn and wnt 2 l clr over 1f out: kpt on but hdd and no ex nr fin* **33/1**	72
	3	3 ¾	**Larkham (USA)** 2-9-3 0 ... GeorgeBaker 9 (R M Beckett) *in tch: shkn up and unable qck over 1f out: kpt on same pce fnl f: wnt 3rd cl home* **13/2**	66+
	4	nk	**Spiritual Art** 2-8-12 0 ... NCallan 1 (S A Callaghan) *s.i.s: hld up in midfield: hdwy 2f out: chsd ldng pair ent fnl f: one pce: lost 3rd cl home* **28/1**	60
	5	¾	**Emirates World (IRE)** 2-9-3 0 ... RHills 5 (Saeed Bin Suroor) *chsd ldrs: rdn over 2f out: outpcd over 1f out: plugged on* **5/1**[2]	63
	6	nk	**Brenthurst (USA)** 2-9-3 0 ... TPQueally 6 (J Noseda) *s.i.s: hld up in midfield: effrt jst over 2f out: no imp over 1f out* **14/1**	62
	7	2 ½	**Baariq** 2-9-3 0 ... AdrianMcCarthy 7 (P W Chapple-Hyam) *s.i.s: sn in tch in midfield: rdn and edgd rt 2f out: sn struggling* **33/1**	54
3	8	1 ½	**Marbled Cat (USA)**[20] [4446] 2-9-3 0 ... GregFairley 3 (M Johnston) *chsd ldr tl over 1f out: wknd qckly fnl f* **6/1**[3]	50
	9	5	**Sharaxia (IRE)** 2-8-12 0 ... IanMongan 10 (C F Wall) *stdd s and dropped in bhd: rdn and btn over 2f out* **33/1**	30
	10	3	**Bright Wire (IRE)** 2-9-3 0 ... RobertHavlin 8 (M L W Bell) *s.i.s: a bhd: rdn and struggling fr 1/2-way* **50/1**	26

1m 14.76s (2.26) **Going Correction** +0.25s/f (Good) — **10** Ran SP% **115.2**

Speed ratings (Par 96): **94,93,88,88,87 86,83,81,74,70**

toteswinger: 1&2 £5.60, 1&3 £3.10, 2&3 £30.30. CSF £50.76 TOTE £2.00: £1.30, £4.20, £1.80; EX 33.20.

Owner Lady Rothschild **Bred** Kincorth Investments Inc **Trained** Manton, Wilts

FOCUS

Not the strongest of maidens with half the field starting at 28-1 or longer. The early pace was very modest too and it developed into something of a sprint, so the form may not add up to much though a couple are entitled to improve.

NOTEBOOK

Greensward, down a furlong from his debut though he does have a high-class sprinting pedigree, was probably not helped by the modest early pace which explains why he made such hard work of cutting down the runner-up. He should continue to improve though, and is almost certainly capable of better given a truly run race. (op 5-4 tchd 10-11& 11-8 in places)

Miss Tango Hotel, beaten a long way on her Newbury debut, very much had her own way at the head of affairs and very nearly pulled off a major shock, but the favourite cut her down near the line. The way the race was run puts a big question mark against this effort, but this was still undeniably a big improvement.

Larkham(USA) ◆, a $125,000 yearling and 44,000gns two-year-old, is a half-brother to five winners including the top-class sprinter Les Arcs. He was unable to respond when the pace quickened over a furlong from home but was noted staying on steadily in the latter stages to snatch third without by any means being knocked about. He looks capable of a good deal better. (op 10-1 tchd 6-1)

Spiritual Art, a 130,000gns half-brother to three winners including the enigmatic Jomus, made an effort towards the far side of the field entering the last couple of furlongs, but could never really land a blow. The market did not suggest that a great deal was expected from him on this debut and the best of him may be seen in handicap company in due course. (op 16-1)

Emirates World(IRE), a half-brother to two juvenile winners, was up there early but did not find very much once off the bridle. He may appreciate another furlong, but it seems highly unlikely that he is the best Godolphin two-year-old around. (op 4-1 tchd 6-1)

5100 LLOYDS TSB CARDNET H'CAP — 1m 4f
2:25 (2:26) (Class 4) (0-85,85) 3-Y-O+ — **£6,476** (£1,927; £963; £481) **Stalls** Centre

Form				RPR
-025	1		**Ascalon**[77] [2591] 4-9-11 **82** ... NCallan 5 (Pat Eddery) *chsd ldr tl led 4f out: rdn and drew wl clr 2f out: in n.d after* **7/1**	102
-102	2	10	**Sleepy Hollow**[20] [4448] 3-8-8 **78** ... TravisBlock(3) 1 (H Morrison) *hld up in midfield: hdwy 4f out: rdn to chse wnr 2f out: no prog u.p over 1f out* **4/1**[2]	82
1-03	3	7	**Jadaara**[44] [3649] 3-9-0 **81** ... GregFairley 7 (M Johnston) *t.k.h: chsd ldng pair: wnt 2nd wl over 3f out: rdn and outpcd by wnr over 2f out: lost 2nd 2f out: wl btn after* **9/1**	74
4310	4	1	**Coyote Creek**[49] [3505] 4-10-0 **85** ... (b[1]) GeorgeBaker 9 (E F Vaughan) *hld up towards rr: rdn and effrt 3f out: wl outpcd over 2f out: no ch fnl f* **10/1**	76
2014	5	2	**She's Our Lass (IRE)**[6] [4894] 7-9-5 **76** ... DNolan 6 (D Carroll) *hld up in last pair: hdwy over 4f out: rdn and btn over 2f out: no ch after* **20/1**	64
-036	6	9	**Just Two Numbers**[30] [4131] 4-9-7 **78** ... J-PGuillambert 11 (W Jarvis) *t.k.h: hld up towards rr: rdn 4f out: wknd wl over 2f out* **9/1**	52
0055	7	3	**Mikao (IRE)**[13] [4662] 7-9-4 **75** ... (b) PaulMulrennan 10 (M H Tompkins) *stdd s: hld up in midfield: rdn over 3f out: wl btn over 2f out: t.o* **11/1**	44
0042	8	20	**Invasian (IRE)**[14] [4645] 7-10-0 **85** ... JohnEgan 2 (P W D'Arcy) *led: rdn and hdd 4f out: sn wknd: t.o and eased fr over 1f out* **6/1**[3]	22
-350	9	7	**Winter Bloom (USA)**[67] [2920] 3-8-13 **80** ... TPQueally 4 (H R A Cecil) *t.k.h: chsd ldrs tl lost pl qckly 4f out: t.o and eased last 2f* **10/3**[1]	6
5100	10	hd	**Moment's Notice**[37] [3875] 3-9-1 **85** ... LukeMorris(3) 8 (R W Price) *stdd s: a wl bhd: rdn and lost tch 4f out: t.o and eased last 2f* **25/1**	10

2m 31.63s (-1.27) **Going Correction** +0.25s/f (Good)

WFA 3 from 4yo+ 10lb — **10** Ran SP% **115.9**

Speed ratings (Par 105): **114,107,102,102,100 94,92,79,74,74**

toteswinger: 1&2 £15.10, 1&3 £15.40, 2&3 £4.30. CSF £34.92 CT £256.54 TOTE £11.50: £2.80, £1.60, £2.60; EX 46.20 Trifecta £230.00 Part won. Pool £310.82 - 0.40 winning units..

Owner P J J Eddery, Mrs John Magnier, M Tabor **Bred** Patrick Eddery Ltd **Trained** Nether Winchendon, Bucks

FOCUS

With habitual trailblazer Invasian in the field, a strong pace was always likely and this race was run at a proper end-to-end gallop. The runners made straight for the far rail on reaching the home straight and the field finished spread out all over Newmarket Heath. The winning time was also very smart. The easy winner is rated up 12lb, but this was a strange result and there are doubts over how reliable the form will be.

Mikao(IRE) Official explanation: jockey said gelding stopped quickly

Invasian(IRE) Official explanation: jockey said gelding was unable to get an uncontested lead

Winter Bloom(USA) Official explanation: trainer had no explanation for the poor form shown

Moment's Notice Official explanation: jockey said gelding was never travelling

5101 SOCCER SATURDAY SUPER 6 GREY HORSE H'CAP — 6f
2:55 (2:56) (Class 4) (0-85,83) 3-Y-O+ — **£12,462** (£3,732; £1,866; £934; £466; £234) **Stalls** High

Form				RPR
0450	1		**Finsbury**[52] [3383] 5-8-0 **59** ... NickyMackay 15 (J S Goldie) *hld up bhd: hdwy 2f out: rdn to ld jst ins fnl f: hld on wl last 100yds* **13/2**[3]	65
5403	2	½	**Star Strider**[9] [4772] 4-7-11 **61** ... DavidProbert(5) 13 (Miss Gay Kelleway) *s.i.s: sn swtchd lft: racd in midfield: hdwy 2f out: rdn over 1f out: chsd wnr and ev ch ins fnl f: hung rt and no ex nr fin* **8/1**	65
3500	3	nse	**Mogok Ruby**[23] [4341] 4-9-5 **78** ... PatDobbs 11 (L Montague Hall) *stdd s: hld up bhd: rdn and gd hdwy jst over 1f out: ev ch ins fnl f: hung rt and no ex nr fin* **40/1**	82
4066	4	1 ¼	**Charlotte Grey**[2] [5007] 4-7-6 **58** oh12 ow1 ... AndreaAtzeni(7) 3 (P J McBride) *wnt rt s: sn chsng ldrs: ev ch and edgd lft ent fnl f: one pce u.p last 100yds* **33/1**	58
0144	5	shd	**Witchry**[44] [3626] 6-8-4 **63** ... JohnEgan 14 (A G Newcombe) *hld up towards rr: hdwy wl over 1f out: swtchd rt jst over 1f out: chsd ldrs ent fnl f: one pce* **15/2**	63
5051	6	1	**Grey Boy (GER)**[21] [4414] 7-8-4 **66** ... LukeMorris(3) 5 (A W Carroll) *s.i.s: sn pushed up to chse ldrs: rdn to ld over 1f out: hdd jst ins fnl f: wknd last 50yds* **6/1**[2]	62
505	7	1 ½	**Pic Up Sticks**[29] [4154] 9-8-5 **64** ... GregFairley 9 (B G Powell) *in tch in midfield: rdn and effrt over 1f out: no imp fnl f* **11/1**	56
0056	8	½	**Sands Of Barra (IRE)**[33] [4018] 5-8-2 **61** ... PatrickMathers 2 (I W McInnes) *in tch in midfield: rdn wl over 1f out: wkng whn sltly hmpd ent fnl f* **20/1**	51
002-	9	hd	**Certain Justice (USA)**[303] [6278] 10-8-11 **70** ... MickyFenton 6 (Stef Liddiard) *sn pushed along towards rr: kpt on u.p fnl f: nvr trbld ldrs* **10/1**	59
22	10	¾	**Secret Night**[21] [4407] 5-9-4 **77** ... (p) EddieAhern 10 (C G Cox) *hld up bhd: rdn and effrt over 1f out: n.d* **9/2**[1]	64
1040	11	nk	**Zowington**[15] [4601] 6-9-10 **83** ... IanMongan 8 (C F Wall) *t.k.h: hld up towards rr: rdn 2f out: nvr trbld ldrs* **11/1**	69

5100 **12** 3/4 **Lunces Lad (IRE)**30 4103 4-9-3 **76**................................ TPO'Shea 7 60
(M R Channon) *in tch: rdn wl over 1f out: wkng whn edgd lft ent fnl f* **16/1**

4002 **13** 3/4 **Our Fugitive (IRE)**8 4824 6-8-1 **60**..........................(p) ChrisCatlin 1 41
(C Gordon) *led tl over 2f out: wknd qckly u.p over 1f out* **14/1**

010- **14** 3/4 **Sarah's Art (IRE)**269 6895 5-7-12 **57** oh2..............(t) AdrianMcCarthy 12 36
(Stef Liddiard) *in tch: rdn and effrt over 1f out: sn wknd* **25/1**

0550 **15** *nk* **Walragnek**8 4812 4-8-0 **59** oh7 ow2..........................(v1) DavidKinsella 4 37
(J G M O'Shea) *s.i.s: sn chsng ldr: rdn to ld over 2f out: hdd over 1f out: sn wknd* **66/1**

0150 **16** 3/4 **Leading Edge (IRE)**7 4864 3-8-7 **76**.................. MatthewDavies(7) 16 52
(M R Channon) *chsd ldrs: rdn 2f out: wknd over 1f out* **25/1**

1m 13.46s (0.96) **Going Correction** +0.25s/f (Good)
WFA 3 from 4yo+ 3lb **16** Ran SP% **126.3**
Speed ratings (Par 105): **103,102,102,100,100 99,97,96,96,95 94,93,92,91,91 90**
toteswinger: 1&2 £14.30, 1&3 £108.00, 2&3 £102.50. CSF £55.55 CT £1308.99 TOTE £8.20: £2.30, £2.50, £9.00, £6.40; EX 93.60 TRIFECTA Not won..

Owner M Mackay & S Bruce **Bred** O Pointing **Trained** Uplawmoor, E Renfrews

FOCUS

The sixth running of this race and although it was an ordinary handicap, it was also very competitive. The runners raced centre to far side for most of the way, though by the time they reached the line they were spread out over almost the full width of the track. Modest form, with the fourth casting doubts.

Secret Night Official explanation: jockey said mare ran flat

Walragnek Official explanation: jockey said gelding ran too free

5102 LLOYDS TSB COMMERCIAL BANKING H'CAP 6f

3:30 (3:31) (Class 2) (0-105,98) 3-Y-O

£18,693 (£5,598; £2,799; £1,401; £699; £351) **Stalls** High

Form RPR

1000 **1** **Thebes**21 4405 3-8-7 **84**.. GregFairley 13 94
(M Johnston) *chsd ldr tl led over 2f out: sn rdn: edgd lft fr over 1f out: hld on u.p towards fin* **16/1**

2450 **2** 1/2 **Royal Intruder**16 4553 3-8-13 **90**.. PatDobbs 5 98
(R Hannon) *in tch: rdn and effrt jst over 2f out: chsd wnr ins fnl f: kpt on u.p last 100yds but nvr quite getting to wnr* **9/1**

4210 **3** 2 1/2 **Wise Melody**38 3850 3-8-10 **87**.. LiamJones 9 87
(W J Haggas) *hld up towards rr: hdwy 2f out: nt clr run briefly over 1f out: styd on u.p fnl f: wnt 3rd nr fin: nvr trble ldng pair* **20/1**

1030 **4** *nk* **Tawaash (USA)**16 4553 3-9-7 **98**.......................................(b1) RHills 1 97
(M A Jarvis) *chsd ldrs: chsd wnr 2f out: sn rdn: no imp 1f out: fdd last 100yds* **9/2**1

1556 **5** 1/2 **Always Ready**21 4423 3-8-4 **81**.. NickyMackay 12 78
(C E Brittain) *bhd: niggled along 1/2-way: stl bhd and swtchd rt jst over 1f out: r.o wl ins fnl f: nvr nr ldrs* **16/1**

1361 **6** 1 **Marvellous Value (IRE)**21 4416 3-9-2 **93**.................. TonyHamilton 4 87
(M Dods) *t.k.h: rdn over 2f out: keeping on same pce whn edgd lft ent fnl f: no threat to ldrs after* **9/2**1

0525 **7** *nk* **Spitfire**7 4842 3-9-7 **98**.. EddieAhern 14 91
(J R Jenkins) *hld up bhd: hdwy 1/2-way: effrt u.p wl over 1f out: no prog fnl f* **10/1**

61 **8** *nk* **The Game**22 4375 3-8-3 **80**.. RichardKingscote 7 72
(Tom Dascombe) *taken down early: hld up towards rr: hdwy over 2f out: no imp fnl f* **5/1**2

3564 **9** *shd* **Rash Judgement**15 4591 3-8-9 **86**.. ChrisCatlin 8 78
(W S Kittow) *rrd s and slowly away: bhd: rdn wl over 2f out: edgd lft ent fnl f: r.o past btn horses ins fnl f: n.d* **8/1**3

5461 **10** 1 3/4 **Piscean (USA)**15 4591 3-7-12 **80**..............................(b) DavidProbert(5) 6 66
(T Keddy) *s.i.s: hld up in midfield: rdn and effrt jst over 2f out: no real hdwy: wl btn fnl f* **16/1**

1620 **11** 1 3/4 **Victorian Bounty**38 3850 3-9-3 **94**.................................. MickyFenton 10 75
(Stef Liddiard) *led tl over 2f out: wknd u.p wl over 1f out* **22/1**

3-44 **12** 2 **Exhibition (IRE)**84 2409 3-9-2 **98**................. Louis-PhilippeBeuzelin(5) 2 72
(S A Callaghan) *in tch in midfield: rdn over 2f out: wknd wl over 1f out and wl btn after* **16/1**

124 **13** 8 **Rubirosa (IRE)**21 4408 3-8-8 **85**.................................. PaulMulrennan 11 34
(M Dods) *in tch in midfield: rdn 1/2-way: wknd ent fnl 2f: wl bhd fnl f* **16/1**

1m 13.37s (0.87) **Going Correction** +0.25s/f (Good) **13** Ran SP% **121.8**
Speed ratings (Par 106): **104,103,100,99,98 97,97,96,96,94 92,89,78**
toteswinger: 1&2 £40.50, 1&3 £44.10, 2&3 £30.20. CSF £156.05 CT £3005.62 TOTE £16.00: £5.70, £3.50, £5.40; EX 241.50 TRIFECTA Not won..

Owner Sheikh Hamdan Bin Mohammed Al Maktoum **Bred** Whitsbury Manor Stud And Mrs M E Slade **Trained** Middleham Moor, N Yorks

FOCUS

A decent sprint handicap for three-year-olds and the time was fractionally faster than the older horses in the greys' race, though that was to be expected given the difference in class. This time the field came down the centre. The winner reproduced his early sand form, with the second up 7lb and the third to form.

NOTEBOOK

Thebes ◆, dropped 4lb after finishing no better than tenth in his previous three outings on turf, was always up there until taking it up approaching the last couple of furlongs. Despite hanging away to his left and ending up against the far rail, he was always doing just enough and now that he has broken his duck on turf he may be capable of more. This is his trip and it now seems that he does not want the ground too quick. Official explanation: trainer said he had no explanation for the apparent improvement in form (tchd 14-1)

Royal Intruder, back down in trip after finishing unplaced on his first attempt at 7f last time, was never too far away and really found his stride up the hill to pull clear of the rest, but the winner had got first run on him. On this evidence he may be worth another try over the extra furlong. (op 11-1)

Wise Melody ◆, last of 20 here last time when behind several of these including Thebes, performed much better this time and was finishing to some effect. This suggests that she is not handicapped out of things just yet and a return to faster ground will help her. (op 14-1)

Tawaash(USA), well backed in the first-time blinkers, had every chance but the winner had the legs of him starting up the final hill. He does appear better over 7f. (op 15-2)

Always Ready, racing over a trip this short for the first time since his second start at two, had the blinkers left off this time and he stayed on strongly from off the pace without ever quite managing to get there. He does not have much in the way of scope, but he is back on a winning mark now and a return to further will help. (op 20-1)

Marvellous Value(IRE), raised 6lb for his Newcastle victory, raced keenly and could only find one pace off the bridle. (op 5-1 tchd 11-2)

Spitfire, who had several of these behind when runner-up here last month, could never land a blow and it may be that performance flatters him. (op 8-1)

5103 LLOYDS TSB CORPORATE MARKETS NURSERY 5f

4:05 (4:05) (Class 4) 2-Y-O

£6,476 (£1,927; £963; £481) **Stalls** High

Form RPR

250 **1** **Mythical Blue (IRE)**18 4497 2-7-9 **68**.........................(t) DavidProbert(5) 4 74
(S C Williams) *chsd ldr: led over 1f out: edgd lft ins fnl f: stened and r.o wl last 100yds* **9/4**1

105 **2** 1 1/4 **Waffle (IRE)**7 4857 2-9-7 **89**.. TPQueally 1 90
(J Noseda) *stdd after s: t.k.h: hld up in last: hdwy and squeezed through over 1f out: ev ch ent fnl f: edgd lft and unable qck last 100yds* **9/4**1

4241 **3** *nk* **Ruby Tallulah**4 4942 2-8-7 **75** 6ex.............................. KirstyMilczarek 5 75
(N P Littmoden) *t.k.h: hld up in tch: hdwy 2f out: ev ch ent fnl f: one pce last 100yds* **13/2**3

2414 **4** 5 **Red Rossini (IRE)**7 4857 2-8-11 **79**.................................... PatDobbs 3 61
(R Hannon) *in tch: effrt to press ldrs and rdn over 1f out: wknd fnl f* **7/2**2

050 **5** 4 **Mattamia (IRE)**29 4164 2-8-7 **75**.. JohnEgan 2 43
(B R Millman) *in tch: rdn 1/2-way: wknd over 1f out* **12/1**

1064 **6** 5 **Skruton (IRE)**9 4768 2-8-7 **75**.. TPO'Shea 6 25
(M G Quinlan) *led tl hdd and rdn over 1f out: wknd qckly ent fnl f* **10/1**

59.91 secs (0.81) **Going Correction** +0.25s/f (Good) **6** Ran SP% **113.9**
Speed ratings (Par 96): **103,101,100,92,86 78**
toteswinger: 1&2 £2.20, 1&3 £3.00, 2&3 £2.00. CSF £7.65 TOTE £3.80: £1.70, £2.00; EX 8.40.

Owner Chris Watkins And David N Reynolds **Bred** John O'Dowd **Trained** Newmarket, Suffolk

■ Stewards' Enquiry : T P Queally one-day ban: careless riding (Aug 30)

FOCUS

A small field for this nursery, but the pace was good and the time was decent. The runners stayed against the stands' rail this time and the front three pulled miles clear of the others.

NOTEBOOK

Mythical Blue(IRE), well backed for this nursery debut and dropped right back down to the minimum trip in a first-time tongue tie, travelled really well behind the leader and, after taking it up, he showed good resolution to keep his two challengers at bay. This is his trip and he still has some scope. Official explanation: trainer said, regarding apparent improvement in form, that in its previous race, the colt was not suited by the 7 1/2f and the uphill finish. (op 7-2)

Waffle(IRE), held up at the back, was momentarily stopped when trying to squeeze his way through starting up the hill, but he was still through in plenty of time had he been good enough and the winner was just too determined. (op 2-1 tchd 5-2 in places)

Ruby Tallulah, carrying a 6lb penalty for her Lingfield Polytrack victory four days earlier, travelled well behind the leaders towards the stands' side and came through to hold every chance. She went down with all guns blazing and looks capable of winning a race like this on turf too. (op 11-2)

Red Rossini(IRE) had every chance, but did not get up the hill. He may need a sharper track and a drop in the weights. (tchd 4-1)

Mattamia(IRE), making his nursery debut after finishing unplaced in three maidens, was easily seen off and has probably been given too stiff a mark. (op 9-1)

Skruton(IRE) set the pace, but dropped out very tamely once headed. She does not seem to be progressing. (op 9-1 tchd 14-1)

5104 SCOTTISH WIDOWS H'CAP 1m

4:40 (4:40) (Class 4) (0-85,85) 3-Y-O

£6,476 (£1,927; £963; £481) **Stalls** High

Form RPR

-502 **1** **Rochefort (IRE)**10 4731 3-9-7 **82**................................ RobertHavlin 4 94+
(J H M Gosden) *mde all: set stdy gallop: rdn and qcknd clr 2f out: in n.d fr over 1f out: easily* **2/1**1

24-2 **2** 3 3/4 **Alwaabel**127 1295 3-9-4 **79**.. RHills 9 82
(J L Dunlop) *stdd s: hld up in rr: hdwy and n.m.r over 1f out: chsd wnr jst ins fnl f: no imp* **4/1**2

0000 **3** 3 **Jebel Tara**23 4341 3-9-4 **79**.. LiamJones 1 75
(C E Brittain) *plld hrd: chsd wnr: rdn and unable qck 2f out: no ch w wnr over 1f out: lost 2nd jst ins fnl f* **20/1**

0-10 **4** 3/4 **Indian Skipper (IRE)**121 1421 3-9-5 **80**.................... PaulMulrennan 3 74
(M H Tompkins) *plld hrd: hld up in tch: hdwy over 2f out: disp 2nd but no ch w wnr ent fnl f: wknd ins fnl f* **7/1**

3230 **5** 4 **Ocean Legend (IRE)**10 4731 3-9-1 **76**................................ JohnEgan 7 61
(Miss J Feilden) *chsd ldrs: rdn 3f out: struggling over 2f out: no ch last 2f* **11/2**3

6-60 **6** 3/4 **Mujaadel (USA)**87 2302 3-9-7 **82**................................ EddieAhern 5 65
(E A L Dunlop) *hld up in rr: hdwy 3f: rdn and btn whn short of room and snatched up over 1f out: no ch after* **12/1**

0140 **7** 2 **Burnbrake**38 3855 3-8-11 **72**.. TPO'Shea 2 51
(J A R Toller) *t.k.h: hld up in tch: rdn over 2f out: sn btn* **12/1**

1044 **8** 4 1/2 **Kiwi Bay**6 4893 3-9-9 **84**.. TonyHamilton 6 53
(M Dods) *taken down early: t.k.h: hld up towards rr: rdn over 2f out: sn edgd lft and no rspnse: wl btn after* **6/1**

1m 43.4s (3.40) **Going Correction** +0.25s/f (Good) **8** Ran SP% **115.7**
Speed ratings (Par 102): **93,89,86,85,81 80,78,74**
toteswinger: 1&2 £2.00, 1&3 £7.30, 2&3 £11.50. CSF £10.12 CT £121.95 TOTE £2.60: £1.30, £1.60, £4.10; EX 10.20.

Owner H R H Princess Haya Of Jordan **Bred** John Fielding **Trained** Newmarket, Suffolk

FOCUS

An ordinary handicap and the slow early pace set by the winner resulted in a few pulling and a moderate winning time. The field raced centre to far side on this occasion. This probably did not take much winning.

5105 LLOYDS TSB "FOR THE JOURNEY" H'CAP 1m 2f

5:15 (5:15) (Class 5) (0-70,70) 3-Y-O+

£3,885 (£1,156; £577; £288) **Stalls** Centre

Form RPR

-011 **1** **Lilac Moon (GER)**23 4331 4-9-8 **64**........................ RichardKingscote 12 71
(N J Vaughan) *mde all: racd alone on stands' rail fr 8f out: rdn jst over 2f out: hld on gamely u.p ins fnl f* **4/1**2

0-0 **2** *nk* **Mac Don (IRE)**17 4546 4-9-12 **68**..(p) NCallan 3 74
(Eamon Tyrrell, Ire) *hld up in midfield: hdwy 4f out: rdn and hung rt fr over 2f out: chsd wnr over 1f out: styd on to chal wl ins fnl f: hld nr fin* **9/1**

0502 **3** 1 1/2 **Silent Applause**29 4156 5-9-6 **65**................................ LukeMorris(3) 4 68
(Dr J D Scargill) *hld up towards rr: rdn 4f out: hdwy whn hmpd over 2f out: chsd ldrs and carried sltly lft ent fnl f: kpt on same pce last 100yds* **7/1**

0020 **4** *shd* **Hawk Flight (IRE)**28 4179 3-9-3 **67**................................ TPQueally 10 70
(W R Muir) *chsd ldrs: rdn over 3f out: edgd out lft ent fnl f: kpt on u.p* **18/1**

453 **5** 5 **Just Intersky (USA)**8 4829 5-9-3 **59**..........................(p) J-PGuillambert 9 52
(V Smith) *stdd s: t.k.h: hld up bhd: rdn wl over 3f out: swtchd lft wl over 1f out: plugged on u.p: nvr nr ldrs* **12/1**

-520 **6** 1 **Berry Baby (IRE)**17 4527 3-8-7 **62**............... Louis-PhilippeBeuzelin(5) 8 53
(G A Butler) *chsd ldr: rdn over 3f out: lost 2nd over 2f out: hrd rdn and wknd over 1f out* **3/1**1

-200 **7** *shd* **Pop Music (IRE)**10 4727 5-8-12 **61**..........................(v1) SophieDoyle(7) 6 52
(Ms J S Doyle) *taken down early: t.k.h: chsd ldrs: chsd wnr and hung rt over 2f out: wknd over 1f out* **33/1**

5661 **8** *2 ¼* **Krugerrand (USA)**8 4829 9-10-0 **70**.......................... StephenDonohoe 2 55
(W J Musson) *v.s.a: hld up bhd: hdwy and hmpd over 2f out: swtchd lft and effrt u.p over 1f out: fdd fnl f* **9/1**

0606 **9** *2 ¼* **Barley Moon**8 4820 4-8-2 **51** oh6............................(b) AndreaAtzeni(7) 1 32
(T Keddy) *stdd after s: hld up towards rr: rdn and effrt 3f out: wknd 2f out* **66/1**

5000 **10** *2 ¼* **Sunny Spells**74 2695 3-8-5 **55**.. NeilPollard 5 31
(S C Williams) *awkward leaving stalls: hld up bhd: hdwy and rdn 3f out: wknd 2f out: wl btn and eased fnl f* **6/1**3

42 **11** *14* **Night Orbit**10 4739 4-9-12 **68**.. JohnEgan 7 16
(Miss J Feilden) *in tch in midfield: rdn over 3f out: wkng whn sltly hmpd over 2f out: wl btn and eased ins fnl f: t.o* **7/1**

4052 **12** *½* **Meohmy**9 4774 5-8-9 **51** oh4.. TPO'Shea 11 —
(M R Channon) *hld up in midfield: rdn 4f out: sn dropped out: t.o over 1f out* **16/1**

2m 8.13s (2.63) **Going Correction** +0.25s/f (Good)
WFA 3 from 4yo+ 8lb 12 Ran SP% **127.6**
Speed ratings (Par 103): **99,98,97,97,93 92,92,90,88,86 75,75**
toteswinger: 1&2 £8.30, 1&3 £8.00, 2&3 £14.70. CSF £43.63 CT £257.68 TOTE £5.70: £2.10, £3.30, £2.90; EX 45.60 Place 6 £ 257.73, Place 5 £ 162.25.
Owner A Black **Bred** Graf Und Grafin Von Stauffenberg **Trained** Hampton, Cheshire
■ Stewards' Enquiry : Sophie Doyle four-day ban: careless riding (Aug 30-Sep 2)

FOCUS
An ordinary handicap and a messy contest, with the bulk of the field coming down the centre of the track whilst the winner stayed against the stands' rail. How much that affected the result is anyone's guess, but the form does look rather dubious even so. The first four finished clear.
T/Plt: £699.00 to a £1 stake. Pool: £84,659.04. 88.41 winning tickets. T/Qpdt: £229.20 to a £1 stake. Pool: £4,399.57. 14.20 winning tickets. SP

4685

RIPON (R-H)

Saturday, August 16

OFFICIAL GOING: Good to soft
Wind: Light, across Weather: Sunny periods

5106 ARK DE TRIUMPH MAIDEN AUCTION STKS 6f
2:15 (2:17) (Class 4) 2-Y-O **£3,885** (£1,156; £577; £288) **Stalls** Centre

Form RPR

1 **More Than Many (USA)** 2-8-10 0.......................... JamieMoriarty(3) 12 62
(R A Fahey) *green and towards rr far side: rdn along 1/2-way: hdwy 2f out: swtchd lft over 1f out: swtchd rt ins fnl f: styd on strly to ld last 75yds* **8/1**

5 **2** *¾* **Our Apolonia (IRE)**50 3432 2-7-11 0.......................... CharlotteKerton(7) 8 50
(A Berry) *prom far side: rdn along 2f out and ev ch: drvn ins fnl f: kpt on wl towards fin: 2nd in gp* **80/1**

63 **3** *nse* **Abbey Steps (IRE)**20 4449 2-8-13 0.......................... DavidAllan 6 59
(T D Easterby) *cl up far side: led that gp 1/2-way: overall ldr 2f out and sn rdn: drvn ent fnl f: hdd and no ex last 75yds: 3rd in gp* **11/2**3

0 **4** *4* **Home Before Dark**29 4169 2-8-12 0.................. MichaelJStainton(3) 10 49
(R M Whitaker) *prom far side: rdn along over 2f out: grad wknd appr fnl f: 4th in gp* **14/1**

524 **5** *nk* **Sea Crest**18 4499 2-8-4 71.. TWilliams 3 37+
(M Brittain) *led stands' side gp and overall ldr to 1/2-way: rdn along over 2f out: edgd rt towards far side wl over 1f out: drvn and wknd appr fnl f: 1st in gp* **5/1**2

5 **6** *1 ¾* **Senor Berti**17 4536 2-9-3 0.. TomEaves 1 45+
(B Smart) *cl up stands' side: rdn along 2f out: sn drvn and kpt on same pce: no ch w far side: 2nd in gp* **9/1**

000 **7** *shd* **Look For Value**10 4734 2-8-4 43.................................. KimTinkler 2 32+
(N Tinkler) *chsd ldrs stands' side: rdn along 2f out: sn one pce: 3rd in gp* **100/1**

5 **8** *5* **Royal Salsa (IRE)**14 4616 2-8-6 0.......................... PaulHanagan 5 19+
(R A Fahey) *dwlt: in rr stands' side: rdn along 2f out: sme late hdwy: 4th in gp* **11/2**3

6 **9** *1* **Bob's Smithy**15 4593 2-9-1 0.......................... RobertWinston 4 25+
(T P Tate) *cl up stands' side: ev ch 2f out: sn rdn and edgd rt towards far side: drvn and wknd appr fnl f: 5th in gp* **3/1**1

40 **10** *nk* **Castle Myth (USA)**21 4415 2-8-4 0.......................... AnthonyBetts(7) 11 20
(B Ellison) *led far side: pushed along and hdd 1/2-way: drvn 2f out and sn wknd: 5th in gp* **16/1**

0 **11** *nk* **Hawkeyethenoo (IRE)**21 4415 2-8-9 0.......................... DaleGibson 7 17+
(M W Easterby) *swtchd to r stands' side: in tch: rdn along wl over 2f out and sn wknd: 6th in gp* **11/1**

1m 16.26s (3.26) **Going Correction** +0.35s/f (Good) 11 Ran SP% **116.7**
Speed ratings (Par 96): **92,91,90,85,85 82,82,76,74,74 73**
toteswinger: 1&2 £38.70, 1&3 £44.50, 2&3 £47.20. CSF £464.52 TOTE £9.40: £2.30, £12.30, £2.00; EX 764.80 TRIFECTA Not won..
Owner The Rumpole Partnership **Bred** Wall Street Thoroughbreds **Trained** Musley Bank, N Yorks

FOCUS
A modest-looking maiden. The runner-up was absolutely thrashed on her debut, so may limit the form, with the third and seventh also helping with the level.

NOTEBOOK
More Than Many(USA) came up the far-side rail and, after taking a little time to find his stride, ran on strongly inside the final furlong to win comfortably. This was not a great race but he is a big, scopey horse and he could hardly have been expected to do more on his racecourse debut. (op 14-1)
Our Apolonia(IRE) showed absolutely nothing on her debut, so this looked like a massive improvement. It is far too early, however, to know if this run can be trusted but there looked little fluke in the effort.
Abbey Steps(IRE), stepping back up in trip again, had every chance but did not quite get home as strongly as the first two. One would imagine his immediate future will be in nurseries. (op 7-1 tchd 15-2)
Home Before Dark definitely made progress from his debut effort and is one to keep an eye on when moved into handicaps. (op 16-1)
Sea Crest, stepping up in trip, spoiled her chances by hanging across the course, ending up with the far-side group having raced with the stands-side bunch for the first half of the race. Official explanation: jockey said filly hung right-handed (op 4-1)
Bob's Smithy chased Sea Crest down the stands' side early but drifted badly to his right over two furlongs out and was never going to get involved thereafter. Official explanation: jockey said gelding hung right-handed from half-way (op 4-1 tchd 9-2)

5107 A. RHODES HAULAGE RIPON HORN BLOWER CONDITIONS STKS 6f
2:50 (2:51) (Class 3) 2-Y-O **£6,938** (£2,076; £1,038; £519; £258) **Stalls** Centre

Form RPR

31 **1** **Zuzu (IRE)**29 4164 2-9-0 82.......................... PhilipRobinson 3 93
(M A Jarvis) *mde all: rdn along over 1f out: drvn ins fnl f: edgd lft and kpt on wl towards fin* **10/11**1

15 **2** *½* **Deadly Secret (USA)**36 3920 2-9-5 0.......................... PaulHanagan 6 96
(R A Fahey) *chsd wnr: rdn along wl over 1f out: drvn and styd on ins fnl f* **3/1**2

413 **3** *6* **Lakeman (IRE)**14 4628 2-9-5 76.......................... TomEaves 2 78
(B Ellison) *prom: rdn along over 2f out: sn one pce* **11/1**

163 **4** *10* **Prime Delivery (USA)**21 4402 2-9-5 97.......................... JimCrowley 1 48
(R M H Cowell) *wnt lft s: sn chsng ldrs: rdn along over 2f out: sn drvn and wknd wl over 1f out* **9/2**3

5 *25* **Danderdandan** 2-8-8 0.......................... JamieMoriarty(3) 5 —
(P T Midgley) *sn rdn along in rr: bhd fr 1/2-way* **20/1**

6 *hd* **Miss Thippawan (USA)** 2-8-6 0.......................... PaulFessey 4 —
(P T Midgley) *dwlt: sn chsng ldrs: rdn along 1/2-way: sn wknd and bhd* **80/1**

1m 14.47s (1.47) **Going Correction** +0.35s/f (Good) 6 Ran SP% **109.9**
Speed ratings (Par 98): **104,103,95,82,48 48**
toteswinger: 1&2 £1.40, 1&3 £1.30, 2&3 £30.50. CSF £3.64 TOTE £1.80: £1.20, £2.20; EX 3.60.
Owner Stephen Dartnell **Bred** Bryan Ryan **Trained** Newmarket, Suffolk
■ Stewards' Enquiry : Paul Hanagan one-day ban: used whip with excessive frequency (Aug 30)

FOCUS
The whole field went to the far side and the first two look very useful.

NOTEBOOK
Zuzu(IRE) ◆, a keen-going filly, quickly secured the far-side rail position and travelled strongly throughout the race. However, inside the last she had to be asked a serious question and, inclined to hang a little to her right, she had to pull out all the stops to keep the runner-up at bay. She is going the right way and would not be too inconvenienced by a drop in trip. (op 11-10 tchd 6-5 in places)
Deadly Secret(USA) ◆, who was far from disgraced in a Group 2 last time, got slightly outpaced just inside the two-furlong marker, but he regained his momentum approaching the last and produced a spirited finish without looking like quite overhauling the winner. The fact that he finished six lengths clear of the rest speaks volumes for his performance, and that of the winner. (op 11-4 tchd 7-2)
Lakeman(IRE), beaten in a nursery last time off a mark of 77, was firmly put in his place in the closing stages. (tchd 8-1)
Prime Delivery(USA), dropping down in trip by a furlong, found it very tough against a couple of decent sprinters but, even so, was disappointing. His official mark looks much too high and he will probably struggle for the rest of the season, although a return to a quicker surface may help him. (op 7-2 tchd 3-1)

5108 EUROPEAN BREEDERS' FUND STOWE FAMILY LAW FILLIES' H'CAP 1m 1f 170y
3:25 (3:25) (Class 4) (0-80,80) 3-Y-O+ **£6,308** (£1,888; £944; £472; £235) **Stalls** Low

Form RPR

4213 **1** **La Sarrazine (FR)**9 4791 3-10-0 **80**.......................... RobertWinston 5 90+
(J R Fanshawe) *trckd ldng pair: hdwy 3f out: rdn to ld 2f out: kpt on wl u.p ins fnl f* **11/8**1

4256 **2** *3 ½* **Feisty Royale**18 4500 3-9-6 **72**.......................... RoystonFfrench 7 75
(M Johnston) *led 4f: cl up tl led again 3f out: sn rdn and hdd 2f out: drvn appr fnl f and kpt on same pce* **15/2**

31 **3** *1 ¾* **St Trinians**39 3823 3-9-11 **77**.......................... JimCrowley 3 77
(E F Vaughan) *trckd ldrs: hdwy over 3f out: rdn 2f out and sn no imp* **4/1**2

5 **4** *2 ¼* **Bois Joli (IRE)**31 4082 3-9-13 **79**.......................... JimmyQuinn 6 74
(M Botti) *t.k.h: trckd ldrs: effrt 3f out and sn rdn: drvn 2f and sn btn* **9/2**3

0-00 **5** *1 ¾* **Tender Moments**15 4597 4-9-2 **60**.......................... TomEaves 2 52
(B Smart) *a in rr* **25/1**

0230 **6** *16* **Italian Goddess**13 4669 3-8-9 **61**.......................... HayleyTurner 4 21
(M L W Bell) *t.k.h: trckd ldrs tl hdwy to ld after 4f: rdn along 4f out: hdd 3f out and grad wknd* **4/1**2

2m 9.27s (3.87) **Going Correction** +0.35s/f (Good)
WFA 3 from 4yo 8lb 6 Ran SP% **115.9**
Speed ratings (Par 102): **98,95,93,92,90 77**
toteswinger: 1&2 £3.80, 1&3 £1.90, 2&3 £8.00. CSF £13.29 TOTE £2.30: £1.40, £3.40; EX 14.80.
Owner Mr & Mrs Duncan Davidson **Bred** Benedikt Fassbender **Trained** Newmarket, Suffolk

FOCUS
A fair handicap run at a respectable pace in the ground. The form is weakish for the grade but sound enough.
Italian Goddess Official explanation: jockey said filly ran too free

5109 WILLIAM HILL GREAT ST WILFRID STKS (HERITAGE H'CAP) 6f
4:00 (4:02) (Class 2) (0-105,104) 3-Y-O+
£37,386 (£11,196; £5,598; £2,802; £1,398; £702) **Stalls** Centre

Form RPR

-310 **1** **Tajneed (IRE)**105 1809 5-8-12 **92**.......................... AdrianTNicholls 11 103
(D Nicholls) *trckd ldr far side: rdn over 1f out: styd on to ld ins fnl f: drvn and hld on gamely* **17/2**

0501 **2** *hd* **Valery Borzov (IRE)**7 4854 4-9-4 **98**.......................... FrancisNorton 16 108
(D Nicholls) *trckd ldrs far side: hdwy 2f out: rdn over 1f out: edgd rt and styd on strly towards fin: 2nd in gp* **11/2**1

2500 **3** *nk* **Tamagin (USA)**21 4437 5-9-3 **97**..........................(p) FergalLynch 9 106
(K A Ryan) *qckly away and swtchd to far side: overall ldr: rdn along 2f out: drvn over 1f out: hdd and no ex ins fnl f: 3rd in gp* **28/1**

0001 **4** *¾* **Conquest (IRE)**14 4624 4-9-6 **100**.......................... HayleyTurner 12 107
(W J Haggas) *chsd ldrs far side: hdwy over 2f out: rdn and ch over 1f out: tl drvn and nt qckn wl ins fnl f: 4th in gp* **14/1**

4600 **5** *3 ¼* **Confuchias (IRE)**14 4624 4-9-6 **100**.......................... JimCrowley 8 96
(K R Burke) *cl up stands' side: led that gp 1/2-way: rdn over 2f out: drvn and kpt on ins fnl f: no ch w far side: 1st in gp* **33/1**

0-00 **6** *1* **Patavellian (IRE)**14 4624 10-9-3 **97**..........................(b) PhilipRobinson 18 90
(R Charlton) *prom far side: rdn along 2f out: drvn over 1f out: sn one pce: 5th in gp* **14/1**

3002 **7** *½* **Fullandby (IRE)**26 4240 6-9-7 **104**.......................... LeeVickers(3) 20 95
(T J Etherington) *hld up towards rr far side: hdwy 2f out: sn rdn and styd on ins fnl f: nt rch ldrs: 6th in gp* **8/1**3

-564 **8** *hd* **Hogmaneigh (IRE)**70 2828 5-9-7 **101**.......................... SaleemGolam 15 92
(S C Williams) *towards rr far side: hdwy 2f out: rdn and styd on ins fnl f: nrst fin: 7th in gp* **10/1**

0034 **9** 3/4 **Joseph Henry**[7] 4854 6-8-9 **89**.............................. PaulFessey 4 77
(D Nicholls) *chsd ldrs stands' side: rdn along over 2f out: grad wknd: 2nd in gp* **25/1**
5622 **10** *nse* **Baby Strange**[15] 4586 4-9-3 **97**.......................... DarrenWilliams 17 85
(D Shaw) *towards rr far side: hdwy 2f out: sn rdn and no imp appr fnl f: 8th in gp* **6/1**[2]
2020 **11** 1/2 **Dhaular Dhar (IRE)**[15] 4587 6-9-7 **101**........................ DanielTudhope 13 88
(J S Goldie) *racd far side: in tch: rdn 2f out: sn drvn and no imp appr fnl f: 9th in gp* **16/1**
0104 **12** *nk* **Viking Spirit**[32] 4059 6-9-8 **102**..............................(p) AdamKirby 3 88
(W R Swinburn) *led stands' side gp: hdd 1/2-way: cl up tl rdn wl over 1f out and grad wknd: 3rd in gp* **22/1**
2000 **13** *hd* **Hinton Admiral**[14] 4624 4-8-7 **94**.............................. FrederikTylicki(3) 10 79
(R A Fahey) *in tch far side: effrt over 2f out: sn rdn and no imp: 10th in gp* **22/1**
416 **14** 1 1/2 **Knot In Wood (IRE)**[14] 4624 6-9-9 **103**.......................... PaulHanagan 1 83
(R A Fahey) *a towards rr stands' side: 4th in gp* **16/1**
4500 **15** 1 1/4 **Rising Shadow (IRE)**[14] 4624 7-8-10 **95**................ AshleyHamblett(5) 7 71
(N Wilson) *a towards rr stands' side: 5th in gp* **28/1**
0-00 **16** 1/2 **Protector (SAF)**[14] 4624 7-9-1 **95**..............................(t) RobertWinston 5 70
(A G Foster) *a towards rr stands' side: 6th in gp* **50/1**
4250 **17** 4 **Northern Dare (IRE)**[15] 4586 4-8-7 **90**.................... AndrewMullen(3) 2 52
(D Nicholls) *chsd ldrs stands' side: rdn along over 2f out: sn wknd: 7th in gp* **14/1**
4601 **18** *nse* **Bond City (IRE)**[12] 4687 6-8-10 **90**.............................. TomEaves 6 52
(G R Oldroyd) *a towards rr stands' side: 8th in gp* **33/1**
430 **19** 8 **Ebraam (USA)**[20] 4445 5-8-13 **93**.............................. JimmyQuinn 19 29
(P Howling) *a towards rr far side: 11th in gp* **16/1**
0050 **20** 6 **Ajigolo**[12] 4687 5-8-12 **92**.............................. SamHitchcott 14 9
(M R Channon) *in tch far side: rdn along over 2f out: sn wknd: 12th in gp* **28/1**

1m 13.75s (0.75) **Going Correction** +0.35s/f (Good) **20** Ran SP% **128.8**
Speed ratings (Par 109): **109,108,108,107,103 101,101,100,99,99 99,98,98,96,94 94,88,88,77,69**
toteswinger: 1&2 £19.70, 1&3 £116.80, 2&3 £61.50. CSF £49.46 CT £1328.08 TOTE £11.00: £2.70, £2.00, £5.50, £3.40; EX 67.30 Trifecta £3746.60 Pool: £1,9745.82 - 3.90 w/u..
Owner AlexNichollsRobertGilmartinFinolaDevaney **Bred** R Hodgins **Trained** Sessay, N Yorks
■ A 1-2 for David Nicholls.
■ Stewards' Enquiry : Fergal Lynch caution: used whip down shoulder in forehand position

FOCUS
A predictably competitive race for this valuable and historic handicap, though the draw clearly had a major effect. With the field splitting into two groups, the far side, which had the majority of runners, had the advantage. The usual solid form for this sort of race, rated through the third and fourth.

NOTEBOOK
Tajneed(IRE), a course-and-distance winner, had the ground in his favour and bounced back from a 105-day break to get home by the skin of his teeth. Lightly raced this season, since joining David Nicholls for only 4,000gns from Dermot Weld, he remains a horse of interest, especially with some give underfoot. (op 8-1 tchd 9-1)
Valery Borzov(IRE) really hit full stride about a furlong from home and would have got up in another few strides. Winner of a good Haydock handicap last time off a 6lb lower mark, he went down fighting and is one to keep in mind for all the big sprint handicaps for the rest of the season. (op 7-1)
Tamagin(USA), back in cheekpieces, deserves plenty of praise as he was drawn in single figures, but still managed to dash across to the far side and take his rivals along at a rate of knots. Headed inside the final furlong, he kept on well to the line and only just missed out in a driving finish. (op 33-1)
Conquest(IRE), the long-priced winner of the Stewards' Cup, came through to have every chance but lacked the finishing kick of a couple of those in front of him. However, he was hardly disgraced off a 5lb higher mark and seems to be enjoying life a bit more again.
Confuchias(IRE) ran a belter from a low draw and deserves plenty of credit. This looked to be his best effort for some time and he would be interesting next time if building on the run. (op 40-1)
Patavellian(IRE) ran well from an advantageous draw but one would suspect that he will always find at least a couple of rivals too good for him now in this sort of race at the age of ten. (op 16-1)
Fullandby(IRE) had the best of the draw but is much too high in the weights to have an obvious winning chance.
Joseph Henry did not run as badly as his final position suggests, as he came down the unfavoured stands'-side rail.
Baby Strange had lots of things in his favour, despite being high in the weights, so it was disappointing to see him never pose a threat. (tchd 13-2 and 7-1 in places)
Knot In Wood(IRE) had no chance from his draw and might as well have stayed at home. (op 14-1)

5110 E-TECH GROUP GEOFF JEWSON MEMORIAL MAIDEN STKS 5f
4:35 (4:38) (Class 5) 3-Y-O+ **£3,885** (£1,156; £577; £288) **Stalls** Centre

Form RPR
505 **1** **Nabeeda**[22] 4379 3-9-0 **55**.............................. MarkLawson(3) 8 58
(M Brittain) *chsd ldrs: rdn wl over 1f out: drvn and styd on ins fnl f to ld nr fin* **12/1**
2000 **2** *nk* **Paddy Jack**[7] 4852 3-9-3 **56**..............................(p) RobertWinston 12 57
(J R Weymes) *chsd ldr: rdn and hdwy to ld over 1f out: drvn ins fnl f: hdd and no ex nr fin* **10/1**
0 **3** 1/2 **Half A Crown (IRE)**[71] 2786 3-9-3 **0**.............................. FergalLynch 11 55
(D W Barker) *in tch: hdwy on inner wl over 1f out: styd on strly ins fnl f* **7/1**
-020 **4** *nk* **Until When (USA)**[22] 4385 4-9-5 **67**..............................(v) TomEaves 7 54
(B Smart) *in tch and sn rdn along: drvn to chse ldrs 2f out: kpt on same pce u.p ins fnl f* **4/1**[1]
0 **5** 1 1/2 **Molly Two**[42] 3712 3-8-9 **0**.............................. DuranFentiman(3) 4 44
(L A Mullaney) *sn led and clr: rdn 2f out: hdd over 1f out: wknd ins fnl f* **33/1**
30- **6** 1 1/4 **Imperial Quest**[306] 6238 4-9-0 **0**.............................. JimmyQuinn 9 39
(E J Alston) *chsd ldrs: rdn along 2f out: drvn and no imp ent fnl f* **13/2**[3]
6-2 **7** 3/4 **Billberry**[17] 4523 3-9-3 **0**.............................. SaleemGolam 10 42
(S C Williams) *midfield: rdn along and hdwy 2f out: no imp appr fnl f* **4/1**[1]
6020 **8** 2 1/2 **Admiral Bond (IRE)**[14] 4615 3-9-3 **67**..............................(v) DanielTudhope 5 33
(G R Oldroyd) *hmpd s and bhd tl sme late hdwy* **5/1**[2]
0000 **9** 3/4 **Lovely Lilling**[27] 4216 3-8-12 **35**..............................(p) PaulFessey 2 25
(P T Midgley) *midfield: rdn along over 2f out: n.d* **100/1**
3500 **10** *hd* **Recent Times**[12] 4684 3-8-12 **54**..............................(b[1]) DavidAllan 6 24
(T D Easterby) *chsd ldrs: rdn along 2f out: grad wknd* **10/1**
-04 **11** *hd* **Meinardus (IRE)**[20] 4454 3-9-0 **0**.............................. NeilBrown(3) 1 28
(T D Barron) *a towards rr* **16/1**
12 3 3/4 **Lifetime Endeavour** 4-8-12 **0**.............................. BMcHugh(7) 14 15
(R E Barr) *v.s.a and a bhd* **40/1**
0 **13** 1 1/2 **Red Wind (IRE)**[22] 4379 3-8-12 **0**.............................. AshleyHamblett(5) 13 9
(N Wilson) *a towards rr* **33/1**
4060 **14** 2 1/2 **Wave Hill (IRE)**[71] 2803 3-8-12 **54**.............................. SladeO'Hara(5) 3 —
(A Berry) *in tch on outer: rdn along over 2f out: sn wknd* **40/1**

62.13 secs (1.43) **Going Correction** +0.35s/f (Good)
WFA 3 from 4yo 2lb **14** Ran SP% **126.0**
Speed ratings (Par 103): **102,101,100,100,97 95,94,90,89,89 88,82,80,76**
toteswinger: 1&2 £28.40, 1&3 £14.50, 2&3 £10.60. CSF £128.84 TOTE £19.00: £4.70, £2.50, £2.90; EX 139.40 TRIFECTA Not won..
Owner Mel Brittain **Bred** Mrs S Clifford **Trained** Warthill, N Yorks

FOCUS
A very modest maiden. Winners may emerge from the race but, on balance, the form looks weak judged on the winner's and runner-up's previous efforts, if sound enough.

5111 I'ANSONS - BRITISH HORSE FEEDS H'CAP 1m 4f 10y
5:10 (5:10) (Class 3) (0-95,90) 3-Y-O **£7,569** (£2,265; £1,132; £566; £282) **Stalls** Low

Form RPR
-021 **1** **Blimey O'Riley (IRE)**[85] 2363 3-8-5 **74**.............................. JimmyQuinn 1 86
(M H Tompkins) *chsd ldr: hdwy 3f out: rdn to ld 2f out: drvn and edgd lft over 1f out: kpt on strly* **8/1**
-121 **2** 2 **Inchwood (IRE)**[46] 3586 3-9-6 **89**.............................. PhilipRobinson 5 98+
(M A Jarvis) *hld up in rr: pushed along and outpcd whn pce qcknd over 4f out: rdn to chse ldrs over 2f out and sn hung rt: drvn to chse wnr whn hung bdly rt ins fnl f* **11/8**[1]
0413 **3** 3 3/4 **Sweet Lightning**[44] 3633 3-9-7 **90**.............................. FrancisNorton 4 93
(W R Muir) *trckd ldng pair: hdwy 3f out: rdn and ev ch over 2f out: sn rdn and sltly hmpd over 1f out: sn one pce* **11/4**[2]
1014 **4** 7 **Jabal Tariq**[28] 4205 3-9-4 **87**.............................. PaulHanagan 6 79
(B W Hills) *led: qcknd over 4f out: rdn and qcknd again 3f out: hdd 2f out: sn drvn and wknd* **7/2**[3]
164- **5** 1 **Keenes Day (FR)**[310] 6120 3-8-11 **80**.............................. RoystonFfrench 3 70
(M Johnston) *hld up in tch: rdn along 4f out: sn outpcd and bhd* **12/1**

2m 40.31s (3.61) **Going Correction** +0.35s/f (Good) **5** Ran SP% **109.8**
Speed ratings (Par 104): **101,99,97,92,91**
CSF £19.56 TOTE £7.40: £2.50, £1.30; EX 16.30 Place 6 £ 223.04, Place 5 £ 45.78.
Owner Trevor Benton **Bred** Mrs Ann Kennedy **Trained** Newmarket, Suffolk

FOCUS
A fair small-field handicap run at a respectable pace. The wiiner is improving and the second and third ran to form.

NOTEBOOK
Blimey O'Riley(IRE), not seen since May, struck for home early in the home straight and stayed on well to land a brave victory. He is the sort to thrive in the autumn, as he has not been over-raced and handles soft ground. (op 11-2)
Inchwood(IRE) kept on really well but never gave her rider much help, as she hung under pressure and could not be kept straight. A flatter track may well help her next time. (op 5-4 tchd 6-4 and 6-5 in places)
Sweet Lightning ranged up alongside the winner over two furlongs from home but could not sustain his effort. This run suggests that the handicapper has him about right now. (op 7-2)
Jabal Tariq did all the hard work in front but had no response to the finishers once joined. (op 5-1)
Keenes Day(FR) was struggling as soon as they swung into the home straight and probably needs a much quicker surface to be at his best. (op 10-1)
T/Plt: £649.20 to a £1 stake. Pool: £72,674.90. 81.71 winning tickets. T/Qpdt: £76.60 to a £1 stake. Pool: £4,814.65. 46.50 winning tickets. JR

5038 DEAUVILLE (R-H)
Saturday, August 16
OFFICIAL GOING: Turf course - good to soft; all-weather - standard

5112a PRIX DE LA VALLEE D'AUGE (LISTED RACE) 5f
1:10 (1:09) 2-Y-O **£20,221** (£8,088; £6,066; £4,044; £2,022)

RPR
1 **Treasure (FR)**[28] 2-8-8 .... DBoeuf 4 98
(Mme C Head-Maarek, France)
2 *nk* **Raggle Taggle (IRE)**[28] 4190 2-8-8 .... DBonilla 2 97
(R M Beckett) *cl up: pushed along 1 1/2f out: rdn over 1f out: ev ch fnl f: styd on* **12/1**[2]
3 1 1/2 **Ares Choix**[21] 4403 2-8-8 .... CSoumillon 1 92
(P C Haslam) *cl up: pushed along 1 1/2f out: cl 3rd 1f out: no ex fnl stages* **21/10**[1]
4 3 **Bluster (FR)**[63] 3052 2-8-11 .... OPeslier 3 84
(Robert Collet, France)
5 3 **Caparroso (FR)**[20] 4472 2-8-8 ....(b) C-PLemaire 5 70
(T Lemer, France)

59.10 secs (1.60) **5** Ran SP% **40.0**
PARI-MUTUEL: WIN 2.70; PL 1.70, 4.90; SF 23.60.
Owner Mme Alec Head **Bred** Alec & Mme Ghislaine Head **Trained** Chantilly, France

NOTEBOOK
Raggle Taggle(IRE) was always well placed and challenged for the lead throughout the final furlong but could never get to the winner. He stuck to his guns to the bitter end.
Ares Choix was waited with and still had plenty to do at the halfway stage. She made her run up the stands' rail and finished really well, and possibly a longer trip will be of benefit in the future.

5113a LE GALOP HERMES 1ERE MANCHE (STRAIGHT) 6f 110y(S)
2:15 (2:18) 4-Y-O+ **£14,706** (£5,882; £4,412; £2,941; £1,471)

RPR
1 **Desert Ocean (IRE)**[11] 4-8-11 .... MDemuro 90
(G Collet, France)
2 1 **Anisakis (FR)**[7] 4-8-11 .... DBonilla 87
(N Clement, France)
3 *shd* **El Vettorio (GER)**[83] 5-9-1 .... OPeslier 91
(C Sprengel, Germany)
4 1/2 **Celtie Rod (IRE)**[6] 4-9-1 90
(X Nakkachdji, France)
5 1/2 **Air Bag (FR)**[11] 4-8-8 81
(Mme C Barande-Barbe, France)
6 *snk* **Skyteam (FR)**[28] 4-8-11 84
(Mme C Head-Maarek, France)
7 3 **Kilometre Neuf (FR)**[291] 5-8-11 75
(F Doumen, France)
8 1 **Biniou (IRE)**[56] 3248 5-8-11 .... IMendizabal 73
(R M H Cowell) *plld hrd in mid-div: pushed along 2f out: n.d* **29/4**[1]
9 *shd* **Objeto De Arte (BRZ)**[40] 5-8-11 72
(P Bary, France)

10 nk **Up And Coming (IRE)**[28] 4-8-11 71
(J E Pease, France)
0 **Alendha (GER)**[31] 5-8-8 .... —
(T Clout, France)
U **Alternative**[17] 4-8-11 .... —
(Jorge Romero, U.S.A)
1m 17.3s (0.10) **12** Ran SP% **12.1**
PARI-MUTUEL: WIN 21.10; PL 5.90, 3.70, 4.00; DF 51.80.
Owner N Lemaire **Bred** Mrs H Owen **Trained** France

5114a PRIX GONTAUT-BIRON (GROUP 3) 1m 2f
2:45 (2:46) 4-Y-0+ **£29,412** (£11,765; £8,824; £5,882; £2,941)

RPR

1 **Boris De Deauville (IRE)**[24] 4320 5-8-11 .... DBoeuf 2 117
(S Wattel, France) *mde all: drvn and r.o fnl f: drvn out* **43/10**[2]
2 1 **Crossharbour**[28] 4212 4-9-1 .... SPasquier 3 119
(A Fabre, France) *racd in 4th: drvn 2f out: hdwy to go 2nd over 1f out: r.o fnl f: nt rch wnr* **1/1**[1]
3 3 **Eradicate (IRE)**[18] 4504 4-8-9 .... JoeFanning 1 107
(M Johnston) *racd in 3rd: drvn st: styd on u.p to line: nt trble ldrs* **18/1**
4 2 1/2 **Light Green (BRZ)**[28] 4212 4-8-5 .... C-PLemaire 5 98
(A De Royer-Dupre, France) *hld up in last: styd on in centre fr appr fnl f: fin wl clsng stages to take 4th nr fin* **16/1**
5 1 1/2 **Terra Incognita**[21] 4-8-10 ow2.................. CSoumillon 6 100
(Y De Nicolay, France) *prom in 2nd: pushed along st: styd in 2nd tl rdn and wknd fr over 1f out* **13/2**[3]
6 3/4 **Russian Desert (IRE)**[16] 4-8-9 .... MGuyon 8 98
(A Fabre, France) *disp 5th: 6th st: rdn 2f out: unable qck* **74/10**
7 nk **Elasos (FR)**[46] 3595 6-8-9 .... DBonilla 4 97
(D Sepulchre, France) *disp 5th: 5th st: effrt over 1 1/2f out: no imp* **40/1**
8 3/4 **Atlantic Air (FR)**[16] 6-8-9 .... OPeslier 7 95
(A De Mieulle,) *racd in 7th: n.d* **89/10**
2m 6.70s (-3.50) **Going Correction** -0.025s/f (Good) **8** Ran SP% **117.8**
Speed ratings: **113,112,109,107,106 106,105,105**
PARI-MUTUEL: WIN 5.30; PL 1.40, 1.20, 3.00; DF 3.30.
Owner Mme M Bryant & L Haegel **Bred** Petra Bloodstock Agency Ltd **Trained** France

NOTEBOOK
Boris De Deauville(IRE) had a new jockey aboard and was ridden more positively, and the change in tactics certainly paid dividends. He quickened things up considerably soon after entering the straight and, although challenged by the favourite, he always had a little in hand. This soft-ground specialist will now be aimed at the Prix Dollar for the third time.
Crossharbour tried in vain to give a kilo and a half to the winner. Raced just behind the leaders in the early part of the race, he looked dangerous at the two-furlong marker but never really got a blow in. He just stayed on one-paced and would have probably preferred better ground.
Eradicate(IRE) was slightly unlucky in the straight and never looked like catching the winner and runner-up. Although probably a little out of his depth, he was putting in his best work at the finish.
Light Green(BRZ) ran on really well in the straight. She now appears to have adapted to racing in France and will definitely be one worth following in the future. Her trainer was certainly delighted with this effort.

5115a LE GALOP HERMES 2EME MANCHE (ALL-WEATHER) 1m 1f 110y
3:15 (3:19) 4-Y-0+ **£14,706** (£5,882; £4,412; £2,941; £1,471)

RPR

1 **Roi (FR)**[93] 7-8-11 ....(b) GMosse 85
(J Rossi, France)
2 snk **Ilie Nastase (FR)**[6] 4913 4-9-1 .... DBoeuf 89
(R Gibson, France)
3 nk **Gloria De Campeao (BRZ)**[140] 1092 5-9-4 .... IMendizabal 91
(P Bary, France) **11/4**[1]
4 1 1/2 **Slickly Royal (FR)**[11] 4-8-11 82
(P Demercastel, France)
5 snk **Menestrol (FR)**[86] 6-9-4 88
(D Prod'Homme, France)
6 nk **Kingvati (FR)**[248] 7128 6-8-11 81
(S Wattel, France)
7 hd **Beau Vengerov (IRE)**[22] 4401 4-8-11 80
(D Smaga, France)
8 3/4 **De Zephyr (FR)**[6] 4913 6-9-1 83
(Robert Collet, France)
9 nse **Troque (FR)**[65] 4-8-11 79
(F Doumen, France)
10 3/4 **Salsa De La Tour (FR)**[14] 4-8-11 77
(P Demercastel, France)
0 **Woolfall Blue (IRE)**[458] 1767 5-8-11 .... CSoumillon —
(G G Margarson) *led after 2f: hdd 2 1/2f out: 2nd and u.p st: sn wknd and qckly eased* **29/1**[2]
0 **Thunder Storm Cat (USA)**[36] 4-9-1 ....(b) —
(M Rulec, Germany)
0 **Fontcia (FR)**[46] 3595 4-8-8 .... —
(D Sepulchre, France)
0 **Pur Sucre (FR)**[36] 4-8-11 .... —
(R Pritchard-Gordon, France)
0 **Becher**[325] 5744 4-9-4 ....(b) —
(A De Mieulle,)
0 **Arlanda (GER)**[16] 7-8-8 .... —
(S Smrczek, Germany)
2m 0.30s (120.30) **16** Ran SP% **30.0**
PARI-MUTUEL: WIN 18.70; PL 5.70, 6.10, 2.20; DF 174.60.
Owner G Lheritier **Bred** A & Mme A Head **Trained** France

4762 BATH (L-H)
Sunday, August 17

OFFICIAL GOING: Good to soft (6.9)
Wind: Breezy, half-against. Weather: showery

5116 HUNTERS LAND ROVER BRISTOL MAIDEN AUCTION STKS 5f 11y
2:30 (2:33) (Class 6) 2-Y-O **£1,942** (£578; £288; £144) **Stalls** Centre

Form RPR

0203 1 **Shiva Adiva**[20] 4486 2-8-4 72.................. RichardKingscote 1 60
(Tom Dascombe) *mde all: rdn over 1f out: hrd pressed ent fnl f: outbattled runner up last 100yds* **8/11**[1]
0440 2 1/2 **Song Of Praise**[12] 4706 2-8-8 60.................. FrancisNorton 7 62
(M Blanshard) *in tch: chsd wnr 1/2-way: rdn over 1f out: upsides wnr ent fnl f: nt run on and btn last 100yds* **11/2**[3]
30 3 hd **Queen Sally (IRE)**[29] 4176 2-8-7 0.................. TolleyDean(3) 4 63
(J L Spearing) *taken down early: in tch: rdn to chse ldng pair over 1f out: kpt on u.p ins fnl f* **7/2**[2]
5600 4 3 1/4 **Call Me Courageous (IRE)**[29] 4185 2-8-13 62.................. JohnEgan 6 55
(A B Haynes) *chsd ldrs: rdn 1/2-way: wknd fnl f* **7/1**
000 5 nk **Haulit**[52] 3417 2-8-8 58.................. KevinGhunowa(3) 5 52
(R A Harris) *chsd wnr tl 1/2-way: wknd u.p over 1f out* **20/1**
0 6 2 1/4 **Erris Lady**[10] 4763 2-8-6 0.................. LiamJones 2 38
(Mrs L Williamson) *wnt rt s: t.k.h: hld up in tch: lost pl and hung rt 1/2-way: no ch last 2f* **25/1**
66.10 secs (3.60) **Going Correction** +0.575s/f (Yiel) **6** Ran SP% **116.6**
Speed ratings (Par 92): **94,93,92,87,87 83**
toteswinger: 1&2 £1.40, 1&3 £1.30, 2&3 £1.90. CSF £5.78 TOTE £1.60: £1.30, £2.40; EX 5.10.
Owner Stephen Bayless **Bred** S & Mrs M Bayless **Trained** Lambourn, Berks
■ Edgeworth (5/1) was withdrawn (saddle slipped on way to s, ran free and eventually uns rdr.) R4 applies, deduct 15p in the £.

FOCUS
A routine maiden, with the odds-on winner only scrambling home and well below form in victory. Limited form.

NOTEBOOK
Shiva Adiva, an above-average sort at this level in the paddock, knuckled down well after the runner-up had drawn alongside passing the furlong pole. The Handicapper is not likely to rate this performance too highly, but she looks the type to improve a bit and will be interesting in handicaps from now on, with Kingscote praising her battling attitude. (op 5-6 tchd 10-11 and evens in a place)
Song Of Praise came as close as she ever has to winning in maiden company, but Shiva Adiva was probably not at her best. Her prospects back in nurseries will depend upon how the Handicapper views her proximity to the more highly-rated winner. (op 9-1)
Queen Sally(IRE) has the ability to win a run-of-the-mill maiden, but her future lies in nurseries. Five furlongs suits her well at present, but she should stay 6f on better ground than she encountered at Haydock. (op 4-1 tchd 5-1)
Call Me Courageous(IRE) was well beaten in his only nursery, but that looks a more likely home for him from now on. (op 14-1 tchd 20-1)
Haulit needs to switch to nurseries to improve his prospects of success. (op 50-1)
Erris Lady has plenty of winners in the family, but she cost only 7,000gns and looks as if she needs more time. Her dam, Mysterious Plans, won over 1m2f as a three-year-old, and she has produced four previous winners who have become more effective as they have matured. (op 66-1)

5117 PLATINUM MOTOR GROUP & WELLSWAY LTD MAIDEN STKS 1m 3f 144y
3:00 (3:04) (Class 5) 3-Y-O+ **£2,590** (£770; £385; £192) **Stalls** Low

Form RPR

432 1 **King O'The Gypsies (IRE)**[23] 4372 3-9-3 84.................. SteveDrowne 12 87
(R Charlton) *in tch: chsd ldr 3f out: sn led: rdn clr and hung lft over 1f out: easily* **1/2**[1]
2-35 2 8 **French Riviera**[49] 3530 3-9-3 79.................. JimmyFortune 6 74
(Sir Michael Stoute) *chsd ldr: led 3f out: sn hdd and rdn: no ch w wnr fnl f* **3/1**[2]
0 3 5 **Extreme Pleasure (IRE)**[24] 4342 3-8-12 0.................. RichardKingscote 10 61
(W J Knight) *hld up in midfield: hdwy over 4f out: chsd ldng pair u.p over 2f out: edgd rt and no hdwy after* **66/1**
55 4 7 **Go On Ahead (IRE)**[45] 3637 8-9-13 0.................. ChrisCatlin 5 55
(W S Kittow) *s.i.s: sn led: hdd and rdn 3f out: sn wknd* **25/1**
5 1 **Auction Belle** 3-8-12 0.................. GregFairley 8 48
(P A Blockley) *hld up in midfield: rdn and wknd 4f out* **66/1**
6 4 1/2 **Darfen (IRE)**[28] 5-9-10 0.................. KevinGhunowa(3) 7 46
(J L Flint) *v.s.a: t.k.h: hld up bhd: hdwy 7f out: rdn and wknd 4f out* **16/1**[3]
7 25 **Frankly Fantastic**[63] 4-9-13 0..................(bt[1]) FrankieMcDonald 13 6
(Jean-Rene Auvray) *hld up in midfield: hdwy 6f out: rdn and wknd qckly over 4f out: t.o* **100/1**
8 1 **It's Early Days** 3-9-3 0.................. FrancisNorton 14 5
(W R Muir) *s.i.s: sn rdn along in rr: lost tch 5f out: t.o* **33/1**
9 36 **Mr Grumble (USA)** 3-8-12 0.................. RichardEvans(5) 9 —
(P D Evans) *v.s.a: rdn along in rr: t.o last 4f* **33/1**
0/0 10 1 3/4 **Topsy Maite**[99] 2015 4-9-3 0.................. GabrielHannon(5) 4 —
(P A Blockley) *chsd ldrs tl wknd rapidly 4f out: t.o* **100/1**
2m 36.45s (5.85) **Going Correction** +0.575s/f (Yiel)
WFA 3 from 4yo+ 10lb **10** Ran SP% **112.2**
Speed ratings (Par 103): **103,97,94,89,89 86,69,68,44,43**
toteswinger: 1&2 £1.10, 1&3 £8.60, 2&3 £9.60. CSF £1.78 TOTE £1.40: £1.10, £1.10, £8.70; EX 2.30 Trifecta £31.90 Pool £311.59 - 7.20 winning units..
Owner B E Nielsen **Bred** Premier Bloodstock **Trained** Beckhampton, Wilts
■ Inquest was withdrawn after proving unruly in the stalls (9/1, deduct 10p in the £).

FOCUS
Two expensive purchases filled the first two places, but on the whole this was a modest event which took little winning.
Darfen(IRE) Official explanation: jockey said gelding missed the break
It's Early Days Official explanation: jockey said gelding was unbalanced throughout

5118 BATHWICK TYRES H'CAP 1m 2f 46y
3:30 (3:31) (Class 4) (0-80,77) 3-Y-O+ **£4,857** (£1,445; £722; £360) **Stalls** Low

Form RPR

0043 1 **Dr Brass**[29] 4179 3-9-1 72..................(b[1]) EddieAhern 2 81
(H J L Dunlop) *t.k.h: chsd ldr after 1f: rdn to ld over 2f out: styd on wl u.p fr over 1f out* **4/1**[3]
6042 2 1 1/4 **Master Mahogany**[5] 4953 7-9-0 63.................. SteveDrowne 4 69
(R J Hodges) *t.k.h: chsd ldr for 1f: chsd wnr over 2f out: kpt on same pce u.p fnl f* **11/4**[2]
0343 3 1/2 **Penang Cinta**[14] 4662 5-9-3 66..................(p) JimCrowley 3 71
(P D Evans) *t.k.h: hld up in midfield: hdwy to chse ldng pair over 2f out: kpt on u.p but nvr gng pce to chal ldng pair* **13/2**
3201 4 9 **Latin Scholar (IRE)**[27] 4254 3-9-5 76.................. DaneO'Neill 5 63
(A King) *stdd after s: hld up in last pair: hdwy over 3f out: chsd ldrs and hrd rdn over 2f out: wknd qckly ent fnl f* **2/1**[1]
0042 5 hd **Scary Movie (IRE)**[55] 3333 3-8-11 68.................. JohnEgan 8 55
(D J Coakley) *stdd s: hld up in last pl: brief effrt 3f out: wl btn last 2f: eased ins fnl f* **9/1**
3140 6 5 **Friends Hope**[30] 4152 7-9-11 77.................. KevinGhunowa(3) 9 54
(P A Blockley) *plld hrd: hld up in midfield: rdn 3f out: sn outpcd and wl btn* **12/1**

000- 7 26 **Kapellmeister (IRE)**[255] 7046 5-9-11 77.....................(p) TolleyDean(3) 7 2
(M S Saunders) *led: rdn and hdd 3f out: wknd 2f out: virtually p.u ins fnl f: t.o* 22/1

2m 15.46s (4.46) **Going Correction** +0.575s/f (Yiel)
WFA 3 from 4yo+ 8lb 7 Ran SP% **115.4**
Speed ratings (Par 105): **105,104,103,96,96 92,71**
toteswinger: 1&2 £3.30, 1&3 £4.20, 2&3 £3.90. CSF £15.74 CT £69.21 TOTE £6.20: £2.50, £2.20; EX 20.10 Trifecta £115.90 Pool £369.82 - 2.36 winning units..
Owner Normandie Stud Ltd **Bred** Normandie Stud Ltd **Trained** Lambourn, Berks
■ Stewards' Enquiry : John Egan three-day ban: failed to ride out for 4th place (Aug 31-Sep 2)

FOCUS
A moderate contest, but the winner looked progressive in first-time blinkers.

5119 BRISTOL & BATH HONDA FILLIES' H'CAP 1m 5y
4:00 (4:01) (Class 5) (0-70,69) 3-Y-O+ **£2,914** (£867; £433; £216) **Stalls** Low

Form RPR
0026 1 **Liberally (IRE)**[27] 4253 3-9-8 **69**.. EddieAhern 12 81
(B J Meehan) *chsd ldr: rdn to ld over 1f out: r.o wl ins fnl f: readily* 14/1
1344 2 3 ¼ **Jollyhockeysticks**[11] 4724 3-9-2 **63**.............................. SamHitchcott 2 67
(M R Channon) *t.k.h: hld up in midfield: rdn and unable qck 3f out: styd on u.p over 1f out: swtchd rt ins fnl f: wnt 2nd last strides: nvr nr wnr* 9/1
0010 3 shd **Very Well Red**[7] 4895 5-9-8 **68**.............................. WilliamCarson(5) 8 72
(P W Hiatt) *led: clr over 3f out: rdn over 2f out: hdd over 1f out: wknd ins fnl f: lost 2nd last strides* 16/1
4444 4 ½ **Granary**[34] 4022 4-9-11 **66**.. DaneO'Neill 6 69
(H Candy) *chsd ldrs: swtchd rt and effrt u.p over 2f out: hrd rdn and chsd ldrs over 1f out: no prog fnl f* 3/1[1]
005 5 2 **Bramalea**[55] 3333 3-8-11 **58**.. LiamJones 9 55
(B W Duke) *chsd ldng pair: rdn over 3f out: wknd over 1f out* 20/1
1435 6 2 **Dancing Storm**[22] 4428 5-9-9 **64**.............................. ChrisCatlin 13 58+
(W S Kittow) *wl bhd: c wd and rdn 3f out: styd on fr over 1f out: nvr trbld ldrs* 11/2[2]
3030 7 2 ¾ **Poppets Sweetlove**[12] 4708 4-9-5 **60**.............................. DavidKinsella 14 47
(A B Haynes) *in tch: drvn wl over 2f out: sn struggling and n.d after* 12/1
01 8 nk **Make Amends (IRE)**[12] 4709 3-9-8 **69**.............................. SteveDrowne 15 54+
(R J Hodges) *bhd: rdn 3f out: swtchd rt 2f out: sme modest late hdwy: nvr nr ldrs* 11/2[2]
9 2 ½ **Margot Mine (IRE)**[83] 3-8-2 **52**.............................. LukeMorris(3) 3 32
(J S Moore) *s.i.s: bhd: rdn over 3f out: nvr a factor* 14/1
0462 10 3 ¼ **Bauhaus Bourbon (USA)**[11] 4727 3-9-7 **68**.............................. JimmyFortune 5 40
(P F I Cole) *racd in midfield: rdn 3f out: sn struggling and wl btn* 8/1[3]
-605 11 nk **Siryena**[12] 4708 3-8-3 **50**..(t) CatherineGannon 11 22
(B I Case) *s.i.s: hld up bhd: rdn 3f out: n.d* 33/1
035 12 2 ¼ **Veni Bidi Vici**[17] 4566 3-8-6 **58**..(v[1]) DavidProbert(5) 7 25
(A M Balding) *hld up in midfield: rdn 3f out: sn wknd* 14/1
000 13 6 **Park Run**[27] 4249 3-8-5 **52**.. FrancisNorton 1 5
(A W Carroll) *s.i.s: a bhd: no ch and eased fnl f: t.o* 50/1
13-0 14 8 **Heavenly Saint**[14] 4669 3-9-0 **61**.............................. JimCrowley 10 —
(R J Price) *chsd ldrs: rdn over 3f out: wknd over 2f out: wl bhd and eased fnl f: t.o* 20/1
31P0 15 2 **Ten Spot (IRE)**[138] 1128 3-8-10 **60**..(tp) TolleyDean(3) 4 —
(Stef Liddiard) *s.i.s: a bhd: t.o* 40/1

1m 45.25s (4.45) **Going Correction** +0.575s/f (Yiel)
WFA 3 from 4yo+ 6lb 15 Ran SP% **127.3**
Speed ratings (Par 100): **100,96,96,96,94 92,89,89,86,83 83,80,74,66,64**
toteswinger: 1&2 £10.70, 1&3 £63.90, 2&3 £46.10. CSF £133.94 CT £2120.56 TOTE £16.20: £4.40, £2.80, £8.20; EX 114.70 Trifecta £304.30 Part won..
Owner Andrew Rosen **Bred** Waterford Hall Stud **Trained** Manton, Wilts

FOCUS
A modest event, but the winner looks progressive.
Poppets Sweetlove Official explanation: jockey said filly had no more to give

5120 EUROPEAN BREEDERS' FUND DICK HERN FILLIES' STKS (LISTED RACE) 1m 5y
4:30 (4:31) (Class 1) 3-Y-O+
£22,708 (£8,608; £4,308; £2,148; £1,076; £540) **Stalls** Low

Form RPR
0451 1 **Lady Deauville (FR)**[4] 4977 3-8-13 106.............................. FrancisNorton 6 113+
(P A Blockley) *racd keenly: trckd ldrs: wnt 2nd over 3f out: led gng wl over 2f out: rdn over 1f out: styd on strly: readily* 3/1[2]
0602 2 2 **Eva's Request (IRE)**[29] 4189 3-8-8 99.............................. EdwardCreighton 2 103
(M R Channon) *s.i.s: hld up in tch: hdwy 4f out: rdn to chse wnr wl over 1f out: kpt on u.p but nvr able to chal wnr* 11/2[3]
1-01 3 5 **Perfect Star**[8] 4845 4-9-5 95.. AdamKirby 8 97
(C G Cox) *hld up in tch: hdwy on outer over 2f out: chsd ldng pair over 1f out: no imp* 5/2[1]
1001 4 2 ½ **Nans Joy (IRE)**[8] 4841 4-9-5 95.............................. ChrisCatlin 10 91
(E J O'Neill) *s.i.s: bhd: pushed along 1/2-way: kpt on past btn horses fnl f: nvr nr ldrs* 12/1
-260 5 nk **Cruel Sea (USA)**[60] 3124 3-8-9 95 ow1.............................. EddieAhern 9 86
(B W Hills) *t.k.h: hld up in tch on outer: effrt 3f out: no hdwy 2f out and wl btn after* 16/1
560- 6 2 **Lady Jane Digby**[299] 6416 3-8-8 99.............................. GregFairley 3 80
(M Johnston) *t.k.h: chsd ldrs: rdn 3f out: wknd 2f out* 16/1
0541 7 ¾ **Cape Velvet (IRE)**[16] 4583 4-9-0 74.............................. DaneO'Neill 4 79
(H J L Dunlop) *led tl rdn and hdd over 2f out: wknd wl over 1f out* 28/1
-623 8 1 ¼ **Nolas Lolly (IRE)**[46] 3623 4-9-0 96.............................. JohnEgan 1 76
(M Botti) *hld up in tch on inner: edgd out rt over 2f out: sn rdn: no hdwy and wl btn whn hmpd over 1f out* 16/1
2126 9 10 **Melodramatic (IRE)**[43] 3742 3-8-8 101.............................. SteveDrowne 5 53+
(R Charlton) *s.i.s: sn in tch: rdn and nt clr run over 2f out: sn swtchd rt: nt clr run again and lost pl 2f out: no ch after: eased fnl f* 3/1[2]
0-00 10 3 ½ **Treat**[23] 4395 4-9-0 95..(p) JimmyFortune 7 45
(E A L Dunlop) *chsd ldr tl over 3f out: sn rdn: wknd over 2f out: t.o* 33/1

1m 43.16s (2.36) **Going Correction** +0.575s/f (Yiel)
WFA 3 from 4yo 6lb 10 Ran SP% **125.7**
Speed ratings (Par 108): **111,109,104,101,101 99,98,97,87,83**
toteswinger: 1&2 £5.00, 1&3 £3.00, 2&3 £2.90. CSF £21.95 TOTE £3.80: £1.60, £2.40, £1.50; EX 28.40 Trifecta £53.00 Pool £677.57 - 9.45 winning units..
Owner P J Hughes Developments Ltd **Bred** Aerial Bloodstock Et Al **Trained** Lambourn, Berks

FOCUS
A very good race for the track, with the winner a regular winner at this level.

NOTEBOOK
Lady Deauville(FR) has not yet been able to win at Group level, but this was her fourth win in Listed grade and she is clearly very smart in this sort of company. She is scheduled for another Listed race at Tralee on Friday but, if she continues to go as well as this, she should find a Group 3 in due course, with softish ground always likely to be in her favour. (tchd 11-4)
Eva's Request(IRE) is back in form following an indifferent spell, and this was a good effort to chase home the useful winner with the rest a long way behind. Though finding suitable opportunities may not be easy, she deserves to win at Listed level or in smart handicap company. (op 13-2 tchd 8-1)
Perfect Star, making the step into non-handicap Listed company for the first time, found herself falling short of what was required. Though making an effort in the middle of the track, she was never quite able to get to grips with the first two, but she should remain a potent force in high-class handicaps. (op 3-1)
Nans Joy(IRE) is a smart sort, but her only win at Listed level was in Germany and she never got into contention here after yet again being sluggish out of the stalls. However, the return to a mile showed her versatility as regards distance, and on this evidence a return to even longer trips would not be a problem. (op 9-1)
Cruel Sea(USA), forced to make her effort very wide, was never quite getting there. She has been rather disappointing at 1m in her last two races, so a return to 1m2f would seem like a good move. (op 20-1)
Lady Jane Digby, pitched in deep on this seasonal debut, showed enough to suggest she retains the ability to be competitive in slightly lower grade. (op 20-1 tchd 10-1)
Cape Velvet(IRE) did reasonably well considering her official rating was way below her rivals. She can be more effective back in handicaps. (tchd 25-1)
Melodramatic(IRE), running for the first time in easy conditions, did not get an ideal passage in the home straight, but it did not make a huge difference so she cannot be considered unlucky. However, the market support suggests she can do better. (op 5-1 tchd 6-1)

5121 LUCY AND STEVE'S WEDDING APPRENTICE H'CAP 5f 161y
5:00 (5:00) (Class 5) (0-75,75) 3-Y-O+ **£2,914** (£867; £433; £216) **Stalls** Centre

Form RPR
2431 1 **Desperate Dan**[24] 4324 7-9-0 **69**.. PNolan(7) 7 77
(A B Haynes) *bhd: rdn 1/2-way: hdwy on outer ent fnl f: edgd lft wl ins fnl f: r.o wl to ld nr fin* 14/1
0640 2 nk **Don Pele (IRE)**[17] 4563 6-9-3 **70**..(p) DavidProbert(5) 10 77
(R A Harris) *racd wd: bhd: hdwy 2f out: rdn and ev ch ins fnl f: led wl ins fnl f: edgd lft and hdd nr fin* 8/1
5312 3 1 ¾ **Matterofact (IRE)**[5] 4958 5-9-0 **62**.............................. TolleyDean 2 63
(M S Saunders) *chsd ldr: rdn to ld over 1f out: hdd wl ins fnl f: fdd towards fin* 11/4[2]
3500 4 shd **Kyllachy Storm**[30] 4154 4-8-3 **56** oh5........... Louis-PhilippeBeuzelin(5) 6 57
(R J Hodges) *in tch: rdn jst over 2f out: pressed ldrs ins fnl f: no ex last 100yds* 15/2
5651 5 nk **Memphis Man**[8] 4858 5-9-6 **73**.............................. RichardEvans(5) 9 73
(P D Evans) *taken down early: stdd s: swtchd to inner and hld up bhd: rdn over 2f out: squeezed through on inner jst ins fnl f: swtchd rt wl ins fnl f: nvr able to chal* 2/1[1]
3040 6 1 ¾ **Stamford Blue**[37] 3905 7-9-10 **75**..(b) HaddenFrost(3) 1 69
(R A Harris) *led: rdn jst over 2f out: hdd over 1f out: wknd ins fnl f* 13/2[3]
2004 7 1 ½ **Harrison's Flyer (IRE)**[9] 4812 7-8-8 **56** oh1.......(p) RussellKennemore 3 45
(J M Bradley) *chsd ldrs: rdn 1/2-way: wknd over 1f out: wl hld whn bmpd jst ins fnl f* 11/1
0030 8 shd **Thabaat**[18] 4535 4-9-0 **62**..(b) LukeMorris 5 50
(J M Bradley) *chsd ldrs: rdn 1/2-way: wknd over 1f out* 14/1
5300 9 1 ½ **Summer Recluse (USA)**[7] 4903 9-8-3 **56**..........................(t) BillyCray(5) 4 39
(J M Bradley) *stdd s: a bhd* 20/1

1m 14.38s (3.18) **Going Correction** +0.575s/f (Yiel) 9 Ran SP% **122.6**
Speed ratings (Par 103): **101,100,98,98,97 95,93,93,91**
toteswinger: 1&2 £17.20, 1&3 £4.40, 2&3 £8.10. CSF £127.57 CT £409.82 TOTE £9.50: £1.60, £3.30, £1.60; EX 117.20 Trifecta £266.60 Pool £500.78 - 1.39 winning units. Place 6 £81.83, Place 5 £57.63..
Owner Joe McCarthy **Bred** Sheikh Amin Dahlawi **Trained** Limpley Stoke, Bath

FOCUS
A typical Bath sprint and fair form.
T/Jkpt: Part won. £7,100.00 to a £1 stake. Pool: £10,000.00. 0.50 winning tickets. T/Plt: £43.40 to a £1 stake. Pool: £88,343.68. 1,485.48 winning tickets. T/Qpdt: £37.40 to a £1 stake. Pool: £4,084.88. 80.70 winning tickets. SP

4739 PONTEFRACT (L-H)
Sunday, August 17
5122 Meeting Abandoned - Waterlogged

5129 - (Foreign Racing) - See Raceform Interactive

4352 LEOPARDSTOWN (L-H)
Sunday, August 17

OFFICIAL GOING: Soft to heavy (heavy in places) changing to heavy after race 1 (2.15pm)
The Patrick P.O'Leary, Debutante and Royal Whip Stakes were all rescheduled from the waterlogged Curragh fixture a week earlier.

5130a PATRICK P.O'LEARY MEMORIAL PHOENIX SPRINT STKS (GROUP 3) 6f
2:45 (2:46) 3-Y-O+ **£35,845** (£10,477; £4,963; £1,654)

RPR
1 **Snaefell (IRE)**[57] 3247 4-9-5 110.. RPCleary 5 113
(M Halford, Ire) *chsd ldrs: cl 5th 2f out: 3rd 1f out: styd on wl to ld ins fnl f* 3/1[2]
2 hd **Georgebernardshaw (IRE)**[36] 3982 3-9-1 109.................. JMurtagh 6 111+
(A P O'Brien, Ire) *hld up in tch: rdn on outer st: 4th 1f out: styd on wl fnl f: jst failed* 11/8[1]
3 ½ **Kyniska (IRE)**[322] 5843 3-8-12 97.............................. PShanahan 8 107
(Tracey Collins, Ire) *chsd ldrs: rdn in 2nd 1f out: kpt on same pce fnl f* 20/1
4 shd **Rock Moss (IRE)**[12] 4712 3-9-1 106.............................. KJManning 4 109
(J S Bolger, Ire) *hld up in tch: rdn 1 1/2f out: kpt on wl fnl f: nvr nrr* 10/1
5 hd **Masta Plasta (IRE)**[17] 4550 5-9-5.............................. CDHayes 2 110
(D Nicholls) *led: rdn and strly pressed fr 1 1/2f out: hdd ins fnl f: no ex and dropped to 5th cl home* 11/2[3]
6 3 ½ **Age Of Chivalry (IRE)**[21] 4467 3-9-1 106.............................. MJKinane 1 98
(John M Oxx, Ire) *chsd ldrs: 3rd 1/2-way: no imp fr 1 1/2f out* 11/2[3]

7 2 **Miss Gorica (IRE)**[21] 4467 4-9-2 101 .... DPMcDonogh 7 89
(Ms Joanna Morgan, Ire) *chsd ldr in 2nd: rdn 1 1/2f out: wknd fnl f* **16/1**

1m 18.2s (4.10) **Going Correction** +1.025s/f (Soft)
WFA 3 from 4yo+ 3lb 8 Ran SP% **117.6**
Speed ratings: **113,112,112,111,111 107,104**
CSF £7.90 TOTE £4.50: £2.90, £1.50; DF 8.50.
Owner Lady Clague **Bred** Newberry Stud Farm **Trained** the Curragh, Co Kildare

NOTEBOOK

Snaefell(IRE), a very consistent performer at Listed level over the last couple of seasons, gained a deserved success at this level and considering he had never raced around a bend before it was a fair performance. Sitting behind the leaders most of the way, his rider found the door closing on him early in the straight and had to manoeuvre a bit to find a gap, but when it came the gelding quickened up well on his favourite surface to get his head in front well inside the last. The Flying Five in a couple of weeks' time was nominated by his trainer as the next target. (op 3/1 tchd 7/2)

Georgebernardshaw(IRE) had most things in his favour, but realistically 6f even on this sort of ground is the minimum he needs, and coming up against a genuine stakes performer he just was not quite good enough on the day. Held up in rear, he always travelled quite sweetly and moved up on the outer to deliver his challenge a furlong out, and while he kept on well inside the last half-furlong he just did not have the finishing burst possessed by the winner. (op 2/1 tchd 5/4)

Kyniska(IRE), despite being out for almost 11 months, ran a cracker. Tracking the leaders early on, she was ridden to close early in the straight but sustained her effort until well inside the final furlong and looked the likely winner about a furlong out. She could not quite sustain it, but was entitled to get a bit tired close home and should come on for this and for a step back up in trip.

Rock Moss(IRE) was probably the only one of the first four that never really looked like winning, but that is not to take away from a very good run. Held up early, he was fairly tight to the inside rail most of the way but could never quite get there. He kept on well inside the last to be nearest at the finish.

Masta Plasta(IRE) cut out the donkey work and was unlucky not to get a share of the prizemoney. For a horse whose best form is over the minimum trip, he lasted out in front until he tired well inside the final furlong and was run out of it. (op 5/1 tchd 6/1)

Age Of Chivalry(IRE) was prominent most of the way before weakening inside the last. (op 11/2 tchd 6/1)

Miss Gorica(IRE) faced a stiff enough task at the weights and dropped away inside the last furlong or so having shown some early dash.

5132a BALLYGALLON STUD DEBUTANTE STKS (GROUP 2) 7f

3:45 (3:47) 2-Y-O **£59,742** (£17,463; £8,272; £2,757)

RPR

1 **Again (IRE)**[21] 4468 2-8-12 .... JMurtagh 10 108+
(David Wachman, Ire) *mid-div: 5th 3f out: rdn in 2nd 2f out: led 1f out: kpt on wl* **9/2**[3]

2 3 **Oui Say Oui (IRE)**[36] 3979 2-8-12 .... WMLordan 9 99
(T Stack, Ire) *hld up: prog after 1/2-way: rdn in 3rd 2f out: 2nd 1f out: kpt on* **9/1**

3 1 1/2 **Rare Ransom**[19] 4513 2-8-12 .... PJSmullen 3 95
(D K Weld, Ire) *trckd ldr in 2nd: led 3f out: rdn 1 1/2f out: hdd 1f out: no ex* **10/3**[2]

4 4 1/2 **Beauthea (IRE)**[49] 3534 2-8-12 .... CDHayes 6 84
(H Rogers, Ire) *hld up: prog fr 1/2-way: rdn in 5th 1f out: kpt on same pce* **50/1**

5 1 1/2 **Baliyana (IRE)**[36] 3979 2-8-12 .... MJKinane 4 80
(John M Oxx, Ire) *mid-div: 6th 3f out: pushed along and kpt on same pce fr 1 1/2f out* **11/2**

6 7 **Beth**[11] 4759 2-8-12 .... DPMcDonogh 7 62
(Andrew Oliver, Ire) *chsd ldrs: 2nd 3f out: no imp fr 2f out* **25/1**

7 5 **Ceist Eile (IRE)**[12] 4711 2-8-12 .... MHarley 8 50
(J S Bolger, Ire) *sn led: rdn and hdd 3f out: sn no imp* **66/1**

8 10 **Cuis Ghaire (IRE)**[24] 4353 2-8-12 106 .... KJManning 2 25
(J S Bolger, Ire) *chsd ldrs: rdn along 1/2-way: wknd on inner bef st* **7/4**[1]

9 2 1/2 **Spira (IRE)**[21] 4468 2-8-12 .... JAHeffernan 5 19
(A P O'Brien, Ire) *mid-div on inner: wknd fr 3f out: trailing st* **16/1**

1m 33.1s (2.80) **Going Correction** +0.625s/f (Yiel) 10 Ran SP% **116.2**
Speed ratings: **109,105,103,98,97 89,83,71,69**
CSF £43.77 TOTE £4.90: £1.80, £2.70, £1.50; DF 18.80.
Owner Michael Tabor **Bred** Southern Bloodstock **Trained** Goolds Cross, Co Tipperary

NOTEBOOK

Again(IRE), winner of a Curragh maiden on her second start, has looked a potentially decent filly from day one, acts on any ground, and there could be a good bit more to come from her as there is no doubt that it took a smart performance to win this race as she did, as this was run at a proper gallop on testing ground. Having tracked the leaders in mid-division, she came wide with the rest of the field, quickened to challenge a furlong and a half out, and once going to the front she put the result beyond doubt quite quickly. She is very smart, already gets 1m and is completely versatile as to ground conditions, and there is no reason why she cannot go very far indeed. (op 11/2 tchd 4/1)

Oui Say Oui(IRE) took the step up in class from her Curragh maiden success very much in her stride. She handled cut in the ground that day and what was most noteworthy here was how the step up in trip did not bother her and she looks certain to get 1m even at this stage. Held up in rear, she ran on well from the two-furlong pole and kept going all the way to the line. She was not good enough to trouble the winner, but time may tell that this was no disgrace whatsoever. (op 7/1)

Rare Ransom, prominent throughout, went for her race a furlong and a half out but had no chance with the winner and was eventually outstayed for second place. Winner of a Galway maiden on her previous start, she is a decent filly and appeared to handle the ground well enough. There is a nice race to be won with her. (op 11/4)

Beauthea(IRE) can claim to be just about the best maiden filly around. She might well appreciate the drop in class back to maiden company, but having not blown the start this represented her best run to date. She never looked like winning once the race developed in earnest from the top of the straight, but she ran on well under pressure inside the final furlong to be nearest at the finish.

Baliyana(IRE), whom by all accounts a good bit is thought of, never really threatened, but she was not at all knocked about and there should be a bit more to come. The stable are really starting to hit a bit of form as well, and she looks well capable of at least winning her maiden. (op 13/2)

Beth, supplemented for this race following her win at Sligo a couple of weeks ago, broke well before being settled in mid-division and appeared to be travelling well to about the 3f point before weakening in the straight. She is probably better than this showing.

Cuis Ghaire(IRE) was obviously the biggest disappointment. She tracked the leaders towards the inside in the very early stages, but was being ridden and came under pressure before the turn into the straight and was the first filly beaten. Her trainer said the filly was fine and just did not act on the ground, although she was found to be clinically abnormal when examined by the Turf Club vet. Official explanation: jockey said filly did not handle the heavy ground, vet said filly was clinically abnormal post-race (op 7/4 tchd 13/8)

Spira(IRE) was never a factor. (op 20/1)

5134a DESMOND STKS (GROUP 3) 1m

4:45 (4:45) 3-Y-O+ **£33,455** (£9,779; £4,632; £1,544)

RPR

1 **Carribean Sunset (IRE)**[43] 3807 3-9-3 111 .... PJSmullen 1 113
(D K Weld, Ire) *sn in tch in last: rdn to ld over 2f out: clr 1f out: styd on wl: easily* **5/2**[2]

2 4 1/2 **Blythe Knight (IRE)**[22] 4436 8-9-10 .... GrahamGibbons 5 105
(J J Quinn) *chsd ldrs in 4th: rdn in 2nd fr 2f out: kpt on same pce wout threatening wnr fnl f* **7/2**[3]

3 1 3/4 **Deauville Vision (IRE)**[4] 4997 5-9-4 103 .... RPCleary 4 95
(M Halford, Ire) *chsd ldrs in 3rd: rdn fr 2f out: kpt on same pce over 1f out* **5/1**

4 7 **Kitty Matcham (IRE)**[59] 3153 3-9-3 104 .... JMurtagh 2 85
(A P O'Brien, Ire) *racd in 2nd: rdn fr 2 1/2f out: no imp fr 1 1/2f out* **6/1**

5 21 **Jumbajukiba**[7] 4915 5-9-12 114 .... (b) FMBerry 3 82+
(Mrs John Harrington, Ire) *led on inner: rdn fr 3f out: hdd over 2f out: sn wknd and eased* **9/4**[1]

1m 44.3s (3.10) **Going Correction** +0.725s/f (Yiel)
WFA 3 from 5yo+ 6lb 7 Ran SP% **112.5**
Speed ratings: **113,108,106,99,78**
CSF £11.73 TOTE £3.60: £1.70, £2.40; DF 17.50.
Owner Dr R Lambe **Bred** Barronstown Stud **Trained** The Curragh, Co Kildare

NOTEBOOK

Carribean Sunset(IRE) has progressed tremendously well since her last run on heavy ground in March and was the only one in the race with Group 1 form. She did this in the style of a good filly, racing at the rear of a tightly bunched quintet, moving through stylishly to deliver her challenge well over a furlong out and going clear inside the final furlong. She still didn't look totally at ease on this surface but was just too classy for the opposition. The Matron Stakes here next month looks a target with the ultimate target being the Breeders' Cup Filly And Mare Turf. (op 5/2 tchd 11/4)

Blythe Knight(IRE), who has form on this ground in the past, ran a fine race. He travelled well throughout and kept on well inside the last furlong without having any chance with the winner. He has been an admirable servant to his connections and seemingly isn't losing any of his ability. (op 4/1)

Deauville Vision(IRE) also appreciated the underfoot conditions and this is about as good as she is. She travelled as well as anything turning in and maybe they didn't quite go quick enough for her. She was unable to quicken with the winner and just kept on at the same pace. (op 6/1)

Kitty Matcham(IRE) has been disappointing this season and this wasn't really any better. What factor the ground played in this performance is open to question but, having raced close to the pace and leading the quartet that raced centre to stands' side for most of the journey, she was quickly beaten once coming under pressure well over a furlong out. (op 5/1)

Jumbajukiba was having his seventh run of the season, and the tactic of sticking to the inside rail on the more churned-up ground didn't help, but even that can't explain fully the way he folded so tamely. He led to the turn into the straight, but once headed by the winner a furlong and a half out he dropped right away and was eased right down. He was found to be post-race normal on examination by the Turf Club vet. Official explanation: trainer said gelding ran flat throughout (op 9/4 tchd 5/2)

5135a ROYAL WHIP STKS (GROUP 2) 1m 2f

5:15 (5:15) 3-Y-O+ **£56,985** (£17,463; £8,272; £2,757; £1,838)

RPR

1 **King Of Rome (IRE)**[24] 4356 3-9-0 111 .... JMurtagh 2 112
(A P O'Brien, Ire) *trckd ldrs in 3rd: mod 3rd and pushed along fr 1/2-way: clsd appr st: led 1 1/2f out: styd on wl: comf* **9/10**[1]

2 3 1/2 **Alarazi (IRE)**[16] 4614 4-9-9 106 .... (b) MJKinane 4 106
(John M Oxx, Ire) *racd mod 4th: rdn in clsr 3rd 1 1/2f out: wnt 2nd over 1f out: kpt on wout threatening wnr* **7/1**

3 1 3/4 **Zulu Chief (USA)**[39] 3861 3-9-0 .... JAHeffernan 5 102
(A P O'Brien, Ire) *racd in last: clsr in 3rd 2 1/2f out: sn rdn: 2nd 1 1/2f out: no ex and dropped to 3rd fnl f* **5/2**[2]

4 11 **Moiqen (IRE)**[58] 3193 3-9-0 106 .... DPMcDonogh 1 80
(Kevin Prendergast, Ire) *t.k.h and led after 2f: rdn ent st: hdd 1 1/2f out: wknd* **6/1**[3]

5 7 **King Of Westphalia (USA)**[24] 4356 3-9-0 94 .... CO'Donoghue 3 66
(A P O'Brien, Ire) *led: hdd after 2f: rdn and wknd fr 3f out: bhd over 1f out* **20/1**

2m 12.8s (4.60) **Going Correction** +0.725s/f (Yiel)
WFA 3 from 4yo 8lb 5 Ran SP% **112.8**
Speed ratings: **110,107,105,97,91**
CSF £8.20 TOTE £1.90: £1.20, £3.20; DF 6.10.
Owner Derrick Smith **Bred** The Amizette Partnership **Trained** Ballydoyle, Co Tipperary

NOTEBOOK

King Of Rome(IRE) followed up on his Group 3 success over the same course and trip last month. The pace was strong for the ground conditions and the winner picked up well to lead one and a half furlongs out before stretching clear inside the final furlong. He might be kept to this trip in the immediate future but the Irish Champion Stakes here on September 6 is an option. He coped with the conditions although connections feel that he is a better horse on quicker ground. (op 11/8)

Alarazi(IRE), a proven performer on testing ground, was dropping back in trip having failed to stay 1m6f in lesser company at Galway on his previous start. He stayed on to win the race for second place without ever troubling the winner. (op 6/1)

Zulu Chief(USA), a 20-length winner of a maiden at Naas last month, was stepping up in class and encountering this sort of ground for the first time. Held up in rear, he moved up promisingly turning for home but began to falter early in the final furlong and tired in the testing conditions. (op 9/4)

5136a BALLYROAN STKS (GROUP 3) 1m 4f

5:45 (5:45) 3-Y-O+ **£33,455** (£9,779; £4,632; £1,544)

RPR

1 **Mores Wells**[50] 3513 4-9-10 111 .... (t) DPMcDonogh 2 118
(Kevin Prendergast, Ire) *chsd ldrs: 3rd 3f out: led over 2f out: styd on wl fnl f: easily* **5/1**[3]

2 3 1/2 **Washington Irving (IRE)**[49] 3535 3-8-11 113 .... JMurtagh 9 110
(A P O'Brien, Ire) *trckd ldrs: mod 2nd 1/2-way: clsr 2nd 3f out: sn rdn: mod 3rd over 1f out: wnt 2nd wout threatening wnr cl home* **7/2**[2]

3 1/2 **Profound Beauty (IRE)**[32] 4100 4-9-4 108 .... PJSmullen 4 106
(D K Weld, Ire) *trckd ldrs: rdn in 3rd 2 1/2f out: mod 2nd over 1f out: sn no ex: lost 2nd cl home* **7/4**[1]

4 2 **Prima Luce (IRE)**[9] 4832 3-8-11 107 .... KJManning 1 106
(J S Bolger, Ire) *hld up: rdn in 4th 2 1/2f out: sn no imp* **6/1**

5 5 **Arch Rebel (USA)**[71] 2854 7-9-7 110 .... (p) FMBerry 10 98
(Noel Meade, Ire) *mid-div: 6th 1/2-way: rdn and no imp fr 3f out* **12/1**

6 1/2 **Sail (IRE)**[9] 4833 3-8-8 105 .... JAHeffernan 7 94
(A P O'Brien, Ire) *led: rdn and hdd over 2f out: sn wknd* **20/1**

7 3 **Via Galilei (IRE)**[322] 5845 3-8-11 96 DJMoran 3 92
(J S Bolger, Ire) *towards rr: no imp fr 3f out* **33/1**
8 25 **Consulate (IRE)**[351] 5056 4-9-7 103 PShanahan 8 52
(D K Weld, Ire) *a bhd: no imp bef st: eased fnl f: t.o* **20/1**
9 7 **Raydiya (IRE)**[32] 4100 3-8-8 100 MJKinane 5 38
(John M Oxx, Ire) *trckd ldrs: rdn and wknd fr 3f out: eased fnl f: t.o* **12/1**

2m 40.2s (4.90) **Going Correction** +0.725s/f (Yiel)
WFA 3 from 4yo+ 10lb 10 Ran SP% **117.4**
Speed ratings: **112,109,109,108,104 104,102,85,81**
CSF £22.65 TOTE £2.70: £1.30, £1.90, £1.40; DF 18.70.
Owner Iona Equine Syndicate **Bred** Cliveden Stud Ltd & Ocean Bloo **Trained** Friarstown, Co Kildare

NOTEBOOK
Mores Wells repeated his win in this race a year ago with a decisive victory. After tracking the leaders, he challenged on the stands'-side rail in the straight and led well over a furlong out before keeping on well. His trainer will let him take his chance in the Irish St Leger in which he was third last year. (op 4/1)
Washington Irving(IRE) remains one of the better three-year-old maidens around and is a possible for the St Leger. He ran a solid race here against the older horses, racing prominently and keeping on quite well, without troubling the winner, inside the final furlong after disputing the lead into the straight. (op 7/2 tchd 4/1)
Profound Beauty(IRE) was being pushed along to try and close leaving the back straight and kept plugging away on ground which was far from ideal for her. (op 2/1)
Prima Luce(IRE), proven on testing ground albeit over 7f, had finished seventh in the Irish Oaks on her previous attempt over this trip. Fifth into the straight, she kept on under pressure without ever posing a serious threat. (op 6/1 tchd 13/2)
T/Jkpt: @7,753.80. Pool of @20,677.00 - 2 winning units. T/Plt: @64.30. Pool of @21,959.00.
II

5133 - 5136a (Foreign Racing) - See Raceform Interactive

4911 COLOGNE (R-H)
Sunday, August 17

OFFICIAL GOING: Good

5137a RHEINLAND-POKAL DER SPARKASSE KOLNBONN (GROUP 1) 1m 4f
4:15 (4:44) 3-Y-0+ £73,529 (£24,265; £11,029; £5,147)

RPR
1 7 **Kamsin (GER)**[42] 3773 3-8-8 AStarke 6 105
(P Schiergen, Germany) *racd in 2nd thrght: rdn over 2f out: no imp: fin 2nd, 7l: subseq awrdd r* **3/1**[2]
2 ½ **Papal Bull**[22] 4406 5-9-6 RyanMoore 4 106
(Sir Michael Stoute) *hld up in 3rd or 4th: 4th st: swtchd to middle: nvr nr to chal: fin 3rd, 7l & 1/2l: plcd 2nd* **4/9**[1]
3 5 **Akiem (IRE)**[42] 3773 3-8-8 ASuborics 2 96
(Andreas Lowe, Germany) *disp 3rd: 3rd fr bef 1/2-way: rdn over 2f out: kpt on one pce: fin 4th, plcd 3rd* **20/1**
4 6 **First Stream (GER)**[34] 4041 4-9-6 ADeVries 5 88
(Mario Hofer, Germany) *last most of way: fin 5th, plcd 4th* **28/1**
5 7 **Prinz (GER)**[49] 3540 4-9-6 EPedroza 3 77
(A Wohler, Germany) *racd in 5th to st: nvr a factor: fin 6th, plcd 5th* **33/1**
D **Oriental Tiger (GER)**[84] 2440 5-9-6 (b) THellier 1 118
(U Ostmann, Germany) *mde all: sn clr: 15 l clr at 1/2-way: 6 l up 2f out: drvn out: fin 1st: subseq disq* **13/2**[3]

2m 26.76s (-6.14)
WFA 3 from 4yo+ 10lb 6 Ran SP% **118.7**
PARI-MUTUEL: WIN 56; PL 21, 17; SF 221.
Owner Stall Blankenese **Bred** Gestut Karlshof **Trained** Germany
FOCUS
Oriental Tiger was subsequently disqualified after testing positive for a banned substance. The race was awarded to Kamsin.
NOTEBOOK
Kamsin(GER), the German Derby winner, ran a decent race on only his fourth start and taking on his elders for the first time.
Papal Bull was very disappointing, failing to run anywhere near his King George form. His rider blamed the tight turns at this track for the below-par effort.
Oriental Tiger(GER) poached an early lead and the others were just unable to drag him back. He is dangerous when left alone in front and has a good record at this course, but he is not as effective on a left-handed track so will not run in the Grosser Preis von Baden. The Arc remains a possibility, though.

5112 DEAUVILLE (R-H)
Sunday, August 17

OFFICIAL GOING: Turf course - good to soft; all-weather - standard

5138a PRIX DU HARAS DE FRESNAY-LE-BUFFARD - JACQUES LE MAROIS (GROUP 1) (C&F) (STRAIGHT) 1m
2:50 (2:54) 3-Y-0+ £252,088 (£100,853; £50,426; £25,191; £12,618)

RPR
1 **Tamayuz**[35] 4010 3-8-11 DBonilla 5 125+
(F Head, France) *trckd ldr tl led 2f out: drvn out* **11/8**[1]
2 2½ **Natagora (FR)**[14] 4674 3-8-8 YTake 4 116
(P Bary, France) *a in tch: wnt 3rd 1/2-way: chsd wnr fr wl over 1f out: rdn over 1f out: one pce fnl f* **9/2**[3]
3 3 **Major Cadeaux**[18] 4518 4-9-3 RichardHughes 3 113
(R Hannon) *restrained in rr: pulling early: swtchd to outside 1 1/2f out: hdwy to go 3rd 150yds out: kpt on same pce* **7/1**
4 ¾ **Sageburg (IRE)**[61] 3100 4-9-3 CSoumillon 7 112
(A De Royer-Dupre, France) *hld up in rr: hdwy on outside over 2f out: 3rd appr fnl f: one pce* **5/2**[2]
5 1½ **Runaway**[70] 2876 6-9-3 TJarnet 8 108
(R Pritchard-Gordon, France) *mid-div: disp 3rd briefly over 1f out: one pce* **66/1**
6 3 **Arcadia's Angle (USA)**[35] 4010 3-8-11 C-PLemaire 6 100
(P Bary, France) *disp 5th: btn 2f out* **25/1**
7 6 **Racinger (FR)**[29] 4212 5-9-3 OPeslier 2 87
(F Head, France) *led to 2f out: eased whn btn fnl f* **12/1**
8 10 **Sindajan (IRE)**[34] 4042 3-8-11 TGillet 1 63
(A De Royer-Dupre, France) *racd in 3rd: sn pushed along: wknd 1/2-way* **150/1**

1m 36.4s (-4.60) **Going Correction** -0.15s/f (Firm)
WFA 3 from 4yo+ 6lb 8 Ran SP% **115.1**
Speed ratings: **117,114,111,110,109 106,100,90**
PARI-MUTUEL: WIN 1.90 (coupled with Racinger); PL 1.10, 1.40, 1.70; DF 5.30.
Owner Hamdan Al Maktoum **Bred** Shadwell Estate Company Limited **Trained** France
FOCUS
Tamayuz is rated up a length on his Prix Jean Prat form and the equal of Raven's Pass for now. Natagora ran to form, with the next two not at their best.
NOTEBOOK
Tamayuz, strictly on a line of form through Raven's Pass, is superior to Henrythenavigator. He completely outclassed his seven rivals in this Group 1 event and the race had been well planned by his bang in-form trainer. Considering the ground, the pacemaker set a strong pace but he had given all before the two-furlong marker. At this point Tamayuz took complete control of the race and soon after there was never a question of defeat. A constantly improving colt, he was winning his second Group 1 race and will now be aimed at the Queen Elizabeth II Stakes at Ascot and probably the Breeders' Cup Mile in October. His rider felt that on faster ground he would have been even more impressive.
Natagora(FR) looked in superb shape considering that she had only had a Group 1 outing two weeks ago, and she went down beautifully to post. She raced in third place in the early stages and shadowed the winner, but when he kicked for home she was left struggling and was finally a well beaten runner-up. Connections are now thinking about a run in the Queen Elizabeth II but a more likely target now is the 7f Prix de la Foret.
Major Cadeaux was given plenty to do and had an enormous task at the two-furlong marker where things quickened up. Once top gear was engaged, he ran on well but never had the slightest chance with the winner and runner-up. He could turn out for the Celebration Mile at Goodwood and his trainer thinks he is at his best over 7f.
Sageburg(IRE) was alright in the paddock but by the time he reached the start he was completely sweating up. He was given a waiting race but just did not fire on this occasion. It was a disappointing effort from this Group 1 winner and his trainer felt that he was not at all suited to the straight track, so he is now likely to be aimed at the Prix du Moulin de Longchamp. He is not an easy individual but a talented one when he is on song.

5139a PRIX FRANCOIS BOUTIN (LISTED RACE) (STRAIGHT) 7f
3:15 (3:25) 2-Y-O £20,221 (£8,088; £6,066; £4,044; £2,022)

RPR
1 **Soul City (IRE)**[18] 4517 2-9-2 RichardHughes 7 103+
(R Hannon) **6/4**[1]
2 2 **Denomination (USA)**[43] 2-8-13 TGillet 3 95
(Mme C Head-Maarek, France) **4/1**[2]
3 2½ **Temple Lord (FR)**[34] 4039 2-9-2 CSoumillon 6 92
(Y De Nicolay, France) **10/1**
4 2½ **Jukebox Jury (IRE)**[15] 4625 2-9-2 JoeFanning 4 86
(M Johnston) **5/1**
5 3 **Rain Of Melody (IRE)**[55] 2-9-2 OPeslier 2 78
(Robert Collet, France) **25/1**
6 1½ **Los Gigantes (FR)**[43] 2-9-2 C-PLemaire 5 74
(J-C Rouget, France) **9/2**[3]
7 1½ **Morning Smile (IRE)**[39] 2-9-2 FBlondel 1 71
(Robert Collet, France) **20/1**

1m 26.6s (2.10) 7 Ran SP% **112.5**
PARI-MUTUEL: WIN 2.70; PL 1.70, 2.80; SF 14.10.
Owner Patrick J Fahey **Bred** Peter Thome **Trained** East Everleigh, Wilts

NOTEBOOK
Soul City(IRE) made virtually every yard of the running and dominated the race inside the final furlong. He has now won two of his four races and looks progressive. His trainer has now marked down the Goffs Million in September and then possibly a return to France for the Prix Jean-Luc Lagardere.
Jukebox Jury(IRE) tried vainly to get on terms with the winner and runner-up from two out but eventually had to settle for fourth position. He was the only one to make his run up the stands' rail.

5086 LINGFIELD (L-H)
Monday, August 18

OFFICIAL GOING: Standard
Wind: strong and gusty behind Weather: overcast, showers threatening

5140 SPELDHURST RATING RELATED MAIDEN STKS 1m (P)
2:30 (2:30) (Class 5) 3-4-Y-O £3,238 (£963; £481; £240) Stalls High

Form RPR
0200 1 **Storm Sir (USA)**[23] 4423 3-9-1 73 (t) RyanMoore 2 86
(B J Meehan) *chsd ldng pair: rdn to chal wl over 1f out: drew wl clr fnl f: easily* **13/2**[3]
6043 2 8 **King's Wonder**[3] 5052 3-9-1 76 MartinDwyer 1 68
(W R Muir) *chsd ldr tl led after 1f: rdn 2f out: hdd ent fnl f: edgd rt and no ch w wnr after* **3/1**[2]
4323 3 ½ **Seventh Cavalry (IRE)**[17] 4606 3-9-1 74 TedDurcan 3 66
(H R A Cecil) *s.i.s: hld up in last pl: hdwy on outer over 2f out: outpcd over 1f out: no ch w wnr fnl f* **3/1**[2]
6204 4 3¾ **Meydan Dubai (IRE)**[7] 4927 3-9-1 80 JimCrowley 5 58
(J R Best) *t.k.h: led for 1f: chsd ldr after tl wl over 1f out: wknd u.p over 1f out* **11/10**[1]

1m 36.65s (-1.55) **Going Correction** -0.05s/f (Stan) 4 Ran SP% **111.0**
Speed ratings (Par 103): **105,97,96,92**
CSF £24.65 TOTE £6.40; EX 16.30.
Owner Saleh Al Homaizi & Imad Al Sagar **Bred** Calumet Farm **Trained** Manton, Wilts
FOCUS
A modest maiden for three-year-olds, with each of the four runners having something to prove. It was run at a sound pace and the winner outclassed his rivals but this is not form to take too literally.

5141 FELBRIDGE H'CAP 5f (P)
3:00 (3:00) (Class 6) (0-60,60) 3-Y-O £2,914 (£867; £433; £216) Stalls High

Form RPR
-000 1 **Edie Superstar (USA)**[68] 2946 3-9-4 60 (v) RyanMoore 6 69
(M A Magnusson) *led for 1f: chsd ldr after tl led again 2f out: hung rt u.p fnl f: styd on wl* **11/2**[2]
4603 2 1 **Spic 'n Span**[12] 4725 3-8-10 55 (b) KevinGhunowa(3) 3 61
(R A Harris) *s.i.s: sn rdn up to chse ldrs: hdwy to chal ent fnl f: rdn: hung lft and nt qckn last 100yds* **11/4**[1]

5040 **3** 1 **Nawaaff**[14] 4684 3-8-13 55 (v[1]) TPO'Shea 5 57
(M R Channon) *s.i.s: towards rr: rdn 2f out: styd on u.p fnl f: wnt 3rd nr fin: nt rch ldng pair* **8/1**[3]

165 **4** nk **Stoneacre Pat (IRE)**[9] 4852 3-8-13 55 PatrickMathers 1 56
(Peter Grayson) *bhd on inner: rdn and hdwy ent fnl 2f: chsd ldng pair jst ins fnl f: wknd towards fin* **8/1**[3]

0-00 **5** 1 1/4 **Rocheport**[27] 4268 3-8-6 53 WilliamCarson(5) 7 50
(G C H Chung) *bhd after 1f: c wd bnd 2f out: rdn wl over 1f out: r.o fnl f: nvr trbld ldrs* **20/1**

3450 **6** 2 3/4 **Town And Gown**[16] 4639 3-9-1 57 (p) NCallan 9 44
(S C Williams) *chsd ldrs: rdn wl over 1f out: wknd tamely ent fnl f* **8/1**[3]

0405 **7** 3 3/4 **Jalons Bridewell**[19] 4523 3-9-3 59 (v) RobertHavlin 4 32
(M Quinn) *pushed up to ld after 1f: hdd 2f out: wknd qckly 1f out* **10/1**

5061 **8** 2 **Hot Bertie**[90] 2268 3-9-3 59 LPKeniry 2 25
(Peter Grayson) *racd in midfield: rdn 3f out: wknd over 1f out* **8/1**[3]

003 **9** nk **Gower Belle**[11] 4779 3-9-2 58 MartinDwyer 8 23
(W R Muir) *towards rr: rdn over 2f out: wknd 2f out* **11/2**[2]

58.71 secs (-0.09) **Going Correction** -0.05s/f (Stan) 9 Ran SP% **115.7**
Speed ratings (Par 98): **98,96,94,94,92 87,81,78,78**
toteswinger: 1&2 £5.30, 1&3 £10.60, 2&3 £3.70. CSF £21.06 CT £121.05 TOTE £7.30: £2.40, £1.10, £3.40; EX 26.50 Trifecta £133.50 Pool: £322.99 - 1.79 winning units..
Owner Eastwind Racing & Mountgrange Stud **Bred** Brylynn Farm, Inc **Trained** Upper Lambourn, Berks
■ Stewards' Enquiry : Kevin Ghunowa two-day ban: careless riding (Sep 1-2)

FOCUS
A tricky sprint handicap, run at a sound pace and the form looks fairly solid rated through the second.

5142 MARSH GREEN FILLIES' H'CAP 6f (P)
3:30 (3:30) (Class 5) (0-75,73) 3-Y-O **£3,885** (£1,156; £577; £288) **Stalls** Low

Form RPR

0322 **1** **Artistic License (IRE)**[5] 4988 3-9-6 72 TPO'Shea 3 86
(M R Channon) *hld up towards rr on inner: hdwy 2f out: swtchd rt over 1f out: chsd ldr 1f out: str run to ld wl ins fnl f: readily* **9/2**[2]

0-13 **2** 1 **Valatrix (IRE)**[33] 4090 3-9-2 73 JackMitchell(5) 6 84
(C F Wall) *taken down early: led for 1f: chsd ldr after tl led again wl over 1f out: sn rdn clr: 3 l ld 1f out: hdd and no ex wl ins fnl f* **3/1**[1]

4353 **3** 5 **Fly Kiss**[11] 4773 3-9-4 70 (b[1]) RyanMoore 8 65
(C E Brittain) *s.i.s: bhd: rdn and hdwy jst over 2f out: styd on to chse ldng pair last 100yds: nvr a threat* **6/1**

0066 **4** 1 1/4 **Acquifer**[27] 4277 3-8-13 65 TedDurcan 7 56
(J L Dunlop) *s.i.s: bhd: effrt on outer 3f out: outpcd and swtchd to inner bnd 2f out: kpt on past btn horses fnl f: nvr nr ldrs* **10/1**

5221 **5** 3/4 **Bahamian Bliss**[40] 3847 3-8-13 65 KirstyMilczarek 1 54
(J A R Toller) *s.i.s: hdwy to chse ldrs over 4f out: rdn and wknd over 1f out* **8/1**

0000 **6** 1/2 **Applesnap (IRE)**[14] 4696 3-8-10 67 DavidProbert(5) 9 54
(Miss Amy Weaver) *sn pushed up to chse ldrs: rdn and lost pl wl over 2f out: n.d after* **8/1**

5504 **7** nk **Asian Lady**[23] 4413 3-8-11 63 (v) SteveDrowne 2 49
(R Charlton) *chsd ldr tl led after 1f: rdn and hdd wl over 1f out: sn outpcd by ldr: wknd fnl f* **5/1**[3]

-460 **8** nk **Wavertree Princess (IRE)**[82] 2506 3-9-3 69 JamesDoyle 4 54
(N P Littmoden) *t.k.h: in tch: rdn to chse ldrs over 2f out: wknd 2f out: no ch fnl f* **14/1**

50-0 **9** 3 1/4 **Eastern Pride**[101] 1964 3-7-9 54 oh2 SophieDoyle(7) 5 29
(P A Blockley) *t.k.h: hld up towards rr: rdn and struggling over 2f out: wl bhd over 1f out* **33/1**

1m 11.1s (-0.80) **Going Correction** -0.05s/f (Stan) 9 Ran SP% **115.1**
Speed ratings (Par 97): **103,101,95,93,92 91,91,90,86**
toteswinger: 1&2 £3.90, 1&3 £5.00, 2&3 £6.70. CSF £18.33 CT £81.41 TOTE £4.10: £1.60, £1.80, £2.40; EX 19.30 Trifecta £53.60 Pool: £296.79 - 4.09 winning units..
Owner Wood Street Syndicate IV **Bred** Mountarmstrong Stud **Trained** West Ilsley, Berks

FOCUS
A modest fillies' handicap which saw the first pair come well clear in the home straight. Both look a cut above this grade but there was little depth to this.

5143 ASHURST WOOD NOVICE STKS 7f (P)
4:00 (4:01) (Class 4) 2-Y-O **£4,415** (£1,321; £660; £330; £164) **Stalls** Low

Form RPR

1 **1** **War Native (IRE)**[17] 4598 2-9-5 0 ShaneKelly 1 97+
(J Noseda) *wnt rt s: plld hrd: hld up in 3rd pl: chsd ldr and hung rt bnd 2f out: hung bdly rt over 1f out: rdn to ld last 100yds: sn in command* **2/5**[1]

22 **2** 1 1/4 **Fullback (IRE)**[9] 4861 2-8-12 0 LPKeniry 6 85
(J S Moore) *chsd ldr: led over 2f out: sn rdn clr: 3 l ld ent fnl f: wknd ins fnl f: hdd last 100yds: sn btn* **9/2**[2]

12 **3** 2 1/4 **Laahig**[24] 4374 2-9-2 0 HayleyTurner 2 83
(G A Butler) *stdd s: bhd: rdn wl over 2f out: chsd ldng pair over 1f out: nvr pce to chal* **5/1**[3]

56 **4** 7 **Fisher Hill (USA)**[37] 3939 2-8-12 0 NCallan 4 62
(K A Ryan) *wnt lft s: led: rdn and hdd over 2f out: outpcd wl over 1f out: wl btn after* **20/1**

5 2 **Mr Deal** 2-8-8 0 StephenCarson 7 53
(Eve Johnson Houghton) *s.i.s: bhd: rdn 4f out: wl bhd last 2f* **40/1**

1m 25.07s (0.27) **Going Correction** -0.05s/f (Stan) 5 Ran SP% **113.5**
Speed ratings (Par 96): **96,94,92,84,81**
toteswinger: 1&2 £3.20. CSF £2.85 TOTE £1.40: £1.10, £1.50; EX 3.10.
Owner Ballygallon Stud Limited **Bred** Ballygallon Stud Limited **Trained** Newmarket, Suffolk

FOCUS
An interesting novice event. It was run at a modest pace and War Native is value for a little further, with the placed horses helping to set the level. Fullback should soon get off the mark.

NOTEBOOK
War Native(IRE) proved all the rage in the betting ring to follow up his ready Newmarket debut success 17 days previously. He duly obliged on this switch to Polytrack, but was only workmanlike in doing so and did not overly impress with his attitude. Due to the average early pace he again took time to settle and momentarily looked in trouble when asked for maximum effort in the home straight, showing a tendency to hang. He eventually stamped his authority on the race and looked to have something up his sleeve passing the post, with this extra furlong proving well within his compass. It will be interesting to see where he goes next as he is well entered up, but while he looks a very useful prospect he is still clearly learning his trade. (op 8-15 after 8-13 in a place)
Fullback(IRE), a runner-up on his previous two outings at the track, was not surprisingly given a positive ride on this drop back a furlong and made the favourite work hard for his success. He was again a clear second best and richly deserves to find a race now, which should not prove much trouble in the coming weeks. He now also has the option of nurseries. (op 15-2)
Laahig, taking another step up in trip, was off the bridle and being ridden before the final bend and ultimately stayed on too late from off the pace. This was a little disappointing, but is it probable the best of him has yet to be seen and he deserves to be ridden more handily over this trip in the future. (op 3-1)
Fisher Hill(USA) again dropped out after making the early running and needed this for an official mark. (op 25-1)
Mr Deal was faced with a stiff introduction and was the first off the bridle. This half-brother to the stout stayer Som Tala looks to need more experience and will enjoy another furlong before too long. (op 50-1)

5144 FOREST ROW H'CAP 7f (P)
4:30 (4:30) (Class 4) (0-80,80) 4-Y-O+ **£6,308** (£1,888; £944; £472; £235) **Stalls** Low

Form RPR

0266 **1** **Fiefdom (IRE)**[27] 4284 6-8-10 69 PatrickMathers 6 78
(I W McInnes) *s.i.s: sn in midfield: rdn over 2f out: hdwy u.p over 1f out: r.o wl to ld nr finsh* **14/1**

0130 **2** nk **Glencalvie (IRE)**[40] 3840 7-9-1 77 (p) TolleyDean(3) 9 85
(J Akehurst) *w ldr tl led over 4f out: rdn jst over 2f out: kpt on wl u.p tl hdd nr fin* **16/1**

0643 **3** nk **Cativo Cavallino**[9] 4865 5-8-7 71 NataliaGemelova(5) 8 78
(J E Long) *chsd ldrs: rdn jst over 2f out: kpt on u.p ins fnl f: nt quite pce to rch ldng pair* **8/1**[3]

0040 **4** 1 1/2 **Wavertree Warrior (IRE)**[37] 3972 6-9-3 76 (b) JamesDoyle 3 79
(N P Littmoden) *in tch: rdn wl over 2f out: kpt on u.p fr over 1f out: nvr quite pce to chal ldrs* **14/1**

0452 **5** 1/2 **H Harrison (IRE)**[9] 4862 8-8-4 63 GregFairley 7 65
(I W McInnes) *led tl over 4f out: pressed ldr after: rdn jst over 2f out: lost 2nd ins fnl f: fdd towards fin* **10/1**

2063 **6** 3/4 **Jake The Snake (IRE)**[24] 4393 7-9-4 77 KirstyMilczarek 4 77
(A W Carroll) *hld up in midfield on inner: rdn and effrt over 1f out: kpt on but nvr pce to threaten ldrs* **11/4**[1]

1150 **7** 1 **My Learned Friend (IRE)**[52] 3443 4-8-11 75 DavidProbert(5) 10 72
(A M Balding) *hld up in midfield: rdn and effrt 2f out: kpt on one pce after* **9/2**[2]

5210 **8** 1 3/4 **Napoletano (GER)**[33] 4081 7-8-10 69 (p) IanMongan 13 61
(S Dow) *rrd s: sn swtchd lft and hld up in rr: t.k.h: rdn jst over 2f out: modest late hdwy: nvr nr ldrs* **14/1**

11-0 **9** hd **Sweet Gale (IRE)**[35] 4022 4-9-1 74 StephenCarson 12 66
(Mike Murphy) *hld up towards rr on outer: rdn and no prog wl over 1f out* **33/1**

0506 **10** nse **Flying Goose (IRE)**[10] 4809 4-8-11 73 KevinGhunowa(3) 1 65
(R A Harris) *v.s.a: t.k.h: hld up wl bhd: hanging lft fr 3f out: sltly hmpd bnd jst over 2f out: modest late hdwy: nvr a factor* **14/1**

2304 **11** 1/2 **Teasing**[30] 4181 4-8-13 72 (p) RobertHavlin 2 62
(J Pearce) *stdd s: hld up in rr: nvr a factor* **16/1**

2402 **12** 1/2 **Guildenstern (IRE)**[33] 4084 6-8-2 61 oh3 ChrisCatlin 5 50
(P Howling) *a bhd: no ch last 2f* **14/1**

00-6 **13** 1 1/4 **Princess Valerina**[39] 3892 4-9-0 73 TedDurcan 14 59
(H R A Cecil) *t.k.h: chsd ldrs tl rdn and wknd jst over 2f out: no ch and eased ins fnl f* **10/1**

1200 **14** 18 **Danetime Lord (IRE)**[30] 4186 5-9-7 80 (b[1]) NCallan 11 17
(J R Gask) *racd in midfield: rdn and struggling over 2f out: wl bhd and eased fnl f: t.o* **20/1**

1m 23.91s (-0.89) **Going Correction** -0.05s/f (Stan) 14 Ran SP% **126.9**
Speed ratings (Par 105): **103,102,102,100,100 99,98,96,95,95 95,94,93,72**
toteswinger: 1&2 £57.10, 1&3 £31.90, 2&3 £35.00. CSF £232.55 CT £1939.88 TOTE £15.40: £4.30, £3.90, £2.40; EX 406.30 TRIFECTA Not won..
Owner Stephen Hackney **Bred** Kildaragh Stud **Trained** Catwick, E Yorks

FOCUS
An open handicap for the ordinary class, with plenty of previous course form on offer and the race should work out.
Flying Goose(IRE) Official explanation: jockey said gelding missed the break
Princess Valerina Official explanation: jockey said filly had no more to give

5145 THREE BRIDGES H'CAP 1m 2f (P)
5:00 (5:00) (Class 6) (0-60,60) 3-Y-O+ **£2,914** (£867; £433; £216) **Stalls** Low

Form RPR

0525 **1** **Kings Topic (USA)**[2] 5087 8-9-3 58 (p) PNolan(7) 4 67+
(A B Haynes) *t.k.h: hld up in tch: hdwy to trck ldrs over 1f out: nt clr run ent fnl f: gap opened and rdn to ld ins fnl f: r.o wl* **9/2**[2]

-020 **2** 3/4 **Everyman**[28] 4254 4-8-12 49 TolleyDean(3) 6 56
(A W Carroll) *chsd ldr: rdn to ld ent fnl f: hdd and unable qck ins fnl f* **16/1**

0030 **3** nk **Golden Brown (IRE)**[4] 5020 4-8-9 48 DavidProbert(5) 12 54
(David Pinder) *chsd ldrs: rdn jst over 2f out: ev ch u.p ent fnl f: unable qck last 100yds* **9/1**

0-50 **4** 3/4 **Zalkani (IRE)**[27] 4267 8-8-13 50 JerryO'Dwyer(3) 10 55+
(J Pearce) *stdd s: t.k.h: hld up bhd: hdwy over 1f out: nt clr run and swtchd lft ent fnl f: r.o but nvr able to chal* **16/1**

0004 **5** 1/2 **Josr's Magic (IRE)**[7] 4936 4-9-10 58 KirstyMilczarek 5 63+
(H J Collingridge) *t.k.h: hld up in midfield: hdwy jst over 2f out: chsd ldrs and styng on whn nt clr run fnl f: nvr able to chal* **7/1**[3]

0300 **6** shd **Strike Force**[21] 4491 4-9-9 57 ChrisCatlin 7 61
(K F Clutterbuck) *in tch in midfield: rdn to chse ldrs 2f out: kpt on u.p but nt pce to chal ldrs* **25/1**

6000 **7** 1 **Spiritofthestorm (USA)**[49] 3562 3-9-0 56 StephenCarson 1 58
(R A Teal) *led: rdn jst over 2f out: hdd ent fnl f: wknd last 100yds* **25/1**

4302 **8** 3 1/2 **Stark Contrast (USA)**[7] 4936 4-9-11 59 NCallan 2 54
(M D I Usher) *in tch: effrt to chse ldrs jst over 2f out: wkng whn hmpd ins fnl f: eased last 100yds* **11/4**[1]

0600 **9** 1 1/2 **King After**[6] 4946 6-9-6 54 (v) RobertHavlin 9 46
(J R Best) *t.k.h: hld up in midfield: rdn over 2f out: no imp last 2f* **14/1**

00-0 **10** 3/4 **Fareeha**[173] 712 3-9-4 60 ShaneKelly 13 50
(B R Johnson) *t.k.h: hld up towards rr on outer: rdn and effrt jst over 2f out: sn struggling: wknd over 1f out* **25/1**

4-00 **11** 1 **Blitzen (IRE)**[19] 4524 3-9-4 60 JamesDoyle 8 48
(Tom Dascombe) *t.k.h: hld up bhd: rdn over 3f out: no ch last 2f* **14/1**

-060 **12** 1/2 **Muraco**[10] 4811 4-9-12 60 DavidKinsella 3 47
(A M Hales) *s.i.s: hld up in midfield: rdn 4f out: wknd wl over 2f out* **16/1**

506 **13** 2 **Magpie (IRE)**[21] 4484 3-9-3 59 TQuinn 14 42
(B G Powell) *s.i.s: tk keen hokld: hld up in last: nvr a factor* **8/1**

0106 **14** *6* **Paparaazi (IRE)**[4] 5008 6-9-3 **51**.............................(p) PatrickMathers 11 22
(I W McInnes) *s.i.s: hld up in rr: rdn and struggling over 3f out: wl btn after* **9/1**

2m 7.03s (0.43) **Going Correction** -0.05s/f (Stan)
WFA 3 from 4yo+ 8lb **14** Ran SP% **131.0**
Speed ratings (Par 101): **96,95,95,94,94 94,93,90,89,88 87,87,85,81**
toteswinger: 1&2 £17.90, 1&3 £11.80, 2&3 £32.50. CSF £80.32 CT £639.69 TOTE £5.80: £1.90, £6.00, £3.70; EX 102.20 TRIFECTA Not won..
Owner Ms C Berry **Bred** Marvin Delfiner And Fred Seitz **Trained** Limpley Stoke, Bath
■ Stewards' Enquiry : Jerry O'Dwyer two-day ban: careless riding (Sep 1-2)

FOCUS
A moderate handicap, run at a steady early pace. The first three ran to form so the form makes a fair bit of sense.
Josr's Magic(IRE) Official explanation: jockey said gelding was denied a clear run
T/Plt: £527.30 to a £1 stake. Pool: £69,526.18. 96.25 winning tickets. T/Qpdt: £43.70 to a £1 stake. Pool: £5,018.97. 84.90 winning tickets. SP

4925 WINDSOR (R-H)
Monday, August 18

OFFICIAL GOING: Good to soft (good in places)
Wind: Blustery, across Weather: Overcast, rain race 3

5146 GET ON WITH WILLIAM HILL - 0800 444040 APPRENTICE H'CAP 1m 2f 7y
5:30 (5:30) (Class 5) (0-75,72) 3-Y-0 **£3,070** (£906; £453) **Stalls** Centre

Form RPR
1406 **1** **Animator**[18] 4571 3-9-0 **67**............................ AshleyMorgan(5) 1 75
(P F I Cole) *hld up in last: prog on wd outside over 3f out: rdn to chse ldr 2f out: styd on u.p to ld fnl 100yds* **10/1**
1111 **2** *1 1/4* **Aleatricis**[25] 4334 3-9-5 **72**..(b[1]) RosieJessop(5) 7 78
(Sir Mark Prescott) *s.s: racd freely and led after 1f: clr over 3f out: styd against nr side rail fr over 2f out: hrd rdn over 1f out: hdd fnl 100yds* **5/4**[1]
-054 **3** *3/4* **Mistress Eva**[15] 4669 3-9-3 **68**............................ WilliamCarson(3) 2 72
(P Winkworth) *chsd ldr after 3f to 2f out: nt qckn u.p: kpt on ins fnl f* **7/2**[2]
004 **4** *3 3/4* **No Wonga**[13] 4709 3-8-7 **58**.. RichardEvans(3) 3 55
(P D Evans) *settled in 5th: effrt on outer over 3f out: rdn to chse ldrs 2f out: wknd fnl f* **6/1**[3]
-511 **5** *1* **A Dream Come True**[178] 665 3-9-7 **69**............................ JackMitchell 5 64
(D K Ivory) *hld up bhd ldrs: outpcd fr 4f out and sn rdn: no real imp after* **14/1**
005- **6** *4 1/2* **Cool The Heels (IRE)**[346] 5186 3-9-3 **65**........................ HaddenFrost 4 51
(J S Moore) *led 1f: chsd ldr to 7f out: rdn in 3rd 4f out: sn btn* **16/1**
0010 **7** *3/4* **Themwerethedays**[42] 3799 3-9-1 **68**........................ MatthewBirch(5) 6 52
(S Kirk) *hld up in last pair: outpcd 4f out: struggling fnl 3f* **11/1**

2m 8.52s (-0.18) **Going Correction** +0.05s/f (Good) **7** Ran SP% **110.9**
Speed ratings (Par 100): **102,101,100,97,96 93,92**
toteswinger: 1&2 £4.80, 1&3 £4.20, 2&3 £1.10. CSF £21.70 TOTE £16.00: £5.30, £1.30; EX 26.10.
Owner Strategic Thoroughbred Racing **Bred** Stowell Park Stud **Trained** Whatcombe, Oxon
■ Stewards' Enquiry : Ashley Morgan three-day ban: used whip above shoulder height (Sep 1-2 & 25 (latter for remedial training)

FOCUS
Following 6mm of overnight rain the ground was changed to good to soft, good in places. This looked a modest and uncompetitive apprentice handicap with over half the field starting at 10-1 or longer. The winner was back to form after two poor efforts on fast ground, and the next three ran close to their marks.

5147 EUROPEAN BREEDERS' FUND MAIDEN FILLIES' STKS 6f
6:00 (6:01) (Class 5) 2-Y-0 **£3,885** (£1,156; £577; £288) **Stalls** High

Form RPR
32 **1** **Tropical Paradise (IRE)**[76] 2691 2-9-0 0............................ JimCrowley 5 85
(P Winkworth) *racd centre: mde virtually all: rdn clr fr 2f out: styd on strly fnl f* **4/1**[2]
45 **2** *4 1/2* **Solitary**[31] 4149 2-9-0 0.. DaneO'Neill 12 72
(H Candy) *racd centre: mostly chsd wnr: outpcd fr 2f out: styd on but n.d after* **7/1**
3 *2 1/4* **Albertine Rose** 2-9-0 0... MartinDwyer 14 65
(W R Muir) *racd centre: wl in tch: rn green and outpcd fr 2f out: styd on steadily fnl f* **22/1**
0 **4** *2* **Equinine (IRE)**[19] 4521 2-9-0 0.. SteveDrowne 9 59
(B W Hills) *settled wl in rr: stdy prog over 2f out: styd on fnl f: nrst fin* **25/1**
5 *1/2* **My Superstar** 2-9-0 0.. RyanMoore 15 57
(Sir Michael Stoute) *dwlt: racd centre: rn green towards rr and pushed along after 2f: edgd lft 2f out: nvr on terms but kpt on* **9/2**[3]
6 *nk* **Moonlife (IRE)** 2-9-0 0... TedDurcan 11 56
(Saeed Bin Suroor) *dwlt: rcvrd to trck ldrs: taken to far side over 2f out: nt on terms w ldrs over 1f out* **12/1**
62 **7** *1 1/4* **Peninsula Girl (IRE)**[16] 4643 2-9-0 0............................ EdwardCreighton 16 53
(M R Channon) *racd centre: pressed ldrs to 2f out: steadily wknd* **9/4**[1]
8 *2 1/4* **It's Dubai Dolly** 2-9-0 0.. WandersonD'Avila 4 46
(A J Lidderdale) *racd centre: pressed ldrs: edgd lft fr 2f out and steadily wknd* **100/1**
9 *nse* **Assent (IRE)** 2-9-0 0... FergusSweeney 10 46
(B R Millman) *dwlt: wl in rr: stylish prog to trck ldrs over 2f out: rn green and wknd over 1f out* **50/1**
10 *1/2* **Dream Date (IRE)** 2-9-0 0... LiamJones 6 44
(W J Haggas) *dwlt: rn v green and sn rdn in rr: nvr a factor* **12/1**
11 *1* **Champion Girl (IRE)** 2-9-0 0.. GregFairley 8 41
(D Haydn Jones) *a in rr: pushed along after 2f: brief effrt 2f out: sn wknd* **20/1**
12 *nk* **Caught On Camera** 2-9-0 0... HayleyTurner 2 40
(M L W Bell) *dwlt: sn pushed along in rr: nvr on terms w ldrs* **20/1**
13 *1 3/4* **Especially Special (IRE)** 2-9-0 0.. LPKeniry 7 35
(S Kirk) *trckd ldrs: gng wl enough over 2f out: wknd rapidly over 1f out* **40/1**
14 *1 1/2* **Zellers** 2-9-0 0.. TPO'Shea 13 31
(W J Haggas) *dwlt: sn pushed along in rr: nvr a factor* **33/1**
15 *7* **Braishfield Lass** 2-8-9 0.. GabrielHannon(5) 3 10
(B G Powell) *s.s: a detached in last* **100/1**

1m 13.25s (0.25) **Going Correction** +0.05s/f (Good) **15** Ran SP% **123.9**
Speed ratings (Par 91): **100,94,91,88,87 87,85,82,82,81 80,80,77,75,66**
toteswinger: 1&2 £12.00, 1&3 £35.00, 2&3 £38.50. CSF £29.36 TOTE £5.80: £1.90, £2.90, £5.60; EX 36.60.
Owner R Lovelace & R Muddle **Bred** George E McMahon **Trained** Chiddingfold, Surrey

FOCUS
A fair maiden on paper featuring four Group 1 entries, and an impressive winner. The standard is set through the time and the runner-up.

NOTEBOOK
Tropical Paradise(IRE) ran out a most convincing winner. Returning from a little break, she showed good speed to be at the head of affairs throughout, and drew well clear inside the last, so much so that her rider was able to ease down close home. Softish ground clearly holds no terrors and, while she holds a couple of entries for valuable sales races in the next few weeks, her trainer apparently plans to keep her to a more modest level for the time being. (op 11-2 tchd 6-1)
Solitary kept on well to chase the easy winner home and, having shown a consistent level of ability in three maidens, she will now be eligible to run in nursery company. (op 15-2)
Albertine Rose is by Namid out of a mare who won on fast and soft ground over this trip, so she was never going to have any problems with conditions. She ran green here and hails from a stable whose juveniles invariably improve for their debuts. (op 25-1 tchd 20-1)
Equinine(IRE), another daughter of Namid, proved all the better for her debut effort in a stronger maiden at Goodwood and did best of those entered in the big autumn Group 1 races. She looks one for nurseries after one more run. (op 20-1 tchd 16-1)
My Superstar, who holds a Fillies' Mile entry and is out of a prolific winning sprinter on dirt in the US, is bred to want further than this and the way she ran confirmed that impression. She should come on for the experience. (tchd 7-2 and 5-1)
Moonlife(IRE), a half-sister to a triple winner in Italy, ended up racing next to the far-side rail which probably was not the best place to be. She cost 120,000gns but holds no fancy entries. (op 9-1)
Peninsula Girl(IRE) looked the one to beat on her second at Newmarket last time, but the easier ground may not have suited. (op 11-4 tchd 3-1)
Assent(IRE) was too green to do herself true justice, but showed ability.

5148 TRADITIONAL PASTY & PIE CO LTD (S) STKS 1m 3f 135y
6:30 (6:30) (Class 6) 3-Y-0+ **£2,047** (£604; £302) **Stalls** Centre

Form RPR
0033 **1** **A One (IRE)**[8] 4910 9-8-12 **48**............................ SophieDoyle(7) 15 55
(H J Manners) *mde most: styd alone against nr side rail fr 3f out: hld on gamely fnl f* **16/1**
6350 **2** *nk* **Soldiers Quest**[16] 4635 4-9-5 **47**............................ DaneO'Neill 14 54
(Peter Grayson) *dwlt: hld up wl in rr: rdn and prog in centre fr 3f out: led gp over 1f out: styd on u.p: jst hld* **16/1**
5053 **3** *1* **Black Falcon (IRE)**[4] 5003 8-9-10 **51**............................ JimCrowley 16 58
(John A Harris) *trckd ldrs: effrt 3f out: cl up in centre 2f out: styd on same pce fnl f* **9/2**[2]
660 **4** *1 1/4* **Jafaru**[25] 4343 4-9-5 **61**..(b) HayleyTurner 8 51
(G A Butler) *t.k.h early: mostly chsd wnr to over 2f out: nt qckn wl over 1f out: kpt on* **7/2**[1]
/000 **5** *shd* **Robbie Can Can**[32] 4123 9-9-5 **42**............................ CatherineGannon 4 50
(A W Carroll) *dwlt: wl in rr: rdn and prog over 3f out: chalng in centre 2f out: one pce over 1f out* **50/1**
0500 **6** *1 1/4* **Tamrai Dancer**[9] 4859 3-8-4 **54**............................(b[1]) KirstyMilczarek 10 43
(R M Beckett) *settled midfield: prog 4f out: led centre gp over 2f out to over 1f out: wknd fnl f* **8/1**
62 **7** *1 1/4* **Pairumani Pat (IRE)**[13] 4698 3-8-9 0............................ ChrisCatlin 11 46
(J Pearce) *dwlt: sn rdn in last: nvr on terms: plugged on fnl 2f* **6/1**[3]
3206 **8** *nse* **Dickie Valentine**[139] 1130 3-8-9 **46**............................(p) FergusSweeney 12 46
(M R Bosley) *t.k.h early: hld up in rr: prog to trck ldrs gng strly 3f out: wknd over 1f out* **33/1**
4354 **9** *1 1/4* **Converti**[14] 4691 4-9-2 **50**.. KevinGhunowa(3) 2 44
(H J Manners) *trckd ldrs: cl enough in centre 2f out: steadily wknd* **8/1**
0604 **10** *1* **Film Queen (IRE)**[30] 4182 4-9-0 **45**............................(t) IanMongan 13 37
(Mrs L J Mongan) *hld up in midfield: effrt over 3f out: wdst of all over 2f out and nvr quite on terms: wknd over 1f out* **20/1**
3545 **11** *hd* **Missie Baileys**[12] 4722 6-9-0 **47**............................(p) LPKeniry 6 37
(Mrs L J Mongan) *trckd ldrs: wknd fr over 2f out* **7/1**
-040 **12** *8* **Lenouska (IRE)**[27] 4280 3-8-4 **50**............................ MartinDwyer 9 23
(J W Hills) *pressed ldrs to 3f out: sn wknd* **20/1**
5560 **13** *3/4* **Mtoto Girl**[80] 2561 4-9-0 **42**.. RichardSmith 5 22
(B R Johnson) *pressed ldrs to 3f out: wknd rapidly* **33/1**
14 *nse* **Defectivedetective**[15] 4-9-5 0.. RichardThomas 7 27
(Dr J D Scargill) *dwlt: hld up wl in rr: no prog 3f out: wknd 2f out* **100/1**
050- **15** *19* **Dickie Deano**[243] 7189 4-9-5 **36**.. GregFairley 1 —
(J M Bradley) *a in rr: detached and struggling over 4f out: t.o* **66/1**
0000 **16** *6* **War Feather**[197] 415 6-9-0 **32**............................(t) JackMitchell(5) 3 —
(G C Bravery) *prom tl wknd rapidly over 3f out: t.o* **50/1**

2m 31.79s (2.29) **Going Correction** +0.05s/f (Good)
WFA 3 from 4yo+ 10lb **16** Ran SP% **123.0**
Speed ratings (Par 101): **94,93,93,92,92 91,90,90,89,89 88,83,83,83,70 66**
toteswinger: 1&2 £33.80, 1&3 £10.10, 2&3 £30.40. CSF £234.65 TOTE £19.80: £5.00, £5.50, £1.90; EX 228.50.There was no bid for the winner. Jafaru was claimed by W Knight for £5,000. Pairumani Pat was subject to a friendly claim of £5,000. Soldiers Quest was claimed by P D Evans for £5,000.
Owner H J Manners **Bred** Humphrey Okeke **Trained** Highworth, Wilts

FOCUS
An ordinary seller in which the winner is rated to his recent best.

5149 GET A BONUS AT WILLIAMHILLCASINO.COM FILLIES' H'CAP 1m 67y
7:00 (7:00) (Class 4) (0-85,83) 3-Y-0+ **£5,375** (£1,599; £799; £399) **Stalls** High

Form RPR
3453 **1** **Montrachet**[17] 4596 4-9-8 **72**.. SteveDrowne 4 80
(M L W Bell) *a in ldng trio: shkn up to ld narrowly jst over 1f out: punched out fnl f: shade cosily* **11/4**[1]
0234 **2** *1/2* **Mekong Melody (IRE)**[17] 4583 3-9-6 **76**............................ IanMongan 3 82
(C G Cox) *led: hanging lft bnd over 5f out and reminders: stl hanging lft over 2f out: narrowly hdd over 1f out: kpt on wl but readily hld* **11/2**[3]
6166 **3** *2 1/4* **Lekita**[12] 4731 3-9-4 **74**.. AdamKirby 7 75
(W R Swinburn) *sn restrained into last trio: effrt over 2f out: chsd ldng pair and cl enough jst over 1f out: no ex* **11/4**[1]
0612 **4** *2* **Talk Of Saafend (IRE)**[9] 4872 3-9-6 **76**............................ RyanMoore 5 72
(R Hannon) *hld up in last pair: prog on wd outside fr 3f out: cl enough 2f out: wknd fnl f* **7/2**[2]
4200 **5** *1/2* **Challow Hills (USA)**[45] 3672 3-8-11 **67**............................ ChrisCatlin 6 62
(B W Hills) *hld up and sn last: pushed along over 3f out: sn struggling and btn: plugged on fnl f* **9/1**
1-06 **6** *1* **Miss Emma May (IRE)**[24] 4395 3-9-13 **83**............................(v) TQuinn 2 76
(D R C Elsworth) *t.k.h: hld up bhd ldrs: rdn over 2f out: fdd wl over 1f out* **9/1**

160 7 1 1/2 **Maybe I Will (IRE)**[32] 4104 3-8-12 68 .... HayleyTurner 1 57
(S Dow) *mostly chsd ldr tl wknd u.p over 2f out* **20/1**

1m 44.54s (-0.16) **Going Correction** +0.05s/f (Good)
WFA 3 from 4yo 6lb **7 Ran SP% 115.7**
Speed ratings (Par 102): **102,101,99,97,96 95,94**
toteswinger: 1&2 £4.30, 1&3 £2.60, 2&3 £3.80. CSF £18.80 CT £44.77 TOTE £4.10: £1.90, £2.90; EX 19.50.
Owner Mr & Mrs G Middlebrook **Bred** G And Mrs Middlebrook **Trained** Newmarket, Suffolk

FOCUS
A competitive fillies' handicap on paper, and the form seems sound enough.

5150 GET YOUR CHIPS AT WILLIAMHILLPOKER.COM MAIDEN STKS 1m 67y
7:30 (7:30) (Class 5) 3-4-Y-O £2,729 (£806; £403) Stalls High

Form RPR
22 1 **French Art**[7] 4929 3-9-3 84 .... RyanMoore 1 78
(D R C Elsworth) *mde all and sn 3 l clr: nvr chal: pushed out fnl f* **4/11**[1]
06 2 6 **Black Coffee**[7] 4929 3-9-3 0 .... TPO'Shea 7 65
(W J Musson) *hld up in 4th: rdn 3f out: plugged on to take 2nd over 1f out: nt remotest threat to wnr* **15/2**[3]
4 3 2 **Mazaris (IRE)**[28] 4255 3-9-3 0 .... DaneO'Neill 8 60
(L M Cumani) *hld up and sn last: effrt 3f out: disp 2nd wl over 1f out: one pce after* **5/1**[2]
0 4 1 3/4 **Summer Loving (IRE)**[12] 4730 4-9-4 0 .... LPKeniry 5 51
(Mrs L C Jewell) *chsd wnr to wl over 1f out: n.d and sn wknd* **50/1**
04 5 1 1/4 **Sponge**[34] 4057 3-9-3 0 .... JimCrowley 6 53
(P R Chamings) *chsd ldng pair to 2f out: wknd* **33/1**

1m 44.2s (-0.50) **Going Correction** +0.05s/f (Good)
WFA 3 from 4yo 6lb **5 Ran SP% 106.6**
Speed ratings (Par 103): **104,98,96,94,93**
toteswinger: 1&2 £1.10. CSF £3.36 TOTE £1.30: £1.10, £1.80; EX 2.90.
Owner Matthew Green **Bred** Newsells Park Stud Limited **Trained** Newmarket, Suffolk

FOCUS
A weak maiden especially with three non-runners. The first two were again separated by 6l as they had been in a course-and-distance maiden last week, although seemed to run slightly better here, and the fourth and fifth may limit this form.

5151 READING 107FM H'CAP 5f 10y
8:00 (8:00) (Class 4) (0-85,85) 3-Y-O+ £5,375 (£1,599; £799; £399) Stalls High

Form RPR
2231 1 **Equuleus Pictor**[6] 4958 4-8-10 77 6ex .... JackDean(5) 7 87
(J L Spearing) *mde virtually all: hrd rdn over 1f out: hld on wl fnl f* **4/1**[2]
0231 2 1/2 **Judge 'n Jury**[5] 4981 4-9-2 81 6ex .... (t) KevinGhunowa(3) 3 89
(R A Harris) *prom: mostly pressed wnr fr 1/2-way: hrd rdn over 1f out: kpt on but a jst hld* **4/1**[2]
1021 3 1/2 **Regal Royale**[9] 4865 5-8-5 67 .... (v) KirstyMilczarek 9 73
(Peter Grayson) *pressed ldrs thrght: edgd lft fr 2f out: nt qckn 1f out but styd on* **7/1**[3]
4132 4 hd **Make My Dream**[14] 4693 5-8-8 70 .... TPO'Shea 8 75+
(J Gallagher) *pressed ldrs: lost pl sltly after 2f: kpt on again fnl f* **7/2**[1]
-004 5 3/4 **The Tatling (IRE)**[5] 4962 11-9-9 85 .... PaulFitzsimons 2 88
(J M Bradley) *off the pce in last pair: prog on wd outside over 1f out: pressed ldrs ins fnl f: nt qckn fnl 100yds* **12/1**
0355 6 shd **Hereford Boy**[15] 4668 4-8-10 77 .... JackMitchell(5) 4 81+
(D K Ivory) *off the pce in rr: urged along and prog 2f out: cl up bhd ldrs whn nt clr run fnl f: nt rcvr* **8/1**
0060 7 nk **Liberty Belle (IRE)**[12] 4749 3-8-4 68 .... HayleyTurner 5 69
(J R Best) *chsd ldrs: u.p fr 1/2-way: nvr quite pce to chal but kpt on* **16/1**
3400 8 3/4 **Monsieur Reynard**[9] 4854 3-8-11 75 .... StephenDonohoe 1 74
(Ian Williams) *hld up in rr and off the pce: kpt on fr over 1f out but no real imp on ldrs* **25/1**
6600 9 3/4 **Golden Dixie (USA)**[17] 4586 9-9-3 84 .... HaddenFrost(5) 10 80
(R A Harris) *sn rdn to stay in tch in midfield: no prog 2f out: one pce after* **8/1**
6105 10 6 **Caribbean Coral**[39] 3890 9-9-2 78 .... SteveDrowne 6 52
(A B Haynes) *hld up in last pair and wl off the pce: no prog 2f out: eased whn no ch* **16/1**

59.92 secs (-0.38) **Going Correction** +0.05s/f (Good)
WFA 3 from 4yo+ 2lb **10 Ran SP% 120.2**
Speed ratings (Par 105): **105,104,103,103,101 101,101,100,98,89**
toteswinger: 1&2 £2.80, 1&3 £6.90, 2&3 £10.80. CSF £21.17 CT £113.16 TOTE £6.00: £1.80, £2.00, £2.80; EX 21.20 Place 6: £82.00, Place 5: £49.35..
Owner Masonaires **Bred** A J And Mrs L Brazier **Trained** Kinnersley, Worcs

FOCUS
Various lines of form suggested that there was little between many of these, but it was the two penalised runners who came to the fore. Equuleus Pictor continues to progress and the form seems solid.
T/Plt: £98.30 to a £1 stake. Pool: £63,947.76. 474.51 winning tickets. T/Qpdt: £23.40 to a £1 stake. Pool: £6,452.80. 203.40 winning tickets. JN

4931 WOLVERHAMPTON (A.W) (L-H)
Monday, August 18

OFFICIAL GOING: Standard
Racing delayed half an hour because of a problem with the public address.
Wind: Fresh behind Weather: Overcast turning showery after the 2nd race

5152 TOTEPLACEPOT H'CAP 5f 216y(P)
2:15 (2:46) (Class 6) (0-50,50) 3-Y-O+ £2,729 (£806; £403) Stalls Low

Form RPR
4055 1 **Welcome Approach**[18] 4561 5-8-9 50 .... JamieMoriarty(3) 2 61
(J R Weymes) *prom: rdn 1/2-way: led wl ins fnl f: edgd rt: styd on* **15/2**
0060 2 hd **Willhewiz**[37] 3948 8-8-10 48 ow1 .... EddieAhern 8 59
(W M Brisbourne) *chsd ldrs: rdn over 2f out: ev ch wl ins fnl f: r.o* **4/1**[1]
5U40 3 2 1/4 **Gone'N'Dunnett (IRE)**[12] 4749 9-8-9 47 ow1 .... (v) StephenDonohoe 10 51
(Mrs C A Dunnett) *broke wl and led early: sn lost pl: rdn over 2f out: r.o ins fnl f: nt rch ldrs* **16/1**
0000 4 1/2 **Tadlil**[8] 4903 6-8-9 50 .... (v) TravisBlock(3) 3 52
(J M Bradley) *prom: chsd ldr over 2f out: led over 1f out: edgd lft: rdn and hdd wl ins fnl f: no ex* **40/1**
0000 5 shd **Rosie Cross (IRE)**[10] 4812 4-8-8 49 .... PatrickHills(3) 11 51
(Eve Johnson Houghton) *mid-div: hdwy u.p over 2f out: edgd lft over 1f out: styd on* **20/1**
0000 6 1/2 **Empire Dancer (IRE)**[16] 4653 5-8-10 48 .... (p) RoystonFfrench 1 48
(I W McInnes) *s.i.s: hld up: hdwy u.p over 1f out: nt rch ldrs* **8/1**
3000 7 4 **Hla Tun (USA)**[19] 4531 3-8-9 50 .... PaulHanagan 9 37
(W R Swinburn) *broke wl: sn outpcd: last over 2f out: r.o ins fnl f* **8/1**
3640 8 2 1/2 **Puskas (IRE)**[8] 4903 5-8-9 50 .... (b) RussellKennemore(3) 4 29
(J M Bradley) *sn led: rdn and hdd over 1f out: wknd ins fnl f* **12/1**
0306 9 1 3/4 **Polar Force**[65] 3033 8-8-11 49 .... PatCosgrave 5 23
(Mrs C A Dunnett) *mid-div: hdwy over 2f out: rdn and wknd over 1f out* **14/1**
-004 10 3/4 **Piccolo Diamante (USA)**[19] 4542 4-8-11 49 .... TonyCulhane 6 20
(S Parr) *dwlt: outpcd* **6/1**[3]
5403 11 3 **Stargazy**[133] 1248 4-8-3 48 .... MatthewDavies(7) 12 10
(W G M Turner) *hld up: rdn over 2f out: sn wknd* **9/1**
0240 12 17 **Mujma**[5] 4967 4-8-12 50 .... (b[1]) AdamKirby 7 —
(S Parr) *sn chsng ldr: rdn over 2f out: wknd over 1f out* **5/1**[2]

1m 16.3s (1.30) **Going Correction** +0.20s/f (Slow)
WFA 3 from 4yo+ 3lb **12 Ran SP% 122.4**
Speed ratings (Par 101): **99,98,95,95,94 94,88,85,83,82 78,55**
toteswinger: 1&2 £10.00, 1&3 £31.70, 2&3 £21.50. CSF £38.81 CT £490.27 TOTE £9.80: £2.90, £1.70, £5.10; EX 46.00.
Owner T A Scothern **Bred** P Wyatt And Ranby Hall **Trained** Middleham Moor, N Yorks

FOCUS
A moderate if competitive sprint handicap and a couple were very well backed. Not easy form to pin down, with the fourth perhaps the best guide.
Mujma Official explanation: jockey said gelding had no more to give

5153 TOTESWINGER NURSERY 5f 216y(P)
2:45 (3:16) (Class 4) (0-85,84) 2-Y-O £4,533 (£1,348; £674; £336) Stalls Low

Form RPR
141 1 **Crystal Moments**[19] 4525 2-9-7 84 .... EddieAhern 5 86
(E A L Dunlop) *chsd ldrs: rdn over 1f out: edgd lft and led wl ins fnl f* **4/5**[1]
2535 2 1/2 **Gone Hunting**[10] 4822 2-8-13 81 .... JackDean(5) 4 82
(W G M Turner) *chsd ldr tl led over 2f out: rdn and edgd lft over 1f out: hung rt and hdd wl ins fnl f* **25/1**
516 3 1 3/4 **Ridgeway Silver**[37] 3941 2-8-4 67 .... JimmyQuinn 1 64+
(M D I Usher) *a.p: rdn over 1f out: styng on same pce whn hmpd wl ins fnl f* **16/1**[3]
504 4 3 3/4 **Helpmeronda**[12] 4720 2-8-3 66 .... RoystonFfrench 2 50
(S A Callaghan) *sn pushed along in rr: rdn over 2f out: n.d* **4/1**[2]
5046 5 3 3/4 **Abhainn (IRE)**[13] 4706 2-8-11 74 .... CatherineGannon 3 47
(B Palling) *led: rdn and hdd over 2f out: wknd over 1f out* **16/1**[3]
434 6 7 **Sparkling Crystal (IRE)**[15] 4666 2-8-8 71 .... PaulHanagan 6 23
(B W Hills) *chsd ldrs: rdn over 2f out: sn wknd* **4/1**[2]

1m 16.67s (1.67) **Going Correction** +0.20s/f (Slow) **6 Ran SP% 111.2**
Speed ratings (Par 96): **96,95,93,88,83 73**
toteswinger: 1&2 £3.00, 1&3 £2.90, 2&3 £8.90. CSF £22.95 TOTE £1.70: £1.40, £5.50; EX 17.50.
Owner Mohammed Jaber **Bred** Lady Jennifer Green And John Eyre **Trained** Newmarket, Suffolk

FOCUS
Only a small field for this nursery and fairly uncompetitive as they bet 16-1 bar three, but the time was only fractionally slower than the opening older-horse handicap. The winner is progressive and the runner-up sets the level.

NOTEBOOK
Crystal Moments is not that big and it looked halfway up the straight as if the weight had anchored her, but she responded to pressure to get up near the line, just as she had done at Kempton on her previous start. Her dam won numerous races under all disciplines and this filly is following family tradition. She looks as if she will appreciate another furlong before much longer. (op 10-11)
Gone Hunting, a Polytrack winner who ran well in a good race for the grade last time, was making his handicap debut and did nothing wrong, taking over entering the straight and making the best of his way home, only to be run down near the line by the favourite, so may find a small race before long. (op 20-1)
Ridgeway Silver was making her debut on this surface but had won on fast ground on turf and it seemed to suit. She travelled upsides the winner for much of the way but was just getting the worst of things when the runner-up came across her in the closing stages. (tchd 14-1)
Helpmeronda was getting plenty of weight from the principals on this handicap debut, but was dropping back in trip on this first encounter with the surface and was struggling to go the pace from the outset. Official explanation: jockey said filly never travelled (op 3-1)
Abhainn(IRE) took them along at a good early gallop but was brushed aside and folded pretty quickly once headed. (op 11-1)
Sparkling Crystal(IRE) raced close to the pace early, but dropped away from the turn in. (op 5-1 tchd 7-2)

5154 TOTEQUADPOT H'CAP 1m 5f 194y(P)
3:15 (3:47) (Class 6) (0-65,65) 3-Y-O+ £2,729 (£806; £403) Stalls Low

Form RPR
0112 1 **Swords**[7] 4935 6-9-1 57 .... AshleyHamblett(5) 4 71
(R E Peacock) *hld up: hdwy over 3f out: led over 1f out: sn rdn and edgd lft: styd on gamely* **4/1**[2]
4444 2 nk **Natural Action**[33] 4087 4-10-0 65 .... JimmyFortune 13 78
(W Jarvis) *hld up: hdwy over 3f out: led over 2f out: rdn and hdd over 1f out: styd on u.p* **7/2**[1]
4033 3 11 **Adage**[35] 4029 5-9-3 54 .... (t) J-PGuillambert 8 52
(David Pinder) *hld up: hdwy over 3f out: sn rdn: hung lft and wknd over 1f out* **7/2**[1]
-003 4 3/4 **Spume (IRE)**[53] 3399 4-9-12 63 .... (tp) TonyCulhane 2 60
(S Parr) *plld hrd and prom: rdn over 2f out: wknd over 1f out* **20/1**
5233 5 3/4 **Sir Sandicliffe (IRE)**[9] 4848 4-9-9 60 .... TGMcLaughlin 3 56
(W M Brisbourne) *sn pushed along in rr: outpcd over 3f out: swtchd rt over 1f out: nvr nrr* **8/1**
060 6 1 1/4 **Amir Pasha (UAE)**[32] 4124 3-9-1 64 .... AdamKirby 12 58
(W R Swinburn) *trckd ldr: rdn and ev ch over 2f out: wknd over 1f out: hung rt ins fnl f* **7/1**[3]
0622 7 3 **Parkview Love (USA)**[14] 4690 7-9-0 54 .... LeeVickers(3) 9 44
(J G Given) *sn led: rdn and hdd over 2f out: wknd over 1f out* **14/1**
0315 8 2 1/4 **Looks The Business (IRE)**[10] 4811 7-9-4 60 .... (tp) JackDean(5) 1 47
(W G M Turner) *hld up: racd keenly: rdn over 3f out: n.d* **16/1**
5-00 9 shd **Sharmy (IRE)**[14] 4691 12-9-9 60 .... StephenDonohoe 10 47
(Ian Williams) *prom: rdn over 2f out: sn wknd* **66/1**
1345 10 3 1/2 **Naughty Thoughts (IRE)**[12] 4751 4-9-12 63 .... RichardKingscote 11 45
(Tom Dascombe) *hld up: hdwy 3f out: sn rdn and wknd* **14/1**
0460 11 3/4 **Pearl (IRE)**[13] 4704 4-9-5 56 .... (b[1]) TomEaves 5 37
(I A Wood) *chsd ldrs: rdn over 3f out: wknd over 2f out* **40/1**
156- 12 1 1/4 **Stagecoach Emerald**[293] 6564 6-9-12 63 .... JimmyQuinn 7 42
(R W Price) *hld up: bhd fnl 5f* **16/1**

5000 **13** *31* **Kirkie (USA)**[5] 4972 3-8-13 **65** TravisBlock(3) 6 —
(S Parr) *led early: reminded handy tl rdn and wknd over 3f out* **20/1**

3m 9.60s (3.60) **Going Correction** +0.20s/f (Slow)
WFA 3 from 4yo+ 12lb **13** Ran SP% **126.6**
Speed ratings (Par 101): **97,96,90,90,89 88,87,85,85,83 83,82,65**
toteswinger: 1&2 £4.90, 1&3 £4.50, 2&3 £3.90. CSF £18.88 CT £56.81 TOTE £4.50: £1.90, £1.80, £1.70; EX 21.30.
Owner J Babb **Bred** Mrs A Yearley **Trained** Kyre Park, Worcs

FOCUS
A very modest staying handicap and, with no-one keen to go on early, the pace was very moderate. The first two came clear in a thrilling finish with the winner posting a personal best and the second rated to his recent turf form.

5155 TOTEEXACTA MAIDEN FILLIES' STKS 1m 4f 50y(P)
3:45 (4:17) (Class 5) 3-Y-O+ **£3,238** (£963; £481; £240) **Stalls** Low

Form RPR
0432 **1** **Rio Guru (IRE)**[9] 4860 3-8-12 73 TonyCulhane 4 77
(M R Channon) *hld up: hdwy over 1f out: rdn to ld ins fnl f: r.o* **8/1**
00-3 **2** *2 1/4* **Babilu**[14] 4689 3-8-10 70 ow1 LeeVickers(3) 7 74
(J G Given) *hld up in tch: led over 1f out: rdn: edgd rt and hdd ins fnl f: styd on same pce* **14/1**
0030 **3** *shd* **Pure Song**[31] 4170 3-8-12 72 EddieAhern 6 73
(J L Dunlop) *chsd ldrs: rdn and hmpd over 1f out: styd on* **9/1**
50- **4** *1 3/4* **Incarnation (IRE)**[324] 5801 3-8-12 0 PatCosgrave 8 70
(J G Given) *hld up: hdwy over 2f out: rdn and edgd lft over 1f out: styd on* **33/1**
4 **5** *3/4* **Mvuto**[77] 2681 3-8-12 0 AdamKirby 10 69
(C G Cox) *hld up in tch: pushed along 7f out: rdn over 3f out: swtchd lft over 1f out: no ex ins fnl f* **9/2**[3]
6 *3/4* **Princess Rainbow (FR)** 3-8-12 0 JimmyQuinn 3 68
(Jennie Candlish) *s.s: hld up: hdwy over 1f out: nt trble ldrs* **50/1**
0230 **7** *3 1/4* **Stormy View (USA)**[40] 3841 3-8-12 71 (b[1]) JimmyFortune 9 63
(J H M Gosden) *chsd ldr tl led over 3f out: rdn and hdd over 1f out: wknd ins fnl f* **3/1**[1]
0 **8** *28* **River Naiad**[31] 4161 3-8-12 0 (b[1]) J-PGuillambert 5 18
(J A R Toller) *hld up: last and rdn 1/2-way: sn wknd* **50/1**
5 **9** *5* **Lazeyma**[9] 4871 3-8-12 0 PhilipRobinson 1 10
(M A Jarvis) *led: rdn and hdd over 3f out: sn wknd* **7/2**[2]
42 **10** *2 3/4* **Sibi Saba (USA)**[14] 4689 3-8-12 0 RoystonFfrench 12 —
(Saeed Bin Suroor) *chsd ldrs: hung rt: rdn over 4f out: wknd 3f out* **7/2**[2]

2m 41.86s (0.76) **Going Correction** +0.20s/f (Slow)
WFA 3 from 5yo 10lb **10** Ran SP% **122.3**
Speed ratings (Par 100): **105,103,103,102,101 101,99,80,77,75**
toteswinger: 1&2 £12.10, 1&3 £6.60, 2&3 £16.20. CSF £116.37 TOTE £8.40: £2.40, £3.90, £3.00; EX 115.70.
Owner Mrs T G Trant **Bred** Des Vere Hunt Farm Co Ltd & Jack Moclair **Trained** West Ilsley, Berks

FOCUS
This maiden fillies' race looked quite competitive on paper and the betting amongst the first four was quite open but none of them finished in the frame. Not form to take too seriously.
Mvuto Official explanation: jockey said filly hung left
Sibi Saba(USA) Official explanation: jockey said filly hung right throughout

5156 TOTETRIFECTA H'CAP 1m 141y(P)
4:15 (4:46) (Class 4) (0-80,79) 3-Y-O+ **£6,476** (£1,927; £963; £481) **Stalls** Low

Form RPR
0562 **1** **Bold Cross (IRE)**[8] 4895 5-8-13 **66** PaulFitzsimons 6 73
(E G Bevan) *hld up: hdwy over 2f out: hung lft over 1f out: r.o u.p to ld post* **14/1**
4230 **2** *hd* **Prince Noel**[11] 4785 4-8-12 **70** AshleyHamblett(5) 10 76
(N Wilson) *chsd ldrs: rdn and edgd lft over 1f out: r.o to ld last stride: hdd post* **20/1**
-500 **3** *shd* **Officer**[12] 4723 4-9-10 **77** (bt) GeorgeBaker 11 83
(G L Moore) *led and sn clr: rdn over 1f out: hung lft ins fnl f: hdd last stride* **8/1**[3]
0212 **4** *2* **Glenridding**[10] 4813 4-9-8 **75** PatCosgrave 2 76
(J G Given) *stmbld s: chsd clr ldr: rdn over 1f out: styd on* **11/2**[2]
5450 **5** *nk* **Gold Prospect**[18] 4568 4-9-12 **79** PaulHanagan 8 80
(M L W Bell) *hld up: hdwy over 1f out: r.o: nt rch ldrs* **16/1**
1043 **6** *1 1/2* **Dancing Deano (IRE)**[7] 4934 6-8-9 **65** RussellKennemore(3) 9 62
(R Hollinshead) *hld up in tch: outpcd over 2f out: hung lft and styd on u.p fnl f* **20/1**
4065 **7** *3/4* **Carmenero (GER)**[25] 4345 5-9-5 **72** EddieAhern 5 68
(W R Muir) *hld up: hdwy over 1f out: nt trble ldrs* **16/1**
1101 **8** *2 1/4* **Wisdom's Kiss**[7] 4934 4-9-7 **74** 6ex (b) JimmyQuinn 4 64
(J D Bethell) *hld up in tch: rdn over 3f out: wknd over 1f out* **15/8**[1]
-1P3 **9** *2 3/4* **Trifti**[24] 4390 7-9-5 **72** SimonWhitworth 7 56
(Miss Jo Crowley) *s.i.s: hld up: n.d* **14/1**
111 **10** *3* **Willie Ever**[24] 4390 4-9-5 **72** J-PGuillambert 3 49
(B Ellison) *trckd ldrs: racd keenly: rdn over 3f out: wknd over 1f out eased* **11/2**[2]
3316 **11** *1/2* **Harare**[17] 4602 7-9-3 **70** (v) DanielTudhope 1 46
(R J Price) *hld up: a in rr: eased whn no ch over 1f out* **10/1**
50P0 **12** *3 3/4* **Haroldini (IRE)**[19] 4542 6-9-2 **69** (p) DavidAllan 12 36
(J Balding) *sn pushed along in rr: wknd 3f out* **50/1**

1m 51.22s (0.72) **Going Correction** +0.20s/f (Slow) **12** Ran SP% **122.3**
Speed ratings (Par 105): **104,103,103,101,101 100,99,97,95,92 92,88**
toteswinger: 1&2 £32.80, 1&3 £23.80, 2&3 £32.90. CSF £272.90 CT £2427.02 TOTE £17.60: £5.10, £5.30, £2.60; EX 456.00.
Owner E G Bevan **Bred** M Hosokawa **Trained** Ullingswick, H'fords
■ Stewards' Enquiry : Ashley Hamblett one-day ban: failed to ride to draw (Sep 1)
George Baker one-day ban: used whip without allowing colt time to respond (Sep 1)

FOCUS
Not a bad little handicap and they went a furious pace. The first two produced career bests, with the form rated through the third.
Willie Ever Official explanation: trainer's rep said gelding scoped dirty on return

5157 TOTEPOOL H'CAP 1m 141y(P)
4:45 (5:16) (Class 6) (0-55,61) 3-Y-O+ **£2,729** (£806; £403) **Stalls** Low

Form RPR
0000 **1** **Tous Les Deux**[30] 4182 5-9-3 **54** GeorgeBaker 6 66+
(G L Moore) *hld up: hdwy over 2f out: led over 1f out: sn rdn and hung lft: r.o* **7/2**[1]
0401 **2** *1 3/4* **Time To Regret**[7] 4919 8-9-10 **61** 6ex (p) DanielTudhope 3 69
(I W McInnes) *hld up in tch: rdn over 1f out: styd on same pce ins fnl f* **9/1**
0-00 **3** *1* **Confide In Me**[25] 4349 4-9-1 **52** (t) DavidAllan 2 58
(G A Butler) *hld up: hdwy over 3f out: led over 2f out: rdn and hdd over 1f out: no ex ins fnl f* **7/1**
0000 **4** *6* **First Tracks (IRE)**[23] 4431 3-8-11 **55** SimonWhitworth 4 47
(J W Hills) *hld up and bhd: hdwy over 2f out: rdn and hung lft fr over 1f out: wknd ins fnl f* **28/1**
-500 **5** *2* **Run Free**[17] 4597 4-8-13 **55** (v[1]) AshleyHamblett(5) 5 42
(N Wilson) *chsd ldrs: nt clr run 2f out: sn rdn: wknd fnl f* **14/1**
4-05 **6** *6* **Beck**[17] 4597 4-9-1 **52** TGMcLaughlin 13 25
(W M Brisbourne) *mid-div: hdwy over 5f out: rdn and ev ch 2f out: wknd fnl f* **8/1**
0400 **7** *1* **Wadnagin (IRE)**[9] 4862 4-8-13 **50** TomEaves 11 21
(I A Wood) *sn pushed along in rr: n.d* **7/1**
3052 **8** *2* **Straight Face (IRE)**[8] 4891 4-9-2 **53** EddieAhern 10 20
(Miss Gay Kelleway) *s.i.s: hld up: n.d* **6/1**[3]
30-0 **9** *shd* **Almora Guru**[21] 4491 4-8-13 **50** (p) PaulHanagan 9 16
(W M Brisbourne) *trckd ldrs: racd keenly: nt clr run over 2f out: rdn and wknd over 1f out* **25/1**
00-0 **10** *2 1/4* **Lights Of Vegas**[56] 3311 4-9-4 **55** RichardKingscote 8 16
(S Kirk) *prom: rdn 3f out: wknd 2f out* **40/1**
4-40 **11** *4* **Murrisk**[71] 2648 4-9-4 **55** StephenDonohoe 7 7
(Eamon Tyrrell, Ire) *sn pushed along to ld: rdn and hdd over 2f out: wknd wl over 1f out* **8/1**
6003 **12** *1 3/4* **Kansas Gold**[18] 4567 5-9-4 **55** (v) RoystonFfrench 12 3
(J Mackie) *s.i.s: hdwy over 5f out: rdn and wknd wl over 1f out* **11/2**[2]
0000 **13** *22* **To The Max (IRE)**[47] 3612 4-8-13 **50** (v) PatCosgrave 1 —
(Mrs C A Dunnett) *mid-div: rdn and wknd over 2f out* **40/1**

1m 51.77s (1.27) **Going Correction** +0.20s/f (Slow)
WFA 3 from 4yo+ 7lb **13** Ran SP% **128.0**
Speed ratings (Par 101): **102,100,99,94,92 87,86,84,84,82 78,77,57**
toteswinger: 1&2 £11.40, 1&3 £10.40, 2&3 £20.60. CSF £37.56 CT £220.01 TOTE £3.90: £1.90, £2.70, £3.40; EX 42.40 Place 6: £744.90, Place 5: £255.74..
Owner A Grinter **Bred** G And Mrs Middlebrook **Trained** Woodingdean, E Sussex
■ Stewards' Enquiry : Ashley Hamblett two-day ban: careless riding (Sep 2-3)

FOCUS
A moderate handicap, but reasonable for the grade and solid form.
T/Jkpt: Not won. T/Plt: £1,622.70 to a £1 stake. Pool: £72,578.09. 32.65 winning tickets. T/Qpdt: £183.40 to a £1 stake. Pool: £4,858.47. 19.60 winning tickets. CR

4986 YARMOUTH (L-H)
Monday, August 18

OFFICIAL GOING: Good to soft
Wind: Light across Weather: overcast

5158 GREAT YARMOUTH TOURISM MEDIAN AUCTION MAIDEN STKS 6f 3y
5:20 (5:23) (Class 6) 2-Y-O **£2,072** (£616; £308; £153) **Stalls** High

Form RPR
265 **1** **Coconut Shy**[37] 3959 2-8-12 64 (t) AdrianMcCarthy 3 71
(G Prodromou) *mde all: rdn clr ins fnl f: jst hld on* **33/1**
02 **2** *hd* **Brazilian Art**[12] 4734 2-9-3 0 WilliamBuick 1 75
(P W Chapple-Hyam) *cl up: rdn and sltly outpcd 2f out: rallied and str run to go 2nd ins fnl f: jst failed* **9/2**[2]
4 **3** *1* **Nizhoni Dancer**[11] 4792 2-8-12 0 AlanMunro 4 67
(C F Wall) *pressed wnr: rdn and lost 2nd ins fnl f: kpt on steadily* **8/1**
32 **4** *4* **Doctor Parkes**[25] 4346 2-9-3 0 JamieSpencer 16 60
(E F Vaughan) *midfield: effrt over 2f out: sn hung rt: one pce and nvr rchd ldng trio* **1/1**[1]
3 **5** *nk* **Chasing Amy**[18] 4562 2-8-9 0 DominicFox(3) 6 54
(M G Quinlan) *stdd s: rn green but stdy prog fnl 2f: styng on at fin but no ch w ldrs* **20/1**
6 *3 1/4* **General Zhukov** 2-9-3 0 LukeMorris(3) 9 49
(J M P Eustace) *nvr bttr than midfield: rdn and btn 2f out* **50/1**
7 *1 1/4* **Dice (IRE)** 2-8-10 0 MJMurphy(7) 8 46
(L M Cumani) *sn bdly outpcd: passed btn horses ins fnl f: no ch* **33/1**
8 *3/4* **Dream Of Mine** 2-8-12 0 LDettori 15 38
(Saeed Bin Suroor) *chsd ldrs: rdn and struggling wl over 1f out* **6/1**[3]
9 *1 1/2* **Outland (IRE)** 2-9-3 0 PaulMulrennan 2 39
(M H Tompkins) *s.i.s: bdly outpcd tl styd on stoutly ins fnl f* **80/1**
10 *1/2* **Arteus** 2-9-3 0 RobertWinston 5 37
(G G Margarson) *cl up tl rdn and lost pl over 2f out* **66/1**
11 *1* **Captain Churchill (IRE)** 2-9-3 0 JohnEgan 7 34
(D R Lanigan) *struggling in rr after 2f* **50/1**
0 **12** *2 1/2* **Bubses Boy**[12] 4734 2-9-3 0 MickyFenton 10 27
(M L W Bell) *struggling 1/2-way: hmpd and swvd rt over 1f out* **66/1**
0 **13** *1/2* **Highland River**[10] 4826 2-9-0 0 MarcHalford(3) 14 25
(D R C Elsworth) *outpcd 1/2-way: struggling whn bmpd over 1f out* **16/1**
14 *nk* **Al Wujood (IRE)** 2-9-3 0 RichardMullen 12 24
(D M Simcock) *wknd 1/2-way: hanging bdly rt fr wl over 1f out* **40/1**
15 *2 1/2* **Ditto Ditto** 2-9-3 0 TPQueally 13 17
(D R Lanigan) *plld hrd: a bhd* **40/1**
00 **16** *10* **Fawaz**[12] 4747 2-9-3 0 SaleemGolam 11 —
(Mrs C A Dunnett) *brief early spd: rdn and labouring after 2f* **150/1**

1m 16.07s (1.67) **Going Correction** +0.075s/f (Good) **16** Ran SP% **123.8**
Speed ratings (Par 92): **91,90,89,84,83 79,77,76,74,74 72,69,68,68,64 51**
toteswinger: 1&2 £9.70, 1&3 £34.10, 2&3 £13.60. CSF £172.42 TOTE £53.50: £8.70, £1.80, £2.50; EX 194.30.
Owner F Butler **Bred** Burns Farm Stud **Trained** East Harling, Norfolk

FOCUS
A modest maiden in which the winner perhaps didn't need to improve too much on her previous effort where she had raced alone.

NOTEBOOK
Coconut Shy, runner-up in a course-and-distance seller on debut, had struggled in two subsequent starts in maiden company, including when finishing a well-beaten fifth at Nottingham last time. Blasted out in front here, she was kicked clear over a furlong out and just found enough to hold on from the fast-finishing Brazilian Art. The application of a first-time tongue tie clearly made all the difference and she is the type to pay her way in nurseries.
Brazilian Art left his debut running behind when finishing second in a soft-ground maiden at Newcastle last time, so conditions were not expected to present a problem. Niggled to hold his early position, he came under strong pressure from two out and responded well, but was unable to quite get there. A slow surface is evidently the key to him and he will get an extra furlong on this evidence. (tchd 4-1 and 5-1)
Nizhoni Dancer, who out-ran her 50/1 odds to finish a close fourth behind a useful sort over course and distance on her recent debut, comes from a yard who tend to do well with their runners at this venue and she ran well back in third, keeping on without ever looking likely to win the race. A small race should come her way on this evidence. (tchd 15-2 and 17-2)

Doctor Parkes had shown more than enough in two previous tries to suggest this was his for the taking, with the step back up to 6f expected to be in his favour. However, despite a good showing on good to soft ground on his Ascot debut, he did not look happy on the surface and was floundering from two out. He deserves another chance, as this was clearly not his form, and it will be interesting to see what handicap mark he gets. (op 6-4 tchd 13-8)
Chasing Amy, third in a fairly low-key event at Nottingham on debut, made a little late headway, having again showed signs of inexperience, and is more of a nursery type. (op 16-1)
General Zhukov, a half-brother to smart sprinter Angus Newz, made a little late headway and should know more next time. (op 40-1)
Dice(IRE), a 35,000gns son of Kalanisi who is related to several winners, made a little late headway, suggesting he has a future.
Dream Of Mine, a £180,000 purchase who is a half-sister to smart three-year-old Rosa Grace, holds no notable entries and, having raced keenly early on, she found little for pressure. (op 4-1 tchd 7-1)
Captain Churchill(IRE) Official explanation: jockey said gelding ran very green
Ditto Ditto Official explanation: jockey said gelding was unsuited by the good to soft ground

5159 DIGIBET.COM CLAIMING STKS — 6f 3y
5:50 (5:51) (Class 6) 2-Y-O — £2,201 (£655; £327; £163) Stalls High

Form	Pos	Dist	Horse / details	RPR
120	1		**Simple Rhythm**[23] [4434] 2-8-8 78 .... DominicFox(3) 1	64+
			(M G Quinlan) *cl up: led over 2f out: a holding rival fnl f: pushed out* **4/1**[3]	
050	2	½	**Bold Account (IRE)**[45] [3670] 2-8-11 45 .... AndrewElliott 4	62
			(K R Burke) *chsd wnr over 2f out: ev ch fnl 100yds: rdn and no imp* **12/1**	
131	3	10	**Silent Treatment (IRE)**[5] [4986] 2-8-1 56....(t) Louis-PhilippeBeuzelin(5) 5	27+
			(Miss Gay Kelleway) *taken down early: s.i.s: sn led: sddle slipped and hdd over 2f out: no ch after* **6/4**[1]	
5123	4	6	**Faraway Sound (IRE)**[18] [4558] 2-9-5 77 .... PaulMulrennan 3	22+
			(P C Haslam) *plld hrd and cl up tl rdn over 2f out: sn racing awkwardly and dropped rt out* **13/8**[2]	
066	5	1¼	**Persian Tomcat (IRE)**[11] [4769] 2-8-11 52 .... AmyBaker(5) 2	15
			(Miss J Feilden) *s.i.s: labouring in last after 1f* **25/1**	

1m 15.99s (1.59) **Going Correction** +0.075s/f (Good) — 5 Ran SP% **109.6**
Speed ratings (Par 92): **92,91,78,70,68**
CSF £41.17 TOTE £4.90: £1.90, £5.00; EX 53.40.
Owner P T Quinlan **Bred** P Quinlan **Trained** Newmarket, Suffolk

FOCUS
A poor claimer and a rather messy contest that did not work out as many expected, with neither Faraway Sound, nor Silent Treatment, whose saddle slipped, playing a hand in the finish.

NOTEBOOK
Simple Rhythm, all-the-way winner of a course seller back in May, brought the best single piece of form into this, having finished second to the useful Rievaulx World at Redcar last month, although she did have to leave behind a poorer effort at York last time. She had a question to answer over the suitability of the ground, but travelled up strongly and assumed control two out, always just doing enough. She reversed form from earlier in the season with Faraway Sound and clearly improved for the extra furlong, but will be kept to this sort of grade according to her trainer, as her handicap mark is too high. (op 7-2 tchd 11-2)
Bold Account(IRE), backed at large odds beforehand, had been well held in sellers on all three previous starts, but an improved showing was clearly expected and, having switched to the winner's outside over a furlong out, he stuck on right the way to the line. He is clearly very moderate, but looks capable of winning at claiming/selling level. (op 20-1)
Silent Treatment(IRE) has appreciated the drop into sellers, winning two of her last three, including when showing a good attitude in soft ground over course and distance just last week. This was tougher, but she never really had a chance to show what she could do as, having recovered from an awkward start to lead, it emerged her saddle had slipped. Official explanation: jockey said saddle slipped (op 9-4)
Faraway Sound(IRE), an easy winner in this grade at Musselburgh back in June, has twice run gallantly in defeat off an estimated mark of 74 in nurseries and he set a strong standard on this drop back in grade. The return to 6f was not expected to prove a problem, however the slower ground seemed to do for his chance and he was beaten fully two furlongs out. He probably deserves another chance back at 5f on fast ground. Official explanation: jockey said colt never travelled (op 11-10)

5160 REGGIE HOLE MEMORIAL MAIDEN STKS — 6f 3y
6:20 (6:21) (Class 5) 3-4-Y-O — £2,775 (£830; £415; £207; £103) Stalls High

Form	Pos	Dist	Horse / details	RPR
0	1		**Prescription**[5] [4987] 3-8-12 0 .... PaulMulrennan 7	75+
			(Sir Mark Prescott) *prom: rdn over 2f out: led over 1f out: kpt on wl* **6/1**[3]	
-	2	2	**War And Peace (IRE)**[303] [6351] 4-9-6 72 .... JohnEgan 9	74
			(Jane Chapple-Hyam) *chsd ldrs: rdn after 2f: effrt to ld over 2f out: hdd over 1f out: nt qckn fnl f* **10/3**[1]	
4	3	¾	**Baby Rock**[26] [4301] 3-9-3 0 .... AlanMunro 1	72
			(C F Wall) *tubed: chsd ldrs: rdn and ch 1f out: one pce after* **6/1**[3]	
3	4	½	**Onemoreandstay**[5] [4987] 3-8-9 0 .... LukeMorris(3) 3	65
			(R W Price) *midfield: mod 5th and rdn over 1f out: r.o gamely wout chalng ldrs* **7/2**[2]	
0	5	2	**Truly Divine**[30] [4195] 3-9-3 0 .... LDettori 2	64
			(E A L Dunlop) *prom tl rdn and wknd 1f out* **9/1**	
0	6	3	**Bedloe's Island (IRE)**[26] [4301] 3-9-3 0 .... DeanMcKeown 4	54
			(R C Guest) *slowly away: plld hrd in rr: effrt 1/2-way: one pce and btn wl over 1f out* **100/1**	
0	7	2¼	**Johnny McGurk**[60] [3161] 3-9-3 0 .... RobertWinston 6	47
			(M E Rimmer) *cl up: rdn after 2f out: wknd 2f out* **50/1**	
5	8	nk	**State Function (IRE)**[67] [2981] 3-9-3 0 .... DMylonas 12	46
			(G Prodromou) *t.k.h: led tl hdd over 2f out: hanging lft after and qckly lost pl* **8/1**	
0-4	9	4	**Senorita Parkes**[97] [2067] 3-8-12 0 .... RichardMullen 13	28
			(E F Vaughan) *midfield: drvn 1/2-way: sn struggling* **18/1**	
	10	4½	**Wilby (IRE)** 3-9-0 0 .... MarcHalford(3) 8	19
			(Mrs C A Dunnett) *chsd ldrs tl rdn and fdd over 2f out: eased 1f out* **50/1**	
00	11	1¼	**Savanna's Gold**[56] [3318] 4-9-1 0 .... SaleemGolam 14	10
			(G Prodromou) *struggling 1/2-way: t.o* **100/1**	
	12	¾	**Ashton Heights** 3-8-10 0 .... KylieManser(7) 10	12
			(Miss Gay Kelleway) *rdn 1/2-way: racd awkwardly and labouring after: t.o* **50/1**	
6-	13	2½	**Kara Tau**[410] [3233] 3-9-3 0 .... MickyFenton 11	4
			(Stef Liddiard) *s.s: a wl bhd: t.o* **10/1**	
3	14	1	**Flying Free**[16] [4638] 3-9-3 0 .... JamieSpencer 5	—
			(J R Fanshawe) *s.s: racd awkwardly and wl bhd: t.o* **25/1**	

1m 15.97s (1.57) **Going Correction** +0.075s/f (Good)
WFA 3 from 4yo 3lb — 14 Ran SP% **121.0**
Speed ratings (Par 103): **92,89,88,87,85 81,78,77,72,66 64,63,60,58**
toteswinger: 1&2 £7.40, 1&3 £15.30, 2&3 £1.40. CSF £25.71 TOTE £6.20: £2.70, £1.90, £1.90; EX 33.50.
Owner Cheveley Park Stud **Bred** Cheveley Park Stud Ltd **Trained** Newmarket, Suffolk

FOCUS
These 3yo-plus sprint maidens are not usually that informative, but this could work out to be a reasonable contest, for all that the time was only 0.02 seconds quicker than the previous 2yo claimer. Big improvement from the winner to reverse debut form with the fourth.

5161 ROY ALLEN ENGINEERING H'CAP — 1m 3y
6:50 (6:51) (Class 6) (0-65,65) 3-Y-0+ — £2,072 (£616; £308; £153) Stalls High

Form	Pos	Dist	Horse / details	RPR
0003	1		**Lilburn (IRE)**[18] [4569] 3-9-6 64 .... JamieSpencer 4	74+
			(J R Fanshawe) *dropped out in last pl: gd prog 2f out: swtchd rt over 1f out: led ins fnl f: drvn out* **16/1**	
4162	2	1½	**Libre**[13] [4710] 8-9-9 61 .... TPQueally 1	67
			(F Jordan) *hld up: prog on bit 3f out: led over 2f out: clr whn rdn and idled ins fnl f: sn hdd: kpt on again cl home* **13/2**[2]	
0136	3	1	**Al Rayanah**[11] [4797] 5-9-1 53 ....(p) SaleemGolam 7	57
			(G Prodromou) *stdd in rr: prog on stands rails 2f out: chal 1f out: drvn and hung lft: sn btn* **16/1**	
5033	4	1	**Complete Frontline (GER)**[23] [4413] 3-8-11 55 .... AndrewElliott 16	56
			(K R Burke) *cl up: rdn and ch 1f out: nt qckn after* **12/1**	
1622	5	5	**Navene (IRE)**[9] [4863] 4-9-13 65 .... AlanMunro 2	55
			(C F Wall) *led 2f: remained prom tl rdn and wknd 1f out* **15/2**[3]	
1511	6	1¼	**Kimono My House**[11] [4797] 4-9-9 61 .... LDettori 9	48
			(J G Given) *chsd ldrs: rdn 2f out: btn over 1f out* **15/8**[1]	
4660	7	6	**Life's A Whirl**[27] [4282] 6-8-8 46 ....(p) JohnEgan 5	20
			(Mrs C A Dunnett) *midfield: btn over 2f out: poor 7th 1f out* **16/1**	
0-00	8	3¼	**Tarraburn (USA)**[21] [4478] 4-9-1 60 .... AndreaAtzeni(7) 8	26
			(G C H Chung) *midfield: rdn and wknd 2f out* **33/1**	
004	9	4½	**Gee Ceffyl Bach**[12] [4746] 4-8-13 51 .... DaleGibson 10	7
			(John A Harris) *rdn and struggling bdly 2f out: t.o* **16/1**	
6030	10	5	**Wodhill Schnaps**[23] [4428] 7-9-5 57 .... RichardMullen 15	1
			(D Morris) *struggling in rr 1/2-way: t.o* **25/1**	
0006	11	1¾	**Squire Boldwood (IRE)**[27] [4278] 3-8-11 58 .... MarcHalford(3) 3	—
			(D R C Elsworth) *cl up: rdn 1/2-way: lost pl tamely: t.o and eased over 1f out* **25/1**	
0030	12	nk	**Mick Is Back**[13] [4710] 4-9-6 58 ....(vt) RobertWinston 13	—
			(G G Margarson) *struggling 1/2-way: t.o* **12/1**	
6030	13	1¼	**Djalalabad (FR)**[10] [4825] 4-8-7 52 ....(t) DonnaCaldwell(7) 12	—
			(Mrs C A Dunnett) *led after 2f: rdn and hdd over 2f out: lost pl rapidly: eased and t.o* **33/1**	
4363	14	7	**Bartercard (USA)**[5] [4991] 7-9-12 64 .... MickyFenton 14	—
			(Stef Liddiard) *lost pl 1/2-way: t.o and virtually p.u fnl f* **14/1**	
-430	15	¾	**Princess Gee**[31] [4156] 3-9-6 64 .... PaulEddery 11	—
			(B J McMath) *bhd fnl 3f: t.o* **40/1**	
0000	16	1½	**Farsighted**[21] [4477] 3-8-12 59 ....(b[1]) LukeMorris(3) 6	—
			(J M P Eustace) *chsd ldrs: drvn and lost pl 1/2-way: t.o* **66/1**	

1m 43.49s (2.89) **Going Correction** +0.075s/f (Good)
WFA 3 from 4yo+ 6lb — 16 Ran SP% **123.0**
Speed ratings (Par 101): **88,86,85,84,79 78,72,69,64,59 57,57,56,49,48 46**
toteswinger: 1&2 £9.30, 1&3 not won, 2&3 £19.50. CSF £110.78 CT £1726.60 TOTE £24.00: £3.70, £2.10, £3.70, £3.60; EX 75.30.
Owner Mr & Mrs Duncan Davidson **Bred** Denis J Reddan **Trained** Newmarket, Suffolk

FOCUS
A very moderate winning time to this modest handicap. The first four came clear and the winner is on the upgrade, but the form is only ordinary.
Kimono My House Official explanation: jockey said filly ran flat
Life's A Whirl Official explanation: jockey said mare had no more to give
Mick Is Back Official explanation: jockey said gelding hung left
Bartercard(USA) Official explanation: jockey said gelding moved badly

5162 FIRSTBET £50 MATCHED TELEPHONE BETTING 0800 230 0800 H'CAP — 7f 3y
7:20 (7:20) (Class 5) (0-70,70) 3-Y-O — £2,719 (£809; £404; £202) Stalls High

Form	Pos	Dist	Horse / details	RPR
0-43	1		**Jennie Jerome (IRE)**[30] [4194] 3-9-0 70 .... MJMurphy(7) 3	81+
			(L M Cumani) *hld up travelling wl in rr: shkn up and prog over 2f out: rdn to ld 130yds out: sn in command: lost hind shoe* **85/40**[1]	
2143	2	1¼	**All In The Red (IRE)**[76] [2705] 3-9-7 70 ....(b[1]) AlanMunro 7	75
			(Miss Gay Kelleway) *prom: rdn to ld but hld hd high over 1f out: passed and outbattled ins fnl f* **7/2**[2]	
0435	3	2¾	**Just Jimmy (IRE)**[24] [4369] 3-8-10 59 .... JohnEgan 6	57
			(P D Evans) *bhd and sn pushed along: hdwy 2f out: wnt 3rd ins fnl f: unable to chal* **11/2**[3]	
050	4	4	**Writingonthewall (IRE)**[16] [4641] 3-9-3 66 ....(v[1]) TPQueally 2	53
			(M L W Bell) *t.k.h trcking ldrs: shkn up over 1f out: immediately reluctant and nt run on* **15/2**	
0000	5	½	**Wooden King (IRE)**[3] [5045] 3-7-13 51 oh4 ....(v[1]) LukeMorris(3) 10	36
			(P D Evans) *midfield: pushed along 1/2-way: btn wl over 1f out* **33/1**	
5354	6	1	**Easy Wonder (GER)**[11] [4773] 3-8-0 54 .....(p) Louis-PhilippeBeuzelin(5) 5	37
			(I A Wood) *chsd ldrs: rdn 1/2-way: sn btn: plugged on* **12/1**	
0403	7	1¼	**Merrion Tiger (IRE)**[24] [4377] 3-8-9 58 ....(v[1]) AndrewElliott 1	37
			(K R Burke) *plld hrd in ld: rdn over 2f out: hdd and lost pl qckly over 1f out* **15/2**	
4100	8	½	**Zaarmit (IRE)**[19] [4533] 3-9-2 65 ....(b[1]) RichardMullen 4	43
			(D M Simcock) *t.k.h: cl up tl rdn and gave up qckly 2f out* **25/1**	
0504	9	3	**Sazerac (USA)**[97] [2074] 3-8-5 54 .... SaleemGolam 8	24
			(P Howling) *stdd in last pl: rdn 3f out: hung lft and nt run on* **20/1**	
4000	10	7	**Ramblin Bob**[19] [4535] 3-8-2 51 .... PaulEddery 11	2
			(W J Musson) *last and struggling over 2f out: t.o* **20/1**	
5000	11	2¼	**Miss Tilen**[11] [4794] 3-8-3 52 oh6 ow1 ....(v[1]) MatthewHenry 9	—
			(V Smith) *drvn and reluctant in last pair over 2f out: t.o* **100/1**	

1m 29.93s (3.33) **Going Correction** +0.075s/f (Good) — 11 Ran SP% **118.1**
Speed ratings (Par 100): **83,81,78,73,73 72,70,70,66,58 56**
toteswinger: 1&2 £1.80, 1&3 £2.20, 2&3 £2.30. CSF £8.69 CT £36.05 TOTE £3.10: £1.30, £1.70, £1.70; EX 11.00.
Owner The Honorable Earle I Mack **Bred** Old Carhue Stud **Trained** Newmarket, Suffolk

FOCUS
A modest handicap in which six of the field wore first-time headgear and the winning time was moderate. The winner is rated up 12lb with the form rated through the runner-up.
Wooden King(IRE) Official explanation: jockey said gelding jumped left at start

Miss Tilen Official explanation: jockey said filly was unsuited by the good to soft ground

5163 FIRSTBET.COM ONLINE SPORTSBOOK £50 IN FREE BETS MAIDEN H'CAP 1m 6f 17y

7:50 (7:52) (Class 5) (0-70,70) 3-Y-0+ **£2,719** (£809; £404; £202) **Stalls** High

Form RPR

0444 **1** **Broken Moon**[25] 4344 3-9-5 **70** .... JamieSpencer 11 79
(J R Fanshawe) *t.k.h in midfield: reminders to cl 4f out: led 3f out: rdn and in command fnl f* **6/4**[1]

0-00 **2** 2 1/2 **Lindy Lou**[81] 2533 4-9-7 **60** .... AlanMunro 8 65
(C F Wall) *t.k.h in rr: hdwy 4f out: chsd wnr 3f out: sn rdn: kpt on gamely tl no match for wnr fnl f* **8/1**

2466 **3** 1/2 **Compton Falcon**[30] 4193 4-9-3 **61** .... Louis-PhilippeBeuzelin(5) 13 66
(G A Butler) *settled in rr: rdn over 3f out: sn hanging lft: plugged on but would nt keep st after* **7/1**[3]

620 **4** 2 1/2 **Kritzia**[9] 4871 3-8-7 **58** ow1 .... TPQueally 3 59
(H R A Cecil) *prom: rdn 3f out: plodded on and btn over 1f out* **11/2**[2]

40/3 **5** 1 1/2 **Palace Walk (FR)**[24] 4366 6-8-11 **50** .... MickyFenton 12 49
(B G Powell) *sn drvn into ld: rdn and hdd 3f out: btn 2f out but kpt trying* **10/1**

0P-6 **6** 3 **Very Green (FR)**[13] 4704 6-8-11 **57** .... KylieManser(7) 2 52
(Mrs A L M King) *nvr bttr than midfield: short lived effrt over 3f out* **12/1**

2000 **7** 1 **National Day (IRE)**[7] 4930 4-9-4 **60** .... MarcHalford(3) 4 53
(D R C Elsworth) *chsd ldrs tl rdn and wknd 3f out* **14/1**

003/ **8** 8 **Pacific Ocean (ARG)**[1456] 5002 9-8-10 **49** oh4........(bt) SaleemGolam 9 31
(Miss Z C Davison) *a bhd: no ch fnl 4f* **40/1**

604 **9** 10 **Major Promise**[17] 4581 3-9-1 **66** .... RobertWinston 10 34
(G G Margarson) *slowly away: rdn to rch midfield 1/2-way: wknd 3f out: eased and t.o* **16/1**

0-40 **10** 1/2 **Blue Admiral**[34] 4067 3-9-2 **67** .... PaulMulrennan 6 34
(M H Tompkins) *pushed along in midfield 1/2-way: no rspnse: btn 4f out: eased and t.o* **33/1**

00-0 **11** nk **Al Mogeer (IRE)**[33] 4085 3-7-5 **49** oh4........(vt[1]) AndreaAtzeni(7) 5 16
(P J McBride) *t.k.h: cl up tl wknd 4f out: eased and t.o* **80/1**

3/00 **12** 3/4 **Berkeley Castle (USA)**[37] 3965 4-10-0 **67**........(p) JohnEgan 1 33
(E F Vaughan) *midfield: rdn and wknd 3f out: eased and t.o* **33/1**

3m 10.34s (2.74) **Going Correction** +0.275s/f (Good)
WFA 3 from 4yo+ 12lb **12** Ran SP% **117.9**
Speed ratings (Par 103): **103,101,101,99,99 97,96,92,86,86 85,85**
toteswinger: 1&2 £3.00, 1&3 £4.40, 2&3 £12.50. CSF £13.41 CT £67.35 TOTE £2.70: £1.50, £2.80, £1.90; EX 20.70 Place 6: £222.92, Place 5: £82.00, Place 5: 60.57..
Owner Chippenham Lodge Stud Limited **Bred** Chippenham Lodge Stud Ltd **Trained** Newmarket, Suffolk

FOCUS
Moderate stuff rated through the second and third. The winner is up 5lb but does not look to have a progressive profile.
Berkeley Castle(USA) Official explanation: jockey said gelding had no more to give
T/Plt: £198.90 to a £1 stake. Pool: £55,626.62. 204.10 winning tickets. T/Qpdt: £12.00 to a £1 stake. Pool: £6,280.43. 384.40 winning tickets. IM

SARATOGA (R-H)
Friday, August 15

OFFICIAL GOING: Yielding

5164a LAKE PLACID STKS (GRADE 2) (FILLIES) (INNER TURF) 1m 1f

9:56 (9:57) 3-Y-0

£45,226 (£15,075; £7,538; £3,769; £2,261; £503)

RPR

1 **Backseat Rhythm (USA)**[41] 3807 3-8-4 .... JJCastellano 6 109
(Patrick L Reynolds, U.S.A) **62/10**

2 3 1/4 **Rosa Grace**[33] 4006 3-8-6 .... JRLeparoux 2 104
(Rae Guest) *held up in last, good headway 2f out, close 3rd straight, soon went 2nd, no chance with winner SP 11-1* **12/1**

3 1 1/4 **Raw Silk (USA)**[41] 3807 3-8-8 ....(b) AGarcia 8 103
(Thomas Albertrani, U.S.A) **47/10**[3]

4 1 3/4 **Namaste's Wish (USA)**[27] 3-8-6 .... KDesormeaux 4 97
(William Mott, U.S.A) **73/10**

5 1 **I Lost My Choo (USA)**[27] 3-8-8 .... EPrado 3 97
(Philip M Serpe, U.S.A) **49/20**[1]

6 2 1/4 **Encanto Park (USA)**[48] 3-8-4 ....(b) JChavez 1 88
(Henry Collazo, U.S.A) **44/1**

7 3/4 **Zaskar**[41] 3807 3-8-4 ....(b) JRVelazquez 7 86
(John Terranova II, U.S.A) **78/10**

8 1 1/2 **Much Obliged (USA)**[48] 3-8-6 .... SXBridgmohan 5 84
(Malcolm Pierce, Canada) **31/10**[2]

1m 50.69s (110.69) **8** Ran SP% **118.1**
PARI-MUTUEL (Including $2 stake): WIN 14.40; PL (1-2) 6.80, 11.40;SHOW (1-2-3) 5.30, 6.70, 5.00; SF 180.00.
Owner Paul P Pompa Jr **Bred** Hill 'N' Dale Farm & Spast Farm **Trained** USA

NOTEBOOK
Rosa Grace was readily outpointed by the winner in the straight but it should be remembered that Backseat Rhythm boasts top-class juvenile and turf form in the States.

4806 BRIGHTON (L-H)
Tuesday, August 19

OFFICIAL GOING: Good to soft (good in places)
Wind: Strong, half against Weather: Cool and cloudy

5165 EUROPEAN BREEDERS' FUND MEDIAN AUCTION MAIDEN STKS 6f 209y

2:00 (2:02) (Class 5) 2-Y-0 **£3,561** (£1,059; £529; £264) **Stalls** Low

Form RPR

1 **Al Sabaheya** 2-8-12 0 .... LiamJones 8 74+
(C E Brittain) *chsd ldrs: led wl over 1f out: rdn clr: readily* **16/1**

0325 **2** 3 3/4 **Today's The Day**[20] 4525 2-8-12 75........(p) J-PGuillambert 10 64
(M A Jarvis) *chsd ldrs on outside: carried rt over 2f out: rdn and hung lft fr wl over 1f out: styd on to take 2nd ins fnl f* **13/2**[3]

3 1 3/4 **Popiel** 2-9-3 0 .... ChrisCatlin 6 68+
(Saeed Bin Suroor) *s.s: bhd: pushed along 4f out: in rr of main gp whn bdly hmpd wl over 1f out: stydon wl fnl f: nrst fin* **8/1**

400 **4** nk **Imperial Skylight**[18] 4589 2-9-3 64 .... TPO'Shea 3 64
(M R Channon) *dwlt: hld up in midfield: effrt over 2f out: rdn to chse ldrs over 1f out: styd on same pce* **25/1**

6620 **5** hd **Deal Clincher**[34] 4079 2-8-12 70 .... JimCrowley 1 63+
(P Winkworth) *hld up in rr: effrt and sme hdwy whn bdly hmpd wl over 1f out: styd on fnl f: nt rch ldrs* **12/1**

0 **6** hd **Arrogance**[28] 4274 2-9-3 0 .... GeorgeBaker 4 63
(G L Moore) *mid-div: rdn and hdwy on rail 2f out: chsd wnr over 1f out tl no ex ins fnl f* **33/1**

632 **7** 3 **Andhaar**[13] 4728 2-9-3 78 .... SebSanders 7 56
(E A L Dunlop) *w ldrs: led over 4f out tl wl over 1f out: hrd rdn: sn wknd* **3/1**[2]

0 **8** 2 **Honorable Endeavor**[59] 3267 2-8-12 0 .... DavidProbert(5) 5 50
(E F Vaughan) *w ldrs tl hrd rdn and wknd over 1f out* **50/1**

0 **9** 10 **Tallulah's Secret**[20] 4530 2-8-12 0 .... FergusSweeney 2 20
(J Gallagher) *s.s: towards rr: swtchd wd and rdn 3f out: n.d: bhd and eased 1f out* **100/1**

43 **10** 1/2 **Night Lily (IRE)**[10] 4870 2-8-9 0 .... LukeMorris(3) 9 39+
(J Jay) *led over 2f: hung rt over 2f out: hung lft: bmpd and squeezed out wl over 1f out: nt rcvr: eased whn no ch* **11/8**[1]

1m 25.8s (2.70) **Going Correction** +0.325s/f (Good) **10** Ran SP% **114.9**
Speed ratings (Par 94): **97,92,90,90,90 89,86,84,72,72**
toteswinger: 1&2 £24.00, 1&3 £14.70, 2&3 £8.90. CSF £111.34 TOTE £19.50: £3.60, £2.00, £2.60; EX 153.40 Trifecta £322.20 Pool: £435.43 - 1.00 winning units..
Owner Saeed Manana **Bred** Genesis Green Stud Ltd **Trained** Newmarket, Suffolk
■ Stewards' Enquiry : Luke Morris two-day ban: careless riding (Sep 2-3)

FOCUS
An ordinary maiden in which the strong crosswind would have made it a fair test for juveniles. The runner-up was below par. The field went off at a solid early pace and were spread across the track at the top of the home straight, before they edged over to the far side inside the final furlong.

NOTEBOOK
Al Sabaheya, related to winners from 5f to 1m4f, impressed with the way she went about her business and ran out a clear-cut winner. She travelled nicely in a handy position through the first half of the race and lengthened clear when the gap appeared nearing the final furlong. The easy ground was clearly in her favour, as was the distance, and she looks a useful prospect. She was also a welcome winner for her stable and, while she has just a sales race entry to date, no doubt her trainer will now be eyeing some future Group-race engagements for her. (op 25-1 tchd 28-1)
Today's The Day, whose last three outings have been at Kempton, was soon in a prominent position and had her chance. The application of cheekpieces with the step up to this trip helped bring about a more encouraging effort, and with an official rating of 75 she helps to put the form into perspective. There should be a small race within her compass before too long. (op 7-1 tchd 15-2)
Popiel, a brother to the formerly very useful juvenile Queen Of Poland, was very easy to back ahead of this racecourse bow and showed his inexperience by failing to go the early pace. He certainly caught the eye staying on at the finish, however, and should really come on a bundle for the experience. Official explanation: jockey said colt suffered interference in running (tchd 7-1)
Imperial Skylight posted a much-improved effort on this switch back to maiden company and returned to the sort of form that saw him go close on his debut at Kempton back in March. The easier ground helped him and he looks worth sticking back in a nursery now. Official explanation: jockey said gelding suffered interference in running (op 33-1)
Deal Clincher ran better than her finishing position suggests as she was involved in a barging match with the disappointing Night Lily around the final furlong marker and took time to get re-organised before running on again late in the day. This proves she gets the trip. (op 10-1)
Andhaar was handy enough if good enough in the home straight and eventually weakened disappointingly. He does look flattered by an official mark of 78, but perhaps a return to a sounder surface will see him back in a better light. (op 5-2 tchd 9-4)
Night Lily(IRE) was well backed on the promise of her previous two outings over this trip at Newmarket, but the way in which she began to fold before the trouble would suggest she could have found it coming too soon after her latest effort. She now has the option of nurseries. (op 7-4 tchd 2-1)

5166 3663 (S) STKS 6f 209y

2:35 (2:36) (Class 6) 3-Y-0+ **£1,942** (£578; £288; £144) **Stalls** Low

Form RPR

0034 **1** **Seneschal**[10] 4863 7-9-6 65 .... SteveDrowne 3 71
(A B Haynes) *chsd ldrs: got through on rail and led over 1f out: idled in front: rdn clr* **11/2**[1]

0060 **2** 2 **Banjo Patterson**[32] 4162 6-9-1 59........(b) ShaneKelly 7 60
(M G Quinlan) *s.i.s: sn in tch: rdn and hung lft ins fnl 2f: disp 2nd ins fnl f: nt qckn* **20/1**

4004 **3** shd **Billy Hot Rocks (IRE)**[38] 3960 3-8-10 60 .... SebSanders 6 58
(R M Beckett) *sn in tch: effrt and hrd rdn 2f out: disp 2nd ins fnl f: kpt on same pce* **11/2**[1]

4065 **4** 1 **Jal Music**[26] 4324 3-8-12 57 .... KevinGhunowa(3) 1 60
(R A Harris) *led tl over 1f out: hrd rdn: one pce* **14/1**

6005 **5** 1/2 **Compulsion**[14] 4707 5-8-10 44 .... PaulEddery 15 51
(Pat Eddery) *towards rr: rdn and hdwy 2f out: sn in tch: styd on same pce appr fnl f* **20/1**

0126 **6** 1/2 **Mannello**[11] 4808 5-9-1 52........(p) RichardThomas 14 55
(Jim Best) *towards rr: rdn and hdwy 2f out: kpt on: nt pce to chal* **10/1**

5401 **7** 2 1/2 **Who's Winning (IRE)**[11] 4808 7-9-6 59........(t) TQuinn 9 53
(B G Powell) *hld up in tch: rdn 3f out: no imp fnl 2f* **13/2**[2]

6322 **8** 3 **Razzano (IRE)**[11] 4808 4-8-3 50 .... AndreaAtzeni(7) 8 35
(A M Hales) *hld up in midfield: sme hdwy and in tch whn brought wd st: rdn and hung lft 2f out: sn wknd* **11/2**[1]

0006 **9** 1 3/4 **Royal Choir**[13] 4748 4-8-10 44 .... LiamJones 10 30
(C E Brittain) *bhd: rdn over 3f out: nvr nr ldrs* **50/1**

00-0 **10** 3 1/4 **Nashharry (IRE)**[41] 3839 4-8-10 50 .... DaneO'Neill 11 21
(R A Harris) *mid-div on outside: brought wd st: rdn and wknd over 2f out* **33/1**

2223 **11** 6 **Fairly Honest**[26] 4322 4-8-10 51 .... WilliamCarson(5) 4 10
(P W Hiatt) *prom tl hrd rdn and wknd wl over 1f out: eased whn no ch fnl f* **7/1**[3]

-600 **12** 1 1/4 **Mamichor**[35] 4053 5-9-1 47........(p) RichardSmith 2 7
(B R Johnson) *pressed ldr: hung lft over 2f out: sn wknd: wl btn whn hmpd on rail and eased over 1f out* **28/1**

6205 **13** 3 **Fly In Johnny (IRE)**[19] 4569 3-8-10 56 .... ChrisCatlin 5 —
(M R Hoad) *in tch tl wknd qckly over 2f out* **33/1**

6200 **14** 2 **Apache Dawn**[14] 4707 4-9-1 63........(b) GeorgeBaker 12 —
(G L Moore) *bhd: brought wd st: sn rdn: no ch fnl 2f* **10/1**

1m 25.13s (2.03) **Going Correction** +0.325s/f (Good)
WFA 3 from 4yo+ 5lb **14** Ran SP% **117.7**
Speed ratings (Par 101): **101,98,98,97,96 96,93,90,88,84 77,76,72,70**
toteswinger: 1&2 £23.50, 1&3 £6.20, 2&3 £24.60. CSF £119.31 TOTE £6.30: £2.30, £5.20, £2.00; EX 142.50 Trifecta £190.50 Pool: £334.75 - 1.30 winning units..There was no bid for the winner. Billy Hot Rocks was claimed by Miss Gay Kelleway for £6000.
Owner P Cook **Bred** Michael E Broughton **Trained** Limpley Stoke, Bath

FOCUS
A typically moderate seller, run at an average pace. The winner is a decent type for the grade and looks the best guide to the form.
Nashharry(IRE) Official explanation: jockey said filly had no more to give
Apache Dawn Official explanation: jockey said gelding hung right

5167 MALSAR KEST H'CAP 7f 214y
3:10 (3:10) (Class 6) (0-65,63) 3-Y-O £2,201 (£655; £327; £163) Stalls Low

Form RPR
0030 1 **Space Pirate**[11] 4810 3-8-10 **52**.....................(p) RobertHavlin 7 58
(J Pearce) *bhd: hrd rdn and rapid hdwy over 1f out: edgd lft ins fnl f: styd on wl to ld nr fin* **11/1**
6000 2 *nk* **Lady Florence**[36] 4028 3-8-0 **45**..................... LukeMorris(3) 10 50
(A B Coogan) *prom: led wl over 1f out: hrd rdn and hld on wl fnl f tl hdd and nt qckn nr fin* **33/1**
4064 3 *½* **Croeso Cusan**[35] 4049 3-7-10 **45**..................... SophieDoyle(7) 11 49
(J L Spearing) *hld up in midfield: smooth hdwy 2f out: promising chal 1f out: faltered and nt qckn fnl 50yds* **11/1**
6051 4 *1* **Spent**[11] 4806 3-9-5 **61**..................... ChrisCatlin 6 63
(Mouse Hamilton-Fairley) *towards rr: hdwy 2f out: drvn to chse ldrs 1f out: nt qckn fnl 75yds* **5/1**[1]
2600 5 *2 ¼* **Bury Treasure (IRE)**[26] 4332 3-9-2 **63**..................... NicolPolli(5) 1 59
(Miss Gay Kelleway) *mid-div: rdn along over 4f out: hdwy 2f out: hrd drvn and no imp over 1f out* **20/1**
0006 6 *nk* **Loyal Knight (IRE)**[13] 4732 3-9-6 **62**..................... GeorgeBaker 2 58
(S Kirk) *in tch: effrt over 2f out: one pce appr fnl f* **11/2**[2]
5000 7 *6* **Darley Star**[12] 4772 3-8-9 **51**..................... LiamJones 8 33
(C E Brittain) *chsd ldrs: rdn and lost pl 4f out: kpt on past btn horses fnl f* **18/1**
5420 8 *½* **Mganga**[11] 4810 3-9-4 **60**..................... TPO'Shea 3 41
(M R Channon) *dwlt: bhd: rdn and hdwy over 2f out: sn in tch: wknd wl over 1f out* **8/1**
-240 9 *1* **The Willowy Wigeon**[54] 3397 3-9-4 **60**..................... JimCrowley 4 38
(P Winkworth) *chsd ldrs: drvn along 5f out: wknd over 2f out* **13/2**[3]
1000 10 *1 ½* **King Of Cadeaux (IRE)**[54] 3395 3-8-10 **52**..........(b) FergusSweeney 14 27
(M A Magnusson) *led tl wl over 1f out: sn wknd* **14/1**
3000 11 *nk* **Silky Steps (IRE)**[43] 3799 3-9-5 **61**..................... EddieAhern 5 35+
(P J Makin) *t.k.h: hld up in tch: n.m.r over 2f out: sn lost pl* **15/2**
0000 12 *nk* **It's Josr**[16] 4664 3-8-10 **52**.....................(v) RichardThomas 15 26
(I A Wood) *in tch tl wknd over 2f out* **16/1**
0500 13 *1 ¼* **Miss Clarice (USA)**[14] 4708 3-9-3 **59**..................... SebSanders 9 37+
(B J Meehan) *towards rr: effrt on outside over 2f out: hung bdly lft: eased* **22/1**
0000 14 *1* **Azzaamm**[15] 4684 3-7-12 **45**..................... Louis-PhilippeBeuzelin(5) 12 14
(C A Dwyer) *a towards rr: drvn along and no ch fnl 2f* **66/1**
5060 15 *6* **Sacred Flame (USA)**[16] 4669 3-8-13 **55**..................... DaneO'Neill 16 10
(B J Meehan) *prom: hrd rdn over 2f out: sn wknd: eased whn no ch 1f out* **9/1**

1m 38.39s (2.39) **Going Correction** +0.325s/f (Good) **15 Ran SP% 126.3**
Speed ratings (Par 98): **101,100,100,99,96 96,90,90,89,87 87,87,85,84,78**
toteswinger: 1&2 £100.80, 1&3 £23.20, 2&3 £88.30. CSF £352.37 CT £4074.14 TOTE £13.50: £4.50, £11.00, £3.80; EX 558.40 TRIFECTA Not won..
Owner Oceana racing **Bred** W E A Fox And S Frisby **Trained** Newmarket, Suffolk

FOCUS
This was a weak, but open handicap. Very ordinary form. It was run at a sound pace and the field again elected to stay more towards the far side.
Silky Steps(IRE) Official explanation: jockey said filly suffered interference in running
Miss Clarice(USA) Official explanation: jockey said filly hung left
Azzaamm Official explanation: jockey said gelding suffered interference in running

5168 3663 H'CAP 1m 1f 209y
3:45 (3:47) (Class 5) (0-70,70) 3-Y-O+ £2,978 (£886; £442; £221) Stalls High

Form RPR
5506 1 **Shesha Bear**[40] 3886 3-9-1 **66**..................... DavidProbert(5) 4 75
(W R Muir) *hld up in 5th: rdn 3f out: hdwy 2f out: led over 1f out: veered rt ins fnl f: drvn to get on top fnl 75yds* **13/2**
3321 2 *1 ¾* **Gracechurch (IRE)**[13] 4721 5-9-8 **60**..................... SteveDrowne 5 65
(R J Hodges) *hld up in 6th: brought wd and hdwy 2f out: chal over 1f out: hrd rdn ent fnl f: faltered and no ex fnl 75yds* **7/4**[1]
5542 3 *2 ¾* **Fantasy Crusader**[11] 4819 9-8-10 **48** ow1..................... DaneO'Neill 6 48
(R M H Cowell) *plld hrd: trckd ldng pair: rdn to chal 2f out: outpcd fnl f* **5/1**[3]
0000 4 *1 ½* **Sunny Spells**[3] 5105 3-8-9 **55**..................... J-PGuillambert 3 52
(S C Williams) *led tl over 1f out: no ex fnl f* **12/1**
6223 5 *shd* **Thunder Gorge (USA)**[13] 4724 3-9-10 **70**..................... ChrisCatlin 7 66
(Mouse Hamilton-Fairley) *t.k.h: sn chsng ldr: hrd rdn and wknd jst over 1f out* **3/1**[2]
020 6 *12* **Lordship (IRE)**[8] 4927 4-9-11 **66**..................... JamesMillman(3) 2 38
(A W Carroll) *bhd: rdn over 3f out: n.d fnl 2f* **8/1**
04-0 7 *21* **Grand Symphony**[11] 4825 4-9-5 **57**.....................(t) TPO'Shea 1 —
(B I Case) *handy 4th tl wknd over 2f out: bhd and eased 1f out* **33/1**

2m 7.54s (3.94) **Going Correction** +0.325s/f (Good)
WFA 3 from 4yo+ 8lb **7 Ran SP% 113.1**
Speed ratings (Par 103): **97,95,93,92,92 82,65**
toteswinger: 1&2 £3.40, 1&3 £4.40, 2&3 £2.00. CSF £17.95 CT £61.19 TOTE £7.50: £3.80, £1.40; EX 18.10 Trifecta £96.40 Pool: £1058.59 - 8.12 winning units..
Owner Joe Bear Racing **Bred** Beechgrove Stud Farm Ltd & Catridge Farm Stud **Trained** Lambourn, Berks

FOCUS
This very modest handicap was run at a steady pace. Improvement from the winner with the second rated to this year's form.

5169 ARMY BENEVOLENT FUND H'CAP 1m 3f 196y
4:20 (4:24) (Class 5) (0-70,67) 3-Y-O £2,978 (£886; £442; £221) Stalls High

Form RPR
3201 1 **Soundbyte**[11] 4811 3-9-0 **60**..................... FergusSweeney 5 73
(J Gallagher) *hld up and bhd: hdwy 4f out: brought wd and led 3f out: styd on u.p: a holding runner-up* **2/1**[1]
1102 2 *3 ¼* **Ambrose Princess (IRE)**[13] 4722 3-8-6 **55**............ KevinGhunowa(3) 9 63
(R A Harris) *in tch: rdn 4f out: chsd wnr over 2f out: edgd lft: styd on same pce: a hld* **12/1**
00-3 3 *1 ¾* **Limelight (USA)**[6] 4992 3-8-7 **53** ow1..................... SebSanders 8 58
(Sir Mark Prescott) *chsd ldrs: rdn 4f out: hung bdly lft in st: one pce* **9/4**[2]
2505 4 *5* **Dancing Dik**[17] 4646 3-9-5 **65**..................... JimCrowley 3 62
(Mrs A J Perrett) *chsd ldrs: rdn 4f out: n.m.r 3f out: sn btn* **10/1**
0420 5 *9* **Cossack Prince**[35] 4067 3-9-5 **65**.....................(p) DaneO'Neill 4 48
(B J Meehan) *disp ld: led 4f out tl 3f out: wknd over 2f out* **15/2**
320 6 *26* **Pinnacle Point**[14] 4704 3-8-13 **59**..................... StephenCarson 2 —
(G L Moore) *disp ld tl 4f out: wknd 3f out: bhd and eased over 1f out* **11/2**[3]
4505 7 *22* **I Certainly May**[69] 2931 3-8-6 **52**.....................(b[1]) NickyMackay 6 —
(S Dow) *stood in stalls and lost 15 l: a t.o* **33/1**
065 8 *12* **Waarid**[61] 3168 3-9-7 **67**..................... GeorgeBaker 7 —
(G L Moore) *bhd: drvn along after 4f: no ch fnl 7f: eased over 2f out* **20/1**
2030 9 *9* **Persian Wish (IRE)**[49] 3574 3-8-11 **57**..................... ChrisCatlin 1 —
(J W Mullins) *towards rr of main gp: lost tch 1/2-way: sn wl bhd: eased over 2f out* **40/1**

2m 35.93s (3.23) **Going Correction** +0.325s/f (Good) **9 Ran SP% 118.2**
Speed ratings (Par 100): **102,99,98,95,89 72,57,49,43**
toteswinger: 1&2 £3.80, 1&3 £2.40, 2&3 £5.10. CSF £27.27 CT £59.40 TOTE £3.10: £1.30, £2.80, £1.30; EX 33.80 Trifecta £69.00 Pool: £955.75 - 10.25 winning units..
Owner Oliver Parsons **Bred** Mrs R J Gallagher **Trained** Moreton-in-Marsh, Gloucs

FOCUS
A moderate handicap for three-year-olds, run at a decent pace, and the first three came nicely clear. Fair form for the grade, with the winner capable of a bit better still.
Pinnacle Point Official explanation: jockey said gelding hung right
I Certainly May Official explanation: jockey said gelding planted itself in the stalls
Waarid Official explanation: jockey said gelding never travelled
Persian Wish(IRE) Official explanation: jockey said colt had no more to give

5170 KING'S TROOP ROYAL HORSE ARTILLERY H'CAP 6f 209y
4:50 (4:53) (Class 5) (0-70,70) 3-Y-O+ £2,978 (£886; £442; £221) Stalls Low

Form RPR
0500 1 **Shamrock Lady (IRE)**[36] 4022 3-9-7 **70**..................... TPO'Shea 1 76
(J Gallagher) *sltly sluggish s: sn led: mde rest: hld on gamely u.p fnl f* **8/1**
1004 2 *nk* **Ten To The Dozen**[11] 4807 5-8-13 **57**..................... ChrisCatlin 8 64
(P W Hiatt) *bhd: hdwy over 2f out: drvn to chal fnl f: r.o gamely: jst hld* **4/1**[2]
606P 3 *2 ¼* **Torquemada (IRE)**[28] 4268 7-9-2 **60**.....................(t) KirstyMilczarek 7 61
(M J Attwater) *hld up in midfield: squeezed through and hdwy 2f out: promising chal over 1f out: fnd little ins fnl f* **12/1**
3200 4 *2* **Magroom**[6] 4979 4-9-12 **70**..................... SteveDrowne 10 66
(R J Hodges) *hld up in rr: effrt over 2f out: hung lft: nt pce to chal* **15/2**[3]
00-0 5 *2 ½* **Tyzack (IRE)**[53] 3457 7-9-11 **69**..................... MickyFenton 9 58
(Stef Liddiard) *hld up towards rr: short-lived effrt over 2f out: edgd lft: nt knocked abt whn btn* **20/1**
6500 5 *dht* **Proud Killer**[22] 4478 5-8-13 **57**.....................(v) EddieAhern 3 46
(J R Jenkins) *dwlt: sn prom: hrd rdn and wknd 2f out* **9/1**
0360 7 *7* **China Cherub**[11] 4831 5-9-12 **70**.....................(p) SebSanders 2 40
(S Dow) *in tch: effrt over 2f out: wknd wl over 1f out* **4/1**[2]
0 8 *11* **Desert Clover (USA)**[55] 3376 3-9-7 **70**.....................(b[1]) NelsonDeSouza 4 8
(P F I Cole) *prom: hrd rdn 3f out: sn wknd* **9/1**
0321 9 *35* **Steig (IRE)**[11] 4807 5-9-12 **70**..................... JamesDoyle 6 —
(Carl Llewellyn) *chsd ldrs: rdn and wknd 3f out: sn bhd and eased: b.b.v* **10/3**[1]

1m 25.25s (2.15) **Going Correction** +0.325s/f (Good)
WFA 3 from 4yo+ 5lb **9 Ran SP% 118.4**
Speed ratings (Par 103): **100,99,97,94,91 91,83,71,31**
toteswinger: 1&2 £10.60, 1&3 £20.30, 2&3 £10.70. CSF £41.11 CT £392.45 TOTE £14.00: £3.30, £1.60, £3.90; EX 57.70 TRIFECTA Not won..
Owner Mrs Irene Clifford **Bred** Mrs Irene Clifford **Trained** Moreton-in-Marsh, Gloucs

FOCUS
Another moderate handicap which was run at a fair pace and the field came more towards the middle of the track in the home straight. the winner is rated back to her 2yo best.
Steig(IRE) Official explanation: vet said gelding had bled from the nose

5171 FRIDAY-AD H'CAP 5f 59y
5:20 (5:20) (Class 6) (0-65,65) 3-Y-O+ £2,266 (£674; £337; £168) Stalls Low

Form RPR
0-12 1 **Drumming Party (USA)**[12] 4765 6-9-9 **65**.....................(t) GeorgeBaker 6 74
(J R Boyle) *sltly hmpd s: hld up in rr: smooth hdwy 2f out: led 1f out: rdn along and hld on narrowly nr fin* **9/4**[1]
3340 2 *hd* **Hart Of Gold**[20] 4535 4-9-4 **65**..................... HaddenFrost(5) 7 73
(R A Harris) *prom towards outside: effrt over 1f out: r.o fnl f: grad clsd: jst hld* **15/2**
3143 3 *shd* **Night Prospector**[11] 4812 8-9-1 **60**.....................(p) KevinGhunowa(3) 4 68
(R A Harris) *chsd ldrs: chal and hrd rdn over 1f out: kpt on wl* **8/1**
-110 4 *2 ¾* **Croeso Bach**[33] 4106 4-9-0 **63**..................... SophieDoyle(7) 1 61
(J L Spearing) *led tl 1f out: no ex fnl f* **7/1**[3]
6221 5 *½* **Miss Firefly**[26] 4325 3-9-7 **65**..................... KirstyMilczarek 2 61
(R J Hodges) *prom 3f: 5th and wkng whn bdly squeezed over 1f out* **8/1**
1600 6 *shd* **Musical Script (USA)**[6] 4981 5-9-1 **57**.....................(b) ChrisCatlin 8 53
(Mouse Hamilton-Fairley) *hld up towards rr: effrt 2f out: no imp whn hung lft 1f out* **11/1**
6051 7 *3 ¼* **Jayanjay**[11] 4812 9-9-0 **56**..................... RichardSmith 10 40
(B R Johnson) *wd: in tch tl hrd rdn and wknd 2f out* **5/1**[2]
2266 8 *½* **Black Moma (IRE)**[7] 4958 4-8-12 **61**..................... PNolan(7) 9 43
(A B Haynes) *awkward s and slowly away: a in rr gp: drvn along and n.d fnl 2f* **15/2**

64.15 secs (1.85) **Going Correction** +0.325s/f (Good)
WFA 3 from 4yo+ 2lb **8 Ran SP% 114.0**
Speed ratings (Par 101): **98,97,97,93,92 92,86,86**
toteswinger: 1&2 £5.10, 1&3 £4.50, 2&3 £9.20. CSF £19.56 CT £113.77 TOTE £2.90: £1.40, £2.20, £2.70; EX 26.60 Trifecta £167.20 Pool: £598.79 - 2.65 winning units. Place 6: £485.94 Place 5: £117.52.
Owner M Khan X2 **Bred** Robert N Clay, Et Al **Trained** Epsom, Surrey

FOCUS
This was not a bad sprint handicap for the class and it saw a cracking finish between the first three, who came nicely clear. A carre best from the winner.
Hart Of Gold Official explanation: jockey said gelding hung left
T/Plt: £1,226.20 to a £1 stake. Pool: £109,687.54. 65.30 winning tickets. T/Qpdt: £54.40 to a £1 stake. Pool: £11,715.23. 159.08 winning tickets. IM

4434 YORK (L-H)
Tuesday, August 19

5172 Meeting Abandoned - Waterlogged

The first four-day Ebor meeting, and the last scheduled fixture at York before the track was to close for drainage work, proved a complete washout.

4679 CARLISLE (R-H)
Wednesday, August 20
5176 Meeting Abandoned - Waterlogged

4774 FOLKESTONE (R-H)
Wednesday, August 20
OFFICIAL GOING: Good to soft (soft in places on round course)
Wind: Fresh, half behind Weather: cloudy with sunny intervals

5182 STONE OF FOLCA MAIDEN STKS — 1m 1f 149y
5:25 (5:26) (Class 5) 3-Y-O+ — £2,590 (£770; £385; £192) Stalls Centre

Form — RPR
4023 1 **Celt**[32] 4205 3-9-3 80 — PatCosgrave 3 — 80+
(L M Cumani) *trckd ldrs: led 2f out: sn in command: comf* **4/9**[1]
05 2 4 1/2 **Plaisterer**[11] 4860 3-8-12 0 — IanMongan 9 — 66
(C F Wall) *in mid-div: hdwy fr over 1f out to go 2nd ins fnl f: no ch w wnr* **20/1**
53 3 1/2 **Cheeky Download (IRE)**[33] 4166 3-8-12 0 — EddieAhern 8 — 65
(E A L Dunlop) *trckd ldr and chsd wnr fr 2f out tl no ex ins fnl f* **13/2**[2]
344 4 4 1/2 **Almonafis (IRE)**[16] 4689 3-8-10 75 — (v) JPHamblett(7) 1 — 61
(Sir Michael Stoute) *trckd ldrs: rdn over 2f out: sn btn* **13/2**[2]
5 3 1/2 **Al Asayl Rose (USA)** 3-8-12 0 — SteveDrowne 7 — 48
(H J L Dunlop) *mid-div: kpt on one pce fnl 2f* **14/1**[3]
00 6 1/2 **American Madness (USA)**[11] 4871 3-9-3 0 — SimonWhitworth 4 — 52
(M G Quinlan) *in rr: rdn 3f out: nvr got into r* **66/1**
7 2 **Search Me**[31] 6-9-11 0 — AdamKirby 2 — 48
(C Gordon) *slowly away: mde sme late hdwy* **100/1**
0 8 1 1/4 **Walhalla (IRE)**[14] 4730 3-9-3 0 — PatDobbs 6 — 45
(M P Tregoning) *mid-div: reminders 6f out: sn struggling in rr* **40/1**
0 9 8 **Brave Knave (IRE)**[34] 4124 3-9-3 0 — JamesDoyle 5 — 28
(B De Haan) *t.k.h: led tl hdd 2f out: wknd qckly* **100/1**
10 nse **Capeleira (IRE)** 3-9-3 0 — ChrisCatlin 11 — 28
(R Rowe) *s.i.s: a bhd* **40/1**
0 11 62 **Hard To Resist (IRE)**[16] 4695 3-9-0 0 — TolleyDean(3) 10 — —
(P R Webber) *in rr: rdn 1/2-way: virtually p.u ins fnl 2f: t.o* **40/1**

2m 6.50s (1.60) **Going Correction** +0.15s/f (Good)
WFA 3 from 6yo 8lb — **11** Ran SP% **118.1**
Speed ratings (Par 103): **99,95,95,91,88 88,86,85,79,79 29**
toteswinger: 1&2 £1.80, 1&3 £1.10, 2&3 £3.10. CSF £16.48 TOTE £1.40: £1.02, £8.40, £1.70; EX 9.40.
Owner Aristocracy Racing Club **Bred** Fittocks Stud **Trained** Newmarket, Suffolk

FOCUS
A moderate maiden with only three of these having previously made the frame, but at least the pace was sound. The winner set a decent standard.
Search Me Official explanation: jockey said gelding missed the break

5183 ROMNEY MARSH H'CAP — 1m 4f
5:55 (5:55) (Class 5) (0-70,71) 3-Y-O+ — £2,590 (£770; £385; £192) Stalls Low

Form — RPR
001 1 **Right Stuff (FR)**[9] 4930 5-10-1 71 6ex — PatDobbs 7 — 78+
(G L Moore) *hld up in rr: gd hdwy over 2f out: styd on to ld towards fin: won gng away* **3/1**[1]
0400 2 1 1/4 **Good Effect (USA)**[12] 4820 4-9-6 62 — SteveDrowne 1 — 67
(C P Morlock) *sn led: rdn over 1f out: kpt on but hdd towards fin* **16/1**
3533 3 nk **Fourth Dimension (IRE)**[36] 4067 9-9-12 68 — AdamKirby 12 — 73
(Miss T Spearing) *in tch: wnt 2nd 2f out: rdn and ev ch ent fnl f tl fnl 50yds* **8/1**
066 4 1 1/2 **Cruise Director**[28] 4299 8-10-0 70 — StephenDonohoe 5 — 72
(Ian Williams) *trckd ldrs: wnt 3rd over 3f out: no ex ins fnl f* **15/2**
0454 5 nse **Bienheureux**[12] 4811 7-8-13 60 — (t) DavidProbert(5) 3 — 62
(Miss Gay Kelleway) *towards rr: hdwy over 2f out: nvr nr to chal* **15/2**
000- 6 1 1/2 **Lemon Silk (IRE)**[17] 6235 4-9-4 65 — HaddenFrost(5) 8 — 65
(D E Pipe) *in tch: effrt over 2f out: kpt on one pce after* **16/1**
666 7 3/4 **Amical Risks (FR)**[16] 4690 4-8-11 53 — NeilPollard 14 — 51
(W J Musson) *in rr: effrt over 2f out: nvr nr to chal* **9/1**
0626 8 1/2 **Capistrano**[27] 4343 5-8-9 51 oh3 — (b) PaulEddery 9 — 49
(G D Blake) *in rr: effrt over 2f out but nvr got into r* **22/1**
0 9 1 1/4 **Tapaellya (IRE)**[58] 3321 4-9-2 58 — RichardThomas 13 — 54
(J E Long) *trckd ldrs: wnt 2nd over 4f out: wknd wl over 1f out* **50/1**
301 10 1 **Shenandoah Girl**[6] 5003 5-8-10 59 6ex — (p) KylieManser(7) 11 — 53
(Miss Gay Kelleway) *slowly away: nvr gng wl and a bhd* **7/1**[3]
/0-0 11 13 **Irish Whispers (IRE)**[34] 4105 5-8-8 55 — GabrielHannon(5) 4 — 28
(B G Powell) *mid-div: rdn 5f out: sn struggling in rr* **22/1**
5030 12 6 **Icannshift (IRE)**[29] 4275 8-8-9 51 — FrankieMcDonald 10 — 15
(T M Jones) *trckd ldr to over 4f out: wknd qckly* **13/2**[2]

2m 41.76s (0.86) **Going Correction** +0.15s/f (Good) — **12** Ran SP% **117.9**
Speed ratings (Par 103): **103,102,101,100,100 99,99,99,98,97 88,84**
toteswinger: 1&2 £63.80, 1&3 £5.20, 2&3 £29.20. CSF £54.66 CT £355.43 TOTE £3.90: £1.90, £5.10, £2.50; EX 99.50.
Owner The Ashden Partnership & Partners **Bred** N P Bloodstock Ltd **Trained** Woodingdean, E Sussex
■ Stewards' Enquiry : Adam Kirby caution: careless riding

FOCUS
An ordinary though fairly competitive handicap and the pace was solid enough. The third looks the best guide to the form.
Icannshift(IRE) Official explanation: jockey said gelding hung right throughout

5184 SANDGATE MAIDEN AUCTION STKS — 7f (S)
6:25 (6:27) (Class 5) 2-Y-O — £2,590 (£770; £385; £192) Stalls Low

Form — RPR
0 1 **Tombov (FR)**[13] 4780 2-8-8 0 — TravisBlock(3) 13 — 73
(A King) *racd 4th in gp of 5 on far side: chal 2f out: overall ldr 1f out: jst hld on* **20/1**
63 2 nse **Penton Hook**[28] 4304 2-8-9 0 — FrankieMcDonald 14 — 71
(P Winkworth) *led far side gp of 5: hdd 1f out: rallied gamely ins fnl f: jst failed* **6/1**[3]
2 3 1 1/4 **Never Lose**[14] 4747 2-8-6 0 — LiamJones 5 — 65
(C E Brittain) *chsd ldrs on stands' side and led that gp over 1f out: styd on fnl f but no imp on first two on far side* **4/1**[1]
0 4 hd **King's La Mont (IRE)**[20] 4570 2-9-2 0 — DarryllHolland 2 — 74
(Mrs A J Perrett) *chsd ldrs stands' side: styd on to go 2nd of that gp ins fnl f* **13/2**
63 5 1 3/4 **Spit And Polish**[13] 4769 2-8-13 0 — EddieAhern 4 — 67
(J L Dunlop) *led stands' side gp tl over 1f out: wknd ins fnl f* **4/1**[1]
6 1 **Acting Lady (USA)** 2-8-8 0 — SteveDrowne 11 — 60
(J R Best) *last of far side gp of 5: styd on but nvr on terms* **16/1**
0 7 1 3/4 **Laraffelle (GR)**[16] 4692 2-8-8 0 — NeilPollard 6 — 55
(E A L Dunlop) *a towards rr on stands' side* **66/1**
8 2 1/2 **Bertie Smalls** 2-8-11 0 — SaleemGolam 1 — 52
(M H Tompkins) *slowly away on stands' side: a in rr* **25/1**
63 9 nk **Ashwinder (IRE)**[12] 4827 2-8-8 0 — GabrielHannon(5) 9 — 53
(B J Meehan) *w ldrs on stands' side tl wknd over 1f out* **11/2**[2]
00 10 3 3/4 **Reel Hope**[27] 4337 2-8-4 0 — KirstyMilczarek 12 — 35
(J R Best) *chsd ldr far side tl wknd 2f out* **16/1**
0 11 nk **Cabo Polonio (IRE)**[10] 4907 2-8-8 0 — PatDobbs 10 — 38
(S Kirk) *3rd of far side tl wknd 2f out* **16/1**
005 12 1 1/2 **Buckers Beauty (IRE)**[10] 4907 2-8-4 0 — ChrisCatlin 8 — 30
(P D Evans) *chsd ldrs stands' side: wknd 2f out* **16/1**
13 4 1/2 **Miss Jodarah (USA)** 2-8-4 0 — RichardThomas 3 — 19
(J R Best) *a in rr on stands' side* **33/1**
0 14 3 1/4 **Abner**[28] 4296 2-9-2 0 — (b[1]) PatCosgrave 7 — 23
(W J Haggas) *in tch stands' side: rdn 3f out: sn btn* **25/1**

1m 27.66s (0.36) **Going Correction** -0.125s/f (Firm) — **14** Ran SP% **123.4**
Speed ratings (Par 94): **92,91,90,90,88 87,85,82,81,77 77,75,70,66**
toteswinger: 1&2 £0.00, 1&3 £0.00, 2&3 £5.20. CSF £133.28 TOTE £28.40: £8.00, £2.40, £1.60; EX 139.60.
Owner Mr And Mrs J D Cotton **Bred** Olivier Tricot **Trained** Barbury Castle, Wilts

FOCUS
A modest maiden auction event, and the field split into two. The main group of nine stayed on the stands' side, while a smaller group of five went over to the far side, but although there wasn't a great deal between the two groups at the line, the far side did provide the first two home. Average form for the grade and track.

NOTEBOOK
Tombov(FR) had been a springer in the market on his Haydock debut when ending up well beaten, but he gave plenty of trouble before the start that day and this effort confirmed the ability he had obviously been showing at home. He should come on again for this, but the form is probably only modest and he may be one for nurseries. (op 22-1 tchd 16-1)
Penton Hook was always up with the pace on the far side and went down with all guns blazing. He looked happier on this straight track, after looking awkward around the bends on the Lingfield Polytrack last time, and there should be a small race in him. (op 11-2 tchd 5-1)
Never Lose fared best of those on the stands' side, and though she probably did not step up from the form of her Yarmouth debut, she can probably find a small race. (op 7-2 tchd 9-2)
King's La Mont(IRE) looked a very awkward ride and took an age to respond to pressure on the stands' side, but he was finishing to some effect. Out of a half-sister to Montjeu, he may need more time and a longer trip, so looks one for later on (op 8-1 tchd 5-1)
Spit And Polish had every chance in the stands'-side group and will have more opportunities now that he qualifies for a nursery mark. (tchd 9-2)
Acting Lady(USA) fared best of the John Best trio and she should improve both for the experience and a longer trip. (tchd 14-1)

5185 MAYER DE ROTHSCHILD H'CAP — 7f (S)
6:55 (6:56) (Class 4) (0-80,80) 3-Y-O — £4,731 (£1,416; £708; £354; £176) Stalls Low

Form — RPR
5102 1 **Portodora (USA)**[18] 4641 3-9-5 78 — IanMongan 4 — 89+
(H R A Cecil) *trckd ldr: led 1/2-way: in command fr over 1f out even though sddle slipped sn after s* **2/1**[1]
4554 2 3 **Bere Davis (FR)**[16] 4682 3-8-13 72 — TGMcLaughlin 5 — 75
(P D Evans) *chsd ldrs: rdn 3f out: styd on u.p to go 2nd fnl 100yds* **13/2**[3]
0005 3 2 1/4 **Sofia's Star**[28] 4310 3-8-9 68 — FrankieMcDonald 7 — 65
(P Winkworth) *led to 1/2-way: chsd wnr tl no ex and lost 2nd fnl 100yds* **7/1**
6030 4 1 1/2 **Eternal Luck (IRE)**[42] 3840 3-9-7 80 — (b) PhilipRobinson 1 — 73
(M A Jarvis) *chsd ldrs: rdn over 2f out: one pce after* **8/1**
1010 5 hd **Divine Power**[7] 4983 3-9-7 80 — JamesDoyle 8 — 72
(R M Beckett) *swtchd lft s: hld up: styd on fnl 2f but nvr on terms* **17/2**
-450 6 2 **Andaman Sunset**[32] 4194 3-8-13 72 — (p) SteveDrowne 2 — 59
(G Wragg) *in tch tl wknd over 2f out* **10/1**
-500 7 2 3/4 **Dry Speedfit (IRE)**[14] 4731 3-9-2 75 — EddieAhern 3 — 55
(G G Margarson) *a in rr* **14/1**
3101 8 1 1/2 **Benedetto**[25] 4413 3-9-3 76 — (p) DarryllHolland 6 — 51
(Mrs A J Perrett) *in tch: rdn 3f out: wknd 2f out* **9/2**[2]

1m 25.54s (-1.76) **Going Correction** -0.125s/f (Firm) — **8** Ran SP% **114.7**
Speed ratings (Par 102): **105,101,99,97,97 94,91,89**
toteswinger: 1&2 £3.00, 1&3 £14.40, 2&3 £52.00. CSF £15.47 CT £75.75 TOTE £2.80: £1.30, £2.00, £3.00; EX 12.70.
Owner K Abdulla **Bred** Juddmonte Farms Inc **Trained** Newmarket, Suffolk

FOCUS
The best race on the card, and in this smaller field they all decided to stay stands' side. The pace looked no more than ordinary, but very few ever got into it. Portodora won easily and the form is rated around the runner-up.

5186 BENVENUE H'CAP — 6f
7:25 (7:27) (Class 6) (0-65,63) 3-Y-O — £1,325 (£1,325; £302) Stalls Low

Form — RPR
0000 1 **Hawk Eyed Lady (IRE)**[18] 4639 3-9-1 57 — (b) SteveDrowne 11 — 63
(J A Osborne) *overall ldr on far side: rdn fnl f: jnd on line* **10/1**
5204 1 dht **Bye Baby Bunting**[14] 4725 3-8-4 46 ow1 — RichardSmith 6 — 52
(B R Johnson) *racd far side tl hung lft over 1f out bef led stands' side drvn and r.o to dead heat line* **10/1**
0500 3 1 1/2 **Pasta Prayer**[11] 4862 3-8-12 54 — (b[1]) ChrisCatlin 2 — 55
(S A Callaghan) *led stands' side gp of 5 to over 1f out: no ex ins fnl f* **25/1**
0044 4 1 3/4 **Outside Edge (IRE)**[11] 4865 3-9-7 63 — (t[1]) AdamKirby 8 — 59
(W R Swinburn) *in rr on far side: rdn 2f out: kpt on but n.d* **10/3**[2]
-245 5 1 **My Flame**[36] 4044 3-8-12 54 — EddieAhern 1 — 46
(J R Jenkins) *hld up on stands' side: kpt on one pce fnl 2f* **3/1**[1]
054 6 3 3/4 **Celtic Spring (IRE)**[42] 3847 3-9-4 60 — PatCosgrave 10 — 40
(J R Boyle) *racd far side: rdn over 2f out: wknd fnl f* **8/1**
1030 7 3/4 **Rich Harvest (USA)**[5] 5045 3-9-0 56 — TGMcLaughlin 5 — 34
(P D Evans) *chsd ldrs stands' side: wknd appr fnl f* **7/1**[3]
00-2 8 5 **Royal Sovereign (IRE)**[12] 4806 3-9-4 60 — OscarUrbina 4 — 22
(G C H Chung) *s.i.s: hld up on stands' side: nvr on terms* **7/1**[3]
0056 9 2 **Santa Clara**[7] 4990 3-8-5 47 — (p) SaleemGolam 3 — —
(P Leech) *chsd ldrs stands' side to 1/2-way: sn wknd* **33/1**
0000 10 1/2 **Zeeran**[27] 4338 3-8-3 45 — LiamJones 7 — —
(C E Brittain) *racd far side: struggling fr 1/2-way: a bhd* **16/1**

0540 **11** ¾ **Heron (IRE)**[14] 4725 3-7-10 **45**.......... AndreaAtzeni(7) 9 —
(M R Hoad) *chsd ldrs far side tl hung lft and wknd over 1f out* **33/1**

-520 **12** 14 **Forever Changes**[99] 2074 3-9-1 **57**.......... PatDobbs 12 —
(L Montague Hall) *chsd ldrs far side tl wknd 1/2-way: t.o* **18/1**

1m 13.32s (0.62) **Going Correction** -0.125s/f (Firm) 12 Ran SP% **123.2**
Speed ratings (Par 98): **90,90,88,85,84 79,78,71,69,68 67,48**
WIN: HEL £5.80, BBB £7.00, PL: HEL £4.40, BBB £3.60, £10.50. CSF: HEL/BBB £54.19 BBB/HEL £54.19. TC: H/B/P £1237.44 B/H/P £1237.44; toteswinger: HEL/BB £52.30, HEI/PP £52.30, BB/PP £52.30..
Owner A D Spence **Bred** James Burns And A Moynan **Trained** Upper Lambourn, Berks
Owner Mrs A M Upsdell **Bred** The National Stud **Trained** Ashtead, Surrey

FOCUS
A dead-heat in this very moderate handicap, contested by horses which had only managed two victories between them prior to this and one of those was in a seller. Not form to be too positive about. The field soon split into two, with the larger group of seven going far side, while the other five stayed towards the stands' side.
Outside Edge(IRE) Official explanation: jockey said gelding hung right

5187 SPADE HOUSE H'CAP 5f
7:55 (7:57) (Class 5) (0-75,73) 3-Y-O+ £2,590 (£770; £385; £192) Stalls Low

Form RPR
0622 **1** **Gentle Guru**[7] 4981 4-9-11 **73**.......... SteveDrowne 2 86
(R T Phillips) *hld up in tch: shkn up to ld over 1f out: sn clr: r.o wl* **10/11**[1]

3430 **2** 3 ¼ **Malapropism**[17] 4668 8-9-11 **73**.......... DarryllHolland 6 74
(M R Channon) *in tch: wnt 2nd 1f out: no imp on wnr fnl f* **3/1**[2]

000 **3** 2 **Bookiesindex Boy**[36] 4064 4-8-9 **62**..........(v) DavidProbert(5) 3 56
(J R Jenkins) *led tl rdn and and hdd over 1f out: one pce after* **15/2**

3462 **4** 1 ¾ **Azygous**[12] 4812 5-9-0 **62**..........(p) EddieAhern 5 50
(J Akehurst) *trckd ldr to over 1f out: wknd qckly* **4/1**[3]

59.93 secs (-0.07) **Going Correction** -0.125s/f (Firm)
WFA 3 from 4yo+ 2lb 4 Ran SP% **115.8**
Speed ratings (Par 103): **95,89,86,83**
toteswinger: 1&2 £2.10. CSF £3.93 TOTE £1.80; EX 4.40 Place 6: £131.32 Place 5: £108.45.
Owner Flying Tiger Partnership **Bred** R Phillips And Tweenhills Farm And Stud **Trained** Adlestrop, Gloucs

FOCUS
A modest sprint handicap made even less competitive by the three non-runners including the previous day's Brighton scorer, Drumming Party, and then decimated further by the late withdrawal of Captain Kir, who got loose before the start (14/1, deduct 5p in the £ under Rule 4). Despite there only been four remaining runners, they didn't hang about. The form is rated through the runner-up.
T/Jkpt: Not won. T/Plt: £176.80 to a £1 stake. Pool: £87,081.14. 359.41 winning tickets. T/Qpdt: £91.40 to a £1 stake. Pool: £6,070.89. 49.10 winning tickets. JS

4967 HAMILTON (R-H)
Wednesday, August 20
5188 Meeting Abandoned - Waterlogged

4434 YORK (L-H)
Wednesday, August 20
5194 Meeting Abandoned - Waterlogged

4658 CHESTER (L-H)
Thursday, August 21

OFFICIAL GOING: Soft (good to soft in places; 6.4)
The rail was out, adding 18 yards to race distances.
Wind: Light, half-against Weather: overcast

5198 ALEXANDER EVENTS APPRENTICE H'CAP 7f 122y
5:40 (5:42) (Class 6) (0-65,65) 3-Y-O+ £2,729 (£806; £403) Stalls Low

Form RPR
5034 **1** **Zennerman (IRE)**[10] 4919 5-8-12 **57**..........(b) FrederikTylicki(5) 4 72+
(G A Swinbank) *trckd ldrs: led over 1f out: pushed clr* **5/2**[1]

3015 **2** 3 ½ **Tanforan**[6] 5045 6-9-1 **60**.......... BillyCray(5) 8 66
(B P J Baugh) *hld up in midfield: hdwy over 2f out: styd on fnl f: tk 2nd post* **8/1**[2]

6412 **3** shd **Leptis Magna**[7] 5008 4-9-7 **61**.......... MarcHalford 12 66
(D R C Elsworth) *s.i.s: hdwy on outside over 2f out: wnt 2nd ins fnl f: kpt on same pce* **8/1**[2]

4040 **4** 3 ½ **Unlimited**[45] 3797 6-9-6 **65**.......... SoniaEaton(5) 9 61
(A W Carroll) *mid-div: effrt over 2f out: kpt on one pce* **16/1**

0560 **5** ½ **Sands Of Barra (IRE)**[5] 5101 5-9-4 **61**.......... KellyHarrison(3) 13 56
(I W McInnes) *trckd ldrs: fdd appr fnl f* **16/1**

402- **6** 2 ¼ **Eternal Legacy (IRE)**[218] 6638 6-9-3 **57**.......... MichaelJStainton 1 46
(E J Alston) *t.k.h: trckd ldrs: lost pl over 1f out* **9/1**[3]

6000 **7** 1 ¾ **Gilded Youth**[79] 2703 4-9-6 **65**.......... StacyRenwick(5) 6 50
(G F Bridgwater) *led tl over 1f out: sn wknd* **40/1**

3-10 **8** 1 ¼ **Tri Chara (IRE)**[103] 2007 4-9-3 **62**..........(v[1]) ClGillies(5) 3 43
(R Hollinshead) *hld up in midfield: effrt over 2f out: wknd appr fnl f* **16/1**

4-00 **9** shd **Kirstys Lad**[7] 5008 6-9-0 **59**.......... RossAtkinson(5) 10 40
(M Mullineaux) *in rr: nvr a factor* **33/1**

0430 **10** 1 **Danzig Fox**[18] 4661 3-8-13 **64**.......... GarryWhillans(5) 2 42
(M Mullineaux) *rrd star: a towards rr* **9/1**[3]

0440 **11** 1 ½ **Obe Royal**[26] 4440 4-9-8 **65**..........(b) RichardEvans(3) 15 40
(P D Evans) *hld up in rr: nvr on terms* **16/1**

5005 **12** 2 ½ **Alseraaj (USA)**[13] 4814 3-9-2 **62**..........(t) DNolan 11 30
(Ian Williams) *drvn along and swtchd lft sn after s: mid-div: lost pl 3f out* **50/1**

3144 **13** 1 ¾ **Machinate (USA)**[124] 1486 6-9-6 **65**.......... DeanHeslop(5) 7 29
(W M Brisbourne) *a in rr* **22/1**

4014 **14** 7 **Feeling Fresh (IRE)**[17] 4684 3-9-5 **65**.......... WilliamBuick 5 10
(Paul Green) *in rr: sme hdwy 3f out: lost pl wl over 1f out: bhd whn eased ins fnl f* **8/1**[2]

5565 **F** **Cheery Cat (USA)**[16] 4700 4-9-4 **58**.......... NeilBrown 14 —
(D W Barker) *in rr: stmbld and fell 3f out* **16/1**

1m 38.76s (4.96) **Going Correction** +0.675s/f (Yiel)
WFA 3 from 4yo+ 6lb 15 Ran SP% **123.0**
Speed ratings (Par 101): **102,98,98,94,94 92,90,89,89,88 86,84,82,75,—**
toteswinger: 1&2 £5.60, 1&3 £4.90, 2&3 £6.10. CSF £21.12 CT £150.01 TOTE £3.10: £1.60, £3.20, £3.10; EX 25.40.
Owner Shropshire Wolves **Bred** Eurostrait Ltd **Trained** Melsonby, N Yorks
■ Stewards' Enquiry : Sonia Eaton caution: careless riding
Richard Evans two-day ban: used whip when out of contention (Sep 4-5)

FOCUS
Just a moderate handicap restricted to apprentices. The winner will still be well treated on last year's form after this, and the plcaed horses were close to their recent form.

5199 ERNST & YOUNG H'CAP 1m 4f 66y
6:10 (6:10) (Class 4) (0-85,84) 3-Y-O+ £5,504 (£1,637; £818; £408) Stalls Low

Form RPR
5005 **1** **Dzesmin (POL)**[29] 4299 6-9-7 **78**.......... FrederikTylicki(7) 9 89
(R A Fahey) *trckd ldrs: led 2f out: rdn and edgd lft 1f out: hld on towards fin* **5/1**[2]

0001 **2** ½ **Ainama (IRE)**[19] 4645 4-10-0 **78**.......... ShaneKelly 8 88+
(M Wigham) *hld up in rr: smooth hdwy on ins over 3f out: wnt 3rd over 1f out: styd on wl: nt quite rch wnr* **14/1**

3322 **3** 1 **First Avenue**[38] 4021 3-9-10 **84**.......... PhilipRobinson 2 93
(M A Jarvis) *led: hdd 2f out: hmpd and swtchd rt jst ins fnl f: kpt on* **11/10**[1]

0000 **4** 9 **Overrule (USA)**[20] 4603 4-9-4 **68**.......... J-PGuillambert 5 62
(B Ellison) *hld up in rr: hdwy and n.m.r over 2f out: kpt on: nvr nr ldrs* **18/1**

20-0 **5** 1 **Leslingtaylor (IRE)**[15] 4742 6-9-10 **74**.......... GrahamGibbons 4 67
(J J Quinn) *chsd ldrs: sn pushed along: one pce fnl 3f* **7/1**[3]

00-0 **6** 5 **Compton Dragon (USA)**[72] 2908 9-8-9 **59** oh1.......... KirstyMilczarek 6 44
(W M Brisbourne) *hld up in rr: effrt 3f out: nvr on terms* **40/1**

0145 **7** 2 **She's Our Lass (IRE)**[5] 5100 7-9-12 **76**.......... DNolan 3 57
(D Carroll) *hld up in midfield: hdwy over 3f out: one pce fnl 2f* **20/1**

5615 **8** 14 **Colorado Blue (IRE)**[28] 4350 3-9-5 **79**..........(tp) StephenDonohoe 7 38
(C E Longsdon) *chsd ldrs: lost pl 3f out* **50/1**

3126 **9** 21 **Prelude**[18] 4662 7-9-8 **72**.......... TGMcLaughlin 10 —
(W M Brisbourne) *hld up towards rr: rn in snatches: shkn up 7f out: lost pl over 2f out: bhd and eased over 1f out* **12/1**

620P **10** 3 **Command Marshal (FR)**[12] 4866 5-9-11 **75**.......... WilliamBuick 11 —
(M J Scudamore) *w ldrs: drvn over 4f out: lost pl 3f out: bhd and eased over 1f out* **33/1**

3102 **11** 3 **Altitude**[16] 4699 3-9-6 **80**..........(b) SebSanders 1 —
(Sir Mark Prescott) *sn chsng ldrs: wkng whn n.m.r over 3f out: bhd and eased over 1f out* **8/1**

2m 46.26s (6.36) **Going Correction** +0.675s/f (Yiel)
WFA 3 from 4yo+ 10lb 11 Ran SP% **119.6**
Speed ratings (Par 105): **105,104,104,98,97 94,92,83,69,67 65**
toteswinger: 1&2 £19.50, 1&3 £2.70, 2&3 £3.90. CSF £70.52 CT £130.90 TOTE £7.30: £1.90, £4.20, £1.30; EX 84.50.
Owner JAS Partnership **Bred** Marian Pokrywka **Trained** Musley Bank, N Yorks
■ Stewards' Enquiry : Frederik Tylicki four-day ban: careless riding (Sept 4-5, 7, 25 (latter for remedial training))

FOCUS
A fair handicap with the winner rated back to something like his best and the favourite to form.

5200 VIRGIN ATLANTIC MEDIAN AUCTION MAIDEN STKS 6f 18y
6:40 (6:40) (Class 5) 2-Y-O £3,238 (£963; £481; £240) Stalls Low

Form RPR
04 **1** **Cyflymder (IRE)**[19] 4616 2-9-3 0.......... SebSanders 5 78
(J G Given) *sn chsng ldr: hrd rdn and styd on fnl f: led last stride* **10/3**[2]

2360 **2** hd **Kyllachy Star**[19] 4626 2-9-3 77.......... PaulHanagan 1 77
(R A Fahey) *led: rdn over 1f out: hdd post* **11/8**[1]

652 **3** 4 **Key To Love (IRE)**[16] 4705 2-8-12 67.......... JamesDoyle 8 60
(H J L Dunlop) *chsd ldrs: effrt 3f out: wnt modest 3rd over 1f out* **10/3**[2]

366 **4** 11 **Tillers Satisfied (IRE)**[28] 4321 2-8-12 61.......... GrahamGibbons 4 27
(R Hollinshead) *chsd ldrs: wknd over 1f out* **11/1**

5 12 **Mister Wilberforce** 2-9-0 0.......... AndrewMullen(3) 6 —
(Mrs L Williamson) *s.i.s: reminders and lost pl over 3f out: sn bhd* **25/1**

6 5 **Jaq's Sister** 2-8-12 0.......... KirstyMilczarek 3 —
(M Blanshard) *s.i.s: sn t.o in last* **9/1**[3]

1m 19.6s (5.80) **Going Correction** +0.90s/f (Soft) 6 Ran SP% **110.4**
Speed ratings (Par 94): **97,96,91,76,60 54**
toteswinger: 1&2 £1.40, 1&3 £2.10, 2&3 £1.10. CSF £8.06 TOTE £3.50: £2.70, £1.70; EX 8.60.
Owner R S G Jones & Amblestock Partnership **Bred** Miss Laura G F Ferguson **Trained** Willoughton, Lincs
■ Stewards' Enquiry : Seb Sanders one-day ban: used whip with excessive frequency (Sep 4)

FOCUS
A modest, uncompetitive juvenile maiden that only concerned two horses from about halfway.

NOTEBOOK
Cyflymder(IRE) stepped up significantly on the form he showed on his debut when fourth behind three fair types at Doncaster last time and he progressed again to get off the mark at the third attempt. However, he looked held for much of the way up the straight and it took all of the joint-champion's strength to force his head in front on the line. For all that he is clearly progressive, he looked to have a hard race and might not be one to back to follow up if turned out too soon. (op 5-2 tchd 9-4)
Kyllachy Star did absolutely nothing wrong, showing good speed and handling the track well, but he was just caught in the final few strides. He has had a few chances now, and an official mark of 77 is probably stiff enough, but he ought to find a similar race eventually. (op 7-4 tchd 15-8)
Key To Love(IRE), just pegged back over 5f on similar ground at Chepstow on her previous start, seemed to lack the pace of the front two and was never a threat. This sharp track probably didn't suit. (op 3-1)
Tillers Satisfied(IRE) was well beaten and may not have handled the ground, the softest she has encountered to date. (op 12-1 tchd 10-1)

5201 TECHNAL H'CAP 5f 16y
7:10 (7:11) (Class 6) (0-65,65) 3-Y-O+ £2,729 (£806; £403) Stalls Low

Form RPR
6022 **1** **Grudge**[10] 4922 3-9-5 **63**.......... FrancisNorton 4 74
(D W Barker) *mde all: styd on wl fnl 2f* **5/2**[2]

0040 **2** 2 **Littledodayno (IRE)**[22] 4542 5-9-3 **59**.......... SebSanders 6 63
(M Wigham) *sn chsng ldrs: styd on to take 2nd ins fnl f: no real imp* **12/1**

3443 **3** 1 ½ **Kings College Boy**[15] 4743 8-9-2 **65**..........(b) FrederikTylicki(7) 1 64
(R A Fahey) *chsd wnr: chal 2f out: kpt on same pce* **2/1**[1]

1654 **4** ¾ **Stoneacre Pat (IRE)**[3] 5141 3-8-11 **55**.......... KirstyMilczarek 10 51+
(Peter Grayson) *s.s: kpt on fnl 2f: nvr rchd ldrs* **14/1**

1000 **5** ½ **Lambrini Lace (IRE)**[14] 4767 3-8-11 **58**.................... AndrewMullen(3) 9 52
(Mrs L Williamson) *chsd ldrs: kpt on one pce fnl 2f* **33/1**

0041 **6** ¾ **Dalarossie**[17] 4686 3-9-7 **65**.. ShaneKelly 11 57
(E J Alston) *prom: outpcd over 2f out: edgd lft and kpt on fnl f* **16/1**

5010 **7** ½ **Guto**[6] 5074 5-8-9 **56**.. KellyHarrison(5) 13 46
(W J H Ratcliffe) *chsd ldrs on outer: one pce fnl 2f* **15/2**

0535 **8** ½ **Yerevan**[11] 4891 4-8-11 **60**..(t) RossAtkinson(7) 3 48
(M Mullineaux) *trckd ldrs on inner: effrt 2f out: one pce* **11/2**[3]

3303 **9** 5 **Kalligal**[7] 5028 3-9-7 **65**.. StephenDonohoe 7 35
(R Ingram) *gave problems bef s: hmpd s: bhd and eased fnl f* **16/1**

65.34 secs (4.34) **Going Correction** +0.90s/f (Soft)
WFA 3 from 4yo+ 2lb **9** Ran SP% **118.1**
Speed ratings (Par 101): **101,97,95,94,93 92,91,90,82**
toteswinger: 1&2 £4.20, 1&3 £1.10, 2&3 £4.20. CSF £33.55 CT £71.70 TOTE £3.00: £1.40, £2.00, £1.50; EX 25.10.
Owner Mark Sumner & Partners I **Bred** D H Brailsford **Trained** Scorton, N Yorks

FOCUS
A modest sprint handicap. The winner made all in a modest time and the form is not entirely convincing.

5202 ALMOND RESORTS H'CAP — 1m 2f 75y
7:40 (7:40) (Class 4) (0-85,89) 3-Y-O **£4,371** (£1,300; £650; £324) **Stalls** High

Form RPR

5222 **1** **Just Rob**[39] 3996 3-8-13 **77**.. GrahamGibbons 3 85+
(R Hollinshead) *hld up towards rr: stdy hdwy 3f out: wnt 2nd on inner 1f out: styd on to ld post* **9/2**[2]

013 **2** *nse* **Eton Fable (IRE)**[15] 4741 3-8-6 **70**.. FergalLynch 8 78
(W J H Ratcliffe) *sn led: kpt on wl fnl 2f: hdd last stride* **16/1**

4504 **3** 3 **Resounding Glory (USA)**[13] 4818 3-8-12 **76**................ PaulHanagan 2 78+
(R A Fahey) *led early: trckd ldrs: nt clr run over 3f out: styd on same pce fnl 2f* **11/1**

0025 **4** ½ **The Oil Magnate**[33] 4205 3-9-1 **79**.. TonyHamilton 9 80
(M Dods) *hld up towards rr: effrt over 3f out: sn chsng ldrs: one pce fnl 2f* **12/1**

2141 **5** ½ **Craigstown**[5] 5098 3-9-6 **89** 6ex...................... Louis-PhilippeBeuzelin(5) 7 89
(Saeed Bin Suroor) *hld up in midfield: effrt and chsng ldrs 3f out: wnt 2nd 2f out: hung bdly rt 1f out: kpt on same pce* **11/10**[1]

0462 **6** 13 **Master Spy**[28] 4335 3-9-7 **85**..(b) JimmyFortune 1 59
(J H M Gosden) *t.k.h: sn trcking ldrs: chal 6f out: hung lft and wknd over 1f out* **7/1**[3]

-550 **7** 3 ¾ **Thunderstruck**[90] 2378 3-8-9 **73**.. ShaneKelly 5 40
(K A Ryan) *in rr: reminders and detached 6f out: nvr a factor* **25/1**

420 **8** 3 ¼ **Cathedral Walk (USA)**[19] 4621 3-8-8 **72**....................(v[1]) AndrewElliott 6 32
(K R Burke) *chsd ldrs: rdn 5f out: lost pl over 2f out* **12/1**

661 **9** 8 **Mont Cervin**[73] 2885 3-8-11 **75**.. StephenDonohoe 4 19
(P C Haslam) *t.k.h: trckd ldrs: chal 4f out: wknd 2f out* **18/1**

2m 20.34s (8.14) **Going Correction** +0.90s/f (Soft) **9** Ran SP% **117.0**
Speed ratings (Par 102): **103,102,100,100,99 89,86,83,77**
toteswinger: 1&2 £9.60, 1&3 £10.00, 2&3 £61.10. CSF £73.53 CT £750.37 TOTE £4.80: £1.30, £4.00, £3.00; EX 92.20.
Owner Mrs Dianne E Edwards **Bred** S L Edwards **Trained** Upper Longdon, Staffs

FOCUS
A fair three-year-old handicap and quite competitive, but they went an ordinary gallop early on. The first two improved but the favourite disappointed.
Craigstown Official explanation: jockey said colt hung badly right from 2f out

5203 SARTORI MENSWEAR MAIDEN FILLIES' STKS — 7f 122y
8:10 (8:11) (Class 5) 3-Y-O+ **£3,070** (£906; £453) **Stalls** Low

Form RPR

-222 **1** **Rhadegunda**[31] 4253 3-8-12 74.. JimmyFortune 5 71+
(J H M Gosden) *trckd ldrs: effrt and 2nd over 2f out: led over 1f out: edgd lft and drvn clr: eased nr fin* **2/7**[1]

2 4 ½ **Nawaahi (IRE)**[93] 3-8-12 68.. JamesDoyle 3 59
(K A Morgan) *led tl over 1f out: kpt on same pce* **16/1**[3]

4624 **3** ½ **Hydrophonic**[15] 4737 3-8-12 65.. PaulHanagan 1 58
(R A Fahey) *sn trcking ldrs: effrt over 2f out: one pce appr fnl f* **5/1**[2]

4 ½ **Ishiadancer** 3-8-12 0.. ShaneKelly 4 56
(E J Alston) *s.s: hdwy over 4f out: styd on same pce fnl 2f* **20/1**

63-6 **5** *shd* **Eternal Optimist (IRE)**[20] 4596 3-8-12 56.................. StephenDonohoe 8 56
(Paul Green) *prom: effrt 3f out: one pce* **16/1**[3]

6 6 **Jonquille (IRE)**[356] 5021 3-8-12 0.. KirstyMilczarek 7 40
(R Ford) *trckd ldrs: wknd appr fnl f* **20/1**

R00 **7** 4 ½ **Tot Hill**[22] 4523 5-8-11 0.. RossAtkinson(7) 9 29
(C N Kellett) *s.i.s: in rr: drvn over 5f out: lost pl over 2f out* **150/1**

6000 **8** 3 ¾ **Madame Rio (IRE)**[55] 3436 3-8-8 42 ow3.................. GarryWhillans(7) 10 22
(M Mullineaux) *in rr: effrt 3f out: sn wknd* **33/1**

6000 **9** 6 **Arrabiata**[22] 4531 3-8-12 43..(b[1]) TGMcLaughlin 6 3
(C N Kellett) *t.k.h: trckd ldrs: drvn over 2f out: lost pl over 1f out* **66/1**

1m 40.81s (7.01) **Going Correction** +0.90s/f (Soft)
WFA 3 from 5yo 6lb **9** Ran SP% **120.8**
Speed ratings (Par 100): **100,95,95,94,94 88,83,80,74**
toteswinger: 1&2 £2.80, 1&3 £1.60, 2&3 £2.60. CSF £7.05 TOTE £1.30: £1.02, £2.70, £1.40; EX 8.10 Place 6 £12.06, Place 5 £6.78.
Owner A E Oppenheimer **Bred** Hascombe And Valiant Studs **Trained** Newmarket, Suffolk

FOCUS
A modest, uncompetitive fillies' maiden, as one would expect for the time of year, and they went steady for much of the way. The winner was fuly entitled to win in the style she did.
T/Jkpt: £9,476.10 to a £1 stake. Pool: £26,693.49. 2.00 winning tickets. T/Plt: £10.30 to a £1 stake. Pool: £82,427.85. 5,835.60 winning tickets. T/Qpdt: £4.00 to a £1 stake. Pool: £5,549.40. 1,009.70 winning tickets. WG

5015 GREAT LEIGHS (A.W) (L-H)
Thursday, August 21

OFFICIAL GOING: Standard
Wind: fresh behind Weather: bright spells, overcast

5204 GOOSE GREEN NURSERY — 5f (P)
2:05 (2:05) (Class 4) (0-85,84) 2-Y-O **£3,885** (£1,156; £577; £288) **Stalls** Low

Form RPR

2101 **1** **The Magic Of Rio**[14] 4768 2-9-7 **84**.. LiamJones 1 88
(W J Haggas) *wnt rt s: chsd ldrs: rdn to chse ldr wl over 1f out: styd on wl fnl f: led last stride* **7/1**

0332 **2** *shd* **Red Cell (IRE)**[9] 4942 2-8-0 **63**..(b) ChrisCatlin 4 67
(E J O'Neill) *led: rdn over 1f out: kpt on wl tl hdd last stride* **6/1**[3]

21 **3** *nk* **Leftontheshelf (IRE)**[24] 4486 2-9-4 **84**.. TolleyDean(3) 3 87+
(J L Spearing) *sn bustled along and outpcd in rr: hdwy on inner over 1f out: r.o wl fnl f: nt quite rch ldng pair* **4/1**[2]

3022 **4** 2 **Kate The Great**[14] 4768 2-9-3 **80**.. EddieAhern 6 76
(M J Wallace) *towards rr: hdwy 3f out: chsd ldrs and rdn jst over 2f out: kpt on same pce fnl f* **15/2**

5561 **5** *nk* **First Choice (IRE)**[21] 4557 2-8-9 **72**..(p) NCallan 10 67
(K A Ryan) *wnt rt s: racd wd: rdn jst over 2f out: kpt on same pce u.p fnl f* **14/1**

643 **6** ¾ **Imaginary Diva**[16] 4705 2-7-12 **61** oh2.. AdrianMcCarthy 7 53
(G G Margarson) *chsd ldrs: rdn jst over 2f out: wknd jst ins fnl f* **40/1**

5020 **7** *shd* **Sweet Applause (IRE)**[26] 4403 2-9-4 **81**.. DarrenWilliams 8 75+
(A P Jarvis) *hld up bhd rdn and effrt wl over 1f out: styng on whn nt clr run 1f out tl ins fnl f: swtchd rt ins fnl f: nvr able to chal* **9/1**

31 **8** 2 **Zelos Girl (IRE)**[17] 4681 2-8-5 **68**.. SaleemGolam 2 52
(Rae Guest) *racd keenly: chsd ldr tl wl over 1f out: wknd over 1f out: btn whn edgd rt ent fnl f* **2/1**[1]

5010 **9** *nk* **Time Loup**[9] 4956 2-7-8 **62**.. DavidProbert(5) 5 45
(S R Bowring) *in tch tl lost pl 3f out: n.d after* **40/1**

3106 **10** 1 ¼ **Barbee (IRE)**[19] 4640 2-9-2 **79**.. JoeFanning 9 58
(E A L Dunlop) *s.i.s: hld up bhd: c wd and rdn 2f out: no prog* **16/1**

61.04 secs (0.84) **Going Correction** +0.125s/f (Slow) **10** Ran SP% **119.3**
Speed ratings (Par 96): **98,97,97,94,93 92,92,89,88,86**
toteswinger: 1&2 £11.00, 1&3 £3.80, 2&3 £6.20. CSF £49.86 CT £169.71 TOTE £7.70: £2.70, £2.60, £1.40; EX 41.10 Trifecta £325.50 Part won. Pool: £439.87. 0.90 winning units..
Owner M Scotney/ D Asplin/ A Symonds **Bred** R F And S D Knipe **Trained** Newmarket, Suffolk

FOCUS
A modest nursery. The first three came clear and the form makes sense.

NOTEBOOK
The Magic Of Rio confirmed her Brighton running with Red Cell despite the 5lb rise by just doing enough to reel in that rival at the line. She had shown on her second outing this term that she handles an artificial surface and this was her third win from her last four outings, the one defeat coming in the Super Sprint at Newbury. This obviously rates another career-best effort and she really is a tough, likeable sort. (op 15-2 tchd 8-1)
Red Cell(IRE) has to rate as unfortunate as he did well to prevail in the battle for the early lead and only again got run out of it at the business end. This consistent gelding does richly deserve to go one better again, but obviously still holds little in hand of the Handicapper. (op 13-2)
Leftontheshelf(IRE) was unable to dominate on this switch to the All-Weather as she did when winning nicely at Yarmouth 24 days previously and was not travelling that well through the first few furlongs. She kept on well for pressure inside the final furlong and was not disgraced, yet does look to have begun life in this sphere on a stiff enough mark. (op 7-2 tchd 9-2 in a palce)
Kate The Great was very closely matched with the first pair on Brighton form, for which she had been raised 3lb, and may need another furlong now. (tchd 8-1)
Sweet Applause(IRE) met some support in the betting ring for this drop back in trip and grade and was beginning to make a move from off the pace prior to meeting trouble. She must be rated better than the bare form and is worth another chance from this mark. (op 14-1 tchd 8-1)
Zelos Girl(IRE) had won a Carlisle race which looked decent with the placed horses winning next time out and, looking well treated on a mark of 68, she was well backed to follow up on this switch to the sand. However, she took time to settle early on and faded tamely in the home straight.
Official explanation: jockey said filly ran too free (tchd 5-2)

5205 HATFIELD PERVERAL MAIDEN FILLIES' STKS — 6f (P)
2:40 (2:40) (Class 5) 3-Y-O+ **£2,590** (£770; £385; £192) **Stalls** Low

Form RPR

5 **1** **Ethaara**[30] 4277 3-8-12 0.. RHills 1 91
(W J Haggas) *trckd ldng pair: chsd ldr wl over 1f out: sn ev ch: led 1f out: r.o wl* **5/4**[1]

42- **2** 1 ¼ **Anne Of Kiev (IRE)**[294] 6601 3-8-12 0.. LDettori 5 87
(J H M Gosden) *led after 1f: rdn and clr w wnr over 1f out: hdd 1f out: one pce: eased whn btn towards fin* **7/4**[2]

0 **3** 22 **Xandra (IRE)**[8] 4987 3-8-7 0.. JackMitchell(5) 8 17
(C F Wall) *fly-jmpd and v awkward s: hld up bhd: hdwy 3f out: sn wl outpcd: wnt poor 3rd over 1f out* **33/1**

4 4 **Motivated Choice** 3-8-12 0.. PatCosgrave 6 —
(L M Cumani) *fly-jmpd s and slowly away: t.k.h and sn in tch: rdn and wknd over 2f out* **20/1**

3-42 **5** 2 **Orchestrion**[19] 4651 3-8-12 62.. RobertWinston 4 —
(G A Swinbank) *awkward leaving stalls: in tch in midfield: rdn and wknd 1/2-way: t.o* **6/1**[3]

0-00 **6** ½ **Rahaan (USA)**[33] 4194 3-8-12 53.. JoeFanning 9 —
(C E Brittain) *bhd and rdn over 3f out: sn lost tch: t.o* **40/1**

7 ½ **Ruby Rocks** 3-8-12 0.. HayleyTurner 3 —
(P S McEntee) *led for 1f: chsd ldr after tl wl over 1f out: wknd rapidly: t.o* **66/1**

4-53 **8** 5 **Royal Encore**[42] 3867 4-9-1 59.. EddieAhern 2 —
(J R Fanshawe) *in tch tl lost pl and rdn 1/2-way: wl bhd last 2f: t.o* **11/1**

1m 13.44s (-0.26) **Going Correction** +0.125s/f (Slow)
WFA 3 from 4yo+ 3lb **8** Ran SP% **115.1**
Speed ratings (Par 100): **106,104,75,69,67 66,65,59**
toteswinger: 1&2 £1.10, 1&3 £14.20, 2&3 £17.70. CSF £3.52 TOTE £2.30: £1.10, £1.30, £5.50; EX 4.00 Trifecta £61.70 Pool: £372.47. 4.46 winning units..
Owner Hamdan Al Maktoum **Bred** Shadwell Estate Company Limited **Trained** Newmarket, Suffolk

FOCUS
A weak maiden overall in which the two market leaders came well clear in the home straight. The form is rated around the runner-up.
Orchestrion Official explanation: jockey said filly anticipated the gates opening and never travelled thereafter

5206 HIGHAM H'CAP — 5f (P)
3:15 (3:15) (Class 3) (0-90,90) 3-Y-O- **£7,569** (£2,265; £1,132; £566; £282) **Stalls** Low

Form RPR

1111 **1** **Cheveton**[18] 4668 4-9-6 **87**.. JimCrowley 5 96+
(R J Price) *chsd ldr: rdn wl over 1f out: led ins fnl f: r.o wl* **7/2**[1]

0324 **2** 1 ¼ **Harry Up**[29] 4294 7-9-1 **82**..(p) NCallan 2 86
(K A Ryan) *led: rdn ent fnl 2f: 2 l ld wl over 1f out: hdd ins fnl f:* **11/1**

340 **3** ¾ **Tia Mia**[33] 4198 3-9-2 **85**..(p) TPQueally 11 86
(M Botti) *chsd ldrs: rdn over 2f out: chsd ldng pair over 1f out: kpt on fnl f but nvr pce to rch ldng pair* **12/1**

/6-0 **4** 1 **Doctor Hilary**[203] 378 6-9-4 **85**..(v) RobertHavlin 9 83
(A B Haynes) *racd in midfield: c wd 2f out: r.o fnl f: nt rch ldrs* **50/1**

4616 **5** 1 **Dvinsky (USA)**[9] 4944 7-9-1 **82**..(b) IanMongan 13 76+
(P Howling) *grad dropped in after s: bhd: hdwy over 1f out: edgd lft ent fnl f: styd on but no threat to ldrs* **20/1**

0244 **6** *hd* **Brandywell Boy (IRE)**[6] 5046 5-8-4 **71** oh2.. LiamJones 1 64
(D J S Ffrench Davis) *chsd ldrs: rdn wl over 2f out: unable qck 2f out: plugged on same pce* **11/1**

4610 **7** ¾ **Piscean (USA)**[5] 5102 3-8-11 **80**........ MickyFenton 6 71+
(T Keddy) *s.i.s: bhd: sme hdwy whn nt clr run and swtchd rt ins fnl f: nvr nr ldrs* **14/1**

1110 **8** ¾ **Whiskey Junction**[31] 4240 4-9-7 **88**........ LPKeniry 10 76
(A M Balding) *chsd ldng pair tl over 1f out: wknd u.p ent fnl f* **7/1**[3]

300 **9** ¾ **Luscivious**[42] 3881 4-9-9 **90**........(b) PatCosgrave 7 75
(A J McCabe) *dwlt: a towards rr: rdn over 3f out: nvr able to chal* **11/1**

0501 **10** ¾ **Hadaf (IRE)**[55] 3462 3-9-5 **88**........ RHills 4 71+
(M P Tregoning) *a bhd: hmpd 4f out: nvr a factor* **4/1**[2]

0000 **11** ¾ **Canadian Danehill (IRE)**[33] 4201 6-9-8 **89**........(p) EddieAhern 8 69
(R M H Cowell) *racd in midfield: drvn 3f out: sn struggling: no ch whn nt clr run ins fnl f: eased after* **10/1**

6354 **12** *nk* **Tony The Tap**[18] 4668 7-8-13 **80**........ RichardMullen 3 59
(W R Muir) *a towards rr: nvr a factor* **8/1**

60.04 secs (-0.16) **Going Correction** +0.125s/f (Slow)
WFA 3 from 4yo+ 2lb 12 Ran SP% **121.0**
Speed ratings (Par 107): **106,104,102,101,99 99,98,96,95,94 93,92**
toteswinger: 1&2 £9.60, 1&3 £14.40, 2&3 £23.30. CSF £43.82 CT £433.74 TOTE £4.60: £2.20, £3.60, £4.50; EX 47.80 Trifecta £226.50 Part won. Pool: £306.12. 0.50 winning units..
Owner Mrs K Oseman **Bred** Miss K Rausing **Trained** Ullingswick, H'fords

FOCUS
A typically competitive sprint handicap for the grade, run at a decent clip and few really got into it from off the pace. Cheveton continues to progress.

NOTEBOOK
Cheveton landed the five-timer with another ready display and fully confirmed his adaptability for underfoot conditions. Racing from another 4lb higher mark, he was always up with the pace and did not need to be fully extended to get on top inside the final furlong. He is still improving fast and further prizes look within his grasp, with the Portland Handicap at Doncaster next month looking a viable target. (tchd 4-1)
Harry Up had been held in claiming company on turf of late, but his previous two outings on the All-Weather were winning ones and he showed he is best on an artificial surface with a solid effort from the front. (op 12-1 tchd 14-1)
Tia Mia, 3lb lower and tried in cheekpieces, was another always on the pace and posted an improved effort for the drop back in trip. She has taken time to really find her feet this term, but could build on this now. (op 11-1)
Doctor Hilary registered an encouraging performance considering it was his first outing for 203 days. His new stable has really hit form in the past week and, looking potentially well treated on his previous best efforts, he should come on nicely for the run.
Dvinsky(USA) was having his first outing over the minimum trip since 2004 and really found this too sharp a test, but was not disgraced and goes some way to helping set the level. (tchd 22-1)
Piscean(USA), a runner-up on both his previous starts on sand, fell out of the gates and had to come from behind as a result. He was coming with an effort prior to meeting trouble around the final furlong pole and the manner in which he ran on would suggest he is still on a fair mark. Granted he may not be straightforward, but it was the first time he had taken on his elders and he is a bit better than this (op 16-1)
Hadaf(IRE), who had won his only previous start on the All-Weather, had been upped 6lb for his narrow Newmarket success in June. He never looked like getting involved from off the pace and now has questions to answer. (op 9-2 tchd 5-1)
Tony The Tap Official explanation: jockey said gelding did not act on the track

5207 WICKHAM BISHOPS H'CAP 1m (P)
3:50 (3:51) (Class 3) (0-90,90) 3-Y-O+ **£7,569** (£2,265; £1,132; £566; £282) **Stalls** Centre

Form RPR

50 **1** **Irish Mayhem (USA)**[14] 4783 3-9-1 **84**........ EddieAhern 3 98
(B J Meehan) *t.k.h: hld up towards rr: hdwy and rdn over 2f out: led ins fnl f: sn clr: readily* **12/1**

003 **2** *3* **Yarqus**[19] 4642 5-9-13 **90**........(b) LiamJones 5 98
(C E Brittain) *in tch: rdn 3f out: chsd ldrs ent fnl f: kpt on wl u.p to go 2nd wl ins fnl f: no ch w wnr* **12/1**

2024 **3** *hd* **Hazzard County (USA)**[26] 4407 4-9-10 **87**........ RichardMullen 4 95+
(D M Simcock) *t.k.h in midfield tl stdd to rr after 1f: hdwy 2f out: r.o wl fnl f: wnt 3rd nr fin: nvr a threat to wnr* **7/1**[3]

6102 **4** *nk* **Mount Hermon (IRE)**[7] 5018 4-8-11 **77**........(b) TravisBlock(3) 16 84+
(H Morrison) *hld up in tch on outer: hdwy 3f out: ev ch over 1f out: led jst ins fnl f: sn hdd and one pce* **13/2**[2]

4226 **5** ½ **Trans Siberian**[19] 4642 4-9-9 **86**........ JoeFanning 8 92
(P F I Cole) *led: rdn and hdd over 1f out: ev ch tl one pce jst ins fnl f* **9/1**

04-3 **6** *1* **Furnace (IRE)**[36] 4089 4-9-11 **88**........ HayleyTurner 15 91
(M L W Bell) *stdd s: swtchd sharply lft after s: bhd: hdwy 3f out: hrd drvn 2f out: kpt on to chse ldrs ent fnl f: no imp after* **12/1**

4160 **7** ½ **Kings Point (IRE)**[23] 4509 7-9-10 **87**........ AdrianTNicholls 14 89
(D Nicholls) *chsd ldr: rdn to ld over 1f out: hdd jst ins fnl f: btn whn n.m.r fnl 100yds* **16/1**

1163 **8** *3* **Grand Vizier (IRE)**[42] 3887 4-9-0 **82**........ JackMitchell(5) 13 77
(C F Wall) *sn bustled along in rr: edgd out rt off of rail 2f out: kpt on u.p: nvr trbld ldrs* **8/1**

4514 **9** *hd* **Count Ceprano (IRE)**[15] 4723 4-9-5 **87**........ DavidProbert(5) 6 82
(M D I Usher) *stdd s: hld up: effrt and nt clr run briefly wl over 1f out: nvr trbld ldrs* **10/1**

6116 **10** *6* **Dear Maurice**[45] 3800 4-9-8 **85**........ TPQueally 9 66
(E A L Dunlop) *dwlt: hld up in midfield on outer: rdn and no hdwy over 2f out: wl bhd fnl f* **5/1**[1]

1100 **11** *3* **Always A Rock (IRE)**[21] 4553 3-9-4 **87**........ GregFairley 11 60
(M Johnston) *chsd ldrs: drvn 3f out: sn struggling: no ch fr over 1f out* **12/1**

0564 **12** ¾ **Neardown Beauty (IRE)**[9] 4945 5-9-8 **85**........(p) PatCosgrave 1 57
(A J McCabe) *hld up in midfield on inner: rdn and no prog over 2f out: wl bhd over 1f out* **33/1**

0602 **13** *2½* **Gallantry**[20] 4602 6-9-11 **88**........ IanMongan 2 55
(P Howling) *chsd ldrs: rdn 3f out: wknd over 1f out: eased ins fnl f* **20/1**

3101 **14** *nse* **Choreography**[15] 4723 5-9-4 **81**........(p) PaulDoe 12 48
(Jim Best) *in tch tl rdn and struggling 1/2-way: no ch fnl 2f* **16/1**

15 **15** *11* **Flying Valentino**[20] 4583 4-8-11 **77**........ PJMcDonald(3) 10 18
(G A Swinbank) *racd in midfield: rdn over 3f out: sn lost pl: no ch fnl 2f: eased ins fnl f: t.o* **25/1**

1m 40.26s (0.36) **Going Correction** +0.125s/f (Slow)
WFA 3 from 4yo+ 6lb 15 Ran SP% **126.8**
Speed ratings (Par 107): **103,100,99,99,99 98,97,94,94,88 85,84,82,82,71**
toteswinger: 1&2 £48.90, 1&3 £33.80, 2&3 £18.00. CSF £152.14 CT £753.35 TOTE £16.30: £5.30, £5.00, £3.00; EX 149.50 TRIFECTA Not won..
Owner Dean Fleming **Bred** Heaven Trees Farm **Trained** Manton, Wilts

FOCUS
This was an open handicap, run at a fair pace. The form looks good for the grade with a personal best from the winner.

NOTEBOOK
Irish Mayhem(USA) had lost his way after winning a decent handicap at Yarmouth in April and was making his All-Weather bow. He was given time to find his feet from off the pace before making his move nearing the final bend and ran on strongly when asked for maximum effort. He ultimately scored with a good deal up his sleeve and, considering his US pedigree, it is not the biggest surprise that the switch to this surface worked the oracle. It is fair to expect connections to now search for a suitable for him under a penalty and he will be high on confidence again now. (op 14-1 tchd 16-1)
Yarqus has proved himself on the All-Weather in the past and he turned in a brave effort under his big weight. He holds no secrets from the Handicapper and rates the benchmark for this form, but few would argue he richly deserves to find another opening. (op 14-1)
Hazzard County(USA) stayed on stoutly having been set a fair amount to do from off the pace and is another who gives the form a sound look. He confirmed course-and-distance running with Furnace.
Mount Hermon(IRE) was not really at his best and was certainly not helped by being housed in the outside stall. (op 15-2)
Trans Siberian enjoyed the return to this surface and posted a solid effort from the front considering he took time to settle through the early parts. This was a lot better from him. (op 10-1)
Furnace(IRE) was taken to the inside after a sluggish start and emerged with a chance in the home straight, only to find the same pace.
Kings Point(IRE) was given a very positive ride from his wide draw and kept on gamely enough under maximum pressure down the home straight. (op 14-1)
Grand Vizier(IRE), who was unbeaten on each of his three previous outings on the all-weather, was given a lot to do from off the pace and was always getting there too late down the home straight. He was still not helped by his outside stall, but a return to more slightly positive handling now looks in order. (op 10-1)
Dear Maurice, returning from a 45-day break, was forced to race wide on this first taste of the all-weather and his effort proved short-lived. He now has something to prove. (tchd 6-1)

5208 MARKS HALL CONDITIONS STKS 1m (P)
4:25 (4:25) (Class 3) 3-Y-O+ **£7,569** (£2,265; £1,132; £566; £282) **Stalls** Centre

Form RPR

3000 **1** **Royal Power (IRE)**[20] 4587 5-9-1 96........ AdrianTNicholls 5 108+
(D Nicholls) *stdd s: hld up bhd: gng wl and nt clr run 2f out: sn swtchd rt and nt clr run again: sn swtchd sharply lft: rdn and qcknd to ld ins fnl f: readily* **12/1**

-136 **2** *1¾* **Igor Protti**[168] 817 6-9-1 109........(b) LDettori 3 104
(Saeed Bin Suroor) *t.k.h: chsd ldng pair: hdwy to ld over 2f out: rdn wl over 1f out: hdd and nt pce of wnr fnl 100yds* **11/1**

2232 **3** *hd* **Masaalek**[20] 4587 3-8-12 106........ RHills 6 106
(M P Tregoning) *dwlt: bhd: rdn over 3f out: hdwy u.p jst over 2f out: edgd lft and ev ch ent fnl f: nt qckn and outpcd fnl 100yds* **4/6**[1]

3305 **4** *2¼* **Vanderlin**[40] 3946 9-8-10 100........ DavidProbert(5) 9 98
(A M Balding) *awkward s: racd off the pce in midfield: rdn to chse ldr wl over 1f out tl jst over 1f out: btn whn short of room wl ins fnl f* **8/1**[3]

-104 **5** *6* **Jack Junior (USA)**[28] 4330 4-9-4 95........ TQuinn 2 88+
(B J Meehan) *stall nt open fully: v.s.a: wl detached in last: r.o past btn horses fnl f: no ch* **14/1**

3006 **6** ¾ **Azarole (IRE)**[40] 3946 7-9-1 96........ JohnEgan 8 83
(Jane Chapple-Hyam) *hld up bhd: rdn over 2f out: wknd over 1f out* **20/1**

1230 **7** ½ **Xpres Maite**[82] 2593 5-9-1 92........(v) MickyFenton 7 82
(S R Bowring) *led and sn clr: rdn over 3f out: hdd over 2f out: wkng whn edgd rt over 1f out* **33/1**

6105 **8** ¾ **Scartozz**[12] 4845 6-8-8 97........(b) AndreaAtzeni(7) 4 80
(M Botti) *chsd ldr tl 2f out: rdn and edgd lft over 1f out: struggling whn hmpd ent fnl f: no ch after* **20/1**

2-20 **9** *1½* **Hurricane Hymnbook (USA)**[63] 3155 3-8-9 97........ EddieAhern 1 77
(B J Meehan) *racd in midfield: rdn and effrt over 2f out: wknd over 1f out: wl btn whn eased fnl f* **9/2**[2]

1m 40.94s (1.04) **Going Correction** +0.125s/f (Slow)
WFA 3 from 4yo+ 6lb 9 Ran SP% **124.4**
Speed ratings (Par 107): **99,97,97,94,88 88,87,86,85**
toteswinger: 1&2 £23.50, 1&3 £5.20, 2&3 £4.50. CSF £139.39 TOTE £18.20: £3.40, £2.80, £1.10; EX 172.80 Trifecta £239.50 Pool: £579.46. 1.79 winning units..
Owner D Nicholls **Bred** Denis McDonnell **Trained** Sessay, N Yorks

FOCUS
A decent conditions event that was run at a solid pace. The first four came clear and the winner is rated back to his best.

NOTEBOOK
Royal Power(IRE) ran out a ready winner on this switch to the all-weather and can be rated value for a little further than the winning margin. He swung into the home straight and had to switch twice for his effort after finding trouble. His response when asked to win the race up the far rail was most positive and this surface clearly suits, as he had finished second to Asset in the Easter Stakes at Kempton on his only other previous outing on sand back in 2006. His third in this year's Royal Hunt Cup confirmed he still has an engine and he had been drawn out of things the next twice, so this was deserved. A likely rise in the ratings will now likely dictate a move back up into Listed company is on the cards for him, but he did win the German 2000 Guineas when trained by Mick Channon and could well make his mark at that level now. (op 14-1)
Igor Protti, having his first outing for 168 days, proved very easy to back on this comeback yet ran very encouragingly. With an official mark of 109 he was the highest rated and could have been expected to score, but the run was likely needed and he ought to come on a deal for this. (op 6-1)
Masaalek was very well backed for this return to the All-Weather and looked the one to beat after his recent placed efforts in some of the hottest handicaps of the year to date. He came with every chance in the home straight, but he did not find a great deal when push really came to shove. He had to come wide into the home straight, but the fact he failed to get on top of the runner-up would suggest he may just have some temperament. The application of some headgear could now prove a wise move. (op Evens)
Vanderlin had to race wide from his outside stall, but he still ran close to his recent level in defeat and helps to set the standard of the form. (tchd 15-2)
Jack Junior(USA)'s stall failed to open with the rest of the field and he lost around eight lengths at the start. He is obviously forgiven this run. Official explanation: starter said, regarding why stall failed open with other stalls, he was satisfied they all released at once and a false start was not necessary but in his view colt's nose had been caught in the bars of the gates; jockey said, having anticipated the start, colt then sat back as one half of the gates opened, preventing him from exiting the stalls (op 16-1 tchd 12-1)
Hurricane Hymnbook(USA) has been gelded since disappointing in the Britannia in June, but after travelling nicely enough off the pace his response when asked to make up his ground was very limited. It may be that he did not act on the new surface, but this effort still leaves him with a good deal to prove. (op 7-1)

5209 FAIRSTEAD H'CAP 1m 2f (P)
5:00 (5:00) (Class 4) (0-85,89) 3-Y-O+ **£4,857** (£1,445; £541; £541) **Stalls** Low

Form RPR

5403 **1** **Legislation**[22] 4539 3-9-4 **82**........(b) LDettori 6 92
(J H M Gosden) *mde all: rdn wl over 1f out: clr ins fnl f: eased towards fin* **6/1**[2]

3023 **2** *2* **Del Mar Sunset**[14] 4771 9-9-4 **74**........ LiamJones 7 80
(W J Haggas) *t.k.h: hld up towards rr: hdwy 2f out: plld out and rdn over 1f out: styd on u.p fnl f: wnt 2nd nr fin but nvr chal wnr* **17/2**
4201 **3** *3/4* **Mazaaya (USA)**[11] 4894 3-9-11 **89** 6ex........ TedDurcan 1 94
(D R Lanigan) *chsd ldr tl 5f out: styd handy: kpt on same pce u.p fr over 1f out* **13/2**[3]
2155 **3** *dht* **Formation (USA)**[17] 4694 3-9-6 **84**........ EddieAhern 8 89
(E A L Dunlop) *t.k.h: hld up in midfield: hdwy 3f out: chsd wnr over 1f out: flashed tail and edgd lft: fnd nil and no imp fnl f* **8/1**
1422 **5** *1 3/4* **Ornella**[9] 4945 4-8-13 **72**........ TravisBlock(3) 4 73
(H Morrison) *hld up in midfield: n.m.r over 2f out: drvn and effrt over 1f out: plugged on same pce fnl f* **9/2**[1]
4P10 **6** *1/2* **Alfie Tupper (IRE)**[14] 4791 5-8-5 **66**........ JackMitchell(5) 2 66
(J R Boyle) *in tch on inner: rdn over 2f out: keeping on same pce whn hit on nose by rivals whip 1f out: one pce* **20/1**
1233 **7** *1/2* **Hilbre Court (USA)**[15] 4731 3-9-4 **82**........ RobertWinston 13 81
(B J Meehan) *chsd ldrs: wnt 2nd 5f out: rdn and chal 3f out: lost 2nd over 1f out: hld whn short of room ins fnl f* **8/1**
2631 **8** *7* **Finmore Queen (USA)**[33] 4183 3-9-1 **79**........ AdamKirby 11 64
(J R Fanshawe) *hld up in midfield: hdwy over 4f out: rdn andn struggling over 2f out: no ch fnl 2f* **9/2**[1]
5000 **9** *hd* **Risque Heights**[43] 3836 4-9-2 **72**........ PatCosgrave 14 57
(J R Boyle) *stdd s: hld up bhd: nvr on terms* **16/1**
-206 **10** *shd* **King Columbo (IRE)**[35] 4128 3-9-2 **83**........ RussellKennemore(3) 3 67
(Miss J Feilden) *chsd ldrs: rdn along 8f out: reminders over 4f out: drvn 3f out: wknd over 2f out* **16/1**
550 **11** *3/4* **Shake On It**[55] 3440 4-9-9 **79**........ JimCrowley 10 62
(Eve Johnson Houghton) *a towards rr: nvr a factor* **16/1**
6060 **12** *9* **Tilapia (IRE)**[11] 4894 4-9-7 **84**........ KylieManser(7) 9 49
(Miss Gay Kelleway) *stdd s: hld up bhd: lost tch over 3f out* **40/1**
-000 **13** *3 1/2* **Abydos**[35] 4131 4-9-3 **73**........(p) TPQueally 5 31
(A P Stringer) *stdd s: t.k.h: hld up bhd: no ch whn rn v wd bnd 2f out: t.o* **33/1**

2m 8.39s (-0.21) **Going Correction** +0.125s/f (Slow)
WFA 3 from 4yo+ 8lb **13** Ran SP% **124.5**
Speed ratings (Par 105): **105,103,102,102,101 101,100,95,94,94 94,86,84**PL: Maz £1.40, W. Formation £1.50. TC: M £176.51; WF £211.73 toteswinger: L&DMS £9.10, L&M £6.10, L&F £4.40, DMS&M £5.80, DMS&F £5.70. TRIFECTA: £109.10 (M): Part won. 0.79 w/u. £131.00 (WF) 1.20 w/u. Pool: £354.12. Place 6: £96.67, Place 5: £46.79. CSF £57.7927 CT £Owner TOTE £H R H Princess Haya Of Jordan: £Bred, £Elsdon Farms, £Trained, £Newmarket, Suffolk .

FOCUS
A fair handicap for the class which was run at an uneven pace. The form can be rated through the solid runner-up with the winner up 5lb.
Abydos Official explanation: jockey said gelding hung right up the straight
T/Plt: £103.60 to a £1 stake. Pool: £76,074.01. 536.01 winning tickets. T/Qpdt: £40.20 to a £1 stake. Pool: £5,091.12. 93.70 winning tickets. SP

4434 YORK (L-H)
Thursday, August 21
5210 Meeting Abandoned - Waterlogged

5116 BATH (L-H)
Friday, August 22
OFFICIAL GOING: Good to soft (7.2)
Wind: Moderate, half-against

5213 BATH ALES HOP POLE MAIDEN AUCTION STKS 5f 161y
5:30 (5:30) (Class 5) 2-Y-O **£2,590** (£770; £385; £192) **Stalls** Centre

Form RPR
1 **Peking Prince** 2-8-3 0........ DavidProbert(5) 2 76+
(A M Balding) *stdd s: sn mid-div: hdwy on ins 2f out: pushed out fnl f: comf* **20/1**
03 **2** *2 3/4* **Blackwater Fort (USA)**[32] 4243 2-8-8 0........ FergusSweeney 14 64
(J Gallagher) *nvr far away on outside: rdn to chse wnr appr fnl f: no imp ins fnl f* **22/1**
0 **3** *1/2* **Lady Mulligan**[73] 2916 2-8-4 0 ow5........ JackDean(5) 11 63+
(M Blanshard) *mid-div: rdn 2f out: prom whn hung lft over 1f out: styd on ins fnl f* **66/1**
5 **4** *shd* **Perfect Friend**[8] 5021 2-8-3 0........ RichardThomas 9 57
(S Kirk) *s.i.s: sn in tch: rdn 2f out: kpt on one pce fnl f* **16/1**
04 **5** *1 1/4* **Mr Flannegan**[9] 4973 2-8-9 0........ DaneO'Neill 7 59
(H Candy) *trckd ldr: led over 2f out: hung lft and hdd appr fnl f: wknd ins fnl f* **9/1**
6 *3/4* **Perfect Class** 2-8-11 0........ AdamKirby 6 58
(C G Cox) *s.i.s: sn in tch: ev ch over 2f out: sn rdn: wknd ins fnl f* **6/1**[3]
3 **7** *3/4* **Edgeworth (IRE)**[21] 4579 2-8-10 0........ CatherineGannon 13 55
(B G Powell) *in rr: kpt on past btn horses fr over 1f out* **16/1**
005 **8** *nk* **Spring Quartet**[11] 4926 2-9-0 0........ ChrisCatlin 12 58
(Pat Eddery) *a towards rr* **25/1**
9 *3 1/4* **Jessy Jones** 2-8-0 0........ DominicFox(3) 1 36
(R Brotherton) *slowly away: a bhd* **100/1**
04 **10** *2* **Rockfella**[43] 3888 2-9-1 0........ TPO'Shea 10 42
(D J Coakley) *a bhd* **12/1**
3 **11** *2 3/4* **Safari Guide**[12] 4907 2-8-11 0........ StephenCarson 3 29
(P Winkworth) *led for 2f: sn wknd* **6/1**[3]
0323 **12** *2 1/4* **My Best Man**[28] 4367 2-8-12 75........ TGMcLaughlin 5 22
(B R Millman) *in tch: rdn over 2f out: wkng whn hmpd over 1f out* **8/1**
3 **13** *3 1/4* **Ziggy Lee**[55] 3485 2-8-10 0........ JamesDoyle 8 9
(S C Williams) *mid-div: rdn 1/2-way: wknd over 1f out* **5/1**[2]
3603 **14** *3 1/2* **Riflessione**[10] 4942 2-8-9 75........(p) LukeMorris(3) 4 —
(J S Moore) *prom: rdn whn hmpd and stmbld over 1f out: lost all ch and eased* **3/1**[1]

1m 14.93s (3.73) **Going Correction** +0.45s/f (Yiel) **14** Ran SP% **126.2**
Speed ratings (Par 94): **93,89,88,88,86 85,84,84,80,77 73,70,66,61**
toteswinger: 1&2 £18.50, 1&3 £50.20, 2&3 £50.20. CSF £402.02 TOTE £27.90: £5.20, £8.00, £22.60; EX 798.50.
Owner Kingsclere Racing CLub **Bred** Kingsclere Stud **Trained** Kingsclere, Hants
■ Stewards' Enquiry : Dane O'Neill two-day ban: careless riding (Sep 5 & 7)

FOCUS
A modest event.

NOTEBOOK
Peking Prince failed to attract much interest at the sales, going for just £1,700, and has already been gelded, but put up a decent performance on his debut. He was always well positioned, squeezed through on the far rail and quickened to win with plenty in hand. The form looks a bit suspect but he is a long-striding individual who should improve for this experience. (op 18-1 tchd 22-1)
Blackwater Fort(USA) looked a big threat at the furlong pole but could not cope with the potentially decent newcomer. This was however a pleasing effort on his debut for a new yard after being claimed for £6,000 last time. (op 16-1)
Lady Mulligan, whose rider's overweight nullified his claim, caught the eye staying on late after being trapped for room in the closing stages and stepped up significantly on her modest debut run in June.
Perfect Friend was denied a run on a couple of occasions but stayed on steadily and probably ran a bit better than the result suggests. (op 11-1)
Mr Flannegan raced up with the pace and showed up well for a long way. A drop to 5f on an easier track could suit and he may be able to make an impact when switched to nursery company. (op 8-1 tchd 10-1)
Perfect Class was prominent in the betting, travelled well for a long way and ran a promising race on her debut. (op 9-2)
Safari Guide Official explanation: jockey said colt stopped very quickly
Riflessione was a bit keen early, never looked entirely comfortable and was in serious trouble when stumbling. Official explanation: jockey said colt had clipped heels (op 5-1)

5214 E.B.F./BATH ALES SALAMANDER MAIDEN FILLIES' STKS 5f 11y
6:00 (6:02) (Class 5) 2-Y-O **£3,561** (£1,059; £529; £264) **Stalls** Centre

Form RPR
4 **1** **Happy Forever (FR)**[44] 3837 2-8-9 0........ JackMitchell(5) 8 79+
(M Botti) *mde all: pushed out and in command fnl f* **6/1**[3]
4 **2** *2* **Yanza**[15] 4763 2-8-9 0........ DavidProbert(5) 4 72
(J R Gask) *chsd wnr thrght: rdn over 1f out: no imp fnl f* **12/1**
0 **3** *1 1/4* **Smokey Ryder**[15] 4786 2-9-0 0........ FergusSweeney 13 67
(G L Moore) *mid-div: rdn and hdwy 2f out: chsd ldrs over 1f out: kpt on fnl f* **16/1**
2423 **4** *5* **Sterling Sound (USA)**[23] 4521 2-9-0 76........ DaneO'Neill 12 49
(M P Tregoning) *in tch: rdn 2f out: edgd lft and fdd fnl f* **5/2**[1]
0 **5** *nk* **Luvmedo (IRE)**[60] 3315 2-9-0 0........ RichardSmith 9 48
(R Hannon) *s.i.s: sn mid-div: rdn over 2f out: wknd over 1f out* **40/1**
04 **6** *3/4* **On The Feather**[37] 4088 2-9-0 0........ StephenCarson 7 45
(P Winkworth) *trckd ldrs tl rdn and wknd over 1f out* **10/1**
7 *shd* **Rathlin Light (USA)** 2-9-0 0........ AdamKirby 10 45
(W R Swinburn) *chsd ldrs: rdn 2f out: wknd fnl f* **6/1**[3]
0 **8** *1* **Midnight Fantasy**[34] 4202 2-9-0 0........ ChrisCatlin 1 41
(Rae Guest) *in tch on ins tl rdn and wknd over 1f out* **11/1**
9 *3/4* **Final Rhapsody** 2-9-0 0........ RichardThomas 2 39
(J A Geake) *s.i.s: towards rr whn swtchd lft over 2f out: nvr on terms* **20/1**
02 **10** *nk* **Always There (IRE)**[9] 4980 2-9-0 0........ SebSanders 15 37
(R Hannon) *sn prom on outside: rdn and wknd over 1f out* **11/4**[2]
00 **11** *1/2* **Emerald Lass**[39] 4020 2-9-0 0........ TPO'Shea 3 36
(D J Coakley) *mid-div: rdn over 2f out: wknd over 1f out* **100/1**
12 *3 3/4* **Aine's Delight (IRE)** 2-9-0 0........ AlanDaly 6 22
(Andrew Turnell) *slowly away: a bhd* **80/1**
0 **13** *3/4* **Abacus House (IRE)**[17] 4705 2-8-9 0........ JackDean(5) 5 19
(W G M Turner) *spd to 1/2-way* **100/1**
14 *5* **Micro Chip** 2-8-9 0........ GabrielHannon(5) 14 —
(B G Powell) *slowly away and a outpcd* **50/1**
0 **15** *3 3/4* **Definite Honey**[58] 3358 2-8-7 0........ PNolan(7) 16 —
(A B Haynes) *slowly away: a bhd* **100/1**
40 **16** *19* **Red Myth**[28] 4387 2-9-0 0........(b[1]) TGMcLaughlin 11 —
(Karen George) *a bhd: t.o* **100/1**

64.77 secs (2.27) **Going Correction** +0.45s/f (Yiel) **16** Ran SP% **129.2**
Speed ratings (Par 91): **99,95,93,85,85 84,83,82,81,80 79,73,72,64,58 28**
toteswinger: 1&2 £21.70, 1&3 £32.60, 2&3 Not won. CSF £78.57 TOTE £7.60: £2.30, £5.10, £7.20; EX 134.80.
Owner Mrs R J Jacobs **Bred** Newsells Park Stud **Trained** Newmarket, Suffolk

FOCUS
They went a decent pace.

NOTEBOOK
Happy Forever(FR) showed plenty of speed, seemed to appreciate the give in the ground and got off the mark in decisive style under an enterprising ride. The precocious sort should continue to be campaigned at 5f, has scope for further improvement and should have some realistic opportunities in nursery company this autumn. Official explanation: jockey said filly hung right-handed (op 7-1 tchd 8-1)
Yanza was backed from 20-1 to 12-1, showed good tactical pace against the inside rail from a decent draw and stepped up considerably on her debut form. She should be able to win a similar event. (op 20-1)
Smokey Ryder was a springer in the market. She never really got into a threatening position but did knuckle down well in the closing stages to be nearest at the finish and gave the impression that a step up in trip would suit. (op 40-1 tchd 14-1)
Sterling Sound(USA) had a strong chance on form but could only plug on in the closing stages and was well held. It is possible, though, that the slow ground and drop down to 5f did not suit and she may be worth another chance on quicker ground next time. (op 2-1 tchd 11-4 in a place)
Always There(IRE) had decent claims on the form of her second on soft ground at Sandown last week and managed to get into a good position from a difficult draw, but dropped away quickly when pressure was applied. (op 5-2 tchd 10-3)

5215 BATH ALES WILD HARE ORGANIC ALE (S) STKS 1m 3f 144y
6:30 (6:32) (Class 6) 3-4-Y-O **£1,942** (£578; £288; £144) **Stalls** Low

Form RPR
3100 **1** **Lady Jinks**[16] 4722 3-8-11 52........ HayleyTurner 10 64
(M D I Usher) *trckd ldrs: led over 2f out: rdn clr fnl f* **3/1**[1]
0-50 **2** *3 3/4* **Corking (IRE)**[35] 4173 3-8-6 63........ ChrisCatlin 6 52
(Eve Johnson Houghton) *a.p: led over 4f out: hdd over 2f out: swtchd rt ent fnl f: no imp after* **9/2**[3]
4530 **3** *10* **Balais Folly (FR)**[28] 4366 3-8-6 48........ MCGeran(5) 7 40
(B Palling) *led tl hdd over 4f out: rdn 2f out: wandered u.p fnl f* **13/2**
0230 **4** *4* **Royal Soverin**[16] 4750 3-8-11 50........(v) DaneO'Neill 1 33
(M J Wallace) *mid-div: hdwy 4f out: rdn over 2f out: eased whn lost action appr fnl f* **10/3**[2]
0000 **5** *3 1/2* **Lady Maya**[14] 4807 3-8-2 41 ow3........(v) MatthewCosham(7) 4 25
(Dr J R J Naylor) *in rr: rdn and edgd rt but styd on past btn horses ins fnl 2f* **25/1**
300- **6** *2* **My Beautaful**[8] 6147 4-9-2 53........(t) VinceSlattery 3 19
(Miss J S Davis) *hld up: hdwy over 5f out: chsd ldrs 3f out: wknd over 1f out* **25/1**
0060 **7** *2 1/4* **Xaravella (IRE)**[14] 4810 3-8-3 45........(v[1]) LukeMorris(3) 11 15
(J G M O'Shea) *s.i.s: a towards rr* **9/1**

0-06 **8** *9* **Demure Princess**30 4298 3-8-4 49 ow3........................(p) JackDean(5) 5 3
(W G M Turner) *plld hrd: prom tl rdn and wknd over 3f out* **9/1**
000 **9** *8* **Evianne**17 4698 4-9-2 35............................... TGMcLaughlin 8 —
(P W Hiatt) *in tch: rdn over 2f out: wknd and eased over 1f out* **22/1**
4020 **10** *49* **Paul The Carpet (UAE)**40 3687 3-9-2 45.................. RichardHughes 2 —
(G L Moore) *hld up in rr: eased over 3f out: t.o* **8/1**
000 **11** *14* **Dungleddy Star**17 4707 3-8-6 15.......................... CatherineGannon 14 —
(J M Bradley) *in rr: rdn 1/2-way: sn lost tch: t.o* **50/1**
2m 36.69s (6.09) **Going Correction** +0.45s/f (Yiel)
WFA 3 from 4yo 10lb **11** Ran SP% **124.7**
Speed ratings (Par 101): **97,94,87,85,82 81,80,74,68,36 26**
toteswinger: 1&2 £5.80, 1&3 £3.20, 2&3 £3.80. CSF £17.16 TOTE £3.60: £1.70, £2.60, £2.30; EX 32.70.The winner was sold to D Charlesworth for 7,000gns. Corking was claimed by T. A. Jones for £6,000.
Owner The High Jinks Partnership **Bred** A B Barraclough **Trained** Upper Lambourn, Berks
■ Stewards' Enquiry : Matthew Cosham two-day ban: careless riding (Sep 5, 7)

FOCUS
A modest seller in which the winner showed improved form, although there are doubts over what else ran their race.
Xaravella(IRE) Official explanation: jockey said filly hit its head leaving stalls

5216 BATH ALES SPA H'CAP — 1m 5f 22y
7:00 (7:00) (Class 5) (0-70,70) 3-Y-O — £3,367 (£1,002; £500; £250) Stalls High

Form RPR
006 **1** **Look To This Day**32 4249 3-9-7 70.......................... HayleyTurner 10 79+
(R Charlton) *hld up: hdwy 2f out: edgd lft but led 1f out: rdn clr* **11/1**
523 **2** *3* **Dubai Petal (IRE)**15 4762 3-9-4 70.............................. LukeMorris(3) 9 74+
(J S Moore) *in tch: hdwy 4f out: led briefly over 1f out: squeezed out and swtchd rt jst ins fnl f: r.o to regain 2nd* **2/1**1
0456 **3** *1 1/4* **Abstract Colours (IRE)**71 2977 3-8-10 64.................. DavidProbert(5) 7 66
(A M Balding) *led after 1f: hdd over 1f out: edgd rt and no ex ins fnl f* **9/2**2
0344 **4** *1/2* **Capstan**35 4173 3-9-5 68... DaneO'Neill 1 69
(L M Cumani) *mid-div: rdn over 2f out: kpt on one pce* **9/2**2
044 **5** *1 1/2* **Purely By Chance**54 3521 3-8-13 62..........................(v1) SebSanders 3 61
(R M Beckett) *led for 1f: styd in tch: rdn over 2f out: n.m.r over 1f out: wknd ins fnl f* **11/1**
-423 **6** *1/2* **Berrynarbor**19 4669 3-8-6 55.. FergusSweeney 8 53
(A G Newcombe) *w.w: rdn and hdwy over 2f out: hld whn bmpd over 1f out* **15/2**3
0245 **7** *5* **Kiho**36 4112 3-9-1 64.. StephenCarson 4 55
(Eve Johnson Houghton) *mid-div: hdwy on outside 4f out: rdn over 2f out: hld whn hmpd over 1f out* **10/1**
2000 **8** *1 1/2* **Bainisteoir**8 5020 3-8-2 51 oh2................................(b) CatherineGannon 2 40
(S Kirk) *hld up: rdn 5f out: nvr on terms* **28/1**
3-53 **9** *30* **Foresight**38 4057 3-9-2 65..(b1) JimCrowley 5 9
(Mrs A J Perrett) *t.k.h: sn trckd ldr: wknd over 3f out: eased: t.o* **12/1**
2m 59.33s (7.33) **Going Correction** +0.45s/f (Yiel) **9** Ran SP% **118.4**
Speed ratings (Par 100): **95,93,92,92,91 90,87,86,68**
toteswinger: 1&2 £7.80, 1&3 £11.50, 2&3 £1.20. CSF £34.24 CT £119.22 TOTE £9.40: £2.80, £1.50, £1.60; EX 47.00.
Owner A Parker (London) **Bred** Alan Parker **Trained** Beckhampton, Wilts
■ Stewards' Enquiry : Luke Morris three-day ban: careless riding (Sep 5, 7-8)
Hayley Turner two-day ban: careless riding (Sep 5,7)

FOCUS
The early pace was reasonable but it slackened, and the race developed into a bit of a sprint in the closing stages. The winner is rated up a stone and the form looks pretty sound.
Look To This Day Official explanation: trainer said, regarding running, that the filly was very well at present and may have been suited by the step up in trip.

5217 BATH ALES GEM H'CAP — 5f 11y
7:30 (7:30) (Class 5) (0-70,69) 3-Y-O — £2,719 (£809; £404; £202) Stalls Centre

Form RPR
4240 **1** **Pennyspider (IRE)**10 4958 3-8-13 61.......................... TGMcLaughlin 7 69
(M S Saunders) *mde all: clr whn edgd lft ins fnl f* **6/1**3
0262 **2** *3 1/4* **Towy Boy (IRE)**15 4793 3-9-2 64...............................(t) CatherineGannon 1 60
(I A Wood) *sn rdn in tch: kpt on to chse wnr ins fnl f* **4/1**2
2215 **3** *1/2* **Miss Firefly**3 5171 3-8-12 65...................................... MCGeran(5) 6 60
(R J Hodges) *chsd wnr tl rdn and one pce ins fnl f* **13/2**
451 **4** *2 1/2* **Our Acquaintance**12 4904 3-8-12 65..........................(b) DavidProbert(5) 3 51
(W R Muir) *bmpd leaving stalls: chsd ldrs to 1/2-way: nt qckn after* **1/1**1
362 **5** *1 1/4* **Our Kally**12 4904 3-7-9 50 oh5...................................... BillyCray(7) 4 31
(M D I Usher) *bmpd leaving stalls: rdn and no hdwy fnl 2f* **11/1**
0503 **6** *1* **Meridian Line (IRE)**10 4943 3-9-2 69..........................(b) JackMitchell(5) 5 46
(J G Portman) *slowly away: a bhd* **16/1**
5600 **7** *2 3/4* **Swindon Town Flyer (IRE)**29 4325 3-8-8 63..............(b) GihanArnolda(7) 2 31
(A B Haynes) *swvd rt leaving stalls: in tch to 1/2-way* **25/1**
64.62 secs (2.12) **Going Correction** +0.45s/f (Yiel) **7** Ran SP% **115.7**
Speed ratings (Par 100): **101,95,95,91,89 87,83**
toteswinger: 1&2 £12.30, 1&3 £5.70, 2&3 £4.20. CSF £30.74 TOTE £6.80: £3.80, £3.10; EX 34.30.
Owner Chris Scott **Bred** Tally-Ho Stud **Trained** Green Ore, Somerset
■ Stewards' Enquiry : M C Geran caution: careless riding

FOCUS
A moderate handicap and the form has not been rated too positively.
Meridian Line(IRE) Official explanation: jockey said filly missed the break

5218 BATH ALES BARNSTORMER H'CAP — 1m 5y
8:00 (8:02) (Class 6) (0-65,65) 3-Y-O — £2,266 (£674; £337; £168) Stalls Low

Form RPR
0000 **1** **It's Josr**3 5167 3-8-8 52..(b1) CatherineGannon 16 61
(I A Wood) *led after 1f: rdn 2f out: clr fnl f* **18/1**
442 **2** *2 1/4* **Jollyhockeysticks**5 5119 3-9-5 63.............................. SamHitchcott 10 67
(M R Channon) *mid-div: rdn and hdwy over 1f out: edgd lft but r.o to go 2nd wl ins fnl f* **2/1**1
0055 **3** *1/2* **Bramalea**5 5119 3-9-0 58... JamesDoyle 6 61
(B W Duke) *led for 1f: styd w ldr tl rdn and one pce ins fnl f* **10/1**
-040 **4** *1 1/2* **Encore Belle**29 4349 3-8-10 59................................ DavidProbert(5) 14 59
(Mouse Hamilton-Fairley) *prom: rdn 2f out: sltly hmpd and one pce ins fnl f* **11/1**
034 **5** *3/4* **Duty Doctor**14 4806 3-9-4 62...................................... RichardHughes 15 60
(S Kirk) *hld up: rdn and hdwy over 1f out: one pce fnl f* **5/1**2
000 **6** *5* **Mick's Dancer**20 4637 3-8-11 55................................ HayleyTurner 4 41
(W R Muir) *trckd ldrs: rdn over 2f out: wknd over 1f out* **16/1**
6050 **7** *hd* **Copperwood**13 4863 3-8-12 56.................................. FergusSweeney 2 42
(M Blanshard) *in tch tl wknd appr fnl f* **9/1**

0004 **8** *3/4* **Flying Flute**9 4979 3-9-2 60.. DaneO'Neill 9 44
(H Candy) *s.i.s: a bhd* **7/1**3
3036 **9** *1 1/4* **Christophers Quest**63 3221 3-9-4 65........................ EmmettStack(3) 1 46
(A W Carroll) *mid-div: rdn 3f out: wknd over 1f out* **14/1**
0000 **10** *nse* **Lekezia (IRE)**27 4429 3-8-6 55 ow5.......................... GabrielHannon(5) 7 36
(J W Hills) *mid-div: bhd fnl 3f* **50/1**
-005 **11** *18* **Red Twist**23 4527 3-9-2 63.. TravisBlock(3) 13 3
(H Morrison) *in tch tl lost pl over 3f out: t.o* **8/1**
006 **12** *1/2* **Age Of Miracles (IRE)**45 3823 3-8-1 52.................. MatthewDavies(7) 5 —
(G A Ham) *s.i.s: a bhd: t.o* **50/1**
0-00 **13** *8* **Promised Gold**23 4527 3-8-5 52................................(p) LukeMorris(3) 11 —
(J A Geake) *a bhd: t.o* **40/1**
1m 44.33s (3.53) **Going Correction** +0.45s/f (Yiel) **13** Ran SP% **125.2**
Speed ratings (Par 98): **100,97,97,95,95 90,89,89,87,87 69,69,61**
toteswinger: 1&2 £46.50, 1&3 Not won, 2&3 £10.60. CSF £56.29 CT £426.44 TOTE £25.70: £5.70, £1.60, £2.40; EX 75.90 Place 6 £2730.81, Place 5 £80.32..
Owner G R Jones **Bred** Dr A Ramkaran **Trained** Upper Lambourn, Berks
■ Stewards' Enquiry : Sam Hitchcott caution: careless riding

FOCUS
Only a couple of runners arrived here in decent form and the unexposed types had not done much to enthuse about, but the first five did finish some way clear of the rest.The form does look quite sound, with the winner back to his 2yo best.
Flying Flute Official explanation: jockey said gelding hung left
T/Plt: £6,645.30 to a £1 stake. Pool: £60,991.53. 6.70 winning tickets. T/Qpdt: £21.30 to a £1 stake. Pool: £7,913.70. 274.80 winning tickets. JS

4967

HAMILTON (R-H)
Friday, August 22

OFFICIAL GOING: Soft (7.1)
Wind: Nil Weather: Overcast

5219 MCKENNA / FRIEL MAIDEN AUCTION FILLIES' STKS — 6f 5y
5:50 (5:51) (Class 5) 2-Y-O — £3,885 (£1,156; £577; £288) Stalls Low

Form RPR
035 **1** **Lady Salama**19 4658 2-8-13 64.................................... AndrewElliott 3 64
(K R Burke) *chsd ldrs: effrt over 1f out: rdr dropped whip ins fnl f: styd on to ld last 50yds* **2/1**1
0 **2** *1* **Asserting**39 4014 2-8-4 0... AdrianTNicholls 8 52
(A G Foster) *led: rdn over 1f out: hdd and no ex last 50yds* **9/2**3
3 *4* **Highly Acclaimed** 2-8-4 0.. AndrewMullen(3) 2 43
(Mrs A Duffield) *in tch: hdwy 1/2-way: effrt over 1f out: sn outpcd* **2/1**1
02 **4** *5* **Miss Scarlet**22 4562 2-8-11 0...................................... FergalLynch 6 32
(K A Ryan) *cl up tl rdn and wknd fr 2f out* **4/1**2
00 **5** *3 1/2* **Kilsyth (IRE)**9 4965 2-8-11 0 ow2.................................. LeeEnstone 5 22
(S Parr) *in tch tl hung rt and wknd over 2f out* **12/1**
1m 16.36s (4.16) **Going Correction** +0.475s/f (Yiel) **5** Ran SP% **112.5**
Speed ratings (Par 91): **91,89,84,77,73**
toteswinger: 1&2 £3.70. (Only 5 ran) CSF £11.61 TOTE £3.20: £1.10, £3.40; EX 16.10.
Owner S Marley & S Hyypia **Bred** David John Brown **Trained** Middleham Moor, N Yorks

FOCUS
This looked a very maiden, only marginally better than selling class.

NOTEBOOK
Lady Salama, whose trainer has a 26 per cent strike-rate with his juveniles at this track, in the end saw the trip out just that bit better than the runner-up. She was dropping back in distance from 7f and as a result she settled better, but the soft ground over this stiff 6f also made it quite a test. She wore down the leader inside the last despite her rider dropping his whip, and on this evidence she will ultimately be happier back over 7f. (tchd 15-8 and 9-4 and 5-2 in a place)
Asserting was always behind and finished last on her debut at Ayr, but she had clearly learned plenty for that experience and, showing good pace from the off, coped well with conditions and looked the winner a furlong out. She should be able to find a little race if continuing to progress. (op 10-1)
Highly Acclaimed came in for good support on this debut, but she ran green and did not help her rider by hanging to her right in the closing stages. She has a speedy pedigree and will know more next time. Faster ground will also be in her favour. (op 7-2 tchd 4-1)
Miss Scarlet drifted badly in the market beforehand and failed miserably to run to her Nottingham form on this softer ground. Nurseries are now an option for her. Official explanation: trainer said filly was unsuited by the soft ground (op 13-8)
Kilsyth(IRE) has now had three starts and has yet to beat a single rival. (op 14-1 tchd 16-1)

5220 TARMAC H'CAP — 5f 4y
6:20 (6:20) (Class 5) (0-70,70) 3-Y-O+ — £3,885 (£1,156; £577; £288) Stalls Low

Form RPR
1035 **1** **Rothesay Dancer**9 4971 5-9-4 70.............................. KellyHarrison(5) 4 77
(J S Goldie) *hld up in tch: smooth hdwy over 1f out: led ins fnl f: pushed out* **3/1**2
101 **2** *1* **By The Edge (IRE)**8 5007 4-8-12 66 6ex.................. DeanHeslop(7) 2 69
(T D Barron) *chsd ldrs: effrt 2f out: led briefly ent fnl f: kpt on towards fin* **11/10**1
5510 **3** *2 3/4* **Mr Rooney (IRE)**13 4846 5-8-8 60................................ SladeO'Hara(5) 3 54
(A Berry) *led: hung rt thrght: hdd ent fnl f: one pce* **9/2**3
5464 **4** *1 1/2* **Howards Prince**9 4967 5-8-6 60 oh6 ow9.................... PaulPickard(7) 1 48
(D A Nolan) *dwlt: bhd: hdwy over 1f out: no imp fnl f* **10/1**
0045 **5** *3* **Seafield Towers**10 4950 8-8-4 51 oh1..........................(p) AndrewElliott 5 28
(D A Nolan) *chsd ldrs tl edgd rt and no ex wl over 1f out* **8/1**
0600 **6** *1 1/4* **Percy Douglas**10 4950 8-8-4 56 oh6 ow5....................(p) AnnStokell(5) 7 29
(Miss A Stokell) *in tch: outpcd 1/2-way: n.d after* **25/1**
0000 **7** *12* **Mister Marmaduke**10 4950 7-8-5 59 oh6 ow8...........(t) JamesRogers(7) 6 —
(D A Nolan) *missed break: nvr on terms* **200/1**
0000 **8** *1/2* **Sokoke**20 4632 7-8-0 52 oh6 ow1.................................. PatrickDonaghy(5) 9 —
(D A Nolan) *chsd ldrs tl wknd over 2f out* **150/1**
62.13 secs (2.13) **Going Correction** +0.475s/f (Yiel) **8** Ran SP% **116.0**
Speed ratings (Par 103): **101,99,95,92,87 85,66,65**
toteswinger: 1&2 £1.80, 1&3 £2.80, 2&3 £2.30. CSF £6.77 CT £13.56 TOTE £3.60: £1.10, £1.20, £1.80; EX 8.20.
Owner Highland Racing **Bred** Frank Brady **Trained** Uplawmoor, E Renfrews

FOCUS
With only three in the handicap proper this looked a rather uncompetitive contest. The form is rated around the first two.

5221 HAMILTON-PARK.CO.UK CLAIMING STKS — 1m 1f 36y
6:50 (6:50) (Class 4) 3-5-Y-O — £6,476 (£1,927; £963; £481) Stalls High

Form RPR
0260 **1** **Moody Tunes**41 3972 5-9-4 77.................................. DarrenWilliams 4 75
(K R Burke) *cl up: led over 2f out: drvn out* **2/1**1

0561 **2** *1* **Sweet World**[12] 4899 4-8-10 50 PaulMulrennan 1 65
(B J Llewellyn) *led to over 2f out: drvn and rallied over 1f out: kpt on towards fin* **15/2**

0010 **3** *1 1/4* **Grethel (IRE)**[15] 4785 4-8-8 62 ow2 SladeO'Hara(5) 6 65
(A Berry) *sn chsng ldrs: rdn over 2f out: kpt on same pce fnl f* **7/1**

5652 **4** *2* **Jamieson Gold (IRE)**[27] 4419 5-9-2 75 (p) PaulFessey 5 64
(Miss L A Perratt) *hld up in tch: drvn and outpcd 4f out: rallied over 1f out: nvr rchd ldrs* **7/2**[3]

6002 **5** *2* **White Deer (USA)**[20] 4627 4-9-9 82 (b[1]) AdrianTNicholls 3 66
(D Nicholls) *plld hrd: hld up in tch: drvn 4f out: edgd rt and no imp fr 2f out* **3/1**[2]

3364 **6** *3* **Bourse (IRE)**[10] 4952 3-7-13 64 ow1 PatrickDonaghy(5) 2 48
(R Johnson) *in tch: rdn 4f out: sn outpcd: n.d after* **14/1**

2m 3.81s (4.11) **Going Correction** +0.60s/f (Yiel)
WFA 3 from 4yo+ 7lb **6** Ran SP% **111.5**
Speed ratings (Par 105): **105,104,103,101,99 96**
toteswinger: 1&2 £5.10, 1&3 £3.40, 2&3 £9.70. CSF £17.13 TOTE £2.80: £1.60, £2.80; EX 15.30.
Owner Geoffrey Hamilton **Bred** Llety Stud **Trained** Middleham Moor, N Yorks

FOCUS
A competitive claimer on paper and not a bad race of its type. The whole field came towards the stands' side in the straight. The winner made hard work of it and the third looks the best guide to the form.

5222 OFFICER AND A GENTLEMAN H'CAP 6f 5y
7:20 (7:21) (Class 4) (0-80,80) 3-Y-0+ **£7,123** (£2,119; £1,059; £529) **Stalls** Low

Form RPR

2600 **1** **Mister Hardy**[19] 4661 3-9-0 **80** FrederikTylicki(7) 4 89
(R A Fahey) *cl up: led over 2f out: hld on wl fnl f* **8/1**[2]

2133 **2** *nk* **Grazeon Gold Blend**[18] 4687 5-9-4 **77** PJMcDonald(3) 7 85
(J J Quinn) *in midfield: effrt 2f out: chsd wnr ins fnl f: kpt on fin* **7/1**[1]

0500 **3** *1* **Ice Planet**[28] 4393 7-9-6 **76** AdrianTNicholls 8 81
(D Nicholls) *towards rr: swtchd rt and hdwy over 1f out: r.o fnl f* **8/1**[2]

5515 **4** *3/4* **Makshoof (IRE)**[40] 3998 4-9-6 **76** FergalLynch 5 78+
(K A Ryan) *in midfield: effrt 2f out: kpt on ins fnl f* **8/1**[2]

4000 **5** *1/2* **Dickie Le Davoir**[26] 4460 4-9-10 **80** J-PGuillambert 9 81
(John A Harris) *towards rr: hdwy 2f out: one pce fnl f* **20/1**

0204 **6** *shd* **Yorkshire Blue**[13] 4875 9-8-5 **66** KellyHarrison(5) 2 66
(J S Goldie) *dwlt: bhd tl styd on fnl f: nrst fin* **10/1**

5132 **7** *1 1/4* **Katie Boo (IRE)**[9] 4971 6-9-3 **73** PaulMulrennan 12 69
(A Berry) *in tch: effrt 2f out: one pce appr fnl f* **8/1**[2]

0440 **8** *hd* **Paris Bell**[32] 4239 6-8-7 **66** DuranFentiman(3) 11 62
(T D Easterby) *dwlt: bhd: hdwy over 1f out: r.o: no imp* **9/1**

0060 **9** *3/4* **Ingleby Arch (USA)**[33] 4218 5-9-9 **79** PaulFessey 14 72
(T D Barron) *bhd on outside: drvn 1/2-way: sme late hdwy: n.d* **14/1**

0061 **10** *2* **Lucayos**[17] 4700 5-9-7 **77** DarrenWilliams 3 64
(K R Burke) *chsd ldrs tl wknd over 1f out: eased whn btn ins fnl f* **9/1**

0245 **11** *shd* **Hotham**[13] 4854 5-9-2 **77** SladeO'Hara(5) 1 64
(N Wilson) *prom: rdn and hung rt wl over 1f out: sn btn* **17/2**[3]

6-01 **12** *1* **Angle Of Attack (IRE)**[9] 4971 3-8-10 **76** 6ex JamesRogers(7) 6 60
(A D Brown) *led to over 2f out: wknd over 1f out* **9/1**

6004 **13** *7* **Steel City Boy (IRE)**[9] 4971 5-8-4 **65** ow2 AnnStokell(5) 13 26
(Miss A Stokell) *bhd: struggling 1/2-way: eased whn no ch fnl f* **16/1**

51-2 **14** *6* **Seta Pura**[51] 3601 3-8-6 **68** AndrewMullen(3) 10 10
(Mrs A Duffield) *chsd ldrs tl wknd over 2f out* **20/1**

1m 14.16s (1.96) **Going Correction** +0.475s/f (Yiel)
WFA 3 from 4yo+ 3lb **14** Ran SP% **128.6**
Speed ratings (Par 105): **105,104,103,102,101 101,99,99,98,95 95,94,85,77**
toteswinger: 1&2 £27.50, 1&3 £24.70, 2&3 £16.60. CSF £67.59 CT £476.43 TOTE £12.50: £4.00, £3.20, £2.60; EX 112.90.
Owner The Cosmic Cases **Bred** Mrs M Bryce **Trained** Musley Bank, N Yorks

FOCUS
A wide-open handicap in which they went 7-1 the field. Solid form for the grade with the winner back to his 2-y-o best.
Hotham Official explanation: trainer said gelding was unsuited by the soft ground
Steel City Boy(IRE) Official explanation: jockey said gelding never travelled

5223 FRANK FLYNN & CO ACCOUNTANTS 25TH ANNIVERSARY RATING RELATED MAIDEN STKS 1m 4f 17y
7:50 (7:50) (Class 6) 3-5-Y-0 **£2,388** (£705; £352) **Stalls** High

Form RPR

4300 **1** **Prince Rhyddarch**[78] 2750 3-9-0 51 PaulFessey 7 69
(Miss L A Perratt) *prom: led over 3f out: pushed clr fr over 2f out* **7/1**

5220 **2** *18* **River Kent**[49] 3666 3-9-0 55 PaulMulrennan 1 44
(Mrs A Duffield) *chsd ldrs: rdn and hung rt 3f out: sn chsng wnr: sn no imp* **11/2**[3]

0-52 **3** *5* **Suite Francaise**[15] 4762 3-8-11 58 J-PGuillambert 5 34
(Sir Mark Prescott) *t.k.h: mde most to over 3f out: wknd over 2f out* **8/13**[1]

40 **4** *9* **Martingrange Lass (IRE)**[21] 4607 3-8-11 49 (p) DaleGibson 4 21
(S Parr) *hld up: outpcd over 5f out: n.d after* **40/1**

0660 **5** *2 3/4* **Scanno (IRE)**[10] 4952 3-8-8 47 ow1 GarryWhillans(7) 6 22
(M Mullineaux) *w ldr tl wknd fr 3f out* **66/1**

000- **6** *20* **Jumpin Johnnie**[265] 6998 3-8-7 47 DeanHeslop(7) 2 —
(M Mullineaux) *prom: outpcd 1/2-way: sn n.d* **40/1**

0023 **7** *7* **Afton View (IRE)**[10] 4952 3-9-0 57 (bt) LeeEnstone 3 —
(S Parr) *hld up: shortlived effrt 4f out: sn wknd* **9/2**[2]

2m 45.44s (6.84) **Going Correction** +0.60s/f (Yiel) **7** Ran SP% **114.4**
Speed ratings (Par 101): **101,89,85,79,77 64,59**
toteswinger: 1&2 £3.20, 1&3 £1.40, 2&3 £1.40. CSF £43.52 TOTE £11.10: £3.70, £2.20; EX 57.90.
Owner Hamilton Park Members Syndicate II **Bred** Ian Murray Tough **Trained** Carluke, S Lanarks

FOCUS
A poor maiden on paper but it was won in runaway style by Prince Rhyddarch. He has obviously improved for the soft ground but there are clear doubts over quite what he achieved.

5224 FIRST INDEPENDENT FINANCE H'CAP 1m 65y
8:20 (8:20) (Class 5) (0-70,70) 3-Y-0 **£3,885** (£1,156; £577; £288) **Stalls** Low

Form RPR

4520 **1** **Casino Night**[32] 4241 3-8-2 **58** DeanHeslop(7) 3 64
(R Johnson) *hld up: smooth hdwy to ld over 3f out: rdn and hld on wl fnl f* **14/1**

0345 **2** *3/4* **Doon Haymer (IRE)**[19] 4663 3-9-4 **70** PJMcDonald(3) 9 74
(Miss L A Perratt) *led to over 3f out: sn rdn: rallied over 1f out: kpt on ins fnl f* **4/1**[3]

5003 **3** *shd* **Rossini's Dancer**[8] 5008 3-8-2 **54** AndrewMullen(3) 5 58
(R A Fahey) *hld up in tch: drvn and outpcd over 3f out: hdwy over 1f out: kpt on ins fnl f* **11/4**[1]

5412 **4** *3 1/2* **Tamasou (IRE)**[34] 4180 3-9-4 **67** DaleGibson 2 63
(Garry Moss) *cl up: ev ch over 2f out: wknd ins fnl f* **7/2**[2]

0201 **5** *1 3/4* **Red Skipper (IRE)**[10] 4952 3-8-8 **62** 6ex SladeO'Hara(5) 8 54
(N Wilson) *chsd ldrs tl edgd rt and wknd over 1f out* **4/1**[3]

0050 **6** *3/4* **Pequeno Dinero (IRE)**[37] 4077 3-7-12 **52** oh5 ow1 KellyHarrison(5) 7 42
(C W Fairhurst) *prom tl rdn and wknd over 2f out* **18/1**

1100 **7** *3* **Natural Rhythm (IRE)**[9] 4964 3-8-9 **61** (b) MichaelJStainton(3) 1 44
(Mrs R A Carr) *plld hrd in tch: effrt and cl up over 3f out: wknd over 2f out* **12/1**

056 **8** *8* **Kargan (IRE)**[16] 4738 3-8-7 **61** PatrickDonaghy(5) 6 26
(R Johnson) *missed break: bhd: struggling over 3f out: sn btn* **10/1**

1m 52.69s (4.29) **Going Correction** +0.60s/f (Yiel) **8** Ran SP% **117.6**
Speed ratings (Par 100): **102,101,101,97,95 95,92,84**
toteswinger: 1&2 £8.80, 1&3 £6.10, 2&3 £3.90. CSF £71.13 CT £206.69 TOTE £12.20: £3.30, £1.60, £1.60; EX 83.20 Place 6 £71.13, Place 5 £38.49..
Owner Barry Robson **Bred** Kingsmead Breeders **Trained** Newburn, Tyne & Wear
■ Stewards' Enquiry : Dean Heslop two-day ban: used whip with excessive frequency (Sep 5,7)
P J McDonald one-day ban: used whip with excessive frequency (Sep 5)

FOCUS
A tight little handicap and once again the field came across to the stands' side in the straight. Ordinary for, but sound enough.
T/Plt: £206.50 to a £1 stake. Pool: £61,181.00. 216.20 winning tickets. T/Qpdt: £152.40 to a £1 stake. Pool: £4,799.00. 23.30 winning tickets. RY

5092 NEWBURY (L-H)
Friday, August 22

OFFICIAL GOING: Good to soft (good in places; 6.9)
Wind: Virtually nil

5225 RE PERSONNEL MEDIAN AUCTION MAIDEN STKS (DIV I) 7f (S)
1:10 (1:14) (Class 5) 2-Y-0 **£4,209** (£1,252; £625; £312) **Stalls** Centre

Form RPR

0 **1** **Felday**[35] 4151 2-9-0 0 TravisBlock(3) 11 84+
(H Morrison) *in tch: led over 2f out: rdn and edgd lft over 1f out: leant on runner -up and bmpd whn pressed ins fnl f: pushed out towards fin: jst hld on* **9/1**

2 *nse* **Latin Tinge (USA)** 2-8-12 0 GregFairley 7 79+
(P F I Cole) *w ldr and racd keenly: upsides and rdn whn edgd rt and bmpd ins fnl f: r.o wl towards fin: jst denied* **14/1**

2 **3** *5* **Dr Jameson (IRE)**[23] 4536 2-9-3 0 PaulHanagan 16 71
(R A Fahey) *hld up: hdwy 3f out: rdn wl over 1f out: styd on but nt pce of front pair fnl f* **11/2**[3]

4 *nk* **Omnium Duke (IRE)** 2-9-3 0 JamesDoyle 13 70+
(J W Hills) *hld up: pushed along over 2f out: gd prog 1f out: r.o ins fnl f: promising* **12/1**

5 *1/2* **Mabuya (UAE)** 2-9-3 0 NCallan 10 69
(P J Makin) *midfield: effrt 2f out: hdwy to chse ldrs over 1f out: kpt on ins fnl f wout pce to chal* **20/1**

6 *1/2* **Truism** 2-9-3 0 JimCrowley 3 68
(Mrs A J Perrett) *s.i.s: sn in midfield: hdwy to chse ldrs over 2f out: rdn over 1f out: one pce ins fnl f* **12/1**

02 **7** *1/2* **Very Distinguished**[29] 4337 2-8-12 0 SaleemGolam 14 62
(M G Quinlan) *hld up: effrt whn nt clr run over 2f out: styd on ins fnl f: no imp on ldrs fnl 75yds* **4/1**[2]

8 *1 3/4* **Screaming Brave** 2-9-3 0 TPO'Shea 1 62
(M R Channon) *hld up: rdn and sme hdwy over 1f out: kpt on ins fnl f: nvr able to chal* **25/1**

9 *hd* **Law And Order** 2-9-3 0 PaulFitzsimons 4 62
(Miss J R Tooth) *prom: rdn over 1f out: sn outpcd by ldrs: btn ins fnl f* **33/1**

0 **10** *hd* **Brad's Luck (IRE)**[12] 4890 2-9-3 0 KirstyMilczarek 12 61
(M Blanshard) *midfield: rdn over 2f out: no imp over 1f out* **16/1**

00 **11** *3/4* **Harry Raffle**[8] 5021 2-8-12 0 HaddenFrost(5) 2 59
(S Kirk) *in tch: pushed along 2f out: outpcd over 1f out* **66/1**

12 *1* **Timpanist** 2-8-12 0 HayleyTurner 5 52
(P W Chapple-Hyam) *missed break: sn in midfield: rdn and lost pl 3f out: n.d after* **11/1**

00 **13** *2* **Blue Bogey (USA)**[9] 4974 2-9-3 0 DaneO'Neill 8 52
(R Charlton) *sn led: hdd over 2f out: sn rdn: wknd 1f out* **16/1**

14 *3* **Ready For Battle (IRE)** 2-9-3 0 RichardMullen 15 44+
(C G Cox) *misded break: in rr: u.p over 1f out: nvr on terms* **3/1**[1]

15 *2 1/4* **Levitation (IRE)** 2-8-12 0 FergusSweeney 9 34
(W S Kittow) *prom tl rdn and wknd 3f out* **33/1**

0 **16** *4 1/2* **Dicksons Delight (USA)**[16] 4728 2-9-3 0 (t) OscarUrbina 6 27
(D K Ivory) *prom: rdn and wknd over 2f out: bhd over 1f out* **200/1**

1m 28.98s (3.28) **Going Correction** +0.30s/f (Good) **16** Ran SP% **129.0**
Speed ratings (Par 94): **93,92,87,86,86 85,85,83,82,82 81,80,78,75,72 67**
toteswinger: 1&2 £25.60, 1&3 £4.70, 2&3 £14.20. CSF £129.10 TOTE £10.20: £3.00, £5.50, £2.00; EX 116.40.
Owner Mrs R C A Hammond **Bred** Rockwell Bloodstock **Trained** East Ilsley, Berks

FOCUS
This was probably just an average juvenile maiden, run at a sound enough pace and it saw the first two come well clear in a driving finish.

NOTEBOOK
Felday showed the benefit of his initial experience over course and distance 35 days previously and ran out a gutsy winner. He had got worked up before his debut and made a sluggish start, but showed a totally different attitude here and was soon racing on the early pace. He did not do the runner-up many favours by edging into that rival inside the final furlong, but he stuck his head out where it mattered and no doubt his previous experience won him the day. This was his stable's first juvenile winner of the season and he looks sure to progress further as he is faced with a stiffer test in due course. (op 7-1 tchd 10-1)
Latin Tinge(USA) ◆, despite racing freely through the early parts, was the only one to go with the winner when it mattered and only just lost out. She was not helped when that rival drifted into her late on, but rallied gamely under pressure and was in front soon after the line. A half-sister to the very useful Malt Or Mash, she will relish a longer trip as she matures and deserved compensation should not be too far off. (op 12-1)
Dr Jameson(IRE) helps to set the level for this form. His debut second on quicker ground at Redcar has worked out okay with the third winning next time out and he got the extra furlong well enough, but simply found the first pair too good. He will be eligible for nurseries after his next assignment and should come on again for this experience. (op 7-2 tchd 6-1)

Omnium Duke(IRE), whose dam won over 1m, did not go without support on this racecourse bow and posted a fair effort, looking better the further he went. He should know more next time. (op 22-1 tchd 25-1)

Mabuya(UAE), whose dam was a dual 7f-1m4f winner, turned in a pleasing enough display and was another who looked to be getting the hang of things late on. (op 14-1)

Truism is bred to appreciate a stiffer test as a three-year-old and was not given too hard a time of things so should benefit for this debut experience. (op 9-1 tchd 15-2)

Very Distinguished found just the same pace after travelling nicely enough through the first half of the contest. She may prefer quicker ground and now has the option of nurseries. (op 7-1 tchd 15-2)

Ready For Battle(IRE), whose pedigree suggests a mix of speed and stamina, was well backed, but he blew his chances with a slow start and proved too green to do himself justice. (op 5-1)

5226 IRISH THOROUGHBRED MARKETING GIMCRACK STKS (GROUP 2) (C&G) 6f 8y

1:45 (1:45) (Class 1) 2-Y-O

£39,739 (£15,064; £7,539; £3,759; £1,883; £945) **Stalls** Centre

Form RPR

1035 **1** **Shaweel**[23] 4517 2-8-12 104 GregFairley 13 112+
(M Johnston) *trckd ldrs: led ins fnl 2f: drvn and styd on strly fnl f* **16/1**

11 **2** *2 1/4* **Master Noverre (IRE)**[49] 3663 2-8-12 0 PaulHanagan 8 105+
(R A Fahey) *broke wl: stdd mid-div: hrd rdn 2f out: styd on strly fnl f to take 2nd ins fnl f but no imp on wnr* **16/1**

31 **3** *1 1/4* **Jobe (USA)**[13] 4847 2-8-12 0 NCallan 4 102+
(K A Ryan) *chsd ldrs: chal 3f out: led appr fnl 2f: hdd ins fnl 2f: styd on ins fnl f to dispute 2nd 1f out: one pce ins fnl f* **8/1**[3]

2114 **4** *1/2* **Saxford**[21] 4588 2-8-12 99 ShaneKelly 5 100
(Mrs L Stubbs) *chsd ldrs: rdn over 2f out: styd on fnl f but nvr gng pce to trble ready wnr* **12/1**

113 **5** *2* **Able Master (IRE)**[76] 2826 2-8-12 91 RobertWinston 6 94
(B Smart) *in tch: rdn after 2f: styd promonent: hrd drvn fr 2f out: kpt on same pce fnl f* **40/1**

21 **6** *1 1/4* **Deposer (IRE)**[44] 3848 2-8-12 0 LPKeniry 2 90
(J R Best) *t.k.h: chsd ldrs: rdn and green 2f out: styd on same pce fr over 1f out* **20/1**

1 **7** *shd* **Marine Boy (IRE)**[19] 4665 2-8-12 0 RichardKingscote 11 90
(Tom Dascombe) *led tl hdd over 2f out: wknd over 1f out* **11/8**[1]

1112 **8** *nk* **Art Connoisseur (IRE)**[26] 4465 2-9-1 112 JamieSpencer 1 92
(M L W Bell) *in rr but in tch: stdy hdwy 3f out to chse ldrs 2f out: sn rdn: wknd over 1f out* **3/1**[2]

4134 **9** *3* **Tagula Breeze (IRE)**[20] 4626 2-8-12 80 (t) SebSanders 9 80
(I W McInnes) *in rr: rdn 3f out and sme prog over 2f out: nvr in contention and wknd over 1f out* **100/1**

3105 **10** *7* **Sun Ship (IRE)**[50] 3634 2-8-12 92 RichardHughes 7 59
(R Hannon) *rdn over 3f out: a bhd* **40/1**

5103 **11** *hd* **Dabbers Chief (USA)**[50] 3634 2-8-12 93 PhilipRobinson 3 58
(B W Hills) *chsd ldrs over 3f* **33/1**

1125 **12** *1* **Spin Cycle (IRE)**[24] 4507 2-8-12 106 RichardMullen 10 55
(B Smart) *outpcd most of the way* **16/1**

1m 13.92s (0.92) **Going Correction** +0.30s/f (Good) **22** Ran SP% **117.1**
Speed ratings (Par 106): **105,102,100,99,97 95,95,94,90,81 81,79**
toteswinger: 1&2 £16.30, 1&3 £11.10, 2&3 £7.90. CSF £230.67 TOTE £19.30: £4.00, £4.00, £2.10; EX 266.30 Trifecta £328.80 Part won. Pool £444.36. 0.30 winning units..
Owner Sheikh Ahmed Al Maktoum **Bred** P C Hunt **Trained** Middleham Moor, N Yorks
■ This race was transferred from York after the abandonment of the Ebor meeting. Greg Fairley's first Group winner.

FOCUS
One of the races salvaged from the washed-out Ebor meeting at York and, despite the prize-money being halved, the field size increased from 9 to 12, the biggest turnout since 2005. This looked a decent renewal beforehand, but Marine Boy and Art Connoisseur were both below their best and the bare results suggests this is very ordinary form for the grade. That said, Shaweel is progressive and an up-to-scratch winner. They seemed to go an even gallop and, after racing up the middle of the track through the early stages, the majority edged across towards the stands' rail, which is where the main action took place in the closing stages.

NOTEBOOK
Shaweel had struggled a little in good company since winning his maiden at Ayr on his second start, but he had been improving steadily - he reversed Superlative Stakes form with Firth Of Fifth in the Vintage Stakes - and he progressed again on this drop back to 6f. He was well beaten on his last try at this trip when ridden from the front in the Coventry Stakes, but is a much better horse now and, after breaking better than has sometimes been the case, he showed good speed to race handy. He was then able to grab the stands' rail when the field began to edge in that direction inside the last three furlongs and ran on really strongly for pressure. Interestingly enough, he had been scheduled to contest the Prix Morny instead of this, and Mark Johnston had declared the once-raced maiden winner Weatherstaff for this before the race was switched from York. The winner may now be stepped back up to 7f for the Champagne Stakes and, although this is ordinary form for the grade, he continues to improve. (op 20-1)

Master Noverre(IRE), the winner of his first two starts in minor company over 5f on quick ground, was well away from the stalls, but he raced a little freely early on and his rider seemed keen to get him some cover. However, he probably switched off just a bit too much and was caught a bit flat footed when the pace increased passing the three-furlong pole, losing a couple of lengths on the eventual winner and third in the process. He was given numerous stern reminders in an attempt to focus his mind and he eventually ran on strongly to claim a fast-finishing second. Like the winner, he is in the Champagne Stakes, but he is now likely to be aimed at the £250,000 sales race at Newmarket in October. (tchd 14-1)

Jobe(USA) ◆, a very impressive seven-length maiden winner at Ayr on his previous start, was representing the same trainer/owner combination that landed this race with Amadeus Wolf in 2005. He ran a strange sort of race, as having travelled really sweetly in a share of the lead with Marine Boy, he looked likely to drop away when headed inside the final two furlongs, but then ran on again in the closing stages. It is interesting to note that he only picked up when he had the stands' rail to run against, which makes sense as he was tight against a rail last time, and also hung badly right on his racecourse debut. He's clearly very talented, and one suspects even better than he showed on this occasion, but having a right-handed rail to run against may be crucial to his chances unless that slight quirk can be ironed out. Although it would mean dropping in grade, the Group 3 Sirenia Stakes at Kempton could be absolutely made for him, and being by Johannesburg he should handle the sand. (op 10-1 tchd 13-2)

Saxford, fourth in the Richmond Stakes on his previous start, looked to run his race once again and is probably a good guide to the strength of the form. (op 14-1 tchd 11-1)

Able Master(IRE) had been off the track since running third in the Listed Woodcote Stakes at Epsom in June, but this was a satisfactory return faced with his toughest task to date. (op 100-1 tchd 33-1)

Deposer(IRE), who found the smart Amour Propre too good on his debut before winning on the Polytrack at Lingfield, was far too keen for his own good early on and made his move out wider than most, so he did well to finish so close. (op 16-1)

Marine Boy(IRE), who won by seven lengths over this course and distance on his debut, was really well backed but he failed to give his running. He won pretty much unchallenged first-time up, but was pressed for the lead on this occasion and may just have been found out by his inexperience. He can be given another chance to confirm that initial promise, but it remains to be seen whether he needs to dominate to be at his best. Official explanation: trainer had no explanation for the poor form shown (op 13-8)

Art Connoisseur(IRE), who appeared to finish very tired when losing his unbeaten record in the Phoenix Stakes last time, had a 3lb penalty to contend with here. He looked very laboured when asked to quicken and was well below par, but it transpired that he had cracked his off-fore cannonbone, which will keep him out for the rest of the season. Official explanation: jockey said colt never travelled (op 2-1 tchd 7-2 and 4-1 in a place)

Tagula Breeze(IRE) only has an official mark of 80, but he looks better than that. He travelled well to a point, but seemed to be hanging left in the closing stages and his rider was unable to get that serious.

5227 RE PERSONNEL MEDIAN AUCTION MAIDEN STKS (DIV II) 7f (S)

2:20 (2:21) (Class 5) 2-Y-O **£4,209** (£1,252; £625; £312) **Stalls** Centre

Form RPR

3 **1** **Midnight Cruiser (IRE)**[14] 4826 2-9-3 0 RichardHughes 3 81+
(R Hannon) *racd keenly: mde all: rdn ins fnl f: r.o wl and in command clsng stages* **7/4**[1]

2 *2* **Kouloura (IRE)** 2-8-12 0 KirstyMilczarek 16 69
(M Botti) *midfield: rdn and hdwy 2f out: hung lft fr over 1f out: wnt 2nd ins fnl f but nt pce of wnr* **16/1**

3 **3** *3/4* **Champagne Fizz (IRE)**[27] 4430 2-8-9 0 TravisBlock(3) 1 67
(Miss Jo Crowley) *racd keenly: a.p: rdn to chal wnr over 1f out: nt qckn fnl 100yds* **16/1**

3 **4** *shd* **Polly's Mark (IRE)**[42] 3913 2-8-12 0 PhilipRobinson 5 67
(C G Cox) *racd keenly: w wnr tl rdn and nt qckn over 1f out: carried lft ins fnl f: styd on u.p but a hld* **13/2**[3]

4 **5** *3/4* **Bagber**[35] 4150 2-9-3 0 JamesDoyle 4 71+
(H J L Dunlop) *trckd ldrs: rdn over 1f out: keeping on u.p whn nt clr run and checked sltly 150yds out: styd on same pce after* **10/1**

6 *nse* **Water Hen (IRE)** 2-8-12 0 FergusSweeney 7 65+
(R Charlton) *dwlt: midfield: pushed along over 1f out: prog ins fnl f: gng on at fin: promising* **22/1**

03 **7** *1/2* **Lucky Score (IRE)**[9] 4982 2-8-7 0 DavidProbert(5) 13 64
(Mouse Hamilton-Fairley) *cl up: rdn over 1f out: styng on u.p whn n.m.r 150yds out: no ex towards fin* **16/1**

0 **8** *3/4* **D'Artagnans Dream**[13] 4861 2-9-3 0 OscarUrbina 12 67
(G D Blake) *midfield: effrt over 1f out: one pce ins fnl furlong* **150/1**

9 *3/4* **Eddie Boy** 2-9-3 0 HayleyTurner 11 65
(M L W Bell) *missed break: in rr: rn green: pushed along briefly 4f out: pushed along over 2f out: styd on fnl f: nt pce to get competitive* **16/1**

10 *2* **Deuce** 2-8-12 0 StephenCarson 8 55
(Eve Johnson Houghton) *missed break: sn in midfield: rdn over 1f out: nvr able to chal* **40/1**

11 *3 1/2* **Hurakan (IRE)** 2-9-3 0 JimCrowley 9 51
(Mrs A J Perrett) *in rr: rdn 1/2-way: nvr on terms* **20/1**

12 *1* **Melange (USA)** 2-9-3 0 NCallan 6 49
(P F I Cole) *prom: rdn 2f out: wknd over 1f out* **7/2**[2]

13 *1 3/4* **Buddha O' Neil** 2-9-3 0 TPO'Shea 15 44
(M R Channon) *missed break: hld up: rdn over 1f out: nvr on terms* **66/1**

14 *12* **Venture Capitalist** 2-9-3 0 DaneO'Neill 10 14
(L M Cumani) *missed break: rdn over 2f out: a bhd* **12/1**

15 *4* **Lambourn Genie (UAE)** 2-9-3 0 RichardKingscote 14 4
(Tom Dascombe) *missed break: hld up: rdn 3f out: lft bhd 2f out* **18/1**

1m 29.05s (3.35) **Going Correction** +0.30s/f (Good) **15** Ran SP% **131.2**
Speed ratings (Par 94): **92,89,88,88,87 87,87,86,85,83 79,78,76,62,57**
toteswinger: 1&2 £16.10, 1&3 £7.60, 2&3 £62.90. CSF £36.31 TOTE £2.80: £1.40, £8.40, £4.50; EX 52.90.
Owner Michael Pescod **Bred** Vincent Hannon **Trained** East Everleigh, Wilts

FOCUS
The second division of the juvenile maiden, run in a marginally slower time than the first, but it looked the stronger of the pair and the form appears sound enough rated through the third.

NOTEBOOK
Midnight Cruiser(IRE) ◆, the only runner in the field thought classy enough at this stage to hold a Group-race entry, had finished third in what should prove to be a decent maiden at Newmarket a fortnight previously and he opened his account at the second attempt in dogged fashion. Always on the pace, he lengthened clear nicely when asked to win his race and was always holding his pursuers at the business end. He was well suited by being able to race prominently this time, which he could not do on debut after an awkward start, and he is clearly a colt going in the right direction. A step up to another furlong will also be within his range before too long and, while he will have to step up markedly on this form to be competitive in Group company, he is in the right hands to progress to a higher level. (op 13-8 tchd 11-8)

Kouloura(IRE), who has mainly speed in her pedigree, was supported at decent odds ahead of this debut and she justified the confidence with a pleasing effort. She had little trouble with the trip and looks capable of being placed to strike now she has this run under her belt. (op 25-1)

Champagne Fizz(IRE) had finished third on quick ground on her debut at Salisbury 27 days previously and that form looks good with the runner-up being successful next time. She ran a sound race in defeat, staying the extra furlong without much fuss, and evidently has a future. (tchd 14-1)

Polly's Mark(IRE), whose stable took this event last term, had her chance and probably ran to a similar level as her debut third over course and distance six weeks ago. Surprisingly her stable have yet to hit the target with their juveniles this season and she now looks the sort to fare better when qualifying for a mark after her next outing. (op 5-1 tchd 9-2)

Bagber, who belied odds of 100-1 when fourth on debut over course and distance in July, ran a similar sort of race and is another who should fare better after qualifying for nurseries after his next assignment. (op 9-1 tchd 17-2)

Water Hen(IRE) took time to really get the hang of things yet was staying on towards the finish. Her yard has a decent enough strike-rate with their second-time-out juveniles and she should be expected to go close on her next run. (op 40-1 tchd 50-1)

Melange(USA), whose connections' runner was just touched off in the first division, met strong support in the betting ring yet failed to live up to market expectations and looks to need more time. With his US pedigree a switch to the sand may also suit him better. (op 7-1)

5228 BATHWICK TYRES ANDOVER NURSERY 6f 8y

2:50 (2:52) (Class 4) 2-Y-O **£4,533** (£1,348; £674; £336) **Stalls** Centre

Form RPR

4562 **1** **Kingswinford (IRE)**[12] 4905 2-7-11 68 ow2 LukeMorris(3) 1 72
(P D Evans) *chsd ldrs: rdn to ld jst ins fnl 2f: styd on u.p ins fnl f* **15/2**[2]

61 **2** *1/2* **Belle Des Airs (IRE)**[23] 4534 2-8-11 79 SebSanders 4 81
(R M Beckett) *led: rdn and hdd jst ins fnl 2f: styd chsng wnr and rallied u.p ins fnl f: coming bk at fin but a hld* **9/1**

104 **3** *nk* **Versaki (IRE)**[43] 3879 2-9-10 **92**.................... RichardHughes 2 93
(R Hannon) *hld up in rr: hdwy 3f out: styd on to chse ldrs ins fnl f: fin wl u.p but a hld* **11/1**

13 **4** *nk* **Dove Mews**[28] 4374 2-8-13 **81**.................... HayleyTurner 7 81
(M L W Bell) *in rr: hdwy 3f out: styd on to chse ldrs fr 2f out: kpt on fnl f but nvr gng pce to chal* **12/1**

31 **5** *1 ¾* **Hip Hip Hooray**[11] 4925 2-7-12 **66** 6ex oh3.............. CatherineGannon 9 61
(L A Dace) *s.i.s: sn rcvrd: chsd ldrs 3f oiut and sn rdn: kpt on same pce ins fnl f* **16/1**

3013 **6** *¾* **Asian Tale (IRE)**[75] 2859 2-8-9 **77** ow1.................... TGMcLaughlin 6 70+
(A B Haynes) *slowly away: bhd: rdn and hdwy 2f out: swtchd lft 1f out and r.o wl clsng stages but nvr in contention* **20/1**

6344 **7** *2 ¾* **Paymaster In Chief**[17] 4706 2-7-7 **66** oh4.................. DavidProbert(5) 5 50
(M D I Usher) *chsd ldrs: rdn 1/2-way: styd on same pce fnl 2f* **16/1**

61 **8** *¾* **Proclaim**[19] 4658 2-8-13 **81**.................... GregFairley 10 63
(M Johnston) *pressed ldrs: rdn over 2f out: wknd fnl f* **5/1**[1]

512 **9** *shd* **Diggeratt (USA)**[20] 4628 2-8-11 **79**.................... PaulHanagan 8 61
(R A Fahey) *chsd ldrs: rdn over 2f out: wknd over 1f out* **5/1**[1]

01 **10** *1 ½* **Tartan Turban (IRE)**[39] 4024 2-8-5 **73**.................... RichardMullen 14 50
(R Hannon) *in rr: rdn 1/2-way: effrt over 2f and no imp* **8/1**[3]

060 **11** *1 ½* **Protiva**[20] 4643 2-7-13 **74** ow7.................... MatthewDavies(7) 13 47
(A P Jarvis) *racd alone stands' side for 3f and upsides to that point: btn 2f out* **10/1**

500 **12** *1 ¼* **Polly's Choice (IRE)**[42] 3913 2-7-12 **66** oh1.......... FrankieMcDonald 15 35
(R Hannon) *chsd ldrs tl wknd qckly 2f out* **12/1**

3153 **13** *hd* **Dubai's Gazal**[34] 4185 2-8-12 **80**.................... TPO'Shea 12 49
(M R Channon) *rdn over 3f out and a in rr* **12/1**

6000 **14** *4* **Louie's Lad**[9] 4975 2-7-9 **66** oh9.................... DominicFox(3) 3 23
(J A Geake) *chsd ldrs tl rdn 1/2-way and sn wknd* **100/1**

1m 14.89s (1.89) **Going Correction** +0.30s/f (Good) **14** Ran SP% **124.2**
Speed ratings (Par 96): **99,98,97,97,95 94,90,89,89,87 85,83,83,78**
toteswinger: 1&2 £20.10, 1&3 £15.60, 2&3 £13.60. CSF £75.97 CT £536.51 TOTE £8.70: £2.70, £3.60, £4.00; EX 138.60.
Owner Nick Shutts **Bred** J Costello **Trained** Pandy, Monmouths

FOCUS
Plenty of runners, but it was easy to pick holes in the form of most of these and this was an ordinary nursery. The winning time was 0.97 seconds slower than the Gimcrack Stakes won by Shaweel and the winner of this carried 17lb less (including his rider's claim). They raced middle to stands' side.

NOTEBOOK
Kingswinford(IRE) was not inconvenienced by stall one, as he raced close to the pace up the centre of the track and had plenty of company. He looked to have hit the front soon enough, but found plenty and was always holding on. He came into this a maiden after 11 starts and looking thoroughly exposed but, following his recent second in a Windsor maiden, he was 5lb well-in, even after his rider's 2lb overweight had been taken into account. This was a good effort, but he lacks size and does not appeal as one to back to follow up. (op 10-1)
Belle Des Airs(IRE), the winner of a weak maiden at Leicester on her previous start, was soon the overall leader after breaking well, but she could not respond immediately when passed by the eventual winner around two out and briefly looked intimidated by that rival. She was closing again at the finish, but was never going to get there and, although she clearly has plenty of ability, she might just be the type who needs keeping sweet. (op 15-2 tchd 10-1)
Versaki(IRE) has struggled since winning a Goodwood maiden on his debut, including when only fourth of five in a conditions contest on the July course last time and, on a stiff-looking mark, he had no easy task conceding upwards of 11lb all round. As it turned out, he acquitted himself with real credit, especially as the two who finished in front of him got first run, but it is worth remembering this was not a great race for the grade. (tchd 9-1 and 12-1)
Dove Mews very much looks a galloper rather than a quickener and she promised to be suited by the ground, the easiest she has encountered to date, but her run just flattened out a little late on. She looks the type to do better when she strengthens up and she should make a three-year-old. (op 10-1)
Hip Hip Hooray, well suited by easy ground when winning on her nursery debut in a weak race at Windsor, ran a respectable race in this more competitive contest under her penalty. Not for the first time she was slowly away, but she recovered to have her chance and gave the impression she is ready for 7f now. (tchd 14-1)
Asian Tale(IRE), carrying 1lb overweight, was stuck behind a wall of horses after completely fluffing the start, but she finished quite nicely once in the clear and looked to appreciate the easy ground. (op 25-1 tchd 16-1)
Paymaster In Chief, 4lb out of the handicap, is a little better than he was able to show as he was badly bumped around two furlongs. (op 11-1)
Proclaim had a lot going for him when winning a 7f maiden at Chester on his previous start and he could not repeat that form in this more competitive contest, although he did make his move against the stands' rail, away from the principals. (op 7-1)
Diggeratt(USA) looked to be struggling two furlongs out and did not seem happy on the loose ground. (op 6-1)
Tartan Turban(IRE) was unable to build on his surprise Windsor maiden success. (op 12-1)
Louie's Lad Official explanation: jockey said gelding hung left-handed throughout

5229 TOTESPORT NEWBURGH (HERITAGE H'CAP) 1m 5f 61y
3:25 (3:28) (Class 2) 3-Y-0+
£62,310 (£18,660; £9,330; £4,670; £2,330; £1,170) **Stalls** Low

Form RPR

1-40 **1** **All The Good (IRE)**[13] 4844 5-9-0 **100**.................... DaneO'Neill 7 114
(Saeed Bin Suroor) *hld up in midfield and a shade keen: swtchd rt and hdwy on wd outside over 2f out: led over 1f out: sn shot clr: edgd lft ins fnl f: r.o wl* **25/1**

-201 **2** *3 ¼* **Tropical Strait (IRE)**[7] 5054 5-8-7 **93** 4ex.................. FergusSweeney 6 102+
(D W P Arbuthnot) *in tch: nt clr run and lost pl over 2f out: sn rdn: rallied over 1f out: styd on to take 2nd ins fnl f: no imp on wnr* **9/1**[3]

0051 **3** *1 ½* **Yellowstone (IRE)**[41] 3975 4-9-10 **110**....................(p) JohnEgan 19 117+
(Jane Chapple-Hyam) *in tch: impr to ld over 2f out: sn rdn: hdd over 1f out: sn outpcd by wnr: lost 2nd ins fnl f: styd on same pce after* **14/1**

2040 **4** *hd* **Pevensey (IRE)**[26] 4444 6-8-8 **94**.................... GrahamGibbons 1 101
(J J Quinn) *missed break: sn in midfield: pushed along briefly 7f out: rdn 3f out: hdwy 2f out: styd on u.p to chal for pls ins fnl f* **25/1**

0422 **5** *½* **Young Mick**[26] 4444 6-9-1 **101**....................(v) RobertWinston 2 112+
(G G Margarson) *midfield: nt clr run and bmpd over 2f out: sn rdn: prog whn nt clr run again over 1f out: styd on ins fnl f but unable to fully rcvr* **11/2**[1]

1353 **6** *1 ¼* **Formax (FR)**[13] 4844 6-8-5 **91**.................... RichardMullen 8 95
(M P Tregoning) *midfield: swtchd rt over 2f out: hdwy over 1f out: styd on wl on outside to chse ldrs ins fnl f: run flattened out towards fin* **14/1**

-002 **7** *hd* **Bauer (IRE)**[24] 4508 5-9-3 **103**.................... RichardHughes 10 107+
(L M Cumani) *trckd ldrs: rdn whn bmpd over 2f out: ch over 1f out: no ex fnl 100yds* **8/1**[2]

30R0 **8** *½* **Carte Diamond (USA)**[21] 4585 7-9-4 **104**.................... TPO'Shea 13 107
(B Ellison) *led: rdn 4f out: hdd over 2f out: hld whn n.m.r ins fnl f: n.d after* **40/1**

4-0 **9** *1 ¾* **Minkowski**[24] 4504 5-8-7 **93**.................... HayleyTurner 20 93
(J Noseda) *stmbld sn after s: hld up: nt clr run over 2f out: swtchd lft and hdwy wl over 1f out: styd on u.p: nvr able to trble ldrs* **18/1**

-601 **10** *½* **Pippa Greene**[26] 4444 4-8-10 **96** 4ex.................... ShaneKelly 14 96
(P F I Cole) *hld up: rdn over 2f out: snatched up whn nt clr run over 1f out: kpt on: nvr able to rch ldrs* **12/1**

2/0- **11** *1 ¼* **Salute Him (IRE)**[21] 4611 5-8-6 **92**.................... PhilipRobinson 3 90
(A J Martin, Ire) *missed break: sn in midfield: hdwy gng wl over 3f out: chsd ldrs 2f out: rdn over 1f out: wknd ins fnl f* **16/1**

2002 **12** *2 ¾* **Record Breaker (IRE)**[13] 4844 4-8-9 **95**.................... GregFairley 4 89
(M Johnston) *prom: rdn over 3f out: wknd over 1f out* **16/1**

1-16 **13** *½* **Milne Graden**[24] 4508 4-8-12 **98**.................... NCallan 15 91
(J Noseda) *hld up: nt clr run over 2f out: sn rdn: hung lft over 1f out: nvr able to trble ldrs* **11/1**

2030 **14** *hd* **Camps Bay (USA)**[26] 4444 4-8-12 **98**.................... JimCrowley 16 91
(Mrs A J Perrett) *hld up: rdn 4f out: nvr able to get on terms* **16/1**

604 **15** *hd* **Wing Collar**[41] 3975 7-8-7 **93**....................(p) TonyCulhane 12 85
(T D Easterby) *midfield: rdn and hdwy to chse ldrs over 2f out: wknd ins fnl f* **33/1**

0/10 **16** *1* **Bureaucrat**[26] 4444 6-8-2 **93** ow1.................... JackMitchell(5) 18 84
(P J Hobbs) *pushed along early: hld up after: rdn over 3f out: nvr on terms* **25/1**

0004 **17** *2* **Players Please (USA)**[24] 4508 4-8-4 **93**.................... PatrickHills(3) 9 81
(M Johnston) *trckd ldrs: rdn 3f out: losing pl whn n.m.r over 2f out: n.d after* **16/1**

1150 **18** *nk* **Ajaan**[48] 3743 4-9-0 **100**....................(b) TPQueally 17 87
(H R A Cecil) *hld up: hdwy over 3f out: rdn whn chsd ldrs over 2f out: wknd over 1f out* **11/1**

4540 **19** *1 ½* **Smart Instinct (USA)**[62] 3249 4-8-8 **94**.................... PaulHanagan 5 79
(R A Fahey) *in tch: rdn 3f out: wknd wl over 1f out* **40/1**

1211 **20** *21* **Wicked Daze (IRE)**[28] 4362 5-8-10 **96** 4ex.................... SebSanders 11 50
(Sir Mark Prescott) *prom: rdn whn chalng over 3f out: wknd under 2f out* **14/1**

2m 52.05s (0.05) **Going Correction** +0.30s/f (Good) **62** Ran SP% **129.0**
Speed ratings (Par 109): **111,109,108,107,107 106,106,106,105,105 104,102,102,102,102 101,100,100,99,86**
toteswinger: 1&2 £63.90, 1&3 £75.10, 2&3 £26.00. CSF £231.12 CT £3308.71 TOTE £31.90: £6.40, £2.60, £4.20, £8.00; EX 336.80 TRIFECTA Not won..
Owner Godolphin **Bred** Mount Coote Partnership **Trained** Newmarket, Suffolk
■ This race was run as a replacement for the abandoned Ebor Handicap but with a different title and over a slightly shorter trip.

FOCUS
The rescheduled running of the Ebor and a different race altogether, with the ground riding a lot faster than it would have been, 13 of the original line-up in attendance and the prize-money being £110,000 less than the York showpiece offered. There were still similarities in the track and draw bias, however, plus the line-up ensured it was still a highly competitive staying handicap. It was run at a solid early gallop and the winner is rated up 5lb with the fourth the best guide.

NOTEBOOK
All The Good(IRE) shot clear of his rivals when getting a crack with the whip nearing the final furlong and soon put the race to bed. Not entered for the original version of this race earlier in the week, he had been very disappointing on his second outing for his powerful connections at the Shergar Cup meeting 13 days previously, but that probably came too soon for him as there was no denying the authority in which he took this. He would have won by further had he not veered left over to the far rail late on, but that was probably due to him having been in front sooner than may have been ideal. He will surely be kept to staying races from now on and it will be very interesting to see whether he can now step up on this at a higher level, as he should really still have more to offer this term. Official explanation: trainer's rep had no explanation for the apparent improvement in form
Tropical Strait(IRE), penalised for his decisive win over course and distance a week previously, would have been suited by this return to the track and he ran a career-best race in defeat. He had to wait to make his challenge around two furlongs out and the winner got first run on him, but it made no difference to the overall result. (op 10-1)
Yellowstone(IRE), who had repaid some of his large purchase price when winning a Listed handicap 41 days previously, ran well under his big weight. He fared best of those to race up with the decent early pace and kept on bravely under maximum pressure. His effort is made even more meritorious as he was drawn in 19. (op 16-1 tchd 18-1)
Pevensey(IRE), who finished last in the 2007 Ebor, missed the kick and tended to run in snatches yet he eventually came through to post a much-improved effort in defeat, reversing recent form with Young Mick, although that one was denied a clear run. (op 33-1)
Young Mick endured a particularly troubled passage down the home straight and was unlucky not to have finished closer, being rated as finishing second. He now richly deserves to find another winning turn. (op 6-1)
Formax(FR), back up in trip, again got going all too late in the day. The manner in which connections choose to ride him out the back early on does dictate he will always need things to fall right in his races (op 20-1)
Bauer(IRE), who was originally scratched earlier in the week due to the testing ground, fitted the profile of previous winners and was from a yard with a good record in the race. He travelled sweetly, but failed to quicken when asked for maximum effort. Perhaps a return to more patient tactics could help him. (op 6-1)
Carte Diamond(USA) was a sitting duck from two furlongs out yet ran one of his better races in defeat. (op 66-1)
Minkowski, fourth in last year's Ebor off the same mark, turned in a better effort for the step back up in trip without ever threatening. (tchd 16-1 and 22-1)
Pippa Greene was burdened with a 4lb penalty for winning at Ascot where he finished in front of today's winner and looked a player on this return to the longer trip. He was ridden way off the pace, however, and simply got going too late in the day. (op 10-1 tchd 9-1)
Salute Him(IRE) travelled nicely until finding just the same pace when push eventually came to shove. A drop back to 1m4f can see him find a race. (tchd 14-1)
Milne Graden never looked like getting involved from off the pace. (op 10-1)
Wicked Daze(IRE) proved friendless in the betting ring and eventually dropped out to finish a bitterly disappointing last. (op 8-1)

5230 BATHWICK TYRES CLAIMING STKS 1m 2f 6y
3:55 (3:56) (Class 4) 3-4-Y-0 **£4,857** (£1,445; £722; £360) **Stalls** Low

Form RPR

6061 **1** **La Columbina**[6] 5086 3-7-9 73....................(v) CharlesEddery(7) 4 68
(R Hannon) *t.k.h: trckd ldrs tl led jst ins fnl 3f: shkn up ins fnl f: two reminders to assert cl home* **15/8**[1]

5100 **2** *nk* **North Parade**[7] 5054 3-9-6 88....................(t) RichardHughes 6 85
(B J Meehan) *hld up in rr: hdwy over 2f out: styd on u.p to chse wnr fnl f: clsng nr fin but a hld* **15/2**

0256 **3** *4* **Eagle Nebula**[37] 4081 4-8-13 63.. JohnEgan 3 62
(B R Johnson) *in rr: rdn and hdwy over 2f out: styd on fnl f but no ch w ldng duo* **8/1**

611 **4** *1* **Addikt (IRE)**[36] 4112 3-9-1 83.. HaddenFrost(5) 8 75
(S Kirk) *t.k.h: led: narrowly hdd jst ins fnl 3f: wknd over 1f out* **9/4**[2]

0506 **5** *2 ¾* **No To Trident**[6] 5098 3-8-13 78..(v[1]) TGMcLaughlin 5 63
(P D Evans) *t.k.h: chsd ldrs: rdn 3f out: wknd 2f out* **13/2**[3]

4020 **6** *½* **Mouse White**[29] 4332 3-8-3 52.. FrankieMcDonald 1 52
(H Candy) *t.k.h early: chsd ldrs: rdn over 4f out: wknd over 2f out* **16/1**

00 **7** *8* **Brathay (IRE)**[49] 3687 4-8-13 0.. JimCrowley 7 38
(Ian Williams) *chsd ldr to 4f out: wknd 3f out* **18/1**

2m 12.89s (4.09) **Going Correction** +0.30s/f (Good)
WFA 3 from 4yo 8lb 7 Ran SP% **112.9**
Speed ratings (Par 105): **95,94,91,90,88 88,81**
toteswinger: 1&2 £3.60, 1&3 £3.70, 2&3 £4.80. CSF £16.14 TOTE £3.10: £1.70, £2.40; EX 14.20.The winner was claimed by G Harker for £12,000. Addikt was claimed by G Harker for £25,000.
Owner Raymond Tooth **Bred** P And Mrs A G Venner **Trained** East Everleigh, Wilts

FOCUS
A decent claimer, but they went a steady pace for much of the way and the form is a little muddling. The first two home raced away from the far rail in the straight.

5231 BATHWICK TYRES SWINDON MAIDEN FILLIES' STKS 1m 2f 6y
4:25 (4:25) (Class 5) 3-Y-O+ **£4,533** (£1,348; £674; £336) **Stalls** Low

Form RPR

-633 **1** **Belotto (IRE)**[58] 3362 3-8-12 73.. HayleyTurner 1 81
(R Charlton) *stdd s: hld up in rr: swtchd off rail to outside 2f out: smooth hdwy to ld over 1f out: sn clr: v easily* **13/2**[3]

2 *6* **Vine Street (IRE)** 3-8-12 0.. PhilipRobinson 7 69
(M A Jarvis) *chsd ldrs: rdn over 2f out: chsd wnr fnl f: nvr any ch but readily 2nd best* **7/2**[2]

-450 **3** *1 ½* **Sovereign's Honour (USA)**[64] 3153 3-8-12 97.......... RichardHughes 4 66
(Sir Michael Stoute) *led: rdn and hdd over 1f out sn no ch w wnr: no ex and wknd into 3rd fnl f* **8/11**[1]

0-6 **4** *½* **Bet Noir (IRE)**[60] 3326 3-8-12 0.. SaleemGolam 6 65
(W R Swinburn) *in rr but in tch: rdn and styd on 2f out: hung lft u.p over 1f out: kpt on again nr fin* **14/1**

06 **5** *¾* **Miss Pelling (IRE)**[35] 4166 3-8-9 0.. PatrickHills(3) 5 64
(B J Meehan) *chsd ldr: rdn over 2f out: wknd appr fnl f* **16/1**

6 *½* **Alvee (IRE)** 3-8-12 0.. RobertWinston 2 63
(J R Fanshawe) *chsd ldrs: hrd rdn over 2f out: wknd over 1f out* **12/1**

7 *4* **Won More Night**[25] 6-9-6 0.. VinceSlattery 3 55
(D J Wintle) *nvr in contention* **50/1**

2m 11.01s (2.21) **Going Correction** +0.30s/f (Good)
WFA 3 from 6yo 8lb 7 Ran SP% **115.7**
Speed ratings (Par 100): **103,98,97,96,96 95,92**
toteswinger: 1&2 £2.50, 1&3 £2.30, 2&3 £1.30. CSF £30.07 TOTE £6.40: £2.20, £2.10; EX 23.40.
Owner Lady Rothschild **Bred** The Rt Hon Lord Rothschild **Trained** Beckhampton, Wilts
■ Stewards' Enquiry : Robert Winston jockey said, regarding why he failed to ride out to the line, he considered that he would have clipped the heels of Sovereigns Honour if he had done so

FOCUS
The odds-on favourite, Sovereign's Honour, was clearly well below her official mark of 97 and this was just a fair fillies' maiden. It was run at a stady pace.

5232 BATHWICK TYRES DEVIZES FILLIES' H'CAP 1m 4f 5y
4:55 (4:55) (Class 5) (0-70,69) 3-Y-O+ **£3,238** (£963; £481; £240) **Stalls** Low

Form RPR

2635 **1** **Adorabella (IRE)**[22] 4568 5-9-5 62.. HaddenFrost(5) 10 77
(A King) *hld up in tch: smooth hdwy to ld 2f out: drvn clr fnl f* **3/1**[1]

1045 **2** *7* **Trysting Grove (IRE)**[7] 5058 7-9-1 53.. PaulFitzsimons 11 57
(E G Bevan) *slowly away: bhd tl hdwy 3f out: chsd ldrs and rdn 2f out: chsd wnr fnl f but nvr any ch* **15/2**

0511 **3** *1 ¼* **Wogan's Sister**[9] 4991 3-9-0 65 6ex.. MarcHalford(3) 3 67
(D R C Elsworth) *led 5f: led again travelling wl 3f out: hdd and rdn 2f out: no ch w wnr over 1f out: wknd and lost 2nd sn after* **7/2**[2]

/00- **4** *3 ¾* **Dawn At Sea**[493] 767 6-9-0 55.. LeeVickers(3) 5 51
(Mrs K Waldron) *in rr: hrd drvn and sme prog over 2f out: styd on u.p fnl f but nvr any ch w ldng trio* **66/1**

0023 **5** *nk* **Etain (IRE)**[12] 4892 4-10-0 66.. SaleemGolam 8 61
(W R Swinburn) *chsd ldr tl led after 5f: hdd 3f out: wknd u.p fr 2f out* **7/1**

0640 **6** *6* **Requia**[26] 4457 3-8-10 65.. AmyScott(7) 2 51
(H Candy) *chsd ldrs: rdn 3f out: wknd over 2f out* **14/1**

6400 **7** *4* **April's Daughter**[22] 4572 3-8-11 62.. TravisBlock(3) 4 41
(B R Millman) *rdn over 3f out: a towards rr* **10/1**

0006 **8** *1 ¼* **Rosy Dawn**[15] 4774 3-7-13 47 oh2..(v) FrankieMcDonald 1 24
(J J Bridger) *chsd ldrs: rdn over 4f out: wknd 3f out* **33/1**

-053 **9** *1 ½* **Snowy Indian**[12] 4902 3-9-2 69.. Louis-PhilippeBeuzelin(5) 9 44
(Sir Michael Stoute) *a in rr* **11/2**[3]

1-45 **10** *6* **Ashwell Rose**[101] 2091 6-9-3 55..(v) JimCrowley 6 20
(J R Jenkins) *in tch: rdn 4f out: sn wknd* **14/1**

0506 **11** *15* **Silver Surprise**[8] 5027 4-8-2 47 oh2.. BillyCray(7) 7 —
(J J Bridger) *racd on outside: in tch tl wd and wknd bnd 5f out* **16/1**

2m 38.2s (2.70) **Going Correction** +0.30s/f (Good)
WFA 3 from 4yo+ 10lb 11 Ran SP% **119.6**
Speed ratings (Par 100): **103,98,97,95,94 90,88,87,86,82 72**
toteswinger: 1&2 £6.50, 1&3 £4.40, 2&3 £7.60. CSF £26.57 CT £83.80 TOTE £4.20: £1.60, £2.60, £1.50; EX 30.20.
Owner Mrs Carol Hawkins **Bred** J Hawkins **Trained** Barbury Castle, Wilts

FOCUS
A modest fillies' handicap and they finished strung out. Most of these were happy to avoid the far rail in the straight. The winner has had plenty of chances off this sort of mark but won well and could defy a penalty.

5233 BATHWICK TYRES NEWBURY APPRENTICE H'CAP 6f 8y
5:25 (5:25) (Class 5) (0-75,79) 3-Y-O+ **£2,914** (£867; £433; £216) **Stalls** Centre

Form RPR

6221 **1** **Gentle Guru**[2] 5187 4-10-3 79 6ex.. Louis-PhilippeBeuzelin 4 92+
(R T Phillips) *trckd ldrs: led jst ins fnl 2f: drvn clr ins fnl f* **11/4**[1]

6515 **2** *2 ¼* **Memphis Man**[5] 5121 5-9-11 73.. RichardEvans 7 79
(P D Evans) *in rr but in tch: rdn and hdwy fr 2f out: styd on to chse wnr ins fnl f but nvr any ch* **5/1**[2]

5005 **3** *½* **Proud Killer**[3] 5170 5-8-9 57..(b[1]) JPHamblett 5 61
(J R Jenkins) *led tl hdd jst ins fnl 2f: hung rt u.p 1f out: outpcd and lost 2nd sn after* **12/1**

050 **4** *1 ¼* **Cheap Street**[46] 3797 4-9-7 69.. MatthewDavies 3 69
(J G Portman) *in tch: rdn and styd on to chse ldrs ins fnl f but nvr gng pce to be competitive* **6/1**[3]

2104 **5** *3* **Kelamon**[11] 4928 4-9-11 73.. BillyCray 1 64
(M D I Usher) *chsd ldrs: rdn 1/2-way: wknd fr 2f out* **11/4**[1]

6010 **6** *4 ½* **Boldinor**[23] 4535 5-8-13 61.. KylieManser 6 37
(M R Bosley) *a outpcd* **12/1**

4000 **7** *7* **Dazed And Amazed**[50] 3646 4-9-8 75.. CharlesEddery(5) 8 59+
(R Hannon) *trckd ldrs tl wknd 2f out: eased whn no ch fnl f* **7/1**

1m 14.44s (1.44) **Going Correction** +0.30s/f (Good) 7 Ran SP% **112.2**
Speed ratings (Par 103): **102,99,98,96,92 86,77**
toteswinger: 1&2 £2.90, 1&3 £7.00, 2&3 £10.30. CSF £16.08 CT £136.77 TOTE £3.10: £2.00, £2.90; EX 11.00 Place 6: £1,627.49, Place 5: £440.61..
Owner Flying Tiger Partnership **Bred** R Phillips And Tweenhills Farm And Stud **Trained** Adlestrop, Gloucs
■ Stewards' Enquiry : Louis-Philippe Beuzelin caution: used whip in incorrect place.

FOCUS
A modest handicap restricted to apprentices who had not ridden more than 25 winners. They raced up the middle of the track. The form is solid with the runner-up the best guide.
Dazed And Amazed Official explanation: jockey said gelding hung left-handed
T/Jkpt: Not won. T/Plt: £1,524.80 to a £1 stake. Pool: £88,880.41. 42.55 winning tickets. T/Qpdt: £107.90 to a £1 stake. Pool: £8,156.50. 55.90 winning tickets. ST

4733 NEWCASTLE (L-H)
Friday, August 22
5234 Meeting Abandoned - Waterlogged

5099 NEWMARKET (JULY) (R-H)
Friday, August 22

OFFICIAL GOING: Good (8.3)
Wind: Light, half behind, becoming fresher after Race 4 (2.05) Weather: Cloudy with sunny spells

5240 EUROPEAN BREEDERS' FUND MAIDEN FILLIES' STKS (DIV I) 7f
12:25 (12:30) (Class 4) 2-Y-O **£4,857** (£1,445; £722; £360) **Stalls** High

Form RPR

1 **Anice Stellato (IRE)** 2-9-0 0.. TomEaves 5 81+
(R M Beckett) *w'like: scope: athletic: lw: chsd ldrs: rdn to ld ins fnl f: r.o* **11/2**[3]

2 *1* **Capitelli (IRE)** 2-9-0 0.. RyanMoore 14 78+
(R Hannon) *w'like: scope: lw: chsd ldrs: rdn over 1f out: n.m.r ins fnl f: r.o* **10/1**

3 *½* **Greenisland (IRE)** 2-9-0 0.. RobertHavlin 15 77+
(H Morrison) *w'like: plld hrd and prom: led over 5f out: rdn: edgd rt and hdd over 1f out: r.o* **33/1**

5 **4** *¾* **Purple Sage (IRE)**[13] 4870 2-9-0 0.. MichaelHills 11 75
(B W Hills) *w'like: scope: lengthy: led: hdd over 5f out: chsd ldrs: rdn to ld over 1f out: hdd and unable qck ins fnl f* **4/1**[1]

5 *2 ¾* **Mooteeah (IRE)** 2-9-0 0.. RHills 12 68+
(M A Jarvis) *w'like: bit bkwd: hld up: hdwy over 1f out: nt rch ldrs* **9/2**[2]

6 *½* **Light Dubai (IRE)** 2-9-0 0.. EdwardCreighton 13 67+
(M R Channon) *w'like: lengthy: dwlt: hld up: hdwy over 1f out: nvr nrr* **11/1**

7 *1* **Haakima (USA)** 2-9-0 0.. LiamJones 6 64
(C E Brittain) *leggy: s.i.s: hdwy 5f out: rdn and ev ch over 2f out: wknd fnl f* **20/1**

00 **8** *¾* **Lake Kalamalka (IRE)**[22] 4554 2-9-0 0.. EddieAhern 17 63
(J L Dunlop) *chsd ldrs: led briefly over 5f out: rdn and wknd over 1f out* **25/1**

9 *1 ¾* **Rock Art (IRE)** 2-9-0 0.. JimmyFortune 16 58
(B J Meehan) *leggy: scope: s.s: hdwy over 5f out: wknd over 1f out* **12/1**

10 *1 ½* **Sworn (USA)** 2-9-0 0.. ShaneKelly 7 54
(J Noseda) *unf: scope: sn pushed along in rr: hdwy over 1f out: n.d* **20/1**

0 **11** *¾* **Free Falling**[13] 4870 2-8-7 0.. MJMurphy(7) 10 53
(L M Cumani) *rangy: on toes: hld up in tch: rdn and wknd over 1f out* **28/1**

12 *2* **Morning Calm** 2-9-0 0.. SteveDrowne 4 48
(R Charlton) *w'like: scope: lengthy: mid-div: hdwy over 2f out: edgd lft and wknd over 1f out* **10/1**

13 *1 ¼* **Arabian Moonlight** 2-9-0 0.. JoeFanning 3 44
(E F Vaughan) *lengthy: scope: prom: rdn and ev ch over 2f out: wknd over 1f out* **33/1**

14 *1* **Timeless Dream** 2-9-0 0.. AlanMunro 9 42
(P W Chapple-Hyam) *w'like: bit bkwd: mid-div: sn pushed along: wknd 2f out* **12/1**

15 *1* **First Passage (USA)** 2-9-0 0.. TedDurcan 2 39
(B J Meehan) *w'like: scope: bit bkwd: mid-div: rdn over 2f out: sn hung lft and wknd* **12/1**

16 *1 ½* **Inis Boffin** 2-9-0 0.. MartinDwyer 1 36
(S Kirk) *leggy: s.s: outpcd and bhd: hdwy 2f out: sn wknd and eased* **66/1**

17 *23* **Cobos** 2-9-0 0.. IanMongan 8 —
(Miss J R Gibney) *w'like: str: dwlt: outpcd* **66/1**

1m 24.66s (-1.04) **Going Correction** -0.225s/f (Firm) 17 Ran SP% **128.8**
Speed ratings (Par 93): **96,94,94,93,90 89,88,87,85,84 83,80,79,78,77 75,49**
toteswinger: 1&2 £11.70, 1&3 £60.40, 2&3 £76.90. CSF £57.06 TOTE £7.00: £2.50, £4.10, £18.00; EX 75.20.
Owner Clipper Logistics **Bred** Irish National Stud **Trained** Whitsbury, Hants

FOCUS
Very few in this big field had racecourse experience and the time was 0.65 secs slower than the second division.

NOTEBOOK
Anice Stellato(IRE) ◆, a 70,000-euro first foal of a 6f winner from the family of Definite Article, Salford Express and Salford City, was well backed and knew her job, as she raced in the leading group throughout. Eaves gave her a good ride, as he held on to her when the favourite committed and did not make an effort until hitting the rising ground, from which point she picked up well to score a shade cosily. She has a Fillies' Mile entry but her trainer will not rush her this year and expects her to stay 1m2f to 1m4f in time. This race has produced such good fillies as Short Skirt and Playful Act in recent years and she could be in that league once mature. (op 10-1)
Capitelli(IRE), a market drifter on this debut, tracked the leaders from the start and stayed on well in the closing stages. A 60,000gns half-sister to a 1m1f juvenile winner from the family of Sleepytime, she is likely to be stepped up to 1m next time. (op 17-2 tchd 11-1)

Greenisland(IRE) ◆, the first foal of a half-sister to Luchiroverte from the family of Green Lucia, was very keen on this debut and made the early running, but after looking likely to drop away she ran on again in the closing stages and looks more than capable of winning good races provided she learns to settle.
Purple Sage(IRE) was very excitable beforehand and easy in the market. She travelled well in the race, though, and looked the winner meeting the rising ground, but she had nothing more to offer and was run out of the places in the last furlong. (op 11-4)
Mooteeah(IRE), a half-sister to Honolulu out of the top-class Cerulean Sky, also has a Fillies' Mile entry but the race may come too soon for her. She was doing her best work in the closing stages and should be better for the experience. (op 15-2)
Light Dubai(IRE), a 40,000gns first foal of a 7f juvenile winner; was another doing good work in the closing stages and should come on for the experience. (op 18-1)
Haakima(USA), a $160,000 half-sister to two winners out of a champion filly in Brazil, was backed at long prices and showed ability before fading up the hill. (op 33-1)
Lake Kalamalka(IRE), the most experienced in the line-up, had finished out the back in a decent contest at Goodwood last time and probably offers a fair line to the form. (op 28-1 tchd 33-1)
Rock Art(IRE), a 120,000euros half-sister to a couple of decent sorts from the family of Gothenberg, looked as if this experience was needed but got the hang of things late on and should come on considerably for the outing.
Cobos Official explanation: jockey said filly missed the break

5241 EUROPEAN BREEDERS' FUND MAIDEN FILLIES' STKS (DIV II) 7f

12:55 (12:59) (Class 4) 2-Y-O **£4,857** (£1,445; £722; £360) **Stalls** High

Form	Pos	Btn	Horse	Jockey	RPR
	1		**Golden Stream (IRE)** 2-9-0 0	RyanMoore 6	89+
			(Sir Michael Stoute) *unf: scope: led 2f: led over 2f out: styd on wl*	**10/1**[3]	
	2	1	**Uvinza** 2-9-0 0	PaulDoe 10	87+
			(W J Knight) *w'like: scope: bit bkwd: s.i.s: in rr: hdwy 2f out: styd on wl fnl f: nt rch wnr*	**66/1**	
0	3	shd	**Midday**[22] 4554 2-9-0 0	TedDurcan 5	86+
			(H R A Cecil) *lw: mid-div: effrt over 3f out: edgd rt: kpt on same pce ins fnl f: eased nr fin*	**11/8**[1]	
	4	2 3/4	**Multiplication** 2-9-0 0	SteveDrowne 8	79+
			(R Charlton) *w'like: mid-div: sn drvn along: edgd rt 2f out: styd on wl ins fnl f*	**16/1**	
5	5	3/4	**Simplification**[22] 4570 2-9-0 0	PatCosgrave 16	78
			(R Hannon) *in rr: hdwy 4f out: hung lft and kpt on fnl f*	**10/1**[3]	
	6	1/2	**King's Starlet** 2-9-0 0	RobertHavlin 13	76
			(H Morrison) *unf: scope: edgy: t.k.h: sn trcking ldrs: kpt on same pce appr fnl f*	**50/1**	
	7	3	**Super Sleuth (IRE)** 2-9-0 0	AlanMunro 12	69
			(B J Meehan) *w'like: scope: bit bkwd: s.s: styd on fnl 2f: nvr nr ldrs*	**12/1**	
	8	1	**Badiat Alzaman (IRE)** 2-9-0 0	StephenDonohoe 17	66
			(D M Simcock) *led after 2f: hdd over 2f out: sn wknd*	**11/1**	
30	9	1	**Triple Cee (IRE)**[42] 3913 2-9-0 0	EdwardCreighton 15	64
			(M R Channon) *in tch: outpcd over 2f out: kpt on fnl f*	**10/1**[3]	
2	10	1 1/4	**Plotting**[36] 4109 2-9-0 0	DarryllHolland 11	61
			(K A Ryan) *chsd ldrs: wknd 2f out*	**8/1**[2]	
06	11	4	**Dream Huntress**[29] 4337 2-9-0 0	JimmyFortune 9	51
			(B J Meehan) *in tch: lost pl over 1f out*	**16/1**	
35	12	3/4	**Black Nun**[37] 4080 2-9-0 0	PatDobbs 7	49
			(R Hannon) *lw: a towards rr*	**16/1**	
	13	1 1/4	**Deckchair** 2-9-0 0	DavidKinsella 14	46
			(V Smith) *w'like: cl cpld: a outpcd and in rr*	**100/1**	
	14	1 1/4	**Act Green** 2-9-0 0	MartinDwyer 4	43
			(M L W Bell) *w'like: scope: rangy: chsd ldrs: drvn over 3f out: lost pl over 1f out*	**16/1**	
0	15	3	**Varsa (IRE)**[67] 3085 2-9-0 0	RoystonFfrench 1	35
			(K R Burke) *w'like: chsd ldrs: lost pl over 2f out*	**80/1**	
	16	3/4	**Labisa (IRE)** 2-9-0 0	JimmyQuinn 3	33
			(H Morrison) *w'like: s.s: a in rr*	**28/1**	
	17	12	**Ocean Countess (IRE)** 2-8-11 0	RussellKennemore(3) 2	3
			(Miss J Feilden) *leggy: scope: s.s: in rr and drvn along: bhd fnl 2f*	**100/1**	

1m 24.01s (-1.69) **Going Correction** -0.225s/f (Firm) 2y crse rec **17** Ran SP% **130.2**
Speed ratings (Par 93): **100,98,98,95,94 94,90,89,88,87 82,81,80,78,75 74,60**
toteswinger: 1&2 £57.80, 1&3 £4.50, 2&3 £27.50. CSF £601.34 TOTE £8.80: £3.00, £8.90, £1.40; EX 433.20.
Owner The Queen **Bred** The Queen **Trained** Newmarket, Suffolk

FOCUS

The better of the two divisions and in all likelihood a strong fillies' maiden from which a number of winners will emerge. Again the field shunned the stands' rail and came down the centre. It was run in a time over half a second faster than division one, breaking the juvenile track record.

NOTEBOOK

Golden Stream(IRE) ◆, whose trainer's juveniles have not tended to be at their sharpest first time out this year, was one of the exceptions and clearly knew her job. She bounced out of the stalls but was given a lead after a couple of furlongs before moving back to the front and completing the job with something in hand. Her dam Phantom Gold, a Ribblesdale winner in the royal colours, has produced four previous winners, notably Flight Of Fancy, who won first time out at two and went on to finish second in the Oaks. Golden Stream is bred to stay 1m4f and makes some appeal at this early stage for the Epsom Classic in which Short Skirt, who won this maiden for Stoute three years ago, finished third. She looks to have the raw ability, and showed none of the temperament other members of the family have displayed. The Fillies' Mile at Ascot in a month or so may tell us more. (op 7-1)
Uvinza was one of the slowest away and palpably green in the early stages, but she really found her feet in the closing stages and came home well to snatch second on the post. The half-sister to ordinary winners at 1m and 1m3f was very cheaply retained as a yearling and comes from a relatively small yard, but she has plenty of ability.
Midday had shaped with promise on her debut when seventh at Glorious Goodwood and she was well supported for this second assignment. She raced on the far side of the pack, away from the main pace in the race, came under pressure at halfway and, after edging over to her right, had her chance, just lacking the pace of the winner inside the last furlong. A maiden will soon come her way. (op 6-4 tchd 5-4 and 13-8 in places)
Multiplication ◆ was being niggled along from a relatively early stage but, switched for a clear run on the stands' side of the bunch, she flew up the hill for fourth. The 110,000gns yearling is a half-sister to several winners, including the smart and versatile Black Monday, who has recently rejoined the Roger Charlton yard. Another furlong will suit her at this stage and she looks sure to shed her maiden tag soon. (op 25-1 tchd 33-1 in places)
Simplification, fifth against colts at Sandown on her debut, ran another sound race despite getting involved in some scrimmaging. (op 11-1 tchd 7-1)
King's Starlet ◆ is out of a maiden half-sister to Oaks winner Lady Carla. She did not settle early on but tracked the leaders travelling well on the near side before gradually fading once taken up. She looks sure to build on this promising introduction.
Super Sleuth(IRE), who is closely related to decent 6f winner Duelling, holds a Fillies' Mile entry and made a pleasing debut. Official explanation: jockey said filly hung right (op 20-1)
Badiat Alzaman(IRE), showed some of the pace that saw her fetch 120,000gns at the breeze-ups before weakening in the closing stages. (op 10-1 tchd 14-1)
Triple Cee(IRE) ran respectably and is now qualified for nurseries. (tchd 14-1)
Plotting, runner-up on her debut at Doncaster, had her chance and was a little disappointing, tracking the leaders on the favoured side of the pack but dropping away under pressure. (op 6-1 tchd 11-2)
Labisa(IRE), a half-sister to the yard's Free Handicap winner Stimulation, was always towards the back but can be expected to do better in time. (op 33-1 tchd 40-1)

5242 MICK ELLIOTT NURSERY 1m

1:30 (1:30) (Class 4) 2-Y-O **£5,180** (£1,541; £770; £384) **Stalls** High

Form	Pos	Btn	Horse	Jockey	RPR
326	1		**Highland Storm**[20] 4625 2-8-7 72	AlanMunro 14	78+
			(J G Given) *a.p: rdn over 1f out: edgd lft and led ins fnl f: r.o*	**11/1**	
4154	2	3/4	**Roly Boy**[21] 4589 2-9-1 80	RyanMoore 9	84+
			(R Hannon) *hld up: hdwy over 2f out: rdn over 1f out: r.o*	**5/2**[1]	
3213	3	1 1/4	**Jazacosta (USA)**[21] 4589 2-9-1 80	OPeslier 5	81
			(Mrs A J Perrett) *lw: chsd ldrs: rdn to ld and edgd lft 1f out: sn hdd and unable qckn*	**6/1**[2]	
261	4	1/2	**Calahonda**[16] 4747 2-8-7 72	EddieAhern 6	72
			(P W D'Arcy) *a.p: led over 1f out: sn rdn and hdd: no ex ins fnl f*	**20/1**	
3500	5	1 1/2	**In Transit (IRE)**[20] 4626 2-8-10 75	DarryllHolland 13	72
			(M R Channon) *led: racd keenly: rdn and hdd over 1f out: no ex whn rdr dropped whip ins fnl f*	**20/1**	
61	6	nse	**Zaaqya**[36] 4109 2-8-10 75	RHills 3	72
			(J L Dunlop) *lw: chsd ldrs: rdn over 2f out: styd on same pce fnl f*	**6/1**[2]	
0044	7	1	**Silent Hero**[14] 4828 2-8-0 65	WilliamBuick 2	60
			(M A Jarvis) *trckd ldrs: racd keenly: ev ch 2f out: sn rdn and hung lft: no ex ins fnl f: eased nr fin*	**7/1**	
51	8	1/2	**Cool Art (IRE)**[101] 2086 2-8-11 76	LDettori 1	69
			(S A Callaghan) *wnt lft s: hld up: hdwy over 1f out: sn rdn: wknd ins fnl f*	**13/2**[3]	
4011	9	1/2	**Shadow Bay (IRE)**[10] 4956 2-8-2 74 6ex	RossAtkinson(7) 7	66
			(Tom Dascombe) *hld up: rdn over 2f out: sn hung lft: n.d*	**9/1**	
5415	10	2	**Wohaida (IRE)**[20] 4640 2-8-5 70	EdwardCreighton 12	58
			(M R Channon) *lw: hld up: plld hrd: rdn over 1f out: a in rr*	**20/1**	
054	11	2	**Siciliando**[50] 3651 2-8-5 70	LiamJones 10	54
			(M L W Bell) *lw: s.i.s: hld up: rdn over 2f out: a in rr*	**20/1**	
040	12	7	**Kaada**[13] 4861 2-7-12 63 oh5	(b[1]) NickyMackay 4	31
			(C E Brittain) *hld up: swtchd lft over 3f out: rdn and wknd wl over 1f out*	**50/1**	

1m 39.4s (-0.60) **Going Correction** -0.225s/f (Firm) **12** Ran SP% **122.3**
Speed ratings (Par 96): **94,93,92,91,90 89,88,88,87,85 83,76**
toteswinger: 1&2 £7.80, 1&3 £13.70, 2&3 £4.70. CSF £36.99 CT £194.24 TOTE £14.70: £3.00, £1.50, £2.40; EX 50.10.
Owner D J Fish **Bred** D P Martin **Trained** Willoughton, Lincs

FOCUS

A decent nursery in which they seemed to go an even gallop. Roly Boy and Jazacosta ran pretty close to their previous form, suggesting this race is solid enough.

NOTEBOOK

Highland Storm, who was on his toes in the parade ring, travelled well on this handicap debut and picked up in the closing stages to get the better of the more experienced placed horses. He had apparently been struck into on his second start, which affected him on his third run, and, still a little green, he is likely to return here for another nursery. (op 12-1 tchd 10-1)
Roly Boy had finished a length and a quarter behind today's third at Goodwood last time but was 3lb better off and was backed into favourite to reverse the form. He was held up before delivering his effort over a furlong out, but found the winner finishing too strongly. (op 4-1)
Jazacosta(USA), who had finished just over a length ahead of Roly Boy at Goodwood, could not confirm the form on 3lb worse terms but is pretty consistent and again ran his race. (op 9-1)
Calahonda, who got off the mark when stepped up to 7f on her turf debut last time, ran a decent race and briefly looked the winner before her effort petered out up the hill. Perhaps she found the longer trip and stiffer track too much. (op 8-1)
In Transit(IRE), who was warm in the paddock, was stepping up two furlongs in trip and was backed at long prices but, after making the early running, he faded late on. He was not given a hard time once beaten and could be interesting in similar races over shorter trips. (op 50-1 tchd 18-1)
Zaaqya is relatively inexperienced and appeared to hit a flat spot when the race began in earnest before staying on again. (tchd 7-1)
Silent Hero was ridden more positively this time but carried his head awkwardly under pressure and may be happier on easier ground. (op 13-2 tchd 6-1)
Cool Art(IRE) was reappearing after a 101-day absence and briefly flattered before fading. (op 15-2 tchd 11-2)

5243 DARLEY YORKSHIRE OAKS (GROUP 1) (F&M) 1m 4f

2:05 (2:06) (Class 1) 3-Y-O+
£93,670 (£35,508; £17,770; £8,860; £4,438; £2,227) **Stalls** Centre

Form	Pos	Btn	Horse	Jockey	RPR
1512	1		**Lush Lashes**[20] 4623 3-8-11 0	KJManning 2	119+
			(J S Bolger, Ire) *lw: hld up: effrt over 3f out: led fnl 150yds: comf*	**1/1**[1]	
3311	2	1 1/4	**Dar Re Mi**[8] 5039 3-8-11 107	OPeslier 3	117
			(J H M Gosden) *lw: hld up: hdwy to ld over 2f out: hdd and no ex ins fnl f*	**15/2**	
0101	3	3 1/2	**Michita (USA)**[64] 3153 3-8-11 109	JimmyFortune 5	111
			(J H M Gosden) *trckd ldrs: hrd drvn 2f out: kpt on same pce appr fnl f*	**10/3**[2]	
1-04	4	2 3/4	**Allegretto (IRE)**[64] 3154 5-9-7 112	(v) RyanMoore 6	107
			(Sir Michael Stoute) *w ldr: led over 3f out: hdd over 2f out: sn outpcd: kpt on fnl f*	**14/1**	
4013	5	3/4	**Passage Of Time**[20] 4623 4-9-7 115	TedDurcan 1	105
			(H R A Cecil) *hld up: hdwy over 2f out: sn rdn and hung rt: wknd over 1f out*	**6/1**[3]	
2603	6	7	**Cape Amber (IRE)**[9] 4977 3-8-11 104	LDettori 4	94
			(P W Chapple-Hyam) *t.k.h: led tl over 3f out: lost pl over 1f out*	**25/1**	

2m 25.11s (-7.79) **Going Correction** -0.225s/f (Firm) course record
WFA 3 from 4yo+ 10lb **14** Ran SP% **109.6**
Speed ratings (Par 117): **116,115,112,111,110 105**
toteswinger: 1&2 £2.70, 1&3 £1.60, 2&3 £2.50. CSF £8.77 TOTE £1.80: £1.40, £2.60; EX 8.30.
Owner Mrs J S Bolger **Bred** Mrs A M Jenkins **Trained** Coolcullen, Co Carlow
■ This race was transferred after York's Ebor meeting was abandoned. The prize money was considerably reduced.

FOCUS

An interesting renewal of this prestigious event, but not a vintage one despite a top-notch winner, with such as Look Here, Moonstone and Promising Lead all missing. The pace was pretty solid despite the small field and the runners again made for the centre of the track, keeping away from the inside rail.

NOTEBOOK

Lush Lashes would have missed the race due to the testing ground had the Ebor meeting beaten the elements, but things fell right for her and she gained a deserved victory following her unlucky defeat in the Nassau at Goodwood. Held up in last place, she was switched to the near side of the sextet in preparation for the drive to the line, clearly travelling well, but was carried slightly to her right as Allegretto edged over on Michita. She was soon straightened up and ran on well to withstand the challenge of Dar Re Mi. She saw out the 1m4f well enough, having appeared not to stay in a fast-run Oaks on her only previous attempt at the trip, and is unfortunate not to have top-level wins to her name now at 1m, 1m2f and 1m4f. Her versatility looks sure to bring her further Group 1 success, with races like the Prix de l'Opera, Sun Chariot Stakes and Hong Kong Cup potential targets. (op 6-5 tchd 5-4 and 11-8 in places)

Dar Re Mi landed Deauville's Prix Minerve in soft ground and would not have been inconvenienced by underfoot conditions at York. She tracked the pace this time, having made all in France, and was the last to be let down. She ran on determinedly up the hill, but the Irish filly always had her measure. She is well worth another crack at this grade and may go for the Prix Vermeille at Longchamp, where Look Here could be in opposition. (op 8-1 tchd 7-1)

Michita(USA), a stablemate of the runner-up, had been targeted for this race since her impressive Ribblesdale win in June. She sweated up in the preliminaries but settled in fourth place in the race. After momentarily coming a bit close with the winner, she was unable to quicken up, but there seemed no real excuse and her third was the best placing achieved by the last eight Ribblesdale winners to contest the Yorkshire Oaks. The Prix de Royallieu at the Arc meeting looks a suitable target. (op 11-4 tchd 5-2 and 7-2 in places)

Allegretto(IRE), visored again, made the frame in the race for the third year in a row, after her third to Alexandrova in 2006 and second behind Peeping Fawn last year. She raced up with the pace in an attempt to utilise her stamina and plugged on willingly but lacked the turn of foot of her younger rivals. She could bid for a repeat victory in the Prix Royal-Oak, with the Doncaster Cup, a race her dam won, another possibility. (op 16-1 tchd 12-1)

Passage Of Time, who finished just a head behind Lush Lashes in a steadily run Nassau Stakes, was the disappointment of the race. She was always in the last pair, failed to find anything under pressure and is again left with something to prove, including her stamina for this trip, although she did seem to get home when last tried over 1m4f in last season's Vermeille. (tchd 13-2)

Cape Amber(IRE), rather keen in her previous three races, was taken to post early. She was allowed to bowl along in front but could not hold on once tackled and faded to finish last, the position she was booked for on official figures. She is a smart filly but not up to this class. (tchd 20-1)

5244 DBS £300000 ST LEGER YEARLING STKS — 6f

2:35 (2:40) (Class 2) 2-Y-O

£160,620 (£64,261; £32,130; £16,049; £8,024; £8,024) **Stalls** High

Form				RPR
41	**1**		**Elnawin**[27] 4430 2-8-11 0 ... PatDobbs 15 (R Hannon) *lw: w ldr tl led over 2f out: rdn out* **25/1**	104+
12	**2**	*2*	**Bonnie Charlie**[24] 4507 2-8-11 0 ... RyanMoore 14 (R Hannon) *lw: a.p: rdn to chse wnr over 1f out: no imp ins fnl f* **13/8**[1]	97
43	**3**	*2*	**Frognal (IRE)**[24] 4510 2-8-11 0 ... LDettori 17 (B J Meehan) *lw: hld up: hdwy over 1f out: sn rdn: styd on same pce ins fnl f* **12/1**	91
1	**4**	*3/4*	**Damien (IRE)**[25] 4480 2-8-11 0 ... MichaelHills 9 (B W Hills) *chsd ldrs: rdn over 1f out: edgd rt and styd on same pce ins fnl f* **14/1**	89+
22	**5**	*hd*	**Fitz Flyer (IRE)**[32] 4237 2-8-11 0 ... RoystonFfrench 10 (D H Brown) *lw: s.i.s and hmpd s: hld up: plld hrd: outpcd 2f out: r.o ins fnl f: nt rch ldrs* **9/1**	88+
141	**6**	*1/2*	**Anglezarke (IRE)**[27] 4434 2-8-6 0 ... DavidAllan 16 (T D Easterby) *a.p: rdn over 2f out: styd on* **8/1**[3]	82
2263	**7**	*1*	**Noble Jack (IRE)**[20] 4626 2-8-11 0 ... PatCosgrave 20 (R Hannon) *chsd ldrs: rdn over 2f out: styd on same pce appr fnl f* **20/1**	84
4123	**8**	*shd*	**Indian Art (IRE)**[53] 3553 2-8-11 87 ... OPeslier 19 (R Hannon) *hld up in tch: rdn and hung lft over 1f out: styd on same pce* **25/1**	83
321	**9**	*1/2*	**Ouqba**[43] 3879 2-8-11 0 ... RHills 4 (B W Hills) *chsd ldrs: rdn and edgd rt over 1f out: no ex ins fnl f* **11/2**[2]	82+
1206	**10**	*hd*	**Harwalla (IRE)**[34] 4190 2-8-11 87 ... MartinDwyer 18 (M Johnston) *lw: chsd ldrs: rdn over 1f out: wknd fnl f* **16/1**	81
4624	**11**	*1 3/4*	**Heliodor (USA)**[9] 4974 2-8-11 74 ... (b[1]) SteveDrowne 13 (R Hannon) *chsd ldrs: rdn over 2f out: wknd over 1f out* **100/1**	76
164	**12**	*3/4*	**Full Of Nature**[57] 3412 2-8-6 84 ... JoeFanning 8 (K A Ryan) *mid-div: sn pushed along: lost pl over 3f out: n.d after* **66/1**	69+
423	**13**	*nk*	**Mister Green (FR)**[28] 4389 2-8-11 83 ... (v[1]) EddieAhern 11 (M J Wallace) *chsd ldrs: rdn over 2f out: wknd fnl f* **33/1**	73
6451	**14**	*1 3/4*	**Klynch**[16] 4729 2-8-11 85 ... (b) JimmyFortune 6 (B J Meehan) *prom: rdn over 2f out: wknd and eased fnl f* **40/1**	68+
0001	**15**	*shd*	**Shampagne**[25] 4475 2-9-2 100 ... TedDurcan 2 (P F I Cole) *hld up in tch: plld hrd: rdn and wknd over 1f out* **28/1**	72+
2313	**16**	*nse*	**Evelyn May (IRE)**[14] 4822 2-8-6 0 ... WilliamBuick 5 (B W Hills) *hld up: effrt over 2f out: hung lft and wknd sn after* **40/1**	62+
0232	**17**	*shd*	**Olympic Dream**[16] 4740 2-8-11 0 ... JamieMoriarty 12 (R A Fahey) *led over 3f: rdn and wknd over 1f out* **50/1**	67
4101	**18**	*1*	**Burning Flute**[30] 4297 2-8-11 78 ... TomEaves 7 (B J Meehan) *lw: hld up: plld hrd: in rr whn nt clr run over 1f out* **33/1**	67+
2231	**19**	*2 1/2*	**Secret Venue**[28] 4384 2-8-11 0 ... TonyHamilton 1 (Jedd O'Keeffe) *lw: prom: rdn over 2f out: wknd over 1f out* **100/1**	56+

1m 10.35s (-2.15) **Going Correction** -0.225s/f (Firm) 2y crse rec **19** Ran SP% **126.9**

Speed ratings (Par 100): **105,102,99,98,98 97,96,96,95,95 93,92,91,89,89 89,88,87,84**

toteswinger: 1&2 £19.50, 1&3 £54.40, 2&3 £7.50. CSF £61.93 TOTE £37.00: £9.20, £1.30, £4.00; EX 145.50 Trifecta £307.30 Pool: £830.75. 2.00 winning units..

Owner Noodles Racing **Bred** D R Tucker **Trained** East Everleigh, Wilts

■ Another race rescheduled from the Ebor meeting.

FOCUS

Not a strong renewal of this valuable sales race but the time was good, helped by a tail wind. The runner-up was way below his Molecomb figure. They raced virtually all across the track but those who raced centre to stands' side dominated, with the first three drawn 15, 14 and 17 and the other one who raced with them early on, drawn 16, finishing sixth. The race was a triumph for Richard Hannon - surprisingly, winning it for the first time - who was responsible for the first two.

NOTEBOOK

Elnawin, who had improved on his debut effort when beating a subsequent winner in a Salisbury maiden, was proven over the trip and on the ground. He was on the pace throughout, went clear running into the Dip and scored with a bit in hand. He could well go for the Horris Hill Stakes, but he may well be kept to this trip for the time being. (op 50-1 tchd 22-1)

Bonnie Charlie, touched off in the Molecomb, was a hot favourite and got a good lead into the race from his stablemate. He was not disgraced, coming clear of the rest, and it would be no surprise if he was dropped back to 5f for races such as the Flying Childers and the Cornwallis Stakes. (op 6-4 tchd 7-4, 15-8 in places and 2-1 in a place)

Frognal(IRE) stepped up on his previous efforts and was possibly helped by getting a tow from the principals. He should be winning races before long. (op 14-1)

Damien(IRE), who was representing last year's winning connections, was noisy in the paddock but ran a fine race for one so inexperienced. He did best of those drawn in single figures and should improve with racing. (tchd 16-1)

Fitz Flyer(IRE), who got rid of his rider on the way to the start, was staying on nicely in the closing stages. He had been a narrowly beaten second in both starts on a sound surface before this and should be winning before long on this evidence.

Anglezarke(IRE), one of only three fillies in the line-up, showed up well for a long way with the first three before tiring in the closing stages. She is unbeaten in two runs at 5f but beaten on both tries over 6f and is another who is likely drop back in trip, with races like the Harry Rosebery at Ayr looking suitable. (op 11-1)

Noble Jack(IRE) raced closer to the stands' rail than the first three and the would probably have appreciated more give in the ground. (op 40-1)

Ouqba, who had some good form in the spring before having a break, had shown his well-being when scoring on his previous start but was not helped by racing more towards the far side of the track and can be rated better than the bare result suggests. (op 13-2)

5245 COOLMORE NUNTHORPE STKS (GROUP 1) — 5f

3:05 (3:12) (Class 1) 2-Y-O+

£93,670 (£35,508; £17,770; £8,860; £4,438; £2,227) **Stalls** High

Form				RPR
2223	**1**		**Borderlescott**[20] 4624 6-9-11 109 ... PatCosgrave 12 (R Bastiman) *chsd ldrs: styd on gamely to ld wl ins fnl f* **12/1**	121
10-6	**2**	*1/2*	**National Colour (SAF)**[66] 3101 6-9-8 0 ... KShea 10 (S Tarry, South Africa) *w ldrs: edgd lft and led over 2f out: hdd and no ex fnl 75yds* **9/1**	116
-015	**3**	*1*	**Kingsgate Native (IRE)**[42] 3922 3-9-9 120 ... RyanMoore 11 (J R Best) *in rr: hdwy 2f out: styd on strly ins fnl f* **4/1**[2]	116
3-21	**4**	*1 3/4*	**Equiano (FR)**[66] 3101 3-9-9 0 ... OPeslier 8 (B W Hills) *mid-div: effrt 2f out: hung lft: styd on wl fnl f* **10/3**[1]	109
5020	**5**	*1/2*	**Benbaun (IRE)**[42] 3922 7-9-11 111 ... (v) TedDurcan 13 (M J Wallace) *sn wl bhd: hdwy over 1f out: styd on strly ins fnl f* **14/1**	108
0-00	**6**	*1/2*	**Moorhouse Lad**[22] 4550 5-9-11 110 ... RoystonFfrench 5 (B Smart) *chsd ldrs: kpt on same pce appr fnl f* **33/1**	106
-043	**7**	*1 3/4*	**Dandy Man (IRE)**[22] 4550 5-9-11 114 ... (t) LDettori 14 (Saeed Bin Suroor) *hld up in rr: hdwy stands' side 2f out: kpt on fnl f* **13/2**[3]	99
0200	**8**	*1 3/4*	**Prime Defender**[20] 4624 4-9-11 113 ... MichaelHills 7 (B W Hills) *lw: mid-div: edgd lft over 2f out: nvr trbld ldrs* **25/1**	93
3030	**9**	*nk*	**Desert Lord**[22] 4550 8-9-11 106 ... (b) DarryllHolland 6 (K A Ryan) *b: chsd ldrs: edgd lft over 1f out: sn wknd* **33/1**	92
3214	**10**	*1/2*	**Shyrl**[7] 5055 2-7-12 101 ... AdrianMcCarthy 1 (S A Callaghan) *chsd ldrs: fdd appr fnl f* **66/1**	79
1-14	**11**	*2 3/4*	**Captain Gerrard (IRE)**[82] 2652 3-9-9 114 ... TomEaves 3 (B Smart) *led over 2f: hung lft and wknd over 1f out* **16/1**	80
1112	**12**	*2*	**Percolator**[26] 4472 2-7-12 0 ... WilliamBuick 4 (P F I Cole) *chsd ldrs: lost pl over 1f out* **18/1**	62
3146	**13**	*nk*	**Flashmans Papers**[24] 4507 2-8-1 105 ... JimmyQuinn 2 (J R Best) *mid-div: drvn over 2f out: n.d* **25/1**	64
5-20	**14**	*41*	**Sakhee's Secret**[62] 3247 4-9-11 120 ... SteveDrowne 9 (H Morrison) *lw: s.i.s: detached in last: virtually p.u 2f out: dismntd after line* **15/2**	—

56.09 secs (-3.01) **Going Correction** -0.225s/f (Firm) course record **17** Ran SP% **118.7**

Speed ratings: **115,114,112,109,109 108,105,102,102,101 96,93,93,27**

toteswinger: 1&2 £19.80, 1&3 £12.80, 2&3 £8.80. CSF £108.63 TOTE £14.60: £3.30, £2.70, £2.00; EX 152.10 Trifecta £1434.00 Part won. Pool: £1937.97. 0.40 winning units..

Owner James Edgar & William Donaldson **Bred** James Clark **Trained** Cowthorpe, N Yorks

■ This race, transferred after the abandonment of York's Ebor meeting, was the first Group race run over 5f on the July Course.

FOCUS

The switch of tracks changed the complexion of the race to a stiffish test at the trip on good ground from what would have been testing conditions over the usually easy five at York. The prize money was considerably reduced. This was an intriguing renewal in which many of the leading 5f performers were present, exceptions being Fleeting Spirit and Enticing, plus Takeover Target, who would not have turned up even before his injury. July Cup second US Ranger was taken out after the race was switched from York. With the fifth, seventh and fourteenth not at their best this year it was probably only an ordinary renewal, but the pace was strong and, with the aid of a tail wind, the track record was broken by over a second. A high draw seemed a definite advantage, with the first three drawn 12, ten and 11, and not many got into the race.

NOTEBOOK

Borderlescott is at home in soft ground, unlike some of his rivals, and his chance seemed to have been dented by the change of venue, but he has plenty of form on decent ground too. He chased the mare through the early stages, remained well in touch and came through under a well-judged ride to pick her off close home. This was his first Group victory and since winning the 2006 Stewards' Cup he had only a Musselburgh conditions race win to his name, to go with 12 placed efforts. He is a great credit to his trainer and could bid for further Group 1 laurels in the Prix de l'Abbaye. (op 10-1)

National Colour(SAF) has remained in Britain since finishing sixth to Equiano in the King's Stand at Ascot in June, her first run for well over a year. The grey is suited by fast ground and showed fine pace to get most of the field on the stretch but, after drifting over to the centre of the track, she could not hold off the winner. This was an excellent effort. (op 12-1)

Kingsgate Native(IRE) was a surprise winner of this race last year when in receipt of a hefty juvenile weight allowance, but showed that to be no fluke when landing the Golden Jubilee Stakes at Ascot. He was fifth in the July Cup here last time and ran another solid race, slightly outpaced by the leaders through the early parts but coming home strongly. It might be that he is most effective over the extra furlong now and the Betfred Sprint Cup at Haydock is his next target. (tchd 7-2 and 9-2 in places)

Equiano(FR) left Madrid-based trainer Mauricio Delcher Sanchez immediately after his King's Stand win to join Barry Hills. He showed decent pace in the centre of the pack but rather hung to his left when the pressure was on before knuckling down to claim fourth close home. He handles most types of ground and it would be no surprise to see him aimed at the Abbaye. (op 4-1 tchd 9-2 in a place)

Benbaun(IRE), drawn on what turned out to be the right side, could not go the early pace but came home with a flourish. No doubt the Abbaye figures on his agenda again but he looks ready for a return to 6f. (op 16-1)

Moorhouse Lad ran an encouraging race in the King George at Goodwood and he performed respectably again, relegated two places close home after chasing the pace throughout. This was only his third run of the campaign and he will be fresher than most in the autumn, although he does need a sound surface. (op 40-1)

Dandy Man(IRE) has proved notoriously expensive to follow and remains without a Group-race win since May 2006. He was unable to cash in on what was probably the best of the draw, ending up racing on his own near the stands' rail and keeping on but no threat to the principals. (op 8-1 tchd 6-1)

Prime Defender, behind Borderlescott when disappointing in the Stewards' Cup last time, had run well here in the July Cup but was well below that level over this sharper trip.

Desert Lord, runner-up in this last year, performed better than he had at Goodwood, where he lost a couple of shoes, but could not sustain his pace in the final furlong. (tchd 28-1)

Shyrl did best of the three juveniles, but she raced on the wrong flank of the pack and was no threat late on.

Captain Gerrard(IRE), who was on his toes beforehand, had been off the track since finishing fourth to Equiano at Chantilly at the beginning of June, and was another to drop out after showing bright pace towards the far side of the pack.
Percolator, who was in receipt of 27lb from the older males, was another inconvenienced by being drawn low but did travel well to a point. (op 14-1 tchd 20-1)
Flashmans Papers, a stablemate of Kingsgate Native and bidding to repeat that colt's feat in this race, was always struggling to go the speed. (op 20-1 tchd 16-1)
Sakhee's Secret, last year's July Cup winner, was on a retrieval mission with underfoot conditions to suit after a poor effort at Ascot. He missed the break, trailed throughout and was eased right off two furlongs out. He was dismounted after the line and it turned out that he had pulled muscles in his back, probably as he exited the stalls. Official explanation: jockey said colt came out of stalls awkwardly; vet said colt was lame (op 5-1)

5246 RENAULT MASTER E B F MAIDEN STKS (C&G) 7f
3:40 (3:47) (Class 4) 2-Y-O £5,180 (£1,541; £770; £384) Stalls High

Form RPR

2 1 **Delegator**[14] 4826 2-9-0 0 .... JimmyFortune 15 85+
(B J Meehan) *lw: hld up in tch: led over 1f out: rdn clr and hung lft ins fnl f: eased and edgd rt towards fin* **8/11**[1]

2 *1* **Palavicini (USA)** 2-9-0 0 .... EddieAhern 9 85+
(J L Dunlop) *w'like: scope: lw: hld up: rdn over 2f out: edgd lft and r.o ins fnl f: no ch w wnr* **10/1**[3]

3 *2 1/4* **Four Winds** 2-9-0 0 .... JamieSpencer 2 75+
(M L W Bell) *w'like: scope: chsd ldrs: rdn over 1f out: styd on same pce fnl f* **11/2**[2]

4 *hd* **Kaolak (USA)** 2-9-0 0 .... NeilPollard 10 74
(J Ryan) *rangy: scope: lw: s.s: hdwy to chse ldrs over 5f out: rdn over 1f out: styd on* **100/1**

5 *1/2* **Contretemps (USA)** 2-9-0 0 .... LDettori 5 73
(Saeed Bin Suroor) *rangy: lw: led: rdn and hdd over 1f out: no ex ins fnl f* **11/1**

6 *1 1/2* **Sumbe (USA)** 2-9-0 0 .... MartinDwyer 7 69
(M P Tregoning) *w'like: bit bkwd: chsd ldrs: rdn over 2f out: no ex fnl f* **25/1**

7 *1 1/4* **Take The Micky** 2-9-0 0 .... PaulDoe 12 66
(W J Knight) *leggy: hld up: hdwy over 2f out: hung rt over 1f out: wknd fnl f* **50/1**

8 *2* **Cry For The Moon (USA)** 2-9-0 0 .... OPeslier 18 61+
(Mrs A J Perrett) *leggy: lengthy: scope: hld up: plenty to do 2f out: r.o ins fnl f: nvr nr to chal* **33/1**

9 *nse* **Cornish Castle (USA)** 2-9-0 0 .... TedDurcan 16 61
(H R A Cecil) *w'like: hld up: rdn over 2f out: sn hung lft: n.d* **16/1**

10 *hd* **Crowded House** 2-9-0 0 .... DarryllHolland 3 61+
(B J Meehan) *str: bit bkwd: s.s: hld up: shkn up over 2f out: n.d* **25/1**

11 *1* **Salomo (GER)** 2-9-0 0 .... RHills 6 58
(J L Dunlop) *unf: attr: hld up in tch: rdn over 2f out: wknd fnl f* **25/1**

12 *1 1/4* **Jack Cool (IRE)** 2-9-0 0 .... AlanMunro 11 55
(P W Chapple-Hyam) *unf: scope: sn pushed along in rr: n.d* **33/1**

13 *1/2* **Kattar** 2-9-0 0 .... StephenDonohoe 13 54
(D M Simcock) *w'like: athletic: sn outpcd* **66/1**

14 *nk* **Royal Trooper (IRE)** 2-9-0 0 .... TomEaves 1 53
(J G Given) *w'like: bit bkwd: chsd ldrs: rdn and wknd over 1f out* **66/1**

15 *1 1/4* **Recession Proof (FR)** 2-9-0 0 .... RobertHavlin 20 50
(S A Callaghan) *w'like: bit bkwd: hld up: rdn 1/2-way: a in rr* **100/1**

16 *2 1/2* **Muhim** 2-9-0 0 .... LiamJones 14 44
(C E Brittain) *leggy: prom: rdn 1/2-way: wknd over 1f out* **66/1**

17 *4 1/2* **Aziz (IRE)** 2-9-0 0 .... (b[1]) PaulEddery 19 32
(Miss D Mountain) *leggy: dwlt: outpcd* **100/1**

18 *24* **Riptide** 2-9-0 0 .... IanMongan 17 —
(C F Wall) *w'like: bit bkwd: s.s: outpcd* **50/1**

19 *11* **Stanley Rigby** 2-9-0 0 .... PatCosgrave 4 —
(C F Wall) *w'like: bit bkwd: s.s: outpcd* **100/1**

1m 24.86s (-0.84) **Going Correction** -0.225s/f (Firm) **19** Ran SP% **126.4**
Speed ratings (Par 96): **95,93,91,91,90 88,87,85,85,84 83,82,81,81,79 77,71,44,31**
toteswinger: 1&2 £6.00, 1&3 £3.10, 2&3 £15.30. CSF £7.78 TOTE £1.70: £1.20, £2.90, £2.00; EX 10.60.
Owner Mrs P Good **Bred** Mrs P Good **Trained** Manton, Wilts

FOCUS
Another big field for this colts' maiden and only the winner had previous experience. The time was slower than the two divisions of the fillies' race over the trip earlier in the day although they did tend to race more towards the far side of the track on this occasion.

NOTEBOOK
Delegator ◆, out of a half-sister to the top-class performers Tomba and Holding Court, ran green when runner-up in a 7f maiden on easy ground here on his debut, but that race had already been boosted by Midnight Cruiser's win at Newbury earlier in the afternoon and he duly improved enough to get off the mark. He cruised to the front two furlongs from home and soon stormed clear but what looked like being an impressive victory became less so as the runner-up made serious inroads into his advantage. He looks a nice sort and the trainer thinks he could make up into a stakes-class performer. (op 11-10)
Palavicini(USA) ◆, on his toes in the paddock, was the real eyecatcher and should not be long in getting off the mark on this evidence. The first foal of a dual 1m4f winner from the family of Son Of Sharp Shot and Oath, he was surprisingly well backed beforehand, considering he is from a yard that is not noted for having first-time-out juvenile winners, so he had clearly been showing a certain amount of precocity at home. (op 25-1)
Four Winds, a half-brother to several middle-distance winners from the family of Blueprint, showed up throughout on this debut and, although no match for the first two in the closing stages, was by no means disgraced. He holds a Royal Lodge and Derby entry so is another who is clearly well thought-of. (op 6-1)
Kaolak(USA), a cheaply-bought half-brother to three minor US winners, ran well considering he missed the break before being keen and pulling his way into contention, then staying on well in the closing stages.
Contretemps(USA) a 170,000gns half-brother to Latif, travelled well up with the pace before tiring up the hill and should be better for the outing. (op 8-1)
Sumbe(USA) ◆, an attractive 290,000gns half-brother to six winners including Summoner and Compton Admiral, was another to run well. He also has a Derby entry and, although he may not get quite that far ultimately, looks a decent prospect nonetheless. (op 22-1)
Take The Micky, whose trainer had a long-priced runner-up in the second division of the fillies' race, will have been pleased with the debut effort of the first foal of the multiple winning miler Ailincala and looks the sort who could emulate his dam if able to build on this initial effort. (op 66-1 tchd 100-1)
Cry For The Moon(USA), a $190,000 half-brother to four winners in the USA, was coltish in the paddock but showed some promise. Official explanation: jockey said, regarding running and riding, his orders were to settle the colt and do his best, adding that it is weak and backward and showed signs of greenness, particularly in the early stages, further adding that it became tired, only staying on through beaten horses. (op 16-1)
Crowded House, a 75,000gns half-brother to several winners including Heron Bay, has a Derby entry and did not do too badly after missing the break. (op 28-1 tchd 33-1)
Salomo(GER), an attractive 430,000 euros yearling from a high-class German family; should do better with this outing under his belt. (op 20-1 tchd 16-1)

5247 RENAULT TRAFIC H'CAP 6f
4:10 (4:16) (Class 4) (0-85,84) 3-Y-O+ £6,476 (£1,927; £963; £481) Stalls High

Form RPR

2511 1 **Earlsmedic**[7] 5067 3-8-8 76 6ex .... (v) WilliamCarson(5) 14 88+
(S C Williams) *lw: mde all towards stands' side: kpt on wl fnl f* **9/4**[1]

3626 2 *1 3/4* **Rockfield Lodge (IRE)**[15] 4773 3-8-12 75 .... JoeFanning 7 81
(M E Rimmer) *stdd s: tk fierce hold: swtchd rt after 2f: hdwy over 2f out: styd on fnl f: tk 2nd towards fin* **40/1**

015 3 *hd* **Romany Nights (IRE)**[6] 5088 8-8-5 65 .... (bt) LiamJones 15 70
(Miss Gay Kelleway) *chsd ldrs stands' side: edgd lft over 1f out: kpt on same pce ins fnl f* **16/1**

0160 4 *1/2* **Wyatt Earp (IRE)**[13] 4854 7-9-7 81 .... (b) TonyHamilton 12 85
(R A Fahey) *chsd ldrs: kpt on same pce fnl f* **16/1**

3603 5 *1 1/4* **Gift Horse**[7] 5067 8-9-10 84 .... (p) JamieSpencer 6 84
(D Nicholls) *lw: s.i.s: swtchd rt after s: bhd tl hdwy over 1f out: kpt on wl: nt rch ldrs* **7/1**[2]

5000 5 *dht* **Special Day**[22] 4555 4-9-9 83 .... MichaelHills 17 83
(B W Hills) *in rr-div stands' side: hdwy over 2f out: nvr rchd ldrs* **11/1**

5236 7 *shd* **Cornus**[7] 5067 6-9-4 78 .... (be) PatCosgrave 2 77
(A J McCabe) *hld up towards rr: hdwy far side over 1f out: hrd rdn and styd on ins fnl f* **18/1**

0000 8 *nk* **Obe Brave**[13] 4869 5-9-8 82 .... JamieMoriarty 3 80
(R A Fahey) *chsd ldrs: fdd appr fnl f* **16/1**

030 9 *hd* **Tudor Prince (IRE)**[40] 3998 4-8-13 73 .... LDettori 8 71
(A W Carroll) *w ldrs: wknd 1f out* **25/1**

2010 10 *1/2* **Rocker**[21] 4586 4-8-9 69 ow3 .... (b) RyanMoore 4 65
(G L Moore) *w ldrs: wknd 1f out* **16/1**

3042 11 *3/4* **John Keats**[7] 5067 5-9-4 78 .... DanielTudhope 5 72
(J S Goldie) *mid-div: effrt over 2f out: wknd over 1f out* **9/1**[3]

2415 12 *1* **Liberation Spirit (USA)**[20] 4641 3-9-5 82 .... (v[1]) WilliamBuick 11 73
(J Noseda) *lw chsd ldrs: lost pl over 1f out* **10/1**

0000 13 *5* **Brunelleschi**[7] 5067 5-8-13 73 .... (b) AlanMunro 1 48
(P L Gilligan) *in rr: hdwy far side over 2f out: wknd fnl f* **25/1**

2246 14 *1 3/4* **Realt Na Mara (IRE)**[13] 4865 5-8-11 71 .... SteveDrowne 16 40
(H Morrison) *chsd ldrs: edgd lft over 1f out: sn wknd* **20/1**

1600 15 *nk* **Imperial Echo (USA)**[11] 4928 7-8-13 73 .... IanMongan 9 41
(P Howling) *a towards rr* **33/1**

0025 16 *5* **Pacific Pride**[9] 4962 5-9-4 78 .... (p) DarryllHolland 13 30
(J J Quinn) *w wnr: wknd over 1f out: eased ins fnl f* **16/1**

0000 17 *12* **Lawyer To World**[36] 4123 4-7-12 65 oh20 .... DonnaCaldwell(7) 10 —
(Mrs C A Dunnett) *in rr: eased over 1f out* **100/1**

1m 10.23s (-2.27) **Going Correction** -0.225s/f (Firm)
WFA 3 from 4yo+ 3lb **17** Ran SP% **124.2**
Speed ratings (Par 105): **106,103,103,102,101 101,100,100,100,99 98,97,90,88,87 81,65**
toteswinger: 1&2 £28.10, 1&3 £15.70, 2&3 £99.90. CSF £130.07 CT £1277.04 TOTE £3.30: £1.50, £6.30, £4.10, £3.30; EX 131.00.
Owner Mad Man Plus One **Bred** W N Greig **Trained** Newmarket, Suffolk

FOCUS
This fair sprint was competitive numbers-wise, but it revolved around the progressive winner who ran basically to form in landing the hat-trick. The runner-up showed improvement.
Pacific Pride Official explanation: vet said gelding had bled from the nose

5248 RENAULT KANGOO CLAIMING STKS 7f
4:40 (4:43) (Class 5) 3-Y-O £3,885 (£1,156; £577; £288) Stalls High

Form RPR

0610 1 **Bellomi (IRE)**[64] 3155 3-9-9 92 .... EddieAhern 7 85+
(W J Haggas) *hld up: swtchd lft 2f out: hdwy on bit over 1f out: edgd rt: shkn up to ld ins fnl f: readily* **4/6**[1]

321 2 *1/2* **Spin Again (IRE)**[20] 4637 3-9-3 74 .... GeorgeBaker 3 78
(R M Beckett) *swtg: led after 1f: rdn and edgd lft over 1f out: hdd ins fnl f: r.o* **11/4**[2]

2403 3 *7* **Zeffirelli**[45] 3817 3-8-12 59 .... ShaneKelly 8 54
(M Quinn) *led 1f: chsd ldr tl rdn over 1f out: wknd ins fnl f* **20/1**

0400 4 *3/4* **Young Ivanhoe**[8] 5015 3-8-8 52 .... (t) JimmyQuinn 4 48
(C A Dwyer) *plld hrd and prom: rdn over 1f out: wknd ins fnl f* **50/1**

0164 5 *1* **Royal Applord**[9] 4969 3-9-4 68 .... (p) DarryllHolland 9 55
(K A Ryan) *chsd ldrs: shkn up over 2f out: rdn and wknd fnl f* **10/1**[3]

042 6 *3* **Rankayo Hitam (USA)**[34] 4181 3-9-9 73 .... JoeFanning 2 52
(P F I Cole) *lw: hld up: hdwy 2f out: sn rdn and edgd lft: wknd fnl f* **20/1**

45-0 7 *2 1/2* **Calypso Charms**[68] 3064 3-8-8 73 .... LiamJones 6 31
(M L W Bell) *lw: plld hrd and prom: rdn and wknd over 1f out* **33/1**

1m 24.5s (-1.20) **Going Correction** -0.225s/f (Firm) **7** Ran SP% **110.2**
Speed ratings (Par 100): **97,96,88,87,86 83,80**
toteswinger: 1&2 £1.30, 1&3 £4.00, 2&3 £5.10. CSF £2.29 TOTE £1.70: £1.40, £1.60; EX 3.00.The winner was claimed by Gay Kelleway for £20,000. Spin Again was claimed by D Nicholls for £14,000.
Owner Hit The Beach Partnership **Bred** Barronstown Stud **Trained** Newmarket, Suffolk

FOCUS
A reasonable if uncompetitive claimer in which the favourite appeared to have plenty in hand judged on official ratings. The race worked out as the market suggested and the form is rated through the runner-up.
Royal Applord Official explanation: jockey said gelding was unsuited by the good ground

5249 BREHENY H'CAP 1m 6f 175y
5:15 (5:15) (Class 3) (0-95,91) 3-Y-O+ £9,066 (£2,697; £1,348; £673) Stalls Centre

Form RPR

2111 1 **Askar Tau (FR)**[16] 4751 3-8-6 82 .... MartinDwyer 10 97+
(M P Tregoning) *lw: chsd ldrs: shkn up over 7f out: styd on to ld over 1f out: styd on strly: readily* **11/4**[1]

3431 2 *3 1/4* **Ollie George (IRE)**[63] 3209 5-9-11 88 .... LPKeniry 12 94
(A M Balding) *lw: led: hung lft and hdd over 1f out: kpt on: no ch w wnr* **10/1**

4113 3 *1/2* **Rajeh (IRE)**[24] 4508 5-10-0 91 .... LiamJones 7 97
(J L Spearing) *chsd ldrs: rdn over 2f out: styd on same pce appr fnl f* **14/1**

2664 4 *3 3/4* **Trenchtown (IRE)**[23] 4519 3-8-8 84 .... SteveDrowne 1 85+
(R Charlton) *hld up in rr: hdwy 3f out: kpt on same pce: nvr rchd ldrs* **5/1**[2]

3131 5 *1 1/2* **Any Given Day (IRE)**[26] 4448 3-8-5 81 .... JimmyQuinn 4 80+
(D M Simcock) *hld up in rr: drvn along 7f out: styd on fnl 2f: nvr trbld ldrs* **8/1**

0110 6 *3/4* **Always Bold (IRE)**[23] 4519 3-8-11 87 .... JoeFanning 11 85
(M Johnston) *chsd ldrs: one pce fnl 2f* **10/1**

43-1 **7** *1 ¼* **Armure**[51] 3611 3-8-3 **79** .... WilliamBuick 5 75
(M A Jarvis) *mid-div: t.k.h: lost pl 6f out: hdwy on outer over 3f out: wknd over 1f out* **11/2**[3]

0102 **8** *3* **Birkside**[16] 4742 5-9-12 **89** .... DNolan 8 82
(D Carroll) *lw: hld up in rr: hdwy 7f out: wknd over 1f out* **20/1**

0-20 **9** *11* **Horseford Hill**[42] 3925 4-9-9 **86** .... AlanMunro 2 64
(D R C Elsworth) *sn chsng ldrs: lost pl over 3f out* **22/1**

2514 **10** *1* **Paktolos (FR)**[55] 3505 5-9-11 **88** ....(b) JamieSpencer 13 65
(A King) *hld up in rr: effrt over 3f out: wknd 2f out* **16/1**

6512 **11** *11* **Sea Chorus**[8] 5024 3-7-12 **74** oh3................(t) DavidKinsella 6 37
(M L W Bell) *swtg: w ldrs: rdn over 3f out: lost pl over 2f out: sn bhd* **12/1**

1334 **12** *49* **Pass The Port**[50] 3630 7-9-3 **80** .... TedDurcan 3 —
(D Haydn Jones) *hld up in rr: lost pl over 2f out: sn bhd: virtually p.u: hopelessly t.o* **20/1**

3m 4.60s (-6.70) **Going Correction** -0.225s/f (Firm)
WFA 3 from 4yo+ 13lb **12** Ran SP% **122.1**
Speed ratings (Par 107): **108,106,106,104,103 102,102,100,94,94 88,62**
toteswinger: 1&2 £8.30, 1&3 £6.30, 2&3 £13.90. CSF £31.39 CT £341.57 TOTE £3.30: £1.60, £3.70, £3.30; EX 34.10.
Owner Nurlan Bizakov **Bred** Gestut Zoppenbroich & Aerial Bloodstock **Trained** Lambourn, Berks

FOCUS
A good handicap run at a decent pace, and the form should prove solid. The runners came down the centre of the track up the long home straight and not many got into it. The winner continues on the upgrade.

NOTEBOOK
Askar Tau(FR) ◆ has looked a most progressive colt in recent weeks and he completed a four-timer with what was ultimately a ready win. No less than 25lb higher than when getting off the mark at Haydock last month, he was always well placed but rather ran in snatches from halfway, coming off the bridle for a few strides at times. That proved deceptive, as once he was in front he powered away from his pursuers, eased up in the final half furlong with the race in the bag. He will go up again for this but the Handicapper will have his work cut out to stop him extending his sequence. This extra furlong was not a problem and he should stay a bit further too, with easier ground also likely to suit him. The Cesarewitch would appear a tempting target, and in the longer term he is regarded as a potential Cup horse. (op 7-2)
Ollie George(IRE) made all at Goodwood and tried to repeat the dose off this 4lb higher mark, racing with his head to one side out in front. He had no answers to the progressive winner in the end, but stuck on for second despite edging left and loses nothing in defeat. (op 12-1 tchd 14-1)
Rajeh(IRE) ran a solid race under top weight, always up with the pace and keeping on for third, but the Handicapper might just have him now. (op 12-1 tchd 16-1)
Trenchtown(IRE) stayed on well enough on this rise in trip but, while consistent, remains hard to find the key to. (op 9-2 tchd 11-2 in places)
Any Given Day(IRE) was 5lb higher than when scoring at Ascot, his second win in his last three starts, and was held up over this longer trip. He seemed to stay it well enough but was never quite able to make his presence felt. (op 15-2 tchd 13-2)
Always Bold(IRE) was 4lb higher than when winning over course and distance a month ago and he was never able to land a telling blow. (op 12-1)
Armure, making her handicap debut having landed a 1m3f maiden on Kempton's Polytrack seven weeks ago, raced keenly early on and lost her pitch before halfway. She improved again in the straight before the effort flattened out and probably didn't quite stay. (op 9-2 tchd 6-1 in places)
Paktolos(FR) Official explanation: jockey said gelding had no more to give
Sea Chorus had looked well worth a try over this sort of trip but, after racing rather keenly close to the pace, she weakened rather tamely. (op 16-1 tchd 11-1)
Pass The Port Official explanation: jockey said gelding stopped quickly

5250 RENAULT UK H'CAP 5f
5:45 (5:46) (Class 4) (0-85,85) 3-Y-0+ **£6,476** (£1,927; £963; £481) **Stalls** High

Form RPR

0602 **1** **Lord Of The Reins (IRE)**[27] 4418 4-9-6 **80** .... JamieSpencer 5 91
(J G Given) *hld up: last whn swtchd rt over 1f out: r.o u.p ins fnl f to ld nr fin* **8/1**[2]

0000 **2** *½* **Fantasy Explorer**[26] 4445 5-9-6 **80** ....(p) JimmyQuinn 3 89
(J J Quinn) *hld up in tch: edgd rt fr over 1f out: rdn to ld ins fnl f: hdd nr fin* **8/1**[2]

6322 **3** *1* **Even Bolder**[22] 4555 5-8-13 **73** .... LiamJones 11 78
(E A Wheeler) *led: hdd over 3f out: sn hung lft: rdn over 1f out: hung rt ins fnl f: styd on same pce* **6/1**[1]

1660 **4** *½* **Mango Music**[21] 4601 5-9-9 **83** .... ShaneKelly 8 87
(M Quinn) *chsd ldrs: rdn over 1f out: styd on* **20/1**

505 **5** *¾* **Thoughtsofstardom**[14] 4809 5-7-11 **64** oh4................ SophieDoyle(7) 12 65
(P S McEntee) *a.p: racd keenly: rdn over 1f out: kpt on* **33/1**

0022 **6** *½* **Steelcut**[24] 4502 4-8-8 **75** .... BMcHugh(7) 18 74+
(R A Fahey) *mid-div: sn pushed along: hung lft 1/2-way: nt clr run over 1f out: hdwy u.p fnl f: nt trble ldrs* **11/1**

0520 **7** *hd* **Namir (IRE)**[9] 4962 6-9-1 **75** ....(vt) TedDurcan 9 73
(D Shaw) *s.i.s: sn prom: rdn over 1f out: kpt on* **12/1**

2022 **8** *nk* **Nomoreblondes**[22] 4561 4-8-7 **67** ....(p) JoeFanning 15 68+
(P T Midgley) *chsd ldrs: hung lft thrght: led over 1f out: hdd and no ex ins fnl f* **14/1**

1100 **9** *nse* **What Do You Know**[41] 3945 5-9-4 **78** ....(b) DavidKinsella 6 75
(A M Hales) *hld up: hdwy u.p fnl f: nt trble ldrs* **25/1**

4315 **10** *¾* **Royal Envoy (IRE)**[91] 2359 5-9-6 **80** .... IanMongan 2 74
(P Howling) *sn outpcd: nvr nrr* **20/1**

0-53 **11** *1 ¼* **Handsome Cross (IRE)**[46] 3787 7-9-1 **75** .... PatCosgrave 14 65
(Mrs A Duffield) *chsd ldrs: ev ch over 1f out: sn rdn and hung lft: wknd ins fnl f* **10/1**[3]

2204 **12** *hd* **Requisite**[13] 4864 3-9-7 **83** .... RyanMoore 17 72+
(I A Wood) *sn pushed along in rr: nt clr run fr over 1f out: eased whn no ch ins fnl f* **11/1**

000 **13** *½* **Multahab**[20] 4639 9-8-4 **64** oh6................(t) NickyMackay 4 51
(M Wigham) *sn pushed along in rr: n.d* **66/1**

0050 **14** *nk* **Gwilym (GER)**[59] 3352 5-8-9 **69** .... MichaelHills 19 55
(D Haydn Jones) *s.i.s: sn pushed along in rr: sme hdwy over 1f out: n.m.r and wknd fnl f* **20/1**

3216 **15** *1 ¼* **Nusoor (IRE)**[22] 4563 5-8-8 **68** ....(v) KirstyMilczarek 13 50
(Peter Grayson) *s.i.s: rcvrd to ld over 3f out: rdn and hdd over 1f out: hmpd sn after: wkng whn hmpd ins fnl f* **12/1**

3026 **16** *¾* **Ocean Blaze**[22] 4555 4-9-8 **82** .... AlanMunro 10 61
(B R Millman) *chsd ldrs: rdn over 1f out: sn wknd and eased* **6/1**[1]

57.96 secs (-1.14) **Going Correction** -0.225s/f (Firm)
WFA 3 from 4yo+ 2lb **16** Ran SP% **121.2**
Speed ratings (Par 105): **100,99,97,96,95 94,94,94,93,92 90,90,89,87,87 85**
toteswinger: 1&2 £10.40, 1&3 £6.90, 2&3 £13.90. CSF £63.37 CT £437.16 TOTE £4.90: £2.00, £2.80, £1.70, £4.60; EX 111.40 Place 6: £117.89, Place 5: £19.00..
Owner Danethorpe Racing Partnership **Bred** C Farrell **Trained** Willoughton, Lincs

FOCUS
A fair sprint handicap featuring several regulars in similar contests and something of a rough race. The field came towards the stands' side. Sound form.

Fantasy Explorer Official explanation: jockey said gelding hung right
Nomoreblondes Official explanation: jockey said filly hung left
T/Plt: £171.40 to a £1 stake. Pool: £85,281.18. 363.16 winning tickets. T/Qpdt: £11.10 to a £1 stake. Pool: £7,570.50. 500.60 winning tickets. CR

4434 YORK (L-H)
Friday, August 22
5251 Meeting Abandoned - Waterlogged

5003 BEVERLEY (R-H)
Saturday, August 23
OFFICIAL GOING: Soft (heavy in places)
Wind: Virtually nil Weather: Sunny periods

5256 EUROPEAN BREEDERS' FUND "SPECIOSA" MAIDEN FILLIES' STKS 7f 100y
1:50 (1:52) (Class 4) 2-Y-O **£5,018** (£1,493; £746; £372) **Stalls** High

Form RPR

03 **1** **Amethyst Dawn (IRE)**[29] 4394 2-9-0 0................ DavidAllan 8 77
(T D Easterby) *sn led: qcknd clr 2f out: rdn ent fnl f: kpt on* **10/3**[2]

0 **2** *1* **Choral Festival**[8] 5048 2-9-0 0................ J-PGuillambert 2 75+
(Sir Mark Prescott) *midfield: hdwy 3f out: chsd wnr 2f out and sn rdn: drvn and edgd rt ins fnl f: styd on strly towards fin* **10/1**

4 **3** *nk* **Chilly Filly (IRE)**[12] 4921 2-9-0 0................ JoeFanning 7 74+
(M Johnston) *midfield: pushed along and hdwy 3f out: rdn to chse ldng pair over 1f out: drvn and edgd rt ins fnl f: kpt on* **4/1**[3]

3 **4** *4 ½* **Moneycantbuymelove (IRE)**[21] 4643 2-9-0 0................ MickyFenton 11 63
(M L W Bell) *chsd ldrs: effrt 3f out and sn rdn along: drvn wl over 1f out and sn no imp* **11/4**[1]

2 **5** *8* **Izzy Lou (IRE)**[13] 4896 2-9-0 0................ FergalLynch 3 45
(K A Ryan) *cl up: rdn along 3f out: drvn 2f out and grad wknd* **9/2**

4 **6** *½* **Diesis Of Cloyne (USA)**[18] 4697 2-9-0 0................ DarrenWilliams 4 43
(K R Burke) *chsd ldrs: rdn along over 2f out: drvn and wknd wl over 1f out* **18/1**

04 **7** *1 ¼* **Sardan Dansar (IRE)**[38] 4072 2-8-11 0................ AndrewMullen(3) 10 40
(Mrs A Duffield) *cl up on inner: rdn along 3f out: grad wknd fnl 2f* **33/1**

8 *nse* **Lomica** 2-9-0 0................ TomEaves 12 40
(Miss J A Camacho) *stdd s and hld up in rr tl sme late hdwy* **40/1**

03 **9** *nse* **Game Roseanna**[20] 4658 2-9-0 0................ RoystonFfrench 13 40
(W M Brisbourne) *nvr nr ldrs* **18/1**

0 **10** *1* **Staceys Girl**[30] 4328 2-9-0 0................ DNolan 5 38
(T P Tate) *in tch on inner: rdn along 1/2-way: sn wknd* **100/1**

11 *8* **Amba** 2-9-0 0................ LPKeniry 9 19
(Joss Saville) *s.i.s: a in rr* **80/1**

12 *¾* **Le Petit Vigier** 2-8-11 0................(t) DuranFentiman(3) 1 17
(P Beaumont) *a in rr* **80/1**

000 **13** *hd* **Smoke Me A Kipper (IRE)**[38] 4072 2-9-0 48................ PaulFessey 6 17
(Mrs A Duffield) *a bhd* **100/1**

1m 37.54s (3.74) **Going Correction** +0.55s/f (Yiel) **13** Ran SP% **117.4**
Speed ratings (Par 93): **100,98,98,93,84 83,82,82,82,80 71,70,70**
toteswinger: 1&2 £7.40, 1&3 £4.00, 2&3 £11.80. CSF £35.09 TOTE £4.30: £1.70, £3.00, £1.90; EX 39.20.
Owner D A West **Bred** W Kane **Trained** Great Habton, N Yorks
■ Stewards' Enquiry : J-P Guillambert caution: careless riding.

FOCUS
A fair maiden and the form seems to make sense. Jockeys in this opener reported the ground to be heavy, although the times suggested it was not as testing as that and the runners appeared to be getting through it well enough, and the pace was fair. They stayed on the inside rail in the straight rather than making for the centre of the track as they often do in soft ground at Beverley.

NOTEBOOK
Amethyst Dawn(IRE), third at York after making the running, again set off in front. Kicking clear from the two pole, she looked to have the race safely in the bag but she began to tie up inside the last, changing her legs, and needed the line when it came. She has some filling out to do and is regarded as the type to do better still at three. (op 11-2 tchd 3-1)
Choral Festival, who is out of a half-sister to the smart filly Chorist, had shaped better than her finishing position would suggest on her debut on Kempton's Polytrack. She was closing on the winner throughout the final furlong and there should be a race to be won with her, although she is rather lightly made. (op 14-1 tchd 16-1)
Chilly Filly(IRE), who ran green on her debut, raced a little keenly held up on this second start. She began to improve down the outside in the straight and kept staying on to the line in company with the runner-up. (op 11-2)
Moneycantbuymelove(IRE) had made a promising debut when third at Newmarket, but that form has taken some knocks since with defeats for the second and fourth. A drifter here, she was close enough turning in but was already held when tightened up slightly over 2f out. She is a leggy, lightly made individual and does not have much scope for physical improvement. (op 7-4 tchd 13-8)
Izzy Lou(IRE), green when runner-up on her debut, tracked the winner before gradually fading once the pressure was on in the straight. (op 4-1 tchd 7-2)
Diesis Of Cloyne(USA) faded after racing prominently and did not get home in the conditions. (op 20-1 tchd 25-1)

5257 TOTESCOOP6 HERITAGE H'CAP 1m 1f 207y
2:20 (2:21) (Class 2) (0-105,96) 3-Y-O **£25,904** (£7,708; £3,852; £1,924) **Stalls** High

Form RPR

5032 **1** **Drill Sergeant**[14] 4856 3-9-7 **96** .... JoeFanning 2 106
(M Johnston) *mde all: qcknd over 2f out: rdn over 1f out: drvn ins fnl f and styd on strly* **11/4**[1]

1405 **2** *1 ¾* **Albaqaa**[16] 4783 3-8-8 **83** .... PaulHanagan 1 89+
(R A Fahey) *t.k.h early: hld up towards rr: gd hdwy over 3f out: chsd wnr over 1f out: sn rdn and ev ch ins fnl f tl drvn: edgd rt and no ex last 100yds* **7/1**

5060 **3** *1 ½* **Meeriss (IRE)**[21] 4622 3-9-7 **96** .... DavidAllan 10 99
(M R Channon) *trckd wnr: effrt over 2f out and sn rdn: drvn over 1f out: kpt on same pce ins fnl f* **25/1**

2116 **4** *1 ½* **My Aunt Fanny**[24] 4519 3-8-12 **87** .... LPKeniry 5 87
(A M Balding) *trckd ldrs: hdwy on outer 3f out: rdn along over 2f out: drvn and hung bdly rt over 1f out: kpt on u.p ins fnl f* **4/1**[2]

3144 **5** *1 ¼* **Shaloo Diamond**[29] 4392 3-8-2 **77** .... PaulQuinn 9 75
(R M Whitaker) *chsd ldrs on inner: rdn along over 2f out: drvn over 1f out and sn one pce* **13/2**[3]

2102 **6** *1 3/4* **Conquisto**[16] 4790 3-9-1 **90** .... TomEaves 7 84
(C G Cox) *t.k.h: hld up in rr: hdwy over 2f out: sn rdn and no imp* **7/1**

2002 **7** *13* **Unbreak My Heart (IRE)**[16] 4783 3-9-3 **92** .... MickyFenton 4 60
(R Charlton) *hld up towards rr: effrt and sme hdwy on outer 3f out: sn rdn and btn 2f out* **8/1**

-153 **8** *3/4* **By Command**[15] 4830 3-9-6 **95** .... RoystonFfrench 8 62
(J L Dunlop) *trckd ldrs on inner: hdwy 4f out: rdn along over 2f out and sn wknd* **16/1**

0604 **9** *shd* **Tiger Dream**[14] 4867 3-8-7 **82** .... FergalLynch 6 48
(K A Ryan) *chsd wnr: rdn along wl over 2f out: drvn 2f out and sn wknd* **11/1**

2m 10.51s (3.51) **Going Correction** +0.55s/f (Yiel) **9** Ran SP% **114.2**
Speed ratings (Par 106): **107,105,104,103,102 100,90,89,89**
toteswinger: 1&2 £7.30, 1&3 £16.20, 2&3 £44.50. CSF £22.10 CT £392.19 TOTE £3.50: £1.80, £2.70, £6.70; EX 28.90 Trifecta £225.00 Pool: £547.50, 1.80 winning units..
Owner J Barson **Bred** D G Hardisty Bloodstock **Trained** Middleham Moor, N Yorks

FOCUS
A decent line-up for this valuable heritage handicap, although all the runners came here fairly exposed. The winner got the run of the race from the front and the form is only ordinary for the grade.

NOTEBOOK
Drill Sergeant's rider was determined to secure the early lead and the colt made all the running, winding up the pace in the straight and staying on grittily to repel his pursuers. He is a typically tough Johnston handicapper and his latest second at Haydock had proved his effectiveness in testing ground. (tchd 3-1)
Albaqaa had his stamina to prove at this trip but appeared to stay well enough. Racing rather keenly, he improved once into the straight and went after the winner from the two pole, staying on but at the same time hanging into the rail and never really looking likely to bridge the gap. (op 8-1)
Meeriss(IRE) ran a decent race under top weight, never far from the pace and sticking on for third after the runner-up had rather leaned in on him. He has proved somewhat difficult to place this year after winning a Listed race at two. (op 22-1)
My Aunt Fanny plugged on in the straight despite appearing to hang, as she had last time. The Handicapper does look in charge now after her brace of wins at Chester earlier in the summer. (op 9-2)
Shaloo Diamond had no excuses on account of the ground and, while performing respectably, is another who looks a few pounds too high at present. (op 8-1 tchd 6-1)
Conquisto was put up 7lb for his good second at Sandown and, after taking a keen hold early, could never get into the action. (op 8-1)
Unbreak My Heart(IRE) has a good record in soft conditions, but found himself trapped out wide and was always towards the rear. This was not his running. (op 11-2)
By Command, again rather keen, did improve into a modest fourth place turning in but was soon back-pedalling. He needs to settle a lot better. (op 12-1 tchd 20-1)
Tiger Dream continues to make no real impact in handicaps and faded in the straight after turning for home in a prominent position. (op 14-1)

5258 TOTESPORTGAMES.COM H'CAP 7f 100y
2:50 (2:50) (Class 5) (0-75,72) 3-Y-O+ **£2,914** (£867; £433; £216) **Stalls** High

Form RPR

002 **1** **Mr Toshiwonka**[14] 4877 4-9-3 **62** .... AdrianTNicholls 9 69
(D Nicholls) *hld up in rr: effrt over 2f out and sn pushed along: rdn over 1f out: swtchd outside and drvn ent fnl f: styd on strly to ld last 50yds* **8/1**

0425 **2** *nk* **Handsome Falcon**[14] 4875 4-9-12 **71** .... PaulHanagan 6 77
(R A Fahey) *hld up towards rr: hdwy 3f out: rdn along 2f out: drvn ent fnl f: styd on wl towards fin* **7/2**[1]

5005 **3** *1/2* **Jonny Lesters Hair (IRE)**[19] 4682 3-9-3 **67** .... DavidAllan 8 70
(T D Easterby) *led: pushed clr 2f out: rdn over 1f out: drvn ins fnl f: hdd & wknd last 50yds* **5/1**[3]

2363 **4** *nk* **Johnny Friendly**[18] 4702 3-8-12 **62** .... DarrenWilliams 1 64
(K R Burke) *cl up: rdn along and sltly outpcd 2f out: drvn over 1f out: styd on u.p ins fnl f: no ex towards fin* **11/1**

1-36 **5** *3/4* **San Silvestro (IRE)**[33] 4248 3-9-1 **68** .... AndrewMullen(3) 4 68
(Mrs A Duffield) *hld up in rr: hdwy over 2f out: rdn over 1f out: styng on whn sltly hmpd and swtchd rt ins fnl f: nrst fin* **16/1**

2321 **6** *1/2* **Ubenkor (IRE)**[18] 4702 3-9-8 **72** .... TomEaves 2 73+
(B Smart) *chsd ldng pair: hdwy to chse ldr wl over 2f out: rdn over 1f out: drvn and ev ch ent fnl f: wkng whn n.m.r last 75yds* **5/1**[3]

3600 **7** *3* **The Twelve Steps**[17] 4741 3-9-3 **70** .... PJMcDonald(3) 10 61
(G A Swinbank) *in tch: rdn along wl over 2f out: drvn and wknd over 1f out* **10/1**

0001 **8** *1* **Trans Sonic**[13] 4898 5-9-0 **59** ....(v) RoystonFfrench 5 50
(A J Lockwood) *trckd ldres: hdwy over 3f out: rdn over 2f out: sn drvn and wknd over 1f out* **4/1**[2]

-305 **9** *36* **Planet Queen**[48] 3753 3-8-5 **55** ....(v) AndrewElliott 3 —
(K R Burke) *t.k.h: in tch on outer whn hung lft and rn wd on bnd after 3f: rdn along 3f out and sn wknd: eased* **12/1**

1m 37.89s (4.09) **Going Correction** +0.55s/f (Yiel)
WFA 3 from 4yo+ 5lb **9** Ran SP% **117.7**
Speed ratings (Par 103): **98,97,97,96,95 95,91,90,49**
toteswinger: 1&2 £5.20, 1&3 £9.90, 2&3 £4.80. CSF £36.89 CT £157.63 TOTE £8.70: £2.60, £1.70, £1.90; EX 41.20.
Owner Ian Guise & Warren Smith **Bred** Mrs P A Clark **Trained** Sessay, N Yorks
■ Stewards' Enquiry : Adrian T Nicholls two-day ban: careless riding (Sep 7-8); two-day ban: used whip down shoulder in forehand position (Sep 9-10)
Paul Hanagan caution: used whip with excessive frequency

FOCUS
Just a modest handicap, but an exciting finish, although with so many in close proximity at the end the form may not prove too reliable. The form is rated through the runner-up to this year's form.

5259 TOTESPORT BETXTRA BEVERLEY BULLET SPRINT STKS (LISTED RACE) 5f
3:20 (3:22) (Class 1) 3-Y-O+ **£23,704** (£8,964; £4,480; £2,240) **Stalls** High

Form RPR

1416 **1** **Look Busy (IRE)**[20] 4660 3-8-11 **104** .... SladeO'Hara 8 111
(A Berry) *trckd ldrs: hdwy and cl up 1/2-way: rdn to ld over 1f out: kpt on wl u.p ins fnl f* **11/2**[3]

5542 **2** *1* **Advanced**[49] 3722 5-9-0 **104** .... FergalLynch 7 109
(K A Ryan) *trckd ldrs: swtchd lft and hdwy 2f out: rdn over 1f out: styd on ins fnl f* **7/1**

0020 **3** *1/2* **Fullandby (IRE)**[7] 5109 6-9-0 **104** .... RoystonFfrench 4 107
(T J Etherington) *chsd ldrs: rdn along and sltly outpcd over 2f out: styd on u.p ent fnl f: nrst fin* **11/2**[3]

-611 **4** *1/2* **Peace Offering (IRE)**[11] 4957 8-9-0 **108** .... AdrianTNicholls 5 105
(D Nicholls) *led: rdn along 2f out: hdd over 1f out: grad wknd ins fnl f* **7/4**[1]

2220 **5** *3 1/4* **Sudden Impact (IRE)**[14] 4842 3-8-7 **92** .... RussellKennemore 3 89
(Paul Green) *chsd ldrs: rdn along 1/2-way: wknd and hung lft wl over 1f out* **25/1**

011- **6** *1* **Fonthill Road (IRE)**[307] 6363 8-9-0 **106** .... PaulHanagan 2 90
(R A Fahey) *sn pushed along: rdn along and outpcd after 2f: a in rr* **11/1**

5536 **7** *1 3/4* **Hoh Mike (IRE)**[36] 4159 4-9-0 **112** .... MickyFenton 6 84
(M L W Bell) *sn outpcd and a in rr* **9/2**[2]

000 **8** *3/4* **Luscivious**[2] 5206 4-9-0 **86** ....(b) JoeFanning 1 81
(A J McCabe) *in tch on outer: effrt to chse ldrs over 2f out: sn rdn and wknd over 1f out* **25/1**

64.82 secs (1.32) **Going Correction** +0.55s/f (Yiel)
WFA 3 from 4yo+ 2lb **8** Ran SP% **113.8**
Speed ratings (Par 111): **111,109,108,107,102 101,98,97**
toteswinger: 1&2 £7.40, 1&3 £5.10, 2&3 £5.50. CSF £42.87 TOTE £7.00: £1.70, £2.80, £1.70; EX 43.20.
Owner A Underwood **Bred** Tom And Hazel Russell **Trained** Cockerham, Lancs
■ Stewards' Enquiry : Royston Ffrench two-day ban: used whip with excessive force (Sep 7-8)
Russell Kennemore one-day ban: careless riding (Sep 7)

FOCUS
A competitive Listed sprint run at a decent pace in the conditions. Look Busy produced another improved run, the form rated around the first two and the fifth.

NOTEBOOK
Look Busy(IRE), whose rider was unable to claim his usual 5lb allowance, tracked the pace closest to the rail before going on with over a furlong to run. Her lead was being reduced inside the last but she was always going to hold on. Suited by the return to this trip, this admirably tough and consistent filly was winning for the second time in this grade and may bid for Group 3 honours at the Curragh next time. (tchd 5-1 and 6-1)
Advanced ran on strongly inside the last, passing a couple of rivals late on and cutting into the winner's advantage at the line. He is well capable of winning at this level but, as befits an Ayr Gold Cup winner, is perhaps most effective in big fields over 6f. (op 6-1 tchd 8-1)
Fullandby(IRE), like Advanced, is probably happier over a bit further. He likes this ground and ran a solid race, putting him right for another crack at the Portland at Doncaster over an intermediate trip next month. (op 8-1 tchd 5-1)
Peace Offering(IRE) came here on a hat-trick following wins at Newmarket and Nottingham. Well away and again attempting to make all, he could not fend off the filly and was relegated two further places close home as his stamina waned in the soft ground. (op 15-8 tchd 13-8, 2-1 in a place)
Sudden Impact(IRE) had plenty on at these terms and ran as well as could be expected, already held when a bit short of room over a furlong out. (op 28-1 tchd 33-1)
Fonthill Road(IRE) had not been out since last October and he is entitled to improve for this reappearance. He will appreciate an extra furlong and there is still life in him yet. (op 10-1 tchd 17-2)
Hoh Mike(IRE) was soon outpaced in rear and never picked up. He is a smart 5f specialist when on song, fifth in the King's Stand in June, but he has not run up to that form since and has become one to be wary of. (tchd 5-1)
Luscivious, making a quick reappearance, faded quickly in the final furlong. (op 33-1)

5260 TOTESPORT 0800 221 221 H'CAP 5f
3:55 (3:56) (Class 5) (0-75,74) 3-Y-O+ **£2,849** (£847; £423; £211) **Stalls** High

Form RPR

3511 **1** **Highland Warrior**[11] 4950 9-9-6 **70** .... MickyFenton 13 81
(P T Midgley) *dwlt and towards rr: gd hdwy 1/2-way: rdn to ld over 1f out: styd on strly* **11/2**[1]

0200 **2** *3/4* **Winthorpe (IRE)**[33] 4246 8-8-9 **66** .... JamieKyne(7) 11 74
(J J Quinn) *towards rr: hdwy over 2f out: rdn over 1f out: styd on to chse wnr ins fnl f* **16/1**

4230 **3** *1* **Rabbit Fighter (IRE)**[10] 4962 4-9-9 **73** ....(v) DarrenWilliams 3 78
(D Shaw) *hld up and bhd: hdwy wl over 1f out: swtchd rt and rdn ent fnl f: kpt on: nrst fin* **10/1**

6110 **4** *hd* **Steel Blue**[8] 5067 8-9-7 **71** ....(p) J-PGuillambert 6 75
(R M Whitaker) *bhd: hdwy wl over 1f out: sn rdn and styd on strly ins fnl f: nrst fin* **8/1**

4200 **5** *2* **Royal Composer (IRE)**[29] 4393 5-8-9 **59** ....(b) DavidAllan 15 56
(T D Easterby) *cl up on inner rail: rdn along 2f out: drvn over 1f out: kpt on same pce* **8/1**

503 **6** *nk* **Tender Process (IRE)**[11] 4958 5-8-9 **59** ....(b) PaulHanagan 10 55
(E S McMahon) *in rr: hdwy wl over 1f out: rdn and kpt on ins fnl f: nt rch ldrs* **6/1**[2]

4433 **7** *1/2* **Kings College Boy**[2] 5201 8-8-8 **65** ....(b) BMcHugh(7) 9 59
(R A Fahey) *cl up: rdn wl over 1f out and ev ch tl drvn and wknd ent fnl f* **7/1**[3]

6604 **8** *1/2* **Wicked Wilma (IRE)**[18] 4703 4-8-4 **54** oh3 .... JoeFanning 2 46
(A Berry) *wnt lft s: in tch on outer: hdwy to chse ldrs 2f out: sn rdn and grad wknd* **20/1**

1325 **9** *3* **The Geester**[141] 1189 4-8-4 **54** oh4 ....(b) DaleGibson 4 35
(S R Bowring) *chsd ldrs on outer: rdn along 2f out: grad wknd* **20/1**

2242 **10** *3* **Orpen's Art (IRE)**[52] 3609 3-9-5 **74** .... RussellKennemore(3) 12 45
(Evan Williams) *led: rdn along 2f out: drvn and hdd over 1f out: wknd* **20/1**

034 **11** *1 3/4* **Never Without Me**[25] 4502 8-8-8 **58** .... AdrianTNicholls 5 22
(J F Coupland) *towards rr: swtchd lft and effrt 2f out: sn rdn and no hdwy* **14/1**

-000 **12** *1* **Making Music**[17] 4743 5-8-5 **58** ....(t) DuranFentiman(3) 7 19
(T D Easterby) *midfield: rdn along 1/2-way and sn wknd* **20/1**

2503 **13** *hd* **Colorus (IRE)**[8] 5044 5-9-1 **65** .... FergalLynch 8 25
(W J H Ratcliffe) *chsd ldrs: rdn along over 2f out and sn wknd* **11/1**

0665 **14** *9* **Desert Opal**[8] 5046 8-8-9 **62** ....(b) TolleyDean(3) 14 —
(C R Dore) *prom: rdn along over 2f out: sn drvn and wknd* **8/1**

65.54 secs (2.04) **Going Correction** +0.55s/f (Yiel)
WFA 3 from 4yo+ 2lb **14** Ran SP% **124.5**
Speed ratings (Par 103): **105,103,102,101,98 98,97,96,91,87 84,82,82,67**
toteswinger: 1&2 £15.30, 1&3 £18.30, 2&3 £31.90. CSF £90.52 CT £868.25 TOTE £6.80: £2.40, £5.20, £3.80; EX 153.30.
Owner Frank & Annette Brady **Bred** Rowcliffe Stud **Trained** Westow, N Yorks

FOCUS
A modest but competitive sprint. The winner is rated back to his best form of last summer, with the overall form solid.
Never Without Me Official explanation: jockey said gelding was unsuited by the soft (heavy in places) ground; vet said gelding finished distressed

5261 TOTESPORTCASINO.COM MAIDEN STKS 5f
4:30 (4:34) (Class 5) 3-Y-O+ **£2,752** (£818; £409; £204) **Stalls** High

Form RPR

0450 **1** **First Swallow**[27] 4453 3-9-3 **60** .... PaulHanagan 2 64
(R A Fahey) *chsd ldrs: hdwy 2f out: rdn over 1f out: led ins fnl f: drvn out* **12/1**

2-60 **2** *1/2* **Royal Degree**[22] 4595 3-9-3 **65** .... TomEaves 11 62
(B Smart) *chsd ldrs: effrt 2f out and sn rdn: styd on u.p to chal ins fnl f: drvn and no ex towards fin* **7/2**[2]

3 1 1/4 **Minnola** 3-8-12 0 SaleemGolam 9 53+
(Rae Guest) *in tch: hdwy on inner 2f out: rdn over 1f out: kpt on ins fnl f: nrst fin* **14/1**

05 **4** 1 1/4 **Molly Two**7 5110 3-8-9 0 DuranFentiman(3) 4 48
(L A Mullaney) *led and sn clr: rdn over 1f out: drvn and hdd ins fnl f: wknd last 100yds* **20/1**

0 **5** 1/2 **Master Of Light**106 1960 3-9-3 0 J-PGuillambert 6 51+
(P A Blockley) *hld up towards rr: hdwy over 1f out: styd on strly ins fnl f: nrst fin* **20/1**

30 **6** 1 **Onebidkintymill (IRE)**29 4388 3-8-10 0 GarryWhillans(7) 7 48
(M Mullineaux) *chsd ldrs: rdn and hung lft wl over 1f out: sn drvn and one pce* **33/1**

206 **7** 3/4 **Safaseef (IRE)**10 4987 3-8-12 56 PaulFessey 10 40
(K A Morgan) *prom: rdn along 2f out: sn drvn and grad wknd* **8/1**3

3300 **8** 1 1/2 **Miss Taboo (IRE)**9 5007 4-9-0 47 (b1) MickyFenton 12 35
(P T Midgley) *prom: rdn along 2f out: drvn and wknd appr fnl f* **12/1**

3 **9** 1 1/2 **Vienna Affair**84 2620 3-8-12 0 OscarUrbina 5 29
(J R Fanshawe) *dwlt: hld up towards rr: effrt 2f out: sn rdn and no hdwy* **11/10**1

0- **10** 6 **County Crystal**393 3915 3-9-3 0 DavidAllan 1 13
(T D Easterby) *wnt lft s: in tch: rdn along 2f out and sn wknd* **50/1**

11 1 **Dontpaytheferryman (USA)**357 5054 3-9-3 0 (tp) AdrianTNicholls 3 9
(Evan Williams) *a in rr* **20/1**

-000 **12** 5 **Ronnies Girl**11 4950 4-8-7 9 JamieKyne(7) 8 —
(C J Teague) *a bhd* **200/1**

66.52 secs (3.02) **Going Correction** +0.55s/f (Yiel)
WFA 3 from 4yo 2lb 12 Ran SP% **122.7**
Speed ratings (Par 103): **97,96,94,92,91 89,88,86,83,74 72,64**
toteswinger: 1&2 £9.80, 1&3 £9.90, 2&3 £8.30. CSF £52.03 TOTE £15.70: £3.10, £1.90, £2.90; EX 81.90.
Owner The Secret Seven Partnership **Bred** A K Smeaton **Trained** Musley Bank, N Yorks
■ Stewards' Enquiry : Tom Eaves two-day ban: used whip with excessive frequency (Sep 7,8)

FOCUS
A weak sprint maiden, particularly with the favourite running poorly, and not form to be too interested in. The winner is rated up 9lb
Vienna Affair Official explanation: trainer had no explanation for the poor form shown

5262 PERTEMPS PEOPLE DEVELOPMENT "HANDS AND HEELS" APPRENTICE MAIDEN H'CAP 1m 1f 207y
5:00 (5:02) (Class 6) (0-65,63) 4-Y-0+ **£2,201** (£655; £327; £163) **Stalls** High

Form RPR

40-2 **1** **White Moss (IRE)**13 4902 4-9-6 61 AshleyMorgan 2 67
(M H Tompkins) *hld up in tch: smooth hdwy over 3f out: led over 1f out: kpt on ins fnl f* **9/4**1

0300 **2** 1 **Jiminor Mack**39 4048 5-8-4 45 (p) DeclanCannon 8 49
(W J H Ratcliffe) *sn led: hdd after 4f: cl up on inner tl led again over 3f out: rdn along over 2f out: hdd over 1f out: kpt on* **7/1**

6306 **3** 1 1/2 **Bollin Freddie**10 4966 4-8-1 45 JamieKyne(3) 3 46
(A J Lockwood) *rrd s and s.i.s: sn prom: rdn along over 2f out and kpt on same pce appr fnl f* **9/2**3

0463 **4** 1 1/4 **Ghufa (IRE)**16 4797 4-9-8 63 BMcHugh 6 62
(E A L Dunlop) *trckd ldrs: hdwy over 3f out: rdn to chal over 2f out: sn one pce* **11/4**2

62-0 **5** 7 **Pugnacity**66 3131 4-8-2 46 TobyAtkinson(3) 1 31
(A Berry) *in rr: wd st: rdn along over 2f out and nvr nr ldrs* **40/1**

0030 **6** 1 1/4 **Right You Are (IRE)**25 4501 8-8-5 49 AntiocoMurgia(3) 7 31
(Paul Green) *racd wd: trckd ldrs: effrt 4f out: sn rdn along and wknd wl over 2f out* **11/1**

6050 **7** 1/2 **Trireme (IRE)**10 4991 4-8-11 52 BillyCray 5 33
(K A Morgan) *a in rr* **12/1**

2550 **8** 7 **Cape Dancer (IRE)**20 3113 4-8-1 45 MatthewLawson(3) 4 12
(J S Wainwright) *t.k.h: cl up tl led after 4f: pushed along and hdd over 3f out: sn rdn and wknd* **10/1**

2m 13.39s (6.39) **Going Correction** +0.55s/f (Yiel) 8 Ran SP% **115.7**
Speed ratings (Par 101): **96,95,94,93,87 86,86,80**
toteswinger: 1&2 £4.50, 1&3 £3.90, 2&3 £5.40. CSF £18.99 CT £65.69 TOTE £2.80: £1.60, £1.50, £1.70; EX 17.90 Place 6 £ 202.91, Place 5 £ 107.37.
Owner Mr & Mrs G Middlebrook **Bred** G And Mrs Middlebrook **Trained** Newmarket, Suffolk

FOCUS
A very weak race confined to apprentices who had yet to ride ten winners. The pace was only steady and the runners were spread right across the track in the home straight. The form does seem to make a fair bit of sense.
T/Plt: £371.10 to a £1 stake. Pool: £61,639.87. 121.25 winning tickets. T/Qpdt: £87.80 to a £1 stake. Pool: £3,501.50. 29.50 winning tickets. JR

4621 GOODWOOD (R-H)
Saturday, August 23

OFFICIAL GOING: Good to soft (good in places on round course; 7.4)
Wind: moderate across

5263 LADBROKES GREAT VOLTIGEUR STKS (GROUP 2) (C&G) 1m 4f
2:10 (2:10) (Class 1) 3-Y-O **£56,770** (£21,520; £10,770; £5,370; £2,690) **Stalls** High

Form RPR

1400 **1** **Centennial (IRE)**40 4042 3-8-12 105 (b) JimmyFortune 3 114
(J H M Gosden) *bustled into ld and mde virtually all: styd on gamely u.p whn chal fr over 2f out: asserted wl fnl f* **12/1**

4333 **2** 1 1/2 **Top Lock**48 3773 3-8-12 110 MartinDwyer 1 111
(A M Balding) *chsd wnr thrght: drvn along 3f out and upsides u.p over 2f out: no ex and one pce ins fnl f* **9/2**3

0025 **3** 2 **Scintillo**25 4505 3-8-12 109 RichardHughes 4 108
(R Hannon) *racd in 3rd most of way tl rdn and one pce over 2f out: styd on to retake 3rd ins fnl f* **16/1**

3211 **4** 1 **Patkai (IRE)**64 3196 3-8-12 109 RobertWinston 5 106
(Sir Michael Stoute) *hld up in tch: rdn 3f out and hdwy to chal 2f out: sn no ex and btn whn edgd rt 1f out* **8/11**1

311 **5** 3 **Meydan City (USA)**15 4830 3-8-12 0 LDettori 2 102+
(Saeed Bin Suroor) *hld up in tch: drvn and qckndto press ldrs wl over 2f out: wknd wl over 1f out* **4/1**2

2m 41.7s (3.30) **Going Correction** +0.225s/f (Good) 26 Ran SP% **109.7**
Speed ratings (Par 112): **98,97,95,95,93**
CSF £60.40 TOTE £15.10: £4.40, £2.00; EX 57.10.
Owner Michael O'Flynn **Bred** W Lazy T Ltd **Trained** Newmarket, Suffolk
■ This St Leger trial was salvaged from the abandoned Ebor meeting at York.
■ Stewards' Enquiry : Robert Winston caution: careless riding

FOCUS
Another race salvaged from the abandoned Ebor meeting, and all five of these had been due to take their chance at York, but disappointingly, the three Aidan O'Brien horses who featured among the original declarations were missing. A field of five represented the smallest turnout since the same number lined up in 2000, although that year's race still produced the St Leger runner-up and a subsequent Arc winner. This year's race looked a reasonable contest, but they went no pace and the first three home filled those positions from the off, so the form needs treating with caution. The winner is rated up 5lb, with Patkai below par.

NOTEBOOK
Centennial(IRE) was a Derby fancy earlier in the year and won the Sandown Classic Trial from the front on his reappearance, but he had seemingly had his limitations exposed since then, finding a few too good in the Dante, the Irish Derby and the Grand Prix de Paris. However, this was much easier than those recent assignments and, sent to the front for the first time since his Sandown success, he was gifted the lead. Having taken them along at a very modest pace for much of the way, he was strongly challenged early in the straight, but had the benefit of the rail to run against and kept responding to pressure when Top Lock got to within around half a length passing the furlong pole, eventually seeing off that one's effort to win in clear-cut fashion. The blinkers (second time) clearly help, and there is no doubt he is very talented when things fall right, but he does look flattered by the bare result. He should stay 1m6f, but needs to be supplemented for the St Leger. His trainer is apparently happy to let him take his chance, but the final decision will rest with his owner. (tchd 11-1 and 14-1)
Top Lock ◆, third in the German Derby on his latest start, tracked the winner throughout and ranged almost upsides around a furlong out, but Centennial had saved something in front for the final furlong. His connections reported afterwards that he should come on for this run, suggesting he was using this race as a genuine prep for the St Leger, and he now heads to Doncaster. He'll have something to find in the final Classic of the season, but gives the impression we have yet to see the best of him and a strongly run 1m6f should suit ideally, so he could run well at a big price. (op 4-1)
Scintillo has struggled a little in good company this season, but this was better than his recent course-and-distance effort in the Gordon Stakes. He won a Group 1 in Italy last year and may need to go abroad again for further Pattern-race success.
Patkai(IRE), who came into this off the back of a seven-length success in the Queen's Vase at Royal Ascot, was looking to enhance his St Leger claims, but he completely blew out and was a major disappointment. The way he ran suggests he probably would have struggled no matter how the race was run, but the tactics used do have to be questioned. He had Robert Winston taking over in the saddle, with his regular partner Ryan Moore in action at Newmarket, and presumably his jockey was riding to orders by holding his mount up well out the back. However, considering there was no pace on and the horse was dropping half a mile in trip, it seemed a strange decision and such a stout stayer was always going to find a relative dash to the line tough going. He looked briefly dangerous around three furlongs out, but quickly began to struggle and looked rather ungainly under pressure, not appearing comfortable on the track. He should be able to leave this form behind granted a stiffer test of stamina back on a galloping track, but his St Leger odds were pushed out and he could not be backed at Doncaster with any confidence. (op 10-11 tchd evens in a place)
Meydan City(USA) earned a shot at a race like this with an easy win in a conditions race on the July course last time. Like the favourite, he was at a disadvantage being held up off a slow pace, but he was up two furlongs in trip and ran like a non-stayer.

5264 WINDFLOWER MARCH STKS (LISTED RACE) 1m 6f
2:45 (2:45) (Class 1) 3-Y-0+
£28,385 (£10,760; £5,385; £2,685; £1,345; £675) **Stalls** High

Form RPR

032 **1** **Tungsten Strike (USA)**23 4551 7-9-7 105 (p) DarryllHolland 6 110
(Mrs A J Perrett) *s.i.s and sn drvn to ld: 6 l clr after 2f: rdn along 3f out: hdd ins fnl 2f: styd pressing ldr and r.o gamely u.p to ld again fnl 25yds* **5/2**2

6036 **2** 1/2 **Petara Bay (IRE)**28 4406 4-9-7 105 JimCrowley 1 109
(T G Mills) *trckd wnr 7f out: drvn to ld jst ins fnl 2f: kpt on u.p tl hdd and no ex fnl 25yds* **6/1**3

-000 **3** 3 1/4 **Shahin (USA)**22 4585 5-9-7 98 (v) MartinDwyer 2 105
(M P Tregoning) *in rr tl hdwy and rdn 4f out: hung rt u.p 3f out: styd on again fnl 2f and chsd ldr duo fnl f but nvr any ch* **12/1**

-341 **4** shd **Sanbuch**25 4508 4-9-7 110 (b) DaneO'Neill 3 105
(L M Cumani) *chsd clr ldng duo 5f out and sn drvn along: kpt on u.p fnl 2f but nvr in contention* **6/4**1

0540 **5** 2 3/4 **Heron Bay**84 2625 4-9-7 100 SteveDrowne 4 101
(G Wragg) *hld up in rr: rdn and hdwy fr 3f out: styd on fnl 2f but nvr in contention* **12/1**

1324 **6** nk **Susie May**23 4549 4-9-2 85 LDettori 9 95
(G L Moore) *hld up off pce in rr: rdn and hdwy fr 3f out but nvr gng pce to rch ldrs: wknd fnl f* **14/1**

7 47 **Valentino Rossi (BRZ)**98 6-9-10 98 RichardHughes 7 38
(J M P Eustace) *chsd wnr to 1/2-way: wknd qckly fr 3f out: t.o* **16/1**

3-00 **8** 9 **Veenwouden**99 2169 4-9-2 100 ShaneKelly 5 17
(E F Vaughan) *chsd ldrs to 1/2-way: t.o* **22/1**

3m 6.28s (2.68) **Going Correction** +0.225s/f (Good) 8 Ran SP% **115.1**
Speed ratings (Par 111): **101,100,98,98,97 97,70,65**
toteswinger: 1&2 £3.00, 1&3 £7.30, 2&3 £11.20. CSF £18.15 TOTE £3.60: £1.40, £2.40, £3.70; EX 16.40 Trifecta £123.80 Pool: £803.40, 4.80 winning units..
Owner John Connolly **Bred** Minster Stud **Trained** Pulborough, W Sussex

FOCUS
This race used to be a St Leger trial but it was opened up to older horses in 1998 and for the second time since 2003 this year's field didn't feature any three-year-olds. It certainly wasn't the strongest of renewals, with many of the participants looking hopelessly out of form coming into the race, but it produced a thrilling finish nonetheless. The form is questionable.

NOTEBOOK
Tungsten Strike(USA), winner of this race last year, was unsurprisingly sent to the front early on by Darryll Holland, although he had to be ridden to get there. He then dictated a steady pace for most of the contest, with the other jockeys opting not to go after him, which was reminiscent of the Goodwood Cup last month when only Yeats beat him home. When they entered the straight, Petara Bay emerged from the pack as the only danger under a confident-looking Jim Crowley, who even looked over his shoulder to see if anything was coming from behind as he appeared to be travelling much the better of the pair, but Tungsten Strike battled on gamely against the far rail, getting back up within 100 yards of the line. (op 11-4 tchd 3-1)
Petara Bay(IRE) has mainly been running at Group level this season, including a sixth place last time out in the King George, and he clearly does have a race in him at this level. However, he will always need some luck in running, as he needs to be produced very late. He probably got to the front sooner than he would have liked and he may also have just failed to get home. (op 11-2)
Shahin(USA), whose stable won this race with Mubtaker in 2005 and Jadalee in 2006, has done most of his running over 1m4f and this was the longest trip he has tried. He did run on late to snatch third but it is too soon to say if this represents a return to form. (op 16-1)
Sanbuch, who rarely runs a bad race, was one of the few runners with a progressive profile and he was stepping up to Listed company for the first time. He was well backed before the off but was travelling on and off the bridle throughout the contest and could not quicken when Tungsten Strike kicked for home. This has to rate as slightly disappointing, although he would probably have preferred a much stronger gallop. (tchd 11-8)

The Form Book, Raceform Ltd, Compton, RG20 6NL

Heron Bay has achieved very little since winning the King George V Handicap at Royal Ascot last year and he simply plugged on into fifth. (tchd 14-1)
Susie May has been contesting handicaps off marks in the 60s this season, but finished fourth at 40-1 in a Group 3 Fillies' race over course and distance last month, although well beaten. She was always going to struggle in this company, but she is in foal to Shirocco and this race may well have been her swansong. (op 12-1)

5265 TOTESPORT.COM CELEBRATION MILE (GROUP 2) 1m

3:15 (3:18) (Class 1) 3-Y-O+ **£56,770** (£21,520; £10,770; £5,370; £2,690) **Stalls** High

Form RPR

4222 **1** **Raven's Pass (USA)**[24] 4518 3-8-9 122 .... JimmyFortune 4 125+
(J H M Gosden) *mde all: qcknd 2f out: drvn to assert over 1f out: in command thrght fnl f: comf* **1/2**[1]

1152 **2** *1* **Bankable (IRE)**[35] 4192 4-9-1 117 .... DaneO'Neill 2 123
(L M Cumani) *trckd ldrs in 4th: hdwy 3f out and chsd wnr jst ins fnl 2f: kpt on ins fnl f but a readily hld* **3/1**[2]

2115 **3** *9* **Third Set (IRE)**[9] 5025 5-9-1 112 .... LDettori 5 102
(Saeed Bin Suroor) *chsd ldrs in 3rd most of way: rdn 3f out: disp wl hld 2nd 2f out: wknd sn after* **11/1**[3]

0433 **4** *1* **Dubai's Touch**[22] 4587 4-9-1 104 .... DarryllHolland 1 100
(M Johnston) *chsd wnr: rdn to dispute wl hld 2nd 2f out: wknd sn after* **16/1**

4420 **5** *½* **Docofthebay (IRE)**[64] 3197 4-9-1 107 ....(b) ShaneKelly 3 99
(J A Osborne) *awkward stalls and s.i.s: rdn 3f out: a bhd* **16/1**

1m 39.3s (-0.60) **Going Correction** +0.225s/f (Good)
WFA 3 from 4yo+ 6lb **5** Ran SP% **111.8**
Speed ratings (Par 115): **112,111,102,101,100**
CSF £2.34 TOTE £1.50: £1.20, £1.50; EX 2.40.
Owner Stonerside Stable Llc **Bred** Stonerside Stable **Trained** Newmarket, Suffolk

FOCUS
The Celebration Mile rarely attracts a big field, but even so a field of five, the smallest since the same number lined up in 1999, represented a disappointing turnout. The overall quality of the field was also less than inspiring, with just the one previous Group-race winner among them (Raven's Pass in last season's Solario Stakes), but the first two pulled a long way clear and it will probably pay to be very positive about those two, who are several notches above the other three runners. Raven's Pass has been rated as basically running to his best.

NOTEBOOK
Raven's Pass(USA) ◆, who many people felt should have had more use made of him when a fast-finishing second to the top-class Henrythenavigator in the Sussex Stakes over course and distance on his previous start, was ridden from the front this time with no guaranteed pacesetter in opposition. The gallop seemed just steady through the first couple of furlongs, but Dubai's Touch kept the eventual winner honest up front and the pace soon noticeably increased. He travelled easily throughout and, still going well early in the straight, his rider didn't have to go for everything at any stage, just getting a little more busy in the last furlong to keep to Bankable at bay, before easing off a few yards from the line. This was much more comfortable than the official winning margin suggests and, although the race lacked strength in depth, this performance should not be underestimated, as Bankable is improving rapidly. He will now go for the Queen Elizabeth II Stakes at Ascot if the ground is good, and the Breeders' Cup Mile is his longer-term aim. He should go well in both, particularly given he has now proven he is versatile with regards running style. (op 8-15 tchd 8-13 in places)
Bankable(IRE) ◆ emerges with loads of credit in second. Settled off the pace early on, he was produced with his effort in the straight and picked up really well to pull a long way clear of the remainder, although he is probably just a touch flattered by his proximity, as he was never going to pick that rival up. He had been a beaten favourite on both his starts since hacking up in a Listed race over this course and distance in May, firstly when beaten by the draw in the Hunt Cup, then when possibly outstayed by Passage Of Time at Newbury last month, but he remains hugely progressive. A giant of a horse, there should be even better to come next year and it looks just a matter of time before he breaks through at Group level. (tchd 10-3)
Third Set(IRE) found this tougher than the Group 3 he contested at Salisbury a week earlier on his first start back after a successful spell in Dubai. On this evidence, he needs his sights lowered a little. (op 9-1 tchd 8-1)
Dubai's Touch's latest effort was a third placing off a mark of 100 in the Totesport Mile handicap over course and distance at the Glorious meeting, and he is simply not up to this level.
Docofthebay(IRE) started rather awkwardly and was never seen with chance. Although he had something to find at this level, he could still have been expected to run a good race, as he has plenty of natural talent, but he is not straightforward and seems to save his best for big fields. (op 33-1)

5266 TOTESWINGER PRESTIGE STKS (GROUP 3) (FILLIES) 7f

3:45 (3:48) (Class 1) 2-Y-O
£31,223 (£11,836; £5,923; £2,953; £1,479; £742) **Stalls** High

Form RPR

1 **1** **Fantasia**[43] 3923 2-9-0 0 .... DaneO'Neill 4 105+
(L M Cumani) *bmpd stalls: hld up in rr: gd hdwy on outside over 2f out to ld 1f out: pushed out: readily* **9/4**[1]

415 **2** *1* **Rose Diamond (IRE)**[28] 4403 2-9-0 92 .... SteveDrowne 2 101
(R Charlton) *towards rr but in tch: hdwy fr 2f out: styd on wl fnl f to chse wnr cl home but a readily hld* **6/1**[3]

2524 **3** *1* **April Pride**[28] 4403 2-9-0 94 .... RichardHughes 5 98
(R Hannon) *hld up in rr: rapid hdwy on outside over 1f out: styd on strly fnl f but a hld by ldng duo* **8/1**

0511 **4** *1 ¾* **Lahaleeb (IRE)**[17] 4733 2-9-0 90 .... SamHitchcott 8 94
(M R Channon) *in rr but in tch: rdn and hdwy on ins over 1f out: styng on whn hit over hd and faltered 110yds out: kpt on again cl home* **7/1**

2101 **5** *nk* **Souter's Sister (IRE)**[21] 4640 2-9-0 83 .... JimCrowley 6 93
(R Hannon) *sn chsng ldr: rdn to chal 2f out: stl upsides over 1f out: wknd ins fnl f* **25/1**

1 **6** *hd* **Faraway Flower (USA)**[57] 3437 2-9-0 0 .... MichaelHills 10 92
(B W Hills) *t.k.h: chsd ldrs: edgd rt fr 3f out: n.m.r sn after: lost pl and rr 2f out: styd on again fnl f but nvr a threat* **15/2**

41 **7** *¾* **Seradim**[13] 4896 2-9-0 0 .... ShaneKelly 1 91
(P F I Cole) *chsd ldrs: ev ch fr 2f out: wknd ins fnl f* **20/1**

221 **8** *¾* **Qalahari (IRE)**[30] 4321 2-9-0 96 .... TPO'Shea 3 89
(D J Coakley) *wnt rt s: sn led: rdn over 2f out: hdd & wknd 1f out* **7/1**

41 **9** *1 ¼* **Pachattack (USA)**[23] 4554 2-9-0 0 .... LDettori 7 86
(G A Butler) *chsd ldrs: rdn over 2f out: sn btn* **11/2**[2]

620 **10** *1 ¾* **Shaws Diamond (USA)**[30] 4348 2-9-0 78 .... TGMcLaughlin 9 81
(D Shaw) *s.i.s: rdn over 3f out: a towards rr* **40/1**

1m 29.49s (2.09) **Going Correction** +0.225s/f (Good) **10** Ran SP% **119.4**
Speed ratings (Par 101): **97,95,94,92,92 92,91,90,89,87**
toteswinger: 1&2 £4.30, 1&3 £2.40, 2&3 £5.80. CSF £15.85 TOTE £3.00: £1.40, £1.80, £2.50; EX 18.40 Trifecta £153.00 Pool: £951.30, 4.60 winning units..
Owner Fittocks Stud & Andrew Bengough **Bred** Ronchalon Racing Uk Ltd **Trained** Newmarket, Suffolk

FOCUS
The bare form of this year's Prestige Stakes looks modest by Group 3 standards, but there was a lot to like about Fantasia who has plenty more to offer.

NOTEBOOK
Fantasia ◆ continues to follow in the footsteps of Luca Cumani's 2001 winner, Gossamer, having started off with a win in the same 6f Newmarket maiden. Having been held up early on, she was brought wide with her challenge in the straight and gradually picked up to record a decisive, if unspectacular success. She still looked green but her rider seemed keen to educate her rather than given her an unnecessarily hard ride, and she also gave the impression she was not totally home on this uneven track. Considering she is a Sadler's Wells filly, out of a 1m2f winner, this level of form over these sorts of trips as a juvenile mark her down as a potentially high-class three-year-old. But before then, she will continue to try and emulate Gossamer by taking in the Fillies' Mile at Ascot. Her trainer is apparently already thinking ahead to next year's 1,000 Guineas at Newmarket (for which she is now around 12-1), showing just how well regarded she is while also suggesting he believes the filly to have plenty of speed. Her immediate pedigree points more towards the Oaks, but the dam is a daughter of Queen Mary and Cheveley Park winner Blue Duster. (op 3-1 tchd 10-3 in a place)
Rose Diamond(IRE), upped a furlong in trip after running fifth in the Group 3 Princess Margaret Stakes at Ascot, was kept in by the eventual winner and did not enjoy the clearest of runs, but she was out in the open for long enough if good enough. She should continue to run well in similar company. (tchd 11-2)
April Pride had Rose Diamond three quarters of a length behind when fourth at Ascot last time, but she could not confirm form over this longer trip. Having been held up last, she stayed on nicely under pressure in the straight without quite managing to get there and this rates as another solid effort in defeat. (tchd 15-2)
Lahaleeb(IRE) ◆ was taking a big step up in class after consecutive wins in nursery company over this trip off marks of 72 and 74, but at least she came into the race in great form. She looked unlucky not to finish considerably closer as was stuck behind the tiring Qalahari for much of the way up the straight and the first three had already made their moves by the time she got into the clear. Added to that, she was hit over the head by a rival jockey's whip quite violently inside the final furlong, but she showed real guts to regain her momentum and run on for fourth. Clearly a really tough sort, there could be more to come. (op 13-2)
Souter's Sister(IRE), successful in a 6f nursery at the July course off a mark of 79 on her previous start, found this much tougher, but ran with credit.
Faraway Flower(USA), winner of a 6f maiden at Doncaster on her debut, is much better than she showed as she was continually kept in when looking to make her move and ended up being shuffled back to nearly last, before staying on again. (op 11-2)
Seradim found this much harder than the Redcar maiden she won on her previous start. (op 25-1)
Qalahari(IRE), who bolted up in a weak maiden over an extended 5f maiden at Bath, went off in front, but was soon in trouble in the straight and this trip probably stretched her in this company. (op 9-1)
Pachattack(USA), a course-and-distance maiden winner last time, failed to pick up when asked and might not have appreciated the easy ground. Official explanation: trainer said filly did not handle the good to soft (good in places) ground (op 5-1)
Shaws Diamond(USA) has plenty of ability, but she is not up to this level. (op 66-1)

5267 PICNIC STKS (H'CAP) 7f

4:20 (4:20) (Class 5) (0-70,71) 3-Y-O+ **£3,238** (£963; £481; £240) **Stalls** High

Form RPR

3200 **1** **Batchworth Blaise**[16] 4772 5-8-0 **51** .... SophieDoyle(7) 4 60
(E A Wheeler) *hld up in rr: swtchd lft to outside and rapid hdwy fnl f: led fnl 50yds: won gng away* **16/1**

303 **2** *¾* **Crataegus**[18] 4709 3-8-13 **62** .... DaneO'Neill 3 67
(H Candy) *in rr tl hdwy fr 2f out: str run ins fnl f to take 2nd clsng stakes but no imp on wnr* **8/1**

30B0 **3** *nk* **Imperium**[16] 4772 7-8-13 **57** ....(p) TPO'Shea 9 63
(Jean-Rene Auvray) *chsd ldrs: rdn to ld jst ins fnl f: hdd fnl 50yds and lost 2nd cl home* **25/1**

6613 **4** *¾* **Castano**[7] 5088 4-9-5 **66** ....(p) JamesMillman(3) 8 70
(B R Millman) *chsd ldrs: rdn and styd on fnl f but nvr quite gng pce to chal* **5/1**[2]

1000 **5** *hd* **Vanadium**[28] 4428 6-8-13 **64** .... JemmaMarshall(7) 2 67
(G L Moore) *plld hrd: pressed ldr after 1f: stl upsides 1f out: one pce fnl 50yds* **16/1**

0000 **6** *1 ¼* **Zazous**[7] 5088 7-8-4 **51** oh3 .... MarcHalford(3) 13 51
(J J Bridger) *chsd ldrs: rdn over 2f out: kpt on same pce ins fnl f* **20/1**

2531 **7** *½* **Viscountess (IRE)**[10] 4989 3-9-7 **70** .... DarryllHolland 11 67
(M Johnston) *led: rdn over 2f out: hdd jst ins fnl f and edgd rt u.p: sn btn* **4/1**[1]

0636 **8** *1* **Dr Synn**[13] 4910 7-8-7 **51** .... KirstyMilczarek 10 47
(M J Attwater) *chsd ldrs: rdn over 2f out: wknd ins fnl f* **12/1**

1003 **9** *½* **Shot To Fame (USA)**[14] 4862 9-9-11 **69** ....(t) JimCrowley 5 64
(S Kirk) *in rr: rdn and sme prog fnl 2f but nvr gng pce to be competitive* **10/1**

2100 **10** *¾* **Napoletano (GER)**[5] 5144 7-9-11 **69** ....(p) ShaneKelly 7 62+
(S Dow) *hdwy to trck ldrs on ins 3f out: n.m.r 2f out: styng on same pce whn hmpd 1f out and sn btn* **8/1**

6645 **11** *1 ¾* **Starlight Gazer**[14] 4865 5-9-12 **70** ....(t) RichardThomas 6 58
(J A Geake) *rdn over 2f out: a towards rr* **15/2**[3]

0341 **12** *2* **Seneschal**[4] 5166 7-9-6 **71** 6ex .... PNolan(7) 14 54
(A B Haynes) *chsd ldrs: rdn over 2f out: wknd over 1f out* **9/1**

100/ **13** *4 ½* **Spirit's Awakening**[1396] 6445 9-8-5 **52** .... LukeMorris(3) 12 22
(M J Attwater) *outpcd most of way* **14/1**

1m 29.86s (2.46) **Going Correction** +0.225s/f (Good)
WFA 3 from 4yo+ 5lb **13** Ran SP% **124.5**
Speed ratings (Par 103): **94,93,92,91,91 90,89,88,88,87 85,82,77**
toteswinger: 1&2 £51.70, 1&3 £128.10, 2&3 £55.40. CSF £144.39 CT £3319.36 TOTE £32.00: £7.00, £2.70, £8.80; EX 294.20.
Owner Astrod TA Austin Stroud & Co **Bred** Mrs D Price **Trained** Whitchurch-on-Thames, Oxon

FOCUS
A modest but competitive handicap run at a fair pace. A few of these were kept away from the far rail in the straight and the winner made his move up the middle of the track. The first two both came from the rear. Ordinary form.
Shot To Fame(USA) Official explanation: jockey said gelding had been struck into behind

5268 GOODWOOD.CO.UK MEDIAN AUCTION MAIDEN STKS 6f

4:55 (4:57) (Class 5) 3-4-Y-O **£3,238** (£963; £481; £240) **Stalls** Low

Form RPR

3 **1** **Triumphant Welcome**[29] 4388 3-8-10 0 .... StacyRenwick(7) 7 68
(G F Bridgwater) *trckd ldrs tl led wl over 1f out: pushed clr ins fnl f: easily* **8/1**[2]

0225 **2** *2* **Diego Rivera**[16] 4782 3-9-0 69 .... TravisBlock(3) 3 62
(P J Makin) *chsd ldrs: rdn and styd on to chse wnr ins fnl f but nvr any ch* **6/4**[1]

4665 **3** *2 ¾* **Flying Seasons**[31] 4301 3-9-0 50 .... JamesMillman(3) 2 53
(B R Millman) *led: rdn and hung lft fr over 2f out: hdd wl over 1f out and sn btn* **14/1**

0 **4** *6* **Casela Park (IRE)**[9] 5023 3-9-3 0 .... JimCrowley 1 34
(S Kirk) *t.k.h: chsd ldr: rdn to chal over 2f out: wknd ins fnl 2f* **8/1**[2]

5 **5** *6* **Soviet Cat (IRE)**[58] 3419 3-9-3 0 SamHitchcott 8 15
(D W P Arbuthnot) *veered rt s and slowly away: plld hrd in rr: no ch whn rdn and hung bdly lft fr over 2f out* **12/1**[3]

-400 **6** *1/2* **St Michael's Mount**[94] 2311 3-9-3 63 MartinDwyer 6 13
(M P Tregoning) *spd over 3f: sn wknd* **8/1**[2]

1m 14.08s (1.88) **Going Correction** +0.35s/f (Good) **6** Ran SP% **87.7**
Speed ratings (Par 103): **101,98,94,86,78 78**
toteswinger: 1&2 £1.80, 1&3 £6.90, 2&3 £3.30. CSF £12.41 TOTE £7.30: £2.30, £1.20; EX 11.30.
Owner C J Shelton **Bred** C J Shelton **Trained** Shrewley, Warwicks
■ Melt (9/2, kicked in stalls) and Silver Moonshine (7/1, unruly in stalls) were withdrawn. Deduct 25p in the £ under Rule 4.

FOCUS
Two withdrawals just before the start after some trouble in the stalls further weakened what was already a very modest sprint maiden. They raced towards the stands' rail. The winner reversed Wolverhampton form with the disappointing runner-up and the third casts some doubt over the form.

5269 TURFTV IS FOR BETTING SHOPS MAIDEN STKS (H'CAP) 2m
5:30 (5:31) (Class 5) (0-70,71) 3-Y-O **£3,238** (£963; £481; £240) **Stalls** High

Form RPR

5654 **1** **Hamsat Elqamar**[39] 4067 3-9-4 **65** MartinDwyer 3 75
(J H M Gosden) *led 4f: styd chsng ldr: drvn and grad plugged on fr 3f out tl fnlly got hd in front fnl strides* **6/1**[2]

0430 **2** *hd* **Tobago Bay**[41] 940 3-8-1 **51** oh1 (b) DominicFox(3) 8 60
(Miss Sheena West) *led after 4f: rdn 6f out: styd on u.p fnl 3f: ct fnl strides* **7/1**[3]

5342 **3** *7* **Silk Hall (UAE)**[10] 4985 3-9-10 **71** DaneO'Neill 9 72
(D W P Arbuthnot) *mid-div: rdn and hdwy fr 4f out: styd on one pce u.p fnl 3f: tk wl hld 3rd fnl f* **7/4**[1]

4606 **4** *3/4* **Blue Citadel (USA)**[15] 4821 3-9-9 **70** JimCrowley 6 70
(Mrs A J Perrett) *chsd ldrs: but nvr bttr than 3rd: rdn and no imp 3f out: wknd fr 2f out: lost mod 3rd fnl f* **17/2**

3005 **5** *nk* **Kalokairi (IRE)**[14] 4859 3-8-13 **60** (b[1]) SamHitchcott 1 60
(J L Dunlop) *in rr: rdn and sme prog fr 4f out but nvr anywhere nr ldrs: no ch fr over 2f out* **8/1**

6334 **6** *hd* **King Of Pentacles**[30] 4334 3-8-11 **61** (b[1]) TravisBlock(3) 12 61
(H Morrison) *t.k.h: hdwy to cl on ldrs 6f out: nvr in contention and no ch fnl 2f* **12/1**

0004 **7** *3 1/2* **Eddie Dowling**[28] 4410 3-8-10 **57** TPO'Shea 7 52
(M R Channon) *chsd ldrs: rdn over 4f out: wknd fr 3f out* **12/1**

0004 **8** *7* **Poppy Gregg**[29] 4366 3-7-13 **51** oh6 (b) AmyBaker(5) 13 38
(Dr J R J Naylor) *in rr: rdn and mod prog into mid-div 4f out but nvr anywhere nr ldrs* **33/1**

0652 **9** *2 1/4* **Miss Cruisecontrol**[8] 5077 3-8-4 **51** oh6 KirstyMilczarek 15 35
(J R Best) *s.i.s: a towards rr* **10/1**

0-00 **10** *15* **Amouretta**[17] 4750 3-8-4 **54** oh6 ow3 MarcHalford(3) 2 20
(T T Clement) *chsd ldrs: rdn 6f out: sn wknd* **80/1**

5050 **11** *26* **I Certainly May**[4] 5169 3-8-5 **55** ow3 PatrickHills(3) 10 —
(S Dow) *bhd fr 1/2-way* **33/1**

0000 **12** *16* **In Decorum**[52] 3611 3-7-13 **51** oh6 NataliaGemelova(5) 14 —
(J A Geake) *s.i.s: a in rr* **100/1**

006 **13** *16* **Lovespell (USA)**[60] 3350 3-8-11 **58** TGMcLaughlin 5 —
(Ms J S Doyle) *sn bhd* **33/1**

-600 **14** *18* **Starfinch**[7] 5086 3-8-2 **56** oh6 ow5 RossAtkinson(7) 4 —
(J J Bridger) *a in rr* **66/1**

0-00 **15** *3 3/4* **Dancing Ellie**[110] 1876 3-8-1 **51** oh2 LukeMorris(3) 11 —
(P M Phelan) *chsd ldrs tl wknd qckly 6f out* **40/1**

3m 33.04s (-0.16) **Going Correction** +0.225s/f (Good) **15** Ran SP% **124.2**
Speed ratings (Par 100): **109,108,105,105,104 104,103,99,98,90 77,69,61,52,51**
toteswinger: 1&2 £8.00, 1&3 £4.00, 2&3 £4.70. CSF £47.30 CT £106.87 TOTE £7.40: £2.30, £2.90, £1.40; EX 54.10.
Owner Hamdan Al Maktoum **Bred** Shadwell Estate Company Limited **Trained** Newmarket, Suffolk

FOCUS
As you might expect from a maiden handicap for three-year-olds, this race featured very few in-form runners and it is hard to envisage too many future winners emerging from this contest. Several of these will probably end up going over hurdles in the autumn. The pace was reasonable and the form is rated around the third.
Miss Cruisecontrol Official explanation: jockey said filly never travelled
I Certainly May Official explanation: jockey said gelding hung left
In Decorum Official explanation: vet said filly had finished tied up

5270 GOODWOOD REVIVAL MEETING STKS (H'CAP) 6f
6:00 (6:02) (Class 3) (0-95,93) 3-Y-0+ **£7,771** (£2,312; £1,155; £577) **Stalls** Low

Form RPR

3542 **1** **Osiris Way**[12] 4928 6-9-4 **87** JimCrowley 2 96
(P R Chamings) *trckd ldrs: led wl over 1f out: hld on all out* **5/1**[3]

6026 **2** *1/2* **Mujood**[7] 5096 5-9-4 **90** (b) LukeMorris(3) 6 97
(Eve Johnson Houghton) *sn drvn along in rr: hrd rdn 2f out: styd on u.p fnl f and tk 2nd cl home but nt rch wnr* **8/1**

1501 **3** *hd* **Seamus Shindig**[15] 4831 6-8-10 **86** AmyScott(7) 9 92
(H Candy) *trckd ldrs: shkn up and styd on to press wnr ins fnl f: no ex and lost 2nd cl home* **15/2**

5640 **4** *3/4* **Rash Judgement**[7] 5102 3-8-9 **84** TravisBlock(3) 5 88
(W S Kittow) *s.i.s: in rr: effrt whn n.m.r on ins over 1f out: swtchd rt and r.o ins fnl f: nt rch ldrs* **15/2**

0001 **5** *3/4* **Thebes**[7] 5102 3-9-5 **91** MichaelHills 1 93+
(M Johnston) *slt ld: rdn over 2f out: hdd wl over 1f out: wknd ins fnl f* **4/1**[1]

0550 **6** *3* **Berbice (IRE)**[14] 4842 3-9-1 **90** (t) PatrickHills(3) 7 82
(R Hannon) *sn chsng ldrs: rdn over 2f out: wknd ins fnl f* **16/1**

25 **7** *3/4* **Sir Edwin Landseer (USA)**[183] 670 8-9-10 **93** RichardThomas 4 83
(Christian Wroe) *s.i.s: rdn and sme prog over 2f out: wknd fnl f* **25/1**

4320 **8** *4 1/2* **Merlin's Dancer**[23] 4555 8-9-0 **86** JamesMillman(3) 3 61
(S Dow) *w ldr 4f: wknd over 1f out* **14/1**

6154 **9** *1 1/2* **Film Maker (IRE)**[22] 4601 3-9-0 **86** MartinDwyer 8 56
(B J Meehan) *outpcd most of way* **9/2**[2]

3155 **10** *nse* **Idle Power (IRE)**[12] 4928 10-9-0 **83** AmirQuinn 10 53
(J R Boyle) *hld up in rr: effrt on outside over 2f out: sn wknd* **7/1**

1m 13.11s (0.91) **Going Correction** +0.35s/f (Good)
WFA 3 from 5yo+ 3lb **10** Ran SP% **118.4**
Speed ratings (Par 107): **107,106,106,105,104 100,99,93,91,91**
toteswinger: 1&2 £9.20, 1&3 £6.90, 2&3 £15.00. CSF £45.47 CT £308.05 TOTE £5.10: £1.80, £2.70, £2.20; EX 49.20 Place 6 £ 286.58, Place 5 £ 42.94.
Owner Mrs Alexandra J Chandris **Bred** Whitsbury Manor Stud **Trained** Baughurst, Hants
■ Stewards' Enquiry : Luke Morris one-day ban: used whip with excessive frequency (Sep 9)

FOCUS
A good sprint handicap and they went a strong pace throughout. The form looks sound and should prove reliable. They raced middle to stands' side, but the main action took place away from the near rail.

NOTEBOOK
Osiris Way ran into a big improver when second at Windsor on his previous start, but he showed he is very much going the right way himself with a determined effort. His jockey believes there is even more to come and thinks he could be one for some of the big sprint handicaps next season. (tchd 9-2)
Mujood, dropped back in trip, needed strong driving to move into a threatening position, but he eventually responded and finished strongly. It is easy to see why he has been campaigned over further lately. (op 10-1)
Seamus Shindig, the winner of three of his last five starts, ran right up to form off a mark 3lb higher than when winning at Newmarket last time. (op 8-1)
Rash Judgement stayed on after being switched around the weakening Thebes, but was not unlucky. However, he did most of his racing against the stands' rail, which may not have been the place to be. (op 8-1)
Thebes, 7lb higher than when winning at Newmarket on his previous start, is probably better than he showed as he raced tight against the stands' rail throughout, whereas the principals more towards the middle. (tchd 7-2)
Film Maker(IRE) Official explanation: jockey said colt ran too free
Idle Power(IRE) Official explanation: jockey said gelding banged its head on leaving stalls
T/Plt: £305.10 to a £1 stake. Pool: £85,784.63. 205.20 winning tickets. T/Qpdt: £22.50 to a £1 stake. Pool: £5,178.00. 169.75 winning tickets. ST

5240
NEWMARKET (JULY) (R-H)
Saturday, August 23

OFFICIAL GOING: Good to firm (9.2)
Wind: Light, half behind Weather: Cloudy with sunny spells

5271 EUROPEAN BREEDERS' FUND MAIDEN STKS 6f
12:50 (12:51) (Class 4) 2-Y-O **£5,180** (£1,541; £770; £384) **Stalls** Low

Form RPR

5 **1** **Absent Pleasure (USA)**[8] 5053 2-9-3 0 AlanMunro 13 83+
(B J Meehan) *trckd ldrs: edgd lft over 1f out: styd on to ld fnl strides* **5/1**[3]

2 *shd* **Huntdown (USA)** 2-9-3 0 RobertHavlin 1 83+
(J H M Gosden) *chsd ldrs: led over 1f out: hdd post* **6/1**

32 **3** *shd* **Kingship Spirit (IRE)**[71] 2999 2-9-3 0 JMurtagh 5 82+
(J Noseda) *trckd ldrs: styd on wl ins fnl f: jst hld* **9/4**[1]

4 *3/4* **Adorn** 2-8-12 0 WilliamBuick 12 75+
(J Noseda) *sn chsng ldrs: styd on wd outside: styd on appr fnl f: fin wl* **16/1**

4 **5** *3/4* **Invincible Heart (GR)**[15] 4826 2-9-3 0 JohnEgan 9 78+
(Jane Chapple-Hyam) *w ldr: led over 2f out: hdd over 1f out: kpt on same pce* **4/1**[2]

0 **6** *2 1/4* **Capeability (IRE)**[21] 4625 2-9-3 0 TonyCulhane 2 71
(M R Channon) *led tl over 2f out: fdd fnl f* **12/1**

7 *2 1/2* **Hula King (GER)** 2-9-3 0 RyanMoore 3 64
(B J Meehan) *prom: sn pushed along: wknd over 1f out* **25/1**

8 *3/4* **Sioux Rising (IRE)** 2-8-12 0 TonyHamilton 14 56
(R A Fahey) *chsd ldrs: wknd over 1f out* **50/1**

9 *5* **Cheviot (USA)** 2-9-3 0 PhilipRobinson 11 46
(M A Jarvis) *chsd ldrs: wknd over 1f out* **8/1**

10 *2 1/4* **Broughtons Paradis (IRE)** 2-8-12 0 StephenDonohoe 7 35
(W J Musson) *s.s: a in rr* **100/1**

11 *1 1/2* **Destiny Quest (USA)** 2-9-3 0 GeorgeBaker 8 35
(L M Cumani) *mid-div: lost pl over 2f out* **16/1**

12 *2 1/4* **Valkyrie (IRE)** 2-8-12 0 TPQueally 6 23
(N P Littmoden) *s.s: sn drvn along in rr* **66/1**

5 **13** *1 1/4* **Bold Hawk**[100] 2117 2-9-3 0 PatCosgrave 4 25
(Mrs C A Dunnett) *sn outpcd and in rr* **100/1**

14 *nk* **Dontforgeturshovel** 2-9-3 0 JimmyQuinn 15 24
(J Pearce) *s.s: t.k.h: a in rr* **100/1**

15 *4 1/2* **Sir Isaac** 2-9-3 0 LiamJones 10 10
(W J Haggas) *s.s: outpcd and in rr: bhd fnl 2f* **33/1**

1m 12.29s (-0.21) **Going Correction** -0.05s/f (Good) **15** Ran SP% **125.5**
Speed ratings (Par 96): **99,98,98,97,96 93,90,89,82,79 77,74,73,72,66**
toteswinger: 1&2 £9.00, 1&3 £4.00, 2&3 £6.70. CSF £35.59 TOTE £5.60: £1.70, £2.60, £1.30; EX 29.00.
Owner Bill Hinge & John Searchfield 1 **Bred** Darley **Trained** Manton, Wilts

FOCUS
A decent maiden that should produce winners. The form looks rock solid through the third and fifth.

NOTEBOOK
Absent Pleasure(USA), a Dewhurst entry, stepped up markedly on his recent debut effort to land some good bets. Too inexperienced to get involved when fifth of nine behind a highly-regarded stablemate Nasri at Newbury last week (6f, good to soft), he started to be niggled three out, but was switched towards onto the far rail racing into the final quarter mile and stayed on strongly under Munro. The step up to 7f is expected to see him improve again and there is plenty of scope for physical improvement. (tchd 9-2 and 11-2)
Huntdown(USA) ◆, a half-brother to a couple of 6f winners in Vainglory and Wingbeat, holds a Racing Post Trophy entry and is clearly expected to stay further in time. He seemed to know his job, travelling strongly just in behind the speed, and he struck on about a furlong and half out, but in the end was run out of it. This was a promising start and he should find a similar race. (op 9-2)
Kingship Spirit(IRE), twice beaten at a short price earlier in the season when runners from the yard were not going so well, was expected to prove suited by the return to 6f. He raced quite keenly early on, but it did not seem to affect his performance and he stuck on right the way to the line, having also been switched more towards the far rail. There is a maiden in him, but he will remain vulnerable to classier types. (tchd 11-4)
Adorn ◆'s breeding is nothing to get excited about and she holds no notable entries, but she ran a race full of promise back in fourth. Chasing the pace more towards the centre of the track, she looked a big danger when looming up on the outer with two to run, but just lacked that change of gear and stuck on without being given a hard time. Improvement should be forthcoming and her action suggested a little cut in the ground may not go amiss. (op 22-1)
Invincible Heart(GR), dismissed in betting when a promising fourth in a CD maiden earlier in the month (both second and third won on Friday) shaped as though a drop to this distance would not go amiss that day and his breeding backs that up. Soon up with the pace, he started to be ridden over two out and had every chance racing into the final furlong, but was unable to quicken. His debut effort came on slower ground and perhaps he found this surface a shade quick.
Capeability(IRE) stepped up on his debut effort at Goodwood, leading for quite a long way on this drop to 6f, and will be qualified for nurseries following another run. (tchd 11-1 and 14-1)
Hula King(GER) ◆, from the same yard as the winner, cost 55,000gns as a 2yo and he shaped with definite promise under a considerate ride.
Sioux Rising(IRE) Official explanation: jockey said filly hung left

The Form Book, Raceform Ltd, Compton, RG20 6NL

Cheviot(USA), the first foal of a half-sister to Gossamer, comes from a yard more than capable of readying one first time, but it looked significant he lacks any big-race entries and, having been up there early, he dropped away from two out. (op 16-1)
Destiny Quest(USA), a Royal Lodge entrant whose sales price more than doubled to $150,000, was the owner's second-string and he shaped with little immediate promise for the future. (op 25-1)

5272 THOROUGHBRED BREEDERS' ASSOCIATION LOWTHER STKS (GROUP 2) (FILLIES) 6f

1:25 (1:25) (Class 1) 2-Y-O

£34,062 (£12,912; £6,462; £3,222; £1,614; £810) **Stalls** Low

Form				RPR
612	**1**		**Infamous Angel**[35] 4190 2-8-12 87 EddieAhern 4 (R Hannon) *hld up: hdwy over 1f out: r.o u.p to ld post* **11/2**[3]	105
1120	**2**	*nse*	**Penny's Gift**[35] 4190 2-8-12 99 RyanMoore 5 (R Hannon) *chsd ldrs: rdn over 1f out: edgd lft ins fnl f: r.o* **7/2**[2]	105
121	**3**	*hd*	**Langs Lash (IRE)**[66] 3123 2-9-1 102 AlanMunro 3 (M G Quinlan) *led: rdn over 1f out: hdd post* **8/1**	107
110	**4**	*2*	**Danehill Destiny**[66] 3123 2-8-12 101 JMurtagh 1 (W J Haggas) *a.p: nt clr run 2f out: sn swtchd rt and chsng ldr: rdn fnl f: styng on same pce whn nt clr run towards fin* **13/2**	98
101	**5**	*1 3/4*	**Please Sing**[45] 3851 2-9-1 103 EdwardCreighton 6 (M R Channon) *hld up: hdwy over 2f out: rdn over 1f out: edgd lft and styd on same pce fnl f* **10/1**	96
241	**6**	*1/2*	**African Skies**[28] 4403 2-8-12 102 NCallan 7 (K A Ryan) *chsd ldr tl rdn over 1f out: wknd ins fnl f* **7/4**[1]	92
125	**7**	*5*	**Maggie Lou (IRE)**[28] 4441 2-8-12 87 TedDurcan 2 (K A Ryan) *dwlt: outpcd* **18/1**	77

1m 11.65s (-0.85) **Going Correction** -0.05s/f (Good) 7 Ran SP% **112.8**
Speed ratings (Par 103): **103,102,102,100,97 97,90**
toteswinger: 1&2 £3.70, 1&3 £7.20, 2&3 £5.50. CSF £24.26 TOTE £7.10: £3.40, £2.10; EX 24.50.
Owner Geoff Howard-Spink & Peter Marshall **Bred** Bricklow Stud **Trained** East Everleigh, Wilts
■ Another important race transferred from the abandoned York Ebor meeting.
■ Stewards' Enquiry : J Murtagh two-day ban: careless riding (Sep 7-8)

FOCUS

This was a very weak renewal, although the first two deserve credit for their improvement.

NOTEBOOK

Infamous Angel, who would have won the Super Sprint in another stride, came in for plenty of support beforehand and a bold bid was clearly expected. Waited with through the early stages, she took a while to pick up but really grabbed the rising ground inside the final 100 yards. She is reportedly thriving physically and there is every chance of further progress. The Cheveley Park is an obvious end-of-season target and connections plan on supplementing her. (op 7-1)
Penny's Gift has been a rapid improver, finding only Cuis Ghaire too good in her bid for a hat-trick in the Albany, before getting no luck at all when a fast-finishing seventh in the Super Sprint. The step back up to 6f was in her favour and the only surprise about her performance was that she did not show more speed. She started to be niggled just under halfway, but kept finding for strong pressure and gives every indication she will stay 7f now. (op 4-1)
Langs Lash(IRE) improved on her York Listed second when springing a surprise in the Queen Mary, making just about all on the best ground, and this required another step forward, up to 6f for the first time and having to concede a 3lb penalty. Very quickly into stride, she settled nicely on the rail and gradually wound up the tempo under a well-judged ride, momentarily looking to have them all beaten, but the final climb to the line found her out. This was a brave effort and she emerges as the best horse at the weights. (op 6-1)
Danehill Destiny ◆ looked a top-notch juvenile on her first couple of starts, winning her maiden impressively before beating subsequent Richmond winner Prolific at Windsor, but failed to run her race on the fastest ground she has encountered in the Queen Mary (bumped start) and there was again a question over the suitability of this surface. The step up to 6f was certainly going to suit and she travelled strongly, tucked in behind Langs Lash on the rails. However, having been switched out to challenge with just under two to run, she seemed reluctant to let herself down on the ground and could not quicken, already being beaten when squeezed out close home. She is clearly in need of a slower surface and remains a filly of some potential. (op 9-2 tchd 4-1)
Please Sing left behind her Royal Ascot disappointment behind some of these when quickening well to win the Cherry Hinton over CD last month and the return to a faster surface was not expected to be a problem. She too had a 3lb penalty to shoulder though and came up short in this stronger contest, coming wide with her challenge and never looking likely to pick them up. (op 15-2)
African Skies confirmed the promise of her Royal Ascot fourth in Albany (one place behind Penny's Gift) when winning the Group 3 Princess Margaret Stakes back at Ascot and she was strongly supported. However, having held an ideal early position, she came under pressure from over two furlongs out and was left behind in the final furlong. (op 11-4)
Maggie Lou(IRE), who could only manage fourth in a 5f Listed contest at Vichy last month, was always likely to struggle and never got into it, having been restrained right at the back early on. (op 20-1)

5273 CHRIS BLACKWELL MEMORIAL H'CAP 7f

2:00 (2:04) (Class 3) (0-90,89) 3-Y-O **£9,066** (£2,697; £1,348; £673) **Stalls** Low

Form				RPR
-133	**1**		**Relative Order**[23] 4553 3-9-7 87 SebSanders 4 (J R Best) *chsd ldrs: drvn over 2f out: styd on to ld 1f out: hld on wl* **11/4**[1]	98+
2323	**2**	*1*	**Ellemujie**[28] 4423 3-9-7 87 RichardKingscote 10 (D K Ivory) *in rr: hdwy on outer over 2f out: hung lft 1f out: styd on to take 2nd towards fin* **5/1**[2]	95
4-11	**3**	*1/2*	**Aromatherapy**[86] 2532 3-9-7 87 TedDurcan 3 (H R A Cecil) *uns rdr gng to s: rn v free loose for 5f: sn chsng ldrs: led over 2f out: hdd 1f out: kpt on same pce* **10/1**	94+
2251	**4**	*2 1/4*	**Dunn'o (IRE)**[10] 4983 3-9-6 86 AdamKirby 2 (C G Cox) *led tl over 2f out: kpt on one pce* **8/1**	87
1144	**5**	*1/2*	**Stevie Thunder**[16] 4783 3-9-9 89 PaulMulrennan 12 (G A Swinbank) *hld up in rr: effrt on outer over 2f out: kpt on fnl f* **8/1**	88
4004	**6**	*1 3/4*	**Cat Whistle**[13] 4900 3-8-7 73 TonyHamilton 9 (R A Fahey) *t.k.h in rr: effrt over 2f out: kpt on: nvr nr ldrs* **28/1**	68
530	**7**	*2 3/4*	**Coachhouse Lady (USA)**[13] 4893 3-8-12 78 NCallan 6 (K A Ryan) *w ldrs: wknd 1f out* **25/1**	65
4-21	**8**	*3/4*	**Credit Swap**[63] 3268 3-9-2 82 GeorgeBaker 8 (L M Cumani) *hld up in mid-div: drvn over 3f out: lost pl 2f out* **7/1**	67
3311	**9**	*nk*	**Persian Sea (UAE)**[37] 4110 3-9-6 86 PhilipRobinson 5 (M A Jarvis) *chsd ldrs: wknd 2f out* **13/2**[3]	70
0003	**10**	*3 3/4*	**Jebel Tara**[7] 5104 3-8-11 77 LiamJones 1 (C E Brittain) *w ldrs: rdn over 2f out: sn wknd* **16/1**	51
16-6	**11**	*1 1/4*	**Mistress Greeley (USA)**[99] 2170 3-9-8 88 RyanMoore 11 (Sir Michael Stoute) *in rr: rdn over 2f out: nvr on terms: eased ins fnl f* **14/1**	59

1m 23.57s (-2.13) **Going Correction** -0.05s/f (Good) 11 Ran SP% **120.3**
Speed ratings (Par 104): **110,108,108,105,105 103,100,99,98,94 93**
toteswinger: 1&2 £4.70, 1&3 £6.50, 2&3 £13.00. CSF £16.29 CT £125.20 TOTE £3.90: £1.50, £2.40, £2.50; EX 19.10 Trifecta £526.20 Part won. Pool: £711.20, 0.30 winning units..
Owner One Carat Partnership **Bred** John And Mrs Caroline Penny **Trained** Hucking, Kent

FOCUS

A fair handicap. Solid form.

NOTEBOOK

Relative Order got plenty of cover early on and burst through with a decisive turn of foot. He is progressive and had been knocking on the door in better races, notably at Goodwood last time when poorly drawn, so this was a well-deserved success. He is due to be shipped off to Hong Kong to join a new stable, but looks set to have another race for John Best, as, if he can get upto a rating of 100, it will open up his options when going abroad. (op 10-3 tchd 7-2)
Ellemujie continues to run well but is now on a losing run which stretches back 17 starts. He ran on down the centre of the track and finished well, so a step back up to 1m may be called for, but he will continue to struggle against less exposed types. (op 8-1 tchd 17-2 in places)
Aromatherapy, who took part despite disposing of Ted Durcan and running loose before the start, had won her two starts this term, both at Great Leighs over 1m, and she produced a sound effort in third, having raced up against the far rail most of the way. She is open to improvement. (op 8-1)
Dunn'o(IRE) was always prominent until finding just the one pace late on. He did win over 7f at Sandown last time but he may do better over slightly shorter. (tchd 10-1)
Stevie Thunder, whose form was closely matched with Relative Order and Ellemujie on their running behind Duntulm over 1m last month, is admirably consistent, but he may need to drop a few pounds before regaining the winning thread. He may also benefit from a step back up to 1m. (op 12-1)
Cat Whistle ◆, who has been slipping down the weights, confirmed the promise of her recent run at Redcar and ran an eyecatching race. She may do better when stepped up to 1m. (op 33-1)
Credit Swap was making his handicap debut but never threatened. (tchd 6-1)
Persian Sea(UAE) gradually faded, having been prominent early on. (op 9-2)
Mistress Greeley(USA) was always struggling and has plenty to prove. Official explanation: jockey said filly never travelled (op 12-1 tchd 11-1)

5274 ADNAMS EAST GREEN NURSERY 7f

2:35 (2:35) (Class 2) 2-Y-O **£12,952** (£3,854; £1,926; £962) **Stalls** Low

Form				RPR
4236	**1**		**Gal Aloud (USA)**[43] 3924 2-9-0 78 RyanMoore 13 (R Hannon) *hld up in tch: rdn over 1f out: r.o to ld post* **16/1**	81+
301	**2**	*hd*	**Perfect Citizen (USA)**[17] 4728 2-9-5 83 AdamKirby 17 (W R Swinburn) *chsd ldrs: rdn over 2f out: led over 1f out: sn edgd lft: hung rt and lft ins fnl f: hdd post* **14/1**	86
023	**3**	*1/2*	**Royal Executioner (USA)**[28] 4415 2-8-13 77 AlanMunro 14 (P W Chapple-Hyam) *hld up: nt clr run over 1f out: r.o and swtchd lft ins fnl f: nt rch ldrs* **16/1**	78+
21	**4**	*1/2*	**Diddums**[21] 4616 2-9-0 78 LiamJones 11 (W J Haggas) *hld up: hdwy over 2f out: rdn and ev ch ins fnl f: hung rt and bmpd ins fnl f: no ex nr fin* **6/1**[2]	78+
441	**5**	*2*	**Stirling Castle**[14] 4861 2-9-6 84 TedDurcan 8 (M J Wallace) *s.i.s: hld up: running on whn nt clr run ins fnl f: nvr able to chal* **14/1**	79+
61	**6**	*2*	**Sultans Way (IRE)**[18] 4697 2-8-7 71 WilliamBuick 12 (P F I Cole) *prom: racd keenly: rdn and ev ch over 1f out: no ex ins fnl f* **8/1**[3]	61
3021	**7**	*hd*	**Pegasus Lad (USA)**[23] 4570 2-9-7 85 JMurtagh 10 (M Johnston) *led: rdn: hung lft and hdd over 1f out: styd on same pce* **7/2**[1]	75
420	**8**	*3/4*	**Tepmokea (IRE)**[21] 4625 2-8-12 76 FergusSweeney 16 (K R Burke) *hld up: pushed along 1/2-way: r.o ins fnl f: nvr nrr* **16/1**	64+
066	**9**	*1 1/4*	**Sericus (IRE)**[40] 4020 2-7-13 68 DavidProbert(5) 18 (W Jarvis) *hld up: effrt over 2f out: n.d* **9/1**	53
0451	**10**	*1/2*	**Richo**[28] 4415 2-9-0 78 PaulMulrennan 6 (D H Brown) *chsd ldrs: rdn and ev ch whn hmpd over 1f out: wknd ins fnl f* **12/1**	61+
041	**11**	*1/2*	**Bobbie Soxer (IRE)**[30] 4337 2-9-0 78 SebSanders 9 (J L Dunlop) *s.i.s: sn hld up in tch: rdn and ev ch whn hmpd over 1f out: wknd ins fnl f* **8/1**[3]	60+
233	**12**	*2 1/4*	**Raise All In (IRE)**[30] 4337 2-8-9 73 PatDobbs 7 (R Hannon) *s.i.s: hld up: hdwy 3f out: rdn and nt clr run over 1f out: sn wknd* **25/1**	49+
3542	**13**	*3/4*	**Digger Derek (IRE)**[9] 5006 2-8-1 65 JimmyQuinn 4 (R A Fahey) *trckd ldrs: plld hrd: n.m.r and lost pl over 2f out: wknd over 1f out* **10/1**	40+
525	**14**	*9*	**Flyit (IRE)**[51] 3651 2-8-10 74 TonyCulhane 15 (M R Channon) *hld up: a in rr: wkng whn hung lft over 1f out* **33/1**	26
301	**15**	*hd*	**Swingfire (USA)**[29] 4373 2-8-1 65 (p) NickyMackay 3 (R M H Cowell) *chsd ldrs: rdn over 2f out: ev ch whn hmpd over 1f out: sn wknd* **20/1**	17

1m 25.54s (-0.16) **Going Correction** -0.05s/f (Good) 15 Ran SP% **128.0**
Speed ratings (Par 100): **98,97,97,96,94 92,91,90,89,88 88,85,84,74,74**
toteswinger: 1&2 £47.50, 1&3 £20.60, 2&3 £25.00. CSF £231.03 CT £3655.76 TOTE £22.40: £5.30, £5.50, £3.80; EX 354.10 TRIFECTA Not won..
Owner Mrs J K Powell **Bred** Tony Holmes **Trained** East Everleigh, Wilts
■ Stewards' Enquiry : J Murtagh one-day ban: careless riding (Sep 9)

FOCUS

A hugely competitive nursery which should be a good source of winners. The third and fourth set the level, which should prove reliable.

NOTEBOOK

Gal Aloud(USA), whose trainer's juveniles can do little wrong at present, relished the stiff finish and took advantage of the runner-up's waywardness. Her sire was a top-class 1m performer in the US and this scopey filly may well improve further for a step up to that distance.
Perfect Citizen(USA) would have won had he run straight under pressure. Off the mark at the third attempt in a 7f Kempton maiden, he was starting out nursery life off a reasonable mark. Out wide, more towards the centre of the track, he was driven into the lead just over a furlong out, but hung both left and right under pressure. There is clearly a good deal of ability there, but it remains to be seen whether this was down to greenness.
Royal Executioner(USA) ◆ had just come up short in a couple of northern maidens over 7f and he showed improved form on this nursery debut, really flying home having been quite well back early. He clearly has it in him to win off this sort of mark and should stay 1m.
Diddums, a rather fortunate winner of a 6f maiden at Doncaster, was keeping on well when the runner-up barged into him, but he would not have won. He may well do better back at 6f. (op 13-2 tchd 7-1)
Stirling Castle ran well on this handicap debut, keeping on despite getting slightly impeded, without suggesting the drop back from 1m was in his favour.
Sultans Way(IRE) left his debut running behind on fast ground at Thirsk last time and he looked a real threat over a furlong out, but he had raced a shade freely early on and did not get home. (op 15-2)
Pegasus Lad(USA) had won in good fashion at Sandown last time, but found this a bit too competitive off a mark of 85. (op 5-1)
Tepmokea(IRE) looked on a stiff enough mark for this nursery debut, but ran on well. (op 25-1)
Sericus(IRE), another handicap debutant, was wide throughout and kept on without threatening. Official explanation: jockey said colt was unsuited by the good to firm ground (op 10-1 tchd 8-1)
Richo Official explanation: trainer said gelding suffered interference in running

Digger Derek(IRE) Official explanation: jockey said colt ran too free
Flyit(IRE) Official explanation: jockey said colt moved badly

5275 COUNTRYWIDE STEEL AND TUBES HOPEFUL STKS (LISTED RACE) 6f

3:05 (3:06) (Class 1) 3-Y-O+

£24,978 (£9,468; £4,738; £2,362; £1,183; £594) **Stalls** Low

Form				RPR
1050	**1**		**Edge Closer**[21] 4624 4-9-4 109........(t) RyanMoore 14	117
			(R Hannon) *chsd ldrs stands' side: led over 1f out: styd on wl* **16/1**	
1030	**2**	¾	**Balthazaar's Gift (IRE)**[13] 4915 5-9-4 110........(p) GeorgeBaker 10	115+
			(L M Cumani) *hld up in rr: effrt 2f out: styd on to take 2nd nr fin* **12/1**	
5054	**3**	½	**Strike The Deal (USA)**[35] 4188 3-8-11 106........(v[1]) SebSanders 4	109
			(J Noseda) *chsd ldrs: wnt 2nd over 1f out: edgd rt and no ex fnl f* **12/1**	
-140	**4**	1 ¾	**Salsa Steps (USA)**[43] 3927 4-8-9 100........(t) RobertHavlin 3	98
			(H Morrison) *chsd ldrs towards far side: kpt on wl fnl f* **25/1**	
3162	**5**	½	**Damika (IRE)**[20] 4660 5-9-0 106........JMurtagh 5	102+
			(R M Whitaker) *in rr: reminders over 2f out: styd on wl fnl f* **11/1**	
-601	**6**	hd	**Pearly Wey**[22] 4586 5-9-0 99........PhilipRobinson 12	101
			(C G Cox) *chsd ldrs: kpt on same pce appr fnl f* **22/1**	
5302	**7**	nse	**King's Apostle (IRE)**[21] 4624 4-9-0 106........LiamJones 15	101+
			(W J Haggas) *hld up in rr stands' side: effrt 2f out: kpt on: nvr rchd ldrs* **3/1**[2]	
1-04	**8**	¾	**Winker Watson**[24] 4518 3-8-11 115........AlanMunro 18	99+
			(P W Chapple-Hyam) *hld up in rr stands' side: effrt 2f out: kpt on: nvr rchd ldrs* **15/8**[1]	
5300	**9**	2 ½	**Sakhee's Song (IRE)**[14] 4841 4-8-9 92........TQuinn 13	86
			(D R C Elsworth) *mid-div: effrt 2f out: nvr a threat* **100/1**	
-130	**10**	hd	**Cartimandua**[43] 3927 4-8-13 104........GrahamGibbons 8	89
			(E S McMahon) *chsd ldrs: wknd appr fnl f* **20/1**	
04-1	**11**	hd	**Battle Paint (USA)**[21] 4617 4-9-0 108........TedDurcan 11	89
			(J H M Gosden) *trckd ldrs: effrt 2f out: sn btn* **9/1**[3]	
1400	**12**	nk	**Sonny Red (IRE)**[82] 2680 4-9-0 106........(p) EddieAhern 6	88
			(R Hannon) *hld up in rr: last and shkn up 1f out: swtchd lft: r.o towards fin* **20/1**	
0600	**13**	nse	**Judd Street**[42] 3943 6-9-4 97........StephenCarson 17	92
			(Eve Johnson Houghton) *chsd ldrs: wknd appr fnl f* **66/1**	
2400	**14**	¾	**Day By Day**[42] 3948 4-8-9 94........(b) WilliamBuick 2	81
			(B J Meehan) *mde most tl hdd & wknd over 1f out* **100/1**	
11-5	**15**	shd	**Floristry**[21] 4617 3-8-6 103........RichardMullen 16	80
			(Saeed Bin Suroor) *hld up towards stands' side: rdn 2f out: sn btn* **20/1**	
2052	**16**	3 ¼	**Al Muheer (IRE)**[14] 4842 3-8-11 100........NCallan 7	75
			(C E Brittain) *w ldrs: wknd 2f out* **33/1**	
05-0	**17**	½	**Monaazalah (IRE)**[72] 2967 3-8-6 79........JimmyQuinn 1	68
			(Rae Guest) *s.i.s: effrt far side over 2f out: sn wknd* **100/1**	

1m 10.32s (-2.18) **Going Correction** -0.05s/f (Good)
WFA 3 from 4yo+ 3lb **17** Ran SP% **129.3**
Speed ratings (Par 111): **112,111,110,108,107 107,107,106,102,102 102,101,101,100,100 96,95**
toteswinger: 1&2 £32.30, 1&3 £35.60, 2&3 £19.40. CSF £187.57 TOTE £22.30: £5.30, £4.00, £4.30; EX 309.20 Trifecta £1706.40 Part won. Pool: £2306.00, 0.20 winning unit..
Owner Lady Whent And Friends **Bred** Caroline Wilson **Trained** East Everleigh, Wilts

FOCUS
A fascinating Listed sprint where all the attention was on Winker Watson, but he flopped in a major way and it was Richard Hannon who collected yet another valuable prize, courtesy of Edge Closer. Decent form by Listed standards, although there is a question mark over its solidity.

NOTEBOOK
Edge Closer, well drawn in stall 14 and sporting a first-time tongue tie, was one of several up there in the early firing line and impressed with the change of pace he showed to skip clear over a furlong out. The breathing aid clearly made a difference and he will now be stepped back up to Group company. (op 25-1)
Balthazaar's Gift(IRE) does not have the win record he should, but he is capable of popping up in these events and won in this grade at Windsor earlier in the season. Outclassed in the Prix Maurice De Gheest last time, he came with a strong late run, but Edge Closer had already poached a winning lead. (op 11-1)
Strike The Deal(USA) has come right back to his best of late and this was a further step forward in first-time visor. Unlike the front two, he was drawn low, but he got himself into a challenging position and had every chance. He will find a race at this sort of level before long. (tchd 11-1)
Salsa Steps(USA) ran above herself back in fourth, never being too far away and staying on under pressure. (op 20-1)
Damika(IRE), a fast-finishing second in this grade at Chester earlier in the month, came from too far back and the principals had flown by the time he hit top stride. (tchd 10-1)
Pearly Wey, who made it back-to-back wins in the Stewards' Cup consolation race earlier in the month, needed to pull out quite a bit more on this rise in grade and he ran about as well as could have been expected. (op 20-1)
King's Apostle(IRE), a tough and progressive handicapper who ran a career-best when just losing out in the Stewards' Cup, looked well worth his place at this level. He had a good draw, but was under pressure over two furlongs out and just stayed on at the one pace. (op 5-1)
Winker Watson, a leading sprint juvenile who had had this year's campaign restricted to just two runs, both over 1m in the top company, finished a highly creditable fourth behind Henrythenavigator in the Sussex Stakes and was a stand-out at this level if coping with the drop back to 6f. The Peter Chapple-Hyam team have hardly been firing though and he was never travelling as well as his rider would have liked. He is better than this, but it seems clear now that 6f is too sharp. (op 9-4)
Battle Paint(USA)was a very smart performer up to 1m in France and made a winning debut for connections in a 6f conditions event at Doncaster, but he had yet to run on ground this quick and he struggled. (op 15-2 tchd 10-1)
Sonny Red(IRE) Official explanation: jockey said colt was unsuited by the good to firm ground

5276 JUDDMONTE INTERNATIONAL STKS (GROUP 1) 1m 2f

3:35 (3:43) (Class 1) 3-Y-O+

£141,925 (£53,800; £26,925; £13,425; £6,725; £3,375) **Stalls** Centre

Form				RPR
1111	**1**		**Duke Of Marmalade (IRE)**[28] 4406 4-9-5 0........JMurtagh 4	128+
			(A P O'Brien, Ire) *chsd ldrs: led 3f out: edgd lft ins fnl f: drvn out* **4/6**[1]	
1222	**2**	¾	**Phoenix Tower (USA)**[49] 3741 4-9-5 117........TedDurcan 9	126
			(H R A Cecil) *trckd ldrs: nt clr run 2f out: swtchd lft over 1f out: rdn to chse wnr fnl f: styd on* **12/1**[3]	
-221	**3**	2 ½	**New Approach (IRE)**[77] 2829 3-8-11 0........KJManning 10	121
			(J S Bolger, Ire) *stdd s: hld up: plld hrd: hdwy over 2f out: rdn and hung rt over 1f out: styd on ins fnl f* **2/1**[2]	
3331	**4**	1 ¼	**Pipedreamer**[28] 4436 4-9-5 117........SebSanders 11	119
			(J H M Gosden) *hld up: hdwy 3f out: rdn over 1f out: no ex ins fnl f* **14/1**	
504	**5**	4	**Halicarnassus (IRE)**[28] 4436 4-9-5 110........TonyCulhane 3	111
			(M R Channon) *s.i.s: hld up: rdn over 2f out: n.d* **80/1**	
1005	**6**	1 ¾	**Championship Point (IRE)**[14] 4855 5-9-5 110........EdwardCreighton 7	107
			(M R Channon) *hld up: rdn over 2f out: n.d* **66/1**	
-304	**7**	8	**Red Rock Canyon (IRE)**[28] 4406 4-9-5 0........CO'Donoghue 8	91
			(A P O'Brien, Ire) *led: rdn and edgd lft 4f out: hdd 3f out: hmpd and wknd over 1f out* **66/1**	
/205	**8**	10	**Rob Roy (USA)**[49] 3741 6-9-5 113........RyanMoore 6	71
			(Sir Michael Stoute) *hld up in tch: rdn over 2f out: wknd over 1f out* **25/1**	
-644	**9**	26	**Cat Junior (USA)**[41] 4010 3-8-11 115........(t) NCallan 1	19
			(B J Meehan) *chsd ldr tl rdn over 3f out: wknd over 1f out* **33/1**	

2m 1.53s (-3.97) **Going Correction** -0.05s/f (Good)
WFA 3 from 4yo+ 8lb **9** Ran SP% **118.7**
Speed ratings (Par 117): **113,112,110,109,106 104,98,90,69**
toteswinger: 1&2 £3.30, 1&3 £1.50, 2&3 £2.80. CSF £11.03 TOTE £1.60: £1.02, £2.20, £1.40; EX 7.50 Trifecta £31.40 Pool: £29,124.93, 684.77 winning units..
Owner Mrs John Magnier & M Tabor **Bred** Southern Bloodstock **Trained** Ballydoyle, Co Tipperary
■ This Group 1 was salvaged from the abandoned York Ebor meeting, but the race distance was slightly shorter.
■ Stewards' Enquiry : J Murtagh seven-day ban: breach of Rule 220 (iii) (Oct 8-14)
C O'Donoghue seven-day ban: breach of Rule 153 (iv) (Oct 8-14)
Ted Durcan two-day ban: careless riding (Sep 7-8)

FOCUS
Following a rollercoaster week of will they or won't they, the hugely-anticipated clash between the leaders of their respective generations Duke Of Marmalade and New Approach finally took place at Newmarket rather than York, and with the latter never really getting into it, 'The Duke' was able to register his fifth Group 1 victory of the season. The form looks up to scratch, with the winner confirming his position at the head of the turf rankings, although he was left with a straightforward task with New Approach refusing to settle and running only to the fast-ground level of the Irish Guineas.

NOTEBOOK
Duke Of Marmalade(IRE) is officially the highest-rated turf performer in the world and has not looked back this year, and following a career-best rout in in the Prince Of Wales's Stakes, he saw out the 1m4f trip of the King George in gritty fashion to make it four wins from four at the top level in 2008. In front travelling strongly three out after his stablemate had moved off the rail and allowed him through, it was always going to take an enormous effort to deny him and he was not for passing, staying on strongly as they climbed for the line, despite edging away from the rail. He has it all - speed, stamina, a determined attitude and a strong constitution - and he also seems to act on any ground, which leaves connections with any number of options for the remainder of the season. There was talk of dropping him back to 1m, as a Group 1 win at that distance would make him even more attractive as a stallion, but he excels at 1m2f to 1m4f and the Irish Champion Stakes, where he could meet New Approach again, looks the obvious target. It is hard to see him meeting with defeat there, and perhaps a bigger test will come if asked to compete in races such as the Arc and at the Breeders' Cup, whether it be the Turf or Classic. (op 8-11 tchd 4-5 in places)
Phoenix Tower(USA) has never run a bad race, winning his first four starts before finishing runner-up in a trio of top Group 1 contests, and he ran another blinder here. He got closer to the winner than he had done at Ascot, but unfortunately it was again not quite good enough. After having to force his way out past Red Rock Canyon to get a run he delivered a strong challenge, but he was always just coming off worse. This effort confirmed him to be one of the best around and his best chance of Group 1 success this season is likely to come in the Champion Stakes.
New Approach(IRE), whose Derby win has not really worked out, was unable to step up to the mark against his elders. Not expected to have any problems with the drop in trip, having been a dual Guineas runner-up behind Henrythenavigator earlier in the season, he came into this fresh, having been forced to miss the Irish Derby with muscle soreness, and he had the advantage of not having travelled over to York earlier in the week. However, whereas his stablemate Lush Lashes had shown her versatility by winning the rescheduled Yorkshire Oaks on Friday, things did not really go to plan for him, as he refused to settle and came pressure from three out. He had to mount his challenge in the centre of the track, away from the main action, and he could only stay on in rather laboured fashion to beat Pipedreamer for third. This faster ground did not look to suit and connections will be hoping conditions are more in his favour for round two with the winner in the Irish Champion Stakes, where his trainer is predicting we will see a different horse. (op 9-4)
Pipedreamer took his form to another level by finishing third behind Duke Of Marmalade at Royal Ascot and again filling that position in the Eclipse. Slightly more positive tactics saw him off the mark for the season in a Group 2 at York last time and the change of venue was certainly a plus for him, with the fast ground being more in his favour than it would have been back at York. He came to have every chance and again ran really well, but could not reverse form with either of his old rivals and was run out of third late on. He is to be given a break before returning to the Rowley course for the Champion Stakes.
Halicarnassus(IRE) was ridden with an eye to nicking a place if they fell apart up front, but that never happened and he did as well as could have been expected in fifth. (op 66-1 tchd 100-1)
Championship Point(IRE) ran a similar race to Halicarnassus, keeping on without any hope of challenging. (tchd 100-1)
Red Rock Canyon(IRE) once again performed his duties to satisfaction.
Rob Roy(USA) continues to fall short in top company. (op 28-1)
Cat Junior(USA), not beaten far behind Tamayuz in a French Group 1 last month, dropped right out and clearly failed to run his race.

5277 DBS ST LEGER YEARLING STKS 6f

4:10 (4:12) (Class 2) 2-Y-O

£21,665 (£8,668; £4,334; £2,164; £1,082; £1,082) **Stalls** Low

Form				RPR
35	**1**		**Dark Lane**[12] 4923 2-8-11 0........RyanMoore 15	71+
			(T D Barron) *chsd ldrs towards stands' side: hung lft over 1f out: led 1f out: hld on towards fin* **10/3**[1]	
43	**2**	nk	**Defector (IRE)**[40] 4027 2-8-11 0........SebSanders 9	70
			(W R Muir) *wnt lft s: hld up: hdwy over 2f out: swtchd rt over 1f out: kpt on wl: no ex towards fin* **4/1**[2]	
5	**3**	¾	**Veroon (IRE)**[17] 4740 2-8-11 0........TPQueally 4	68
			(J G Given) *chsd ldrs towards far side: swtchd rt and nt clr run over 1f out and ins fnl f: swtchd lft: r.o strly towards fin* **10/1**	
030	**4**	hd	**Mymateeric**[28] 4425 2-8-11 0........JimmyQuinn 17	67
			(J Pearce) *in rr: hdwy stands' side over 2f out: styd on wl fnl f* **40/1**	
00	**5**	2 ¼	**Pansy Potter**[7] 5097 2-8-6 0........NickyMackay 14	56
			(B J Meehan) *in rr: styd on fnl 2f: nvr trbld ldrs* **50/1**	
4240	**6**	shd	**Misty Glade**[18] 4706 2-8-6 0........(b) RobertHavlin 16	55
			(B J Meehan) *led tl 1f out: wknd ins fnl f* **33/1**	
00	**7**	1 ¾	**Fly Butterfly**[36] 4149 2-8-6 0........(b[1]) WilliamBuick 12	50
			(B J Meehan) *chsd ldrs: fdd appr fnl f* **25/1**	
20	**8**	1 ¾	**Whisky Jack**[35] 4176 2-8-11 0........DO'Donohoe 7	50
			(W R Muir) *chsd ldrs towards far side: kpt on same pce appr fnl f* **12/1**	
4	**9**	1 ½	**Dark Echoes**[15] 4815 2-8-11 0........TonyHamilton 3	45
			(Jedd O'Keeffe) *chsd ldrs far side: wknd over 1f out* **11/1**	
6210	**10**	½	**Sloop Johnb**[14] 4874 2-8-11 76........JamieMoriarty 5	44
			(R A Fahey) *prom: rdn and edgd rt over 2f out: grad wknd* **9/1**	
2103	**11**	nse	**Cutting Comments**[15] 4816 2-8-11 75........LiamJones 1	44
			(M Dods) *chsd ldrs far side: wknd over 1f out* **15/2**[3]	
5556	**12**	4 ½	**Sharav**[10] 4975 2-8-11 0........RichardMullen 13	30
			(Eve Johnson Houghton) *sn outpcd and in rr* **16/1**	

The Form Book, Raceform Ltd, Compton, RG20 6NL

505 **13** 1 1/4 **Fyelehk (IRE)**[49] 3735 2-8-11 0..(t) AlanMunro 11 26
(B R Millman) *in rr: hung lft over 2f out: nvr on terms* **33/1**

05 **14** 7 **Lyonesse**[16] 4769 2-8-6 0.. EddieAhern 8 —
(R Hannon) *crowded s: in rr: bhd fnl 2f* **16/1**

0365 **15** 2 3/4 **Scrapper Smith (IRE)**[35] 4185 2-8-11 68........................(v[1]) PatCosgrave 2 —
(E F Vaughan) *w ldrs far side: hung lft 2f out: sn wknd* **25/1**

0 **16** 2 **Going Going Gone**[12] 4926 2-8-11 0........................ RichardKingscote 10 —
(Tom Dascombe) *unruly in stalls: rrd s: a bhd* **25/1**

1m 12.75s (0.25) **Going Correction** -0.05s/f (Good) **16** Ran SP% **123.5**
Speed ratings (Par 100): **96,95,94,94,91 91,88,86,84,83 83,77,76,66,63 60**
toteswinger: 1&2 £3.80, 1&3 £9.90, 2&3 £9.40. CSF £14.82 TOTE £4.10: £1.70, £2.00, £3.20; EX 13.70.
Owner David W Armstrong **Bred** David Jamison Bloodstock **Trained** Maunby, N Yorks
■ Stewards' Enquiry : D O'Donohoe caution: careless riding

FOCUS
A poor renewal of this race, with the 16 runners mustering just two wins from 46 starts between them. The form is unbelievably weak for a race of such value.

NOTEBOOK
Dark Lane was a deserving winner, having travelled well in a prominent position. He was probably favoured by the draw, as most of the horses to contest the finish raced on the near side, but he showed a willing attitude once sent to the front and held on in determined fashion. Ryan Moore was an eyecatching booking for David Barron and his record for the stable is now seven wins from 23 rides. Dark Lane, who handled the ground better than expected, has suffered from sore shins, and there may be more to come from him. (op 4-1 tchd 3-1)
Defector(IRE) had also made a favourable impression in two previous outings and was challenging the winner all the way to the line. The half-brother to Stubbs Art should improve again and looks sure to benefit from a step up in trip. (op 5-1 tchd 11-2)
Veroon(IRE), drawn in stall four, was switched to the near side and was only just denied, despite losing momentum at a crucial stage. He confirmed the promise he showed in a Pontefract maiden this month and can improve. (op 11-1)
Mymateeric, who was tailed off in a course-and-distance maiden a month ago, posted an encouraging effort in fourth, albeit from a good draw. He looks ready for a step up in trip, as he was responding to pressure late on. (op 33-1)
Pansy Potter ran on into fifth, which was a vast improvement on her earlier efforts in maidens. (op 33-1)
Misty Glade broke well and was travelling with plenty of dash before wandering around under pressure. (tchd 40-1)
Fly Butterfly was wearing first-time blinkers, having beaten just one of 29 rivals in two 6f maidens at Newbury last month. This was a slight improvement but she was still well beaten in what was essentially a weak race. (op 22-1)
Sloop Johnb, top rated on official figures, ran disappointingly and he doesn't look to be progressing. He will continue to struggle in nurseries on this evidence. (op 7-1)
Going Going Gone played up in the stalls for the second successive time and he has questions to answer on temperament. (op 20-1 tchd 33-1 in places)

5278 UNIVERSITY OF CAMBRIDGE VETERINARY SCHOOL TRUST MAIDEN STKS (HOPE APPEAL FOR CANCER THERAPY UNIT) 1m
4:45 (4:46) (Class 4) 3-Y-0+ **£5,180** (£1,541; £770; £384) **Stalls** Low

Form RPR

2 **1** **Mawatheeq (USA)**[17] 4730 3-9-3 0.. PatDobbs 2 90+
(M P Tregoning) *a.p: rdn to ld 1f out: r.o wl* **6/4**[1]

0 **2** 2 3/4 **Blessing (USA)**[21] 4620 3-8-12 0.. JMurtagh 11 79
(J Noseda) *hld up in tch: rdn over 1f out: styd on* **9/2**[2]

5 **3** shd **I'm Sensational**[63] 3275 3-8-12 0.. TPQueally 12 79
(H R A Cecil) *chsd ldrs: led 2f out: rdn: edgd rt and hdd 1f out: styd on same pce* **8/1**

4 4 1/2 **Pension Policy (USA)** 3-8-12 0.. KShea 8 68+
(R Charlton) *hld up: hdwy and hung lft over 1f out: wknd ins fnl f* **33/1**

0- **5** 3 1/2 **Intabih (USA)**[353] 5140 3-9-3 0.. PaulDoe 5 65+
(C E Brittain) *hld up: outpcd over 2f out: kpt on fr over 1f out* **50/1**

5 **6** 1 1/4 **Mutawahej (USA)**[30] 4349 4-9-9 0.. RobertHavlin 16 62
(J H M Gosden) *s.i.s: hld up: hdwy and hung lft over 1f out: nt trble ldrs* **8/1**

3-2 **7** 1/2 **Rahere (IRE)**[23] 4566 3-9-3 0.. GregFairley 17 61+
(M Johnston) *plld hrd: led: rdn and hdd 2f out: wknd fnl f* **7/1**[3]

8 3 **Desert Kiss** 3-8-12 0.. AdamKirby 4 49
(W R Swinburn) *wnt lft s: hld up: hung lft 3f out: sn wknd: hung rt ins fnl f* **33/1**

60 **9** 3 3/4 **Eleonora (FR)**[19] 4695 3-8-12 0..(p) LiamJones 1 41
(W J Haggas) *prom: rdn over 3f out: wknd wl over 1f out* **33/1**

55 **10** 1 1/4 **Gaelic Dancer (IRE)**[8] 5076 3-9-3 0.. PatCosgrave 14 43
(J G Given) *chsd ldrs: rdn over 3f out: wknd 2f out* **25/1**

54 **11** 4 1/2 **Flight Of Fashion (IRE)**[9] 5031 3-8-12 0.. TQuinn 3 28+
(Dr J D Scargill) *hmpd s: hld up plld hrd: hmpd 3f out: sn wknd* **66/1**

12 1 3/4 **Spice Run** 5-9-9 0.. PhilipRobinson 9 29+
(C G Cox) *prom: shkn up over 2f out: wknd wl over 1f out: eased fnl f* **12/1**

50 **13** 1 3/4 **Amaakin (USA)**[14] 4871 3-9-3 0.. SebSanders 15 25+
(P W Chapple-Hyam) *chsd ldrs tl rdn and wknd over 2f out: eased ins fnl f* **20/1**

400- **14** 2 **Lord Of Esteem**[299] 6536 3-9-3 55.. VinceSlattery 10 20
(J Ryan) *a in rr: bhd fr 1/2-way* **100/1**

0 **15** 1/2 **Tomatina**[10] 4987 3-8-12 0.. StephenCarson 13 14
(C F Wall) *s.i.s: hld up: wknd over 2f out* **80/1**

1m 37.47s (-2.53) **Going Correction** -0.05s/f (Good)
WFA 3 from 4yo+ 6lb **15** Ran SP% **123.7**
Speed ratings (Par 105): **110,107,107,102,99 97,97,94,90,89 84,83,81,79,78**
toteswinger: 1&2 £3.20, 1&3 £4.90, 2&3 £9.80. CSF £7.22 TOTE £2.30: £1.50, £2.10, £2.30; EX 10.60.
Owner Hamdan Al Maktoum **Bred** Shadwell Farm LLC **Trained** Lambourn, Berks

FOCUS
An ordinary maiden by the course's standards, but Mawatheek's all-weather debut set a good standard and he won well in the end, showing slight improvement. Sound form overall.
Rahere(IRE) Official explanation: jockey said colt ran too free
Flight Of Fashion(IRE) Official explanation: jockey said filly suffered interference in running

5279 JIM BAMFORTH MEMORIAL H'CAP 1m 2f
5:15 (5:17) (Class 3) (0-95,95) 3-Y-0+ **£9,066** (£2,697; £1,348; £673) **Stalls** Centre

Form RPR

0-20 **1** **Unshakable (IRE)**[49] 3740 9-9-9 90.. PaulEddery 3 99
(Bob Jones) *hld up: hdwy over 1f out: rdn to ld ins fnl f: r.o* **20/1**

5512 **2** 1/2 **Presvis**[30] 4350 4-9-6 87.. GeorgeBaker 7 98+
(L M Cumani) *hld up: nt clr run over 2f out: swtchd lft and hdwy over 1f out: sn rdn: r.o* **3/1**[1]

-303 **3** 1 **Samsons Son**[14] 4867 4-9-4 85.. JimmyQuinn 4 91
(J R Best) *hld up: hdwy over 2f out: led over 1f out: hdd and unable qck ins fnl f* **22/1**

4035 **4** 1 3/4 **Rayhani (USA)**[27] 4443 5-9-10 91.. JMurtagh 14 94+
(M P Tregoning) *hld up: hdwy and nt clr run over 1f out: sn rdn: styd on* **12/1**

00-4 **5** 3/4 **Lundy's Lane (IRE)**[205] 381 8-10-0 95.. WilliamBuick 13 96+
(A M Balding) *hld up: swtchd lft over 3f out: nt clr run and swtchd rt over 1f out: r.o ins fnl f: nvr nr to chal* **12/1**

5645 **6** 1/2 **Prince Forever (IRE)**[14] 4867 4-10-0 95.. PhilipRobinson 5 95
(M A Jarvis) *hld up: swtchd lft over 2f out: hdwy over 1f out: edgd rt and no ex ins fnl f* **12/1**

4-13 **7** 4 1/2 **Last Three Minutes (IRE)**[14] 4876 3-8-11 86........................ SebSanders 18 77
(E A L Dunlop) *prom: rdn and ev ch over 1f out: wknd ins fnl f* **17/2**

4010 **8** 1/2 **Upton Grey (IRE)**[23] 4552 3-9-3 92.. RobertHavlin 20 82
(J H M Gosden) *chsd ldrs: led over 6f out: rdn and hdd over 1f out: wknd fnl f* **8/1**[3]

1130 **9** 2 1/2 **Hunting Country**[23] 4552 3-9-1 90.. GregFairley 10 75
(M Johnston) *prom: rdn over 2f out: n.m.r over 1f out: sn wknd* **11/1**

-400 **10** hd **Fool's Wildcat (USA)**[25] 4509 3-8-12 87.. EddieAhern 12 72
(B J Meehan) *s.i.s: hdwy over 8f out: wkng whn hmpd over 1f out* **33/1**

1001 **11** 1 3/4 **Tri Nations (UAE)**[23] 4565 3-8-10 85.. TQuinn 15 66
(J W Hills) *led: hdd over 6f out: rdn over 2f out: wknd fnl f* **12/1**

120 **12** 3 1/4 **Just Lille (IRE)**[35] 4191 5-9-8 89..(p) PaulMulrennan 11 64
(Mrs A Duffield) *chsd ldrs: rdn over 3f out: wknd over 1f out* **25/1**

423 **13** nk **Hustle (IRE)**[59] 3382 3-8-12 87.. PatDobbs 6 61
(R Hannon) *hld up: hdwy over 3f out: rdn and wknd over 1f out* **20/1**

120- **14** 7 **Gremlin**[408] 3460 4-9-3 84.. FergusSweeney 2 44
(A King) *hld up: hdwy over 3f out: wknd over 1f out* **18/1**

6404 **15** 2 1/4 **Paveroc**[15] 4830 3-8-13 88..(p) FrankieMcDonald 1 44
(Jane Chapple-Hyam) *hld up: hdwy over 3f out: sn rdn: wknd over 1f out* **50/1**

1-01 **16** 17 **Bee Sting**[21] 4642 4-9-7 88.. AdamKirby 16 10
(W R Swinburn) *mid-div: rdn over 4f out: wknd 2f out* **7/1**[2]

/05- **17** 4 **Monreale (GER)**[90] 4-9-12 93.. VinceSlattery 9 7
(G Brown) *hld up: plld hrd: bhd fnl 4f* **66/1**

3246 **18** 8 **Royal Fantasy (IRE)**[28] 4435 5-9-0 81.. TonyCulhane 17 —
(N Tinkler) *chsd ldrs: rdn and wknd over 2f out* **50/1**

2m 3.61s (-1.89) **Going Correction** -0.05s/f (Good)
WFA 3 from 4yo+ 8lb **18** Ran SP% **129.6**
Speed ratings (Par 107): **105,104,103,102,101 101,97,97,95,95 93,91,91,85,83 70,66,60**
toteswinger: 1&2 £20.70, 1&3 £40.00, 2&3 £18.10. CSF £77.48 CT £1423.81 TOTE £21.20: £4.00, £1.20, £5.70, £3.30; EX 126.40 Place 6 £ 449.72, Place 5 £ 270.94.
Owner Unshakable Partnership **Bred** Timothy Coughlan **Trained** Wickhambrook, Suffolk

FOCUS
A competitive handicap, but it got a bit messy and several shaped better than the bare form. The runner-up looked unlucky and has been rated a length winner, while the fourth and fifth were among others who did not enjoy the best of runs.

NOTEBOOK
Unshakable(IRE) was still 4lb higher than when last winning at Epsom last year but had gone close to winning that race again off a 1lb lower mark in June and had not run too badly in a good handicap at Sandown last time. Dropped in from his wide draw, settling a length or so behind the favourite, the gaps opened for him and he was able to get first run, leading just inside the final furlong and doing enough. He will struggle to defy much of a rise but has the Cambridgeshire as his target. (op 16-1)
Presvis ◆, unsurprisingly slammed by the Handicapper for bolting up by nine lengths on his handicap debut at Sandown, had little go right there seven days later when attempting to make light of a penalty and, though significantly higher here, looked of obvious interest in the hands of a senior jockey for the first time. Dropped out well in rear, Baker started to look for a run from over three out, and had one door slammed shut in his face passing the two. He eventually found daylight but while some may argue he had enough time to pick up the winner, there is no doubting he would have won had he been able to build some momentum sooner. He has been rated as having won and, though he will go up for this, he looks capable of better again. Official explanation: jockey said gelding was denied a clear run (op 4-1 tchd 11-4)
Samsons Son, a well-beaten third here last time, was off the same mark and ran well, hitting the front over a furlong out and sticking on willingly. This represented an improved performance. (tchd 25-1)
Rayhani(USA) is far from straightforward and ideally needs further than this. He ran on for fourth and is probably capable of winning off this mark, but would not be one to place maximum trust in. (tchd 14-1 in places)
Lundy's Lane(IRE) ◆ had not run since finishing fourth at Nad Al Sheba way back in January and he looked vulnerable under joint top-weight. He ran well though, staying on late after having to be switched several times, and he may well strip fitter next time. (op 14-1)
Prince Forever(IRE) is not straightforward and could find no extra, having come with his challenge out wide. Official explanation: jockey said colt hung right (tchd 14-1)
Last Three Minutes(IRE), dropped 1lb having only managed third on his handicap debut at Redcar, fared best of the 3yo's, but again gave the impression this sort of mark is beyond him at present. (op 11-1)
Upton Grey(IRE), 6lb higher than when winning over CD two starts back, was taken down the centre of the track in the straight and gave it his best shot, but could find no more from a furlong out. (op 10-1)
Tri Nations(UAE) Official explanation: jockey said gelding had no more to give
Royal Fantasy(IRE) Official explanation: jockey said mare became fired up at the start and in the early stages
T/Jkpt: Not won. T/Plt: £664.70 to a £1 stake. Pool: £104,394.00. 114.64 winning tickets. T/Qpdt: £112.40 to a £1 stake. Pool: £7,626.00. 50.20 winning tickets. CR

4896

REDCAR (L-H)
Saturday, August 23
5280 Meeting Abandoned - Waterlogged

5146 WINDSOR (R-H)

Saturday, August 23

OFFICIAL GOING: Good to firm (good in places)

Wind: virtually nil Weather: overcast

5286 EUROPEAN BREEDERS' FUND NOVICE MEDIAN AUCTION STKS 6f

5:20 (5:20) (Class 5) 2-Y-O **£3,885** (£1,156; £577; £288) **Stalls** High

Form RPR

4105 **1** **Imperial Guest**[15] 4828 2-9-6 85 .... JohnEgan 6 83
(G G Margarson) *hld up in tch: edgd out lft 3f out: rdn over 2f out: hdwy u.p over 1f out: led ins fnl f: jst hld on* **8/1**

2103 **2** *shd* **Brae Hill (IRE)**[44] 3879 2-9-4 94 .... JimmyFortune 5 81
(M L W Bell) *led: hrd pressed and rdn over 2f out: hdd ins fnl f: rallied gamely towards fin: jst hld* **1/1**[1]

5 **3** *1 3/4* **Piazza San Pietro**[52] 3603 2-8-7 0 .... WilliamCarson(5) 4 70
(C G Cox) *hld up in last pair: hdwy to chse ldr 3f out: ev ch and rdn over 2f out: one pce fnl f* **7/2**[2]

00 **4** *hd* **All Spin (IRE)**[43] 3895 2-8-12 0 .... DavidKinsella 2 69
(A P Jarvis) *t.k.h: sn chsd ldr tl 3f out: rdn and lost pl 2f out: kpt on fnl f* **40/1**

5 *1 3/4* **Moscow Eight (IRE)** 2-8-8 0 .... ChrisCatlin 3 60
(E J O'Neill) *t.k.h early: in tch: hdwy over 3f out: ev and rdn over 2f out: fdd ins fnl f* **9/2**[3]

6 *20* **Little Blacknumber** 2-8-3 0 .... FrancisNorton 7 —
(R Hannon) *s.i.s: bhd: lost tch 1/2-way* **10/1**

1m 11.69s (-1.31) **Going Correction** -0.35s/f (Firm) **6** Ran SP% **113.0**

Speed ratings (Par 94): **94,93,91,91,88 62**

toteswinger: 1&2 £1.80, 1&3 £6.00, 2&3 £1.50. CSF £16.89 TOTE £9.30: £3.90, £1.60; EX 14.70.

Owner John Guest **Bred** John Guest Racing Ltd **Trained** Newmarket, Suffolk

FOCUS

A decent little median auction race which produced a good finish between the two most experienced runners after five were virtually in line at the quarter-mile pole.

NOTEBOOK

Imperial Guest, who ran well under top weight in decent 7f nursery last time, was dropping in trip and a market drifter. He tracked the leader early before being pulled around his field to take the advantage entering the final furlong then just held the renewed challenge of the favourite. He was the stable's first winner since the spring and he will now be aimed at a Sandown nursery. (op 15-2 tchd 7-1)

Brae Hill(IRE), too keen when upped to this trip on easy ground last time, was happier on this surface. After dictating the early pace, he looked beaten when taken on soon after halfway but rallied well and would have been in front in another stride or two. He deserves compensation but is quite high in the handicap, so may be better sticking to conditions races for the time being. (op 6-5)

Piazza San Pietro was a well-backed second favourite to build on his promising debut effort and made a decisive move soon after halfway. However, he was unable to establish a decisive advantage and was run out of it by the more experienced pair inside the final furlong. He should be capable of winning races on this evidence. (op 4-1 tchd 9-2)

All Spin(IRE) had been well beaten on his two previous starts and pulled hard early, but he kept going quite well and now qualifies for a handicap mark. (op 50-1)

Moscow Eight(IRE), the first foal of a half-sister to Hurricane Alan and Aaim To Prosper, is from a yard that often has its juveniles ready first time. He travelled well and challenged the third over a quarter of a mile out, but he ran out of steam inside the last. He has ability and will have learnt a fair amount from this. (op 4-1)

Little Blacknumber, a 57,000gns daughter of an unraced half-sister to Baltic King, missed the break and was always struggling on this debut. (op 8-1)

5287 TOTEEXACTA (S) STKS 5f 10y

5:50 (5:56) (Class 6) 2-Y-O **£2,047** (£604; £302) **Stalls** High

Form RPR

0033 **1** **August Days (IRE)**[16] 4764 2-8-6 57 .... ChrisCatlin 1 57
(R M Beckett) *wnt lft s: sn w ldr: rdn jst over 2f out: led 1f out: styd on wl u.p* **9/1**

2351 **2** *1* **Like For Like (IRE)**[16] 4764 2-8-6 68 .... MCGeran(5) 4 58
(R J Hodges) *stdd s: hld up in tch: hdwy 2f out: swtchd lft over 1f out: chsd wnr u.p ins fnl f: a hld* **3/1**[1]

004 **3** *1/2* **Turn To Dreams**[18] 4705 2-8-6 59 .... JohnEgan 3 51
(P D Evans) *led: rdn 2f out: hung lft after: hdd 1f out: kpt on same pce fnl f* **9/2**

024 **4** *4 1/2* **Black Skirt**[26] 4482 2-8-7 55 ow1 .... RichardHughes 5 36
(R Hannon) *in tch rdn and effrt u.p 2f out: wknd fnl f* **7/2**[2]

5 *9* **Itshim** 2-8-6 0 .... WilliamCarson(5) 7 8
(S C Williams) *s.i.s: t.k.h: sn chsng ldrs: rdn 2f out: sn btn: eased ins fnl f* **3/1**[1]

3060 **6** *1 3/4* **Satwa Boy**[16] 4768 2-8-11 60 .... JimmyFortune 6 —
(E A L Dunlop) *in tch: rdn and wknd jst over 2f out: eased ins fnl f* **4/1**[3]

60.30 secs **Going Correction** -0.35s/f (Firm) **6** Ran SP% **120.4**

Speed ratings (Par 92): **86,84,83,76,62 59**

toteswinger: 1&2 £3.10, 1&3 £9.90, 2&3 £2.40. CSF £38.73 TOTE £12.60: £3.10, £2.10; EX 50.60.There was no bid for the winner.

Owner Pump & Plant Services Ltd **Bred** Pump And Plant Services Ltd **Trained** Whitsbury, Hants

FOCUS

The feature of this run-of-the-mill seller was the gamble on the Stuart Williams-trained debutant Itshim, who was backed from 14-1 into favourite. However, the gamble went astray. The winner and runner-up set just a modest level for the grade.

NOTEBOOK

August Days(IRE), who had been beaten by today's runner-up on easy ground at Bath, was 5lb better off and reversed the form on this better ground. (op 10-1 tchd 12-1)

Like For Like(IRE) had shown signs of temperament in the past and unseated her jockey on the way to the start, although she did not get loose. However, she did nothing wrong in the race on this first start for new connections and should remain competitive at this level. (tchd 5-2 and 10-3)

Turn To Dreams, who had been well beaten in two 6f maidens on fast ground here, had put up a better effort over 5f on soft ground last time. She ran pretty well from the front on this drop in grade. Official explanation: jockey said filly hung left and right-handed (op 3-1)

Black Skirt chased the leaders throughout but could never land an effective blow. (op 11-4)

Itshim, who was backed from 14-1 into favourite, missed the break then took a fierce hold before looking quite disorganised under pressure. He seems to have a bit of size about him and can do better in future, but the cat is out of the bag now. (op 14-1)

5288 TOTEPOOL AUGUST STKS (LISTED RACE) 1m 3f 135y

6:20 (6:23) (Class 1) 3-Y-O+

£22,708 (£8,608; £4,308; £2,148; £1,076; £540) **Stalls** High

Form RPR

1663 **1** **Spanish Moon (USA)**[14] 4855 4-9-7 108 .... RyanMoore 9 113
(Sir Michael Stoute) *chsd ldr: ev ch and rdn fr over 2f out: led ins fnl f: hld on gamely nr fin* **9/2**[1]

1102 **2** *nk* **Ronaldsay**[20] 4667 4-9-2 100 .... RichardHughes 3 108
(R Hannon) *stdd s: hld up in last trio: rdn over 3f out: swtchd rt over 1f out: str chal ins fnl f: unable qck nr fin* **12/1**

0000 **3** *1* **Hattan (IRE)**[14] 4855 6-9-9 112 .... (b[1]) DarryllHolland 1 113
(C E Brittain) *racd freely: led: hung lft fr 3f out: hdd over 2f out: led again u.p over 1f out: continued to hang lft and hdd ins fnl f: nt rcvr* **14/1**

200 **4** *1* **Supersonic Dave (USA)**[42] 3975 4-9-2 105 .... JimmyFortune 2 104
(B J Meehan) *hld up in midfield: rdn and unable qck jst over 2f out: edgd rt ent fnl f: r.o fnl 100yds: nt pce to rch ldrs* **14/1**

54-0 **5** *3/4* **Foxhaven**[22] 4585 6-9-2 105 .... FrancisNorton 7 103
(P R Chamings) *chsd ldrs: rdn and hdwy to join ldr over 3f out: led narrowly over 2f out tl over 1f out: fdd fnl 100yds* **10/1**[3]

3-06 **6** *nk* **Dansili Dancer**[27] 4444 6-9-2 101 .... IanMongan 10 102
(C G Cox) *hld up in tch: hdwy over 3f out: ev ch and rdn wl over 2f out tl jst ins fnl f: fdd fnl 100yds* **8/1**[2]

5410 **7** *2 1/4* **Humungous (IRE)**[25] 4504 5-9-2 101 .... (b) ChrisCatlin 8 99
(C R Egerton) *stdd s: t.k.h: hld up in rr: effrt over 2f out: no real hdwy: wl hld whn swtchd lft ins fnl f* **10/1**[3]

-164 **8** *3 1/4* **Book Of Music (IRE)**[177] 740 5-9-2 108 .... (v) LDettori 5 93
(Saeed Bin Suroor) *stdd s: hld up in rr: hdwy over 3f out: drvn and effrt over 2f out: btn 1f out: eased ins fnl f* **8/1**[2]

2m 24.83s (-4.67) **Going Correction** -0.35s/f (Firm) **8** Ran SP% **79.6**

Speed ratings (Par 111): **101,100,100,99,98 98,97,95**

toteswinger: 1&2 £5.70, 1&3 £3.70, 2&3 £20.10. CSF £26.71 TOTE £3.00: £1.80, £1.40, £3.20; EX 18.60.

Owner K Abdulla **Bred** Juddmonte Farms Inc **Trained** Newmarket, Suffolk

■ Tranquil Tiger (7/4F) was withdrawn after proving unruly in the stalls. Rule 4 applies, deduction 35p in the £.

FOCUS

This established Listed contest was devalued a touch by the withdrawal of the favourite Tranquil Tiger, who reared up and burst the stalls just as they were about to open. The winner has been rated to the level of the bare form of his Ascot win, while the runner-up continues to improve steadily and was up another 4lb here.

NOTEBOOK

Spanish Moon(USA), wearing the second colours of Khalid Abdullah, whose first silks were on the withdrawn favourite, but the task did not prove that easy and Moore had to be at his strongest to get the better of Ronaldsay and Hattan in a desperate finish. He should have appreciated the slight drop in grade having contested a Group 3 on his previous start, but his jockey was having to get after him almost half a mile from home and he only just wore down the filly near the finish. (op 4-1)

Ronaldsay, whose wins have been at 1m2f, is suited by a flat track and proved she stays this trip, although she would probably have preferred easier ground. She should find easier opportunities against her own sex before the end of the season. (op 11-1)

Hattan(IRE) was wearing blinkers for the first time and they caused him to race keenly in front, but he responded well when challenged, only to drift left in the closing stages. (op 20-1)

Supersonic Dave(USA), who was dropping in trip having struggled over 1m6f, tracked the leaders early but then appeared to hit a flat spot before finishing well to snatch fourth. He may benefit from a slightly longer trip or a stiffer track over this distance. (op 12-1)

Foxhaven had the trip and ground to suit but seems to save his best form for Chester. (op 9-1)

Dansili Dancer, better known as handicapper and held in two previous tries at this level, made his bid for home soon after crossing the intersection but his effort flattened out in the last furlong. (op 9-1)

5289 TOTESWINGER WINTER HILL STKS (GROUP 3) 1m 2f 7y

6:50 (6:52) (Class 1) 3-Y-O+

£39,739 (£15,064; £7,539; £3,759; £1,883; £945) **Stalls** High

Form RPR

5660 **1** **Stotsfold**[22] 4585 5-9-4 114 .... AdamKirby 11 119
(W R Swinburn) *stdd s: t.k.h: hld up in rr: hdwy on outer 3f out: rdn 2f out: r.o to ld wl ins fnl f* **5/1**

0320 **2** *hd* **Traffic Guard (USA)**[97] 2234 4-9-0 110 .... JohnEgan 5 115
(Jane Chapple-Hyam) *hld up in tch: hdwy 4f out: ev ch and rdn over 2f out: unable qck fnl 100yds: wnt 2nd fnl strides* **14/1**

1210 **3** *nk* **Unnefer (FR)**[65] 3156 3-8-6 111 .... TedDurcan 8 114
(H R A Cecil) *chsd ldr: ev ch and rdn jst over 2f out: led jst over 1f out: hdd and no ex wl ins fnl f: lost 2nd last strides* **9/2**[3]

0021 **4** *1 1/2* **Gulf Express (USA)**[25] 4504 4-9-0 105 .... (v) RyanMoore 7 111
(Sir Michael Stoute) *dwlt: t.k.h: hld up in tch: hdwy 4f out: chsd ldrs and drvn over 1f out: one pce fnl f* **7/2**[2]

1-12 **5** *1/2* **Silver Pivotal (IRE)**[161] 906 4-8-11 105 .... LDettori 10 108+
(G A Butler) *hld up in midfield: hdwy over 3f out: chsd ldrs and rdn 2f out: keeping on same pce whn nt clr run ins fnl f: unable to chal* **11/4**[1]

3321 **6** *1/2* **Drumfire (IRE)**[8] 5070 4-9-0 104 .... DarryllHolland 9 109
(M Johnston) *dwlt: chsd ldrs: rdn and outpcd wl over 2f out: swtchd lft and rallied 1f out: kpt on but nvr pce to rch ldrs* **8/1**

3103 **7** *5* **Supaseus**[28] 4436 5-9-0 111 .... SteveDrowne 1 99
(H Morrison) *led: rdn over 2f out: hdd jst over 1f out: eased whn btn wl ins fnl f* **7/1**

3000 **8** *2 1/4* **Diamond Quest (SAF)**[22] 4585 7-9-0 107 .... LPKeniry 3 95
(A M Balding) *stdd s: t.k.h: hld up in rr: rdn and effrt over 2f out: no hdwy: btn and eased ins fnl f* **33/1**

2m 5.06s (-3.64) **Going Correction** -0.35s/f (Firm)

WFA 3 from 4yo+ 8lb **8** Ran SP% **117.0**

Speed ratings (Par 113): **100,99,99,98,98 97,93,91**

toteswinger: 1&2 £5.80, 1&3 £13.20, 2&3 £18.90. CSF £71.72 TOTE £6.60: £2.50, £3.30, £1.60; EX 68.10.

Owner Exors Of The Late Mrs P W Harris **Bred** Pendley Farm **Trained** Aldbury, Herts

FOCUS

A fair Group 3 which has been dominated by Sir Michael Stoute and Saeed bin Suroor in recent years, although only the former was represented by Gulf Express. The pace was a bit messy, but the form looks pretty sound.

NOTEBOOK

Stotsfold had the highest official rating coming into this race, the trip and the ground suited and he appreciated the slightly easier company having been taking on Group 1 horses of late. The key with him is getting him to settle, and this was a good effort under the penalty. Connections are now thinking in terms of the Dubai Carnival early next year for him. (op 11-2 tchd 9-2)

Traffic Guard(USA) ◆ had not won beyond 1m and had not run since competing at Kranji in May. However, he ran a fine race on this return to action and should not be long in winning at this sort of level. (op 16-1)

Unnefer(FR), another returning from a break, is a pretty reliable sort, ran his race and should be able to pay his way for the rest of the season. (op 11-2)

Gulf Express(USA) has been progressive in handicaps and came to have his chance at around the two-furlong pole, but he was unable to sustain his effort against this better opposition. (op 9-4 tchd 4-1 in places)

Silver Pivotal(IRE), a progressive filly on Polytrack last winter, was another returning from a break, in her case since March. She ran reasonably well but should come on for the outing and looks the sort who will be contesting the Churchill Stakes at Lingfield later in the year. (tchd 3-1 and 7-2 in a place)

Drumfire(IRE), whose form is at a lower level or shorter trips, could only keep on at one pace in the closing stages. (op 9-1 tchd 10-1)

Supaseus set a steady pace and did not quicken things up until about a half a mile from home, but he was in trouble at the quarter-mile pole. (op 10-1)

Diamond Quest(SAF) has yet to find his form since coming to this country and the drop in trip here did not help. (op 66-1 tchd 100-1 in places)

5290 TOTETRIFECTA H'CAP — 1m 67y

7:20 (7:21) (Class 4) (0-85,85) 3-Y-O+ — **£5,180** (£1,541; £770; £384) **Stalls** High

Form — RPR

311 **1** **Grande Annee (USA)**[28] 4423 3-9-6 **84**.............................. ShaneKelly 2 — 94+
(J Noseda) *stdd s: hld up in last trio: rdn and effrt over 3f out: hdwy 2f out: swtchd rt over 1f out: r.o wl to ld nr fin* — **10/11**[1]

1402 **2** *hd* **Nightjar (USA)**[9] 5033 3-9-2 **80**.................................... DarryllHolland 14 — 87
(M Johnston) *chsd ldng trio: rdn and clsd over 3f out: led over 1f out: battled on wl tl hdd last strides* — **5/1**[2]

2500 **3** *1* **Woodcote Place**[17] 4723 5-9-5 **77**............................... AlanMunro 8 — 83
(P R Chamings) *stdd s: t.k.h: hld up in rr: hdwy 3f out: ev ch and hrd rdn 1f out: wknd towards fin* — **9/1**

-000 **4** *2* **Hawaana (IRE)**[70] 3031 3-8-13 **77**............................ StephenCarson 10 — 77
(Eve Johnson Houghton) *hld up off the pce in midfield: hdwy over 3f out: chsd ldrs over 1f out: kpt on same pce u.p fnl f* — **16/1**

2140 **5** *½* **Irony (IRE)**[8] 5051 9-9-4 **81**.................................. DavidProbert(5) 4 — 81
(A M Balding) *chsd ldr tl led and c to centre 3f out: sn rdn: hdd over 1f out: wknd last 100yds* — **8/1**[3]

0600 **6** *1 ¾* **Trafalgar Square**[12] 4927 6-9-3 **75**..........................(p) KirstyMilczarek 1 — 71
(M J Attwater) *t.k.h: chsd ldrs: ev ch and c centre 3f out: sn rdn: wknd ins fnl f* — **20/1**

3060 **7** *¾* **Lord Theo**[17] 4723 4-9-3 **75**... SteveDrowne 11 — 70
(N P Littmoden) *stdd s: hld up off the pce in midfield: rdn and effrt over 2f out: chsd ldrs over 1f out: wknd ent fnl f* — **20/1**

00-0 **8** *8* **Hopeful Purchase (IRE)**[110] 1857 5-9-10 **82**....................(b) JohnEgan 9 — 58
(J R Gask) *led at gd gallop: hdd 3f out: wknd u.p wl over 1f out* — **33/1**

0403 **9** *3 ½* **Man Of Gwent (UAE)**[32] 4276 4-8-12 **75**.................. RichardEvans(5) 6 — 43
(P D Evans) *a bhd: lost tch 1/2-way* — **12/1**

0-05 **P** **Marajaa (IRE)**[22] 4602 6-9-8 **80**.............................. StephenDonohoe 7 — —
(W J Musson) *hld up in rr: lost tch over 3f out: p.u and dismntd ins fnl f* — **14/1**

1m 40.88s (-3.82) **Going Correction** -0.35s/f (Firm)
WFA 3 from 4yo+ 6lb — **10** Ran SP% **122.9**
Speed ratings (Par 105): **105,104,103,101,101 99,98,90,87,—**
toteswinger: 1&2 £1.30, 1&3 £8.10, 2&3 £2.50. CSF £5.82 CT £29.38 TOTE £1.90: £1.10, £1.50, £2.50; EX 6.00 Trifecta £80.40 Pool: £500.10, 4.60 winning units..
Owner Tom Ludt **Bred** Grapestock Llc **Trained** Newmarket, Suffolk

FOCUS
A decent handicap although slightly devalued by four non-runners. The front pair were less exposed than most, and the form looks sound.
Hopeful Purchase(IRE) Official explanation: jockey said gelding had no more to give
Marajaa(IRE) Official explanation: jockey said gelding lost its action

5291 READING EVENING POST FILLIES' H'CAP — 1m 67y

7:50 (7:50) (Class 5) (0-75,75) 3-Y-O+ — **£3,070** (£906; £453) **Stalls** High

Form — RPR

0132 **1** **Rescue Me**[13] 4910 3-9-1 **69**.. RichardHughes 7 — 78+
(R Hannon) *hld up in midfield: rdn and gd hdwy 2f out: chsd ldng pair ent fnl f: led fnl 100yds: sn clr: readily* — **3/1**[1]

004 **2** *1 ¾* **Angels Quest**[26] 4484 3-8-4 **58**.................................... FrancisNorton 11 — 63
(A W Carroll) *chsd ldrs: rdn over 2f out: ev ch u.p ent fnl f: kpt on to go 2nd wl ins fnl f but nt pce of wnr* — **16/1**

5210 **3** *½* **Run For Ede'S**[19] 4694 4-9-0 **67**................................ JackDean(5) 5 — 72
(P M Phelan) *stdd s: hld up in rr: rdn and effrt 2f out: hdwy u.p over 1f out: kpt on to go 3rd wl ins fnl f: nt trble wnr* — **12/1**

0022 **4** *¾* **Bikini**[22] 4583 3-9-4 **72**.. DaneO'Neill 10 — 74
(H Candy) *chsd ldr: rdn over 2f out: ev ch u.p ent fnl f: wknd last 100yds* — **10/3**[2]

0030 **5** *nk* **Ci Vediamo (IRE)**[18] 4708 3-8-10 **64**....................... RichardKingscote 12 — 65
(R M Beckett) *led: rdn ent fnl 2f: hrd pressed ent fnl f: hdd fnl 100yds: wknd* — **25/1**

0000 **6** *1 ½* **Dalkey Girl (IRE)**[63] 3272 3-9-6 **74**.............................. JohnEgan 3 — 72
(M Botti) *hld up bhd: rdn over 3f out: hdwy on outer over 2f out chsd ldrs 2f out: wknd fnl f* — **14/1**

4200 **7** *hd* **Onenightinlisbon (IRE)**[16] 4789 4-9-1 **70**.................. HarryPoulton(7) 1 — 69
(J R Boyle) *hld up wl bhd in last pl: hdwy and rdn over 1f out: styd on fnl f: nvr nr ldrs* — **14/1**

-505 **8** *1* **Ever Dreaming (USA)**[30] 4326 3-7-13 **58**.................. DavidProbert(5) 4 — 53
(A M Balding) *hld up in midfield: rdn and hdwy on outer over 2f out: chsd ldrs 2f out: wknd ent fnl f* — **7/1**

6002 **9** *½* **Brave Mave**[16] 4795 3-8-13 **67**..(b) AlanMunro 2 — 61
(W Jarvis) *s.i.s: t.k.h: chsd ldrs after 2f: rdn over 3f out: wknd wl over 1f out* — **10/1**

-050 **10** *½* **Princess India (IRE)**[12] 4930 3-8-12 **66**...................... StephenCarson 6 — 59
(P Winkworth) *taken down early: rdn and hdwy over 3f out: chsd ldrs on outer 2f out: wknd over 1f out* — **25/1**

1-4 **11** *9* **Delta Diva (USA)**[31] 4300 3-9-6 **74**............................ JimmyFortune 8 — 46
(P F I Cole) *t.k.h: chsd ldrs tl over 3f out: sn struggling: wl bhd and eased ins fnl f* — **4/1**[3]

000 **12** *16* **Baby Princess (BRZ)**[65] 3163 4-9-13 **75**........................ TedDurcan 9 — 11
(J W Hills) *hld up in midfield: rdn and struggling 3f out: wl bhd fnl 2f: t.o and eased ins fnl f* — **33/1**

1m 41.42s (-3.28) **Going Correction** -0.35s/f (Firm)
WFA 3 from 4yo 6lb — **12** Ran SP% **127.2**
Speed ratings (Par 100): **102,100,99,99,98 97,97,96,95,95 86,70**
toteswinger: 1&2 £18.70, 1&3 £2.50, 2&3 £29.60. CSF £56.35 CT £544.61 TOTE £3.60: £1.90, £5.30, £4.80; EX 104.90 Place 6: £73.86, Place 5: £46.28..
Owner P D Merritt **Bred** Raimon Bloodstock **Trained** East Everleigh, Wilts

FOCUS
A modest fillies' handicap but solid form.
Dalkey Girl(IRE) Official explanation: jockey said filly had no more to give
Delta Diva(USA) Official explanation: jockey said filly stopped very quickly
T/Plt: £95.90 to a £1 stake. Pool: £64,109.81. 487.51 winning tickets. T/Qpdt: £20.50 to a £1 stake. Pool: £7,413.80. 267.30 winning tickets. SP

4463 CURRAGH (R-H)

Saturday, August 23

OFFICIAL GOING: Heavy

5294a TATTERSALLS IRELAND SALE STKS — 6f

3:05 (3:08) 2-Y-O

£108,088 (£41,911; £25,367; £14,338; £4,411; £2,205)

RPR

1 **Choose Me (IRE)**[65] 3184 2-8-11 88.............................. CDHayes 14 — 92+
(Kevin Prendergast, Ire) *mid-div: 7th and hdwy fr 2f out: chal u.p and led ins fnl f: styd on wl* — **7/1**

2 *2* **Heart Of Fire (IRE)**[41] 4005 2-9-2 96........................... DPMcDonogh 10 — 91
(Kevin Prendergast, Ire) *trckd ldrs: in front over 2f out: hdd over 1f out: no imp and kpt on ins fnl f* — **11/2**[3]

3 *¾* **What's Up Pussycat (IRE)**[19] 4883 2-8-11 85................ WMLordan 15 — 84
(David Wachman, Ire) *trckd ldrs: clsr in 4th over 2f out: rdn to chal and ld over 1f out: hdd and kpt on same pce ins fnl f* — **9/2**[1]

4 *1 ¼* **Slant (IRE)**[24] 4521 2-8-11 .... MJKinane 3 — 80+
(Eve Johnson Houghton) *towards rr: swtchd towards outside fr 2f out: rdn to go 4th and kpt on wout threatening ins fnl f* — **10/1**

5 *3 ½* **Jhinga Palak (IRE)**[83] 2638 2-8-11 .... PBBeggy 4 — 70
(P D Evans) *chsd ldrs: 8th fr 2f out: sn no imp u.p: kpt on wout threatening ins fnl f* — **33/1**

6 *shd* **Calypso Girl (IRE)**[86] 2541 2-8-11 .... PShanahan 12 — 69
(P D Evans) *trckd ldrs: 6th fr 2f out: sn no imp u.p and kpt on same pce* — **11/1**

7 *shd* **Duaisbhanna (IRE)**[104] 2020 2-8-11 .... DJMoran 13 — 69
(J S Bolger, Ire) *cl up: sn led: 2nd over 2f out: sn rdn and rdr dropped whip: no imp and kpt on same pce fr over 1f out* — **5/1**[2]

8 *1 ½* **Fong's Alibi**[22] 4589 2-8-11 .... WJSupple 2 — 65
(J S Moore) *mid-div: kpt on wout threatening fr under 2f out* — **20/1**

9 *1 ¾* **Buckers Beauty (IRE)**[3] 5184 2-8-11 .... WJLee 8 — 59
(P D Evans) *towards rr: kpt on wout threatening fr under 2f out* — **50/1**

10 *hd* **Flawless Diamond (IRE)**[15] 4823 2-8-11 ....(b) RPCleary 5 — 59
(J S Moore) *prom early: kpt on same pce fr under 2f out* — **25/1**

11 *1 ½* **Jeremiah (IRE)**[32] 4274 2-9-2 .... JamesDoyle 1 — 59
(J G Portman) *prom: 5th fr 2f out: sn no imp u.p* — **16/1**

12 *nk* **Cerito**[19] 4685 2-9-2 .... PJSmullen 16 — 58
(M R Channon) *cl up: 3rd fr 2f out: sn no ex u.p* — **10/1**

13 *7* **Lucky Larkin (IRE)** 2-9-2 .... DMGrant 17 — 37
(J T Gorman, Ire) *towards rr: no imp fr 2f out* — **33/1**

14 *shd* **Nicokellhann (USA)** 2-8-11 .... MCHussey 11 — 32
(J T Gorman, Ire) *nvr bttr than mid-div* — **33/1**

15 *½* **July Days (IRE)**[8] 5079 2-8-11 ....(t) FMBerry 9 — 31
(David Marnane, Ire) *cl up: lost pl and no ex fr under 2f out* — **14/1**

16 *7* **Roshina (IRE)**[41] 4008 2-8-11 72....................................(tp) MHarley 7 — 10
(J S Bolger, Ire) *nvr bttr than mid-div* — **16/1**

17 *2 ½* **Unconsoled**[63] 3284 2-8-11 71..................................(t) NGMcCullagh 19 — —
(K J Condon, Ire) *a towards rr* — **33/1**

18 *nk* **Warrior Nation (FR)**[17] 4753 2-9-2 74..............................(b[1]) KLatham 6 — 6
(G M Lyons, Ire) *mid-div: no ex fr 2f out: eased ins fnl f* — **25/1**

19 *13* **Come On Buckers (IRE)**[51] 3652 2-9-2 ....(b[1]) JAHeffernan 18 — —
(E J Creighton) *nvr bttr than mid-div: dropped bhd and eased fnl f* — **20/1**

1m 20.28s (5.78) **Going Correction** +1.075s/f (Soft) — **19** Ran SP% **138.6**
Speed ratings: **104,101,100,98,94 93,93,91,89,89 87,86,77,77,76 67,63,63,46**
CSF £45.18 TOTE £7.50: £2.10, £1.60, £1.50, £3.20; DF 57.30.
Owner Mrs W Whitehead **Bred** Owenstown Stud **Trained** Friarstown, Co Kildare

NOTEBOOK

Choose Me(IRE) came out best to lead home a stable one-two. In truth, it simply seemed to be a case of the daughter of Choisir handling the conditions that bit better and she was the proven stayer of the two. She closed up behind the leaders two furlongs out and made her challenge between horses inside the last before drawing clear inside the last half-furlong. She had not been seen out since June but looks to be improving and there is every chance she could land a stakes race in similar conditions.

Heart Of Fire(IRE) broke well and was up there throughout, travelling like a winner two furlongs out when going to the front. It looked as though he got there a bit soon and in the conditions he could not last it out. (op 5/1)

What's Up Pussycat(IRE) raced just behind the leaders towards the centre of the track, closing up inside the final two furlongs and had every chance inside the last. Despite her pedigree suggesting she should not have had much of an issue with this ground, she just did not seem to get home on it and was readily overhauled by the winner inside the final half-furlong. (op 7/1)

Slant(IRE) moved towards the centre of the track to try and make her challenge inside the final fulrong but could not get there and was not really good enough to do so. She was not beaten that far and will probably appreciate further.

Jhinga Palak(IRE) raced quite handily most of the way and basically just ran on at one pace inside the last furlong.

Calypso Girl(IRE) also just kept on at one pace from a handy position. (op 10/1)

Duaisbhanna(IRE) raced prominently and probably a bit too keenly until she was headed over two furlongs out. (op 4/1 tchd 6/1)

5296a GALILEO EUROPEAN BREEDERS FUND FUTURITY STKS (GROUP 2) 7f

4:15 (4:19) 2-Y-O **£55,147** (£17,463; £8,272; £2,757; £1,838; £919)

RPR

1 **Arazan (IRE)**^{87} 2515 2-9-1 .... MJKinane 1 115+
(John M Oxx, Ire) *sn trckd ldrs: 3rd 1/2-way: chal and led 1 1/2f out: rdn clr and r.o wl fr over 1f out: comf* **4/1**^{2}

2 4 **Ryehill Dreamer (IRE)**^{24} 4517 2-9-1 105.......... WMLordan 4 104
(T Stack, Ire) *chsd ldrs: 5th 1/2-way: rdn to go mod 2nd and kpt on same pce fr over 1f out* **10/1**

3 3 **Grand Ducal (IRE)**^{43} 3920 2-9-1 102.......... WJSupple 2 97
(A P O'Brien, Ire) *prom: 2nd 1/2-way: 4th and no imp u.p fr over 1f out: kpt on same pce* **20/1**

4 ½ **Driving Snow**^{16} 4804 2-9-1 97.......... CDHayes 7 96
(Kevin Prendergast, Ire) *mid-div: 7th 1/2-way: rdn to go mod 5th and kpt on same pce fr over 1f out* **16/1**

5 nk **Drumbeat (IRE)**^{10} 4993 2-9-1 95.......... DavidMcCabe 6 95
(A P O'Brien, Ire) *towards rr: hdwy into mod 6th over 1f out: kpt on u.p wout threatening* **9/1**^{3}

6 ¾ **Gluteus Maximus (IRE)**^{21} 4654 2-9-1 91.......... PJSmullen 9 93
(A P O'Brien, Ire) *chsd ldrs: 6th 1/2-way: rdn to go mod 3rd and no ex fr over 1f out* **25/1**

7 8 **Westphalia (IRE)**^{16} 4804 2-9-1 110.......... JAHeffernan 11 74
(A P O'Brien, Ire) *towards rr: no imp u.p fr over 1f out* **4/5**^{1}

8 2 **Sawtooth Mountain (USA)**^{16} 4804 2-9-1 101.......... SMLevey 3 69
(A P O'Brien, Ire) *sn led: hdd 1 1/2f out: no ex* **20/1**

9 1 **Prayer Boat (IRE)**^{26} 4492 2-9-1 .... DMGrant 8 67
(John Joseph Murphy, Ire) *trckd ldr in 2nd: 4th 1/2-way: no ex fr over 1f out* **66/1**

10 13 **Vilasol (IRE)**^{19} 4883 2-9-1 102..........(b^{1}) DPMcDonogh 10 36
(Kevin Prendergast, Ire) *s.i.s and reminders early: a towards rr: no ex fr 1 1/2f out* **20/1**

1m 33.61s (6.51) **Going Correction** +1.075s/f (Soft) **10** Ran SP% **120.2**
Speed ratings: **105,100,97,96,96 95,86,83,82,67**
CSF £40.23 TOTE £3.70: £1.60, £2.30, £6.90; DF 27.90.
Owner H H Aga Khan **Bred** Hh The Aga Khan's Studs Sc **Trained** Currabeg, Co Kildare

FOCUS
The winner leaps into second place in the two-year-old rankings and is clearly an exciting type. He was very impressive and the form looks solid rated through the placed horses.

NOTEBOOK
Arazan(IRE), a half-brother to Azamour, easily dismissed his rivals here. Racing handily and always travelling well, when sent on by Mick Kinane over two furlongs out the response was immediate as he quickened clear for an impressive success. The way he handled this ground was equally impressive, especially as his pedigree suggests that quick ground will be his forte, and he certainly looks ready to take the step up into Group 1 company. He adds to the wealth of juvenile talent prevalent on this side of the Irish Sea. (op 7/2)
Ryehill Dreamer(IRE) ran well below his best at Goodwood last time but returned to his best here. He had previously shown his ability to handle this ground, and the evidence of this would suggest he should handle a mile without a problem. Attempting to make his challenge towards the stands'-side rail, he kept on well but had no chance with the winner and this is about as good as he probably is.
Grand Ducal(IRE) was an improving two-year-old in the early part of the summer on fast ground. It is hard to come to the conclusion that he did not handle the ground, but having been up there most of the way what is pretty certain is that he failed to quicken in this testing ground as the winner left him standing. He is another that is likely to appreciate a mile on better ground.
Driving Snow moved through to try and go in pursuit of the winner over two furlongs out. It was briefly a threatening-looking run but he was not quite able to sustain it inside the final furlong. This very testing ground over this trip just appeared to stretch his stamina ever so slightly.
Drumbeat(IRE) has not looked the most straightforward of characters. On the book this represented his best run to date, but he did not run like a straightforward one today either. Held up off the pace, he looked to be going absolutely nowhere and was a candidate to finish last a furlong and a half out, but somehow he grabbed hold of the bit inside the final furlong and flew home on the testing ground to be nearest at the finish. He is a horse with tons of ability but is not exactly free of quirks. (op 8/1)
Gluteus Maximus(IRE) did not run badly at all. Having been prominent for most of the journey, he weakened inside the final furlong or so and basically ran as well as he was entitled to.
Westphalia(IRE) was bitterly disappointing, especially as he had shown an ability to handle ground of this nature in the past. Held up towards the rear, he found nothing when asked a question inside the final two furlongs. He is capable of much better than this and the ground was unlikely to have been a factor in this display. Official explanation: jockey said colt never travelled on today's ground (op 1/1 tchd 11/10)

5295 - 5299a (Foreign Racing) - See Raceform Interactive

5138 DEAUVILLE (R-H)

Saturday, August 23

OFFICIAL GOING: Turf course - good; all-weather - standard

5300a CRITERIUM DU FONDS EUROPEEN DE L'ELEVAGE (LISTED RACE) (ROUND COURSE) 1m (R)

2:15 (2:16) 2-Y-O **£44,853** (£17,941; £13,456; £8,971; £4,485)

RPR

1 **Sokar (FR)**^{24} 4548 2-8-11 .... MAndrouin 10 100
(J Boisnard, France)

2 snk **Canwinn (IRE)**^{11} 4954 2-8-11 .... GMosse 4 100
(M R Channon) *trckd ldr on ins in 3rd: 4th and pushed along ent st: swtchd lft jst ins fnl f: drvn to take 2nd fnl 70yds* **5/1**^{2}

3 1½ **Faylan (FR)**^{18} 2-8-11 .... OPeslier 3 96
(C Baillet, France)

4 1 **Full Snow Moon (USA)**^{24} 4548 2-8-8 .... C-PLemaire 6 91
(J-C Rouget, France)

5 5 **Jet D'Eau (FR)**^{40} 4039 2-8-8 ....(b) THuet 5 80
(R Pritchard-Gordon, France) **10/1**^{3}

6 1 **Belle Jeanne (FR)**^{20} 2-8-8 .... CSoumillon 7 78
(C Ferland, France) **4/1**^{1}

7 1½ **Voie De Printemps (FR)**^{24} 4548 2-8-8 .... DBoeuf 8 75
(D Smaga, France)

8 2½ **Drawn At Dawn (IRE)**^{26} 2-8-8 .... DBonilla 2 69
(C Boutin, France)

9 3 **Yes Mate (FR)**^{24} 4548 2-8-8 .... MaximeFoulon 9 63
(R Gibson, France)

1m 43.6s (2.60) **Going Correction** +0.15s/f (Good) **9** Ran SP% **45.8**
Speed ratings: **93,92,91,90,85 84,82,80,77**
PARI-MUTUEL: WIN 11.40; PL 3.10, 2.40, 2.20; DF 32.10.
Owner J Uzel **Bred** Mme D De La Heronniere **Trained** France

■ Stewards' Enquiry : C Soumillon €300 fine: failed to ride out for best possible placing; €150 fine: heavier than registered weight
M Androuin €100 fine: whip abuse

NOTEBOOK
Canwinn(IRE), finally off the mark at Nottingham last time, coped well with the rise in grade and responded well to pressure to just miss out, never quite getting to the winner.

5301a PRIX DU CALVADOS - HARAS DES CAPUCINES (GROUP 3) (FILLIES) (STRAIGHT COURSE) 7f

2:45 (2:45) 2-Y-O **£29,412** (£11,765; £8,824; £5,882)

RPR

1 **Elusive Wave (IRE)**^{40} 4039 2-8-9 .... C-PLemaire 1 103
(J-C Rouget, France) *racd in 2nd: pushed along to ld 1 1/2f out: rdn out clsng stages: comf* **17/10**^{2}

2 ½ **Ana Americana (FR)**^{18} 2-8-9 .... SPasquier 2 102
(P Demercastel, France) *led: rdn 1 1/2f out: hdd 1f out: styd on gamely to hold 2nd while strly pressed fnl 110yds* **11/10**^{1}

3 hd **Queen America (FR)**^{24} 4548 2-8-9 .... OPeslier 4 101
(Robert Collet, France) *racd in 3rd: hrd rdn to chal for 2nd 110yds out: no ex cl home* **54/10**

4 3 **Article Rare (USA)**^{26} 2-8-9 .... ACrastus 3 94
(E Lellouche, France) *last thrght: outpcd fnl 1 1/2f* **9/2**^{3}

1m 26.2s (1.70) **Going Correction** +0.15s/f (Good) **4** Ran SP% **118.5**
Speed ratings: **96,95,95,91**
PARI-MUTUEL: WIN 2.70; PL 1.20, 1.20; SF 5.00.
Owner M De Chambure **Bred** Pier House Stud **Trained** Pau, France

NOTEBOOK
Elusive Wave(IRE), second for much of the 7f, was extracted to challenge at the furlong marker and then stayed on well to the line. This ex-English filly is now unbeaten in three races and she may well now head to the Prix Marcel Boussac although connections might have a look at the Cheveley Park Stakes.
Ana Americana(FR) attempted to make all but was tackled by the winner at the furlong marker. She did not go down without a fight and the front running tactics were forced on her by the small field. Still looks like a Group 3 filly and the Prix d'Aumale could be a target next time out.
Queen America(FR), third for much of the race, was extracted to challenge at the furlong marker and looked really dangerous when making her effort up the centre of the track. She only just failed to take second.
Article Rare(USA) was last throughout the race and never threatened to land a blow, but she is better than this performance suggests.

5302a PRIX GUILLAUME D'ORNANO (GROUP 2) 1m 2f

3:15 (3:20) 3-Y-O **£54,485** (£21,029; £10,037; £6,691; £3,346)

RPR

1 **Russian Cross (IRE)**^{26} 3-8-12 .... JVictoire 1 118
(A Fabre, France) *racd in 5th on ins: 3rd st: slipped through on ins to ld over 1 1/2f out: drvn out* **11/2**^{3}

2 1½ **River Proud (USA)**^{21} 4622 3-8-12 .... CSoumillon 7 115
(P F I Cole) *racd in 2nd: led over 2f out to over 1 1/2f out: kpt on same pce* **23/10**^{1}

3 nk **City Leader (IRE)**^{27} 4473 3-8-12 .... DBonilla 4 114
(B J Meehan) *racd in 4th: squeezed up and hmpd over 2 1/2f out: 4th st: wnt 3rd over 1f out: styd on fnl f* **42/10**^{2}

4 1½ **Chinchon (IRE)**^{27} 4473 3-8-12 .... MBlancpain 3 111
(C Laffon-Parias, France) *hld up in 7th: 5th st: disp 3rd over 1 1/2f out to over 1f out: one pce* **89/10**

5 2 **Blue Bresil (FR)**^{11} 4959 3-8-12 .... WMongil 8 107
(L Larrigade, France) *reluctant to enter stalls: led: edgd rt over 2 1/2f out: hdd over 2f out: one pce* **33/1**

6 2½ **Starlish (IRE)**^{60} 3356 3-8-12 .... ACrastus 2 102
(E Lellouche, France) *hld up in last: nvr a factor* **30/1**

7 nk **Twice Over**^{27} 4473 3-9-2 .... SPasquier 5 106
(H R A Cecil) *racd in 3rd: squeezed up and bdly hmpd over 2 1/2f out: 6th st: sltly hmpd over 1 1/2f out: nt pushed fr over 1f out* **23/10**^{1}

8 5 **Change The World (IRE)**^{40} 4042 3-8-12 .... IMendizabal 6 92
(J-C Rouget, France) *racd in 6th: 7th st: wknd 2f out* **15/1**

2m 8.50s (-1.70) **Going Correction** +0.15s/f (Good) **8** Ran SP% **117.7**
Speed ratings: **112,110,110,109,107 105,105,101**
PARI-MUTUEL: WIN 6.50; PL 1.90, 1.90, 1.60; DF 10.30.
Owner Baron Edouard De Rothschild **Bred** Societe Civile De L'Ecurie De Meautry **Trained** Chantilly, France

NOTEBOOK
Russian Cross(IRE) was given a fine ride by his young jockey. Mid division for much of the race, which was not run at a great pace, he found a gap on the rail early in the straight and then ran on really well to win with something in hand. This colt had training problems early in the season, but the patience of his trainer is being rewarded. There is a strong possibility he will go directly for the Arc, but if the ground came up heavy he might well be diverted to the Champion Stakes at Newmarket. He is certainly one worth following during the autumn.
River Proud(USA) was not suited by a lack of early pace, which can so often happen in France. Dropped into second place soon after the start, he went to the head of affairs early in the straight and looked a likely winner until the furlong marker. He then stayed on one paced and was certainly not suited by the way the race turned out. There are no particular plans for him at the moment, but he will be kept to 1m2f.
City Leader(IRE), dropped in just behind the leaders, did not look very happy at the end of the turn into the straight. He then ran on well and would have probably been second but for getting hampered.
Chinchon(IRE) was waited with and then came with a progressive run up the centre of the track. He never really looked like getting on terms with the first three. He will not be pushed too much for the rest of the season as he is likely to stay in training as a four-year-old.
Twice Over did not have the run of the race. He was hampered when leaving the stalls and again just before the straight. He never really recovered and stayed on one paced. This race is best forgotten.

5256

BEVERLEY (R-H)

Sunday, August 24

OFFICIAL GOING: Soft (heavy in places)

Wind: moderate, half against Weather: overcast but mainly fine

5303 JOHN JENKINS MEMORIAL CLAIMING STKS — 7f 100y

2:00 (2:00) (Class 5) 3-Y-0+ — **£2,590** (£770; £385; £192) **Stalls** High

Form — RPR

0140 **1** — **West End Lad**[17] 4785 5-9-3 62 .... (b) ChrisCatlin 4 — 71
(S R Bowring) *mid-div: hdwy centre over 2f out: led over 1f out: drew clr* — **4/1**[2]

0210 **2** *6* **Efidium**[29] 4440 10-8-11 66 .... NeilBrown(3) 9 — 52
(N Bycroft) *mid-div: hdwy centre over 2f out: kpt on to take 2nd ins fnl f* — **4/1**[2]

0400 **3** *2* **Ming Vase**[15] 4878 6-9-1 45 .... JamieMoriarty 14 — 48
(P T Midgley) *chsd ldrs: effrt on ins over 2f out: kpt on same pce fnl f* — **16/1**

6053 **4** *nk* **Scotty's Future (IRE)**[11] 4961 10-8-10 48 .... SladeO'Hara(5) 7 — 47
(A Berry) *sn drvn along in rr: hdwy on ins to chse ldrs over 2f out: one pce appr fnl f* — **9/1**

6101 **5** *2 1/2* **Le Chiffre (IRE)**[11] 4961 6-9-0 63 .... (p) J-PGuillambert 3 — 40
(John A Harris) *trckd ldr: led centre 3f out: hdd over 1f out: sn wknd* **7/2**[1]

0-00 **6** *1/2* **Apache Point (IRE)**[13] 4919 11-9-1 47 .... KimTinkler 8 — 39
(N Tinkler) *in rr-div: hdwy on outside over 2f out: hung rt and kpt on fnl f* — **20/1**

4350 **7** *1/2* **Admiralcollingwood**[20] 4680 3-8-7 50 .... DominicFox(3) 6 — 36
(T P Tate) *in rr: effrt on wd outside over 2f out: nvr nr ldrs* — **14/1**

60 **8** *3/4* **Poppy Day**[11] 4961 5-8-7 0 .... NSLawes(7) 10 — 35
(M W Easterby) *dwlt: sn in tch: outpcd inner over 2f out: kpt on fnl f* **18/1**

0500 **9** *nk* **Brutus Maximus**[66] 3182 5-9-0 42 .... (b) MarkLawson(3) 12 — 37
(I W McInnes) *chsd ldrs: wandered centre 2f out: sn wknd* — **66/1**

6-65 **10** *shd* **Invincible Rose (IRE)**[36] 4207 3-8-3 43 .... PaulHanagan 11 — 24
(M E Sowersby) *led tl hdd 3f out: styd towards far side: sn wknd* — **25/1**

2420 **11** *2* **Wizby**[37] 4168 5-8-11 51 .... RussellKennemore(3) 5 — 29
(Ms Deborah J Evans) *s.i.s: t.k.h in rr: hdwy inner over 2f out: wknd over 1f out* — **14/1**

1645 **12** *6* **Royal Applord**[2] 5248 3-9-0 68 .... PaulMulrennan 2 — 16
(K A Ryan) *chsd ldrs: c wd st: lost pl wl over 1f out* — **15/2**[3]

1m 38.65s (4.85) **Going Correction** +0.60s/f (Yiel)

WFA 3 from 4yo+ 5lb — **12** Ran SP% **118.6**

Speed ratings (Par 103): **96,89,86,86,83 83,82,81,81,81 78,72**

toteswinger: 1&2 £3.90, 1&3 £17.90, 2&3 £21.30. CSF £19.95 TOTE £4.40: £1.40, £2.30, £5.10; EX 25.50.

Owner K Nicholls **Bred** Keith Nicholls **Trained** Edwinstowe, Notts

FOCUS

A modest claimer and, with very few at home on the testing ground, this is not a race to dwell on, although the winner did it well. They were spread out across the track in the straight, but the main action took place up the middle, well away from the far rail.

Royal Applord Official explanation: jockey said gelding ran flat

5304 E B F OLD CROSSLEYANS RUGBY CLUB MAIDEN STKS — 1m 100y

2:30 (2:31) (Class 5) 2-Y-0 — **£3,668** (£1,091; £545; £272) **Stalls** High

Form — RPR

5 **1** — **Sergeant Pink (IRE)**[15] 4861 2-9-3 0 .... PaulHanagan 6 — 73
(S Gollings) *chsd ldrs: swtchd lft over 1f out: styd on to ld fnl 75yds* **6/1**[3]

06 **2** *1/2* **Huxaar**[17] 4780 2-9-3 0 .... CatherineGannon 3 — 72
(Mrs L Stubbs) *drvn along to chse ldr: led over 1f out: hdd and no ex wl ins fnl f* — **8/1**

54 **3** *6* **Heading East (IRE)**[26] 4497 2-9-3 0 .... JoeFanning 4 — 59
(K A Ryan) *swtchd rt after s: led tl over 1f out: sn wknd* — **13/8**[1]

60 **4** *3 1/2* **King's Counsel (IRE)**[37] 4150 2-9-3 0 .... TomEaves 7 — 52
(B Smart) *mid-div: hdwy over 2f out: one pce* — **12/1**

6 **5** *1/2* **Baileys Red**[34] 4256 2-9-3 0 .... PaulMulrennan 2 — 51
(J G Given) *dwlt: sn chsng ldrs: one pce fnl 2f* — **8/1**

004 **6** *2 1/4* **Kingaroo (IRE)**[50] 3706 2-9-3 47 .... AndrewElliott 8 — 46
(Garry Moss) *in rr: kpt on fnl 3f: nvr a factor* — **28/1**

7 *8* **Anotherbottleteddy** 2-8-12 0 .... PatrickMathers 10 — 24
(I W McInnes) *s.i.s: rn green and sn bhd* — **33/1**

60 **8** *2 1/4* **Captain Cromby (IRE)**[60] 3365 2-9-3 0 .... DeanMcKeown 9 — 25
(J R Weymes) *in rr: bhd fnl 4f* — **50/1**

9 *2 3/4* **It's Me Again** 2-9-3 0 .... ChrisCatlin 11 — 19
(E J O'Neill) *t.k.h in rr: lost pl after 2f: bhd fnl 4f* — **5/1**[2]

10 *2* **Star Of Sophia (IRE)** 2-8-9 0 .... AndrewMullen(3) 5 — 10
(Mrs A Duffield) *s.i.s: trckd ldrs: lost pl 4f out: sn bhd* — **16/1**

5 **11** *9* **Danderdandan**[8] 5107 2-9-3 0 .... JamieMoriarty 1 — —
(P T Midgley) *prom on outside: drvn 4f out: sn lost pl* — **25/1**

1m 54.32s (6.72) **Going Correction** +0.60s/f (Yiel) — **11** Ran SP% **117.0**

Speed ratings (Par 94): **90,89,83,80,79 77,69,67,64,62 53**

toteswinger: 1&2 £7.60, 1&3 £2.80, 2&3 £4.90. CSF £50.98 TOTE £7.30: £1.90, £2.40, £1.30; EX 70.70.

Owner P J MArtin **Bred** Ring Pink Partnership **Trained** Scamblesby, Lincs

FOCUS

No more than a fair juvenile maiden and an extended mile in this ground proved quite a test for these youngsters. They raced up the middle of the track in the straight and the first two pulled nicely clear.

NOTEBOOK

Sergeant Pink(IRE) ◆ was well beaten into fifth when a 40-1 shot on his debut over 1m on the Lingfield Polytrack, but his trainer felt the track did not suit that day and feels the horse needs a galloping course. A decent-sized colt with plenty of scope, he handled the testing ground well enough and responded really gamely to strong pressure in the straight to run out a narrow winner, improving significantly on that initial effort. He had to be switched left, around both Huxaar and the tiring Heading East, but although he did not lose any momentum, he still looked inexperienced. He probably had a hard enough race, so might need a bit of time before his next outing, and things are likely to get tougher as this was just an ordinary maiden, but he very much looks the type who can progress as he continues to fill his frame and strengthen up. (op 9-1)

Huxaar, who showed he handles soft ground when sixth over this trip at Haydock on his previous start, ran a game race in defeat and pulled a long way clear of the remainder. Having raced on the pace close to the favourite from the outset, he really had to battle to see that rival off early in the straight and was just softened up by the time the winner made his move. He is another who looked to have a tough race, but is progressing with every run and now has the option of nurseries. (op 7-1 tchd 6-1)

Heading East(IRE) took them along early and seemed to travel okay, but this trip on such testing ground seemed to stretch his stamina. Entries in both the Royal Lodge and the Racing Post Trophy suggest he is well regarded, but he probably wants less of a test of stamina for the time being and better ground will help in that respect. (tchd 6-4)

King's Counsel(IRE) was never involved on this step up in trip, but he will have more options now he is qualified for a handicap mark. (tchd 14-1)

Baileys Red should have been suited by the ground, being a son of Diktat, but his dam was a dual 5f winner and this trip surely stretched his stamina. He might be one for handicaps over shorter a little bit further down the line. (op 7-1 tchd 17-2)

Danderdandan Official explanation: trainer said colt failed to stay the trip

5305 CHARLES ELSEY MEMORIAL H'CAP — 1m 4f 16y

3:05 (3:05) (Class 5) (0-75,74) 3-Y-0+ — **£3,076** (£915; £457; £228) **Stalls** High

Form — RPR

021 **1** — **Red Fama**[11] 4966 4-8-9 54 .... ChrisCatlin 5 — 73
(N Bycroft) *hld up in rr: smooth hdwy to ld 2f out: rdn wl clr: eased nr fin* — **4/1**[3]

4313 **2** *11* **Master Nimbus**[20] 4690 8-9-2 61 .... GrahamGibbons 2 — 62
(J J Quinn) *sn trcking ldrs on outer: drvn over 3f out: kpt on to take modest 2nd appr fnl f* — **3/1**[2]

2012 **3** *1 1/4* **Channel Crossing**[14] 4892 6-9-10 69 .... JoeFanning 4 — 68
(S Wynne) *t.k.h and led after 1f: qckd over 4f out: hdd 2f out: one pce* — **15/2**

3253 **4** *6* **Mister Fizzbomb (IRE)**[26] 4501 5-9-8 67 .... DNolan 3 — 57
(J S Wainwright) *led 1f: chsd ldrs: wknd over 1f out* — **9/1**

1635 **5** *3/4* **Hepburn Bell (IRE)**[10] 5024 3-9-5 74 .... EddieAhern 1 — 63
(J R Fanshawe) *trckd ldrs: rdn and wandered over 2f out: sn btn* — **13/8**[1]

114- **6** *31* **Paradise Walk**[287] 5523 4-9-11 70 .... PaulHanagan 7 — 9
(E W Tuer) *t.k.h in rr: hung rt thrght: hdwy over 5f out: lost pl over 2f out: sn bhd and eased: t.o* — **16/1**

2m 46.88s (5.98) **Going Correction** +0.60s/f (Yiel)

WFA 3 from 4yo+ 10lb — **6** Ran SP% **110.7**

Speed ratings (Par 103): **104,96,95,91,91 70**

toteswinger: 1&2 £2.70, 1&3 £4.60, 2&3 £5.50. CSF £15.86 TOTE £5.20: £2.20, £2.20; EX 16.60.

Owner B F Rayner **Bred** N Bycroft **Trained** Brandsby, N Yorks

FOCUS

A small field for what was no more than a fair middle-distance handicap and Red Fama absolutely routed his five rivals. They all raced up the middle of the track, continuing the theme of the earlier races. The winner is rated up a stone but it is questionable how literally this form should be taken.

Paradise Walk Official explanation: jockey said filly hung right throughout

5306 IT'S ALL OVER NOW NURSERY — 5f

3:40 (3:40) (Class 4) (0-85,82) 2-Y-0 — **£5,180** (£1,541; £770; £384) **Stalls** High

Form — RPR

332 **1** — **Captain Scooby**[13] 4923 2-8-8 72 .... MichaelJStainton(3) 5 — 75
(R M Whitaker) *trckd ldrs: led over 1f out: r.o strly* — **9/4**[1]

403 **2** *1 1/2* **Mo Mhuirnin (IRE)**[53] 3598 2-8-11 72 .... PaulHanagan 4 — 70
(R A Fahey) *t.k.h: effrt: n.m.r and swtchd lft 2f out: kpt on wl fnl f* — **5/1**[3]

4011 **3** *nse* **Visterre (IRE)**[24] 4558 2-9-4 79 .... TomEaves 2 — 76
(B Smart) *led tl hdd over 1f out: kpt on same pce* — **13/2**

041 **4** *12* **Dispol Grand (IRE)**[12] 4948 2-8-4 65 .... PaulFessey 1 — 19
(P T Midgley) *chsd ldrs: hung rt and lost pl over 1f out* — **5/2**[2]

3450 **5** *1/2* **Mesyaal**[11] 4975 2-8-7 68 .... (v[1]) ChrisCatlin 7 — 20
(M R Channon) *chsd along: w ldrs: lost pl over 1f out* — **7/1**

2534 **6** *2* **What A Fella**[38] 4113 2-8-5 69 .... AndrewMullen(3) 3 — 14
(Mrs A Duffield) *t.k.h: hdwy to trck ldrs 3f out: lost pl over 1f out* — **9/1**

66.97 secs (3.47) **Going Correction** +0.60s/f (Yiel) — **6** Ran SP% **111.8**

Speed ratings (Par 96): **96,93,93,74,73 70**

toteswinger: 1&2 £3.40, 1&3 £2.30, 2&3 £2.30. CSF £13.67 TOTE £3.00: £1.70, £2.70; EX 10.30.

Owner Paul Davies & David Horner **Bred** Hellwood Stud Farm & Paul Davies (h'Gate) **Trained** Scarcroft, W Yorks

FOCUS

Just the six lined up, but this looked a reasonable nursery and the first three pulled well clear. They raced middle to stands' side. The winning time was 1.93 seconds quicker than the following three-year-old 46-60 handicap.

NOTEBOOK

Captain Scooby stepped up on the form he showed in three runs in maiden company to get off the mark on his nursery debut. Niggled along to stay in touch early on, he made his move out wide, furthest away from the stands' rail, but picked up well to record a decisive success. His sire, Captain Rio, loved easy ground and he proved well suited by the conditions, although his connections apparently think he doesn't necessarily need it soft. He should make up into a useful sprinter. (op 5-2 tchd 2-1)

Mo Mhuirnin(IRE) looked to improve on the form she showed in maiden company, but found one too strong. She was a little keen early and, after having to switch to get into the clear, her run just flattened out a little late on. She gives the impression she is still learning her job and there ought to be more to come. (op 3-1)

Visterre(IRE) came into this following two wins on a quick surface at Musselburgh, firstly a maiden and then a nursery off 74. She seemed to go through this very different ground well enough and looked to have her chance, but she gives the impression she is ready for 6f now. (op 5-1 tchd 9-2)

Dispol Grand(IRE) was below the form he showed when winning a lesser race under similar conditions off a 4lb lower mark at Musselburgh on his previous start (op 7-2)

Mesyaal offered nothing in a first-time visor and probably wants better ground. (op 9-1 tchd 13-2)

What A Fella finished last of all on his nursery bow. (op 14-1)

5307 BEVERLEY LIONS H'CAP — 5f

4:15 (4:16) (Class 6) (0-60,60) 3-Y-0 — **£2,900** (£856; £428) **Stalls** High

Form — RPR

3060 **1** — **Dubai To Barnsley**[9] 5074 3-8-2 47 .... DuranFentiman(3) 1 — 51
(Garry Moss) *w ldrs on wd outside: styd on to ld towards fin* — **12/1**

0000 **2** *nk* **Myriola**[11] 4987 3-8-4 46 .... ChrisCatlin 11 — 49
(S Gollings) *chsd ldrs: styd on to ld wl ins fnl f: hdd nr fin* — **16/1**

154 **3** *nk* **Select Committee**[15] 4852 3-9-3 59 .... (v) GrahamGibbons 9 — 61
(J J Quinn) *t.k.h: led: bmpd after 1f: edgd lft over 1f out: hdd wl ins fnl f: no ex* — **9/4**[1]

1060 **4** *1/2* **Foreign Rhythm (IRE)**[17] 4782 3-8-11 53 .... (v) KimTinkler 6 — 53
(N Tinkler) *s.i.s: in rr: hdwy 2f out: chsng ldrs ins fnl f: no ex* — **9/1**

051 **5** *1* **Nabeeda**[8] 5110 3-8-12 57 .... MarkLawson(3) 16 — 54+
(M Brittain) *bolted to post: s.i.s: in rr: nt clr run over 1f out: fin wl* — **8/1**[3]

0010 **6** *1 1/4* **Bahamian Princess**[17] 4770 3-9-1 60 .... RussellKennemore(3) 13 — 52
(R Hollinshead) *mid-div: hdwy and edgd rt over 1f out: kpt on: nt rch ldrs* — **16/1**

0000 **7** *2 3/4* **Mill Creek**[20] 4686 3-8-4 46 oh1 .... AndrewElliott 8 — 28
(Jedd O'Keeffe) *chsd ldrs: edgd rt and hmpd over 1f out: one pce* — **66/1**

0320 **8** *hd* **Handsinthemist (IRE)**[35] 4216 3-8-11 **53**..................(p) JamieMoriarty 7 34
(P T Midgley) *chsd ldrs: n.m.r over 2f out: kpt on same pce* **14/1**

0-46 **9** *3 1/4* **Hits Only Time**[72] 2991 3-8-13 **55**.............................. DeanMcKeown 12 25
(P A Blockley) *hmpd s: s.i.s: bhd: swtchd stands' side over 2f out: kpt on fnl f* **7/1**[2]

0002 **10** *3/4* **Paddy Jack**[8] 5110 3-9-0 **56**..................................(p) TonyHamilton 3 23
(J R Weymes) *chsd ldrs: lost pl over 1f out* **7/1**[2]

4006 **11** *2 1/2* **Tanley**[19] 4703 3-8-12 **54**..(p) JoeFanning 5 12
(J F Coupland) *w ldrs: lost pl over 1f out* **8/1**[3]

4000 **12** *3/4* **Note Perfect**[20] 4684 3-8-4 **46** oh1...................................(b) DaleGibson 17 —
(M W Easterby) *t.k.h and hung lft: w ldrs: wnt lft and bmpd after 1f: lost pl over 1f out* **12/1**

0600 **13** *2 3/4* **Wave Hill (IRE)**[8] 5110 3-8-10 **57** ow7..........................(t) SladeO'Hara(5) 4 2
(A Berry) *a in rr* **66/1**

68.90 secs (5.40) **Going Correction** +0.60s/f (Yiel) **13** Ran SP% **124.8**
Speed ratings (Par 98): **80,79,79,78,76 74,70,69,64,63 59,58,53**
toteswinger: 1&2 £52.50, 1&3 £13.20, 2&3 £12.90. CSF £198.64 CT £617.94 TOTE £21.30: £4.60, £5.50, £1.60; EX 446.80.
Owner J A Bower **Bred** J A Bower **Trained** Loughborough, Leics

FOCUS
A weak sprint handicap in which they raced middle to stands' side. The form is rated through the runner-up. The time was 1.93 seconds slower than the previous 0-85 nursery.
Nabeeda Official explanation: jockey said gelding bolted to post and missed the break
Hits Only Time Official explanation: jockey said colt was hampered at the stasrt
Note Perfect Official explanation: jockey said filly hung left-handed throughout

5308 RACING AGAIN ON 9TH SEPTEMBER FILLIES' H'CAP — 1m 1f 207y
4:50 (4:50) (Class 6) (0-65,65) 3-Y-O+ **£2,752** (£818; £409; £204) **Stalls** High

Form RPR

3040 **1** **Jenny Soba**[15] 4879 5-8-9 **46** oh1.................................... DNolan 10 55
(Lucinda Featherstone) *in rr and sn pushed along: hdwy on stands' side over 2f out: led ins fnl f: hld on towards fin* **14/1**

-005 **2** *1/2* **Tender Moments**[8] 5108 4-9-1 **52**.............................. TomEaves 11 60
(B Smart) *in rr: hdwy over 2f out: hrd rdn and edgd rt ins fnl f: styd on: jst hld* **16/1**

5603 **3** *1 1/4* **Piverina (IRE)**[20] 4680 3-8-1 **49**............................ AndrewMullen(3) 1 55
(Miss J A Camacho) *w ldrs: led over 2f out: hdd and no ex ins fnl f* **12/1**

3002 **4** *2 1/2* **Jiminor Mack**[1] 5262 5-8-4 **46** oh1......................(p) PatrickDonaghy(5) 6 47
(W J H Ratcliffe) *s.i.s: hdwy on inner over 2f out: one pce appr fnl f* **6/1**[3]

2153 **5** *3/4* **Coral Shores**[11] 4964 3-9-6 **65**.................................. ChrisCatlin 7 64
(P W Hiatt) *led 1f: chsd ldrs: kpt on same pce appr fnl f* **6/1**[3]

0003 **6** *3/4* **Sudden Impulse**[19] 4701 7-9-12 **63**............................. AndrewElliott 13 61
(A D Brown) *t.k.h in rr: checked over 7f out: hdwy over 2f out: kpt on fnl f* **15/2**

5443 **7** *2 1/2* **Giddywell**[40] 4048 4-8-13 **53**............................ RussellKennemore(3) 4 46
(R Hollinshead) *chsd ldrs on outer: led over 4f out tl over 2f out: edgd rt and wknd over 1f out* **9/2**[2]

4014 **8** *5* **Jemima's Art**[11] 4964 3-8-9 **54**..................................(b) PaulMulrennan 9 37
(M W Easterby) *trckd ldrs: n.m.r on inner over 3f out: edgd lft and wknd over 1f out* **4/1**[1]

2300 **9** *16* **Kayflaa (IRE)**[73] 2982 3-9-1 **60**.............................. GrahamGibbons 2 11
(T D Walford) *mid-div: lost pl over 2f out: sn bhd* **16/1**

050/ **10** *15* **Strathtay**[689] 243 6-8-10 **47**....................................... PaulHanagan 8 —
(M G Rimell) *prom: lost pl over 3f out: sn bhd* **33/1**

5402 **11** *1 3/4* **Cecina Marina**[14] 4899 5-8-9 **46** oh1.............................. JoeFanning 5 —
(Mrs K Walton) *chsd ldrs on outer: lost pl over 2f out: sn bhd* **14/1**

5500 **12** *3/4* **Cape Dancer (IRE)**[1] 5262 4-8-9 **46** oh1..................... TonyHamilton 3 —
(J S Wainwright) *led after 1f tl over 4f out: lost pl 3f out: sn bhd* **14/1**

2m 14.63s (7.63) **Going Correction** +0.60s/f (Yiel)
WFA 3 from 4yo+ 8lb **12** Ran SP% **120.9**
Speed ratings (Par 98): **93,92,91,89,89 88,86,82,69,57 56,55**
toteswinger: 1&2 £24.70, 1&3 £28.10, 2&3 £26.30. CSF £223.66 CT £2768.04 TOTE £19.60: £5.20, £4.80, £3.80; EX 278.00 Place 6: £248.52, Place 5: £117.35..
Owner J Roundtree **Bred** Theakston Stud **Trained** Atlow, Derbyshire

FOCUS
A moderate fillies' handicap and the leaders went off pretty quick in the conditions, setting this up for those held up. They all seemed to be heading for the stands' side early in the straight, but most of these ended up racing up the middle of the track. Weak form, with the winner the worst-in runner.
Jemima's Art Official explanation: jockey said filly was unsuited by the soft (heavy in places) ground
T/Plt: £405.10 to a £1 stake. Pool: £55,953.07. 100.81 winning tickets. T/Qpdt: £212.30 to a £1 stake. Pool: £3,013.50. 10.50 winning tickets. WG

5263 GOODWOOD (R-H)
Sunday, August 24

OFFICIAL GOING: Soft (6.4)
Wind: medium, against Weather: brightening after rain, sunny spells

5309 SOUTH COAST STKS (H'CAP) — 1m 1f
2:10 (2:11) (Class 4) (0-85,85) 3-Y-O **£6,476** (£1,927; £963; £481) **Stalls** High

Form RPR

2241 **1** **Mr Hichens**[24] 4566 3-8-13 **77**..................................... TPO'Shea 10 86
(B J Meehan) *mde all: rdn over 2f out: gng clr whn swvd lft 2f out: in command and wandered lft and rt fnl f: rdn out* **10/1**

1-32 **2** *2* **Roaring Forte (IRE)**[29] 4423 3-9-7 **85**......................... TonyCulhane 7 90
(W J Haggas) *t.k.h: hld up in last pl: hdwy over 3f out: chsd wnr u.p over 1f out: plugged on but nvr threatened wnr* **9/4**[1]

2031 **3** *1/2* **Gross Prophet**[14] 4910 3-8-4 **75**............................ RossAtkinson(7) 9 79
(Tom Dascombe) *chsd ldng pair: wnt 2nd 4f out: rdn over 2f out: kpt on same pce fnl f* **7/2**[2]

-316 **4** *1 3/4* **Wikaala (USA)**[22] 4621 3-9-2 **80**................................ MartinDwyer 1 80
(M P Tregoning) *in tch in midfield: chsd ldrs and rdn wl over 2f out: no imp fnl f* **11/2**[3]

14 **5** *5* **Summerstrand (IRE)**[20] 4694 3-9-2 **80**....................... PhilipRobinson 8 69
(M A Jarvis) *chsd ldr tl 4f out: rdn over 2f out: wknd wl over 1f out* **7/1**

16 **6** *8* **Paint The Town Red**[10] 5018 3-8-12 **76**........................ DarryllHolland 3 47
(H J Collingridge) *t.k.h: hld up towards rr on outer: rdn over 3f out: sn struggling and wl btn* **10/1**

21-4 **7** *12* **Benhavis**[133] 1348 3-9-4 **82**...(t) SebSanders 5 27
(J L Dunlop) *t.k.h: hld up in tch: rdn over 3f out: sn lost tch: t.o* **20/1**

0000 **8** *4* **Missioner (USA)**[9] 5051 3-9-2 **80**.................................(b) GregFairley 4 16
(M Johnston) *towards rr: rdn over 3f out: sn lost tch: t.o* **17/2**

2m 1.89s (5.59) **Going Correction** +0.75s/f (Yiel) **8** Ran SP% **114.3**
Speed ratings (Par 102): **105,103,102,101,96 89,79,75**
toteswinger: 1&2 £5.70, 1&3 £6.10, 2&3 £2.20. CSF £32.90 CT £96.44 TOTE £11.20: £3.00, £1.40, £1.80; EX 37.90.
Owner Mrs J & D E Cash **Bred** C A Green **Trained** Manton, Wilts

FOCUS
After 8.5mm of rain overnight the ground was changed to soft. There was also a slight headwind up the straight. A fair handicap to kick things off. They came up the centre of the track in the straight and it looked pretty hard work in the testing conditions. The form seems sound enough despite the ground.
Summerstrand(IRE) Official explanation: vet said filly finished distressed

5310 EBF CHICHESTER OBSERVER FILLIES' STKS (H'CAP) — 6f
2:45 (2:46) (Class 3) (0-95,94) 3-Y-O+ **£9,714** (£2,890; £1,444; £721) **Stalls** Low

Form RPR

0001 **1** **Perfect Flight**[15] 4864 3-8-5 **77**.......................... KirstyMilczarek 7 89
(M Blanshard) *hld up in tch on stands' side: swtchd rt and hdwy over 2f out: chal 2f out: led over 1f out: edgd lft but drew clr fnl f* **10/1**

2151 **2** *3* **Superduper**[34] 4252 3-8-10 **82**.............................. RichardHughes 12 84
(R Hannon) *racd in centre pair tl crossed over to join stands' side gp 1/2-way: led over 2f out: rdn and hdd over 1f out: wknd ins fnl f: hld on for 2nd* **7/2**[2]

-141 **3** *shd* **Maimoona (IRE)**[48] 3794 3-9-3 **89**............................ MartinDwyer 10 91+
(W J Haggas) *led centre pair tl lft to r alone fr over 3f out: a handy overall: ev ch 2f out: wknd ins fnl f* **6/4**[1]

6-0 **4** *3 3/4* **Janina**[46] 3849 3-9-6 **92**.. MichaelHills 1 82
(B W Hills) *stdd s: hld up in tch stands' side: hdwy over 2f out: chsd ldrs and rdn wl over 1f out: wknd qckly 1f out* **9/1**

1300 **5** *2* **Angus Newz**[21] 4660 5-9-9 **92**...................................(v) SebSanders 5 76
(M Quinn) *dwlt and hmpd s: sn rcvrd and led overall on stands' side: rdn and hdd over 2f out: sn struggling: no ch fnl f* **9/1**

03 **6** *6* **Temple Of Thebes (IRE)**[36] 4198 3-9-2 **88**............. StephenDonohoe 2 52
(E A L Dunlop) *chsd ldrs on stands' side: rdn over 2f out: sn struggling: eased whn wl btn fnl f* **6/1**[3]

616 **7** *9* **Mondovi**[64] 3252 4-9-5 **88**... JohnEgan 3 24
(N J Vaughan) *wnt rt s: plld hrd: chsd ldr on stands' side tl wknd qckly over 2f out: no ch and eased fr over 1f out: t.o* **12/1**

1m 16.2s (4.00) **Going Correction** +0.75s/f (Yiel)
WFA 3 from 4yo+ 3lb **7** Ran SP% **113.3**
Speed ratings (Par 104): **103,99,98,93,91 83,71**
toteswinger: 1&2 £4.70, 1&3 £4.60, 2&3 £1.70. CSF £43.90 CT £82.35 TOTE £10.70: £3.30, £1.90; EX 39.50.
Owner John Drew **Bred** Biddestone Stud **Trained** Upper Lambourn, Berks
■ Stewards' Enquiry : Kirsty Milczarek four-day ban (includes three deferred days): careless riding (Sep 12,14-17)

FOCUS
There was a difference of opinion as to where the best ground was here, and the field split into two, with the bigger group staying towards the stands'-side rail, while Superduper and Maimoona raced more towards the centre of the track. \n\x\x After two furlongs Superduper tacked over to join the stands'-side bunch but the favourite continued racing up the middle. Improved form from the winner.

NOTEBOOK
Perfect Flight had conditions very much to suit as she loves to get her toe in and, because she does not like to be crowded, racing on the outer of the main field suited her. This was a tougher race than she normally competes in, though, and the form of her last-time-out Lingfield success did not look too hot in the context of this race. She saw it out strongly, however, and could well be in for a productive autumn if conditions remain like this. (op 9-1)
Superduper has a progressive profile at this distance and ran a solid race off a career-high mark. She has twice won on fast ground and twice finished second on soft now, showing her versatility with regard to conditions. (op 5-1)
Maimoona(IRE) has been in cracking form of late, her previous success at Ripon confirming how comfortable she is with plenty of cut in the ground, and an 8lb higher mark looked far from insurmountable. She may have been at a disadvantage racing isolated up the centre of the track so it could be worth giving this progressive daughter of Pivotal the benefit of the doubt. (op 2-1 tchd 9-4 in a place)
Janina is bred to be a mud-loving sprinter, being by Namid out of that speedy filly Lady Dominatrix, so the drop back from 7f looked likely to suit her. She was also entitled to have come on for her belated seasonal reappearance at Newmarket. In the circumstances this was a bit disappointing, as having threatened to get involved inside the final two furlongs she got quite tired in the closing stages. (op 13-2 tchd 6-1)
Angus Newz acts on soft ground, but she had enough on at the weights and is at her best when dominating. She never got any peace in front this time. (op 7-1)
Temple Of Thebes(IRE) was disappointing and presumably the ground was to blame. Official explanation: jockey said filly stumbled 2f out (tchd 5-1)
Mondovi, a 5f fast-ground winner, had her stamina to prove over this longer trip. She showed early pace but was beaten over two furlongs out. Official explanation: jockey said filly had no more to give (op 11-1 tchd 10-1)

5311 EBF ALICE KEPPEL STKS (FILLIES' H'CAP) (LISTED RACE) — 1m 1f 192y
3:20 (3:20) (Class 1) (0-110,105) 3-Y-O+
£24,978 (£9,468; £4,738; £2,362; £1,183; £594) **Stalls** High

Form RPR

-211 **1** **Crystal Capella**[29] 4435 3-8-10 **93**.................................. JimmyQuinn 5 102
(Sir Michael Stoute) *hld up in midfield: shkn up over 3f out: hdwy and rdn over 2f out: drvn and ev ch over 1f out: styd on wl to ld wl ins fnl f* **2/1**[1]

1142 **2** *shd* **Casilda (IRE)**[23] 4582 3-8-3 **86** oh6.................................... PaulDoe 2 95
(W J Knight) *led after 1f: hrd pressed and rdn 3f out: kpt on gamely u.p: edgd rt fnl 100yds: hdd and no ex wl ins fnl f* **12/1**

-0U4 **3** *2* **Les Fazzani (IRE)**[21] 4667 4-9-11 **100**............................... ShaneKelly 3 105
(M J Wallace) *hld up wl in tch: effrt to join ldr 3f out: ev ch after tl wandered ent fnl f: no ex ins fnl f* **8/1**

1054 **4** *1/2* **Farley Star**[25] 4520 4-9-2 **91**...................................... SteveDrowne 6 95
(R Charlton) *hld up in midfield: rdn and effrt wl over 2f out: hdwy u.p 2f out: kpt on same pce fnl f* **5/1**[3]

4011 **5** *3/4* **Quirina**[9] 5075 3-8-5 **88**.. RichardMullen 9 91
(J H M Gosden) *led for 1f: chsd ldr after tl over 3f out: styd handy: ev ch u.p 2f out: wknd ins fnl f* **9/2**[2]

2140 **6** *2* **Princess Taylor**[36] 4189 4-8-11 **86** oh4..............................(t) JohnEgan 10 85
(M Botti) *hld up in tch: hdwy over 3f out: rdn wl over 2f out: kpt on same pce u.p fnl 2f* **16/1**

4-13 **7** *3 1/2* **Asfurah's Dream (IRE)**[25] 4520 3-8-3 **86** oh3................ MartinDwyer 1 78
(M P Tregoning) *chsd ldrs on outer: hdwy and pressing ldrs 4f out: rdn 3f out: wkng whn edgd rt wl over 1f out* **8/1**

4321 **8** 1 1/2 **Rio Guru (IRE)**[6] 5155 3-8-3 **86** oh13 .... TPO'Shea 11 75
(M R Channon) *hld up in last trio: rdn 3f out: no prog whn swtchd lft wl over 1f out: nvr nr ldrs* **20/1**

4406 **9** 2 1/4 **Ivory Lace**[15] 4841 7-8-11 **86** oh7 .... JimCrowley 8 70
(S Woodman) *hld up in last trio: n.d* **25/1**

6340 **10** 1 3/4 **Don't Forget Faith (USA)**[81] 2743 3-8-12 **95** .... PhilipRobinson 12 76
(C G Cox) *stdd after s: hld up in last pl: rdn and struggling 3f out: hanging rt and wl bhd fnl 2f* **8/1**

2m 13.34s (5.34) **Going Correction** +0.75s/f (Yiel)
WFA 3 from 4yo+ 8lb **10** Ran SP% **123.7**
Speed ratings (Par 108): **108,107,106,105,105 103,100,99,97,96**
toteswinger: 1&2 £7.90, 1&3 £5.60, 2&3 £21.30. CSF £31.03 CT £171.27 TOTE £2.70: £1.50, £4.30, £2.80; EX 27.20.
Owner Sir Evelyn De Rothschild **Bred** Southcourt Stud **Trained** Newmarket, Suffolk

FOCUS
Not a strong race for the class, with half the field racing from out of the handicap. The runner-up was 6lb wrong but the third is a solid guide, and the winner is rated up 3lb. They did not go a mad gallop early and once again the field crossed over to race middle to stands' side in the straight.

NOTEBOOK
Crystal Capella only got home narrowly but maintained her progressive profile. She had been put up 13lb for her easy win at York last month, but that looked perfectly fair, especially considering that the third that day Suzi's Decision has since gone and won a Listed race at Newbury, and with her dam a winner in this grade on soft ground there had to be a good chance she would handle conditions. However, while she got the job done, she was a bit laboured and it is likely that she will be even better back on fast ground, and on this evidence another couple of furlongs should be within her compass. She is likely to stay in training as a four-year-old. (op 5-2)
Casilda(IRE), proven in the conditions, ran a brave race from the front and came back at the winner after being headed. She had looked held off marks around 80 so this performance from 6lb wrong does put a question mark on the value of the form. However, it is always possible that this lightly-raced filly simply improved for the testing ground. She completed a one-two in the race for her sire Cape Cross. (op 16-1)
Les Fazzani(IRE) appreciated the return to 1m2f and, most importantly, soft ground. She kept on well next to the stands' rail, posting a solid effort under top weight. (tchd 15-2)
Farley Star was unlucky in running here last month but had no such excuse this time. Whether this ground suited her ideally is open to question, but it is just as possible that the Handicapper just about has her measure now. (op 6-1)
Quirina has looked a progressive type this season, but she had to prove she could go on this sort of ground. Her two best siblings Quito and Quarter Note both won on soft and heavy ground, so that was encouraging, but in the event she was beaten with over a furlong to run. (op 4-1)
Princess Taylor, who was 4lb wrong at the weights, was running on at the finish, which was surprising given that she does most of her racing over distances around a mile.
Asfurah's Dream(IRE), who was 3lb out of the handicap, failed to handle these much softer conditions. (tchd 9-1)
Rio Guru(IRE) had plenty on at the weights. (op 16-1 tchd 14-1)
Don't Forget Faith(USA), returning from a mid-season break, went without the visor she wore when well beaten in France last time, but she failed to improve on her mediocre form this season. She appears to have simply failed to train on. (op 9-1)

5312 FEGENTRI WORLD CUP OF NATIONS STKS (AMATEUR RIDERS H'CAP) (IN MEMORY OF LATE JOHN CIECHANOWSKI) 1m 1f

3:55 (3:56) (Class 5) (0-75,73) 3-Y-O+ **£6,246** (£1,937; £968; £484) **Stalls** High

Form RPR

0422 **1** **Master Mahogany**[7] 5118 7-11-2 **63** .... MissCBurri 3 69
(R J Hodges) *chsd ldrs: rdn over 1f out: r.o ins fnl f to ld fnl 75yds* **6/1**[3]

0634 **2** 1 1/4 **Admirals Way**[13] 4920 3-10-6 **60** .... MmeRUnrath 6 63
(C N Kellett) *led to s: led tl 4f out: chsd ldr after: rdn over 1f out: ev ch ins fnl f: no ex fnl 75yds: snatched 2nd nr fin* **7/1**

131 **3** nk **Western Roots**[21] 4664 7-11-9 **70** .... MrYMergirie 9 73
(A M Balding) *chsd ldr tl led 4f out: rdn wl over 1f out: kpt on gamely: hdd and no ex fnl 75yds: lost 2nd nr fin* **7/2**[2]

406B **4** 2 1/2 **Bollywood (IRE)**[25] 4529 5-10-7 **54** oh9 .... MissGMO'Callaghan 2 51
(J J Bridger) *in tch: rdn and outpcd 3f out: kpt on again fnl f: nt threaten ldrs* **33/1**

5441 **5** 1/2 **Merrymadcap (IRE)**[9] 5059 6-11-7 **68** .... MissCAllen 4 64
(M Blanshard) *in tch: hdwy and rdn 2f out: wknd u.p ent fnl f* **3/1**[1]

0006 **6** 1 1/2 **Mythical Charm**[9] 5059 9-10-7 **54** oh9 .... (t) MrSWalker 5 47
(J J Bridger) *stdd after s: hld up in rr: hdwy 4f out: rdn 2f out: wknd u.p over 1f out* **12/1**

0032 **7** 6 **Red Current**[9] 5059 4-11-0 **61** .... MrFDePaola 1 40
(R A Harris) *racd wd in midfield: rdn wl over 2f out: no hdwy: no ch fnl f* **8/1**

0300 **8** 2 3/4 **Bold Phoenix (IRE)**[10] 5020 7-10-7 **54** oh9 .... (t) MrRO'Sullivan 10 27
(Miss Amy Weaver) *hld up bhd: n.d* **28/1**

0320 **9** 6 **Blacktoft (USA)**[32] 4309 5-11-12 **73** .... (e) MissMPenman 8 33
(S C Williams) *towards rr: rdn and struggling 3f out: sn wl bhd* **14/1**

0000 **10** 14 **Ruffie (IRE)**[9] 5059 5-10-7 **54** oh9 .... (e) MlleDGarcia-Dubois 7 —
(Miss J Feilden) *towards rr: c to centre over 3f out: sn wl bhd: t.o* **40/1**

5354 **11** 56 **Danetime Panther (IRE)**[10] 5033 4-11-12 **73** .... MsVRodenbusch 11 —
(P F I Cole) *hld up towards rr: wknd 3f out: t.o whn virtually p.u ins fnl f* **7/1**

2m 5.86s (9.56) **Going Correction** +0.75s/f (Yiel)
WFA 3 from 4yo+ 7lb **11** Ran SP% **120.8**
Speed ratings (Par 103): **87,85,85,83,82 81,76,73,68,56 6**
toteswinger: 1&2 £10.30, 1&3 £4.10, 2&3 £6.40. CSF £48.28 CT £175.30 TOTE £7.20: £2.50, £2.60, £1.80; EX 52.80.
Owner Villagers Five **Bred** C J Hill **Trained** Charlton Mackrell, Somerset
■ A winner on her first ride in Britain for Swiss jockey Christine Burri.

FOCUS
The fourth leg of the Fegentri World Cup of Nations for amateur riders from around the world, but to all intents and purposes an ordinary handicap, albeit a fairly competitive one. The form is questionable although the winner and third were close to their recent marks. They stayed towards the far side to centre in the straight.
Bold Phoenix(IRE) Official explanation: trainer said gelding had a breathing problem
Danetime Panther(IRE) Official explanation: jockey said saddle slipped

5313 TURFTV.CO.UK STKS (H'CAP) 7f

4:30 (4:31) (Class 2) (0-105,105) 3-Y-O+
£12,462 (£3,732; £1,866; £934; £466; £234) **Stalls** High

Form RPR

0342 **1** **Signor Peltro**[10] 5030 5-8-8 **85** .... DaneO'Neill 13 96
(H Candy) *stdd s: hld up bhd: hdwy over 3f out: rdn wl over 1f out: chal ent fnl f: hung lft after: led fnl 100yds: r.o wl* **7/1**

2113 **2** 1 **Little White Lie (IRE)**[15] 4869 4-9-12 **103** .... DarryllHolland 9 111
(J R Jenkins) *hld up in midfield: hdwy and rdn 3f out: drvn and edging rt over 1f out: kpt on fnl f to go 2nd nr fin: nt pce to rch wnr* **10/3**[1]

0466 **3** 1/2 **Fathsta (IRE)**[24] 4553 3-8-8 **90** .... LPKeniry 12 94
(S Kirk) *t.k.h: hld up in midfield: hdwy over 3f out: rdn 2f out: led ent fnl f: hdd fnl 100yds: no ex: lost 2nd towards fin* **16/1**

0100 **4** 2 3/4 **Masai Moon**[15] 4869 4-8-12 **92** .... JamesMillman(3) 18 91
(B R Millman) *in tch: hdwy wl over 2f out: led 2f out: hdd ent fnl f: keeping on same pce and btn whn short of room wl ins fnl f* **16/1**

0041 **5** hd **Nezami (IRE)**[14] 4893 3-8-7 **89** .... WilliamBuick 11 85
(B J Meehan) *hld up towards rr: hdwy 3f out: nt clr run 2f out tl over 1f out: sn rdn and no imp* **12/1**

0040 **6** 1 **Dubai Dynamo**[50] 3744 3-8-12 **94** .... JohnEgan 7 88
(P F I Cole) *stdd after s: hld up in last pair: rdn and no hdwy 3f out: styd on past btn horses fnl f: nvr trbld ldrs* **9/1**

0022 **7** 2 1/2 **Zakhaaref**[14] 4893 3-8-12 **94** .... MartinDwyer 14 81
(M Johnston) *chsd ldng pair: rdn 3f out: wknd u.p wl over 1f out: no ch fnl f* **7/1**

3235 **8** 3 3/4 **Guilded Warrior**[21] 4661 5-8-7 **87** .... TravisBlock(3) 3 66
(W S Kittow) *t.k.h: chsd ldr: drvn 3f out: wknd 2f out: eased whn no ch ins fnl f* **13/2**[3]

4004 **9** 1/2 **Salient**[10] 5030 4-8-7 **84** oh1 .... KirstyMilczarek 15 62
(M J Attwater) *led: rdn wl over 2f out: hdd 2f out: wknd qckly jst over 1f out* **16/1**

1120 **10** 1/2 **Commander Cave (USA)**[66] 3155 3-9-2 **98** .... RichardHughes 6 72
(R Hannon) *in tch: rdn and unable qck wl over 2f out: wknd wl over 1f out* **5/1**[2]

4030 **11** 1 **Presumptive (IRE)**[29] 4405 8-9-3 **94** .... SteveDrowne 10 67
(R Charlton) *stdd s: hld up bhd: rdn and no rspnse 3f out* **10/1**

1m 30.88s (3.48) **Going Correction** +0.75s/f (Yiel)
WFA 3 from 4yo+ 5lb **11** Ran SP% **122.5**
Speed ratings (Par 109): **110,108,108,105,104 103,100,96,96,95 94**
toteswinger: 1&2 £6.60, 1&3 £23.30, 2&3 £13.90. CSF £31.91 CT £374.95 TOTE £9.20: £2.50, £1.60, £5.10; EX 32.20.
Owner First Of Many Partnership **Bred** R D And J S Chugg & The Overbury Partnership **Trained** Kingston Warren, Oxon
■ Stewards' Enquiry : Dane O'Neill one-day ban (Sep 8); further two-day ban: (Sep 9-10): careless riding

FOCUS
Despite a host of non-runners this was still a competitive handicap and Salient ensured it was run at a strong gallop. The form looks pretty sound.

NOTEBOOK
Signor Peltro, a confirmed hold-up performer, runs his best races over 7f off a good pace, and as he is also perfectly effective with give in the ground, he had conditions pretty much to suit. He came with his challenge up the centre of the track, getting to the front inside the last and drawing steadily clear close home. Whether he can cope with a rise in the weights remains to be seen, as the last time he won off this mark last summer, he struggled somewhat off marks in the high 80s subsequently.
Little White Lie(IRE), who is very much at home on soft ground, has done nothing but improve since leaving Ireland and joining John Jenkins, and the Bunbury Cup winner ran another fine race under top weight, staying on well next to the stands' rail in the closing stages. Over this trip a stiffer track probably suits him better. (op 4-1 tchd 3-1)
Fathsta(IRE) may be thoroughly exposed but he rarely runs a bad race, and again did not go down without a fight. He is a keen going sort and will always be seen at his best when able to settle off a strong gallop like he had here. (op 14-1)
Masai Moon has a good record over this trip and ran well, but he is high in the weights now and vulnerable in these competitive handicaps.
Nezami(IRE) confirmed Leicester form with Zakhaaref despite being 2lb worse off with the Mark Johnston-trained colt. He did, however, again have the race run to suit, with the leaders going off too quick. Whether this soft ground was ideal, though, is open to question. (op 14-1)
Dubai Dynamo comes from a yard responsible for three of the last nine winners of this race, so had to be of interest simply on that statistic. However, he ran poorly on his last start at Sandown and this effort was a long way below the form of his Britannia fourth on quicker ground. (op 12-1)
Zakhaaref once again paid for racing too close to a strong pace, just like at Leicester last time. (tchd 6-1)
Guilded Warrior had never previously finished out of the places in eight starts when the word soft or heavy appeared in the going description, but he had no chance of getting home here having chased the fast pace set by Salient. Official explanation: jockey said gelding lost a front shoe (op 8-1)
Commander Cave(USA), having his first run since finishing in mid-division in the Britannia, proved very disappointing. (op 9-2)
Presumptive(IRE) was always towards the rear. (tchd 11-1)

5314 GG CLUB MAIDEN AUCTION STKS 1m

5:05 (5:07) (Class 5) 2-Y-O **£3,238** (£963; £481; £240) **Stalls** High

Form RPR

0 **1** **Orsippus (USA)**[15] 4861 2-8-10 0 .... SamHitchcott 17 75
(M R Channon) *bhd: hdwy 5f out: rdn over 2f out: styd on to ld over 1f out: rn green ent fnl f fnd ex whn hrd pressed wl ins fnl f* **20/1**

40 **2** hd **Perfect Shot (IRE)**[36] 4184 2-8-12 0 .... MartinDwyer 9 77
(J L Dunlop) *bhd: hdwy 3f out: rdn over 2f out: gd hdwy 2f out: str chal ins fnl f: hld nr fin* **13/2**

0 **3** 1 1/4 **La Diosa (IRE)**[32] 4296 2-8-9 0 .... MichaelHills 4 71
(W J Haggas) *bhd: hdwy 3f out: rdn over 2f out: styd on to press ldrs ins fnl f: no ex fnl 100yds* **16/1**

5 **4** 7 **Mr Udagawa**[32] 4305 2-9-0 0 .... SebSanders 6 60
(R M Beckett) *in tch: hdwy over 3f out: ev ch and rdn over 2f out: fdd fnl f* **7/2**[1]

0 **5** nk **Flashgun (USA)**[17] 4780 2-9-0 0 .... ShaneKelly 15 60
(M G Quinlan) *s.i.s: t.k.h: hld up in midfield: hdwy 3f out: chsd ldrs and drvn whn nt clr run and swtchd rt over 1f out: no imp after* **14/1**

03 **6** 1 1/4 **Peter Grimes (IRE)**[10] 5022 2-8-12 0 .... FrancisNorton 3 55
(H J L Dunlop) *chsd ldrs: rdn and effrt 3f out: ev ch u.p ent fnl 2f: wkng whn hmpd over 1f out: wl btn fnl f* **9/2**[2]

0 **7** shd **Sequillo**[16] 4826 2-9-1 0 .... RichardHughes 1 58
(R Hannon) *t.k.h: chsd ldrs: led 3f out: rdn over 2f out: edgd lft wl over 1f out: sn hdd: wknd qckly fnl f* **11/2**[3]

00 **8** nk **Vien (IRE)**[64] 3267 2-8-10 0 .... PatDobbs 5 52
(R Hannon) *racd in midfield on outer: rdn and effrt over 3f out: no prog and wl hld fnl 2f* **33/1**

0 **9** 2 **Foxtrot Charlie**[18] 4728 2-8-10 0 .... StephenCarson 16 48
(P Winkworth) *rn green: in tch tl bustled along and lost pl 5f out: plugged on fnl 2f: nvr trbld ldrs* **20/1**

10 shd **Aurorian (IRE)** 2-8-11 0 .... PatrickHills(3) 13 52
(R Hannon) *s.i.s: sn rcvrd and in tch: hdwy over 3f out: ev ch and rdn over 2f out: keeping on same pce whn hmpd wl over 1f out: no ch after: eased fnl f* **16/1**

000 **11** *4 1/2* **Daily Planet (IRE)**[24] 4570 2-8-10 0.................................... JohnEgan 11 38
(B W Duke) *chsd ldrs: rdn 1/2-way: struggling fr 3f out: no ch and eased ins fnl f* **66/1**

64 **12** *1/2* **Mykingdomforahorse**[10] 5021 2-8-10 0.................................... TPO'Shea 2 37
(M R Channon) *a bhd: sme late hdwy: nvr a factor* **9/1**

13 *nk* **Wilfred Pickles (IRE)** 2-9-0 0.................................... JimCrowley 18 40
(Mrs A J Perrett) *in tch: rdn over 2f out: wkng whn hmpd over 1f out: wl btn after: tired and eased ins fnl f* **10/1**

0505 **14** *1/2* **Forster Island**[13] 4933 2-8-9 53.................................(b) JimmyQuinn 12 34
(M Blanshard) *racd in midfield: effrt and rdn 3f out: no hdwy whn nt clr run and swtchd rt over 1f out: no ch after* **33/1**

00 **15** *2* **My Choice**[18] 4728 2-8-9 0.................................... SteveDrowne 8 29
(A P Jarvis) *a bhd: lost tch 1/2-way* **66/1**

16 *1/2* **Lily Of The Nile (UAE)** 2-8-6 0 ow5.................................... JackDean(5) 10 30
(J G Portman) *s.i.s: hdwy into midfield after 2f: struggling and rdn 1/2-way: no ch after* **28/1**

50 **17** *1 3/4* **Killmarnock**[60] 3372 2-9-0 0.................................... DaneO'Neill 7 29
(R A Teal) *racd freely: led tl 4f out: sn wknd: t.o and eased fnl f* **16/1**

000 **18** *11* **Craft (FR)**[52] 3645 2-8-12 48.................................(b1) WilliamBuick 14 3
(B J Meehan) *racd keenly: chsd ldr tl led 4f out: hdd 3f out: sn wknd: t.o fnl f* **33/1**

1m 45.63s (5.73) **Going Correction** +0.75s/f (Yiel) **18 Ran SP% 137.3**
Speed ratings (Par 94): **101,100,99,92,92 91,90,90,88,88 84,83,83,82,80 80,78,67**
toteswinger: 1&2 £45.90, 1&3 £95.80, 2&3 £33.10. CSF £151.06 TOTE £37.30: £9.80, £2.20, £8.20; EX 371.20.
Owner Mrs M Findlay **Bred** Stephen H Batchelder & Gainesway Farm **Trained** West Ilsley, Berks
■ Stewards' Enquiry : Dane O'Neill one-day ban: improper riding - struck gelding at the start (Sep 11)

FOCUS
Some decent horses have won this maiden in recent years, the best of them being Youmzain in 2005, but this looked a weak event in comparison.

NOTEBOOK
Orsippus(USA) did not show a great deal on his debut on the Polytrack at Lingfield, but he ran very green that day, and clearly that experience had taught him plenty as he was far more professional this time, finding plenty for driving and battling on well when strongly challenged inside the last. This was probably not a great race but he clearly enjoyed the ground, stays well and has the right attitude, so he should pay his way in handicap company, especially next year. (op 25-1)
Perfect Shot(IRE) was towards the rear turning into the straight, but stamina had looked his strong suit in his previous two starts and the extra furlong here saw him in a better light. A half-brother to six winners, he should not be too harshly treated when making his nursery debut, and looks one for middle-distance handicaps next year. (op 8-1)
La Diosa(IRE) was another who did not show a great deal on her debut, but shaped far more encouragingly this time. The colts just saw it out that bit better inside the last half furlong, but she finished well in front of the rest and clearly has a future. (op 25-1)
Mr Udagawa, for whom a Royal Lodge entry now looks a bit optimistic, had his chance from two furlongs out and, while he was on the stands' rail and the place to be all day had been a few horse widths off it, this was still a bit disappointing. (op 4-1)
Flashgun(USA), who travelled well into the straight, has a dirt pedigree and will be interesting if given an entry on the All-Weather. (op 12-1)
Peter Grimes(IRE) has now had the requisite three runs for a mark and may do a bit better in nursery company. (tchd 4-1)
Sequillo, who made his debut in a stronger race than this, failed to get home after having plenty of use made of him. (tchd 5-1, 13-2 and 15-2 in a place)
Aurorian(IRE) was in the process of running a promising race when badly hampered a furlong and a half out. He would have finished closer with a clear run and this son of Fantastic Light out of a mare who was able to win over 1m2f at two looks the type to do better over further as he gets older. Official explanation: jockey said colt suffered interference in running (op 14-1 tchd 20-1)

5315 TURFTV FOR BETTING SHOPS APPRENTICE STKS (H'CAP) 6f
5:40 (5:40) (Class 5) (0-70,70) 3-Y-O+ **£3,238** (£963; £481; £240) **Stalls** Low

Form RPR

5004 **1** **Kyllachy Storm**[7] 5121 4-8-3 51.................................... WilliamCarson(5) 9 64
(R J Hodges) *in tch: rdn and hdwy ent fnl 2f: drvn to ld over 1f out: styd on wl u.str.p fnl 100yds* **4/1**[1]

1155 **2** *3/4* **Linda Green**[17] 4767 7-9-3 65.................................... MCGeran(5) 1 76
(M R Channon) *hld up bhd: hdwy jst over 1f out: gd hdwy 1f out: chsd wnr ins fnl f: no imp fnl 50yds* **12/1**

3402 **3** *1 3/4* **Hart Of Gold**[5] 5171 4-9-3 65.................................... RichardEvans(5) 11 70
(R A Harris) *chsd ldrs: rdn over 2f out: carried rt and swtchd lft wl over 1f out: kpt on same pce ins fnl f* **9/2**[2]

0054 **4** *1/2* **Kempsey**[37] 4154 6-8-8 51 oh2.................................(b) MarcHalford 7 55
(J J Bridger) *sn pushed up to ld: rdn and hung rt fr jst over 2f out: hdd over 1f out: no ex ins fnl f* **20/1**

6002 **5** *nk* **Dualagi**[10] 5026 4-9-6 63.................................... WilliamBuick 3 66
(M R Bosley) *plld hrd: hld up bhd: grad edgd out rt over 2f out: rdn wl over 1f out: kpt on u.p fnl 100yds: nt pce to rch ldrs* **15/2**

0404 **6** *nse* **Unlimited**[3] 5198 6-9-8 65.................................... KirstyMilczarek 5 68
(A W Carroll) *stdd and bmpd s: plld hrd: hld up bhd: rdn 2f out: swtchd lft ins fnl f: r.o fnl 100yds: nt threaten ldrs* **15/2**

6402 **7** *1/2* **Don Pele (IRE)**[7] 5121 6-9-8 70.................................(p) RossAtkinson(5) 4 71
(R A Harris) *chsd ldr: ev ch and rdn 2f out: edgd rt over 1f out: wknd fnl 100yds* **6/1**[3]

-220 **8** *3/4* **Desert Pride**[29] 4431 3-9-8 68.................................... JamesMillman 10 67
(W S Kittow) *hmpd sn after s: hld up in tch: n.m.r over 1f out: sn rdn: no prog* **16/1**

5500 **9** *shd* **Contented (IRE)**[8] 5088 6-8-7 53.................................(v1) JackDean(3) 6 51
(Mrs L C Jewell) *wnt lft s: hld up in tch: hdwy over 2f out: chsd ldrs and rdn wl over 1f out: wknd jst ins fnl f* **15/2**

0000 **10** *5* **Ishibee (IRE)**[11] 4979 4-8-3 51 oh6.................................(p) SophieDoyle(5) 12 33
(J J Bridger) *hld up in tch in midield: rdn 2f out: wknd jst over 1f out* **33/1**

0044 **11** *6* **Bobby Rose**[16] 4824 5-9-1 58.................................... TravisBlock 2 21
(D K Ivory) *t.k.h: hld up in midfield: rdn and effrt jst over 2f out: wknd over 1f out: eased ins fnl f* **8/1**

1m 15.97s (3.77) **Going Correction** +0.75s/f (Yiel)
WFA 3 from 4yo+ 3lb **11 Ran SP% 120.2**
Speed ratings (Par 103): **104,103,100,100,99 99,98,97,97,91 83**
toteswinger: 1&2 £15.70, 1&3 £4.50, 2&3 £6.50. CSF £54.07 CT £232.74 TOTE £5.20: £1.90, £2.50, £2.10; EX 84.10 Place 6: £223.47, Place 5: £152.86..
Owner Mrs Angela Hart **Bred** Sir Eric Parker **Trained** Charlton Mackrell, Somerset
■ Stewards' Enquiry : William Carson seven-day ban: used whip with excessive frequency (Sep 8-14)

FOCUS
A modest handicap for apprentices in which only one of the runners had won a race in its last three starts, although it was still probably a fair race for the grade and the form has been rated slightly positively.
T/Jkpt: Not won. T/Plt: £347.20 to a £1 stake. Pool: £98,673.16. 207.45 winning tickets. T/Qpdt: £46.60 to a £1 stake. Pool: £5,499.50. 87.20 winning tickets. SP

[5158]YARMOUTH (L-H)
Sunday, August 24

OFFICIAL GOING: Good to soft (7.4)
Wind: Fresh, half against Weather: Overcast giving way to sunny spells from race 2 onwards

5316 E B F & EDP "MAKES NORFOLK LIFE COMPLETE" MAIDEN STKS 6f 3y
2:20 (2:21) (Class 5) 2-Y-O **£3,784** (£1,132; £566; £283; £141) **Stalls** High

Form RPR

420 **1** **Donativum**[68] 3105 2-9-3 87.................................... RobertHavlin 5 88+
(J H M Gosden) *chsd ldrs: led 1/2-way: rdn over 1f out: styd on wl* **2/1**[2]

24 **2** *1 1/4* **Magaling (IRE)**[26] 4510 2-9-3 0.................................... PatCosgrave 1 84
(L M Cumani) *hld up: hdwy to chse wnr over 2f out: rdn and ev ch over 1f out: styd on same pce fnl f* **10/11**[1]

5 **3** *8* **Tarzan (IRE)**[57] 3476 2-9-3 0.................................... RoystonFfrench 9 60
(M Johnston) *chsd ldrs: rdn over 2f out: sn hung lft: wknd over 1f out* **9/1**[3]

4 *hd* **Spinight (IRE)** 2-8-10 0.................................... AndreaAtzeni(7) 2 60
(M Botti) *hld up in tch: rdn and wknd over 1f out* **14/1**

50 **5** *4 1/2* **Mr Redford**[9] 5066 2-9-3 0.................................... TGMcLaughlin 6 46
(N P Littmoden) *hld up: rdn over 2f out: sn wknd* **28/1**

6 *1/2* **Celtic Rebel (IRE)** 2-9-3 0.................................... TPQueally 3 45
(S A Callaghan) *s.i.s: hld up: effrt over 2f out: sn wknd* **12/1**

0 **7** *4 1/2* **Strongarm**[16] 4826 2-9-3 0.................................... TedDurcan 8 31
(A Bailey) *hld up: hdwy over 3f out: wknd over 2f out* **33/1**

00 **8** *1* **Flamboyant Red (IRE)**[9] 5066 2-8-10 0.................................... KylieManser(7) 7 28
(Miss Gay Kelleway) *s.i.s and rdr lost iron s: racd keenly and led 5f out: hdd 1/2-way: sn rdn and wknd* **100/1**

00 **9** *5* **Minenotyours (IRE)**[27] 4474 2-9-3 0.................................... HayleyTurner 4 13
(D E Cantillon) *led 1f: chsd ldrs tl rdn and wknd over 2f out* **50/1**

1m 14.7s (0.30) **Going Correction** +0.15s/f (Good) **9 Ran SP% 119.4**
Speed ratings (Par 94): **104,102,91,91,85 84,78,77,70**
toteswinger: 1&2 £1.30, 1&3 £2.90, 2&3 £2.00. CSF £4.22 TOTE £3.20: £1.20, £1.10, £1.80; EX 3.90 Trifecta £3.70 Pool: £132.67, 25.90 winning units..
Owner H R H Princess Haya Of Jordan **Bred** Stratford Place Stud **Trained** Newmarket, Suffolk

FOCUS
An ordinary maiden.

NOTEBOOK
Donativum, not seen since finishing a highly creditable seventh in the Windsor Castle at Royal Ascot, had earlier showed useful form in defeat in maidens and the gelding operation he has undergone clearly made a difference. Always travelling strongly, Robert Havlin never had to get serious, just giving him a couple of slaps down the neck with the whip, and it will be interesting to see how he gets on in nurseries, with the promise of better to come. The slower ground apparently suited. (tchd 9-4)
Magaling(IRE) improved on his debut effort when a close fourth in a decent Goodwood maiden last month, and was solid at the head of the market. Running on slow ground for the first time, he was encouraged to take closer order at halfway and came through to hold every chance, but the winner was always doing too much. Clear of the third, an ordinary maiden is his for the taking, but connections now also have the option of nurseries. (op 5-4)
Tarzan(IRE) did best of the rest, keeping on at the one pace to just grab third. This was an improvement on his first effort and he still showed signs of greenness, so should progress again. He will be one to watch out for in 7f nurseries later in the season. (op 15-2 tchd 7-1)
Spinight(IRE), a 6,000gns son of Spinning World, fared best of the newcomers. Keen early on, he made headway travelling well over two out and kept on right the way to the line, but was no match for the front pair. He should learn from this and can probably find a modest maiden. (op 20-1 tchd 25-1)
Mr Redford should do better now eligible for handicaps. (tchd 33-1)
Celtic Rebel(IRE), a half-brother to the useful Celtic Sultan, was slowly away and never really threatened but should know more next time. (op 9-1)

5317 EVENING NEWS CHAMPIONS FILLIES' H'CAP 7f 3y
2:55 (2:55) (Class 5) (0-75,74) 3-Y-O+ **£2,838** (£637; £637; £212; £105) **Stalls** High

Form RPR

533 **1** **Shindy (FR)**[23] 4583 3-9-7 69.................................... TedDurcan 8 74
(J A R Toller) *hld up in tch: rdn to ld wl ins fnl f: r.o* **11/2**[2]

1000 **2** *1/2* **Debonnaire**[52] 3636 3-9-12 74.................................... RoystonFfrench 3 78
(M Johnston) *led: rdn over 1f out: hdd wl ins fnl f* **12/1**

0050 **2** *dht* **Dancing Duo**[158] 938 4-8-7 50.................................(v) SaleemGolam 4 56
(D Shaw) *hld up: hdwy over 2f out: sn rdn and hung rt: ev ch ins fnl f: kpt on* **25/1**

0504 **4** *1* **Savannah Poppy (IRE)**[9] 5073 3-9-11 73.................................... HayleyTurner 1 74
(M L W Bell) *hld up: hdwy u.p fr over 1f out: nt rch ldrs* **11/2**[2]

0300 **5** *3 1/4* **Djalalabad (FR)**[6] 5161 4-8-9 52.................................(t) AdrianTNicholls 7 47
(Mrs C A Dunnett) *hld up: hdwy and edgd lft over 1f out: sn rdn: wknd ins fnl f* **20/1**

61-5 **6** *1* **Rosy Alexander**[10] 5032 3-9-10 72.................................... AdamKirby 2 62
(S A Callaghan) *chsd ldrs: lost pl 1/2-way: n.d after* **11/1**

0435 **7** *1 1/4* **Selsey**[24] 4572 3-9-3 70.................................... Louis-PhilippeBeuzelin(5) 12 56
(Sir Michael Stoute) *prom: rdn over 1f out: edgd lft: wknd fnl f* **11/2**[2]

0001 **8** *1 1/2* **Convallaria (FR)**[16] 4825 5-8-13 56.................................(b) RobertHavlin 5 40
(G Wragg) *trckd ldrs: hmpd 2f out: sn rdn and wknd* **10/1**[3]

-041 **9** *1 1/4* **Siren Party**[11] 4987 3-9-11 73.................................... PatCosgrave 10 52
(L M Cumani) *s.i.s: hld up: hdwy over 2f out: shkn up and edgd lft over 1f out: sn wknd* **9/4**[1]

2040 **10** *7* **Bookiebasher Babe (IRE)**[17] 4795 3-9-4 66.................................... TPQueally 11 26
(M Quinn) *w ldr tl rdn 3f out: hmpd and wknd 2f out* **20/1**

005 **11** *9* **Star Acclaim**[44] 3916 3-9-8 70.................................... TGMcLaughlin 6 6
(T Keddy) *hld up: hdwy 1/2-way: sn rdn and wknd* **20/1**

1m 28.93s (2.33) **Going Correction** +0.15s/f (Good)
WFA 3 from 4yo+ 5lb **11 Ran SP% 120.2**
Speed ratings (Par 100): **92,91,91,90,86 85,84,82,80,72 62**
PL: Shindy £2.30, Debonnaire £4.40, Dancing Duo £5.60. EX: S&D £40.20, S&DD £95.00. CSF: S&D £33.07, S&DD £70.87. TRICAST: S-D-DD £778.89; S-DD-D £809.51. toteswinger: S&D £20.10, S&DD £29.10, D&DD £41.20. TOTE £6.90 TRIFECTA Not won..
Owner P C J Dalby & R Schuster **Bred** David Michael Adams **Trained** Newmarket, Suffolk
■ Stewards' Enquiry : Ted Durcan one-day ban: careless riding (Sep 9)

FOCUS
A tricky fillies' handicap, though it was no surprise to see the three-year-olds come out on top. Modest form.

Convallaria(FR) Official explanation: jockey said mare hung right

5318 GREAT YARMOUTH MERCURY H'CAP — 1m 3y

3:30 (3:32) (Class 6) (0-60,60) 3-Y-O+ **£2,266** (£674; £337; £168) **Stalls** Low

Form RPR

6600 **1** **Life's A Whirl**[6] 5161 6-8-10 **46**...............................(p) TGMcLaughlin 7 57
(Mrs C A Dunnett) *s.i.s: hld up: swtchd lft and hdwy over 2f out: rdn to ld and hung rt fr over 1f out: r.o* **12/1**

5060 **2** *2¾* **Circadian Rhythm**[17] 4796 3-8-8 **50**................................ RoystonFfrench 8 54
(S C Williams) *prom: swtchd rt over 6f out: chsd ldr 1/2-way: led over 2f out: rdn and hdd over 1f out: styd on same pce ins fnl f* **20/1**

0300 **3** *1½* **Poppets Sweetlove**[7] 5119 4-9-10 **60**................................ DavidKinsella 2 62
(A B Haynes) *hmpd s: hld up: hdwy 3f out: sn rdn: nt clr run over 1f out: styd on same pce ins fnl f* **8/1**

1363 **4** *¾* **Al Rayanah**[6] 5161 5-9-3 **53**...............................(p) SaleemGolam 1 53
(G Prodromou) *edgd rt s: hld up: hdwy over 2f out: rdn over 1f out: styd on* **5/1**[1]

-000 **5** *¾* **Ducal Pip Squeak**[16] 4806 4-8-7 **50**.............................. PNolan(7) 14 48
(A B Haynes) *sn led: rdn and hdd over 2f out: no ex ins fnl f* **20/1**

0200 **6** *1¼* **Charlie Bear**[8] 5088 7-8-12 **48**................................ AdamKirby 6 43
(Miss Z C Davison) *chsd ldrs: rdn over 2f out: no ex ins fnl f* **14/1**

0U40 **7** *1½* **Dawn Wind**[11] 4991 3-8-4 **46** oh1............................ RichardThomas 10 37
(I A Wood) *sn pushed along in rr: rdn over 2f out: styd on ins fnl f: nvr nrr* **28/1**

1 **8** *5* **Blue Savannah (FR)**[47] 3817 3-9-4 **60**........................ AdrianTNicholls 12 39
(G J Smith) *s.i.s: sn pushed along in rr: rdn over 3f out: n.d* **7/1**[2]

000 **9** *2¼* **Lavender And Lace**[17] 4774 3-8-4 **46** oh1..........(tp) FrankieMcDonald 5 20
(T Keddy) *chsd ldrs: rdn over 3f out: wknd over 1f out* **50/1**

0-00 **10** *4* **Too Hot To Handle (IRE)**[32] 4301 3-8-10 **55**.............. LukeMorris(3) 4 20
(J M P Eustace) *hld up: rdn over 3f out: sn edgd rt: n.d* **16/1**

0050 **11** *½* **Rain Stops Play (IRE)**[9] 5069 6-9-3 **53**.......................... PatCosgrave 9 18
(M Quinn) *chsd ldrs: rdn 1/2-way: sn wknd* **5/1**[1]

040 **12** *1¾* **Gee Ceffyl Bach**[6] 5161 4-8-8 **51**..........................(p) StacyRenwick(7) 15 12
(John A Harris) *chsd ldrs: rdn over 3f out: sn wknd* **14/1**

5051 **13** *3* **Josephine Malines**[43] 3963 4-9-10 **60**............................ TPQueally 16 14
(Mrs A Duffield) *prom: rdn 1/2-way: wknd 3f out* **15/2**[3]

0030 **14** *2¼* **Glitz (IRE)**[75] 2915 3-8-3 **52**...............................(v[1]) MatthewDavies(7) 13 —
(George Baker) *chsd ldrs: rdn and wknd over 3f out* **10/1**

00-0 **15** *7* **Jolie Fleur**[36] 4195 3-8-4 **46** oh1............................ HayleyTurner 11 —
(D E Cantillon) *sn pushed along in rr: bhd fr 1/2-way* **22/1**

1m 42.83s (2.23) **Going Correction** +0.15s/f (Good)
WFA 3 from 4yo+ 6lb **15** Ran SP% **124.0**
Speed ratings (Par 101): **94,91,89,89,88 87,85,80,78,74 73,72,69,66,59**
toteswinger: 1&2 £56.70, 1&3 £34.10, 2&3 £55.70. CSF £242.60 CT £2051.72 TOTE £18.90: £4.90, £12.50, £3.00; EX 315.10 TRIFECTA Not won..
Owner Life's a Whirl Partnership **Bred** The Queen **Trained** Hingham, Norfolk
■ Stewards' Enquiry : T G McLaughlin one-day ban: careless riding (Sep 7)

FOCUS
A competitive handicap in which all but two of the field were fillies or mares. Weak form which has not been rated too positively.
Charlie Bear Official explanation: jockey said horse was unsuited by the good to soft ground
Rain Stops Play(IRE) Official explanation: jockey said gelding lost a shoe

5319 WE LOVE YARMOUTH MERCURY H'CAP — 5f 43y

4:05 (4:07) (Class 5) (0-70,69) 3-Y-O+ **£1,844** (£1,844; £424; £212; £105) **Stalls** High

Form RPR

0035 **1** **Russian Rocket (IRE)**[74] 2950 6-8-8 **54**..................... AdrianTNicholls 5 64
(Mrs C A Dunnett) *hld up in tch: rdn and ev ch fr over 1f out: r.o to join ldr post* **10/1**

002 **1** *dht* **Diane's Choice**[17] 4767 5-9-8 **68**.. KShea 6 78
(Miss Gay Kelleway) *dwlt: hld up: hdwy to ld over 1f out: sn rdn: jnd post* **8/1**

0010 **3** *2* **Taboor (IRE)**[19] 4703 10-8-6 **52**................................ SaleemGolam 4 55
(R M H Cowell) *trckd ldrs: led briefly wl over 1f out: sn rdn: styd on same pce ins fnl f* **16/1**

411 **4** *hd* **Hurricane Harriet**[11] 4988 3-9-3 **65**.............................. TedDurcan 1 67
(R M H Cowell) *trckd ldrs: rdn and ev ch over 1f out: styd on same pce ins fnl f* **2/1**[1]

0620 **5** *shd* **Twosheetstothewind**[20] 4693 4-9-0 **60**.......................... HayleyTurner 9 62
(C R Dore) *mde most over 3f: edgd lft and styd on same pce ins fnl f* **10/1**

4311 **6** *2* **Desperate Dan**[7] 5121 7-9-9 **69**..............................(p) TGMcLaughlin 7 64
(A B Haynes) *chsd ldrs: rdn 1/2-way: ev ch wl over 1f out: no ex fnl f* **5/1**[3]

0201 **7** *1¼* **Tyrannosaurus Rex (IRE)**[9] 5074 4-9-2 **62**............... DarrenWilliams 8 52
(D Shaw) *chsd ldrs: rdn and ev ch wl over 1f out: wknd ins fnl f* **7/2**[2]

0-53 **8** *1¼* **Smiddy Hill**[24] 4561 6-8-4 **50** oh2............................ RoystonFfrench 2 36
(R Bastiman) *w ldr tl rdn 2f out: wknd fnl f* **14/1**

64.31 secs (2.11) **Going Correction** +0.15s/f (Good)
WFA 3 from 4yo+ 2lb **8** Ran SP% **114.1**
Speed ratings (Par 103): **89,89,85,85,85 82,80,78**WIN: Diane's Choice £4.10, Russian Rocket £6.00. PL: DC £2.00, RR £2.70, Taboor £4.20. EX: DC&RR £32.70, RR&DC £31.10. CSF: DC&RR £41.37, RR&DC £42.77. TRICAST: DC-RR-T £621.59; RR-DC-T £633.72. toteswinger: DC&RR £9.60, DC&T £22.60, RR&T £15.40. 27 Trifecta £Owner Mrs Christine Dunnett Bred.
Owner The Dark Side **Bred** Green Pastures Farm **Trained** Exning, Suffolk

FOCUS
A field of largely exposed sprinters, but the form has been rated slightly positively.
Hurricane Harriet Official explanation: jockey said filly had no more to give
Tyrannosaurus Rex(IRE) Official explanation: jockey said gelding hung left-handed throughout

5320 EVENING NEWS LOCAL LIFE CLAIMING STKS — 1m 2f 21y

4:40 (4:40) (Class 6) 3-Y-O **£2,201** (£655; £327; £163) **Stalls** Low

Form RPR

2524 **1** **Golden Bishop**[17] 4796 3-9-3 65................................ HayleyTurner 6 69
(M L W Bell) *chsd ldr tl led over 7f out: pushed clr over 1f out: eased fnl strides* **5/4**[1]

0000 **2** *½* **Testimonial**[25] 4527 3-8-7 62.. TedDurcan 4 58
(E A L Dunlop) *hld up: rdn over 1f out: hung lft and r.o ins fnl f: nt rch wnr* **14/1**

0440 **3** *1¼* **Sparkling Montjeu (IRE)**[34] 4247 3-8-4 55.............. RoystonFfrench 2 53
(George Baker) *hld up: plld hrd: hdwy 1/2-way: rdn over 2f out: styd on* **9/2**[3]

4062 **4** *2¼* **Flash Of Fire (USA)**[11] 4990 3-8-6 51..................(b) LukeMorris(3) 3 53
(J M P Eustace) *prom: rdn over 2f out: hung lft over 1f out: no ex ins fnl f* **7/1**

6141 **5** *1¾* **Maddy**[11] 4990 3-8-5 56.. FrankieMcDonald 7 46
(G J Smith) *hld up in tch: chsd wnr over 3f out: rdn and edgd rt over 1f out: hmpd and no ex ins fnl f* **5/2**[2]

00-0 **6** *19* **Where To Now**[66] 3161 3-8-10 45.............................. RichardThomas 8 13
(Mrs C A Dunnett) *led: hdd over 7f out: rdn and wknd over 2f out* **40/1**

00 **7** *25* **Unique (IRE)**[56] 3530 3-9-1 0... TGMcLaughlin 5 —
(N P Littmoden) *s.i.s: hdwy over 8f out: rdn 1/2-way: wknd over 3f out* **33/1**

2m 10.52s (0.02) **Going Correction** +0.15s/f (Good) **7** Ran SP% **115.7**
Speed ratings (Par 98): **105,104,103,101,100 85,65**
toteswinger: 1&2 £4.80, 1&3 £2.40, 2&3 £6.50. CSF £21.74 TOTE £2.30: £1.60, £5.20; EX 25.00 Trifecta £131.70 Part won. Pool: £177.98, 0.74 winning units..The winner was claimed by S L Walker for £14,000. Flash of Fire was claimed by P R Chamings for £6,000. Testimonial was claimed by B G Powell for £9,000.

Owner Sir Thomas Pilkington **Bred** Sir Thomas Pilkington **Trained** Newmarket, Suffolk

FOCUS
An ordinary claimer in which the third and fourth look the best guides to the form.
Maddy Official explanation: jockey said filly had no more to give

5321 FIRSTBET £50 MATCHED TELEPHONE BETTING 0800 230 0800 APPRENTICE H'CAP — 1m 2f 21y

5:15 (5:15) (Class 6) (60-92,66) 4-Y-O+ **£2,072** (£616; £308; £153) **Stalls** Low

Form RPR

2244 **1** **Astrolibra**[40] 4054 4-8-13 **54**.. AshleyMorgan 5 60
(M H Tompkins) *hld up: hdwy over 3f out: rdn to ld over 1f out: edgd rt ins fnl f: r.o* **7/2**[1]

0-25 **2** *1½* **Wicked Lady (UAE)**[17] 4774 5-8-12 **53**.......................... MatthewDavies 4 56
(B J McMath) *trckd ldrs: led 2f out: rdn and hdd over 1f out: hung lft ins fnl f: styd on same pce* **11/2**

-140 **3** *1½* **Credential**[27] 4485 6-8-10 **54**.. BMcHugh(3) 2 54
(John A Harris) *led 1f: chsd ldr tl led over 3f out: rdn and hdd 2f out: styng on same pce whn hmpd ins fnl f* **5/1**[3]

160 **4** *nk* **Ruwain**[10] 5020 4-8-3 **49**... AndreaAtzeni(5) 7 48
(P J McBride) *prom: racd keenly: rdn and hung lft over 2f out: styd on* **13/2**

-006 **5** *hd* **Peas 'n Beans (IRE)**[18] 4751 5-8-2 **46** oh1...............(t) RosieJessop(3) 1 45
(T Keddy) *chsd ldrs: outpcd over 3f out: styd on fnl f* **25/1**

6-35 **6** *4* **Baan (USA)**[221] 185 5-9-7 **65**.. PNolan(3) 9 56
(P W D'Arcy) *hld up: hdwy over 2f out: hung lft and wknd over 1f out* **4/1**[2]

0-60 **7** *4* **Yab Adee**[24] 4568 4-8-13 **61**.. TalibHussain(7) 8 44
(M P Tregoning) *s.s: rdn 1/2-way: a in rr* **11/2**

0000 **8** *2½* **General Flumpa**[40] 4048 7-8-4 **50**................................. AmyScott(5) 10 28
(Miss Tor Sturgis) *led after 1f: rdn and hdd over 3f out: wknd over 2f out* **9/1**

2m 11.52s (1.02) **Going Correction** +0.15s/f (Good) **8** Ran SP% **116.8**
Speed ratings (Par 101): **101,99,98,98,98 95,91,89**
toteswinger: 1&2 £3.30, 1&3 £4.80, 2&3 £7.10. CSF £23.59 CT £96.35 TOTE £4.20: £1.80, £1.80, £1.80; EX 16.50 Trifecta £80.80 Pool: £173.74, 1.59 winning units..

Owner Mystic Meg Limited **Bred** Mystic Meg Limited **Trained** Newmarket, Suffolk

■ Stewards' Enquiry : Matthew Davies caution: careless riding

FOCUS
A weak handicap run in a slow time, and very limited form.

5322 EASTERN DAILY PRESS SHOP LOCAL H'CAP — 1m 6f 17y

5:50 (5:51) (Class 6) (0-65,65) 3-Y-O+ **£2,266** (£674; £337; £168) **Stalls** Low

Form RPR

-050 **1** **Rutba**[34] 4247 3-8-9 **46**...(v[1]) TedDurcan 11 60
(M P Tregoning) *chsd ldrs: rdn over 1f out: styd on to ld nr fin* **9/1**

0016 **2** *nk* **Benhego**[24] 4573 3-9-11 **62**.. SaleemGolam 7 76
(S C Williams) *chsd ldrs: led on bit over 3f out: rdn and hdd nr fin* **5/2**[1]

-424 **3** *5* **Red Lily (IRE)**[48] 3793 3-10-0 **65**................................. PatCosgrave 1 72
(J R Fanshawe) *broke wl: stdd and lost pl after 1f: hdwy over 4f out: rdn over 2f out: no ex fnl f* **5/2**[1]

03/0 **4** *3¾* **Pacific Ocean (ARG)**[6] 5163 9-9-6 **45**........................(bt) AdamKirby 3 46
(Miss Z C Davison) *hld up: rdn over 3f out: sn hung rt: styd on: nt trble ldrs* **20/1**

3316 **5** *1¾* **Chiff Chaff**[13] 4924 4-9-6 **48**...................................... TolleyDean(3) 9 47
(C R Dore) *chsd ldrs: rdn over 2f out: wknd ins fnl f* **8/1**[3]

-033 **6** *1* **Bruki (IRE)**[9] 5077 3-9-4 **62**...................................(bt) AndreaAtzeni(7) 10 60
(M Botti) *hld up in tch: rdn over 2f out: n.m.r over 1f out: sn wknd* **11/2**[2]

0305 **7** *1* **Miss Serena**[9] 5077 3-9-4 **55**................................. AdrianTNicholls 2 51
(Mrs P Sly) *hld up: hdwy and nt clr run over 1f out: nt rcvr* **9/1**

0000 **8** *6* **Bunty Malenoir**[11] 4991 3-8-8 **45**............................... TGMcLaughlin 6 33
(Mrs C A Dunnett) *chsd ldrs: rdn over 3f out: wknd 2f out: eased fnl f* **33/1**

000 **9** *¾* **Cwm Rhondda (USA)**[22] 4620 3-9-10 **61**........................ HayleyTurner 5 48
(P W Chapple-Hyam) *sn led: hdd over 3f out: rdn over 2f out: wknd over 1f out* **12/1**

0-00 **10** *6* **Al Mogeer (IRE)**[6] 5163 3-8-3 **45**.............................(bt[1]) NicolPolli(5) 8 23
(P J McBride) *hld up: rdn over 5f out: wknd over 3f out* **80/1**

6060 **11** *8* **Barley Moon**[8] 5105 4-9-6 **45**...(b) TPQueally 4 12
(T Keddy) *hld up: rdn over 4f out: sn wknd* **33/1**

3m 9.29s (1.69) **Going Correction** +0.15s/f (Good)
WFA 3 from 4yo+ 12lb **11** Ran SP% **123.2**
Speed ratings (Par 101): **101,100,97,95,94 94,93,90,89,86 81**
toteswinger: 1&2 9.50, 1&3 £9.10, 2&3 £2.80. CSF £32.48 CT £77.30 TOTE £11.00: £3.10, £1.60, £1.60; EX 40.00 Trifecta £144.80 Pool: £203.62, 1.04 winning units. Place 6: £681.83, Place 5: £624.38..

Owner William Lea Screed Mac's Plaster & Home **Bred** Shadwell Estate Company Limited **Trained** Lambourn, Berks

FOCUS
Two came clear in a weak handicap. The first three came here not fully exposed but there was plenty of dead wood in behind.

Rutba Official explanation: trainer's rep said, regarding running, filly benefited from a reduction in trip, being raced in first-time visor and appeared to be suited by the good to soft ground.

T/Plt: £977.20 to a £1 stake. Pool: £61,913.29. 46.25 winning tickets. T/Qpdt: £112.50 to a £1 stake. Pool: £4,789.80. 31.50 winning tickets. CR

5323 - 5328a (Foreign Racing) - See Raceform Interactive

BREMEN

Sunday, August 24

OFFICIAL GOING: Soft

5329a WALTHER J JACOBS-STUTENPREIS (GROUP 3) (F&M) — 1m 3f

4:10 (4:18) 3-Y-O+ **£23,529** (£7,353; £3,676; £2,206)

RPR

1 **Ashantee (GER)**[51] [3705] 3-8-8 .... DPorcu 8 102
(M Rulec, Germany) *hld up in rr: 9th st: hdwy over 2f out: led over 1 1/2f out: r.o wl* **41/10**[3]

2 *3/4* **Goathemala (GER)**[22] [4657] 3-8-8 .... AStarke 6 101
(P Schiergen, Germany) *a in tch: 6th st: hdwy 2f out: chsd wnr fr over 1f out: kpt on steadily* **21/10**[1]

3 *1 3/4* **Dawn Dew (GER)**[21] [4675] 3-8-8 .... JiriPalik 9 98
(P Schiergen, Germany) *hld up in rr: 8th st: brought wdst: rdn and hung lft 2f out: hdwy over 1f out: styd on fnl f* **11/1**

4 *nk* **Hobby**[66] [3153] 3-8-8 .... JamesDoyle 7 97
(R M Beckett) *a.p: 3rd st: kpt on steadily on far rail fnl 2f* **44/10**

5 *3 1/2* **Counterclaim**[35] [4234] 3-8-8 .... MGuyon 4 92
(H-A Pantall, France) *a in tch: 4th st: nvr able to chal* **33/10**[2]

6 *3/4* **Servenya (GER)**[70] [3073] 3-8-8 .... (b) WPanov 2 90
(J Hirschberger, Germany) *disp ld early: settled in 4th: 5th st: kpt on one pce fnl f* **132/10**

7 *nse* **Silver Mitzva (IRE)**[21] [4667] 4-9-5 .... (b) ASuborics 1 92
(M Botti) *hld up: 7th st: nvr a factor* **21/1**

8 *2* **Night Heart (IRE)** 3-8-8 .... ABest 5 87
(W Baltromei, Germany) *last to st: a bhd* **51/1**

9 *1 1/4* **Ianapourna (GER)**[21] [4675] 3-8-9 ow1 .... WMongil 10 86
(J Hirschberger, Germany) *led to over 1 1/2f out* **81/10**

10 *19* **Leni Riefenstahl (IRE)**[288] [6768] 3-8-8 .... StefanieHofer 3 52
(Mario Hofer, Germany) *trckd ldr: 2nd st: sn wknd* **22/1**

2m 22.04s (142.04)
WFA 3 from 4yo 9lb — 10 Ran SP% **130.8**
(including 10 euro stakes): WIN 51; PL 15, 14, 23; SF 181.
Owner Gestut Graditz **Bred** Gestut Graditz **Trained** Germany

NOTEBOOK
Hobby has been running against some top fillies in Britain this year and it was a shade disappointing she was unable to fare any better in this Group 3 contst. She was always well positioned, but could not quicken under pressure.
Silver Mitzva(IRE) could never get into the race on this step up in grade.

5300 DEAUVILLE (R-H)

Sunday, August 24

OFFICIAL GOING: Turf course - good to soft; all-weather - standard

5330a DARLEY PRIX MORNY (GROUP 1) (C&F) (STRAIGHT) — 6f

2:15 (2:18) 2-Y-O **£147,051** (£58,831; £29,415; £14,695; £7,360)

RPR

1 **Bushranger (IRE)**[28] [4465] 2-9-0 .... JMurtagh 11 116+
(David Wachman, Ire) *trckd ldrs: clsd up over 2f out: rdn 1 1/2f out: drvn to ld 150yds out: all out* **9/2**[1]

2 *1/2* **Gallagher**[23] [4588] 2-9-0 .... JimmyFortune 13 115
(B J Meehan) *a cl up: led wl over 1f out to 150yds out: kpt on u.str.p* **8/1**

3 *2 1/2* **Lord Shanakill (USA)**[25] [4517] 2-9-0 .... FergusSweeney 7 107
(K R Burke) *led over 3f out to over 1f out: one pce* **8/1**

4 *2* **Milanais (FR)**[21] [4677] 2-9-0 .... TJarnet 10 101+
(B De Montzey, France) *towards rr tl hdwy 1 1/2f out: r.o u.str.p to take 4th last strides* **50/1**

5 *hd* **Naaqoos**[22] 2-9-0 .... DBonilla 14 100
(F Head, France) *hld up towards rr: rdn over 2f out: hdwy to rch 4th 150yds out: one pce* **7/1**

6 *3* **Light The Fire (IRE)**[51] [3681] 2-9-0 .... LDettori 8 91
(B J Meehan) *a in tch: 4th 1 1/2f out: wknd fnl f* **16/1**

7 *3* **Silver Frost (IRE)**[21] [4673] 2-9-0 .... OPeslier 3 82
(Y De Nicolay, France) *in tch tl one pce fnl 2f* **7/1**

8 *1/2* **Ladouce (FR)**[26] 2-8-11 .... C-PLemaire 4 78
(Robert Collet, France) *mid-div: styng on whn hmpd 1 1/2f out: kpt on one pce* **40/1**

9 *2* **Classic Blade (IRE)**[45] [3876] 2-9-0 .... RichardKingscote 6 75
(Tom Dascombe) *pressed ldrs 4f* **6/1**[3]

10 *shd* **Lui Rei (ITY)**[28] [4472] 2-9-0 .... DVargiu 2 75
(A Renzoni, Italy) *mid-div towards stands' side: rdn and btn 2f out* **5/1**[2]

11 *snk* **Matwan (FR)**[29] [4441] 2-8-11 .... MickaelForest 15 71
(C Boutin, France) *cl up on outside tl wl over 2f out* **66/1**

12 *3* **Exceptional Art**[13] [4926] 2-9-0 .... CSoumillon 1 65
(P W Chapple-Hyam) *racd nr stands' rails: outpcd fr 1/2-way* **17/2**

13 *1/2* **Rileyskeepingfaith**[14] [4908] 2-9-0 .... EdwardCreighton 5 64
(M R Channon) *pressed ldrs: rdn and btn over 2f out* **40/1**

14 *2 1/2* **Baby Wood (FR)**[41] [4039] 2-9-0 .... SPasquier 12 56
(S Loeuillet, France) *led over 2f: wknd 2f out: eased fnl f* **25/1**

69.90 secs (-1.30) **Going Correction** -0.075s/f (Good) — 14 Ran SP% **124.9**
Speed ratings: **105,104,101,98,98 94,90,89,86,86 86,82,81,78**
PARI-MUTUEL: WIN 5.30; PL 2.20, 3.40, 4.20; DF 25.20.
Owner Derrick Smith **Bred** Tally-Ho Stud **Trained** Goolds Cross, Co Tipperary
■ Stewards' Enquiry : J Murtagh €200 fine: whip abuse
Jimmy Fortune €200 fine: whip abuse

FOCUS
The majority of Prix Mornys tend to promise more than they deliver, in that the prize's recent winners have, with a handful of notable exceptions, failed to build on their Group 1 triumph. However, this was an unusual Morny in a number of ways, not least because a 15-runner field turned up - the biggest since 1972 - and the race was not staged on a summer seaside swamp. Although it was no more than an average renewal in terms of the strength of the form, the front two were both significant improvers.

NOTEBOOK
Bushranger(IRE), whose jockey bided his time, did not make his challenge until one and a half out. Knuckling down to his task to take over the lead well nside the final furlong, he was put under strong pressure but responded well. A gutsy individual who has never been out of the first three in five races, he is engaged in all the top races and is likely to stay further. His owners have plenty of two-year-olds to place but they will not find a more genuine one among their large string. He equalled the race record on good to soft ground, which was very creditworthy.
Gallagher was dropped in behind the leading group and came to the head of affairs one and a half out, looking the likely winner at the furlong marker. He responded well to pressure but could not hold the winner. He is now likely to be aimed at the Middle Park Stakes, and the Mill Reef might well be taken on before.
Lord Shanakill(USA) was well up from the start but proved rather one-paced when things quickened up 300 yards from the line, although he was never seriously challenged for third. He may well do better over a longer distance in the future.
Milanais(FR), behind at the half way stage, was hampered one and a half out, but ran on well in the final stages without looking a threat to the first three. He can be considered a little unlucky.
Naaqoos was racing for only the second time, and it showed. Slow to get into his stride, he then found himself in the rear and, though he did make headway through the race, he looked green and never threatened. He is better than he showed here.
Light The Fire(IRE) settled behind the leading group, he tried to go with the others when things quickened up a furlong and a half out and was then one paced for the rest of the race.
Classic Blade(IRE), well up from the start, was already feeling the pace at the two-furlong marker. He just stayed on at the same pace and never really looked dangerous.
Exceptional Art, slowly into his stride, was never a danger but might be worth another chance. (op 8-1)
Rileyskeepingfaith was smartly away and went with the leaders until the two furlong pole, then gradually dropped away.

5331a DARLEY PRIX DE LA NONETTE (GROUP 3) (FILLIES) — 1m 2f

2:45 (2:50) 3-Y-O **£29,412** (£11,765; £8,824; £5,882; £2,941)

RPR

1 **Lady Marian (GER)**[21] [4675] 3-9-0 .... DBoeuf 10 116
(W Baltromei, Germany) *hld up: 9th st: gd hdwy 1 1/2f out: led jst ins fnl f: drvn out* **8/1**

2 *1/2* **Treat Gently**[56] [3543] 3-9-0 .... SPasquier 5 115
(A Fabre, France) *4th st: swtchd to rails and hmpd wl over 1f out: 2nd appr fnl f: r.o wl* **9/4**[1]

3 *2 1/2* **Albisola (IRE)**[22] [4657] 3-9-0 .... C-PLemaire 7 110
(Robert Collet, France) *s.i.s: 6th st: hdwy 2f out: disp 2nd 1 1/2f out: kpt on same pce u.p fnl f* **6/1**

4 *1 1/2* **Turning For Home (FR)**[28] 3-9-0 .... GMosse 9 107
(H-A Pantall, France) *hld up: last st: brought to outside and hdwy 2f out: rdn 1 1/2f out: one pce* **20/1**

5 *3* **Changing Skies (IRE)**[22] [4657] 3-9-0 .... LDettori 3 101
(B J Meehan) *led: rdn and hung rt wl over 1f out: hdd jst ins fnl f: one pce* **5/1**[3]

6 *1* **Belle Allure (IRE)**[77] [2877] 3-9-0 .... DBonilla 1 99
(R Pritchard-Gordon, France) *7th st: hdwy 2f out: one pce fr over 1f out* **8/1**

7 *3* **Muthabara (IRE)**[22] [4623] 3-9-0 .... RHills 8 93
(J L Dunlop) *sn cl up: 3rd st: rdn and btn over 1 1/2f out* **4/1**[2]

8 *3* **Yarastar**[51] [3705] 3-9-0 .... JVictoire 2 87
(H-A Pantall, France) *5th st: btn 1 1/2f out* **33/1**

9 *3* **Classic Remark (IRE)**[22] [4623] 3-9-0 .... MickyFenton 4 81
(H J L Dunlop) *trckd ldr: 2nd st: sn btn* **12/1**

10 *3* **Tremoto**[56] [3544] 3-9-0 .... (b) MDemuro 6 75
(F & L Camici, Italy) *7th st: nvr a factor: eased fnl f* **50/1**

2m 6.70s (-3.50) **Going Correction** -0.075s/f (Good) — 10 Ran SP% **121.3**
Speed ratings: **111,110,108,107,105 104,101,99,97,94**
PARI-MUTUEL: WIN 8.00; PL 1.90, 1.40, 1.60; DF 8.90.
Owner Rennstall Gestut Hachtsee **Bred** Count & Countess Von Stauffenberg **Trained** Germany
■ Stewards' Enquiry : L Dettori €300 fine: careless riding

NOTEBOOK
Lady Marian(GER) showed improved form for the change of tactics. She was held up in last but one as the field entered the straight. The filly then quickened well from one and a half out up the middle of the track and she took the lead running into the final furlong. This was a good performance by this German-trained filly and she will now be prepared for the Prix de L'Opera.
Treat Gently can be considered unlucky. She was well placed behind the leaders early on but had to be snatched up on the rail at the two furlong marker. Once balanced, she ran on again but never looked like going to the head of affairs. This distance was short of her best and she will now be aimed at the Prix Vermeille. (op 5-2)
Albisola(IRE) still had plenty to do coming into the straight and then looked dangerous when challenging for the lead a furlong and a half from the post. She did not go through with her challenge but it was still a decent effort. This filly is a mudlark and when the going changes in her favour later in the year, she should be followed.
Turning For Home(FR), held up for much of the race, came with a late effort up the centre of the track but was never a danger to the first three past the post.
Changing Skies(IRE) was asked to go from pillar to post and was still going well on entering the straight. She then hung to the left when apparently being frightened by an advertising panel and caused interference to the runner up. She was one paced throughout the last furlong and a half and her jockey was fined €300 for the problems the filly caused to several others.
Muthabara(IRE), quickly into her stride and well up from the start, was still well there entering the straight, but her effort petered out soon after. (op 7-2)
Classic Remark(IRE), another close to the leader in the early stages, was going nowhere soon after entering the straight.

5332a DARLEY PRIX JEAN ROMANET (GROUP 2) (F&M) — 1m 2f

3:15 (3:19) 4-Y-O+ **£54,485** (£21,029; £10,037; £6,691; £3,346)

RPR

1 **Folk Opera (IRE)**[24] [4549] 4-8-12 .... LDettori 9 111
(Saeed Bin Suroor) *mde all: qcknd over 1f out: drvn out* **11/4**[1]

2 *1 1/2* **Fair Breeze (GER)**[28] [4470] 5-9-0 .... J-PCarvalho 5 110
(Mario Hofer, Germany) *a cl up: 2nd st: chal fr 1 1/2f out: r.o u.p fnl f but could nvr worry wnr* **11/4**[1]

3 *1/2* **Hapsburg (FR)**[32] [4320] 4-8-12 .... IMendizabal 2 107
(E Libaud, France) *a in tch: 6th st on ins: 4th 1 1/2f out: styd on fnl f* **4/1**[2]

4 *shd* **Bahia Breeze**[15] [4855] 6-8-12 .... RyanMoore 4 107
(Rae Guest) *a in tch: 5th st: followed 2nd tl swtchd out over 1f out: styd on fnl f* **15/2**[3]

5 *snk* **Guardia (GER)**[24] 4-8-12 .... JVictoire 8 107
(A Fabre, France) *trckd wnr: 3rd st: styd on one pce fr wl over 1f out* **9/1**

6 *nk* **Altamira**[69] 4-8-12 .... ACrastus 3 106
(E Lellouche, France) *8th st: hdwy wl over 1f out: 5th ins fnl f: one pce* **20/1**

7	3/4	**Sweet Lilly**[11] 4977 4-8-12 ... EdwardCreighton 1 (M R Channon) *hld up in last to st: nvr able to chal* **14/1**	104
8	1/2	**Alix Road (FR)**[14] 4914 5-8-12 ... AlexisBadel 7 (Mme M Bollack-Badel, France) *dwlt: sn in tch: 7th st: nvr a factor* **22/1**	103
9	2 1/2	**Jalmira (IRE)**[16] 4832 7-8-12 ... WJLee 10 (C F Swan, Ire) *4th st: sn btn* **12/1**	98

2m 10.7s (0.50) **Going Correction** -0.075s/f (Good) **9** Ran SP% **118.6**
Speed ratings: **95,93,93,93,93 92,92,91,89**
PARI-MUTUEL: WIN 3.60; PL 1.30, 1.20, 1.40; DF 4.50.
Owner Godolphin **Bred** Abbeville And Meadow Court Partners **Trained** Newmarket, Suffolk

NOTEBOOK
Folk Opera(IRE) was really on song in this event. Taken into the lead soon after the start, she did not set a very fast pace but did quicken things up early in the straight. She never looked like being caught and finally won with something in hand. A very consistent individual and also a versatile one, she may well come back to France for the Prix Vermeille next month.
Fair Breeze(GER) gave 2lb to the winner and lost nothing in defeat. Never far from the head of affairs, she challenged consistently for the lead from one and a half out but could never make it to the lead. She has already won two Group races in France this season and has been marked down for the Prix de L'Opera. (tchd 5-2)
Hapsburg(FR), waited with in the early part of this race, made her challenge on the far rail in the straight. She was outpaced for a bit and then ran on again as the race came to an end. Certainly still on the upgrade, she is another to be aimed at the Opera.
Bahia Breeze, fifth rounding the final turn, was caught for speed early in the straight before running on again inside the final furlong. If the race had been truly run, she might well have taken second place.
Sweet Lilly was well behind for much of the time before running on one paced in the straight. Another who was surely unsuited by the race was run.

5333a DARLEY PRIX KERGORLAY (GROUP 2) 1m 7f
3:45 (3:49) 3-Y-O+ **£54,485** (£21,029; £10,037; £6,691; £3,346)

			RPR
1		**Ponte Tresa (FR)**[41] 4041 5-9-1 ... OPeslier 9 (Y De Nicolay, France) *hld up: 9th st: brought to stands' side: hrd rdn to ld 100yds out: drvn out* **25/1**	112
2	snk	**Mad Rush (USA)**[50] 3721 4-9-4 ... C-PLemaire 1 (L M Cumani) *mid-div: cl 7th st: brought wd and chal 1 1/2f out: drvn and ev ch fnl f tl unable qck last 80yds* **9/2**[2]	115
3	2 1/2	**Coastal Path**[66] 3154 4-9-6 ... SPasquier 2 (A Fabre, France) *a cl up: 4th st: led 1 1/2f out to 100yds out: one pce* **4/6**[1]	114
4	1	**Hi Calypso (IRE)**[24] 4549 4-9-3 ... RyanMoore 8 (Sir Michael Stoute) *hld up: last st: hdwy wl over 1f out: one pce fnl f* **16/1**	110
5	1	**Caudillo (GER)**[41] 4041 5-9-4 ... J-PCarvalho 3 (Dr A Bolte, Germany) *mid-div on outside: 5th st: brought wd and hrd rdn 2f out: kpt on one pce u.p* **16/1**	110
6	3	**Green Tango (FR)**[27] 4496 5-9-4 ... JCrocquevieille 10 (P Van De Poele, France) *hld up in rr: 8th st: styd on far side: kpt on one pce* **50/1**	106
7	2 1/2	**Royal And Regal (IRE)**[87] 2542 4-9-4 ... LDettori 7 (M A Jarvis) *a cl up: wnt 2nd on outside wl over 3f out: led ent st to 1 1/2f out: sn wknd* **6/1**[3]	103
8	6	**Varevees**[41] 4041 5-9-1 ... CSoumillon 4 (R Gibson, France) *a cl up: 3rd st: hrd rdn wl over 1f out: one pce* **20/1**	93
9	6	**Finalmente**[50] 3743 6-9-6 ... RHills 6 (S A Callaghan) *led after 2f tl ent st: wknd wl over 1f out* **25/1**	91
10	4	**Limatus (GER)**[27] 4496 7-9-4 ... DBoeuf 5 (P Vovcenko, Germany) *led 2f: reminders over 4f out: 3rd st: sn wknd: eased* **25/1**	84

3m 12.1s (-7.00) **Going Correction** -0.075s/f (Good) **10** Ran SP% **122.5**
Speed ratings: **115,114,113,113,112 110,109,106,103,101**
PARI-MUTUEL: WIN 17.90; PL 2.40, 2.10, 1.10; DF 78.60.
Owner Mme E Hilger **Bred** Paul Hilger **Trained** France
■ Stewards' Enquiry : O Peslier €200 fine: whip abuse

NOTEBOOK
Ponte Tresa(FR), third in this race last year, was bang on form on this occasion. The mare still had plenty to do coming into the straight and was brought right across to the stands side to make her final challenge. She quickened well and joined the battle for the lead at the furlong marker, then ran on gamely to the line. She will have just one more outing, in the Prix du Cadran, before being retired to stud.
Mad Rush(USA) was towards the tail of the field in the early stages and ran a fine race for a handicapper. He was brought a little wide to challenge coming into the straight and looked the likely winner when taking the lead just before the furlong marker. Although he battled on really gamely, he could not quite hold off the eventual winner, but he has certainly made his mark at Group level and will now be trained for the Melbourne Cup.
Coastal Path was a little disappointing but had not been out since his third place in the Ascot Gold Cup. Never far from the leading group, he made his challenge up the centre of the track but looked rather one paced during the final stages. He was giving weight to the winner and runner-up and this race will have done him good. He could be another for the Cadran.
Hi Calypso(IRE), last year's Park Hill winner, still had plenty to do coming into the straight and began to make a forward move from one and a half out. It looks as if she might be coming back to her best.
Royal And Regal(IRE) was quickly up with the leader and took the lead early in the straight, but he was a beaten force soon after. It was rather a disappointing effort from this rather one paced individual.
Finalmente went into the lead soon after the start but was beaten early in the straight.

4675 DUSSELDORF (R-H)
Sunday, August 24

OFFICIAL GOING: Good

5334a GROSSER PREIS DER STADTSPARKASSE DUSSELDORF (LISTED RACE) (F&M) 7f
3:50 (3:56) 3-Y-O+ **£13,235** (£5,515; £2,206; £1,103)

			RPR
1		**Chantilly Tiffany**[15] 4841 4-9-2 ... TMundry 10 (E A L Dunlop) *4th st: led on outside over 1f out: sn clr: rdn out* **3/1**[2]	103
2	4	**Zaya (GER)**[42] 4011 3-8-7 ... EPedroza 9 (A Wohler, Germany) **68/10**	88
3	1 1/2	**Atalia (GER)**[42] 4011 3-8-7 ... ASchikora 6 (Mario Hofer, Germany) **29/1**	84
4	3/4	**The Fairy (GER)**[28] 4-9-0 ... ADeVries 7 (J Hirschberger, Germany) **18/1**	84
5	shd	**Mona Lisa (GER)**[42] 4011 3-8-9 ... KatharinaWerning 3 (Mario Hofer, Germany) **77/10**	84
6	1 1/4	**Chamara (GER)** 3-8-9 ... FilipMinarik 2 (P Schiergen, Germany) **49/10**[3]	80
7	1/2	**Topkapi Diamond (IRE)**[41] 3-8-7 ... MCadeddu 1 (E Kurdu, Germany) **27/1**	77
8	1	**Alexa (GER)**[42] 4011 4-9-0 ... VSchulepov 11 (H J Groschel, Germany) **103/10**	76
9	3 1/2	**Flashing Colour (GER)**[35] 4233 4-9-4 ... THellier 5 (J Hirschberger, Germany) **8/5**[1]	71
10	nk	**Etoile Nocturne (FR)**[15] 4881 4-9-0 ... WCahill 4 (W Baltromei, Germany) **37/1**	66
11	11	**Sasphee (GER)**[64] 4-9-0 ... J-LSilverio 8 (E Kurdu, Germany) **25/1**	36

1m 26.32s (86.32)
WFA 3 from 4yo 5lb **11** Ran SP% **132.2**
WIN 40; PL 22, 28, 55; SF 404.
Owner Ballygallon Stud Limited **Bred** Ballygallon Stud Limited **Trained** Newmarket, Suffolk

NOTEBOOK
Chantilly Tiffany, who came right back to her best when finishing second at Ascot last time, had been found a relatively weak race for the grade and she sprinted clear to win with plenty in hand.

4578 OVREVOLL (R-H)
Sunday, August 24

OFFICIAL GOING: Good to soft

5335a MARIT SVEEAS MINNELOP (GROUP 3) 1m 1f
2:20 (2:20) 3-Y-O+ **£92,507** (£24,052; £11,001; £6,660; £4,440)

			RPR
1		**Appel Au Maitre (FR)**[82] 2708 4-9-4 ... FJohansson 11 (Wido Neuroth, Norway) *mid-div: hdwy 3f out: led wl over 1f out: drvn out* **9/4**[1]	95
2	1	**Tertullus (FR)**[33] 5-9-4 ... FDiaz 14 (Rune Haugen, Norway) *broke wl: stdd in tch: hdwy 4f out: kpt on same pce u.p fnl f* **137/10**	93
3	1	**Peas And Carrots (DEN)**[21] 4676 5-9-6 ... MSantos 9 (L Reuterskiold Jr, Sweden) *racd in 5th: stdy prog to go 3rd 1f out: kpt on one pce* **9/2**[3]	93
4	3 1/2	**Volo Cat (FR)**[21] 4-9-4 ... NCordrey 13 (B Olsen, Denmark) *s.i.s: hld up: rdn over 2f out: styd on fnl f: nrest at fin* **61/1**	84
5	hd	**The Pirate (DEN)**[17] 5-9-4 ... EspenSki 6 (Niels Petersen, Norway) *midfield: outpcd 4f out: styd on again fr over 1f out* **10/1**	84
6	1 1/2	**Regime (IRE)**[43] 3983 4-9-6 ... JamieSpencer 10 (M L W Bell) *hld up in midfield: hdwy 4f out: rdn and no ex fr over 1f out* **26/10**[2]	83
7	1	**Fly Society (DEN)**[21] 7-9-4 ... KAndersen 12 (S Jensen, Denmark) *in rr early: clsd up after 3f: btn wl over 1f out* **21/1**	79
8	2 1/2	**Dan Tucket**[21] 4676 3-8-11 ... JacobJohansen 15 (B Olsen, Denmark) *hld up in midfield: hrd rdn wl over 2f out: sn btn* **114/10**	74
9	1	**Angel De Madrid (CHI)**[70] 7-9-4 ... DPSanchez 7 (Rune Haugen, Norway) *s.s: rdn over 2f out: n.d* **36/1**	72
10	1	**Miss The Boat**[38] 6-8-13 ... PPinto 3 (A Lund, Norway) *chsd ldr: rdn 3f out: wknd over 1f out* **108/10**	65
11	8	**Alpacco (IRE)**[21] 4676 6-9-4 ... LennartHammer-Hansen 1 (L Kelp, Denmark) *chsd ldrs tl wkng over 2f out* **22/1**	54
12	8	**Hovman (DEN)**[24] 4578 9-9-4 ... LSantos 8 (Ms C Erichsen, Norway) *led: rdn 3f out: hdd & wknd wl over 1f out* **29/1**	38

1m 50.3s (0.40)
WFA 3 from 4yo+ 7lb **12** Ran SP% **125.7**
TOTE: WIN 3.26; PL 1.59, 2.68, 1.42; DF 44.61.
Owner Stall Perlen **Bred** Gilles & Aliette Forien **Trained** Norway

NOTEBOOK
Regime(IRE), a winner at this level earlier in the season, likes plenty of cut in the ground and he looked set to take the beating, but having crept into it, the response was limited and he could find no more.

5336a ERIK O STEENS MEMORIAL (LISTED RACE) (F&M) 1m 4f
5:00 (5:00) 3-Y-O+ **£18,501** (£9,251; £4,440; £2,960; £1,850)

			RPR
1		**Dancing Abbie (USA)**[36] 4196 3-8-13 ... JamieSpencer 4 (M L W Bell) *hld up: hdwy 3f out: led 1f out: drvn out* **28/10**[2]	87
2	1	**Hot Fudge (SWE)**[21] 4676 5-9-0 ... FJohansson 6 (L Reuterskiold Jr, Sweden) **31/10**[3]	76
3	1/2	**Novasky (SWE)**[14] 4917 6-9-13 ... ManuelMartinez 2 (T Gustafsson, Sweden) **111/10**	88
4	4	**Will Be (IRE)**[82] 5-9-4 ... P-AGraberg 1 (B Bo, Sweden) **109/10**	73
5	5	**What Budget**[683] 5906 4-9-4 ... (b) TinaSmith 3 (A Lund, Norway) **17/1**	65
6	2 1/2	**Negra Del Oro (GER)**[343] 5-9-0 ... LennartHammer-Hansen 8 (A Lund, Norway) **19/10**[1]	57
7	1 1/2	**Distant Star (FR)** 3-8-13 ... FDiaz 7 (W Neuroth) **94/10**	64
8	hd	**Lumen (FR)**[21] 4676 6-9-4 ... MLarsen 5 (O Larsen, Sweden) **97/10**	58

2m 37.5s (3.40)
WFA 3 from 4yo+ 10lb **8** Ran SP% **126.4**
TOTE: WIN 3.80; PL 2.59, 1.94, 3.00; DF 17.02.
Owner Sheikh Marwan Al Maktoum **Bred** Ttee Of Hines Family Trust **Trained** Newmarket, Suffolk

NOTEBOOK
Dancing Abbie(USA), third in a Group 3 at San Siro on her penultimate outing, has form on similar ground and she came through to lead over a furlong out, always doing enough once in front. This is her level.

[4704]CHEPSTOW (L-H)

Monday, August 25

5337 Meeting Abandoned - Waterlogged

[5046]KEMPTON (A.W) (R-H)

Monday, August 25

OFFICIAL GOING: Standard
Wind: Moderate, across

5344 BET US OPEN TENNIS - BETDAQ E B F MEDIAN AUCTION MAIDEN STKS — 7f (P)

2:10 (2:10) (Class 5) 2-Y-O — **£3,885** (£1,156; £577; £288) **Stalls** High

Form — RPR

1 **Captain Ramius (IRE)** 2-9-3 0 .... JamieSpencer 3 — 80+
(M J Wallace) *trckd ldr: rdn and qcknd to ld over 1f out: pushed clr* **13/2**[3]

0 **2** *2½* **Ysing Yi**[12] 4960 2-9-3 0 .... TedDurcan 5 — 70+
(K A Ryan) *chsd ldrs: outpcd 2f out: rdn and r.o fnl f to go 2nd towards fin* **9/1**

3 *½* **Cheam Forever (USA)** 2-9-3 0 .... SteveDrowne 4 — 69+
(R Charlton) *s.i.s: sn mid-div: hdwy appr fnl f: r.o: nvr nrr* **12/1**

6 **4** *hd* **Shooting Party (IRE)**[22] 4665 2-9-3 0 .... RichardHughes 12 — 68
(R Hannon) *mid-div: outpcd 2f out: hdwy appr fnl f: styd on* **9/4**[1]

2 **5** *3* **Learo Dochais (USA)**[48] 3821 2-9-3 0 .... EddieAhern 9 — 61
(M J Wallace) *trckd ldrs: rdn 2f out: one pce fnl f* **11/4**[2]

0 **6** *1* **Primo Dilettante**[18] 4776 2-9-3 0 .... ShaneKelly 7 — 58
(W J Knight) *led tl rdn and hdd over 1f out: wknd fnl f* **16/1**

7 *1½* **Tobond (IRE)** 2-8-10 0 .... AndreaAtzeni(7) 6 — 54+
(M Botti) *pushed along in rr: nvr nr to chal* **16/1**

8 *1½* **Sunshine Ellie** 2-8-12 0 .... AdamKirby 11 — 46
(C G Cox) *towards rr: no hdwy fnl 2f* **14/1**

00 **9** *1½* **Monte Mayor Eagle**[70] 3085 2-8-12 0 .... FrancisNorton 2 — 42
(D Haydn Jones) *t.k.h: prom on outside to 1/2-way: lost tch 2f out* **66/1**

10 *2* **Royal Toerag** 2-9-3 0 .... PaulDoe 1 — 42
(W J Knight) *v.s.a: rdn over 2f out: nvr on terms* **25/1**

11 *2* **Kessraa (IRE)** 2-9-3 0 .... TPO'Shea 10 — 37
(M R Channon) *slowly away: sn pushed along in rr and nvr got into r* **12/1**

1m 28.45s (2.45) **Going Correction** +0.025s/f (Slow) — **11** Ran SP% **119.9**
Speed ratings (Par 94): **87,84,83,83,79 78,77,75,73,71 69**
toteswinger: 1&2 £6.90, 1&3 £4.50, 2&3 £7.90. CSF £65.19 TOTE £7.70: £2.20, £2.80, £3.00; EX 67.20.
Owner Mrs Clodagh McStay **Bred** P G Lyons **Trained** Newmarket, Suffolk

FOCUS
A fair juvenile maiden, but they went a modest pace early on and as a result there was not the usual advantage to high drawn horses. The winning time was 2.72 seconds slower than the following 56-75 handicap for three-year-olds and upwards. The first two are likely improvers although the time limits the race for now.

NOTEBOOK
Captain Ramius(IRE) set punters a bit of a poser, as he had Spencer booked for his debut, yet his trainer also sent out Learo Dochais, who had already shown ability and had been forecast to go off as favourite, but this colt proved the answer. An 80,000euros purchase as a foal, half-brother to very smart multiple 6f-7f winner Kingsgate Prince, and 1m winner Smuggler's Bay and fitted with a cross-noseband, he showed a nice turn of foot when asked to go in the straight. He very much had the run of the race, so it would be unwise to get carried away, but he was given a good education by Spencer before easing up close home, and there should be more to come. His trainer thinks he will make up into a nice horse next year. (op 5-1 tchd 7-1)
Ysing Yi showed very limited form on his debut over an extended 7f on easy ground at Beverley, but that experience has clearly brought him on and this was better. Having travelled well to a point just off the leaders, he did not pick immediately when asked, but kept on to grab second in a bunch finish for that position. (op 12-1 tchd 8-1)
Cheam Forever(USA), a 40,000gns half-brother to a modest winner over 1m plus in the US, out of a winner on the turf in the States, did not help his chance by racing keenly early on, but he kept on in the straight and showed ability. He is entitled to come on for this, but one would want to see him settle better next time. (op 8-1)
Shooting Party(IRE) was strongly supported to improve on his debut sixth over 6f at Newbury, but he did not make use of his favourable high draw and was stuck in about sixth, a few lengths off the pace at halfway. He ran on in the straight, but could not muster the pace to land a telling blow. (op 9-2)
Learo Dochais(USA) proved easy to back, but still went off a shorter price than his winning stablemate. He was well placed early, but failed to pick up in the straight and could not build on his debut second over this trip at Wolverhampton. (op 9-4 tchd 3-1 in places)
Primo Dilettante had the run of the race in front and can have no excuses. (op 20-1)
Tobond(IRE), a son of Tobougg, ran green early on after missing the break and will have learnt plenty. (op 20-1)
Kessraa(IRE), a 150,000euros son of Kheleyf, was coltish beforehand and seemed to find this first experience all too much. (op 10-1 tchd 9-1)

5345 BRENDANPOWELLRACING.COM H'CAP — 7f (P)

2:45 (2:45) (Class 5) (0-75,75) 3-Y-O+ — **£3,238** (£963; £481; £240) **Stalls** High

Form — RPR

5456 **1** **Landucci**[34] 4268 7-9-1 **67** ....(v1) PatrickHills(3) 6 — 81
(J W Hills) *t.k.h in mid-div: rdn and hdwy to ld appr fnl f: sn clr* **14/1**

1432 **2** *2¾* **All In The Red (IRE)**[7] 5162 3-9-2 **70** ....(b) JimmyFortune 10 — 75
(Miss Gay Kelleway) *hmpd sn after s: mid-div: hdwy over 1f out: r.o to go 2nd wl ins fnl f* **11/2**[3]

404 **3** *1* **Blow Hole (USA)**[19] 4730 3-9-4 **72** .... ShaneKelly 9 — 74
(J Noseda) *a.p: rdn to chal appr fnl f: nt qckn ins fnl f* **4/1**[2]

0650 **4** *¾* **Carmenero (GER)**[7] 5156 5-9-9 **72** .... MartinDwyer 12 — 74
(W R Muir) *hmpd sn after s: mid-div: on terms whn squeezed out wl over 1f out: r.o fnl f* **14/1**

1060 **5** *1* **Divertimenti (IRE)**[39] 4121 4-9-11 **74** ....(p) SebSanders 7 — 73
(C R Dore) *chsd ldrs: led over 2f out: hdd appr fnl f: no ex* **25/1**

0020 **6** *2¾* **Adantino**[14] 4934 9-9-4 **67** ....(b) GeorgeBaker 11 — 59
(B R Millman) *towards rr: effrt over 2f out: wknd fnl f* **16/1**

0501 **6** *dht* **Royal Island (IRE)**[20] 4707 6-9-12 **75** .... JamieSpencer 14 — 67
(M G Quinlan) *hmpd sn after s: in rr whn swtchd lft over 2f out: r.o but nvr nr to chal* **10/3**[1]

0033 **8** *1* **Sedge (USA)**[21] 4679 8-9-2 **65** ....(b) EddieAhern 1 — 54
(P T Midgley) *towards rr: mde sme late hdwy* **20/1**

0046 **9** *¾* **Last Of The Line**[10] 5052 3-9-1 **69** ....(v) SteveDrowne 2 — 54
(H J L Dunlop) *hld up: sme hdwy 2f out: nvr on terms* **40/1**

0625 **10** *¾* **Bold Argument (IRE)**[23] 4639 5-8-11 **65** .... JackMitchell(5) 8 — 50
(Mrs P N Dutfield) *a towards rr* **16/1**

0224 **11** *2* **Don Pietro**[20] 4710 5-9-7 **70** ....(b) FrancisNorton 4 — 50
(P A Blockley) *t.k.h: carried rt sn after s: chsd ldr tl wknd over 1f out* **12/1**

0005 **12** *2¾* **Dickie Le Davoir**[3] 5222 4-9-11 **74** .... PatCosgrave 5 — 46
(John A Harris) *in rr: effrt over 2f out: wknd appr fnl f* **10/1**

2014 **13** *1* **Sovereignty (JPN)**[21] 4696 6-9-3 **66** .... JimCrowley 13 — 35
(D K Ivory) *prom tl wknd 2f out* **8/1**

0005 **14** *8* **Namid Reprobate (IRE)**[39] 4129 5-9-4 **67** ....(b) RichardHughes 3 — 15
(P F I Cole) *c over to stands' side fr wd draw and led tl hdd over 2f out: wknd qckly and eased* **25/1**

1m 25.73s (-0.27) **Going Correction** +0.025s/f (Slow)
WFA 3 from 4yo+ 5lb — **14** Ran SP% **126.3**
Speed ratings (Par 103): **102,98,97,96,95 92,92,91,90,89 87,84,83,74**
toteswinger: 1&2 £16.10, 1&3 £19.90, 2&3 £4.10. CSF £89.92 CT £380.57 TOTE £16.20: £5.50, £2.10, £1.90; EX 79.90.
Owner R J Tufft **Bred** D J And Mrs Deer **Trained** Upper Lambourn, Berks

■ Stewards' Enquiry : Richard Hughes four-day ban: careless riding (Sep 8-11)
Shane Kelly two-day ban: careless riding (Sep 8-9)

FOCUS
Just a fair handicap contested by mainly exposed sorts and rated through the winner to his early season form with the third to maiden form. The winning time was 2.72 seconds quicker than the opening two-year-old maiden.

5346 HAPPY BIRTHDAY TOPNAPS.COM H'CAP — 6f (P)

3:20 (3:22) (Class 5) (0-75,78) 3-Y-O — **£3,238** (£963; £481; £240) **Stalls** High

Form — RPR

6004 **1** **Geoffdaw**[19] 4745 3-9-0 **68** ....(v1) EddieAhern 11 — 78
(M J Wallace) *chsd ldrs: rdn over 1f out: led ins fnl f: sn clr* **10/1**

5523 **2** *2½* **Dan Chillingworth (IRE)**[12] 4989 3-9-4 **72** .... JamieSpencer 1 — 74
(J R Fanshawe) *in tch on outside: outpcd over 2f out: r.o strly fnl f to go 2nd cl home* **6/1**[3]

3131 **3** *nk* **Bazguy**[10] 5050 3-9-2 **70** ....(b) JimmyFortune 10 — 71
(P D Evans) *led: rdn over 1f out: nt qckn: hdd ins fnl f and lost 2nd cl home* **9/2**[1]

1066 **4** *shd* **Vigano (IRE)**[10] 5056 3-9-4 **72** .... RichardHughes 5 — 73
(S Kirk) *stdd s: hld up towards rr: styd on fnl f: nvr nrr* **9/1**

3200 **5** *2½* **Prime Factor**[16] 4864 3-9-7 **75** .... TedDurcan 12 — 68
(B W Hills) *s.i.s: rdn and sn in tch: rdn over 2f out: one pce fnl f* **9/2**[1]

0133 **6** *1* **River Bounty**[11] 5026 3-8-11 **65** .... SebSanders 8 — 55
(A P Jarvis) *disp 2nd to 2f out: nt qckn and fdd ins fnl f* **11/2**[2]

3221 **7** *½* **Artistic License (IRE)**[7] 5142 3-9-10 **78** 6ex .... TPO'Shea 2 — 66+
(M R Channon) *in rr: rdn over 2f out: one pce after* **9/2**[1]

3-30 **8** *1* **Fabuleux Cherie**[10] 5046 3-8-13 **67** .... MartinDwyer 6 — 52
(W R Muir) *trckd ldr tl rdn and one pce fnl 2f* **25/1**

-340 **9** *nk* **A Wish For You**[21] 4693 3-9-3 **71** .... JimCrowley 7 — 55
(D K Ivory) *t.k.h in rr: hung rt fr over 2f out and nvr on terms* **33/1**

0001 **10** *2½* **Deal Flipper**[13] 4943 3-8-11 **65** .... FrankieMcDonald 4 — 41
(P Winkworth) *a in rr* **14/1**

5066 **11** *6* **Miss Clonyn (IRE)**[30] 4431 3-9-6 **74** .... RichardThomas 9 — 31
(Christian Wroe) *mid-div tl outpcd over 2f out: wknd over 1f out* **40/1**

1m 13.14s (0.04) **Going Correction** +0.025s/f (Slow) — **11** Ran SP% **119.2**
Speed ratings (Par 100): **100,96,96,96,92 91,90,89,89,85 77**
toteswinger: 1&2 £15.40, 1&3 £13.40, 2&3 £7.40. CSF £68.74 CT £318.69 TOTE £13.40: £3.70, £2.10, £2.20; EX 105.70.
Owner Mike & Denise Dawes **Bred** Barton Stud Partnership **Trained** Newmarket, Suffolk

FOCUS
A reasonable three-year-old sprint handicap. They went a strong pace and the winning time was only 0.85 seconds slower than the following 86-105 handicap for three-year-olds and upwards and the form looks pretty ordinary.

5347 BETDAQ THE BETTING EXCHANGE H'CAP — 6f (P)

3:55 (3:56) (Class 2) (0-105,105) 3-Y-O+
£11,215 (£3,358; £1,679; £840; £419; £210) **Stalls** High

Form — RPR

546- **1** **Warsaw (IRE)**[346] 5377 3-9-2 **100** ....(b1) KShea 8 — 109
(M F De Kock, South Africa) *a in tch: rdn 2f out: r.o to ld fnl 110yds* **16/1**

300 **2** *¾* **Ebraam (USA)**[9] 5109 5-9-3 **98** .... IanMongan 3 — 105
(P Howling) *trckd ldrs: led 2f out: rdn hdd fnl 110yds* **20/1**

0240 **3** *¾* **Mastership (IRE)**[30] 4405 4-9-1 **96** ....(v1) GrahamGibbons 12 — 101
(J J Quinn) *t.k.h in rr: hdwy 2f out: rn on to go 3rd ins fnl f* **11/4**[1]

4111 **4** *hd* **Shifting Star (IRE)**[16] 4842 3-9-1 **99** .... AdamKirby 9 — 103+
(W R Swinburn) *t.k.h in rr: hdwy 2f out: kpt on fnl f* **4/1**[2]

-150 **5** *nk* **Oldjoesaid**[29] 4445 4-9-10 **105** .... DaneO'Neill 2 — 108
(H Candy) *t.k.h in mid-div: rdn 2f out: r.o fnl f* **8/1**

4234 **6** *1¼* **Crystany (IRE)**[72] 3041 3-8-11 **95** .... TedDurcan 11 — 94
(E A L Dunlop) *a mid-div: rdn 2f out: kpt on fnl f* **12/1**

3500 **7** *nk* **Ashdown Express (IRE)**[23] 4624 9-9-0 **95** .... PaulDoe 6 — 93
(W J Knight) *s.i.s: plld hrd in rr though mde sme late hdwy* **20/1**

3050 **8** *¾* **Eisteddfod**[22] 4660 7-9-8 **103** .... NelsonDeSouza 5 — 99
(P F I Cole) *trckd ldr to 2f out: rdn and wknd ins fnl f* **20/1**

4056 **9** *nse* **Mac Gille Eoin**[16] 4840 4-9-3 **98** .... JimCrowley 1 — 93
(J Gallagher) *trckd ldrs on outside: rdn over 2f out: wknd fnl f* **13/2**[3]

0600 **10** *1¼* **New Freedom (BRZ)**[16] 4840 7-9-2 **97** .... EddieAhern 10 — 88
(D R Lanigan) *led tl hdd 2f out: wknd 1f out* **12/1**

-000 **11** *½* **Mutamared (USA)**[57] 3532 8-9-2 **97** .... FrancisNorton 7 — 87
(K A Ryan) *t.k.h in rr: no hdwy fnl 2f* **12/1**

11-6 **12** *¾* **Exclamation**[131] 1400 3-9-4 **102** .... JamieSpencer 4 — 89
(B J Meehan) *s.i.s: hung lft fnl 2f: a bhd* **8/1**

1m 12.29s (-0.81) **Going Correction** +0.025s/f (Slow)
WFA 3 from 4yo+ 3lb — **12** Ran SP% **125.5**
Speed ratings (Par 109): **106,105,104,103,103 101,101,100,100,98 97,96**
toteswinger: 1&2 £43.70, 1&3 £10.30, 2&3 £23.10. CSF £314.70 CT £1160.06 TOTE £13.70: £3.00, £8.10, £1.60; EX 231.00.
Owner Sheikh Mohammed Bin Khalifa Al Maktoum **Bred** Redpender Stud Ltd **Trained** South Africa

FOCUS
A decent, competitive sprint handicap and the form looks pretty sound rated around those in the frame behind the winner. They didn't go as quick as one might have expected early on and the winning time was only 0.85 seconds quicker than the previous three-year-old 56-75 handicap.

NOTEBOOK

Warsaw(IRE) was a decent early-season two-year-old for Aidan O'Brien last year, winning a Listed event on his second start, but he looked to have his limitations exposed in better company thereafter, and had not been seen since beating only two home in the Group 2 Flying Childers last September. Now with Mike de Kock, he had not been showing much in his homework according to jockey Kevin Shea, so he was tried in first-time blinkers and had his first start for new connections on Polytrack, a surface he had apparently taken a liking to. As it turned out, his master trainer got it absolutely spot-on, as the colt raced enthusiastically just in behind the speed and ran on strongly when asked to extend in the straight, recording a victory more decisive than the official margin suggests. He is a likely type for the Dubai Carnival. (tchd 14-1 and 20-1)

Ebraam(USA) was forced to race three wide from his low stall, but he was always close up and had every chance. He was well suited by the return to Polytrack, very much his favoured surface, and he probably ran into a pretty decent type for the level.

Mastership(IRE) tends to need cover in his races, so he could not take full advantage of his rails draw in the first-time visor (has worn blinkers). He travelled strongly just in behind the leaders, but was short of room and had to switch in the straight, by which time the first two had already been sent of their way. His run flattened out late on and he is the type who needs everything to fall right. (op 3-1)

Shifting Star(IRE) came into this searching for a four-timer following a hat-trick on turf, but he was up a further 7lb for his recent Shergar Cup success and 18lb higher than for his only previous try on sand, a close third over this trip at Lingfield in May. Produced with his challenge against the far rail in the straight, he fared best of those held up, but was never really getting there and probably would have preferred an even stronger pace to run at. (op 3-1)

Oldjoesaid has not had things go his way since winning a decent handicap at Newbury on his reappearance and stall two was no help this time. Stepping up from 5f, he would have preferred a stronger pace to run at as well, so he remains one to keep on-side. (tchd 17-2)

Crystany(IRE), the only filly in the line up, seemed unsuited by the less than frantic pace and gave the impression 5f, or a stronger-run race will suit better. (op 14-1)

Ashdown Express(IRE) would also have preferred a stronger pace. (op 25-1)

Mac Gille Eoin is better than he showed as he was forced to race widest of all. (op 10-1)

New Freedom(BRZ) has a tendency to hang right, so this track promised to suit, but he dropped out tamely and has not gone on since running well in the Wokingham on his British debut.

Mutamared(USA) was keen early and is another who would have preferred a better pace. (op 16-1)

Exclamation, a decent two-year-old last year who was having his first start since running sixth in the Free Handicap in April, was always out the back and hung right in the straight, proving virtually unsteerable. Official explanation: jockey said colt did not face the kickback (op 11-1)

5348 BETDAQ.CO.UK E B F CONDITIONS STKS 1m 3f (P)

4:30 (4:30) (Class 3) 3-Y-O+

£8,598 (£2,575; £1,287; £644; £321; £161) Stalls High

Form				RPR
2221	1		**Many Volumes (USA)**[52] 3683 4-9-8 111 ... TedDurcan 2 (H R A Cecil) *s.i.s: sn trckd ldr: rdn to ld over 1f out: in command fnl f* **2/1**[1]	119
2140	2	2 1/2	**Gravitas**[149] 1091 5-9-3 113 ... LDettori 1 (Saeed Bin Suroor) *t.k.h: disp 3rd pl: rdn and hdwy 2f out: kpt on to chse wnr fnl f* **6/1**	110
6-36	3	1 1/2	**Hearthstead Maison (IRE)**[30] 4436 4-9-3 114 ... GregFairley 5 (M Johnston) *led tl rdn and hdd over 1f out: one pce fnl f* **4/1**[3]	107
1004	4	1/2	**Dansant**[24] 4585 4-9-8 110 ... EddieAhern 3 (G A Butler) *hld up: rdn over 2f out: kpt on one pce* **9/4**[2]	111
-060	5	5	**Big Robert**[80] 2791 4-9-3 103 ... MartinDwyer 4 (W R Muir) *hld up: effrt 2f out: no hdwy after* **33/1**	98
1030	6	4	**Kandidate**[44] 3940 6-9-8 105 ... (t) JimmyFortune 6 (C E Brittain) *trckd ldrs: rdn 3f out: bhd fnl 2f* **8/1**	96

2m 19.09s (-2.81) **Going Correction** +0.025s/f (Slow) 6 Ran SP% 112.4

Speed ratings (Par 107): **111,109,108,107,104 101**

toteswinger: 1&2 £2.00, 1&3 £2.50, 2&3 £4.70. CSF £14.42 TOTE £2.90: £1.70, £2.90; EX 9.60.

Owner K Abdulla **Bred** Juddmonte Farms Inc **Trained** Newmarket, Suffolk

FOCUS

A really good conditions contest and the sort of field one would hope to see line up for a Listed event. However, the early pace was not that strong, resulting in the winning time being 0.55 slower than the following 71-90 handicap and those held up struggled to land a blow, so the form cannot be taken too literally with the runner-up and fourth the best guides. The main action took place closer to the stands' side in the straight.

NOTEBOOK

Many Volumes(USA) has improved from three to four and he supplemented his recent Sandown Listed success over 1m2f on this drop in grade over an extra furlong. He raced in a clear second for much of the way, tracking the sensible pace, and ran on strongly once taking over around two furlongs out, despite edging over towards the stands' rail. He deserves a step back up in grade and the Group 3 September Stakes back here over 1m4f, in which last year's winner of this went on to finish second, could be a suitable target. (op 9-4 tchd 5-2 in a place)

Gravitas, the winner of a Dubai Carnival handicap off a mark of 105 this year, was having his first start since finishing down the field in the Group 1 Sheema Classic in March and he ran about as well as could have been expected. He was keen enough off the modest pace in around mid-division, but finished well to take a respectable second. He switched around Many Volumes about a furlong out, but he was getting 5lb from that rival and was by no means unlucky. (tchd 11-2 and 5-1 in a place)

Hearthstead Maison(IRE) had run well on both his starts so far this year and he looked dangerous having escaped a penalty for last year's Group 3 success but, despite enjoying a very soft lead, he was below his best. This was his first experience of Polytrack and, on this evidence, he is better suited to turf. (tchd 7-2 and 9-2)

Dansant had won all three of his previous starts on Polytrack, with each victory being gained in Listed company, and he shaped well at Goodwood on his latest start, but he proved rather disappointing this time. His trainer could probably be in better form but, to be fair, stamina looks to be his strong suit, so the steady pace over a trip shorter than ideal was against him. (op 2-1 tchd 5-2 in a place)

Big Robert offered little on his first start since June.

Kandidate was unbeaten in three previous runs on the Kempton Polytrack, winning a decent handicap, a Group 3 and, most recently, a Listed contest. However, he came into this out of form having failed to beat a rival at Ascot on his latest start and he ran no sort of race, even allowing for the unsuitable steady pace. (op 9-1)

5349 BET PREMIER LEAGUE FOOTBALL - BETDAQ H'CAP 1m 3f (P)

5:05 (5:06) (Class 3) (0-90,90) 3-Y-O+

£7,477 (£2,239; £1,119; £560; £279; £140) Stalls High

Form				RPR
3-10	1		**Muhannak (IRE)**[45] 3929 4-9-13 89 ... SebSanders 5 (R M Beckett) *towards rr: hdwy on outside 2f out: drvn and r.o wl to ld fnl 50yds* **8/1**	101+
5100	2	1 1/4	**Tomintoul Flyer**[23] 4621 3-9-5 90 ... (v[1]) TedDurcan 10 (H R A Cecil) *trckd ldrs: led over 1f out: rdn and hdd fnl 50yds* **9/2**[2]	100
0-22	3	3	**Tastahil (IRE)**[103] 2103 4-9-13 89 ... MartinDwyer 3 (B W Hills) *sn mid-div: hdwy over 1f out: r.o to go 3rd nr fin* **3/1**[1]	94
3416	4	hd	**Downhiller (IRE)**[37] 4205 3-9-3 88 ... EddieAhern 2 (J L Dunlop) *chsd ldrs: rdn over 2f out: kpt on one pce* **12/1**	92
4114	5	3/4	**Press The Button (GER)**[31] 4363 5-9-0 83 ... HarryPoulton[(7)] 13 (J R Boyle) *led tl rdn and hdd over 1f out: wknd ins fnl f* **16/1**	86
3064	6	2 3/4	**Haarth Sovereign (IRE)**[18] 4771 4-9-2 78 ... AdamKirby 1 (W R Swinburn) *towards rr: styd on steadily ins fnl 2f* **8/1**	76
0150	7	1/2	**Calakanga**[51] 3720 3-9-4 89 ... RichardHughes 4 (C E Brittain) *in rr tl hdwy over 1f out: styd on: nvr nrr* **20/1**	87
0600	8	5	**Northern Spy (USA)**[10] 5051 4-9-2 78 ... DaneO'Neill 7 (S Dow) *in rr: mde sme late hdwy* **20/1**	67
3214	9	2	**Coin Of The Realm (IRE)**[22] 4662 3-8-13 84 ... JimmyFortune 11 (E A L Dunlop) *trckd ldrs to over 2f out: sn wknd* **14/1**	70
0600	10	1/2	**Master Pegasus**[11] 5033 5-8-9 71 ... PatCosgrave 6 (J R Boyle) *a bhd: rdn over 2f out but no hdwy* **33/1**	56
1013	11	1/2	**Safari Sundowner (IRE)**[19] 4726 4-9-4 85 ... WilliamCarson[(5)] 12 (P Winkworth) *mid-div: rdn over 2f out: wknd over 1f out* **8/1**	69
0104	12	1 1/2	**Obrigado (USA)**[28] 4481 8-8-9 71 ... (bt[1]) SteveDrowne 8 (G L Moore) *t.k.h: a in rr* **16/1**	52
3006	13	2	**Rationale (IRE)**[18] 4771 5-9-4 80 ... JimCrowley 9 (S C Williams) *mid-div: rdn and wknd 3f out* **7/1**[3]	58
1100	14	7	**Polish Power (GER)**[16] 4844 8-10-0 90 ... TPO'Shea 14 (J S Moore) *prom: sn rdn along: wknd over 1f out: eased* **20/1**	56+

2m 18.54s (-3.36) **Going Correction** +0.025s/f (Slow)

WFA 3 from 4yo+ 9lb 14 Ran SP% 132.4

Speed ratings (Par 107): **113,112,109,109,109 107,106,103,101,101 101,99,98,93**

toteswinger: 1&2 £9.70, 1&3 £4.50, 2&3 £10.20. CSF £46.06 CT £141.16 TOTE £12.70: £4.00, £2.00, £1.80; EX 63.10.

Owner R A Pegum **Bred** Mount Coote Stud **Trained** Whitsbury, Hants

■ Stewards' Enquiry : T P O'Shea caution: allowed horse to coast home

FOCUS

A good middle-distance handicap and solid form rated around the third, fourth and fifth. They went a decent pace and the winning time was 0.55 seconds quicker than the previous conditions contest.

NOTEBOOK

Muhannak(IRE), who was having his first start since leaving Mick Easterby, was held well off the pace for much of the way, but was taken widest of all by Sanders early in the straight and produced one sustained effort to get up near the line. He showed his latest running at York to be all wrong, when he was clearly unsuited by testing ground, and this surface or quick turf suits much better. (op 9-1 tchd 10-1)

Tomintoul Flyer, fitted with a visor for the first time having failed to progress in two runs on turf after winning a decent 1m2f handicap round here in June, travelled well just off the pace for much of the way and the race looked his for the taking in the straight, but he ruined his chance by continually hanging right. His rider was able to get more serious by the time he mastered long-time leader Press The Button just over a furlong out, when the horse had the rail to run against, but the damage was already done and he was picked off late on. (op 6-1 tchd 4-1)

Tastahil(IRE), a maiden winner here in 2006 on his only previous try on Polytrack, kept on without threatening and is entitled to come on for this first run in over three months. (op 11-4 tchd 7-2)

Downhiller(IRE) ran a reasonable first race on Polytrack, but he probably wants a stiffer test of stamina. (op 20-1)

Press The Button(GER) set a decent enough pace, but crucially he was left alone up front and he ran a good race. He has yet to win on Polytrack, but the surface clearly suits.

5350 GO RACING WITH BRENDAN POWELL RACING H'CAP 1m (P)

5:40 (5:41) (Class 4) (0-80,80) 3-Y-O+ £5,180 (£1,541; £770; £384) Stalls High

Form				RPR
413	1		**Cave Lion (USA)**[25] 4571 3-9-6 80 ... JimmyFortune 6 (J H M Gosden) *t.k.h: a.p: wnt 2nd 1/2-way: led over 1f out: rdn clr* **11/2**[2]	93+
1233	2	3	**Moonlight Man**[11] 5018 7-9-11 79 ... (t) SebSanders 12 (C R Dore) *chsd ldrs: rdn 2f out: wnt 2nd ins fnl f: no ch w wnr* **11/1**	86
2021	3	1 3/4	**Totally Focussed (IRE)**[61] 3376 3-9-6 80 ... IanMongan 5 (S Dow) *mid-div: hdwy over 1f out: r.o fnl f: nvr nrr* **4/1**[1]	82
0204	4	nk	**Prince Of Thebes (IRE)**[11] 5018 7-9-10 78 ... AdamKirby 14 (M J Attwater) *a.p rdn over 2f out: kpt on one pce* **14/1**	80
3401	5	nk	**Murrin (IRE)**[13] 4946 4-9-2 75 ... JackMitchell[(5)] 1 (T G Mills) *s.i.s: in rr tl hdwy 2f out: r.o: nrst fin* **10/1**	77+
5003	6	nk	**Officer**[7] 5156 4-9-9 77 ... (b) GeorgeBaker 7 (G L Moore) *led after 1f: rdn over 1f out: nt qckn fnl f* **4/1**[1]	78
4403	7	shd	**Jo'Burg (USA)**[33] 4310 4-9-6 74 ... JimCrowley 2 (Mrs A J Perrett) *s.i.s: in rr whn rdn over 3f out: sme late hdwy* **20/1**	75
5210	8	1 3/4	**Millfield (IRE)**[19] 4723 5-9-6 74 ... TedDurcan 13 (P R Chamings) *v.s.a: in rr: mde sme late hdwy* **12/1**	71+
3221	9	nk	**Golden Penny**[19] 4731 3-9-2 76 ... SteveDrowne 8 (H Morrison) *led for 1f: trckd ldr to 1/2-way: wknd appr fnl f* **8/1**	71
065	10	1/2	**Cross The Line (IRE)**[17] 4364 6-9-7 75 ... RichardHughes 9 (A P Jarvis) *mid-div: rdn over 2f out: no hdwy after* **15/2**[3]	70
3200	11	1 3/4	**Our Kes (IRE)**[11] 5018 6-9-4 72 ... KirstyMilczarek 11 (P Howling) *a in rr* **33/1**	63
6230	12	5	**Lawyers Choice**[11] 5018 4-9-10 78 ... EddieAhern 3 (Pat Eddery) *chsd ldrs on outside: rdn 3f out: wknd 2f out* **25/1**	57
006	13	3 3/4	**Rock Anthem (IRE)**[59] 3457 4-9-4 72 ... ShaneKelly 4 (Mike Murphy) *a towards rr* **20/1**	43

1m 38.86s (-0.94) **Going Correction** +0.025s/f (Slow)

WFA 3 from 4yo+ 6lb 13 Ran SP% 126.4

Speed ratings (Par 105): **105,102,100,99,99 99,99,97,97,96 94,89,86**

toteswinger: 1&2 £11.20, 1&3 £6.70, 2&3 £13.40. CSF £65.26 CT £287.71 TOTE £6.50: £2.80, £3.50, £2.10; EX 66.20 Place 6: £213.91, Place 5: £42.64..

Owner H R H Princess Haya Of Jordan **Bred** Darley **Trained** Newmarket, Suffolk

FOCUS

A fair, competitive handicap run at a good pace and best rated around the placed horses.

Our Kes(IRE) Official explanation: jockey said mare spread a plate

T/Jkpt: Not won. T/Plt: £488.20 to a £1 stake. Pool: £68,952.91. 103.10 winning tickets. T/Qpdt: £37.80 to a £1 stake. Pool: £4,457.40. 87.10 winning tickets. JS

4733 NEWCASTLE (L-H)

Monday, August 25

5351 Meeting Abandoned - Waterlogged

[5106]RIPON (R-H)

Monday, August 25

OFFICIAL GOING: Good to soft (7.8)

Wind: Virtually nil Weather: Overcast

5357 SOLBERGE HALL IS A THOROUGHBRED HOTEL (S) STKS 6f

2:25 (2:26) (Class 6) 2-Y-O **£2,729** (£806; £403) **Stalls** Low

Form RPR

0502 **1** **Bold Account (IRE)**[7] 5159 2-9-2 45 AndrewElliott 1 66+
(K R Burke) *mde all: rdn over 1f out: kpt on strly* **11/8**[1]

0520 **2** 3 **Nchike**[10] 5041 2-9-2 53 (v) AdrianTNicholls 5 56
(D Nicholls) *a chsng wnr: rdn over 2f out: drvn over 1f out: kpt on same pce* **7/2**[3]

000 **3** 7 **Look For Value**[9] 5106 2-8-11 43 KimTinkler 7 29
(N Tinkler) *dwlt and towards rr: rdn along 1/2-way: kpt on u.p to take poor 3rd ent fnl f* **28/1**

0540 **4** 3½ **Royal Premium**[19] 4734 2-8-9 50 (p) KrishGundowry(7) 6 22
(H A McWilliams) *chsd ldng pair: rdn 1/2-way: drvn and hung lft over 1f out: wknd* **16/1**

3002 **5** 3 **El Portet**[10] 5041 2-9-2 63 TomEaves 4 13
(G M Moore) *dwlt: rdn along and in tch after 2f: drvn along 1/2-way: no imp whn n.m.r over 1f out* **5/2**[2]

0440 **6** 14 **Conakry**[24] 4604 2-9-2 53 TonyCulhane 3 —
(M R Channon) *sn outpcd and a in rr* **9/1**

0 **7** 7 **Any Luck (IRE)**[10] 5041 2-9-2 0 PatrickMathers 8 —
(I W McInnes) *s.i.s: reminders sn after s: a bhd* **80/1**

1m 15.54s (2.54) **Going Correction** +0.325s/f (Good) **7** Ran SP% **113.5**
Speed ratings (Par 92): **96,92,82,78,74 55,46**
toteswinger: 1&2 £1.30, 1&3 £6.20, 2&3 £10.20. CSF £6.45 TOTE £2.50: £1.80, £1.90; EX 6.50 Trifecta £62.20 Pool: £587.59, 6.99 winning units..There was no bid for the winner.
Owner Mrs Elaine M Burke **Bred** G Loftus **Trained** Middleham Moor, N Yorks

FOCUS
After a dry night the ground was officially good to soft. This looked a weak seller as not one of the runners had won a race before but the winner is clearly improved with the runner-up setting the level.

NOTEBOOK
Bold Account(IRE), representing a stable with a 24 per cent strike-rate with its two-year-olds at the track, had posted an improved effort when chasing home a 78-rated rival in a Yarmouth claimer last time, and he showed that was no fluke. Drawn best of all and with the stands' rail to help, he made every yard of the running, and while Nchike threatened to make a race of it, he was readily brushed aside from a furlong out. His improvement has coincided with getting to race on softish ground. (op 6-4 tchd 5-4)
Nchike, whose stable is in good form at the moment, ran a better race back over 6f having failed to get home over a furlong further at Catterick last time. (op 5-1 tchd 11-2)
Look For Value, who was dropping into a seller for the first time having cut little ice in maiden company, was representing a stable that had won this race twice in the past nine years. She struggled to go the early pace but did plug on to take third. (op 20-1 tchd 33-1)
Royal Premium, wearing cheekpieces instead of a visor this time, paid the price for trying to match the pace of the first two in the early stages. (op 12-1 tchd 20-1)
El Portet was best in strictly at the weights, but he got 7f well at Catterick last time and the drop back to 6f was not sure to suit. He was hampered next to the rail when trying to stay on inside the final two furlongs and his rider was not too serious with him afterwards. (op 11-4)
Conakry never looked happy on the ground. (op 15-2 tchd 7-1 and 10-1)
Any Luck(IRE) sat in the stalls as the gates opened and was always towards the rear. (op 50-1 tchd 40-1)

5358 BILLY NEVETT MEMORIAL H'CAP 6f

3:00 (3:00) (Class 4) (0-85,84) 3-Y-O **£4,857** (£1,445; £722; £360) **Stalls** Low

Form RPR

2056 **1** **Baldemar**[30] 4416 3-9-7 84 AndrewElliott 2 91
(K R Burke) *cl up: effrt 2f out: rdn to ld ent fnl f: styd on wl* **11/2**[3]

0060 **2** ¾ **Northern Bolt**[25] 4553 3-9-1 78 AdrianTNicholls 3 83
(D Nicholls) *led: rdn along 2f out: drvn and hdd ent fnl f: kpt on u.p* **7/1**

0034 **3** 1 **Errigal Lad**[10] 5056 3-8-13 76 (b[1]) PaulMulrennan 6 78
(K A Ryan) *a.p: rdn along 2f out: drvn appr fnl f: kpt on same pce* **5/1**[2]

5150 **4** 2½ **Artsu**[16] 4854 3-8-13 76 MickyFenton 9 70
(M L W Bell) *hld up: hdwy on outer 1/2-way: rdn to chal and ch wl over 1f out: sn edgd lft and wknd* **15/2**

063 **5** 1 **Hazelrigg (IRE)**[24] 4595 3-8-12 75 DavidAllan 4 66
(T D Easterby) *squeezed out s: sn chsng ldrs: pushed along 1/2-way and sn hanging rt: drvn and btn wl over 1f out* **9/4**[1]

3000 **6** 6 **Montaquila**[21] 4682 3-9-1 78 (t) RobertWinston 7 49
(J Howard Johnson) *chsd ldrs: rdn along and hung bdly rt over 2f out: sn btn* **16/1**

4040 **7** 1½ **Mey Blossom**[30] 4416 3-9-7 84 TomEaves 8 51
(R M Whitaker) *a in rr* **18/1**

5105 **8** ¾ **Everything**[43] 3999 3-8-7 70 ow1 TonyCulhane 1 34
(P T Midgley) *chsd ldrs: rdn along 1/2-way and sn wknd* **20/1**

2301 **9** 1¼ **Moonage Daydream (IRE)**[15] 4900 3-8-3 69 (bt) DuranFentiman(3) 5 29
(T D Easterby) *sn rdn along and a in rr* **7/1**

1m 14.62s (1.62) **Going Correction** +0.325s/f (Good) **9** Ran SP% **115.5**
Speed ratings (Par 102): **102,101,99,96,95 87,85,84,82**
toteswinger: 1&2 £11.80, 1&3 £6.70, 2&3 £8.80. CSF £43.61 CT £206.78 TOTE £5.80: £2.00, £2.30, £2.00; EX 34.10 Trifecta £524.80 Part won. Pool: £709.31, 0.90 winning units..
Owner A Rhodes Haulage And P Timmins **Bred** Hellwood Stud Farm **Trained** Middleham Moor, N Yorks

FOCUS
This handicap has been won by some smart performers in recent seasons, notably Borderlescott and Al Qasi, but it is unlikely that this year's race contained a sprinter of that quality. The form looks sound rated around the first three.
Hazelrigg(IRE) Official explanation: trainer said gelding was unsuited by the track

5359 RIPON CHAMPION TWO YRS OLD TROPHY, 2008 (LISTED RACE) 6f

3:35 (3:36) (Class 1) 2-Y-O

£17,031 (£6,456; £3,231; £1,611; £807; £405) **Stalls** Low

Form RPR

11 **1** **Desert Phantom (USA)**[15] 4908 2-9-2 0 RichardMullen 1 95
(D M Simcock) *led: rdn along 2f out: hdd and drvn over 1f out: rallied u.p ins fnl f to ld on line* **1/1**[1]

1301 **2** nk **Favourite Girl (IRE)**[16] 4857 2-8-11 82 DavidAllan 5 89
(T D Easterby) *cl up: rdn 2f out: led over 1f out and sn edgd rt: drvn ins fnl f and edgd rt: ct on line* **5/1**[3]

614 **3** hd **Zezao**[15] 4908 2-9-2 91 RobertWinston 2 93
(B J Meehan) *stdd s: trckd ldrs: pushed along and sltly outpcd 2f out: sn rdn and hung lft: sn swtchd rt and drvn: styd on wl fnl f* **9/1**

031 **4** 4 **Come And Go (UAE)**[17] 4815 2-9-2 86 PaulMulrennan 6 81
(G A Swinbank) *cl up: effrt over 2f out: sn rdn and ev ch tl drvn and wknd ent fnl f* **10/1**

2111 **5** 6 **Talking Hands**[30] 4402 2-9-5 96 PaulHanagan 4 66
(S Kirk) *sn rdn along and a in rr* **4/1**[2]

212 **6** 2¼ **Sunset Crest**[37] 4175 2-8-11 82 AndrewMullen 3 51
(Mrs A Duffield) *in tch: rdn along bef 1/2-way: sn outpcd and bhd* **16/1**

1m 15.03s (2.03) **Going Correction** +0.325s/f (Good) **6** Ran SP% **111.6**
Speed ratings (Par 102): **99,98,98,93,85 82**
toteswinger: 1&2 £1.50, 1&3 £2.00, 2&3 £6.60. CSF £6.32 TOTE £1.90: £1.40, £2.40; EX 5.40.
Owner Ahmad Al Shaikh **Bred** John R Penn & Frank Penn **Trained** Newmarket, Suffolk
■ Stewards' Enquiry : David Allan one-day ban: used whip with excessive frequency (Sep 8)

FOCUS
A Listed race for juveniles that rarely attracts a big field, and this looked a typical renewal with the runner-up the best guide to the form.

NOTEBOOK
Desert Phantom(USA) came into the race unbeaten in his previous two starts, including when successful at Windsor last time out, where he got the better of five previous winners. A proven liking for ease underfoot was also in his favour, and with the box draw to boot, it was easy to see why he was heavily favoured in the market. In the end, he made hard work of it, despite having the rail to help, and his trainer is now inclined to step him up in trip to 7f, and have him ridden more patiently in future. (op 6-5 tchd 5-4)
Favourite Girl(IRE) gave the winner a real fright despite not looking entirely happy on the track. Steadily progressive, she showed that she handles a testing surface well when picking up a heavy-ground nursery at Haydock last time, and the return to 6f caused her no problems at all. She could well go one better in Listed company against her own sex. (op 13-2 tchd 9-2)
Zezao could finish only fourth behind Desert Phantom at Windsor last time and he was re-opposing on the same terms, so it looked to face a stiff task, but he did not settle that day, and while he was again a touch keen, he had conserved enough energy to play a part in the finish this time. Entered in the Mill Reef and Middle Park, we have yet to see the best of him, and a return to faster ground ought to suit. (op 8-1)
Come And Go(UAE) showed early speed but was drawn widest of all and never had the advantage of the favoured rail. He is bred to need further than this and stepping up to 7f in nursery company might be an idea. (op 8-1 tchd 12-1)
Talking Hands had to give weight all round as a result of his win in a similar race over 7f at Ascot last month. The worry for him was that he would get outpaced on this drop back in trip on this easier track, and that concern seemed to be borne out. Official explanation: jockey said gelding was unsuited by the track (op 7-2 tchd 9-2)
Sunset Crest hails from a stable that is having a bad season and whose current form remains in question. Official explanation: jockey said filly hung right-handed (op 14-1)

5360 RIPON ROWELS H'CAP 1m

4:10 (4:11) (Class 2) (0-100,98) 3-Y-O+

£12,462 (£3,732; £1,866; £934; £466; £234) **Stalls** High

Form RPR

113 **1** **Osteopathic Remedy (IRE)**[23] 4649 4-9-4 87 TomEaves 17 100
(M Dods) *t.k.h: a cl up: effrt 2f out: rdn to ld 1f out: styd on wl* **15/2**[3]

1-43 **2** 1¾ **Webbow (IRE)**[16] 4853 6-9-6 89 DavidAllan 15 98
(T D Easterby) *trckd ldrs on inner: smooth hdwy 3f out: effrt over 1f out: swtchd lft and rdn ent fnl f: kpt on* **6/1**[1]

006 **3** 1 **Cobo Bay**[16] 4869 3-9-6 98 (p) NeilBrown(3) 8 103
(K A Ryan) *trckd ldrs: hdwy 4f out: rdn along and outpcd over 2f out: styd on u.p ins fnl f* **14/1**

5465 **4** nse **Collateral Damage (IRE)**[16] 4876 5-8-8 80 (bt) DuranFentiman(3) 7 86
(T D Easterby) *sn led: rdn along wl over 2f out: drvn and hdd 1f out: wknd ins fnl f: lost 3rd cl home* **16/1**

5610 **5** 1 **Nevada Desert (IRE)**[19] 4744 8-8-9 78 DeanMcKeown 16 82
(R M Whitaker) *chsd ldrs: rdn along over 2f out: drvn over 1f out: kpt on same pce* **20/1**

0500 **6** nk **Lucky Dance (BRZ)**[16] 4856 6-9-3 86 RobertWinston 14 89
(A G Foster) *prom: rdn along 3f out: drvn and wkng whn n.m.r over 1f out* **33/1**

0514 **7** ¾ **Blue Spinnaker (IRE)**[37] 4206 9-8-7 83 BradleyRoper(7) 1 85
(M W Easterby) *hld up towards rr: hdwy wl over 2f out: rdn and styd on ins fnl f: nt rch ldrs* **16/1**

04-4 **8** 1 **Bolodenka (IRE)**[27] 4512 6-9-11 94 PaulHanagan 13 93
(R A Fahey) *in tch: effrt over 3f out: rdn over 2f out and sn no imp* **9/1**

1100 **9** 1 **Summon Up Theblood (IRE)**[25] 4553 3-9-4 93 TonyCulhane 2 89
(M R Channon) *s.i.s and bhd: hdwy 3f out: swtchd ins and rdn wl over 1f out: kpt on ins fnl f* **33/1**

-506 **10** ½ **Kinsya**[16] 4845 5-9-9 92 SaleemGolam 11 88
(M H Tompkins) *midfield: rdn along over 3f out: no hdwy* **11/1**

5016 **11** nse **Mountain Pride (IRE)**[27] 4509 3-8-13 88 RichardMullen 6 83
(J L Dunlop) *midfield: hdwy on outer 3f out: sn rdn along to chse ldrs: wknd wl over 1f out* **12/1**

4650 **12** 2 **Raptor (GER)**[24] 4587 5-9-13 96 AndrewElliott 12 87
(K R Burke) *midfield: rdn along 4f out: n.d* **14/1**

1130 **13** ¾ **Jaser**[67] 3155 3-8-13 93 AshleyHamblett(5) 4 81
(P W Chapple-Hyam) *a towards rr* **9/1**

1042 **14** ½ **Exit Smiling**[16] 4876 6-9-6 89 MickyFenton 9 77
(P T Midgley) *a towards rr* **14/1**

3231 **15** 3 **Mangham (IRE)**[18] 4783 3-8-8 83 PaulMulrennan 3 63
(D H Brown) *chsd ldrs on outer: rdn along wl over 2f out: sn drvn and wknd* **7/1**[2]

0030 **16** 4½ **Minority Report**[68] 3142 8-8-13 82 AdrianTNicholls 10 53
(D Nicholls) *v.s.a and a bhd* **20/1**

1m 41.59s (0.19) **Going Correction** +0.25s/f (Good)
WFA 3 from 4yo+ 6lb **16** Ran SP% **121.7**
Speed ratings (Par 109): **109,107,106,106,105 104,104,103,102,101 101,99,98,98,95 90**
toteswinger: 1&2 £4.60, 1&3 £25.00, 2&3 £23.60. CSF £49.25 CT £649.80 TOTE £8.10: £2.30, £2.10, £4.10, £3.70; EX 34.80 Trifecta £650.70 Pool: £967.26, 1.10 winning units..
Owner Kevin Kirkup **Bred** Airlie Stud **Trained** Denton, Co Durham
■ Stewards' Enquiry : Duran Fentiman ten-day ban: failed to ride out for 3rd place (Sep 8-17)

FOCUS
A competitive handicap in which a high draw and racing prominently predictably proved a big advantage. The form looks sound enough.

NOTEBOOK
Osteopathic Remedy(IRE) saw his winning run come to an end at Thirsk last time, but he regained the thread despite being another 2lb higher in the weights. He was plenty keen enough in the early stages after being rushed up from the highest stall, but on the plus side he was able to hold a good position on the inside into the turn. In a race in which few got involved, he stayed on well close home to score fairly comfortably, and while things undoubtedly fell perfectly for him this time, he remains a progressive handicapper. A strong pace will help him settle better, and he will go to Ayr next for a similar event. (op 13-2)

Webbow(IRE), another with a favourable high draw, arrived fresher than most as he had had only two previous outings this season. On the rail most of the way, Tom Eaves on the winner denied him an easy way through when looking for a gap between the leader and Osteopathic Remedy inside the final two furlongs, and in the end he was forced to switch wide. As a result the winner got first run on him and he was unable to bridge the gap. He remains capable of better. (op 11-2)
Cobo Bay did best of those drawn low and forced to race wide. A previous course and distance winner in similar conditions, he ran a sound race off what remains a stiff mark. (op 16-1)
Collateral Damage(IRE), who had the blinkers back on and ground to suit, showed good speed to get over from stall seven to lead. He tired in the closing stages but still finished fourth, showing the advantage of racing prominently and saving ground on the rail over this trip. His rider was given a ten-day ban for dropping his hands three yards from the line and losing third place.
Nevada Desert(IRE), who was racing off a mark only 3lb higher than when successful at Beverley two starts back, ran a sound race against this tougher opposition, but he was another blessed with a favourable high draw. (tchd 18-1)
Lucky Dance(BRZ) was another who had a decent draw. Never too far off the pace, he ran his best race so far in this country.
Blue Spinnaker(IRE), poorly drawn in stall one, swung widest into the straight and struggled to get involved from off the pace. (op 14-1)
Bolodenka(IRE) has done all winning on good ground or faster, but he does handle cut. He won this race last year off a 6lb lower mark and has looked held by the assessor since. (tchd 10-1)
Jaser Official explanation: jockey said colt never travelled
Mangham(IRE) was unable to get to the front from his low draw and, forced to race wide, was beaten some way out. (op 10-1)

5361 SOLBERGE SILKS BRASSERIE MAIDEN STKS — 1m

4:45 (4:46) (Class 5) 3-4-Y-O — £2,914 (£867; £433; £216) Stalls High

Form	Pos	Dist	Horse / details	RPR
-2	1		**Taaresh (IRE)**^{32} 4349 3-9-3 0 ... RichardMullen 7 (J L Dunlop) *trckd ldrs: hdwy 3f out: shkn up to ld and edgd rt over 1f out: rdn out* **4/11**^{1}	69+
	2	1 1/2	**Top Tribute** 3-9-3 0 ... MickyFenton 8 (T P Tate) *led: rdn along over 2f out: hdd over 1f out: kpt on u.p ins fnl f* **20/1**	66+
4	3	3/4	**Proficiency**^{56} 3556 3-8-9 0 ... DuranFentiman$^{(3)}$ 10 (T D Walford) *trckd ldrs on inner: hdwy 3f out: rdn 2f out: drvn and one pce ent fnl f* **16/1**^{3}	59
	4	4	**Lachafinna (IRE)**^{343} 5490 3-8-12 0 ... DavidAllan 4 (D Carroll) *chsd ldr: rdn along 3f out: drvn 2f out: sn one pce* **66/1**	50
0	5	2 3/4	**Predictable (IRE)**^{16} 4877 3-8-5 0 ... BradleyRoper$^{(7)}$ 9 (M W Easterby) *chsd ldrs: rdn along over 2f out: sn one pce* **125/1**	44
32-0	6	1 1/2	**Cozy Tiger (USA)**^{116} 1748 3-9-3 75 ... TonyCulhane 2 (W J Musson) *t.k.h: hld up towards rr: smooth hdwy 3f out: swtchd rt over 2f out: kpt on ins fnl f* **10/1**^{2}	45
40	7	nk	**Fell Pack**^{21} 4689 4-9-9 0 ... PaulMulrennan 5 (J J Quinn) *t.k.h: hld up in rr: swtchd outside 2f out: styd on strly ins fnl f: nrst fin* **50/1**	46+
	8	1/2	**Arikinui** 3-8-12 0 ... AndrewElliott 3 (K R Burke) *chsd ldrs: effrt 3f out: sn rdn along and wknd wl over 1f out* **16/1**^{3}	38
	9	2 1/4	**Drumadoon Bay (IRE)**^{39} 4140 4-9-9 54 ... RobertWinston 6 (G A Swinbank) *t.k.h: hld up: a in rr* **10/1**^{2}	39
0	10	4	**Dolly Royal (IRE)**^{16} 4877 3-8-12 0 ... PaulHanagan 1 (K A Ryan) *wnt lft s: racd wd and alway bhd* **33/1**	24
	11	3/4	**Miss Ferney** 4-9-4 0 ... TomEaves 12 (A Kirtley) *t.k.h: hld up: a in rr* **125/1**	23
000/	12	124	**Amaretto Venture**^{714} 5237 4-9-4 40 ... AdrianTNicholls 11 (R Johnson) *rn green: sn outpcd and bhd after 1f* **200/1**	—

1m 44.54s (3.14) **Going Correction** +0.25s/f (Good)
WFA 3 from 4yo 6lb — **12** Ran SP% **116.5**
Speed ratings (Par 103): **94,92,91,87,85 83,83,82,80,76 75,—**
toteswinger: 1&2 £4.50, 1&3 £3.60, 2&3 £17.50. CSF £14.03 TOTE £1.30: £1.10, £3.40, £3.10; EX 10.60 Trifecta £91.60 Pool: £755.66, 6.10 winning units..
Owner Hamdan Al Maktoum **Bred** Shadwell Estate Company Limited **Trained** Arundel, W Sussex

FOCUS
A weak maiden run at a steady early pace that provided a straightforward opportunity for the favourite. The form looks messy and is limited by the proximity of the fourth and fifth.
Drumadoon Bay(IRE) Official explanation: trainer said colt was unsuited by the track
Amaretto Venture Official explanation: jockey said filly bucked for first furlong

5362 R. H. EMSLEY & SONS H'CAP — 1m 1f 170y

5:20 (5:22) (Class 5) (0-70,70) 3-Y-O — £2,914 (£867; £433; £216) Stalls High

Form	Pos	Dist	Horse / details	RPR
062	1		**Shaylee**^{21} 4680 3-8-4 **53** ... SilvestreDeSousa 1 (T D Walford) *in tch: hdwy over 3f out: led 2f out and sn rdn: drvn and edgd rt ent fnl f: kpt on wl* **12/1**	58
3050	2	1 1/2	**Plenilune (IRE)**^{83} 2699 3-9-3 **66** ... TWilliams 9 (M Brittain) *hld up in tch: hdwy over 4f out: cl up 3f out: rdn and ev ch 2f out: swtchd lft and drvn ent fnl f: kpt on* **25/1**	68
0450	3	1	**Mill Beattie**^{19} 4741 3-8-6 **55** ... PaulHanagan 2 (G M Moore) *trckd ldrs: hdwy 3f out: rdn 2f out: kpt on u.p fnl f* **40/1**	55
0132	4	1/2	**Eton Fable (IRE)**^{4} 5202 3-9-7 **70** ... JamieMoriarty 10 (W J H Ratcliffe) *chsd ldng pair on inner: rdn along 3f out: drvn wl over 1f out and kpt on same pce* **15/8**^{1}	69
534	5	4 1/2	**Joinedupwriting**^{22} 4663 3-9-4 **67** ... DeanMcKeown 6 (R M Whitaker) *hld up in tch: smooth hdwy to trck ldrs 3f out: rdn wl over 1f out: wknd appr fnl f* **11/2**	56
0551	6	nk	**Devinius (IRE)**^{14} 4920 3-9-1 **64** ... RobertWinston 7 (G A Swinbank) *hld up in rr: sme hdwy over 2f out: sn rdn and no imp* **10/3**^{2}	53
040	7	6	**Doctor Delta**^{21} 4689 3-8-4 **53** ow1 ... AdrianTNicholls 3 (M Brittain) *cl up: rdn along 3f out: sn wknd* **20/1**	29
0344	8	1/2	**Manuka Bee**^{19} 4738 3-8-7 **56** ... PaulMulrennan 4 (J Howard Johnson) *led: rdn along 3f out: hdd 2f out and sn wknd* **11/1**	31
3-63	9	30	**Soggy Dollar**^{58} 3484 3-9-7 **70** ... SaleemGolam 5 (M H Tompkins) *chsd ldrs: rdn along over 3f out and sn wknd* **5/1**^{3}	—

2m 9.60s (4.20) **Going Correction** +0.25s/f (Good) — **9** Ran SP% **117.0**
Speed ratings (Par 100): **93,91,91,90,87 86,81,81,57**
toteswinger: 1&2 £38.00, 1&3 £38.80, 2&3 £35.10. CSF £267.50 CT £11008.16 TOTE £9.30: £1.90, £6.40, £8.80; EX 198.50 Trifecta £670.50 Part won. Pool: £906.19, 0.50 winning units. Place 6 £439.58, Place 5 £270.83..
Owner L C And A E Sigsworth **Bred** L C And Mrs A E Sigsworth **Trained** Sheriff Hutton, N Yorks

FOCUS
An ordinary handicap for three-year-olds and the form looks modest rated around the placed horses.
Soggy Dollar Official explanation: vet said gelding finished lame behind

T/Plt: £419.60 to a £1 stake. Pool: £67,855.83. 118.05 winning tickets. T/Qpdt: £75.10 to a £1 stake. Pool: £3,759.60. 37.00 winning tickets. JR

3888 WARWICK (L-H)

Monday, August 25

OFFICIAL GOING: Soft (good to soft in places; 6.1)
Wind: Fresh behind Weather: Cloudy with sunny spells

5363 TURFTV NURSERY — 5f 110y

1:30 (1:33) (Class 5) (0-75,75) 2-Y-O — £3,238 (£963; £481; £240) Stalls Centre

Form	Pos	Dist	Horse / details	RPR
651	1		**Coconut Shy**^{7} 5158 2-9-2 **70** 6ex ... (t) AdrianMcCarthy 2 (G Prodromou) *mde virtually all: rdn clr fnl f: jst hld on* **7/1**^{3}	75
051	2	nk	**Golden Destiny (IRE)**^{15} 4907 2-9-1 **74** ... DavidProbert$^{(5)}$ 7 (P J Makin) *a.p: rdn to chse wnr over 1f out: sn edgd rt: r.o* **8/1**	78
432	3	1	**Lookafternumberone (IRE)**^{10} 5072 2-9-0 **68** ... TPQueally 11 (J G Given) *sn outpcd: hdwy over 1f out: rdn and nt clr run 1f out: r.o* **7/1**^{3}	69
3233	4	6	**Titus Andronicus (IRE)**^{30} 4434 2-9-6 **74** ... TQuinn 9 (K A Ryan) *chsd wnr: rdn 1/2-way: wknd fnl f* **3/1**^{1}	55
006	5	1 3/4	**Courageous Nature (IRE)**^{72} 3020 2-8-3 **57** ... WilliamBuick 8 (B J Meehan) *bmpd s: sn chsng ldrs: rdn: hung lft and wknd over 1f out* **8/1**	32
4604	6	1	**Rio Cobolo (IRE)**^{37} 4175 2-8-4 **58** ... DavidKinsella 6 (Paul Green) *prom: lost pl over 3f out: n.d after* **12/1**	30
6060	7	shd	**Neo's Mate (IRE)**^{76} 2903 2-8-1 **55** ... PaulQuinn 10 (Paul Green) *sn outpcd: nvr nrr* **50/1**	27
335	8	1 1/4	**Cash In The Attic**^{12} 4980 2-8-9 **63** ow1 ... DarryllHolland 4 (M R Channon) *mid-div: sn pushed along: n.d* **11/2**^{2}	30
5402	9	1	**Nativity**^{39} 4101 2-8-12 **66** ... LiamJones 12 (J L Spearing) *s.i.s: sn outpcd* **10/1**	30
004	10	nk	**Goodenough Magic**^{32} 4321 2-8-2 **56** ow1 ... HayleyTurner 1 (Andrew Turnell) *chsd ldrs: lost pl over 3f out: hung rt 1/2-way: sn bhd* **20/1**	19
544	11	3 1/2	**Chimbonda**^{14} 4923 2-9-3 **71** ... (b^{1}) ChrisCatlin 13 (S Parr) *chsd ldrs: rdn 1/2-way: wknd over 1f out* **12/1**	23

67.54 secs (1.64) **Going Correction** +0.125s/f (Good) — **11** Ran SP% **118.8**
Speed ratings (Par 94): **94,93,92,84,81 80,80,78,77,77 72**
toteswinger: 1&2 £8.80, 1&3 £9.30, 2&3 £5.00. CSF £62.69 CT £420.72 TOTE £9.00: £2.60, £3.00, £2.30; EX 55.90.
Owner F Butler **Bred** Burns Farm Stud **Trained** East Harling, Norfolk

FOCUS
This was an ordinary nursery over an in-between trip, but there was a fair amount of market activity. The first three drew clear and the form looks solid.

NOTEBOOK
Coconut Shy, a 6f winner on easy ground when fitted with a first-time tongue-tie, had a 6lb penalty for that win but she is clearly on the upgrade and, making virtually all the running, established a clear lead early in the straight and had enough in hand to hold off the runner-up. Her trainer thinks a lot of her and a quick hat-trick could be on the cards providing there is cut in the ground. (tchd 11-2)
Golden Destiny(IRE), a daughter of Captain Rio and another whose best effort was when winning her maiden over 6f on easy ground, chased the leaders from the start and was gradually reeling in the winner through the last furlong. She should remain competitive at this level. (op 6-1)
Lookafternumberone(IRE), making his handicap debut, did best of those to come from off the pace and maintained his record of being in the frame on all of his starts. Nurseries probably offer his best chance of losing his maiden tag. (op 11-2)
Titus Andronicus(IRE) raced up with the pace from the start but was in trouble soon after turning for home. (op 10-3 tchd 7-2)
Courageous Nature(IRE) was making his handicap debut on his first start for 72 days and was supported in the market. He chased the leaders into the straight but could make no impression from that point. (op 12-1)
Cash In The Attic, another making her handicap debut, was also backed but lost a good early pitch before the turn and only ran on past beaten horses. (op 8-1)
Chimbonda was a market drifter despite the first-time blinkers and, after racing keenly, faded right out of things in the straight. (op 17-2)

5364 RACING UK MAIDEN AUCTION STKS (DIV I) — 7f 26y

2:00 (2:03) (Class 5) 2-Y-O — £2,914 (£867; £433; £216) Stalls Low

Form	Pos	Dist	Horse / details	RPR
6	1		**Advertise**^{95} 2324 2-8-9 0 ... LPKeniry 10 (A M Balding) *chsd ldr: led over 1f out: rdn and hung rt ins fnl f: r.o* **9/4**^{1}	74
0	2	1 3/4	**Chalk Hill Blue**^{32} 4337 2-8-4 0 ... HayleyTurner 5 (Eve Johnson Houghton) *hld up in tch: rdn over 1f out: r.o* **13/2**^{3}	65
00	3	1/2	**Rocksy**^{47} 3848 2-8-6 0 ... JoeFanning 8 (D J Coakley) *trckd ldrs: racd keenly: rdn over 1f out: styd on* **20/1**	65
	4	nse	**Aahaykid (IRE)** 2-9-0 0 ... FergusSweeney 12 (K R Burke) *a.p: rdn and wandered over 1f out: styd on* **16/1**	73+
	5	1	**Glan Lady (IRE)** 2-8-4 0 ... LiamJones 1 (J L Spearing) *hld up: hmpd 3f out: r.o ins fnl f: nt rch ldrs* **12/1**	61+
00	6	1/2	**Jul's Lad (IRE)**^{37} 4176 2-9-0 0 ... RobertHavlin 9 (Paul Green) *led: rdn and hdd over 1f out: no ex ins fnl f* **20/1**	70
	7	4	**Oriental Cavalier** 2-8-8 0 ... RussellKennemore$^{(3)}$ 6 (R Hollinshead) *s.i.s: hld up: carried rt over 2f out: hmpd over 1f out: wknd fnl f* **33/1**	57
000	8	1/2	**Fleur De'Lion (IRE)**^{15} 4905 2-8-9 49 ... WilliamBuick 4 (S Kirk) *hld up: hmpd 3f out: n.d* **20/1**	53
0	9	hd	**Al Wujood (IRE)**^{7} 5158 2-8-11 0 ... StephenDonohoe 7 (D M Simcock) *hld up: effrt and hung rt over 2f out: wknd fnl f* **50/1**	55
0	10	14	**What A Day**^{18} 4780 2-8-13 0 ... TQuinn 11 (J J Quinn) *chsd ldrs: rdn 1/2-way: wknd 2f out* **4/1**^{2}	22
	11	3/4	**Major Potential (USA)** 2-9-1 0 ... TPQueally 3 (R M H Cowell) *s.s: outpcd* **14/1**	22

1m 26.45s (1.85) **Going Correction** +0.20s/f (Good) — **11** Ran SP% **103.5**
Speed ratings (Par 94): **97,95,94,94,93 92,88,87,87,71 70**
toteswinger: 1&2 £3.60, 1&3 £12.10, 2&3 £26.90. CSF £11.71 TOTE £2.60: £1.30, £1.50, £4.80; EX 11.20.
Owner Kingsclere Racing CLub **Bred** Kingsclere Stud **Trained** Kingsclere, Hants

FOCUS
An ordinary-looking maiden auction and those that had run had limited experience. There is not much strength in depth to the form.

NOTEBOOK
Advertise was a well-backed favourite though and duly scored in straightforward fashion, having been close to the pace throughout. He showed promise on his debut on fast ground but had been absent for over three months since then and clearly this easier surface was in his favour. (op 5-2 tchd 11-4)

Chalk Hill Blue, who showed promise on her debut over 7f on fast ground after missing the break, handled this easier surface and stayed on under pressure to grab second. She is likely to make her mark in handicaps after one more run (tchd 6-1)

Rocksy, who had been well beaten two runs on Polytrack and fast ground at 6f but had been backed on the first occasion and to some extent showed why this time, although she could have settled better early on this step up in trip. (op 40-1)

Aahaykid(IRE), a half-brother to several winners between 6f and 1m2f out of a 7f winner, did best of the newcomers and, sure to benefit from the experience, looks capable of winning races in time. (tchd 14-1)

Glan Lady(IRE), the first foal of a 5f winner who is a half-sister to several winners including the speedy Lake Chini, did not appear to handle the home turn very well but stayed on quite nicely without being given a hard race and will know more next time. Official explanation: jockey said filly lost its action (op 14-1)

Jul's Lad(IRE) made the running and did not drop away too far once headed and he now qualifies for a handicap mark. (op 22-1)

Oriental Cavalier Official explanation: jockey said colt hung right-handed

Al Wujood(IRE) Official explanation: jockey said colt hung right-handed on the final bend

What A Day, a half-brother to Systematic, failed to build on the promise of his debut on this drop in trip. Official explanation: jockey said colt had no more to give (op 9-2 tchd 3-1)

5365 RACING UK MAIDEN AUCTION STKS (DIV II) 7f 26y

2:35 (2:38) (Class 5) 2-Y-O £2,914 (£867; £433; £216) Stalls Low

Form				RPR
62	1		**Blazing Buck**[11] 5022 2-8-13 0 ... TPQueally 6 (H J L Dunlop) *a.p: chsd ldr over 1f out: rdn to ld wl ins fnl f* **13/8**[1]	76
0322	2	1	**Hameildaeme**[18] 4769 2-7-13 68 ... DavidProbert(5) 8 (S C Williams) *prom: chsd ldr over 5f out tl led 2f out: sn rdn and edgd lft: hdd wl ins fnl f* **11/4**[2]	64
	3	3	**Lady Francesca** 2-8-9 0 ... DO'Donohoe 5 (W R Muir) *hld up in tch: rdn over 1f out: styd on same pce fnl f* **8/1**	62+
	4	1	**Seaquel** 2-8-6 0 ... DavidKinsella 7 (A B Haynes) *s.s: edgd lft and r.o ins fnl f: nvr nrr* **25/1**	56
60	5	1	**Tax Dodger (IRE)**[11] 5021 2-8-9 0 ... LiamJones 3 (J L Spearing) *trckd ldrs: racd keenly: n.m.r over 4f out: rdn over 1f out: edgd rt and styd on same pce fnl f* **16/1**	57
	6	1 1/2	**Strathcal** 2-9-0 0 ... RobertHavlin 4 (H Morrison) *s.s: in rr: shkn up over 2f out: n.d* **16/1**	58
	7	1 3/4	**Canmoss (USA)** 2-9-0 0 ... ChrisCatlin 11 (E J O'Neill) *hld up: last and pushed along 4f out: n.d* **13/2**[3]	53
000	8	1	**Harry Raffle**[3] 5225 2-9-0 0 ... LPKeniry 10 (S Kirk) *chsd ldrs: rdn 1/2-way: wknd 2f out* **20/1**	51
	9	3 1/2	**Russian Saint** 2-8-6 0 ... WilliamBuick 9 (T J Pitt) *led: hdd 2f out: wknd fnl f* **14/1**	34

1m 28.31s (3.71) **Going Correction** +0.20s/f (Good) **9** Ran SP% **116.2**
Speed ratings (Par 94): **86,84,81,80,79 77,75,74,70**
toteswinger: 1&2 £2.30, 1&3 £4.10, 2&3 £4.40. CSF £6.06 TOTE £2.40: £1.20, £1.50, £2.20; EX 7.50.
Owner Stephen J Buckmaster **Bred** Charlock Stud **Trained** Lambourn, Berks
■ Stewards' Enquiry : William Buick two-day ban: careless riding (Sep 8-9)

FOCUS
The second division of this maiden auction was run 1.86secs slower than the first leg. The market leaders fought out the finish clear of the rest and the runner-up sets the level.

NOTEBOOK
Blazing Buck, whose dam was a 6f-1m winner and is a half-sister nine winners in Germany, built on his debut effort when runner-up over 7f at Salisbury on easy ground and the same conditions enabled him to get off the mark, although he was made to work quite hard by the runner-up. (op 7-4 tchd 2-1)

Hameildaeme, who had placed form in maidens on a sound surface but is progressing with racing and handled the softer ground well. She lost little in defeat and may be able to win a small nursery on this evidence. (op 5-2)

Lady Francesca, a 21,000gns half-sister to Jeer out of a 7f winner, came wider into the straight but kept on steadily on this debut and should appreciate longer distances in time. (tchd 9-1)

Seaquel caught the eye on this debut as, after missing the break, she was held up at the back of the field before keeping on quite nicely once in line for home. She is a sister to a 7f juvenile winner and a half-sister to the multiple winners Keltic Bard and Seneschal, so is bred to win races. (op 28-1)

Tax Dodger(IRE) had been well beaten in both his starts but was backed at long prices and ran better, although he did not help his cause by being a little keen early. (op 28-1 tchd 12-1)

Strathcal, a half-brother to several winners including Bannister and Roo, missed the break on this debut and never figured. (op 12-1)

Canmoss(USA), a $45,000 half-brother to a couple of dirt sprint winners in the USA, was making his debut for a yard that often does well with its newcomers. He was another who was well supported but never figured and was in the rear and being pushed along before the turn. (op 11-1 tchd 12-1)

5366 WARWICKRACECOURSE.CO.UK MAIDEN STKS 7f 26y

3:10 (3:12) (Class 5) 3-Y-O+ £3,238 (£963; £481; £240) Stalls Low

Form				RPR
04-5	1		**Cigalas**[52] 3694 3-9-3 85 ... MichaelHills 3 (B W Hills) *mde all: hung rt fnl f: eased last 50yds* **11/4**[2]	80+
3	2	6	**Shakedown**[31] 4378 3-9-3 0 ... StephenDonohoe 1 (E S McMahon) *a.p: chsd wnr over 2f out: rdn and hung lft over 1f out: wknd ins fnl f* **7/1**	65
2	3	nk	**Surprise Package (FR)**[11] 5023 3-9-3 0 ... TPQueally 8 (H J L Dunlop) *chsd wnr tl rdn over 2f out: styd on same pce appr fnl f* **2/1**[1]	64
0-	4	5	**Arganil (USA)**[339] 5580 3-9-3 0 ... DarryllHolland 4 (K A Ryan) *awkward leaving stalls: hld up: r.o ins fnl f: nvr nrr* **8/1**	51+
3	5	3/4	**Mr Burton**[31] 4379 4-9-1 0 ... GarryWhillans(7) 9 (M Mullineaux) *prom: rdn 1/2-way: wknd wl over 2f out* **16/1**	51
	6	2 1/2	**Historical Giant (USA)**[458] 2013 3-9-3 0 ... LPKeniry 2 (E F Vaughan) *hld up: rdn 1/2-way: n.d* **9/2**[3]	43
0-5	7	1	**Timocracy**[24] 4606 3-9-3 0 ... JoeFanning 11 (M Johnston) *prom: rdn 1/2-way: wknd over 2f out* **14/1**	40
	8	1 1/2	**Interchoice Star** 3-9-3 0 ... FergusSweeney 7 (K G Wingrove) *prom: rdn 1/2-way: wknd over 2f out* **40/1**	36
	9	3 3/4	**Smart Tazz** 3-9-3 0 ... ChrisCatlin 6 (H J Evans) *s.s: a bhd* **28/1**	26

1m 25.38s (0.78) **Going Correction** +0.20s/f (Good)
WFA 3 from 4yo 5lb **9** Ran SP% **120.2**
Speed ratings (Par 103): **103,96,95,90,89 86,85,83,79**
toteswinger: 1&2 £4.50, 1&3 £2.30, 2&3 £3.60. CSF £23.63 TOTE £4.10: £1.60, £2.50, £1.40; EX 33.10.
Owner Mrs A Gurney, Lord Vestey, Cavendish Inv **Bred** Stowell Park Stud **Trained** Lambourn, Berks

FOCUS
A modest contest run 1.07secs faster than the quicker of the earlier juvenile events over the same trip and the form is a bit shaky behind the clear-cut winner.

5367 SYD MERCER MEMORIAL H'CAP 2m 39y

3:45 (3:47) (Class 5) (0-70,68) 3-Y-O+ £3,238 (£963; £481; £240) Stalls Low

Form				RPR
05/0	1		**Tagula Blue (IRE)**[10] 5058 8-9-9 63 ... StephenDonohoe 6 (Ian Williams) *hld up: hdwy 6f out: rdn to ld and edgd lft 1f out: jst hld on* **14/1**	72
2304	2	nse	**Mister Completely (IRE)**[26] 4526 7-8-13 53 ...(v) JamesDoyle 2 (Ms J S Doyle) *hld up: hdwy over 2f out: rdn and hung lft over 1f out: styd on wl* **8/1**	62
3155	3	1 1/2	**Moonshine Beach**[31] 4391 10-9-3 57 ... LiamJones 5 (P W Hiatt) *led after 1f: hdd over 12f out: chsd ldrs: n.m.r and stmbld over 3f out: sn rdn: styd on u.p* **7/1**[3]	64
006	4	1/2	**Munlochy Bay**[15] 4909 4-8-12 52 ... FergusSweeney 11 (W S Kittow) *prom: outpcd 4f out: rallied and hung lft over 1f out: styd on* **66/1**	59
2344	5	3/4	**Right Option (IRE)**[25] 4193 4-9-9 68 ... DavidProbert(5) 10 (J L Flint) *a.p: rdn to ld and edgd rt over 1f out: sn hdd: no ex ins fnl f* **6/1**[2]	74
-500	6	1 1/2	**Historic Place (USA)**[14] 4935 8-8-12 52 ...(p) TQuinn 4 (J A Geake) *led 1f: remained handy: rdn and ev ch 2f out: no ex fnl f* **16/1**	56
600/	7	3	**Irish Legend (IRE)**[131] 6267 8-8-5 52 oh6 ... MJMurphy(7) 8 (C Roberts) *hld up: rdn over 2f out: n.d* **9/2**[1]	52
1621	8	2 1/4	**Squirtle (IRE)**[14] 4924 5-9-6 67 ... DeanHeslop(7) 13 (W M Brisbourne) *s.s: outpcd: hdwy 1/2-way: rdn over 2f out: wknd fnl f* **6/1**[2]	65
3130	9	hd	**Whaxaar (IRE)**[68] 3137 4-9-7 61 ... RobertHavlin 12 (R Ingram) *hld up: hdwy 10f out: rdn over 2f out: sn wknd* **8/1**	58
5/06	10	1 1/4	**Mohawk Star (IRE)**[11] 5003 7-9-0 54 ... TPQueally 3 (I A Wood) *hld up: hmpd 12f out: hdwy 4f out: rdn and wknd 2f out* **20/1**	50
P-66	11	hd	**Very Green (FR)**[7] 5163 6-9-0 57 ... RussellKennemore(3) 1 (Mrs A L M King) *hld up: n.d* **16/1**	53
1000	12	1 1/2	**Arabian Sun**[14] 4935 4-9-0 54 ...(v) ChrisCatlin 16 (M J Attwater) *led over 12f out: hdd 9f out: led again over 4f out: rdn: hdd & wknd over 1f out* **16/1**	48
0440	13	1 3/4	**Archimboldo (USA)**[14] 4935 5-8-12 52 oh2 ...(b) WilliamBuick 15 (T Wall) *chsd ldrs: rdn over 3f out: ev ch over 2f out: wknd sn after* **16/1**	44
06	14	12	**Ashmolian (IRE)**[40] 4087 5-8-12 52 oh4 ... LPKeniry 14 (Miss Z C Davison) *prom: led 9f out: hdd over 4f out: rdn and wknd over 2f out* **16/1**	29

3m 39.07s (5.27) **Going Correction** +0.20s/f (Good) **14** Ran SP% **123.8**
Speed ratings (Par 103): **94,93,93,92,92 91,90,89,89,88 88,87,86,80**
toteswinger: 1&2 £22.90, 1&3 £23.00, 2&3 £9.80. CSF £125.27 CT £871.55 TOTE £18.20: £4.40, £2.80, £3.00; EX 113.00.
Owner Boston R S Ian Bennett **Bred** Michael Conlon **Trained** Portway, Worcs

FOCUS
A big field for this well-established staying handicap but full of moderate, exposed performers and jumpers, and it was one of the latter group that just prevailed. The first two came from off the pace but the form makes sense rated around the placed horses.
Moonshine Beach Official explanation: jockey said gelding was denied a clear run

5368 WARWICK CONDITIONS STKS 7f 26y

4:20 (4:22) (Class 3) 3-Y-O+ £7,641 (£2,273; £1,136; £567) Stalls Low

Form				RPR
/21-	1		**Icelandic**[106] 6-9-0 0 ...(t) OscarUrbina 6 (Frank Sheridan) *hld up: hmpd over 1f out: hdwy sn after: led ins fnl f: shkn up and r.o wl* **8/1**[3]	104
-406	2	1 1/4	**Caldra (IRE)**[11] 5025 4-8-11 100 ... WilliamBuick 1 (S Kirk) *chsd ldrs: outpcd over 2f out: swtchd rt over 1f out: sn rdn: r.o* **11/4**[1]	98
4000	3	3/4	**Fishforcompliments**[16] 4845 4-8-11 91 ... TonyHamilton 4 (R A Fahey) *chsd ldr: rdn 1/2-way: led over 1f out: hdd and unable qckn ins fnl f* **8/1**[3]	96
4140	4	1	**Barons Spy (IRE)**[22] 4661 7-8-11 87 ... HayleyTurner 5 (R J Price) *stdd s: hld up: outpcd over 2f out: sn rdn: styd on: nt pce to chal* **12/1**	93
3022	5	nk	**Pawan (IRE)**[16] 4869 8-8-6 90 ...(b) AnnStokell(5) 7 (Miss A Stokell) *prom: rdn over 2f out: hmpd over 1f out: kep on* **5/1**[2]	92
-236	6	nk	**Law Lord**[179] 745 4-8-11 106 ... DarryllHolland 8 (Saeed Bin Suroor) *hld up: hdwy over 2f out: rdn whn hmpd over 1f out: one pce fnl f* **5/1**[2]	91
1610	7	1/2	**Tasdeer (USA)**[44] 3946 3-9-7 105 ... RHills 3 (M A Jarvis) *led: qcknd over 2f out: rdn and hdd over 1f out: wknd towards fin* **11/4**[1]	103

1m 25.14s (0.54) **Going Correction** +0.20s/f (Good)
WFA 3 from 4yo+ 5lb **7** Ran SP% **116.6**
Speed ratings (Par 107): **104,102,101,100,100 99,99**
toteswinger: 1&2 £4.50, 1&3 £8.40, 2&3 £4.40. CSF £31.31 TOTE £11.40: £3.90, £2.40; EX 40.20.
Owner Scuderia A4/5 **Bred** Cheveley Park Stud Ltd **Trained** Stoke Heath, Shropshire
■ Stewards' Enquiry : William Buick one-day ban: careless riding (Sep 10)

FOCUS
An interesting conditions stakes with the winner running up to his Italian form and the fourth close to his best.

NOTEBOOK
Icelandic came from last to first to win in comfortable fashion. A Group 3 winner in Italy, he acts well on good and softer ground and, coming right down the stands' side as the field fanned out, he cruised in and is clearly capable of scoring at a higher level. His trainer has recently moved from Italy to Shropshire and he may be forced to campaign Icelandic back in Listed or Group company after this performance. (op 5-1)

Caldra(IRE) was well backed on this drop in grade having struggled in Pattern company since returning from a long absence at about this time last year. He ran his race but could not match the acceleration of the winner and would have probably preferred the ground a little softer. (op 7-2)

Fishforcompliments had a pretty stiff task judged on official ratings but, after having had to be driven to take a prominent position early on, stuck on really well. However, this performance will not help to ease his current rating in handicaps. (op 10-1)

Barons Spy(IRE) is a pretty reliable performer and likes a turning track, although he was a little out of his depth judged on official ratings he did not run too badly and is probably a reasonable guide to the level of the form. (op 14-1 tchd 10-1)

Pawan(IRE), who has been most consistent of late and goes well on this track, but did not help his cause by getting involved in some scrimmaging. (op 7-1 tchd 9-2)

Law Lord goes well fresh but was a market drifter. He moved up looking a danger on this first run since Dubai in February but his effort proved short-lived. (op 3-1)

Tasdeer(USA) stays further than this so set out to make it a test of stamina but was unable to resist the challengers in the straight. (op 9-2)

5369 WARWICK RACECOURSE FOR CONFERENCES H'CAP 1m 4f 134y
4:55 (4:57) (Class 5) (0-75,74) 3-Y-O+ £3,238 (£963; £481; £240) Stalls Low

Form RPR
201 1 **Ragdollianna**[24] 4581 4-9-11 **71**........ LPKeniry 1 85+
(Norma Twomey) *hld up: hdwy over 2f out: led and edgd lft over 1f out: r.o wl: eased towards fin* **5/1**[3]
46 2 3 1/2 **Moonshine Creek**[17] 4811 6-8-9 **55** oh1........ ChrisCatlin 2 60
(P W Hiatt) *chsd ldr: rdn and ev ch over 1f out: no ex ins fnl f* **13/2**
5144 3 2 1/2 **Great View (IRE)**[21] 4690 9-9-8 **68**........(p) LiamJones 4 69
(Mrs A L M King) *prom: outpcd over 3f out: rallied over 1f out: no imp fnl f* **8/1**
1003 4 3 **Bolckow**[28] 4477 5-8-7 **56** oh4 ow1........ RussellKennemore(3) 3 52
(J T Stimpson) *prom: led over 3f out: rdn and hdd over 1f out: wknd fnl f* **11/1**
0003 5 6 **Rudry World (IRE)**[12] 4972 5-8-11 **64**........ GarryWhillans(7) 5 51
(M Mullineaux) *hld up: sme hdwy 3f out: sn rdn and wknd* **4/1**[2]
0221 6 1 **Olimpo (FR)**[17] 4820 7-9-9 **72**........ JamesMillman(3) 7 57
(B R Millman) *led: hdd over 3f out: sn rdn: wknd over 1f out* **4/1**[2]
-325 7 8 **Ethereal Flame**[62] 3350 3-9-1 **72**........ TPQueally 9 44
(H R A Cecil) *chsd ldrs: rdn over 3f out: sn wknd* **10/3**[1]
00/0 P **Esenin**[11] 5030 9-8-11 **64** oh10 ow9........ JWStevenson(7) 10 —
(Mrs Tracey Barfoot-Saunt) *hld up: bhd fnl 5f: t.o whn p.u and dismntd ins fnl f* **100/1**

2m 48.91s (4.31) **Going Correction** +0.20s/f (Good)
WFA 3 from 4yo+ 11lb 8 Ran SP% **113.5**
Speed ratings (Par 103): **94,91,90,88,84 84,79,—**
toteswinger: 1&2 £4.90, 1&3 £6.50, 2&3 £4.70. CSF £36.59 CT £253.98 TOTE £4.90: £2.10, £1.70, £2.00; EX 36.60.
Owner D M & Mrs M A Newland **Bred** Mrs M Newland **Trained** Rockley, Wilts

FOCUS
An ordinary handicap in which those at the head of the market disappointed. The winner is value for five lengths with the runner-up close to previous course form.

5370 ENTERTAIN CLIENTS AT WARWICK RACECOURSE H'CAP 1m 2f 188y
5:30 (5:32) (Class 4) (0-80,80) 3-Y-O+ £4,857 (£1,445; £722; £360) Stalls Low

Form RPR
101 1 **Rowan Rio**[49] 3793 3-9-4 **79**........ LiamJones 1 90+
(W J Haggas) *chsd ldr 2f: remained handy: led wl over 2f out: sn rdn and edgd lft: r.o wl* **13/8**[1]
-060 2 1 1/4 **Lunar Promise (IRE)**[11] 5033 6-9-3 **69**........ StephenDonohoe 7 78
(Ian Williams) *s.i.s: hld up: hdwy over 3f out: chsd wnr 2f out: sn rdn: r.o* **6/1**
3562 3 6 **Spirit Of Adjisa (IRE)**[22] 4662 4-9-11 **77**........(b) TPQueally 11 75
(Pat Eddery) *prom: rdn over 2f out: sn edgd lft: wknd fnl f* **11/2**[3]
1420 4 nk **Shabahar (IRE)**[25] 4567 4-9-6 **72**........ LPKeniry 10 69
(M J McGrath) *hld up: hdwy over b2f out: sn rdn: wknd fnl f* **20/1**
4045 5 2 **Giant Love (USA)**[15] 4894 3-8-13 **74**........ JoeFanning 2 68
(M Johnston) *prom: rdn over 2f out: wknd over 1f out* **4/1**[2]
6125 6 nk **Gallego**[11] 5008 6-9-1 **67**........ HayleyTurner 8 60
(R J Price) *s.i.s: hld up: rdn over 2f out: n.d* **14/1**
1040 7 1/2 **Dove Cottage (IRE)**[18] 4771 6-9-9 **75**........ ChrisCatlin 4 67
(W S Kittow) *prom: chsd ldr 9f out tl rdn over 2f out: wknd over 1f out* **15/2**
3001 8 5 **Snowed Under**[26] 4532 7-10-0 **80**........ DarryllHolland 3 63+
(J D Bethell) *led: rdn and hdd wl over 2f out: wknd over 1f out: eased ins fnl f* **8/1**

2m 25.77s (4.67) **Going Correction** +0.20s/f (Good)
WFA 3 from 4yo+ 9lb 8 Ran SP% **122.1**
Speed ratings (Par 105): **91,90,85,85,84 83,83,79**
toteswinger: 1&2 £4.00, 1&3 £2.80, 2&3 £9.00. CSF £13.06 CT £46.90 TOTE £2.30: £1.20, £2.80, £2.00; EX 22.90 Place 6 £ 81.93, Place 5 £ 22.45.
Owner Rowan Stud Partnership 1 **Bred** Rowan Farm Stud **Trained** Newmarket, Suffolk

FOCUS
Several non-runners in this fair handicap but the form looks reasonable rated around the placed horses.
Snowed Under Official explanation: jockey said gelding was unsuited by the soft (good to soft in places) ground
T/Plt: £35.00 to a £1 stake. Pool: £49,478.08. 1,030.81 winning tickets. T/Qpdt: £9.40 to a £1 stake. Pool: £2,872.75. 225.50 winning tickets. CR

5371 - 5373a (Foreign Racing) - See Raceform Interactive

5204 GREAT LEIGHS (A.W) (L-H)
Tuesday, August 26

OFFICIAL GOING: Standard
Wind: fresh, half behind Weather: overcast, breezy

5374 DOVER COURT (S) STKS 5f (P)
2:30 (2:31) (Class 5) 3-Y-O+ £2,590 (£770; £385; £192) Stalls Low

Form RPR
5304 1 **Pegasus Dancer (FR)**[14] 4950 4-9-0 61........(p) FrancisNorton 5 67
(K A Ryan) *taken down early: pressed ldr: rdn to ld ent fnl f: jst hld on* **9/2**[1]
400 2 nse **Monte Major (IRE)**[11] 5074 7-9-0 57........(v) JimmyQuinn 10 67
(D Shaw) *hld up in tch: rdn and hdwy over 2f out: str chal ins fnl f: jst hld* **7/1**[3]
502 3 3 1/4 **Rann Na Cille (IRE)**[35] 4285 4-9-1 51........ DO'Donohoe 4 56
(P T Midgley) *led: rdn 2f out: hdd ent fnl f: wknd last 100yds* **5/1**[2]
2030 4 3/4 **Smirfys Gold (IRE)**[21] 4703 4-9-0 49........(v) DarryllHolland 6 52
(E S McMahon) *chsd ldng pair: rdn 2f out: wknd ent fnl f* **8/1**
1501 5 1 1/4 **Game Lady**[10] 5090 4-9-1 54........ CatherineGannon 8 49
(I A Wood) *sn pushed along in midfield: kpt on steadily u.p fnl f: nvr trbld ldrs* **8/1**
5436 6 1 **Wynberg (IRE)**[11] 5046 3-9-4 64........ ChrisCatlin 3 50
(S A Callaghan) *t.k.h: hld up in midfield: rdn and effrt over 1f out: edgd lft and no prog 1f out* **9/2**[1]
6400 7 nk **Puskas (IRE)**[8] 5152 5-8-11 48........(b) TravisBlock(3) 13 43
(J M Bradley) *bhd: rdn over 2f out: pluged on fnl f: n.d* **20/1**
300 8 hd **Loyal Royal (IRE)**[38] 4186 5-8-11 62........(p) KevinGhunowa(3) 12 43
(J M Bradley) *stdd s: sn swtchd lft and dropped in bhd: nvr trbld ldrs* **14/1**
0505 9 1 3/4 **Mollyatti**[11] 5074 3-8-7 52........(b[1]) EdwardCreighton 2 31
(Miss V Haigh) *s.i.s: a bhd* **8/1**
6000 10 2 1/4 **Safranine (IRE)**[16] 4903 11-8-5 40 ow1........ AnnStokell(5) 1 24
(Miss A Stokell) *chsd ldrs: rdn 1/2-way: wknd 2f out* **50/1**
0060 11 4 1/2 **River Gleam (IRE)**[92] 2463 3-8-7 42........ RichardThomas 11 7
(A P Jarvis) *a towards rr: rdn 1/2-way: no ch last 2f* **40/1**
5100 12 8 **Montzando**[57] 3565 5-9-3 55........(v) JamesMillman(3) 9 —
(B R Millman) *sn pushed along in rr: rdn 3f out: wl bhd last 2f: eased fnl f* **20/1**

60.61 secs (0.41) **Going Correction** +0.225s/f (Slow)
WFA 3 from 4yo+ 2lb 12 Ran SP% **119.5**
Speed ratings (Par 103): **105,104,99,98,96 94,94,94,91,87 80,67**
toteswinger: 1&2 £7.90, 1&3 £5.00, 2&3 £8.00. CSF £34.67 TOTE £5.00: £1.60, £3.60, £2.20; EX 39.70.There was no bid for the winner
Owner Rievaulx Racing Syndicate **Bred** Jean-Claude Campos Et Al **Trained** Hambleton, N Yorks

FOCUS
The first seller to be run at Great Leighs and quite an open betting heat. The most notable aspect to this race was how few ever got into it as the front four were at the sharp end throughout. The third offers the best guide to the level.
Mollyatti Official explanation: jockey said filly missed the break
Safranine(IRE) Official explanation: jockey said mare hung right on both bends
Montzando Official explanation: jockey said gelding was never travelling

5375 CHRIS WOTTON CUP NOVICE AUCTION STKS 6f (P)
3:00 (3:00) (Class 5) 2-Y-O £2,914 (£867; £433; £216) Stalls Low

Form RPR
5410 1 **Fazbee (IRE)**[17] 4868 2-8-8 86........ DarryllHolland 3 87+
(P W D'Arcy) *led for 2f: trckd ldng pair after: shkn up to ld over 1f out: sn pushed clr: eased towards fin* **6/5**[1]
1 2 4 **Noodles Blue Boy**[42] 4045 2-9-0 0........ FrancisNorton 2 77
(Ollie Pears) *hld up in tch: swtchd ins and rdn over 1f out: chsd wnr ins fnl f: no ch w wnr* **2/1**[2]
1 3 1/2 **Leadenhall Lass (IRE)**[29] 4482 2-8-9 0........ IanMongan 6 71
(P M Phelan) *hld up in tch: rdn and effrt wl over 1f out: wnt 3rd ins fnl f: no ch w wnr* **7/2**[3]
1506 4 2 1/4 **Calley Ho**[39] 4143 2-8-11 68........ CatherineGannon 4 66
(Mrs L Stubbs) *dwlt: sn pushed up to chse ldr: led 4f out: rdn over 2f out: hdd over 1f out: sn outpcd by wnr: wknd and lost 2 pls fnl f* **16/1**
05 5 6 **Lady Angelica**[29] 4486 2-8-4 0........ RichardThomas 5 41
(Dr J D Scargill) *pressed ldrs on outer: hanging rt on bnd over 3f out: wknd over 2f out: wl bhd fnl f* **33/1**

1m 14.91s (1.21) **Going Correction** +0.225s/f (Slow) 5 Ran SP% **109.8**
Speed ratings (Par 94): **100,94,94,91,83**
toteswinger: 1&2 £2.70 CSF £3.85 TOTE £2.00: £1.10, £1.80; EX 3.70.
Owner Mrs Dot Burlton **Bred** Stuart McPhee Bloodstock & Morton Bstock **Trained** Newmarket, Suffolk

FOCUS
A fair little novice auction event with four of the five runners previous winners. The form is anchored by the fourth.

NOTEBOOK
Fazbee(IRE) had faced some stiff tasks in her short career including when beaten a long way over 7f on soft ground in the Sweet Solera last time, but she found this much easier despite the different surface. Although she broke well and set the early pace, her rider was happy to drop the filly in and take a lead from Calley Ho and Lady Angelica, but once the latter hung away to her right on the home bend, she was soon through the resulting gap and away and clear. She is likely to remain in low-key events in the near future, but she may have another go at gaining some black type next year. (op 5-4 tchd 11-8 in places)
Noodles Blue Boy, something of a surprise winner on his Beverley debut, was backed against the favourite. Dropped in on the inside, he tried to launch an effort tight against the inside up the home straight but although he battled on well for second, he was never anywhere near the filly. He remains unexposed. (op 11-4)
Leadenhall Lass(IRE) was ridden very differently to when successful on her Windsor debut, but although she plugged on late she could never land a blow. The extra furlong was not a problem and she remains open to a bit more improvement. (op 5-2)
Calley Ho had every chance from the front, but was swept aside when the winner was produced. He had 21lb to find with the favourite on official ratings which demonstrates the task he faced.
Lady Angelica, who had shown little in her two previous starts, showed up for a while but started to hang badly off the final bend and was soon totally outclassed. Official explanation: jockey said filly hung right

5376 TIPTREE H'CAP 1m 6f (P)
3:30 (3:30) (Class 4) (0-80,78) 3-Y-O+ £5,180 (£1,541; £770; £384) Stalls Low

Form RPR
3-02 1 **City Stable (IRE)**[11] 5042 3-9-1 **77**........ RyanMoore 9 86+
(Sir Michael Stoute) *hld up in last pair: rdn and outpcd 4f out: hdwy u.p wl over 1f out: chsd ldr ins fnl f: styd on to ld cl home* **9/4**[1]
4442 2 hd **Natural Action**[8] 5154 4-9-1 **65**........(b[1]) JimmyFortune 7 74
(W Jarvis) *wnt lft s: reminder sn after: led after 1f: squeezed along and qcknd clr wl over 3f out: 3l clr and hld hd high over 1f out: sn hrd drvn: kpt on tl hdd cl home* **3/1**[2]
2361 3 2 1/4 **Casual Affair**[21] 4699 5-9-13 **77**........ JimmyQuinn 6 83
(J D Bethell) *t.k.h: chsd ldrs: rdn and unable qckn wl over 3f out: styd on u.p to chse ldr briefly 1f out: kpt on same pce after* **4/1**[3]
0540 4 3/4 **Generous Jem**[19] 4771 5-9-10 **77**........ LukeMorris(3) 2 82
(G G Margarson) *hld up in last trio: rdn and outpcd wl over 3f out: plugged on u.p fr over 1f out: nvr nr ldrs* **16/1**
4625 5 3 1/2 **Alfie Noakes**[16] 4892 6-9-7 **71**........ JimCrowley 5 71
(Mrs A J Perrett) *hld up in midfield: rdn and outpcd wl over 3f out: plugged on but nvr pce to trble ldrs* **12/1**
0015 6 2 3/4 **Clear Reef**[17] 4866 4-9-13 **77**........(p) TGMcLaughlin 8 73
(Jane Chapple-Hyam) *stdd s: t.k.h: hld up in rr: nvr nr ldrs* **9/1**
441 7 3/4 **Darksideofthemoon (IRE)**[18] 4821 6-10-0 **78**........ PaulDoe 4 73
(N J Gifford) *led for 1f: chsd ldr after: rdn and unable qck wl over 3f out: lost 2nd 1f out: wknd* **14/1**
-422 8 1 3/4 **Callisto Moon**[34] 4314 4-9-6 **70**........(p) ChrisCatlin 1 63
(Ian Williams) *chsd ldrs: rdn over 4f out: bhd last 2f* **15/2**
6602 9 17 **Irish Quest (IRE)**[20] 4751 4-9-4 **75**........ MartinGuest(7) 3 44
(M A Jarvis) *hld up in midfield: rdn over 4f out: wl bhd over 2f out: eased fnl f: t.o* **12/1**

3m 7.37s (4.17) **Going Correction** +0.225s/f (Slow)
WFA 3 from 4yo+ 12lb 9 Ran SP% **125.5**
Speed ratings (Par 105): **97,96,95,95,93 91,91,90,80**
toteswinger: 1&2 £3.10, 1&3 £3.80, 2&3 £3.80. CSF £10.04 CT £27.25 TOTE £4.10: £1.70, £1.70, £1.80; EX 13.00.
Owner Ballymacoll Stud **Bred** Ballymacoll Stud Farm Ltd **Trained** Newmarket, Suffolk
■ Stewards' Enquiry : Jimmy Fortune one-day ban: used whip with excessive force (Sep 9)
Ryan Moore one-day ban: used whip with excessive frequency (Sep 9)

FOCUS
A fair staying handicap and a thrilling finish for a race which again showed that the best ride does not always end up with a win. The third and fourth are rated as having run close to form.

5377 BIRCH GREEN CLAIMING STKS — 1m (P)
4:00 (4:00) (Class 6) 3-Y-O — **£1,942** (£578; £288; £144) **Stalls** Centre

Form | | | | RPR
2330 **1** **Hilbre Court (USA)**[5] 5209 3-9-7 82 .... RyanMoore 1 — 83
(B J Meehan) *hld up wl bhd: hdwy on outer wl over 2f out: edgd rt wl over 1f out: led ent fnl f: drvn out* **4/9**[1]

1206 **2** *1* **Hasty Lady**[15] 4919 3-8-5 61 .... (p) FrancisNorton 7 — 65
(K A Ryan) *chsd clr ldng pair: rdn over 2f out: clsd 2f out: ev ch ent fnl f: kpt on same pce fnl f* **8/1**[3]

1065 **3** *7* **Sistos Fascination**[38] 4181 3-8-1 61 .... (p) AndreaAtzeni(7) 8 — 52
(M Botti) *hld up in main gp: rdn and effrt 3f out: ev ch ent fnl f: sn outpcd and wl btn* **16/1**

426 **4** *¾* **Rankayo Hitam (USA)**[4] 5248 3-9-5 77 .... NelsonDeSouza 2 — 61
(P F I Cole) *bmpd s: bustled along early: t.k.h after 1f: bhd: effrt on inner wl over 2f out: nt clr run over 1f out: sn swtchd lft and hrd rdn: nvr nr ldrs* **5/1**[2]

0 **5** *1* **Diktat Tempo**[10] 5086 3-8-0 0 .... DavidProbert(5) 3 — 45
(I A Wood) *s.i.s: sn bustled along: rdn and effrt 3f out: nvr pce to trble ldrs* **14/1**

0110 **6** *1 ¼* **The Hoofer (IRE)**[19] 4772 3-8-3 59 .... (b) CatherineGannon 10 — 40
(I A Wood) *sn clr w ldr: led 6f out: rdn 2f out: hdd ent fnl f: wknd* **14/1**

0000 **7** *2 ¾* **Harlequinn Danseur (IRE)**[18] 4810 3-8-8 40 .... (b) FergusSweeney 6 — 39
(G L Moore) *hld up in main gp: rdn and struggling wl over 3f out* **50/1**

00 **8** *14* **Alabjar**[47] 3870 3-8-12 0 .... SimonWhitworth 5 — 11
(J R Jenkins) *racd off the pce in midfield: rdn and struggling 1/2-way: t.o* **66/1**

0020 **9** *¾* **Micheals Boy (IRE)**[18] 4806 3-8-8 58 .... (b[1]) PatCosgrave 4 — 5
(J R Boyle) *racd freely: led for 2f: chsd ldr after tl wl over 1f out: wkng whn bmpd over 1f out: eased fnl f: t.o* **25/1**

1m 42.15s (2.25) **Going Correction** +0.225s/f (Slow) **9** Ran SP% **123.5**
Speed ratings (Par 98): **97,96,89,88,87 86,83,69,68**
toteswinger: 1&2 £2.30, 1&3 £3.90, 2&3 £8.20. CSF £5.63 TOTE £1.50: £1.02, £2.30, £3.70; EX 6.40.
Owner E H Jones (paints) Ltd **Bred** Richard Nip & Omar Trevino **Trained** Manton, Wilts

FOCUS
A very modest claimer and two went off at a scorching pace early with the first-time blinkered Micheals Boy and the blinkered The Hoofer setting each other alight. Not surprisingly, neither figured in the finish and the form is ordinary with the runner-up the best guide.

5378 LITTLE OAKLEY H'CAP — 1m (P)
4:30 (4:33) (Class 6) (0-65,65) 3-Y-O — **£1,942** (£578; £288; £144) **Stalls** Centre

Form | | | | RPR
0553 **1** **Bramalea**[4] 5218 3-9-0 **58** .... JamesDoyle 4 — 62
(B W Duke) *led for 2f: chsd ldrs after: rdn to ld again over 1f out: styd on wl fnl f* **15/2**

6263 **2** *1 ½* **Ride A White Swan**[24] 4632 3-9-4 **62** .... DarrenWilliams 6 — 63
(D Shaw) *stdd s: plld v hrd: hld up towards rr: hdwy jst over 2f out: chsd wnr ins fnl f: no imp last 100yds* **14/1**

0025 **3** *¾* **Dream Of Olwyn (IRE)**[15] 4920 3-9-5 **63** .... RyanMoore 1 — 62
(J G Given) *hld up in tch: rdn and hdwy 2f out: chsd wnr ent fnl f: kpt on same pce: lost 2nd ins fnl f* **13/2**[3]

0610 **4** *¾* **Whaston (IRE)**[27] 4533 3-9-2 **60** .... (v) JimmyQuinn 3 — 58
(J D Bethell) *dwlt: sn in tch: rdn over 2f out: hung rt ent fnl f: kpt on fnl f: nt pce to trble ldrs* **16/1**

040 **5** *½* **Cape Roberto (IRE)**[20] 4730 3-9-2 **60** .... RobertHavlin 2 — 56
(Jamie Poulton) *hld up in midfield: rdn and gd hdwy on inner wl over 1f out: kpt on but nvr getting to ldrs* **16/1**

1 **6** *hd* **Wallonia (IRE)**[24] 4651 3-9-7 **65** .... FrancisNorton 16 — 61+
(K A Ryan) *towards rr: pushed along and hdwy over 2f out: n.m.r over 1f out: r.o but nvr trbld ldrs* **7/1**

006 **7** *½* **King Of Sparta (USA)**[61] 3419 3-8-1 **50** .... DavidProbert(5) 15 — 45
(T J Fitzgerald) *hld up towards rr on outer: hdwy over 3f out: kpt on same pce fr over 1f out* **14/1**

000 **8** *nk* **Rumline**[22] 4695 3-8-3 **54** .... HollyHall(7) 14 — 48+
(S A Callaghan) *stdd and swtchd lft after s: bhd: c wd bnd 2f out: edgd lft but styd on steadily fnl f: nvr nr ldrs* **50/1**

0531 **9** *¾* **Mr Fantozzi (IRE)**[53] 3690 3-8-13 **64** .... (b) AndreaAtzeni(7) 5 — 56
(M Botti) *t.k.h: chsd ldr tl led 6f out: rdn 2f out: hdd over 1f out: wknd fnl f* **11/2**[2]

0562 **10** *½* **Welsh Opera**[12] 5019 3-8-12 **56** .... JimCrowley 7 — 47
(Mrs A J Perrett) *squeezed after s: hld up in midfield: rdn and effrt over 2f out: no imp fr over 1f out* **4/1**[1]

0030 **11** *1* **Alfredtheordinary**[72] 3065 3-9-2 **60** .... SamHitchcott 11 — 49
(M R Channon) *bhd: rdn and hdwy jst over 2f out: no hdwy fnl f: nvr trbld ldrs* **25/1**

000 **12** *¾* **Trinkila (USA)**[25] 4607 3-9-4 **62** .... NelsonDeSouza 8 — 49
(P F I Cole) *squeezed after s: a bhd: n.d* **12/1**

000 **13** *nk* **Tapas Lad (IRE)**[27] 4533 3-8-8 **55** .... (v) KevinGhunowa(3) 13 — 42
(G J Smith) *t.k.h: chsd ldrs: rdn over 2f out: wkng whn carried rt ent fnl f* **25/1**

35-0 **14** *1 ½* **Southern Mistral**[102] 2161 3-9-5 **63** .... NickyMackay 12 — 46
(M Wigham) *a towards rr: nvr a factor* **25/1**

-230 **15** *2 ¾* **Rowan Dancer**[26] 4572 3-8-11 **55** .... PatCosgrave 9 — 32
(J R Boyle) *edgd lft sn after s: racd in midfield: rdn wl over 3f out: bhd last 2f* **9/1**

0613 **16** *5* **Grit (IRE)**[13] 4990 3-9-5 **63** .... TPO'Shea 10 — 28
(M R Channon) *chsd ldrs: wnt 2nd over 5f out: drvn 3f out: wknd 2f out: wl bhd and eased fnl f* **9/1**

1m 42.52s (2.62) **Going Correction** +0.225s/f (Slow) **16** Ran SP% **139.3**
Speed ratings (Par 98): **95,93,92,92,91 91,90,90,89,89 88,87,87,85,82 77**
toteswinger: 1&2 £19.30, 1&3 £11.40, 2&3 £11.80. CSF £120.12 CT £538.64 TOTE £9.30: £2.50, £3.50, £2.50, £4.60; EX 183.60.
Owner P J Cave **Bred** P J Cave **Trained** Lambourn, Berks
■ Stewards' Enquiry : Pat Cosgrave three-day ban: careless riding (Sep 9-11)

FOCUS
A moderate handicap, but still quite competitive and there were still a whole host of horses in with a chance starting up the home straight. Those drawn low seemed to hold the advantage and they dominated the finish. The form is sound but limited.

Grit(IRE) Official explanation: jcokey said gelding had no more to give

5379 WALTON-ON-THE-NAZE H'CAP — 1m 2f (P)
5:00 (5:02) (Class 6) (0-50,50) 3-Y-O — **£1,942** (£578; £288; £144) **Stalls** Low

Form | | | | RPR
0602 **1** **Circadian Rhythm**[2] 5318 3-8-12 **50** .... J-PGuillambert 1 — 60+
(S C Williams) *hld up towards rr: hdwy 5f out: chsd ldrs jst over 2f out: rdn to chal 1f out: led ins fnl f: r.o wl* **4/1**[2]

-005 **2** *1 ¼* **Epsom Salts**[18] 4810 3-8-12 **50** .... IanMongan 7 — 57
(P M Phelan) *hld up bhd: hdwy 5f out: chal 2f out: sn led: kpt on u.p tl hdd and no ex ins fnl f* **9/1**

0030 **3** *½* **Templetuohy Max (IRE)**[30] 4457 3-8-12 **50** .... (v) JimmyQuinn 9 — 56
(J D Bethell) *hld up in tch: hdwy over 3f out: ev ch and rdn 2f out: unable qckn u.p fr over 1f out: btn last 100yds* **7/1**

0-00 **4** *6* **Fleur De Montjeu (IRE)**[20] 4721 3-8-11 **49** .... AdamKirby 3 — 43
(W R Swinburn) *hld up in midfield: hdwy over 4f out: rdn and outpcd over 3f out: plugged on u.p and hung lft wl over 1f out: nvr pce to threaten ldrs* **6/1**[3]

-004 **5** *2 ½* **Toballa**[13] 4992 3-8-10 **48** .... DarryllHolland 4 — 37
(H J Collingridge) *led for 1f: styd handy: nt clr run on inner 3f out tl swtchd rt 2f out: no imp u.p after* **7/1**

5263 **6** *½* **Pretty Officer (USA)**[18] 4810 3-8-7 **50** .... DavidProbert(5) 14 — 38
(Rae Guest) *hld up in tch: hdwy over 3f out: wnt 2nd over 2f out: led 2f out: sn hdd and btn: fdd tamely* **5/2**[1]

0-00 **7** *10* **Victory Shout (USA)**[223] 184 3-8-10 **48** .... LPKeniry 12 — 16
(J R Best) *towards rr: rdn over 7f out: sme hdwy u.p over 4f out: wknd 3f out: wl bhd last 2f* **25/1**

0000 **8** *1 ¾* **House Of Tudor**[33] 4334 3-8-12 **50** .... (b) FergusSweeney 15 — 15
(David Pinder) *led after 1f: rdn and hdd 2f out: sn wknd and wl btn* **20/1**

0500 **9** *hd* **Princess Raya**[11] 5077 3-8-11 **49** .... (t) FrancisNorton 11 — 13
(M E Rimmer) *hld up in last trio: nvr a factor* **18/1**

P0-0 **10** *nk* **Valentine Blue**[20] 4724 3-8-12 **50** .... (t) RobertHavlin 6 — 14
(A B Haynes) *s.i.s: a wl bhd* **33/1**

000 **11** *3* **La Rochette**[11] 5076 3-8-12 **50** .... AdrianMcCarthy 8 — 8
(P W Chapple-Hyam) *chsd ldr after 1f tl over 2f out: sn drvn and wknd* **16/1**

0-00 **12** *2 ¾* **Riorun (IRE)**[27] 4533 3-8-12 **50** .... JimCrowley 13 — —
(Ian Williams) *dwlt: hld up in rr: nvr a factor* **25/1**

00-0 **13** *1* **Bellalatino (IRE)**[37] 3611 3-8-6 **49** .... JackMitchell(5) 2 — —
(Norma Twomey) *hld up in midfield: hmpd bnd 7f out: rdn and struggling 4f out: wl bhd last 3f* **50/1**

0-40 **14** *nse* **Dareios (GER)**[29] 4477 3-8-8 **49** .... KevinGhunowa(3) 10 — —
(G J Smith) *chsd ldrs: rdn 5f out: wknd qckly 3f out: wl bhd last 2f: t.o* **40/1**

0340 **15** *22* **Our Dolly**[16] 4891 3-8-11 **49** .... SaleemGolam 5 — —
(Garry Moss) *racd in midfield rdn and edgd lft bnd 7f out: wl bhd last 3f: t.o* **25/1**

2m 10.74s (2.14) **Going Correction** +0.225s/f (Slow) **15** Ran SP% **132.6**
Speed ratings (Par 98): **100,99,98,93,91 91,83,82,81,81 79,77,76,76,58**
toteswinger: 1&2 £10.90, 1&3 £7.90, 2&3 £14.00. CSF £40.95 CT £262.55 TOTE £5.30: £2.40, £3.30, £2.10; EX 69.10 Place 6 £ 32.28, Place 5 £ 16.25.
Owner Circadian **Bred** Red House Stud **Trained** Newmarket, Suffolk

FOCUS
A very moderate handicap with none of these having tasted success before and just 2lb covered the entire field. The pace was a fair one though and they finished spread out all over Essex, but it will take a leap of faith to imagine some of these ever winning a race. The form is rated around the placed horses.
Toballa Official explanation: jockey said filly was denied a clear run
Our Dolly Official explanation: jockey said filly was never travelling
T/Jkpt: £13,213.70 to a £1 stake. Pool: £37,221.96. 2.00 winning tickets. T/Plt: £51.20 to a £1 stake. Pool: £82,208.21. 1,170.99 winning tickets. T/Qpdt: £18.90 to a £1 stake. Pool: £4,656.80. 182.10 winning tickets. SP

5357 RIPON (R-H)
Tuesday, August 26

OFFICIAL GOING: Good to soft (7.7)
Wind: Virtually nil Weather: Overcast

5380 CLARO (S) STKS — 1m 1f 170y
2:15 (2:15) (Class 5) 3-4-Y-O — **£2,590** (£770; £385; £192) **Stalls** High

Form | | | | RPR
3 **1** **Sorrento Moon (IRE)**[16] 4901 4-8-12 43 .... PJMcDonald(3) 2 — 52
(G M Moore) *hld up towards rr: hdwy 3f out: swtchd ins and rdn along 2f out: drvn and styd on to ld ent fnl f: sn edgd lft and kpt on wl towards fin* **7/2**[2]

00 **2** *hd* **Baileys Benchmark**[22] 4689 3-8-7 0 .... TomEaves 1 — 52
(M E Sowersby) *in rr: hdwy on outer wl over 2f out: rdn to chse ldrs over 1f out: drvn and ev ch ins fnl f: edgd rt and kpt on towards fin* **12/1**

5361 **3** *hd* **Intersky Melody (USA)**[10] 3230 3-9-4 57 .... DeanMcKeown 7 — 62
(R M Whitaker) *trckd ldrs: hdwy over 4f out: rdn to ld wl over 1f out: drvn and hdd ent fnl f: kpt on u.p* **5/2**[1]

4004 **4** *3* **Carry On Cleo**[22] 4680 3-8-9 54 ow1 .... (v) SladeO'Hara(5) 9 — 52
(A Berry) *cl up: led over 4f out: rdn along 3f out: hdd wl over 1f out and sn drvn: wknd ins fnl f* **7/1**

0000 **5** *4* **Take To The Skies (IRE)**[48] 3839 4-9-3 46 .... MichaelJStainton(3) 4 — 41
(Miss Tracy Waggott) *chsd ldrs: rdn along over 2f out: sn one pce* **25/1**

0-0 **6** *6* **Glenisland**[49] 3810 4-8-12 46 .... RussellKennemore(3) 8 — 24
(Mrs L Williamson) *chsd ldrs: rdn along 3f out: drvn and wknd 2f out* **20/1**

50-2 **7** *16* **Viscaya (IRE)**[54] 3640 3-8-4 55 .... AndrewMullen(3) 10 — —
(Mrs A Duffield) *towards rr: pushed along 1/2-way: nvr a factor* **9/2**[3]

0000 **8** *5* **Carlton Mac**[32] 4381 3-8-9 41 .... (b) NeilBrown(3) 3 — —
(N Bycroft) *a towards rr* **14/1**

0-06 **9** *18* **Bond Scissorsister (IRE)**[54] 3640 3-8-7 47 .... SilvestreDeSousa 5 — —
(G R Oldroyd) *in tch: rdn along 4f out and sn wknd* **9/1**

00-0 **10** *76* **Caffrey Kelly**[50] 3791 3-8-5 16 .... PNolan(7) 11 — —
(A Kirtley) *t.k.h: sn led: pushed along and hdd over 4f out: sn wknd* **100/1**

2m 12.42s (7.02) **Going Correction** +0.65s/f (Yiel)
WFA 3 from 4yo 8lb **10** Ran SP% **115.4**
Speed ratings (Par 103): **97,96,96,94,91 86,73,69,55,—**
toteswinger: 1&2 £9.50, 1&3 £3.30, 2&3 £5.60. CSF £43.35 TOTE £5.10: £2.00, £3.50, £1.40; EX 57.80 Trifecta £276.10 Pool: £447.75, 1.20 winning units.There was no bid for the winner. Viscaya was claimed by M J Bourn for £6,000
Owner Mrs S Sunderland **Bred** John Cullinan **Trained** Middleham Moor, N Yorks
■ Stewards' Enquiry : P J McDonald three-day ban: used whip with excessive frequency (Sep 9-11)

The Form Book, Raceform Ltd, Compton, RG20 6NL

Silvestre De Sousa two-day ban: careless riding (Sep 9-10)
Tom Eaves two-day ban: used whip with excessive force (Sep 9-10)

FOCUS
A weak seller and it looked pretty hard work for the runners up the home straight. The first two are both rated as up 3lb.
Viscaya(IRE) Official explanation: jockey said filly suffered interference entering the bottom bend

5381 RIPON LAND ROVER NURSERY 6f
2:45 (2:46) (Class 4) 2-Y-O **£4,533** (£1,348; £674; £336) **Stalls** Low

Form RPR
5303 **1** **Coleorton Choice**[17] 4857 2-8-8 **70**............................... RobertWinston 4 78+
(K A Ryan) *mde all stands' side: rdn wl over 1f out: kpt on ins fnl f* **11/2**[3]
31 **2** ½ **Needwood Lad**[20] 4734 2-9-0 **76**..................................... PaulHanagan 10 81+
(R A Fahey) *in rr far side and pushed along after 2f: hdwy 2f out: swtchd to ins and rdn over 1f out: styd on strly to ld that gp ins fnl f: kpt on* **7/4**[1]
5313 **3** 2¾ **Lisburn (IRE)**[14] 4956 2-8-11 **73**.............................. AlanMunro 12 69
(M Brittain) *led far side gp: rdn along 2f out: drvn and hdd ins fnl f: kpty on same pce: 2nd in gp* **9/2**[2]
421 **4** 3 **Fitzolini**[11] 5043 2-8-13 **75**.......................................(p) SilvestreDeSousa 6 62
(A D Brown) *chsd wnr stands' side: rdn along 2f out: grad wknd: 2nd in gp* **12/1**
6626 **5** ½ **Veronicas Boy**[41] 4072 2-8-8 **73**.............................. PJMcDonald(3) 5 59
(G M Moore) *in rr stands' side: hdwy 1/2-way: swtchd wd and pushed along 2f out: kpt on ins fnl f: nrst fin: 3rd in gp* **25/1**
1340 **6** 2 **Toby Tyler**[20] 4733 2-8-11 **73**..................................... JamieMoriarty 2 53
(P T Midgley) *towards rr stands' side: pushed along 1/2-way: hdwy 2f out: sn rdn and no imp appr last: 4th in gp* **14/1**
5216 **7** nse **Harriet's Girl**[59] 3496 2-9-3 **79**.................................. AndrewElliott 11 59
(K R Burke) *chsd ldr far side: rdn along 2f out: drvn and wknd appr fnl f: 3rd in gp* **14/1**
1224 **8** 6 **Madame Jourdain (IRE)**[39] 4143 2-7-13 **66**.......... PatrickDonaghy(5) 8 28
(N Wilson) *chsd ldrs stands' side: rdn along over 2f out: grad wknd: 5th in gp* **14/1**
1550 **9** hd **Deadly Encounter (IRE)**[17] 4857 2-9-7 **83**.................. TonyHamilton 9 44
(R A Fahey) *a in rr stands' side: 6th in gp* **20/1**
550 **10** ½ **Tagula Sunset (IRE)**[103] 2134 2-7-5 **60** oh5................. JamieKyne(7) 13 20
(P T Midgley) *chsd ldng pair far side: rdn along over 2f out: sn wknd: 4th in gp* **50/1**
456 **11** 3½ **Pacific Bay (IRE)**[55] 3597 2-8-3 **68**........................ AndrewMullen(3) 7 17
(Mrs A Duffield) *chsd ldrs stands' side: rdn along over 2f out and sn wknd: 7th in gp* **50/1**
633 **12** 1 **Abbey Steps (IRE)**[10] 5106 2-8-2 **67**...................... DuranFentiman(3) 3 13
(T D Easterby) *a towards rr stands' side: 8th in gp* **9/1**

1m 16.54s (3.54) **Going Correction** +0.15s/f (Good) **12** Ran SP% **120.2**
Speed ratings (Par 96): **82,81,77,73,73 70,70,62,62,61 56,55**
toteswinger: 1&2 £2.10, 1&3 £5.00, 2&3 £2.60. CSF £15.12 CT £48.56 TOTE £6.60: £2.00, £1.40, £1.90; EX 16.50 Trifecta £35.90 Pool: £419.02, 8.63 winning units.
Owner Coleorton Moor Racing **Bred** A Holmes **Trained** Hambleton, N Yorks
■ Stewards' Enquiry : Alan Munro one-day ban: failed to ride to draw (Sep 9)
Andrew Elliott one-day ban: failed to ride to draw (Sep 9)

FOCUS
A fair nursery but the winning time was very slow for a race like this. They split into two groups, but there seemed no real bias.

NOTEBOOK
Coleorton Choice had proved himself on testing ground when a close third at Haydock last time, for which he had been raised 2lb, and was opening his account at the fifth time of asking. The return to this extra furlong proved right up his street as he was able to race more handily and there can be no faulting his attitude when put under maximum pressure. He was a long way clear of the remainder of the near-side group and there should still be more to come, despite another weight rise for this. (tchd 5-1)
Needwood Lad, a ready maiden winner on similar ground at Newcastle 20 days previously, met plenty of market support for this switch to a nursery. He raced on the far side and looked to be in trouble around two furlongs out, but he eventually motored home inside the closing stages. He only just failed to reel in the winner and finished a clear second best, but while he looks to have begun life in this sphere on a good mark, he may need a stiffer test now. (tchd 15-8 and 2-1 in a place)
Lisburn(IRE) took the far-side group along through the early stages and, while proving no match for the first pair at the business end, she kept on gamely enough when headed. She rates a sound enough benchmark for the form. (op 11-2 tchd 6-1)
Fitzolini had won very well at Catterick 11 days previously and he had his chance here, but an 11lb rise now looks to have put him firmly in the Handicapper's grip. (op 11-1)
Veronicas Boy could find only the same pace on this drop back a furlong and really looks to want a stiffer test. (op 33-1)

5382 CITY OF RIPON STKS (H'CAP) 1m 1f 170y
3:15 (3:16) (Class 3) (0-90,90) 3-Y-O+
£8,723 (£2,612; £1,306; £653; £326; £163) **Stalls** High

Form RPR
12-2 **1** **Rose Street (IRE)**[27] 4528 4-9-10 **87**........................... PhilipRobinson 7 101+
(M A Jarvis) *trckd ldng pair: hdwy 3f out: rdn wl over 1f out: styd on to ld fnl 100yds* **11/8**[1]
5050 **2** 2 **Veiled Applause**[22] 4688 5-9-6 **83**........................... GrahamGibbons 2 92
(J J Quinn) *in rr: pushed along 1/2-way: stdy hdwy on inner 3f out: rdn to chse ldrs wl over 1f out: swtchd lft and drvn ent fnl f: kpt on towards fin* **16/1**
5230 **3** ¾ **Suits Me**[17] 4856 5-9-9 **86**.. MickyFenton 8 94
(T P Tate) *led: rdn along 3f out: drvn wl over 1f out: hdd and no ex last 100yds* **8/1**[3]
505 **4** 4 **Intersky Charm (USA)**[40] 4111 4-8-12 **75**.................. DeanMcKeown 3 74
(R M Whitaker) *in tch: hdwy to trck ldrs 4f out: rdn over 2f out: sn drvn and no imp* **20/1**
2026 **5** 2¾ **Eglevski (IRE)**[17] 4867 4-9-7 **84**.....................................(b[1]) SebSanders 10 78
(J L Dunlop) *hld up: stdy hdwy on outer 4f out: effrt over 2f out and sn ev ch: rdn and hung lft and rt wl over 1f out: sn wknd* **9/2**[2]
134 **6** nk **Magic Echo**[13] 4970 4-9-7 **87**...................................... NeilBrown(3) 4 80
(M Dods) *cl up: rdn along 3f out: drvn over 2f out and grad wknd* **9/1**
3524 **7** 3¼ **Motafarred (IRE)**[12] 5005 6-9-0 **77**............................ PaulMulrennan 12 63
(Micky Hammond) *trckd ldrs on inner: effrt over 3f out: sn rdn and wknd* **14/1**
400- **8** 9 **Harvest Warrior**[284] 5623 6-9-0 **77**............................... DavidAllan 5 44
(T D Easterby) *s.i.s: a in rr* **33/1**
00 **9** 2¾ **Turfshuffle (GER)**[17] 4853 5-9-13 **90**.................... StephenDonohoe 11 52
(Ian Williams) *towards rr: rdn along over 3f out and sn bhd* **50/1**
0143 **10** 40 **Kingsdale Orion (IRE)**[12] 5005 4-9-10 **87**......................(tp) TomEaves 6 —
(B Ellison) *in tch: rdn along over 4f out and sn wknd* **9/1**
0060 **11** 33 **Charlie Tokyo (IRE)**[17] 4856 5-9-11 **88**.........................(b) PaulHanagan 1 —
(R A Fahey) *prom: pushed along over 4f out: sn lost pl and bhd: lost action and eased fnl 3f* **14/1**

2m 10.0s (4.60) **Going Correction** +0.65s/f (Yiel) **11** Ran SP% **120.3**
Speed ratings (Par 107): **107,105,104,101,99 99,96,89,87,55 28**
toteswinger: 1&2 £7.80, 1&3 £3.70, 2&3 £16.30. CSF £27.61 CT £141.88 TOTE £2.30: £1.10, £5.30, £2.50; EX 31.20 Trifecta £163.00 Pool: £639.15, 2.90 winning units.
Owner Mr & Mrs Raymond Anderson Green **Bred** Margaret Conlon **Trained** Newmarket, Suffolk

FOCUS
A good handicap for the grade run at a sound pace and the form looks solid using the placed horses as a guide.

NOTEBOOK
Rose Street(IRE) resumed winning ways on this return from the All-Weather and looked better the further she went on this step back up in trip. She had to be given a wake-up call by her jockey passing the three-furlong pole and still looks to be learning her trade, but her class eventually told where it really mattered. This imposing filly ought to have no trouble staying further and really does look a progressive sort, so a likely weight rise may well not be enough to scupper a follow-up bid. (op 6-5 tchd 13-8)
Veiled Applause was never going to get to the winner, but this was a much-improved effort from him at a track he clearly likes. He is versatile as regards underfoot conditions. (tchd 14-1)
Suits Me, who came unstuck on testing ground at Haydock last time, had won this event last term from a 15lb lower mark and he put up a bold display from the front. He can be rated a little better than the bare form as he was hardly left alone in the lead, but still looks weighted to around his best in any case. (op 10-1)
Intersky Charm(USA) had yet to encounter ground this easy on turf and he was not disgraced. He ran close to his course-and-distance form with the runner-up and the track evidently suits him. (op 25-1)
Eglevski(IRE) reached for the first-time blinkers and it is not hard to see just why, as he looked most unwilling when put under pressure in the home straight. He is now one to avoid. (op 15-2)
Magic Echo was given a positive ride and had her chance, but she eventually felt the pinch nearing the final furlong and was well beaten off. She needs some further respite from the Handicapper on this evidence, but may get it now. (op 12-1)
Motafarred(IRE) was never a serious threat and is this trip on such ground really stretches his stamina to the limit. (op 16-1 tchd 12-1)
Kingsdale Orion(IRE) is proven on a soft surface and had run a sound race when third from this mark at Beverley 12 days previously. He was ultimately beaten at the three-furlong pole, however, and something presumably went amiss. (op 17-2 tchd 8-1)
Charlie Tokyo(IRE) Official explanation: jockey said gelding stumbled on the bend

5383 SAPPER CONDITIONS STKS 5f
3:45 (3:45) (Class 3) 2-Y-O **£6,542** (£1,959; £979; £490) **Stalls** Low

Form RPR
2 **1** **Magic Cat**[30] 4456 2-9-0 0.. AndrewElliott 2 97+
(K R Burke) *trckd ldng pair: hdwy wl over 1f out: swtchd rt and rdn ent fnl f: rdn to ld last 100yds: r.o* **7/2**[3]
3100 **2** 1½ **Thunderous Mood (USA)**[28] 4507 2-9-4 97......................... JohnEgan 4 96
(P F I Cole) *cl up: rdn along 1/2-way: drvn and slt ld over 1f out: hdd and no ex last 100yds* **15/8**[2]
2251 **3** ½ **Caranbola**[19] 4781 2-9-1 92.. AlanMunro 1 91
(M Brittain) *led: rdn along 1/2-way: drvn and hdd over 1f out: one pce ins fnl f* **1/1**[1]
4 27 **Alibar's Surprise (IRE)** 2-8-9 0 ow8.......................... SladeO'Hara(5) 3 —
(A Berry) *s.i.s: a outpcd and bhd* **80/1**

61.67 secs (0.97) **Going Correction** +0.15s/f (Good) **4** Ran SP% **108.2**
Speed ratings (Par 98): **98,95,94,51**
CSF £10.28 TOTE £4.50; EX 9.40.
Owner Ray Bailey **Bred** R Bailey **Trained** Middleham Moor, N Yorks

FOCUS
This decent little conditions event was run at a strong early pace and the two form principals, Thunderous Mood and Caranbola, looked to cut each other's throats in the battle for the lead. However, they set the level with the winner looking up to Listed level.

NOTEBOOK
Magic Cat was suited by the strong pace and eventually came through to break his duck at the second time of asking. He had only just failed on debut at Pontefract a month previously when bustling up a 1-5 shot, but he showed that to be no fluke and did the job well in this higher grade. He also acted without fuss on the much softer ground and is clearly well thought of by his trainer, as he was the only runner in this field to currently hold a Group entry (Mill Reef). He looks the sort to make his mark in a better company and, considering his dam was a triple 6f winner, he should get another furlong before too long. However, he may just be better off keeping to the minimum trip for the short term. (op 3-1 tchd 11-4)
Thunderous Mood(USA) had been beaten only four lengths in the Molecomb last-time out and was best in according to adjusted official ratings. He held every chance and was not helped by being hassled for the lead, really looking to go off too quick. The softer ground was probably not ideal for him either, but a mark of 97 dictates he is not going to prove simple to place successfully now. (op 2-1 tchd 9-4)
Caranbola has proved herself a game filly this season and acts on such ground, but she also looked to go off too fast early on. She showed a tendency to hang left despite having the stands' rail to race against and was not quite at her best. (op 11-10 tchd 6-5 and 5-4 in a place)
Alibar's Surprise(IRE), whose claiming rider put up 8lb overweight, was outclassed on her debut. (op 50-1)

5384 DESTINATION HARROGATE FILLIES' MAIDEN AUCTION STKS 5f
4:15 (4:16) (Class 5) 2-Y-O **£2,914** (£867; £433; £216) **Stalls** Low

Form RPR
2 **1** **Blades Princess**[28] 4499 2-8-7 0.............................. GrahamGibbons 12 79+
(E S McMahon) *cl up gng wl: led 1f out: edgd rt and qcknd clr ins fnl f* **2/1**[1]
5245 **2** 3 **Sea Crest**[10] 5106 2-8-4 70.. TWilliams 4 62+
(M Brittain) *led: rdn along and hdd 1/2-way: cl up whn n.m.r and swtchd rt 1f out: sn drvn and kpt on: no ch w wnr* **3/1**[2]
2 **3** nk **Whispering Spirit (IRE)**[52] 3714 2-8-4 0................. AndrewMullen(3) 6 64
(Mrs A Duffield) *chsd ldrs: rdn and n.m.r over 1f out: styd on ins fnl f to take 3rd nr line* **4/1**[3]
004 **4** nk **Bubbly Baby**[13] 4965 2-8-1 62................................... DuranFentiman(3) 5 60
(T D Easterby) *cl up: led 1/2-way: rdn 2f out: drvn: wandered and hdd 1f out: wknd ins fnl f* **10/1**
6660 **5** 5 **That Boy Ronaldo**[17] 4857 2-8-0 56......................... CharlotteKerton(7) 2 45
(A Berry) *in tch: rdn along 2f out: sn one pce* **25/1**
04 **6** hd **Feeling Stylish (IRE)**[11] 5072 2-8-7 0.............................. KimTinkler 10 44
(N Tinkler) *racd wd: towards rr tl sme late hdwy* **50/1**
3 **7** 1½ **Sensacion Sensual**[11] 5072 2-8-11 0................................ TPQueally 8 43
(J G Given) *dwlt and towards rr: hdwy and in tch 1/2-way: sn rdn and wknd* **13/2**
0 **8** 1½ **Following Wind**[20] 4734 2-8-11 0................................. RobertWinston 9 38
(K A Ryan) *a towards rr* **20/1**

9 *hd* **Angelsbemine** 2-8-4 0 .... PaulHanagan 1 30
(J R Norton) *a in rr* **66/1**

6 **10** *3/4* **Miss Thippawan (USA)**[10] 5107 2-8-4 0 .... SilvestreDeSousa 7 27
(P T Midgley) *chsd ldrs: rdn along 1/2-way: sn wknd* **40/1**

11 *13* **Perfect Honour (IRE)** 2-8-4 0 .... RoystonFfrench 11 —
(Joss Saville) *s.i.s: a outpcd and bhd* **40/1**

62.53 secs (1.83) **Going Correction** +0.15s/f (Good) **11** Ran SP% **117.7**
Speed ratings (Par 91): **91,86,85,85,77 76,74,72,71,70 49**
toteswinger: 1&2 £2.70, 1&3 £3.10, 2&3 £3.90. CSF £7.44 TOTE £3.40: £1.30, £1.70, £2.00; EX 10.00 Trifecta £21.30 Pool: £616.09, 21.36 winning units.

Owner R L Bedding **Bred** Mrs J McMahon **Trained** Lichfield, Staffs

■ Stewards' Enquiry : Andrew Mullen one-day ban: used whip with excessive frequency and without giving filly time to respond (Sep 9)

FOCUS
A modest juvenile fillies' maiden, run at a sound pace and the runners elected to race on the near side through the first half of the contest. the runner-up is the best guide to the form.

NOTEBOOK
Blades Princess confirmed the promise of her debut second at Beverley 28 days previously and came home to go one better in good style. She showed a much more professional attitude, looked well suited by the slower ground, and could really have been called the winner soon after passing the two-furlong marker. A filly with some scope, she should come on again for the experience and it will be interesting to see how the Handicapper now assesses her effort. (op 15-8 tchd 5-2)

Sea Crest was the subject of strong market support on this drop back to the minimum, but she was not helped by being taken on for the early lead and wanted to hang left when racing up the stands' rail. She kept to her task and picked up again when switched wide inside the final furlong, but she does appear the type who needs to be left alone out in front. With an official mark of 70 she could also be better off switching to a nursery now. (op 13-2)

Whispering Spirit(IRE) had shown promise when second on her debut at Carlisle on easy ground, but had been off for 52 days subsequently and she was ultimately doing all of her best work towards the finish. Another furlong may now prove ideal for her or perhaps the return to a stiffer track at this distance, but she does have the ability to win in maiden company. (tchd 7-2)

Bubbly Baby, officially rated 62 after her three previous runs, helped to force the early pace on the near side and probably ran to her previous level in defeat. (op 11-1 tchd 12-1)

That Boy Ronaldo was never in the hunt from off the pace. (op 33-1)

Feeling Stylish(IRE) needed this in order to qualify for a nursery mark.

Sensacion Sensual failed to run to the level of her debut on this more testing surface and drop in trip. Official explanation: trainer said filly was unsuited by the good to soft ground (op 11-2 tchd 9-2)

Miss Thippawan(USA) Official explanation: trainer said filly was unsuited by the good to soft ground

Perfect Honour(IRE) Official explanation: jockey said filly missed the break

5385 WAKEMAN STAYERS H'CAP 2m
4:45 (4:46) (Class 6) (0-65,65) 3-Y-O+ £2,590 (£770; £385; £192) Stalls Low

Form RPR

3165 **1** **Chiff Chaff**[2] 5322 4-8-9 49 oh1 .... TolleyDean(3) 2 60
(C R Dore) *a.p: hdwy to ld 3f out: rdn wl over 1f out: drvn and edgd rt ins fnl f: hld on wl* **25/1**

62 **2** *3/4* **Stoop To Conquer**[40] 4105 8-9-11 62 .... TonyCulhane 6 72
(A W Carroll) *in tch: hdwy 3f out: rdn to chse ldrs 2f out: drvn to chse wnr and ev ch ins fnl f: kpt on same pce towards fin* **13/2**[2]

-354 **3** *5* **Aleron (IRE)**[60] 2701 10-9-10 61 .... (p) GrahamGibbons 17 65
(J J Quinn) *hld up in midfield: hdwy on inner 3f out: rdn to chse ldrs 2f out: n.m.r and swtchd lft over 1f out: drvn and kpt on same pce ins fnl f* **9/1**

116- **4** *2 1/4* **Kentucky Boy (IRE)**[192] 5906 4-9-8 59 .... TonyHamilton 9 60
(Jedd O'Keeffe) *chsd ldrs on inner: rdn along 3f out: drvn 2f out and kpt on same pce* **22/1**

4/03 **5** *nse* **Restart (IRE)**[47] 3863 7-9-0 51 .... LiamJones 16 52
(Lucinda Featherstone) *hld up towards rr: gd hdwy on wd outside over 2f out and sn rdn: drvn over 1f out: kpt on ins fnl f: nrst fin* **7/1**[3]

1062 **6** *1 1/2* **Sendali (FR)**[15] 4924 4-8-13 50 .... AlanMunro 15 49
(J D Bethell) *hld up towards rr: hdwy over 3f out: rdn along 2f out: plugged on same pce appr fnl f: nt rch ldrs* **8/1**

50-2 **7** *3 1/2* **Rightful Ruler**[14] 4947 6-8-7 49 .... AshleyHamblett(5) 3 47+
(N Wilson) *led: clr 1/2-way: rdn along 4f out: hdd 3f out: sn drvn and wknd 2f out: eased appr fnl f* **10/1**

0063 **8** *1/2* **Nelsons Column (IRE)**[21] 4698 5-9-1 55 .... PJMcDonald(3) 10 50
(G M Moore) *chsd ldr: rdn along 4f out: drvn wl over 2f out and grad wknd* **18/1**

5405 **9** *3 1/4* **Rocknest Island (IRE)**[17] 4848 5-8-12 49 .... (p) RoystonFfrench 11 40
(P D Niven) *hld up towards rr: hdwy 4f out: sn rdn along and nvr nr ldrs* **12/1**

-355 **10** *5* **Industrial Star (IRE)**[24] 4652 7-10-0 65 .... (v[1]) SebSanders 1 50
(Micky Hammond) *reminders after s and sn chsng ldrs: rdn along 3f out and sn wknd* **20/1**

6414 **11** *10* **Jackday (IRE)**[20] 4735 3-8-7 58 .... DavidAllan 8 31
(T D Easterby) *chsd ldrs: effrt over 3f out: rdn along wl over 2f out and sn wknd* **4/1**[1]

2164 **12** *4 1/2* **Mister Pete (IRE)**[15] 4924 5-8-12 52 .... DominicFox(3) 4 19
(W Storey) *chsd ldrs: rdn along 3f out: drvn over 2f out and sn wknd* **12/1**

0002 **13** *1* **Lodgician (IRE)**[30] 4452 6-9-0 51 .... PaulHanagan 7 17
(K G Reveley) *hld up: a in rr* **20/1**

1 **14** *26* **Spiders Star**[21] 4698 5-9-2 53 ow3 .... MHNaughton 13 —
(Miss Kate Milligan) *a bhd* **25/1**

6063 **15** *30* **Lady Killer Queen**[15] 4924 4-9-6 57 .... (v) DNolan 12 —
(D Carroll) *hld up: a towards rr* **25/1**

3m 40.16s (8.36) **Going Correction** +0.65s/f (Yiel)
WFA 3 from 4yo+ 14lb **15** Ran SP% **122.1**
Speed ratings (Par 101): **105,104,102,101,100 100,98,98,96,94 89,86,86,73,58**
toteswinger: 1&2 £41.80, 1&3 £65.20, 2&3 £14.70. CSF £167.47 CT £1590.35 TOTE £30.30: £9.90, £2.80, £3.90; EX 397.30 TRIFECTA Not won. Place 6 £ 68.90, Place 5 £ 47.17.

Owner J A Higson & Castles UK **Bred** Sir Thomas Pilkington **Trained** West Pinchbeck, Lincs

FOCUS
This moderate staying handicap was run at a sound gallop and the first pair eventually came clear of the remainder. The placed horses set the level of the form, which looks sound.

Rightful Ruler Official explanation: jockey said gelding had no more to give

Jackday(IRE) Official explanation: trainer had no explanation for the poor form shown

Spiders Star Official explanation: trainer said mare was unsuited by the good to soft ground

T/Plt: £75.30 to a £1 stake. Pool: £90,254.29. 874.47 winning tickets. T/Qpdt: £40.10 to a £1 stake. Pool: £4,862.50. 89.60 winning tickets. JR

5386 - (Foreign Racing) - See Raceform Interactive

4846

AYR (L-H)
Wednesday, August 27

OFFICIAL GOING: Soft (good to soft in places in home straight)
Wind: Breezy, across Weather: Overcast

5387 VLADIVAR VODKA E B F MAIDEN STKS 7f 50y
2:10 (2:15) (Class 4) 2-Y-O £5,828 (£1,734; £866; £432) Stalls Low

Form RPR

3 **1** **Zafisio (IRE)**[13] 5029 2-9-3 0 .... GrahamGibbons 10 80
(P A Blockley) *in tch: effrt 2f out: styd on wl fnl f: led cl home* **9/2**[2]

3 **2** *hd* **Henderson Park**[38] 4214 2-8-10 0 .... FrederikTylicki(7) 13 80
(A G Foster) *cl up: led over 2f out: kpt on fnl f: hdd cl home* **5/1**[3]

3 *3 3/4* **High Office** 2-8-10 0 .... BMcHugh(7) 7 71
(R A Fahey) *t.k.h in midfield: effrt over 2f out: kpt on u.p fnl f* **33/1**

6 **4** *2 3/4* **Island Chief**[16] 4921 2-9-0 0 .... MichaelJStainton(3) 14 64+
(K A Ryan) *prom: effrt 3f out: no ex appr fnl f* **13/2**

0 **5** *2* **Mister Bombastic (IRE)**[32] 4415 2-9-0 0 .... NeilBrown(3) 9 59
(M Dods) *trckd ldrs: ev ch over 2f out: hung lft and wknd over 1f out* **100/1**

6 *1 1/4* **Hard Luck Story** 2-9-3 0 .... SilvestreDeSousa 11 56+
(Miss L A Perratt) *s.i.s: bhd tl sme late hdwy: n.d* **66/1**

7 *shd* **Tartan Gunna** 2-9-3 0 .... J-PGuillambert 8 56+
(M Johnston) *missed break: bhd: effrt 3f out: no imp fr 2f out* **5/2**[1]

52 **8** *2 1/2* **Atabaas Allure (FR)**[20] 4788 2-8-12 0 .... RoystonFfrench 1 45
(M Johnston) *slt ld to over 2f out: wknd over 1f out* **6/1**

5 **9** *hd* **New Tricks**[37] 4237 2-8-12 0 .... GaryBartley(5) 12 49
(Miss L A Perratt) *bhd: drvn and outpcd 3f out: n.d after* **33/1**

40 **10** *15* **Postman**[33] 4394 2-9-3 0 .... TomEaves 5 13
(B Smart) *midfield: drvn and outpcd 3f out: sn btn* **9/1**

0 **11** *12* **Thatwasthepension (IRE)**[18] 4847 2-9-3 0 .... AndrewElliott 2 —
(B Storey) *w ldr tl wknd over 2f out* **200/1**

12 *1* **Olympian Order (IRE)** 2-9-3 0 .... DeanMcKeown 4 —
(G A Swinbank) *s.i.s: bhd: drvn 1/2-way: nvr on terms* **33/1**

5 **13** *19* **Lady Dunhill (IRE)**[18] 4847 2-8-12 0 .... DanielTudhope 6 —
(J S Goldie) *bhd: struggling 1/2-way: nvr on terms* **25/1**

1m 38.0s (4.60) **Going Correction** +0.725s/f (Yiel) **13** Ran SP% **117.2**
Speed ratings (Par 96): **102,101,97,94,92 90,90,87,87,70 56,55,33**
toteswinger: 1&2 £5.10, 1&3 £30.20, 2&3 £22.00. CSF £25.42 TOTE £5.10: £2.10, £2.10, £7.20; EX 27.80.

Owner H Downs **Bred** Airlie Stud And Sir Thomas Pilkington **Trained** Lambourn, Berks

FOCUS
An ordinary miaden. The runners made for the centre of the track once into the home straight. A decent winning time for a race like this given the conditions, 0.25 seconds faster than the later handicap for older horses and the form looks solid.

NOTEBOOK
Zafisio(IRE) had run green on his debut at Sandown, but still shaped with definite promise in finishing third of five. Sent a long way north for this second appearance, he was slow to find his stride in common with several of his rivals. Coming under pressure with over 2f to run, he stayed on to get to the leader almost on the line. The return to 1m will suit and he is clearly well at home in this sort of ground. (tchd 4-1)

Henderson Park, third on his debut at Redcar in a race that has been working out quite well, went for home in the straight and stuck his neck out willingly, only to be pipped in the last couple of strides. He is capable of going one better if kept to a realistic level. (op 7-2)

High Office, already gelded, is bred to come into his own over further than this in time and stayed on in a pleasing manner for third. He should certainly make the grade. (op 50-1)

Island Chief stepped up on the form of his debut at Thirsk, where he looked sorely in need of the experience, and there could be further improvement in him still after this second run. (op 12-1)

Mister Bombastic(IRE) showed little first time and this was much more encouraging, although he is the type who will not be seen to best effect until further down the line. (tchd 66-1)

Hard Luck Story fell out of the stalls and did well to reach his finishing position. He is entitled to come on considerably for this. (op 50-1 tchd 80-1)

Tartan Gunna was very slow to break and, although closing down the outside in the straight, he ran green and never looked like seriously getting involved. Not knocked about in a hopeless cause, this half-brother to the useful duo Fondled and Caressed will probably be worth another chance. (tchd 9-4 and 11-4 in places)

Atabaas Allure(FR) weakened in the latter stages but is now eligible for handicaps. (op 11-2 tchd 5-1)

Postman has failed to build on the promise of his debut effort but the ground was a plausible excuse here. (op 12-1)

5388 COKE ZERO H'CAP 1m 2f
2:40 (2:41) (Class 6) (0-65,63) 3-Y-O £2,590 (£770; £385; £192) Stalls Low

Form RPR

-602 **1** **Bosamcliff (IRE)**[19] 4810 3-9-4 60 .... J-PGuillambert 8 69+
(A B Haynes) *in tch: smooth hdwy over 2f out: led over 1f out: pushed out* **5/2**[2]

4564 **2** *3* **Always Brave**[14] 4991 3-9-7 63 .... RoystonFfrench 6 66
(M Johnston) *trckd ldrs: effrt and ev ch over 1f out: kpt on same pce fnl f* **10/3**[3]

0-25 **3** *2 3/4* **Bollin Greta**[23] 4689 3-9-7 63 .... DanielTudhope 3 61
(T D Easterby) *hld up: niggled 1/2-way: effrt and hdwy over 2f out: kpt on same pce fnl f* **9/1**

3060 **4** *20* **Fantastic Lass**[27] 4564 3-8-6 55 .... FrederikTylicki(7) 7 13
(R A Fahey) *cl up: ev ch 2f out: sn rdn and wknd* **9/4**[1]

0035 **5** *4* **Orpen Bid (IRE)**[14] 4967 3-8-6 48 .... AndrewElliott 4 —
(A M Crow) *led to over 1f out: sn btn* **11/1**

6006 **6** *7* **Howards Hope**[23] 4680 3-8-6 48 .... SilvestreDeSousa 9 —
(Miss L A Perratt) *hld up in tch: struggling 3f out: sn btn* **22/1**

530- **7** *16* **World Tour**[292] 6740 3-9-6 62 .... TomEaves 5 —
(Miss L A Perratt) *bhd: lost tch fr 1/2-way* **14/1**

2m 20.06s (8.06) **Going Correction** +0.725s/f (Yiel) **7** Ran SP% **111.8**
Speed ratings (Par 98): **96,93,91,75,72 66,53**
toteswinger: 1&2 £2.30, 1&3 £2.60, 2&3 £3.60. CSF £10.74 CT £60.33 TOTE £3.10: £1.80, £2.10; EX 8.60.

Owner T Samuel, D Burns & W Clifford **Bred** London Thoroughbred Services Ltd **Trained** Limpley Stoke, Bath

FOCUS
A very modest handicap in which again the jockeys made for the centre of the track in the home straight. The time was nearly 14 seconds outside standard and the first three finished a long way clear. The winner is rated a slight improver.

5389 TENNENTS LAGER H'CAP 7f 50y
3:10 (3:10) (Class 6) (0-65,64) 3-Y-0+ £2,590 (£770; £385; £192) Stalls Low

Form RPR
02-6 **1** **Eternal Legacy (IRE)**[6] 5198 6-9-5 **57**........................ GrahamGibbons 5 70
(E J Alston) *mde all: qcknd clr 2f out: unchal* **7/1**
0305 **2** *3 1/2* **Trimlestown (IRE)**[18] 4858 5-9-9 **64**..................(tp) MichaelJStainton(3) 2 68
(K A Ryan) *hld up: hdwy to chse wnr over 1f out: kpt on fnl f: no imp* **4/1**[1]
5605 **3** *1* **Sands Of Barra (IRE)**[6] 5198 5-9-6 **58**........................ PatrickMathers 7 59
(I W McInnes) *hld up: hdwy over 2f out: kpt on ins fnl f* **13/2**[3]
5005 **4** *3 3/4* **Botham (USA)**[15] 4951 4-8-8 **51**........................ GaryBartley(5) 11 42
(J S Goldie) *hld up in tch: c wd st: kpt on fnl 2f: no imp* **14/1**
-060 **5** *1 3/4* **Hypnotic**[63] 3366 6-9-8 **60**.....................................(vt) SilvestreDeSousa 10 46
(D Nicholls) *hld up: hdwy over 2f out: wknd over 1f out* **13/2**[3]
4023 **6** *1/2* **The Salwick Flyer (IRE)**[23] 4683 5-9-8 **60**........................ RoystonFfrench 9 45
(Miss L A Perratt) *prom: c wd st: effrt over 2f out: sn no ex* **6/1**[2]
0-00 **7** *3 1/2* **Domesday (UAE)**[80] 2866 7-8-3 **48**........................ DeanHeslop(7) 14 23
(W G Harrison) *pressed wnr tl wknd fr 2f out* **100/1**
2523 **8** *1* **A Big Sky Brewing (USA)**[12] 5045 4-9-4 **59**..............(b) NeilBrown(3) 13 32
(T D Barron) *prom: c wd st: rdn and wknd fr 2f out* **6/1**[2]
3050 **9** *1/2* **Planet Queen**[4] 5258 3-8-12 **55**........................ AndrewElliott 1 26
(K R Burke) *trckd ldrs tl rdn and wknd fr 2f out* **28/1**
30-6 **10** *1 1/4* **Imperial Quest**[11] 5110 4-8-12 **50**........................ J-PGuillambert 12 18
(E J Alston) *t.k.h: prom tl wknd fr 2f out* **7/1**
0454 **11** *16* **Beaumont Boy**[51] 3789 4-9-1 **53**...(p) TomEaves 6 —
(A G Foster) *bhd and sn pushed along: lost tch fr 1/2-way* **16/1**

1m 38.25s (4.85) **Going Correction** +0.725s/f (Yiel)
WFA 3 from 4yo+ 5lb 11 Ran SP% **117.2**
Speed ratings (Par 101): **101,97,95,91,89 89,85,83,83,81 63**
toteswinger: 1&2 £7.30, 1&3 £13.60, 2&3 £5.80. CSF £34.99 CT £193.57 TOTE £8.40: £2.40, £1.80, £2.60; EX 28.90.
Owner Derrick Mossop **Bred** Colin Kennedy **Trained** Longton, Lancs

FOCUS
A moderate handicap that looks fairly solid rated around the placed horses. There was a difference of opinion among the jockeys as to where the best ground was to be found in the home straight, with the winner leading the majority of the field down the centre of the track but three rivals opting to come down the stands' rail.

5390 KOPPARBERG CIDER H'CAP 1m
3:40 (3:41) (Class 4) (0-80,80) 3-Y-0+ £6,476 (£1,927; £963; £481) Stalls Low

Form RPR
4252 **1** **Handsome Falcon**[4] 5258 4-8-11 **71**........................ FrederikTylicki(7) 13 79
(R A Fahey) *prom: effrt over 2f out: led ins fnl f: hld on wl* **11/4**[1]
0050 **2** *nk* **Moheebb (IRE)**[39] 4204 4-8-11 **67**........................(b) MichaelJStainton(3) 9 74
(Mrs R A Carr) *hld up: hdwy 2f out: pressed wnr wl ins fnl f: r.o* **13/2**[3]
4422 **3** *2* **Ancient Cross**[28] 4538 4-9-1 **68**........................ DaleGibson 12 71
(M W Easterby) *bhd tl hdwy 2f out: kpt on fnl f: nrst fin* **15/2**
1200 **4** *1/2* **Ninefineirishmen (IRE)**[23] 4682 3-9-0 **73**..................(p) AndrewElliott 4 74
(K R Burke) *led: rdn over 2f out: hdd ins fnl f: no ex* **20/1**
1100 **5** *1 1/4* **Spinning**[18] 4876 5-9-10 **80**...(b) NeilBrown(3) 1 79+
(T D Barron) *dwlt: hld: hdwy and edgd lft 2f out: kpt on fnl f: no imp* **8/1**
1610 **6** *1 3/4* **Shy Glance (USA)**[18] 4850 6-9-3 **70**........................ TomEaves 8 65
(P Monteith) *hld up in midfield: effrt over 2f out: nvr able to chal* **25/1**
6321 **7** *6* **Alexander Huricane (IRE)**[21] 4736 4-9-9 **76**........................ NCallan 5 57
(K A Ryan) *prom tl rdn and wknd fr 2f out* **6/1**[2]
0260 **8** *5* **Wovoka (IRE)**[18] 4876 5-9-8 **75**........................ DanielTudhope 2 44
(D W Barker) *trckd ldrs gng wl: rdn 2f out: sn btn* **10/1**
4525 **9** *15* **Chin Wag (IRE)**[14] 4969 4-8-1 **61** oh1........................(p) DeanHeslop(7) 10 —
(J S Goldie) *cl up tl wknd over 2f out* **10/1**
3334 **10** *3 1/4* **Atabaas Pride**[53] 3709 3-9-4 **77**........................ RoystonFfrench 7 3
(M Johnston) *trckd ldrs tl wknd over 2f out* **12/1**
55-0 **11** *12* **Govenor Eliott (IRE)**[12] 5069 3-8-7 **66**........................ J-PGuillambert 3 —
(M Johnston) *midfield: struggling 1/2-way: sn btn* **20/1**

1m 48.44s (4.64) **Going Correction** +0.725s/f (Yiel)
WFA 3 from 4yo+ 6lb 11 Ran SP% **116.4**
Speed ratings (Par 105): **105,104,102,102,100 99,93,88,73,69 57**
toteswinger: 1&2 £5.30, 1&3 £3.90, 2&3 £13.10. CSF £19.17 CT £111.76 TOTE £3.20: £1.80, £2.50, £2.10; EX 22.50.
Owner B Shaw **Bred** Miss D Fleming **Trained** Musley Bank, N Yorks
■ Stewards' Enquiry : Frederik Tylicki three-day ban: used whip with excessive frequency (Sep 10-12)

FOCUS
A fair handicap run at a moderate pace but pretty sound form rated through the fourth. This time the whole field came down the centre.

5391 BACARDI RUM H'CAP 1m 2f
4:10 (4:10) (Class 4) (0-85,83) 3-Y-0+
£7,352 (£2,201; £1,100; £551; £274; £138) Stalls Low

Form RPR
1210 **1** **Deep Winter**[25] 4621 3-8-6 **76**........................ FrederikTylicki(7) 2 88+
(R A Fahey) *trckd ldrs: led wl over 1f out: edgd lft u.p ins fnl f: hld on wl* **4/1**[2]
1000 **2** *hd* **Bajan Parkes**[24] 4662 5-9-9 **83**........................ GaryBartley(5) 8 92
(E J Alston) *led to wl over 1f out: rallied u.p: kpt on fnl f: jst hld* **25/1**
1010 **3** *nk* **Tarkheena Prince (USA)**[44] 4021 3-9-6 **83**........................ NCallan 9 91
(G A Swinbank) *hld up: pushed along over 3f out: rallied wl over 1f out: kpt on wl fnl f* **7/2**[1]
0442 **4** *4 1/2* **Vicious Warrior**[13] 5005 9-9-6 **75**........................ DeanMcKeown 11 74
(R M Whitaker) *trckd ldr tl rdn and outpcd fr 2f out* **9/2**[3]
3033 **5** *3 1/4* **Dar Es Salaam**[34] 4331 4-9-2 **71**........................ DanielTudhope 3 64
(J S Goldie) *hld up in tch: effrt over 2f out: wknd over 1f out* **11/1**
2101 **6** *shd* **Lochiel**[63] 3368 4-9-6 **78**........................ NeilBrown(3) 6 71
(Mrs S C Bradburne) *in tch: effrt over 3f out: rdn and wknd wl over 1f out* **9/2**[3]
35-0 **7** *4 1/2* **Crow Wood**[24] 4662 9-9-12 **81**........................ GrahamGibbons 5 65
(J J Quinn) *midfield: outpcd over 3f out: sn n.d* **16/1**
10-1 **8** *3/4* **Honorable Love**[137] 1329 4-9-8 **77**........................ TomEaves 1 59
(M Dods) *dwlt: hld up: rdn over 3f out: sn btn* **8/1**
0100 **9** *16* **Trouble Mountain (USA)**[46] 3965 11-8-10 **65**.............(t) DaleGibson 10 15
(M W Easterby) *prom: drvn over 3f out: sn wknd* **33/1**
602 **10** *3 1/4* **Greyfriarsblessing (IRE)**[13] 5031 3-8-3 **66**........................ RoystonFfrench 7 10
(M Johnston) *sn drvn in rr: nvr on terms* **14/1**

2m 18.16s (6.16) **Going Correction** +0.725s/f (Yiel)
WFA 3 from 4yo+ 8lb 10 Ran SP% **117.4**
Speed ratings (Par 105): **104,103,103,100,97 97,93,93,80,77**
toteswinger: 1&2 £23.80, 1&3 £4.60, 2&3 £25.10. CSF £97.60 CT £386.18 TOTE £5.10: £1.70, £8.30, £1.90; EX 121.60.
Owner R A Fahey **Bred** Gainsborough Stud Management Ltd **Trained** Musley Bank, N Yorks

FOCUS
A decent handicap, but one that not many got into. The runner-up is rated to his previous best.

5392 BELL'S ORIGINAL H'CAP 6f
4:40 (4:43) (Class 5) (0-70,70) 3-Y-0+ £2,914 (£867; £433; £216) Stalls High

Form RPR
0601 **1** **Woodsley House (IRE)**[17] 4903 6-8-13 **62**........................ NeilBrown(3) 17 76
(A G Foster) *hld up stands' side: gd hdwy to ld ins fnl f: sn clr* **9/1**
0006 **2** *2 1/2* **Avontuur (FR)**[15] 4951 6-8-7 **56**........................ MichaelJStainton(3) 8 62+
(Mrs R A Carr) *overall ldr in centre tl hdd ins fnl f: kpt on same pce* **22/1**
3030 **3** *1/2* **Rainbow Fox**[26] 4605 4-8-11 **64**........................ FrederikTylicki(7) 7 68
(R A Fahey) *prom in centre: drvn over 2f out: kpt on u.p fnl f* **11/2**[1]
0022 **4** *3/4* **Imperial Sword**[18] 4846 5-8-6 **59**........................(b) DeanHeslop(7) 5 61
(T D Barron) *bhd and outpcd in centre: hdwy and edgd lft 2f out: nvr rchd ldrs* **7/1**[3]
0603 **5** *3/4* **Blazing Heights**[14] 4971 5-9-5 **70**........................ GaryBartley(5) 6 70
(J S Goldie) *hld up in tch: hdwy over 1f out: no ex ins fnl f* **16/1**
6154 **6** *nk* **Royal Challenge**[16] 4934 7-9-4 **64**........................ PatrickMathers 9 63
(I W McInnes) *hld up in tch: effrt 2f out: no imp fnl f* **20/1**
2432 **7** *1/2* **Obe One**[17] 4903 8-8-6 **52**........................ SilvestreDeSousa 3 49
(A Berry) *cl up in centre tl rdn and wknd over 1f out* **10/1**
4001 **8** *hd* **Almost Married (IRE)**[18] 4846 4-8-13 **59**........................ DanielTudhope 4 55
(J S Goldie) *cl up in centre: rdn 1/2-way: wknd over 1f out* **6/1**[2]
-300 **9** *nk* **Cross Of Lorraine (IRE)**[61] 3454 5-8-6 **59**..................(b) BMcHugh(7) 2 54
(C Grant) *sn drvn bhd centre ldrs: no imp fnl 2f* **40/1**
2046 **10** *1 1/4* **Yorkshire Blue**[5] 5222 9-9-6 **66**........................ J-PGuillambert 16 57
(J S Goldie) *chsd stands' side ldr: effrt over 2f out: btn fnl f* **8/1**
0003 **11** *1 1/4* **Argentine (IRE)**[18] 4846 4-8-9 **55**........................ DeanMcKeown 10 42
(L Lungo) *cl up in centre to 2f out: sn rdn and btn* **12/1**
4-50 **12** *1/2* **Howards Way**[93] 2466 3-9-0 **63**........................ TomEaves 14 49
(Miss L A Perratt) *bhd stands' side: rdn and edgd lft 2f out: nvr on terms* **20/1**
-605 **13** *1 1/4* **Lake Chini (IRE)**[51] 3787 6-9-3 **63**................................(b) DaleGibson 12 45
(M W Easterby) *gd spd stands' side tl wknd over 1f out* **20/1**
4450 **14** *3/4* **Orotund**[18] 4858 4-8-5 **51** oh4........................ RoystonFfrench 1 30
(T D Easterby) *cl up in centre tl wknd fr 2f out* **20/1**
0316 **15** *11* **Mafaheem**[11] 5091 6-9-10 **70**................................(b) NCallan 11 14
(A B Haynes) *chsd stands' side ldrs tl edgd lft and wknd fr 2f out* **8/1**

1m 15.23s (1.63) **Going Correction** +0.375s/f (Good)
WFA 3 from 4yo+ 3lb 15 Ran SP% **122.9**
Speed ratings (Par 103): **104,100,100,99,98 97,96,96,96,94 92,92,90,89,74**
toteswinger: 1&2 £53.20, 1&3 £11.80, 2&3 £34.40. CSF £202.24 CT £1230.35 TOTE £11.50: £4.00, £6.00, £2.30; EX 209.40.
Owner Mrs V L Davis **Bred** Roger G English **Trained** Cousland, Midlothian
■ Stewards' Enquiry : Dean Heslop one-day ban: careless riding (Sep 10)

FOCUS
They split into two groups in this routine sprint handicap, with five coming stands' side and the rest sticking more towards the centre. The form looks sound enough overall.

5393 LIME GROVE H'CAP 5f
5:10 (5:11) (Class 6) (0-65,65) 3-Y-0 £2,729 (£806; £403) Stalls High

Form RPR
3346 **1** **Andrasta**[18] 4852 3-7-11 **48**........................ CharlotteKerton(7) 5 54
(A Berry) *prom: led over 1f out: pushed out* **12/1**
1543 **2** *1 1/4* **Select Committee**[3] 5307 3-9-1 **59**........................(v) GrahamGibbons 3 61
(J J Quinn) *in tch: effrt over 2f out: chsd wnr 1f out: r.o* **7/4**[1]
6542 **3** *3/4* **Stoneacre Chris (USA)**[18] 4852 3-8-6 **50**........................ PatrickMathers 2 49
(Peter Grayson) *in tch: effrt and swtchd rt over 1f out: r.o fnl f* **11/2**[3]
2303 **4** *3 1/2* **Killer Class**[18] 4852 3-9-0 **63**........................ GaryBartley(5) 1 49
(J S Goldie) *hld up: smooth hdwy to chse ldrs over 1f out: sn rdn: fnd little* **4/1**[2]
0416 **5** *1/2* **Dalarossie**[6] 5201 3-9-7 **65**........................ DeanMcKeown 7 49
(E J Alston) *w ldrs tl wknd appr fnl f* **7/1**
6000 **6** *1 1/4* **Swindon Town Flyer (IRE)**[5] 5217 3-9-5 **63**..................(b) NCallan 9 43
(A B Haynes) *w ldrs: led over 2f out: edgd lft and hdd over 1f out: sn wknd* **8/1**
4-06 **7** *13* **Ingleby Star (IRE)**[15] 4950 3-9-0 **65**........................(b[1]) DeanHeslop(7) 8 —
(T D Barron) *led to over 2f out: sn rdn and wknd* **20/1**

62.47 secs (2.37) **Going Correction** +0.375s/f (Good) 7 Ran SP% **107.8**
Speed ratings (Par 98): **96,94,92,87,86 84,63**
toteswinger: 1&2 £5.20, 1&3 £9.10, 2&3 £2.40. CSF £29.76 CT £113.80 TOTE £11.50: £4.60, £1.40; EX 39.40 Place 6: £104.89, Place 5: £32.52..
Owner A B Parr **Bred** Peter Barclay **Trained** Cockerham, Lancs
■ Stewards' Enquiry : Charlotte Kerton two-day ban: used whip with excessive frequency and in incorrect place (Sep 10-11)

FOCUS
A weak handicap in which the three leaders went off too fast, allowing the finishers to come through and eventually filling the last three places. The first four home had all contested a very similar race here earlier in the month won by Cheshire Rose, but the outcome was different this time. The form looks very ordinary rated around the first three.
T/Plt: £225.00 to a £1 stake. Pool: £70,169.32. 227.62 winning tickets. T/Qpdt: £27.00 to a £1 stake. Pool: £4,868.50. 133.30 winning tickets. RY

5040 CATTERICK (L-H)
Wednesday, August 27

OFFICIAL GOING: Good (good to firm in places; 9.3)
Wind: Strong across Weather: Overcast with brighter periods

5394 RACINGUK.TV MEDIAN AUCTION MAIDEN STKS 5f
2:20 (2:22) (Class 6) 2-Y-0 £2,388 (£705; £352) Stalls Low

Form RPR
324 **1** **Doctor Parkes**[9] 5158 2-9-3 0........................ GregFairley 6 76
(E F Vaughan) *cl up: rdn wl over 1f out: drvn and slt advantage whn edgd lft ent fnl f: edgd rt and hdd ins fnl f: kpt on u.p to ld nr fin* **13/8**[1]

6 **2** *hd* **Kheleyf's Silver (IRE)**[21] 4734 2-8-12 0 RobertWinston 1 71
(B Smart) *slt ld: rdn along 2f out: drvn: bmpd and hdd ent fnl f: sn edgd rt and led again ins fnl f: hmpd and hdd nr fin* **5/1**[2]

06 **3** *3/4* **Inthawain**[26] 4579 2-8-12 0 TonyCulhane 10 68+
(M R Channon) *chsd ldrs: effrt 2f out and sn rdn: kpt on ins fnl f: nrst fin* **16/1**

32 **4** *1/2* **Paddy Bear**[41] 4113 2-9-3 0 JamieMoriarty 15 71+
(R A Fahey) *wnt rt s: sn pushed along and hdwy 1/2-way: rdn to chse ldrs whn hung lft over 1f out: n.m.r on inner ins fnl f: nrst fin* **8/1**[3]

5 *1/2* **Swiss Lake Sweetie (USA)** 2-8-12 0 DO'Donohoe 8 67+
(George Baker) *s.i.s and sn in rr: hdwy wl over 1f out: styd on ins fnl f: nrst fin* **9/1**

6436 **6** *3 1/2* **Imaginary Diva**[6] 5204 2-8-12 60 SebSanders 11 52
(G G Margarson) *chsd ldrs: effrt 2f out: sn rdn and kpt on same pce* **8/1**[3]

06 **7** *2 1/4* **Elsie Jo (IRE)**[36] 4270 2-8-12 0 NickyMackay 9 44
(M Wigham) *nvr bttr than midfield* **66/1**

53 **8** *1* **Capo Regime**[33] 4384 2-9-3 0 AdrianTNicholls 14 45
(D Nicholls) *nvr bttr than midfield* **5/1**[2]

9 *1 1/4* **Call Me Naan (IRE)** 2-8-12 0 DarrenWilliams 3 35
(K R Burke) *nvr nr ldrs* **22/1**

10 *hd* **James Junior** 2-9-3 0 DNolan 4 40
(D Carroll) *s.i.s: a in rr* **66/1**

0050 **11** *1/2* **El Bobby (IRE)**[18] 4874 2-9-3 59 StephenDonohoe 13 38
(J R Weymes) *a towards rr* **100/1**

6 **12** *hd* **Smitain**[85] 2702 2-9-3 0 PAspell 5 37
(Mrs S Lamyman) *chsd ldrs: rdn along over 2f out and sn wknd* **200/1**

53 **13** *3 3/4* **Dotty's Brother**[137] 1341 2-9-0 0 AndrewMullen(3) 7 24
(Mrs A Duffield) *sn outpcd and a in rr* **28/1**

61.98 secs (2.18) **Going Correction** +0.125s/f (Good) **13** Ran SP% **121.8**
Speed ratings (Par 92): **87,86,85,84,83 78,74,73,71,70 69,69,63**
toteswinger: 1&2 £3.70, 1&3 £8.50, 2&3 £17.80. CSF £9.45 TOTE £2.30: £1.10, £1.80, £3.70; EX 11.40.

Owner Joseph Heler **Bred** Joseph Heler **Trained** Newmarket, Suffolk

FOCUS
Probably no more than a fair maiden, but it was competitive enough and has been rated positively as it looked better than average for the track and grade. It should produce a few winners at the right level. The first two home went off pretty quick, but had built up enough of a lead over the remainder to hang on.

NOTEBOOK
Doctor Parkes had been a beaten favourite on both his starts since running third on his debut at Ascot, including over 6f at Yarmouth on his latest start, but he proved suited by this drop back in trip and was just good enough. He went off plenty quick enough, chasing Kheleyf's Silver throughout, and he had to work hard to get by that one in the straight, forcing his head in front only close home. He should have more to offer over this trip in nurseries as well as handicaps next year. (op 15-8 tchd 2-1 in a place)

Kheleyf's Silver(IRE) was hassled throughout by Doctor Parkes and set a strong enough pace trying to see off that rival, but she was eventually pegged back. This was a big improvement on the form she showed on her debut over 6f at Newcastle and she should be hard to beat in similar company next time, especially if able to dominate. (op 9-2)

Inthawain was well placed just off the strong gallop and stayed on in the straight, but she was not quite good enough. She is now qualified for nurseries and may find things easier in that sphere. (op 22-1)

Paddy Bear had the worst draw of all in stall 15 and to make matters worse he was pushed wide soon after the start. Having then been dropped in, he steadily made ground but was never going to reach the leaders. He is also now qualified for a handicap and should be able to win a race or two for the Fahey team on a more galloping course. Official explanation: jockey said colt was hampered at start and hung left (op 7-1)

Swiss Lake Sweetie(USA) ◆, who was backed at big prices, was undoubtedly the eye-catcher of the race. A daughter of Action This Day, first foal of an unraced half-sister to the very smart triple 5f winner Swiss Lake, she had only one behind her after starting awkwardly and was soon a good eight or so lengths off the pace. However, despite her rider not being over hard on her (particularly in the last furlong when she was inclined to edge left), she finished her race in quite taking fashion in the straight, suggesting she may well have done better had she broken on terms. There should be loads of improvement to come and she might be worth a bet in similar company next time. Official explanation: jockey said, regarding running and riding, his orders were to get a good break, ride the filly handily and to finish as well as possible, adding that it put its head up leaving stalls and missed the break, ran green early, only to do best work in the latter stages. (op 25-1)

Elsie Jo(IRE) is likely to prove better suited by 6f, or maybe even 7f, and she should leave this form behind in time now she is qualified for a handicap mark. (op 50-1)

Capo Regime was never competitive, but he could do better over 6f on slightly easier ground now he is qualified for a handicap mark. Official explanation: jockey said colt hung both ways (op 4-1 tchd 7-2)

5395 WEATHERBYS BLOODSTOCK INSURANCE MAIDEN STKS 5f 212y
2:50 (2:50) (Class 5) 3-Y-O+ **£2,590** (£770; £385; £192) **Stalls** Low

Form RPR

5 **1** **Chosen One (IRE)**[18] 4877 3-9-3 0 RobertWinston 1 66
(B Smart) *mde all: rdn along 2f out: drvn over 1f out: kpt on gamely ins fnl f* **7/2**[2]

3046 **2** *2* **Gioacchino (IRE)**[54] 3678 3-9-0 58 KevinGhunowa(3) 7 60
(R A Harris) *in tch: hdwy 2f out: rdn to chal whn hung lft ent fnl f: sn drvn and kpt on same pce* **3/1**[1]

0-60 **3** *nk* **Pride Of Northcare (IRE)**[21] 4727 4-9-6 53 DarrenWilliams 12 59
(D Shaw) *stdd and swtchd lft s: hld up in rr: gd hdwy 2f out: rdn and ev ch whn nt clr run ins fnl f: kpt on* **12/1**

-336 **4** *1 1/4* **Carmine Rock**[50] 3818 3-8-9 52 RussellKennemore(3) 11 50
(R Hollinshead) *towards rr: stdy hdwy on outer 2f out: rdn to chse ldrs whn edgd lft ent fnl f: sn drvn and one pce* **16/1**

4046 **5** *nk* **Tugalu (IRE)**[13] 5015 3-9-3 59 (p) FrancisNorton 8 54
(K A Ryan) *hld up in tch: hdwy 2f out: rdn to chse ldrs whn n.m.r and swtchd rt ent fnl f: sn drvn and no imp* **5/1**

0200 **6** *5* **Admiral Bond (IRE)**[11] 5110 3-9-3 65 (b[1]) DavidAllan 2 38
(G R Oldroyd) *chsd ldrs on inner: rdn along 2f out: drvn and wknd over 1f out* **4/1**[3]

0 **7** *1 3/4* **Lifetime Endeavour**[11] 5110 4-9-3 0 MarkLawson(3) 6 32
(R E Barr) *cl up: rdn over 2f out: drvn and wknd over 1f out: n.m.r and hmpd ent fnl f* **100/1**

0 **8** *6* **Trusted Friend (USA)**[204] 441 3-9-3 0 GregFairley 5 13
(M Johnston) *dwlt: sn rdn along and bhd fr 1/2-way* **10/1**

5000 **9** *5* **Recent Times**[11] 5110 3-8-12 50 TonyCulhane 9 —
(T D Easterby) *a in rr: bhd fr 1/2-way* **12/1**

00 **10** *5* **Idle Court**[31] 4451 3-8-12 0 TWilliams 10 —
(Bruce Hellier) *prom: rdn along wl over 2f out and sn wknd* **100/1**

1m 14.46s (0.86) **Going Correction** +0.125s/f (Good)
WFA 3 from 4yo 3lb **10** Ran SP% **116.2**
Speed ratings (Par 103): **99,96,95,94,93 87,84,76,70,63**
toteswinger: 1&2 £3.40, 1&3 £9.10, 2&3 £8.90. CSF £14.38 TOTE £4.00: £1.70, £1.10, £4.50; EX 17.10.

Owner Ceffyl Racing **Bred** Carl Holt **Trained** Hambleton, N Yorks

■ Stewards' Enquiry : Francis Norton one-day ban: careless riding (Sep 10)

FOCUS
Three of the first four came into this officially rated in the 50s, so this was clearly a very moderate sprint maiden. The runner-up and fourth are the best guides to the form.

Trusted Friend(USA) Official explanation: jockey said colt ran green

5396 SWALE H'CAP 1m 7f 177y
3:20 (3:20) (Class 5) (0-70,68) 3-Y-O+ **£2,729** (£806; £403) **Stalls** Low

Form RPR

2111 **1** **Let It Be**[14] 4963 7-9-7 68 ClGillies(7) 8 76+
(K G Reveley) *hld up in rr: stdy hdwy 5f out: trckd ldrs over 2f out: led 1 1/2f out: comf* **5/1**[2]

123 **2** *1 3/4* **Mr Crystal (FR)**[89] 2577 4-9-13 67 RobertWinston 4 73
(Micky Hammond) *trckd ldrs: effrt 3f out and sn rdn: drvn to chse ldrs over 1f out: kpt on ins fnl f* **7/1**[3]

4100 **3** *hd* **Abstract Folly (IRE)**[28] 4516 6-9-12 66 SebSanders 10 72
(J D Bethell) *hld up in rr: hdwy 3f out: rdn to chse ldrs on outer wl over 1f out: kpt on u.p ins fnl f* **8/1**

2003 **4** *2 1/2* **Wulimaster (USA)**[18] 4879 5-8-12 52 oh2 FrancisNorton 6 55
(D W Barker) *hld up and bhd: stdy hdwy 4f out: rdn 2f out: drvn over 1f out: kpt on same pce ins fnl f* **10/1**

3302 **5** *nk* **Court Of Appeal**[13] 5003 11-8-12 59 (tp) LanceBetts(7) 9 61
(B Ellison) *trckd ldrs: hdwy to chse ldng pair 4f out: rdn 3f out: drvn wl over 1f out and kpt on same pce* **12/1**

1310 **6** *1/2* **Silver Seeker (USA)**[28] 4516 8-9-9 63 JamieMoriarty 11 65
(Miss P Robson) *t.k.h: trckd ldrs: hdwy over 3f out: rdn along 2f out: sn drvn and kpt on same pce* **9/2**[1]

7 *nse* **Rare Ruby (IRE)**[326] 3832 4-9-11 65 LiamTreadwell 3 67
(Jennie Candlish) *midfield: hdwy 3f out: rdn along on inner 2f out: sn drvn and no imp* **66/1**

-026 **8** *2 1/2* **Mcqueen (IRE)**[26] 3642 8-9-4 61 RussellKennemore(3) 5 60
(J T Stimpson) *prom: hdwy and cl up over 4f out: led 3f out and sn rdn: drvn and hdd 1 1/2f out: sn wknd* **8/1**

5432 **9** *2 1/2* **Dechiper (IRE)**[21] 4735 6-9-8 67 PatrickDonaghy(5) 7 63
(R Johnson) *hld up in rr: effrt and sme hdwy on outer over 2f out: sn rdn and n.d* **17/2**

0-05 **10** *2 1/4* **Boxhall (IRE)**[19] 4817 6-8-7 52 oh2 AshleyHamblett(5) 1 45
(N Wilson) *led and sn clr: rdn along and jnd over 4f out: sn hdd and drvn: wknd 2f out* **8/1**

0004 **11** *9* **Matinee Idol**[22] 4698 5-8-5 52 oh7 (b) JamieKyne(7) 12 34
(Mrs S Lamyman) *a towards rr* **100/1**

/023 **12** *2* **Depraux (IRE)**[19] 4817 5-9-7 61 DO'Donohoe 2 41
(G M Moore) *chsd ldrs: rdn along over 4f out and sn wknd* **9/1**

3m 32.08s (0.08) **Going Correction** +0.125s/f (Good) **12** Ran SP% **120.5**
Speed ratings (Par 103): **104,103,103,101,101 101,101,100,98,97 93,92**
toteswinger: 1&2 £4.70, 1&3 £12.10, 2&3 £10.60. CSF £40.74 CT £281.80 TOTE £4.80: £1.90, £2.60, £2.90; EX 22.80.

Owner A Frame **Bred** Sir Eric Parker **Trained** Lingdale, Redcar & Cleveland

FOCUS
A modest staying handicap. but a most progressive winner in the form of Let It Be, who comfortably completed a four-timer. They went a good pace from the off thanks to Boxhall, who was soon in a clear lead and the form looks sound rated around the placed horses.

Mcqueen(IRE) Official explanation: jockey said gelding failed to get the trip

5397 WEATHERBYS FINANCE H'CAP 7f
3:50 (3:51) (Class 4) (0-80,80) 3-Y-O **£4,857** (£1,445; £722; £360) **Stalls** Low

Form RPR

1156 **1** **Willkandoo (USA)**[19] 4818 3-8-11 70 (p) FrancisNorton 9 78
(K A Ryan) *chsd ldrs: hdwy over 2f out: rdn to chse ldr over 1f out: styd on to ld ins fnl f: kpt on* **6/1**

0053 **2** *1* **Jonny Lesters Hair (IRE)**[4] 5258 3-8-8 67 DavidAllan 4 72
(T D Easterby) *cl up: led 3f out: rdn wl over 1f out: drvn and hdd ins fnl f: no ex* **11/4**[1]

1313 **3** *2* **Dream Express (IRE)**[23] 4682 3-9-3 76 JamieMoriarty 2 76
(M Dods) *chsd ldng pair: hdwy 3f out: rdn to chse ldr wl over 1f out: sn drvn and kpt on same pce* **5/1**[2]

2030 **4** *shd* **Dancing Maite**[25] 4615 3-8-6 65 PaulEddery 3 65+
(S R Bowring) *in tch: hdwy to chse ldrs over 2f out: sn rdn and kpt on same pce ent fnl f* **15/2**

0054 **5** *2* **Style Award**[16] 4922 3-8-13 77 PatrickDonaghy(5) 7 71
(W J H Ratcliffe) *towards rr: hdwy over 2f out and sn rdn: drvn over 1f out: kpt on ins fnl f: nrst fin* **25/1**

0321 **6** *1* **Tartan Gigha (IRE)**[31] 4454 3-9-7 80 GregFairley 5 72
(M Johnston) *sn outpcd and rr tl styd on fnl 2f: nrst fin* **11/2**[3]

3050 **7** *shd* **Blindspin**[23] 4682 3-9-2 75 RobertWinston 10 66
(M Dods) *dwlt and rr: hdwy on outer over 2f out: sn rdn and no imp fr over 1f out* **9/1**

-040 **8** *7* **Sam's Cross (IRE)**[32] 4408 3-9-5 78 AdrianTNicholls 8 50
(K R Burke) *nvr nr ldrs* **7/1**

0006 **9** *2* **Baronovici (IRE)**[49] 3833 3-8-2 61 oh1 NickyMackay 6 28
(D W Barker) *chsd ldrs: rdn along 3f out: wknd over 2f out* **40/1**

6500 **10** *20* **Dhhamaan (IRE)**[16] 4920 3-8-10 69 (b) SebSanders 1 —
(Mrs R A Carr) *led: rdn along and hdd 3f out: sn wknd* **22/1**

1m 26.94s (-0.06) **Going Correction** +0.125s/f (Good) **10** Ran SP% **117.9**
Speed ratings (Par 102): **105,103,101,101,99 98,97,89,87,64**
toteswinger: 1&2 £5.10, 1&3 £6.10, 2&3 £3.90. CSF £22.66 CT £92.14 TOTE £8.10: £2.40, £1.30, £1.40; EX 26.40.

Owner M Forsyth,J Turner And M F Logistics Ltd **Bred** Craig Singer **Trained** Hambleton, N Yorks

■ Stewards' Enquiry : Paul Eddery caution: careless riding

FOCUS
A fair three-year-old handicap run at a strong pace from the off. The form looks straightforward with the third the best guide.

Sam's Cross(IRE) Official explanation: jockey said colt hung left-handed in straight

5398 CATTERICKBRIDGE.CO.UK H'CAP 5f
4:20 (4:21) (Class 6) (0-65,65) 3-Y-0+ £2,388 (£705; £352) Stalls Low

Form RPR
-000 1 **Haajes**[15] 4958 4-9-8 **64**....(t) TonyCulhane 2 82
(S Parr) *in tch on inner: hdwy 2f out: rdn to ld ent fnl f: edgd rt and sn clr* **8/1**[3]
1000 2 3 ¾ **Metal Guru**[33] 4370 4-9-1 **60**....(p) RussellKennemore[(3)] 6 64
(R Hollinshead) *wnt rt s: sn in rr: rdn along and hdwy 2f out: drvn over 1f out: styd on ins fnl f* **16/1**
4040 3 hd **Trinculo (IRE)**[11] 5091 11-9-4 **63**....(b) KevinGhunowa[(3)] 1 66
(R A Harris) *led: rdn along 2f out: hdd over 1f out: drvn and kpt on same pce fnl f* **10/1**
1433 4 nk **Night Prospector**[8] 5171 8-8-13 **60**....(p) RichardEvans[(5)] 12 62+
(R A Harris) *towards rr: hdwy wl over 1f out: sn rdn and styd on wl appr fnl f: nrst fin* **9/1**
3102 5 ¾ **Raccoon (IRE)**[35] 4294 8-9-8 **64**.... SebSanders 4 64
(Mrs R A Carr) *cl up: rdn to ld over 1f out: drvn and hdd ent fnl f: wknd* **5/1**[1]
5103 6 nk **Mr Rooney (IRE)**[5] 5220 5-8-13 **60**.... SladeO'Hara[(5)] 11 58
(A Berry) *midfield: hdwy to chse ldrs 2f out: sn rdn and kpt on same pce appr fnl f* **14/1**
2141 7 nse **Whinhill House**[35] 4294 8-9-9 **65**....(v) RobertWinston 14 63+
(D W Barker) *chsd ldrs on wd outside: rdn along 2f out: drvn and wknd appr fnl f* **11/1**
0360 8 ½ **Yungaburra (IRE)**[48] 3868 4-9-6 **65**....(tp) TolleyDean[(3)] 10 61
(S Parr) *in rr tl sme late hdwy* **20/1**
0000 9 ¾ **Jakeini (IRE)**[31] 4462 5-8-13 **55**....(p) StephenDonohoe 8 49
(E S McMahon) *hmpd s: a towards rr* **40/1**
0020 10 hd **Darcy's Pride (IRE)**[27] 4561 4-9-4 **60**.... FrancisNorton 3 57+
(D W Barker) *prom: effrt and nt clr run wl over 1f out and again ent fnl f: eased* **11/2**[2]
0100 11 ½ **Guto**[6] 5201 5-8-9 **56**.... PatrickDonaghy[(5)] 9 47
(W J H Ratcliffe) *a midfield* **12/1**
0100 12 1 ¾ **Toy Top (USA)**[33] 4385 5-9-6 **62**....(b) JamieMoriarty 7 47
(M Dods) *bdly hmpd s: a in rr* **20/1**
4065 13 shd **Windjammer**[35] 4291 4-9-7 **63**....(b) DavidAllan 13 48
(T D Easterby) *chsd ldrs: rdn along 2f out: n.m.r wl over 1f out and sn wknd* **9/1**
5054 14 2 ¾ **El Potro**[44] 4025 6-9-1 **57**.... GregFairley 5 32
(J R Holt) *in tch: rdn along 1/2-way: sn wknd* **10/1**
0650 15 13 **Hawaii Prince**[48] 3868 4-8-13 **55**....(v[1]) AdrianTNicholls 15 —
(S T Mason) *s.i.s: a in rr* **28/1**

60.33 secs (0.53) **Going Correction** +0.125s/f (Good) 15 Ran SP% **125.3**
Speed ratings (Par 101): **100,94,93,93,92 91,91,90,89,89 88,85,85,80,60**
toteswinger: 1&2 £42.40, 1&3 £24.40, 2&3 £39.10. CSF £127.90 CT £1317.16 TOTE £12.00: £3.80, £6.60, £3.20; EX 187.50.
Owner Willie McKay **Bred** Irish National Stud **Trained** Bawtry, S Yorks

FOCUS
Plenty of runners, but this was a modest sprint handicap. They finished in a bunch behind the clear-cut winner but the form still looks sound.
Darcy's Pride(IRE) Official explanation: jockey said filly was denied a clear run
El Potro Official explanation: jockey said gelding was unsuited by the good to firm ground

5399 GO RACING AT RIPON ON SATURDAY H'CAP 1m 3f 214y
4:50 (4:50) (Class 6) (0-60,60) 3-Y-0 £2,388 (£705; £352) Stalls High

Form RPR
0400 1 **Banquet (IRE)**[18] 4879 3-8-12 **54**....(b[1]) JamieMoriarty 11 61
(T D Walford) *led: rdn along 1/2-way: drvn and hdd 3f out: rallied u.p over 1f out: swtchd rt and led ent fnl f: edgd rt and kpt on* **10/1**
1022 2 1 **Ambrose Princess (IRE)**[8] 5169 3-8-10 **55**.... KevinGhunowa[(3)] 6 60
(R A Harris) *trckd ldrs: effrt 3f out: rdn along 2f out: drvn and styd on wl fnl f* **4/1**[2]
2405 3 2 ¾ **Top Man Dan (IRE)**[17] 4902 3-8-12 **54**.... DavidAllan 9 55
(D Carroll) *trckd ldrs: hdwy 4f out: pushed along 3f out: styd on to chal over 1f out and ev ch tl rdn and one pce fnl f* **14/1**
0443 4 shd **Sabancaya**[14] 4966 3-9-2 **58**.... AdrianTNicholls 12 59
(Mrs P Sly) *prom: led 3f out: rdn along 2f out: drvn and hdd ent fnl f: one pce* **7/2**[1]
6F20 5 3 ¾ **Lizzie Wiggins**[17] 4898 3-8-9 **56**.... PatrickDonaghy[(5)] 5 51
(Mrs Marjorie Fife) *trckd ldrs: hdwy 3f out: rdn along 2f out: sn drvn and wknd over 1f out* **9/1**
530 6 1 ½ **Paddy Rielly (IRE)**[30] 4485 3-8-12 **59**.... RichardEvans[(5)] 10 51
(P D Evans) *bhd tl sme late hdwy* **6/1**[3]
0333 7 nk **Zaplamation (IRE)**[21] 4738 3-8-4 **46** oh1.... FrancisNorton 7 38
(D W Barker) *in tch: rdn along over 4f out: wknd over 2f out* **13/2**
0-40 8 2 ¼ **Terrasini (FR)**[37] 4247 3-9-4 **60**.... RobertWinston 8 48
(J Howard Johnson) *chsd ldrs: rdn along over 4f out: drvn over 2f out: wkng whn n.m.r over 1f out* **8/1**
-066 9 3 ¼ **Uncle Harry**[14] 4964 3-8-6 **48**.... DO'Donohoe 3 31
(J J Quinn) *a towards rr* **25/1**
2450 10 17 **Caught In Paradise (IRE)**[23] 4680 3-8-7 **49**.... GregFairley 4 5
(D W Thompson) *a towards rr* **28/1**
0040 P **Light Sea (IRE)**[12] 5077 3-8-13 **55**.... TonyCulhane 1 —
(M R Channon) *hld up towards rr: pushed along and lost pl over 5f out: bhd whn p.u 2 1/2f out* **14/1**

2m 39.89s (0.99) **Going Correction** +0.125s/f (Good) 11 Ran SP% **120.7**
Speed ratings (Par 98): **101,100,98,98,95 94,94,93,91,79** —
toteswinger: 1&2 £12.40, 1&3 £25.00, 2&3 £10.80. CSF £51.15 CT £577.52 TOTE £14.80: £4.40, £1.40, £4.30; EX 50.30.
Owner P Willis I & V A Brown V Chapman **Bred** R Fagan **Trained** Sheriff Hutton, N Yorks

FOCUS
A moderate three-year-old middle-distance handicap and not a race to be positive about.
Paddy Rielly(IRE) Official explanation: jockey said, regarding running and riding, his orders were to get the gelding balanced as it is tall and leggy and try to obtain the best possible placing, adding that he was struggling to get balanced round home turn into back straight and became detached, running on in the closing stages; trainer's rep added that gelding was unsuited by the course

5400 RACING AGAIN ON FRIDAY 5TH SEPTEMBER H'CAP 5f 212y
5:20 (5:21) (Class 5) (0-75,75) 3-Y-0+ £2,590 (£770; £385; £192) Stalls Low

Form RPR
6223 1 **Turn Me On (IRE)**[26] 4605 5-9-1 **69**.... DuranFentiman[(3)] 5 80
(T D Walford) *trckd ldrs: hdwy wl over 1f out: rdn ent fnl f: styd on wl to ld fnl 75yds* **9/2**[2]
5152 2 ¾ **Memphis Man**[5] 5233 5-9-3 **73**.... RichardEvans[(5)] 12 82
(P D Evans) *in tch: rdn along on outer 2f out: drvn over 1f out: kpt on u.p ins fnl f* **7/1**
5320 3 shd **Mr Wolf**[21] 4743 7-9-6 **71**....(p) FrancisNorton 10 79
(D W Barker) *led: rdn 2f out: drvn over 1f out: hdd and no ex fnl 75yds* **9/1**
2002 4 1 **Winthorpe (IRE)**[4] 5260 8-8-8 **66**.... JamieKyne[(7)] 4 71
(J J Quinn) *hld up towards rr: hdwy 2f out: rdn and edgd lft over 1f out: kpt on u.p ins fnl f* **8/1**
2200 5 2 ½ **Westport**[18] 4849 5-9-8 **73**.... DO'Donohoe 11 70
(K A Ryan) *chsd ldr: rdn 2f out and ev ch tl drvn ent fnl f and wknd* **18/1**
5014 6 1 **Lethal**[22] 4700 5-9-5 **70**.... JamieMoriarty 6 64
(R A Fahey) *chsd ldrs: rdn along 2f out: drvn over 1f out and sn wknd* **13/2**[3]
-005 7 ½ **Apollo Shark (IRE)**[26] 4608 3-9-2 **70**.... PAspell 7 62
(J Howard Johnson) *a towards rr* **40/1**
4351 8 2 ½ **Mandelieu (IRE)**[51] 3782 3-9-2 **70**.... RobertWinston 8 54
(Ollie Pears) *hld up towards rr: hdwy 1/2-way: rdn 2f out and sn no imp* **8/1**
0406 9 nk **Stamford Blue**[10] 5121 7-9-7 **75**....(b) KevinGhunowa[(3)] 3 58
(R A Harris) *a in rr* **14/1**
1061 10 ½ **Guest Connections**[12] 5044 5-9-3 **68**....(v) AdrianTNicholls 1 50
(D Nicholls) *dwlt: a in rr* **4/1**[1]
4525 11 3 **H Harrison (IRE)**[9] 5144 8-9-2 **70**.... LeeVickers[(3)] 2 42
(I W McInnes) *chsd ldrs: rdn along 1/2-way: sn wknd* **10/1**

1m 14.18s (0.58) **Going Correction** +0.125s/f (Good)
WFA 3 from 5yo+ 3lb 11 Ran SP% **119.7**
Speed ratings (Par 103): **101,100,99,98,95 93,93,89,89,88 84**
toteswinger: 1&2 £6.90, 1&3 £10.50, 2&3 £11.00. CSF £36.88 CT £281.98 TOTE £5.60: £1.60, £2.10, £3.50; EX 39.50 Place 6: £132.31, Place 5: £80.70..
Owner Ms M Austerfield **Bred** Brendan Lavery **Trained** Sheriff Hutton, N Yorks

FOCUS
A modest but competitive sprint handicap. The winning time was 0.28 seconds quicker than the earlier maiden for three-year-olds and upwards and the form is pretty solid rated around the placed horses.
Guest Connections Official explanation: jockey said gelding never travelled
T/Jkpt: Not won. T/Plt: £176.80 to a £1 stake. Pool: £66,767.45. 275.56 winning tickets. T/Qpdt: £118.20 to a £1 stake. Pool: £3,547.30. 22.20 winning tickets. JR

5374 GREAT LEIGHS (A.W) (L-H)
Wednesday, August 27

OFFICIAL GOING: Standard
Wind: fresh, half behind Weather: overcast but dry

5401 DEBDEN H'CAP 5f (P)
2:30 (2:31) (Class 5) (0-70,70) 3-Y-0+ £2,590 (£770; £385; £192) Stalls Low

Form RPR
6000 1 **Spoof Master (IRE)**[15] 4958 4-8-13 **63**....(p) LukeMorris[(3)] 2 73
(C R Dore) *s.i.s: sn mid-div: rdn and hdwy over 1f out: sn chal: led fnl 100yds: r.o wl: rdn out* **15/2**
5055 2 ½ **Thoughtsofstardom**[5] 5250 5-8-13 **60**.... HayleyTurner 12 68
(P S McEntee) *mid-div: hdwy 2f out: sn rdn: tk narrow advantage ent fnl f: drifted lft: hdd fnl 100yds: no ex* **10/1**
2343 3 1 **Cosmic Destiny (IRE)**[19] 4809 6-9-8 **69**.... LPKeniry 5 74
(E F Vaughan) *mid-div: rdn and hdwy wl over 1f out: chal ent fnl f: kpt on* **8/1**
2010 4 shd **Tyrannosaurus Rex (IRE)**[3] 5319 4-9-1 **62**.... AdamKirby 4 66
(D Shaw) *mid-div: rdn and hdwy 2f out: ev ch ent fnl f: hld whn sltly short of room towards fin* **4/1**[2]
000 5 1 ¼ **Multahab**[5] 5250 9-9-0 **61**....(t) JimmyQuinn 11 61+
(M Wigham) *racd wd: towards rr: rdn and styd on fr over 1f out: nt rch ldrs* **22/1**
0300 6 nk **Bluebok**[12] 5046 7-9-0 **61**....(bt) DaneO'Neill 1 60
(J M Bradley) *led: rdn 2f out: hdd ent fnl f: no ex* **14/1**
0003 7 1 ½ **Lithaam (IRE)**[12] 5074 4-8-5 **52**....(p) ChrisCatlin 6 45
(J M Bradley) *hld up towards rr: sme late prog: nvr a danger* **20/1**
3000 8 1 **Brazilian Brush (IRE)**[17] 4904 3-9-2 **68**.... TravisBlock[(3)] 9 58
(H Morrison) *a towards rr* **16/1**
0000 9 1 ¾ **Hollow Jo**[42] 4084 8-8-12 **59**.... MickyFenton 8 42
(J R Jenkins) *a towards rr* **20/1**
0261 10 ¾ **Mac Dalia**[36] 4272 3-9-3 **66**....(p) PatCosgrave 10 47
(A J McCabe) *mid-div: effrt 2f out: wknd appr fnl f* **8/1**
5032 11 ½ **Feelin Foxy**[27] 4563 4-9-9 **70**.... TPQueally 7 49
(J G Given) *chsd ldrs: rdn over 2f out: wkng whn short of room over 1f out* **7/2**[1]
6205 12 3 ¾ **Twosheetstothewind**[3] 5319 4-8-10 **57**.... LiamJones 3 22
(C R Dore) *prom: rdn over 2f out: wknd over 1f out* **13/2**[3]

60.30 secs (0.10) **Going Correction** +0.10s/f (Slow)
WFA 3 from 4yo+ 2lb 12 Ran SP% **125.1**
Speed ratings (Par 103): **103,102,100,100,98 97,95,93,91,89 89,83**
toteswinger: 1&2 £31.20, 1&3 £17.90, 2&3 £20.90. CSF £82.41 CT £641.60 TOTE £8.80: £2.80, £3.80, £2.90; EX 86.70 TRIFECTA Not won..
Owner Mrs Jennifer Marsh **Bred** Chris McHale And Oghill House Stud **Trained** West Pinchbeck, Lincs
■ Stewards' Enquiry : Hayley Turner one-day ban: careless riding (Sep 10)

FOCUS
A modest sprint handicap and weakened further by the withdrawal of the horses that would have started from the two outside stalls. The form is ordinary for the grade with the runner-up the best guide.

5402 RODING MAIDEN FILLIES' STKS 6f (P)
3:00 (3:00) (Class 5) 3-Y-0+ £2,590 (£770; £385; £192) Stalls Low

Form RPR
2432 1 **Ivory Silk**[14] 4987 3-9-0 70.... ChrisCatlin 5 78
(D K Ivory) *chsd ldrs: bmpd 3f out: rdn to ld wl over 1f out: drew clr fnl f: r.o wl* **5/2**[1]
5445 2 6 **Lake Sabina**[14] 4987 3-9-0 66.... DarryllHolland 4 59
(E S McMahon) *prom: lft in ld 3f out: sn rdn: hdd wl over 1f out: kpt on but nt pce of wnr* **4/1**[3]
-365 3 4 **Siren Sound**[73] 3061 3-8-11 66.... TravisBlock[(3)] 9 46
(H Morrison) *broke wl: sn restrained bhd ldrs: rdn 2f out: kpt on same pce* **8/1**
034 4 ¾ **Poyle Dee Dee**[13] 5023 3-9-0 70....(v[1]) RyanMoore 8 44
(R M Beckett) *sn pushed along in chsng gp: nvr gng pce to get on terms* **3/1**[2]

00 **5** 3 ¾ **Miss Riviera Chic**[65] 3318 3-9-0 0 .... TedDurcan 2 32
(G Wragg) *s.i.s: sn in tch: rdn 2f out: sn wknd* **66/1**
03 **6** 10 **Xandra (IRE)**[6] 5205 3-8-9 0 .... JackMitchell(5) 1 —
(C F Wall) *led for 1f: chsd ldrs: rdn over 2f out: wknd over 1f out* **25/1**
0 **7** 10 **Ruby Rocks**[6] 5205 3-9-0 0 .... HayleyTurner 7 —
(P S McEntee) *s.i.s: a outpcd in rr* **66/1**
3344 **P** **Theory**[25] 4651 3-9-0 69 .... (b) RobertHavlin 3 —
(J H M Gosden) *led after 1f: injured and p.u 3f out* **3/1**[2]

1m 13.14s (-0.56) **Going Correction** +0.10s/f (Slow) **8** Ran SP% **116.5**
Speed ratings (Par 100): **107,99,93,92,87 74,61,—**
toteswinger: 1&2 £2.90, 1&3 £5.00, 2&3 £8.20. CSF £13.12 TOTE £4.20: £1.40, £1.60, £2.10; EX 12.50 Trifecta £84.30 Pool £355.57, 3.12 winning units..
Owner K T Ivory **Bred** K T Ivory **Trained** Radlett, Herts

FOCUS
A very modest contest, as maidens for older fillies tend to be at this stage of the season, and marred by the tragic accident which befell Theory when John Gosden's filly was still in front at around halfway. This was a far from solid race and not form to be taken too literally.

5403 THAMES H'CAP 6f (P)
3:30 (3:30) (Class 3) (0-95,93) 3-Y-O
£7,477 (£2,239; £1,119; £560; £279; £140) **Stalls** Low

Form RPR
1540 **1** **Film Maker (IRE)**[4] 5270 3-9-0 86 .... TPO'Shea 8 96
(B J Meehan) *hld up: stdy prog fr over 2f out: swtchd rt wl over 1f out: sn rdn: led jst ins fnl f: r.o strly: readily* **5/1**[2]
2103 **2** 2 ¼ **Wise Melody**[11] 5102 3-9-1 87 .... LiamJones 7 90
(W J Haggas) *mid-div: hdwy over 2f out: sn rdn: tk narrow advantage over 1f out: hdd jst ins fnl f: kpt on but sn hld by wnr* **4/1**[1]
4442 **3** 1 **Sparton Duke (IRE)**[17] 4900 3-8-8 80 .... (p) RichardMullen 6 80+
(K A Ryan) *hld up bhd: rdn and hdwy wl over 1f out: wnt 3rd ins fnl f: styd on* **5/1**[2]
0600 **4** 2 ½ **C'Mon You Irons (IRE)**[18] 4864 3-8-5 77 .... (b[1]) AdrianMcCarthy 1 69
(M R Hoad) *chsd ldr: rdn 2f out: ev ch ent fnl f: no ex* **25/1**
300 **5** ½ **Loose Caboose (IRE)**[17] 4900 3-8-6 78 .... (p) JamesDoyle 3 68
(A J McCabe) *chsd ldrs: rdn and ev ch over 1f out: fdd ins fnl f* **20/1**
0206 **6** 2 **Sophie's Girl**[35] 4312 3-9-2 88 .... JimmyQuinn 13 72
(C A Dwyer) *nvr bttr than mid-div* **20/1**
21-0 **7** 1 **Messias Da Silva (USA)**[76] 2967 3-8-10 82 .... ShaneKelly 12 62
(J Noseda) *towards rr: rdn over 2f out: sme late prog: nvr a threat* **12/1**
0115 **8** nk **Onceaponatime (IRE)**[65] 3324 3-8-12 84 .... RyanMoore 9 63
(E A L Dunlop) *mid-div: rdn over 2f out: no imp* **4/1**[1]
600- **9** nk **Captain Royale (IRE)**[305] 6486 3-8-11 83 .... TPQueally 5 61
(J Noseda) *a towards rr* **20/1**
1102 **10** ½ **Mister New York (USA)**[162] 926 3-8-9 81 .... KirstyMilczarek 4 58
(Noel T Chance) *a towards rr* **15/2**[3]
6200 **11** nk **Victorian Bounty**[11] 5102 3-9-7 93 .... (b[1]) MickyFenton 2 69
(Stef Liddiard) *led: set gd pce: rdn whn hung rt and hdd over 1f out: wknd* **16/1**
6006 **12** 3 **We Have A Dream**[18] 4864 3-8-8 80 .... MartinDwyer 11 46
(W R Muir) *chsd ldrs: rdn over 3f out: sn btn* **25/1**

1m 13.0s (-0.70) **Going Correction** +0.10s/f (Slow) **12** Ran SP% **120.7**
Speed ratings (Par 104): **108,105,103,100,99 97,95,95,94,94 93,89**
toteswinger: 1&2 £9.10, 1&3 £8.00, 2&3 £6.20. CSF £23.46 CT £105.84 TOTE £7.00: £2.10, £2.20, £2.20; EX 30.00 Trifecta £135.80 Pool £190.96, 1.04 winning units..
Owner Bayardo **Bred** Mountarmstrong Stud **Trained** Manton, Wilts

FOCUS
A decent and competitive sprint handicap, though the time was just 0.14 seconds faster than the preceding fillies' maiden. Those drawn in the three lowest stalls dominated the early part of the race, but they may have gone off too quick as none of them figured in the finish. The form is ordinary for the grade and best rated around the first two.

NOTEBOOK
Film Maker(IRE) ◆ had put in a modest effort on soft ground on turf last time, but he was running well before that and he clicked on this quicker surface at the first time of asking. He could be spotted travelling well behind the leaders from a long way out and, once switched to the wide outside, he found plenty. There is probably more to come from him on Polytrack. (op 6-1)
Wise Melody, backed earlier in the day, had been generally running well on turf lately and was a winner over this trip on Polytrack on her second start at two. Although she pinged the gates, her rider was content to settle her just off the pace but she was produced to hold every chance and just ran into a better horse on the day. There are more races to be won with her on Polytrack. (tchd 9-2)
Sparton Duke(IRE), another supported earlier in the day, has put together a string of good performances in handicaps since winning a maiden over this trip at Kempton in January. He was staying on well late in the day and this was another decent effort. (op 9-2)
C'Mon You Irons(IRE) had only shown patchy form for his current yard this year, but this was a very creditable sand debut in the first-time blinkers, especially as he fared best of those that raced up with the pace early.
Loose Caboose(IRE), a winner over course and distance and returning to Polytrack after two modest efforts on turf, was not disgraced but she is still 6lb higher than for her last win. (op 16-1)
Onceaponatime(IRE), a dual winner for Peter Chapple-Hyam including over this trip on Polytrack, was making his debut for his new yard but he was weak in the market earlier in the day and never got involved at any stage. Official explanation: jockey said gelding had no more to give
Victorian Bounty Official explanation: jockey said gelding hung right

5404 ORWELL EBF MAIDEN STKS 1m (P)
4:00 (4:02) (Class 4) 2-Y-O **£4,533** (£1,348; £674; £336) **Stalls** Centre

Form RPR
0323 **1** **Thunderball**[21] 4733 2-9-3 76 .... PatCosgrave 3 77+
(A J McCabe) *a.p: led over 3f out: rdn clr 2f out: drifted rt and idled fr over 1f out: r.o wl: comf* **4/1**[2]
0 **2** 3 ¾ **Excelsior Academy**[12] 5068 2-9-3 0 .... MartinDwyer 1 69
(B J Meehan) *led tl over 3f out: chsd wnr: rdn 2f out: kpt on but sn hld by wnr: jst hung on for 2nd* **9/1**
0 **3** hd **Worth A King'S**[60] 3495 2-9-3 0 .... RyanMoore 6 70+
(Sir Michael Stoute) *hmpd leaving stalls: bhd: rdn over 2f out: swtchd rt over 1f out: fin strly: snatched 3rd fnl stride* **7/2**[1]
04 **4** hd **Blue Dynasty (USA)**[13] 5029 2-9-3 0 .... JimCrowley 7 68
(Mrs A J Perrett) *awkward leaving stalls: sn chsng ldrs: rdn over 2f out: kpt on same pce fr over 1f out* **16/1**
5 ½ **Guestofthenation (USA)** 2-9-3 0 .... JoeFanning 4 67+
(M Johnston) *hld up towards rr: rdn over 2f out: styd on fr over 1f out* **20/1**
4 **6** nk **Doncosaque (IRE)**[20] 4776 2-9-3 0 .... TedDurcan 10 66+
(H R A Cecil) *hld up in mid-div: hdwy over 2f out: sn rdn: kpt on same pce fr over 1f out* **13/2**
0 **7** ¾ **Forte Dei Marmi**[19] 4826 2-9-3 0 .... DaneO'Neill 13 64+
(L M Cumani) *s.i.s: hld up towards rr: hdwy on outer over 2f out: rdn over 1f out: no further imp fnl f* **8/1**

05 **8** 2 **Kayfiar (USA)**[17] 4890 2-9-3 0 .... JimmyQuinn 11 60
(P F I Cole) *mid-div: rdn and hdwy over 2f out: fdd fnl f* **6/1**[3]
9 1 ¼ **Pure Crystal** 2-8-9 0 .... JerryO'Dwyer(3) 2 52
(M E Rimmer) *hld up towards rr: short-lived effrt on inner wl over 1f out* **66/1**
10 ½ **Samba Mirander** 2-8-12 0 .... (p) RobertHavlin 8 51
(C Drew) *mid-div: rdn 3f out: wknd over 1f out* **100/1**
5 **11** 1 ¾ **Andean Margin (IRE)**[26] 4600 2-9-3 0 .... HayleyTurner 14 52
(S A Callaghan) *sn struggling: a towards rr* **11/1**
12 11 **Billy Smart (IRE)** 2-9-3 0 .... LPKeniry 5 28
(D J S Ffrench Davis) *mid-div: rdn over 4f out: wknd wl over 1f out* **33/1**
00 **13** 1 **Storm Mist (IRE)**[40] 4151 2-9-3 0 .... (t) ShaneKelly 12 26
(P F I Cole) *in tch: rdn 3f out: wknd wl over 1f out* **66/1**
6 **14** 1 ¼ **Got Flash (FR)**[21] 4728 2-9-3 0 .... ChrisCatlin 9 23
(E J O'Neill) *chsd ldrs: rdn 3f out: wknd wl over 1f out* **20/1**

1m 42.0s (2.10) **Going Correction** +0.10s/f (Slow) **14** Ran SP% **128.0**
Speed ratings (Par 96): **93,89,89,88,88 88,87,85,84,83 81,70,69,68**
toteswinger: 1&2 £9.80, 1&3 £4.70, 2&3 £12.70. CSF £41.63 TOTE £4.70: £1.70, £4.50, £1.90; EX 51.10 Trifecta £296.80 Part won. Pool £401.16, 0.10 winning units..
Owner Paul J Dixon & Brian Morton **Bred** Mrs Yvette Dixon **Trained** Babworth, Notts

FOCUS
A fair maiden on paper and experience told as it was won in comprehensive style by the most exposed runner in the field who ran basically to form.

NOTEBOOK
Thunderball, already officially rated 76, had been placed in a couple of maidens and a nursery on turf and his rider made the most of his experience. Kicking clear off the home bend, he was never in any danger from then on and there could be more to come from him in nurseries on this surface. (op 7-2 tchd 10-3)
Excelsior Academy had only beaten one home on his Newmarket debut, but this was much better and, although his Group 1 entries may be a bit optimistic, there do appear to be races to be won with him. (op 8-1)
Worth A King'S was well backed despite finishing last of 11 on his Newmarket debut, but he ran a rather strange race. Given a great deal to do, he finished with a rare rattle down the wide outside and although probably not amongst the very best in the Stoute yard, it will be disappointing if he can't find a race. (op 11-2)
Blue Dynasty(USA) who had only shown modest form in two Sandown maidens, was never far away and stayed on to the line. He will have more options now that he qualifies for a nursery mark.
Guestofthenation(USA), who fetched 85,000euros at the breeze-ups and is related to several winners in France on the dam's side, did not enjoy the smoothest of passages but showed enough to suggest that he has a future. (op 7-1 tchd 13-2)
Forte Dei Marmi, who finished in mid-division in a Newmarket maiden on his debut that has produced winners, threatened to get into it down the outside off the home bend, but his effort soon flattened out. He may be one for handicaps further down the line. (op 15-2)
Kayfiar(USA), making his All-Weather bow, will look of greater interest now he is eligible for a nursery mark. (op 13-2 tchd 8-1)

5405 KINGG OF WATCHES H'CAP 1m (P)
4:30 (4:32) (Class 3) (0-90,89) 3-Y-O+
£7,477 (£2,239; £1,119; £560; £279; £140) **Stalls** Centre

Form RPR
1- **1** **Riggins (IRE)**[488] 1282 4-9-4 80 .... DaneO'Neill 4 92
(L M Cumani) *mid-div: tk clsr order over 2f out: rdn to ld over 1f out: hrd pressed: styd on wl to assert towards fin: rdn out* **13/8**[1]
3004 **2** 1 ½ **Big Noise**[18] 4869 4-9-11 87 .... RichardThomas 8 96
(Dr J D Scargill) *mid-div: rdn and hdwy 2f out: edgd lft over 1f out: ev ch ins fnl f: hld towards fin* **7/1**[3]
5502 **3** 2 ¼ **Murfreesboro**[12] 5051 5-9-11 87 .... AdamKirby 5 91
(D Shaw) *hld up bhd: rdn over 2f out: hung lft fr over 1f out: styd on fnl f: wnt 3rd towards fin* **10/1**
3-12 **4** nk **Diamond Yas (IRE)**[75] 3002 3-8-13 81 .... TedDurcan 1 83
(H R A Cecil) *mid-div: rdn over 2f out: styd on same pce fr over 1f out* **11/2**[2]
2360 **5** 1 **Vainglory (USA)**[32] 4405 4-9-12 88 .... RichardMullen 3 89
(D M Simcock) *sn pumped along: towards rr: styd on fr over 1f out: nvr trbld ldrs* **11/2**[2]
2202 **6** nse **Mesbaah (IRE)**[29] 4500 4-9-9 85 .... TonyHamilton 6 86
(R A Fahey) *chsd ldrs: rdn over 3f out: one pce fr over 1f out* **16/1**
3125 **7** nk **Rainbow Mirage (IRE)**[18] 4853 4-9-8 84 .... DarryllHolland 7 84
(E S McMahon) *chsd ldrs: led over 2f out: rdn and hdd over 1f out: sn one pce* **12/1**
331 **8** 1 ¾ **Golden Desert (IRE)**[32] 4407 4-9-8 89 .... JackMitchell(5) 10 85
(T G Mills) *t.k.h: trckd ldrs: rdn and ev ch over 1f out: wknd fnl f* **15/2**
3143 **9** ½ **Froissee**[18] 4841 4-9-6 82 .... TPO'Shea 2 77
(S A Callaghan) *hld up bhd: nt clr run and swtchd rt over 1f out: sn rdn but no imp* **20/1**
2504 **10** 11 **Captain Jacksparra (IRE)**[43] 4060 4-9-9 85 .... JoeFanning 9 55
(K A Ryan) *racd keenly: led: hdd over 2f out: sn rdn: wknd over 1f out: eased whn btn* **16/1**

1m 40.43s (0.53) **Going Correction** +0.10s/f (Slow)
WFA 3 from 4yo+ 6lb **10** Ran SP% **126.4**
Speed ratings (Par 107): **101,99,97,96,95 95,95,93,93,82**
toteswinger: 1&2 £5.20, 1&3 £5.80, 2&3 £10.30. CSF £15.08 CT £96.78 TOTE £2.50: £1.50, £3.40, £2.80; EX 16.00 Trifecta £119.50 Pool £369.91, 2.29 winning units..
Owner Scuderia Rencati Srl **Bred** Compagnia Generale S R L **Trained** Newmarket, Suffolk

FOCUS
A decent handicap which totally revolved around how the favourite would fare on his first start since bolting up in a Wolverhampton maiden in April of last year. The answer was very positive and the form looks pretty sound rated around the runner-up and fourth.

NOTEBOOK
Riggins(IRE) ◆, on his first start since bolting up in a Wolverhampton maiden in April of last year, had to battle hard to fend off the runner-up but he knuckled down well to the task and saw his race out nicely. His absence had been due to him splitting a pastern when winning on his debut and then suffering further problems in the spring, whilst his trainer believed he was only 90 per cent fit for this. He is in the Cambridgeshire, but it later transpired that he will not be qualified for that. This run is sure to have brought him on though, and he really still could be anything. (op 6-4 tchd 11-8 and 7-4, tchd 2-1 in a place and 15-8 in a place)
Big Noise, who had run well in his only previous try on this surface, made his effort wide and might have given the favourite more to think about had he not tended to wander about. This was his first attempt at the trip and in view of how well he ran it is hard to be critical at all, but it does look to be right on the limit of his stamina. (op 8-1 tchd 9-1)
Murfreesboro, who had been raised 4lb for finishing second on his debut for his current yard at Kempton last time, finished strongly down the outside, but he was never getting there and is without a win in almost three years. Official explanation: jockey said horse hung left
Diamond Yas(IRE), who ran a fair handicap debut last time after an easy win in a Warwick maiden that has not worked out, was the only three-year-old in the field and ran with credit against her elders after holding every chance. (op 6-1)

Vainglory(USA) attracted market support despite still being 8lb above his last winning mark last November, but he does look better over further and he he could never get into the race from off the pace. (op 9-1 tchd 10-1)

Mesbaah(IRE), whose first try on this surface was inconclusive, has been running well in headgear on turf recently but they were left off here. He was off the bridle on the home bend and is still to show that he appreciates Polytrack.

Captain Jacksparra(IRE) pulled like a train out in front early and that told against him well before stamina became an issue. Official explanation: jockey said gelding ran too free (tchd 18-1)

5406 COLNE H'CAP 2m (P)
5:00 (5:02) (Class 5) (0-75,75) 3-Y-O £2,590 (£770; £385; £192) Stalls Centre

Form RPR

0162 1 **Benhego**[3] 5322 3-8-8 **62** SaleemGolam 9 77
(S C Williams) *trckd ldrs: led 4f out: sn wl clr: kpt up to work: v easily* **5/2**[1]

0105 2 *11* **Tyrrells Wood (IRE)**[14] 4985 3-8-12 **71** JackMitchell(5) 8 73
(T G Mills) *mid-div: hdwy 4f out: sn rdn: wnt 2nd over 3f out but nvr any danger to easy wnr* **7/1**

5344 3 *18* **Mushtaaq (USA)**[19] 4821 3-9-7 **75** (b) RHills 6 55
(M A Jarvis) *sn pushed along: led after 2f: hdd 4f out: sn rdn: lost 2nd over 3f out: wknd over 2f out* **7/2**[2]

6064 4 *8* **Blue Citadel (USA)**[4] 5269 3-9-2 **70** (v[1]) JimCrowley 5 41
(Mrs A J Perrett) *led for 2f: trckd ldrs: rdn over 4f out: wknd over 2f out* **12/1**

311 5 *9* **Trip The Light**[18] 4879 3-9-3 **71** (v) TonyHamilton 4 31
(R A Fahey) *nvr travelling in rr: drvn along after 4f: nvr on terms: t.o* **7/1**

0655 6 *18* **It's A Date**[27] 4573 3-9-7 **75** DaneO'Neill 1 13
(A King) *in tch: rdn over 5f out: wknd 3f out: t.o* **9/2**[3]

5310 7 *dist* **Beautiful Lady (IRE)**[18] 4859 3-9-2 **70** JoeFanning 2 —
(P F I Cole) *mid-div: struggling over 6f out: sn btn and eased: t.o* **5/1**

0066 P **Hold That Call (USA)**[15] 4943 3-8-2 **59** oh11 ow3 EmmettStack(3) 3 —
(A J Chamberlain) *t.k.h early: hld up: reminders 1/2-way: rdn over 6f out: sn lost tch: t.o and p.u over 1f out* **66/1**

3m 30.54s (0.54) **Going Correction** +0.10s/f (Slow) **8** Ran SP% **119.8**
Speed ratings (Par 100): **102,96,87,83,79 70,—,—**
toteswinger: 1&2 £5.10, 1&3 £3.20, 2&3 £7.40. CSF £22.03 CT £63.06 TOTE £3.40: £1.30, £2.90, £1.70; EX 23.90 Trifecta £343.90 Pool £557.80, 1.20 winning units..

Owner Essex Racing Club **Bred** Old Mill Stud **Trained** Newmarket, Suffolk

FOCUS
An ordinary handicap, but with some unexposed stayers on show. The pace was a fair one and this proved too much of a test for many of these and it's rare for the runners in a Flat race to be separated by such margins. The runner-up to his latest mark is the best guide.

Trip The Light Official explanation: jockey said gelding never travelled

Beautiful Lady(IRE) Official explanation: jockey said filly never travelled

5407 AVON APPRENTICE H'CAP 1m 2f (P)
5:30 (5:30) (Class 6) (0-60,64) 3-Y-0+ £1,942 (£578; £288; £144) Stalls Low

Form RPR

5251 1 **Kings Topic (USA)**[9] 5145 8-10-0 **64** 6ex (p) PNolan(5) 13 77
(A B Haynes) *sn prom: led wl over 3f out: rdn and hdd over 1f out: rallied to regain ld ent fnl f: kpt on gamely: drvn out* **5/1**[3]

3006 2 *3/4* **Strike Force**[9] 5145 4-9-9 **57** JackMitchell(3) 12 69
(K F Clutterbuck) *hld up towards rr: smooth hdwy over 4f out: rdn into ld over 1f out: hdd ent fnl f: kpt on: hld towards fin* **10/1**

0045 3 *6* **Josr's Magic (IRE)**[9] 5145 4-9-11 **56** KirstyMilczarek 7 56
(H J Collingridge) *in tch: cl up 3f out: effrt 2f out: kpt on same pce* **3/1**[1]

0000 4 *1 3/4* **Havanavich**[14] 4978 3-8-8 **54** MatthewBirch(7) 14 50
(S Kirk) *hld up bhd: rdn over 3f out: styd on steadily fr over 1f out: wnt 4th ins fnl f* **12/1**

0610 5 *1 1/2* **Rampant Ronnie (USA)**[20] 4796 3-9-7 **60** LukeMorris 6 53
(P W D'Arcy) *mid-div: rdn over 2f out: sn one pce* **13/2**

1250 6 *3* **Autumn Charm**[43] 4049 3-8-11 **57** ow2 MrJPFeatherstone(7) 1 44
(Lucinda Featherstone) *prom: rdn 3f out: wknd over 1f out* **14/1**

5000 7 *1* **Tewin Green**[39] 4182 3-8-11 **55** (p) BillyCray(5) 9 40
(M D Squance) *mid-div: hdwy 7f out: rdn 3f out: wknd over 1f out* **33/1**

6000 8 *5* **King After**[9] 5145 6-9-0 **52** (v) AndreaAtzeni(7) 11 27
(J R Best) *rrd leaving stalls: rdn over 4f out: a towards rr* **12/1**

0-05 9 *3 1/4* **Golden Horus (USA)**[32] 4412 3-8-9 **53** Louis-PhilippeBeuzelin(5) 8 22
(J P O'Gorman) *trckd ldrs: jnd ldrs 4f out: rdn over 2f out: wknd wl over 1f out* **20/1**

0350 10 *nk* **Veni Bidi Vici**[10] 5119 3-9-2 **58** (v) DavidProbert(3) 5 26
(A M Balding) *mid-div tl wknd over 3f out* **11/1**

1225 11 *12* **Sceilin (IRE)**[26] 4596 4-9-9 **57** (t) HaddenFrost(3) 2 —
(J Mackie) *led tl wl over 3f out: grad fdd* **7/2**[2]

6650 12 *5* **Pure Inspiration**[54] 3692 3-8-1 **45** RossAtkinson(5) 10 —
(A G Newcombe) *rrd leaving stalls: a towards rr* **40/1**

00-0 13 *47* **Lord Of Esteem**[4] 5278 3-9-2 **55** MarcHalford 3 —
(J Ryan) *s.i.s: a towards rr: lost tch over 5f out* **50/1**

2m 10.22s (1.62) **Going Correction** +0.10s/f (Slow)
WFA 3 from 4yo+ 8lb **13** Ran SP% **128.8**
Speed ratings (Par 101): **97,96,91,90,89 86,85,81,79,78 69,65,27**
toteswinger: 1&2 £15.60, 1&3 £6.10, 2&3 £10.30. CSF £57.18 CT £183.74 TOTE £5.30: £2.50, £3.40, £1.60; EX 69.90 Trifecta £163.80 Part won. Pool £221.48, 0.74 winning units. Place 6: £49.95, Place 5: £8.00..

Owner Ms C Berry **Bred** Marvin Delfiner And Fred Seitz **Trained** Limpley Stoke, Bath

FOCUS
A modest if fairly competitive apprentice handicap and they went a decent pace, though ultimately this developed into a two-horse race. The form looks somewhat suspect.

Josr's Magic(IRE) Official explanation: jockey said gelding had no more to give

Sceilin(IRE) Official explanation: jockey said filly never travelled

T/Plt: £73.20 to a £1 stake. Pool: £60,854.01. 606.35 winning tickets. T/Qpdt: £6.10 to a £1 stake. Pool: £4,486.00. 541.20 winning tickets. TM

5387 AYR (L-H)
Thursday, August 28

OFFICIAL GOING: Soft (good to soft in places in home straight; 6.3)

The ground was riding similar to the previous day here, that is to say rather more testing than the official going description.

Wind: Breezy, against Weather: Overcast

5414 COSGROVE RESPITE NURSERY 6f
2:10 (2:11) (Class 6) (0-65,65) 2-Y-O £2,914 (£867; £433; £216) Stalls High

Form RPR

5021 1 **Bold Account (IRE)**[3] 5357 2-8-7 **51** 6ex AndrewElliott 3 66+
(K R Burke) *mde all: pushed clr fnl 2f* **30/100**[1]

5404 2 *7* **Royal Premium**[3] 5357 2-8-6 **50** (p) RoystonFfrench 4 44
(H A McWilliams) *prom: effrt and edgd lft 2f out: chsd wnr ins fnl f: no imp* **40/1**

004 3 *2 1/2* **Imperial Skylight**[9] 5165 2-9-6 **64** TonyCulhane 2 51
(M R Channon) *pressed wnr: outpcd over 1f out: lost 2nd ins fnl f* **7/1**[2]

646 4 *1 3/4* **Bella's Story**[45] 4014 2-8-12 **61** GaryBartley(5) 5 42
(J S Goldie) *bhd and outpcd: sme late hdwy: nvr on terms* **10/1**[3]

0405 5 *5* **Port Ronan (USA)**[32] 4456 2-9-4 **65** MarkLawson(3) 1 31
(J S Wainwright) *cl up tl rdn and wknd fr 2f out* **28/1**

0564 6 *2 1/4* **Wee Bizzom**[16] 4948 2-7-13 **50** CharlotteKerton(7) 6 10
(A Berry) *trckd ldrs tl hung lft and wknd fr 2f out* **16/1**

1m 19.37s (5.77) **Going Correction** +0.50s/f (Yiel) **6** Ran SP% **110.3**
Speed ratings (Par 92): **81,71,68,66,59 56**
toteswinger: 1&2 £4.40, 1&3 £1.60, 2&3 £9.80. CSF £16.24 TOTE £1.30: £1.02, £13.30; EX 15.30.

Owner Mrs Elaine M Burke **Bred** G Loftus **Trained** Middleham Moor, N Yorks

FOCUS
A very slow winning time, 1.56 seconds slower than the later juvenile maiden auction event. A weakly contested nursery which presented a straightforward opportunity to Bold Account who has been a revelation of late.

NOTEBOOK
Bold Account(IRE), penalised for his selling win at Ripon on Monday but still 9lb ahead of the handicapper, was bounced out of the stalls to claim the stands' rail and, clear entering the final furlong, blitzed this very modest opposition. He is an improved performer since getting the opportunity to tackle soft ground. (op 4-11 tchd 4-9 in a place and 2-5 in places)
Royal Premium plugged on for second to finish closer to Bold Account on these revised terms than he had at Ripon earlier in the week.
Imperial Skylight, like the winner, was officially well in, in his case by 4lb, but he will struggle off this revised mark if this effort is to be taken literally.The drop in trip should not have been a problem in these conditions. (op 6-1)
Bella's Story, a half-sister to the Goldie yards's decent sprint handicappers Geojimali and Blazing Heights, showed little in three maidens over this course and distance and not much more on this nursery debut, although she did stay on past a couple of rivals late on. She had become a little upset in the stalls.
Port Ronan(USA) went freely to post and did not last long in the race in this ground. (op 33-1)
Wee Bizzom raced off 9lb lower than when an improved fourth at Musselburgh but did not get home over this extra furlong. (op 14-1)

5415 COSGROVE CONNECTIONS FOR LIFE H'CAP 1m 5f 13y
2:40 (2:40) (Class 6) (0-65,64) 3-Y-0+ £2,914 (£867; £433; £216) Stalls Low

Form RPR

0003 1 **Always Best**[16] 4947 4-8-9 **45** TonyHamilton 14 55
(R Allan) *chsd ldr: led over 5f out: kpt on strly fnl 2f* **9/1**

-162 2 *2 3/4* **Signalman**[19] 4848 4-9-5 **55** RoystonFfrench 1 61
(P Monteith) *in tch: effrt and chsd wnr over 2f out: edgd lft over 1f out: kpt on same pce fnl f* **15/8**[1]

0356 3 *14* **Asrar**[16] 4947 6-8-2 **45** LanceBetts(7) 9 30
(Miss Lucinda V Russell) *s.i.s: bhd tl styd on fr 3f out: no ch w first two* **66/1**

4004 4 *1/2* **Stravonian**[16] 4947 8-8-9 **45** MickyFenton 5 29
(D A Nolan) *bhd: hdwy over 2f out: kpt on: nvr able to chal* **28/1**

005- 5 *nse* **Quicuyo (GER)**[126] 5586 5-8-7 **46** NeilBrown(3) 4 30
(P Monteith) *in tch tl rdn and outpcd fr over 2f out* **11/2**[3]

5300 6 *5* **Blue Jet (USA)**[39] 4220 4-9-0 **50** DeanMcKeown 2 27
(R M Whitaker) *cl up: effrt over 3f out: wknd fr 2f out* **12/1**

-000 7 *10* **Templet (USA)**[57] 3204 8-8-6 **45** (v) DuranFentiman(3) 15 7
(W G Harrison) *midfield: drvn and outpcd 1/2-way: n.d after* **100/1**

2/64 8 *2 3/4* **Nevsky Bridge**[19] 4879 6-8-9 **45** (p) TomEaves 3 3
(M Todhunter) *prom: drvn over 4f out: sn btn* **18/1**

05-0 9 *3/4* **Catherines Cafe (IRE)**[24] 4683 5-8-9 **48** PJMcDonald(3) 13 4
(A C Whillans) *hld up: stdy hdwy over 4f out: rdn and wknd over 3f out* **33/1**

0505 10 *3 3/4* **Don Jose (USA)**[27] 4592 5-8-3 **46** (be) StacyRenwick(7) 12 —
(N J Vaughan) *led to over 5f out: wknd over 3f out* **11/1**

6043 11 *14* **Lisbon Lion (IRE)**[19] 4859 3-8-12 **59** SamHitchcott 11 —
(N J Vaughan) *s.i.s: bhd: drvn over 5f out: nvr on terms* **4/1**[2]

/0-5 12 *32* **English City (IRE)**[12] 4850 5-9-1 **51** DO'Donohoe 6 —
(Mrs L B Normile) *bhd: lost tch 1/2-way: nvr on terms* **14/1**

3m 5.93s (9.33) **Going Correction** +0.80s/f (Soft)
WFA 3 from 4yo+ 11lb **12** Ran SP% **117.0**
Speed ratings (Par 101): **103,101,92,92,92 89,83,81,80,78 70,50**
toteswinger: 1&2 £3.90, 1&3 £67.90, 2&3 £28.70. CSF £25.36 CT £1083.14 TOTE £11.70: £2.80, £1.30, £12.50; EX 36.70.

Owner Michael Wares **Bred** Mrs R D Peacock **Trained** Duns, Scottish Borders

FOCUS
A weak handicap which proved a searching test in the conditions. The runners came over to the stands' side in the home straight. The time was a hefty 18.93 seconds outside standard. Not many got into the race and the first two pulled clear of a couple who were out of the handicap. The winner is rated back to his latter 3yo form.

Lisbon Lion(IRE) Official explanation: jockey said colt was unsuited by the soft (good to soft places) ground

5416 COSGROVE KIDS MAIDEN AUCTION STKS 6f
3:10 (3:11) (Class 5) 2-Y-O £3,238 (£963; £481; £240) Stalls High

Form RPR

332 1 **Happy Anniversary (IRE)**[16] 4956 2-8-1 **75** DuranFentiman(3) 8 76
(Miss V Haigh) *mde all: rdn and styd on wl fnl f* **1/1**[1]

0 2 *1* **Jatman**[19] 4847 2-8-11 **0** TomEaves 4 80
(Mrs L Stubbs) *dwlt: sn prom: effrt over 1f out: chsd wnr and edgd lft ins fnl f: r.o* **25/1**

22 **3** *3 ½* **Dean Iarracht (IRE)**[40] 4203 2-8-9 0.............................. TonyHamilton 3 68
(M Dods) *prom on outside: chsd wnr over 1f out to ins fnl f: sn btn* **2/1**[2]
4 *6* **Ursula (IRE)** 2-8-10 0.............................. AndrewElliott 6 51
(K R Burke) *pressed wnr to over 1f out: sn wknd* **5/1**[3]
5 *2 ½* **Distinctive Spirit (IRE)** 2-9-1 0.............................. RoystonFfrench 7 48
(K A Ryan) *dwlt: sn rdn in rr: struggling fnl 2f* **16/1**
6 *25* **Grissom (IRE)** 2-8-11 0 ow5.............................. SladeO'Hara[(5)] 5 —
(A Berry) *chsd ldrs tl hung lft and wknd 2f out: t.o* **40/1**

1m 17.81s (4.21) **Going Correction** +0.50s/f (Yiel) **6** Ran SP% **112.2**
Speed ratings (Par 94): **91,89,85,77,73 40**
toteswinger: 1&2 £6.00, 1&3 £1.40, 2&3 £5.70. CSF £27.29 TOTE £2.00: £1.20, £8.40; EX 25.20.
Owner R J Budge **Bred** Thomastown Stud **Trained** Wiseton, Notts

FOCUS
A fair maiden run in a time 1.56 seconds quicker than the earlier nursery. The winner ran to form.

NOTEBOOK
Happy Anniversary(IRE) was much the most experienced runner and she set a fair standard, placed on each of her last four starts and officially rated 75. Making all against the rail and ridden out to see off the runner-up, her Fillies' Mile entry is obviously fanciful but she should prove competitive in nurseries. (tchd 5-4)
Jatman ◆ showed little on his debut over course and distance three weeks ago but had clearly derived considerable benefit and ran a lot better, running on well inside the last to bustle up the winner. There should be a maiden to be won with him. (op 16-1)
Dean Iarracht(IRE) was making his debut for the Dods yard after finishing runner-up in a couple of sellers when trained by John Upson. Happy Anniversary had his measure on a line through Shadow Bay, who beat the filly at Nottingham and him at Ripon, but he ran a fair race and looks the type for nurseries now that he is eligible. (op 11-4)
Ursula(IRE), by a sprinter but from a decent middle-distance family on the dam's side, fared best of the newcomers and is entitled to improve on this. (op 11-2)
Distinctive Spirit(IRE), whose dam won over this trip at two, had been withdrawn from his intended debut nearly three months ago after proving unruly in the stalls. He was never able to get into contention after breaking slowly and appearing to hit the rails before halfway. (op 12-1 tchd 20-1)
Grissom(IRE) showed some early pace but hung badly when the pressure was on and finished up well beaten. Official explanation: jockey said colt had a breathing problem and lost its left front shoe (op 33-1)

5417 CORUM H'CAP 5f
3:40 (3:40) (Class 4) (0-80,78) 3-Y-O **£5,180** (£1,541; £770; £384) **Stalls** High

Form RPR
3034 **1** **Killer Class**[1] 5393 3-8-1 **63**.............................. KellyHarrison[(5)] 4 70
(J S Goldie) *hld up: nt clr run and swtchd lft appr fnl f: led gng wl ins fnl f: shkn up and kpt on wl* **13/2**
3461 **2** *1 ½* **Andrasta**[1] 5393 3-7-9 **59** 6ex oh5.............................. CharlotteKerton[(7)] 3 61
(A Berry) *prom: led appr fnl f to ins fnl f: kpt on same pce* **10/1**
-010 **3** *3* **Angle Of Attack (IRE)**[6] 5222 3-9-7 **78**.............................. SilvestreDeSousa 6 69
(A D Brown) *led to appr fnl f: sn no ex* **3/1**[2]
1303 **4** *2 ½* **Wotashirtfull (IRE)**[17] 4922 3-9-6 **77**..............................(p) JamieMoriarty 7 59
(K A Ryan) *w ldrs tl rdn and wknd appr fnl f* **4/1**[3]
5233 **5** *hd* **Rio Sands**[34] 4397 3-8-11 **71**.............................. MichaelJStainton[(3)] 5 52
(R M Whitaker) *prom: drvn over 2f out: wknd 1f out* **11/4**[1]
5041 **6** *6* **Cheshire Rose**[19] 4852 3-8-5 **69**.............................. DeanHeslop[(7)] 2 28
(T D Barron) *w ldrs tl rdn and wknd wl over 1f out* **5/1**

62.32 secs (2.22) **Going Correction** +0.50s/f (Yiel) **6** Ran SP% **110.8**
Speed ratings (Par 102): **102,99,94,90,90 80**
toteswinger: 1&2 £3.30, 1&3 £11.20, 2&3 £32.40. CSF £61.71 CT £223.73 TOTE £9.20: £3.30, £4.00; EX 42.20.
Owner Frank Brady **Bred** Jonayro Investments **Trained** Uplawmoor, E Renfrews

FOCUS
Quite an interesting 3yo handicap, run in a decent time for the conditions. Both the first two had run in a class 6 race over course and distance less than 24 hours earlier. The winner is rated to her previous best plus the rider's claim.
Cheshire Rose Official explanation: jockey said filly having gone to post early boiled over at start

5418 WINDSAVE LTD H'CAP 1m 1f 20y
4:10 (4:10) (Class 4) (0-85,85) 4-Y-O+ **£6,476** (£1,927; £963; £481) **Stalls** Low

Form RPR
1010 **1** **Persian Peril**[12] 5092 4-8-5 **72**.............................. PJMcDonald[(3)] 5 79
(G A Swinbank) *hld up in tch: hdwy over 2f out: led ent fnl f: drvn out* **4/1**[2]
6524 **2** *¾* **Jamieson Gold (IRE)**[6] 5221 5-8-11 **75**..............................(b[1]) RoystonFfrench 6 80
(Miss L A Perratt) *trckd ldrs: effrt and ev ch ins fnl f: r.o* **8/1**
4110 **3** *2 ½* **Supercast (IRE)**[39] 4219 5-8-11 **75**.............................. SamHitchcott 8 75
(N J Vaughan) *led to ent fnl f: kpt on same pce* **5/1**
0361 **4** *2* **Major Magpie (IRE)**[22] 4744 6-9-3 **81**.............................. TomEaves 3 77
(M Dods) *hld up in tch: effrt over 2f out: no imp over 1f out* **9/2**[3]
6105 **5** *3 ¼* **Nevada Desert (IRE)**[3] 5360 8-9-0 **78**.............................. DeanMcKeown 7 66
(R M Whitaker) *prom: effrt 2f out: sn rdn and wknd* **7/2**[1]
0 **6** *15* **Solis (GER)**[139] 1308 5-8-11 **78**.............................. NeilBrown[(3)] 2 34
(P Monteith) *bhd: struggling over 3f out: sn btn* **22/1**
0330 **7** *nse* **My Paris**[26] 4649 7-9-3 **81**.............................. TonyHamilton 4 37
(Ollie Pears) *tracled ldrs tl rdn and wknd over 2f out* **9/2**[3]

2m 4.43s (6.03) **Going Correction** +0.80s/f (Soft) **7** Ran SP% **110.7**
Speed ratings (Par 105): **105,104,102,100,97 83,83**
toteswinger: 1&2 £8.90, 1&3 £5.80, 2&3 £6.00. CSF £32.69 CT £153.56 TOTE £6.70: £3.10, £3.00; EX 51.20.
Owner Mrs J Porter **Bred** Mrs P Lewis **Trained** Melsonby, N Yorks

FOCUS
A fair handicap run at just a reasonable pace. The runners tacked over to the stands' side once into the home straight. The form is rated through the winner and this is probably not form to take too positively.

5419 WALTON FOUNDATION H'CAP 7f 50y
4:40 (4:41) (Class 4) (0-85,85) 3-Y-O+ **£6,476** (£1,927; £963; £481) **Stalls** Low

Form RPR
124 **1** **Amicus Meus (IRE)**[13] 5067 4-9-1 **73**.............................. MickyFenton 11 86+
(A Bailey) *trckd ldrs: led over 1f out: r.o strly* **7/2**[2]
2114 **2** *3 ½* **Esoterica (IRE)**[26] 4649 5-9-5 **77**..............................(b) DanielTudhope 10 81
(J S Goldie) *bhd: styd alone far side ent st: chsd wnr ins fnl f: r.o* **10/1**
1522 **3** *1 ½* **Ink Spot**[41] 4167 3-9-5 **85**..............................(v) PJMcDonald[(3)] 9 85
(M L W Bell) *bhd tl styd on fr 2f out: nrst fin* **11/2**
1341 **4** *½* **Zabeel Tower**[16] 4951 5-9-1 **73**..............................(p) TonyHamilton 3 72
(R Allan) *led to over 1f out: no ex ins fnl f* **5/1**[3]
6402 **5** *2 ¾* **Charles Parnell (IRE)**[22] 4736 5-9-4 **76**.............................. JamieMoriarty 1 68
(M Dods) *prom: effrt 2f out: sn no ex* **11/1**
0020 **6D** **The Osteopath (IRE)**[19] 4853 5-9-5 **84**.............................. FrederikTylicki[(7)] 7 67
(M Dods) *trckd ldrs: effrt over 2f out: sn lost pl: fin 6th, 3½l subs disq* **5/2**[1]
2406 **6** *3 ¾* **Alqaahir (USA)**[19] 4876 6-9-1 **73**.............................. RobertWinston 5 55
(J S Wainwright) *w ldr tl wknd fr 2f out: fin 7th, nk: placed 6th* **14/1**
0352 **7** *3 ¼* **Countdown**[33] 4417 6-9-11 **83**..............................(b) DavidAllan 6 56
(T D Easterby) *hld up: pushed along 1/2-way: nvr on terms: fin 8th, plcd 7th* **9/1**

1m 38.15s (4.75) **Going Correction** +0.80s/f (Soft)
WFA 3 from 4yo+ 5lb **8** Ran SP% **116.9**
Speed ratings (Par 105): **104,100,98,97,94 90,90,86**
toteswinger: 1&2 £7.60, 1&3 £4.20, 2&3 £8.40. CSF £38.76 CT £168.88 TOTE £4.60: £1.30, £2.10, £1.90; EX 44.40.
Owner North Cheshire Trading & Storage Ltd **Bred** John Egan **Trained** Newmarket, Suffolk

FOCUS
A decent handicap which produced a taking winner in Amicus Meus who can rate higher. The Osteopath was subsequently disqualified from sixth place (prohibited substance in sample).
The Osteopath(IRE) Official explanation: trainer had no explanation for the poor form shown

5420 COSGROVE EMPLOYABILITY OPEN APPRENTICE H'CAP 1m
5:10 (5:10) (Class 6) (0-60,59) 4-Y-O+ **£2,590** (£770; £385; £192) **Stalls** Low

Form RPR
0051 **1** **Wednesdays Boy (IRE)**[19] 4851 5-9-0 **54**..............................(p) ClGillies 10 61+
(P D Niven) *hld up: hdwy over 2f out: led and hung lft 1f out: r.o* **11/2**[3]
0445 **2** *1 ½* **Apache Nation (IRE)**[19] 4851 5-9-2 **56**..............................(b[1]) FrederikTylicki 9 60
(M Dods) *prom: led over 2f out to 1f out: kpt on u.p* **10/3**[1]
0001 **3** *shd* **Distant Pleasure**[24] 4683 4-8-12 **57**.............................. JohnCavanagh[(5)] 11 61
(M Dods) *s.i.s: bhd tl styd on fr 2f out: nrst fin* **8/1**
3041 **4** *nse* **Grandad Bill (IRE)**[19] 4850 5-9-4 **58**.............................. DeanHeslop 3 62+
(J S Goldie) *hld up: styd far side w one other ent st: hdwy over 1f out: r.o fnl f* **4/1**[2]
053 **5** *2 ¼* **Kielty's Folly**[18] 4898 4-8-2 **47**.............................. MatthewLawson[(5)] 8 45
(B P J Baugh) *prom: effrt over 2f out: edgd lft and no ex over 1f out* **9/1**
0050 **6** *1 ½* **Polish Star**[16] 4949 4-7-12 **45**..............................(b) SFeeney[(7)] 2 40
(Miss L A Perratt) *hld up: effrt and styd far side w one other ent st: wknd over 1f out* **28/1**
0000 **7** *nk* **Mangano**[17] 4919 4-8-3 **48** ow3.............................. KrishGundowry[(5)] 4 42
(A Berry) *hld up in midfield: effrt over 2f out: wknd appr fnl f* **25/1**
2503 **8** *nk* **Anduril**[17] 4919 7-8-8 **51**..............................(b) BMcHugh[(3)] 6 45
(I W McInnes) *midfield: drvn and outpcd over 3f out: no imp fnl 2f* **11/1**
0000 **9** *2 ½* **Baylaw Star**[15] 4961 7-8-0 **45**.............................. JamieKyne[(5)] 13 33
(I W McInnes) *led to over 2f out: sn rdn and wknd* **25/1**
0433 **10** *2 ¾* **Oeuf A La Neige**[15] 4967 8-9-1 **55**.............................. LanceBetts 5 37
(Miss L A Perratt) *trckd ldrs tl wknd over 2f out* **7/1**
0000 **11** *1 ¼* **Linden's Lady**[13] 5045 8-8-5 **45**..............................(v) DeclanCannon 7 24
(J R Weymes) *plld hrd: prom tl wknd over 2f out* **50/1**
000 **12** *2* **Tom Tower (IRE)**[19] 4846 4-8-6 **51** ow4.............................. BradleyRoper[(5)] 1 25
(A C Whillans) *t.k.h: trckd ldrs tl wknd over 2f out* **50/1**

1m 50.86s (7.06) **Going Correction** +0.80s/f (Soft) **12** Ran SP% **115.5**
Speed ratings (Par 101): **96,94,94,94,92 90,90,90,87,84 83,81**
toteswinger: 1&2 £5.30, 1&3 £7.80, 2&3 £7.60. CSF £22.20 CT £130.62 TOTE £6.60: £2.00, £1.60, £3.00; EX 27.80 Place 6: £592.47, Place 5: £473.55..
Owner The Wednesday Club **Bred** Sean Collins **Trained** Barton-le-Street, N Yorks
■ Stewards' Enquiry : Frederik Tylicki one-day ban: used whip with excessive frequency (Sep 14)

FOCUS
A low-grade handicap restricted to apprentices with no more than 25 winners to their name. The pace was only steady and the bulk of the field came stands' side in the straight, the two exceptions, who raced up the far rail, finishing fourth and sixth. The form should hold up at a lowly level and the winner is rated back to his 3yo best.
T/Plt: £404.60 to a £1 stake. Pool: £61,940.19. 111.75 winning tickets. T/Qpdt: £97.40 to a £1 stake. Pool: £3,272.10. 24.85 winning tickets. RY

5401

GREAT LEIGHS (A.W) (L-H)
Thursday, August 28

OFFICIAL GOING: Standard
Wind: virtually nil Weather: sunny and rather warm

5421 GREEN DRAGON H'CAP 6f (P)
2:30 (2:30) (Class 6) (0-60,60) 3-Y-O **£2,590** (£770; £385; £192) **Stalls** Low

Form RPR
0532 **1** **Penrice Castle**[27] 4580 3-8-8 **50** ow1.............................. RyanMoore 4 58
(R Hannon) *mid-div: gd hdwy on inner 2f out: rdn to ld jst over 1f out: kpt on wl: rdn out* **7/1**[2]
5003 **2** *½* **Pasta Prayer**[8] 5186 3-8-12 **54**..............................(b) ChrisCatlin 1 60
(S A Callaghan) *chsd ldrs: rdn 3f out: chsd wnr fr over 1f out: styd on u.str.p fnl f* **10/1**
0403 **3** *1 ¼* **Nawaaff**[10] 5141 3-8-13 **55**..............................(v) TPO'Shea 3 57
(M R Channon) *s.i.s: towards rr: hdwy over 2f out: sn rdn: wnt 2rd ent fnl f: styd on* **8/1**[3]
5500 **4** *1 ¾* **Charmel's Lad**[21] 4777 3-8-12 **59**..............................(t) DavidProbert[(5)] 10 55+
(W R Swinburn) *hld up towards rr: hdwy over 2f out: c wd ent st: sn rdn: styd on but hung lft fr over 1f out* **8/1**[3]
5402 **5** *nk* **Westwood Dawn**[14] 5015 3-8-6 **48**..............................(v) DMylonas 2 43
(Mrs N Macauley) *chsd ldrs: nt clr run over 2f out: sn rdn: hmpd over 1f out: kpt on same pce fnl f* **20/1**
4302 **6** *shd* **The Little Fizzer (IRE)**[22] 4725 3-8-11 **53**.............................. TGMcLaughlin 7 48
(P D Evans) *chsd ldrs: rdn whn swtchd rt over 1f out: kpt on same pce fnl f* **4/1**[1]
5063 **7** *½* **Linnet Park**[14] 5015 3-8-2 **51**.............................. RosieJessop[(7)] 8 45
(J G Given) *led: rdn and hdd jst over 1f out: no ex* **12/1**
625 **8** *3 ½* **Our Kally**[6] 5217 3-8-4 **53**.............................. SeanPalmer[(7)] 11 35
(M D I Usher) *s.i.s: bhd: sme hdwy u.p 2f out: edgd rt and wknd over 1f out* **20/1**
3000 **9** *5* **Karky Schultz (GER)**[52] 3799 3-9-4 **60**..............................(b[1]) SebSanders 12 26
(J M P Eustace) *s.i.s: towards rr: hdwy on outer over 2f out: sn rdn: wknd over 1f out* **7/1**[2]
3452 **10** *½* **Bilboa**[29] 4531 3-8-13 **55**..............................(p) DaneO'Neill 9 20
(J M Bradley) *mid-div on outer: gd hdwy over 2f out: sn rdn: ev ch whn jinked lft over 1f out: wknd* **4/1**[1]
0000 **11** *2 ½* **King Of Cadeaux (IRE)**[9] 5167 3-8-12 **54**..............................(b) JamieSpencer 14 11
(M A Magnusson) *prom: rdn over 2f out: wkng whn hmpd and snatched up over 1f out* **10/1**
0000 **12** *14* **Solemn**[47] 3960 3-8-9 **54**..............................(p) TravisBlock[(3)] 6 —
(J M Bradley) *a towards rr: eased whn btn fr over 1f out* **50/1**

1m 14.43s (0.73) **Going Correction** +0.05s/f (Slow) **12** Ran SP% **124.6**
Speed ratings (Par 98): **97,96,94,92,91 91,91,86,79,79 75,57**
toteswinger: 1&2 £4.80, 1&3 £7.50, 2&3 £17.40. CSF £77.35 CT £436.71 TOTE £4.70: £1.80, £4.60, £2.80; EX 59.70.
Owner D J Deer **Bred** D J And Mrs Deer **Trained** East Everleigh, Wilts

FOCUS
A very weak opening handicap for three-year-olds in which a low draw proved to be a real advantage. The winner and third had slipped to good marks and the form makes sense.

5422 CHURCH END NURSERY 6f (P)
3:00 (3:02) (Class 4) (0-85,85) 2-Y-O **£3,885** (£1,156; £577; £288) **Stalls** Low

Form RPR
01 **1** **Athania (IRE)**[14] 5022 2-8-4 **68** .... RichardThomas 1 76+
(A P Jarvis) *a little slowly away: sn nudged into ld: shkn up over 1f out: r.o wl: eased towards fin* **2/1**[1]
3435 **2** *3 1/2* **River Rye (IRE)**[22] 4729 2-8-12 **76** .... RyanMoore 3 71
(R Hannon) *broke wl: sn settled bhd ldng pair: rdn 2f out: kpt on to go 2nd ent fnl f: no ch w wnr* **7/2**[2]
5163 **3** *3/4* **Ridgeway Silver**[10] 5153 2-8-3 **67** .... JimmyQuinn 2 60
(M D I Usher) *broke wl: sn settled bhd ldng pair: rdn over 2f out: wnt 2nd briefly over 1f out: kpt on same pce fnl f* **4/1**[3]
0100 **4** *2 1/4* **Asaint Needs Brass (USA)**[40] 4190 2-9-7 **85** .... SebSanders 4 71
(R M Beckett) *a little slowly away: sn w wnr: rdn over 2f out: one pce and lost 2nd over 1f out* **2/1**[1]

1m 14.31s (0.61) **Going Correction** +0.05s/f (Slow) **4** Ran SP% **108.9**
Speed ratings (Par 96): **97,92,91,88**
CSF £8.98 TOTE £2.90; EX 8.00.
Owner Mrs Ann Jarvis **Bred** Mrs Anne Marie Burns **Trained** Twyford, Bucks

FOCUS
Despite the small turnout this was still an open nursery. It was run at a solid early pace and the form looks straightforward enough, with the winner building on her Salisbury win and with the winning time being 0.12 secs faster than the preceding handicap for three-year-olds.

NOTEBOOK
Athania(IRE) ◆ followed up her Salisbury maiden success a fortnight previously and ran out a very ready winner. She was sensibly ridden aggressively on this drop back in trip and already had the race sewn up when passing the 1f pole. This different surface evidently posed her no problem and, value for further than her winning margin, it would be no big surprise to see her bag the hat-trick now. (op 6-4 tchd 9-4)
River Rye(IRE), 2lb lower, kept on for pressure inside the final furlong to win the race for second, but she has to rate flattered by her proximity to the winner. (op 3-1 tchd 4-1)
Ridgeway Silver, third over this trip at Wolverhampton ten days previously, met support in the betting ring and ran her race. She helps to set the level of this form as she does look held by the Handicapper. (op 6-1 tchd 7-2)
Asaint Needs Brass(USA) had won both his previous outings on the all-weather at Kempton and looked a big player on this drop down in grade. He tried to go with the winner early on, but was a spent force before the final furlong and simply failed to see out the extra furlong. He may be better when going right-handed and looks worth dropping back a furlong, but still has questions to answer now. (op 9-4 tchd 15-8)

5423 SHOWGROUND H'CAP 1m 6f (P)
3:30 (3:30) (Class 3) (0-95,93) 3-Y-O+
£7,477 (£2,239; £1,119; £560; £279; £140) **Stalls** Low

Form RPR
3203 **1** **Jagger**[13] 5054 8-9-2 **84** .... TolleyDean(3) 6 93
(G A Butler) *mid-div: hdwy on outer over 2f out: sn rdn: led ins fnl f: styd on wl* **7/1**[3]
2423 **2** *1 3/4* **Fregate Island (IRE)**[40] 4200 5-9-2 **81** .... RHills 11 88
(A G Newcombe) *led: rdn 2f out: hdd ins fnl f: kpt on but no ex* **15/2**
1106 **3** *3/4* **Always Bold (IRE)**[6] 5249 3-8-10 **87** .... JoeFanning 3 93
(M Johnston) *trckd ldrs: wnt 2nd 3f out: sn rdn: lost 2nd ent fnl f: kpt on same pce* **15/2**
-105 **4** *1* **Crete (IRE)**[40] 4191 6-9-9 **88** .... MichaelHills 12 93
(W J Haggas) *hld up towards rr: rdn and stdy hdwy 2f out: styd on fnl f* **6/1**[2]
0010 **5** *1 1/2* **Boz**[22] 4742 4-9-9 **88** ....(b) JamieSpencer 9 90
(L M Cumani) *mid-div: rdn and hdwy 2f out: edgd lft and styd on same pce fnl f* **8/1**
6-14 **6** *4* **Shimoni**[14] 5024 4-9-4 **83** .... RyanMoore 2 80
(G L Moore) *mid-div: rdn over 4f out: effrt on inner 2f out: wknd fnl f* **12/1**
0426 **7** *1/2* **Candle**[19] 4844 5-10-0 **93** .... DaneO'Neill 7 89
(H Candy) *trckd ldrs: rdn over 3f out: wknd fnl f* **7/1**[3]
04-3 **8** *1/2* **La Estrella (USA)**[35] 735 5-9-3 **82** ....(b) ChrisCatlin 10 77
(D E Cantillon) *chsd ldr tl 3f out: sn rdn: wknd fnl f* **16/1**
-000 **9** *5* **Jadalee (IRE)**[34] 4362 5-9-11 **90** ....(t) SebSanders 4 78
(G A Butler) *mid-div: rdn whn nt clr run briefly over 2f out: effrt over 1f out: wknd ent fnl f* **33/1**
0004 **10** *3 1/2* **Kasthari (IRE)**[33] 4439 9-9-6 **85** ....(v) DarryllHolland 1 69
(J D Bethell) *s.i.s: a towards rr* **16/1**
140 **11** *9* **Tighnabruaich (IRE)**[54] 3719 3-8-10 **87** .... PhilipRobinson 5 58
(M A Jarvis) *a towards rr* **9/2**[1]
-000 **12** *1/2* **Duty Free (IRE)**[44] 4046 4-9-2 **81** .... TedDurcan 8 51
(C R Egerton) *rdn over 3f out: a towards rr* **14/1**

3m 1.83s (-1.37) **Going Correction** +0.05s/f (Slow)
WFA 3 from 4yo+ 12lb **12** Ran SP% **121.2**
Speed ratings (Par 107): **105,104,103,103,102 99,99,99,96,94 89,89**
toteswinger: 1&2 £10.00, 1&3 £19.30, 2&3 £12.70. CSF £60.13 CT £413.84 TOTE £9.40: £2.40, £2.10, £3.60; EX 46.90.
Owner C McFadden **Bred** Mrs M Lavell **Trained** Newmarket, Suffolk

FOCUS
A good staying handicap, run at a solid gallop and few really landed a blow from off the pace. The form looks sound with the first three close to their recent best.

NOTEBOOK
Jagger finally ended a losing run that dated back to 2005 and he rates a much-deserved winner. He has run some solid races in defeat this term on both turf and this surface, plus he was able to race from a 1lb lower mark than when running third at Newbury 13 days previously on an unsuitably easy going. That form looked decent with the winner finishing second in the rescheduled Ebor last week and everything went according to plan for him this time. His overall profile does dictate he should be taken on from a higher mark next time, but this should still serve his confidence very well and he will no doubt continue to pay his way. (op 6-1)
Fregate Island(IRE) set a good clip out in front and did not go down easily when the challengers emerged. He holds no secrets from the Handicapper, but has developed into a very consistent performer this year and does deserve to go one better once more. (op 8-1)
Always Bold(IRE) was always well placed just off the pace and returned to the sort of form that saw him win at Newmarket in July. He looks up to finding a race from this mark. (op 9-1)
Crete(IRE) fared best of those to come from behind and again showed a liking for the all-weather. He may not be the most straightforward, but has the talent to defy this mark when things go his way and looks well worth a more positive ride over this longer trip. (tchd 13-2)
Boz had the blinkers replacing the visor for this return to a course and distance he has won over. He was given his chance, but was never a serious threat to the winner and does look handicapped to his best at present. (op 7-1)
Kasthari(IRE) Official explanation: jockey said gelding missed the break
Tighnabruaich(IRE) was making his all-weather bow after a 54-day break. He was ridden very patiently on this step up in trip, but was ultimately beaten turning for home, before the longer distance really came into play. It may have been the surface was to blame and this was not a race where it was an advantage to be held up, but he still has quite a bit to prove now. Official explanation: jockey said colt gurgled (tchd 5-1)

5424 HATFIELD HEATH H'CAP 6f (P)
4:00 (4:02) (Class 3) (0-95,94) 3-Y-O+
£7,477 (£2,239; £1,119; £560; £279; £140) **Stalls** Low

Form RPR
5013 **1** **Diriculous**[17] 4928 4-8-13 **88** .... JackMitchell(5) 2 103
(T G Mills) *mid-div: hdwy over 2f out: sn swtchd rt: led ent fnl f: r.o wl: comf* **2/1**[1]
4336 **2** *3 1/4* **Orpenindeed (IRE)**[17] 4928 5-9-6 **90** ....(t) SebSanders 10 95
(M Botti) *chsd ldrs: rdn 2f out: led briefly jst over 1f out: nt pce of wnr* **7/1**
1050 **3** *1/2* **Carcinetto (IRE)**[19] 4841 6-8-12 **87** .... RichardEvans(5) 7 90
(P D Evans) *mid-div: rdn 3f out: no imp tl r.o ins fnl f: wnt 3rd nr fin* **16/1**
2233 **4** *1 3/4* **Dingaan (IRE)**[14] 5030 5-9-3 **87** .... FrancisNorton 8 84
(A M Balding) *trckd ldr: rdn and ev ch over 1f out: kpt on same pce fnl f* **7/2**[2]
6165 **5** *1/2* **Dvinsky (USA)**[7] 5206 7-8-12 **82** ....(b) JimmyQuinn 1 78
(P Howling) *chsd ldrs: effrt 2f out: kpt on same pce fnl f* **12/1**
2410 **6** *1/2* **Everymanforhimself (IRE)**[41] 4145 4-9-8 **92** .... JamieSpencer 9 86
(K A Ryan) *towards rr: sme late prog: nvr a factor* **11/2**[3]
2300 **7** *hd* **Xpres Maite**[7] 5208 5-9-8 **92** ....(v) DaneO'Neill 3 86
(S R Bowring) *chsd ldrs: rdn 3f out: wknd over 1f out* **16/1**
1322 **8** *1/2* **Peter Island (FR)**[20] 4809 5-8-5 **75** ....(v) ChrisCatlin 12 67
(J Gallagher) *led: rdn and hdd over 1f out: fdd fnl f* **12/1**
0000 **9** *1 1/4* **Vhujon (IRE)**[18] 4893 3-9-0 **87** .... TGMcLaughlin 6 75
(P D Evans) *s.i.s: racd wd: a bhd* **25/1**
0200 **10** *1 1/4* **Dressed To Dance (IRE)**[19] 4841 4-9-2 **86** .... RyanMoore 11 70
(P D Evans) *s.i.s: a outpcd in rr* **18/1**
5025 **11** *1* **Prior Warning**[24] 4687 4-9-10 **94** ....(t) PaulEddery 5 75
(Miss D Mountain) *a towards rr* **16/1**

1m 12.55s (-1.15) **Going Correction** +0.05s/f (Slow)
WFA 3 from 4yo+ 3lb **11** Ran SP% **125.6**
Speed ratings (Par 107): **109,104,104,101,101 100,100,99,97,96 94**
toteswinger: 1&2 £6.10, 1&3 £20.70, 2&3 £27.80. CSF £18.00 CT £193.11 TOTE £3.10: £1.80, £2.40, £7.40; EX 24.30.
Owner Sherwoods Transport Ltd **Bred** Sherwoods Transport Ltd **Trained** Headley, Surrey

FOCUS
This good quality sprint handicap was run at a strong early pace and that played right into the hands of the winner, who is progressive. The placed horses set the level, both rated to their sand marks.

NOTEBOOK
Diriculous relished the strong early pace and motored home inside the final furlong to score with plenty in hand. He got going too late at Windsor last time, but was given a sensible ride from his claiming jockey and this does rate as a career-best effort. He is also now unbeaten in two outings over course and distance, so clearly loves it here and no doubt his connections will now be very keen to find him a suitable opportunity under a penalty before the handicapper can strike. (op 5-2)
Orpenindeed(IRE) was having his first run on the all-weather this year and he ran right up to par, rating a benchmark for the form (tchd 8-1)
Carcinetto(IRE), back in trip, also helps to set the level of this form as she had been beaten in similar fashion by the winner on her only previous outing over the course and distance in July. This was better from her, but she ideally wants a stiffer finish over this distance.
Dingaan(IRE), rated 5lb higher on the all-weather, was ridden more prominently than is often the case and ran a little below his recent turf level. He is very hard to actually win with. (op 4-1)
Dvinsky(USA) had run creditably over the minimum at this track a week previously and he again ran respectably without really threatening. He too ran close enough to his previous course-and-distance form with the winner. (op 14-1)
Everymanforhimself(IRE) was making his all-weather debut and failed to seriously get into the race, but he still did best of those to be given waiting rides. (tchd 5-1)
Vhujon(IRE) Official explanation: jockey said gelding hung right

5425 WILLOW GREEN H'CAP 1m (P)
4:30 (4:34) (Class 3) (0-95,94) 3-Y-O
£7,477 (£2,239; £1,119; £560; £279; £140) **Stalls** Centre

Form RPR
-130 **1** **Slam**[49] 3877 3-9-3 **90** .... MichaelHills 4 100
(B W Hills) *cl up: wnt 2nd over 3f out: rdn to ld over 1f out: sn hrd pressed: kpt on gamely: all out* **10/1**
5312 **2** *nk* **Acrostic**[15] 4976 3-9-3 **90** .... DaneO'Neill 3 99
(L M Cumani) *s.i.s: sn cl up: rdn to chal and wandered u.p fr over 1f out: ev ch thrght fnl f: hld fnl strides* **9/1**
1261 **3** *4 1/2* **Born Tobouggie (GER)**[24] 4694 3-9-2 **89** .... TedDurcan 8 88
(H R A Cecil) *hld up last: rdn over 2f out: hung lft fr 2f out: styd on to go 3rd ins fnl f: nvr able to mount chal* **13/2**
21 **4** *2 1/4* **Once A Gulch (USA)**[22] 4730 3-8-13 **86** .... SebSanders 2 79
(J Noseda) *hld up bhd ldrs: rdn and hdwy 3f out: disp cl 3rd over 1f out: wknd ins fnl f* **6/4**[1]
4100 **5** *1* **Mukhber**[21] 4783 3-8-13 **86** ....(b[1]) RHills 6 77
(J H M Gosden) *led: rdn over 2f out: hdd over 1f out: wknd fnl f* **7/1**
5565 **6** *8* **Always Ready**[12] 5102 3-8-7 **80** ....(b) LiamJones 1 53
(C E Brittain) *w ldr: rdn over 3f out: wknd 2f out* **14/1**
4604 **7** *20* **Flawed Genius**[29] 4522 3-9-6 **93** .... RyanMoore 5 20
(Sir Michael Stoute) *s.i.s: hld up bhd ldrs: rdn 3f out: wknd 2f out: sn virtually p.u* **9/2**[2]
6243 **8** *1 3/4* **Kal Barg**[40] 4197 3-9-7 **94** .... PhilipRobinson 7 17
(M A Jarvis) *chsd ldrs: rdn over 3f out: sn btn: virtually p.u over 1f out* **5/1**[3]

1m 39.7s (-0.20) **Going Correction** +0.05s/f (Slow) **8** Ran SP% **126.4**
Speed ratings (Par 104): **103,102,98,95,94 86,66,65**
toteswinger: 1&2 £9.10, 1&3 £13.40, 2&3 £5.50. CSF £104.28 CT £651.00 TOTE £11.70: £3.60, £2.80, £2.40; EX 99.30.
Owner K Abdulla **Bred** Juddmonte Farms Ltd **Trained** Lambourn, Berks

FOCUS
This was an interesting three-year-old handicap for the grade with some unexposed performers amongst those better known. It was run at a sound early pace and the first pair came clear, with both progressing.

NOTEBOOK

Slam was ridden handily and eventually just did enough to repel the runner-up towards the finish. He had found things too hot in a strong handicap at Newmarket last time, but had won his maiden over course and distance on his seasonal bow in May and the return to this track worked the oracle. Showing a willing attitude when pressed late on, he now faces a rise up the weights, but may just find some further improvement for a step up in trip. He holds an entry in the Cambridgeshire and the extra furlong there should really suit were he to make that valuable target in October. (op 12-1)

Acrostic ◆ ran a big race in defeat on this sand debut and was the only one to give the winner a serious race inside the final furlong. He is no doubt still progressing and his shrewd outfit can place him to deservedly go one better again before long. It is very interesting that he too holds an entry in the Cambrigeshire. (op 7-1)

Born Tobouggie(GER) , another newcomer to the all-weather, had been officially raised 6lb for her Windsor success 24 days previously. She did not look totally at ease on the surface down the home straight, but still ran creditably and remains open to a little further improvement. (op 6-1)

Once A Gulch(USA) failed to really fire on this handicap debut and never looked like justifying strong support in the betting ring. He had been beaten around three lengths by the winner on his debut in May, so it is obviously disappointing that he failed to reverse that form on these better terms. It is still too soon to be writing him off, however. (op 9-4 tchd 5-2)

Mukhber, equipped with first-time blinkers for this switch to the all-weather, got a bit warm beforehand and paid late on for running freely at the head of affairs (op 11-1)

Always Ready Official explanation: jockey said colt hung left

Flawed Genius was not that surprisingly without the visor he had worn at Goodwood last time. While the new surface may have been against him, he simply ran no sort of race from off the pace and has it all to prove after this. Official explanation: jockey said gelding lost its action

Kal Barg, a winner on his only previous run on an artificial surface, dropped out from the final bend and ran too badly to be true. Official explanation: trainer had no explanation for the poor form shown (op 9-2)

5426 BLAKE END MEDIAN AUCTION MAIDEN STKS 1m (P)

5:00 (5:03) (Class 6) 3-5-Y-O £2,590 (£770; £385; £192) Stalls Centre

Form RPR

00 **1** **Lady Brora**[37] 4277 3-8-12 0 FrancisNorton 7 68
(A M Balding) *in tch: rdn over 2f out: led ent fnl f: r.o wl: readily* **11/2**

43 **2** 2 ½ **Mazaris (IRE)**[10] 5150 3-9-3 0 DaneO'Neill 8 67
(L M Cumani) *trckd ldr: chal 2f out: sn wandered u.p: ev ch ent fnl f: kpt on but nt pce of wnr* **7/2**[3]

3233 **3** ½ **Seventh Cavalry (IRE)**[10] 5140 3-9-3 74 (v) TedDurcan 10 66
(H R A Cecil) *s.i.s: bmpd after 1f: sn trcking ldrs: rdn into narrow advantage wl over 1f out: hdd ent fnl f: no ex* **2/1**[1]

4 1 ½ **Time To Play** 3-9-3 0 KirstyMilczarek 5 62
(T T Clement) *trckd ldrs: rdn 3f out: kpt on same pce fnl 2f* **25/1**

24 **5** 2 ½ **Crafty Dealer (IRE)**[13] 5049 3-9-3 0 JamesDoyle 2 56
(J W Hills) *mid-div: rdn 3f out: kpt on same pce fnl 2f* **5/2**[2]

6 **6** 3 ¼ **Tampopo (IRE)**[14] 5023 3-9-3 0 LiamJones 3 49
(D J S Ffrench Davis) *in tch: rdn 3f out: one pce fnl 2f* **33/1**

0500 **7** 3 ½ **Marvin Gardens**[20] 4806 5-9-4 42 DavidProbert[(5)] 11 41
(P S McEntee) *led: rdn and hdd wl over 1f out: fdd fnl f* **40/1**

00 **8** 9 **Johnny McGurk**[10] 5160 3-9-3 0 ChrisCatlin 9 20
(M E Rimmer) *mid-div: rdn over 3f out: wknd 2f out* **33/1**

0 **9** 1 ¾ **Wrecker's Moon (IRE)**[34] 4378 3-8-10 0 ow1 LeeVickers[(3)] 1 12
(T J Etherington) *sn towards rr* **66/1**

5060 **10** 3 ¾ **Plum Asset (USA)**[61] 3507 3-8-12 62 SebSanders 6 —
(R M Beckett) *s.i.s: a in rr* **6/1**

0 **11** 2 **Emily's Secret**[26] 4651 3-8-12 0 SaleemGolam 4 —
(G C Bravery) *mid-div: drvn 4f out: wknd over 2f out* **25/1**

000- **12** 11 **Spoilt Madame**[308] 6454 3-8-12 41 (v[1]) TGMcLaughlin 12 —
(P D Evans) *a bhd* **50/1**

1m 41.98s (2.08) **Going Correction** +0.05s/f (Slow)
WFA 3 from 5yo 6lb 12 Ran SP% **133.3**
Speed ratings (Par 101): **91,88,88,86,84 80,77,68,66,62 60,49**
toteswinger: 1&2 £5.20, 1&3 £4.80, 2&3 £3.20. CSF £27.17 TOTE £8.50: £2.20, £1.90, £1.30; EX 27.80 Place 6: £611.12, Place 5: £158.40..
Owner W Aeberhard **Bred** Kingsclere Stud **Trained** Kingsclere, Hants

FOCUS

A weakish maiden for three-year-olds and the winning time was very moderate, 2.28 seconds slower than the preceding handicap. The favourite disappointed and this is not form to be too positive about.

Crafty Dealer(IRE) Official explanation: jockey said gelding missed the break
Tampopo(IRE) Official explanation: jockey said gelding became unbalanced on final bend
Plum Asset(USA) Official explanation: jockey said filly missed the break

T/Plt: £223.20 to a £1 stake. Pool: £66,794.73. 218.37 winning tickets. T/Qpdt: £23.20 to a £1 stake. Pool: £4,512.40. 143.40 winning tickets. TM

5140 LINGFIELD (L-H)

Thursday, August 28

OFFICIAL GOING: Turf course - good (good to firm in places); all weather - standard

Turf course: the jockeys were of the opinion that the ground was good, or perhaps just on the easy side of good in the home straight.
Wind: Moderate, half behind Weather: Overcast

5427 HOLLOW LANE APPRENTICE H'CAP 1m 2f

2:20 (2:20) (Class 6) (0-65,65) 4-Y-O+ £2,047 (£604; £302) Stalls Low

Form RPR

2151 **1** **Action Impact (ARG)**[12] 5087 4-9-10 65 JemmaMarshall 3 72+
(G L Moore) *settled in abt 6th: clsd on ldrs 2f out: rdn over 1f out: led jst ins fnl f: styd on strly* **7/2**[2]

3212 **2** ¾ **Gracechurch (IRE)**[9] 5168 5-9-6 60 Louis-PhilippeBeuzelin 9 67
(R J Hodges) *hld up in abt 8th: prog 3f out: sn rdn: clsd on ldrs over 1f out: styd on to take 2nd nr fin: a hld* **5/2**[1]

0202 **3** ½ **Everyman**[10] 5145 4-8-9 49 MCGeran 2 55
(A W Carroll) *trckd ldrs: gng strly 3f out: wnt 2nd 2f out: upsides ent fnl f: one pce fnl 100yds* **8/1**[3]

2000 **4** 1 ¼ **Pop Music (IRE)**[12] 5105 5-9-7 61 (v) SophieDoyle 10 64
(Ms J S Doyle) *t.k.h early: led after 2f: rdn over 2f out: hdd and fdd jst ins fnl f* **20/1**

0555 **5** 2 **Dubai Shadow (IRE)**[44] 4055 4-8-3 48 DebraEngland[(5)] 8 47
(C E Brittain) *t.k.h early: trckd ldrs: gng easily over 2f out: cl enough over 1f out: folded tamely* **9/1**

/02- **6** nse **Lucefer (IRE)**[436] 2745 10-8-5 45 WilliamCarson 11 44
(G C H Chung) *hld up in last pair: stl there ovfer 2f out gng wl enough: sn outpcd and rdn: styd on fr over 1f out: nvr nrr* **25/1**

0520 **7** 1 ½ **Meohmy**[12] 5105 5-8-7 47 MatthewDavies 7 43
(M R Channon) *hld up in last trio: rdn over 3f out: no prog tl styd on fr over 1f out: n.d* **18/1**

4-00 **8** 2 ¾ **Royal Indulgence**[32] 4458 8-9-5 59 AshleyMorgan 6 49
(W M Brisbourne) *dwlt: hld up in last pair: rdn 3f out: no prog tl kpt on fnl f* **12/1**

5423 **9** ½ **Fantasy Crusader**[9] 5168 9-8-2 47 AndreaAtzeni[(5)] 12 36
(R M H Cowell) *prom: chsd ldr 4f out to 2f out: wknd* **8/1**[3]

0010 **10** 4 ½ **Muffett's Dream**[14] 5024 4-8-10 50 RossAtkinson 4 30
(J J Bridger) *led 2f: chsd ldr top 4f out: wknd over 2f out* **9/1**

000 **11** 4 ½ **Alright Chuck**[38] 4249 4-8-5 45 AmyBaker 1 16
(P W Hiatt) *t.k.h early: hld up in 9th: no prog over 2f out: wknd wl over 1f out* **100/1**

066/ **12** 14 **Black Draft**[1167] 2698 6-8-5 45 BillyCray 5 —
(B Forsey) *t.k.h early: prom tl wknd over 3f out: t.o* **66/1**

2m 10.79s (0.29) **Going Correction** +0.075s/f (Good) 12 Ran SP% **117.1**
Speed ratings (Par 101): **101,100,100,99,97 97,96,93,93,89 86,75**
toteswinger: 1&2 £2.70, 1&3 £5.10, 2&3 £3.60. CSF £12.04 CT £65.00 TOTE £4.00: £1.90, £1.70, £1.90; EX 11.20 Trifecta £68.60 Pool: £381.34, 4.11 winning units..
Owner T Bowley **Bred** Santa Maria De Araras **Trained** Woodingdean, E Sussex

FOCUS

A moderate apprentice handicap, though a couple did come into it in reasonable form. The form is sound. The pace was only steady and there were five in a line across the track with every chance passing the furlong pole.

5428 WEATHERBYS BANK H'CAP 1m 2f

2:50 (2:51) (Class 5) (0-75,75) 3-Y-O £2,590 (£770; £385; £192) Stalls Low

Form RPR

0261 **1** **Liberally (IRE)**[11] 5119 3-9-7 75 6ex EddieAhern 6 81
(B J Meehan) *prom: rdn in 3rd whn pce lifted 4f out: clsd u.p fr 2f out: styd on wl to ld nr fin* **2/1**[1]

0306 **2** nk **Title Role**[35] 4344 3-9-4 72 GregFairley 7 77
(P F I Cole) *t.k.h early: led 2f: w ldr to 4f out: chsng after: rdn to chal over 1f out: upsides 75yds out: jst outpcd* **10/1**

2654 **3** nk **Politeia (USA)**[29] 4527 3-9-1 69 (v[1]) RichardHughes 5 73
(R Hannon) *led after 2f: qcknd 4f out: hrd rdn 2f out: worn down nr fin* **7/1**[3]

6122 **4** 2 **Houri (IRE)**[25] 4669 3-9-7 75 (p) AdamKirby 3 77+
(R M Beckett) *trckd ldrs: outpcd 4f out: clsd fr over 2f out: tried to chal 1f out: hld whn no room fnl 100yds* **6/1**[2]

3254 **5** ¾ **Flam**[29] 4532 3-9-4 72 JimCrowley 13 71
(J R Fanshawe) *cl up: outpcd over 3f out and rdn: kpt on fnl 2f: nvr able to chal* **14/1**

01-6 **6** 1 ¼ **Desert Thistle (IRE)**[15] 4984 3-9-5 73 IanMongan 9 69+
(H J L Dunlop) *hld up in rr: outpcd 4f out: effrt on outer over 2f out: hanging lft over 1f out: kpt on: nvr rchd ldrs* **20/1**

1-03 **7** 2 ¾ **Ballora (FR)**[15] 4976 3-9-7 75 WilliamBuick 2 66
(S Kirk) *stdd s: hld up in rr: outpcd 4f out: rdn and one pce fnl 3f: no imp* **8/1**

6-05 **8** ½ **Eseej (USA)**[13] 5047 3-8-9 68 WilliamCarson[(5)] 8 58
(P W Hiatt) *hld up in rr: awkward downhill 4f out and outpcd: struggling on outer over 2f out: modest late prog* **80/1**

0144 **9** ¾ **Stage Acclaim (IRE)**[21] 4766 3-9-0 71 ow1 (p) JamesMillman[(3)] 4 59
(B R Millman) *t.k.h: hld up in midfield: stl pulling 4f out but outpcd: pushed along and no imp after* **16/1**

0430 **10** shd **Clovis**[15] 4978 3-9-2 70 (b) ShaneKelly 12 58
(N P Mulholland) *dwlt: sn in midfield: outpcd 4f out: nvr on terms after* **33/1**

4002 **11** 1 ½ **Seventh Hill**[15] 4978 3-8-11 65 SteveDrowne 10 50
(M Blanshard) *a towards rr: wl outpcd in last pair 4f out: no ch after* **14/1**

4050 **12** 7 **Drum Major (IRE)**[21] 4790 3-9-3 71 (b[1]) GeorgeBaker 1 42
(G L Moore) *dwlt: a in rr: outpcd 4f out: bhd after* **16/1**

0003 **13** nk **Harting Hill**[22] 4732 3-8-3 57 oh1 ow1 MartinDwyer 11 28
(M P Tregoning) *t.k.h early: prom: outpcd 4f out: wknd 3f out: eased* **16/1**

2m 11.16s (0.66) **Going Correction** +0.075s/f (Good) 13 Ran SP% **120.2**
Speed ratings (Par 100): **100,99,99,97,97 96,94,93,93,93 91,86,86**
toteswinger: 1&2 £6.90, 1&3 £4.40, 2&3 £14.70. CSF £22.47 CT £123.44 TOTE £3.10: £1.60, £3.50, £2.00; EX 27.20 Trifecta £179.80 Pool: £340.34, 1.40 winning units..
Owner Andrew Rosen **Bred** Waterford Hall Stud **Trained** Manton, Wilts

FOCUS

Another ordinary handicap, this time restricted to three-year-olds, and the early pace was moderate with the winning time 0.37 seconds slower than than the opening apprentice handicap. The most notable aspect of this contest was how very few ever got into it and the first three home were on the pace throughout. The form might not prove the most solid.

Eseej(USA) Official explanation: jockey said gelding ran too free
Harting Hill Official explanation: jockey said gelding lost its action

5429 TANDRIDGE LANE (S) STKS 1m 1f

3:20 (3:20) (Class 6) 3-Y-O+ £1,978 (£584; £292) Stalls Low

Form RPR

44 **1** **Old Romney**[12] 5087 4-9-6 58 (b[1]) RichardHughes 4 67+
(M Wigham) *prom: wnt 2nd 3f out: cruising after: shkn up to ld jst over 1f out and swtchd to rail: sn clr* **13/8**[1]

42 **2** 3 ¼ **The Gaikwar (IRE)**[23] 4707 9-9-3 50 (b) HaddenFrost[(3)] 8 60
(R A Harris) *trckd ldrs: rdn 3f out: wnt 3rd 2f out: r.o to take 2nd fnl 150yds and sn clr of rest: no ch w wnr* **8/1**

0000 **3** 3 ¾ **Appointment**[29] 4527 3-8-8 53 IanMongan 11 47
(Mrs L J Mongan) *chsd ldr to 3f out: sn outpcd: kpt on to take 3rd nr fin* **16/1**

0-00 **4** nk **Fareeha**[10] 5145 3-8-8 60 ShaneKelly 9 46
(B R Johnson) *led: kicked on 3f out: drvn and hdd jst over 1f out: hmpd sn after: sn lost 2nd: wknd and lost 3rd nr fin* **14/1**

3505 **5** ½ **Danish Monarch**[13] 5059 7-8-13 49 BillyCray[(7)] 13 50
(David Pinder) *prom: outpcd 3f out: urged along and kpt on one pce fnl 2f* **8/1**

4000 **6** 1 ¼ **Terminate (GER)**[20] 4813 6-9-12 58 StephenDonohoe 2 53
(Ian Williams) *hld up in rr: drvn over 2f out: nvr on terms: modest prog fr over 1f out* **11/2**[2]

0060 **7** 1 ¼ **Royal Choir**[9] 5166 4-9-1 44 EddieAhern 12 39
(C E Brittain) *wl in tch in midfield: outpcd 3f out: no prog after* **50/1**

-046 **8** ¾ **Artistic Light**[20] 4810 3-8-8 54 MartinDwyer 3 38
(W R Muir) *t.k.h early: hld up in midfield on inner: outpcd 3f out: nvr on terms after* **13/2**[3]

0060 **9** ¾ **Coup D'Etat**[20] 4808 6-9-3 50 (v[1]) KevinGhunowa[(3)] 10 41
(R A Harris) *plld hrd: hld up in rr: hrd rdn and no rspnse over 2f out* **20/1**

5600 **10** *nk* **Mtoto Girl**[10] 5148 4-8-12 42............................ MarcHalford(3) 5 36
(J J Bridger) *a towards rr: outpcd 3f out: struggling after* **66/1**
5530 **11** *1* **Scientific**[37] 4281 3-8-13 53..................(b) CatherineGannon 1 38
(G Prodromou) *s.s and drvn in last early: nvr a factor* **25/1**
0/00 **12** *5* **Pickled Again**[19] 4860 4-9-1 45.................................. PaulDoe 14 22
(S Dow) *tool t.k.h early: hld up in rr: outpcd 3f out: no ch after* **66/1**
5060 **13** *9* **Ledgerwood**[37] 4275 3-9-2 54.......................... EmmettStack(3) 6 14
(A J Chamberlain) *towards rr: effrt on wd outside 1/2-way: wd bnd over 3f out: wknd over 2f out: t.o* **33/1**

1m 57.45s (0.85) **Going Correction** +0.075s/f (Good)
WFA 3 from 4yo+ 7lb **13** Ran SP% **118.1**
Speed ratings (Par 101): **99,96,92,92,92 90,89,89,88,88 87,82,74**
toteswinger: 1&2 £3.30, 1&3 £11.20, 2&3 £32.40. CSF £13.69 TOTE £2.20: £1.20, £2.60, £7.10; EX 12.70 Trifecta £220.50 Part won. Pool: £297.99, 0.40 winning units..The winner was bought in for 10,400gns. Appointment was claimed by Sheena West for £6,000.
Owner James Crickmore **Bred** Gainsborough Stud Management Ltd **Trained** Newmarket, Suffolk
■ Stewards' Enquiry : Richard Hughes 14-day ban (takes into account previous offences; three days deferred): careless riding (Sep 12-22)

FOCUS
A weak seller and ultimately a one-horse race woth Old Romney not having to improve on his recent form. The first four were always prominent but the form looks sound enough.
Scientific Official explanation: jockey said gelding hung left

5430 DRYHILL MEDIAN AUCTION MAIDEN STKS (DIV I) 6f (P)
3:50 (3:51) (Class 6) 2-Y-O **£1,706** (£503; £252) **Stalls** Low

Form RPR
0 **1** **Fleeting Star (USA)**[89] 2627 2-8-12 0.......................... TPQueally 8 80+
(J Noseda) *trckd ldng pair: green briefly over 1f out: plenty to do after: wnt 2nd ent fnl f: rdn and r.o wl to ld nr fin: won w smething to spare* **9/4**[1]
6 **2** *1/2* **Master Lightfoot**[35] 4346 2-9-3 0............................ AdamKirby 3 80+
(W R Swinburn) *led at str pce: rdn 2f out: clr ins fnl f: hdd nr fin* **7/2**[2]
3 **3** *5* **Dannios**[21] 4778 2-9-3 0.................................... PatCosgrave 4 65
(L M Cumani) *chsd ldrs: rdn over 2f out: outpcd wl over 1f out: kpt on to take 3rd last strides* **8/1**[3]
43 **4** *nse* **Nizhoni Dancer**[10] 5158 2-8-12 0.......................... AlanMunro 1 60
(C F Wall) *chsd ldrs: rdn and outpcd 2f out: kpt on fnl f* **7/2**[2]
6 **5** *hd* **Tricky Trev (USA)**[26] 4616 2-9-3 0.............................. PaulDoe 2 64
(S Curran) *pressed ldr and clr of rest to 1/2-way: drvn over 2f out: wknd ent fnl f* **12/1**
4 **6** *1 3/4* **Edith's Boy (IRE)**[66] 3315 2-9-3 0......................... IanMongan 11 59+
(S Dow) *in tch at rr of main gp: outpcd 2f out: nudged along and kpt on steadily fnl f* **33/1**
20 **7** *1/2* **Louidor**[18] 4907 2-9-3 0.................................... GeorgeBaker 9 58
(J R Boyle) *in tch at rr of main gp: outpcd 2f out: shkn up and hanging over 1f out: plugged on* **12/1**
6 **8** *6* **Dance Club (IRE)**[93] 2479 2-8-12 0.................... J-PGuillambert 10 35+
(W Jarvis) *dwlt: rdn and outpcd in last trio: nvr a factor* **8/1**[3]
5 **9** *3/4* **Phoenix Enforcer**[21] 4763 2-8-12 0.......................... MartinDwyer 7 32+
(George Baker) *sn wl detached in last: nvr in it: kpt on fnl f* **50/1**
60 **10** *1* **Tasman Gold**[37] 4274 2-9-3 0..............................(t) WilliamBuick 6 34
(A M Balding) *sn outpcd and bhd in last trio: wd into st 2f out: no prog* **50/1**

1m 11.31s (-0.59) **Going Correction** -0.05s/f (Stan) 2y crse rec **10** Ran SP% **119.7**
Speed ratings (Par 92): **101,100,93,93,93 91,90,82,81,80**
toteswinger: 1&2 £3.40, 1&3 £5.70, 2&3 £6.90. CSF £10.30 TOTE £3.10: £1.40, £1.90, £1.70; EX 14.30 Trifecta £32.80 Pool: £448.32, 10.11 winning units..
Owner The Searchers **Bred** Jilsie's Gigalo Stables Inc Et Al **Trained** Newmarket, Suffolk

FOCUS
An ordinary maiden on paper, though they all had racecourse experience and a few had previously made the frame. They went a serious early pace in this with both Master Lightfoot and Tricky Trev soon well clear of the others and that resulted in a very smart winning time, 2.21 seconds faster than the second division. The first two both built on their debut form.

NOTEBOOK
Fleeting Star(USA), given a break since stopping very quickly on her York debut in May, did very well to pick up the leader as she still looked very green, so it's reasonable to expect that this $490,000 filly is capable of a good deal more. (op 5-2)
Master Lightfoot's rider did not go for the whip when it mattered and he was just pegged back. He had finished last of six on his Sandown debut, but this much-improved effort showed why he was well backed that day. In view of his speedy pedigree and the way he ran here, he may be worth dropping back to the minimum. (tchd 10-3 and 4-1)
Dannios, who was green when a well-beaten third on his Folkestone debut, plugged on to grab third but may need a bit more time and an extra furlong. (op 9-1)
Nizhoni Dancer followed up her two good efforts in Yarmouth maidens with another fair effort here and now qualifies for a mark. (op 5-2 tchd 9-4 and 4-1)
Tricky Trev(USA) kept on well enough considering how much he had done early and he looks to possess some ability. He needs one more run for a nursery mark. (op 22-1 tchd 25-1)
Louidor is yet to confirm the promise of his Windsor debut, though to be fair he didn't look at all happy on this track and was inclined to hang all the way up the home straight. (tchd 14-1)

5431 DRYHILL MEDIAN AUCTION MAIDEN STKS (DIV II) 6f (P)
4:20 (4:23) (Class 6) 2-Y-O **£1,706** (£503; £252) **Stalls** Low

Form RPR
026 **1** **Cat Patrol**[13] 5055 2-8-12 74.................................. EddieAhern 8 70+
(H J L Dunlop) *reluctant to go to post tl dismntd and led: reluctant to enter stalls: trckd ldr to 1/2-way: styd cl up: effrt to ld jst ins fnl f: won gng away* **8/11**[1]
35 **2** *1 3/4* **Chasing Amy**[10] 5158 2-8-12 0.............................. ShaneKelly 9 65
(M G Quinlan) *dwlt: sn prom: wnt 2nd 1/2-way: chal 2f out: upsides ent fnl f: sn lft bhd by wnr* **9/2**[2]
00 **3** *1/2* **Strike Command (USA)**[17] 4926 2-9-3 0..................... SteveDrowne 3 68
(R Charlton) *led: hrd pressed over 2f out: hdd jst ins fnl f: fdd* **10/1**
4 *1/2* **Piccolinda** 2-8-12 0.. MartinDwyer 4 62+
(W R Muir) *in tch: effrt over 2f out: chsd ldng trio over 1f out: shkn up and styd on* **33/1**
0 **5** *1 3/4* **Clerk's Choice (IRE)**[77] 2979 2-9-3 0................. J-PGuillambert 6 62+
(W Jarvis) *dwlt: in tch but racd wd thrght: lost grnd bnd 2f out: green but kpt on* **8/1**[3]
6 *1* **May Need A Spell** 2-9-0 0.............................. LukeMorris(3) 5 59
(J G M O'Shea) *dwlt: hld up in last pair: sme prog over 2f out: chsng ldrs over 1f out but nt on terms: one pce* **50/1**
7 *nk* **Indian Tonic (IRE)** 2-8-12 0.............................. AlanMunro 12 53+
(W Jarvis) *hld up in detached last: stl there 2f out: nudged along and styd on stylishly fnl f* **14/1**
0 **8** *3/4* **Baby Josr**[15] 4973 2-9-3 0.......................(t) CatherineGannon 7 55
(I A Wood) *sn rdn to stay in tch towards rr: struggling fr 1/2-way: plugged on* **25/1**
9 *hd* **Fortunate Bid (IRE)** 2-9-3 0.............................. WilliamBuick 1 55
(B W Hills) *dwlt: hld up in last trio: rdn over 2f out: kpt on fnl f: nvr a factor* **11/1**
10 *1 1/2* **Kutanga (USA)** 2-8-12 0.................................... OscarUrbina 11 45
(R M H Cowell) *chsd ldrs: rdn over 2f out: wknd over 1f out* **20/1**
0 **11** *2 1/4* **Igotim**[18] 4907 2-9-3 0.. JimCrowley 2 44
(J Gallagher) *in tch in midfield: rdn over 2f out: wknd over 1f out* **66/1**

1m 13.52s (1.62) **Going Correction** -0.05s/f (Stan) **11** Ran SP% **126.3**
Speed ratings (Par 92): **87,84,84,83,81 79,79,78,78,76 73**
toteswinger: 1&2 £2.10, 1&3 £4.20, 2&3 £5.10. CSF £4.37 TOTE £1.90: £1.30, £1.70, £2.80; EX 4.40 Trifecta £16.00 Pool: £377.23, 17.42 winning units..
Owner Normandie Stud Ltd **Bred** Normandie Stud Ltd **Trained** Lambourn, Berks

FOCUS
Something of a contrast to the first division as only around half the field had seen the racecourse before. The early pace was nothing like as strong as the other division either, and the winning time was 2.21 seconds slower. A weakish race in which the winner probably beat little.

NOTEBOOK
Cat Patrol, who had already shown that she handled this surface when runner-up in a 5f maiden here this month, was totally out of her depth in Listed company last time, but found this rather easier. She did give plenty of trouble before the start here so obviously has a mind of her own, but she travelled well during in the race and picked up very well when asked. Already rated 74, her future is probably in nurseries. (op 10-11 tchd Evens)
Chasing Amy was always up with the pace and had every chance, but found the hot favourite much too strong late on. She now qualifies for a mark. (op 4-1)
Strike Command(USA) had only shown a small amount of ability on turf, but his US breeding suggested he might appreciate the switch to sand and he put in a much-improved effort. He also now qualifies for a mark and may be best kept to this surface. (op 14-1)
Piccolinda put in some decent late work up the inside rail and fared much the best of the newcomers. Although by a sprinter, her dam was a multiple winner at up to 1m7f, so it would be no surprise to see her improve over further. (op 33-1)
Clerk's Choice(IRE), gelded since beating only one home on his Yarmouth debut, can be given a bit of extra credit as he was very wide into the home straight and looks capable of better. (op 20-1)
May Need A Spell wasn't disgraced on this racecourse debut. Out of a winning sister to the smart Obe Gold, he should improve for the experience.

5432 JACKSBRIDGE NURSERY 7f (P)
4:50 (4:53) (Class 5) (0-75,73) 2-Y-O **£2,590** (£770; £385; £192) **Stalls** Low

Form RPR
2335 **1** **Woolston Ferry (IRE)**[55] 3669 2-9-7 73.................. EdwardCreighton 4 76
(M R Channon) *chsd ldrs: shkn up over 2f out: prog over 1f out: got through to ld jst ins fnl f: battled on wl* **7/1**[2]
0513 **2** *hd* **Striding Edge (IRE)**[47] 3967 2-8-12 64...................... MartinDwyer 9 67
(W R Muir) *t.k.h: hld up on outer in midfield: rdn and prog 2f out: clsd to chal 1f out: w wnr 100yds out: outbattled* **8/1**[3]
4030 **3** *2* **Temperence Hall (USA)**[17] 4933 2-9-5 71.................. SteveDrowne 14 69
(J R Best) *pressed ldr: rdn 4f out: led jst over 2f out: hdd jst ins fnl f: one pce* **20/1**
505 **4** *3/4* **Hum Cat (IRE)**[34] 4367 2-8-12 67......................... LukeMorris(3) 13 63
(J S Moore) *dwlt: racd wd towards rr: rdn 3f out: gd prog wl over 1f out: effrt flattened out fnl f* **25/1**
044 **5** *1 3/4* **Tae Kwon Do (USA)**[26] 4636 2-9-2 68......................... EddieAhern 7 59
(E A L Dunlop) *hld up wl in rr: gng wl 3f out: shuffled along and kpt on steadily fr over 1f out: nvr nr ldrs* **8/1**[3]
066 **6** *1/2* **Welcome Applause (IRE)**[21] 4792 2-8-12 67......... JerryO'Dwyer(3) 11 57
(M G Quinlan) *hld up in last pair: stl there 2f out: pushed along and styd on wl fr over 1f out: nrst fin* **16/1**
256 **7** *3/4* **Straitjacket**[64] 3378 2-9-3 69..................................(b[1]) RichardHughes 2 57
(R Hannon) *hld up in midfield: nt clr run briefly over 2f out: prog over 1f out: sn rdn and nt qckn* **5/2**[1]
0304 **8** *1/2* **Mymateeric**[5] 5277 2-8-13 65.............................. RobertHavlin 5 52
(J Pearce) *nvr beyond midfield: struggling u.p 2f out* **7/1**[2]
011 **9** *1/2* **Rocket Rob (IRE)**[17] 4933 2-8-12 64............................ TPO'Shea 10 50
(S A Callaghan) *t.k.h: hld up in rr on inner: plenty to do 2f out: appeared to be hanging and no prog* **5/2**[1]
300 **10** *1* **Damassin**[18] 4905 2-8-13 65.............................. StephenCarson 8 48
(Eve Johnson Houghton) *prom: 3rd and rdn 2f out: wknd over 1f out* **33/1**
5200 **11** *1* **Going Time (USA)**[14] 5006 2-8-13 65........................ GregFairley 12 46
(M Johnston) *led at decent pce: hdd jst over 2f out: wknd rapidly fnl f* **20/1**
006 **12** *9* **Heartsease**[24] 4692 2-8-13 65................................ PatCosgrave 3 23
(J G Portman) *sn prom: wknd on inner over 2f out: t.o* **20/1**

1m 25.3s (0.50) **Going Correction** -0.05s/f (Stan) **12** Ran SP% **131.3**
Speed ratings (Par 94): **95,94,92,91,89 89,88,87,87,85 84,74**
toteswinger: 1&2 £12.50, 1&3 £19.30, 2&3 £23.40. CSF £63.62 CT £1131.09 TOTE £8.90: £2.50, £2.40, £5.10; EX 82.30 Trifecta £227.90 Part won. Pool: £308.03, 0.40 winning units..
Owner Capital **Bred** Tim Taylor **Trained** West Ilsley, Berks

FOCUS
Quite a competitive nursery and a couple were well backed. The form is sound.

NOTEBOOK
Woolston Ferry(IRE), making his sand and nursery debuts, hadn't built on a narrow defeat on his Goodwood debut, but he had been gelded since his last run and the operation has apparently done the trick. He can't be put up too much for this and he looks worth persevering with on this surface. (op 15-2 tchd 6-1)
Striding Edge(IRE), who handled Polytrack well when beating a subsequent winner in a Great Leighs maiden two starts ago, was up in trip for this nursery debut. It wasn't the extra furlong that beat him here, but a more determined rival.
Temperence Hall(USA), who had shown promise in maidens before a poor effort on his nursery debut last time, performed much better here and deserves credit for keeping on for third considering he had to do a lot of early running in order to get across and gain a handy position from the outside stall. (op 14-1 tchd 12-1)
Hum Cat(IRE), up in trip and on sand for the first time for this nursery debut, stayed on up the home straight and was another to run well from a wide draw.
Tae Kwon Do(USA), another making his nursery debut whose best effort so far had come in a course-and-distance maiden two starts back, was noted staying on well up the home straight without being given a hard time. He looks capable of better. (op 9-1)
Welcome Applause(IRE) was another noted making good late headway from the back of the field. Another making her sand and nursery debuts, she is also one to keep an eye on. (op 12-1)
Straitjacket was the subject of quite a punt beforehand in the first-time blinkers, but although close enough coming to the last furlong she could make no impression from there and has been very disappointing since her promising Goodwood debut. (op 13-2)

Rocket Rob(IRE), up 2lb and on a hat-trick after wins in a Yarmouth seller and Wolverhampton nursery, was well backed earlier in the day but he did not really look happy at any stage and never got involved. (op 7-2)

5433 FORD MANOR ROAD H'CAP — 6f (P)
5:20 (5:20) (Class 4) (0-80,80) 3-Y-0+ — **£4,727** (£1,406; £702; £351) — **Stalls** Low

Form				RPR
5222	**1**		**Vintage (IRE)**[16] 4944 4-9-3 **72** ... IanMongan 6 (J Akehurst) *pressed ldr: led jst over 2f out: hanging jst over 1f out but clr: kpt on wl* **11/4**[1]	85
0610	**2**	1 1/2	**Lucayos**[6] 5222 5-9-10 **79** ... DarrenWilliams 4 (K R Burke) *chsd ldrs: pushed along fr 1/2-way: rdn to chse wnr jst over 1f out: kpt on but nvr able to chal* **9/2**[2]	87
5055	**3**	1 1/2	**Buy On The Red**[16] 4944 7-9-6 **75** ...(p) MartinDwyer 5 (W R Muir) *stmbld s: in tch in midfield: wnt 4th over 2f out: styd on to take 3rd ins fnl f: nvr able to chal* **12/1**	78
2150	**4**	1	**Mandarin Spirit (IRE)**[20] 4809 8-8-13 **68** ... OscarUrbina 7 (G C H Chung) *hld up in rr: sme prog 2f out: kpt on same pce fnl f: nvr on terms* **14/1**	68
4160	**5**	nse	**Resplendent Alpha**[13] 5067 4-9-4 **73** ... ShaneKelly 1 (P Howling) *hld up in rr: 9th 2f out: taken to outer and shuffled along: styd on wl: nvr nr ldrs* **12/1**	73
4000	**6**	1 1/4	**Sand Cat**[15] 4981 5-9-3 **72** ...(b) GeorgeBaker 3 (G L Moore) *nvr bttr than midfield: outpcd fr 2f out: no real imp after* **5/1**[3]	68
00	**6**	dht	**Garstang**[22] 4743 5-8-10 **65** ... PatrickMathers 8 (Peter Grayson) *t.k.h early: hld up in last: stl there 2f out: urged along over 1f out: r.o last 150yds: nrst fin* **20/1**	61
4310	**8**	hd	**Chjimes (IRE)**[16] 4944 4-9-5 **74** ... TPQueally 2 (C R Dore) *chsd ldrs: lost pl over 2f out: no prog and btn over 1f out* **13/2**	69
0-45	**9**	3/4	**Legal Eagle (IRE)**[85] 2732 3-9-8 **80** ... RobertHavlin 10 (J H M Gosden) *led to jst over 2f out: wknd rapidly fnl f* **6/1**	73
0/0-	**10**	6	**Beau Jazz**[389] 4204 7-8-5 **60** oh15 ... PaulDoe 9 (W De Best-Turner) *chsd ldrs and racd wd: wknd rapidly 2f out* **100/1**	33

1m 11.05s (-0.85) **Going Correction** -0.05s/f (Stan)
WFA 3 from 4yo+ 3lb — **10** Ran SP% **116.9**
Speed ratings (Par 105): **103,101,99,97,97 95,95,95,94,86**
toteswinger: 1&2 £4.80, 1&3 £3.50, 2&3 £10.40. CSF £14.89 CT £127.55 TOTE £3.00: £1.50, £2.30, £2.80; EX 18.70 Trifecta £231.10 Part won. Pool: £312.40, 0.80 winning units. Place 6: £25.83, Place 5: £17.78..
Owner Sheldon Homes Ltd **Bred** Mountarmstrong Stud **Trained** Epsom, Surrey

FOCUS
A tight little Polytrack sprint and they went a reasonable pace. Progressive form from the winner.
T/Jkpt: £2,840.00 to a £1 stake. Pool: £10,000.00. 2.50 winning tickets. T/Plt: £26.20 to a £1 stake. Pool: £61,948.10. 1,721.68 winning tickets. T/Qpdt: £11.20 to a £1 stake. Pool: £3,207.30. 210.40 winning tickets. JN

5434 - 5437a (Foreign Racing) - See Raceform Interactive

4802 TIPPERARY (L-H)
Thursday, August 28

OFFICIAL GOING: Round course - soft; sprint course - first half heavy second half soft

5438a DANEHILL DANCER TIPPERARY STKS (LISTED RACE) — 5f
4:55 (4:57) 2-Y-0 — **£28,720** (£8,426; £4,014; £1,367)

			RPR
1		**Senor Mirasol**[32] 4472 2-9-1 ... NCallan 7 (K A Ryan) *mde all: rdn to assert over 1f out: kpt on strly fnl f: comf* **4/5**[1]	106+
2	2 1/2	**Nubar Lady (IRE)**[32] 4463 2-8-12 97 ...(t) WMLordan 3 (T Stack, Ire) *chsd ldrs: 2nd 1/2-way: rdn and no imp on ldr over 1f out: kpt on same pce* **5/1**[3]	93
3	3/4	**Roof Fiddle (USA)**[15] 4965 2-8-12 ... DPMcDonogh 4 (Kevin Prendergast, Ire) *trckd ldrs: 5th 1/2-way: 4th 2f out: rdn and no ex 1 1/2f out: kpt on same pce fr over 1f out* **7/1**	90
4	3/4	**Arfajah (IRE)**[70] 3185 2-8-12 87 ... CDHayes 8 (Kevin Prendergast, Ire) *towards rr: rdn into 5th 1 1/2f out: kpt on same pce fr over 1f out* **14/1**	88
5	3/4	**Call Me Alice (USA)**[32] 4463 2-8-12 97 ...(t) JMurtagh 5 (David Wachman, Ire) *chsd ldrs on inner: rdn in 3rd 1 1/2f out: no ex over 1f out: kpt on one pce* **4/1**[2]	85
6	11	**Sleepy Dreams (IRE)**[15] 4993 2-8-12 75 ... FMBerry 6 (David Marnane, Ire) *chsd ldr early: rdn in 4th 1/2-way: sn no ex and wknd* **25/1**	45
7	nk	**Aoibhinn**[23] 4711 2-8-12 ... DMGrant 2 (Patrick J Flynn, Ire) *a towards rr* **100/1**	44
8	1 1/4	**Douze Points (IRE)**[15] 4993 2-9-1 85 ... PJSmullen 1 (Joseph G Murphy, Ire) *chsd ldrs early: rdn in 6th and no ex 1/2-way: sn wknd* **8/1**	43

60.89 secs (1.89) — **8** Ran SP% **127.3**
CSF £6.44 TOTE £1.50: £1.10, £2.20, £2.30; DF 6.40.
Owner Mrs Margaret Forsyth **Bred** P C Hunt **Trained** Hambleton, N Yorks

FOCUS
There could be better to come from the winner.

NOTEBOOK
Senor Mirasol had finished third in the Super Sprint on his penultimate outing, a race which has worked out nicely so far, and in Group 1 company in France last time out. He showed himself to be an improving colt with a clear-cut win from the front on ground that held no fears. There is no reason why he will not get another furlong and the Group 1 Middle Park could figure in his plans. (op 5/4 tchd 11/8)
Nubar Lady(IRE), whose two wins over the trip included one over this course and distance, had shown her ability to cope with testing ground and she acquitted herself well without making any impression on the winner. She helps to rate this form. (op 11/2)
Douze Points(IRE) Official explanation: trainer's rep said colt swallowed its tongue in running

5439 - 5444a (Foreign Racing) - See Raceform Interactive

5198 CHESTER (L-H)
Friday, August 29

OFFICIAL GOING: Good to firm (good in places)
Wind: Almost nil Weather: Warm and overcast

5445 RACECOURSE APARTMENTS BY DAVID MCLEAN HOMES MAIDEN FILLIES' STKS — 1m 2f 75y
2:20 (2:23) (Class 5) 3-Y-0+ — **£3,561** (£1,059; £529; £264) — **Stalls** High

Form				RPR
-323	**1**	nse	**Time Control**[20] 4871 3-8-12 81 ... JamieSpencer 4 (L M Cumani) *trckd ldrs: moved upsides to chal under 3f out: tk narrow ld briefly 2f out: carried hd awkwardly whn stl upsides and carried rt fr over 1f out: nt look keen: jst btn: fin 2nd, nse: awrdd r* **2/9**[1]	69
-564	**2**		**Hamalka (IRE)**[19] 4909 3-8-12 68 ... MichaelHills 5 (B W Hills) *mde virtually all: rdn and edgd rt whn pressed fr over 1f out: all out: fin 1st: disq & plcd 2nd* **15/2**[2]	69
40	**3**	2 1/4	**Chatanoogachoochoo**[42] 4161 3-8-12 0 ... RobertWinston 3 (G A Swinbank) *racd keenly: in tch: effrt to chal on outside 3f out: sltly outpcd by front pair 2f out: rallied ent fnl f: no ex towards fin* **22/1**	64
04-	**4**	19	**Tamdiid (USA)**[338] 5727 3-8-12 0 ... MickyFenton 6 (C E Brittain) *sn chsd wnr: pushed along 4f out: wknd over 2f out* **11/1**[3]	26
	5	4 1/2	**Fleetwood Flame** 3-8-12 0 ... TPO'Shea 1 (W M Brisbourne) *missed break: bhd: pushed along over 7f out: wl outpcd and lost tch over 4f out* **40/1**	17
0-6	**6**	6	**Ghizlaan (USA)**[60] 3556 3-8-12 0 ... DarryllHolland 2 (M Johnston) *missed break: rn green and bhd: wl outpcd and lost tch over 4f out* **20/1**	5

2m 11.24s (-0.96) **Going Correction** -0.10s/f (Good) — **6** Ran SP% **113.5**
Speed ratings (Par 100): **98,99,97,81,78 73**
toteswinger: 1&2 £1.50, 1&3 £2.80, 2&3 £4.50. CSF £2.48 TOTE £1.20: £1.10, £2.50; EX 2.40.
Owner Merry Fox Stud Limited **Bred** W & R Barnett Ltd And Globe Bloodstock **Trained** Newmarket, Suffolk

■ Stewards' Enquiry : Michael Hills two-day ban: careless riding (Sep 12,14)

FOCUS
After a dry night and a humid morning the ground was officially changed to good to firm, good in places. There was as usual an excellent cover of grass and the riders reported it was just on the quick side of good. This was a weak maiden fillies' race, best rated through Hamalka with Time Control lucky to get the race.

5446 TRITON HOLIDAYS H'CAP — 7f 2y
2:55 (2:55) (Class 3) (0-95,95) 3-Y-0 **£8,831** (£2,643; £1,321; £660; £329) — **Stalls** Low

Form				RPR
0201	**1**		**Keep Discovering (IRE)**[15] 5030 3-9-5 **93** ... DarryllHolland 3 (M Johnston) *trckd ldrs: 2nd over 3f out: hung lft whn str chal over 1f out: led narrowly post u.str ride* **4/1**[1]	101+
0210	**2**	shd	**Heywood**[80] 2905 4-9-4 **87** ...(p) SilvestreDeSousa 14 (D Nicholls) *racd keenly w ldr: led over 5f out: rdn whn strly pressed fr over 1f out: hdd narrowly post* **28/1**	97
1600	**3**	2 1/2	**Kings Point (IRE)**[8] 5207 7-9-4 **87** ... AdrianTNicholls 13 (D Nicholls) *led: hdd over 5f out: remained prom: rdn over 1f out: nt qckn ins fnl f* **14/1**	90
0241	**4**	1 1/4	**The Kiddykid (IRE)**[26] 4661 8-9-2 **85** ... StephenDonohoe 2 (P D Evans) *in tch: pushed along 3f out: styd on same pce fr over 1f out* **6/1**[2]	85
4520	**5**	1/2	**South Cape**[20] 4869 5-9-5 **88** ... TPO'Shea 8 (M R Channon) *in tch: pushed along 3f out: rdn to chse ldrs 2f out: one pce ins fnl 100yds* **8/1**[3]	87
2003	**6**	3/4	**King's Bastion (IRE)**[13] 5096 4-9-3 **86** ... JamieSpencer 6 (M L W Bell) *hld up: rdn and swtchd rt over 1f out: prog on outside ent fnl f: nt rch ldrs: eased fnl 75yds* **8/1**[3]	83+
6001	**7**	1	**Sir Xaar (IRE)**[34] 4417 5-9-6 **89** ...(v) TomEaves 1 (B Smart) *midfield: pushed along 3f out: rdn 1f out: nvr able to chal* **10/1**	83
0060	**8**	4 1/2	**Daaweitza**[26] 4661 5-9-2 **85** ... RobertWinston 10 (B Ellison) *dwlt: towards rr: nvr really gng wl* **25/1**	67
2514	**9**	nk	**Kafuu (IRE)**[38] 4269 4-9-5 **88** ...(p) SebSanders 7 (S A Callaghan) *midfield: effrt 3f out: no imp on ldrs: hung lft over 1f out: sn wknd* **8/1**[3]	69
4663	**10**	4 1/2	**Fathsta (IRE)**[5] 5313 3-9-2 **90** ... ChrisCatlin 4 (S Kirk) *missed break: a bhd* **4/1**[1]	57
0600	**11**	30	**Dabbers Ridge (IRE)**[49] 3921 6-9-12 **95** ... MichaelHills 5 (B W Hills) *a bhd: struggling 4f out: eased fnl 2f* **14/1**	—

1m 24.4s (-2.10) **Going Correction** -0.10s/f (Good)
WFA 3 from 4yo+ 5lb — **11** Ran SP% **117.3**
Speed ratings (Par 107): **108,107,105,103,103 102,101,95,95,90 56**
toteswinger: 1&2 £21.70, 1&3 £13.20, 2&3 £38.50. CSF £124.91 CT £1458.49 TOTE £5.10: £2.10, £7.50, £4.60; EX 148.70.
Owner Sheikh Hamdan Bin Mohammed Al Maktoum **Bred** Kilfrush Stud **Trained** Middleham Moor, N Yorks

FOCUS
Fast and furious stuff and the first three were one-two-three throughout. The winner continues to progress but the form may not work out.

NOTEBOOK
Keep Discovering(IRE), raised 4lb for his defeat of a subsequent winner at Sandown, has since been re-assessed another 2lb higher. He kept tabs on the leader but looked somewhat unhappy on the tight track going into the final turn. He never flinched and put his head in front right on the line. (op 5-1)
Heywood, tried in cheekpieces but worst drawn, was racing from a mark 5lb higher than when successful at Catterick in June. Absent for 11 weeks, he was soon taking them along and in the end did not really deserve to lose. (op 25-1)
Kings Point(IRE), drawn one from the outside, jumped off first and deserves credit for the way he stuck to his guns in the home straight. (op 22-1)
The Kiddykid(IRE), 3lb higher than his all-the-way win over this course and distance a month earlier, was drawn one off the inside but on this occasion could not dominate. (op 15-2)
South Cape likes it round here but he is creeping up the ratings and never threatened to land a blow. (op 9-1)
King's Bastion(IRE), very weak beforehand, made his effort on the wide outside once in line for home. He was not persevered with in the closing stages and is better than the bare result indicates. Official explanation: jockey said gelding jumped left at start (op 11-2)
Fathsta(IRE), a winner and runner-up on his two previous outings here, missed the break slightly and was always struggling. He has already had quite a taxing season. (tchd 7-2)

Dabbers Ridge(IRE), who has gone very well here in the past, never went a yard on this occasion and was tailed off in the final quarter-mile.

5447 SURRENDA-LINK NURSERY 7f 2y
3:30 (3:31) (Class 3) 2-Y-O £8,418 (£2,505; £1,251; £625) Stalls Low

Form RPR

4212 **1** **Night Of Fortune**[32] 4475 2-9-1 **80** SebSanders 6 85
(Sir Mark Prescott) *racd keenly: mde all: rdn over 1f out: kpt on gamely ins fnl f* **7/2**[2]

0132 **2** ½ **River Dee (IRE)**[16] 4975 2-8-5 **70** AdrianTNicholls 2 76+
(Miss Amy Weaver) *midfield: hdwy over 3f out: pushed along whn nt clr run 2f out: wnt 2nd over 1f out: clsd on wnr ins fnl 100yds: nvr gng to get there* **4/1**[3]

012 **3** 2½ **Quatermain**[23] 4733 2-9-3 **82** TomEaves 1 80
(B Smart) *trckd ldrs: rdn and nt qckn over 1f out: styd on same pce ins fnl f* **3/1**[1]

3300 **4** *hd* **Custard Cream Kid (IRE)**[23] 4733 2-8-1 **66** SilvestreDeSousa 5 63
(R A Fahey) *prom: rdn 2f out: one pce fnl 75yds* **22/1**

31 **5** 6 **Beautiful Breeze (IRE)**[16] 4960 2-9-2 **81** DarryllHolland 11 63
(M Johnston) *in tch: sn in niggled along: outpcd 3f out: no imp after* **9/1**

3210 **6** 1½ **Wilbury Star (IRE)**[21] 4828 2-9-4 **83** JamieSpencer 3 61+
(R Hannon) *racd keenly: n.m.r after 1f and dropped to midfield: effrt on outside over 2f out: no imp on ldrs* **8/1**

014 **7** 1 **Red Humour (IRE)**[23] 4729 2-9-1 **80** MichaelHills 8 56
(B W Hills) *prom: rdn over 1f out: sn wknd* **12/1**

5452 **8** *nk* **Yokozuna**[45] 4063 2-7-13 **69** ow3 (b) KellyHarrison(5) 12 44
(Mrs R A Carr) *s.i.s: hld up: no imp whn n.m.r on ins over 1f out: nvr on terms* **40/1**

5364 **9** 2½ **Tapis Wizard**[23] 4733 2-8-9 **74** RobertWinston 10 43
(M W Easterby) *missed break: hld up: hdwy over 2f out: no imp on ldrs: edgd lft whn wkng over 1f out* **16/1**

4531 **10** 3½ **Polish Pride**[21] 4816 2-9-7 **86** ChrisCatlin 9 46
(M Brittain) *a bhd* **14/1**

031 **11** *nk* **Captain Imperial (IRE)**[18] 4921 2-8-11 **76** MickyFenton 7 35+
(T P Tate) *nt much after 1f: sn lost pl and towards rr: racd wd wl over 2f out: nvr on terms w ldrs: wl btn over 1f out* **14/1**

1m 26.03s (-0.47) **Going Correction** -0.10s/f (Good) **11** Ran SP% **122.0**
Speed ratings (Par 98): **98,97,94,94,87 85,84,84,81,77 77**
toteswinger: 1&2 £5.10, 1&3 £3.70, 2&3 £4.30. CSF £18.76 CT £48.13 TOTE £4.90: £1.60, £2.30, £1.80; EX 23.00.
Owner P J McSwiney - Osborne House **Bred** Gainsborough Stud Management Ltd **Trained** Newmarket, Suffolk

FOCUS
This was a decent nursery and the first four finished clear. Again it paid to race up with what was a strong pace.

NOTEBOOK
Night Of Fortune, 10lb higher than his Kempton success, had a subsequent winner some way adrift when narrowly denied at Southwell next time. Keen early, he soon showed ahead and stuck on in most willing fashion. He was always holding the challenge of the runner-up and a grand, big type, he will be suited by a more galloping track and should continue to give a good account of himself, with the mile nursery at Doncaster's St Leger meeting on the agenda. (op 4-1 tchd 9-2 in places)
River Dee(IRE), placed on his first two starts in nursery company, had a 3lb higher mark to contend with. He travelled nicely and went in pursuit of the winner once in line for home. He always looked like being held but deserves to add to his selling-race success for his young trainer. (op 9-2 tchd 13-2)
Quatermain, runner-up in a nursery at Newcastle which has worked out well, was heavily backed to add to his Redcar maiden-race victory. He had the best of the draw but always looked held in the home straight. (op 9-2)
Custard Cream Kid(IRE), over seven lengths behind Quatermain at Redcar, had a 16lb pull and finished a creditable fourth. (op 25-1 tchd 20-1)
Beautiful Breeze(IRE), drawn one from the outside, had to be driven along to hold a handy position. He still looks inexperienced and his Beverley maiden-race success came on soft ground. Official explanation: jockey said colt never travelled (op 15-2)
Wilbury Star(IRE) was fighting a losing battle when he was tightened up on the first turn. Official explanation: jockey said bit slipped through colt's mouth
Tapis Wizard Official explanation: jockey said colt was unsuited by the good to firm (good in places) ground

5448 EUROPEAN BREEDERS' FUND COMBERMERE FILLIES' CONDITIONS STKS 6f 18y
4:05 (4:07) (Class 2) 2-Y-O £12,616 (£3,776; £1,888; £944) Stalls Low

Form RPR

3305 **1** **Aspen Darlin (IRE)**[14] 5055 2-9-1 91 (p) MickyFenton 2 94
(A Bailey) *s.i.s: trckd ldrs: rdn to take 2nd 1f out: r.o to ld post* **7/1**[3]

133 **2** *nse* **Excellerator (IRE)**[34] 4403 2-8-12 98 JamieSpencer 1 91
(George Baker) *led: shkn up over 1f out: rdn ins fnl f: ct post* **2/5**[1]

402 **3** 3¾ **Aahaygirl (IRE)**[26] 4659 2-8-12 84 FergusSweeney 5 80
(K R Burke) *chsd ldr: chal 2f out: rdn over 1f out: sn lost 2nd: no ex ins fnl f* **10/1**

221 **4** ½ **Acquiesced (IRE)**[25] 4692 2-9-1 81 SebSanders 4 81
(R Hannon) *trckd ldrs: rdn and wanted to lug lft whn nt qckn over 1f out: nvr able to chal* **5/1**[2]

1m 14.59s (0.79) **Going Correction** -0.10s/f (Good) **4** Ran SP% **109.7**
Speed ratings (Par 97): **90,89,84,84**
CSF £10.87 TOTE £9.30; EX 12.10.
Owner Indian Haven Syndicate **Bred** Miss Annmarie Burke **Trained** Newmarket, Suffolk
■

FOCUS
A decent fillies' event though the time was modest for the grade. The winner and third set the level and the runner-up was 6lb off her Ascot figure.

NOTEBOOK
Aspen Darlin(IRE), rated 13lb behind the favourite, made her effort on the inside coming off the final turn and, very persistent, put her head in front right on the line. This was her seventh start and she is very tough and a credit to her trainer. She now heads for the Group 3 Firth Of Clyde Stakes at Ayr's Western meeting. (tchd 13-2)
Excellerator(IRE), a good third in a Group 3 at Ascot, was sent off a warm order and everything looked to be going to plan when Jamie Spencer pushed her almost a length clear a furlong out, but the winner had other ideas. On the face of things she had no excuse but she is all speed and 5f looks her trip. (op 4-6 tchd 8-11)
Aahaygirl(IRE), already twice behind Aspen Girl, was very weak in the market and after looking the main threat was quickly put in her place. (op 6-1)
Acquiesced(IRE), narrow winner of an ordinary maiden at Windsor, had a lot more on her plate. She travelled well but didn't pick up in the home straight. Far from disgraced, her nursery mark might well shoot up as a result. (op 7-2 tchd 3-1)

5449 AXON RESOURCING H'CAP 1m 2f 75y
4:40 (4:41) (Class 3) (0-90,88) 3-Y-O £8,831 (£2,643; £1,321; £660; £329) Stalls High

Form RPR

4114 **1** **Prince Kalamoun (IRE)**[42] 4160 3-9-7 **88** RobertWinston 4 99+
(G A Swinbank) *hld up: hdwy over 2f out: led on outside over 1f out: r.o wl and in command ins fnl f* **4/1**[3]

4022 **2** 3¼ **Nightjar (USA)**[6] 5290 3-8-13 **80** DarryllHolland 5 84
(M Johnston) *dwlt: prom after 2f: rdn to chal 2f out: no answer to wnr ins fnl f* **9/4**[1]

3-30 **3** ½ **Dauberval (IRE)**[29] 4552 3-9-5 **86** SebSanders 8 89
(S Kirk) *hld up: pushed along 2f out: n.m.r briefly over 1f out: rdn and r.o ins fnl f: nt quite pce to chal ldrs* **11/1**

-100 **4** 1¼ **Porthole (USA)**[29] 4552 3-9-5 **86** MichaelHills 2 87
(B W Hills) *led: rdn and hung rt over 1f out: sn hdd: wknd ins fnl f* **3/1**[2]

5103 **5** ¾ **Never Ending Tale**[31] 4500 3-9-2 **83** JamieSpencer 3 82
(W Jarvis) *trckd ldrs: bmpd 2f out: nt clr run and swtchd rt over 1f out: sn no rspnse* **4/1**[3]

-410 **6** 1 **Sweet Sara**[42] 4170 3-8-7 **74** SaleemGolam 9 71
(C E Brittain) *broke wl: hld up: pushed along over 4f out: hmpd over 1f out: nvr able to chal* **20/1**

4262 **7** 2½ **Grey Command (USA)**[23] 4737 3-8-3 **70** ChrisCatlin 6 62
(M Brittain) *prom: pushed along over 5f out: lost pl over 2f out: wknd over 1f out* **10/1**

2m 10.06s (-2.14) **Going Correction** -0.10s/f (Good) **7** Ran SP% **118.0**
Speed ratings (Par 104): **104,101,101,100,99 98,96**
toteswinger: 1&2 £2.60, 1&3 £7.00, 2&3 £5.30. CSF £14.13 CT £92.21 TOTE £5.30: £2.60, £2.10; EX 11.70.
Owner Jonathan Dixon **Bred** Michael Pitt **Trained** Melsonby, N Yorks
■ Stewards' Enquiry : Robert Winston one-day ban: careless riding (Sep 12)
Jamie Spencer one-day ban: careless riding (Sep 12)

FOCUS
A sound gallop to this decent three-year-old handicap. Prince Kalamoun remains progressive but there are slight doubts over how solid this form is.

NOTEBOOK
Prince Kalamoun(IRE) made it three wins from his last four starts, quickening up in good style to hit the front coming to the final furlong and in the end running out a decisive winner. He has made great strides and is a credit to his trainer, but is unlikely to make the cut in the Cambridgeshire and connections are looking at the John Smith's Handicap at Newbury on September 20. (op 9-2)
Nightjar(USA), due to run from a 4lb higher higher mark in future after his good effort when runner-up at Windsor, was stepping up two furlongs in trip. He missed a beat at the start but was soon hunting up the leader, but in the end did not see it out anywhere near as well as the winner. (tchd 11-4)
Dauberval(IRE), Listed placed at two, has been dropped 4lb. He stayed on from off the pace and, though fully exposed, is worth a try over 1m4f. (op 10-1 tchd 9-1)
Porthole(USA) was keen to lead and wound up the gallop in the final half-mile, but in the end he was simply not good enough. (op 4-1 tchd 9-2 in places)
Never Ending Tale, back up in trip, travelled sweetly on the inner. Jamie Spencer had all sorts of traffic problems turning in but when he switched his mount to the outside the gelding carried his head very high and looked somewhat reluctant.

5450 BOLLINGER CHAMPAGNE CHALLENGE SERIES H'CAP (FOR GENTLEMAN AMATEUR RIDERS) 1m 4f 66y
5:10 (5:11) (Class 5) (0-75,75) 3-Y-O+ £3,435 (£1,065; £532; £266) Stalls Low

Form RPR

5231 **1** **Sand Repeal (IRE)**[25] 4691 6-10-5 **63** MrRBirkett(5) 11 68
(Miss J Feilden) *trckd ldrs: led over 2f out: sn edgd lft: hdd narrowly 1f out: regained advantage 75yds out: kpt on wl* **15/2**

0615 **2** *hd* **Desert Hawk**[15] 5020 7-9-11 **55** oh3 (b) MrHarryChalloner(5) 4 60
(W M Brisbourne) *midfield after 2f: hdwy 3f out: led narrowly 1f out: hdd 75yds out: kpt on* **14/1**

1020 **3** 5 **York Cliff**[14] 5040 10-9-9 **55** oh5 MrLWard(7) 1 52
(W M Brisbourne) *towards rr: hdwy on outside 3f out: wnt 3rd 1f out: nt trble front pair* **25/1**

0346 **4** ¾ **Thorny Mandate**[28] 4592 6-10-2 **55** MrSDobson 3 51
(W M Brisbourne) *stdd s: hld up: hdwy whn nt clr run wl over 1f out: styd on ins fnl f: nt pce to chal ldrs* **5/1**[2]

3635 **5** ¾ **Elk Trail (IRE)**[30] 4532 3-10-9 **75** MrDFDevereux(3) 2 70
(T P Tate) *prom: led over 4f out: sn rdn and hdd: one pce fnl f* **15/2**

5060 **6** 5 **Chapter (IRE)**[39] 4261 6-10-1 **61** oh10 ow6 (p) MrOJMurphy(7) 6 48
(Mrs A L M King) *missed break: bhd: rdn over 1f out: sme hdwy sn after: nvr a danger* **40/1**

1260 **7** *shd* **Prelude**[8] 5199 7-11-2 **72** MrBenBrisbourne(3) 7 58
(W M Brisbourne) *bustled along early: nt clr run after 1f: bustled along sn after and hdwy to ld after 4f: hdd over 4f out: remained handy: rdn and wknd over 1f out* **7/1**[3]

4462 **8** 2 **Baltimore Jack (IRE)**[30] 4537 4-10-4 **62** MrJoshuaMoore(5) 9 45
(M W Easterby) *led: hdd after 4f: remained handy: wknd over 3f out* **7/1**[3]

6163 **9** *nse* **Opera Writer (IRE)**[37] 4299 5-10-2 **60** (p) MrStephenHarrison(5) 5 43
(R Hollinshead) *hld up: forced wd after 1f: racd keenly: hdwy to trck ldrs after 3f: led 4f out: hdd over 2f out: sn squeezed out: wknd over 1f out* **8/1**

4225 **10** 5 **Spanish Diva**[23] 4721 4-11-5 **72** MrSWalker 10 47
(S C Williams) *hld up: stdy hdwy fr 7f out: chsd ldrs 4f out tl wknd 2f out* **4/1**[1]

563- **11** 1¼ **Woodcraft**[13] 5870 4-11-2 **74** MrBJToomey(5) 8 47
(D McCain Jnr) *trckd ldrs for 2f: sn dropped to midfield: wknd over 4f out* **16/1**

2m 39.27s (-0.63) **Going Correction** -0.10s/f (Good)
WFA 3 from 4yo+ 10lb **11** Ran SP% **115.1**
Speed ratings (Par 103): **98,97,94,94,93 90,90,88,88,85 84**
toteswinger: 1&2 £13.60, 1&3 £48.20, 2&3 £46.80. CSF £105.08 CT £2471.17 TOTE £8.20: £2.40, £4.30, £5.80; EX 99.70 Place 6: £615.34 Place 5: £576.71 .
Owner The Sultans of Speed **Bred** Don Commins **Trained** Exning, Suffolk

FOCUS
A modest gentleman amateur riders' handicap run at just a steady pace to halfway. Very ordinary form.
Chapter(IRE) Official explanation: jockey said gelding missed the break and saddle slipped
T/Plt: £642.40 to a £1 stake. Pool: £80,791.58. 91.80 winning tickets. T/Qpdt: £141.40 to a £1 stake. Pool: £4,377.50. 22.90 winning tickets. DO

5219 HAMILTON (R-H)

Friday, August 29

OFFICIAL GOING: Good to soft

Wind: Almost nil Weather: Overcast

5451 PRESTIGE SCOTLAND NURSERY — 6f 5y

2:30 (2:30) (Class 5) (0-75,75) 2-Y-O — **£4,209** (£1,252; £625; £312) **Stalls** Low

Form | | | | RPR
354 **1** **Go Go Green (IRE)**[37] 4289 2-9-5 **73**........ TonyCulhane 3 — 74
(S Parr) *t.k.h: mde all: rdn and edgd rt over 1f out: hld on wl fnl f* **4/1**[3]

323 **2** *nk* **Count Almaviva (USA)**[18] 4923 2-9-4 **72**........ RoystonFfrench 6 — 72
(K A Ryan) *prom: hung rt: n.m.r and lost pl over 2f out: rallied to chse wnr wl ins fnl f: r.o* **2/1**[1]

01 **3** *2* **Toledo Gold (IRE)**[30] 4536 2-9-7 **75**........ DavidAllan 5 — 69
(E J Alston) *stdd bhd ldrs: effrt and hdwy over 1f out: one pce ins fnl f* **8/1**

0344 **4** *½* **Rossett Rose (IRE)**[21] 4816 2-9-1 **69**........ TWilliams 7 — 62
(M Brittain) *in tch on outside: effrt over 2f out: one pce fnl f* **14/1**

100 **5** *hd* **Fathey (IRE)**[28] 4594 2-9-7 **75**........(b[1]) JamieMoriarty 2 — 67
(R A Fahey) *trckd ldrs: effrt over 2f out: one pce fnl f* **7/2**[2]

0351 **6** *5* **Lady Salama**[7] 5219 2-9-2 **70** 6ex........ AndrewElliott 4 — 47
(K R Burke) *cl up untl wknd over 1f out* **4/1**[3]

1m 15.86s (3.66) **Going Correction** +0.40s/f (Good) **6** Ran SP% **113.3**

Speed ratings (Par 94): **91,90,87,87,87 80**

toteswinger: 1&2 £4.60, 1&3 £7.30, 2&3 £7.40. CSF £12.68 TOTE £5.60: £2.10, £1.40; EX 14.90.

Owner S Bolland P Holling **Bred** Edmond And Richard Kent **Trained** Bawtry, S Yorks

■ Stewards' Enquiry : Jamie Moriarty three-day ban: used whip with excessive frequency (Sep 12,14,15)

FOCUS

This open nursery was run at just an average early pace and the first two were coming clear at the finish. Straightforward form.

NOTEBOOK

Go Go Green(IRE) lost his maiden tag at the fourth attempt on this handicap debut and did the job in determined fashion. He pulled his way to the early lead and took time to settle, but showed a willing attitude when getting organised. He was always just holding the fast-finishing runner-up and proved he gets all of this trip, as it was the most testing surface he had raced on. (op 6-1)

Count Almaviva(USA), another nursery newcomer, had been placed on each of his previous three starts and was well backed. He ran a strange race because he looked like folding after the three-furlong pole, but picked up strongly nearing the final furlong and was only just held in the end. He did get a little warm beforehand and, on this evidence, has begun life in this sphere on a good mark. However, he now has temperament issues to overcome and connections may opt for some form of headgear after this. (op 7-4)

Toledo Gold(IRE) proved very easy to back. He was never quite getting there on this return to an easier surface, but was not disgraced by any means and most likely does need a sound surface. He has more scope than most of these and is not one to give up on. (op 6-1 tchd 11-2)

Rossett Rose(IRE) was ridden with greater restraint and failed to get any cover on the outside of the pack. She ran close to her recent level, again looking in need of some respite from the handicapper, and helps to put the form into perspective. (op 12-1 tchd 11-1)

Fathey(IRE), 4lb lower, had every chance against the stands' rail and ran a slightly improved race in the first-time blinkers. (op 5-1 tchd 13-2)

Lady Salama dropped right out inside the final furlong and rates disappointing under her penalty. A stronger end-to-end gallop over this trip is probably what she really wants, however. (op 9-2 tchd 7-2)

5452 ESCAPE RECRUITMENT H'CAP — 5f 4y

3:05 (3:05) (Class 6) (0-55,53) 3-Y-O+ — **£2,388** (£705; £352) **Stalls** Low

Form | | | | RPR
40 **1** **Miacarla**[69] 3260 5-8-8 **50**........(t) NeilBrown(3) 12 — 61
(H A McWilliams) *hld up: hdwy 2f out: squeezed through to ld ins fnl f: sn clr: comf* **14/1**

3304 **2** *2¼* **Whozart (IRE)**[14] 5044 5-8-10 **49** ow1........ DanielTudhope 7 — 52
(A Dickman) *prom: effrt 2f out: ev ch ins fnl f: kpt on same pce* **4/1**[1]

560 **3** *1* **Distant Vision (IRE)**[43] 4118 5-8-6 **45**........ PaulFessey 13 — 44
(H A McWilliams) *hld up on outside: effrt over 1f out: r.o fnl f* **16/1**

0552 **4** *½* **Gelert (IRE)**[25] 4686 3-8-5 **45**........ PatrickMathers 4 — 43
(Peter Grayson) *cl up: led over 1f out to ins fnl f: sn no ex* **8/1**

6506 **5** *1¼* **Jojesse**[29] 4561 4-8-6 **45**........ PaulQuinn 5 — 38
(G A Swinbank) *bhd tl hdwy fnl f: nrst fin* **13/2**[3]

6040 **6** *¾* **Wicked Wilma (IRE)**[6] 5260 4-8-12 **51**........ TonyCulhane 9 — 41
(A Berry) *hld up: hdwy over 1f out: no imp fnl f* **5/1**[2]

4644 **7** *1* **Howards Prince**[7] 5220 5-8-6 **45**........ AndrewElliott 6 — 31
(D A Nolan) *midfield: drvn 1/2-way: no imp over 1f out* **8/1**

0006 **8** *¾* **She's Our Beauty (IRE)**[14] 5044 5-8-3 **45**........(v) DuranFentiman(3) 1 — 29
(S T Mason) *led to over 1f out: sn btn* **28/1**

6030 **9** *¾* **Valiant Romeo**[46] 4013 8-8-7 **46**........(v) RoystonFfrench 8 — 27
(R Bastiman) *bhd and sn pushed along: nvr able to chal* **10/1**

100- **10** *1½* **Jadan (IRE)**[303] 6594 7-9-0 **53**........(b) DavidAllan 11 — 29
(E J Alston) *chsd ldrs tl wknd over 1f out* **12/1**

0455 **11** *½* **Seafield Towers**[7] 5220 8-8-8 **47**........(p) NickyMackay 10 — 21
(D A Nolan) *midfield: drvn and outpcd 2f out: sn btn* **18/1**

000 **12** *1¾* **Throw The Dice**[14] 5044 6-7-13 **45**........(v) CharlotteKerton(7) 3 — 13
(A Berry) *in tch tl rdn and wknd 2f out* **16/1**

0/0- **13** *7* **Stylistic (IRE)**[314] 6347 7-8-6 **45**........ DaleGibson 2 — —
(W A Murphy, Ire) *dwlt: a bhd* **20/1**

61.11 secs (1.11) **Going Correction** +0.40s/f (Good)

WFA 3 from 4yo+ 2lb **13** Ran SP% **120.9**

Speed ratings (Par 101): **107,103,101,101,99 97,96,95,93,91 90,87,76**

toteswinger: 1&2 £18.90, 1&3 £52.70, 2&3 £21.70. CSF £70.02 CT £967.91 TOTE £18.80: £7.10, £1.70, £7.50; EX 132.50.

Owner J D Riches **Bred** Primrose Cottage **Trained** Cockerham, Co Durham

■ The first winner for trainer Tony McWilliams in more than five years.

FOCUS

A typically poor sprint handicap for the grade, but it was still wide open. The winner has slipped back to a good mark and the form is rated through the third.

Miacarla Official explanation: trainer said, regarding apparent improvement in form, mare benefited from fitting of a tongue strap for the first time

Valiant Romeo Official explanation: jockey said gelding never travelled

Throw The Dice Official explanation: jockey said gelding bled from the nose

5453 AVONHILL LTD MAIDEN STKS — 1m 1f 36y

3:40 (3:41) (Class 5) 3-Y-O+ — **£3,412** (£1,007; £504) **Stalls** High

Form | | | | RPR
1 **Ozone Trustee (NZ)**[345] 4-9-7 0........ PJMcDonald(3) 2 — 85
(G A Swinbank) *chsd ldrs: stdy hdwy stands' side over 2f out: rdn to ld appr fnl f: r.o strly* **14/1**[3]

2522 **2** *6* **Buddhist Monk**[17] 4941 3-9-3 77........ J-PGuillambert 6 — 72
(Sir Mark Prescott) *led: clr whn c to stands' side ent st: carried hd high and hdd over 1f out: nt run on* **1/5**[1]

40 **3** *14* **Kings Maiden (IRE)**[14] 5042 5-9-5 0........ RoystonFfrench 5 — 36
(James Moffatt) *in tch: drvn and effrt stands' side over 3f out: qckly lft bhd by front two over 2f out* **33/1**

0 **4** *¾* **Oscar Wild**[14] 5042 6-9-10 0........ PAspell 1 — 40
(James Moffatt) *bhd: drvn stands' side over 4f out: nvr able to chal* **80/1**

5 *1* **Gargano (IRE)** 3-9-3 0........ GregFairley 3 — 37
(M Johnston) *s.i.s: sn prom: effrt far side over 3f out: drifted lft and wknd fr over 2f out* **5/1**[2]

6605 **6** *16* **Scanno (IRE)**[7] 5223 3-8-10 43........(t) GarryWhillans(7) 4 — —
(M Mullineaux) *cl up: rdn centre over 4f out: sn wknd* **100/1**

2m 1.55s (1.85) **Going Correction** +0.40s/f (Good)

WFA 3 from 4yo+ 7lb **6** Ran SP% **111.8**

Speed ratings (Par 103): **107,101,89,88,87 73**

toteswinger: 1&2 £1.90, 1&3 £13.10, 2&3 £4.30. CSF £17.93 TOTE £13.50: £4.40, £1.02; EX 21.10.

Owner W J Gredley **Bred** Emblem Ltd **Trained** Melsonby, N Yorks

FOCUS

No strength in depth to this maiden, in which the runner-up set a good standard. The first two finished clear and the form is rated through the time.

5454 SITE SERVICES PLANT LTD H'CAP — 1m 65y

4:15 (4:19) (Class 5) (0-70,70) 4-Y-O+ — **£3,412** (£1,007; £504) **Stalls** High

Form | | | | RPR
0500 **1** **Superior Star**[20] 4850 5-8-8 **57**........(b) JamieMoriarty 6 — 65
(N Wilson) *hld up in midfield: smooth hdwy over 2f out: rdn to ld ins fnl f: r.o* **7/1**

5302 **2** *3¼* **Primo Way**[16] 4969 7-8-11 **63**........ NeilBrown(3) 1 — 63
(Miss L A Perratt) *cl up: led over 3f out: hdd ins fnl f: kpt on same pce* **7/1**

2411 **3** *hd* **Five Wishes**[16] 4969 4-9-1 **67**........(be) PJMcDonald(3) 2 — 67
(M Dods) *hld up in tch: effrt over 2f out: kpt on u.p fnl f* **11/2**[3]

6042 **4** *1* **Mystical Ayr (IRE)**[17] 4949 6-8-7 **56**........ RoystonFfrench 5 — 54
(Miss L A Perratt) *hld up: rdn 3f out: effrt over 1f out: one pce fnl f* **10/3**[2]

0511 **5** *½* **Wednesdays Boy (IRE)**[1] 5420 5-8-5 **54**........(p) DO'Donohoe 7 — 51
(P D Niven) *bhd and sn drvn along: hdwy over 1f out: nrst fin* **2/1**[1]

0043 **6** *2½* **Apres Ski (IRE)**[19] 4903 5-7-13 **51** oh3........ DuranFentiman(3) 3 — 42
(J F Coupland) *missed break: sn cl up: rdn over 2f out: no ex over 1f out* **20/1**

2-00 **7** *2* **Augustus John (IRE)**[19] 4902 5-9-6 **69**........ TonyCulhane 4 — 55
(S Parr) *trckd ldrs tl rdn and wknd fr 2f out* **14/1**

00 **8** *½* **Middlemarch (IRE)**[20] 4876 8-9-2 **70**........(p) GaryBartley(5) 8 — 55
(J S Goldie) *hld up: rdn and edgd rt over 2f out: sn btn* **12/1**

-505 **9** *16* **Sydneyroughdiamond**[23] 4746 6-8-2 **51** oh6........ TWilliams 9 — —
(M Mullineaux) *t.k.h: led to over 3f out: sn lost pl* **100/1**

1m 51.61s (3.21) **Going Correction** +0.40s/f (Good) **9** Ran SP% **116.9**

Speed ratings (Par 103): **99,95,95,94,94 91,89,89,73**

toteswinger: 1&2 £10.60, 1&3 £7.70, 2&3 £3.70. CSF £55.77 CT £293.54 TOTE £10.80: £2.80, £2.10, £1.60; EX 58.70.

Owner B Plows P M Watson J Owen **Bred** R F And Mrs Knipe **Trained** Flaxton, N Yorks

FOCUS

This was a moderate handicap, run at an average pace. The placed horses ran to their recent form.

Wednesdays Boy(IRE) Official explanation: jockey said gelding never travelled

5455 SODEXO STOP HUNGER CHARITY H'CAP — 6f 5y

4:50 (4:50) (Class 4) (0-80,80) 3-Y-O+ — **£7,123** (£2,119; £1,059; £529) **Stalls** Low

Form | | | | RPR
0333 **1** **Bid For Gold**[20] 4875 4-8-8 **64**........ AndrewElliott 1 — 72
(Jedd O'Keeffe) *cl up: led over 2f out: edgd lft 1f out: hld on gamely* **11/2**[3]

1500 **2** *hd* **The Nifty Fox**[39] 4240 4-9-10 **80**........ DavidAllan 6 — 87
(T D Easterby) *hld up bhd ldng gp: hdwy over 1f out: r.o wl fnl f: jst hld* **18/1**

1340 **3** *hd* **Ingleby Princess**[20] 4858 4-8-9 **65**........ PaulFessey 10 — 71+
(T D Barron) *bhd tl hdwy over 1f out: kpt on wl fnl f* **12/1**

1332 **4** *1* **Grazeon Gold Blend**[7] 5222 5-9-4 **77**........ PJMcDonald(3) 4 — 80
(J J Quinn) *prom: effrt over 1f out: one pce fnl f* **2/1**[1]

4501 **5** *nse* **Finsbury**[13] 5101 5-8-5 **61**........ NickyMackay 7 — 64
(J S Goldie) *hld up: hdwy to chse ldrs over 1f out: one pce fnl f* **5/1**[2]

0440 **6** *2½* **Glasshoughton**[14] 5067 5-9-9 **79**........ RoystonFfrench 5 — 74
(M Dods) *trckd ldrs tl rdn and no ex over 1f out* **13/2**

3160 **7** *¾* **Optical Illusion (USA)**[23] 4736 4-8-5 **61** oh2........ DaleGibson 8 — 54
(R A Fahey) *trckd ldrs: effrt over 2f out: wknd over 1f out* **16/1**

4541 **8** *3½* **Angel Voices (IRE)**[16] 4967 5-8-5 **68**........(p) DeclanCannon(7) 2 — 49
(K R Burke) *led to over 2f out: wknd over 1f out* **8/1**

515 **9** *½* **Nabeeda**[5] 5307 3-8-2 **61** oh4........ TWilliams 9 — 41
(M Brittain) *prom tl rdn and wknd over 2f out* **11/1**

1m 13.84s (1.64) **Going Correction** +0.40s/f (Good)

WFA 3 from 4yo+ 3lb **9** Ran SP% **117.0**

Speed ratings (Par 105): **105,104,104,103,103 99,98,94,93**

toteswinger: 1&2 £21.50, 1&3 £8.20, 2&3 £20.10. CSF £98.08 CT £1148.41 TOTE £6.90: £2.10, £4.80, £2.50; EX 131.20.

Owner Paul Chapman And Ba'Tat Investments **Bred** B Minty **Trained** Middleham Moor, N Yorks

FOCUS

A fair handicap for the grade and run at a solid pace. The form looks sound enough with the winner, second and fifth rated to this year's best.

5456 STRATHCLYDE PLANT LTD H'CAP — 1m 3f 16y

5:20 (5:20) (Class 6) (0-65,61) 3-Y-O+ — **£2,388** (£705; £352) **Stalls** High

Form | | | | RPR
0603 **1** **Three Strings (USA)**[22] 4785 5-9-8 **55**........(p) DO'Donohoe 7 — 63
(P D Niven) *set stdy pce: rdn over 2f out: hld on wl fnl f* **6/1**[3]

-002 **2** *shd* **Edas**[16] 4966 6-9-10 **60**........ NeilBrown(3) 9 — 68
(J J Quinn) *prom: stdy hdwy over 2f out: ev ch fnl f: jst hld* **6/1**[3]

01-0 **3** *1½* **Mayadeen (IRE)**[146] 1219 6-9-1 **48**........ JamieMoriarty 4 — 53
(R A Fahey) *hld up in tch: effrt over 2f out: one pce fnl f* **14/1**

0064 4 1 3/4 **Fever**[20] 4878 4-10-0 **61** PAspell 8 63
(M W Easterby) *hld up: rdn and edgd rt 2f out: kpt on fnl f: nvr able to chal* **10/1**
3001 5 shd **Prince Rhyddarch**[7] 5223 3-9-1 **57** 6ex PaulFessey 1 59
(Miss L A Perratt) *trckd ldrs: rdn and outpcd over 2f out: rallied fnl f: r.o* **2/1**[1]
0002 6 3/4 **Ulysees (IRE)**[27] 4630 9-9-3 **50** DNolan 5 51
(Miss L A Perratt) *hld up: drvn 3f out: no imp over 1f out* **12/1**
1 7 2 1/4 **Follow The Sun (IRE)**[19] 4902 4-9-4 **58** BMcHugh(7) 2 55
(Ronald O'Leary, Ire) *plld hrd: cl up tl wknd over 1f out* **10/3**[2]
6504 8 10 **Qaasi (USA)**[15] 5003 6-8-13 **46** RoystonFfrench 6 26
(M Brittain) *hld up in tch: rdn 3f out: sn btn* **12/1**

2m 30.6s (5.00) **Going Correction** +0.40s/f (Good)
WFA 3 from 4yo+ 9lb **8 Ran SP% 116.1**
Speed ratings (Par 101): **97,96,95,94,94 93,92,85**
toteswinger: 1&2 £6.50, 1&3 £10.10, 2&3 £8.30. CSF £42.24 CT £485.03 TOTE £7.70: £1.80, £2.20, £4.60; EX 33.90.
Owner The Wednesday Club **Bred** Gaucho Ltd **Trained** Barton-le-Street, N Yorks

FOCUS
This ordinary handicap was run at just a moderate early pace and again the runners came to the stands' side in the home straight. Very modest form.
Qaasi(USA) Official explanation: trainer said gelding finished lame on its left fore and left hind

5457 TRAINERMAGAZINE.COM H'CAP 6f 5y
5:50 (5:51) (Class 6) (0-55,55) 3-Y-O £2,388 (£705; £352) Stalls Low

Form RPR
0346 1 **Many Welcomes**[54] 3753 3-8-7 **46** oh1 AndrewElliott 4 52+
(B P J Baugh) *hld up: hdwy and cl up whn bdly hmpd over 1f out: rcvrd and led ins fnl f: r.o wl* **12/1**
0260 2 1/2 **Swallow Forest**[28] 4609 3-9-0 **53** (b) PaulFessey 5 58
(T D Barron) *hld up in tch: rdn: hung rt and squeezed through over 1f out: ev ch ins fnl f: r.o* **11/2**[2]
0060 3 2 3/4 **Tanley**[5] 5307 3-8-12 **54** (p) DuranFentiman(3) 7 50
(J F Coupland) *hld up in midfield: hdwy and cl up whn hmpd over 1f out: ev ch ins fnl f* **8/1**[3]
065 4 1/2 **Mensadil**[22] 4794 3-8-0 **46** oh1 KristinStubbs(7) 3 40
(Mrs L Stubbs) *led to ins fnl f: no ex* **20/1**
-040 5 3/4 **Meinardus (IRE)**[13] 5110 3-8-12 **54** NeilBrown(3) 1 46
(T D Barron) *hld up: hdwy and cl up over 1f out: one pce fnl f* **10/1**
5600 6 1 3/4 **Scots W'Hae**[129] 1533 3-8-11 **50** JamieMoriarty 13 36
(Miss L A Perratt) *cl up: effrt and ev ch over 1f out: wknd ins fnl f* **8/1**[3]
-301 7 3/4 **Glenveagh (IRE)**[25] 4684 3-9-2 **55** (p) RoystonFfrench 10 39+
(K A Ryan) *chsd ldrs: drvn over 2f out: bmpd over 1f out: sn btn* **6/4**[1]
0000 8 3/4 **Amber Ridge**[67] 3333 3-8-7 **46** oh1 TonyCulhane 2 28
(B P J Baugh) *prom: drvn and outpcd 1/2-way: n.d after* **16/1**
0006 9 1 1/4 **Captain Turbot (IRE)**[71] 3172 3-8-5 **47** oh1 ow1 PJMcDonald(3) 8 25+
(D W Barker) *hld up: hdwy over 2f out: checked and wknd over 1f out* **18/1**
0000 10 3 1/2 **Mujada**[41] 4207 3-8-7 **46** TWilliams 11 12
(M Brittain) *prom tl rdn and wknd fr 2f out* **28/1**
465 11 12 **Heavenly Encounter**[190] 635 3-8-0 **46** oh1 DeclanCannon(7) 9 —
(K R Burke) *dwlt: sn chsng ldrs: rdn and wknd over 2f out* **28/1**

1m 14.97s (2.77) **Going Correction** +0.40s/f (Good) **11 Ran SP% 117.2**
Speed ratings (Par 98): **97,96,92,92,91 88,87,86,85,80 64**
toteswinger: 1&2 £6.80, 1&3 £9.60, 2&3 £7.50. CSF £74.65 CT £563.94 TOTE £14.90: £2.90, £2.30, £2.60; EX 66.20 Place 6: £256.72 Place 5: £153.00 .
Owner Gang Of Four **Bred** Mrs F Wilson **Trained** Audley, Staffs
■ Stewards' Enquiry : Paul Fessey five-day ban: careless riding (Sep 12-16); three-day ban: used whip with excessive frequency (Sep 17-19)

FOCUS
A poor handicap, this time for three-year-olds, in which five raced from out of the handicap. The winner is rated up 8lb with the runner-up to her best.
T/Plt: £450.00 to a £1 stake. Pool: £53,021.59. 86.00 winning tickets. T/Qpdt: £39.90 to a £1 stake. Pool: £3,465.40. 64.20 winning tickets. RY

5021 SALISBURY (R-H)
Friday, August 29

OFFICIAL GOING: Good to firm (8.9)
Wind: Nil

5458 BATHWICK TYRES LADY RIDERS' SERIES H'CAP 1m
4:00 (4:03) (Class 5) (0-70,70) 3-Y-O+ £3,123 (£968; £484; £242) Stalls High

Form RPR
2231 1 **South Wales**[54] 3763 3-9-1 **59** MissMHugo(7) 1 68
(R W Price) *racd wd: chsd ldrs: chal 3f out: slt advantage 2f out: pushed out fnl f* **10/1**
5201 2 1 1/4 **Uhuru Peak**[15] 5008 7-9-9 **54** (bt) MissSBrotherton 4 61
(M W Easterby) *racd wd: slt ld 3f out: narrowly hdd 2f out: kpt on but nt pce of wnr fnl f* **8/1**[3]
1066 3 1 1/2 **Sir Boss (IRE)**[19] 4895 3-10-2 **70** MissMSowerby(3) 7 73
(D E Cantillon) *chsd ldrs: rdn and ev ch over 2f out: styd on same pce fr over 1f out* **9/2**[2]
3400 4 nk **Shaded Edge**[20] 4862 4-9-11 **56** MissGDGracey-Davison 12 59
(D W P Arbuthnot) *mid-div: rdn 3f out: styd on fnl f: nt trble ldng duo* **11/1**
2601 5 nk **Barathea Dreams (IRE)**[24] 4710 7-10-8 **67** MrsSMoore 10 69
(J S Moore) *in rr: rdn 1/2-way: styd on u.p fnl 2f and gng on cl home but n.d* **12/1**
-022 6 1 3/4 **She's So Pretty (IRE)**[14] 5058 4-9-7 **57** (b) MissHayleyMoore(5) 9 55
(G L Moore) *mid-div: rdn 3f out: styd on fnl f: nt trble ldrs* **4/1**[1]
0404 7 shd **Gracie's Gift (IRE)**[21] 4813 6-9-7 **52** MissFayeBramley 11 50
(A G Newcombe) *pressed ldrs: slt ld over 3f out: sn hdd: wknd ins fnl f* **8/1**[3]
6300 8 3/4 **Corlough Mountain**[20] 4865 4-9-11 **63** ow2 (tp) MissMBryant(7) 2 59
(P Butler) *racd wd: in tch: rdn to chse ldrs 3f out: one pce fnl 2f* **40/1**
2200 9 5 **Haasem (USA)**[19] 4895 5-10-2 **68** MissCHobson(7) 14 53
(J R Jenkins) *chsd ldrs: rdn over 3f out: wknd 2f out* **11/1**
-040 10 1/2 **Daring Dream (GER)**[21] 4829 3-9-12 **68** MissLEBurke(5) 5 52
(A P Jarvis) *chsd ldrs: rdn to chal over 3f out: wknd over 2f out* **8/1**[3]
230 11 5 **Valentino Swing (IRE)**[51] 3842 5-10-10 **69** MissEJJones 8 41
(Miss T Spearing) *chsd ldrs over 5f* **20/1**
0301 12 1 1/4 **Lopinot (IRE)**[22] 4772 5-9-6 **58** (p) MissRachelKing(7) 3 27
(M R Bosley) *racd wd and sn led: hdd over 3f out and wknd qckly sn after* **18/1**
4305 13 2 3/4 **High 'n Dry (IRE)**[17] 4946 4-9-13 **65** (p) MissVJBaalham(7) 13 28
(M A Allen) *slowly away: a bhd* **25/1**
5060 14 4 1/2 **Magpie (IRE)**[11] 5145 3-9-8 **64** ow5 MissCLWills(5) 6 16
(B G Powell) *slowly away: a bhd* **50/1**

1m 44.39s (0.89) **Going Correction** -0.075s/f (Good)
WFA 3 from 4yo+ 6lb **14 Ran SP% 123.2**
Speed ratings (Par 103): **92,90,89,88,88 86,86,86,81,80 75,74,71,67**
CSF £86.77 CT £432.31 TOTE £8.70: £2.90, £2.70, £2.00; EX 50.20.
Owner Dhafi Al Marri **Bred** Usk Valley Stud **Trained** Newmarket, Suffolk
■ The first training success for former jockey Russell Price, and the first winner under Rules for rider Michelle Hugo.

FOCUS
A wide-open affair, as is often the case in these lady-rider handicaps, and it was those who raced down the centre of the course that came out on top. The form looks ordinary with the runner-up the best guide.

5459 FRANCIS CLARK CHARTERED ACCOUNTANTS MAIDEN AUCTION STKS (DIV I) 6f
4:35 (4:35) (Class 5) 2-Y-O £3,238 (£963; £481; £240) Stalls High

Form RPR
00 1 **Bermondsey Bob (IRE)**[19] 4905 2-8-6 **0** TolleyDean(3) 13 75
(J L Spearing) *s.i.s: drvn to chse ldrs after 1f: chal fr 3f out: edgd lft 2f out and again whn chalng 1f out: drvn to ld fnl 75yds: hld on wl* **150/1**
002 2 nk **Hi Shinko**[19] 4907 2-8-9 **79** TedDurcan 2 74
(B R Millman) *sn led: stl travelling wl whn pushed lft 2f out: rdn and pushed lft again 1f out: hdd and no ex fnl 75yds* **4/1**[3]
653 3 1 1/2 **Admiral Sandhoe (USA)**[16] 4974 2-8-13 **79** JimCrowley 10 74
(Mrs A J Perrett) *lw: in rr: drvn and hdwy 2f out: styng on whn checked and swtchd rt 1f out: styd on ins fnl f: nt pce to rch ldng duo* **15/8**[1]
4 3 1/2 **Barood (IRE)** 2-8-11 **0** SamHitchcott 12 61+
(M R Channon) *w'like: leggy: in rr: pushed along and plenty to do over 2f out: styd on strly thrght fnl f: gng on cl home* **20/1**
5 3/4 **Security Joan (IRE)** 2-8-8 **0** RichardHughes 6 56+
(R Hannon) *w'like: strong: bit bkwd: in rr: off the pce and plenty to do 3f out: rdn 2f out: styd on wl fr over 1f out: fin fast* **9/1**
6 nk **Dametime (IRE)**[6] 5292 2-7-13 **0** DavidProbert(5) 4 51
(Daniel Mark Loughnane, Ire) *chsd ldrs: rdn and effrt 2f out: nvr quite on terms: wknd fnl f* **15/2**
0 7 3/4 **Wetherby Place (IRE)**[27] 4643 2-8-11 **0** RichardKingscote 1 56
(R M Beckett) *lengthy: lw: s.i.s: sn chsng ldrs: rdn 3f out: wknd over 1f out* **14/1**
00 8 1 3/4 **Red Robert**[38] 4274 2-8-9 **0** MartinDwyer 7 50+
(J L Dunlop) *lw: towards rr: rdn and sme prog over 2f out: nvr rchd ldrs* **25/1**
9 1 **Speedy Guru** 2-8-4 **0** FrankieMcDonald 3 40
(H Candy) *b.hind: lengthy: chsd ldrs: rdn over 2f out: sn btn* **28/1**
10 2 3/4 **Boundless Applause** 2-8-6 **0** CatherineGannon 5 34
(I A Wood) *w'like: bit bkwd: chsd ldrs: rdn over 3f out: sn btn* **33/1**
40 11 69 **Millway Beach (IRE)**[27] 4625 2-8-11 **0** ShaneKelly 9 —
(Pat Eddery) *lw: in rr whn virtually p.u over 2f out: t.o* **11/4**[2]

1m 14.92s (0.12) **Going Correction** -0.075s/f (Good) **11 Ran SP% 125.5**
Speed ratings (Par 94): **96,95,93,88,87 87,86,84,82,79** —
CSF £703.60 TOTE £58.60: £9.30, £2.00, £1.30; EX 487.00.
Owner A A Campbell **Bred** Pier House Stud **Trained** Kinnersley, Worcs
■ Stewards' Enquiry : Tolley Dean one-day ban: careless riding (Sep 12)

FOCUS
This looked just a moderate maiden on paper and the shock victory of 150-1 shot Bermondsey Bob, who had to survive a stewards' enquiry, did nothing to alter that view. The placed horses were both close to their marks though, so the form can be rated somewhere near face value.

NOTEBOOK
Bermondsey Bob(IRE), having managed to beat just one home in two previous attempts, sprung a big surprise. He bounced out of the stalls and soon bagged the lead, being harried by the runner-up, but managed to fend them all off, despite showing distinct signs of greenness and twice hanging into that rival. Handicaps will be next on the agenda and only then will we learn whether this was a fluke. Official explanation: trainer said, regarding apparent improvement in form, gelding was slowly away and raced lazily at Windsor, whereas he was ridden more positively this time (op 100-1)
Hi Shinko, who nearly registered a shock himself at Windsor last time, looked a big player in this and was soon helping to force the pace. Although done no favours by the winner, he had every chance both before and after the interference to get past, but was making no impression as they crossed the line. His future is in handicaps. (op 11-2)
Admiral Sandhoe(USA), a fast finisher over course and distance latest, gave the front two plenty of ground and still had several lengths to make up with two to run. Switched inside the final furlong, he was making no further inroads on the front pair as they crossed the line and needs a return to 7f on this evidence. (op 5-2 tchd 3-1)
Barood(IRE), a gelded son of Xaar, who was found wanting for pace. He looked more likely to finish last at one stage though and the fact he managed to stay on for third should give connections some encouragement. (op 18-1 tchd 22-1)
Security Joan(IRE), related to several juvenile winners, was another who struggled early on this racecourse debut before making late headway, and she should know a lot more next time. (op 15-2 tchd 6-1)
Dametime(IRE), who finished sixth at the Curragh just the other day, is now qualified for a handicap mark and should fare better in that sphere. (op 5-1)
Red Robert is the type to do better in nurseries now that he is qualified. (op 18-1)
Millway Beach(IRE), strongly supported beforehand, had the bit slip through his mouth and was allowed to come home in his own time. Official explanation: jockey said bit pulled through colt's mouth (op 9-2 tchd 11-2)

5460 SETSQUARE RECRUITMENT CONSTRUCTION PERSONNEL SOUTHAMPTON NURSERY 1m
5:05 (5:07) (Class 5) (0-75,73) 2-Y-O £3,238 (£963; £481; £240) Stalls High

Form RPR
006 1 **Red Reef**[23] 4720 2-8-8 **60** JohnEgan 1 64+
(D J Coakley) *in rr: rdn along 3f out and sn hunging rt: hdwy over 2f out: swtchd lft to outside over 1f out and fin strly to ld fnl 20yds* **25/1**
2113 2 1 **Rose Of Coma (IRE)**[15] 5006 2-8-0 **57** DavidProbert(5) 9 59
(Miss Gay Kelleway) *b.hind: w ldr tl drvn to take slt advantage appr fnl f: kpt on whn strly chal ins fnl f: ct fnl 20yds* **13/2**[3]
0062 3 hd **Pokfulham (IRE)**[21] 4827 2-8-10 **62** (v) DarrenWilliams 4 64
(A P Jarvis) *sn slt ld: kpt narrow advantage tl hdd appr fnl f: styd chalng u.p ins fnl f: no ex fnl 20yds* **14/1**
030 4 1/2 **Arushore (IRE)**[22] 4788 2-8-13 **65** PatDobbs 14 65
(R Hannon) *chsd ldrs: rdn to chal appr fnl f: styd pressing ldrs ins fnl f: no ex nr fin* **11/1**

045 **5** ½ **Supernoverre (IRE)**[61] 3519 2-9-4 70 .... TedDurcan 13 71+
(Mrs A J Perrett) *lw: towards rr and drvn along over 3f out: hdwy 2f out: styng on whn nt clr run and swtchd lft ins fnl f: stl no room fnl 100yds and nt rcvr* **9/1**

01 **6** 2¼ **Dazinski**[39] 4256 2-9-7 73 .... JimmyQuinn 11 67
(M H Tompkins) *w'like: towards rr tl hdwy and drvn into mid-div 3f out: styd on u.p fnl f but nvr gng pce to be competitive* **9/2**[2]

000 **7** ½ **Captain Walcot**[29] 4570 2-8-10 62 ....(p) RichardMullen 8 55
(R Hannon) *chsd ldrs: rdn over 2f out: no imp on ldrs whn checked ins fnl f: sn wknd* **14/1**

2320 **8** 2¼ **Hold The Bucks (USA)**[15] 5006 2-8-4 59 .... LukeMorris(3) 5 47
(J S Moore) *lw: in rr: rdn and sme prog on outer over 2f out: nvr gng pce to chal and wknd fnl f* **12/1**

0300 **9** 2¼ **Calypso Prince**[17] 4956 2-8-4 56 .... MartinDwyer 2 39
(M D I Usher) *chsd ldrs: rdn fr 4f out: wknd 2f out* **40/1**

0021 **10** 2¼ **Sienna Lake (IRE)**[21] 4827 2-8-10 62 .... RichardHughes 6 40
(R Hannon) *chsd ldrs: rdn over 2f out: sn btn* **11/4**[1]

6300 **11** 2 **Duke Of Aquitaine (USA)**[23] 4729 2-9-3 69 .... JoeFanning 12 43
(P F I Cole) *t.k.h early: sn bhd* **12/1**

0005 **12** 11 **Ba Globetrotter**[14] 5041 2-8-4 56 .... CatherineGannon 7 6
(M R Channon) *sn rdn and a in rr* **22/1**

0062 **13** 5 **Josiah Bartlett (IRE)**[18] 4933 2-8-9 61 .... FrankieMcDonald 3 —
(J W Hills) *chsd ldrs: rdn 3f out: wknd qckly over 2f out* **12/1**

1m 43.84s (0.34) **Going Correction** -0.075s/f (Good) **13 Ran SP% 123.6**
Speed ratings (Par 94): **95,94,93,92 90,90,87,85,83 81,70,65**
CSF £183.29 CT £2491.44 TOTE £29.50: £5.40, £2.20, £4.00; EX 218.40.
Owner Scarlet Racing **Bred** Preston Lodge Stud **Trained** West Ilsley, Berks
■ Stewards' Enquiry : Darren Williams two-day ban: used whip with excessive frequency (Sep 12,14)

FOCUS
A most competitive nursery and another surprise winner.

NOTEBOOK
Red Reef had shaped with a degree of promise on each of her three starts in maidens, despite getting upset before the race at Brighton last time, and the step up to 1m was clearly the making of her. Well in rear early, she took an age to pick up, but really started to motor from a furlong out got there in plenty of time. She is likely to get trips beyond on this in time and may well be capable of further improvement. Official explanation: trainer said, regarding running, filly is highly strung, and had become upset by a band playing near the parade ring on its last run, and had also appreciated the extra furlong here (op 20-1)
Rose Of Coma(IRE) has been in good form at a lower level and ran well off this mark when finishing third at Beverley last time. Never too far away, she looked to be going best at one stage and kept battling, but had no answer to the swooping winner. This goes down as a personal best. (op 15-2 tchd 8-1)
Pokfulham(IRE) showed improved form when finishing second in a 7f seller at Newmarket last time (first-time visor) and he improved again on that for third in this much stronger contest. He saw the 1m out well, but travelled strongly in the lead for a long way, and may be best back at 7f for now. (tchd 12-1 and 16-1)
Arushore(IRE) well behind a useful sort at Sandown last time, was always likely to do better once handicapping and he fared best of the Hannon brigade, just lacking a change of pace late on. (op 10-1)
Supernoverre(IRE) can be rated better than the bare form as he was denied a clear run close home, having been switched. Up in trip for this nursery debut, he started to stay on having been badly outpaced and could be of interest in a similar contest. (tchd 12-1)
Dazinski, narrow winner of a modest 7f Yarmouth maiden, needed to improve to win this off a mark of 73 and he was not up to it, getting outpaced on this faster ground and just keeping on at the same pace. (op 5-1 tchd 7-2)
Captain Walcot, sporting first-time cheekpieces for this nursery debut, showed enough before getting hampered to suggest he can find a small race. (op 12-1)
Sienna Lake(IRE), who had beaten Pokfulham at Newmarket last time, failed to run her race on this faster ground. (op 3-1 tchd 4-1)

5461 FRANCIS CLARK CHARTERED ACCOUNTANTS MAIDEN AUCTION STKS (DIV II) 6f
5:35 (5:40) (Class 5) 2-Y-O **£3,238** (£963; £481; £240) **Stalls** High

Form RPR

02 **1** **Perfect Pride (USA)**[42] 4149 2-8-8 0 .... IanMongan 6 77
(C G Cox) *chsd ldrs: rdn over 2f out: styd on u.p to ld fnl 100yds: hld on wl whn hrd pressed cl home* **9/2**[3]

3060 **2** *nse* **Amosite**[24] 4705 2-7-13 72 .... DavidProbert(5) 5 73
(J R Jenkins) *pressed ldrs: drvn to chal fr 2f out: slt ld appr fnl f: narrowly hdd fnl 100yds: styd upsides: no ex last strides* **28/1**

252 **3** 1¼ **Forward Feline (IRE)**[13] 5097 2-8-6 78 .... CatherineGannon 10 71
(B Palling) *sn slt ld: hdd over 3f out: slt advantage again 2f out: hdd appr fnl f: outpcd ins fnl f* **8/1**

23 **4** *nk* **Poyle Meg**[22] 4786 2-8-11 0 .... RichardKingscote 3 75
(R M Beckett) *towards rr and drvn along over 3f out: styng on whn nt clr run and swtchd rt fnl 100yds: no imp on ldng duo cl home* **5/2**[1]

34 **5** 2¼ **Rumble Of Thunder (IRE)**[19] 4907 2-8-11 0 .... ShaneKelly 12 69+
(D W P Arbuthnot) *chsd ldrs: styng on whn hmpd fnl 100yds: nt rcvr and one pce* **14/1**

5 **6** 1½ **Floor Show**[30] 4530 2-8-9 0 .... RichardMullen 7 62
(E S McMahon) *rangy: pressed ldr and t.k.h: led and j. path over 3f out: sn rdn and green: hdd over 2f out: wknd fnl f* **16/1**

332 **7** ½ **Sunny Future (IRE)**[15] 5021 2-8-10 81 .... TolleyDean(3) 13 64
(M S Saunders) *s.i.s: sn in tch: drvn to chse ldrs over 3f out: wknd fnl f* **7/2**[2]

03 **8** ¾ **D'Nurse (IRE)**[26] 4665 2-8-8 0 .... RichardHughes 9 57+
(R Hannon) *chsd ldrs: rdn and hung lft 2f out: wknd over 1f out* **10/1**

54 **9** 2½ **Kings Ace (IRE)**[26] 4665 2-8-13 0 .... DarrenWilliams 2 55
(A P Jarvis) *towards rr: hdwy on outside whn pushed lft 2f out: no further prog and sn wknd* **28/1**

06 **10** 9 **Catenaccio (IRE)**[64] 3392 2-8-9 0 .... JimCrowley 8 24
(P Winkworth) *t.k.h in rr whn stmbld bdly over 3f out: sn lost tch* **40/1**

11 7 **Every Little Helps** 2-8-5 0 ow1 .... JoeFanning 4 —
(J Gallagher) *w'like: slowly away: a wl bhd* **50/1**

1m 14.87s (0.07) **Going Correction** -0.075s/f (Good) **11 Ran SP% 113.0**
Speed ratings (Par 94): **96,95,94,93,90 88,88,87,83,71 62**
CSF £110.02 TOTE £5.60: £1.60, £5.90, £2.50; EX 131.00.
Owner Dr Bridget Drew & E E Dedman **Bred** Camelia Casby **Trained** Lambourn, Berks
■ Kuanyao (9/1) was withdrawn after proving unruly at the start. R4 applies, deduct 10p in the £.
■ Stewards' Enquiry : Ian Mongan two-day ban: used whip with excessive frequency (Sep 18-19)

FOCUS
Although the first division of this maiden was won by a 150-1 shot, it is hard to say this was much better, with the hugely exposed Amosite going down by the minimum margin. She helps to dictate the level. The time was only marginally quicker than division one.

NOTEBOOK
Perfect Pride(USA), who had shown fair form in two previous attempts at Newbury, did well to win as she got worked up beforehand, pulling hard to post and unshipping Mongan down at the start having been wound up by the antics of Kuanyao. She picked up well, but did not do a lot once seeing clear daylight and ultimately just edged it in a head-bobber. It is likely there is more to come and perhaps she will do more in front as she gains further experience. (op 7-2)
Amosite showed some fair form earlier in the season, but she has not really progressed and had run poorly on each of the last two occasions. Going without the usual headgear, this was a return to something like her best form, improving for the step up to 6f, but she is likely to continue remain vulnerable in maidens. (op 40-1)
Forward Feline(IRE), runner-up on three of her five previous starts, got a little warm beforehand and showed plenty of speed. She was looking vulnerable inside the final quarter mile though and, despite keeping on right the way to the line, was unable to match the front pair.
Poyle Meg, a promising second over 6f on her Windsor debut, found the drop to 5f against her when a beaten favourite at Sandown last time, and she was again found wanting for pace. Given reminders with just under three to run, she did not give in and kept grinding away, but was never reaching the principals. There is a moderate maiden in her, but she now has the option of nurseries. (op 7-2)
Rumble Of Thunder(IRE) was a shade disappointing in fifth, although this run sees him also qualified for handicaps. He will stay further than this.
Floor Show improved on his debut effort, showing good early pace, but is still quite green and may do better on a slower surface. (tchd 14-1)
Sunny Future(IRE) was the disappointment of the race. He had shown a decent level of ability on all three previous attempts over 7f and was expected to have no trouble with this drop in trip. However, he was unable to quicken when asked for his effort and just plugged on at the same pace. (op 10-3 tchd 3-1)

5462 WEATHERBYS BANK STONEHENGE STKS (LISTED RACE) 1m
6:05 (6:09) (Class 1) 2-Y-O
£17,031 (£6,456; £3,231; £1,611; £807; £405) **Stalls** High

Form RPR

4031 **1** **Snoqualmie Girl (IRE)**[20] 4870 2-8-8 88 .... TQuinn 8 97
(D R C Elsworth) *chsd ldrs: hung rt on far rail 2f out and racd alone fr over 1f out: styd on to ld fnl 110yds: rdn out* **7/1**

31 **2** ½ **On Our Way**[22] 4788 2-8-13 86 .... TedDurcan 1 100+
(H R A Cecil) *lw: rangy: gd sort: pressed ldrs: chal 2f out: hung lft fr 1f out and stl upsides: tk 2nd fnl 110yds but a hld by wnr on far side* **15/8**[1]

41 **3** ½ **Derbaas (USA)**[35] 4360 2-8-13 0 .... MartinDwyer 7 99
(E A L Dunlop) *lw: wnt lft s: t.k.h and led 1f: styd chsng ldrs: slt ld 2f out: hung lft u.p fr 1f out: hdd fnl 110yds: lost 2nd sn after* **5/1**[3]

511 **4** 1½ **Sohcahtoa (IRE)**[28] 4589 2-8-13 90 .... RichardHughes 2 96
(R Hannon) *in tch: drvn to press ldrs fr 2f out: edgd lft fr over 1f out: wknd ins fnl f* **4/1**[2]

3121 **5** ½ **Measurement (IRE)**[49] 3924 2-8-13 92 .... PatDobbs 5 95
(R Hannon) *wnt rt s: in rr: rdn 3f out: sme prog 2f out but nvr gng pce to chal ldrs* **13/2**

2316 **6** 4 **Maid For Music (IRE)**[36] 4348 2-8-8 84 .... RichardMullen 4 81
(E S McMahon) *chsd ldr after 1f: rdn over 2f out: wknd over 1f out* **22/1**

115 **7** 2¾ **Doctor Crane (USA)**[34] 4402 2-8-13 94 .... RobertHavlin 6 80
(J H M Gosden) *bmpd s: drvn to ld after 1f: hdd 2f out: sn btn* **12/1**

5 **8** 1¾ **Ayrus (USA)**[41] 4199 2-8-13 0 .... SteveDrowne 3 76
(B J Meehan) *w'like: strong: sn bhd* **28/1**

1m 42.47s (-1.03) **Going Correction** -0.075s/f (Good) **8 Ran SP% 112.8**
Speed ratings (Par 102): **102,101,101,99,99 95,92,90**
CSF £19.98 TOTE £9.00: £2.10, £1.40, £1.80; EX 19.50.
Owner J C Smith **Bred** Littleton Stud **Trained** Newmarket, Suffolk

FOCUS
Only a fair race for the grade, but there were a few nice long-term prospects on show. The likes of the fourth and fifth help set the level. The time was significantly quicker than that recorded by Red Reef in the earlier nursery over the same distance.

NOTEBOOK
Snoqualmie Girl(IRE), whose trainer/owner combination took this three years ago, has taken a while to come to herself but confirmed the promise of her third behind Rainbow View at Newmarket when winning back there in soft ground last time. Up to 1m for the first time, she was only going to improve for it on breeding and, having travelled nicely in behind the leaders, found plenty for pressure against the far-side rail, as the others drifted towards the stands' side. She was initially hanging left under pressure, but got straightened out and gives the impression there is more to come, something that was backed up by her trainer. (op 8-1)
On Our Way ◆, who confirmed previous promise when winning his maiden at Sandown last time, was solid at the head of the market. A fine, big sort, he travelled strongly throughout and came to have every chance, but wandered towards the stands' side, having been intimidated by the hanging Derbaas, and was not quite on terms with the winner as they crossed the line. He holds plenty of big entries and has a bright future, with the best of him unlikely to be seen until next season. (tchd 2-1 tchd 85-40 in a place)
Derbaas(USA) is entered in all the big races and confirmed the promise of his debut fourth when winning a fair maiden at Ascot (flashed tail under pressure). Up to 1m for the first time, he again showed signs of inexperience, hanging left under pressure, and was unable to pick up close home. It is possible the extra furlong proved beyond him at this stage of his career, but ahe does not look good enough to take up any of his Group-race engagements yet. (tchd 9-2 and 11-2)
Sohcahtoa(IRE), who needed all of the 7f trip when winning on his nursery debut at Goodwood, faced a stiffer task on this rise in grade, but was entitled to improve again for 1m (sire won Breeders' Cup Mile). Held up early on, he travelled well and looked a big threat over a furlong out, but was another carried slightly left under pressure and he could find no more. He may have been another who found the 1m a shade too far at this stage. (op 7-2)
Measurement(IRE), like stablemate Sohcahtoa, was stepping up in grade having won a nursery last time, and he too looked set to be suited by the step up to 1m. However, he was very awkward coming out of the stalls and ran rather flat, only being able to make some laboured late headway. He can probably be rated a little better than the bare form, but is not going to be the easiest to place. (op 8-1)
Maid For Music(IRE), a course-and-distance maiden winner who seemed to find the rise to this level beyond her at Sandown last time, was up a furlong in trip, but that made no difference and, having been up there early, she dropped away from two out. (op 18-1)
Doctor Crane(USA), who flopped in a Listed contest at Ascot last time when bidding for a hat-trick, had earlier looked a useful sort and was up to 1m for first time. He was done no favours by Measurement's awkward start and recovered quickly to lead, but found little once asked for maximum effort and dropped right out. This effort leaves him with plenty to prove. (tchd 9-1)
Ayrus(USA) shaped promisingly when fifth on his debut at Newmarket, but this was a big step up and he was too green to do himself justice. Easier opportunities will present themselves. (op 33-1 tchd 25-1)

5463 BATHWICK TYRES MAIDEN STKS 1m 1f 198y
6:40 (6:42) (Class 5) 3-4-Y-O **£3,885** (£1,156; £577; £288) **Stalls** High

Form RPR

345- **1** **Bazergan (IRE)**[312] 6382 3-9-3 102 ....(tp) LiamJones 8 81
(C E Brittain) *chsd ldrs: rdn 3f out: qcknd to ld over 1f out: hung bdly rt u.p fnl 100yds: styd on wl* **8/1**

3 **2** 1½ **Star Rocker**[27] 4620 3-9-3 0 ..... RobertHavlin 10 80+
(J H M Gosden) *lw: w'like: sn led: rdn 2f out: hdd over 1f out: styng on whn bdly hmpd and snatched up fnl 100yds: rallied to retake 2nd last strides but stl nt rcvr* **5/6**[1]
3 **3** nk **Wellington Square**[25] 4695 3-9-3 0 ..... SteveDrowne 7 77
(H Morrison) *strong: chsd ldrs: rdn and outpcd over 3f out: rallied to press ldrs over 1f out: styng on whn hmpd fnl 100yds but lft 2nd: no imp and pipped bk to 3rd last strides* **7/2**[2]
0232 **4** hd **Special Reserve (IRE)**[39] 4249 3-9-3 77 ..... RichardHughes 3 77
(R Hannon) *lw: trckd ldrs: rdn 2f out: swtchd lft to outside and kpt on ins fnl f: r.o cl home but nvr gng pce to chal* **9/2**[3]
0-0 **5** 1 **Colour Trooper (IRE)**[113] 1926 3-9-3 0 ..... StephenCarson 9 75
(P Winkworth) *sn chsng ldr: rdn and ev ch 2f out: wknd ins fnl f* **66/1**
6 4½ **Streets Apart (USA)** 3-8-12 0 ..... AdamKirby 2 61
(W R Swinburn) *w'like: scope: bit bkwd: wnt rt after 1f: in tch 1/2-way: rdn 3f out: sn outpcd* **20/1**
55 **7** nk **Chioroscuro**[28] 4581 3-9-3 0 ..... MartinDwyer 6 65
(J L Dunlop) *hmpd in rr after 1f: sme prog fnl 2f: nvr in contention* **40/1**
8 7 **Watercolours (IRE)** 3-8-12 0 ..... JimCrowley 4 46
(G L Moore) *w'like: bit bkwd: a towards rr* **33/1**
9 ½ **Tignello (IRE)** 3-9-3 0 ..... TQuinn 1 50
(D R C Elsworth) *rangy: bit bkwd: slowly away: a bhd* **33/1**
10 57 **Quick Flash** 3-8-12 0 .....(t) RichardKingscote 5 —
(R M Beckett) *leggy: scope: lw: in tch: rdn over 4f out: sn wknd: eased over 2f out: t.o* **33/1**

2m 11.0s (1.10) **Going Correction** +0.15s/f (Good) 10 Ran SP% **123.6**
Speed ratings (Par 103): **101,99,99,99,98 95,94,89,88,43**
CSF £15.50 TOTE £10.00: £2.30, £1.10, £1.50; EX 20.20.
Owner Saeed Manana **Bred** Darley **Trained** Newmarket, Suffolk
■ Stewards' Enquiry : Liam Jones four-day ban: careless riding (Sep 12,14-16)

FOCUS
A fair maiden but pretty sound form with the fourth the best guide backed up by the placed horses.
Quick Flash Official explanation: jockey said filly stumbled on road crossing and he didn't persevere thereafter

5464 STEPHEN & JENNIFER TILLEY MEMORIAL H'CAP 1m 4f
7:10 (7:11) (Class 4) (0-85,83) 3-Y-O **£4,857** (£1,445; £722; £360) **Stalls** High

Form RPR
3115 **1** **Fair Gale**[19] 4906 3-9-7 83 ..... RichardHughes 2 89
(S Kirk) *lw: mde all: shkn up 2f out: drvn and hld on wl thrght fnl f* **14/1**
4405 **2** 1¼ **Trianon**[27] 4619 3-8-11 73 .....(vt[1]) SteveDrowne 6 77
(R Charlton) *rdn s: t.k.h and sn chsng wnr: rdn over 2f out: nvr quite on terms w wnr and hung lft u.p fnl f but hld on all out for 2nd* **16/1**
4531 **3** ¾ **Killcara Boy**[27] 4619 3-9-6 82 ..... DaneO'Neill 8 85+
(H Candy) *chsd ldrs tl rdn and lost position over 3f out: styd on u.p fnl 2f and fin wl fnl f to cl on 2nd but no ch w wnr* **7/2**[2]
2112 **4** hd **Cosmea**[27] 4621 3-9-0 79 ..... TravisBlock(3) 4 81
(A King) *in tch: chsd ldrs 4f out: styng on whn carried lft fr 1f out: sn swtchd rt and kpt on same pce cl home* **7/4**[1]
1110 **5** shd **Precision Break (USA)**[53] 3793 3-9-0 76 ..... JohnEgan 3 78
(P F I Cole) *in rr: rdn over 2f out: styd on fr over 1f out and gng on cl home but nvr gng pce to be competitive* **9/1**
0120 **6** nk **Celtic Dragon**[63] 3459 3-9-0 76 ..... JimCrowley 1 78
(Mrs A J Perrett) *chsd ldrs: rdn over 2f out: styd wl there tl outpcd ins fnl f* **20/1**
0514 **7** 1 **Spider Silk**[19] 4906 3-9-2 78 ..... ShaneKelly 9 78
(W Jarvis) *in tch early: rdn and in rr 4f out: hung rt whn hrd drvn over 2f out: styd on fr over 1f out and kpt on wl cl home but nvr in contention* **12/1**
3131 **8** 2½ **Victoria Montoya**[36] 4351 3-9-4 80 .....(p) FrancisNorton 7 76
(A M Balding) *lw: hld up in rr: rdn and hdwy fr 3f out: nvr gng pce to be competitive and wknd fr 2f out* **13/2**[3]
140 **9** 1¾ **Mon Plaisir (USA)**[22] 4771 3-8-12 74 ..... TedDurcan 5 67
(J L Dunlop) *chsd ldrs: rdn 3f out: wknd 2f out* **17/2**

2m 38.69s (0.69) **Going Correction** +0.15s/f (Good) 9 Ran SP% **117.4**
Speed ratings (Par 102): **103,102,101,101,101 101,100,98,97**
CSF £215.67 CT £962.87 TOTE £16.50: £3.20, £4.50, £1.80; EX 230.10.
Owner Norman Ormiston **Bred** Hesmonds Stud Ltd **Trained** Upper Lambourn, Berks

FOCUS
A good handicap made up of largely progressive runners. The form could rate higher but the runner-up is the best guide for now.
Mon Plaisir(USA) Official explanation: jockey said colt had no more to give

5465 WESTOVER GROUP H'CAP 1m 6f 21y
7:40 (7:40) (Class 5) (0-70,70) 3-Y-O+ **£3,238** (£963; £481; £240)

Form RPR
6253 **1** **Colonel Flay**[34] 4432 4-9-9 70 ..... JackMitchell(5) 9 75
(Mrs P N Dutfield) *hld up in rr: rapid hdwy on outside over 2f out to ld appr fnl f: drvn out* **7/1**[3]
1343 **2** ½ **Hadron Collider (FR)**[15] 5027 3-9-2 70 ..... RichardHughes 2 74+
(R Hannon) *in tch: hdwy and rdn over 2f out: styd on wl to chse wnr ins fnl f: kpt on but a hld* **13/2**[2]
4364 **3** nk **Wester Ross (IRE)**[14] 5058 4-9-6 65 ..... LukeMorris(3) 12 69
(J M P Eustace) *in rr: hdwy over 2f out: rdn and hung lft whn styng on ins fnl f: kpt on cl home but a hld* **16/1**
0/ **4** 1 **Meneur (FR)**[167] 6-9-12 68 ..... GeorgeBaker 10 71
(G L Moore) *in tch: hdwy to press ldrs fr 3f out and slt ld ins fnl 2f: hdd appr fnl f: one pce ins fnl f* **8/1**
5333 **5** ½ **Fourth Dimension (IRE)**[9] 5183 9-9-12 68 ..... AdamKirby 5 72+
(Miss T Spearing) *in rr tl hdwy fr 3f out: styng on whn pushed lft and hmpd over 1f out: styd on whn hmpd again ins fnl f: kpt on again cl home* **12/1**
6225 **6** 1¼ **Urban Warrior**[15] 5027 4-9-9 65 ..... RichardMullen 8 65
(Ian Williams) *chsd ldrs tl led over 3f out: hdd ins fnl 2f: wknd fnl f* **8/1**
6330 **7** 3 **Rock Peak (IRE)**[16] 4985 3-9-2 70 ..... SteveDrowne 14 66
(H Morrison) *chsd ldrs: rdn 3f out: sn one pce but styd wl there: wknd fnl f* **11/4**[1]
533 **8** 1½ **Is It Me (USA)**[29] 4410 5-9-8 64 ..... TedDurcan 4 58
(A W Carroll) *led tl hdd 10f out: styd pressing ldrs to 3f out: wknd ins fnl 2f* **9/1**
010 **9** 3¼ **Shenandoah Girl**[9] 5183 5-8-12 61 .....(p) KylieManser(7) 1 50
(Miss Gay Kelleway) *in rr tl rapid hdwy fr 3f out to chse ldrs over 2f out: hung lft and wknd over 1f out* **16/1**
1533 **10** 1¼ **Lapina (IRE)**[22] 4775 4-9-4 60 .....(p) ShaneKelly 7 48
(Pat Eddery) *towards rr most of way* **8/1**
40/0 **11** nk **Towerofcharlemagne (IRE)**[44] 4078 5-9-4 60 .....(p) PatDobbs 3 47
(Miss E C Lavelle) *chsd ldrs: chal 3f out: wknd qckly 2f out* **40/1**
6530 **12** 15 **Ocean Avenue (IRE)**[21] 4820 9-9-2 58 .....(p) TQuinn 13 24
(C A Horgan) *plld hrd: led 10f out: hdd over 3f out: sn btn* **14/1**

3m 8.26s (0.86) **Going Correction** +0.15s/f (Good)
WFA 3 from 4yo+ 12lb 12 Ran SP% **124.4**
Speed ratings (Par 103): **103,102,102,101,101 100,99,98,96,95 95,87**
CSF £54.79 CT £724.53 TOTE £10.10: £2.60, £2.20, £5.90; EX 64.80 Place 6 £142.23, Place 5 £48.36.
Owner John Boswell **Bred** Mrs Nerys Dutfield **Trained** Axmouth, Devon

FOCUS
An open handicap in which any number could be given a chance. The form looks sound with the placed horses to their marks.
Fourth Dimension(IRE) Official explanation: jockey said gelding hung right-handed in the straight
T/Plt: £152.10 to a £1 stake. Pool: £43,372.64. 208.15 winning tickets. T/Qpdt: £53.80 to a £1 stake. Pool: £3,130.80. 43.00 winning tickets. ST

5028 SANDOWN (R-H)
Friday, August 29

OFFICIAL GOING: Sprint course - good to firm (good in places); round course - good (good to firm in places)
Wind: Almost nil Weather: Overcast, humid

5466 SIGN UP BONUS AT BETINTERNET.COM NURSERY 5f 6y
2:10 (2:11) (Class 4) 2-Y-O **£6,476** (£1,927; £963; £481) **Stalls** High

Form RPR
2501 **1** **Mythical Blue (IRE)**[13] 5103 2-8-1 74 .....(t) DavidProbert(5) 13 75
(S C Williams) *led to jst over 2f out: sn rdn: styd on to ld again 150yds out: jst hld on* **15/8**[1]
01 **2** hd **Lady Master**[34] 4411 2-8-4 72 ..... FrankieMcDonald 6 74+
(H Candy) *chsd ldrs: cl up whn nt clr run ent fnl f: eased out and r.o fnl 100yds: jst failed* **25/1**
4100 **3** hd **Fault**[17] 4942 2-9-2 84 ..... SteveDrowne 14 84
(R Charlton) *racd against rail: pressed ldr: led jst over 2f out: drvn and hdd last 150yds: no ex* **20/1**
2231 **4** 2 **Timeteam (IRE)**[28] 4579 2-8-9 77 ..... PatDobbs 7 70
(S Kirk) *chsd ldrs: drvn 2f out: nt qckn 1f out: one pce fnl f* **14/1**
5023 **5** ¾ **You've Been Mowed**[34] 4411 2-8-2 70 ..... AdrianMcCarthy 8 60
(D K Ivory) *sn off the pce towards rr: rdn 1/2-way: styd on ins fnl f: nrst fin* **20/1**
310 **6** ¾ **Tishtar**[27] 4626 2-9-4 86 ..... RichardHughes 11 73
(R Hannon) *settled in rr: outpcd and struggling bef 1/2-way: no ch after: kpt on fnl f* **11/2**[3]
201 **7** ½ **Aakef (IRE)**[22] 4792 2-9-1 83 ..... RHills 2 69
(M A Jarvis) *cl up: rdn to press ldng pair on outer over 1f out: wknd ins fnl f* **5/1**[2]
2005 **8** 1 **Pocket's Pick (IRE)**[22] 4768 2-8-13 81 ..... RyanMoore 10 63+
(G L Moore) *restrained s: hld up in rr: bdly outpcd after 2f and struggling: kpt on fnl f: no ch* **17/2**
0200 **8** dht **Sweet Applause (IRE)**[8] 5204 2-8-5 80 ..... MatthewDavies(7) 5 62
(A P Jarvis) *chsd ldrs: hrd rdn 2f out: wknd jst over 1f out* **25/1**
4144 **10** 2¼ **Red Rossini (IRE)**[13] 5103 2-8-10 78 ..... EddieAhern 9 52
(R Hannon) *dwlt: last whn hmpd on inner wl over 3f out: detached after and no ch: kpt on steadily fnl f* **12/1**
3241 **11** 10 **Mazzola**[27] 4628 2-9-3 85 ..... SamHitchcott 1 23
(M R Channon) *s.i.s: rcvrd to press ldrs on outer: wknd rapidly 2f out: t.o* **20/1**
0204 **12** 8 **Court Approval (IRE)**[19] 4905 2-8-5 73 ..... WilliamBuick 12 —
(T G Mills) *prom 1f: lost pl bdly and sn bhd: t.o* **16/1**

62.61 secs (1.01) **Going Correction** +0.15s/f (Good) 12 Ran SP% **119.6**
Speed ratings (Par 96): **97,96,96,93,91 90,89,88,88,84 68,55**
toteswinger: 1&2 £19.40, 1&3 £18.20, 2&3 £109.30. CSF £65.26 CT £738.15 TOTE £2.80: £1.40, £6.90, £5.70; EX 74.70.
Owner Chris Watkins And David N Reynolds **Bred** John O'Dowd **Trained** Newmarket, Suffolk

FOCUS
A competitive nursery which produced an exciting finish. The majority of the runners were fairly exposed, but five had won on their previous start.

NOTEBOOK
Mythical Blue(IRE), who appreciated the drop to 5f when landing a gamble in a first-time tongue tie at Newmarket, took a while to pick up after travelling well up with the pace from a good draw, but showed plenty of tenacity. He had little to spare but should not go up much and his good cruising speed and determination should enable him to win again. (op 2-1 tchd 9-4)
Lady Master ◆ had to wait to find a gap against the far rail, but quickened well when seeing daylight and just failed to supplement her front-running Lingfield maiden success. She looks a quick learner, has scope for further progress and is one to note in a similar race next time. (op 22-1 tchd 20-1)
Fault has been a bit disappointing since his Bath nursery win off 2lb lower in July, but got back on track here, showing good pace throughout and being only narrowly beaten by two progressive types.
Timeteam(IRE) had an easy time up front when winning at Bath last time. He was ridden more patiently here, in a race involving some very precocious types, but stayed on steadily and ran a solid race.
You've Been Mowed was in trouble some way out but did stay on fairly well and gave the impression that an extra furlong could suit.
Tishtar disappointed again, but connections were adamant that the ground, which Richard Hughes insisted was much softer than advertised, was to blame. (op 9-2)
Aakef(IRE) has a host of big-race entries and looked potentially well treated. Although well held, he deserves some credit because he had to use up a fair amount of energy from his difficult draw to get into the race. He could be worth another chance. (op 9-2 tchd 4-1)
Pocket's Pick(IRE) was reported by his rider to have run too free. Official explanation: jockey said colt ran too free (op 12-1)
Court Approval(IRE) was reported to have moved poorly throughout. Official explanation: jockey said colt moved poorly throughout

5467 BEST ODDS GUARANTEED AT BETINTERNET.COM H'CAP 5f 6y
2:45 (2:45) (Class 5) (0-75,75) 3-Y-O+ **£4,857** (£1,445; £722; £360) **Stalls** High

Form RPR
3223 **1** **Even Bolder**[7] 5250 5-9-7 73 ..... StephenCarson 7 88
(E A Wheeler) *w ldng pair: led jst over 2f out: sn rdn clr: in n.d whn edgd lft ins fnl f* **9/2**[2]
050 **2** 3¼ **Pic Up Sticks**[13] 5101 9-8-10 62 ..... RHills 2 65
(B G Powell) *settled in last pair: rdn and prog 2f out: chsd wnr 1f out: no imp at all: jst hld on for 2nd* **14/1**

0226 3 shd **Steelcut**[7] 5250 4-9-2 **75**........ FrederikTylicki(7) 6 78
(R A Fahey) *rdn towards rr after 2f: effrt u.p over 1f out: styd on to press for 2nd nr fin* **5/1**[3]

1/3- 4 ½ **Gold Express**[447] 2479 5-9-3 **69**........ AlanMunro 11 70+
(P J O'Gorman) *trckd ldrs: n.m.r fr 2f out: got through ins fnl f: styd on one pce* **15/2**

0346 5 1¾ **Replicator**[65] 3374 3-9-2 **70**........ PatDobbs 4 65+
(Pat Eddery) *stdd s: hld up in fnl pair: prog on inner over 1f out: short of room ent fnl f: swtchd lft 100yds out and styd on* **25/1**

4504 6 1¼ **Bertie Southstreet**[16] 4981 5-9-2 **68**........(b) SteveDrowne 12 58
(J R Best) *racd against rail: w ldr: rdn 1/2-way: outpcd over 1f out: wknd ins fnl f* **5/1**[3]

0100 6 dht **Rocker**[7] 5247 4-9-0 **66**........(b) RyanMoore 8 56
(G L Moore) *mde most to jst over 2f out: chsd wnr to 1f out: wknd* **7/2**[1]

5131 8 7 **Night Rocket (IRE)**[15] 5026 4-9-4 **70**........(t) FrancisNorton 5 35
(A M Balding) *chsd ldrs on outer: wknd rapidly fr 2f out: bhd fnl f* **7/1**

021 9 1½ **Diane's Choice**[5] 5319 5-9-8 **74** 6ex........ KShea 9 33
(Miss Gay Kelleway) *chsd ldrs: losing pl whn bdly hmpd over 1f out: eased* **10/1**

62.12 secs (0.52) **Going Correction** +0.15s/f (Good)
WFA 3 from 4yo+ 2lb **9** Ran SP% **117.6**
Speed ratings (Par 103): **101,95,95,94,92 90,90,78,76**
toteswinger: 1&2 £11.00, 1&3 £6.30, 2&3 £14.80. CSF £65.99 CT £332.30 TOTE £5.20: £1.70, £3.20, £2.30; EX 78.50.
Owner Astrod TA Austin Stroud & Co **Bred** Raffin Bloodstock **Trained** Whitchurch-on-Thames, Oxon

FOCUS
This looked a wide-open contest but was run at a steady pace and the winner scored decisively. The form is best rated around the first two.
Night Rocket(IRE) Official explanation: jockey said filly ran flat
Diane's Choice Official explanation: vet said mare returned with cut to left-fore

5468 BETINTERNET.COM E B F MAIDEN STKS (DIV I) 7f 16y
3:20 (3:21) (Class 4) 2-Y-O £4,857 (£1,445; £722; £360) **Stalls** High

Form RPR

1 **Anmar (USA)** 2-9-3 0........ LDettori 4 81+
(Saeed Bin Suroor) *sn trckd ldr: led 3f out to 2f out: led again jst over 1f out: rdn out* **5/1**[2]

2 ½ **Souter Point (USA)** 2-9-3 0........ SteveDrowne 7 80+
(R Charlton) *dwlt: wl in rr: shkn up over 2f out: taken to outer and gd prog over 1f out: r.o to take 2nd nr fin* **16/1**

3 nk **Liberation (IRE)** 2-9-3 0........ PatCosgrave 10 79+
(M Johnston) *sn towards rr: effrt and nt clr run over 2f out: prog over 1f out: drvn and r.o fnl f: nrst fin* **8/1**[3]

4 hd **Ra Junior (USA)** 2-9-3 0........ WilliamBuick 2 79+
(B J Meehan) *dwlt: rn green in rr on outer: rapid prog fr 3f out to ld 2f out: unable to sustain effrt and hdd jst over 1f out: lost 2 pls nr fin* **10/1**

5 1 **Lonely Star (IRE)** 2-8-12 0........ TPQueally 5 73+
(D R Lanigan) *wl in rr: gd prog on outer over 2f out: looked dangerous over 1f out: one pce fnl f* **20/1**

6 1¾ **Alazeyab (USA)** 2-9-3 0........ RHills 13 72+
(M A Jarvis) *trckd ldng pair to over 2f out: sn outpcd: pushed along and kpt on steadily fr over 1f out* **8/1**[3]

7 1 **Glass Harmonium (IRE)** 2-9-3 0........ RyanMoore 11 69+
(Sir Michael Stoute) *settled in midfield: pushed along 2f out: styd on steadily fr over 1f out: nvr on terms: bttr for r* **8/1**[3]

8 ½ **Durgan** 2-9-3 0........ PhilipRobinson 1 68
(C G Cox) *led at mod pce to 3f out: wknd jst over 1f out* **20/1**

9 1¾ **Roman Glory (IRE)** 2-9-3 0........ EddieAhern 16 64+
(B J Meehan) *trckd ldrs: lost pl over 2f out: shuffled bk again over 1f out: pushed along briefly fnl f and styd on* **14/1**

6 10 nk **Hydrant**[42] 4151 2-9-3 0........ AlanMunro 6 63+
(P W Chapple-Hyam) *chsd ldrs: rdn over 2f out: no prog whn nt clr run sn after: n.d* **3/1**[1]

11 ½ **Charlie Smirke (USA)** 2-9-3 0........ GeorgeBaker 9 62+
(G L Moore) *wl enough plcd in midfield: nt clr run 2f out and again over 1f out: pushed along and kpt on steadily* **33/1**

12 1½ **Classic Vintage (USA)** 2-9-3 0........ AdamKirby 14 58
(Mrs A J Perrett) *s.s: wl in rr: brief effrt over 2f out: sn no real prog* **33/1**

13 1 **Gtaab** 2-9-3 0........ NeilPollard 3 56+
(E A L Dunlop) *dwlt: a in rr: no prog fnl 2f: bttr for r* **50/1**

14 2½ **Manolito Montoya (IRE)** 2-8-12 0........(b[1]) GabrielHannon(5) 12 49
(J W Hills) *t.k.h: cl up tl wknd wl over 1f out* **66/1**

3 15 2¼ **Spinning Waters**[22] 4776 2-9-3 0........ StephenCarson 15 44
(Eve Johnson Houghton) *trckd ldrs: rdn and lost pl over 2f out: sn no ch* **14/1**

16 2¼ **Mojeerr** 2-9-3 0........ DaneO'Neill 8 38
(M P Tregoning) *rn green in midfield: wknd over 2f out* **25/1**

1m 33.05s (3.55) **Going Correction** +0.15s/f (Good) **16** Ran SP% **126.0**
Speed ratings (Par 96): **85,84,84,83,82 80,79,79,77,76 76,74,73,70,67 65**
toteswinger: 1&2 £22.50, 1&3 £6.60, 2&3 £32.80. CSF £78.89 TOTE £5.90: £2.20, £5.40, £3.00; EX 136.10.
Owner Godolphin **Bred** Shadwell Farm LLC **Trained** Newmarket, Suffolk

FOCUS
Hydrant set a fair standard but faced several well-bred and expensive rivals making their debut. The only newcomer to attract notable support was the eventual winner Anmar. Despite a moderate winning time which was 1.44 seconds slower than the second division, the form could be very decent and is worth following.

NOTEBOOK
Anmar(USA) ◆ was always well positioned near the steady pace, showed a gritty attitude to keep responding for pressure and put in a really promising performance on his debut. He has a good physique, looked likely to improve for this experience and holds entries in the Dewhurst and Racing Post Trophy. He is one to keep a close eye on this autumn. (op 13-2)
Souter Point(USA) ◆ fetched $160,000 at the breeze-ups and ran a really encouraging race on his debut, staying on really well from an unpromising position and just failing to reel in the winner.
Liberation(IRE) ◆ had to weave his way through the field after being held up but knuckled down really well to be nearest at the finish. He is a half-brother to the smart middle-distance performer Subtle Power and should improve with time and a more demanding test. (op 11-1)
Ra Junior(USA) raced wide, swept into contention and looked a likely winner at one stage, but could not quite sustain his effort. This was still a very pleasing debut from a comparatively cheap 50,000gns purchase. (op 16-1)
Lonely Star(IRE) ◆ showed good tactical pace for a long way and performed admirably against the colts on her debut. She will have learned a lot from this experience and should have no trouble winning a maiden at this trip. (op 16-1)
Alazeyab(USA) got a good position against the far rail and showed ability staying on steadily. (tchd 9-1)
Glass Harmonium(IRE) ◆, who looked in need of the race, ran green but stuck to his task. He could step up significantly on this next time. (op 11-2)
Roman Glory(IRE) wasn't given at all a hard time and is another who can do a lot better. Official explanation: jockey said colt was denied a clear run (op 20-1 tchd 25-1)
Hydrant failed to improve on his Newbury debut but may well be capable of better when the stable returns to form. (op 10-3 tchd 11-4 and 7-2 in a place)

5469 BETINTERNET.COM E B F MAIDEN STKS (DIV II) 7f 16y
3:55 (3:57) (Class 4) 2-Y-O £4,857 (£1,445; £722; £360) **Stalls** High

Form RPR

30 1 **Brief Candle**[29] 4554 2-8-12 0........(t) AdamKirby 6 82+
(W R Swinburn) *settled midfield: nt clrest of runs fr over 2f out: weaved through fr over 1f out: styd on wl to ld fnl strides* **10/1**

2 2 nk **Summers Target (USA)**[35] 4360 2-9-3 0........ AlanMunro 13 84
(B J Meehan) *sn trckd ldr: shkn up to ld 2f out: rdn fnl f: hdd fnl strides* **4/5**[1]

3 2¼ **Sayyaaf** 2-9-3 0........ WilliamBuick 11 78
(B W Hills) *coltish paddock: wl plcd on inner: prog 2f out: chsd ldr jst over 1f out and looked dangerous: one pce fnl f* **33/1**

4 1 **Ithbaat (USA)** 2-9-3 0........ RHills 16 77+
(J H M Gosden) *s.i.s: wl in rr: nt clr run over 2f out: stdy prog on inner over 1f out: pushed along and styd on: nrst fin* **8/1**[3]

5 nse **Spring Of Fame (USA)** 2-9-3 0........ TPQueally 5 76
(M A Magnusson) *wl in rr: shuffled along 3f out: prog fr 2f out: styd on wl fnl f: nrst fin* **40/1**

6 ½ **Cabernet Sauvignon** 2-9-3 0........ EddieAhern 3 75+
(J W Hills) *dwlt: wl in rr: pushed along and prog fr jst over 2f out: kpt on fnl f: nrst fin* **66/1**

0 7 1½ **Qelaan (USA)**[14] 5048 2-8-12 0........ HayleyTurner 7 66
(M P Tregoning) *led at fair pce to 2f out: wknd fnl f* **50/1**

8 nk **Block Party** 2-9-3 0........ SteveDrowne 2 70+
(R Charlton) *s.s: last and sn wl bhd: shkn up 3f out: styd on fnl 2f: nrst fin* **33/1**

9 ¾ **Causeway King (USA)** 2-9-3 0........ LDettori 8 68
(M Johnston) *trckd ldrs: shkn up over 2f out: wknd over 1f out* **12/1**

10 1 **Cygnet** 2-9-3 0........ DaneO'Neill 9 66
(L M Cumani) *in tch in midfield on outer: rdn over 2f out: wknd over 1f out* **33/1**

04 11 ½ **Hambledon Hill**[22] 4788 2-9-0 0........ PatrickHills(3) 10 64
(R Hannon) *chsd ldrs: rdn over 2f out: steadily wknd fr wl over 1f out* **25/1**

12 2¾ **Herschel (IRE)** 2-9-3 0........ GeorgeBaker 4 58+
(G L Moore) *disp 2nd pl: stl cl up 2f out: fdd over 1f out: eased* **40/1**

5 13 4½ **Mr Deal**[11] 5143 2-9-3 0........ StephenCarson 1 46
(Eve Johnson Houghton) *nvr on terms w ldrs: struggling in rr over 2f out* **66/1**

14 1 **December** 2-9-3 0........ RyanMoore 12 44+
(Sir Michael Stoute) *trckd ldrs: shkn up 2f out: lost pl over 1f out: eased whn btn fnl f* **4/1**[2]

1m 31.61s (2.11) **Going Correction** +0.15s/f (Good) **14** Ran SP% **125.9**
Speed ratings (Par 96): **93,92,90,88,88 88,86,86,85,84 83,80,75,74**
toteswinger: 1&2 £4.80, 1&3 £53.10, 2&3 £14.80. CSF £18.19 TOTE £17.70: £3.70, £1.10, £9.60; EX 35.30.
Owner Exors Of The Late Mrs P W Harris **Bred** Pendley Farm **Trained** Aldbury, Herts

FOCUS
A very interesting event. Summers Target set a decent standard on form but faced a number of newcomers with six-figure price-tags and multiple Group entries. The field generally looked a bit more tuned up than the runners in the earlier division and the time was 1.44 seconds quicker.

NOTEBOOK
Brief Candle ◆ had an excuse when stumbling and racing keenly from a difficult draw at Goodwood last time but put in an impressive performance here, with a tongue tie applied for the first time. She was always travelling sweetly, was denied a run on several occasions but eventually quickened up well to catch the favourite in the dying strides. She is value for more than the winning margin, looks useful prospect and her next target is likely to be the Fillies' Mile at Ascot. (op 8-1)
Summers Target(USA) ◆, the form of whose narrow defeat at Ascot last month has worked out really well, almost justified strong market support here. He travelled smoothly near the pace and was just reeled in by a useful rival. The first two finished a little way clear of the third, and he can gain compensation next time. (op 11-10 tchd 8-11 tchd 5-4 and 6-5 in a place)
Sayyaaf is entered in the Derby and ran a promising race on his debut, particularly as he was unfancied. (op 50-1)
Ithbaat(USA) ◆ got behind at an early stage and looked inexperienced, but found a decent finishing effort and would be very interesting in a similar race next time. (op 14-1)
Spring Of Fame(USA) ◆ cost $170,000 and holds some high-profile entries. He looked like this experience would do him good and showed quite a bit of ability, staying on steadily from a difficult position. (op 66-1)
Cabernet Sauvignon ◆, whose pedigree suggests a stiffer test might ideally suit, also stayed on steadily. (tchd 50-1)
Block Party's sales price rose from 58,000gns to 140,000gns as a yearling. He had a difficult task from a tough draw on his debut and was almost detached at an early stage, but found a really good burst down the outside to be nearest at the finish. (op 40-1)
Causeway King(USA) ◆ showed up well for a long way on his debut and should do better next time. (op 8-1)

5470 PLAY LIVE CASINO AT BETINTERNET.COM H'CAP 1m 14y
4:30 (4:37) (Class 3) (0-90,90) 3-Y-O+
£9,346 (£2,799; £1,399; £700; £349; £175) **Stalls** High

Form RPR

1004 1 **Fervent Prince**[29] 4553 3-9-8 **90**........ TravisBlock(3) 8 102
(H Morrison) *settled wl in rr: rdn wl over 2f out: prog fr 2f out and gd run through: r.o to ld fnl 75yds* **8/1**

2141 2 ¾ **Isphahan**[22] 4789 5-9-2 **75**........ WilliamBuick 2 86
(A M Balding) *racd towards outer in midfield: rdn and prog over 2f out: led over 1f out: kpt on fnl f: hdd fnl 75yds* **13/2**[3]

4141 3 1¼ **Ebn Malk (IRE)**[15] 5032 3-9-3 **82**........ RHills 7 89
(M A Jarvis) *settled towards rr: taken to outer and prog wl over 1f out: tried to chal jst ins fnl f: nt qckn and sn hld* **5/1**[2]

2000 4 1¾ **Danehillsundance (IRE)**[27] 4649 4-9-12 **85**........ EddieAhern 11 89+
(S Parr) *led after 1f: drvn and hdd over 1f out: grad fdd* **16/1**

6011 5 shd **Admiral Dundas (IRE)**[23] 4741 3-9-2 **81**........ LDettori 9 90+
(W Jarvis) *hld up in midfield: trapped bhd wkng rival fr over 2f out and lost pl completely: last over 1f out: styd on again ins fnl f* **7/1**

105 6 1¼ **Rattan (USA)**[50] 3880 3-9-9 **88**........ TPQueally 10 88
(H R A Cecil) *trckd ldrs on inner: drvn and nt qckn wl over 1f out: one pce after* **8/1**

1201 7 2½ **Carlitos Spirit (IRE)**[28] 4603 4-9-8 **81**........ AlanMunro 3 76
(B R Millman) *t.k.h early: cl up: grad wknd fr wl over 1f out* **12/1**

2322 **8** *nse* **Billy Dane (IRE)**[29] 4576 4-9-1 **81**..........................(p) FrederikTylicki[(7)] 4 76
(R A Fahey) *hld up in midfield and racd wd: prog over 2f out: clsd and looked a threat over 1f out: edgd rt and wknd fnl f* **9/2**[1]

2044 **9** *2 1/4* **Prince Of Thebes (IRE)**[4] 5350 7-9-5 **78**.............................. PaulDoe 6 68
(M J Attwater) *led 1f: chsd ldr to over 2f out: wknd wl over 1f out* **14/1**

6006 **10** *nk* **Southandwest (IRE)**[15] 5030 4-9-12 **85**.............................. GeorgeBaker 12 77+
(J S Moore) *stdd s: towards rr on inner: rdn over 2f out: no prog over 1f out: eased ins fnl f* **33/1**

4-00 **11** *nse* **Eastern Gift**[113] 1923 3-9-9 **88**.............................. RyanMoore 1 76
(R Hannon) *a in rr: last and detached 1/2-way: effrt u.p 2f out: no hdwy 1f out: wknd* **33/1**

5254 **12** *2* **Aye Aye Digby (IRE)**[13] 5096 3-9-11 **90**.............................. DaneO'Neill 5 74
(H Candy) *t.k.h early: hld up in rr on outer: rdn and no real prog over 2f out: wknd ins fnl f* **15/2**

1m 43.04s (-0.26) **Going Correction** +0.15s/f (Good)
WFA 3 from 4yo+ 6lb **12** Ran SP% **120.8**
Speed ratings (Par 107): **107,106,105,103,103 101,99,99,97,96 96,94**
toteswinger: 1&2 £14.80, 1&3 £11.80, 2&3 £7.40. CSF £60.45 CT £294.57 TOTE £10.60: £3.40, £2.70, £1.90; EX 85.10 Trifecta £501.40 Pool: £813.10 - 1.20 winning units..
Owner Thurloe Finsbury II **Bred** Fonthill Stud **Trained** East Ilsley, Berks

FOCUS
An open contest that produced another tight finish and at least one hard-luck story. Despite that the form looks reasonably solid rated through the third.

NOTEBOOK
Fervent Prince had looked on a prohibitive mark since two 7f wins in the spring, but benefited from the step up to 1m and found further improvement to pounce late under an accomplished ride. He should not go up much for this win and could have some more room to successfully operate, particularly now that he has conclusively proved his ability to stay this trip. He is one for the big handicaps next year, and in the interim possibly the Dubai Carnival. (tchd 9-1 in places)
Isphahan managed to win fairly decisively over the course and distance last time despite some steering problems. He ran much straighter here and put in a bold bid to follow up, producing a personal best. He should continue to run well and his ability to handle slow ground could be a valuable asset this autumn. (op 7-1)
Ebn Malk(IRE) had registered two wins on taxing ground on his last three starts. He coped fairly well with this faster surface and still looks on a feasible mark, so could manage a third win this season. (tchd 9-2)
Danehillsundance(IRE) had gone off the boil since registering three wins last season, but is now 4lb lower than his last winning mark and gave a hint of revival switched to more positive tactics. He seems to appreciate a sound surface. (tchd 20-1)
Admiral Dundas(IRE) ◆ kept finding his path blocked all the way up the straight and was forced back into last position at one point. He was unlucky not to have finished much closer in his bid to complete a hat-trick since being gelded. Official explanation: jockey said gelding was denied a clear run (tchd 6-1)
Rattan(USA) could not really pick up but ran a respectable race. He has produced his best form on good to soft and could do much better on easier ground next time. (op 7-1)
Southandwest(IRE) Official explanation: jockey said gelding suffered interference
Eastern Gift has been gelded since his last run but ran no sort of race. (op 25-1)

5471 CELEBRATING 10 YEARS AT BETINTERNET.COM MAIDEN FILLIES' STKS 1m 14y
5:00 (5:06) (Class 5) 3-Y-O **£3,885** (£1,156; £577; £288) **Stalls** High

Form RPR

-025 **1** **Lambda (USA)**[50] 3866 3-9-0 78.............................. RyanMoore 8 78
(Sir Michael Stoute) *trckd ldng pair: led over 2f out: sn rdn wl clr: eased nr fin* **5/4**[1]

6 **2** *7* **Turfwolke (GER)**[14] 5057 3-9-0 0.............................. EddieAhern 4 60
(J W Hills) *s.i.s: sn in tch: lft in 3rd 3f out: drvn and outpcd over 2f out: kpt on to take 2nd last 100yds* **25/1**

4032 **3** *1 1/2* **Marraasi (USA)**[41] 4183 3-9-0 67.............................. RHills 6 57
(M P Tregoning) *trckd ldr: led 3f out: hdd over 2f out: wknd and lost 2nd fnl 100yds* **9/4**[2]

0006 **4** *5* **Amyann (IRE)**[24] 4702 3-9-0 47.............................. SimonWhitworth 7 44
(J R Holt) *chsd ldrs: outpcd fr 3f out: no ch after* **66/1**

50 **5** *1* **Katy Kitten (UAE)**[58] 3611 3-9-0 0.............................. WilliamBuick 1 42
(G L Moore) *in tch towards rr: rdn and lft wl bhd fr over 2f out* **33/1**

2 **6** *1 3/4* **Classic Lass**[38] 4283 3-9-0 0.............................. AlanMunro 3 37
(Rae Guest) *towards rr: rdn and struggling over 3f out: sn no ch* **6/1**

7 *1 1/4* **Actress Annie** 3-9-0 0.............................. HayleyTurner 2 34
(Mike Murphy) *s.v.s: a last and wl adrift* **50/1**

5026 **P** **Queen's Speech (IRE)**[15] 5019 3-9-0 72..........................(b) LDettori 5 —
(J H M Gosden) *racd wd early: led: hdd and broke down 3f out: p.u* **9/2**[3]

1m 45.69s (2.39) **Going Correction** +0.15s/f (Good) **8** Ran SP% **117.9**
Speed ratings (Par 97): **94,87,85,80,79 77,76,—**
toteswinger: 1&2 £7.30, 1&3 £1.60, 2&3 £7.70. CSF £38.50 TOTE £2.30: £1.30, £3.80, £1.10; EX 34.60.
Owner Niarchos Family **Bred** Flaxman Holdings Ltd **Trained** Newmarket, Suffolk

FOCUS
An ordinary looking maiden won decisively by the favourite. The pace was only modest and the poor fourth is the best guide to the form.

5472 BETINTERNET.COM H'CAP 1m 2f 7y
5:30 (5:45) (Class 4) (0-80,78) 3-Y-O **£7,123** (£2,119; £1,059; £529) **Stalls** High

Form RPR

0361 **1** **Kingdom Of Fife**[16] 4984 3-9-7 **76**.............................. RyanMoore 8 84+
(Sir Michael Stoute) *hld up in last pair: prog on wd outside over 2f out: drvn to ld 1f out: all out but hld on wl* **7/2**[2]

0066 **2** *1/2* **Fitzroy Crossing (USA)**[32] 4489 3-9-6 **75**.............................. RHills 1 82
(M Johnston) *trckd ldr: led 3f out: drvn and hdd over 1f out: kpt on wl fnl f* **12/1**

0-05 **3** *shd* **Falcativ**[27] 4620 3-8-9 **71**.............................. MJMurphy[(7)] 12 78+
(L M Cumani) *t.k.h early: hld up in midfield: lost pl 1/2-way: renewed effrt over 2f out: r.o to chal 1f out: styd on same pce* **10/1**

5206 **4** *nse* **Danamight (IRE)**[21] 4819 3-8-6 **61**.............................. WilliamBuick 10 68+
(J L Dunlop) *hld up towards rr: trbld passage fr 3f out: trying to cl whn nt clr run 1f out: swtchd lft: r.o wl last 100yds: gaining fin* **16/1**

1133 **5** *4* **Storyland (USA)**[63] 3433 3-9-7 **76**.............................. LDettori 9 75
(W J Haggas) *last early: prog on outer 7f out: chsd ldrs over 2f out: drvn and hdwy to chal over 1f out: n.m.r ent fnl f: wknd* **10/3**[1]

1544 **6** *2* **Palmerin**[16] 4984 3-9-6 **78**.............................. PatrickHills[(3)] 2 73
(R Hannon) *hld up in rr on outer: prog over 2f out: rdn to ld over 1f out: fnd nil in front and immediately gave up* **5/1**[3]

3015 **7** *1* **Sinbad The Sailor**[27] 4621 3-9-6 **75**.............................. AlanMunro 7 68+
(J W Hills) *hld up in midfield: trbld passage fr 3f out: clsng on ldrs u.p whn no room 1f out: eased* **8/1**

1540 **8** *1 1/2* **House Of Lords (USA)**[19] 4906 3-9-8 **77**.............................. HayleyTurner 4 67
(M L W Bell) *trckd ldng pair: hrd rdn over 2f out: wknd over 1f out* **12/1**

2501 **9** *1/2* **Flying Applause**[32] 4481 3-9-8 **77**.............................. EddieAhern 5 74+
(A King) *led to 3f out: cl up but hld whn hmpd on inner over 1f out: eased* **8/1**

1000 **10** *3/4* **Stock Market (USA)**[55] 3736 3-9-7 **76**..........................(vt[1]) PatCosgrave 6 64
(E A L Dunlop) *trckd ldng trio: u.str.p and no rspnse 2f out: wknd and eased* **25/1**

5115 **11** *3 1/4* **A Dream Come True**[11] 5146 3-8-9 **69**....... Louis-PhilippeBeuzelin[(5)] 11 50
(D K Ivory) *dropped to last over 6f out: struggling after* **25/1**

2m 10.7s (0.20) **Going Correction** +0.15s/f (Good) **11** Ran SP% **122.2**
Speed ratings (Par 102): **105,104,104,104,101 99,98,97,97,96 94**
toteswinger: 1&2 £9.80, 1&3 £7.80, 2&3 £20.40. CSF £47.48 CT £390.03 TOTE £4.30: £1.90, £4.20, £3.20; EX 55.20 Place 6: £78.98 Place 5: £38.24 .
Owner The Queen **Bred** The Queen **Trained** Newmarket, Suffolk
■ Stewards' Enquiry : Ryan Moore caution: careless riding

FOCUS
They only went a fair pace and the field was tightly bunched in the early stages. They finished in a bit of a heap, with several enjoying little luck and the runner-up is the best guide to the level.
Sinbad The Sailor Official explanation: jockey said colt was denied a clear run
Flying Applause Official explanation: jockey said gelding suffered interference in running
T/Jkpt: Not won. T/Plt: £215.30 to a £1 stake. Pool: £73,700.41. 249.78 winning tickets. T/Qpdt: £23.40 to a £1 stake. Pool: £4,107.60. 129.40 winning tickets. JN

5152 WOLVERHAMPTON (A.W) (L-H)
Friday, August 29
OFFICIAL GOING: Standard
Wind: Light, behind Weather: Overcast

5473 HOTEL & CONFERENCING AT WOLVERHAMPTON CLAIMING STKS 5f 216y(P)
6:50 (6:50) (Class 5) 2-Y-O **£2,914** (£867; £433; £216) **Stalls** Low

Form RPR

644 **1** **Alphabeth**[14] 5043 2-8-4 67.............................. MCGeran[(5)] 9 64
(M R Channon) *chsd ldr tl led 5f out: hdd wl over 3f out: rdn over 1f out: styd on u.p to ld post* **5/1**[3]

201 **2** *hd* **Simple Rhythm**[11] 5159 2-8-11 78.............................. DominicFox[(3)] 10 68
(M G Quinlan) *led 1f: chsd ldr tl led wl over 3f out: rdn clr over 1f out: hdd post* **3/1**[2]

0366 **3** *3 3/4* **Herring Senior (IRE)**[22] 4776 2-9-3 63.............................. JerryO'Dwyer[(3)] 1 63
(P F I Cole) *mid-div: sn pushed along: hdwy u.p over 1f out: nt rch ldrs* **12/1**

0645 **4** *1 1/4* **Jaslyn (IRE)**[20] 4873 2-8-7 47 ow1.............................. TonyHamilton 2 46
(J R Weymes) *hld up: hdwy over 1f out: nvr nrr* **50/1**

000 **5** *2 1/4* **Sonett**[68] 3292 2-8-6 59.............................. JamesDoyle 8 39
(A J McCabe) *trckd ldrs: rdn 2f out: hung lft and wknd over 1f out* **40/1**

3244 **6** *2* **Frame And Cover**[22] 4764 2-8-5 54..........................(b[1]) AdrianMcCarthy 3 32
(R A Harris) *s.i.s: hld up: hdwy u.p over 2f out: wknd wl over 1f out* **14/1**

150 **7** *4 1/2* **Royal Raider**[34] 4403 2-8-9 82.............................. RichardEvans[(5)] 5 27
(P D Evans) *chsd ldrs: rdn over 2f out: sn wknd* **10/11**[1]

00 **8** *hd* **Mfi'Ve**[19] 4905 2-9-0 0.............................. TPO'Shea 11 27
(B R Millman) *chsd ldrs: sn pushed along: lost pl wl over 3f out: wknd over 2f out* **40/1**

000 **9** *2* **Liliaceae**[18] 4931 2-8-8 20..........................(t) TomEaves 6 15
(D Shaw) *sn outpcd* **80/1**

162 **10** *1/2* **Missus Christie**[21] 4823 2-8-7 61.............................. StephenDonohoe 4 12
(Ian Williams) *chsd ldrs: rdn 1/2-way: wknd wl over 1f out* **6/1**

0 **11** *14* **Rahzeena**[67] 3309 2-8-12 0.............................. EdwardCreighton 7 —
(R Brotherton) *s.i.s: sn outpcd: wknd 1/2-way* **66/1**

1m 15.74s (0.74) **Going Correction** +0.075s/f (Slow) **11** Ran SP% **132.3**
Speed ratings (Par 94): **98,97,92,91,88 85,79,79,76,75 57**
.Simple Rhythm was claimed by N. Tinkler for £15,000.\n\x\x
Owner The Lord Ilsley Racing Club **Bred** A C M Spalding **Trained** West Ilsley, Berks

FOCUS
The times of the first two races suggest the track may have been riding slower than usual. This was a reasonable juvenile claimer and the winning time was only 0.83 seconds slower than the following 46-60 handicap for three-year-olds and upwards. They looked to go a decent pace throughout, but very few got involved. The winner, second and fourth set the level.

NOTEBOOK
Alphabeth, although holding her form well, has just been finding a few too good lately and the drop in grade did the trick. She was given a good ride by her apprentice, who didn't panic when Simple Rhythm was sent into a clear lead, and she was able to peg that rival back in the final stride. Although well exposed, she is clearly very tough. (op 6-1 tchd 9-2)
Simple Rhythm was given every chance and looked to have this in the bag when sent into a clear lead at about halfway, but she was pegged back.
Herring Senior(IRE), dropped in class and trip, was never going and his rider had to work hard to get him up for third, although this was still a reasonable effort strictly on the figures. He might not have faced the kickback on this first try on sand, but he basically seemed to lack the speed of some of these and will probably be happier back over 7f. (op 14-1)
Jaslyn(IRE) was another who struggled to lay up early. She is a half-sister to dual 1m winner Emotive and looks to need further. (op 66-1)
Sonett was well placed early, but did not pick up and looks very moderate.
Frame And Cover Official explanation: jockey said filly hung right on final bend
Royal Raider, who had the useful Mythical Blue behind when winning a Chepstow seller on her debut, was lowered in class after being out of her depth in Listed company and a Group 3, but she was never seen with a chance and was a huge disappointment. The track seemed to be riding on the slow side and perhaps she wants a quicker surface. (op 6-4 tchd 13-8)
Rahzeena Official explanation: jockey said gelding hung right

5474 SPONSOR A RACE BY CALLING 01902 390009 H'CAP 5f 216y(P)
7:20 (7:20) (Class 6) (0-60,60) 3-Y-O+ **£2,388** (£705; £352) **Stalls** Low

Form RPR

0402 **1** **Littledodayno (IRE)**[8] 5201 5-9-5 **59**.............................. SebSanders 11 70
(M Wigham) *broke wl and led early: sn stdd and lost pl: hdwy over 1f out: r.o u.p to ld nr fin* **6/1**[3]

0415 **2** *1/2* **Ryedane (IRE)**[19] 4903 6-9-2 **56**.............................. ChrisCatlin 12 65
(T D Easterby) *sn led: rdn over 1f out: hdd nr fin* **13/2**

2056 **3** *1 1/4* **Gilded Cove**[20] 4858 8-9-3 **60**.............................. RussellKennemore[(3)] 5 65
(R Hollinshead) *hld up: hdwy and swtchd lft over 1f out: r.o: nt rch ldrs* **6/1**[3]

2300 **4** *shd* **All You Need (IRE)**[18] 4934 4-9-4 **58**..........................(p) FergusSweeney 4 63
(R Hollinshead) *chsd ldrs: rdn over 1f out: styd on* **7/1**

0552 **5** *1 3/4* **Thoughtsofstardom**[2] 5401 5-9-1 **60**.............................. KellyHarrison[(5)] 6 59
(P S McEntee) *prom: hmpd 5f out: rdn and hung lft over 1f out: styd on same pce* **5/1**[2]

0050 **6** *nk* **Dasheena**[52] 3826 5-9-0 **59**............(be) MCGeran(5) 3 58
(A J McCabe) *hld up: rdn over 2f out: hdwy over 1f out: nt trble ldrs* **20/1**

4353 **7** *nse* **Just Jimmy (IRE)**[11] 5162 3-8-11 **59**............ RichardEvans(5) 9 57
(P D Evans) *mid-div: sn pushed along: lost pl over 3f out: styd on u.p ins fnl f* **10/1**

313 **8** *1* **Avoca Dancer (IRE)**[167] 898 5-9-3 **57**............ DarryllHolland 8 52
(Miss Gay Kelleway) *chsd ldrs: rdn over 1f out: styd on same pce* **4/1**[1]

5043 **9** *shd* **Epidaurian King (IRE)**[119] 1780 5-9-5 **59**............(v) TomEaves 10 54
(D Shaw) *hld up: rdn over 2f out: n.d* **10/1**

5230 **10** *hd* **Cape Of Storms**[27] 4639 5-9-6 **60**............(b) RobertWinston 7 54
(R Brotherton) *mid-div: racd keenly: hdwy to trck ldr 5f out: rdn 2f out: wknd ins fnl f* **12/1**

04-0 **11** *1 ¾* **Comrade Cotton**[20] 4862 4-8-10 **57**............ DannyDunnachie(7) 13 46
(J Ryan) *s.i.s: sn prom: rdn over 2f out: wknd over 1f out* **50/1**

5060 **12** *5* **Mambazo**[21] 4824 6-8-13 **58**............(p) WilliamCarson(5) 2 31
(S C Williams) *s.i.s: hld up: hdwy u.p over 2f out: wknd wl over 1f out* **12/1**

1m 14.91s (-0.09) **Going Correction** +0.075s/f (Slow)
WFA 3 from 4yo+ 3lb 12 Ran SP% **131.4**
Speed ratings (Par 101): **103,102,100,100,98 97,97,96,96,96 93,87**
CSF £50.09 CT £261.93 TOTE £8.40: £2.10, £3.10, £3.00; EX 65.80.
Owner John Williams P'Ship Have Ago Syndicate **Bred** Lodge Park Stud **Trained** Newmarket, Suffolk

FOCUS
A modest but competitive sprint handicap, run in a time 0.83 seconds quicker than the earlier juvenile claimer. Sound enough form.

5475 NAME A RACE TO ENHANCE YOUR BRAND FILLIES' (S) STKS 5f 20y(P)
7:50 (7:51) (Class 6) 2-Y-0 **£2,047** (£604; £302) **Stalls** Low

Form RPR

52 **1** **Pressed For Time (IRE)**[16] 4986 2-8-12 0............(t) EdwardCreighton 7 61
(E J Creighton) *chsd ldr tl led 1/2-way: rdn out* **5/1**

4366 **2** *¾* **Imaginary Diva**[2] 5394 2-8-12 60............ AdrianMcCarthy 6 58
(G G Margarson) *a.p: rdn to chse wnr and hung lft over 1f out: styd on* **4/1**[3]

005 **3** *1 ½* **Franchesca's Gold**[34] 4411 2-8-12 51............ TPO'Shea 10 53
(B R Millman) *s.i.s: sn pushed along in rr: hdwy u.p over 1f out: hung lft ins fnl f: r.o* **33/1**

1134 **4** *nk* **Just The Lady**[29] 4558 2-9-4 64............ TonyHamilton 5 58
(Ollie Pears) *led: rdn and hdd 1/2-way: styd on same pce fnl f* **15/8**[1]

06 **5** *1 ½* **Bold Ring**[22] 4763 2-8-12 0............ FergusSweeney 9 47
(D W P Arbuthnot) *hld up: hdwy 1/2-way: rdn over 1f out: sn edgd lft: styd on* **11/1**

0440 **6** *¾* **Premier Krug (IRE)**[30] 4525 2-8-12 57............ StephenDonohoe 2 44+
(P D Evans) *s.i.s: sn pushed along in rr: r.o ins fnl f: nvr nrr* **8/1**

04 **7** *nse* **Lemon Dash**[25] 4681 2-8-12 0............ RobertWinston 8 44
(J J Quinn) *prom: rdn 1/2-way: wknd fnl f* **10/1**

0331 **8** *2 ½* **August Days (IRE)**[6] 5287 2-9-4 57............ SebSanders 1 41
(R M Beckett) *chsd ldrs: rdn over 3f out: wknd over 1f out* **3/1**[2]

00 **9** *1* **Killyea**[32] 4474 2-8-9 0............ KevinGhunowa(3) 4 31
(R A Harris) *s.i.s: a in rr* **33/1**

0 **10** *1* **Abitofaboost (IRE)**[21] 4823 2-8-7 0............ KellyHarrison(5) 3 27
(Peter Grayson) *hld up: rdn 1/2-way: a in rr* **33/1**

62.78 secs (0.48) **Going Correction** +0.075s/f (Slow) 10 Ran SP% **133.8**
Speed ratings (Par 89): **99,97,95,94,92 91,91,87,85,84**
CSF £29.16 TOTE £6.10: £1.40, £2.00, £9.10; EX 40.30.The winner was bought in for 9,500gns.
Owner P Cafferty **Bred** Richard O' Hara **Trained** Mill Hill, London NW7

FOCUS
Just a fillies' seller, but a reasonable race for the grade.

NOTEBOOK
Pressed For Time(IRE) had run her best race since coming over from Ireland when second in this grade over this trip on the soft at Yarmouth and she built on that with a tongue-tie fitted for the first time to get off the mark at the sixth attempt. She showed good speed to take over after around a couple of furlongs and ran to the line, despite looking to get tired late on. A penalty in this grade will make things tougher. (tchd 9-2 and 11-2)
Imaginary Diva had her chance on this drop in grade but just found one too good. (op 6-1)
Franchesca's Gold, drawn worst of all, was never travelling towards the outside early on but ran on strongly in the straight to grab third. She could do better back over 6f, but this was a weak race, so it would probably be unwise to get carried away.
Just The Lady showed good early speed, but offered disappointingly little when joined by the eventual winner at around halfway and was nowhere near her official mark of 64. (op 5-2 tchd 11-4)
Bold Ring was never a threat on this drop in grade, but is still learning and might be capable of a little better back on turf. (op 14-1)
Premier Krug(IRE) only ran on when the race was all over and probably wants both some headgear back on and a return to a longer trip.
August Days(IRE) never travelled and was well below the form she showed when winning a seller at Windsor last time. (op 11-4 tchd 10-3)

5476 BEATTIES, HOUSE OF FRASER, WOLVERHAMPTON, H'CAP 1m 4f 50y(P)
8:20 (8:20) (Class 5) (0-70,68) 3-Y-0+ **£3,238** (£963; £481; £240) **Stalls** Low

Form RPR

1121 **1** **Swords**[11] 5154 6-9-1 **62** 6ex............ AshleyHamblett(5) 11 69
(R E Peacock) *chsd ldrs: rdn to ld and edgd lft 1f out: styd on gamely* **13/2**[3]

1-01 **2** *nk* **Master At Arms**[18] 4935 5-9-8 **67**............ JerryO'Dwyer(3) 5 73
(Daniel Mark Loughnane, Ire) *hld up: hdwy over 7f out: chsd ldr over 5f out: rdn to ld over 1f out: sn hdd: styd on u.p* **5/2**[2]

1152 **3** *shd* **Auntie Mame**[32] 4485 4-9-6 **62**............ TPO'Shea 7 68
(D J Coakley) *hld up in tch: rdn and edgd lft fr over 1f out: styd on u.p* **9/1**

6351 **4** *2* **Adorabella (IRE)**[7] 5232 5-9-12 **68** 6ex............ JamieSpencer 4 71
(A King) *hld up: hdwy over 3f out: rdn and hung lft over 1f out: styd on same pce fnl f* **9/4**[1]

53-0 **5** *1 ¼* **Stalking Tiger (IRE)**[136] 1383 4-9-10 **66**............ FergusSweeney 6 67
(R Charlton) *hld up: plld hrd: hdwy to ld over 6f out: rdn and hdd over 1f out: no ex ins fnl f* **12/1**

6/0- **6** *hd* **Cash On (IRE)**[285] 5500 6-9-11 **67**............(p) DarryllHolland 2 67
(Karen George) *s.s: hld up: styd on ins fnl f: nvr nrr* **66/1**

6121 **7** *hd* **Granary Girl**[28] 4599 6-9-4 **60**............ ChrisCatlin 10 60
(J Pearce) *a.p: rdn over 1f out: styd on same pce fnl f* **16/1**

1550 **8** *hd* **Fenners (USA)**[16] 4966 5-8-12 **61**............ BradleyRoper(7) 8 61
(M W Easterby) *chsd ldrs: rdn over 2f out: no ex fnl f* **25/1**

6104 **9** *3* **Royal Premier (IRE)**[19] 4892 5-9-12 **68**............(v) SebSanders 9 63
(H J Collingridge) *led: hdd over 6f out: rdn over 1f out: n.m.r and wknd sn after* **20/1**

0563 **10** *3* **Bold Adventure**[18] 4930 4-9-6 **62**............ StephenDonohoe 1 52
(W J Musson) *hld up: shkn up over 2f out: nvr nr to chal* **10/1**

0/ **11** *3* **Aura Of Calm (IRE)**[361] 5106 6-9-2 **58**............(t) TonyHamilton 12 43
(Ronald O'Leary, Ire) *hld up: hdwy u.p over 2f out: wknd wl over 1f out* **16/1**

0000 **12** *1 ½* **Eva Soneva So Fast (IRE)**[15] 5017 6-9-9 **65**............ VinceSlattery 3 48
(G F Bridgwater) *hld up in tch: lost pl over 5f out: rdn over 3f out: sn wknd* **50/1**

2m 46.04s (4.94) **Going Correction** +0.075s/f (Slow) 12 Ran SP% **123.3**
Speed ratings (Par 103): **86,85,85,84,83 83,83,83,81,79 77,76**
CSF £23.32 CT £154.45 TOTE £9.50: £2.20, £1.70, £3.00; EX 19.40.
Owner J Babb **Bred** Mrs A Yearley **Trained** Kyre Park, Worcs

FOCUS
A good race for the grade, although they went no pace for the first circuit, which meant that several were inconvenienced and there was a bit of a bunch finish. The winner did not need to reproduce his best form and the second was some 6lb off his best.
Stalking Tiger(IRE) Official explanation: jockey said gelding hung right throughout

5477 BOOK TICKETS ONLINE MEDIAN AUCTION MAIDEN STKS 1m 1f 103y(P)
8:50 (8:50) (Class 6) 3-4-Y-O **£2,047** (£604; £302) **Stalls** Low

Form RPR

022- **1** **Long Distance (FR)**[315] 6303 3-9-3 75............ JamieSpencer 6 76+
(J R Fanshawe) *hld up in tch: shkn up to ld and edgd lft ins fnl f: comf* **8/13**[1]

033 **2** *1 ¼* **Street Crime**[17] 4941 3-9-3 67............ ChrisCatlin 2 66
(A M Balding) *hld up in tch: plld hrd: led 7f out: rdn and hdd ins fnl f: styd on same pce* **7/2**[2]

0425 **3** *½* **Scary Movie (IRE)**[12] 5118 3-9-3 68............ TPO'Shea 1 65
(D J Coakley) *a.p: chsd ldr over 5f out: rdn and hung lft over 1f out: styd on* **7/1**[3]

2200 **4** *8* **John Potts**[36] 4332 3-9-3 59............ HayleyTurner 4 48
(B P J Baugh) *led: hdd 7f out: chsd ldrs: rdn over 2f out: wknd over 1f out* **7/1**[3]

5 *2 ½* **Royal Flyer (IRE)**[179] 4-9-10 0............ FergusSweeney 3 43
(R A Farrant) *s.s: hld up: rdn over 2f out: wkng whn hung lft over 1f out* **33/1**

0 **6** *7* **Alltheclews**[27] 4620 3-8-10 0............ MatthewDavies(7) 5 28
(B J McMath) *hld up in tch: rdn over 3f out: wknd over 2f out* **66/1**

06- **7** *14* **Clare Park**[10] 3903 4-9-0 0............ SophieDoyle(5) 8 —
(H J Manners) *wnt rt s: hld up: rdn over 3f out: sn wknd* **66/1**

2m 4.84s (3.14) **Going Correction** +0.075s/f (Slow)
WFA 3 from 4yo 7lb 7 Ran SP% **115.1**
Speed ratings (Par 101): **89,87,87,80,78 71,59**
CSF £3.14 TOTE £1.70: £1.30, £2.30; EX 2.70.
Owner Simon Gibson **Bred** Petra Bloodstock Agency Ltd **Trained** Newmarket, Suffolk

FOCUS
A weak maiden run at just a modest pace and the form is far from solid. However, the winner had something in hand and loks a likely improver.

5478 DINE IN STYLE IN THE HORIZONS RESTAURANT H'CAP 1m 141y(P)
9:20 (9:20) (Class 6) (0-65,65) 3-Y-0+ **£2,388** (£705; £352) **Stalls** Low

Form RPR

3225 **1** **Nesno (USA)**[34] 4419 5-9-7 **63**............(p) DarryllHolland 13 72
(J D Bethell) *mde all: rdn over 1f out: styd on wl* **4/1**[2]

1064 **2** *1 ¼* **Lunar River (FR)**[14] 5059 5-9-8 **64**............(t) FergusSweeney 9 71+
(David Pinder) *s.i.s: hld up: hdwy over 2f out: rdn over 1f out: n.m.r sn after: r.o: nt rch wnr* **7/1**[3]

-000 **3** *1 ¼* **St Petersburg**[18] 4927 8-9-7 **63**............ EdwardCreighton 2 66
(J R Boyle) *hld up: hdwy over 2f out: rdn and edgd lft 1f out: styd on same pce* **22/1**

0000 **4** *¾* **Fort Amhurst (IRE)**[69] 3261 4-9-9 **65**............ RobertWinston 4 67
(M W Easterby) *a.p: chsd wnr over 3f out: rdn over 1f out: hung lft and no ex ins fnl f* **8/1**

2023 **5** *1 ½* **Kangrina**[38] 4267 6-9-6 **62**............ JamieSpencer 8 60
(George Baker) *hld up: hdwy 2f out: sn rdn: one pce fnl f* **10/3**[1]

-000 **6** *2 ½* **Kirstys Lad**[8] 5198 6-8-9 **58**............ SoniaEaton(7) 3 50
(M Mullineaux) *hld up: rdn over 2f out: r.o ins fnl f: nvr nrr* **25/1**

0300 **7** *1 ¼* **Wodhill Schnaps**[11] 5161 7-9-9 **65**............(b) AdrianMcCarthy 6 54
(D Morris) *sn pushed along in rr: rdn over 2f out: styd on ins fnl f: nvr nrr* **33/1**

0040 **8** *1* **Samuel Charles**[18] 4919 10-9-6 **62**............ SebSanders 5 49
(C R Dore) *mid-div: hdwy 5f out: rdn and wknd over 1f out* **7/1**[3]

0436 **9** *1* **Dancing Deano (IRE)**[11] 5156 6-9-5 **64**............ RussellKennemore(3) 12 49
(R Hollinshead) *chsd ldrs: rdn over 3f out: wknd 2f out* **12/1**

3020 **10** *hd* **Stark Contrast (USA)**[11] 5145 4-9-6 **62**............ HayleyTurner 10 46
(M D I Usher) *hld up: hdwy over 2f out: sn rdn: wknd over 1f out* **12/1**

0034 **11** *4 ½* **Spume (IRE)**[11] 5154 4-9-7 **63**............ ChrisCatlin 1 37
(S Parr) *prom: rdn over 3f out: wknd over 2f out* **8/1**

000 **12** *1 ½* **Sion Hill (IRE)**[18] 4934 7-9-0 **61**............(p) KellyHarrison(5) 11 32
(John A Harris) *trckd ldrs: racd keenly: wknd 2f out* **33/1**

3340 **13** *3* **Wahoo Sam (USA)**[19] 4895 8-9-3 **64**............ RichardEvans(5) 7 28
(P D Evans) *chsd ldrs: rdn over 2f out: wknd over 1f out* **14/1**

1m 49.43s (-1.07) **Going Correction** +0.075s/f (Slow) 13 Ran SP% **126.4**
Speed ratings (Par 101): **107,105,104,104,102 100,99,98,97,97 93,92,89**
CSF £32.97 CT £584.38 TOTE £5.90: £1.80, £3.60, £5.60; EX 43.50 Place 6 £115.89, Place 5 £48.04 .
Owner Elliott Brothers **Bred** Elisabeth Fabre **Trained** Middleham Moor, N Yorks

FOCUS
A moderate handicap. The winner, who got a good front running ride from a difficult draw, is rated to his recent best and the runner-up was also to form.
T/Plt: £131.20 to a £1 stake. Pool: £66,746.70. 371.30 winning tickets. T/Qpdt: £16.70 to a £1 stake. Pool: £5,946.20. 262.60 winning tickets. CR

5479 - 5485a (Foreign Racing) - See Raceform Interactive

5330 DEAUVILLE (R-H)
Friday, August 29

OFFICIAL GOING: Turf course - good; all-weather - standard

5486a PRIX DU HARAS DE LA HUDERIE (LISTED RACE) (STRAIGHT) 7f
1:50 (1:49) 2-Y-O **£20,221** (£8,088; £6,066; £4,044; £2,022)

RPR

1 **Homebound (USA)**[48] 2-8-13............ C-PLemaire 5 99
(J-C Rouget, France)

2 1 **Higha (FR)**[33] 4472 2-8-13 .... SPasquier 3 97
(P Demercastel, France) 5/1[2]
3 ¾ **Wildcat Wizard (USA)**[34] 4402 2-9-2 .... CSoumillon 6 98
(P F I Cole) *pressed ldrs on outside: led wl over 2f out: hung rt wl over 1f out: rdn and hdd 150yds out: one pce* 6/4[1]
4 2 ½ **Easy Sundae (IRE)**[55] 2-8-13 .... THuet 1 88
(J E Pease, France)
5 2 **Cotes D'Armor (FR)**[30] 4548 2-8-13 .... JVictoire 4 83
(H-A Pantall, France)
6 3 **Singapore Treat (FR)**[12] 2-8-13 .... OPeslier 2 76
(Robert Collet, France)
1m 23.8s (-0.70) 6 Ran SP% **56.7**
PARI-MUTUEL: WIN 2.70; PL 1.50, 2.10; SF 7.20.
Owner Joseph Allen **Bred** Joseph Allen **Trained** Pau, France

NOTEBOOK
Wildcat Wizard(USA), a keen sort who was sent off favourite on the strength of a decent effort in this grade at Ascot, raced up with the pace as usual but after taking the lead started to hang and was run out of it inside the last furlong.

5213 BATH (L-H)
Saturday, August 30

OFFICIAL GOING: Good (8.0)
Wind: Slight, half behind Weather: Warm and sunny

5487 TOTESPORT.COM NOVICE STKS 5f 161y
5:15 (5:19) (Class 4) 2-Y-0 **£4,857** (£1,445; £722; £360) **Stalls** Centre

Form RPR
1 1 **Triple Aspect (IRE)**[37] 4346 2-9-4 0 .... LiamJones 5 101+
(W J Haggas) *in tch: rdn 2f out: hdwy over 1f out: led ins fnl f: r.o* **11/10**[1]
2 2 2 ½ **Cavera (USA)**[17] 4973 2-8-6 0 .... FrancisNorton 4 81
(A M Balding) *s.i.s: sn trckd ldr: led appr fnl f: hdd ins fnl f: nt pce of wnr* **9/2**
213 3 1 ¼ **Leftontheshelf (IRE)**[9] 5204 2-8-5 87 .... TolleyDean(3) 3 78
(J L Spearing) *led tl rdn and hdd appr fnl f: no ex ins fnl f* **7/2**[2]
13 4 3 **Ginobili (IRE)**[20] 4908 2-9-1 0 .... PatrickHills(3) 6 78
(R Hannon) *chsd ldrs: rdn and hld whn hmpd appr fnl f: no ex after* **4/1**[3]
5 28 **May Boy** 2-8-6 0 .... MCGeran(5) 2 —
(R J Hodges) *sn outpcd: no ch fr 1/2-way: t.o* **33/1**
6 6 **River Style (IRE)** 2-8-6 0 .... RichardThomas 1 —
(A P Jarvis) *v.s.a: a wl bhd and virtually p.u fnl f: t.o* **66/1**
1m 10.66s (-0.54) **Going Correction** -0.05s/f (Good) 6 Ran SP% **112.5**
Speed ratings (Par 96): **101,97,96,92,54 46**
toteswinger: 1&2 £1.10, 1&3 £2.00, 2&3 £2.30. CSF £6.61 TOTE £1.90: £1.40, £1.60; EX 5.00.
Owner Mrs M Findlay **Bred** Noel O'Callaghan **Trained** Newmarket, Suffolk

FOCUS
The ground had dried out slightly and was basically Good all over. A decent novice event with three of the six runners previous winners, and strong form for the grade.

NOTEBOOK
Triple Aspect(IRE) ◆, who beat a subsequent winner when making a successful debut at Sandown last month, needed to be niggled along to stay in touch with the leaders at one stage here on this sharper track, despite the slightly longer trip, but once he picked up down the wide outside he was always going to win. A sound surface seems to be the key to him and he is likely to turn out for a Group race at Chantilly in a couple of weeks' time. With further improvement likely, he will certainly not be out of place there. (op 6-4 tchd Evens)
Cavera(USA) missed the break slightly, but was soon travelling strongly up with the pace and she battled on well even after the favourite went past her. She has now finished runner-up in both of her starts and deserves to go one better. (op 4-1 tchd 7-2)
Leftontheshelf(IRE), who missed the nursery at Sandown the previous day due to travel problems, was the most experienced in the field and tried to make every yard, but she had no answer to the front pair. Already rated 87, she provides the benchmark for the form but may be better off back in nurseries. Official explanation: jockey said filly banged its head on the stalls (op 4-1 tchd 3-1)
Ginobili(IRE), third behind a subsequent Listed winner at Windsor last time, was fairly weak in the market beforehand and, although he was close enough for most of the way, he never really looked like picking up the leaders. Official explanation: jockey said colt hung left throughout (op 3-1 tchd 9-2)
May Boy, out of a multiple winner on the Flat at up to 7f who was also later successful over hurdles, was soon struggling on this racecourse debut. (op 50-1)
River Style(IRE), an 8,000euros half-sister to a couple of winners at up to 1m, walked out of the stalls and showed nothing.

5488 HEROS "TO PASTURES NEW" CLAIMING STKS 5f 11y
5:45 (5:45) (Class 6) 2-Y-0 **£2,719** (£809; £404; £202) **Stalls** Centre

Form RPR
0000 1 **Barcode**[22] 4827 2-8-6 50 .... FrancisNorton 3 56
(R Hannon) *towards rr and nt gng pce: rdn and plenty to do whn swtchd rt 1f out: r.o wl to ld cl home* **15/2**[3]
0043 2 nk **Turn To Dreams**[7] 5287 2-8-4 55 .... CatherineGannon 4 53
(P D Evans) *prom: rdn and led over 1f out: r.o: hdd cl home* **11/4**[2]
6550 3 ½ **Buddy Marvellous (IRE)**[22] 4827 2-8-4 57 .... PatrickHills(3) 2 54
(R Hannon) *w ldr: rdn and ev ch ent fnl f: no ex towards fin* **9/1**
005 4 4 **Hatchet Man**[83] 2859 2-8-11 70 ....(p) LiamJones 6 44
(P Winkworth) *trckd ldrs: rdn 2f out: one pce fr over 1f out* **8/1**
1044 5 4 **Officer Mor (USA)**[28] 4628 2-9-2 71 .... DarrenWilliams 5 34
(K R Burke) *led: rdn 1/2-way: hdd over 1f out: sn wknd* **11/8**[1]
6 1 ¾ **Fruitful Job (IRE)** 2-8-9 0 ....(p) SamHitchcott 1 21
(A G Newcombe) *wnt lft s and sn outpcd* **22/1**
00 7 nk **Dark Desert**[22] 4815 2-8-11 0 .... ChrisCatlin 7 22
(A G Newcombe) *outpcd thrght* **14/1**
63.46 secs (0.96) **Going Correction** -0.05s/f (Good) 7 Ran SP% **112.7**
Speed ratings (Par 92): **90,89,88,82,75 73,72**
toteswinger: 1&2 Not won, 1&3 Not won, 2&3 £3.80. CSF £27.57 TOTE £9.30: £3.70, £1.70; EX 38.60.Buddy Marvellous was claimed by R Harris for £6,000.
Owner A J Ilsley & G Battocchi **Bred** Norman Court Stud **Trained** East Everleigh, Wilts

FOCUS
A weak juvenile claimer with only a couple of these having shown much form previously. The early pace was strong with almost four in a line across the track for much of the way, but they may have done too much and set it up for a closer.

NOTEBOOK
Barcode had not shown much worthwhile form prior to this, including in selling company, and for a long time it seemed that she would not play a part here either as she was completely taken off her feet and struggling to stay in touch. However, she was taking a big drop in trip having raced over 7f the last twice, and with the leaders wilting she found reserves of stamina from somewhere to snatch the race near the line. She had quite a bit to find with a couple of these at the weights, so her future may depend on how the Handicapper views this. (op 8-1 tchd 7-1)
Turn To Dreams, whose third in a Windsor seller last time was still just about the best recent form on show here, was quite weak in the market beforehand but she ran well up with the strong pace and battled on all the way to the line. She should be up to winning a similar event. (op 9-4 tchd 4-1)
Buddy Marvellous(IRE), who finished well behind Barcode when tailed off in a Newmarket seller last time, finished much closer to his stable-companion on this quicker ground after racing up with the pace throughout. He is only modest, but he was claimed by Ron Harris for £6,000 subsequently and he may be able to find a small race on a sound surface. (op 7-1)
Hatchet Man, not seen since appearing to lose his action at Brighton in June, had cheekpieces on for the first time. He ran with credit and had every chance, but he was always seeing plenty of daylight down the wide outside and that may have eventually counted against him. (op 5-1)
Officer Mor(USA), dropping in class having been disappointing since showing plenty of ability in the spring, was very well backed beforehand but after showing good early pace, he dropped away tamely. It is now back to the drawing board with him. (op 5-2 tchd 11-10)
Fruitful Job(IRE), a relatively cheap half-brother to three fair performers at up to 1m4f, was sporting cheekpieces for this racecourse debut, but he could never get into the race after missing the break. He is bred to need much further than this though. (op 20-1)
Dark Desert was always struggling and is yet to show much in the way of ability. (tchd 12-1)

5489 TRAINERS AFFILIATION SCHEME SUPPORTS HEROS (TAS) H'CAP 1m 3f 144y
6:15 (6:16) (Class 6) (0-55,56) 3-Y-0+ **£2,914** (£867; £433; £216) **Stalls** Low

Form RPR
62 1 **Moonshine Creek**[5] 5369 6-9-6 54 .... ChrisCatlin 3 64
(P W Hiatt) *a gng wl bhd ldrs: led over 3f out: rdn out fnl f* **5/1**[2]
2500 2 ¾ **Bob's Your Uncle**[16] 5027 5-9-1 52 .... TolleyDean(3) 7 61
(J G Portman) *mid-div: styd on fr 3f out to chse wnr over 1f out: kpt on fnl f* **13/2**[3]
006 3 11 **Beckenham's Secret**[37] 4322 4-8-12 46 .... FergusSweeney 16 36
(A W Carroll) *mid-div: rdn and hdwy on outside fr 3f out: styd on but nvr nr to chal* **20/1**
0-10 4 2 ½ **The Composer**[25] 4704 6-9-6 54 .... SteveDrowne 15 40
(M Blanshard) *in tch: hdwy 3f out: one pce after* **14/1**
0222 5 nk **Ambrose Princess (IRE)**[3] 5399 3-8-9 56 .... KevinGhunowa(3) 12 42
(R A Harris) *in tch tl rdn and wknd over 1f out* **9/2**[1]
0533 6 1 **Black Falcon (IRE)**[12] 5148 8-8-13 50 .... PatrickHills(3) 2 34
(John A Harris) *in tch: chsd wnr over 2f out tl wknd over 1f out* **9/1**
4433 7 4 **The Grey One (IRE)**[16] 5020 5-8-13 50 ....(p) TravisBlock(3) 8 27
(J M Bradley) *nvr bttr than mid-div* **9/1**
0331 8 7 **A One (IRE)**[12] 5148 9-8-9 48 .... RichardEvans(5) 5 13
(H J Manners) *led tl hdd over 3f out: wknd qckly* **16/1**
0000 9 1 ½ **Black Or Red (IRE)**[61] 3563 3-8-11 55 .... CatherineGannon 17 18
(I A Wood) *chsd ldrs tl wknd over 3f out* **33/1**
0000 10 2 **General Flumpa**[6] 5321 7-9-2 50 ....(v[1]) RichardThomas 9 9
(Miss Tor Sturgis) *a towards rr* **50/1**
-001 11 4 **Hallings Overture (USA)**[16] 5020 9-9-2 50 ....(p) RichardKingscote 14 2
(C A Horgan) *t.k.h in mid-div: rdn 3f out: sn wknd* **7/1**
0-00 12 2 ½ **Vehari**[15] 5059 5-9-2 50 .... StephenDonohoe 13 —
(Ian Williams) *a bhd* **40/1**
2105 13 ½ **Nimello (USA)**[57] 3687 12-8-12 46 ....(p) DaneO'Neill 11 —
(A G Newcombe) *towards rr: lost tch over 3f out* **16/1**
000 14 72 **Misselliebee**[20] 4909 3-8-11 55 .... LiamJones 10 —
(J W Hills) *a bhd: t.o whn virtually p.u over 1f out* **40/1**
0606 P **Saloon (USA)**[87] 2715 4-9-7 55 .... PaulDoe 1 —
(S Curran) *bmpd and rdr lost iron leaving stalls: sn p.u* **12/1**
0100 P **Camera Shy (IRE)**[46] 4055 4-9-1 49 ....(p) AdamKirby 6 —
(K A Morgan) *chsd ldr tl wknd over 3f out: p.u over 1f out* **9/1**
2m 31.31s (0.71) **Going Correction** +0.10s/f (Good)
WFA 3 from 4yo+ 10lb 16 Ran SP% **131.3**
Speed ratings (Par 101): **101,100,93,91,91 90,87,83,82,80 78,76,76,28,— —**
toteswinger: 1&2 £3.00, 1&3 £38.20, 2&3 £38.20. CSF £38.91 CT £634.69 TOTE £6.10: £2.10, £2.10, £4.40, £4.10; EX 39.40.
Owner P W Hiatt **Bred** Lawrence Shepherd **Trained** Hook Norton, Oxon

FOCUS
A very moderate handicap and the pace appeared no more than ordinary, but they still finished very well spread out and the front pair pulled a long way clear of the rest. They are the best guides to the level.
Black Or Red(IRE) Official explanation: jockey said gelding had no more to give
General Flumpa Official explanation: trainer said gelding would not face the first time visor
Nimello(USA) Official explanation: jockey said gelding moved poorly
Saloon(USA) Official explanation: jockey said gelding lost an iron leaving stalls
Camera Shy(IRE) Official explanation: jockey said gelding lost its action and stopped quickly

5490 BATHWICK TYRES H'CAP 5f 161y
6:45 (6:46) (Class 4) (0-85,83) 3-Y-0 **£6,799** (£2,023; £1,011; £505) **Stalls** Centre

Form RPR
1412 1 **Pretty Bonnie**[16] 5007 3-8-2 69 .... NataliaGemelova(5) 11 87
(A E Price) *hld up: hdwy 2f out: hung lft fr over 1f out but r.o to ld wl ins fnl f* **7/1**[3]
0-20 2 3 ¼ **First In Command (IRE)**[33] 4494 3-9-0 79 ....(t) JerryO'Dwyer(3) 5 86
(Daniel Mark Loughnane, Ire) *in tch: rdn to ld 1f out: hdd wl ins fnl f* **14/1**
2331 3 ¾ **Polar Annie**[15] 5056 3-9-2 78 .... TGMcLaughlin 6 82
(M S Saunders) *trckd ldrs: rdn 2f out: kpt on fnl f* **7/2**[1]
0056 4 1 ¼ **Our Piccadilly (IRE)**[16] 5028 3-8-7 69 ow1 .... FergusSweeney 1 69
(W S Kittow) *led tl rdn and hdd 1f out: wknd ins fnl f* **16/1**
2115 5 2 ¼ **Billion Dollar Kid**[15] 5056 3-9-4 83 ....(t) KevinGhunowa(3) 9 76
(R A Harris) *mid-div: rdn 2f out: nt pce to chal* **7/2**[1]
2040 6 3 ½ **Requisite**[8] 5250 3-9-6 82 .... CatherineGannon 4 63
(I A Wood) *s.i.s: effrt over 1f out: sn btn* **8/1**
1112 7 1 ½ **Speedy Senorita (IRE)**[64] 3462 3-8-11 73 .... DarrenWilliams 7 49
(K R Burke) *trckd ldr: ev ch 2f out: rdn and wknd fnl f* **7/1**[3]
0040 8 hd **Harlech Castle**[29] 4595 3-9-0 76 .... ChrisCatlin 10 51
(P F I Cole) *a in rr* **5/1**[2]
4000 9 6 **Monsieur Reynard**[12] 5151 3-8-11 73 .... StephenDonohoe 8 27
(Ian Williams) *in tch tl rdn and wknd over 1f out* **14/1**
1500 10 1 ¾ **Leading Edge (IRE)**[14] 5101 3-8-6 75 .... MatthewDavies(7) 3 24
(M R Channon) *mid-div: rdn and lost pl 1/2-way* **18/1**
1m 10.59s (-0.61) **Going Correction** -0.05s/f (Good) 10 Ran SP% **121.7**
Speed ratings (Par 102): **102,97,96,95,92 87,85,85,77,74**
toteswinger: 1&2 £7.70, 1&3 £7.50, 2&3 Not won. CSF £104.20 CT £417.60 TOTE £10.10: £2.50, £4.50, £1.70; EX 104.00.
Owner N Field **Bred** P And Mrs A G Venner & Alpha Bloodstock Ltd **Trained** Leominster, H'fords

FOCUS
The best race on the card and quite a few of this came into the race at the top of their game. They went a decent pace too and the third and fourth are rated to recent marks.

5491 HEROS "BECAUSE ALL HORSES DESERVE A FUTURE" MAIDEN STKS — 1m 5y
7:15 (7:18) (Class 5) 3-Y-O+ — **£4,118** (£1,225; £612; £305) **Stalls** Low

Form	Pos	Dist	Horse / Trainer / Comment	Jockey	SP	RPR
36	1		**Hall Hee (IRE)**[52] 3854 3-8-12 0 (M P Tregoning) *trckd ldr: rdn to ld over 1f out: drvn out*	MartinDwyer 13	9/4[2]	78+
24	2	nk	**Expresso Star (USA)**[98] 2413 3-9-3 0 (J H M Gosden) *led: rdn 2f out: hdd over 1f out: rallied ins fnl f*	JimmyFortune 4	6/5[1]	82+
630/	3	7	**Wrecking Crew (IRE)**[819] 2218 4-9-9 65 (B R Millman) *trckd ldrs: rdn 2f out: one pce but kpt on after*	RichardKingscote 1	66/1	66
	4	2	**Mubrook (USA)** 3-9-3 0 (L M Cumani) *mid-div: rdn over 2f out: kpt on but nvr a danger*	DaneO'Neill 7	25/1	61+
2433	5	2 ¾	**Barricado (FR)**[29] 4582 3-9-3 73 (R Charlton) *t.k.h in mid-div: hdwy on ins 2f out but nvr on terms*	(b) SteveDrowne 6	6/1[3]	54
6-0	6	4	**Institute**[40] 4249 3-9-3 0 (Sir Michael Stoute) *in tch: rdn 2f out: sn btn*	RyanMoore 3	8/1	44
000/	7	5	**Jose Bove**[103] 6429 6-9-9 45 (R Dickin) *trckd ldrs: rdn 3f out: wknd 2f out*	TGMcLaughlin 12	150/1	32
-642	8	¾	**Holden Eagle**[22] 4818 3-9-3 73 (A G Newcombe) *s.i.s: a bhd*	StephenDonohoe 5	12/1	31
0	9	½	**Nyumba (IRE)**[73] 3133 3-8-12 0 (P R Chamings) *mid-div tl lost pl 3f out*	CatherineGannon 14	100/1	24
	10	2	**Otis May (IRE)**[66] 4-9-9 0 (A W Carroll) *mid-div: rdn 3f out: sn wknd*	VinceSlattery 8	150/1	25
00	11	9	**Walhalla (IRE)**[10] 5182 3-8-10 0 (M P Tregoning) *a bhd*	KatiaScallan(7) 9	100/1	3
06	12	1 ¼	**Rose Of Torridge**[25] 4709 3-8-12 0 (A G Newcombe) *mid-div: rdn 3f out: wknd over 3f out*	FergusSweeney 15	200/1	—
030	13	29	**Bluebird Chariot**[25] 4709 5-9-6 45 (J M Bradley) *a bhd: t.o fnl 2f*	TolleyDean(3) 2	150/1	—

1m 42.11s (1.31) **Going Correction** +0.10s/f (Good)
WFA 3 from 4yo+ 6lb — **13 Ran SP% 119.1**
Speed ratings (Par 103): **97,96,89,87,84 80,75,75,74,72 63,62,33**
toteswinger: 1&2 £1,40, 1&3 Not won, 2&3 Not won. CSF £5.25 TOTE £3.70: £1.30, £1.02, £10.50; EX 7.40.
Owner Sheikh Ahmed Al Maktoum **Bred** Hawthorn Villa Stud **Trained** Lambourn, Berks

FOCUS
A big field of maidens, but less than half of these had shown any worthwhile form beforehand and few could be given any realistic chance. The pace was a fair one and it paid to race handy as the principals were to the fore throughout and the front two came right away; they set the level. This was also a race where the market got it right.

Barricado(FR) Official explanation: jockey said colt hung left in early stages

Institute Official explanation: jockey said colt hung right

Bluebird Chariot Official explanation: jockey said horse ran too free

5492 "NEW START" H'CAP — 1m 5y
7:45 (7:46) (Class 5) (0-75,75) 3-Y-O+ — **£4,533** (£1,348; £674; £336) **Stalls** Low

Form	Pos	Dist	Horse / Trainer / Comment	Jockey	SP	RPR
2625	1		**Sotik Star (IRE)**[23] 4789 5-9-9 72 (P J Makin) *t.k.h in mid-div: rdn and hdwy over 1f out: kpt on u.p to ld post*	CatherineGannon 9	17/2	79+
2004	2	shd	**Magroom**[11] 5170 4-9-5 68 (R J Hodges) *a.p: rdn to ld wl ins fnl f: hdd post*	SteveDrowne 4	20/1	75
5410	3	¾	**Cape Velvet (IRE)**[13] 5120 4-9-11 74 (H J L Dunlop) *trckd ldr: led over 2f out: rdn: hdd and lost 2nd wl ins fnl f*	JamesDoyle 2	11/1	79
5621	4	nk	**Bold Cross (IRE)**[12] 5156 5-9-6 69 (E G Bevan) *stdd s: sn mid-div: rdn over 1f out: r.o fnl f*	PaulFitzsimons 1	15/2[3]	73
1321	5	nk	**Rescue Me**[7] 5291 3-9-6 75 (R Hannon) *slowly away and in rr tl hdwy 2f out: r.o fnl f: nvr nrr*	RyanMoore 15	5/2[1]	78+
5542	6	hd	**Bere Davis (FR)**[10] 5185 3-9-4 73 (P D Evans) *prom on outside: rdn 3f out: kpt on ins fnl 2f*	TGMcLaughlin 16	14/1	75
0103	7	hd	**Very Well Red**[13] 5119 5-9-6 69 (P W Hiatt) *led tl hdd over 2f out: rdn and one pce fnl f*	ChrisCatlin 13	14/1	72
0100	8	1 ½	**Eastern Emperor**[24] 4723 4-9-10 73 (W R Swinburn) *trckd ldrs: rdn 2f out: wknd appr fnl f*	(p) AdamKirby 10	9/1	72
0243	9	¾	**Palmetto Point**[23] 4789 4-9-2 68 (H Morrison) *in tch: rdn 3f out: wknd 2f out*	(tp) TravisBlock(3) 8	6/1[2]	65
4415	10	4 ½	**Merrymadcap (IRE)**[6] 5312 6-9-0 68 (M Blanshard) *in tch: rdn over 2f out: wknd over 1f out*	JackDean(5) 11	11/1	55
02-5	11	1 ¼	**Rydal (USA)**[21] 4862 7-9-5 68 (Miss Jo Crowley) *hld up: rdn over 3f out: no hdwy after*	FergusSweeney 7	20/1	52
/03-	12	20	**Ghost Dancer**[476] 1684 4-9-11 74 (L M Cumani) *t.k.h in mid-div: rdn 3f out: sn btn: eased fnl f: t.o*	DaneO'Neill 6	8/1	10

1m 42.64s (1.84) **Going Correction** +0.10s/f (Good)
WFA 3 from 4yo+ 6lb — **12 Ran SP% 125.8**
Speed ratings (Par 103): **94,93,93,92,92 92,92,90,89,85 84,64**
toteswinger: 1&2 £6.60, 1&3 Not won, 2&3 Not won. CSF £175.81 CT £1915.49 TOTE £13.50: £4.10, £3.90, £3.80; EX 181.20 Place 6 £237.55, Place 5 £157.76.
Owner D Ladhams M Holland J Ritchie R P Marchant **Bred** Holborn Trust Co **Trained** Ogbourne Maisey, Wilts

FOCUS
A modest handicap to end the evening, but still fairly competitive. They only went a steady early pace though, and a few of the leaders were inclined to take a hold. The winning time was 0.53 seconds slower than the preceding maiden and the first seven finished in a heap, suggesting the form, rate around the placed horses, may be suspect.

Eastern Emperor Official explanation: jockey said gelding hung left

T/Plt: £460.50 to a £1 stake. Pool: £44,765.16. 70.95 winning tickets. T/Qpdt: £133.00 to a £1 stake. Pool: £5,015.50. 27.90 winning tickets. JS

5445 CHESTER (L-H)
Saturday, August 30

OFFICIAL GOING: Good to firm (good in places; 8.3)
Wind: Light, behind Weather: Overcast

5493 CORBETTCASINO.COM H'CAP — 5f 16y
2:20 (2:22) (Class 4) (0-85,84) 3-Y-O+ — **£5,504** (£1,637; £818; £408) **Stalls** Low

Form	Pos	Dist	Horse / Trainer / Comment	Jockey	SP	RPR
4166	1		**Supermassive Muse (IRE)**[19] 4922 3-8-13 79 (E S McMahon) *led for 1f: chsd ldr after: pushed along 1/2-way: rdn over 1f out: r.o to ld 150yds out: won a shade comf*	(p) DarryllHolland 2	14/1	90
0000	2	½	**Bo McGinty (IRE)**[17] 4962 7-8-11 80 (R A Fahey) *chsd ldrs: rdn 2f out: r.o ins fnl f: tk 2nd fnl strides*	(b) FrederikTylicki(5) 8	6/1[3]	89
3203	3	½	**Mr Wolf**[3] 5400 7-8-7 71 (D W Barker) *led after 1f: rdn 1f out: hdd 150yds out: hld fnl strides*	TonyHamilton 3	11/4[1]	78
-300	4	¾	**Topflightcoolracer**[21] 4854 4-9-0 78 (Mrs G S Rees) *chsd ldrs: nt clr run over 1f out: rdn and styd on ins fnl f: nt quite pce to chal*	DaleGibson 1	15/2	82
0006	5	nk	**The Jobber (IRE)**[18] 4957 7-9-6 84 (M Blanshard) *in tch: nt clr run and swtchd rt over 1f out: rdn and hung lft ins fnl f: r.o towards fin: nt rch ldrs*	JamieSpencer 6	9/1	87
3300	6	½	**Mambo Spirit (IRE)**[30] 4555 4-9-1 79 (J G Given) *s.i.s: swtchd lft s: towards rr: hdwy over 1f out: styd on ins fnl f: nt pce to chal ldrs*	SebSanders 10	12/1	80+
-254	7	¾	**Maryolini**[70] 3256 3-8-4 75 (N J Vaughan) *chsd ldrs: n.m.r 1/2-way: rdn over 1f out: bmpd ins fnl f: one pce towards fin*	Louis-PhilippeBeuzelin(5) 7	22/1	74
1112	8	2 ¾	**Methaaly (IRE)**[29] 4601 5-9-6 84 (M Mullineaux) *restless in stalls: s.i.s: bhd: sme prog ins fnl f: nvr on terms w ldrs*	(be) RichardMullen 11	11/1	73
000	9	½	**Jilly Why (IRE)**[15] 5073 7-8-9 76 (Paul Green) *bhd: sn pushed along: nvr gng pce to get on terms*	(b) RussellKennemore(3) 13	50/1	63
0130	10	shd	**Mandurah (IRE)**[24] 4743 4-8-7 71 (D Nicholls) *reminders jst after s: midfield: rdn whn n.m.r over 1f out: eased whn no imp fnl 75yds*	AdrianTNicholls 5	4/1[2]	58+
0050	11	2 ¼	**Magic Glade**[30] 4555 9-8-9 73 (Peter Grayson) *midfield: effrt 1/2-way: no imp on ldrs: wknd ins fnl f*	PatrickMathers 9	33/1	52
4440	12	2 ¾	**Foxy Music**[17] 4962 4-9-2 80 (E J Alston) *stdd s: hld up: hung rt fr 3f out: c wd ent st wl over 1f out: nvr on terms*	PatCosgrave 14	20/1	49
1-03	13	shd	**Really Really Wish**[15] 5046 3-8-5 71 (J R Best) *midfield: lost pl 3f out: bhd after*	HayleyTurner 12	33/1	39

60.74 secs (-0.26) **Going Correction** -0.15s/f (Firm)
WFA 3 from 4yo+ 2lb — **13 Ran SP% 122.4**
Speed ratings (Par 105): **96,95,94,93,92 91,90,86,85,85 81,77,77**
toteswinger: 1&2 £19.40, 1&3 £11.70, 2&3 £5.90. CSF £92.75 CT £308.19 TOTE £16.60: £4.30, £2.60, £1.80; EX 147.20 Trifecta £476.20 Part won. Pool: £643.52 - 0.70 winning units..
Owner Nick Hughes **Bred** Richard O' Hara **Trained** Lichfield, Staffs
■ Stewards' Enquiry : Jamie Spencer caution: careless riding

FOCUS
A decent sprint handicap where the draw, as is often the case in sprints here, played a major part. The riders reported that the going was a little faster than it had been the previous afternoon.

Foxy Music Official explanation: jockey said gelding hung right

5494 CORBETTSPORTS.COM CHESTER H'CAP (LISTED RACE) — 1m 5f 89y
2:50 (2:51) (Class 1) (0-110,109) 3-Y-O+
£24,978 (£9,468; £4,738; £2,362; £1,183; £594) **Stalls** Low

Form	Pos	Dist	Horse / Trainer / Comment	Jockey	SP	RPR
5453	1		**Red Gala**[63] 3497 5-9-9 107 (Sir Michael Stoute) *s.i.s: midfield: hdwy over 3f out: rdn to ld wl over 1f out: sn hung lft: hld on wl towards fin*	RichardMullen 7	11/2[2]	114
-001	2	½	**Strategic Mount**[21] 4844 5-9-2 100 (P F I Cole) *hld up: hdwy over 2f out: rdn over 1f out: sn edgd lft: chal wnr ins fnl f: looked hld cl home*	DavidAllan 2	7/1[3]	106
-123	3	1 ¼	**Cool Judgement (IRE)**[50] 3925 3-8-0 95 (M A Jarvis) *a.p: n.m.r and hmpd jst over 3f out: rdn 2f out: ev ch ins fnl f: nt qckn towards fin*	HayleyTurner 3	3/1[1]	99
0102	4	2 ½	**Mull Of Dubai**[50] 3929 5-8-11 95 oh1 (T P Tate) *hld up: hmpd over 3f out: hdwy on outer over 1f out: styd on ins fnl f: unable to rch ldrs*	MickyFenton 6	11/1	95
0020	5	1	**Record Breaker (IRE)**[8] 5229 4-8-12 96 (M Johnston) *prom: chsd ldr after 2f: led 4f out: rdn and hdd wl over 1f out: wknd fnl 100yds*	DarryllHolland 12	17/2	95
0520	6	¾	**Greenwich Meantime**[21] 4843 8-8-11 95 oh4 (R A Fahey) *midfield: effrt over 2f out: nvr able to chal ldrs: one pce over 1f out*	TonyHamilton 1	14/1	93
4343	7	2 ¼	**New Guinea**[184] 740 5-9-5 103 (Saeed Bin Suroor) *prom: chal 2f out: hung lft and wknd appr fnl f*	JamieSpencer 9	7/1[3]	97
6165	8	1	**Sahrati**[21] 4844 4-8-11 95 oh6 (C E Brittain) *hld up: reminders over 6f out: niggled along whn hmpd over 3f out: nvr on terms*	(b) AdrianTNicholls 5	40/1	88
1-00	9	68	**Solent (IRE)**[29] 3975 6-9-0 98 (J J Quinn) *led: hdd 4f out: wknd qckly 3f out: eased wl over 1f out: t.o*	PatCosgrave 8	16/1	—
2121	F		**Sir Duke (IRE)**[44] 4111 4-8-11 95 oh5 (P W D'Arcy) *trckd ldrs: rdn whn fell over 3f out: dead*	PatDobbs 4	9/1	—
2113	B		**Cheshire Prince**[21] 4856 4-8-11 95 oh6 (W M Brisbourne) *hld up: b.d over 3f out*	DeanHeslop 10	14/1	—
-345	B		**Speed Gifted**[47] 4041 4-9-11 109 (L M Cumani) *racd keenly in midfield: pushed along whn b.d over 3f out*	SebSanders 13	11/2[2]	—

2m 49.9s (-5.80) **Going Correction** -0.15s/f (Firm)
WFA 3 from 4yo+ 11lb — **12 Ran SP% 131.3**
Speed ratings (Par 111): **111,110,109,108,107 107,105,105,63,— —,—**
toteswinger: 1&2 £10.70, 1&3 £8.60, 2&3 £11.70. CSF £49.05 CT £144.54 TOTE £7.70: £2.50, £3.20, £2.00; EX 72.80 Trifecta £280.10 Pool: £454.33 - 1.20 winning units.
Owner Cheveley Park Stud **Bred** Cheveley Park Stud Ltd **Trained** Newmarket, Suffolk
■ Stewards' Enquiry : Hayley Turner caution: used whip with excessive frequency

FOCUS
A decent Listed contest but the limited weight range meant that nearly half the field were out of the handicap and the form is rated around the runner-up and fourth. However, there was a dramatic incident over half a mile out when Sir Duke, who was being ridden to improve around the outside of his field, clipped heels and came down, along with Speed Gifted and Cheshire Prince, who were in his slipstream and could not avoid being brought down. Seb Sanders suffered a broken leg which will rule him out for the rest of the season.

NOTEBOOK
Red Gala, three times a winner on fast and easy ground in 2007, had yet to win above Class 2 level and had not scored beyond 1m2f. However, he had looked as if he stayed 1m4f in the past and travelled well behind the leading group. He made his ground off the bend and established sufficient advantage to hold of the late challengers. (op 7-1)
Strategic Mount ◆, raised 6lb for his win at the Shergar Cup meeting, he is clearly in good form at present, came from the back of the field in the straight, and was closing down the winner all the way to the line. A return to a stiffer track could well enable him to add to his score while in such good heart. (op 15-2 tchd 8-1)
Cool Judgement(IRE) ◆, whose trainer won this with New Guinea two years ago, was the only three-year-old in the line-up. He ran well having been slightly checked on the home turn and this lightly-raced colt remains progressive. (op 5-1 tchd 11-2)
Mull Of Dubai, a course winner here in May, ran well from a pound out of the handicap having had to come from off the pace and is another in good form at present. (op 9-1 tchd 8-1)
Record Breaker(IRE), took over in front after the melee, but he had already done a lot of running to hold his position and had nothing in reserve once the challenges were delivered in the straight. (op 16-1)
Greenwich Meantime has not scored since winning the Chester Cup here in May 2007, but is suited by a sound surface and did not run too badly over a trip short of his optimum from 4lb out of the handicap. (op 16-1)
New Guinea, who won this two years ago when with Michael Jarvis, was 12lb higher and having his first run since Nad Al Sheba in February and he faded in the straight after racing prominently. (tchd 15-2 and 8-1 in places)
Solent(IRE) made much of the running, but was in trouble and headed soon after the drama 4f out.

5495 CORBETTPOKER.COM STKS (HERITAGE H'CAP) 7f 122y
3:25 (3:28) (Class 2) 3-Y-O+

£24,924 (£7,464; £3,732; £1,868; £932; £468) **Stalls** Low

Form				RPR
4-36	**1**		**Furnace (IRE)**[9] 5207 4-8-1 **86** ...... HayleyTurner 13	95
			(M L W Bell) *midfield: hdwy over 4f out: rdn to ld over 1f out: hdd narrowly 150yds out: rallied gamely to regain ld fnl strides* **16/1**
3054	**2**	*shd*	**Vanderlin**[9] 5208 9-8-9 **94** ...... LPKeniry 6	103
			(A M Balding) *in tch: gng wl over 2f out: prog on outer to ld narrowly 150yds out: hdd fnl strides* **5/1**[2]
0004	**3**	*¾*	**Extraterrestrial**[21] 4853 4-8-6 **91** ow1 ...... (p) TonyHamilton 16	98+
			(R A Fahey) *towards rr: sn niggled along: hdwy over 1f out: r.o and gaining towards fin* **20/1**
0015	**4**	*hd*	**Thebes**[7] 5270 3-8-0 **91** ...... NickyMackay 7	97
			(M Johnston) *a.p: rdn 2f out: chalng whn n.m.r over 1f out: sn hung lft: nt qckn towards fin* **12/1**
1201	**5**	*½*	**Underworld**[14] 5096 3-8-8 **99** ...... DarryllHolland 4	107+
			(M Johnston) *in tch: n.m.r and hmpd 2f out: sn rdn and swtchd rt: r.o ins fnl f: gaining whn changed legs towards fin* **11/4**[1]
5010	**6**	*1¾*	**Adversity**[30] 4553 3-7-11 **93** ...... Louis-PhilippeBeuzelin(5) 10	93
			(Sir Michael Stoute) *chsd ldrs: rdn to chal whn bmpd over 1f out: one pce fnl 150yds* **5/1**[2]
6630	**7**	*nk*	**Fathsta (IRE)**[1] 5446 3-7-6 **90** ...... CharlesEddery(7) 15	94+
			(S Kirk) *hld up: nt clr run 4f out: nt clr run again over 1f out: gd prog ins fnl f: fin wl* **25/1**
0520	**8**	*1¼*	**Al Muheer (IRE)**[7] 5275 3-8-9 **100** ...... JamieSpencer 8	96
			(C E Brittain) *bmpd s: bhd: rdn and sme hdwy on wd outside over 1f out: nt rch ldrs* **20/1**
0225	**9**	*3*	**Pawan (IRE)**[5] 5368 8-8-3 **93** ow3 ...... (b) AnnStokell(5) 3	83
			(Miss A Stokell) *missed break: midfield: pushed along 4f out: n.m.r over 1f out: no imp fnl f* **18/1**
5000	**10**	*2¼*	**Dream Theme**[29] 4586 5-8-3 **88** ...... AdrianTNicholls 1	76
			(D Nicholls) *dwlt: bustled along to sn ld: hdd over 1f out: sn hmpd: wknd and eased ins fnl f* **10/1**
0000	**11**	*2½*	**Hinton Admiral**[14] 5109 4-8-5 **90** ...... (p) DaleGibson 5	68
			(R A Fahey) *midfield: pushed along over 2f out: wknd over 1f out* **20/1**
1500	**12**	*nse*	**Celtic Sultan (IRE)**[56] 3740 4-9-1 **100** ...... MickyFenton 9	78
			(T P Tate) *sn chsd ldr: lost 2nd 2f out: wknd over 1f out* **8/1**[3]
0202	**13**	*14*	**Troubadour (IRE)**[36] 4364 7-8-0 **85** ...... (b) AdrianMcCarthy 11	28
			(W Jarvis) *missed break: sn in midfield: wknd over 2f out* **28/1**
0012	**14**	*shd*	**Dream Lodge (IRE)**[34] 4459 4-9-1 **100** ...... (v) PatCosgrave 17	42
			(J G Given) *reminders sn after s: racd in midfield on outside: nvr looked happy: wknd over 2f out* **16/1**

1m 31.66s (-2.14) **Going Correction** -0.15s/f (Firm)
WFA 3 from 4yo+ 6lb **14** Ran SP% **126.5**
Speed ratings (Par 109): **104,103,103,102,102 100,100,99,96,93 91,91,77,77**
toteswinger: 1&2 £20.90, 1&3 £48.70, 2&3 £25.70. CSF £91.61 CT £1706.65 TOTE £23.70: £6.50, £2.30, £5.10; EX 146.00 Trifecta £391.90 Part won. Pool: £529.70 - 0.20 winning units..
Owner Highclere Thoroughbred Racing XXXV **Bred** Barouche Stud Ireland Ltd **Trained** Newmarket, Suffolk
■ Stewards' Enquiry : Hayley Turner caution: used whip with excessive frequency

FOCUS
A good, competitive heritage handicap and a good finish with Furnace just getting the better of last year's winner Vanderlin. The form is rated around the placed horses.

NOTEBOOK
Furnace(IRE) had not won since his debut two years ago but acts on a sound surface and had been gradually dropping in handicap. Back on turf following two runs on Polytrack after a year's absence, he travelled well throughout and found plenty under pressure to hold off his more battle-hardened rival. (op 14-1)
Vanderlin, who won this last year off a mark of 100, had not scored since but had dropped to 94. Effective on fast ground and better drawn this year, he came to have every chance in the straight but could not get past the winner. (op 7-1)
Extraterrestrial, who was better off with both Celtic Sultan and Dream Lodge compared with their running here in May, had struggled since and had a wide draw to overcome. He weaved his way through but finished well and will not be inconvenienced by a return to 1m.
Thebes, the stable companion of the favourite, was easy in the market but ran pretty well, although he drifted left and could find no more in the straight. (tchd 16-1)
Underworld was held up on the rail, but did not settle and probably was unsuited by the track. However, he was doing his best work at the finish and will be better back on a more conventional course. (op 4-1)
Adversity, a winner over 7f here in June, was 10lb higher and appeared to have his chance but looks in the Handicapper's grip now. (tchd 9-2 and 11-2)
Fathsta(IRE) was held up out the back and ran on in the wake of the third, but never got into contention. He has been on the go for a long time and, although he keeps running well, his earlier improvement seems to have plateaued. (op 20-1)
Pawan(IRE) has not run over a trip this far for over two years, but was keeping on at the end. (op 20-1)
Dream Theme made the early running but faded quickly in the straight. Official explanation: jockey said gelding hung right (op 9-1)
Celtic Sultan(IRE) was unable to dominate and was on the retreat before the home turn. (op 17-2)
Dream Lodge(IRE) Official explanation: jockey said colt hung left

5496 CORBETT CHARITY DONATION NIGHTINGALE HOUSE HOSPICE E B F CONDITIONS STKS (C&G) 6f 18y
4:00 (4:01) (Class 2) 2-Y-O **£9,777** (£2,926; £1,463; £731; £364) **Stalls** Low

Form				RPR
2214	**1**		**Viva Ronaldo (IRE)**[51] 3876 2-9-1 99 ...... TonyHamilton 1	99+
			(R A Fahey) *n.m.r sn after s: trckd ldrs: qcknd up on inner to ld 1f out: r.o wl and in command after* **9/4**[2]
3341	**2**	*2½*	**Parisian Pyramid (IRE)**[28] 4626 2-8-12 82 ...... AdrianTNicholls 2	89
			(D Nicholls) *led: rdn and hdd 1f out: nt pce of wnr ins fnl f* **7/4**[1]
2400	**3**	*nk*	**Effort**[32] 4507 2-9-1 97 ...... DarryllHolland 8	91+
			(M Johnston) *hld up: hdwy whn hung lft over 1f out: racd on outer whn chsd ldrs ins fnl f: r.o cl home* **11/2**[3]
1050	**4**	*shd*	**Sun Ship (IRE)**[8] 5226 2-9-1 92 ...... PatDobbs 5	90
			(R Hannon) *racd keenly: a.p: chal 2f out: rdn and stl ev ch 1f out: nt qckn ins fnl f* **16/1**
1010	**5**	*6*	**Burning Flute**[8] 5244 2-9-1 88 ...... JamieSpencer 3	72
			(B J Meehan) *s.i.s: bhd: swtchd rt over 1f out: no imp on ldrs: eased ins fnl f* **7/1**
4551	**6**	*1¾*	**Elegant Cad (CAN)**[19] 4931 2-8-12 90 ...... LPKeniry 6	64
			(J R Best) *trckd ldrs: rdn and lost pl over 2f out: btn whn bmpd over 1f out* **15/2**

1m 13.92s (0.12) **Going Correction** -0.15s/f (Firm) **6** Ran SP% **112.7**
Speed ratings (Par 100): **93,89,89,89,81 78**
toteswinger: 1&2 £1.10, 1&3 £3.40, 2&3 £2.50. CSF £6.66 TOTE £2.40: £1.50, £1.70; EX 4.40.
Owner Aykroyd And Sons Ltd **Bred** Thomas Foy **Trained** Musley Bank, N Yorks

FOCUS
A good juvenile conditions stakes and the highest-rated runner in the race scored in decisive fashion. This is strong form for a conditions race with the winner up to Listed level.

NOTEBOOK
Viva Ronaldo(IRE) ◆, officially the highest-rated runner in the race, scored in decisive fashion. He got a lead from the runner-up Parisian Pyramid early but was able to squeeze through on the inside at the point where the false rail ended and once in the clear kept on strongly to record his first success over this trip. Connections are thinking in terms of the Weatherbys Insurance Sales race at Doncaster's St Leger meeting next. (op 2-1 tchd 15-8)
Parisian Pyramid(IRE), who had put up a fine time performance when winning a nursery at Goodwood last time, was stepping up in class and had a stone to find with the winner judged on official ratings. He ran pretty well but once the winner got through on his inside he had nothing in reserve with which to respond. (op 5-2 tchd 11-4 and 3-1 in places)
Effort, who had two-and-a-quarter lengths to find with the winner compared with their running in the July Stakes, ran pretty close to that form, especially considering he had the outside draw, suggesting the form is pretty solid. (op 6-1 tchd 9-2)
Sun Ship(IRE), dropping in class after running in Group and Listed races, showed up from the start and did as well as he was entitled to judged on official marks. (op 10-1)
Burning Flute struggled to go the early pace and never got involved. Official explanation: jockey said colt hung right-handed (op 8-1 tchd 10-1)
Elegant Cad(CAN), who had been held at Group and Listed level prior to getting off the mark in a Polytrack maiden, dropped away turning for home. (op 6-1 tchd 8-1)

5497 RAYMOND CORBETT E B F MAIDEN STKS 7f 2y
4:35 (4:36) (Class 3) 2-Y-O **£7,317** (£2,177; £1,088; £543) **Stalls** Low

Form				RPR
22	**1**		**Full Toss**[28] 4625 2-9-3 0 ...... PatDobbs 2	88+
			(R Hannon) *chsd ldr tl over 4f out: wnt 2nd again wl over 1f out: led appr fnl f: pushed out and in command sn after* **4/6**[1]
0222	**2**	*2*	**Cosmic Sun**[17] 4960 2-8-12 80 ...... FrederikTylicki(5) 4	81
			(R A Fahey) *in tch: nt clr run 2f out: sn rdn: styd on to take 2nd towards fin: nt pce to trble wnr* **10/3**[2]
553	**3**	*½*	**The Kyllachy Kid**[17] 4960 2-9-3 77 ...... MickyFenton 5	80
			(T P Tate) *led: rdn and hdd appr fnl f: kpt on same pce after* **16/1**
52	**4**	*7*	**Layer Cake**[19] 4931 2-9-3 0 ...... JamieSpencer 6	62
			(J W Hills) *in tch: pushed along 2f out: looked ill at ease on trck: wknd over 1f out* **8/1**[3]
33	**5**	*3¾*	**Aladdin's Lamp (IRE)**[21] 4847 2-9-3 0 ...... DarryllHolland 3	53
			(M Johnston) *chsd ldrs: wnt 2nd over 4f out: pushed along over 2f out: wknd over 1f out* **9/1**
0	**6**	*11*	**Piccolo Express**[31] 4530 2-9-3 0 ...... TonyHamilton 1	25
			(B P J Baugh) *hld up: bdly outpcd wl over 1f out* **100/1**
7	*19*	**Nut Hand (IRE)** 2-9-3 0 ...... DavidAllan 8	—
			(T D Easterby) *in rr: pushed along over 3f out: hung bdly rt on bnd and lost tch wl over 1f out* **33/1**

1m 26.31s (-0.19) **Going Correction** -0.15s/f (Firm) **7** Ran SP% **114.0**
Speed ratings (Par 98): **95,92,92,84,79 67,45**
toteswinger: 1&2 £1.60, 1&3 £4.10, 2&3 £4.80. CSF £3.11 TOTE £1.80: £1.30, £2.00; EX 3.70.
Owner The Queen **Bred** The Queen **Trained** East Everleigh, Wilts

FOCUS
A fair maiden and the second and third help establish the strength of the form. The winner stepped forward slightly on his sound Goodwood run.

NOTEBOOK
Full Toss, who got a good lead into the contest, swept to the front halfway up the straight to score pulling up. He had shown his appreciation of a sound surface when finishing a close second at Goodwood and this confidence booster should set him up for handicaps, where he is likely to get a mark in the mid-to-high 80s using the placed horses as a guide. (op 4-5 after 5-6 in places and 10-11 in a place)
Cosmic Sun, who had been narrowly beaten in his last three starts, ran on late to finish second again. Although no match for the winner, he did not appear to do much wrong and deserves to win a race before long. (op 4-1 tchd 9-2)
The Kyllachy Kid had a length to find with the runner-up compared with their meeting on easy ground at Beverley and, after making the running, reduced the margin by half on this sounder surface. (op 12-1)
Layer Cake had lost out narrowly to Elegant Cad, who failed to advertise the form in the preceding contest, on his previous start on Polytrack and faded out of things once in line for home. He now qualifies for a nursery mark. (op 11-2 tchd 5-1)
Aladdin's Lamp(IRE) was shown up as just modest on this occasion, but at least he also now qualifies for handicaps. (tchd 10-1)

Nut Hand(IRE) Official explanation: jockey said gelding hung right turning into home straight

5498 WILLIAM T CORBETT "IN RUNNING" H'CAP — 1m 7f 195y

5:05 (5:05) (Class 4) (0-85,82) 3-Y-0+ **£5,504** (£1,637; £818; £408) **Stalls** Low

Form RPR

0012 1 **Ainama (IRE)**[9] 5199 4-10-0 **82** ... JamieSpencer 1 90+
(M Wigham) *confidently rdn off the pce: hdwy over 2f out: led pulling double over 1f out: v cheekily* **2/1**[1]

-460 2 *1* **Dr Sharp (IRE)**[65] 3414 8-9-7 **75** ... MickyFenton 4 77
(T P Tate) *chsd ldr: led wl over 7f out: rdn and hdd over 1f out: styd on same pce and chalng for pls thrght fnl f: no ch w wnr* **10/1**

0313 3 *shd* **Hawridge King**[38] 4314 6-9-9 **80** ... JamesMillman(3) 8 82
(W S Kittow) *midfield: tk clsr order 9f out: wnt 2nd 4f out: rdn to chal 2f out: kpt on same pce and chal for pls thrght fnl f: no ch w wnr* **7/1**[3]

6210 4 *hd* **Squirtle (IRE)**[5] 5367 5-8-13 **67** ... PatCosgrave 6 69
(W M Brisbourne) *s.i.s: midfield: lost pl 5f out: rallied u.p over 1f out: styd on to chal for pls towards fin: no ch w wnr* **10/1**

-210 5 *hd* **Mighty Moon**[32] 4511 5-9-2 **75** ... FrederikTylicki(5) 9 77
(R A Fahey) *hld up: hdwy 5f out: rdn to chse ldrs over 1f out: kpt on u.p whn chalng for pls thrght fnl f: no ch w wnr* **5/2**[2]

2353 6 *10* **Thewhirlingdervish (IRE)**[34] 4452 10-8-12 **66** oh1 ... DavidAllan 3 56
(T D Easterby) *chsd ldrs tl rdn and wknd 2f out* **9/1**

5100 7 *¾* **Mister Arjay (USA)**[17] 4963 8-8-12 **73** ... LanceBetts(7) 5 62
(B Ellison) *led: hdd wl over 7f out: rdn whn stl chsd ldrs over 3f out: wknd wl over 1f out* **20/1**

4246 8 *nse* **Inspirina (IRE)**[66] 3368 4-9-4 **72** ... HayleyTurner 7 61
(R Ford) *hld up: effrt on outside over 2f out: no imp on ldrs: wknd over 1f out* **8/1**

3m 25.47s (-4.43) **Going Correction** -0.15s/f (Firm) 8 Ran SP% **118.5**

Speed ratings (Par 105): **105,104,104,104,104 99,98,98**

toteswinger: 1&2 £5.10, 1&3 £4.60, 2&3 £5.50. CSF £24.16 CT £121.72 TOTE £2.80: £1.50, £2.50, £2.30; EX 24.40 Place 6: £24.84 Place 5: £12.19.

Owner R Morecombe & D Morrison **Bred** Roundhill Stud And A Stroud **Trained** Newmarket, Suffolk

FOCUS

A fair staying handicap, but run at a good pace and, although the first five finished in something of a heap, it bore no relationship to the superiority of the winner who is rated value for five lengths with the placed horses setting the standard.

T/Plt: £46.80 to a £1 stake. Pool: £110,790.88. 1,725.71 winning tickets. T/Qpdt: £10.40 to a £1 stake. Pool: £4,527.40. 321.30 winning tickets. DO

5380 RIPON (R-H)

Saturday, August 30

OFFICIAL GOING: Good (good to firm in places; 8.4)

Wind: Fresh, half behind Weather: Cloudy

5499 UREDALE MAIDEN STKS (DIV I) — 6f

1:40 (1:44) (Class 5) 2-Y-0 **£3,561** (£1,059; £529; £264) **Stalls** Low

Form RPR

52 1 **Quanah Parker (IRE)**[21] 4847 2-9-3 0 ... DeanMcKeown 2 81
(R M Whitaker) *mde all: rdn over 1f out: kpt on strly fnl f* **7/1**

3 2 *2 ¼* **Montmorency (IRE)**[14] 5089 2-9-3 0 ... NCallan 12 74
(Saeed Bin Suroor) *cl up: effrt and edgd rt over 1f out: kpt on same pce fnl f* **4/1**[2]

60 3 *3 ¼* **Count Paris (USA)**[15] 5053 2-9-3 0 ... RoystonFfrench 15 65
(M Johnston) *trckd ldrs: effrt over 2f out: nt qckn over 1f out* **10/1**

0 4 *5* **Spinners End (IRE)**[43] 4164 2-9-3 0 ... AndrewElliott 11 50
(K R Burke) *towards rr: rdn over 2f out: kpt on fnl f: no imp* **13/2**[3]

5 *3 ¼* **Darcey** 2-8-12 0 ... JamieMoriarty 10 35
(R A Fahey) *dwlt: bhd tl sme late hdwy: nvr on terms* **22/1**

00 6 *4* **Acclaben (IRE)**[60] 3590 2-9-0 0 ... PJMcDonald(3) 6 28
(G A Swinbank) *hld up: pushed along 1/2-way: nvr rchd ldrs* **33/1**

34 7 *½* **Aathaar**[20] 4890 2-9-3 0 ... RobertWinston 8 26
(Sir Michael Stoute) *prom: sn drvn along: rdn and wknd 2f out: eased whn btn ins fnl f* **11/10**[1]

04 8 *1 ½* **Miss Xu Xia**[78] 3008 2-8-12 0 ... DanielTudhope 7 17
(G R Oldroyd) *in midfield: outpcd after 2f: n.d after* **100/1**

00 9 *½* **Silver Sceptre (IRE)**[47] 4024 2-9-3 0 ... NeilPollard 3 20
(W J Musson) *hld up: pushed along 1/2-way: n.d* **100/1**

10 *1 ¼* **Rebel Radio (USA)** 2-9-3 0 ... TomEaves 13 17
(J Howard Johnson) *dwlt: sn prom: rdn and wknd fr 1/2-way* **25/1**

11 *20* **Oneofthesedayz (IRE)** 2-8-9 0 ... NeilBrown(3) 1 —
(Miss V Haigh) *uns rdr and loose bef s: dwlt: sn wl bhd* **80/1**

1m 13.35s (0.35) **Going Correction** +0.05s/f (Good) 11 Ran SP% **116.9**

Speed ratings (Par 94): **99,96,91,85,80 75,74,72,72,70 43**

toteswinger: 1&2 £3.50, 1&3 £5.30, 2&3 £7.30. CSF £33.34 TOTE £8.70: £2.00, £1.70, £2.60; EX 40.30 Trifecta £76.50 Pool: £479.88 - 4.64 winning units..

Owner Robert Macgregor **Bred** M Fahy **Trained** Scarcroft, W Yorks

FOCUS

An interesting maiden with some top stables represented.

NOTEBOOK

Quanah Parker(IRE), a rangy, imposing sort, broke smartly from his low draw to hug the stands' rail and always had the others struggling, winning with authority. He may go to Ayr before taking his chance in the Two-Year-Old Trophy at Redcar in October and looks promising. (op 8-1 tchd 9-1)

Montmorency(IRE) was bustled early to get to the rail from his wide draw and that early effort possibly told as, though he pulled clear with the winner, he was always looking a bit stretched for speed. He improved again on his debut when third of four in a Lingfield maiden last time, and should continue to progress. He holds an entry for the Dewhurst in October. (op 5-1)

Count Paris(USA) was also drawn high and was driven up with the pace, but had to race further from the rail than the first two and was outpaced from two furlongs out but still stayed on. He has been running in competitive races at Goodwood and Newbury, and should pick up a maiden, especially if his sights are lowered a little. (op 8-1 tchd 11-1)

Spinners End(IRE) holds several entries for some top two-year-old races later in the season, but he will need to improve to feature in those on this evidence for he was never going the pace. (op 7-1 tchd 6-1)

Darcey made some late headway without threatening and will come on for this. (op 25-1 tchd 20-1)

Aathaar, a smallish colt, was a well-backed favourite to atone for his defeat when fading over 7f in a more competitive race last time, but though he had every chance on the rail, he was never going the pace and again faded. This was a disappointing run. Official explanation: jockey said colt never travelled (tchd Evens and 5-4)

5500 UREDALE MAIDEN STKS (DIV II) — 6f

2:10 (2:11) (Class 5) 2-Y-0 **£3,561** (£1,059; £529; £264) **Stalls** Low

Form RPR

6 1 **Mary Mason**[60] 3590 2-8-12 0 ... TPO'Shea 13 73
(Mrs A Duffield) *sn led: pushed along over 2f out: rdn wl over 1f out: kpt on u.p ins fnl f* **20/1**

2 *1 ¼* **Bajan Tryst (USA)** 2-9-3 0 ... NCallan 8 75+
(K A Ryan) *chsd wnr: effrt 2f out: sn rdn and ev ch ent fnl f: sn drvn and kpt on same pce towards fin* **7/1**[3]

22 3 *½* **Prime Mood (IRE)**[30] 4557 2-9-3 0 ... TomEaves 3 73+
(B Smart) *wnt rt s: chsd ldrs: rdn along and hanging rt after 2f: drvn 2f out: styd on ins fnl f* **5/6**[1]

60 4 *2 ¼* **Shaker Style (USA)**[41] 4214 2-9-3 0 ... (b[1]) GrahamGibbons 10 66
(J D Bethell) *chsd ldng pair: rdn along 2f out: drvn and one pce appr fnl f* **12/1**

5 *1 ½* **Embsay Crag** 2-9-0 0 ... NeilBrown(3) 14 62
(Mrs K Walton) *in tch on outer: rdn along 2f out: kpt on same pce* **80/1**

6 *1 ½* **Holberg (UAE)** 2-9-3 0 ... RoystonFfrench 6 57
(M Johnston) *wnt lft s: sn rdn along and outpcd towards rr: hdwy over 2f out: styd on u.p appr fnl f: nrst fin* **13/2**[2]

50 7 *3* **Royal Salsa (IRE)**[14] 5106 2-8-5 0 ... BMcHugh(7) 11 43
(R A Fahey) *in midfield: rdn along over 2f out: no hdwy* **33/1**

0 8 *13* **Venetian Lady**[43] 4169 2-8-9 0 ... AndrewMullen(3) 12 —
(Mrs A Duffield) *in tch: rdn along bef 1/2-way: sn wknd* **100/1**

9 *nse* **Paddythefish (USA)** 2-9-3 0 ... AndrewElliott 2 9
(K R Burke) *sn rdn along and a outpcd in rr* **7/1**[3]

10 *shd* **Lady Zena** 2-8-5 0 ... BradleyRoper(7) 4 —
(M W Easterby) *hmpd s: a in rr* **66/1**

11 *17* **Eyesore** 2-8-12 0 ... (e[1]) PAspell 5 —
(R C Guest) *hmpd s: a in rr* **50/1**

05 12 *22* **Tee Gee Cee**[76] 3055 2-9-0 0 ... DuranFentiman(3) 9 —
(T D Easterby) *a towards rr* **25/1**

0 13 *23* **Arteus**[12] 5158 2-9-3 0 ... TonyCulhane 7 —
(G G Margarson) *a in rr* **50/1**

1m 14.46s (1.46) **Going Correction** +0.05s/f (Good) 13 Ran SP% **119.8**

Speed ratings (Par 94): **92,90,89,86,84 82,78,61,61,61 38,9,—**

toteswinger: 1&2 £26.20, 1&3 £8.00, 2&3 £3.70. CSF £148.18 TOTE £22.80: £3.70, £2.30, £1.10; EX 258.80 TRIFECTA Not won..

Owner R R Whitton **Bred** R R Whitton **Trained** Constable Burton, N Yorks

■ Stewards' Enquiry : T P O'Shea one-day ban: not riding to draw (Sep 14)

FOCUS

The weaker of the two divisions of the maiden, run in a time over one second slower than the first.

NOTEBOOK

Mary Mason broke smartly from her wide draw and made straight for the stands' rail, got the lead and was never headed. She made late progress on her debut at Thirsk two months ago but the change of tactics certainly worked on this track.

Bajan Tryst(USA) attempted to get to the lead on the rail but was outpaced early by the winner, then challenged three-wide one furlong out without looking likely to get there. The stable have a 37 per cent strike rate with their juveniles at Ripon this season, so he might have been expected to do a little better, but he should be able to pick up a maiden. (op 13-2)

Prime Mood(IRE) was again a warm order to make amends for his flop at short odds at Musselburgh over 5f last time, and though he showed early speed he was outpaced by halfway before staying on again. If anything, the Choisir colt might need to step up in trip. On this evidence his entries in the valuable two-year-old races at Doncaster and Redcar look a little ambitious. (op 10-11 tchd Evens)

Shaker Style(USA), another holding an entry for Redcar in October, had looked outpaced in his first two races at 6f and 7f and, tried in first-time blinkers, he showed more early speed before tiring in the final furlong. (op 14-1)

Embsay Crag headed the chasing pack and stayed on towards the finish without threatening. Considering his stable are 0-15 with their juveniles, he should improve given time. (op 66-1)

Holberg(UAE) was never going the pace on his debut, but is likely to be seen to better effect as a three-year-old. Official explanation: jockey said colt missed the break (op 7-1 tchd 6-1)

Paddythefish(USA) Official explanation: jockey said colt missed the break

Arteus Official explanation: jockey said colt had a breathing problem

5501 HAPPY 80TH BIRTHDAY GEORGE SIMPSON APPRENTICE (S) STKS — 6f

2:40 (2:40) (Class 6) 3-4-Y-0 **£2,590** (£770; £385; £192) **Stalls** Low

Form RPR

-200 1 **Varinia (IRE)**[40] 4241 3-8-8 46 ... JohnCavanagh(5) 1 55
(M Brittain) *towards rr: hdwy over 1f out: led ins fnl f: edgd rt: kpt on wl* **25/1**

-303 2 *¾* **Pintano**[36] 4381 3-9-4 65 ... (b) ClGillies 10 57
(J Howard Johnson) *cl up: rdn to ld over 2f out: edgd rt and hdd ins fnl f: kpt on u.p* **5/2**[1]

2-00 3 *nse* **Mickleberry (IRE)**[45] 4073 4-9-2 49 ... RossAtkinson 15 52
(M Brittain) *prom: effrt over 2f out: ev ch and edgd rt ins fnl f: r.o* **12/1**

604 4 *1 ¾* **Foreign Rhythm (IRE)**[6] 5307 3-9-4 53 ... (v) StacyRenwick 6 51
(N Tinkler) *bhd tl hdwy over 1f out: nrst fin* **6/1**[3]

-002 5 *¾* **Missus Molly Brown**[73] 3139 4-8-13 42 ... BMcHugh(3) 9 44
(R A Fahey) *dwlt: outpcd tl hdwy over 1f out: kpt on same pce ins fnl f* **9/2**[2]

6000 6 *1 ¼* **Veronicas Way**[70] 3281 3-8-13 48 ... AmyBaker 5 40
(G M Moore) *in tch: outpcd over 2f out: no imp fnl f* **14/1**

0000 7 *1 ¾* **Cool Fashion (IRE)**[26] 4686 3-8-8 44 ... (b) AnthonyBetts(5) 8 34
(Ollie Pears) *bmpd s: prom: drvn and outpcd over 2f out: n.d after* **12/1**

00 8 *3 ¾* **Red Wind (IRE)**[14] 5110 3-9-4 0 ... (b[1]) JPHamblett 14 27
(N Wilson) *led to over 2f out: wknd over 1f out* **40/1**

6400 9 *hd* **Nufoudh (IRE)**[15] 5045 4-9-2 49 ... JamieKyne(5) 13 27
(Miss Tracy Waggott) *dwlt: rdn in rr on outside 1/2-way: nvr rchd ldrs* **15/2**

-002 10 *nk* **Head To Head (IRE)**[15] 5044 4-9-2 54 ... JamesRogers(5) 11 26
(A D Brown) *in tch tl rdn and wknd over 2f out* **14/1**

00-0 11 *1 ¾* **Ruby's Rainbow (IRE)**[28] 4615 3-8-8 30 ... MatthewLawson(5) 2 15
(J Balding) *bhd and rdn along: nvr on terms* **50/1**

00 12 *2* **Porto Santana (IRE)**[17] 4962 3-8-13 75 ... (v[1]) BradleyRoper(5) 4 14
(D Nicholls) *chsd ldrs: rdn 1/2-way: wknd 2f out* **7/1**

The Form Book, Raceform Ltd, Compton, RG20 6NL

0000 **13** *5* **Ourbelle**[26] 4684 3-8-8 29 RichardRowe(5) 12 —
(Miss Tracy Waggott) *in midfield on outside: hung rt 1/2-way: sn wknd* **80/1**

1m 15.26s (2.26) **Going Correction** +0.05s/f (Good)
WFA 3 from 4yo 3lb 13 Ran SP% **123.5**
Speed ratings (Par 101): **86,85,84,82,81 79,77,72,72,71 69,66,60**
toteswinger: 1&2 £3.00, 1&3 £23.20, 2&3 £6.80. CSF £88.73 TOTE £30.00: £5.50, £1.50, £3.70; EX 136.00 TRIFECTA Not won..
Owner Northgate Black **Bred** John Grogan **Trained** Warthill, N Yorks
■ Stewards' Enquiry : Ross Atkinson caution: careless riding
B McHugh two-day ban: used whip with excessive frequency (Sep 14-15)

FOCUS
A weak seller full of disappointing 3yos, although the third and fourth give the form some sense. A very moderate time even for a seller, slower than both divisions of the two-year-old maiden.

5502 WENSLEYDALE H'CAP 1m 1f 170y
3:15 (3:15) (Class 4) (0-80,80) 3-Y-O **£6,938** (£2,076; £1,038; £519; £258) **Stalls** High

Form RPR
143 **1** **Closertobelieving**[17] 4984 3-9-7 **80** GeorgeBaker 3 91+
(D R C Elsworth) *hld up in rr: hdwy 3f out: swtchd rt and rdn to chal whn hung rt over 1f out: led ent fnl f: drvn out* **3/1**[1]
1240 **2** *nk* **St Jean Cap Ferrat**[28] 4621 3-9-6 **79** (v) TPO'Shea 2 90
(G Wragg) *trckd ldrs: hdwy over 4f out: rdn to chal 2f out and ev ch tl drvn ent fnl f and no ex towards fin* **7/1**
1233 **3** *2 1/4* **Mezzanisi (IRE)**[28] 4619 3-9-4 **80** PJMcDonald(3) 7 86
(M L W Bell) *hld up towards rr: hdwy over 4f out: rdn to ld 2f out: drvn and hdd ent fnl f: one pce* **10/3**[2]
0121 **4** *9* **Highland Love**[17] 4964 3-8-10 **72** MichaelJStainton(3) 4 60
(Jedd O'Keeffe) *trckd ldr: hdwy 3f out and sn cl up: rdn and ev ch 2f out: drvn and hld whn hmpd over 1f out: wknd after* **7/2**[3]
2562 **5** *7* **Feisty Royale**[14] 5108 3-8-13 **72** RoystonFfrench 1 46
(M Johnston) *chsd ldng pair: rdn along over 3f out: sn drvn and wknd 2f out* **7/1**
510 **6** *7* **Totoman**[64] 3459 3-9-1 **74** TonyCulhane 5 34
(G G Margarson) *trckd ldrs: effrt 4f out: rdn along wl over 2f out and sn btn* **16/1**
1542 **7** *9* **Black Dahlia**[15] 5075 3-9-3 **76** NCallan 8 18
(A J McCabe) *set stdy pce: rdn and qcknd over 4f out: drvn and hdd 2f out: sn drvn and wkng whn hmpd over 1f out* **7/1**

2m 3.77s (-1.63) **Going Correction** +0.05s/f (Good) 7 Ran SP% **113.7**
Speed ratings (Par 102): **108,107,105,98,93 87,80**
toteswinger: 1&2 £5.00, 1&3 £4.50, 2&3 £6.00. CSF £23.89 CT £72.48 TOTE £3.40: £2.30, £3.30; EX 15.00 Trifecta £68.80 Pool: £232.77 - 2.50 winning units..
Owner Gordon Li **Bred** Cheveley Park Stud Ltd **Trained** Newmarket, Suffolk
■ Stewards' Enquiry : George Baker four-day ban: careless riding (Sep 14-17)

FOCUS
A competitive handicap featuring several in-form runners. The first three were the last trio turning in and the winner is nicely progressive.
Black Dahlia Official explanation: jockey said filly suffered interference in running

5503 RIPON CATHEDRAL CITY OF THE DALES H'CAP 6f
3:50 (3:50) (Class 2) (0-100,100) 4-Y-0+
£12,462 (£3,732; £1,866; £934; £466; £234) **Stalls** Low

Form RPR
512 **1** **Bel Cantor**[21] 4854 5-8-0 **84** (p) KellyHarrison(5) 14 95
(W J H Ratcliffe) *mde all far side: drvn and kpt on strly fnl f* **9/1**
0230 **2** *1 3/4* **Swift Princess (IRE)**[40] 4240 4-8-5 **84** (v) AndrewElliott 4 89
(K R Burke) *led stands' side gp: rdn and r.o fnl f: nt rch far side wnr: 1st of 10 in gp* **18/1**
0000 **3** *1/2* **Northern Fling**[28] 4624 4-9-7 **100** SilvestreDeSousa 16 104
(D Nicholls) *cl up far side: rdn over 2f out: kpt on fnl f: 2nd of 6 in gp* **11/2**[1]
0340 **4** *1 1/4* **Joseph Henry**[14] 5109 6-8-6 **88** AndrewMullen(3) 17 88+
(D Nicholls) *cl up far side: rdn and hung bdly lft wl over 1f out: ev ch stands' side gp ins fnl f: one pce: 2nd of 10 in gp* **13/2**[3]
0100 **5** *hd* **Zomerlust**[21] 4854 6-8-11 **90** GrahamGibbons 19 89
(J J Quinn) *in tch far side: effrt over 2f out: kpt on u.p fnl f: 3rd of 6 in gp* **18/1**
4115 **6** *nk* **Inter Vision (USA)**[93] 2538 8-9-4 **97** DanielTudhope 18 95
(A Dickman) *midfield far side: drvn over 2f out: one pce fnl f: 4th of 6 in gp* **14/1**
0500 **7** *2 1/4* **Fremen (USA)**[49] 3972 8-8-9 **88** PaulQuinn 11 79
(D Nicholls) *swtchd to r far side sn after s: hld up: pushed along 2f out: kpt on fnl f: no imp: 5th of 6 in gp* **22/1**
2000 **8** *3/4* **High Curragh**[21] 4854 5-8-2 **81** PaulFessey 9 70
(K A Ryan) *cl up stands' side tl rdn and no ex over 1f out: 3rd of 10 in gp* **18/1**
05-0 **9** *3/4* **Majuro (IRE)**[81] 2905 4-8-10 **92** NeilBrown(3) 13 78
(M W Easterby) *hld up far side: rdn 2f out: nvr rchd ldrs: last of 6 in gp* **25/1**
1040 **10** *nse* **Barney McGrew (IRE)**[28] 4624 5-9-0 **93** TomEaves 8 79+
(M Dods) *taken early to post: dwlt: hld up stands' side: rdn 2f out: nvr rchd ldrs: 4th of 10 in gp* **14/1**
6010 **11** *1 1/4* **Bond City (IRE)**[14] 5109 6-8-8 **90** MichaelJStainton(3) 2 72
(G R Oldroyd) *prom: drvn along 1/2-way: btn over 1f out: 5th of 10 in gp* **14/1**
2150 **12** *shd* **He's A Humbug (IRE)**[17] 4962 4-8-5 **84** (p) SaleemGolam 12 66
(K A Ryan) *cl up stands' side tl wknd wl over 1f out: 6th of 10 in gp* **33/1**
5403 **13** *3 1/4* **Gallery Girl (IRE)**[17] 4962 5-7-13 **81** oh2 DuranFentiman(3) 7 52
(T D Easterby) *prom stands' side tl wknd fr 2f out: 7th of 10 in gp* **25/1**
3605 **14** *2 1/2* **Stevie Gee (IRE)**[35] 4437 4-8-6 **88** PJMcDonald(3) 3 51
(G A Swinbank) *hld up stands' side: rdn over 2f out: n.d: 8th of 10 in gp* **15/2**
010 **15** *4* **My Gacho (IRE)**[35] 4437 6-8-5 **84** (b) RoystonFfrench 1 35
(M Johnston) *towards rr stands' side: drvn over 3f out: nvr on terms: 9th of 10 in gp* **10/1**
2331 **16** *3* **Total Impact**[30] 4555 5-8-7 **86** JamieMoriarty 10 27
(R A Fahey) *hld up outer of stands' side gp: rdn 1/2-way: nvr on terms: last of 10 in gp* **6/1**[2]

1m 11.87s (-1.13) **Going Correction** +0.05s/f (Good) 16 Ran SP% **124.6**
Speed ratings (Par 109): **109,106,106,104,104 103,100,99,98,98 96,96,92,89,83 79**
toteswinger: 1&2 £46.60, 1&3 £17.90, 2&3 £20.30. CSF £157.37 CT £1029.05 TOTE £12.40: £2.50, £4.20, £1.90, £2.00; EX 167.40 Trifecta £418.40 Part won. Pool: £565.44 - 0.10 winning units..
Owner W J H Ratcliffe **Bred** Henry And Mrs Rosemary Moszkowicz **Trained** Wensley, N Yorks

FOCUS
A good handicap. The field split into two groups, and though a high draw is an advantage here, racing prominently and running against the rail are also significant factors. The winner and runner-up both made all on their side.

NOTEBOOK
Bel Cantor came into this race in grand form after a win and a second place recently, and though he was up in class and on a career-high mark, he led on the far-side rail and never saw a rival. He is entered at Ayr next month. (op 15-2)
Swift Princess(IRE) led the stands'-side group and was gaining on the winner near the finish. Usually better in smaller fields, she capitalised on her low weight here and could go one better especially if dropped a little in grade. (op 20-1)
Northern Fling, who tried to chase the winner on the far side from several lengths off the pace, was driven two furlongs out and responded well, but there was no catching the lowly weighted winner on this track today. He has been pitched into some big sprint handicaps this season, and ran well against a bad draw in the Stewards' Cup last time. He should again run a good race if taking up his engagement at Ayr. (op 13-2 tchd 5-1)
Joseph Henry ran an interesting race. Prominent in the far-side group, he began to veer left across the course two furlongs out, ending up chasing home Swift Princess on the stands' side. His record is now 0-18 over 6f, but if he can get a rail to run against stepped up to a mile he should gain compensation. Official explanation: jockey said gelding hung left (tchd 15-2)
Zomerlust ran respectably on the far side considering he prefers softer ground. (op 20-1 tchd 22-1)
Inter Vision(USA) ran respectably, staying on late without ever threatening. Most of his best form has been following a recent race, and he will come on for this. (op 16-1)
My Gacho(IRE) Official explanation: jockey said gelding lost its action
Total Impact Official explanation: trainer had no explanation for the poor form shown

5504 COVERDALE H'CAP 1m
4:25 (4:25) (Class 4) (0-80,78) 3-Y-O **£6,938** (£2,076; £1,038; £519; £258) **Stalls** High

Form RPR
4423 **1** **Reel Buddy Star**[23] 4783 3-9-2 **73** TomEaves 3 81
(G M Moore) *cl up: led after 2f: pushed along over 3f out: rdn over 2f out: drvn ins fnl f and styd on gamely* **7/2**[2]
2006 **2** *nk* **Applaude**[30] 4560 3-8-13 **70** RobertWinston 1 77
(G A Swinbank) *prom: cl up 1/2-way: rdn along over 2f out: drvn over 1f out and ev ch tl no ex wl ins fnl f* **33/1**
3210 **3** *nk* **Lee Miller (IRE)**[31] 4520 3-9-7 **78** GeorgeBaker 9 84+
(L M Cumani) *hld up: hdwy 3f out: rdn to chse ldng pair 2f out: drvn and edgd rt ent fnl f: styd on wl towards fin* **11/4**[1]
1445 **4** *6* **Shaloo Diamond**[7] 5257 3-9-2 **76** MichaelJStainton(3) 2 69
(R M Whitaker) *trckd ldrs: hdwy on outer over 3f out: rdn 2f out: drvn and edgd rt appr last: sn no imp* **4/1**[3]
2015 **5** *2 1/2* **Red Skipper (IRE)**[8] 5224 3-8-2 **64** KellyHarrison(5) 5 51
(N Wilson) *chsd ldrs: effrt and hdwy 3f out: rdn over 2f out: drvn and wknd over 1f out* **16/1**
5241 **6** *3 3/4* **Romantic Destiny**[36] 4379 3-9-2 **73** NCallan 8 51
(K A Ryan) *chsd ldrs: rdn along over 3f out: sn drvn and wknd over 2f out* **8/1**
153 **7** *nk* **Shadowtime**[56] 3709 3-8-13 **70** DeanMcKeown 11 47
(Miss Tracy Waggott) *led 2f: chsd ldrs tl rdn along 3f out and sn wknd* **17/2**
5310 **8** *shd* **Viscountess (IRE)**[7] 5267 3-8-13 **70** RoystonFfrench 6 47
(M Johnston) *cl up on inner: rdn along over 3f out: drvn over 2f out and sn wknd* **17/2**
30-0 **9** *4* **Lecanvey**[33] 4494 3-8-7 **64** JamieMoriarty 10 32
(R A Fahey) *a towards rr* **10/1**
0-50 **10** *nse* **Bonjour Allure (IRE)**[56] 3716 3-8-12 **72** AndrewMullen(3) 7 40
(Mrs A Duffield) *s.i.s: a in rr* **33/1**

1m 41.37s (-0.03) **Going Correction** +0.05s/f (Good) 10 Ran SP% **121.9**
Speed ratings (Par 102): **102,101,101,95,92 89,88,88,84,84**
toteswinger: 1&2 £12.50, 1&3 £2.90, 2&3 £16.70. CSF £113.78 CT £373.83 TOTE £3.60: £2.10, £5.10, £1.50; EX 114.30 TRIFECTA Not won..
Owner J W Armstrong & M J Howarth **Bred** M Pennell **Trained** Middleham Moor, N Yorks

FOCUS
Quite a competitive handicap, and once again it helped to race against the rail in the home straight. Not many got into the race and the first two were to the fore almost throughout.
Lee Miller(IRE) Official explanation: jockey said filly was hampered going into bend leaving back straight

5505 TRAINERMAGAZINE.COM MAIDEN STKS 1m 1f 170y
4:55 (4:57) (Class 5) 3-Y-0+ **£3,885** (£1,156; £577; £288) **Stalls** High

Form RPR
0-52 **1** **Crystal Rock (IRE)**[68] 3326 3-9-3 75 NCallan 6 82+
(B W Hills) *trckd ldrs: led over 3f out: drew clr fr 2f out: eased wl ins fnl f* **11/4**[2]
2 *7* **Nexus (IRE)** 3-9-3 0 RobertWinston 7 66+
(Saeed Bin Suroor) *missed break: hdwy 1/2-way: effrt over 2f out: hung rt over 1f out: chsd wnr ins fnl f: r.o: no ch w wnr* **10/3**[3]
525 **3** *2* **Crusoe's Return**[26] 4695 3-9-3 79 GeorgeBaker 3 62
(L M Cumani) *trckd ldrs: effrt over 2f out: edgd lft and one pce over 1f out: lost 2nd ins fnl f* **7/4**[1]
4 *2 3/4* **Turjuman (USA)**[67] 3-9-3 0 NeilPollard 4 56
(W J Musson) *prom: effrt 3f out: one pce fr 3f out* **14/1**
44 **5** *1/2* **Sirvino**[88] 2700 3-9-3 0 PaulFessey 1 55
(T D Barron) *chsd ldng gp: pushed along 3f out: one pce* **16/1**
0455 **6** *1/2* **Defies Logic**[24] 4738 3-9-3 51 RoystonFfrench 14 54
(J G Given) *led to over 3f out: no ex fr 2f out* **16/1**
05 **7** *4 1/2* **Predictable (IRE)**[5] 5361 3-8-5 0 BradleyRoper(7) 5 40
(M W Easterby) *prom tl wknd fr 2f out* **66/1**
8 *18* **Rimsky Korsakov (IRE)**[86] 6369 4-9-11 0 TonyCulhane 11 9
(Micky Hammond) *bhd: struggling 1/2-way: nvr on terms* **20/1**
00 **9** *1 3/4* **Bertie Boo**[15] 5042 3-9-3 0 TomEaves 12 6
(B Smart) *towards rr: struggling 4f out: sn btn* **33/1**
0-0 **10** *4 1/2* **Tiegan An Josh**[52] 3835 3-8-7 0 KellyHarrison(5) 10 —
(A Crook) *cl up tl rdn and wknd over 3f out* **200/1**
11 *7* **Mill Annie** 3-8-9 0 PJMcDonald(3) 13 —
(G M Moore) *missed break: a bhd* **33/1**
0 **12** *4 1/2* **Ma Nadri**[20] 4901 3-8-12 0 JamieMoriarty 8 —
(S T Mason) *s.i.s: nvr on terms* **100/1**
U **13** *140* **Mandrake Miss**[20] 4901 4-9-3 0 AndrewMullen(3) 2 —
(C R Wilson) *s.s: sn wl bhd* **100/1**

2m 5.84s (0.44) **Going Correction** +0.05s/f (Good)
WFA 3 from 4yo 8lb 13 Ran SP% **119.2**
Speed ratings (Par 103): **100,94,92,90,90 89,86,71,70,66 61,57,—**
toteswinger: 1&2 £2.50, 1&3 £1.80, 2&3 £2.10. CSF £11.42 TOTE £3.90: £1.70, £1.70, £1.30; EX 14.70 Trifecta £16.00 Pool: £246.25 - 11.37 winning units. Place 6: £73.87 Place 5: £19.98.

Owner Triermore Stud **Bred** Triermore Stud **Trained** Lambourn, Berks
■ The Little Master was withdrawn (14/1, veterinary advice). Deduct 5p in the £ under R4.

FOCUS
A mixed bag for this maiden, with well-bred expensive purchases running against hurdlers and bumper runners. It did not take too much winning but Crystal Rock did it well.
T/Plt: £47.20 to a £1 stake. Pool: £58,787.77. 908.94 winning tickets. T/Qpdt: £13.60 to a £1 stake. Pool: £3,385.80. 184.10 winning tickets. RY

5466 SANDOWN (R-H)
Saturday, August 30

OFFICIAL GOING: Good (good to firm in places)
Wind: nil Weather: warm and sunny

5506 IVECO ATALANTA STKS (LISTED RACE) (F&M) — 1m 14y
2:05 (2:07) (Class 1) 3-Y-O+
£22,708 (£8,608; £4,308; £2,148; £1,076; £540) **Stalls** High

Form — RPR

2353 **1** **Shabiba (USA)**[29] 4590 3-8-8 99 .... RHills 6 101
(M P Tregoning) *sn in mid-div: hdwy fr 3f out: pushed along to ld wl over 1f out: drvn and styd on strly ins fnl f* **17/2**

6-14 **2** *1 1/4* **Ada River**[106] 2149 3-8-8 93 .... WilliamBuick 3 98
(A M Balding) *lw: stdd s but sn trcking ldrs: pushed along over 2f out: styd on wl u.p to chse wnr fnl f: kpt on but a hld* **20/1**

2165 **3** *nk* **Ghaidaa (IRE)**[31] 4520 3-8-8 90 .... MartinDwyer 1 97
(M A Jarvis) *in rr: rdn along 3f out: styd on u.p fnl 2f and tk 3rd ins fnl f: clsng on 2nd but no ch w wnr* **22/1**

6226 **4** *1 1/2* **Barshiba (IRE)**[27] 4674 4-9-0 110 .... TQuinn 10 94
(D R C Elsworth) *plld hrd: chsd ldrs and stdd after 4f: drvn and lost pl over 2f out: styd on again u.p fr over 1f out: gng on again cl home* **7/2**[1]

6022 **5** *1 1/4* **Eva's Request (IRE)**[13] 5120 3-8-8 99 .... EdwardCreighton 13 91
(M R Channon) *chsd ldrs: rdn 3f out and pressing ldr 2f out: stl wl there 1f out: wknd ins fnl f* **6/1**[3]

2342 **6** *1* **Mekong Melody (IRE)**[12] 5149 3-8-8 76 .... IanMongan 9 88?
(C G Cox) *sn chsng ldr: rdn and ev ch 2f out: wknd qckly 1f out* **50/1**

-100 **7** *1* **Raymi Coya (CAN)**[7] 4674 3-8-12 102 .... TedDurcan 12 90
(M Botti) *in tch: rdn and outpcd 3f out: styd on again fr over 1f out but nvr in contention* **12/1**

1051 **8** *1/2* **Rosaleen (IRE)**[56] 3742 3-8-12 99 .... AlanMunro 4 89
(B J Meehan) *in rr: stl plenty to do whn plld to outside and pushed along over 2f out: styd on fnl f but nvr in contention* **12/1**

1211 **9** *1* **Lindelaan (USA)**[42] 4189 3-8-8 96 .... (b[1]) RyanMoore 8 83
(Sir Michael Stoute) *lw: in rr: pushed along and mod prog 3f out: nvr in contention after* **4/1**[2]

23-5 **10** *2 3/4* **In The Light**[17] 4977 4-9-0 0 .... JimmyFortune 11 76
(Sir Michael Stoute) *lw: chsd ldrs: rdn 3f out: wknd 2f out* **14/1**

4054 **11** *7* **Selinka**[17] 4977 4-9-0 104 .... (v[1]) RichardHughes 7 60
(R Hannon) *in tch: rdn 3f out: sn btn* **9/1**

0 **12** *3* **Que Piensa Cat (ARG)**[27] 4660 4-9-0 100 .... LDettori 5 53
(Saeed Bin Suroor) *led: rdn 2f out: hdd & wknd qckly wl over 1f out: hung rt and hit rails whn no ch ins fnl f: eased* **14/1**

1m 41.32s (-1.98) **Going Correction** -0.025s/f (Good)
WFA 3 from 4yo+ 6lb — **12 Ran** SP% **116.8**
Speed ratings (Par 111): **108,106,106,104,103 102,101,101,100,97 90,87**
toteswinger: 1&2 £36.20, 1&3 £37.50, 2&3 £55.40. CSF £166.98 TOTE £9.90: £2.70, £6.30, £8.00; EX 201.70 TRIFECTA Not won..
Owner Hamdan Al Maktoum **Bred** Shadwell Farm LLC **Trained** Lambourn, Berks

FOCUS
A decent enough Listed contest, although it attracted its share of underachievers and the form, rated around the first three, may be suspect, with several leading fancies underperforming and the sixth too close for comfort.

NOTEBOOK
Shabiba(USA)'s strong-finishing third in a Group 3 at Goodwood was a step in the right direction and she won this decisively. Her rider had to be patient, but when he asked her to go to the front inside the last two furlongs she found plenty and was in charge through the final furlong. (op 9-1 tchd 10-1)
Ada River, one of the least exposed in the field after just three runs, needed to improve to figure and did so, racing handily on the outside and sticking on better than the other prominently ridden fillies. A particularly good effort considering her 106-day absence.
Ghaidaa(IRE) had not confirmed the promise of her Newbury win, but she came from well off the pace to challenge for second place and was another who appeared to improve. (tchd 25-1)
Barshiba(IRE) was the clear form pick and this looked an ideal opportunity, but she is not one to count on and threw her chance away by refusing to settle, although she was going on again when the race was all over. (tchd 3-1 tchd4-1 in places)
Eva's Request(IRE) came here in good form, but she had her chance and was beaten fair and square. (op 8-1)
Mekong Melody(IRE) finished a bit too close for comfort, as she had no realistic chance, having been beaten in handicaps off marks in the mid 70s.
Raymi Coya(CAN) was dropped considerably in class but could only make a bit of headway after getting outpaced. This was a moderate effort. (tchd 11-1)
Lindelaan(USA), wearing blinkers instead of the visor, was always struggling to get involved and never picked up.
In The Light, having her first start since leaving Andre Fabre, seemed to find the competition too hot and may not be the easiest to place. (op 16-1)
Selinka failed to give her running in the first-time visor. (op 10-1)
Que Piensa Cat(ARG), a disappointment on her recent British debut, made the running until the winner took over, then dropped away so quickly that something may have been amiss. She has yet to beat a rival home in two starts for the yard. Official explanation: jockey said filly stopped quickly (op 12-1)

5507 BETINTERNET.COM SOLARIO STKS (GROUP 3) — 7f 16y
2:35 (2:41) (Class 1) 2-Y-O
£28,385 (£10,760; £5,385; £2,685; £1,345; £675) **Stalls** High

Form — RPR

1 **1** **Sri Putra**[79] 2972 2-9-0 0 .... PhilipRobinson 7 105+
(M A Jarvis) *chsd ldrs: drivn along over 2f out: styd on u.p to ld fnl 75yds: all out* **8/1**

1 **2** *1/2* **The Cheka (IRE)**[49] 3939 2-9-0 0 .... TQuinn 3 104+
(Eve Johnson Houghton) *lw: fly-jmpd stalls: sn trcking ldr: drvn to ld ins fnl 2f: styd on u.p fnl f: hdd and one pce fnl 75yds* **4/1**[2]

1 **3** *nk* **Patrician's Glory (USA)**[43] 4151 2-9-0 0 .... JohnEgan 2 103
(Jane Chapple-Hyam) *in rr: drvn along 4f out: hdwy on outside fr 3f out: hung lft over 2f out: styd on strly u.p to cl on ldrs ins fnl f but nvr quite gng pce to chal: styd on wl* **25/1**

1115 **4** *1 1/4* **Talking Hands**[5] 5359 2-9-0 96 .... AdamKirby 1 100+
(S Kirk) *in rr: stl plenty to do whn drvn along over 2f out: styd on wl u.p fr over 1f out: gng on cl home* **25/1**

4014 **5** *shd* **Nashmiah (IRE)**[21] 4868 2-8-11 93 .... KShea 10 97
(C E Brittain) *in tch: rdn over 2f out and styd on fr over 1f out: kpt on nr fin but nvr gng pce to be competitive* **50/1**

1 **6** *shd* **Prince Siegfried (FR)**[49] 3968 2-9-0 0 .... MartinDwyer 4 100
(A M Balding) *lw: chsd ldrs: hrd drvn fr 2f out: styd on same pce ins fnl f* **9/2**[3]

106 **7** *2 1/2* **Instalment**[31] 4517 2-9-0 102 .... RichardHughes 8 93
(R Hannon) *hld up in rr and t.k.h: hmpd over 2f out: sme prog ins fnl f but nvr in contention* **12/1**

11 **8** *1/2* **Cry Of Freedom (USA)**[14] 5093 2-9-0 0 .... LDettori 6 92
(M Johnston) *lw: led: rdn and hdd ins fnl 2f: wknd 1f out* **5/2**[1]

1634 **9** *hd* **Prime Delivery (USA)**[14] 5107 2-9-0 93 .... ShaneKelly 5 92
(R M H Cowell) *s.i.s: in rr: styd on fnl 2f but nvr anyhere nr ldrs* **66/1**

012 **10** *3/4* **Oratory (IRE)**[42] 4187 2-9-0 92 .... RyanMoore 9 90
(R Hannon) *s.i.s: in tch 1/2-way: rdn 3f out: sn no imp and wknd fr 2f out* **11/1**

1 **11** *1 1/2* **Parisian Art (IRE)**[35] 4421 2-9-0 0 .... (b) JimmyFortune 11 86
(J Noseda) *plld hrd: chsd ldrs tl ins fnl 3f: wknd 2f out: no ch whn n.m.r and eased fnl f* **7/1**

1m 29.13s (-0.37) **Going Correction** -0.025s/f (Good) — **11 Ran** SP% **117.5**
Speed ratings (Par 104): **101,100,100,98,98 98,95,95,94,93 92**
toteswinger: 1&2 £9.40, 1&3 £21.80, 2&3 £22.80. CSF £38.92 TOTE £9.50: £2.10, £1.70, £5.40; EX 64.60 Trifecta £768.30 Part won. Pool: £1,038.32 - 0.60 winning tickets..
Owner H R H Sultan Ahmad Shah **Bred** Glebe Stud And Partners **Trained** Newmarket, Suffolk

FOCUS
This Group 3 has gone to some smart colts in recent years, notably last year's runaway winner Raven's Pass and the shock 1999 winner Best Of The Bests, and this looked a strong renewal although the time and the exposed ninth hold down the form. Three of the unbeaten runners occupied the first three places at the finish, and they can all go on to better things.

NOTEBOOK
Sri Putra had a hiccup at home after making a good impression on his debut, so he was expected to be better for the race, while Philip Robinson said the colt was doing all his best work at the finish, after going a bit flat when first asked to pick up, and that suggests there will be more improvement when he steps up to 1m. That will probably be the limit of his stamina, but he may yet prove a live 2000 Guineas outsider. He is well entered but in the short term heads to Newmarket for the 7f Tattersalls Timeform Million. (tchd 9-1)
The Cheka(IRE) could hardly have impressed more at Ascot, but wide margin wins can be flattering there so he still had it to prove. In front sooner than intended when Cry Of Freedom weakened, he looked the likely winner but was just run out of it. He is clearly a smart colt, but perhaps not the star he looked on his debut. (op 7-2)
Patrician's Glory(USA) is held in high regard despite his long odds here, and he ran a blinder in third. John Egan said the youngster just found the ground a bit tacky, and he would have been happier racing near the rail. (op 22-1)
Talking Hands has made his way through the nursery ranks and had disappointed when upped in class, but he left behind his below-par effort at Ripon on Monday and did best of those trying to come from off the pace. The return to 7f was clearly a factor. (op 28-1)
Nashmiah(IRE), the only filly in the race and fourth in a Group 3 last time, appeared to run well.
Prince Siegfried(FR), so impressive at Salisbury, was up markedly in grade and ran well enough without suggesting he will be taking up his Dewhurst entry. He is well regarded but proved disappointingly one paced, with no obvious explanation. (op 4-1 tchd 5-1 in a place)
Instalment was again too keen and has now been beaten three times in Group company. (op 11-1)
Cry Of Freedom(USA), unbeaten in two races, including a Listed event at Newbury, was keen to post and unseated Frankie Dettori on the way down, although luckily he did not get loose. He soon got to the front but was brushed aside unusually quickly for one from the Mark Johnston stable. This wasn't his running. (op 3-1 tchd 10-3)
Oratory(IRE) never got into it following a slow start, but he is a fine, big animal and will do better as a three-year-old. (op 12-1)
Parisian Art(IRE), an impressive winner in the blinkers on debut, failed to settle and dropped out tamely on this rise in grade. He is evidently not straightforward. (op 9-1 tchd 10-1 in a place)

5508 BEST ODDS GUARANTEED AT BETINTERNET.COM STKS (HERITAGE H'CAP) — 1m 2f 7y
3:10 (3:12) (Class 2) 3-Y-O+
£62,310 (£18,660; £9,330; £4,670; £2,330; £1,170) **Stalls** High

Form — RPR

-141 **1** **Ask The Butler**[35] 4422 4-8-11 95 .... DaneO'Neill 10 108+
(L M Cumani) *towards rr and stl plenty to do whn rdn 3f out: hdwy 2f out and swtchd lft over 1f out: styd on strly to ld and edgd lft fnl 100yds: rdn out* **6/1**[1]

2000 **2** *3/4* **Lang Shining (IRE)**[29] 4587 4-9-0 98 .... RyanMoore 15 110
(Sir Michael Stoute) *lw: mid-div: rdn and hdwy over 2f out: styd on u.p to ld jst ins fnl f: hdd and one pce fnl 100yds* **12/1**

-212 **3** *2* **Swop (IRE)**[32] 4509 5-8-11 95 .... LDettori 6 103+
(L M Cumani) *lw: hld up in rr: hdwy on outside fr 3f out: drvn to chse ldrs over 1f out: styng on whn pushed lft and one pce fnl 100yds* **6/1**[1]

1031 **4** *1* **Tazeez (USA)**[21] 4867 4-9-3 101 .... MartinDwyer 11 107
(J H M Gosden) *chsd ldrs: rdn to chal ins fnl 2f: slt ld over 1f out: hdd jst ins fnl f: wknd nr fin* **14/1**

4160 **5** *nk* **Proponent (IRE)**[32] 4504 4-8-12 96 .... SteveDrowne 17 101
(R Charlton) *lw: chsd ldrs: rdn and styd on fr over 2f out: one pce fnl f* **13/2**[2]

4302 **6** *1/2* **Pinpoint (IRE)**[32] 4504 6-9-10 108 .... AdamKirby 1 112
(W R Swinburn) *lw: in rr: rdn over 3f out: hdwy on ins fr 2f out: kpt on fnl f but nvr in contention* **10/1**[3]

3411 **7** *3/4* **Australia Day (IRE)**[37] 4350 5-8-8 92 .... TedDurcan 16 94
(P R Webber) *led: rdn and styd on to keep slt advantage fr over 3f out: hdd over 1f out: wknd ins fnl f* **14/1**

-231 **8** *2* **Nanton (USA)**[28] 4618 6-8-7 91 .... JimmyQuinn 8 89
(J S Goldie) *in rr: hdwy on ins over 3f out: nvr quite gng pce to rch ldrs: wknd ins fnl f* **20/1**

2600 **9** *2 3/4* **Benandonner (USA)**[32] 4512 5-8-7 96 .... JackMitchell(5) 5 89
(R A Fahey) *sn prom: drvn and lost position over 3f out: nvr in contention after* **25/1**

2130 **10** *1/2* **Luberon**[32] 4504 5-8-10 94 .... JoeFanning 14 86
(M Johnston) *chsd ldr: chal fr over 3f out tl ins fnl 2f: sn wknd* **25/1**

0421 **11** *2* **Love Galore (IRE)**[31] 4519 3-8-10 102 .... GregFairley 4 90
(M Johnston) *t.k.h: chsd ldrs: rdn 3f out: wknd 2f out* **10/1**[3]

3536 **12** *1 1/2* **King Charles**[56] 3721 4-9-1 99 .... JimmyFortune 3 84
(E A L Dunlop) *in tch: rdn 3f out: sn btn* **14/1**

1503 **13** *1 3/4* **Watamu (IRE)**[32] 4504 7-9-4 105 .... (v) TravisBlock(3) 13 86
(P J Makin) *chsd ldrs: wknd 3f out: no ch whn hmpd ins fnl 2f* **14/1**

0101 **14** ½ **Re Barolo (IRE)**[77] 3046 5-9-2 **100**....(t) JohnEgan 12 80
(M Botti) *a towards rr* **22/1**

0036 **15** *23* **Capable Guest (IRE)**[21] 4856 6-8-7 **91**.... ChrisCatlin 7 25
(M R Channon) *a bhd: no ch whn bdly hmpd ins fnl 2f* **33/1**

2212 **P** **Kaateb (IRE)**[34] 4443 5-8-12 **96**....(v) RHills 9 —
(W J Haggas) *towards rr: no ch whn broke leg and p.u ins fnl 2f: destroyed* **10/1**[3]

2m 7.15s (-3.35) **Going Correction** -0.025s/f (Good)
WFA 3 from 4yo+ 8lb **16** Ran SP% **123.3**
Speed ratings (Par 109): **112,111,109,109,108 108,107,106,103,103 101,100,99,98,80** —
toteswinger: 1&2 £23.90, 1&3 £5.20, 2&3 £20.90. CSF £71.67 CT £461.85 TOTE £5.30: £1.70, £3.00, £2.10, £3.50; EX 115.80 Trifecta £1020.10 Pool: £17,645.77 - 12.80 winning tickets..
Owner R J Baines **Bred** Skymarc Farm Inc **Trained** Newmarket, Suffolk

FOCUS
The usual big field for this lucrative affair, and a field of quality, with the top weight a solid yardstick racing off 108 and almost the entire field running from marks in the mid-90s and upwards. The pace was strong and the form looks solid.

NOTEBOOK
Ask The Butler has made tremendous strides with Luca Cumani and looked to have plenty going for him here despite another 6lb hike up the handicap. As in his previous Newmarket wins, he did his best work in the last two furlongs, and there's a strong suggestion he is still capable of better. He was cut to 10-1 favourite for the Cambridgeshire in some lists but it will be ground dependent, as he has to have it on top. The strong pace there would suit him, but it will be no surprise to see him returned to further one day. (tchd 13-2)
Lang Shining(IRE) came from a similar position in midfield. Much better behaved this time, he was eased out with his challenge in plenty of time and did nothing wrong, getting the longer trip and appreciating the good ground. He, too, is a likely Cambridgeshire type, but this form will be taken into account when the weights are published and, like the winner and the other principals, he will go up a few pounds. (tchd 14-1 in a place)
Swop(IRE), a stablemate of the winner, is very much an intended Cambridgeshire runner, and this was another excellent effort from the rear of the field. He may just have found the longer trip stretching him, and as this was only his fifth appearance he could well go on improving for a while yet. (tchd 13-2)
Tazeez(USA), who raced more prominently, ran right up to form in fourth, but he had his chance. (op 16-1)
Proponent(IRE) was found wanting for a chance of pace and remains a shade high in the weights. (tchd 7-1)
Pinpoint(IRE) was always going to be up against it from stall one under topweight, but he stayed on under strong pressure . (op 11-1 tchd 9-1)
Australia Day(IRE), who is now 24lb higher than for the first of two recent wins, gave it a bold go off the front end, but had nothing left to give from a furlong out. He is still a maiden over hurdles and, given his recent rapid improvement, would be a fascinating prospect returned to obstacles. (op 16-1)
Love Galore(IRE) was too keen for his own good and failed to run to his Goodwood form. (tchd 11-1)

5509 MCGEE GROUP H'CAP 5f 6y
3:45 (3:47) (Class 2) (0-100,100) 3-Y-0+
£12,462 (£3,732; £1,866; £934; £466; £234) **Stalls** High

Form RPR

2000 **1** **Hoh Hoh Hoh**[28] 4624 6-9-11 **100**.... JimCrowley 1 108
(R J Price) *stdd s: gd hdwy 2f out: styd on strly thrght fnl f to ld fnl stride* **20/1**

1105 **2** *nse* **Crimson Fern (IRE)**[21] 4840 4-9-5 **94**.... TGMcLaughlin 16 102
(M S Saunders) *led: rdn 2f out: hung bdly lft 1f out but kpt on gamely thrght fnl f: ct fnl stride* **5/1**[2]

2324 **3** *hd* **Safari Mischief**[34] 4445 5-8-10 **88**.... LukeMorris(3) 17 95
(P Winkworth) *lw: chsd ldrs: hrd rdn thrght fnl f: no ex cl home* **4/1**[1]

0640 **4** ½ **Matsunosuke**[34] 4445 6-9-4 **93**.... AlanMunro 13 98
(A B Coogan) *chsd ldrs: rdn and styd on wl fr over 1f out: kpt on nr fin but nvr quite gng pce to chal* **16/1**

2563 **5** *nse* **Cake (IRE)**[29] 4591 3-9-0 **91**.... RichardHughes 7 96
(R Hannon) *lw: in tch 1/2-way: drvn and hdwy over 1f out: squeezed through ins fnl f: fin wl* **12/1**

-160 **6** *1* **Little Edward**[19] 4928 10-9-2 **91**.... SteveDrowne 2 92
(R J Hodges) *in rr: rdn and hdwy over 1f out: fin strly fnl 100yds: nt rch ldrs* **33/1**

060 **7** *shd* **Fyodor (IRE)**[34] 4445 7-9-4 **93**.... DaneO'Neill 15 94
(W J Haggas) *in tch on ins: rdn 2f out: styd on ins fnl f: kpt on cl home* **14/1**

110- **8** *hd* **Loch Verdi**[331] 5953 5-9-9 **98**.... WilliamBuick 6 98
(A M Balding) *chsd ldrs: rdn 2f out: nt qckn ins fnl f* **16/1**

3026 **9** *hd* **Little Pete (IRE)**[21] 4842 3-9-1 **92**.... MartinDwyer 10 92
(A M Balding) *in tch: rdn and styng on whn n.m.r 1f out: styd on cl home* **16/1**

0100 **10** ¾ **Sohraab**[28] 4624 4-9-4 **96**.... TravisBlock(3) 9 93
(H Morrison) *chsd ldrs: nudged along 3f out: styd prom tl n.m.r and wknd fnl f* **20/1**

1406 **11** *hd* **Good Gorsoon (USA)**[29] 4591 3-8-13 **90**.... MichaelHills 12 86
(B W Hills) *stdd s: hdwy 1/2-way: n.m.r over 1f out: kpt on again cl home* **12/1**

1114 **12** ½ **Misaro (GER)**[42] 4201 7-9-0 **92**....(b) KevinGhunowa(3) 8 86
(R A Harris) *in rr: rdn 2f out: styd on wl cl home but nvr in contention* **20/1**

0120 **13** *hd* **Tabaret**[34] 4445 5-9-4 **93**....(p) TedDurcan 5 87
(R M Whitaker) *in tch: rdn 1/2-way: styd on same pce fnl f* **12/1**

0050 **14** *nk* **The Trader (IRE)**[21] 4840 10-9-1 **90**....(b) FergusSweeney 3 83
(M Blanshard) *hld up in rr: mod late prog* **40/1**

2-20 **15** *nk* **Cute Ass (IRE)**[30] 4550 3-9-8 **99**.... RyanMoore 14 91
(K R Burke) *in rr: drvn along 2f out and sme prog fnl f but nvr in contention* **7/1**[3]

6010 **16** *nk* **Dubai Princess (IRE)**[29] 4586 3-9-6 **97**.... ShaneKelly 4 87
(J A Osborne) *sn outpcd* **33/1**

4000 **17** *2 ¾* **Elhamri**[30] 4555 4-8-12 **87**.... JimmyFortune 11 68
(S Kirk) *stdd s: a in rr* **12/1**

60.39 secs (-1.21) **Going Correction** -0.025s/f (Good)
WFA 3 from 4yo+ 2lb **17** Ran SP% **126.9**
Speed ratings (Par 109): **108,107,107,106,106 105,104,104,104,103 102,102,101,101,100 100,95**
toteswinger: 1&2 £10.70, 1&3 £22.30, 2&3 £19.20. CSF £112.86 CT £518.05 TOTE £26.60: £4.40, £1.70, £1.80, £4.20; EX 205.00 Trifecta £718.50 Pool: £1,262.40 - 1.30 winning tickets..
Owner Multi Lines 2 **Bred** D R Botterill **Trained** Ullingswick, H'fords
■ Stewards' Enquiry : Luke Morris one-day ban: used whip with excessive frequency with arm above shoulder height (Sep 14)

FOCUS
A massive field for this nice prize, and inevitably there were some traffic problems. The first five were close to their marks and the form looks solid.

NOTEBOOK
Hoh Hoh Hoh overcame stall 1 in a tight finish. This was not undeserved after some near misses in similar company, and he now heads for the Portland, provided the ground is on top, but he will be up 3lb or 4lb on this mark of 100, and he was well down the field last year off 96. (tchd 22-1)
Crimson Fern(IRE), a rapid improver this term who has registered two course and distance victories, avoided any trouble by racing in front up the rail from stall 16, but she edged off of it and was collared right on the line. She is holding her form remarkably well. (op 9-2)
Safari Mischief was the only runner drawn higher than Crimson Fern, and he put in a strong effort on the far side. He is raced sparingly but is very consistent for a sprint handicapper. (op 9-2 tchd 5-1)
Matsunosuke is suited by a stiff track and he showed clear signs of a return to form in fourth (op 12-1)
Cake(IRE) came home strongly having been forced to wait for a run and could soon become of interest. (op 40-1)
Little Edward raced up the wide outside like the winner, but got going too late.
Loch Verdi, fit enough for this return, showed up very well on this first run in nearly 11 months and she could well improve enough to win another nice race this autumn, although she won't want it too soft.
Sohraab Official explanation: jockey said gelding suffered interference in running
Good Gorsoon(USA) was among those who did not enjoy the best of runs, but he is the type who always needs luck in running. (tchd 11-1)

5510 VARIETY CLUB CHILDREN'S CHARITY H'CAP 5f 6y
4:15 (4:19) (Class 4) (0-80,80) 3-Y-O **£6,476** (£1,927; £963; £481) **Stalls** High

Form RPR

2021 **1** **Ridge Wood Dani (IRE)**[23] 4787 3-9-4 **75**.... RichardHughes 1 84+
(E J Alston) *hld up trcking ldrs: edgd lft to centre of crse ins fnl f: shkn up and qcknd to ld fnl 100yds: comf* **8/1**

-132 **2** ¾ **Valatrix (IRE)**[12] 5142 3-9-1 **77**.... JackMitchell(5) 4 83
(C F Wall) *lw: trckd ldrs: drvn to ld ins fnl 2f: kpt on wl u.p: edgd lft to centre of crse: hdd and outpcd fnl 100yds* **9/2**[2]

0210 **3** *1* **Tadalavil**[15] 5056 3-9-4 **75**.... TedDurcan 3 78
(M R Channon) *s.i.s: towards rr but in tch: rdn and hdwy over 1f out: styd on ins fnl f and edgd lft to centre: kpt on cl home* **14/1**

1141 **4** *nk* **Filligree (IRE)**[23] 4773 3-9-4 **80**.... WilliamCarson(5) 12 82+
(Rae Guest) *lw: trckd ldrs: nt clr run whn effrt 1f out and ins fnl f: swtchd lft ins fnl f and fin wl but nt pce of ldng trio* **8/1**

6113 **5** ½ **Muftarres (IRE)**[15] 5056 3-9-6 **77**.... RHills 10 77
(Sir Michael Stoute) *lw: in rr: rdn along 1/2-way: hdwy ins fnl f and kpt on wl but nt rch ldrs* **4/1**[1]

2116 **6** *nk* **Heaven**[23] 4787 3-9-8 **79**.... LDettori 8 78
(P J Makin) *chsd ldrs: rdn to chal over 1f out: swtchd rt sn after and hung rt ins fnl f: wknd fnl 100yds* **12/1**

6100 **7** *1 ¼* **Piscean (USA)**[9] 5206 3-9-8 **79**.... ShaneKelly 11 73+
(T Keddy) *slowly away: bhd: sme hdwy 1/2-way: n.m.r over 1f out: styd on same pce ins fnl f* **9/1**

4422 **8** *nk* **Blue Jack**[23] 4787 3-9-8 **79**.... MartinDwyer 7 72
(W R Muir) *in tch: sme hdwy over 1f out: c towards centre of crse u.p ins fnl f and sn wknd* **6/1**[3]

2036 **9** *nk* **Maggie Kate**[20] 4904 3-8-8 **65**.... RobertHavlin 9 57
(R Ingram) *pressed ldr: stl upsides over 1f out: one pce whn hmpd and wknd sn after* **25/1**

3405 **10** *1 ½* **Mistress Cooper**[17] 4988 3-8-5 **62**.... JohnEgan 13 49
(W J Musson) *chsd ldrs: one pce whn hmpd and wknd ins fnl f* **17/2**

-040 **11** ½ **Thunder Bay**[35] 4418 3-9-8 **79**.... JimmyQuinn 2 64
(R A Fahey) *in rr: sme hdwy 2f out: one pce whn n.m.r and hmpd over 1f out* **16/1**

6050 **12** *5* **Extreme North (USA)**[16] 5028 3-8-1 **59**....(b) LukeMorris(3) 5 28
(Miss V Haigh) *led: hdd u.p ins fnl 2f: rdr dropped whip over 1f out and sn wknd* **50/1**

61.11 secs (-0.49) **Going Correction** -0.025s/f (Good) **12** Ran SP% **121.3**
Speed ratings (Par 102): **102,100,99,98,97 97,95,94,94,92 91,83**
toteswinger: 1&2 £10.70, 1&3 £22.30, 2&3 £19.20. CSF £44.92 CT £395.08 TOTE £9.20: £2.90, £2.50, £4.70; EX 40.90.
Owner Con Harrington **Bred** Con Harrington **Trained** Longton, Lancs
■ Stewards' Enquiry : L Dettori two-day ban: careless riding (Sep 14-15)

FOCUS
Another sprint winner from stall one, bucking the usual trend. Indeed the first three were all drawn low and ended up racing apart from the rest towards the stands' side. The form looks pretty sound overall.
Piscean(USA) Official explanation: jockey said colt missed the break

5511 VARIETY CLUB GOLDEN ANNIVERSARY NURSERY 7f 16y
4:50 (4:55) (Class 4) (0-85,84) 2-Y-O **£6,476** (£1,927; £963; £481) **Stalls** High

Form RPR

615 **1** **Swift Chap**[29] 4589 2-9-0 **77**.... AlanMunro 9 81
(B R Millman) *in rr tl plld to outside and hdwy over 2f out: str run u.p fnl f and upsides fnl 100yds: led last stride* **7/1**[2]

521 **2** *shd* **Key Signature**[15] 5048 2-9-2 **79**.... ShaneKelly 11 83
(Pat Eddery) *lw: in tch: drvn and hdwy over 2f out to ld appr fnl f: kpt on gamely u.p: ct last stride* **7/1**[2]

021 **3** *2* **Oil Man (IRE)**[23] 4776 2-9-7 **84**.... JimCrowley 8 85+
(P Winkworth) *lw: in rr: gd hdwy over 2f out and sn clr run and checked sn after: styd on again ins fnl f: gng on cl home but nt rch ldng duo* **7/2**[1]

421 **4** ½ **Starry Sky**[24] 4720 2-9-0 **77**.... J-PGuillambert 7 75
(Sir Mark Prescott) *in rr: rdn and hdwy 3f out: n.m.r 2f out: styd on u.p fr over 1f out and kpt on cl home* **7/1**[2]

0043 **5** *2* **Super Fourteen**[22] 4828 2-8-1 **64**.... DavidKinsella 12 57
(R Hannon) *led after 2f: rdn fr over 2f out and kpt narrow advantage tl hdd over 1f out: sn btn* **22/1**

004 **6** *1* **Dubai Crest**[30] 4570 2-8-5 **68**.... JoeFanning 15 60+
(Mrs A J Perrett) *lw: in tch tl rdn: n.m.r and outpcd 3f out: styd on again over 1f out: kpt on again cl home* **14/1**

51 **7** ½ **Papa Meilland**[17] 4982 2-8-13 **76**.... StephenCarson 16 65
(Eve Johnson Houghton) *led 2f: styd chsng ldrs tl wknd ins fnl f* **14/1**

642 **8** *1* **Granski (IRE)**[17] 4982 2-8-9 **72**.... RichardHughes 2 58
(R Hannon) *chsd ldrs and rn wd into bnd after 2f: sn chsng ldr: travelling wl 2f out: btn whn hmpd ins fnl f* **15/2**[3]

524 **9** *1 ½* **Bouggie Daize**[29] 4593 2-8-9 **72**.... PhilipRobinson 3 55
(C G Cox) *racd wd bnd after 2f: chsd ldrs: rdn and styng on whn bdly hmpd ins fnl f: nt rcvr* **14/1**

5210 **10** ½ **Suruor (IRE)**[29] 4589 2-8-12 **75**.... RHills 10 64+
(M Johnston) *in rr tl hdwy on ins fr 3f out: repeatedly denied clr run fr over 2f out and nt rcvr* **16/1**

01 **11** *2 ½* **Tidal Force (USA)**[35] 4425 2-8-13 **76**.... GregFairley 6 51
(P F I Cole) *a towards rr* **16/1**

1300 **12** ¾ **Motor Home**[29] 4589 2-9-0 **77**.....................(p) WilliamBuick 1 50
(A M Balding) *racd wd bnd after 2f: chsd ldrs: rdn 2f out: btn over 1f out: btn whn nt clr ins fnl f* **33/1**

5201 **13** 6 **Cavendish Road (IRE)**[23] 4769 2-9-0 **77**..................... LDettori 5 35
(W R Muir) *racd wd bnd after 2f: chsd ldrs to 1/2-way* **11/1**

15 **14** 2 **Rafiqa (IRE)**[23] 4781 2-9-2 **79**..................... TedDurcan 14 32
(C F Wall) *w'like: a towards rr: eased whn no ch fnl f* **14/1**

440 **15** 3½ **Minder**[66] 3358 2-8-6 **69**..................... JamesDoyle 13 13
(J G Portman) *a in rr* **33/1**

503 **P** **Danzadil (IRE)**[19] 4926 2-8-2 **65**..................... JimmyQuinn 4 —
(R A Teal) *sn t.o: p.u after 2f: lame* **33/1**

1m 29.53s (0.03) **Going Correction** -0.025s/f (Good) **16** Ran SP% **131.4**
Speed ratings (Par 96): **98,97,95,95,92 91,91,89,88,87 84,83,77,74,70** —
toteswinger: 1&2 £12.00, 1&3 £10.40, 2&3 £7.70. CSF £57.79 CT £207.51 TOTE £9.30: £2.70, £2.00, £1.80, £2.30; EX 91.10.
Owner M A Swift **Bred** D R Tucker **Trained** Kentisbeare, Devon

FOCUS
A most competitive nursery, contested largely by lightly raced and unexposed yougsters, but there were traffic problems and several can be rated a good bit better than their finishing positions.

NOTEBOOK
Swift Chap , whose Goodwood fifth represented solid nursery form, came with a strong challenge and got there in the final stride.Rod Millman, who was full of praise for Alan Munro, plans to give him just one more run in another nursery this year. (op 8-1 tchd 9-1)
Key Signature, a winner on the All-Weather at Kempton, went on approaching the furlong marker and was clear of the rest, but was collared on the line by Swift Chap. (tchd 15-2)
Oil Man(IRE) ◆ had beaten a poor lot by a wide margin at Folkestone, but Racing Post Ratings gave him a good chance despite top weight and he'd have gone close with better luck in running. He had to wriggle through from an unpromising position and was running on well at the finish. (op 5-1 tchd6-1 in aplace)
Starry Sky, another leading fancy, was also staying on well after being a bit tight for room. (tchd 6-1)
Super Fourteen weakened after making much of the running, but has a race in him at a slightly lesser level. (op 25-1)
Dubai Crest was going on well at the finish, having been outpaced and short of room. (op 12-1)
Granski(IRE) was among those who were wide early on. He looked to be going as well as any two out but didn't find much and was weakening when hampered. (op 9-1 tchd 10-1)
Bouggie Daize ◆ was just beginning to get going when stopped dead in her tracks. Official explanation: jockey said filly suffered interference in running (op 16-1)
Suruor(IRE) ◆ failed to get any sort of run inside the final quarter mile and crossed the line with plenty left in the tank. Official explanation: jockey said colt was denied a clear run
Motor Home Official explanation: jockey said colt suffered interference in running
Rafiqa(IRE) Official explanation: jockey said filly was denied a clear run
Danzadil(IRE) Official explanation: jockey said filly pulled up lame

5512 VARIETY CLUB AMATEUR DERBY (A H'CAP FOR GENTLEMAN AMATEUR RIDERS) 1m 2f 7y
5:25 (5:26) (Class 5) (0-75,74) 4-Y-0+ **£6,246** (£1,937; £968; £484) **Stalls** High

Form RPR

1F53 **1** **Dragon Slayer (IRE)**[18] 4953 6-11-5 **69**..................... MrSDobson 5 79
(John A Harris) *mid-div: hdwy 3f out: sn hrd drvn: 4l down appr fnl f but styd on gamely to ld last stride* **12/1**

2210 **2** *nse* **Wee Charlie Castle (IRE)**[23] 4771 5-11-4 **68**..................... MrSWalker 3 77
(G C H Chung) *chsd ldrs: led 2f out: drvn 4 l clr 1f out: wknd and ct last stride* **3/1**[1]

5230 **3** 2 **Potentiale (IRE)**[28] 4645 4-11-8 **72**.....................(p) MrJDeletombe 10 78
(J W Hills) *in rr: stl plenty to do whn pushed along 3f out: styd on wl fr over 1f out and clsng on ldrs nr fin* **10/1**

426 **4** 1¾ **Roodolph**[77] 3029 4-11-10 **74**..................... MrLoekVanDerHam 11 76
(Eve Johnson Houghton) *in rr: hdwy fr 3f out and sn rdn: kpt on fnl f but nt rch ldrs* **8/1**

4243 **5** 4 **Bavarica**[18] 4945 6-11-2 **66**..................... MrDMacAuley 6 60
(Miss J Feilden) *in rr tl hdwy 3f out: kpt on fnl 2f: nt rch ldrs* **12/1**

5034 **6** 5 **Prime Number (IRE)**[24] 4726 6-11-1 **65**..................... MrBenBrisbourne 8 49
(J Akehurst) *in rr tl styd on fnl 3f: nt rch ldrs* **15/2**[3]

1313 **7** *nk* **Western Roots**[6] 5312 7-11-6 **70**..................... MrOGreenall 4 53
(A M Balding) *chsd ldrs: led over 3f out: hdd 2f out: wknd over 1f out* **7/2**[2]

3301 **8** 3 **Megalala (IRE)**[15] 5058 7-10-6 **56**..................... MrPCollington 1 33
(J J Bridger) *led tl hdd over 3f out: sn btn* **10/1**

-000 **9** 5 **Robert The Brave**[39] 3258 4-11-6 **70**..................... CWallis 12 37
(P R Webber) *towards rr: hdwy into mid-div 1/2-way: rdn and no ch fr 3f out* **14/1**

2-52 **10** ½ **Twist Bookie (IRE)**[43] 3084 8-10-6 **56**..................... MrlPopham 7 22
(S Lycett) *chsd ldrs to 3f out* **16/1**

234- **11** 13 **Mount Usher**[38] 2136 6-11-8 **72**..................... MrNPearce 9 12
(M J Gingell) *slowly away: a in rr* **33/1**

-050 **12** ¾ **Cormorant Wharf (IRE)**[22] 4819 8-10-13 **63**.....................(p) MrDavidTurner 2 2
(T E Powell) *chsd ldrs: rdn over 3f out: sn btn* **25/1**

2m 10.26s (-0.24) **Going Correction** -0.025s/f (Good) **12** Ran SP% **123.0**
Speed ratings (Par 103): **99,98,97,95,92 88,88,86,82,81 71,70**
toteswinger: 1&2 £9.00, 1&3 £30.30, 2&3 £9.30. CSF £49.72 CT £393.08 TOTE £16.50: £3.80, £1.50, £3.30; EX 68.50 Place 6: £865.61 Place 5: £99.20.
Owner Carl Would **Bred** Arandora Star Syndicate **Trained** Eastwell, Leics
■ Stewards' Enquiry : Mr Ben Brisbourne two-day ban: used whip when out of contention (Sep 16,23)

FOCUS
They looked to go too fast here, and the winner came from off the pace to lead on the line after the leaders tired one after another. Nevertheless, the form looks pretty solid.
T/Jkpt: Not won. T/Plt: £793.10 to a £1 stake. Pool: £153,794.97. 141.55 winning tickets. T/Qpdt: £14.40 to a £1 stake. Pool: £8,743.70. 449.30 winning tickets. ST

5521 - 5527a (Foreign Racing) - See Raceform Interactive

2440 BADEN-BADEN (L-H)
Saturday, August 30

OFFICIAL GOING: Good

5528a PREIS DER SPARKASSEN-FINANZGRUPPE (GROUP 3) 1m 2f
4:00 (4:19) 4-Y-0+ **£24,265** (£10,294; £3,676; £2,206)

RPR

1 **Prince Flori (GER)**[41] 4232 5-9-0..................... AStarke 7 111
(S Smrczek, Germany) *hld up: hdwy appr st: chal 1 1/2f out: drvn to ld 100yds out: drvn out* **24/10**[2]

2 1¼ **Lord Hill (GER)**[30] 4-9-0..................... J-PCarvalho 11 108
(C Zeitz) *led: pushed along st: r.o fr 2f out tl hdd 100yds out* **16/1**

3 ½ **Wiesenpfad (FR)**[34] 4470 5-9-2..................... ADeVries 10 109
(W Hickst, Germany) *hld up: hdwy on ins over 1 1/2f out: tk 3rd cl home: nrest at fin* **17/10**[1]

4 5 **Wassiljew (IRE)**[209] 423 4-9-0..................... J-MBreux 6 97
(K Schafflutzel, Switzerland) *mid-div: styd on at one pce fr over 1 1/2f out* **57/1**

5 ½ **Pont Des Arts (FR)**[315] 6353 4-9-0..................... OPlacais 8 96
(K Schafflutzel, Switzerland) *mid-div: nvr in chalng position* **30/1**

6 ½ **Dwilano (GER)**[60] 3595 5-8-12..................... LennartHammer-Hansen 5 93
(P Remmert, Germany) *hld up towards rr: n.d* **50/1**

7 7 **Lilia (GER)**[27] 4-8-9..................... AHelfenbein 3 76
(Frau E Mader, Germany) *in tch: 5th 1/2-way: nvr nrr* **14/1**

8 5 **Supaseus**[7] 5289 5-9-0..................... ASuborics 2 71
(H Morrison) *pushed along to r in 2nd: wknd 1 1/2f out: eased fnl f* **32/10**[3]

9 2 **Simon Magus (GER)**[48] 4012 4-8-12..................... FilipMinarik 1 65
(W Hickst, Germany) *in tch: u.p 5f out and lost pl: btn bef st* **87/10**

10 5 **Allanit (GER)**[27] 4-9-0..................... THellier 4 57
(J Hirschberger, Germany) *in tch: 4th 1/2-way: lost pl appr st: sn btn* **88/10**

2m 1.46s (-3.53) **10** Ran SP% **130.2**
(Including 10 Euros stake): WIN 34; PL 15, 27, 14; SF 405.
Owner Stall Reni **Bred** H A Wacek **Trained** Germany

NOTEBOOK
Supaseus has gone up in the ratings since winning the Wolferton Handicap at Ascot and has not found things easy in Group company since. He was eased down after fading from his prominent early pitch.

CLAIREFONTAINE (R-H)
Saturday, August 30

OFFICIAL GOING: Good

5529a GRAND PRIX DE CLAIREFONTAINE - HARAS DU LOGIS (LISTED RACE) 1m 4f
2:30 (2:29) 3-Y-0 **£20,221** (£8,088; £6,066; £4,044; £2,022)

RPR

1 **Buenos Dias (IRE)**[30] 4577 3-8-12..................... ACrastus 6 97
(E Lellouche, France)

2 *nk* **Chirango (FR)**[35] 4442 3-8-12..................... IMendizabal 2 97
(P Demercastel, France)

3 *snk* **Shawnee Saga (FR)**[18] 3-8-12..................... DBoeuf 7 97
(W Baltromei, Germany)

4 1 **Resplendent Light**[66] 3380 3-8-12..................... DO'Donohoe 4 95
(W R Muir) *racd in 3rd: pushed along ent st: styd on at one pce* **58/10**[1]

5 1½ **Torrid Hell (FR)**[30] 4577 3-8-12..................... CSoumillon 5 93
(Y De Nicolay, France)

6 2½ **All The Winds (GER)**[27] 3-8-12..................... OPeslier 3 89
(A Wohler, Germany)

7 1 **Cinq Cinq (FR)**[35] 4442 3-9-2..................... FBlondel 1 91
(J P Sabatino, France)

2m 31.0s (-6.90) **7** Ran SP% **14.7**
PARI-MUTUEL (Including 1 Euro stake): WIN 2.30; PL 1.60, 4.00;DF 20.60.
Owner Ecurie Wildenstein **Bred** Dayton Investments Ltd **Trained** Lamorlaye, France

NOTEBOOK
Resplendent Light, returning from a break having been in good form in the early summer, ran a creditable race but found this step up in grade beyond him. He was brave to the end by totally unsuited by a lack of early pace.

5182 FOLKESTONE (R-H)
Sunday, August 31

OFFICIAL GOING: Good to firm (8.1)
Wind: virtually nil Weather: overcast, muggy

5530 GRACE TURNER MEDIAN AUCTION MAIDEN STKS 5f
2:10 (2:11) (Class 6) 2-Y-0 **£2,388** (£705; £352) **Stalls** Low

Form RPR

03 **1** **Smokey Ryder**[9] 5214 2-8-12 0..................... RyanMoore 1 74+
(G L Moore) *mde all on stands' rail: rdn 2f out: clr and edgd rt fnl f: r.o strly* **7/2**[3]

032 **2** 3¼ **Blackwater Fort (USA)**[9] 5213 2-9-3 67..................... JimCrowley 6 67
(J Gallagher) *chsd wnr thrght: ev ch and rdn 2f out: outpcd by wnr over 1f out: kpt on* **10/1**

4402 **3** 1½ **Peper Harow (IRE)**[24] 4786 2-8-12 81..................... WilliamBuick 5 57
(M D I Usher) *chsd ldng pair: rdn wl over 1f out: sn outpcd by wnr: kpt on same pce* **15/8**[1]

000 **4** ½ **Silver Salsa**[26] 4705 2-8-12 49..................... ChrisCatlin 3 55
(J R Jenkins) *chsd ldng trio: rdn and outpcd wl over 1f out: kpt on ins fnl f* **100/1**

32 **5** 1½ **Frank Street**[18] 4974 2-9-3 0..................... StephenCarson 4 55
(Eve Johnson Houghton) *dwlt: short of room sn after s: racd in midfield: swtchd rt and rdn wl over 1f out: no imp* **2/1**[2]

060 **6** 1½ **Rapanui Belle**[46] 4088 2-8-12 49..................... SteveDrowne 10 44
(G L Moore) *bhd: styd on steadily fr over 1f out: nvr trbld ldrs* **66/1**

66 **7** ½ **Place The Duchess**[26] 4705 2-8-12 0..................... DaneO'Neill 9 42
(D W P Arbuthnot) *t.k.h early: lost pl after 2f: effrt on outer 2f out: sn outpcd and wl btn* **18/1**

55 **8** ¾ **Itsher**[24] 4776 2-8-12 0..................... SaleemGolam 8 40
(S C Williams) *s.i.s: a bhd: rdn and struggling 1/2-way* **20/1**

0 **9** ¾ **Jiggalong**[57] 3735 2-8-12 0..................... AdrianMcCarthy 11 37
(G G Margarson) *s.i.s: towards rr: hdwy 1/2-way: rdn and wknd wl over 1f out* **28/1**

000 **10** 4½ **Flamboyant Red (IRE)**[7] 5316 2-8-10 0..................... KylieManser(7) 7 26
(Miss Gay Kelleway) *dwlt: t.k.h: hld up towards rr: rdn 2f out: wknd qckly over 1f out* **66/1**

5 **11** 8 **Itshim**[8] 5287 2-8-12 0..................... WilliamCarson(5) 2 —+
(S C Williams) *t.k.h: sddle slipped after 1f: a bhd* **25/1**

60.40 secs (0.40) **Going Correction** -0.025s/f (Good) **11** Ran SP% **120.7**
Speed ratings (Par 92): **95,89,87,86,84 81,81,79,78,71 58**
toteswinger: 1&2 £4.60, 1&3 £5.20, 2&3 £2.80. CSF £36.11 TOTE £4.90: £1.80, £3.20, £1.10; EX 21.20 Trifecta £110.60 Part won. Pool: £149.47, 0.50 winning units..

Owner Pleasure Palace Racing **Bred** Jeremy Hinds **Trained** Woodingdean, E Sussex

FOCUS

A modest maiden auction but a clear winner.

NOTEBOOK

Smokey Ryder broke well from her favourable draw to hug the stands' rail and make all. She quickened the pace from over one furlong out and, though hanging away from the rail, stretched right away. Gary Moore was worried that the trip might not suit, but decided to make the best of her good draw and said the winner is now heading for nurseries. (op 9-2)

Blackwater Fort(USA) tracked Smokey Ryder on her outside but, despite keeping on, was readily outpaced. Claimed from David Barron at Beverley last month, he is still improving. (tchd 9-1 and 11-1)

Peper Harow(IRE), officially rated 14lb higher than the best of the others with ratings, had been overmatched previously at Ascot and Newmarket over 6f. She was keen tracking the winner three off the rail but at the 2f pole she was again very one-paced and looks to need further. (op 9-4)

Silver Salsa tracked the winner on the rail and ran better than her three no-shows previously, but she looks modest.

Frank Street, who holds an entry for the valuable auction stakes at Newmarket in October, had improved on his debut run last time at Salisbury. In mid-division away from the rail, he looked poised to strike two out but could make no impression and in the end was disappointing. (op 7-4 tchd 9-4)

Itsher Official explanation: jockey said filly hung left

Itshim was backed from 14-1 to 3-1 on his debut. Conversely, in this stronger race he drifted slightly but was always in rear after his saddle slipped. Official explanation: jockey said saddle slipped (op 18-1)

5531 BRIAN JAMES CLAW MEMORIAL H'CAP — 5f

2:40 (2:40) (Class 5) (0-75,73) 3-Y-O — £2,590 (£770; £385; £192) Stalls Low

Form — RPR

4245 **1** **Barraland**[21] 4904 3-9-5 **71** .... TPO'Shea 3 — 76
(M R Channon) *racd in stands' side gp: in tch: hdwy over 2f out: led stands' side gp over 1f out: r.o wl: 1st of 4 in gp* — **4/1**[2]

2050 **2** *½* **Magical Speedfit (IRE)**[38] 4347 3-9-6 **72** .... RyanMoore 10 — 75
(G G Margarson) *racd in far side gp: chsd ldrs: hdwy to ld far side gp 1f out: r.o but hld by wnr towards fin: 1st of 5 in gp* — **5/1**[3]

4651 **3** *3* **Enodoc**[17] 5015 3-9-2 **68** .... (t) DO'Donohoe 2 — 60
(W R Muir) *led stands' side gp tl over 1f out: outpcd u.p fnl f: 2nd of 4 in gp* — **7/2**[1]

0001 **4** *nk* **Hawk Eyed Lady (IRE)**[11] 5186 3-8-9 **61** .... (b) ShaneKelly 9 — 52
(J A Osborne) *led far side gp: hdd and hung lft 1f out: sn outpcd: 2nd of 5 in gp* — **15/2**

4600 **5** *hd* **Wavertree Princess (IRE)**[13] 5142 3-9-0 **66** .... JamesDoyle 1 — 57
(N P Littmoden) *racd stands' side: hld up in tch: rdn and effrt 2f out: no imp over 1f out: 3rd of 4 in gp* — **6/1**

3000 **6** *¾* **Chinese Temple (IRE)**[30] 4595 3-9-4 **70** .... AlanMunro 5 — 58
(M G Quinlan) *racd stands' side: chsd ldr stands' side tl wl over 1f out: wknd over 1f out: 4th of 4 in gp* — **8/1**

0005 **7** *1* **Regal Step**[38] 4347 3-9-4 **70** .... EddieAhern 8 — 54
(R M H Cowell) *racd far side: chsd ldr far side: rdn and hld high hd high wl over 1f out: btn whn hmpd jst ins fnl f: 3rd of 5 in gp* — **16/1**

0030 **8** *6* **Ten Down**[24] 4787 3-8-13 **72** .... RosieJessop(7) 7 — 35
(Miss Gay Kelleway) *racd alone in centre: led overall: rdn and hung rt over 2f out: hdd and jnd far side gp over 1f out: wknd: 4th of 5 in gp* — **8/1**

5-05 **9** *14* **Sinead Of Aglish (IRE)**[19] 4943 3-8-8 **60** .... (b) LPKeniry 6 — —
(Peter Grayson) *awkward s and v.s.a: racd far side: effrt and hung rt 2f out: sn wl btn: 5th of 5 in gp* — **16/1**

59.89 secs (-0.11) **Going Correction** -0.025s/f (Good) — **9** Ran SP% **118.9**

Speed ratings (Par 100): **99,98,93,92,92 91,89,80,57**

toteswinger: 1&2 £6.10, 1&3 £22.30, 2&3 £5.60. CSF £25.20 CT £77.96 TOTE £4.50: £1.40, £2.50, £1.80; EX 22.60 Trifecta £102.50 Part won. Pool: £138.62, 0.85 winning units..

Owner Box 41 **Bred** Tattersalls Scoundrels & Trickledown Stud **Trained** West Ilsley, Berks

FOCUS

A competitive enough handicap for the grade with all the runners having won at least one race, but most of the field are regressive. The field split into two groups for this sprint with the stands' side just prevailing.

5532 LICENSED TRADE TRUSTEE H'CAP — 6f

3:10 (3:10) (Class 5) (0-75,75) 3-Y-O+ — £2,590 (£770; £385; £192) Stalls Low

Form — RPR

1504 **1** **Mandarin Spirit (IRE)**[3] 5433 8-8-10 **64** .... (b) WilliamCarson(5) 8 — 77
(G C H Chung) *t.k.h: hld up in tch: hdwy wl over 1f out: led jst over 1f out: rdn clr fnl f: eased nr fin* — **7/1**[3]

4022 **2** *2¾* **Alfresco**[15] 5091 4-9-10 **73** .... (v) RyanMoore 6 — 78
(I A Wood) *chsd ldrs: effrt and ev ch 2f out: nt pce of wnr fnl f* — **11/4**[2]

4660 **3** *1¼* **Billy Red**[39] 4313 4-8-6 **55** .... (b) ChrisCatlin 1 — 56
(J R Jenkins) *in tch: n.m.r on stands' rail and swtchd rt wl over 1f out: kpt on same pce fnl f* — **8/1**

4013 **4** *1* **Overwing (IRE)**[16] 5073 5-9-9 **72** .... EddieAhern 2 — 70+
(R M H Cowell) *led tl rdn and hdd 2f out: n.m.r and lost pl jst over 1f out: swtchd rt 1f out: plugged on* — **5/2**[1]

0213 **5** *¾* **Regal Royale**[13] 5151 5-9-4 **67** .... (v) AdamKirby 3 — 62
(Peter Grayson) *sn bustled up to press ldr: rdn to ld: 2f out: hdd over 1f out: wknd ins fnl f* — **5/2**[1]

6305 **6** *4* **Ben Ami**[18] 4976 3-9-3 **69** .... IanMongan 5 — 52
(Miss J R Gibney) *in tch in rr: rdn and outpcd 1/2-way: edgd rt and sme hdwy u.p over 1f out: wknd ent fnl f* — **22/1**

1m 12.08s (-0.62) **Going Correction** -0.025s/f (Good)

WFA 3 from 4yo+ 3lb — **6** Ran SP% **111.8**

Speed ratings (Par 103): **103,99,97,96,95 90**

toteswinger: 1&2 £2.20, 1&3 £9.50, 2&3 £2.80. CSF £26.21 CT £154.73 TOTE £6.60: £1.70, £2.00; EX 17.40 Trifecta £118.50 Pool: £160.26, 1.00 winning units..

Owner Peter Tsim **Bred** W Haggas And W Jarvis **Trained** Newmarket, Suffolk

FOCUS

A competitive handicap featuring some in-form runners and a couple of confirmed pacesetters. The form seems to make sense at face value but the leaders did appear to go too fast.

Regal Royale Official explanation: jockey said gelding had no more to give

5533 WESTENHANGER (S) STKS — 7f (S)

3:40 (3:41) (Class 6) 3-Y-O+ — £2,047 (£604; £302) Stalls Low

Form — RPR

-021 **1** **Singleb (IRE)**[21] 4891 4-9-10 62 .... DaneO'Neill 11 — 65+
(George Baker) *racd on far side: mde all: hung bdly lft fr 2f out: jnd stands' side gp over 2f out: styd on wl* — **2/1**[1]

0042 **2** *¾* **Ten To The Dozen**[12] 5170 5-9-10 60 .... ChrisCatlin 7 — 63
(P W Hiatt) *racd stands' side: chsd ldrs: led stands' side gp over 2f out: chsd wnr fnl f: kpt on same pce* — **6/1**[3]

0000 **3** *1¼* **Naughty Girl (IRE)**[25] 4748 8-8-7 41 .... SoniaEaton(7) 6 — 50
(John A Harris) *racd stands' side: chsd ldrs: kpt on same pce u.p fr wl over 1f out* — **40/1**

5004 **4** *nse* **Border Artist**[47] 4052 9-9-5 50 .... RyanMoore 3 — 54
(J Pearce) *racd on stands' side: hld up: hdwy over 2f out: chsd ldrs and rdn over 1f out: kpt on same pce fnl f* — **12/1**

1015 **5** *¾* **Le Chiffre (IRE)**[7] 5303 6-9-10 63 .... (p) J-PGuillambert 4 — 57
(John A Harris) *racd on stands' side: hld up in midfield: effrt 2f out: edgd rt and kpt on same pce u.p fnl f* — **9/2**[2]

00 **6** *7* **Lauras Joy (IRE)**[47] 4052 5-9-0 40 .... AdamKirby 1 — 29
(G P Enright) *racd stands' side: bhd: rdn 1/2-way: sme hdwy u.p 2f out: wknd over 1f out* — **50/1**

4010 **7** *3* **Who's Winning (IRE)**[12] 5166 7-9-10 59 .... (t) GeorgeBaker 12 — 30
(B G Powell) *racd on far side: chsd wnr over 2f out: sn wl outpcd: no ch fnl f* — **7/1**

0602 **8** *2¼* **Banjo Patterson**[12] 5166 6-9-5 57 .... (b) ShaneKelly 2 — 19
(M G Quinlan) *racd stands' side: dwlt: sn in tch: rdn and wknd qckly over 1f out* — **8/1**

0300 **9** *1¼* **Mick Is Back**[13] 5161 4-9-10 57 .... (vt) EddieAhern 13 — 21
(G G Margarson) *chsd wnr on far side tl over 2f out: sn wl btn* — **10/1**

0060 **10** *5* **Bahamian Blue (IRE)**[23] 4806 3-9-0 45 .... (b) JamesDoyle 8 — —
(P G Murphy) *racd on stands' side: led stands' side tl over 2f out: wknd qckly over 1f out* — **66/1**

-040 **11** *6* **Bakers Boy**[36] 4412 4-9-5 40 .... (b[1]) RichardThomas 10 — —
(J E Long) *racd far side: a bhd: no ch last 2f* — **66/1**

2400 **12** *½* **Only If I Laugh**[36] 4414 7-9-5 43 .... IanMongan 5 — —
(M J Attwater) *racd stands' side: stdd s: a wl bhd* — **33/1**

5400 **13** *50* **Heron (IRE)**[11] 5186 3-8-9 43 .... NicolPolli(5) 9 — —
(M R Hoad) *racd far side: a bhd: virtually p.u fr over 1f out: t.o* — **66/1**

1m 27.46s (0.16) **Going Correction** -0.025s/f (Good)

WFA 3 from 4yo+ 5lb — **13** Ran SP% **118.0**

Speed ratings (Par 101): **98,97,95,95,94 86,83,80,79,73 66,66,9**

toteswinger: 1&2 £3.40, 1&3 £34.40, 2&3 £51.20. CSF £13.29 TOTE £2.80: £1.50, £2.20, £6.10; EX 13.30 Trifecta £31.50 Pool: £213.07, 5.00 winning units..The winner was sold to R A Green for 9,400gns.

Owner The Betfair Radioheads **Bred** Spratstown Stud Gm **Trained** Moreton Morrell, Warwicks

FOCUS

The runners again split into two groups and five on the stands' side pulled clear of the field. The form is straightforward.

Mick Is Back Official explanation: jockey said gelding hung badly left

Only If I Laugh Official explanation: jockey said gelding hung right throughout

5534 EUROPEAN BREEDERS' FUND MAIDEN FILLIES' STKS (DIV I) — 7f (S)

4:10 (4:12) (Class 4) 2-Y-O — £5,204 (£1,557; £778; £389; £193) Stalls Low

Form — RPR

5 **1** **My Superstar**[13] 5147 2-9-0 0 .... RyanMoore 2 — 76+
(Sir Michael Stoute) *mde all on stands' rail: rdn clr over 1f out: r.o strly: readily* — **7/2**[2]

45 **2** *4½* **Caster Sugar (USA)**[21] 4896 2-9-0 0 .... DaneO'Neill 5 — 66+
(L M Cumani) *hld up towards rr: hdwy over 2f out: nt clr run and swtchd lft jst ins fnl f: kpt on to go 2nd last 50yds: no ch w wnr* — **10/1**[3]

3 *nk* **Daylumney (IRE)**[73] 3184 2-9-0 0 .... ChrisCatlin 11 — 64
(E J O'Neill) *t.k.h: hld up in tch: hdwy over 2f out: kpt on u.p fnl f: wnt 3rd nr fin: no ch w wnr* — **12/1**

06 **4** *½* **Jewelled Reef (IRE)**[41] 4251 2-9-0 0 .... StephenCarson 7 — 63
(Eve Johnson Houghton) *racd in midfield: rdn 1/2-way: hdwy u.p 2f out: disp 2nd ent fnl f: kpt on same pce after* — **50/1**

0 **5** *shd* **Impressionist Art (USA)**[44] 4157 2-9-0 0 .... AlanMunro 8 — 63
(B J Meehan) *chsd wnr: rdn 2f out: outpcd by wnr jst over 1f out: lost 3 pls last 50yds* — **16/1**

6 *1½* **Fongoli** 2-9-0 0 .... TQuinn 4 — 59+
(B G Powell) *in tch in midfield: rdn over 2f out: keeping on whn nt clr run and hmpd ent fnl f: nvr able to chal* — **50/1**

7 *¾* **Praise Of Folly** 2-9-0 0 .... JimCrowley 9 — 57
(P Winkworth) *chsd ldrs: rdn to chse ldng pair over 2f out: wknd ent fnl f* — **33/1**

0 **8** *1* **Demand**[25] 4740 2-9-0 0 .... LiamJones 6 — 57+
(W J Haggas) *chsd ldrs: rdn 1/2-way: wknd over 1f out: btn whn hmpd jst ins fnl f* — **14/1**

9 *1¼* **Dazzel** 2-9-0 0 .... HayleyTurner 3 — 52+
(D R Lanigan) *rn green: sn pushed along in rr: n.d* — **33/1**

10 *1½* **Pure Rhythm** 2-9-0 0 .... J-PGuillambert 1 — 48
(S C Williams) *s.i.s: a bhd: n.d* — **50/1**

0 **11** *24* **Tinkerbelle (IRE)**[68] 3349 2-9-0 0 .... DO'Donohoe 13 — —
(J L Dunlop) *dropped in after s: bhd: rdn whn bdly hmpd wl over 2f out: no ch after: t.o fnl f* — **50/1**

02 **P** **Careless Whisper**[31] 4554 2-9-0 0 .... MichaelHills 12 — —
(J W Hills) *in tch tl injured and p.u wl over 2f out: dead* — **4/6**[1]

1m 28.16s (0.86) **Going Correction** -0.025s/f (Good) — **12** Ran SP% **125.3**

Speed ratings (Par 93): **94,88,88,87,87 86,85,84,82,80 53,—**

toteswinger: 1&2 £4.80, 1&3 £5.50, 2&3 £9.20. CSF £38.74 TOTE £4.70: £1.40, £2.50, £3.60; EX 18.00 Trifecta £112.90 Part won. Pool: £152.60, 0.65 winning units..

Owner Mrs R J Jacobs **Bred** Newsells Park Stud Limited **Trained** Newmarket, Suffolk

FOCUS

The field tracked over to the stands' side for this maiden, which the winner turned into an end-to-end romp. The race was marred when hot favourite Careless Whisper broke down when travelling well.

NOTEBOOK

My Superstar, after breaking smartly and getting to the rail, fought off an early challenger and powered home. She certainly built on her debut run at Windsor over softer ground where connection felt she was green, and she relished the longer trip. She holds a Group 1 Fillies' Mile entry but is not certain to run. However, she will get further. (tchd 3-1)

Caster Sugar(USA) was held up early and still looked a little green. She was driven 2f out and began to stay on when slightly checked in her run, but was then switched to the outside and ran on again close home. Her dam was a top-class middle-distance filly for the same stable and her future also looks to be over further. (op 14-1 tchd 16-1)

Daylumney(IRE) was quite keen early and was chased along to challenge five wide 2f from home before her run flattened out. Having her first run for a stable that has succeeded with three of her relatives, she will win in due course. (tchd 14-1)

Jewelled Reef(IRE) made headway to challenge four wide 2f out and looks set to make her mark in nurseries. (tchd 66-1)

Impressionist Art(USA) disputed the lead early, but faded in the final furlong. (op 20-1)

Fongoli Official explanation: jockey said filly was denied a clear run

Careless Whisper unfortunately suffered a fatal injury when still travelling well. (op 10-11 tchd Evens in places)

5535 EUROPEAN BREEDERS' FUND MAIDEN FILLIES' STKS (DIV II) 7f (S)
4:40 (4:42) (Class 4) 2-Y-O £5,204 (£1,557; £778; £389; £193) Stalls Low

Form RPR

0 **1** **Silver Games (IRE)**[15] [5097] 2-9-0 0 .... EdwardCreighton 9 82+
(M R Channon) *hld up in midfield: hdwy 4f out: trckd ldrs fr 1/2-way: chsd ldr over 1f out: led jst ins fnl f: edgd rt but r.o strly: readily* **7/1**[3]

0 **2** *2 ¾* **Damini (USA)**[16] [5048] 2-9-0 0 .... RyanMoore 4 75
(Sir Michael Stoute) *chsd ldrs: bustled along to ld 4f out: rdn wl over 2f out: clr w wnr 1f out: hdd jst ins fnl f: nt pce of wnr* **11/4**[2]

4 **3** *4 ½* **Perception (IRE)**[43] [4184] 2-9-0 0 .... SteveDrowne 10 64
(R Charlton) *racd in midfield: rdn 3f out: hdwy over 2f out: kpt on to go modest 3rd ins fnl f: no ch w ldng pair* **5/4**[1]

0 **4** *2 ½* **Golden Games (IRE)**[29] [4643] 2-9-0 0 .... DaneO'Neill 11 58+
(J L Dunlop) *bhd: rdn over 2f out: styd on steadily past btn horses fr over 1f out: nvr trbld ldrs* **25/1**

000 **5** *1 ½* **Hosanna**[44] [4157] 2-9-0 53 .... EddieAhern 1 54
(B J Meehan) *s.i.s: t.k.h: sn trcking ldrs: chsd ldr wl over 2f out tl over 1f out: sn wknd* **25/1**

6 *1 ½* **Age Of Couture** 2-9-0 0 .... AlanMunro 7 50
(W Jarvis) *v.s.a: wl bhd: hdwy wl over 2f out: swtchd rt 2f out: styd on past btn horses fnl f: nvr nr ldrs* **40/1**

4 **7** *6* **Money Money Money**[16] [5048] 2-9-0 0 .... JimCrowley 12 35
(P Winkworth) *chsd ldrs for 2f out: rdn and struggling 1/2-way: no ch after* **15/2**

8 *½* **Chic Retreat (USA)** 2-9-0 0 .... HayleyTurner 6 34
(M L W Bell) *prom: chsd ldr 4f out tl over 2f out: sn wknd* **20/1**

6 **9** *6* **Spinning Belle (IRE)**[16] [5048] 2-9-0 0 .... MichaelHills 8 19
(J W Hills) *t.k.h: chsd ldr tl 4f out: struggling fr 1/2-way* **16/1**

0 **10** *6* **My Les**[22] [4861] 2-9-0 0 .... LPKeniry 2 4
(J R Best) *a struggling in rr: t.o* **50/1**

11 *7* **Dicey Affair** 2-9-0 0 .... AdamKirby 5 —
(G L Moore) *s.i.s: a outpcd in rr: t.o* **50/1**

03 **12** *nk* **Rebounding**[34] [4488] 2-9-0 0 .... SaleemGolam 3 —
(S C Williams) *led tl 4f out: wknd qckly u.p over 2f out: t.o* **22/1**

0 **13** *17* **Micro Chip**[9] [5214] 2-8-9 0 .... GabrielHannon(5) 13 —
(B G Powell) *rrd over and uns rdr bef s: a outpcd: t.o last 3f* **100/1**

1m 27.65s (0.35) **Going Correction** -0.025s/f (Good) **13 Ran SP% 125.4**
Speed ratings (Par 93): **97,93,88,85,84 82,75,75,68,61 53,52,33**
toteswinger: 1&2 £5.90, 1&3 £4.90, 2&3 £2.40. CSF £25.88 TOTE £8.90: £2.50, £1.30, £1.30; EX 33.40 TRIFECTA Not won..
Owner Box 41 **Bred** Ceka Ireland Limited **Trained** West Ilsley, Berks

FOCUS
The second division of the maiden was run at a strong pace in a time over half a second quicker than the first. The runners again headed for the stands' rail, they finished strung out, and the form looks solid.

NOTEBOOK
Silver Games(IRE) had been green on her debut at Newbury, but she was much more accomplished here. Quite keen early in mid-division off the rail, she quickened to challenge two furlongs out and won going away. Connections were very encouraged by this run as she is considered one of the better two-year-olds in the yard, and she will get further. A half-sister to Nahoodh, she is entered for the Group 1 Fillies' Mile and surely has to take her chance there. (op 12-1)
Damini(USA) helped set up the early pace racing towards the centre and though she stayed on well she had no answer to the ready winner, but this was still a good run. At home she works with My Superstar, the winner of the first division of the maiden, and might not be as good but she is still improving. (op 5-1)
Perception(IRE) was a warm order to build on her debut when staying on late to finish fourth at Lingfield in a strong race. She plugged on rather than making late progress and was a bit disappointing, though she might be better on slightly easier ground. (op 10-11 tchd 5-6)
Golden Games(IRE), who was well beaten on her Newmarket debut early this month, stayed on at one pace and might be better over further. (tchd 33-1)
Hosanna had every chance racing against the rail, but was not good enough to take advantage. She is only moderate, having beaten just three rivals in her previous three starts, and is rated just 53. (op 22-1)
Chic Retreat(USA) was prominent until driven 2f out and was eased when beaten. She might be better next season. (tchd 18-1)

5536 EUROPEAN BREEDERS' FUND FILLIES' H'CAP 1m 1f 149y
5:10 (5:10) (Class 3) (0-90,83) 3-Y-O+
£9,346 (£2,799; £1,399; £700; £349; £175) Stalls Centre

Form RPR

5413 **1** **Moon Sister (IRE)**[17] [5024] 3-9-0 78 .... AlanMunro 8 86
(W Jarvis) *mde all: rdn 2f out: styd on strly and a in command after* **10/3**[2]

-403 **2** *2* **Fantasy Princess (USA)**[22] [4872] 3-8-7 76 .. Louis-PhilippeBeuzelin(5) 1 80
(G A Butler) *s.i.s: bhd tl rapid hdwy to chse wnr over 6f out: rdn ent fnl 2f: kpt on same pce* **12/1**

0313 **3** *1* **Fountains Abbey (USA)**[27] [4694] 3-9-1 79 .... RyanMoore 5 81
(Sir Michael Stoute) *chsd wnr tl over 6f out: rdn and unable qck jst over 2f out: plugged on same pce u.p* **10/3**[2]

3066 **4** *½* **Baylini**[17] [5033] 4-9-10 80 .... JamesDoyle 6 81
(Ms J S Doyle) *hld up in tch: effrt jst over 2f out: swtchd lft and rdn over 1f out: kpt on but nvr pce to rch ldrs* **12/1**

0546 **5** *2 ½* **Free Offer**[32] [4520] 4-9-8 83 .... AshleyHamblett(5) 3 79
(J L Dunlop) *s.i.s: t.k.h: hld up in rr: wanting to hang and nt clr run 2f out tl ent fnl f: swtchd lft: kpt on: nvr trbld ldrs* **3/1**[1]

1124 **6** *1* **Amicable Terms**[16] [5075] 3-8-11 80 .... WilliamCarson(5) 2 74
(Rae Guest) *hld up in rr: effrt and edgd rt jst over 2f out: no imp fr over 1f out* **11/1**

2453 **7** *nse* **Candy Mountain**[21] [4894] 4-9-9 79 .... DaneO'Neill 7 73
(L M Cumani) *chsd ldrs: rdn and unable qck 2f out: wknd fnl f* **8/1**

3321 **8** *4 ½* **Luck Will Come (IRE)**[19] [4945] 4-9-0 70 .... ChrisCatlin 4 55
(H J Collingridge) *t.k.h: hld up towards rr: rdn and effrt over 2f out: wknd wl over 1f out* **7/1**[3]

2m 2.13s (-2.77) **Going Correction** -0.20s/f (Firm)
WFA 3 from 4yo 8lb **8 Ran SP% 118.5**
Speed ratings (Par 104): **103,101,100,100,98 97,97,93**
toteswinger: 1&2 £10.40, 1&3 £3.50, 2&3 £9.70. CSF £43.78 CT £145.45 TOTE £4.70: £1.70, £3.40, £1.30; EX 44.20 Trifecta £114.40 Pool: £201.12, 1.30 winning units..
Owner Abdullah Saeed Belhab **Bred** Darley **Trained** Newmarket, Suffolk

FOCUS
A decent contest, but the winner made her inside stall position count under a positive ride. This is perhaps not form to take too literally.

NOTEBOOK
Moon Sister(IRE) broke well from the inside stall, tracked over to the inside rail and led all the way, easily repelling her sole challenger around the turn and staying on well. She did not stay 1m4f at Salisbury last time and this drop in trip was clearly more suitable. Her trainer had been worried about the going, but she handled it well and should be a filly to follow in the autumn. (op 5-1 tchd 11-2)
Fantasy Princess(USA) ran well considering she had the outside stall to overcome and had to make her challenge wide. She was the only one that looked likely to trouble the winner at any stage, but could not make up the ground. Stepping up in trip, stamina was not a problem and she can win soon. (tchd 14-1)
Fountains Abbey(USA), who won a maiden at Windsor last month, was also stepping up from 1m. Tracking the winner, she had every chance but never really picked up and might be better over shorter after all. (op 3-1 tchd 4-1)
Baylini, who has been struggling in Listed and Group 3 class recently, made some late headway but her three previous wins have been on the All-Weather. (op 11-1 tchd 10-1 and 14-1)
Free Offer, still 5lb above her last winning mark, not for the first time met trouble in running but she also again showed that she is not an easy ride and is becoming less and less convincing. (op 10-3 tchd 11-4)

5537 LYMPNE H'CAP 1m 4f
5:40 (5:40) (Class 6) (0-65,64) 3-Y-O £2,047 (£604; £302) Stalls Low

Form RPR

0650 **1** **Fearless Warrior**[29] [4646] 3-9-0 57 .... (b[1]) EddieAhern 3 69
(J L Dunlop) *hld up in midfield: hdwy 4f out: chsd ldng pair and rdn jst over 2f out: chal between horses wl over 1f out: led jst over 1f out: styd on wl* **9/1**

5054 **2** *3* **Dancing Dik**[12] [5169] 3-9-5 62 .... JimCrowley 14 69
(Mrs A J Perrett) *led: rdn over 2f out: hdd jst over 1f out: no ex fnl f* **5/1**[3]

4404 **3** *2 ½* **Ba Dreamflight**[18] [4978] 3-8-4 47 .... WilliamBuick 13 50
(H Morrison) *reminder sn after s: chsd ldr: rdn to chal over 2f out: ev ch tl wknd fnl f* **14/1**

0-33 **4** *1 ½* **Limelight (USA)**[12] [5169] 3-8-9 52 .... J-PGuillambert 2 52
(Sir Mark Prescott) *sn bustled up to chse ldrs: rn wd bnd after 3f: rdn to chse ldng pair wl over 2f out tl over 2f out: plugged on same pce after* **9/4**[1]

3000 **5** *7* **West Lorne (USA)**[111] [2041] 3-8-13 56 .... ChrisCatlin 12 44
(E J O'Neill) *t.k.h: hld up in midfield: rdn over 3f out: sn outpcd: wl btn fnl 2f* **40/1**

500 **6** *1 ½* **Etta Place**[27] [4695] 3-9-2 59 .... AlanMunro 6 45
(P W Chapple-Hyam) *bmpd after s: wl bhd: outpcd 4f out: plugged on past btn horses fnl 2f: swtchd lft over 1f out: nvr nr ldrs* **25/1**

0505 **7** *2 ½* **Dixie Dean (USA)**[24] [4796] 3-8-13 56 .... (v) RyanMoore 4 38
(Sir Michael Stoute) *hld up towards rr: rdn over 3f out: little rspnse and n.d* **7/1**

0606 **8** *¾* **Amir Pasha (UAE)**[13] [5154] 3-9-4 61 .... (v[1]) AdamKirby 11 41
(W R Swinburn) *chsd ldrs: rdn over 3f out: sn struggling: wl btn fnl 2f* **10/1**

0412 **9** *½* **Star Grazer**[18] [4992] 3-9-2 64 .... JackMitchell(5) 8 43
(C F Wall) *hld up towards rr on outer: hmpd 8f out: rdn and no hdwy over 3f out: no ch fnl 2f* **4/1**[2]

6105 **10** *2 ¼* **Rampant Ronnie (USA)**[4] [5407] 3-9-3 60 .... ShaneKelly 9 36
(P W D'Arcy) *hld up in midfield: lost pl 1/2-way: no ch fnl 3f* **16/1**

0000 **11** *4* **Ubiquitous**[24] [4774] 3-8-3 46 .... SaleemGolam 1 15
(S Dow) *stdd and dropped in bhd after s: plld hrd: rapid hdwy and plld wd 8f out: sn chsng ldrs: rdn and wknd qckly over 2f out* **22/1**

0006 **12** *3 ¾* **Ray Diamond**[32] [4527] 3-8-3 46 .... (p) AdrianMcCarthy 5 8
(M Madgwick) *stdd s: hld up in rr: rdn and outpcd 4f out: wl bhd fnl 3f* **40/1**

2m 38.19s (-2.71) **Going Correction** -0.20s/f (Firm) **12 Ran SP% 124.6**
Speed ratings (Par 98): **101,99,97,96,91 90,89,88,88,86 84,81**
toteswinger: 1&2 £6.90, 1&3 £22.10, 2&3 £10.70. CSF £54.56 CT £644.19 TOTE £11.10: £3.50, £1.90, £4.70; EX 44.50 Trifecta £196.70 Part won. Pool: £265.88, 0.65 winning units. Place 6: £47.93, Place 5: £29.96..
Owner Mrs I H Stewart-Brown & M J Meacock **Bred** I Stewart-Brown And M Meacock **Trained** Arundel, W Sussex

FOCUS
A moderate handicap with three horses setting the early pace, which might not have been as strong as it looked for, though they were all beaten by a rejuvenated winner, no other hold-up horses got into it. The form is probably worth taking at face value.
T/Plt: £38.90 to a £1 stake. Pool: £58,313.12. 1,092.30 winning tickets. T/Qpdt: £21.30 to a £1 stake. Pool: £3,424.55. 118.70 winning tickets. SP

4947 MUSSELBURGH (R-H)
Sunday, August 31

OFFICIAL GOING: Good (good to firm in places) changing to good (good to soft in places) after race 2 (2.50)
Wind: Virtually nil Weather: Raining

5538 STRATHALLAN SCHOOL APPRENTICE H'CAP 1m
2:20 (2:20) (Class 6) (0-60,60) 4-Y-O+ £2,590 (£770; £385; £192) Stalls High

Form RPR

4036 **1** **Shunkawakhan (IRE)**[72] [3211] 5-9-2 57 .... (p) AndrewMullen 1 65
(Miss L A Perratt) *trckd ldrs: hdwy and cl up 5f out: effrt to chal 2f out and sn rdn: drvn to ld ins fnl f: jst hld on* **25/1**

3314 **2** *shd* **Silly Gilly (IRE)**[21] [4898] 4-8-9 55 .... DeclanCannon(5) 9 63
(R E Barr) *sn led: rdn along over 2f out: drvn over 1f out: hdd ins fnl f: rallied nr fin: jst failed* **10/1**

6053 **3** *hd* **Sands Of Barra (IRE)**[4] [5389] 5-9-0 58 .... KellyHarrison(3) 12 66+
(I W McInnes) *a.p: effrt whn nt clr run wl over 1f out: swtchd lft and rdn ent fnl f: styd on strly: jst failed* **11/2**[2]

4330 **4** *2 ½* **Oeuf A La Neige**[3] [5420] 8-8-7 55 .... JamieKyne(7) 4 57
(Miss L A Perratt) *hld up and bhd: hdwy wl over 2f out: rdn wl over 1f out: swtchd ins ent fnl f and styd on strly: nrst fin* **14/1**

5620 **5** *hd* **Polish Corridor**[21] [4898] 9-9-5 60 .... NeilBrown 10 61
(M Dods) *chsd ldrs: rdn along over 2f out: drvn over 1f out and sn no imp* **10/1**

000 **6** *1 ¼* **Social Rhythm**[42] [4215] 4-8-9 57 ow6 .... GarryWhillans(7) 2 55
(A C Whillans) *in tch on outer: effrt and hdwy 3f out: rdn 2f out: kpt on u.p ins fnl f* **25/1**

4052 **7** *nse* **Pianoforte (USA)**[21] [4898] 6-9-4 59 .... (b) DNolan 7 57
(E J Alston) *hld up in midfield: hdwy over 2f out: rdn wl over 1f out: sn one pce* **11/1**

 The Form Book, Raceform Ltd, Compton, RG20 6NL

0146 **8** *hd* **Sarraaf (IRE)**[18] 4969 12-8-9 **53**.......................... PatrickDonaghy(3) 6 51+
(Miss L A Perratt) *hld up towards rr: hdwy over 2f out: sn rdn and kpt on ins fnl f: nt rch ldrs* **33/1**

5030 **9** *1 1/4* **Anduril**[3] 5420 7-8-5 **51**..(p) BMcHugh(5) 8 46
(I W McInnes) *in tch: effrt over 3f out: rdn along over 2f out and grad wknd* **20/1**

4452 **10** *1/2* **Apache Nation (IRE)**[3] 5420 5-9-1 **56**......................(b) DuranFentiman 3 50
(M Dods) *trckd ldrs: effrt 3f out: sn rdn along: drvn 2f out and sn btn* **5/1**[1]

-603 **11** *1 1/4* **Barataria**[44] 4168 6-9-0 **55**.. MichaelJStainton 14 46
(R Bastiman) *s.i.s: a in rr* **8/1**

0003 **12** *nk* **Kirkby's Treasure**[19] 4949 10-9-1 **56**............................ JamieMoriarty 5 46
(A Berry) *hld up towards rr: swtchd outside and sme hdwy wl over 2f out: sn rdn and wknd* **14/1**

4162 **13** *nse* **Papa's Princess**[22] 4851 4-9-0 **58**............................. GaryBartley(3) 13 48
(J S Goldie) *s.i.s: a in rr* **6/1**[3]

0005 **14** *2 3/4* **Forzarzi (IRE)**[29] 4632 4-8-7 **53**................................ LanceBetts(5) 11 37
(H A McWilliams) *chsd ldrs: rdn alongh over 3f out: sn wknd* **8/1**

1m 41.41s (0.21) **Going Correction** +0.075s/f (Good) **14** Ran SP% **123.8**
Speed ratings (Par 101): **101,100,100,98,98 96,96,96,95,94 93,93,93,90**
toteswinger: 1&2 £28.40, 1&3 £31.10, 2&3 £10.50. CSF £255.09 CT £1636.82 TOTE £29.10: £7.70, £3.20, £2.50; EX 233.10.
Owner Partick Thistle Racing Club **Bred** Matthew Duffy **Trained** Carluke, S Lanarks
■ Stewards' Enquiry : Jamie Kyne one-day ban: careless riding (Sep 14)

FOCUS
After light rain throughout the morning and more persistent rain in the hour before racing, the meeting started on ground officially described as good, good to firm in places. This low-grade apprentice handicap was not run at a strong pace and the time suggested the rain had not yet got into the ground. The first three occupied those positions throughout.

5539 LTSB SCOTLAND COMMERCIAL BANKING AND FINANCE MAIDEN AUCTION STKS 7f 30y
2:50 (2:51) (Class 6) 2-Y-O **£2,266** (£674; £337; £168) **Stalls** High

Form RPR

032 **1** **Tale Of Silver (IRE)**[36] 4415 2-8-11 77......................... PJMcDonald(3) 8 81+
(G A Swinbank) *trckd ldng pair: smooth hdwy on inner to ld wl over 2f out: sn clr: easily* **10/11**[1]

33 **2** *4* **Hel's Angel (IRE)**[71] 3277 2-8-2 0............................ AndrewMullen(3) 10 60
(Mrs A Duffield) *led: rdn along and edgd lft 3f out: sn hdd: drvn wl over 1f out: kpt on: no ch w wnr* **9/2**[2]

3 **3** *5* **Denton Diva**[20] 4921 2-8-5 0.. DaleGibson 6 48
(M Dods) *in tch: hdwy over 3f out: rdn over 2f out: kpt on same pce u.p ent fnl f* **13/2**[3]

0 **4** *4* **Yeoman Of England (IRE)**[20] 4921 2-8-13 0.................... TomEaves 2 46
(B Smart) *in tch: hdwy to chse ldrs 3f out: rdn over 2f out and sn one pce* **20/1**

02 **5** *1/2* **Haulage Lady (IRE)**[21] 4897 2-8-4 0........................... PaulHanagan 1 35
(Karen McLintock) *in rr: rdn along 3f out: styd on appr fnl f: n.d* **15/2**

00 **6** *3* **Nino Zachetti (IRE)**[30] 4593 2-8-12 0........................ GrahamGibbons 4 36
(E J Alston) *chsd ldrs: rdn along 3f out: drvn and wknd over 2f out* **66/1**

7 *1/2* **Saving Grace** 2-8-7 0 ow1... DavidAllan 5 30
(E J Alston) *a in rr* **20/1**

52 **8** *2 1/4* **Our Apolonia (IRE)**[15] 5106 2-8-5 0............................... JoeFanning 3 22+
(A Berry) *cl up: pushed along whn bmpd 3f out and sn rdn: wknd 2f out: eased* **9/1**

00 **9** *8* **Cleard For Action**[57] 3707 2-9-1 0............................... TonyHamilton 7 12
(J R Weymes) *a in rr* **100/1**

0 **10** *16* **Valdemar**[34] 4474 2-8-10 0.. PaulMulrennan 9 —
(A D Brown) *t.k.h: dwlt: sn in tch on inner: rdn along 3f out and sn wknd* **50/1**

1m 30.79s (0.49) **Going Correction** +0.075s/f (Good) **10** Ran SP% **119.6**
Speed ratings (Par 92): **100,95,89,85,84 81,80,78,68,50**
toteswinger: 1&2 £2.40, 1&3 £3.30, 2&3 £4.50. CSF £5.07 TOTE £2.20: £1.30, £1.90, £2.00; EX 6.40.
Owner Mrs I Gibson **Bred** Audrey Frances Stynes **Trained** Melsonby, N Yorks

FOCUS
The rain continued to fall and the ground was starting to ease. A weak maiden.

NOTEBOOK
Tale Of Silver(IRE) had easily the best credentials and was well backed. Rated 77 after missing out by a head on his third start at Newcastle five weeks earlier, he travelled smoothly and nipped through on the inside of the leader and coming clear for a very easy success. A nice type with size and scope, he will be interesting in handicap company. (op 5-4 tchd 11-8 in a place)
Hel's Angel(IRE), absent for ten weeks and from a stable swinging back into action, set a good pace but she left the running rail, leaving the door open for the winner. She is now qualified for a nursery mark. (op 10-3)
Denton Diva, third in another weak event on her debut at Thirsk, stuck on to finish a creditable third. She looks a likely nursery type but needs another outing to qualify (op 6-1)
Yeoman Of England(IRE), clueless on his debut, again showed signs of inexperience, edging left under pressure. There is better to come especially on a more galloping track.
Haulage Lady(IRE), 100/1 when runner-up at Redcar, had the worst of the draw. She was towards the rear turning in but stuck on in her own time. Stoutly-bred on her dam's side, she will not be seen at her best until next year. (op 9-1)
Saving Grace, a likeable newcomer, is a daughter of the speedy Damalis who served this yard so well. After a tardy start she stayed on in pleasing fashion and will have learnt a fair bit. (tchd 16-1)
Our Apolonia(IRE), 80/1 when second at Ripon, raced up with the pace, but she persisted in hanging badly right and in the end her rider had to just sit and suffer. Official explanation: jockey said filly hung right-handed in home straight (op 14-1)

5540 ALAN J. BAIN CONTRACTORS H'CAP 1m 6f
3:20 (3:20) (Class 5) (0-75,73) 3-Y-O+ **£3,885** (£1,156; £577; £288) **Stalls** High

Form RPR

5343 **1** **Danzatrice**[18] 4963 6-9-5 **65**....................................... PJMcDonald(3) 4 71+
(C W Thornton) *hld up in rr: hdwy on bit 3f out: cl up appr last: shkn up to ld last 100yds: styd on strly* **2/1**[1]

6413 **2** *1 3/4* **Nero West (FR)**[44] 4146 7-10-0 **71**..................................(b) TomEaves 7 74
(Miss L A Perratt) *led: pushed along 3f out: rdn 2f out: drvn over 1f out: hdd and no ex last 100yds* **10/3**[3]

0251 **3** *3/4* **Kyber**[19] 4947 7-9-1 **63**... GaryBartley(5) 6 65
(J S Goldie) *hld up in tch: hdwy 3f out: rdn along 2f out: kpt on u.p fnl f* **5/2**[2]

-455 **4** *1* **Flamed Amazement**[108] 1773 4-9-7 **64**.............................. PaulHanagan 2 65
(L Lungo) *chsd ldr: rdn along 3f out: drvn 2f out: kpt on one pce* **15/2**

10/0 **5** *13* **Shankly Bond (IRE)**[22] 4848 6-8-13 **63**........................ BMcHugh(7) 8 46
(Mrs L B Normile) *chsd ldrs: rdn along 3f out: drvn over 2f out and sn wknd* **9/1**

6 *4 1/2* **Pegasus Mondrianus (GER)**[32] 8-9-1 **58**..............(v[1]) PaulMulrennan 1 35
(Mrs S C Bradburne) *chsd ldrs: rdn along over 4f out: wknd 3f out* **25/1**

0000 **7** *22* **Ceduna Roadhouse (IRE)**[48] 4019 3-7-10 **54** oh8 ow1 DuranFentiman(3) 5 —
(A M Crow) *a in rr: bhd fnl 3f* **100/1**

3m 4.76s (-0.54) **Going Correction** +0.075s/f (Good)
WFA 3 from 4yo+ 12lb **7** Ran SP% **111.6**
Speed ratings (Par 103): **104,103,102,102,94 92,79**
toteswinger: 1&2 £2.50, 1&3 £1.90, 2&3 £2.20. CSF £8.53 CT £15.60 TOTE £3.50: £1.90, £2.70; EX 10.00.
Owner 980 Racing **Bred** G G A Gregson **Trained** Middleham Moor, N Yorks

FOCUS
The rain persisted and before this race the ground was changed to good, good to soft in places. The runner-up set a fair pace and the form is rated around the third and fourth.

5541 SAN ROSSORE TURF CLUB (S) STKS 5f
3:50 (3:51) (Class 6) 2-Y-O **£1,942** (£578; £288; £144) **Stalls** Low

Form RPR

0654 **1** **Compton Ford**[41] 4243 2-8-11 61................................ PaulMulrennan 7 56
(M Dods) *prom: effrt 1/2-way: led 2f out: rdn clr ent fnl f: kpt on* **7/1**[2]

534 **2** *2 3/4* **Chicken Momo**[18] 4986 2-8-11 49................................ DarrenWilliams 1 46
(K R Burke) *trckd ldrs: hdwy 2f out: rdn to chse wnr ent fnl f: sn drvn and kpt on same pce* **11/1**[3]

000 **3** *1 1/4* **Future Gem**[20] 4923 2-8-6 30.. PaulHanagan 5 37
(A Dickman) *prom: rdn along and outpcd 1/2-way: styd on u.p ins fnl f* **66/1**

0500 **4** *1/2* **El Bobby (IRE)**[4] 5394 2-8-11 59.................................... TomEaves 2 40
(J R Weymes) *in rr: rdn along 2f out: hdwy over 1f out: drvn and kpt on ins fnl f: nrst fin* **18/1**

5646 **5** *1/2* **Wee Bizzom**[3] 5414 2-8-6 50.. JoeFanning 6 33
(A Berry) *chsd ldrs: effrt 2f out and ev ch tl drvn and wknd ent fnl f* **14/1**

2104 **6** *1 3/4* **Predict**[19] 4942 2-8-12 78.. DavidAllan 8 33
(Sir Mark Prescott) *sn led: rdn along 1/2-way: hdd 2f out: sn drvn and wknd* **1/3**[1]

61.83 secs (1.43) **Going Correction** +0.075s/f (Good) **6** Ran SP% **109.3**
Speed ratings (Par 92): **91,86,84,83,83 80**
toteswinger: 1&2 £2.30, 1&3 £11.10, 2&3 £10.80. CSF £69.23 TOTE £9.00: £2.50, £2.80; EX 42.00.There was no bid for the winner
Owner Septimus Racing Group **Bred** A J Coleing **Trained** Denton, Co Durham

FOCUS
A poor event even by selling race standards which took little winning with the favourite a flop.

NOTEBOOK
Compton Ford, rated 61 and with 16lb to find with the long odds-on favourite, was descending to selling company for the first time. He seized the initiative against the stands' rail and took this poor event in decisive fashion. No doubt his trainer will now aim him at low-grade nurseries. (op 5-1)
Chicken Momo had finished a well beaten fourth in selling company at Yarmouth and is rated just 49 (op 12-1)
Future Gem, rated just 30, seemed to improve on her first try at the bottom grade. (op 50-1 tchd 100-1)
El Bobby(IRE) struggled to go the pace and made his effort on the wide outside. Six furlongs will suit him better but he will need to find plenty to make any real impression even at the lowest level. (op 16-1)
Predict, officially rated 78 but well held when in two tried in nursery company, seemed to face a simple task. Loaded with a blanket, she was drawn on the wide outside. She was soon taking them along against the stands' side running rail but when challenged she found nothing and eventually finished last of all. After this she is one to have severe reservations about. Official explanation: trainer's rep had no explanation for the poor form shown (op 2-5 tchd 3-10)

5542 DAILY RECORD GARRY OWEN H'CAP 5f
4:20 (4:23) (Class 3) (0-95,92) 3-Y-O+ **£9,066** (£2,697; £1,348; £673) **Stalls** Low

Form RPR

3504 **1** **Ishetoo**[50] 3973 4-9-9 **92**.. SilvestreDeSousa 7 103
(A Dickman) *prom: effrt 2f out: rdn to chal over 1f out: drvn ins fnl f: led last 75yds* **9/2**[1]

2043 **2** *1/2* **Princess Ellis**[39] 4291 4-9-2 **85**.................................. GrahamGibbons 14 94
(E J Alston) *led: rdn over 1f out: drvn ins fnl f: hdd and nt qckn last 75yds* **6/1**[2]

0000 **3** *3 3/4* **Sunrise Safari (IRE)**[36] 4437 5-9-9 **92**......................(v) PaulHanagan 8 88
(R A Fahey) *midfield: hdwy on outer 2f out: sn rdn and kpt on u.p ins fnl f: nrst fin* **9/1**[3]

1043 **4** *nk* **Sandwith**[26] 4700 5-8-6 **78** ow3.. PJMcDonald(3) 4 72
(R Johnson) *in tch: hdwy 2f out: swtchd rt and rdn over 1f out: kpt on ins fnl f: nrst fin* **10/1**

00 **5** *1 1/2* **Blue Tomato**[36] 4437 7-9-1 **87**.. NeilBrown(3) 5 76+
(D Nicholls) *dwlt and sltly hmpd s: towards rr: hdwy 2f out: rdn and styd on ins fnl f: nrst fin* **12/1**

0055 **6** *nk* **Fol Hollow (IRE)**[30] 4591 3-9-3 **91**............................. AndrewMullen(3) 2 79
(D Nicholls) *prom: rdn along 2f out: swtchd rt and drvn over 1f out: wknd ent fnl f* **9/1**[3]

0605 **7** *2* **Curtail (IRE)**[41] 4239 5-8-4 **78**.................................. PatrickDonaghy(5) 13 59
(Miss L A Perratt) *midfield: effrt over 2f out: sn rdn and no imp* **22/1**

0351 **8** *shd* **Rothesay Dancer**[9] 5220 5-8-0 **74**................................. KellyHarrison(5) 3 54
(J S Goldie) *in tch: rdn along 2f out: drvn and wknd over 1f out* **16/1**

3021 **9** *1* **Captain Dunne (IRE)**[20] 4922 3-8-12 **83**............................ DavidAllan 9 60
(T D Easterby) *awkward s: a in rr* **9/2**[1]

2303 **10** *3/4* **River Thames**[30] 4608 5-8-9 **78**..................................(b[1]) JamieMoriarty 6 52
(K A Ryan) *a towards rr* **20/1**

0651 **11** *3 3/4* **Divine Spirit**[18] 4962 7-8-10 **79**.................................... PaulMulrennan 1 40
(M Dods) *hld up: a towards rr* **10/1**

0431 **12** *2 3/4* **First Order**[36] 4418 7-9-0 **83**...(v) TomEaves 12 34
(Miss L A Perratt) *prom: rdn along 2f out: sn drvn and wknd* **18/1**

0146 **13** *7* **Geojimali**[27] 4687 6-9-0 **83**.. JoeFanning 11 8
(J S Goldie) *s.i.s: a in rr* **12/1**

59.76 secs (-0.64) **Going Correction** +0.075s/f (Good)
WFA 3 from 4yo+ 2lb **13** Ran SP% **124.5**
Speed ratings (Par 107): **108,107,101,100,98 97,94,94,92,91 85,81,70**
toteswinger: 1&2 £8.60, 1&3 £13.40, 2&3 £16.50. CSF £31.70 CT £250.50 TOTE £6.30: £2.40, £2.60, £3.80; EX 39.30.
Owner John H Sissons **Bred** Longdon Stud Ltd **Trained** Sandhutton, N Yorks

FOCUS
A highly competitive sprint handicap run in a fast time in the deteriorating underfoot conditions. Not many got into it. The winner's progress had seemed to level out but he is rated up 7lb here.

NOTEBOOK
Ishetoo, much improved and a winner five times last year, was running off a mark 7lb higher than his final win at Thirsk in September. Keeping tabs on the pacesetter, he mastered her inside the last and was right on top at the line. This was his first outing for seven weeks and it tees him up nicely for a possible tilt at the Silver Cup at Ayr, but easier ground there would be a problem (op 5-1 tchd 11-2 in a place)

Princess Ellis had the worst of the draw but she showed blinding speed to take them along, soon racing hard against the stands'-side rail. Worn down in the end, she finished clear of the remainder in a hotly contested handicap and can run from the same mark if she reappears at Doncaster next week. (op 8-1)

Sunrise Safari(IRE) is still 4lb above his last winning mark. He is finding his feet in his new stable and stuck on in willing fashion to claim third spot, albeit well beaten by the first two. (op 12-1)

Sandwith, a winner three times over this course and distance, ran really well from a mark 11b higher than his last success including his rider's overweight. (op 12-1)

Blue Tomato stayed on nicely on his first outing for seven weeks and this will have put an edge on him. Official explanation: jockey said gelding was denied a clear run

Fol Hollow(IRE), taking on his elders, could never take a serious hand. (op 12-1)

Captain Dunne(IRE), another youngster taking on older established sprinters, couldn't dominate this time and ended up making his effort on the wide outside. Things did not go his way here and there will be another day. Official explanation: jockey said gelding missed the break (op 13-2 tchd 4-1)

Divine Spirit was soon in a poor position on the stands'-side rail. He was short of room at a crucial stage and was not persevered with. This is best overlooked. Official explanation: jockey said gelding hung right-handed from halfway (op 7-1)

Geojimali Official explanation: jockey said gelding missed the break

5543 MOLLY MCGARRITY H'CAP — 1m 4f
4:50 (4:51) (Class 6) (0-65,63) 3-Y-O+ — **£2,914** (£867; £433; £216) **Stalls** High

Form — RPR

0036 **1** **Sudden Impulse**[7] 5308 7-9-13 **63** .... SilvestreDeSousa 10 — 73
(A D Brown) *a.p: hdwy to chse ldr over 3f out: rdn to ld 1 1/2f out: drvn ins fnl f and styd on wl* — **5/1**[3]

1524 **2** 1 3/4 **Chookie Hamilton**[18] 4972 4-9-8 **58** .... TomEaves 14 — 65
(Miss L A Perratt) *chsd ldr: effrt 3f out: rdn and ev ch 2f out: drvn and kpt on ins fnl f* — **9/2**[2]

2300 **3** 1/2 **Forrest Flyer (IRE)**[22] 4848 4-8-10 **53** .... LanceBetts(7) 11 — 59
(Miss L A Perratt) *led and sn clr: pushed along over 3f out: rdn over 2f out: drvn and hdd 1 1/2f out: kpt on same pce u.p ins fnl f* — **7/2**[1]

6020 **4** 1/2 **Saluscraggie**[16] 5040 6-9-2 **59** .... ClGillies(7) 3 — 64
(R E Barr) *hld up: hdwy on outer 5f out: rdn to chse ldrs 2f out: sn drvn: edgd rt and kpt on same pce ins fnl f* — **14/1**

140- **5** 3 **Karlani (IRE)**[249] 5257 5-9-9 **62** .... PJMcDonald(3) 5 — 63
(G A Swinbank) *hld up: hdwy over 3f out: rdn along over 2f out: kpt on same pce* — **9/2**[2]

5225 **6** nk **Calcutta Cup (UAE)**[25] 4737 5-9-12 **62** .... (p) PaulHanagan 13 — 62
(Karen McLintock) *hld up in rr: hdwy on inner over 2f out: sn rdn and no imp appr fnl f* — **11/2**

1/1- **7** 3 1/4 **Ifatfirst (IRE)**[587] 212 5-9-10 **60** .... DanielTudhope 12 — 55
(J S Goldie) *a in rr* — **10/1**

6325 **8** 9 **Snow Dancer (IRE)**[29] 4630 4-9-5 **60** .... (p) PBradley(5) 8 — 41
(H A McWilliams) *trckd ldrs on inner: effrt and hdwy 3f out: rdn along over 2f out: sn wknd* — **8/1**

4050 **9** 33 **Northgate Maisie**[61] 3580 3-7-10 **45** .... DuranFentiman(3) 6 — —
(Jedd O'Keeffe) *chsd ldrs: rdn along 4f out: sn wknd* — **66/1**

2m 40.6s (0.90) **Going Correction** +0.075s/f (Good)
WFA 3 from 4yo+ 10lb — **9** Ran SP% **119.0**
Speed ratings (Par 101): **100,98,98,98,96 95,93,87,65**
toteswinger: 1&2 £5.30, 1&3 £4.30, 2&3 £4.70. CSF £28.72 CT £90.28 TOTE £5.90: £2.30, £1.80, £1.70; EX 15.20.
Owner Mrs Glen E Salt & S Nellis **Bred** Sagittarius Bloodstock Associates Ltd **Trained** Pickering, York

FOCUS
A low-grade handicap run at a sound pace. Weak form, the winner taking advantage of a good mark.

5544 WILSON-HENDERSON WEDDING H'CAP — 1m
5:20 (5:21) (Class 5) (0-70,67) 3-Y-O — **£3,885** (£1,156; £577; £288) **Stalls** High

Form — RPR

5365 **1** **Talon (IRE)**[21] 4901 3-8-4 **50** .... (tp) PaulQuinn 11 — 59
(G A Swinbank) *mde all: qcknd 3f out: rdn and qcknd wl over 1f out: drvn ins fnl f and kpt on wl* — **12/1**

0041 **2** 3/4 **Mr Lu**[31] 4560 3-8-11 **60** .... DuranFentiman(3) 4 — 68
(Miss L A Perratt) *chsd ldrs: hdwy 3f out: rdn to chse wnr over 1f out: drvn ent fnl f and kpt on* — **8/1**

0033 **3** 2 1/2 **Rossini's Dancer**[9] 5224 3-8-8 **54** .... PaulHanagan 6 — 56+
(R A Fahey) *hld up and bhd: hdwy on inner 3f out: rdn 2f out: swtchd lft and drvn over 1f out: kpt on same pce* — **2/1**[1]

0354 **4** nk **Take It Easee (IRE)**[82] 2911 3-9-1 **64** .... PJMcDonald(3) 9 — 65
(G A Swinbank) *chsd wnr: rdn along over 2f out: drvn over 1f out and kpt on same pce* — **11/2**[3]

4054 **5** 4 1/2 **Miss Understanding**[41] 4241 3-8-2 **48** oh3 .... (b) SilvestreDeSousa 5 — 39
(J R Weymes) *hld up towards rr: hdwy 3f out: rdn to chse ldrs 2f out: sn drvn and no imp* — **20/1**

4222 **6** 2 1/2 **Willyn (IRE)**[19] 4952 3-8-3 **54** .... (p) KellyHarrison(5) 13 — 39
(J S Goldie) *dwlt: sn chsng ldrs on inner: rdn along wl over 2f out and sn wknd* — **7/2**[2]

0020 **7** 1 3/4 **Stormin Heart (USA)**[24] 4797 3-8-6 **52** .... GregFairley 7 — 33
(M Johnston) *midfield: effrt and sme hdwy 3f out: sn rdn and n.d* — **8/1**

3320 **8** 3/4 **Just Sam (IRE)**[26] 4702 3-8-7 **53** .... TonyHamilton 2 — 32
(D W Barker) *hld up in rr: effrt and sme hdwy on wd outside over 2f out: sn rdn and n.d* — **12/1**

6000 **9** nk **Jim Martin**[61] 3592 3-9-4 **64** .... PaulMulrennan 3 — 43
(Miss L A Perratt) *a in rr* — **33/1**

0355 **10** 3 1/4 **Orpen Bid (IRE)**[4] 5388 3-8-2 **48** .... AndrewElliott 8 — 19
(A M Crow) *hld up in rr: effrt and hdwy 3f out: rdn over 2f out and sn wknd* — **14/1**

1m 43.26s (2.06) **Going Correction** +0.075s/f (Good) — **10** Ran SP% **122.9**
Speed ratings (Par 100): **92,91,88,88,83 81,79,78,78,75**
toteswinger: 1&2 £14.10, 1&3 £7.10, 2&3 £5.20. CSF £109.92 CT £286.09 TOTE £17.40: £3.30, £2.10, £1.50; EX 175.80 Place 6 £ 127.28, Place 5 £ 23.99.
Owner S S Anderson **Bred** Mrs C L Weld **Trained** Melsonby, N Yorks

FOCUS
The rain continued to fall but the ground was only verging on good to soft. The actual top-weight was 6lb below the race ceiling in this modest event. Not much got into it and the winner is rated up 3lb.

Talon(IRE) Official explanation: trainer's rep said, regarding apparent improvement in form, gelding benefited from the first-time cheek pieces

T/Plt: £138.00 to a £1 stake. Pool: £59,942.74. 317.05 winning tickets. T/Qpdt: £22.10 to a £1 stake. Pool: £3,963.44. 132.50 winning tickets. JR

5545 - 5552a (Foreign Racing) - See Raceform Interactive

5292 CURRAGH (R-H)
Sunday, August 31

OFFICIAL GOING: Soft

5546a GO AND GO ROUND TOWER STKS (GROUP 3) — 6f
2:45 (2:45) 2-Y-O — **£38,294** (£11,235; £5,352; £1,823)

RPR

1 **Maoineach (USA)** 2-8-12 .... KJManning 7 — 100
(J S Bolger, Ire) *towards rr on outer: hdwy 2f out: disp ld over 1f out: led ins fnl f: kpt on wl* — **14/1**

2 1 1/4 **Silver Shoon (IRE)**[24] 4802 2-8-12 95 .... (b) PJSmullen 3 — 96
(D K Weld, Ire) *settled in rr: hdwy on outer 2f out: 4th 1f out: styd on wl to go 2nd cl home* — **7/1**

3 nk **Cristal Island (IRE)**[30] 4610 2-8-12 75 .... DMGrant 8 — 95
(Thomas Mullins, Ire) *trckd ldrs: hdwy to dispute ld briefly over 1f out: hdd and no ex ins fnl f: dropped to 3rd cl home* — **25/1**

4 1/2 **Like Magic (IRE)**[27] 4883 2-9-1 97 .... DPMcDonogh 6 — 97
(Patrick Martin, Ire) *disp ld: led 2f out: rdn and hdd over 1f out: sn no ex and dropped bk to 4th ins fnl f* — **10/3**[2]

5 2 **Kamado**[49] 4005 2-9-1 .... CDHayes 5 — 91
(Edward Lynam, Ire) *trckd ldrs: rdn and no imp in 6th over 1f out: kpt on* — **7/4**[1]

6 1 1/2 **Gluteus Maximus (IRE)**[8] 5296 2-9-1 98 .... JAHeffernan 2 — 86
(A P O'Brien, Ire) *racd keenly early: trckd ldrs: 5th and no ex fr 1 1/2f out* — **6/1**[3]

7 2 **Three Way Stretch (IRE)**[77] 3067 2-9-1 94 .... FMBerry 4 — 80
(J T Gorman, Ire) *disp ld: rdn and hdd 2f out: sn no ex and wknd* — **7/1**

8 1 **Zero Point Seven (USA)** 2-8-12 .... DJMoran 1 — 74
(J S Bolger, Ire) *mid-div on inner: dropped to rr and no ex fr 2f out* — **33/1**

1m 15.76s (1.26) **Going Correction** 0.0s/f (Good) — **8** Ran SP% **112.2**
Speed ratings: **92,90,89,89,86 84,81,80**
CSF £103.05 TOTE £18.30: £4.50, £2.20, £4.30; DF 160.00.
Owner Mrs J S Bolger **Bred** WinStar Farm LLC **Trained** Coolcullen, Co Carlow

NOTEBOOK
Maoineach(USA), a daughter of Congaree, a former top-class dirt performer in the US, belied her inexperience when getting her head in front inside the final furlong and got her career off to a superb start. She was purchased at the Calder Breeze-up Sales earlier this year and reportedly clocked 10.1 seconds for a furlong on firm ground before changing hands. She is entered in the Prix Marcel Boussac, "should handle any ground", and "has a future", according to her trainer. She is generally quoted at 25-1 for next year's 1000 Guineas and she should hopefully go on to better things with more improvement likely from this debut. (op 12/1)

Silver Shoon(IRE) had every chance entering the final furlong, but was unable to go with the eventual winner on this tacky ground. She is arguably the best maiden filly in Ireland and should really shed that tag when she encounters a sounder surface. (op 6/1)

5547a DANCE DESIGN STKS (LISTED RACE) (FILLIES) — 1m 1f
3:15 (3:16) 3-Y-O+ — **£28,720** (£8,426; £4,014; £1,367)

RPR

1 **Beach Bunny (IRE)**[49] 4007 3-8-12 101 .... CDHayes 8 — 102+
(Kevin Prendergast, Ire) *trckd ldrs in 4th: 3rd and chal early st: led over 1f out: styd on strly* — **3/1**[2]

2 2 1/2 **Deauville Vision (IRE)**[14] 5134 5-9-5 103 .... (p) RPCleary 6 — 96
(M Halford, Ire) *trckd ldrs: 2nd appr st: prog to ld briefly under 2f out: sn hdd and no ch w wnr ins fnl f* — **11/2**[3]

3 4 **Finsceal Beo (IRE)**[53] 3852 4-9-5 117 .... KJManning 4 — 88
(J S Bolger, Ire) *towards rr: 5th on outer ent st: wnt 3rd 1f out: no ex ins fnl f* — **4/5**[1]

4 shd **Varsity**[16] 5084 5-9-5 87 .... (t) WJLee 9 — 87
(C F Swan, Ire) *settled in rr: sme hdwy ent st: 5th over 1f out: kpt on wl wout threatening ldrs* — **16/1**

5 3 1/2 **End Of The Affair (IRE)**[18] 5000 4-9-5 76 .... NGMcCullagh 1 — 80
(V C Ward, Ire) *trckd ldr early: led bef 1/2-way: hdd under 2f out: 4th and no ex 1f out* — **25/1**

6 2 1/2 **Crossing**[49] 4007 7-9-5 99 .... DPMcDonogh 3 — 75
(William J Fitzpatrick, Ire) *sn led: hdd bef 1/2-way: dropped to 4th early st: no ex fr 2f out* — **16/1**

7 5 1/2 **Glowing (IRE)**[77] 3070 3-8-12 89 .... (t) FMBerry 5 — 63
(Charles O'Brien, Ire) *a towards rr* — **20/1**

2m 3.44s (8.54) **Going Correction** +0.775s/f (Yiel)
WFA 3 from 4yo+ 7lb — **7** Ran SP% **116.3**
Speed ratings: **93,90,87,87,84 81,76**
CSF £20.42 TOTE £4.50: £2.00, £2.90; DF 21.60.
Owner Lady O'Reilly **Bred** D G Hardisty Bloodstock & Mars **Trained** Friarstown, Co Kildare

NOTEBOOK
Beach Bunny(IRE) settled well in what was a slowly-run affair and having raced in mid-division, was sent to the front with just under 2f to race. The further she went, the better she looked and, on this evidence, this progressive filly looks capable of picking up a Group race. (op 3/1 tchd 7/2)

Deauville Vision(IRE) ran her best race for some time. She is well suited by an ease in the ground and led briefly until headed by the winner with just under 2f to go. She kept on well without ever threatening the winner and she can be placed to win again at this level. (op 9/2)

Finsceal Beo(IRE) was well suited by the race conditions and looked a picture beforehand. However, she did not pick up the way she can and, on this evidence, could now be in decline. However, it would be unwise to write her off yet and she is one that would prefer much better ground. (op 4/6)

5549a MOYGLARE STUD STKS (GROUP 1) (FILLIES) — 7f
4:15 (4:16) 2-Y-O
£123,970 (£42,352; £20,294; £7,058; £4,852; £2,647)

RPR

1 **Again (IRE)**[14] 5132 2-8-12 108 .... JAHeffernan 4 — 110
(David Wachman, Ire) *mid-div: clsd 2f out: sn disp ld: advantage 1f out: edgd rt and kpt on wl ins fnl f* — **6/4**[1]

2 1/2 **Shimah (USA)**[65] 3466 2-8-12 .... DPMcDonogh 2 — 109
(Kevin Prendergast, Ire) *settled in mid-div: hdwy under 2f out: chal fr 1f out: carried sltly rt ins fnl f: kpt on wout rching wnr* — **11/4**[2]

3 2 1/2 **Beyond Our Reach (IRE)**[14] 5131 2-8-12 .... MJKinane 6 — 103
(T Stack, Ire) *mid-div: hdwy to disp ld briefly 1 1/2f out: hdd 1f out: no ex* — **10/1**

4 hd **Aaroness (USA)**[46] 4095 2-8-12 98.....................(t) DJMoran 5 102
(J S Bolger, Ire) *prom in chsng gp: tk clsr order in 4th 3f out: rdn and kpt on one pce fr over 1f out* **50/1**

5 1 1/4 **Sugar Free (IRE)**[24] 4802 2-8-12 100..................... JamieSpencer 3 99
(T Stack, Ire) *hld up in rr: hdwy into 5th under 2f out: kpt on fnl f wout threatening ldrs* **9/1**

6 8 **Baileys Cacao (IRE)**[64] 3496 2-8-12..................... RichardHughes 7 79
(R Hannon) *mid-div: 7th 3f out: no ex fr over 1f out: wknd fnl f* **10/1**

7 hd **Beauthea (IRE)**[14] 5132 2-8-12 91..................... CDHayes 8 78
(H Rogers, Ire) *towards rr: clsr 2f out: no ex fr over 1f out* **66/1**

8 2 **Marina Of Venice (IRE)**[24] 4804 2-8-12 95..................... KJManning 1 73
(J S Bolger, Ire) *chsd ldrs: clsr in 3rd 3f out: no ex and wknd appr fnl f* **16/1**

9 nk **Rare Ransom**[14] 5132 2-8-12 99..................... PJSmullen 9 73
(D K Weld, Ire) *hld up: sme hdwy 2f out: no ex and wknd over 1f out* **8/1**[3]

10 3 1/2 **Marquesa (USA)**[16] 5079 2-8-12 97..................... FMBerry 12 64
(David Wachman, Ire) *prom: led bef 1/2-way tl jnd under 2f out: sn wknd* **25/1**

11 3 1/2 **Hello Bunclody (IRE)**[39] 4316 2-8-12..................... MHarley 11 55
(J S Bolger, Ire) *led early: 2nd fr bef 1/2-way tl wknd under 2f out* **100/1**

12 2 **Bay Swallow (IRE)**[26] 4711 2-8-12..................... DMGrant 10 50
(Patrick J Flynn, Ire) *a in rr: trailing fr over 2f out* **200/1**

1m 28.83s (1.73) **Going Correction** +0.35s/f (Good) 12 Ran SP% **120.6**
Speed ratings: **104,103,100,100,98 89,89,87,86,82 78,76**
CSF £5.46 TOTE £2.20: £1.10, £1.70, £3.40; DF 6.10.
Owner Michael Tabor **Bred** Southern Bloodstock **Trained** Goolds Cross, Co Tipperary

NOTEBOOK
Again(IRE), who ran out an impressive winner of the Debutante Stakes a fortnight ago, is a much-improved performer and credited David Wachman with his second Group 1 victory in the space of a week. She appreciated what was a generous gallop and weaved her way into the race from the two pole. She quickened up well and despite drifting to her right with 200 yards to go, she was always holding the runner-up. She is generally now a 10-1 shot with most firms for next season's Newmarket 1000 Guineas. Her dam is a half-sister to Montjeu, so she is bred to get further and this Danehill Dancer filly is clearly an exciting prospect who could well get the Oaks trip. (op 6/4 tchd 5/4)
Shimah(USA) shed her unbeaten tag, but lost little in defeat. She came there with every chance at the furlong pole and was carried right when the winner drifted inside the final furlong. She is bred to appreciate a sounder surface, but she stuck to her task well and is clearly a talented filly who deserves to be as short as 14-1 for the 1000 Guineas. (op 3/1 tchd 7/2)
Beyond Our Reach(IRE) ran a fine race for a maiden. She was handy and held every chance at the furlong pole, keeping on at the one pace and is clearly a smart type who can pay her way well at stakes level. (op 10/1 tchd 9/1)
Baileys Cacao(IRE), who was stepping into Group 1 company after winning a Listed contest at Newmarket, could never land a serious blow yet was still not disgraced on ground she found plenty soft enough. (op 8/1)

5550a HACKETTS EUROPEAN BREEDERS FUND IRISH CAMBRIDGESHIRE (PREMIER H'CAP) 1m
4:45 (4:46) 3-Y-0+

£53,029 (£16,852; £8,029; £2,735; £1,852; £970)

RPR

1 **Tis Mighty (IRE)**[31] 4575 5-8-1 87..................... EJMcNamara(7) 8 97+
(P J Prendergast, Ire) *trckd ldrs: 2nd travelling wl over 2f out: sent to the front 1f out: kpt on wl* **16/1**

2 1 **Amarama (IRE)**[32] 4547 3-8-1 89 oh4..................... PBBeggy(3) 7 96+
(David P Myerscough, Ire) *a.p: 3rd and rdn 2f out: kpt on wl u.p to go 2nd cl home* **20/1**

3 1 3/4 **Zero Tolerance (IRE)**[22] 4853 8-9-0 93..................... JamieSpencer 6 97
(T D Barron) *trckd ldr: led 2 1/2f out: hdd 1f out: no ex and dropped to 3rd cl home* **10/3**[1]

4 3 **Miranda's Girl (IRE)**[31] 4575 3-8-4 89 oh6.....................(p) CDHayes 5 85
(Thomas Cleary, Ire) *mid-div: smooth hdwy into 5th over 2f out: rdn 1 1/2f out: no ex fnl f* **20/1**

5 3 **Settigano (IRE)**[33] 4512 5-9-12 105.....................(p) JAHeffernan 3 95
(Michael Joseph Fitzgerald, Ire) *chsd ldrs: 6th 2f out: no ex and kpt on one pce fr over 1f out* **7/1**[2]

6 1 3/4 **Celtic Dane (IRE)**[33] 4512 4-9-1 104..................... SHJames(10) 10 90
(Kevin Prendergast, Ire) *prom thrght: rdn in 4th 2f out: no ex fr over 1f out* **10/1**[3]

7 1 3/4 **Alone He Stands (IRE)**[14] 5133 8-8-5 84 ow1..................... KLatham 1 66
(J C Hayden, Ire) *towards rr: kpt on fnl 2fs wout threatening ldrs* **33/1**

8 1 **Ready To Rocknroll (IRE)**[26] 4712 3-7-11 89 oh6.......... DEMullins(7) 2 68
(J T Gorman, Ire) *chsd ldrs: no ex fr 2f out: kpt on* **25/1**

9 hd **Holly Hawk (IRE)**[18] 4995 3-7-13 89 oh13..................... SFoley(5) 16 67
(Kevin F O'Donnell, Ire) *towards rr: kpt on fr over 2f out* **50/1**

10 2 1/2 **Dane Blue (IRE)**[18] 4995 6-8-5 91..................... BACurtis(7) 4 65
(S J Treacy, Ire) *led: hdd 2 1/2f out: sn no ex and wknd* **16/1**

11 3 **Drunken Sailor (IRE)**[7] 5324 3-7-13 89 oh8..............(bt[1]) MHarley(5) 11 55
(Paul W Flynn, Ire) *nvr bttr than mid-div* **20/1**

12 nk **Castle Bar Sling (USA)**[26] 4716 3-7-13 89 oh1............ MACleere(5) 20 54
(T J O'Mara, Ire) *chsd ldrs: no ex fr over 2f out: kpt on* **20/1**

13 12 **Festival Princess (IRE)**[27] 4885 3-8-7 92..................... RPCleary 12 29
(M Halford, Ire) *mid-div: rdn over 2f out: wknd* **12/1**

14 1 **Shayrazan (IRE)**[18] 4995 7-8-10 89.....................(t) DMGrant 17 25
(James Leavy, Ire) *nvr a factor* **20/1**

15 1 **Central Station (IRE)**[46] 4098 3-9-4 103.....................(b) PJSmullen 13 36
(D K Weld, Ire) *prom: no ex fr 3f out: sn wknd* **7/1**[2]

16 1 1/4 **Reload (IRE)**[18] 4995 5-8-8 90..................... SMGorey(3) 18 21
(Thomas Mullins, Ire) *nvr a factor* **12/1**

17 10 **Ridge Boy (IRE)**[46] 4098 7-8-8 87.....................(b) NGMcCullagh 19 —
(Mrs John Harrington, Ire) *chsd ldrs: no threat fr 3f out* **16/1**

18 4 **Ard Fheis (IRE)**[14] 5133 3-8-3 91..................... DJMoran(3) 21 —
(J S Bolger, Ire) *chsd ldrs: lost tch after 1/2-way* **20/1**

19 hd **Adajal (IRE)**[7] 1700 5-9-9 102.....................(t) FMBerry 9 —
(C F Swan, Ire) *dwlt and a towards rr* **14/1**

20 18 **Dul Ar An Ol (IRE)**[31] 4576 7-8-4 83 oh2..................... MCHussey 14 —
(Peter Henley, Ire) *a bhd: eased fnl f* **25/1**

21 5 **Phoenix Ice (IRE)**[50] 3991 4-8-9 88..................... CO'Donoghue 15 —
(M J P O'Brien, Ire) *nvr a factor: eased fnl f* **11/1**

1m 42.99s (1.09) **Going Correction** +0.35s/f (Good)
WFA 3 from 4yo+ 6lb 21 Ran SP% **146.4**
Speed ratings: **109,108,106,103,100 98,96,95,95,93 90,89,77,76,75 74,64,60,60,42 37**
CSF £328.10 TOTE £17.00: £3.60, £6.10, £1.90, £6.40; DF 493.30.
Owner Joseph P Daly **Bred** Farrington Bloodstock **Trained** Melitta Lodge, Co Kildare
■ Stewards' Enquiry : P B Beggy three-day ban: used whip with excessive frequency (Sep 14-16)

NOTEBOOK
Tis Mighty(IRE) had what appeared to be a competitive handicap wrapped up some way from home. She appeared to idle in front.
Zero Tolerance(IRE), who returned to near his best when winning easily in testing conditions at Haydock 20 days previously, was very well backed for this second outing of the season in Ireland and he was produced with every chance. He probably hit the front sooner than ideal, but this was still another solid effort. (op 5/1)

5551a CILL DARA SECURITY FLYING FIVE STKS (GROUP 3) 5f
5:15 (5:15) 3-Y-0+ **£35,882** (£10,514; £5,000; £1,691)

RPR

1 **Look Busy (IRE)**[8] 5259 3-8-12..................... SladeO'Hara 5 113+
(A Berry) *hld up on rail: swtchd to outer 1/2-way: hdwy to chal under 2f out: led 1f out: kpt on wl* **7/2**[2]

2 1 1/4 **Masta Plasta (IRE)**[14] 5130 5-9-3..................... CDHayes 1 111
(D Nicholls) *led: strly pressed and hdd 1f out: no ex and kpt on* **6/4**[1]

3 shd **Wi Dud**[43] 4188 4-9-3.....................(b[1]) NCallan 3 111
(K A Ryan) *trckd ldrs on rail: no ex in 4th appr 1f out: kpt on wl u.p fnl f* **7/1**

4 3/4 **Fathom Five (IRE)**[22] 4840 4-9-3..................... PJSmullen 2 108
(B Smart) *trckd ldr: chal fr 1 1/2f out: 3rd and no ex ins fnl f* **12/1**

5 1 1/4 **Snaefell (IRE)**[14] 5130 4-9-6 110..................... RPCleary 6 107
(M Halford, Ire) *chsd ldrs: no imp fr over 1f out: kpt on* **5/1**[3]

6 3 1/2 **Chief Editor**[19] 4957 4-9-3..................... JamieSpencer 4 91
(M J Wallace, Australia) *a in rr: eased whn btn fnl f* **11/2**

60.70 secs (-1.70) **Going Correction** 0.0s/f (Good)
WFA 3 from 4yo+ 2lb 6 Ran SP% **114.5**
Speed ratings: **113,111,110,109,107 102**
CSF £9.48 TOTE £4.50: £2.60, £1.80; DF 10.80.
Owner A Underwood **Bred** Tom And Hazel Russell **Trained** Cockerham, Lancs

NOTEBOOK
Look Busy(IRE) took her already fine season to new heights with a ready first success in Group company. This was her sixth win of the year, the race was run to suit her, and her versatility as regards underfoot conditions is a notable plus. She may not have finished winning yet.
Masta Plasta(IRE), back in trip, showed his usual early dash and ran close to his previous level in defeat. He helps to set the level of this form, but has had a busy time of it this term and may benefit from a little break. (op 6/4 tchd 13/8)
Wi Dud turned in his best effort of the current campaign and the first-time blinkers had a positive effect. (op 8/1)
Fathom Five(IRE) posted a personal-best effort in defeat on ground he loves, but still found things too hot. (op 8/1)
Snaefell(IRE), the only domestic challenger, had beaten the runner-up over 6f last time so this was obviously a backward step. (op 6/1)
Chief Editor, whose trainer had sent out Benbaun to win the last three running of this race, was taking a big step up in grade and simply got found out. (op 5/1)

5548 - 5552a (Foreign Racing) - See Raceform Interactive

5528 BADEN-BADEN (L-H)
Sunday, August 31

OFFICIAL GOING: Good

5553a BESTWETTEN.DE 138TH GOLDENE PEITSCHE (GROUP 2) 6f
4:00 (4:13) 3-Y-0+ **£30,882** (£12,500; £5,147; £2,941)

RPR

1 **Overdose**[57] 3752 3-8-11..................... ASuborics 2 119
(S Ribarszki, Hungary) *mde all: two l clr st: r.o wl: unchal* **11/8**[1]

2 2 1/2 **Abbadjinn (GER)**[21] 4912 4-9-2..................... TMundry 4 113
(P Rau, Germany) *trckd wnr: kpt on fnl f but nvr able to chal* **6/1**[3]

3 1 1/4 **Starlit Sands**[31] 4550 3-8-7..................... AStarke 5 103
(Sir Mark Prescott) *5th st: hdwy to go 3rd appr fnl f: edgd lft 1f out: kpt on same pce* **6/1**[3]

4 1/2 **Intrepid Jack**[21] 4915 6-9-2..................... THellier 3 108
(H Morrison) *4th st: nvr able to chal* **5/1**[2]

5 3 1/2 **Abbashiva (GER)**[21] 4916 3-8-11..................... EPedroza 1 95
(P Rau, Germany) *outpcd fr 1/2-way: last st* **16/1**

6 1/2 **Contat (GER)**[21] 4912 5-9-2..................... RJuracek 6 96
(P Vovcenko, Germany) *racd wd of the others in the middle: 5th st: nvr a factor* **33/1**

68.21 secs (-2.08)
WFA 3 from 4yo+ 3lb 6 Ran SP% **96.2**
TOTE: WIN 15; PL 13, 15; SF 39.
Owner S C H Racing Team **Bred** Mr & Mrs G Robinson **Trained** Hungary

NOTEBOOK
Starlit Sands, fourth in the King George Stakes last time, was up a furlong in distance and it was expected to suit. However, she did not really improve on her Goodwood run.
Intrepid Jack is the type who needs the leaders to fall in a hole. He never got close enough to land a blow this time.

5486 DEAUVILLE (R-H)
Sunday, August 31

OFFICIAL GOING: Turf course - good; all-weather- standard

5555a PRIX QUINCEY LUCIEN BARRIERE (GROUP 3) (STRAIGHT COURSE) 1m
2:15 (2:17) 3-Y-0+ **£29,412** (£11,765; £8,824; £5,882; £2,941)

RPR

1 **Laa Rayb (USA)**[17] 5025 4-9-2..................... RoystonFfrench 9 117
(M Johnston) *sn disputing 2nd on outside: led 3f out: rdn and hung lft jst ins fnl f: sn clr: drvn out* **5/1**[3]

2 5 **Athanor (FR)**[37] 4401 6-9-2..................... DBonilla 8 105
(F Head, France) *hld up: hdwy on outside over 2f out: drvn to chse wnr fr over 1f out: no imp fnl f* **9/2**[2]

3 1 1/2 **Holocene (USA)**[26] 4-9-2..................... C-PLemaire 7 102
(P Bary, France) *disp 5th: drvn to go 3rd over 1f out: kpt on one pce* **7/1**

4 2 **Celebrissime (IRE)**[57] 3750 3-8-8..................... OPeslier 6 95
(F Head, France) *led to 3f out: one pce fr wl over 1f out* **8/1**

5 1 1/2 **Echoes Rock (GER)**[37] 4401 5-9-0..................... SPasquier 5 92
(A Fabre, France) *disp 2nd to over 3f out: one pce fnl 2f* **9/1**

6 3 **Hello Morning (FR)**[35] 4473 3-8-10 .... IMendizabal 2 87
(Mme C Head-Maarek, France) *a outpcd* **7/1**

7 4 **Stop Making Sense**[21] 4913 6-9-0 .... JVictoire 3 75
(A Fabre, France) *racd in 4th: rdn and btn 2f out: eased fnl f* **20/1**

8 1 1/2 **Calming Influence (IRE)**[26] 4719 3-8-8 .... LDettori 4 72
(Saeed Bin Suroor) *plld early: restrained in rr: drvn 2f out: no hdwy* **11/4**[1]

1m 36.8s (-4.20) **Going Correction** -0.20s/f (Firm)
WFA 3 from 4yo+ 6lb **8** Ran SP% **112.4**
Speed ratings: **113,108,106,104,103 100,96,94**
PARI-MUTUEL: WIN 6.50; PL 2.40, 1.80, 2.50; DF 15.20.
Owner Sheikh Ahmed Al Maktoum **Bred** Darley **Trained** Middleham Moor, N Yorks
■ Stewards' Enquiry : D Bonilla €200 fine: whip abuse

NOTEBOOK
Laa Rayb(USA) completely outclassed seven useful performers in this straight mile having taken the advantage two and a half furlongs from the post. He had been given a good lead up that point and the time of the race was very fast considering the ground. Once asked to lengthen, the colt did it in fine style and is certainly improving with every race. There are no definite plans but it would be no surprise if he lined up for the Prix de la Foret on October 4th, although an alternative would be the Daniel Wildenstein the following day.
Athanor(FR), given a waiting ride, did not come on to the scene until the furlong and a half marker, but never for a moment looked likely to peg back the winner. He is a reliable performer who rarely lets down his connections.
Holocene(USA) has been rather disappointing since a second in a Group 1 event just over a year ago although he did win well on the all-weather at Deauville in August. He was in mid-division for much of the mile but could not quicken when things warmed up and just stayed on one paced. Better ground would have been more to his liking.
Celebrissime(IRE) was smartly away and held the lead until two and a half out but had no answer to the acceleration of the eventual winner. He just kept going one paced and is not quite up to this standard.
Calming Influence(IRE) was always behind and never played a role on this occasion. He certainly ran below his best and should be given another chance.

5556a LUCIEN BARRIERE PRIX DE MEAUTRY (GROUP 3) 6f
2:50 (2:49) 3-Y-O+ £29,412 (£11,765; £8,824; £5,882; £2,941)

RPR

1 **Tiza (SAF)**[21] 4915 6-9-1 .... CSoumillon 10 114
(A De Royer-Dupre, France) *hld up: hdwy on outside 2f out: led 1f out: rdn out* **3/1**[1]

2 1 **Inxile (IRE)**[22] 4881 3-8-11 .... AdrianTNicholls 7 110
(D Nicholls) *led to 1f out: r.o* **5/1**[3]

3 1 1/2 **Mariol (FR)**[21] 4915 5-9-5 .... SMaillot 6 111
(Robert Collet, France) *mid-div: hdwy on outside wl over 1f out: hrd rdn to dispute 2nd ins fnl f: no ex* **7/1**

4 shd **Stern Opinion (USA)**[51] 3938 3-8-11 .... SPasquier 2 105
(P Bary, France) *s.i.s: plld hrd in rr first 2f: hdwy wl over 1f out: drvn to take 4th 120yds out: fin wl* **10/3**[2]

5 2 **Salut L'Africain (FR)**[26] 4719 3-8-11 .... DBoeuf 3 99
(Robert Collet, France) *disp 4th: clsd up over 2f out: rdn over 1f out: one pce* **16/1**

6 2 **Isanous (FR)**[25] 3-8-8 .... IMendizabal 1 90
(J-C Rouget, France) *nvr nr to chal* **10/1**

7 1 1/2 **Derison (USA)**[22] 4881 6-9-1 ....(b) TJarnet 5 90
(P Van De Poele, France) *chsd ldr tl wknd over 1f out* **9/1**

8 1 1/2 **Lumiere Noire (FR)**[49] 4011 4-8-11 .... TRicher 9 81
(R Gibson, France) *disp 2nd: wknd over 1 1/2f out* **10/1**

9 8 **Calbuco (FR)**[91] 2652 4-9-1 .... WMongil 8 61
(Mme E Holmey, France) *disp 4th to over 2f out: btn wl over 1f out* **16/1**

10 6 **Loyalist (SAF)**[71] 7-9-1 .... JVictoire 4 43
(S Seemar, France) *a outpcd* **40/1**

69.90 secs (-1.30)
WFA 3 from 4yo+ 3lb **10** Ran SP% **119.6**
PARI-MUTUEL: WIN 4.80; PL 1.80, 2.10, 2.70; DF 16.90.
Owner J C Seroul & R Plersch **Bred** Daytona Stud (pty) Ltd **Trained** Chantilly, France

NOTEBOOK
Tiza(SAF) well behind in the early stages of this event from his outside draw, he did not really engage top gear until the furlong and a half marker. He then quickened well to take the lead inside the final furlong and finally won with a little in hand. Not the most consistent of individuals, he is very useful when on song and could go for the Petit Couvert over 5f as a prep for the Prix de L'Abbaye de Longchamp.
Inxile(IRE), still inexperienced compared with most of his older rivals, put up a fine performance over a distance which is currently just a little far for him. He broke well, was soon at the head of affairs and looked in total control a furlong and a half out. He battled on gamely as his stamina began to wane in the last 100yds but it was still and excellent performance. He is still learning and looks to have an excellent future and will be aimed at the Abbaye next year.
Mariol(FR), a consistent sprinter, was mid-division in the early stages and began a forward move up the centre of the track a furlong and a half out. He never looked like reaching the first two but was giving 2kg to the winner on this occasion.
Stern Opinion(USA) completely missed the start and was last in the early stages. Did not have the clearest of runs at a crucial stage but then just stayed on one paced. He was certainly unable to show his best on this occasion and this race is better forgotten.

5557a LUCIEN BARRIERE GRAND PRIX DE DEAUVILLE (GROUP 2) 1m 4f 110y
3:20 (3:20) 3-Y-O+ £83,824 (£32,353; £15,441; £10,294; £5,147)

RPR

1 **Getaway (GER)**[63] 3542 5-9-6 .... LDettori 8 118+
(A Fabre, France) *wnt 2nd over a m out: led wl over 1f out: sn rdn: pushed out fnl f and a holding 2nd* **11/8**[1]

2 1 **Doctor Dino (FR)**[63] 3542 6-9-10 .... OPeslier 7 120+
(R Gibson, France) *a in tch: disp 3rd fr 1/2-way: rdn over 1f out: chsd wnr fnl f: r.o same pce u.p* **15/8**[2]

3 1 **Poseidon Adventure (IRE)**[48] 4041 5-9-3 ....(b) DBoeuf 4 111
(W Figge, Germany) *racd in 6th to st: rdn and trcking 2nd wl over 1f out: drvn to take 3rd fnl 100yds* **33/1**

4 hd **Candy Gift (ARG)**[22] 4880 5-9-6 .... SPasquier 2 114
(A Fabre, France) *hld up in rr: last st: r.o fr over 1f out: nrest at fin* **40/1**

5 1 1/2 **Sommertag (GER)**[35] 5-9-3 .... JVictoire 5 109
(J Hirschberger, Germany) *set mod pce: qcknd over 2f out: hdd wl over 1f out: kpt on steadily* **150/1**

6 1 1/2 **Magadino (FR)**[22] 4880 7-9-3 .... FBlondel 1 106
(Mme Brigitte Renk, Switzerland) *mid-div: disp 5th st: nvr able to chal* **20/1**

7 nk **Loup Breton (IRE)**[74] 3121 4-9-6 .... ACrastus 6 109
(E Lellouche, France) *racd in 3rd to st: wknd over 1f out* **6/1**[3]

8 5 **Avanti Polonia (GER)**[21] 4914 4-9-3 .... DBonilla 3 98
(F Head, France) *7th st: a in rr* **8/1**

2m 48.2s (1.80) **Going Correction** +0.525s/f (Yiel) **8** Ran SP% **113.1**
Speed ratings: **115,114,113,113,112 111,111,108**
PARI-MUTUEL: WIN 2.80 (coupled with Sommertag): PL 1.40, 1.10, 2.90;DF 2.70.
Owner Baron G Von Ullmann **Bred** Baron G Von Ullmann **Trained** Chantilly, France

NOTEBOOK
Getaway(GER) seems to like this track and also appears to show his best when going right handed and this was an excellent trial for the Arc de Triomphe. His pacemaker did a good job early on and took him to the 2f marker and the further he went the better he got, holding the runner-up easily. Certainly not fully wound up, he will strip much fitter for the Arc, having been fourth in the race last year, and looks an excellent each-way prospect.
Doctor Dino(FR), whose trainer was worried about the state of the ground before the race, lost nothing in defeat. He stalked the first winner for much of the race and looked extremely dangerous one and a half out but did not quite go through with his challenge. It was another decent effort from this consistent six-year-old and he will now start his international campaign with the next target the Canadian International afollowed by the Hong Kong Vase.
Poseidon Adventure(IRE) arrived late on the scene after being towards the tail of the field early on. He finished so fast he nearly ran up the backside of the runner-up and there was a Stewards; enquiry. This was a much-improved effort and he will now be aimed at the Preis von Europa at Cologne on September 28th.
Candy Gift(ARG), an ex-Argentine horse, put up a really decent effort and looks to be coming back to the form which gave him Group 1 success before being sent to France. Considerable improvement can be expected and the target now is the Prix du Conseil de Paris in October, although he has been entered in the Arc. He is certainly one to watch during the autumn.

5451 HAMILTON (R-H)
Monday, September 1

OFFICIAL GOING: Good to soft (7.1) changing to soft after race 6 (4.20)
Wind: Light across Weather: Sunny periods

5559 HAMILTON-PARK.CO.UK AMATEUR RIDERS' H'CAP 1m 5f 9y
1:50 (1:51) (Class 6) (0-65,65) 4-Y-O+ £2,307 (£709; £354) Stalls High

Form RPR

1640 1 **Mister Pete (IRE)**[6] 5385 5-10-8 52 .... MissPRobson 4 64
(W Storey) *trckd ldrs: hdwy over 4f out: led 2 1/2f out: rdn wl over 1f out: drvn ins fnl f: hld on wl* **12/1**

1621 2 nse **Elite Land**[17] 5040 5-11-2 60 .... MissARyan 1 72
(K A Ryan) *trckd ldrs: hdwy 3f out: swtchd rt and effrt to chal 2f out: sn rdn: drvn ins fnl f and ev ch: jst hld* **9/4**[1]

2335 3 4 1/2 **Sir Sandicliffe (IRE)**[14] 5154 4-10-11 58 .... MrBenBrisbourne(3) 10 63
(W M Brisbourne) *trckd ldrs: hdwy 4f out: rdn to chse ldng pair 3f out: sn rdn and no imp* **11/2**[3]

5561 4 3 1/4 **Zed Candy (FR)**[13] 4817 5-11-0 58 .... MrDRCook 6 58
(J T Stimpson) *hld up in rr: stdy hdwy 5f out: chsd ldxers 3f out: sn rdn and wknd over 1f out* **5/1**[2]

00-1 5 2 1/2 **Front Rank (IRE)**[9] 3399 8-10-6 55 .... MissECSayer(5) 2 51
(Mrs Dianne Sayer) *led 5f: cl up tl led again over 4f out: rdn 3f out: sn hdd and grad wknd* **15/2**

6250 6 5 **Coronado's Gold (USA)**[15] 2467 7-10-9 58 .... MrDaleSwift(5) 11 47
(B Ellison) *towards rr: sme hdwy over 3f out: rdn over 2f out: sn no imp* **33/1**

043 7 5 **Jane Of Arc (FR)**[30] 4630 4-10-7 51 oh5 ....(p) MrsCBartley 3 32
(J S Goldie) *cl up: led after 5f: pushed along and hdd over 4f out: sn rdn and wknd 3f out* **9/1**

3563 8 8 **Asrar**[4] 5415 6-10-2 51 oh6 .... MrBJToomey(5) 7 20
(Miss Lucinda V Russell) *dwlt: a towards rr* **33/1**

-000 9 12 **Hurricane Thomas (IRE)**[33] 4537 4-11-0 65 .... MissPhillipaTutty(7) 8 16
(R E Barr) *chsd ldrs: rdn along over 4f out and sn wknd* **33/1**

0035 10 2 1/2 **Rudry World (IRE)**[7] 5369 5-11-1 64 .... MissMMullineaux(5) 9 12
(M Mullineaux) *hld up: a in rr* **10/1**

0400 11 9 **Bed Fellow (IRE)**[48] 4048 4-10-10 61 .... MissJKWilson(7) 5 —
(Paul Murphy) *midfield: rdn along 4f out: wknd 3f out* **100/1**

3m 3.96s (10.06) **Going Correction** +0.70s/f (Yiel) **11** Ran SP% **111.2**
Speed ratings (Par 101): **97,96,94,92,90 87,84,79,72,70 65**
toteswinger: 1&2 £7.60, 1&3 £17.50, 2&3 £3.80. CSF £36.27 CT £163.48 TOTE £13.20: £2.90, £1.30, £2.40; EX 43.40.
Owner W Storey **Bred** Tom Radley **Trained** Muggleswick, Co Durham

FOCUS
Despite a fair amount of overnight rain at the track the ground was described as good to soft, good in places. A moderate amateur riders' handicap in which the first two came clear and are rated improvers.

5560 SCOTTISH RACING BUSINESS CLUB TWO YEAR OLD CLAIMING STKS 6f 5y
2:20 (2:20) (Class 6) 2-Y-O £2,266 (£674; £337; £168) Stalls Centre

Form RPR

4301 1 **Scenic Pass**[23] 4873 2-8-4 60 .... PaulHanagan 1 72+
(E S McMahon) *wnt rt s: mde all: rdn over 1f out: styd on strly and sn clr* **13/8**[1]

4553 2 7 **Digit**[17] 5041 2-8-3 65 .... RoystonFfrench 6 49
(B Smart) *cl up: rdn 2f out: sn drvn and kpt on: no ch w wnr* **11/4**[3]

4430 3 1 3/4 **Little Tokyo (USA)**[26] 4733 2-8-10 65 ....(b[1]) PaulMulrennan 5 51
(J Howard Johnson) *dwlt and rr: hdwy over 2f out: rdn and kpt on ins fnl f: nrst fin* **14/1**

014 4 3/4 **Haven't A Clue**[21] 4933 2-8-12 84 ....(b) TomEaves 4 51
(Sir Mark Prescott) *trckd ldng pair: effrt over 2f out: sn rdn: hung lft and btn wl over 1f out* **9/4**[2]

4042 5 7 **Royal Premium**[4] 5414 2-8-9 50 ....(p) DavidAllan 3 27
(H A McWilliams) *in tch: rdn along 1/2-way and sn wknd* **14/1**

00 6 1 1/4 **Moroccan Party**[59] 3689 2-8-7 0 .... DaleGibson 2 21
(M W Easterby) *prom: rdn along after 2f: wknd 1/2-way* **100/1**

1m 15.32s (3.12) **Going Correction** +0.45s/f (Yiel) **6** Ran SP% **109.9**
Speed ratings (Par 93): **97,87,85,84,75 73**
toteswinger: 1&2 £1.40, 1&3 £3.40, 2&3 £3.80. CSF £6.12 TOTE £2.50: £1.20, £2.30; EX 6.50.
Owner A McWilliam/J Yorston **Bred** Norman Court Stud **Trained** Lichfield, Staffs

FOCUS
The ground was unsurprisingly officially changed to good to soft, soft in places before this race. A modest juvenile claimer that took little winning but a clear-cut success for the improving winner while the runner-up is the key to the form.

NOTEBOOK

Scenic Pass could do no more than win as she did on this debut for her new connections. She was smartly into stride and soon at the head of affairs, which is a style of running that evidently suits her. She had the race won at the furlong pole and, on this evidence, is a good bit better than a plater. Her confidence will be high at present and this confirms she goes on most ground, but her handicap mark will now probably suffer. (op 5-2)

Digit, dropping back a furlong, met some support as the favourite drifted out and she ran close to her recent level in defeat. (op 7-2)

Little Tokyo(USA) was having his first run in this lower grade and sported first-time blinkers. He was outpaced for most of the contest before running on late to grab third and, clearly not that straightforward, has now found his level. (op 11-1)

Haven't A Clue, who was easily the best in according to official figures, took a walk in the market, however, and the betting proved to be correct as she performed well below her previous level, looking unwilling under pressure. This effort leaves her with it all to prove, despite it being the most testing surface she had raced on to date. (op 5-4)

Royal Premium struggled to go the pace on this drop back a furlong and likely found it coming too soon. (op 25-1 tchd 33-1)

5561 AVONHILL LTD MAIDEN STKS — 6f 5y

2:50 (2:52) (Class 5) 3-4-Y-O — **£3,238** (£963; £481; £240) **Stalls** Centre

Form — RPR

0-4 **1** **Arganil (USA)**[7] 5366 3-9-3 0 ... SilvestreDeSousa 10 — 85
(K A Ryan) *sn led: rdn wl over 1f out: styd on strly* **10/1**

-5 **2** *2 ½* **Eton Rifles (IRE)**[79] 3051 3-9-3 0 ... PaulMulrennan 8 — 77
(J Howard Johnson) *trckd ldrs: hdwy to chse wnr 1/2-way: rdn wl over 1f out: sn drvn and no imp ins fnl f* **11/4**[1]

05 **3** *4* **Truly Divine**[14] 5160 3-9-3 0 ... PaulHanagan 1 — 64
(E A L Dunlop) *in tch: hdwy to chse ldng pair over 2f out and sn rdn: drvn wl over 1f out and kpt on same pce* **5/1**

00-0 **4** *2* **Barkass (UAE)**[45] 4162 4-9-5 69 ... TonyHamilton 9 — 58
(B Ellison) *towards rr: hdwy 2f out: sn rdn and kpt on: nrst fin* **4/1**[3]

4 **5** *¾* **Ishiadancer**[11] 5203 3-8-12 0 ... DavidAllan 6 — 50
(E J Alston) *in rr: hdwy 1/2-way: rdn 2f out: sn no imp* **8/1**

666 **6** *8* **Ros Cuire (IRE)**[17] 5082 3-9-3 0 ... DaleGibson 5 — 30
(W A Murphy, Ire) *a in rr* **25/1**

050 **7** *1 ½* **Warm Tribute (USA)**[60] 3638 4-9-0 45 ... KellyHarrison(5) 7 — 25
(A G Foster) *cl up: rdn along 1/2-way: sn wknd* **66/1**

6025 **8** *½* **Virtuality (USA)**[51] 3960 3-8-12 62 ... TomEaves 4 — 18
(B Smart) *dwlt: in tch 1/2-way: sn rdn and wknd over 2f out* **3/1**[2]

1m 14.43s (2.23) **Going Correction** +0.45s/f (Yiel)
WFA 3 from 4yo 2lb — **8** Ran SP% **113.9**
Speed ratings (Par 103): **103,99,94,91,90 80,78,77**
toteswinger: 1&2 £6.70, 1&3 £4.70, 2&3 £3.80. CSF £37.44 TOTE £10.60: £3.20, £1.40, £1.60; EX 48.20.
Owner The Big Moment **Bred** Colt Neck Stables, Llc **Trained** Hambleton, N Yorks

FOCUS
A weak maiden with the highest rated officially on 69. In keeping with the preceding two-year-old race the field came down the middle of the track and the first pair eventually came clear. There is little to go on formwise and the race could be a few pounds out either way.
Virtuality(USA) Official explanation: jockey said filly became upset in the stalls

5562 AUTUMN FINALE CLAIMING STKS — 6f 5y

3:20 (3:20) (Class 6) 3-Y-O+ — **£2,388** (£705; £352) **Stalls** Centre

Form — RPR

0000 **1** **Obe Brave**[10] 5247 5-9-7 80 ... PaulHanagan 4 — 74+
(R A Fahey) *chsd clr ldr: hdwy 2f out: rdn to ld jst ins fnl f: drvn and hld on wl towards fin* **7/4**[2]

6035 **2** *½* **Gift Horse**[10] 5247 8-9-7 83 ... (p) AdrianTNicholls 3 — 73+
(D Nicholls) *hld up: hdwy over 1f out: swtchd lft and rdn ent fnl f: styd on towards fin* **11/8**[1]

0460 **3** *shd* **Yorkshire Blue**[5] 5392 9-8-11 65 ... DanielTudhope 2 — 62+
(J S Goldie) *in tch: hdwy wl over 1f out: swtchd lft and rdn ent fnl f: nt qckn towards fin* **3/1**[3]

005 **4** *4 ½* **Geordie Dancer (IRE)**[23] 4849 6-8-2 45 ... (b) CharlotteKerton(7) 6 — 46
(A Berry) *led and sn clr: rdn over 1f out hdd jst ins fnl f and sn wknd* **16/1**

1m 15.86s (3.66) **Going Correction** +0.45s/f (Yiel) — **4** Ran SP% **109.4**
Speed ratings (Par 101): **93,92,92,86**
toteswinger: 1&2 £2.80. CSF £4.60 TOTE £2.30; EX 5.40.
Owner Mrs J Penman **Bred** Helshaw Grange Stud, E Kent & Mrs E Connelly **Trained** Musley Bank, N Yorks

FOCUS
A modest winning time, slower than both the maiden and the juvenile claimer and the form looks messy.

5563 SCOTTISH RACING ON BIG SCREEN H'CAP — 1m 3f 16y

3:50 (3:50) (Class 5) (0-75,75) 4-Y-O+ — **£4,533** (£1,348; £674; £336) **Stalls** High

Form — RPR

4251 **1** **Hurlingham**[25] 4785 4-9-4 **75** ... PaulMulrennan 1 — 84
(M W Easterby) *hld up in tch: smooth hdwy over 3f out: chal wl over 1f out: rdn to ld ent fnl f: sn hung bdly rt and hdd: drvn and hung lft: rallied under stgrong press to ld nr fin* **11/4**[2]

2522 **2** *hd* **Gordonsville**[45] 4146 5-9-2 **73** ... DanielTudhope 9 — 82
(J S Goldie) *hld up: hdwy 3f out: chal wl over 1f out: rdn to ld jst ins fnl f: sn drvn: hdd and no ex nr fin* **2/1**[1]

0123 **3** *2 ¾* **Channel Crossing**[8] 5305 6-8-12 **69** ... GregFairley 3 — 73
(S Wynne) *led: set stdy pce: rdn and qcknd 3f out: jnd and drvn 2f out: hdd ent fnl f: wknd* **6/1**[3]

3155 **4** *8* **Dan Tucker**[28] 4690 4-8-10 **67** ... TonyCulhane 8 — 58
(N Tinkler) *in tch: effrt over 3f out and sn rdn: plugged on same pce fnl 2f* **7/1**

3-30 **5** *1 ¼* **Tsaroxy (IRE)**[98] 2447 6-9-3 **74** ... TomEaves 7 — 63
(J Howard Johnson) *hld up in rr: effrt and sme hdwy 3f out: sn rdn and no imp* **12/1**

42/ **6** *20* **Auenmoon (GER)**[681] 5863 7-8-10 **70** ... NeilBrown(3) 5 — 25
(P Monteith) *midfield: hdwy to chse ldng pair after 3f: rdn along over 3f out and sn wknd* **9/1**

7 *3 ½* **Daraybad (FR)**[28] 6-9-0 **74** ... PJMcDonald(3) 4 — 23
(A Crook) *chsd ldr: rdn along 3f out and sn wknd* **16/1**

2m 34.48s (8.88) **Going Correction** +0.70s/f (Yiel) — **7** Ran SP% **110.4**
Speed ratings (Par 103): **95,94,92,87,86 71,69**
toteswinger: 1&2 £2.40, 1&3 £3.00, 2&3 £3.80. CSF £8.02 CT £26.07 TOTE £3.00: £1.80, £2.00; EX 10.90.
Owner A G Black **Bred** Aston Mullins Stud **Trained** Sheriff Hutton, N Yorks
■ Stewards' Enquiry : Paul Mulrennan two-day ban: used whip with excessive frequency and in incorrect place (Sep 15-16)

FOCUS
This modest handicap was run at a sound early pace thanks to the front-running Channel Crossing and the field elected to come down the centre of the track in the home straight. There was a cracking finish and the top weight just stuck his head out where it mattered. The form is sound rated around the first three.

5564 RBS SCOTTISH TROPHY SERIES FINAL STKS (H'CAP) — 1m 1f 36y

4:20 (4:20) (Class 3) 3-Y-O+ — **£9,714** (£2,890; £1,444; £721) **Stalls** High

Form — RPR

0061 **1** **King Of The Moors (USA)**[20] 4949 5-8-1 64 ... (p) PaulFessey 9 — 77
(T D Barron) *in tch: hdwy over 4f out: led 2f out and sn rdn: styd on strly fnl f* **8/1**[2]

5100 **2** *4 ½* **Moonstreaker**[66] 3450 5-8-0 63 ... PaulQuinn 3 — 66
(R M Whitaker) *dwlt and towards rr: stdy hdwy over 3f out: rdn to chse wnr over 1f out: drvn and kpt on same pce ins fnl f* **9/1**[3]

1411 **3** *3 ½* **Wind Shuffle (GER)**[30] 4633 5-8-12 75 ... DanielTudhope 12 — 71
(J S Goldie) *chsd ldrs: hdwy 3f out: chsd wnr 2f out and sn rdn: drvn and one pce appr fnl f* **11/4**[1]

0424 **4** *2* **Mystical Ayr (IRE)**[3] 5454 6-7-9 61 oh5 ... DuranFentiman(3) 8 — 53
(Miss L A Perratt) *in tch: chsd ldrs over 3f out: sn rdn: drvn and kpt on same pce fnl 2f* **12/1**

6433 **5** *hd* **Regent's Secret (USA)**[9] 4633 8-7-13 62 ow1 ... (p) PaulHanagan 6 — 53
(J S Goldie) *towards rr: hdwy over 2f outr: sn rdn and kpt on ins fnl f: nrst fin* **8/1**[2]

4320 **6** *2 ½* **Dechiper (IRE)**[5] 5396 6-7-13 67 ... (p) KellyHarrison(5) 10 — 53
(R Johnson) *towards rr: effrt and sme hdwy 3f out: sn rdn and no imp fnl 2f* **8/1**[2]

1206 **7** *1 ¼* **Keisha Kayleigh (IRE)**[19] 4970 5-8-9 72 ... (p) TomEaves 7 — 56
(B Ellison) *dwlt and towards rr: effrt and sme hdwy 3f out: sn rdn and no imp* **10/1**

0103 **8** *2* **Grethel (IRE)**[10] 5221 4-7-6 62 ... CharlotteKerton(7) 5 — 41
(A Berry) *prom: rdn along 3f out: sn wknd* **20/1**

3022 **9** *3* **Primo Way**[3] 5454 7-8-0 63 ... RoystonFfrench 1 — 36
(Miss L A Perratt) *prom: hdwy to chse ldr after 2f: styd alone far rail in st and ev ch tl rdn 2f over 2f out and sn wknd* **10/1**

1100 **10** *15* **El Dececy (USA)**[23] 4876 4-9-10 87 ... TonyCulhane 2 — 29
(S Parr) *led and sn clr: wd to stands rail st: rdn 3f out: hdd 2f out and sn wknd* **12/1**

5250 **11** *hd* **Chin Wag (IRE)**[5] 5390 4-8-1 67 oh1 ow6 ... AndrewMullen(3) 11 — 8
(J S Goldie) *a in rr* **14/1**

2m 4.36s (4.66) **Going Correction** +0.70s/f (Yiel) — **11** Ran SP% **115.0**
Speed ratings (Par 107): **107,103,99,98,97 95,94,92,90,76 76**
toteswinger: 1&2 £12.60, 1&3 £5.00, 2&3 £7.70. CSF £76.23 CT £248.71 TOTE £8.80: £3.10, £3.40, £1.60; EX 112.20.
Owner G Fawcett **Bred** Frank Brown, Hedberg Hall & K Hernandez **Trained** Maunby, N Yorks

FOCUS
This was just a fair handicap for the class, run at a solid early pace. There was divided opinion as they came into the home straight, with the runners spread across the track, and it was pretty much slow motion stuff in the final two furlongs. The winner can defy a penalty.

NOTEBOOK

King Of The Moors(USA) confirmed himself to be right back at the top of his game and followed up his Musselburgh with another improved display. He relished underfoot conditions and was well on top inside the final furlong, rating value for further than the bare margin. Another likely rise in weight will put him near or higher than his previous highest winning mark of 68, but while he remains in this sort of form he may not have stopped winning yet. (op 7-1)

Moonstreaker, having his first run for 66 days, came out of the pack to rate the clear danger to the winner yet was eventually put in his place. This was better from him and he was nicely clear of the remainder. (op 12-1)

Wind Shuffle(GER) had been successful on his last two outings over the course and distance and was bidding for his fifth win from his last six outings. He was unable to dictate this time, but still had his chance and could muster only the same pace in the last two furlongs. (tchd 3-1)

Mystical Ayr(IRE), unplaced at the track three days previously, failed to land a serious blow from off the pace and never looked like reversing Musselburgh form with the winner on these 2lb better terms. This was still no real disgrace from 5lb out of the weights. (op 14-1)

Regent's Secret(USA) was near last at the two-furlong pole, but he stayed on dourly when others had cried enough and only just missed out on fourth place. He ran a little below his course-and-distance form with the third and does seem at his happiest on a sound surface. (op 5-1)

5565 FINAL FLING H'CAP — 1m 65y

4:50 (4:51) (Class 6) (0-60,60) 3-Y-O — **£2,266** (£674; £337; £168) **Stalls** High

Form — RPR

5201 **1** **Casino Night**[10] 5224 3-8-11 **60** ... DeanHeslop(7) 6 — 71+
(R Johnson) *hld up: hdwy over 3f out: rdn to ld wl over 1f out: styd on strly fnl f* **11/4**[2]

1000 **2** *3 ¾* **Natural Rhythm (IRE)**[10] 5224 3-9-4 **60** ... (b) PaulMulrennan 3 — 61
(Mrs R A Carr) *led: rdn along 3f out: drvn 2f out: sn hdd and kpt on same pce* **8/1**

0333 **3** *½* **Rossini's Dancer**[1] 5544 3-8-12 **54** ... PaulHanagan 9 — 54
(R A Fahey) *hld up: hdwy 3f out: rdn to chse ldng pair wl over 1f out: sn drvn and no imp* **15/8**[1]

0506 **4** *6* **Pequeno Dinero (IRE)**[10] 5224 3-7-13 **46** oh1 ... (v[1]) KellyHarrison(5) 1 — 32
(C W Fairhurst) *chsd ldrs: hdwy to chse wnr 3f out: sn rdn along and wknd 2f out* **15/2**[3]

0000 **5** *4 ½* **Snake Catcher**[17] 5077 3-8-4 **46** oh1 ... (b[1]) DaleGibson 8 — 22
(M W Easterby) *s.i.s and rr: hdwy 1/2-way: rdn along to chse ldrs 3f out: drvn and wknd 2f out* **33/1**

6-06 **6** *20* **Pinewood Lulu**[30] 4650 3-9-4 **60** ... PAspell 7 — —
(R C Guest) *a in rr* **10/1**

0000 **7** *1 ½* **Paint Stripper**[22] 4903 3-8-8 **50** ... SilvestreDeSousa 2 — —
(W Storey) *chsd ldrs: rdn along over 3f out: drvn over 2f out and sn wknd* **12/1**

0066 **8** *¾* **Howards Hope**[5] 5388 3-8-7 **49** ow1 ... TomEaves 4 — —
(Miss L A Perratt) *chsd ldr: rdn along over 3f out and sn wknd* **12/1**

1m 55.44s (7.04) **Going Correction** +0.875s/f (Soft) — **8** Ran SP% **111.7**
Speed ratings (Par 99): **99,95,94,88,84 64,62,62**
toteswinger: 1&2 £4.10 1&3 £2.60, 2&3 £3.60. CSF £23.71 CT £49.00 TOTE £3.70: £1.30, £2.00, £1.20; EX 17.00.
Owner Barry Robson **Bred** Kingsmead Breeders **Trained** Newburn, Tyne & Wear

FOCUS
The ground was again changed, this time to soft, before this moderate handicap. The runners came to the stands' side in the home straight, it saw a clear-cut winner and the form appears sound.

5566 TRAINERMAGAZINE.COM H'CAP — 5f 4y
5:20 (5:20) (Class 6) (0-65,70) 4-Y-0+ — **£2,266** (£674; £337; £168) **Stalls** Centre

Form — RPR

4320 **1** — **Obe One**[5] 5392 8-8-5 **52** .... PaulHanagan 1 — 57
(A Berry) *trckd ldrs: effrt and nt clr run wl over 1f out: swtchd rt ent fnl f: rdn and qcknd to ld nr fin* — **5/1**[3]

4326 **2** *nk* **Rainbow Bay**[27] 4700 5-8-7 **54** .... (v) SilvestreDeSousa 4 — 58
(Miss Tracy Waggott) *wnt rt s: led: rdn along 2f out: drvn ent fnl f: hdd and nt qckn nr fin* — **8/1**

0060 **3** *1 ¾* **She's Our Beauty (IRE)**[3] 5452 5-8-1 **51** oh6 .... (v) DuranFentiman[(3)] 5 — 49
(S T Mason) *sltly hmpd s: trckd ldrs: hdwy 2f out and sn ev ch tl rdn and one pce ent fnl f* — **33/1**

0001 **4** *1 ¾* **Haajes**[5] 5398 4-9-9 **70** 6ex .... TonyCulhane 6 — 61+
(S Parr) *in rr and pushed along 1/2-way: sn rdn and kpt on same pce ins fnl f: n.d* — **5/2**[2]

01 **5** *½* **Miacarla**[3] 5452 5-8-7 **57** 6ex ow1 .... (t) NeilBrown[(3)] 2 — 47+
(H A McWilliams) *hld up in rr: smooth hdwy 2f out: chal over 1f out and ev ch: rdn ins fnl f and sn wknd* — **15/8**[1]

5350 **6** *4 ½* **Yerevan**[11] 5201 4-8-4 **56** .... KellyHarrison[(5)] 7 — 29
(M Mullineaux) *cl up on outer: effrt 2f out: sn rdn and wknd over 1f out* — **10/1**

3000 **7** *7* **Pickering**[26] 4743 4-9-4 **65** .... (b[1]) DavidAllan 9 — 13
(E J Alston) *cl up: rdn along 2f out: sn wknd* — **8/1**

63.23 secs (3.23) **Going Correction** +0.675s/f (Yiel) — **7** Ran SP% **114.3**
Speed ratings (Par 101): **101,100,97,94,94 86,75**
toteswinger: 1&2 £3.70, 1&3 £10.60, 2&3 £16.20. CSF £43.19 CT £1181.16 TOTE £5.20: £2.20, £4.50; EX 41.70 Place 6: £27.12 Place 5: £16.59 .
Owner A P Shandley **Bred** R And Mrs Kent **Trained** Cockerham, Lancs

FOCUS
A modest sprint which was dominated by the three at the bottom of the handicap and the form, rated around the first two, looks worth treating with some caution.
T/Plt: £63.10 to a £1 stake. Pool: £51,778.42. 598.75 winning tickets. T/Qpdt: £25.50 to a £1 stake. Pool: £4,038.70. 117.10 winning tickets. JR

5344 KEMPTON (A.W) (R-H)
Monday, September 1

OFFICIAL GOING: Standard
Wind: Strong, behind Weather: Fine but cloudy

5567 BET US OPEN TENNIS - BETDAQ NURSERY — 5f (P)
2:30 (2:31) (Class 6) (0-65,65) 2-Y-0 — **£2,047** (£604; £302) **Stalls** High

Form — RPR

0005 **1** — **Agnes Love**[20] 4942 2-8-12 **56** .... MartinDwyer 7 — 58
(J Akehurst) *mde virtually all: hrd rdn and gained upper hand fnl f: drifted lft but kpt on wl* — **9/1**

050 **2** *1* **Val De Flores**[18] 5004 2-9-4 **62** .... JamieSpencer 11 — 60
(E F Vaughan) *chsd ldng pair: drvn over 1f out: kpt on fnl f to take 2nd nr fin: unable to chal* — **7/1**

0050 **3** *¾* **Claphands**[33] 4525 2-8-11 **55** .... RyanMoore 10 — 51
(G L Moore) *chsd ldrs but nt on terms: styd on fnl f to snatch 3rd last strides* — **4/1**[2]

0432 **4** *hd* **Amber Sunset**[40] 4297 2-9-7 **65** .... NCallan 12 — 60
(J Jay) *w wnr: clr of rest over 1f out: hld ins fnl f: lost 2 pls nr fin* — **7/2**[1]

313 **5** *2* **Silent Treatment (IRE)**[14] 5159 2-9-6 **64** .... (t) DarryllHolland 5 — 52
(Miss Gay Kelleway) *chsd ldng pair: drvn and no imp over 1f out: one pce after* — **8/1**

0035 **6** *1 ½* **Gemini Jive (IRE)**[20] 4956 2-9-5 **63** .... RichardMullen 2 — 45+
(M G Quinlan) *s.i.s: nvr on terms w ldrs: styd on fnl f: nrst fin* — **20/1**

000 **7** *1* **Short Cut**[19] 4980 2-8-11 **55** .... AdamKirby 4 — 34
(S Kirk) *reminder after 1f: forced to r wd: effrt in midfield 1/2-way: no prog over 1f out: fdd* — **20/1**

6640 **8** *1 ¾* **The Saucy Snipe**[44] 4185 2-8-13 **57** .... JimCrowley 6 — 29
(P Winkworth) *sn bhd in last pair: stl there over 1f out: kpt on fnl f* — **20/1**

350 **9** *1 ¾* **Cash In The Attic**[7] 5363 2-9-4 **62** .... EdwardCreighton 8 — 28
(M R Channon) *chsd ldrs: u.p and outpcd 1/2-way: n.d after: fdd* — **7/1**

2410 **10** *1* **Sub Prime (IRE)**[25] 4768 2-8-12 **56** .... ChrisCatlin 9 — 19
(J A Osborne) *dwlt: nvr on terms: rdn and no prog 2f out* — **13/2**[3]

243 **11** *½* **Grand Plan (USA)**[53] 3889 2-9-3 **61** .... TPQueally 1 — 22
(J A Osborne) *forced to r wd: nvr on terms: struggling fr 1/2-way* — **16/1**

0046 **12** *1 ½* **Usual Suspects**[30] 4628 2-8-10 **54** .... PatrickMathers 3 — 9
(Peter Grayson) *s.i.s: mostly in last pair and nvr a factor* — **50/1**

61.39 secs (0.89) **Going Correction** +0.025s/f (Slow) — **12** Ran SP% **123.8**
Speed ratings (Par 93): **93,91,90,89,86 84,82,79,77,75 74,72**
toteswinger: 1&2 £18.40, 1&3 £11.30, 2&3 £6.00. CSF £70.28 CT £300.49 TOTE £15.10: £3.50, £2.50, £1.90; EX 135.30.
Owner David S M Caplin **Bred** Paul Sweeting **Trained** Epsom, Surrey

FOCUS
A modest nursery in which the pace was sound and the form looks moderate.

NOTEBOOK
Agnes Love, who showed her first worthwhile form on her all-weather debut last month, had the run of the race and showed a decent attitude to get off the mark. She should not be going up too much for this but will have to improve again to follow up. Official explanation: trainer said, regarding running, the race was a drop in class for the filly, and in its previous run at Lingfield, its first for the trainer, it was out of the handicap (op 8-1 tchd 10-1 tchd 12-1 in a place)
Val De Flores had shown ability at a modest level on turf but bettered those efforts from a good draw on this all-weather and nursery debut. She should have no problems with an extra furlong and is capable of picking up a similar event. (op 10-1)
Claphands attracted a bit of support from her favourable draw on this first run for Gary Moore and shaped as though the return to 6f would be in her favour. She is likely to win a race for this yard. (op 5-1)
Amber Sunset has been a consistent sort on turf and all-weather and she was far from disgraced from the plum draw after enjoying the rub of things. Effective over 6f, she has little margin for error from her current mark.
Silent Treatment(IRE) was soon well placed from her stall five draw but had her limitations exposed back in trip on this nursery debut. (op 6-1)
Gemini Jive(IRE) shaped as though the return to 6f would suit and this unexposed sort is not one to write off yet. (op 25-1)
Short Cut was not disgraced on his nursery debut after racing wide from his low draw and he too shaped as though a stiffer test of stamina would be in his favour. Official explanation: jockey said colt failed to handle the bend (op 14-1)

5568 BETDAQPOKER.CO.UK MEDIAN AUCTION MAIDEN STKS — 1m 2f (P)
3:00 (3:01) (Class 6) 3-5-Y-0 — **£2,047** (£604; £302) **Stalls** High

Form — RPR

1 — **Rotative** 3-8-12 0 .... AdamKirby 4 — 70+
(W R Swinburn) *awkward s and bustled along: rn green in last: stl only 7th over 1f out: picked up and r.o wl fnl f: led fnl strides* — **6/1**

0632 **2** *nk* **Azure Mist**[25] 4797 3-8-12 64 .... JimmyQuinn 6 — 65
(M H Tompkins) *prom: wnt 2nd wl over 3f out: drvn wl over 1f out: kpt on to ld ins fnl f but all out: hdd fnl strides* — **2/1**[1]

3002 **3** *½* **Speyside (IRE)**[48] 4061 3-9-0 70 .... (b[1]) PatrickHills[(3)] 3 — 69
(J W Hills) *in tch: chsd ldng pair over 3f out: drvn and nt no rspnse over 1f out: plugged on ins fnl f* — **11/2**

6623 **4** *shd* **Cheney Manor**[23] 4860 3-9-3 70 .... MichaelHills 9 — 69
(B W Hills) *led: gng strly 2f out: drvn over 1f out: tired and hdd ins fnl f: lost 2 pls nr fin* — **9/2**[3]

-050 **5** *2 ½* **Eseej (USA)**[4] 5428 3-9-3 68 .... DarrenWilliams 5 — 64
(P W Hiatt) *t.k.h: hld up in last trio: effrt over 2f out: hanging and fnd nil over 1f out: clsd reluctantly on ldrs fnl f* — **14/1**

6 **6** *7* **Candy Rose**[23] 4860 3-8-12 0 .... MartinDwyer 7 — 45
(M P Tregoning) *in tch: rdn over 3f out: sn struggling: no ch over 1f out* — **14/1**

-40 **7** *2* **Sensible**[39] 4342 3-8-12 68 .... JamieSpencer 8 — 41
(M J Wallace, Australia) *trckd ldr: rdn wl over 3f out: sn lost pl: n.d over 1f out* — **7/2**[2]

0000 **8** *46* **Eau Sauvage**[65] 3484 4-9-2 30 .... LukeMorris[(3)] 2 — —
(M J Attwater) *rdn after 2f: lost tch 4f out: sn t.o: virtually p.u* — **100/1**

2m 7.63s (-0.37) **Going Correction** +0.025s/f (Slow)
WFA 3 from 4yo 7lb — **8** Ran SP% **117.7**
Speed ratings (Par 101): **102,101,101,101,99 93,92,55**
toteswinger: 1&2 £3.80, 1&3 £8.90, 2&3 £3.20. CSF £19.05 TOTE £7.10: £2.30, £1.30, £2.30; EX 24.90.
Owner Exors Of The Late Mrs P W Harris **Bred** Pendley Farm **Trained** Aldbury, Herts

FOCUS
A modest maiden and the bare form is ordinary, although the winner looks a likely improver.

5569 BETDAQ.CO.UK H'CAP — 1m 2f (P)
3:30 (3:30) (Class 3) (0-95,95) 3-Y-0+
£7,477 (£2,239; £1,119; £560; £279; £140) **Stalls** High

Form — RPR

1500 **1** — **Bahar Shumaal (IRE)**[23] 4853 6-9-6 **92** .... NCallan 12 — 103
(C E Brittain) *mde all: set sensible pce: upped tempo over 2f out: drvn and clr over 1f out: unchal* — **14/1**

3-30 **2** *2* **King's Event (USA)**[23] 4856 4-8-13 **85** .... RyanMoore 1 — 92
(Sir Michael Stoute) *awkward s: pushed up fr wd draw to trck wnr: rdn over 2f out: no imp: kpt on but nvr able to chal after* — **11/4**[1]

6000 **3** *½* **Olympic City (BRZ)**[17] 5071 5-9-6 **92** .... KShea 2 — 98+
(M F De Kock, South Africa) *settled in midfield: 7th over 2f out: prog wl over 1f out: wnt 3rd ent fnl f: clsd on runner-up nr fin* — **20/1**

0405 **4** *2* **Beauchamp Viceroy**[17] 5051 4-8-13 **90** .... Louis-PhilippeBeuzelin[(5)] 4 — 92+
(G A Butler) *hld up in rr: 9th and plenty to do whn pushed along over 3f out: stl same pl over 1f out: r.o wl fnl f: nrst fin* — **16/1**

4110 **5** *1 ¾* **Goodwood Starlight (IRE)**[33] 4519 3-9-2 **95** .... EddieAhern 10 — 94
(J L Dunlop) *settled wl in tch: 6th and rdn over 2f out: nt qckn over 1f out: one pce after* — **10/3**[2]

1050 **6** *¾* **Scartozz**[11] 5208 6-9-6 **95** .... (p) TedDurcan 7 — 92
(M Botti) *trckd ldrs: rdn in 4th over 2f out: no imp over 1f out: fdd* — **33/1**

5405 **7** *hd* **Jeer (IRE)**[30] 4642 4-9-3 **89** .... JimmyFortune 9 — 86
(E A L Dunlop) *trckd ldng pair 2f: styd handy: rdn in 5th over 2f out: fdd over 1f out* — **16/1**

3300 **8** *2* **Mystery Star (IRE)**[25] 4790 3-8-3 **82** .... JimmyQuinn 3 — 75
(M H Tompkins) *settled in last trio: rdn in 12th over 2f out: nvr on terms: plugged on* — **11/2**[3]

4305 **9** *nk* **Kayak (SAF)**[38] 4363 6-9-6 **92** .... RichardMullen 8 — 84
(D M Simcock) *dwlt: nvr beyond midfield: drvn and struggling in 8th over 3f out: no prog* — **16/1**

1100 **10** *1* **Algarade**[33] 4520 4-9-0 **86** .... DO'Donohoe 13 — 76
(Sir Mark Prescott) *chsd ldng pair after 2f: drvn over 2f out: wknd over 1f out* — **10/1**

3236 **11** *9* **Bobski (IRE)**[26] 4723 6-8-10 **82** .... DarryllHolland 11 — 54
(Miss Gay Kelleway) *a in rr: rdn in 10th over 2f out: no prog: t.o* — **20/1**

3103 **12** *1* **Crossbow Creek**[65] 3480 10-9-0 **86** .... JamieSpencer 6 — 56
(M G Rimell) *stdd s: hld up in last: nvr a factor: t.o* — **16/1**

00-0 **13** *9* **Ofaraby**[23] 4867 8-9-0 **86** .... MatthewHenry 5 — 38
(M A Jarvis) *hld up in last trio: wl off the pce over 3f out: t.o* — **50/1**

2m 5.76s (-2.24) **Going Correction** +0.025s/f (Slow)
WFA 3 from 4yo+ 7lb — **13** Ran SP% **118.8**
Speed ratings (Par 107): **109,107,107,105,104 103,103,101,101,100 93,92,85**
toteswinger: 1&2 £11.40, 1&3 £43.60, 2&3 £10.90. CSF £49.96 CT £799.66 TOTE £21.60: £5.20, £2.00, £2.50; EX 62.30.
Owner Saeed Manana **Bred** Airlie Stud And Sir Thomas Pilkington **Trained** Newmarket, Suffolk

FOCUS
Few in-form sorts in this reasonable handicap and the form is best rated around the first two.

NOTEBOOK
Bahar Shumaal(IRE) is a better horse on Polytrack than on turf and he returned to something like his best to register a convincing success. However, he was very much allowed to do his own thing in front against the inside rail and it's likely he'll need similar leeway if he is to follow up after reassessment on this surface.
King's Event(USA) was bogged down in testing ground on his previous start but was always ideally placed and fared much better on this all-weather debut. Things were in his favour this time but he is only relatively lightly raced sort from a top stable and he appeals as the sort to win races this term. (op 5-2 tchd 3-1 in a place)
Olympic City(BRZ) form has been patchy this year but he ran creditably upped in distance to come from just behind the gallop in a race where the leaders did not come back. A stiffer test of stamina over this trip is going to suit and he is sure to win a race for Mike de Kock. (op 25-1)
Beauchamp Viceroy has not won since 2006 and has not been the most reliable since his last victory but he again found himself in a race that was not run to suit and fared better than the bare form. A stronger gallop will suit and he is worth another chance, despite that inconsistency.
Goodwood Starlight(IRE) had not been at his best over 1m4f in a competitive Goodwood handicap on his previous start but performed better on this all-weather debut. A much stronger overall gallop would have suited and he may be worth another try over that longer trip. (op 4-1)
Scartozz had the run of the race and was not disgraced but a mark of 95 offers him little room for manoeuvre. Official explanation: jockey said horse hung right-handed

Jeer(IRE) has yet to run up to his best turf form on Polytrack and was below his best for the third time in a row.
Mystery Star(IRE) Official explanation: jockey said colt missed the break
Crossbow Creek Official explanation: jockey said gelding missed the break

5570 BET MULTIPLES - BETDAQ MAIDEN FILLIES' STKS (DIV I) 1m (P)
4:00 (4:03) (Class 4) 2-Y-O **£3,561** (£1,059; £529; £264) **Stalls** High

Form RPR
5 **1** **Simple Solution (USA)**[30] 4643 2-9-0 0 MichaelHills 3 81+
(B W Hills) *sn prom: stdy prog gng wl to ld jst over 2f out: shkn up and drew clr fnl f* **15/8**[2]
0 **2** *4* **Sri Kandi**[30] 4643 2-9-0 0 ChrisCatlin 6 73
(P F I Cole) *trckd ldng pair to 3f out: nt qckn 2f out: kpt on u.p to take 2nd ins fnl f* **7/1**[3]
3 *1 1/4* **Sussex Dancer (IRE)** 2-9-0 0 TPQueally 8 70
(J A Osborne) *hld up bhd ldrs: plld out and prog over 2f out: looked possible danger over 1f out: effrt petered out fnl f* **20/1**
4 **4** *1 1/4* **Fen Spirit (IRE)**[23] 4870 2-9-0 0 JimmyFortune 10 67
(J H M Gosden) *led: rdn and hdd jst over 2f out: wknd and lost 2 pls fnl f* **1/1**[1]
5 *3 3/4* **Loulou (USA)** 2-9-0 0 JamieSpencer 7 59+
(S A Callaghan) *s.i.s: reluctant early and detached in last: jnd main gp over 4f out: outpcd fr 3f out: plugged on steadily* **14/1**
0 **6** *2 3/4* **Anaasheed**[52] 3913 2-9-0 0 MartinDwyer 1 53
(J L Dunlop) *hld up in rr: outpcd fr 3f out: pushed along and nvr on terms after* **25/1**
06 **7** *nk* **Save The Day**[22] 4896 2-9-0 0 JoeFanning 5 52
(M Johnston) *chsd ldr to wl over 2f out: sn wknd* **12/1**
00 **8** *3 1/2* **Laraffelle (GR)**[12] 5184 2-9-0 0 TedDurcan 2 44
(E A L Dunlop) *settled in rr: outpcd and reminder over 2f out: nvr nr ldrs after* **50/1**
0 **9** *5* **Guilin (IRE)**[30] 4643 2-9-0 0 NCallan 9 33
(P F I Cole) *a wl in rr: lost tch 3f out: bhd after* **33/1**
0 **10** *8* **Braishfield Lass**[14] 5147 2-9-0 0 MickyFenton 4 16
(B G Powell) *prom 2f: sn dropped to midfield: wknd over 2f out w legs moving in all directions: t.o* **100/1**

1m 40.68s (0.88) **Going Correction** +0.025s/f (Slow) **10** Ran SP% **126.1**
Speed ratings (Par 94): **96,92,90,89,85 83,82,79,74,66**
toteswinger: 1&2 £3.20, 1&3 £7.90, 2&3 £13.40. CSF £16.32 TOTE £3.00: £1.30, £2.00, £4.00; EX 17.50.
Owner K Abdulla **Bred** Juddmonte Farms Inc **Trained** Lambourn, Berks

FOCUS
Just a fair winning time despite being 1.29 seconds faster than the second division but the form looks sound with the fourth to her debut form.

NOTEBOOK
Simple Solution(USA) ◆ had shaped well on her debut over 7f on turf and confirmed that promise over this extra furlong. She travelled strongly, responded well once asked for an effort and, although edging off a true line in the closing stages, left the impression that she would be able to progress again in nursery company. (op 9-4 tchd 11-4)
Sri Kandi, who attracted support and ran well for a long way onher racecourse debut, was again nibbled at in the market and turned in an improved display. She is open to further improvement on this surface and looks more than capable of picking up a race. (op 12-1)
Sussex Dancer(IRE) holds an entry in the Group 1 Fillies' Mile but, while that looks optimistic, she showed more than enough on this racecourse debut to suggest a race can be found. She is entitled to improve a fair bit for this run and is one to keep an eye on in similar company. (op 25-1 tchd 28-1)
Fen Spirit(IRE) was keen both on the way to post and in the race itself and, although allowed to set an ordinary gallop from her good draw, she folded tamely once pressure was applied. She has ability but lacks physical scope and is going to have to settle better if she is to progress. (tchd 8-11 and 11-10)
Loulou(USA) has several winners in her pedigree and also holds an entry in the Fillies' Mile but was easy to back and too green to do herself justice after a tardy start on this racecourse debut. She should be able to improve on this bare form and looks more of a handicap prospect. (op 12-1)
Anaasheed hadn't shown much in soft ground on her debut and, although again well beaten on this all-weather debut, she did hint at ability without being knocked about and may do better in ordinary handicaps in due course. (op 33-1)
Guilin(IRE) Official explanation: jockey said filly hung left-handed

5571 BET MULTIPLES - BETDAQ MAIDEN FILLIES' STKS (DIV II) 1m (P)
4:30 (4:33) (Class 4) 2-Y-O **£3,561** (£1,059; £529; £264) **Stalls** High

Form RPR
26 **1** **High Heeled (IRE)**[32] 4554 2-9-0 0 MichaelHills 1 79+
(B W Hills) *trckd ldrs: stdy prog on outer to ld jst over 2f out: sn shkn up and drew clr: comf* **6/4**[1]
2 *2 1/2* **Speedy Cleaners (IRE)** 2-9-0 0 PatDobbs 10 73
(R Hannon) *trckd ldrs: effrt over 2f out: kpt on wl enough to claim 2nd fnl f: no ch w wnr* **25/1**
5 **3** *hd* **Kaloni (IRE)**[18] 5029 2-9-0 0 MickyFenton 4 72
(Mrs P Sly) *trckd ldrs: effrt and hanging rt over 2f out: prog over 1f out to dispute 2nd ent fnl f: kpt on steadily* **33/1**
0 **4** *1 1/2* **Mitra Jaan (IRE)**[45] 4157 2-9-0 0 AdamKirby 3 69
(W R Swinburn) *led to jst over 2f out: stl disputing 2nd 1f out: wknd ins fnl f* **7/1**
04 **5** *nk* **Silk Cotton (USA)**[22] 4896 2-9-0 0 RyanMoore 2 68
(E A L Dunlop) *mostly trckd ldr to wl over 2f out: effrt again to dispute 2nd over 1f out: wknd ins fnl f* **8/1**
6 *4* **Holamo (IRE)** 2-9-0 0 DarryllHolland 5 59
(M Botti) *s.i.s: sn in tch: reminders on outside and wl outpcd 3f out: kpt on fnl 2f* **7/2**[2]
7 *6* **Rio Carnival (USA)** 2-9-0 0 JimmyFortune 6 46
(J H M Gosden) *hld up in rr: shkn up 3f out: sn outpcd and bhd* **9/2**[3]
8 *1 1/4* **Always Rocking (FR)** 2-9-0 0 PaulEddery 9 43
(G D Blake) *mostly in last pair: rdn 3f out: sn bhd* **25/1**
0 **9** *1 3/4* **Clodazone (IRE)**[44] 4199 2-8-9 0 NicolPolli(5) 7 40
(M G Quinlan) *hld up in last pair: pushed along 3f out: sn lost tch and bhd* **100/1**
0 **10** *nse* **Sutania**[30] 4643 2-9-0 0 ChrisCatlin 8 39
(P F I Cole) *trckd ldrs tl wknd rapidly over 2f out* **25/1**

1m 41.97s (2.17) **Going Correction** +0.025s/f (Slow) **10** Ran SP% **119.5**
Speed ratings (Par 94): **90,87,87,85,85 81,75,74,72,72**
toteswinger: 1&2 £6.90, 1&3 £11.90, 2&3 £27.00. CSF £51.72 TOTE £2.60: £1.10, £5.80, £5.80; EX 42.00.
Owner Mr And Mrs Steven Jenkins **Bred** Ballylinch Stud **Trained** Lambourn, Berks

FOCUS
A modest winning time, 1.29 seconds slower than the first division but the winner and fifth set a fairly solid level.

NOTEBOOK
High Heeled(IRE) ◆ was the clear form choice on her debut second in a race that worked out well at Newmarket. Although she again saw plenty of daylight after racing three deep from her low draw, the filly settled much better than at Goodwood and showed a decent turn of foot to win with more in hand than the official margin suggested. It will be interesting to see what the Handicapper does with her and she looks the type to win more races. (op 10-11 tchd 7-4 in a place)
Speedy Cleaners(IRE) is out of a dual sprint winner but, after proving easy to back, had no problems with this trip on her racecourse debut. With the exception of the winner, this form is nothing special and, although entitled to improve, ordinary handicaps may provide her best chance of success. (op 33-1)
Kaloni(IRE) was well beaten on her debut at Sandown but she fared much better on this Polytrack surface. She looked less than an easy ride once pressure was applied but she may fare better again once qualified for a mark. (op 50-1)
Mitra Jaan(IRE) had the run of the race against the inside rail at a meeting that has favoured those that raced up with the pace. She is in good hands and will be of more interest after her next run.
Silk Cotton(USA) was always well placed but again had her limitations exposed over this longer trip on this all-weather debut. She is likely to continue to look vulnerable in this type of event. (op 9-1 tchd 10-1)
Holamo(IRE) is related to a useful turf/dirt performer in the US but only hinted at ability on this racecourse debut. (op 8-1)
Rio Carnival(USA) took the eye on pedigree, is going to have to show a good deal more before she is a betting proposition. (tchd 4-1)

5572 GET YOUR PRINTING@OPTICHROME.COM MAIDEN STKS 6f (P)
5:00 (5:03) (Class 4) 2-Y-O **£3,885** (£1,156; £577; £288) **Stalls** High

Form RPR
0 **1** **Cheviot (USA)**[9] 5271 2-9-3 0 NCallan 3 77+
(M A Jarvis) *pressed ldr: led over 2f out: rdn clr over 1f out: tired fnl f: jst hld on* **6/1**[3]
2 *hd* **Audemar (IRE)** 2-9-3 0 JamieSpencer 7 76
(E F Vaughan) *trckd ldrs: c v wd in st: rdn to go 2nd over 1f out: clsd on wnr wl fnl f: jst failed* **10/1**
3 *1* **Caerus (USA)** 2-9-3 0 PaulDoe 8 73
(W J Knight) *s.i.s: sn in tch: effrt and c v wd in st: prog to dispute 2nd over 1f out: kpt on same pce fnl f* **7/1**
30 **4** *1 3/4* **Marbled Cat (USA)**[16] 5099 2-9-3 0 JoeFanning 11 68
(M Johnston) *led to over 2f out: sn outpcd and btn: one pce fnl f* **11/4**[1]
5 *2 3/4* **Ascendant** 2-9-3 0 DO'Donohoe 5 60+
(Sir Mark Prescott) *dwlt: rn green in last pair: sme prog fnl 2f: nvr on terms but kpt on* **14/1**
5 **6** *1 3/4* **Scottish Affair**[17] 5072 2-9-3 0 NeilPollard 12 55
(E A L Dunlop) *wl in rr: sme prog 2f out: no hdwy after and no ch* **16/1**
6 **7** *1 3/4* **Overbright (IRE)**[19] 4980 2-9-3 0 PatDobbs 6 49
(G L Moore) *a towards rr: outpcd over 2f out: no ch after* **12/1**
4 **8** *nk* **Spiritual Art**[16] 5099 2-8-12 0 RyanMoore 1 43
(S A Callaghan) *wnt lft s: rushed up on outer to join ldng pair: nt qckn over 2f out: sn wknd* **7/2**[2]
0 **9** *2 1/2* **Kaikoura**[42] 4251 2-8-12 0 PaulEddery 10 36
(G D Blake) *w ldrs: lost pl after 2f: wknd over 2f out* **33/1**
10 *1 3/4* **Residency (IRE)** 2-9-3 0 TedDurcan 2 36
(M J Wallace, Australia) *wnt lft s: nrly rn off the crse bnd 4f out: wl bhd after* **7/1**

1m 14.11s (1.01) **Going Correction** +0.025s/f (Slow) **10** Ran SP% **120.4**
Speed ratings (Par 97): **94,93,92,90,86 84,81,81,78,75**
toteswinger: 1&2 £11.70, 1&3 £9.90, 2&3 £16.10. CSF £66.73 TOTE £7.00: £1.80, £2.30, £2.70; EX 77.40.
Owner Sheikh Ahmed Al Maktoum **Bred** Darley **Trained** Newmarket, Suffolk

FOCUS
Not much solid form to go on but a decent gallop this time and the form is assessed through the fourth backed up by the sixthand seventh.

NOTEBOOK
Cheviot(USA) ◆ looks a bit better than the bare form of his narrow win. A big sort with plenty of scope who proved a bit disappointing after attracting support on his debut (turf), he handled this track really well and had his race won soon after the intersection. It's a fair bet that there's plenty more to come and he is one to keep on the right side in nurseries. (op 11-2 tchd 5-1)
Audemar(IRE) needed a bit of assistance to get into the stalls but he ran creditably on this racecourse debut. As his dam won over 1m6f, it's fair to assume that he should have no problems with longer distances and he should improved for this initial experience. (op 11-1)
Caerus(USA), who hails from a yard that has done well with its all-weather runners, is out of a multiple sprint dirt winner in the US and he showed ability on this racecourse debut. He too is entitled to improve. (op 8-1)
Marbled Cat(USA) tried to match strides with the winner against the inside rail for a long way on this all-weather debut and fared better than on his previous start. He may do better in handicaps and is not one to write off yet. (op 4-1 tchd 9-2 in a place)
Ascendant ◆ shaped with promise over a trip that, on pedigree alone, was always going to be on the sharp side on this racecourse debut. After a tardy start, he kept on without being knocked about and he will be of much more interest over 7f further in due course. (op 11-1)
Scottish Affair again showed ability on this all-weather debut without being unduly punished and who will be suited by another furlong. (op 22-1)
Spiritual Art ran creditably on her debut on turf but failed to match that effort on this Polytrack debut. (op 5-2 tchd 4-1 in a place)
Residency(IRE) Official explanation: jockey said colt failed to handle the bend

5573 DAY TIME, NIGHT TIME, GREAT TIME H'CAP 1m 4f (P)
5:30 (5:33) (Class 3) (0-95,95) 3-Y-O
£7,477 (£2,239; £1,119; £560; £279; £140) **Stalls** Centre

Form RPR
3-21 **1** **Starfala**[39] 4342 3-8-4 **78** WilliamBuick 7 89
(P F I Cole) *hld up in last trio: rapid prog over 2f out and swtchd to inner: led jst over 1f out: rdn clr* **20/1**
1610 **2** *2 1/4* **Inventor (IRE)**[25] 4784 3-9-6 **94** JimmyFortune 10 101
(B J Meehan) *hld up towards rr: prog over 2f out: drvn and styd on fnl f to take 2nd nr fin: no ch w wnr* **7/1**
122 **3** *1/2* **Reclamation (IRE)**[62] 3586 3-8-6 **80** DO'Donohoe 8 86
(Sir Mark Prescott) *trckd ldr: rdn 4f out: stl pressing 2f out: chsd wnr 1f out: outpcd: lost 2nd nr fin* **12/1**
4133 **4** *1* **Sweet Lightning**[16] 5111 3-9-0 **88** RyanMoore 2 93
(W R Muir) *hld up in last trio: prog over 2f out: nt pce to chal fr over 1f out but styd on* **13/2**[3]
1412 **5** *nk* **Slip**[25] 4791 3-8-11 **85** MartinDwyer 1 89
(M P Tregoning) *trckd ldrs: rdn and hung bdly lft over 2f out: kpt on one pce after* **11/1**
2263 **6** *1* **Midships (USA)**[36] 4443 3-9-7 **95** JimCrowley 6 98
(Mrs A J Perrett) *led: rdn over 2f out: hdd jst over 1f out: wknd last 100yds* **10/1**

2120 **7** *hd* **Fiulin**[74] 3157 3-9-2 **90**.......... TedDurcan 3 94+
(M Botti) *hld up towards rr: effrt whn hmpd over 2f out: rallied over 1f out: tried to cl on ldrs but no ch to rcvr: eased last 50yds* **9/1**

3011 **8** *shd* **Dance The Star (USA)**[40] 4303 3-8-9 **83**.......... RichardMullen 5 85
(D M Simcock) *hld up in last trio: rdn and hmpd over 2f out: sme prog over 1f out: keeping on whn swtchd sharply lft nr fin* **13/2**[3]

212 **9** *6* **Meshtri (IRE)**[25] 4784 3-9-1 **89**.......... PhilipRobinson 9 81+
(M A Jarvis) *hld up in midfield: effrt and sltly hmpd over 2f out: trying to cl whn bdly hmpd over 1f out: wknd and eased* **3/1**[1]

0-60 **10** *9* **Safari Sunup (IRE)**[93] 2610 3-9-0 **88**.......... StephenCarson 11 66
(P Winkworth) *mostly trckd ldng pair to 2f out: wknd rapidly* **25/1**

314 **11** *7* **Checklow (USA)**[30] 4618 3-9-0 **88**..........(v[1]) LDettori 4 55
(J Noseda) *reluctant to enter stalls: dwlt and rousted along to go prom: rdn over 3f out: wandered bdly over 2f out: gave up and eased* **4/1**[2]

2m 31.08s (-3.42) **Going Correction** +0.025s/f (Slow) **11** Ran SP% **127.9**
Speed ratings (Par 105): **112,110,110,109,109 108,108,108,104,98 93**
toteswinger: 1&2 £37.60, 1&3 £23.50, 2&3 £19.40. CSF £166.81 CT £1802.00 TOTE £25.40: £5.50, £2.90, £4.50; EX 224.00.
Owner Ben & Sir Martyn Arbib **Bred** Arbib Bloodstock Partnership **Trained** Whatcombe, Oxon

FOCUS
A useful handicap run in a good time and the form is rated fairly positively through the runner-up with the next three home close to their best.

NOTEBOOK
Starfala, only had a course-and-distance maiden win to her name but turned in a much improved effort to win on this handicap debut after getting a good run through near the inside rail. She is a progressive sort who should stay further and it will be surprising if she isn't able to win again this season.
Inventor(IRE) did not get home over 1m6f on soft on his previous start but returned to form on this all-weather debut. He shaped as though an even stiffer test of stamina over this trip would have been more to his liking but he did show a tendency to edge off a true line and is vulnerable to the more progressive sorts from his current mark. (op 10-1)
Reclamation(IRE) was up in the weights and in grade and, although showing a tendency to go in snatches, she kept plugging away to finish the best of those that raced up with the pace. She will be worth a try over 1m6f and possibly a try in headgear and is the type to win again for this yard. (op 8-1)
Sweet Lightning is a consistent sort who seemed to give it his best shot returned to Polytrack and he looks a good guide to the worth of this form. He should continue to give a good account either on turf or all-weather. (op 10-1)
Slip was not disgraced in terms of form over this longer trip and did not fail through lack of stamina from this 5lb higher mark but looked less than an easy ride once asked for an effort. (op 12-1 tchd 10-1)
Midships(USA) was allowed a fairly easy time of it on this all-weather debut but did not seem to get home on this first run over 1m4f. The return to shorter should suit but he has little margin for error from his current mark. (op 16-1)
Fiulin, a fairly unexposed sort who was trying Polytrack for the first time, carries his head high and was under pressure a long way out but looks better than the bare form after meeting trouble.
Official explanation: jockey said colt was denied a clear run (op 14-1)
Meshtri(IRE) looked a progressive sort judging on his turf form but was not travelling particularly well when badly hampered after the intersection. He is worth another chance back on grass. (op 4-1 tchd 9-2 in places)
Checklow(USA) proved the disappointment of the race on this all-weather debut. Sporting first-time blinkers, he missed a beat at the start before finding precious little off the bridle. Although eased when clearly held, this lightly raced colt looks one to tread carefully with at present. (op 5-2 tchd 9-2 in a place)

5574 BACK OR LAY AT BETDAQ CLASSIFIED STKS 7f (P)
6:00 (6:02) (Class 6) 3-Y-0+ **£2,047** (£604; £302) **Stalls High**

Form RPR

6-20 **1** **Billberry**[16] 5110 3-8-12 54..........(t) SaleemGolam 2 62+
(S C Williams) *bmpd s: hld up in midfield: effrt and nt clr run briefly 2f out: prog over 1f out: hrd rdn and r.o to ld fnl 100yds: hung lft but kpt on* **5/1**[2]

0-65 **2** *nse* **Melt (IRE)**[25] 4772 3-8-12 55.......... RyanMoore 1 58
(R Hannon) *hld up in last pair: brought to wd outside in st: prog 2f out: r.o to chal last 100yds: nt qckn nr fin* **10/1**

0603 **3** *1 ½* **Tallest Peak (USA)**[67] 3397 3-8-12 53.......... JamieSpencer 6 54
(M G Quinlan) *wl in rr: brought to outer in st: hrd rdn and prog 2f out: styd on to take 3rd fnl strides* **5/2**[1]

0-00 **4** *hd* **Milne Bay (IRE)**[111] 2079 3-8-12 55.......... RichardMullen 10 53
(D M Simcock) *dwlt: sn midfield: effrt and racd awkwardly over 2f out: prog to ld over 1f out: looked wnr but floundered in front: hdd last 100yds* **33/1**

0026 **5** *4 ½* **Lucky Character**[48] 4044 3-8-12 47..........(vt) RichardKingscote 5 41
(N J Vaughan) *w ldrs: chal over 2f out: upsides wl over 1f out: wknd fnl f* **25/1**

3-63 **6** *1 ¾* **Ginger Minx (IRE)**[189] 702 3-8-9 53.......... LukeMorris[(3)] 13 37
(N J Vaughan) *cl up: effrt over 2f out: nt qckn over 1f out: wknd fnl f* **16/1**

-060 **7** *¾* **Todber**[33] 4524 3-8-12 55.......... MartinDwyer 11 35
(M P Tregoning) *trckd ldrs: cl up 2f out: sn nt qckn and btn* **9/1**

0032 **8** *nk* **Pasta Prayer**[4] 5421 3-8-12 54..........(b) ChrisCatlin 7 34
(S A Callaghan) *w ldrs: led over 2f out to over 1f out: wknd qckly* **13/2**[3]

0060 **9** *nk* **Squire Boldwood (IRE)**[14] 5161 3-8-12 55..........(b) DO'Donohoe 12 33
(D R C Elsworth) *nt wl away: mostly in last trio: struggling over 2f out: brief effrt sn after: no hdwy over 1f out* **20/1**

0235 **10** *3 ½* **Charming Tale (USA)**[48] 4061 3-8-12 55..........(b) EddieAhern 3 23
(B J Meehan) *wnt lft s: wl in rr: rdn 1/2-way: limited prog u.str.p 2f out: sn btn* **5/1**[2]

0-00 **11** *7* **Nisbah**[95] 2549 3-8-12 47.......... J-PGuillambert 4 5
(C E Brittain) *sn pushed along in midfield: wknd over 1f out* **66/1**

6-05 **12** *5* **Celtic Charlie (FR)**[39] 4333 3-8-12 55.......... IanMongan 9 —
(P M Phelan) *w ldr to over 2f out: wknd rapidly* **8/1**

0403 **13** *16* **Coup De Torchon (FR)**[25] 4770 3-8-12 55.......... TPQueally 14 —
(J A Osborne) *mde most to over 2f out: wknd v rapidly and t.o* **14/1**

1m 26.53s (0.53) **Going Correction** +0.025s/f (Slow)
WFA 3 from 4yo 4lb **13** Ran SP% **131.0**
Speed ratings (Par 101): **97,96,95,95,89 87,87,86,86,82 74,68,50**
toteswinger: 1&2 £8.10, 1&3 £4.40, 2&3 £5.80. CSF £58.07 TOTE £7.60: £2.60, £2.20, £2.10; EX 40.50 Place 6: £203.57 Place 5: £69.31.
Owner Pascoe, Enticknap & Sullivan **Bred** G Deacon **Trained** Newmarket, Suffolk

FOCUS
A tight classified stakes on paper and a decent gallop saw those held up coming to the fore in the closing stages. The placed horses set the standard.
T/Jkpt: Not won. T/Plt: £351.10 to a £1 stake. Pool: £58,777.27. 122.20 winning tickets. T/Qpdt: £88.00 to a £1 stake. Pool: £3,938.10. 33.10 winning tickets. JN

5427 LINGFIELD (L-H)
Monday, September 1

OFFICIAL GOING: Turf course - good (good to firm in places); all-weather - standard
There was a big bias towards the stands'-side rail on the turf course.
Wind: fresh behind Weather: overcast

5575 TAGWORLDWIDE.COM APPRENTICE H'CAP 1m (P)
2:10 (2:10) (Class 6) (0-55,56) 3-Y-0+ **£2,590** (£770; £385; £192) **Stalls High**

Form RPR

6021 **1** **Circadian Rhythm**[6] 5379 3-9-1 **56** 6ex.......... JamieKyne[(3)] 2 62
(S C Williams) *in tch: hdwy over 2f out: rdn to chal wl over 1f out: led ins fnl f: hld on wl* **3/1**[1]

0334 **2** *shd* **Complete Frontline (GER)**[14] 5161 3-8-13 **54**...(p) CharlesEddery[(3)] 10 60
(K R Burke) *chsd ldrs: rdn to chal wl over 1f out: led narrowly 1f out: hdd ins fnl f: nt qckn fnl 100yds* **4/1**[3]

3600 **3** *¾* **Nikki Bea (IRE)**[24] 4825 5-9-2 **52**.......... DebraEngland[(3)] 3 58+
(Jamie Poulton) *hld up in midfield: hdwy 3f out: chsd ldrs gng wl 2f out: nt clr run over 1f out tl swtchd rt jst ins fnl f: r.o wl but nvr quite getting to ldng pair* **8/1**

0-40 **4** *3* **Janet's Delight**[41] 4278 3-9-1 **53**.......... RosieJessop 5 50
(S Curran) *s.i.s: hld up bhd: hdwy over 3f out: kpt on same pce fr over 1f out* **12/1**

2230 **5** *nk* **Fairly Honest**[13] 5166 4-8-13 **51**.......... MJMurphy[(5)] 4 49
(P W Hiatt) *led tl over 3f out: pressed ldr after tl wknd jst ins fnl f* **8/1**

0002 **6** *shd* **Turfani (IRE)**[18] 5019 3-9-0 **55**.......... AndreaAtzeni[(3)] 9 51
(W J Knight) *hld up towards rr: hdwy over 3f out: rdn over 2f out: kpt on same pce fr wl over 1f out* **7/2**[2]

0000 **7** *2 ¼* **Franksalot (IRE)**[62] 3593 8-9-5 **52**..........(b) BMcHugh 1 44
(I W McInnes) *t.k.h: chsd ldr tl led over 3f out: rdn jst over 2f out: hdd 1f out: wknd* **14/1**

5300 **8** *4* **Scientific**[4] 5429 3-8-8 **53**..........(t) HollyHall[(7)] 6 35
(G Prodromou) *bhd: detached in last pl after 2f: no ch last 3f* **33/1**

4/0- **9** *6* **Ohana**[74] 144 5-8-10 **48**.......... MrJPFeatherstone[(5)] 8 17
(N J Gifford) *racd wd: bhd: rdn and struggling 4f out: no ch last 3f* **9/1**

1m 38.71s (0.51) **Going Correction** +0.025s/f (Slow)
WFA 3 from 4yo+ 5lb **9** Ran SP% **116.7**
Speed ratings (Par 101): **98,97,97,94,93 93,91,87,81**
toteswinger: 1&2 £3.30, 1&3 £6.30, 2&3 £4.10. CSF £15.31 CT £87.20 TOTE £3.40: £1.70, £1.70, £2.10; EX 12.90 Trifecta £42.30 Pool: £329.89 - 5.77 winning units..
Owner Circadian **Bred** Red House Stud **Trained** Newmarket, Suffolk

FOCUS
A very moderate handicap restricted to apprentices who had not ridden more than ten winners. The pace was just modest through the first furlong or two, but Fairly Honest and Franksalot ended up taking each other on, ruining their chance and setting this up for those waited with. The runner-up is rated to form with the winner up 6lb.

5576 BAKER TILLY H'CAP 1m 4f (P)
2:40 (2:40) (Class 5) (0-70,70) 3-Y-0+ **£3,238** (£963; £481; £240) **Stalls Low**

Form RPR

4254 **1** **Mr Napoleon (IRE)**[166] 941 6-9-9 **68**.......... FergusSweeney 6 73
(G L Moore) *t.k.h: hld up in last trio: hdwy over 3f out: str run on outer over 1f out: led ins fnl f: r.o wl* **9/1**

0053 **2** *1 ½* **Vinces**[18] 5017 4-9-6 **65**.......... RobertHavlin 8 68
(T D McCarthy) *dwlt: sn rcvrd: t.k.h: chsd ldrs: hdwy to ld 3f out: rdn jst over 2f out: hdd ins fnl f: one pce* **9/2**[2]

1-63 **3** *shd* **Ommadawn (IRE)**[97] 2482 4-9-5 **64**..........(t) RobertWinston 5 67
(J R Fanshawe) *hld up in midfield: hdwy over 3f out: chal wl over 1f out: ev ch tl one pce u.p ins fnl f* **11/2**[3]

0005 **4** *3 ½* **Afram Blue**[16] 5086 3-9-2 **70**..........(t) PaulDoe 7 67
(W J Knight) *dwlt: sn in midfield: rdn over 3f out: chsd ldrs u.p wl over 1f out: wknd fnl f* **8/1**

4630 **5** *½* **Apache Fort**[25] 4771 5-9-8 **67**.......... ShaneKelly 3 63
(T Keddy) *in tch: nt clr run over 2f out: swtchd to inner and effrt wl over 1f out: no imp ent fnl f* **5/2**[1]

4450 **6** *2* **Generous Lad (IRE)**[83] 2921 5-9-3 **62**..........(p) PatCosgrave 2 55
(A B Haynes) *t.k.h: hld up in rr: rdn and effrt wl over 2f out: nvr trbld ldrs* **9/1**

1300 **7** *2 ¾* **Prince Charlemagne (IRE)**[16] 5087 5-9-2 **61**..........(b) DaneO'Neill 1 50
(R M Stronge) *t.k.h: hld up in midfield: rdn and no prog over 2f out* **8/1**

00-0 **8** *5* **Kapellmeister (IRE)**[15] 5118 5-9-3 **62**..........(p) TGMcLaughlin 9 43
(M S Saunders) *led for 2f: chsd ldr after: rdn over 4f out: wknd qckly over 1f out* **40/1**

000 **9** *3 ¼* **Mister Right (IRE)**[68] 3375 7-9-11 **70**.......... RichardHughes 4 46
(D J S Ffrench Davis) *hld up bhd: nvr a factor* **12/1**

0-00 **10** *¾* **Siena**[61] 3611 3-8-5 **59**.......... HayleyTurner 11 33
(Mrs C A Dunnett) *dwlt: sn rcvrd: led after 2f: rdn and hdd 3f out: wknd jst over 2f out* **33/1**

2m 32.34s (-0.66) **Going Correction** +0.025s/f (Slow)
WFA 3 from 4yo+ 9lb **10** Ran SP% **117.4**
Speed ratings (Par 103): **103,102,101,99,99 97,96,92,90,90**
toteswinger: 1&2 £3.40, 1&3 £12.80, 2&3 £4.20. CSF £49.65 CT £248.34 TOTE £7.40: £2.40, £1.70, £2.10; EX 41.20 Trifecta £158.70 Pool: £302.45 - 1.41winning units..
Owner Jason Gibbons **Bred** Forenaghts Stud **Trained** Woodingdean, E Sussex
■ Stewards' Enquiry : T G McLaughlin one-day ban: failed to ride to draw (Sep 15)

FOCUS
A reasonable race for the grade, but as usual over this sort of trip at Lingfield, the early pace was just modest. The form looks reasonable rated around the placed horses.
Mister Right(IRE) Official explanation: jockey said gelding had no more to give

5577 MARSH GREEN CLAIMING STKS 1m 2f (P)
3:10 (3:11) (Class 6) 3-Y-0+ **£2,590** (£770; £385; £192) **Stalls Low**

Form RPR

16/0 **1** **What's Up Doc (IRE)**[32] 4576 7-9-9 75.......... JackMitchell[(3)] 8 69
(Mrs T J Hill) *t.k.h: chsd ldr tl led 3f out: rdn over 2f out: 2l clr 1f out: drvn out* **11/4**[2]

1101 **2** *nk* **Nawamees (IRE)**[46] 4123 10-9-12 79..........(p) FergusSweeney 3 68
(G L Moore) *s.i.s: pushed along early: settled in tch: effrt to chse ldrs and rdn 2f out: little imp tl r.o wl last 100yds: nt quite rch wnr* **4/5**[1]

3320 **3** *¾* **My Mirasol**[18] 5018 4-9-5 62.......... DaneO'Neill 6 60
(D E Cantillon) *in tch: chsd wnr 3f out: rdn over 2f out: kpt on same pce fnl f* **7/1**[3]

The Form Book, Raceform Ltd, Compton, RG20 6NL

6000 **4** 4 1/2 **Mtoto Girl**[4] 5429 4-8-4 36 MarcHalford(3) 1 39
(J J Bridger) *chsd ldrs: rdn over 2f out: outpcd by ldng trio wl over 1f out* **66/1**

460 **5** 1 **Has To Be Abacus (IRE)**[44] 4182 3-8-9 48 PatCosgrave 10 46
(A B Haynes) *stdd s: hld up bhd: hdwy 3f out: nt clr run bnd jst over 2f out: no ch w ldrs after* **20/1**

3000 **6** nk **Bold Phoenix (IRE)**[8] 5312 7-9-8 46 (t) HayleyTurner 9 51
(Miss Amy Weaver) *hld up in last trio: hdwy and rdn 3f out: wl outpcd 2f out: no ch w ldrs after* **20/1**

0-50 **7** 6 **Height Of Spirits**[89] 392 6-8-12 41 RobertHavlin 7 29
(T D McCarthy) *mounted on crse: t.k.h: hld up in midfield: effrt 3f out: wkng whn hung lft bnd jst over 2f out: no ch after* **20/1**

4-00 **8** 4 1/2 **Grand Symphony**[13] 5168 4-8-9 53 (tp) TPO'Shea 4 17
(B I Case) *stdd s: hld up bhd: nvr a factor* **33/1**

0060 **9** 6 **Lady Lorins**[21] 4932 4-8-7 39 AlanDaly 2 3
(Andrew Turnell) *sn rdn along to ld: hdd 3f out: wknd qckly over 2f out* **50/1**

2m 5.56s (-1.04) **Going Correction** +0.025s/f (Slow)
WFA 3 from 4yo+ 7lb **9** Ran SP% **115.4**
Speed ratings (Par 101): **105,104,104,100,99 99,94,91,86**
toteswinger: 1&2 £2.00, 1&3 £1.10, 2&3 £1.80. CSF £4.88 TOTE £2.90: £1.50, £1.02, £1.50; EX 5.80 Trifecta £25.40 Pool: £757.15 - 22.02 winning units..
Owner Andrew Barr **Bred** James J Monaghan **Trained** Aston Rowant, Oxon

FOCUS
A modest claimer than only really concerned three horses. They went just an ordinary pace and the first two appeared to be well below last year's best form using the fourth to sixth as guides.

5578 ONE TO ONE OFFICE SOLUTIONS MAIDEN STKS (DIV I) 7f
3:40 (3:44) (Class 5) 2-Y-O **£3,238** (£963; £481; £240) **Stalls** High

Form RPR

0 **1** **Aurorian (IRE)**[8] 5314 2-9-3 0 RichardHughes 11 81
(R Hannon) *mde all on stands' side: rdn over 1f out: in command fnl f* **11/1**[3]

22 **2** 1 3/4 **Imaam**[45] 4151 2-9-3 0 RHills 10 77
(J L Dunlop) *chsd wnr thrght: rdn wl over 1f out: one pce after* **2/5**[1]

0 **3** 4 **Aqwaal (IRE)**[24] 4826 2-9-3 0 DaneO'Neill 1 69+
(E A L Dunlop) *racd off the pce in midfield: hdwy on outer over 2f out: chsd ldng pair over 1f out: no imp* **16/1**

4 4 **Sgt Roberts (IRE)** 2-9-3 0 SimonWhitworth 9 59+
(J S Moore) *awkward s and slowly away: wl bhd: hdwy over 2f out: r.o fnl f: wnt modest 4th nr fin* **50/1**

5 nk **Calligrapher (USA)** 2-9-3 0 PhilipRobinson 2 56
(M A Jarvis) *chsd ldrs: rdn over 3f out: chsd ldng pair over 2f out: no imp and wl btn fnl f* **8/1**[2]

0 **6** 3 **Beaubrav**[80] 3001 2-9-3 0 AlanMunro 6 49
(P W D'Arcy) *racd off the pce in midfield: rdn and outpcd over 2f out: n.d* **14/1**

7 3 1/4 **Some Time Good (IRE)** 2-9-3 0 TPO'Shea 5 41
(M R Channon) *hld up in midfield: rdn and struggling over 2f out: no ch after* **33/1**

8 1 1/2 **Remaah (IRE)** 2-9-3 0 LiamJones 3 37+
(W J Haggas) *s.i.s: a bhd* **20/1**

9 3 1/2 **Double Act** 2-9-3 0 ShaneKelly 7 28
(J Noseda) *towards rr: rdn after 2f: nvr a factor* **12/1**

10 2 **Ma Patrice** 2-8-12 0 RobertHavlin 4 18
(T D McCarthy) *v.s.a: a wl bhd* **66/1**

11 3 **Green Onions** 2-8-12 0 GabrielHannon(5) 8 16
(D J S Ffrench Davis) *sddle slipped on way to s: racd freely: pressed ldrs tl wknd qckly over 2f out* **50/1**

1m 23.36s (0.06) **Going Correction** -0.125s/f (Firm) **11** Ran SP% **124.2**
Speed ratings (Par 95): **94,92,87,82,82 79,75,73,69,67 63**
toteswinger: 1&2 £3.40, 1&3 £5.20, 2&3 £6.50. CSF £16.31 TOTE £14.20: £2.70, £1.02, £3.90; EX 22.60 Trifecta £261.00 Pool: £691.56 - 1.96 winning units..
Owner Martin Mitchell **Bred** Richard Moses Bloodstock **Trained** East Everleigh, Wilts

FOCUS
The draw played its part with Aurorian, next to the stands' rail in stall 11, being followed home by the odds-on favourite, Imaam, who was in ten, although they were the best two horses in the race. The winning time was 2.46 seconds quicker than the second division, although that is misleading as this race was run at a much stronger pace. The form is rated at face value for now.

NOTEBOOK
Aurorian(IRE) ◆, whose stable won a division of this race last year, improved significantly on the form he showed when finishing down the field after being hampered on his debut over 1m on the soft at Goodwood. While he obviously had the run of the race on the best ground, he is a horse with plenty of size and scope and it would be silly to underestimate him. He is bred to come into his own over middle-distances next year and rates as a very useful prospect. (op 9-1 tchd 12-1)
Imaam found one too good for the third race in succession (and the second as favourite). He didn't seem to do much wrong and is probably even a little better than he showed as the winner had the benefit of the favoured rail, but he was always being outstayed by that rival. He finished nicely clear of the remainder and obviously gets this trip, but there is plenty of speed in his pedigree and he gives the impression he might be worth a try over 6f when there is bit of cut in the ground. (op 8-15 tchd 4-7 in a place)
Aqwaal(IRE), whose trainer won a division of this race last year, was well held in third, but emerges with plenty of credit as he was drawn worst of all in stall one. This was a big improvement on the form he showed first-time up at Newmarket and he gives the impression he is still learning, so there should be better to come again. (op 20-1 tchd 14-1)
Sgt Roberts(IRE), a 26,000gns gelded son of Diktat and half-brother to the stable's regular middle-distance all-weather winner Sgt Schultz, out of a 1m juvenile winner, showed ability on his debut. He was green early, but plugged on into fourth and will know a lot more next time. Easier ground may also suit better. (op 40-1)
Calligrapher(USA), a son of Rahy, chased the pace but weakened rather tamely and probably needed this. (tchd 17-2 and 9-1 in places)
Remaah(IRE), a son of Green Desert who was carrying his owner's third colours, did not enjoy the clearest of runs but basically looked in need of the experience. (op 25-1)
Double Act, whose trainer won the following division with a well-backed newcomer, was a first runner trained by Jeremy Noseda for Highclere Thoroughbred Racing, but he showed little. He will want further next year. (op 10-1 tchd 9-1)

5579 ONE TO ONE OFFICE SOLUTIONS MAIDEN STKS (DIV II) 7f
4:10 (4:13) (Class 5) 2-Y-O **£3,238** (£963; £361; £361) **Stalls** High

Form RPR

1 **Sans Frontieres (IRE)** 2-9-3 0 ShaneKelly 9 73+
(J Noseda) *t.k.h: hld up in tch: grad edgd out lft fr over 1f out: rdn to ld wl ins fnl f: pushed out* **5/6**[1]

2 nk **Rafaan (USA)** 2-9-3 0 J-PGuillambert 8 72+
(M Johnston) *hld up in rr of main gp: swtchd lft and hdwy jst over 1f out: n.m.r thrght fnl f: r.o to go 2nd last strides* **10/1**

0 **3** nk **Admirable Duque (IRE)**[30] 4625 2-9-3 0 TQuinn 7 68
(D J S Ffrench Davis) *stdd and bmpd s: hld up in midfield: hdwy and rdn wl over 1f out: pressed ldrs ins fnl f: unable qckn nr fin* **11/1**

3 dht **Beat Up** 2-9-3 0 LPKeniry 3 68
(P R Chamings) *s.i.s: hld up in tch: plld out and hdwy jst over 2f out: rdn to ld 1f out: hdd and no ex wl ins fnl f* **50/1**

5 **5** 1 1/4 **Fajita**[74] 3158 2-9-3 0 RobertWinston 11 65
(M G Quinlan) *led at stdy gallop: rdn jst over 2f out: hdd 1f out: kpt on same pce last 100yds* **12/1**

0 **6** 1 1/2 **Rawaaj**[93] 2592 2-9-3 0 RHills 10 63+
(Sir Michael Stoute) *hld up in bhd ldrs: rdn wl over 1f out: n.m.r ent fnl f: kpt on same pce* **8/1**[3]

7 1 1/4 **Fieriness (IRE)** 2-9-3 0 LDettori 4 58
(Saeed Bin Suroor) *in tch: hdwy to press ldrs 4f out: ev ch and rdn 2f out: wknd ins fnl f* **4/1**[2]

0 **8** 1 1/4 **Roar Of Applause**[17] 5072 2-9-3 0 AlanMunro 1 55
(B J Meehan) *chsd ldr: ev ch and rdn over 2f out: wknd ins fnl f* **25/1**

9 3 **Merdaam** 2-9-3 0 TPO'Shea 6 48
(J L Dunlop) *wnt lft s: rn green and a in last pair* **20/1**

10 1/2 **Urban Space** 2-9-3 0 StephenDonohoe 2 46+
(B G Powell) *s.i.s: rn green and a bhd* **40/1**

1m 25.82s (2.52) **Going Correction** -0.125s/f (Firm) **10** Ran SP% **123.8**
Speed ratings (Par 95): **80,79,79,79,77 76,74,73,69,69**
Place AD £1.00, BU £4.90. Trif: SF/R/AD £166.70, SF/R/BU £203.30, Pool: £549.72 AD 1.22 w/u, BU 0.81 w/u; toteswinger: 1&2 £4.50, 1&AD £2.20, 2&AD £7.10, 1&BU £11.30, 2&BU £21.40 CSF £11.19 TOTE £2.10: £1.10, £2.80; EX 12.30.
Owner Sir Robert Ogden **Bred** The Lavington Stud **Trained** Newmarket, Suffolk

FOCUS
Plenty of nice types from big stables took their chance, and this looked a fair maiden beforehand, but they went steady, resulting in a bunch finish and the form looks modest. The winning time was 2.46 seconds slower than the first division, as a result of the slow pace, and the form needs treating with caution, although the race should still produce its share of winners. There wasn't the same bias to those on the rail as there had appeared to be in the previous race.

NOTEBOOK
Sans Frontieres(IRE) ◆, a Galileo half-brother to among others smart miler Kootenay, out of a 7f juvenile winner who was later useful over 1m2f, has a host of big-race entries from 7f upwards and was all the rage beforehand. He justified the support, but things hardly panned out ideally as, having raced keenly, he was stuck behind horses and had to be switched wide to get a clear run inside the final two furlongs. However, once in the open, his jockey always looked confident and he is a fair bit better than the bare form suggests. He may now be aimed at a conditions race over 7f or 1m, after which his trainer will decide whether he tackles something better this season. (op 5-4 tchd 6-4)
Rafaan(USA) ◆, a son of Gulch, does not have any big-race entries and he carried his owner's third colours, but he shaped with a deal of promise. He ran green mid-race, but came back on the bridle inside the final three furlongs, only to be denied a clear run when trying to make a move. He weaved his way through and picked up nicely in the circumstances, but the line was always coming too soon. He should win a similar event next time, especially if given a positive ride. (op 8-1)
Beat Up, a gelded son of Beat Hollow, travelled nicely out wide for much of the way and this was a very pleasing introduction. It would be unwise to get carried away, as this was a slowly run race, but he clearly has a fair amount of ability. (op 33-1 tchd 10-1)
Admirable Duque(IRE), backed at big prices, improved significantly on the form he showed on his debut at Salisbury with a very creditable effort, especially as he made his move out widest and was not given too hard a time once his winning chance had gone. There should be more to come. (op 33-1 tchd 10-1)
Fajita, a beaten favourite on his debut over 6f at Great Leighs, very much had the run of the race against the rail and as such may be flattered. He might to better back over 6f and will have the option of taking the handicap route after one more run. (op 8-1)
Rawaaj, the owner's first string on jockey bookings/colours, improved significantly on the form he showed on his debut over 6f at Doncaster and is even better than the bare result, as he was another who was denied a clear run. (op 7-1 tchd 10-1)
Fieriness(IRE), a gelded son of Pivotal, was well held and an entry in a Brighton maiden suggests he is not one of his stable's better juveniles. (op 3-1)

5580 SCOTS GROUP H'CAP 7f
4:40 (4:40) (Class 4) (0-85,85) 3-Y-O **£6,308** (£1,888; £944; £472; £235) **Stalls** High

Form RPR

5343 **1** **Noble Citizen (USA)**[22] 4893 3-8-13 80 StephenDonohoe 8 93
(D M Simcock) *mde virtually all: rdn 2f out: styd on wl fnl f* **6/1**[2]

5123 **2** 1 1/2 **Arabian Spirit**[19] 4983 3-9-4 85 RichardHughes 11 94
(E A L Dunlop) *chsd ldrs: swtchd lft and rdn 2f out: chsd wnr over 1f out: kpt on same pce u.p fnl f* **2/1**[1]

4162 **3** 2 1/2 **Badweia (USA)**[17] 5073 3-8-10 77 RHills 7 79
(J L Dunlop) *s.i.s: sn pushed along and outpcd in rr: rdn and hdwy over 1f out: styd on fnl f: wnt 3rd wl ins fnl f: nvr trbld ldrs* **8/1**[3]

5255 **4** nk **Astrodonna**[33] 4539 3-8-8 75 AlanMunro 2 76
(M H Tompkins) *stdd s: bhd: hdwy 3f out: jostled over 2f out: sn rdn: swtchd lft ent fnl f: wnt 3rd wl ins fnl f tl nr fin* **10/1**

1030 **5** nk **Lodi (IRE)**[17] 5056 3-8-13 80 (t) IanMongan 1 81
(J Akehurst) *racd on outer: bhd: hdwy and jostled over 2f out: chsd ldng pair over 1f out: no imp after: lost 2 pls wl ins fnl f* **16/1**

4605 **6** 2 3/4 **Amylee (IRE)**[51] 3977 3-8-3 75 DavidProbert(5) 9 68
(C G Cox) *in tch: rdn 4f out: no imp fr wl over 1f out* **8/1**[3]

1010 **7** 1/2 **Benedetto**[12] 5185 3-8-8 75 (p) PatCosgrave 10 67
(Mrs A J Perrett) *s.i.s: in tch in midfield: rdn over 2f out: no hdwy* **12/1**

4311 **8** 1 3/4 **Stand In Flames**[16] 5088 3-8-6 80 CharlesEddery(7) 5 67
(Pat Eddery) *stdd s: racd on outer: hld up in midfeld: rdn and brief effrt wl over 1f out: no ch fnl f* **6/1**[2]

0400 **9** 1 3/4 **Sam's Cross (IRE)**[5] 5397 3-8-11 78 (p) DarrenWilliams 4 60
(K R Burke) *racd keenly: sn pressing ldr: rdn over 2f out: wknd wl over 1f out* **25/1**

0006 **10** 9 **Solent Ridge (IRE)**[52] 3897 3-9-3 84 LPKeniry 3 42
(J S Moore) *chsd ldrs: rdn and struggling 3f out: wl bhd fr over 1f out* **16/1**

1m 21.59s (-1.71) **Going Correction** -0.125s/f (Firm) **10** Ran SP% **116.5**
Speed ratings (Par 103): **104,102,99,99,98 95,95,93,91,80**
toteswinger: 1&2 £3.70, 1&3 £6.50, 2&3 £3.90. CSF £18.33 CT £98.03 TOTE £8.70: £2.00, £1.40, £2.90; EX 23.00 Trifecta £153.90 Pool: £368.29 - 1.77 winning units..
Owner Khalifa Dasmal **Bred** Don M Robinson **Trained** Newmarket, Suffolk

FOCUS
A fair handicap but, just as in the first division of the juvenile maiden, the stands' rail looked a big advantage. The winner is rated a 4lb improver with the runner-up to his mark.

5581 ASHFORD ENVIRONMENTAL NURSERY — 6f
5:10 (5:10) (Class 6) (0-65,65) 2-Y-O — **£2,590** (£770; £385; £192) **Stalls** High

Form — RPR

010 **1** — **Swingfire (USA)**[9] [5274] 2-8-13 **64**............................(p) AndreaAtzeni(7) 7 — 66
(R M H Cowell) *hld up bhd: swtchd lft and hdwy 2f out: rdn to ld 1f out: hung lft fnl f: r.o wl* **6/1**[3]

0110 **2** 1/2 **Rocket Rob (IRE)**[4] [5432] 2-9-6 **64**............................ StephenDonohoe 10 — 65
(S A Callaghan) *s.i.s: hld up bhd: edgd out lft and hdwy 2f out: drvn over 1f out: ev ch ins fnl f: edgd rt and no ex nr fin* **3/1**[2]

505 **3** 1 3/4 **Ray Of Joy**[22] [4905] 2-9-3 **61**............................ RobertWinston 8 — 57+
(J R Jenkins) *hld up in midfield: hdwy over 2f out: rdn to ld over 1f out: hdd 1f out: keeping on one pce and hld whn short of room and snatched up nr fin* **17/2**

002 **4** 5 **Intrepid Lady (IRE)**[25] [4764] 2-9-1 **62**............................ TravisBlock(3) 1 — 42
(J C Tuck) *in tch in midfield: hdwy over 2f out: ev ch and drvn over 1f out: wknd fnl f* **20/1**

6004 **5** 1 1/2 **Call Me Courageous (IRE)**[15] [5116] 2-9-7 **65**............................ PatCosgrave 4 — 41
(A B Haynes) *bmpd s: sn rcvrd and w ldr: rdn and hung lft fr over 2f out: wknd ent fnl f* **20/1**

454 **6** 1 3/4 **Street Of Hope (USA)**[70] [3331] 2-9-6 **64**............................ DaneO'Neill 2 — 35
(George Baker) *wnt rt s: bhd on outer: rdn 3f out: nvr trbld ldrs* **15/2**

0010 **7** 1 **Flawless Diamond (IRE)**[9] [5294] 2-9-3 **61**............................(b) LPKeniry 6 — 29
(J S Moore) *wnt rt s: chsd ldrs: rdn over 2f out: sn struggling: wl bhd over 1f out* **12/1**

0006 **8** 1/2 **Join Up**[26] [4729] 2-8-12 **61**............................(p) DavidProbert(5) 5 — 27
(W R Swinburn) *led and sn crossed to stands rail: rdn 2f out: hdd over 1f out: wknd qckly ent fnl f* **13/2**

0102 **9** 6 **Anacaona (IRE)**[27] [4706] 2-9-3 **61**............................ RichardHughes 11 — 9
(R Hannon) *in tch in midfield: rdn 3f out: wl bhd last 2f* **11/4**[1]

1m 10.58s (-0.62) **Going Correction** -0.125s/f (Firm) — **9** Ran SP% **118.8**
Speed ratings (Par 93): **99,98,96,89,87 85,83,83,75**
toteswinger: 1&2 £5.60, 1&3 £12.10, 2&3 £9.60. CSF £25.12 CT £152.44 TOTE £8.70: £2.40, £1.20, £2.40; EX 30.90 Trifecta £242.00 Part won. Pool: £242 - 0.10 winning units..
Owner Prestige Racing **Bred** Mike G Rutherford **Trained** Six Mile Bottom, Cambs
■ Stewards' Enquiry : Andrea Atzeni two-day ban: careless riding (Sep 15-16)

FOCUS
Just a modest nursery and not that much strength in depth, so the form is best treated cautiously. The first three home came from well off the pace, suggesting that the leaders may have gone off a little too quick. The stands' rail again looked to be a help.

NOTEBOOK
Swingfire(USA) failed to beat a single rival in a much better race than this at Newmarket on his previous start, but he returned to the sort of form that saw him successful at that very track two starts back, winning off a 4lb higher mark this time. He did much of his racing against the favoured rail and picked up well when getting a clear run through, still towards the stands' side. Considering everything went his way, he appeals as one to oppose off a higher mark next time. (op 7-1)
Rocket Rob(IRE) failed to give his true running on the Polytrack here four days earlier, but this was better. His effort is all the more creditable considering he made his move much wider than the winner. (op 7-2)
Ray Of Joy ran with credit on her nursery debut after showing some ability in maidens. She was slightly squeezed up by the front two close home, but was held at the time. (op 12-1 tchd 8-1)
Intrepid Lady(IRE), picked up out of Mick Channon's yard after running second in a Bath seller on her latest start, ran with credit in this tougher company. She might be capable of even better back on easy ground. (op 14-1)
Call Me Courageous(IRE) is another who might want easy ground. (op 16-1)
Street Of Hope(USA), who has left John Hills since she was last seen over two months previously, was never really travelling after starting awkwardly. (op 8-1 tchd 7-1)
Anacaona(IRE) was nowhere near the form she showed when runner-up in a similar event at Chepstow on her previous start. Official explanation: vet said filly pulled up stiff (op 3-1 tchd 10-3)

5582 PREMIER SHOWFREIGHT H'CAP — 6f
5:40 (5:40) (Class 6) (0-50,55) 3-Y-O+ — **£2,729** (£806; £403) **Stalls** High

Form — RPR

2204 **1** — **Music Box Express**[17] [5074] 4-8-7 **50**............................(t) MatthewDavies(7) 10 — 66
(George Baker) *mde all on stands' rail: clr fr 1/2-way: rdn over 1f out: wl clr fnl f: eased towards fin* **11/4**[1]

0302 **2** 6 **Norcroft**[26] [4749] 6-8-13 **49**............................(p) TGMcLaughlin 2 — 46
(Mrs C A Dunnett) *short of room sn after s: sn bustled along in rr: hdwy u.p over 1f out: snatched 2nd fnl strides: no ch w wnr* **4/1**[2]

5321 **3** shd **Penrice Castle**[4] [5421] 3-9-0 **55** 6ex............................ HaddenFrost(3) 4 — 51
(R Hannon) *in tch: rdn to chse wnr wl over 1f out: no imp: lost 2nd last stride* **6/1**[3]

0005 **4** shd **Rosie Cross (IRE)**[14] [5152] 4-8-5 **48**............................ DanielBlackett(7) 3 — 44
(Eve Johnson Houghton) *short of room sn after s: hld up in midfield: hdwy over 2f out: kpt on fnl f: nvr nr wnr* **14/1**

030 **5** hd **Lost All Alone**[224] [255] 4-8-6 **49**............................ ChrisHough(7) 1 — 45
(D M Simcock) *hld up bhd: hdwy on outer 1/2-way: rdn over 1f out: kpt on but nvr nr wnr* **14/1**

2045 **6** hd **Miracle Baby**[24] [4825] 6-8-12 **48**............................ RobertHavlin 5 — 43
(J A Geake) *chsd wnr: rdn 1/2-way: lost 2nd wl over 1f out: one pce after* **8/1**

0002 **7** nk **Mr Forthright**[17] [5074] 4-8-12 **48**............................(b) PatCosgrave 6 — 42
(J M Bradley) *in tch in midfield: rdn 1/2-way: drvn and kpt on same pce fr wl over 1f out* **16/1**

2144 **8** 2 **Mr Loire**[208] [445] 4-9-0 **50**............................(b) DeanMcKeown 9 — 38
(K G Wingrove) *hld up bhd: n.d* **14/1**

0544 **9** nk **Kempsey**[8] [5315] 6-8-10 **49**............................(b) MarcHalford(3) 7 — 36
(J J Bridger) *chsd ldrs: rdn 1/2-way: no ch fr over 1f out* **6/1**[3]

6000 **10** 3 1/4 **Sherjawy (IRE)**[111] [2075] 4-8-13 **49**............................(b) SamHitchcott 11 — 25
(Miss Z C Davison) *hld up bhd: swtchd lft and rdn over 2f out: no prog* **14/1**

1m 10.22s (-0.98) **Going Correction** -0.125s/f (Firm)
WFA 3 from 4yo+ 2lb — **10** Ran SP% **118.9**
Speed ratings (Par 101): **101,93,92,92,92 92,91,89,88,84**
toteswinger: 1&2 £3.70, 1&3 £4.90, 2&3 £4.60. CSF £13.73 CT £63.05 TOTE £4.30: £1.90, £1.50, £2.90; EX 19.00 Trifecta £66.10 Pool: £401.30 - 4.49 winning units. Place 6: £7.31 Place 5: £4.36.
Owner The Betfair Radioheads **Bred** Dachel Stud **Trained** Moreton Morrell, Warwicks

FOCUS
A moderate sprint handicap and they finished in a heap behind Music Box Express, who was soon in front against the greatly advantageous stands' rail and never looked back. The winner is rated to last winter's best with the third to recent turf form.
Sherjawy(IRE) Official explanation: trainer said gelding was unsuited by the good ground

T/Plt: £7.50 to a £1 stake. Pool: £52,132.18. 5,055.59 winning tickets. T/Qpdt: £2.50 to a £1 stake. Pool: £3,585.40. 1,050.80 winning tickets. SP

5309 GOODWOOD (R-H)
Tuesday, September 2

OFFICIAL GOING: Soft
A total of 24.6mm of overnight rain resulted in a host of non-runners throughout the card. The stands' rail was a big advantage in the straight.
Wind: fresh half against Weather: heavy rain this morning now dry and brightening up

5583 BOLLINGER CHAMPAGNE CHALLENGE SERIES H'CAP (FOR GENTLEMAN AMATEUR RIDERS) — 1m 3f
2:00 (2:00) (Class 5) (0-70,70) 4-Y-O+ — **£3,123** (£968; £484; £242) **Stalls** High

Form — RPR

0005 **1** — **Fort Churchill (IRE)**[27] [4739] 7-11-2 **70**............................(bt) MrDaleSwift(5) 8 — 76
(B Ellison) *in tch: hdwy to chse ldr over 3f out: led over 2f out: edgd lft over 1f out: styd on wl* **11/1**

6200 **2** 2 **Optimus (USA)**[18] [5069] 6-11-6 **69**............................ MrSWalker 1 — 71
(B G Powell) *chsd ldrs: wnt 2nd 6f out: led 3f out: sn hdd: swtchd rt over 1f out: kpt on same pce fnl f* **12/1**

0203 **3** hd **York Cliff**[4] [5450] 10-10-4 **56** oh6............................ MrBenBrisbourne(3) 14 — 58
(W M Brisbourne) *hld up towards rr: hdwy over 2f out: styd on u.p fr over 1f out: wnt 3rd nr fin: nt rch wnr* **14/1**

6152 **4** 1 **Desert Hawk**[4] [5450] 7-10-2 **56** oh4............................(b) MrHarryChalloner(5) 7 — 56
(W M Brisbourne) *hld up in midfield: hdwy 4f out: chsd ldng pair 2f out: hung rt u.p and kpt on same pce after: lost 3rd nr fin* **13/2**

2311 **5** 3/4 **Sand Repeal (IRE)**[4] [5450] 6-10-13 **67** 6ex............................ MrRBirkett(5) 4 — 66
(Miss J Feilden) *chsd ldr tl 6f out: lost pl and swtchd rt over 2f out: sn rdn: kpt on but nvr pce to threaten ldrs* **4/1**[2]

545 **6** 2 3/4 **Bienheureux**[13] [5183] 7-10-4 **58**............................(t) MrBJToomey(5) 3 — 52
(Miss Gay Kelleway) *hld up in rr: effrt towards centre over 3f out: kpt on same pce fr over 1f out* **8/1**

06B4 **7** shd **Bollywood (IRE)**[9] [5312] 5-10-2 **56** oh11............................ MrRyanBird(5) 12 — 50
(J J Bridger) *t.k.h: chsd ldrs early: grad stdd into midfield: rdn and effrt over 2f out: wknd wl over 1f out* **33/1**

006/ **8** 7 **Wujood**[33] [1373] 6-10-7 **56** oh1............................(t) MrDRCook 10 — 38
(Mrs L J Young) *hld up towards rr: rdn and struggling over 3f out: no ch after* **14/1**

0226 **9** 1 1/4 **She's So Pretty (IRE)**[4] [5458] 4-10-3 **57**............................(b) MrJoshuaMoore(5) 9 — 37
(G L Moore) *hld up in rr: shkn up over 3f out: no prog: wl btn fr over 2f out* **11/4**[1]

6002 **10** 4 **Balnagore**[25] [4829] 4-11-4 **67**............................ MrSDobson 13 — 40
(J L Dunlop) *sn led: hdd 3f out: sn dropped out: no ch and eased ins fnl f* **11/2**[3]

05P/ **11** 11 **Cosmic Messenger (FR)**[707] [5587] 5-10-0 **56** oh1...(t) MrTJCannon(7) 2 — 11
(L A Dace) *bhd: rdn and lost tch 4f out: wl bhd and eased ins fnl f* **66/1**

2m 42.64s (14.34) **Going Correction** +1.00s/f (Soft) — **11** Ran SP% **120.3**
Speed ratings (Par 103): **87,85,85,84,84 82,82,76,76,73 65**
toteswinger: 1&2 £19.80, 1&3 £25.50, 2&3 £21.40. CSF £138.78 CT £1870.50 TOTE £12.40: £2.90, £3.70, £4.30; EX 87.90.
Owner Black and White Diamond Partnership **Bred** P H Betts **Trained** Norton, N Yorks

FOCUS
Just a modest amateur riders' handicap and weak form with the third and fourth both out of the handicap. They seemed to go an even pace, but the winning time was over 20sec slower than standard, confirming the ground to be testing, even allowing for these horses carrying more weight than in a conventional race. They headed over towards the stands side in the straight and the near rail looked advantageous.

5584 EUROPEAN BREEDERS' FUND COMPTON MEDIAN AUCTION MAIDEN FILLIES' STKS — 6f
2:35 (2:35) (Class 5) 2-Y-O — **£3,561** (£1,059; £529; £264) **Stalls** Low

Form — RPR

3 **1** — **Lady Rusty (IRE)**[29] [4692] 2-9-0 0............................ JimCrowley 12 — 73+
(P Winkworth) *chsd ldrs: wnt 2nd over 3f out: rdn to ld wl over 1f out: styd on wl to forge ahd last 50yds* **3/1**[1]

04 **2** 1 1/4 **Equinine (IRE)**[15] [5147] 2-9-0 0............................ MichaelHills 10 — 69
(B W Hills) *bmpd and short of room s: bustled along early: hdwy on outer 1/2-way: ev ch and rdn wl over 1f out: w wnr tl tired and btn last 50yds* **8/1**

03 **3** 1/2 **Brooksby**[23] [4905] 2-9-0 0............................ RyanMoore 3 — 67+
(R Hannon) *in tch: lost pl 1/2-way: swtchd rt and rdn over 2f out: r.o ins fnl f: wnt 3rd last 75yds: nt rch ldng pair* **4/1**[2]

0 **4** 1 1/2 **Assent (IRE)**[15] [5147] 2-9-0 0............................ FergusSweeney 4 — 63
(B R Millman) *s.i.s: t.k.h: hld up in tch: hdwy over 2f out: ev ch over 1f out: wknd ins fnl f* **14/1**

5 1 1/2 **Ailsa Craig (IRE)** 2-9-0 0............................ RichardHughes 7 — 58+
(R Hannon) *s.i.s: bhd and pushed along: styd on steadily ins fnl f: nvr trbld ldrs* **8/1**

64 **6** nk **Bella Rowena**[33] [4554] 2-9-0 0............................ WilliamBuick 8 — 57+
(A M Balding) *led: rdn over 2f out: hdd wl over 1f out: wknd ent fnl f* **5/1**

3 **7** hd **Albertine Rose**[15] [5147] 2-9-0 0............................ MartinDwyer 13 — 57
(W R Muir) *t.k.h: hld up in tch: hdwy over 2f out: ev ch and rdn over 1f out: wknd ins fnl f: tired last 100yds* **9/2**[3]

00 **8** nk **Sapphire Rose**[24] [4870] 2-9-0 0............................ RichardKingscote 2 — 56
(J G Portman) *in tch in midfield: rdn 1/2-way: n.d after* **40/1**

9 6 **Rebetica** 2-9-0 0............................ DaneO'Neill 9 — 38
(H Candy) *wnt rt s: sn chsng ldr: rdn over 3f out: wknd u.p over 2f out* **20/1**

1m 18.41s (6.21) **Going Correction** +0.85s/f (Soft) — **9** Ran SP% **115.9**
Speed ratings (Par 92): **92,90,89,87,85 85,85,84,76**
toteswinger: 1&2 £5.20, 1&3 £3.50, 2&3 £5.50. CSF £27.92 TOTE £4.70: £1.50, £2.50, £1.80; EX 37.30.
Owner Mrs I Russell **Bred** Corduff Stud **Trained** Chiddingfold, Surrey

FOCUS
The bare form of this juvenile fillies' maiden looks just fair, but there were some interesting types for the future and the race should produce winners. They raced stands' side and the winner had the benefit of the rail in the final furlong.

NOTEBOOK
Lady Rusty(IRE) improved on the form she showed when third in an ordinary Windsor maiden on her debut with a battling success. She showed a good attitude under pressure, having been on the pace from the outset, although she did have the benefit of the stands' rail, whereas the runner-up was out wide throughout. She is clearly game and handles testing ground well. (op 7-2)

Equinine(IRE), whose trainer won this last year, improved on the form she showed on her first two starts, reversing recent Windsor placings with Albertine Rose, and emerges with plenty of credit as she was stuck out wide throughout. She was suited by the soft ground and, although not up to her Cheveley Park entry, she should win a race or two this year. She now has the option of nurseries. (op 7-1 tchd 13-2)
Brooksby ◆ stayed on again after getting outpaced mid-race. Just as when third over this trip at Windsor last time, she shaped as though in need of another furlong and will be interesting if switched to nursery company and stepped up to 7f on easy ground. (op 9-2 tchd 7-2)
Assent(IRE) improved on the form she showed when down the field on her debut at Windsor, but was a little too keen early. She looked inexperienced and there ought to be more to come. (op 33-1)
Ailsa Craig(IRE) ◆, a 55,000euros daughter of Chevalier, was well off the pace early but ran on nicely late on despite not being given a hard time. She will know a lot more next time and should be hard to beat in similar company. (tchd 9-1)
Bella Rowena was another not given too hard a time once her chance had gone and she will be interesting when switching to nurseries. (op 4-1)
Albertine Rose shaped well when third on her debut at Windsor, but she was unable to confirm form with Equinine or Assent and finished tired. (tchd 5-1)
Sapphire Rose Official explanation: trainer said filly was unsuited by the soft ground

5585 SEPTEMBER NURSERY STKS (H'CAP) 1m

3:10 (3:10) (Class 4) (0-85,81) 2-Y-O **£3,885** (£1,156; £577; £288) **Stalls** High

Form RPR
004 **1** **Lethal Glaze (IRE)**[19] 5022 2-8-8 **68**............................ RichardHughes 7 70
(R Hannon) *s.i.s: in rr: rdn over 3f out: drvn over 2f out: str run ins fnl f: led last stride* **3/1**[1]
12 **2** *shd* **High Alert**[20] 4968 2-9-7 **81**...(b) LDettori 11 83
(J Noseda) *led: pushed clr over 1f out: rdn ins fnl f: tired last 100yds: ct fnl stride* **10/3**[2]
502 **3** *1* **Miss Sophisticat**[19] 5029 2-8-13 **73**.. PaulDoe 2 73
(W J Knight) *chsd ldr: rdn 3f out: kpt on same pce u.p last 2f* **7/1**
6240 **4** *nk* **Heliodor (USA)**[11] 5244 2-9-6 **80**....................................... RyanMoore 6 79
(R Hannon) *hld up in rr: effrt whn hanging rt and nt clr run 2f out: edgd rt u.p ent fnl f: styd on: nt pce to rch ldrs* **15/2**
306 **5** *1 ½* **Mawjaat (IRE)**[18] 5066 2-8-8 **68**.. RHills 9 64
(J L Dunlop) *hld up in midfield: hdwy 3f out: chsd ldrs and rdn wl over 1f out: wknd ins fnl f* **10/1**
4133 **6** *4* **Lakeman (IRE)**[17] 5107 2-9-3 **77**.. TomEaves 4 64
(B Ellison) *chsd ldrs: rdn over 2f out: wknd qckly ent fnl f* **13/2**
2133 **7** *7* **Jazacosta (USA)**[11] 5242 2-9-7 **81**..................................... JimCrowley 3 52+
(Mrs A J Perrett) *chsd ldrs: rdn over 3f out: wknd qckly over 2f out: eased ins fnl f* **9/2**[3]
630 **8** *14* **Innactualfact**[69] 3373 2-8-4 **64**.................................... CatherineGannon 5 5+
(L A Dace) *stdd s: bhd: rdn over 3f out: wknd over 2f out: t.o and eased fnl f* **50/1**

1m 48.35s (8.45) **Going Correction** +1.00s/f (Soft) **8** Ran SP% **114.9**
Speed ratings (Par 97): **97,96,95,95,94 90,83,69**
toteswinger: 1&2 £3.60, 1&3 £5.80, 2&3 £4.60. CSF £13.28 CT £63.35 TOTE £4.60: £1.60, £1.30, £2.00; EX 13.90.
Owner Nigel Morris **Bred** B Kennedy **Trained** East Everleigh, Wilts

FOCUS

Probably just an ordinary nursery for the grade with the fourth the best guide. The eventual runner-up looked to set a reasonable pace considering the conditions, although he was left alone and was able to gradually wind up the tempo. They raced stands side in the straight and those towards the rail again looked to be at an advantage.

NOTEBOOK

Lethal Glaze(IRE) was a beaten favourite in an ordinary maiden over 7f at Salisbury on his previous start, but he proved well suited by this step up in trip and showed himself on a fair mark on his nursery debut. His sire Verglas, who also sired the winner of the previous race (confirming his progeny are suited by soft ground), was a speedy type, but his dam was a 1m4f winner and he needed every yard of this trip, staying on well from off the pace to get up virtually on the line. He is considered a lazy individual, so there should be more to come, but he is probably going to want at least 1m2f at some point, possibly even this season according to connections. (tchd 10-3 and 7-2 in places)
High Alert won a weak maiden on his debut at Lingfield and had been a beaten favourite last time in a four-runner contest under similar conditions to those he encountered again here, but this was his best effort yet. Although setting a reasonable pace, he was very much allowed the run of the race and also had the benefit of the stands' rail in the straight. He looked the winner inside the final quarter, but just got tired late on. (op 3-1 tchd 7-2)
Miss Sophisticat, making her nursery debut, came under pressure a fair way out but kept plugging on. She might be better suited by a return to a more galloping track. (op 6-1 tchd 8-1)
Heliodor(USA), with the blinkers left off this time, did not enjoy the best of runs and, although not unlucky, is a little better than he was able to show. (op 10-1)
Mawjaat(IRE), upped in trip on here nursery debut, was representing a trainer who had won this race twice in the last seven years. She should be rated a little better than the bare form as she made her move very wide in the straight. (op 9-1 tchd 11-1)
Jazacosta(USA) probably wants quicker ground. (op 5-1)

5586 KBC SUPREME STKS (GROUP 3) 7f

3:45 (3:47) (Class 1) 3-Y-O+ **£36,900** (£13,988; £7,000; £3,490; £1,748) **Stalls** High

Form RPR
230 **1** **Express Wish**[32] 4586 4-8-13 92.. ShaneKelly 1 111
(J Noseda) *hld up in tch: hdwy jst over 2f out: upsides ldr gng wl over 1f out: led ins fnl f: rdn clr: comf* **7/1**
4416 **2** *2 ½* **Welsh Emperor (IRE)**[17] 5095 9-8-13 107..................... TonyCulhane 8 104
(T P Tate) *led: rdn 3f out: jnd over 1f out: hdd ins fnl f: no ch w wnr after* **15/8**[1]
2003 **3** *2* **Beaver Patrol (IRE)**[17] 5095 6-8-13 108..................(v) StephenCarson 7 99
(Eve Johnson Houghton) *chsd ldr: swtchd rt and rdn wl over 2f out: btn over 1f out: plugged on u.p fnl f* **11/4**[2]
1344 **4** *nk* **Appalachian Trail (IRE)**[37] 4459 7-8-13 108..................(b) TomEaves 2 98
(Miss L A Perratt) *s.i.s: hld up in last pl: hdwy on rail over 2f out: hanging rt over 1f out: no imp ent fnl f: wknd fnl 100yds* **7/2**[3]
0640 **5** *31* **Excusez Moi (USA)**[17] 5095 6-8-13 97...........................(b) LiamJones 9 14
(C E Brittain) *led to s: chsd ldng pair tl jst over 2f out: sn wknd: t.o fnl f* **6/1**

1m 32.75s (5.35) **Going Correction** +1.00s/f (Soft)
WFA 3 from 4yo+ 4lb **5** Ran SP% **110.5**
Speed ratings (Par 113): **109,106,103,103,68**
toteswinger: 1&2 £7.40. CSF £20.62 TOTE £7.50: £2.50, £1.70; EX 24.10.
Owner Peter Mitchell **Bred** Cranford Stud **Trained** Newmarket, Suffolk

FOCUS

Four non-runners left a very weak field by Group 3 standards and this was more the sort of line-up one would expect to see for a Listed race or even a conditions contest. They went a good pace in the conditions, with Beaver Patrol hassling Welsh Emperor up front, and that compromised both their chances to further devalue the form. Once again, they raced stands' side in the straight and the rail looked advantageous. The winner is rated a 9lb improver.

NOTEBOOK

Express Wish came into this rated just 92, but he has always looked a horse with plenty of talent. He had not run over 7f or on soft ground since making his racecourse debut, but the combination brought about an improved performance. His jockey was exuding confidence halfway up the straight, looking over both shoulders for dangers, and he found plenty when eventually asked. He will face much tougher tests at this level, but will be one to respect when getting these conditions. Official explanation: trainer had no explanation for the apparent improvement in form (op 13-2 tchd 15-2)
Welsh Emperor(IRE) has not looked quite as good this season as in previous years and he was no match for the winner, who came into this rated 15lb inferior, but he did well to plug on for second considering he was not left alone up front. (op 9-4 tchd 5-2 in a place)
Beaver Patrol(IRE) has looked as good as ever this season, but this ground was probably softer than he wants and he could not sustain his effort after keeping Welsh Emperor honest up front. (op 3-1 tchd 10-3 and 7-2 in places)
Appalachian Trail(IRE) tried to squeezed through against the inside rail in the straight, but he could never muster the pace to pose a serious threat and probably wants better ground. (op 11-4)
Excusez Moi(USA), who had the blinkers back on for the first time since March 2007, was mulish before the start and offered very little in the race. (op 7-1 tchd 11-2)

5587 TURFTV MAIDEN STKS 1m 1f 192y

4:20 (4:22) (Class 5) 3-Y-O **£3,238** (£963; £481; £240) **Stalls** High

Form RPR
-334 **1** **Moville (IRE)**[29] 4695 3-9-3 80.. MichaelHills 4 79+
(B W Hills) *mde all: rdn and drew clr over 1f out: easily* **6/4**[1]
0 **2** *3 ½* **Inquest**[29] 4695 3-9-3 0.. JimCrowley 3 72
(Mrs A J Perrett) *hld up in tch: chsd wnr wl over 2f out: rdn over 2f out: wl hld fnl f* **5/2**[2]
04 **3** *4* **Hammer**[18] 5047 3-9-3 0.. MartinDwyer 8 64
(M P Tregoning) *hld up in tch: rdn and chsd ldng pair over 2f out: wknd 2f out* **5/1**[3]
03 **4** *8* **Mister Ross**[22] 4929 3-9-3 0... GeorgeBaker 1 48
(G L Moore) *chsd ldr tl wl over 2f out: sn btn* **11/2**
0 **5** *65* **Deer Lake (IRE)**[95] 2571 3-9-3 0.. ShaneKelly 6 —
(J Noseda) *in tch tl dropped to last over 6f out: drvn and reluctant 4f out: sn lost tch: virtually p.u fr over 1f out: wl t.o* **9/1**

2m 16.4s (8.40) **Going Correction** +1.00s/f (Soft) **5** Ran SP% **110.6**
Speed ratings (Par 101): **106,103,100,93,41**
toteswinger: 1&2 £4.40. CSF £5.53 TOTE £2.20: £1.60, £1.50; EX 5.70.
Owner John C Grant **Bred** Eclipse Bloodstock **Trained** Lambourn, Berks

FOCUS

Several non-runners weakened what had looked quite an interesting maiden and this turned out be a modest, uncompetitive contest. They again came stands' side in the straight and the best ground looked to be on the rail. The time was very decent given the conditions although the winner probably did not need to improve to score.

5588 BETTING SHOPS BACK TURFTV STKS (H'CAP) 1m

4:55 (4:55) (Class 4) (0-80,79) 3-Y-O+ **£4,857** (£1,445; £722; £360) **Stalls** High

Form RPR
2235 **1** **Thunder Gorge (USA)**[14] 5168 3-8-8 **70**......................... WilliamBuick 2 76
(Mouse Hamilton-Fairley) *t.k.h: chsd ldr: rdn to chal jst over 2f out: led 1f out: drvn fnl f: hld on nr fin* **8/1**
0055 **2** *nk* **Heroes**[19] 5018 4-9-8 **79**... GeorgeBaker 6 85
(C F Wall) *hld up in tch: swtchd rt 3f out: chsd ldng pair jst over 2f out: chal ent fnl f: nt qckn and hld nr fin* **7/2**[2]
3212 **3** *2* **Rum Jungle**[22] 4927 4-9-7 **78**.. DaneO'Neill 5 79
(H Candy) *led: rdn over 2f out: hdd over 1f out: wknd jst ins fnl f* **15/8**[1]
1014 **4** *7* **Monashee Rock (IRE)**[26] 4789 3-8-13 **75**.................. TGMcLaughlin 1 59
(M Salaman) *rrd and wnt lft s: bhd: rdn over 4f out: no ch fr over 2f out* **12/1**
0055 **5** *2 ¼* **Miss Bootylishes**[24] 4872 3-8-13 **75**................................ SteveDrowne 7 54
(A B Haynes) *in tch: rdn over 3f out: wknd over 2f out: no ch after* **12/1**
6006 **6** *6* **Trafalgar Square**[10] 5290 6-8-10 **72**.......................(p) DavidProbert[(5)] 13 38
(M J Attwater) *t.k.h: chsd ldrs: rdn 3f out: wknd qckly jst over 2f out* **9/2**[3]
0146 **7** *1* **Scarlet Oak**[18] 5073 4-8-1 **65** oh2......................................(p) BillyCray[(7)] 8 29
(D J S Ffrench Davis) *hld up in rr: rdn and brief effrt wl over 2f out: wl btn last 2f* **8/1**

1m 48.32s (8.42) **Going Correction** +1.00s/f (Soft)
WFA 3 from 4yo+ 5lb **7** Ran SP% **112.8**
Speed ratings (Par 105): **97,96,94,87,85 79,78**
toteswinger: 1&2 £7.30, 1&3 £3.40, 2&3 £2.00. CSF £34.97 CT £73.93 TOTE £9.20: £3.60, £2.30; EX 40.20.
Owner Bramshill Racing **Bred** Camelia Casby **Trained** Bramshill, Hants
■ Stewards' Enquiry : William Buick three-day ban: used whip with excessive frequency (Sep 16-18)

FOCUS

An ordinary handicap for the grade and they didn't go that quick, so not a race to be too positive about. The stands' side was again the place to be in the straight.
Monashee Rock(IRE) Official explanation: trainer's rep said filly banged its head leaving stalls

5589 BEST UK RACING ON TURFTV STKS (H'CAP) 7f

5:30 (5:30) (Class 4) (0-85,85) 3-Y-O+ **£4,857** (£1,445; £722; £360) **Stalls** High

Form RPR
0106 **1** **Koraleva Tectona (IRE)**[27] 4745 3-8-6 **72**......................... SteveDrowne 2 79
(Pat Eddery) *chsd ldrs: wnt 2nd over 2f out: rdn to ld over 1f out: hdd fnl 100yds: rallied to ld again on post* **3/1**[2]
0000 **2** *nse* **Compton's Eleven**[17] 5096 7-9-5 **81**......................... EdwardCreighton 6 89
(M R Channon) *stdd after s: bhd: pushed along over 4f out: hdwy over 2f out: rdn and ev ch ent fnl f: led last 100yds: hdd on post* **7/2**[3]
0040 **3** *2* **Salient**[9] 5313 4-9-7 **83**.. PaulDoe 5 86
(M J Attwater) *led at gd gallop: rdn over 2f out: hdd over 1f out: wknd ins fnl f* **4/1**
0053 **4** *2 ¼* **Sofia's Star**[13] 5185 3-8-3 **69** oh2..................................(b) WilliamBuick 4 66
(P Winkworth) *t.k.h: chsd ldr tl over 2f out: hung rt over 1f out: no prog after* **9/2**
0040 **5** *¾* **Purus (IRE)**[74] 3222 6-9-6 **82**... GeorgeBaker 8 77
(R A Teal) *taken down early: hld up wl in tch: rdn over 2f out: fnd little and no prog* **11/4**[1]

1m 35.46s (8.06) **Going Correction** +1.00s/f (Soft)
WFA 3 from 4yo+ 4lb **5** Ran SP% **112.1**
Speed ratings (Par 105): **93,92,90,88,87**
toteswinger: 1&2 £7.90. CSF £13.85 TOTE £4.30: £2.20, £2.00; EX 15.40 Place 6: £202.80 Place 5 £12.31 .
Owner Pat Eddery Racing (Ramruma) **Bred** Cathal Ryan **Trained** Nether Winchendon, Bucks

FOCUS
Only five were left after all the non-runners had been taken out and this was an ordinary handicap. The leaders appeared to go off too quickly, setting this up for those coming from off the pace. They raced towards the stands' side in the straight and Koraleva Tectona was tight against the rail, which probably made the difference as the runner-up was stuck out mid-track. the runner-up is the best guide to the form.
T/Jkpt: Not won. T/Plt: £201.70 to a £1 stake. Pool: £94,724.73. 342.70 winning tickets. T/Qpdt: £13.40 to a £1 stake. Pool: £6,734.46. 370.90 winning tickets. SP

4474 SOUTHWELL (L-H)
Tuesday, September 2

OFFICIAL GOING: Standard
Wind: Light across Weather: Overcast

5590 FREE CASINO CHIPS @ FREEBETS.CO.UK MAIDEN STKS — 1m (F)
2:10 (2:14) (Class 5) 2-Y-0 — **£3,885** (£1,156; £577; £288) **Stalls** Low

Form — RPR

00 **1** — **Ever Loved (USA)**[23] 4896 2-8-12 0 .... TedDurcan 8 — 75+
(Saeed Bin Suroor) *chsd ldr tl led 7f out: hdd over 5f out: led again 3f out: rdn and edgd rt fr over 1f out: r.o* — **8/1**[3]

02 **2** 2 ½ **Choral Festival**[10] 5256 2-8-12 0 .... J-PGuillambert 10 — 71+
(Sir Mark Prescott) *chsd ldrs: rdn and edgd rt over 3f out: styd on to go 2nd ins fnl f: no ch w wnr* — **11/10**[1]

02 **3** 4 **Ysing Yi**[8] 5344 2-9-3 0 .... NCallan 9 — 66+
(K A Ryan) *led 1f: led again over 5f out: hdd 3f out: rdn and edgd lft over 1f out: wknd ins fnl f* — **5/2**[2]

0 **4** 3 ¼ **Amazing Blue Sky**[64] 3568 2-9-3 0 .... ChrisCatlin 5 — 59
(E J O'Neill) *sn outpcd: hdwy u.p over 2f out: nt trble ldrs* — **33/1**

0 **5** 2 **Age Of Magic (USA)**[27] 4740 2-8-12 0 .... GregFairley 13 — 49
(M Johnston) *chsd ldrs: rdn over 2f out: wknd over 1f out* — **11/1**

6 nk **Upton Seas** 2-8-9 0 .... PJMcDonald(3) 14 — 49
(R D E Woodhouse) *s.i.s: outpcd: styd on appr fnl f: nvr nrr* — **66/1**

7 ½ **Largem** 2-9-3 0 .... FrankieMcDonald 1 — 53
(Jane Chapple-Hyam) *mid-div: pushed along 1/2-way: wknd over 2f out* — **33/1**

0 **8** 1 ¼ **Duar Mapel (USA)**[25] 4826 2-9-3 0 ....(b[1]) PaulEddery 7 — 50
(G D Blake) *prom: rdn over 3f out: wkng whn hung lft 2f out* — **50/1**

0 **9** 12 **Pure Crystal**[6] 5404 2-8-12 0 .... TPQueally 2 — 19
(M E Rimmer) *mid-div: sn pushed along: outpcd over 5f out: wknd over 3f out* — **14/1**

00 **10** hd **Kidson (USA)**[23] 4890 2-9-3 0 .... DO'Donohoe 12 — 23
(George Baker) *sn outpcd* — **40/1**

0 **11** 2 **Star Of Sophia (IRE)**[9] 5304 2-8-9 0 .... AndrewMullen(3) 3 — 14
(Mrs A Duffield) *mid-div: sn pushed along: lost pl over 5f out: wknd 1/2-way* — **100/1**

0 **12** 1 ½ **Noble Artist**[39] 4384 2-9-3 0 ....(b[1]) PaulMulrennan 11 — 15
(D H Brown) *s.i.s: sn outpcd* — **80/1**

00 **13** 15 **Susurrayshaan**[20] 4960 2-9-3 0 .... PaulHanagan 6 — —
(Mrs G S Rees) *prom: lost pl over 6f out: sn bhd* — **125/1**

0 **14** 6 **Curtain Up**[60] 3689 2-9-3 0 .... DaleGibson 4 — —
(M W Easterby) *s.i.s: sn outpcd* — **100/1**

1m 42.2s (-1.50) **Going Correction** -0.25s/f (Stan) — **14** Ran SP% **118.1**
Speed ratings (Par 95): **97,94,90,87,85 84,84,83,71,71 69,67,52,46**
toteswinger: 1&2 £3.20, 1&3 £3.10, 2&3 £1.80. CSF £16.42 TOTE £9.10: £2.20, £1.10, £1.30; EX 18.60 Trifecta £34.50 Pool: £403.13 - 8.63 winning units..
Owner Godolphin **Bred** Macdonald Stables Llc **Trained** Newmarket, Suffolk

FOCUS
A moderate maiden in which only a couple had shown any previous signs of ability, while the vast majority of those with racecourse experience had demonstrated very little. This trip on a deep surface would have provided quite a test for these two-year-olds and they were spread out all over Nottinghamshire by halfway, while those that raced up with the pace duly dominated.

NOTEBOOK
Ever Loved(USA), who cost 250,000gns as a two-year-old, had shown little in two turf outings but she is related to several dirt winners in the US and the switch to this surface made all the difference. Always up with the pace, she ran straight and true up the middle of the track and saw her race out much better than her main challenger, but this was not a great race and her future probably lies in all-weather nurseries.
Choral Festival, a staying-on second over the extended 7f on soft ground at Beverley last time, was never far off the pace but she failed to find the required turn of foot when first asked and was merely plugging on once again. She looks to need an even greater test of stamina than this, so may be suited by the 1m2f juvenile events that will start to take place within the next month or two. She now qualifies for a mark. (op 6-5)
Ysing Yi helped force the pace, but he couldn't stay with the winner over the last couple of furlongs and he hung over to the inside rail as he got tired. His previous second came in a slowly run Kempton maiden last month and this extra furlong on a more testing surface seemed to find him out. He also now qualifies for nurseries. (op 11-4)
Amazing Blue Sky made up some ground over the last couple of furlongs and this was much better than his Wolverhampton debut effort. A half-brother to a couple of winning stayers including Legend Erry, who has been successful a couple of times around here, he is entitled to improve again and could be interesting back here in modest company.
Age Of Magic(USA) was another to race prominently early, but while this was a small improvement from her Pontefract debut she does not look anything special. (op 10-1 tchd 12-1 in places)
Upton Seas, from a yard not noted for two-year-old winners, didn't have much to recommend her on pedigree but she made a little late headway and may not be a hopeless cause.
Pure Crystal came in for some support but was never seen with any sort of a chance. (op 25-1)

5591 FREE BETTING @ FREEBETS.CO.UK NURSERY — 7f (F)
2:45 (2:46) (Class 5) (0-70,70) 2-Y-0 — **£3,753** (£1,108; £554) **Stalls** Low

Form — RPR

0440 **1** — **Silent Hero**[11] 5242 2-9-1 64 .... NCallan 10 — 68+
(M A Jarvis) *s.i.s: hdwy over 5f out: rdn and hung lft fr over 2f out: led over 1f out: styd on* — **7/2**[1]

000 **2** nk **Dark Oasis**[48] 4072 2-8-8 57 ....(b[1]) PaulHanagan 12 — 60
(K A Ryan) *chsd ldrs: rdn over 2f out: r.o wl nr fin* — **20/1**

025 **3** 2 **Iorek Byrnison**[20] 4965 2-8-8 57 .... AdrianTNicholls 9 — 55
(D Nicholls) *led: rdn and hdd over 1f out: edgd lft ins fnl f: styd on same pce* — **9/1**

0055 **4** shd **Russian Art**[47] 4119 2-8-9 58 ....(t) EddieAhern 14 — 56+
(R M Beckett) *s.i.s: hld up: rdn and hung rt over 4f out: r.o wl fnl f: nt rch ldrs* — **5/1**[2]

4520 **5** 5 **Yokozuna**[4] 5447 2-8-12 66 ....(b) KellyHarrison(5) 6 — 52
(Mrs R A Carr) *s.i.s hld up: rdn 1/2-way: nvr nrr* — **8/1**

420 **6** nk **Identity**[32] 4593 2-9-7 70 .... ChrisCatlin 1 — 55
(E J O'Neill) *chsd ldr tl rdn over 2f out: wknd edgd lft over 1f out* — **10/1**

500 **7** 1 **Isabella Romee (IRE)**[17] 5097 2-9-4 67 .... FrankieMcDonald 2 — 49
(Jane Chapple-Hyam) *hld up: hdwy 1/2-way: rdn over 2f out: wknd over 1f out* — **6/1**[3]

0013 **8** 3 **Nun Today (USA)**[22] 4933 2-8-13 62 ....(b) SimonWhitworth 3 — 37
(J S Moore) *mid-div: hdwy 1/2-way: rdn and wknd over 1f out* — **11/1**

005 **9** 1 ¼ **Real Dandy**[25] 4815 2-9-6 69 .... TPQueally 8 — 41
(J G Given) *prom: lost pl 6f out: sn drvn along: n.d after* — **9/1**

0100 **10** hd **Time Loup**[12] 5204 2-8-10 59 .... MickyFenton 7 — 30
(S R Bowring) *prom: rdn 1/2-way: wknd over 1f out* — **40/1**

643 **11** ½ **Weet In Nerja**[22] 4931 2-9-5 68 .... LPKeniry 5 — 38
(R Hollinshead) *sn outpcd* — **14/1**

646 **12** 2 ½ **Winsome Hearts**[20] 4960 2-8-10 59 .... PaulMulrennan 13 — 23
(M W Easterby) *sn pushed along and prom: rdn 1/2-way: wknd wl over 2f out* — **12/1**

1m 30.04s (-0.26) **Going Correction** -0.25s/f (Stan) — **12** Ran SP% **123.3**
Speed ratings (Par 95): **91,90,88,88,82 82,81,77,76,75 75,72**
toteswinger: 1&2 £18.70, 1&3 £6.60, 2&3 £30.90. CSF £82.59 CT £603.50 TOTE £4.60: £1.50, £6.00, £3.60; EX 81.10 Trifecta £243.90 Part won. Pool: £329.06 - 0.56 winning units..
Owner Mrs P Good **Bred** Mrs P Good **Trained** Newmarket, Suffolk

FOCUS
An ordinary nursery, though several were making their debuts in this type of event following the prerequisite number of outings in maidens. The pace looked solid enough, but not many ever got into it and the third and fourth set the level.

NOTEBOOK
Silent Hero, making his sand debut, was delivered with his effort widest and although hanging away to his left late on, something he has done before, he was always doing just enough. This looks to be his trip for the time being and he can probably improve a bit more. (op 9-2)
Dark Oasis, well beaten in three turf maidens, had been gelded since last seen and was tried in first-time blinkers for this nursery debut. He put up a much better effort and deserves credit for coming again after looking likely to drop away. He should be able to find a race like this if the headgear continues to work. (op 16-1)
Iorek Byrnison, runner-up in a seller here in July, was racing beyond the minimum trip for this first time on this nursery debut, but he wasn't ridden as though stamina was thought to be an issue and he kept on battling until well inside the last furlong. He still doesn't look the finished article, as he had to be given a few taps down the shoulder to keep his mind on the job rounding the home bend and he still looked green in the latter stages, so he may well be capable of better. Official explanation: jockey said colt hung right round final bend (op 17-2 tchd 8-1)
Russian Art, up a furlong and tried in a tongue tie for this sand debut, ran a strange race as he was out the back and going nowhere rounding the home bend, but he suddenly took off inside the last 2f and would have been third in another stride. To be fair the outside stall would have done him few favours and there is a race like this in him when things go more his way. (op 9-2 tchd 4-1)
Yokozuna tried to come from even further back, but his best form to date came in a seller and he was the most exposed in the field. Official explanation: trainer said gelding was unsuited by the kickback (op 12-1)
Identity, another making her sand and nursery debuts, helped set the early pace but failed to get home over this extra furlong. (op 12-1)

5592 FREE POKER CHIPS @ FREEBETS.CO.UK H'CAP — 5f (F)
3:20 (3:20) (Class 5) (0-70,70) 3-Y-0 — **£3,753** (£1,108; £554) **Stalls** High

Form — RPR

2522 **1** — **Shakespeare's Son**[60] 3678 3-8-6 61 .... DuranFentiman(3) 1 — 68
(H J Evans) *chsd ldrs: shkn up to ld over 1f out: sn rdn: jst hld on* — **11/4**[1]

1056 **2** hd **Bishopbriggs (USA)**[37] 4450 3-9-2 68 .... EddieAhern 6 — 74
(S Parr) *chsd ldrs: rdn over 1f out: hung lft ins fnl f: r.o* — **13/2**[2]

4025 **3** 1 ½ **Westwood Dawn**[5] 5421 3-7-13 56 oh8 ....(v) KellyHarrison(5) 11 — 57
(Mrs N Macauley) *mid-div: hdwy 1/2-way: rdn and hung lft over 1f out: r.o* — **25/1**

5104 **4** 2 ½ **Mr Funshine**[23] 4904 3-8-5 60 ow2 .... JackMitchell(3) 4 — 52
(Mrs P N Dutfield) *chsd ldrs: rdn and ev ch fr over 1f out: no ex ins fnl f* — **13/2**[2]

5050 **5** 1 ¼ **Mollyatti**[7] 5374 3-8-0 57 oh4 ow1 ....(b) PatrickDonaghy(5) 7 — 44
(Miss V Haigh) *s.s: outpcd: r.o wl ins fnl f: nvr nrr* — **20/1**

6434 **6** hd **Kinout (IRE)**[48] 4074 3-9-4 70 ....(p) NCallan 2 — 56
(K A Ryan) *led: rdn and hdd over 1f out: wknd ins fnl f* — **11/4**[1]

2610 **7** 2 ½ **Mac Dalia**[6] 5401 3-8-11 66 ....(p) TolleyDean(3) 3 — 43
(A J McCabe) *w ldr tl rdn 1/2-way: wknd over 1f out* — **7/1**[3]

4634 **8** 1 ¾ **Valhillen**[19] 5028 3-9-0 69 .... TravisBlock(3) 12 — 40
(M D I Usher) *sn outpcd* — **14/1**

3005 **9** ¾ **Diademas (USA)**[25] 4830 3-8-10 62 ....(v) StephenDonohoe 10 — 30
(M J Gingell) *sn outpcd* — **25/1**

0-00 **10** nse **Ruby's Rainbow (IRE)**[3] 5501 3-8-4 56 oh11 .... DaleGibson 5 — 24
(J Balding) *sn outpcd: drvn along in rr whn hung lft 1/2-way* — **100/1**

58.85 secs (-0.85) **Going Correction** -0.125s/f (Stan) — **10** Ran SP% **112.6**
Speed ratings (Par 101): **101,100,98,94,92 91,87,85,83,83**
toteswinger: 1&2 £6.30, 1&3 £4.70, 2&3 £13.90. CSF £19.49 CT £367.40 TOTE £3.40: £1.30, £2.50, £3.00; EX 21.50 TRIFECTA Not won..
Owner ownaracehorse.co.uk (Shakespeare) **Bred** T C Chiang **Trained** Honeybourne, Worcs

FOCUS
An ordinary sprint handicap and, as is normal over this straight 5f, those drawn low who raced down the middle of the track held the advantage. The form looks weak and is rated around the principals.
Mollyatti Official explanation: jockey said filly missed the break

5593 FREEBETS.CO.UK H'CAP — 1m 4f (F)
3:55 (3:55) (Class 6) (0-60,60) 3-Y-0+ — **£2,558** (£755; £378) **Stalls** Low

Form — RPR

5306 **1** — **Paddy Rielly (IRE)**[6] 5399 3-8-8 59 ....(p) RichardEvans(5) 10 — 68
(P D Evans) *hld up: hdwy over 3f out: rdn to ld ins fnl f: sn edgd rt: jst hld on* — **9/2**[1]

5336 **2** shd **Black Falcon (IRE)**[3] 5489 8-9-9 60 .... RobertWinston 12 — 68
(John A Harris) *hld up in tch: edgd lft wl over 3f out: sn swtchd rt: rdn to ld over 1f out: edgd lft and hdd ins fnl f: styd on gamely* — **5/1**[2]

00-3 **3** ½ **Summer Lodge**[22] 4936 5-9-0 58 .... MrJPFeatherstone(7) 13 — 66
(A J McCabe) *hld up in tch: hung lft over 2f out: sn rdn: styd on* — **9/1**

0034 **4** 3 ¾ **Bolckow**[8] 5369 5-8-9 51 .... PatrickDonaghy(5) 2 — 53
(J T Stimpson) *sn led: hdd over 8f out: chsd ldr tl led again over 4f out: rdn and hdd over 1f out: no ex ins fnl f* — **9/2**[1]

0401 **5** nk **Jenny Soba**[9] 5308 5-9-0 51 6ex .... DNolan 5 — 52
(Lucinda Featherstone) *sn pushed along in rr: rdn 1/2-way: styd on appr fnl f: nvr nrr* — **16/1**

4636 **6** ¾ **Viscount Rossini**[52] 3965 6-8-11 48 ....(b[1]) ChrisCatlin 9 — 48
(S Gollings) *chsd ldrs: rdn over 2f out: styd on same pce appr fnl f* — **12/1**

0-64 **7** 1 1/2 **Stravita**[50] 4031 4-9-2 **56** .... RussellKennemore(3) 8 54
(R Hollinshead) *chsd ldr tl led over 8f out: hdd over 4f out: sn rdn: wknd fnl f* **33/1**
40-4 **8** 5 **Silver Mont (IRE)**[16] 1779 5-9-2 **53** ....(v) MickyFenton 14 43
(S R Bowring) *s.i.s: sn pushed along in rr: rdn 1/2-way: n.d* **8/1**[3]
0-00 **9** 8 **Sweet Seville (FR)**[78] 3089 4-8-10 **47** .... DaleGibson 11 24
(Mrs G S Rees) *plld hrd and prom: rdn over 3f out: wkng whn hung lft 2f out* **100/1**
0440 **10** 8 **Love Empire (USA)**[36] 4477 3-8-9 **55** ....(v) GregFairley 1 19
(M Johnston) *chsd ldrs: rdn 1/2-way: wknd over 3f out* **16/1**
3160 **11** 7 **Cragganmore Creek**[113] 2053 5-8-10 **52** ..... Louis-PhilippeBeuzelin(5) 4 5
(D Morris) *hld up: rdn 1/2-way: sn bhd* **12/1**
0250 **12** 49 **Kanisorn (SWE)**[55] 3137 6-9-4 **58** ....(bt) TolleyDean(3) 7 —
(Mike Hammond) *s.s and rel to r: a bhd: t.o fnl 8f* **16/1**
0060 **13** 2 1/4 **Iron Cross (IRE)**[24] 4859 3-8-5 **51** .... PaulHanagan 3 —
(Sir Mark Prescott) *hld up: hmpd 9f out: sn bhd: t.o fnl 7f* **16/1**
-010 **14** 10 **Ricci De Mare**[151] 1193 3-9-0 **60** .... NCallan 6 —
(A B Haynes) *prom: rdn over 4f out: hmpd and wknd over 3f out: t.o* **16/1**

2m 38.0s (-3.00) **Going Correction** -0.25s/f (Stan)
WFA 3 from 4yo+ 9lb **14** Ran SP% **122.9**
Speed ratings (Par 101): **100,99,99,97,96 96,95,92,86,81 76,44,42,35**
toteswinger: 1&2 £7.20, 1&3 £13.00, 2&3 £12.70. CSF £26.78 CT £201.26 TOTE £6.10: £2.00, £2.60, £3.20; EX 30.50 Trifecta £63.10 Pool: £287.46 - 3.37 winning units..
Owner P D Evans **Bred** Kilfrush Stud **Trained** Pandy, Monmouths

FOCUS
An ordinary middle-distance handicap, full of the usual suspects. They went a fair pace and the front three pulled clear of the rest. The third is the best guide to the level.
Black Falcon(IRE) Official explanation: jockey said gelding hung left
Iron Cross(IRE) Official explanation: jockey said gelding was hampered round first bend

5594 FREE SPORTS BETS @ FREEBETS.CO.UK H'CAP 6f (F)
4:30 (4:32) (Class 4) (0-80,80) 3-Y-O+ **£5,828** (£1,734; £866; £432) **Stalls** Low

Form RPR
4-10 **1** **Crying Aloud (USA)**[139] 1401 3-9-6 **80** .... StephenDonohoe 6 94
(P A Blockley) *hld up: hdwy over 1f out: rdn to ld wl ins fnl f: r.o* **16/1**
2460 **2** 1/2 **Realt Na Mara (IRE)**[11] 5247 5-8-9 **70** .... TravisBlock(3) 10 82
(H Morrison) *chsd ldrs: rdn over 2f out: led ins fnl f: sn hdd: r.o* **8/1**
5154 **3** 1 1/2 **Makshoof (IRE)**[11] 5222 4-9-4 **76** ....(p) NCallan 1 83
(K A Ryan) *trckd ldrs: led over 1f out: edgd rt: hdd ins fnl f: styd on same pce* **7/1**[3]
5355 **4** 1 1/2 **Baunagain (IRE)**[18] 5067 3-9-6 **80** .... PatCosgrave 11 82
(M J Wallace, Australia) *prom: rdn over 2f out: no ex ins fnl f* **17/2**
0600 **5** nk **Ingleby Arch (USA)**[11] 5222 5-9-5 **77** .... PaulFessey 2 78
(T D Barron) *chsd ldrs: rdn over 2f out: no ex fnl f* **5/1**[2]
503 **6** 2 **Cerebus**[21] 4944 6-9-3 **78** ....(bt) TolleyDean(3) 7 73
(A J McCabe) *led: rdn and hdd over 1f out: hmpd sn after: edgd lft and wknd ins fnl f* **20/1**
1004 **7** 1 3/4 **Flying Bantam (IRE)**[21] 4951 7-9-0 **72** .... PaulHanagan 9 61
(R A Fahey) *chsd ldrs: rdn over 2f out: wknd over 1f out* **20/1**
1522 **8** 3/4 **Memphis Man**[6] 5400 5-8-10 **73** .... RichardEvans(5) 12 60
(P D Evans) *hld up: r.o ins fnl f: nvr nrr* **12/1**
0050 **9** 2 1/2 **Dickie Le Davoir**[8] 5345 4-9-2 **74** .... ChrisCatlin 13 53
(John A Harris) *hld up: rdn over 2f out: wknd over 1f out* **14/1**
2500 **10** nk **Jord (IRE)**[39] 4390 4-9-0 **72** .... JamesDoyle 5 50
(A J McCabe) *mid-div: rdn 1/2-way: wknd wl over 1f out* **50/1**
6260 **11** 5 **Weet A Surprise**[26] 4767 3-9-0 **74** .... LPKeniry 4 36
(R Hollinshead) *sn pushed along in rr: hdwy 1/2-way: sn rdn: wknd wl over 1f out* **66/1**
-011 **12** 2 1/2 **Elusive Hawk (IRE)**[56] 3819 4-9-2 **74** .... TPQueally 3 28
(A P Stringer) *dwlt: hld up: rdn over 2f out: a in rr* **5/2**[1]
1104 **13** 3/4 **Another Genepi (USA)**[166] 949 5-8-12 **75** ....(b) ShaneCreighton(5) 14 27
(E J Creighton) *rrd s and nrly uns rdr: outpcd* **22/1**

1m 14.96s (-1.54) **Going Correction** -0.25s/f (Stan)
WFA 3 from 4yo+ 2lb **13** Ran SP% **116.9**
Speed ratings (Par 105): **100,99,97,95,94 92,89,88,85,85 78,75,74**
toteswinger: 1&2 £19.00, 1&3 £19.10, 2&3 £82.30. CSF £127.32 CT £1017.84 TOTE £22.10: £5.30, £2.30, £2.30; EX 197.30 TRIFECTA Not won..
Owner M J Wiley **Bred** Eric Heitzmann & Darley **Trained** Lambourn, Berks

FOCUS
A very decent sprint handicap in which 11 of these were previous course winners, nine of them over this trip and the form looks solid rated around those in the frame behind the winner. With so many trailblazers in opposition a strong pace was assured and with Cerebus winning the battle for the early lead, that is what we got. However, as things turned out it had the effect of setting things up perfectly for a closer.
Elusive Hawk(IRE) Official explanation: jockey said, regarding running, that the gelding missed the break

5595 FREE BETS @ FREEBETS.CO.UK H'CAP 1m (F)
5:05 (5:05) (Class 5) (0-75,75) 3-Y-O **£3,691** (£1,098; £548; £274) **Stalls** Low

Form RPR
0216 **1** **Mahadee (IRE)**[37] 4448 3-8-12 **69** ....(b) NCallan 5 79
(C E Brittain) *prom: sn pushed along and led over 6f out: rdn: hung lft and hdd 2f out: rallied to ld ins fnl f: styd on* **6/1**[3]
4545 **2** 1 **Indy Driver**[36] 4481 3-9-1 **72** .... RobertWinston 4 79
(J R Fanshawe) *chsd ldrs: rdn over 2f out: ev ch ins fnl f: kpt on* **4/1**[2]
2305 **3** nk **Ocean Legend (IRE)**[17] 5104 3-9-2 **73** .... SaleemGolam 6 79
(Miss J Feilden) *led: hdd over 6f out: chsd ldr tl led 2f out: sn rdn and edgd lft: hdd and unable qckn ins fnl f* **10/3**[1]
5245 **4** 1 1/2 **Saleima (IRE)**[19] 5019 3-9-1 **72** .... TPQueally 9 75
(P W Chapple-Hyam) *s.i.s: sn pushed along in rr: hdwy over 2f out: rdn over 1f out: styd on same pce ins fnl f* **7/1**
313 **5** 3/4 **St Trinians**[17] 5108 3-9-4 **75** .... LPKeniry 11 76+
(E F Vaughan) *hld up: hdwy u.p over 1f out: nt trble ldrs* **8/1**
0402 **6** 6 **Green Diamond**[21] 4946 3-8-13 **70** .... GregFairley 2 57
(M Johnston) *chsd ldrs: rdn over 2f out: wknd over 1f out* **13/2**
5100 **7** 2 **Redarsene**[39] 4377 3-8-9 **69** .... TravisBlock(3) 3 51
(M G Quinlan) *hld up: rdn over 3f out: n.d* **20/1**
5400 **8** 7 **King's Icon (IRE)**[82] 2976 3-8-13 **70** .... NickyMackay 10 36
(M Wigham) *hld up: rdn 1/2-way: wknd 3f out* **20/1**
4003 **9** 5 **Royal Straight**[17] 5086 3-8-8 **68** .... RussellKennemore(3) 8 23
(B N Pollock) *mid-div: hdwy 1/2-way: rdn and wknd over 2f out* **20/1**
03-3 **10** 9 **Climaxtackledotcom**[123] 1781 3-9-1 **72** .... PaulMulrennan 7 6
(M W Easterby) *chsd ldrs: hung rt fr over 5f out: rdn and wknd over 3f out* **9/1**

1m 41.77s (-1.93) **Going Correction** -0.25s/f (Stan) **10** Ran SP% **119.5**
Speed ratings (Par 101): **99,98,97,96,95 89,87,80,75,66**
toteswinger: 1&2 £7.20, 1&3 £6.80, 2&3 £5.20. CSF £30.09 CT £91.79 TOTE £7.80: £2.40, £2.50, £1.70; EX 55.30 TRIFECTA Not won. Place 6: £49.38 Place 5: £44.73 .
Owner Saeed Manana **Bred** Darley **Trained** Newmarket, Suffolk

FOCUS
Just a reasonable handicap, though a couple were open to a bit more improvement on the surface and only one of these had raced here before. The form looks sound enough despite the modest time.
Climaxtackledotcom Official explanation: jockey said gelding hung right
T/Plt: £139.60 to a £1 stake. Pool: £63,251.15. 330.52 winning tickets. T/Qpdt: £121.90 to a £1 stake. Pool: £3,493.80. 21.20 winning tickets. CR

5553 BADEN-BADEN (L-H)
Tuesday, September 2
OFFICIAL GOING: Soft

5596a DARLEY OETTINGEN-RENNEN (GROUP 2) 1m
3:55 (3:56) 3-Y-O+ **£40,401** (£14,706; £7,353; £3,676)

RPR
1 **Lovelace**[53] 3921 4-9-1 .... JamieSpencer 2 113
(M Johnston) *hld up in rr: 7th st: str run down outside to ld 150yds out: rdn out* **19/10**[2]
2 1 3/4 **Peace Royale (GER)**[30] 4675 3-8-4 .... ASuborics 8 103
(A Wohler, Germany) *hld up towards rr: 5th st: rdn and edgd lft 1 1/2f out: tk 2nd 200yds out* **13/10**[1]
3 3/4 **Sehrezad (IRE)**[44] 4233 3-8-8 .... JiriPalik 1 105
(Andreas Lowe, Germany) *hld up towards rr: 6th st: styd in u.p fr over 1f out to take 3rd on line* **117/10**
4 shd **Setareh (GER)**[45] 3-8-8 .... FilipMinarik 5 105
(P Olsanik, France) *led racing freely: set str pce: 6 l clr 1/2-way: hdd 150yds out: lost 3rd on line* **19/2**
5 2 **Waky Love (GER)**[23] 4916 4-8-11 .... ADeVries 3 98
(Frau Jutta Mayer, Germany) *racd in 3rd: hrd rdn 1 1/2f out: sn one pce* **135/10**
6 1 1/2 **Vinea Federspiel (IRE)**[62] 3623 4-8-11 ....(b) GBocskai 6 95
(C Bocksai, Germany) *a bhd* **33/1**
7 nk **King Jock (USA)**[70] 3357 7-9-4 .... RMBurke 7 101
(R J Osborne, Ire) *racd in 4th: hrd rdn to press for 2nd whn carried lft 1 1/2f out: sn btn* **137/10**
8 13 **Briseida**[30] 4674 3-8-7 .... AStarke 4 65
(P Schiergen, Germany) *chsd clr ldr: wkng whn hmpd 1 1/2f out: eased* **42/10**[3]

1m 39.85s (0.74)
WFA 3 from 4yo+ 5lb **8** Ran SP% **131.2**
(including 10 Euro stake): WIN 29; PL 14, 12, 20; SF 58.
Owner Hamad Suhail **Bred** Mrs Mary Taylor **Trained** Middleham Moor, N Yorks

NOTEBOOK
Lovelace was held up in the rear until being asked for his effort in the straight and swept past virtually the whole field to score going away. He may take his chance in the Prix du Moulin but his ultimate aim is the Hong Kong Mile.

4039 LONGCHAMP (R-H)
Tuesday, September 2
OFFICIAL GOING: Good to soft

5597a PRIX DE LIANCOURT (LISTED RACE) (FILLIES) 1m 2f 110y
1:50 (1:49) 3-Y-O **£20,221** (£8,088; £6,066; £4,044; £2,022)

RPR
1 **Astrologie (FR)**[19] 5039 3-9-2 .... SPasquier 5 109
(A Fabre, France) **37/10**[2]
2 2 **Tres Rapide (IRE)**[30] 4675 3-8-12 .... JVictoire 4 101
(H-A Pantall, France) **87/10**[3]
3 1 1/2 **Balladeuse (FR)**[93] 2650 3-9-2 .... OPeslier 1 102
(A Fabre, France) **12/1**
4 1/2 **Salve Germania (IRE)**[30] 4675 3-8-12 .... CSoumillon 2 97
(W Hickst, Germany)
5 1/2 **For Joy**[50] 4040 3-8-12 .... C-PLemaire 6 96
(J-M Beguigne, France)
6 shd **Saturnine (IRE)**[44] 4234 3-8-12 .... TThulliez 3 96
(N Clement, France)
7 1 1/2 **Icon Project (USA)**[45] 4196 3-8-12 .... AlanMunro 7 93
(B J Meehan) *trckd ldr to st: sn pushed along: rdn over 1 1/2f out: wknd fr over 1f out* **9/10**[1]
8 3/4 **L'Etoile De Moscou**[44] 4234 3-8-12 .... ACrastus 10 92
(E Lellouche, France)
9 1 1/2 **Vraiment Rouge (FR)**[20] 5001 3-8-12 .... MBlancpain 8 89
(C Laffon-Parias, France)
10 10 **Seal Bay (IRE)**[93] 2650 3-8-12 .... DBoeuf 9 70
(D Smaga, France)

2m 15.8s (2.80) **Going Correction** +0.40s/f (Good) **10** Ran SP% **91.9**
Speed ratings: **105,103,102,102,101 101,100,100,98,91**
PARI-MUTUEL: WIN 4.70; PL 1.80, 2.50, 3.30; DF 14.50.
Owner Famille De Moussac **Bred** Ship Commodoties Intern Inc **Trained** Chantilly, France

NOTEBOOK
Icon Project(USA), the odds on favourite, was given every possible chance, but she could not go the pace in the straight and ran below her best.

5165 BRIGHTON (L-H)

Wednesday, September 3

OFFICIAL GOING: Good (good to firm in places)

Wind: Fresh, half against Weather: Mostly sunny

5599 E B F TRAINERMAGAZINE.COM MAIDEN STKS — 6f 209y

2:30 (2:31) (Class 5) 2-Y-O **£3,784** (£1,132; £566; £283; £141) **Stalls** Low

Form RPR

00 **1** **My Kingdom (IRE)**[70] 3372 2-9-0 0 ....(t) TravisBlock(3) 4 75+
(H Morrison) *stdd s in rr tl hdwy after 3f: led over 2f out: clr whn hung lft over 1f out: r.o st ins fnl f: easily* **40/1**

3 **2** *6* **Popiel**[15] 5165 2-9-3 0 .... ChrisCatlin 1 57
(Saeed Bin Suroor) *j. path after 1f: trckd ldrs: chsd wnr but no ch fnl f* **7/4[1]**

4 **3** *nk* **Rio Gael (IRE)**[33] 4579 2-9-3 0 .... TGMcLaughlin 8 57
(M S Saunders) *in tch on outside: outpcd 2f out: styd on fnl f* **14/1[2]**

00 **4** *2 ½* **Honorable Endeavor**[15] 5165 2-8-12 0 .... DavidProbert(5) 6 50
(E F Vaughan) *in rr: mde sme late hdwy* **50/1**

00 **5** *1 ¼* **Old Street**[24] 4890 2-9-3 0 .... SteveDrowne 5 47
(R Charlton) *stmbld path after 1f: trckd ldr to over 2f out: sn btn* **25/1[3]**

00 **6** *12* **Fantastic Fred (IRE)**[42] 4305 2-9-3 0 .... MartinDwyer 2 16
(J A Osborne) *led tl hdd over 2f out: wknd over 1f out* **50/1**

P4 **7** *7* **Rigged**[103] 2349 2-9-3 0 .... WilliamBuick 3 —
(J A Osborne) *plld hrd: dropped in rr after 3f* **50/1**

1m 26.66s (3.56) **Going Correction** +0.225s/f (Good) **7 Ran SP% 55.2**
Speed ratings (Par 95): **88,81,80,77,76 62,54**
toteswinger: 1&2 £3.80, 1&3 £8.80, 2&3 £1.10. CSF £23.84 TOTE £27.40: £5.10, £1.10; EX 34.80 Trifecta £78.80 Part won. Pool: £106.52 - 0.81 winning units..
Owner Wood Street Syndicate V **Bred** Irish National Stud **Trained** East Ilsley, Berks
■ Noble Jack withdrawn (4/6F, broke out of stalls). Deduct 55p in the £ under R4.

FOCUS
The complexion of this juvenile maiden totally changed just before the off when the warm favourite Noble Jack was withdrawn. It looks weakish form rated around the third and fourth, but the winner won very well and produced a massively-improved effort.

NOTEBOOK
My Kingdom(IRE) had shown little on his two previous outings earlier in the season, but was returning from a 70-day break and he has clearly improved a bundle having been gelded in the meantime. He travelled sweetly into contention before taking up the running and, despite hanging markedly right when in front, came home to score with any amount in hand. His prospective handicap mark will suffer as a result of this, but he looks a useful prospect indeed and looks one to side with on his next outing. (op 33-1)
Popiel, third over course and distance on debut, has to rate as somewhat disappointing in the circumstances, but he is still very much learning his trade and should find his feet when qualifying for a nursery mark after his next run. (op 2-1 tchd 9-4 in a place)
Rio Gael(IRE) posted a fair effort in defeat and got the longer trip well enough. He will look more interesting when becoming eligible for an official rating after his next assignment. (op 10-1 tchd 16-1)
Honorable Endeavor kept on steadily under a more patient ride and finished closer to the runner-up than was the case over course and distance last time. He now qualifies for a handicap mark. (op 33-1 tchd 80-1)
Old Street showed more early dash than had been the case on his previous two starts, but was cooked before the final furlong. He looks only modest, but should find his right level now he has the option of nurseries. (op 20-1)
Rigged Official explanation: jockey said colt was unsuited by the track

5600 BET365 BEST ODDS GUARANTEED ON EVERY RACE H'CAP — 6f 209y

3:00 (3:02) (Class 5) (0-75,75) 3-Y-O+ **£2,838** (£849; £424; £212; £105) **Stalls** Low

Form RPR

4550 **1** **Buxton**[19] 5067 4-9-5 72 ....(t) RobertHavlin 1 83
(R Ingram) *trckd ldrs: led 2f out: pressed thrght fnl f: jst hld on* **17/2**

5250 **2** *nk* **H Harrison (IRE)**[7] 5400 8-8-10 70 .... BMcHugh(7) 8 80
(I W McInnes) *a.p on ins: wnt 2nd 2f out: pressed wnr thrght fnl f: jst failed* **22/1**

1000 **3** *¾* **Napoletano (GER)**[11] 5267 7-9-1 68 ....(p) NCallan 16 76
(S Dow) *in rr: mde hdwy fr 2f out: r.o to go 3rd nr fin* **14/1**

3533 **4** *½* **Fly Kiss**[16] 5142 3-8-11 68 ....(t) HayleyTurner 9 73
(C E Brittain) *s.i.s: in rr tl rdn and hdwy over 2f out: kpt on u.p fnl f* **9/1**

1500 **5** *nse* **My Learned Friend (IRE)**[16] 5144 4-9-3 75 .... DavidProbert(5) 5 82
(A M Balding) *led tl hdd 2f out: styd prom: no ex towards fin* **15/2[2]**

0230 **6** *3 ¼* **Scarlet Flyer (USA)**[116] 1996 5-9-3 70 ....(p) GeorgeBaker 4 68
(G L Moore) *mid-div: rdn and no hdwy fr over 1f out* **10/1**

0506 **7** *1 ¼* **Support Fund (IRE)**[19] 5069 4-9-3 70 .... StephenCarson 15 64
(Eve Johnson Houghton) *stdd s: in rr whn swtchd rt over 2f out: kpt on one pce* **16/1**

0600 **8** *3 ½* **Lord Theo**[11] 5290 4-9-6 73 .... SteveDrowne 3 58
(N P Littmoden) *mid-div: outpcd over 2f out* **14/1**

5001 **9** *nk* **Shamrock Lady (IRE)**[15] 5170 3-9-3 74 .... J-PGuillambert 7 56
(J Gallagher) *trckd ldr to over 2f out: sn btn* **12/1**

5305 **10** *1 ¾* **Blue Java**[21] 4979 7-8-10 66 .... TravisBlock(3) 13 45
(H Morrison) *prom on outside tl wknd over 2f out* **12/1**

5030 **11** *½* **Tender The Great (IRE)**[19] 5071 5-9-4 71 .... ChrisCatlin 11 49
(V Smith) *a towards rr* **8/1[3]**

0000 **12** *1* **Brunelleschi**[12] 5247 5-9-0 72 ....(b) WilliamCarson(5) 2 47
(P L Gilligan) *slowly away: a bhd* **33/1**

2122 **13** *2* **Greystoke Prince**[19] 5052 3-9-0 71 ....(p) AdamKirby 10 39
(W R Swinburn) *mid-div tl wknd over 2f out* **13/2[1]**

2404 **14** *5* **Prince Of Delphi**[50] 4051 5-9-0 67 ....(b[1]) RichardKingscote 14 23
(R M Beckett) *in tch tl wknd over 2f out* **11/1**

406 **15** *38* **Madame Hoi (IRE)**[53] 3944 3-9-2 73 .... DarryllHolland 12 —
(M R Channon) *in tch tl rdn 1/2-way: qckly lost pl: virtually p.u fnl f: t.o* **14/1**

1m 24.15s (1.05) **Going Correction** +0.225s/f (Good)
WFA 3 from 4yo+ 4lb **15 Ran SP% 122.7**
Speed ratings (Par 103): **103,102,101,101,101 97,96,92,91,89 89,87,85,79,36**
toteswinger: 1&2 £41.90, 1&3 £38.30, 2&3 £91.30. CSF £184.78 CT £2654.50 TOTE £11.20: £3.30, £5.70, £4.10; EX 230.70 TRIFECTA Not won..
Owner Peter J Burton **Bred** Sharon Ingram **Trained** Epsom, Surrey
■ Stewards' Enquiry : Robert Havlin four-day ban: used whip with excessive frequency (Sep 17-20)

FOCUS
This was a modest handicap, but still wide open affair. The runners were pretty much spread across the home straight and the first five finished clear of the remainder. The four behind the winner were close to their marks suggesting the form is solid.

Shamrock Lady(IRE) Official explanation: jockey said filly had no more to give

5601 IAN CARNABY (S) STKS — 5f 213y

3:30 (3:32) (Class 6) 3-Y-O+ **£1,942** (£578; £288; £144) **Stalls** Low

Form RPR

3130 **1** **Avoca Dancer (IRE)**[5] 5474 5-9-0 57 ....(p) NCallan 3 65
(Miss Gay Kelleway) *in tch on ins: swtchd rt over 1f out: led ins fnl f: drvn out* **10/1**

0403 **2** *¾* **Trinculo (IRE)**[7] 5398 11-9-2 63 ....(b) HaddenFrost(3) 1 68
(R A Harris) *trckd ldr: led over 2f out: rdn and hdd ins fnl f: kpt on* **9/1[3]**

5036 **3** *¾* **Meridian Line (IRE)**[12] 5217 3-8-7 64 ....(b) RichardKingscote 4 56
(J G Portman) *s.i.s: hdwy on ins whn n.m.r 2f out: hmpd and plld out wd over 1f out: r.o wl ins fnl f* **16/1**

2041 **4** *1* **Music Box Express**[2] 5582 4-8-12 50 ....(t) MatthewDavies(7) 6 62
(George Baker) *led tl hdd over 2f out: one pce fr over 1f out* **4/1[1]**

4256 **5** *½* **Oi Vay Joe (IRE)**[25] 4863 4-9-0 64 ....(b) J-PGuillambert 8 56
(W Jarvis) *prom: nt qckn fr over 1f out* **6/1[2]**

0054 **6** *1* **Caustic Wit (IRE)**[55] 3872 10-9-5 60 ....(p) TGMcLaughlin 16 58
(M S Saunders) *in rr: rdn and hdwy over 1f out: nvr nr to chal* **12/1**

0012 **7** *hd* **Exit Strategy (IRE)**[18] 5090 4-9-2 56 ....(b) KevinGhunowa(3) 5 57
(R A Harris) *mid-div tl rdn and outpcd ½-way: kpt on fnl f but nvr a danger* **9/1[3]**

-006 **8** *3 ¾* **River Kirov (IRE)**[18] 5090 5-9-0 61 .... NickyMackay 7 40
(M Wigham) *in rr: effrt over 1f out: nvr on terms* **16/1**

0100 **9** *½* **Who's Winning (IRE)**[3] 5533 7-9-5 59 ....(t) GeorgeBaker 9 43
(B G Powell) *a towards rr* **4/1[1]**

0000 **10** *5* **Cracking Nick (IRE)**[20] 5015 3-8-12 59 .... AdamKirby 12 22
(W R Swinburn) *prom tl wknd 2f out* **18/1**

0010 **11** *4 ½* **Deal Flipper**[9] 5346 3-8-12 65 .... FrankieMcDonald 10 8
(P Winkworth) *slowly away: a bhd* **18/1**

0200 **12** *2 ¾* **Micheals Boy (IRE)**[8] 5377 3-8-12 58 ....(b) PatCosgrave 13 —
(J R Boyle) *s.i.s: sn prom on outside: wknd over 2f out* **33/1**

6033 **13** *2 ½* **Cleveland**[26] 4808 6-9-2 52 .... RussellKennemore(3) 14 —
(R Hollinshead) *racd wd in tch tl wknd over 1f out* **16/1**

1m 12.63s (2.43) **Going Correction** +0.425s/f (Yiel)
WFA 3 from 4yo+ 2lb **13 Ran SP% 122.2**
Speed ratings (Par 101): **100,99,98,96,96 94,94,89,88,82 76,72,69**
toteswinger: 1&2 £19.60, 1&3 £37.10, 2&3 £38.60. CSF £99.35 TOTE £13.30: £3.00, £3.90, £6.10; EX 112.20 TRIFECTA Not won..There was no bid for the winner.
Owner Mrs Donna Joslyn **Bred** Frank Towey **Trained** Exning, Suffolk

FOCUS
Quite a competitive seller, run at a sound pace. The field migrated more towards the far side in the home straight and the form is straightforward through the runner-up.
Who's Winning(IRE) Official explanation: jockey said gelding never travelled
Cleveland Official explanation: jockey said gelding hung right

5602 MATTHEW CLARK WINES & SPIRITS FILLIES' H'CAP — 1m 1f 209y

4:00 (4:01) (Class 5) (0-70,70) 3-Y-O+ **£2,775** (£830; £415; £207; £103) **Stalls** High

Form RPR

600 **1** **Maybe I Will (IRE)**[16] 5149 3-9-5 66 .... NCallan 6 73
(S Dow) *mid-div: gd hdwy to ld over 2f out: hung rt over 1f out: straightened up fnl f: rdn out* **12/1**

5061 **2** *¾* **Shesha Bear**[15] 5168 3-9-4 70 .... DavidProbert(5) 9 76
(W R Muir) *stdd s: in rr tl hdwy over 3f out: rdn to chse wnr fnl f* **4/1[2]**

000 **3** *4* **Trinkila (USA)**[8] 5378 3-9-1 62 .... MartinDwyer 2 60
(P F I Cole) *led tl hdd 6f out: trckd wnrover 2f out: tl wknd fnl f* **14/1**

0603 **4** *1 ½* **Blur**[27] 4774 3-8-2 49 .... HayleyTurner 10 44
(R Hannon) *trckd ldrs: rdn over 3f out: one pce fr over 1f out* **15/2**

0404 **5** *½* **Encore Belle**[12] 5218 3-8-11 58 .... SteveDrowne 13 52
(Mouse Hamilton-Fairley) *t.k.h: in rr: one pce fnl 2f* **13/2**

3210 **6** *3 ¾* **Emshabb**[139] 1412 3-9-9 70 .... LiamJones 7 56
(W J Haggas) *in rr: nvr nr to chal* **6/1[3]**

1460 **7** *4 ½* **Little Firecracker**[24] 4898 3-8-12 59 ow1 .... AdamKirby 12 36
(Miss M E Rowland) *a in rr* **14/1**

0602 **8** *½* **Royal Tender (IRE)**[33] 4599 4-8-9 49 oh4 ....(v) WilliamBuick 14 25
(V Smith) *prom on outside: c over to stands' side 3f out: sn btn* **25/1**

163 **9** *1 ½* **Jemiliah**[28] 4721 3-8-12 59 .... TQuinn 4 32
(B G Powell) *trckd ldr: led 6f out: hdd over 2f out: sn wknd* **9/1**

6321 **10** *1 ¾* **Solo River**[26] 4810 3-9-0 61 .... ChrisCatlin 11 31
(P J Makin) *trckd ldrs: rdn and wknd over 2f out* **3/1[1]**

2m 7.56s (3.96) **Going Correction** +0.425s/f (Yiel)
WFA 3 from 4yo+ 7lb **10 Ran SP% 119.3**
Speed ratings (Par 100): **101,100,97,96,95 92,89,88,87,86**
toteswinger: 1&2 £11.00, 1&3 £13.80, 2&3 £13.60. CSF £61.00 CT £698.23 TOTE £14.40: £2.70, £2.10, £5.60; EX 69.20 Trifecta £245.80 Part won: Pool: £332.27 - 0.60 winning units..
Owner Mrs Alicia Aldis **Bred** Cheval Court Stud **Trained** Epsom, Surrey

FOCUS
A moderate handicap run at an average pace. The first two pulled clear with the third rated to this year's form.
Little Firecracker Official explanation: jockey said filly hung right

5603 MATTHEW CLARK WINES & SPIRITS CLAIMING STKS — 1m 1f 209y

4:30 (4:30) (Class 6) 3-4-Y-O **£1,942** (£578; £288; £144) **Stalls** High

Form RPR

6050 **1** **Siryena**[17] 5119 3-8-0 48 ....(tp) DavidProbert(5) 10 55
(B I Case) *stdd s: hld up in tch: led 2f out: hung lft over 1f out: rdn out* **20/1**

0000 **2** *1* **Tank Commander**[19] 5077 3-8-9 46 .... MartinDwyer 9 57
(W R Muir) *hld up in rr: hdwy over 3f out: sn rdn wnt 2nd over 1f out: kpt on fnl f* **25/1**

0260 **3** *4 ½* **Trawlerman (IRE)**[30] 4691 3-8-6 71 ....(b[1]) AshleyMorgan(7) 6 52
(M H Tompkins) *in rr: hdwy on ins: kpt on to go 3rd over 1f out* **7/2[2]**

0452 **4** *5* **Nikolaievich (IRE)**[24] 4901 3-9-2 60 .... ChrisCatlin 4 45
(P F I Cole) *hld up in tch: rdn 2f out: one pce after* **5/2[1]**

0 **5** *1 ¾* **External Force (IRE)**[47] 4161 3-8-11 0 .... WilliamBuick 3 37
(S A Callaghan) *mid-div: no hdwy fnl 2f* **9/1**

43-0 **6** *1 ¾* **War Anthem**[23] 4930 4-9-6 66 ....(b) PatCosgrave 8 35
(J R Boyle) *trscked ldrs: ev ch 2f out: rdn whn bmpd over 1f out: wknd* **9/2[3]**

000- **7** *22* **Lady Charlemagne**[315] 6433 3-8-8 54 .... SteveDrowne 2 —
(N P Littmoden) *trckd ldrs: wknd wl over 2f out* **25/1**

5612 **8** *5* **Sweet World**[12] 5221 4-9-5 60 .... NCallan 5 —
(B J Llewellyn) *led tl hdd 2f out: hung bdly rt: sn btn and eased* **7/2[2]**

/000 **9** *17* **Pickled Again**[6] 5429 4-8-9 45 .... HayleyTurner 7 —
(S Dow) *trckd ldrs: wknd over 2f out: eased over 1f out* **50/1**

2m 7.70s (4.10) **Going Correction** +0.425s/f (Yiel)
WFA 3 from 4yo 7lb **9** Ran SP% **115.6**
Speed ratings (Par 101): **100,99,95,91,90 88,71,67,53**
.Siryena was claimed by G. Baker for £9000. Trawlerman was claimed by M. Gates for £12000.\n\x\x
Owner Patrick Milmo **Bred** C R Mason **Trained** Edgcote, Northants

FOCUS
This weak claimer was run at a sound pace and the first pair eventually came clear. The form is rated around the time with the winner rated back to his best.
Sweet World Official explanation: jockey said gelding hung right

5604 BET365 BEST ODDS GUARANTEED ON EVERY RACE APPRENTICE H'CAP 7f 214y
5:00 (5:02) (Class 6) (0-60,60) 4-Y-0+ **£1,942** (£578; £288; £144) **Stalls** Low

Form RPR
422 **1** **The Gaikwar (IRE)**[6] 5429 9-9-0 **55** ow5 ....(b) HaddenFrost 8 67
(R A Harris) *a in tch: led over 1f out: drvn out* **6/1**[2]
0000 **2** *2* **Franksalot (IRE)**[2] 5575 8-8-6 **52** ....(p) BMcHugh(5) 4 59
(I W McInnes) *hld up: hdwy 2f out: rn to go 2nd wl ins fnl f* **16/1**
054 **3** *3 ¼* **Colton**[44] 4261 5-8-12 **53** .... DavidProbert 6 53
(J M P Eustace) *hld up in tch: swtchd lft 2f out: r.o wl fnl f to go 3rd nr fin* **9/2**[1]
3216 **4** *hd* **Prince Valentine**[27] 4772 7-8-9 **53** ....(p) JemmaMarshall(3) 12 52
(G L Moore) *prom: led over 2f out: hdd over 1f out: wknd ins fnl f* **12/1**
0403 **5** *¾* **Astroangel**[26] 4806 4-8-11 **55** .... AshleyMorgan(3) 13 52
(M H Tompkins) *racd on outside: rdn and ev ch over 1f out: one pce fnl f* **10/1**
0000 **6** *¾* **Evianne**[12] 5215 4-8-0 **46** oh1 .... AndreaAtzeni(5) 7 42
(P W Hiatt) *mid-div: hdwy whn edgd rt over 2f out: rdn and no hdwy fr over 1f out* **66/1**
2001 **7** *½* **Batchworth Blaise**[11] 5267 5-8-11 **55** .... SophieDoyle(3) 1 49
(E A Wheeler) *in rr: mde sme late hdwy* **8/1**[3]
30-3 **8** *2 ¾* **Night Wolf (IRE)**[50] 4053 8-9-3 **58** .... MCGeran 2 46
(S Curran) *hld up: hdwy 3f out: wknd over 1f out* **8/1**[3]
4012 **9** *4* **Time To Regret**[16] 5157 8-9-2 **60** ....(p) LanceBetts(3) 9 39
(I W McInnes) *trckd ldrs tl wknd wl over 1f out* **9/1**
5106 **10** *8* **Parthenope**[28] 4727 5-8-12 **53** .... JackDean 5 14
(J A Geake) *a in rr* **10/1**
3010 **11** *2 ¼* **Lopinot (IRE)**[5] 5458 5-9-3 **58** ....(p) KellyHarrison 10 13+
(M R Bosley) *trckd ldr: chalng whn wnt lft over 2f: hmpd and lost action: no ch after* **8/1**[3]
0045 **12** *16* **Nothingtodeclaire**[36] 3614 4-8-5 **46** oh1 ....(v) NicolPolli 11 —+
(V Smith) *led tl hdd over 2f out: wkng whn bdly hmpd sn after* **25/1**
250- **13** *64* **Tarkamara (IRE)**[344] 5714 4-9-2 **60** .... WilliamCarson(3) 3 —
(P F I Cole) *slowly away: rdn 3f out: sn lost tch: eased over 1f out: t.o* **16/1**

1m 39.07s (3.07) **Going Correction** +0.425s/f (Yiel) **13** Ran SP% **118.8**
Speed ratings (Par 101): **101,99,95,95,94 94,93,90,86,78 76,60,—**
toteswinger: 1&2 £23.70, 1&3 £4.20, 2&3 £20.50. CSF £97.80 CT £477.10 TOTE £7.10: £2.60, £4.70, £2.10; EX 88.40 Trifecta £308.30 Part won. Pool: £416.64 - 0.20 winning units. Place 6: £1150.00 Place 5: £1163.05 .
Owner Leeway Group Limited **Bred** Burton Agnes Stud Co Ltd **Trained** Earlswood, Monmouths

FOCUS
A poor-quality handicap, confined to apprentice riders, but it was another open heat. The form makes sense and appears sound.
Night Wolf(IRE) Official explanation: jockey said gelding missed the break
Lopinot(IRE) Official explanation: trainer said gelding lost a shoe
Tarkamara(IRE) Official explanation: jockey said filly never travelled
T/Jkpt: Not won. T/Plt: £3,048.50 to a £1 stake. Pool: £70,366.50. 16.85 winning tickets. T/Qpdt: £503.80 to a £1 stake. Pool: £5,038.93. 7.40 winning tickets. JS

5567 KEMPTON (A.W) (R-H)
Wednesday, September 3

OFFICIAL GOING: Standard
Wind: Brisk, behind

5605 PANORAMIC BAR & RESTAURANT H'CAP 1m 2f (P)
6:20 (6:26) (Class 5) (0-75,75) 3-Y-0 **£2,590** (£770; £385; £192) **Stalls** High

Form RPR
5332 **1** **Dark Prospect**[64] 3573 3-8-13 **70** .... PhilipRobinson 6 79
(M A Jarvis) *trckd ldr: led ins fnl 2f: drvn clr ins fnl f: readily* **9/2**[2]
3062 **2** *1 ½* **Title Role**[6] 5428 3-9-1 **72** .... GregFairley 13 78
(P F I Cole) *sn led and t.k.h: rdn 3f out: hdd ins fnl 2f: outpcd by wnr ins fnl f* **7/2**[1]
54 **3** *½* **Bois Joli (IRE)**[18] 5108 3-9-3 **74** .... JohnEgan 8 79
(M Botti) *chsd ldrs: rdn over 2f out: styd on fr over 1f out and kpt on u.p cl home but nvr gng pce to trble wnr* **12/1**
120 **4** *2 ½* **Vilna (USA)**[20] 5017 3-9-4 **75** ....(v) RyanMoore 12 75
(S A Callaghan) *chsd ldrs: rdn over 2f out: wknd fnl f* **13/2**[3]
0061 **5** *6* **Bushy Dell (IRE)**[28] 4732 3-8-11 **73** .... AmyBaker(5) 5 61
(Miss J Feilden) *mid-div: pushed along 3f out: no ch fr over 2f out but mod prog ins fnl f* **10/1**
504 **6** *nse* **Opera De Luna**[25] 4871 3-8-11 **68** .... DarrenWilliams 11 56
(D Shaw) *in rr tl moderate prog fnl 2f* **14/1**
-030 **7** *3 ½* **Ballora (FR)**[6] 5428 3-9-4 **75** .... JimmyFortune 1 56
(S Kirk) *t.k.h: chsd ldrs tl wknd qckly 2f out* **12/1**
5000 **8** *¾* **Dry Speedfit (IRE)**[14] 5185 3-8-13 **70** .... TPQueally 4 49
(G G Margarson) *s.i.s: sn in tch and wd bnd after 2f: wknd ins fnl 3f* **50/1**
0350 **9** *¾* **Filun**[21] 4984 3-9-2 **73** ....(b[1]) DaneO'Neill 10 51
(L M Cumani) *mid-div: rdn and effrt over 3f out: wknd over 2f out* **14/1**
50-6 **10** *3 ¾* **Lobby**[66] 3521 3-8-10 **67** ....(t) JimCrowley 9 37
(Mrs A J Perrett) *t.k.h: a in rr* **20/1**
546 **11** *18* **Canyon Colours (USA)**[25] 4871 3-9-0 **71** ....(b[1]) HayleyTurner 3 5
(G A Butler) *a in rr* **20/1**
-520 **12** *32* **Smooth As Silk (IRE)**[81] 3023 3-8-10 **67** .... ShaneKelly 2 —
(C R Egerton) *s.i.s: wd bnd after 2f: a towards rr: virtually p.u fnl 2f* **22/1**

2m 6.27s (-1.73) **Going Correction** -0.05s/f (Stan) **12** Ran SP% **107.4**
Speed ratings (Par 101): **104,102,102,100,95 95,92,92,91,88 74,48**
toteswinger: 1&2 £2.80, 1&3 £10.90, 2&3 £11.20. CSF £15.94 CT £128.89 TOTE £4.30: £1.80, £1.40, £2.90; EX 14.00.
Owner Michael Hill **Bred** Bearstone Stud **Trained** Newmarket, Suffolk

FOCUS
This looked competitive enough beforehand but very few got into it and it paid to race prominently. The form makes sense rated around the runner-up and fourth.
Ballora(FR) Official explanation: jockey said filly hung right in straight
Smooth As Silk(IRE) Official explanation: jockey said filly stopped quickly

5606 DIGIBET.COM NURSERY 1m (P)
6:50 (6:54) (Class 6) (0-65,65) 2-Y-0 **£2,047** (£604; £302) **Stalls** High

Form RPR
662 **1** **Bright Enough**[27] 4776 2-9-5 **63** .... ChrisCatlin 11 79
(E J O'Neill) *mde virtually all: drvn clr over 1f out: rdn out ins fnl f* **5/1**[1]
3200 **2** *8* **Hold The Bucks (USA)**[5] 5460 2-9-1 **59** .... JamesDoyle 4 57
(J S Moore) *chsd ldrs: wd into st and chsd wnr 2f out: kpt on but sn no ch: drvn out to hold wl btn 2nd* **5/1**[1]
044 **3** *½* **Extremely So**[57] 3821 2-9-2 **60** .... RyanMoore 7 57
(P J McBride) *in rr: rdn and stl plenty to do whn swtchd lft over 2f out: styd on wl appr fnl f and clsng on wl hld 2nd cl home* **8/1**
005 **4** *½* **Pansy Potter**[11] 5277 2-9-4 **62** .... NCallan 10 58
(B J Meehan) *chsng ldrs whn bmpd after 2f and dropped to mid-div: drvn 3f out: styd on fnl 2f and kpt on ins fnl f but nvr in contention* **13/2**[3]
0620 **5** *2* **Josiah Bartlett (IRE)**[5] 5460 2-9-3 **61** .... LiamJones 12 52
(J W Hills) *s.i.s: rdn 3f out: styd on fr 2f and kpt on ins fnl f but nvr in contention* **10/1**
4400 **6** *2* **Lucky Punt**[90] 2759 2-9-4 **62** .... TQuinn 13 49
(B G Powell) *in rr: tl sme prog fnl 2f* **16/1**
050 **7** *¾* **Against The Rules**[26] 4827 2-9-4 **62** .... OscarUrbina 8 47
(P Howling) *in rr tl sme prog fnl 2f* **25/1**
006 **8** *hd* **Starlight Wish**[42] 4304 2-9-5 **63** ....(p) LPKeniry 14 48
(E F Vaughan) *chsd ldrs: rdn and wknd 2f out* **11/1**
000 **9** *2* **Blue Bogey (USA)**[12] 5225 2-9-1 **59** ....(b[1]) SteveDrowne 1 40
(R Charlton) *sn drvn to press wnr: upsides fr 4f out: rdn 3f out: wknd qckly 2f out* **16/1**
0500 **10** *8* **Buckers Beauty (IRE)**[11] 5294 2-9-2 **60** .... JohnEgan 6 23
(P D Evans) *chsd ldrs: rdn 3f out: wknd over 2f out* **14/1**
060 **11** *6* **Dream Huntress**[12] 5241 2-9-7 **65** .... JimmyFortune 9 15
(B J Meehan) *chsd ldrs: bmpd after 2f: wd bnd 3f out and sn wknd* **6/1**[2]
0005 **12** *2* **Haulit**[17] 5116 2-8-13 **60** .... KevinGhunowa(3) 3 5
(R A Harris) *restless stalls: chsd ldrs 5f* **50/1**
3050 **13** *½* **Entrancer (IRE)**[49] 4079 2-9-6 **64** ....(b[1]) MartinDwyer 2 8
(W R Muir) *a in rr* **20/1**
034 **14** *5* **Superstitious Me (IRE)**[23] 4931 2-9-3 **61** .... CatherineGannon 5 —
(B Palling) *in rr: no ch whn wd bnd 3f out* **20/1**

1m 40.6s (0.80) **Going Correction** -0.05s/f (Stan) **14** Ran SP% **123.2**
Speed ratings (Par 93): **94,86,85,85,83 81,80,80,78,70 64,62,61,56**
toteswinger: 1&2 £5.30, 1&3 £4.60, 2&3 £13.30. CSF £28.04 CT £209.37 TOTE £4.10: £1.70, £2.60, £2.50; EX 22.00.
Owner Mrs Joya Burns **Bred** Whitsbury Manor Stud And Mrs M E Slade **Trained** Averham Park, Notts
■ Stewards' Enquiry : Steve Drowne two-day ban: careless riding (Sep 17-18)

FOCUS
Plenty of unexposed juveniles in this line-up, with most making their handicap debuts and stepping up to a mile for the first time. The winner was impressive and the form is rated at face value around the placed horses.

NOTEBOOK
Bright Enough, a half-sister to that decent handicapper Smart Enough, had run with promise in three starts over 7f and, being by Fantastic Light there was always a good chance she would improve for the step up to a mile. Well drawn, she was quickly away, soon had the best position next to the rail, and drew clear for a convincing success. She is obviously a well-handicapped filly and if she turns out under a penalty at Bath on Monday she will take the beating. (op 9-2)
Hold The Bucks(USA) came in for some market support but he had an awkward draw to overcome. Wide around the turn into the straight, he ran a sound race, appreciating the return to Polytrack. (op 8-1)
Extremely So, with Ryan Moore a rare booking for this yard, saw her race out strongly and looks capable of better. (tchd 7-1)
Pansy Potter had shaped as though she would appreciate a longer trip in each of her three previous starts over 6f, but having travelled well through the race she did not quite see this mile out. A drop back to 7f could be the answer. (tchd 6-1)
Josiah Bartlett(IRE), one of the more experienced runners in the line-up, forfeited any advantage his high draw may have given him by being slowly away. He did keep on from off the pace, though. (tchd 9-1)
Lucky Punt has a fairly speedy pedigree and is not really bred for this trip.
Blue Bogey(USA), racing in first-time blinkers, was drawn worst of all and had plenty of use made of him to get up and contest the lead with the eventual winner. He paid for his early effort in the latter stages.
Buckers Beauty(IRE) Official explanation: jockey said filly hung right-handed
Dream Huntress Official explanation: jockey said filly suffered interference in running

5607 DIGIBET CLAIMING STKS 1m (P)
7:20 (7:22) (Class 6) 3-Y-0 **£2,047** (£604; £302) **Stalls** High

Form RPR
6124 **1** **Talk Of Saafend (IRE)**[16] 5149 3-9-2 75 .... RichardHughes 5 78
(R Hannon) *t.k.h: hld up towards rr: impr 3f out: shkn up and hung rt 2f out: rapid hdwy sn after and led appr fnl f: sn in command: readily* **7/2**[2]
0055 **2** *1 ¼* **Too Grand**[27] 4777 3-7-12 49 .... DavidProbert(5) 1 62
(J J Bridger) *in rr: hdwy on outside 3f out: rapid hdwy fr 2f out and chsd wnr insde last but a hld* **40/1**
6054 **3** *4* **Smokey Rye**[19] 5052 3-9-0 72 ....(b) RyanMoore 9 64
(G L Moore) *chsd ldrs: rdn 3f out: styd on to take wl-hld 3rd fnl f* **4/1**[3]
3301 **4** *¾* **Hilbre Court (USA)**[8] 5377 3-9-7 80 .... JimmyFortune 11 69
(B J Meehan) *chsd ldrs: rdn and wnt 2nd 2f out: wknd fnl f* **1/1**[1]
0 **5** *½* **Desert Clover (USA)**[15] 5170 3-9-2 67 .... NCallan 6 63
(P F I Cole) *sn led: rdn over 2f out: hdd & wknd appr fnl f* **16/1**
0206 **6** *8* **Mouse White**[12] 5230 3-8-6 52 .... FergusSweeney 10 35
(H Candy) *sn pushed along to chse ldrs: rdn 3f out: wknd 2f out* **33/1**
2446 **7** *1 ½* **Regal Veil**[21] 4988 3-8-8 48 .... EdwardCreighton 7 33
(R W Price) *towards rr most of way* **33/1**
6000 **8** *2 ½* **Starfinch**[11] 5269 3-8-3 37 ....(p) ChrisCatlin 2 22
(J J Bridger) *bhd most of way* **100/1**
0550 **9** *shd* **Quinzey's Best (IRE)**[34] 4572 3-8-8 56 .... PaulDoe 8 27
(W J Knight) *slowly away: a towards rr* **20/1**
1106 **10** *5* **The Hoofer (IRE)**[8] 5377 3-8-4 59 ....(b) MartinDwyer 3 12
(I A Wood) *plld hrd: chsd ldr untl wknd qckly appr fnl 2f* **20/1**

1m 39.48s (-0.32) **Going Correction** -0.05s/f (Stan) **10** Ran SP% **116.9**
Speed ratings (Par 99): **99,97,93,93,92 84,83,80,80,75**
toteswinger: 1&2 £10.00, 1&3 £2.50, 2&3 £14.90. CSF £138.07 TOTE £5.10: £1.50, £4.40, £1.20; EX 120.90.
Owner J B R Leisure Ltd **Bred** Michael Dalton **Trained** East Everleigh, Wilts

FOCUS
They did not go much of a pace in the early stages of this claimer and the winning time was only 1.12sec quicker than the nursery earlier on the card. The proximity of the runner-up raises doubts about the form.
The Hoofer(IRE) Official explanation: jockey said filly ran too free

5608 DIGIBET CASINO MAIDEN STKS 7f (P)
7:50 (7:50) (Class 5) 3-Y-O+ £2,590 (£770; £385; £192) Stalls High

Form RPR
0- **1** **Cadre (IRE)**[334] 5971 3-9-3 0........................ JimmyFortune 4 87+
(J H M Gosden) *mid-div: hdwy over 2f out: drvn and qcknd wl over 1f out to ld ins fnl f: sn clr* **4/1**[2]
34 **2** 3 ¼ **Pivka**[19] 5076 3-8-12 0........................ RyanMoore 13 70
(Sir Michael Stoute) *chsd ldrs: rdn to ld appr fnl f: hdd and outpcd ins fnl f* **5/1**
5 **3** *hd* **Uncle Fred**[20] 5023 3-9-3 0........................ JimCrowley 6 74
(P R Chamings) *sn chsng ldr: rdn and outpcd ins fnl 2f: styd on again fnl f and kpt on wl cl home* **25/1**
0-3 **4** 2 **Pride Of India (USA)**[124] 1763 3-9-3 0........................ ShaneKelly 10 69
(J Noseda) *led: rdn over 2f out: hdd appr fnl f: wknd ins fnl f* **7/2**[1]
03 **5** ¾ **Aegean Pride**[20] 5023 3-8-12 0........................ RichardHughes 2 62
(R Hannon) *towards rr early: hdwy over 2f out: qcknd to chse ldrs over 1f out: no ex ins fnl f* **15/2**
6 ¾ **Gold Again (USA)** 3-8-12 0........................ AdamKirby 7 60+
(W R Swinburn) *towards rr: hdwy fr 2f out: kpt on fnl f but nvr gng ace to be competitive* **9/2**[3]
34 **7** *hd* **Onemoreandstay**[16] 5160 3-8-12 0........................ EdwardCreighton 1 59
(R W Price) *chsd ldrs: rdn over 2f out: wknd over 1f out* **9/1**
0 **8** 5 **James Pollard (IRE)**[23] 4929 3-9-3 0........................ TQuinn 12 51+
(D R C Elsworth) *sn t.k.h in rr: sme prog on ins whn hmpd over 2f out: nvr in contention after* **33/1**
0- **9** 1 **Pretty Orchid**[330] 6087 3-8-12 0........................ OscarUrbina 14 43
(G C H Chung) *in rr: sme prog on ins whn hmpd over 2f out: nvr in contention after* **50/1**
3 **10** 2 ¼ **Rightcar Dominic**[188] 734 3-9-3 0........................ LPKeniry 9 42
(Peter Grayson) *chsd ldrs: rdn 3f out: wknd 2f out* **33/1**
0-0 **11** 3 ½ **Shybutwilling (IRE)**[89] 2772 3-8-9 0........................ JackMitchell(3) 8 28
(Mrs P N Dutfield) *chsd ldrs: rdn 3f out: wknd over 2f out* **100/1**
56 **12** *nse* **Danesman**[109] 2207 3-9-3 0........................ GeorgeBaker 11 33
(G L Moore) *a towards rr* **11/1**
13 7 **Hilltop Legacy** 5-9-2 0........................ JohnEgan 5 9
(S W James) *s.i.s: a towards rr* **25/1**

1m 26.86s (0.86) **Going Correction** -0.05s/f (Stan)
WFA 3 from 5yo 4lb **13** Ran SP% **123.7**
Speed ratings (Par 103): **93,89,89,86,85 85,84,79,77,75 71,71,63**
toteswinger: 1&2 £1.60, 1&3 £44.30, 2&3 £23.30. CSF £23.85 TOTE £5.60: £2.00, £1.70, £7.60; EX 34.50.
Owner H R H Princess Haya Of Jordan **Bred** Mrs Eithne Hamilton **Trained** Newmarket, Suffolk

FOCUS
A fair maiden for the time of year, but the early pace was steady. The form looks reasonable with the placed horses and the fifth close to their marks.
Pretty Orchid Official explanation: jockey said, regarding the running and riding, his orders were to jump off where filly was happy, adding that she jumped slowly and he was further back than he wanted to be in the early stages, further adding that filly stayed on at one pace on entering home straight; vet said filly was sore after race

5609 EUROPEAN BREEDERS' FUND MEDIAN AUCTION MAIDEN STKS 6f (P)
8:20 (8:21) (Class 5) 2-Y-O £3,561 (£1,059; £529; £264) Stalls High

Form RPR
433 **1** **Frognal (IRE)**[12] 5244 2-9-3 95........................ JamieSpencer 5 81+
(B J Meehan) *wnt lft s: trckd ldrs: qcknd: hung rt and led 2f out: hung rt again over 1f out: shkn up: easily* **4/9**[1]
3056 **2** 1 ½ **I Am The Best**[20] 5021 2-9-3 95........................ RichardMullen 10 75
(D M Simcock) *led: rdn and hdd 2f out: crossed: swtchd lft and lost 2nd 1f out: rallied to retake 2nd last stride but no ch w wnr* **4/1**[2]
54 **3** *nse* **Retro (IRE)**[43] 4274 2-9-3 0........................ RichardHughes 8 75
(R Hannon) *t.k.h: chsd ldrs: rdn to go 2nd 1f out: sn no ch w wnr: lost 2nd last stride* **9/1**
06 **4** 3 ¼ **Arrogance**[15] 5165 2-9-3 0........................ GeorgeBaker 6 64
(G L Moore) *chsd ldr 4f out: rdn and one pce 2f out: kpt on fnl f* **20/1**
4 **5** ½ **Bartica (IRE)**[23] 4926 2-9-3........................ RyanMoore 7 63
(R Hannon) *chsd ldrs 1/2-way: rdn over 2f out: wknd over 1f out* **8/1**[3]
6 4 **Chosen Son (IRE)** 2-9-3 0........................ AlanMunro 4 51
(P J O'Gorman) *bmpd s: s.i.s: outpcd but kpt on fnl f* **25/1**
0 **7** 1 ¾ **Ditto Ditto**[16] 5158 2-9-3 0........................ TedDurcan 2 45
(D R Lanigan) *wnt rt s: plld hrd and chsd ldrs after 1f: wknd over 2f out* **66/1**
0 **8** 1 ½ **Zellers**[16] 5147 2-8-12 0........................ LiamJones 9 36
(W J Haggas) *outpcd* **33/1**
6 **9** 25 **Group Leader (IRE)**[33] 4598 2-9-3 0........................(v[1]) JimCrowley 1 —
(J R Jenkins) *a in rr* **100/1**

1m 14.13s (1.03) **Going Correction** -0.05s/f (Stan) **9** Ran SP% **124.4**
Speed ratings (Par 95): **91,89,88,83,83 77,75,73,40**
toteswinger: 1&2 £1.30, 1&3 £1.70, 2&3 £4.60. CSF £2.79 TOTE £1.40: £1.10, £1.10, £1.70; EX 3.70.
Owner Raymond Tooth **Bred** Bryan Ryan **Trained** Manton, Wilts

FOCUS
Both the winner and runner-up seemed to run well below their official marks of 95 and this was not a strong maiden.

NOTEBOOK
Frognal(IRE) found this a suitable opportunity to get off the mark at the fourth attempt. With his main market rival, I Am The Best, seemingly regressive, he confirmed the promise he had shown on his last two starts, including when third in the rearranged St Leger Yearling Stakes at Newmarket, although he did not have to run up to his official mark of 95. He was a little keen early, but picked up well in the straight and settled matters quickly enough, despite drifting to his right. He did not seem to be doing a great deal in front, and one would imagine that if he is stepped up to Pattern company next time, he will be held on to for a bit longer. Decent ground is thought to be required for him on turf. (op 1-2 after 8-15 in places and 4-7 in a place)
I Am The Best, who stumbled leaving the stalls and was apparently unsuited by the easy ground at Salisbury last time, was looking to bounce back to form - his best efforts when running well in the Coventry and July Stakes appeared to give him every chance – but despite having the best draw and being up there throughout in a steadily run race, he was easily put in his place by the winner. His mark of 95 means he is likely to continue to prove difficult to place. (tchd 9-2)
Retro(IRE), who was having his third run, looked to have secured second place inside the last but his rider appeared to take things a bit easy close home. Edged out of second in a photo by the rallying I Am The Best, he nevertheless ran well enough to suggest that he should pay his way in nurseries.
Arrogance did not seem to get home over 7f at Brighton last time and was outpaced from the turn this time over this shorter trip. He will find his level in lesser handicap company. (op 14-1)
Bartica(IRE) showed promise on his debut and, while not improving on that effort, he was not given a hard race and no doubt better will be see of him once he is eligible for handicaps after one more run.

5610 TOPNAPS.CO.UK H'CAP 6f (P)
8:50 (8:50) (Class 6) (0-65,65) 3-Y-O+ £2,047 (£604; £302) Stalls High

Form RPR
1-61 **1** **Tubby Isaacs**[26] 4824 4-9-6 65........................ NCallan 2 82+
(P J Makin) *trckd ldrs: wnt 2nd over 3f out: hung rt 2f out: drvn to ld appr fnl f: pushed out* **5/2**[1]
0064 **2** 2 **Rhapsilian**[46] 4186 4-8-12 57........................ DaneO'Neill 4 65
(J A Geake) *in rr: hdwy and hung rt over 2f out: styd on to chse wnr fnl f but nvr any ch* **8/1**
6006 **3** ¾ **Musical Script (USA)**[15] 5171 5-8-10 55........................(b) ChrisCatlin 1 61
(Mouse Hamilton-Fairley) *plld hrd: led after 2f: rdn over 2f out: hdd over 1f out: one pce ins fnl f* **16/1**
4020 **4** 2 **Guildenstern (IRE)**[16] 5144 6-8-13 58........................ JimmyQuinn 12 57+
(P Howling) *hmpd and dropped in rr after 2f: hdwy on ins whn nt clr run over 2f out: styd on again fnl f but nvr in contention* **6/1**[2]
3140 **5** ½ **Arfinnit (IRE)**[43] 4273 7-8-9 54........................(p) TedDurcan 8 52
(Mrs A L M King) *led 2f: styd chsng ldrs to 2f out: wknd over 1f out* **20/1**
0343 **6** ½ **Sheriff's Silk**[37] 4478 4-9-4 63........................(b) PaulEddery 3 59
(G D Blake) *in tch: rdn and sme prog over 2f out: nvr gng pce to be competitive* **10/1**
0660 **7** *shd* **Muktasb (USA)**[50] 4058 7-9-6 65........................(v) AdamKirby 7 61
(D Shaw) *bumpered s: rr: styd on fr over 1f out: nvr in contention* **16/1**
1250 **8** 1 **Forced Upon Us**[43] 4284 4-9-3 62........................(b) RichardHughes 9 54
(P J McBride) *in rr: shkn up over 2f out: no imp: eased whn no ch ins fnl f* **15/2**[3]
1552 **9** ½ **Linda Green**[10] 5315 7-9-6 65........................ EdwardCreighton 6 56
(M R Channon) *outpcd* **8/1**
1565 **10** 2 **Diminuto**[20] 5026 4-9-0 62........................ PatrickHills(3) 5 46
(M D I Usher) *chsd ldrs: rdn over 3f out: wknd 2f out* **25/1**
1432 **11** *hd* **Bentley**[28] 4746 4-9-3 62........................ TPQueally 11 46
(J G Given) *wnt lft s: chsd ldrs to 2f out: sn wknd* **6/1**[2]
0-56 **12** 1 ½ **Gambling Jack**[54] 3916 3-8-13 60........................ ShaneKelly 10 39
(A W Carroll) *hmpd s: a bhd* **20/1**

1m 12.59s (-0.51) **Going Correction** -0.05s/f (Stan)
WFA 3 from 4yo+ 2lb **12** Ran SP% **125.4**
Speed ratings (Par 101): **101,98,97,94,94 93,93,91,91,88 88,86**
toteswinger: 1&2 £9.20, 1&3 £12.80, 2&3 £0.00. CSF £23.59 CT £243.95 TOTE £3.60: £2.20, £4.00, £9.90; EX 32.10.
Owner John Khan & Arnold Bros **Bred** J W Ford **Trained** Ogbourne Maisey, Wilts

FOCUS
A field made up mainly of exposed sprinters, but the one exception was the lightly raced Tubby Isaacs who scored well with the placed horses running close to previous course and distance form.
Guildenstern(IRE) Official explanation: jockey said gelding was denied a clear run
Bentley Official explanation: jockey said gelding stumbled leaving stalls

5611 WEATHERBYS BLOODSTOCK INSURANCE APPRENTICE H'CAP (ROUND 10) 1m 3f (P)
9:20 (9:20) (Class 6) (0-60,60) 3-Y-O+ £2,047 (£604; £302) Stalls High

Form RPR
5324 **1** **Mixing**[23] 4930 6-9-8 56........................ DavidProbert 5 63
(M J Attwater) *chsd ldrs: led 2f out: styd on wl whn strly chal thrght fnl f* **8/1**
6545 **2** *hd* **Citron Presse (USA)**[33] 4607 3-9-1 60.....(p) Louis-PhilippeBeuzelin(3) 1 67
(J H M Gosden) *towards rr and wd bnd after 2f: hdwy 4f out: styd on u.p to press wnr wl ins fnl f: no ex last strides* **15/2**[3]
0306 **3** ½ **Garafena**[18] 5087 5-9-11 59........................ HaddenFrost 4 65
(B G Powell) *chsd ldrs: rdn to chal over 2f out: stl upsides ins fnl f: no ex cl home* **14/1**
500 **4** ¾ **Oasis Sun (IRE)**[43] 4267 5-9-1 54........................(b) AndreaAtzeni(5) 6 59
(J R Best) *mid-div 1/2-way: hdwy fr 3f out: styd on wl fr 2f out and gng on ins fnl f: nt rch ldng trio* **25/1**
606P **5** 2 **Saloon (USA)**[4] 5489 4-9-4 55........................ WilliamCarson(3) 10 56+
(S Curran) *chsd ldrs: lost position 4f out: rdn and styd on again fr over 2f out: kpt on ins fnl f: one pce nr fin* **5/2**[1]
5003 **6** 2 ¼ **Shouldntbethere (IRE)**[32] 4635 4-9-2 53........................ JPHamblett(3) 8 51
(Mrs P N Dutfield) *in rr: hdwy 2f out: styd on fnl f* **20/1**
0642 **7** 1 ½ **Noah Jameel**[23] 4919 6-9-5 53........................ JackDean 3 48+
(A G Newcombe) *stmbld bnd after 2f: rr: sme prog fnl 2f* **9/2**[2]
0305 **8** ½ **Hatch A Plan (IRE)**[23] 4936 7-8-13 52........................ PNolan(5) 12 46
(Mouse Hamilton-Fairley) *chsd ldrs: rdn 3f out: wknd 2f out* **14/1**
00 **9** 1 **Harveys Spirit (IRE)**[34] 4564 3-8-13 58........................ RichardEvans(3) 9 51
(S Curran) *mid-div: rdn over 3f out: no ch w ldrs fnl 2f* **33/1**
4600 **10** 2 ¼ **Pearl (IRE)**[16] 5154 4-9-4 52........................(b) KellyHarrison 2 41
(I A Wood) *chsd ldrs: led over 5f out: hdd 2f out and sn wknd* **25/1**
2206 **11** *hd* **Medieval Maiden**[34] 4568 5-9-8 56........................ MCGeran 7 44
(Mrs L J Mongan) *s.i.s: nvr bttr then mid-div* **8/1**
2120 **12** 22 **Check Up (IRE)**[19] 5058 7-9-6 57........................ HarryPoulton(3) 11 8
(J L Flint) *led 2f: styd pressing ldrs to 3f out* **8/1**
-260 **13** 3 ½ **Highly Regal (IRE)**[49] 4086 3-9-1 60........................ AshleyMorgan(3) 14 5
(R A Teal) *led after 2f: hdd over 5f out: wknd 4f out* **16/1**
0500 **14** *nk* **Ramprakash**[18] 5087 3-9-1 60........................ BillyCray(3) 13 5
(M L W Bell) *chsd ldrs: rdn 1/2-way: wknd 4f out* **14/1**

2m 21.07s (-0.83) **Going Correction** -0.05s/f (Stan)
WFA 3 from 4yo+ 8lb **14** Ran SP% **133.1**
Speed ratings (Par 101): **101,100,100,99,98 96,95,95,94,93 92,76,74,74**
toteswinger: 1&2 £12.10, 1&3 £14.10, 2&3 £13.90. CSF £71.22 CT £867.10 TOTE £5.20: £1.70, £3.20, £5.70; EX 56.60 Place 6: £52.35 Place 5: £29.16.
Owner Canisbay Bloodstock **Bred** Juddmonte Farms **Trained** Epsom, Surrey
■ David Probert is the series winner.

FOCUS
An ordinary apprentice handicap but sound enough form rated around the placed horses.
Harveys Spirit(IRE) Official explanation: jockey said filly suffered interference at start
T/Plt: £28.40 to a £1 stake. Pool: £82,425.44. 2,113.03 winning tickets. T/Qpdt: £14.70 to a £1 stake. Pool: £6,178.36. 309.20 winning tickets. ST

5575 **LINGFIELD** (L-H)

Wednesday, September 3

OFFICIAL GOING: Turf course - soft (good to soft in places); all-weather - standard

Wind: Brisk, behind Weather: Fine

5612 BETLIVE & IN-RUNNING @ WILLIAMHILL.CO.UK MAIDEN STKS 1m 3f 106y

2:20 (2:21) (Class 5) 3-Y-0+ **£2,590** (£770; £385; £192) **Stalls** High

Form RPR

622 **1** **Fortune City (UAE)**[26] 4821 3-9-3 76........ LDettori 4 81+
(Saeed Bin Suroor) *mde all: forged clr fr 3f out: shkn up and flashed tail over 1f out: unchal* **9/4**[2]

2 **2** *7* **Vine Street (IRE)**[12] 5231 3-8-12 0........ PhilipRobinson 7 65+
(M A Jarvis) *trckd wnr 3f: wnt 2nd again over 3f out: sn rdn and lft bhd: no ch fnl 2f* **8/11**[1]

60 **3** *2* **Mary Athena (FR)**[19] 5042 3-8-7 0........ NicolPolli(5) 1 58
(M G Quinlan) *hld up: last and outpcd 4f out: prog after: rdn and kpt on to take modest 3rd over 1f out: no ch* **40/1**

0 **4** *1/2* **Euroceleb (IRE)**[24] 4909 3-8-12 0........ EdwardCreighton 3 57+
(H Morrison) *towards rr: rdn and outpcd 4f out: 7th and struggling 3f out: picked up 2f out: styd on wl: nrst fin* **50/1**

00 **5** *6* **Sleepy Mountain**[26] 4821 4-9-4 0........ HarryPoulton(7) 6 53
(A Middleton) *chsd wnr after 3f to over 4f out: hrd rdn and wknd over 2f out* **66/1**

00 **6** *1 3/4* **Water Violet**[41] 4342 3-8-12 0........ RobertWinston 11 45
(J R Fanshawe) *prom: chsd wnr over 4f out to over 3f out: sn wknd u.p* **25/1**

6 **7** *19* **Colourful Move**[62] 3654 3-9-3 0........ TedDurcan 8 19
(H R A Cecil) *trckd ldrs: outpcd 4f out: struggling 3f out: virtually p.u over 1f out: t.o* **14/1**

3 **8** *1/2* **Winter Miss (USA)**[19] 5047 3-8-12 0........ RichardHughes 10 14+
(J Noseda) *stdd s: hld up in last: sme prog 4f out but already outpcd: shkn up briefly 3f out: sn heavily eased: t.o: sddle slipped* **8/1**[3]

00 **9** *22* **Hard To Resist (IRE)**[14] 5182 3-9-3 0........(b[1]) DaneO'Neill 5 —
(P R Webber) *dwlt: in tch tl wknd u.p over 4f out: wl t.o* **66/1**

2m 35.19s (3.69) **Going Correction** +0.425s/f (Yiel)
WFA 3 from 4yo+ 8lb **9** Ran SP% **117.7**
Speed ratings (Par 103): **103,97,96,96,91 90,76,76,60**
toteswinger: 1&2 £1.30, 1&3 £10.40, 2&3 £9.90. CSF £4.19 TOTE £4.00: £1.30, £1.10, £5.60; EX 5.00.
Owner Godolphin **Bred** Darley **Trained** Newmarket, Suffolk

FOCUS
A fairly interesting maiden but it is doubtful whether the winner had to improve to score and the third is the best guide to the level.
Euroceleb(IRE) Official explanation: jockey said filly ran green
Winter Miss(USA) Official explanation: jockey said saddle slipped

5613 WILLIAM HILL ON 0800 44 40 40 H'CAP 2m

2:50 (2:51) (Class 6) (0-65,68) 3-Y-0+ **£2,047** (£604; £302) **Stalls** Low

Form RPR

0501 **1** **Rutba**[10] 5322 3-8-5 52 6ex........(v) RichardMullen 17 62
(M P Tregoning) *dwlt and pushed up to go prom: wnt 2nd 4f out: drvn 3f out: led over 1f out: asserted fnl 150yds* **9/2**[1]

1651 **2** *1 1/2* **Chiff Chaff**[8] 5385 4-9-3 54 6ex........ TolleyDean(3) 11 62
(C R Dore) *trckd ldr: led 5f out: drvn over 3f out: hdd over 1f out: no ex fnl 100yds* **10/1**

2134 **3** *1/2* **Kokkokila**[20] 5027 4-9-13 61........ RyanMoore 4 68
(Lady Herries) *hld up in rr: smooth prog over 4f out: drvn and nt qckn over 2f out: kpt on fnl f: nrst fin* **5/1**[2]

22 **4** *1/2* **Stoop To Conquer**[8] 5385 8-10-0 62........ TonyCulhane 12 69
(A W Carroll) *hld up towards rr: smooth prog 4f out: drvn and nt qckn 3f out: plugged on one pce fnl 2f* **13/2**[3]

4115 **5** *1* **Trigger's Friend**[27] 4775 4-9-8 56........ JohnEgan 2 62
(Jamie Poulton) *trckd ldrs: rdn 5f out: stl chsng and wl in tch 2f out: one pce u.p* **7/1**

0055 **6** *2 3/4* **Kalokairi (IRE)**[11] 5269 3-8-11 58........(b) TedDurcan 6 60
(J L Dunlop) *hld up towards rr: stdy prog over 4f out: chsd ldrs 3f out: sn rdn and nt qckn: fdd over 1f out* **9/1**

644 **7** *9* **Brave Bugsy (IRE)**[32] 4652 5-9-8 56........ LPKeniry 1 48
(A M Balding) *dwlt and rousted along early: in tch in midfield: rdn 5f out: wknd fr 3f out* **9/1**

505- **8** *7* **Openide**[103] 4531 7-9-4 52........(p) JoeFanning 5 35
(B W Duke) *rn in snatches in last pair: t.o 4f out: styd on fnl 2f* **18/1**

4602 **9** *1 3/4* **Brave Boogie**[44] 4247 3-8-9 56........(b) MickyFenton 16 37
(H J L Dunlop) *led to 5f out: wknd u.p 3f out* **16/1**

3042 **10** *12* **Mister Completely (IRE)**[9] 5367 7-9-5 53........(v) JamesDoyle 10 20
(Ms J S Doyle) *settled in rr: rdn and no prog over 3f out: wl btn after: t.o* **11/1**

5341 **11** *9* **Sonnengold (GER)**[40] 4366 7-9-7 55........ JimCrowley 9 11
(B J Llewellyn) *prom but nvr gng wl: dropped to last bef 1/2-way: t.o 4f out* **10/1**

3m 42.18s (7.38) **Going Correction** +0.425s/f (Yiel)
WFA 3 from 4yo+ 13lb **11** Ran SP% **118.3**
Speed ratings (Par 101): **98,97,97,96,96 94,90,86,86,80 75**
toteswinger: 1&2 £11.30, 1&3 £5.60, 2&3 £14.10. CSF £49.95 CT £236.22 TOTE £4.70: £1.50, £5.10, £2.30; EX 48.40.
Owner William Lea Screed Mac's Plaster & Home **Bred** Shadwell Estate Company Limited **Trained** Lambourn, Berks

FOCUS
The pace looked fair considering the going, but quite a few of them seemed to have a chance as they started up the home straight. The form looks sound with the majority of the first six close to their marks.
Mister Completely(IRE) Official explanation: jockey said gelding was unsuited by the good (good to soft places) ground

5614 WILLIAMHILLCASINO.COM (S) STKS 6f (P)

3:20 (3:22) (Class 6) 2-Y-0 **£1,978** (£584; £292) **Stalls** Low

Form RPR

0065 **1** **Courageous Nature (IRE)**[9] 5363 2-8-11 57........ EddieAhern 9 62
(B J Meehan) *in tch: prog to trck ldrs 1/2-way: effrt 2f out: drvn to ld ins fnl f: kpt on wl* **8/1**

2330 **2** *1/2* **Raise All In (IRE)**[11] 5274 2-8-6 70........ RichardSmith 1 55
(R Hannon) *w ldrs 2f: settled cl up on inner: effrt 2f out: led 1f out: sn hdd: styd on but hld last 75yds* **4/5**[1]

503 **3** *2 1/4* **Handcuff**[43] 4270 2-8-11 67........ ShaneKelly 2 53
(J A Osborne) *w ldrs: led over 2f out: hdd 1f out: fdd* **5/1**[2]

630 **4** *3 1/4* **Ashwinder (IRE)**[14] 5184 2-8-6 56........ GabrielHannon(5) 4 44
(B J Meehan) *dwlt: wl in rr: outpcd overe 2f out: bmpd along and kpt on steadily fr over 1f out* **6/1**[3]

00 **5** *nk* **Abitofaboost (IRE)**[5] 5475 2-8-7 0 ow1........ LPKeniry 11 39
(Peter Grayson) *wl away fr wd draw to join ldrs: led after 2f to over 2f out: wknd over 1f out* **66/1**

00 **6** *2* **Dancing Delta**[57] 3821 2-8-6 0........(b[1]) RichardMullen 7 32
(W R Muir) *awkward s: keen and hld up: green and wd bnd 4f out: prog to join ldrs over 2f out: wknd over 1f out* **25/1**

0045 **7** *8* **Premier Demon (IRE)**[29] 4706 2-8-6 53........ JohnEgan 8 8
(P D Evans) *already rdn in rr whn forced wd bnd 4f out: prog and in tch 1/2-way: sn wknd* **14/1**

0050 **8** *1 3/4* **Free To Choose (IRE)**[20] 5021 2-8-11 43........ AndrewElliott 6 7
(A P Jarvis) *t.k.h early: cl up: trapped bhd wkng rival 1/2-way: lost pl completely and sn gave up* **33/1**

9 *nk* **Lucky In Love (IRE)** 2-8-3 0........ DominicFox(3) 10 1
(Mark Gillard) *dwlt: a in rr: outpcd fr 1/2-way: sn bhd* **25/1**

00 **10** *6* **Abacus House (IRE)**[12] 5214 2-8-6 0 ow3........ TolleyDean(3) 5 —
(W G M Turner) *led 2f: wknd rapidly bef 1/2-way: t.o* **50/1**

1m 12.88s (0.98) **Going Correction** -0.025s/f (Stan) **10** Ran SP% **118.4**
Speed ratings (Par 93): **92,91,88,84,83 80,70,67,67,59**
toteswinger: 1&2 £2.90, 1&3 £3.20, 2&3 £2.30. CSF £14.59 TOTE £9.30: £1.90, £1.20, £1.40; EX 18.90.The winner was sold to A. McCabe for 7,000gns. Handcuff was claimed by J. Gallagher for £6000. Raise All In was claimed by J R. Owen for £6000.
Owner N B Attenborough **Bred** Matthew Duffy **Trained** Manton, Wilts

FOCUS
The first three home were all trying the grade for the first time and went home with new connections after the auction. The form could be better than rated but the proximity of the fifth limits things.

NOTEBOOK
Courageous Nature(IRE), having his first start on the all-weather, attracted a bit of market support last time after a break but ultimately was a little disappointing in nursery company. Dropped in grade, he was always travelling nicely behind the pace and forged his way to the front inside the final furlong. He seems sure to get another furlong. (op 7-1 tchd 6-1)
Raise All In(IRE) broke well from her low draw but eventually dropped slightly off the leaders after being prominent. She got to the lead again up the home straight and was only worried out of it in the final half a furlong. Nicely clear of the third, she should win a race before too long. (op 10-11 tchd Evens and 11-10 in places)
Handcuff, who has only raced on artificial surfaces, showed a lot of early pace but did not quite get home. This effort came after a lay-off, so he can improve a little for the run. (op 11-2)
Ashwinder(IRE) got badly outpaced three furlongs from home but kept on quite well through runners up the straight. His ideal distance is not easy to gauge at the moment, as he had looked to not stay seven furlongs before but was doing all his best work at the finish in this. (op 15-2)
Abitofaboost(IRE) showed a lot of early pace but was another not to get home. She is bred for sprinting and will surely be found a race in time.
Dancing Delta pulled a bit in the early stages and did not look completely straightforward under pressure in first-time blinkers. (tchd 33-1)

5615 WILLIAMHILLPOKER.COM NOVICE STKS 7f (P)

3:50 (3:52) (Class 5) 2-Y-0 **£3,238** (£963; £481; £240) **Stalls** Low

Form RPR

1 **1** **Playfellow (IRE)**[46] 4176 2-9-5 0........ PhilipRobinson 5 93+
(M A Jarvis) *pressed ldr: shkn up to ld over 1f out: drew clr fnl f: readily* **11/8**[1]

2 *2 1/4* **Musleh (USA)** 2-8-8 0........ LDettori 2 75+
(Saeed Bin Suroor) *wl in tch: prog to go 3rd jst over 2f out: shkn up over 1f out: kpt on fnl f to take 2nd fnl strides* **7/2**[2]

214 **3** *shd* **Spanish Cygnet (USA)**[41] 4348 2-9-0 85........ JimCrowley 7 81
(Mrs A J Perrett) *led at stdy pce: rdn over 2f out: hdd and one pce over 1f out* **6/1**

06 **4** *2 1/4* **Dalradian (IRE)**[21] 4974 2-8-12 0........ PaulDoe 3 73
(W J Knight) *t.k.h early and restrained into last pair: prog over 2f out: rdn over 1f out: kpt on one pce* **20/1**

5 *2 1/2* **Comadoir (IRE)**[82] 3011 2-8-12 0........ FergusSweeney 1 67
(Miss Jo Crowley) *cl up: rdn 3f out: steadily outpcd fr 2f out* **20/1**

214 **6** *1 1/4* **Kentish Dream**[30] 4685 2-9-5 86........ DaneO'Neill 6 71
(S A Callaghan) *trckd ldng pair: rdn wl over 2f out: wknd wl over 1f out* **10/1**

1230 **7** *3/4* **Indian Art (IRE)**[12] 5244 2-9-2 86........ RichardHughes 8 66
(R Hannon) *racd wd in rr: reminder 4f out: outpcd fr over 2f out: no ch after* **5/1**[3]

8 *6* **King's Sabre** 2-8-8 0........ RichardMullen 4 43
(W R Muir) *dwlt: a in last trio: wknd 2f out* **66/1**

1m 25.16s (0.36) **Going Correction** -0.025s/f (Stan) **8** Ran SP% **115.4**
Speed ratings (Par 95): **96,93,93,90,87 86,85,78**
toteswinger: 1&2 £2.10, 1&3 £2.80, 2&3 £6.10. CSF £6.16 TOTE £2.40: £1.10, £1.80, £2.00; EX 7.60.
Owner Sheikh Ahmed Al Maktoum **Bred** Darley **Trained** Newmarket, Suffolk

FOCUS
This looked the best race on the card. Half of them had already managed a win, so this should turn out to be fairly strong form despite the pace looking ordinary in the early stages and the winning time being modest. The form looks strong and the race has been rated positively.

NOTEBOOK
Playfellow(IRE), who apparently came to the Jarvis stable with a bit of a reputation from pre-training, created a good impression when sluicing through the mud at Haydock in the middle of July and built on that win to come home a comfortable winner. He holds a Group 1 Middle Park Stakes entry later in the season and looks the sort to ply his trade at a higher level. (op 6-4 tchd 5-4 and 13-8 in places)
Musleh(USA) has a very American pedigree, being by one of the most sought-after stallions in the US and out of a top-class racemare, who won a Grade 1 handicap in 2004. His entries suggested that connections believed he was fairly useful on what they had seen at home and he showed enough on his debut to suggest that they were right. A horse with a bit of substance, he should improve for the run and win next time if kept to a sensible level. (tchd 4-1)
Spanish Cygnet(USA), the only filly in the race, looked unlucky not to finish much closer in a Listed event last time after the winner hung right across her, which meant her jockey had to snatch her up sharply. This was another good effort against some promising-looking sorts. One would imagine she could win again this season if kept on the go. (op 8-1)
Dalradian(IRE), whose six siblings have all won at least one race on the Flat, showed plenty of promise on his debut but looked much too keen last time when fancied to reach the winner's enclosure on his second start. Held up, he stayed on well late in the day and looks a winner waiting to happen, possibly in nurseries for which he is now qualified. (op 22-1 tchd 25-1 and 16-1)

Comadoir(IRE) was on the go early for Jim Bolger, for whom he finished second on five of his six starts. Having his first run for Jo Crowley, he was not completely disgraced but never looked likely to play a part. (tchd 16-1)
Kentish Dream disappointed last time when dropped in trip after winning a race at Lingfield (on the turf over 7f) that has produced plenty of winners. He got completely outpaced about three furlongs from home and never got back on terms. (op 7-1)
Indian Art(IRE), who finished second in the Listed Woodcote Stakes at Epsom at the Derby meeting, was not beaten that far in a big sales race last time, but he received a reminder almost four furlongs out and never gave his supporters much hope of collecting. (op 6-1 tchd 13-2)
King's Sabre was out of his depth on his first start.

5616 WILLIAMHILLBINGO.COM H'CAP — 7f (P)
4:20 (4:21) (Class 6) (0-65,65) 3-Y-O — £2,047 (£604; £302) Stalls Low

Form				RPR
4004	1		**Lawton**50 4061 3-9-2 **63** PaulFitzsimons 14	68
			(Miss J R Tooth) *trckd ldrs: hung wd bnd 2f out: prog over 1f out: drvn to ld last 150yds: jst hld on* **25/1**	
3433	2	*nk*	**Gulch's Rose (USA)**43 4284 3-9-3 **64** RyanMoore 13	68+
			(J Noseda) *hld up in rr: c wd bnd 2f out and only 11th wl over 1f out: drvn and r.o strly fnl f: jst failed: too much to do* **5/2**1	
6002	3	¾	**Feasible**35 4524 3-9-3 **64** (b1) JamesDoyle 3	66
			(J G Portman) *w ldrs: led 3f out: hrd pressed fr 2f out: hdd last 150yds: kpt on* **9/1**	
0444	4	*shd*	**Outside Edge (IRE)**14 5186 3-9-1 **62** (p) JamieSpencer 4	64
			(W R Swinburn) *hld up in midfield: prog on inner wl over 1f out: styd on fnl f: nvr quite pce to chal* **13/2**3	
360	5	½	**Seasonal Cross**28 4730 3-8-13 **60** JohnEgan 5	60
			(S Dow) *hld up towards rr on inner: prog over 2f out: effrt over 1f out: kpt on same pce fnl f* **25/1**	
3166	6	¾	**Rio L'Oren (IRE)**22 4952 3-9-2 **63** LDettori 6	61
			(N J Vaughan) *mostly in midfield: bustled along and prog over 2f out: chsng ldrs and wl in tch over 1f out: nt qckn* **11/1**	
4-0	7	½	**Street Diva (USA)**31 4669 3-9-3 **64** EddieAhern 8	61
			(P A Blockley) *pressed ldrs: stl cl up 2f out: nt qckn over 1f out: fdd ins fnl f* **33/1**	
2226	8	1½	**Great Knight (IRE)**35 4538 3-9-3 **64** TonyCulhane 10	57
			(W J Haggas) *hld up in last pair: stl there over 2f out: pushed along and kpt on fr over 1f out: nvr nr ldrs* **11/1**	
2444	9	¾	**Rondeau (GR)**32 4637 3-9-4 **65** JimCrowley 1	56
			(P R Chamings) *s.s: in tch in last trio: effrt over 2f out: no imp on ldrs over 1f out: one pce* **8/1**	
0664	10	2	**Acquifer**16 5142 3-9-2 **63** TedDurcan 7	49
			(J L Dunlop) *dwlt: hld up in rr: sme prog into midfield over 2f out: no hdwy wl over 1f out: fdd* **12/1**	
4600	11	2¼	**Connor's Choice**27 4773 3-9-4 **65** MichaelHills 12	44
			(Andrew Turnell) *w ldrs: led 4f out to 3f out: wknd wl over 1f out* **16/1**	
3634	12	5	**Johnny Friendly**11 5258 3-9-1 **62** AndrewElliott 2	28
			(K R Burke) *led to 4f out: lost pl and struggling 3f out* **4/1**2	
6660	13	*nk*	**Cotton Reel**27 4777 3-9-2 **63** JoeFanning 11	28
			(P F I Cole) *stdd s: racd wd and a wl in rr: v wd bnd 2f out: bhd after* **33/1**	
60-0	14	6	**Rakeekah**172 899 3-9-3 **64** LPKeniry 9	13
			(J S Moore) *pushed along in midfield over 4f out: sn struggling: bhd 2f out: t.o* **66/1**	

1m 24.55s (-0.25) **Going Correction** -0.025s/f (Stan) — **14** Ran SP% **128.3**
Speed ratings (Par 99): **100,99,98,98,98 97,96,94,94,91 89,83,83,76**
toteswinger: 1&2 £24.70, 1&3 £48.00, 2&3 £6.80. CSF £89.50 CT £671.36 TOTE £36.90: £8.40, £1.60, £3.00; EX 204.00.
Owner Raymond Tooth **Bred** Raymond Clive Tooth **Trained** Upper Lambourn, Berks

FOCUS
A modest-looking handicap but sound form with the third, fourth and sixth close to previous marks.
Seasonal Cross Official explanation: vet said filly lost a shoe

5617 REALTIME RADIO @ WILLIAMHILL.CO.UK H'CAP — 6f (P)
4:50 (4:51) (Class 5) (0-70,74) 3-Y-O — £2,590 (£770; £385; £192) Stalls Low

Form				RPR
0041	1		**Geoffdaw**9 5346 3-9-8 **74** 6ex (v) EddieAhern 3	79
			(M J Wallace, Australia) *chsd ldrs: hrd rdn over 2f out: disp 2nd 1f out: styd on wl u.p to ld last strides* **7/2**1	
3514	2	*nk*	**Little Knickers**125 1738 3-9-1 **67** (b) EdwardCreighton 8	71
			(E J Creighton) *pushed along in midfield over 3f out: no prog after tl styd on wl fr over 1f out: grabbed 2nd on post* **16/1**	
660	3	*nk*	**Night Premiere (IRE)**26 4824 3-8-4 **56** oh2 JimmyQuinn 1	59
			(R Hannon) *led at str pce: hdd over 4f out: led again over 2f out: drew at least 2l clr fnl f: wknd and hdd last strides* **12/1**	
0460	4	*hd*	**Last Of The Line**9 5345 3-9-3 **69** (v) JamesDoyle 11	71
			(H J L Dunlop) *wl in rr: outpcd fr 1/2-way and rdn: styd on wl fnl f: gaining at fin* **16/1**	
3236	5	*nk*	**Nice Dream**78 3118 3-8-9 **61** JoeFanning 2	62
			(C E Brittain) *pressed ldrs: rdn over 2f out: stl disputing 2nd 1f out: fdd last 100yds* **14/1**	
-304	6	½	**Laureldean Dream (USA)**21 4987 3-9-1 **67** (t) AlanMunro 5	67
			(P W Chapple-Hyam) *hld up in midfield: prog on inner over 2f out: effrt over 1f out: nt qckn and hld ins fnl f* **10/1**	
31	7	*hd*	**Triumphant Welcome**11 5268 3-8-8 **67** StacyRenwick(7) 4	66
			(G F Bridgwater) *trckd ldrs: clsd gng wl enough 2f out: hanging and fnd nil over 1f out* **4/1**2	
0010	8	1	**Minwir (IRE)**49 4090 3-8-7 **59** ow1 (v) ShaneKelly 7	55
			(M Quinn) *hld up in rr: outpcd fr over 3f out: sme prog 1f out: hanging and no hdwy ins fnl f* **16/1**	
2540	9	2¾	**Gainshare**32 4615 3-8-13 **65** RyanMoore 9	52
			(T D Barron) *a in rr and racd towards outer: struggling fr 1/2-way: n.d after* **9/2**3	
5500	10	¾	**Affirmatively**121 1867 3-8-13 **65** TonyCulhane 12	50
			(A W Carroll) *blasted off fr wd draw and led over 4f out: hdd over 2f out: wkng whn n.m.r ins fnl f* **40/1**	
3045	11	1¼	**Blue Zenith (IRE)**19 5050 3-8-7 **59** LPKeniry 6	40
			(J S Moore) *fast away: w ldrs 1f: sn lost pl and rdn: struggling in rr over 2f out* **11/1**	
2400	12	7	**Salt Of The Earth (IRE)**96 2555 3-9-4 **70** MichaelHills 10	28
			(T G Mills) *racd wd: a wl in rr: t.o* **15/2**	

1m 12.0s (0.10) **Going Correction** -0.025s/f (Stan) — **12** Ran SP% **124.0**
Speed ratings (Par 101): **98,97,97,96,96 95,95,94,90,89 87,78**
toteswinger: 1&2 £12.70, 1&3 £12.50, 2&3 £39.00. CSF £64.81 CT £636.50 TOTE £4.60: £2.00, £3.70, £4.90; EX 51.80 Place 6: £13.02 Place 5: £11.08.
Owner Mike & Denise Dawes **Bred** Barton Stud Partnership **Trained** Australia

FOCUS
This looked a difficult race to weigh up as, despite the form figures of most of them, a lot of the field looked to be running up to scratch recently. The form is ordinary.
T/Plt: £8.20 to a £1 stake. Pool: £56,141.26. 4,958.47 winning tickets. T/Qpdt: £4.70 to a £1 stake. Pool: £2,962.93. 466.31 winning tickets.

5618 - 5622a (Foreign Racing) - See Raceform Interactive

4577 CHANTILLY (R-H)
Wednesday, September 3

OFFICIAL GOING: Soft

5623a PRIX DES TOURELLES (LISTED RACE) (F&M) — 1m 4f
3:05 (3:15) 3-Y-O+ — £19,118 (£7,647; £5,735; £3,824; £1,912)

			RPR
1		**Sell Out**18 5094 4-9-2 GMosse 2	104
		(G Wragg) *trckd ldr in 3rd to st: narrow ldr fr 2f out: rdn out and r.o wl* **47/10**1	
2	½	**Alix Road (FR)**10 5332 5-9-2 AlexisBadel 6	103
		(Mme M Bollack-Badel, France) **9/1**2	
3	¾	**Winkle (IRE)**28 3-8-7 CSoumillon 4	102
		(M Delzangles, France)	
4	2½	**Shake The Moon (GER)**87 3-8-7 SPasquier 3	98
		(A Fabre, France)	
5	1½	**Cymbal (IRE)**21 5001 3-8-7 JVictoire 5	95
		(H-A Pantall, France)	
6	10	**She Hates Me (IRE)**21 5001 3-8-7 ACrastus 1	79
		(E Lellouche, France)	

2m 32.2s (1.60) **Going Correction** +0.35s/f (Good)
WFA 3 from 4yo+ 9lb — **6** Ran SP% **27.5**
Speed ratings: **108,107,107,105,104 97**
PARI-MUTUEL: WIN 5.70; PL 3.00, 4.80; SF 34.40.
Owner T D Rootes **Bred** Shutford Stud **Trained** Newmarket, Suffolk

NOTEBOOK
Sell Out sat in third on the rail for much of the race just behind the leaders. Asked to quicken one and a half out, she hit the front and stayed on gamely, battling to the line and holding off the persistent challenge of the eventual second. This race was always the aim for her and no future plans are in the pipeline for the time being.

5596 BADEN-BADEN (L-H)
Wednesday, September 3

OFFICIAL GOING: Soft (4pm); heavy (5.15pm)

5624a FURSTENBERG-RENNEN (GROUP 3) — 1m 2f
4:00 (4:02) 3-Y-O — £22,059 (£9,191; £3,676; £1,838)

			RPR
1		**Liang Kay (GER)**59 3773 3-9-2 THellier 2	113
		(U Ostmann, Germany) *hld up in rr to st: c over towards stands' rails: smooth prog to ld over 1f out: sn clr: pushed out and r.o wl* **4/5**1	
2	5	**Redolent (IRE)**20 5025 3-8-12 PatDobbs 1	99
		(R Hannon) *led after 3f to over 1f out: kpt on same pce* **29/10**2	
3	½	**Duellant (IRE)**52 4012 3-8-12 AStarke 5	98
		(P Schiergen, Germany) *led 3f: pressed ldr: 2nd st: sn hrd rdn: kpt on same pce u.p* **11/2**	
4	6	**Walzertraum (USA)**59 3773 3-9-0 FJohansson 4	88
		(J Hirschberger, Germany) *racd in 3rd: 4th st: btn wl over 1f out* **67/10**	
5	5	**Satier (FR)**24 3-8-12 AHelfenbein 3	76
		(Mario Hofer, Germany) *disp 3rd: 3rd st: sn wknd* **34/10**3	

2m 11.42s (6.43) — **5** Ran SP% **132.3**
(including ten euro stakes): WIN 18: PL 13, 18: SF 43.
Owner Stall Emina **Bred** Frau I Zimmermann **Trained** Germany

NOTEBOOK
Redolent(IRE), who finished runner-up on his previous visit to Germany and his only other try at this trip, was no match for the winner, who had finished fourth in the Deutsches Derby on his previous start. Richard Hannon's colt has now been placed in all five tries in Group company and deserves to win one.

5625a KABA BADENER STEHER-CUP (LISTED RACE) — 1m 6f
5:15 (5:09) 3-Y-O+ — £11,029 (£4,412; £1,838; £1,103)

			RPR
1		**Valdino (GER)**24 4911 3-8-8 J-PCarvalho 7	111
		(U Ostmann, Germany) **14/10**1	
2	7	**Brisant (GER)**24 4911 6-9-2 WMongil 3	99
		(M Trybuhl, Germany) **64/10**3	
3	3½	**Eiswind**38 4-9-0 AStarke 9	92
		(P Schiergen, Germany) **79/10**	
4	2½	**Waldvogel (IRE)**64 3596 4-9-4 EPedroza 10	93
		(A Wohler, Germany) **6/1**2	
5	4	**Si Belle (IRE)**24 4911 3-8-0 FilipMinarik 11	81
		(Rae Guest) *mid-div: 6th st: btn wl over 1f out* **6/1**2	
6	1¼	**Sapiranga (GER)**24 4911 4-8-9 LennartHammer-Hansen 5	77
		(Frau Marion Rotering, Germany) **116/10**	
7	15	**Foreign Music (FR)**19 4-8-9 ABest 2	58
		(H J Groschel, Germany) **134/10**	
8	2½	**Dragon Fly (GER)**64 3596 6-9-0 TMundry 4	60
		(Frau Jutta Mayer, Germany) **30/1**	
9	28	**Alleviate (IRE)**24 4911 4-8-9 (b) ASuborics 6	18
		(Sir Mark Prescott) *led to jst bef st: wknd qckly: eased* **68/10**	
10	6	**Princess Petra (FR)** 4-8-11 AHelfenbein 8	12
		(M Rulec, Germany) **23/1**	

3m 6.04s (186.04)
WFA 3 from 4yo+ 11lb — **10** Ran SP% **130.1**
WIN 24; PL 13, 27, 23; SF 170.
Owner Frau H Endres **Bred** Gestut Auenquelle **Trained** Germany

NOTEBOOK
Si Belle(IRE), who finished runner-up to Valdino at Cologne, was 4lb better off for two lengths this time but ran well below that form. She handled soft ground last time but perhaps this ground found her out.
Alleviate(IRE) finished fourth behind the winner at Cologne, but ran a long way below that effort, dropping out rapidly after leading and being eased in the straight.

The Form Book, Raceform Ltd, Compton, RG20 6NL

[5421]GREAT LEIGHS (A.W) (L-H)

Thursday, September 4

OFFICIAL GOING: Standard

This was the first meeting at Great Leighs to take place under floodlights.
Wind: blustery, behind Weather: dry but showers threatening, blustery

5626 MUSCO LIGHTING AT GREAT LEIGHS H'CAP 5f (P)

6:50 (6:51) (Class 6) (0-60,60) 3-Y-O+ £2,590 (£770; £385; £192) Stalls Low

Form RPR

6650 **1** **Desert Opal**[12] 5260 8-9-2 **60**..............................(b) LukeMorris(3) 1 73
(C R Dore) *chsd ldng pair: hanging rt fr 2f out: styd on u.p to ld over 1f out: drvn out* **6/1**

6603 **2** *3/4* **Billy Red**[4] 5532 4-9-0 **55**..............................(b) AdrianMcCarthy 5 65
(J R Jenkins) *chsd ldr: rdn and ev ch 2f out: no ex u.p ins fnl f* **9/1**

4002 **3** *1 1/4* **Monte Major (IRE)**[9] 5374 7-9-2 **57**..............................(v) GeorgeBaker 9 63
(D Shaw) *chsd ldrs: rdn 2f out: nt clr run and swtchd rt over 1f out: kpt on but nvr pce to rch ldng pair* **7/2**[1]

023 **4** *3* **Rann Na Cille (IRE)**[9] 5374 4-8-10 **51**.............................. MickyFenton 3 46
(P T Midgley) *led: rdn jst over 2f out: hdd over 1f out: wknd fnl f* **9/2**[2]

300- **5** *2 3/4* **Desert Dust**[424] 3347 5-8-5 **46** oh1..............................(p) NickyMackay 8 31
(R M H Cowell) *stdd s: hld up in tch: rdn and outpcd wl over 1f out: no ch w ldrs fnl f* **33/1**

0602 **6** *nk* **Overstayed (IRE)**[49] 4107 5-8-9 **57**..............................(t) AndreaAtzeni(5) 10 41
(P J McBride) *towards rr: hdwy over 3f out: rdn and edgd lft over 1f out: no prog fnl f* **13/2**

0103 **7** *1* **Taboor (IRE)**[11] 5319 10-8-11 **52**.............................. ShaneKelly 13 32
(R M H Cowell) *dropped in bhd after s: racd wd: nvr trbld ldrs* **20/1**

0000 **8** *1 3/4* **The Real Guru**[22] 4979 3-8-13 **55**..............................(v) FergusSweeney 2 29
(Miss Tor Sturgis) *in tch in midfield: rdn and struggling over 2f out: no ch fr over 1f out* **50/1**

0440 **9** *1/2* **Bobby Rose**[11] 5315 5-8-12 **58**..............................(b) Louis-PhilippeBeuzelin(5) 6 30
(D K Ivory) *v.s.a: bhd: gd hdwy on inner over 3f out: chsd ldrs and rdn over 2f out: wknd over 1f out* **7/1**

6050 **10** *1* **Jucebabe**[20] 5074 5-8-8 **49**..............................(p) DavidKinsella 7 17
(J L Spearing) *a towards rr: rdn and struggling fr 1/2-way* **14/1**

5440 **11** *1 1/2* **Kempsey**[3] 5582 6-8-5 **49**..............................(v) MarcHalford(3) 4 12
(J J Bridger) *sn bustled along: chsd ldrs for 2f: steadily lost pl: bhd last 2f* **11/2**[3]

0-40 **12** *nse* **Senorita Parkes**[17] 5160 3-9-1 **57**.............................. LPKeniry 11 20
(E F Vaughan) *s.i.s: bhd: rdn and struggling fr 1/2-way* **50/1**

60.31 secs (0.11) **Going Correction** +0.05s/f (Slow)
WFA 3 from 4yo+ 1lb **12** Ran SP% **124.2**
Speed ratings (Par 101): **101,99,97,93,88 88,86,83,82,81 78,78**
toteswinger: 1&2 £31.40, 1&3 £16.30, 2&3 £8.80. CSF £60.12 CT £225.27 TOTE £7.60: £3.20, £4.30, £1.80; EX 76.40.
Owner Mrs Louise Marsh **Bred** Juddmonte Farms **Trained** West Pinchbeck, Lincs
■ Stewards' Enquiry : Luke Morris one-day ban: used whip above shoulder height (Sep 18)

FOCUS
A race run in driving rain and there was standing water on parts of the track, possibly making it even harder than usual to make up significant amounts of ground, and that was certainly the case in this race. Just a moderate sprint handicap and the first three home, who were never far away, raced up the centre of the track. All three had slipped to good marks.
Desert Opal Official explanation: trainer said, regarding apparent improvement in form, on its last run the gelding was short of room early and thereafter resented being behind horses, but this time it benefited from a clear run and being raced prominently

5627 MUSCO GREEN GENERATION LIGHTING MEDIAN AUCTION MAIDEN STKS 6f (P)

7:20 (7:20) (Class 6) 3-5-Y-O £2,590 (£770; £385; £192) Stalls Low

Form RPR

020 **1** **Al Gillani (IRE)**[28] 4793 3-9-3 57.............................. GeorgeBaker 4 73
(J R Boyle) *chsd ldrs: wnt 2nd over 2f out: carried rt ent fnl f: led fnl 100yds: eased nr fin* **3/1**[2]

0226 **2** *1 3/4* **Wreningham**[20] 5049 3-9-3 66.............................. ShaneKelly 5 67
(T Keddy) *chsd ldr tl led over 4f out: rdn 2f out: hung rt fr over 1f out: hdd fnl 100yds: sn btn* **7/2**[3]

04 **3** *1 1/4* **Casela Park (IRE)**[12] 5268 3-9-3 0.............................. LPKeniry 3 63+
(S Kirk) *s.i.s: t.k.h: hld up bhd: hdwy and nt clr run over 3f out: swtchd rt 3f out: chsd ldng pair over 1f out: edgd rt but kpt on fnl f* **14/1**

4 *14* **Light The Light (IRE)** 3-8-12 0.............................. ChrisCatlin 8 13
(M J Wallace, Australia) *s.i.s: bhd: outpcd 4f out: plugged on to go modest 4th ins fnl f: n.d* **15/2**

60 **5** *3/4* **Mr Rio (IRE)**[96] 2620 3-9-3 0.............................. DarrenWilliams 2 16
(A P Jarvis) *sn led: hdd over 4f out: rdn and struggling over 2f out: wknd wl over 1f out* **4/1**

5032 **6** *2 1/2* **Red Amaryllis**[39] 5002 3-8-12 60.............................. EddieAhern 1 —
(H J L Dunlop) *chsd ldr tl rdn and outpcd 4f out: wl btn fr 1/2-way* **11/4**[1]

0 **7** *3 1/4* **Interchoice Star**[10] 5366 3-9-3 0.............................. FergusSweeney 7 —
(K G Wingrove) *racd in midfield: outpcd 4f out: no ch w ldrs after: t.o* **33/1**

000 **8** *21* **Super Al**[20] 5049 3-9-3 0.............................. NickyMackay 6 —
(M Wigham) *s.i.s: bhd: outpcd 4f out: wl t.o fr over 1f out* **50/1**

1m 12.8s (-0.90) **Going Correction** +0.05s/f (Slow) **8** Ran SP% **117.2**
Speed ratings (Par 101): **108,105,104,85,84 81,76,48**
toteswinger: 1&2 £2.10, 1&3 £22.60, 2&3 £16.00. CSF £14.42 TOTE £4.90: £1.80, £1.30, £5.80; EX 22.40.
Owner The Paddock Space Partnership **Bred** Sean Finnegan **Trained** Epsom, Surrey
■ k.

FOCUS
A moderate older-horse sprint maiden and the first three home pulled a long way clear. It again paid to be on the pace and once more the main action took place up the centre of the track in the straight. The form is rated through the second and may have been underrated, although the quick time could have been due to the wet track.
Red Amaryllis Official explanation: jockey said filly was outpaced throughout
Interchoice Star Official explanation: jockey said gelding hung left
Super Al Official explanation: jockey said gelding suffered interference in running

5628 MUSCO LIGHTING E B F MAIDEN STKS 5f (P)

7:50 (7:54) (Class 4) 2-Y-O £5,180 (£1,541; £770; £384) Stalls Low

Form RPR

0 **1** **Especially Special (IRE)**[17] 5147 2-8-12 0.............................. EddieAhern 2 75+
(S Kirk) *chsd ldr: led over 2f out: rdn 2f out: clr ent fnl f: eased towards fin: easily* **25/1**

3 **2** *2 1/4* **Brief Encounter (IRE)**[49] 4126 2-9-3 0.............................. LPKeniry 4 74+
(A M Balding) *chsd ldrs: rdn wl over 3f out: lost pl 3f out: bhd 2f out: hdwy over 1f out: edgd lft but r.o fnl f: wnt 2nd towards fin: no ch w wnr* **4/5**[1]

6 **3** *1/2* **Fortune In Faith (USA)**[28] 4786 2-8-12 0.............................. PhilipRobinson 6 65
(C G Cox) *led: hdd and rdn over 2f out: no ch w wnr fnl f: lost 2nd nr fin* **12/1**

30 **4** *3/4* **Eagles Call (USA)**[28] 4792 2-9-3 0.............................. ChrisCatlin 8 68
(P W Chapple-Hyam) *chsd ldrs: hung rt bnd wl over 3f out: chsd ldng pair and rdn jst over 2f out: kpt on but no ch w wnr fnl f* **15/2**[3]

42 **5** *1* **Florentia**[21] 5004 2-8-12 0.............................. J-PGuillambert 5 59
(Sir Mark Prescott) *s.i.s: sn rdn along: a bhd: no ch last 2f* **11/4**[2]

6 *1* **Vamos (IRE)** 2-9-0 0.............................. LukeMorris(3) 1 60
(J R Gask) *s.i.s: racd in midfield: rdn over 3f out: wkng whn edgd rt over 1f out* **33/1**

7 *nk* **Art Fund (USA)** 2-9-3 0.............................. GeorgeBaker 7 59
(G L Moore) *s.i.s: bhd: swtchd rt and rdn wl over 1f out: nvr nr ldrs* **16/1**

30 **8** *17* **Sorrel Ridge (IRE)**[104] 2362 2-9-3 0.............................. DO'Donohoe 3 —
(M G Quinlan) *s.i.s: t.k.h: hld up in midfield: rdn 1/2-way: wl bhd over 1f out* **40/1**

60.92 secs (0.72) **Going Correction** +0.05s/f (Slow) **8** Ran SP% **116.8**
Speed ratings (Par 97): **96,92,91,90,88 87,86,59**
toteswinger: 1&2 £10.80, 1&3 £15.90, 2&3 £1.40. CSF £46.42 TOTE £26.80: £4.10, £1.10, £3.10; EX 125.50.
Owner Lady Davis **Bred** Austin Lyons **Trained** Upper Lambourn, Berks

FOCUS
The bare form of this juvenile sprint maiden is probably just fair at best, but the winner was a cut above her rivals. They stayed towards the inside this time, but once again the pace bias was evident as very few made up significant amounts of ground. The winning time was 0.61 seconds slower than the earlier 46-60 handicap for three-year-olds and upwards. The runner-up and fourth help set the level of the fourth.

NOTEBOOK
Especially Special(IRE) ◆ showed little on her debut when a 40-1 shot over 6f on easy ground at Windsor, but a Group 1 Cheveley Park entry suggests she is well regarded and she left that initial effort well behind, taking this in the style of an above-average filly. It is true that she was always in the best place considering the way this track is currently riding, but she showed loads of natural speed to earn her place in front and actually seemed to quicken away from her rivals at the top of the straight. She still looked very green when coming under pressure inside the final 2f and just tired a little late on, allowing her rivals to finish a length or two closer than had looked likely at one stage. She looks all speed. (op 22-1 tchd 20-1)
Brief Encounter(IRE) did all his best work late on. He is still learning his job and gave the impression he might benefit from another furlong for the time being. (op 13-8)
Fortune In Faith(USA) soon lost the early lead to the eventual winner, but she did not drop away and plugged on for a respectable third. This was an improvement on the form she showed first-time up at Sandown. (op 10-1)
Eagles Call(USA) was stuck wide and never really got in a telling blow, but this was still a creditable effort. He now has the option of nurseries and might to better over a little further. (op 8-1 tchd 7-1)
Florentia, a beaten favourite when second over this trip at Beverley last time, lacked the pace of some of these and was soon driven along, but she stuck to her task. There is loads of speed on her dam's side, but she probably wants a little further and it will be no surprise if she leaves this form behind when taking the handicap route. (op 2-1)
Vamos(IRE), a £44,000 two-year-old and half-brother to a winning juvenile, showed a little ability on this debut. (op 20-1)
Art Fund(USA), a £60,000 two-year-old with a speedy American dirt pedigree, wore a cross noseband and has already been gelded. He did most of his racing out wide and will know more next time. (op 9-1)

5629 MUSCO MOBILE LIGHTING H'CAP 6f (P)

8:20 (8:21) (Class 5) (0-70,67) 3-Y-O+ £3,561 (£1,059; £529; £264) Stalls Low

Form RPR

0006 **1** **Applesnap (IRE)**[17] 5142 3-9-1 **64**..............................(b[1]) DO'Donohoe 6 76
(Miss Amy Weaver) *s.i.s: sn pushed along: hdwy over 2f out: r.o wl to ld fnl 100yds: sn clr* **20/1**

4343 **2** *2 1/2* **Our Blessing (IRE)**[20] 5050 4-8-13 **60**.............................. DarrenWilliams 7 64
(A P Jarvis) *w ldr: rdn 2f out: ev ch tl nt pce of wnr fnl 100yds* **5/1**[2]

4400 **3** *1* **Hammer Of The Gods (IRE)**[23] 4944 8-9-6 **67**..........(bt) GeorgeBaker 5 68
(G C Bravery) *sn pushed up to ld narrowly: rdn over 2f out: hdd fnl 100yds: wknd and lost 2nd towards fin* **5/1**[2]

1030 **4** *1* **Perlachy**[58] 3825 4-8-5 **55**..............................(v) LukeMorris(3) 8 53
(Mrs N Macauley) *racd in midfield: rdn and lost pl 1/2-way: bhd and c wd bnd 2f out: styd on fnl f: nt rch ldrs* **25/1**

1235 **5** *1/2* **Rosie Says No**[79] 3118 3-9-1 **64**.............................. ShaneKelly 2 60
(R M H Cowell) *hld up in midfield: effrt towards inner wl over 1f out: kpt on same pce fnl f* **11/2**[3]

131- **6** *1* **Ruman (IRE)**[290] 6870 6-9-6 **67**.............................. EddieAhern 3 60
(M J Attwater) *chsd ldrs: rdn over 2f out: wknd ent fnl f* **7/2**[1]

6056 **7** *1/2* **Blackmalkin (USA)**[20] 5050 4-8-11 **58**.............................. MickyFenton 9 49
(M Quinn) *stdd and dropped in after s: hld up bhd: rdn and effrt over 1f out: nvr pce to trble ldrs* **16/1**

0140 **8** *3/4* **Sovereignty (JPN)**[10] 5345 6-9-5 **66**.............................. ChrisCatlin 10 55
(D K Ivory) *in tch tl rdn and lost pl 1/2-way: rdn 2f out: kpt on same pce* **10/1**

0001 **9** *2 1/2* **Cool Sands (IRE)**[38] 4478 6-9-2 **63**..............................(v) TPQueally 1 44
(J G Given) *chsd ldrs: rdn 1/2-way: wknd wl over 1f out: eased towards fin* **7/2**[1]

1m 13.91s (0.21) **Going Correction** +0.05s/f (Slow)
WFA 3 from 4yo+ 2lb **9** Ran SP% **116.7**
Speed ratings (Par 103): **100,96,95,94,93 92,91,90,87**
toteswinger: 1&2 £8.70, 1&3 £2.60, 2&3 £16.10. CSF £118.12 CT £590.68 TOTE £26.00: £8.70, £1.20, £1.80; EX 156.90.
Owner Michael Bringloe **Bred** Rathasker Stud **Trained** Newmarket, Suffolk

FOCUS
A modest sprint handicap. Although the winner came from off the pace, the speed bias was still evident, as the two leaders managed to finish second and third, despite taking each other on throughout. They raced towards the inside in the straight. The winner is rated back to his best.

5630 MUSCO "WE MAKE IT HAPPEN" H'CAP 1m 2f (P)

8:50 (8:50) (Class 5) (0-75,75) 3-Y-O+ £3,561 (£1,059; £529; £264) Stalls Low

Form RPR

2502 **1** **Cupid's Glory**[27] 4820 6-9-3 **69**.............................. GeorgeBaker 10 83+
(G L Moore) *stdd after s: hld up bhd: smooth hdwy on outer over 3f out: trckd ldrs gng wl 2f out: sn led: clr 1f out: eased towards fin: easily* **5/2**[1]

0341 **2** *3 1/2* **Suzi Spends (IRE)**[21] 5019 3-8-13 **72**.............................. JohnEgan 9 79
(H J Collingridge) *hld up towards rr: hdwy 4f out: rdn and edgd lft wl over 2f out: r.o to chse wnr ent fnl f: kpt on but no imp on wnr* **11/2**[3]

0016 **3** 1 1/4 **Resplendent Ace (IRE)**[29] 4726 4-9-9 **75**........................ JimmyQuinn 4 79
(P Howling) *t.k.h: hld up bhd: hdwy on outer 3f out: r.o u.p to go 3rd ins fnl f: no ch w wnr* **7/1**

1000 **4** 1 3/4 **Always Certain (USA)**[45] 4244 3-8-6 **65**..................... RoystonFfrench 3 66
(M Johnston) *in tch in midfield: rdn over 4f out: lost pl over 3f out: rallied u.p over 1f out plugged on but nvr a threat to ldrs* **12/1**

-404 **5** 2 **Crystal Prince**[19] 4299 4-9-5 **71**..............................(b[1]) FergusSweeney 6 68
(C E Longsdon) *hld up towards rr: rdn and effrt wl over 3f out: no real hdwy: plugged on fnl f: n.d* **25/1**

51-6 **6** nk **Sir Haydn**[230] 212 8-8-4 **61**.. DavidProbert[(5)] 5 57
(J R Jenkins) *hld up bhd: hdwy over 3f out: rdn wl over 2f out: nvr trbld ldrs* **14/1**

5113 **7** 1/2 **Wogan's Sister**[13] 5232 3-8-8 **70**.................................... MarcHalford[(3)] 8 65
(D R C Elsworth) *led: rdn and hdd wl over 1f out: sn no ch w wnr: wknd fnl f* **10/1**

-352 **8** hd **French Riviera**[18] 5117 3-8-11 **75**.............. Louis-PhilippeBeuzelin[(5)] 11 70
(Sir Michael Stoute) *in tch: swtchd to inner and trckd ldng pair 6f out: rdn and fnd little wl over 1f out: wl btn fnl f* **3/1**[2]

022- **9** 12 **Can Can Star**[342] 5774 5-9-6 **72**.. ShaneKelly 2 43
(A W Carroll) *chsd ldr tl rdn 2f out: wknd qckly over 1f out* **16/1**

0000 **10** 3/4 **Abydos**[14] 5209 4-9-0 **66**.. TPQueally 7 35
(A P Stringer) *t.k.h: hld up in tch: rdn and struggling over 3f out: wkng whn hmpd wl over 2f out: no ch after* **20/1**

3300 **11** 67 **Watchmaker**[118] 1963 5-9-1 **67**.. ChrisCatlin 1 —
(Miss Tor Sturgis) *chsd ldrs tl lost pl qckly 1/2-way: wl t.o and virtually p.u last 2f* **20/1**

2m 7.76s (-0.84) **Going Correction** +0.05s/f (Slow)
WFA 3 from 4yo+ 7lb 11 Ran SP% **124.2**
Speed ratings (Par 103): **105,102,101,99,98 97,97,97,87,87 33**
toteswinger: 1&2 £3.50, 1&3 £36.00, 2&3 £48.10. CSF £17.14 CT £90.48 TOTE £5.30: £1.50, £1.90, £2.70; EX 19.50.

Owner K Johnson, K Jessup **Bred** Cheveley Park Stud Ltd **Trained** Woodingdean, E Sussex

FOCUS
A modest handicap run in a time 1.19 seconds quicker than the following 46-50 contest. This is probably a reasonable race for the grade. They seemed to go just an ordinary pace early but, unlike in the earlier sprint races, there was no advantage in racing handy.

Watchmaker Official explanation: jockey said gelding lost its action; vet said gelding returned lame

5631 MUSCO ARENA SHOWLIGHT H'CAP 1m 2f (P)
9:20 (9:20) (Class 6) (0-50,56) 3-Y-O+ £2,590 (£770; £385; £192) **Stalls** Low

Form RPR

2023 **1** **Everyman**[7] 5427 4-9-0 **50**.. LukeMorris[(3)] 2 63
(A W Carroll) *s.i.s: sn in midfield: hdwy over 3f out: led wl over 1f out: drew clr fnl f* **5/1**[2]

0211 **2** 2 1/2 **Circadian Rhythm**[3] 5575 3-9-2 **56** 6ex........................ J-PGuillambert 9 64
(S C Williams) *hld up in midfield: hdwy 4f out: chal and ev ch 2f out: rdn over 1f out: no ex ins fnl f* **5/4**[1]

0004 **3** 3 **Play Up Pompey**[33] 4635 6-9-2 **49**.................................. GeorgeBaker 7 51
(J J Bridger) *stdd s: hld up in midfield: hdwy and nt clr run over 2f out: styd on u.p to go 3rd ins fnl f: nvr trbld ldng pair* **16/1**

4000 **4** nk **Barry Island**[21] 5008 9-8-13 **49**...................................... MarcHalford[(3)] 14 50
(D R C Elsworth) *stdd and dropped in bhd after s: hdwy on outer over 3f out: styd on steadily fr over 1f out: nvr rchd ldrs* **25/1**

0034 **5** 2 1/4 **Marie Tempest**[66] 3555 3-8-7 **47**...................................... ChrisCatlin 4 44
(B W Hills) *stdd after s: hld up in rr: hdwy over 2f out: nt clr run and swtchd lft over 1f out: styd on but nvr trbld ldrs* **7/1**[3]

0303 **6** 1 **Golden Brown (IRE)**[17] 5145 4-9-1 **48**.......................... FergusSweeney 11 43
(David Pinder) *hld up in tch: rdn over 2f out: wknd jst over 1f out* **16/1**

5200 **7** nk **Meohmy**[7] 5427 5-8-9 **47**.. MCGeran[(5)] 8 41
(M R Channon) *towards rr and niggled along: hdwy 4f out: edgd rt u.p over 1f out: no real imp* **28/1**

2534 **8** 1 1/4 **Magic Amigo**[21] 5020 7-8-8 **46**...........................(b) DavidProbert[(5)] 12 38
(J R Jenkins) *chsd ldrs: rdn 3f out: sn struggling: wl btn over 1f out* **8/1**

-504 **9** 1/2 **Zalkani (IRE)**[17] 5145 8-9-0 **50**.................................... JerryO'Dwyer[(3)] 3 41
(J Pearce) *hld up bhd: nvr plcd to chal* **14/1**

0060 **10** 9 **Rosy Dawn**[13] 5232 3-8-6 **46**..(v) JohnEgan 15 19
(J J Bridger) *chsd ldr tl led 4f out: sn rdn hdd wl over 1f out: btn and eased fnl f* **50/1**

4003 **11** 2 3/4 **Ming Vase**[11] 5303 6-8-13 **46** oh1.................................... MickyFenton 6 13
(P T Midgley) *t.k.h: chsd ldrs: rdn to chse ldr 4f out tl 2f out: wknd qckly* **16/1**

6640 **12** 1 3/4 **Morestead (IRE)**[32] 4664 3-8-10 **50**................................ TQuinn 5 14
(B G Powell) *s.i.s: sn in tch in midfield: rdn and struggling over 3f out: no ch and eased fnl f* **25/1**

0500 **13** 7 **Rain Stops Play (IRE)**[11] 5318 6-9-1 **48**........................ ShaneKelly 10 —
(M Quinn) *led tl 4f out: wknd wl over 2f out: eased fnl f* **18/1**

000 **14** 1 1/4 **Savanna's Gold**[17] 5160 4-8-13 **46** oh1.......................... AdrianMcCarthy 1 —
(G Prodromou) *chsd ldrs: rdn 4f out: wknd 3f out: wl bhd over 1f out* **66/1**

0000 **15** 4 1/2 **Lekezia (IRE)**[13] 5218 3-8-6 **51** ow3.......................... GabrielHannon[(5)] 16 —
(J W Hills) *stdd and dropped in after s: plld hrd: hld up in rr: sddle slipped over 7f out: no ch last 3f* **33/1**

2m 8.95s (0.35) **Going Correction** +0.05s/f (Slow)
WFA 3 from 4yo+ 7lb 15 Ran SP% **131.8**
Speed ratings (Par 101): **100,98,95,95,93 92,92,91,91,83 81,80,74,73,70**
toteswinger: 1&2 £3.30, 1&3 £13.10, 2&3 £12.20. CSF £11.90 CT £107.51 TOTE £6.90: £5.70, £1.30, £5.90; EX 17.80 Place 6 £46.04, Place 5 £18.90.

Owner M Woodall **Bred** Natton House Thoroughbreds & Mark Woodall **Trained** Cropthorne, Worcs

FOCUS
A moderate event, but quite competitive and the pace was solid enough. The form appears sound.

Zalkani(IRE) ◆ Official explanation: jockey said gelding was denied a clear run

Rosy Dawn Official explanation: jockey said filly had no more to give

Morestead(IRE) Official explanation: jockey said gelding never travelled

Lekezia(IRE) Official explanation: jockey said saddle slipped

T/Plt: £24.70 to a £1 stake. Pool: £87,472.35. 2,578.10 winning tickets. T/Qpdt: £6.20 to a £1 stake. Pool: £7,214.81. 853.10 winning tickets. SP

4896 REDCAR (L-H)
Thursday, September 4

OFFICIAL GOING: Good to soft (soft in places)
Wind: Moderate, half behind Weather: Overcast

5632 CONSTANT SECURITY NURSERY 7f
2:00 (2:01) (Class 5) (0-75,74) 2-Y-O £2,590 (£770; £385; £192) **Stalls** High

Form RPR

4036 **1** **One Cool Kitty**[41] 4373 2-8-10 **66**.................................... DominicFox[(3)] 8 70
(M G Quinlan) *hld up: hdwy 2f out: edgd lft and styd on ins fnl f to ld last stride* **20/1**

4323 **2** shd **Lookafternumberone (IRE)**[10] 5363 2-9-1 **68**........ GrahamGibbons 14 72
(J G Given) *prom: led over 1f out: sn rdn: kpt on fnl f: hdd last stride* **8/1**[3]

2035 **3** 1 1/4 **Becausewecan (USA)**[26] 4874 2-9-5 **72**.......................... GregFairley 13 73
(M Johnston) *cl up: effrt and ev ch over 1f out: no ex wl ins fnl f* **14/1**

1030 **4** 1 1/4 **Cutting Comments**[12] 5277 2-9-6 **73**.............................. TomEaves 17 71
(M Dods) *in tch: n.m.r over 2f out and wl over 1f out: kpt on u.p ins fnl f* **25/1**

1322 **5** shd **River Dee (IRE)**[6] 5447 2-9-3 **70**.................................. AdrianTNicholls 10 67
(Miss Amy Weaver) *hld up: hdwy wl over 1f out: kpt on same pce fnl f* **7/2**[1]

002 **6** 1/2 **Classic Contours (USA)**[30] 4697 2-8-13 **66**........................ PJMcDonald 5 62+
(G A Swinbank) *in tch: drvn over 2f out: kpt on fnl f: no imp* **14/1**

0506 **7** 1 **Woteva**[21] 5006 2-8-3 **63**.. LanceBetts[(7)] 6 57
(B Ellison) *towards rr: hdwy over 2f out: kpt on fnl f: nvr rchd ldrs* **25/1**

0600 **8** 1 1/2 **Cool Sonata (IRE)**[51] 4045 2-7-12 **51** oh6.......................... PaulQuinn 12 41
(M Brittain) *led to over 1f out: sn rdn and btn* **100/1**

1 **9** 1/2 **More Than Many (USA)**[19] 5106 2-9-0 **67**........................ PaulHanagan 2 56
(R A Fahey) *prom: lost pl over 2f out: n.d after* **9/2**[2]

3444 **10** nse **Rossett Rose (IRE)**[6] 5451 2-9-2 **69**.................................... TWilliams 1 57
(M Brittain) *chsd ldrs: effrt and ev ch over 1f out: sn no ex* **40/1**

6304 **11** nk **Ay Tay Tate (IRE)**[29] 4740 2-9-6 **73**.............................. PatrickMathers 15 61
(I W McInnes) *midfield: outpcd over 2f out: r.o fnl f: no imp* **20/1**

0006 **12** 1/2 **Dark Moment**[29] 4733 2-8-9 **62**.. DaleGibson 20 48
(A Dickman) *in tch: outpcd over 2f out: sn btn* **66/1**

3406 **13** 1 **Toby Tyler**[9] 5381 2-9-6 **73**.. JamieMoriarty 7 57
(P T Midgley) *dwlt: t.k.h and sn midfield: effrt over 2f out: btn over 1f out* **25/1**

6265 **14** 2 1/2 **Veronicas Boy**[9] 5381 2-9-6 **73**.................................... DanielTudhope 11 51
(G M Moore) *early reminders in rr: drvn 1/2-way: n.d* **16/1**

000 **15** nk **Missou Maiden**[26] 4870 2-8-7 **60**.................................... JimmyQuinn 19 37
(M H Tompkins) *dwlt: bhd: effrt over 2f out: sn btn* **20/1**

544 **16** 1 1/2 **Mabait**[36] 4530 2-9-5 **72**.. PatCosgrave 16 45
(L M Cumani) *bhd: pushed along over 2f out: nvr on terms* **8/1**[3]

406 **17** 1 **Igneous**[26] 4847 2-8-3 **56** ow2.. AndrewElliott 9 27
(K R Burke) *dwlt: bhd and rdn 1/2-way: nvr on terms* **28/1**

045 **18** 2 3/4 **The Kilkenny Kat (IRE)**[79] 3107 2-8-10 **63**.......................... JohnEgan 18 27
(T D Easterby) *chsd ldrs to over 2f out: sn btn* **20/1**

4162 **19** 2 1/4 **Sweet Smile (IRE)**[27] 4816 2-9-7 **74**.............................. PaulMulrennan 4 32
(K A Ryan) *towards rr: hdwy over 2f out: btn over 1f out* **22/1**

006 **20** 1 1/4 **Ten Cents A Dance**[72] 3334 2-7-9 **51** oh4..................(b[1]) DuranFentiman[(3)] 3 6
(T D Easterby) *towards rr on outside: drvn 3f out: sn btn* **100/1**

1m 27.77s (3.27) **Going Correction** +0.30s/f (Good) 20 Ran SP% **126.1**
Speed ratings (Par 95): **93,92,91,90,89 89,88,86,85,85 85,84,83,80,80 78,77,74,72,70**
toteswinger: 1&2 £40.70, 1&3 £111.50, 2&3 £32.00. CSF £152.08 CT £2352.49 TOTE £29.20: £4.90, £1.90, £4.20, £6.30; EX 336.50.

Owner Roger Turner **Bred** Hunscote House Farm Stud **Trained** Newmarket, Suffolk

FOCUS
A hugely competitive nursery and any number looked in with a chance as they passed the two-furlong marker. The winner is an improver with the runner-up backing up his Warwick form.

NOTEBOOK
One Cool Kitty, off since failing to make any impression on her handicap debut at Newmarket in July, she had been eased 4lb and seemed to appreciate the easier going. The extra furlong was clearly the making of her and there may well be more to come. (op 22-1)
Lookafternumberone(IRE) had already proven his effectiveness in this ground, having finished third off this mark at Warwick the other day. Another stepping up in trip, he was produced to have every chance and went on over a furlong out, but just got run out of it. He stayed the seventh furlong well and can continue to progress under similar conditions. (op 9-1 tchd 15-2)
Becausewecan(USA) was always likely to improve for this first crack at 7f and he left behind his recent course effort (nursery debut) by going down fighting in third. He is only modest and has not displayed any consistency in his five-race career, but clearly has a race in him. (op 16-1)
Cutting Comments, unsuited by the fast ground in a sales race at Newmarket last time, was 2lb lower than when dead-heating at Musselburgh earlier in the season and he seemed to have no problems with this longer trip, sticking on right the way to the line. A slow surface is evidently important to him. (op 33-1)
River Dee(IRE), a selling winner who has progressed well without scoring since running in nurseries, looked unlucky at Chester the other day and was understandably fancied to gain compensation off the same mark. Although his win came on fast ground, he had run well with some cut at Salisbury, so it was a little disappointing he failed to take hand in the finish, just keeping on at the one pace inside the final furlong. (op 4-1)
Classic Contours(USA), making his nursery debut, has never run on ground this soft before and he was found wanting for a change of pace. (op 11-1)
Woteva is exposed and ran as well as could have been expected.
Cool Sonata(IRE) hung in there for longer than expected and posted an improved performance.
More Than Many(USA), who overcame greenness to score on his Ripon debut, had been handed a fair mark and looked set to be suited by the extra furlong. However, he seemed to find this a bit too much so early in his career and, having lost his position at halfway, could only plod on at the one pace. This was not the best of him and he deserves another chance. (op 11-2 tchd 4-1 and 6-1 in a place)
Rossett Rose(IRE), up in trip, is on a stiff enough mark and, having been there with a chance over a furlong out, could find no more. (op 50-1)
Mabait had to be respected on this nursery debut, hailing from a top Newmarket yard, but he failed to reproduce the form he showed in maidens and may have had a problem with the ground, despite being bred to go on it (op 15-2)
The Kilkenny Kat(IRE) Official explanation: jockey said gelding was unsuited by the good to soft (soft in places) ground

5633 REDCARRACING.CO.UK MAIDEN AUCTION STKS 5f
2:30 (2:32) (Class 6) 2-Y-O £2,388 (£705; £352) **Stalls** High

Form RPR

3243 **1** **Sir Geoffrey (IRE)**[22] 4965 2-8-11 **73**.............................. PatCosgrave 7 74
(A J McCabe) *mde all: edgd rt ins fnl f: hld on towards fin* **11/4**[2]

2 3/4 **Silent Wonder** 2-8-9 0 .... TomEaves 5 69
(R M H Cowell) *hmpd s: sn w ldrs: edgd rt over 1f out: styd on wl towards fin* **22/1**

5334 3 1 1/4 **Desert Falls**[29] 4734 2-8-13 70 .... DeanMcKeown 8 69
(R M Whitaker) *chsd ldrs: kpt on same pce appr fnl f* **8/1**

324 4 1/2 **Paddy Bear**[8] 5394 2-8-9 0 .... PaulHanagan 6 63
(R A Fahey) *swvd lft s: sn chsng ldrs: kpt on same pce appr fnl f* **15/8**[1]

5 3 1/4 **Lady Gem** 2-8-8 0 .... PaulMulrennan 9 50
(D H Brown) *prom: kpt on same pce fnl 2f* **12/1**

00 6 nse **Miss Gibboa (IRE)**[29] 4734 2-8-8 0 .... PJMcDonald 12 50
(G A Swinbank) *prom: outpcd 2f out: kpt on ins fnl f* **40/1**

2452 7 1 **Sea Crest**[9] 5384 2-8-4 70 .... TWilliams 13 43
(M Brittain) *chsd ldrs on inner: one pce appr fnl f: rdr dropped whip ins fnl f* **4/1**[3]

0 8 1/2 **Flaming Ruby**[126] 1749 2-8-1 0 .... KellyHarrison(5) 2 43
(N Tinkler) *sn trcking ldrs on outer: wknd over 1f out* **66/1**

9 2 **Wrens Hope** 2-8-4 0 .... JimmyQuinn 11 34
(N Bycroft) *mid-div: sn drvn along: nvr a factor* **25/1**

0 10 hd **James Junior**[8] 5394 2-8-9 0 .... DNolan 10 38
(D Carroll) *mid-div: sn drvn along: wknd 2f out* **125/1**

11 2 1/4 **Shining Times (IRE)** 2-8-10 0 .... TonyHamilton 4 31
(D W Barker) *hmpd s: a in rr* **66/1**

12 1/2 **Katie Girl** 2-8-4 0 .... DaleGibson 3 23
(Mrs G S Rees) *s.i.s: a in rr* **40/1**

13 1 **No Quarter Given (IRE)** 2-9-1 0 .... PaulFessey 1 30
(Mrs A Duffield) *chsd ldrs: lost pl 2f out* **33/1**

60.43 secs (1.83) **Going Correction** +0.30s/f (Good) **13 Ran SP% 120.0**
Speed ratings (Par 93): **97,95,93,93,87 87,86,85,82,81 78,77,75**
toteswinger: 1&2 £16.90, 1&3 £3.60, 2&3 £22.70. CSF £68.07 TOTE £3.70: £1.10, £4.50, £2.10; EX 82.70.
Owner Dixon, Howlett & The Chrystal Maze Ptn **Bred** P Rabbitte **Trained** Babworth, Notts

FOCUS
A modest maiden and not many got into it. The form is rated around the winner and third.

NOTEBOOK
Sir Geoffrey(IRE) soon took it up and was never headed. He had shown fair form in Polytrack maidens and, although a shade disappointing on his turf debut at Beverley, made no mistake here. Strongly driven from over a furlong out, he was always holding the newcomer Silent Wonder and may progress further in nurseries. (op 4-1 tchd 9-2)
Silent Wonder, who cost just £800, is bred to handle some cut in the ground and he made a pleasing debut. Hailing from a yard whose juvenile often need a run, he seemed to know his job and stuck on right the way to the line, suggesting a minor maiden can come his way. (op 16-1)
Desert Falls, back down in trip having raced keenly at Newcastle last time, was unable to match the front pair, but stayed on under pressure and should stand more of a chance in nurseries. (op 7-1 tchd 13-2)
Paddy Bear got going all too late having tried to overcome a bad draw at Catterick last time and he held strong claims. Not many by his sire enjoy soft ground, however,and he was struggling from over a furlong out, just keeping on at the one pace. He deserves another chance back on faster ground. (op 2-1 tchd 13-8 and 9-4 in a place)
Lady Gem, a 157,000gns daughter of Captain Rio, seemed to know her job well enough and kept on under pressure. (op 14-1 tchd 16-1)
Miss Gibboa(IRE) is now qualified for a handicap mark and should fare better in that sphere. (op 33-1)
Sea Crest was the disappointment of the race. She has twice finished second this season, but the change of tactics did not seem to work and she would not have finished much closer even if her rider hadn't dropped his whip (tchd 7-2)

5634 WEDDINGS AT REDCAR H'CAP 6f
3:00 (3:01) (Class 5) (0-75,72) 3-Y-O+ **£2,590** (£770; £385; £192) **Stalls** High

Form RPR

6011 1 **Woodsley House (IRE)**[8] 5392 6-8-13 68 6ex .... NeilBrown(3) 6 76+
(A G Foster) *hld up: swtchd and hdwy stands' side 2f out: kpt on to ld wl ins fnl f* **3/1**[1]

-2 2 1 **War And Peace (IRE)**[17] 5160 4-9-6 72 .... JohnEgan 11 77
(Jane Chapple-Hyam) *cl up: edgd lft and led briefly ins fnl f: r.o* **6/1**[2]

6443 3 shd **Coleorton Dancer**[56] 3890 6-8-13 65 .... (b) PaulHanagan 10 70
(K A Ryan) *prom: effrt over 2f out: kpt on fnl f* **8/1**

4400 4 1 **Paris Bell**[13] 5222 6-8-9 64 .... DuranFentiman(3) 4 65
(T D Easterby) *t.k.h in midfield: effrt 2f out: r.o fnl f* **8/1**

0050 5 1/2 **Elkhorn**[46] 4218 6-9-2 68 .... (b) TonyHamilton 9 68
(Miss J A Camacho) *dwlt: sn midfield: effrt over 1f out: nrst fin* **12/1**

0/01 6 1/2 **Keys Of Cyprus**[20] 5045 6-8-11 63 .... AdrianTNicholls 14 61+
(D Nicholls) *hld up: effrt over 2f out: r.o fnl f: nrst fin* **7/1**[3]

0361 7 nk **Uace Mac**[26] 4877 4-8-10 65 .... MarkLawson(5) 2 62
(N Bycroft) *led after 1f: edgd lft and hdd ins fnl f: no ex* **14/1**

1104 8 hd **Steel Blue**[12] 5260 8-9-5 71 .... (p) PaulMulrennan 12 68
(R M Whitaker) *prom: shkn up over 1f out: no imp fnl f* **11/1**

3010 9 2 1/4 **Moonage Daydream (IRE)**[10] 5358 3-9-1 69 .... (bt) DavidAllan 1 58
(T D Easterby) *trckd ldrs tl edgd lft and wknd ent fnl f* **9/1**

4/00 10 3/4 **Bon News (IRE)**[49] 4117 4-8-7 59 .... TomEaves 8 46
(B Smart) *taken early to post: bhd: drvn 1/2-way: nvr on terms* **50/1**

0200 11 nk **Darcy's Pride (IRE)**[8] 5398 4-8-8 60 .... PJMcDonald 3 46
(D W Barker) *led 1f: cl up tl wknd over 1f out* **16/1**

2400 12 shd **Royal Acclamation (IRE)**[30] 4700 3-8-12 66 .... SilvestreDeSousa 13 52
(G A Harker) *hld up: drvn 1/2-way: n.d* **22/1**

6/00 13 3/4 **Fitzwarren**[30] 4700 7-7-13 58 oh13 .... JamesRogers(7) 7 41
(A D Brown) *awkward s: a bhd* **150/1**

1m 13.0s (1.20) **Going Correction** +0.30s/f (Good)
WFA 3 from 4yo+ 2lb **13 Ran SP% 119.6**
Speed ratings (Par 103): **104,102,102,101,100 99,99,99,96,95 94,94,93**
toteswinger: 1&2 £6.20, 1&3 £9.60, 2&3 £6.60. CSF £19.62 CT £133.75 TOTE £4.20: £1.90, £2.00, £3.20; EX 21.60.
Owner Mrs V L Davis **Bred** Roger G English **Trained** Cousland, Midlothian
■ Stewards' Enquiry : John Egan one-day ban: failed to ride to draw (Sep 18)

FOCUS
An open handicap and straightforward form with the winner to his latest mark backed up by the placed horses.
Steel Blue Official explanation: jockey said gelding hung right-handed throughout

5635 BODDINGTONS REDCAR STRAIGHT-MILE CHAMPIONSHIP (QUALIFIER) (H'CAP) 1m
3:35 (3:35) (Class 4) (0-85,85) 3-Y-O+ **£4,857** (£1,445; £722; £360) **Stalls** High

Form RPR

1150 1 **Medici Pearl**[32] 4661 4-8-12 76 .... DavidAllan 11 86
(T D Easterby) *hld up in midfield: hdwy outer over 2f out: styd on to ld last 75yds* **8/1**

051 2 3/4 **Brasingaman Hifive**[27] 4818 3-8-8 77 .... DaleGibson 2 84
(Mrs G S Rees) *trckd ldrs towards outer: edgd rt over 1f out: led jst ins fnl f: hdd and no ex wl ins fnl f* **22/1**

5U60 3 1 1/2 **Red Romeo**[55] 3928 7-8-8 72 .... PaulHanagan 3 77
(G A Swinbank) *w ldrs on outer: kpt on same pce ins fnl f* **22/1**

5016 4 3 1/2 **Royal Island (IRE)**[10] 5345 6-8-11 75 .... DanielTudhope 10 72
(M G Quinlan) *hld up in rr: hdwy on outer over 2f out: kpt on: nt rch ldrs* **7/1**[3]

-011 5 1/2 **Borasco (USA)**[26] 4875 3-8-13 82 .... PaulFessey 9 77
(T D Barron) *led towards stands' side: edgd lft and hdd jst ins fnl f: sn wknd* **9/2**[1]

0301 6 2 1/2 **Charlie Tipple**[26] 4876 4-9-2 80 .... (p) PaulMulrennan 6 70
(T D Easterby) *rrd s: hdwy outer to chse ldrs 4f out: wknd over 1f out* **9/1**

2500 7 2 1/4 **Bold Marc (IRE)**[33] 4649 6-8-12 76 .... AndrewElliott 5 61
(K R Burke) *chsd ldrs on outer: wknd over 1f out* **16/1**

5P0 8 4 1/2 **Bid For Glory**[26] 4867 4-9-7 85 .... JimmyQuinn 12 60
(H J Collingridge) *dwlt: hld up in rr: hdwy on ins over 2f out: wknd over 1f out* **22/1**

2601 9 nk **Moody Tunes**[13] 5221 5-8-13 77 .... PatCosgrave 7 51
(K R Burke) *chsd ldrs centre: wknd over 1f out* **9/1**

4220 10 1 1/2 **Follow The Flag (IRE)**[26] 4875 4-8-8 72 .... NeilPollard 4 42
(A J McCabe) *mid-div on outer: effrt over 2f out: nvr nr ldrs* **18/1**

2460 11 3/4 **Royal Fantasy (IRE)**[12] 5279 5-8-13 77 .... JohnEgan 1 46
(N Tinkler) *trckd ldrs on wd outside: edgd lft and lost pl over 1f out* **28/1**

645 12 nse **Goodbye**[71] 3369 4-9-6 84 .... PJMcDonald 14 53
(G A Swinbank) *chsd ldrs stands' side: wknd over 1f out* **13/2**[2]

6630 13 1 **Passion Fruit**[26] 4875 7-8-13 77 .... DeanMcKeown 15 43
(C W Fairhurst) *in rr: hdwy on ins over 2f out: wknd over 1f out* **20/1**

14 3 1/2 **Smarty Socks (IRE)**[139] 1464 4-8-13 77 .... JamieMoriarty 8 35
(P T Midgley) *a towards rr in centre* **66/1**

1000 15 1 1/2 **Always A Rock (IRE)**[14] 5207 3-9-2 85 .... GregFairley 17 39
(M Johnston) *chsd ldrs on ins: sn drvn along: lost pl over 2f out* **14/1**

4610 16 1/2 **Boy Blue**[28] 4783 3-9-1 84 .... TonyHamilton 13 37
(D W Barker) *mid-div stands' side: lost pl over 2f out* **22/1**

610 17 3 1/2 **Mooted (UAE)**[92] 2714 3-8-7 76 ow1 .... TomEaves 16 21
(Miss J A Camacho) *in rr: bhd fnl 2f* **20/1**

1m 40.81s (2.81) **Going Correction** +0.30s/f (Good)
WFA 3 from 4yo+ 5lb **17 Ran SP% 124.8**
Speed ratings (Par 105): **97,96,94,91,90 88,86,81,81,79 78,78,77,74,72 72,68**
toteswinger: 1&2 £36.10, 1&3 £82.40, 2&3 £51.10. CSF £179.68 CT £3857.41 TOTE £8.90: £2.10, £4.10, £5.80, £2.00; EX 172.20.
Owner Ryedale Partners No 3 **Bred** Larkwood Stud **Trained** Great Habton, N Yorks

FOCUS
Few could be discounted in this tricky handicap and the form looks pretty straightforward with the winner back to form.

5636 SUBSCRIBE TO RACING UK MAIDEN STKS 6f
4:05 (4:05) (Class 5) 3-Y-O+ **£2,590** (£770; £385; £192) **Stalls** High

Form RPR

3333 1 **Strawberry Moon (IRE)**[28] 4782 3-8-12 65 .... TomEaves 2 68
(B Smart) *missed break: bhd tl hdwy over 2f out: led appr fnl f: kpt on strly* **9/4**[1]

02- 2 1 1/4 **Tito (IRE)**[318] 6384 3-9-3 0 .... PaulFessey 5 69
(T D Barron) *midfield: effrt over 2f out: chsd wnr appr fnl f: kpt on same pce ins fnl f* **12/1**

0 3 3 3/4 **Cullybackey (IRE)**[26] 4877 3-8-12 0 .... PJMcDonald 1 52
(G A Swinbank) *hld up: shkn up and hdwy 2f out: rdn and kpt on fnl f: nvr nr ldrs* **33/1**

03 4 3/4 **Half A Crown (IRE)**[19] 5110 3-9-3 0 .... TonyHamilton 6 55
(D W Barker) *prom: effrt over 2f out: one pce fnl f* **10/1**

05 5 nk **Master Of Light**[12] 5261 3-9-3 0 .... GrahamGibbons 10 54
(P A Blockley) *prom: drvn over 2f out: one pce over 1f out* **9/1**

4540 6 nk **Beaumont Boy**[8] 5389 4-9-2 53 .... (b) NeilBrown(3) 7 53
(A G Foster) *prom: effrt over 2f out: no ex ent fnl f: eased nr fin* **28/1**

7 2 1/2 **Barley Bree (IRE)** 3-8-12 0 .... PaulMulrennan 4 40
(Mrs A Duffield) *cl up: led over 2f out to appr fnl f: sn wknd* **14/1**

4 8 1 3/4 **Lachafinna (IRE)**[10] 5361 3-8-12 0 .... DavidAllan 12 34
(D Carroll) *dwlt: sn pushed along in rr: nvr rchd ldrs* **40/1**

6500 9 1/2 **Sharp Indian**[85] 2928 4-8-9 49 .... KellyHarrison(5) 9 32
(W J H Ratcliffe) *chsd ldrs tl rdn and wknd fr 2f out* **80/1**

00 10 1 1/2 **Lifetime Endeavour**[8] 5395 4-8-12 0 .... BMcHugh(7) 3 33
(R E Barr) *bhd: pushed along 1/2-way: nvr on terms* **100/1**

3 11 3/4 **Minnola**[12] 5261 3-8-12 0 .... SaleemGolam 8 25
(Rae Guest) *prom 2f: sn lost pl: n.d after* **5/1**[3]

12 2 1/4 **Colonel Sherman (USA)** 3-9-3 0 .... PatCosgrave 11 23
(Jane Chapple-Hyam) *dwlt: rdn in rr over 2f out: nvr on terms* **33/1**

5040 13 2 1/4 **Mozayada (USA)**[40] 4420 4-9-0 45 .... TWilliams 13 11
(M Brittain) *led to over 2f out: sn wknd* **50/1**

43 14 4 1/2 **Baby Rock**[17] 5160 3-9-3 0 .... GregFairley 15 1
(C F Wall) *t.k.h: chsd ldrs tl wknd over 2f out* **10/3**[2]

/005 15 9 **Frill A Minute**[39] 4454 4-9-0 40 .... PaulQuinn 14 —
(Miss L C Siddall) *sn towards rr: struggling fr 1/2-way* **150/1**

1m 14.5s (2.70) **Going Correction** +0.30s/f (Good)
WFA 3 from 4yo 2lb **15 Ran SP% 120.6**
Speed ratings (Par 103): **94,92,87,86,85 85,82,79,79,77 76,73,70,64,52**
toteswinger: 1&2 £6.70, 1&3 £16.40, 2&3 £49.40. CSF £29.86 TOTE £3.20: £1.40, £3.40, £10.30; EX 39.10.
Owner Mrs Julie Martin **Bred** Gerrardstown House Stud **Trained** Hambleton, N Yorks
■ Stewards' Enquiry : Neil Brown ten-day ban: failed to ride out for 4th place (Sep 18-27)

FOCUS
A typically weak three-year-old plus sprint maiden but the form looks sound enough with the runner-up, fourth and sixth close to their marks..

5637 REDCAR CONFERENCE CENTRE H'CAP 1m 6f 19y
4:40 (4:40) (Class 6) (0-65,63) 3-Y-O+ **£2,388** (£705; £352) **Stalls** Low

Form RPR

211 1 **Red Fama**[11] 5305 4-9-11 60 6ex .... JimmyQuinn 2 79+
(N Bycroft) *in tch gng wl: smooth hdwy to ld 2f out: shkn up and sn clr: easily* **9/4**[1]

-631 2 6 **Hawk Mountain (UAE)**[20] 5077 3-9-1 61 .... GrahamGibbons 15 69
(J J Quinn) *mid-div: pushed along 9f out: hdwy 4f out: styd on wl fnl f to take 2nd last stride* **3/1**[2]

0-06 3 shd **Compton Dragon (USA)**[14] 5199 9-9-1 55 .... KellyHarrison(5) 12 62
(W M Brisbourne) *in rr-div: hdwy over 2f out: tk 2nd ins fnl f: kpt on same pce* **20/1**

-002 **4** 1 ¾ **Lindy Lou**[17] 5163 4-9-12 **61** GregFairley 3 66
(C F Wall) *rrd s: edgd rt and hdwy over 3f out: kpt on same pce appr fnl f* **9/1**

3006 **5** 2 **Blue Jet (USA)**[7] 5415 4-9-1 **50** DeanMcKeown 9 52
(R M Whitaker) *trckd ldrs: styd on same pce fnl 2f* **16/1**

0031 **6** 1 ½ **Always Best**[7] 5415 4-9-2 **51** 6ex TonyHamilton 5 51
(R Allan) *chsd ldr: led 3f out: hdd 2f out: wknd fnl f* **7/1**[3]

0402 **7** 7 **Bond Casino**[26] 4879 4-9-3 **52** SilvestreDeSousa 1 42
(G R Oldroyd) *led tl 3f out: wknd over 1f out* **11/1**

3556 **8** 3 ¼ **Its Moon (IRE)**[33] 4652 4-10-0 **63** PaulMulrennan 16 49
(T D Walford) *chsd ldrs: reminders 7f out: lost pl over 2f out* **14/1**

000 **9** 1 ¾ **Unawatuna**[31] 4689 3-8-8 **54** AndrewElliott 8 37
(Mrs K Walton) *in rr: reminders 6f out: nvr a factor* **100/1**

0630 **10** ¾ **Lady Killer Queen**[9] 5385 4-9-8 **57** (v) DNolan 6 39
(D Carroll) *hld up in rr: nvr on terms* **40/1**

0436 **11** ½ **Trance (IRE)**[26] 4848 8-9-3 **59** DeanHeslop(7) 10 41
(T D Barron) *in rr: sme hdwy 6f out: nvr a factor* **16/1**

000- **12** 4 **Shekan Star**[455] 2391 6-9-0 **49** PaulHanagan 14 25
(K G Reveley) *hld up in rr: nvr a factor* **50/1**

0006 **13** 1 ¾ **Clueless**[22] 4963 6-9-13 **62** NeilPollard 13 36
(A J McCabe) *in tch: effrt 4f out: wandered: lost pl over 1f out* **20/1**

0600 **14** ¾ **College Land Boy**[46] 4217 4-8-10 **45** TWilliams 4 17
(A Kirtley) *chsd ldrs: drvn 6f out: lost pl 3f out* **100/1**

000- **15** 3 ½ **Starbougg**[247] 5906 4-9-3 **52** TomEaves 11 20
(K G Reveley) *in rr-div: bhd fnl 4f* **66/1**

0055 **16** ¾ **Notnowrosie (IRE)**[48] 4147 3-8-3 **49** DaleGibson 7 16
(A G Foster) *in tch: lost pl 3f out* **100/1**

3m 8.23s (3.53) **Going Correction** +0.30s/f (Good)
WFA 3 from 4yo+ 11lb **16** Ran SP% **123.4**
Speed ratings (Par 101): **101,97,97,96,95 94,90,88,87,87 86,84,83,83,81 80**
toteswinger: 1&2 £3.40, 1&3 £14.50, 2&3 £18.70. CSF £8.14 CT £110.19 TOTE £2.80: £1.30, £1.60, £5.00, £2.10; EX 11.50.
Owner B F Rayner **Bred** N Bycroft **Trained** Brandsby, N Yorks

FOCUS
This was very much a case of Red Fama first the rest nowhere. The form looks sound through the fourth.
Clueless Official explanation: jockey said gelding had no more to give

5638 "GO RACING" IN YORKSHIRE APPRENTICE H'CAP 7f
5:10 (5:11) (Class 5) (0-70,70) 3-Y-O+ **£2,590** (£770; £385; £192) **Stalls** High

Form RPR

0331 **1** **Shotley Mac**[25] 4901 4-9-5 **65** (b) DuranFentiman 9 76
(N Bycroft) *pressed ldr: led gng wl over 2f out: rdn out fnl f* **11/4**[1]

0-11 **2** 3 **Sea Salt**[26] 4849 5-9-4 **69** BMcHugh(5) 3 72
(A J McCabe) *prom: rdn over 2f out: wandered and chsd wnr ins fnl f: r.o* **7/2**[2]

0610 **3** 1 ½ **Mister Jingles**[45] 4245 5-9-1 **61** RussellKennemore 7 60
(R M Whitaker) *led to over 2f out: no ex and lost 2nd ins fnl f* **17/2**

0000 **4** 1 **My Kaiser Chief**[34] 4609 3-8-13 **66** KellyHarrison(3) 10 60
(W J H Ratcliffe) *hld up: hdwy 2f out: one pce fnl f* **10/1**

3300 **5** 1 ½ **Young Gladiator (IRE)**[51] 4044 3-8-11 **61** DNolan 8 51
(Miss J A Camacho) *prom tl rdn and no ex fr 2f out* **8/1**[3]

2062 **6** shd **Hasty Lady**[9] 5377 3-8-11 **61** (p) JamieMoriarty 11 51
(K A Ryan) *in tch: drvn and outpcd over 2f out: n.d after* **8/1**[3]

0010 **7** nk **Trans Sonic**[12] 5258 5-8-6 **59** (v) JamieKyne(7) 5 50
(A J Lockwood) *hld up in tch: effrt over 2f out: wknd over 1f out* **8/1**[3]

1540 **8** 2 ¾ **Lujiana**[21] 5007 3-8-3 **60** AdamCarter(7) 2 42
(M Brittain) *hld up: rdn over 2f out: nvr on terms* **20/1**

6210 **9** 1 **To Bubbles**[26] 4782 3-8-10 **60** NeilBrown 1 39
(T D Barron) *dwlt: drvn over 2f out: sn btn* **14/1**

-100 **10** 18 **Nortune (USA)**[117] 2002 3-9-3 **70** (v[1]) GaryBartley(3) 4 —
(B Smart) *cl up tl wknd qckly fr 2f out: eased whn no ch fnl f* **14/1**

1m 27.2s (2.70) **Going Correction** +0.30s/f (Good)
WFA 3 from 4yo+ 4lb **10** Ran SP% **119.9**
Speed ratings (Par 103): **96,92,90,89,88 87,87,84,83,62**
toteswinger: 1&2 £3.20, 1&3 £6.10, 2&3 £7.90. CSF £12.59 CT £75.37 TOTE £3.20: £1.40, £2.10, £2.90; EX 8.60 Place 6: £257.10, Place 5: £55.43..
Owner J A Swinburne **Bred** N Bycroft **Trained** Brandsby, N Yorks

FOCUS
A modest handicap with the placed horses close to recent form.
Nortune(USA) Official explanation: jockey said colt was unsuited by the good to soft (soft in places) ground
T/Jkpt: Not won. T/Plt: £254.60 to a £1 stake. Pool: £65,341.93. 187.30 winning tickets. T/Qpdt: £22.00 to a £1 stake. Pool: £5,042.57. 169.40 winning tickets. RY

5458 SALISBURY (R-H)
Thursday, September 4

OFFICIAL GOING: Good (good to soft in places; 8.7)
Wind: Quite strong against Weather: Overcast

5639 AXMINSTER CARPETS APPRENTICE H'CAP (WHIPS SHALL BE CARRIED BUT NOT USED) 1m
1:40 (1:43) (Class 5) (0-70,69) 3-Y-O+ **£3,238** (£963; £481; £240) **Stalls** High

Form RPR

6032 **1** **Effigy**[28] 4789 4-9-1 **65** AmyScott(5) 5 76
(H Candy) *mid-div: smooth hdwy 4f out: led 3f out: edgd rt ins fnl f: kpt on wl: pushed out* **5/2**[1]

31 **2** 1 ½ **Straight Sets (IRE)**[20] 5057 4-9-9 **68** MatthewDavies 2 76
(M R Channon) *lw: trckd ldrs: rdn over 2f out: styd on ins fnl f: wnt 2nd towards fin* **9/2**[2]

4032 **3** ½ **Star Strider**[19] 5101 4-8-11 **61** AndreaAtzeni(5) 12 67
(Miss Gay Kelleway) *t.k.h in mid-div: rdn and hdwy over 2f out: styd on fnl f: wnt 3rd fnl stride* **13/2**[3]

5003 **4** nse **Hobson**[42] 4333 3-8-5 **60** DanielBlackett(5) 11 66
(Eve Johnson Houghton) *led tl 3f out: sn rdn to chse wnr: no ex and lost 2 pls nr fin* **20/1**

0100 **5** 3 ½ **Themwerethedays**[17] 5146 3-8-11 **66** MatthewBirch(5) 10 64
(S Kirk) *hld up: rdn and sme prog into midfield over 2f out: kpt on same pce fnl f* **20/1**

3053 **6** 2 ½ **Takitwo**[22] 4979 5-8-4 **54** oh2 TobyAtkinson(5) 4 46
(P D Cundell) *in tch: rdn over 2f out: fdd fnl f* **10/1**

0050 **7** 5 **Naval Review (USA)**[48] 4158 3-9-5 **69** (t) JPHamblett 1 50
(Sir Michael Stoute) *in tch: rdn 3f out: wknd 2f out* **11/1**

2004 **8** hd **Fantasy Parkes**[25] 4901 4-9-6 **65** (t) ByronMoorcroft 9 46
(K Bishop) *mid-div: rdn over 3f out: wknd 2f out* **25/1**

54/0 **9** shd **Cover Drive (USA)**[28] 4789 5-9-7 **66** BillyCray 7 46
(Christian Wroe) *rrd leaving stalls: hung rt fr 3f out: a towards rr* **33/1**

153 **10** hd **Romany Nights (IRE)**[13] 5247 8-9-7 **66** (bt) KylieManser 8 46
(Miss Gay Kelleway) *s.i.s: a towards rr* **12/1**

2346 **11** 2 ¼ **Interactive (IRE)**[135] 1541 5-9-9 **68** RossAtkinson 3 43
(Andrew Turnell) *t.k.h: trckd ldrs: rdn 3f out: wknd 2f out* **25/1**

6015 **12** shd **Barathea Dreams (IRE)**[6] 5458 7-9-8 **67** SophieDoyle 6 41
(J S Moore) *rrd leaving stalls: a bhd* **13/2**[3]

1m 44.98s (1.48) **Going Correction** +0.025s/f (Good)
WFA 3 from 4yo+ 5lb **12** Ran SP% **118.7**
Speed ratings (Par 103): **93,91,91,90,87 84,79,79,79,79 77,77**
toteswinger: 1&2 £3.00, 1&3 £4.30, 2&3 £5.70. CSF £11.91 CT £67.48 TOTE £3.20: £1.40, £1.90, £2.30; EX 13.30.
Owner The Earl Cadogan **Bred** The Earl Cadogan **Trained** Kingston Warren, Oxon

FOCUS
A fair handicap for the class, confined to apprentice riders, in which whips were carried but not to be used. They went an average pace and the first four finished clear of the remainder, so the form looks sound enough with the third, fourth and fifth close to this year's marks.
Barathea Dreams(IRE) Official explanation: jockey said gelding reared as stalls opened

5640 EUROPEAN BREEDERS' FUND QUIDHAMPTON MAIDEN FILLIES' STKS (DIV I) 6f 212y
2:10 (2:15) (Class 4) 2-Y-O **£6,476** (£1,927; £963; £481) **Stalls** High

Form RPR

56 **1** **Fanditha (IRE)**[19] 5097 2-9-0 0 RichardHughes 9 79+
(R Hannon) *lw: mde most: hdd briefly 3f out: rdn 2f out: sn narrowly hdd: rallied to regain ld and edgd lft ins fnl f: kpt on gamely: drvn out* **14/1**

2 **2** nk **Bouvardia**[26] 4870 2-9-0 0 TedDurcan 12 78+
(H R A Cecil) *w'like: scope: lw: trckd wnr: rdn over 2f out: tk narrow advantage over 1f out: hdd ins fnl f: no ex nr fin* **4/7**[1]

5 **3** 3 **Fallen In Love**[48] 4157 2-9-0 0 EddieAhern 10 71+
(J L Dunlop) *unf: lw: trckd ldrs: rdn over 2f out: kpt on but nt pce to chal* **13/2**[2]

6 **4** 1 ¼ **Al Tamooh (IRE)**[33] 4643 2-9-0 0 RHills 2 67
(J L Dunlop) *w'like: leggy: mid-div: rdn 3f out: no imp tl styd on fnl f* **10/1**[3]

364 **5** ¾ **Slant (IRE)**[12] 5294 2-9-0 0 StephenCarson 14 65
(Eve Johnson Houghton) *in tch: rdn 3f out: one pce fnl 2f* **10/1**[3]

50 **6** 1 **Virginia's Choice**[20] 5048 2-9-0 0 FrankieMcDonald 7 63
(Jane Chapple-Hyam) *trckd wnr: led briefly 3f out: sn rdn: one pce fnl f* **100/1**

7 ½ **Ariadnes Filly (IRE)** 2-9-0 0 JimCrowley 6 62
(Mrs A J Perrett) *leggy: s.i.s: sn mid-div: rdn 3f out: no imp* **66/1**

0 **8** 1 ½ **Ja One (IRE)**[35] 4554 2-9-0 0 RyanMoore 5 58
(B W Hills) *lw: sme late prog: mainly towards rr* **25/1**

9 2 ½ **Breadstick** 2-8-11 0 TravisBlock(3) 11 51
(H Morrison) *w'like: str: lw: s.i.s: a towards rr* **33/1**

65 **10** 1 **Ageebah**[31] 4692 2-9-0 0 LiamJones 4 49
(C E Brittain) *s.i.s: a towards rr* **50/1**

11 ¾ **Lyra's Daemon** 2-9-0 0 MartinDwyer 1 47
(W R Muir) *w'like: bit bkwd: in tch: rdn 3f out: wknd 2f out* **100/1**

6 **12** nk **Water Hen (IRE)**[13] 5227 2-9-0 0 SteveDrowne 3 46
(R Charlton) *lw: a towards rr* **16/1**

0 **13** 1 ¼ **Inis Boffin**[13] 5240 2-9-0 0 RichardKingscote 13 43
(S Kirk) *s.i.s: sn mid-div: rdn 3f out: wknd 2f out* **125/1**

1m 29.62s (0.62) **Going Correction** +0.025s/f (Good) **13** Ran SP% **120.7**
Speed ratings (Par 94): **97,96,93,91,90 89,89,87,84,83 82,82,80**
toteswinger: 1&2 £5.10, 1&3 £8.90, 2&3 £2.90. CSF £22.32 TOTE £17.80: £3.10, £1.10, £1.90; EX 34.80.
Owner A P Patey **Bred** Lynch Bages Ltd & Samac Ltd **Trained** East Everleigh, Wilts

FOCUS
The first division of the juvenile fillies' maiden and it looked an above-average heat on paper with five of the runners holding Group 1 entries. The first pair came clear but the proximity of the sixth tempers enthusiasm for the form.

NOTEBOOK
Fanditha(IRE) had struggled to go the early pace on her first two starts, but was soon to the fore on this first try over the extra furlong and showed a very professional attitude when challenged inside the final furlong. This 140,000euros purchase has a deal of speed in her pedigree, but clearly also stays well and is in the right hands to keep progressing. She holds an entry in the Goffs Fillies' Million at the Curragh later this month and she is an intended runner there. (tchd 12-1)
Bouvardia was well placed from her favourably high draw and was produced with every chance, but simply lacked the resolution of the winner. This will be considered disappointing and she may not have improved from her initial run, but she was still well clear of the remainder at the finish. No doubt she can be placed to find compensation, but her Cheveley Park entry looks to be flying high on this evidence. (op 8-13 tchd 4-6)
Fallen In Love, entered in the Fillies' Mile, proved one paced when it really mattered yet still kept on to post another pleasing effort in defeat. She may just benefit further from another furlong now. (op 7-1 tchd 11-2)
Al Tamooh(IRE) saw little really go her way as she was unable to get any cover from her low draw and was always playing catch up with the leaders. This rates as a step in the right direction and she should learn again for the experience. (op 12-1 tchd 14-1)
Slant(IRE), far from disgraced in a valuable sales race at the Curragh 12 days previously, got the longer trip well enough yet lacked the pace to land a serious blow. She helps to set the level of this form and can find less competitive assignments. (tchd 11-1)
Inis Boffin Official explanation: jockey said filly hung badly left-handed

5641 E B F PORTWAY NOVICE STKS 1m
2:40 (2:44) (Class 4) 2-Y-O **£4,695** (£1,397; £698; £348) **Stalls** High

Form RPR

2 **1** **Cityscape**[20] 5068 2-8-12 0 SteveDrowne 6 104+
(R Charlton) *w'like: scope: gd sort: chsd ldr: chal 3f out: led 2f out: forged clr fnl f: readily* **11/10**[1]

1 **2** 9 **Such Optimism**[21] 5021 2-8-11 0 RichardKingscote 4 82
(R M Beckett) *led: rdn 3f out: hdd 2f out: kpt on but no ch w wnr fnl f* **9/4**[2]

6 **3** 4 **Akhenaten**[19] 5093 2-8-12 0 SamHitchcott 2 74
(M R Channon) *bmpd s: sn trcking ldrs: rdn 3f out: kpt on same pce* **10/1**

4 ¾ **Forty Thirty (IRE)** 2-8-8 0 DarryllHolland 3 69
(M R Channon) *w'like: leggy: hld up: effrt 3f out: sn one pce: wnt 4th jst ins fnl f* **16/1**

043 **5** 2 ¼ **Versaki (IRE)**[13] 5228 2-9-5 **94** RichardHughes 7 75
(R Hannon) *hld up: effrt 3f out: wknd over 1f out* **9/2**[3]

00 **6** 2 **Chiberta King**[48] 4151 2-8-12 0 MartinDwyer 5 63
(A M Balding) *chsd ldrs: rdn 3f out: sn btn* **33/1**

6 7 4 **Sumani (FR)**[26] 4861 2-8-12 0 ..... IanMongan 1 54
(S Dow) *t.k.h bhd ldrs: dropped to last 4f out: nvr bk on terms* **50/1**

1m 44.02s (0.52) **Going Correction** +0.025s/f (Good) **7** Ran SP% **116.4**
Speed ratings (Par 97): **98,89,85,84,82 80,76**
toteswinger: 1&2 £1.40, 1&3 £4.20, 2&3 £5.10. CSF £3.92 TOTE £2.10: £1.40, £1.80; EX 4.20.

Owner K Abdulla **Bred** Juddmonte Farms Ltd **Trained** Beckhampton, Wilts

FOCUS

Cityscape took this novice event in most impressive fashion and looks a smart colt in the making.

NOTEBOOK

Cityscape ◆ showed himself to be a highly progressive colt with a very impressive display to go one better. He took time to really find his stride, but once asked to reel in the eventual runner-up nearing the final furlong he shot clear and ultimately came home with any amount left up his sleeve. This half-brother to his stable's progressive miler Scuffle, he clearly possesses more stamina than his sibling, despite his sire's influence suggesting otherwise. It is also very encouraging that his half-sister and dam took until their three-year-old careers to come good and he looks sure to improve physically with a winter over his back. He has no fancy entries at this stage, so it will be fascinating to see where he is pitched in next and no doubt it will take a smart sort to lower his colours wherever he does turn up. (tchd Evens and 6-5)

Such Optimism had run out a decisive maiden winner over 7f at the track 21 days previously and looked a big player in this, despite that race not working out so well to date. Given a positive ride over this longer trip, she proved no match for the winner once that rival asserted for home, but still stayed on to finish a clear second-best. There will be other days for her. (op 3-1)

Akhenaten, sixth over 7f on his debut in Listed company19 days previously, was never a serious threat to the first pair yet still showed he has an engine. He should not be too long in finding a race. (op 8-1 tchd 14-1)

Forty Thirty(IRE) is bred to make his mark over further in time and he recorded a nice debut effort in this taxing company. He should know a deal more next time. (tchd 18-1)

Versaki(IRE)was ridden to get the longer trip and failed to get seriously involved. A drop back to around 7f looks a wise move, but he is not simple to place from his current rating. (tchd 5-1)

5642 EUROPEAN BREEDERS' FUND DICK POOLE FILLIES' STKS (LISTED RACE) 6f

3:15 (3:18) (Class 1) 2-Y-O

£20,437 (£7,747; £3,877; £1,933; £968; £486) **Stalls** High

Form RPR

1 **1** **Serious Attitude (IRE)**[25] 4905 2-8-12 0 ..... JimmyFortune 14 105+
(Rae Guest) *unf: scope: trckd ldrs: nt clr run over 2f out: squeezed through gap to ld ent fnl f: r.o strly: readily* **9/2**[1]

312 **2** 3 **Sneak Preview**[28] 4781 2-8-12 94 ..... RichardMullen 8 96
(E S McMahon) *trckd ldrs: rdn over 2f out: led over 1f out tl ent fnl f: nt pce of wnr* **9/2**[1]

410 **3** ½ **Seradim**[12] 5266 2-8-12 88 ..... JoeFanning 10 95
(P F I Cole) *squeezed out sn after s: mid-div: hdwy on rails over 2f out: sn rdn: swtchd lft over 1f out: r.o* **20/1**

1015 **4** 1 **Souter's Sister (IRE)**[12] 5266 2-8-12 93 ..... RyanMoore 13 92
(R Hannon) *in tch: rdn over 2f out: swtchd lft over 1f out: kpt on* **15/2**

2102 **5** 1 **Art Princess (USA)**[57] 3851 2-8-12 99 ..... MichaelHills 15 89
(B W Hills) *lw: led: rdn and hdd over 1f out: no ex ins fnl f* **11/2**[3]

3102 **6** ½ **Kerrys Requiem (IRE)**[20] 5055 2-8-12 101 ..... TPO'Shea 2 87
(M R Channon) *hld up towards rr: prog whn n.m.r and snatched up over 2f out: sn swtchd lft and rdn: hdwy over 1f out: hung rt and kpt on same pce fnl f* **11/1**

10 **7** 2¼ **Queen Of Thebes (IRE)**[49] 4108 2-8-12 80 ..... TedDurcan 4 80
(G L Moore) *hld up towards rr: styd on fr over 1f out: nvr a danger* **33/1**

1356 **8** ¾ **Calypso Girl (IRE)**[12] 5294 2-8-12 77 ..... TGMcLaughlin 5 78
(P D Evans) *mid-div: rdn over 3f out: no imp* **50/1**

01 **9** ¾ **Ballyalla**[48] 4149 2-8-12 82 ..... RichardHughes 12 76
(R Hannon) *prom: rdn 3f out: wknd over 1f out:* **5/1**[2]

0401 **10** 3 **Blushing Maid**[71] 3358 2-8-12 70 ..... SteveDrowne 1 67
(H S Howe) *a bhd* **100/1**

1 **11** ½ **Cut The Cackle (IRE)**[28] 4786 2-8-12 0 ..... JimCrowley 9 65
(P Winkworth) *lw: trckd ldrs: rdn 3f out: wknd 2f out* **10/1**

140 **12** 1¼ **Oasis Breeze**[40] 4403 2-8-12 87 ..... LDettori 6 62
(G D Blake) *a towards rr* **14/1**

33 **13** 3¾ **Champagne Fizz (IRE)**[13] 5227 2-8-12 0 ..... TravisBlock 3 50
(Miss Jo Crowley) *mid-div tl 3f out* **66/1**

1 **14** 1¾ **Rowayton**[101] 2462 2-8-12 0 ..... PhilipRobinson 11 45
(J D Bethell) *w'like: scope: mid-div: rdn whn swtchd lft over 2f out: sn wknd* **16/1**

1m 14.62s (-0.18) **Going Correction** +0.025s/f (Good) **14** Ran SP% **122.3**
Speed ratings (Par 100): **102,98,97,96,94 94,91,90,89,85 84,82,77,75**
toteswinger: 1&2 £6.30, 1&3 £22.40, 2&3 £23.70. CSF £23.81 TOTE £6.00: £2.00, £1.80, £7.30; EX 27.90.

Owner The Purple & Yellow Partnership 1 **Bred** Paddy Twomey **Trained** Newmarket, Suffolk

FOCUS

This was an open heat and not the strongest of races for a Listed event. It was run at a strong pace, however, and still produced a taking winner. The form looks solid rated around those in the frame behind her.

NOTEBOOK

Serious Attitude(IRE) ◆, an easy Windsor maiden winner 25 days previously, confirmed herself to be a filly of real promise with a decisive success and rates value for better than the bare margin. It was clear she was the one to beat nearing the furlong pole and, once quickening to the front, soon had the race sewn up. Considering she is by Mtoto and out of a mare who won twice over 1m at three, it is fair to expect her to keep improving as she steps up in trip. Another rise in class is now on the cards, perhaps in the £250,000 Tattersalls October Auction Stakes at Newmarket, and she can be expected to make a bold bid for the hat-trick. (op 11-2 after 13-2 in a place)

Sneak Preview again did nothing wrong in defeat on this first foray into such company and had every chance, but was no match for the winner's turn of foot. She helps to set the level of this form and has developed into a likeable filly (tchd 6-1)

Seradim, given a mark of 88 after finishing down the field in Group 3 company last time, showed up well on this drop back a furlong and is another who helps to put the form into perspective (op 33-1)

Souter's Sister(IRE), the most experienced runner in this field, ran her race on this drop back a furlong yet failed to confirm Goodwood form with the third and really looks more of a nursery type. She will not prove easy to place in that sphere from a mark of 93, however. (op 12-1 tchd 7-1)

Art Princess(USA), the Cherry Hinton second, again had her own way out in front, but she eventually proved a sitting duck and paid for setting the generous early pace. (op 9-2)

Ballyalla Official explanation: jockey said filly ran flat

Rowayton Official explanation: jockey said filly became unbalanced

5643 EUROPEAN BREEDERS' FUND QUIDHAMPTON MAIDEN FILLIES' STKS (DIV II) 6f 212y

3:45 (3:53) (Class 4) 2-Y-O

£6,476 (£1,927; £963; £481) **Stalls** High

Form RPR

2 **1** **Intense**[36] 4521 2-9-0 0 ..... MichaelHills 5 84+
(B W Hills) *lw: prom: rdn to ld wl over 1f out: r.o wl: comf* **11/8**[1]

2 **2** 1¾ **Three Moons (IRE)**[20] 5048 2-9-0 0 ..... LDettori 4 78
(H J L Dunlop) *prom: led 3f out tl wl over 1f out: kpt on but sn hld by wnr* **11/2**[3]

4 **3** 1 **Multiplication**[13] 5241 2-9-0 0 ..... SteveDrowne 13 75
(R Charlton) *led for 1f: trckd ldrs: rdn over 2f out: swtchd lft over 1f out: kpt on ins fnl f: wnt 3rd nr fin* **7/2**[2]

4 ¾ **Ave** 2-9-0 0 ..... RyanMoore 1 73
(Sir Michael Stoute) *unf: scope: bit bkwd: s.i.s: steadily rcvrd to get in tch: hdwy 3f out: rdn and ev ch 2f out: kpt on same pce: lost 3rd towards fin* **10/1**

5 5 **Mejala (IRE)** 2-9-0 0 ..... RHills 14 64+
(J L Dunlop) *w'like: s.i.s: towards rr: pushed along whn nt clr run on rails over 2f out: styd on fr over 1f out whn gap appeared: edgd lft: nvr threatened ldrs* **8/1**

6 2¾ **Cumana Bay** 2-9-0 0 ..... JimmyFortune 10 53
(R Hannon) *w'like: scope: bit bkwd: led after 1f: hdd 3f out: sn rdn: wknd over 1f out* **25/1**

7 ½ **Heart Of Tuscany** 2-9-0 0 ..... PaulDoe 7 52+
(W J Knight) *w'like: hld up towards rr: sme late prog: nvr a danger* **80/1**

8 3½ **Highland Burn** 2-9-0 0 ..... TQuinn 9 43
(D R C Elsworth) *w'like: bit bkwd: s.i.s: a towards rr* **50/1**

0 **9** ½ **Sunshine Ellie**[10] 5344 2-9-0 0 ..... PhilipRobinson 8 42+
(C G Cox) *trckd ldrs: squeezed out over 3f out: sn rdn and btn* **50/1**

10 nk **In Secret** 2-9-0 0 ..... EddieAhern 3 41
(J L Dunlop) *unf: scope: bit bkwd: mid-div: rdn and hung lft over 2f out: sn wknd* **33/1**

11 1½ **Diktalina** 2-9-0 0 ..... MartinDwyer 2 37
(W R Muir) *leggy: mid-div: rdn over 2f out: sn wknd* **40/1**

12 1 **Arlene Phillips** 2-9-0 0 ..... RichardHughes 12 35
(R Hannon) *leggy: scope: mid-div: rdn over 3f out: wknd 2f out: sn hung lft* **16/1**

13 2 **Wish You Luck** 2-9-0 0 ..... TedDurcan 6 30
(D R Lanigan) *leggy: bkwd: hmpd over 1f out: a towards rr* **50/1**

1m 30.06s (1.06) **Going Correction** +0.025s/f (Good) **13** Ran SP% **122.1**
Speed ratings (Par 94): **94,92,90,90,84 81,80,76,76,75 73,72,70**
toteswinger: 1&2 £3.20, 1&3 £2.50, 2&3 £4.30. CSF £8.95 TOTE £2.40: £1.30, £1.90, £1.80; EX 12.40.

Owner K Abdulla **Bred** Juddmonte Farms Ltd **Trained** Lambourn, Berks

FOCUS

This second division of the fillies' maiden had just one runner boasting a Group 1 entry, the unplaced Mejala, and it was run in a time 0.44secs slower than the first division. The form looks straightforward and sound.

NOTEBOOK

Intense showed the benefit of her debut second at Goodwood in July and got off the mark with a professional display. The extra furlong proved right up her street and she was always in command through the final 200 yards. She is not entered in the Fillies' Mile, but looks well worth her place in better company now and should really relish yet another furlong before the season's end. She should also have little trouble with 1m2f and beyond next year (op 2-1)

Three Moons(IRE) ◆ stepped up on the level of her debut second at Kempton and was the only one to make the winner work inside the final furlong. She deserves a little extra credit as she had to race wider than that rival and is clearly a useful prospect. (op 7-1 tchd 5-1)

Multiplication had her chance from the front, but lacked the tactical pace of the first pair. This rates a step forward from her debut effort at Newmarket and she can be placed to strike before long. (op 3-1)

Ave ◆ fared best of the debutantes and showed more than enough to suggest she ought to go close next time now she has this experience under her belt. (op 9-2)

Mejala(IRE), a half-sister to his stable's smart Sudoor, was always playing catch up after a tardy start and had to be switched for her run nearing the furlong pole. She kept on without being given too hard a time and should prove sharper next time out. (op 20-1)

Sunshine Ellie Official explanation: jockey said filly ran green and hung left-handed

5644 EUROPEAN BREEDERS' FUND LOCHSONG FILLIES' STKS (H'CAP) 6f 212y

4:20 (4:22) (Class 2) (0-100,97) 3-Y-O+

£16,823 (£5,038; £2,519; £1,260; £629; £315) **Stalls** High

Form RPR

2246 **1** **Just Like A Woman**[20] 5071 3-8-4 79 oh1 ..... HayleyTurner 4 87
(M L W Bell) *b: b.hind: chsd ldrs on nr side: rdn to chal 2f out: led ins fnl f: drvn out* **7/2**[1]

3666 **2** nk **Kay Es Jay (FR)**[36] 4522 3-8-12 87 ..... MichaelHills 5 94
(B W Hills) *racd in centre: hld up: jnd nr side gp 4f out: hdwy over 2f out: rdn to ld wl over 1f out: sn hung lft: hdd ins fnl f: kpt on* **8/1**

0505 **3** 2 **Vital Statistics**[26] 4841 4-8-13 84 ..... LDettori 1 88
(D R C Elsworth) *hld up on nr side: rdn and hdwy 2f out: kpt on same pce fnl f* **4/1**[2]

4000 **4** ¾ **Silca Chiave**[20] 5071 4-9-2 87 ..... DarryllHolland 2 89
(M R Channon) *led nr side gp: rdn over 2f out: hdd wl over 1f out: kpt on same pce* **11/1**

5640 **5** 2¼ **Highland Daughter (IRE)**[57] 3849 3-8-12 87 ..... PhilipRobinson 6 80
(C G Cox) *racd in centre: prom: jnd nr side gp 4f out: rdn over 2f out: wknd jst over 1f out* **11/2**[3]

0503 **6** 3 **Carcinetto (IRE)**[7] 5424 6-9-2 87 ..... TGMcLaughlin 9 74
(P D Evans) *chsd ldng pair on far side: rdn over 2f out: wknd over 1f out* **11/1**

0010 **7** 1¾ **Dubai Power**[40] 4424 3-8-12 87 ..... LiamJones 7 67
(C E Brittain) *chsd ldrs towards far side tl wknd over 1f out* **16/1**

5116 **8** 8 **Clifton Dancer**[34] 4590 3-9-8 97 ..... RichardKingscote 10 56
(Tom Dascombe) *led far side trio tl 3f out: sn btn: eased fnl f* **7/2**[1]

1m 28.85s (-0.15) **Going Correction** +0.025s/f (Good)
WFA 3 from 4yo+ 4lb **8** Ran SP% **113.5**
Speed ratings (Par 96): **101,100,98,97,94 91,89,80**
toteswinger: 1&2 £6.10, 1&3 £2.80, 2&3 £5.30. CSF £31.28 CT £114.98 TOTE £4.50: £1.30, £2.40, £1.80; EX 31.40 Trifecta £119.70 Pool: £699.24, 4.32 winning units..

Owner Mascalls Stud **Bred** Mascalls Stud **Trained** Newmarket, Suffolk

FOCUS

Just an average fillies' handicap for the class and it saw divided opinion with all bar three of the runners coming over the stands' side in the home straight. The first two came clear and the form is rated around the third and fourth.

NOTEBOOK

Just Like A Woman finally got her head back in front under a strong ride against the near rail. She has been consistent in the main this season, but had flopped last time and become expensive to follow. There was no faulting her attitude here though, easy ground looks to suit her ideally, and it rates a decent effort from 1lb out of the weights. (op 9-2)

Kay Es Jay(FR) was quickly settled out the back and was one of the last to come over to the near side. She was produced with a strong late challenge, but could not get past the winner try as she might. She deserves to find another opening now. (op 13-2)

Vital Statistics received a very patient ride and posted another sound enough effort in defeat, but is the type who needs things to fall just right in her races. (op 10-3 tchd 9-2)

Silca Chiave ran very close to her Newmarket form with the runner-up and needs further respite in the weights. (op 14-1 tchd 10-1)

Clifton Dancer was really beaten too far out for this to be her true running. (op 4-1)

5645 SYDENHAMS H'CAP — 5f

4:50 (4:53) (Class 5) (0-70,69) 3-Y-O+ — **£3,238** (£963; £481; £240) **Stalls** High

Form — RPR

6250 **1** **Bold Argument (IRE)**[10] 5345 5-8-13 **65** .... JackMitchell(3) 6 — 74
(Mrs P N Dutfield) *s.i.s and squeezed out: sn drvn along in rr: hdwy over 1f out: styd on to ld ins fnl f: drvn out* **11/2**[2]

3123 **2** *nk* **Matterofact (IRE)**[18] 5121 5-9-2 **65** .... TGMcLaughlin 3 — 73
(M S Saunders) *travelled wl bhd ldrs: nt clr run and swtchd rt fr over 1f out: sn rdn: ev ch ins fnl f: kpt on* **3/1**[1]

4334 **3** *1* **Night Prospector**[8] 5398 8-8-10 **62** .... (p) KevinGhunowa(3) 10 — 66
(R A Harris) *chsd ldrs: rdn to ld over 1f out: hdd ins fnl f: no ex* **6/1**[3]

020 **4** *1 1/4* **Blessed Place**[39] 4462 8-8-13 **62** .... TQuinn 1 — 62
(D J S Ffrench Davis) *prom: led after 1f: rdn whn hdd over 1f out: kpt on same pce* **7/1**

0030 **5** *2 1/2* **Joss Stick**[20] 5046 3-9-0 **67** .... (p) TravisBlock(3) 4 — 58
(P J Makin) *chsd ldrs: rdn over 2f out: wknd fnl f* **16/1**

624 **6** *hd* **Azygous**[15] 5187 5-8-13 **62** .... (p) MartinDwyer 9 — 52
(J Akehurst) *lw: wnt lft s: led for 1f: prom: rdn and ev ch over 1f out: wknd fnl f* **8/1**

61.96 secs (1.16) **Going Correction** +0.025s/f (Good)
WFA 3 from 4yo+ 1lb — **6** Ran SP% **84.2**
Speed ratings (Par 103): **91,90,88,86,82 82**
toteswinger: 1&2 £3.10, 1&3 £3.80, 2&3 £2.50. CSF £12.42 CT £33.81 TOTE £5.20: £2.30, £1.40; EX 12.90.

Owner Simon Dutfield **Bred** K S Lee **Trained** Axmouth, Devon

■ Drumming Party was withdrawn (9/4F, deduct 30p in the £ under R4).

■ Stewards' Enquiry : T G McLaughlin caution: used whip with excessive frequency

FOCUS

Despite the late withdrawal of the in-form Drumming Party, who refused to load, this modest sprint handicap was a still tight affair with just 6lb covering the entire field. They went a frantic early pace and the placed horses were close to their recent marks in a solid handicap.

5646 IRISH THOROUGHBRED MARKETING 'PERSIAN PUNCH' CONDITIONS STKS — 1m 6f 21y

5:20 (5:21) (Class 2) 3-Y-O+

£12,462 (£3,732; £1,866; £934; £466; £234) **Stalls** Far side

Form — RPR

2365 **1** **Regal Flush**[35] 4551 4-9-2 109 .... LDettori 6 — 103+
(Saeed Bin Suroor) *lw: trckd ldr: led after 3f: qcknd 3f out: styd on strly: comf* **11/10**[1]

-640 **2** *3* **Hawridge Prince**[79] 3104 8-9-2 92 .... JimCrowley 2 — 99
(B R Millman) *trckd ldrs: wnt 2nd over 3f out: sn rdn: kpt on but a hld by wnr* **22/1**

4260 **3** *hd* **Balkan Knight**[19] 5094 8-9-2 108 .... JimmyFortune 4 — 99
(D R C Elsworth) *lw: hld up: hdwy 3f out: sn rdn to dispute 2nd: kpt on same pce fnl f* **7/2**[2]

105- **4** *10* **Juniper Girl (IRE)**[333] 6044 5-8-11 102 .... HayleyTurner 5 — 80
(M L W Bell) *led at stdy pce for 3f: trckd wnr tl over 3f out: rdn over 2f out: wknd fnl f* **8/1**

-066 **5** *1/2* **Dansili Dancer**[12] 5288 6-9-2 100 .... IanMongan 1 — 84
(C G Cox) *lw: hld up: effrt over 2f out: wknd over 1f out* **8/1**

060- **6** *3 1/2* **Land 'n Stars**[320] 6335 8-9-2 96 .... PaulDoe 7 — 79
(Jamie Poulton) *trckd ldrs: rdn over 3f out: wknd over 1f out* **25/1**

-522 **7** *15* **Munsef**[41] 4376 6-9-2 105 .... RHills 8 — 58
(J L Dunlop) *hld up: short-lived effrt over 2f out: eased whn btn* **6/1**[3]

3m 13.55s (6.15) **Going Correction** +0.025s/f (Good) — **7** Ran SP% **114.5**
Speed ratings (Par 109): **83,81,81,75,75 73,64**
toteswinger: 1&2 £6.20, 1&3 £2.10, 2&3 £12.30. CSF £29.37 TOTE £2.00: £1.60, £6.70; EX 24.90 Place 6: £4.14, Place 5: £3.07..

Owner Godolphin **Bred** Cheveley Park Stud Ltd **Trained** Newmarket, Suffolk

FOCUS

There were no starting stalls for this race. A decent staying event, it was run at a stop-start pace. The winner dictated and outclassed his rivals with the runner-up rated to this year's form and the rest below their best.

NOTEBOOK

Regal Flush, beaten in the Gold Cup and Goodwood Cup on the last two occasions, relished the drop into this grade and outclassed his rivals by making all. His jockey has few peers when able to boss his races from the front and he set just a modest early pace before quickening things up around 3f out. This ground would have been easy enough for him, but he was always in command inside the final furlong and should be high on confidence now for a return to Pattern company. (tchd 6-4)

Hawridge Prince posted his best effort for quite some time and enjoyed this easier surface. It was a solid effort in defeat on the back of a 79-day break and he could be an interesting sort for the Cesarewitch if consenting to build on this. (op 20-1 tchd 28-1)

Balkan Knight, a winner over course and distance on his sole outing at the track, travelled kindly off the pace yet lacked a change of gear when it mattered. He is the most reliable guide to this form. (op 4-1 tchd 3-1)

Juniper Girl(IRE), last year's Northumberland Plate heroine, posted a pleasing seasonal return over a test plenty sharp enough and should come on a bundle for the run. (tchd 7-1)

Dansili Dancer should have enjoyed the early pace set by the winner, but he never got into it and really wants quicker ground. (op 17-2 tchd 10-1)

Land 'n Stars was one of the first beaten, but this was his first outing of the current campaign and it should do him a world of good. (tchd 33-1)

Munsef faded tamely when push came to shove and obviously ran one of his poorer races. (op 7-1 tchd 9-2)

T/Plt: £7.70 to a £1 stake. Pool: £53,356.35. 5,000.54 winning tickets. T/Qpdt: £6.00 to a £1 stake. Pool: £3,113.71. 378.70 winning tickets. TM

[5363] WARWICK (L-H)

Thursday, September 4

OFFICIAL GOING: Soft (heavy in places; 6.6)

Wind: Slight behind Weather: Showers 2.20, 2.50 and 3.25

5647 WARWICKRACECOURSE.CO.UK NURSERY — 5f 110y

2:20 (2:21) (Class 5) (0-75,78) 2-Y-O — **£3,238** (£963; £481; £240) **Stalls** Centre

Form — RPR

336 **1** **Noble Storm (USA)**[24] 4923 2-9-7 **74** .... StephenDonohoe 3 — 82
(E S McMahon) *mde all: rdn and edgd rt fr over 1f out: r.o wl* **7/1**[3]

0466 **2** *2* **Jubilee Juggins (IRE)**[23] 4942 2-8-10 **63** .... CatherineGannon 8 — 64
(N P Littmoden) *a.p: rdn wl over 1f out: ev ch whn carried rt ins fnl f: nt qckn: jst hld on for 2nd* **22/1**

0512 **3** *shd* **Golden Destiny (IRE)**[10] 5363 2-9-0 **72** .... DavidProbert(5) 7 — 73
(P J Makin) *chsd wnr tl hung lft over 1f out: kpt on same pce fnl f: jst failed to retake 2nd* **13/8**[1]

3321 **4** *3* **Captain Scooby**[11] 5306 2-9-8 **78** 6ex .... MichaelJStainton(3) 2 — 69
(R M Whitaker) *hld up in mid-div: rdn and no real prog fr over 1f out* **3/1**[2]

0646 **5** *nk* **Skruton (IRE)**[19] 5103 2-9-6 **73** .... RobertWinston 5 — 63
(M G Quinlan) *s.i.s: hld up and bhd: hdwy wl over 1f out: sn rdn: edgd rt and wknd ins fnl f* **28/1**

4402 **6** *8* **Song Of Praise**[18] 5116 2-9-4 **71** .... FrancisNorton 1 — 35
(M Blanshard) *t.k.h: prom: wkng whn edgd rt wl over 1f out* **50/1**

010 **7** *3 3/4* **Tartan Turban (IRE)**[13] 5228 2-9-6 **73** .... PatDobbs 4 — 24
(R Hannon) *chsd ldr: rdn over 3f out: wknd 2f out* **10/1**

045 **8** *1 1/2* **Mr Flannegan**[13] 5213 2-9-0 **67** .... DaneO'Neill 6 — 13
(H Candy) *a towards rr* **15/2**

3246 **9** *1/2* **Sills Vincero**[37] 4499 2-9-3 **70** .... AlanMunro 9 — 15
(P W Chapple-Hyam) *a towards rr* **12/1**

69.36 secs (3.46) **Going Correction** +0.475s/f (Yiel) — **9** Ran SP% **113.9**
Speed ratings (Par 95): **95,92,92,88,87 77,72,70,69**
toteswinger: 1&2 £24.40, 1&3 £4.20, 2&3 £12.60. CSF £141.67 CT £367.50 TOTE £8.20: £1.90, £5.00, £1.60; EX 195.70.

Owner R L Bedding **Bred** Brereton C Jones **Trained** Lichfield, Staffs

FOCUS

A reasonable nursery in which the runners came mid-track in the home straight. The third is below recent course form.

NOTEBOOK

Noble Storm(USA) settled much better allowed to lead on this handicap debut and, while he drifted to his left in the latter stages plus also jumped a path in the straight, won with a bit to spare in the end. He has a bit of scope and there be more improvement to come from him. (op 6-1 tchd 11-2)

Jubilee Juggins(IRE) had shown very modest form in his four previous outings, all on Polytrack, but the drastically different underfoot conditions brought about an improved showing. Racing widest into the straight, he soon posed a threat to the winner but was slightly intimidated by him drifting to his right and could not get by. (op 18-1 tchd 25-1)

Golden Destiny(IRE) arrived here in good form and was officially 5lb ahead of the Handicapper. Always well placed, she had her chance but could not pick up the winner in the straight, hanging to her left before keeping on and just missing out on second. (op 7-4 tchd 2-1)

Captain Scooby had no problem with the ground, but could not pick up the leaders in the straight. (op 11-4)

5648 WARWICK RACECOURSE FOR CONFERENCES H'CAP — 6f

2:50 (2:52) (Class 4) (0-85,84) 3-Y-O+ — **£6,476** (£1,927; £963; £481) **Stalls** Centre

Form — RPR

2100 **1** **Nobilissima (IRE)**[90] 2773 4-9-1 **82** .... MarcHalford(3) 1 — 88
(J L Spearing) *led over 3f: rdn wl over 1f out: led ins fnl f: r.o* **8/1**

0000 **2** *3/4* **Charles Darwin (IRE)**[27] 4831 5-9-0 **78** .... NCallan 14 — 82
(M Blanshard) *t.k.h in mid-div: rdn over 1f out: r.o wl towards fin: nt rch wnr* **20/1**

0040 **3** *3/4* **Steel City Boy (IRE)**[13] 5222 5-8-5 **74** oh8 ow4 .... AnnStokell(5) 8 — 75
(Miss A Stokell) *a.p: ev ch fr over 1f out: nt qckn towards fin* **20/1**

-420 **4** *3/4* **Corridor Creeper (FR)**[124] 1802 11-8-8 **77** .... (p) DavidProbert(5) 6 — 76
(J M Bradley) *chsd ldr: led over 2f out: rdn over 1f out: hdd and no ex ins fnl f* **20/1**

6102 **5** *1/2* **Lucayos**[7] 5433 5-8-13 **77** .... FergusSweeney 3 — 74
(K R Burke) *t.k.h: chsd ldrs: n.m.r and checked wl over 1f out: sn rdn: hld whn hmpd towards fin* **6/1**[3]

2303 **6** *shd* **Rabbit Fighter (IRE)**[12] 5260 4-8-9 **73** .... (v) DarrenWilliams 12 — 70
(D Shaw) *s.i.s and hmpd s: bhd: rdn wl over 1f out: r.o ins fnl f: nvr nrr* **9/2**[1]

0202 **7** *1* **North South Divide (IRE)**[68] 3502 4-8-13 **77** .... (p) DaneO'Neill 11 — 71
(R A Teal) *wnt sltly rt s: prom on outside: rdn wl over 1f out: wknd ins fnl f* **8/1**

0300 **8** *hd* **Tudor Prince (IRE)**[13] 5247 4-8-7 **71** .... FrancisNorton 4 — 64
(A W Carroll) *s.i.s: sn chsng ldrs: lost pl over 2f out: rdn over 1f out: no hdwy* **5/1**[2]

0045 **9** *1 1/2* **The Tatling (IRE)**[17] 5151 11-9-6 **84** .... PaulFitzsimons 2 — 72
(J M Bradley) *s.i.s: sn chsng ldrs on ins: rdn and wknd ins fnl f* **16/1**

0020 **10** *2 1/2* **Street Star (USA)**[42] 4345 3-9-4 **84** .... JamieSpencer 7 — 64
(J R Fanshawe) *dropped out s: t.k.h in rr: rdn 2f out: no rspnse: eased ins fnl f* **16/1**

410- **11** *12* **No Page (IRE)**[332] 6052 3-8-11 **77** .... TPQueally 13 — 19
(B P J Baugh) *bmpd s: a bhd: rdn over 2f out: eased whn no ch fnl f* **25/1**

1045 **12** *1 1/4* **Kelamon**[13] 5233 4-8-8 **72** .... WilliamBuick 5 — 10
(M D I Usher) *hld up in mid-div: pushed along 3f out: sn bhd: eased fnl f* **13/2**

3150 **13** *2 1/2* **Royal Envoy (IRE)**[13] 5250 5-9-0 **78** .... RobertWinston 10 — 8
(P Howling) *wnt sltly rt s: chsd ldrs 3f: eased whn no ch fnl f* **14/1**

1m 15.72s (3.92) **Going Correction** +0.65s/f (Yiel)
WFA 3 from 4yo+ 2lb — **13** Ran SP% **121.3**
Speed ratings (Par 105): **99,98,97,96,95 95,93,93,91,88 72,70,67**
toteswinger: 1&2 £49.50, 1&3 £46.70, 2&3 £85.80. CSF £164.27 CT £3170.06 TOTE £11.60: £3.50, £7.50, £6.30; EX 173.40.

Owner Nine Traders Syndicate **Bred** Sea Syndicate **Trained** Kinnersley, Worcs

■ Stewards' Enquiry : Jamie Spencer one-day ban: careless riding (Sep 18)

FOCUS

An open handicap and the form does not look that solid with the third the best guide from out of the handicap. The field came over to the stands' side in the straight and finished in something of a heap.

Royal Envoy(IRE) Official explanation: jockey said gelding was unsuited by the soft (heavy patches) ground

5649 EUROPEAN BREEDERS' FUND MAIDEN STKS 7f 26y
3:25 (3:28) (Class 5) 2-Y-O £3,885 (£1,156; £577; £288) Stalls Low

Form RPR

4 **1** **Aahaykid (IRE)**[10] 5364 2-9-0 0 FergusSweeney 2 87+
(K R Burke) *a gng wl: led 2f out: sn qcknd clr and edgd rt: easily* **5/2**[1]

2 *3 ¾* **Light Sleeper** 2-9-0 0 AlanMunro 1 75+
(P W Chapple-Hyam) *prom: lost pl over 5f out: hdwy 2f out: wnt 2nd over 1f out: no ch w wnr* **11/1**

3 *3 ½* **Time Medicean** 2-9-0 0 EdwardCreighton 9 66+
(M R Channon) *s.i.s: sn hld up in tch: rdn and edgd lft over 1f out: wknd ins fnl f* **12/1**

0 **4** *2* **Squad**[25] 4890 2-9-0 0 NCallan 8 61
(Pat Eddery) *s.i.s: sn hld up in tch: rdn and hung lft over 1f out: wknd ins fnl f* **7/2**[2]

5 *1 ½* **Land Hawk (IRE)** 2-9-0 0 StephenDonohoe 4 57
(J Pearce) *s.i.s: in rr: sme late prog: nvr nr ldrs* **8/1**

0 **6** *½* **Ready For Battle (IRE)**[13] 5225 2-9-0 0 JamieSpencer 5 56
(C G Cox) *led: rdn and hdd 2f out: sn wknd* **17/2**

03 **7** *¾* **Kersivay**[29] 4720 2-9-0 0 AdamKirby 7 54
(W R Swinburn) *prom tl rdn and wknd over 1f out* **7/1**

8 *nk* **Rainbow Seeker** 2-9-0 0 TonyCulhane 3 53
(W J Haggas) *prom tl wknd over 1f out* **13/2**[3]

0 **9** *18* **Bright Wire (IRE)**[19] 5099 2-9-0 0 RobertHavlin 6 8
(M L W Bell) *a bhd: pushed along over 5f out: lost tch over 2f out* **50/1**

1m 29.0s (4.40) **Going Correction** +0.55s/f (Yiel) **9** Ran SP% **116.3**
Speed ratings (Par 95): **96,91,87,85,83 83,82,81,61**
toteswinger: 1&2 £6.70, 1&3 £8.90, 2&3 £18.90. CSF £31.71 TOTE £3.10: £1.30, £3.80, £3.40; EX 34.20.
Owner Mrs Maura Gittins **Bred** Moyglare Stud Farm Ltd **Trained** Middleham Moor, N Yorks

FOCUS
An interesting maiden, won in clear-cut style by a colt who can rate higher.

NOTEBOOK
Aahaykid(IRE) ◆, fourth on his debut over course and distance in similar ground, led going easily and came over towards the stands' side in the straight before clearing away from his rivals. He looks worth a crack at something a bit better (op 2-1)
Light Sleeper, related to winners from 6-10f, lost his prominent early pitch and had only two behind him turning in, but he stayed on nicely down what was probably the worst ground in the straight for second. He should better this next time. (op 9-1)
Time Medicean, the first foal of a juvenile debut winner, made a pleasing debut, keeping on nearest the stands' fence up the straight after a slow start. (op 25-1 tchd 28-1)
Squad, well backed, was slow to break and could only stick on at the one pace after hanging to his left in the straight. He remains capable of better. (op 8-1)
Land Hawk(IRE) ◆ was slowly away and soon trailing, but he picked up very nicely late on and is sure to improve with this experience behind him. (op 12-1 tchd 14-1)
Rainbow Seeker, who is out of a half-sister to the dam of Rock Of Gibraltar, ran better than his eventual finishing position suggests. (op 9-1 tchd 10-1)

5650 EUROPEAN BREEDERS' FUND MAIDEN FILLIES' STKS 7f 26y
3:55 (3:57) (Class 5) 2-Y-O £3,885 (£1,156; £577; £288) Stalls Low

Form RPR

5 **1** **La Adelita (IRE)**[19] 5097 2-9-0 0 JamieSpencer 1 76+
(M L W Bell) *mde all: pushed clr fnl f: coasted home* **4/5**[1]

0 **2** *1 ¼* **It's Dubai Dolly**[17] 5147 2-9-0 0 WandersonD'Avila 10 71+
(A J Lidderdale) *chsd wnr: rdn and outpcd over 1f out: r.o towards fin: flattered* **25/1**

3 *7* **Nawojka (IRE)** 2-9-0 0 TPQueally 3 53
(J G Given) *s.i.s: sn in tch: lost pl bnd 3f out: styd on to take 3rd ins fnl f* **17/2**[3]

0 **4** *1* **Wanted (GER)**[45] 4251 2-9-0 0 AlanMunro 8 51
(B R Millman) *t.k.h: prom tl wknd over 1f out* **12/1**

5 *1 ¼* **My Best Bet** 2-9-0 0 EdwardCreighton 12 48
(M R Channon) *s.i.s: towards rr: hdwy 3f out: edgd lft and wknd over 1f out* **16/1**

0 **6** *3 ¾* **Valentine Bay**[21] 5004 2-9-0 0 RobertHavlin 13 38
(M Mullineaux) *hld up in tch: wnt 2nd briefly over 3f out: edgd lft and wknd over 1f out* **66/1**

7 *nk* **Mekong Miss** 2-9-0 0 RobertWinston 4 38
(J Jay) *mid-div: btn over 1f out* **16/1**

8 *¾* **Kiyari** 2-9-0 0 NCallan 5 36
(M Botti) *s.i.s: sn mid-div: hdwy 4f out: hung lft and wknd wl over 1f out* **6/1**[2]

9 *1* **Nesayem (IRE)** 2-9-0 0 StephenDonohoe 9 33
(D M Simcock) *s.s: a in rr* **16/1**

10 *8* **No Sting** 2-8-9 0 JackDean(5) 2 13
(W G M Turner) *prom: n.m.r whn stmbld and lost pl over 4f out: sn bhd* **40/1**

0 **11** *8* **Velox Vixen (IRE)**[42] 4339 2-9-0 0 JamesDoyle 11 —
(M Blanshard) *a in rr* **100/1**

1m 29.78s (5.18) **Going Correction** +0.55s/f (Yiel) 11 Ran SP% **114.5**
Speed ratings (Par 92): **92,90,82,81,80 75,75,74,73,64 55**
toteswinger: 1&2 £4.80, 1&3 £3.00, 2&3 £18.90. CSF £30.15 TOTE £1.60: £1.10, £4.70, £2.00; EX 21.70.
Owner Mrs Melba Bryce **Bred** David J Brown **Trained** Newmarket, Suffolk

FOCUS
Not much strength in depth to this fillies' maiden, run in a time about three-quarters of a second slower than the earlier colts' and geldings' equivalent. The winner was the pre-race form choice and won well.

NOTEBOOK
La Adelita(IRE) had run a pleasing race on her Newbury debut and this step up in trip was expected to suit. Making all and dictating the pace, she came over towards the stands' side in the straight and won a good deal more easily than the actual margin would appear to indicate. She is a nice prospect and is likely to head for a valuable sales race at Newmarket now. (op 8-11)
It's Dubai Dolly was beaten a long way when 100-1 for her debut at Windsor, but she ran a big race over this extra furlong and was gaining on the easing winner near the line. She was flattered by her proximity, but still finished seven lengths clear of the remainder. (op 33-1)
Nawojka(IRE), who started slowly, was the only one of the principals not to race prominently. She stayed on steadily in the straight as befits a filly who is bred to make a middle-distance performer at three. (tchd 8-1 and 9-1)
Wanted(GER), who raced rather keenly, was another to improve on a less than convincing debut effort. (op 16-1)

5651 BOOK YOUR CHRISTMAS AT WARWICK RACECOURSE H'CAP 1m 6f 213y
4:30 (4:31) (Class 5) (0-75,74) 3-Y-O+ £3,238 (£963; £481; £240) Stalls Low

Form RPR

2341 **1** **Kiribati King (IRE)**[26] 4859 3-8-13 71 TonyCulhane 12 75
(M R Channon) *hld up in tch: hdwy over 8f out: pushed along over 4f out: led ent fnl f: drvn out* **9/2**[2]

5-60 **2** *½* **Simone Martini (IRE)**[19] 5098 3-8-8 66 (bt[1]) RobertHavlin 1 69
(R Charlton) *hld up in mid-div: smooth hdwy over 4f out: led over 2f out: rdn and reluctant over 1f out: hdd ent fnl f: styd on to take 2nd nr fin* **12/1**

0622 **3** *hd* **Sphere (IRE)**[29] 4751 3-8-13 71 JamieSpencer 11 74
(J R Fanshawe) *hld up in mid-div: stdy hdwy 8f out: rdn over 3f out: ev ch 1f out: nt qckn and lost 2nd nr fin* **3/1**[1]

445 **4** *1 ¼* **Purely By Chance**[13] 5216 3-8-2 60 (v) WilliamBuick 6 61
(R M Beckett) *led: rdn and hdd over 2f out: hung rt to stands' rail wl over 1f out: ev ch ins fnl f: no ex towards fin* **9/1**

1443 **5** *3 ¼* **Great View (IRE)**[10] 5369 9-9-8 68 (v) NCallan 10 65
(Mrs A L M King) *stdd s: hld up in rr: hdwy over 4f out: rdn and hung lft over 1f out: eased whn hld wl ins fnl f* **14/1**

0300 **6** *3 ¾* **Sister Agnes (IRE)**[15] 3697 4-8-5 56 (b) DavidProbert(5) 3 48
(M F Harris) *hld up towards rr: styd on fr over 1f out: nvr nr ldrs* **28/1**

5046 **7** *2* **Synonymy**[24] 4935 5-8-10 56 oh2 (b) FrancisNorton 8 46
(M Blanshard) *prom: lost pl 5f out: n.d after* **12/1**

45-1 **8** *2 ¾* **Flying Grey (IRE)**[16] 4704 4-8-13 59 (t) DaneO'Neill 9 45
(Tim Vaughan) *hld up towards rr: hdwy 6f out: wknd over 4f out* **9/2**[2]

3031 **9** *11* **Zeloso**[14] 3710 10-8-10 56 oh3 (v) CatherineGannon 14 28
(M F Harris) *in rr: rdn and struggling over 5f out* **33/1**

6412 **10** *16* **Captain Mainwaring**[92] 2719 3-8-7 65 JamesDoyle 5 16
(N P Littmoden) *chsd ldr to 4f out: wknd over 2f out* **8/1**[3]

-400 **11** *15* **Dareios (GER)**[9] 5379 3-7-7 58 oh7 ow2 StacyRenwick(7) 4 —
(G J Smith) *towards rr: struggling 6f out: t.o* **200/1**

0-00 **12** *4* **Great Man (FR)**[24] 4936 7-8-10 56 oh3 RobertWinston 2 —
(K M Prendergast) *t.k.h towards rr: sme hdwy over 4f out: mid-div whn awkward on ins bnd over 3f out: sn lost pl: t.o* **28/1**

-000 **13** *29* **Tusculum (IRE)**[47] 4200 5-9-0 60 TPQueally 7 —
(A P Stringer) *prom tl wknd over 6f out: t.o* **10/1**

3m 29.57s (10.57) **Going Correction** +0.725s/f (Yiel)
WFA 3 from 4yo+ 12lb **13** Ran SP% **124.0**
Speed ratings (Par 103): **100,99,99,98,97 95,94,92,86,78 70,68,52**
toteswinger: 1&2 £22.00, 1&3 £4.20, 2&3 £13.70. CSF £58.50 CT £192.97 TOTE £5.70: £1.70, £4.10, £1.60; EX 83.20.
Owner Box 41 **Bred** Noel Finnegan **Trained** West Ilsley, Berks

FOCUS
A modest handicap which proved quite a test in the conditions. The third and fourth are the best guides to the form.

5652 RACING UK MEDIAN AUCTION MAIDEN STKS 1m 22y
5:00 (5:03) (Class 6) 3-4-Y-O £2,729 (£806; £403) Stalls Low

Form RPR

42 **1** **Spotty Muldoon (IRE)**[47] 4195 3-9-3 0 WilliamBuick 10 77
(R M Beckett) *hld up in mid-div: hdwy over 3f out: rdn over 2f out: hung lft over 1f out: hung rt and led wl ins fnl f: r.o* **15/8**[1]

2333 **2** *1 ½* **Seventh Cavalry (IRE)**[7] 5426 3-9-3 72 (b[1]) TPQueally 2 74
(H R A Cecil) *impr to ld after 1f: clr over 2f out: rdn over 1f out: hdd and no ex wl ins fnl f* **9/4**[2]

5 **3** *5* **Superior Duchess**[24] 4929 3-8-12 0 FrankieMcDonald 12 57
(Jane Chapple-Hyam) *led 1f: a.p: rdn 3f out: wknd jst over 1f out* **7/1**

4 *1 ¾* **Psycho Killer** 3-8-12 0 AdamKirby 9 53
(R M Beckett) *dwlt: hdwy over 2f out: one pce* **16/1**

0550 **5** *6* **Isabella's Fancy**[51] 4044 3-8-12 50 JamieSpencer 13 39
(J R Fanshawe) *hld up in mid-div: hdwy over 4f out: rdn over 3f out: sn wknd* **16/1**

00 **6** *2 ½* **Brave Knave (IRE)**[15] 5182 3-9-3 0 (t) PatDobbs 1 38
(B De Haan) *hld up in tch: wknd wl over 2f out* **66/1**

0065 **7** *8* **Bewdley**[43] 4298 3-8-10 45 ow1 LeeVickers(3) 4 16
(Mrs K Waldron) *hld up in tch: wknd wl over 2f out* **50/1**

534 **8** *1* **Unbiased (IRE)**[26] 4877 3-9-3 67 (b[1]) DaneO'Neill 11 18
(J L Dunlop) *wnt rt s: racd wd: hld up in mid-div: lost pl over 3f out: rdn over 2f out: no rspnse* **9/2**[3]

0 **9** *nk* **Smart Tazz**[10] 5366 3-9-3 0 SimonWhitworth 8 17
(H J Evans) *s.s: a bhd* **100/1**

50 **10** *11* **Billy Cadiz**[41] 4388 3-9-3 0 RobertWinston 3 —
(E J O'Neill) *sn chsng ldr: rdn 3f out: wknd qckly over 1f out* **33/1**

6-00 **11** *½* **Green Wonder (GER)**[25] 4909 3-8-12 45 StephenDonohoe 7 —
(D M Simcock) *rdn over 4f out: a bhd* **50/1**

0 **12** *115* **Karibu Blue**[58] 3823 4-9-3 0 TonyCulhane 6 —
(C F Wall) *s.i.s: a in rr: t.o whn virtually p.u over 3f out* **66/1**

1m 47.51s (6.51) **Going Correction** +0.725s/f (Yiel)
WFA 3 from 4yo 5lb **12** Ran SP% **118.8**
Speed ratings (Par 101): **96,94,89,87,81 79,71,70,69,58 58,—**
toteswinger: 1&2 £2.10, 1&3 £5.20, 2&3 £5.30. CSF £6.03 TOTE £2.40: £1.10, £1.20, £2.40; EX 7.30.
Owner Axis Partnership **Bred** Liam Queally **Trained** Whitsbury, Hants
■ Stewards' Enquiry : William Buick three-day ban: used whip with excessive frequency and force (Sep 19-21)

FOCUS
A modest event in which very few could be seriously fancied. The form looks a bit shaky with the placed horses the best guides.
Unbiased(IRE) Official explanation: jockey said colt was unsuited by the soft (heavy patches) ground
Karibu Blue Official explanation: jockey said filly hung throughout

5653 TURFTV APPRENTICE H'CAP 1m 2f 188y
5:30 (5:34) (Class 6) (0-58,57) 3-Y-O+ £2,047 (£604; £302) Stalls Low

Form RPR

4015 **1** **Jenny Soba**[2] 5593 5-8-13 51 6ex MrJPFeatherstone(5) 5 63
(Lucinda Featherstone) *hmpd sn after s: hld up in mid-div: hdwy over 4f out: wnt 2nd over 1f out: styd on to ld ins fnl f: sn clr* **6/1**[2]

0044 **2** *5* **No Wonga**[17] 5146 3-8-11 55 JemmaMarshall(3) 2 58
(P D Evans) *in rr: nt clr run and swtchd lft over 2f out: hdwy over 1f out: styd on to take 3rd cl home* **8/1**

4330 **3** *½* **The Grey One (IRE)**[5] 5489 5-9-3 50 (p) MCGeran 8 52
(J M Bradley) *s.i.s: in rr: hdwy on outside over 3f out: sn rdn: styd on ins fnl f* **8/1**

4430 **4** *shd* **Giddywell**[11] 5308 4-9-1 **53** .... SoniaEaton(5) 13 55
(R Hollinshead) *led: clr over 6f out: ct ins fnl f: wknd* **8/1**

0344 **5** *3* **Bolckow**[2] 5593 5-9-4 **51** .... PatrickDonaghy 16 48
(J T Stimpson) *hld up in tch: chsd clr ldr 3f out tl over 1f out: wknd fnl f* **5/1**[1]

/00- **6** *6* **Head To Kerry (IRE)**[31] 578 8-8-7 **45** .... (t) MJMurphy(5) 10 31
(D J S Ffrench Davis) *s.i.s: in rr: styd on fr over 1f out: nvr nr ldrs* **14/1**

0-00 **7** *3 1/4* **Aston Boy**[24] 4929 3-9-0 **55** .... HaddenFrost 11 35
(M Blanshard) *sn towards rr: pushed along over 5f out: sme hdwy over 3f out: wknd wl over 1f out* **25/1**

0052 **8** *2 1/2* **Sendefaa (IRE)**[29] 4750 3-8-7 **53** .... (b) PNolan(5) 3 28
(S Lycett) *rdn after s: sn in tch: wnt 2nd briefly over 3f out: wknd wl over 1f out* **15/2**[3]

0000 **9** *7* **Park Run**[18] 5119 3-8-5 **49** .... StacyRenwick(3) 6 12
(A W Carroll) *hld up in mid-div: rdn and wknd over 3f out* **66/1**

0-14 **10** *2 1/2* **It's No Problem (IRE)**[63] 3631 4-9-2 **52** ow3 .... HarryPoulton(3) 9 10
(Mrs N S Evans) *prom: chsd clr ldr over 5f tl over 3f out: wknd over 2f out* **20/1**

0000 **11** *12* **General Flumpa**[5] 5489 7-9-3 **50** .... SladeO'Hara 12 —
(Miss Tor Sturgis) *s.i.s: sn mid-div: bhd fnl 4f* **14/1**

100 **12** *2 1/4* **Having A Ball**[121] 1898 4-9-5 **57** .... TobyAtkinson(5) 7 —
(P D Cundell) *hld up in tch: wknd 4f out* **16/1**

0300 **13** *21* **Glitz (IRE)**[11] 5318 3-8-8 **52** .... MatthewDavies(3) 4 —
(George Baker) *rdn to chse ldr: lost 2nd over 5f out: wknd over 4f out: t.o* **25/1**

2m 28.72s (7.62) **Going Correction** +0.725s/f (Yiel)
WFA 3 from 4yo+ 8lb **13** Ran SP% **109.2**
Speed ratings (Par 101): **101,97,97,96,94 90,88,86,81,79 70,68,53**
toteswinger: 1&2 £7.90, 1&3 £6.00, 2&3 £9.60. CSF £42.04 CT £287.11 TOTE £5.10: £1.80, £2.80, £2.20; EX 45.90 Place 6: £68.70, Place 5: £43.83..
Owner J Roundtree **Bred** Theakston Stud **Trained** Atlow, Derbyshire
■ Credential (7/1) was withdrawn after breaking out of the stalls. R4 applies, deduct 10p in the £.

FOCUS
A typical low-grade apprentice handicap, run at a decent pace. The form is a bit messy with the third and fourth setting the level.
T/Plt: £85.60 to a £1 stake. Pool: £51,523.83. 439.25 winning tickets. T/Qpdt: £4.40 to a £1 stake. Pool: £4,239.21. 698.80 winning tickets. KH

5654 - 5657a (Foreign Racing) - See Raceform Interactive

5394 CATTERICK (L-H)
Friday, September 5
5658 Meeting Abandoned - Waterlogged

4704 CHEPSTOW (L-H)
Friday, September 5
5665 Meeting Abandoned - Waterlogged

5605 KEMPTON (A.W) (R-H)
Friday, September 5

OFFICIAL GOING: Standard
Wind: Brisk behind

5671 SUNRISE RADIO NURSERY — 6f (P)
6:20 (6:24) (Class 5) (0-70,70) 2-Y-O — **£2,590** (£770; £385; £192) **Stalls** High

Form — RPR

1102 **1** **Rocket Rob (IRE)**[4] 5581 2-9-1 **64** .... JamieSpencer 12 68+
(S A Callaghan) *s.i.s: sn trckd ldrs: hdwy on ins whn hmpd 2f out: styd on strly to ld fnl 110yds: hld on all out* **15/8**[1]

346 **2** *hd* **Sparkling Crystal (IRE)**[18] 5153 2-9-5 **68** .... MichaelHills 3 71
(B W Hills) *pressed ldr: rdn over 2f out: chal u.p ins fnl f and stl upsides wnr fnl 75yds: no ex last strides* **7/1**

5064 **3** *1/2* **Calley Ho**[10] 5375 2-9-5 **68** .... DarryllHolland 8 70
(Mrs L Stubbs) *trckd ldrs: rdn and str run appr fnl f: pressed ldrs fnl 100yds: no ex cl home* **33/1**

055 **4** *1/2* **Daily Double**[30] 4728 2-9-0 **63** .... RyanMoore 7 63+
(R Hannon) *wnt rt s: towards rr: rdn over 2f out: hdwy over 1f out: str run ins fnl f: gng on cl home but nt rch ldrs* **13/2**[3]

6523 **5** *shd* **Key To Love (IRE)**[15] 5200 2-9-1 **64** .... JamesDoyle 11 64
(H J L Dunlop) *led: rdn and edgd rt 2f out: hdd & wknd fnl 110yds* **7/1**

046 **6** *2* **Reel Ale**[29] 4778 2-9-3 **66** .... StephenCarson 9 60
(P Winkworth) *in rr: pushed along 1/2-way: styd on fnl f but nvr in contention* **25/1**

0303 **7** *3 1/4* **Temperence Hall (USA)**[8] 5432 2-9-7 **70** .... LPKeniry 2 54
(J R Best) *chsd ldrs: pushed along 1/2-way: wknd fr 2f out* **12/1**

045 **8** *1/2* **Al Mukaala (IRE)**[38] 4510 2-9-7 **70** .... (t) LiamJones 10 53
(C E Brittain) *chsd ldrs: pushed along 1/2-way: wknd 2f out* **5/1**[2]

000 **9** *3/4* **Kyle Of Bute**[44] 4296 2-9-3 **66** .... TedDurcan 4 47
(J L Dunlop) *s.i.s: outpcd* **25/1**

0600 **10** *2 1/4* **Protiva**[14] 5228 2-9-0 **63** .... RichardThomas 5 37
(A P Jarvis) *bmpd s: a in rr* **14/1**

1m 13.19s (0.09) **Going Correction** -0.075s/f (Stan) **10** Ran SP% **114.8**
Speed ratings (Par 95): **96,95,95,94,94 91,87,86,85,82**
toteswinger: 1&2 £3.80, 1&3 £7.30, 2&3 £31.40. CSF £14.11 CT £289.63 TOTE £2.30: £1.40, £2.30, £6.90; EX 16.70.
Owner Bill Hinge, J Searchfield & N Callaghan **Bred** Mrs Marita Rogers **Trained** Newmarket, Suffolk
■ Rich Red was withdrawn on veterinary advice (14/1, deduct 5p in the £ under R4).

FOCUS
A fair nursery in which it was hard to make ground.

NOTEBOOK
Rocket Rob(IRE), despite taking a keen hold early, stayed on best. Already a dual winner this season, he was runner-up off this mark at Lingfield earlier in the week and carried that good form over. He briefly got checked by Key To Love when heading to the rail just after the intersection, but had plenty of time to find his stride and this progressive son of Danetime can continue to pay his way. (op 7-4 tchd 2-1)
Sparkling Crystal(IRE), dropped 3lb having run as though something was amiss at Wolverhampton last time, had earlier run creditably at Newbury, and she made the favourite pull out all the stops. She had an ideal sit throughout and battled on right to the line. There is a minor race in her off this sort of mark. (op 8-1)
Calley Ho has not found things easy since winning his maiden and this goes down as an improved effort. He is exposed, but came with a strong challenge inside the final 2f and looks worth another try at 7f.
Daily Double, back in trip having looked a non-stayer over 7f at this course last time, was a bit too far back early, having been tardy out of the gate, and still showed signs of greenness. He stayed on well though and is of definite interest for a similar contest. (op 6-1 tchd 7-1)
Key To Love(IRE) made full use of her high draw on this handicap debut and return to sand and ran well for a long way, but could find no extra inside the final furlong. (op 10-1)
Reel Ale never got into it on this nursery debut, staying on all too late (op 33-1)
Temperence Hall(USA) was unable to repeat his recent Lingfield effort and dropped away tamely. (op 10-1 tchd 9-1)
Al Mukaala(IRE), making his handicap debut, was under pressure from the home bend and dropped out tamely in the final furlong and half. The first-time tongue tie evidently had little effect. (op 8-1)

5672 BETDAQ THE BETTING EXCHANGE E B F MAIDEN STKS — 1m (P)
6:50 (6:57) (Class 4) 2-Y-O — **£5,180** (£1,541; £770; £384) **Stalls** High

Form — RPR

0 **1** **Crowded House**[14] 5246 2-9-3 0 .... JamieSpencer 11 93+
(B J Meehan) *sn pushed along to take slt ld: kpt narrow advantage whn chal fr 4f out tl over 2f out: pushed clr wl over 1f out: eased nr fin* **11/4**[1]

6 **2** *3 1/4* **Custody (IRE)**[91] 2796 2-9-3 0 .... RyanMoore 9 78
(Sir Michael Stoute) *chsd ldrs: rdn to chse wnr 2f out but sn no ch: styd on fnl f for clr but wl hld 2nd* **11/1**

3 *2 3/4* **Alwaary (USA)** 2-9-3 0 .... RHills 2 72
(J H M Gosden) *towards rr tl stdy hdwy over 2f out: styd on wl thrght fnl f wout ever looking likely to trble easy wnr and clr 2nd* **11/4**[1]

52 **4** *5* **Zelloof (IRE)**[34] 4636 2-8-12 0 .... LDettori 3 56
(Saeed Bin Suroor) *in tch: rdn and hdwy fr 3f out: no ch w ldrs whn edgd rt over 2f out and sn btn* **7/2**[2]

0 **5** *1/2* **Muhim**[14] 5246 2-9-3 0 .... LiamJones 13 60
(C E Brittain) *unruly bef s: in rr: hrd drvn 3f out: styd on wl u.p fnl 2f and gng on fnl f but nvr any ch* **66/1**

6 *2 1/2* **Cut And Thrust (IRE)** 2-9-3 0 .... DarryllHolland 5 54
(M A Jarvis) *w ldrs: drvn to chal fr over 4f out tl over 2f out: sn wknd* **20/1**

0 **7** *shd* **Murhee (USA)**[28] 4826 2-9-3 0 .... TedDurcan 12 54
(D R Lanigan) *in tch: pushed along and effrt over 2f out: nvr in contention and sn wknd* **8/1**[3]

00 **8** *2 1/2* **D'Artagnans Dream**[14] 5227 2-9-3 0 .... PaulEddery 10 48
(G D Blake) *in tch: rdn to chse ldrs over 3f out: wknd qckly over 2f out* **66/1**

9 *2* **Inflammable** 2-8-12 0 .... J-PGuillambert 14 39
(Sir Mark Prescott) *s.i.s: nvr in contention* **20/1**

10 *1 3/4* **Step Fast (USA)** 2-8-12 0 .... RoystonFfrench 4 35
(M Johnston) *a towards rr* **25/1**

6 **11** *hd* **By Precedence (USA)**[41] 4421 2-9-3 0 .... SteveDrowne 7 40
(H J L Dunlop) *w ldr to 4f out: wknd qckly 3f out* **16/1**

12 *3/4* **Orthology (IRE)** 2-9-3 0 .... JimmyQuinn 8 38
(M H Tompkins) *s.i.s: a towards rr* **66/1**

00 **13** *3/4* **Hesketh (IRE)**[33] 4665 2-9-3 0 .... EddieAhern 1 36
(R M Beckett) *sn bhd* **25/1**

1m 39.42s (-0.38) **Going Correction** -0.075s/f (Stan) **13** Ran SP% **122.6**
Speed ratings (Par 97): **98,94,92,87,86 84,83,81,79,77 77,76,75**
toteswinger: 1&2 £5.10, 1&3 £3.40, 2&3 £5.30. CSF £33.37 TOTE £3.30: £1.70, £3.40, £1.80; EX 37.30.
Owner Mrs Carmen Burrell & Jonathan Harvey **Bred** Car Colston Hall Stud **Trained** Manton, Wilts

FOCUS
A decent maiden.

NOTEBOOK
Crowded House ◆, slowly away and never involved on his recent Newmarket debut, was always likely to come on a good deal for the run and Jamie Spencer was keen to bag the lead. Always travelling strongly, he quickly put daylight between himself and the others and had the luxury of being eased close home. A Racing Post Trophy entrant, he is held in high regard and should progress again from this. Connections view him as a long-term prospect and he will not be given a hard time at two. (op 3-1 tchd 5-2 and 100-30 in places)
Custody(IRE) has been gelded since disappointing on his debut at Goodwood in early June and he showed a lot more here. The extra quarter-mile undoubtedly helped this son of Oaks winner Shahtoush, and, although no match for the winner, he should progress again as he goes up in trip. (op 8-1 tchd 12-1)
Alwaary(USA) ◆, a fine, big colt whose dam was an unraced sister to the yard's 1,000 Guineas winner Lahan, holds Dewhurst and Racing Post Trophy entries and it was easy to see why he was fancied, with his yard having a good course record with their juveniles. However, his inexperience was evident and, having handed the winner a healthy lead, he was unable to get near him. He stayed on takingly though, not being given a hard time, and should know a lot more next time. (op 7-2 tchd 4-1)
Zelloof(IRE), found wanting late on over slightly shorter at Lingfield last time, was always likely to come up short in a much stronger heat and she was no match for the front trio. A drop to 7f may help and she is now qualified for nurseries. (op 3-1)
Muhim stepped up on his debut effort and will be of interest once handicapping. (tchd 50-1)
Cut And Thrust(IRE), an 85,000gns son of Haafhd who has already been gelded, has plenty of speed in his pedigree and it was a slight worry to see him starting out over this trip. He failed to get home and may do better at 7f. (tchd 22-1)
Murhee(USA), sent off short on his debut at Newmarket, was again nibbled at, but is clearly failing to do it on the course. (op 12-1)
Inflammable, a daughter of Montjeu, comes from a yard whose juveniles often need a run and she should know more next time. (op 14-1)
Step Fast(USA), an American-bred, was always struggling. (op 18-1)

5673 BETDAQ.CO.UK E B F MAIDEN FILLIES' STKS — 6f (P)
7:20 (7:24) (Class 4) 2-Y-O — **£5,180** (£1,541; £770; £384) **Stalls** High

Form — RPR

4 **1** **Adorn**[13] 5271 2-9-0 0 .... RyanMoore 7 85+
(J Noseda) *mde all: qcknd clr 2f out: v easily* **5/6**[1]

0 **2** *6* **Dream Of Mine**[18] 5158 2-9-0 0 .... LDettori 9 67
(Saeed Bin Suroor) *cl 3rd tl chsd wnr 3f out: no ch fr over 2f out but hld on wl for 2nd whn hrd pressed nr fin* **14/1**

6 **3** *3/4* **Stylish Dream (USA)**[70] 3456 2-9-0 0 .... JamieSpencer 6 65
(J R Fanshawe) *chsd wnr to 3f out: sn rdn and dropped bk to 3rd: rallied and kpt on fnl f to repress for 2nd cl home but nvr and ch w v easy wnr* **11/4**[2]

0 **4** *1/2* **Dream Date (IRE)**[18] 5147 2-9-0 0 .... MichaelHills 4 63
(W J Haggas) *towards rr tl drvn 3f out: hdwy over 2f out: kpt on thrght fnl f but nvr a danger* **33/1**

02 **5** *3/4* **Dubai Legend**[32] 4692 2-9-0 0 .... RichardMullen 5 61
(D M Simcock) *chsd ldrs: rdn and one pce ins fnl 3f: styd on again fr over 1f out* **15/2**[3]

6 3¾ **Good For Her** 2-9-0 0 .... EddieAhern 12 50+
(J L Dunlop) *towards rr: pushed along and sme prog 2f out: nvr in contention* **33/1**

00 7 4 **Halaak (USA)**[66] 3584 2-8-11 0 .... MarcHalford[(3)] 2 38
(D M Simcock) *awkward stalls: bhd: sme prog fr 2f out* **100/1**

0 8 3¼ **Ruby Best**[23] 4980 2-9-0 0 .... JimCrowley 10 28
(D K Ivory) *chsd ldrs over 3f* **66/1**

9 1¾ **Clodoline** 2-9-0 0 .... JoeFanning 3 23
(P F I Cole) *plld hrd early: a bhd* **11/1**

06 10 1¾ **Mount Ella**[39] 4482 2-9-0 0 .... ShaneKelly 1 18
(J A Osborne) *a in rr* **66/1**

1m 12.44s (-0.66) **Going Correction** -0.075s/f (Stan) **10** Ran SP% **117.8**
Speed ratings (Par 94): **101,93,92,91,90 85,80,75,73,71**
toteswinger: 1&2 £6.20, 1&3 £1.20, 2&3 £7.50. CSF £15.38 TOTE £1.70: £1.10, £2.90, £1.20; EX 13.10.
Owner Cheveley Park Stud **Bred** Cheveley Park Stud Ltd **Trained** Newmarket, Suffolk

FOCUS
Not the most competitive of maidens and Adorn turned it into a procession, winning in a quicker time than that recorded by Rocket Rob in the opening nursery.

NOTEBOOK
Adorn ◆, a highly promising fourth over the trip on her debut at Newmarket (trapped wide throughout), knew a lot more this time and Ryan Moore was quick to bag the rail. Setting her own tempo, she quickened immediately when asked, and stretched away impressively to score in the manner of a smart filly. She holds no major entries, but will be of interest regardless of where she turns up next. (tchd 4-5 and 10-11 in a place)
Dream Of Mine, who offered little on her debut at Yarmouth, held an ideal stalking position and tried to go in pursuit of the winner over two out, but that was soon a lost cause. This faster surface was clearly to her liking and a modest maiden can come her way. (op 12-1)
Stylish Dream(USA), a Cheveley Park entry who shaped with plenty of promise on her debut at Newmarket back in June, was badly outpaced when the winner started to go clear, but she kept plugging away and held third. A seventh furlong is required on this evidence. (op 3-1 tchd 100-30 in a place)
Dream Date(IRE), too green to do herself justice on her debut, again displayed signs of inexperience and lacked the pace to challenge over this trip. This was a step up on her first effort and she is another for whom 7f should suit.
Dubai Legend was beaten a nose at Windsor last time, improving markedly on her debut effort, but she was unable to go on again. She is now qualified for a handicap mark.
Good For Her, a daughter of Rock Of Gibraltar, comes from a yard whose juveniles usually need their first run and she shaped well enough, keeping on having come from the rear.

5674 E B F SEEABILITY SAVING SIGHT FILLIES' CONDITIONS STKS 7f (P)
7:50 (7:51) (Class 3) 2-Y-O **£7,477** (£2,239; £1,119; £560) **Stalls** High

Form RPR

6 1 **Moonlife (IRE)**[18] 5147 2-8-12 0 .... LDettori 3 85+
(Saeed Bin Suroor) *mde all: shkn up 2f out: kpt on whn strly chal ins fnl f and a in command* **10/3**[3]

2 ½ **Say No Now (IRE)** 2-8-12 0 .... TedDurcan 1 84+
(D R Lanigan) *racd in cl 3rd tl trckd wnr ins fnl 3f: drvn to chal ins fnl f: kpt on wl but a hld* **6/4**[1]

3 1¾ **Applause (IRE)** 2-8-12 0 .... ShaneKelly 4 79+
(J Noseda) *s.i.s: sn cl 4th: outpcd but 3rd 2f out: kpt on again fnl f and gng on cl home* **10/3**[3]

5 4 12 **Security Joan (IRE)**[7] 5459 2-8-12 0 .... RichardHughes 2 49
(R Hannon) *chsd wnr tl ins fnl 3f: wknd sn after* **3/1**[2]

1m 26.1s (0.10) **Going Correction** -0.075s/f (Stan) **4** Ran SP% **111.2**
Speed ratings (Par 96): **96,95,93,79**
CSF £8.97 TOTE £3.20; EX 9.00.
Owner Godolphin **Bred** M Parola **Trained** Newmarket, Suffolk

FOCUS
Only the four runners for this conditions event but it looked a fair contest and the race should produce winners.

NOTEBOOK
Moonlife(IRE), sixth of 15 from the wrong side at Windsor on debut, was put to good use, and, having set a decent tempo, she battled on gamely to hold the well regarded newcomer Say No Now. Always travelling kindly, the daughter of Invincible Spirit saw the seventh furlong out well and should progress again on a sound surface. She holds no notable entries. (op 4-1 tchd 9-2 in a place)
Say No Now(IRE) is engaged in the Group 1 Fillies' Mile and, although unable to make a winning debut, it was still a promising effort. A daughter of Refuse To Bend, she seemed to know her job well enough and briefly looked the winner when nipping up Moonlife's inside two out, but was never able to get alongside. An ordinary maiden should be hers for the taking. (op 13-8 tchd 7-4 and 15-8 in places)
Applause(IRE) ◆ has a few middle-distance winners in the family and there was a suspicion this trip was going to be a bit sharp for her debut. Another Fillies' Mile entrant, she ran green throughout and was being shoved along some way from the finish. She kept running on though, suggesting a lot more will be known next time, and she too should have little trouble winning a maiden. (op 5-2)
Security Joan(IRE), who had shaped with a good deal of promise at Salisbury a week earlier, running on strongly over 6f, went completely the wrong way and ran too bad to be true. There may well have been something amiss. (op 10-3 tchd 7-2)

5675 WEATHERBYS PRINTING APPRENTICE H'CAP (FINAL ROUND) 1m (P)
8:20 (8:20) (Class 4) (0-85,86) 3-Y-O+
£6,231 (£1,866; £933; £467; £233; £117) **Stalls** High

Form RPR

1630 1 **Grand Vizier (IRE)**[15] 5207 4-9-2 **80** .... JPHamblett[(3)] 2 91
(C F Wall) *chsd ldrs: drvn and outpcd ins fnl 3f: hdwy fr 2f out: rdn to take slt ld 1f out: styd on strly cl home* **8/1**

3540 2 2 **Danetime Panther (IRE)**[12] 5312 4-8-9 **73** .... AshleyMorgan[(3)] 6 79
(P F I Cole) *led after 1f: rdn over 2f out: narrowly hdd 1f out: kpt on same pce to hold 2nd ins fnl f* **20/1**

4131 3 1¼ **Cave Lion (USA)**[11] 5350 3-9-3 **86** 6ex .... Louis-PhilippeBeuzelin[(3)] 4 88
(J H M Gosden) *chsd ldrs: rdn and styd on to chal 1f out: no ex ins fnl f* **11/10**[1]

403 4 hd **Titan Triumph**[21] 5051 4-9-0 **75** .... (t) DavidProbert 8 78
(W J Knight) *chsd ldrs: rdn over 2f out: chal appr fnl f: wknd fnl 110yds* **7/2**[2]

-304 5 ¾ **Hallingdal (UAE)**[22] 5032 3-8-4 **73** .... SophieDoyle[(3)] 1 73
(Ms J S Doyle) *in rr: hdwy over 2f out: chsd ldrs and n.m.r over 1f out: sn one pce* **20/1**

6103 6 ½ **Premier Danseur (IRE)**[42] 4392 3-9-3 **83** ....(b[1]) AshleyHamblett 5 82
(M Johnston) *led 1f: styd pressing ldrs: rdn 3f out: wknd fnl f* **13/2**[3]

5140 7 5 **Count Ceprano (IRE)**[15] 5207 4-9-7 **85** .... HarryPoulton[(3)] 7 74
(M D I Usher) *a in rr* **10/1**

0600 8 1 **Tilapia (IRE)**[15] 5209 4-9-3 **81** .... KylieManser[(3)] 3 67
(Miss Gay Kelleway) *s.i.s: a in rr* **33/1**

1m 38.87s (-0.93) **Going Correction** -0.075s/f (Stan)
WFA 3 from 4yo 5lb **8** Ran SP% **115.8**
Speed ratings (Par 105): **101,99,97,97,96 96,91,90**
toteswinger: 1&2 £10.10, 1&3 £3.50, 2&3 £6.40. CSF £146.20 CT £313.74 TOTE £12.70: £2.60, £2.90, £1.20; EX 180.90.
Owner Hintlesham SP Partners **Bred** Yeomanstown Stud **Trained** Newmarket, Suffolk
■ Stewards' Enquiry : Ashley Morgan one day ban: used whip with whip arm above shoulder height (Sep 19)

FOCUS
The rain really started to come down hard before this race and remained throughout the rest of the evening. The pace was not particularly strong for this fair handicap and the form might not be the most solid. The winner is rated up 6lb.

5676 BET HAYDOCK SPRINT - BETDAQ H'CAP 2m (P)
8:50 (8:51) (Class 5) (0-70,66) 4-Y-O+ **£2,590** (£770; £385; £192) **Stalls** High

Form RPR

/060 1 **Mohawk Star (IRE)**[11] 5367 7-8-9 **54** ....(v[1]) MartinDwyer 9 63
(I A Wood) *in rr: stl plenty to do whn rdn and hdwy over 2f out: str run to chse wnr 1f out: styd on u.p to ld last stride* **20/1**

1553 2 nse **Moonshine Beach**[11] 5367 10-8-12 **57** .... JimCrowley 1 66
(P W Hiatt) *led: rdn 3f out: 4 l clr 2f out: hld on fnl f tl ct last stride* **3/1**[1]

200 3 3½ **Irish Ballad**[28] 4811 6-8-3 **48** .... NickyMackay 10 53
(S Dow) *chsd ldrs: rdn and styd on same pce fnl 2f* **12/1**

/4-2 4 ½ **Colophony (USA)**[49] 3321 8-9-4 **66** .... JackMitchell[(3)] 4 70
(K A Morgan) *in rr: rdn and hdwy on ins fr 3f out: styd on fnl 2f but nvr gng pce to be competitive* **9/1**

554 5 8 **Go On Ahead (IRE)**[19] 5117 8-9-3 **65** .... TravisBlock[(3)] 7 59
(W S Kittow) *chsd ldrs: rdn and btn whn hmpd over 2f out* **14/1**

1300 6 2¼ **Whaxaar (IRE)**[11] 5367 4-9-2 **61** .... RobertHavlin 2 53
(R Ingram) *mid-div: rdn and sme prog 3f out: sn wknd* **5/1**[3]

50/0 7 4½ **Strathtay**[12] 5308 6-7-11 **47** oh2 .... NicolPolli[(5)] 3 33
(M G Rimell) *slowly away: a towards rr* **50/1**

0420 8 ¾ **Mister Completely (IRE)**[2] 5613 7-9-4 **63** ....(v) JamesDoyle 6 48
(Ms J S Doyle) *chsd ldrs: rdn over 3f out: wknd 2f out* **4/1**[2]

3562 9 1 **Daring Racer (GER)**[29] 4775 5-8-13 **58** .... IanMongan 8 42
(Mrs L J Mongan) *chsd ldrs: rdn over 3f out: wknd qckly 2f out* **4/1**[2]

5060 10 13 **Silver Surprise**[14] 5232 4-7-11 **47** oh2 .... DavidProbert[(5)] 5 16
(J J Bridger) *chsd ldrs 12f* **25/1**

3m 31.24s (1.14) **Going Correction** -0.075s/f (Stan) **10** Ran SP% **116.6**
Speed ratings (Par 103): **94,93,92,91,87 86,84,84,83,77**
toteswinger: 1&2 £12.90, 1&3 £33.20, 2&3 £8.30. CSF £78.26 CT £777.64 TOTE £15.60: £3.40, £1.40, £2.60; EX 79.80.
Owner Richard Abbott & Mario Stavrou **Bred** Mrs T V Ryan **Trained** Upper Lambourn, Berks
■ Stewards' Enquiry : Martin Dwyer three-day ban: careless riding (Sep 20-22)

FOCUS
A modest winning time for the grade. A moderate staying handicap that produced a cracking finish. The winner is rated up 9lb on this year's form, and the form makes sense rated around the second and fourth.

5677 BETDAQ.CO.UK H'CAP 1m 3f (P)
9:20 (9:22) (Class 3) (0-95,94) 3-Y-O+
£7,477 (£2,239; £1,119; £560; £279; £140) **Stalls** High

Form RPR

22-0 1 **Ajhar (USA)**[139] 1468 4-9-9 **92** .... RHills 2 107
(M P Tregoning) *hld up in rr: stdy hdwy over 2f out: drvn and qcknd over 1f out: led fnl 75yds: kpt on strly* **9/2**[2]

5521 2 1¼ **Ascot Lime**[29] 4790 3-8-7 **84** .... RyanMoore 6 97
(Sir Michael Stoute) *chsd ldrs: rdn 3f out: edgd rt and led over 2f out: styd on u.p whn chal fnl f: hdd and outpcd fnl 75yds* **2/1**[1]

0050 3 1½ **Royal Jet**[30] 4742 6-9-5 **88** .... DarryllHolland 10 98
(M R Channon) *chsd ldrs: rdn to chal ins fnl f: wknd nr fin* **12/1**

4000 4 5 **Night Crescendo (USA)**[38] 4508 5-9-9 **92** .... JimCrowley 5 94
(Mrs A J Perrett) *in tch: chsd ldrs over 3f out: wknd ins fnl 2f* **14/1**

3033 5 5 **Samsons Son**[13] 5279 4-9-5 **88** .... LPKeniry 1 81
(J R Best) *sn bhd: rdn over 3f out: mod prog through btn horses fnl f* **14/1**

3202 6 3 **Pinch Of Salt (IRE)**[48] 4191 5-9-10 **93** .... MartinDwyer 8 81
(A M Balding) *in rr whn bmpd bnd after 2f: rdn over 4f out and no rspnse* **5/1**[3]

2006 7 ¾ **Ramona Chase**[36] 4552 3-9-3 **94** .... RichardHughes 7 81
(S Kirk) *chsd ldrs: rdn 3f out: wknd over 2f out* **6/1**

3256 8 nk **William Blake**[22] 5005 3-8-11 **88** .... RoystonFfrench 4 75
(M Johnston) *chsd ldr: rdn over 3f out: wknd 2f out* **12/1**

0420 9 3¼ **Invasian (IRE)**[20] 5100 7-9-2 **85** .... ShaneKelly 9 66
(P W D'Arcy) *led tl hdd & wknd over 2f out* **33/1**

0-23 10 13 **Guardian Of Truth (IRE)**[20] 5092 4-8-5 **79** oh4.......(p) DavidProbert[(5)] 3 38
(G L Moore) *a in rr* **14/1**

2m 17.74s (-4.16) **Going Correction** -0.075s/f (Stan)
WFA 3 from 4yo+ 8lb **10** Ran SP% **120.8**
Speed ratings (Par 107): **112,111,110,106,102 100,100,99,97,87**
toteswinger: 1&2 £3.40, 1&3 £12.80, 2&3 £9.20. CSF £14.44 CT £104.47 TOTE £6.00: £1.70, £1.60, £2.90; EX 19.90 Place 6: £58.33, Place 5: £28.69..
Owner Hamdan Al Maktoum **Bred** Shadwell Farm LLC **Trained** Lambourn, Berks

FOCUS
A good handicap and the pace-setting Invasian ensured there was a really decent clip on. Ajhar set a new course record. This was a decent handicap for the grade and a positive view has been taken of the form. The first two are progressive and the winner is smart.

NOTEBOOK
Ajhar(USA) had been off the track since finishing down the field in the Group 3 John Porter Stakes at Newbury in May, but the fact he was running in that race boded well for his chance here, as did his form in handicaps from last season, and he ran down Ascot Lime in the final furlong. He had been slowly away and took a while to warm to his task, so it would come as no surprise to see him prove a lot sharper next time. There may well be more to come. (op 6-1)
Ascot Lime, who had been raised 7lb for last month's narrow Sandown victory, showed he is progressing with a cracking effort in second. He looked the winner when going on two out, but in the end was unable to repel Ajhar. Perhaps the extra furlong found him out. (op 9-4)
Royal Jet finds himself back on a decent mark and he ran his best race for a while, pulling clear with the front pair. He could soon be winning again. (tchd 14-1)
Night Crescendo(USA), back down in trip, is another back on a fair mark these days and he travelled well into the straight, but could not race on with the front trio.
Samsons Son was attempting to come from too far back and never got into it. (op 16-1)
Pinch Of Salt(IRE), who has gone well here in the past, was being ridden turning in and never picked up. (op 4-1)
Ramona Chase failed to settle early and was unable to capitalise on this drop in grade. (op 8-1)
T/Plt: £75.70 to a £1 stake. Pool: £102,634.29. 988.75 winning tickets. T/Qpdt: £19.80 to a £1 stake. Pool: £6,876.36. 256.30 winning tickets. ST

5612 LINGFIELD (L-H)

Friday, September 5

OFFICIAL GOING: Standard

Wind: Moderate, behind Weather: Rainy, brightening after Race 2

5678 WITHYHAM MEDIAN AUCTION MAIDEN STKS 1m (P)

2:20 (2:22) (Class 6) 2-Y-O **£2,729** (£806; £403) **Stalls** High

Form				RPR
0	1		**Hurakan (IRE)**[14] 5227 2-9-3 0 JimCrowley 8 (Mrs A J Perrett) *w ldr: led over 1f out: hdd ins fnl f: strly rdn to ld again towards fin* **20/1**	74
5	2	hd	**Free Thinker**[21] 5068 2-9-3 0 JohnEgan 11 (P W D'Arcy) *trckd ldrs: rdn to ld ins fnl f: hdd towards fin* **6/1**[2]	74
0	3	hd	**Sandor**[30] 4728 2-9-3 0 EddieAhern 9 (P J Makin) *prom: rdn 2f out: swtchd lft over 1f out and pressed first 2 thrght fnl f* **8/1**	74
00	4	3 1/4	**Sequillo**[12] 5314 2-9-3 0 RichardHughes 12 (R Hannon) *towards rr: hdwy wl over 1f out: nvr nr to chal* **9/1**	68+
0	5	1 1/4	**Persian Buddy**[21] 5066 2-9-3 0 RobertHavlin 6 (Jamie Poulton) *s.i.s: sn in tch: rdn and outpcd over 1f out* **100/1**	64
	6	nk	**Penang Princess** 2-8-12 0 MartinDwyer 5 (R M Beckett) *mid-div: rdn 2f out: sltly hmpd appr fnl f and no ch after* **7/1**[3]	58
	7	1	**Candilejas** 2-8-12 0 TPO'Shea 10 (D J Coakley) *s.i.s: in rr: kpt on but nvr in contention* **33/1**	56
44	8	1/2	**Bad Baron (IRE)**[29] 4769 2-9-3 0 StephenCarson 4 (Eve Johnson Houghton) *in rr: rdn over 3f out: nvr on terms* **8/1**	60
02	9	1	**Beraimi (IRE)**[36] 4570 2-9-3 0 PhilipRobinson 1 (M A Jarvis) *s.i.s: sn led: rdn and hdd over 1f out: wknd qckly* **6/5**[1]	58+
0	10	1 3/4	**Bertie Smalls**[16] 5184 2-9-3 0 JimmyQuinn 3 (M H Tompkins) *s.i.s: rdn over 3f out: a bhd* **50/1**	54
	11	11	**Doran's Lodge (IRE)** 2-9-3 0 EdwardCreighton 2 (M R Channon) *in rr and sn outpcd* **33/1**	29

1m 38.79s (0.59) **Going Correction** -0.05s/f (Stan) **11** Ran SP% **118.1**

Speed ratings (Par 93): **95,94,94,91,90 89,88,88,87,85 74**

toteswinger: 1&2 £23.20, 1&3 £25.20, 2&3 £5.40. CSF £131.85 TOTE £22.70: £4.70, £1.90, £2.90; EX 187.70 Trifecta £259.10 Part won. Pool: £350.24 - 0.41 winning units..

Owner Lady Clague **Bred** Newberry Stud Company **Trained** Pulborough, W Sussex

FOCUS

A moderate median auction event in which only a couple had shown any worthwhile form, but it provided a thrilling finish with little covering the front three at the line.

NOTEBOOK

Hurakan(IRE), given a much more positive ride than when well beaten at Newbury on his debut, looked likely to be swallowed up when coming under pressure after swinging into the straight, but he kept finding a bit more and ground out a game victory. The half-brother to five winners at up to 1m6f, including the useful pair Chartres and Pugin, was unlikely to fail through lack of stamina and he should continue to progress as he goes up in trip. (op 33-1 tchd 18-1)

Free Thinker, who showed some promise at Newmarket on his debut in a maiden that is just starting to work out, looked as though he had come to win his race when delivered down the outside, but found the winner very game. He should not take long in going one better. (op 5-1)

Sandor, a bit of a handful beforehand, is bred to have been suited by this extra furlong and he kept battling away up the inside rail right to the line. (tchd 13-2)

Sequillo ◆ ran an interesting race. He travelled really well off the pace for much of the way but did not see much daylight up the home straight when trying to get closer and ended up a fair way behind the leading trio. His rider was not hard on him at all though and he now qualifies for nurseries. (tchd 8-1)

Persian Buddy was tailed off at Newmarket on his debut, but he performed much better here and there may be even better to come, especially when he qualifies for a mark.

Penang Princess, a springer in the market, was close enough against the inside rail turning in, but although she did not have much room, it would be pushing it to say she would have troubled the front three with a clear run. Her dam scored at up to 1m5f, so she ought to progress as she goes up in trip. (op 14-1)

Candilejas, a half-sister to Mexican Venture, showed some promise on this debut especially as she missed the break. (op 25-1)

Bad Baron(IRE) Official explanation: jockey said colt hung badly left

Beraimi(IRE) had the best form coming into this, but although ridden positively he was given no peace by the eventual winner and that seemed to find him out. Official explanation: jockey had no explanation for the poor form shown (op 11-10 tchd 11-8)

5679 HOLTYE MEDIAN AUCTION MAIDEN STKS 5f (P)

2:50 (2:50) (Class 6) 3-5-Y-O **£2,729** (£806; £403) **Stalls** High

Form				RPR
-603	1		**Pride Of Northcare (IRE)**[9] 5395 4-9-1 53 DarrenWilliams 4 (D Shaw) *a.p: led over 1f out: drvn out* **11/4**[2]	63
0	2	1	**Green Velvet**[37] 4523 3-8-9 0 RichardSmith 2 (P J Makin) *hld up: hdwy 2f out: rdn and r.o wl to go 2nd ins fnl f* **20/1**	54
6305	3	3 3/4	**Shatter Resistant (IRE)**[22] 5015 3-9-0 51 (p) JohnEgan 6 (M D Squance) *led tl rdn and hdd over 1f out: fdd ins fnl f* **8/1**	46
5400	4	1	**Tittle**[30] 4725 3-8-9 53 FergusSweeney 8 (H Candy) *in tch: sn pushed along: outpcd 2f out: kpt on ins fnl f* **9/2**[3]	37
0600	5	shd	**Cherries On Top (IRE)**[30] 4725 3-9-0 44 JimCrowley 7 (I A Wood) *awkward leaving stalls: in rr mde sme late hdwy fr over 1f out* **20/1**	42
5000	6	hd	**Hucking Harmony (IRE)**[29] 4793 3-8-9 45 SteveDrowne 10 (J R Best) *racd wd: w ldr: wknd ent fnl f* **20/1**	36
423	7	3/4	**Stoneacre Chris (USA)**[9] 5393 3-8-9 50 LPKeniry 9 (Peter Grayson) *pressed ldrs tl wknd appr fnl f* **5/2**[1]	34
0000	8	1 3/4	**Abitofafath (IRE)**[32] 4686 3-9-0 46 (b) TPQueally 3 (J G Given) *chsd ldrs tl rdn and wknd over 1f out* **33/1**	32
	9	3	**Rare Old Bird** 3-8-9 0 LiamJones 1 (J F Panvert) *outpcd thrght* **40/1**	16
0	10	9	**Stoneacre Paddy (IRE)**[190] 734 3-9-0 0 ChrisCatlin 5 (Peter Grayson) *s.i.s and sn outpcd* **10/1**	—

58.62 secs (-0.18) **Going Correction** -0.05s/f (Stan)

WFA 3 from 4yo 1lb **10** Ran SP% **113.3**

Speed ratings (Par 101): **99,97,91,89,89 89,88,85,80,66**

toteswinger: 1&2 £14.70, 1&3 £4.60, 2&3 £23.20. CSF £60.03 TOTE £3.60: £1.30, £5.20, £2.60; EX 78.70 Trifecta £266.60 Part won. Pool: £360.28 - 0.80 winning units..

Owner George Houghton **Bred** Mrs L Miller **Trained** Danethorpe, Notts

FOCUS

A very poor older-horse maiden, with the two officially highest-rated contestants just 53. The winner has been rated as running basically to form. The pace was a fair one, with a trio battling for the lead for much of the way.

Cherries On Top(IRE) Official explanation: jockey said gelding missed the break

5680 NUTLEY NURSERY 5f (P)

3:20 (3:22) (Class 4) (0-85,83) 2-Y-O **£5,046** (£1,510; £755; £377; £188) **Stalls** High

Form				RPR
5520	1		**Azwa**[30] 4729 2-8-6 68 MartinDwyer 2 (E A L Dunlop) *a in tch on ins: led 1f out: drvn out* **16/1**	71
01	2	3/4	**Olynard (IRE)**[34] 4634 2-9-7 83 GeorgeBaker 1 (R M Beckett) *in tch whn checked on ins over 3f out: sn rdn: hung lft fr over 1f out but r.o ins fnl f to go 2nd towards fin* **4/6**[1]	85+
0051	3	1/2	**Agnes Love**[4] 5567 2-7-9 62 6ex DavidProbert(5) 3 (J Akehurst) *led tl rdn and hdd 1f out: stl ev ch but lost 2nd towards fin* **12/1**	61
2000	4	1 3/4	**Sweet Applause (IRE)**[7] 5466 2-9-2 78 RichardThomas 4 (A P Jarvis) *trckd ldrs: rdn over 1f out: fdd ins fnl f* **20/1**	70
11	5	5	**Fangfoss Girls**[116] 2049 2-8-11 73 RichardMullen 6 (D M Simcock) *s.i.s: nvr in contention* **10/1**[3]	47
3322	6	2	**Red Cell (IRE)**[15] 5204 2-8-5 67 (b) ChrisCatlin 8 (E J O'Neill) *prom on outside tl wknd over 1f out* **5/1**[2]	34
616	7	4 1/2	**Lesley's Choice**[27] 4857 2-8-13 75 StephenDonohoe 7 (P A Blockley) *sn outpcd and a bhd* **12/1**	26

58.78 secs (-0.02) **Going Correction** -0.05s/f (Stan) **7** Ran SP% **111.8**

Speed ratings (Par 97): **98,96,96,93,85 82,74**

toteswinger: 1&2 £5.10, 1&3 £20.80, 2&3 £3.00. CSF £26.27 CT £142.44 TOTE £15.10: £5.00, £1.20; EX 31.80 Trifecta £458.40 Part won. Pool: £619.56 - 0.91 winning units..

Owner Hamdan Al Maktoum **Bred** Shadwell Estate Company Limited **Trained** Newmarket, Suffolk

■ Stewards' Enquiry : Martin Dwyer one-day ban: careless riding (Sep 19)

FOCUS

A fair nursery, but a race with some controversy as the well-backed favourite Olynard failed to hold his place from the inside draw and was squeezed out after a furlong, then failed to get a clear run in the straight before finishing strongly.

NOTEBOOK

Azwa took full advantage of the problems which beset the favourite, although she was partly responsible for the vicissitudes he suffered in that she was drawn next to him and closed the gap on the rail as those on her outside cut across. She then edged right as she went to the front, which was partly responsible for Olynard being denied a clear run in the straight, but essentially neither her nor her rider did much wrong. Well beaten on her nursery debut and dropped 2lb since, the shorter trip seemed to suit her and she was able to find enough to establish a winning advantage, but whether she can follow up off a higher mark remains to be seen. (tchd 14-1)

Olynard(IRE) looked unlucky, but to some extent contributed to his own misfortune. He jumped well enough from his inside stall but his rider did not commit him or rein him back and as a result he got squeezed for room on the rail and lost momentum. However, he recovered well enough to be on the heels of the leaders turning in and still looked the most likely winner, but when his jockey tried to pull him out into the gap that was developing between the eventual third and fourth, he tended to lug back in and the gap quickly closed. He was then presented with an opening on the inner as the two leaders drifted right and ran on, but too late to catch the winner. He was clearly unlucky, but does not look the most straightforward of rides. (op 10-11 tchd 8-13 and evens in a place)

Agnes Love has proved much better on the All-Weather than on turf and ran quite well off a 6lb penalty for her win at Kempton. She was carried right by the winner in the closing stages, but it did not affect the result. (tchd 11-1)

Sweet Applause(IRE) arguably put up her best previous effort on her sole try on Polytrack and was right in the mix until weakening over a furlong out. (op 25-1)

Fangfoss Girls, who had won two claimers in the spring, was running for her third trainer in three starts, but she was a market drifter on this return from nearly four months off and lost her chance with a tardy start. (op 6-1)

Red Cell(IRE), who had Agnes Love three lengths behind two runs previously, had been raised 4lb since his latest outing but on that evidence should have been involved in the finish. The fact that this front-runner had a high draw and could never get to the lead is probably the reason for this disappointing effort. (op 9-2 tchd 11-2)

Lesley's Choice was never able to go the pace. Official explanation: jockey said colt never travelled (op 14-1)

5681 BURSTOW H'CAP 6f (P)

3:50 (3:50) (Class 3) (0-95,94) 3-Y-O+

£7,477 (£2,239; £1,119; £560; £279; £140) **Stalls** Low

Form				RPR
1215	1		**Benllech**[71] 3394 4-9-0 87 RichardMullen 1 (D M Simcock) *trckd ldrs on ins: led 1f out: r.o wl* **10/1**	96
0040	2	1/2	**Halsion Chancer**[24] 4944 4-8-11 84 SteveDrowne 7 (J R Best) *trckd ldr to over 1f out: r.o wl to regain 2nd cl home* **14/1**	92
0131	3	hd	**Diriculous**[8] 5424 4-9-4 94 6ex JackMitchell(3) 4 (T G Mills) *prom: rdn and sltly outpcd 2f out: rdn and r.o wl ins fnl f* **15/8**[1]	101+
6115	4	nk	**Markab**[139] 1469 5-9-6 93 JimCrowley 2 (K A Morgan) *led tl rdn and hdd 1f out: kpt on but nt qckn towards fin* **15/2**[3]	99
6160	5	1 1/2	**Mondovi**[12] 5310 4-9-1 88 ChrisCatlin 3 (N J Vaughan) *nvr bttr than mid-div: nt qckn fnl f* **20/1**	89
03-0	6	1 1/4	**Russian Reel**[40] 4466 3-8-8 83 (t) EdwardCreighton 5 (E J Creighton) *a towards in rr* **66/1**	80
0200	7	1/2	**Bazroy (IRE)**[20] 5096 4-9-3 90 (b) StephenDonohoe 8 (P D Evans) *a in rr* **12/1**	86
5401	8	2	**Film Maker (IRE)**[9] 5403 3-9-2 91 6ex TPO'Shea 9 (B J Meehan) *s.i.s: towards rr: rdn 1/2-way and nvr gng wl* **9/4**[2]	80
0-00	9	4	**El Bosque (IRE)**[25] 4928 4-9-1 88 AlanMunro 12 (B R Millman) *a outpcd in rr* **20/1**	64
0006	10	1 1/4	**Free Tussy (ARG)**[40] 4443 4-9-0 87 RichardHughes 6 (G L Moore) *towards rr and no ch after outpcd over 2f out* **33/1**	59

1m 10.41s (-1.49) **Going Correction** -0.05s/f (Stan) course record

WFA 3 from 4yo+ 2lb **10** Ran SP% **114.7**

Speed ratings (Par 107): **107,106,106,105,103 102,101,98,93,91**

toteswinger: 1&2 £6.90, 1&3 £3.40, 2&3 £5.10. CSF £128.61 CT £382.65 TOTE £10.10: £2.20, £3.50, £1.30; EX 91.80 Trifecta £340.70 Pool: £465.01 - 1.01 winning units..

Owner Trillium Place Racing **Bred** Speedlith Group **Trained** Newmarket, Suffolk

FOCUS

A decent sprint handicap and more competitive than 15-2 bar two would suggest, but with pace holding up well at the meeting it was crucial to race handily and the first four home were at the sharp end throughout. The form is sound enough with a personal bset from the winner.

NOTEBOOK

Benllech, a four-time winner over course and distance since December, was making his debut for the yard, having been given a short break since an ordinary effort at Great Leighs, and the return to his favourite venue did the trick. He travelled well behind the two leaders and made full use of the gap that presented itself on the inside as Markab hung away from the rail on the home bend. Things got tight late on, but he always looked like hanging on and in view of his great record here it would be brave to say he cannot win again despite another inevitable rise. (op 8-1)

Halsion Chancer, a six-time winner here previously and back on the same mark as when last successful, had been well below his best recently but this was much more like it and he battled all the way to the line, having been up there from the off. (tchd 16-1)

Diriculous, winner of seven of his 11 previous starts on sand and carrying a 6lb penalty for his recent Great Leighs victory, was making his debut at this track and connections were concerned that the race might come a bit soon. Never far away, he finished well down the outside, though he was never quite getting there in time, but in view of how narrowly he was beaten it would be hard to blame fatigue. Things will not get any easier for him in the near future though, as he is due to go up another 3lb. (op 7-4 tchd 2-1)

Markab, returning from a five-month break and racing over a trip this short for the first time in well over two years, was sent straight to the front to utilise his stamina and he took some passing. This was a decent return effort and it will be interesting to see if connections let him take his chance in the Cambridgeshire. (op 17-2 tchd 10-1)

Mondovi, a winner on sand in Germany but making her debut on an artificial surface in Britain, was always in about the same place, but she was quite keen in the first half of the contest and could not pick up the leaders when asked. This effort suggests she is worth another try back here though.

Russian Reel, well beaten in two outings at the Curragh in July, was making his debut for the yard in a first-time tongue tie and was not completely disgraced given that he was another who tried to come from off the pace.

Film Maker(IRE), carrying a 6lb penalty for his recent impressive Great Leighs victory, was in trouble some way out. One possible excuse is that anything held up in the race never had a prayer, so he is probably worth another chance even though he is due to go up another 2lb. Official explanation: jockey said colt ran flat (op 5-2 tchd 15-8)

5682 JACKSON LIFT GROUP H'CAP — 1m 2f (P)

4:20 (4:23) (Class 3) (0-90,90) 3-Y-O

£7,477 (£2,239; £1,119; £560; £279; £140) **Stalls** Low

Form — RPR

31 **1** **Crackentorp**[27] 4860 3-8-8 **80** FergusSweeney 11 — 93+
(G L Moore) *broke wl: swtchd lft sn after s: sn trckd ldrs: led appr fnl f: rdn clr* **8/1**[3]

230 **2** 3 1/4 **Hustle (IRE)**[13] 5279 3-9-1 **87** RichardHughes 10 — 91
(R Hannon) *hmpd after 1f and sn bhd: hdwy wl over 1f out: r.o to go 2nd ins fnl f: no ch w wnr* **12/1**

3000 **3** 1/2 **Mystery Star (IRE)**[4] 5569 3-8-10 **82** AlanMunro 8 — 85
(M H Tompkins) *s.i.s: hdwy over 2f out: r.o fnl f* **16/1**

1002 **4** nk **Tomintoul Flyer**[11] 5349 3-9-4 **90** (v) TedDurcan 14 — 92
(H R A Cecil) *racd wd on outside in mid-div: hdwy 2f out: rdn and edgd lft over 1f out: kpt on* **4/1**[2]

210 **5** 1/2 **Navajo Joe (IRE)**[41] 4404 3-9-0 **86** MartinDwyer 6 — 87
(B J Meehan) *hmpd after 1f: trckd ldr 1m out: ev ch ent fnl f: wknd inwd* **12/1**

1500 **6** 1/2 **Calakanga**[11] 5349 3-9-3 **89** LiamJones 2 — 89
(C E Brittain) *hld up in mid-div: hdwy over 2f out: one pce fr over 1f out* **40/1**

2-50 **7** 2 **Points Of View**[26] 4918 3-9-0 **86** DO'Donohoe 12 — 82
(Sir Mark Prescott) *in rr: hdwy on ins over 1f out: nvr nr to chal* **14/1**

4031 **8** 3/4 **Legislation**[15] 5209 3-9-3 **89** (b) JimmyFortune 4 — 84
(J H M Gosden) *sn led: rdn and hdd appr fnl f: sn wknd* **10/1**

4000 **9** 1 1/4 **Fool's Wildcat (USA)**[13] 5279 3-9-1 **87** EddieAhern 9 — 79
(B J Meehan) *a towards rr and nvr gng wl* **25/1**

-644 **10** 2 1/2 **Ellmau**[97] 2610 3-9-0 **86** ChrisCatlin 1 — 73
(E J O'Neill) *trckd ldrs tl rdn over 3f out: wknd over 1f out* **14/1**

2-31 **11** 6 **Sortita (GER)**[34] 4620 3-9-0 **86** RHills 5 — 61
(M A Jarvis) *sn prom: rdn and wknd 2f out* **7/4**[1]

5510 **12** 3 **Bencoolen (IRE)**[34] 4621 3-8-13 **85** (p) SteveDrowne 3 — 54
(R Charlton) *prom tl lost pl over 4f out: nvr on terms after* **20/1**

0226 **13** 3 1/4 **American Art (IRE)**[29] 4790 3-9-2 **88** (t) MichaelHills 7 — 51
(B W Hills) *trckd ldrs tl lost pl over 3f out and sn bhd* **14/1**

2m 4.33s (-2.27) **Going Correction** -0.05s/f (Stan) **13** Ran SP% **128.9**
Speed ratings (Par 105): **107,104,104,103,103 102,101,100,99,97 92,90,87**
toteswinger: 1&2 £14.90, 1&3 £25.50, 2&3 £48.70. CSF £106.29 CT £1539.89 TOTE £7.30: £2.20, £4.10, £5.50; EX 106.10 TRIFECTA Not won..

Owner Mrs Charles Cyzer **Bred** C A Cyzer **Trained** Woodingdean, E Sussex

■ Stewards' Enquiry : Fergus Sweeney five-day ban: careless riding (Sep 19-23)

FOCUS

A competitive handicap with only a 10lb weight range, but the betting suggested it was less open. However, this was quite a rough race in the early stages, with the favourite Sortita one of those affected, but not as badly as Hustle and, worst of all, Navajo Joe. The pace was only steady and the bare form is pretty ordinary although the winner could rate higher.

NOTEBOOK

Crackentorp ◆, well backed in the morning but a drifter nearer the off, was responsible for some of the problems as he cut across from his high draw to get a good early pitch, which landed his rider in hot water with the stewards. However, once settled just off the pace he was always travelling well and, taking the advantage early in the straight, came away for an authoritative success. Out of a mare who won five times and a half-brother to middle-distance Polytrack winner Boot'N Toot, he had scored over course and distance on his previous start and looks a useful performer in the making and one to keep on-side, especially on this surface. (op 11-2 tchd 5-1)

Hustle(IRE) was one of the major sufferers in the early troubles and was in the rear until staying on quite nicely in the straight, although without having any chance of catching the winner. Proven on this surface, he also showed the longer trip was no problem for him. (op 14-1 tchd 16-1)

Mystery Star(IRE), a winner on Polytrack as a juvenile, missed a beat at the start but stuck to the inside and got a dream run through to have a chance over a furlong out. However, the inside is not always the place to be in the straight here and he could find no more from the furlong pole. (tchd 25-1)

Tomintoul Flyer ran creditably considering he was forced to race four or five horses wide throughout. He did stay on quite well in the straight, but he is due to go up 6lb so will not find things easy from his new mark. (op 5-1 tchd 7-1)

Navajo Joe(IRE) was the worst sufferer in the early scrimmaging and got lit up as a result, not settling until he was almost upsides the leader. He remained in contention until fading in the straight and can be given credit considering the amount of early running he did. He is also worth another try over this trip. (op 10-1 tchd 14-1)

Calakanga was on the heels of the leaders and was keeping on quite nicely at the finish. Her previous success was gained over 1m4f and a return to that longer distance will be in her favour. Official explanation: jockey said filly was denied a clear run (op 33-1)

Ellmau has been running over longer trips of late, but this shorter distance appeared likely to suit. He has dropped 14lb since the start of the season and is running well enough to suggest he will become competitive if he falls a little further in the ratings. (tchd 16-1)

Sortita(GER), heavily backed, appeared to fly-leap as the stalls opened and missed the break, as a result of which she was short of room on the first bend. However, she soon had a good pitch towards the outside of the leaders which she held until starting to struggle as the pace picked up approaching the home turn. She dropped away tamely and her rider subsequently reported that she ran too free and then lost her action. Official explanation: jockey said filly ran too free and lost its action (op 10-3)

5683 HARTFIELD FILLIES' H'CAP — 1m 2f (P)

4:50 (4:52) (Class 4) (0-85,83) 3-Y-O+ **£5,677** (£1,699; £849; £424; £211) **Stalls** Low

Form — RPR

4621 **1** **Oat Cuisine**[49] 4162 4-8-11 **76** DavidProbert(5) 3 — 83
(M L W Bell) *trckd ldrs: rdn over 2f out: led 1f out: drvn out* **9/2**[3]

3210 **2** 1 1/4 **Rio Guru (IRE)**[12] 5311 3-8-11 **78** EdwardCreighton 4 — 82
(M R Channon) *hld up in rr: hdwy on ins over 1f out: r.o to go 2nd ins fnl f* **12/1**

0102 **3** hd **Albarouche**[23] 4984 3-8-13 **80** (tp) PhilipRobinson 8 — 84
(M A Jarvis) *trckd ldr: rdn over 1f out: kpt on b ut lost 2nd wl ins fnl f* **11/4**[2]

2122 **4** hd **Tableau Vivant (IRE)**[21] 5071 3-9-2 **83** JimmyFortune 7 — 86
(Sir Michael Stoute) *led: rdn 2f out: hdd 1f out: kpt on one pce* **9/4**[1]

6331 **5** 1 **Belotto (IRE)**[14] 5231 3-8-11 **78** SteveDrowne 9 — 79
(R Charlton) *hld up in rr: c wd into strt: r.o ins fnl f but nvr nrr* **5/1**

4060 **6** nk **Ivory Lace**[12] 5311 7-9-1 **75** JimCrowley 6 — 76
(S Woodman) *in tch: rdn over 1f out: no hdwy fnl f* **16/1**

6005 **R** **Lisathedaddy**[24] 4945 6-9-9 **83** GeorgeBaker 2 — —
(B G Powell) *ref to r* **22/1**

2m 9.62s (3.02) **Going Correction** -0.05s/f (Stan)
WFA 3 from 4yo+ 7lb **7** Ran SP% **110.2**
Speed ratings (Par 102): **85,84,83,83,82 82,—**
toteswinger: 1&2 £8.90, 1&3 £4.70, 2&3 £3.40. CSF £50.24 CT £163.15 TOTE £5.70: £4.20, £3.70; EX 51.10 Trifecta £157.10 Pool: £212.39 - 1.00 winning units..

Owner Mrs G Rowland-Clark **Bred** Glebe Stud & J F Dean **Trained** Newmarket, Suffolk

FOCUS

A fair fillies' handicap, despite the small field, and a few came into it in decent form. However, it was rather spoilt by an early dawdle and the race rather developed into a three-furlong sprint. The winning time was 5.29 seconds slower than the preceding handicap. Despite the lack of pace the form does make some sense at face value.

5684 COLEMANS HATCH H'CAP — 7f (P)

5:20 (5:20) (Class 6) (0-55,60) 3-Y-O **£2,590** (£770; £385; £192) **Stalls** Low

Form — RPR

-201 **1** **Billberry**[4] 5574 3-9-5 **60** 6ex (t) GeorgeBaker 9 — 76+
(S C Williams) *hld up: smooth hdwy 2f out: led on bit ins fnl f: easily* **11/10**[1]

000 **2** 1 **Headache**[45] 4278 3-8-4 **52** (t) AmyScott(7) 3 — 57
(B W Duke) *in tch: led over 2f out: rdn and hdd ins fnl f but no ch w wnr* **33/1**

5040 **3** 2 **Sazerac (USA)**[18] 5162 3-8-12 **53** IanMongan 8 — 53
(P Howling) *slowly away: hdwy on ins over 1f out: nt qckn fnl f* **20/1**

0000 **4** 4 1/2 **Spiritofthestorm (USA)**[18] 5145 3-8-12 **53** JimCrowley 2 — 41
(R A Teal) *led tl hdd over 2f out: wknd ins fnl f* **8/1**[3]

2455 **5** nk **My Flame**[16] 5186 3-8-11 **52** EddieAhern 11 — 39
(J R Jenkins) *t.k.h: prom tl wknd over 1f out* **11/1**

060 **6** 1 3/4 **Hawa Khana (IRE)**[42] 4386 3-8-7 **51** RussellKennemore(3) 1 — 33
(N P Littmoden) *trckd ldrs: rdn over 2f out: wknd over 1f out* **50/1**

5602 **7** 1/2 **Scruffy Skip (IRE)**[94] 2704 3-8-11 **55** JackMitchell(3) 12 — 36
(Mrs C A Dunnett) *t.k.h: racd wd in tch: rdn and wknd over 1f out* **16/1**

4033 **8** 1 1/4 **Nawaaff**[8] 5421 3-8-12 **53** (v) TPO'Shea 14 — 31
(M R Channon) *stdd s: effrt 2f out: sn btn* **7/1**[2]

0063 **9** hd **Jay Gee Wigmo**[42] 4369 3-8-9 **53** TolleyDean(3) 4 — 30
(A W Carroll) *mid-div: rdn 4f out: nvr on terms* **20/1**

4406 **10** 3/4 **Evenstorm (USA)**[71] 3397 3-8-8 **54** DavidProbert(5) 13 — 29
(B Gubby) *racd wd in rr: effrt 2f out: sn btn* **25/1**

4004 **11** 2 1/4 **Young Ivanhoe**[14] 5248 3-8-11 **52** (t) JimmyQuinn 6 — 21
(C A Dwyer) *mid-div: rdn 4f out: nvr on terms* **16/1**

0300 **12** 4 1/2 **Rich Harvest (USA)**[16] 5186 3-8-13 **54** (t) StephenDonohoe 10 — 11
(P D Evans) *mid-div: rdn and wknd over 3f out* **12/1**

2050 **13** 1 **Fly In Johnny (IRE)**[17] 5166 3-8-12 **53** ChrisCatlin 7 — 7
(M R Hoad) *a outpcd in rr* **50/1**

6653 **P** **Flying Seasons**[13] 5268 3-9-0 **55** (p) AlanMunro 5 — —
(B R Millman) *in rr whn broke down and p.u over 3f out* **16/1**

1m 25.08s (0.28) **Going Correction** -0.05s/f (Stan) **14** Ran SP% **125.1**
Speed ratings (Par 99): **96,94,92,87,87 85,84,83,82,82 79,74,73,—**
toteswinger: 1&2 £21.70, 1&3 £17.00, 2&3 £120.10. CSF £62.39 CT £557.50 TOTE £2.30: £1.30, £12.00, £6.70; EX 77.60 Trifecta £226.20 Part won. Pool: £305.68 - 0.20 winning units. Place 6: £235.85 Place 5: £63.43 .

Owner Pascoe, Enticknap & Sullivan **Bred** G Deacon **Trained** Newmarket, Suffolk

FOCUS

A moderate handicap and not as competitive as the size of the field would suggest with most of these regressive or disappointing. The market said this was a one-horse race and it was proved right. The winner has been rated value for 4l.

T/Plt: £1,170.90 to a £1 stake. Pool: £101,211.08. 63.10 winning tickets. T/Qpdt: £77.70 to a £1 stake. Pool: £12,589.87. 119.80 winning tickets. JS

5597 LONGCHAMP (R-H)

Friday, September 5

OFFICIAL GOING: Good to soft

5685a PRIX DE LUTECE (GROUP 3) — 1m 7f

1:50 (1:56) 3-Y-O **£29,412** (£11,765; £8,824; £5,882; £2,941)

RPR

1 3/4 **Shemima**[22] 5039 3-8-8 CSoumillon 7 — 106
(A De Royer-Dupre, France) *hld up in 6th: hdwy 1 1/2f out: chalng 1f out whn crossed and snatched up: drvn and r.o to line: fin 2nd, 3/4l: awrdd r* **29/10**[2]

2 **Americain (USA)**[24] 4959 3-8-9 OPeslier 5 — 107
(A Fabre, France) *led after 3f: r.o ent st: rdn 1 1/2f out: strly pressed whn wnt lft 1f out: drvn out: fin 1st: disq: plcd 2nd* **46/10**[3]

3 1 1/2 **Watar (IRE)**[24] 4959 3-8-11 DBonilla 1 — 107
(F Head, France) *prom: disputing 3rd 1/2-way: 3rd st: pushed along and nt clr run: rdn and wnt 2nd over 1f out: ev ch fnl f: styd on* **6/4**[1]

4 6 **Tsar De Russie (IRE)**[24] 4959 3-8-9 ....(b) ACrastus 4 99
(E Lellouche, France) *hld up in last: drvn over 1f out: styd on steadily to take 4th post* **21/1**

5 ½ **Donegal (USA)**[20] 5094 3-8-11 .... WilliamBuick 6 100
(A M Balding) *prom: 2nd 1/2-way: pushed along st: rdn and 4th over 1f out: no ex* **63/10**

6 1 ½ **Classic Swain (USA)**[27] 4880 3-8-9 .... JVictoire 2 97
(A Fabre, France) *first to show: led 3f: disputing cl 3rd 1/2-way: 4th st: effrt 1 1/2f out: sn no ex* **28/1**

7 6 **Track Record**[36] 4577 3-8-9 .... SPasquier 3 90
(A Fabre, France) *in tch: 4th 1/2-way: 5th st: drvn 1 1/2f out: no imp* **7/1**

3m 20.0s (4.00) **Going Correction** +0.60s/f (Yiel) **7 Ran SP% 117.7**
Speed ratings: **112,113,111,108,108 107,104**
PARI-MUTUEL: WIN 3.90; PL 2.20, 2.30; SF 19.50.
Owner H H Aga Khan **Bred** H H The Aga Khan's Studs S C **Trained** Chantilly, France

NOTEBOOK
Shemima, towards the tail of the field early on, came with a run up the centre of the track but was badly hampered at the furlong marker. She never really recovered and finally went under by three parts of a length, and the Stewards subsequently awarded her the race. This consistent daughter of Dalakhani will now be aimed at the Prix de Royallieu on October 4th.
Americain(USA) was soon at the head of affairs and still going well at the entrance to the straight. Once under pressure he began to hang to the left and badly hampered the runner-up, who was making a forward move. It was no surprise the Stewards changed the finishing order but the jockey tried his best to keep him straight so was not given a suspension.
Watar(IRE) once again did not have the best of runs as he had nowhere to go halfway up the straight then just stayed on as the race came to an end. He is certainly better than this performance suggests and has been entered in the Prix de Chaudenay over the course and distance on October 4th.
Donegal(USA) was close to the leader from the start but appeared to be outpaced early in the straight and was never able to get in a blow from then on. He is a possible for the Chaudenay and may well be schooled over hurdles before the end of the year.

5624 BADEN-BADEN (L-H)
Friday, September 5

OFFICIAL GOING: Soft

5686a 135TH MAURICE LACROIX-TROPHY (GROUP 3) 7f
4:00 (4:01) 2-Y-O **£40,441** (£14,706; £7,353; £3,676)

RPR

1 **Serienhoehe (IRE)** 2-8-12 .... FilipMinarik 6 —
(P Schiergen, Germany) *hld up: 6th st: hdwy wl over 1f out: rdn to ld ins fnl f: pushed out fnl 100yds and a holding 2nd* **22/10**[2]

2 1 ¼ **Mambo Light (USA)**[112] 2160 2-8-12 .... EPedroza 2 —
(A Wohler, Germany) *racd in 3rd bhd clr ldr: clsd up appr st: led wl over 1f out to 1f out: ins fnl f: one pce* **52/10**

3 4 **Takhir (IRE)** 2-9-2 .... AStarke 1 —
(P Schiergen, Germany) *racd in 5th to st: ev ch over 1f out: one pce* **19/10**[1]

4 1 ½ **Lautenspielerin (GER)** 2-8-12 .... LennartHammer-Hansen 4 —
(Frau Marion Rotering, Germany) *last to st: rdn and effrt over 1f out: sn one pce* **77/10**

5 1 ¼ **Lacy Sunday (USA)**[26] 2-8-12 .... ADeVries 3 —
(A Trybuhl, Germany) *hdwy on outside and 4th st: rdn and ev ch wl over 1f out: sn one pce* **19/1**

6 5 **Spirit Of Duke (GER)** 2-9-2 .... TMundry 7 —
(C Von Der Recke, Germany) *first to show: trckd clr ldr: hdwy and cl 2nd st: wknd wl over 1f out* **88/10**

7 29 **Zarrado (GER)**[26] 2-9-2 ....(b) THellier 5 —
(U Ostmann, Germany) *sn clr: hdd & wknd wl over 1f out* **7/2**[3]

1m 29.49s (5.59) **7 Ran SP% 130.8**
(Including 10 Euros stake): WIN 32; PL 13, 17, 13; SF 182.
Owner Gestut Wittekindshof **Bred** Gestut Wittekindshof **Trained** Germany

4853 HAYDOCK (L-H)
Saturday, September 6

5687 Meeting Abandoned - Waterlogged
Sprint Cup transferred to Doncaster on September 13.

5671 KEMPTON (A.W) (R-H)
Saturday, September 6

OFFICIAL GOING: Standard
Wind: Fresh behind Weather: mostly cloudy

5693 TOTESWINGER SIRENIA STKS (GROUP 3) 6f (P)
2:20 (2:21) (Class 1) 2-Y-O
£28,385 (£10,760; £5,385; £2,685; £1,345; £675) **Stalls** High

Form RPR

411 1 **Elnawin**[15] 5244 2-9-0 106 .... PatDobbs 10 108+
(R Hannon) *mid-div: hdwy 2f out: rdn and rdr dropped reins ins fnl f but kpt on to ld cl home* **6/4**[1]

301 2 hd **Square Eddie (CAN)**[46] 4274 2-9-0 86 .... SteveDrowne 2 107+
(J R Best) *lw: prom: led 2f out: kpt on u.p: hdd cl home* **9/1**[3]

1 3 hd **Weatherstaff (USA)**[47] 4237 2-9-0 0 .... JoeFanning 12 107+
(M Johnston) *str: prom: pressed ldrs 2f out and ev ch tl wl ins fnl f* **9/2**[2]

0110 4 2 **Khor Dubai (IRE)**[36] 4588 2-9-0 96 .... LDettori 3 101
(Saeed Bin Suroor) *lw: stdd s: in rr tl hdwy on outside over 1f out: r.o fnl f: nvr nrr* **12/1**

1460 5 nk **Flashmans Papers**[15] 5245 2-9-0 104 .... MartinDwyer 7 100
(J R Best) *mid-div: rdn and hung lft fr over 1f out: kpt on one pce fnl f* **9/1**[3]

216 6 1 ½ **Deposer (IRE)**[15] 5226 2-9-0 94 .... LPKeniry 8 95
(J R Best) *led tl rdn and hdd 2f out: wknd over 1f out* **9/1**[3]

6143 7 ½ **Zezao**[12] 5359 2-9-0 91 .... JimmyFortune 9 94
(B J Meehan) *s.i.s: in rr: mde sme late hdwy* **9/1**[3]

4510 8 ½ **Klynch**[15] 5244 2-9-0 89 ....(b) EddieAhern 11 92
(B J Meehan) *in rr effrt over 1f out: nvr on terms* **25/1**

0323 9 ½ **Missile Dodger (USA)**[31] 4729 2-9-0 89 ....(v) AdamKirby 6 91
(R M Beckett) *in tch: effrt over 2f out: wknd over 1f out* **40/1**

012 10 hd **Keeptheboatafloat (USA)**[68] 3553 2-9-0 92 .... DarrenWilliams 5 90
(K R Burke) *a in rr* **20/1**

0026 11 hd **White Shift (IRE)**[64] 3681 2-8-11 91 .... TQuinn 4 87
(P D Evans) *b: trckd ldr tl rdn and wknd 2f out* **66/1**

1m 11.91s (-1.19) **Going Correction** -0.025s/f (Stan) **11 Ran SP% 118.4**
Speed ratings (Par 105): **106,105,105,102,102 100,99,99,98,98 97**
toteswinger: 1&2 £3.90, 1&3 £2.90, 2&3 £9.10. CSF £15.44 TOTE £2.30: £1.10, £2.90, £2.20; EX 16.70 Trifecta £49.30 Pool: £1,141.41 - 17.10 winning units..
Owner Noodles Racing **Bred** D R Tucker **Trained** East Everleigh, Wilts
■ Stewards' Enquiry : Pat Dobbs three-day ban: used whip in the incorrect place (Sep 20-22)

FOCUS
The third running of this race on Polytrack and, considering the official figures, this looked the best renewal since it was moved from the turf. The pace was good, as you would expect, and the winner lowered Dhanyata's course record for two-year-olds. However, it is worth noting that the deluge of rain that has fallen recently probably quickened up the surface.

NOTEBOOK
Elnawin ◆ came through with a strong challenge, after travelling strongly in midfield, to just hold off the runner-up, despite his rider losing his reins. He had made a decent start to his career, finishing fourth before landing a minor event at Salisbury. However, he surpassed all of that by landing the £300,000 St Leger Yearlings Stakes last time (albeit at odds of 25-1) and made the next step up the ladder in style. Connections are unsure whether he will be seen again this season, but he looks sure to make up into a nice sort next season. (op 7-4)
Square Eddie(CAN) ◆ got off the mark last time after a respectable effort at Royal Ascot in the Coventry Stakes. Always well positioned during the race, he made Elnawin fight hard for victory and lost little caste in defeat. He has an entry in a valuable sales race soon and the Group 1 Dewhurst Stakes later in the year (op 10-1 tchd 8-1)
Weatherstaff(USA) ◆ was said to be very green and noisy before his debut so, in those circumstances, probably did well to just prevail. He finished in front of a couple of subsequent winners that day (Jobe went on to be third in the Gimcrack) and improvement looked likely. A rangy-looking sort, he battled on bravely under pressure in the final furlong to not be beaten very far. He seems sure to continue improving. (op 5-1)
Khor Dubai(IRE), who had looked promising before his effort in the Group 2 Richmond Stakes at Goodwood last time, did not break too smartly and never featured until finishing strongly inside the final furlong. He is probably up to Group 3 standard but may need further. (tchd 14-1)
Flashmans Papers arguably had the best form coming into this race. His defeat of Bushranger at Royal Ascot looks very good after that horse's subsequent efforts. However, he failed to figure on his first start at 6f, and hung away from the inside rail up the home straight. (op 8-1)
Deposer(IRE) won nicely at Lingfield in July over 6f and was not disgraced in an ordinary-looking Gimcrack last time after taking a good grip in the early stages. He was much too keen again (this time in front) and failed to see the trip out. (op 10-1 tchd 11-1)
Zezao, beaten by David Simcock's Desert Phantom on his last two starts, kept on well from the two-furlong marker but only ran through some beaten horses. (op 8-1)

5694 TOTESPORT.COM SEPTEMBER STKS (GROUP 3) 1m 4f (P)
2:50 (2:51) (Class 1) 3-Y-O+
£36,900 (£13,988; £7,000; £3,490; £1,748; £877) **Stalls** Centre

Form RPR

0003 1 **Hattan (IRE)**[14] 5288 6-9-7 110 ....(v[1]) NCallan 8 116
(C E Brittain) *lw: a in tch: rdn to ld appr fnl f: edgd lft: r.o wl* **16/1**

000 2 nk **Illustrious Blue**[22] 5070 5-9-4 103 .... PaulDoe 1 113
(W J Knight) *hld up in rr: hdwy 2f out: r.o strly u.p to go 2nd ins fnl f: no ex cl home* **33/1**

1200 3 3 ¼ **Mourilyan (IRE)**[111] 2234 4-9-4 113 .... GeorgeBaker 12 107
(G L Moore) *w'like: mid-div: hdwy 2f out: rdn and styd on to go 3rd cl home* **12/1**

2211 4 hd **Many Volumes (USA)**[12] 5348 4-9-4 111 .... TPQueally 10 107
(H R A Cecil) *lw: led tl hdd appr fnl f: no ex ins fnl f* **5/2**[1]

1430 5 1 **Lion Sands**[21] 5094 4-9-4 111 .... JimmyFortune 4 105
(L M Cumani) *hld up: mde hdwy over 1f out but nvr nr to chal* **9/1**[2]

-302 6 ½ **Galactic Star**[36] 4585 5-9-4 112 .... RyanMoore 3 105
(Sir Michael Stoute) *trckd ldrs: rdn over 2f out: wknd fnl f* **5/2**[1]

40-2 7 ½ **Blue Monday**[22] 5070 7-9-4 108 .... SteveDrowne 6 104
(R Charlton) *racd in snatches: effrt over 3f out: mde sme late hdwy* **10/1**[3]

004 8 6 **Supersonic Dave (USA)**[14] 5288 4-9-4 102 .... RHills 2 94
(B J Meehan) *trckd ldr: rdn over 2f out: sn wknd* **25/1**

4225 9 4 **Young Mick**[15] 5229 6-9-4 103 ....(v) TQuinn 7 88
(G G Margarson) *t.k.h in rr: nvr nr to chal* **9/1**[2]

045 10 6 **Halicarnassus (IRE)**[14] 5276 4-9-4 110 .... TonyCulhane 11 78
(M R Channon) *lw: in tch: rdn over 2f out: sn btn* **14/1**

4100 11 3 ¾ **Humungous (IRE)**[14] 5288 5-9-4 100 ....(b) ChrisCatlin 5 72
(C R Egerton) *s.i.s: hdwy on outside after 3f: wknd over 2f out* **66/1**

1340 12 52 **Al Shemali**[49] 4192 4-9-4 108 ....(t) LDettori 9 —
(Saeed Bin Suroor) *lw: mid-div: dropped out to rr over 3f out: eased over 2f out: t.o* **11/1**

2m 30.5s (-4.00) **Going Correction** -0.025s/f (Stan) **12 Ran SP% 123.1**
Speed ratings (Par 113): **112,111,109,109,108 108,108,104,101,97 95,60**
toteswinger: 1&2 £73.20 1&3 £38.90, 2&3 £62.10. CSF £470.81 TOTE £16.60: £4.70, £9.00, £3.70; EX 541.60 Trifecta £1747.90 Part won. Pool: £2,362.09 - 0.30 winning units..
Owner Saeed Manana **Bred** Darley **Trained** Newmarket, Suffolk

FOCUS
After a couple of smallish fields for this race since its move to the all-weather, plenty of solid types lined up for the good prize on offer, and it looked to be right up to the sort of standard you would hope to see in a Group 3 event. The pace set by Many Volumes did not look strong by any means, which meant plenty had chances as they turned in. The form is rated around the first two.

NOTEBOOK
Hattan(IRE), fitted with a visor for the first time after running too freely in blinkers last time, and the only runner carrying a 3lb penalty, handles Polytrack really well, as he showed when taking this year's Winter Derby. He eventually settled nicely behind the leaders and came through with his effort at around the two-furlong marker, picking off the long-time leader. However, he made things a little difficult for himself by edging away from the rail when in front and only just held off the fast-finishing runner-up. Placed in Group 1 and Group 2 company, he is a fine servant to all connected with him and continues to hold his own at a decent level. (tchd 20-1 in a place)
Illustrious Blue, who was behind Blue Monday at Newmarket last time, has been running without a great deal of success in 2008 but has regularly faced stiff tasks. Quickly settled at the rear of the field, he still had plenty to give rounding the final bend in last place before meeting a little bit of traffic about two furlongs from home, although his jockey never stopped riding. Flying home under a strong ride, he gave Hattan plenty to think about and went down fighting. (tchd 28-1)
Mourilyan(IRE) ◆, having his first start for Gary Moore, was an improving sort for John Oxx at the end of last year and the start of this one. That progression saw him run in two Group 1 races (the latter for another trainer) before his absence and he shaped with any amount of promise on his return to the track. With normal progression and a step back up to 1m4f, he looks set to go even closer next time. Connections are looking to aim him at the Canadian International. (op 10-1)

Many Volumes(USA) had really got his act together after a frustrating run of second places, albeit in good company. He won over 1m3f last time at this course, in a small conditions race, and had his own way out in front. It was slightly disappointing that he could not quicken away from his rivals better than he did, and he was caught for third approaching the line. (tchd 11-4 & 3-1 in places)

Lion Sands, third in this race last year, probably did not like the ground last time at Newbury but had been fairly consistent before. He tried to come from off the pace but did not get going quickly enough and failed to trouble the leaders. (op 8-1 tchd 11-1)

Galactic Star, who sweated up a bit, was well positioned but could not accelerate when his jockey needed a response and was arguably dossing. It would not be a huge surprise to see him in some headgear soon. (op 7-2)

Blue Monday failed to really shine down in Australia (although his seventh in last year's Melbourne Cup was far from disgraceful) but ran really well on his return to this country last time. However, this time he appeared to run in snatches and was on and off the bridle a couple of times during the race. He stayed on well through some beaten horses and possibly will be better over further. (tchd 11-1)

Young Mick did not seem to have any excuses this time and looked beaten on merit. Official explanation: jockey said gelding hung right (tchd 8-1)

Al Shemali Official explanation: jockey said colt had a breathing problem

5695 TOTESCOOP6 LONDON MILE HERITAGE H'CAP (SERIES FINAL) 1m (P)

3:25 (3:26) (Class 2) 3-Y-O+

£30,825 (£9,280; £4,640; £2,315; £1,160; £585) **Stalls** High

Form				RPR
1-01	1		**Premio Loco (USA)**[38] 4528 4-9-10 **99** ... GeorgeBaker 16 (C F Wall) *lw: a in tch on ins: shkn up to ld appr fnl f: qcknd clr: readily* **2/1**[1]	114+
4140	2	2 ½	**Cape Hawk (IRE)**[28] 4845 4-9-5 **94** ... RichardHughes 2 (R Hannon) *led for 1f: styd prom: rdn 2f out: chal ent fnl f: nt pce of wnr* **11/1**	103
1553	3	¾	**Formation (USA)**[16] 5209 3-8-3 **83** ... HayleyTurner 8 (E A L Dunlop) *lw: hld up: hdwy 2f out: r.o wl ins fnl f: nvr nrr* **20/1**	89
1132	4	2 ¼	**The Fifth Member (IRE)**[28] 4853 4-8-6 **81** ... MartinDwyer 13 (J R Boyle) *in tch: hdwy 2f out: r.o ins fnl f* **6/1**[2]	83
0213	5	¾	**Totally Focussed (IRE)**[12] 5350 3-8-0 **80** ... NickyMackay 3 (S Dow) *in rr tl hdwy over 1f out: r.o: nvr nrr* **14/1**	79
4550	6	nk	**Nice To Know (FR)**[42] 4407 4-8-6 **81** ow1 ... SteveDrowne 11 (G L Moore) *slowly away: kpt on fr rr ins fnl 2f: nvr nr to chal* **33/1**	81+
1041	7	1	**Russki (IRE)**[22] 5051 4-9-7 **96** ...(b) RichardMullen 4 (D M Simcock) *led after 1f: hdd 4f out: led again over 2f out tl hdd appr fnl f: wknd ins fnl f* **16/1**	93
2212	8	nse	**Willow Dancer (IRE)**[33] 4694 4-8-10 **85** ...(p) AdamKirby 1 (W R Swinburn) *lw: trckd ldr to over 4f out: rdn 2f out: one pce after* **16/1**	82
3225	9	1 ¾	**Mumbleswerve (IRE)**[23] 5030 4-7-11 **77** ...(b[1]) DavidProbert[(5)] 10 (W Jarvis) *lw: prom: led 4f out to over 4f out: hung lft and btn over 1f out* **12/1**	70
4000	10	1 ¼	**Samarinda (USA)**[38] 4528 5-9-4 **93** ... TonyCulhane 7 (Mrs P Sly) *burst out of stalls but sn hdd: rdn 3f out: wknd 2f out* **50/1**	83
4400	11	1	**Electric Warrior (IRE)**[111] 2233 5-8-8 **90** ... DeclanCannon[(7)] 15 (K R Burke) *mid-div: rdn and wknd 2f out* **50/1**	78
0222	12	¾	**Alfresco**[6] 5532 4-9-1 **90** ... NCallan 12 (I A Wood) *mid-div: reminders 3f out: wknd 2f out* **16/1**	76
1413	13	nk	**Ebn Malk (IRE)**[8] 5470 3-8-3 **83** ow1 ... JoeFanning 5 (M A Jarvis) *lw: towards rr: c wd into strt and nvr on terms* **16/1**	68
-100	14	2	**Red Rumour (IRE)**[115] 2104 3-8-11 **91** ...(b[1]) EddieAhern 14 (R M Beckett) *slowly away: a bhd* **20/1**	71
5021	15	2 ¾	**Rochefort (IRE)**[21] 5104 3-8-10 **90** ... JimmyFortune 9 (J H M Gosden) *mid-div: wknd over 2f out* **7/1**[3]	64
262	16	1 ½	**Mujood**[14] 5270 5-8-4 **79** ...(v) ChrisCatlin 6 (Eve Johnson Houghton) *outpcd 1/2-way: a bhd* **20/1**	50

1m 37.39s (-2.41) **Going Correction** -0.025s/f (Stan)
WFA 3 from 4yo+ 5lb **16** Ran SP% **127.5**
Speed ratings (Par 109): **111,108,107,105,104 104,103,103,101,100 99,98,98,96,93 92**
toteswinger: 1&2 £11.10, 1&3 £14.40, 2&3 £58.30. CSF £23.60 CT £383.91 TOTE £3.70: £1.20, £2.80, £4.10, £2.00; EX 36.80 Trifecta £1051.30 Pool: £2,557.32 - 1.80 winning units..
Owner Bernard Westley **Bred** Kidder, Cole & Griggs **Trained** Newmarket, Suffolk

FOCUS
The third running of this valuable handicap, featuring a maximum field and several complex lines of form with many of these having already met each other in the qualifiers. The betting did not suggest this was as competitive as the numbers would suggest though, as punters only wanted to know one horse. Premio Loco continues on the upgrade and this is solid form which should work out.

NOTEBOOK
Premio Loco(USA) ◆, who went off at a very skinny-looking 2-1, does look something of a nervous type and, having become full of himself in the paddock, he was taken to the start early and was the last to be loaded into the stalls. Once under way, however, he travelled very nicely just off the pace on the inside before edging his way towards the outside on reaching the home straight. Showing a decent turn of speed, not even getting a bump from Mumbleswerve could stop his momentum and he was in no danger after hitting the front. This was a decent effort off a 7lb higher mark than for his last win and he gives the impression that there is a lot more to come provided his nerves don't get the better of him. He picks up a 4lb penalty for the Cambridgeshire and the way he won this the extra furlong will not be a problem, but at this stage it looks more likely that he will go to Dubai this winter. (op 9-4 tchd 5-2 in places)

Cape Hawk(IRE), a three-time winner over course and distance, was 10lb higher than when fourth in this race a year ago. Richard Hughes did very well to get him across to race prominently from his wide draw and he ran a cracker. He had every chance and just had the misfortune to run into a potentially classy individual on the day. (op 10-1 tchd 12-1)

Formation(USA) finished well despite some trademark flashes of the tail and on this evidence probably needs a return to 1m2f.

The Fifth Member(IRE), winner of his last two starts over this course and distance and running well on turf in the meantime, was always close to the pace and kept on to record another decent performance at this track. (op 7-1 tchd 15-2)

Totally Focussed(IRE), whose only previous win came in a qualifier for this in June, was drawn out wide but was noted putting in some decent late work up the inside and deserves to add to his tally. Official explanation: jockey said gelding ran too free (op 16-1)

Nice To Know(FR) ◆ completely fluffed the start and was soon in a detached last, but she was finishing very strongly and is definitely one for the notebook.

Russki(IRE) blazed a trail as he usually does, but he had to do quite a bit of running early in order to get across from his low draw and that counted against him late on. (op 14-1)

Willow Dancer(IRE), who had it to do from the outside stall, was always close to the pace and ran well under the circumstances. (op 20-1)

Mumbleswerve(IRE), sporting first-time blinkers, ran well for a long way and was still bang in the firing line entering the last 2f, but then started to hang as he got tired. (op 14-1)

Samarinda(USA), 2lb higher than when beaten less than a length into third in this race a year ago, anticipated the start and burst his stall but ran well until weakening approaching the last quarter-mile.

Electric Warrior(IRE) ran better than his finishing position might suggest on this return from nearly four months off

Rochefort(IRE) was very disappointing off this 8lb higher mark and it does seem that he needs to dominate in order to show his best.

5696 TOTESPORT 0800 221 221 CONDITIONS STKS (C&G) 7f (P)

4:00 (4:02) (Class 3) 2-Y-O **£6,854** (£2,052; £1,026; £513; £256) **Stalls** High

Form				RPR
1	1		**Captain Ramius (IRE)**[12] 5344 2-8-12 0 ... JamieSpencer 3 (M J Wallace, Australia) *unf: mde all: wnt lft nrly 2f out and again edgd lft ins fnl f: drvn out* **15/8**[1]	82
1	2	¾	**Ashram (IRE)**[22] 5066 2-9-2 0 ... TQuinn 1 (J W Hills) *str: lw: trckd wnr: carried lft nrly 2f out: checked and swtchd rt ins fnl f: jst hld on for 2nd* **15/8**[1]	84+
	3	hd	**Sir Al (IRE)** 2-8-12 0 ... DarrenWilliams 5 (K R Burke) *w'like: leggy: s.i.s: hld up: hdwy over 1f out: r.o wl ins fnl f* **16/1**[3]	80
	4	2 ½	**Standpoint** 2-8-12 0 ... RyanMoore 6 (Sir Michael Stoute) *unf: scope: tall: lw: trckd first 2f: rdn and chal on ins 2f out: one pce fnl f* **9/4**[2]	73
0	5	5	**Paddythefish (USA)**[7] 5500 2-8-12 0 ... FergusSweeney 2 (K R Burke) *w'like: str: racd in 4th pl tl wknd over 2f out* **25/1**	61

1m 27.8s (1.80) **Going Correction** -0.025s/f (Stan) **5** Ran SP% **110.1**
Speed ratings (Par 99): **88,87,86,84,78**
toteswinger: 1&2 £3.20. CSF £5.72 TOTE £2.80: £1.60, £1.40; EX 5.80.
Owner Mrs Clodagh McStay **Bred** P G Lyons **Trained** Australia

FOCUS
Only a small turnout for some reasonable prize money. Previous runnings of this race have not produced too much of note, so it remains to be seen how good these turn out to be. The pace looked sensible.

NOTEBOOK
Captain Ramius(IRE), wearing a cross noseband, broke smartly and always held an easy lead. He appeared to have things in hand as the runner-up started to be niggled turning in, but he gave his rivals a chance of catching him when edging towards the stands' side just inside the two-furlong marker, which hampered Ashram, and once again inside the final furlong, impeding John Hills's runner again. All things considered, he was probably just about the best horse in the race, but surely would have been in danger of being demoted had the winning margin been less. Connections are aiming him towards a Listed race next. (op 7-4 tchd 13-8)

Ashram(IRE), a strong-looking sort who played up a little before going into the stalls, endured a nightmare run up the home straight. It is difficult to say with any certainty that he would have won, but it was a decent-enough effort when he was allowed a clear passage, although there is a suspicion that he might have quirks and he is not one to be backing at short odds. (op 7-4 tchd 2-1)

Sir Al(IRE) ◆, who looked a bit unfurnished, really caught the eye on his debut, finishing strongly after being behind in the early stages. If building on the effort, he can win an ordinary maiden. (op 10-1)

Standpoint, who had a handler at the start and wore a blanket for stalls entry, was far from disgraced on his first start and kept on nicely, without being unduly punished, up the inside rail. He should improve mentally for the run. (op 7-2)

Paddythefish(USA) did not show much on his debut and was readily left behind here when the tempo increased. (op 20-1)

5697 BET TOTEPOOL IN UK AND IRELAND H'CAP 7f (P)

4:30 (4:31) (Class 4) (0-85,85) 3-Y-O+ **£4,727** (£1,054; £1,054; £351) **Stalls** High

Form				RPR
51	1		**Ethaara**[16] 5205 3-8-10 **77** ... RHills 15 (W J Haggas) *b.hind: lw: wnt rt s: towards rr on ins: short of room over 2f out: sn mde hdwy: r.o strly fr over 1f out to ld cl home* **2/1**[1]	88+
5003	2	nk	**Woodcote Place**[14] 5290 5-9-2 **79** ... GeorgeBaker 7 (P R Chamings) *stdd s: hdwy over 2f out: fin fast to dead heat for 2nd cl home* **8/1**[3]	86
-000	2	dht	**Lone Wolfe**[42] 4417 4-9-8 **85** ... JimmyFortune 5 (Jane Chapple-Hyam) *lw: led: clr over 1f out: rdn and hdd cl home* **16/1**	92
0431	4	1	**Minus Fifteen (IRE)**[22] 5052 3-8-13 **80** ... NCallan 2 (K A Ryan) *t.k.h: trckd ldr to 2f out: r.o fnl f* **12/1**	82
2565	5	½	**Wigram's Turn (USA)**[24] 4983 3-8-13 **85** ... DavidProbert[(5)] 11 (A M Balding) *lw: mid-div: short of room and swtchd lft over 1f out: r.o fnl f* **9/2**[2]	86+
4410	6	hd	**Opus Maximus (IRE)**[28] 4876 3-8-12 **79** ... JoeFanning 16 (M Johnston) *hmpd sn after s: in rr: short of rooom2f out: r.o wl fnl f: nvr nrr* **14/1**	79+
1-00	7	½	**Sweet Gale (IRE)**[19] 5144 4-8-9 **72** ... TonyCulhane 6 (Mike Murphy) *t.k.h: in tch: effrt over 2f out: kpt on fnl f* **33/1**	73
-000	8	hd	**Eastern Gift**[8] 5470 3-8-10 **77** ... RyanMoore 8 (R Hannon) *towards rr: hdwy over 1f out: nvr nrr* **20/1**	76
20	9	½	**Secret Night**[21] 5101 5-9-5 **82** ...(p) AdamKirby 4 (C G Cox) *mid-div: effrt over 2f out: one pce after* **16/1**	81
2005	10	½	**Prime Factor**[12] 5346 3-8-6 **73** ...(b[1]) EddieAhern 3 (B W Hills) *trckd ldrs: rdn over 1f out: wknd ins fnl f* **25/1**	69
1135	11	hd	**Autumn Blades (IRE)**[27] 4893 3-8-9 **76** ... TQuinn 9 (J W Hills) *lw: stdd s: in rr whn swtchd lft to avoid trble over 1f out: kpt on one pce fnl f* **14/1**	71+
0605	12	nk	**Divertimenti (IRE)**[12] 5345 4-8-10 **73** ...(p) LPKeniry 1 (C R Dore) *in rr whn hmpd and stmbld over 1f out: nvr on terms* **33/1**	69+
6460	13	nk	**I Confess**[22] 5056 3-8-6 **73** ... SteveDrowne 13 (P D Evans) *swtg: in tch: effrt 2f out: sn wknd* **33/1**	67
034	14	1 ½	**Resplendent Nova**[24] 4989 6-9-7 **84** ... JimmyQuinn 14 (P Howling) *b: mid-div rdn 2f out: wknd fnl f* **10/1**	76
6446	15	3	**Phluke**[33] 4694 7-8-11 **74** ... StephenCarson 12 (Eve Johnson Houghton) *trckd ldrs tl wknd 2f out* **14/1**	58
000-	16	4 ½	**Rhuepunzel**[315] 6497 4-8-12 **75** ... NelsonDeSouza 10 (P F I Cole) *mid-div: wknd over 2f out* **33/1**	46

1m 25.5s (-0.50) **Going Correction** -0.025s/f (Stan)
WFA 3 from 4yo+ 4lb **16** Ran SP% **131.5**
Speed ratings (Par 105): **101,100,100,99,98 98,98,97,97,96 96,96,95,94,90 85**
toteswinger: 1&LW £12.40, 1&WP £6.40, 2&3 £34.50. TOTE £2.90 TRIFECTA WIN £2.90 PL £1.30, LW £4.40, WP £2.10, E2.70 EX: E/LW £26.20, E/WP £13.80 CSF E/LW £19.17, E/WP £8.97 TRIC E/LW/WP £117.64, E/WP/L.
Owner Hamdan Al Maktoum **Bred** Shadwell Estate Company Limited **Trained** Newmarket, Suffolk

■ Stewards' Enquiry : David Probert four-day ban: careless riding (Sep 20-23)
R Hills five-day ban: careless riding (Sep 20-24)

FOCUS
A decent handicap with another maximum field and fiercely competitive. It provided a dramatic finish too. The pace was steady, though, and the form is somewhat messy. Ethaara is rated as better than the bare form.

5698 TOTESPORTCASINO.COM H'CAP 2m (P)
5:00 (5:03) (Class 4) (0-80,79) 3-Y-O £4,727 (£1,406; £702; £351) Stalls High

Form RPR
1105 **1** **Precision Break (USA)**[8] 5464 3-9-4 **76** .... JimmyFortune 8 84
(P F I Cole) *trckd ldr: led 6f out: hdd 1f out: strly rdn to ld again post* **5/1**[3]
1262 **2** *nse* **Borrowdale**[37] 4564 3-8-3 **61** .... ChrisCatlin 3 69
(J A Osborne) *led tl hdd 6f out: rdn to nose ahd 1f out: hdd post* **10/1**
64-5 **3** *1 3/4* **Keenes Day (FR)**[21] 5111 3-9-5 **77** .... JoeFanning 2 83+
(M Johnston) *mid-div: lost pl 4f out: styd on again ins fnl 2f to go 3rd nr fin* **14/1**
0316 **4** *1/2* **Swingkeel (IRE)**[28] 4866 3-9-7 **79** .... EddieAhern 7 84
(J L Dunlop) *lw: mid-div: chsd first 2 over 1f out: lost 3rd cl home* **6/1**
3031 **5** *7* **Deer Daylami (IRE)**[30] 4762 3-9-4 **76** .... TonyCulhane 9 73
(M R Channon) *prom: rdn 4f out: one pce fnl 2f* **13/2**
4441 **6** *1* **Broken Moon**[19] 5163 3-9-5 **77** .... JamieSpencer 5 73
(J R Fanshawe) *a towards rr* **4/1**[2]
1004 **7** *1 1/2* **Eventide**[23] 5017 3-8-4 **67** .... DavidProbert(5) 1 61
(W J Knight) *hld up: a behiond* **20/1**
3432 **8** *7* **Hadron Collider (FR)**[8] 5465 3-8-12 **70** .... RyanMoore 4 55
(R Hannon) *lw: hld up: rdn over 5f out: a bhd* **3/1**[1]
1125 **9** *6* **Sea Admiral**[42] 4432 3-9-2 **74** ....(b) SteveDrowne 6 52
(R Charlton) *trckd ldrs: rdn 5f out: wknd 3f out* **14/1**

3m 27.66s (-2.44) **Going Correction** -0.025s/f (Stan) 9 Ran SP% **116.5**
Speed ratings (Par 103): **105,104,104,103,100 99,99,95,92**
toteswinger: 1&2 £10.00, 1&3 £14.40, 2&3 £13.80. CSF £54.20 CT £658.90 TOTE £6.40: £2.00, £3.00, £3.10; EX 64.50.
Owner JMH Lifestyle Ltd **Bred** Gainesway Thoroughbreds Ltd **Trained** Whatcombe, Oxon
FOCUS
A decent staying handicap and it was Precision Break who got the better of Borrowdale in a ding-dong battle up the straight, with both Jimmy Fortune and Chris Catlin deserving credit for astute rides. The form looks sound.

5699 TOTESPORTGAMES.COM H'CAP 1m 3f (P)
5:30 (5:32) (Class 4) (0-85,85) 3-Y-O+ £4,727 (£1,406; £702; £351) Stalls High

Form RPR
3-10 **1** **Armure**[15] 5249 3-8-5 **79** .... DavidProbert(5) 11 89
(M A Jarvis) *lw: trckd ldrs: rdn to ld over 1f out: hld on wl* **9/2**[3]
6620 **2** *3/4* **Quince (IRE)**[27] 4894 5-9-4 **79** ....(v) AdamKirby 1 88
(J Pearce) *mid-div: rdn and styd on to chse wnr 1f out: hld towards fin* **20/1**
3116 **3** *1 1/4* **Royal Amnesty**[91] 2839 5-8-11 **72** ....(b) TonyCulhane 9 79
(Miss L A Perratt) *slowly away: hld up in rr: styd on fr 2f out to go 3rd ins fnl f* **14/1**
3221 **4** *nk* **Pediment**[59] 3841 3-8-13 **82** .... EddieAhern 7 88
(J R Fanshawe) *mid-div: hdwy whn hung rt fr over 1f out: nvr nrr* **9/4**[1]
2221 **5** *1/2* **King Supreme (IRE)**[30] 4771 3-8-9 **78** ....(b) RyanMoore 3 84
(R Hannon) *lw: in tch: chal over 1f out: nt qckn ins fnl f* **7/2**[2]
-200 **6** *1 1/2* **Horseford Hill**[15] 5249 4-9-9 **84** .... GeorgeBaker 8 87
(D R C Elsworth) *hld up in rr: styd on fnl 2f: nvr nr to chal* **8/1**
3165 **7** *1 3/4* **Aegean Prince**[35] 4645 4-9-4 **79** .... JimmyFortune 10 79
(R Hannon) *hld up: hdwy 2f out: wknd fnl f* **14/1**
-066 **8** *1/2* **Black Rain**[24] 4985 3-8-7 **76** ....(v) JoeFanning 2 75
(P J McBride) *trckd ldr: rdn and hdd over 1f out: wknd fnl f* **16/1**
0130 **9** *6* **Safari Sundowner (IRE)**[12] 5349 4-9-5 **85** .... WilliamCarson(5) 5 74
(P Winkworth) *lw: mid-div: rdn and hdwy on outside 5f out: ev ch 2f out: wknd over 1f out* **14/1**
4505 **10** *5* **Gold Prospect**[19] 5156 4-9-3 **78** .... JamieSpencer 4 58
(M L W Bell) *stdd s: a in rr* **16/1**
3246 **11** *2 1/2* **Dawn Sky**[50] 4146 4-9-9 **84** ....(b) MartinDwyer 12 60
(D R Lanigan) *led tl hdd 3f out: sn wknd* **20/1**
00 **12** *33* **Daltaban (FR)**[81] 3104 4-9-7 **82** ....(b) SteveDrowne 6 —
(Miss E C Lavelle) *mid-div: rdn over 4f out: sn dropped out: t.o* **33/1**

2m 18.83s (-3.07) **Going Correction** -0.025s/f (Stan)
WFA 3 from 4yo+ 8lb 12 Ran SP% **126.5**
Speed ratings (Par 105): **110,109,108,108,107 106,105,105,100,97 95,71**
toteswinger: 1&2 £27.00, 1&3 £10.40, 2&3 £24.80. CSF £99.54 CT £1207.37 TOTE £5.80: £1.80, £6.40, £3.00; EX 135.00 Place 6: £359.27 Place 5: £241.47 .
Owner Sarah J Leigh and Robin S Leigh **Bred** Sarah J Leigh And Robin S Leigh **Trained** Newmarket, Suffolk
FOCUS
A decent handicap and they went a good pace, but the picture changed dramatically in the closing stages as the pair that led the field past the 2f pole ultimately ended up finishing eighth and ninth. Sound form with the winner up 10lb on her maiden win here and the next four close to their marks.
T/Jkpt: £31,810.20 to a £1 stake. Pool: £112,007.92. 2.50 winning tickets. T/Plt: £449.20 to a £1 stake. Pool: £260,455.14. 423.20 winning tickets. T/Qpdt: £26.90 to a £1 stake. Pool: £17,368.05. 476.31 winning tickets. JS

4919 THIRSK (L-H)
Saturday, September 6
5700 Meeting Abandoned - Waterlogged

5473 WOLVERHAMPTON (A.W) (L-H)
Saturday, September 6
OFFICIAL GOING: Standard
Wind: Light, behind Weather: Overcast with the odd shower

5708 OPEN A HILLS ACCOUNT - 0800 44 40 40 CLAIMING STKS 7f 32y(P)
6:50 (6:50) (Class 5) 3-Y-O+ £3,238 (£963; £481; £240) Stalls High

Form RPR
0155 **1** **Le Chiffre (IRE)**[6] 5533 6-8-9 63 ....(p) MickyFenton 3 68
(John A Harris) *chsd ldrs: rdn to ld ins fnl f: r.o* **6/1**[1]
1204 **2** *1* **Doubtful Sound (USA)**[21] 5091 4-9-1 65 ....(p) KevinGhunowa(3) 4 74
(R A Harris) *sn led: rdn 1f out: hdd and unable qck ins fnl f* **12/1**
6211 **3** *1 1/4* **One More Round (USA)**[68] 3567 10-9-1 71 ....(b) TPQueally 7 68
(Ollie Pears) *hld up: hdwy 1/2-way: rdn over 1f out: styd on same pce ins fnl f* **6/1**[1]
4420 **4** *2* **Swinbrook (USA)**[36] 4586 7-9-4 73 ....(v) JamieMoriarty 8 66
(R A Fahey) *hld up: rdn 1/2-way: styd on appr fnl f: nt rch ldrs* **13/2**[2]
1R33 **5** *3 1/4* **Claret And Amber**[28] 4878 6-9-1 65 .... HayleyTurner 10 54+
(W K Goldsworthy) *hld up: nt clr run over 2f out: r.o ins fnl f: nrst fin* **9/1**
3122 **6** *hd* **No Grouse**[32] 4700 8-9-7 68 .... DavidAllan 9 58
(E J Alston) *broke wl: sn lost pl: r.o ins fnl f: nt trble ldrs* **15/2**[3]
264 **7** *hd* **Rankayo Hitam (USA)**[11] 5377 3-9-9 75 .... ShaneKelly 1 63
(P F I Cole) *prom: rdn 1/2-way: styd on same pce fnl 2f* **16/1**
1056 **8** *1/2* **Royal Storm (IRE)**[31] 4744 9-9-4 66 .... JamesMillman(3) 6 56
(B R Millman) *prom: rdn 1/2-way: wknd over 1f out* **8/1**
5-50 **9** *1 3/4* **Ochre Bay**[26] 4934 5-9-1 65 ....(p) RussellKennemore(3) 5 48
(R Hollinshead) *mid-div: nt clr run 5f out: sn rdn: nt trble ldrs* **17/2**
052 **10** *15* **Zippi Jazzman (USA)**[25] 4943 3-9-3 70 ....(v) RichardKingscote 12 11
(R M Beckett) *prom: rdn over 2f out: sn wknd* **16/1**
0000 **11** *3* **Gilded Youth**[16] 5198 4-8-5 63 .... StacyRenwick(7) 11 —
(G F Bridgwater) *s.i.s: hld up: plld hrd: rdn 1/2-way: sn wknd* **50/1**
3400 **12** *3/4* **Wahoo Sam (USA)**[8] 5478 8-8-9 62 .... TGMcLaughlin 2 —
(P D Evans) *chsd ldr tl rdn 1/2-way: wknd over 2f out: eased over 1f out* **12/1**

1m 30.63s (1.03) **Going Correction** +0.175s/f (Slow)
WFA 3 from 4yo+ 4lb 12 Ran SP% **114.4**
Speed ratings (Par 103): **101,99,98,96,91 91,91,90,88,71 68,67**
toteswinger: 1&2 £31.60, 1&3 £14.30, 2&3 £15.00. CSF £74.36 TOTE £8.50: £2.20, £4.40, £1.60; EX 84.10.The winner was subject to a friendly claim.
Owner Stan Wright Shaun Taylor **Bred** Agricola Del Parco **Trained** Eastwell, Leics
FOCUS
27mm of rain fell overnight and the course was hit by torrential rain about an hour before the first race. A competitive race of its type and one in which those held up could never land a blow in a race run at just an ordinary gallop. The winner raced just off the inside rail throughout. This is not really a race to view positively.
Ochre Bay Official explanation: jockey said gelding was denied a clear run

5709 GET A BONUS AT WILLIAMHILLCASINO.COM H'CAP 5f 216y(P)
7:20 (7:21) (Class 6) (0-65,67) 3-Y-O+ £2,388 (£705; £352) Stalls Low

Form RPR
1546 **1** **Royal Challenge**[10] 5392 7-9-5 **63** .... PatrickMathers 12 74
(I W McInnes) *dwlt: hld up: stl last and plenty to do 2f out: swtchd rt over 1f out: str run u.p to ld wl ins fnl f: edgd lft nr fin* **16/1**
5221 **2** *1 1/2* **Shakespeare's Son**[4] 5592 3-9-4 **67** 6ex........ DuranFentiman(3) 8 73
(H J Evans) *hld up: racd keenly: hdwy over 1f out: sn rdn: r.o* **11/2**[2]
006 **3** *hd* **Garstang**[9] 5433 5-9-4 **62** .... HayleyTurner 6 67
(Peter Grayson) *hld up: nt clr run ins fnl f: swtchd lft: r.o strly: nrst fin* **12/1**
5625 **4** *nk* **Morse (IRE)**[21] 5091 7-9-0 **58** ....(p) ShaneKelly 13 62
(J A Osborne) *chsd ldrs: rdn and hung rt over 1f out: ev ch ins fnl f: styd on* **16/1**
0000 **5** *1/2* **Sion Hill (IRE)**[8] 5478 7-8-9 **58** ....(p) KellyHarrison(5) 7 61
(John A Harris) *trckd ldrs: plld hrd: rdn to ld ins fnl f: sn hdd and unable qck* **50/1**
0554 **6** *3/4* **Back In The Red (IRE)**[25] 4958 4-9-3 **64** .... KevinGhunowa(3) 11 64
(R A Harris) *chsd ldrs: rdn 1/2-way: ev ch ins fnl f: styd on same pce* **16/1**
5040 **7** *nk* **Grimes Faith**[28] 4846 5-9-2 **60** ....(b) SilvestreDeSousa 5 59
(K A Ryan) *chsd ldrs: rdn over 2f out: no ex ins fnl f* **16/1**
4152 **8** *hd* **Ryedane (IRE)**[8] 5474 6-9-1 **59** ....(b) DavidAllan 9 58
(T D Easterby) *led 5f out: rdn over 1f out: hdd and no ex ins fnl f* **10/3**[1]
0010 **9** *1/2* **Cool Sands (IRE)**[2] 5629 6-9-5 **63** ....(v) TPQueally 1 60
(J G Given) *hld up: hdwy and swtchd rt over 1f out: hmpd ins fnl f: nt trble ldrs* **9/1**
4300 **10** *nse* **Danzig Fox**[16] 5198 3-8-7 **60** .... DeanHeslop(7) 2 57
(M Mullineaux) *s.i.s: sn pushed along in rr: styd on ins fnl f: nvr nrr* **22/1**
163 **11** *3/4* **Hamaasy**[40] 4476 7-9-3 **61** .... TGMcLaughlin 4 56
(R A Harris) *hld up: hdwy over 2f out: rdn over 1f out: wknd ins fnl f* **28/1**
3004 **12** *2 3/4* **All You Need (IRE)**[8] 5474 4-9-0 **58** ....(v) LPKeniry 3 44
(R Hollinshead) *led 1f: chsd ldrs: rdn over 1f out: wknd ins fnl f: fin 13th: plcd 12th* **8/1**
4021 **D** *shd* **Littledodayno (IRE)**[8] 5474 5-9-6 **64** .... NickyMackay 10 —
(M Wigham) *broke wl: chsd ldrs: rdn 1/2-way: wknd ins fnl f: fin 12th: disq & plcd last* **6/1**[3]

1m 15.39s (0.39) **Going Correction** +0.175s/f (Slow)
WFA 3 from 4yo+ 2lb 13 Ran SP% **114.8**
Speed ratings (Par 101): **104,102,101,101,100 99,99,99,98,98 97,93,97**
toteswinger: 1&2 £20.90, 1&3 £41.80, 2&3 Not won. CSF £96.01 CT £1141.04 TOTE £16.80: £3.40, £2.30, £2.20; EX 164.80.
Owner Truck Export **Bred** Capt A L Smith-Maxwell **Trained** Catwick, E Yorks
■ Stewards' Enquiry : Shane Kelly two-day ban: careless riding (Sep 20-21)
Nicky Mackay three-day ban: weighed in 2lb light (Sep 20-22)
Hayley Turner caution: careless riding
FOCUS
A competitive handicap in which the pace was sound throughout but the winning time was nearly two seconds above standard. The winner came down the centre of the track in the straight. Solid if ordinary form.

5710 ALL THE BALLS AT WILLIAMHILLBINGO.COM (S) STKS 1m 4f 50y(P)
7:50 (7:51) (Class 6) 3-5-Y-O £1,978 (£584; £292) Stalls Low

Form RPR
0000 **1** **Ruby Delta**[78] 3206 3-8-10 52 ow1........(v[1]) VinceSlattery 5 56
(A G Juckes) *hld up: rdn over 5f out: bmpd sn after: hdwy over 3f out: rdn and hung lft fr over 1f out: styd on u.p to ld ins fnl f* **33/1**
000 **2** *nk* **Well Informed**[71] 3455 3-8-4 68 .... NickyMackay 3 50
(E J O'Neill) *hld up: hdwy over 3f out: sn rdn: hung lft and ev ch ins fnl f: styd on* **8/1**
005 **3** *1 3/4* **Run Free**[19] 5157 4-8-13 52 ....(p) AshleyHamblett(5) 10 52
(N Wilson) *chsd ldrs: led over 4f out: rdn over 1f out: hdd and no ex ins fnl f* **7/1**
5640 **4** *nk* **Ask Nicely**[31] 4722 3-8-4 50 ....(b[1]) LiamJones 9 47
(W R Muir) *dwlt: plld hrd: hdwy over 10f out: rdn over 2f out: nt clr run over 1f out: hung lft and styd on ins fnl f* **11/2**[3]
0440 **5** *7* **Floodlight Fantasy**[23] 5003 5-9-9 55 ....(b) HayleyTurner 7 45
(Dr R D P Newland) *hld up: racd keenly: hdwy over 4f out: rdn and ev ch over 2f out: wknd fnl f* **9/2**[2]
5303 **6** *1 1/4* **Balais Folly (FR)**[15] 5215 3-8-6 46 .... LukeMorris(3) 11 38
(B Palling) *chsd ldrs: rdn over 3f out: wknd fnl f* **13/2**

0000 **7** *42* **Grafty Green (IRE)**[40] 4490 5-9-4 40 TGMcLaughlin 1 —
(W M Brisbourne) *hld up: rdn and hung lft over 4f out: hmpd over 3f out: sn wknd* **16/1**

8 *10* **Celtic Jazz (IRE)**[62] 3355 5-8-13 30 (p) NeilPollard 8 —
(A J McCabe) *prom: racd keenly early: rdn 8f out: hung lft and wknd over 4f out* **66/1**

1415 **9** *3/4* **Maddy**[13] 5320 3-8-6 56 (p) KevinGhunowa(3) 2 —
(G J Smith) *chsd ldrs: rdn over 3f out: sn wknd* **9/4**[1]

10 *13* **Leo's Girl (IRE)**[60] 3828 3-7-13 35 KellyHarrison(5) 6 —
(D Carroll) *led over 7f: rdn and wknd wl over 3f out* **25/1**

2m 44.79s (3.69) **Going Correction** +0.175s/f (Slow)
WFA 3 from 4yo+ 9lb **10 Ran SP% 115.4**
Speed ratings (Par 101): **94,93,92,92,87 86,58,52,51,43**
toteswinger: 1&2 Not won, 1&3 £25.50, 2&3 £8.50. CSF £271.68 TOTE £30.00: £6.70, £3.20, £2.00; EX 165.20.There was no bid for the winner. Maddy was claimed by George Baker for £6,000.
Owner A G Juckes **Bred** Mrs Jennie Loriston-Clarke **Trained** Abberley, Worcs
■ Stewards' Enquiry : Nicky Mackay one-day ban: used whip with excessive frequency (Sep 23)

FOCUS
A weak race, even for the grade and the steady pace means this bare form is dubious.
Maddy Official explanation: jockey said filly never travelled

5711 GET YOUR CHIPS AT WILLIAMHILLPOKER.COM NOVICE AUCTION STKS 1m 141y(P)
8:20 (8:20) (Class 5) 2-Y-O **£2,729** (£806; £403) **Stalls Low**

Form RPR

41 **1** **Poster (IRE)**[27] 4890 2-9-5 85 DaneO'Neill 5 94+
(L M Cumani) *chsd ldr tl led over 2f out: rdn and edgd lft over 1f out: sn clr: eased wl ins fnl f* **11/10**[1]

222 **2** *4 1/2* **Fullback (IRE)**[19] 5143 2-8-9 90 LPKeniry 4 73+
(J S Moore) *chsd ldrs: rdn over 2f out: styd on same pce appr fnl f* **15/8**[2]

01 **3** *3/4* **Orsippus (USA)**[13] 5314 2-9-1 78 EdwardCreighton 1 76
(M R Channon) *hld up: rdn over 2f out: styd on ins fnl f: nvr nrr* **7/1**[3]

4 *1* **Granny McPhee** 2-7-13 0 NicolPolli(5) 2 63
(A Bailey) *led: rdn: hung rt and hdd over 2f out: hung lft over 1f out: wknd ins fnl f* **33/1**

2115 **5** *9* **Solo Attempt**[44] 4348 2-8-13 84 Louis-PhilippeBeuzelin(5) 3 58
(M Botti) *prom: rdn over 2f out: wkng whn hung rt over 1f out* **9/1**

1m 51.7s (1.20) **Going Correction** +0.175s/f (Slow) **5 Ran SP% 107.8**
Speed ratings (Par 95): **101,97,96,95,87**
CSF £3.21 TOTE £2.20: £1.80, £1.10; EX 3.60.
Owner Scuderia Archi Romani **Bred** Sc Archi Romani **Trained** Newmarket, Suffolk

FOCUS
The highlight of the evening quality wise but a steady gallop on ground that looked on the slow side of standard resulted in a time nearly four seconds above the Racing Post standard.

NOTEBOOK
Poster(IRE) ◆ was always well placed in a muddling event but pulled away from his rivals in a matter of strides to win with more in hand than the official margin suggested over this longer trip on his AW debut. His rider stated he is a laid back type with a good attitude and this progressive sort appeals as the type to hold his own in stronger company. (tchd Evens and 11-8)
Fullback(IRE), who had shown steadily progressive form on his three previous starts, failed to settle in a messy race but was not disgraced against an improving rival. He is starting to look exposed but will be suited by a more strongly run race and remains capable of picking up an ordinary maiden. (op 9-4)
Orsippus(USA), a soft-ground maiden winner over 1m, was not disgraced after being set plenty to do in a muddling race back on Polytrack. A stiffer test of stamina should suit and he is worth another chance on this surface. (op 6-1 tchd 4-1)
Granny McPhee showed ability on her racecourse debut but may be flattered by her proximity given the way things panned out. However she will be of more interest in uncompetitive maiden company.
Solo Attempt failed to settle in a race that was not really run to suit and proved a disappointment returned to Polytrack and upped in trip. A more strongly run race over shorter may suit better but she has something to prove judging by the way she dropped out of contention. (op 8-1 tchd 10-1)

5712 REAL TIME RADIO AT WILLIAMHILL.CO.UK H'CAP 1m 141y(P)
8:50 (8:50) (Class 6) (0-60,64) 3-Y-O+ **£2,388** (£705; £352) **Stalls Low**

Form RPR

0062 **1** **Strike Force**[10] 5407 4-9-3 59 JackMitchell(3) 9 69+
(K F Clutterbuck) *hld up: hdwy on outside over 1f out: edgd lft and r.o to ld towards fin* **4/1**[2]

2611 **2** *3/4* **Rowan Lodge (IRE)**[28] 4878 6-9-4 57 (b) JamieMoriarty 10 65
(Ollie Pears) *hld up: racd keenly: hdwy over 3f out: rdn to ld and hung lft ins fnl f: hdd and unable qck towards fin* **13/2**[3]

5060 **3** *hd* **Convivial Spirit**[47] 4261 4-9-7 60 (t) LPKeniry 6 67
(E F Vaughan) *hld up: swtchd lft and hdwy over 1f out: r.o u.p* **14/1**

2311 **4** *nk* **South Wales**[8] 5458 3-9-2 64 LukeMorris(3) 7 71
(R W Price) *s.i.s: sn pushed along in rr: hdwy over 2f out: rdn and hung lft fr over 1f out: styd on* **7/2**[1]

0340 **5** *2 3/4* **Spume (IRE)**[8] 5478 4-9-6 59 (t) TonyCulhane 12 60
(S Parr) *hld up: hdwy over 5f out: rdn to ld and hung lft 1f out: sn hdd and no ex* **16/1**

0-00 **6** *1 1/4* **Corrib (IRE)**[22] 5059 5-9-6 59 CatherineGannon 2 57
(B Palling) *prom: chsd ldr 6f out: rdn and nt clr run over 1f out: styd on same pce* **25/1**

0005 **7** *1/2* **Komreyev Star**[55] 4001 6-9-5 58 HayleyTurner 5 55+
(R E Peacock) *hld up: nt clr run 2f out: r.o ins fnl f: nvr nrr* **25/1**

00/3 **8** *1 1/4* **Uncle Bulgaria (IRE)**[90] 2866 6-9-2 55 AdamKirby 3 49
(G C Bravery) *prom: rdn over 3f out: wknd fnl f* **16/1**

0064 **9** *3/4* **Joshua's Gold (IRE)**[25] 4949 7-9-4 57 (v) DavidAllan 11 49
(D Carroll) *plld hrd and prom: rdn over 3f out: wknd fnl f* **9/1**

5531 **10** *nk* **Bramalea**[11] 5378 3-9-4 63 JamesDoyle 8 54
(B W Duke) *sn led: rdn over 2f out: hdd & wknd 1f out* **13/2**[3]

0034 **11** *3 1/4* **Motu (IRE)**[60] 3826 7-9-7 60 (v) PatrickMathers 4 44
(I W McInnes) *hld up in tch: racd keenly: nt clr run over 2f out: sn rdn: wknd fnl f* **14/1**

-100 **12** *4* **Tri Chara (IRE)**[16] 5198 4-9-4 60 (p) RussellKennemore(3) 1 35
(R Hollinshead) *chsd ldrs: rdn over 3f out: wknd over 1f out* **11/1**

1m 52.1s (1.60) **Going Correction** +0.175s/f (Slow)
WFA 3 from 4yo+ 6lb **12 Ran SP% 120.0**
Speed ratings (Par 101): **99,98,98,97,95 94,93,92,92,91 88,85**
toteswinger: 1&2 £12.80, 1&3 £5.00, 2&3 £14.60. CSF £30.76 CT £331.62 TOTE £5.70: £1.80, £3.00, £5.60; EX 47.70.
Owner Miss A L Hutchinson **Bred** Cheveley Park Stud Ltd **Trained** Exning, Suffolk

FOCUS
Three previous winners in a run-of-the-mill handicap. The early pace was only fair and the winner was another to race in the centre of the track in the straight. The winner confirmed his recent return to form and the form overall is sound.

5713 BET ONLINE AT WILLIAMHILL.CO.UK H'CAP 7f 32y(P)
9:20 (9:20) (Class 5) (0-75,75) 3-Y-O **£3,885** (£1,156; £577; £288) **Stalls High**

Form RPR

0-03 **1** **Spate River**[22] 5049 3-9-1 72 GeorgeBaker 3 79+
(C F Wall) *a.p: chsd ldr 4f out: rdn over 1f out: r.o to ld nr fin* **6/1**[2]

0432 **2** *nk* **King's Wonder**[19] 5140 3-9-3 74 RichardMullen 5 80
(W R Muir) *sn led: rdn over 1f out: edgd rt ins fnl f: hdd nr fin* **8/1**

5005 **3** *1/2* **Rockfield Tiger (IRE)**[42] 4429 3-9-2 73 ShaneKelly 12 78
(J A Osborne) *hld up: hdwy over 2f out: rdn over 1f out: r.o* **25/1**

5232 **4** *1/2* **Dan Chillingworth (IRE)**[12] 5346 3-9-1 72 AdamKirby 8 75
(J R Fanshawe) *hld up in tch: outpcd over 2f out: rallied and hung lft fnl f: r.o* **10/3**[1]

0630 **5** *hd* **King Kenny**[25] 4951 3-9-4 75 TonyCulhane 4 78
(S Parr) *hld up: hdwy u.p over 1f out: r.o* **8/1**

3333 **6** *shd* **Montiboli (IRE)**[26] 4920 3-9-1 72 SilvestreDeSousa 1 74
(K A Ryan) *chsd ldrs: rdn over 2f out: styd on* **7/1**[3]

2-00 **7** *1* **Regal Bird (USA)**[77] 3270 3-9-1 72 TPQueally 2 72
(M A Magnusson) *hld up in tch: rdn over 2f out: styd on* **16/1**

0601 **8** *nk* **Kinnego Bay (IRE)**[30] 4777 3-8-13 70 ChrisCatlin 9 69
(B W Hills) *prom: rdn over 2f out: styd on same pce* **8/1**

5044 **9** *1/2* **Savannah Poppy (IRE)**[13] 5317 3-9-2 73 HayleyTurner 10 71
(M L W Bell) *hld up: stl last and plenty to do turning for home: nvr nrr* **9/1**

410 **10** *1* **Candela Bay (IRE)**[42] 4408 3-9-4 75 LiamJones 11 70
(W J Haggas) *hld up: rdn 1/2-way: lost pl over 2f out: bhd whn hung lft over 1f out* **12/1**

0664 **11** *shd* **Vigano (IRE)**[12] 5346 3-9-1 72 RichardKingscote 7 67
(S Kirk) *chsd ldrs: rdn 1/2-way: wknd fnl f* **11/1**

1m 30.36s (0.76) **Going Correction** +0.175s/f (Slow) **11 Ran SP% 119.0**
Speed ratings (Par 101): **102,101,101,100,100 100,99,98,98,96 96**
toteswinger: 1&2 £41.60, 1&3 £41.60, 2&3 £19.80. CSF £54.09 CT £1149.68 TOTE £5.70: £2.40, £3.10, £8.50; EX 73.60 Place 6 £505.37, Place 5 £205.73.
Owner Firman Webster Racing **Bred** Firman And Webster Bloodstock **Trained** Newmarket, Suffolk

FOCUS
An ordinary handicap in which the pace was soon fair but a race in which winner and second (who both raced towards the centre in the straight) filled the first two positions throughout. The runner-up is the best guide to the form and the winner is unexposed.
T/Plt: £1,005.70 to a £1 stake. Pool: £138,191.98. 100.30 winning tickets. T/Qpdt: £75.10 to a £1 stake. Pool: £8,294.66. 81.71 winning tickets. CR

4919 THIRSK (L-H)
Sunday, September 7

OFFICIAL GOING: Soft (heavy in places)
Wind: Moderate, half-behind Weather: fine

5714 TURFTV H'CAP 6f
2:00 (2:00) (Class 5) (0-75,75) 3-Y-O **£4,274** (£1,271; £635; £317) **Stalls High**

Form RPR

6000 **1** **The Twelve Steps**[15] 5258 3-8-10 67 (t) PJMcDonald 10 79
(G A Swinbank) *dwlt: sn trcking ldrs: led over 1f out: hung lft and sn drew clr* **7/1**

3112 **2** *3 1/2* **Mandalay King (IRE)**[34] 4684 3-8-4 66 KellyHarrison(5) 11 67+
(Mrs Marjorie Fife) *trckd ldrs: effrt and wnt 2nd 1f out: no ch w wnr* **5/2**[1]

3314 **3** *2* **Whiteoak Lady (IRE)**[25] 4988 3-9-1 72 LiamJones 5 66
(J L Spearing) *led: edgd rt and hdd over 1f out: kpt on same pce* **5/1**[3]

6235 **4** *1/2* **Capone (IRE)**[32] 4745 3-8-13 70 DaleGibson 3 63
(Garry Moss) *dwlt: in rr: hdwy 2f out: kpt on: nt rch ldrs* **14/1**

1050 **5** *6* **Everything**[13] 5358 3-8-8 65 (p) MickyFenton 12 39
(P T Midgley) *dwlt: sn w ldrs: edgd lft and wknd appr fnl f* **16/1**

000 **6** *hd* **Distant Rock**[26] 4952 3-8-1 61 oh3 (t) DuranFentiman(3) 9 34
(D Carroll) *mid-div: sn drvn along: nvr a threat* **66/1**

4612 **7** *1* **Andrasta**[10] 5417 3-8-4 61 oh2 FrancisNorton 2 31
(A Berry) *chsd ldrs: wknd over 1f out* **9/1**

006- **8** *6* **Dark Tara**[317] 6462 3-8-11 68 JamieMoriarty 6 19
(R A Fahey) *dwlt: in rr and sn drvn along: bhd fnl 2f* **16/1**

6205 **9** *1 1/2* **La Chicaluna**[23] 5052 3-9-4 75 PaulHanagan 8 21
(J G Given) *w ldrs: lost pl 2f out* **7/2**[2]

3250 **10** *1 3/4* **Peter's Storm (USA)**[36] 4615 3-8-10 67 PaulMulrennan 4 7
(K A Ryan) *chsd ldrs on outer: hung lft and lost pl 2f out* **16/1**

1m 16.09s (3.39) **Going Correction** +0.575s/f (Yiel) **10 Ran SP% 115.8**
Speed ratings (Par 101): **100,95,92,92,84 83,82,74,72,70**
toteswinger: 1&2 £3.20, 1&3 £7.70, 2&3 £4.10. CSF £24.62 CT £99.03 TOTE £8.40: £2.00, £1.30, £2.20; EX 25.90.
Owner D N Green **Bred** Wickfield Farm Partnership **Trained** Melsonby, N Yorks

FOCUS
A modest sprint handicap but the early leaders appeared to go too fast on what was the softest part of the track and left the way clear for those settled off the pace. The form is rated around the first two.

5715 JOHN BOTTERILL (S) STKS 6f
2:30 (2:32) (Class 5) 2-Y-O **£4,274** (£1,271; £635; £317) **Stalls High**

Form RPR

5202 **1** **Nchike**[13] 5357 2-8-11 56 (v) SilvestreDeSousa 18 67+
(D Nicholls) *mde all: styd on strly fnl f* **7/2**[2]

5 **2** *2* **Glan Lady (IRE)**[13] 5364 2-8-6 0 LiamJones 13 56
(J L Spearing) *chsd wnr: kpt on same pce fnl f* **15/8**[1]

05 **3** *4* **Jessica Mary (IRE)**[62] 3792 2-8-1 0 KellyHarrison(5) 17 44
(D Carroll) *mid-div: hdwy 2f out: styd on fnl f* **9/2**[3]

0003 **4** *3/4* **Future Gem**[7] 5541 2-8-6 30 PaulHanagan 19 42
(A Dickman) *chsd ldrs: kpt on same pce fnl 2f* **20/1**

1000 **5** *5* **Time Loup**[5] 5591 2-8-12 59 DavidProbert(5) 5 38
(S R Bowring) *swtchd lft after s and racd alone far side: w ldrs: rdn over 2f out: wknd over 1f out* **16/1**

50 **6** *1* **Danderdandan**[14] 5304 2-8-11 0 JamieMoriarty 11 29
(P T Midgley) *in rr: kpt on fnl 2f: nvr a factor* **66/1**

6055 **7** *shd* **Samba Queen (IRE)**[25] 4986 2-8-6 45 FrancisNorton 15 23
(J L Spearing) *chsd ldrs: wknd over 2f out* **25/1**

5050 **8** *hd* **Kneesy Earsy Nosey**[24] 5006 2-8-12 48 (v[1]) KimTinkler 14 29
(N Tinkler) *wnt rt s: towards rr: nvr on terms* **25/1**

344 **9** ½ **Forever's Girl**[28] 4897 2-8-7 0 ow1 PJMcDonald 7 22
(G R Oldroyd) *chsd ldrs: wknd 2f out* **20/1**

2000 **10** ¾ **Dancing Wave**[23] 5066 2-7-13 50 AndreaAtzeni(7) 6 19
(M C Chapman) *chsd ldrs: wknd 2f out* **20/1**

00 **11** *nse* **Ishiquick**[64] 3707 2-8-7 0 ow1 (b[1]) DavidAllan 8 20
(T D Easterby) *sn outpcd and in rr* **50/1**

040 **12** *nk* **Miss Xu Xia**[8] 5499 2-8-3 43 DuranFentiman(3) 2 18
(G R Oldroyd) *s.i.s: sn mid-div: wknd over 2f out* **50/1**

4640 **13** *15* **Tito Gobbi**[46] 4292 2-8-11 49 PaulMulrennan 1 —
(Mrs Marjorie Fife) *swtchd rt after s: tk fierce grip: effrt over 2f out: sn wknd: bhd whn eased fnl f* **11/1**

00 **14** *45* **Staceys Girl**[15] 5256 2-8-7 0 ow1 TonyCulhane 12 —
(T P Tate) *sn bhd: t.o fnl 3f* **33/1**

1m 16.79s (4.09) **Going Correction** +0.575s/f (Yiel) 14 Ran SP% **119.7**
Speed ratings (Par 95): **95,92,87,86,79 78,77,77,76,75 75,75,55,—**
toteswinger: 1&2 £2.60, 1&3 £4.30, 2&3 £3.50. CSF £8.93 TOTE £4.00: £1.80, £1.40, £2.20; EX 12.30.The winner was bought in for 8,000gns.

Owner Middleham Park Racing XXXVII **Bred** J And Mrs S Cleeve **Trained** Sessay, N Yorks

■ Stewards' Enquiry : David Allan one-day ban: used whip when out of contention & filly showing no response (Sep 21)

FOCUS
A big field for this juvenile seller and the time was 0.7 secs slower than the preceding three-year-old handicap. Despite the number of runners the market suggested this was a three-horse race and those three filled the placings. They were drawn 18, 13 and 17 respectively and backed up the impression from the first race that near the rail was the place to be.

NOTEBOOK
Nchike, who is best at this trip, made virtually all from his high draw and drew away nicely in the last furlong. A straight, flattish track suits and connections obviously feel he has more to offer as they retained him at the subsequent auction. (op 4-1 tchd 10-3)

Glan Lady(IRE) was made favourite following her debut effort when she did not appear to handle the home turn very well but stayed on quite nicely. She was dropping in grade and, although she ran her race and handled conditions, the winner proved too strong. She should be capable of winning a race at this level. (op 2-1 tchd 9-4 & 85-40 in a place)

Jessica Mary(IRE), another who was dropping in grade, came in for market support but, after tracking the leaders, appeared to hit a flat spot at around halfway before keeping on again in the closing stages. (op 6-1 tchd 4-1)

Future Gem, whose best effort came when dropped to a seller last time, had the lowest mark of those with official ratings and showed up until tiring in the last furlong and a half. (op 16-1)

Time Loup, the only previous winner in the field and the highest rated, was the only one to switch across to the far rail and did not do too badly in the circumstances. (op 14-1)

Tito Gobbi was the subject of late market support but never figured and finished well behind. (op 18-1)

5716 E B F DR SUSAN HARRIS'S RETIREMENT MAIDEN STKS 1m
3:00 (3:03) (Class 4) 2-Y-0 **£5,666** (£1,686; £842; £420) **Stalls** Low

Form RPR

5 **1** **Guestofthenation (USA)**[11] 5404 2-9-3 0 JoeFanning 8 79+
(M Johnston) *chsd ldrs: led over 2f out: hung lft: clr 1f out: eased towards fin* **5/2**[2]

2 3½ **Peaceful Rule (USA)** 2-9-3 0 SilvestreDeSousa 11 69
(D Nicholls) *s.i.s: in rr: hdwy over 2f out: styd on to take 2nd towards fin* **9/1**[3]

062 **3** *1* **Huxaar**[14] 5304 2-9-3 73 CatherineGannon 7 67
(Mrs L Stubbs) *t.k.h: led tl 5f out: led 3f out: sn hdd: wknd towards fin* **15/8**[1]

0 **4** *1* **Lomica**[15] 5256 2-8-12 0 TonyHamilton 5 60+
(Miss J A Camacho) *chsd ldrs: drvn over 4f out: one pce fnl 3f* **9/1**[3]

0046 **5** *2* **Kingaroo (IRE)**[14] 5304 2-9-3 50 DaleGibson 6 60
(Garry Moss) *chsd ldrs: one pce fnl 2f* **40/1**

6 *8* **Dreamonandon (IRE)** 2-9-3 0 PJMcDonald 10 43
(G A Swinbank) *s.i.s: kpt on fnl 2f: nvr on terms* **12/1**

0 **7** *2* **Nayessence**[44] 4394 2-9-3 0 PaulMulrennan 2 38
(M W Easterby) *chsd ldrs: wknd over 2f out* **80/1**

8 2½ **Saffron's Son (IRE)** 2-9-3 0 MickyFenton 13 33
(P T Midgley) *mid-div: lost pl over 4f out: bhd whn swtchd rt over 1f out* **33/1**

0 **9** 1¼ **Addison De Witt**[25] 4960 2-9-3 0 PaulHanagan 1 30
(Micky Hammond) *s.i.s: lost pl over 4f out: sn bhd* **50/1**

0 **10** *15* **Accumulation (UAE)**[28] 4897 2-8-9 0 DuranFentiman(3) 12 —
(M W Easterby) *sn drvn along and in rr: bhd fnl 2f* **66/1**

00 **11** *2* **Thatwasthepension (IRE)**[11] 5387 2-9-3 0 AndrewElliott 4 —
(B Storey) *trckd ldrs: led 5f out tl 3f out: sn wknd and bhd* **150/1**

1m 46.12s (6.02) **Going Correction** +0.50s/f (Yiel) 11 Ran SP% **101.8**
Speed ratings (Par 97): **89,85,84,83,81 73,71,69,67,52 50**
toteswinger: 1&2 £4.90, 1&3 £1.40, 2&3 £4.10. CSF £18.26 TOTE £3.00: £1.40, £2.50, £1.40; EX 25.50.

Owner Claire Riordan And Kieran Coughlan **Bred** Tracy Farmer **Trained** Middleham Moor, N Yorks

■ Distant Memories was withdrawn (13/2, unruly in stalls). Deduct 10p in the £ under Rule 4.

■ Stewards' Enquiry : Catherine Gannon caution: used whip down shoulder in forehand position

FOCUS
A mile maiden that looked a stiff test for these juveniles in the conditions and very few got involved. It was run in a very moderate time for the type of contest.

NOTEBOOK
Guestofthenation(USA), a scopey son of Gulch, made 85,000euros at the breeze-ups and is related to several winners in France. He had obviously come on for his promising debut over this trip on Polytrack and, having no problem with the ground, always had matters in hand once striking the front. There should be more to come from him in nurseries. (op 11-4 tchd 10-3)

Peaceful Rule(USA), a 50,000gns half-brother to winners on dirt and turf in USA, has a Derby entry but there are sprinters on the dam's side of his pedigree. He missed the break on this debut before staying on in pleasing fashion in the straight. He should come on a fair amount for the experience. (op 8-1)

Huxaar had the best previous form in the race and, proven on the ground, was sent off market leader. Always up with the pace, he had every chance in the straight but proved no match for the winner and lost out on the runner-up spot near the finish. (op 6-4 tchd 2-1)

Lomica, who made some late headway on debut over slightly shorter on soft, showed the benefit of that by running her race and keeping on all the way to the line. She could win a maiden against her own sex but will probably make her mark in handicaps after another outing. (op 14-1 tchd 8-1)

Kingaroo(IRE) finished closer to Huxaar than at Beverley without ever looking the likely winner. (tchd 33-1)

Dreamonandon(IRE) lost his chance at the start when slowly away. (op 9-1 tchd 14-1)

Thatwasthepension(IRE) made the early running but was there on sufferance and, once the market principals swept past at around the three-furlong pole, his race was over. (tchd 100-1)

5717 CALVERTS CARPETS STKS (H'CAP) 7f
3:30 (3:30) (Class 4) (0-85,87) 3-Y-O+ **£5,569** (£1,657; £828; £413) **Stalls** Low

Form RPR

6003 **1** **Kings Point (IRE)**[9] 5446 7-9-10 87 JoeFanning 8 97
(D Nicholls) *trckd ldrs: led over 2f out: rdn out* **13/2**

2044 **2** 1½ **Hiccups**[67] 3599 8-9-0 77 DanielTudhope 6 83
(M Dods) *hld up towards rr: effrt over 3f out: styd on to go 2nd 1f out: no real imp* **9/2**[2]

5145 **3** ¾ **Ezdeyaad (USA)**[43] 4417 4-8-13 76 PaulMulrennan 3 80
(G A Swinbank) *trckd ldr: led 3f out: sn hdd: styd on same pce* **8/1**

2444 **4** *hd* **Violent Velocity (IRE)**[29] 4876 5-8-8 78 JamieKyne(7) 4 81
(J J Quinn) *chsd ldrs: outpcd over 3f out: styd on same pce fnl 2f* **5/2**[1]

0025 **5** 3½ **White Deer (USA)**[16] 5221 4-9-3 80 SilvestreDeSousa 1 74
(D Nicholls) *trckd ldrs: swtchd rt over 1f out: one pce* **11/1**

3000 **6** 3¼ **Xpres Maite**[10] 5424 5-8-12 78 (v) MichaelJStainton(3) 5 63
(S R Bowring) *s.i.s: styd on fnl 2f: nvr nr ldrs* **20/1**

00-0 **7** *7* **Roman Maze**[35] 4661 8-9-6 83 DavidAllan 7 49
(W M Brisbourne) *in rr: hung lft and bhd fnl 2f* **16/1**

14- **8** 4½ **Salingers Star (IRE)**[379] 4819 3-8-9 76 PJMcDonald 10 28
(G A Swinbank) *trckd ldrs: t.k.h: lost pl over 3f out* **16/1**

1312 **9** 1¼ **Horatio Carter**[26] 4951 3-8-13 80 (p) PaulHanagan 2 28
(K A Ryan) *led tl 3f out: wknd and eased over 1f out* **5/1**[3]

1m 29.83s (2.63) **Going Correction** +0.50s/f (Yiel)
WFA 3 from 4yo+ 4lb 9 Ran SP% **112.7**
Speed ratings (Par 105): **104,102,101,101,97 93,85,80,78**
toteswinger: 1&2 £5.60, 1&3 £8.50, 2&3 £9.10. CSF £34.83 CT £237.50 TOTE £7.80: £1.80, £1.90, £2.50; EX 38.20.

Owner WRB 61 (The Claire King Syndicate) **Bred** John Costello **Trained** Sessay, N Yorks

FOCUS
A decent handicap and fairly competitive with only 11lb between the field on official ratings. However, they went a decent pace in the conditions and not many got into it. The form looks solid.
Horatio Carter Official explanation: jockey said gelding was unsuited by the soft (heavy in places) ground

5718 BLACK SWAN HELMSLEY H'CAP 2m
4:00 (4:01) (Class 4) (0-85,83) 4-Y-O+ **£5,569** (£1,657; £828; £413) **Stalls** Low

Form RPR

2313 **1** **Bollin Felix**[29] 4866 4-9-9 83 (b) DavidAllan 7 97
(T D Easterby) *mid-div: sn pushed along: gd hdwy 6f out: led over 2f out: drvn clr: eased towards fin* **7/4**[1]

0424 **2** *5* **Sphinx (FR)**[25] 4963 10-9-4 78 PaulMulrennan 2 86
(E W Tuer) *hld up in tch: effrt over 4f out: chal over 2f out: kpt on same pce* **14/1**

-633 **3** *6* **Mith Hill**[39] 4516 7-8-13 73 StephenDonohoe 8 74
(Ian Williams) *chsd ldrs: one pce fnl 2f* **12/1**

0040 **4** *14* **Kasthari (IRE)**[10] 5423 9-9-9 83 (p) GrahamGibbons 9 67
(J D Bethell) *s.i.s: sn chsng ldrs: led over 8f out: hdd over 2f out: wknd over 1f out* **20/1**

4646 **5** *7* **Numero Due**[43] 4439 6-9-7 81 JoeFanning 3 57
(G M Moore) *drvn 5f out: lost pl over 3f out* **12/1**

2104 **6** *6* **Squirtle (IRE)**[8] 5498 5-8-7 67 LiamJones 1 35
(W M Brisbourne) *s.i.s: drvn 9f out: lost pl 5f out: sn bhd* **8/1**

4602 **7** *10* **Dr Sharp (IRE)**[8] 5498 8-9-1 75 MickyFenton 10 31
(T P Tate) *led: hdd over 8f out: lost pl over 2f out: bhd and eased over 1f out* **6/1**[3]

610 **8** *8* **Winged D'Argent (IRE)**[57] 3942 7-9-9 83 (b) FrancisNorton 5 30
(B J Llewellyn) *sn drvn along in rr: lost pl 7f out: bhd fnl 5f* **5/1**[2]

1/50 **9** *5* **Toldo (IRE)**[58] 3929 6-9-6 80 DanielTudhope 6 21
(G M Moore) *hld up in rr on outer: sme hdwy 7f out: lost pl 5f out: sn bhd* **9/1**

2325 **10** *29* **Hollins**[23] 5042 4-8-13 73 PaulHanagan 4 —
(Micky Hammond) *chsd ldrs: lost pl over 7f out: sn bhd: virtually p.u: t.o* **50/1**

3m 39.04s (5.64) **Going Correction** +0.50s/f (Yiel) 10 Ran SP% **117.2**
Speed ratings (Par 105): **105,102,99,92,89 86,81,77,74,60**
toteswinger: 1&2 £8.30, 1&3 £7.60, 2&3 £17.00. CSF £29.79 CT £233.89 TOTE £2.60: £1.30, £4.00, £2.70; EX 36.40.

Owner Sir Neil Westbrook **Bred** Sir Neil & Exors Of Late Lady Westbrook **Trained** Great Habton, N Yorks

FOCUS
A fair staying handicap in which they went a good gallop from the start despite the soft ground. The winner is rated up another 5lb.
Hollins Official explanation: jockey said gelding was unsuited by the soft (heavy in places) ground

5719 COURSE ELECTRICIAN'S APPRENTICE STKS (H'CAP) 5f
4:30 (4:30) (Class 5) (0-75,72) 3-Y-O+ **£4,274** (£1,271; £635; £317) **Stalls** High

Form RPR

6050 **1** **Lake Chini (IRE)**[11] 5392 6-8-5 60 (b) LanceBetts(3) 6 72
(M W Easterby) *chsd ldrs on outer: styd on to ld jst ins fnl f: edgd rt and kpt on* **11/1**

6310 **2** 1¾ **Baybshambles (IRE)**[49] 4218 4-8-11 68 BMcHugh(5) 4 74
(R E Barr) *mid-div: hdwy 2f out: styd on same pce fnl f* **13/2**

0000 **3** *nk* **King Of Swords (IRE)**[32] 4743 4-8-10 67 AndreaAtzeni(5) 9 72
(N Tinkler) *chsd ldrs on inner: led appr fnl f: hdd and no ex last 150yds* **20/1**

6035 **4** 1¼ **Blazing Heights**[11] 5392 5-9-3 69 GaryBartley 5 69+
(J S Goldie) *hld up off the pce: effrt: n.m.r and swtchd lft 1f out: styd on: nt rch ldrs* **3/1**[1]

2325 **5** *1* **Fire Up The Band**[23] 5044 9-8-12 64 SladeO'Hara 8 61
(A Berry) *led tl appr fnl f: fdd* **5/1**[2]

0650 **6** *nk* **Windjammer**[11] 5398 4-8-9 61 (b) KellyHarrison 7 57
(T D Easterby) *trckd ldrs: nt clr run over 1f out: kpt on same pce ins fnl f* **13/2**

0010 **7** *nk* **Inspainagain (USA)**[43] 4418 4-9-6 72 DavidProbert 1 67
(T D Barron) *swtchd rt after s: sn outpcd and detached in last: hdwy over 1f out: nvr trbld ldrs* **13/2**

2303 **8** 3¼ **The Bear**[43] 4418 5-9-5 71 PatrickDonaghy 2 54
(R Johnson) *chsd ldrs: lost pl over 1f out* **6/1**[3]

1400 **9** 2¾ **The History Man (IRE)**[25] 4981 5-8-9 66 (be) GarryWhillans(5) 3 39
(M Mullineaux) *chsd ldrs on wd outside: lost pl over 1f out* **12/1**

62.10 secs (2.50) **Going Correction** +0.575s/f (Yiel) 9 Ran SP% **116.7**
Speed ratings (Par 103): **103,100,99,97,96 95,95,89,85**
toteswinger: 1&2 £12.90, 1&3 £20.40, 2&3 £24.10. CSF £81.26 CT £1429.78 TOTE £13.30: £3.40, £2.70, £5.50; EX 101.90 Place 6 £72.55, Place 5 £49.35.

Owner Mrs Jean Turpin **Bred** Paul McEnery **Trained** Sheriff Hutton, N Yorks
■ Stewards' Enquiry : Lance Betts two-day ban: careless riding (Sep 21,25)

FOCUS
A modest apprentices' sprint handicap. The form is rated around the runner-up but the third lends doubts.
Lake Chini(IRE) Official explanation: trainer's rep had no explanation for the apparent improvement in form
T/Plt: £76.40 to a £1 stake. Pool: £75,692.15. 723.03 winning tickets. T/Qpdt: £38.30 to a £1 stake. Pool: £4,668.54. 90.00 winning tickets. WG

5720 - 5728a (Foreign Racing) - See Raceform Interactive

5129
LEOPARDSTOWN (L-H)
Sunday, September 7

OFFICIAL GOING: Yielding (yielding to soft in places)
The meeting was put back 24 hours after the track was waterlogged on the Saturday. The ground was certainly riding better than was anticipated.

5729a AT THE RACES KILTERNAN STKS (GROUP 3) 1m 2f
2:10 (2:10) 3-Y-O+ **£47,794** (£13,970; £6,617; £2,205)

RPR
1 **The Bogberry (USA)**[78] 3287 3-9-1 104 CO'Donoghue 4 111
(A P O'Brien, Ire) *hld up in rr: hdwy on outer early st: rdn to ld under 1f out: kpt on wl* **9/1**[3]
2 ½ **Famous Name**[98] 2654 3-9-4 120 PJSmullen 5 113
(D K Weld, Ire) *hld up in 6th: impr into 4th travelling wl ent st: sn chal: led narrowly over 1f out: hdd under 1f out: kpt on* **2/5**[1]
3 ¾ **Mr Medici (IRE)**[8] 5517 3-9-1 104 DPMcDonogh 7 108
(Kevin Prendergast, Ire) *trckd ldrs in 4th: 3rd and chal st: led over 1 1/2f out: hdd over 1f out: kpt on u.p* **9/1**[3]
4 nk **Arch Rebel (USA)**[21] 5136 7-9-8 108 (p) FMBerry 3 107
(Noel Meade, Ire) *s.i.s: sn in tch: 5th 1/2-way: cl 6th appr st: 4th whn nt clr run over 1f out: swtchd to outer: kpt on* **12/1**
5 4 **Prima Luce (IRE)**[21] 5136 3-9-1 107 KJManning 6 99
(J S Bolger, Ire) *broke wl: settled 2nd: cl up travelling wl 3f out: rdn appr st: no ex fr 1 1/2f out* **8/1**[2]
6 nk **Superius (IRE)**[62] 3805 3-9-1 98 WJLee 1 99
(T Stack, Ire) *settled 3rd: dropped to 5th appr st: sn no ex* **25/1**
7 1 ¾ **Sail (IRE)**[21] 5136 3-8-12 104 JAHeffernan 8 92
(A P O'Brien, Ire) *sn led: edgd clr appr 1/2-way: drvn along and strly pressed 3f out: hdd & wknd early st* **16/1**

2m 8.60s (0.40) **Going Correction** +0.25s/f (Good)
WFA 3 from 7yo 7lb 7 Ran SP% **120.0**
Speed ratings: **108,107,107,106,103 103,101**
CSF £13.99 TOTE £10.60: £3.70, £1.10; DF 15.70.
Owner Mrs E M Stockwell **Bred** March Thoroughbreds **Trained** Ballydoyle, Co Tipperary

FOCUS
The winner ran a personal best but the third limits the form.

NOTEBOOK
The Bogberry(USA) evidently relished the easy surface and posted a career-best effort to score. He has not been that easy to predict, but does not have many miles on the clock and could still have more to offer this term. (op 7/1)
Famous Name, just denied in the Prix du Jockey Club on his previous start, performed well below that level yet still ran right up to the form of his course-and-distance win at the start of the season. He looked the one beat turning in, but got tired inside the final furlong and probably needed the run. He is better than this, but does still have a little to prove now. (op 1/2)
Mr Medici(IRE) ran right up to his best in defeat, but he has been exposed in Listed company this term and so his proximity limits the form. (op 12/1)

5730a COOLMORE FUSAICHI PEGASUS MATRON STKS (GROUP 1) (F&M) 1m
2:40 (2:45) 3-Y-O+ **£119,485** (£34,926; £16,544; £5,514)

RPR
1 **Lush Lashes**[16] 5243 3-8-12 119 KJManning 2 116
(J S Bolger, Ire) *sellted 2nd: chal ent st: led 2f out: strly pressed ins fnl f: styd on wl u.p* **9/4**[1]
2 nk **Nahoodh (IRE)**[35] 4674 3-8-12 MJKinane 4 115
(M Johnston) *trckd ldrs in 6th: 5th and prog early st: 3rd on inner under 1f out: sn chal: ev ch cl home: jst failed* **6/1**
3 ½ **Halfway To Heaven (IRE)**[36] 4623 3-8-12 113 JAHeffernan 11 114
(A P O'Brien, Ire) *trckd ldrs in 3rd: rdn early st: cl 2nd and chal wl ins fnl f: no ex cl home* **4/1**[3]
4 ½ **You'resothrilling (USA)**[381] 4744 3-8-12 106 WMLordan 5 113
(A P O'Brien, Ire) *hld up: towards rr early st: 7th and hdwy over 1f out: styd on cl home* **20/1**
5 1 **Listen (IRE)**[344] 5796 3-8-12 117 CO'Donoghue 7 110+
(A P O'Brien, Ire) *hld up towards rr: 6th and hdwy on outer early st: 4th over 1f out: kpt on same pce* **8/1**
6 ½ **Psalm (IRE)**[10] 5441 3-8-12 106 SMLevey 8 109
(A P O'Brien, Ire) *s.i.s and hld up towards rr: kpt on wout threatening fr over 1f out* **16/1**
7 ½ **Lady Gloria**[60] 3852 4-9-3 TedDurcan 3 109
(J G Given) *sn led: strly pressed st: hdd 2f out: no ex u.p fnl f* **25/1**
8 nk **Carribean Sunset (IRE)**[21] 5134 3-8-12 113 PJSmullen 12 107
(D K Weld, Ire) *broke wl and restrained: 5th early: 4th 1/2-way: tk clsr oder appr st: rdn and no imp fr 2f out: one pce* **10/3**[2]
9 nk **Baharah (USA)**[44] 4361 4-9-3 RobertWinston 6 108+
(G A Butler) *hld up in 8th: kpt on same pce on outer fr 2f out* **20/1**
10 7 **Cheyenne Star (IRE)**[37] 4590 5-9-3 107 DPMcDonogh 1 92
(Ms F M Crowley, Ire) *4th early: 5th 1/2-way: wknd ent st* **25/1**

1m 40.73s (-0.47) **Going Correction** +0.25s/f (Good)
WFA 3 from 4yo+ 5lb 10 Ran SP% **122.3**
Speed ratings: **112,111,111,110,109 109,108,108,108,101**
CSF £16.25 TOTE £2.70: £1.50, £1.70, £1.40; DF 18.50.
Owner Mrs J S Bolger **Bred** Mrs A M Jenkins **Trained** Coolcullen, Co Carlow

FOCUS
The form is rated through Halfway To Heaven with Lush Lashes and Nahoodh just shy of their best.

NOTEBOOK
Lush Lashes, dropping back from 1m4f, displayed real class and guts to land her fourth win of the current campaign. This was also a third straight success at the top level and the attitude she displayed to repel her challengers inside the final furlong was most taking. This very adaptable filly reversed her Naasau form with the third (where she was most unlucky not to have won) and just got away with this dead ground. She still has a host of options this year, with the Prix de l'Opera on Arc weekend her next likely port of call and there is also the Breeder's Cup to consider. She has also been confirmed as staying in training next year and her first intended target for 2009 will be in the Dubai Duty Free at Nad Al Sheba. (op 5/2)
Nahoodh(IRE) emerged with every chance up the inside in the final furlong, but could not get past the determined winner try as she might. She ran very close to her best and, considering the winner will likely miss out the Sun Chariot, she would take some beating in that Group 1 on Champions Day next month. (op 8/1)
Halfway To Heaven(IRE) failed to confirm her Nassau form with Lush Lashes, but she was not as well drawn as that rival here and still performed right up to her best in defeat on this drop back in trip. (op 7/2)
You'resothrilling(USA), last year's Cherry Hinton winner, turned in a very pleasing belated seasonal bow after picking up an injury in the winter and was doing all of her best work at the finish. She should come on a bundle for the run and clearly retains all of her ability.
Listen(IRE), last season's Fillies' Mile heroine, was far from disgraced on this first run of the year after meeting with a setback in April and, like her stable companion in fourth, is also entitled to improve a great deal for the outing.
Lady Gloria set a sound early pace in front, but was not surprisingly a sitting duck in the home straight. She probably ran the race of her life in defeat, however.
Carribean Sunset(IRE) was the main disappointment of the race, falling a long way short of the overall form that made her a strong contender on paper. The ground ought not to have been a problem. (op 7/2 tchd 3/1)
Baharah(USA) was stepping up from a Listed win at Ascot in July and she could make no impression from off the pace. She still ran close enough to her previous form, however, and really needs a quicker surface to shine.

5731a LEOPARDSTOWN PAVILION SEPTEMBER H'CAP (PREMIER HANDICAP) 7f
3:15 (3:18) 3-Y-O+ **£47,867** (£14,044; £6,691; £2,279)

RPR
1 **Rain Rush (IRE)**[35] 4670 5-9-5 93 JAHeffernan 2 101
(David Marnane, Ire) *dwlt: hld up in tch: 10th 3f out: hdwy on inner ent st: 3rd and chal over 1f out: led 100yds out: styd on wl* **20/1**
2 ¾ **Maundy Money**[38] 4576 5-9-3 91 CO'Donoghue 1 97
(David Marnane, Ire) *mid-div: 8th and hdwy on outer ent st: 3rd 1f out: kpt on wl cl home* **8/1**[2]
3 1 ¼ **Thebes**[8] 5495 3-8-13 91 MJKinane 9 92
(M Johnston) *a.p: 4th 1/2-way: 2nd and chal early st: led under 1 1/2f out: hdd 100yds out: no ex cl home* **6/1**[1]
4 1 ¼ **Nanotech (IRE)**[21] 5133 4-8-13 87 WJLee 11 87
(Jarlath P Fahey, Ire) *trckd ldrs: 7th appr 1/2-way: 9th 3f out: styd on fr 2f out* **8/1**[2]
5 ½ **Russian Empress (IRE)**[10] 5441 4-9-4 95 PBBeggy(3) 8 93
(David P Myerscough, Ire) *trckd ldrs in 5th: 4th and effrt early st: no imp fnl f: kpt on same pce* **6/1**[1]
6 ¾ **Thoughtless Moment (IRE)**[35] 4670 4-9-10 98 (b[1]) PJSmullen 10 94
(D K Weld, Ire) *hld up towards rr: prog on inner ent st: 7th over 1f out: kpt on* **10/1**[3]
7 1 ¼ **Nastrelli (IRE)**[23] 5081 5-8-13 87 (p) JohnEgan 7 80
(M Halford, Ire) *towards rr: kpt on wout threatening fr 2f out* **14/1**
8 2 ½ **Dedo (IRE)**[21] 5133 3-8-13 91 DPMcDonogh 15 75
(Kevin Prendergast, Ire) *in rr of mid-div: kpt on one pce st* **16/1**
9 ½ **Empirical Power (IRE)**[23] 5081 7-9-4 95 SMGorey(3) 18 80
(Edward Lynam, Ire) *led: strly pressed st: hdd under 1 1/2f out: sn no ex* **25/1**
10 ½ **Newgate Lodge (IRE)**[49] 4229 4-8-4 83 (p) SFoley(5) 17 66
(M Halford, Ire) *towards rr: 11th and prog on outer appr st: no imp fr 2f out* **20/1**
11 nk **Fit The Cove (IRE)**[14] 5133 8-8-11 85 (t) PShanahan 3 68
(H Rogers, Ire) *trckd ldrs on inner: 6th 1/2-way: cl 5th and effrt ent st: no ex over 1f out: eased* **16/1**
12 ½ **Majestic Times (IRE)**[21] 5133 8-8-8 89 JPFahy(7) 6 70
(Liam McAteer, Ire) *mid-div: 9th bef 1/2-way: no imp st* **25/1**
13 nk **Alone He Stands (IRE)**[7] 5550 8-8-9 83 ow1 RobertWinston 4 63
(J C Hayden, Ire) *in rr: sn pushed along: no imp fr 3f out* **10/1**[3]
14 ½ **Fourpenny Lane**[23] 5081 3-9-6 98 (p) WMLordan 14 75
(Ms Joanna Morgan, Ire) *prom: 2nd 1/2-way: 3rd appr st: sn no ex and wknd* **14/1**
15 shd **Impossible Dream (IRE)**[21] 5133 4-9-6 94 TedDurcan 16 73
(A Kinsella, Ire) *in tch: 8th 1/2-way: wknd st* **10/1**[3]
16 nk **Le Citadel (USA)**[8] 5517 3-8-5 90 DEMullins(7) 5 66
(P D Deegan, Ire) *a bhd* **16/1**
17 ½ **Baggio (IRE)**[23] 5081 7-9-6 94 FMBerry 13 71
(Charles O'Brien, Ire) *a bhd* **14/1**
18 2 ½ **Ireland's Call (IRE)**[23] 5081 7-9-3 96 OCasey(5) 12 66
(Peter Casey, Ire) *prom: 3rd 1/2-way: wknd early st* **20/1**

1m 27.9s (-2.40) **Going Correction** -0.10s/f (Good)
WFA 3 from 4yo+ 4lb 18 Ran SP% **137.7**
Speed ratings: **109,108,106,105,104 103,102,99,99,98 98,97,97,96,96 96,95,92**
CSF £179.15 CT £1149.36 TOTE £25.20: £5.80, £2.20, £1.80, £2.60; DF 67.70.
Owner Ms Melanie Marnane **Bred** Miss Gemma Cunningham **Trained** Bansha, Co Tipperary

NOTEBOOK
Rain Rush(IRE), who runs his best races here, held the challenge of his shorter-priced stablemate.
Maundy Money, twice a winner at the Galway Festival, found only his stablemate too good. (op 9/1)
Thebes was produced to lead nearing the final furlong, but he was collared by the first two in the final 100yards. He fared best of the three-year-olds and it rates another sound effort on ground he would have likely found soft enough. (op 13/2 tchd 7/1)

5732a TATTERSALLS MILLIONS IRISH CHAMPION STKS (GROUP 1) 1m 2f
3:50 (3:52) 3-Y-O+
£425,735 (£138,970; £65,441; £21,323; £13,970; £6,617)

RPR
1 **New Approach (IRE)**[15] 5276 3-9-0 125 KJManning 5 122
(J S Bolger, Ire) *racd keenly early: settled 2nd: rdn to ld ent st: kpt on wl u.p fnl f* **8/13**[1]
2 ½ **Traffic Guard (USA)**[15] 5289 4-9-7 JohnEgan 1 121
(Jane Chapple-Hyam) *trckd ldrs: 5th 3f out: rdn st: 2nd ins fnl f: styd on wl cl home* **50/1**

3 1 1/4 **Mores Wells**21 5136 4-9-7 115 (t) DPMcDonogh 7 118
(Kevin Prendergast, Ire) *trckd ldrs: 3rd 4f out: rdn st: 2nd 1 1/2f out: kpt on fnl f* **8/1**
4 shd **Multidimensional (IRE)**29 4855 5-9-7 TedDurcan 3 118
(H R A Cecil) *trckd ldrs in 4th: rdn 3f out: 3rd over 1f out: kpt on u.p* **6/1**3
5 3 **Lord Admiral (USA)**45 4356 7-9-7 112 (b) MJKinane 2 112
(Charles O'Brien, Ire) *hld up towards rr: kpt on wout threatening st* **33/1**
6 1 **Red Rock Canyon (IRE)**15 5276 4-9-7 113 CO'Donoghue 4 110
(A P O'Brien, Ire) *led: rdn and hdd ent st: no ex fr over 1f out* **25/1**
7 1 3/4 **She's Our Mark**25 4997 4-9-4 108 PJSmullen 9 103
(Patrick J Flynn, Ire) *hld up towards rr: no imp st* **50/1**
8 2 1/2 **King Of Rome (IRE)**21 5135 3-9-0 112 JAHeffernan 6 101
(A P O'Brien, Ire) *trckd ldrs in 5th: 6th and rdn under 3f out: no ex early st* **11/2**2

2m 7.57s (-0.63) **Going Correction** +0.25s/f (Good)
WFA 3 from 4yo+ 7lb 8 Ran SP% **113.4**
Speed ratings: **112,111,110,110,108 107,105,103**
CSF £51.79 TOTE £1.50: £1.10, £7.70, £1.90; DF 60.20.
Owner H R H Princess Haya Of Jordan **Bred** Lodge Park Stud **Trained** Coolcullen, Co Carlow

FOCUS
With Duke Of Marmalade a non-runner because of the ground, this looked a straightforward task for New Approach and he was below his best in victory. The form is rated through the third.

NOTEBOOK
New Approach(IRE) did not have to be at his best to get back in the winning groove following his defeat in the Juddmonte. Jim Bolger was on record as saying that a lot of work had been done in trying to get New Approach to settle in the run-up to this. However, the difficulty in perfecting the racing technique of this richly talented colt was still in evidence as he raced keenly in the early part of the race. Having settled adequately in second, he travelled strongly to take the lead but failed to produce any real fireworks in the straight, merely carving out a workmanlike win. It is not hard to pick holes in the form of the race as a genuine Group 1 test. (op 8/13 tchd 4/6)
Traffic Guard(USA) had run well against Phoenix Tower in the Earl Of Sefton and was in front of Multidimensional there, but there was little in his form to suggest that he could be a serious player at this level. And yet, he gave supporters of the odds-on favourite a moment or two of anxiety in staying on to good effect through the final furlong as he stayed on stoutly. Considering that his best form has been evident on quickish ground, it was a revelatory display by the very experienced four-year-old, and it will be fascinating to see whether he can repeat it. (op 66/1)
Mores Wells, a four-time winner at the track and effective on soft, really needs 1m4f to show his best form, but the ground and a pace that was reasonable in view of the conditions brought his stamina into play, helping him to achieve an honourable third.\n\x\x \bMultidimensional\p, another for whom the ground held no fears, can be rated a genuine Group 2-standard performer on his Hardwicke second. From that perspective, his fourth placing represents one of the more reassuring angles to the form, though his degree of impact was not particularly emphatic.
Multidimensional(IRE), another for whom the ground held no fears, can be rated a genuine Group 2-standard performer on his Hardwicke second. From that perspective, his fourth placing represents one of the more reassuring angles to the form, though his degree of impact was not particularly emphatic. (op 11/2)
King Of Rome(IRE) never looked like making his presence felt as deputy for the absent Duke Of Marmalade, failing to sustain the progression of recent starts. (op 11/2 tchd 5/1)

5733 - 5735a (Foreign Racing) - See Raceform Interactive

5686 BADEN-BADEN (L-H)
Sunday, September 7

OFFICIAL GOING: Soft

5736a 136TH GROSSER MERCEDES-BENZ PREIS VON BADEN (GROUP 1) 1m 4f
4:00 (4:04) 3-Y-O+ **£110,294** (£44,118; £18,382; £11,029)

RPR
1 **Kamsin (GER)**21 5137 3-8-9 JVictoire 1 119
(P Schiergen, Germany) *hld up sharing last pl but a wl in tch: hdwy over 2f out: rdn to ld ins fnl f: r.o wl* **9/2**2
2 2 1/2 **Adlerflug (GER)**49 4232 4-9-6 FJohansson 3 117
(J Hirschberger, Germany) *racd in 4th: hdwy over 3f out: led wl over 2f out: drvn wl over 1f out: hdd ins fnl f: one pce* **4/5**1
3 5 **It's Gino (GER)**49 4232 5-9-6 EPedroza 5 109
(P Vovcenko, Germany) *hld up sharing last pl but a wl in tch: clsd up on outside 5f out: brought wdst and 2nd st: ev ch over 1f out: one pce* **9/1**
4 3/4 **Ostland (GER)**63 3773 3-8-9 ADeVries 2 106
(P Schiergen, Germany) *racd in 3rd: cl 5th st: sn rdn and one pce* **20/1**
5 11 **Lucarno (USA)**43 4406 4-9-6 JimmyFortune 4 90
(J H M Gosden) *led to wl over 2f out: 4th and btn st* **11/2**3
6 26 **Tempelstern (GER)**22 5094 4-9-6 (b) TPQueally 6 49
(H R A Cecil) *trckd ldr tl wkng wl over 3f out: sn wl bhd* **10/1**

2m 37.68s (4.22)
WFA 3 from 4yo+ 9lb 6 Ran SP% **113.0**
(including ten euro stakes): WIN 43; PL 16, 13; SF 63.
Owner Stall Blankenese **Bred** Gestut Karlshof **Trained** Germany

NOTEBOOK
Kamsin(GER), who won the Deutsches Derby but had been well behind the subsequently disqualified Oriental Tiger at Cologne, proved too strong for last year's Deutsches Derby winner in what developed into match in the straight. He will probably go for the Gran Premio del Jockey-Club at San Siro next month.
Adlerflug(GER), a runaway winner at Dusseldorf when last seen, had every chance but was unable to cope with the winner in the final furlong. It is yet to be decided if he takes his chance in the Arc.
Lucarno(USA) made the running but his rider was unable to get a breather into him and he dropped right out in the straight. This ground was probably more testing than he likes.
Tempelstern(GER), who is well suited by soft ground, was stepping up in class and found the oppostion too strong, but was so far behind that something may have been amiss.

5737a PREIS DER PETER DEILMANN REEDEREI (EX GONTARD-RENNEN) (LISTED RACE) (FILLIES) 1m 2f
5:15 (5:18) 3-Y-O **£11,029** (£4,412; £1,838; £1,103)

RPR
1 **Adolfina (GER)**42 3-8-12 ASchikora 7 104
(W Figge, Germany) **66/10**
2 1 1/4 **Themelie Island (IRE)**35 4675 3-8-9 ADeVries 5 98
(A Trybuhl, Germany) **7/2**1
3 2 **Bittersweetsymfony (GER)**28 3-8-9 MSuerland 2 94
(Frau E Mader, Germany) **136/10**
4 5 **Inquisitive Look**28 4909 3-8-9 AlanMunro 12 84
(P W Chapple-Hyam) *a.p: 3rd st: sn rdn: wknd appr fnl f* **38/10**3
5 1 **Elba (GER)** 3-8-9 FJohansson 11 82
(C Von Der Recke, Germany) **186/10**
6 3 1/2 **Sina (GER)**322 6371 3-9-2 THellier 8 82
(W Hickst, Germany) **61/10**
7 22 **Auentime (GER)**35 4675 3-8-9 (b) J-PCarvalho 1 31
(U Ostmann, Germany) **36/10**2
8 6 **Khandaar (IRE)** 3-9-2 AHelfenbein 3 26
(Werner Glanz, Germany) **103/10**

2m 8.95s (3.96) 8 Ran SP% **112.8**
TOTE: WIN 66; PL 19, 19, 26; DF 256.
Owner F W Holtkotter **Bred** F W Holtkotter **Trained** Germany

NOTEBOOK
Inquisitive Look, a lightly raced filly who got off the mark in a Windsor maiden on easy ground last time, raced up with the pace but had nothing in reserve in the closing stages.

5685 LONGCHAMP (R-H)
Sunday, September 7

OFFICIAL GOING: Good to soft

5738a PRIX DU PIN (GROUP 3) 7f
2:15 (2:16) 3-Y-O+ **£29,412** (£11,765; £8,824; £5,882; £2,941)

RPR
1 **Captain's Lover (SAF)**246 4-8-11 SPasquier 5 109
(A Fabre, France) *sn trcking ldr: 2nd st: led 120yds out: r.o wl* **88/10**
2 3/4 **Spirito Del Vento (FR)**50 4212 5-9-5 IMendizabal 6 115
(J-M Beguigne, France) *hld up: last st: hdwy on outside fnl 2f: tk 2nd last strides* **13/10**1
3 hd **Alnadana (IRE)**42 4471 3-8-8 C-PLemaire 2 107
(A De Royer-Dupre, France) *broke wl: racd in 3rd to st: r.o one pce fnl f: lost 2nd last strides* **8/1**
4 snk **Mariol (FR)**7 5556 5-9-5 JMurtagh 7 114
(Robert Collet, France) *7th st: hdwy over 2f out: styng on whn nt clr run bhd wkng ldr wl ins fnl f: swtchd lft: kpt on* **21/1**
5 1/2 **Belliflore (FR)**28 4915 4-8-11 TJarnet 8 104
(Mlle S-V Tarrou, France) *mid-div: 7th st: hdwy on outside to go 4th over 1f out: kpt on same pce fnl f* **56/10**2
6 hd **Garnica (FR)**28 4915 5-9-5 DBonilla 9 112
(D Nicholls) *drawn on outside: led after 1f: set str pce: hdd 120yds out: no ex* **76/10**3
7 3 **Salut L'Africain (FR)**7 5556 3-8-11 DBoeuf 4 100
(Robert Collet, France) *racd in 4th to st: btn appr fnl f* **23/1**
8 snk **Prince Fasliyev**28 4912 4-9-1 MGuyon 1 99
(H-A Pantall, France) *broke wl: settled in 5th: disp 4th ins fnl 2f: sn one pce* **36/1**
9 1/2 **Royal God (USA)**33 4719 3-8-11 OPeslier 3 98
(F Head, France) *9th st: a in rr* **12/1**
10 snk **Battle Paint (USA)**15 5275 4-9-1 GMosse 10 97
(J H M Gosden) *8th st: effrt on outside over 2f out: btn 1f out* **16/1**

1m 20.3s (-0.60) **Going Correction** +0.25s/f (Good)
WFA 3 from 4yo+ 4lb 10 Ran SP% **116.6**
Speed ratings: **113,112,111,111,111 110,107,107,106,106**
PARI-MUTUEL: WIN 9.80; PL 2.50, 1.30, 2.20; DF 11.70.
Owner Team Valor **Bred** W J Engelbrecht **Trained** Chantilly, France

NOTEBOOK
Captain's Lover(SAF), an ex-South African filly put up a fine performance on her first run in France and her first since the beginning of January. She was dropped in behind the early leader and started her run two out to take the lead at the furlong marker. She stayed on well in the final stages and further improvement can be expected and she is now likely to go for the Group 1 Prix de la Foret over the course and distance on October 4th.
Spirito Del Vento(FR), who he had not been out since mid-July, produced a decent run and it will have put him spot on for another successful autumn campaign. He was dropped out last early on and was not asked for a forward move until one and a half out, then came with his normal late run but could not peg back the winner. He was not given a hard time and he will now be aimed at either the Foret or the Prix Daniel Wildenstein, which he took last year.
Alnadana(IRE), tucked in behind the leading group, she was always well up and began her effort 2f out. She just stayed on one paced throughout the final stages and a longer trip and better ground should be beneficial in the future. Something like the Prix Perth later in the year could be on the cards and she will be campaigned in Dubai early next year.
Mariol(FR), checked inside the final furlong, might well have finished closer. He was given a waiting ride but made progress up the far rail and was finishing best of all; it will be no surprise to see him in the Foret line up.
Garnica(FR) was smartly away and soon at the head of affairs. Still going well at the entrance to the straight, he began to tie up at the furlong marker but was only beaten just over a length he might have been closer on deeper ground.
Battle Paint(USA) was never seen with a chance and made virtually no progress in the straight.

5739a PRIX LA ROCHETTE (GROUP 3) 7f
2:50 (2:50) 2-Y-O **£29,412** (£11,765; £8,824; £5,882; £2,941)

RPR
1 **Soul City (IRE)**21 5139 2-8-11 RichardHughes 2 110
(R Hannon) *mde all: rdn out and r.o wl* **7/4**1
2 1/2 **Milanais (FR)**14 5330 2-8-11 TJarnet 3 109
(B De Montzey, France) *hld up in 4th: hdwy on outside wl over 1f out: r.o* **5/1**3
3 3/4 **Jukebox Jury (IRE)**21 5139 2-8-11 JMurtagh 1 107
(M Johnston) *disp 2nd on ins: looking for room over 2f out: sn rdn and outpcd: kpt on to take 3rd ins fnl f* **10/1**
4 1 1/2 **Cafe Racer (IRE)**41 2-8-11 SPasquier 4 103
(A Fabre, France) *trckd wnr: chal 2f out: no ex fnl f* **10/3**2
5 1 **Queen America (FR)**15 5301 2-8-8 OPeslier 5 98
(Robert Collet, France) *hld up in 5th: nvr able to chal* **7/1**
6 1 1/2 **Racingisdreaming (USA)**30 2-8-11 C-PLemaire 6 97
(J-C Rouget, France) *last thrght* **5/1**3

1m 22.7s (1.80) **Going Correction** +0.25s/f (Good) 6 Ran SP% **114.4**
Speed ratings: **99,98,97,95,94 93**
PARI-MUTUEL: WIN 3.40; PL 2.10, 2.20; SF 16.70.
Owner Patrick J Fahey **Bred** Peter Thome **Trained** East Everleigh, Wilts

NOTEBOOK

Soul City(IRE) appears to be going from strength to strength and made every yard of the running in this 7f contest. He quickened well when asked and then gamely held off the late challenge of the runner-up but finally won with a little in hand. This was his second victory in France this season and the plan now is to run in the Goffs Million at the Curragh at the end of the month. The Prix Jean-Luc Lagardere may also be taken into consideration as it will be run over this course and distance.

Milanais(FR) put up another decent performance. He was fourth in the early stages and looked to have a double handful halfway up the straight. Although he quickened well the winner pulled out just that little bit extra inside the final furlong. His provincial trainer feels that he might be better suited by a mile but he looks certain now to come back for the Jean-Luc Lagardere on October 5th.

Jukebox Jury(IRE) was tucked in just behind the leaders early on but appeared outpaced early in the straight before running on well again up the far rail inside the final furlong. He was much closer to the winner when they met at Deauville and a longer trip may well suit in the future.

Cafe Racer(IRE), second in the early part of the race, tried to tackle the leader a furlong and a half out but was one paced thereafter.

5740a PRIX DU MOULIN DE LONGCHAMP (GROUP 1) (C&F) — 1m

3:20 (3:23) 3-Y-O+ **£168,059** (£67,235; £33,618; £16,794; £8,412)

RPR

1 **Goldikova (IRE)**[35] 4674 3-8-8 .... OPeslier 2 123
(F Head, France) *trckd ldrs on ins: 3rd st: led over 2f out: rdn over 1f out: drvn out and a holding 2nd* **34/10**[2]

2 ½ **Darjina (FR)**[35] 4674 4-8-12 .... GMosse 5 121
(A De Royer-Dupre, France) *a cl up: 4th st: wnt 2nd 2f out: sn rdn: r.o u.p fnl f but unable to cl on wnr* **9/2**[3]

3 1 **Paco Boy (IRE)**[22] 5095 3-8-11 .... RichardHughes 7 122+
(R Hannon) *mid-div: 7th st: hdwy over 2f out: 3rd wl over 1f out: r.o same pce u.p* **10/1**

4 ½ **Sageburg (IRE)**[21] 5138 4-9-2 .... SPasquier 8 122
(A De Royer-Dupre, France) *hld up: 8th st: hdwy on outside 2f out: rdn over 1f out: kpt on u.p* **13/1**

5 snk **Henrythenavigator (USA)**[39] 4518 3-8-11 .... JMurtagh 11 120+
(A P O'Brien, Ire) *hld up: 9th st: hdwy trcking 4th on outside: rdn wl over 1f out: kpt on: nrst fin* **11/10**[1]

6 2½ **Natagora (FR)**[21] 5138 3-8-8 .... C-PLemaire 9 112
(P Bary, France) *mid-div: 6th st: disp 3rd over 1f out: one pce* **12/1**

7 2½ **Lovelace**[5] 5596 4-9-2 .... JamieSpencer 10 110
(M Johnston) *hld up in last: 10th st: nvr a factor* **84/1**

8 10 **Forthe Millionkiss (GER)**[28] 4916 4-9-2 .... WMongil 1 87
(Uwe Ostmann, Germany) *cl up: 5th st: btn 2f out* **40/1**

9 15 **Sarissa (BRZ)**[29] 4881 5-8-12 .... GBenoist 3 48
(P Bary, France) *led to over 2f out* **12/1**

10 snk **Honoured Guest (IRE)**[82] 3100 4-9-2 .... DavidMcCabe 6 52
(A P O'Brien, Ire) *pressed ldrs on outside: edgd rt over 3f out: 2nd st: btn over 2f out* **11/10**[1]

11 8 **Pas Seule (FR)**[63] 3775 3-8-8 .... DBonilla 4 30
(F Head, France) *pressed ldr: hmpd and wknd qckly over 3f out: moved outside and sn wl bhd* **34/10**[2]

1m 36.7s (-2.10) **Going Correction** +0.25s/f (Good)
WFA 3 from 4yo+ 5lb — 11 Ran SP% **194.1**
Speed ratings: **120,119,118,118,117 115,112,102,87,87 79**
PARI-MUTUEL: WIN 4.40 (coupled with Pas Seule); PL 2.00, 2.00, 3.30;DF 11.70.
Owner Wertheimer Et Frere **Bred** Wertheimer Et Frere **Trained** France
■ Stewards' Enquiry : G Mosse €100 fine: whip abuse

FOCUS

A high-class renewal, contested by four individual winners at the top level who had accrued seven Group 1 victories between them this year. The most notable absentee among the season's top milers was the Prix Jacques le Marois winner Tamayuz. The failure of Henrythenavigator to give his running does hold down the form, although otherwise it seems sound. With three pacemakers in the field, the race was run at a generous gallop, but in common with most recent runnings of this event it proved difficult to make much ground from off the pace.

NOTEBOOK

Goldikova(IRE), a stablemate of Tamayuz, arrived here with a progressive profile, having got the better of Darjina on her first assignment at Group 1 level in last month's Prix Rothschild at Deauville, but she was taking on the colts for the first time. Racing keenly, perfectly positioned on the heels of the pacemakers, she went on with around 2f to run and kicked for home, holding the runner-up with a bit to spare. The fourth three-year-old filly to win in the last half-dozen renewals, following Nebraska Tornado, Grey Lilas and Darjina, she should continue on the upgrade and has the choice of either the Mile or the Filly and Mare Turf at the Breeders' Cup at Santa Anita.

Darjina(FR), successful from Ramonti and George Washington in this event last year, is without a win since and has now finished second on all five of her appearances this year, but it is not for want of trying. Beaten by Goldikova at Deauville last time, she never let her old rival get too far ahead and gave chase throughout the last couple of furlongs without being able to close the gap. This was a fine effort considering that the ground was softer than ideal for her and she may take her chance in the Queen Elizabeth II Stakes at Ascot.

Paco Boy(IRE), who incurred his only previous defeat this term when meeting trouble in running in the French Guineas here in May, has reverted to 7f with great success since, principally in the Hungerford Stakes last time. The soft ground was not a problem and neither was the return to a mile, and he did best of the hold-up horses, running on well but held in third when becoming a little short of room on the inside close home. The Prix de la Foret looks the obvious target but he could take in the Breeders' Cup Mile.

Sageburg(IRE) took the measure of his stable companion Darjina in the Prix d'Ispahan over an extra furlong here in the spring but things have not gone his way since in the Queen Anne at Ascot (trapped wide) and the Jacques le Marois (given too much to do). He ran a solid race on ground that he likes, sticking on gamely without quite getting to the principals and is likely to go for the Prix Dollar at the Arc meeting next.

Henrythenavigator(USA), whose trainer had serious misgivings about the soft ground and gave the go-ahead for the colt to run less than an hour before the race, was bidding to emulate stable companion Rock Of Gibraltar in 2002 by adding this race to the Newmarket and Curragh Guineas, St James's Palace Stakes and Sussex Stakes, but Aidan O'Brien's fears over ground conditions proved well founded as the brilliant colt lost his unbeaten record for the season. Dropped in from his outside stall, and held up one from the back, he never looked at ease on the surface and could not quicken up when the winner went for home, although to his credit he was closing on the four in front of him when the race was all but over. He is undefeated on a sound surface but has now been beaten on all three of his runs on soft ground, twice as a two-year-old at the Curragh. He could run in the Queen Elizabeth II later this month and the Breeders' Cup Classic remains his long-term target.

Natagora(FR), whose stablemate Sarissa carried out pacemaking duties, was settled in midfield but lacked the speed of the principals in the last couple of furlongs. She is an admirable filly, but since her 1000 Guineas win four months ago she has just fallen short at the highest level. She was beaten further by Goldikova here than she was by Tamayuz in the Jacques le Marois.

Lovelace, stepping out of handicaps when an easy winner of a Group 2 at Baden-Baden as recently as Tuesday, had an awful lot on his plate in this company and, although he ran on from the rear, he never promised to get to the principals. There should be another nice prize in him this autumn.

Forthe Millionkiss(GER), a German challenger who won a Hanover Grade 2 last month, was biting off more than he could chew here.

5743 VELIEFENDI

Sunday, September 7

OFFICIAL GOING: Good

5741a BOSPHORUS CUP (TURKISH GROUP 2) — 1m 4f

7:15 (7:18) 3-Y-O+ **£201,005** (£80,402; £40,201; £20,101)

RPR

1 **Inspector (TUR)** 4-9-6 .... (b) HKaratas 5 117
(U Bekmezci, Turkey) *soon racing in 2nd, 2nd straight, led 2f out, ridden over 1f out, went clear last half furlong, ran on well* **2/1**[2]

2 2½ **Out Of Control (TUR)** 5-9-6 .... FCakar 3 113
(M Yigiter, Turkey) *led, 3 lengths clear for a long way, headed 2f out, every chance inside final f, no extra last half furlong* **129/10**

3 ½ **Dickens (GER)**[37] 4585 5-9-6 .... ASuborics 6 112
(H Blume, Germany) *held up, last straight, headway over 2f out, reached 3rd inside final f, ran on steadily* **66/10**

4 1½ **Buccellati**[44] 4363 4-9-6 .... (b) WilliamBuick 2 110
(A M Balding) *disputed 3rd, 4th straight, kept on under pressure from over 1f out, never able to challenge* **183/20**

5 1½ **Love Galore (IRE)**[8] 5508 3-8-10 .... RHills 1 106
(M Johnston) *with leader over 1f, restrained disputing 3rd, 3rd straight, ridden well over 1f out, weakened final f* **196/10**

6 1 **Gravitas**[13] 5348 5-9-6 .... LDettori 4 106
(Saeed Bin Suroor) *held up sharing last, 6th straight, effort on outside 2f out, never able to challenge* **2/5**[1]

7 6 **Tiramisu (TUR)**[316] 5-9-3 .... (b) SKaya 7 93
(S Tasbek, Turkey) *raced in 5th, closed up on outside over 3f out to dispute 3rd, close 5th straight, weakened well over 1f out* **109/20**[3]

2m 27.35s (-1.45)
WFA 3 from 4yo+ 9lb — **7** Ran SP% **155.3**
(including one lira stakes): WIN 3.00; DF 11.95; SF 26.65 [no place betting].
Owner H Dogan **Bred** H Yavas **Trained** Turkey

NOTEBOOK

Buccellati, a decent handicapper but held in two previous starts in Listed and Group company, ran reasonably but does not look up to this class.

Love Galore(IRE), another stepping up in grade, had the ground to suit but was out of his depth.

Gravitas, who ran well at Kempton on his return from five months off at the end of August, was disappointing under a hold-up ride.

5742a TOPKAPI TROPHY (TURKISH GROUP 2) — 1m

8:45 (8:48) 3-Y-O+ **£301,508** (£120,603; £60,302; £30,151)

RPR

1 **Pressing (IRE)**[42] 4470 5-9-6 .... NCallan 8 118
(M A Jarvis) *led 1f, tracked leader til led entering straight well over 2f out, 3 lengths clear 2f out, soon ridden, driven out* **8/1**

2 1½ **Linngari (IRE)**[42] 4470 6-9-6 .... RyanMoore 6 114
(Sir Michael Stoute) *went left start, mid-division, 7th straight, headway on outside from over 2f out, reached 2nd 100yds out, ran on but could never reach winner* **23/20**[1]

3 hd **Stimulation (IRE)**[40] 4506 3-8-12 .... DarryllHolland 5 111
(H Morrison) *always well in touch, 5th straight, headway over 2f out, driven & reached 2nd at distance, lost 2nd 100yds out, ran on* **208/10**

4 1 **Kurtiniadis (IRE)**[343] 5-9-6 .... SKaya 7 112
(S Kulak, Turkey) *bumped start, raced in 8th, 9th straight, headway on outside over 1f out, stayed on to take 4th last strides* **37/10**[3]

5 ¾ **Collection (IRE)**[42] 4473 3-8-12 .... LDettori 2 107
(W J Haggas) *mid-division, 6th straight, kept on steadily final 2f* **53/10**

6 nse **In Chambers**[42] 4473 3-8-12 .... ASuborics 3 107
(M Delzangles, France) *held up, 8th straight, headway over 2f out, stayed on under pressure to dispute 4th in last half furlong* **35/1**

7 ½ **Gris De Gris (IRE)**[98] 2656 4-9-6 .... TThulliez 4 109
(J-M Capitte, France) *tracked leaders, close 4tth straight, 2nd 2f out to distance, one pace* **20/1**

8 ½ **Fifteen Love (USA)**[37] 4587 3-8-12 .... SteveDrowne 1 105
(R Charlton) *tracked leaders, 3rd straight, disputed 2nd well over 1f out, weakened inside final f* **22/1**

9 nse **Sabirli (TUR)**[321] 7-9-6 .... HKaratas 10 107
(C Kurt, Turkey) *last most of way, stayed on final f* **14/10**[2]

10 13 **My Sacrifice (TUR)** 3-8-9 .... GYildiz 9 72
(C Kurt, Turkey) *led after 1f, headed entering straight well over 2f out, weakened 2f out* **46/1**

1m 33.65s (-1.68)
WFA 3 from 4yo+ 5lb — **10** Ran SP% **155.0**
WIN 9.00; PL 1.60, 1.15 [only two place dividends]; DF 7.70; SF 50.90.
Owner Gary A Tanaka **Bred** Azienda Agricola Del Parco **Trained** Newmarket, Suffolk

NOTEBOOK

Pressing(IRE), who was at his best at the end of last season, got off the mark for the year on this drop back to a mile under a positive ride. He went clear turning for home and never looked like being reeled in, reversing recent Munich running with the favourite in the process.He is likely to be aimed at the Hong Kong Mile at the end of the year.

Linngari(IRE), who beat the winner over an extra 2f at Munich, is full effective at this trip but reportedly found the ground too fast and also hit a false patch of ground.

Stimulation(IRE), who was trying this trip for only the second time, ran well and did best of the three-year-olds. He could drop back to 7f for the Prix de la Foret next and Hong Kong may also be on the agenda.

Collection(IRE), dropping in trip and up in grade, ran quite well and was not beaten far. He is improving and should be up to holding his own in Group company on this evidence.

Fifteen Love(USA), who has been in good form in competitive handicaps this season, found this step up in grade too much for him.

VELIEFENDI

Saturday, September 6

OFFICIAL GOING: Standard

5743a ANATOLIA STKS (TURKISH GROUP 2) (FIBRESAND) 1m 2f

8:15 (8:19) 3-Y-O+ **£125,628** (£50,251; £30,151; £15,075)

RPR

1 **Harputlu Gaggos (TUR)** 4-9-6 ....(b) SKaya 2 113
(R Tasdemir, Turkey) *held up in rear but always well in touch, headway 3f out, 4th straight, challenged on outside over 1f out, driven to lead 150yds out, ran on well* **123/20**[3]

2 3½ **Fairson (TUR)**[363] 5265 5-9-6 ....(b) EYavuz 9 107
(K Ozturk, Turkey) *towards rear early, closed up on outside before half-way, 3rd straight, led over 1f out to 150yds out, one pace* **31/10**[2]

3 7 **Familiar Territory**[191] 742 5-9-6 .... DBonilla 8 94
(Saeed Bin Suroor) *tracked leader, led approaching straight over 2f out, headed & weakened over 1f out* **3/20**[1]

4 9 **Oglumemre (TUR)** 3-8-11 .... MGunduzeli 3 76
(Sab Arslan, Turkey) *led 2f, pushed along over 3f out, 5th straight, kept on one pace final 2f* **72/10**

5 5 **Santiago (GER)**[41] 4470 6-9-6 .... ASuborics 4 69
(H Blume, Germany) *held up, last straight, some progress 2f out, never near to challenge* **31/2**

6 3 **Happy Boy (BRZ)**[49] 4192 5-9-6 .... DO'Donohoe 5 64
(Saeed Bin Suroor) *broke well, restrained to race in mid-division, 6th straight, never a factor* **3/20**[1]

7 1¼ **Hearthstead Maison (IRE)**[12] 5348 4-9-6 .... GregFairley 6 62
(M Johnston) *led after 2f to over 2f out, 2nd straight, soon weakened* **104/10**

8 1½ **Thunder Storm Cat (USA)**[21] 5115 4-9-6 ....(b) J-MBreux 7 59
(M Rulec, Germany) *raced in 4th to 3f out, 6th & beaten straight* **21/1**

2m 10.14s (130.14)
WFA 3 from 4yo+ 7lb **8 Ran SP% 243.9**
(including one lira stakes): WIN 7.15; DF 7.20; SF 14.15 [no place betting].
Owner F Serpil Ataman **Bred** F Serpil Ataman **Trained** Turkey

NOTEBOOK
Familiar Territory raced close to the pace and went to the front turning for home but was soon brushed aside by the principals.
Happy Boy(BRZ) was held up early but failed to pick up from the home turn.
Hearthstead Maison(IRE) made the running as he likes to do but, once the eventual third took him on, he was soon in trouble. He looks more effective on turf than sand.

4887 ARLINGTON (L-H)

Saturday, September 6

OFFICIAL GOING: All-weather - fast; turf course - soft

5744a PUCKER UP STKS (GRADE 3) (FILLIES) (TURF) 1m 1f

10:55 (11:12) 3-Y-O

£55,477 (£18,492; £10,171; £5,548; £2,774; £1,005)

RPR

1 **Closeout (USA)**[28] 3-8-6 .... HJTheriotII 9 99
(Thomas F Proctor, U.S.A) **42/10**[3]

2 ½ **Lucky Copy (USA)** 3-8-6 .... GKGomez 2 98
(Todd Pletcher, U.S.A) **28/10**[1]

3 1¼ **Clear Pond (USA)** 3-8-4 .... EBaird 5 93
(George R Arnold II, U.S.A) **305/10**

4 ½ **Tight Precision (USA)**[71] 3-8-4 .... RBaze 4 92
(Thomas F Proctor, U.S.A) **77/10**

5 nse **Much Obliged (USA)**[22] 5164 3-8-10 .... CEmigh 8 98
(Malcolm Pierce, Canada) **66/10**

6 hd **Gone Theatrical (USA)** 3-8-4 .... JAlvarado 12 92
(Austin Smith, U.S.A) **80/1**

7 3½ **Mushka (USA)**[21] 3-8-6 .... RRDouglas 10 86
(William Mott, U.S.A) **104/10**

8 hd **Jazz Jam**[38] 4520 3-8-6 .... RAlbarado 6 86
(P F I Cole) *mid-division, 8th straight, stayed on but never able to challenge* **224/10**

9 ½ **Apple Martini (USA)**[35] 3-8-8 .... EPerez 3 87
(Chris Block, U.S.A) **50/1**

10 2¾ **Bel Air Sizzle (USA)**[21] 3-8-10 .... RBejarano 1 83
(Barry Abrams, U.S.A) **32/10**[2]

11 1½ **Dreaming Of Liz (USA)**[35] 3-8-8 ....(b) EarlieFires 7 78
(Wayne Catalano, U.S.A) **217/10**

12 10¼ **Return To Paradise (USA)**[397] 3-8-6 ....(b) JamesGraham 13 54
(Todd Pletcher, U.S.A) **362/10**

13 2½ **Nijinsky Ballet (USA)**[49] 3-8-4 .... JFerrer 11 47
(Robert Gorham, U.S.A) **116/1**

1m 53.22s (113.22) **13 Ran SP% 121.4**
PARI-MUTUEL (including $2 stakes): WIN 10.40; PL (1-2) 4.80, 4.60; SHOW (1-2-3) 3.80, 4.20, 12.40; SF 66.00.
Owner Glen Hill Farm **Bred** Glen Hill Farm **Trained** USA

NOTEBOOK
Jazz Jam, who has form at Listed level, is probably better on a faster surface but also may be in need of a step up in trip.

4235 BELMONT PARK (L-H)

Saturday, September 6

OFFICIAL GOING: Turf course - yielding; dirt course - sloppy

5745a GARDEN CITY STKS (GRADE 1) (FILLIES) (INNER TURF) 1m 1f (T)

7:03 (6:52) 3-Y-O

£75,377 (£25,126; £12,563; £6,281; £3,769; £838)

RPR

1 **Backseat Rhythm (USA)**[22] 5164 3-8-8 .... JJCastellano 4 110
(Patrick L Reynolds, U.S.A) **49/10**[3]

2 ½ **Pure Clan (USA)**[63] 3807 3-8-10 ....(b) JRLeparoux 5 111
(Robert E Holthus, U.S.A) **1/1**[1]

3 nk **Ariege (USA)**[28] 3-8-6 .... AGarcia 7 106
(Robert Frankel, U.S.A) **1/1**[1]

4 1 **My Princess Jess (USA)**[43] 3-8-8 .... ECoa 2 106
(Barclay Tagg, U.S.A) **43/10**[2]

5 2 **Raw Silk (USA)**[22] 5164 3-8-8 ....(b) EPrado 1 102
(Thomas Albertrani, U.S.A) **94/10**

6 1¼ **Alwajeeha (USA)**[43] 3-8-6 .... JRVelazquez 3 97
(Kiaran McLaughlin, U.S.A) **196/10**

7 nse **Shaker (IRE)**[43] 4361 3-8-5 ow1 .... CVelasquez 6 96
(M L W Bell) *always in the last two, closed up 3f out, 7th straight on outside, kept on same pace* **65/1**

8 3¾ **Satan's Circus (USA)**[21] 3-8-7 ow3 .... CNakatani 8 90
(Christophe Clement, U.S.A) **49/10**[3]

1m 51.82s (111.82) **8 Ran SP% 168.8**
PARI-MUTUEL (including $2 stakes): WIN 11.80; PL (1-2) 4.30, 2.40, 2.40; SHOW (1-2-3) 3.90, 2.60, 2.60; SF 32.00 (winner with Pure Clan & Ariege).
Owner Paul P Pompa Jr **Bred** Hill 'N' Dale Farm & Spast Farm **Trained** USA

NOTEBOOK
Shaker(IRE) who had been running respectably but had been held in all her runs (all in Listed company), had the ground to suit but found the step up in grade too much for her.

5487 BATH (L-H)

Monday, September 8

OFFICIAL GOING: Soft (5.8)
Wind: Light against Weather: Fine

5746 EVENING POST MAIDEN AUCTION FILLIES' STKS 5f 11y

2:10 (2:16) (Class 6) 2-Y-O **£2,266** (£674; £337; £168) **Stalls** Centre

Form RPR

54 1 **Perfect Friend**[17] 5213 2-7-12 0 .... Louis-PhilippeBeuzelin(5) 5 66+
(S Kirk) *in rr: sddle sn slipped: hdwy 2f out: rdn ins fnl f: str run to ld nr fin* **8/1**

60 2 ½ **Caledonia Princess**[41] 4499 2-7-10 0 .... ManavNem(7) 7 64
(P A Blockley) *hld up in tch: pushed along to ld wl over 1f out: hdd nr fin* **50/1**

42 3 hd **Yanza**[17] 5214 2-8-4 0 .... DavidProbert(5) 1 69
(J R Gask) *led: hdd wl over 1f out: sn rdn: ev ch ins fnl f: kpt on* **6/5**[1]

000 4 3¾ **Caressing**[66] 3674 2-8-11 59 .... RyanMoore 2 58
(R Hannon) *chsd ldrs: wknd over 1f out* **13/2**[3]

4023 5 5 **Peper Harow (IRE)**[8] 5530 2-8-7 81 .... TQuinn 9 36
(M D I Usher) *w ldrs tl wknd over 1f out* **9/4**[2]

0606 6 6 **Rapanui Belle**[8] 5530 2-8-3 49 .... AdrianMcCarthy 6 10
(G L Moore) *tk keen early: chsd ldrs: wknd over 2f out* **50/1**

6605 7 1¾ **That Boy Ronaldo**[13] 5384 2-8-9 56 .... FrancisNorton 3 10
(A Berry) *w ldr tl rdn and wknd over 2f out* **16/1**

6 8 4½ **River Style (IRE)**[9] 5487 2-8-5 0 .... RichardThomas 8 —
(A P Jarvis) *s.i.s: a in rr* **50/1**

65.61 secs (3.11) **Going Correction** +0.65s/f (Yiel) **8 Ran SP% 112.4**
Speed ratings (Par 90): **101,100,99,93,85 76,73,66**
toteswinger: 1&2 £27.60, 1&3 £2.20, 2&3 £15.80. CSF £325.81 TOTE £7.90: £2.10, £7.30, £1.10; EX 399.10.
Owner Lady Davis **Bred** Speedlith Group **Trained** Upper Lambourn, Berks

FOCUS
This weak juvenile fillies maiden was little better than a seller. It was run at a strong early pace and it saw the field come down the middle of the home straight.

NOTEBOOK
Perfect Friend still had a lot of ground to make up on the eventual placed horses entering the final furlong. As that pair began to wilt she really found her stride, however, and swept past in the closing stages to win a little cosily in the end. Her rider also deserves a lot of credit as the saddle looked to slip after a furlong. On this evidence, she should relish another furlong and ought not to be overburdened when switching to nurseries. (op 15-2)
Caledonia Princess, having her first run for 41 days, came with a strong challenge at the furlong pole and at one stage looked set to score, but she could not sustain her effort. This was her most encouraging effort to date, the softer ground evidently held no fears, and she is now eligible for a nursery mark. Stronger handling when switching to that sphere can see her off the mark.
Yanza, runner-up over course and distance 17 days previously, travelled nicely on the early pace and held every chance. She most likely paid for going so hard through the first few furlongs and is no doubt up to winning a race or two, but probably needs slightly better ground. She too now qualifies for an official mark. (op 5-4 tchd 11-8)
Caressing was nibbled at in the betting ring on this return from a 66-day break, but lacked the pace to land a significant blow over the shorter trip. A switch to nurseries and a step back up to 6f should further help her cause. (op 10-1)
Peper Harow(IRE) is rated 81 and was most disapppointing, helping to force the early pace but dropping out tamely before the final furlong. While her half-brother is a mud lover, this was by far the deepest surface she has raced on so far and it could have been to blame. She still has something to prove now all the same. (op 5-2)

5747 WESTERN DAILY PRESS NURSERY 1m 5y

2:40 (2:40) (Class 5) (0-75,73) 2-Y-O **£2,914** (£867; £433; £216) **Stalls** Low

Form RPR

001 1 **River Captain (IRE)**[26] 4975 2-9-4 70 .... RichardKingscote 4 74+
(S Kirk) *a.p: rdn to ld and edgd rt over 1f out: r.o* **2/1**[1]

2341 2 2 **Musical Maze**[25] 5006 2-9-0 66 .... TGMcLaughlin 5 66
(W M Brisbourne) *a.p: rdn and ev ch over 2f out: kpt on u.p ins fnl f* **9/2**[3]

3026 3 hd **Cherry Belle (IRE)**[24] 5041 2-8-3 55 ....(v) CatherineGannon 3 55
(P D Evans) *towards rr: rdn and hdwy over 2f out: kpt on ins fnl f* **12/1**

0304 **4** 2 1/4 **Arushore (IRE)**[10] 5460 2-9-0 **66** RyanMoore 7 61
(R Hannon) *led early: hld up in tch: led over 2f out: rdn and hdd over 1f out: fdd ins fnl f* **11/2**

050 **5** 4 1/2 **Lyonesse**[16] 5277 2-7-10 **55** CharlesEddery(7) 9 40
(R Hannon) *in rr: pushed along 3f out: no real prog fnl 2f* **16/1**

6621 **6** 12 **Bright Enough**[5] 5606 2-9-3 **69** 6ex ChrisCatlin 1 27
(E J O'Neill) *sn led: hdd over 6f out: led over 4f out tl over 2f out: wknd wl over 1f out* **7/2[2]**

005 **7** 5 **In Transit (IRE)**[17] 5242 2-9-7 **73** EdwardCreighton 8 20
(M R Channon) *a in rr: struggling over 2f out* **10/1**

0000 **8** 1/2 **Daily Planet (IRE)**[15] 5314 2-8-1 **60** (v[1]) AmyScott(7) 2 6
(B W Duke) *sn w ldr: led over 6f out: rn sltly wd and hdd bnd over 4f out: wknd over 2f out* **80/1**

1m 48.25s (7.45) **Going Correction** +0.85s/f (Soft) **8 Ran SP% 113.0**
Speed ratings (Par 95): **96,94,93,91,87 75,70,69**
toteswinger: 1&2 £3.70, 1&3 £6.10, 2&3 £9.50. CSF £10.93 CT £82.29 TOTE £3.10: £1.40, £1.60, £3.40; EX 11.20.
Owner S J McCay **Bred** Sean Finnegan **Trained** Upper Lambourn, Berks

FOCUS
A modest nursery, run at a solid early pace and the field came more towards the stands' side in the final two furlongs. The second and third help set the level.

NOTEBOOK
River Captain(IRE) followed up his Salisbury win with a ready effort despite racing from a 7lb higher mark. He travelled kindly into the home straight, before knuckling down to settle the issue from the furlong pole. The longer trip and even softer ground proved right up his street and he has no doubt begun life in this sphere at the right end of the handicap. A bold bid for the hat-trick can be expected from this progressive colt despite another likely rise up the weights. (op 9-4 tchd 15-8)
Musical Maze, 5lb higher than when winning at Beverley, ran a solid race in defeat without seriously troubling the winner. She is a likeable filly and helps to set the level of the form. (op 5-1)
Cherry Belle(IRE), the subject of some late support, proved suited to the decent early pace and was doing most of her best work inside the final furlong. This would have been the most testing ground she had raced on, so she got the longer trip well enough and this rates an improved effort. (op 25-1)
Arushore(IRE) made a positive move around two furlongs out and came furthest to the stands' rail, but he ultimately got outstayed by the principals. He is handicapped about right, but should get a little closer when reverting to a slightly sharper test. (op 5-1 tchd 7-1)
Bright Enough was not able to dictate as was the case when successful at Kempton five days previously and, on this vastly different surface, it was evident at the top of the home straight that she was done with. (op 5-2)
In Transit(IRE) Official explanation: jockey said colt was unsuited by the soft ground

5748 THISISBRISTOL.CO.UK (S) STKS 1m 5y
3:10 (3:10) (Class 6) 3-4-Y-0 **£1,260** (£1,260; £288; £144) **Stalls** Low

Form RPR

000 **1** **Mick Is Back**[8] 5533 4-9-9 57 (p) AdamKirby 3 58
(G G Margarson) *hld up in mid-div: hdwy over 2f out: hrd rdn to ld wl ins fnl f: r.o: jnd post* **7/1[3]**

00- **1** dht **Pembo**[313] 6591 3-8-10 0 KevinGhunowa(3) 4 52
(R A Harris) *a.p: sltly outpcd over 3f out: hrd rdn over 2f out: sustained chal ins fnl f: jnd ldr post* **66/1**

0020 **3** 1/2 **Fun In The Sun**[33] 4746 4-9-9 52 StephenDonohoe 8 57
(A B Haynes) *hld up in tch: rdn to ld wl over 1f out: hdd wl ins fnl f: r.o* **11/1**

2000 **4** hd **Apache Dawn**[20] 5166 4-9-4 60 RyanMoore 11 51
(G L Moore) *hld up towards rr: hdwy over 2f out: nt clr run and swtchd rt over 1f out: styd on u.p ins fnl f* **7/1[3]**

66 **5** 3 3/4 **Tampopo (IRE)**[11] 5426 3-8-13 0 RichardThomas 16 42
(D J S Ffrench Davis) *led: hdd wl over 1f out: sn hung rt: wknd ins fnl f* **14/1**

0000 **6** 3 3/4 **The Name Is Frank**[66] 3678 3-8-13 60 ChrisCatlin 12 33
(J W Mullins) *w ldr: rdn and ev ch over 2f out: wknd ins fnl f* **8/1**

-004 **7** 1/2 **Road To Recovery**[14] 4891 4-9-4 45 (p) SamHitchcott 10 33
(D J Wintle) *s.i.s: bhd: rdn and hdwy over 2f out: no further prog* **16/1**

-000 **8** 7 **Purple Ransom (IRE)**[81] 3183 3-8-13 47 (t) VinceSlattery 1 16
(D J Wintle) *bhd: rdn over 2f out: nvr nr ldrs* **66/1**

00-0 **9** 1/2 **Shavoulin (USA)**[23] 5091 4-9-4 52 EdwardCreighton 5 16
(Christian Wroe) *led to post: t.k.h: prom: rdn over 2f out: sn wknd* **33/1**

2605 **10** nk **Highland Homestead**[26] 4978 3-8-13 58 (b) TGMcLaughlin 13 14
(B R Millman) *chsd ldrs: rdn over 3f out: wknd wl over 1f out* **7/2[1]**

0000 **11** 1 1/2 **House Of Tudor**[13] 5379 3-8-8 47 (b) DavidProbert(5) 6 11
(David Pinder) *s.s: rdn over 4f out: a bhd* **20/1**

0004 **12** 3 3/4 **First Tracks (IRE)**[21] 5157 3-8-13 52 TQuinn 14 2
(J W Hills) *prom: rdn over 2f out: sn wknd: sddle slipped* **10/1**

0-00 **13** 6 **Les Allues (IRE)**[46] 4326 3-8-8 43 CatherineGannon 15 —
(H S Howe) *s.i.s: sn prom: wknd over 2f out* **100/1**

05 **14** 3 1/4 **External Force (IRE)**[5] 5603 3-8-8 0 Louis-PhilippeBeuzelin(5) 9 —
(S A Callaghan) *hld up in mid-div: rdn and struggling 3f out: hung rt 2f out* **13/2[2]**

066 **15** 30 **Saafend Geezer**[14] 4901 3-8-13 43 FrancisNorton 2 —
(A Berry) *anticipated s and fly-jmpd: a in rr: lost tch 4f out: eased fnl 2f* **14/1**

1m 49.24s (8.44) **Going Correction** +0.85s/f (Soft)
WFA 3 from 4yo 5lb **15 Ran SP% 120.0**
Speed ratings (Par 101): **91,91,90,90,86 82,82,75,74,74 73,69,63,60,30**
WIN: Mick Is Back £3.40, Pembo £48.00. PL: MIB £2.30, P £16.20, Fun In The Sun £5.00. EX: MIB-P £174.30, P-MIB £381.00. CSF: MIB-P £215.75, P-MIB £237.23. toteswinger: M&P £65.90, M&F £15.60, P&F £91.00..There was no bid for Mick Is Back. Pembo was bought in for 5,000gns.
Owner Five To Follow **Bred** Mrs D Hughes **Trained** Earlswood, Monmouths
Owner M Jenner & G Margarson **Bred** J E Abbey **Trained** Newmarket, Suffolk

FOCUS
A dead-heat to this ordinary seller. The form makes sense. The runners again elected to come more towards the near side up the home straight.
House Of Tudor Official explanation: jockey said gelding never travelled
First Tracks(IRE) Official explanation: jockey said saddle slipped

5749 JOBSITE.CO.UK MAIDEN STKS 5f 161y
3:40 (3:44) (Class 5) 3-Y-0+ **£2,590** (£770; £385; £192) **Stalls** Centre

Form RPR

-450 **1** **Belle Bellino (FR)**[75] 3381 3-8-12 60 RyanMoore 5 64
(R M Beckett) *hld up and bhd: hdwy 3f out: edgd rt wl over 1f out: led ent fnl f: rdn and r.o wl* **9/2**

0462 **2** 3 1/2 **Gioacchino (IRE)**[12] 5395 3-9-0 58 KevinGhunowa(3) 9 58
(R A Harris) *s.i.s: sn mid-div: hdwy over 3f out: rdn over 1f out: chsd wnr fnl f: no imp* **3/1[2]**

0040 **3** hd **Vogarth**[23] 5090 4-9-2 45 JamesMillman(3) 4 57
(B R Millman) *in rr: rdn and hdwy over 1f out: kpt on ins fnl f* **9/1**

-335 **4** 8 **Chelsea Girl**[91] 2898 3-8-12 66 PhilipRobinson 11 26
(C G Cox) *prom: chsd ldr over 2f out tl over 1f out: wknd ins fnl f* **11/4[1]**

000 **5** 1/2 **Professor Malone**[45] 4388 3-9-3 50 ChrisCatlin 6 29
(J C Tuck) *t.k.h. early: in tch: lost pl over 3f out: no hdwy fnl 2f* **14/1**

6032 **6** 1 **Spic 'n Span**[21] 5141 3-8-12 55 (b) DavidProbert(5) 8 26
(R A Harris) *t.k.h: a.p: led over 3f out: hdd ent fnl f: sn wknd* **4/1[3]**

-406 **7** 2 1/4 **Alto Singer (IRE)**[25] 5026 3-8-12 60 TGMcLaughlin 1 13
(B R Millman) *prom: lost pl over 3f out: n.d after* **16/1**

0-00 **8** 1 1/4 **Amber Bamber**[24] 5049 3-8-12 45 FrancisNorton 3 9
(D Haydn Jones) *a bhd* **50/1**

-300 **9** 3 1/4 **Rose De Rita**[46] 4324 3-8-5 31 RichardRowe(7) 10 —
(L P Grassick) *chsd ldr tl over 2f out: sn wknd* **150/1**

-000 **10** 4 1/2 **Fervent**[65] 3733 4-9-5 38 (b) StephenDonohoe 2 —
(J M Bradley) *in rr: sltly hmpd and checked 3f out: sn struggling* **100/1**

4000 **11** 2 1/4 **Sempre Libera (IRE)**[31] 4825 3-8-12 45 (b[1]) TQuinn 7 —
(R T Phillips) *led: hdd over 3f out: wknd 2f out* **33/1**

44 **12** 16 **Heroic Fool**[139] 1536 3-9-3 0 SamHitchcott 12 —
(Miss Z C Davison) *s.i.s: hdwy over 3f out: rdn over 2f out: sn wknd* **40/1**

1m 15.18s (3.98) **Going Correction** +0.65s/f (Yiel)
WFA 3 from 4yo 2lb **12 Ran SP% 121.4**
Speed ratings (Par 103): **99,94,94,83,82 81,78,76,72,66 63,42**
toteswinger: 1&2 £4.20, 1&3 £10.60, 2&3 £9.10. CSF £18.62 TOTE £6.40: £2.10, £1.80, £3.20; EX 22.10.
Owner Terry Cooper **Bred** Newsells Park Stud Ltd **Trained** Whitsbury, Hants

FOCUS
A typically poor sprint maiden for the time of year. The winner may rate a little higher.

5750 MITIE ENGINEERING MAIDEN FILLIES' STKS 1m 3f 144y
4:10 (4:13) (Class 5) 3-Y-0+ **£2,719** (£809; £404; £202) **Stalls** Low

Form RPR

0222 **1** **Syvilla**[29] 4909 3-8-12 82 ChrisCatlin 11 80
(Rae Guest) *t.k.h in tch: lost pl over 4f out: smooth prog 3f out: led on bit over 1f out: rdn clr ins fnl f* **1/1[1]**

2254 **2** 7 **Shy**[33] 4732 3-8-12 75 StephenCarson 7 68
(P Winkworth) *led: rdn and hdd over 1f out: sn btn* **9/2[2]**

03 **3** 2 3/4 **Extreme Pleasure (IRE)**[22] 5117 3-8-12 0 PaulDoe 6 64
(W J Knight) *hld up in mid-div: rdn over 3f out: hdwy over 2f out: one pce fnl f* **14/1**

6 **4** 1 1/4 **Alvee (IRE)**[17] 5231 3-8-12 0 RobertWinston 2 62
(J R Fanshawe) *hld up towards rr: stdy hdwy on ins over 5f out: rdn over 2f out: one pce* **9/1**

0 **5** 2 **Watercolours (IRE)**[10] 5463 3-8-12 0 AdamKirby 12 59
(G L Moore) *hld up in tch: jnd ldr 5f out: ev ch over 2f out: sn rdn: wknd fnl f* **33/1**

6 3/4 **Sakheela** 3-8-12 0 PaulEddery 3 58
(Pat Eddery) *s.i.s: hld up in rr: rdn 3f out: nvr nr ldrs* **25/1**

0530 **7** 3 **Winners Chant (IRE)**[26] 4985 3-8-12 70 RyanMoore 1 53
(Sir Michael Stoute) *rdn leaving stalls: sn prom: rdn and wknd over 3f out* **5/1[3]**

0 **8** 1 **Won More Night**[17] 5231 6-9-7 0 EdwardCreighton 10 51
(D J Wintle) *t.k.h: sn bhd: hdwy on ins over 4f out: ev ch 3f out: sn rdn: wknd over 1f out* **80/1**

5 **9** shd **Al Asayl Rose (USA)**[19] 5182 3-8-12 0 FrancisNorton 9 51
(H J L Dunlop) *t.k.h: lost pl over 7f out: sn bhd* **33/1**

00- **10** 1 **Prima Ballerina**[486] 1639 4-9-7 0 RichardKingscote 4 49
(J G Portman) *hld up in tch: rdn and wknd over 2f out* **40/1**

11 46 **Honeypot Splenda**[50] 3-8-12 0 CatherineGannon 8 —
(H S Howe) *prom tl wknd qckly over 5f out: t.o fnl 4f* **150/1**

2m 41.52s (10.92) **Going Correction** +0.85s/f (Soft)
WFA 3 from 4yo+ 9lb **11 Ran SP% 115.6**
Speed ratings (Par 100): **97,92,90,89,88 87,85,85,85,84 53**
toteswinger: 1&2 £2.20, 1&3 £4.60, 2&3 £7.80. CSF £5.08 TOTE £2.00: £1.10, £1.50, £2.90; EX 5.90.
Owner T J Cooper **Bred** T J Cooper **Trained** Newmarket, Suffolk

FOCUS
The winner outclassed her rivals in this steadily run, modest maiden and the form is rated through the third and fourth.

5751 SOS LEGAL SOFTWARE H'CAP 5f 161y
4:40 (4:40) (Class 5) (0-75,75) 3-Y-0+ **£2,914** (£867; £433; £216) **Stalls** Centre

Form RPR

1445 **1** **Witchry**[23] 5101 6-8-7 **62** SamHitchcott 6 71
(A G Newcombe) *hld up: hdwy over 2f out: rdn to ld and hung lft ins fnl f: r.o* **4/1[2]**

4020 **2** 1 1/4 **Don Pele (IRE)**[15] 5315 6-8-13 **71** (b) KevinGhunowa(3) 8 76
(R A Harris) *sn w ldrs: led over 3f out: rdn over 1f out: hdd and hung lft ins fnl f: nt qckn* **7/1**

210 **3** 4 **Diane's Choice**[10] 5467 5-8-12 **72** (p) DavidProbert(5) 5 64
(Miss Gay Kelleway) *hld up and bhd: rdn and hdwy over 1f out: no ex ins fnl f* **5/1[3]**

1310 **4** nk **Night Rocket (IRE)**[10] 5467 4-9-1 **70** (t) FrancisNorton 4 61
(A M Balding) *prom: rdn over 1f out: fdd fnl f* **5/1[3]**

3000 **5** nk **Tudor Prince (IRE)**[4] 5648 4-9-2 **71** PhilipRobinson 7 61
(A W Carroll) *led: hdd over 3f out: rdn over 1f out: fdd fnl f* **11/4[1]**

0206 **6** 2 **Digital**[26] 4981 11-9-6 **75** ChrisCatlin 1 58
(M R Channon) *bhd: hdwy over 2f out: wknd over 1f out* **8/1**

4030 **7** 10 **Apple Pie Order (IRE)**[30] 4865 3-7-13 **61** oh1 Louis-PhilippeBeuzelin(5) 3 11
(R J Hodges) *hld up and bhd: rdn 2f out: sn struggling* **16/1**

0040 **8** 1 1/2 **Harrison's Flyer (IRE)**[22] 5121 7-7-13 **61** oh7 (p) PietroRomeo(7) 2 6
(J M Bradley) *t.k.h: w ldr 2f: styd far side and racd alone fr 3f out: wknd 2f out* **25/1**

1m 14.63s (3.43) **Going Correction** +0.65s/f (Yiel)
WFA 3 from 4yo+ 2lb **8 Ran SP% 113.3**
Speed ratings (Par 103): **103,101,96,95,95 92,79,77**
toteswinger: 1&2 £5.30, 1&3 £4.40, 2&3 £7.30. CSF £31.28 CT £140.91 TOTE £6.80: £1.80, £2.40, £1.80; EX 37.10.
Owner M K F Seymour **Bred** Darley **Trained** Yarnscombe, Devon

FOCUS
An ordinary sprint which saw the first pair come clear. The form is rated through the first two.

5752 BOLLINGER CHAMPAGNE CHALLENGE SERIES MAIDEN H'CAP (FOR GENTLEMAN AMATEUR RIDERS) 1m 5f 22y
5:10 (5:12) (Class 5) (0-70,64) 3-Y-O+ £2,623 (£813; £406; £203) Stalls High

Form RPR
5065 1 **Wyeth**35 4691 4-11-5 56........................(p) MrJoshuaMoore(5) 12 64
(G L Moore) *hld up in rr: hdwy 3f out: rdn to ld over 1f out: sn wandered: drvn and hld on towards fin* 7/1³
0064 2 *nk* **Munlochy Bay**14 5367 4-11-6 52........................ MrSWalker 8 59
(W S Kittow) *hld up and bhd: rdn and hdwy into mid-div 5f out: styd on over 1f out: hung lft ins fnl f: sn ev ch: r.o* 3/1¹
5006 3 *1* **Historic Place (USA)**14 5367 8-11-1 50..............(p) MrDFDevereux(3) 2 56
(J A Geake) *led: hdd 3f out: sn rdn: styd on ins fnl f* 6/1²
-660 4 *6* **Very Green (FR)**14 5367 6-10-11 50..............(p) MrOJMurphy(7) 1 48
(Mrs A L M King) *a.p: wnt 2nd 7f out: led 3f out: rdn and hung rt 2f out: hdd over 1f out: wknd ins fnl f* 8/1
6600 5 *4 ½* **Code Violation**72 3483 3-10-7 56........................ MrHGMiller(7) 4 47
(Jean-Rene Auvray) *hld up in tch: rdn over 2f out: sn wknd* 12/1
4563 6 *6* **Abstract Colours (IRE)**17 5216 3-11-3 64.............. MrNdeBoinville(5) 10 47
(A M Balding) *dwlt: towards rr: no ch whn hung bdly lft 1f out* 3/1¹
304- 7 *7* **Lap Of The Gods**299 6808 4-10-8 45........................ MrDColeman(5) 9 18
(Miss Z C Davison) *hld up in mid-div: hdwy over 5f out: rdn over 4f out: wknd over 2f out* 50/1
044- 8 *4* **Pertemps Power**347 5755 4-10-13 50........................ MrIPopham(5) 3 18
(A D Smith) *hld up in mid-div: rdn 3f out: sn struggling* 25/1
0222 9 *1* **Bocciani (GER)**31 4814 3-10-12 61........................ MrThomasHogg(7) 5 27
(A Berry) *hld up in rr: no ch fnl 3f* 10/1
/6-0 10 *6* **Pips Assertive Way**25 4322 7-10-10 45........................ MrMJJSmith(3) 7 3
(A W Carroll) *chsd ldr tl over 7f out: wknd over 5f out: no ch fnl 3f* 33/1
02-0 11 *7* **Hill Cloud**30 4879 6-10-10 45........................ MrBenBrisbourne(3) 11 —
(W M Brisbourne) *hld up in tch: wknd 3f out* 28/1
3m 7.99s (15.99) **Going Correction** +0.85s/f (Soft)
WFA 3 from 4yo+ 10lb 11 Ran SP% 116.9
Speed ratings (Par 103): **84,83,83,79,76 73,68,66,65,61 57**
toteswinger: 1&2 £5.70, 1&3 £11.40, 2&3 £5.50. CSF £27.18 CT £135.80 TOTE £9.30: £2.70, £1.70, £2.30; EX 30.40 Place 6: £81.51, Place 5: 48.86..
Owner D R Hunnisett **Bred** Lael Stables **Trained** Woodingdean, E Sussex

FOCUS
A weak handicap for the grade, confined to gentleman amateur riders, with the top weight rated just 56.The second and third ran to their Warwick latest.
T/Jkpt: Not won. T/Plt: £38.20 to a £1 stake. Pool: £85,887.74. 1,640.71 winning tickets. T/Qpdt: £15.20 to a £1 stake. Pool: £5,615.61. 272.00 winning tickets. KH

5530 FOLKESTONE (R-H)
Monday, September 8

OFFICIAL GOING: Soft (heavy in places; 5.9)
Wind: Fairly modest Weather: Bright, partly cloudy

5753 HYTHE MEDIAN AUCTION MAIDEN STKS (DIV I) 7f (S)
2:20 (2:21) (Class 5) 2-Y-O £2,914 (£867; £433; £216) Stalls Low

Form RPR
022 1 **Brazilian Art**21 5158 2-9-3 78........................ AlanMunro 9 78+
(P W Chapple-Hyam) *led far side gp after 2f: clr of that gp fr 1/2-way: rdn over 3f out: led overall ins fnl f: r.o wl: 1st of 4 in gp* 1/1¹
0323 2 *½* **Zebrano**47 4305 2-9-3 78........................ MickyFenton 4 77
(Miss E C Lavelle) *led stands' side gp and overall ldr: rdn over 1f out: hdd and no ex ins fnl f: 1st of 6 in gp* 3/1²
0 3 *1 ¾* **Destiny Quest (USA)**16 5271 2-9-3 0........................ GeorgeBaker 1 72
(L M Cumani) *racd stands' side: stdd s: hld up in rr: hdwy to chse stands' side ldr 4f out: rdn and hung rt ent fnl f: kpt on same pce after: 2nd of 6 in gp* 12/1
00 4 *10* **Bubses Boy**21 5158 2-9-3 0........................ HayleyTurner 3 47
(M L W Bell) *racd stands' side: a bhd: sme modest late hdwy: 3rd of 6 in gp* 50/1
00 5 *2* **Marcus Crassus (IRE)**25 5021 2-9-3 0........................ JimmyQuinn 5 42
(H J L Dunlop) *racd stands' side: sn wl bhd: modest late hdwy: 4th of 6 in gp* 66/1
6 *nse* **Attainable** 2-8-12 0........................ JimCrowley 2 37
(Mrs A J Perrett) *racd stands' side: chsd ldr on stands' side tl 4f out: sn struggling: wl btn fnl 2f: 5th of 6 in gp* 16/1
7 *4* **North Cape (USA)** 2-9-3 0........................ FergusSweeney 11 32
(H Candy) *racd far side: a wl bhd: nvr a factor: 2nd of 4 in gp* 10/1
00 8 *shd* **Dark Ranger**33 4747 2-9-3 0........................ RobertHavlin 8 32
(M J Wallace, Australia) *racd far side: chsd wnr far side 3f out: no imp: wknd 2f out: 3rd of 4 in gp* 50/1
5 9 *1* **Googoobarabajagal (IRE)**25 5022 2-9-3 0........................ SteveDrowne 7 30
(W S Kittow) *racd far side: s.i.s: sn led far side tl 5f out: struggling 1/2-way: no ch last 2f: 4th of 4 in gp* 15/2³
50 10 *26* **Itshim**8 5530 2-9-3 0........................ SaleemGolam 6 —
(S C Williams) *racd stands' side: racd keenly: chsd ldrs tl wknd qckly 3f out: virtually p.u fnl f: t.o: 6th of 6 in gp* 33/1
1m 30.48s (3.18) **Going Correction** +0.40s/f (Good) 10 Ran SP% 117.8
Speed ratings (Par 95): **97,96,94,83,80 80,76,75,74,45**
toteswinger: 1&2 £1.10, 1&3 £3.90, 2&3 £8.80. CSF £3.91 TOTE £1.70: £1.10, £1.10, £3.70; EX 4.50 Trifecta £32.50 Pool: £384.21, 8.74 winning units..
Owner Matthew Green **Bred** Mrs D Du Feu And Trickledown Stud **Trained** Newmarket, Suffolk

FOCUS
The course had taken 70mm of rain over the past week, but a dry night and a strong wind in the morning led to a change in the official going to soft, heavy in places. It was predictably tacky and testing, though. They split into two groups and there appeared to be no strong bias. Four went to the far-side rail, and it was from that group that the winner Brazilian Art emerged. He could progress again.

NOTEBOOK
Brazilian Art, narrowly beaten last time out by a filly who won a nursery off 70 on her next start, looked to have a solid chance on that effort. He already had form in the book on soft ground so it was just a question of whether he would get this extra furlong, but the way he stayed on at the end of his last two starts over 6f gave plenty of encouragement on that front. He beat the rest on his side by a long way but did not have much in hand over Zebrano, who came out on top on the stands' side. (op 5-6)
Zebrano had to prove he could handle ground this soft having never raced on anything like it before, but he is bred to stay well and he got the trip well enough. Quickly away, he had the stands' rail to help throughout and came out on top on his side. (op 10-3 tchd 4-1)
Destiny Quest(USA), who is a half-brother to three winners and holds a Royal Lodge entry, finished down the field in a Newmarket maiden on his debut, but the ground was softer this time and he had another furlong to run. He shaped with a bit of promise and looks one for handicaps after one more run. (op 18-1)
Bubses Boy, who finished a long way behind Brazilian Art at Yarmouth last time, was again well beaten by that rival. He has not shown a great deal in his three starts to date but is at least now eligible for a mark. (op 66-1)
Marcus Crassus(IRE), who does at least come from a family that knows how to win, is another now eligible for handicaps.
Attainable took the eye on paper as she is a daughter of Kalanisi out of a sister to Dancing Brave, but the ground may have been plenty soft enough for her. She should be better for the experience, though. (tchd 14-1)
Itshim showed up well, away from the stands' rail, for a fair way. He was well backed but disappointed on his debut, has ability and can do better in handicap company. (tchd 28-1)

5754 HYTHE MEDIAN AUCTION MAIDEN STKS (DIV II) 7f (S)
2:50 (2:53) (Class 5) 2-Y-O £2,914 (£867; £433; £216) Stalls Low

Form RPR
5 1 **Mishrif (USA)**31 4826 2-9-3 0........................ AlanMunro 4 90+
(P W Chapple-Hyam) *mde virtually all: rdn jst over 2f out: drew clr ent fnl f: r.o wl: comf* 11/10¹
22 2 *4* **Captain Ellis (USA)**44 4438 2-9-3 0........................ FergusSweeney 10 80
(K R Burke) *hld up in tch: swtchd rt and hdwy 2f out: chsd wnr over 1f out: hung lft ent fnl f: outpcd fnl f* 4/1³
45 3 *3 ¼* **Bagber**17 5227 2-9-3 0........................ EddieAhern 7 72
(H J L Dunlop) *w ldr tl rdn 2f out: plugged on same pce after* 10/3²
4 *4* **Star Links (USA)** 2-9-3 0........................ SteveDrowne 11 62+
(R Hannon) *chsd ldrs: rdn to chse wnr briefly 2f out: wknd ent fnl f* 16/1
5 *nk* **Cool Strike (UAE)** 2-9-3 0........................ LPKeniry 3 61+
(A M Balding) *s.i.s: sn bustled along: wl bhd: styd on steadily fr over 1f out: nvr on terms* 25/1
0 6 *1 ¼* **Congenial**46 4339 2-8-12 0........................ JimCrowley 1 53
(J R Fanshawe) *hld up in tch: edgd out rt and effrt 2f out: sn wknd: wl btn fnl f* 20/1
7 *2 ½* **Royal Willy (IRE)** 2-9-3 0........................ J-PGuillambert 2 52
(W Jarvis) *dwlt: sn pressing ldrs: rdn over 2f out: wknd qckly 2f out* 25/1
8 *6* **Merton Lad** 2-9-3 0........................ MichaelHills 6 37
(T G Mills) *s.i.s: rn green and sn detached in last: nvr a factor* 25/1
0 9 *6* **Dontforgetturshovel**16 5271 2-9-0 0........................ JerryO'Dwyer(3) 8 22
(J Pearce) *a towards rr: sn bustled along: struggling fr 1/2-way: wl bhd after* 100/1
5 10 *5* **Katie Higgins**64 3754 2-8-9 0........................ TolleyDean(3) 5 —
(J L Spearing) *s.i.s: rdn and struggling 4f out: t.o* 33/1
00 11 *33* **Orangeleg**32 4778 2-9-3 0........................ SaleemGolam 9 —
(S C Williams) *s.i.s: rdn and struggling 4f out: t.o* 100/1
1m 29.94s (2.64) **Going Correction** +0.40s/f (Good) 63 Ran SP% 117.8
Speed ratings (Par 95): **100,95,91,87,86 85,82,75,68,63 25**
toteswinger: 1&2 £2.60, 1&3 £1.10, 2&3 £3.30. CSF £5.12 TOTE £2.10: £1.20, £1.50, £1.10; EX 7.10 Trifecta £10.50 Pool: £518.31, 36.40 winning units..
Owner Sheik Ahmad Yousuf Al Sabah **Bred** Mr & Mrs Theodore Kuster Et Al **Trained** Newmarket, Suffolk

FOCUS
They all stayed stands' side on this occasion, and the time was just over half a second quicker than the first division. This is very strong maiden form for the track.

NOTEBOOK
Mishrif(USA), whose debut fifth came in a decent Newmarket maiden that has been working out well, with the second and third winning next time, had far more testing conditions to deal with here but he coped well, racing prominently throughout and drawing clear in the closing stages. He looks a useful prospect. (op 6-4 tchd 7-4)
Captain Ellis(USA), who holds Group 1 entries in the National Stakes and Racing Post Trophy, looked a threat a furlong and a half out but just could not go with the winner late on. He coped with the ground well enough, despite reservations on breeding, and the extra furlong certainly suited. He could now run in nurseries, but is clearly up to winning a similar race to this. (op 9-4 tchd 2-1)
Bagber looks a solid guide to the level of the form as he had put up two solid efforts over this trip at Newbury previously. By soft-ground sire Diktat, he plugged on well for third and is another now eligible for nurseries. (op 13-2)
Star Links(USA), an American-bred newcomer, shaped quite well racing four wide for much of the way. Quicker ground is likely to suit him and he can be expected to come on for his first run. (op 14-1)
Cool Strike(UAE), who was a cheap purchase and is already a gelding, ran pretty green but was putting in some good work at the finish. He should come into his own over middle distances next term.
Congenial, who did not face the kickback on her debut at Kempton, is by Kyllachy out of a Sadler's Wells mare so it was reasonable to expect better from her on this switch to turf. She could never really pick up in this ground, though. (op 16-1)

5755 GARDEN COAST H'CAP 7f (S)
3:20 (3:22) (Class 6) (0-65,65) 3-Y-O+ £2,914 (£867; £433; £216) Stalls Low

Form RPR
4004 1 **Hucking Harkness**32 4777 3-8-9 56........................ LPKeniry 12 63
(J R Best) *racd far side: mde all: rdn wl over 1f out: styd on wl: 1st of 3 in gp* 14/1
0001 2 *1 ¾* **Palais Polaire**32 4770 6-8-10 53........................(p) RobertHavlin 3 57
(J A Geake) *racd stands' side: led stands' side: rdn over 1f out: kpt on same pce: 1st of 9 in gp* 10/1
300 3 *½* **Affrettando (IRE)**54 4081 4-9-5 62........................ EddieAhern 6 65+
(J A R Toller) *racd stands' side: s.i.s: bhd: rdn 4f out: hdwy u.p 2f out: styd on to go 3rd overall fnl 100yds: nvr trbld ldrs: 2nd of 9 in gp* 14/1
005 4 *2 ¾* **Vanadium**16 5267 6-9-6 63........................ GeorgeBaker 7 58
(G L Moore) *racd stands' side: t.k.h: hld up in midfield: hdwy 4f out: chsd ldr stands' side over 2f out: rdn and one pce fr wl over 1f out: 3rd of 9 in gp* 5/1²
3410 5 *2 ¼* **Seneschal**16 5267 7-9-8 65........................ SteveDrowne 2 54
(A B Haynes) *racd stands' side: chsd ldrs: rdn wl over 1f out: wknd over 1f out: 4th of 9 in gp* 8/1
050 6 *1 ½* **Kappalyn (IRE)**25 5023 3-8-5 52........................ HayleyTurner 10 35
(R Hannon) *racd far side: last of far side trio: rdn and struggling over 2f out: wnt 2nd of gp 1f out: no ch w wnr: 2nd of 3 in gp* 20/1
3032 7 *3 ¼* **Crataegus**16 5267 3-9-3 64........................ FergusSweeney 1 38
(H Candy) *racd stands' side: rdn 1/2-way: sn struggling: no ch last 2f: 5th of 9 in gp* 4/1¹
0652 8 *1 ½* **Hits Only Cash**23 5088 6-9-8 65........................(p) JimmyQuinn 5 37
(J Pearce) *wnt freely to post: racd stands' side: s.i.s: bhd: rdn 1/2-way: nvr nr ldrs: 6th of 9 in gp* 7/1

0043 **9** ¾ **Island Treasure**[37] 4637 3-8-13 **60**........................ TravisBlock 13 28
(H Morrison) *racd far side: chsd wnr: rdn over 2f out: no ch w wnr last 2f: 3rd of 3 in gp* **9/1**

0104 **10** 1½ **Pragmatist**[31] 4825 4-9-6 **63**........................ JimCrowley 9 29
(P Winkworth) *racd stands' side: chsd ldrs stands' side tl over 2f out: wknd qckly 2f out: 7th of 9 in gp* **6/1**[3]

0600 **11** 9 **Turkish Sultan (IRE)**[90] 2917 5-8-9 **52**........................(p) MickyFenton 8 —
(J M Bradley) *racd stands' side: in tch in midfield: rdn and wknd qckly over 2f out: 8th of 9 in gp* **33/1**

0430 **12** 26 **Harryana To**[32] 4793 3-8-9 **56**........................ JohnEgan 4 —
(B J McMath) *racd stands' side: sn pushed along and nvr travelling: wl bhd last 3f: t.o* **33/1**

1m 30.13s (2.83) **Going Correction** +0.40s/f (Good)
WFA 3 from 4yo+ 4lb **12** Ran SP% **117.6**
Speed ratings (Par 101): **99,97,96,93,90 89,85,83,82,81 70,41**
toteswinger: 1&2 £21.20, 1&3 £24.70, 2&3 £26.30. CSF £142.69 CT £2019.51 TOTE £13.70: £2.90, £3.40, £3.90; EX 168.10 TRIFECTA Not won..
Owner Hucking Horses **Bred** Darley **Trained** Hucking, Kent

FOCUS
An ordinary handicap and this time they split into two groups, with the smaller one heading for the far-side rail. It was from that trio that the winner came, though. The winner and runner-up made all on their respective sides and the form looks pretty modest.
Crataegus Official explanation: jockey said gelding never travelled
Harryana To Official explanation: jockey said filly was unsuited by the soft ground

5756 GARDEN OF ENGLAND NOVICE STKS 6f
3:50 (3:50) (Class 4) 2-Y-O **£3,885** (£1,156; £577; £288) **Stalls** Low

Form RPR

1 **1** **Portugese Caddy (IRE)**[77] 3323 2-9-2 0........................ JimCrowley 1 79
(P Winkworth) *mde all: rdn wl over 1f out: hld on gamely fnl f* **3/1**[3]

2 shd **Sign Of Approval** 2-8-8 0........................ FergusSweeney 3 72+
(K R Burke) *stdd s: t.k.h: hld up in tch: squeezed through to chal 1f out: str chal but a jst hld fnl f: sddle slipped and uns rdr after fin* **2/1**[2]

3 4½ **Confucius Captain (IRE)** 2-8-8 0........................ EddieAhern 4 57+
(J R Boyle) *in tch: rdn and effrt 2f out: ev ch over 1f out: outpcd fnl f* **5/1**

1051 **4** ½ **Imperial Guest**[16] 5286 2-9-9 88........................ JohnEgan 2 71
(G G Margarson) *chsd ldr: rdn and ev ch wl over 1f out tl outpcd fnl f* **7/4**[1]

1m 16.85s (4.15) **Going Correction** +0.40s/f (Good) **4** Ran SP% **111.4**
Speed ratings (Par 97): **88,87,81,81**
CSF £9.50 TOTE £5.20; EX 7.00.
Owner Mrs Tessa Winkworth **Bred** N H Bloodstock Ltd **Trained** Chiddingfold, Surrey

FOCUS
This did not look that strong a race on paper, with the most experienced runner in the race Imperial Guest, who has a rating of 88, having to give 7lb to Portugese Caddy and 15lb to the unraced duo. The winner built on his Windsor win and the next two have improvement in him.

NOTEBOOK
Portugese Caddy(IRE), who sprang a surprise when taking a modest 6f maiden on fast ground on his debut at Windsor back in June, had the stands' rail to help throughout and rallied close home after being strongly challenged by the newcomer Sign Of Approval well inside the last. There are apparently no great plans for him and his immediate future depends on the handicapper's reaction. (op 5-2)
Sign Of Approval is a half-brother to four winners, including Italian Listed race winner Green Room, and he is entered in the Mill Reef and Middle Park Stakes. Tracking the eventual winner on the rail, things got a bit tight as he went for a gap between horses approaching the final furlong, but he got through alright and looked like he was coming with a successful challenge inside the last until the winner rallied on the rail. It was a promising debut, albeit in receipt of plenty of weight, and he can improve for the experience. Sweeney was unseated after the finish and was unable to weigh in. (tchd 9-4)
Confucius Captain(IRE), another newcomer, is by Captain Rio so should not have had any problems with the ground. A half-brother to five winners, he probably was not helped by racing widest, away from the favoured stands' rail, for most of the way. (op 6-1 tchd 15-2)
Imperial Guest had plenty on his plate giving weight all round and this ground may not have been his cup of tea anyway. He was done no favours approaching the furlong marker either. Official explanation: trainer said colt lost a shoe and was unsuited by the soft (heavy in places) ground (op 9-4 tchd 13-8)

5757 CLIVE PARKER 50TH BIRTHDAY H'CAP 5f
4:20 (4:21) (Class 4) (0-85,84) 3-Y-O+ **£5,361** (£1,604; £802; £401; £199) **Stalls** Low

Form RPR

2135 **1** **Regal Royale**[8] 5532 5-8-5 **70** oh3........................(v) PatrickMathers 6 74
(Peter Grayson) *reminders sn after s: chsd ldrs: drvn to chal over 1f out: led last strides* **8/1**

4506 **2** hd **Irish Pearl (IRE)**[26] 4962 3-9-2 **82**........................ JimCrowley 2 85
(K R Burke) *hld up in tch: plld out and hdwy wl over 1f out: rdn to ld ent fnl f: hdd last strides* **4/1**[2]

2311 **3** 1¼ **Equuleus Pictor**[21] 5151 4-8-11 **81**........................ JackDean(5) 8 80
(J L Spearing) *led: rdn over 1f out: hdd ent fnl f: kpt on same pce* **9/4**[1]

4361 **4** 1 **Woodcote (IRE)**[24] 5046 6-9-2 **81**........................(vt) GeorgeBaker 5 76
(P R Chamings) *chsd ldr: rdn 2f out: nt qckn ent fnl f: btn fnl 100yds* **11/2**

0400 **5** 1½ **Zowington**[23] 5101 6-9-2 **81**........................(v[1]) IanMongan 3 71
(C F Wall) *bhd: rdn 1/2-way: nvr trbld ldrs* **5/1**[3]

0450 **6** 2¾ **The Tatling (IRE)**[4] 5648 11-9-5 **84**........................ PaulFitzsimons 4 64
(J M Bradley) *s.i.s: sn pushed along and struggling to go pce: nvr trbld ldrs* **8/1**

1045 **7** 11 **Cape Royal**[26] 4981 8-8-12 **77**........................(bt) SteveDrowne 7 17
(J M Bradley) *s.i.s: hdwy to chse ldrs over 3f out: wknd qckly wl over 1f out: eased ins fnl f* **9/1**

61.41 secs (1.41) **Going Correction** +0.40s/f (Good)
WFA 3 from 4yo+ 1lb **7** Ran SP% **115.0**
Speed ratings (Par 105): **104,103,101,100,97 93,75**
toteswinger: 1&2 £7.70, 1&3 £3.40, 2&3 £2.90. CSF £40.19 CT £96.37 TOTE £8.40: £3.10, £2.70; EX 53.90 Trifecta £177.10 Pool: £387.89, 1.62 winning units..
Owner S Kamis And Mrs S Grayson **Bred** Cheveley Park Stud Ltd **Trained** Formby, Lancs

FOCUS
A pretty competitive sprint handicap on paper, and they all came up the stands' rail. The pace was ordinary. The winner was 3lb wrong and the favourite disappointed, but the form has been taken at face value.

5758 WESTENHANGER H'CAP 1m 4f
4:50 (4:50) (Class 5) (0-70,70) 3-Y-O **£3,238** (£963; £481; £240) **Stalls** Low

Form RPR

6501 **1** **Fearless Warrior**[8] 5537 3-8-11 **63** 6ex........................(b) EddieAhern 1 73+
(J L Dunlop) *hld up in tch: chsd ldng pair 8f out: trckd ldr gng wl 3f out: led 2f out: rdn clr over 1f out: eased ins fnl f* **11/4**[2]

4410 **2** 4 **China Pink**[24] 5077 3-8-4 **56**........................ DO'Donohoe 7 57
(Sir Mark Prescott) *led at gd gallop: rdn 3f out: hdd 2f out: no ch w wnr after: plugged on* **9/2**[3]

1-66 **3** 3¼ **Desert Thistle (IRE)**[11] 5428 3-9-4 **70**........................ SteveDrowne 5 67
(H J L Dunlop) *sn niggled along in last pair: wnt modest 4th 4f out: chsd ldng pair 3f out: no imp* **9/2**[3]

0623 **4** 2 **Carmela Maria**[40] 4527 3-8-8 **60**........................ AlanMunro 3 53
(C F Wall) *chsd ldr after 1f tl 3f out: sn rdn: wknd jst over 2f out* **7/1**

0543 **5** 13 **Mistress Eva**[21] 5146 3-9-2 **68**........................ JimCrowley 8 40
(P Winkworth) *chsd ldr for 1f: lost pl and rdn over 6f out: btn whn sltly hmpd over 4f out: no ch after* **5/2**[1]

6040 **6** 40 **Major Promise**[21] 5163 3-8-11 **63**........................ JohnEgan 6 —
(G G Margarson) *s.i.s: rn wd bnd 9f out: bhd: rdn over 6f out: hung rt over 4f out: t.o fnl 2f: eased fnl f* **16/1**

2m 45.47s (4.57) **Going Correction** +0.475s/f (Yiel) **6** Ran SP% **110.0**
Speed ratings (Par 101): **103,100,98,96,88 61**
toteswinger: 1&2 £3.20, 1&3 £1.20, 2&3 £3.10. CSF £14.66 CT £48.19 TOTE £3.20: £1.80, £2.60; EX 16.70 Trifecta £49.20 Pool: £421.71, 6.33 winning units..
Owner Mrs I H Stewart-Brown & M J Meacock **Bred** I Stewart-Brown And M Meacock **Trained** Arundel, W Sussex

FOCUS
An ordinary handicap run at a fair pace. The winner is rated value for 6l with the runner-up to form.
Mistress Eva Official explanation: trainer had no explanation for the poor form shown

5759 STONE OF FOLCA H'CAP 1m 1f 149y
5:20 (5:20) (Class 4) (0-85,83) 3-Y-O+ **£5,361** (£1,604; £802; £401; £199) **Stalls** Centre

Form RPR

2411 **1** **Mr Hichens**[15] 5309 3-9-3 **82**........................ TPO'Shea 4 91+
(B J Meehan) *chsd ldr tl led 8f out: mde rest: pushed along in command fr over 1f out: eased nr fin* **9/4**[1]

02 **2** 1½ **Air Chief**[51] 4179 3-8-6 **71**........................ JimmyQuinn 7 75
(H J L Dunlop) *racd keenly: led tl 8f out: chsd wnr after tl over 2f out: sn rdn: regained 2nd ins fnl f: nt pce to threaten wnr* **4/1**[3]

3033 **3** 1 **Greylami (IRE)**[37] 4621 3-9-2 **81**........................ MichaelHills 1 83
(T G Mills) *s.i.s: hld up in last trio: hdwy 4f out: rdn and unable qck 2f out: styd on fnl 100yds to go 3rd nr fin: nt pce to trble wnr* **7/2**[2]

-124 **4** hd **Diamond Yas (IRE)**[12] 5405 3-9-1 **80**........................ TPQueally 2 82
(H R A Cecil) *chsd ldng pair: chsd wnr over 2f out: rdn 2f out: unable qck: lost 2 pls ins fnl f* **7/1**

0612 **5** shd **Higgy's Boy (IRE)**[29] 4906 3-9-4 **83**........................ SteveDrowne 3 85+
(R Hannon) *hld up in last pair: rdn over 2f out: no hdwy tl r.o ins fnl f: nvr trbld wnr* **9/1**

0431 **6** 1 **Dr Brass**[22] 5118 3-8-12 **77**........................(b) EddieAhern 8 77
(H J L Dunlop) *hld up in midfield: rdn and effrt 2f out: fnd little and plugged on same pce* **6/1**

4454 **7** 10 **Sonny Parkin**[24] 5069 6-9-0 **75**........................(p) JerryO'Dwyer(3) 5 55
(J Pearce) *hld up in last: hdwy over 3f out: shkn up and no rspnse over 2f out: eased ins fnl f* **16/1**

2m 9.13s (4.23) **Going Correction** +0.475s/f (Yiel)
WFA 3 from 4yo+ 7lb **7** Ran SP% **115.7**
Speed ratings (Par 105): **102,100,100,99,99 98,90**
toteswinger: 1&2 £3.80, 1&3 £2.70, 2&3 £4.30. CSF £11.79 CT £30.11 TOTE £3.20: £1.40, £2.80; EX 13.40 Trifecta £91.50 Pool: £324.02, 2.62 winning units. Place 6: £319.74, Place 5: £255.42..
Owner Mrs J & D E Cash **Bred** C A Green **Trained** Manton, Wilts

FOCUS
A fairly competitive heat on paper. The winner was allowed to set an ordinary pace but otherwise the form makes sense.
Higgy's Boy(IRE) Official explanation: jockey said colt was denied a clear run which prevented him riding out near line
T/Plt: £470.40 to a £1 stake. Pool: £80,851.04. 125.45 winning tickets. T/Qpdt: £262.60 to a £1 stake. Pool: £4,472.01. 12.60 winning tickets. SP

4733 NEWCASTLE (L-H)
Monday, September 8
5760 Meeting Abandoned - Waterlogged

5766 - 5769a (Foreign Racing) - See Raceform Interactive

5303 BEVERLEY (R-H)
Tuesday, September 9

OFFICIAL GOING: Heavy
Wind: Light across Weather: Rain

5770 FIONA'S SIGNIFICANT BIRTHDAY H'CAP 5f
2:00 (2:06) (Class 6) (0-50,51) 3-Y-O+ **£2,104** (£626; £312; £156) **Stalls** High

Form RPR

0406 **1** **Wicked Wilma (IRE)**[11] 5452 4-8-8 **51** ow2........................ SladeO'Hara(5) 15 63
(A Berry) *cl up centre: led 1/2-way: rdn over 1f out: edgd lft ent fnl f: sn drvn and kpt on* **9/1**

3042 **2** 1¼ **Whozart (IRE)**[11] 5452 5-8-12 **50**........................ DanielTudhope 17 57
(A Dickman) *in tch: hdwy over 2f out: rdn to chse wnr over 1f out: drvn ent fnl f: no imp towards fin* **4/1**[1]

0000 **3** 3¼ **Morristown Music (IRE)**[56] 4047 4-8-12 **50**........................(v[1]) TonyHamilton 13 45
(J S Wainwright) *towards rr: pushed along and hdwy 2f out: sn rdn: styd on ent fnl f: nrst fin* **12/1**

0025 **4** 1 **Missus Molly Brown**[10] 5501 4-8-8 **46** oh1........................ PaulHanagan 8 38
(R A Fahey) *cl up: rdn along 2f out: drvn over 1f out and kpt on same pce* **12/1**

5524 **5** ½ **Gelert (IRE)**[11] 5452 3-8-2 **46** oh1........................(b) KellyHarrison(5) 12 36
(Peter Grayson) *chsd ldrs: rdn along 2f out: sn drvn and kpt on same pce* **7/1**[3]

3000 **6** 2 **Miss Taboo (IRE)**[17] 5261 4-8-8 **46**........................ JamieMoriarty 10 29
(P T Midgley) *in rr: rdn along 1/2-way: styd on u.p ins fnl f: nrst fin* **20/1**

0020 **7** hd **Head To Head (IRE)**[10] 5501 4-8-3 **48**........................ JamesRogers(7) 6 30
(A D Brown) *dwlt: sn rdn along and outpcd in rr: swtchd rt and hdwy 2f out: styd on u.p ins fnl f: nrst fin* **33/1**

00-0 **8** 3 **Sunley Sovereign**[29] 4919 4-8-8 **46** oh1........................(b[1]) PaulFessey 14 17
(Mrs R A Carr) *prom centre: rdn along 1/2-way: drvn wl over 1f out and grad wknd* **50/1**

5606 **9** 2¼ **Fan Club**[39] 4609 4-8-8 **46** oh1........................(b) DaleGibson 16 9
(Mrs R A Carr) *s.i.s and bhd tl sme hdwy u.p fnl 2f* **16/1**

0023 **10** 1 ½ **Monte Major (IRE)**5 5626 7-8-11 **49**........................(v) RobertWinston 2 7
(D Shaw) *in tch: effrt 2f out: sn rdn and n.d* **6/1**2

0601 **11** ¾ **Dubai To Barnsley**16 5307 3-8-11 **50**.............................. LeeEnstone 5 5
(Garry Moss) *in tch: rdn along 1/2-way: nvr a factor* **10/1**

0002 **12** *nk* **Myriola**16 5307 3-8-9 **48**.. ChrisCatlin 3 2
(S Gollings) *a in rr* **12/1**

3430 **13** 2 **Mormeatmic**35 4703 5-8-12 **50**............................... PaulMulrennan 7 —
(M W Easterby) *racd nr stands' rail: led to 1/2-way: sn rdn along: wknd wl over 1f out* **9/1**

0060 **14** ½ **Captain Turbot (IRE)**11 5457 3-8-7 **46** oh1............... RoystonFfrench 9 —
(D W Barker) *wnt lft s: a towards rr* **50/1**

5-50 **15** 3 ½ **Height Of Esteem**27 4961 5-8-8 **46** oh1.............................. TPO'Shea 4 —
(W M Brisbourne) *chsd ldr stands' rail: rdn along 1/2-way: sn wknd* **125/1**

66.79 secs (3.29) **Going Correction** +0.70s/f (Yiel)
WFA 3 from 4yo+ 1lb **15** Ran SP% **117.3**
Speed ratings (Par 101): **101,99,93,92,91 88,87,83,79,77 75,75,72,71,65**
toteswinger: 1&2 £16.00, 1&3 £23.30, 2&3 £12.40. CSF £41.67 CT £343.14 TOTE £13.00: £4.20, £2.00, £4.10; EX 44.20.
Owner Auldyn Stud Ltd **Bred** Gerry O'Sullivan **Trained** Cockerham, Lancs

FOCUS
This was a decidedly moderate sprint. The majority of runners came over to the near side after 2f, but the main action eventually developed down the middle of the track. The form seems to make sense.
Dubai To Barnsley Official explanation: jockey said gelding ran flat

5771 EDWARD FROST "SORRY" MAIDEN AUCTION STKS 1m 100y
2:30 (2:30) (Class 6) 2-Y-O **£1,942** (£578; £288; £144) **Stalls** High

Form RPR
0623 **1** **Huxaar**2 5716 2-8-11 73.. TonyHamilton 3 72
(Mrs L Stubbs) *cl up: led 1/2-way: rdn over 2f out: drvn over 1f out: kpt on wl* **4/1**2

43 **2** 2 ¼ **Chilly Filly (IRE)**17 5256 2-8-7 0............................ RoystonFfrench 5 63
(M Johnston) *trckd ldrs: hdwy to chal over 3f out: rdn 2f out: sn drvn: edgd lft and one pce* **2/5**1

3 4 **Miss Cracklinrosie** 2-8-6 0.. ChrisCatlin 6 54+
(J R Weymes) *hld up and sn wl bhd: rdn along 1/2-way: hdwy over 2f out: styd on wl u.p appr fnl f: nrst fin* **25/1**

000 **4** 3 **Aven Mac (IRE)**29 4921 2-7-13 35................................ KellyHarrison(5) 1 46
(N Bycroft) *chsd ldrs: rdn along over 3f out: drvn over 2f out and sn one pce* **100/1**

0465 **5** ½ **Kingaroo (IRE)**2 5716 2-8-10 50...................................... NickyMackay 8 51
(Garry Moss) *led 1f: cl up: rdn along 3f out: drvn and hung lft 2f out: sn wknd* **14/1**3

00 **6** 7 **Noble Artist**7 5590 2-8-11 0... PaulMulrennan 4 37
(D H Brown) *a in rr: bhd fnl 3f* **100/1**

7 *shd* **Dance Society** 2-8-10 0.. DavidAllan 2 36
(T D Easterby) *a in rr: bhd fnl 3f* **22/1**

00 **8** 24 **Venetian Lady**10 5500 2-8-7 0...................................... PaulFessey 7 —
(Mrs A Duffield) *t.k.h: led after 1f: hdd 1/2-way: sn rdn and wknd wl over 2f out* **50/1**

1m 56.52s (8.92) **Going Correction** +0.90s/f (Soft) **8** Ran SP% **110.2**
Speed ratings (Par 93): **91,88,84,81,81 74,74,50**
toteswinger: 1&2 £2.00, 1&3 £3.70, 2&3 £3.20. CSF £5.57 TOTE £3.60: £1.10, £1.02, £4.30; EX 8.10.
Owner Tyme Partnership **Bred** Mrs J A Chapman **Trained** Norton, N Yorks

FOCUS
A weak juvenile maiden. The ground found most out and the fourth and fifth put the form into perspective.

NOTEBOOK
Huxaar, beaten favourite at Thirsk just two days previously, settled a lot better and showed his true colours with a determined success. He displayed a game attitude when pressed by the eventual runner-up around 2f out, looking right at home on the testing ground, and basically outstayed his main rival. The fact he put a lot more daylight between himself and the fifth, who was not that far behind him at Thirsk, indicates he was not on his game there. With an official mark of 73 already he will not want to be going up too much for this when switching to nurseries, but he is a likeable performer who will continue to pay his way. (op 9-2 tchd 5-1)
Chilly Filly(IRE) was all the rage in the betting to open her account at the third attempt and she travelled up looking a likely winner at the 2f pole, but she failed to pick up when push came to shove, not looking the most resolute. That said, this was still the stiffest task she has faced to date and it was probably more a case of her being outstayed by the winner. She now has the option of nurseries.
Miss Cracklinrosie is bred to appreciate soft ground, but her pedigree suggested this may be a trip too far. Having been near last turning in, she eventually made up a lot of ground to grab a place and it is fair to expect a deal of improvement now she has this initial experience under her belt. (tchd 22-1)
Aven Mac(IRE) hails from an in-form yard and, finishing closer to the runner-up this time, kept on to post her best form to date. With an official mark of just 35, however, she puts the form into perspective. (tchd 80-1)

5772 BAY, FILEY, PREMIER COASTAL HOLIDAY VILLAGE H'CAP 1m 100y
3:00 (3:00) (Class 3) (0-95,91) 3-Y-O+ **£9,714** (£2,890; £1,444; £721) **Stalls** High

Form RPR
1250 **1** **Rainbow Mirage (IRE)**13 5405 4-8-13 **83**................ GrahamGibbons 7 92
(E S McMahon) *trckd ldng pair: smooth hdwy 3f out: rdn to ld 2f out: drvnand edgd rt ent fnl f: kpt on wl* **9/2**2

0420 **2** 1 **Exit Smiling**15 5360 6-9-3 **87**.................................. JamieMoriarty 6 94
(P T Midgley) *hld up in tch: hdwy 3f out: rdn to chse wnr wl over 1f out: drvn ins fnl f and kpt on* **16/1**

3220 **3** 6 **Billy Dane (IRE)**11 5470 4-8-11 **81**..............................(p) PaulHanagan 2 74
(R A Fahey) *led after 1f: rdn along and hdd 2f out: sn drvn and wknd over 1f out* **11/2**

1055 **4** 1 ½ **Nevada Desert (IRE)**12 5418 8-8-7 **77** oh1................ DeanMcKeown 4 67
(R M Whitaker) *trckd ldrs: hdwy 3f out: swtchd rt and rdn wl over 1f out: sn one pce* **13/2**

4231 **5** 4 **Reel Buddy Star**10 5504 3-8-2 **77**................................ ChrisCatlin 8 58
(G M Moore) *led 1f: cl up tl rdn along wl over 2f out and grad wknd* **11/2**

1430 **6** 1 ¾ **Kingsdale Orion (IRE)**14 5382 4-9-3 **87**........................ TPO'Shea 3 64
(B Ellison) *hld up in rr: hdwy on outer over 3f out: rdn along over 2f out: sn drvn and wknd* **5/1**3

3605 **7** 4 ½ **Vainglory (USA)**13 5405 4-9-3 **87**............................ RichardMullen 1 53
(D M Simcock) *in tch: effrt 3f out: sn rdn along and wknd over 2f out* **7/2**1

-100 **8** 2 ¾ **Best Prospect (IRE)**114 2218 6-9-7 **91**........................(t) PaulMulrennan 9 51
(M Dods) *hld up: a in rr* **14/1**

1m 53.27s (5.67) **Going Correction** +0.90s/f (Soft)
WFA 3 from 4yo+ 5lb **8** Ran SP% **113.7**
Speed ratings (Par 107): **107,106,100,98,94 92,88,85**
toteswinger: 1&2 £14.00, 1&3 £8.20, 2&3 £11.30. CSF £70.04 CT £404.14 TOTE £7.20: £1.90, £3.70, £2.10; EX 88.90.
Owner R L Bedding **Bred** Neville O'Byrne And Roderick Ryan **Trained** Lichfield, Staffs
■ Stewards' Enquiry : Jamie Moriarty caution: used whip in the incorrect place

FOCUS
The first pair came clear in this open handicap and they seemed to gain an advantage by keeping towards the middle to far side down the home straight. The form can be rated through the runner-up, but it is probably wise not to take it too literally.

NOTEBOOK
Rainbow Mirage(IRE) bounced right back to form on this return to turf and kept up the excellent recent form of his stable. He was always handy and, picking up strongly when asked for maximum effort, was always doing enough to hold off the runner-up despite his rider losing the whip around the furlong marker. This rates a career-best effort and, on this evidence, he could find a little further improvement when stepping up to 1m2f. (op 6-1 tchd 13-2)
Exit Smiling showed his previous lacklustre effort to be wrong and returned to form with a solid effort, finishing a clear second-best. He is just weighted to his best now. (op 11-1)
Billy Dane(IRE) has been in good form this term and he posted a fair effort from the front considering he set a sound early pace in the conditions. This would have stretched his stamina to the limit. (op 8-1 tchd 5-1)
Nevada Desert(IRE) took time to settle, but still performed close enough to his previous level at a track he likes. (op 6-1 tchd 11-2)
Vainglory(USA) had finished just in front of the winner on the all-weather 13 days previously, but he was floundering from off the pace a fair way out and failed to run up to par, most likely on account of the ground. Official explanation: jockey said colt was unsuited by the heavy ground (op 9-2)

5773 WEATHERBYS PRINTING H'CAP 1m 1f 207y
3:30 (3:30) (Class 4) (0-80,80) 3-Y-O+ **£4,727** (£1,406; £702; £351) **Stalls** High

Form RPR
1450 **1** **She's Our Lass (IRE)**19 5199 7-9-6 **76**........................ NeilBrown(3) 10 87
(K A Ryan) *hld up towards rr: gd hdwy on inner 3f out: led over 1f out: rdn clr ent fnl f* **8/1**

1360 **2** 4 ½ **Top Ticket (IRE)**27 4984 3-9-3 **77**.............................. RichardMullen 2 79
(D M Simcock) *in tch: hdwy to chse ldrs on outer over 3f out: rdn along over 2f out: drvn over 1f out: edgd rt and styd on ins fnl f: tk 2nd nr fiunish* **14/1**

5043 **3** ½ **Resounding Glory (USA)**19 5202 3-9-2 **76**................. PaulHanagan 3 77
(R A Fahey) *hld up towards rr: hdwy on outer 3f out: swtchd rt and pushed along over 2f out: sn rdn and styng on whn n.m.r over 1f out: swtchd to inner and kpt on strly ins fnl f: nrst fin* **17/2**

5623 **4** *nk* **Spirit Of Adjisa (IRE)**15 5370 4-9-9 **76**..................(b) GrahamGibbons 4 76
(Pat Eddery) *prom: led over 3f out: rdn and hdd over 2f out: sn drvn and kpt on same pce fr wl over 1f out* **15/2**3

00-0 **5** 1 **Harvest Warrior**14 5382 6-9-7 **74**................................... DavidAllan 8 72
(T D Easterby) *hld up towards rr: gd hdwy on inner 3f out: led over 2f out and sn rdn: hdd over 1f out: wknd ent fnl f* **14/1**

0215 **6** 1 ¾ **Sacrilege**54 4128 3-9-3 **77**.. DO'Donohoe 1 72
(D R C Elsworth) *hld up: hdwy to chse ldrs over 3f out: sn rdn and wknd 2f out* **3/1**1

-033 **7** ½ **Jadaara**24 5100 3-9-6 **80**.. RoystonFfrench 6 74
(M Johnston) *chsd ldrs: rdn along 3f out: drvn over 2f out and grad wknd* **12/1**

0611 **8** 2 **King Of The Moors (USA)**8 5564 5-9-3 **70** 6ex............(p) PaulFessey 9 60
(T D Barron) *trckd ldrs: effrt 3f out: sn rdn along and wknd over 2f out* **4/1**2

5054 **9** 2 ¼ **Intersky Charm (USA)**14 5382 4-9-6 **73**..................... DeanMcKeown 7 58
(R M Whitaker) *hld up: effrt and sme hdwy over 3f out: sn rdn and wknd* **10/1**

6205 **10** 3 ½ **New Beginning (IRE)**38 4618 4-9-9 **76**..................... RobertWinston 5 54
(Mrs S Lamyman) *racd wd: led and clr: pushed along and jnd wl over 3f out: sn hdd & wknd* **22/1**

410 **11** 34 **Portrush Storm**91 2907 3-8-9 **69** ow2................................. DNolan 12 —
(D Carroll) *hld up: hdwy over 4f out: rdn to chse ldrs over 3f out: sn drvn and wknd* **28/1**

2m 18.35s (11.35) **Going Correction** +1.00s/f (Soft)
WFA 3 from 4yo+ 7lb **11** Ran SP% **116.3**
Speed ratings (Par 105): **94,90,90,89,88 87,87,85,83,80 53**
toteswinger: 1&2 £32.70, 1&3 £11.70, 2&3 £22.70. CSF £112.94 CT £978.46 TOTE £9.80: £2.50, £5.50, £3.00; EX 177.00.
Owner John Walsh & Reuben Glynn **Bred** Illuminatus Investments **Trained** Hambleton, N Yorks
■ Stewards' Enquiry : Paul Hanagan one-day ban: careless riding (Sep 23)

FOCUS
This modest handicap was run at a solid early pace in the conditions. It was a moderate winning time for the class, even allowing for the ground, but the form seems to make sense.
King Of The Moors(USA) Official explanation: trainer had no explanation for the poor form shown

5774 GEORGE SWIERS "THE TAXMAN" NURSERY 7f 100y
4:00 (4:01) (Class 6) (0-65,64) 2-Y-O **£1,942** (£578; £288; £144) **Stalls** High

Form RPR
5060 **1** **Woteva**5 5632 2-9-6 **63**..(p) DavidAllan 11 68+
(B Ellison) *trckd ldrs on inner: hdwy 3f out: swtchd lft and rdn to chal over 1f out: led ins fnl f and drvn clr* **11/2**3

560 **2** 2 ¼ **Shifting Gold (IRE)**37 4658 2-9-0 **57**........................ RobertWinston 14 57
(K A Ryan) *led: rdn along 3f out: jnd 2f out: sn drvn: hdd and one pce ins fnl f* **12/1**

0364 **3** 1 ¼ **Dispol Diva**26 5006 2-8-11 **54**...............................(v) JamieMoriarty 7 51
(P T Midgley) *midfield: hdwy 3f out: swtchd outside and rdn to chse ldrs wl over 1f out: drvn and edgd rt ins fnl f: kpt on* **7/1**

050 **4** 1 ½ **Royal Max (IRE)**43 4474 2-8-13 **56**.............................. PaulHanagan 5 49
(R A Fahey) *chsd ldrs: rdn along and outpcd 1/2-way: hdwy 2f out: swtchd rt and drvn over 1f out: kpt on ins fnl f: nrst fin* **4/1**2

6460 **5** ½ **Winsome Hearts**7 5591 2-9-2 **59**............................ PaulMulrennan 8 51
(M W Easterby) *hld up: hdwy 3f out: rdn to chse ldrs over 2f out: drvn and one pce appr fnl f* **16/1**

1132 **6** 6 **Rose Of Coma (IRE)**11 5460 2-9-2 **59**............................ ChrisCatlin 12 37
(Miss Gay Kelleway) *hld up in tch: hdwy over 3f out: chal 2f out: sn rdn and ev ch tl drvn and wknd over 1f out* **7/2**1

000 **7** 1 ¾ **Bitza Baileys (IRE)**47 4328 2-8-12 **55**.................... GrahamGibbons 2 29
(J G Given) *a towards rr* **12/1**

0666 **8** *5* **Welcome Applause (IRE)**[12] 5432 2-9-4 **64**............ JerryO'Dwyer(3) 4 26
(M G Quinlan) *towards rr: hdwy on inner 3f out: rdn along over 2f out: drvn and wknd wl over 1f out* **6/1**

3000 **9** *hd* **Eilean Eeve**[101] 2592 2-8-12 **55**........................ RichardMullen 3 17
(A J McCabe) *chsd ldrs: rdn along 3f out: grad wknd* **16/1**

003 **10** *1 1/2* **Look For Value**[15] 5357 2-8-2 **45**........................ KimTinkler 1 3
(N Tinkler) *a towards rr* **28/1**

0000 **11** *5* **Smoke Me A Kipper (IRE)**[17] 5256 2-8-5 **48**...............(v[1]) TPO'Shea 13 —
(Mrs A Duffield) *cl up: rdn along 3f out: wknd over 2f out* **33/1**

0005 **12** *61* **Hunch**[50] 4257 2-8-2 **45**........................ NickyMackay 10 —
(Garry Moss) *a in rr* **100/1**

1m 41.93s (8.13) **Going Correction** +1.00s/f (Soft) **12** Ran SP% **118.9**
Speed ratings (Par 93): **93,90,89,87,86 79,77,72,71,70 64,—**
toteswinger: 1&2 £14.10, 1&3 £10.70, 2&3 £8.70. CSF £69.20 CT £479.80 TOTE £6.90: £2.40, £3.60, £2.50; EX 66.50.
Owner M Laverack **Bred** Oakhill Stud **Trained** Norton, N Yorks

FOCUS
A modest nursery with provided a thorough test of stamina. The winner is rated back towards her early-season form.

NOTEBOOK
Woteva, the subject of market support, got off the mark at the eighth attempt with a clear-cut win. She picked up gamely for pressure in the home straight and, looking better the further she went, rates value for more than the bare margin. Despite having looked exposed in this sphere of late, the step up to the stiffer test, in addition to first-time cheekpieces, worked the oracle. She reportedly now heads to Ayr next week to try to follow up under a penalty. (op 7-1)
Shifting Gold(IRE) ◆ ran a promising race considering he did all the donkey work and he has evidently started life in this division on a good mark. He stays well and looks up to going one better now. (op 9-1)
Dispol Diva, whose only win to date came over the minimum trip at this track in April, ran another fair race and seems to have benefited for the recent application of a visor. She helps to set the level of this form. (op 8-1)
Royal Max(IRE), another making his nursery debut, was doing his best work at the finish and already looks in need of a stiffer test. He can build on this. (op 9-2)
Rose Of Coma(IRE) found this too testing and failed to confirm her course-and-distance form with the third on 4lb worse terms. Official explanation: jockey said filly was unsuited by the heavy ground (op 4-1)

5775 SIMON WOOD "THE MESSENGER" H'CAP 5f
4:30 (4:31) (Class 5) (0-70,68) 3-Y-0+ **£4,209** (£1,252; £625; £312) **Stalls** High

Form RPR

0501 **1** **Lake Chini (IRE)**[2] 5719 6-8-11 **60**........................(b) DaleGibson 8 71
(M W Easterby) *trckd ldrs: hdwy on inner 1/2-way: rdn to ld wl over 1f out: clr ins fnl f: rdn out* **13/8**[1]

0001 **2** *1 1/2* **Spoof Master (IRE)**[13] 5401 4-9-1 **67**........................(p) TolleyDean(3) 9 73
(C R Dore) *led: rdn along 2f out: sn hdd: kpt on u.p ins fnl f* **11/2**[3]

0024 **3** *3/4* **Winthorpe (IRE)**[13] 5400 8-8-12 **68**........................(p) JamieKyne(7) 3 71
(J J Quinn) *in tch: pushed along 1/2-way: rdn and hdwy wl over 1f out: kpt on ins fnl f* **8/1**

140 **4** *3 1/2* **Ursus**[36] 4684 3-8-6 **56**........................ RoystonFfrench 5 47
(C R Wilson) *prom: rdn along 2f out: sn drvn and kpt on same pce appr fnl f* **14/1**

2622 **5** *1 1/4* **Soto**[27] 4967 5-9-2 **65**........................(b) PaulMulrennan 1 51
(M W Easterby) *cl up: rdn along 1/2-way: drvn and wknd wl over 1f out* **3/1**[2]

046- **6** *1/2* **Joyeaux**[314] 6594 6-9-4 **67**........................ PaulHanagan 4 51
(L R James) *chsd ldrs: rdn along 2f out: edgd rt and wknd over 1f out* **20/1**

0540 **7** *11* **El Potro**[13] 5398 6-8-7 **56**........................ ChrisCatlin 2 1
(J R Holt) *towards rr: rdn along and outpcd fr 1/2-way* **9/1**

67.95 secs (4.45) **Going Correction** +1.00s/f (Soft)
WFA 3 from 4yo+ 1lb **7** Ran SP% **111.0**
Speed ratings (Par 103): **104,101,100,94,92 92,74**
toteswinger: 1&2 £3.60, 1&3 £3.70, 2&3 £5.60. CSF £10.30 CT £50.91 TOTE £2.70: £1.70, £3.20; EX 10.90.
Owner Mrs Jean Turpin **Bred** Paul McEnery **Trained** Sheriff Hutton, N Yorks

FOCUS
A modest sprint for the grade, but the form makes sense.

5776 SAWFISH SOFTWARE LADY RIDERS' H'CAP (FOR LADY AMATEUR RIDERS) 1m 1f 207y
5:00 (5:01) (Class 6) (0-55,56) 3-Y-0+ **£2,637** (£811; £405) **Stalls** High

Form RPR

3063 **1** **Bollin Freddie**[17] 5262 4-9-12 **46** oh1........................ MissADeniel 16 52
(A J Lockwood) *mde all: sn clr: rdn 2f out: drvn and edgd lft ent fnl f: jst hld on* **12/1**

005- **2** *nse* **Dark Planet**[295] 6866 5-9-9 **48**........................(v) MissHCuthbert(5) 9 54
(D W Thompson) *chsd ldrs: hdwy over 2f out and sn rdn: kpt on wl u.p ins fnl f: jst failed* **40/1**

0030 **3** *nse* **Ming Vase**[5] 5631 6-9-8 **47**........................ MissWGibson(5) 2 53
(P T Midgley) *hld up towards rr: hdwy 3f out: rdn 2f out: swtchd rt and drvn over 1f out: kpt on strly u.p ins fnl f: jst hld* **33/1**

4304 **4** *5* **Giddywell**[5] 5653 4-9-11 **52**........................ MissStefaniaGandola(7) 10 48
(R Hollinshead) *in tch: hdwy 3f out: rdn to chse ldrs 2f out: drvn and one pce ent fnl f* **6/1**[3]

600 **5** *1 1/4* **Poppy Day**[16] 5303 5-9-13 **52**........................ MissJoannaMason(5) 6 46
(M W Easterby) *bhd: rdn 3f out: styng on whn hung bdly lft over 1f out: kpt on wl fnl f: nrst fin* **33/1**

0024 **6** *nse* **Jiminor Mack**[16] 5308 5-9-12 **46**........................(p) MissGDGracey-Davison 17 39
(W J H Ratcliffe) *hld up towards rr: hdwy wl over 2f out: swtchd rt and rdn over 1f out: kpt on u.p ins fnl f: nrst fin* **14/1**

/000 **7** *2 3/4* **Woody Valentine (USA)**[7] 4679 7-10-1 **56** ow1........(p) MissNSayer(7) 4 44
(Mrs Dianne Sayer) *towards rr: hdwy on inner 3f out and sn rdn: no imp appr fnl f* **33/1**

0140 **8** *3 1/4* **Jemima's Art**[16] 5308 3-9-9 **53**........................(b) MissJCoward(3) 15 34
(M W Easterby) *chsd wnr: rdn along 3f out: drvn 2f out and sn wknd* **9/1**

3362 **9** *1 1/2* **Black Falcon (IRE)**[7] 5593 8-10-0 **48**........................ MissARyan 12 26
(John A Harris) *prom: effrt 3f out: rdn 2f out and sn wknd* **7/2**[2]

1060 **10** *3* **Paparaazi (IRE)**[22] 5145 6-10-2 **55**........................(p) MissKSharp(5) 13 27
(I W McInnes) *chsd ldrs: rdn along 3f out: sn wknd* **28/1**

-325 **11** *1* **Lady Valentino**[81] 3201 4-10-4 **52**........................ MissPRobson 1 22
(M Dods) *a towards rr* **12/1**

0151 **12** *2 3/4* **Jenny Soba**[5] 5653 5-10-3 **51**........................ MissSBrotherton 3 16
(Lucinda Featherstone) *a in rr* **5/2**[1]

0003 **13** *31* **Naughty Girl (IRE)**[9] 5533 8-9-12 **46** oh1........................ MrsMMorris 5 —
(John A Harris) *a bhd* **50/1**

0534 **U** **Scotty's Future (IRE)**[16] 5303 10-9-9 **48**........ MissBeverleyKendall(5) 8 —
(A Berry) *swvd lft and uns rdr leaving stalls* **16/1**

2m 20.96s (13.96) **Going Correction** +1.00s/f (Soft)
WFA 3 from 4yo+ 7lb **14** Ran SP% **119.7**
Speed ratings (Par 101): **84,83,83,79,78 78,76,74,72,70 69,67,42,—**
toteswinger: 1&2 £60.90, 1&3 £63.00, 2&3 £96.90. CSF £438.84 CT £14335.69 TOTE £18.20: £3.30, £11.20, £9.70; EX 547.70 Place 6: £190.92, Place 5: £73.02..
Owner Highgreen Partnership **Bred** Sir Neil & Exors Of Late Lady Westbrook **Trained** Brawby, N Yorks

FOCUS
A poor handicap, confined to lady amateur riders, run at a strong pace. It saw a cracking three-way finish and the form should be treated with caution with the winner allowed to build up a huge lead.
Paparaazi(IRE) Official explanation: jockey said gelding was unsuited by the heavy ground
T/Plt: £305.50 to a £1 stake. Pool: £77,328.51. 184.77 winning tickets. T/Qpdt: £144.10 to a £1 stake. Pool: £4,208.50. 21.60 winning tickets. JR

[4890]LEICESTER (R-H)
Tuesday, September 9

OFFICIAL GOING: Heavy (6.2)
Wind: Light behind Weather: Raining

5777 EUROPEAN BREEDERS' FUND APOLLO MAIDEN STKS 7f 9y
2:20 (2:21) (Class 4) 2-Y-O **£5,180** (£1,541; £770; £384) **Stalls** Low

Form RPR

1 **Parthenon** 2-9-3 0........................ GregFairley 5 71+
(M Johnston) *s.i.s: rcvrd to ld after 1f out: rdn and hdd over 1f out: rallied to ld ins fnl f: edgd rt: r.o* **3/1**[2]

2 *1/2* **Imposing** 2-8-12 0........................ Louis-PhilippeBeuzelin(5) 2 70+
(Sir Michael Stoute) *prom: outpcd 3f out: swtchd rt and hdwy over 1f out: r.o wl* **10/3**[3]

3 *nk* **Hunterview** 2-9-3 0........................ PhilipRobinson 1 69+
(M A Jarvis) *led 1f: chsd ldr: shkn up 1/2-way: outpcd over 1f out: r.o wl ins fnl f* **7/2**

53 **4** *1/2* **Piazza San Pietro**[17] 5286 2-9-3 0........................ IanMongan 6 68
(C G Cox) *s.i.s: hld up in tch: led over 1f out: sn rdn: hdd ins fnl f: unable qck towards fin* **11/4**[1]

5 *11* **Kinigi (IRE)** 2-8-12 0........................ StephenDonohoe 3 36
(S A Callaghan) *chsd ldrs: rdn over 2f out: wknd over 1f out* **8/1**

1m 32.41s (6.21) **Going Correction** +0.375s/f (Good) **5** Ran SP% **108.1**
Speed ratings (Par 97): **79,78,78,77,64**
toteswinger: 1&2 £3.70. CSF £12.61 TOTE £4.30: £1.50, £1.90; EX 12.60.
Owner Sheikh Hamdan Bin Mohammed Al Maktoum **Bred** Darley **Trained** Middleham Moor, N Yorks

FOCUS
A very moderate winning time even allowing for the conditions, nearly three seconds slower than the seller, and the first four finished in a heap. The bare form is only fair but the race should produce winners.

NOTEBOOK
Parthenon ◆, who is related to several soft-ground lovers, is bred to stay well and he ground it out best. Soon in front, he settled nicely into his stride and picked up strongly once headed over a furlong out by Piazza San Pietro, showing an attitude typical of runners from this yard. He is definitely going to get further and, being a fine, big sort, there is a strong chance of further improvement. Connections will now aim a little higher. (op 5-2 tchd 10-3)
Imposing ◆ ran a race full of promise in second. A Derby entry who cost 170,000gns, he was outpaced from well over two furlongs out and showed signs of greenness, but stuck on well for pressure and was closing nicely at the line. He should know more next time and win an ordinary maiden. (op 11-4)
Hunterview, whose pedigree is a blend of speed and stamina, was happy to take a tow in behind the winner, but he too found himself tapped for toe from someway out. He put in some good late work, not getting beaten far at all in the end, and should improve for 1m. (op 10-3 tchd 3-1)
Piazza San Pietro, the one runner with previous experience, was up a furlong in trip and had plenty to prove in the ground, being a son of Compton Place. He travelled up nicely and went on over a furlong out, but had raced free early on and did not get home. He should get this trip on fast ground, although needs to settle better. (op 9-2)
Kinigi(IRE), a daughter of Verglas, showed up well to a point, but dropped right out in the end and may have found the ground too testing. (op 9-1 tchd 7-1)

5778 RANCLIFFE (S) STKS 7f 9y
2:50 (2:52) (Class 6) 2-Y-O **£1,942** (£578; £288; £144) **Stalls** Low

Form RPR

0044 **1** **Hollow Green (IRE)**[25] 5041 2-8-0 51........................ AndreaAtzeni(7) 18 60
(P D Evans) *racd far side: prom: chsd ldr 4f out: led overall over 2f out: rdn and hung lft over 1f out: styd on wl* **7/1**[3]

000 **2** *3* **Bounty Reef**[47] 4337 2-8-7 54........................ FrankieMcDonald 2 53
(P D Evans) *racd centre: prom: rdn over 2f out: styd on u.p to ld that side ins fnl f: no ch w wnr: 1st of 12 in gp* **12/1**

00 **3** *3 1/4* **Transfered (IRE)**[50] 4256 2-8-7 0........................ EdwardCreighton 15 44
(M G Quinlan) *racd centre: hld up in tch: rdn over 2f out: styd on: 2nd of 12 in gp* **11/1**

4666 **4** *nk* **Mr Clearview**[29] 4933 2-8-9 52........................ KevinGhunowa(3) 11 49
(B R Millman) *overall ldr in centre tl over 2f out: sn rdn: wknd fnl f: 3rd of 12 in gp* **14/1**

0044 **5** *4* **Heaven Or Hell (IRE)**[43] 4475 2-8-12 55........................ RichardEvans(5) 4 44
(P D Evans) *racd centre: chsd ldrs: rdn over 2f out: wknd over 1f out: 4th of 12 in gp* **9/1**

000 **6** *4* **Mfi'Ve**[11] 5473 2-8-12 48........................ StephenDonohoe 7 29
(B R Millman) *racd centre: chsd ldrs: rdn over 2f out: sn wknd: 5th of 12 in gp* **16/1**

05 **7** *5* **Jimwasright (IRE)**[33] 4764 2-8-12 0........................ RobertHavlin 16 16
(P D Evans) *racd far side: prom: rdn over 2f out: sn wknd: 2nd of 4 in gp* **25/1**

0506 **8** *5* **Positive Opinion**[32] 4823 2-8-7 54........................ PaulDoe 3 —
(B R Millman) *racd centre: s.i.s: sn pushed along: bhd fr 1/2-way: 6th of 12 in gp* **11/1**

40 **9** *3/4* **Svindal (IRE)**[25] 5072 2-8-12 0........................ FrancisNorton 9 2
(K A Ryan) *racd centre: mid-div: sn drvn along: wknd over 2f out: 7th of 12 in gp* **12/1**

64 **10** *1* **Heaven Knows When (IRE)**[32] 4827 2-8-7 0........................ TQuinn 17 —
(B W Hills) *s.i.s: hung lft trhoughout: c to centre gp over 4f out: a in rr: 8th of 12 in gp* **4/1**[1]

0025 **11** *6* **El Portet**[15] 5357 2-8-12 60........................ GregFairley 12 —
(G M Moore) *rel to r: a t.o in centre: 9th of 12 in gp* **6/1**[2]

06 **12** 3 ¼ **Moon Warrior**[108] 2392 2-8-12 0.. MickyFenton 6 —
(C Smith) *wnt rt s: racd centre: sn chsng ldrs: rdn and wknd over 2f out: 10th of 12 in gp* **50/1**

13 3 **Maverick's Magic** 2-8-7 0.. JackDean(5) 1 —
(W G M Turner) *racd centre: sn pushed along in rr: bhd fr 1/2-way: 11th of 12 in gp* **33/1**

540 **14** ½ **Scarlet Blade**[66] 3706 2-8-9 45..............................(v) JackMitchell(3) 5 —
(Mrs A Duffield) *racd centre: mid-div: rdn 1/2-way: sn wknd: last of 12th in gp* **33/1**

5 **15** 1 ½ **May Boy**[10] 5487 2-8-7 0.. MCGeran(5) 13 —
(R J Hodges) *racd far side: chsd ldr tl led that gp 4f out: hdd & wknd over 2f out: 3rd of 4 in gp* **28/1**

00 **16** 37 **Rahzeena**[11] 5473 2-8-12 0.. LiamJones 14 —
(R Brotherton) *sn led far side: hdd 4f out: wknd 3f out: last of 4 in gp* **100/1**

1m 29.56s (3.36) **Going Correction** +0.375s/f (Good) **16** Ran SP% **117.5**
Speed ratings (Par 93): **95,91,87,87,82 78,72,66,66,64 58,54,50,50,48 6**
toteswinger: 1&2 £24.00, 1&3 £24.50, 2&3 £46.80. CSF £79.74 TOTE £8.70: £3.30, £5.20, £4.10; EX 116.10 TRIFECTA Not won..There was no bid for the winner. Transfered was claimed by Lucinda Featherstone for £6,000.
Owner Raymond N R Auld **Bred** R N Auld **Trained** Pandy, Monmouths
■ Stewards' Enquiry : Andrea Atzeni three-day ban: used whip with excessive frequency (Sept 23-25)

FOCUS
These sellers are often competitive, but they actually finished well strung-out, the heavy ground playing its part, and David Evans was responsible for the one-two. They split into two groups and, despite the larger number coming middle to stands' side, it was one of the five that raced in the far ground who emerged best. The form makes sense.

NOTEBOOK
Hollow Green(IRE), who raced more towards the far side, got well on top from over a furlong out. She had finished fourth in this grade last time and this looked a fair effort, considering how far behind the rest were in her group. (op 17-2)
Bounty Reef, beaten a long way in maiden company latest, improved for the testing ground and 'won' her race up the middle. She was no match for her stablemate, but should find a small race in this grade when the going is soft. (tchd 11-1)
Transfered(IRE) stayed on for third, improving on her recent Yarmouth effort. She handled the ground just fine and may well get 1m. (op 8-1 tchd 16-1)
Mr Clearview set the pace in the main group and gave it a really bold go, but could find no extra inside the final furlong. He may be helped by a return to 6f. (op 18-1)
Heaven Or Hell(IRE),a stablemate of the first two, did best of the rest, but is not progressing and has little scope. (op 11-1 tchd 8-1)
Heaven Knows When(IRE) was unable to build on her recent Newmarket fourth and clearly failed to cope with the ground. (op 9-2 tchd 5-1)
El Portet did not seem in the mood for it and lost many lengths at the stalls. Official explanation: jockey said gelding missed the break (op 5-1 tchd 9-2)

5779 SIS H'CAP 7f 9y
3:20 (3:21) (Class 5) (0-70,70) 3-Y-0+ **£3,238** (£963; £481; £240) **Stalls** Low

Form RPR

4444 **1** **Granary**[23] 5119 4-8-11 **66**.. AmyScott(7) 2 76
(H Candy) *s.i.s: hdwy over 4f out: led over 2f out: hdd and hung rt fr over 1f out: styd on to ld post* **13/2**[3]

6134 **2** *hd* **Castano**[17] 5267 4-9-0 **65**.. JamesMillman(3) 18 74
(B R Millman) *mid-div: hdwy 1/2-way: edgd rt over 2f out: rdn to ld over 1f out: hdd post* **6/1**[2]

1401 **3** 3 ¼ **West End Lad**[16] 5303 5-9-1 **63**..............................(b) PhilipRobinson 3 63
(S R Bowring) *dwlt: hld up: swtchd rt 1/2-way: hdwy over 1f out: sn rdn: nt rch ldrs* **5/1**[1]

6450 **4** 7 **Starlight Gazer**[17] 5267 5-9-6 **68**..............................(t) RichardThomas 8 49
(J A Geake) *s.s: hld up: hdwy and hung rt over 2f out: nt run on* **9/1**

0004 **5** ¾ **Dakota Rain (IRE)**[41] 4535 6-9-2 **64**..............................(p) SamHitchcott 6 43
(Jennie Candlish) *chsd ldrs: led 1/2-way: rdn and hdd over 2f out: wknd wl over 1f out* **16/1**

4603 **6** 2 **Kensington (IRE)**[30] 4895 7-9-3 **70**.. RichardEvans(5) 11 44
(P D Evans) *chsd ldrs: rdn 1/2-way: wknd wl over 1f out* **10/1**

6000 **7** ¾ **Imperial Echo (USA)**[18] 5247 7-9-3 **70**........ Louis-PhilippeBeuzelin(5) 13 42
(P Howling) *prom: rdn 1/2-way: wknd wl over 1f out* **20/1**

3656 **8** 1 ½ **Pelham Crescent (IRE)**[180] 874 5-8-13 **61**.......... CatherineGannon 10 29
(B Palling) *mid-div: sn pushed along: effrt over 2f out: sn wknd* **40/1**

300 **9** 1 **Valentino Swing (IRE)**[11] 5458 5-9-3 **65**.......................... LiamJones 15 30
(Miss T Spearing) *s.i.s: hld up: rdn over 4f out: hdwy over 2f out: wknd wl over 1f out* **16/1**

1104 **10** ½ **High Five Society**[33] 4785 4-8-9 **57** ow1............(bt) StephenDonohoe 12 21
(S R Bowring) *prom: rdn and wknd 2f out* **8/1**

0000 **11** 6 **Naledi**[52] 4207 4-8-1 **56** oh11.. AndreaAtzeni(7) 14 4
(J R Norton) *mid-div: hdwy 1/2-way: wknd over 2f out* **100/1**

3430 **12** 13 **Orphan (IRE)**[36] 4690 6-8-8 **56** oh4.. GregFairley 7 —
(G M Moore) *chsd ldrs: rdn over 4f out: wknd over 2f out* **14/1**

2-61 **13** 19 **Eternal Legacy (IRE)**[13] 5389 6-9-2 **64**.. MickyFenton 17 —
(E J Alston) *led: rdn and hdd 1/2-way: wknd over 2f out* **6/1**[2]

1m 29.64s (3.44) **Going Correction** +0.575s/f (Yiel)
WFA 3 from 4yo+ 4lb **13** Ran SP% **115.4**
Speed ratings (Par 103): **103,102,99,91,90 87,87,85,84,83 76,61,40**
toteswinger: 1&2 £8.90, 1&3 £5.80, 2&3 £6.00. CSF £42.95 CT £218.44 TOTE £7.70: £2.20, £2.20, £2.40; EX 57.90 Trifecta £129.30 Part won. Pool: £174.78, 0.40 winning units..
Owner Major M G Wyatt **Bred** W And R Barnett Ltd **Trained** Kingston Warren, Oxon

FOCUS
Another race that looked wide-open beforehand, but the first two ended up drawing clear. The time was slow, though, and this is not form to take too literally.
Eternal Legacy(IRE) Official explanation: trainer had no explanation for the poor form shown

5780 LEICESTERSHIRE MAIDEN STKS 1m 1f 218y
3:50 (3:50) (Class 5) 3-Y-0+ **£3,238** (£963; £481; £240) **Stalls** High

Form RPR

2 **1** **Torphichen**[99] 2681 3-9-3 0.. PhilipRobinson 4 84+
(M A Jarvis) *chsd ldrs: led 2f out: edgd rt and shkn up over 1f out: sn clr: eased ins fnl f* **4/6**[1]

0- **2** 4 ½ **Distinctive Image (USA)**[313] 6602 3-9-0 0........ RussellKennemore(3) 2 68
(R Hollinshead) *hld up in tch: rdn over 2f out: styd on same pce appr fnl f* **12/1**[3]

5332 **3** 2 ½ **Hawk House**[34] 4721 3-9-3 66.. TQuinn 6 63
(B W Hills) *chsd ldr tl led over 2f out: sn rdn and hdd: wknd ins fnl f* **15/8**[2]

4 6 **Scania Classic**[47] 7-9-5 0.. JackDean(5) 1 51
(M J Scudamore) *s.i.s: hld up: hdwy over 3f out: sn rdn: wknd wl over 1f out* **125/1**

35 **5** 6 **Mr Burton**[15] 5366 4-9-3 0.. DeanHeslop(7) 3 39
(M Mullineaux) *led: rdn and hdd over 2f out: wknd wl over 1f out* **25/1**

4 **6** 59 **Pas De Roland**[49] 4283 3-9-3 0.. MickyFenton 5 —
(S W Hall) *s.s: hld up: plld hrd: bhd fr 1/2-way* **100/1**

2m 17.37s (9.47) **Going Correction** +0.90s/f (Soft)
WFA 3 from 4yo+ 7lb **6** Ran SP% **108.1**
Speed ratings (Par 103): **98,94,92,87,82 35**
toteswinger: 1&2 £2.20, 1&3 £1.10, 2&3 £1.90. CSF £9.09 TOTE £1.80: £1.20, £5.30; EX 7.20.
Owner Thomas Barr **Bred** Mount Coote Stud And M H Dixon **Trained** Newmarket, Suffolk

FOCUS
A weak maiden in which the easy winner was value for 8l. The third was 9lb off his recent fast-ground form.

5781 PRESTWOLD CONDITIONS STKS 5f 2y
4:20 (4:20) (Class 3) 3-Y-0+ **£7,477** (£2,239; £1,119; £560) **Stalls** Low

Form RPR

3005 **1** **Angus Newz**[16] 5310 5-8-10 90.. FrancisNorton 1 96
(M Quinn) *mde all: set stdy pce: qcknd 2f out: rdn 1f out: r.o wl* **7/4**[2]

6604 **2** 1 ¼ **Mango Music**[18] 5250 5-8-7 83.. EdwardCreighton 4 89
(M Quinn) *w wnr: plld hrd: rdn and ev ch ins fnl f: styd on same pce* **9/2**[3]

0500 **3** 4 **The Trader (IRE)**[10] 5509 10-8-9 88..............................(b) LiamJones 3 76
(M Blanshard) *chsd ldrs: swtchd rt 1/2-way: rdn over 1f out: wknd ins fnl f* **13/2**

00 **4** 7 **Biniou (IRE)**[24] 5113 5-8-9 100.. RobertHavlin 2 51
(R M H Cowell) *trckd ldrs: rdn and wknd over 1f out* **6/4**[1]

62.81 secs (2.81) **Going Correction** +0.575s/f (Yiel) **4** Ran SP% **107.9**
Speed ratings (Par 107): **100,98,91,80**
CSF £9.16 TOTE £2.30; EX 4.90.
Owner M J Quinn **Bred** Henry And Mrs Rosemary Moszkowicz **Trained** Newmarket, Suffolk

FOCUS
This was not much of a race and with Biniou running poorly and The Trader struggling for form the winner did not have much to beat. The form is rated through the winner.

NOTEBOOK
Angus Newz, a good, honest mare who likes soft ground, made all against the stands' rail. She has often performed above herself in small-field conditions/Listed events and everything looked to be in her favour. Going withoutthe usual visor, she was able to slow it up in front and was always doing enough inside the final furlong. She will continue to be a threat in similar races when conditions suit. (tchd 13-8, 15-8 in a place)
Mango Music has been coming up shy off marks in the 80s and she found this a bit easier. She was up there with the winner and stuck on well in second, but was always coming off worse. (op 5-1 tchd 11-2)
The Trader(IRE) was once a smart sprinter and he still offers the odd glimpse of his old ability, but he has become incredibly hard to win with and was well held in third. (op 5-1 tchd 9-2)
Biniou(IRE) was a big disappointment. Winner of a weak Listed race in France last year, he is something of an underachiever and was left flat-footed when the winner kicked. He did not have a gallop in him and it is back to the drawing board for connections. (op 13-8 tchd 2-1)

5782 E B F FILBERT MAIDEN FILLIES' STKS 1m 60y
4:50 (4:50) (Class 4) 2-Y-0 **£5,180** (£1,541; £770; £384) **Stalls** High

Form RPR

00 **1** **Le Grand Amour (IRE)**[60] 3913 2-9-0 0.. PhilipRobinson 4 69+
(B W Hills) *mde all: shkn up and c clr over 1f out: comf* **4/7**[1]

6 **2** 4 ½ **Fongoli**[9] 5534 2-9-0 0.. TQuinn 2 57
(B G Powell) *hld up in tch: plld hrd: rdn and ev ch over 2f out: edgd rt over 1f out: styd on same pce* **2/1**[2]

3 5 **Jaubertie** 2-8-9 0.. JackDean(5) 3 47
(W G M Turner) *w wnr tl rdn over 2f out: wknd over 1f out* **16/1**[3]

0 **4** 3 ¼ **Amatara (IRE)**[68] 3632 2-9-0 0.. StephenDonohoe 1 40
(B G Powell) *trckd ldrs: racd keenly: rdn and ev ch over 2f out: wknd over 1f out* **20/1**

1m 55.12s (10.02) **Going Correction** +0.90s/f (Soft) **4** Ran SP% **107.6**
Speed ratings (Par 94): **85,80,75,72**
CSF £1.92 TOTE £1.60; EX 2.30.
Owner Lady Bamford **Bred** Lady Bamford **Trained** Lambourn, Berks

FOCUS
A disappointing turnout for this fillies' maiden and hot favourite Le Grand Amour had little trouble winning. She could clearly be much better than rated but the gound was bad and there was little strengh in depth to this.

NOTEBOOK
Le Grand Amour(IRE) has shaped with promise on each of her first two starts and was always likely to be suited by this step up to 1m, being by Montjeu. She dominated at her own tempo under Philip Robinson and raced clear in the final quarter mile, coping adequately with the ground. There should be more to come in nurseries. (op 8-11)
Fongoli, who may well have finished second but for meeting trouble on her debut at Folkestone, should have been suited by the step up in trip, but she was keen early and did not seem overly happy in the ground. She can be given another chance to build on that debut promise. Official explanation: jockey said filly hung right (tchd 9-4)
Jaubertie, whose dam was a staying performer, ran well to a point and plugged on at the one pace in third. She should know more next time, but it is likely she will ply her trade at claiming/selling level. (op 9-1)
Amatara(IRE) travelled up well, but as was the case on her debut, could not see it out. She is reportedly still quite weak and more of a three-year-old prospect. (tchd 16-1)

5783 BETFAIR APPRENTICE TRAINING SERIES H'CAP 1m 1f 218y
5:20 (5:20) (Class 5) (0-70,69) 3-Y-0+ **£3,238** (£963; £481; £240) **Stalls** High

Form RPR

5116 **1** **Kimono My House**[22] 5161 4-9-1 **61**.. RosieJessop(3) 2 71
(J G Given) *trckd ldrs: rdn and hung rt over 1f out: led ins fnl f: hung lft: styd on* **8/1**

3041 **2** *nk* **Princess Flame (GER)**[77] 3347 6-9-6 **63**.. KylieManser 4 73
(B G Powell) *s.s: sn chsng ldrs: rdn to ld over 1f out: hdd and hung lft ins fnl f: styd on* **16/1**

4533 **3** 2 ¾ **Under Fire (IRE)**[46] 4365 5-9-0 **57**.. JemmaMarshall 5 61
(A W Carroll) *led: racd keenly: rdn and hdd over 1f out: styd on same pce ins fnl f* **25/1**

6610 **4** 2 **Krugerrand (USA)**[24] 5105 9-9-7 **69**.. DebraEngland(5) 1 69
(W J Musson) *stdd s: hld up: hdwy over 2f out: rdn over 1f out: styd on same pce* **14/1**

0305 **5** *nse* **Hucking Heat (IRE)**[35] 4710 4-8-10 **56**.. SoniaEaton(3) 7 56
(R Hollinshead) *hld up: plld hrd: hdwy over 2f out: sn lost pl: rallied and edgd rt over 1f out: styd on same pce ins fnl f* **16/1**

426 **6** 1 ¼ **Princelywallywogan**[44] 4458 6-9-7 **67**.. BMcHugh(3) 3 64
(John A Harris) *plld hrd: sn trcking ldr: rdn over 2f out: wknd fnl f* **9/2**[2]

2122 **7** 2 ¼ **Gracechurch (IRE)**[12] 5427 5-9-5 **62**.......... Louis-PhilippeBeuzelin 11 55
(R J Hodges) *hld up: nt clr run 4f out: hdwy 3f out: rdn and edgd rt over 1f out: wknd fnl f* **11/4**[1]

0100 **8** *1 ¼* **Shenandoah Girl**[11] 5465 5-8-9 **57**..........................(p) AndreaAtzeni(5) 12 47
(Miss Gay Kelleway) *dwlt: hld up: hdwy over 3f out: rdn over 1f out: sn wknd* **10/1**

155 **9** *nse* **Ryan's Future (IRE)**[100] 2640 8-9-6 **63**.................................. JackDean 6 53
(J S Moore) *hld up: racd keenly: hdwy over 3f out: rdn and wknd over 1f out* **5/1**[3]

4503 **10** *1 ½* **Mill Beattie**[15] 5362 3-8-5 **55** oh2.. AmyBaker 8 42
(G M Moore) *prom: lost pl over 4f out: sn rdn: wkng whn hung lft fr over 1f out* **25/1**

3533 **11** *2 ½* **Jackie Kiely**[34] 4739 7-9-6 **63**...(t) MCGeran 9 45
(R Brotherton) *s.i.s: sn prom: rdn over 2f out: sn wknd* **14/1**

2m 15.93s (8.03) **Going Correction** +0.90s/f (Soft)
WFA 3 from 4yo+ 7lb **11** Ran SP% **114.5**
Speed ratings (Par 103): **103,102,100,98,98 97,96,95,95,93 91**
toteswinger: 1&2 £30.30, 1&3 £28.00, 2&3 £38.10. CSF £124.81 CT £2998.13 TOTE £8.80: £2.70, £3.90, £6.40; EX 143.10 TRIFECTA Not won. Place 6: £85.00, Place 5: £44.77..
Owner Beadle Booth Bloodstock Limited **Bred** G And Mrs Middlebrook **Trained** Willoughton, Lincs
■ Stewards' Enquiry : Kylie Manser caution: careless riding

FOCUS
They went just a steady gallop in this moderate handicap although this was the pick of the three round-course times. The winner improved to the level of her sand form.
Ryan's Future(IRE) Official explanation: jockey said horse ran too free
Jackie Kiely Official explanation: jockey said gelding was unsuited by the heavy ground
T/Plt: £157.20 to a £1 stake. Pool: £59,852.80. 277.82 winning tickets. T/Qpdt: £14.30 to a £1 stake. Pool: £4,092.90. 211.60 winning tickets. CR

5678 LINGFIELD (L-H)

Tuesday, September 9

OFFICIAL GOING: Turf course - soft (5.9); all-weather - standard
It rained steadily for much of the afternoon but the ground on the turf course, which was changed from heavy before racing, remained soft.
Wind: Behind, moderate races 1-4, almost nil after Weather: Overcast, drizzly

5784 EUROPEAN BREEDERS' FUND MEDIAN AUCTION MAIDEN STKS 6f
2:10 (2:12) (Class 6) 2-Y-O **£2,914** (£867; £433; £216) **Stalls** High

Form RPR

52 **1** **Definightly**[25] 5053 2-9-3 0.. SteveDrowne 2 91+
(R Charlton) *mde all and sn crossed towards nr side rail: shkn up over 1f out: drew rt away fnl f* **8/15**[1]

2 *5* **Keep Dancing (IRE)** 2-8-7 0.. DavidProbert(5) 5 68
(A M Balding) *sn chsd wnr: kpt on wl enough for 2nd but easily lft bhd fnl f* **20/1**

0 **3** *1 ¾* **Dice (IRE)**[22] 5158 2-9-3 0.. EddieAhern 11 68
(L M Cumani) *chsd ldrs: pushed along 1/2-way: wl outpcd fr over 1f out* **10/1**

0 **4** *1* **Fortunate Bid (IRE)**[12] 5431 2-9-3 0................................ MichaelHills 8 65
(B W Hills) *trckd ldrs: pushed along 1/2-way: effrt 2f out: sn outpcd and btn* **25/1**

0 **5** *4 ½* **Arachnophobia (IRE)**[96] 2759 2-9-3 0............................ JimCrowley 4 53+
(Pat Eddery) *dwlt: detached in last trio: pushed along over 2f out: nvr any ch but kpt on steadily fr over 1f out* **33/1**

03 **6** *1 ½* **Lady Mulligan**[18] 5213 2-8-12 0...................................... JimmyQuinn 13 42
(M Blanshard) *t.k.h: cl up: shkn up and wknd tamely 2f out* **9/1**[3]

P40 **7** *1 ½* **Rigged**[6] 5599 2-9-3 0.. TPQueally 10 42
(J A Osborne) *in tch to 1/2-way: sn struggling* **66/1**

4 **8** *3 ¾* **Spinight (IRE)**[16] 5316 2-9-3 0.. JohnEgan 7 31
(M Botti) *t.k.h early: chsd ldrs to 1/2-way: wknd* **6/1**[2]

9 *22* **Contemplate** 2-8-12 0.. JoeFanning 12 —
(Dr J D Scargill) *s.s: a wl bhd: t.o* **33/1**

10 *14* **Chicory Cottage** 2-9-3 0... GeorgeBaker 1 —
(G L Moore) *awkward to post: s.s: a bhd: already t.o whn heavily eased over 1f out* **25/1**

1m 14.23s (3.03) **Going Correction** +0.60s/f (Yiel) **10** Ran SP% **118.4**
Speed ratings (Par 93): **103,96,94,92,86 84,82,77,48,29**
toteswinger: 1&2 £8.80, 1&3 £2.00, 2&3 £24.90. CSF £19.74 TOTE £1.40: £1.02, £7.90, £2.80; EX 18.40.
Owner S Emmet And Miss R Emmet **Bred** S Emmet And Miss R Emmet **Trained** Beckhampton, Wilts

FOCUS
Just an ordinary maiden. They raced stands' side and the winner soon had the rail to run against. He won decisively, building on his good debut effort. It proved hard to make up significant amounts of ground.

NOTEBOOK
Definightly ◆, a good second at Newbury on his latest start, found this a straightforward opportunity to get off the mark at the third attempt. With nothing else particularly keen to lead, he was able to get to the head of affairs from stall two and grab the favoured rail. Despite not looking a natural front-runner and still showing signs of greenness, pricking his ears soon after the start, he was too good for this lot and came clear in the closing stages. Like so many of Diktat's progeny, he relished the soft ground and should continue to progress when getting these sorts of conditions. (op 4-7)
Keep Dancing(IRE), a daughter of Distant Music, half-sister to 5f three-year-old winner Mickleberry, showed up well throughout and this was a pleasing debut.
Dice(IRE) stepped up on the form he showed on his debut at Yarmouth, but was still well held. He is going to want further and will be one to keep in mind once he is qualified for a handicap mark. (op 12-1)
Fortunate Bid(IRE) is another who should be suited by a step up in trip and is likely to do better when handicapped. (op 22-1)
Arachnophobia(IRE) was soon off the bridle and never threatened, but he made some late headway and is gradually getting the hang of things. (op 50-1)
Lady Mulligan Official explanation: jockey said filly ran too free
Spinight(IRE) was keen early on and could not build on the promise he showed when fourth on his debut at Yarmouth. (op 7-1)
Chicory Cottage Official explanation: jockey said colt lost its action

5785 TEENOSO NURSERY 7f
2:40 (2:41) (Class 5) (0-75,75) 2-Y-O **£3,238** (£963; £481; £240) **Stalls** High

Form RPR

603 **1** **Count Paris (USA)**[10] 5499 2-8-13 **67**................................. JoeFanning 4 69
(M Johnston) *racd wdst of trio disputing ld: shkn up over 2f out: def advantage over 1f out: jst hld on* **9/2**[2]

522 **2** *shd* **My Sweet Georgia (IRE)**[69] 3603 2-9-6 **74**...................... MichaelHills 5 76
(B W Hills) *disp ld: grabbed nr side rail over 2f out: hdd over 1f out: rallied fnl f: jst failed* **8/1**

036 **3** *3 ¾* **Daddy's Gift (IRE)**[39] 4589 2-9-6 **74**.................................... EddieAhern 3 66
(R Hannon) *trckd ldng trio: rdn and nt qckn 2f out: no imp after: jst hld on for 3rd* **5/1**[3]

3040 **4** *hd* **Mymateeric**[12] 5432 2-9-5 **73**.. JimmyQuinn 2 65+
(J Pearce) *wl in rr: outpcd and rdn sn after 1/2-way: r.o fnl f: fin wl* **33/1**

3222 **5** *¾* **Hameildaeme**[15] 5365 2-8-8 **67**.................................... DavidProbert(5) 8 57
(S C Williams) *hld up in rr: trapped bhd reluctant rival and lost grnd 1/2-way: prog wl over 2f out: hrd rdn and no imp over 1f out* **11/4**[1]

532 **6** *12* **Auld Arty (FR)**[29] 4926 2-9-7 **75**.. JohnEgan 10 35
(T G Mills) *rrd bef stalls opened and dwlt: sn rcvrd: disp ld to 3f out: dropped out tamely u.p* **7/1**

0660 **7** *2 ½* **Sericus (IRE)**[17] 5274 2-8-13 **67**.. TPQueally 11 21
(W Jarvis) *dwlt: a in rr: floundering by 1/2-way: no ch after* **11/2**

003 **8** *37* **Gilbertian**[32] 4815 2-9-5 **73**... GeorgeBaker 13 —
(R M Beckett) *racd awkwardly: reluctant and lost grnd bef 1/2-way: t.o* **8/1**

1m 28.31s (5.01) **Going Correction** +0.60s/f (Yiel) **8** Ran SP% **114.6**
Speed ratings (Par 95): **95,94,90,90,89 75,72,30**
toteswinger: 1&2 £12.10, 1&3 £4.40, 2&3 £5.50. CSF £39.93 CT £185.86 TOTE £5.30: £1.90, £2.20, £2.10; EX 45.50.
Owner Sheikh Hamdan Bin Mohammed Al Maktoum **Bred** Darley **Trained** Middleham Moor, N Yorks

FOCUS
A modest but competitive nursery and they went a good pace considering the conditions, but it still proved hard to make up much ground. They raced stands' side but, unlike in the previous race, the winner did not race against the rail. The winning time was only 0.10 seconds slower than the following maiden for three-year-old and upwards. The first two finished clear and the form looks sound.

NOTEBOOK
Count Paris(USA) had shown some ability in three runs in maiden company over 6f and he improved for this step up in trip on his nursery debut. Although stuck out widest of all, he showed good speed and sustained his effort to the line. He looked set to win by a length or two inside the final furlong but seemed to get tired late on and the runner-up was coming back at him. Although he ultimately had nothing in hand, he should remain competitive off higher marks. (tchd 5-1)
My Sweet Georgia(IRE), being by Royal Applause, was not sure to be suited by 7f on soft ground, but there is stamina on her dam's side and she ran well on her nursery debut after over two months off. She looked held inside the final furlong, but saw her race out well and might have got back up in another stride or two. (op 15-2 tchd 9-1 and 10-1 in places)
Daddy's Gift(IRE) seemed to travel well just in behind the leaders, but she looked to be outstayed by the front two. (op 4-1)
Mymateeric stayed on when the race was all over and was never a danger. He ran as though he wants 1m, but would be an unlikely stayer on breeding. (op 25-1)
Hameildaeme struggled to get a position against the stands' rail early but she looked to be coming back on the bridle when short of room at about halfway. She made a brief effort when switched wide, but could not sustain her challenge and things just didn't really fall right for her on this occasion. (op 4-1)
Auld Arty(FR) recovered from an awkward start to help force the pace against the rail but was beaten a long way out. Official explanation: trainer's rep said the colt was unsuited by the soft ground (op 6-1)

5786 APRIL THE FIFTH MAIDEN STKS 7f
3:10 (3:12) (Class 5) 3-Y-O+ **£2,590** (£770; £385; £192) **Stalls** High

Form RPR

53 **1** **I'm Sensational**[17] 5278 3-8-12 0.. JimmyQuinn 3 79+
(H R A Cecil) *t.k.h early: racd on outer: cl up: led jst over 2f out: rdn and styd on wl fr over 1f out* **6/4**[1]

6252 **2** *3* **Cape Rock**[25] 5056 3-9-3 72... GeorgeBaker 1 76
(C A Horgan) *racd wd: t.k.h early: hld up in tch: effrt to press wnr 2f out: styd on but readily hld fnl f* **7/2**[2]

222- **3** *3 ¾* **Izzibizzi**[347] 5766 3-8-12 81.. TGMcLaughlin 4 61
(E A L Dunlop) *racd on outer: trckd ldrs: outpcd 2f out: kpt on to take 3rd ins fnl f* **7/1**

4 **4** *3 ¼* **Pension Policy (USA)**[17] 5278 3-8-12 0............................. SteveDrowne 6 52
(R Charlton) *stmbld s: mostly in last pair tl prog over 2f out: no real imp fr over 1f out* **6/1**[3]

0040 **5** *1* **Flying Flute**[18] 5218 3-9-3 56.. AdamKirby 8 54
(H Candy) *mde most to jst over 2f out: sn no ch w ldng pair: wknd fnl f* **16/1**

6 *8* **Shamali** 3-9-3 0.. DarryllHolland 11 33
(W J Haggas) *w ldrs to 3f out: rn green and sn wl outpcd: wknd fnl f* **13/2**

0 **7** *13* **Faintly Hopeful**[26] 5023 3-9-3 0... LPKeniry 9 —
(R A Teal) *restless in stalls and s.s: t.k.h and sn cl up: wknd 1/2-way: t.o* **66/1**

0 **8** *2 ½* **Curly Brown**[25] 5076 3-8-10 0.. DannyDunnachie(7) 7 —
(A Bailey) *dwlt: rcvrd to join ldr and racd against rail: rdn and lost pl fr 3f out: t.o* **100/1**

9 *6* **Elisiario (IRE)** 3-9-3 0... JimCrowley 10 —
(J R Boyle) *cl up tl wknd rapidly 3f out: t.o* **25/1**

1m 28.21s (4.91) **Going Correction** +0.60s/f (Yiel)
WFA 3 from 4yo 4lb **9** Ran SP% **114.6**
Speed ratings (Par 103): **95,91,87,83,82 73,58,55,48**
toteswinger: 1&2 £2.90, 1&3 £3.30, 2&3 £4.90. CSF £6.58 TOTE £2.30: £1.10, £1.20, £2.10; EX 7.20.
Owner Niarchos Family **Bred** Bloomsbury Stud **Trained** Newmarket, Suffolk

FOCUS
An ordinary, uncompetitive maiden. The runner-up is the best guide to the form. The winning time was only 0.10 seconds quicker than the previous 0-75 nursery.

5787 MID-DAY SUN (S) STKS 1m 2f (P)
3:40 (3:41) (Class 6) 3-Y-O+ **£1,978** (£584; £292) **Stalls** Low

Form RPR

0000 **1** **Jelly Mo**[33] 4774 3-8-6 52..(p) EddieAhern 7 50
(J W Hills) *hld up wl in rr: sme prog over 2f out: plenty to do over 1f out: gd prog after: edgd lft but r.o wl to ld fnl 50yds* **8/1**[3]

6613 **2** *½* **Tabulate**[24] 5087 5-9-4 60.. JimmyQuinn 13 54+
(P Howling) *dropped in fr wd draw and hld up wl in rr: plenty to do over 2f out: trbld passage through wl over 1f out: styd on strly fnl f to take 2nd nr fin* **1/1**[1]

2305 **3** *½* **Fairly Honest**[8] 5575 4-9-4 51.. JimCrowley 8 53
(P W Hiatt) *trckd ldr: led over 3f out: drvn over 1f out: collared fnl 50yds* **7/1**[2]

4600 **4** *nse* **Tenement (IRE)**[32] 4811 4-9-4 42.. SteveDrowne 3 53
(Jamie Poulton) *settled towards rr: sme prog 2f out: drvn over 1f out: styng on but hld whn no room fnl 50yds* **16/1**

0460 **5** 1 ¾ **Artistic Light**[12] 5429 3-8-6 51 MartinDwyer 5 45
(W R Muir) *trckd ldrs: gng strly 3f out: chsd ldr over 2f out: hrd rdn and nt qckn over 1f out: lost pls fnl 75yds* **9/1**

5055 **6** 1 ¾ **Danish Monarch**[12] 5429 7-8-13 48 DavidProbert(5) 1 53+
(David Pinder) *trckd ldrs: rdn whn trapped bhd wkng rival over 2f out and lost all ch: styd on again fnl f* **17/2**

-004 **7** ½ **Fareeha**[12] 5429 3-8-7 53 ow1 JohnEgan 2 44+
(B R Johnson) *hld up in midfield: prog over 2f out: chsd ldng pair over 1f out: no imp: wkng whn no room fnl 50yds and eased* **16/1**

2060 **8** 8 **Dickie Valentine**[22] 5148 3-8-12 45 ow1 (p) AdamKirby 9 30
(M R Bosley) *pressed ldrs on outer: hrd rdn over 3f out: wknd over 1f out* **20/1**

-006 **9** 2 **Our Glenard**[45] 4409 9-8-13 35 NataliaGemelova(5) 11 25
(J E Long) *s.s: nvr gng wl in last: lost tch over 3f out: no ch after* **66/1**

-060 **10** ½ **Demure Princess**[18] 5215 3-8-6 45 (p) SaleemGolam 4 19
(W G M Turner) *led to over 2f out: wknd rapidly over 2f out* **66/1**

0000 **11** 15 **The Slider**[33] 4772 4-8-13 35 (v[1]) LPKeniry 12 —
(Mrs L C Jewell) *racd wd in midfield: hrd rdn over 4f out: wknd over 3f out: t.o* **50/1**

2-00 **12** ½ **Mairead's Boy (IRE)**[101] 2613 3-8-11 57 (vt) RichardKingscote 10 —
(P Butler) *hmpd by loose horse after 1f and wl in rr: drvn and wknd 3f out: t.o* **25/1**

060- **U** **Captain Jack Black**[382] 4755 3-8-11 0 StephenCarson 6 —
(M R Bosley) *uns rdr sn after s* **66/1**

2m 5.91s (-0.69) **Going Correction** 0.0s/f (Stan)
WFA 3 from 4yo+ 7lb 13 Ran SP% **120.9**
Speed ratings (Par 101): **102,101,101,101,99 98,97,91,89,89 77,77,—**
toteswinger: 1&2 £5.00, 1&3 £9.70, 2&3 £2.50. CSF £15.82 TOTE £12.30: £2.90, £1.20, £2.10; EX 25.20.There was no bid for the winner. Tabulate was subject to a friendly claim.
Owner Over The Moon Racing & Partner **Bred** Cheveley Park Stud Ltd **Trained** Upper Lambourn, Berks
■ Stewards' Enquiry : Eddie Ahern two day ban: careless riding (Sept 23-24)

FOCUS
A typically moderate seller and there was plenty of trouble in running. The third and fourth look the best guides and the favourite is rated a stone off her recent best.
Danish Monarch Official explanation: jockey said gelding was denied a clear run
Dickie Valentine Official explanation: jockey said gelding hung left

5788 EUROPEAN BREEDERS' FUND MAIDEN FILLIES' STKS 7f (P)
4:10 (4:14) (Class 5) 2-Y-O **£3,885** (£1,156; £577; £288) **Stalls** Low

Form RPR

23 **1** **Feeling Fab (FR)**[35] 4697 2-9-0 0 JoeFanning 7 84+
(M Johnston) *trckd ldr: led 2f out: scooted clr over 1f out: v comf* **13/2**

54 **2** 4 **Purple Sage (IRE)**[18] 5240 2-9-0 0 MichaelHills 10 74+
(B W Hills) *nt that wl away: t.k.h and rcvrd grnd on outer after 3f: prog 2f out: chsd wnr over 1f out: hanging and fnd v little* **15/8**[1]

3 ½ **Featherweight (IRE)** 2-9-0 0 DarryllHolland 12 73+
(B W Hills) *settled midfield: shkn up over 2f out: nudged along and styd on takingly fr over 1f out: nrst fin* **40/1**

53 **4** 2 **Syrinx (IRE)**[25] 5066 2-9-0 0 EddieAhern 6 68
(J Noseda) *prom: chsd wnr briefly wl over 1f out: wknd ins fnl f* **7/2**[2]

00 **5** 1 **First Queen**[54] 4109 2-9-0 0 MartinDwyer 5 65+
(L M Cumani) *hld up wl in rr: nt clr run on inner over 2f out: 10th over 1f out: shuffled along and styd on steadily fnl f* **25/1**

6 1 **Lindy Hop (IRE)** 2-9-0 0 AdamKirby 1 63
(W R Swinburn) *settled midfield: cl enough 2f out: shkn up and one pce over 1f out* **16/1**

55 **7** hd **Simplification**[18] 5241 2-9-0 0 SteveDrowne 8 62+
(R Hannon) *hld up in midfield: chsng ldrs and in tch 2f out: outpcd over 1f out* **5/1**[3]

0 **8** 1 ½ **Aula**[31] 4870 2-9-0 0 NeilPollard 4 59
(E A L Dunlop) *uns rdr and bolted 6f bef s: cl up: stl pressing ldrs 2f out: fnd nil over 1f out* **66/1**

00 **9** nk **Suakin Dancer (IRE)**[24] 5097 2-9-0 0 TravisBlock 2 58
(H Morrison) *dwlt: wl in rr: nvr on terms: plugged on over 1f out* **22/1**

0 **10** 1 ¾ **Miss Tikitiboo (IRE)**[30] 4907 2-9-0 0 LPKeniry 11 53
(E F Vaughan) *settled in last trio: nvr a factor: plugged on fnl f* **100/1**

11 2 ½ **Honours Stride (IRE)** 2-8-9 0 JPHamblett(5) 9 47
(Sir Michael Stoute) *rn green and a wl in rr: struggling over 2f out* **14/1**

0 **12** 2 **Mill Pond**[102] 2584 2-9-0 0 J-PGuillambert 3 42
(M Johnston) *led to 2f out: immediately hanging and gave up* **40/1**

0 **13** 7 **Maisie Mouse**[30] 4905 2-9-0 0 SaleemGolam 13 25
(S C Williams) *trckd ldrs on outer: lost pl rapidly over 2f out: sn bhd* **100/1**

1m 24.96s (0.16) **Going Correction** 0.0s/f (Stan) 13 Ran SP% **116.1**
Speed ratings (Par 92): **99,94,93,91,90 89,89,87,87,85 82,79,71**
toteswinger: 1&2 £4.60, 1&3 £16.90, 2&3 £15.30. CSF £17.63 TOTE £5.50: £2.00, £1.20, £7.60; EX 21.50.
Owner A D Spence **Bred** Alain Decrion & Sunland Holdings Ltd **Trained** Middleham Moor, N Yorks

FOCUS
A reasonable fillies' maiden with plenty of big stables represented and this race ought to produce a few winners. The winning time was only 0.19 seconds slower than the following handicap won by a six-year-old rated 73. The winner can rate higher.

NOTEBOOK
Feeling Fab(FR) failed to build on her debut second at Thirsk when not looking entirely straightforward and turned over at 4/11 at Catterick last time, but her connections felt she was unsuited by the undulating track that day. She left that effort well behind with a most decisive success, extending well in the straight having been in a good position from the off. She looked to carry her head a little to the right, but was certainly trying hard enough. It remains to be seen where she will go next. (op 11-2 tchd 7-1)
Purple Sage(IRE), a beaten favourite at Newmarket on her previous start, is a little better than she showed, as she was stuck out very wide for most of the way, particularly on the bends. She seemed to be hanging in the straight but, although no match for the winner, she did enough to hold on for second. (op 9-4 tchd 5-2)
Featherweight(IRE), a 27,000gns daughter of Fantastic Light, half-sister to quite useful 7f juvenile winner Feathers Flying, out of a 1m scorer, made a pleasing debut. She got rid of her rider in the paddock when possibly being spooked by something, but was fine in the race itself. She came very wide into the straight, but kept on steadily and was not given a hard ride once her chance had gone. She will know more next time. (op 50-1)
Syrinx(IRE) seemed to be well enough placed if good enough, but did not pick up in the straight. Perhaps she will be worth another try over 6f. (op 9-4 tchd 4-1)
First Queen ◆ stayed on from a long way back when the race was all over, despite not getting the best of runs through, and caught the eye in fifth. She is now qualified for a handicap mark and will be one to keep in mind when stepped up in trip. (op 33-1)
Lindy Hop(IRE), a daughter of Danehill Dancer, showed some ability and should come on for this. (op 25-1)
Simplification is now qualified for a handicap mark and might do better over a little further. (op 6-1 tchd 9-2)
Aula got loose before the start and bolted for around six furlongs.
Maisie Mouse is a little better than she showed as she seemed to lose her action when squeezed up turning for home, although she was weakening at the time.

5789 PARTHIA H'CAP 7f (P)
4:40 (4:42) (Class 4) (0-80,80) 3-Y-O+ **£4,604** (£1,378; £689; £344; £171) **Stalls** Low

Form RPR

2661 **1** **Fiefdom (IRE)**[22] 5144 6-9-1 73 PatrickMathers 4 80
(I W McInnes) *trckd ldng pair: effrt to go 2nd ent fnl f: drvn to ld fnl 100yds: styd on wl* **6/1**[3]

-421 **2** ½ **Silent Master (USA)**[190] 772 3-9-3 79 JoeFanning 3 83
(M Johnston) *led: drvn over 1f out: kpt on wl: hdd and outpcd fnl 100yds* **9/2**[1]

0-00 **3** ½ **Hopeful Purchase (IRE)**[17] 5290 5-9-2 79 (b) DavidProbert(5) 7 83
(J R Gask) *t.k.h early: chsd ldr tl ent fnl f: styd on same pce after* **16/1**

0-60 **4** ½ **Princess Valerina**[22] 5144 4-8-13 71 TPQueally 10 74
(H R A Cecil) *mostly in midfield on outer: drvn over 2f out: styd on fnl f: nvr able to chal* **12/1**

1040 **5** nse **Perfect Treasure (IRE)**[34] 4723 5-9-4 76 EddieAhern 8 79
(J A R Toller) *hld up in midfield: gng wl enough 2f out: n.m.r over 1f out: styd on: nvr able to chal* **10/1**

6433 **6** nk **Cativo Cavallino**[22] 5144 5-8-10 73 NataliaGemelova(5) 1 75
(J E Long) *cl up on inner: rdn over 2f out: stl pressing jst over 1f out: nt qckn and btn fnl f* **5/1**[2]

5041 **7** hd **Mandarin Spirit (IRE)**[9] 5532 8-8-8 73 6ex (p) AshleyMorgan(7) 13 75
(G C H Chung) *hld up in rr: effrt 2f out: drvn and styd on fnl f: no ch to threaten ldrs* **11/1**

1655 **8** ¾ **Dvinsky (USA)**[12] 5424 7-9-8 80 (b) JimmyQuinn 9 80
(P Howling) *pressed ldrs on outer: drvn over 2f out: nt qckn over 1f out: wknd and lost pls fnl 100yds* **11/1**

600 **9** shd **Lend A Grand (IRE)**[62] 3840 4-9-0 72 TravisBlock 11 71
(Miss Jo Crowley) *dwlt: hld up in last trio: pushed along over 1f out: styd on fnl 150yds: nvr nr ldrs* **28/1**

2060 **10** nk **Summer Dancer (IRE)**[39] 4603 4-9-2 74 MartinDwyer 12 73
(D R C Elsworth) *plld v hrd: hld up in last pair: stl there and drvn over 1f out: kpt on but no ch* **13/2**

1-00 **11** ½ **Messias Da Silva (USA)**[13] 5403 3-9-3 79 SteveDrowne 2 74
(J Noseda) *wl in tch in midfield: rdn over 2f out: wknd jst over 1f out* **10/1**

5200 **12** 2 ¼ **Hessian (IRE)**[88] 2993 4-9-1 73 SaleemGolam 6 64
(M D Squance) *dwlt: hld up in last trio: gng wl enough 2f out: pushed along and no prog sn after: eased fnl 75yds* **20/1**

1m 24.77s (-0.03) **Going Correction** 0.0s/f (Stan)
WFA 3 from 4yo+ 4lb 12 Ran SP% **119.1**
Speed ratings (Par 105): **100,99,98,98,98 97,97,96,96,96 95,93**
toteswinger: 1&2 £7.00, 1&3 £28.70, 2&3 £17.90. CSF £33.29 CT £418.27 TOTE £7.80: £2.50, £1.40, £6.10; EX 37.50.
Owner Stephen Hackney **Bred** Kildaragh Stud **Trained** Catwick, E Yorks

FOCUS
A fair, typically competitive Polytrack handicap. The winning time was 0.19 seconds quicker than the previous juvenile fillies' maiden.
Summer Dancer(IRE) Official explanation: jockey said gelding ran too free

5790 TULYAR MEDIAN AUCTION MAIDEN STKS 1m (P)
5:10 (5:10) (Class 6) 3-4-Y-O **£2,047** (£604; £302) **Stalls** High

Form RPR

0-05 **1** **Colour Trooper (IRE)**[11] 5463 3-9-3 75 StephenCarson 7 67+
(P Winkworth) *trckd ldng pair: pushed along over 2f out: chal wd over 1f out: led ins fnl f: drvn out* **11/4**[2]

2- **2** ½ **Girl Of Pangaea (GER)**[303] 6777 3-8-12 0 LDettori 8 61+
(E A L Dunlop) *hld up towards rr: prog on outer 3f out: wdst of all bnd 2f out: chal over 1f out: pressed wnr ins fnl f: jst hld* **3/1**[3]

432 **3** ½ **Mazaris (IRE)**[12] 5426 3-9-3 71 GeorgeBaker 4 64+
(L M Cumani) *led: drvn and kpt on wl over 1f out: hdd and outpcd ins fnl f* **11/8**[1]

425 **4** 2 **Caro George (USA)**[95] 2772 3-8-12 69 SteveDrowne 3 55
(R Charlton) *trckd ldng pair: nt qckn 2f out: effrt again on inner over 1f out: kpt on one pce* **13/2**

66 **5** 1 ½ **Candy Rose**[8] 5568 3-8-5 0 KatiaScallan(7) 6 51
(M P Tregoning) *pressed ldr: chal over 2f out: upsides over 1f out: fdd* **33/1**

-050 **6** 1 **Follow The Band**[33] 4772 3-9-0 46 PatrickHills(3) 5 54
(R Hannon) *sn dropped to last pair: u.p 3f out: sn outpcd: no ch after* **50/1**

00 **7** nk **Mayfair's Future**[29] 4929 3-9-3 0 EddieAhern 2 53
(J R Jenkins) *hld up towards rr: outpcd over 2f out: nudged along and n.d after* **66/1**

5/5 **8** nk **Charming Escort**[38] 4644 4-9-8 0 AdamKirby 1 53
(T T Clement) *stdd s: a in last pair: outpcd over 2f out: no ch after* **50/1**

1m 38.37s (0.17) **Going Correction** 0.0s/f (Stan)
WFA 3 from 4yo 5lb 8 Ran SP% **115.5**
Speed ratings (Par 101): **99,98,98,96,94 93,93,92**
toteswinger: 1&2 £3.20, 1&3 £2.60, 2&3 £1.70. CSF £11.40 TOTE £4.40: £1.30, £1.10, £1.10; EX 15.80 Place 6: £14.34, Place 5: £10.74..
Owner Kennet Valley Thoroughbreds I **Bred** P D Savill **Trained** Chiddingfold, Surrey

FOCUS
A pretty ordinary maiden which was steadily run. There is some doubt over the reliability of the form with the sixth close enough.

T/Jkpt: £5,712.50 to a £1 stake. Pool: £24,137.63. 3.00 winning tickets. T/Plt: £7.90 to a £1 stake. Pool: £75,247.71. 6,896.94 winning tickets. T/Qpdt: £2.90 to a £1 stake. Pool: £4,059.20. 1,009.70 winning tickets. JN

[4615]DONCASTER (L-H)

Wednesday, September 10

OFFICIAL GOING: Soft (good to soft in places on round course)

Rail realignment added circa 12yds to race distances on round course. A new-look and low-key opening day of the St Leger meeting.

Wind: Light against Weather: Sunny periods

5791 FLAKT WOODS NURSERY 7f

1:30 (1:31) (Class 3) (0-95,87) 2-Y-O **£9,714** (£2,890; £1,444; £721) **Stalls** High

Form RPR

10 **1** **Ballantrae (IRE)**[32] 4868 2-9-3 **83** ... JamieSpencer 16 93+
(M L W Bell) *w'like: leggy: stdd s: hld up and bhd stands' side: hdwy over 2f out: swtchd lft and effrt over 1f out: sn rdn and styd on to ld ins fnl f: 1st in gp* **12/1**

603 **2** *1 1/2* **Mister Dee Bee (IRE)**[27] 5021 2-8-12 **78** ... MichaelHills 2 84+
(B W Hills) *lw: trckd ldrs far side: hdwy over 2f out: rdn to ld that gp and overall ldr over 1f out: drvn and hdd ins fnl f: kpt on: 1st in gp* **28/1**

031 **3** *hd* **Cook's Endeavour (USA)**[42] 4530 2-8-10 **76** ... NCallan 14 82+
(K A Ryan) *trckd ldrs stands' side: hdwy over 2f out: swtchd rt and rdn over 1f out: kpt on u.p ins fnl f: 2nd in gp* **15/2**[3]

31 **4** *1/2* **Satwa Laird**[26] 5072 2-9-3 **83** ... JimmyFortune 8 88
(E A L Dunlop) *w'like: str: lw: hld up in tch stands' side: hdwy over 2f out: rdn and ev ch over 1f out: kpt on u.p ins fnl f 3rd in gp* **8/1**

031 **5** *4* **Amethyst Dawn (IRE)**[18] 5256 2-8-11 **77** ... DavidAllan 11 72
(T D Easterby) *cl up stands' side: effrt 2f out and ev ch tl rdn and wknd appr fnl f: 4th in gp* **9/1**

122 **6** *shd* **High Alert**[8] 5585 2-9-1 **81** ... (b) LDettori 5 75
(J Noseda) *lw: overall ldr far side: rdn along 2f out: drvn and hdd appr fnl f: sn wknd: 2nd in gp* **9/2**[1]

0314 **7** *2* **Come And Go (UAE)**[16] 5359 2-9-6 **86** ... MartinDwyer 12 75
(G A Swinbank) *w'like: lengthy: led stands' side gp: rdn over 2f out: sn drvn and grad wknd appr last: 5th in gp* **20/1**

3541 **8** *3/4* **Go Go Green (IRE)**[12] 5451 2-8-12 **78** ... AlanMunro 9 65
(S Parr) *prom stands' side: rdn along over 2f out: sn drvn and wknd over 1f out: 6th in gp* **40/1**

3112 **9** *2 1/4* **Lucky Redback (IRE)**[38] 4666 2-9-7 **87** ... RyanMoore 17 69
(R Hannon) *trckd ldrs on stands' rail: hdwy over 2f out and sn rdn: drvn and no imp whn n.m.r appr fnl f: 7th in gp* **14/1**

621 **10** *1/2* **Blazing Buck**[16] 5365 2-8-12 **78** ... TPQueally 13 59
(H J L Dunlop) *chsd ldrs stands' side: rdn along and outpcd 1/2-way: 8th in gp* **20/1**

4221 **11** *2 3/4* **Inheritor (IRE)**[43] 4497 2-9-2 **82** ... PaulMulrennan 10 56
(B Smart) *cl up stands' side: rdn along wl over 2f out: sn drvn and wknd: 9th in gp* **25/1**

112 **12** *3 1/4* **Fol Liam**[40] 4594 2-9-1 **81** ... StephenDonohoe 4 47
(Ian Williams) *w'like: a towards rr far side: 3rd in gp* **20/1**

1640 **13** *1 1/2* **Full Of Nature**[19] 5244 2-8-13 **79** ... RobertWinston 6 41
(K A Ryan) *t.k.h: prom far side: rdn along over 2f out and sn wknd: 4th in gp* **66/1**

61 **14** *2 1/4* **Advertise**[16] 5364 2-8-9 **75** ... LPKeniry 1 31
(A M Balding) *dull in coat: t.k.h: prom far side tl rdn along over 2f out and sn wknd: 5th in gp* **10/1**

312 **15** *4 1/2* **Needwood Lad**[15] 5381 2-9-2 **82** ... PaulHanagan 15 27
(R A Fahey) *athletic: lw: a towards rr stands' side: 10th in gp* **11/2**[2]

315 **16** *1* **Beautiful Breeze (IRE)**[12] 5447 2-9-1 **81** ... RoystonFfrench 7 23
(M Johnston) *in tch far side: swtchd rt to join stands' side gp whn stmbld after 1 1/2f: a in rr after: 11th in gp* **25/1**

1m 29.51s (3.21) **Going Correction** +0.375s/f (Good) **16** Ran SP% **119.2**

Speed ratings (Par 99): **96,94,94,93,88 88,86,85,83,82 79,75,73,71,66 65**

toteswinger: 1&2 £55.00, 1&3 £22.50, 2&3 £49.00. CSF £314.88 CT £2786.55 TOTE £15.60: £2.90, £6.70, £2.80, £2.60; EX 687.20 TRIFECTA Not won..

Owner Sheikh Marwan Al Maktoum **Bred** Darley **Trained** Newmarket, Suffolk

FOCUS

This was a very competitive nursery and all bar one of these was a previous winner. The field split into two with the five lowest drawn going far side, whilst the main bulk of the field came up the stands' rail. There did not appear to be much between the two groups at the line though, despite the winner coming stands' side, as two from the much smaller far-side group finished in the first six. The first four finished clear and this is solid form.

NOTEBOOK

Ballantrae(IRE) ◆, proven in soft ground and making her nursery debut after being outclassed in the Sweet Solera, was switched off right out the back early. She travelled like a dream though and was still on the bridle passing the 2f pole whilst her rivals were all under the pump, so that the only question was how much she would find when Jamie Spencer eventually got after her. The answer was plenty and throughout the last furlong her only conceivable danger was racing on the other flank. She obviously loves to get her toe in and looks more than capable of finding something even better when conditions are in her favour.

Mister Dee Bee(IRE) ◆, the only maiden in the field, was making his nursery debut and he ran a blinder, ultimately pulling a long way clear of the other quartet that raced up the far rail. He is improving with every race and should not take long in breaking his duck. (op 33-1)

Cook's Endeavour(USA) was encountering softer ground and attempting an extra furlong on this nursery debut, though a Racing Post Trophy entry did not suggest he was thought to have stamina issues. That was the way it looked too, as he stayed on all the way to the line, and he should be able to find further success even though he is already due to go up another 3lb. (op 6-1)

Satwa Laird, one of the least exposed in the field, was another trying an extra furlong and racing on softer ground than he had encountered before. He was produced to hold every chance entering the last 2f, but as soon as the winner was unleashed there was little he could do about it. This was only his third start, so he is entitled to still have some improvement left in him.

Amethyst Dawn(IRE), proven on soft ground after winning a fillies' maiden at Beverley, was making her nursery debut and she ran with plenty of credit having been close to the pace from the off.

High Alert, a winner over this trip on Polytrack on his debut, had performed well enough in similar conditions in a couple of starts over 1m on turf in the meantime. He was given a positive ride in the far-side group, but was made to look very one-paced when the eventual runner-up swept past him. He may be worth another chance on better ground. (op 5-1tchd 11-2 in a place)

Come And Go(UAE), making his nursery debut and trying this trip for the first time, made much of the running against the stands' rail but did not appear to get home in the ground. (op 25-1)

Lucky Redback(IRE) ◆ was probably the unlucky horse of the race as he was staying on nicely when running into serious trouble when trying for a gap between Come And Go and Cook's Endeavour approaching the last furlong. He was eased right off after that and would have been a lot closer otherwise. Official explanation: jockey said colt was denied a clear run

Full Of Nature Official explanation: jockey said filly was unsuited by the soft (good to soft in places) ground

Needwood Lad was well backed earlier in the day, but after walking out of the stalls he never managed to get into the race at all. Official explanation: jockey said colt never travelled (op 9-2)

Beautiful Breeze(IRE) Official explanation: jockey said colt lost its action

5792 HIRE FROM HEWDEN CONDITIONS STKS 1m 2f 60y

2:00 (2:00) (Class 2) 3-5-Y-0 **£12,462** (£3,732; £1,866) **Stalls** Low

Form RPR

3001 **1** **Perks (IRE)**[32] 4856 3-8-9 **102** ... JimmyQuinn 2 114+
(J L Dunlop) *lw: trckd ldr gng wl: smooth hdwy over 2f out: shkn up to ld wl over 1f out: rdn and edgd rt ent fnl f: styd on strly* **10/11**[1]

4114 **2** *3* **With Interest**[26] 5070 5-9-2 **107** ... LDettori 4 110+
(Saeed Bin Suroor) *stdd s: hld up in tch: swtchd outside and gd hdwy 2f out: rdn to chal over 1f out and ev ch tl nt qckn ins fnl f* **5/2**[2]

1144 **3** *8* **Flying Clarets (IRE)**[32] 4855 5-9-1 **111** ... PaulHanagan 3 91
(R A Fahey) *set stdy pce: qcknd 1/2-way: rdn along over 3f out: hdd wl over 1f out and sn outpcd* **3/1**[3]

2m 15.41s (4.21) **Going Correction** +0.65s/f (Yiel)

WFA 3 from 4yo+ 7lb **3** Ran SP% **106.0**

Speed ratings (Par 109): **109,106,100**

CSF £3.28 TOTE £1.90; EX 3.20.

Owner Benny Andersson **Bred** Chess Racing Ab **Trained** Arundel, W Sussex

FOCUS

A very small field for this conditions contest, but all three are smart performers and this was a decent race. The pace, although not strong by any means, was reasonable enough considering the lack of runners. The form is muddling but the winner, value for 2l, is rated up 5lb.

NOTEBOOK

Perks(IRE) looked a different horse when upped to this sort of trip for the first time in a hot handicap at Haydock on his previous start, thrashing subsequent winner Drill Sergeant in a time over a second quicker than Multidimensional clocked in a Group 3 over 35 minutes earlier, and he confirmed the immense promise of that effort with another taking performance. Having travelled well throughout, he was asked to pick up when the early leader Flying Clarets began to weaken and With Interest tried to draw upsides inside the final two furlongs. Although he took a few strides to really going get going, he was always doing enough and gradually drew clear for a convincing success. As well as improving for this longer trip, plenty of give underfoot also seems crucial and he looked to relish the testing conditions. Provided conditions are suitable, he will surely now be aimed the Cambridgeshire, for which he has incurred a 4lb penalty. While the drop back to 1m1f will not be ideal, a strong pace will suit and soft ground will help bring his stamina into play. He can still be backed at 10-1 and that looks a fair price if you are happy to gamble on the ground. (op Evens and 11-10 in places)

With Interest was held up last of the three for much of the way, but he was close enough if good enough in the straight. He remains lightly raced, but is capable of smart form and this was a solid effort conceding 7lb to the rapidly improving winner. (op 9-4 tchd 2-1)

Flying Clarets(IRE), this season's John Smith's Cup winner, very much had the run of the race out in front, which is where she likes to be, but she offered no resistance when both her rivals loomed up passing the two-furlong pole and her recent exertions may just have taken the edge off her. (tchd 10-3 in a place)

5793 CONSTRUCTION NEWS SCARBROUGH STKS (LISTED RACE) 5f

2:35 (2:35) (Class 1) 2-Y-0+ **£26,667** (£10,084; £5,040; £2,520) **Stalls** High

Form RPR

0040 **1** **Galeota (IRE)**[98] 2712 6-9-9 **101** ... RyanMoore 8 102
(R Hannon) *trckd ldrs: hdwy to ld wl over 1f out: sn rdn and styd on strly fnl f* **3/1**[2]

10-0 **2** *3/4* **Loch Verdi**[11] 5509 5-9-4 **97** ... LPKeniry 6 95
(A M Balding) *lw: led: rdn along over 2f out: hdd wl over 1f out: rallied wl u.p ins fnl f to take 2nd nr line* **7/1**

006 **3** *nk* **Moorhouse Lad**[19] 5245 5-9-9 **109** ... RoystonFfrench 3 99+
(B Smart) *plld hrd: trckd ldrs tl n.m.r and lost pl over 2f out: hdwy over 1f out: rdn and qcknd to chse wnr ins fnl f: drvn and no ex fnl 50yds: lost 2nd nr line* **5/1**[3]

412 **4** *1* **Hypnosis**[39] 4631 5-9-4 **78** ... TonyHamilton 9 90?
(D W Barker) *b: chsd ldrs: rdn along wl over 1f out: kpt on same pce ins fnl f* **40/1**

5140 **5** *nk* **Turn On The Style**[195] 741 6-9-9 **105** ... (b) PaulMulrennan 7 94
(J Balding) *b.hind: s.i.s: sn in tch: hdwy to chse ldrs 2f out: sn rdn and kpt on same pce ins fnl f* **20/1**

0205 **6** *3/4* **Benbaun (IRE)**[19] 5245 7-9-9 **110** ... (v) PJSmullen 4 91
(M J Wallace, Australia) *lw: in rr and reminders after 1f: hdwy on outer 2f out and sn rdn: drvn to chse ldrs over 1f out: wknd ins fnl f* **9/4**[1]

0432 **7** *4 1/2* **Princess Ellis**[10] 5542 4-9-4 **85** ... DavidAllan 2 70
(E J Alston) *lw: cl up: rdn along over 2f out: sn edgd rt and wknd wl over 1f out* **11/1**

0300 **8** *8* **Desert Lord**[19] 5245 8-9-9 **106** ... (b) NCallan 5 46
(K A Ryan) *b: sn cl up: rdn along 2f out and sn wknd* **8/1**

61.84 secs (1.34) **Going Correction** +0.375s/f (Good) **8** Ran SP% **111.6**

Speed ratings: **104,102,102,100,100 99,91,79**

toteswinger: 1&2 £6.00, 1&3 £4.00, 2&3 £4.20. CSF £22.97 TOTE £3.60: £1.30, £2.10, £2.00; EX 25.10 Trifecta £129.70 Pool: £631.00, 3.60 winning units..

Owner Robin Blunt **Bred** W Maxwell Ervine **Trained** East Everleigh, Wilts

FOCUS

This looked a decent Listed sprint with four of these having been successful at an even higher level, but several also had a question mark against their ability to handle this sort of ground, so the form may not be totally reliable. The fourth also lends doubts. Galeota did not need to be at his best to score.

NOTEBOOK

Galeota(IRE) was proven on an easy surface and boasted a perfect three from three record at the track coming into this, including this contest last year. Always travelling well behind the leaders, he had to fight hard to get on top of the early leader Loch Verdi, but once he did so the race was always going to be his. He had not been at his best so far this season, although his performance on his Polytrack debut at Kempton in his previous start was too bad to be true, but this return to his favourite venue obviously did the trick. He is still in Saturday's Portland for which he incurs a 6lb penalty, but he is unlikely to take up that option and may be aimed at the Bentinck Stakes at Newmarket next month in which he finished third last year.

Loch Verdi, all the better for her belated return to action at Sandown 11 days earlier, could have 'bounced' from that effort, but she actually did the opposite and stepped up from it, making most of the running and fighting back well when headed. She was one of those with a major doubt over the ground, so this was a decent effort and she can go one better at this level, especially back against her own sex. (op 9-1)

Moorhouse Lad ◆ travelled powerfully behind the leaders, but then got into trouble behind Desert Lord and Princess Ellis, especially as the former began to weaken, and he soon had a mountain to climb. He finished well once out in the clear, but had too much ground to make up. This would not have been his sort of ground either and there will be other days for him back on a sound surface. (op 13-2 tchd 7-1 in a place)

Hypnosis had no chance at these weights so she ran with a huge amount of credit, especially as her best form has been on quicker ground, but form shown in these types of races can be very misleading and she could be in trouble if the handicapper takes this effort at face value. (op 66-1)

Turn On The Style, racing for the first time since Nad Al Sheba in February, deserves a lot of credit as he messed about as the stalls opened and gave his rivals a start. Even though he has winning form on soft ground, he still did very well to finish as close as he did and he has the ability to win a race like this. Official explanation: jockey said gelding missed the break

Benbaun(IRE), whose connections were concerned about the ground beforehand, never looked happy once under way. It was only his class that enabled him to finish so close and he should not be judged too harshly on this. (op 15-8)

Princess Ellis found herself rather marooned towards the outside of the field, but she had a lot to do at the weights and probably performed as well as she was entitled to on ground that would have been much softer than ideal. (op 12-1 tchd 14-1 and 10-1)

Desert Lord is yet another best on a sound surface, but even so the way he dropped out tamely after showing early speed was still very disappointing. (tchd 9-1)

5794 CONSTRUCTION INDEX CONDITIONS STKS 6f
3:10 (3:10) (Class 2) 2-Y-O

£10,904 (£3,265; £1,632; £817; £407; £204) **Stalls High**

Form RPR

122 **1** **Bonnie Charlie**[19] 5244 2-8-13 **109** .... RyanMoore 3 97+
(R Hannon) *lw: chsd ldrs: pushed along 1/2-way: swtchd outside and rdn 2f out: drvn to chal over 1f out: led ent fnl f: kpt on* **10/11**[1]

16 **2** *hd* **Faraway Flower (USA)**[18] 5266 2-8-8 **0** .... MichaelHills 2 92+
(B W Hills) *unf: lengthy: scope: cl up: effrt 2f out: rdn to ld wl over 1f out: drvn and hdd ent fnl f: kpt on wl u.p towards fin* **7/2**[2]

45 **3** *1 1/2* **Invincible Heart (GR)**[18] 5271 2-8-11 **0** .... JamieSpencer 4 90
(Jane Chapple-Hyam) *edgy: warm: stdd s: hld up in rr: hdwy 2f out: rdn over 1f out: ev ch ent fnl f: sn drvn and no ex* **25/1**

225 **4** *3/4* **Fitz Flyer (IRE)**[19] 5244 2-8-11 **93** .... PaulMulrennan 5 88
(D H Brown) *lw: cl up gng wl: effrt 2f out: sn rdn and ev ch tl drvn and nt qckn ent fnl f* **6/1**[3]

10 **5** *1 1/2* **Parisian Art (IRE)**[11] 5507 2-8-13 **95** ....(b) TPQueally 6 86
(J Noseda) *lw: dwlt: hld up in rr: hdwy 2f out: swtchd lft and rdn over 1f out: kpt on same pce ins fnl f* **14/1**

2513 **6** *3 1/4* **Caranbola**[15] 5383 2-8-8 **92** .... AlanMunro 7 69
(M Brittain) *led: rdn along 2f out: sn hdd and grad wknd* **8/1**

1340 **7** *12* **Tagula Breeze (IRE)**[19] 5226 2-8-11 **83** ....(t) PatrickMathers 1 36
(I W McInnes) *prom: rdn along over 2f out and sn wknd* **66/1**

1m 15.55s (1.95) **Going Correction** +0.375s/f (Good) 7 Ran SP% **112.0**

Speed ratings (Par 101): **102,101,99,98,96 91,75**

toteswinger: 1&2 £1.90, 1&3 £4.30, 2&3 £6.20. CSF £4.06 TOTE £1.80: £1.40, £1.90; EX 4.10.

Owner Thurloe Thoroughbreds XXII **Bred** C D S Bryce And Mrs M Bryce **Trained** East Everleigh, Wilts

FOCUS

A decent juvenile conditions contest and it was certainly competitive. Listed-class form. They raced stands' side.

NOTEBOOK

Bonnie Charlie was the clear form pick having run second in both the Group 3 Molecomb Stakes and a valuable sales race over this trip at the July course since winning on his debut at Windsor, but he was made to work hard to land the odds. Having tracked the pace, he was forced to switch out widest of all with his challenge, which was not ideal, and he was pushed all the way to the line by Faraway Flower. This still rates as a smart effort, however, as the runner-up was better than she showed in a Group 3 at Goodwood on her previous start. He has no fancy entries, but deserves a chance in Listed or Group 3 company if he is to be kept on the go this season. (op 5-6 tchd evens in places)

Faraway Flower(USA), a course-and-distance winner on her debut before looking unlucky not to finish closer than sixth in the Prestige Stakes at Goodwood, ran a game race in defeat. Always on the speed, she kept finding for pressure once coming off the bridle around two furlongs out and was coming back at the winner close home. She is entered in the Cheveley Park, showing her connections believe her to have both plenty of speed and class, but on this evidence she might be worth another try back over 7f. (op 4-1 tchd 9-2)

Invincible Heart(GR) ◆ was a shade disappointing when dropped back to this trip on quick ground in a maiden on the July course last time, but he proved well suited by the underfoot conditions and ran a big race in defeat. Held up last early on, he moved into contention travelling as well as anything at about halfway and looked dangerous, but his effort just flattened out a touch late on. He should have no trouble winning his maiden before stepping back up in class and the speed he showed this time suggests he will be worth a try over 5f when the ground is on the easy side.

Fitz Flyer(IRE), around three lengths behind today's winner when fifth in a sales race at Newmarket on his previous start, got a little closer this time and posted a solid effort in defeat. He will probably benefit from a return to maiden company to try and gain a confidence-boosting success. (op 7-1)

Parisian Art(IRE) had to switch off the rail to get past the tiring Caranbola and never looked like getting involved. His maiden win was gained over 7f on quick ground, although it wasn't much of a race. (op 11-1 tchd 9-1)

Caranbola dropped away rather tamely and a busy season may be catching up with her. (op 12-1)

Tagula Breeze(IRE) would appear to need his sights lowering for the time being.

5795 HEATING AND VENTILATION NEWS H'CAP 7f
3:45 (3:47) (Class 2) (0-100,99) 3-Y-O

£12,462 (£3,732; £1,866; £934; £466; £234) **Stalls High**

Form RPR

3000 **1** **Slugger O'Toole**[46] 4405 3-8-7 **88** .... ChrisCatlin 11 100
(B W Hills) *trckd ldrs: hdwy over 2f out: rdn to ld over 1f out: styd on strly ins fnl f* **20/1**

3116 **2** *2 1/4* **Harrison George (IRE)**[40] 4586 3-8-7 **88** .... PaulHanagan 4 94
(R A Fahey) *chsd ldrs: swtchd rt and hdwy 2f out: rdn to chse wnr ent fnl f: kpt on u.p* **7/1**[3]

6300 **3** *hd* **Fathsta (IRE)**[11] 5495 3-8-9 **90** .... JamieSpencer 8 95
(S Kirk) *lw: dwlt and rr: swtchd lft and hdwy over 2f out: rdn to chse ldrs over 1f out: drvn and kpt on ins fnl f* **10/1**

2211 **4** *2 1/4* **Carniolan**[54] 4158 3-8-11 **92** .... AdamKirby 15 91
(W R Swinburn) *in tch on stands' rail: hdwy over 2f out: rdn to chse ldrs over 1f out: sn drvn and one pce ins fnl f* **3/1**[1]

063 **5** *4 1/2* **Cobo Bay**[16] 5360 3-9-3 **98** ....(p) NCallan 6 85
(K A Ryan) *cl up: rdn 2f out: drvn and wknd over 1f out* **14/1**

2514 **6** *2 1/4* **Dunn'o (IRE)**[18] 5273 3-8-0 **86** .... Louis-PhilippeBeuzelin(5) 12 67
(C G Cox) *chsd ldrs: rdn along 2f out: drvn and wknd over 1f out* **12/1**

2011 **7** *nk* **Keep Discovering (IRE)**[12] 5446 3-9-4 **99** .... DarryllHolland 9 79
(M Johnston) *lw: prom: rdn along over 2f out: grad wknd* **12/1**

6404 **8** *1 3/4* **Rash Judgement**[18] 5270 3-8-4 **85** ow1 .... RoystonFfrench 2 61
(W S Kittow) *in touch on outer: effrt over 2f out: sn rdn and no imp* **20/1**

0-00 **9** *nk* **Broken Applause (IRE)**[100] 2666 3-8-11 **92** .... TonyHamilton 3 67
(R A Fahey) *bit bkwd: in rr: hdwy over 2f out: rdn along and styng on whn n.m.r ent fnl f: no imp after* **66/1**

0321 **10** *shd* **The Jostler**[26] 5071 3-8-6 **87** .... MichaelHills 13 62
(B W Hills) *on toes: midfield: effrt 2f out: sn rdn and no imp* **16/1**

0025 **11** *3 1/4* **Cristal Clear (IRE)**[46] 4416 3-8-5 **86** .... JimmyQuinn 10 50
(T D Easterby) *in tch: effrt whn n.m.r 2f out: sn wknd* **33/1**

0020 **12** *8* **Unbreak My Heart (IRE)**[18] 5257 3-8-11 **92** .... SteveDrowne 14 35
(R Charlton) *in tch: rdn along 1/2-way: drvn and wknd wl over 2f out* **14/1**

5-10 **13** *3/4* **Royalist (IRE)**[125] 1923 3-8-5 **86** ow1 .... PhilipRobinson 5 27
(M A Jarvis) *lw: t.k.h: led: rdn along over 2f out: drvn and edgd rt wl over 1f out: sn hdd & wknd* **9/2**[2]

4502 **14** *2 3/4* **Royal Intruder**[25] 5102 3-9-0 **95** .... RyanMoore 1 28
(R Hannon) *lw: in tch: rdn along on outer wl over 2f out and sn wknd* **12/1**

1m 28.14s (1.84) **Going Correction** +0.375s/f (Good) 14 Ran SP% **121.0**

Speed ratings (Par 107): **104,101,101,98,93 90,90,88,88,88 83,74,73,70**

toteswinger: 1&2 £44.10, 1&3 £43.90, 2&3 £14.60. CSF £150.31 CT £1546.65 TOTE £28.80: £6.90, £2.40, £3.50; EX 186.30 Trifecta £912.00 Part won. Pool: £1,232.47, 0.40 winning units..

Owner R J Crothers, Phil Cunningham **Bred** Harts Farm And Stud **Trained** Lambourn, Berks

FOCUS

A competitive handicap in which the whole field raced centre to stands' side and the pace looked decent. The front four pulled well clear of the others and the form looks solid with the winner up 7lb.

NOTEBOOK

Slugger O'Toole ◆, disappointing since winning twice in the spring, was racing on the softest ground he had ever encountered and he absolutely relished it. Once brought through to lead, he pulled right away from his field and with his ability to act on soft ground now proven, he looks set for a good autumn. (op 25-1)

Harrison George(IRE), backed earlier in the day, has winning form in heavy ground and was produced with his effort at the right time, but the winner proved far too strong for him late on. He is consistent and should continue to give a good account. (op 8-1)

Fathsta(IRE) is being kept very busy as this was his 20th start of the year. Supported in the market beforehand, he was switched off out the back early but was produced to hold every chance. Despite coming under strong pressure, he was never quite doing enough. (op 14-1)

Carniolan, bidding for a hat-trick off a 6lb higher mark, looked as if he could be made fitter following a short break and was fairly weak in the market. He was produced with a dangerous-looking effort against the stands' rail, but did not appear to quite get home in this ground. (op 11-4 tchd 7-2)

Cobo Bay, very much in his element in this sort of ground, was always up there but could not stop the front four from running away from him in the last furlong. He is still 6lb above his last winning mark and may be best over 1m these days. Official explanation: jockey said colt hung right-handed throughout (op 16-1)

Dunn'o(IRE), who looked dull in his coat, established his usual prominent position, but he was making hard work of it before halfway and he could only plug on at one pace.

Keep Discovering(IRE), bidding for a hat-trick off a 6lb higher mark, was very keen up with the pace early and eventually paid for it. (op 11-1 tchd 10-1)

Royalist(IRE), the least exposed in the field, had not been seen since disappointing at the Chester May meeting though his maiden win here in April showed that he could go well fresh. Popular in the market, he was soon in front but he took far too strong a hold in this ground and had blown up before reaching the 2f pole. Official explanation: jockey said colt ran too free (op 5-1 tchd 4-1)

5796 EMAP GLENIGAN SPRINT H'CAP 5f
4:20 (4:21) (Class 4) (0-85,85) 3-Y-O+ **£6,476** (£1,927; £963; £481) **Stalls High**

Form RPR

2312 **1** **Judge 'n Jury**[23] 5151 4-9-0 **83** ....(t) KevinGhunowa(3) 14 91
(R A Harris) *a.p: rdn to ld over 1f out: drvn ins fnl f and kpt on wl* **7/1**[1]

2110 **2** *hd* **Rasaman (IRE)**[41] 4555 4-8-13 **79** ....(tp) NCallan 5 86
(K A Ryan) *lw: a.p: rdn 2f out and ev ch tl drvn ins fnl f and nt qckn nr fin* **20/1**

0602 **3** *nk* **Northern Bolt**[16] 5358 3-8-13 **80** .... PaulMulrennan 20 86
(D Nicholls) *a.p nr stands' rail: effrt 2f out and sn rdn: drvn ins fnl f and kpt on wl* **8/1**[2]

0354 **4** *nk* **Blazing Heights**[3] 5719 5-8-0 **71** oh2 .... KellyHarrison(5) 6 76
(J S Goldie) *hld up: gd hdwy 2f out: rdn over 1f out: chal ent fnl f and ev ch tl drvn and nt qckn fnl 50yds* **9/1**[3]

1324 **5** *nse* **Make My Dream**[23] 5151 5-8-5 **71** oh1 .... DO'Donohoe 8 76
(J Gallagher) *lw: a chsng ldrs: effrt and hdwy wl over 1f out: n.m.r ent fnl f: sn drvn and kpt on wl towards fin* **16/1**

1500 **6** *nk* **He's A Humbug (IRE)**[11] 5503 4-8-13 **82** ....(p) NeilBrown(3) 7 86
(K A Ryan) *s.i.s and towards rr: hdwy 2f out: rdn and styng on whn n.m.r ins fnl f: kpt on wl towards fin* **28/1**

6000 **7** *nk* **Golden Dixie (USA)**[23] 5151 9-9-1 **81** .... PhilipRobinson 13 84
(R A Harris) *midfield: hdwy wl over 1f out: sn rdn and styd on ins fnl f: nrst fin* **20/1**

2450 **8** *nse* **Hotham**[19] 5222 5-8-9 **75** .... JimmyQuinn 16 77+
(N Wilson) *midfield: effrt and n.m.r wl over 1f out: swtchd rt and rdn jst over 1f out: kpt on u.p ins fnl furlnog: nrst fin* **16/1**

5113 **9** *shd* **Invincible Lad (IRE)**[41] 4563 4-8-5 **71** oh4 .... AndrewElliott 11 73
(E J Alston) *bit bkwd: cl up: rdn along 2f out: sn drvn and one pce appr fnl f* **16/1**

065 **10** *hd* **The Jobber (IRE)**[11] 5493 7-9-3 **83** .... PaulHanagan 4 84
(M Blanshard) *lw: midfield: hdwy 2f out: rdn over 1f out: styd on ins fnl f: nrst fin* **10/1**

6021 **11** *3/4* **Lord Of The Reins (IRE)**[19] 5250 4-9-5 **85** .... JamieSpencer 9 84+
(J G Given) *dwlt and bhd: hdwy 2f out: swtchd outside and rdn over 1f out: kpt on ins fnl f: nrst fin* **8/1**[2]

0014 **12** *1/2* **Haajes**[9] 5566 4-8-8 **74** ....(t) AlanMunro 10 71+
(S Parr) *chsd ldrs: rdn along 2f out: sn drvn and grad wknd* **18/1**

0002 **13** *shd* **Fantasy Explorer**[19] 5250 5-9-3 **83** .... DarryllHolland 15 85+
(J J Quinn) *midfield: hdwy 2f out: nt clr run over 1f out: nt rcvr* **10/1**

0-00 **14** *hd* **Jack Rackham**[78] 3336 4-8-13 **79** .... RoystonFfrench 12 75
(B Smart) *chsd ldrs: rdn along and outpcd 1/2-way: kpt on u.p ins fnl f* **40/1**

0221 **15** *1/2* **Grudge**[20] 5201 3-8-4 **71** oh1 .... MartinDwyer 18 65
(D W Barker) *led: rdn along over 2f out: drvn and hdd over 1f out: sn wknd* **12/1**

3600 **16** *1/2* **Yungaburra (IRE)**[14] 5398 4-8-0 **71** oh9...(t) Louis-PhilippeBeuzelin(5) 19 63
(S Parr) *towards rr fr 1/2-way* **33/1**

514 **17** *1* **Know No Fear**[47] 4397 3-8-10 **77** .... RobertWinston 17 77+
(J J Quinn) *s.i.s and rr: hdwy on stands' rails whn nt clr run over 1f out: no ch after* **18/1**

4302 **18** *2* **Malapropism**[21] 5187 8-8-6 **72** .... TPO'Shea 1 53
(M R Channon) *chsd ldrs: rdn along over 2f out: grad wknd* **20/1**

2640 **19** *2* **Wibbadune (IRE)**[26] 5046 4-8-7 **73** .... ChrisCatlin 3 47
(D Shaw) *in tch on outer: effrt to chse ldrs 2f out: sn rdn and wknd* **50/1**

0210 **20** 9 **Captain Dunne (IRE)**[10] 5542 3-9-2 **83**........................ DavidAllan 2 25+
(T D Easterby) *lw: racd alone far side: prom tl rdn along and wknd over 2f out* **16/1**

61.71 secs (1.21) **Going Correction** +0.375s/f (Good)
WFA 3 from 4yo+ 1lb **20** Ran SP% **129.7**
Speed ratings (Par 105): **105,104,104,103,103 103,102,102,102,102 100,100,99,99,98 98,96,93,90,75**
toteswinger: 1&2 £29.40, 1&3 £9.70, 2&3 £48.00. CSF £151.23 CT £1199.59 TOTE £8.60: £2.60, £6.80, £2.20, £2.50; EX 233.50 TRIFECTA Not won. Place 6: £152.30, Place 5: £46.72..
Owner Mrs Ruth M Serrell **Bred** C A Cyzer **Trained** Earlswood, Monmouths

FOCUS
A really competitive sprint handicap and the first ten were covered by only around a length and a half. With the exception of Captain Dunne, who was alone against the far rail, they raced middle to stands' side and there seemed no real draw bias. Sound if ordinary form.
Lord Of The Reins(IRE) Official explanation: jockey said gelding missed the break
Fantasy Explorer Official explanation: jockey said gelding was denied a clear run
T/Jkpt: Not won. T/Plt: £240.20 to a £1 stake. Pool: £121,889.05. 370.37 winning tickets. T/Qpdt: £28.50 to a £1 stake. Pool: £8,494.00. 219.80 winning tickets. JR

5693 KEMPTON (A.W) (R-H)

Wednesday, September 10

OFFICIAL GOING: Standard
Wind: Moderate, behind Weather: Fine but cloudy

5797 MIX BUSINESS WITH PLEASURE H'CAP 7f (P)

6:20 (6:20) (Class 6) (0-50,50) 3-Y-O+ £2,047 (£604; £302) Stalls High

Form RPR

6360 **1** **Dr Synn**[18] 5267 7-8-8 **49**........................(p) DavidProbert(5) 7 57
(M J Attwater) *sn pushed up to press ldng pair: drvn over 2f out: prog over 1f out: edgd rt but r.o to ld last 50yds* **13/2**[3]

0500 **2** ½ **Mulberry Lad (IRE)**[111] 2337 6-8-12 **48**........................ JamesDoyle 10 55
(S Curran) *t.k.h early: trckd ldrs: effrt over 2f out: rdn to ld last 150yds: hdd fnl 50yds* **8/1**

4000 **3** 1 **Wadnagin (IRE)**[23] 5157 4-8-11 **47**........................ JimCrowley 1 51+
(I A Wood) *stdd s: dropped in fr outside draw to r on inner: hld up in last: prog 2f out: r.o to take 3rd nr fin* **6/1**[2]

5500 **4** ½ **Follow Your Spirit**[92] 2922 3-8-10 **50**........................ CatherineGannon 3 51
(B Palling) *led at stdy pce for 3f: hrd pressed fr 2f out: hdd and outpcd last 150yds* **22/1**

006 **5** nk **Moverra (IRE)**[30] 3201 4-8-7 **50**........................(v[1]) HollyHall(7) 8 52
(M J Gingell) *pressed ldr: rdn to chal 2f out: awkward and nt qckn over 1f out: lost pl fnl f* **50/1**

0054 **6** ¾ **Rosie Cross (IRE)**[9] 5582 4-8-5 **48**........................ DanielBlackett(7) 5 48
(Eve Johnson Houghton) *mostly in midfield on outer: pushed along and outpcd 2f out: kpt on steadily fr over 1f out: nrst fin* **16/1**

0552 **7** 1 ½ **Megalo Maniac**[26] 5045 5-9-0 **50**........................(p) JamieMoriarty 13 46
(R A Fahey) *cl up on inner: effrt over 2f out: cl enough u.p jst over 1f out: wknd last 150yds* **5/1**[1]

0006 **8** ¾ **Zazous**[18] 5267 7-8-9 **48**........................ MarcHalford(3) 12 48+
(J J Bridger) *dwlt: t.k.h early and hld up towards rr: hrd rdn over 2f out: prog over 1f out: keeping on but hld whn hmpd on inner jst ins fnl f* **5/1**[1]

3005 **9** 1 ¾ **Djalalabad (FR)**[17] 5317 4-9-0 **50**........................(t) JohnEgan 11 39
(Mrs C A Dunnett) *t.k.h early: hld up in midfield: outpcd by ldrs fr 2f out: no imp after* **8/1**

3220 **10** hd **Razzano (IRE)**[22] 5166 4-8-6 **49**........................ AndreaAtzeni(7) 6 37
(A M Hales) *racd wd in midfield: lost grnd bnd 3f out: drvn and no prog over 2f out* **17/2**

0004 **11** 3 ¾ **Tadlil**[23] 5152 6-8-11 **47**........................(v) TravisBlock 2 25
(J M Bradley) *stdd s: hld up and racd wd: nvr on terms: lost tch 2f out* **20/1**

0006 **12** 2 ½ **Empire Dancer (IRE)**[23] 5152 5-8-11 **47**........................(p) MickyFenton 9 19
(I W McInnes) *dwlt: hld up and t.k.h early: outpcd over 2f out: shkn up and no prog: b.b.v* **12/1**

2000 **13** 1 ¼ **Tenancy (IRE)**[25] 5088 4-9-0 **50**........................(e) TGMcLaughlin 4 18
(R C Guest) *stdd s but plld like a maniac: rchd midfield after 3f: wknd 2f out* **25/1**

4030 **14** ½ **Stargazy**[23] 5152 4-8-5 **48**........................ MatthewDavies(7) 14 15
(W G M Turner) *plld hrd early and hemmed in against rail: prog 3f out: rdn and wknd 2f out* **12/1**

1m 26.99s (0.99) **Going Correction** 0.0s/f (Stan)
WFA 3 from 4yo+ 4lb **14** Ran SP% **129.9**
Speed ratings (Par 101): **94,93,92,91,91 90,88,87,85,85 81,78,77,76**
toteswinger: 1&2 £16.60, 1&3 £7.40, 2&3 £24.10. CSF £60.03 CT £351.59 TOTE £6.70: £1.80, £3.50, £3.30; EX 95.50.
Owner Canisbay Bloodstock **Bred** Collin Stud **Trained** Epsom, Surrey

FOCUS
A typically poor handicap for the grade, but it had an open look on paper. It was run at an average early pace and there were still numerous chances at the furlong pole. Moderate form.
Empire Dancer(IRE) Official explanation: vet said gelding had bled from the nose
Stargazy Official explanation: jockey said gelding ran too free

5798 PANORAMIC BAR & RESTAURANT MAIDEN STKS 7f (P)

6:50 (6:52) (Class 5) 2-Y-O £2,590 (£770; £385; £192) Stalls High

Form RPR

1 **Mafaaz** 2-9-3 0........................ SteveDrowne 8 83+
(J H M Gosden) *sn in midfield: stdy prog over 2f out: shkn up and wnt 2nd over 1f out: pushed along and r.o wl to ld last strides* **8/1**[3]

3 **2** nk **Sayyaaf**[12] 5469 2-9-3 0........................ RHills 10 82+
(B W Hills) *led 2f: trckd ldr: led over 2f out: at least 3 l clr and pushed along over 1f out: rdn ins fnl f: hdd last strides* **8/13**[1]

3 ½ **Evasive** 2-9-3 0........................ RyanMoore 11 81+
(Sir Michael Stoute) *reluctant to enter stalls: sn lost pl: scrubbed along in midfield over 4f out and over 3f out: prog over 2f out: r.o wl fnl f: gaining fin* **7/2**[2]

4 9 **Noordhoek Kid** 2-9-3 0........................ ShaneKelly 9 58
(C R Egerton) *dwlt: wl in rr and off the pce: stl only modest 9th over 1f out: styd on wl to take 4th nr fin* **33/1**

5 ½ **Seek The Fair Land** 2-9-3 0........................ FergusSweeney 6 57
(J R Boyle) *dwlt: sn chsd ldrs: rdn to dispute 3rd over 2f out: no imp: wknd fnl f* **66/1**

6 1 ½ **Hit The Switch** 2-9-3 0........................ JamieMoriarty 2 53
(R A Fahey) *wnt violently rt s: chsd ldrs: rdn to dispute 3rd over 2f out: no imp: wknd fnl f* **20/1**

7 1 ¼ **Saturn Way (GR)** 2-9-3 0........................ JimCrowley 4 50
(P R Chamings) *dwlt: t.k.h and rcvrd to ld after 2f: hdd over 2f out: wknd over 1f out* **33/1**

8 ¾ **Winterbrook King** 2-9-3 0........................ LPKeniry 13 48
(J R Best) *mostly in midfield and nt on terms: no prog over 2f out: wknd over 1f out* **33/1**

9 1 ½ **Dr Valentine (FR)** 2-9-3 0........................ AdamKirby 1 45
(S Kirk) *s.s: wl in rr: sme prog over 2f out but nvr on terms: reminder over 1f out: wknd fnl f* **16/1**

10 2 ¼ **Duke's Emerald** 2-9-3 0........................ RobertHavlin 14 39
(J A R Toller) *s.s: mostly in last and nvr a factor* **50/1**

11 2 ¼ **Queen Of Burlesque (USA)** 2-8-12 0........................ EddieAhern 7 28
(B J Meehan) *hmpd s: a wl in rr: nvr a factor* **20/1**

1m 26.66s (0.66) **Going Correction** 0.0s/f (Stan) **11** Ran SP% **122.9**
Speed ratings (Par 95): **96,95,95,84,84 82,81,80,78,75 73**
toteswinger: 1&2 £1.50, 1&3 £1.40, 2&3 £1.10. CSF £13.22 TOTE £9.90: £1.90, £1.02, £1.80; EX 17.90.
Owner Hamdan Al Maktoum **Bred** The Complimentary Pass Partnership **Trained** Newmarket, Suffolk

FOCUS
The first three came clear in this maiden and all look useful. The form should work out and could be rated up to 8lb better. Only the runner-up had previous experience.

NOTEBOOK
Mafaaz, a 400,000gns half-brother to most notably the useful juvenile Gweebarra, proved easy to back for this racecourse bow and showed inexperience by running keen through the first half of the race. He got the hang of it down the home straight, however, and picked up strongly inside the final furlong to just get up.\n\x\x There was a lot in this performance to suggest the winner will learn a great deal for the experience, and he looks a very useful prospect, with another furlong likely to be within his range before the season's end. He holds numerous big-race entries, so it will be very interesting to see where connections will pitch him next. (op 6-1)
Sayyaaf was the only runner with a previous start to his name and seemed sure to improve on his initial third at Sandown 12 days previously. He was soon on the early lead and ran a little freely, but looked all over Mafaaz nearing the final furlong as he stretched on. He received only hands-and-heels riding through most of the final furlong, until it became clear he was wilting, and he eventually just got reeled in. Time may tell there was no disgrace in this performance, and a drop back to 6f should really see him go one better. (op 5-4)
Evasive clearly has an aversion to the stalls as he was blanketed and took an age to load up. He jumped okay once the gates opened, but proved too green for his own good and became outpaced turning for home. The manner in which he eventually stayed on when the penny dropped was most encouraging and, with this debut experience now under his belt, he ought to prove very hard to beat next time out. (op 9-4 tchd 2-1)
Noordhoek Kid cost 150,000gns and his dam scored over this trip at three. He proved clueless through the first half of the race, but stayed on encouragingly to bag fourth, and is another who should know a lot more next time. (op 50-1)
Duke's Emerald Official explanation: jockey said gelding missed the break

5799 DIGIBET CLAIMING STKS 1m (P)

7:20 (7:22) (Class 6) 3-Y-O+ £2,047 (£604; £151; £151) Stalls High

Form RPR

3200 **1** **Blacktoft (USA)**[17] 5312 5-9-12 **71**........................(e) J-PGuillambert 5 77
(S C Williams) *hld up towards rr: prog over 2f out: swtchd to inner and drvn to ld last 150yds: sn 2 l clr: eased fnl strides* **5/1**[2]

4000 **2** 1 **Yes Eighteen (IRE)**[25] 5086 3-8-13 **58**........................ TQuinn 9 66
(J W Hills) *dwlt: detached in last and nt gng wl: effrt and nt clr run wl over 2f out and swtchd lft: prog over 1f out: stl only 6th 100yds out: fin strly* **40/1**

1551 **3** 1 **Le Chiffre (IRE)**[4] 5708 6-8-9 **63** ow1........................(p) MickyFenton 7 55
(John A Harris) *pressed ldr: led wl over 2f out: hrd pressed over 1f out: hdd & wknd last 150yds* **15/8**[1]

1406 **3** dht **Mountain Pass (USA)**[32] 4878 6-8-8 **58**........................(p) DavidProbert(5) 12 59
(B J Llewellyn) *wl plcd: chsd ldng pair over 3f out: rdn to chal over 2f out: nt qckn and hld 1f out* **12/1**

3040 **5** ¾ **Teasing**[23] 5144 4-9-7 **70**........................(p) RobertHavlin 8 66
(J Pearce) *hld up towards rr: prog over 2f out: chsng ldrs over 1f out: nt qckn: kpt on last 100yds* **14/1**

200 **6** nk **Cathedral Walk (USA)**[20] 5202 3-9-7 **70**........................(v) DarrenWilliams 13 69
(K R Burke) *mde most to wl over 2f out: styd cl up: grad fdd ins fnl f* **6/1**[3]

1000 **7** 12 **Sun Catcher (IRE)**[47] 4390 5-9-4 **72**........................(p) SteveDrowne 3 34
(P G Murphy) *chsd ldrs to 1/2-way: wd bnd 3f out and struggling: sn lost tch* **14/1**

4316 **8** 1 ½ **Pab Special (IRE)**[94] 2863 5-9-2 **58**........................ JohnEgan 14 29
(B R Johnson) *prom on inner: wknd over 2f out: eased over 1f out* **10/1**

1060 **9** 3 **The Hoofer (IRE)**[7] 5607 3-8-4 **57**........................ JoeFanning 2 14
(I A Wood) *racd wd in midfield: prog over 3f out: in tch over 2f out: sn wknd* **40/1**

0004 **10** 1 ¼ **Pop Music (IRE)**[13] 5427 5-9-0 **60**........................(v) JamesDoyle 4 17
(Ms J S Doyle) *racd v wd: cl up tl lost grnd bnd 3f out: sn wknd* **16/1**

05 **11** 1 ½ **Diktat Tempo**[15] 5377 3-8-8 0........................(p) CatherineGannon 6 12
(I A Wood) *struggling in last pair fr 1/2-way: no ch fnl 3f* **50/1**

1201 **12** 1 ¼ **Party In The Park**[42] 4531 3-9-4 **68**........................ AndrewMullen(3) 1 22
(Miss J A Camacho) *racd wd in midfield: rdn over 3f out: lost tch w ldrs over 2f out: wknd* **11/1**

4000 **13** 13 **Wahoo Sam (USA)**[4] 5708 8-8-10 **62**........................(b) TGMcLaughlin 10 —
(P D Evans) *sn prom: wknd over 3f out: eased fnl 2f: t.o* **20/1**

1m 39.61s (-0.19) **Going Correction** 0.0s/f (Stan)
WFA 3 from 4yo+ 5lb **13** Ran SP% **121.7**
Speed ratings (Par 101): **100,99,98,98,97 96,84,83,80,79 77,76,63**
Place: Le Chiffre £0.50, Mountain Pass £2.40. toteswinger: 1&2 £33.40, 1&3 (B/MP) £9.90 (B/LC) £1.20, 2&3 (YE/MP) £31.80 (YE/LC) £11.40. CSF £204.71 TOTE £5.70: £2.00, £14.60; EX 158.40.Le Chiffre was claimed by Miss Sheena West for £5,000.
Owner Chris Watkins And David N Reynolds **Bred** Paradigm Thoroughbreds Inc **Trained** Newmarket, Suffolk

FOCUS
Not a bad claimer. The form is rated around the winner with the runner-up casting some doubts.
Pop Music(IRE) Official explanation: jockey said gelding hung left

5800 DIGIBET.COM H'CAP 1m (P)

7:50 (7:51) (Class 5) (0-75,75) 3-Y-O+ £2,590 (£770; £385; £192) Stalls High

Form RPR

3045 **1** **Hallingdal (UAE)**[5] 5675 3-9-0 **73**........................ JamesDoyle 4 81
(Ms J S Doyle) *dwlt: hld up in last pair: rapid prog 2f out: squeezed through between ldng pair to ld last 150yds: sn clr* **14/1**

4043 **2** 1 ¾ **Blow Hole (USA)**[16] 5345 3-8-13 **72**........................ ShaneKelly 13 76
(J Noseda) *pressed ldr after 3f: sustained chal fr 3f out: fnlly led ent fnl f: immediately hdd and outpcd* **4/1**[1]

2100 **3** *hd* **Millfield (IRE)**[16] 5350 5-9-5 **73** GeorgeBaker 11 78+
(P R Chamings) *dwlt: hld up in last trio: effrt on inner and n.m.r over 2f out: gd prog over 1f out: styd on wl and nrly snatched 2nd* **6/1**

6030 **4** *1 1/4* **Blue Charm**[26] 5059 4-9-0 **68** LPKeniry 8 70
(S Kirk) *chsd ldrs: rdn over 2f out: disp 3rd over 1f out: one pce fnl f* **33/1**

4015 **5** *nse* **Murrin (IRE)**[16] 5350 4-9-4 **75** JackMitchell(3) 7 77
(T G Mills) *hld up in rr: rdn and n.m.r over 2f out: prog wl over 1f out: styd on wl fnl f: nrst fin* **5/1**[2]

1400 **6** *nk* **Daniel Thomas (IRE)**[47] 4364 6-9-7 **75** JimCrowley 3 76
(Mrs A L M King) *stdd s: t.k.h early: hld up in rr: progs fr 3f out: chsng ldrs but nt on terms over 1f out: styd on: unable to chal* **33/1**

1663 **7** *1 1/4* **Lekita**[23] 5149 3-9-0 **73** (p) AdamKirby 10 70
(W R Swinburn) *led: hrd pressed fr over 2f out: hdd & wknd ent fnl f* **11/2**[3]

4030 **8** *nk* **Man Of Gwent (UAE)**[18] 5290 4-9-1 **74** RichardEvans(5) 14 71
(P D Evans) *a in midfield: pushed along in 7th 3f out: nt rch ldrs over 1f out: fading nr fin* **25/1**

111 **9** *1 3/4* **Ogre (USA)**[35] 4724 3-9-2 **75** TGMcLaughlin 6 67
(P D Evans) *t.k.h: hld up in midfiield: rdn and fnd nil over 2f out: btn after* **10/1**

0042 **10** *nk* **Magroom**[11] 5492 4-9-1 **69** SteveDrowne 12 62
(R J Hodges) *chsd ldr 2f: styd prom: nt qckn 2f out: wknd rapidly fnl f* **12/1**

4365 **11** *1 1/2* **Game Park (USA)**[75] 3457 3-9-0 **73** EddieAhern 2 61
(J R Fanshawe) *chsd ldrs: lost pl and struggling over 2f out: sn no ch* **9/1**

0460 **12** *3/4* **My Shadow**[63] 3840 3-9-2 **75** TQuinn 9 62
(S Dow) *a wl in rr: struggling wl over 2f out* **33/1**

446- **13** *2 1/2* **Ambrosiano**[325] 3707 4-9-0 **73** DavidProbert(5) 1 55
(Miss E C Lavelle) *stdd s: dropped in fr wd draw: plld hrd and hld up in last pair: rdn and no prog 3f out* **33/1**

0006 **14** *1/2* **Dalkey Girl (IRE)**[18] 5291 3-8-13 **72** JohnEgan 5 52
(M Botti) *chsd ldr after 2f tl after 3f: wknd 3f out* **12/1**

1m 39.03s (-0.77) **Going Correction** 0.0s/f (Stan)
WFA 3 from 4yo+ 5lb **14** Ran SP% **123.1**
Speed ratings (Par 103): **103,101,101,99,99 99,98,97,96,95 94,93,91,90**
toteswinger: 1&2 £24.80, 1&3 £15.60, 2&3 £5.00. CSF £67.55 CT £387.62 TOTE £17.30: £5.00, £2.40, £2.00; EX 128.60.
Owner W Wood **Bred** Darley **Trained** Eastbury, Berks

FOCUS
This was competitive enough for the class but the form looks pretty ordinary with Hallingdal a surprise winner on profile.
My Shadow Official explanation: jockey said gelding was denied a clear run

5801 DIGIBET CASINO H'CAP 6f (P)
8:20 (8:21) (Class 6) (0-60,63) 3-Y-O+ **£2,047** (£604; £302) **Stalls** High

Form RPR

201 **1** **Al Gillani (IRE)**[6] 5627 3-9-7 **63** 6ex GeorgeBaker 7 79
(J R Boyle) *pressed ldng pair: waited tl asked to ld over 1f out: sn in command: comf* **15/8**[1]

0642 **2** *2 1/4* **Rhapsilian**[7] 5610 4-9-3 **57** SteveDrowne 4 66
(J A Geake) *hld up towards rr and off the pce: prog fr over 2f out: styd on to take 2nd ins fnl f: no ch w wnr* **11/2**[2]

1301 **3** *1/2* **Avoca Dancer (IRE)**[7] 5601 5-9-1 **62** 6ex (p) KylieManser(7) 8 69
(Miss Gay Kelleway) *dwlt: outpcd and wl in rr: swtchd to inner and gd prog 2f out: styd on to dispute 2nd fnl f: no ch w wnr* **14/1**

4400 **4** *3* **Bobby Rose**[6] 5626 5-9-0 **57** (p) PatrickHills(3) 11 55
(D K Ivory) *chsd ldr: clsd fr 1/2-way: led 2f out: sn hdd: wknd fnl f* **8/1**

0B03 **5** *nk* **Imperium**[18] 5267 7-9-4 **58** TPO'Shea 3 55
(Jean-Rene Auvray) *stdd s and swtchd towards inner: wl off the pce in last pair: hanging and reminders 2f out: styd on steadily fnl f: nvr nr ldrs* **14/1**

0106 **6** *1/2* **Boldinor**[19] 5233 5-9-6 **60** JimCrowley 10 57+
(M R Bosley) *chsd clr ldrs: clsd over 2f out: no imp whn n.m.r 1f out: wknd* **14/1**

0155 **7** *1 1/4* **Tilsworth Charlie**[26] 5073 5-8-13 **58** (b) DavidProbert(5) 6 49
(J R Jenkins) *chsd clr ldrs: clsd fr 1/2-way and in tch 2f out: wknd over 1f out* **12/1**

0020 **8** *1 1/2* **Our Fugitive (IRE)**[25] 5101 6-9-6 **60** (p) AdamKirby 12 47
(C Gordon) *blasted off in front and sn clr: hdd & wknd 2f out* **13/2**[3]

0204 **9** *1/2* **Guildenstern (IRE)**[7] 5610 6-9-4 **58** JimmyQuinn 2 43
(P Howling) *a in last pair and nvr gng the pce: wd and hanging bnd 3f out: no ch after* **8/1**

-240 **10** *5* **Scuba (IRE)**[94] 2869 6-9-2 **56** (b) TravisBlock 9 25
(H Morrison) *sn furiously rdn to stay even modestly in tch: bhd fnl 2f* **16/1**

1m 11.93s (-1.17) **Going Correction** 0.0s/f (Stan)
WFA 3 from 4yo+ 2lb **10** Ran SP% **119.3**
Speed ratings (Par 101): **107,104,103,99,98 98,96,94,93,87**
toteswinger: 1&2 £2.00, 1&3 £7.20, 2&3 £12.60. CSF £12.24 CT £115.03 TOTE £2.50: £1.10, £2.30, £3.30; EX 14.40.
Owner The Paddock Space Partnership **Bred** Sean Finnegan **Trained** Epsom, Surrey

FOCUS
A moderate handicap, but it was run at a solid pace and produced a decent winning time for the class. The form has been rated on the positive side, with improvement from the winner.

5802 TOPNAPS.CO.UK H'CAP 1m 4f (P)
8:50 (8:52) (Class 6) (0-60,60) 3-Y-O+ **£2,047** (£604; £302) **Stalls** Centre

Form RPR

0350 **1** **Formidable Guest**[25] 5087 4-9-3 **52** RobertHavlin 1 62
(J Pearce) *stdd s: hld up wl in rr: prog gng strly over 3f out: swooped to ld 2f out: styd on wl fnl f* **14/1**

3241 **2** *3/4* **Mixing**[7] 5611 6-9-2 **56** DavidProbert(5) 10 65
(M J Attwater) *wl plcd bhd ldrs: effrt to chal jst over 2f out but surprised by wnr: chsng after: styd on but a hld* **2/1**[1]

0/00 **3** *1 1/4* **Towerofcharlemagne (IRE)**[12] 5465 5-9-8 **57** (v[1]) MickyFenton 5 64
(Miss E C Lavelle) *nt gng wl in last pair: stl there and rdn 3f out: prog on outer 2f out: styd on to take 3rd ins fnl f* **20/1**

2563 **4** *1 1/2* **Eagle Nebula**[19] 5230 4-9-11 **60** JohnEgan 11 64
(B R Johnson) *hld up in rr: prog 3f out: trying to cl whn carried rt 2f out: kpt on one pce over 1f out* **7/1**[2]

6056 **5** *3/4* **Fateful Attraction**[35] 4722 5-9-10 **59** (t) GeorgeBaker 6 62
(I A Wood) *settled wl in rr: rdn over 3f out: stl at the bk over 2f out: prog u.p after: kpt on: nvr able to chal* **10/1**[3]

6000 **6** *1 1/2* **Pearl (IRE)**[7] 5611 4-9-3 **52** (v[1]) EddieAhern 8 53
(I A Wood) *led: hdd and hung rt 2f out: nt qckn: fdd fnl f* **16/1**

0453 **7** *nk* **Josr's Magic (IRE)**[14] 5407 4-9-7 **56** JimmyQuinn 14 56
(H J Collingridge) *hld up in midfield: rdn and effrt 3f out: n.m.r 2f out: kpt on same pce after* **12/1**

-103 **8** *1/2* **Soviet Sceptre (IRE)**[20] 4704 7-9-5 **54** (tp) TravisBlock 9 54+
(Tim Vaughan) *hld up in midfield on inner: lost pl over 3f out: prog again over 2f out: snatched up over 1f out: nt on terms after* **10/1**[3]

2425 **9** *3 1/2* **Compton Charlie**[30] 4930 4-9-6 **58** TolleyDean(3) 12 52
(J G Portman) *mostly in midfield: u.p wl over 3f out: stl chsng but no imp over 1f out: wknd ins fnl f* **10/1**[3]

0240 **10** *1* **Mix N Match**[39] 4635 4-9-5 **54** JimCrowley 7 46
(R M Stronge) *s.s: last for much of way: shkn up and slt prog over 2f out: sn no ch* **16/1**

P600 **11** *2 3/4* **Jarvo**[34] 4797 7-9-4 **53** PatrickMathers 3 41
(I W McInnes) *chsd ldrs: u.p wl over 3f out: wknd 2f out* **50/1**

000 **12** *1 1/4* **National Day (IRE)**[23] 5163 4-9-7 **56** StephenDonohoe 4 42
(D R C Elsworth) *sn trckd ldr: wknd rapidly jst over 2f out* **16/1**

5-00 **13** *1/2* **Govenor Eliott (IRE)**[14] 5390 3-9-2 **60** JoeFanning 2 45
(M Johnston) *pressed ldrs tl wknd tamely over 2f out* **16/1**

2060 **14** *1 1/4* **Medieval Maiden**[7] 5611 5-9-7 **56** AmirQuinn 13 39
(Mrs L J Mongan) *prom: drvn to try to chal on inner over 2f out: wknd rapidly wl over 1f out* **14/1**

2m 34.23s (-0.27) **Going Correction** 0.0s/f (Stan)
WFA 3 from 4yo+ 9lb **14** Ran SP% **124.4**
Speed ratings (Par 101): **100,99,98,97,97 96,95,95,93,92 90,89,89,88**
toteswinger: 1&2 £12.00, 1&3 £64.80, 2&3 £14.50. CSF £43.32 CT £605.28 TOTE £18.60: £3.50, £1.60, £7.80; EX 61.00.
Owner Macniler Racing Partnership **Bred** Kingwood Bloodstock **Trained** Newmarket, Suffolk

FOCUS
A modest handicap. The form looks pretty muddling overall.
Josr's Magic(IRE) Official explanation: jockey said gelding suffered interference in running

5803 DAY TIME, NIGHT TIME, GREAT TIME H'CAP 1m 3f (P)
9:20 (9:22) (Class 6) (0-65,65) 3-Y-O **£2,047** (£604; £302) **Stalls** High

Form RPR

0505 **1** **Shraayef**[34] 4797 3-8-10 **57** JohnEgan 12 61+
(M Botti) *t.k.h early: hld up wl in rr: effrt whn no room and swtchd lft 2f out: gd prog over 1f out: styd on wl to ld last 75yds* **33/1**

5030 **2** *3/4* **Eureka Moment**[51] 4254 3-9-4 **65** EddieAhern 3 67
(E A L Dunlop) *hld up in rr and racd wd: prog on outer over 2f out: edgd rt but styd on wl fnl f to take 2nd last stride* **16/1**

5-00 **3** *hd* **Southern Mistral**[15] 5378 3-8-13 **60** NickyMackay 5 62
(M Wigham) *hld up in midfield: prog 2f out: got through to chse ldr fnl f: nt qckn last 100yds* **25/1**

0542 **4** *nse* **Dancing Dik**[10] 5537 3-9-1 **62** JimCrowley 2 64
(Mrs A J Perrett) *led after 1f to 6f out: effrt on inner to ld again over 2f out: drvn and hdd last 75yds* **10/3**[1]

003 **5** *nk* **Trinkila (USA)**[7] 5602 3-8-12 **59** JoeFanning 9 61+
(P F I Cole) *trckd ldrs: lost pl on inner over 3f out: prog over 2f out: clsng whn nt clr run and swtchd lft 1f out: kpt on* **16/1**

3633 **6** *1* **Dusk**[33] 4811 3-9-3 **64** (b) JimmyQuinn 14 63+
(J L Dunlop) *hld up in last pair: tried to make prog fr over 2f out but repeatedly denied clr run: fin w plenty lft* **7/2**[2]

04-4 **7** *1 1/4* **Tamdiid (USA)**[12] 5445 3-8-13 **60** LiamJones 8 57
(C E Brittain) *prom: drvn fr 4f out: stl cl up 2f out but edging rt: fdd ins fnl f* **14/1**

0500 **8** *1/2* **Princess India (IRE)**[18] 5291 3-9-2 **63** StephenCarson 11 59
(P Winkworth) *hld up towards rr: effrt 2f out: chsng ldrs and cl enough jst over 1f out: fdd* **16/1**

0-64 **9** *nk* **Bet Noir (IRE)**[19] 5231 3-9-3 **64** AdamKirby 1 60+
(W R Swinburn) *dwlt: hld up in last pair: effrt over 2f out but sn rn into trble: rdn but nowhere to go over 1f out: no ch after* **7/1**[3]

6021 **10** *1/2* **Bosamcliff (IRE)**[14] 5388 3-9-4 **65** GeorgeBaker 13 62+
(A B Haynes) *hld up in rr: effrt over 2f out: stl at bk of tightly gped pack over 1f out: no prog* **7/2**[2]

5040 **11** *1 3/4* **Dubai Samurai**[33] 4820 3-9-2 **63** (b[1]) TQuinn 10 58+
(J W Hills) *t.k.h early: trckd ldr after 2f: upsides over 2f out: stl gng wl but lost pl sn after: shuffled bk in scrimmaging over 1f out: coasted home* **10/1**

000 **12** *2 1/4* **Civitas Filius (USA)**[37] 4695 3-9-2 **63** RichardMullen 7 51+
(D M Simcock) *led 1f: styd cl up: nt clr run over 2f out and lost pl: nowhere to go over 1f out and btn after* **14/1**

-000 **13** *20* **Siena**[9] 5576 3-8-12 **59** TGMcLaughlin 6 13
(Mrs C A Dunnett) *s.i.s: t.k.h in rr: allowed to charge past field and ld 6f out: hdd & wknd rapidly over 2f out: t.o* **66/1**

2m 21.66s (-0.24) **Going Correction** 0.0s/f (Stan) **13** Ran SP% **128.4**
Speed ratings (Par 99): **100,99,99,99,99 98,97,97,96,96 95,93,79**
toteswinger: 1&2 £98.50, 1&3 £98.50, 2&3 £80.70. CSF £516.86 CT £12671.96 TOTE £41.30: £9.20, £5.70, £6.70; EX 729.10 Place 6 £29.92, Place 5 £7.77.
Owner Saif Misfer **Bred** Launceston Stud **Trained** Newmarket, Suffolk
■ Stewards' Enquiry : Nicky Mackay five-day ban: careless riding (Sep 24-27, 29)

FOCUS
A modest three-year-old handicap which became very messy in the straight off a quickening pace. Several found troubled passages and have to be rated better than the bare form.
Shraayef Official explanation: trainer's rep said, regarding the apparent improvement in form, that filly seemed well suited by the all-weather surface.
Dusk ◆ Official explanation: jockey said gelding was denied a clear run
Dubai Samurai Official explanation: jockey said colt suffered interference in running
T/Plt: £42.50 to a £1 stake. Pool: £90,237.14. 1,549.61 winning tickets. T/Qpdt: £7.40 to a £1 stake. Pool: £7,055.00. 699.50 winning tickets. JN

5647 WARWICK (L-H)
Wednesday, September 10
5804 Meeting Abandoned - Waterlogged

5599 BRIGHTON (L-H)

Thursday, September 11

OFFICIAL GOING: Soft (good to soft in places)

This meeting replaced the Chepstow fixture which had been abandoned due to waterlogging.

Wind: Light, half-against Weather: Dull and damp, with some late sunshine

5811 E.B.F. TIMEFORM JURY TELEPHONE TIPPING SERVICE NOW LIVE MAIDEN STKS 6f 209y

2:10 (2:10) (Class 5) 2-Y-O £3,885 (£1,156; £577; £288) Stalls Low

Form				RPR
3	1		**Liberation (IRE)**[13] 5468 2-9-3 0 ... RoystonFfrench 8 (M Johnston) *racd keenly: pressed ldrs: led 3f out: hrd rdn and hung lft jst ins fnl f: hld on wl* **1/2**[1]	79+
00	2	1 ½	**Appraisal**[40] 4625 2-9-3 0 ... LPKeniry 3 (R Hannon) *pressed ldrs: hrd rdn over 1f out: carried lft jst ins fnl f: one pce fnl f* **10/1**	75
5	3	1 ¼	**Ascendant**[10] 5572 2-9-3 0 ... J-PGuillambert 9 (Sir Mark Prescott) *dwlt: sn in tch: rdn to press ldrs over 2f out: drvn and btn over 1f out: easing down whn styd on again nr fin* **8/1**[3]	72
500	4	8	**Killmarnock**[18] 5314 2-9-3 60 ...(t) GeorgeBaker 6 (R A Teal) *prom tl wknd over 2f out: btn whn hmpd jst ins fnl 2f* **50/1**	52
06	5	nk	**Adios Juan**[27] 5068 2-9-3 0 ... TGMcLaughlin 2 (S C Williams) *in rr: rdn and lost tch over 2f out: styng on against stands' rail at fin* **11/2**[2]	51
4	6	¾	**Barood (IRE)**[13] 5459 2-9-3 0 ... ChrisCatlin 7 (M R Channon) *in rr: rdn and no prog over 2f out: nvr rchd ldrs* **14/1**	50
00	7	shd	**Medlock**[32] 4890 2-9-3 0 ... TPQueally 4 (J Noseda) *led 4f: carried rt and crowded for room over 2f out: sn wknd* **16/1**	49
00	8	3 ¾	**Zaruschka**[61] 3968 2-8-9 0 ... JackMitchell(3) 1 (R M Beckett) *s.i.s: t.k.h towards rr: rdn and sme hdwy over 2f out: wknd over 1f out* **66/1**	35

1m 27.08s (3.98) **Going Correction** +0.425s/f (Yiel) 8 Ran SP% **118.3**

Speed ratings (Par 95): **94,92,90,81,81 80,80,76**

toteswinger: 1&2 £1.80, 1&3 £1.50, 2&3 £6.60. CSF £7.32 TOTE £1.50: £1.02, £2.70, £2.30; EX 9.60.

Owner Sheikh Hamdan Bin Mohammed Al Maktoum **Bred** Epona Bloodstock Ltd **Trained** Middleham Moor, N Yorks

FOCUS

They went a steady pace in this modest maiden, the field moved to the stands' rail in the straight and the first three finished a long way clear of the rest. The winner is basically rated to form with improvement from the placed colts.

NOTEBOOK

Liberation(IRE) had done well to finish third after meeting interference at a crucial stage on his debut in a potentially useful Sandown maiden, involving a number of well-related runners with multiple Group entries. He was always well positioned, but he still showed signs of inexperience and had to work hard to eventually assert in the closing stages. The form of this race does not look strong, but it is possible that he won in spite of the ground and remains an interesting prospect. (op 4-7 tchd 4-6)

Appraisal seemed to appreciate the testing ground, travelled well for a long way and stepped up considerably on his first two efforts. This was an encouraging run against a potentially decent rival. He should have no problem winning a similar event, but it is worth noting that he was reluctant to enter the stalls on his debut and does have some close relatives who showed signs of temperament. (op 17-2 tchd 8-1)

Ascendant looked more professional than he had on his debut, shaped with plenty of promise and finished a long way clear of the fourth without being given a hard time. He looks steadily progressive and, like many of his stablemates, will be suited by a stiffer test. He should be capable of winning races. (op 15-2)

Killmarnock had looked regressive on three previous starts. He did a bit better with a tongue-tie applied for the first time, but did not do enough to suggest he will make an impact in handicaps off a current mark of 60. Official explanation: jockey said gelding hung badly right (op 66-1)

Adios Juan was backed from 12-1 to 11-2, but he put in a laboured effort and may not have coped with the arduous conditions. (op 12-1)

5812 TOTE IRELAND NOW AT BETFAIR MEDIAN AUCTION MAIDEN STKS 7f 214y

2:45 (2:46) (Class 5) 2-Y-O £2,719 (£809; £404; £202) Stalls Low

Form				RPR
	1		**Alcalde** 2-9-3 0 ... RoystonFfrench 5 (M Johnston) *led 1f: chsd ldr after tl led again ins fnl 2f: pushed clr 1f out: comf* **9/2**[3]	82+
0	2	7	**Timpanist**[20] 5225 2-8-12 0 ... TPQueally 11 (P W Chapple-Hyam) *s.s: hdwy 3f out: swtchd lft over 1f out: styd on to take 2nd ins fnl f: no ch w wnr* **3/1**[2]	62
00	3	2	**Crystallize**[54] 4184 2-9-3 0 ... RobertHavlin 4 (A B Haynes) *prom: rdn over 2f out: no ex over 1f out* **40/1**	62
06	4	1 ¾	**Primo Dilettante**[17] 5344 2-9-3 0 ... StephenDonohoe 2 (W J Knight) *led after 1f and racd freely: hdd ins fnl 2f: wknd over 1f out* **8/1**	58
0	5	1	**Efficiency**[71] 3610 2-8-12 0 ... J-PGuillambert 10 (M Blanshard) *chsd ldrs: rdn over 2f out: wknd over 1f out* **12/1**	51
0	6	½	**Herschel (IRE)**[13] 5469 2-9-3 0 ... GeorgeBaker 8 (G L Moore) *towards rr: sme hdwy in centre and rdn 2f out: wknd over 1f out* **9/4**[1]	55
0	7	2	**Every Little Helps**[13] 5461 2-8-9 0 ... JackMitchell(3) 6 (J Gallagher) *mid-div: outpcd 1/2-way: sn drvn along and struggling* **50/1**	46
	8	15	**Welsh Passion** 2-8-5 0 ... RobbieEgan(7) 9 (D Flood) *sn bhd: drvn and no ch fr 1/2-way* **12/1**	13
0	9	7	**Royal Arthur**[55] 4150 2-9-3 0 ... TGMcLaughlin 1 (L A Dace) *s.s: a bhd: drvn and no ch fr 1/2-way* **80/1**	2
0	10	33	**Buddha O' Neil**[20] 5227 2-9-3 0 ... ChrisCatlin 7 (M R Channon) *sn bhd: t.o fr 1/2-way* **11/1**	—

1m 40.35s (4.35) **Going Correction** +0.425s/f (Yiel) 10 Ran SP% **114.4**

Speed ratings (Par 95): **95,88,86,84,83 82,80,65,58,25**

toteswinger: 1&2 £5.00, 1&3 £31.00, 2&3 £43.40. CSF £17.91 TOTE £3.20: £1.30, £1.30, £7.40; EX 20.00.

Owner Sheikh Hamdan Bin Mohammed Al Maktoum **Bred** Miss K Rausing And Mrs S Rogers **Trained** Middleham Moor, N Yorks

FOCUS

An ordinary maiden which saw an emphatic winner. He beat little but is obviously a nice prospect.

NOTEBOOK

Alcalde was weak in the market and a bit keen early on, but he swept into the lead at the two-furlong pole, responded really well to pressure and absolutely pulverised his rivals. The form of this debut win is nothing to get excited about but the style was impressive. He is closely related to Alambic, who won five in a row at 1m4f-1m6f as a three-year-old, is from a family that seems versatile as far as ground is concerned and looks to have a bright future. (op 11-4)

Timpanist was trapped for room on a couple of occasions and Alcalde had already gone clear when she saw daylight, but she did stay on fairly well to beat the rest comfortably. She should continue to progress and is a half-sister to the useful Sunley Peace, who was highly progressive over staying trips at three. (op 4-1)

Crystallize had been beaten around 19 lengths on both his two previous starts, so holds the form down a bit, but the soft ground probably encouraged some improvement, and he will face more realistic targets in nurseries. (op 66-1)

Primo Dilettante had form to be strongly competitive here, but he took a strong hold, probably went off too quickly on the taxing ground and was a spent force some way out. Official explanation: jockey said colt ran too free (op 11-2)

Herschel(IRE) was well backed and looked a threat in the straight, but it was a bit disappointing that he could not sustain his effort, particularly as there is plenty of stamina on the dam's side of his pedigree. (op 7-2)

5813 BET ON TOTE AT BETFAIR (S) STKS 1m 1f 209y

3:20 (3:26) (Class 6) 3-Y-O £1,942 (£578; £288; £144) Stalls High

Form				RPR
0565	1		**Ministerofinterior**[51] 4281 3-8-9 57 ... JackMitchell(3) 3 (C F Wall) *led and set mod pce: hdd 5f out: regained slt ld over 2f out: drvn clr fnl f* **6/4**[1]	53
0000	2	2 ¾	**Oronsay**[28] 5023 3-8-7 45 ...(t) ChrisCatlin 4 (B R Millman) *plld hrd in rr: hdwy to join wnr over 2f out: nt qckn fnl f* **28/1**	42
6560	3	3	**Fleurs De Censier**[52] 4259 3-8-4 52 ... MarcHalford(3) 6 (D M Simcock) *dwlt: sn in mid-div: rdn 3f out: effrt and drvn fnl 2f: no imp on first 2* **10/1**	36
0-00	4	½	**Valentine Blue**[16] 5379 3-8-12 47 ...(t) RobertHavlin 7 (A B Haynes) *t.k.h: chsd ldrs tl outpcd fnl 2f* **20/1**	40
0002	5	2	**Tank Commander**[8] 5603 3-8-12 46 ... LPKeniry 9 (W R Muir) *in tch tl dropped towards rr 1/2-way: effrt and hrd rdn 2f out: nt pce to chal* **11/4**[2]	36
0040	6	13	**Fareeha**[2] 5787 3-8-7 53 ... SimonWhitworth 5 (B R Johnson) *t.k.h: w ldrs tl wknd 2f out* **5/1**[3]	5
	7	1 ¾	**Cadeaux Fax** 3-8-12 ... TGMcLaughlin 1 (A B Haynes) *carried lft s: bhd: rdn 5f out: hdwy and wnt for stands' rail 3f out: wknd over 2f out* **14/1**	7
0000	8	11	**Bobster**[26] 5086 3-8-7 45 ... NickyMackay 2 (B R Millman) *wnt lft s: prom: led 5f out tl outpcd and n.m.r over 2f out: sn lost pl* **14/1**	—

2m 12.2s (8.60) **Going Correction** +0.625s/f (Yiel) 8 Ran SP% **114.0**

Speed ratings (Par 99): **90,87,85,85,83 73,71,62**

toteswinger: 1&2 £11.70, 1&3 £4.30, 2&3 £31.80. CSF £47.71 TOTE £2.60: £1.10, £4.70, £2.20; EX 47.30.The winner was sold for 6,400gns to D Hunnisett.

Owner Ms Aida Fustoq **Bred** Deerfield Farm **Trained** Newmarket, Suffolk

FOCUS

A weak seller and a slow winning time, even for a race like this. The winner did not have to run much above his last couple of disappointing efforts.

Tank Commander Official explanation: trainer's rep said gelding was unsuited by the soft (good to soft places) ground

Bobster Official explanation: trainer's rep said filly was unsuited by the soft (good to soft places) ground

5814 TIMEFORM JURY MAIDEN STKS 1m 3f 196y

3:55 (3:58) (Class 5) 3-Y-O £2,719 (£809; £404; £202) Stalls High

Form				RPR
4303	1		**Red Merlin (IRE)**[27] 5058 3-9-3 71 ...(v[1]) J-PGuillambert 2 (C G Cox) *plld hrd: chsd ldrs: drvn to ld ins fnl f: edgd lft: styd on* **3/1**[2]	74
0204	2	1 ½	**Hawk Flight (IRE)**[26] 5105 3-9-3 68 ... GeorgeBaker 3 (W R Muir) *chsd ldrs: hung lft and led over 1f out: continued to drift bdly lft and hdd ins fnl f: one pce* **10/1**[3]	72
32	3	3 ½	**Star Rocker**[13] 5463 3-9-3 ... RobertHavlin 6 (J H M Gosden) *led and set mod pce: qcknd over 3f out: hdd over 1f out: no ex* **1/2**[1]	66
-305	4	3	**Basanti (USA)**[34] 4821 3-8-12 72 ... ChrisCatlin 1 (B W Hills) *hld up in 5th: rdn and outpcd 3f out: sn btn* **10/1**[3]	57
6406	5	7	**Requia**[20] 5232 3-8-12 62 ... SimonWhitworth 7 (H Candy) *chsd ldr: rdn 3f out: sn wknd* **25/1**	45
	6	20	**Dontellempike** 3-9-3 ... LPKeniry 4 (J Gallagher) *in rr: hrd rdn over 5f out: sn wl bhd* **66/1**	18
0	7	9	**Percyslavenderblue**[32] 4909 3-8-12 ... TPQueally 5 (J Gallagher) *t.k.h towards rr: wknd 3f out: sn bhd* **100/1**	—

2m 42.2s (9.50) **Going Correction** +0.625s/f (Yiel) 7 Ran SP% **116.2**

Speed ratings (Par 101): **93,92,89,87,83 69,63**

toteswinger: 1&2 £2.80, 1&3 £1.10, 2&3 £2.20. CSF £31.50 TOTE £3.60: £1.60, £2.80; EX 41.30.

Owner Reid's Allstars **Bred** Keatly Overseas Ltd **Trained** Lambourn, Berks

FOCUS

A fairly interesting maiden run in a modest winning time. Two of the contenders had an official rating in the low 70s, but appeared to have a bit to find with the less exposed Star Rocker. The winner probably didn't need to improve.

5815 BETFAIR - BETTING AS IT SHOULD BE H'CAP 1m 1f 209y

4:30 (4:32) (Class 6) (0-65,65) 3-Y-O £2,072 (£616; £308; £153) Stalls High

Form				RPR
0-50	1		**Timocracy**[17] 5366 3-9-2 63 ... RoystonFfrench 1 (M Johnston) *led for 2f: chsd ldrs: pushed along 5f out: rdn 3f out: led ent fnl f: sn forged clr: eased nr fin* **16/1**	75+
0000	2	5	**Cwm Rhondda (USA)**[18] 5322 3-8-9 59 ...(t) JackMitchell(3) 4 (P W Chapple-Hyam) *awkward leaving stalls: sn w ldrs: led 3f out: hrd rdn and hdd ent fnl f: kpt on but sn hld by wnr* **11/1**	61
1535	3	3	**Coral Shores**[18] 5308 3-9-4 65 ...(v) ChrisCatlin 3 (P W Hiatt) *plld hrd: led after 2f: rdn and hdd 3f out: one pce fnl 2f* **4/1**[2]	61
0210	4	3	**Bosamcliff (IRE)**[1] 5803 3-9-4 65 ... J-PGuillambert 7 (A B Haynes) *wnt rt s: cl up: rdn 3f out: sn edgd lft: nt pce to chal* **11/4**[1]	55
0020	5	3 ½	**Seventh Hill**[14] 5428 3-9-3 64 ... LPKeniry 6 (M Blanshard) *cl up: nudged along 5f out: rdn 3f out: sn one pce* **6/1**[3]	47
-366	6	2 ½	**Pharaohs Queen (IRE)**[111] 2376 3-9-4 65 ... TPQueally 9 (E A L Dunlop) *hld up: rdn 4f out: nvr pce to get on terms* **12/1**	43
44	7	3 ¾	**Bon Ton Roulet**[42] 4569 3-7-11 51 oh1 ... CharlesEddery(7) 8 (R Hannon) *v awkward leaving stalls and wnt lft: t.k.h in rr: rdn 4f out: no imp* **11/1**	22

6005 **8** *4* **Bury Treasure (IRE)**[23] 5167 3-8-8 62.......................... KylieManser[(7)] 5 25
(Miss Gay Kelleway) *t.k.h early: mid-div tl hung bdly lft and wknd over 3f out* **14/1**
0301 **9** *4* **Space Pirate**[23] 5167 3-8-9 56............................(p) RobertHavlin 2 11
(J Pearce) *hld up: rdn over 3f out: sme hdwy for effrt over 2f out: wknd over 1f out: eased whn btn* **13/2**
2m 9.78s (6.18) **Going Correction** +0.625s/f (Yiel) **9** Ran SP% **111.2**
Speed ratings (Par 99): **100,96,93,91,88 86,83,80,77**
toteswinger: 1&2 £15.50, 1&3 £5.60, 2&3 £9.40. CSF £168.88 CT £821.86 TOTE £13.30: £3.30, £4.70, £1.40; EX 139.70.
Owner Sheikh Hamdan Bin Mohammed Al Maktoum **Bred** Gainsborough Stud Management Ltd **Trained** Middleham Moor, N Yorks

FOCUS
Ordinary handicap form. The winner is unexposed and rated up a stone with the runner-up setting the standard.
Timocracy Official explanation: trainer said he had no explanation for the apparent improvement in form
Bury Treasure(IRE) Official explanation: jockey said gelding lost its action
Space Pirate Official explanation: jockey said colt had no more to give

5816 BETFAIR SP H'CAP 7f 214y
5:00 (5:00) (Class 6) (0-65,65) 3-Y-O+ **£2,072** (£616; £308; £153) **Stalls** Low

Form RPR
0643 **1** **Croeso Cusan**[23] 5167 3-7-13 51 oh4.......................... SophieDoyle[(5)] 1 63+
(J L Spearing) *stdd s: patiently rdn fr rr: gd hdwy in centre fr 2f out: led jst ins fnl f: easily drew clr* **4/1**[1]
0406 **2** *3 ½* **Out Of Nothing**[29] 4979 5-8-9 58............. AmyKathleenParsons[(7)] 9 63
(K M Prendergast) *2nd most of way: rdn over 2f out: nt pce of wnr fnl f* **10/1**[3]
0405 **3** *1 ¼* **Paradise Island (IRE)**[36] 4727 3-9-1 62.................(b[1]) TPQueally 8 63
(E A L Dunlop) *led: c to stands' rail st: drvn along and hung lft over 1f out: hdd jst ins fnl f: no ex* **12/1**
0-00 **4** *3* **Surprise Act**[107] 2477 4-9-3 59.. LPKeniry 2 54
(P R Chamings) *prom: styd far side w one rival st: wknd over 1f out* **11/1**
0433 **5** *½* **Timber Creek**[27] 5069 3-8-9 63....................................... AmyScott[(7)] 10 56
(H Candy) *in tch: rdn over 2f out: no imp* **9/2**[2]
0406 **6** *2 ¾* **Quaglino Way (GR)**[45] 4481 4-9-7 63......................... GeorgeBaker 7 51
(P R Chamings) *in tch: rdn over 2f out: sn wknd* **9/2**[2]
0514 **7** *hd* **Spent**[23] 5167 3-9-0 61.. ChrisCatlin 4 47
(Mouse Hamilton-Fairley) *in tch: styd far side w one rival st: wknd over 1f out* **4/1**[1]
0000 **8** *3* **Regal Dream (IRE)**[56] 4125 6-8-6 51 oh4....................... JackMitchell[(3)] 6 31
(J W Unett) *hld up towards rr: hdwy and prom over 2f out: wknd over 1f out* **12/1**
00-0 **9** *1 ¾* **Dowlleh**[31] 4934 4-9-4 60.. RobertHavlin 5 36
(T T Clement) *stdd s: t.k.h in rr: rdn and lost tch over 2f out* **22/1**
1m 40.61s (4.61) **Going Correction** +0.625s/f (Yiel)
WFA 3 from 4yo+ 5lb **9** Ran SP% **113.5**
Speed ratings (Par 101): **101,97,96,93,92 90,89,86,85**
toteswinger: 1&2 £9.40, 1&3 £9.60, 2&3 £11.50. CSF £43.46 CT £439.52 TOTE £4.00: £1.40, £3.30, £3.20; EX 47.90.
Owner Mrs Richard Evans **Bred** Richard Evans Bloodstock **Trained** Kinnersley, Worcs

FOCUS
A tight handicap run at a modest pace. For the first time during the afternoon the runners were spread across the track in the straight. The form is a bit suspect because several compromised their chance by racing keenly, and the placed horses are not that consistent, but the winner was impressive.

5817 CANARY WHARF SPORTS EXCHANGE 1ST ANNIVERSARY H'CAP 5f 59y
5:30 (5:30) (Class 6) (0-65,65) 3-Y-O+ **£2,072** (£616; £308; £153) **Stalls** Low

Form RPR
1232 **1** **Matterofact (IRE)**[7] 5645 5-9-5 65........................... TGMcLaughlin 9 73
(M S Saunders) *prom: rdn to ld jst ins fnl f: strly pressed by runner-up nr fin: jst got home* **11/4**[1]
1006 **2** *hd* **Rocker**[13] 5467 4-9-5 65... GeorgeBaker 10 72
(G L Moore) *in tch: drvn to chse ldrs over 1f out: rn to almost join wnr nr fin: jst hld* **9/2**[3]
3030 **3** *½* **Kalligal**[21] 5201 3-9-2 63... RobertHavlin 1 68
(R Ingram) *led tl jst ins fnl f: hrd rdn: kpt on* **16/1**
3262 **4** *1 ½* **Rainbow Bay**[10] 5566 5-8-5 54...........................(v) JackMitchell[(3)] 2 54
(Miss Tracy Waggott) *prom: drvn along and sltly outpcd whn short of room 2f out: kpt on fnl f* **4/1**[2]
0510 **5** *1 ½* **Jayanjay**[23] 5171 9-8-10 56.. TPQueally 11 50
(B R Johnson) *hld up in tch on outer: rdn 2f out: no imp* **12/1**
0063 **6** *¾* **Musical Script (USA)**[8] 5610 5-8-9 55....................(b) ChrisCatlin 7 47
(Mouse Hamilton-Fairley) *s.i.s: mid-div after 2f: outpcd 2f out: n.d after* **17/2**
0546 **7** *4* **Caustic Wit (IRE)**[8] 5601 10-9-0 60............................ MickyFenton 8 37
(M S Saunders) *sn pushed along towards rr: sme hdwy and hrd rdn ins fnl 2f: sn wknd* **8/1**
6000 **8** *2* **George The Second**[107] 2478 5-7-12 51 oh1................. RossAtkinson[(7)] 5 21
(Miss Tor Sturgis) *nvr gng pce* **12/1**
2606 **9** *2 ½* **Jonny Ebeneezer**[38] 4696 9-8-7 60.......................... CharlesEddery[(7)] 3 21
(D Flood) *bhd: mod effrt on rail 2f out: sn hrd rdn and wknd* **14/1**
65.41 secs (3.11) **Going Correction** +0.625s/f (Yiel)
WFA 3 from 4yo+ 1lb **9** Ran SP% **114.4**
Speed ratings (Par 101): **100,99,98,96,94 92,86,83,79**
toteswinger: 1&2 £4.00, 1&3 £8.90, 2&3 £8.90. CSF £14.84 CT £164.19 TOTE £2.70: £1.30, £2.30, £5.50; EX 18.30 Place 6: £166.40 Place 5: £133.45.
Owner Prempro Racing **Bred** Tony Gleeson **Trained** Green Ore, Somerset

FOCUS
They raced more towards the centre and far side for this sprint, and few got into it from behind. Ordinary form, and it is doubtful whether the winner had to improve.
Musical Script(USA) Official explanation: jockey said gelding missed the break
T/Plt: £200.00 to a £1 stake. Pool: £56,111.52. 204.80 winning tickets. T/Qpdt: £41.10 to a £1 stake. Pool: £3,080.00. 55.45 winning tickets. LM

4704 CHEPSTOW (L-H)
Thursday, September 11
5818 Meeting Abandoned - Waterlogged

5791 DONCASTER (L-H)
Thursday, September 11

OFFICIAL GOING: Soft (6.7)
Wind: Light against Weather: Cloudy

5825 CROWNHOTEL-BAWTRY.COM CONDITIONS STKS 7f
1:30 (1:30) (Class 3) 2-Y-O
£9,346 (£2,799; £1,399; £700; £349; £175) **Stalls** High

Form RPR
1 **Secrecy** 2-8-9 0.. PhilipRobinson 3 94+
(M A Jarvis) *unf: scope: dwlt: sn trcking ldrs: hdwy on outer over 2f out: rdn to ld 1f out: hung lft ins fnl f: styd on wl* **12/1**
15 **2** *2 ¼* **Courageous (IRE)**[26] 5093 2-9-2 87............................ TomEaves 4 93
(B Smart) *lw: t.k.h: trckd ldrs: effrt 2f out: swtchd lft and rdn wl over 1f out: styd on ins fnl f: tk 2nd nr fin* **16/1**
20 **3** *½* **Yorksters Girl (IRE)**[33] 4868 2-8-7 0.................... RobertWinston 1 83
(M G Quinlan) *leggy: prom: hdwy to ld 2f out and sn rdn: drvn and hdd 1f out: no ex ins fnl f: lost 2nd towards fin* **13/2**[3]
31 **4** *3 ¼* **Midnight Cruiser (IRE)**[20] 5227 2-9-0 88................... RyanMoore 2 82
(R Hannon) *t.k.h: cl up: led after 1f: rdn along and hdd 2f out: drvn and wknd ent fnl f* **4/6**[1]
5 *4 ½* **Bigalo's Star (IRE)** 2-8-4 0........................... KellyHarrison[(5)] 6 65
(L A Mullaney) *w'like: bit bkwd: s.i.s and bhd: swtchd lft and hdwy over 2f out: sn rdn and no imp* **150/1**
323 **6** *5* **Crackdown (IRE)**[30] 4954 2-8-12 92............................. JoeFanning 5 56
(M Johnston) *led 1f: cl up tl rdn along 3f out and sn wknd* **7/2**[2]
0 **7** *3 ¼* **Chief Red Cloud (USA)**[59] 4014 2-8-12 0............... DarrenWilliams 7 48
(K R Burke) *w'like: leggy: a towards rr: rdn along 3f out and sn outpcd* **28/1**
1m 29.26s (2.96) **Going Correction** +0.30s/f (Good) **7** Ran SP% **113.2**
Speed ratings (Par 99): **95,92,91,88,83 77,73**
toteswinger: 1&2 £9.60, 1&3 £6.40, 2&3 £5.00. CSF £167.63 TOTE £11.80: £3.50, £5.40; EX 177.80.
Owner Sheikh Ahmed Al Maktoum **Bred** Whatton Manor Stud **Trained** Newmarket, Suffolk

FOCUS
This was a decent conditions event, but it was run at an average early pace and the majority of runners proved keen through the first two furlongs. A taking debut from Secrecy and improvement from Courageous in a race in which the third helps set the level of the form.

NOTEBOOK
Secrecy ◆, an 80,000gns purchase whose dam scored over 6f, got his career off to a perfect start with a fairly taking display. He took time to get organised through the first half of the race, but was kept wide of his rivals and asked for maximum effort in between the final two furlongs. His response was most positive and, if anything, he looked better the further he went. Already gelded, being by King's Best it is not surprising that he enjoyed the soft ground and he does appear to have a bright future. He holds no big-race entries, but it is worth noting that his stable's winner of this event in 2003, Sabbeeh, subsequently took in the Group 3 Horris Hill at Newbury in October, and that could be on the agenda next. (tchd 14-1)
Courageous(IRE), conceding weight all round, hit a flat spot nearing the final furlong, but he responded to pressure and eventually saw the race out well. He was again free early on, but this was much more like it and he looks set to benefit for another furlong in due course. (op 14-1)
Yorksters Girl(IRE), who came unstuck behind Rainbow View in the Sweet Solera last time, travelled kindly until feeling the pinch approaching the final furlong. She just looked to find this too testing on the ground and a drop into maiden company should see her off the mark. (op 8-1)
Midnight Cruiser(IRE) proved all the rage to follow up his Newbury maiden win but ran freely early on, which probably cost him at the business end. He should make up into a nice three-year-old and a drop back in trip may help him in the short term. (op 8-11 tchd 4-5, 5-6 in a place)
Crackdown(IRE) failed to fire on this drop back in trip and faded tamely when it got serious. He did not look at all suited by this soft ground, however. (op 4-1)

5826 GOFFS/DBS PARK HILL STKS (GROUP 2) (F&M) 1m 6f 132y
2:00 (2:00) (Class 1) 3-Y-O+
£56,770 (£21,520; £10,770; £5,370; £2,690; £1,350) **Stalls** Low

Form RPR
-044 **1** **Allegretto (IRE)**[20] 5243 5-9-4 108.............................. RyanMoore 4 108+
(Sir Michael Stoute) *trckd ldrs: smooth hdwy over 3f out: led over 2f out: sn clr: easily* **7/4**[1]
0000 **2** *6* **Perihelion (IRE)**[19] 5293 3-8-6 0................................ TQuinn 2 100
(A P O'Brien, Ire) *w'like: str: lw: in tch: hdwy on inner over 3f out: swtchd rt and rdn 2f out: styd on wl u.p ins fnl f: no ch w wnr* **66/1**
055 **3** *2 ½* **Hold Me Love Me (IRE)**[19] 5293 3-8-6 0...................... MartinDwyer 1 97
(A P O'Brien, Ire) *unf: scope: led: pushed along 4f out: rdn 3f out: hdd over 2f out: sn drvn and wandered: one pce fr over 1f out* **9/1**
1321 **4** *3 ¾* **Gravitation**[42] 4549 3-8-6 108.................................... AlanMunro 6 91
(W Jarvis) *trckd ldr: effrt over 3f out and sn rdn: drvn over 2f out and sn wknd* **11/4**[2]
3463 **5** *2 ½* **Presbyterian Nun (IRE)**[39] 4667 3-8-6 96.................. RichardMullen 3 88
(J L Dunlop) *hld up towards rr: effrt 4f out: sn rdn along and outpcd fr 3f out* **20/1**
2200 **6** *41* **Under The Rainbow**[77] 3415 5-9-4 100.............................(p) LDettori 8 30
(B W Hills) *hld up and bhd: hdwy over 4f out: shqalken up 3f out: sn btn and eased* **14/1**
4635 **7** *9* **Queen Of Naples**[42] 4549 3-8-6 102.............................(b) SteveDrowne 7 18
(J H M Gosden) *lw: towards rr: rdn along over 5f out: sn wknd and eased* **14/1**
520 **R** **Gull Wing (IRE)**[39] 4667 4-9-4 99................................ JamieSpencer 5 —
(M L W Bell) *ref to r* **9/2**[3]
3m 13.31s (6.61) **Going Correction** +0.60s/f (Yiel)
WFA 3 from 4yo+ 12lb **8** Ran SP% **110.8**
Speed ratings (Par 115): **106,102,101,99,98 76,71,—**
toteswinger: 1&2 £19.40, 1&3 £5.20, 2&3 £19.10. CSF £102.63 TOTE £2.80: £1.20, £9.00, £1.60; EX 101.20 Trifecta £285.00 Pool: - £874.38 - 2.27 winning units..
Owner Cheveley Park Stud **Bred** Miss K Rausing And Airlie Stud **Trained** Newmarket, Suffolk

FOCUS
This didn't look the most competitive Park Hill, but with the ground much more testing than normal it became a stiff test of stamina, even though the gallop was not especially strong. The form is hard to pin down, but it has provisionally been rated through the third.

NOTEBOOK
Allegretto(IRE) is a proven stayer at the highest level, and while the ordinary pace would not necessary have been ideal the ground would have helped bring her stamina into play. She has had some niggling foot problems this year, but she was back to her best here and once Ryan Moore pressed the button the race was all over. She may now bid for a repeat win in the Prix Royal-Oak before being retired to stud. (op 13-8 tchd 2-1 and 15-8 in places)

Perihelion(IRE), whose only previous win came in a Bellewstown maiden, was worst-in on official ratings and had 15 lengths to find with her stable-companion Hold Me Love Me on their recent meeting at the Curragh, but she belied both that formline and her odds with a huge effort. However, while she didn't have a lot of room to play with at one point, she wouldn't have bothered the favourite even with a clear run. She should be able to win a Listed race.

Hold Me Love Me(IRE) did look very much the stable's number one and she has shown that she can handle this sort of ground, but despite getting the run of the race out in front she was easy picked off by the winner and could not even confirm recent form with her stable companion. (op 10-1)

Gravitation, who was nominated for this race straight after finishing third in the Queen's Vase at Royal Ascot, was in a decent position throughout, just behind the leader, but when asked for her effort she did not find as much as had looked likely. Connections were concerned by the soft ground and also pointed out that she had had quite a hard season. She didn't see the racecourse until April of this year though, so there is every reason to believe that she will be an even better filly next season. (op 5-2 tchd 3-1)

Presbyterian Nun(IRE), whose only previous attempt on soft ground resulted in her fourth in the Italian Oaks, was trying beyond 1m4f for the first time. On her toes beforehand, she had every chance starting up the long home straight, but soon came under strong pressure and there was nothing more to come. (op 16-1)

Under The Rainbow, still looking for her first win since her final start at two, had not shown anything in her last couple of starts and had been given a short break since. Back in cheekpieces on ground that would not have been a problem to her, she was switched right off but floundered almost as soon as she was asked for an effort. (op 16-1)

Queen Of Naples, whose only previous win came in a Wolverhampton maiden, has run well on soft ground before but she had almost nine lengths to find with Gravitation on their meeting at Glorious Goodwood. On her toes in the paddock, she was in big trouble rounding the long home turn and then dropped right out. Even allowing for the stiff task she faced this was too bad to be true. (tchd 16-1)

Gull Wing(IRE), well backed, took one step out of the stalls and then stopped. (op 6-1)

5827 WEATHERBYS INSURANCE £300,000 2-Y-O STKS 6f 110y

2:35 (2:39) (Class 2) 2-Y-O

£147,720 (£59,100; £29,550; £14,760; £7,380; £7,380) **Stalls** High

Form RPR

1631 **1** **Awinnersgame (IRE)**[41] 4600 2-8-9 97 LDettori 16 108+
(J Noseda) *lw: hld up stands' side: gd hdwy over 2f out: rdn and ev ch over 1f out: drvn ins fnl f and styd on to ld nr fin* **8/1**

14 **2** *nk* **Damien (IRE)**[20] 5244 2-8-6 MichaelHills 17 104+
(B W Hills) *hld up stands' side: gd hdwy over 2f out: rdn to ld 1f out: drvn ins fnl f: hdd and no ex nr fin: 2nd in gp* **11/2**[1]

1032 **3** *5* **Brae Hill (IRE)**[19] 5286 2-8-3 91 HayleyTurner 9 87
(M L W Bell) *led far side gp and overall ldr: rdn wl over 1f out: drvn and hdd 1f out: kpt on same pce:1st in gp* **25/1**

22 **4** *1/2* **Cavera (USA)**[12] 5487 2-8-7 FrancisNorton 2 90
(A M Balding) *hld up towards rr far side: hdwy over 2f out: sn rdn and kpt on ins fnl f: nrst fin: 2nd in gp* **25/1**

1154 **5** *nk* **Talking Hands**[12] 5507 2-8-9 96 JamieSpencer 11 91+
(S Kirk) *dwlt: hld up and bhd stands' side: hdwy 2f out: sn rdn and styd on ins fnl f: nrst fin: 3rd in gp* **7/1**[3]

2141 **6** *1 1/2* **Viva Ronaldo (IRE)**[12] 5496 2-8-9 99 PaulHanagan 13 87
(R A Fahey) *led stands' side gp: rdn 2f out and ev ch tl drvn and one pce appr fnl f: 4th in gp* **9/1**

223 **7** *shd* **Prime Mood (IRE)**[12] 5500 2-8-9 TomEaves 8 87
(B Smart) *prom far side: effrt 2f out and ch tl drvn and wknd fr over 1f out: 3rd in gp* **33/1**

130 **8** *4* **Mister Laurel**[33] 4857 2-8-6 81 TonyHamilton 20 73
(R A Fahey) *hld up towards rr stands' side: gd hdwy 2f out: sn rdn and kpt on ent fnl f: nt rch ldrs: 5th in gp* **50/1**

152 **9** *1 1/4* **Deadly Secret (USA)**[26] 5107 2-9-2 97 JamieMoriarty 19 79
(R A Fahey) *hld up in rr stands' side: hdwy 2f out: sn rdn and no imp: 6th in gp* **16/1**

1030 **10** *3/4* **Dabbers Chief (USA)**[20] 5226 2-8-6 93 AlanMunro 18 67
(B W Hills) *chsd ldrs stands' side: rdn along over 2f out: sn drvn and wknd: 7th in gp* **33/1**

2300 **11** *3/4* **Indian Art (IRE)**[8] 5615 2-8-9 86 (v[1]) RichardMullen 14 68
(R Hannon) *in tch stands' side: rdn along over 2f out: grad wknd: 8th in gp* **40/1**

13 **12** *hd* **Foundation Room (IRE)**[105] 2541 2-7-12 DavidProbert 3 57
(A M Balding) *chsd ldrs far side: rdn along over 2f out: sn wknd: 4th in gp* **8/1**

2404 **13** *1/2* **Heliodor (USA)**[9] 5585 2-8-3 80 DavidKinsella 1 60
(R Hannon) *trckd ldrs far side: effrt over 2f out: sn rdn and btn: 5th in gp* **50/1**

3320 **14** *1/2* **Sunny Future (IRE)**[13] 5461 2-8-3 81 AdrianTNicholls 21 59
(M S Saunders) *chsd ldrs stands' side: rdn along 1/2-way: sn wknd: 8th in gp* **66/1**

021 **15** *1/2* **Perfect Pride (USA)**[13] 5461 2-8-11 PhilipRobinson 22 66
(C G Cox) *a towards rr stands' side: 10th in gp* **33/1**

1135 **16** *shd* **Able Master (IRE)**[20] 5226 2-8-9 97 PaulMulrennan 6 63
(B Smart) *hld up far side: a in rr: 6th in gp* **22/1**

2060 **17** *1/2* **Harwalla (IRE)**[20] 5244 2-8-6 96 RHills 4 59
(M Johnston) *lw: prom far side: rdn along 1/2-way: sn wknd: 7th in gp* **18/1**

0142 **18** *1* **Zaffaan**[28] 5016 2-8-12 92 MartinDwyer 10 62
(E A L Dunlop) *cl up stands' side: rdn along over 2f out and grad wknd: 11th in gp* **20/1**

0101 **19** *1/2* **Pure Poetry (IRE)**[48] 4374 2-8-7 100 ow1 RyanMoore 12 56
(R Hannon) *prom stands' side: effrt over 2f out and sn ev ch tl rdn and wknd qckly wl over 1f out: 12th in gp* **6/1**[2]

1025 **20** *2 1/2* **Art Princess (USA)**[7] 5642 2-8-1 99 WilliamBuick 7 43
(B W Hills) *in tch far side: rdn along 1/2-way: sn wknd: 8th in gp* **12/1**

0504 **21** *1 3/4* **Sun Ship (IRE)**[12] 5496 2-8-9 92 SteveDrowne 5 46
(R Hannon) *chsd ldrs far side: rdn along 1/2-way and sn wknd: 9th in gp* **66/1**

1m 21.26s (1.36) **Going Correction** +0.30s/f (Good) **21** Ran SP% **128.2**

Speed ratings (Par 101): **104,103,97,97,97 95,95,90,89,88 87,87,86,86,85 85,84,83,83,80 78**

toteswinger: 1&2 £5.90, 1&3 £23.70, 2&3 £40.50. CSF £45.69 TOTE £9.00: £2.90, £2.70, £8.30; EX 56.10 Trifecta £981.20 Pool: £1326.01 - 1.00 winning units..

Owner Saeed Suhail **Bred** J Joyce **Trained** Newmarket, Suffolk

FOCUS

Europe's richest juvenile event and a highly competitive race. It was run at a sound pace and, with the field electing to shun both rails, the first two put up smart efforts in pulled clear down the middle of the track.

NOTEBOOK

Awinnersgame(IRE) ◆ had been kept for this after winning at Newmarket 41 days previously and he registered his third win of the season with a game display. He looked held by Damien as that rival moved to the front going nicely entering the final furlong, but he dug deep under maximum pressure and eventually got on top. His sire's progeny have shown a liking for soft ground and he had no trouble at all with it. Always well regarded by his shrewd outfit, he is evidently now at the top of his game and further improvement still looks on the cards. (op 10-1)

Damien(IRE) ◆ took time to find his stride through the early stages, but he joined the leaders travelling easily after the two-furlong pole and looked the likely victor. He responded positively when his rider asked him to win the race and hit the front, but ultimately appeared to be outstayed by the winner. He has done very little wrong in his three outings to date, is versatile as regards the going, and finished well clear of the remainder. He would not look totally out of place in the Mill Reef at Newbury later this month and, while the winner is also entered in that, the drop back to 6f should suit him much the better. It is well worth remembering his connections took that event last year with Dark Angel. (op 13-2)

Brae Hill(IRE) was given an aggressive ride and fared best of those who stayed towards the far side. He has developed into a consistent performer and it looks a personal-best effort on ground he probably found easy enough (op 33-1)

Cavera(USA), whose stable landed this last season with the smart Dream Eater, was another to register a career-best display and she enjoyed the softer ground. An ordinary maiden should be hers for the taking in the coming weeks. (op 33-1)

Talking Hands was dropping in grade after finishing fourth in the Solario 12 days previously and met support. Not that surprisingly he struggled to go the early pace and had a lot to do 2f out, but he finished with a flourish. This was no doubt an inadequate test and the best of him has probably still to be seen. (op 12-1)

Viva Ronaldo(IRE) was always up with the pace and he kept on to record a respectable effort in defeat. He is a likeable colt who helps to set the level of this form and will probably prove happier again when back on a quicker surface. (op 8-1 tchd 10-1)

Foundation Room(IRE) was never a serious player under her feather weight and may have needed this first run for 105 days. (tchd 15-2)

Perfect Pride(USA) Official explanation: jockey said filly did not like the soft ground

Able Master(IRE) Official explanation: jockey said colt was keen early

Pure Poetry(IRE) faded after racing on the pace down the middle of the track and was later reported to have lost his action. Official explanation: jockey said colt lost its action (op 5-1)

Art Princess(USA), who had a chance on official figures, was ridden a lot more conservatively than is often the case and was never in the hunt.

5828 ROBIN HOOD AIRPORT DONCASTER SHEFFIELD MAY HILL STKS (GROUP 2) (FILLIES) 1m (S)

3:10 (3:12) (Class 1) 2-Y-O

£45,416 (£17,216; £8,616; £4,296; £2,152; £1,080) **Stalls** High

Form RPR

11 **1** **Rainbow View (USA)**[33] 4868 2-9-1 0 JimmyFortune 8 112+
(J H M Gosden) *hld up in rr: smooth hdwy on outer over 2f out: led on bit appr fnl f: easily* **1/3**[1]

0311 **2** *2* **Snoqualmie Girl (IRE)**[13] 5462 2-8-12 96 TQuinn 3 102
(D R C Elsworth) *hld up in tch: hdwy 3f out: rdn to ld briefly wl over 1f out: sn drvn and hdd over 1f out: kpt on same pce* **10/1**[3]

5114 **3** *1 1/2* **Lahaleeb (IRE)**[19] 5266 2-8-12 94 SamHitchcott 4 98
(M R Channon) *cl up: led over 3f out: rdn over 2f out: hdd and drvn wl over 1f out: kpt on same pce* **25/1**

4152 **4** *nk* **Rose Diamond (IRE)**[19] 5266 2-8-12 99 SteveDrowne 7 98
(R Charlton) *hld up towards rr: hdwy on outer wl over 2f out: rdn to chse ldrs wl over 1f out: drvn and edgd lft ins fnl f: sn no imp* **12/1**

2 **5** *1* **Uvinza**[20] 5241 2-8-12 0 PaulDoe 6 95
(W J Knight) *lw: trckd ldrs: hdwy 1/2-way and sn cl up: rdn over 2f out and grad wknd* **50/1**

54 **6** *3 3/4* **Aaroness (USA)**[11] 5549 2-8-12 0 (t) KJManning 2 87
(J S Bolger, Ire) *w'like: leggy: sn trcking ldrs: hdwy and cl up 1/2-way: rdn along and ch over 2f out: sn wknd* **9/1**[2]

2 **7** *shd* **Latin Tinge (USA)**[20] 5225 2-8-12 0 LDettori 5 87
(P F I Cole) *unf: scope: led: hdd over 3f out: sn rdn along and wknd* **20/1**

1m 42.42s (3.12) **Going Correction** +0.30s/f (Good) **7** Ran SP% **112.4**

Speed ratings (Par 104): **96,94,92,92,91 87,87**

toteswinger: 1&2 £2.00, 1&3 £4.40, 2&3 £9.90. CSF £4.21 TOTE £1.30: £1.10, £3.20; EX 4.20 Trifecta £45.80 Pool: £1007.85 - 16.25 winning units..

Owner George Strawbridge **Bred** Augustin Stable **Trained** Newmarket, Suffolk

■ Stewards' Enquiry : Paul Doe caution: used whip down the shoulder

FOCUS

The soft ground might have made this an even greater test of stamina for these young fillies, but as it turned out the early pace was very modest. Rainbow View was tremendously impressive again and the form looks sound, rated through the time and the balance of form shown by her three closest pursuers. She is easily the best 2-y-o filly seen so far.

NOTEBOOK

Rainbow View(USA) ◆ travelled like a dream, having been dropped out last. Switched to make her effort towards the far side of the group, she quickened up well without having to be asked a serious question and was able to take things very easy in the last half-furlong. She had been very impressive in both of her previous victories on varying ground, including when running away with the Sweet Solera last month, and having proved she stays 1m and seems able to cope with any ground, she is the one to beat in next year's 1,000 Guineas provided she trains on. She may now go to Ascot to try to complete the May Hill/Fillies' Mile double achieved by her stable-companion Playful Act four years ago. (op 4-11 tchd 4-9 in a place and 2-5 in places)

Snoqualmie Girl(IRE), proven in soft ground and the only one of these to have already been successful over this trip, had over six lengths to find with Rainbow View on Newmarket running in July. She was produced with every chance passing the 2f pole, but her old rival loomed alongside at the same time and it proved an unequal struggle. She did narrow the gap from their Newmarket meeting and still seems to be improving, but connections see her as more of an Oaks filly. (tchd 11-1)

Lahaleeb(IRE), the most experienced in the field and proven in the ground, was always up there and kept on for third, though she was firmly put in her place by the front pair. She did at least reverse recent Goodwood running with Rose Diamond. (op 20-1)

Rose Diamond(IRE) tried to get into the race when switched stands' side entering the last quarter-mile but could then make little impression. Her trainer had expressed concern over the soft ground beforehand, so she is probably worth another chance back on a sounder surface. (tchd 14-1)

Uvinza, runner-up at 66-1 on her Newmarket debut when looking very green, probably stepped up on that as she plugged on to finish close behind a couple of fillies with proven Pattern-race form. She should have little difficulty in finding a maiden with further improvement likely. (op 40-1)

Aaroness(USA), fourth in a first-time tongue tie in the Moyglare Stud on soft ground last time, ended up well beaten, which might be seen as a knock to The Curragh form, but that is probably unfair as she almost certainly did too much early here. (op 11-1)

Latin Tinge(USA), promising on her Newbury debut, is bred to appreciate this extra furlong, being a half-sister to the November Handicap winner Malt Or Mash, but she was also too keen in front early. She still has scope and may well come into her own when stepped up to middle distances next season. (op 16-1)

5829 JAPAN RACING ASSOCIATION SCEPTRE STKS (LISTED RACE) (F&M) 7f

3:45 (3:46) (Class 1) 3-Y-O+ **£26,667** (£10,084; £5,040; £2,520) **Stalls** High

Form RPR

0005 **1** **Royal Confidence**[41] 4590 3-8-10 103 .... MichaelHills 12 103
(B W Hills) *lw: hld up towards rr: gd hdwy 2f out: rdn ent fnl f: styd on wl u.p to ld nr fin* **4/1**[2]

4021 **2** *nk* **Chantilly Tiffany**[18] 5334 4-9-3 98 .... JimmyFortune 9 107
(E A L Dunlop) *hld up in tch: smooth hdwy 3f out: rdn to ld over 1f out: drvn and edgd lft ins fnl f: hdd nr fin* **12/1**

253- **3** *¾* **Festoso (IRE)**[342] 5973 3-8-10 106 .... SteveDrowne 6 100+
(H J L Dunlop) *s.i.s: sn in tch: hdwy over 2f out: swtchd lft and rdn to chal ent fnl f: drvn and nt qckn towards fin* **8/1**

2114 **4** *nse* **Red Dune (IRE)**[41] 4590 3-8-10 98 .... PhilipRobinson 2 100+
(M A Jarvis) *lw: t.k.h: led: rdn along 2f out: drvn and hdd over 1f out: one pce ins fnl f* **7/2**[1]

5000 **5** *1½* **Spinning Lucy (IRE)**[41] 4590 3-8-10 95 .... WilliamBuick 5 96
(B W Hills) *midfield: hdwy and in tch over 2f out: sn rdn and styd on ins fnl f: nrst fin* **16/1**

2330 **6** *½* **Kylayne**[58] 4059 3-8-10 100 .... RobertWinston 10 94
(P W D'Arcy) *chsd ldrs on outer: rdn along over 2f out: drvn and one pce appr fnl f* **16/1**

1-50 **7** *nse* **Floristry**[19] 5275 3-8-10 100 .... LDettori 3 94
(Saeed Bin Suroor) *t.k.h: trckd ldrs: hdwy 2f out: rdn over 1f out: one pce ent fnl f* **9/1**

6050 **8** *1¾* **Nijoom Dubai**[41] 4590 3-8-10 103 .... TPO'Shea 11 89
(M R Channon) *a towards rr* **9/1**

3000 **9** *2* **Sakhee's Song (IRE)**[19] 5275 4-9-0 92 .... TQuinn 4 86
(D R C Elsworth) *hld up towards rr: effrt over 2f out: sn rdn and nvr a factor* **50/1**

-204 **10** *½* **Dream Day**[97] 2793 3-8-10 99 .... RyanMoore 7 83
(R Hannon) *hld up towards rr: gd hdwy over 2f out: rdn to chse ldrs whn n.m.r over 1f out and sn wknd* **5/1**[3]

1143 **11** *1* **Candle Sahara (IRE)**[55] 4153 3-8-10 95 .... SamHitchcott 8 80
(M R Channon) *prom: rdn along wl over 2f out: drvn and wkng whn edgd lft over 1f out* **25/1**

4531 **12** *¾* **Montrachet**[24] 5149 4-9-0 76 .... JamieSpencer 1 80
(M L W Bell) *prom: rdn along wl over 2f out: sn wknd* **16/1**

1m 28.66s (2.36) **Going Correction** +0.30s/f (Good)
WFA 3 from 4yo 4lb **12** Ran SP% **121.1**
Speed ratings (Par 111): **98,97,96,96,95 94,94,92,90,89 88,87**
toteswinger: 1&2 £6.50, 1&3 £6.50, 2&3 £8.40. CSF £52.97 TOTE £4.80: £1.90, £3.60, £3.10; EX 60.80 Trifecta £223.50 Pool: £888.10 - 2.94 winning units.
Owner D M James **Bred** D M James **Trained** Lambourn, Berks

FOCUS
Just a fair renewal of this fillies' Listed prize and ordinary form for the grade, although it provided a cracking finish between the first four. With the fifth running much her best race of the year and the sixth below par on her last two starts there is a slight doubt over the value of the form.

NOTEBOOK
Royal Confidence arrived late in the day to record a first win since landing a valuable nursery over the course and distance at this meeting last year. She still had a lot of rivals to pass 2f out, but once she hit top gear inside the final furlong she always looked like getting up. This was a deserved success for a filly that was not beaten far in the 1,000 Guineas and the trip looks ideal for her now. Now she has confirmed a liking for soft ground, she looks worth chancing again when stepping back up to Group company. (tchd 7-2, 9-2 in places)

Chantilly Tiffany came into this on the back of a Listed success in Germany and only just failed to follow up. She again travelled sweetly for most of the race and only got reeled in near the line. This rates another improved effort under her penalty. (op 11-1)

Festoso(IRE) ◆ was making her belated seasonal return but looked fit enough beforehand. She has to rate as somewhat unlucky, as she fell out of the gates and ultimately lost more ground than she was eventually beaten by. She got the longer distance well and, providing she comes out of this without hitch, there still looks to be a decent prize within her compass. (op 12-1)

Red Dune(IRE) was given her now customary positive ride and held every chance. She just failed to see the race out as well as the principals on this easier surface, but did fare the best of those to race on the early pace. (op 4-1 tchd 9-2)

Spinning Lucy(IRE) turned in her most encouraging effort of the current campaign and saw out the trip well enough. She could be ready to build on this. (tchd 20-1)

Dream Day Official explanation: jockey said filly had no more to give

5830 TOTESUPER7 H'CAP 1m 2f 60y

4:20 (4:20) (Class 2) (0-110,102) 3-Y-O+ **£12,952** (£3,854; £1,926; £962) **Stalls** Low

Form RPR

1310 **1** **Wasan**[63] 3877 3-9-3 95 .... RHills 2 104+
(E A L Dunlop) *hld up in tch: hreadway 2f out: swtchd rt and rdn ent fnl f: styd on wl u.p to ld nr fin* **4/1**[2]

143 **2** *shd* **Allied Powers (IRE)**[35] 4784 3-9-0 92 .... RyanMoore 1 101
(M L W Bell) *lw: trckd ldr: hdwy over 2f out: led wl over 1f out: rdn ent fnl f: sn drvn: hdd nr line* **7/2**[1]

3 *1½* **Satu (IRE)**[27] 5084 4-9-1 86 .... KJManning 8 92
(David P Myerscough, Ire) *hld up towards rr: hdwy on outer over 2f out: rdn over 1f out: kpt on u.p ins fnl f* **25/1**

3400 **4** *½* **Feared In Flight (IRE)**[63] 3877 3-9-7 99 .... MichaelHills 5 104
(B W Hills) *trckd ldrs: hdwy 3f out: rdn wl over 1f out: kpt on same pce u.p ins fnl f* **10/1**

1410 **5** *¾* **Swinging Sixties (IRE)**[43] 4519 3-9-2 94 .... PhilipRobinson 6 98
(M A Jarvis) *trckd ldng pair: hdwy 3f out: rdn along 2f out: drvn and n.m.r ent fnl f: kpt on same pce* **8/1**

10 **6** *nk* **Secret Dancer (IRE)**[89] 3045 3-8-12 90 .... JamieSpencer 3 93
(J R Fanshawe) *dwlt: hld up in rr: swtchd outside and hdwy 2f out: rdn over 1f out: kpt on ins fnl f: nrst fin* **6/1**

2-04 **7** *1½* **Filios (IRE)**[33] 4844 4-9-11 96 .... LDettori 7 96
(Saeed Bin Suroor) *trckd ldrs: hdwy over 2f out: swtchd lft and rdn over 1f out: sn drvn and wknd ins fnl f* **6/1**

4-40 **8** *½* **Bolodenka (IRE)**[17] 5360 6-9-7 92 .... PaulHanagan 4 91
(R A Fahey) *trckd ldrs: hdwy over 2f out: rdn and edgd rt over 1f out: wknd ent fnl f* **20/1**

0321 **9** *4½* **Drill Sergeant**[19] 5257 3-9-10 102 .... JoeFanning 9 92
(M Johnston) *lw: led: rdn along 3f out: hdd wl over 1f out: wkng whn hmpd appr fnl f* **5/1**[3]

2m 14.88s (3.68) **Going Correction** +0.60s/f (Yiel)
WFA 3 from 4yo+ 7lb **9** Ran SP% **116.3**
Speed ratings (Par 109): **109,108,107,107,106 106,105,104,101**
toteswinger: 1&2 £3.80, 1&3 £18.90, 2&3 £21.40. CSF £18.58 CT £308.14 TOTE £4.80: £1.60, £1.90, £5.20; EX 18.80 Trifecta £488.80 Part won. Pool: £660.56 - 0.20 winning units..
Owner Hamdan Al Maktoum **Bred** Belgrave Bloodstock **Trained** Newmarket, Suffolk

FOCUS
A decent handicap and the solid pace set by Drill Sergeant meant that this was a good test of stamina in the ground. It was noticeable that the runners spurned the inside rail by shifting out towards the centre of the track on reaching the home straight. The form has been rated fairly positively.

NOTEBOOK
Wasan, who was returning from a short break since losing his action at Newmarket, was buried away in the pack for most of the way. He had to wait a while until a gap appeared for him, but once through it he responded very well to pressure to get up right on the line. He was cut from 33-1 to 20-1 for the Cambridgeshire which is a possibility, though he would need soft ground. (op 5-1)

Allied Powers(IRE), proven in testing ground, was taking a major drop in trip and sat in the leader's slipstream for most of the way. Once committed approaching the last 2f, he looked to have the race in the bag, but despite keeping on very bravely he had the prize snatched from him on the post. He is still currently 10lb above his last winning mark, but this effort shows that he is up to it. (tchd 10-3)

Satu(IRE), proven on soft ground in Ireland, responded to pressure to stay on for third and this was certainly an improvement on his last couple of starts. (op 33-1)

Feared In Flight(IRE), who ran very badly on his handicap debut last time, performed much better off a 3lb lower mark here and he had every chance. He may not be as good as was hoped after his third in last season's Racing Post Trophy and the Sandown Classic Trial, but he is dropping to the sort of handicap mark he can win off. (op 14-1)

Swinging Sixties(IRE), who did too much too soon when stepped up to 1m4f at Goodwood last time, was trying soft ground for the first time here. He was close enough running up the home straight, but lacked a turn of foot and will probably prefer a return to a faster surface. (op 9-1)

Secret Dancer(IRE) ◆, very disappointing when lady amateur-ridden last time after winning on his racecourse debut, was the least exposed in the field. Switched right off out the back early, he plugged on after being switched to the stands' side but was never getting there. This was only his third start though and he is probably still capable of better, especially back on a sound surface. (op 13-2 tchd 11-2)

Filios(IRE), down in trip, had run well on his return from eight months off at Ascot last month and he probably ran a bit better than his fnishing position here would suggest, as he briefly looked dangerous towards the far side of the field passing the 2f pole. He may still have just needed it and is another that may appreciate a return to a quicker surface. (op 7-1 tchd 11-2)

Bolodenka(IRE), whose only previous try over this trip was two years ago, has run well on soft ground before. He had his chance, but did not appear to see out the trip in the ground this time. (op 16-1)

Drill Sergeant, raised 6lb for his Beverley win on soft ground last month when making all, attempting the same tactics here but despite getting the run of the race he did not get home and was already beaten when hampered. (op 4-1)

5831 STATE CLUB H'CAP 6f

4:50 (4:53) (Class 3) (0-90,90) 3-Y-O+ **£9,714** (£2,890; £1,444; £721) **Stalls** High

Form RPR

113 **1** **Main Aim**[50] 4312 3-9-4 90 .... RyanMoore 16 108+
(Sir Michael Stoute) *lw: hld up in rr: hdwy 2f out: sn swtchd lft: rdn and hung lft over 1f out: led ins fnl f: drvn out* **5/1**[1]

0352 **2** *1½* **Gift Horse**[10] 5562 8-8-10 83 .... (p) NeilBrown(3) 18 96
(D Nicholls) *lw: hld up in rr: hdwy wl over 1f out: swtchd rt and rdn to chse wnr ins fnl f: drvn and no imp last 75yds* **12/1**

3404 **3** *3½* **Joseph Henry**[12] 5503 6-9-3 87 .... SilvestreDeSousa 2 89
(D Nicholls) *a.p: effrt 2f out: sn rdn and ev ch tl drvn and one pce jst ins fnl f* **10/1**[3]

3324 **4** *hd* **Grazeon Gold Blend**[13] 5455 5-8-10 80 .... (p) GrahamGibbons 17 81
(J J Quinn) *hld up: hdwy 2f out: rdn and n.m.r over 1f out: kpt on u.p ins fnl f: nrst fin* **20/1**

4112 **5** *nk* **Atlantic Story (USA)**[118] 2172 6-9-6 90 .... (bt) AlanMunro 10 90
(M W Easterby) *a.p: rdn to ld over 1f out: drvn and hdd ins fnl f: wknd* **16/1**

1000 **6** *½* **El Dececy (USA)**[10] 5564 4-8-12 87 .... DavidProbert(5) 8 86
(S Parr) *lw: prom: rdn along 2f out: sn drvn and kpt on same pce appr fnl f* **40/1**

6050 **7** *¾* **Stevie Gee (IRE)**[12] 5503 4-9-3 87 .... (b[1]) RobertWinston 22 83
(G A Swinbank) *trckd ldrs: effrt 2f out: sn rdn and grad wknd appr fnl f* **10/1**[3]

1604 **8** *½* **Wyatt Earp (IRE)**[20] 5247 7-8-11 81 .... (b) JamieMoriarty 12 76
(R A Fahey) *towards rr: hdwy wl over 1f out: rdn and kpt on ins fnl f: nt rch ldrs* **25/1**

0006 **9** *1¾* **Bonnie Prince Blue**[33] 4854 5-8-10 80 .... (b) MichaelHills 20 69
(B W Hills) *lw: hld up in rr: hdwy wl over 1f out: kpt on ins fnl f: n.d* **16/1**

5111 **10** *¾* **Earlsmedic**[20] 5247 3-8-10 82 .... (v) SaleemGolam 1 69
(S C Williams) *in tch: effrt to chse ldrs 2f out: rdn along whn hmpd over 1f out and sn wknd* **8/1**[2]

2104 **11** *¾* **Great Charm (IRE)**[38] 4687 3-9-2 88 .... JamieSpencer 15 72
(M L W Bell) *in tch: rdn along 1/2-way: edgd lft and drvn over 1f out: no imp* **10/1**[3]

5-00 **12** *½* **Majuro (IRE)**[12] 5503 4-9-5 89 .... PaulMulrennan 11 72
(M W Easterby) *s.i.s: a in rr* **33/1**

6001 **13** *¾* **Mister Hardy**[20] 5222 3-8-5 84 .... BMcHugh(7) 13 64
(R A Fahey) *nvr bttr than midfield* **20/1**

3310 **14** *¾* **Total Impact**[12] 5503 5-9-2 86 .... PaulHanagan 6 64
(R A Fahey) *trckd ldrs: effrt 2f out: rdn whn sltly hmpd over 1f out and sn wknd* **20/1**

2500 **15** *½* **Northern Dare (IRE)**[26] 5109 4-9-4 88 .... AdrianTNicholls 21 64
(D Nicholls) *lw: chsd ldrs: rdn along 2f out: sn hung rt and wknd* **8/1**[2]

2060 **16** *¾* **Obe Gold**[41] 4586 6-9-5 89 .... (p) JoeFanning 14 63
(D Nicholls) *hld up towards rr: swtchd wd and hdwy 2f out: sn rdn and wknd over 1f out* **33/1**

160 **17** *1½* **Not My Choice (IRE)**[75] 3472 3-9-0 86 .... (t) FrancisNorton 4 55
(S Parr) *chsd ldrs: rdn along over 2f out: wkng whn sltly hmpd over 1f out* **66/1**

5002 **18** *1½* **The Nifty Fox**[13] 5455 4-8-12 82 .... DavidAllan 9 46
(T D Easterby) *in tch: rdn along over 2f out: sn wknd* **28/1**

0000 **19** *1¾* **Luscivious**[19] 5259 4-9-1 85 .... (b) MartinDwyer 3 44
(A J McCabe) *led: rdn 2f out: drvn and hdd whn hmpd over 1f out: sn wknd* **40/1**

2302 **20** *¾* **Swift Princess (IRE)**[12] 5503 4-9-1 85 .... (v) AndrewElliott 7 41
(K R Burke) *cl up: rdn along over 2f out and sn wknd* **11/1**

000- **21** *8* **Roker Park (IRE)**^{386} 4724 3-9-4 **90**............................ DarrenWilliams 5 21
(K R Burke) *midfield: rdn along over 2f out: sn wknd* **66/1**

1m 14.28s (0.68) **Going Correction** +0.30s/f (Good)
WFA 3 from 4yo+ 2lb **21** Ran SP% **129.3**
Speed ratings (Par 107): **107,105,100,100,99 99,98,97,95,94 93,92,91,90,89 88,86,84,82,81 70**
toteswinger: 1&2 £21.80, 1&3 £10.80, 2&3 £6.30. CSF £56.98 CT £611.24 TOTE £5.80: £2.30, £3.40, £3.00, £5.90; EX 94.40 Trifecta £722.90 Part won. Pool: £977.00 - 0.40 winning units. Place 6: £969.09 Place 5: £30.83.
Owner K Abdulla **Bred** Juddmonte Farms Ltd **Trained** Newmarket, Suffolk

FOCUS
This was a very tight sprint, with 8lb covering the field, and it was very competitive. Not that surprisingly, the main action eventually developed down the centre of the track and the first pair came clear late on. Strong handicap form.

NOTEBOOK
Main Aim ◆ made it three wins from four career starts and did the job in great style, finding an immediate turn of foot once he saw daylight. This was his first run on soft ground and if anything it really suited him over this shorter trip. It will be interesting to see how the handicapper now assesses this effort as he is in the right hands to keep climbing the sprinting ladder. (tchd 11-2)
Gift Horse, just denied in a claimer ten days previously, was travelling as well as any passing the 2f pole but allowed the winner first run. He evidently has his own ideas these days, but the engine evidently remains and he was nicely clear of the remainder. This should put him spot on for the Ayr Gold Cup. (op 14-1)
Joseph Henry ran his usual sort of race and, holding no secrets from the Handicapper, rates the best guide to this form. (op 12-1)
Grazeon Gold Blend, 3lb higher for finishing fourth last time, showed improved form in the first-time cheekpieces and is up to winning from this sort of mark when encountering a sounder surface once again. (op 22-1)
Atlantic Story(USA) ran a very encouraging race on the back of a 118-day break and was not at all disgraced under top weight. He should come on nicely for the outing. (op 18-1)
Earlsmedic was racing from a 6lb higher mark in this quest for the four-timer. He was not allowed to dominate, however, and this would have been his hardest task to date by some way.
Northern Dare(IRE) Official explanation: jockey said gelding hung right
Swift Princess(IRE) Official explanation: jockey said filly lost its action
T/Jkpt: Not won. T/Plt: £634.50 to a £1 stake. Pool: £117,873.88. 135.60 winning tickets. T/Qpdt: £12.40 to a £1 stake. Pool: £10,094.20. 601.50 winning tickets. JR

5626 GREAT LEIGHS (A.W) (L-H)
Thursday, September 11

OFFICIAL GOING: Standard
Wind: virtually nil Weather: overcast

5832 SUDBURY APPRENTICE H'CAP 6f (P)
6:50 (6:53) (Class 6) (0-50,50) 3-Y-O+ **£2,590** (£770; £385; £192) **Stalls** Low

Form RPR
0040 **1** **Piccolo Diamante (USA)**^{24} 5152 4-8-12 **48**...................(t) TolleyDean 4 59
(S Parr) *a.p: rdn to ld wl over 1f: r.o wl* **16/1**
0664 **2** *1 ½* **Charlotte Grey**^{26} 5101 4-8-7 **50**.................................. AndreaAtzeni(7) 3 56
(P J McBride) *chsd ldrs: rdn over 2f out: chsd wnr over 1f out: kpt on but a hld* **3/1**^{1}
0006 **3** *¾* **Peopleton Brook**^{48} 4370 6-8-8 **47**.................................... MCGeran(3) 7 51
(B G Powell) *mid-div: rdn and hdwy fr 2f out: wnt 3rd ent fnl f: styd on* **8/1**^{3}
0 **4** *2 ¼* **Margot Mine (IRE)**^{25} 5119 3-8-12 **50**............................(tp) LukeMorris 5 47
(J S Moore) *sn pushed along in mid-div: styd on fr over 1f out: wnt 4th ins fnl f: nt pce to get on terms* **14/1**
6-56 **5** *nk* **Accolation**^{101} 2664 4-8-5 **46** oh1.............................. AshleyMorgan(5) 14 42
(Pat Eddery) *mid-div: hdwy over 2f out: sn rdn: kpt on same pce fr over 1f out* **10/1**
0000 **6** *1* **Ramblin Bob**^{24} 5162 3-8-3 **48**................................(t) DebraEngland(7) 10 40
(W J Musson) *broke wl: sn settled bhd ldrs: effrt over 2f out: kpt on same pce* **10/1**
1440 **7** *nk* **Mr Loire**^{10} 5582 4-8-9 **50**..........................(b) Louis-PhilippeBeuzelin(5) 13 41
(K G Wingrove) *s.i.s: a towards rr* **14/1**
2041 **8** *1 ½* **Bye Bye Bunting**^{22} 5186 3-8-12 **50**.............................. TravisBlock 11 37
(B R Johnson) *mid -div: effrt 2f out: one pce fnl f* **9/1**
-600 **9** *¾* **Halsion Challenge**^{47} 4409 3-8-3 **46** oh1...........(t) JemmaMarshall(5) 15 30
(J R Best) *a mid-div* **33/1**
4460 **10** *1* **Regal Veil**^{8} 5607 3-8-7 **48**... JackDean(3) 2 29
(R W Price) *v.s.a: a towards rr* **20/1**
0500 **11** *shd* **The Young Fella**^{50} 4301 3-8-12 **50**...............................(v¹) PatrickHills 6 31
(S A Callaghan) *prom: rdn and ev ch 2f out: sn wknd* **5/1**^{2}
0000 **12** *1 ¾* **Talamahana**^{36} 4725 3-8-10 **48**..............................(p) MarcHalford 12 23
(A B Haynes) *sn outpcd: a bhd* **25/1**
3364 **13** *6* **Carmine Rock**^{15} 5395 3-8-12 **50**.................................. RussellKennemore 1 6
(R Hollinshead) *led narrowly after 1f: rdn over 2f out: hdd & wknd over 1f out* **14/1**

1m 13.65s (-0.05) **Going Correction** 0.0s/f (Stan)
WFA 3 from 4yo+ 2lb **13** Ran SP% **118.4**
Speed ratings (Par 101): **100,98,97,94,93 92,91,89,88,87 87,85,77**
toteswinger: 1&2 £11.50, 1&3 £30.00, 2&3 £4.10. CSF £56.40 CT £328.70 TOTE £19.20: £5.80, £1.10, £3.60; EX 77.00.
Owner W Mckay, D Cornan, M Morris, P Reid **Bred** Pamela Linahan **Trained** Bawtry, S Yorks
■ Lost All Alone (8/1) was withdrawn (ducked under stalls, rdr inj). R4 applies, deduct 10p in the £.
■ Stewards' Enquiry : Patrick Hills two-day ban: careless riding (Sept 25-26)

FOCUS
A poor handicap and not much got into it. The winner returned to form with the next two close to their recent turf form.
Carmine Rock Official explanation: vet said filly returned lame

5833 GREAT YELDAM H'CAP 1m 6f (P)
7:20 (7:26) (Class 6) (0-65,65) 3-Y-O+ **£2,590** (£770; £385; £192) **Stalls** Low

Form RPR
6204 **1** **Kritzia**^{24} 5163 3-8-8 **56**.. TedDurcan 1 73+
(H R A Cecil) *trckd ldrs: led over 2f out: sn shkn up to go clr v easily* **9/2**^{1}
5456 **2** *8* **Bienheureux**^{9} 5583 7-9-7 **58**......................................(t) NCallan 10 58
(Miss Gay Kelleway) *hld up towards rr: hdwy whn nt clr run on rails over 2f out: styd on wl fr over 1f out but no ch w wnr* **11/1**
333 **3** *½* **Adage**^{24} 5154 5-9-1 **52**...(t) TravisBlock 14 52
(David Pinder) *hld up bhd: rdn and hdwy on outer fr over 3f out: wnt 2nd briefly ent fnl f but no ch w wnr* **5/1**^{2}
4663 **4** *1 ½* **Compton Falcon**^{24} 5163 4-9-5 **61**............. Louis-PhilippeBeuzelin(5) 15 59
(G A Butler) *hld up bhd: rdn over 2f out: hdwy on outer over 2f out: hung lft but styd on: wnt 4th ins fnl f* **7/1**^{3}
0000 **5** *½* **Black Or Red (IRE)**^{12} 5489 3-8-3 **51**.................(b¹) CatherineGannon 12 48
(I A Wood) *mid-div: lost pl 5f out: rdn whn n.m.r over 2f out: swtchd rt and styd on fr over 1f out* **20/1**
4020 **6** *2 ¾* **Bond Casino**^{7} 5637 4-9-0 **51**.. DanielTudhope 2 44
(G R Oldroyd) *led: rdn and hdd over 2f out: sn no ch w wnr: lost 2nd ent fnl f* **10/1**
1023 **7** *1 ¾* **Hoar Frost**^{42} 4564 3-8-2 **50**....................................... AdrianMcCarthy 16 41
(M R Channon) *mid-div: hdwy over 4f out: effrt over 2f out: one pce after* **20/1**
-125 **8** *shd* **Fantasy Ride**^{29} 4991 6-9-10 **64**................................ JerryO'Dwyer(3) 13 54
(J Pearce) *trckd ldrs: rdn over 2f out: one pce fr over 1f out* **12/1**
6034 **9** *½* **Blur**^{8} 5602 3-8-2 **50** ow1.. HayleyTurner 5 40
(R Hannon) *mid-div: effrt over 2f out: wknd over 1f out* **18/1**
1260 **10** *½* **Prince Of Medina**^{35} 4775 5-8-8 **52**............................ AndreaAtzeni(7) 9 41
(J R Best) *hld up towards rr: sme hdwy on rails over 2f out: nvr trbld ldrs* **20/1**
6260 **11** *10* **Capistrano**^{22} 5183 5-8-9 **46**.. PaulEddery 6 21
(G D Blake) *s.i.s: sn mid-div: rdn over 2f out: wknd over 1f out* **16/1**
0360 **12** *2 ½* **Sonny Sam (IRE)**^{52} 4247 3-8-8 **56**.................................. JimmyQuinn 8 28
(M H Tompkins) *mid-div: rdn over 3f out out: wknd over 1f out* **7/1**^{3}
0235 **13** *4 ½* **Etain (IRE)**^{20} 5232 4-9-13 **64**..(p) RichardMullen 7 29
(W R Swinburn) *trckd ldr tl wl over 2f out: sn rdn: wknd wl over 1f out* **10/1**
56-0 **14** *21* **Stagecoach Emerald**^{24} 5154 6-9-9 **60**....................(tp) SamHitchcott 11 —
(R W Price) *s.i.s: reminders: sn mid-div: rn in snatches tl dropped in rr 3f out: sn lost tch* **20/1**
-000 **15** *42* **Victory Shout (USA)**^{16} 5379 3-7-12 **46**.......................... NickyMackay 4 —
(J R Best) *chsd ldrs: rdn over 6f out: wknd 3f out: sn virtually p.u* **50/1**

3m 2.66s (-0.54) **Going Correction** 0.0s/f (Stan)
WFA 3 from 4yo+ 11lb **15** Ran SP% **126.2**
Speed ratings (Par 101): **101,96,96,95,95 93,92,92,92,91 86,84,82,70,15**
toteswinger: 1&2 £16.50, 1&3 £2.00, 2&3 £24.80. CSF £51.79 CT £267.45 TOTE £5.90: £2.10, £4.20, £2.60; EX 53.90.
Owner Lordship Stud **Bred** Lordship Stud **Trained** Newmarket, Suffolk
■ Stewards' Enquiry : Louis-Philippe Beuzelin caution: careless riding

FOCUS
A moderate race largely contested by exposed stayers, but Kritzia was an exception. She was value for 12l, but it is doubtful if anything else ran to form.
Compton Falcon Official explanation: jockey said gelding hung left

5834 GROTON NURSERY 5f (P)
7:50 (7:54) (Class 5) (0-70,70) 2-Y-O **£3,885** (£1,156; £577; £288) **Stalls** Low

Form RPR
521 **1** **Pressed For Time (IRE)**^{13} 5475 2-8-10 **59**..........(t) EdwardCreighton 7 62
(E J Creighton) *chsd ldrs: rdn to ld jst over 1f out: edgd lft but r.o wl: rdn out* **11/2**^{3}
5615 **2** *1 ¼* **First Choice (IRE)**^{21} 5204 2-9-7 **70**..................................(p) NCallan 4 69
(K A Ryan) *bmpd s: sn chsng ldrs: rdn wl over 2f out: kpt on to go 2nd ins fnl f* **3/1**^{2}
0000 **3** *nk* **Clerical (USA)**^{34} 4828 2-7-8 **50**..............................(p) AndreaAtzeni(7) 6 47+
(M J Gingell) *mid-div: rdn 3f out: edgd lft and r.o fnl f: nvr able to chal* **33/1**
3226 **4** *1* **Red Cell (IRE)**^{6} 5680 2-8-13 **67**...................................(b) MCGeran(5) 8 61
(E J O'Neill) *sn led at decent pce: rdn and hdd jst over 1f out: no ex* **13/2**
0432 **5** *¾* **Turn To Dreams**^{12} 5488 2-8-6 **55**................................ DeanMcKeown 5 46
(P D Evans) *wnt rt s: chsd ldrs: outpcd over 2f out: styd on again fnl f* **15/2**
0415 **6** *½* **Adozen Dreams**^{42} 4558 2-9-2 **65**.................................... DanielTudhope 1 54
(G R Oldroyd) *squeezed out s: outpcd sn after: sme late prog: nvr able to get on terms* **20/1**
640 **7** *½* **Captain Kallis (IRE)**^{77} 3417 2-7-13 **48**..................... FrankieMcDonald 3 36
(D J S Ffrench Davis) *squeezed out s: a towards rr* **25/1**
5055 **8** *½* **Impressible**^{28} 5004 2-9-3 **66**.. ShaneKelly 9 52
(E J Alston) *hld up: rn wd on bnd 3f out: nvr able to get on terms* **15/2**
0502 **9** *nk* **Val De Flores**^{10} 5567 2-8-13 **62**.. LPKeniry 2 47
(E F Vaughan) *sn pushed along: nvr pce to chal: wknd fnl f* **11/4**^{1}

61.36 secs (1.16) **Going Correction** 0.0s/f (Stan) **9** Ran SP% **115.5**
Speed ratings (Par 95): **90,88,87,85,84 83,83,82,81**
toteswinger: 1&2 £4.50, 1&3 £27.00, 2&3 £0.00. CSF £21.84 CT £497.33 TOTE £5.20: £2.00, £1.80, £11.40; EX 24.20.
Owner P Cafferty **Bred** Richard O' Hara **Trained** Mill Hill, London NW7

FOCUS
They went a fast gallop in this modest nursery. The first two were always prominent and the winner was slightly above her recent plating form.

NOTEBOOK
Pressed For Time(IRE) took a while to get off the mark, winning in selling company at Wolverhampton last time (wore first-time tongue tie) and she showed she had speed to burn here. Always well positioned, she hit the front just inside the final furlong and, despite getting a little tired, was always doing enough. She has a bit of size and may well improve again. (op 9-2)
First Choice(IRE) was another to chase the early leader and she deserves some credit, for she looked almost certain to be swallowed up for third just inside the final furlong, but stuck her neck out and kept on well to take second. (tchd 11-4)
Clerical(USA), last from 12lb out of the handicap on his recent nursery debut over 7f at Newmarket, was running off his correct mark here and ran a lot better. The first-time cheekpieces also seemed to help and he may improve for an extra furlong. (op 40-1)
Red Cell(IRE) could not keep up the gallop in the straight and was run out of the places. He is all about speed and is likely to remain vulnerable at the end of his races. (op 5-1)
Turn To Dreams, twice placed at a lower level, kept on at one pace for fifth and it will probably take a return to selling level for her to score. (op 7-1)
Captain Kallis(IRE), making his nursery debut, was squeezed out at the start and proceeded to take a keen hold. He can be given another chance. Official explanation: jockey said colt suffered interference in running (tchd 33-1)
Val De Flores, second off this mark at Kempton last week, was a bit tight for room in the early stages and found herself behind. She made no impression in the straight, but looked a future winner at Kempton and can be given another chance. (op 4-1)

5835 E B F RIVER CROUCH MAIDEN FILLIES' STKS 6f (P)
8:20 (8:22) (Class 4) 2-Y-O **£4,857** (£1,445; £722; £360) **Stalls** Low

Form RPR
1 **Rosy Mantle** 2-9-0 0.. DO'Donohoe 5 74
(W R Muir) *chsd ldrs: rdn wl over 2f out: swtchd rt over 1f out: led ins fnl f: edgd lft: r.o wl* **16/1**

2 2 **Strictly** 2-9-0 0 NCallan 4 68
(Sir Michael Stoute) *chsd ldrs: wnt 2nd over 2f out: sn rdn: led briefly ins fnl f: edgd lft: nt pce of wnr* **10/3[2]**

04 **3** 1 3/4 **Dream Date (IRE)**[6] 5673 2-9-0 0 MichaelHills 11 63+
(W J Haggas) *chsd ldrs: rdn over 2f out: kpt on fnl f* **3/1[1]**

45 **4** nse **Chatterszaha**[31] 4931 2-9-0 0 RobertHavlin 1 64+
(C Drew) *led: edgd lft u.p over 1f out: hdd ins fnl f: no ex* **50/1**

5 3 **Minute Limit (IRE)** 2-9-0 0 ShaneKelly 13 54
(J A Osborne) *s.i.s: sn mid-div: rdn and hdwy over 1f out: no further imp fnl f* **25/1**

0 **6** shd **Romantic Queen**[89] 3027 2-9-0 0 TedDurcan 9 56+
(E A L Dunlop) *mid-div: hdwy 2f out: nt clr run and swtchd twice over 1f out: kpt on: nvr trbld ldrs* **4/1[3]**

7 1 **Beautiful Filly** 2-9-0 0 RichardMullen 3 51
(D M Simcock) *chsd ldrs: rdn over 2f out: one pce fr over 1f out* **5/1**

0 **8** 3/4 **Broughtons Paradis (IRE)**[19] 5271 2-9-0 0 StephenDonohoe 16 48
(W J Musson) *a in mid-div* **50/1**

6 **9** 1 **Princess Rebecca**[45] 4486 2-9-0 0 LPKeniry 2 45
(E F Vaughan) *cl up: rdn over 2f out: wknd fnl f* **50/1**

3 **10** nk **Le Reve Royal**[28] 5004 2-9-0 0 DanielTudhope 7 44+
(G R Oldroyd) *towards rr: sme late prog: nvr a factor* **13/2**

11 hd **Fleuron** 2-9-0 0 TQuinn 14 44+
(D R C Elsworth) *s.i.s: racd green: sme late prog ent fnl f but mainly towards rr* **20/1**

12 nk **Supera (IRE)** 2-9-0 0 JimmyQuinn 12 43
(M H Tompkins) *s.i.s: a towards rr* **50/1**

30 **13** shd **Sensacion Sensual**[16] 5384 2-9-0 0 TPQueally 10 43
(J G Given) *in tch: rdn 3f out: wknd over 1f out* **20/1**

14 hd **Jonah's Cruising (IRE)** 2-9-0 0 ChrisCatlin 6 42
(M J Wallace, Australia) *a towards rr* **33/1**

15 2 **Honestly (USA)** 2-9-0 0 (t) EddieAhern 15 36
(B J Meehan) *mid-div tl wknd 2f out* **14/1**

16 5 **Myttons Maid** 2-9-0 0 MickyFenton 8 21
(A Bailey) *a towards rr* **50/1**

1m 13.59s (-0.11) **Going Correction** 0.0s/f (Stan) **16** Ran SP% **136.7**
Speed ratings (Par 94): **100,97,95,94,90 90,89,88,87,86 86,86,85,85,83 76**
toteswinger: 1&2 £2.20, 1&3 £15.60, 2&3 £3.80. CSF £71.74 TOTE £14.20: £5.50, £2.50, £1.50; EX 48.80.
Owner Foursome Thoroughbreds **Bred** Foursome Thoroughbreds **Trained** Lambourn, Berks

FOCUS
A fair fillies' maiden that was run in a new record time for the distance. Not an easy race to rate accurately.

NOTEBOOK
Rosy Mantle, whose trainer William Muir is hardly renowned for his debut winners, is a half-sister to one who did manage to score at the first time of asking for him, Suki Bear, and she too seemed to know her job. Never too far from the lead, she picked up strongly once switched just over a furlong out and was well on top close home. The Watership Down Stud sales race at Ascot later in the month is her next target. Her trainer thinks a bit of her and she is expected to stay further. (op 10-1)
Strictly, a half-sister to speedy two-year-old Dance Away, knew her job and was soon just in behind the pace travelling strongly. Driven into the lead over a furlong out, she looked the winner, but could find no extra when Rosy Mantle came alongside. This was a pleasing start and she should be able to win an ordinary maiden. (op 2-1)
Dream Date(IRE) fared best of those with experience and now looks ready for a step up to 7f. Having her second run in a week, she could not match the front pair, but was trapped wide throughout and will certainly have more to give in nurseries. (op 5-1)
Chatterszaha set a decent gallop on this first crack at 6f and was still in front a furlong and a half out, but could find no extra. This was a fair effort against classier types and she too should find a race in nurseries. (op 40-1)
Minute Limit(IRE), a 90,000gns daughter of Pivotal, comes from a yard that has endured a tough year and she was always going to do well to figure from her high draw. She stayed on nicely without being given anything like a hard time, just grabbing fifth, and will be of obvious interest for a similar race. (op 28-1)
Romantic Queen has twice come up short of market expectations and perhaps the best of her will be seen in handicaps over further. (op 8-1)
Beautiful Filly, a 60,000gns daughter of Oasis Dream, was up there early, but came under pressure from the end of the back straight and gradually faded. (op 12-1)
Le Reve Royal Official explanation: jockey said filly was hampered leaving stalls
Fleuron, a half-sister to a couple of smart performers, was slowly into stride, but put in some good late work and should know more next time.

5836 EASTWICK H'CAP — 1m (P)
8:50 (8:57) (Class 5) (0-70,75) 3-Y-O — £3,885 (£1,156; £577; £288) Stalls Centre

Form — RPR

4422 **1** **Jollyhockeysticks**[20] 5218 3-8-12 **64** SamHitchcott 11 71
(M R Channon) *mid-div on outer: rdn over 4f out: r.o strly ent fnl f: led nr fin* **10/1**

2161 **2** hd **Mahadee (IRE)**[9] 5595 3-9-9 **75** 6ex (b) NCallan 8 82
(C E Brittain) *trckd ldrs: rdn over 2f out: kpt on to ld wl ins fnl f: hdd nr fin* **4/1[1]**

6364 **3** nse **Sir Ike (IRE)**[47] 4412 3-8-8 **60** (t) ShaneKelly 16 67
(W S Kittow) *hld up towards rr: swtchd rt wl over 1f out: sn rdn and hung lft: r.o fnl f: fin wl* **25/1**

5210 **4** 1 1/4 **Sabre Light**[36] 4721 3-9-4 **70** MickyFenton 5 74
(A Bailey) *in tch: rdn over 2f out: ch enetering fnl f: kpt on* **20/1**

6342 **5** 1/2 **Admirals Way**[18] 5312 3-8-6 **58** JimmyQuinn 2 61
(C N Kellett) *led: rdn 2f out: hdd wl ins fnl f: no ex* **8/1[3]**

330 **6** 1/2 **Saintly Gaze**[31] 4929 3-8-13 **65** AdamKirby 7 67
(W R Swinburn) *mid-div: rdn and hdwy fr 2f out: hung rt and no ex ins fnl f* **16/1**

050 **7** 1/2 **Mischief Lady**[29] 4987 3-9-0 **66** EddieAhern 13 67
(E A L Dunlop) *hld up towards rr: swtchd lft and styd on fr over 1f out: nt rch ldrs* **12/1**

0253 **8** 2 **Dream Of Olwyn (IRE)**[16] 5378 3-8-11 **63** TPQueally 10 65+
(J G Given) *w ldr: rdn over 2f out: disputing cl 3rd whn squeezed out ins fnl f: no ch after* **16/1**

2103 **9** 1/2 **Loveinanelevator**[35] 4795 3-9-3 **69** HayleyTurner 3 64
(M L W Bell) *mid-div: effrt on rails over 1f out: one pce fnl f* **11/2[2]**

5-00 **10** 1/2 **Double Duty (IRE)**[70] 3628 3-8-7 **59** ow1 (b[1]) RobertHavlin 14 53
(B J Meehan) *mid-div: rdn over 2f out: wknd fnl f* **33/1**

2040 **11** 3/4 **Sheer Bluff (IRE)**[36] 4745 3-9-1 **67** TQuinn 6 59
(D R C Elsworth) *t.k.h: in tch whn snatched up after 1f: rdn over 2f out: wknd fnl f* **14/1**

2632 **12** 1 1/4 **Ride A White Swan**[16] 5378 3-8-12 **64** TonyCulhane 1 53
(D Shaw) *t.k.h in rr: nt clr run 3f out: sn rdn: no imp fr 2f out* **9/1**

0400 **13** 1/2 **Bookiebasher Babe (IRE)**[18] 5317 3-9-0 **66** ChrisCatlin 12 54
(M Quinn) *chsd ldrs: rdn 3f out: wknd over 1f out* **16/1**

-416 **14** 41 **Longevity**[104] 2563 3-9-4 **70** J-PGuillambert 9 —
(W Jarvis) *wnt rt and stmbld leaving stalls: sn mid-div: rdn 5f out: wknd 3f out: virtually p.u* **11/2[2]**

1m 40.74s (0.84) **Going Correction** 0.0s/f (Stan) **14** Ran SP% **124.5**
Speed ratings (Par 101): **95,94,94,93,93 92,92,90,89,89 88,87,86,37**
toteswinger: 1&2 £9.80, 1&3 £43.40, 2&3 £0.00. CSF £50.28 CT £1038.84 TOTE £7.70: £2.00, £1.80, £9.10; EX 59.70.
Owner J P Coggan **Bred** J P Coggan **Trained** West Ilsley, Berks

FOCUS
A modest handicap and the form is muddling with something of a bunch finish. The winner probably only had to match her recent form.
Sheer Bluff(IRE) Official explanation: jockey said gelding suffered interference in running
Ride A White Swan Official explanation: jockey said gelding ran too free
Longevity Official explanation: jockey said colt stumbled in stalls; vet said colt returned lame

5837 WALTHAM ABBEY CLASSIFIED STKS — 1m 2f (P)
9:20 (9:26) (Class 6) 3-Y-O+ — £2,729 (£806; £403) Stalls Low

Form — RPR

6356 **1** **Valdan (IRE)**[38] 4679 4-9-4 55 DeanMcKeown 12 63
(P D Evans) *cl up: led 2f out: sn rdn: styd on strly: comf* **5/1[2]**

0004 **2** 2 1/4 **Sunny Spells**[23] 5168 3-8-11 52 SaleemGolam 13 59
(S C Williams) *mid-div: hdwy 3f out: sn rdn: styd on fr over 1f out: wnt 2nd ins fnl f* **11/1**

6353 **3** 2 3/4 **Ready To Crown (USA)**[120] 2100 4-9-4 53 ChrisCatlin 8 53
(Andrew Turnell) *trckd ldrs: nt clr run briefly over 2f out: sn rdn to chse wnr: kpt on same pce: lost 2nd ins fnl f* **11/4[1]**

-550 **4** 1 1/2 **Stand Guard**[181] 879 4-9-4 53 TonyCulhane 7 50+
(P Howling) *hld up bhd: making gd hdwy whn nt clr run and snatched up over 2f out: styd on but no ch after: wnt 4th ins fnl f* **14/1**

500 **5** 3/4 **High Coincidence**[69] 3694 3-8-11 54 AlanDaly 16 49
(Andrew Turnell) *reminders and sn in tch on outer: reminders 5f out: rdn over 3f out: kpt on same pce fnl 2f* **20/1**

0002 **6** 4 **Rockjumper**[34] 4807 3-8-8 55 EmmettStack(3) 4 41
(H Morrison) *trckd ldrs: led 3f out: rdn and hdd 2f out: wknd 1f out* **9/1**

5300 **7** 3/4 **Bobal Girl**[34] 4810 3-8-4 55 AndreaAtzeni(7) 6 39
(E F Vaughan) *hld up towards rr: rdn and sme hdwy2f out: no further imp* **16/1**

0600 **8** 1 1/2 **Magpie (IRE)**[13] 5458 3-8-11 55 TQuinn 5 36
(B G Powell) *hld up bhd: hdwy and swtchd rt 2f out: sn rdn and hung lft: no further imp* **25/1**

060- **9** 12 **Stateside (CAN)**[393] 4487 3-8-11 52 TonyHamilton 3 12
(R A Fahey) *mid-div tl wknd 2f out* **16/1**

000- **10** 3 3/4 **Up The Chimney**[351] 5738 4-9-4 54 ShaneKelly 9 5
(A P Jarvis) *a towards rr* **33/1**

0000 **11** 4 1/2 **Rumline**[16] 5378 3-8-11 52 StephenDonohoe 1 —
(S A Callaghan) *led tl 3f out: grad fdd* **20/1**

4556 **12** 4 **Defies Logic**[12] 5505 3-8-11 55 TPQueally 15 —
(J G Given) *trckd ldrs: rdn 3f out: wknd 2f out* **9/1**

0605 **13** 5 **Sleeping**[35] 4795 3-8-11 55 JimmyQuinn 10 —
(M H Tompkins) *a towards rr* **16/1**

0004 **14** 20 **Lady Petrus**[35] 4774 3-8-11 54 NCallan 14 —
(H J L Dunlop) *mid-div tl 3f out: sn bhd* **7/1[3]**

2m 7.05s (-1.55) **Going Correction** 0.0s/f (Stan)
WFA 3 from 4yo 7lb **14** Ran SP% **124.8**
Speed ratings (Par 101): **106,103,102,100,100 97,96,95,85,82 79,75,71,55**
toteswinger: 1&2 £0.00, 1&3 £5.60, 2&3 £9.90. CSF £58.34 TOTE £9.00: £4.40, £4.20, £2.20; EX 69.00 Place 6: £62.46 Place 5: £31.13 .
Owner D Maloney **Bred** Herbertstown Stud Ltd **Trained** Pandy, Monmouths

FOCUS
A weak event run at just a steady gallop with the winner the best guide to the form.
T/Plt: £33.60 to a £1 stake. Pool: £107,125.04. 2,327.01 winning tickets. T/Qpdt: £12.30 to a £1 stake. Pool: £7,887.68. 470.94 winning tickets. TM

5506 SANDOWN (R-H)
Thursday, September 11

OFFICIAL GOING: Soft (good to soft in places on round course; heavy in places on sprint course; round 6.8; sprint 6.0)
Wind: Light, half against Weather: Cloudy becoming bright

5838 SODEXO PRESTIGE MEDIAN AUCTION MAIDEN FILLIES' STKS — 5f 6y
2:20 (2:21) (Class 5) 2-Y-O — £3,885 (£1,156; £577; £288) Stalls High

Form — RPR

0 **1** **Top Town Girl**[26] 5097 2-9-0 0 RichardKingscote 1 83
(R M Beckett) *trckd ldng pair in centre: prog to ld gp 2f out and overall ldr over 1f out: drvn out* **12/1**

023 **2** 1 3/4 **Aahaygirl (IRE)**[13] 5448 2-9-0 84 NCallan 6 76+
(K R Burke) *overall ldr against far side rail: rdn 1/2-way: hdd over 1f out: plugged on* **11/10[1]**

5 **3** 3/4 **Intikama (IRE)**[35] 4792 2-9-0 0 JimmyQuinn 5 74
(M H Tompkins) *dwlt: sn swtchd to centre and last of gp: effrt 2f out: wnt 3rd fnl f: kpt on* **6/1[3]**

063 **4** 3 1/4 **Inthawain**[15] 5394 2-9-0 69 DarryllHolland 3 62+
(M R Channon) *led gp of 4 in centre: hdd u.p 1/2-way: sn btn* **8/1**

020 **5** nse **Always There (IRE)**[20] 5214 2-9-0 65 EddieAhern 2 62
(R Hannon) *chsd ldr in centre: led gp 1/2-way to 2f out: wknd rapidly fnl f* **11/2[2]**

5 **6** 15 **Swiss Lake Sweetie (USA)**[15] 5394 2-9-0 0 DO'Donohoe 4 8+
(George Baker) *trckd ldr far side: wknd rapidly 2f out: virtually p.u fnl f* **7/1**

66.79 secs (5.19) **Going Correction** +0.85s/f (Soft) **6** Ran SP% **108.6**
Speed ratings (Par 92): **92,89,88,82,82 58**
toteswinger: 1&2 £4.30, 1&3 £9.10, 2&3 £2.20. CSF £24.33 TOTE £18.30: £6.80, £1.30; EX 36.50.
Owner Landmark Racing Limited **Bred** Lady Whent, Mrs B Burchett & R Hannon **Trained** Whitsbury, Hants

FOCUS
A reasonable juvenile fillies' maiden, despite the small field. The winning time was 1.35 seconds slower than the following 71-85 handicap for three-year-olds. They split into two groups early, with the eventual second and sixth racing against the far rail, whilst the majority raced more up the middle. However, they merged as one in the closing stages. The favourite was a little below form so it is possible the winner could be flattered.

NOTEBOOK

Top Town Girl ◆ did not show much first time up over 6f at Newbury, but she clearly learnt plenty from that and produced a much improved performance, taking this in tidy fashion. It might be that she was at an advantage in racing closest to the near side but this was still a likeable effort. She relished the conditions and will be worthy of respect in better company when there is give underfoot. \n\x\x \bAahaygirl\p should not have minded the ground, but she might have been at a disadvantage in racing towards the far side and the only filly to take that route finished tailed off. She probably ran a little way below her official mark of 84, and that rating looks high enough, but she ought to find a weak race at some point, possibly back up north. (tchd 14-1)

Aahaygirl(IRE) should not have minded the ground, but she might have been at a disadvantage in racing towards the far side and the only filly to take that route finished tailed off. She probably ran a little way below her official mark of 84, and that rating looks high enough, but she ought to find a weak race at some point, possibly back up north. (op evens tchd 5-4)

Intikama(IRE), well backed, improved on the form she showed on her debut over 6f at Yarmouth, but still looked a little green and gave the impression she will be suited by a step back up in trip. (op 10-1 tchd 11-1)

Inthawain failed to pick up and may have been unsuited by the testing ground. (op 10-1 tchd 15-2)

Always There(IRE) showed she handles these sort of conditions when runner-up over course and distance two starts previously, but although attracting strong market support she proved disappointing this time. (op 7-1)

Swiss Lake Sweetie(USA) really caught the eye when fifth in an ordinary maiden at Catterick on her debut, but having been easy to back this time she failed to confirm that promise and appeared totally unsuited by the soft ground. She broke much better on this occasion and travelled enthusiastically towards the far side, but she looked ill at ease when coming off the bridle and was heavily eased inside the final furlong. (op 7-2)

5839 SODEXO PRESTIGE H'CAP — 5f 6y

2:55 (2:55) (Class 4) (0-85,82) 3-Y-O — **£6,476** (£1,927; £963; £481) **Stalls** High

Form — RPR

4121 **1** **Pretty Bonnie**[12] 5490 3-8-9 **78** ... NataliaGemelova(5) 3 — 86
(A E Price) *led: rdn 2f out: hdd over 1f out: rallied to ld again ins fnl f* **7/2**[2]

1155 **2** *nk* **Billion Dollar Kid**[12] 5490 3-9-1 **82** ... (t) KevinGhunowa(3) 4 — 89
(R A Harris) *cl up: led over 1f out: urged along and carried hd high: hdd and nt qckn ins fnl f* **9/2**

103 **3** *1* **Tadalavil**[12] 5510 3-8-10 **74** ... DarryllHolland 1 — 77
(M R Channon) *cl up: rdn and nt qckn 2f out: kpt on fnl f but nvr able to chal* **6/4**[1]

1512 **4** *2* **Superduper**[18] 5310 3-9-4 **82** ... EddieAhern 2 — 78
(R Hannon) *cl up to 1/2-way: hanging and struggling wl over 1f out: nt on terms after* **4/1**[3]

-030 **5** *½* **Really Really Wish**[12] 5493 3-8-4 **68** ... JimmyQuinn 5 — 62
(J R Best) *mostly last: hrd rdn and effrt 2f out: no prog 1f out: fdd* **10/1**

65.45 secs (3.85) **Going Correction** +0.85s/f (Soft) — **5** Ran SP% **109.5**
Speed ratings (Par 103): **103,102,100,97,96**
CSF £18.46 TOTE £4.90: £2.10, £1.80; EX 19.60.

Owner N Field **Bred** P And Mrs A G Venner & Alpha Bloodstock Ltd **Trained** Leominster, H'fords

■ Stewards' Enquiry : Natalia Gemelova caution: used whip with excessive frequency

FOCUS

Only five runners for this three-year-old sprint handicap, but it looked a fair enough contest. They raced up the middle of the track and the winning time was 1.35 seconds quicker than the previous juvenile fillies' maiden. Another improved run from Pretty Bonnie.

5840 FAUCETS FOR HANSGROHE FORTUNE STKS (LISTED RACE) — 7f 16y

3:30 (3:30) (Class 1) 3-Y-O+ — **£22,708** (£8,608; £4,308; £2,148; £1,076) **Stalls** High

Form — RPR

-123 **1** **Atlantic Sport (USA)**[40] 4622 3-8-12 105 ... EdwardCreighton 3 — 109
(M R Channon) *hld up in 4th: rousted along and effrt over 2f out: led over 1f out: gained upper hand ins fnl f* **9/4**[2]

2221 **2** *1 ¼* **Dijeerr (USA)**[40] 4644 4-9-2 109 ... (v) TedDurcan 6 — 107
(Saeed Bin Suroor) *led: hdd and nt qckn u.p 2f out: kpt on fnl f to take 2nd fnl stride* **7/4**[1]

21-1 **3** *nse* **Icelandic**[17] 5368 6-9-2 0 ... (t) MDemuro 7 — 107
(Frank Sheridan) *std s: hld up in last: effrt over 2f out: drvn to chal ent fnl f: sn hld: lost 2nd last stride* **7/1**

1625 **4** *2 ¾* **Damika (IRE)**[19] 5275 5-9-2 105 ... JimCrowley 5 — 99
(R M Whitaker) *cl up: rdn to ld 2f out: hdd over 1f out: wknd fnl f* **5/1**[3]

1040 **5** *shd* **Captain Marvelous (IRE)**[61] 3946 4-9-5 104 ... NCallan 4 — 102
(B W Hills) *mostly trckd ldr to over 2f out: sn lost pl u.p* **13/2**

1m 32.48s (2.98) **Going Correction** +0.475s/f (Yiel)
WFA 3 from 4yo+ 4lb — **5** Ran SP% **109.6**
Speed ratings (Par 111): **101,99,99,96,96**
toteswinger: 1&2 £3.50. CSF £6.54 TOTE £3.00: £1.80, £1.40; EX 6.00.

Owner Jaber Abdullah **Bred** Gainsborough Farm Llc **Trained** West Ilsley, Berks

FOCUS

Just the five runners and this was an ordinary Listed contest for the grade and not form to be too positive about. The early pace was just ordinary, but the winning time was 1.28 seconds quicker than the following 71-85 handicap for three-year-olds. They raced towards the near side in the straight, but the best ground looked to be off the rail, more towards the middle.

NOTEBOOK

Atlantic Sport(USA) is really well regarded and it looks as though he is now getting his act together judged by the way he knuckled down in the relative sprint to the line. He has plenty of speed, so the modest gallop would not have inconvenienced him too much and he picked up well having raced off the leaders through the early stages. He looked to find 1m stretching his stamina when third in a Listed race at Goodwood last time, so the trip and the ground, the softest he has encountered to date, were absolutely fine. This was only his sixth career start and Edward Creighton is of the opinion he is still improving. It would be fascinating to see him dropped back to 6f at some point. (op 3-1)

Dijeerr(USA), although able to set an ordinary pace, was pestered by the free-running Captain Marvelous and failed to pick up immediately when asked for his effort in the straight. He just looked swamped for speed when the race got serious and might be happier back over further. (op 13-8 tchd 6-4)

Icelandic, who landed a decent conditions contest on similar ground at Warwick on his British debut, ran well in this tougher heat. Having been held up off the ordinary pace, he was produced with his effort out widest in the straight, which looked the place to be, and only just lost second. It transpired he had lost a shoe at the start and pulled up lame afterwards, so he was perhaps unlucky not to go even closer. (op 5-1 tchd 9-2)

Damika(IRE) had the ground to suit but was below par and all his best form has come in double-figure fields. (op 11-2 tchd 6-1 in places)

Captain Marvelous(IRE) was too keen for his own good and might not have been on the best ground when taken to the stands' rail in the straight. (op 8-1 tchd 17-2)

5841 FOR A QUALITY BETTING EXPERIENCE CHOOSE BETTER H'CAP — 7f 16y

4:05 (4:07) (Class 4) (0-85,84) 3-Y-O — **£6,476** (£1,927; £963; £481) **Stalls** High

Form — RPR

5012 **1** **Myanmar (IRE)**[29] 4989 3-8-9 **75** ... ShaneKelly 5 — 80
(J Noseda) *prog fr rr into midfield 1/2-way: rdn over 2f out and styd in centre: clsng whn hung lft ent fnl f: r.o to ld last 100yds* **11/4**[1]

6002 **2** *1* **Jeninsky (USA)**[29] 4983 3-9-4 **84** ... JimmyQuinn 1 — 86
(Rae Guest) *hld up towards rr but wl in tch: prog over 2f out on nr side: rdn to ld over 1f out: hdd fnl 100yds: jst hld on for 2nd* **9/1**

015 **3** *hd* **Amber Queen (IRE)**[34] 4818 3-9-0 **80** ... NCallan 3 — 82
(B W Hills) *t.k.h early: cl up: effrt to chal over 1f out: nt qckn ent fnl f: kpt on again nr fin* **4/1**[2]

0000 **4** *shd* **Eastern Gift**[5] 5697 3-9-0 **83** ... PatrickHills(3) 8 — 84
(R Hannon) *t.k.h early: trckd ldrs: rdn and effrt over 2f out: kpt on u.p fnl f: nvr quite able to chal* **16/1**

4322 **5** *3 ¼* **All In The Red (IRE)**[17] 5345 3-8-4 **73** ow3 ... (b) KevinGhunowa(3) 6 — 69+
(Miss Gay Kelleway) *prom: styd in centre st: almost on terms 2f out: drvn and looked hld whn bmpd ent fnl f* **4/1**[2]

3110 **6** *shd* **Stand In Flames**[10] 5580 3-9-0 **80** ... DarryllHolland 11 — 72
(Pat Eddery) *racd freely in ld: c to nr side in st: hdd & wknd over 1f out* **17/2**

0100 **7** *1* **Benedetto**[10] 5580 3-8-9 **75** ... (p) JimCrowley 4 — 65
(Mrs A J Perrett) *settled in rr: rdn and no imp on ldrs over 2f out: btn after* **25/1**

00-0 **8** *3 ½* **Captain Royale (IRE)**[15] 5403 3-9-0 **80** ... TedDurcan 7 — 60
(J Noseda) *dwlt: plld hrd early: hld up in last: rdn and struggling 3f out: n.d after* **16/1**

5331 **9** *1 ¾* **Shindy (FR)**[18] 5317 3-8-6 **72** ... EddieAhern 10 — 70+
(J A R Toller) *mostly chsd ldr to 3f out: styd in centre in st: renewed effrt and trying to cl whn knocked sideways ent fnl f: eased* **8/1**[3]

1020 **10** *8* **Mister New York (USA)**[15] 5403 3-9-0 **80** ... JamesDoyle 9 — 34
(Noel T Chance) *in tch in rr tl wknd rapidly jst over 2f out* **33/1**

1m 33.76s (4.26) **Going Correction** +0.475s/f (Yiel) — **10** Ran SP% **116.9**
Speed ratings (Par 103): **94,92,92,92,88 88,87,83,81,72**
toteswinger: 1&2 £4.70, 1&3 £3.10, 2&3 £9.60. CSF £28.69 CT £96.30 TOTE £3.90: £1.30, £2.50, £1.80; EX 27.10.

Owner D Smith, Mrs J Magnier, M Tabor **Bred** Mrs Jacqueline Donnelly **Trained** Newmarket, Suffolk

FOCUS

A fair handicap run in a time 1.28sec slower than the earlier Listed race. Once again they came towards the stands' side in the straight, although the winner raced towards the outside of the bunch more towards the centre of the track. The unexposed winner is rated to form.

Shindy(FR) Official explanation: jockey said filly suffered interference in running

5842 SODEXO PRESTIGE E B F MAIDEN STKS — 1m 14y

4:40 (4:44) (Class 4) 2-Y-O — **£5,180** (£1,541; £770; £384) **Stalls** High

Form — RPR

0 **1** **Classic Vintage (USA)**[13] 5468 2-9-3 0 ... JimCrowley 4 — 82
(Mrs A J Perrett) *hld up bhd ldrs: prog on outer fr 2f out: chal 1f out: rdn to ld last 75yds* **20/1**

2 *½* **Montaff** 2-9-3 0 ... EdwardCreighton 9 — 81
(M R Channon) *hld up in midfield: prog on wd outside over 2f out: narrow ld over 1f out: hdd and hld last 75yds* **16/1**

03 **3** *1 ¾* **Khan Tengri (IRE)**[35] 4788 2-9-3 0 ... NCallan 8 — 77
(M P Tregoning) *sn trckd ldr: led 2f out and tried to kick on: hdd and nt qckn over 1f out* **3/1**[2]

0 **4** *1 ¼* **King Of Wands**[34] 4826 2-9-3 0 ... EddieAhern 7 — 74+
(J L Dunlop) *cl up: pushed along and no imp 2f out: kpt on one pce fnl f* **6/4**[1]

0 **5** *shd* **Takaatuf (IRE)**[103] 2592 2-9-3 0 ... DarryllHolland 2 — 74+
(M Johnston) *trckd ldrs: shkn up over 2f out: sn nt qckn and hld: plugged on* **7/1**[3]

0 **6** *4 ½* **Gtaab**[13] 5468 2-9-3 0 ... TedDurcan 3 — 64
(E A L Dunlop) *rn in snatches in midfield: stl in tch 2f out: sn wknd* **25/1**

7 *1 ½* **Directorship** 2-9-3 0 ... JimmyQuinn 5 — 61+
(P R Chamings) *reluctant to enter stalls: s.i.s: hld up in last pair: lft bhd fr 3f out: pushed along and kpt on steadily* **50/1**

50 **8** *1 ¾* **Andean Margin (IRE)**[15] 5404 2-9-3 0 ... OscarUrbina 12 — 57
(S A Callaghan) *hld up in rr gp: shkn up 3f out: no prog* **50/1**

0 **9** *½* **Recession Proof (FR)**[20] 5246 2-9-3 0 ... StephenDonohoe 11 — 56
(S A Callaghan) *a in rr gp: lft bhd fr 3f out* **66/1**

05 **10** *1* **Flashgun (USA)**[18] 5314 2-9-3 0 ... ShaneKelly 6 — 54
(M G Quinlan) *sn led and set modest pce: hdd & wknd rapidly 2f out* **16/1**

00 **11** *4* **Achromatic**[32] 4890 2-9-3 0 ... AdamKirby 10 — 45
(W R Swinburn) *a in rr gp: pushed along and lft bhd fr over 2f out: wknd over 1f out* **9/1**

1m 50.39s (7.09) **Going Correction** +0.475s/f (Yiel) — **11** Ran SP% **113.3**
Speed ratings (Par 97): **83,82,80,79,79 74,73,71,71,70 66**
toteswinger: 1&2 £24.30, 1&3 £12.70, 2&3 £4.30. CSF £279.84 TOTE £26.80: £4.50, £2.30, £1.40; EX 230.00.

Owner R & P Scott A & J Powell Gallagher Stud **Bred** Gallagher's Stud **Trained** Pulborough, W Sussex

FOCUS

Although some of these will improve this was probably an ordinary maiden by Sandown's standards and the form needs to be treated with caution, as the first two looked to be on the best ground up the middle of the track in the straight, whereas the majority were taken towards the stands' side. In addition the early pace was noticeably steady. The winning time was very slow, even allowing for the conditions.

NOTEBOOK

Classic Vintage(USA) was well held in a better race than this over 7f on his debut, but he had clearly learnt from that and handled the testing ground well to provide his trainer with her third winner in this race since 2002. Along with the runner-up, he was probably racing on the best ground, but he is obviously open to more improvement and should make a nice three-year-old.

Montaff ◆, a son of Montjeu, half-brother to a dual sprint juvenile winner, out of a triple 7f winner at two and three who was also fairly useful at 1m2f, has been entered in the Racing Post Trophy and ran a big race on his debut. He briefly looked the winner when brought out wide with his effort in the straight, but he was just pegged back by a rival who had the benefit of previous racecourse experience. Even though he was probably racing on the best ground, he showed enough to suggest he can win a maiden before trying something better. (op 20-1)

Khan Tengri(IRE), although not as wide as the first two, was still some way off the near rail and had his chance. He had shown ability when third over course and distance on his previous start and this was another solid effort. He now has the option of nurseries. (op 15-8)

King Of Wands ◆ was bumped at the top of the straight and still looked green, but he kept on in pleasing fashion. This Racing Post Trophy entrant showed ability on his debut over 7f at Newmarket and should make a nice horse over middle-distances next season. (op 2-1 tchd 9-4 and 5-2 in a place)
Takaatuf(IRE), upped from 6f, could not sustain his effort but very much gave the impression he will come on again for the experience. (op 8-1 tchd 9-1)
Gtaab, Hamdan Al Maktoum's second string, improved on his debut effort but was still beaten a long way. (op 33-1)
Directorship made a satisfactory debut on ground that his breeding suggested would suit. (op 40-1)
Andean Margin(IRE) should do better back on a quicker surface now he is qualified for a handicap mark.

5843 SODEXO PRESTIGE AT SANDOWN PARK H'CAP — 1m 2f 7y

5:10 (5:15) (Class 3) (0-90,89) 3-Y-O+ **£7,771** (£2,312; £1,155; £577) **Stalls High**

Form — RPR

2622 **1** **Redesignation (IRE)**[40] 4642 3-9-4 **88** .... JimCrowley 1 98
(R Hannon) *trckd ldrs: effrt over 2f out: drvn to chal over 1f out: pressed ldr ins fnl f: led fnl stride* **7/1**[3]

0335 **2** *nse* **Dar Es Salaam**[15] 5391 4-8-11 **74** oh4 .... JimmyQuinn 12 84
(J S Goldie) *t.k.h early: wl in tch: effrt 2f out: disp ld jst over 1f out: narrow advantage ins fnl f: hdd post* **20/1**

6013 **3** *1* **Howdigo**[43] 4519 3-8-11 **81** .... RichardKingscote 9 89
(J R Best) *hld up towards rr: prog on wd outside fr 3f out: rdn to dispute ld jst over 1f out: nt qckn ins fnl f* **9/2**[1]

0265 **4** *½* **Eglevski (IRE)**[16] 5382 4-9-4 **81** ....(b) EddieAhern 3 88
(J L Dunlop) *t.k.h early: hld up towards rr: effrt over 2f out: styd on to press ldrs ins fnl f: hld whn short of room nr fin* **8/1**

5222 **5** *1* **Show Winner**[36] 4726 5-9-5 **82** .... NCallan 11 87
(A M Balding) *t.k.h early: in ldng trio: led over 2f out: hdd and fdd jst over 1f out* **5/1**[2]

-010 **6** *2 ½* **Bee Sting**[19] 5279 4-9-11 **88** ....(v[1]) AdamKirby 6 88
(W R Swinburn) *ldng trio: hrd rdn to chal over 2f out: rdr dropped whip wl over 1f out: wknd fnl f* **10/1**

0-30 **7** *½* **Killena Boy (IRE)**[27] 5051 6-9-1 **83** .... JPHamblett(5) 10 82
(W Jarvis) *hld up in midfield: prog over 4f out: pressed ldrs over 2f out: grad wknd towards nr side over 1f out* **8/1**

1026 **8** *½* **Conquisto**[19] 5257 3-9-5 **89** .... TedDurcan 4 87
(C G Cox) *hld up in rr: effrt on outer 3f out: drvn and nt qckn 2f out: wl hld after* **9/2**[1]

4424 **9** *12* **Vicious Warrior**[15] 5391 9-8-12 **75** .... DeanMcKeown 7 49
(R M Whitaker) *mde most at decent pce to over 2f out: wknd rapidly* **11/1**

20-0 **10** *16* **Gremlin**[19] 5279 4-9-5 **82** .... ShaneKelly 2 24
(A King) *a in last pair: bhd over 3f out: t.o* **16/1**

05-0 **11** *8* **Monreale (GER)**[19] 5279 4-9-10 **87** .... VinceSlattery 8 13
(G Brown) *a in rr: wl bhd over 3f out: t.o* **66/1**

2m 13.4s (2.90) **Going Correction** +0.475s/f (Yiel)
WFA 3 from 4yo+ 7lb **11** Ran SP% **117.3**
Speed ratings (Par 107): **107,106,106,105,104 102,102,102,92,79 73**
toteswinger: 1&2 £18.80, 1&3 £5.20, 2&3 £18.50. CSF £136.65 CT £702.05 TOTE £6.60: £2.50, £5.10, £2.10; EX 120.70 Place 6: £65.90 Place 5: £46.86 .
Owner Fergus Jones **Bred** D G Iceton **Trained** East Everleigh, Wilts

FOCUS
A decent handicap, and sound form despite the runner-up being 4lb wrong. They raced up the middle for much of the straight, but ended up towards the stands' side.

NOTEBOOK
Redesignation(IRE) had never previously raced on ground this soft, but he handled the conditions well and narrowly gained a deserved victory following some good efforts in defeat. He is quite versatile and should remain competitive off higher marks. (op 11-2 tchd 9-2)
Dar Es Salaam has not always convinced on this sort of ground, but he handled the conditions and was just denied from 4lb out of the handicap. His connections will probably want to get him out off his correct mark before he is reassessed. (op 16-1)
Howdigo made his move out widest and kept on well for pressure, but he just found a couple too strong. He is holding his form well. (op 11-2 tchd 6-1)
Eglevski(IRE) looked a little unlucky as he was continually denied a clear run in the straight, although it was probably a case that he was simply unable to muster the required speed to take some tight gaps. His jockey had to stop riding late on, although by that time the damage was already done. (op 10-1)
Show Winner had the ground to suit for his return to turf, but he was a little keen early and could not sustain his effort. (tchd 4-1)
Conquisto looked to have conditions to suit, but he was well held off a mark 6lb higher than when a close second in a similar event over course and distance two starts back. (op 15-2)
T/Plt: £39.30 to a £1 stake. Pool: £52,906.77. 981.98 winning tickets. T/Qpdt: £6.00 to a £1 stake. Pool: £3,557.90. 435.50 winning tickets. JN

5844 - 5849a (Foreign Racing) - See Raceform Interactive

[5622] CHANTILLY (R-H)

Thursday, September 11

OFFICIAL GOING: Good

5850a PRIX D'ARENBERG (GROUP 3) — 5f 110y

1:20 (1:20) 2-Y-O **£29,412** (£11,765; £8,824; £5,882; £2,941)

RPR

1 **Triple Aspect (IRE)**[12] 5487 2-8-11 .... LiamJones 3 105
(W J Haggas) *cl up on ins: 4th 1/2-way: chal 2f out: led over 1 1/2f out: drvn and r.o fnl f: drvn out* **17/10**[1]

2 *1* **Thunderous Mood (USA)**[16] 5383 2-8-11 ....(b) JohnEgan 6 102
(P F I Cole) *hld up in tch: 7th 1/2-way: rdn and r.o in centre 2f out: chal and ev ch fnl f: r.o* **15/1**

3 *nk* **Treasure (FR)**[26] 5112 2-8-8 .... DBoeuf 8 98
(Mme C Head-Maarek, France) *hld up: last 1/2-way: pushed along over 2f out: rdn and r.o fnl f: nrst at fin* **18/10**[2]

4 *hd* **Privalova (IRE)**[28] 2-8-8 .... TJarnet 4 97
(R Pritchard-Gordon, France) *cl up: 2nd 1/2-way: pushed along to dispute ld 1 1/2f out: no ex u.p fnl 100yds* **9/1**

5 *1* **Anyaar (IRE)**[28] 2-8-8 .... DBonilla 7 94
(F Head, France) *in tch: disputing 5th 1/2-way: pushed along to chse ldrs 1 1/2f out: styd on same pce* **10/1**

6 *1 ½* **Ladouce (FR)**[18] 5330 2-8-8 .... CSoumillon 9 89
(Robert Collet, France) *last early: disputing 5th 1/2-way: rdn on ins 1 1/2f out: no imp* **62/10**[3]

7 *2* **Matwan (FR)**[18] 5330 2-8-8 .... RMarcelli 2 82
(C Boutin, France) *led to over 1 1/2f out: one pce fnl f* **27/1**

8 *20* **Rahan (FR)**[47] 4441 2-8-11 .... WSaraiva 5 19
(G Bailly, France) *prom: 3rd and pushed along 1/2-way: outpcd fr over 1 1/2f out* **62/1**

64.10 secs (-0.40) **8** Ran SP% **117.1**
PARI-MUTUEL: WIN 2.70; PL 1.30, 2.30, 1.20; DF 12.40.
Owner Mrs M Findlay **Bred** Noel O'Callaghan **Trained** Newmarket, Suffolk

NOTEBOOK
Triple Aspect(IRE) landed his hat-trick with something in reserve. He was given a fine ride and was settled just behind the leaders near the rail before making a forward move which took him into the lead one and a half out. He stayed on well and looks progressive and capable of getting further, and connections are now looking at either the Mill Reef, Middle Park or Cornwallis Stakes for him.
Thunderous Mood(USA), blinkered for the first time, ran free early on towards the outside of the pack. He came with a run from one and a half out but never looked a threat to the winner. He was unsuited by the lack of early pace and it was a creditable performance.
Treasure(FR) pulled in the early stages when one but last. She then took time to become balanced but was putting in her best work at the finish and would have been second in a few more strides.
Privalova(IRE), always well up with the pace, had every chance at the furlong marker but could not go with the winner and runner- up and was caught for third place just before the line.

5851 - (Foreign Racing) - See Raceform Interactive

[5825] DONCASTER (L-H)

Friday, September 12

OFFICIAL GOING: Soft (good to soft in places; 6.7)
Wind: Moderate, half behind Weather: Overcast, light rain

5852 POLYPIPE FLYING CHILDERS STKS (GROUP 2) — 5f

1:35 (1:36) (Class 1) 2-Y-O
£45,416 (£17,216; £8,616; £4,296; £2,152; £1,080) **Stalls High**

Form — RPR

5241 **1** **Madame Trop Vite (IRE)**[28] 5055 2-8-11 104 .... TedDurcan 11 104+
(K A Ryan) *trckd ldrs: hdwy wl over 1f out: rdn ins fnl f: qcknd to ld nr fin* **11/1**

1416 **2** *nk* **Anglezarke (IRE)**[21] 5244 2-8-11 90 .... DavidAllan 7 103
(T D Easterby) *cl up: led 1/2-way: rdn and hdd over 1f out: rallied to ld wl ins fnl f: hdd and nt qckn nr fin* **14/1**

1 **3** *hd* **Mythical Border (USA)**[126] 1955 2-8-11 0 .... LDettori 6 102+
(J Noseda) *in tch: gd hdwy 2f out: led over 1f out: sn rdn and hdd wl ins fnl f: no ex* **10/1**[3]

1104 **4** *¾* **Danehill Destiny**[20] 5272 2-8-11 102 .... JMurtagh 9 100
(W J Haggas) *hld up: hdwy 2f out: rdn over 1f out: styd on strly ins fnl f: nrst fin* **7/2**[2]

1323 **5** *1 ¼* **Lord Shanakill (USA)**[19] 5330 2-9-0 108 .... FergusSweeney 10 100+
(K R Burke) *dwlt: t.k.h and hld up towards rr: hdwy 2f out: nt clr run and swtchd lft over 1f out: sn rdn and kpt on ins fnl f* **7/2**[2]

21 **6** *nk* **Doncaster Rover (USA)**[128] 1914 2-9-0 0 .... JohnEgan 5 99+
(S Parr) *cl up: rdn along whn bdly hmpd over 1f out: rallied ins fnl f: gng on towards fin* **12/1**

2140 **7** *1* **Shyrl**[21] 5245 2-8-11 95 .... TPQueally 2 90
(S A Callaghan) *cl up on outer: rdn along 2f out and sn wknd* **25/1**

6511 **8** *nk* **Coconut Shy**[18] 5363 2-8-11 75 ....(t) AdrianMcCarthy 4 89
(G Prodromou) *led: hdd 1/2-way and sn rdn: drvn: edgd rt and hld whn sltly hmpd over 1f out: sn wknd* **66/1**

1520 **9** *½* **Saucy Brown (IRE)**[42] 4588 2-9-0 94 .... JimmyFortune 3 90
(R Hannon) *in tch: effrt 2f out: sn rdn and grad wknd* **25/1**

1026 **10** *½* **Kerrys Requiem (IRE)**[8] 5642 2-8-11 102 .... TPO'Shea 1 86
(M R Channon) *s.i.s and bhd tl styd on appr fnl f* **40/1**

1043 **11** *2* **Bahamian Babe**[41] 4648 2-8-11 93 .... HayleyTurner 8 78
(M L W Bell) *lw: cl up: rdn along 2f out and sn wknd* **20/1**

1331 **12** *3* **Senor Mirasol**[15] 5438 2-9-0 108 .... NCallan 12 71
(K A Ryan) *lw: cl up on stands' rail: rdn and ev ch 2f out: drvn and wknd over 1f out* **3/1**[1]

60.22 secs (-0.28) **Going Correction** +0.125s/f (Good) **12** Ran SP% **117.6**
Speed ratings (Par 107): **107,106,106,105,103 102,100,100,99,98 95,90**
toteswinger: 1&2 £29.60, 1&3 £11.00, 2&3 £39.20. CSF £142.88 TOTE £13.70: £3.80, £5.20, £2.40; EX 209.70 TRIFECTA Not won..
Owner Mrs T Marnane **Bred** Mark & Pippa Hackett **Trained** Hambleton, N Yorks
■ Stewards' Enquiry : Fergus Sweeney one-day ban: careless riding (Sep 26)

FOCUS
An ordinary renewal of the Flying Childers, and rated as such, but it was run at a strong pace. Recent winners of this have tended to struggle at three, with the Group 2 penalty proving a hindrance in the first part of the campaign, but last year's winner, Fleeting Spirit, went some way to bucking that trend with her win in the Temple Stakes. The finish here was dominated by fillies, who comprised two-thirds of the field.

NOTEBOOK
Madame Trop Vite(IRE) had made all in a Listed race confined to her own sex at Newbury, but different tactics were adopted here, as she tracked her stablemate Senor Mirasol near the stands' fence. It momentarily looked as if she might not get a run, but a gap quickly appeared and she quickened up well to catch the two in front of her near the line. She may go for the Cheveley Park Stakes next, and the return to 6f will not a problem. Easy ground would suit her there. (op 14-1)
Anglezarke(IRE), on her toes beforehand, ran a big race on this drop back to 5f. She was always up with the pace and, after seeing off the challenge of the third, only succumbed late on to Madame Trop Vite. She could revert to 6f in the Redcar Two-Year-Old Trophy next month. (op 25-1)
Mythical Border(USA) ◆, representing the yard successful with Fleeting Spirit, could prove the nicest long-term prospect among these. Off the track since her winning debut at Lingfield four months ago, she made eyecatching headway to challenge Anglezarke, but then ran green when asked to battle and could not quite get her head in front. This outing should have taught her a good deal. (op 15-2)
Danehill Destiny, reverting to the minimum trip and suited by the soft ground, ran on well late and was closing on the three in front of her at the line. An easy 6f may suit her. (tchd 4-1)
Lord Shanakill(USA), whose placed efforts in the Coventry Stakes, Vintage Stakes (over 7f) and Prix Morny represented the best form on offer, was down to 5f for the first time since his debut. He was switched left for a run, inconveniencing Doncaster Rover, before finishing to some purpose. A return to 6f looks in order. Official explanation: jockey said colt missed the break (op 4-1 tchd 9-2 and 10-3)
Doncaster Rover(USA) had just come under pressure and was struggling to hold his position when he was hampered between Lord Shanakill and Coconut Shy, but he picked himself up and finished well. He has undergone something of a growth spurt, which explains his absence since his win in the Lily Agnes at Chester in May, and on this evidence should soon be making up for lost time. (tchd 11-1, 14-1 in a place)
Shyrl showed speed down the wide outside of the pack, but she could not sustain her effort inside the last. She has not progressed.
Coconut Shy, who came here off the back of a nursery win from a mark of 70, was on her toes beforehand. She showed good initial speed on this big step up in class.
Saucy Brown(IRE) displayed early pace out wide, but he had lost his pitch by halfway.

Kerrys Requiem(IRE), who had been just under three lengths second to today's winner at Newbury two starts back and was 3lb better off here, was slow to break and never figured.
Senor Mirasol, who was successful in a 5f Listed event on soft ground last time following his third at Group 2 level in the Prix Robert Papin, was the choice of Neil Callan over stablemate Madame Trop Vite, but he faded out of the picture after showing dash against the rail. This ground was against him. Official explanation: trainer had no explanation for the poor form shown (tchd 10-3)

5853 LADBROKES MALLARD STKS (H'CAP) 1m 6f 132y
2:05 (2:06) (Class 2) (0-110,98) 3-Y-O+ **£32,380** (£9,635; £4,815; £2,405) **Stalls** Low

Form RPR
3031 **1** **The Betchworth Kid**[31] 4955 3-8-10 **90**.......................... HayleyTurner 6 103
(M L W Bell) *drvn along early: in rr: smooth hdwy on outside over 3f out: hung lft and led over 1f out: styd on strly: eased towards fin* **10/1**
3131 **2** *3* **Bollin Felix**[5] 5718 4-9-7 **89** 6ex..........................(b) DavidAllan 13 98
(T D Easterby) *s.i.s: hdwy on outside 6f out: led over 2f out: hung lft and hdd over 1f out: styd on same pce* **5/1**[1]
1205 **3** *1 1/4* **La Vecchia Scuola (IRE)**[34] 4843 4-9-1 **88**.............. KellyHarrison(5) 4 95
(J S Goldie) *in tch: effrt over 2f out: styd on same pce fnl 2f* **20/1**
1024 **4** *2 1/2* **Mull Of Dubai**[13] 5494 5-9-12 **94**.......................... JohnEgan 5 98
(T P Tate) *hld up in rr: stdy hdwy on inner over 3f out: chal over 2f out: fdd fnl f* **16/1**
0051 **5** *hd* **Dzesmin (POL)**[22] 5199 6-9-3 **85**.......................... PaulHanagan 12 88
(R A Fahey) *prom: effrt over 3f out: one pce fnl 2f* **18/1**
-P00 **6** *hd* **The Last Drop (IRE)**[69] 3721 5-9-4 **86**.......................... WilliamBuick 3 89
(B W Hills) *hld up in rr: hdwy 4f out: kpt on same pce fnl 2f* **33/1**
0363 **7** *11* **Burnt Oak (UAE)**[41] 4652 6-8-10 **78** oh9.......................... TedDurcan 2 66
(C W Fairhurst) *dwlt: effrt on inner over 4f out: lost pl 3f out* **80/1**
1233 **8** *hd* **Cool Judgement (IRE)**[13] 5494 3-9-4 **98**.......................... PhilipRobinson 7 85
(M A Jarvis) *lw: chsd ldrs: led 3f out: sn hdd & wknd* **5/1**[1]
351/ **9** *6* **Mikado**[45] 5962 7-9-13 **95**.......................... JimCrowley 17 74
(Jonjo O'Neill) *swtchd lft after s: in rr: drvn 6f out: nvr a factor* **50/1**
0405 **10** *2 1/2* **Akarem**[28] 5054 7-9-4 **86**.......................... FergusSweeney 16 61
(K R Burke) *trckd ldrs on outer: lost pl over 2f out* **20/1**
3000 **11** *7* **Swan Queen**[62] 3942 5-9-5 **87**.......................... JimmyQuinn 14 53
(J L Dunlop) *trckd ldrs on outer: lost pl over 2f out* **12/1**
2121 **12** *4 1/2* **Laterly (IRE)**[55] 4205 3-9-2 **96**.......................... MickyFenton 10 55
(T P Tate) *lw: led tl 3f out: wknd over 1f out* **9/1**
2012 **13** *3/4* **Tropical Strait (IRE)**[21] 5229 5-10-0 **96**.......................... AlanMunro 15 54
(D W P Arbuthnot) *mid-div on outer: lost pl over 3f out* **8/1**[3]
2332 **14** *6* **Bogside Theatre (IRE)**[34] 4843 4-9-11 **93**.............. DanielTudhope 11 43
(G M Moore) *lw: chsd ldrs on outer: lost pl over 2f out* **15/2**[2]
0205 **15** *5* **Record Breaker (IRE)**[13] 5494 4-9-13 **95**.......................... GregFairley 8 38
(M Johnston) *swtg: chsd ldrs: drvn 7f out: lost pl over 3f out* **33/1**
6010 **16** *15* **Pippa Greene**[21] 5229 4-10-0 **96**.......................... ShaneKelly 1 18
(P F I Cole) *sn trcking ldrs: lost pl 3f out: eased and sn bhd* **9/1**

3m 10.23s (3.53) **Going Correction** +0.325s/f (Good)
WFA 3 from 4yo+ 12lb **16** Ran SP% **122.7**
Speed ratings (Par 109): **103,101,100,99,99 99,93,93,90,88 84,82,82,78,76 68**
toteswinger: 1&2 £14.20, 1&3 £61.50, 2&3 £27.70. CSF £55.62 CT £1009.31 TOTE £12.80: £3.20, £1.70, £4.90, £3.30; EX 87.90 TRIFECTA Not won..
Owner W H Ponsonby **Bred** R P Williams **Trained** Newmarket, Suffolk

FOCUS
A false rail was removed from the previous day to give 4.5 metres of fresh ground from the bottom of Rose Hill into the straight. Cool Judgement, the highest rated horse in the field, came into the race with a rating of 98, well below the ceiling of 110, but this is usually a decent handicap and the form looks solid. Seven of the previous ten winners were three-year-olds, and once again that age group provided the winner. They went a good gallop and the principals all came from off the pace.

NOTEBOOK
The Betchworth Kid ran well in some tough 1m4f handicaps on fast ground earlier this season, but he has always looked a stayer in the making, and the combination of a step up in trip and soft ground - he is after all by Tobougg - saw him off the mark for the year at Nottingham last time. A 5lb higher mark did not look too much of a burden, and as a hold-up horse in a race that was always likely to be run at a good gallop, he had conditions very much to suit. Travelling best of all from some way out, it was just a question of how much he would find off the bridle, and once in front he just had to be kept up to his work to draw clear for an easy win. He looks the type to improve further in this division next season, when 2m will pose him few problems. (op 12-1)
Bollin Felix is engaged in the Cesarewitch. He looked well in under his penalty following his easy win at Thirsk five days earlier, and with ground conditions to suit he posted a sound effort behind the unexposed three-year-old. A little further probably suits him ideally nowadays. (tchd 11-2)
La Vecchia Scuola(IRE) has had a fine season, translating her improved hurdling form to the Flat and progressing from a 66-rated filly in the spring to running here off 88. She seems to handle most ground, but a bit quicker probably suits her best, and she is another likely to take her chance in the Cesarewitch. (tchd 25-1)
Mull Of Dubai looks handicapped right up to his best at the moment, but he is pretty reliable, and as a confirmed hold-up performer he had the race run to suit. (tchd 18-1)
Dzesmin(POL) was racing off a 7lb higher mark than when winning at Chester last time and was missing the valuable 7lb claim of Frederik Tylicki, so he did not run badly in the circumstances. (op 20-1)
The Last Drop(IRE), a former St Leger runner-up, has been out of sorts for some time, but he has dropped to a very attractive mark and hinted at a return to form here.
Burnt Oak(UAE) was racing from 9lb out of the handicap, but he did at least benefit from being held up in what was a strongly run race.
Cool Judgement(IRE) had stamina questions to answer and appeared not to get home. He did race handily throughout, though, and given that his fellow pacesetters all failed to see it out as well, it looks very much as though they simply went too fast early. (op 6-1)
Laterly(IRE) was not sure to stay beforehand and setting a decent gallop meant it proved impossible. (op 10-1)
Bogside Theatre(IRE) Official explanation: jockey said filly ran flat
Pippa Greene, another who was never too far off the pace, travelled well through the race but dropped out tamely inside the final half-mile with his rider looking down as though something had gone amiss. Official explanation: trainer had no explanation for the poor form shown (op 11-1 tchd 17-2)

5854 NATIONAL EXPRESS DONCASTER CUP (GROUP 2) 2m 2f
2:40 (2:40) (Class 1) 3-Y-O+
£56,770 (£21,520; £10,770; £5,370; £2,690; £1,350) **Stalls** Low

Form RPR
-416 **1** **Honolulu (IRE)**[43] 4551 4-9-1 0.......................... JMurtagh 1 117
(A P O'Brien, Ire) *trckd ldrs: hdwy 4f out: chsd ldr over 2f out: rdn to ld 1f out: sn edgd lft and clr* **15/8**[1]
2603 **2** *4* **Balkan Knight**[8] 5646 8-9-1 108.......................... JimmyFortune 2 113
(D R C Elsworth) *b.hind: lw: hld up and bhd: hdwy over 3f out: rdn wl over 1f out: styd on ins fnl f to take 2nd nr fin* **16/1**
1230 **3** *1/2* **Royal And Regal (IRE)**[19] 5333 4-9-1 114.......................... NCallan 11 113
(M A Jarvis) *sn led and set medium pce: qcknd over 3f out: rdn along 2f out: drvn and hdd 1f out: sn wknd* **2/1**[2]
05-4 **4** *5* **Juniper Girl (IRE)**[8] 5646 5-8-12 102.......................... HayleyTurner 7 104
(M L W Bell) *trckd ldr: effrt 4f out and sn pushed along: rdn 3f out and kpt on same pce fnl 2f* **10/1**
-140 **5** *1/2* **Bulwark (IRE)**[43] 4551 6-9-1 101..........................(v) JimCrowley 4 106
(Ian Williams) *hld up in tch: hdwy 5f out: rdn alongh to chse ldrs 3f out: drvn and no imp 2f out* **33/1**
0553 **6** *1 1/2* **Sagara (USA)**[43] 4551 4-9-1 110.......................... LDettori 10 105
(Saeed Bin Suroor) *lw: hld up: hdwy and in tch 6f out: effrt over 3f out: sn rdn and btn 2f out* **5/1**[3]
0003 **7** *3 1/4* **Shahin (USA)**[20] 5264 5-9-1 104..........................(v) RHills 5 101
(M P Tregoning) *hld up in tch: effrt over 4f out: sn rdn along and btn wl over 2f out* **20/1**
1040 **8** *25* **Finalmente**[19] 5333 6-9-4 108..........................(p) TPQueally 12 77
(S A Callaghan) *hld up: a in rr* **25/1**
0001 **9** *4* **Baddam**[44] 4516 6-9-1 93.......................... AlanMunro 9 69
(Ian Williams) *lw: chsd ldrs: pushed along 1/2-way: rdn and wknd 5f out: sn bhd* **40/1**

4m 3.40s (5.20) **Going Correction** +0.325s/f (Good)
WFA 3 from 4yo+ 14lb **9** Ran SP% **113.7**
Speed ratings (Par 115): **101,99,99,96,96 95,94,83,81**
toteswinger: 1&2 £5.70, 1&3 £1.20, 2&3 £8.80. CSF £29.56 TOTE £3.00: £1.20, £3.30, £1.20; EX 38.30 Trifecta £80.30 Pool: £1,059.31, 9.75 winning units..
Owner D Smith, Mrs J Magnier, M Tabor **Bred** Kilfrush Stud **Trained** Ballydoyle, Co Tipperary

FOCUS
By no means a vintage edition of this historic race. Both Yeats and last year's winner Septimus are ahead of Honolulu in the stayers' pecking order at Ballydoyle, and he has been rated 4lb off his best here.

NOTEBOOK
Honolulu(IRE) came here following a poor effort in the Goodwood Cup, where he was evidently unsuited by the undulating track. Settled in fourth before going after the leader with three furlongs to run, he showed his customary high head carriage and took a bit of time to get to him, before clearing right away in the final furlong. He had tackled only fast ground this year, but the return to easy underfoot conditions clearly suited. Official explanation: trainer's rep said, regarding apparent improvement in form, that he was unable to offer an explanation for the poor run last time. (op 7-4 tchd 13-8)
Balkan Knight did much the best of those held up at the rear. He was still only sixth with a quarter-mile left, but made up a lot of ground to grab second. Still without a Group win to his name, he appeared to get this trip well enough, but his trainer maintains that he is happiest over 1m6f. The Jockey Club Cup over 2m would appear a valid target.
Royal And Regal(IRE), sharper for his recent run at Deauville, was rather keen early on and was kept wide of his rivals up the home straight on the first circuit. Bringing the field down the centre of the track off the home turn, he tried to kick away, but could not prevent the winner drawing past him at the furlong pole, with both the first two edging over to the inside rail late on. Caught for second close home, he will probably bid to repeat last year's victory in the Jockey Club Cup at Newmarket. (op 11-4)
Juniper Girl(IRE), who was warm and on her toes beforehand, raced prominently and, although left trailing when the race really developed up the straight, she stuck on to regain fourth close home and earn some priceless black type. This tough mare will be fresher than most for a late-season campaign. (tchd 9-1)
Bulwark(IRE) had plenty to find in this company, and he ran respectably, going after the leading pair with three furlongs to run, but being edged out of the frame in the last few strides.
Sagara(USA) had finished a long way ahead of Honolulu at Goodwood and had his ground here, but he has basically proved difficult to place for Godolphin and he never threatened. (op 9-2)
Shahin(USA) is hard to win with, and this longer trip did not provide the answer.
Finalmente, whose Group 2 penalty for his win in a slowly run Henry II Stakes continues to be a millstone around his neck, did not improve for hold-up tactics. (op 33-1)
Baddam was the first beaten. (op 50-1)

5855 EUROPEAN BREEDERS' FUND CARRIE RED FILLIES' NURSERY STKS (H'CAP) 6f 110y
3:15 (3:17) (Class 2) 2-Y-O **£25,904** (£7,708; £3,852; £1,924) **Stalls** High

Form RPR
543 **1** **Dream In Waiting**[49] 4380 2-8-1 **75**.......................... AshleyMorgan(7) 18 83
(P F I Cole) *in rr: hdwy on ins over 2f out: styd on fnl f: led towards fin* **16/1**
321 **2** *1* **Happy Anniversary (IRE)**[15] 5416 2-8-9 **76**.......... EdwardCreighton 15 81
(Miss V Haigh) *chsd ldrs: chal over 1f out: no ex wl ins fnl f* **16/1**
5310 **3** *nk* **Polish Pride**[14] 5447 2-9-4 **85**.......................... AlanMunro 9 89
(M Brittain) *trckd ldrs on outer: led over 1f out: hdd and no ex fnl 50yds* **28/1**
4101 **4** *5* **La Brigitte**[34] 4874 2-9-4 **88**.......................... NeilBrown(3) 6 78
(A J McCabe) *dwlt: hld up towards rr: hdwy on outside over 2f out: sn chsng ldrs: fdd fnl f* **14/1**
061 **5** *3/4* **It's Toast (IRE)**[38] 4705 2-8-3 **70**.......................... HayleyTurner 11 58
(R M Beckett) *lw: dwlt: in rr and sn pushed along: kpt on fnl 2f: nvr nr ldrs* **6/1**[2]
321 **6** *2 3/4* **Tropical Paradise (IRE)**[25] 5147 2-9-4 **85**.......................... JimCrowley 4 66
(P Winkworth) *lw: w ldrs on outer: led 3f out: hdd over 1f out: sn wknd* **9/2**[1]
646 **7** *hd* **Eliza Griffith (IRE)**[34] 4870 2-8-0 **67**.......................... FrancisNorton 1 47
(R Hannon) *lw: chsd ldrs on outer: wknd over 1f out* **20/1**
3133 **8** *nk* **Lisburn (IRE)**[17] 5381 2-8-5 **72**.......................... AdrianTNicholls 12 51
(M Brittain) *led tl over 3f out: wknd over 1f out* **20/1**
4352 **9** *1 1/4* **River Rye (IRE)**[15] 5422 2-8-9 **76**.......................... RichardMullen 16 52
(R Hannon) *in rr-div: nvr a factor* **40/1**
612 **10** *nk* **Belle Des Airs (IRE)**[21] 5228 2-8-12 **82**.......................... JackMitchell(3) 3 57
(R M Beckett) *dwlt: sn chsng ldrs: wknd 2f out* **10/1**
453 **11** *3/4* **Deyas Dream**[65] 3837 2-8-2 **74**.......................... DavidProbert(5) 5 47
(A M Balding) *b.hind: lw: t.k.h: sn trcking ldrs: hung lft and lost pl 2f out* **11/1**
126 **12** *3 1/4* **Sunset Crest**[18] 5359 2-9-1 **82**.......................... RobertWinston 10 45
(Mrs A Duffield) *in rr-div: bhd fnl 2f* **33/1**
134 **13** *1 1/2* **Dove Mews**[21] 5228 2-8-11 **83**.......................... AshleyHamblett(5) 14 41
(M L W Bell) *swtg: sn in rr: bhd fnl 2f* **9/1**
0044 **14** *nk* **Bubbly Baby**[17] 5384 2-8-0 **67**.......................... PaulHanagan 7 25
(T D Easterby) *hld up in midfield: effrt 3f out: sn lost pl* **50/1**
062 **15** *2 1/4* **Norfolk Broads (IRE)**[27] 5089 2-8-2 **69**.......................... RoystonFfrench 13 20
(M Johnston) *in rr-div: bhd fnl 3f* **8/1**[3]
5165 **16** *8* **Golden Rosie (IRE)**[41] 4626 2-8-10 **77**.......................... WilliamBuick 17 6
(B W Hills) *mid-div: lost pl 3f out: sn bhd and eased* **8/1**[3]

1m 20.19s (0.29) **Going Correction** +0.125s/f (Good) **16** Ran SP% **120.9**
Speed ratings (Par 98): **103,101,101,95,94 91,91,91,89,89 88,84,82,82,79 70**
toteswinger: 1&2 £39.80, 1&3 £77.10, 2&3 £64.30. CSF £229.24 CT £7195.55 TOTE £22.90: £4.90, £2.60, £5.00, £3.90; EX 299.40 TRIFECTA Not won..
Owner Pegasus Racing Ltd **Bred** Pegasus Racing **Trained** Whatcombe, Oxon

FOCUS
A very competitive nursery for fillies in which they tended to come up the centre of the track. The winner, however, was drawn widest of all and raced towards the outside of the pack. The form has been rated positively, with the winner lightly raced, the second progressive, and the third best on this ground.

NOTEBOOK
Dream In Waiting had been given a bit of a break since she completed the required three runs for a mark, and she looked far more professional here than at Thirsk on her latest start. She was not going to be beaten for stamina over this extended 6f, and she kept on strongly to score. Her dam was a Group 2 winner over 1m2f and this filly looks the type to progress from two to three, but before then she could well take in the Group 3 Firth of Clyde Stakes at Ayr. (op 14-1)
Happy Anniversary(IRE), who gained a deserved success when winning her maiden at Ayr last time, ran another solid race off what looked a stiff enough mark. She is a tough sort, and apparently connections are considering sending her abroad in search of black type in the coming weeks. (op 20-1)
Polish Pride, who found the ground too fast at Chester last time, was much happier back on a soft surface and, having raced up with the pace throughout, just came out worst in the three-way battle to the line. Her performance suggests that the handicapper was justified in putting her up 13lb for her Haydock win last month, and she could now go for a similar race at Ayr next week. (op 33-1)
La Brigitte raced towards the far side of the pack, which was probably not the ideal place to be, and it is too early to say that the handicapper has her measure. (op 16-1)
It's Toast(IRE) is by Diktat, whose progeny often improve for soft ground, and she is a half-sister to Dream Eater, whose only success so far came over this course and distance in the valuable St Leger 2-y-o Stakes last year. Having won her maiden over 5f last time, this longer trip was a concern, but as it turned out she struggled to go the early pace before staying on. (tchd 11-2, 13-2 in a place)
Tropical Paradise(IRE) looked to have been given a fair mark for her handicap debut. However, having shown up well for a long way, she did not see the trip out in this softer ground. (op 5-1 tchd 4-1)
Eliza Griffith(IRE) raced alongside Tropical Paradise for much of the way and weakened in similar fashion. (tchd 22-1)
Lisburn(IRE), a stablemate of the third, had conditions to suit, but she has been held in lower-grade nurseries recently and so it was always going to be difficult for her here. (op 25-1)
River Rye(IRE) was never a threat. She would not have wanted the ground as soft as this, but is looking exposed now anyway. (op 33-1)
Belle Des Airs(IRE) was a bit disappointing as she had shaped as though this extra half furlong would be in her favour when winning at Newbury last time.
Deyas Dream, returning from a two-month break, raced far too keenly in the early stages. (op 12-1)
Dove Mews Official explanation: jockey said filly never travelled

5856 FRANK WHITTLE PARTNERSHIP CONDITIONS STKS — 1m (S)
3:50 (3:50) (Class 2) 3-Y-O — **£15,577** (£4,665; £2,332; £1,167) **Stalls** High

Form	Pos	Btn	Horse	Jockey	RPR
1-24	1		**Spacious**[84] 3194 3-8-6 112 (J R Fanshawe) *trckd ldrs: hdwy over 2f out: swtchd rt and rdn to chal over 1f out: rdn to ld ins fnl f: drvn and hung lft nr fin: jst hld on* **8/11**[1]	RobertWinston 1	99+
2504	2	nse	**Moyenne Corniche**[41] 4622 3-9-0 105 (G Wragg) *trckd ldr: effrt over 2f out: sn ev ch: rdn over 1f out: drvn ins fnl f edgd rt towards fin and jst hld* **11/2**[3]	AlanMunro 3	107
2020	3	1	**Alexandros**[27] 5095 3-8-11 108 (Saeed Bin Suroor) *lw: set stdy pce: qcknd over 3f out: rdn wl over 1f out: drvn and hdd ins fnl f: jst hld whn hmpd and snatched up nr fin* **5/2**[2]	LDettori 5	103+
2-50	4	13	**Alexander Castle (USA)**[124] 2032 3-8-11 104 (K A Ryan) *chsd ldng pair: pushed along 3f out: rdn over 2f out: sn wknd and eased appr fnl f* **11/1**	NCallan 4	72

1m 40.39s (1.09) **Going Correction** +0.125s/f (Good) — **4** Ran SP% **110.2**
Speed ratings (Par 107): **99,98,97,84**
CSF £5.27 TOTE £1.60; EX 6.10.
Owner Cheveley Park Stud **Bred** Cheveley Park Stud Ltd **Trained** Newmarket, Suffolk

FOCUS
Just the four runners, but a high-class race of its type which produced an exciting finish. However, they raced some way off the stands' rail and with the pace only steady this form may not prove too reliable.

NOTEBOOK
Spacious, who did not look great in her coat beforehand, had been given a break since her Coronation Stakes defeat as connections felt that she wasn't sparkling, but she appeared to face a relatively straightforward task on this marked drop in class. She made heavy weather of landing the odds, though, taking time to master Alexandros then just withstanding Moyenne Corniche's late lunge. In her defence the hold-up tactics off a slow gallop were not ideal and the ground was plenty soft enough. Runner-up to Natagora in the 1,000 Guineas back in May, she will return to Newmarket for the Group 1 Sun Chariot Stakes next month and is set to stay in training at four. (op 4-7 tchd 4-5, 1-2 in places)
Moyenne Corniche's maiden win at Newbury in the spring had come in easy conditions, and he has generally acquitted himself with credit on faster ground since. Despite holding his head rather awkwardly under pressure he ran on well inside the last and would have got up in another stride. He reversed Glorious Goodwood running with Alexandros on these 3lb worse terms and this was a good effort at the weights. (op 13-2 tchd 7-1 and 5-1)
Alexandros set a moderate pace until quickening things past halfway. The favourite eventually got to him inside the last and he was held when the first two combined to squeeze him up on the line. (op 10-3 tchd 7-2 in places)
Alexander Castle(USA) has not had things go to plan since finishing second to McCartney in the Champagne Stakes at this meeting 12 months ago. Gelded since his last appearance when down the field in the French Guineas back in May, he was the first in trouble and hung to the rail when beaten. (op 12-1)

5857 EBF INSPIREPAC MAIDEN STKS (DIV I) — 1m (S)
4:25 (4:27) (Class 4) 2-Y-O — **£6,152** (£1,830; £914; £456) **Stalls** High

Form	Pos	Btn	Horse	Jockey	RPR
2	1		**Kite Wood (IRE)**[33] 4890 2-9-3 0 (M A Jarvis) *w'like: scope: swtg: trckd ldrs: edgd rt and led ins fnl f: hld on wl towards fin* **7/4**[1]	PhilipRobinson 10	87+
	2	1	**La De Two (IRE)** 2-9-3 0 (B W Hills) *w'like: athletic: s.s: in rr: gd hdwy 2f out: styd on wl fnl f: no ex towards fin* **40/1**	WilliamBuick 5	86+
	3	½	**Monitor Closely (IRE)** 2-9-3 0 (P W Chapple-Hyam) *w'like: str: trckd ldrs: chal over 1f out: no ex ins fnl f* **14/1**	AlanMunro 2	84
3	4	1 ¼	**Espiritu (FR)**[28] 5068 2-9-3 0 (J Noseda) *unf: scope: led: hdd and wnt rt ins fnl f: no ex* **7/2**[3]	LDettori 4	81+
	5	2 ¾	**Golden Sword**[15] 5442 2-9-3 0 (A P O'Brien, Ire) *w'like: scope: chsd ldrs: chal over 1f out: fdd ins fnl f* **5/2**[2]	JMurtagh 11	75
0	6	7	**Salomo (GER)**[21] 5246 2-9-3 0 (J L Dunlop) *dwlt: mid-div: outpcd 3f out: edgd rt and kpt on fnl f* **50/1**	RHills 3	60
02	7	nk	**Threestepstoheaven**[85] 3164 2-9-3 0 (B W Hills) *leggy: in rr: drvn 3f out: nvr on terms* **14/1**	DarryllHolland 12	59
	8	1 ¼	**Lively Fling (USA)** 2-9-3 0 (J H M Gosden) *unf: dwlt: hld up in rr: sme hdwy whn edgd lft over 1f out: nvr nr ldrs* **14/1**	JimmyFortune 9	56+
	8	dht	**Ouster (GER)** 2-9-3 0 (D R C Elsworth) *w'like: str: bit bkwd: dwlt: mid-div: carried lft over 1f out: nvr a factor* **80/1**	TQuinn 8	56
	10	½	**Darley Sun (IRE)** 2-9-3 0 (D M Simcock) *w'like: leggy: chsd ldrs: wkng whn hmpd over 1f out* **40/1**	RichardMullen 7	55+
	11	2 ½	**Anthology** 2-9-3 0 (B Smart) *unf: swvd lft s: sn chsng ldrs: wknd 2f out* **66/1**	TedDurcan 1	50
	12	1 ¼	**Swing It Ruby (IRE)** 2-8-12 0 (Miss V Haigh) *unf: trckd ldrs: t.k.h: lost pl 2f out* **100/1**	DanielTudhope 6	42

1m 41.71s (2.41) **Going Correction** +0.125s/f (Good) — **12** Ran SP% **117.7**
Speed ratings (Par 97): **92,91,90,89,86 79,79,77,77,77 74,73**
toteswinger: 1&2 £19.20, 1&3 £8.20, 2&3 £40.50. CSF £90.11 TOTE £2.80: £1.40, £7.00, £3.60; EX 81.30 Trifecta £573.00 Part won. Pool: £774.39, 0.50 winning units..
Owner Thomas Barr **Bred** Elsdon Farms **Trained** Newmarket, Suffolk

FOCUS
This looked a good maiden on paper, with some well-bred newcomers taking on two or three rivals with solid form to their names already. Nice debuts from the second and .

NOTEBOOK
Kite Wood(IRE) had shaped with promise over 7f on his debut at Leicester behind a rival who had since bolted up in a novice event at Wolverhampton. The extra furlong here was always likely to suit this Derby entry and he justified favouritism in good style, staying on strongly despite drifting over to the stands' rail. He holds Group race entries this autumn, but he had a hard enough race here and is probably done for the season. He should make up into a nice middle-distance colt next term, but the general quotes of around 25-1 for Epsom make little appeal. (tchd 2-1)
La De Two(IRE) ◆ is from a stable that had won this maiden three times in the previous ten years. A son of Galileo, he was slowly away and raced towards the back of the field in the early stages, but he really began to motor when his stamina kicked in, only for him to edge left through greenness inside the last. Inexperience denied him a debut win, but he clearly has the ability to win a similar race, and his pedigree suggests he should stay well next year. (op 50-1)
Monitor Closely(IRE) ◆, who cost 140,000gns and is a half-brother to this year's Eclipse winner Mount Nelson, shaped encouragingly on his debut. He does not hold any big-race entries, but on this evidence looks to have a fair amount of ability, and he should be able to win his maiden before the season is out. (op 16-1)
Espiritu(FR), who ran well on his debut in a Newmarket maiden over this trip, was always doing a bit too much in front, and while he still looked to be going well entering the final two furlongs those earlier exertions took their toll. He should do much better back on a decent surface and will be happier getting a lead in future. (tchd 5-2)
Golden Sword, who was third in an ordinary Tipperary maiden on his debut, is well entered up, but he could not go with the first four in the closing stages. A sounder surface may see him in a better light. (tchd 3-1, 9-4 and 10-3 in a place)
Salomo(GER) was detached in the last two furlongs but kept on past beaten horses. He cost 430,000 euros and looks the type to do better in handicaps next season once he has strengthened up.
Threestepstoheaven possibly found this ground too testing but is now eligible to run in nurseries and might do better in that sphere. (tchd 16-1)
Lively Fling(USA), a half-brother to a prolific winner in the US at up to 1m1f, should be better for the experience and will appreciate getting on faster ground. (op 33-1)

5858 FREE £30 BET AT HARINO.COM CLASSIFIED STKS — 1m 2f 60y
4:55 (4:56) (Class 3) 3-Y-O+
£9,346 (£2,799; £1,399; £700; £349; £175) **Stalls** Low

Form	Pos	Btn	Horse	Jockey	RPR
1431	1		**Closertobelieving**[13] 5502 3-8-11 85 (D R C Elsworth) *lw: midfield: hdwy over 2f out: swtchd rt and rdn to ld over 1f out: clr ins fnl f: jst hld on* **7/1**[3]	TQuinn 14	94+
346	2	nse	**Magic Echo**[17] 5382 4-9-1 84 (M Dods) *hld up in midfield: hdwy over 2f out: swtchd outside and rdn over 1f out: styd on strly ins fnl f: jst failed* **25/1**	TomEaves 13	91
31	3	4 ½	**King Olav (UAE)**[28] 5047 3-8-11 84 (M A Jarvis) *lw: midfield: hdwy 3f out: rdn and ev ch over 1f out: drvn and one pce ent fnl f* **6/1**[2]	PhilipRobinson 10	85
5420	4	1 ¼	**Black Dahlia**[13] 5502 3-8-3 76 (A J McCabe) *in tch: hdwy 3f out: rdn 2f out and ev ch tl drvn and wknd appr fnl f* **28/1**	DavidProbert(5) 5	80
4052	5	1	**Albaqaa**[20] 5257 3-8-11 85 (R A Fahey) *midfield: hdwy and in tch 4f out: effrt over 2f out: rdn to ld briefly over 1f out: sn hdd: drvn and one pce ins fnl f* **11/2**[1]	PaulHanagan 8	81
-501	6	hd	**Kings Quay**[29] 5005 6-9-4 84 (J J Quinn) *lw: midfield: hdwy over 2f out: sn rdn and kpt on ins fnl f: nrst fin* **12/1**	(t) GrahamGibbons 19	80
1	7	¾	**Ozone Trustee (NZ)**[14] 5453 4-9-4 85 (G A Swinbank) *in tch: hdwy to chse ldrs over 3f out: rdn over 2f out: drvn and wknd appr fnl f* **9/1**	PJMcDonald 12	79
4221	8	¾	**Demolition**[39] 4688 4-8-13 82 (N Wilson) *midfield: hdwy over 2f out: sn rdn and kpt on: nt rch ldrs* **12/1**	AshleyHamblett(5) 11	77
2303	9	nk	**Suits Me**[17] 5382 5-9-4 85 (T P Tate) *lw: prom: hdwy to ld over 3f out: rdn 2f out: sn drvn and hdd over 1f out: wknd* **9/1**	NCallan 7	77
2315	10	1	**Monfils Monfils (USA)**[27] 5092 6-9-4 78 (A J McCabe) *bhd tl styd on fnl 2f: nvr nr ldrs* **40/1**	ShaneKelly 18	75
4-00	11	¾	**Lets Roll**[132] 1798 7-9-4 79 (C W Thornton) *hld up and bhd tl sme late hdwy* **25/1**	DanielTudhope 1	73
0030	12	9	**Prince Of Light (IRE)**[45] 4509 5-9-4 85 (M Johnston) *prom: rdn along 3f out: grad wknd* **12/1**	GregFairley 6	55
0002	13	1 ¾	**Bajan Parkes**[16] 5391 5-9-4 85 (E J Alston) *t.k.h: prom: led 6f out: rdn along and hdd 4f out: sn wknd* **20/1**	DavidAllan 16	52
003-	14	1	**Mceldowney**[427] 3501 6-9-1 80 (M C Chapman) *nvr bttr than midfield* **100/1**	LeeVickers(3) 15	50
-500	15	1 ¾	**Bright Falcon**[33] 4900 3-8-11 78 (S Parr) *led 4f: cl up tl led again 4f out: rdn along and hdd over 3f out: sn wknd* **66/1**	(t) JohnEgan 3	46
3213	16	¾	**Bowder Stone (IRE)**[33] 4906 3-8-11 82 (M H Tompkins) *trckd ldrs: effrt over 2f out: sn rdn and wknd* **9/1**	JimmyQuinn 4	45
00-1	17	8	**Clear Sailing**[31] 4953 5-9-4 79 (George Baker) *s.i.s: a bhd* **14/1**	DO'Donohoe 9	29

2655 **P** **Dubai Meydan (IRE)**[58] 4089 3-8-11 82........................ DarryllHolland 17 —
(Miss Gay Kelleway) *s.i.s: a bhd: p.u 4f out* **33/1**

2m 12.58s (1.38) **Going Correction** +0.325s/f (Good)
WFA 3 from 4yo+ 7lb **18** Ran SP% **125.7**
Speed ratings (Par 107): **107,106,103,102,101 101,100,100,99,99 98,91,89,89,87 87,80,—**
toteswinger: 1&2 £41.20, 1&3 £12.80, 2&3 £40.20. CSF £183.03 TOTE £7.40: £2.80, £8.40, £2.60; EX 204.80 Trifecta £380.70 Part won. Pool: £514.47, 0.50 winning units..
Owner Gordon Li **Bred** Cheveley Park Stud Ltd **Trained** Newmarket, Suffolk

FOCUS
A competitive and closely matched classified stakes with a number arriving in good form. The pace was reasonable and all bar Prince Of Light, who remained on the inside rail, came down the centre of the track in the home straight. It was a fair test and the first two came from a fair way back. The form makes sense and the winner has been raised 8lb.

NOTEBOOK
Closertobelieving, dropped in from his wide draw, made steady progress down the outside and the race looked over when he forged a couple of lengths clear, but he idled in front at the same time as the runner-up found her stride and the line arrived only just in time. He remains on the upgrade and there should be more to come, although he is set to be switched to Hong Kong at some stage. (op 13-2)
Magic Echo, one of only two fillies in the race, and the pick on official adjusted ratings, took time to get going but finished strongly, just failing to peg back the idling leader. She made all over course and distance in the spring, but had not matched that effort in three starts since. (op 33-1)
King Olav(UAE), a Polytrack maiden winner, was the least experienced member of the field with just two runs behind him, and he still showed signs of greenness. He came to have every chance, but could not go with the winner in the final furlong. Improved form nevertheless. (op 4-1)
Black Dahlia was held by Closertobelieving on their Ripon meeting at the end of last month. Usually a front-runner but held up in touch here, she travelled up strongly, but could not find a change of gear when let down. (op 40-1)
Albaqaa was another who was going well entering the straight but after striking the front he could not hold on. This was another creditable effort. (op 15-2)
Kings Quay ran his race with no apparent excuses other than his wide draw.
Ozone Trustee(NZ) appeared to have plenty in his favour and was close enough if good enough, but he was found wanting. (op 8-1 tchd 10-1)
Demolition was slowly away but he kept staying on up the straight. (op 10-1)
Suits Me struck the front in the straight, but as is often the case, he finished weakly.
Bajan Parkes had company up front and dropped away once tackled. (op 22-1 tchd 25-1)
Dubai Meydan(IRE) Official explanation: jockey said gelding lost its action

5859 EBF INSPIREPAC MAIDEN STKS (DIV II) 1m (S)
5:25 (5:30) (Class 4) 2-Y-O **£6,152** (£1,830; £914; £456) **Stalls** High

Form RPR
0 **1** **The Miniver Rose (IRE)**[34] 4870 2-8-12 0........................ JimCrowley 3 78
(R Hannon) *unf: scope: sltly hmpd sn after s: sn chsng ldrs: edgd rt and styd on to ld wl ins fnl f* **16/1**
2 **2** *1 1/4* **Union Island (IRE)**[36] 4780 2-9-3 0........................ NCallan 8 80
(K A Ryan) *leggy: scope: led: edgd rt over 1f out: hdd and no ex last 75yds* **4/1**[2]
3 *1 1/4* **Headline Act** 2-9-3 0........................ JimmyFortune 9 77+
(J H M Gosden) *w'like: s.i.s: hdwy over 2f out: styd on ins fnl f* **12/1**[3]
6 **4** *1* **Holberg (UAE)**[13] 5500 2-9-3 0........................ GregFairley 4 75
(M Johnston) *w'like: scope: w ldrs: edgd rt and lft fnl f: fdd towards fin* **12/1**[3]
2 **5** *nse* **Mustaqer (IRE)**[27] 5093 2-9-3 0........................ RHills 6 75
(B W Hills) *lw: trckd ldrs: t.k.h: effrt 2f out: kpt on same pce fnl f* **4/6**[1]
0 **6** *4* **Royal Trooper (IRE)**[21] 5246 2-9-3 0........................ TPQueally 11 66
(J G Given) *in rr: hdwy 3f out: nvr rchd ldrs* **50/1**
7 *hd* **Double Rubble (USA)** 2-9-3 0........................ ShaneKelly 7 66
(J Noseda) *leggy: hld up: in rr: hdwy 2f out: nvr trbld ldrs* **25/1**
0 **8** *3/4* **Maybeme**[33] 4896 2-8-9 0........................ NeilBrown(3) 2 59
(N Bycroft) *leggy: unf: swtg: gave problems gng to s: hmpd s: sn prom: wknd over 1f out* **100/1**
9 *10* **Acclaim To Fame (IRE)** 2-9-3 0........................ JMurtagh 10 42
(S Parr) *unf: scope: in rr: drvn and sme hdwy 3f out: wknd over 1f out: eased* **25/1**
10 *13* **Play To Win (IRE)** 2-9-3 0........................ TQuinn 5 13
(D R C Elsworth) *w'like: scope: bit bkwd: s.s: sn outpcd in rr: bhd fnl 3f* **20/1**
025 **11** *12* **Haulage Lady (IRE)**[12] 5539 2-8-12 0........................ AdrianTNicholls 1 —
(Karen McLintock) *swvd rt s: w ldrs: t.k.h: lost pl 2f out: eased and sn bhd* **100/1**

1m 43.32s (4.02) **Going Correction** +0.125s/f (Good) **47** Ran SP% **117.7**
Speed ratings (Par 97): **84,82,81,80,80 76,76,75,65,52 40**
toteswinger: 1&2 £7.60, 1&3 £16.40, 2&3 £3.60. CSF £74.95 TOTE £25.50: £3.70, £1.60, £2.40; EX 111.80 Trifecta £551.10 Pool: £893.83, 1.20 winning units. Place 6: £535.98, Place 5: £51.50..
Owner Mrs J Wood **Bred** Tullamaine Castle & Robert Clay **Trained** East Everleigh, Wilts

FOCUS
The weaker division and it was run in a time 1.61sec slower than the first division, but some nice types and decent maiden form nevertheless.

NOTEBOOK
The Miniver Rose(IRE) settled kindly behind the leaders and responded well when asked to lengthen. A daughter of High Chaparral, she cost 100,000gns and could be useful next season when she steps up to middle distances.
Union Island(IRE) put up a good effort at Haydock on his debut in similar conditions, and this was another sound effort, although it has to be said that he was always well placed in a race not run at a strong gallop. (op 5-1)
Headline Act ◆, a well-bred son of Dalakhani, showed signs of inexperience in the paddock, at the start and at the business end of the race, and he looks sure to improve significantly for this experience. He holds a Royal Lodge entry and is clearly held in some regard. (op 7-1)
Holberg(UAE) made his debut over 6f, shaping as though this longer trip would suit. Up there throughout, he battled on well under pressure and looks to be going the right way. (op 10-1 tchd 9-1)
Mustaqer(IRE), runner-up in the Listed Washington Singer Stakes on his debut, is by Dalakhani and was expected to appreciate the extra furlong here. He appeared to set a pretty high standard for the rest to aim at and it was no surprise that he was sent off a short-priced favourite. However, he never settled and when brought to challenge approaching the furlong marker had little more to give. He is better than this, but will have to learn to settle if he is going to fulfil his potential. Official explanation: jockey said colt ran too free early (op 10-11 tchd Evens in places)
Royal Trooper(IRE), who got warm beforehand, showed more than on his debut, but he looks more of a handicap type for next year.
Double Rubble(USA) is not necessarily bred to be effective in these conditions, and being a son of a triple dirt winner he might be of more interest if turning up on the Polytrack. (op 16-1)
T/Jkpt: Not won. T/Plt: £1,002.60 to a £1 stake. Pool: £138,999.94. 101.20 winning tickets. T/Qpdt: £41.40 to a £1 stake. Pool: £7,889.50. 141.00 winning tickets. JR

5838 SANDOWN (R-H)
Friday, September 12

OFFICIAL GOING: Soft (good to soft in places on round course; heavy in places on sprint course)
Wind: Nil Weather: Bright

5860 SUNGARD EBF MAIDEN STKS 5f 6y
2:15 (2:17) (Class 4) 2-Y-O **£5,180** (£1,541; £770; £384) **Stalls** High

Form RPR
6 **1** **Cumana Bay**[8] 5643 2-8-12 0........................ RyanMoore 9 70
(R Hannon) *in tch: rdn over 2f out: styd on u.p over 1f out: kpt on wl to ld last strides* **6/1**[3]
34 **2** *shd* **Cawdor (IRE)**[46] 4480 2-9-3 0........................ DaneO'Neill 4 75
(H Candy) *chsd ldrs: led over 2f out: styd on u.p fnl f: ct last strides* **3/1**[2]
43 **3** *1* **Hail Promenader (IRE)**[79] 3358 2-9-3 0........................ MartinDwyer 3 71
(B W Hills) *chsd ldrs: rdn over 2f out: chal over 1f out: no ex u.p ins fnl f* **1/1**[1]
4 *1* **Majestic Lady (IRE)** 2-8-12 0........................ ChrisCatlin 5 63+
(B W Hills) *stdd s but in tch: hdwy over 1f out: kpt on ins fnl f but nvr gng pce to rch ldrs* **20/1**
6 **5** *1 1/4* **Perfect Class**[21] 5213 2-8-12 0........................ AdamKirby 11 58+
(C G Cox) *racd alone far side and pressed ldrs: stl ev ch ins fnl f: wknd fnl 100yds* **15/2**
0 **6** *3 3/4* **Winterbourne**[104] 2614 2-8-12 0........................ SteveDrowne 2 45
(M Blanshard) *chsd ldrs: rdn 1/2-way: wknd appr fnl f* **100/1**
0 **7** *2 1/2* **Iachimo**[69] 3735 2-9-3 0........................ AndrewElliott 7 41
(K R Burke) *prssed ldrs: rdn and upsides 2f out: wknd over 1f out* **66/1**
8 *1 3/4* **Allexes (IRE)** 2-8-12 0........................ PatCosgrave 8 30
(J R Boyle) *sn rdn and bhd: no ch whn edgd towards far side over 1f out* **40/1**
9 *5* **Brown Lentic (IRE)** 2-9-3 0........................ GeorgeBaker 10 17
(G L Moore) *chsd ldrs: drvn 2f out: wknd and edgd to far side sn after* **25/1**
10 *1/2* **Night Dancer (IRE)** 2-8-12 0........................ EddieAhern 1 10
(B W Hills) *s.i.s: a bhd* **33/1**
0000 **11** *4 1/2* **Short Cut**[11] 5567 2-9-3 55........................ LPKeniry 6 —
(S Kirk) *sn led: hdd over 2f out and wknd qckly* **66/1**

65.56 secs (3.96) **Going Correction** +0.70s/f (Yiel) **11** Ran SP% **119.0**
Speed ratings (Par 97): **96,95,94,92,90 84,80,77,69,69 61**
toteswinger: 1&2 £4.10, 1&3 £2.80, 2&3 £2.20. CSF £23.52 TOTE £7.40: £2.10, £1.40, £1.10; EX 30.90.
Owner J R Shannon **Bred** J R Shannon **Trained** East Everleigh, Wilts

FOCUS
Not the strongest of Sandown maidens but the first two are improving and the form is rated at face value. Most of the runners raced up the middle of the track whilst only one, Perfect Class, stayed against the far rail throughout.

NOTEBOOK
Cumana Bay was dropping to the minimum trip after failing to see out 7f on her debut at Salisbury eight days earlier when ridden positively. The move proved successful, though it did appear that she needed every yard of this stiff 5f to force her head in front and it may be that 6f will prove her optimum trip for the time being. She had no problem with the ground and looks the type for autumn nurseries. (op 5-1 tchd 9-2)
Cawdor(IRE), a beaten favourite in both of his previous starts and down to the minimum trip for the first time, was always up with the pace and could hardly have done any more without winning. Sprint nurseries may be for him. (op 7-2)
Hail Promenader(IRE), beaten at odds-on last time, had been given a short break since then and he was back on an easier surface. He was always within striking distance but, as hard as he tried, he could never quite get on terms with the front pair. He may need a switch to nursery company now. (op 11-8 tchd 6-4)
Majestic Lady(IRE) ◆ was the eye-catcher of the race, staying on very nicely on meeting the rising ground and faring much the best of the newcomers. A 26,000gns yearling out of a triple winning sprinter in Italy, she will get another furlong and is entitled to improve from this. (op 25-1)
Perfect Class, who showed some promise on her Bath debut last month, was the one to race alone against the far rail having started from the highest stall. She had every chance, but it is impossible to be sure whether the route she took was a help or a hindrance and her next outing should tell us more. (op 7-1 tchd 13-2)
Winterbourne, not seen since showing nothing on her debut back in May, ended up well beaten again but still showed a little bit more this time. (op 80-1 tchd 66-1)
Iachimo, who had finished lame on his debut, showed up for a while but is bred to need further than this. (op 50-1)

5861 LONDON STOCK EXCHANGE H'CAP 5f 6y
2:50 (2:51) (Class 4) (0-80,78) 3-Y-0+ **£5,180** (£1,541; £770; £384) **Stalls** High

Form RPR
204 **1** **Blessed Place**[8] 5645 8-8-5 **64** oh2........................ ChrisCatlin 3 71
(D J S Ffrench Davis) *sn led: rdn 1/2-way: hdd appr fnl f: styd chalng and led again fnl 110yds: gamely* **33/1**
2434 **2** *1/2* **Best One**[57] 4106 4-9-1 **77**........................(b[1]) KevinGhunowa(3) 1 82
(R A Harris) *wnt lft s: chsd ldrs: led appr fnl f: edgd rt ins fnl f: hdd and fnd no ex fnl 110yds* **8/1**
0202 **3** *nk* **Don Pele (IRE)**[4] 5751 6-8-12 **71**........................(b) JoeFanning 13 75
(R A Harris) *in rr: pushed along 1/2-way: hdwy fr 2f out: styd on ins fnl f to take 3rd but a hld by ldng duo* **5/1**[2]
0450 **4** *1 1/4* **Cape Royal**[4] 5757 8-9-4 **77**........................(bt) PatCosgrave 4 77
(J M Bradley) *s.i.s: sn in tch: chsd ldrs halfwway: upsides and rdn over 1f out: wknd ins fnl f* **20/1**
4406 **5** *1 1/4* **Glasshoughton**[14] 5455 5-9-4 **77**........................ PaulMulrennan 8 72
(M Dods) *chsd ldrs: rdn over 2f out: wknd fnl f* **11/2**[3]
0500 **6** *hd* **Dickie Le Davoir**[10] 5594 4-9-5 **78**........................ StephenDonohoe 12 72
(John A Harris) *s.i.s: in rr and sn rdn: kpt on fr over 1f out and styng on cl home wout ever looking a threat* **20/1**
3036 **7** *nk* **Rabbit Fighter (IRE)**[8] 5648 4-9-0 **73**........................(v) AndrewElliott 7 66
(D Shaw) *in tch: rdn 1/2-way and no imp on ldrs* **9/2**[1]
0006 **8** *1* **Sand Cat**[15] 5433 5-8-7 **69**........................(b) MichaelJStainton(3) 14 59
(G L Moore) *chsd ldrs to 1/2-way: wknd over 1f out* **16/1**
0100 **9** *shd* **Inspainagain (USA)**[5] 5719 4-8-6 **72**........................ DeanHeslop(7) 11 61
(T D Barron) *in rr: rdn 1/2-way: mod prog fnl f* **10/1**
310 **10** *1/2* **Triumphant Welcome**[9] 5617 3-8-0 **67**........................ StacyRenwick(7) 6 55
(G F Bridgwater) *chsd ldrs to 1/2-way: wknd over 1f out* **14/1**
3116 **11** *1/2* **Desperate Dan**[19] 5319 7-8-12 **71**........................(b) RyanMoore 9 57
(A B Haynes) *in rr tl mod prog ins fnl f* **8/1**
4204 **12** *1/2* **Corridor Creeper (FR)**[8] 5648 11-9-4 **77**........................(p) SteveDrowne 5 61
(J M Bradley) *chsd ldrs: rdn 1/2-way: wknd fnl f* **14/1**

1000 **13** *22* **What Do You Know**[21] [5250] 5-8-11 **77**..................(b) AndreaAtzeni(7) 10 —
(A M Hales) *pressed ldrs: rdn 1/2-way: wknd qckly fr 2f out* **16/1**

64.37 secs (2.77) **Going Correction** +0.70s/f (Yiel)
WFA 3 from 4yo+ 1lb **13** Ran SP% **119.1**
Speed ratings (Par 105): **105,104,103,101,99 99,98,97,97,96 95,94,59**
toteswinger: 1&2 £34.40, 1&3 £40.10, 2&3 £7.70. CSF £273.06 CT £1626.33 TOTE £48.00: £10.60, £3.10, £2.30; EX 442.50.
Owner S J Edwards **Bred** Mrs W H Gibson Fleming **Trained** Lambourn, Berks

FOCUS
Quite a competitive sprint handicap and the winning time was 1.19 seconds faster than the two-year-old maiden, though that was to be expected. Again the runners came up the middle of the track and with that being the case, a low draw was not the disadvantage it normally is. In fact three of the first four home came from the four lowest stalls. Ordinary form, with the winner 3lb out of the weights.
Glasshoughton Official explanation: jockey said gelding hung right

5862 AIM H'CAP 1m 14y
3:25 (3:25) (Class 3) (0-90,90) 3-Y-O
£9,346 (£2,799; £1,399; £700; £349; £175) **Stalls** High

Form RPR
1000 **1** **Red Rumour (IRE)**[6] [5695] 3-8-12 **84**........................ RichardKingscote 5 92
(R M Beckett) *chsd ldrs: rdn to chal fr 2f out: slt ld 1f out: edgd lft ins fnl f: hld on wl* **28/1**

0115 **2** *hd* **Admiral Dundas (IRE)**[14] [5470] 3-8-9 **81**...................... J-PGuillambert 7 88
(W Jarvis) *towards rr: rdn over 2f out: str run over 1f out to chse wnr ins fnl f: str chal cl home but a jst hld* **4/1**[2]

1035 **3** *1 1/2* **Silver Rime (FR)**[63] [3919] 3-9-1 **87**... RyanMoore 1 91
(R Hannon) *in rr: rdn along 3f out: hdwy 2f out: styng on whn carried lft jst ins fnl f: gng on cl home* **2/1**[1]

4023 **4** *1/2* **Midnight Muse (USA)**[35] [4818] 3-8-8 **80**.................. DeanMcKeown 3 83
(T D Barron) *led: shkn up and hdd 1f out: styd on same pce* **16/1**

2116 **5** *shd* **Topazes**[36] [4783] 3-8-12 **89**.. GaryBartley(5) 8 92
(M L W Bell) *in rr tl hdwy fr 2f out: chsd ldrs over 1f out: kpt on same pce ins fnl f* **12/1**

-130 **6** *shd* **Last Three Minutes (IRE)**[20] [5279] 3-8-13 **85**........... TGMcLaughlin 10 87
(E A L Dunlop) *in tch: rdn over 2f out: styd on to chse ldrs 1f out: one pce ins fnl f* **9/1**

3213 **7** *2 3/4* **Brassini**[30] [4983] 3-9-4 **90**... DaneO'Neill 2 86
(B R Millman) *chsd ldrs: rdn over 2f out: wknd fnl f* **9/1**

105 **8** *2 1/4* **Navajo Joe (IRE)**[7] [5682] 3-9-0 **86**..............................(b[1]) EddieAhern 11 77
(B J Meehan) *plld hrd and reluctant to settle early: hdwy fr 3f out: rdn and effrt 2f out: wknd over 1f out* **17/2**[3]

1530 **9** *shd* **By Command**[20] [5257] 3-9-4 **90**...................................(b[1]) SteveDrowne 4 81
(J L Dunlop) *a towards rr* **33/1**

5125 **10** *2 1/2* **Brave Hawk**[32] [4927] 3-8-6 **78**.......................................(p) MartinDwyer 9 63
(M A Jarvis) *chsd ldrs: rdn over 2f out: wknd sn after* **12/1**

4-15 **11** *1 1/2* **Regal Best (IRE)**[55] [4197] 3-8-13 **85**......................... JoeFanning 6 66
(Mrs A J Perrett) *chsd ldrs: rdn over 3f out: wknd over 2f out* **12/1**

1m 45.78s (2.48) **Going Correction** +0.45s/f (Yiel) **11** Ran SP% **119.2**
Speed ratings (Par 105): **105,104,103,102,102 102,99,97,97,95 93**
toteswinger: 1&2 £32.00, 1&3 £16.70, 2&3 £3.70. CSF £139.12 CT £344.62 TOTE £23.50: £3.80, £2.00, £1.50; EX 207.80.
Owner R Roberts **Bred** Tally-Ho Stud **Trained** Whitsbury, Hants

FOCUS
Quite a competitive handicap and, as was the case on the round course the previous day, the runners came up the middle of the track in the straight. Straightforward form.

NOTEBOOK
Red Rumour(IRE), who has been running poorly since making a winning reappearance including when tried in blinkers last time on his return from being gelded, bounced right back to form with the headgear removed. Never far away, he seemed likely to lose out half a furlong from home but, racing closer to the stands than his main rival, he got back up to score. He seemed to like the ground and he has the option of going back on to sand, but he does seem to have two very distinct ways of running. Official explanation: trainer said, regarding apparent improvement in form, that it had been gelded prior to its previous run where it failed to face the visor. (op 25-1 tchd 33-1)
Admiral Dundas(IRE), possibly unlucky off this mark here in his hat-trick bid last time out, was encountering soft ground for the first time. He was produced with his effort more towards the far side of the track and he looked set to score, but was just run out of it. He coped well enough with the ground which widens his options. (op 9-2)
Silver Rime(FR), who was well backed throughout the day, was returning from a short break. Kept wide of his rivals early on, he was switched towards the stands' side to make his effort entering the last couple of furlongs, but he tended to hang around and was never doing quite enough. (op 3-1)
Midnight Muse(USA), proven on easy ground, tried to make every yard and battled on well when challenged, but he had no more to give inside the last furlong. (op 12-1)
Topazes, disappointing off this mark last time after a string of decent efforts, was switched off out the back early. He did not have a lot of room when trying to get closer halfway up the straight and although he stayed on once in the clear, he was never getting there in time. (op 10-1)
Last Three Minutes(IRE), dropping back in trip after appearing not to stay 1m2f last time, plugged on up the hill but could not make much impression and he may prefer better ground. (tchd 10-1)
Navajo Joe(IRE), who has not looked an easy ride in a couple of his previous starts, had blinkers on for the first time but he gave himself no chance by pulling like a train early. (op 8-1 tchd 9-1)
By Command, disappointing since winning on his reappearance, was tried in first-time blinkers but he never figured at all and continues to disappoint.

5863 MAIN MARKET H'CAP 1m 14y
4:00 (4:04) (Class 4) (0-80,78) 3-Y-0+ **£5,180** (£1,541; £770; £384) **Stalls** High

Form RPR
1344 **1** **Opera Prince**[91] [2998] 3-9-2 **76**.. GeorgeBaker 4 87+
(S Kirk) *hld up in rr: stdy hdwy ins fnl 3f to ld jst ins fnl 2f: pushed clr fnl f: readily* **15/2**

1000 **2** *2* **Eastern Emperor**[13] [5492] 4-9-3 **72**..................................(t) AdamKirby 9 78
(W R Swinburn) *in rr but in tch: rdn over 2f out: styd on to chse wnr fnl f but nvr any ch* **7/1**

0320 **3** *3 1/4* **Marvo**[28] [5040] 4-9-6 **75**.. PaulMulrennan 12 74
(M H Tompkins) *pressed ldrs tl led after 2f: rdn 3f out: hdd jst ins fnl 2f: wknd and lost 2nd fnl f* **16/1**

0004 **4** *1 1/4* **Hawaana (IRE)**[20] [5290] 3-9-1 **75**................................ StephenCarson 11 70
(Eve Johnson Houghton) *chsd ldrs: hrd drvn fr 2f out: styd on fnl f* **8/1**

6214 **5** *nse* **Bold Cross (IRE)**[13] [5492] 5-9-0 **69**........................... PaulFitzsimons 13 65
(E G Bevan) *trckd ldrs: travelling wl 2f out: sn rdn: wknd 1f out* **12/1**

3160 **6** *2 1/4* **Harare**[25] [5156] 7-8-13 **68**..(v) RichardKingscote 10 58
(R J Price) *chsd ldrs: rdn over 2f out: sn btn* **14/1**

4221 **7** *3/4* **Master Mahogany**[19] [5312] 7-8-11 **66**............................. SteveDrowne 14 55
(R J Hodges) *led 2f: styd chsng ldrs: rdn 3f out: wknd fr 2f out* **5/1**[2]

0402 **8** *3 1/4* **Arctic Cape**[28] [5069] 3-9-2 **76**.. JoeFanning 2 56
(M Johnston) *chsd ldrs: rdn 3f out: wknd 2f out: no ch whn n.m.r appr fnl f* **9/2**[1]

1-0 **9** *1/2* **Bigfanofthat (IRE)**[154] [1297] 3-9-4 **78**........................... AndrewElliott 7 57
(K R Burke) *pressed ldrs: rdn to chal fr 3f out: wknd appr fnl 2f* **20/1**

4314 **10** *4* **Penchesco (IRE)**[37] [4741] 3-9-0 **74**.................................. PaulEddery 1 44
(Pat Eddery) *plld hrd: stdd rr: rdn and effrt 3f out: nvr rchd ldrs and wknd ins fnl 2f* **8/1**

3215 **11** *5* **Rescue Me**[13] [5492] 3-9-1 **75**... RyanMoore 5 33
(R Hannon) *sn towards rr: rdn and effrt 3f out: nvr rchd ldrs and wknd fr 2f out* **6/1**[3]

0/0P **12** *20* **Esenin**[18] [5369] 9-8-12 **74** oh19 ow10.............................. JWStevenson(7) 6 —
(Mrs Tracey Barfoot-Saunt) *bhd fr 1/2-way* **200/1**

1m 45.81s (2.51) **Going Correction** +0.45s/f (Yiel)
WFA 3 from 4yo+ 5lb **12** Ran SP% **121.1**
Speed ratings (Par 105): **105,103,99,98,98 96,95,92,91,87 82,62**
toteswinger: 1&2 £14.00, 1&3 £24.00, 2&3 £24.50. CSF £60.61 CT £840.30 TOTE £9.80: £3.00, £2.40, £5.80; EX 68.30.
Owner J C Smith **Bred** Littleton Stud **Trained** Upper Lambourn, Berks

FOCUS
The winning time was only fractionally slower than the preceding handicap confined to three-year-olds. The early pace seemed decent enough, with a few vying for the early lead, and the runners came up the middle of the track. Several were still within a length or so of each other with every chance entering the last couple of furlongs. The form is solid.
Rescue Me Official explanation: jockey said filly was unsuited by the soft (good to soft places) ground

5864 IVECO EUROCARGO MAIDEN STKS 1m 2f 7y
4:35 (4:39) (Class 5) 3-4-Y-0 **£3,885** (£1,156; £577; £288) **Stalls** High

Form RPR
2 **1** **Mumayeza**[86] [3133] 3-8-12 0.. MartinDwyer 6 76+
(Sir Michael Stoute) *mde all: shkn up 2f out: forged clr fnl f: unchal* **13/8**[1]

02 **2** *3* **Inquest**[10] [5587] 3-9-3 0.. GeorgeBaker 2 75
(Mrs A J Perrett) *in tch: hdwy 3f out: chsd wnr fr 2f out but a wl hld* **5/2**[2]

6 **3** *3/4* **Yetholm (USA)**[28] [5076] 3-9-3 0... RyanMoore 7 73
(J R Fanshawe) *towards rr: rdn and hdwy over 2f out: styd on fr over 1f out to take 3rd fnl f but nvr any threat ldng duo* **20/1**

0-30 **4** *1/2* **Crazy About You (IRE)**[118] [2197] 3-8-12 70.................. SteveDrowne 9 67
(B W Hills) *towwards rr: drvn along and hdwy over 2f out: kpt on ins fnl f but nvr gng pce to be competitive* **8/1**

0 **5** *1 1/4* **Jayarbee (IRE)**[66] [3823] 3-8-12 0............................ RichardKingscote 4 65
(P J McBride) *chsd wnr to 2f out: wknd over 1f out* **100/1**

0-5 **6** *3 1/4* **Intabih (USA)**[20] [5278] 3-9-3 0.. JoeFanning 1 63
(C E Brittain) *s.i.s: in rr: effrt fr 3f out: nvr in contention and sn wknd* **12/1**

4 **7** *1 3/4* **Calamansac**[136] [1695] 3-8-12 0.. EddieAhern 8 55
(R M Beckett) *chsd ldrs: rdn over 3f out: wknd over 2f out* **7/2**[3]

- **R** **L'Hirondelle (IRE)** 4-9-10 0... PaulDoe 5 —
(M J Attwater) *ref to r and styd in stalls* **40/1**

2m 15.58s (5.08) **Going Correction** +0.45s/f (Yiel)
WFA 3 from 4yo 7lb **8** Ran SP% **115.9**
Speed ratings (Par 103): **97,94,94,93,92 90,88,—**
toteswinger: 1&2 £1.90, 1&3 £5.10, 2&3 £6.10. CSF £5.87 TOTE £2.40: £1.20, £1.40, £3.40; EX 7.40.
Owner Hamdan Al Maktoum **Bred** Shadwell Estate Company Limited **Trained** Newmarket, Suffolk

FOCUS
A particularly weak older-horse maiden. The early pace set by the winner was moderate and the runners stayed close to the far rail in the home straight, though still away from it. The bare form probably underestimates the winner.
Jayarbee(IRE) Official explanation: jockey said filly lost a near-fore shoe

5865 IVECO ALL BLACKS H'CAP 1m 2f 7y
5:05 (5:09) (Class 4) (0-85,88) 3-Y-0 **£6,476** (£1,927; £963; £481) **Stalls** High

Form RPR
-410 **1** **Dr Livingstone (IRE)**[114] [2311] 3-8-12 **79**........................ SteveDrowne 3 92
(C R Egerton) *hld up towwards rr: stdy hdwy fr 3f out to ld ins fnl 2f: drvn out ins fnl f* **33/1**

441 **2** *1* **Times Vital (IRE)**[55] [4179] 3-8-9 **76**............................. DeanMcKeown 2 87
(E J O'Neill) *s.i.s: t.k.h in rr: stdy hdwy on outside over 2f out: drvn to chse wnr ins fnl f but a hld* **9/2**[3]

-521 **3** *3 1/2* **Crystal Rock (IRE)**[13] [5505] 3-8-13 **80**............................ DaneO'Neill 8 84
(B W Hills) *chsd ldrs: rdn fr 3f out: wknd ins fnl f* **8/1**

4111 **4** *2* **Mr Hichens**[4] [5759] 3-9-7 **88** 6ex...................................... EddieAhern 4 88
(B J Meehan) *led: rdn over 2f out: hdd ins fnl 2f: wknd fnl f* **11/4**[1]

446 **5** *1/2* **Mega Watt (IRE)**[33] [4906] 3-8-9 **76**.............................. RobertHavlin 6 75
(W Jarvis) *in rr: rdn over 2f out: styd on u.p fr over 1f out but nvr in contention* **9/1**

-104 **6** *1 1/2* **Indian Skipper (IRE)**[27] [5104] 3-8-13 **80**................. PaulMulrennan 5 76
(M H Tompkins) *in rr: rdn over 3f out towards outside and nvr in contention* **20/1**

-21 **7** *nk* **Taaresh (IRE)**[18] [5361] 3-9-1 **82**.................................... MartinDwyer 12 77
(J L Dunlop) *stdd in rr after 2f: t.k.h: rdn and no imp on ldrs fr 3f out* **8/1**

5006 **8** *1 1/2* **Calakanga**[7] [5682] 3-9-4 **85**... JoeFanning 7 77
(C E Brittain) *chsd ldrs: rdn 3f out: wknd ins fnl 2f* **16/1**

0304 **9** *7* **Eternal Luck (IRE)**[23] [5185] 3-8-12 **79** ow1.................... AdamKirby 10 57
(M A Jarvis) *rdn over 3f out: a in rr* **25/1**

0555 **10** *6* **Miss Bootylishes**[10] [5588] 3-8-8 **75**............................... LPKeniry 11 41
(A B Haynes) *chsd ldrs to 3f out* **33/1**

621 **11** *9* **Censored**[29] [5031] 3-8-13 **80**... RyanMoore 9 28
(Sir Michael Stoute) *chsd ldrs: rdn and btn over 2f out* **3/1**[2]

2m 12.69s (2.19) **Going Correction** +0.45s/f (Yiel) **11** Ran SP% **122.4**
Speed ratings (Par 103): **109,108,105,103,103 102,101,100,95,90 83**
toteswinger: 1&2 £30.50, 1&3 £31.20, 2&3 £8.70. CSF £177.40 CT £1343.49 TOTE £47.10: £7.70, £1.90, £2.70; EX 200.00 Place 6: £126.37, Place 5: £113.20..
Owner Exors of the Late Mrs E A Hankinson **Bred** Stone Ridge Farm **Trained** Chaddleworth, Berks

FOCUS
This featured five last-time-out winners, and the form is sound. The race was run at a fair pace and all bar one of the runners came away from the far rail starting up the home straight, though they all eventually ended up closer to it than in any of the previous races on the round course. The winning time was nearly three seconds faster than the maiden.
Censored Official explanation: trainers rep had no explanation for the poor form shown
T/Plt: £471.10 to a £1 stake. Pool: £64,405.48. 99.80 winning tickets. T/Qpdt: £92.00 to a £1 stake. Pool: £4,168.70. 33.50 winning tickets. ST

[5708] WOLVERHAMPTON (A.W) (L-H)

Friday, September 12

OFFICIAL GOING: Standard

Wind: Very modest, across Weather: raining

5866 OPEN A HILLS ACCOUNT - 0800 44 40 40 CLAIMING STKS 5f 216y(P)

6:20 (6:21) (Class 5) 2-Y-O £3,070 (£906; £453) Stalls Low

Form RPR

5352 **1** **Gone Hunting**[25] 5153 2-8-9 84........................ JackDean(5) 4 81
(W G M Turner) *racd in midfield: hdwy jst over 2f out: rdn to chse ldr over 1f out: led ins fnl f: r.o wl* **7/2**[2]

1320 **2** *1 3/4* **Night Seed (IRE)**[28] 5055 2-8-10 77........................ FrancisNorton 3 72
(R Hannon) *in tch: effrt on inner and rdn 2f out: pressed ldrs ent fnl f: kpt on to go 2nd nr fin: nt pce of wnr* **10/3**[1]

2410 **3** *hd* **Mazzola**[14] 5466 2-8-13 85........................ EdwardCreighton 1 74
(M R Channon) *led: rdn 2f out: hdd ins fnl f: no ex: lost 2nd nr fin* **10/3**[1]

441 **4** *2 1/4* **Alphabeth**[14] 5473 2-8-1 67 ow1........................ MCGeran(5) 7 60
(M R Channon) *trckd ldng pair: rdn over 1f out: fnd nil and no imp fnl f* **13/2**

4406 **5** *1/2* **Premier Krug (IRE)**[14] 5475 2-8-0 55........................ LukeMorris(3) 10 56
(P D Evans) *sn rdn and struggling to go pce: drvn 1/2-way: kpt on but nvr pce to threaten ldrs* **20/1**

012 **6** *3 1/2* **Simple Rhythm**[14] 5473 2-8-2 72........................ Louis-PhilippeBeuzelin(5) 5 49
(N Tinkler) *chsd ldr: rdn wl over 1f out: lost 2nd over 1f out: wknd qckly fnl f* **4/1**[3]

7 *1 1/2* **Jack's House (IRE)** 2-8-13 0........................(t) TonyCulhane 13 51
(Jane Chapple-Hyam) *sn outpcd in last trio: nvr a factor* **25/1**

6 **8** *15* **Cwmni**[36] 4764 2-8-4 0 ow7........................ MatthewDavies(7) 6 4
(B Palling) *v.s.a: a wl bhd: t.o* **66/1**

0 **9** *7* **Lucky In Love (IRE)**[9] 5614 2-8-2 0........................ RoystonFfrench 2 —
(Mark Gillard) *s.i.s: a bhd: t.o last 2f* **100/1**

1m 15.61s (0.61) **Going Correction** +0.05s/f (Slow) 9 Ran SP% **112.8**

Speed ratings (Par 95): **97,94,94,91,90 86,84,64,54**

CSF £14.69 TOTE £4.90: £1.50, £1.70, £1.10; EX 15.10.

Owner E A Brook **Bred** Norman Court Stud **Trained** Sigwells, Somerset

FOCUS

This was a decent, competitive juvenile claimer and they went a good pace. The winning time was 0.66sec slower than the following 56-70 handicap for three-year-olds and upwards. Solid enough form, although the fifth anchors it to some extent.

NOTEBOOK

Gone Hunting had struggled a little since winning a Polytrack maiden at Lingfield back in April, but he returned to his best last time and was able to take full advantage of this drop in grade. Settled just off the decent pace, he made a big move out wide rounding the turn into the straight and stayed on strongest of all. An official mark of 84 looks stiff enough, so he will probably be best off sticking to this sort of level, but valuable claimers are few and far between unfortunately. (op 10-3)

Night Seed(IRE) was dropping in class from a Listed race at Newbury and was another to benefit from the strong gallop, but having had her chance against the far rail in the straight she found one too strong. She would have been 3lb better off with the winner in a nursery and looked to run right up to form. (op 3-1 tchd 7-2)

Mazzola was the best off at the weights, but he was slightly below form on this first try on Polytrack. Perhaps the surface was not ideal, but he just looked to tee this up for a couple of closers. (tchd 3-1 and 7-2)

Alphabeth found this tougher than the claimer she won over course and distance on her previous start and she found a few too good, but she was still able to confirm form with Simple Rhythm. (op 7-1)

Premier Krug(IRE), who had plenty to find at the weights, was always struggling and got going too late to land a blow. (op 33-1 tchd 16-1)

Lucky In Love(IRE) Official explanation: jockey said filly never travelled

5867 GET A BONUS AT WILLIAMHILLCASINO.COM H'CAP 5f 216y(P)

6:50 (6:50) (Class 5) (0-70,70) 3-Y-O+ £4,209 (£1,252; £625; £312) Stalls Low

Form RPR

5461 **1** **Royal Challenge**[6] 5709 7-9-5 69 6ex........................ PatrickMathers 6 79
(I W McInnes) *taken down early: sn bustled along: racd in midfield: rdn and hdwy over 3f out: chsd clr ldr wl over 1f out: r.o wl u.p to ld towards fin* **6/1**[2]

0552 **2** *1/2* **Fast Freddie**[38] 4703 4-9-1 65........................ TonyCulhane 3 73
(S Parr) *pressed ldr tl led over 3f out: clr and rdn wl over 1f out: hrd drvn fnl f: hdd and no ex towards fin* **10/1**

3160 **3** *1/2* **Mafaheem**[16] 5392 6-9-6 70........................(b) JamesDoyle 1 76
(A B Haynes) *dwlt: bhd: hdwy over 2f out: swtchd lft over 1f out: r.o wl to go 3rd wl ins fnl f: nt rch ldng pair* **11/1**

0403 **4** *1/2* **Steel City Boy (IRE)**[8] 5648 5-8-12 67........................ AnnStokell(5) 8 72+
(Miss A Stokell) *rrd s and s.i.s: bhd: hdwy on outer 2f out: r.o fnl f: nt rch ldrs* **8/1**

4003 **5** *1 1/2* **Hammer Of The Gods (IRE)**[8] 5629 8-9-0 67..........(bt) LukeMorris(3) 4 67
(G C Bravery) *dwlt: sn pushed along: chsd ldng pair after 1f: rdn wl over 1f out: kpt on same pce after* **15/2**[3]

2615 **6** *1/2* **Comptonspirit**[31] 4958 4-9-4 68........................ HayleyTurner 13 66
(B P J Baugh) *racd in midfield on outer: rdn and unable qck 2f out: plugged on u.p fnl f: nt pce to trble ldrs* **14/1**

4602 **7** *2 1/4* **Realt Na Mara (IRE)**[10] 5594 5-9-6 70........................ TravisBlock 11 61
(H Morrison) *chsd ldrs: rdn wl over 3f out: wknd u.p over 1f out* **9/4**[1]

0206 **8** *hd* **Adantino**[18] 5345 9-9-0 67 ow1........................(b) JamesMillman(3) 2 58
(B R Millman) *hld up in midfield on inner: rdn 1/2-way: no prog fr over 1f out* **20/1**

4604 **9** *1 1/2* **Last Of The Line**[9] 5617 3-9-0 66........................(v) FrancisNorton 5 52
(H J L Dunlop) *s.i.s: bhd: modest hdwy fnl f: nvr a factor* **8/1**

2200 **10** *2 1/2* **Desert Pride**[19] 5315 3-9-0 66........................(vt[1]) MickyFenton 12 44
(W S Kittow) *led tl over 3f out: chsd ldr after tl wl over 1f out: wknd qckly* **18/1**

166 **11** *1/2* **Coconut Moon**[57] 4103 6-8-13 70........................(b[1]) RobbieEgan(7) 10 46
(D Flood) *hld up in midfield: nt clr run and swtchd lft over 1f out: no hdwy and wl btn fnl f* **25/1**

6004 **12** *1 3/4* **Tobar Suil Lady (IRE)**[38] 4702 3-9-1 67........................ CatherineGannon 7 38
(K A Ryan) *bhd: rdn over 4f out: no ch fr 1/2-way* **33/1**

1m 14.95s (-0.05) **Going Correction** +0.05s/f (Slow)

WFA 3 from 4yo+ 2lb 12 Ran SP% **119.9**

Speed ratings (Par 103): **102,101,100,100,98 97,94,94,92,88 88,85**

CSF £63.96 CT £662.15 TOTE £7.60: £2.40, £2.90, £5.10; EX 49.60.

Owner Truck Export **Bred** Capt A L Smith-Maxwell **Trained** Catwick, E Yorks

FOCUS

A modest but competitive sprint handicap run in a time 0.66sec quicker than the earlier juvenile claimer. They went a decent pace and the form is sound.

Last Of The Line Official explanation: jockey said colt was hampered at the start

5868 ALL THE BALLS AT WILLIAMHILLBINGO.COM H'CAP 1m 4f 50y(P)

7:20 (7:20) (Class 6) (0-65,65) 3-Y-O £2,388 (£705; £352) Stalls Low

Form RPR

2202 **1** **River Kent**[21] 5223 3-8-5 52........................ CatherineGannon 9 58
(Mrs A Duffield) *t.k.h: stdd and hld up towards rr after 2f: hdwy over 4f out: led wl over 1f out: hung rt fnl f: styd on* **16/1**

0303 **2** *2* **Templetuohy Max (IRE)**[17] 5379 3-8-4 51........................(v) JimmyQuinn 12 54
(J D Bethell) *dropped in bhd after s: t.k.h: hld up wl bhd: hdwy 4f out: chal over 1f out: kpt on same pce fnl f* **7/1**[3]

6543 **3** *2* **The Last Bottle (IRE)**[27] 4663 3-9-0 61........................ JamesDoyle 4 61
(W M Brisbourne) *short of room sn after s: hld up off the pce in midfield: hdwy and rdn over 3f out: styd on u.p to go 3rd 1f out: no imp fnl f* **12/1**

0005 **4** *2* **West Lorne (USA)**[12] 5537 3-8-9 56........................ ChrisCatlin 10 53
(E J O'Neill) *stdd after s: t.k.h: hld up in rr: rdn and hdwy over 3f out: styd on u.p but nvr pce to rch ldrs* **33/1**

0003 **5** *2 1/2* **Catholic Hill (USA)**[52] 4281 3-8-5 52........................ TPO'Shea 1 45
(B J Meehan) *led: clr w rival over 5f out: rdn 4f out: hdd and hung lft over 1f out: wknd fnl f* **2/1**[1]

5065 **6** *3 1/2* **Safebreaker**[30] 4990 3-8-2 54........................ Louis-PhilippeBeuzelin(5) 6 41
(N Tinkler) *hld up in midfield: rdn and lost pl over 5f out: rallied u.p 3f out: sn no imp* **16/1**

-010 **7** *10* **Patthepainter (GER)**[74] 3555 3-7-13 53..........(b) DeclanCannon(7) 2 24
(K R Burke) *awkward s: sn pressing ldr: wnt clr w ldr over 5f out: rdn 2f out: wknd qckly* **11/1**

4120 **8** *17* **Star Grazer**[12] 5537 3-8-13 63........................ JackMitchell(3) 3 7
(C F Wall) *bmpd s: short of room and hmpd after 1f: handy in main gp: rdn 5f out: no ch fnl 3f: t.o* **10/1**

1001 **9** *1 3/4* **Lady Jinks**[21] 5215 3-8-12 59........................ FrancisNorton 5 —
(R J Hodges) *t.k.h: chsd ldrs tl 4f out: sn wknd: t.o* **10/1**

0300 **10** *3 1/2* **Muharjam**[46] 4481 3-9-4 65........................(b) HayleyTurner 11 —
(C E Brittain) *a bhd: rdn and no rspnse 5f out: t.o* **20/1**

623 **11** *1* **Be Free**[227] 350 3-8-12 59........................(b[1]) PatCosgrave 7 —
(Sir Mark Prescott) *s.i.s: t.k.h: sn in midfield: hdwy to chse clr ldng pair 4f out: drvn and stopped to nil 3f out: eased fnl f: t.o* **13/2**[2]

-502 **12** *14* **Corking (IRE)**[21] 5215 3-8-8 58........................ KevinGhunowa(3) 8 —
(J L Flint) *chsd ldrs: rdn and steadily lost pl 8f out: t.o last 3f* **20/1**

2m 41.51s (0.41) **Going Correction** +0.05s/f (Slow) 12 Ran SP% **117.6**

Speed ratings (Par 99): **100,98,97,96,94 92,85,74,72,70 69,60**

CSF £119.83 CT £1407.91 TOTE £21.60: £5.30, £2.90, £3.40; EX 121.10.

Owner Mr & Mrs G Middlebrook **Bred** G And Mrs Middlebrook **Trained** Constable Burton, N Yorks

FOCUS

A moderate middle-distance handicap but quite a test for these three-year-olds as they went off really quickly. The winning time was 0.35 seconds faster than the following 46-50 handicap for three-year-olds and upwards. The winner is the best guide to the form.

Star Grazer Official explanation: jockey said filly never travelled

5869 GET YOUR CHIPS AT WILLIAMHILLPOKER.COM H'CAP 1m 4f 50y(P)

7:50 (7:51) (Class 6) (0-50,50) 3-Y-O+ £2,388 (£705; £352) Stalls Low

Form RPR

5040 **1** **Zalkani (IRE)**[8] 5631 8-9-0 50........................ JerryO'Dwyer(3) 2 61
(J Pearce) *hld up towards rr: hdwy 4f out: chal 2f out: rdn to ld last 100yds: r.o wl* **5/1**[3]

0034 **2** *1* **Wulimaster (USA)**[16] 5396 5-9-3 50........................ RoystonFfrench 11 59
(D W Barker) *dropped in bhd after s: hld up in rr: hdwy over 3f out: rdn to ld 2f out: hdd and unable qck last 100yds* **9/2**[2]

3546 **3** *3 1/4* **Barbirolli**[41] 4630 6-9-0 50........................ LukeMorris(3) 5 54
(W M Brisbourne) *hld up in midfield: jostled 4f out: chsd ldrs and rdn 2f out: unable qck wl over 1f out: rallied u.p fnl f: wnt 3rd nr fin* **8/1**

5430 **4** *1/2* **Personify**[35] 4807 6-9-0 50........................ KevinGhunowa(3) 3 53
(J L Flint) *hld up towards rr: hdwy 4f out: jnd ldr gng wl 2f out: sn rdn and unable qck: kpt on same pce: lost 3rd nr fin* **7/1**

3055 **5** *shd* **Artzola (IRE)**[38] 4704 8-9-1 48........................ HayleyTurner 4 51
(C A Horgan) *stdd and dropped in after s: hld up and bhd: hdwy over 3f out: rdn wl over 1f out: kpt on but nvr pce to rch ldrs* **7/2**[1]

0444 **6** *2* **Hugs Destiny (IRE)**[10] 5040 7-8-10 48........................(t) RichardEvans(5) 12 48
(M A Barnes) *chsd ldrs: rdn jst over 2f out: wknd over 1f out* **8/1**

-050 **7** *hd* **Boxhall (IRE)**[12] 5396 6-8-10 48........................(tp) AshleyHamblett(5) 6 47
(N Wilson) *chsd ldr tl led after 2f: rdn and hdd 2f out: wknd fnl f* **9/1**

6366 **8** *3 1/2* **Viscount Rossini**[10] 5593 6-9-1 48........................(b) ChrisCatlin 7 42
(S Gollings) *hld up in midfield: hdwy to chse ldrs over 2f out: sn rdn and fnd nil: wl hld fnl f* **10/1**

0460 **9** *11* **Bright Sun (IRE)**[29] 5003 7-9-3 50........................ KimTinkler 1 26
(N Tinkler) *led tl 10f out: chsd ldr after: reminder over 4f out: wknd qckly over 2f out* **20/1**

0-00 **10** *23* **Raydan (IRE)**[215] 332 6-9-2 49........................(p) MickyFenton 8 —
(D R Gandolfo) *t.k.h: chsd ldrs: rdn and wkng whn jostled 4f out: wl bhd after: t.o* **40/1**

00-6 **11** *34* **My Beautaful**[21] 5215 4-9-2 49........................(t) VinceSlattery 9 —
(Miss J S Davis) *mounted on crse: racd in midfield: rdn and rapidly lost tch 5f out: wl t.o last 3f* **66/1**

2m 41.86s (0.76) **Going Correction** +0.05s/f (Slow) 11 Ran SP% **119.6**

Speed ratings (Par 101): **99,98,96,95,95 94,94,91,84,69 46**

CSF £27.88 CT £180.99 TOTE £6.80: £1.70, £1.60, £3.40; EX 31.50.

Owner Mrs Lisa Matthews **Bred** His Highness The Aga Khan's Studs S C **Trained** Newmarket, Suffolk

FOCUS

Not bad form for such a low level, rated through the second and fourth. The winning time was 0.35sec slower than the earlier 51-65 handicap for three-year-olds.

5870 REAL TIME RADIO AT WILLIAMHILL.CO.UK MEDIAN AUCTION MAIDEN STKS 1m 141y(P)

8:20 (8:21) (Class 5) 2-Y-O £2,729 (£806; £403) Stalls Low

Form RPR

5 **1** **Stevie Junior**[28] 5066 2-9-3 0........................ AlanMunro 10 86+
(P W Chapple-Hyam) *hld up in tch: hdwy to trck ldrs over 2f out: led over 1f out: rdn and edgd lft ins fnl f: pushed clr* **8/11**[1]

3 **2** *2 3/4* **Daylumney (IRE)**[12] 5534 2-8-12 0........................ ChrisCatlin 7 73
(E J O'Neill) *chsd ldr tl led 4f out: rdn over 2f out: hdd over 1f out: kpt on but nt pce of wnr ins fnl f* **5/1**[3]

3 *2 3/4* **Fin Vin De Leu (GER)** 2-9-3 0........................ RoystonFfrench 8 72+
(M Johnston) *hld up in rr of main gp: rdn and no prog over 3f out: styd on fr over 1f out: wnt 3rd ins fnl f: nvr trbld ldng pair* **11/1**

0 4 1 1/2 **Deuce**[21] 5227 2-8-9 0 .... LukeMorris(3) 11 64
(Eve Johnson Houghton) *racd wd: sn pushed along to go prom: rdn 4f out: outpcd 2f out: plugged on* **25/1**

303 5 nse **Reaction**[41] 4636 2-9-3 79 .... TonyCulhane 9 69
(M R Channon) *chsd ldrs: wnt 2nd wl over 3f out: rdn and ev ch over 2f out: btn jst over 1f out: wknd qckly fnl f* **4/1[2]**

65 6 10 **Baileys Red**[19] 5304 2-9-3 0 .... PatCosgrave 1 48
(J G Given) *in tch: rdn and struggling over 3f out: wl bhd last 2f* **66/1**

0365 7 1 1/4 **Aegean Warning**[37] 4733 2-9-3 62 ....(p) FrancisNorton 3 46
(K A Ryan) *led tl 4f out: wknd qckly over 2f out* **16/1**

8 1/2 **Sampower Quin (IRE)** 2-9-3 0 .... DNolan 2 45
(D Carroll) *dwlt: sn in tch: rdn over 2f out: wknd qckly 2f out: wl bhd fnl f* **66/1**

0000 9 11 **Liliaceae**[14] 5473 2-8-5 20 ....(t) LeeTopliss(7) 4 16
(D Shaw) *s.i.s: a detached in last: t.o last 2f* **100/1**

1m 52.18s (1.68) **Going Correction** +0.05s/f (Slow) **9** Ran SP% **116.6**
Speed ratings (Par 95): **94,91,89,87,87 78,77,77,67**
CSF £4.79 TOTE £2.00: £1.30, £1.90, £2.00; EX 7.20.
Owner S Harris **Bred** Manor Farm Stud (rutland) **Trained** Newmarket, Suffolk

FOCUS
A reasonable juvenile maiden for the course, but the winner did not need to improve to score comfortably.

NOTEBOOK
Stevie Junior ◆ confirmed the promise he showed when fifth over 7f at the Newmarket July course on his debut. The Peter Chapple-Hyam yard has really struck form with their juveniles recently and this one looks capable of holding his own in better company. He will probably be best off going down the handicap route and should not be underestimated. (op 4-5 tchd 4-6)
Daylumney(IRE) had her chance, but probably ran into quite a useful type in the making. She is going the right way and is now qualified for a handicap mark. (op 15-2 tchd 8-1)
Fin Vin De Leu(GER) ◆, a son of Dr Fong whose sales price dropped from 32,000gns as a yearling to 20,000gns this year, is a half-brother to a dual winner in the US, out of high-class multiple 7f-1m4f winner (including the Ribblesdale Stakes) Fairy Queen. He was very green for this racecourse debut and came under strong pressure down the back straight, but he was doing his best work at the finish. He will know more next time and should be good enough to win an ordinary maiden. (op 10-1 tchd 12-1)
Deuce, down the field on her debut over 7f at Newbury, showed ability and should find a race once handicapped. (op 20-1)
Reaction did not see his race out and was below form. The trip should not have been a problem on breeding so this was disappointing.

5871 BET ONLINE AT WILLIAMHILL.CO.UK H'CAP 7f 32y(P)
8:50 (8:51) (Class 6) (0-55,55) 3-Y-0+ £2,388 (£705; £352) Stalls High

Form RPR

500 1 **Sendreni (FR)**[60] 4031 4-9-2 54 .... ChrisCatlin 6 70+
(M Wigham) *racd keenly: chsd ldng pair: led over 1f out: pushed clr fnl f: easily* **10/1**

0620 2 3 1/2 **Elusive Dreams (USA)**[113] 2337 4-9-2 54 ....(v) JimmyQuinn 4 61+
(P Howling) *s.i.s: t.k.h: hld up in rr: hdwy over 1f out: swtchd lft ent fnl f: r.o wl to go 2nd towards fin: no ch w wnr* **8/1**

0304 3 3/4 **Perlachy**[8] 5629 4-9-0 55 ....(v) LukeMorris(3) 9 60
(Mrs N Macauley) *chsd ldr: upsides ldr 3f out: rdn over 2f out: led wl over 1f out: sn hdd: no ch w wnr fnl f: lost 2nd towards fin* **16/1**

3000 4 hd **Summer Recluse (USA)**[26] 5121 9-8-12 53 ....(t) KevinGhunowa(3) 3 57
(J M Bradley) *taken down early: dwlt: hld up in midfield: rdn and lost pl 4f out: rallied u.p over 1f out: kpt on* **40/1**

0006 5 hd **Kirstys Lad**[14] 5478 6-9-2 54 .... AlanMunro 5 58
(M Mullineaux) *chsd ldrs: rdn over 2f out: kpt on same pce u.p last 2f* **6/1[3]**

0040 6 shd **Kingsholm**[66] 3822 6-9-2 54 .... TonyCulhane 7 58+
(K A Ryan) *hld up and bhd: nt clr run jst over 2f out: r.o u.p fnl f: nvr rchd ldrs* **5/1[2]**

0533 7 1 1/4 **Sands Of Barra (IRE)**[12] 5538 5-9-2 54 .... PatrickMathers 2 54
(I W McInnes) *broke wl: sn restrained in midfield: rdn and nt qckn 2f out: plugged on same pce u.p* **7/2[1]**

0502 8 1 **Dancing Duo**[19] 5317 4-9-0 52 ....(v) SaleemGolam 12 50
(D Shaw) *dropped in after s: hld up towards rr: hdwy into midfield 4f out: rdn over 2f out: no prog after* **14/1**

26-0 9 3 **Inka Dancer (IRE)**[241] 165 6-8-10 55 .... MatthewDavies(7) 10 44
(B Palling) *sn led: rdn and jnd over 2f out: hdd wl over 1f out: wknd fnl f* **40/1**

00-0 10 6 **Hurricane Coast**[60] 4031 9-8-9 54 ....(b) RobbieEgan(7) 11 27
(D Flood) *s.i.s: racd in midfield on outer: rdn and btn over 3f out* **33/1**

/010 11 3/4 **Valverde (IRE)**[41] 4653 5-9-1 53 ....(v) DO'Donohoe 1 24
(George Baker) *short of room and shuffled bk sn after s: bhd after: n.d* **13/2**

504 12 11 **Goose Green (IRE)**[38] 4707 4-9-1 53 .... FrancisNorton 8 —
(R J Hodges) *chsd ldrs: rdn and wknd over 3f out: wl bhd over 1f out: t.o* **7/1**

1m 29.82s (0.22) **Going Correction** +0.05s/f (Slow) **12** Ran SP% **119.6**
Speed ratings (Par 101): **100,96,95,94,94 94,93,92,88,81 80,68**
CSF £87.39 CT £1297.12 TOTE £11.60: £4.10, £3.50, £6.30; EX 156.20 Place 6 £319.65, Place 5 £240.01..
Owner Allan Darke **Bred** H H The Aga Khan's Studs Sc **Trained** Newmarket, Suffolk
■ Perlachy was the last runner of trainer Norma Macauley's long career.

FOCUS
This looked like a competitive - if pretty moderate - handicap beforehand, but nothing could live with Sendreni, who bolted up and is rated back to something like his French form. They finished in a bunch in behind.
Elusive Dreams(USA) Official explanation: jockey said gelding missed the break
Summer Recluse(USA) Official explanation: jockey said gelding suffered interference on first bend
T/Plt: £222.70 to a £1 stake. Pool: £86,597.56. 283.83 winning tickets. T/Qpdt: £72.90 to a £1 stake. Pool: £7,452.40. 75.60 winning tickets. SP

5326 CORK (R-H)
Friday, September 12

OFFICIAL GOING: Yielding to soft

5873a DERRINSTOWN STUD APPRENTICE H'CAP 7f
4:40 (4:41) (50-80,76) 3-Y-0+ £6,859 (£1,598; £704; £406)

RPR

1 **Springfort (IRE)**[12] 5545 3-8-8 67 ....(b) JulieBurke(7) 10 75+
(Tracey Collins, Ire) *mde all: strly pressed ent st: rdn clr fr 1 1/2f out: kpt on wl* **11/2[1]**

2 2 **Duck Scary (IRE)**[107] 2519 4-9-3 67 .... EJMcNamara(2) 13 70
(T J O'Mara, Ire) *trckd ldrs in 5th: 4th and rdn early st: 3rd and prog on inner 1f out: kpt on* **16/1**

3 1 **Musical Review (UAE)**[19] 5328 5-8-11 61 ....(p) MACleere(2) 11 61
(G Kennedy, Ire) *settled 2nd: clsd on ldr appr st: rdn to chal over 2f out: no imp fr 1 1/2f out: kpt on* **7/1[3]**

4 shd **Luck Wud Have It (IRE)**[20] 5298 4-9-11 75 .... PTownend(2) 4 75
(Patrick J Flynn, Ire) *chsd ldrs in 6th: rdn on outer st: kpt on fnl f* **10/1**

5 shd **Herbert Crescent**[12] 5545 3-9-3 76 .... SHJames(7) 12 75
(Edward Lynam, Ire) *prom: 4th 1/2-way: 3rd and effrt under 2f out: kpt on same pce* **12/1**

6 1 **Distant Piper (IRE)**[37] 4755 5-9-1 67 .... IJBrennan(4) 9 64
(Adrian McGuinness, Ire) *hld up: prog st: 7th over 1f out: kpt on* **8/1**

7 1 1/2 **Confirm (IRE)**[14] 5480 4-8-0 52 ....(tp) GFCarroll(4) 5 45
(H Rogers, Ire) *hld up in tch: 8th early st: kpt on wout threatening fr 1 1/2f out* **10/1**

8 hd **Littleton Telchar (USA)**[37] 4739 8-9-0 68 .... MHarley(2) 1 56
(S W Hall) *chsd ldrs in 3rd: rdn and no imp st: no ex fr over 1f out* **20/1**

9 1 1/2 **Dragon Lady (IRE)**[20] 5298 3-9-5 73 ....(p) SFoley(2) 6 61
(M Halford, Ire) *hld up in tch: 9th and rdn ent st: kpt on same pce* **8/1**

10 1/2 **Glenconnor Lad (IRE)**[12] 5545 3-9-0 70 .... BACurtis(4) 8 57
(David P Myerscough, Ire) *a towards rr* **8/1**

11 9 **Denanto (IRE)**[14] 5480 4-8-12 60 .... SMGorey 3 22
(P A Fahy, Ire) *a towards rr* **12/1**

12 1 3/4 **Miss Una (IRE)**[16] 5410 6-9-9 71 .... CPGeoghegan 7 29
(Patrick Martin, Ire) *rrd up leaving stalls and lost grnd: a bhd* **6/1[2]**

13 9 **Nightswimmer (IRE)**[15] 5439 3-8-12 68 .... DEMullins(4) 2 1
(David P Myerscough, Ire) *chsd ldrs on outer: wknd appr st* **12/1**

1m 32.0s (-26.90)
WFA 3 from 4yo+ 4lb **13** Ran SP% **127.4**
CSF £100.21 CT £482.98 TOTE £6.90: £1.50, £3.00; DF 539.40.
Owner Mrs C Collins **Bred** Churchland Stud **Trained** The Curragh, Co Kildare

Miss Una(IRE) Official explanation: trainer said mare did not act on the tacky ground

5874 - 5881a (Foreign Racing) - See Raceform Interactive

5493 CHESTER (L-H)
Saturday, September 13

OFFICIAL GOING: Good to soft (soft in places; 7.1)
Rail realignment added about 15yds per circuit to race distances.
Wind: Light, against Weather: Overcast turning bright

5882 HEATHCOTES OUTSIDE EBF MAIDEN STKS 7f 2y
2:30 (2:34) (Class 4) 2-Y-0 £5,504 (£1,637; £818; £408) Stalls Low

Form RPR

63 1 **Akhenaten**[9] 5641 2-9-3 0 .... ChrisCatlin 7 79+
(M R Channon) *chsd ldrs: led over 1f out: rdn clr ins fnl f: r.o wl* **9/4[1]**

2 3 1/2 **Royal Defence (IRE)** 2-9-3 0 .... FrancisNorton 5 70
(D Nicholls) *midfield: hdwy over 3f out: styd on to take 2nd ins fnl f: no imp on wnr* **12/1**

4 3 1/2 **Paqueretza (FR)**[133] 1794 2-8-12 0 .... PaulMulrennan 10 64+
(D H Brown) *chsd ldrs: rdn over 1f out: styd on same pce ins fnl f* **16/1**

55 4 1 **Viking Awake (IRE)**[37] 4780 2-9-3 0 .... MickyFenton 3 67
(J W Unett) *led: rdn and hdd over 1f out: no ex fnl 100yds* **5/1[2]**

5 4 1/2 **Best Bidder (USA)** 2-8-5 0 .... BMcHugh(7) 6 50+
(R A Fahey) *towards rr: rdn and hdwy over 1f out: no imp on ldrs: wknd ins fnl f* **16/1**

6 shd **Northern Acres** 2-9-3 0 .... SilvestreDeSousa 9 55
(D Nicholls) *missed break: sn in midfield: effrt over 3f out: unable to chal ldrs: wknd fnl f* **12/1**

0 7 3 1/2 **Lucy Brown**[43] 4593 2-8-9 0 .... AndrewMullen(3) 4 41
(M W Easterby) *chsd ldr: rdn over 2f out: wknd 1f out: sn hung lft* **50/1**

0 8 1 1/2 **Super Flight**[29] 5068 2-9-3 0 .... AdrianMcCarthy 8 43+
(P W Chapple-Hyam) *in tch: sn pushed along: lost pl over 2f out: eased whn btn over 1f out* **5/1[2]**

0 9 1/2 **Rising Kheleyf (IRE)**[38] 4740 2-9-3 0 .... PJMcDonald 12 41
(G A Swinbank) *a bhd* **8/1**

4 10 10 **Graycliffe (IRE)**[55] 4213 2-9-3 0 .... TonyHamilton 11 16
(R A Fahey) *a bhd* **15/2[3]**

55 B **Antigua Sunrise (IRE)**[50] 4380 2-8-12 0 .... DaleGibson 1 —
(R A Fahey) *sn pushed along in rr: b.d over 4f out* **8/1**

00 F **Nayessence**[6] 5716 2-8-10 0 .... BradleyRoper(7) 2 —
(M W Easterby) *awkward s: midfield: lost pl after 1f: fell over 4f out* **66/1**

1m 31.7s (5.20) **Going Correction** +0.60s/f (Yiel) **12** Ran SP% **120.0**
Speed ratings (Par 97): **94,90,89,88,83 83,79,77,76,65 —,—**
toteswinger: 1&2 £8.60, 1&3 £13.60, 2&3 £14.20. CSF £32.32 TOTE £3.60: £1.80, £4.30, £5.00; EX 38.80.
Owner Box 41 **Bred** Netherfield House Stud **Trained** West Ilsley, Berks

FOCUS
An average-looking maiden for the track. The winner is improving and gave a boost to Cityscape's Salisbury form.

NOTEBOOK
Akhenaten was highly tried on his debut and then ran to the same sort of level in a novice event (beaten 13 lengths by the promising Cityscape). He won this in relatively easy style, but whether he proves good enough to take up any of his big-race entries next season is another matter. (op 11-4 tchd 2-1)
Royal Defence(IRE), a £36,000 half-brother to several winners, including the very useful Pinpoint, ran a really eyecatching race as he travelled well and kept on strongly when asked to chase the winner. He should be capable of winning an ordinary maiden around one of the northern courses. (op 9-1)
Paqueretza(FR), off since a promising effort back in May, kept on in resolute fashion in the final furlong to deny the long-time leader Viking Awake of third place. She will undoubtedly be better for the run and is one to have on your side next time. (tchd 14-1)
Viking Awake(IRE) would have been helped by quicker ground, but will probably also be aided by a drop in trip. A 6f nursery would make him interesting next time. (op 7-1)
Best Bidder(USA), who cost $150,000 as a yearling and is out of a half-sister to several winners in the US, ran with some promise, keeping on well inside the final stages. (op 20-1)
Northern Acres made a satisfactory debut and looks capable of better. (op 16-1)

Graycliffe(IRE)attracted some market support on his first start for the Fahey stable, but he showed very little from a wide draw. (op 12-1)

5883 CHESHIRE LIFE NURSERY 7f 2y

3:00 (3:01) (Class 3) (0-95,87) 2-Y-O **£9,146** (£2,737; £1,368; £684; £340) **Stalls** Low

Form				RPR
14	**1**		**Firebet (IRE)**[56] 4187 2-9-1 **81** .... PaulMulrennan 6 (Mrs A Duffield) *chsd ldrs: wnt 2nd over 1f out: edgd lft ins fnl f: r.o to ld towards fin* **5/1**	85
1336	**2**	*hd*	**Lakeman (IRE)**[11] 5585 2-8-10 **76** .... TonyHamilton 1 (B Ellison) *chsd ldrs: wnt 2nd 2f out: rdn to ld over 1f out: hdd towards fin* **9/2**[3]	79
2100	**3**	*2*	**Suruor (IRE)**[14] 5511 2-8-7 **73** .... WilliamBuick 3 (M Johnston) *in rr: outpcd after 1f tl over 4f out: rdn and hdwy over 1f out: hung lft and chsd ldrs ins fnl f: nt pce to trble front pair* **3/1**[2]	71
4214	**4**	*1 ½*	**Fitzolini**[18] 5381 2-8-9 **75** ....(p) SilvestreDeSousa 2 (A D Brown) *led: rdn and hdd over 1f out: on ex ins fnl f* **9/1**	69
2121	**5**	*6*	**Night Of Fortune**[15] 5447 2-9-7 **87** .... J-PGuillambert 5 (Sir Mark Prescott) *plld hrd: chsd ldr tl 2f out rideen and wknd over 1f out* **11/8**[1]	66
520	**6**	*nk*	**Our Apolonia (IRE)**[13] 5539 2-7-5 **64** oh11 .... CharlotteKerton(7) 4 (A Berry) *in rr: outpcd after 1f tl 4f out: lft bhd over 1f out* **25/1**	43

1m 30.86s (4.36) **Going Correction** +0.60s/f (Yiel) 6 Ran SP% **115.8**
Speed ratings (Par 99): **99,98,96,94,87 87**
toteswinger: 1&2 £2.70, 1&3 £2.40, 2&3 £3.50. CSF £28.20 TOTE £5.90: £2.10, £1.90; EX 32.30.
Owner Mrs H Steel **Bred** Derek Veitch And Saleh Ali Hammadi **Trained** Constable Burton, N Yorks
■ Stewards' Enquiry : Paul Mulrennan five-day ban: used whip with excessive frequency without giving colt sufficient time to respond (Sep 27-Oct 1)

FOCUS
A small field but a case could be made out for virtually all of them, although some had stronger claims than others. The form looks sound.

NOTEBOOK
Firebet(IRE), who had been absent since the middle of July, did not run too badly at Newbury last time (a race that has produced winners) after winning a modest-looking event on his debut. Travelling sweetly in the early stages, he took a while to wear down the runner-up and shaped like a horse who may need a test. He will stay further but the Derby entry he possesses is unlikely to be taken up next season. (op 13-2)
Lakeman(IRE), who won in heavy ground at York earlier in the year, did not seem to stay a mile last time after a respectable effort in the Horn Blower at Ripon. He got to the lead turning into the home straight but just got mugged close to the line, which would suggest 7f is about his limit.
Suruor(IRE) lost some interest in the early stages, but came to have a bit of a chance on the home bend. However, he did not pick up that smartly when asked and was never able to get on terms. (op 7-2)
Fitzolini was one of the most exposed horses in the race, and set the pace. He looked in the grip of the handicapper last time after being raised 11lb for winning, and did nothing to dispel that theory in this. (op 10-1 tchd 8-1)
Night Of Fortune landed his second nursery last time at this course, and was raised 7lb for doing so. A half-brother to the talented but quirky Tam Lin, he pulled much too hard and failed to get home. Official explanation: trainer's rep said colt was unsuited by the good to soft (soft in places) ground (op 5-4 tchd 6-4)
Our Apolonia(IRE), who showed some ability on her second start, never looked like posing a threat. (tchd 22-1 tchd 50-1 in palces)

5884 STOWE FAMILY LAW LLP HENRY GEE FILLIES' STKS (LISTED RACE) 6f 18y

3:30 (3:32) (Class 1) 3-Y-O+

£24,978 (£9,468; £4,738; £2,362; £1,183; £594) **Stalls** Low

Form				RPR
0051	**1**		**Angus Newz**[4] 5781 5-9-0 **90** .... FrancisNorton 1 (M Quinn) *mde all: rdn over 1f out: hrd pressed ins fnl f: hld on wl* **7/2**[2]	96
1611	**2**	*½*	**Look Busy (IRE)**[13] 5551 3-9-3 **106** .... SladeO'Hara 2 (A Berry) *midfield: hdwy 3f out: swtchd rt 2f out: wnt 2nd jst over 1f out: str chal ins fnl f: hld fnl strides* **6/4**[1]	99
0550	**3**	*1*	**Manzila (FR)**[48] 4467 5-9-0 **98** .... SilvestreDeSousa 3 (D Nicholls) *chsd ldrs: wnt 2nd briefly over 1f out: nt qckn ins fnl f* **9/2**[3]	91
3004	**4**	*2 ½*	**Topflightcoolracer**[14] 5493 4-9-0 **77** .... DaleGibson 5 (Mrs G S Rees) *midfield: hdwy over 1f out: kpt on ins fnl f: nt pce to rch ldrs* **25/1**	83
-100	**5**	*1 ½*	**Quiet Elegance**[105] 2606 3-8-12 **92** .... PaulMulrennan 7 (E J Alston) *racd keenly: prom: rdn over 1f out: no ex ins fnl f* **14/1**	78
2346	**6**	*1*	**Crystany (IRE)**[19] 5347 3-8-12 **93** .... ChrisCatlin 9 (E A L Dunlop) *missed break: towards rr: hdwy over 1f out: nt pce to trble ldrs* **14/1**	75
3204	**7**	*hd*	**Tilly's Dream**[65] 3883 5-9-0 **76** .... AndrewMullen 11 (G C Bravery) *towards rr: nt clr run over 2f out: hdwy over 1f out: nt pce to chal* **40/1**	75
2211	**8**	*5*	**Gentle Guru**[22] 5233 4-9-0 **85** .... WilliamBuick 6 (R T Phillips) *a bhd* **15/2**	59
660	**9**	*3*	**Coconut Moon**[1] 5867 6-9-0 **70** ....(b) DNolan 4 (D Flood) *a towards rr* **33/1**	49
4151	**10**	*7*	**Now You See Me**[137] 1706 4-9-0 **56** .... RobbieEgan 8 (D Flood) *chsd ldrs: rdn over 2f out: wknd over 1f out* **66/1**	27
	11	*nk*	**Boule Masquee**[51] 4355 4-9-0 **0** .... J-PGuillambert 10 (David P Myerscough, Ire) *midfield: hdwy 3f out: wknd over 1f out* **33/1**	26

1m 17.72s (3.92) **Going Correction** +0.60s/f (Yiel)
WFA 3 from 4yo+ 2lb 11 Ran SP% **119.2**
Speed ratings (Par 108): **97,96,95,91,89 88,88,81,77,68 67**
toteswinger: 1&2 £1.20, 1&3 £4.50, 2&3 £2.10. CSF £8.86 TOTE £4.90: £1.90, £1.30, £1.90; EX 8.60 Trifecta £33.60 Pool: £599.50 - 13.20 winning units..
Owner M J Quinn **Bred** Henry And Mrs Rosemary Moszkowicz **Trained** Newmarket, Suffolk

FOCUS
Some of these runners definitely deserved to be taking their chance at this level, while others appeared to be having a stab at nicking some black type. The first three finished in draw order and the winner is rated back to her best, but overall this form is ordinary for the grade.

NOTEBOOK
Angus Newz had the perfect starting point for a front-runner (stall 1) and came into the race in good form after landing a small-field conditions race at Leicester in the week. The easy ground was no problem to her and she made every yard for a deserved success. Connections indicated afterwards that she will be sold at the end of the season. (op 9-2 tchd 5-1 in places)
Look Busy(IRE), who had a bit in hand on official figures despite her penalty, has been in tremendous heart this season and produced her best performance so far at the Curragh last time, defeating a decent field in the Flying Five Stakes. From a handy draw, she made her bid off the final bend but could not peg back the winner, who she had beaten when they last met. Tough and game, she is certain to win more races. (op 11-10)
Manzila(FR) was comfortably held in third after holding every chance. She is entitled to be straighter for the run, however, after an absence. (op 6-1)
Topflightcoolracer kept on at the one pace from midfield but never looked like grabbing that valuable third place. (op 33-1)
Quiet Elegance, a half-sister to Reverence, kept tabs on Angus Newz early and paid for that inside the final furlong. (tchd 12-1)
Crystany(IRE) gets a mention as she stayed on well after being slowly away from a wide draw. (op 12-1)
Boule Masquee Official explanation: jockey said filly lost its action

5885 CARLSBERG STAND CUP (LISTED RACE) 1m 4f 66y

4:05 (4:07) (Class 1) 3-Y-O+ **£26,074** (£9,860; £4,928; £2,464) **Stalls** Low

Form				RPR
4-05	**1**		**Foxhaven**[21] 5288 6-9-1 **102** ....(v) FrancisNorton 1 (P R Chamings) *led briefly: prom: led over 1f out: sn hung lft and rdn: styd on wl* **4/1**[3]	111
0R00	**2**	*1 ¾*	**Carte Diamond (USA)**[22] 5229 7-9-1 **100** .... J-PGuillambert 5 (B Ellison) *sn led: hdd over 1f out: sn n.m.r and hmpd: kpt on but unable to chal wnr after* **11/2**	109+
0012	**3**	*2*	**Strategic Mount**[14] 5494 5-9-1 **105** .... PaulMulrennan 6 (P F I Cole) *stdd s: hld up: pushed along and hdwy 2f out: kpt on ins fnl f: nvr able to land blow* **3/1**[2]	105
1-60	**4**	*nse*	**Crime Scene (IRE)**[43] 4585 5-9-1 **109** .... WilliamBuick 2 (Saeed Bin Suroor) *hld up: niggled along over 4f out: chal 3f out: outpcd wl over 1f out: kpt on u.p ins fnl f but no imp on ldrs* **4/1**[3]	105
225-	**5**	*14*	**Veracity**[364] 5408 4-9-1 **112** .... ChrisCatlin 3 (Saeed Bin Suroor) *sn prom: pushed along to chal 3f out: wknd wl over 1f out* **11/4**[1]	83
113B	**6**	*1*	**Cheshire Prince**[14] 5494 4-9-1 **89** .... DeanHeslop 4 (W M Brisbourne) *racd keenly: hld up: brief effrt over 3f out: sn outpcd and lft bhd* **16/1**	81

2m 43.77s (3.87) **Going Correction** +0.60s/f (Yiel) 6 Ran SP% **112.9**
Speed ratings (Par 111): **111,109,108,108,99 98**
toteswinger: 1&2 £4.20, 1&3 £2.80, 2&3 £3.30. CSF £25.76 TOTE £5.30: £2.70, £2.90; EX 24.40.
Owner Mrs Ann Jenkins **Bred** Highclere Stud Ltd **Trained** Baughurst, Hants
■ Stewards' Enquiry : Francis Norton three-day ban: careless riding (Sep 28-30)

FOCUS
There looked to be various reasons to oppose most of these, and this looks ordinary Listed form. The early pace was modest and a sprint developed inside the final 2f, which also tempers enthusiasm.

NOTEBOOK
Foxhaven, the winner of this race in 2006 and second behind Hattan last year when fitted with a visor for the first time, had the headgear back on after a couple of efforts without anything on, and already held a recent verdict over Carte Diamond and Crime Scene after finishing well in front of both of them at Goodwood. Always travelling well, he powered to the front early in the home straight but made things a little complicated by coming across the runner-up well inside the final furlong. He was never going to lose the race and wins in his turn, but is in no way prolific. (op 9-2)
Carte Diamond(USA) had quite a bit to find on official figures against most of his rivals, but he secured a valiant runner-up spot after making most of the running and being hampered in the final stages. (op 10-1)
Strategic Mount managed to win on ground with a bit of ease in it at Ascot two runs ago, but generally looked like a horse that required a decent surface to race on. Not disgraced at this course last time over a bit further, he was given a patient ride but could not get on terms despite quickening, which suggested the early pace was not strong. (op 11-4 tchd 5-2)
Crime Scene(IRE) has won plenty of races in his career, but put up another lacklustre performance.
Veracity, who had not been on the course since running down the field in the St Leger for Michael Jarvis on this day last year, did not look to show a great deal, which was disappointing, but the gallop was not strong enough for him and he was entitled to need the run. It would not be a massive surprise to see him perform much better next time if running over a more suitable trip. (tchd 7-2)
Cheshire Prince had no chance against this lot on official figures, but did at least show he has plenty of heart after being brought down last time around this sharp track. Predictably, he was dropped as the tempo increased. (op 11-1)

5886 HEATHCOTES OUTSIDE H'CAP 5f 16y

4:40 (4:40) (Class 4) (0-85,88) 3-Y-O+ **£5,504** (£1,637; £818; £408) **Stalls** Low

Form				RPR
0002	**1**		**Green Park (IRE)**[31] 4962 5-9-5 **85** ....(b) TonyHamilton 9 (R A Fahey) *stdd s and sn swtchd lft: hld up: rdn and hdwy over 1f out: r.o ins fnl f to get up on line* **9/1**	94
1661	**2**	*nse*	**Supermassive Muse (IRE)**[14] 5493 3-9-2 **83** ....(p) WilliamBuick 6 (E S McMahon) *chsd ldrs: r.o to ld ins fnl f: sn edgd lft: pipped on post* **7/2**[2]	92
0103	**3**	*2*	**Angle Of Attack (IRE)**[16] 5417 3-8-9 **76** .... MickyFenton 4 (A D Brown) *led: rdn and hdd ins fnl f: no ex fnl 50yds* **6/1**	78
003	**4**	*½*	**Ice Planet**[22] 5222 7-8-11 **77** .... SilvestreDeSousa 2 (D Nicholls) *hmpd sn after s and sn bhd: swtchd rt over 1f out: sn rdn: styd on towards fin: nt pce to rch ldrs* **11/4**[1]	77+
3614	**5**	*shd*	**Woodcote (IRE)**[5] 5757 6-9-1 **81** ....(vt) FrancisNorton 5 (P R Chamings) *hld up: hdwy over 1f out: nt clr run ent fnl f: styd on towards fin: nt pce to chal ldrs* **5/1**[3]	81
0400	**6**	*½*	**Thunder Bay**[14] 5510 3-8-10 **77** .... DaleGibson 3 (R A Fahey) *chsd ldrs: rdn and nt qckn 1f out: kpt on same pce ins fnl f* **17/2**	75
3255	**7**	*2 ¼*	**Fire Up The Band**[6] 5719 9-7-12 **71** oh7 .... JamieKyne(7) 7 (A Berry) *chsd ldr tl rdn over 1f out: fading whn edgd lft ins fnl f* **14/1**	61
000	**8**	*½*	**Jilly Why (IRE)**[14] 5493 7-8-7 **76** ow2 ....(b) RussellKennemore(3) 8 (Paul Green) *chsd ldrs: rdn 2f out: wknd fnl f* **20/1**	64
4240	**9**	*1 ¾*	**Tyfos**[62] 3999 3-8-10 **77** .... ChrisCatlin 10 (W M Brisbourne) *hld up: outpcd over 1f out* **25/1**	59

64.27 secs (3.27) **Going Correction** +0.60s/f (Yiel)
WFA 3 from 4yo+ 1lb 9 Ran SP% **115.6**
Speed ratings (Par 105): **97,96,93,92,92 91,88,87,84**
toteswinger: 1&2 £6.20, 1&3 £8.20, 2&3 £4.70. CSF £40.65 CT £208.83 TOTE £9.60: £2.40, £1.50, £2.30; EX 39.40.
Owner G A Fixings Ltd **Bred** James Burns And A Moynan **Trained** Musley Bank, N Yorks

FOCUS
There was 21lb between these on official figures, so this may not have been the strongest event. However, a couple of them did look fairly treated on their best form and the winner may be one to follow in the short-term. He is rated back to his early-season form.

5887 HEATHCOTES @ BANGOR-ON-DEE RACECOURSE H'CAP 1m 7f 195y
5:15 (5:16) (Class 4) (0-80,80) 3-Y-O+ £5,504 (£1,637; £818; £408) Stalls Low

Form RPR
0012 **1** **Okafranca (IRE)**[35] 4859 3-8-0 65 ow1 FrancisNorton 7 75
(W R Muir) *led for 2f: remained prom: led again over 3f out: rdn clr over 1f out: styd on wl* **4/1**[2]
3353 **2** *8* **Sir Sandicliffe (IRE)**[12] 5559 4-8-4 63 oh5 DeanHeslop(7) 4 63
(W M Brisbourne) *hld up: outpcd 4f out: hdwy 3f out: styd on to take 2nd ins fnl f: nt trble wnr* **9/1**
0260 **3** *2* **Basalt (IRE)**[46] 3250 4-10-0 80 (t) WilliamBuick 2 78
(T J Pitt) *midfield: hdwy 6f out: rdn to chse wnr 3f out: outpcd over 1f out: lost 2nd ins fnl f: styd on same pce* **7/2**[1]
003 **4** *½* **River Danube**[29] 5042 5-9-2 68 PaulMulrennan 8 65
(T J Fitzgerald) *hld up: hdwy over 4f out: rdn 2f out: sn one pce* **16/1**
1046 **5** *10* **Squirtle (IRE)**[6] 5718 5-8-10 67 KellyHarrison(5) 1 52
(W M Brisbourne) *s.i.s: hld up: u.p over 5f out: plugged on at one pce fnl 2f: nvr a danger* **15/2**
6115 **6** *3 ½* **Keelung (USA)**[45] 4516 7-9-10 76 MickyFenton 9 57
(R Ford) *led after 2f: rdn and hdd over 3f out: wknd 2f out* **7/2**[1]
51-0 **7** *49* **Gloucester**[126] 309 5-8-13 70 (p) JackDean(5) 3 —
(M J Scudamore) *in tch: pushed along and wknd 4f out: t.o* **9/1**
4052 **8** *2 ¼* **Trianon**[15] 5464 3-8-10 75 (vt) ChrisCatlin 6 —
(R Charlton) *prom tl rdn and wknd over 4f out: t.o* **6/1**[3]
2220 **9** *35* **Bocciani (GER)**[5] 5752 3-7-5 63 oh2 JamieKyne(7) 5 —
(A Berry) *in tch: lost pl 1/2-way: rdn 7f out: t.o fnl 5f* **28/1**

3m 38.09s (8.19) **Going Correction** +0.60s/f (Yiel)
WFA 3 from 4yo+ 13lb **9** Ran SP% **119.8**
Speed ratings (Par 105): **103,99,98,97,92 91,66,65,47**
toteswinger: 1&2 £8.90, 1&3 £4.20, 2&3 £6.90. CSF £41.37 CT £140.45 TOTE £5.30: £1.80, £2.70, £1.70; EX 57.90.
Owner The Eastwood Partnership **Bred** B Kennedy **Trained** Lambourn, Berks

FOCUS
Mainly exposed sorts lined up for this test of stamina and plenty of them were high in the handicap, so the form is unlikely to prove that strong or reliable. Big improvement from the winner, but the runner-up was out of the weights.
Keelung(USA) Official explanation: trainer had no explanation for the poor form shown

5888 HEATHCOTES CATERERS H'CAP 1m 2f 75y
5:50 (5:50) (Class 5) (0-75,75) 3-Y-O £3,561 (£1,059; £529; £264) Stalls High

Form RPR
3523 **1** **Offshore Anna (IRE)**[43] 4607 3-8-10 **67** TonyHamilton 7 76+
(J J Quinn) *midfield: pushed along and outpcd over 2f out: nt clr run wl over 1f out: gd hdwy sn after: swtchd rt ins fnl f: r.o to ld towards fin* **10/3**[1]
0300 **2** *¾* **Ballora (FR)**[10] 5605 3-9-1 **72** WilliamBuick 11 78
(S Kirk) *hld up: hdwy 4f out: rdn 2f out: wnt 2nd over 1f out: r.o to ld ins fnl f: hdd towards fin* **15/2**
0002 **3** *2 ¾* **Natural Rhythm (IRE)**[12] 5565 3-8-4 **61** oh1 (b) SilvestreDeSousa 2 61
(Mrs R A Carr) *led: hdd narrowly jst over 3f out: rdn over 2f out: regained ld wl over 1f out: hdd ins fnl f: no ex fnl 100yds* **13/2**[3]
0062 **4** *hd* **Applaude**[14] 5504 3-9-2 **73** PJMcDonald 3 73
(G A Swinbank) *chsd ldrs: rdn over 1f out: edgd rt ins fnl f: kpt on u.p: nvr able to chal* **11/2**[2]
5500 **5** *1* **Thunderstruck**[23] 5202 3-8-13 **70** (b[1]) FrancisNorton 5 69+
(K A Ryan) *chsd ldr: led narrowly jst over 3f out: hdd wl over 1f out: no ex ent fnl f: eased fnl 75yds* **11/1**
4064 **6** *1 ½* **Bavarian Nordic (USA)**[61] 4017 3-8-7 **67** AndrewMullen(3) 9 62
(Mrs A Duffield) *hld up: effrt 2f out: nvr able to chal* **13/2**[3]
1324 **7** *17* **Eton Fable (IRE)**[19] 5362 3-8-13 **75** KellyHarrison(5) 8 36
(W J H Ratcliffe) *chsd ldrs: rdn along 6f out: wknd 2f out* **10/3**[1]
550 **8** *7* **Gaelic Dancer (IRE)**[21] 5278 3-8-10 **67** PaulMulrennan 1 14
(J G Given) *hld up: struggling 4f out: sn lost tch* **12/1**

2m 18.87s (6.67) **Going Correction** +0.60s/f (Yiel) **8** Ran SP% **116.0**
Speed ratings (Par 101): **97,96,94,94,93 92,78,72**
toteswinger: 1&2 £6.50, 1&3 £6.10, 2&3 £8.90. CSF £29.48 CT £154.74 TOTE £3.20: £1.30, £2.70, £1.70; EX 28.20 Place 6 £204.90, Place 5 £90.49.
Owner Colm McEvoy **Bred** Conor Murphy **Trained** Settrington, N Yorks

FOCUS
This did not look the most competitive race of the day, as most of them had set their level already, which was not that high. However, the early pace looked respectable, which in turn helped to produce a very exciting finish. Modest form that makes sense.
Eton Fable(IRE) Official explanation: jockey said gelding never travelled
T/Plt: £209.80 to a £1 stake. Pool: £65,827.61. 228.95 winning tickets. T/Qpdt: £31.90 to a £1 stake. Pool: £3,622.70. 83.90 winning tickets. DO

5852 DONCASTER (L-H)
Saturday, September 13
OFFICIAL GOING: Soft (good to soft in places; 6.7)
Wind: Light, half behind Weather: fine, becoming sunny and quite warm

5889 KEEPMOAT CHAMPAGNE STKS (GROUP 2) (C&G) 7f
1:35 (1:38) (Class 1) 2-Y-O
£56,770 (£21,520; £10,770; £5,370; £2,690; £1,350) Stalls High

Form RPR
1210 **1** **Westphalia (IRE)**[21] 5296 2-8-12 0 JMurtagh 7 112
(A P O'Brien, Ire) *w'like: str: hld up in tch: effrt and pushed along 2f out: swtchd rt and rdn over 1f out: styd on ins fnl f to ld nr fin* **10/3**[2]
1 **2** *nk* **Zacinto**[71] 3682 2-8-12 0 RyanMoore 8 111+
(Sir Michael Stoute) *lw: trckd ldrs: hdwy 3f out: rdn to ld over 1f out: drvn ins fnl f: hdd and nt qckn nr fin* **13/8**[1]
11 **3** *1* **Playfellow (IRE)**[10] 5615 2-8-12 0 PhilipRobinson 3 108
(M A Jarvis) *w'like: scope: lw: trckd ldng pair: hdwy to ld over 2f out: rdn and hdd over 1f out: drvn and no ex ins fnl f* **7/2**[3]
3210 **4** *½* **Ouqba**[22] 5244 2-8-12 93 RHills 1 107
(B W Hills) *t.k.h: trckd ldrs: hdwy on outer 3f out: rdn and ev ch wl over 1f out: one pce ins fnl f* **20/1**
112 **5** *¾* **Master Noverre (IRE)**[22] 5226 2-8-12 106 PaulHanagan 5 105
(R A Fahey) *trckd ldr: effrt 3f out: rdn along 2f out: drvn and wknd over 1f out* **13/2**
13 **6** *6* **Jazz Police**[28] 5093 2-8-12 0 JimmyFortune 4 90
(R Hannon) *set stdy pce: qcknd 1/2-way: rdn and hdd over 2f out: sn wknd* **25/1**
11 **7** *3 ½* **War Native (IRE)**[26] 5143 2-8-12 0 ShaneKelly 2 81+
(J Noseda) *dwlt: hld up in rr and plld hrd: effrt and sme hdwy over 2f out: sn btn* **10/1**

1m 28.52s (2.22) **Going Correction** +0.30s/f (Good) **7** Ran SP% **114.4**
Speed ratings (Par 107): **99,98,97,96,96 89,85**
toteswinger: 1&2 £2.00, 1&3 £2.90, 2&3 £1.70. CSF £9.19 TOTE £4.60: £2.40, £2.10; EX 9.30 Trifecta £34.50 Pool: £676 - 14.48 winning units..
Owner M Tabor, D Smith & Mrs John Magnier **Bred** Lynch Bages Ltd & Samac Ltd **Trained** Ballydoyle, Co Tipperary
■ Are Can (200/1) was withdrawn at the start on vet's advice.

FOCUS
A mix of two-year-olds with Group race form and less exposed types open to plenty of improvement. The early pace was steady and it turned into a bit of a dash, so the form may not be entirely reliable. However, while it is impossible to rate the principals as highly as usual, they are nice types who can do better in a race more conducive to producing big figures.

NOTEBOOK
Westphalia(IRE) was an odds-on flop in the Futurity Stakes last time out, but the ground was very testing at the Curragh that day and, although soft here, conditions were far less taxing. He had looked progressive prior to that and set a decent standard on his easy win in a Listed race previously. He was a bit keen in the early stages and, not for the first time, put his head in the air when asked to pick up, but while it's an unattractive trait, he is far from ungenuine, and he ran on strongly next to the stands' rail to get up close home. He is likely to take his chance in the Breeders' Cup Juvenile Turf next and, although cut to a best price of 25-1 for the Guineas, his stable looks to hold stronger cards for the race in Mastercraftsman and Rip Van Winkle. (op 9-2 tchd 5-1)
Zacinto, who got a bit warm beforehand, was impressive to the eye when winning on his debut at Sandown, but the form has not worked out and this race on completely different ground was sure to tell us a lot more. Given a nice break since, he did nothing wrong in being narrowly beaten by a more experienced colt from Ballydoyle. A return to faster ground should suit him and he remains open to further improvement in a stronger-run race. The Dewhurst looks a suitable target. (op 6-4 tchd 13-8 in places)
Playfellow(IRE) is a good-looking sort and was proven with plenty of cut in the ground. Philip Robinson kicked on some way out on Playfellow, trying to take advantage of the fact that they had only gone steady early. He was not good enough to hold off the first two but rallied after being headed by Ouqba, and one got the impression that he would have appreciated a stronger gallop. The Horris Hill is next on his agenda. (op 4-1)
Ouqba, whose trainer has won this race three times in the past 11 years and is often represented by his best two-year-old, needed to step up quite a bit on his previous efforts to get in the mix on this step up in class, but he ran well, despite racing keenly in the early stages, briefly threatening down the outside before not quite seeing it out in the ground.
Master Noverre(IRE), second in the rearranged Gimcrack at Newbury last time, was taking on stronger opposition here and was a bit keen early. Perhaps faster ground will suit him, but he does not look quite up to this class. (op 15-2 tchd 8-1)
Jazz Police had only finished third in the Washington Singer Stakes last time out (form which had been let down by the runner-up in a maiden here the previous day) and he looked to face a stiff task. Making the running at a steady enough pace gave him a tactical advantage, but it was not enough in this company. (tchd 20-1)
War Native(IRE), who came into the race with a similar profile to Playfellow, having won his maiden on turf and followed up in novice company on the Polytrack, simply would not settle off the modest pace and failed to run his race. He had looked promising and will be seen to better effect in a race run at a stronger gallop. (op 9-1 tchd 17-2)

5890 LADBROKES PORTLAND (HERITAGE H'CAP) 5f 140y
2:05 (2:08) (Class 2) 3-Y-O+
£46,732 (£13,995; £6,997; £3,502; £1,747; £877) Stalls High

Form RPR
5640 **1** **Hogmaneigh (IRE)**[28] 5109 5-9-6 **100** SaleemGolam 18 112
(S C Williams) *lw: in rr towards stands' side: hdwy 2f out: r.o wl to ld post* **11/1**
0056 **2** *shd* **River Falcon**[49] 4437 8-8-12 **92** DanielTudhope 9 104
(J S Goldie) *in rr centre: gd hdwy over 1f out: r.o wl ins fnl f: jst failed* **14/1**
3300 **3** *nk* **Siren's Gift**[42] 4624 4-8-8 **93** (b[1]) DavidProbert(5) 14 104
(A M Balding) *w ldrs centre: led over all 3f out: hdd last strides* **12/1**
1505 **4** *2* **Oldjoesaid**[19] 5347 4-9-10 **104** DaneO'Neill 21 108+
(H Candy) *lw: dwlt: hdwy on ins over 1f out: styd on wl towards fin* **10/1**[3]
1111 **5** *nk* **Cheveton**[23] 5206 4-8-13 **93** JimCrowley 13 96
(R J Price) *lw: w ldrs on outer: wknd last 75yds* **9/1**[2]
6524 **6** *nk* **Fathom Five (IRE)**[13] 5551 4-9-6 **100** TomEaves 11 102
(B Smart) *lw: chsd ldrs centre: kpt on same pce appr fnl f* **20/1**
4221 **7** *shd* **Strike Up The Band**[35] 4840 5-9-5 **99** RyanMoore 19 101
(D Nicholls) *mid-div stands' side: hdwy 2f out: kpt on: nt rch ldrs* **17/2**[1]
0203 **8** *nk* **Fullandby (IRE)**[21] 5259 6-9-9 **103** GregFairley 6 104
(T J Etherington) *mid-div centre: hdwy over 1f out: kpt on: nt rch ldrs* **14/1**
5003 **9** *nk* **Tamagin (USA)**[28] 5109 5-9-5 **99** (p) NCallan 16 99
(K A Ryan) *led on stands' side: hdd 3f out: styd on same pce fnl f* **9/1**[2]
1156 **10** *½* **Inter Vision (USA)**[14] 5503 8-9-2 **96** JimmyFortune 7 94
(A Dickman) *in rr div centre: hdwy over 1f out: kpt on: nvr nr ldrs* **40/1**
2014 **11** *¾* **Toms Laughter**[44] 4555 4-8-12 **95** (b) KevinGhunowa(3) 22 91
(R A Harris) *w ldrs stands' side: one pce fnl 2f* **14/1**
-205 **12** *1* **Lipocco**[55] 4223 4-9-8 **102** GeorgeBaker 8 95
(R M Beckett) *chsd ldrs towards centre: wknd fnl f* **16/1**
2126 **13** *½* **Chief Editor**[13] 5551 4-9-3 **97** JamieSpencer 17 88+
(M J Wallace, Australia) *hld up in rr: hdwy and nt clr run appr fnl f: nvr nr ldrs* **14/1**
0043 **14** *nse* **Evens And Odds (IRE)**[35] 4840 4-9-3 **97** (bt) LDettori 15 88
(K A Ryan) *chsd ldrs towards stands' side: wknd appr fnl f* **16/1**
0210 **15** *½* **Hamish McGonagall**[54] 4240 3-9-0 **96** DavidAllan 1 85
(T D Easterby) *w ldrs toward far side: wknd over 1f out* **25/1**
0003 **16** *nk* **Northern Fling**[14] 5503 4-9-6 **100** GrahamGibbons 20 88
(D Nicholls) *mid-div stands' side: nvr rchd ldrs* **11/1**
0001 **17** *2 ¾* **Hoh Hoh Hoh**[14] 5509 6-9-9 **103** MartinDwyer 3 82
(R J Price) *lw: dwlt: hdwy far side over 2f out: wknd over 1f out* **25/1**
1130 **18** *4* **Van Bossed (CAN)**[91] 3047 3-8-13 **95** PaulHanagan 5 61
(D Nicholls) *in rr towards far side: sme hdwy over 2f out: lost pl over 1f out* **33/1**
0200 **19** *¾* **Hammadi (IRE)**[42] 4617 3-9-3 **99** (t) DO'Donohoe 4 62
(K A Ryan) *a towards rr far side* **80/1**
-200 **20** *2 ½* **Cute Ass (IRE)**[14] 5509 3-9-2 **98** PatCosgrave 2 53
(K R Burke) *chsd ldrs on outer: wknd over 1f out* **40/1**

5010 **21** *3* **Buachaill Dona (IRE)**[42] 4624 5-9-9 **103**.................. AdrianTNicholls 10 48
(D Nicholls) mid-div towards centre: hung rt and wknd 2f out: bhd and eased ins fnl f **16/1**

68.55 secs (1.15) **Going Correction** +0.30s/f (Good)
WFA 3 from 4yo+ 2lb **21** Ran SP% **129.8**
Speed ratings (Par 109): **104,103,103,100,100 100,99,99,99,98 97,96,95,95,94 94,90,85,84,80 76**
toteswinger: 1&2 £8.80, 1&3 £94.90, 2&3 £86.70. CSF £151.25 CT £1948.55 TOTE £11.50: £3.20, £4.40, £6.10, £2.80; EX 93.20 Trifecta £2322.90 Part won. Pool of £ 3139.09 - 0.20 winning units..
Owner Mrs Lucille Bone **Bred** John Malone **Trained** Newmarket, Suffolk

FOCUS
A competitive and open Portland in which they went 17-2 the field. They raced centre to stands' side in what was a pretty clean and well run affair. Solid form.

NOTEBOOK
Hogmaneigh(IRE) has not been easy to train because of problems with his feet, but some new shoes from America, similar to those that have helped Big Brown, have apparently made things easier, and he was expected to have come on for his run in the Great St Wilfrid. A confirmed hold-up horse who needs a strong pace to be seen at his best, he finished strongly to edge the photo and is a smart sprinter on his day. The Ayr Gold Cup, for which he picks up a 5lb penalty, could be next. (op 9-1)
River Falcon was also held up before coming through with a similarly late flourish. Back down to the mark he last won off, he had conditions to suit and ran a fine race. He will no doubt take his chance in the Ayr Gold Cup, where any cut in the ground will aid his cause.He was sixth in the race last year off a 7lb higher mark.
Siren's Gift, who was wearing blinkers for the first time, ran really well considering the ground was softer than ideal. She showed good pace throughout and it was only in the last half furlong that she began to look vulnerable to a finisher. The headgear seemed to bring about some improvement so she might find a race back over the bare minimum before the season is out. (op 20-1)
Oldjoesaid has a good record on softish ground and ran a fine race under top weight, especially considering he lost a few lengths when slowly away. (op 11-1)
Cheveton has been most progressive this year, winning five on the bounce, but this was another step up in class for him and the extended 5f here has caught many a 5f specialist out in the past. (tchd 8-1)
Fathom Five(IRE), who did not run too badly in a Group 3 race in Ireland last time, reversed Shergar Cup form with Strike Up The Band, but this extended 5f just stretched him.
Strike Up The Band is also happier over the bare five these days. (op 11-1)
Fullandby(IRE), last year's winner, was 6lb higher and ran a sound enough race, but he is vulnerable off his current mark. (op 12-1)
Tamagin(USA), who ran well with the cheekpieces back on at Ripon last time, again showed good speed, but it is difficult to hang on out in front at this track, which usually suits those more patiently ridden. (op 10-1)
Inter Vision(USA) stayed on from off the pace but needs faster ground to be seen at his best.
Lipocco apparently did not have a good journey over to Ireland last time, which explained his disappointing effort in a Listed race there, but this was another ordinary performance.
Chief Editor shaped better than his finishing position. At his best on soft ground and held up off the pace, he had conditions to suit, but he got no luck when his rider was looking for a way through inside the final two furlongs, and the cause was soon given up. Official explanation: jockey said gelding was denied a clear run
Hamish McGonagall, one of only four three-year-olds in the line-up, showed up well to a furlong out but then dropped right out. He will be happier back over a sharp 5f.
Buachaill Dona(IRE) Official explanation: jockey said gelding hung right-handed throughout

5891 LADBROKES SPRINT CUP (GROUP 1) 6f
2:35 (2:38) (Class 1) 3-Y-O+

£93,670 (£35,508; £17,770; £8,860; £4,438; £2,227) **Stalls** High

Form RPR
3-42 **1** **African Rose**[34] 4915 3-8-12 0.............................. SPasquier 12 115+
(Mme C Head-Maarek, France) w'like: scope: hld up towards rr stands' side: hdwy over 2f out: effrt and qcknd over 1f out: rdn to ld jst ins fnl f: edgd lft and hld on wl towards fin **7/2**[1]

1000 **2** *nk* **Assertive**[34] 4915 5-9-3 111...(v[1]) RyanMoore 14 117
(R Hannon) hld up in rr stands' side: swtchd lft and hdwy 2f out: rdn over 1f out: str run ins fnl f: jst hld: 2nd in gp **25/1**

414 **3** *1/2* **Utmost Respect**[34] 4915 4-9-3 112.............................. PaulHanagan 15 115
(R A Fahey) hld up in tch stands' side: effrt 2f out: rdn over 1f out: edgd lft and styd on wl fnl f: nrst fin: 3rd in gp **9/1**[3]

1125 **4** *1/2* **Corrybrough**[35] 4881 3-9-1 110.............................. DaneO'Neill 3 114
(H Candy) trckd ldrs far side: hdwy over 2f out: rdn to chal wl over 1f out and ev ch tl drvn and nt qckn ins fnl f: 1st in gp **10/1**

2000 **5** *shd* **Prime Defender**[22] 5245 4-9-3 111.............................. MichaelHills 8 114
(B W Hills) lw: trckd ldrs far side: hdwy over 2f out: rdn and ev ch wl over 1f out: drvn and kpt on same pce ins fnl f: 2nd in gp **33/1**

6131 **6** *nse* **Ancien Regime (IRE)**[70] 3739 3-9-1 105.............................. PhilipRobinson 2 113
(M A Jarvis) trckd ldr far side: hdwy over 2f out: rdn to ld over 1f out: drvn and hdd jst ins fnl f: edgd lft and one pce ins fnl f: 3rd in gp **20/1**

0065 **7** *1* **Diabolical (USA)**[34] 4915 5-9-3 114.............................. LDettori 11 110
(Saeed Bin Suroor) b: b.hind: lw: trckd ldr stands' side: effrt 2f out: sn rdn and ch tl drvn and one pce ins fnl f: 4th in gp **16/1**

0503 **8** *1* **Reverence**[41] 4660 7-9-3 103.............................. DavidAllan 9 107
(E J Alston) t.k.h: swtchd rt to join stands gp after s: led that gp: ridsden along 2f out: drvn over 1f out and grad wknd: 5th in gp **20/1**

0543 **9** *nk* **Strike The Deal (USA)**[21] 5275 3-9-1 106.....................(v) ShaneKelly 13 106
(J Noseda) in tch stands' side: rdn along over 2f out: grad wknd: 6th in gp **40/1**

0403 **10** *hd* **Wi Dud**[13] 5551 4-9-3 102...(b) NCallan 10 105
(K A Ryan) t.k.h: cl up stands' side: rdn along over 2f out and grad wknd: 7th in gp **33/1**

4525 **11** *1/2* **US Ranger (USA)**[34] 4915 4-9-3 0.............................. JMurtagh 16 104
(A P O'Brien, Ire) lw: hld up: a towards rr stands' side: 8th in gp **4/1**[2]

0302 **12** *1 3/4* **Balthazaar's Gift (IRE)**[21] 5275 5-9-3 110.....................(v[1]) PatCosgrave 6 98
(L M Cumani) swtchd rt after 1f to join stands' side gp: trckd ldrs: rdn along over 2f out and sn wknd: 9th in gp **14/1**

4160 **13** *1* **Knot In Wood (IRE)**[28] 5109 6-9-3 102.............................. JamieMoriarty 1 95
(R A Fahey) in tch far side: rdn along over 2f out: sn drvn and wknd: 4th in gp **66/1**

1045 **14** *1 1/2* **Astronomer Royal (USA)**[34] 4915 4-9-3 0.............................. CO'Donoghue 4 90
(A P O'Brien, Ire) hld up in tch far side: effrt and hdwy 3f out: rdn over 2f out and sn wknd: 5th in gp **16/1**

2000 **15** *1* **Abraham Lincoln (IRE)**[62] 4004 4-9-3 0.............................. JamieSpencer 7 87
(A P O'Brien, Ire) led far side gp and overall ldr: rdn along over 2f out: hdd wl over 1f out and sn wknd: 6th in gp **66/1**

1m 12.81s (-0.79) **Going Correction** +0.30s/f (Good)
WFA 3 from 4yo+ 2lb **22** Ran SP% **104.4**
Speed ratings (Par 117): **117,116,115,115,115 115,113,112,112,111 111,108,107,105,104**
toteswinger: 1&2 £20.20, 1&3 £6.20, 2&3 £42.80. CSF £73.39 TOTE £3.00: £1.40, £8.80, £2.00; EX 86.50 Trifecta £575.30 Pool: £3265.54 - 4.20 winning units..
Owner K Abdulla **Bred** Juddmonte Farms Ltd **Trained** Chantilly, France
■ Ladbrokes replaced Betfred as sponsors when the race was switched from Haydock.

FOCUS
Rescheduled from a week earlier, 14 of the 17 declared for this race when it was due to be staged at Haydock lined up to take part, and it gave some of those who have struggled to cope with Marchand D'Or this season a chance at Group 1 glory. After a furlong or so two groups developed and although they somewhat merged again from a furlong and a half out, the first three home came from the stands'-side group. Fillies had won four of the previous 14 renewals and African Rose, the only one of her sex in this year's field, improved that impressive statistic further. Without needing to improve, she confirmed Marchand D'Or's standing as Europe's top sprinter. Equiano (9/2) was withdrawn after bursting out of his stall. Deduct 15p in the £ under R4.

NOTEBOOK
African Rose, who was slightly on her toes beforehand, had been mown down late when runner-up to Marchand D'Or in the Prix Maurice de Gheest, and this half-furlong shorter trip promised to suit. She got a nice lead in the stands' side group and picked up well once asked to quicken. It looked for a moment as though Assertive might see it out even better inside the last, but in the end she was comfortably holding his challenge. Having started the season running over 1m, she has now found her metier as a sprinter and soft ground clearly suits her well. The Abbaye, which might come a bit quick, and the new Breeders' Cup race, the Turf Sprint, are possible targets, but there are no firm plans for her. (op 4-1 tchd 10-3)
Assertive has struggled in the top sprints since winning the Duke of York Stakes in the spring. He was wearing a visor for the first time, though, and put up a much better display having been held up in the same group as the winner. Finishing strongly, he gave the filly a bit of a fright inside the last but was being held close home.
Utmost Respect has had a successful campaign, improving to win a Group 3 race at Newcastle in June prior to finishing strongly to take fourth in the Prix Maurice de Gheest last time. He had over three lengths to make up on African Rose on that form, so it was a creditable effort to finish within a length of her this time. Soft ground is key to him and it is possible that he could progress further next year. (op 15-2)
Corrybrough got cover to two furlongs out before bursting through to take things up. He could have done with being taken further into the race, but he stayed on well and was always just holding his fellow three-year-old Ancien Regime on the far side. The return to 6f suited him and he can only get better as he strengthens up. The best is yet to come from him.
Prime Defender, who is ideally served by quicker ground, has his limitations but ran a sound enough race. He probably needs to drop back a grade or two, before he is winning again.
Ancien Regime(IRE), who narrowly beat Prime Defender in a 5f Group 3 race at Sandown last time, was pipped by him this time, but he too looks the type who should improve next season, when it would not be a surprise to see him competing in Godolphin blue.
Diabolical(USA) did not run quite as well as in the Maurice de Gheest, but given that his best form is on dirt he has not been running too badly on turf in Europe. He will once again be of obvious interest in the dirt sprints at the Dubai carnival in the new year.
Reverence, who was a bit too keen for his own good, is not the force of old, and while he had ground conditions to suit, this was always going to be a stiff task.
Strike The Deal(USA) has run better since being dropped back to sprinting this term, but he was still up against it in this company.
Wi Dud raced prominently on the stands' side before drifting to the centre of the track as he got tired.
US Ranger(USA) was the major disappointment of the race. He is becoming something of an underachiever, and patently failed to give his running this time. The ground was probably not to his liking but it was still a tame effort.
Balthazaar's Gift(IRE) failed to improve for the fitting of a visor.
Knot In Wood(IRE), who for the most part has been plying his trade in handicaps, was taking a big step up in class.
Astronomer Royal(USA) could not pick up on this ground and needs it faster. He should not be too harshly judged on this and remains capable of better in his new career as a sprinter.
Abraham Lincoln(IRE), who was presumably in the race to ensure a proper gallop for his stablemates, showed pace to a furlong and a half out but then hit the wall.

5892 LADBROKES ST LEGER STKS (GROUP 1) (ENTIRE COLTS & FILLIES) 1m 6f 132y
3:10 (3:13) (Class 1) 3-Y-O

£283,850 (£107,600; £53,850; £26,850; £13,450; £6,750) **Stalls** Low

Form RPR
3121 **1** **Conduit (IRE)**[46] 4505 3-9-0 112.............................. LDettori 5 124
(Sir Michael Stoute) lw: hld up: smooth hdwy 4f out: led over 2f out: edgd rt 1f out: styd on strly **8/1**

1 **2** *3* **Unsung Heroine (IRE)**[36] 4833 3-8-11 0.............................. WMLordan 3 116
(T Stack, Ire) w'like: leggy: hld up in mid-div: hdwy over 3f out: wnt 2nd over 1f out: r.o: no real imp **14/1**

1-21 **3** *3 1/4* **Look Here**[99] 2792 3-8-11 119.............................. EddieAhern 14 112
(R M Beckett) hld up in mid-div: smooth hdwy to chal over 2f out: styd on same pce appr fnl f **11/4**[2]

-440 **4** *5* **Hindu Kush (IRE)**[76] 3535 3-9-0 0.............................. DavidMcCabe 1 108
(A P O'Brien, Ire) w ldr: led after 2f: hdd 3f out: hung lft and kpt on fnl f to take 4th nr fin **200/1**

1564 **5** *nk* **Enroller (IRE)**[32] 4959 3-9-0 103.............................. DO'Donohoe 12 108
(W R Muir) prom: led 3f out: sn hdd: kpt on one pce **100/1**

2502 **6** *nk* **Washington Irving (IRE)**[27] 5136 3-9-0 0.............................. CO'Donoghue 11 107
(A P O'Brien, Ire) trckd ldrs: kpt on one pce fnl 2f **16/1**

-201 **7** *2 1/2* **Frozen Fire (GER)**[76] 3535 3-9-0 0.............................. JMurtagh 8 104
(A P O'Brien, Ire) hld up in rr: effrt over 2f out: kpt on: nvr nr ldrs **9/4**[1]

2144 **8** *4 1/2* **Doctor Fremantle**[61] 4042 3-9-0 116.............................. RyanMoore 13 98+
(Sir Michael Stoute) swtchd lft s: hld up: hdwy to chse ldrs 3f out: wknd over 1f out **13/2**[3]

060 **9** *12* **Bashkirov**[61] 4042 3-9-0 0.............................. JimmyFortune 7 82
(A P O'Brien, Ire) lw: in rr: drvn over 4f out: nvr on terms **66/1**

1636 **10** *4 1/2* **Alessandro Volta**[61] 4042 3-9-0 0.............................. JamieSpencer 10 76
(A P O'Brien, Ire) mid-div: effrt over 3f out: sn btn **15/2**

3332 **11** *1 3/4* **Top Lock**[21] 5263 3-9-0 110.............................. MartinDwyer 2 73
(A M Balding) prom: drvn over 5f out: sn lost pl **14/1**

1-24 **12** *6* **Whistledownwind**[115] 2303 3-9-0 104.............................. GMosse 9 65
(J Noseda) lw: prom: lost pl over 3f out: eased over 1f out **33/1**

2412 **13** *33* **Warringah**[80] 3380 3-9-0 91.............................. RichardMullen 4 21
(Sir Michael Stoute) swtg: chsd ldrs: wknd 3f out: bhd and eased fnl f **33/1**

0 **14** *19* **Maidstone Mixture (FR)**[19] 2829 3-9-0 0.............................. DanielTudhope 6 —
(Paul Murphy) led 2f: drvn and lost pl 8f out: sn bhd: t.o 5f out **200/1**

3m 7.92s (1.22) **Going Correction** +0.30s/f (Good) **14** Ran SP% **122.2**
Speed ratings (Par 115): **108,106,104,102,101 101,100,97,91,89 88,85,67,57**
toteswinger: 1&2 £22.60, 1&3 £6.90, 2&3 £9.40. CSF £113.94 TOTE £7.80: £2.10, £4.20, £2.00; EX 116.80 Trifecta £729.20 Pool: £45816.22 - 46.49 winning units..
Owner Ballymacoll Stud **Bred** Ballymacoll Stud Farm Ltd **Trained** Newmarket, Suffolk
■ A first St Leger winner for Sir Michael Stoute and a fifth for Frankie Dettori.

FOCUS

The largest field assembled since 1982 for this the oldest of Classics, but there was quality as well as quantity, with Irish Derby winner Frozen Fire and Oaks heroine Look Here making it one of the strongest renewals for a while. The Ballydoyle pacemaker Hindu Kush, egged on by Warringah, ensured it was a proper test. Conduit has been rated well up to scratch, but several key runners failed to run their races and even third-placed Look Here has been rated 11lb off her Oaks form.

NOTEBOOK

Conduit(IRE) looked a Group performer in the making when routing handicap opposition off a mark of 85 at Epsom on Derby day, but he had been caught out in a tactical King Edward VII Stakes at Royal Ascot and far from impressive in the Gordon Stakes. This bigger field/faster pace was always going to play to his strengths however, and Frankie Dettori was more than happy to be towards the rear until starting to make headway when they reached the straight. The last one off the bridle, he shot into the lead over two furlongs out, and despite edging right approaching the final furlong ran on right the way to the line. His trainer has run similarly progressive sorts in the race before, but this fellow has a nice change of pace when things work out and the drying ground was a help. Although Leger winners have a mixed record as older horses, he has the profile of one that can improve further. He is unlikely to run again this year but will be back in training in 2009, when his campaign is likely to be geared around middle-distance races. (tchd 17-2 in a place)

Unsung Heroine(IRE), having only the third race of her career, has come a long way in a short space of time. Unraced at two, she went from winning a Fairyhouse maiden to beating some smart older fillies in a 1m4f Group 3 at Cork last month, and this represented another huge step forward. She looked a likely improver for the distance and saw it out well despite being keen through the early stages. Readily making ground to track Conduit through, she briefly looked a major threat, but the winner was always pulling out more. She has a big future and could now be aimed at the new Breeders' Cup Marathon, a race she can go well in, or the Prix de Royallieu.The Melbourne Cup was mentioned for 2009.

Look Here was bidding to become the first filly since User Friendly in 1992 to complete the Oaks/St Leger double. One of the most impressive Oaks winners in recent times, she had not been seen since, a training setback meaning she missed her intended engagement in the Yorkshire Oaks. Bred to stay and not expected to be inconvenienced by this softer ground, she started to make headway, travelling strongly, under half a mile out but could not quicken when asked for her effort. Whether she truly stayed is debatable, but it was not a bad effort considering she had a far from ideal preparation and she will be kept in training at four. There is a possibility she will have one more run in the meantime, back at shorter in Longchamp's Prix de l'Opera. (op 3-1 tchd 10-3 in a place)

Hindu Kush(IRE), who got warm in the paddock, was used effectively as a pace-setter for Frozen Fire in the Irish Derby, and he deserves plenty of credit for this, as he went off hard and stayed on again, having looked set to drop out with three to run. He could be a nice staying prospect for next season.

Enroller(IRE), who finished fifth in the Queen's Vase at Royal Ascot, stays well and likes soft ground, so it was no real surprise to see him run a decent race. He excelled in a strongly run race and is another likely to develop into a useful stayer at four.

Washington Irving(IRE), fifth in the Derby, has always been viewed as a likely sort for this race. He was done for speed when they started to kick for home, but kept plodding away. He is still a maiden and connections will no doubt want to put that right at some stage. (op 20-1)

Frozen Fire(GER), who got warm, was the disappointment of the race. He has not always impressed with his attitude and things rather fell into his lap in the Irish Derby. O'Brien had said he was far from certain about his stamina for this test, and, having been close enough with half a mile to run, it soon became clear it was not going to be his day. In a light career each good run has been followed by a bad one, and though plainly highly talented, he is not one to rely on. (op 5-2 tchd 11-4 in places)

Doctor Fremantle, on his toes beforehand, was another non-stayer. Fourth in the Derby and a stablemate of the winner, with Ryan Moore choosing him over Conduit, he made headway to reach a challenging position but could find no more from over two out. A drop in trip beckons. (tchd 7-1)

Bashkirov never got into it and has not gone on from his promising Irish Derby effort. (op 100-1)

Alessandro Volta ran poorly. A slightly unlucky sixth in the Derby, he has still looked very immature on occasions, and having moved up well straightening for home he soon began to flounder and dropped right out. He has the size and scope to make a better older horse. (op 8-1 tchd 9-1 and 10-1 in a place)

Top Lock was one of the more popular outsiders, but he never featured. (op 16-1 tchd 18-1 in a place)

Whistledownwind did no get home having been up there early. (op 40-1)

5893 NATIONAL EXPRESS PARK STKS (GROUP 2) 7f

3:45 (3:48) (Class 1) 3-Y-O+

£85,155 (£32,280; £16,155; £8,055; £4,035; £2,025) **Stalls** High

Form RPR

5064 **1** **Arabian Gleam**[28] 5095 4-9-4 113 .....(p) JMurtagh 4 119
(J Noseda) *trckd ldrs: effrt over 2f out: rdn: edgd lft and led appr fnl f: sn drvn and edgd rt ins fnl f: kpt on wl u.p* **9/1**

1133 **2** ½ **Major Cadeaux**[27] 5138 4-9-4 115 ..... RyanMoore 5 118
(R Hannon) *lw: in tch: hdwy to trck ldrs 2f out: swtchd rt and effrt to chse wnr ent fnl f: sn rdn and ev ch tl drvn and nt qckn towards fin* **5/4**[1]

0202 **3** 1½ **Al Qasi (IRE)**[28] 5095 5-9-4 109 ..... LDettori 1 114
(P W Chapple-Hyam) *prom: effrt over 2f out: sn rdn and ev ch tl drvn and one pce ins fnl f* **11/2**[3]

4162 **4** 2¾ **Welsh Emperor (IRE)**[11] 5586 9-9-4 104 .....(b) TonyCulhane 2 106
(T P Tate) *led: rdn along over 2f out: drvn and hdd over 1f out: kpt on same pce* **25/1**

333- **5** ¾ **Passager (FR)**[20] 5-9-4 0 ..... SPasquier 3 104
(Mme C Head-Maarek, France) *hld up in rr: hdwy on outer over 2f out: rdn to chse ldrs wl over 1f out: drvn and wknd appr fnl f* **12/1**

1616 **6** 2¼ **Smokey Oakey (IRE)**[35] 4855 4-9-4 110 ..... JimmyQuinn 10 98
(M H Tompkins) *hld up in tch: effrt wl over 2f out: sn rdn and no imp* **10/1**

5121 **7** ¾ **Laa Rayb (USA)**[13] 5555 4-9-4 109 ..... RoystonFfrench 8 96
(M Johnston) *swtg: chsd ldr: rdn along over 2f out: wknd wl over 1f out* **9/2**[2]

05-4 **8** 1¾ **Somnus**[42] 4617 8-9-4 98 .....(t) PaulHanagan 9 91
(J J Quinn) *a in rr* **33/1**

2500 **9** 1 **Bobs Surprise**[70] 3722 3-9-0 102 ..... MichaelHills 6 89
(B W Hills) *swtg: in tch: rdn along 3f out: sn wknd* **16/1**

1m 26.18s (-0.12) **Going Correction** +0.30s/f (Good)
WFA 3 from 4yo+ 4lb **9** Ran SP% **117.5**
Speed ratings (Par 115): **112,111,109,106,105 103,102,100,99**
toteswinger: 1&2 £4.70, 1&3 £6.20, 2&3 £3.10. CSF £21.03 TOTE £12.40: £3.10, £1.20, £1.70; EX 24.30 Trifecta £128.10 Pool: £1301.99 - 7.52 winning units..

Owner Saeed Suhail **Bred** P And Mrs A G Venner **Trained** Newmarket, Suffolk

FOCUS

This was probably not the strongest of Group 2s, although the form looks solid enough. The veteran Welsh Emperor ensured the pace was good, and it was a slight personal best from the winner.

NOTEBOOK

Arabian Gleam, not beaten far in either the Lockinge or Queen Anne earlier in the season, has since struggled under a penalty back down to this level, but he did not have to shoulder one here and first-time cheekpieces helped spark him back into life. Prominent in the chasing group, he travelled up strongly and hit the front over a furlong out, then dug deep when strongly pressed by Major Cadeaux. This is his best distance and he will now head for the Challenge Stakes. (op 8-1 tchd 10-1)

Major Cadeaux, not beaten far behind crack 3-y-o milers Henrythenavigator and Tamayuz on his last two starts, was favourite on this drop in grade and was not expected to have any problems with the return to 7f. Ryan Moore was not in a hurry on him and switched to challenge a furlong a half out, but he could not get past the winner. He would probably have preferred faster ground. (op 6-4 tchd 13-8 in a place)

Al Qasi(IRE), ahead of the winner at Newbury last time, does not have the best win record for a horse of his ability and he again ran well without reward. He had his chance and is likely to continue to come up just shy at this level. (op 7-1)

Welsh Emperor(IRE) is an admirable horse and continues to perform to a high standard. Runner-up in a Group 3 at Goodwood earlier in the month, he ensured they did not crawl and kept battling away, but just lacked the class of a couple of them. He will find easier opportunities.

Passager(FR), who was third in last season's Lockinge on his one previous visit, is not as good as he was and, having won just a minor event at Deauville last month, found this a bit too tough. (op 16-1)

Smokey Oakey(IRE) has had a profitable season, winning both the Lincoln and causing a bit of a shock in the Brigadier Gerard. He ran no sort of race at Haydock last time though and this marked drop in trip counted against him. (op 9-1 tchd 17-2)

Laa Rayb(USA) was disappointing. He has really come into his own this season, twice running crackers off big weights in good handicaps, and easily winning at a Group 3 at Deauville last month. This was another step up, but he found little for pressure and did not appear to like the ground. (op 4-1 tchd 5-1)

5894 KEEPMOAT STKS (H'CAP) 1m 4f

4:15 (4:15) (Class 2) (0-105,105) 3-Y-O+ **£12,952** (£3,854; £1,926; £962) **Stalls** Low

Form RPR

201- **1** **Magicalmysterytour (IRE)**[393] 4572 5-8-11 **91** oh1 ..... EddieAhern 14 104
(W J Musson) *lw: hld up: hdwy 6f out: hung lft and led over 2f out: rdn rt out* **25/1**

-223 **2** 2 **Tastahil (IRE)**[19] 5349 4-8-11 **91** oh1 ..... RHills 7 101
(B W Hills) *lw: hld up towards rr: stdy hdwy over 2f out: wnt 2nd 1f out: styd on: no imp* **7/1**[3]

013- **3** 1½ **Walking Talking**[450] 2790 4-8-11 **91** oh1 ..... JimmyQuinn 4 99+
(H R A Cecil) *hdwy and prom 7f out: drvn and outpcd over 5f out: styd on wl fnl 2f* **9/1**

3430 **4** ½ **New Guinea**[14] 5494 5-9-6 **100** ..... LDettori 3 107
(Saeed Bin Suroor) *mid-div: hdwy over 3f out: kpt on same pce fnl 2f* **8/1**

2120 **5** ½ **Meshtri (IRE)**[12] 5573 3-7-11 **91** oh2 ..... DavidProbert(5) 12 97+
(M A Jarvis) *lw: towards rr: effrt and caqme v wd over 3f out: wandered bdly: styd on fnl f* **6/1**[1]

1000 **6** 4 **Dr Faustus (IRE)**[44] 4552 3-8-9 **98** ..... RyanMoore 10 98
(Sir Michael Stoute) *led 2f: chsd ldrs: led over 3f out: hdd over 2f out: wknd fnl f* **13/2**[2]

5020 **7** 1 **Ladies Best**[48] 4444 4-9-4 **98** ..... DaneO'Neill 6 96
(L M Cumani) *prom: one pce fnl 3f* **14/1**

3-05 **8** nk **Lost Soldier Three (IRE)**[83] 3295 7-8-11 **91** oh1 ..... AdrianTNicholls 9 89
(D Nicholls) *in rr: kpt on fnl 2f: nvr nr ldrs* **50/1**

4050 **9** 2 **Greek Envoy**[35] 4856 4-9-1 **95** ..... TonyCulhane 5 89
(T P Tate) *trckd ldrs: effrt over 3f out: grad wknd* **20/1**

0040 **10** 7 **Players Please (USA)**[22] 5229 4-8-11 **91** ..... GregFairley 8 74
(M Johnston) *lw: w ldrs: t.k.h: lost pl 3f out* **16/1**

0020 **11** 2¾ **Come On Jonny (IRE)**[64] 3925 6-8-11 **91** oh3 ..... MartinDwyer 1 70
(R M Beckett) *led after 2f: hdd over 3f out: sn lost pl* **14/1**

00-5 **12** ½ **Group Captain**[77] 3497 6-9-6 **105** ..... AshleyHamblett(5) 15 83
(H J Collingridge) *in rr: effrt on outer over 3f out: sn wknd* **25/1**

6213 **13** 28 **Moonquake (USA)**[86] 3157 3-8-3 **92** ..... PaulHanagan 11 25
(J H M Gosden) *chsd ldrs on outer: lost pl over 3f out: bhd whn eased fnl f* **6/1**[1]

-160 **14** 14 **Milne Graden**[22] 5229 4-9-2 **96** .....(p) JamieSpencer 13 7
(J Noseda) *s.i.s: hdwy 6f out: rdn over 3f out: hung bdly lft: nt keen: eased and virtually p.u: t.o* **10/1**

2m 34.96s (-0.14) **Going Correction** +0.30s/f (Good)
WFA 3 from 4yo+ 9lb **14** Ran SP% **118.2**
Speed ratings (Par 109): **112,110,109,109,109 106,105,105,104,99 97,97,78,69**
toteswinger: 1&2 £17.20, 1&3 £28.70, 2&3 £15.90. CSF £182.44 CT £1720.43 TOTE £29.40: £6.40, £2.70, £3.50; EX 245.80 TRIFECTA Not won..

Owner M Dunne **Bred** Premier Bloodstock **Trained** Newmarket, Suffolk

FOCUS

A competitive handicap that saw a bit of a shock result. Unlike in most races this week, virtually the whole field stayed towards the far side.

NOTEBOOK

Magicalmysterytour(IRE), who has had several little problems since winning at Newbury last August, was reappearing off a 5lb higher mark and it was easy to see why he was dismissed in the betting, his trainer hardly having the best of times of it. Held up early on, he began to take closer order leaving the back and his lack of a recent run was not evident throughout the final quarter mile. He could make a smart hurdler one day, but has the November Handicap on the agenda first. (tchd 28-1)

Tastahil(IRE) has been going up the handicap without winning and again ran well in defeat. He travelled nicely into the straight and tried to go in pursuit of the winner, but never looked like getting to him. He deserves to find a race, but will probably be nudged up another pound or two for this. (op 6-1)

Walking Talking ◆ looked fit despite returning from a lengthy absence, having last run when third in last season's King George V Handicap at Royal Ascot. Held up on the rail, he was making headway when finding nowhere to go, and, by the time he switched out, the winner had flown. He stayed on well for third, though, and could be an interesting horse for similar races. (op 11-1)

New Guinea, well beaten in a Listed handicap at Chester on his first run back from Dubai, had been dropped 3lb and ran more encouragingly, but is still going to find it tough to win in handicaps.

Meshtri(IRE) ◆ had nothing go right for him at Kempton last time and held an obvious chance, but coming up the middle did not really work as he was wandering all over the place under pressure. Stay on though he did, he was never quite on terms. He remains capable of better. (op 5-1)

Dr Faustus(IRE) looked a possible Group horse when winning off a mark of 89 at Newmarket earlier in the season, but he has not really gone on and the change of tactics failed to work on this step up in trip. (op 9-1)

Moonquake(USA), who ran a cracking race off a 2lb lower mark at Royal Ascot, was not as effective in this softer ground. Official explanation: trainer's rep said colt was unsuited by the soft (good to soft places) ground (op 11-2)

Milne Graden ran poorly in the first-time cheekpieces and continues to regress. Official explanation: jockey said gelding never travelled (op 9-1)

5895 LANDINI TRACTORS NURSERY 1m (S)
4:50 (4:51) (Class 2) 2-Y-O £12,952 (£3,854; £1,926; £962) **Stalls** High

Form RPR

4661 **1** **Battle Of Hastings**[36] 4828 2-8-8 **70** JamieSpencer 2 83+
(M L W Bell) *stdd and swtchd rt s: hld up in rr: hdwy over 2f out: rdn over 1f out: styd on wl u.p ent fnl f: led fnl 100yds* **7/1**[3]

3231 **2** 1 ½ **Thunderball**[17] 5404 2-9-0 **76** PatCosgrave 4 85
(A J McCabe) *cl up: rdn to ld over 2f out: drvn and edgd rt ent fnl f: hdd and no ex fnl 100yds* **16/1**

1542 **3** 1 ¼ **Roly Boy**[22] 5242 2-9-7 **83** RyanMoore 3 90
(R Hannon) *hld up towards rr: hdwy 3f out: rdn to chse ldrs over 1f out: kpt on same pce ins fnl f* **11/2**[2]

51 **4** 2 **Warrior One**[31] 4968 2-9-3 **82** NeilBrown(3) 10 84
(J Howard Johnson) *w'like: scope: lengthy: lw: chsd ldrs: rdn along and sltly outpcd 2f out: kpt on wl u.p appr fnl f* **8/1**

020 **5** 1 ½ **Very Distinguished**[22] 5225 2-8-1 **66** DominicFox(3) 12 65
(M G Quinlan) *s.i.s and bhd: hdwy over 2f out: rdn wl over 1f out: kpt on ins fnl f: nrst fin* **20/1**

01 **6** nse **Punch Drunk**[34] 4897 2-8-11 **73** MartinDwyer 5 72
(J G Given) *w'like: prom on outer: effrt 2f out and ev ch tl rdn and hung bdly lft ent ent fnl f: sn wknd* **20/1**

3040 **7** 1 **Ay Tay Tate (IRE)**[9] 5632 2-8-9 **71** PatrickMathers 8 68+
(I W McInnes) *bhd: hdwy over 2f out: sn rdn and kpt on ins fnl f: nrst fin* **66/1**

2222 **8** ¾ **Cosmic Sun**[14] 5497 2-9-7 **83** JamieMoriarty 15 78
(R A Fahey) *hld up and bhd tl styd on fnl 2f* **16/1**

4200 **9** nse **Tepmokea (IRE)**[21] 5274 2-8-12 **74** DarrenWilliams 1 69
(K R Burke) *in midfield: rdn along over 2f out: n.d* **33/1**

011 **10** ½ **River Captain (IRE)**[5] 5747 2-9-0 **76** 6ex LDettori 16 70
(S Kirk) *hld up: effrt and sme hdwy 3f out: rdn over 2f out and sn no imp* **4/1**[1]

0353 **11** 1 **Becausewecan (USA)**[9] 5632 2-8-12 **74** GregFairley 14 66
(M Johnston) *chsd ldrs: rdn along 3f out and sn wknd* **14/1**

3000 **12** ¾ **Motor Home**[14] 5511 2-8-8 **75** DavidProbert(5) 13 65
(A M Balding) *w'like: a towards rr* **25/1**

0123 **13** 1 ¾ **Quatermain**[15] 5447 2-9-6 **82** TomEaves 7 68
(B Smart) *led: rdn along 3f out: hdd over 2f out and grad wknd* **16/1**

13 **14** nk **Rising Prospect**[31] 4968 2-9-3 **79** JimmyFortune 9 64
(G M Moore) *w'like: prom: rdn along 3f out: sn drvn and grad wknd* **14/1**

51 **15** 1 ¾ **Sergeant Pink (IRE)**[20] 5304 2-8-12 **74** PaulHanagan 6 56
(S Gollings) *str: chsd ldrs: rdn along 3f out: sn wknd* **14/1**

3261 **16** 3 ¼ **Highland Storm**[22] 5242 2-9-2 **78** AlanMunro 11 52
(J G Given) *midfield: pushed along 1/2-way: sn rdn: lost pl and bhd* **10/1**

1m 41.45s (2.15) **Going Correction** +0.30s/f (Good) **16** Ran SP% **123.5**
Speed ratings (Par 101): **101,99,98,96,94 94,93,92,92,92 91,90,88,88,86 83**
toteswinger: 1&2 £27.30, 1&3 £9.60, 2&3 £19.30. CSF £108.05 CT £493.86 TOTE £6.30: £1.70, £3.60, £2.00, £2.30; EX 182.20 Trifecta £349.60 Pool: £514.99 - 1.09 winning units..
Owner R A Green **Bred** Myriad Communications & New England Stud **Trained** Newmarket, Suffolk

FOCUS
A hot nursery which could turn out even better than the impressive provisional figures suggest. The winner started out in nurseries off a good mark and is progressing well, and there was no fluke about the runner-up's improvement. Improvement too from the third, with the fourth to form.

NOTEBOOK
Battle Of Hastings, who earned his handicap mark over sprint distances but improved to win on his nursery debut over 7f in a race that has worked out well, looked sure to do even better on his first go at 1m. Settled off the gallop, he showed signs of inexperience when asked to pick up, but stayed on well to chase the leader down and was really motoring inside the last. In the end he won comfortably and, given his pedigree, looks the type to improve further next season. (op 6-1 tchd 15-2 in a place)
Thunderball, who won an ordinary maiden on the Polytrack last time, came through to lead over two furlongs out and provided a target for the winner to aim at. It was a sound effort in defeat and he clearly stays 1m well.
Roly Boy, who had run solid races in defeat off slightly lower marks on his previous two starts, travelled well and kept on nicely. He is more exposed than some but is consistent and seems to go on any ground. (op 8-1)
Warrior One had no stamina questions to answer and plugged on stoutly. He will thrive when stepped up to middle distances next year.
Very Distinguished, who was running in a handicap for the first time, showed her inexperience by being slowest away, but she came home well and can pick up a nursery at a slightly lower level. (op 16-1)
Punch Drunk, who raced on the outside of the bunch, might have been involved in the battle for the places had she not hung badly left once the whip was used. She did the same when successful at Redcar last time and it might help if she can race next to a left-handed rail in future. (tchd 16-1)
Ay Tay Tate(IRE) has been racing as though he would appreciate this longer trip but did not get the clearest of runs as he was trying to find a way through. He shaped better than the bare form suggests.
Cosmic Sun, who had finished runner-up in his previous four starts in maiden company, was running in a handicap for the first time. This longer trip ought to have suited him, but he never really threatened.
River Captain(IRE) had a lot more to do here than when successful at Bath last time, but given that he was proven under these conditions he had to be of some interest under a penalty. He was well held in the end, though. Official explanation: jockey said colt ran flat having run twice in five-days (op 5-1 tchd 7-2 and 9-2 in a place)

5896 STATE CLUB H'CAP 1m (S)
5:25 (5:25) (Class 2) (0-110,110) 3-Y-0+ £12,952 (£3,854; £1,926; £962) **Stalls** High

Form RPR

-130 **1** **Virtual**[86] 3155 3-8-6 **100** RichardMullen 10 103+
(J H M Gosden) *trckd ldrs: styd on to ld fnl 100yds: kpt on wl* **14/1**

3-14 **2** 1 ½ **Gold Sovereign (IRE)**[35] 4845 4-8-10 **99** LDettori 11 100
(Saeed Bin Suroor) *w ldrs: effrt over 2f out: kpt on same pce fnl f* **11/2**[3]

65 **3** nse **Huzzah (IRE)**[43] 4587 3-8-5 **99** MartinDwyer 3 98
(B W Hills) *s.s: effrt over 2f out: styd on same pce fnl f* **4/1**[1]

2502 **4** hd **The Snatcher (IRE)**[28] 5096 5-8-7 **96** oh7 PaulHanagan 2 96
(R Hannon) *lw: led: qcknd 3f out: edgd lft appr fnl f: hdd and no ex ins fnl f* **16/1**

1316 **5** 1 **Mia's Boy**[99] 2788 4-9-1 **104** JimmyQuinn 9 106+
(C A Dwyer) *lw: hld up: effrt over 2f out: styng on whn bdly hmpd appr fnl f: kpt on towards fin* **7/1**

0500 **6** nk **Steam Cuisine**[28] 5096 4-8-7 **96** oh8 AlanMunro 12 93
(M G Quinlan) *hld up in midfield: effrt over 2f out: kpt on same pce appr fnl f* **20/1**

1615 **7** hd **Duntulm**[42] 4622 3-8-8 **102** DaneO'Neill 6 98
(H Candy) *trckd ldr: effrt over 2f out: edgd rt and kpt on same pce appr fnl f* **5/1**[2]

4002 **8** 2 ½ **Rio Riva**[79] 3413 6-8-10 **99** TomEaves 1 90
(Miss J A Camacho) *hld up towards rr: effrt 3f out: wknd fnl f* **15/2**

5000 **9** 3 ¼ **Pride Of Nation (IRE)**[43] 4587 6-8-9 **98** (t) EddieAhern 4 81
(J W Hills) *hld up in midfield: effrt over 2f out: wknd fnl f* **12/1**

3102 **10** ½ **Blythe Knight (IRE)**[27] 5134 8-9-7 **110** GrahamGibbons 13 92
(J J Quinn) *lw: hld up in midfield: effrt over 2f out: wknd fnl f* **15/2**

3363 **11** 36 **Babodana**[105] 2600 8-8-11 **100** NCallan 8 —
(M H Tompkins) *lw: trckd ldrs: drvn 3f out: sn wknd: bhd whn eased ins fnl f: t.o* **12/1**

1m 40.22s (0.92) **Going Correction** +0.30s/f (Good)
WFA 3 from 4yo+ 5lb **11** Ran SP% **120.8**
Speed ratings (Par 109): **107,105,105,105,104 103,103,101,98,97 61**
toteswinger: 1&2 £11.10, 1&3 £11.10, 2&3 £7.00. CSF £91.65 CT £382.57 TOTE £17.00: £5.10, £2.10, £2.30; EX 99.20 Trifecta £451.20 Part won. Pool: £609.81 - 0.41 winning units. Place 6 £184.19, Place 5 £128.06.
Owner Cheveley Park Stud **Bred** Cheveley Park Stud Ltd **Trained** Newmarket, Suffolk

FOCUS
They did not go much of a gallop and this looks messy form, limited by the proximity of front-running fourth from out of the handicap. Hard to rate the bare form positively, but it was pleasing to see one of the three-year-olds win.

NOTEBOOK
Virtual bounced back from his Royal Ascot disappointment and appreciated the cut in the ground. Always going nicely just in behind the leaders, he was driven to the front inside the final furlong and was nicely on top at the line. Some cut in the ground is key to this attractive son of Pivotal and he could be interesting if allowed to take his chance in the Cambridgeshire (picks up a 4lb penalty) as connections won it last season. (op 12-1)
Gold Sovereign(IRE), fourth off this mark in the Shergar Cup Mile, was faced with similar conditions here and again ran well, but could not match his younger rival. He remains open to further progress. (op 13-2)
Huzzah(IRE), a dual winner earlier in the season, has been running well off this mark in some good handicaps and he stayed on to just miss out on second. (op 5-1 tchd 6-1 and 11-2 in places)
The Snatcher(IRE), who was beaten by a progressive sort at Newbury last time, took them along at just a modest pace and ran well, though probably flattered, from 7lb 'wrong'.
Mia's Boy has been a rapid improver this season, winning five times in handicaps, but had not been seen since coming up short in the Group 3 Diomed Stakes at Epsom in June. He was staying on and would have been in the mix for second had he not been hampered, so can be rated better than the bare form.
Steam Cuisine, back on her last winning mark, was not beaten far and may soon be winning again.
Duntulm has won two valuable handicaps this season, but came up short in a Listed contest at Goodwood last time and he found this mark beyond him. (op 11-2 tchd 6-1)
Pride Of Nation(IRE) travelled well, but found little when it mattered.
Blythe Knight(IRE) was beaten with two furlongs left to run.
T/Jkpt: Not won. T/Plt: £109.80 to a £1 stake. Pool: £197,891.44. 1,314.92 winning tickets.
T/Qpdt: £20.00 to a £1 stake. Pool: £7,541.50. 278.30 winning tickets. JR

5583 GOODWOOD (R-H)
Saturday, September 13

OFFICIAL GOING: Soft (7.0)
Rail realignment added around 15yds to advertised distances on the round course.
Wind: Nil Weather: Fine

5897 SHELL HOUSE STKS (H'CAP) 7f
2:20 (2:22) (Class 2) (0-100,100) 3-Y-0+
£11,215 (£3,358; £1,679; £840; £419; £210) **Stalls** High

Form RPR

5205 **1** **South Cape**[15] 5446 5-8-9 **87** TPO'Shea 1 95
(M R Channon) *prom: chsd ldr after 3f: drvn 2f out: clsd to ld ins fnl f: styd on wl* **12/1**

0403 **2** 1 **Salient**[11] 5589 4-8-8 **86** oh4 PaulDoe 4 91
(M J Attwater) *led: kicked 2 l clr 2f out: collared ins fnl f: kpt on* **20/1**

3421 **3** shd **Signor Peltro**[20] 5313 5-8-11 **89** TQuinn 11 98+
(H Candy) *hld up in last trio: stl covered up 2f out and plenty to do: swtchd rt and prog over 1f out: styd on fnl f: nvr nr enough to chal* **5/2**[1]

4660 **4** 2 ¼ **Flipando (IRE)**[43] 4587 7-8-13 **91** DarryllHolland 2 90
(T D Barron) *stdd s: hld up in rr and racd wd: effrt over 2f out: sme prog but hanging over 1f out: nvr pce to rch ldrs* **15/2**[3]

2540 **5** 1 **Aye Aye Digby (IRE)**[15] 5470 3-8-7 **89** SteveDrowne 10 85
(H Candy) *chsd ldrs: rdn over 2f out: effrt to go 3rd over 1f out: wknd ins fnl f* **15/2**[3]

0500 **6** 1 ¼ **Eisteddfod**[19] 5347 7-9-8 **100** (p) NelsonDeSouza 8 93
(P F I Cole) *t.k.h early: hld up bhd ldrs: rdn on inner 2f out: no imp after* **9/1**

2105 **7** nk **Phantom Whisper**[28] 5096 5-8-13 **94** JamesMillman(3) 7 86
(B R Millman) *hld up in rr and racd wd: rdn over 2f out: no prog and sn btn: plugged on fnl f* **7/1**[2]

1404 **8** ½ **Barons Spy (IRE)**[19] 5368 7-8-7 **90** JPHamblett(5) 3 80
(R J Price) *racd wd in midfield: rdn over 2f out: no imp: wknd over 1f out* **20/1**

0036 **9** nse **King's Bastion (IRE)**[15] 5446 4-8-8 **86** oh1 HayleyTurner 5 76
(M L W Bell) *stdd s: a in rr: rdn and no prog over 2f out* **15/2**[3]

0002 **10** 1 ¾ **Compton's Eleven**[11] 5589 7-8-8 **86** oh3 EdwardCreighton 9 72
(M R Channon) *a in last trio: no prog and struggling 2f out* **14/1**

2250 **11** shd **Pawan (IRE)**[14] 5495 8-8-7 **90** (b) AnnStokell(5) 6 75
(Miss A Stokell) *trckd ldrs: pushed along and steadily wknd fr over 2f out* **12/1**

35-0 **12** ¾ **Mount Pleasure (USA)**[30] 5025 3-9-2 **98** RichardThomas 12 81
(Christian Wroe) *chsd ldr 3f: steadily wknd fr over 2f out* **33/1**

1m 31.33s (3.93) **Going Correction** +0.725s/f (Yiel)
WFA 3 from 4yo+ 4lb **12** Ran SP% **120.9**
Speed ratings (Par 109): **106,104,104,102,101 99,99,98,98,96 96,95**
toteswinger: 1&2 £33.40, 1&3 £9.60, 2&3 £13.60. CSF £235.49 CT £810.84 TOTE £12.60: £4.30, £4.90, £1.70; EX 144.80 Trifecta £415.10 Part won. Pool: £561.00 - 0.40 winning units..
Owner Heart Of The South Racing **Bred** John And Mrs Caroline Penny **Trained** West Ilsley, Berks

FOCUS
Rail realignment added around 15yards to advertised distances on the Round course. This was a competitive enough handicap, but unusual in that all but one of the runners, runner-up Salient who tried to make all, is habitually held up. Few got into it. The runner-up is a slight doubt over the form from 4lb wrong, and the third is rated the narrow winner.

NOTEBOOK

South Cape, who won this last year off a 2lb lower mark, coped with very different conditions to 2007 adequately for another deserved win. Always in the first three, he looked to have the measure of the leader from 2f out and got on top inside the last.

Salient, the only horse in the field not usually held up, made a bold bid to make all despite a moderate draw. His rider had decided before racing that he would hug the far rail up the straight, and expected the majority to switch to the stands' side, but the action surprisingly all took place middle-to-far side, with nothing tacking over. An enterprising ride almost succeeded on the 4-y-o, who was 4lb out of the handicap, but he was cut down inside the last. (op 22-1)

Signor Peltro ◆, a good course-and-distance winner last month on similar ground and heavily backed to follow up, made up so much late ground that he would probably have won had he been ridden just a little handier. Held up at the back of the field, he still only had a couple behind him approaching the furlong marker, but he made up ground hand over fist once in the clear and only just failed to snatch second. He remains one to keep on the right side of. Official explanation: jockey said gelding suffered interference in running (op 10-3 tchd 7-2)

Flipando(IRE) ran well in fourth, but he gets 1m2f and has not won over less than 1m for four years. (op 7-1)

Aye Aye Digby(IRE), a stablemate of the favourite, ran just respectably. (op 8-1 tchd 17-2)

Eisteddfod was tried in cheekpieces here and ran respectably, but is not at his best at present. (tchd 8-1 and 10-1)

Phantom Whisper came widest up the straight, but found no advantage in being up the middle of the track. (op 13-2)

Compton's Eleven Official explanation: jockey said gelding suffered interference in running

5898 BLUEBAY STARDOM STKS (LISTED RACE) 1m

2:50 (2:53) (Class 1) 2-Y-O **£17,031** (£6,456; £3,231; £1,611; £807) **Stalls** High

Form				RPR
31	**1**		**Zafisio (IRE)**[17] 5387 2-9-0 79 .... DarryllHolland 2 (P A Blockley) *led: rdn and narrowly hdd wl over 1f out: led again ent fnl f: asserted fnl 100yds* **9/2**	101
1	**2**	*1 1/4*	**Anmar (USA)**[15] 5468 2-9-0 0 .... TedDurcan 5 (Saeed Bin Suroor) *trckd ldng pair: wnt 2nd over 2f out: pushed into narrow ld wl over 1f out: hdd and rdn ent fnl f: nt qckn* **15/8**[1]	98
1215	**3**	*2 1/4*	**Measurement (IRE)**[15] 5462 2-9-0 95 .... SteveDrowne 4 (R Hannon) *chsd ldng trio: rdn over 3f out: wnt 3rd over 1f out: no imp at all* **3/1**[3]	93
5114	**4**	*1*	**Sohcahtoa (IRE)**[15] 5462 2-9-0 96 .... TPO'Shea 1 (R Hannon) *trckd ldr: rdn over 3f out: lost 2nd over 2f out: fdd* **11/4**[2]	91
0	**5**	*nk*	**Lilly Blue (IRE)**[28] 5097 2-8-9 0 .... EdwardCreighton 3 (M R Channon) *a last: rdn and no prog over 3f out: one pce after* **14/1**	85

1m 46.32s (6.42) **Going Correction** +0.725s/f (Yiel) **5** Ran SP% **111.3**
Speed ratings (Par 103): **96,94,92,91,91**
toteswinger: 1&2 £7.80. CSF £13.54 TOTE £5.90: £2.60, £1.70; EX 14.60.
Owner H Downs **Bred** Airlie Stud And Sir Thomas Pilkington **Trained** Lambourn, Berks

FOCUS

The usual small field for a Listed race that usually goes to a useful juvenile but is seldom won by a future star. Zafisio was a big improver and the form is well up to scratch for the grade. It was another slow time, but the pace was nothing special. This time they all came over to race stands' side.

NOTEBOOK

Zafisio(IRE) had plenty to find on a bare reading of his Ayr win, a performance for which he was given what must have been a tempting nursery mark of 79, but there was no shortage of confidence behind him and it proved well placed when he made the running and fought back well when headed by the favourite. He was well on top in the last 100 yards, and Paul Blockley insists that whatever he does this year is a bonus, as he was still on the green side here and looks very much the type to make a better 3-y-o. The target now is the Group 1 Gran Criterium at San Siro, where he is virtually guaranteed the soft ground that clearly suits him particularly well. We don't know yet if it is a necessity, but Blockley warns he would not want it too firm. (op 8-1)

Anmar(USA) had won what Godolphin had felt was just an average maiden at Sandown, and there was no great confidence behind him. He looked the winner when heading Zafisio narrowly, but there was no apparent excuse. (op 6-4 tchd 2-1 in places)

Measurement(IRE) had soft-ground form, but is relatively exposed and seemed to be beaten fair and square. (op 7-2)

Sohcahtoa(IRE) had to prove himself on the ground, and he was not at his best. When they came across in the straight it looked as if he was going to grab the rail ahead of Zafisio, but he didn't quite have the speed and he was well held in the end. (op 5-2 tchd 3-1)

Lilly Blue(IRE) had been down the field at Newbury on her debut, but she had been declared for the May Hill at Doncaster earlier this week and so her proximity here is not necessarily a negative. She was always last and never dangerous, but it probably wasn't a bad effort. (op 16-1)

5899 STARLIT STKS (LISTED RACE) 6f

3:20 (3:21) (Class 1) 3-Y-O+

£24,978 (£9,468; £4,738; £2,362; £1,183; £594) **Stalls** Low

Form				RPR
2121	**1**		**Lesson In Humility (IRE)**[49] 4437 3-8-7 103 .... AndrewElliott 3 (K R Burke) *mde virtually all: rdn 2f out: tail swishing but forged clr fnl f* **10/3**[3]	110
625-	**2**	*2*	**Asset (IRE)**[329] 6332 5-9-0 111 .... TedDurcan 1 (Saeed Bin Suroor) *w.w in 5th: rdn over 2f out: styd on fr over 1f out to take 2nd fnl 75yds: no ch w wnr* **2/1**[1]	108
1052	**3**	*3/4*	**Crimson Fern (IRE)**[14] 5509 4-8-9 96 .... TGMcLaughlin 5 (M S Saunders) *hld up in 4th: swtchd lft and effrt jst over 2f out: drvn to press wnr over 1f out: btn ent fnl f: lost 2nd fnl 75yds* **11/2**	101
5-00	**4**	*shd*	**Monaazalah (IRE)**[21] 5275 3-8-7 79 .... RobertHavlin 4 (Rae Guest) *stdd s: hld up in last: effrt over 2f out: kpt on fr over 1f out: n.d* **50/1**	101?
5000	**5**	*3*	**Ashdown Express (IRE)**[19] 5347 9-9-0 93 .... PaulDoe 6 (W J Knight) *pressed wnr to over 1f out: wknd fnl f* **10/1**	96
4000	**6**	*7*	**Sonny Red (IRE)**[21] 5275 4-9-0 106 .... (p) SteveDrowne 2 (R Hannon) *chsd ldng pair over 2f: sn lost pl and struggling: t.o* **11/4**[2]	74

1m 14.85s (2.65) **Going Correction** +0.725s/f (Yiel)
WFA 3 from 4yo+ 2lb **6** Ran SP% **109.5**
Speed ratings (Par 111): **111,108,107,107,103 93**
toteswinger: 1&2 £1.70, 1&3 £1.50, 2&3 £2.50. CSF £9.89 TOTE £3.80: £2.00, £1.70; EX 9.40.
Owner M Nelmes-Crocker **Bred** Kevin Quinn **Trained** Middleham Moor, N Yorks
■ Stewards' Enquiry : T G McLaughlin one-day ban: used whip with excessive frequency (Sep 28)

FOCUS

None of the established Group or Listed horses were at their best here, and the value of the form is debatable, especially with the 79-rated Monaazalah uncomfortably close in fourth. The form does make sense around the winner and third.

NOTEBOOK

Lesson In Humility(IRE) was a worthy winner of what was not a strong Listed event. She has improved with every race this year and had won a decent handicap at York off 96 last time, form which gave her every chance in this company. In front throughout, she had them all in trouble soon after halfway, and although she flashed her tail under pressure in the final furlong or so she ran on strongly. She stays in training next year and might not have finished improving. (op 11-4 tchd 7-2)

Asset(IRE) had a good record first time out, and had made a winning reappearance in his last two seasons with Richard Hannon, impressing in the Abernant at the start of a 2007 campaign that ultimately petered out somewhat. It was hard to know what to expect on his debut for Godolphin, and soft ground would not have been to his advantage, but it was still disappointing to see him struggling almost from the off and only running on into second when the race was over. He is likely to continue to struggle this autumn. (op 5-2 tchd 11-4)

Crimson Fern(IRE) has improved even more than the winner this year, and had recorded another career best last time, but she was running at a much lower level when winning at this trip, and most of her improvement has come over 5f. Having looked almost sure to be second she may have found the trip stretching her here. (op 5-1 tchd 9-2)

Monaazalah(IRE) had a lot to find on official figures but her current mark plainly underestimates her. She impressed enough on her debut last year to go off reasonably well fancied for the Queen Mary, and although she had become a bit disappointing, her current trainer has always excelled with fillies. (tchd 40-1)

Ashdown Express(IRE) dead-heated with Moss Vale in this three years ago when with Chris Wall, but that was his last win and he has been in nothing like the same form lately. He went with the winner until inside the last 2f but faded tamely. (op 12-1 tchd 9-1)

Sonny Red(IRE) looks out of love with the game at present and gave up quickly. (op 3-1 tchd 5-2)

5900 CITY FINANCIAL STKS (H'CAP) 1m 4f

3:55 (3:55) (Class 4) (0-85,81) 3-Y-O+ **£7,771** (£2,312; £1,155; £577) **Stalls** Low

Form				RPR
1200	**1**		**Taikoo**[61] 4021 3-8-10 **73** .... RobertHavlin 13 (H Morrison) *trckd ldrs: rdn over 2f out and lost pl sltly: rallied over 1f out: led jst ins fnl f: jst hld on* **25/1**	81
3130	**2**	*hd*	**Cleaver**[56] 4178 7-9-10 **78** .... KShea 11 (Lady Herries) *hld up wl in rr: stdy prog on outer fr 3f out: drvn and r.o to take 2nd fnl 100yds: clsd on wnr: jst failed* **12/1**	86
6661	**3**	*1 1/2*	**Star Of Gibraltar**[30] 5024 3-9-3 **80** .... SteveDrowne 7 (J L Dunlop) *hld up in midfield: prog over 3f out: chsd ldng pair wl over 1f out: nt qckn: kpt on again ins fnl f* **6/1**[3]	85
0526	**4**	*3/4*	**Mae Cigan (FR)**[29] 5058 5-8-13 **67** .... AdamKirby 1 (M Blanshard) *hld up in midfield: lost pl over 3f out: sn rdn: no prog tl styd on wl fnl f: gaining at fin* **14/1**	71+
0011	**5**	*1*	**Right Stuff (FR)**[24] 5183 5-9-7 **75** .... FergusSweeney 14 (G L Moore) *t.k.h early: hld up towards rr: prog 3f out: rdn to chse ldrs 2f out: one pce and no imp fnl f* **3/1**[1]	77
-146	**6**	*nse*	**Shimoni**[16] 5423 4-9-5 **76** .... (v) JackMitchell(3) 8 (G L Moore) *t.k.h early: mostly pressed ldr: upsides fr over 2f out tl ent fnl f: wknd* **16/1**	78
6221	**7**	*shd*	**Fortune City (UAE)**[10] 5612 3-9-3 **80** .... TedDurcan 2 (Saeed Bin Suroor) *mde most: racd against nr side rail in st: jnd over 2f out: drvn over 1f out: hdd & wknd jst ins fnl f* **11/2**[2]	82
-006	**8**	*3/4*	**William's Way**[28] 5092 6-9-10 **78** .... TGMcLaughlin 6 (I A Wood) *hld up in last pair: stdy prog on outer 3f out: rdn over 2f out: kpt on one pce fr over 1f out* **16/1**	79
0230	**9**	*2 1/2*	**Celticello (IRE)**[28] 5092 6-9-2 **75** .... RichardEvans(5) 5 (P D Evans) *hld up in rr: sme prog on outer 3f out: no hdwy u.p 2f out: wknd fnl f* **11/1**	72
122	**10**	*5*	**Outlandish**[175] 970 5-9-7 **75** .... HayleyTurner 9 (Andrew Turnell) *prom: lost pl on inner whn field c to nr side over 3f out: sn wknd* **12/1**	64
664	**11**	*2 1/2*	**Cruise Director**[24] 5183 8-9-0 **68** .... TQuinn 3 (Ian Williams) *trckd ldrs: rdn wl over 2f out: wknd rapidly wl over 1f out* **14/1**	53
0051	**12**	*3/4*	**Fort Churchill (IRE)**[11] 5583 7-9-0 **75** .... (bt) LanceBetts(7) 10 (B Ellison) *trckd ldrs: stl cl up over 2f out: sn wknd u.p* **10/1**	59
0455	**13**	*2 3/4*	**Giant Love (USA)**[19] 5370 3-8-10 **73** .... DarryllHolland 4 (M Johnston) *fractious as stalls opened: t.k.h and sn in ldng trio: wknd rapidly over 3f out* **14/1**	52
/26-	**14**	*3/4*	**Ameeq (USA)**[420] 3509 6-9-13 **81** .... JamieMoore 12 (G L Moore) *hld up in last pair: rdn and no prog over 3f out: sn bhd* **25/1**	59

2m 47.23s (8.83) **Going Correction** +0.725s/f (Yiel)
WFA 3 from 4yo+ 9lb **14** Ran SP% **126.9**
Speed ratings (Par 105): **99,98,97,97,96 96,96,96,94,91 89,88,87,86**
toteswinger: 1&2 £64.70, 1&3 £24.60, 2&3 £16.00. CSF £315.10 CT £2105.36 TOTE £44.60: £9.00, £4.10, £2.30; EX 618.00.
Owner Miss B Swire **Bred** Miss B Swire **Trained** East Ilsley, Berks
■ Stewards' Enquiry : Robert Havlin three-day ban: used whip with excessive frequency (Sep 28-30)

FOCUS

A reasonable handicap in which they again tracked across to race up the stands' side. Sound form.

5901 EUROPEAN BREEDERS' FUND CARD ROOM MAIDEN STKS 1m

4:30 (4:31) (Class 4) 2-Y-O **£4,371** (£1,300; £650; £324) **Stalls** High

Form				RPR
03	**1**		**Aqwaal (IRE)**[12] 5578 2-9-3 0 .... TGMcLaughlin 2 (E A L Dunlop) *hld up in abt 6th: drvn over 2f out: prog over 1f out: gd burst to ld wl ins fnl f: hld on nr fin* **13/2**[3]	75
43	**2**	*shd*	**Silver Print (USA)**[44] 4570 2-9-3 0 .... AdamKirby 1 (W R Swinburn) *trckd ldr: clsd to ld jst over 2f out: hrd pressed after: hdd wl ins fnl f: kpt on wl: jst hld* **7/2**[2]	75
	3	*1 1/4*	**Princability (IRE)** 2-9-3 0 .... DarryllHolland 8 (M R Channon) *hld up in last pair: stdy prog on outer over 2f out: pressed ldrs and looked dangerous 1f out: one pce fnl 100yds* **9/1**	72+
05	**4**	*hd*	**Itlaaq**[31] 4982 2-9-3 0 .... SteveDrowne 4 (J L Dunlop) *trckd ldrs: rdn over 2f out: no imp over 1f out: styd on ins fnl f* **12/1**	72+
0	**5**	*1 1/4*	**Royal Toerag**[19] 5344 2-9-3 0 .... PaulDoe 5 (W J Knight) *wl in tch: prog to chal gng wl 2f out: drvn over 1f out: wknd ins fnl f* **33/1**	69
5	**6**	*nse*	**Mt Kintyre (IRE)**[71] 3682 2-9-3 0 .... TQuinn 6 (M H Tompkins) *cl up: chal over 2f out: upsides but hanging rt over 1f out: wknd ins fnl f* **9/1**	69
4	**7**	*3 1/4*	**Seaquel**[19] 5365 2-8-12 0 .... FergusSweeney 3 (A B Haynes) *hld up in last pair: rdn and struggling over 2f out: no prog after* **18/1**	57
5	**8**	*5*	**Contretemps (USA)**[22] 5246 2-9-3 0 .... TedDurcan 7 (Saeed Bin Suroor) *led: 3 l clr 1/2-way: hdd & wknd tamely jst over 2f out* **6/5**[1]	51

1m 46.62s (6.72) **Going Correction** +0.725s/f (Yiel) **8** Ran SP% **116.9**
Speed ratings (Par 97): **95,94,93,93,92 92,88,83**
toteswinger: 1&2 £3.60, 1&3 £8.90, 2&3 £5.40. CSF £30.23 TOTE £7.60: £1.90, £1.70, £2.10; EX 39.80.
Owner Hamdan Al Maktoum **Bred** Shadwell Estate Company Limited **Trained** Newmarket, Suffolk
■ Stewards' Enquiry : Darryll Holland two-day ban: used whip down neck in forehand position (Sep 28-29)

FOCUS
They finished in a bit of a heap here, having once again crossed over to race up the stands' side, but the time was only marginally slower than that recorded by Zafisio in the earlier Listed race. Improved form from the first two.

NOTEBOOK
Aqwaal(IRE) looked very much a staying type, for he was under strong pressure and going nowhere two out but then picked up well to lead inside the final furlong. He just held the renewed effort of Silver Print up the rail and is improving steadily. (op 9-1 tchd 6-1)
Silver Print(USA), tackling a mile for the first time, produced a renewed effort which was just held. He is progressing, and has the nursery option now. (op 9-2)
Princability(IRE) was a springer in the market and shaped promisingly. Having been held up in last place and still been there into the straight, he stayed on up the outside of the group and had every chance well inside the final furlong. He should have no trouble winning a similar race with this one under his belt. (op 7-1)
Itlaaq, carrying the first colours of the winning owner, ran another sound enough race in fourth, with no apparent excuse, and he is another who is eligible now for nurseries. (op 16-1)
Royal Toerag, well beaten on his Polytrack debut, appeared to show much improved form in fifth.
Mt Kintyre(IRE) is well regarded and looked a possible winner 2f out but faded disappointingly. (op 11-2)
Contretemps(USA), who had shaped reasonably well on his debut, was allowed an easy lead, but having led them across to the stands' rail he was soon joined and capitulated tamely. Official explanation: trainer's rep said colt was unsuited by the soft ground (op 6-4)

5902 GOODWOOD RACEHORSE OWNERS GROUP STKS (H'CAP) 5f
5:05 (5:05) (Class 5) (0-75,76) 3-Y-O **£3,238** (£963; £481; £240) **Stalls** Low

Form RPR
0564 **1** **Our Piccadilly (IRE)**[14] 5490 3-8-9 **66**.......................... FergusSweeney 7 75
(W S Kittow) *pressed ldr: led jst over 2f out: rdn clr fr 1f out* **3/1**[1]
0416 **2** 3 1/4 **Cheshire Rose**[16] 5417 3-8-12 **69**.......................... TedDurcan 8 66
(T D Barron) *trckd ldrs: rdn and nt qckn over 1f out: chsd wnr after: no imp* **4/1**[2]
5-34 **3** 3/4 **Compton Rose**[114] 2341 3-8-4 **68**.......................... AmyScott(7) 4 63
(H Candy) *cl up: rdn to dispute 2nd over 1f out: one pce after* **4/1**[2]
2451 **4** 3 **Barraland**[13] 5531 3-9-5 **76**.......................... TPO'Shea 1 60
(M R Channon) *in tch: rdn 1/2-way: outpcd fr 2f out: plugged on* **5/1**[3]
0014 **5** 1 **Hawk Eyed Lady (IRE)**[13] 5531 3-8-6 **63** ow2............(b) SteveDrowne 5 43
(J A Osborne) *led to jst over 2f out: wknd over 1f out* **6/1**
2401 **6** 8 **Pennyspider (IRE)**[22] 5217 3-8-12 **69**.......................... TGMcLaughlin 3 20
(M S Saunders) *in tch tl wknd u.p 1/2-way* **5/1**[3]
61.37 secs (2.97) **Going Correction** +0.725s/f (Yiel) **6** Ran SP% **112.6**
Speed ratings (Par 101): **105,99,98,93,92 79**
toteswinger: 1&2 £3.40, 1&3 £2.70, 2&3 £2.80. CSF £15.24 CT £46.71 TOTE £4.90: £2.60, £2.30; EX 19.90.
Owner S Kittow, R Perry,the late J Hopkins **Bred** Mrs Hopkins, Mr Kittow And Mrs Perry **Trained** Blackborough, Devon

FOCUS
A weak handicap by Goodwood standards, contested mainly by fillies. The well backed winner is rated to her 2yo best.

5903 SWANS BOTTOM STKS (H'CAP) 1m 1f
5:40 (5:41) (Class 2) (0-100,97) 3-Y-0+
£11,215 (£3,358; £1,679; £840; £419; £210) **Stalls** High

Form RPR
4002 **1** **Siberian Tiger (IRE)**[36] 4830 3-9-1 **96**.......................... EdwardCreighton 1 107
(M R Channon) *trckd ldrs gng wl: eased towards outer over 2f out: led wl over 1f out: hd high but powered away fnl f* **11/2**[3]
0360 **2** 5 **Capable Guest (IRE)**[14] 5508 6-8-9 **91**.................(v) MatthewDavies(7) 7 91
(M R Channon) *hld up in midfield: rdn and prog on outer 3f out: upsides 2f out: chsd wnr over 1f out: sn lft bhd* **14/1**
5060 **3** 3/4 **Kinsya**[19] 5360 5-9-0 **89**.......................... TQuinn 2 87
(M H Tompkins) *t.k.h early: hld up in last pair: nt clr run briefly over 2f out: prog over 1f out but outpcd: kpt on to take 3rd fnl 100yds* **7/1**
4222 **4** 2 **Ace Of Hearts**[35] 4845 9-9-5 **97**.......................... JackMitchell(3) 5 91
(C F Wall) *trckd ldng pair: effrt to chal and upsides 2f out: sn outpcd: wknd fnl f* **4/1**[2]
0100 **5** 1 1/4 **Upton Grey (IRE)**[21] 5279 3-8-10 **91**.......................... RobertHavlin 8 82
(J H M Gosden) *sn led: rdn and hdd wl over 1f out: wknd* **7/2**[1]
0160 **6** 4 1/2 **Mountain Pride (IRE)**[19] 5360 3-8-6 **87** ow1.................. SteveDrowne 4 68
(J L Dunlop) *pressed ldr: hanging fr over 2f out: wknd wl over 1f out* **11/2**[3]
0020 **7** 1 **Orchard Supreme**[46] 4509 5-8-10 **88**.......................... PatrickHills(3) 6 67
(R Hannon) *in tch in midfield: rdn over 2f out: sn wknd* **12/1**
1160 **8** 8 **Dear Maurice**[23] 5207 4-8-8 **83**..........................(b[1]) TedDurcan 3 45
(E A L Dunlop) *hld up in last pair: rdn and wknd over 2f out: t.o* **6/1**
2m 0.48s (4.18) **Going Correction** +0.725s/f (Yiel)
WFA 3 from 4yo+ 6lb **8** Ran SP% **114.1**
Speed ratings (Par 109): **110,105,104,103,102 98,97,90**
toteswinger: 1&2 £14.40, 1&3 £8.40, 2&3 £16.20. CSF £76.38 CT £548.12 TOTE £5.80: £1.40, £4.20, £2.70; EX 57.10 Place 6 £147.46, Place 5 £52.96.
Owner Ridgeway Downs Racing **Bred** Ashley Guest And Mrs John Guest **Trained** West Ilsley, Berks

FOCUS
This was run over the Cambridgeshire distance, and the top four in the handicap are all entered there. It was not the most competitive of handicaps, but the winner showed improved form however one looks at it. The race has provisionally been rated around the placed horses recent efforts.

NOTEBOOK
Siberian Tiger(IRE) burst clear to win by a wide margin and must come well into the Cambridgeshire reckoning now with just a 4lb penalty. That race is definitely his target, and he needs only a handful to come out in order to make the cut. Although he has been struggling somewhat since his highly progressive 2-y-o campaign, he is a smart performer on his day and he had shown plenty when fourth to Conduit at Epsom and again last time in a Newmarket conditions race. He handled this easy ground well, but he is just as effective on a sound surface. (op 8-1 tchd 10-1 in a place)
Capable Guest(IRE), a stablemate of the winner who has had a very busy campaign, plugged on for second. (op 12-1)
Kinsya goes well on soft ground and kept on from off the pace after having nowhere to go briefly when his rider was looking to begin his effort. Official explanation: jockey said gelding was denied a clear run (tchd 13-2)
Ace Of Hearts was weak in the market, which perhaps was not surprising considering all his eight turf wins have been on good to firm or firmer. He has been creeping up the handicap for some cracking efforts in defeat, but the ground looked more of a factor than the weight. (op 11-4)
Upton Grey(IRE) handles this sort of ground and was well backed, but having made the running he did not find a great deal for pressure. (op 9-2)
Mountain Pride(IRE) dropped away disappointingly and was below his recent level. (op 6-1 tchd 13-2)

T/Plt: £351.10 to a £1 stake. Pool: £72,728.36. 151.18 winning tickets. T/Qpdt: £80.60 to a £1 stake. Pool: £3,188.10. 29.25 winning tickets. JN

[5832]GREAT LEIGHS (A.W) (L-H)
Saturday, September 13

OFFICIAL GOING: Standard
Wind: virtually nil Weather: bright and sunny

5904 YELLOW LAPWING MAIDEN AUCTION STKS 5f (P)
2:15 (2:16) (Class 4) 2-Y-O **£5,180** (£1,541; £770; £384) **Stalls** Low

Form RPR
2040 **1** **Court Approval (IRE)**[15] 5466 2-9-1 71.................... StephenDonohoe 1 75
(T G Mills) *mde all: drvn wl over 1f out: styd on wl fnl f* **8/1**[3]
24 **2** 2 **Dakota Hills**[49] 4411 2-8-13 0.......................... LPKeniry 7 66
(J R Best) *chsd ldrs: rdn to chse wiiner 2f out: no imp fnl f* **7/1**[2]
4032 **3** 3/4 **Mo Mhuirnin (IRE)**[20] 5306 2-8-8 72 ow3.................. FrederikTylicki(5) 5 63
(R A Fahey) *s.i.s: hdwy 4f out: chsd ldrs and drvn 2f out: kpt on same pce fnl f* **6/4**[1]
30 **4** hd **The Cuckoo**[42] 4634 2-9-0 0.......................... RichardKingscote 8 63
(M J Wallace, Australia) *chsd ldrs: rdn and effrt wl over 1f out: kpt on same pce fnl f* **8/1**[3]
60 **5** 3 **Miss Thippawan (USA)**[18] 5384 2-8-4 0............... FrankieMcDonald 11 43
(P T Midgley) *s.i.s: bhd: c wd over 1f out: r.o fnl f: nvr trbld ldrs* **100/1**
63 **6** shd **Fortune In Faith (USA)**[9] 5628 2-8-10 0................ RobertWinston 9 48
(C G Cox) *in tch in midfield: rdn and outpcd 1/2-way: drvn and one pce fr over 1f out* **7/1**[2]
46 **7** nse **Edith's Boy (IRE)**[16] 5430 2-8-10 0.......................... NickyMackay 3 48
(S Dow) *rrd s and slowly away: bhd: sme late hdwy: nvr trbld ldrs* **14/1**
3000 **8** hd **Damassin**[16] 5432 2-8-6 60.......................... StephenCarson 10 43
(Eve Johnson Houghton) *s.i.s: bhd and rdn 1/2-way: kpt on fnl f: n.d* **20/1**
56 **9** 1 1/4 **Scottish Affair**[12] 5572 2-9-3 0.......................... NeilPollard 4 50
(E A L Dunlop) *racd in midfield: rdn and outpcd 1/2-way: n.d after* **20/1**
10 1 3/4 **Desert Strike** 2-8-11 0.......................... JoeFanning 2 38
(P F I Cole) *chsd wnr tl 2f out: wkng whn short of room over 1f out: fdd fnl f* **7/1**[2]
11 3 3/4 **Cavitie** 2-8-5 0.......................... MCGeran(5) 6 23
(E J Creighton) *v.s.a: hdwy into midfield over 3f out: sn rdn and struggling: wl bhd fr over 1f out* **33/1**
60.87 secs (0.67) **Going Correction** +0.075s/f (Slow) **11** Ran SP% **119.8**
Speed ratings (Par 97): **97,93,92,92,87 87,87,86,84,82 76**
toteswinger: 1&2 £9.80, 1&3 Not won, 2&3 £5.30. CSF £61.59 TOTE £9.70: £2.20, £2.20, £1.20; EX 72.70.
Owner Mrs L M Askew **Bred** Shadwell Estate Company Limited **Trained** Headley, Surrey

FOCUS
A modest event in which the winner showed speed on the rail all the way. He is rated back to his best and the form could have been rated higher.

NOTEBOOK
Court Approval(IRE) made the most of his inside draw. Breaking well, he made all and never looked likely to be headed. He has looked an in-and-out performer, but his best performances have come when he is able to race prominently. He was not suited by the fast ground at Sandown last time, but the Polytrack surface clearly suited. (op 9-1 tchd 10-1)
Dakota Hills tracked the leader on the rail, was up with the pace around the home turn and was four wide entering the straight, and he just could not peg back the winner. He was outpaced on the turf at Lingfield last time over 5f and is bred to appreciate further, but showed enough speed here to suggest he can pick up a race. (op 6-1)
Mo Mhuirnin(IRE) was slowly away, as she has been in her previous three races. From that position, and running five wide in the straight, she was never able to justify the support. (op 5-2)
The Cuckoo showed early speed but was always on the outside, so he ran respectably in the circumstances. He will be interesting in nurseries. (op 10-1 tchd 11-1)
Edith's Boy(IRE) Official explanation: jockey said colt missed the break

5905 EBF LAPWING MAIDEN STKS 6f (P)
2:45 (2:46) (Class 4) 2-Y-O **£5,180** (£1,541; £770; £384) **Stalls** Low

Form RPR
3343 **1** **Desert Falls**[9] 5633 2-9-3 72.......................... DeanMcKeown 10 82
(R M Whitaker) *broke wl: mde all: edgd rt 2f out: rdn wl over 1f out: styd on wl and in command fnl f* **10/1**
0322 **2** 1 1/2 **Servoca (CAN)**[36] 4815 2-9-3 85.......................... TPQueally 3 78
(B W Hills) *hld up wl in tch: rdn 2f out: chsd wnr 1f out: one pce after* **10/11**[1]
5 **3** 1 1/4 **Comadoir (IRE)**[10] 5615 2-9-3 0.......................... TravisBlock 7 74
(Miss Jo Crowley) *chsd ldr: rdn to chal jst over 2f out: one pce ent fnl f* **7/1**[3]
4 3 1/4 **Mac's Power (IRE)** 2-9-0 0.......................... JerryO'Dwyer(3) 6 64
(P J O'Gorman) *hld up in tch: hdwy to chse ldrs over 2f out: rdn wl over 1f out: wknd fnl f* **12/1**
5 2 3/4 **Chambers (IRE)** 2-9-3 0.......................... JoeFanning 2 56+
(M Johnston) *s.i.s: bhd: hdwy and in tch over 4f out: rdn and outpcd over 2f out: plugged on but n.d after* **5/1**[2]
0 **6** 1 **Pure Rhythm**[13] 5534 2-8-12 0.......................... RichardKingscote 5 48
(S C Williams) *towards rr: rdn and struggling 1/2-way: no ch last 2f* **66/1**
0 **7** 2 1/2 **Law And Order**[22] 5225 2-9-3 0.......................... PaulFitzsimons 8 46
(Miss J R Tooth) *s.i.s: sn rdn: a bhd* **12/1**
8 hd **Point Of Light** 2-9-3 0.......................... StephenDonohoe 4 45
(Sir Mark Prescott) *s.i.s: sn rdn: a bhd* **16/1**
6 **9** 2 1/2 **Celtic Rebel (IRE)**[20] 5316 2-8-12 0............ Louis-PhilippeBeuzelin(5) 9 37
(S A Callaghan) *racd in midfield: ridded and struggling jst over 2f out: wl btn over 1f out: sddle slipped* **25/1**
P **Wicklewood** 2-9-3 0.......................... SamHitchcott 11 —
(Mrs C A Dunnett) *s.i.s: sn bhd: eased over 4f out: p.u 1/2-way: sddle slipped* **66/1**
00 **P** **Arteus**[14] 5500 2-9-3 0.......................... RobertWinston 1 —
(G G Margarson) *in tch: rdn and wknd qckly over 2f out: eased and p.u over 1f out* **66/1**
1m 13.7s **Going Correction** +0.075s/f (Slow) **11** Ran SP% **120.2**
Speed ratings (Par 97): **103,101,99,95,91 90,86,86,83,— —**
toteswinger: 1&2 £4.60, 1&3 £12.20, 2&3 £1.10. CSF £19.71 TOTE £12.30: £1.90, £1.50, £1.70; EX 24.80.
Owner J Barry Pemberton **Bred** Hellwood Farm And J B Pemberton **Trained** Scarcroft, W Yorks

FOCUS
Those with racecourse experience showed the newcomers the way in this maiden. The winner showed improved form but had the run of things from the front. The second is essentially a disappointing sort.

NOTEBOOK

Desert Falls got a flying start from his wide draw and was soon over a length ahead, and though challenged on the home turn he stayed on well to win a little cosily to register a first course win for his trainer and a first all-weather win for his sire Pyrus. Connections were in the dark as to how suited he would be to Polytrack, as he does all his work at home on grass. (op 12-1)

Servoca(CAN) had finished second four times and was a warm order to go one better. He tracked the winner and was switched to the inner in the home straight to deliver a challenge, but he found little under pressure. Although he had been racing in more competitive events, it seems finding the right trip or a winnable race for him might prove problematic. (tchd Evens and 6-5 in a place)

Comadoir(IRE), having his second start for his stable after running some reasonable races in Ireland, went with the pace and briefly headed the winner around the home turn until he was outpaced and hung in the home straight. (op 9-1)

Mac's Power(IRE) ran quite well on this debut, tracking the pace but wide all the way and one-paced in the final stages. He is from a family who do well on the all-weather and will surely pay his way. (op 16-1 tchd 11-1)

Chambers(IRE) was slowly away and lost several lengths but made ground on the home turn before his effort flattened out. This was an encouraging debut. (op 9-2)

Celtic Rebel(IRE) Official explanation: jockey said saddle slipped

Wicklewood Official explanation: jockey said saddle slipped

Arteus Official explanation: trainer said colt had a breathing problem

5906 LINNET H'CAP — 5f (P)

3:15 (3:17) (Class 3) (0-95,95) 3-Y-O+ **£7,771** (£2,312; £1,155; £577) **Stalls** Low

Form — RPR

0000 **1** **Elhamri**[14] 5509 4-8-9 **85** ... RichardKingscote 1 — 95
(S Kirk) *chsd ldr: rdn and ev ch over 2f out: led ins fnl f: r.o wl* **15/2**

655 **2** 1 **Secret Asset (IRE)**[91] 3028 3-8-13 **90** ... LiamJones 2 — 96
(W M Brisbourne) *led: hrd pressed fr 1/2-way: rdn jst over 2f out: hdd and no ex ins fnl f* **20/1**

6404 **3** ½ **Matsunosuke**[14] 5509 6-8-13 **94** ... Louis-PhilippeBeuzelin(5) 7 — 98+
(A B Coogan) *s.i.s: hld up bhd: hdwy on inner 3f out: swtchd rt over 1f out: r.o fnl f: nt quite rch ldng pair* **6/1**[2]

1606 **4** shd **Little Edward**[14] 5509 10-8-9 **90** ... MCGeran(5) 12 — 94
(R J Hodges) *stdd after s: t.k.h: hld up in midfield: hdwy over 2f out: r.o fnl f: nt quite rch ldrs* **10/1**

6000 **5** 2 **Judd Street**[21] 5275 6-9-5 **95** ...(v) StephenCarson 11 — 92
(Eve Johnson Houghton) *sn prom: rdn jst over 2f out: wknd ins fnl f* **14/1**

1140 **6** ½ **Misaro (GER)**[14] 5509 7-9-1 **91** ...(b) JoeFanning 14 — 86
(R A Harris) *racd wd: sn handy: lost pl bnd over 3f out: rallied u.p over 1f out: kpt on* **14/1**

0100 **7** 1¾ **Bond City (IRE)**[14] 5503 6-8-13 **89** ... RobertWinston 6 — 78
(G R Oldroyd) *hld up bhd: hdwy u.p over 1f out: nvr trbld ldrs* **9/1**

1460 **8** ¾ **Efistorm**[33] 4928 7-8-10 **86** ... LPKeniry 10 — 72
(C R Dore) *in tch: rdn and struggling over 3f out: kpt on same pce u.p fr over 1f out* **7/1**[3]

3403 **9** nk **Tia Mia**[23] 5206 3-8-8 **85** ...(p) TPQueally 8 — 70
(M Botti) *hld up towards rr: c wd and effrt wl over 1f out: kpt on but nvr trbld ldrs* **6/1**[2]

1200 **10** shd **Tabaret**[14] 5509 5-9-2 **92** ...(p) DeanMcKeown 3 — 76
(R M Whitaker) *chsd ldrs: wkng whn hung lft over 1f out: wl btn ins fnl f* **5/1**[1]

2000 **11** ¾ **Bazroy (IRE)**[8] 5681 4-8-11 **87** ... StephenDonohoe 9 — 69
(P D Evans) *s.i.s: detached in last: n.d* **12/1**

-040 **12** 6 **Lady Avenger (IRE)**[91] 3028 3-8-9 **89** ... LukeMorris(3) 13 — 49
(J M P Eustace) *racd in midfield tl lost pl bnd wl over 3f out: no ch after: eased towards fin* **40/1**

100- **13** 1 **Obstructive**[350] 5810 4-8-8 **89** ... ShaneCreighton(5) 4 — 46
(E J Creighton) *a towards rr: n.d* **20/1**

3200 **14** 1½ **Merlin's Dancer**[21] 5270 8-8-9 **85** ... NickyMackay 5 — 36
(S Dow) *chsd ldrs: rdn and struggling over 3f out: wl bhd fnl 2f: b.b.v* **14/1**

59.73 secs (-0.47) **Going Correction** +0.075s/f (Slow)
WFA 3 from 4yo+ 1lb — **14** Ran SP% **128.2**
Speed ratings (Par 107): **106,104,103,103,100 99,96,95,94,94 93,84,82,80**
toteswinger: 1&2 £24.60, 1&3 £24.60, 2&3 £24.60. CSF £159.83 CT £1009.76 TOTE £11.00: £6.30, £7.00, £4.80; EX 220.00.
Owner Norman Ormiston **Bred** Highfield Stud Ltd **Trained** Upper Lambourn, Berks
■ Stewards' Enquiry : Luke Morris caution: allowed filly to coast home with no assistance.

FOCUS
Once again early pace prevailed in this fair sprint, and the first two were drawn low and always to the fore. The form is rated to face value.

NOTEBOOK

Elhamri got to the rail from his inside draw but was never seeming to get the better of the pace battle and was driven and headed on the home turn, only to rally to assert in the final furlong. Having shown little form recently – he had not been in the top third of finishers in his last six races – this was obviously an improvement, and the combination of a favourable trip and being back down to his last winning mark made the difference. (op 8-1 tchd 9-1 and 7-1)

Secret Asset(IRE) broke well but could not get the rail and challenged the winner on his outside all the way, leading around the turn before just giving way close home. This was an improved effort, as he has not really built on the promise of his two-year-old season, but the favourable draw was a factor. (op 28-1)

Matsunosuke was in mid-division on the rail before staying on strongly in the straight and almost got to the leaders. His last win was at Lingfield almost a year ago but on this evidence he is coming into form. (op 5-1 tchd 9-2)

Little Edward was one-paced on the home turn before staying on well and ran well from his wide draw. Another all-weather race could still come his way. (tchd 9-1)

Judd Street went with the early pace but from stall 11 he was wide all the way and, not surprisingly, weakened in the home straight. He is dropping in the handicap but has faded in several recent races.

Tia Mia Official explanation: vet said filly returned lame behind

Merlin's Dancer Official explanation: trainer said gelding had bled from the nose

5907 SWALLOW H'CAP — 1m (P)

3:50 (3:50) (Class 2) (0-100,95) 3-Y-O
£11,215 (£3,358; £1,679; £840; £419; £210) **Stalls** Centre

Form — RPR

01 **1** **Irish Mayhem (USA)**[23] 5207 3-9-0 **91** ... NickyMackay 3 — 108
(B J Meehan) *a travelling wl: trckd ldng pair: led over 1f out: clr fnl f: easily* **6/1**[3]

1331 **2** 4 **Relative Order**[21] 5273 3-9-2 **93** ... LPKeniry 7 — 101
(J R Best) *chsd ldrs: edgd out rt and rdn 2f out: no ch w wnr fnl f but plugged on to go 2nd ins fnl f* **4/1**[2]

1301 **3** 1¼ **Slam**[16] 5425 3-9-4 **95** ... IanMongan 10 — 100
(B W Hills) *sn chsng ldr: rdn to ld 2f out: hdd over 1f out: no ch w wnr after: lost 2nd ins fnl f* **7/2**[1]

4-31 **4** 1 **Quotation**[71] 3679 3-9-0 **91** ... RobertWinston 5 — 94+
(Sir Michael Stoute) *hld up bhd: rdn jst over 2f out: nt clr run and swtchd rt over 1f out: kpt on to go 4th ins fnl f: nvr trbld ldrs* **4/1**[2]

0110 **5** 1½ **Gala Casino Star (IRE)**[35] 4876 3-8-8 **90** ow2 ... FrederikTylicki(5) 1 — 89
(R A Fahey) *hld up towards rr: rdn 3f out: nt clr run briefly wl over 2f out: plugged on fnl f: nvr trbld ldrs* **12/1**

3232 **6** ¾ **Ellemujie**[21] 5273 3-8-13 **90** ... RichardKingscote 8 — 88
(D K Ivory) *sn led: rdn and hdd 2f out: wknd over 1f out* **7/1**

0406 **7** nk **Dubai Dynamo**[20] 5313 3-9-2 **93** ... StephenDonohoe 9 — 90
(P F I Cole) *stdd s and dropped in bhd: c wd and rdn 2f out: n.d* **11/1**

-051 **8** 1¼ **Mut'Ab (USA)**[53] 4283 3-9-3 **94** ...(b) LiamJones 2 — 88
(C E Brittain) *in tch: rdn over 2f out: wknd over 1f out:* **16/1**

0100 **9** 5 **Throne Of Power (USA)**[64] 3919 3-9-3 **94** ...(v[1]) TPQueally 4 — 76
(M A Magnusson) *t.k.h: hld up towards rr: rdn 2f out: wl btn whn sltly hmpd over 1f out* **10/1**

1000 **10** 10 **Summon Up Theblood (IRE)**[19] 5360 3-9-1 **92** ... SamHitchcott 6 — 51
(M R Channon) *s.i.s: sn in midfield: rdn over 3f out: wknd over 2f out: wl btn and eased ins fnl f* **20/1**

1m 38.23s (-1.67) **Going Correction** +0.075s/f (Slow) — **10** Ran SP% **124.8**
Speed ratings (Par 107): **111,107,105,104,103 102,102,100,95,85**
toteswinger: 1&2 £2.10, 1&3 £1.70, 2&3 £5.70. CSF £32.57 CT £103.15 TOTE £7.30: £1.40, £1.90, £2.50; EX 27.90.
Owner Dean Fleming **Bred** Heaven Trees Farm **Trained** Manton, Wilts

FOCUS
A good handicap with half the field winners last time out. The time is fast and the form has been rated positively, with the winner up 10lb.

NOTEBOOK

Irish Mayhem(USA) was always travelling well on the rail on the heels of the leaders and came through in the home straight to draw clear under a good ride. A ready winner over course and distance last time, he was raised 7lb and, though up in class here, he still looks to be progressing. (tchd 13-2)

Relative Order was making his all-weather debut and handled the surface well. Racing prominently but on the outside, he was outpaced entering the straight but stayed on a little near the finish. This gives connections options. (op 10-3 tchd 9-2)

Slam was well backed to gain a third course-and-distance win off a 5lb higher mark. Ridden prominently again, he was parked wide around the first turn, remained prominent, then kicked for home early in the straight, perhaps a shade too early. With an inside draw to capitalise on his pacesetting preferences, he can regain the winning thread. (op 11-2)

Quotation, the morning favourite, was easy to back on-course on a 9lb higher mark than when a well-backed winner at Salisbury last time. Held up in the rear early, she had to be switched slightly entering the straight before staying on well, but the interference did not make a material difference. (op 9-4 tchd 2-1)

5908 SWIFT H'CAP — 1m (P)

4:25 (4:25) (Class 3) (0-90,90) 3-Y-O+ **£7,771** (£2,312; £1,155; £577) **Stalls** Centre

Form — RPR

2001 **1** **Storm Sir (USA)**[26] 5140 3-8-8 **80** ...(t) StephenDonohoe 12 — 88
(B J Meehan) *racd in midfield: rdn wl over 2f out: hit by rival's whip wl over 1f out: hdwy u.p over 1f out: led fnl 100yds: hld on cl home* **10/1**

032 **2** shd **Yarqus**[23] 5207 5-9-9 **90** ...(b) LiamJones 5 — 99
(C E Brittain) *hld up towards rr: hdwy over 2f out: looking for gap ent fnl f: burst through ins fnl f: pressed wnr wl ins fnl f: jst hld* **9/2**[3]

0300 **3** 2 **Tender The Great (IRE)**[10] 5600 5-8-12 **82** ... JerryO'Dwyer(3) 14 — 86
(H J Collingridge) *hld up wl in tch: trckd ldrs travellling wl 2f out: rdn to ld ins fnl f: flashed tail u.p: hdd and no ex fnl 100yds* **25/1**

056 **4** 1¼ **Rubacuori (BRZ)**[44] 4565 4-8-8 **78** ... LukeMorris(3) 11 — 81+
(J M P Eustace) *sn bustled along in midfield: hdwy u.p wl over 1f out: chsd ldrs ent fnl f: keeping on same pce whn n.m.r ins fnl f* **40/1**

2120 **5** 1¾ **Decameron (USA)**[35] 4853 3-8-13 **90** ... Louis-PhilippeBeuzelin(5) 4 — 87
(Sir Michael Stoute) *chsd ldrs: wnt 2nd over 2f out: rdn to ld narrowly wl over 1f out: hdd jst ins fnl f: one pce after* **2/1**[1]

0-16 **6** 1¼ **Who's This (IRE)**[34] 4894 4-8-11 **83** ... FrederikTylicki(5) 10 — 78
(W R Swinburn) *racd keenly: sn led: rdn and narrowly hdd wl over 1f out: wknd ins fnl f* **10/1**

3020 **7** 1¼ **Just Bond (IRE)**[35] 4876 6-9-6 **87** ... RobertWinston 7 — 79
(G R Oldroyd) *stdd s: hld up bhd: rdn and effrt 2f out: c wd over 1f out: kpt on but nvr able to chal* **12/1**

6020 **8** ½ **Gallantry**[23] 5207 6-9-5 **86** ... IanMongan 15 — 77
(P Howling) *hld up on outer in midfield: rdn over 2f out: kpt on same pce fr over 1f out* **25/1**

0340 **9** ¾ **Resplendent Nova**[7] 5697 6-9-1 **82** ... TPQueally 1 — 71
(P Howling) *in tch on inner: effrt and rdn wl over 1f out: keeping on same pce whn bmpd ent fnl f: wl hld after* **20/1**

0563 **10** 1½ **Obezyana (USA)**[41] 4661 6-8-10 **77** ... SamHitchcott 8 — 62
(A Bailey) *s.i.s: pushed along in midfield tl 5f out: n.m.r on inner 2f out: no imp after* **14/1**

1024 **11** 4 **Mount Hermon (IRE)**[23] 5207 4-8-12 **79** ...(b) TravisBlock 2 — 55
(H Morrison) *chsd ldng pair: rdn 4f out: nvr looked happy after: wkng whn short of room over 1f out: wl btn afte* **7/2**[2]

0-00 **12** 9 **Roman Maze**[6] 5717 8-8-11 **78** ... RichardKingscote 6 — 34
(W M Brisbourne) *s.i.s: hld up in rr: rdn and no prog over 2f out: n.d* **14/1**

0005 **13** ½ **Silver Hotspur**[82] 3319 4-9-6 **87** ... LPKeniry 3 — 41
(C R Dore) *s.i.s: a bhd* **20/1**

0060 **14** 3¼ **Free Tussy (ARG)**[8] 5681 4-8-13 **80** ... StephenCarson 9 — 27
(G L Moore) *chsd ldr tl over 2f out: sn wknd* **50/1**

1m 39.75s (-0.15) **Going Correction** +0.075s/f (Slow)
WFA 3 from 4yo+ 5lb — **14** Ran SP% **134.6**
Speed ratings (Par 107): **103,102,100,99,97 96,95,94,94,92 88,79,79,75**
toteswinger: 1&2 £11.80, 1&3 £69.70, 2&3 £28.60. CSF £56.85 CT £1185.93 TOTE £16.80: £3.10, £2.00, £9.40; EX 67.50.
Owner Saleh Al Homaizi & Imad Al Sagar **Bred** Calumet Farm **Trained** Manton, Wilts
■ Nightjar was withdrawn on vet's advice (9/1, deduct 10p in the £ under R4). New market formed.
■ Stewards' Enquiry : Luke Morris three-day ban: struck mount in annoyance (Sep 28-30)

FOCUS
A competitive handicap and pretty solid form. The runner-up looks the best guide with the winner up 5lb.

NOTEBOOK

Storm Sir(USA) had to be driven to go the early pace and raced three wide all the way, but he stayed on relentlessly in the home straight and just prevailed. Racing off a 7lb higher mark for winning a four-runner maiden on the Polytrack at Lingfield, the US-bred colt has improved for the switch from turf. Connections were pleased with the way he battled and faced up to the kickback. (old market op 14-1 new market op 12-1)

Yarqus, nibbled at in the market, looked to be travelling so well in the home straight that his jockey had to take a slight pull to make his move as late as possible, which was almost a winning one. Though he has not scored in 13 attempts on the all-weather, this effort suggests he can get off the mark. Official explanation: jockey said gelding weas denied a clear run (old market op 7-1 new market op 11-2)

Tender The Great(IRE), on her debut for the yard, was prominent and given every chance if good enough. She has largely been out of sorts this season but this was an improvement. (old market op 33-1)

Rubacuori(BRZ) looked to be finding the pace too hot from the outset, but he stayed on well to be one of the challengers in the home straight. He had some useful form in Brazil but is only beginning to find his feet for his new stable. (old market op 66-1 new market op 50-1)

Decameron(USA) was well fancied to atone for his heavy-ground flop at Haydock last time. Always prominent, he was the first to challenge entering the straight but his effort flattened out in the closing stages. This was something like his previous good form. (old market op 9-4 tchd 5-2 new market tchd 5-2 in places)

Just Bond(IRE) Official explanation: jockey said gelding hung right

Mount Hermon(IRE) Official explanation: vet said gelding had bled from the nose

Roman Maze Official explanation: jockey said gelding missed the berak

5909 JOHN STAPLEY HAPPY 60TH BIRTHDAY CLAIMING STKS 1m 2f (P)

5:00 (5:00) (Class 5) 2-Y-0 **£3,238** (£963; £481; £240) **Stalls** Low

Form RPR

3131 **1** **Dougie Peel**[29] 5041 2-9-2 67 ... (p) RobertWinston 6 60+
(K A Ryan) *chsd ldrs tl wnt 2nd 7f out: rdn to ld 2f out: hrd drvn and narrowly hdd jst ins fnl f: rallied to ld again towards fin* **6/5**[1]

0050 **2** *nk* **Ba Globetrotter**[15] 5460 2-8-6 62 ... SamHitchcott 4 49+
(M R Channon) *hld up in tch: rdn 3f out: hdwy u.p to chal over 1f out: led narrowly ins fnl f: hdd and no ex towards fin* **11/1**

04 **3** *nk* **Hassadin**[35] 4861 2-9-7 0 ... StephenDonohoe 1 64
(A B Haynes) *chsd ldr tl 7f out: rdn and sltly outpcd jst over 2f out: rallied u.p ent fnl f: ev ch fnl 100yds: no ex nr fin* **9/2**[3]

006 **4** *nk* **Strikemaster (IRE)**[36] 4827 2-8-13 52 ... TPQueally 2 55
(J W Hills) *s.i.s: hld up in last pair: rdn wl over 1f out: hdwy on inner ent fnl f: ev ch fnl 100yds: no ex towards fin* **6/1**

0244 **5** *shd* **Tarawa Atoll**[50] 4387 2-8-6 50 ... JoeFanning 3 48
(M R Channon) *stdd s: hld up in last pair: rdn 3f out: hdwy u.p over 1f out: pressed ldrs ins fnl f: unable qck fnl 100yds* **12/1**

3025 **6** *3* **Gassal**[51] 4340 2-8-10 70 ... RichardKingscote 5 47
(J R Boyle) *led: rdn and hdd 2f out: ev ch after tl wknd ins fnl f* **4/1**[2]

2m 12.78s (4.18) **Going Correction** +0.075s/f (Slow) **6** Ran SP% **113.9**
Speed ratings (Par 95): **86,85,85,85,85 82**
toteswinger: 1&2 £4.10, 1&3 £2.40, 2&3 £4.00. CSF £16.12 TOTE £1.90: £1.10, £4.60; EX 15.10.

Owner Roger Peel **Bred** Brook Stud Bloodstock Ltd **Trained** Hambleton, N Yorks

FOCUS
A long trip for juveniles, and a weak contest featuring just one previous winner, but it produced an exciting finish with the first five in a heap. Modest form, with the principals below their best.

NOTEBOOK
Dougie Peel, stepping up from 7f over which he gained both his previous wins in sellers at Catterick, tracked the leader and went to win his race entering the straight. It then looked like he would be swamped, but he battled back when headed. Admirable fighting qualities aside, this was achieved in very modest company. (op 7-4 tchd 2-1 in a place)

Ba Globetrotter was driven up to challenge around the home turn and was just outbattled. He had been beaten 25 lengths when tried at 1m last time, so this was a bit more encouraging. (tchd 10-1)

Hassadin, like the winner already gelded, was driven to get competitive around the home turn and had every chance. Though comprehensively beaten on both previous starts, this longer trip was more to his liking. (op 7-1)

Strikemaster(IRE) was outpaced in rear before staying on late and looks to need every inch of this trip. (op 9-2)

5910 CIRL BUNTING H'CAP 1m 2f (P)

5:35 (5:35) (Class 4) (0-85,85) 3-Y-0+ **£5,180** (£1,541; £770; £384) **Stalls** Low

Form RPR

-022 **1** **Aboriginie (USA)**[29] 5047 3-8-9 78 ... DavidKinsella 6 85
(J H M Gosden) *mde all: rdn and qcknd clr jst over 2f out: kpt on fnl f: drvn out* **16/1**

4032 **2** *1 1/4* **Fantasy Princess (USA)**[13] 5536 3-8-4 78 .. Louis-PhilippeBeuzelin(5) 2 82
(G A Butler) *chsd ldrs: rdn and unable qck jst over 2f out: kpt on u.p fnl f: wnt 2nd towards fin: unable to chal wnr* **10/1**

1561 **3** *3/4* **Willkandoo (USA)**[17] 5397 3-8-7 76 ... (p) RobertWinston 9 79
(K A Ryan) *chsd wnr: rdn and outpcd by wnr jst over 2f out: kpt on same pce fr over 1f out* **12/1**

0540 **4** *1/2* **Intersky Charm (USA)**[4] 5773 4-8-11 73 ... DeanMcKeown 5 73
(R M Whitaker) *t.k.h: hld up in tch: outpcd 3f out: plugged on u.p but no ch w wnr after: fin 5th, plcd 4th* **10/1**

5534 **5** *hd* **Know The Law**[37] 4791 4-9-3 79 ... (b) IanMongan 10 78
(D R C Elsworth) *stdd and switche dsharply lft after s: hld up bhd: hdwy on inner over 1f out: kpt on but nvr trbld ldrs: fin 6th, plcd 5th* **16/1**

3115 **6** *hd* **Tufton**[30] 5005 5-8-9 76 ... FrederikTylicki(5) 4 75
(R A Fahey) *s.i.s: hld up in midfield: rdn and unable qck over 2f out: kpt on fnl f but nvr pce to rch ldrs: fin 7th, plcd 6th* **6/1**[3]

200 **7** *2 3/4* **Folio (IRE)**[40] 4688 8-9-1 77 ... StephenDonohoe 12 70
(W J Musson) *stdd s: hld up in last: rdn and hdwy over 1f out: nvr trbld ldrs: fin 8th, plcd 7th* **16/1**

0662 **8** *1 1/4* **Fitzroy Crossing (USA)**[15] 5472 3-8-8 77 ... JoeFanning 11 68
(M Johnston) *chsd ldrs: rdn over 3f out: struggling 3f out: wl btn fr wl over 1f out: fin 9th, plcd 8th* **11/1**

1511 **9** *1* **Action Impact (ARG)**[16] 5427 4-8-9 71 oh1 ... StephenCarson 1 60
(G L Moore) *hld up in midfield: rdn and struggling 3f out: n.d after: fn 10th, plcd 9th* **5/1**[2]

3400 **10** *1/2* **Rapid City**[55] 3802 5-9-6 82 ... VinceSlattery 3 70
(D J Wintle) *t.k.h: hld up in rr: n.d: fin 11th, plcd 10th* **33/1**

3552 **11** *nk* **Basra (IRE)**[53] 4276 5-9-9 85 ... TravisBlock 7 72
(Miss Jo Crowley) *t.k.h: hld up towards rr: nvr a factor: fin 12th, plcd 11th* **12/1**

0211 **12** *11* **Certain Promise (USA)**[37] 4795 3-8-8 77 ... TPQueally 8 42
(Sir Michael Stoute) *hld up in midfield on outer: rdn and no rspnse jst over 3f out: wl btn 2f out: eased ins fnl f: fin 13th, plcd 12th* **7/2**[1]

1650 **D** *3/4* **Sahrati**[14] 5494 4-8-11 73 ... (b) LiamJones 13 74+
(C E Brittain) *bhd: rdn and struggling 4f out: hdwy over 1f out: squeezed through and r.o wl fnl f: sddle slipped and uns rdr nr fin: fin 4th, 1 1/4l, 3/4l & 3/4l: disq* **7/1**

2m 7.76s (-0.84) **Going Correction** +0.075s/f (Slow)
WFA 3 from 4yo+ 7lb **13** Ran SP% **128.2**
Speed ratings (Par 105): **106,105,104,103,103 103,100,99,99,98 98,89,103**
toteswinger: 1&2 £43.50, 1&3 £35.80, 2&3 £46.70. CSF £179.30 CT £2026.55 TOTE £16.50: £4.90, £4.20, £4.00; EX 73.30 Place 6 £75.54, Place 5 £47.13.
Owner H R H Princess Haya Of Jordan **Bred** W S Farish & Skara Glen Stables **Trained** Newmarket, Suffolk

FOCUS
A competitive event on paper in which the winner made all under a good ride. Probably not form to be too confident about.
Rapid City Official explanation: vet said gelding had a cut to its left flank
T/Plt: £85.00 to a £1 stake. Pool: £38,497.90. 330.50 winning tickets. T/Qpdt: £54.30 to a £1 stake. Pool: £1,923.00. 26.20 winning tickets. SP

[5797] KEMPTON (A.W) (R-H)

Saturday, September 13

OFFICIAL GOING: Standard
Wind: Nil

5911 BET PREMIER LEAGUE FOOTBALL - BETDAQ H'CAP 5f (P)

6:20 (6:21) (Class 6) (0-60,58) 3-Y-0 **£2,047** (£604; £302) **Stalls** High

Form RPR

0600 **1** **Todber**[12] 5574 3-8-12 52 ... (v1) HayleyTurner 6 65
(M P Tregoning) *mde all: rdn and kpt on whn chal fr 2f out: forged clr ins fnl f* **15/2**

6544 **2** *2 3/4* **Stoneacre Pat (IRE)**[23] 5201 3-8-13 53 ... LPKeniry 9 56
(Peter Grayson) *s.i.s: sn rcvrd to chse ldrs: upsides and rdn 2f out: outpcd by wnr fnl f but kpt on wl for 2nd* **11/2**[3]

3200 **3** *1 3/4* **Handsinthemist (IRE)**[20] 5307 3-8-11 51 ... (p) FrankieMcDonald 7 48
(P T Midgley) *chsd ldrs: rdn 1/2-way: wknd fnl f* **20/1**

0603 **4** *nk* **Tanley**[15] 5457 3-8-11 51 ... (p) JamesDoyle 12 47+
(J F Coupland) *in tch: rdn and outpcd 1/2-way: styd on again fnl f* **5/1**[2]

0330 **5** *nk* **Nawaaff**[8] 5684 3-8-13 53 ... (v) DarryllHolland 8 48
(M R Channon) *in rr early: hdwy 1/2-way: drvn and squeezed through to chse ldrs ins fnl 2f: no imp fnl f* **10/3**[1]

4520 **6** *1/2* **Bilboa**[16] 5421 3-8-10 53 ... (p) KevinGhunowa(3) 3 46
(J M Bradley) *outpcd until mod prog fnl f* **6/1**

063- **7** *1 1/4* **Whiskey Creek**[360] 5529 3-9-2 56 ... CatherineGannon 11 44
(C A Dwyer) *t.k.h towards rr: rdn and styd on fnl f: nvr in contention* **7/1**

-005 **8** *1 1/2* **Rocheport**[26] 5141 3-8-11 51 ... SaleemGolam 2 34
(G C H Chung) *s.i.s: outpcd most of way* **12/1**

4506 **9** *1 1/2* **Town And Gown**[26] 5141 3-9-0 54 ... (t) JimCrowley 5 32
(S C Williams) *in tch early: bhd fr 1/2-way* **9/1**

2250 **10** *8* **Honest Value (IRE)**[123] 2074 3-9-1 55 ... RichardThomas 10 —
(Mrs L C Jewell) *t.k.h: chsd ldrs: wkng whn hmpd ins fnl 2f* **16/1**

60.33 secs (-0.17) **Going Correction** 0.0s/f (Stan) **10** Ran SP% **122.0**
Speed ratings (Par 99): **101,96,93,93,92 92,90,87,85,72**
toteswinger: 1&2 £31.80, 1&3 £31.80, 2&3 £31.80. CSF £50.84 CT £812.12 TOTE £10.60: £1.80, £1.40, £5.30; EX 104.10.
Owner Major & Mrs R B Kennard And Partner **Bred** Stowell Hill Ltd & Major & Mrs R B Kennard **Trained** Lambourn, Berks

FOCUS
A low-grade handicap comprising exposed and inconsistent performers. The early pace set by the winner was not overly strong and, as is often the case over this course and distance, very few got into contention. Not a race to be positive about.
Todber Official explanation: trainer said, regarding the apparent improvement in form, the filly was a late-maturing type and had benefited from the first time visor.

5912 ALFIE HENDRIE 70TH BIRTHDAY H'CAP 1m 2f (P)

6:50 (6:51) (Class 6) (0-50,57) 3-Y-0+ **£2,047** (£604; £302) **Stalls** High

Form RPR

0004 **1** **Havanavich**[17] 5407 3-8-8 50 ... LPKeniry 11 58
(S Kirk) *chsd ldrs: drvn along over 3f out: styd on to chse wnr 1f out: rdn to ld fnl 50yds: kpt on strly* **9/2**[2]

0231 **2** *1/2* **Everyman**[9] 5631 4-9-5 57 ... LukeMorris(3) 3 64
(A W Carroll) *sn chsng ldr: rdn to ld over 1f out: hdd and no ex fnl 50yds* **5/2**[1]

6600 **3** *1 1/2* **Joe Jo Star**[47] 1528 6-8-6 48 ... DeclanCannon(7) 10 52+
(B P J Baugh) *in rr: rdn over 2f out: gd hdwy over 1f out: styd on strly ins fnl f: gng on cl home* **9/1**

0400 **4** *1 1/4* **Kadouchski (FR)**[67] 3820 4-9-0 49 ... (p) TPO'Shea 2 51
(John Berry) *chsd ldrs: rdn over 2f out: wknd ins fnl f* **10/1**

3036 **5** *1/2* **Golden Brown (IRE)**[9] 5631 4-8-6 48 ... BillyCray(7) 6 49
(David Pinder) *chsd ldrs: rdn and outpcd 3f out: styd on again fnl f but nvr a threat* **8/1**[3]

0043 **6** *nk* **Play Up Pompey**[9] 5631 6-9-0 49 ... JimCrowley 8 49
(J J Bridger) *in tch: rdn 3f out: kpt on fnl f: nvr in contention* **8/1**[3]

3303 **7** *1/2* **The Grey One (IRE)**[9] 5653 5-8-11 49 ... (p) KevinGhunowa(3) 9 48
(J M Bradley) *plld hrd in rr: rdn and sme hdwy whn nt clr run and swtchd rt 1f out: kpt on cl home: nvr a threat* **8/1**[3]

3310 **8** *1* **A One (IRE)**[14] 5489 9-8-6 46 ... SophieDoyle(5) 4 43
(H J Manners) *sn led: rdn over 2f out: hdd & wknd over 1f out* **12/1**

505 **9** *nk* **Katy Kitten (UAE)**[15] 5471 3-8-8 50 ... SimonWhitworth 13 46
(G L Moore) *a towards rr* **20/1**

4230 **10** *1/2* **Fantasy Crusader**[16] 5427 9-8-12 47 ... DarryllHolland 14 42
(R M H Cowell) *in rr: rdn and no ch whn wd bnd 2f out* **9/1**

/00- **11** *3/4* **Tinted View (USA)**[392] 4596 4-9-1 50 ... GeorgeBaker 5 44
(W S Kittow) *stdd s: rdn over 2f out: a bhd* **22/1**

0060 **12** *15* **Age Of Miracles (IRE)**[22] 5218 3-8-7 49 ... SaleemGolam 12 13
(G A Ham) *t.k.h: in tch: rdn 3f out: sn wknd* **40/1**

2m 8.95s (0.95) **Going Correction** 0.0s/f (Stan)
WFA 3 from 4yo+ 7lb **12** Ran SP% **128.4**
Speed ratings (Par 101): **96,95,94,93,93 92,92,91,91,90 90,78**
toteswinger: 1&2 £22.80, 1&3 £22.40, 2&3 £13.00. CSF £17.23 CT £105.05 TOTE £6.50: £2.80, £2.10, £3.90; EX 26.60.
Owner M Nicolson, G Doran, A Wilson **Bred** Itchen Valley Stud **Trained** Upper Lambourn, Berks

FOCUS
A weak handicap in which the pace was only fair. Those held up were at a disadvantage and this bare form may not prove reliable.

The Grey One(IRE) Official explanation: jockey said gelding ran too free

5913 GOODBYE & GOOD LUCK VICTORIA CLAIMING STKS 1m 4f (P)
7:20 (7:22) (Class 6) 3-Y-0+ £2,047 (£604; £302) Stalls Centre

Form RPR

1500 1 **Wind Flow**[30] 5017 4-9-6 69 ....(b) CatherineGannon 8 73
(C A Dwyer) *mde all: hrd rdn and edgd rt over 1f out: hld on all out* **11/1**

4500 2 nk **Mustajed**[28] 5092 7-9-5 76 ....(b[1]) JamesMillman[(3)] 14 75
(B R Millman) *chsd ldrs: rdn 3f out: styng on whn hmpd and swtchd lft over 1f out: str run into fnl f to chse wnr cl home: fin wl: nt quite get up* **3/1**[2]

50-0 3 ¾ **Wait For The Light**[31] 4963 4-9-6 70 .... SteveDrowne 5 71
(Mrs S Leech) *sn chsng wnr: rdn and effrt over 2f out: nvr quite on terms: one pce fnl f and lost 2nd cl home* **28/1**

2525 4 ¾ **Red Icon**[43] 4582 3-8-4 73 ....(b) RichardKingscote 11 63
(R M Beckett) *chsd ldrs: rdn over 2f out: styd on u.p ins fnl f but nvr gng pce to chal ldrs* **5/2**[1]

5 3 ½ **Lilac Wine**[23] 5-8-2 0 .... BillyCray[(7)] 12 54
(D J S Ffrench Davis) *in rr: pushed along 3f out: styd on fr over 1f out but nvr in contention* **33/1**

6344 6 nk **Given A Choice (IRE)**[32] 4953 6-9-9 76 ....(p) JerryO'Dwyer[(3)] 3 70
(J Pearce) *s.i.s: in rr: drvn and sme hdwy fnl 2f: nvr in contention* **6/1**

4-10 7 ½ **Tavalu (USA)**[6] 4366 6-9-4 66 ....(b) GeorgeBaker 6 61
(G L Moore) *prom: rdn and effrt over 2f out: nvr in contention* **11/2**[3]

2030 8 1 ¾ **Turner's Touch**[40] 4691 6-9-6 70 ....(b) TedDurcan 10 60
(G L Moore) *s.i.s: sn in mid-div: sme prog 3f out: n.d after* **9/1**

0505 9 2 ½ **Eseej (USA)**[12] 5568 3-8-13 65 .... JimCrowley 13 58
(P W Hiatt) *chsd ldrs tl wknd 2f out* **14/1**

-000 10 2 ½ **Kennyboy**[72] 3637 3-8-5 52 .... WandersonD'Avila 1 46
(P G Murphy) *in rr: no ch whn hung lft over 2f out* **80/1**

11 1 ¾ **Thenford Flyer (IRE)**[87] 8-9-4 0 ....(p) RichardThomas 7 48
(C Roberts) *a towards rr* **66/1**

5- 12 6 **Guerilla (AUS)**[6] 3402 8-9-4 60 .... PAspell 2 38
(R C Guest) *chsd ldrs: rdn 4f out: wknd 3f out* **40/1**

0060 13 dist **Lovespell (USA)**[21] 5269 3-8-4 55 ow2 ....(t) SaleemGolam 9 —
(Ms J S Doyle) *s.i.s: a bhd: t.o* **66/1**

2m 33.69s (-0.81) **Going Correction** 0.0s/f (Stan)
WFA 3 from 4yo+ 9lb **13** Ran SP% **121.3**
Speed ratings (Par 101): **102,101,101,100,98 98,97,96,95,93 92,88,—**
toteswinger: 1&2 £19.10, 1&3 £26.30, 2&3 £18.30. CSF £43.45 TOTE £12.00: £3.80, £1.50, £5.90; EX 90.80.Red Icon was claimed by Miss Sheena West for £10,000.
Owner Super Six Partnership **Bred** Lord Halifax **Trained** Burrough Green, Cambs

FOCUS

A fair claimer on paper but several came here struggling for form and this is not a race to take positively. A modest gallop meant those up with the pace were again favoured.

Eseej(USA) Official explanation: jockey said gelding hung right

5914 STEWART & CO 50TH YEAR ANNIVERSARY NURSERY 1m (P)
7:50 (7:54) (Class 6) (0-65,65) 2-Y-O £2,047 (£604; £302) Stalls High

Form RPR

0046 1 **Dubai Crest**[14] 5511 2-9-7 65 .... JimCrowley 11 70+
(Mrs A J Perrett) *chsd ldrs: hrd drvn over 3f out: styng on whn n.m.r over 1f out: str run u.p fnl f: led cl home* **7/2**[1]

050 2 nk **Victorian Tycoon (IRE)**[37] 4780 2-9-2 60 .... DarryllHolland 9 64
(E J O'Neill) *sn led: hrd rdn and styd on gamely fr over 1f out: hdd and no ex cl home* **12/1**

0554 3 2 **Russian Art**[11] 5591 2-9-1 59 ....(t) GeorgeBaker 3 59
(R M Beckett) *chsd ldrs: rdn and styd on fnl 2f: kpt on same pce ins fnl f* **6/1**[3]

500 4 ¾ **Charismatic Charli (IRE)**[52] 4296 2-9-3 61 ....(v[1]) LPKeniry 13 59
(P W D'Arcy) *chsd ldrs: rdn over 2f out: outpcd ins fnl f* **20/1**

0002 5 nse **Dark Oasis**[11] 5591 2-9-3 61 ....(b) RobertWinston 8 60+
(K A Ryan) *in tch: rdn over 2f out: sn hanging rt: styd on fnl f but nvr in contention* **5/1**[2]

2002 6 ¾ **Hold The Bucks (USA)**[10] 5606 2-8-12 59 .... LukeMorris[(3)] 1 55
(J S Moore) *t.k.h: chsd ldrs: rdn over 2f out: styd on same pce* **17/2**

0445 7 shd **Tae Kwon Do (USA)**[16] 5432 2-9-6 64 .... TedDurcan 7 60
(E A L Dunlop) *hld up in rr: pushed along 2f out: styd on ins fnl f but nvr a threat* **5/1**[2]

0443 8 nse **Extremely So**[10] 5606 2-9-1 59 .... IanMongan 6 55
(P J McBride) *towards rr: rdn and sme hdwy 2f out: no imp u.p fnl f* **10/1**

0405 9 nk **Redhead (IRE)**[41] 4666 2-9-1 62 .... PatrickHills[(3)] 4 57
(R Hannon) *stdd s: hld up in rr: pushed along over 2f out: styd on fnl f: nvr in contention* **16/1**

4006 10 1 **Lucky Punt**[10] 5606 2-8-11 60 .... FrederikTylicki[(5)] 14 53
(B G Powell) *chsd ldrs: rdn 3f out: wknd over 1f out* **25/1**

420 11 11 **Rockinit (IRE)**[43] 4579 2-9-6 64 .... TPO'Shea 5 33
(M R Channon) *rdn over 2f out: a bhd* **25/1**

000 12 1 ¾ **Red Robert**[15] 5459 2-9-1 59 .... PaulDoe 10 24
(J L Dunlop) *in tch: rdn 3f out: sn btn* **16/1**

560 13 2 ¾ **Rio Del Oro (USA)**[42] 4636 2-9-0 58 .... SteveDrowne 2 17
(R Hannon) *a in rr* **14/1**

1m 40.56s (0.76) **Going Correction** 0.0s/f (Stan) **13** Ran SP% **128.0**
Speed ratings (Par 93): **96,95,93,92,92 92,92,92,91,90 79,77,75**
toteswinger: 1&2 £45.60, 1&3 £9.00, 2&3 £45.60. CSF £50.09 CT £263.55 TOTE £6.20: £2.70, £6.20, £2.70; EX 104.20.
Owner A D Spence **Bred** Bearstone Stud **Trained** Pulborough, W Sussex

FOCUS

A couple of unexposed performers in what was a solid but modest nursery. The gallop was less than true and again favoured those racing prominently.

NOTEBOOK

Dubai Crest ◆ unshipped his rider before the start and was the first off the bridle but kept responding to turn in an improved effort on this AW debut and first run over 1m. A stronger gallop over 1m or a longer trip should suit even better, he should not be going up too much for this and is the type to win more races. (op 9-2 tchd 5-1)

Victorian Tycoon(IRE) was allowed an easy lead for this handicap debut but he kept responding to post an improved effort. Although he had the run of the race, he is capable of picking up a similar event on this evidence. (op 16-1)

Russian Art, who ran creditably in a tongue-tie over 7f on his Fibresand debut, was well placed considering the way things unfolded and ran creditably over this longer trip from his low draw with that equipment refitted. He should pick up a small event. (op 5-1 tchd 9-2)

Charismatic Charli(IRE) bettered his turf form on this AW and nursery debut but, while he did have the run of the race from his favourable draw with the first-time visor fitted, he is lightly raced enough to be open to further progress. (op 28-1)

Dark Oasis finished in front of Russian Art at Southwell on his previous start but failed to confirm those placings on this Polytrack debut, although that was not a surprise as he raced keenly on the outside for much of the way. He is worth another chance. (tchd 13-2)

Hold The Bucks(USA) had the run of the race but again underlined his vulnerability in this type of event. (op 10-1)

Tae Kwon Do(USA) was not seen to best effect given the way this race panned out and will be suited by a stiffer test of stamina.

Extremely So Official explanation: jockey said filly missed the break

5915 WILLIAM DEWSALL H'CAP 1m (P)
8:20 (8:22) (Class 5) (0-70,70) 3-Y-O+ £2,590 (£770; £385; £192) Stalls High

Form RPR

4343 1 **Gazboolou**[32] 4946 4-9-4 66 .... FergusSweeney 13 74
(David Pinder) *trckd ldrs: rdn to chal over 1f out: led jst ins fnl f: rdn lost whip cl home and hld on all out* **4/1**[1]

2000 2 hd **Onenightinlisbon (IRE)**[21] 5291 4-9-3 68 .... JackMitchell[(3)] 9 76
(J R Boyle) *chsd ldrs: rdn to ld appr fnl f: hdd jst ins fnl f: rallied u.p: no ex cl home* **11/1**

2241 3 1 ¾ **Dawson Creek (IRE)**[35] 4862 4-9-4 66 .... GeorgeBaker 14 70
(B Gubby) *chsd ldrs: rdn over 2f out: styd on ins fnl f but nvr gng pce to rch ldng duo* **5/1**[2]

2036 4 ¾ **Wrighty Almighty (IRE)**[32] 4946 6-9-5 67 .... JimCrowley 10 69+
(P R Chamings) *t.k.h in rr: effrt whn no much room on ins over 2f out: gd hdwy appr fnl f and fin wl: nt rch ldrs* **14/1**

4620 5 1 **Bauhaus Bourbon (USA)**[27] 5119 3-9-1 68 .... RobertWinston 12 67
(P F I Cole) *in tch: rdn 3f out: hdwy over 1f out: styd on ins fnl f* **9/1**

0516 6 nk **Grey Boy (GER)**[28] 5101 7-9-0 65 .... LukeMorris[(3)] 3 64
(A W Carroll) *hld up in rr: hdwy on outside and pushed along over 2f out: kpt on fnl f but nt rch ldrs* **14/1**

530 7 ¾ **Shadowtime**[14] 5504 3-9-1 68 .... DeanMcKeown 2 65
(Miss Tracy Waggott) *chsd ldr: rdn to chal fr ins fnl 2f tl over 1f out: sn wknd* **25/1**

0023 8 nk **Speyside (IRE)**[12] 5568 3-9-0 70 ....(v) PatrickHills[(3)] 4 66
(J W Hills) *s.i.s: bhd: kpt on fnl 2f: nvr in contention* **14/1**

-324 9 shd **Faithful Ruler (USA)**[220] 452 4-8-13 66 .... FrederikTylicki[(5)] 5 63
(R A Fahey) *s.i.s: in rr: rdn over 2f out: mod prog fnl f* **11/2**[3]

0003 10 2 **St Petersburg**[15] 5478 8-9-1 63 .... TedDurcan 1 55
(J R Boyle) *s.i.s: nvr bttr than mid-div* **14/1**

30/3 11 1 ¼ **Wrecking Crew (IRE)**[14] 5491 4-9-7 69 .... RichardKingscote 11 58
(B R Millman) *led: rdn over 2f out: hdd & wknd qckly over 1f out* **16/1**

6000 12 5 **Smokin Joe**[35] 4862 7-9-5 67 ....(b) LPKeniry 7 45
(J R Best) *t.k.h: a towards rr* **20/1**

/14- 13 10 **Bronte's Hope**[593] 290 4-9-4 66 .... HayleyTurner 8 21
(M P Tregoning) *plld hrd: chsd ldrs: wknd qckly 3f out* **6/1**

1m 39.54s (-0.26) **Going Correction** 0.0s/f (Stan)
WFA 3 from 4yo+ 5lb **13** Ran SP% **125.8**
Speed ratings (Par 103): **101,100,99,98,97 97,96,95,95,93 92,87,77**
toteswinger: 1&2 £9.20, 1&3 £5.80, 2&3 £46.80. CSF £51.77 CT £234.38 TOTE £5.40: £3.40, £3.10, £2.50; EX 21.30.
Owner Mrs Angela Pinder **Bred** Cheveley Park Stud Ltd **Trained** Kingston Lisle, Oxon

FOCUS

Another race run at just an ordinary gallop and one that saw several pulling for their heads early on. As has been the trend this evening, those up with the pace held a big edge and consequently the bare form does not look entirely reliable, although the first three have been rated close to their marks.

Bauhaus Bourbon(USA) Official explanation: jockey said filly had a breathing problem

Wrecking Crew(IRE) Official explanation: jockey said gelding jumped left and ran too free

Smokin Joe Official explanation: jockey said gelding ran too free

Bronte's Hope Official explanation: jockey said filly ran too free

5916 BETDAQ.CO.UK H'CAP 7f (P)
8:50 (8:50) (Class 6) (0-50,50) 3-Y-O+ £2,047 (£604; £302) Stalls High

Form RPR

0050 1 **Djalalabad (FR)**[3] 5797 4-9-0 50 ....(tp) HayleyTurner 1 59
(Mrs C A Dunnett) *in rr: stl plenty to do whn hdwy on outside fr over 2f out to ld appr fnl f: readily* **10/1**

0401 2 1 **Piccolo Diamante (USA)**[2] 5832 4-8-9 48 ....(t) TolleyDean[(3)] 5 54
(S Parr) *chsd ldrs: rdn and styd on to chse wnr fnl 50yds but a readily hld* **3/1**[1]

3020 3 ¾ **Monda**[36] 4813 6-8-9 50 .... AmyBaker[(5)] 7 54
(M Hill) *led: rdn over 2f out: hdd over 1f out: one pce and lost 2nd fnl 50yds* **5/1**[3]

0-00 4 ½ **Lights Of Vegas**[26] 5157 4-9-0 50 .... LPKeniry 11 53
(S Kirk) *chsd ldrs: rdn over 2f out: styd on ins fnl f but nvr gng pce to chal* **25/1**

0040 5 4 **Tadlil**[3] 5797 6-8-8 47 ....(v) KevinGhunowa[(3)] 3 39
(J M Bradley) *sn chsng ldrs: rdn 3f out: styd on same pce sn after* **22/1**

6642 6 ¾ **Charlotte Grey**[2] 5832 4-8-7 50 .... AndreaAtzeni[(7)] 2 40
(P J McBride) *chsd ldrs: rdn over 2f out: wknd fnl f* **11/2**

0060 7 1 **Zazous**[3] 5797 7-8-9 48 .... MarcHalford[(3)] 12 35
(J J Bridger) *sn chsng ldrs: rdn 2f out: eased whn no ch fnl f* **11/2**

4000 8 nk **Puskas (IRE)**[18] 5374 5-8-11 47 ....(b) RobertHavlin 8 33
(J M Bradley) *nvr gng pce to be competitive* **18/1**

4400 9 2 ½ **Kempsey**[9] 5626 6-8-12 48 ....(b) JimCrowley 6 28
(J J Bridger) *nvr bttr than mid-div: bhd fnl 2f* **12/1**

0000 10 1 **Tenancy (IRE)**[3] 5797 4-9-0 50 ....(e) PAspell 10 27
(R C Guest) *hood off slowly: s.i.s: a bhd* **33/1**

0436 11 ½ **Apres Ski (IRE)**[15] 5454 5-8-12 48 .... MickyFenton 13 23
(J F Coupland) *s.i.s: plld hrd in rr: nvr in contention* **9/2**[2]

1m 26.5s (0.50) **Going Correction** 0.0s/f (Stan)
WFA 3 from 4yo+ 4lb **11** Ran SP% **123.8**
Speed ratings (Par 101): **97,95,95,94,89 89,87,87,84,83 82**
toteswinger: 1&2 £8.20, 1&3 £5.40, 2&3 £4.60. CSF £41.48 CT £179.84 TOTE £15.80: £3.90, £1.90, £2.60; EX 86.90.
Owner Far Afield **Bred** Haras De Beauvoir **Trained** Hingham, Norfolk

FOCUS

A low-grade handicap but a better gallop this time, which enabled the winner to come from off the pace and in the centre of the track. She is rated back to her best and this looks a reasonable race for the grade.

Apres Ski(IRE) Official explanation: jockey said gelding missed the break

5917 BET RYDER CUP - BETDAQ H'CAP 2m (P)
9:20 (9:20) (Class 6) (0-60,61) 3-Y-O+ £2,047 (£604; £302) Stalls High

Form RPR

0601 1 **Mohawk Star (IRE)**[8] 5676 7-9-12 58 ....(v) GeorgeBaker 11 73+
(I A Wood) *hld up towards rr: gd hdwy over 3f out: led appr fnl 2f: c clr over 1f out: easily* **8/1**[2]

2003 **2** *2 ¾* **Irish Ballad**[8] 5676 6-9-2 **48**.. NickyMackay 13 56
(S Dow) *chsd ldrs: rdn to ld ins fnl 3f: hdd appr fnl 2f: sn no ch w wnr but kpt on for clr 2nd* **16/1**

5532 **3** *3 ½* **Moonshine Beach**[8] 5676 10-10-1 **61**.. JimCrowley 12 65
(P W Hiatt) *in tch: rdn and hdwy over 3f out: styd on for mod 3rd ins fnl 2f* **8/1**[2]

3006 **4** *2 ¼* **Whaxaar (IRE)**[8] 5676 4-9-13 **59**.. RobertHavlin 2 60
(R Ingram) *hld up in mid-div: rdn and styd on fr 3f out to take mod 4th fnl 2f* **16/1**

/000 **5** *4 ½* **Taxman (IRE)**[55] 1246 6-9-7 **53**..(p) FergusSweeney 5 49
(A G Newcombe) *in rr: hdwy 3f out: one pce fnl 2f* **33/1**

3315 **6** *8* **Dimashq**[32] 4947 6-9-1 **47**.. MickyFenton 4 33
(P T Midgley) *in rr tl mod prog fnl 2f* **10/1**

1200 **7** *6* **Check Up (IRE)**[10] 5611 7-9-7 **56**.. KevinGhunowa(3) 14 35
(J L Flint) *chsd ldrs: rdn 3f out: sn btn* **40/1**

5330 **8** *6* **Is It Me (USA)**[15] 5465 5-9-6 **52**.. TedDurcan 1 24
(A W Carroll) *chsd ldrs to 3f out* **9/1**[3]

6512 **9** *1 ¾* **Chiff Chaff**[10] 5613 4-9-6 **55**.. TolleyDean(3) 6 25
(C R Dore) *a towards rr* **11/1**

0000 **10** *nk* **Arabian Sun**[19] 5367 4-9-0 **46**..(b[1]) IanMongan 7 15
(M J Attwater) *chsd ldrs: led 1m out: hdd ins fnl 3f and sn wknd* **14/1**

140- **11** *17* **Comeintothespace (IRE)**[10] 3927 6-9-2 **55** ow6... ByronMoorcroft(7) 9 4
(K J Burke) *a in rr* **66/1**

/035 **12** *8* **Restart (IRE)**[18] 5385 7-8-13 **52** ow1.................. MrJPFeatherstone(7) 10 —
(Lucinda Featherstone) *chsd ldrs 10f* **7/1**[1]

0003 **13** *3 ½* **Petrosian**[36] 4814 4-8-13 **50**.. NicolPolli(5) 8 —
(T T Clement) *sn led: hdd 1m out: sn wknd* **66/1**

3m 28.27s (-1.83) **Going Correction** 0.0s/f (Stan)
WFA 3 from 4yo+ 13lb **13** Ran SP% **88.9**
Speed ratings (Par 101): **104,102,100,99,97 93,90,87,86,86 77,73,72**
toteswinger: 1&2 £23.60, 1&3 £5.30, 2&3 £5.40. CSF £62.23 CT £308.41 TOTE £5.70: £2.80, £2.20, £2.60; EX 138.60 Place 6 £185.67, Place 5 £34.42.
Owner Richard Abbott & Mario Stavrou **Bred** Mrs T V Ryan **Trained** Upper Lambourn, Berks

FOCUS
A race that lost much of its interest when the progressive Rutba (13/8F, deduct 35p in the £ under R4) was withdrawn after breaking out of the front of the stalls as the last runner was being loaded. Mohawk Star beat the placed horses more easily than he had here last week and is rated back to his 2006 form, value 6l. Solid form for the grade.
T/Plt: £422.60 to a £1 stake. Pool: £65,568.53. 113.25 winning tickets. T/Qpdt: £39.00 to a £1 stake. Pool: £6,423.90. 121.70 winning tickets. ST

5918 - 5919a (Foreign Racing) - See Raceform Interactive

5545 CURRAGH (R-H)
Saturday, September 13
OFFICIAL GOING: Soft to heavy

5920a IRISH NATIONAL STUD BLANDFORD STKS (GROUP 2) (F&M) 1m 2f
3:05 (3:05) 3-Y-0+ **£59,742** (£17,463; £8,272; £2,757)

RPR

1 **Katiyra (IRE)**[31] 4997 3-8-12 109.. MJKinane 3 110+
(John M Oxx, Ire) *trckd ldrs: 4th 1/2-way: impr into cl 3rd ent st: led 2f out: rdn clr fr over 1f out: styd on wl: comf* **1/2**[1]

2 *4* **Beach Bunny (IRE)**[13] 5547 3-8-12 105.. CDHayes 7 102
(Kevin Prendergast, Ire) *chsd ldrs: 5th 1/2-way: impr into cl 4th on outer ent st: 2nd and chal under 2f out: no imp u.p fr over 1f out: eased cl home* **4/1**[2]

3 *4* **Love To Dance (IRE)**[5] 5767 3-8-12 88.. SMLevey 1 94
(A P O'Brien, Ire) *led: rdn and strly pressed ent st: hdd 2f out: 3rd and no ex fr over 1f out* **25/1**

4 *3* **Deauville Vision (IRE)**[13] 5547 5-9-5 101..(p) RPCleary 4 88
(M Halford, Ire) *2nd to 1/2-way: dropped to 5th ent st: kpt on same pce u.p* **12/1**

5 *hd* **Jalmira (IRE)**[20] 5332 7-9-5 107.. WJLee 5 88
(C F Swan, Ire) *hld up in rr: effrt whn nt clr run early st: mod 5th and no imp fr over 1f out* **14/1**

6 *5* **Navajo Moon (IRE)**[36] 4832 4-9-5 106.. DMGrant 6 78
(David Wachman, Ire) *hld up towards rr: no imp st* **14/1**

7 *5* **Sail (IRE)**[6] 5729 3-8-12 102..(b[1]) JAHeffernan 2 68
(A P O'Brien, Ire) *settled 3rd: 2nd 4f out: rdn and wknd early st: eased ins fnl f* **10/1**[3]

2m 14.3s (4.80) **Going Correction** +0.85s/f (Soft)
WFA 3 from 4yo+ 7lb **7** Ran SP% **120.6**
Speed ratings: **114,110,107,105,105 101,97**
CSF £3.24 TOTE £1.40: £1.10, £2.20; DF 2.40.
Owner H H Aga Khan **Bred** Hh The Aga Khan's Stud Sc **Trained** Currabeg, Co Kildare

FOCUS
The third limits the form of this Group 2.

NOTEBOOK
Katiyra(IRE) confirmed she is back at the top of her game and followed up her Group 3 success at Gowran a month previously with a commanding success. She evidently handles this ground without much fuss now and the drop back to this trip has worked the oracle. The form of her third in the Oaks in June looks solid and there is a strong possibility of more to come still from this lightly-raced filly, especially if kept in training as a four-year-old. She will now likely step back up to the top level and the Prix de l'Opera could be her next port of call. (op 4/7)
Beach Bunny(IRE) tried in vain to go with the winner, but was firmly put in her place. This trip on such ground would have stretched her stamina to the limit and she still left the impression she has a Group race in her.
Love To Dance(IRE) had the run of the race out in front, so while her proximity may limit the form somewhat, she is most likely a bit flattered.

5921a IRISH FIELD ST.LEGER (GROUP 1) 1m 6f
3:35 (3:35) 3-Y-0+
£126,176 (£42,352; £20,294; £7,058; £4,852; £2,647)

RPR

1 **Septimus (IRE)**[77] 3513 5-9-11 122.. JAHeffernan 5 121
(A P O'Brien, Ire) *trckd ldrs in mod 3rd: tk clsr order fr 4f out: led early st: sn rdn clr: styd on strly fr 2f out: v easily* **1/3**[1]

2 *13* **New Zealand (IRE)**[14] 5521 3-9-0 94.. PJSmullen 9 104
(A P O'Brien, Ire) *settled in mod 2nd: tk clsr order 4f out: led briefly ent st: 2nd and outpcd under 2f out: 3rd 1f out: kpt on same pce u.p* **40/1**

3 *shd* **Red Moloney (USA)**[21] 5293 4-9-11 105.. CDHayes 7 104
(Kevin Prendergast, Ire) *hld up in rr: prog under 5f out: 5th travelling wl appr st: 3rd over 2f out: mod 2nd 1f out: no ex: one pce* **25/1**

4 *4 ½* **Mores Wells**[6] 5732 4-9-11 117..(t) DPMcDonogh 3 98
(Kevin Prendergast, Ire) *chsd ldrs in mod 5th: clsr 4th appr st: sn rdn and one pce* **7/1**[3]

5 *3 ½* **Hasanka (IRE)**[21] 5293 4-9-8 108.. MJKinane 1 90
(John M Oxx, Ire) *chsd ldrs: mod 6th after 1/2-way: rdn and no imp st* **6/1**[2]

6 *6* **Arch Rebel (USA)**[6] 5729 7-9-11 107..(p) FMBerry 6 86
(Noel Meade, Ire) *hld up: 7th 1/2-way: no imp st* **40/1**

7 *14* **Mikhail Fokine (IRE)**[43] 4612 3-9-0 93.. SMLevey 2 67
(A P O'Brien, Ire) *led and clr: set fast pce: rdn and reduced ld 4f out: hdd & wknd appr st: eased over 1f out* **100/1**

8 *13* **Yellowstone (IRE)**[22] 5229 4-9-11..(p) JohnEgan 10 51
(Jane Chapple-Hyam) *chsd ldrs in mod 4th: rdn 5f out: sn wknd: trailing st* **12/1**

9 *5* **Savannah**[43] 4614 5-9-11 63.. FFDaSilva 8 44
(Luke Comer, Ire) *a bhd: struggling shortly after 1/2-way: trailing st* **200/1**

3m 11.9s (7.20) **Going Correction** +0.85s/f (Soft)
WFA 3 from 4yo+ 11lb **9** Ran SP% **119.7**
Speed ratings: **113,105,105,102,100 97,89,82,79**
CSF £32.43 TOTE £1.40: £1.02, £4.90, £4.90; DF 18.30.
Owner Derrick Smith **Bred** Barronstown Stud & Orpendale **Trained** Ballydoyle, Co Tipperary
■ A clean sweep of the 2008 Irish Classics for Aidan O'Brien. Jack Rogers previously achieved the feat in 1935.

FOCUS
This was not a hot Group 1 by any means, but Septimus could not have been much more impressive in landing his first race at this level.

NOTEBOOK
Septimus(IRE) had the race teed up for him by the pacemaker and, once hitting top gear in the home straight, there was only going to be one outcome. This was his first win at the highest level and, while this may not have been the hottest Group 1 event, he could not have done the job much more impressively. Considering this was just his second run of the year he should still be a fresh horse if, as is expected, travelling to Australia for the Melbourne Cup next. He has been allotted 9st 3lb in that and was not surprisingly promoted to the top of the ante-post bettiing for that with the UK bookmakers. (op 4/11)
New Zealand(IRE), off the mark in a Killarney maiden last time, was no match whatsoever for his winning stable companion, but he kept on to post a personal-best effort in defeat, plugging on to edge second and looking suited by the longer trip. (op 50/1)
Red Moloney(USA) travelled sweetly into the home straight, but he could not sustain his effort in the final two furlongs. He may not be the most resolute, but this was still near to his best and he ideally needs a sounder surface at this distance. (op 20/1)
Mores Wells found this coming too soon after his fourth in the Champion Stakes a week previously and was miles below his best.
Yellowstone(IRE), who put up a sterling effort under top weight in the the rescheduled running of the Ebor last time, had shown a liking for heavy ground when successful at York in July. He was beaten from the home turn, however, and really ran too badly to be true. He is another who is likely to travel down under for the Melbourne Cup.

5922a ST JOVITE RENAISSANCE STKS (GROUP 3) 6f
4:10 (4:10) 3-Y-0+ **£35,845** (£10,477; £4,963; £1,654)

RPR

1 **Rock Of Rochelle (USA)**[29] 5081 3-9-1 95.. RMBurke 7 108
(A Kinsella, Ire) *hld up in tch: hdwy 2f out: led 1 1/2f out: strly pressed ins fnl f: kpt on wl* **16/1**

2 *¾* **Rock Moss (IRE)**[27] 5130 3-9-1 106.. KJManning 2 106
(J S Bolger, Ire) *hld up: 7th on outer 1/2-way: impr into 4th 2f out: cl 3rd 1 1/2f out: 2nd and chal ins fnl f: kpt on u.p* **5/1**[3]

3 *1 ¼* **Senor Benny (USA)**[27] 5133 9-9-3 98.. DPMcDonogh 4 102
(M McDonagh, Ire) *towards rr: hdwy into 4th under 1 1/2f out: 3rd and kpt on ins fnl f* **16/1**

4 *½* **Snaefell (IRE)**[13] 5551 4-9-6 110.. RPCleary 9 104
(M Halford, Ire) *prom: 2nd 1/2-way: led 2 1/2f out: hdd and edgd rt 1 1/2f out: 3rd 1f out: kpt on same pce* **3/1**[1]

5 *7* **Aleagueoftheirown (IRE)**[48] 4467 4-9-0 104..(p) JAHeffernan 6 77
(David Wachman, Ire) *trckd ldrs: 6th appr 1/2-way: kpt on same pce fr over 2f out* **13/2**

6 *nk* **Mooretown Lady (IRE)**[16] 5441 5-9-0 99..(p) CDHayes 3 76
(H Rogers, Ire) *in rr early: sme prog on outer 1/2-way: no imp fr 2f out* **11/1**

7 *4* **Contest (IRE)**[29] 5081 4-9-3 104.. DMGrant 1 67
(David Wachman, Ire) *cl up early: settled 5th: rdn and no imp fr under 2f out* **12/1**

8 *hd* **Kyniska (IRE)**[16] 5441 3-8-12 102.. PShanahan 8 63
(Tracey Collins, Ire) *cl up: 3rd 1/2-way: rdn to chal 2f out: sn wknd* **7/2**[2]

9 *19* **Campfire Glow (IRE)**[16] 5441 3-8-12 104..(b) PJSmullen 5 6
(D K Weld, Ire) *led: rdn and hdd 2 1/2f out: sn wknd: eased fr over 1f out* **10/1**

1m 18.38s (3.88) **Going Correction** +0.70s/f (Yiel)
WFA 3 from 4yo+ 2lb **9** Ran SP% **114.1**
Speed ratings: **102,101,99,98,89 88,83,83,58**
CSF £92.84 TOTE £32.20: £5.70, £1.50, £3.50; DF 168.70.
Owner Her Diamond Necklace Farms FZE **Bred** Beau Cheval L C **Trained** Athy, Co. Kildare

NOTEBOOK
Rock Of Rochelle(USA), a smart two year old last season when his two wins included one at Listed level, had been well beaten on his three previous starts this year and his win here surprised trainer Andrew Kinsella who felt the testing ground would be all against the colt. Beginning his effort over 2f out, he hit the front well over 1f out from where he kept on well when challenged.
Official explanation: trainer said, regarding the apparent improvement in form, that his horses had been running inconsistently and this may have been due to a bad batch of hay; he added gelding had won twice at this track last year and that horses were in better form now, having had a winner the previous day
Rock Moss(IRE) ran right up to his best in defeat and finished a clear second-best.

5924a FLAME OF TARA EUROPEAN BREEDERS FUND STKS (LISTED RACE) 1m
5:10 (5:10) 2-Y-0 **£35,900** (£10,533; £5,018; £1,709)

RPR

1 **Dreamtheimpossible (USA)**[40] 4884 2-8-12.. FMBerry 5 99+
(David Wachman, Ire) *trckd ldrs in 5th: 4th travelling best under 2f out: 2nd and chal 1 1/2f out: led under 1f out: r.o wl: comf* **7/1**[3]

2 *1 ¼* **Forest Storm**[21] 5297 2-8-12.. KJManning 2 96
(J S Bolger, Ire) *settled 2nd: chal 2f out: sn led: hdd under 1f out: kpt on u.p* **9/10**[1]

3 *3* **Tanoura (IRE)**[27] 5131 2-8-12.. MJKinane 1 89
(John M Oxx, Ire) *led: rdn and strly pressed 2f out: sn hdd: 3rd and no ex fnl f* **9/4**[2]

4 1 1/4 **Perfect Truth (IRE)**27 5131 2-8-12 JAHeffernan 6 87
(A P O'Brien, Ire) *hld up in tch: prog into 5th under 2f out: sn rdn: kpt on same pce ins fnl f* **20/1**

5 2 1/2 **Arfajah (IRE)**16 5438 2-8-12 93 DPMcDonogh 3 81+
(Kevin Prendergast, Ire) *settled 3rd: rdn 2f out: no imp: no ex ins fnl f: eased cl home* **14/1**

6 5 **Haaf Ok**17 5408 2-8-12 RPCleary 4 70
(M Halford, Ire) *broke wl: settled 4th: 5th and rdn over 2f out: sn no ex* **10/1**

7 2 1/2 **Petrafied (FR)**17 5408 2-8-12 PBBeggy 7 65
(David P Myerscough, Ire) *hld up towards rr: rdn and effrt over 2f out: sn no ex* **25/1**

1m 54.3s (12.40) **Going Correction** +0.85s/f (Soft) 7 Ran SP% **120.3**
Speed ratings: **72,70,67,66,64 59,56**
CSF £14.77 TOTE £6.80: £2.00, £1.50; DF 20.40.
Owner Mrs John Magnier **Bred** Dromoland Farm **Trained** Goolds Cross, Co Tipperary

FOCUS
The first three are nice types but overall this was not a strong renewal.

NOTEBOOK
Dreamtheimpossible(USA) had shaped with any amount of promise when given an educational ride behind Black Bear Island on her debut at Naas last month. She fully justified the step up to this much higher level with a taking display to get off the mark, handling the more demanding surface without fuss. A filly that stays well, she may have one more run in Pattern company before the season is out and she looks a really nice three-year-old prospect. (op 7/1 tchd 8/1)
Forest Storm had won her maiden easily on similar ground at this venue last month and met plenty of support to follow that up. She was given every chance, but simply failed to see out the extra furlong like the winner and remains a filly of promise. (op 5/4 tchd 6/4)
Tanoura(IRE) was ridden a lot more positively than had been the case when winning her maiden and, while she stepped up on that form, she did not stay the longer trip nearly as well as the first two. (op 7/4)
T/Jkpt: @417.40. Pool of @11,134.00 - 20 winning units. T/Plt: @297.50. Pool of @12,106.00.
II

5923 - 5925a (Foreign Racing) - See Raceform Interactive

BORDEAUX LE BOUSCAT (R-H)
Saturday, September 13

OFFICIAL GOING: Very soft

5926a GRAND PRIX DU SUD-OUEST (LISTED RACE) 1m 4f
3:20 (3:22) 4-Y-O+ £22,059 (£8,824; £6,618; £4,412; £2,206)

RPR

1 **Rento (FR)**48 5-9-0 F-XBertras 2 106
(W Walton, France)

2 shd **Quest For Honor**35 4880 4-9-0 JVictoire 5 106
(A Fabre, France)

3 2 1/2 **Cristobal (USA)**35 4880 4-9-0 (b) IMendizabal 1 102
(J-C Rouget, France)

4 3 **Big Robert**19 5348 4-9-0 DBonilla 3 97
(W R Muir) *racd in last: hdwy 3f out: pushed along and disputing 3rd st: sn rdn: one pce* **17/1**1

5 4 **Libertador (FR)**84 3291 4-9-4 TThulliez 4 95
(J-M Capitte, France)

2m 36.39s (156.39) 5 Ran SP% **5.6**
PARI-MUTUEL (Including 1 Euro stake): WIN 13.60; PL 3.90, 2.00;SF 49.10.
Owner Mme N Walton **Bred** Jean-Pierre Quinson & Mlle Benedicte Cherel **Trained** France

NOTEBOOK
Big Robert never looked dangerous but did make some progress in the straight to take fourth place and some 6,000euros in prizemoney.

5927a GRAND PRIX INTER-REGIONAL DES 3 ANS (LISTED RACE) 1m 4f
3:50 (3:53) 3-Y-O £20,221 (£8,088; £6,066; £4,044; £2,022)

RPR

1 **Polan (FR)**30 3-8-12 CNora 3 97
(R Martin-Sanchez, Spain)

2 hd **Pompeyano (IRE)**32 4959 3-9-2 MBlancpain 5 101
(C Laffon-Parias, France)

3 3/4 **Hopes And Fears (IRE)**48 4473 3-9-2 IMendizabal 6 100
(J-C Rouget, France)

4 shd **Resplendent Light**14 5529 3-8-12 DBonilla 1 96
(W R Muir) *prom: 3rd 1/2-way: pushed along appr st: rdn ent st: styd on same pce* **54/10**1

5 shd **Angelo Minny (FR)**49 4442 3-9-2 JVictoire 2 99
(A Fabre, France)

6 1/2 **Speedy Silver (FR)**60 3-8-12 MGuyon 4 95
(H-A Pantall, France) **14/1**2

2m 42.78s (162.78) 6 Ran SP% **22.3**
PARI-MUTUEL: WIN 13.70; PL 5.40, 3.50; SF 80.10.
Owner Marquesa De Villatoya **Bred** Benedikt Fassbender **Trained** Spain

NOTEBOOK
Resplendent Light, having his second outing in France this year, was unsuited by a lack of early pace. He was given every chance and fought bravely throughout the straight, but was just held at bay.

5897 GOODWOOD (R-H)
Sunday, September 14

OFFICIAL GOING: Soft (7.0)
Wind: Light, across Weather: Fine

5929 EUROPEAN BREEDERS' FUND CELER ET AUDAX MAIDEN STKS 6f
2:00 (2:01) (Class 4) 2-Y-O £4,857 (£1,445; £722; £360) Stalls Low

Form RPR

32 1 **Montmorency (IRE)**15 5499 2-9-3 0 ChrisCatlin 9 77
(Saeed Bin Suroor) *lw: w ldr: def advantage 1f out: drvn out: jst hld on* **3/1**1

4 2 nse **Park Lane**30 5053 2-9-3 0 NCallan 11 77+
(B W Hills) *towards rr: pushed along bef 1/2-way: struggling after: picked up over 1f out: stl only 6th ins fnl f: r.o wl: jst failed* **3/1**1

523 3 1/2 **Forward Feline (IRE)**16 5461 2-8-12 75 CatherineGannon 5 70
(B Palling) *narrow ld to over 1f out: pressed wnr after: jst hld and lost 2nd last strides* **6/1**3

4 nk **Sunniva Duke (IRE)** 2-9-3 0 DaneO'Neill 13 74
(R Hannon) *w'like: wl in rr: stdy prog on outer fr 1/2-way: clsd on ldrs over 1f out: bmpd fnl f and no ex last 100yds* **8/1**

5 nk **Seek N' Destroy (IRE)** 2-9-3 0 DarryllHolland 10 76+
(B W Hills) *w'like: scope: dwlt: off the pce in last pair: prog 1/2-way: hrd rdn fr 2f out: hung rt over 1f out: bmpd rival fnl f and nowhere to go after* **10/1**

4 6 3/4 **Albaseet (IRE)**32 4980 2-9-3 0 RHills 1 71
(M P Tregoning) *lw: pressed ldng pair: rdn and stl ch ent fnl f: no ex and lost pls last 100yds* **5/1**2

7 2 1/4 **Alexander Loyalty (IRE)** 2-8-12 0 ShaneKelly 2 60+
(J Noseda) *w'like: awkward s: sn chsd ldrs: u.p and losing pl 2f out* **12/1**

8 3 1/4 **Hawk's Eye** 2-9-3 0 AlanMunro 3 55
(E F Vaughan) *leggy: s.s: detached in last pair: nvr a factor: plugged on* **25/1**

6 9 1 1/2 **Eager To Bow (IRE)**51 4367 2-9-3 0 LPKeniry 12 50
(P R Chamings) *leggy: in tch in midfield to 1/2-way: sn struggling and rdn: n.d last 2f* **20/1**

10 3/4 **Megasecret** 2-9-3 0 RichardSmith 14 48
(R Hannon) *w'like: in tch over 3f: sn wknd* **25/1**

00 11 6 **Tightrope (IRE)**93 3001 2-9-3 0 KirstyMilczarek 7 30
(T D McCarthy) *chsd ldrs 2f: c to nr side bef 1/2-way: sn wknd* **66/1**

1m 15.23s (3.03) **Going Correction** +0.425s/f (Yiel) 11 Ran SP% **122.8**
Speed ratings (Par 97): **96,95,95,94,94 93,90,86,84,83 75**
toteswinger: 1&2 £4.10, 1&3 £4.00, 2&3 £6.00. CSF £11.50 TOTE £3.70: £1.20, £1.90, £2.30; EX 12.90.
Owner Godolphin **Bred** Frank Dunne **Trained** Newmarket, Suffolk

FOCUS
Those with racing experience did not appear to set that high a standard, but the newcomers were not quite up to taking advantage.

NOTEBOOK
Montmorency(IRE) just held on in something of a bunch finish. He holds a Dewhurst entry, which looks very optimistic, but the form of his run at Ripon last time had been given a boost when the third won a nursery off 67 on his next start, and on that basis he was entitled to win a race of this ordinary nature. He certainly showed the right attitude when tackled on all sides inside the last. (op 7-2 tchd 4-1)
Park Lane really found his stride once he got balanced. He was green on his debut when a promising fourth at Newbury in a race that is working out well, and again shaped as though needing the experience here. Open to further improvement, he is out of a Darshaan mare and will get 7f. (op 4-1)
Forward Feline(IRE), by far the most experienced runner in the line-up, got warm beforehand. She ran a sound race once again but is pretty exposed now and helps set the level of the form. (tchd 5-1 and 7-1)
Sunniva Duke(IRE), representing a stable that is full of juvenile talent, is a half-brother to a 7f two-year-old winner. He did best of the newcomers and should benefit from the outing. (op 10-1)
Seek N' Destroy(IRE), who once held a Champagne Stakes entry, got chopped for room as he was seeking a passage between horses inside the last. He would have finished a little closer with a clear run and is another who should come on for this debut effort. Being by Exceed And Excel, faster ground ought to suit him, too. (op 14-1)
Albaseet(IRE) shaped well on his debut over 5f and promised to be suited by this extra furlong but, having travelled well and looking the likeliest winner 2f out, he was one-paced in the closing stages. (op 4-1 tchd 11-2)
Alexander Loyalty(IRE) is a sister to Bahama Mama, who won three times for Jeremy Noseda at two and was also placed in the Molecomb and Flying Childers. She holds an entry in the Cheveley Park, but was not fancied in the market and, after showing up well to halfway, began to paddle. Quicker ground might help her. (op 9-1)
Tightrope(IRE) Official explanation: trainer said colt was unsuited by the soft ground

5930 DERRICK SMITH'S OURY CLARK FREE BUS PASS STKS (H'CAP) 6f
2:35 (2:35) (Class 2) (0-100,92) 3-Y-O+
£11,215 (£3,358; £1,679; £840; £419; £210) Stalls Low

Form RPR

0011 1 **Perfect Flight**21 5310 3-8-10 84 KirstyMilczarek 7 98
(M Blanshard) *lw: trckd ldrs: smooth prog on outer to ld over 2f out: drifted lft over 1f out but wl in command: styd on wl* **11/2**2

1004 2 2 1/2 **Masai Moon**21 5313 4-9-3 92 JamesMillman(3) 3 98
(B R Millman) *lw: covered up bhd ldng bunch: reminder 1/2-way: effrt but nt clrest of runs over 1f out: wnt 2nd fnl f: styd on wl but no imp on wnr* **7/1**

4530 3 2 1/2 **King's Caprice**29 5096 7-8-13 85 (t) TravisBlock 9 83
(J A Geake) *mde most to over 2f out: sn outpcd u.str.p: kpt on fnl f* **6/1**3

0260 4 1/2 **Little Pete (IRE)**15 5509 3-9-3 91 FrancisNorton 1 87
(A M Balding) *in tch in midfield: rdn over 2f out: styd on fr over 1f out to press for 3rd nr fin* **14/1**

0561 5 1/2 **Baldemar**20 5358 3-9-0 88 AndrewElliott 4 83
(K R Burke) *pressed ldr: upsides over 2f out: nt qckn wl over 1f out: fdd* **15/2**

50 6 3/4 **Sir Edwin Landseer (USA)**22 5270 8-9-4 90 (p) RichardThomas 11 82
(Christian Wroe) *sn outpcd in last pair: styd on fr over 1f out: nrst fin* **20/1**

200 7 hd **Chartist**44 4591 3-8-13 87 DaneO'Neill 2 79
(R Hannon) *t.k.h early: cl up bhd ldrs: gng wl 1/2-way: rdn 2f out: fnd nil* **20/1**

4034 8 2 **Steel City Boy (IRE)**2 5867 5-8-4 81 oh5 ow3 AnnStokell(5) 8 66
(Miss A Stokell) *t.k.h early: pressed ldrs: chalng over 2f out: losing pl whn n.m.r over 1f out: wknd* **16/1**

-000 9 3 **El Bosque (IRE)**9 5681 4-8-12 84 AlanMunro 5 60
(B R Millman) *a wl in rr: struggling fr 1/2-way* **18/1**

5421 10 hd **Osiris Way**22 5270 6-9-4 90 LPKeniry 6 65
(P R Chamings) *lw: pressed ldrs: upsides over 2f out: edgd rt u.p over 1f out: wknd rapidly fnl f* **3/1**1

0400 11 1 1/2 **Sundae**66 3881 4-9-4 90 DarryllHolland 10 60
(C F Wall) *dwlt: a in last trio: gng bdly fr 1/2-way* **8/1**

1m 13.1s (0.90) **Going Correction** +0.425s/f (Yiel)
WFA 3 from 4yo+ 2lb 11 Ran SP% **117.4**
Speed ratings (Par 109): **111,107,104,103,103 102,101,99,95,94 92**
toteswinger: 1&2 £5.10, 1&3 £6.90, 2&3 £8.90. CSF £43.76 CT £241.10 TOTE £5.20: £1.90, £2.20, £2.20; EX 33.30.
Owner John Drew **Bred** Biddestone Stud **Trained** Upper Lambourn, Berks

FOCUS
A decent enough handicap, but the top-weight Masai Moon's handicap mark was 8lb below the ceiling for the race. Just as in the first race they came up the centre of the track. Perfect Flight is rated up another 9lb.

NOTEBOOK

Perfect Flight has been in terrific form of late and notched up the hat-trick in good style. Despite drifting left inside the final 2f, she kept on well and while she remains in such good heart there must be a chance that she can continue defying the handicapper. Getting her on soft ground has been the key and it is possible that while she is in such good heart she could nick a bit of black type somewhere before the season is out. (op 5-1)

Masai Moon has done most of his racing over further, but he is fully effective over this trip and handles soft ground so it was not a surprise to see him run well in what was a weaker race than he has been contesting lately. (op 8-1)

King's Caprice sweated up beforehand, but it did not stop him running a sound race. He pulled too hard over 7f last time and the return to sprinting was in his favour. He rallied after looking likely to drop out 1f out. (op 15-2 tchd 8-1)

Little Pete(IRE) justified the decision to have another go over 6f, seeing out the trip perfectly well, but he has nothing in hand of the handicapper off his current mark. (op 12-1)

Baldemar, who had a draw advantage when winning at Ripon last time, could not cope with a 4lb rise for that success. (tchd 8-1)

Sir Edwin Landseer(USA) kept on past some beaten horses in the closing stages, but was never a threat. Quicker ground suits him best. (tchd 16-1)

Chartist did not help his chances of getting home over this longer trip by racing keenly through the early stages.

Steel City Boy(IRE) faced a stiff task from 5lb out of the handicap, not to mention his rider's 3lb overweight. (op 20-1)

Osiris Way was the disappointment of the race as he was only 3lb higher for his course and distance win last month, on similar ground judging by the winning times. Official explanation: trainer said gelding was unsuited by the soft ground (op 10-3 tchd 7-2)

Sundae Official explanation: jockey said gelding moved poorly

5931 COUNTRYSIDE ALLIANCE MAIDEN STKS — 1m 3f

3:05 (3:08) (Class 5) 3-Y-O — £3,238 (£963; £481; £240) Stalls Low

Form				RPR
042	1		**Lough Diver (IRE)**[36] 4871 3-9-3 83 ... JimmyQuinn 7	71+
			(M H Tompkins) *lw: mde all: clr over 3f out: wandered fr over 2f out: unchal* — 4/6[1]	
0500	2	2	**Drum Major (IRE)**[17] 5428 3-9-3 67 ... FergusSweeney 6	67
			(G L Moore) *trckd ldrs: rdn to chse wnr 3f out: no imp tl kpt on fnl f: nvr able to chal* — 8/1	
53-3	3	5	**Dinarius**[99] 1119 3-9-3 68 ... DarryllHolland 3	59
			(D E Pipe) *chsd wnr to 3f out: steadily fdd fnl 2f* — 14/1	
03	4	6	**Shayera**[35] 4909 3-8-12 0 ... DaneO'Neill 1	43
			(B R Johnson) *nvr on terms w ldrs: lost tch over 3f out* — 7/1[3]	
2	5	1 1/2	**Harlestone Gold**[145] 1539 3-9-3 0 ... RichardMullen 2	46
			(J L Dunlop) *w'like: nvr bttr than midfield: out of tch w ldrs over 3f out: no ch after* — 5/1[2]	
0260	6	1 1/2	**Kijivu**[11] 5077 3-8-12 46 ... WandersonD'Avila 4	38
			(A J Lidderdale) *in tch 7f: sn struggling and btn* — 20/1	
0	7	nk	**Capeleira (IRE)**[25] 5182 3-9-3 0 ... ChrisCatlin 5	43
			(R Rowe) *w'like: a last: struggling fr 4f out* — 66/1	

2m 35.44s (7.14) **Going Correction** +0.425s/f (Yiel) — 7 Ran SP% **113.2**

Speed ratings (Par 101): **91,89,85,81,80 79,79**

toteswinger: 1&2 £1.90, 1&3 £3.70, 2&3 £8.30. CSF £6.75 TOTE £1.50: £1.20, £3.40; EX 6.50.

Owner Sir Thomas Pilkington **Bred** Airlie Stud And Sir Thomas Pilkington **Trained** Newmarket, Suffolk

■ Stewards' Enquiry : Wanderson D'Avila one-day ban: used whip when out of contention (Sep 28)

FOCUS

A weak and steadily run maiden in which the winner did not have to match his previous form.

5932 SELECT RACING UK ON SKY 432 STKS (GROUP 3) — 1m 1f 192y

3:40 (3:43) (Class 1) 3-Y-O+

£36,900 (£13,988; £7,000; £3,490; £1,748; £438) Stalls High

Form				RPR
2100	1		**Lady Gloria**[7] 5730 4-9-0 106 ... TPQueally 1	113
			(J G Given) *sn led: rdn and hrd pressed by eventual 4th 2f out and by runner-up fnl f: battled on wl and asserted nr fin* — 33/1	
1522	2	3/4	**Bankable (IRE)**[22] 5265 4-9-0 117 ... DaneO'Neill 4	112
			(L M Cumani) *dwlt: hld up in last trio: stdy prog over 2f out: chsd wnr jst over 1f out: sn rdn to chal: hld last 75yds* — 8/13[1]	
3216	3	1 1/4	**Drumfire (IRE)**[22] 5289 4-9-0 107 ... RoystonFfrench 3	109
			(M Johnston) *prom: chsd wnr over 5f out to 3f out: outpcd over 2f out: kpt on fnl f to take 3rd last stride* — 20/1	
511	4	hd	**Lady Deauville (FR)**[28] 5120 3-8-4 109 ... FrancisNorton 7	106
			(P A Blockley) *v keen to 1/2-way: cl up: chsd wnr 3f out: drvn to chal 2f out: hld and lost 2nd jst over 1f out: lost 3rd last stride* — 6/1[2]	
1031	5	4 1/2	**Indian Days**[45] 4552 3-8-7 98 ... AlanMunro 2	100
			(J G Given) *lw: hld up in tch: effrt 4f out: rdn and struggling over 2f out: fdd* — 16/1[3]	
0056	6	3/4	**Championship Point (IRE)**[22] 5276 5-9-3 109 ... DarryllHolland 8	102
			(M R Channon) *trckd wnr to over 5f out: rdn and struggling over 3f out: steadily wknd* — 16/1[3]	
0550	6	dht	**Muthabara (IRE)**[21] 5331 3-8-7 109 ... RHills 6	99
			(J L Dunlop) *hld up in last trio: shkn up and no prog over 3f out: sn n.d* — 6/1[2]	
26-0	8	7	**Declaration Of War (IRE)**[150] 1421 3-8-7 115 ... RobertHavlin 5	85
			(P W Chapple-Hyam) *hld up in last trio: effrt 4f out: wknd wl over 2f out* — 16/1[3]	

2m 11.18s (3.18) **Going Correction** +0.425s/f (Yiel)

WFA 3 from 4yo+ 7lb — 8 Ran SP% **115.8**

Speed ratings (Par 113): **104,103,102,102,98 98,98,92**

toteswinger: 1&2 £8.40, 1&3 £16.70, 2&3 £4.30. CSF £55.44 TOTE £37.10: £6.20, £1.10, £3.30; EX 72.00.

Owner M H Tourle **Bred** M H And Mrs G Tourle **Trained** Willoughton, Lincs

FOCUS

Some smart horses have won this race in the last ten years, including five horses, all three-year-olds, who subsequently tasted success at Group 1 level. Bankable disappointed, but the form makes sense otherwise.

NOTEBOOK

Lady Gloria, who was only seventh in the Matron Stakes last time out, looked up against it under her penalty for winning at Epsom earlier in the year, but she loves soft ground and has made a habit of winning when returning to the track after only a short time off. Granted an uncontested lead, she made every yard, and, while strongly challenged inside the final 2f, she kept finding more under pressure and would not be denied. She undoubtedly enjoyed the run of the race, but this was her second success at Group level and connections are now pondering whether to go to Newmarket with her for the Sun Chariot or take her to France for the Prix de l'Opera.

Bankable(IRE), who got a bit warm in the prelims, only found Raven's Pass too strong here in the Group 2 Celebration Mile last time, and that effort strongly suggested he was the one to beat in this weaker affair. However, he was disappointing, failing to find as much as he promised 2f out. He was certainly given a bit to do, having been held up out the back in what was a tactical affair, but in truth he looked a non-stayer. A drop back to a mile should suit him, he remains capable of winning at this level, and could well do better as a five-year-old. (op 4-7 tchd 8-15 and 4-6 in places)

Drumfire(IRE) had a stiff task on the ratings, but he is a consistent sort and, having tracked the leader for most of the way, kept plugging away. He is not the easiest horse to place, but could well be the type to send out to Dubai for the carnival early next year. (op 25-1)

Lady Deauville(FR), whose form in Listed company reads 21111, but in Group company now reads 34230454, may have a class barrier, but she gave herself little chance of getting home here by pulling much too hard. She has been in terrific form of late and relishes soft ground, but she is a keen-going type who wears a cross-noseband and clearly needs a stronger pace in her races. (op 9-2)

Indian Days had the lowest official rating of all in the line-up and the ground was against him. He did not run too badly in the circumstances. (op 25-1)

Championship Point(IRE) likes this track, but he had to give weight all round thanks to a Group 3 penalty he picked up when successful at Chester earlier in the year. (op 8-1)

Muthabara(IRE) had excuses for getting beaten in the top fillies' races earlier in the campaign, but she ran poorly in France last time when appearing to have conditions to suit and this was another disappointing effort. She has questions to answer now. (op 8-1)

Declaration Of War(IRE) held every chance strictly on the ratings, but that was based on his smart two-year-old form and his one outing this season in the Craven left him with plenty to prove, including his stamina for this longer trip. He finished up well held. (op 33-1)

5933 HOLT'S AUCTIONEERS NURSERY STKS (H'CAP) — 5f

4:15 (4:15) (Class 5) (0-75,65) 2-Y-O — £3,238 (£963; £481; £240) Stalls Low

Form				RPR
4662	1		**Jubilee Juggins (IRE)**[10] 5647 2-9-7 65 ... KirstyMilczarek 6	70
			(N P Littmoden) *swtg: trckd ldrs: produced to ld over 1f out: clr fnl f: decisively* — 11/4[2]	
4005	2	2 1/4	**Cocktail Party (IRE)**[34] 4925 2-8-13 57 ... RHills 3	54
			(J W Hills) *lw: t.k.h early: hld up bhd ldrs: nt clr run 2f out: plld out over 1f out: r.o to snatch 2nd last stride: no ch w wnr* — 4/1[3]	
3135	3	hd	**Silent Treatment (IRE)**[13] 5567 2-9-4 62 ... (tp) ChrisCatlin 4	58
			(Miss Gay Kelleway) *swtg: mde most to over 1f out: sn outpcd by wnr: kpt on but lost 2nd last stride* — 5/2[1]	
0000	4	nk	**Louie's Lad**[23] 5228 2-8-8 52 ... DavidKinsella 1	47
			(J A Geake) *w ldrs: stl nrly upsides over 1f out: fnd nil after* — 16/1	
2045	5	3	**Elusive Ronnie (IRE)**[32] 4975 2-9-0 58 ... (p) JimmyQuinn 2	42
			(R A Teal) *lw: settled in last pair: pushed along bef 1/2-way: outpcd fr 2f out: nvr on terms after* — 6/1	
0513	6	9	**Agnes Love**[9] 5680 2-9-5 63 ... DaneO'Neill 5	15
			(J Akehurst) *w ldr to 2f out: wknd rapidly: eased: t.o* — 5/1	

61.42 secs (3.02) **Going Correction** +0.425s/f (Yiel) — 6 Ran SP% **112.1**

Speed ratings (Par 95): **92,88,88,87,82 68**

toteswinger: 1&2 £2.40, 1&3 £2.30, 2&3 £2.50. CSF £14.00 TOTE £3.50: £1.70, £2.60; EX 14.20.

Owner Miss Vanessa Church **Bred** Sunland Holdings Sc **Trained** Newmarket, Suffolk

FOCUS

Not a strong race for the track.

NOTEBOOK

Jubilee Juggins(IRE) showed he handles this sort of ground at Warwick last time and the drop back to the minimum trip caused him no problems at all. He ran out a clear winner in the end and proved difficult to pull up after the line, suggesting there was plenty left in the tank and that a return to 6f will not bother him. Soft conditions clearly bring out the best in him and, while he is in this sort of form, it will not be a surprise to see him defy a penalty. (op 9-4)

Cocktail Party(IRE) took a while to get herself organised, but was staying on well at the finish. A return to 6f looks sure to suit her. (op 5-1)

Silent Treatment(IRE), wearing cheekpieces for the first time, was held by \bAgnes Love\p on their Kempton running last time, but this ground made it a different test and Gay Kelleway's filly, who has a selling-grade win on soft to her name, reversed the form by some margin. (op 7-2 tchd 4-1 in a place)

Louie's Lad had been well beaten in all his previous starts, but this softer ground saw him in a slightly better light. He did not find a great deal in the closing stages, though, and could probably do with some sort of headgear being fitted. (op 20-1)

Elusive Ronnie(IRE) struggled throughout and probably does not want the ground as soft as this. (tchd 11-2)

5934 COUNTRY PARK STKS (H'CAP) — 2m

4:50 (4:50) (Class 5) (0-75,74) 4-Y-O+ — £3,238 (£963; £481; £240) Stalls Low

Form				RPR
2434	1		**Go Amwell**[59] 4105 5-7-11 55 ... DavidProbert(5) 9	64+
			(J R Jenkins) *stdd s: hld up in last trio: stdy prog fr 4f out: wnt 2nd over 2f out: led jst over 1f out: sn wl in command* — 3/1[1]	
1005	2	2	**Rock 'N' Roller (FR)**[32] 4963 4-9-6 73 ... RichardMullen 11	79
			(W R Muir) *hld up in midfield: effrt 4f out: rdn over 2f out: styd on wl fr over 1f out to take 2nd nr fin* — 20/1	
1155	3	1	**Trigger's Friend**[11] 5613 4-8-2 55 ... FrancisNorton 7	60
			(Jamie Poulton) *chsd clr ldr: rdn to cl over 3f out: disp 2nd tl over 2f out: styd on one pce after* — 11/2[3]	
04-4	4	3/4	**Trew Style**[77] 3523 6-9-0 67 ... (e[1]) JimmyQuinn 2	71
			(M H Tompkins) *lw: led and sn 12 l clr: maintained advantage tl c bk fr 4f out: hdd jst over 1f out: wknd and lost 2 pls nr fin* — 14/1	
3643	5	1	**Wester Ross (IRE)**[16] 5465 4-8-12 65 ... MickyFenton 10	68
			(J M P Eustace) *lw: prom in chsng gp: effrt to dispute 2nd 3f out to over 2f out: one pce after* — 10/1	
5/01	6	1 3/4	**Tagula Blue (IRE)**[20] 5367 8-8-13 66 ... StephenDonohoe 6	67
			(Ian Williams) *stdd s: hld up in last trio: effrt 4f out: shkn up over 3f out: edgd lft to nr side over 2f out: nvr on terms w ldrs* — 12/1	
-022	7	8	**Act Three**[31] 5027 4-9-1 68 ... TPQueally 1	59
			(Mouse Hamilton-Fairley) *free to post and t.k.h early: prom in chsng gp: effrt to dispute 2nd over 3f out to over 2f out: wknd over 1f out: v tired fnl f* — 17/2	
4632	8	1 1/2	**Estate**[32] 4963 6-9-7 74 ... DaneO'Neill 3	63
			(E J O'Neill) *hld up in midfield: effrt 4f out: in tch in chsng gp over 2f out: wknd rapidly wl over 1f out* — 7/2[2]	
0532	9	1	**Vinces**[13] 5576 4-8-13 66 ... RobertHavlin 8	54
			(T D McCarthy) *b.hind: hld up in midfield: in tch in chsng gp 3f out: sn wknd* — 12/1	
1500	10	18	**Flame Creek (IRE)**[106] 2621 12-8-4 57 ... ChrisCatlin 4	24
			(E J Creighton) *stdd s: t.k.h early and hld up in last: lost tch over 3f out: t.o* — 20/1	

2/5- **11** *6* **Rio De Janeiro (IRE)**[141] 5924 7-9-7 **74**.............................. AlanMunro 5 33
(Miss E C Lavelle) *bit bwd: chsd clr ldr tl wknd 5f out: t.o* **20/1**

3m 38.55s (5.35) **Going Correction** +0.425s/f (Yiel) **11** Ran SP% **118.6**
Speed ratings (Par 103): **103,102,101,101,100 99,95,95,94,85 82**
toteswinger: 1&2 £18.10, 1&3 £4.60, 2&3 £22.20. CSF £68.75 CT £311.10 TOTE £3.60: £1.50, £4.70, £2.30; EX 78.80.
Owner Robin Stevens **Bred** Michael Ng **Trained** Royston, Herts

FOCUS
An ordinary staying handicap, but thanks to Trew Style it was run at a good gallop. Sound form.
Tagula Blue(IRE) Official explanation: jockey said gelding hung left
Flame Creek(IRE) Official explanation: trainer said gelding did not handle the track

5935 SUSSEX MILITIA STKS (H'CAP) 1m 1f 192y
5:25 (5:27) (Class 5) (0-75,75) 3-Y-O+ **£3,238** (£963; £481; £240) **Stalls** High

Form RPR
3012 **1** **Thumbs Up**[39] 4741 3-9-7 **75**.............................. DaneO'Neill 4 86+
(L M Cumani) *hld up in 5th: smooth prog over 2f out: led wl over 1f out: rdn and styd on stoutly after* **5/2**[1]

400- **2** *1 1/4* **Limbo King**[375] 5131 4-9-9 **70**.............................. AlanMunro 7 78
(J R Fanshawe) *lw: trckd ldr: rdn and nt qckn over 2f out: styd on again fr over 1f out to take 2nd ins fnl f: no real threat to wnr* **14/1**

4064 **3** *2 1/2* **Resonate (IRE)**[54] 4276 10-9-11 **72**.............................. TPQueally 8 75
(A G Newcombe) *t.k.h early: trckd ldng pair: wnt 2nd over 2f out and chalng after: outpcd by wnr over 1f out: one pce and lost 2nd ins fnl f* **8/1**[3]

0612 **4** *1/2* **Shesha Bear**[11] 5602 3-9-0 **73**.............................. DavidProbert(5) 9 75
(W R Muir) *hld up in 7th: effrt 3f out: rdn and kpt on fr over 1f out: nvr pce to threaten* **4/1**[2]

0020 **5** *3/4* **Balnagore**[12] 5583 4-9-5 **66**.............................. RichardMullen 6 67
(J L Dunlop) *led: set modest pce to 4f out: hdd and readily outpcd fr wl over 1f out* **8/1**[3]

4356 **6** *1/2* **Dancing Storm**[28] 5119 5-9-2 **63**.............................. FergusSweeney 5 63
(W S Kittow) *t.k.h early: trckd ldng trio: lost pl and struggling wl over 2f out: plugged on fnl f* **4/1**[2]

4150 **7** *1 1/4* **Merrymadcap (IRE)**[15] 5492 6-9-6 **67**.............................. FrancisNorton 1 64
(M Blanshard) *t.k.h early: hld up in 6th: rdn and no prog over 2f out: struggling after* **9/1**

4204 **8** *1 1/4* **Shabahar (IRE)**[20] 5370 4-9-10 **71**.............................. LPKeniry 2 66
(M J McGrath) *s.v.s: hld up in last pair: rdn and no prog 3f out: one pce after* **20/1**

-010 **9** *1/2* **Serious Choice (IRE)**[59] 4128 3-8-13 **70**.............................. JackMitchell(3) 10 64
(J R Boyle) *dwlt: hld up in last pair: rdn and no prog 3f out* **12/1**

2m 15.43s (7.43) **Going Correction** +0.425s/f (Yiel)
WFA 3 from 4yo+ 7lb **9** Ran SP% **119.9**
Speed ratings (Par 103): **87,86,84,83,83 82,81,80,80**
toteswinger: 1&2 £7.70, 1&3 £5.50, 2&3 £13.80. CSF £42.04 CT £253.92 TOTE £3.20: £1.70, £3.70, £2.30; EX 39.20 Place 6 £25.70, Place 5 £16.89.
Owner Team Spirit **Bred** London Thoroughbred Services Ltd **Trained** Newmarket, Suffolk

FOCUS
A modest handicap that was run at a crawl until past halfway. The winner can do better still and the form seems sound despite the lack of pace.
T/Plt: £44.30 to a £1 stake. Pool: £71,458.20. 1,176.71 winning tickets. T/Qpdt: £21.40 to a £1 stake. Pool: £3,868.52. 133.30 winning tickets. JN

5904 GREAT LEIGHS (A.W) (L-H)
Sunday, September 14

OFFICIAL GOING: Standard
Wind: medium, half against Weather: bright

5936 SHERRY H'CAP 6f (P)
2:25 (2:26) (Class 4) (0-85,86) 3-Y-O+ **£4,857** (£1,445; £722; £360) **Stalls** Low

Form RPR
2210 **1** **Artistic License (IRE)**[20] 5346 3-8-12 **79**.............................. TonyCulhane 14 89+
(M R Channon) *sn outpcd in rr and pushed along: hdwy over 1f out: r.o strly to ld nr fin* **20/1**

51-0 **2** *1/2* **Lochstar**[42] 4668 4-9-1 **80**.............................. WilliamBuick 7 89
(A M Balding) *led: rdn and edgd rt wl over 1f out: kpt on wl tl hdd nr fin* **15/2**

1025 **3** *1/2* **Lucayos**[10] 5648 5-9-1 **80**.............................. RichardKingscote 13 87
(K R Burke) *prom on outer: rdn 2f out: chsd wnr over 1f out: kpt on u.p* **11/1**

4220 **4** *nk* **Blue Jack**[15] 5510 3-8-11 **78**.............................. MartinDwyer 9 84+
(W R Muir) *hld up towards rr: hdwy jst over 2f out: nt clr run briefly jst over 1f out: sn swtchd lft: r.o wl fnl f: nt quite rch ldrs* **14/1**

2221 **5** *nk* **Vintage (IRE)**[17] 5433 4-8-13 **78**.............................. IanMongan 3 83
(J Akehurst) *chsd ldrs: wnt 2nd over 2f out: rdn 2f out: lost 2nd over 1f out: kpt on same pce fnl f* **3/1**[1]

3100 **6** *2* **Chjimes (IRE)**[17] 5433 4-8-8 **73**.............................. JohnEgan 6 72
(C R Dore) *in tch in midfield: effrt on inner wl over 1f out: no imp fnl f* **14/1**

0411 **7** *shd* **Geoffdaw**[11] 5617 3-8-9 **76**..............................(v) EddieAhern 2 74
(M J Wallace, Australia) *in tch: rdn 2f out: no prog over 1f out* **7/1**[3]

5625 **8** *nk* **Feisty Royale**[15] 5502 3-8-4 **71**..............................(b[1]) JoeFanning 8 68+
(M Johnston) *s.i.s: sn wl bhd and rdn: sme late hdwy: n.d* **16/1**

6-04 **9** *1* **Doctor Hilary**[24] 5206 6-9-5 **84**..............................(v) TedDurcan 10 78
(A B Haynes) *hld up wl in tch: rdn wl over 1f out: wknd ent fnl f* **12/1**

1500 **10** *1 1/2* **Royal Envoy (IRE)**[10] 5648 5-8-11 **76**.............................. TGMcLaughlin 1 65
(P Howling) *chsd ldrs: drvn 2f out: wknd jst over 1f out: eased towards fin* **12/1**

0402 **11** *2 1/2* **Halsion Chancer**[9] 5681 4-9-7 **86**.............................. RyanMoore 11 67
(J R Best) *chsd ldr tl over 2f out: wknd wl over 1f out* **13/2**[2]

0161 **12** *3* **Kyle (IRE)**[38] 4765 4-8-11 **79**.............................. TolleyDean(3) 4 51
(C R Dore) *towards rr: rdn and struggling fr 1/2-way* **8/1**

2000 **13** *3 1/2* **Dressed To Dance (IRE)**[17] 5424 4-8-12 **82**..........(v) RichardEvans(5) 5 43
(P D Evans) *s.i.s: a bhd* **25/1**

1m 13.01s (-0.69) **Going Correction** +0.075s/f (Slow) **13** Ran SP% **125.3**
WFA 3 from 4yo+ 2lb
Speed ratings (Par 105): **107,106,105,105,104 102,102,101,100,98 95,91,86**
toteswinger: 1&2 £53.70, 1&3 £61.60, 2&3 £29.50. CSF £170.88 CT £1824.37 TOTE £20.40: £3.50, £5.50, £7.00; EX 224.00 TRIFECTA Not won.
Owner Wood Street Syndicate IV **Bred** Mountarmstrong Stud **Trained** West Ilsley, Berks

FOCUS
A fair sprint handicap run in a time 0.99 seconds quicker than the following fillies' nursery. Unlucky many sprints here the winner came from the rear. The third looks a solid guide to the form.

5937 BRANDY FILLIES' NURSERY 6f (P)
2:55 (2:56) (Class 4) 2-Y-O **£4,731** (£1,416; £708; £354; £176) **Stalls** Low

Form RPR
2142 **1** **Starlarks (IRE)**[43] 4640 2-9-2 **83**.............................. RyanMoore 12 87
(W J Knight) *towards rr: pushed along and hdwy 3f out: swtchd rt and rdn wl over 1f out: str run u.p to ld wl ins fnl f* **11/4**[2]

0261 **2** *1* **Cat Patrol**[17] 5431 2-8-8 **75**.............................. EddieAhern 7 76
(H J L Dunlop) *in tch: chsd ldr over 2f out: rdn to ld over 1f out: hdd and no ex wl ins fnl f* **13/2**

4101 **3** *2 1/4* **Fazbee (IRE)**[19] 5375 2-9-7 **88**.............................. JohnEgan 4 82
(P W D'Arcy) *s.i.s: hld up in midfield: hdwy 1/2-way: rdn to chse ldng pair over 1f out: kpt on same pce fnl f* **5/2**[1]

5000 **4** *1 3/4* **Madison Belle**[72] 3677 2-7-12 **65** oh7.............................. AdrianMcCarthy 2 54
(K R Burke) *towards rr: hdwy on inner 1/2-way: chsd ldrs over 1f out: kpt on same pce fnl f* **33/1**

0005 **5** *1 3/4* **Hosanna**[14] 5535 2-7-12 **65** oh8.............................. WilliamBuick 1 49+
(B J Meehan) *t.k.h: hld up bhd: swtchd rt 1/2-way: c wd and rdn wl over 1f out: edgd lft over 1f out: kpt on but nvr trbld ldrs* **14/1**

2406 **6** *1/2* **Misty Glade**[22] 5277 2-7-12 **65** oh3..............................(b) NickyMackay 5 51
(B J Meehan) *led tl rdn and hdd over 1f out: wknd fnl f* **9/1**

0564 **7** *3* **Anjuna (USA)**[33] 4956 2-7-8 **66** oh13 ow1... Louis-PhilippeBeuzelin(5) 11 39
(J H M Gosden) *s.i.s: sn rdn along in rr: sme hdwy over 1f out: nvr trbld ldrs* **20/1**

1633 **8** *1* **Ridgeway Silver**[17] 5422 2-7-9 **69** ow3.............................. BillyCray(7) 9 39
(M D I Usher) *chsd ldrs: rdn 1/2-way: sn struggling* **10/1**

000 **9** *2 1/4* **Fly Butterfly**[22] 5277 2-7-9 **69** oh7 ow4..............................(b) KMay(7) 8 29
(B J Meehan) *chsd ldrs: wnt 2nd over 3f out tl 2f out: wknd 2f out: btn and edgd lft over 1f out* **20/1**

3560 **10** *9* **Calypso Girl (IRE)**[10] 5642 2-8-6 **78** ow1.............................. RichardEvans(5) 10 15
(P D Evans) *chsd ldr on outer tl over 3f out: sn rdn and struggling: no ch fnl 2f: eased ins fnl f* **11/2**[3]

1m 14.0s (0.30) **Going Correction** +0.075s/f (Slow) **10** Ran SP% **122.2**
Speed ratings (Par 94): **101,99,96,94,92 91,87,86,83,71**
toteswinger: 1&2 £5.80, 1&3 £1.70, 2&3 £1.80. CSF £21.75 CT £52.73 TOTE £4.60: £1.90, £1.60, £1.40; EX 23.90 Trifecta £51.30 Pool: £259.64 - 3.74 winning units..
Owner Mrs W W Fleming **Bred** Stourbank Stud **Trained** Patching, W Sussex

FOCUS
Half the field raced from out of the handicap and this was an ordinary fillies' nursery for the grade. The winning time was 0.99 seconds slower than the earlier 71-85 handicap for three-year-olds and upwards.

NOTEBOOK
Starlarks(IRE) was able to defy a 3lb rise in the weights for her recent close second at the Newmarket July course. She struggled to lay up early, but really found her stride in the straight and ultimately took this in decisive fashion. This galloping track suited and she gives the impression she is ready for a step up to 7f now. (op 10-3 tchd 7-2)
Cat Patrol looked likely to follow up her recent Lingfield maiden success when taking over early in the straight, but she was reeled in late on. It may or may not have been significant that she stuck towards the far rail, whereas the winner made her move out wide. (op 5-1 tchd 7-1)
Fazbee(IRE), winner of a novice event over course and distance on her previous start, had absolutely every chance and this looks as good as she is. (tchd 9-4 and 11-4 in a place)
Madison Belle, trying Polytrack for the first time, ran well from 7lb out of the handicap and this was probably a career best.
Hosanna was 8lb out of the handicap, but she kept on from well off the pace and showed some ability. She looks sure to be suited by a return to 7f and might find a race if turned out off her correct mark. (op 18-1)

5938 MADEIRA H'CAP 1m 6f (P)
3:30 (3:31) (Class 2) (0-100,94) 3-Y-O
£11,215 (£3,358; £1,679; £840; £419; £210) **Stalls** Low

Form RPR
3220 **1** **Detonator (IRE)**[46] 4519 3-9-7 94.............................. JoeFanning 11 106+
(M Johnston) *chsd ldr tl led 5f out: mde rest: styd on wl fnl f: eased nr fin* **9/2**[3]

0145 **2** *1 1/4* **Sevenna (FR)**[38] 4784 3-8-10 83.............................. TedDurcan 9 93
(H R A Cecil) *hld up in midfield: hdwy over 4f out: chsd wnr over 3f out: sn rdn: kpt on same pce u.p fnl f* **8/1**

4164 **3** *hd* **Downhiller (IRE)**[20] 5349 3-9-2 89.............................. EddieAhern 4 99
(J L Dunlop) *hld up in midfield: rdn and effrt 4f out: disp 2nd over 1f out: kpt on same pce fnl f* **11/1**

1334 **4** *7* **Sweet Lightning**[13] 5573 3-9-0 87.............................. MartinDwyer 6 87
(W R Muir) *hld up in rr: hdwy 6f out: chsd ldrs and rdn wl over 2f out: wknd ent fnl f* **8/1**

1310 **5** *1 1/4* **Victoria Montoya**[16] 5464 3-8-7 80..............................(p) WilliamBuick 10 78
(A M Balding) *hld up in rr: rdn and effrt over 3f out: edgd lft over 1f out: plugged on past btn horses but nvr nr ldrs* **14/1**

1206 **6** *2 3/4* **Celtic Dragon**[16] 5464 3-8-3 76.............................. DaleGibson 12 70
(Mrs A J Perrett) *chsd ldrs: rdn wl over 3f out: wknd qckly wl over 1f out* **20/1**

303 **7** *2 1/2* **Dauberval (IRE)**[16] 5449 3-8-13 86.............................. AdamKirby 8 77
(S Kirk) *hld up in last pl: rdn 7f out: nvr nr ldrs: no ch fnl 3f* **20/1**

-021 **8** *hd* **City Stable (IRE)**[19] 5376 3-8-10 83.............................. RyanMoore 7 74
(Sir Michael Stoute) *s.i.s: hld up in rr: drvn and effrt over 3f out: no prog and wl hld after* **3/1**[1]

3141 **9** *7* **Neve Lieve (IRE)**[32] 4992 3-7-11 75.........(v[1]) Louis-PhilippeBeuzelin(5) 1 56
(M Botti) *led tl 5f out: rdn and wknd over 3f out: wl bhd last 2f* **20/1**

1621 **10** *21* **Benhego**[18] 5406 3-8-2 75.............................. SaleemGolam 2 26
(S C Williams) *s.i.s: sn pushed up to chse ldng pair: rdn and wknd qckly over 4f out: sn wl bhd: t.o* **4/1**[2]

12 **11** *3* **Le Brocquy**[65] 3930 3-8-13 86.............................. PaulHanagan 5 33
(M G Quinlan) *s.i.s: hld up in midfield: rdn and struggling 4f out: wl bhd fnl 3f: eased fnl f: t.o* **12/1**

3m 0.73s (-2.47) **Going Correction** +0.075s/f (Slow) **11** Ran SP% **122.4**
Speed ratings (Par 107): **110,109,109,105,104 102,101,101,97,85 83**
toteswinger: 1&2 £12.10, 1&3 £8.30, 2&3 £25.10. CSF £40.87 CT £368.46 TOTE £7.00: £2.40, £1.70, £4.20; EX 51.80 TRIFECTA Not won.
Owner Sheikh Hamdan Bin Mohammed Al Maktoum **Bred** Darley **Trained** Middleham Moor, N Yorks

FOCUS
A decent three-year-old staying handicap run at a fair pace. The first three finished clear and the form has been rated on the positive side, with the winner up 6lb.

NOTEBOOK

Detonator(IRE) probably ran a bit flat at Goodwood on his previous start, as that was his third run in quick succession, but he has clearly been freshened up by over a month off the track and produced a very useful effort to defy top weight. He was travelling really strongly when taking over half a mile from the finish and found plenty when strongly pressed in the straight. He is developing into a smart stayer. (op 7-1)

Sevenna(FR) confirmed she is very much going the right way with a decent effort in defeat. There are races to be won with her. (op 12-1)

Downhiller(IRE) seemed to appreciate the step up in trip and looked to produce a career best, finishing a long way clear of the remainder in third. (op 14-1)

Sweet Lightning looked a threat when produced with his chance at the top of the straight, but he did not see his race out as well as the front three. This was his first try beyond 1m4f and the trip looked to stretch him on this demanding course.

Victoria Montoya was well out the back when coming off the bridle over half a mile out and she could not muster the speed to get into a challenging position. All she does is gallop, so more positive tactics might help in future, and she looks in need of a step up to 2m.

Dauberval(IRE) Official explanation: jockey said gelding never travelled

City Stable(IRE) made hard work of winning a slightly lesser race over course and distance on his previous start and he never looked like defying a 6lb rise. He was in trouble some way out and simply failed to respond to pressure. Official explanation: trainer's rep had no explanation for the poor form shown (op 11-4 tchd 5-2)

Benhego went out like a light when coming under pressure. A 13lb rise for his recent course success over 2m in a lesser race obviously made things tougher, but that doesn't explain this performance. He was reported to have run flat. Official explanation: jockey said gelding ran flat (tchd 9-2 and 7-2)

Le Brocquy Official explanation: jockey said colt hung right

5939 E B F BURGUNDY MEDIAN AUCTION MAIDEN STKS — 6f (P)

4:05 (4:07) (Class 4) 2-Y-O — **£4,857** (£1,445; £722; £360) **Stalls** Low

Form			Horse	Jockey	RPR
4	1		**Piccolinda**[17] 5431 2-8-12 0 (W R Muir) *chsd ldr: chal jst over 2f out: sn rdn: led 1f out: hld on wl towards fin* **7/1**[3]	MartinDwyer 4	67
	2	nk	**Corton Charlemagne (IRE)** 2-8-12 0 (Rae Guest) *s.i.s: sn in midfield: hdwy over 1f out: pressed wnr wl ins fnl f: hld towards fin* **25/1**	SaleemGolam 6	66
0	3	1	**Satwa Street (IRE)**[101] 2754 2-9-0 0 (D M Simcock) *chsd ldrs: nt clr run over 1f out tl 1f out: ev ch ins fnl f: wknd towards fin* **25/1**	MarcHalford(3) 3	68+
00	4	½	**Noverre To Hide (USA)**[32] 4980 2-9-3 0 (J R Best) *led: hrd pressed jst over 2f out: hdd 1f out: ev ch tl wknd wl ins fnl f* **5/1**[2]	TedDurcan 7	67+
40	5	½	**Spinight (IRE)**[5] 5784 2-8-10 0 (M Botti) *trckd ldrs: rdn and effrt over 1f out: unable qck jst ins fnl f: one pce fnl 100yds* **14/1**	AndreaAtzeni(7) 13	65
	6	nk	**Wartime** 2-9-3 0 (J H M Gosden) *reminder sn after s: chsd ldrs: rdn wl over 1f out: kpt on same pce u.p fnl f* **9/2**[1]	(b1) RyanMoore 2	64
	7	¾	**Ucantmissme** 2-9-3 0 (D W P Arbuthnot) *s.i.s: bhd: hdwy on outer wl over 1f out: hanging lft after: kpt on fnl f: nt rch ldrs* **11/1**	WilliamBuick 12	62+
6	8	1	**Chosen Son (IRE)**[11] 5609 2-9-0 0 (P J O'Gorman) *hld up wl in tch on inner: effrt and n.m.r over 1f out: rdn ent fnl f: wknd ins fnl f* **12/1**	JerryO'Dwyer(3) 1	59
	9	1 ¾	**Shirley High** 2-8-12 0 (P Howling) *s.i.s: sn in midfield on outer: lost pl and rdn over 3f out: nt clr run over 1f out: kpt on but nvr pce to trble ldrs* **40/1**	IanMongan 10	49+
33	10	2 ¾	**Dannios**[17] 5430 2-9-3 0 (L M Cumani) *stdd and dropped in bhd after s: n.d* **9/2**[1]	EddieAhern 11	45+
	11	¾	**Miss Jabba (IRE)** 2-8-12 0 (Miss J Feilden) *bhd: nvr trbld ldrs* **40/1**	AdamKirby 8	38
	12	½	**Cooper Island Kid (USA)** 2-9-3 0 (P W D'Arcy) *in tch in midfield: reminder 5f out: rdn and struggling over 2f out: wknd wl over 1f out* **12/1**	JohnEgan 5	42

1m 15.19s (1.49) **Going Correction** +0.075s/f (Slow) — **12** Ran SP% **108.5**

Speed ratings (Par 97): **93,92,91,90,89 89,88,87,84,81 80,79**

toteswinger: 1&2 £13.20, 1&3 £39.90, 2&3 £47.50. CSF £145.11 TOTE £7.30: £2.10, £6.60, £8.20; EX 107.40 TRIFECTA Not won.

Owner North Farm Stud **Bred** North Farm Stud **Trained** Lambourn, Berks

■ Rulesn'Regulations was withdrawn after refusing to enter the stalls 7/1, deduct 10p in the £ under R4).

■ Stewards' Enquiry : Andrea Atzeni one-day ban: failed to ride to draw (Sep 28)

FOCUS

They finished in a bit of a bunch and this was a modest maiden, but there were one or two interesting types among the beaten horses. The winning time was 1.19 seconds slower than the earlier nursery won by a filly rated 83.

NOTEBOOK

Piccolinda improved on the form she showed when fourth in a weak maiden at Lingfield on her debut and gained a narrow success. Her jockey reportedly felt she was idling a little in front, so perhaps she is a little bit better than the bare result, and she should not be harshly treated when switching to nurseries/handicaps. (op 6-1)

Corton Charlemagne(IRE), a half-sister to 5f juvenile winner Argentine, out of a dual winner in South Africa, fared best of the newcomers in a close second and this was a pleasing introduction. She travelled nicely for much of the way and looks capable of winning a similar race. (tchd 20-1)

Satwa Street(IRE) improved significantly on the form he showed when down the field on his debut at Lingfield over three months previously and is entitled to come on again for the run. (op 33-1)

Noverre To Hide(USA), up in trip, had his chance from the front. He now has the option of taking the handicap route. (op 13-2 tchd 9-2)

Spinight(IRE) ran better than at Lingfield on his previous start, confirming the ability he showed first-time up. (tchd 12-1)

Wartime, an 85,000gns son of Bertolini, brother to 1m winner Silly Billy Nick, half-brother to dual 1m2f scorer Fever, out of a dual 5f winner, has already been gelded and was fitted with blinkers for his debut. He was a little short of room late on but did not look unlucky. (op 7-2 tchd 5-1)

Ucantmissme ◆, out of a dual 5f juvenile winner, attracted some support and ran a race full of promise. Having been last of all at halfway, he showed good speed to latch on to the main group early in the straight, but he continued to run green and got going too late once switched towards the inner. Admittedly this was not much of a race, but he should improve significantly for the outing and it will be disappointing if he does not win a maiden. (tchd 12-1)

Shirley High, by Forzando out of a multiple 6f-7f winner, caught the eye a little further down the field and has ability. She might be one to keep in mind once handicapped. (op 33-1)

Dannios was always out the back and was well below the form he showed on his first two starts. However, he was not given too hard a time once his chance had gone and it would be no surprise if he left this run behind when stepped up in trip and sent handicapping. Official explanation: trainer's rep said colt was unsuited by the kickback (op 7-2)

5940 PORT H'CAP — 2m (P)

4:35 (4:36) (Class 2) (0-100,92) 3-Y-O+

£11,215 (£3,358; £1,679; £840; £419; £210) **Stalls** Centre

Form			Horse	Jockey	RPR
1111	1		**Askar Tau (FR)**[23] 5249 3-9-2 92 (M P Tregoning) *in tch: wnt 2nd 4f out: led and edgd lft over 2f out: pushed clr 2f out: eased wl ins fnl f* **4/5**[1]	MartinDwyer 4	106+
-106	2	5	**Desert Sea (IRE)**[36] 4843 5-9-13 90 (D W P Arbuthnot) *t.k.h: hld up in tch: outpcd over 3f out: chsd clr ldng pair over 2f out: kpt on to go 2nd ins fnl f: no ch w wnr* **4/1**[2]	RyanMoore 1	96+
1063	3	1 ¾	**Always Bold (IRE)**[17] 5423 3-8-10 86 (M Johnston) *led: rdn and hdd over 2f out: short of room sn after: no ch w wnr fr wl over 1f out: lost 2nd ins fnl f* **9/2**[3]	JoeFanning 7	90
0060	4	9	**Rationale (IRE)**[20] 5349 5-9-2 79 (S C Williams) *t.k.h: hld up in rr: rdn wl over 3f out: sn outpcd: wl btn last 2f* **20/1**	(t) J-PGuillambert 6	72
30/	5	3	**Absolut Power (GER)**[101] 5974 7-9-8 85 (J A Geake) *s.i.s: early reminders: bhd: drvn 5f out: wl outpcd wl over 3f out: no ch after* **33/1**	(v) AdamKirby 3	75
5206	6	2 ¼	**Greenwich Meantime**[15] 5494 8-10-0 91 (R A Fahey) *chsd ldrs: wnt 2nd 9f out tl 4f out: sn rdn and struggling: wl btn last 3f* **12/1**	PaulHanagan 5	78
3613	7	2 ¼	**Casual Affair**[19] 5376 5-9-1 78 (J D Bethell) *chsd ldr tl 9f out: rdn over 4f out: wknd over 3f out: wl bhd last 2f* **11/1**	TedDurcan 2	62

3m 30.31s (0.31) **Going Correction** +0.075s/f (Slow)

WFA 3 from 5yo+ 13lb — **7** Ran SP% **117.5**

Speed ratings (Par 109): **102,99,98,94,92 91,90**

toteswinger: 1&2 £1.60, 1&3 £1.90, 2&3 £2.70. CSF £4.60 TOTE £2.40: £2.00, £2.10; EX 5.10.

Owner Nurlan Bizakov **Bred** Gestut Zoppenbroich & Aerial Bloodstock **Trained** Lambourn, Berks

FOCUS

A decent staying handicap and Askar Tau took another step forward, rated up 9lb on his latest win.

NOTEBOOK

Askar Tau(FR) ◆ completed a five-timer in fine style. A 10lb rise for his latest success at the Newmarket July course put him on a mark 35lb higher than when beginning his winning run, but he keeps improving and again had plenty in hand. This was his first run beyond an extended 1m6f, but he's a thorough stayer and Martin Dwyer was not afraid to commit him early. Despite looking a touch ungainly as usual, and jinking ever so slightly a couple of times when clear, he ran on powerfully for pressure before being eased near the line. He is now around a 5-1 chance for the Cesarewitch, for which he has picked up a 4lb penalty, and will take some beating if turning up in this form. (op Evens tchd 6-5 in places)

Desert Sea(IRE) seemed to race a little keenly, but he had his chance and was basically just no match for the improving winner. (op 9-2 tchd 10-3)

Always Bold(IRE) took them along, but he had no answer when the winner began to press him about half a mile out and he lost second inside the final furlong. (op 6-1)

Rationale(IRE) is unproven over this trip and did not seem to stay in this company. (op 16-1)

Absolut Power(GER), better known as a hurdler/chaser, offered little on his first Flat outing since 2004. (op 40-1)

Greenwich Meantime had no easy task under top weight but could still have been expected to run better. (op 8-1)

5941 CLARET CONDITIONS STKS — 1m (P)

5:10 (5:10) (Class 3) 3-Y-O+ — **£7,771** (£2,312; £1,155; £577) **Stalls** Centre

Form			Horse	Jockey	RPR
03-3	1		**Eddie Jock (IRE)**[219] 494 4-9-0 110 (Saeed Bin Suroor) *trckd ldr and a travelling wl: led wl over 1f out: rdn and edgd rt ent fnl f: r.o strly* **6/1**	TedDurcan 10	111
4205	2	3 ½	**Docofthebay (IRE)**[22] 5265 4-9-0 107 (J A Osborne) *bhd: hdwy jst over 2f out: rdn wl over 1f out: chsd wnr and hung rt ins fnl f: no imp* **7/2**[2]	ShaneKelly 2	103
1045	3	½	**Jack Junior (USA)**[24] 5208 4-9-0 95 (B J Meehan) *led for 1f: stdd and chsd ldng pair after: drvn over 2f out: chsd wnr over 1f out: no imp ent fnl f: lost 2nd ins fnl f* **12/1**	EddieAhern 7	102
21-5	4	2 ½	**Confront**[148] 1471 3-8-9 108 (Sir Michael Stoute) *hld up in midfield: hdwy to chse ldng trio over 2f out: rdn jst over 2f out: no imp over 1f out: wknd ent fnl f* **15/8**[1]	RyanMoore 9	95
1010	5	3	**Re Barolo (IRE)**[15] 5508 5-9-3 105 (M Botti) *hld up in midfield: rdn and effrt on inner jst over 2f out: nvr wnt pce to rch ldrs: wknd ent fnl f* **4/1**[3]	(t) JohnEgan 1	92
0120	6	1 ½	**Dream Lodge (IRE)**[15] 5495 4-9-3 100 (J G Given) *s.i.s: sn drvn up and led after 1f: rdn over 2f out: hdd wl over 1f out: wknd jst over 1f out* **14/1**	(v) J-PGuillambert 8	89
5400	7	17	**Whitcombe Minister (USA)**[66] 3880 3-8-9 98 (Jamie Poulton) *in tch in midfield: rdn and struggling wl over 3f out: t.o fr over 1f out* **10/1**	JoeFanning 4	46
0406	8	1	**Fly Time**[88] 3128 4-8-4 35 (T T Clement) *in rr: rdn and struggling over 3f out: t.o fr over 1f out* **100/1**	NicolPolli(5) 6	40

1m 38.1s (-1.80) **Going Correction** +0.075s/f (Slow)

WFA 3 from 4yo+ 5lb — **8** Ran SP% **115.7**

Speed ratings (Par 107): **112,108,108,105,102 101,84,83**

toteswinger: 1&2 £3.90, 1&3 £7.70, 2&3 £4.70. CSF £27.66 TOTE £7.30: £1.70, £2.00, £2.50; EX 24.10 Trifecta £280.30 Pool: £378.86 - 1.00 winning unit..

Owner Godolphin **Bred** J Egan, J Corcoran And J Judd **Trained** Newmarket, Suffolk

■ Stewards' Enquiry : J-P Guillambert one-day ban: used whip with excessive force (Sep 28)

FOCUS

A good, competitive conditions contest run at a decent pace. The first three raced up the middle of the track in the straight. The winner was back to something like his best with the third the best guide to the form.

NOTEBOOK

Eddie Jock(IRE) had apparently had some minor problems since running in Dubai in February, but he returned from his absence in great order and was a most decisive winner. In this sort of form he would be worth his place in Listed or Group 3 company, although his connections say he doesn't want the ground too soft. In the longer term, he looks a likely type for next year's Dubai Carnival. (op 13-2 tchd 7-1)

Docofthebay(IRE) was without his usual blinkers for this first try on Polytrack and he was slightly below his best. All of his wins have been gained in double-figure fields. (op 5-1)

Jack Junior(USA) lacks consistency, but he is capable of smart form on his day and is better than his official mark of 95 suggests. This was a solid effort in defeat. (op 11-1)

Confront looked a potential classic horse as a juvenile, but he was disappointing in the Greenham on his reappearance and had been off the track since. Trying Polytrack for the first time, he stuck more towards the far side than the front three in the straight, but that's no real excuse and he basically just ran below expectations. However, it is too early to give up on him and given his trainer's excellent record with older horses there has to be a chance he will come good next year. (op 13-8)
Re Barolo(IRE) has a fine record on sand, but he was not at his best this time. He might not have been helped by sticking towards the far side in the straight. (op 7-2 tchd 10-3)

5942 CIDER H'CAP 1m 2f (P)
5:40 (5:40) (Class 2) (0-100,98) 3-Y-O

£11,215 (£3,358; £1,679; £840; £419; £210) **Stalls** Low

Form				RPR
0550	1		**Yahrab (IRE)**[129] 1922 3-9-4 **98** RyanMoore 7	104
			(C E Brittain) *hld up in tch: rdn and qcknd to ld over 1f out: r.o wl* **8/1**[3]	
0603	2	1 1/4	**Meeriss (IRE)**[22] 5257 3-9-2 **96** TonyCulhane 4	100
			(M R Channon) *chsd ldng pair: rdn wl over 1f out: chsd wnr jst ins fnl f: kpt on same pce* **8/1**[3]	
0060	3	nk	**Ramona Chase**[9] 5677 3-8-13 **93** AdamKirby 6	96
			(S Kirk) *stdd s: t.k.h: hld up in last pair: swtchd rt and drvn over 1f out: disp 2nd ins fnl f: kpt on* **8/1**[3]	
3112	4	1	**Military Power**[45] 4552 3-8-13 **93** EddieAhern 2	94+
			(J W Hills) *hld up in tch: swtchd rt and rdn ent fnl f: kpt on same pce fnl f* **2/1**[2]	
213	5	hd	**Tanto Faz (IRE)**[38] 4790 3-8-5 **85** WilliamBuick 3	86+
			(W J Haggas) *hld up in last: plld out and rdn over 1f out: kpt on but nt pce to chal ldrs* **15/8**[1]	
1004	6	2 3/4	**Porthole (USA)**[16] 5449 3-8-5 **85** MartinDwyer 5	80
			(B W Hills) *s.i.s: t.k.h: sn chsng ldr: upsides ldr and rdn 2f out: wknd jst ins fnl f* **10/1**	
-200	7	5	**Hurricane Hymnbook (USA)**[24] 5208 3-9-1 **95** TedDurcan 8	80
			(B J Meehan) *led at stdy pce: rdn and jnd 2f out: hdd over 1f out: wknd fnl f* **12/1**	

2m 9.68s (1.08) **Going Correction** +0.075s/f (Slow) 7 Ran SP% **118.2**
Speed ratings (Par 107): **98,97,96,95,95 93,89**
toteswinger: 1&2 £7.80, 1&3 £12.40, 2&3 £6.70. CSF £71.03 CT £535.13 TOTE £10.80: £4.30, £2.60; EX 38.60 Trifecta £211.30 Part won. Pool: £285.63 - 0.10 winning units Place 6 £514.33, Place 5 £88.23.
Owner Saif Ali **Bred** Swettenham Stud **Trained** Newmarket, Suffolk

FOCUS
An ordinary handicap for the grade and they went a steady pace for much of the way. The form is a bit muddling and not rated too positively.

NOTEBOOK
Yahrab(IRE) had been off the track since finishing down the field in the Chester Vase in May, but he showed himself on a decent mark on this first attempt in handicap company. He is clearly quite smart and might be forced back up in class before much longer. He had a spell in Dubai earlier in the year and it would be no surprise to see him go back there for next season's Carnival. (op 10-1 tchd 11-1)
Meeriss(IRE), who won a novice event at Lingfield last year on his only previous try on Polytrack, ran with credit behind a horse who was probably well treated. (tchd 7-1)
Ramona Chase would probably have preferred a stronger pace, but he's basically just difficult to win with. (op 7-1)
Military Power had been progressing well on turf lately, but he was not at his best returned to Polytrack for the first time since finishing second in a Wolverhampton maiden earlier in the year. He did not enjoy the best of runs through in the straight, but was not unlucky and basically just seemed unsuited by the modest tempo. (op 9-4 tchd 5-2)
Tanto Faz(IRE) was held up last, so the steady gallop was against him and he was never getting there in the straight. (op 2-1 tchd 9-4)
Hurricane Hymnbook(USA) Official explanation: jockey said gelding stopped very quickly
T/Jkpt: Not won. T/Plt: £1,235.10 to a £1 stake. Pool: £69,796.65. 41.25 winning tickets. T/Qpdt: £80.70 to a £1 stake. Pool: £4,694.15. 43.00 winning tickets. SP

5918 CURRAGH (R-H)
Sunday, September 14

OFFICIAL GOING: Heavy

5944a ASCON ROHCON SOLONAWAY STKS (GROUP 3) 1m
2:40 (2:41) 3-Y-O+ **£35,845** (£10,477; £4,963; £1,654)

			RPR
1		**Jumbajukiba**[28] 5134 5-9-11 114 (b) FMBerry 6	115
		(Mrs John Harrington, Ire) *mde all: rdn clr over 2f out: reduced advantage fnl f: kpt on u.p: all out* **10/3**[3]	
2	1 3/4	**Prima Luce (IRE)**[7] 5729 3-9-1 107 KJManning 5	106
		(J S Bolger, Ire) *trckd ldrs in 3rd: rdn to go 2nd ent st: outpcd 2f out: styd on ins fnl f* **3/1**[2]	
3	11	**Mystical Lady (IRE)**[15] 5517 3-8-12 99 JAHeffernan 4	80+
		(A P O'Brien, Ire) *hld up in rr: swtchd to outer early st: hdwy 2f out: mod 3rd over 1f out: sn no ex* **8/1**	
4	1 1/2	**Zulu Chief (USA)**[28] 5135 3-9-1 105 JMurtagh 1	77+
		(A P O'Brien, Ire) *trckd ldrs in 4th: rdn and outpcd early st: struggling fr over 1f out* **2/1**[1]	
5	3	**Moiqen (IRE)**[28] 5135 3-9-4 106 DPMcDonogh 2	73+
		(Kevin Prendergast, Ire) *settled 5th: rdn and no imp st: struggling fr over 1f out* **13/2**	
6	9	**King Of Westphalia (USA)**[28] 5135 3-9-1 94 SMLevey 7	50+
		(A P O'Brien, Ire) *sn 2nd: rdn and wknd ent st* **20/1**	

1m 49.61s (7.71) **Going Correction** +1.25s/f (Soft)
WFA 3 from 5yo+ 5lb 6 Ran SP% **110.6**
Speed ratings: **111,109,98,96,93 84**
CSF £13.27 TOTE £3.80: £1.70, £2.70; DF 10.90.
Owner J P O'Flaherty **Bred** Woodcote Stud Ltd **Trained** Moone, Co Kildare

NOTEBOOK
Jumbajukiba showed his latest dismal effort to be all wrong and made all to repeat last year's win in this race. He basically handled this ground better than his rivals and has now won five times at this track. Still a five-year-old, he could now be switched to hurdling, and with an official rating of 114 he could rate very highly in that sphere. (op 5/2 tchd 7/2)
Prima Luce(IRE) has shown ability to handle this sort of ground in the past and she was the only one to give the winner a serious race at the business end. This was a solid effort and she finished well clear of the remainder. (op 6/1)
Mystical Lady(IRE) was not at an advantage in being held up off the uneven pace and never got into it. (op 8/1 tchd 9/1)
Zulu Chief(USA), who won his maiden on a testing surface, was one of the first off the bridle and this has to rate as very disappointing. (op 11/10 tchd 9/4)
Moiqen(IRE) simply looked all at sea on this ground. (op 7/1)

5946a BANK OF SCOTLAND (IRELAND) NATIONAL STKS (GROUP 1) (ENTIRE COLTS & FILLIES) 7f
3:45 (3:45) 2-Y-O

£130,441 (£42,205; £20,147; £6,911; £4,705; £2,500)

			RPR
1		**Mastercraftsman (IRE)**[49] 4465 2-9-1 121 JMurtagh 2	118
		(A P O'Brien, Ire) *settled 3rd: 2nd fr 2 1/2f out: rdn to chal on stands' rail fr under 1 1/2f out: disp ld ins fnl f: led last stride: all out* **9/4**[2]	
2	shd	**Shaweel**[23] 5226 2-9-1 GregFairley 6	118
		(M Johnston) *racd in 2nd: led over 3f out: sn rdn: jnd ins fnl f: styd on wl u.p: hdd last stride: jst failed* **12/1**	
3	2 1/2	**Arazan (IRE)**[22] 5296 2-9-1 MJKinane 5	112
		(John M Oxx, Ire) *trckd ldrs in 4th: 3rd and rdn fr over 2f out: no imp fr 1 1/2f out: kpt on wout threatening ins fnl f* **9/10**[1]	
4	7	**Indian Ocean (IRE)**[43] 4656 2-9-1 JAHeffernan 3	94
		(A P O'Brien, Ire) *6th to 1/2-way: prog into 4th over 2f out: rdn and one pce* **7/1**[3]	
5	4 1/2	**Drumbeat (IRE)**[22] 5296 2-9-1 100 PJSmullen 7	83
		(A P O'Brien, Ire) *restrained in rr: 6th and sme prog over 2f out: kpt on same pce fr over 1f out* **20/1**	
6	1/2	**Intense Focus (USA)**[63] 4005 2-9-1 106 (b[1]) KJManning 8	82
		(J S Bolger, Ire) *chsd ldrs in 5th: rdn and no imp fr over 2f out* **16/1**	
7	20	**Sea Of Marmara (USA)**[49] 4465 2-9-1 100 SMLevey 4	32
		(A P O'Brien, Ire) *set fast pce: drvn along and hdd over 3f out: sn wknd: trailing whn eased over 1f out* **66/1**	

1m 37.59s (10.49) **Going Correction** +1.50s/f (Heavy) 7 Ran SP% **115.7**
Speed ratings: **100,99,97,89,83 83,60**
CSF £29.25 TOTE £2.70: £1.70, £3.40; DF 20.50.
Owner Derrick Smith **Bred** Lynch Bages Ltd **Trained** Ballydoyle, Co Tipperary
■ A 20th Group 1 win of the year for Aidan O'Brien and Ballydoyle.

FOCUS
Atrocious conditions, so hard to be dogmatic about the value of the form, but Mastercraftsman has been rated as having shown fractionally better form than in the Phoenix Stakes, and Shaweel has been assessed his equal. Arazan failed to build on his impressive Futurity win, but he may well prove capable of better when conditions are less testing.

NOTEBOOK
Mastercraftsman(IRE) ◆ proved a big market drifter, with his connections genuinely worried about the ground. He took his unbeaten sequence to four, however, with a very gutsy effort and is clearly a very classy performer. His rider's decision to bag the stands' rail paid off and this effort would suggest he will have no trouble at all in staying 1m next year. The Dewhurst would seem his next logical step, but he did have a hard race and it would not come as a big surprise to see him put away now. The world would appear to be his oyster next season. (op 2/1)
Shaweel, the Gimcrack winner, was given a positive ride over this longer trip and made the winner pull out all the stops, showing much improved form again. Like many of his trainer's best horses down the years, he has a healthy appetite for a fight, and his toughness should be enough to ensure that he continues to thrive at a high level. He will seldom have to face conditions as demanding as this, but is likely to prove particularly effective with ease in the ground. (op 12/1 tchd 14/1)
Arazan(IRE) was heavily backed, with his effectiveness for heavy ground having been proven with a taking success in the Futurity Stakes last time. His performance this time makes it apparent that it was his basic superiority to his rivals in that Group 2 event, rather than any marked ground preference, that got him through there with an enhanced reputation. He began to show signs of labouring from around 2f out after his rider had opted to steer a more central course, and while he might have been seen to slightly better effect nearer to the stands' rail, the eventual margin indicates that it made no substantial difference. He remains a very interesting horse for next season. (op 9/10 tchd 1/1)

5945 - 5950a (Foreign Racing) - See Raceform Interactive

2230 CAPANNELLE (R-H)
Sunday, September 14

OFFICIAL GOING: Good to soft

5951a PREMIO DIVINO AMORE TATTERSALLS (LISTED RACE) 5f
3:55 (12:00) 2-Y-O **£14,706** (£6,471; £3,235; £1,765)

			RPR
1		**Mrs Kipling (IRE)**[67] 3851 2-8-8 HayleyTurner 8	98
		(S A Callaghan) *pressed ldrs on outside: led 1/2-way: rdn out (4.66/1)* **47/10**[2]	
2	1/2	**Lan Force (ITY)**[104] 2-8-8 MMonteriso 7	96
		(A Renzoni, Italy)	
3	3 1/2	**Eva Kant**[91] 2-8-8 CFiocchi 1	83
		(R Menichetti, Italy)	
4	1 1/2	**Sweet Hearth (USA)**[84] 3308 2-9-0 PConvertino 5	84
		(R Betti, Italy) **4/5**[1]	
5	4	**Common Market** 2-8-8 PAragoni 6	64
		(A Peraino, Italy)	
6	4	**Blue Klein (IRE)** 2-8-8 PBorelli 9	49
		(Gianluca Bietolini, Italy)	
7	1 3/4	**Mondo Marcio (ITY)** 2-8-11 SDiana 4	46
		(F Natalizi, Italy)	
8	1 3/4	**Capo Carbonara (IRE)**[104] 2-8-11 GBietolini 3	40
		(R Brogi, Italy)	
9	1 3/4	**Diglett (IRE)**[84] 3308 2-9-3 GMarcelli 2	39
		(L Riccardi, Italy)	

58.20 secs (-0.90) 9 Ran SP% **73.1**
(including one euro stakes): WIN 5.66; PL 2.51, 2.57, 2.42; DF 32.76.
Owner Sangster Family & M Green **Bred** J Osborne **Trained** Newmarket, Suffolk

NOTEBOOK
Mrs Kipling(IRE), who pulled too hard when finishing last in the Cherry Hinton, probably benefited from the drop back to the minimum trip and took this in game fashion. The easier ground did not seem to be a problem this time either.

5738 LONGCHAMP (R-H)

Sunday, September 14

OFFICIAL GOING: Good to soft

5952a QATAR PRIX VERMEILLE (GROUP 1) (F&M) 1m 4f

2:25 (2:26) 3-Y-0+ £126,044 (£50,426; £25,213; £12,596; £6,309)

RPR

1 **Zarkava (IRE)**[98] 2877 3-8-8 ... CSoumillon 10 120+
(A De Royer-Dupre, France) *s.v.s: 4 l bhd the rest after 1f: last st: str run on outside fr 2f out: led 60yds out: pushed out* **8/15**[1]

2 2 **Dar Re Mi**[23] 5243 3-8-8 ... C-PLemaire 2 117
(J H M Gosden) *a.p: 5th st: wnt 2nd over 2f out: rdn 1 1/2f out: led 120yds out to 60yds out: one pce* **8/1**[2]

3 ½ **Treat Gently**[21] 5331 3-8-8 ... SPasquier 12 116
(A Fabre, France) *hld up: 9th st: hdwy over 2f out: 4th wl over 1f out: kpt on one pce* **16/1**

4 1 ½ **Michita (USA)**[23] 5243 3-8-8 ... JimmyFortune 4 114
(J H M Gosden) *mid-div: 8th st: hdwy to go 3rd wl over 1f out: kpt on same pce u.p* **18/1**

5 1 ½ **Adored (IRE)**[63] 4006 3-8-8 ... DavidMcCabe 11 111
(A P O'Brien, Ire) *sn led: 6 l clr st: ct 120yds out: one pce* **40/1**

6 1 ½ **Tangaspeed (FR)**[31] 5039 3-8-8 ... TJarnet 3 109
(R Laplanche, France) *mid-div: 6th on ins st: styd on one pce* **100/1**

7 ½ **Gagnoa (IRE)**[63] 4006 3-8-8 ... OPeslier 7 108
(A Fabre, France) *hld up in rr: 11th st: nvr nr to chal* **9/1**[3]

8 1 ½ **Folk Opera (IRE)**[21] 5332 4-9-2 ... LDettori 1 105
(Saeed Bin Suroor) *a cl up: 4th st on ins: swtchd lft over 2f out: one pce* **16/1**

9 2 **Baila Me (GER)**[42] 4675 3-8-8 ... DBoeuf 6 103
(W Baltromei, Germany) *mid-div: 7th st: one pce fnl 2f* **40/1**

10 8 **Turfrose (GER)**[35] 4914 4-9-2 ... JVictoire 5 89
(A Fabre, France) *hld up: 10th st: a bhd* **25/1**

11 dist **Ice Queen (IRE)**[63] 4006 3-8-8 ... CO'Donoghue 8 —
(A P O'Brien, Ire) *prom: 3rd st: wknd wl over 1f out* **11/1**

12 5 **Honoria (IRE)**[6] 5768 3-8-8 ... JamieSpencer 9 —
(A P O'Brien, Ire) *racd in 2nd to st: wknd qckly 2f out* **100/1**

2m 26.0s (-5.20) **Going Correction** -0.10s/f (Good)
WFA 3 from 4yo 9lb **12** Ran SP% **122.4**
Speed ratings: **113,111,111,110,109 108,108,107,105,100 —,—**
PARI-MUTUEL: WIN 1.50; PL 1.10, 2.10, 2.20; DF 9.90.
Owner H H Aga Khan **Bred** His Highness The Aga Khan's Studs S C **Trained** Chantilly, France
■ Stewards' Enquiry : David McCabe €100 fine: whip abuse

FOCUS
Not the strongest of Vermeilles, but there was no hanging about and it was impossible not to be impressed by Zarkava, who produced a dazzling change of pace up the finishing straight to win comfortably and take her unbeaten run to six races. She is understandably a hot favourite to become the first filly to win the Arc since Urban Sea in 1993.

NOTEBOOK
Zarkava(IRE) ◆, half asleep in the stalls, lost many lengths at the start and was trailing the field for a long time in this Group 1 event. She was still last in the straight before being brought with a sweeping late run up the centre of the track. Once in full flight, she mowed down her 11 rivals one by one and was going away in the final 50 yards. It was an outstanding performance by this filly who was racing over 1m4f for the first time in her life. It was her first outing since June 8, so she might have been a little rusty, and this should have put her spot on for the Arc de Triomphe, for which she is now understandably a warm favourite. She will meet male opposition there for the first time, and it's worth bearing in mind she is unproven in Group 1 company on testing ground, in the event of which her awesome finishing speed is unlikely to be as effective. However, connections will make quite sure she does not doze in the stalls there, and if she is in the same sort of form again she will take a deal of beating.
Dar Re Mi put up another fine performance on her third trip to France this year. She was never far behind the leading group and went after the long time leader halfway up the straight, but there was nothing she could do when the winner arrived on the scene. The plan is now to run her in either the EP Taylor at Woodbine or the Group 2 Pride Stakes at Newmarket.
Treat Gently showed much better form over this longer distance. She quickened well but could never quite get to the runner up, who was behind her when the pair met in the Prix de Malleret in June. Something like the Prix de L'Opera could become the next target.
Michita(USA) began her effort running into the final two furlongs and comfortably held fourth place without threatening the first three. Once again she was behind her stable mate Dar Re Mi and her jockey felt she would have been much happier if there had been more cut in the ground.
Adored(IRE) ◆ was seemingly in make the pace for her stablemates, but she is a decent filly in her own right - she was Johnny Murtagh's pick in the Oaks - and nearly nicked this. She looked the winner when sent well clear early in the straight, but she tired noticeably inside the final furlong. It would be no surprise to see Murtagh back on next time, and something like the Prix de L'Opera could be a suitable target.
Folk Opera(IRE), tucked in just behind the leading group, was not much of a factor in the straight when the race quickened up. Her Group 2 success at Deauville was gained over a shorter distance and she was not able to dominate the situation on this occasion.
Ice Queen(IRE) was nowhere near the form she showed when second in the Irish Oaks on her previous start.
Honoria(IRE) was turned out quickly after winning a Listed race over this trip at Galway, but she was well beaten. All she does is gallop and she will probably be capable of better over further in lesser company.

5953a QATAR PRIX NIEL (GROUP 2) (C&F) 1m 4f

3:00 (3:00) 3-Y-0 £54,485 (£21,029; £10,037; £6,691; £3,346)

RPR

1 **Vision D'Etat (FR)**[105] 2654 3-9-2 ... IMendizabal 4 117+
(E Libaud, France) *hld up in 5th: 4th whn rdn over 1f out: tk 3rd 150yds out: styd on wl to ld post* **15/8**[2]

2 nse **Ideal World (USA)**[49] 4473 3-9-2 ... SPasquier 1 116
(A Fabre, France) *racd in 2nd: chal 1 1/2f out: led narrowly 1f out: hdd post* **9/1**[3]

3 1 ½ **Centennial (IRE)**[22] 5263 3-9-2 ... (b) JimmyFortune 6 114
(J H M Gosden) *led: strly pressed 1 1/2f out: hdd 1f out: kpt on gamely tl no ex last 100yds* **10/1**

4 snk **City Leader (IRE)**[22] 5302 3-9-2 ... JamieSpencer 2 114
(B J Meehan) *disp 3rd: 4th st: rdn to go 3rd 2f out: lost 3rd 150yds out: kpt on* **10/1**

5 3 **King Of Rome (IRE)**[7] 5732 3-9-2 ... CO'Donoghue 7 109
(A P O'Brien, Ire) *hld up in last: nvr a factor* **12/1**

6 1 **Prospect Wells (FR)**[62] 4042 3-9-2 ... OPeslier 5 107
(A Fabre, France) *disp 3rd: 3rd st: rdn over 2f out: sn btn* **13/8**[1]

7 1 ½ **Full Of Gold (FR)**[105] 2654 3-9-2 ... TGillet 3 105
(Mme C Head-Maarek, France) *racd in 6th: pushed along 5f out: nvr a factor* **33/1**

2m 27.4s (-3.80) **Going Correction** -0.10s/f (Good) **7** Ran SP% **111.7**
Speed ratings: **108,107,106,106,104 104,103**
PARI-MUTUEL: WIN 2.10; PL 1.60, 2.90; SF 11.40.
Owner J Detre **Bred** Gaetan Gilles **Trained** France
■ Stewards' Enquiry : S Pasquier €400 fine: whip abuse

NOTEBOOK
Vision D'Etat(FR), the French Derby winner who was trying 1m4f for the first time, just got up in a desperate dash to the line. Waiting tactics were used on this colt and he had plenty to do in the straight after not appearing to go down the hill in great style. However, he quickened well from one and a half out and got up literally on the post. His connections were convinced that he wasn't suited by the ground and think he will strip much fitter for the Arc de Triomphe, when they hope soft ground will prevail. He is now unbeaten in six races. Interestingly, his legs were bandaged for his trip back to the Loire valley where he is trained.
Ideal World(USA), well up from the start, went past the long-time leader at the furlong marker and looked the winner until just caught on the line. He stayed the trip well and may be allowed to take his chance in the Arc, although there are no immediate plans for his future.
Centennial(IRE), whose connections chose to run here rather than supplement him for the St Leger, was asked to make all the running and ran with great credit, battling on well for third. His connections felt that the ground was a little lively and he will now have one more run before starting his four-year-old career.
City Leader(IRE) made his run near the far rail but did not have much room in the final stages. He was another considered to have not been at home on the ground and his jockey felt he was unluckly not to have taken third position.
King Of Rome(IRE) proved disappointing in the Irish Champion Stakes the previous weekend and he was again below his best.
Prospect Wells(FR) was ridden closer to the pace this time, but he was far too keen for his own good.

5954a QATAR PRIX FOY (GROUP 2) (C&F) 1m 4f

3:30 (3:32) 4-Y-0+ £54,485 (£21,029; £10,037; £6,691; £3,346)

RPR

1 **Zambezi Sun**[77] 3542 4-9-2 ... SPasquier 4 119
(P Bary, France) *trckd ldr to st: tk narrow advantage over 2f out: edgd rt 1 1/2f out: drvn 1f out: kpt on* **6/4**[1]

2 ½ **Schiaparelli (GER)**[336] 6223 5-9-2 ... LDettori 1 118
(Saeed Bin Suroor) *led to over 2f out: drvn and rallied 1 1/2f out: ev ch tl unable qck fnl 50yds* **11/4**[2]

3 1 ½ **Light Green (BRZ)**[29] 5114 4-8-12 ... CSoumillon 2 112
(A De Royer-Dupre, France) *racd in 3rd to st: cl bhd the first two and nt clr run 2f out: swtchd lft: kpt on u.p* **16/1**

4 ½ **Not Just Swing (IRE)**[77] 3542 4-9-2 ... OPeslier 6 115
(A Fabre, France) *racd in 4th to st: rdn 1 1/2f out: kpt on steadily but nvr able to chal* **12/1**

5 1 **Crossharbour**[29] 5114 4-9-2 ... JVictoire 5 113
(A Fabre, France) *racd in 5th to st: rdn wl over 1f out: nvr able to chal* **10/3**[3]

6 8 **Avanti Polonia (GER)**[14] 5557 4-8-13 ... DBonilla 3 97
(F Head, France) *a bhd* **16/1**

2m 28.8s (-2.40) **Going Correction** -0.10s/f (Good) **6** Ran SP% **109.2**
Speed ratings: **104,103,102,102,101 96**
PARI-MUTUEL: WIN (coupled with Crossharbour) 1.90; PL 1.50, 2.00; SF 9.10.
Owner K Abdulla **Bred** Juddmonte Farms Ltd **Trained** Chantilly, France

NOTEBOOK
Zambezi Sun was always close up in a race run at a steady pace and, after taking over a furlong and a half out, h had to dig deep as the long time leader fought back bravely in the closing stages. He has been entered in the Arc but connections are looking at other options such as the Canadian International and the Japan Cup.
Schiaparelli(GER) ◆, the 2006 German Derby and St Leger winner and successful four times in Group 1 company last year, ran with real promise on his first start for Godolphin after 11 months off. Admittedly he was allowed the run of the race, but there was a lot to like about the way he battled on when headed and he went down fighting. He was apparently short of peak fitness, and would also have preferred softer ground, so there should be much better to come again. He could now take his chance in the Arc de Triomphe, provided there is some cut in the ground and he takes this race okay. He obviously has Zarkava to beat, but this was an ideal trial for the big race as they didn't go that quickly early on, so he's probably not had that hard a time, and he should come on a bundle. At 25/1 (and bigger on Betfair), he appeals as worth taking a chance on for the Arc.
Light Green(BRZ) was third most of the way in a race that was not run at a great gallop early on. Her trainer felt that she is not suited by a right handed tracks, so will try and find a suitable race at a left-handed course. This certainly opens up a campaign in North America or even the Japan Cup if she makes the grade.
Not Just Swing(IRE) is a Group 3 winner over this course and distance and that is probably more his level. There will be plenty of other opportunities for him during the autumn.

5955a QATAR PRIX DU PETIT-COUVERT (GROUP 3) 5f (S)

4:05 (4:04) 3-Y-0+ £29,412 (£11,765; £8,824; £5,882; £2,941)

RPR

1 **Only Answer**[35] 4915 4-8-12 ... OPeslier 4 112
(A Fabre, France) *disp ld tl led over 2f out: rdn 150yds out: rdn out* **5/2**[2]

2 ½ **Rock Harmonie (FR)**[22] 3-8-8 ... C-PLemaire 5 107
(Mme C Head-Maarek, France) *disp ld early: sn relegated to 3rd: rdn to take 2nd ins fnl f: r.o* **14/1**

3 1 ½ **Stern Opinion (USA)**[14] 5556 3-8-11 ... SPasquier 1 105
(P Bary, France) *disp ld tl hdd over 2f out: sn rdn: one pce and lost 2nd ins fnl f* **6/4**[1]

4 snk **Derison (USA)**[14] 5556 6-8-12 ... (b) TJarnet 6 104
(P Van De Poele, France) *last early: wnt 4th after 2f: rdn and outpcd 2f out: kpt on fnl f* **6/1**[3]

5 8 **Calbuco (FR)**[14] 5556 4-8-12 ... WMongil 3 76
(Mme E Holmey, France) *hld up: last and outpcd fr bef 1/2-way: t.o fnl 1 1/2f* **13/2**

P **Raja (IRE)**[16] 3-8-8 ... CSoumillon 2 —
(F Rohaut, France) *prom whn broke down after 1 1/2f: p.u and dismntd* **11/1**

56.30 secs (-0.40) **Going Correction** +0.25s/f (Good)
WFA 3 from 4yo+ 1lb **6** Ran SP% **111.2**
Speed ratings: **113,112,109,109,96 —**
PARI-MUTUEL: WIN 3.50; PL 2.10, 3.40; SF 23.50.
Owner Wertheimer Et Frere **Bred** Wertheimer Et Frere **Trained** Chantilly, France

NOTEBOOK

Only Answer had the favourite beaten by the furlong marker and then had to hold off the late challenge of the runner-up. She is a pretty consistent individual and the only option now is to let her take her chance in the Prix de l'Abbaye where she will come across the likes of Marchand d'Or and African Rose.

Rock Harmonie(FR) ran well for such an inexperienced filly. This performance augurs well for the future and she should make a decent sprinter next year.

Stern Opinion(USA) was again disappointing but on this occasion he was given every possible chance. He was one of the leaders from the start and was still going well at the halfway stage, but his stride began to shorten late on. His trainer felt that possibly he was a little over the top, having run in the sprint just two weeks before at Deauville. He may now be aimed at the Prix de Seine-et-Oise.

Derison(USA) was always thereabouts but was one paced as the race came to an end. He would have been suited by some more cut in the ground.

5956a QATAR PRIX GLADIATEUR (GROUP 3) — 1m 7f 110y

4:35 (4:35) 4-Y-O+ **£29,412** (£11,765; £8,824; £5,882; £2,941)

RPR

1 **Kasbah Bliss (FR)**[28] 6-8-11 .... TThulliez 4 114+
(F Doumen, France) *in rr: last st: angled to outside and hdwy 2f out: qcknd to ld 1 1/2f out: sn clr: v easily* **16/1**

2 *6* **Bannaby (FR)**[30] 5-8-11 .... JGrosjean 7 106+
(M Delcher Sanchez, Spain) *hld up in 5th on ins: no room over 2f out to 1 1/2f out: wnr already wl clr whn split rivals to go 2nd ins fnl f: r.o strly* **7/1**

3 *snk* **High Maintenance (FR)**[48] 4496 4-8-8 .... OPeslier 5 98
(A Fabre, France) *racd in 4th on outside: rdn to press ldrs over 1 1/2f out: one pce fr over 1f out: fin 4th, 6l, 4l & snk: plcd 3rd* **10/1**

4 *3* **Tungsten Strike (USA)**[22] 5264 7-9-0 ....(p) JimCrowley 8 100
(Mrs A J Perrett) *led: narrowly hdd 2f out: stl chalng on ins whn carried rt 1 1/2f out: wknd: fin 5th: plcd 4th* **7/2**[3]

5 *nk* **Noble Prince (GER)**[62] 4041 4-9-0 .... SPasquier 6 100
(A Fabre, France) *racd in 6th: nvr a factor: fin 6th: plcd 5th* **11/4**[2]

6 *6* **Incanto Dream**[62] 4041 4-9-4 .... YLerner 3 97
(C Lerner, France) *racd in 3rd on ins: no room 2f out: wnt for gap on rail whn squeezed up and almost b.d 1 1/2f out: nt rcvr: fin 7th: plcd 6th* **9/4**[1]

D *4* **Harbore (FR)**[20] 4-8-11 .... ACrastus 1 101
(E Lellouche, France) *racd in 2nd: rdn to ld narrowly 2f out: hdd and hung rt 1 1/2f out: lost 2nd ins fnl f: fin 3rd, 6l & 4l: disq: plcd last* **14/1**

3m 14.5s (-7.00) **Going Correction** -0.10s/f (Good) 7 Ran SP% **113.8**
Speed ratings: **113,110,107,106,106 103,108**
PARI-MUTUEL: WIN 8.10; PL 2.50, 2.50, 2.70; DF 27.30.
Owner Henri De Pracomtal **Bred** Haras D'Ecouves Et H De Pracomtal **Trained** Bouce, France
■ Stewards' Enquiry : A Crastus two-day ban: careless riding (Sep 28-29)

NOTEBOOK

Kasbah Bliss(FR) proved he is just as smart on the Flat as he is over hurdles, but he must have decent ground to show his best. He completely outclassed his six rivals in this staying event and passed the post out on his own. He has now earned a tilt at the Prix du Cadran on October 4 and may even be aimed at next year's Ascot Gold Cup. As the ground will change in the autumn he is likely to be rested after the Cadran and then prepared for top hurdle events in the spring.

Bannaby(FR) , trained in Spain, produced a decent performance in defeat considering he did not get the best of runs through. He had a wall of horses in front of him at the furlong and a half marker and then ran on well, but the race for first place was over once he got in the clear. He is turning into a decent stayer.

High Maintenance(FR), mid division in the early stages, was asked to make her challenge early in the straight and was one paced. She was promoted to third place as there was argy bargy at the furlong marker.

Tungsten Strike(USA) tried to make all the running but he never seemed to be going that well. Asked to quicken in the straight, he could only keep on at the same pace and it was a rather disappointing effort for a horse who had his ground. His jockey felt the horse is not a good traveller and prefers to stay at his local tracks. He was a promoted from fifth to fourth position by the stewards.

Harbore(FR) was thrown out for his part in the incident which saw Incanto Dream almost put over the rails.

2708 TABY (R-H)

Sunday, September 14

OFFICIAL GOING: Turf course - yielding; all-weather - standard

5957a TABY OPEN SPRINT CHAMPIONSHIP (GROUP 3) — 5f 165y

3:15 (3:16) 3-Y-O+ **£42,735** (£19,425; £9,324; £6,216; £3,885)

RPR

1 **Calrissian (GER)**[45] 4578 4-9-4 .... ManuelMartinez 12 103
(L Kelp, Denmark) *midfield: rdn to ld 1f out: r.o wl* **93/10**

2 *1 1/2* **Tamburello (ARG)**[35] 5-9-4 .... FJohansson 8 98
(P Wahl, Sweden) *midfield: hdwy 2f out: kpt on but nt rch wnr* **79/10**[3]

3 *nk* **Relampago Plus (ARG)**[35] 8-9-4 .... RSchistl 6 97
(B Bo, Sweden) *towards rr to 1/2-way: late prog to take 3rd on line* **134/10**

4 *hd* **Maxim's (ARG)**[35] 7-9-4 ....(b) MSantos 14 96
(L Reuterskiold Jr, Sweden) *racd in 3rd tl lost 3rd on line* **145/10**

5 *1 1/2* **Master Chef (IRE)**[45] 4578 3-9-2 ....(b) JacobJohansen 7 91
(B Olsen, Denmark) *a.p: one pce fnl f* **109/10**

6 *hd* **Fujisan**[35] 4-9-4 .... YvonneDurant 9 90
(Yvonne Durant, Sweden) *midfield: kpt on same pce fnl f* **31/10**[2]

7 *1* **Steve's Champ (CHI)**[45] 4578 8-9-4 ....(b) FDiaz 4 87
(Rune Haugen, Norway) *cl 2nd to 2f out: grad wknd* **23/10**[1]

8 *1/2* **King Quantas (IRE)**[45] 4578 10-9-4 .... P-AGraberg 13 85
(B Bo, Sweden) *nvr a factor* **24/1**

9 *1 1/2* **Puggy (IRE)**[45] 4578 4-9-0 .... MLarsen 5 76
(Yvonne Durant, Sweden) *led to 1f out: eased whn hdd* **83/10**

10 *nk* **Royal Miswaki (IRE)**[35] 4-9-4 .... CarlosLopez 1 80
(Wido Neuroth, Norway) *last to 1/2-way: no real prog* **31/1**

11 *1 1/2* **Francis**[91] 10-9-4 .... EspenSki 3 75
(Niels Petersen, Norway) *midfield tl wknd 1f out* **185/10**

12 *1/2* **Pipoldchap (CHI)**[103] 8-9-4 ....(b) DinaDanekilde 2 73
(Helena Fylking, Sweden) *a towards rr* **40/1**

13 *7* **Completo (IRE)**[35] 5-9-4 ....(b) GSolis 11 50
(F Castro, Sweden) *prom 2f: t.o fnl f* **26/1**

69.50 secs (2.80)
WFA 3 from 4yo+ 2lb 13 Ran SP% **126.6**
(including 1Skr stake): WIN 10.30; PL 5.50, 3.23, 7.66; DF 64.92.
Owner Provence Hotels Holding **Bred** Graf & Grafin Von Stauffenberg **Trained** Denmark

5958a STOCKHOLM CUP INTERNATIONAL (GROUP 3) — 1m 4f

3:55 (3:55) 3-Y-O+ **£46,620** (£19,425; £9,324; £6,216; £3,885)

RPR

1 **Appel Au Maitre (FR)**[21] 5335 4-9-4 .... FJohansson 9 102
(Wido Neuroth, Norway) *midfield: hdwy to ld 4f out: sn clr: v easily (exact SP 53/100F)* **1/2**[1]

2 *8* **Peas And Carrots (DEN)**[21] 5335 5-9-4 .... MSantos 6 89
(L Reuterskiold Jr, Sweden) *midfield: hdwy to go 2nd 2f out: no ch w wnr* **46/10**[2]

3 *3* **Fricoteiro (ARG)**[73] 5-9-4 ....(b) EspenSki 5 84
(Niels Petersen, Norway) *midfield: nvr nrr* **51/1**

4 *nk* **Volo Cat (FR)**[21] 5335 4-9-4 .... NCordrey 1 84
(B Olsen, Denmark) *a midfield* **178/10**

5 *1* **Alnitak (USA)**[42] 4676 7-9-4 ....(b) JacobJohansen 4 82
(B Olsen, Denmark) *last to 1/2-way: sme late prog* **33/1**

6 *2* **Jagodin (IRE)**[42] 4676 8-9-4 .... CarlosLopez 7 79
(L Reuterskiold Jr, Sweden) *towards rr tl styd on fnl 2f* **94/10**[3]

7 *2 1/2* **Montparnasse (SWE)**[38] 5-9-4 .... MLarsen 11 75
(B Bo, Sweden) *prom to 4f out: grad wknd* **27/1**

8 *18* **Alpacco (IRE)**[21] 5335 6-9-4 .... FDiaz 3 46
(L Kelp, Denmark) *cl 2nd to 1/2-way: wknd fr 3f out* **23/1**

9 *6* **Capto (ARG)** 5-9-4 .... P-AGraberg 8 37
(B Bo, Sweden) *led after 1f to 4f out: remained cl up to 2f out* **106/10**

10 *13* **Farouge (FR)**[352] 7-9-4 .... YvonneDurant 10 16
(Yvonne Durant, Sweden) *a towards rr* **31/1**

11 *26* **Luca Brasi (FR)**[103] 2708 4-9-4 ....(b) ManuelMartinez 2 —
(F Castro, Sweden) *led 1f: prom to 1/2-way: t.o fnl 2f* **31/1**

2m 34.9s (5.70) 11 Ran SP% **126.9**
WIN: 1.53; PL 1.08, 1.38, 3.83; DF 3.66.
Owner Stall Perlen **Bred** Gilles & Aliette Forien **Trained** Norway

5777 LEICESTER (R-H)

Monday, September 15

OFFICIAL GOING: Soft (good to soft in places; 6.8)
Wind: Light behind Weather: Overcast

5959 LADBROKES.COM IBSTOCK MAIDEN AUCTION STKS — 5f 218y

2:30 (2:31) (Class 5) 2-Y-O **£3,238** (£963; £481; £240) **Stalls Low**

Form RPR

0 1 **Dustry (IRE)**[31] 5053 2-8-11 0 .... DaneO'Neill 9 75+
(R Hannon) *s.i.s: sn pushed along in rr: hdwy u.p over 1f out: r.o wl to ld towards fin* **10/1**

0022 2 *1 3/4* **Hi Shinko**[17] 5459 2-8-12 77 .... AlanMunro 12 71
(B R Millman) *sn led: hdd over 2f out: rdn over 1f out: styd on* **3/1**[2]

0 3 *shd* **Speedy Guru**[17] 5459 2-8-5 0 ....(t) MartinDwyer 15 64
(H Candy) *chsd ldrs: led over 2f out: rdn and hdd towards fin* **12/1**

0 4 *hd* **Turkish Lokum**[56] 4251 2-8-6 0 .... LukeMorris(3) 5 67
(J M P Eustace) *prom: rdn over 2f out: styd on* **28/1**

635 5 *1 1/4* **Spit And Polish**[26] 5184 2-9-0 70 ....(b[1]) EddieAhern 11 68
(J L Dunlop) *chsd ldrs: rdn over 1f out: styd on same pce ins fnl f* **9/1**[3]

0423 6 *1 1/4* **Our Day Will Come**[33] 4975 2-8-11 74 .... RyanMoore 14 62
(R Hannon) *chsd ldrs: rdn 1/2-way: styd on same pce appr fnl f* **13/8**[1]

5 7 *1/2* **Distinctive Spirit (IRE)**[18] 5416 2-9-1 0 .... NCallan 4 64
(K A Ryan) *hld up: hdwy u.p over 1f out: nvr nrr* **25/1**

40 8 *1 1/4* **Mr Snowballs**[40] 4728 2-8-9 0 .... RobertHavlin 10 54
(R A Farrant) *hld up in tch: outpcd 1/2-way: styd on ins fnl f* **18/1**

5 9 *shd* **Lost In Paris (IRE)**[88] 3170 2-9-3 0 .... TedDurcan 6 62
(T D Easterby) *s.i.s: swtchd rt 5f out: nvr nrr* **25/1**

0 10 *3/4* **Oneofthesedayz (IRE)**[16] 5499 2-8-5 0 .... GregFairley 8 48
(Miss V Haigh) *chsd ldrs: rdn and wknd over 1f out* **100/1**

00 11 *shd* **Baby Josr**[18] 5431 2-8-9 0 ....(t) CatherineGannon 3 52
(I A Wood) *sn pushed along in rr: n.d* **66/1**

00 12 *2* **Excitable (IRE)**[112] 2462 2-7-13 0 .... DavidProbert(5) 1 41
(Miss V Haigh) *trckd ldrs: racd keenly: rdn over 1f out: sn wknd* **33/1**

00 13 *4 1/2* **El Guevara (IRE)**[57] 4213 2-9-2 0 .... DarryllHolland 7 54+
(K A Ryan) *s.i.s: sn pushed along in rr: sme hdwy u.p over 1f out: eased* **80/1**

60 14 *4* **Lonsdale Lad**[105] 2657 2-8-9 0 .... DeanMcKeown 2 20
(R C Guest) *stdd s: a in rr* **100/1**

15 *3/4* **Ipdipdoo (IRE)** 2-8-5 0 .... HayleyTurner 16 14
(R Hollinshead) *chsd ldrs: rdn and wknd 1/2-way* **40/1**

0 16 *3/4* **Angelsbemine**[20] 5384 2-8-4 0 .... JimmyQuinn 13 11
(J R Norton) *mid-div: lost pl 4f out: sn bhd* **100/1**

1m 14.19s (1.19) **Going Correction** +0.125s/f (Good) 16 Ran SP% **117.4**
Speed ratings (Par 95): **97,94,94,94,92 90,90,88,88,87 87,84,78,73,72 71**
toteswinger: 1&2 £9.50, 1&3 £28.00, 2&3 £11.80. CSF £36.19 TOTE £14.10: £2.40, £1.30, £4.20; EX 55.50 Trifecta £197.60 Part won. Pool: £267.07, 0.30 winning units..
Owner D J Walker **Bred** Tally-Ho Stud **Trained** East Everleigh, Wilts

FOCUS

After a dry night the ground was changed to soft and good to soft in places. The two market leaders in the opening maiden both had BHA ratings in the mid to upper 70s, and set the standard for the others to aim at. Overall this was just a fair race of its type. They raced in the centre to far side of the track and the time was just under three seconds above standard.

NOTEBOOK

Dustry(IRE) was a 20-1 shot when always behind on his debut but he wasn't beaten far in a race that is working out well. He looked the stable second-string behind the favourite, drifted in the betting and had plenty of ground to make up in the final 2f, but responded really well to pressure and eventually won with something in hand. He should be capable of further progress and should stay 7f. (op 7-1)

Hi Shinko lost out by a nose last month, proved that to be no fluke when narrowly beaten at Salisbury last time and gives the form a solid look. He seems to have a decent attitude and has probably been unlucky to meet opponents who have been slightly better. (tchd 11-4 and 10-3)

Speedy Guru showed plenty of speed and looked a possible winner until wandering around a bit and flashing her tail in the closing stages. She responded well to a tongue tie and ran a promising race, getting almost ten lengths closer to Hi Shinko than she had on her debut last time. (op 14-1 tchd 16-1)

Turkish Lokum showed little on her debut but did much better on this slower surface. (op 33-1)

Spit And Polish travelled well for a long way in the first-time blinkers dropped back to 6f. He may be worth a try over shorter with his new headgear reapplied.

Our Day Will Come was heavily backed but was in trouble a long way out and found a limited response. She may have found things happening a bit too quickly dropped down in trip but this was still a disappointing effort. (op 15-8 tchd 2-1 tchd 9-4 in a place)

The Form Book, Raceform Ltd, Compton, RG20 6NL

El Guevara(IRE) Official explanation: jockey said gelding moved poorly
Angelsbemine Official explanation: jockey said filly hung left throughout

5960 LADBROKES.COM DESFORD NURSERY — 7f 9y
3:00 (3:00) (Class 4) (0-80,76) 2-Y-O — **£4,371** (£1,300; £650; £324) **Stalls** Low

Form			Horse	Jockey	RPR
434	**1**		**Nizhoni Dancer**[18] 5430 2-9-1 **70**	AlanMunro 9	74
			(C F Wall) *led: hdd over 5f out: chsd ldr: rdn over 1f out: r.o to ld wl ins fnl f*	**8/1**	
335	**2**	*nk*	**Aladdin's Lamp (IRE)**[16] 5497 2-8-7 **62**	GregFairley 4	65
			(M Johnston) *racd keenly: w ldr tl led over 5f out: rdn over 1f out: hdd wl ins fnl f*	**5/1**[3]	
0435	**3**	*1 ¾*	**Super Fourteen**[16] 5511 2-8-9 **64**	RichardSmith 2	63
			(R Hannon) *chsd ldrs: rdn over 2f out: styd on*	**16/1**	
040	**4**	*shd*	**Hambledon Hill**[17] 5469 2-9-5 **74**	RyanMoore 7	73
			(R Hannon) *s.i.s: hld up: rdn over 2f out: r.o ins fnl f: nrst fin*	**8/1**	
3232	**5**	*nk*	**Lookafternumberone (IRE)**[11] 5632 2-9-3 **72**	TPQueally 6	70
			(J G Given) *trckd ldrs: rdn over 2f out: swtchd rt ins fnl f: styd on*	**4/1**[1]	
4506	**6**	*hd*	**Flying Lady (IRE)**[58] 4187 2-9-1 **70**	TPO'Shea 5	68
			(M R Channon) *hld up: racd keenly: hdwy over 2f out: sn rdn: styd on u.p*	**11/1**	
200	**7**	*1 ¼*	**Whisky Jack**[23] 5277 2-8-11 **66**	MartinDwyer 10	60
			(W R Muir) *s.i.s: hld up: plld hrd: rdn and swtchd lft over 1f out: r.o ins fnl f: nvr nrr*	**16/1**	
556	**8**	*1*	**Bussell Along (IRE)**[32] 5004 2-8-3 **58**	HayleyTurner 1	50
			(M L W Bell) *stdd s: hld up: rdn and hung rt over 1f out: n.d*	**9/2**[2]	
3232	**9**	*2 ¼*	**Count Almaviva (USA)**[17] 5451 2-9-7 **76**	NCallan 3	62
			(K A Ryan) *prom: rdn over 2f out: sn hung rt: wknd fnl f*	**12/1**	
3440	**10**	*nk*	**Paymaster In Chief**[24] 5228 2-7-13 **59**	DavidProbert(5) 11	45+
			(M D I Usher) *chsd ldrs: rdn over 2f out: wknd fnl f*	**14/1**	
01	**11**	*¾*	**Brierty (IRE)**[128] 2011 2-9-1 **70**	DNolan 8	54+
			(D Carroll) *sn prom: rdn 1/2-way: wknd over 1f out*	**33/1**	

1m 27.9s (1.70) **Going Correction** +0.125s/f (Good) — **11** Ran SP% **114.5**
Speed ratings (Par 97): **95,94,92,92,92 91,90,89,86,86 85**
toteswinger: 1&2 £10.10, 1&3 £26.10, 2&3 £16.80. CSF £46.42 CT £638.50 TOTE £10.70: £3.40, £1.60, £3.80; EX 69.70 TRIFECTA Not won..
Owner Don Howlett **Bred** Paramount Bloodstock **Trained** Newmarket, Suffolk

FOCUS
An open-looking event where most of the runners were making their nursery debut. The top-weight Count Almaviva's handicap mark was 4lb below the ceiling for the race. The first two were always prominent and fought out an exciting finish and the form is rated around the second and third.

NOTEBOOK
Nizhoni Dancer travelled sweetly near the pace, saw out the trip really well and showed tenacity to strike on her nursery debut, giving Chris Wall his fifth winner from the last ten runners. She is clearly well suited by slow ground, should be capable of further improvement and would be very interesting off a higher mark or under a penalty next time. (op 7-1 tchd 9-1)
Aladdin's Lamp(IRE) had been slightly regressive in three maiden starts, but got back on track on slower ground on his nursery debut. He wasted some energy by taking a strong hold in the early stages, but showed a feisty attitude to keep battling and was just picked off in the closing stages. He is one to keep a close eye on next time. (op 11-2 tchd 6-1)
Super Fourteen ran another solid race but looks on about the right mark at present and may continue to be vulnerable to more progressive rivals.
Hambledon Hill seemed to appreciate a return to soft ground and deserves some credit for finishing closest of the hold-up performers in a race where few got into it from behind. He should go close next time if exiting the stalls with a bit more urgency. (op 12-1)
Lookafternumberone(IRE) was just collared on the line in a similar nursery at Redcar last time. He was always well positioned but could not land a telling blow off a 4lb higher mark. (tchd 7-2)
Flying Lady(IRE) raced keenly but carried her head high and looked very reluctant when asked for an effort. (op 10-1 tchd 9-1)
Whisky Jack Official explanation: trainer said colt hung left

5961 LADBROKESCASINO.COM CLAIMING STKS — 1m 1f 218y
3:30 (3:30) (Class 5) 3-Y-O+ — **£3,238** (£963; £481; £240) **Stalls** High

Form			Horse	Jockey	RPR
1012	**1**		**Nawamees (IRE)**[14] 5577 10-9-5 73	(p) RyanMoore 11	72
			(G L Moore) *hld up: hdwy over 3f out: led over 2f out: rdn and jnd over 1f out: all out*	**2/1**[1]	
5065	**2**	*nse*	**No To Trident**[24] 5230 3-8-9 73	RichardEvans(5) 5	74
			(P D Evans) *hld up: hdwy over 3f out: chal over 1f out: sn rdn and hung rt: styd on*	**13/2**	
3035	**3**	*3 ¼*	**Prince Samos (IRE)**[40] 4744 6-9-5 70	DarryllHolland 6	65
			(E S McMahon) *hld up: hdwy over 3f out: swtchd lft over 2f out: sn rdn: hung rt over 1f out: styd on same pce fnl f*	**10/3**[2]	
1414	**4**	*5*	**Boundless Prospect (USA)**[87] 3230 9-9-2 68	JamieSpencer 7	55+
			(Ollie Pears) *dwlt: hld up: hdwy over 2f out: nt clr run: lost pl and swtchd lft over 1f out: n.d after*	**6/1**[3]	
600-	**5**	*nk*	**Champagne Dancer**[350] 5858 3-8-5 45	LukeMorris(3) 4	51
			(P D Evans) *chsd ldrs: rdn 1/2-way: outpcd over 2f out: styd on u.p ins fnl f*	**100/1**	
0501	**6**	*nse*	**Siryena**[12] 5603 3-8-7 58	(tp) DavidProbert(5) 2	55
			(George Baker) *hld up: hdwy over 2f out: rdn and edgd rt over 1f out: nt trble ldrs*	**20/1**	
0000	**7**	*2 ¾*	**Better In Heaven**[30] 5087 3-8-7 53	EddieAhern 1	44
			(H J L Dunlop) *w ldrs: rdn over 2f out: wknd over 1f out*	**40/1**	
2050	**8**	*7*	**Miss Porcia**[43] 4664 7-8-11 45	StephenDonohoe 9	27
			(P A Blockley) *w ldrs tl led over 7f out: rdn and hdd over 2f out: wknd over 1f out*	**28/1**	
03-0	**9**	*2*	**Mceldowney**[3] 5858 6-9-4 80	LeeVickers(3) 8	33
			(M C Chapman) *led: hdd over 7f out: rdn over 3f out: sn wknd*	**25/1**	
500-	**10**	*8*	**Gem Bien (USA)**[468] 2343 10-9-5 37	(p) RobertHavlin 12	15
			(T T Clement) *s.i.s: hld up: hdwy over 4f out: sn rdn: wknd over 2f out*	**200/1**	
1440	**11**	*1*	**Stage Acclaim (IRE)**[18] 5428 3-9-1 69	(p) JamesMillman(3) 3	19
			(B R Millman) *hld up: rdn and wknd over 2f out*	**12/1**	
1403	**12**	*12*	**Credential**[22] 5321 6-9-3 53	NCallan 10	—
			(John A Harris) *plld hrd: w ldrs: rdn over 2f out: sn wknd: eased fnl f*	**16/1**	

2m 8.60s (0.70) **Going Correction** +0.125s/f (Good)
WFA 3 from 6yo+ 7lb — **12** Ran SP% **113.6**
Speed ratings (Par 103): **102,101,99,95,95 95,92,87,85,79 78,68**
toteswinger: 1&2 £5.40, 1&3 £2.30, 2&3 £6.90. CSF £13.56 TOTE £2.70: £1.20, £1.60, £1.80; EX 17.50 Trifecta £166.50 Part won. Pool: £225.06, 0.20 winning units..The winner was claimed by P. D. Evans for £10,000. Siryena was claimed by B. I. Case for £15,000
Owner Paul Stamp **Bred** Kilfrush Stud Ltd **Trained** Woodingdean, E Sussex

FOCUS
A reasonable claimer. Six of the contenders had an official rating of 68 or higher, and Nawamees was attempting to win his seventh claimer in his last ten Flat starts. They went a steady pace, the first two were involved in a tight finish and were clear of the third. The principals are rated below their best.
Stage Acclaim(IRE) Official explanation: jockey said gelding never travelled

5962 LADBROKESCASINO.COM H'CAP — 5f 218y
4:00 (4:00) (Class 4) (0-85,82) 3-Y-O — **£4,857** (£1,445; £722; £360) **Stalls** Low

Form			Horse	Jockey	RPR
0343	**1**		**Errigal Lad**[21] 5358 3-8-12 **76**	NCallan 7	87
			(K A Ryan) *chsd ldr tl led 2f out: jnd over 1f out: styd on wl u.p*	**4/1**[1]	
1033	**2**	*1*	**Tadalavil**[4] 5839 3-8-10 **74**	DarryllHolland 5	82
			(M R Channon) *chsd ldrs: rdn over 2f out: sn ev ch: unable qck wl ins fnl f*	**7/1**[3]	
-210	**3**	*1 ¾*	**Credit Swap**[23] 5273 3-9-2 **80**	DaneO'Neill 9	82
			(L M Cumani) *s.i.s: hld up: rdn over 1f out: edgd rt and r.o ins fnl f: nt rch ldrs*	**7/1**[3]	
1504	**4**	*2 ¼*	**Artsu**[21] 5358 3-8-11 **75**	JamieSpencer 11	70
			(M L W Bell) *stdd s: hld up and bhd: hdwy over 1f out: sn hrd rdn: no imp ins fnl f*	**8/1**	
0001	**5**	*nk*	**The Twelve Steps**[8] 5714 3-8-9 **73** 6ex	(t) PJMcDonald 3	67
			(G A Swinbank) *hld up: rdn over 2f out: hdwy over 1f out: hung rt ins fnl f: nt trble ldrs*	**11/2**[2]	
62-1	**6**	*1 ¾*	**Luminous Gold**[137] 1738 3-8-12 **76**	AlanMunro 2	64
			(C F Wall) *chsd ldrs: rdn over 2f out: edgd rt: wknd ins fnl f*	**7/1**[3]	
0000	**7**	*nk*	**Westwood**[33] 4983 3-8-11 **75**	RobertHavlin 4	62
			(D Haydn Jones) *mid-div: rdn 1/2-way: n.d*	**50/1**	
-560	**8**	*½*	**Lord Sandicliffe (IRE)**[72] 3723 3-8-11 **75**	(p) MichaelHills 12	61
			(B W Hills) *mid-div: drvn along thrght: n.d*	**12/1**	
-123	**9**	*1 ¼*	**Mission Impossible**[103] 2732 3-8-13 **77**	LeeEnstone 10	59
			(P C Haslam) *chsd ldrs: rdn over 2f out: wknd and eased fnl f*	**16/1**	
0060	**10**	*½*	**We Have A Dream**[19] 5403 3-9-0 **78**	(b[1]) MartinDwyer 8	58
			(W R Muir) *led: rdn and hdd 2f out: wknd fnl f*	**25/1**	
5062	**11**	*hd*	**Irish Pearl (IRE)**[7] 5757 3-9-4 **82**	HayleyTurner 1	62
			(K R Burke) *prom: rdn over 2f out: wknd fnl f*	**9/1**	
2	**12**	*nk*	**Nawaahi (IRE)**[25] 5203 3-7-13 **68** oh2	DavidProbert(5) 6	47
			(K A Morgan) *mid-div: rdn over 2f out: wknd over 1f out*	**28/1**	

1m 12.94s (-0.06) **Going Correction** +0.125s/f (Good) — **12** Ran SP% **116.8**
Speed ratings (Par 103): **105,103,101,98,97 95,95,94,92,92 91,91**
toteswinger: 1&2 £9.60, 1&3 £15.10, 2&3 £19.40. CSF £30.47 CT £191.30 TOTE £4.30: £1.60, £2.60, £4.30; EX 34.20 Trifecta £281.30 Part won. Pool: £380.16, 0.40 winning units..
Owner Errigal Racing **Bred** Robin Lawson **Trained** Hambleton, N Yorks

FOCUS
A tight sprint handicap and a fair race for the grade. We Have A Dream blasted into the lead and the field raced down the centre of the course. He is rated up 9lb. The time was 1.74sec above standard, suggesting that the ground was drying out.

5963 LADBROKES.COM MAIDEN STKS — 1m 3f 183y
4:30 (4:31) (Class 5) 3-Y-O+ — **£3,238** (£963; £481; £240) **Stalls** High

Form			Horse	Jockey	RPR
3243	**1**		**Factotum**[58] 4178 4-9-7 82	DaneO'Neill 9	85+
			(L M Cumani) *a.p: chsd ldr 7f out: led 3f out: styd on wl*	**5/2**[1]	
6	**2**	*2 ¼*	**Princess Rainbow (FR)**[28] 5155 3-8-7 0	JimmyQuinn 5	76
			(Jennie Candlish) *s.i.s: hld up: plld hrd: hdwy 3f out: sn hung rt: chsd wnr over 1f out: styd on same pce fnl f*	**22/1**	
0-43	**3**	*4 ½*	**Houghton (IRE)**[52] 4372 3-8-12 72	(v[1]) RyanMoore 7	74+
			(Sir Michael Stoute) *sn pushed along in rr: hdwy 7f out: rdn over 2f out: n.m.r and lost pl over 1f out: styd on same pce*	**6/1**	
4220	**4**	*1 ¼*	**Motarid (USA)**[40] 4742 3-8-12 77	NCallan 1	72
			(T D Walford) *prom: rdn 1/2-way: hung rt and wknd over 1f out*	**4/1**[3]	
3456	**5**	*2 ¾*	**Dubai's Wonder (IRE)**[37] 4859 3-8-12 69	MichaelHills 8	68
			(B W Hills) *led: rdn and hdd 3f out: wknd over 1f out*	**13/2**	
/	**6**	*14*	**Ignotus**[149] 6-9-7 0	PJMcDonald 2	45
			(G A Swinbank) *trckd ldr: plld hrd: rdn and wknd over 2f out*	**11/4**[2]	
	7	*17*	**Seconditis** 3-8-12 0	CatherineGannon 4	18
			(Mrs N S Evans) *prom: lost pl 8f out: wknd 5f out*	**100/1**	
	8	*72*	**Prophet's Star** 3-8-12 0	EddieAhern 3	—
			(H J L Dunlop) *hld up: rdn and wknd over 5f out*	**33/1**	
	9	*17*	**Hallys Goal (IRE)**[16] 6-9-7 0	(p) AlanMunro 10	—
			(M Mullineaux) *s.s: sn wl bhd*	**250/1**	

2m 34.75s (0.85) **Going Correction** +0.125s/f (Good)
WFA 3 from 4yo+ 9lb — **9** Ran SP% **111.5**
Speed ratings (Par 103): **102,100,97,96,94 85,74,26,14**
toteswinger: 1&2 £7.50, 1&3 £4.10, 2&3 £12.70. CSF £55.69 TOTE £2.80: £1.30, £4.10, £1.80; EX 41.80 Trifecta £194.70 Pool: £436.79, 1.66 winning units.
Owner Scuderia Rencati Srl & Mrs John Magnier **Bred** Azienda Agricola Francesca **Trained** Newmarket, Suffolk

FOCUS
The market leader for this maiden was a half-brother to Falbrav, who set a decent standard on the pick of his form but had a slightly patchy profile. He faced opposition from a well-related Sir Michael Stoute-trained runner who had headgear applied for the first time and a Grade 2 hurdle winner, making his Flat debut. The winner did not have to be at his best and the form makes sense at face value.

5964 LADBROKES.COM H'CAP — 1m 60y
5:00 (5:02) (Class 5) (0-75,75) 3-Y-O — **£3,885** (£1,156; £577; £288) **Stalls** High

Form			Horse	Jockey	RPR
4150	**1**		**Shanzu**[46] 4572 3-9-1 **72**	DaneO'Neill 2	81
			(H Candy) *led: pushed along and hdd over 3f out: rdn over 1f out: rallied to ld ins fnl f: edgd rt: styd on*	**22/1**	
-452	**2**	*nk*	**Totem Flower (IRE)**[30] 5098 3-8-13 **70**	MartinDwyer 8	78
			(R Charlton) *trckd ldr: plld hrd: led over 3f out: rdn over 1f out: edgd rt and hdd ins fnl f: styd on*	**5/1**[2]	
-431	**3**	*½*	**Jennie Jerome (IRE)**[28] 5162 3-8-10 **74**	MJMurphy(7) 14	81
			(L M Cumani) *hld up: hdwy over 2f out: rdn whn nt clr run and swtchd lft ins fnl f: r.o*	**2/1**[1]	
2005	**4**	*1 ¾*	**Challow Hills (USA)**[28] 5149 3-8-8 **65**	MichaelHills 10	68
			(B W Hills) *chsd ldrs: rdn over 3f out: styd on*	**12/1**	
0060	**5**	*hd*	**We're Delighted**[44] 4650 3-8-11 **68**	PJMcDonald 13	71
			(T D Walford) *hld up: hdwy 1/2-way: rdn over 2f out: styd on*	**20/1**	
543	**6**	*¾*	**Bois Joli (IRE)**[12] 5605 3-9-4 **75**	JimmyQuinn 6	76
			(M Botti) *s.i.s: hld up: hdwy and hmpd over 2f out: nt rch ldrs*	**12/1**	
2-06	**7**	*nk*	**Cozy Tiger (USA)**[21] 5361 3-8-11 **68**	StephenDonohoe 1	68+
			(W J Musson) *s.i.s: hld up: swtchd rt and hdwy over 1f out: nt rch ldrs*	**50/1**	

0031 **8** ½ **Lilburn (IRE)**[28] 5161 3-8-12 **69**........................(p) EddieAhern 4 68
(J R Fanshawe) *hld up: hdwy over 1f out: sn rdn: styd on same pce fnl f* **12/1**

3412 **9** shd **Suzi Spends (IRE)**[11] 5630 3-9-1 **72**........................ JohnEgan 9 71
(H J Collingridge) *chsd ldrs: pushed along over 3f out: no ex ins fnl f* **7/1**[3]

0020 **10** 3¼ **Brave Mave**[23] 5291 3-8-10 **67**........................(b) RyanMoore 3 58
(W Jarvis) *hld up: hung rt over 2f out: styd on ins fnl f: n.d* **8/1**

1144 **11** ¾ **Charlevoix (IRE)**[32] 5019 3-9-0 **71**........................ AlanMunro 7 61
(C F Wall) *chsd ldrs: rdn over 3f out: wknd over 1f out* **20/1**

-540 **12** 2½ **Sunny Sprite**[90] 3117 3-8-7 **67**........................ LukeMorris(3) 11 51
(J M P Eustace) *hld up: hdwy 1/2-way: sn rdn: wknd over 2f out* **66/1**

0200 **13** 1 **Broughtons Flight (IRE)**[47] 4524 3-8-4 **61**........................ TPO'Shea 12 42
(W J Musson) *hld up: rdn and wknd over 1f out* **80/1**

0-35 **14** 23 **Nowzdetime (IRE)**[123] 3-9-0 **71**........................(b1) TPQueally 5 —
(M G Quinlan) *chsd ldrs: rdn and hung lft over 3f out: hung rt and wknd over 2f out* **50/1**

1m 46.21s (1.11) **Going Correction** +0.125s/f (Good) **14** Ran SP% **117.2**
Speed ratings (Par 101): **99,98,98,96,96 95,95,94,94,91 90,88,87,64**
toteswinger: 1&2 £24.70, 1&3 £14.30, 2&3 £4.10. CSF £120.16 CT £335.89 TOTE £29.30: £6.90, £1.20, £1.60; EX 177.50 Trifecta £320.50 Part won. Pool: £433.18, 0.20 winning units. Place 6 £ 58.79, Place 5 £ 18.54.
Owner Baraka Partnership **Bred** Lakin Bloodstock And H And W Thornton **Trained** Kingston Warren, Oxon

FOCUS
Much of the interest in this race centred around clear favourite Jennie Jerome, who was attempting to supplement her stylish handicap debut win at Yarmouth last month. The race was run at a fair pace and the first two were prominent throughout. Ordinary form, but sound.
T/Plt: £95.60 to a £1 stake. Pool: £93,258.23. 711.99 winning tickets. T/Qpdt: £7.60 to a £1 stake. Pool: £6,771.08. 655.60 winning tickets. CR

5538 MUSSELBURGH (R-H)
Monday, September 15

OFFICIAL GOING: Soft (good to soft in places; 7.1)
Wind: Light across Weather: Overcast and showers

5965 ROSIE BELL 40TH BIRTHDAY CELEBRATION H'CAP 7f 30y
2:20 (2:21) (Class 6) (0-65,65) 3-Y-0+ **£2,590** (£770; £385; £192) **Stalls** High

Form RPR

/016 **1** **Keys Of Cyprus**[11] 5634 6-9-4 **63**........................ AdrianTNicholls 6 73
(D Nicholls) *midfield: hdwy over 2f out: rdn over 1f out: styd on ins fnl f to ld last 75yds* **11/2**[2]

0412 **2** ½ **Mr Lu**[15] 5544 3-9-1 **64**........................ RoystonFfrench 4 71
(Miss L A Perratt) *trckd ldrs: hdwy 3f out: rdn to ld 2f out: drvn over 1f out: hdd and no ex last 75yds* **9/1**

0416 **3** ¾ **Grand Diamond (IRE)**[34] 4949 4-9-5 **64**........................(p) DanielTudhope 8 71
(J S Goldie) *midfield: hdwy over 2f out: rdn over 1f out: kpt on u.p ins fnl f* **11/1**

1010 **4** nk **Wisdom's Kiss**[28] 5156 4-9-6 **65**........................(b) GrahamGibbons 7 71
(J D Bethell) *midfield: hdwy on outer over 2f out: rdn to chal over 1f out and ev ch: drvn and edgd lft ent fnl f: kpt on same pce* **10/1**

6130 **5** 1½ **Grit (IRE)**[20] 5378 3-9-0 **63**........................ TonyCulhane 1 63
(M R Channon) *in rr: hdwy 2f out: sn rdn and kpt on ins fnl f: nrst fin* **20/1**

004 **6** ½ **Beetuna (IRE)**[45] 4606 3-9-2 **65**........................ TomEaves 11 64
(B Smart) *bhd: rdn along over 2f out: hdwy over 1f out: styd on wl fnl f: nrst fin* **18/1**

5423 **7** shd **Bold Indian (IRE)**[44] 4629 4-8-11 **59**........................ NeilBrown(3) 10 60
(Miss L A Perratt) *bhd: hdwy 2f out: rdn and kpt on ins fnl f: nrst fin* **9/1**

0303 **8** nk **Rainbow Fox**[19] 5392 4-9-5 **64**........................ PaulHanagan 12 64
(R A Fahey) *towards rr: rdn along over 2f out: styd on u.p appr fnl f: nrst fin* **7/1**[3]

5330 **9** ½ **Sands Of Barra (IRE)**[3] 5871 5-8-10 **60**........................ KellyHarrison(5) 2 58
(I W McInnes) *led for 1f: cl up: rdn along and ev ch over 2f out: drvn and edgd rt over 1f out: wknd* **8/1**

403 **10** ½ **Chatanoogachoochoo**[17] 5445 3-9-1 **64**........................ RobertWinston 3 59
(G A Swinbank) *in rr: pushed along over 2f out: hdwy over 1f out: kpt on ins fnl f* **10/1**

3032 **11** 1 **Pintano**[16] 5501 3-8-11 **65**........................(b) FrederikTylicki(5) 5 57
(J Howard Johnson) *prom: rdn along 3f out: drvn 2f out and grad wknd* **16/1**

5015 **12** nk **Finsbury**[17] 5455 5-9-2 **61**........................ NickyMackay 14 55+
(J S Goldie) *s.i.s and in rr: hdwy on inner over 2f out: rdn to chse ldrs whn n.m.r over 1f out: no imp after* **5/1**[1]

6-06 **13** ½ **Zamalik (USA)**[61] 4073 5-8-12 **60**........................ AndrewMullen(3) 9 52
(Mrs A Duffield) *chsd ldrs on inner: rdn along over 2f out: drvn over 1f out and grad wknd* **25/1**

5000 **14** 5 **Dhhamaan (IRE)**[19] 5397 3-8-13 **65**........................(b) MichaelJStainton(3) 13 42
(Mrs R A Carr) *led after 1f: rdn along 3f out: hdd 2f out: sn drvn and wknd* **66/1**

1m 31.25s (0.95) **Going Correction** +0.175s/f (Good)
WFA 3 from 4yo+ 4lb **14** Ran SP% **123.4**
Speed ratings (Par 101): **101,100,99,99,97 96,96,96,95,95 94,93,93,87**
toteswinger: 1&2 £7.70, 1&3 £16.40, 2&3 £18.60. CSF £54.87 CT £541.03 TOTE £7.20: £2.70, £2.20, £4.60; EX 34.40.
Owner The Beasley Gees **Bred** Juddmonte Farms **Trained** Sessay, N Yorks

FOCUS
This was a wide-open handicap, run at a sound pace, and it saw many in with a chance at the two-furlong pole. The form looks sound.
Bold Indian(IRE) Official explanation: jockey said gelding was denied a clear run

5966 RACING UK THE UK'S BEST RACECOURSES LIVE (S) STKS 7f 30y
2:50 (2:53) (Class 6) 2-Y-0 **£1,942** (£578; £288; £144) **Stalls** High

Form RPR

2021 **1** **Nchike**[8] 5715 2-9-2 56........................(v) AdrianTNicholls 10 67
(D Nicholls) *trckd ldrs: hdwy 3f out: rdn to chse ldr wl over 1f out: drvn and hung lft ent fnl f: styd on u.p to ld nr line* **9/2**[2]

5532 **2** shd **Digit**[14] 5560 2-8-7 60 ow1........................ TomEaves 1 58
(B Smart) *cl up: led 3f out: rdn wl over 1f out and sn hung bdly lft: drvn ins fnl f: hdd and no ex nr fin* **5/1**[3]

400 **3** ¾ **Svindal (IRE)**[6] 5778 2-8-11 0........................(b1) SilvestreDeSousa 2 60
(K A Ryan) *a.p: effrt 3f out: rdn 2f out and ev ch tl drvn and one pce wl ins fnl f* **33/1**

4303 **4** 3 **Little Tokyo (USA)**[14] 5560 2-8-11 63........................(b) RobertWinston 8 53
(J Howard Johnson) *sn led: pushed along and hdd 3f out: drvn wl over 1f out: kpt on same pce* **8/1**

3U03 **5** nk **Just Five (IRE)**[54] 4290 2-8-11 50........................ TonyHamilton 3 52
(M Dods) *s.i.s and bhd: hdwy 3f out: rdn along 2f out: styd on ins fnl f: nrst fin* **20/1**

00 **6** 2¾ **Abuelito John (IRE)**[77] 3568 2-8-11 0........................(v1) PatCosgrave 5 45
(D Carroll) *chsd ldrs: rdn along over 2f out: sn drvn and no imp* **66/1**

053 **7** shd **Jessica Mary (IRE)**[8] 5715 2-8-7 0 ow1........................ DavidAllan 4 41
(D Carroll) *nvr nr ldrs* **9/1**

5004 **8** ½ **El Bobby (IRE)**[15] 5541 2-8-11 50........................ GrahamGibbons 7 44
(J R Weymes) *towards rr: hdwy on inner and in tch 2f out: sn rdn and btn* **33/1**

0000 **9** 6 **Smoke Me A Kipper (IRE)**[6] 5774 2-8-3 48........(v) AndrewMullen(3) 13 24
(Mrs A Duffield) *a towards rr* **100/1**

0450 **10** ½ **The Kilkenny Kat (IRE)**[11] 5632 2-8-11 63........(b1) PaulHanagan 11 28
(T D Easterby) *in tch: hdwy to chse ldrs 3f out: rdn over 2f out and sn btn* **10/1**

4206 **11** 4 **Identity**[13] 5591 2-8-6 67........................ ChrisCatlin 9 13
(E J O'Neill) *sn rdn along and a in rr* **5/2**[1]

0 **12** 6 **Nothing To Worry (IRE)**[84] 3323 2-8-11 0........................ TonyCulhane 12 3
(M R Channon) *a towards rr* **8/1**

1m 33.51s (3.21) **Going Correction** +0.175s/f (Good) **12** Ran SP% **117.9**
Speed ratings (Par 93): **88,87,87,83,83 80,80,79,72,72 67,60**
toteswinger: 1&2 £4.40, 1&3 £28.80, 2&3 £34.20. CSF £25.96 TOTE £4.80: £2.10, £2.00, £7.80; EX 28.80.There was no bid for the winner
Owner Middleham Park Racing XXXVII **Bred** J And Mrs S Cleeve **Trained** Sessay, N Yorks
■ Stewards' Enquiry : Adrian T Nicholls two-day ban: used whip with excessive frequency (Sep 29-30)

FOCUS
A competitive little seller and decent form for the grade with the winner close to the level of his previous win.

NOTEBOOK
Nchike took a while to get off the mark, his recent victory in this grade at Thirsk coming at the tenth attempt, and he again looked a likely player with him being the only previous winner in the field. Back up to 7f, he seemed happy enough to chase the early leaders, but took an age to hit top gear and only got on top close home. He is clearly going the right way. (tchd 4-1)
Digit may well have won had she kept straight and she also carried 1lb overweight. Never far from the lead, she went on readily over two out, but started to wander left and ended up more towards the stands' side. She was just run out of it close home, but can find a race at this level. (op 11-2 tchd 7-1)
Svindal(IRE), beaten out of sight in this grade last week, gave an improved showing back on this less testing ground and was clearly aided by the first-time blinkers. (op 28-1)
Little Tokyo(USA), who stayed on late in a 6f claimer at Hamilton earlier in the month, was probably made too much use of on this step back up in trip and could find no more from a furlong out. (op 9-1)
Just Five(IRE) stayed on down the straight and was going on close home, but did not do enough to suggest he is ready to win. (op 25-1)
Identity, not beaten far in a nursery at Southwell earlier in the month, took a keen hold in rear and never threatened to get into it. The ground should not have been a problem. Official explanation: jockey said filly never travelled (op 11-4)
Nothing To Worry(IRE) lost his position early and looks to have little ability. (op 7-1 tchd 6-1)

5967 TOTESUPER7 H'CAP 1m 6f
3:20 (3:20) (Class 5) (0-75,75) 3-Y-0+ **£3,885** (£1,156; £577; £288) **Stalls** High

Form RPR

-320 **1** **Merchant Of Dubai**[39] 4784 3-8-9 **72**........................ FrederikTylicki(5) 2 88+
(G A Swinbank) *in tch: hdwy to trck ldrs 1/2-way: chsd ldr over 3f out: led over 2f out and sn rdn clr: easily* **9/2**[1]

5560 **2** 7 **Its Moon (IRE)**[11] 5637 4-8-13 **60**........................(b1) GrahamGibbons 5 65
(T D Walford) *prom: hdwy to ld 5f out: rdn along 3f out: sn hdd: drvn and kpt on appr fnl f: no ch w wnr* **10/1**

0560 **3** 1 **Red Wine**[30] 5092 9-9-7 **75**........................ StacyRenwick(7) 12 78
(A J McCabe) *hld up in rr: stdy hdwy on outer wl over 2f out: rdn over 1f out: kpt on ins fnl f* **16/1**

2513 **4** shd **Kyber**[15] 5540 7-8-11 **63**........................ GaryBartley(5) 8 66
(J S Goldie) *trckd ldrs: hdwy on outer 3f out: rdn along 2f out: drvn and kpt on same pce ent fnl f* **7/1**[3]

3115 **5** 3¼ **Trip The Light**[19] 5406 3-8-10 **68**........................(v) PaulHanagan 4 66
(R A Fahey) *midfield: hdwy to chse ldrs 3f out: rdn along over 2f out: drvn and one pce fr wl over 1f out* **8/1**

3431 **6** 6 **Danzatrice**[15] 5540 6-9-9 **70**........................ RobertWinston 3 60
(C W Thornton) *hld up and bhd: hdwy over 3f out: rdn along 2f out: sn no imp* **11/2**[2]

-012 **7** 1½ **Master At Arms**[17] 5476 5-9-11 **72**........................ PatCosgrave 14 60
(Daniel Mark Loughnane, Ire) *a in midfield* **10/1**

1414 **8** 5 **Fossgate**[33] 4966 7-9-5 **66**........................ FrancisNorton 1 47
(J D Bethell) *hld up towards rr: hdwy over 3f out: rdn along over 2f out: sn no imp* **9/1**

9 1 **Zarkozy (IRE)**[11] 5655 3-8-1 **59**........................(b1) SilvestreDeSousa 11 39
(D Broad, Ire) *chsd ldrs on inner: rdn along over 5f out: sn wknd* **16/1**

4554 **10** 1 **Flamed Amazement**[15] 5540 4-9-2 **63**........................(p) TonyHamilton 10 41
(L Lungo) *chsd ldr: pushed along 1/2-way: rdn over 4f out and sn wknd* **12/1**

4132 **11** 11 **Nero West (FR)**[15] 5540 7-9-11 **72**........................(b) TomEaves 6 35
(Miss L A Perratt) *led: rdn along and hdd over 4f out: wknd 3f out* **7/1**[3]

R6 **R** **Kristiansand**[60] 2849 8-8-9 **56** oh3........................ RoystonFfrench 9 —
(P Monteith) *ref to r - tk no part* **25/1**

3m 5.76s (0.46) **Going Correction** +0.175s/f (Good)
WFA 3 from 4yo+ 11lb **12** Ran SP% **121.2**
Speed ratings (Par 103): **105,101,100,100,98 95,94,91,90,90 83,—**
toteswinger: 1&2 £26.40, 1&3 £39.10, 2&3 £53.80. CSF £50.92 CT £675.38 TOTE £6.80: £2.20, £3.80, £4.90; EX 95.40.
Owner Highland Racing 2 **Bred** A Smith **Trained** Melsonby, N Yorks

FOCUS
A modest staying handicap and, while it was another open heat, it could hardly have produced a more decisive winner, rated up 10lb. The form looks sound.
Danzatrice Official explanation: jockey said mare never travelled
Fossgate Official explanation: jockey said gelding never travelled
Zarkozy(IRE) Official explanation: jockey said colt hung right-handed throughout
Nero West(FR) Official explanation: jockey said gelding ran flat

5968 CMYK DIGITAL SOLUTIONS CLAIMING STKS 1m 1f
3:50 (3:51) (Class 5) 3-Y-0+ **£2,590** (£770; £385; £192) **Stalls** High

Form RPR

3255 **1** **Wind Star**[41] 4699 5-9-5 78........................ NeilBrown(3) 3 87+
(G A Swinbank) *trckd ldrs: smooth hdwy to ld 2 1/2f out: clr wl over 1f out: comf* **5/2**[1]

5000 **2** 4 1/2 **Fremen (USA)**[16] 5503 8-10-0 86 .... AdrianTNicholls 13 80
(D Nicholls) *hld up towards rr: hdwy whn n.m.r over 3f out: swtchd lft and rdn 2f out: styd on to chse wnr appr fnl f: sn drvn and no imp* **3/1**[2]

204/ **3** 1 3/4 **Desert Destiny**[262] 5845 8-9-4 85 ....(p) TonyHamilton 2 66
(C Grant) *hld up: hdwy over 3f out: rdn to chse ldrs 2f out: sn drvn and kpt on same pce appr fnl f* **20/1**

430 **4** 1/2 **Jane Of Arc (FR)**[14] 5559 4-8-1 45 ....(p) KellyHarrison(5) 4 53
(J S Goldie) *cl up: rdn along 3f out: drvn 2f out and kpt on same pce* **11/1**

-000 **5** 1 1/4 **Incline (IRE)**[11] 5654 9-8-11 0 .... FrankieMcDonald 8 55+
(R McGlinchey, Ire) *hld up in rr: hdwy whn nt clr run over 2f out: swtchd lft and then rt: several positions after and nt clr run over 1f out: swtchd lft ent fnl f: styd on: nrst fin* **5/1**[3]

000 **6** 3 **Middlemarch (IRE)**[17] 5454 8-9-2 65 ....(v) GaryBartley(5) 11 59
(J S Goldie) *in rr tl sme late hdwy* **16/1**

152 **7** 2 1/2 **Abbondanza (IRE)**[77] 3548 5-9-12 87 ....(p) TomEaves 5 58
(Miss L A Perratt) *t.k.h: prom: effrt 3f out: sn rdn along and wknd 2f out* **5/1**[3]

-000 **8** 1 3/4 **Ignition**[45] 4596 6-8-8 50 ....(p) ChrisCatlin 12 36
(A Kirtley) *led: rdn along 3f out: sn hdd and grad wknd* **66/1**

0044 **9** 1 3/4 **Carry On Cleo**[20] 5380 3-8-1 51 ....(b) FrancisNorton 1 31
(A Berry) *prom: rdn along over 3f out and sn wknd* **20/1**

000 **10** 3 1/4 **Mean Machine (IRE)**[39] 4785 6-9-0 40 ....(t) RobbieEgan(7) 6 38
(D Flood) *in rr fr 1/2-way* **100/1**

060- **11** 21 **Writ (IRE)**[483] 1905 6-9-7 73 .... RoystonFfrench 10 —
(Miss L A Perratt) *chsd ldrs: rdn along over 3f out: sn wknd* **22/1**

2320 **12** 3 1/4 **August Gale (USA)**[74] 3641 3-9-4 72 .... DaleGibson 7 —
(G P Kelly) *chsd ldrs: rdn along pover 3f out and sn wknd* **25/1**

000- **13** 8 **Brace Of Doves**[64] 5838 6-8-10 51 ow6 .... GarryWhillans(7) 9 —
(D W Whillans) *a towards rr* **66/1**

1m 56.77s (2.07) **Going Correction** +0.175s/f (Good)
WFA 3 from 4yo+ 6lb 13 Ran SP% **122.8**
Speed ratings (Par 103): **97,93,91,91,89 87,85,83,81,79 60,57,50**
toteswinger: 1&2 £3.30, 1&3 £14.10, 2&3 £16.70. CSF £9.44 TOTE £3.80: £1.50, £1.50, £6.20; EX 11.40.The winner was claimed by J. Babb for £16,000. Incline was claimed by R. E. R. Williams for £5,000.
Owner B Harker, R Hall & Dr C Emmerson **Bred** Mrs N F M Sampson **Trained** Melsonby, N Yorks

FOCUS
A fair claimer in which the fourth looks the best guide to the form.
Incline(IRE) ◆ Official explanation: jockey said, regarding running and riding, that his orders were to drop the gelding in, make sure it got the trip, do his best to make a run up the home straight, adding that it moved poorly on bend turn into straight and felt he was unable to let it down to the full extent; trainer confirmed, adding that the gelding has suffered from leg problems and that it ran as well as he expected; vet added gelding was found to be lame after two examinations.

5969 BETFAIR SCOTTISH RACING FORTNIGHT NURSERY 5f
4:20 (4:21) (Class 3) (0-90,88) 2-Y-O
£7,477 (£2,239; £1,119; £560; £279; £140) **Stalls** Low

Form RPR

6630 **1** **Cerito**[23] 5294 2-9-0 88 .... MatthewDavies(7) 4 91
(M R Channon) *prom: led 1f out: drvn and hld on wl* **11/2**[3]

0520 **2** nk **Fivefootnumberone (IRE)**[37] 4874 2-9-1 82 ....(v[1]) GrahamGibbons 1 84
(J J Quinn) *prom: drvn wl over 1f out: kpt on wl fnl f but a hld* **6/1**

2322 **3** 3/4 **Majuba (USA)**[34] 4948 2-9-1 82 .... PaulHanagan 6 81
(K A Ryan) *dwlt: bhd: hdwy on outside and ev ch appr fnl f: no ex wl ins fnl f* **4/1**[2]

143 **4** 1 **Go Nani Go**[101] 2775 2-9-5 86 .... TomEaves 2 82
(B Smart) *hld up: hdwy to chse ldrs appr fnl f: rdn and one pce ins fnl f* **10/1**

2431 **5** 1 1/4 **Sir Geoffrey (IRE)**[11] 5633 2-8-10 77 ow1 .... PatCosgrave 10 68
(A J McCabe) *led to 1f out: kpt on same pce* **6/1**

2310 **6** 2 **Secret Venue**[24] 5244 2-8-9 76 .... TonyHamilton 5 60
(Jedd O'Keeffe) *bhd: rdn 1/2-way: effrt u.p over 1f out: no imp fnl f* **7/1**

61 **7** 1 1/2 **Mary Mason**[16] 5500 2-8-8 78 .... AndrewMullen(3) 8 57
(Mrs A Duffield) *cl up tl rdn and wknd over 1f out* **18/1**

5011 **8** 1 **Mythical Blue (IRE)**[7] 5466 2-8-6 78 ....(t) WilliamCarson(5) 7 53
(S C Williams) *chsd ldrs: stmbld after 1f: effrt 2f out: edgd rt and sn wknd* **11/4**[1]

62.24 secs (1.84) **Going Correction** +0.375s/f (Good) 8 Ran SP% **117.5**
Speed ratings (Par 99): **100,99,98,96,94 91,89,87**
toteswinger: 1&2 £7.30, 1&3 £5.30, 2&3 £6.60. CSF £39.33 CT £148.81 TOTE £7.00: £2.00, £2.10, £1.40; EX 38.10.
Owner Mrs M Findlay **Bred** Nicola And Eleanor Kent **Trained** West Ilsley, Berks
■ Stewards' Enquiry : Graham Gibbons one-day ban: used whip with excessive frequency (Sep 29)
Andrew Mullen three-day ban: careless riding (Sep 29-Oct 1)

FOCUS
A good nursery although nothing appeared especially well treated.

NOTEBOOK
Cerito was highly tried after winning his maiden at Bath, running in the Norfolk Stakes and a Listed race at Newbury. Well beaten in heavy ground at the Curragh latest, the less testing conditions here were likely to suit and his capable rider claimed a valuable 7lb. Soon chasing the leaders, he took a narrow lead over a furlong out and stayed on strongly for pressure, always doing enough to hold the runner-up. He will struggle to defy a rise in a better race, though. (op 5-1 tchd 9-2)
Fivefootnumberone(IRE), a good second off a 2lb lower mark at York two starts back, ran poorly at Redcar next time, but came right back to his best here and clearly appreciated the give underfoot. He was closing on the winner and may be worth another try at 6f. (op 15-2)
Majuba(USA), who has finished runner-up in two course-and-distance nurseries, had been nudged up another 3lb, but he again ran well back in third. Held up early, he made his headway wide and deserves to find a race before long. (op 5-1 tchd 11-2)
Go Nani Go has not built on his debut promise and looked on a stiff mark for this nursery debut. He had been off since June, but settled better and was close enough if good enough over a furlong out, in the end being unable to quicken. (op 6-1)
Sir Geoffrey(IRE) needs to improve to win off this sort of mark. (op 7-1 tchd 15-2)
Mythical Blue(IRE) has been transformed by the fitting of a tongue-tie and a drop back to 5f, but he didn't seem to handle the ground and could not complete the hat-trick. Official explanation: trainer said colt was unsuited by the good to soft (soft in places) ground (op 3-1 tchd 7-2)

5970 RECTANGLE GROUP H'CAP 5f
4:50 (4:50) (Class 5) (0-70,69) 3-Y-O+ **£3,885** (£1,156; £577; £288) **Stalls** Low

Form RPR

0003 **1** **King Of Swords (IRE)**[8] 5719 4-9-2 67 .... FrederikTylicki(5) 11 76
(N Tinkler) *chsd ldrs: drvn to ld over 1f out: edgd lft and kpt on strly fnl f* **11/2**[2]

0250 **2** 1/2 **Lambency (IRE)**[44] 4653 5-8-2 53 .... KellyHarrison(5) 13 60
(J S Goldie) *hld up: hdwy 2f out: kpt on wl fnl f: wnt 2nd cl home* **14/1**

0054 **3** 3/4 **Botham (USA)**[19] 5389 4-8-4 50 oh1 .... ChrisCatlin 8 54
(J S Goldie) *bhd: hdwy centre over 1f out: r.o wl fnl f: nrst fin* **10/1**[3]

506 **4** nse **Windjammer**[8] 5719 4-9-1 61 ....(b) DavidAllan 12 65
(T D Easterby) *w ldrs on outside: ev ch over 1f out to ins fnl f: no ex* **10/1**[3]

3544 **5** nk **Blazing Heights**[5] 5796 5-9-9 69 .... DanielTudhope 7 72
(J S Goldie) *hld up: hdwy over 1f out: r.o fnl f: hld nr fin* **7/4**[1]

5065 **6** 1 3/4 **Jojesse**[17] 5452 4-8-4 50 oh5 .... PaulQuinn 10 47
(G A Swinbank) *bhd tl kpt on fnl f: nvr rchd ldrs* **14/1**

1025 **7** 3/4 **Raccoon (IRE)**[19] 5398 8-9-3 63 .... TomEaves 4 57
(Mrs R A Carr) *led to over 1f out: sn rdn and no ex* **12/1**

054 **8** 1/2 **Molly Two**[23] 5261 3-8-5 52 .... AndrewElliott 9 44
(L A Mullaney) *w ldrs tl wknd appr fnl f* **11/2**[2]

6060 **9** 1 3/4 **Jonny Ebeneezer**[4] 5817 9-9-0 60 ....(b) TonyCulhane 2 46
(D Flood) *stdd s: pushed along in rr 2f out: nvr on terms* **18/1**

0005 **10** 1 1/4 **Lambrini Lace (IRE)**[25] 5201 3-8-7 56 ow1 .... RussellKennemore(3) 1 38
(Mrs L Williamson) *prom tl rdn and wknd fr 2f out* **22/1**

1036 **11** 4 1/2 **Mr Rooney (IRE)**[19] 5398 5-8-12 58 .... FrancisNorton 5 23
(A Berry) *midfield: drvn 1/2-way: hung rt and sn wknd* **14/1**

62.11 secs (1.71) **Going Correction** +0.375s/f (Good)
WFA 3 from 4yo+ 1lb 11 Ran SP% **122.6**
Speed ratings (Par 103): **101,100,99,98,98 95,94,93,90,88 81**
toteswinger: 1&2 £15.90, 1&3 £10.80, 2&3 £16.10. CSF £83.49 CT £784.03 TOTE £6.60: £2.20, £3.60, £3.20; EX 109.80.
Owner P Alderson & J Raybould **Bred** Maurice G McAuley **Trained** Langton, N Yorks

FOCUS
Just a moderate sprint handicap. The winner ran to this year's form and the runner-up to his 5f best.
Mr Rooney(IRE) Official explanation: jockey said gelding hung right throughout

5971 SCOTTISH RACING H'CAP 1m 4f
5:20 (5:24) (Class 6) (0-65,65) 3-Y-O+ **£2,590** (£770; £385; £192) **Stalls** High

Form RPR

5242 **1** **Chookie Hamilton**[15] 5543 4-9-4 60 .... TomEaves 13 67
(Miss L A Perratt) *stdd bhd ldrs on ins: lost pl after 4f: hdwy over 2f out: led 1f out: edgd lft ins fnl f: drvn out* **8/1**

3003 **2** 3/4 **Forrest Flyer (IRE)**[15] 5543 4-8-5 54 .... LanceBetts(7) 3 60
(Miss L A Perratt) *led: rdn over 2f out: hdd 1f out: kpt on u.p towards fin* **12/1**

5642 **3** hd **Always Brave**[19] 5388 3-8-12 63 .... RoystonFfrench 11 68
(M Johnston) *in tch: drvn over 3f out: rallied and ev ch ins fnl f: kpt on: hld nr fin* **4/1**[2]

6031 **4** 2 3/4 **Three Strings (USA)**[17] 5456 5-9-2 61 ....(p) NeilBrown(3) 7 62
(P D Niven) *racd wd in midfield: effrt over 2f out: kpt on u.p fnl f* **10/3**[1]

0-33 **5** nk **Summer Lodge**[13] 5593 5-9-5 61 .... PatCosgrave 4 62
(A J McCabe) *hld up: hdwy over 2f out: drifted to far rail fr over 1f out: kpt on fnl f: no imp* **14/1**

6212 **6** shd **Elite Land**[14] 5559 5-9-6 65 .... MissSCheam(3) 6 65
(K A Ryan) *hld up: hdwy on outside 3f out: no imp fr wl over 1f out* **5/1**[3]

0022 **7** 1/2 **Edas**[17] 5456 6-9-2 65 ....(p) JamieKyne(7) 10 65
(J J Quinn) *in tch: smooth hdwy over 2f out: rdn and ev ch over 1f out: wknd ins fnl f* **7/1**

0644 **8** nse **Fever**[17] 5456 4-9-5 61 .... GrahamGibbons 8 61
(M W Easterby) *prom: rdn 3f out: ev ch over 1f out: sn no ex* **5/1**[3]

2534 **9** 14 **Mister Fizzbomb (IRE)**[22] 5305 5-9-9 65 ....(v) RobertWinston 12 42
(J S Wainwright) *t.k.h: cl up tl rdn and wknd fr 2f out: t.o* **16/1**

1144 **10** 19 **Eijaaz (IRE)**[53] 4331 7-9-5 61 .... DO'Donohoe 5 8
(G A Harker) *dwlt: rdn in rr over 4f out: sn struggling: t.o* **20/1**

5240 **11** 20 **Not Now Lewis (IRE)**[88] 3162 4-8-8 55 .... FrederikTylicki(5) 2 —
(F P Murtagh) *t.k.h: chsd ldrs tl rdn and wknd over 2f out: t.o* **28/1**

2m 41.35s (1.65) **Going Correction** +0.175s/f (Good)
WFA 3 from 4yo+ 9lb 11 Ran SP% **128.5**
Speed ratings (Par 101): **101,100,100,98,98 98,97,97,88,75 62**
toteswinger: 1&2 £11.70, 1&3 £6.50, 2&3 £14.40. CSF £109.35 CT £455.26 TOTE £11.90: £3.10, £4.10, £2.10; EX 63.00 Place 6 £ 279.64, Place 5 £ 92.35.
Owner Raeburn Brick Limited **Bred** D And J Raeburn **Trained** Carluke, S Lanarks

FOCUS
Any number were in with a chance in this and they spread out right across the course in the straight. Linda Perratt was responsible for the first two. This is straightforward form.
T/Jkpt: Not won. T/Plt: £2,376.80 to a £1 stake. Pool: £89,703.47. 27.55 winning tickets. T/Qpdt: £90.60 to a £1 stake. Pool: £5,993.50. 48.90 winning tickets. JR

5632 REDCAR (L-H)
Monday, September 15
5972 Meeting Abandoned - Waterlogged

5979 - 5986a (Foreign Racing) - See Raceform Interactive

5850 CHANTILLY (R-H)
Monday, September 15

OFFICIAL GOING: Good

5987a PRIX D'AUMALE (GROUP 3) (FILLIES) 1m
2:05 (2:11) 2-Y-O **£29,412** (£11,765; £8,824; £5,882; £2,941)

RPR

1 **Soneva (USA)**[19] 2-8-9 .... CSoumillon 4 101
(Y De Nicolay, France) *racd in 2nd: pushed along to chal 1 1/2f out: led narrowly fnl strides* **4/1**[3]

2 nse **Article Rare (USA)**[23] 5301 2-8-9 .... ACrastus 1 101
(E Lellouche, France) *led: pushed along 2f out: drvn whn pressed 1 1/2f out: r.o gamely: hdd fnl strides* **14/1**

3 2 1/2 **Denomination (USA)**[29] 5139 2-8-9 .... TGillet 5 95
(Mme C Head-Maarek, France) *in tch: 4th 1/2-way: drvn 1 1/2f out: styd on same pce* **29/10**[2]

4 1 **Ana Americana (FR)**[23] 5301 2-8-9 .... SPasquier 6 93
(P Demercastel, France) *hld up in last: pushed along 2f out: styd on fnl furlnog to take 4th but n.d* **11/10**[1]

5 hd **Jet D'Eau (FR)**[23] 5300 2-8-9 ....(b) THuet 2 93
(R Pritchard-Gordon, France) *in tch: 3rd 1/2-way: drvn 2f out: one pce fr over 1f out* **20/1**

6 2 **Queen America (FR)**[8] 5739 2-8-9 .... OPeslier 3 88
(Robert Collet, France) *hld up in 5th: effrt 1 1/2f out: n.d* **7/1**

1m 41.8s (4.00) 6 Ran SP% **117.2**
PARI-MUTUEL: WIN 5.00; PL 2.90, 4.50; SF 30.50.

Owner A Curty **Bred** Mineola Farm & Dr Houchin & J W Hirshmann **Trained** France

FOCUS
Pretty weak form for the grade.

NOTEBOOK
Soneva(USA) started well on this occasion which was not the case on her previous run at Deauville. She was soon settled in second place and brought with a run from one and a half furlongs out. She joined battle with the long-time leader at the furlong marker and the pair had a battle royal to the line where they were only separated by inches. She is definitely a progressive sort and stays 1m well. The Prix Marcel Boussac is now her main target.
Article Rare(USA) was soon at the head of affairs and still going well on entering the straight. She was tackled inside the final furlong by the winner, but stuck to her guns to the bitter end and only lost the race on the nod
Denomination(USA), behind the leaders from the start, failed to quicken as the race warmed up from one and a half furlongs out, but still stayed on well for third place.
Ana Americana(FR) was a most disappointing favourite and possibly feeling her last race. She was dropped out last on this occasion, but was being niggled at early in the straight and never looked likely to take a hand in the finish. She is probably in need of a break.

4853 HAYDOCK (L-H)
Tuesday, September 16

OFFICIAL GOING: Heavy (soft in places)
Wind: Almost nil Weather: Wet

5988 TAYLORMADE BETTING EBF MAIDEN STKS — 5f
2:30 (2:31) (Class 5) 2-Y-O — **£3,885** (£1,156; £577; £288) **Stalls** Centre

Form — RPR
4 **1** — **Ursula (IRE)**[19] 5416 2-8-12 0 — AndrewElliott 7 — 75+
(K R Burke) *hld up: hdwy 1/2-way: rdn over 1f out: edgd lft and led 150yds out: r.o and in command after* — **8/1**
2 **2** *2* **Silent Wonder**[12] 5633 2-9-3 0 — TomEaves 3 — 73
(R M H Cowell) *chsd ldrs: rdn 2f out: nt qckn over 1f out: swtchd rt fnl 100yds: styd on to take 2nd towards fin: nt pce of wnr* — **13/8**[1]
4 **3** *nk* **Boho Chic**[92] 3085 2-8-12 0 — RichardKingscote 8 — 67
(R M Beckett) *chsd ldr: rdn 2f out: led briefly jst ins fnl f: nt qckn towards fin* — **9/2**[3]
0 **4** *3/4* **Ben's Dream (IRE)**[49] 4510 2-9-3 0 — LPKeniry 6 — 69
(A M Balding) *racd keenly: led: rdn over 1f out: hdd jst ins fnl f: no ex ins fnl 100yds* — **4/1**[2]
0 **5** *6* **Mr Freddy (IRE)**[36] 4923 2-9-3 0 — JamieMoriarty 1 — 48
(R A Fahey) *broke wl: lost pl after 2f: rn green and outpcd after* — **8/1**
6050 **6** *1 1/2* **That Boy Ronaldo**[8] 5746 2-8-8 55 ow1 — SladeO'Hara(5) 5 — 38
(A Berry) *midfield: rdn 1/2-way: wknd wl over 1f out* — **40/1**
6 **7** *8* **Grissom (IRE)**[19] 5416 2-9-3 0 — (t) FrancisNorton 2 — 13
(A Berry) *midfield early: lost pl 1/2-way: sn toiling and rn green: nt on terms after* — **66/1**
2006 **8** *12* **Black Attack (IRE)**[32] 5072 2-9-3 67 — (v1) PaulQuinn 4 — —
(Paul Green) *awkward s: a bhd: sn rdn along: nvr on terms* — **10/1**

62.41 secs (1.91) **Going Correction** +0.25s/f (Good) — **8** Ran SP% **111.5**
Speed ratings (Par 95): **94,90,90,89,79 77,64,45**
toteswinger: 1&2 £4.50, 1&3 £6.60, 2&3 £2.00. CSF £20.37 TOTE £10.50: £2.10, £1.20, £1.30; EX 30.30.
Owner Tweenhills Racing XIV **Bred** Rathbarry Stud **Trained** Middleham Moor, N Yorks

FOCUS
A modest maiden. The first four came clear and the winner showed big improvement from her debut.

NOTEBOOK
Ursula(IRE), fourth on her debut at Ayr over 6f, handled the testing surface with aplomb and got off the mark with a little left up her sleeve. The drop back in distance on such ground proved ideal and, despite still looking green, she was always on top at the business end. She will learn again for this experience, will appreciate stepping up in trip as she matures further, and should not be overburdened when entering nurseries. (op 10-1 tchd 11-1)
Silent Wonder hit a flat spot before picking up again with purpose inside the final 100 yards, only to find the winner gone beyond recall. She has now finished second on both her starts and is well up to winning one of these, but probably wants a sounder surface. (op 7-4 tchd 2-1)
Boho Chic last seen finishing fourth on debut back in June, was faced with a totally contrasting surface for this return. She showed up well under a positive ride and tired only inside the closing stages. Being by Kyllachy, it is not surprising this deeper surface proved to her liking and she looks to be going the right way. (op 3-1)
Ben's Dream(IRE) settled better out in front and stepped up on his Goodwood debut effort 49 days previously. He will be eligible for a nursery mark after his next outing. (op 9-2)
Mr Freddy(IRE) got readily outpaced on the far rail at the 2f pole and was well beaten off. He still hinted at ability, however, and is one to keep an eye on when qualifying for a mark after his next assignment.
Black Attack(IRE) Official explanation: jockey said colt never travelled

5989 CHESSTELECOM.COM EBF MAIDEN STKS — 6f
3:00 (3:02) (Class 5) 2-Y-O — **£3,885** (£1,156; £577; £288) **Stalls** Centre

Form — RPR
02 **1** — **Dubai Hills**[80] 3492 2-9-3 0 — TomEaves 5 — 82+
(B Smart) *racd on far side: chsd ldrs: effrt to chse overall ldrs 2f out: r.o to take overall ld 100yds out: kpt on wl* — **3/1**[2]
5 **2** *1 1/4* **Liberty Diamond**[41] 4734 2-8-12 0 — AndrewElliott 3 — 73
(K R Burke) *racd on far side: overall ldr: rdn over 1f out: hdd 100yds out: hld after: 2nd of 9 in gp* — **8/1**[3]
23 **3** *2* **Dr Jameson (IRE)**[25] 5225 2-9-3 0 — TonyHamilton 15 — 72+
(R A Fahey) *racd on stands' side: in tch: effrt 2f out: led gp jst over 1f out: styd on but no imp on far side ldrs: 1st of 6 in gp* — **15/8**[1]
5 **4** *7* **Lady Gem**[12] 5633 2-8-12 0 — RoystonFfrench 13 — 46+
(D H Brown) *racd on stands' side: chsd ldrs: rdn over 1f out: wnt 2nd of gp ins fnl f: no ch w gp ldr: 2nd of 6 in gp* — **8/1**[3]
00 **5** *1 3/4* **Hawkeyethenoo (IRE)**[31] 5106 2-8-10 0 — BradleyRoper(7) 9 — 46+
(M W Easterby) *pushed along jst after s: racd in rr on stands' side: styd on fr over 1f out: nt pce to trble ldrs: 3rd of 6 in gp* — **40/1**
2623 **6** *3/4* **Musical Bridge**[94] 3019 2-9-0 79 — RussellKennemore(3) 7 — 44
(Mrs L Williamson) *racd on far side: in tch: rdn over 2f out: chsd front pair in gp over 1f out: no imp: 3rd of 9 in gp* — **10/1**
60 **7** *5* **Pollish**[34] 4965 2-8-12 0 — StephenDonohoe 16 — 24+
(A Berry) *racd on stands' side: handy: led gp briefly wl over 1f out: wknd fnl f: 4th of 6 in gp* — **66/1**
006 **8** *1 1/2* **Jul's Lad (IRE)**[22] 5364 2-9-3 70 — PaulQuinn 8 — 24
(Paul Green) *racd on far side: midfield: rdn 2f out: outpcd over 1f out: 4th of 9 in gp* — **12/1**
06 **9** *1 1/2* **Valentine Bay**[12] 5650 2-8-5 0 — DeanHeslop(7) 10 — 15
(M Mullineaux) *racd on far side: towards rr: rdn 1/2-way: plugged on wout threatening: 5th of 9 in gp* — **33/1**
0 **10** *1/2* **Wrens Hope**[12] 5633 2-8-12 0 — JimmyQuinn 14 — 13+
(N Bycroft) *led stands' side gp: rdn and hdd wl over 1f out: sn wknd: 5th of 6 in gp* — **33/1**
0 **11** *1* **Katie Girl**[12] 5633 2-8-12 0 — DavidAllan 11 — 10+
(Mrs G S Rees) *racd on stands' side: in tch: rdn and wknd over 2f out: 6th of 6 in gp* — **50/1**
12 *4 1/2* **Hart House** 2-8-10 0 ow1 — LeeVickers(3) 4 — —
(C J Gray) *racd on far side: in tch: lost pl after 2f: struggling after: 6th of 9 in gp* — **66/1**
13 *1/2* **Top Flight Splash** 2-8-12 0 — DaleGibson 2 — —
(Mrs G S Rees) *racd on far side: prom tl rdn and wknd 2f out: 7th of 9 in gp* — **40/1**
60 **14** *3 1/4* **Bob's Smithy**[31] 5106 2-9-3 0 — TonyCulhane 1 — —
(T P Tate) *racd on far side: prom: rdn and wknd 2f out: 8th of 9 in gp* — **12/1**
15 *2 1/4* **Bill On The Hill** 2-9-3 0 — PJMcDonald 6 — —
(M W Easterby) *swvd bdly lft s: racd far side: a bhd: 9th of 9 in gp* — **40/1**

1m 16.2s (2.20) **Going Correction** +0.25s/f (Good) — **15** Ran SP% **124.6**
Speed ratings (Par 95): **95,93,90,81,79 78,71,69,67,66 65,59,58,54,51**
toteswinger: 1&2 £4.40, 1&3 £3.10, 2&3 £4.10. CSF £26.78 TOTE £3.30: £1.70, £2.30, £1.40; EX 32.50.
Owner H E Sheikh Rashid Bin Mohammed **Bred** A S Denniff **Trained** Hambleton, N Yorks

FOCUS
An ordinary juvenile maiden. The field split into two groups and the first pair eventually finished clear on the far side. The form is rated at face value.

NOTEBOOK
Dubai Hills shed his maiden tag at the third attempt on this return from an 80-day break and did the job in determined fashion. He had shown a liking for soft ground when second at Newcastle on his previous outing and looked better the further he went here, so while his dam's progeny to date have not won over further than this trip, he looks likely to prove an exception. (tchd 7-2 in places)
Liberty Diamond was given an aggressive ride and gave way to the winner only late on. This was a step up on her initial effort at Newcastle and, another likely to enjoy a seventh furlong in time, she looks well up to winning one of these. (op 9-1)
Dr Jameson(IRE) ◆ had been placed on his two previous outings and got very well backed on this drop back a furlong. He ended up racing on the wrong side, but still came well clear of the remainder and should find his feet now he is qualified for an official rating. (op 4-1)
Lady Gem, up in trip, proved one-paced when asked for maximum effort and looks in need of more time. (op 9-1)
Musical Bridge proved very easy to back on this return from a three-month break and, while he ran well below his previous level, this totally different ground looked totally against him. (op 7-1)

5990 AINSCOUGH VANGUARD EBF CLASSIFIED STKS — 6f
3:30 (3:32) (Class 3) 3-Y-O+ — **£10,361** (£3,083; £1,540; £769) **Stalls** Centre

Form — RPR
1000 **1** — **Bond City (IRE)**[3] 5906 6-8-13 89 — PJMcDonald 5 — 96
(G R Oldroyd) *hld up: pushed along and hdwy over 2f out: rdn over 1f out: prog to ld ins fnl f: r.o and wl on top cl home* — **9/1**
2045 **2** *1* **Invincible Force (IRE)**[35] 4957 4-8-13 90 — (b) TPQueally 6 — 93
(Paul Green) *rrd s: led: rdn and hdd 1f out: rallied and continued to chal ins fnl f: hld cl home* — **11/4**[1]
120 **3** *1 3/4* **Methaaly (IRE)**[17] 5493 5-8-6 83 — DeanHeslop(7) 8 — 87
(M Mullineaux) *chsd ldrs: rdn over 2f out: chal ins fnl f: one pce towards fin* — **14/1**
0000 **4** *1 3/4* **Something (IRE)**[45] 4624 6-8-13 90 — SilvestreDeSousa 3 — 82
(D Nicholls) *chsd ldr: rdn to ld 1f out: hdd ins fnl f: no ex fnl 100yds* — **3/1**[2]
1100 **5** *6* **Whiskey Junction**[26] 5206 4-8-13 87 — LPKeniry 2 — 62
(A M Balding) *chsd ldrs: rdn over 2f out: sn wknd* — **9/2**[3]
5003 **6** *3 1/2* **The Trader (IRE)**[7] 5781 10-8-13 88 — FrancisNorton 4 — 51
(M Blanshard) *hld up: pushed along 2f out: nvr on terms* — **8/1**
-101 **7** *3* **Crying Aloud (USA)**[14] 5594 3-8-9 85 ow1 — StephenDonohoe 1 — 40
(P A Blockley) *planted in stalls: lost many l: a wl bhd* — **13/2**

1m 15.54s (1.54) **Going Correction** +0.475s/f (Yiel)
WFA 3 from 4yo+ 2lb — **7** Ran SP% **111.0**
Speed ratings (Par 107): **108,106,104,102,94 89,85**
toteswinger: 1&2 £5.90, 1&3 £9.50, 2&3 £4.60. CSF £31.95 TOTE £11.50: £3.80, £1.80; EX 35.60.
Owner R C Bond **Bred** David Ryan **Trained** Brawby, N Yorks

FOCUS
This was a typically tight classified event. Not surprisingly, after the first two races the runners kept to the far side and it was pretty much slow-motion stuff in the final furlong. The form is muddling with the winner the best guide.

NOTEBOOK
Bond City(IRE) looked held at the furlong marker but dug deep for maximum pressure and eventually mowed down his rivals to score. He has shown form on easy ground in the past, but had raced only once previously on a heavy surface. This was his second success of the season and he remains in good heart, but his profile suggests he is one to oppose again next time. (tchd 8-1)
Invincible Force(IRE) ran freely on the lead and was there to be shot at nearing the final furlong. He kept on most gamely for pressure, however, and was not beaten far in the end. This again shows he handled most ground and he certainly deserves to go one better again. (op 2-1)
Methaaly(IRE), beaten by the draw at Chester last time and without the headgear here, was always in the same sort of place and was not at all disgraced on the most testing ground he has faced to date. (op 10-1)
Something(IRE), well backed, looked the likely winner at the furlong pole yet eventually fell in a hole and really found this ground too demanding. (op 5-1)
Whiskey Junction Official explanation: trainer's rep said gelding was unsuited by the heavy (soft in places) ground

5991 HALLIWELLS CHALLENGE H'CAP — 6f
4:00 (4:00) (Class 4) (0-85,85) 3-Y-O+ — **£5,504** (£1,637; £818; £408) **Stalls** Centre

Form — RPR
1543 **1** — **Makshoof (IRE)**[14] 5594 4-8-8 76 — (p) NeilBrown(3) 10 — 87
(K A Ryan) *midfield: hdwy to ld 1f out: sn dashed away: r.o wl* — **4/1**[2]
0002 **2** *2 1/4* **Charles Darwin (IRE)**[12] 5648 5-9-0 79 — LPKeniry 9 — 83
(M Blanshard) *trckd ldrs travelling wl: rdn over 1f out: styd on to take 2nd towards fin: nt pce of wnr* — **12/1**
5220 **3** *hd* **Memphis Man**[14] 5594 5-8-6 76 ow3 — RichardEvans(5) 5 — 79
(P D Evans) *midfield: rdn over 1f out: hdwy ins fnl f: styd on towards fin* — **6/1**
2000 **4** *3/4* **Lap Of Honour (IRE)**[45] 4650 4-8-7 72 — (p) JimmyQuinn 7 — 73
(Jennie Candlish) *prom: led 2f out: rdn and hdd 1f out: no ex fnl 100yds* — **33/1**

0000 **5** *1* **Dream Theme**[17] 5495 5-9-6 **85** .... SilvestreDeSousa 12 83
(D Nicholls) *hld up: rdn and hdwy 1f out: chsd ldrs ins fnl f: one pce towards fin* **11/2**[3]

0111 **6** *3/4* **Woodsley House (IRE)**[12] 5634 6-8-7 **72** .... PJMcDonald 11 67
(A G Foster) *hld up: rdn over 1f out: kpt on ins fnl f: nvr able to chal* **7/2**[1]

6010 **7** *nk* **Misphire**[61] 4110 5-8-13 **78** .... (p) TonyHamilton 2 72
(M Dods) *trckd ldrs: rdn over 1f out: wknd fnl 100yds* **14/1**

0000 **8** *3* **Monsieur Reynard**[17] 5490 3-8-4 **71** oh1 .... FrancisNorton 6 56
(D Nicholls) *chsd ldrs: rdn over 1f out: wknd ins fnl f* **16/1**

5051 **9** *2 1/4* **Balakiref**[65] 3998 9-8-8 **73** .... TomEaves 3 50
(M Dods) *a towards rr* **7/1**

0110 **10** *5* **Elusive Hawk (IRE)**[14] 5594 4-8-8 **73** .... TPQueally 4 34
(A P Stringer) *missed break: racd off the pce: rdn over 1f out: nvr on terms* **14/1**

350- **11** *2* **Cayman Fox**[411] 4098 3-8-6 **73** .... RoystonFfrench 1 28
(James Moffatt) *led: hdd 2f out: rdn and wknd over 1f out* **66/1**

100 **12** *nk* **Mayoman (IRE)**[53] 4397 3-8-4 **71** oh2 .... PaulQuinn 13 25
(Paul Green) *racd alone stands' side: a struggling to get on terms* **50/1**

1m 16.11s (2.11) **Going Correction** +0.475s/f (Yiel)
WFA 3 from 4yo+ 2lb **12 Ran SP% 117.7**
Speed ratings (Par 105): **104,101,100,99,98 97,97,93,90,83 80,80**
toteswinger: 1&2 £7.50, 1&3 £7.80, 2&3 £12.00. CSF £50.60 CT £288.50 TOTE £4.00: £1.80, £3.60, £1.80; EX 46.20.
Owner F Gillespie **Bred** J Egan **Trained** Hambleton, N Yorks

FOCUS
An open handicap in which all bar one of the runners went far side. The form looks ordinary but sound enough.
Balakiref Official explanation: jockey said gelding ran flat
Elusive Hawk(IRE) Official explanation: jockey said gelding missed the break

5992 PRINCE'S TRUST/BAKER TILLY H'CAP 1m 6f
4:30 (4:30) (Class 4) (0-85,82) 3-Y-O+ **£5,504** (£1,637; £818; £408) **Stalls** Low

Form RPR

1222 **1** **Hits Only Vic (USA)**[63] 4046 4-10-0 **82** .... DavidAllan 8 97+
(D Carroll) *in tch: wnt 2nd on bit over 2f out: led over 1f out: shkn up to draw clr ins fnl f: eased cl home* **3/1**[2]

111 **2** *2 1/2* **Red Fama**[12] 5637 4-9-7 **75** .... JimmyQuinn 7 84
(N Bycroft) *chsd ldr: led over 2f out: rdn and hdd over 1f out: one pce and no ch w wnr fnl f* **15/8**[1]

0646 **3** *2* **Haarth Sovereign (IRE)**[22] 5349 4-9-9 **77** .... SaleemGolam 2 83
(W R Swinburn) *hld up: hdwy over 2f out: styd on ins fnl f: nvr able to chal front two* **8/1**

14/2 **4** *3 3/4* **Souffleur**[165] 981 5-10-0 **82** .... JamieMoore 3 83
(P Bowen) *hld up: hdwy 3f out: chsd ldrs over 2f out: wknd fnl f* **7/2**[3]

2460 **5** *7* **Inspirina (IRE)**[17] 5498 4-9-1 **69** .... TomEaves 6 60
(R Ford) *hld up: rdn over 2f out: nvr able to chal* **15/2**

000 **6** *12* **Turfshuffle (GER)**[21] 5382 5-10-0 **82** .... StephenDonohoe 1 56
(Ian Williams) *led: rdn and hdd over 2f out: sn wknd* **50/1**

3-11 **7** *36* **Me Fein**[127] 2051 4-9-1 **69** .... TPQueally 4 —
(A P Stringer) *chsd ldrs tl rdn and wknd over 3f out: t.o* **16/1**

3m 9.25s (4.95) **Going Correction** +0.525s/f (Yiel) **7 Ran SP% 112.7**
Speed ratings (Par 105): **106,104,103,101,97 90,69**
toteswinger: 1&2 £2.30, 1&3 £5.30, 2&3 £4.00. CSF £8.78 CT £37.83 TOTE £4.30: £2.10, £1.90; EX 10.00.
Owner Kell-Stone & Watson **Bred** Peter E Blum **Trained** Sledmere, E Yorks

FOCUS
An interesting staying handicap, which was run at an average gallop. The winner was value for 5l but overall the race has not been rated too positively.

5993 1ST NORTHERN SIGN COMPANY H'CAP (FOR GENTLEMAN AMATEUR RIDERS) 1m 6f
5:00 (5:00) (Class 5) (0-70,70) 4-Y-O+ **£3,123** (£968; £484; £242) **Stalls** Low

Form RPR

035/ **1** **Hawridge Star (IRE)**[608] 5383 6-10-10 **59** .... MrSWalker 16 73+
(W S Kittow) *hld up: hdwy 5f out: led over 2f out: drew clr over 1f out: styd on wl: eased cl home* **8/1**[3]

4500 **2** *5* **Ursis (FR)**[44] 3613 7-11-2 **70** .... MrTFWoodside(5) 7 75
(S Gollings) *trckd ldrs: w ldr after 4f: led after 6f: rdn and hdd over 3f out: plugged on after: eased whn no ch w wnr fnl 100yds* **14/1**

1622 **3** *hd* **Signalman**[19] 5415 4-10-2 **56** .... MrDColeman(5) 15 61
(P Monteith) *in tch: clsd 3f out: styd on same pce whn chsd ldrs fnl 2f* **4/1**[1]

30-5 **4** *2 3/4* **According To Pete**[152] 778 7-11-2 **70** .... MrKJames(5) 13 71
(J M Jefferson) *midfield: hdwy 7f out: styd on fr 2f out: nvr able to chal ldrs* **8/1**[3]

0063 **5** *1* **Historic Place (USA)**[8] 5752 8-9-11 **51** oh1 .... (p) MrlPopham(5) 9 51
(J A Geake) *w ldr: rdn over 3f out: one pce after* **12/1**

30-4 **6** *nk* **Diktatorship (IRE)**[6] 4477 5-10-2 **51** oh6 .... MrDRCook 14 50
(Jennie Candlish) *trckd ldrs: led over 3f out: hdd over 2f out: no ex fnl f* **33/1**

0002 **7** *1 1/2* **Kalasam**[32] 5040 4-10-13 **67** .... MrOGreenall(5) 5 64
(M W Easterby) *midfield: lost pl over 6f out: rdn and hdwy 3f out: plugged on one pce fnl f* **14/1**

05-5 **8** *1/2* **Quicuyo (GER)**[19] 5415 5-9-11 **51** oh5 .... MrJoshuaMoore(5) 2 48
(P Monteith) *led: hdd after 6f: remained prom: rdn over 2f out: wknd over 1f out* **5/1**[2]

0/ **9** *4 1/2* **Corso Palladio (IRE)**[380] 6-11-2 **70** .... (t) MrBJToomey(5) 1 60
(B P J Baugh) *midfield: lost pl over 7f out: c wd ent st over 4f out: no imp on ldrs fnl 2f* **50/1**

6005 **10** *4 1/2* **Poppy Day**[7] 5776 5-9-10 **52** .... MrJakeGreenall(7) 17 36
(M W Easterby) *hld up: hdwy into midfield after 2f: c wd ent s over 4f out: no imp on ldrs* **20/1**

0405 **11** *1 1/2* **Ronsard (IRE)**[53] 4366 6-9-9 **51** oh6 .... MrTCooper(7) 11 33
(P D Evans) *hld up: hdwy on outer over 6f out: rdn over 4f out: wknd over 2f out* **25/1**

4435 **12** *1 1/2* **Great View (IRE)**[12] 5651 9-10-9 **65** .... (v) MrOJMurphy(7) 12 45
(Mrs A L M King) *missed break: hld up: rdn over 3f out: no imp* **11/1**

4530 **13** *hd* **Markington**[31] 4193 5-10-10 **62** .... (b) MrDFDevereux(3) 10 41
(P Bowen) *midfield: lost pl after 6f: n.d after* **14/1**

0-30 **14** *1/2* **Florentino**[38] 4848 4-9-11 **51** oh5 .... MrDaleSwift(5) 6 30
(C W Thornton) *in tch: rdn and wknd over 3f out* **25/1**

3115 **15** *nse* **Sand Repeal (IRE)**[14] 5583 6-11-0 **68** .... MrRBirkett(5) 8 47
(Miss J Feilden) *trckd ldrs: lost pl over 7f out: clsd over 4f out: wknd over 2f out: eased whn wl btn over 1f out* **12/1**

1/3- **16** *10* **Malakiya (IRE)**[39] 994 5-11-5 **68** .... MrAJBerry 4 33
(Jonjo O'Neill) *missed break: a bhd* **16/1**

000 **17** *27* **Brathay (IRE)**[25] 5230 4-9-11 **51** oh6 .... MrAshleyBird(5) 3 —
(Ian Williams) *hld up: pushed along 5f out: wknd over 4f out* **66/1**

3m 10.64s (6.34) **Going Correction** +0.525s/f (Yiel) **17 Ran SP% 127.3**
Speed ratings (Par 103): **102,99,99,97,96 96,95,95,93,90 89,88,88,88,88 82,67**
toteswinger: 1&2 £35.50, 1&3 £11.40, 2&3 £17.70. CSF £111.40 CT £528.83 TOTE £10.00: £2.50, £3.90, £1.70, £2.20; EX 203.80 Place 6 £25.33, Place 5 £17.83.
Owner Eric Gadsden **Bred** Seamus Murphy **Trained** Blackborough, Devon

FOCUS
A moderate staying handicap, confined to gentleman amateur riders, run at a decent gallop. The winner, returning from a long absence, is rated back to something like his 2006 form.
T/Jkpt: Not won. T/Plt: £20.60 to a £1 stake. Pool: £83,136.46. 2,940.54 winning tickets. T/Qpdt: £13.30 to a £1 stake. Pool: £4,036.98. 223.30 winning tickets. DO

5784 LINGFIELD (L-H)
Tuesday, September 16

OFFICIAL GOING: Standard
Wind: Almost nil Weather: Fine but cloudy

5994 NATIONAL CENTRE FOR YOUNG PEOPLE WITH EPILEPSY CLAIMING STKS 1m 2f (P)
2:20 (2:23) (Class 6) 3-Y-O+ **£1,978** (£584; £292) **Stalls** Low

Form RPR

0030 **1** **Royal Straight**[14] 5595 3-9-0 65 .... NCallan 2 74
(B N Pollock) *lw: hld up in midfield: prog 3f out: rdn to go 3rd sn after 2f out: led 1f out: in command after* **20/1**

110 **2** *1 3/4* **Ogre (USA)**[6] 5800 3-9-0 75 .... TGMcLaughlin 6 70
(P D Evans) *hld up in rr: bk of main gp over 2f out: gd prog on outer over 1f out: styd on wl to take 2nd last stride* **15/2**

352- **3** *hd* **Prize Fighter (IRE)**[40] 6-9-10 0 .... (b) TedDurcan 8 74
(J Dekeyser, Belgium) *cl up on outer: effrt to ld 2f out: hdd and one pce 1f out: lost 2nd on post* **8/1**

2001 **4** *hd* **Blacktoft (USA)**[6] 5799 5-9-11 71 .... (e) J-PGuillambert 5 75
(S C Williams) *lw: hld up: towards rr over 2f out: effrt over 1f out but hanging: styd on fnl f: nrst fin* **5/1**[1]

1311 **5** *1 3/4* **Lucayan Dancer**[42] 4701 8-9-11 76 .... AdrianTNicholls 11 71
(D Nicholls) *hld up: detached in last and str reminders over 4f out: prog fr 3f out: no imp on ldrs over 1f out: plugged on* **13/2**[3]

4530 **5** *dht* **Peruvian Prince (USA)**[45] 4618 6-9-9 78 .... PaulHanagan 1 71+
(R A Fahey) *led at modest pce 2f: cl up tl lost pl on inner over 2f out: nt clr run over 1f out: styd on ins fnl f* **5/1**[1]

1040 **7** *nk* **Obrigado (USA)**[22] 5349 8-9-7 70 .... (t) RyanMoore 10 67
(G L Moore) *s.i.s: hld up towards rr: nt wl plcd 2f out: n.m.r over 1f out: kpt on: n.d* **11/2**[2]

0054 **8** *nse* **Afram Blue**[15] 5576 3-9-1 68 .... (t) PaulDoe 7 66
(W J Knight) *lw: prom: cl enough 2f out: hmpd on inner over 1f out: no ch after* **10/1**

46-0 **9** *1 1/4* **Ambrosiano**[6] 5800 4-9-11 73 .... AdamKirby 4 68+
(Miss E C Lavelle) *lw: hld up: bk of main gp over 2f out whn pce lifted: trapped bhd wall of rivals over 1f out: kpt on but no ch* **25/1**

2113 **10** *nk* **One More Round (USA)**[10] 5708 10-9-2 68 .... (b) SteveDrowne 9 58
(Ollie Pears) *t.k.h: hld up in midfield: cl enough 2f out: edgd lft and nt qckn over 1f out: fdd* **10/1**

5500 **11** *5* **Quinzey's Best (IRE)**[13] 5607 3-8-8 53 .... (tp) MartinDwyer 13 46
(W J Knight) *prom: led 4f out to 2f out: wknd rapidly fnl f* **50/1**

0500 **12** *14* **Hawkstar Express (IRE)**[68] 3873 3-8-13 48 .... (p) JimCrowley 12 23
(J R Boyle) *prog to ld after 2f: hdd 4f out: wknd rapidly over 2f out: t.o* **66/1**

2m 5.53s (-1.07) **Going Correction** -0.05s/f (Stan)
WFA 3 from 4yo+ 6lb **12 Ran SP% 115.2**
Speed ratings (Par 101): **102,100,100,100,98 98,98,98,97,97 93,82**
toteswinger: 1&2 £23.70, 1&3 £28.90, 2&3 £13.40. CSF £154.70 TOTE £24.90: £5.20, £2.30, £3.30; EX 139.20.
Owner McAndrew Utilities Limited **Bred** Brook Stud Bloodstock & Leydens Farm Stud **Trained** Medbourne, Leics
■ Stewards' Enquiry : J-P GuillambertF two-day ban: careless riding (Sep 30-Oct 1)

FOCUS
This looked like a good, competitive claimer on paper, but they went no pace early on and it was a muddling affair, with plenty finding trouble. The winner appeared to improve but this is messy form.
Peruvian Prince(USA) Official explanation: jockey said gelding suffered interference in running
One More Round(USA) Official explanation: jockey said gelding suffered interference in running

5995 BET TOTEPOOL ON ALL UK RACING MAIDEN STKS 7f (P)
2:50 (2:52) (Class 5) 3-Y-O+ **£2,590** (£770; £385; £192) **Stalls** Low

Form RPR

1 **Mutheeb (USA)** 3-9-2 0 .... MartinDwyer 13 77+
(Saeed Bin Suroor) *lengthy: scope: racd wd in rr: prog into midfield 1/2-way: effrt on wd outside 2f out: shkn up to ld jst ins fnl f: green but a in control* **4/1**[2]

2 **2** *1/2* **Party Frock**[32] 5057 3-8-11 0 .... JimmyFortune 9 70
(J H M Gosden) *mostly chsd ldr: rdn to ld wl over 1f out: narrowly hdd jst ins fnl f: styd on but a hld* **5/4**[1]

44 **3** *1 1/4* **Pension Policy (USA)**[7] 5786 3-8-11 0 .... SteveDrowne 8 67
(R Charlton) *lw: b.hind: hld up in midfield: effrt over 2f out: styd on wl fnl f to take 3rd nr fin* **11/1**

00 **4** *1 1/4* **Triple Dream**[52] 4412 3-9-2 0 .... TedDurcan 5 68+
(J L Dunlop) *scope: hld up in rr: shkn up and 9th over 1f out: pushed along and r.o fnl f: nrst fin* **50/1**

4-0 **5** *hd* **Debdene Bank (IRE)**[120] 2257 5-9-0 0 .... MickyFenton 2 64
(Mrs Mary Hambro) *lw: led: rdn and hdd wl over 1f out: fdd and lost pls fnl f* **12/1**

53 **6** *1 1/2* **Uncle Fred**[13] 5608 3-9-2 0 .... JimCrowley 3 64
(P R Chamings) *lw: prom: tried to chal on inner over 1f out: wknd fnl f* **15/2**[3]

6 **7** *nk* **Gold Again (USA)**[13] 5608 3-8-11 0 .... AdamKirby 6 58+
(W R Swinburn) *w'like: bit bkwd: t.k.h early: hld up in tch: trcking ldrs gng wl 2f out: effrt over 1f out: sn fnd nil and wknd* **8/1**

0 **8** *hd* **Spice Run**[24] 5278 5-9-5 0 .... IanMongan 10 63
(C G Cox) *lw: trckd ldrs: effrt on outer and disp 3rd 2f out: wknd jst over 1f out* **66/1**

5 **9** *1 3/4* **Sea Swell (USA)**[33] 5031 3-8-11 0 .... NCallan 1 53
(G A Butler) *s.i.s: sn in tch: rdn over 2f out: fdd over 1f out* **16/1**

10 1/2 **Yvonne Evelyn (USA)** 3-8-11 0 PaulHanagan 4 51
(J R Gask) *tall: scope: dwlt: a in rr gp: detached over 2f out: no prog* **66/1**

00 11 3/4 **James Pollard (IRE)**[13] 5608 3-8-13 0 MarcHalford(3) 12 54
(D R C Elsworth) *t.k.h: hld up: detached in last quartet over 2f out: shuffled along and kpt on steadily fnl f* **40/1**

12 3 1/4 **Tropical Tradition (IRE)** 3-9-2 0 JoeFanning 7 46
(D W P Arbuthnot) *neat: dwlt: a in last gp: detached over 2f out: hanging bdly lft over 1f out* **66/1**

13 7 **Prairie Hawk (USA)**[478] 2063 3-9-2 0 MHNaughton 11 27
(Tim Vaughan) *a in last gp: detached over 2f out: t.o* **25/1**

1m 26.55s (1.75) **Going Correction** -0.05s/f (Stan)
WFA 3 from 5yo 3lb 13 Ran SP% **122.0**
Speed ratings (Par 103): **88,87,86,84,84 82,82,82,80,79 78,74,66**
toteswinger: 1&2 £2.60, 1&3 £7.50, 2&3 £3.70. CSF £9.22 TOTE £5.50: £1.90, £1.20, £2.90; EX 12.20.
Owner Godolphin **Bred** Jayeff 'B' Stables **Trained** Newmarket, Suffolk

FOCUS
No more than a fair maiden and the winning time was slow, even allowing for the steady pace, but there was still plenty to like about the performance of Mutheeb and the form should work out among the principals.
Triple Dream ◆ Official explanation: jockey said gelding hung left in home straight
James Pollard(IRE) Official explanation: jockey said colt ran too free
Tropical Tradition(IRE) Official explanation: jockey said gelding hung left

5996 EBF NITA AND KEITH HAPPY RUBY WEDDING MAIDEN STKS (DIV I) 7f (P)

3:20 (3:24) (Class 5) 2-Y-O £3,238 (£963; £481; £240) **Stalls** Low

Form RPR

54 1 **Dialogue**[32] 5068 2-9-3 0 JoeFanning 10 79+
(M Johnston) *mde all: stdd pce after 3f: kicked on again over 2f out: wd bnd sn after: edgd rt fnl f: urged along and a holding on* **1/1**[1]

03 2 *nk* **Sandor**[11] 5678 2-9-3 0 NCallan 7 78+
(P J Makin) *swtg: pressed wnr: rdn to chal 2f out: wd bnd sn after: edgd rt and carried rt fnl f: nt qckn* **6/1**[3]

3 1 1/4 **Axel Foley (USA)** 2-9-3 0 JimmyFortune 1 75
(J R Best) *mostly in 3rd: styd towards innner bnd 2f out and sn ev ch: kpt on same pce fnl f* **33/1**

4 2 3/4 **Antinori (IRE)** 2-9-3 0 AdamKirby 8 68+
(W R Swinburn) *w'like: scope: str: bit bkwd: s.i.s: hld up in rr: outpcd over 2f out: sme prog over 1f out: shkn up and styd on wl fnl f: nrst fin* **20/1**

54 5 1 3/4 **Mr Udagawa**[23] 5314 2-9-3 0 PaulHanagan 6 64
(R M Beckett) *wl plcd: shkn up to press ldrs 3f out: stl in tch 2f out: wknd fnl f* **9/1**

6 1 **King's Chorister** 2-9-3 0 RyanMoore 4 61+
(Sir Michael Stoute) *w'like: leggy: hld up in midfield: outpcd over 2f out: pushed along and kpt on steadily fr over 1f out* **12/1**

0 7 1 1/2 **Almazar**[59] 4199 2-9-3 0 MartinDwyer 12 57+
(J L Dunlop) *leggy: scope: unf: bit bkwd: hld up in midfield: outpcd fr over 2f out: pushed along and one pce after* **16/1**

3 8 *hd* **Cheam Forever (USA)**[22] 5344 2-9-3 0 SteveDrowne 9 57
(R Charlton) *plld hrd early: cl up: stl pressing ldrs over 2f out: wknd wl over 1f out* **9/2**[2]

0 9 1 1/2 **Clear Hand**[45] 4636 2-9-3 0 TGMcLaughlin 3 53
(B R Millman) *settled in midfield: outpcd over 2f out: no prog on inner over 1f out: fdd* **66/1**

10 7 **Saborido (USA)** 2-9-3 0 JimCrowley 2 36+
(Mrs A J Perrett) *w'like: str: bit bkwd: sn rdn in rr: nvr on terms* **33/1**

11 3/4 **Spinning Joy** 2-8-12 0 J-PGuillambert 13 29
(J R Boyle) *leggy: v s.i.s: a in rr: bhd fnl 2f* **66/1**

12 8 **My Baby Love** 2-8-12 0 IanMongan 5 9
(J Akehurst) *w'like: str: bit bkwd: sn outpcd: a in rr: wknd over 2f out: t.o* **66/1**

1m 26.03s (1.23) **Going Correction** -0.05s/f (Stan) 12 Ran SP% **121.2**
Speed ratings (Par 95): **90,89,88,85,83 81,80,80,78,70 69,60**
toteswinger: 1&2 £2.50, 1&3 £11.40, 2&3 £15.70. CSF £7.04 TOTE £2.10: £1.10, £2.10, £4.40; EX 8.50.
Owner Sheikh Hamdan Bin Mohammed Al Maktoum **Bred** Darley **Trained** Middleham Moor, N Yorks

FOCUS
Probably a fair maiden. The winner did not need to reproduce his Newmarket form to score.

NOTEBOOK
Dialogue, a one-time Royal Lodge entry, confirmed the promise he showed in stronger races on his first two starts, but was made to work hard. Dropped back from 1m and trying Polytrack for the first time, he was allowed the run of the race in front but did not help his chance by hanging right off the home bend and was pressed all the way to the line. He is likely to find things tougher from now on, but can step up on this form if less wayward in future and should be capable of progressing further. (op 11-10 tchd 5-6)
Sandor had his chance, despite being carried right in the straight, but could not get by the winner, who battled on well. He is now qualified for a handicap mark and might be worth another try over 1m. (tchd 13-2)
Axel Foley(USA), a $175,000 son of Officer, knew his job better than some of these and had every chance. He clearly has ability and is entitled to come on for this. (op 25-1 tchd 22-1)
Antinori(IRE) ◆, by Fasliyev, first foal of a 1m6f winner, made a very pleasing debut. He was well out the back early, but gradually got the hang of things and finished well in fourth. He should come on a bundle and ought to get a little further. (op 11-1)
Mr Udagawa, another who was entered in the Royal Lodge earlier in the season, did not really pick up for pressure but will have more options now. (op 14-1)
King's Chorister, an already gelded son of King's Best, first foal of high-class 1m-1m2f performer Chorist, was not given too hard a time once his chance had gone and he should be capable of a fair bit better in time. (op 17-2 tchd 8-1)
Cheam Forever(USA) raced even keener than when third on his debut at Kempton and failed to see his race out. He will need to learn to settle if he is going to fulfil his potential. (op 8-1 tchd 17-2)

5997 TOTESUPER7 NURSERY 6f (P)

3:50 (3:52) (Class 5) (0-75,74) 2-Y-O £3,238 (£963; £481; £240) **Stalls** Low

Form RPR

510 1 **Cool Art (IRE)**[25] 5242 2-9-7 74 JimmyFortune 6 77
(S A Callaghan) *trckd ldrs gng wl: plld out and effrt over 1f out: led ins fnl f: sn pressed: drvn and r.o wl* **7/2**[1]

046 2 *nk* **On The Feather**[25] 5214 2-9-2 69 JimCrowley 8 71
(P Winkworth) *settled in midfield: rdn over 2f out: prog and swtchd ins 1f out: sn chalng: r.o but a hld* **12/1**

0235 3 1 1/2 **You've Been Mowed**[18] 5466 2-9-3 70 J-PGuillambert 5 68
(D K Ivory) *pressed ldr: drvn to ld wl over 1f out: hdd and outpcd ins fnl f* **7/1**[2]

3230 4 *nk* **My Best Man**[25] 5213 2-9-3 70 TGMcLaughlin 10 67+
(B R Millman) *lw: sn midfield: rdn and effrt 3f out: chsd ldrs over 1f out: carried rt sn after: kpt on but nvr able to chal* **25/1**

5250 5 1 1/2 **Flyit (IRE)**[24] 5274 2-9-7 74 TPO'Shea 3 66
(M R Channon) *hld up towards rr: shkn up and no prog 2f out: rdn and styd on wl fnl f: nrst fin* **20/1**

0651 6 *shd* **Courageous Nature (IRE)**[13] 5614 2-9-1 68 JamesDoyle 7 60
(A J McCabe) *wl in rr: rdn over 2f out: styd on fr over 1f out: nrst fin* **12/1**

6465 7 3/4 **Skruton (IRE)**[12] 5647 2-9-3 70 (b[1]) TedDurcan 11 60
(M G Quinlan) *s.s: hld up in last: stl there wl over 1f out: hanging and reminder 1f out: styd on wl fnl f: nvr nr ldrs* **20/1**

560 8 *nk* **Mintoe**[66] 3976 2-9-2 69 NCallan 2 58
(K A Ryan) *lw: chsd ldrs: u.p fr 1/2-way: losing pl 2f out: kpt on again last 100yds* **12/1**

304 9 1 3/4 **Marbled Cat (USA)**[15] 5572 2-9-4 71 JoeFanning 9 55
(M Johnston) *lw: trckd ldng pair: rdn and stl cl up over 1f out: sltly intimidated sn after: wknd* **17/2**

004 10 *nk* **Piste**[31] 5097 2-9-4 71 MartinDwyer 4 54
(B J Meehan) *led to wl over 1f out: wknd rapidly fnl f* **8/1**[3]

401 11 1 1/2 **Princess Hannah**[34] 4973 2-9-3 70 RyanMoore 1 48
(R Hannon) *dwlt: a in rr: rdn and no prog wl over 2f out* **7/2**[1]

003 12 2 1/4 **Strike Command (USA)**[19] 5431 2-9-3 70 SteveDrowne 12 41
(R Charlton) *a in rr and mostly on outer: rdn and struggling wl over 2f out* **20/1**

1m 12.17s (0.27) **Going Correction** -0.05s/f (Stan) 12 Ran SP% **119.8**
Speed ratings (Par 95): **96,95,93,93,91 91,90,89,87,86 84,81**
toteswinger: 1&2 £12.80, 1&3 £5.50, 2&3 £16.10. CSF £45.94 CT £285.68 TOTE £4.40: £1.90, £4.70, £2.60; EX 63.10.
Owner Matthew Green **Bred** Azienda Agricola Robiati Angelo **Trained** Newmarket, Suffolk

FOCUS
An ordinary sprint nursery and not form to rate too positively. The winning time was 0.84sec slower than the following 61-75 handicap for three-year-olds.

NOTEBOOK
Cool Art(IRE) probably failed to see out 1m in a stronger race than this at the Newmarket July course on his previous start and he took advantage of both the drop in trip and class, keeping on well for strong pressure after being switched in the straight. His connections are hopeful he can hold his own in better company, but he had little in hand and strictly on form will have something to find when forced up in class after he is reassessed. (tchd 3-1)
On The Feather ran her best race yet on her nursery debut and showed enough to suggest she can win a small handicap. (op 18-1)
You've Been Mowed was one of the more exposed runners, but she has some reasonable form to her name and ran a solid race in defeat. (op 11-1)
My Best Man was slightly impeded at the furlong pole, but he kept on for pressure to post a respectable effort. (op 40-1)
Flyit(IRE) was doing all his best work at the finish on this drop in trip and first try on Polytrack having been a little short of room rounding the final bend. (op 33-1)
Marbled Cat(USA) once again failed to really see out his race. (op 15-2 tchd 9-1)
Princess Hannah came into this off the back of a success in a weak maiden at Salisbury, but she was immediately out the back after starting slowly and never really travelled. Her jockey reported that she did not face the kickback. Official explanation: jockey said filly could not face the kickback (op 4-1 tchd 9-2)

5998 TOTESWINGER APPRENTICE H'CAP 6f (P)

4:20 (4:20) (Class 5) (0-75,75) 3-Y-O £2,590 (£770; £385; £192) **Stalls** Low

Form RPR

01 1 **Prescription**[29] 5160 3-9-0 73 RosieJessop(3) 2 87+
(Sir Mark Prescott) *lw: plld hrd: hld up in midfield: prog over 1f out: swept into ld ins fnl f: nt extended* **6/4**[1]

5052 2 2 1/2 **Anosti**[41] 4745 3-9-5 75 (p) FrederikTylicki 9 77
(K A Ryan) *sn pressed ldr: rdn to ld over 2f out: hdd and completely outpcd ins fnl f* **3/1**[2]

2215 3 1/2 **Bahamian Bliss**[29] 5142 3-8-8 64 JPHamblett 3 64
(J A R Toller) *trckd ldrs: gng wl enough over 2f out: effrt on inner over 1f out: sn chalng: outpcd fnl f* **16/1**

2540 4 1 1/4 **Maryolini**[17] 5493 3-9-3 73 Louis-PhilippeBeuzelin 7 69
(N J Vaughan) *prom: drvn over 2f out: cl enough over 1f out: one pce after* **15/2**

5142 5 1/2 **Little Knickers**[13] 5617 3-8-12 68 (b) ShaneCreighton 8 62
(E J Creighton) *in tch: effrt and rdn over 2f out: one pce fr over 1f out* **11/1**

0410 6 *hd* **Siren Party**[23] 5317 3-8-12 73 MJMurphy(5) 5 67
(L M Cumani) *dwlt: mostly in last trio: rdn 2f out: kpt on fnl f: no ch* **5/1**[3]

2153 7 2 1/2 **Miss Firefly**[25] 5217 3-8-8 64 WilliamCarson 1 50
(R J Hodges) *led: drvn and hdd over 2f out: wknd fnl f* **16/1**

00 8 *hd* **Street Diva (USA)**[13] 5616 3-8-6 62 MatthewDavies 4 47
(P A Blockley) *stdy: a in last trio: no prog whn rdn over 2f out* **16/1**

0300 9 7 **Apple Pie Order (IRE)**[8] 5751 3-8-5 61 oh1 (b[1]) AshleyMorgan 6 24
(R J Hodges) *squeezed out s: a in last trio: wd bnd 2f out: bhd after* **50/1**

1m 11.33s (-0.57) **Going Correction** -0.05s/f (Stan) 9 Ran SP% **121.4**
Speed ratings (Par 101): **101,97,97,95,94 94,91,90,81**
toteswinger: 1&2 £3.30, 1&3 £8.40, 2&3 £11.10. CSF £6.39 CT £53.09 TOTE £2.40: £1.50, £1.30, £4.40; EX 7.90.
Owner Cheveley Park Stud **Bred** Cheveley Park Stud Ltd **Trained** Newmarket, Suffolk

FOCUS
A modest fillies' sprint handicap, but a very likeable winner. The winning time was 0.84sec quicker than the earlier 0-75 nursery and the form seems sound.
Siren Party Official explanation: jockey said filly suffered interference leaving stalls
Apple Pie Order(IRE) Official explanation: jockey said filly suffered interference leaving stalls

5999 BET TOTEPOOL AT TOTESPORT.COM H'CAP 1m 4f (P)

4:50 (4:50) (Class 5) (0-75,75) 3-Y-O+ £2,590 (£770; £385; £192) **Stalls** Low

Form RPR

2600 1 **War Of The Roses (IRE)**[32] 5058 5-9-12 75 J-PGuillambert 2 83
(R Brotherton) *hld up towards rr: rdn and prog fr over 2f out: sustained effrt fr over 1f out: r.o to ld nr fin* **14/1**

2303 2 *nk* **Potentiale (IRE)**[17] 5512 4-9-9 72 (p) MichaelHills 11 80
(J W Hills) *stdd s: hld up wl in rr: stdy prog on outer fr 3f out: rdn to ld over 1f out: worn down nr fin* **7/1**[3]

0163 3 1 3/4 **Resplendent Ace (IRE)**[12] 5630 4-9-11 74 TGMcLaughlin 3 79
(P Howling) *t.k.h early: hld up wl in rr: rdn over 2f out: prog over 1f out: styd on wl fnl f to take 3rd cl home* **8/1**

1056 4 1 1/4 **Bell Island**[33] 5017 4-9-7 75 (p) Louis-PhilippeBeuzelin(5) 13 78
(Lady Herries) *trckd ldr: led over 2f out to wl over 1f out: sn outpcd on inner: kpt on last 100yds* **14/1**

1P30 **5** ½ **Trifti**[29] 5156 7-9-8 **71**.......................... TravisBlock 5 73
(Miss Jo Crowley) *b: hld up in midfield: rdn and no prog over 2f out: styd on ins fnl f: unable to chal* **11/1**

-633 **6** *nk* **Ommadawn (IRE)**[15] 5576 4-9-2 **65**..........................(t) RyanMoore 6 67
(J R Fanshawe) *trckd ldrs: rdn over 2f out: stl chsng whn forced to switch rt over 1f out: nt qckn and btn after* **9/2**[2]

4106 **7** *nse* **Sweet Sara**[18] 5449 3-9-2 **73**.......................... NCallan 10 75
(C E Brittain) *trckd ldng pair: effrt over 2f out: led briefly wl over 1f out: wknd ins fnl f* **20/1**

-155 **8** *nk* **Monterrico**[75] 3633 3-9-3 **74**.......................... SteveDrowne 8 75
(G Wragg) *lw: trckd ldrs: rdn 3f out: lost pl and struggling 2f out: plugged on* **7/2**[1]

1- **9** 1 ¾ **Veloso (FR)**[227] 6815 6-9-10 **73**.......................... PaulHanagan 9 72
(Ollie Pears) *awkward s: a in rr: struggling over 2f out: plugged on* **10/1**

4000 **10** 3 ¼ **Straight And Level (CAN)**[95] 3004 3-9-0 **71**.......................... AdamKirby 4 64
(Miss Jo Crowley) *b: b.hind: dwlt: a in rr: struggling fr 4f out* **25/1**

1130 **11** 4 ½ **Ovthenight (IRE)**[71] 3793 3-9-0 **71**.......................... MickyFenton 7 57
(Mrs P Sly) *prom: lost pl and rdn over 3f out: wkng whn no room over 2f out* **16/1**

400 **12** 3 **Mon Plaisir (USA)**[18] 5464 3-9-1 **72**..........................(b[1]) TedDurcan 1 53
(J L Dunlop) *led to over 2f out: wknd rapidly over 1f out* **15/2**

2m 30.29s (-2.71) **Going Correction** -0.05s/f (Stan)
WFA 3 from 4yo+ 8lb **12** Ran SP% **121.0**
Speed ratings (Par 103): **107,106,105,104,104 104,104,104,102,100 97,95**
toteswinger: 1&2 £12.60, 1&3 £23.40, 2&3 £6.30. CSF £111.10 CT £855.56 TOTE £15.90: £3.50, £2.90, £2.90; EX 64.20.
Owner P S J Croft **Bred** Mrs Jane Bailey **Trained** Elmley Castle, Worcs

FOCUS
A modest handicap run at a reasonable pace. The form looks solid with the first three to their marks.

6000 EBF NITA AND KEITH HAPPY RUBY WEDDING MAIDEN STKS (DIV II) 7f (P)

5:20 (5:22) (Class 5) 2-Y-O **£3,238** (£963; £481; £240) **Stalls** Low

Form RPR

5 **1** **Spring Of Fame (USA)**[18] 5469 2-9-3 0.......................... PaulHanagan 6 81+
(M A Magnusson) *w'like: scope: str: trckd ldr: led 3f out: drew clr fr 2f out: styd on wl: rdn out* **5/6**[1]

0 **2** 5 **Charlie Smirke (USA)**[18] 5468 2-9-3 0.......................... AdamKirby 12 68
(G L Moore) *w'like: scope: str: wl in tch and racd on outer: outpcd 2f out: shkn up and styd on wl fnl f to snatch 2nd on line* **17/2**

4 **3** *nse* **Wabi Sabi (IRE)**[53] 4359 2-8-12 0.......................... MichaelHills 9 63
(B W Hills) *cl up: rdn to chse wnr over 2f out: kpt on but no ch fr over 1f out* **15/2**[3]

4 *nk* **Son Of The Cat (USA)** 2-9-3 0.......................... MickyFenton 2 67
(B Gubby) *w'like: bit bkwd: str: dwlt: sn chsd ldrs: effrt over 2f out: disp 2nd on inner over 1f out: no ch w wnr* **20/1**

30 **5** 3 ¼ **Edgeworth (IRE)**[25] 5213 2-8-12 0.......................... GabrielHannon(5) 13 59
(B G Powell) *wl in rr: outpcd fr over 2f out: urged along and styd on fr over 1f out* **50/1**

6 *nk* **Curacao** 2-9-3 0.......................... JimCrowley 3 58
(Mrs A J Perrett) *w'like: str: bit bkwd: dwlt: hld up in rr: nudged along and styd on in sme style on inner fr over 1f out: improve* **20/1**

0 **7** *nk* **Rainbow Seeker**[12] 5649 2-9-3 0.......................... RyanMoore 10 58
(W J Haggas) *w'like: str: mostly in midfield: outpcd fr 3f out: no imp on ldrs after* **9/2**[2]

0 **8** 1 ½ **Banda Sea (IRE)**[34] 4973 2-9-3 0.......................... NCallan 4 54
(P J Makin) *chsd ldrs: rdn over 2f out: wknd over 1f out* **20/1**

9 ½ **La Tizona (IRE)** 2-9-3 0.......................... SteveDrowne 8 53
(R Charlton) *leggy: scope: in tch on outer: outpcd fr over 2f out: hanging and green over 1f out: wknd* **20/1**

0 **10** 7 **Mojeerr**[18] 5468 2-9-3 0.......................... MartinDwyer 5 35
(M P Tregoning) *str: led to 3f out: wknd over 2f out* **25/1**

11 1 **Echo Forest** 2-9-0 0.......................... MarcHalford(3) 11 33
(J R Best) *w'like: uns rdr coming on to crse: a towards rr: lost tch over 2f out* **50/1**

12 11 **Red Dagger (IRE)** 2-9-3 0.......................... J-PGuillambert 1 5
(T D McCarthy) *w'like: s.v.s: detached tl latched on to bk of field after 3f: wknd over 2f out: t.o* **66/1**

1m 24.86s (0.06) **Going Correction** -0.05s/f (Stan) **77** Ran SP% **123.3**
Speed ratings (Par 95): **97,91,91,90,87 86,86,84,84,76 75,62**
CSF £7.88 TOTE £1.80: £1.10, £2.50, £2.20; EX 8.90 Place 6 £105.16, Place 5 £14.74.
Owner Eastwind Racing Ltd and Martha Trussell **Bred** Brushwood Stable **Trained** Upper Lambourn, Berks

FOCUS
The winning time was 1.17sec quicker than the first division, and also 1.69sec faster than the earlier older-horse maiden run over this trip. There is better to come from the impressive winner.

NOTEBOOK
Spring Of Fame(USA) ◆ created a big impression and was spoken of in glowing terms afterwards by his trainer, who thinks he will make a "phenomenal three-year-old". Entries in the Royal Lodge, Dewhurst and the Irish Guineas gave a clue as to the regard in which he is held and he duly stepped up on the form he showed when fifth in a decent maiden on his debut at Sandown. He obviously clocked a very decent time and will be worth his place in better company, although his connections said that if he runs again this year he might not be asked too stiff a question. (op Evens)
Charlie Smirke(USA) showed ability on his debut at Sandown and this was a pleasing effort behind a potentially very useful type. (op 12-1)
Wabi Sabi(IRE) stepped up a little on the form she showed over 6f on her debut at Ascot and is going the right way. (op 7-1 tchd 6-1 and 8-1)
Son Of The Cat(USA) hails from a relatively small stable, but cost $100,000 and is a half-brother to, among others, quite useful prolific 7f plus US winner Tales Of Glory, out of a quite useful triple-winning dirt sprinter at two to three. He showed ability on his debut and is entitled to come on for this. (op 40-1tchd 50-1 in a place)
Edgeworth(IRE) showed some ability and is now qualified for a handicap mark. (tchd 66-1)
Curacao, a gelded half-brother to this year's Jersey winner Aqlaam, showed plenty of promise on his debut and appeals as one that will have benefited from the experience. Official explanation: jockey said, regarding running and riding, that his orders were to do his best and finish as close as he could, adding that the gelding was slowly away and short of room in the home straight but ran on well when gap appeared; trainer said the gelding was of a nervous disposition and is bred to want further in time. (op 25-1)
Rainbow Seeker could not improve on the form he showed on his debut at Warwick. (op 4-1)
La Tizona(IRE) Official explanation: jockey said colt hung left
Mojeerr Official explanation: jockey said colt hung left
Echo Forest, who had a bit of size about him, was edgy in the paddock and threw his jockey off as they approached the track. (tchd 66-1)
T/Plt: £258.50 to a £1 stake. Pool: £57,954.69. 163.66 winning tickets. T/Qpdt: £14.60 to a £1 stake. Pool: £4,195.23. 211.80 winning tickets. JN

5316

YARMOUTH (L-H)
Tuesday, September 16

OFFICIAL GOING: Good
Wind: Light, against Weather: Sunny spells

6001 FIRSTBET £50 MATCHED TELEPHONE BET 0800 230 0800 PREMIER CLAIMING STKS 1m 3y

2:10 (2:11) (Class 5) 3-Y-O **£3,154** (£944; £472; £236; £117) **Stalls** High

Form RPR

1241 **1** **Talk Of Saafend (IRE)**[13] 5607 3-8-4 75.......................... HayleyTurner 2 65+
(R Hannon) *trckd ldrs: led on bit over 1f out: shkn up and r.o wl* **4/7**[1]

0322 **2** 2 ½ **Valento**[40] 4777 3-8-10 66.......................... StephenCarson 6 65
(Eve Johnson Houghton) *hld up: rdn over 3f out: hdwy u.p and hung lft over 1f out: wnt 2nd ins fnl f: no ch w wnr* **5/1**[2]

3200 **3** 1 ¾ **Yakama (IRE)**[33] 5020 3-8-4 55..........................(b) DO'Donohoe 7 55
(Mrs C A Dunnett) *chsd ldrs tl led 2f out: hdd over 1f out: no ex ins fnl f* **50/1**

33 **4** *nse* **Gang Show (IRE)**[200] 748 3-8-9 0.......................... EddieAhern 1 60
(W J Musson) *hld up in tch: rdn ins fnl f: styd on same pce* **17/2**[3]

0000 **5** *nk* **Dry Speedfit (IRE)**[13] 5605 3-8-7 65 ow1..........................(b[1]) JohnEgan 5 57
(G G Margarson) *dwlt: hld up: rdn over 3f out: r.o ins fnl f: nvr nrr* **16/1**

0451 **6** 7 **Redsensor**[40] 4794 3-8-3 60.......................... ChrisCatlin 3 37
(M Quinn) *led: hdd over 4f out: rdn and ev ch 2f out: wknd fnl f* **14/1**

40 **7** 6 **Pebble Rock (IRE)**[69] 3854 3-8-5 0..........................(bt[1]) DavidProbert(5) 4 30
(J R Jenkins) *s.s and swvd lft leaving stalls: rel to r and sn given reminders: plld hrd and hdwy to trck ldr 6f out: led over 4f out: sn clr: wknd and hdd 2f out* **25/1**

1m 41.27s (0.67) **Going Correction** -0.075s/f (Good) **7** Ran SP% **109.2**
Speed ratings (Par 101): **93,90,88,88,88 81,75**
toteswinger: 1&2 £1.60, 1&3 £11.00, 2&3 £13.30. CSF £3.28 TOTE £1.60: £1.40, £1.70; EX 3.90.
Owner J B R Leisure Ltd **Bred** Michael Dalton **Trained** East Everleigh, Wilts

FOCUS
A modest claimer overall, with the easy winner the clear form pick. They raced down the centre of the course and the early pace was only steady.
Pebble Rock(IRE) Official explanation: jockey said gelding ran too free

6002 JACQUES CIDER NURSERY (FOR THE JACK LEADER CHALLENGE TROPHY) 7f 3y

2:40 (2:41) (Class 4) (0-85,81) 2-Y-O **£4,037** (£1,208; £604; £302; £150) **Stalls** High

Form RPR

2614 **1** **Calahonda**[25] 5242 2-8-12 **72**.......................... JohnEgan 2 82+
(P W D'Arcy) *a.p: chsd clr ldr over 3f out: led over 1f out: sn rdn: edgd lft ins fnl f: all out* **7/1**[3]

51 **2** *shd* **La Adelita (IRE)**[12] 5650 2-9-0 **74**.......................... JamieSpencer 4 84+
(M L W Bell) *hld up: hdwy over 3f out: hrd rdn and edgd lft fr over 1f out: sn chsng wnr: ev ch ins fnl f: r.o* **13/8**[1]

5332 **3** 6 **Taazur**[45] 4626 2-9-7 **81**.......................... RHills 3 76
(M Johnston) *s.i.s: hld up: rdn over 2f out: hdwy and hung lft over 1f out: no imp fnl f* **11/2**[2]

642 **4** 1 ¾ **Flintlock (IRE)**[44] 4658 2-9-1 **75**..........................(b) RobertHavlin 8 66
(J H M Gosden) *led: clr over 3f out: rdn and hdd over 1f out: wknd ins fnl f* **10/1**

432 **5** 3 ¼ **Defector (IRE)**[24] 5277 2-9-1 **75**.......................... DO'Donohoe 1 58
(W R Muir) *hld up: hdwy over 3f out: rdn over 1f out: sn wknd* **8/1**

2544 **6** 3 **Hawkspur (IRE)**[34] 4975 2-8-11 **71**.......................... DaneO'Neill 5 46
(R Hannon) *hld up: hdwy over 2f out: rdn and wknd over 1f out* **10/1**

001 **7** *nk* **Bermondsey Bob (IRE)**[18] 5459 2-9-1 **78**.......................... TolleyDean(3) 9 52
(J L Spearing) *chsd ldrs: sn pushed along: hung lft 1/2-way: wknd 2f out* **33/1**

510 **8** 1 ¼ **Sapphire Prince (USA)**[67] 3920 2-9-7 **81**.......................... HayleyTurner 6 52
(J R Best) *mid-div: rdn over 3f out: wknd 2f out* **25/1**

430 **9** 3 ¼ **Night Lily (IRE)**[28] 5165 2-9-3 **77**.......................... RobertWinston 10 40
(J Jay) *s.s: in rr whn hmpd over 4f out: n.d* **16/1**

510 **P** **Papa Meilland**[17] 5511 2-9-2 **76**.......................... StephenCarson 7 —
(Eve Johnson Houghton) *chsd ldrs tl broke down and p.u over 4f out: dead* **20/1**

1m 26.59s (-0.01) **Going Correction** -0.075s/f (Good) **10** Ran SP% **112.7**
Speed ratings (Par 97): **97,96,90,88,84 80,80,79,75,—**
toteswinger: 1&2 £3.70, 1&3 £5.20, 2&3 £2.80. CSF £17.62 CT £66.87 TOTE £8.20: £2.80, £1.30, £1.30; EX 20.60 Trifecta £83.50 Pool: £450.43 - 3.99 winning tickets..
Owner Gongolphin & Racing **Bred** Eurostrait Ltd **Trained** Newmarket, Suffolk
■ Stewards' Enquiry : Jamie Spencer two-day ban: careless riding (Sep 30-Oct 1)

FOCUS
A decent nursery run at a strong pace. Not many got into it and the first two came clear to fight out a tight finish. The form should stand up.

NOTEBOOK
Calahonda, fourth off this mark on her nursery debut over Newmarket's stiff mile following her maiden win over this course and distance, was never too far from the pace and showed a good attitude to fend off the other filly through the final furlong. This looks her trip for now and her trainer thinks she is ready for a step up in grade, with the Group 3 C. L. Weld Park Stakes at the Curragh a possibility. (op 8-1)
La Adelita(IRE) impressed in making all in a soft-ground fillies' maiden at Warwick but conditions were different here and she was held up this time. Coming under pressure some way out, she responded and threw down a sustained challenge to the winner that only just failed. She was clear of the rest and remains capable of further progress. (op 11-8)
Taazur, tackling this trip for the first time, and slow to find his stride as he had been on his first two starts, made late progress from the rear to secure third. He remains a maiden but has now been placed on five of his six runs. (op 15-2 tchd 5-1)
Flintlock(IRE) bowled along in front on his nursery debut, racing rather freely, and was half a dozen lengths clear at one stage before being gradually reeled in. He might prefer a drop back to 6f. (op 16-1)
Defector(IRE), runner-up in a Newmarket sales race last time, could never really make his presence felt on this rise in trip. (op 15-2 tchd 7-1)
Night Lily(IRE) Official explanation: jockey said filly was hampered approaching 4f mark

6003 THOMAS PRIOR MEMORIAL MAIDEN STKS 6f 3y

3:10 (3:11) (Class 5) 3-Y-O+ **£2,901** (£868; £434; £217; £108) **Stalls** High

Form RPR

4050 **1** **Doric Lady**[77] 3571 3-8-12 62.......................... KirstyMilczarek 8 70
(J A R Toller) *sn prom: led over 1f out: rdn out* **12/1**

430 **2** 1¼ **Baby Rock**[12] 5636 3-9-3 66 .... AlanMunro 5 71
(C F Wall) *hld up in tch: rdn and ev ch over 1f out: styd on same pce ins fnl f* **9/2**[2]

32 **3** ¾ **Shakedown**[22] 5366 3-9-3 0 .... GrahamGibbons 2 69
(E S McMahon) *trckd ldrs: plld hrd: led 2f out: rdn and hdd over 1f out: no ex ins fnl f* **5/2**[1]

30 **4** 4½ **Vienna Affair**[24] 5261 3-8-12 0 .... RobertWinston 12 49
(J R Fanshawe) *hld up in tch: rdn over 2f out: wknd fnl f* **8/1**[3]

0-34 **5** *nse* **Pride Of India (USA)**[13] 5608 3-9-3 72 .... ShaneKelly 13 54
(J Noseda) *chsd ldrs: rdn over 2f out: wknd fnl f* **9/2**[2]

6 *shd* **Pappoose** 3-8-12 0 .... DaneO'Neill 3 49
(H Candy) *s.i.s: sn prom: rdn over 1f out: wknd fnl f* **12/1**

036 **7** 1½ **Xandra (IRE)**[20] 5402 3-8-9 43 .... JackMitchell(3) 11 44
(C F Wall) *hld up: rdn over 2f out: sn hung rt: nt trble ldrs* **40/1**

- **8** *shd* **Enlightened** 3-8-12 0 .... RobertHavlin 10 44
(J H M Gosden) *s.i.s: hdwy and hung lft over 3f out: rdn and ev ch over 1f out: sn wknd* **9/1**

5000 **9** 1½ **Marvin Gardens**[19] 5426 5-9-0 45 .... DavidProbert(5) 1 44
(P S McEntee) *led: rdn and hdd 2f out: wknd fnl f* **40/1**

00 **10** 1¼ **Tomatina**[24] 5278 3-8-12 0 .... HayleyTurner 9 35
(C F Wall) *sn pushed along: a in rr* **40/1**

0 **11** 5 **Hilltop Legacy**[13] 5608 5-8-11 0 .... LukeMorris(3) 6 19
(S W James) *s.i.s: rdn over 2f out: a in rr* **150/1**

- **12** 2½ **Tophorsnopedigree** 3-9-3 0 .... EdwardCreighton 7 16
(E J Creighton) *prom: rdn 1/2-way: wknd over 2f out* **100/1**

0 **13** 5 **Ashton Heights**[29] 5160 3-8-10 0 .... KylieManser(7) 15 —
(Miss Gay Kelleway) *chsd ldrs: rdn over 3f out: sn wknd* **150/1**

0360 **14** *nk* **Rowaad**[81] 3438 3-9-0 68 .... TolleyDean(3) 16 —
(A E Price) *chsd ldrs: rdn 1/2-way: wknd 2f out* **14/1**

440 **15** 1½ **Heroic Fool**[8] 5749 3-9-3 0 .... SamHitchcott 14 —
(Miss Z C Davison) *s.i.s: sme hdwy over 3f out: sn rdn and wknd* **100/1**

1m 13.7s (-0.70) **Going Correction** -0.075s/f (Good)
WFA 3 from 5yo 2lb **15** Ran SP% **118.7**
Speed ratings (Par 103): **101,99,98,92,92 92,90,90,88,86 79,76,69,69,67**
toteswinger: 1&2 £15.00, 1&3 £9.70, 2&3 £3.80. CSF £63.30 TOTE £16.50: £3.70, £1.90, £1.40; EX 108.00 TRIFECTA Not won..
Owner Buckingham Thoroughbreds I **Bred** Minster Enterprises Ltd **Trained** Newmarket, Suffolk
■ Stewards' Enquiry : Sam Hitchcott one-day ban: used whip when out of contention (Sep 30)

FOCUS
Just an ordinary maiden and there are doubts over the form with the poor seventh and ninth close enough, although the time was decent compared with the later conditions race. The first three finished clear.

6004 NORFOLK NELSON MUSEUM (S) STKS 7f 3y
3:40 (3:43) (Class 6) 3-Y-O **£1,942** (£578; £288; £144) **Stalls** High

Form RPR

4033 **1** **Zeffirelli**[25] 5248 3-8-12 59 .... ShaneKelly 7 59
(M Quinn) *mde all: rdn over 1f out: edgd lft: styd on* **9/2**[1]

006 **2** ¾ **Mick's Dancer**[25] 5218 3-8-12 52 .... DO'Donohoe 4 57
(W R Muir) *hld up in tch: lost pl 1/2-way: hdwy 2f out: nt clr run and swtchd lft 1f out: styd on* **14/1**

5-00 **3** *nk* **Calypso Charms**[25] 5248 3-8-2 68 .... DavidProbert(5) 5 51
(M L W Bell) *s.i.s: hdwy over 4f out: rdn and edgd lft over 1f out: styd on* **15/2**[3]

- **4** ½ **Dazzling Begum** 3-8-7 0 .... RobertHavlin 1 50
(J Pearce) *mid-div: sn pushed along: hdwy 1/2-way: rdn over 1f out: styd on* **10/1**

000 **5** ½ **Johnny McGurk**[19] 5426 3-8-12 50 ....(b[1]) RobertWinston 9 53
(M E Rimmer) *chsd ldrs: rdn and hung rt over 1f out: styd on same pce ins fnl f* **20/1**

1000 **6** 1¾ **Redarsene**[14] 5595 3-9-3 67 .... SamHitchcott 11 54+
(M G Quinlan) *sn pushed along and prom: lost pl 1/2-way: running on whn eased ins fnl f: sddle slipped* **15/2**[3]

0004 **7** 2½ **Dalla Finestra**[40] 4793 3-8-7 51 .... HayleyTurner 14 37
(C F Wall) *hld up: racd keenly: hdwy over 2f out: sn rdn and hung lft: no ex ins fnl f* **9/2**[1]

30-0 **8** 7 **Art Value**[123] 2161 3-8-12 70 .... ChrisCatlin 12 23
(M Wigham) *sn outpcd: nvr nrr* **12/1**

0000 **9** *hd* **Karky Schultz (GER)**[19] 5421 3-8-9 57 ....(b) LukeMorris(3) 13 23
(J M P Eustace) *hld up: hdwy 1/2-way: rdn over 2f out: sn wknd* **9/1**

3010 **10** 2 **Glenveagh (IRE)**[18] 5457 3-9-3 55 ....(p) JohnEgan 16 35+
(K A Ryan) *chsd ldrs: rdn over 2f out: sn hung lft: wknd and eased fnl f* **6/1**[2]

0050 **11** 1½ **Diademas (USA)**[14] 5592 3-8-5 52 ....(p) HollyHall(7) 10 13
(M J Gingell) *chsd ldr untuil rdn 1/2-way: wknd wl over 1f out* **40/1**

0654 **12** 11 **Mensadil**[18] 5457 3-8-5 42 .... KristinStubbs(7) 15 —
(Mrs L Stubbs) *prom: rdn 1/2-way: sn wknd* **66/1**

0000 **13** 3¾ **Her Name Is Rio (IRE)**[97] 2926 3-8-12 42 .... DaneO'Neill 3 —
(Mrs S Lamyman) *chsd ldrs: rdn 1/2-way: sn bhd* **50/1**

0- **14** 1¾ **Princess Namid (IRE)**[464] 2488 3-8-4 0 .... KevinGhunowa(3) 8 —
(R A Harris) *chsd ldrs: rdn over 2f out: wknd wl over 1f out* **100/1**

1m 27.53s (0.93) **Going Correction** -0.075s/f (Good) **14** Ran SP% **119.3**
Speed ratings (Par 99): **91,90,89,89,88 86,83,75,75,73 71,59,54,52**
.The winner was bought in for 5,400gns. Calypso Charms was claimed by M. J. Wallace for £5,000. Mick's Dancer was subject to a friendly claim. Redarsene was claimed by J. Babb for £5,000.
Owner J Henry & J Blake **Bred** J Spearing And Kate Ive **Trained** Newmarket, Suffolk

FOCUS
A very ordinary seller with the winner probably the best guide. Not form to be with.
Redarsene Official explanation: jockey said saddle slipped
Glenveagh(IRE) Official explanation: jockey said gelding had no more to give

6005 AT THE RACES CONDITIONS STKS 6f 3y
4:10 (4:12) (Class 3) 3-Y-O+
£7,477 (£2,239; £1,119; £560; £279; £140) **Stalls** High

Form RPR

-660 **1** **Speedy Dollar (USA)**[101] 2819 3-8-7 87 .... PhilipRobinson 5 100
(M A Jarvis) *mde virtually all: rdn and edgd lft ins fnl f: r.o* **7/1**

5360 **2** ½ **Hoh Mike (IRE)**[24] 5259 4-9-2 110 .... JamieSpencer 8 105
(M L W Bell) *hld up: hdwy over 1f out: sn rdn to chal: hung lft ins fnl f: nt run on* **3/1**[2]

51-0 **3** 1 **Francesca D'Gorgio (USA)**[135] 1830 3-8-2 100 ....(v) HayleyTurner 4 90
(J Noseda) *trckd ldrs: outpcd over 1f out: r.o wl towards fin* **5/1**

620 **4** 1¾ **Mujood**[10] 5695 5-8-9 91 ....(b) StephenCarson 6 89
(Eve Johnson Houghton) *chsd ldrs: rdn and hung rt over 1f out: styd on same pce ins fnl f* **8/1**

2366 **5** 3½ **Law Lord**[22] 5368 4-8-9 106 ....(b[1]) DarryllHolland 7 78
(Saeed Bin Suroor) *dwlt: racd wd and sn prom: jnd ldrs over 3f out: rdn: hung lft and rt over 1f out: wknd ins fnl f* **9/2**[3]

5250 **6** 1 **Spitfire**[31] 5102 3-8-7 97 .... EddieAhern 3 75
(J R Jenkins) *hld up: rdn over 2f out: wknd over 1f out* **11/4**[1]

0000 **7** 36 **Lawyer To World**[25] 5247 4-8-9 35 ....(b) JohnEgan 2 —
(Mrs C A Dunnett) *chsd ldrs tl rdn and wknd over 2f out* **250/1**

1m 12.66s (-1.74) **Going Correction** -0.075s/f (Good)
WFA 3 from 4yo+ 2lb **7** Ran SP% **110.5**
Speed ratings (Par 107): **108,107,106,103,99 97,49**
toteswinger: 1&2 £5.80, 1&3 £6.10, 2&3 £3.70. CSF £26.33 TOTE £9.10: £3.30, £1.90; EX 33.80 Trifecta £86.10 Pool: £751.01 - 6.45 winning tickets..
Owner Stephen Dartnell **Bred** Diamond A Racing Corp **Trained** Newmarket, Suffolk

FOCUS
Quite an interesting conditions sprint, but none of these arrived here in the best of form and four of them were equipped with some headgear. The winner produced what appared to be big improvement, although there was little solid amongst the opposition with the fourth the best guide.

NOTEBOOK
Speedy Dollar(USA) had never run over a trip this short, but he has shown plenty of speed in decent handicaps over 1m and connections were not concerned about the drop back in distance as he is quite a free-going sort. Having his first run for three months, he made a lot of the running and wanted it more than the runner-up when it came down to a fight. This was a good performance at the weights but it will not have helped his handicap mark and he might not be easy to place for the rest of the season (op 9-1)
Hoh Mike(IRE) came through from the rear to issue his challenge but appeared to be outbattled. This was much more encouraging than his latest effort in soft ground at Beverley, with the return to 6f helping, but he remains one to treat with caution. (op 11-4 tchd 7-2)
Francesca D'Gorgio(USA), who had not run since finishing last in the 1,000 Guineas in the spring, ran a reasonable race on this marked drop in class. She was knuckling down well in the end, suggesting that 7f could be her optimum trip. (tchd 11-2)
Mujood, having his 16th race of the year, faced a difficult task on these terms. (op 9-1 tchd 15-2)
Law Lord was slow to break but soon showed pace after being switched to race apart from his rivals towards the stands' rail. Blinkered for the first time, although he has gone well in a visor, he has not recaptured his form yet following a lengthy break. (op 3-1)
Spitfire had a bit to find with some of these and could never land a blow after being held up. Official explanation: jockey said gelding failed to pick up (op 4-1)

6006 PETER DUNNETT MEMORIAL SPRINT H'CAP 5f 43y
4:40 (4:40) (Class 4) (0-85,84) 3-Y-O+ **£5,046** (£1,510; £755; £377; £188) **Stalls** High

Form RPR

650 **1** **The Jobber (IRE)**[6] 5796 7-9-5 83 .... JamieSpencer 1 89
(M Blanshard) *hld up: hdwy over 1f out: sn rdn: led ins fnl f: r.o u.p* **9/2**[2]

0351 **2** *nk* **Russian Rocket (IRE)**[23] 5319 6-8-5 69 oh11 .... HayleyTurner 2 74
(Mrs C A Dunnett) *w ldrs: rdn and ev ch fr over 1f out: r.o* **12/1**

3113 **3** *nk* **Equuleus Pictor**[8] 5757 4-8-12 81 .... JackDean(5) 11 85
(J L Spearing) *led: rdn and hung lft fr over 1f out: hdd ins fnl f: r.o* **7/1**

103 **4** ½ **Diane's Choice**[8] 5751 5-8-3 72 ....(b[1]) DavidProbert(5) 3 74+
(Miss Gay Kelleway) *hld up: swtchd rt 1/2-way: r.o ins fnl f: nt rch ldrs* **11/1**

1211 **5** ¾ **Pretty Bonnie**[5] 5839 3-9-2 84 6ex .... LukeMorris(3) 9 83
(A E Price) *chsd ldrs: rdn 1/2-way: styd on* **8/1**

0000 **6** *hd* **Golden Dixie (USA)**[6] 5796 9-9-0 81 .... KevinGhunowa(3) 10 80
(R A Harris) *chsd ldrs: rdn 1/2-way: outpcd over 1f out: r.o ins fnl f* **9/1**

0220 **7** 1¼ **Bahamian Ballet**[44] 4668 6-8-13 77 .... GrahamGibbons 8 71
(E S McMahon) *s.i.s: sn chsng ldrs: rdn over 1f out: no ex ins fnl f* **13/2**[3]

4506 **8** ¾ **The Tatling (IRE)**[8] 5757 11-9-4 82 .... PatCosgrave 5 74
(J M Bradley) *hld up: effrt over 1f out: n.d* **16/1**

2231 **9** *nse* **Even Bolder**[18] 5467 5-9-2 80 .... StephenCarson 4 71
(E A Wheeler) *prom: racd keenly: rdn over 1f out: no ex* **4/1**[1]

3433 **10** 1½ **Cosmic Destiny (IRE)**[20] 5401 6-8-5 69 .... ChrisCatlin 6 55
(E F Vaughan) *trckd ldrs: plld hrd: rdn over 1f out: wknd ins fnl f* **16/1**

2040 **11** 1½ **Corridor Creeper (FR)**[4] 5861 11-8-5 76 ....(p) BillyCray(7) 7 57
(J M Bradley) *chsd ldrs: rdn 1/2-way: wknd over 1f out* **22/1**

62.58 secs (0.38) **Going Correction** -0.075s/f (Good)
WFA 3 from 4yo+ 1lb **11** Ran SP% **117.3**
Speed ratings (Par 105): **93,92,92,91,90 89,87,86,86,84 81**
toteswinger: 1&2 £6.90, 1&3 £6.90, 2&3 £9.20. CSF £57.43 CT £381.24 TOTE £5.70: £2.20, £2.50, £2.70; EX 58.20 Trifecta £172.10 Pool: £453.69 - 1.95 winning tickets..
Owner Mrs Rosemary Wilkerson & Partners **Bred** Dr T J Molony **Trained** Upper Lambourn, Berks

FOCUS
A competitive handicap contested by several in-form sprinters, with the first two coming out of the two lowest stalls. The runner-up is a slight doubt over the form from 11lb out of the handicap.

6007 VAUXHALL HOLIDAY PARK H'CAP 1m 3f 101y
5:10 (5:10) (Class 5) (0-70,70) 3-Y-O+ **£3,238** (£963; £481; £240) **Stalls** Low

Form RPR

0024 **1** **Lindy Lou**[12] 5637 4-9-2 60 .... AlanMunro 4 72+
(C F Wall) *hld up: hdwy over 2f out: sn swtchd lft: rdn to ld over 1f out: r.o wl* **13/2**[3]

0004 **2** 2¼ **Overrule (USA)**[26] 5199 4-9-8 66 .... DaneO'Neill 14 74
(B Ellison) *hld up: hdwy over 2f out: rdn over 1f out: styd on* **5/1**[2]

621 **3** 2½ **Moonshine Creek**[7] 5489 6-9-3 61 .... ChrisCatlin 5 65
(P W Hiatt) *led: racd keenly: hdd over 9f out: rdn and ev ch over 1f out: styd on same pce* **7/1**

023 **4** 1½ **Silent Applause**[31] 5105 5-9-5 66 .... LukeMorris(3) 10 67
(Dr J D Scargill) *hld up: hdwy u.p and hung lft over 1f out: nt rch ldrs* **12/1**

4634 **5** *nk* **Ghufa (IRE)**[24] 5262 4-9-3 61 .... ShaneKelly 2 62
(E A L Dunlop) *s.i.s: sn mid-div: hdwy 1/2-way: rdn and hung lft ins fnl f: styd on same pce* **14/1**

4243 **6** *nk* **Red Lily (IRE)**[23] 5322 3-9-3 68 .... RobertWinston 13 68
(J R Fanshawe) *chsd ldrs: led over 3f out: rdn and hdd over 1f out: wknd ins fnl f* **9/1**

0361 **7** 2¼ **Sudden Impulse**[16] 5543 7-9-11 69 .... JohnEgan 12 66
(A D Brown) *prom: rdn over 2f out: wknd over 1f out* **16/1**

0045 **8** ½ **Toballa**[21] 5379 3-8-4 55 oh8 .... HayleyTurner 9 51
(H J Collingridge) *hld up: hmpd over 8f out: hdwy over 1f out: nt trble ldrs* **40/1**

3222 **9** ½ **Maha Dubai (USA)**[34] 4964 3-9-5 70 .... RHills 3 65
(M Johnston) *pushed along in mid-div early: hdwy over 1f out: no ex fnl f* **3/1**[1]

1-56 **10** 1 **Rosy Alexander**[23] 5317 3-9-5 70 .... JamieSpencer 1 63
(S A Callaghan) *chsd ldrs: led over 9f out: hdd over 3f out: sn rdn: wknd fnl f* **12/1**

The Form Book, Raceform Ltd, Compton, RG20 6NL

1250 **11** 2 1/2 **Fantasy Ride**[5] 5833 6-9-6 **64**.. JerryO'Dwyer 15 53
(J Pearce) *hld up: hdwy over 7f out: rdn over 2f out: hmpd and wknd sn after* **25/1**

1040 **12** 3 1/2 **Royal Premier (IRE)**[18] 5476 5-9-10 **68**......................(v) DarryllHolland 6 51
(H J Collingridge) *mid-div: rdn over 4f out: wknd over 2f out* **22/1**

00 **13** 5 **Tapaellya (IRE)**[27] 5183 4-8-11 **55** oh1..................... RichardThomas 11 30
(J E Long) *chsd ldrs: rdn over 3f out: wknd over 2f out* **66/1**

4500 **14** 3/4 **Moon Mix (FR)**[36] 4930 5-8-13 **62**...........................(p) DavidProbert(5) 16 35
(J R Jenkins) *hld up: plld hrd: hdwy over 4f out: rdn and wknd over 1f out* **33/1**

20 **15** 3/4 **Night Orbit**[31] 5105 4-9-7 **68**... TolleyDean(3) 7 40
(Miss J Feilden) *hld up in tch: rdn over 3f out: wknd over 2f out* **25/1**

2m 28.07s (-0.63) **Going Correction** -0.075s/f (Good)
WFA 3 from 4yo+ 7lb **15** Ran SP% **124.3**
Speed ratings (Par 103): **99,97,95,94,94 94,92,92,91,90 89,86,82,82,81**
CSF £37.21 CT £243.61 TOTE £8.40: £2.30, £3.00, £3.40; EX 53.20 Trifecta £332.10 Part won.
Pool: £448.91 - 0.30 winning tickets. Place 6 £48.04, Place 5 £43.37.
Owner A H B Hodge **Bred** C A Cyzer **Trained** Newmarket, Suffolk
■ Stewards' Enquiry : Alan Munro one-day ban: careless riding (Sep 30)

FOCUS
The sole race on the card over the round course, it was run at only a steady pace until the final half-mile but three of the first four home came from the rear of the field. The winner is rated up 6lb and a fairly positive view has been taken of the form.
Royal Premier(IRE) Official explanation: jockey said gelding stumbled about 2f out
Tapaellya(IRE) Official explanation: trainer said filly was unsuited by the good ground
T/Plt: £43.10 to a £1 stake. Pool: £66,994.11. 1,133.57 winning tickets. T/Qpdt: £26.60 to a £1 stake. Pool: £3,130.09. 86.80 winning tickets. CR

5770 BEVERLEY (R-H)

Wednesday, September 17

OFFICIAL GOING: Soft (good to soft in places; 6.8)
Wind: light 1/2 behind Weather: overcast, occasional light rain

6008 BEVERLEY RACECOURSE MAIDEN AUCTION STKS (DIV I) 7f 100y

1:30 (1:30) (Class 6) 2-Y-O **£2,590** (£770; £385; £192) **Stalls** High

Form RPR

3 **1** **Ubi Ace**[41] 4780 2-8-11 0.. GrahamGibbons 10 72+
(T D Walford) *mde all: rdn wl over 1f out: drvn and edgd lft ins fnl f: kpt on wl* **6/4**[1]

4 **2** 1 1/4 **Sgt Roberts (IRE)**[16] 5578 2-9-1 0.......................... SimonWhitworth 12 73
(J S Moore) *trckd ldrs on inner: swtchd lft and hdwy wl over 1f out and sn rdn: drvn and edgd lft ins fnl f: kpt on* **9/2**[3]

332 **3** shd **Hel's Angel (IRE)**[17] 5539 2-8-1 66.......................... AndrewMullen(3) 9 62
(Mrs A Duffield) *trckd wnr: effrt to chal over 2f out: rdn and ev ch wl over 1f out: drvn and kpt on same pce fnl f* **4/1**[2]

4 1 1/4 **Hector's House** 2-8-9 0... TonyHamilton 11 64+
(M Dods) *towards rr: hdwy on inner over 2f out: rdn over 1f out: kpt on ins fnl f: nrst fin* **10/1**

55 **5** nk **Fajita**[16] 5579 2-8-8 0.. NeilBrown(3) 1 65
(M G Quinlan) *in rr: hdwy on inner 2f out: rdn over 1f out: kpt on ins fnl f: nrst fin* **11/1**

0U4 **6** 3 1/4 **Chantilly Dancer (IRE)**[42] 4747 2-8-6 0......................... PaulHanagan 6 53
(M J Wallace, Australia) *chsd ldng pair: rdn along over 2f out: grad wknd* **9/1**

00 **7** 4 1/2 **Kladester (USA)**[53] 4415 2-8-11 0....................................(t) TomEaves 8 47
(B Smart) *midfield: effrt 3f out: sn rdn along and no hdwy* **25/1**

0 **8** 2 **Nut Hand (IRE)**[18] 5497 2-9-1 0.. DavidAllan 5 46
(T D Easterby) *in tch: hdwy on outer to chse ldrs 1/2-way: rdn along over 2f out and sn wknd* **50/1**

00 **9** 2 1/2 **James Junior**[13] 5633 2-8-9 0... DNolan 7 35
(D Carroll) *dwlt: towards rr: awkward bnd 1/2-way: nvr a factor* **100/1**

0 **10** 1/2 **Le Petit Vigier**[25] 5256 2-8-4 0.......................................(t) AndrewElliott 4 28
(P Beaumont) *s.i.s: t.k.h and sn in midfield: rdn along over 2f out and sn wknd* **150/1**

00 **11** 6 **Queens Forester**[44] 4692 2-8-8 0.. JoeFanning 2 18
(P F I Cole) *a in rr* **40/1**

12 24 **Political Matters (IRE)** 2-8-11 0...................................... TonyCulhane 3 —
(T P Tate) *in rr: pushed along and outpcd 1/2-way: sn bhd* **22/1**

1m 38.95s (5.15) **Going Correction** +0.65s/f (Yiel) **12** Ran SP% **119.9**
Speed ratings (Par 93): **96,94,94,93,92 88,83,81,78,78 71,43**
toteswinger: 1&2 £4.00, 1&3 £3.50, 2&3 £4.30. CSF £7.86 TOTE £2.50: £1.10, £1.70, £2.10; EX 9.40.
Owner N J Maher **Bred** Steel's Thoroughbred Breeding **Trained** Sheriff Hutton, N Yorks

FOCUS
A modest maiden, although a few had already shown some ability. It was those who dominated the race from the start too, with very little else ever getting into it.

NOTEBOOK
Ubi Ace, a good third in similar ground on his debut in a Haydock maiden which has already produced a couple of winners, was down half a furlong here but he went off a well-backed favourite nonetheless. His rider utilised his stamina to the full, bouncing him out straight into the lead, and he went on to make just about every yard. He obviously relishes this sort of ground and there should be more to come, while a return to further won't bother him at all. In the much longer term he could be a hurdler in the making. (op 9-4)
Sgt Roberts(IRE), well backed, is bred to be suited by this ground being a son of Diktat and he stepped up from his Lingfield debut by staying on to grab second near the line, but the favourite was already away and clear. A half-brother to the multiple middle-distance Polytrack winner Sgt Schultz, he will appreciate a longer trip in due course. (op 11-2 tchd 4-1)
Hel's Angel(IRE) had the best form coming into this, although this would have been the softest ground she had faced and she didn't help her cause by taking a hold early. She had every chance, but her earlier exertions may have told as she didn't quite get home. Her current official rating of 66 provides a benchmark to the form and she may be worth a try in nurseries now. (op 7-2 tchd 9-2)
Hector's House, a relatively cheap yearling whose dam was a winner over this trip at two, did not go off unbacked and he fared much the better of the two newcomers by some way. This was a most pleasing debut and there is a race waiting for him. (op 12-1)
Fajita didn't run at all badly considering he started from the widest stall and tried to come from off the pace in a race otherwise dominated by those that raced handily. He had shown a glimmer of ability in his two previous starts and has more options open to him now that he qualifies for a mark. (op 14-1)
Chantilly Dancer(IRE) raced prominently for a while and now qualifies for a mark. (op 7-1 tchd 6-1)

6009 BEVERLEY ANNUAL BADGEHOLDERS (S) NURSERY 5f

2:00 (2:01) (Class 6) (0-65,63) 2-Y-O **£2,729** (£806; £403) **Stalls** High

Form RPR

1344 **1** **Just The Lady**[19] 5475 2-9-7 **63**..................................... TonyHamilton 14 72
(Ollie Pears) *smartly away: mde all: sn clr: unchal* **7/1**[2]

550 **2** 5 **Sale Or Return (IRE)**[50] 4499 2-8-12 **54**......................(b) DavidAllan 16 45
(T D Easterby) *a chsng wnr: kpt on fnl 2f: nvr a threat* **12/1**

0034 **3** 1 3/4 **Future Gem**[10] 5715 2-7-10 **45**... JamieKyne(7) 5 30+
(A Dickman) *in rr-div: styd on fnl 2f: nrst fin* **11/1**

0000 **4** 1 **Dancing Wave**[10] 5715 2-8-7 **52** ow2................ RussellKennemore(3) 12 33
(M C Chapman) *dwlt: mid-div: kpt on fnl f* **18/1**

0053 **5** 1 **Franchesca's Gold**[19] 5475 2-8-10 **52**...................... GrahamGibbons 13 30
(B R Millman) *chsd ldrs: one pce fnl 2f* **6/1**[1]

0400 **5** dht **Miss Xu Xia**[10] 5715 2-8-3 **45**................................(p) SilvestreDeSousa 11 23
(G R Oldroyd) *chsd ldrs: one pce fnl 2f* **12/1**

600 **7** 2 3/4 **Captain Cromby (IRE)**[24] 5304 2-8-0 **47**................ PatrickDonaghy(5) 9 15
(J R Weymes) *in rr-div: kpt on fnl 2f: nvr a factor* **22/1**

0005 **8** 1 1/2 **Time Loup**[10] 5715 2-8-13 **55**..(t) DeanMcKeown 6 17+
(S R Bowring) *racd towards stands' side: chsd ldr that side: edgd rt and led that gp over 1f out: nvr a threat* **16/1**

040 **9** nk **Lemon Dash**[19] 5475 2-8-7 **49**.. PaulHanagan 15 10
(J J Quinn) *mid-div: kpt on fnl f: nvr a threat* **15/2**[3]

5500 **10** 1/2 **Tagula Sunset (IRE)**[22] 5381 2-8-10 **52**......................... JamieMoriarty 8 11
(P T Midgley) *swvd rt s: nvr a factor* **8/1**

4500 **11** 2 **Rioja Ruby (IRE)**[39] 4873 2-8-6 **48**.................................. AndrewElliott 7 —
(Miss Kate Milligan) *mid-div: nvr a factor* **18/1**

0005 **12** 4 1/2 **Sonett**[19] 5473 2-8-12 **54**...(p) TomEaves 2 —+
(A J McCabe) *led stands' side gp: wknd over 1f out* **12/1**

3004 **13** 4 **Carmanjoe**[39] 4873 2-8-11 **53**.. PaulMulrennan 1 —+
(M W Easterby) *racd towards stands' side: nvr wnt pce* **12/1**

000 **14** 1 1/4 **Ennovy**[78] 3590 2-8-3 **45**.. KimTinkler 10 —
(N Tinkler) *sn outpcd and bhd* **66/1**

005 **15** 14 **Abitofaboost (IRE)**[14] 5614 2-8-2 **49**.......................... KellyHarrison(5) 3 —+
(Peter Grayson) *racd towards stands' side: in rr: wl bhd fnl 2f* **25/1**

2223 **16** 3 3/4 **Lady Fantasie**[62] 4120 2-8-5 **50**.................................. AndrewMullen(3) 4 —+
(Mrs A Duffield) *racd towards stands' side: sn struggling: wl bhd fnl 2f* **10/1**

65.49 secs (1.99) **Going Correction** +0.175s/f (Good) **16** Ran SP% **124.0**
Speed ratings (Par 93): **91,83,80,78,77 77,72,70,69,68 65,58,52,50,27 21**
toteswinger: 1&2 £17.70, 1&3 £11.10, 2&3 £42.20. CSF £88.31 CT £968.96 TOTE £5.00: £1.40, £3.70, £2.90, £4.70; EX 74.80.The winner was sold for 6,000gns to D Nicholls
Owner Ian Bishop **Bred** Mrs Monica Teversham **Trained** Norton, N Yorks

FOCUS
A very moderate selling nursery with 13 of the 16 runners fillies and several of these had already met each other in similarly lowly grade. The draw played its usual major part too, with five of the first six home starting from a double-figure stall. The winner may be flattered by making all on a card where front runners flourished.

NOTEBOOK
Just The Lady managed to bag the early advantage tight against the far rail and it was obvious from a long way out that none of her rivals were travelling well enough to pick her up. Their only hope was that she would empty on this stiff track in the testing ground, but that never looked like happening. (op 4-1)
Sale Or Return(IRE) stepped up on her previous efforts and was always doing her best to bridge the gap to the winner against the far rail. The softer ground didn't seem to be a problem, but she did have the plum draw and that would have helped her quite a bit. (op 16-1)
Future Gem emerges with plenty of credit as not only did she start from a low draw, faring much the best of that group, but she was struggling to go the pace in the early stages before staying on late. She hadn't been disgraced in a couple of recent sellers and can win a race like this when things fall right. (op 10-1 tchd 12-1)
Dancing Wave, beaten miles in all four starts for her current yard, plugged on to finish fourth but was never going to win. This was a better effort though and she had run well in similar conditions at Warwick in April. (op 20-1)
Franchesca's Gold, who showed improved form on her Polytrack debut last time, had the beating of Just A Lady on that form, but she could never get on terms with her old rival on this very different surface. (op 11-2 tchd 13-2)
Miss Xu Xia, a long way behind a couple of these at Thirsk last time, had cheekpieces on for the first time and was not totally disgraced but she will need to improve a lot more if she is to win a race. (op 11-2 tchd 13-2)

6010 GEORGE KILBURN MEMORIAL MAIDEN STKS 5f

2:35 (2:37) (Class 5) 2-Y-O **£2,914** (£867; £433; £216) **Stalls** High

Form RPR

0 **1** **Spiritofthewest (IRE)**[46] 4647 2-9-3 0.................................... JohnEgan 8 83
(S Parr) *mde all: rdn clr wl over 1f out: drvn ins fnl f and kpt on wl* **33/1**

323 **2** 1/2 **Kingship Spirit (IRE)**[25] 5271 2-9-3 87............................. EddieAhern 7 82
(J Noseda) *trckd ldrs: hdwy to chse wnr 2f out: rdn and carried hd high over 1f out: hrd drvn and kpt on ins fnl f: nt rch wnr* **2/5**[1]

3 3 1/4 **York Key Bar** 2-9-3 0... DavidAllan 12 70+
(B Ellison) *midfield: hdwy 1/2-way: rdn wl over 1f out: kpt on ins fnl f: nrst fin* **28/1**

4 2 3/4 **Premier Lad** 2-9-0 0.. NeilBrown(3) 6 60
(T D Barron) *chsd wnr: rdn along 1/2-way: grad wknd fr over 1f out* **33/1**

5 **5** 2 3/4 **Rio Pomba (IRE)**[74] 3714 2-8-12 0... DNolan 10 45
(D Carroll) *chsd ldrs: rdn along over 1f out: n.m.r inner appr fnl f: kpt on same pce* **16/1**

6 nk **Mythicism** 2-8-12 0... TomEaves 15 44
(B Smart) *towards rr: hdwy on inner 1/2-way: rdn over 1f out: kpt on ins fnl f: nrst fin* **6/1**[2]

04 **7** 3 1/2 **Home Before Dark**[32] 5106 2-9-3 0.................................. DeanMcKeown 3 36
(R M Whitaker) *chsd ldrs: rdn along 1/2-way: sn wknd* **20/1**

8 1/2 **Georgie Bee** 2-8-5 0.. PaulPickard(7) 2 30+
(D Carroll) *a towards rr* **100/1**

9 1 **Exopuntia** 2-8-9 0.. MichaelJStainton(3) 11 26
(R M Whitaker) *dwlt: bhd tl sme late hdwy* **33/1**

00 **10** 1 1/4 **Flaming Ruby**[13] 5633 2-8-12 0.. KimTinkler 4 21
(N Tinkler) *a towards rr* **100/1**

11 3/4 **Wunder Strike (USA)** 2-9-3 0.. PaulMulrennan 13 24
(M J Wallace, Australia) *dwlt: a in rr* **12/1**[3]

00 **12** 1 3/4 **Konka (USA)**[39] 4870 2-8-12 0.....................................(t) TonyCulhane 5 12
(E F Vaughan) *a in rr* **80/1**

00 **13** *9* **Valdemar**[17] 5539 2-9-3 0........ PaulHanagan 1 —
(A D Brown) *a in rr* **125/1**

64.94 secs (1.44) **Going Correction** +0.175s/f (Good) 13 Ran SP% **120.3**
Speed ratings (Par 95): **95,94,89,84,80 79,74,73,71,69 68,65,51**
toteswinger: 1&2 £7.70, 1&3 £11.70, 2&3 £6.50. CSF £46.34 TOTE £24.70: £6.50, £1.02, £5.90; EX 27.30.
Owner Bezwell Fixings Limited **Bred** J P Hardiman **Trained** Bawtry, S Yorks

FOCUS
A modest maiden, although the winning time was over half a second quicker than the selling nursery. Spiritofthewest became the third winner on the card to make all against the rail, with the favourite probably runnering to form.

NOTEBOOK
Spiritofthewest(IRE) floored the long odds-on Kingship Spirit and became the third consecutive winner at the meeting to make every yard of the running against the inside rail. He had been very slowly away when finishing last on his Thirsk debut, but his performance here could hardly have been more of a contrast as he bounced out from his central draw and was able to get across to the favoured far rail in front. He did go off at 33-1, but was backed in from double those odds so someone obviously expected a much better effort from him this time. (op 50-1 tchd 66-1 and 100-1 in a place)
Kingship Spirit(IRE), placed in all three of his previous starts at top tracks, appeared to be travelling well enough in the first half of the race and it looked a question of when he would pick the leader up, but when Eddie Ahern first put him under maximum pressure the head went up, something he did in his first two starts, and when he did eventually consent to run on it was always going to be just too late. He had never encountered ground this soft before which could be put forward as an excuse, but he must have a big question mark against him now and he is not going to be easy to place, especially as he is officially rated 87. (op 4-6)
York Key Bar, who cost just 800gns as a yearling, finished a very eye-catching third and was still going forward at the line. The stable don't have many winning debutants, so he can only improve. If he does then a maiden can be found before too long. (op 20-1)
Premier Lad shouldn't have minded the ground being by Tobougg and also made a very commendable debut, especially as he was keen early. There should be a race in him in due course. (op 25-1)
Rio Pomba(IRE), not disgraced behind a couple of subsequent winners on her Carlisle debut, ran a fair race and may be one for nurseries after one more run. (op 14-1)
Mythicism, a 40,000gns half-sister to Stargazy out of the Queen Mary winner Romantic Myth, never got involved but may improve for better ground. (op 11-2)
Home Before Dark, who showed improved form at Ripon last time, was a little disappointing as he was up there early and might have been expected to have performed better, but he does now qualify for a mark. (op 25-1)

6011 SPINKY'S BACK AT 70 H'CAP 5f
3:10 (3:13) (Class 5) (0-75,74) 3-Y-O+ **£3,238** (£963; £481; £240) **Stalls** High

Form RPR
0-41 **1** **Arganil (USA)**[16] 5561 3-9-2 **72**........ SilvestreDeSousa 10 89+
(K A Ryan) *mde all: shkn up and wnt clr over 1f out: eased towards fin* **9/4**[1]
5432 **2** *3 1/2* **Select Committee**[21] 5393 3-7-12 **61**........(v) JamieKyne(7) 13 65
(J J Quinn) *chsd wnr: edgd lft and kpt on same pce appr fnl f* **7/1**
6556 **3** *1 1/4* **Prince Namid**[74] 3713 6-9-1 **70**........ AdrianTNicholls 8 70
(D Nicholls) *mid-div: effrt over 2f out: kpt on same pce fnl f* **11/2**[2]
2600 **4** *1/2* **Weet A Surprise**[15] 5594 3-9-0 **70**........ TonyCulhane 14 68
(R Hollinshead) *prom: n.m.r and lost pl over 3f out: styd on wl fnl f* **20/1**
3201 **5** *1* **Obe One**[16] 5566 8-8-5 **60** oh6........ PaulHanagan 7 54
(A Berry) *in rr: kpt on fnl 2f: nvr trbld ldrs* **18/1**
0031 **6** *hd* **King Of Swords (IRE)**[2] 5970 4-9-4 **73** 6ex........ KimTinkler 4 67
(N Tinkler) *chsd ldrs: one pce fnl 2f* **16/1**
003 **7** *1/2* **Another Socket**[71] 3811 3-8-13 **69**........ JoeFanning 6 61
(E S McMahon) *hld up towards rr: kpt on fnl 2f: nvr nr ldrs* **20/1**
0105 **8** *3/4* **Choisette**[34] 5007 3-8-11 **67**........ TomEaves 2 56
(B Smart) *racd wd: chsd ldrs: fdd over 1f out* **22/1**
4004 **9** *1 1/4* **Paris Bell**[13] 5634 6-8-9 **64**........ DavidAllan 9 49
(T D Easterby) *dwlt: kpt on fnl 2f: nvr a factor* **6/1**[3]
0243 **10** *shd* **Winthorpe (IRE)**[8] 5775 8-8-13 **68**........(p) GrahamGibbons 11 52
(J J Quinn) *chsd wnr: wknd over 1f out* **6/1**[3]
0000 **11** *3/4* **Bertbrand**[44] 4693 3-8-5 **68**........ RobbieEgan(7) 5 50
(D Flood) *mid-div: lost pl over 2f out* **66/1**
012 **12** *1* **By The Edge (IRE)**[26] 5220 4-8-4 **66**........ DeanHeslop(7) 1 44
(T D Barron) *dwlt: a towards rr* **16/1**

63.92 secs (0.42) **Going Correction** +0.175s/f (Good)
WFA 3 from 4yo+ 1lb 12 Ran SP% **119.6**
Speed ratings (Par 103): **103,97,95,94,93 92,91,90,88,88 87,85**
toteswinger: 1&2 £4.90, 1&3 £4.00, 2&3 £6.80. CSF £17.16 CT £80.10 TOTE £2.70: £1.40, £2.20, £2.20; EX 17.80.
Owner The Big Moment **Bred** Colt Neck Stables, Llc **Trained** Hambleton, N Yorks

FOCUS
An ordinary sprint handicap, but quite a competitive one. Another front-running winner, with the first four racing against the rail. The form is rated around the runner-up.

6012 MKM BUILDING SUPPLIES H'CAP 1m 4f 16y
3:45 (3:45) (Class 4) (0-85,85) 3-Y-O **£5,180** (£1,541; £770; £384) **Stalls** High

Form RPR
0254 **1** **The Oil Magnate**[27] 5202 3-8-12 **79**........ TonyHamilton 10 85
(M Dods) *hld up towards rr: hdwy 3f out: chsd ldrs over 1f out and sn rdn: drvn ins fnl f and styd on strly to ld last 50yds* **12/1**
0024 **2** *1 1/4* **Tomintoul Flyer**[12] 5682 3-9-1 **82**........(v) JohnEgan 3 86
(H R A Cecil) *trckd ldr: hdwy to ld wl over 2f out: rdn clr over 1f out: drvn ins fnl f: hdd and no ex last 50yds* **3/1**[1]
6556 **3** *1 1/4* **It's A Date**[21] 5406 3-8-8 **75**........ FrancisNorton 9 77
(A King) *trckd ldng pair: hdwy over 2f out: rdn to chse ldr wl over 1f out: sn drvn and kpt on same pce ins fnl f* **12/1**
-645 **4** *3/4* **Graceful Descent (FR)**[33] 5040 3-8-4 **71** oh1........ PaulHanagan 5 72
(R A Fahey) *dwlt: hld up in rr: hdwy on inner 3f out: rdn to chse ldrs wl over 1f out: drvn and kpt on same pce ins fnl f* **12/1**
6440 **5** *3* **Ellmau**[12] 5682 3-9-3 **84**........ DeanMcKeown 4 80
(E J O'Neill) *led: rdn along over 3f out: hdd wl over 2f out: grad wknd* **9/1**[3]
011 **6** *6* **Rowan Rio**[23] 5370 3-9-4 **85**........ LiamJones 6 71
(W J Haggas) *hld up: swtchd lft and sme hdwy 3f out: rdn over 2f out and sn wknd* **3/1**[1]
22-1 **7** *6* **Long Distance (FR)**[19] 5477 3-8-8 **75**........ OscarUrbina 8 52
(J R Fanshawe) *hld up: a in rr* **11/1**
5011 **8** *1 1/4* **Fearless Warrior**[9] 5758 3-8-6 **73** 6ex ow1........(b) EddieAhern 1 48
(J L Dunlop) *hld up in tch: hdwy to chse ldng pair over 4f out: rdn over 2f out and sn wknd* **10/3**[2]

2m 41.41s (0.51) **Going Correction** +0.125s/f (Good) 8 Ran SP% **114.5**
Speed ratings (Par 103): **103,102,101,100,98 94,90,90**
toteswinger: 1&2 £7.10, 1&3 £10.40, 2&3 £8.30. CSF £48.15 CT £449.76 TOTE £14.80: £2.90, £1.40, £3.30; EX 60.60.
Owner Smith & Allan Racing **Bred** Wheelersland Stud **Trained** Denton, Co Durham

FOCUS
This had the look of a very competitive handicap, as a number of them came into the race either off a win or a decent effort, but the early pace was pretty slow and the form may not be that reliable. It has been rated through the winner and fourth.
Rowan Rio Official explanation: jockey said gelding never travelled
Fearless Warrior Official explanation: trainer's rep said gelding was unsuited by the soft ground

6013 EUROPEAN BREEDERS' FUND MAIDEN FILLIES' STKS 7f 100y
4:20 (4:23) (Class 5) 2-Y-O **£3,885** (£1,156; £577; £288) **Stalls** High

Form RPR
02 **1** **Sri Kandi**[16] 5570 2-9-0 0........ JohnEgan 14 74
(P F I Cole) *trckd ldrs: t.k.h: led over 3f out: kpt on fnl f: jst lasted* **2/1**[1]
5 **2** *nk* **Madamlily (IRE)**[38] 4897 2-9-0 0........ GrahamGibbons 11 73
(J J Quinn) *chsd ldrs: swtchd lft jst ins fnl f: styd on wl: jst hld* **12/1**
0 **3** *2* **Haakima (USA)**[26] 5240 2-9-0 0........ JoeFanning 4 69
(C E Brittain) *trckd ldrs: wnt 2nd over 1f out: kpt on same pce* **9/2**[3]
44 **4** *3 3/4* **Honimiere (IRE)**[111] 2534 2-9-0 0........ PJMcDonald 8 60
(G A Swinbank) *chsd ldrs: rdn and outpcd over 2f out: styd on ins fnl f* **11/2**
5 *nk* **Diamond Surprise** 2-9-0 0........ FrancisNorton 7 59+
(P A Blockley) *mid-div: hdwy over 2f out: sn chsng ldrs: wknd ins fnl f* **20/1**
5 **6** *hd* **Ailsa Craig (IRE)**[15] 5584 2-9-0 0........ EddieAhern 10 59
(R Hannon) *chsd ldrs: effrt over 2f out: one pce* **3/1**[2]
7 *6* **Dillenda** 2-9-0 0........ TomEaves 9 45+
(T D Easterby) *hld up in rr: sme hdwy over 2f out: nvr on terms* **28/1**
8 *2 1/4* **Hawkleaf Flier (IRE)** 2-9-0 0........ DavidAllan 6 39+
(T D Easterby) *in rr: kpt on fnl f: nvr on terms* **20/1**
9 *1* **Elevate Bambina** 2-8-11 0........ MichaelJStainton(3) 1 37
(R M Whitaker) *a towards rr* **50/1**
10 *14* **Hindford Oak Sioux** 2-8-11 0........ RussellKennemore(3) 3 4
(Mrs L Williamson) *mid-div: effrt on outside over 3f out: sn lost pl* **66/1**
0 **11** *1* **Our Bridget**[39] 4873 2-9-0 0........ PaulQuinn 12 2
(C W Fairhurst) *led: hdd over 3f out: lost pl over 2f out* **100/1**
12 *5* **Blushing Dreamer (IRE)** 2-9-0 0........(b[1]) LeeEnstone 13 —
(P A Blockley) *s.i.s: sn prom: lost pl 3f out: sn bhd* **33/1**
13 *4* **Duratwill** 2-9-0 0........ PaulMulrennan 5 —
(M W Easterby) *slowly away: in rr: wl bhd fnl 3f* **40/1**

1m 38.04s (4.24) **Going Correction** +0.65s/f (Yiel) 13 Ran SP% **122.4**
Speed ratings (Par 92): **101,100,98,94,93 93,86,84,82,66 65,60,55**
toteswinger: 1&2 £7.70, 1&3 £2.90, 2&3 £11.20. CSF £26.81 TOTE £2.70: £1.30, £3.40, £2.10; EX 29.10.
Owner Mrs Fitri Hay **Bred** Swettenham Stud **Trained** Whatcombe, Oxon

FOCUS
None of the newcomers caught the eye on paper, so it was not the biggest surprise to see one of those with experience get off the mark. Indeed, the first three home had all run at least once before. This was another race where it paid to be on the speed and the form is only modest.

NOTEBOOK
Sri Kandi was always well positioned towards the front and kept on well up the inside rail to just repel the final thrust of the runner-up. Her future is very much dependent on how the handicapper rates her. (op 10-3 tchd 7-2 in a place)
Madamlily(IRE), whose sales price increased considerably at two, shaped with a little promise on her debut and duly built on it in this. She was possibly a bit unlucky not to make the winner battle a bit harder for success (she was a little short of room inside the final furlong) but can win something similar next time. (op 10-1 tchd 14-1)
Haakima(USA) attracted market support on her debut and showed a bit of ability before fading late on. It was almost a repeat performance in this, as she looked very dangerous with about a couple of furlongs to go before finding her effort flattening out up the incline. (tchd 5-1)
Honimiere(IRE), having her first run since May, kept on quite well once hitting the rising ground after looking a little one-paced. However, she did not completely convince that she is an easy ride. (op 5-1 tchd 13-2)
Diamond Surprise, a half-sister to the very talented Fortunately among others, is definitely the one to take out of the race. She held a few positions during the race and looked a little inexperienced under pressure but she kept on for pressure and will be wiser next time. (op 14-1 tchd 17-2)
Ailsa Craig(IRE) may have been unlucky not to get a bit closer, as she possibly could not get past Madamlily as the tempo increased off the final bend. (op 10-3 tchd 4-1)
Dillenda, a fairly cheap half-sister to 7f winner We're Delighted, looked to have plenty to give coming into the home straight and was given a considerate ride up the hill once it was clear she was not going to play a part in the finish. She is capable of better. (op 25-1 tchd 33-1)

6014 BEVERLEY RACECOURSE MAIDEN AUCTION STKS (DIV II) 7f 100y
4:50 (4:51) (Class 6) 2-Y-O **£2,590** (£770; £385; £192) **Stalls** High

Form RPR
60 **1** **Sharp Sovereign (USA)**[53] 4415 2-8-9 0........ TomEaves 8 71+
(T D Barron) *in tch: pushed along and sltly outpcd 3f out: hdwy on inner over 2f out: swtchd lft and rdn ent fnl f: styd on wl to ld last 75yds* **15/2**[3]
00 **2** *3/4* **What A Day**[23] 5364 2-8-11 0........ GrahamGibbons 11 71
(J J Quinn) *trckd ldrs on inner: hdwy over 2f out: swtchd lft and rdn to ld jst over 1f out: drvn ins fnl f: hdd and nt qckn last 75yds* **8/1**
0 **3** *2 3/4* **Mekong Miss**[13] 5650 2-8-8 0........ PaulQuinn 2 62
(J Jay) *trckd ldrs: hdwy 3f out: rdn 2f out: drvn and kpt on same pce appr fnl f* **33/1**
00 **4** *1 1/2* **Topolski (IRE)**[70] 3853 2-9-1 0........ JoeFanning 1 65+
(M Johnston) *trckd ldrs on outer: pushed along 3f out: rdn over 2f out: sn drvn and kpt on same pce* **7/1**[2]
2 **5** *1 3/4* **Bandanaman (IRE)**[37] 4921 2-9-1 0........ PJMcDonald 5 61+
(G A Swinbank) *dwlt and sn pushed along: hdwy 1/2-way: rdn to chse ldrs 2f out: sn drvn and btn* **8/11**[1]
0 **6** *nse* **Oriental Cavalier**[23] 5364 2-8-8 0........ RussellKennemore(3) 4 57+
(R Hollinshead) *towards rr: hdwy on wd outside over 2f out: sn rdn and no imp* **14/1**
0 **7** *3/4* **Dance Society**[8] 5771 2-8-9 0........ DavidAllan 12 53
(T D Easterby) *led: rdn along and clr over 2f out: drvn and hdd jst over 1f out: wknd qckly* **28/1**
0004 **8** *7* **Aven Mac (IRE)**[8] 5771 2-8-4 35........ FrancisNorton 11 32
(N Bycroft) *a in rr* **33/1**
0 **9** *6* **Santoriney (IRE)**[44] 4692 2-8-4 0........ DaleGibson 9 18
(D Flood) *sn outpcd and a bhd* **66/1**
003 **10** *6* **Chipolini (IRE)**[98] 2924 2-8-11 66........ DNolan 3 11
(D Carroll) *prom: rdn along 1/2-way: sn wknd* **25/1**

1m 37.88s (4.08) **Going Correction** +0.65s/f (Yiel) 10 Ran SP% **114.6**
Speed ratings (Par 93): **102,101,98,96,94 94,93,85,78,71**
toteswinger: 1&2 £7.10, 1&3 £26.60, 2&3 £24.60. CSF £60.20 TOTE £8.20: £1.80, £2.60, £5.50; EX 74.50.
Owner Raymond Miquel **Bred** James Sumter Carter **Trained** Maunby, N Yorks

FOCUS
Another ordinary maiden, though the winning time was 1.07 seconds faster than the first division and 0.16 seconds faster than the fillies' maiden. The principals raced near the speed again.
NOTEBOOK
Sharp Sovereign(USA), who has hinted at ability in both of his previous starts, travelled nicely off the pace and once switched off the rail to make his effort saw his race out well. This stiffer test suited him ideally and he is entitled to carry on improving, whilst his US pedigree suggests that sand might suit him also. (op 8-1 tchd 17-2)
What A Day, a half-brother to the smart Systematic, was always close to the pace and had every chance but the winner saw his race out that much better. He comprehensively turned recent Warwick form around with Oriental Cavalier and he will have more opportunities now that he qualifies for a mark. (op 9-1 tchd 10-1)
Mekong Miss stayed on well in the latter stages and improved on her debut effort. She is bred to appreciate much further than this and she gave the impression she would come on again for the experience. (op 28-1 tchd 25-1)
Topolski(IRE), very green on his debut before finishing last in a hot Newmarket maiden, was weak in the market beforehand and looked rather one-paced here having raced close up from the start. He is bred to appreciate middle-distances next year. (op 4-1)
Bandanaman(IRE), narrowly beaten at Thirsk on his debut in a race that has produced a few placed horses though no winners, was having to be ridden along very early and, when brought wide in order to make his effort, found very little. He may do better once handicapped. Official explanation: trainer said he had no explanation for the poor form shown (op 11-10 tchd 6-5)
Oriental Cavalier was struggling to go the early pace before making a little late headway down the wide outside. He is another whose longer-term future probably lies in handicaps. (op 12-1)
Dance Society very much had the run of the race out in front, but may have done too much and didn't get home. (op 20-1)

6015 RACING AGAIN NEXT TUESDAY APPRENTICE CLASSIFIED STKS 1m 100y
5:20 (5:20) (Class 6) 3-Y-O+ £2,217 (£654; £327) Stalls High

Form RPR
3333 **1** **Rossini's Dancer**[16] 5565 3-8-5 53..............................(p) BMcHugh(5) 11 58
(R A Fahey) *in rr: hdwy u.p 3f out: styd on to ld ins fnl f* **2/1**[1]
5200 **2** *1* **Near The Front**[71] 3817 3-8-8 55 ow1.....................(v[1]) KylieManser(3) 14 57
(Miss Gay Kelleway) *hld up: stdy hdwy on ins over 2f out: nt clr run and swtchd lft 1f out: styd on to take 2nd wl ins fnl f* **16/1**
0510 **3** *1 ½* **Josephine Malines**[24] 5318 4-9-0 55 ow3........................ ClGillies(3) 13 56
(Mrs A Duffield) *trckd ldrs: effrt on inner and hmpd over 1f out: kpt on same pce ins fnl f* **8/1**
0 **4** *1 ¼* **Drumadoon Bay (IRE)**[23] 5361 4-8-11 54................ FrederikTylicki(3) 5 50
(G A Swinbank) *chsd ldr: led over 1f out: hdd ins fnl f: fdd* **10/3**[2]
600 **5** *1 ¾* **Can Can Dancer**[46] 4620 3-8-5 53.......................... RosieJessop(5) 12 46
(J G Given) *hld up in rr: detached over 3f out: styd on strly fnl 2f: nt rch ldrs* **12/1**
6-00 **6** *1 ¼* **Sand Maiden (IRE)**[117] 2367 3-8-5 53.......................... JamieKyne(5) 10 43
(T D Easterby) *led tl over 1f out: sn wknd* **25/1**
3000 **7** *3* **Kayflaa (IRE)**[24] 5308 3-8-10 55.................................. KellyHarrison 8 36
(T D Walford) *trckd ldrs: one pce fnl 2f* **11/1**
1400 **8** *nk* **Jemima's Art**[8] 5776 3-8-7 53......................................(b) LanceBetts(3) 4 35
(M W Easterby) *trckd ldrs: effrt over 2f out: wknd over 1f out* **7/1**[3]
0060 **9** *8* **I Feel Fine**[49] 4537 5-8-11 50.................................. DeanHeslop(3) 7 17
(A Kirtley) *chsd ldrs: lost pl over 2f out* **100/1**
0000 **10** *¾* **Super Al**[13] 5627 3-8-5 21.................................. TobyAtkinson(5) 3 15
(M Wigham) *s.i.s: a bhd* **100/1**
500 **11** *½* **Whipma Whopma Gate (IRE)**[52] 4461 3-8-10 55... PatrickDonaghy 15 14
(D Carroll) *sn bhd* **25/1**
050 **12** *½* **Predictable (IRE)**[18] 5505 3-8-5 48.......................... BradleyRoper(5) 6 13
(M W Easterby) *a in rr* **33/1**
40 **13** *3 ¼* **Lachafinna (IRE)**[13] 5636 3-8-5 54.......................... PaulPickard(5) 9 5
(D Carroll) *in rr-div: sme hdwy on outside over 2f out: sn wknd* **16/1**
-636 **14** *9* **Ginger Minx (IRE)**[16] 5574 3-8-7 50.......................... RossAtkinson(3) 2 —
(N J Vaughan) *swvd lft s: a bhd* **25/1**

1m 52.42s (4.82) **Going Correction** +0.65s/f (Yiel)
WFA 3 from 4yo+ 4lb 14 Ran SP% **124.3**
Speed ratings (Par 101): **101,100,98,97,95 94,91,90,82,82 81,81,77,68**
toteswinger: 1&2 £11.30, 1&3 £5.60, 2&3 £24.70. CSF £37.13 TOTE £2.30: £1.40, £5.40, £2.40; EX 49.30 Place 6 £ 28.67, Place 5 £ 24.13.
Owner Lets Go Racing 1 **Bred** Heather Raw **Trained** Musley Bank, N Yorks
FOCUS
A weak race and ordinary form for the grade, although it does seem sound.
T/Jkpt: Not won. T/Plt: £50.50 to a £1 stake. Pool: £63,086.44. 910.82 winning tickets. T/Qpdt: £21.90 to a £1 stake. Pool: £3,452.89. 116.60 winning tickets. JR

5911 KEMPTON (A.W) (R-H)
Wednesday, September 17

OFFICIAL GOING: Standard
Wind: Moderate, across Weather: Fine but cloudy

6016 DAY TIME, NIGHT TIME, GREAT TIME MEDIAN AUCTION MAIDEN FILLIES' STKS 1m (P)
6:20 (6:20) (Class 6) 2-Y-O £2,047 (£604; £302) Stalls High

Form RPR
1 **Something Perfect (USA)** 2-9-0 0.................................. TPQueally 9 77+
(H R A Cecil) *trckd ldrs: plenty of tail swishing thrght: rdn to go 2nd over 1f out: sustained chal to ld last 50yds despite slipping sddle* **5/1**[3]
53 **2** *½* **Kaloni (IRE)**[16] 5571 2-9-0 0.................................. MickyFenton 8 76
(Mrs P Sly) *mde most: hrd pressed most of way: fought off eventual 3rd over 1f out: kpt on fnl f: hdd last 50yds* **5/1**[3]
2 **3** *2 ½* **Wake Me Now (IRE)**[41] 4763 2-9-0 0.......................... RichardKingscote 2 71
(R M Beckett) *w ldr to over 1f out: steadily outpcd after* **7/2**[2]
2 **4** *1 ¼* **Kouloura (IRE)**[26] 5227 2-9-0 0.......................... KirstyMilczarek 13 68
(M Botti) *trckd ldrs: plld out over 2f out: drifted bdly lft after and nvr able to chal* **2/1**[1]
5 *nk* **Sampi** 2-9-0 0.. JimCrowley 12 67
(Mrs A J Perrett) *sltly tardy s but sn in midfield: effrt to chse ldrs over 2f out: nvr cl enough to chal but kpt on steadily* **17/2**
00 **6** *6* **Miss Tikitiboo (IRE)**[8] 5788 2-9-0 0.......................... GregFairley 14 54
(E F Vaughan) *towards rr: prog 3f out: chsng ldrs but nt on terms 2f out: no imp* **50/1**
4 **7** *1 ¾* **Second To Nun (IRE)**[69] 3869 2-9-0 0.......................... StephenCarson 4 50
(Jean-Rene Auvray) *wl in tch in midfield: outpcd and rdn wl over 2f out: nvr on terms after* **14/1**
0 **8** *nk* **Countess Zara (IRE)**[35] 4974 2-9-0 0.......................... LPKeniry 10 49
(A M Balding) *s.s: wl in rr: rdn over 2f out: plugged on: no ch* **40/1**
6 **9** *1 ½* **Jarrah Bay**[35] 4973 2-9-0 0.................................. JimmyQuinn 6 46
(J G M O'Shea) *t.k.h early: hld up in midfield: outpcd fr over 2f out: wknd over 1f out* **33/1**
0 **10** *1 ¼* **Nesayem (IRE)**[13] 5650 2-9-0 0.......................... StephenDonohoe 5 43
(D M Simcock) *s.i.s: a wl in rr: nvr a factor* **66/1**
0 **11** *2 ¾* **Deckchair**[26] 5241 2-9-0 0.................................. DavidKinsella 3 37+
(H J Collingridge) *racd wd: a towards rr: lost grnd bnd 3f out: sn struggling* **40/1**
04 **12** *6* **Amatara (IRE)**[8] 5782 2-9-0 0.................................. TQuinn 1 24
(B G Powell) *dropped in fr wd draw and hld up in rr: sme prog into midfield over 2f out but nt on terms: wknd rapidly over 1f out* **66/1**
0 **13** *9* **Highams Park (IRE)**[75] 3674 2-9-0 0.......................... JamesDoyle 11 —
(J G Portman) *rdn in midfield bef 1/2-way: sn struggling: t.o* **100/1**
0 **14** *8* **Queen Of Burlesque (USA)**[7] 5798 2-9-0 0.................. MartinDwyer 7 —
(B J Meehan) *chsd ldrs over 4f out: wknd rapidly: t.o* **40/1**

1m 39.9s (0.10) **Going Correction** -0.10s/f (Stan) 14 Ran SP% **122.3**
Speed ratings (Par 90): **95,94,92,90,90 84,82,82,80,79 76,70,61,53**
toteswinger: 1&2 £7.00, 1&3 £3.60, 2&3 £5.00. CSF £29.56 TOTE £4.60: £1.30, £2.20, £2.30; EX 29.40.
Owner The Sticky Wicket Syndicate III **Bred** Arbaway Ventures **Trained** Newmarket, Suffolk
FOCUS
Just an ordinary fillies' maiden. The early pace was pretty steady and the principals were prominent throughout. The form has been rated around the second and fourth.
NOTEBOOK
Something Perfect(USA), a daughter of Lady Angharad, who won five times at up to 1m2f, has apparently not been the easiest to deal with at home, but she travelled well just off the pace and made a winning debut despite showing signs of inexperience, flashing her tail a number of times in the straight. This was not a great race but she won despite a slipping saddle and, as a result of the bare form, the handicapper cannot give her too much to do in nurseries. She could well improve for this. (op 4-1)
Kaloni(IRE), who got some experience of this track when third over the course and distance last time, was soon in front and bagged the rail. She enjoyed the run of the race and can have few excuses, but she is now eligible for a mark and, given her pedigree, should improve with time and distance. (op 15-2)
Wake Me Now(IRE) ran all right over an extended 5f at Bath on her debut, but she had her stamina to prove over this longer trip. Having harried the leader to two furlongs out she did not quite see it out as well as the first two, and perhaps a drop back to 7f will prove the answer. (op 5-1)
Kouloura(IRE) was well drawn and appeared to set a fair standard on her debut second in a Newbury maiden, but she was weak in the betting and raced keenly in the race itself. Once switched off the rail in the straight, she continued to edge left and eventually finished her race near the stands' rail. Official explanation: jockey said filly hung left throughout (op 6-5)
Sampi, who hails from a stable whose juveniles usually need their debuts, did not run too badly and can improve for the experience. (op 12-1 tchd 14-1)
Miss Tikitiboo(IRE) has now had the required three runs for a mark and will be of more interest in moderate handicap company. (op 66-1 tchd 80-1)
Second To Nun(IRE) finished fourth in a soft-ground Folkestone maiden on her debut back in July and the form of that race has worked out well, with the winner, third, sixth and ninth all winning nurseries since. This was a different test and she gave away ground racing wide throughout. She can do better once handicapped and back on soft ground. (op 25-1 tchd 12-1)

6017 PANORAMIC BAR & RESTAURANT NURSERY 6f (P)
6:50 (6:50) (Class 6) (0-65,65) 2-Y-O £2,047 (£604; £302) Stalls High

Form RPR
5053 **1** **Ray Of Joy**[16] 5581 2-9-5 64.................................. JimmyQuinn 4 74+
(J R Jenkins) *trckd ldr: led 2f out and sn kicked clr: in n.d after: r.o wl* **7/1**
4560 **2** *3 ¾* **Pacific Bay (IRE)**[22] 5381 2-9-6 65.......................... DO'Donohoe 5 64
(Mrs A Duffield) *settled towards rr: pushed along and prog on outer over 2f out: shkn up and styd on to take 2nd last strides* **40/1**
211 **3** *nk* **Pressed For Time (IRE)**[6] 5834 2-9-6 65 6ex........(t) EdwardCreighton 3 63
(E J Creighton) *t.k.h early: prom: rdn to chse wnr over 1f out but no ch of threatening: kpt on but lost 2nd last strides* **6/1**[3]
5560 **4** *nk* **Sharav**[25] 5277 2-9-3 62.................................. NCallan 12 59
(Eve Johnson Houghton) *mostly in midfield: rdn wl over 2f out: kpt on u.p fr over 1f out to chal for pls fnl f* **13/2**
2000 **5** *nk* **Going Time (USA)**[20] 5432 2-9-2 61.......................... GregFairley 6 57
(M Johnston) *led to 2f out: sn outpcd: kpt on* **16/1**
0466 **6** *½* **Reel Ale**[12] 5671 2-9-4 63.................................. StephenCarson 9 58
(P Winkworth) *t.k.h early: trckd ldrs: rdn and nt qckn over 2f out: one pce after* **9/2**[2]
5020 **7** *nk* **Val De Flores**[6] 5834 2-9-5 64.......................... JamieSpencer 10 58
(E F Vaughan) *chsd ldng pair: rdn over 2f out: lost pl over 1f out: one pce after* **6/1**[3]
5033 **8** *¾* **Handcuff**[14] 5614 2-9-5 64.................................. JimCrowley 8 56
(J Gallagher) *mostly in last pair: c wd in st: kpt on fr over 1f out but n.d* **14/1**
0554 **9** *shd* **Daily Double**[12] 5671 2-9-4 63.................................. LPKeniry 11 54
(R Hannon) *nrly sat down as stalls opened: in tch in rr but a struggling: no prog u.p 2f out* **5/2**[1]
040 **10** *2 ½* **Twos And Eights (IRE)**[77] 3603 2-9-4 63..................(b[1]) PaulEddery 1 47
(G D Blake) *t.k.h early: hld up: shkn up and no prog over 2f out: fdd* **50/1**

1m 13.3s (0.20) **Going Correction** -0.10s/f (Stan) 10 Ran SP% **118.1**
Speed ratings (Par 93): **94,89,88,88,87 87,86,85,85,82**
toteswinger: 1&2 £65.90, 1&3 £6.00, 2&3 £15.70. CSF £241.94 CT £1286.36 TOTE £10.00: £2.90, £14.30, £1.70; EX 245.50.
Owner Robin Stevens **Bred** D R Tucker **Trained** Royston, Herts
FOCUS
A modest nursery featuring only one previous winner. Ray Of Joy was much improved on this sand debut and the form seems sound enough.
NOTEBOOK
Ray Of Joy ran out a clear-cut winner. She did not have a great draw, but was fast away, soon held a prominent pitch and quickened up well two furlongs out. In no danger in the closing stages, the switch to Polytrack has clearly helped, and she can now expect a decent rise in the weights. Perhaps she can be found an opportunity to follow up under a penalty in the coming days. (tchd 13-2 and 15-2)
Pacific Bay(IRE) had run poorly on her last two starts but she bounced back to the sort of form she showed at Pontefract in June on this, her Polytrack debut. She stayed on from off the pace to come out best in the bunch finish for the places. (op 33-1)
Pressed For Time(IRE) had won her last two starts but she had a penalty to carry this time and an extra furlong to cover. Keen enough, she ran well in the circumstances, but on this evidence she is a 5f specialist. (op 9-2)
Sharav, who was always behind in the St Leger Yearling Stakes last time out, had the best draw and kept on next to the far-side rail, but he was never a serious threat. One suspects he needs further than this. (op 12-1)
Going Time(USA), who has not gone on since her first couple of starts, was down a furlong in distance and again made the running. A half-sister to a high-class US dirt sprinter in Saratoga County, there was hope that she would do better for the switch to Polytrack, but having set a sound pace she was left for dead by the winner two furlongs out. (op 14-1)

Reel Ale confirmed the impression left when last running over this course and distance, which is that he needs further. (op 9-1)
Val De Flores, who was stepping up in distance, travelled well into the straight but did not get home. (op 11-2)
Handcuff Official explanation: jockey said colt hung left
Daily Double sat down in the stalls and was always struggling after a slow start. (op 11-4 tchd 9-4)

6018 DIGIBET.COM MEDIAN AUCTION MAIDEN STKS 1m 4f (P)
7:20 (7:21) (Class 6) 3-4-Y-O **£2,047** (£604; £302) **Stalls** Centre

Form RPR
5222 **1** **Buddhist Monk**[19] 5453 3-9-3 75 ... DO'Donohoe 4 78+
(Sir Mark Prescott) *t.k.h early: hld up: last after 4f: gd prog fr 4f out: brought v wd in st: clsd to ld jst ins fnl f: sn clr and no sign of stopping* **7/4**[2]
2 *2 ¾* **Isabelonabicycle** 3-8-12 0 ... LPKeniry 12 68
(A M Balding) *wl plcd: chsd ldr 3f out to over 1f out: kpt on wl fnl f to snatch 2nd on line* **10/1**
5322 **3** *hd* **Brexca (IRE)**[47] 4581 3-9-3 74 ... (v) AdamKirby 5 73
(C G Cox) *trckd ldr: led over 4f out: hdd and outpcd jst ins fnl f: lost 2nd last strides* **13/8**[1]
0000 **4** *7* **Bluebell Ridge (IRE)**[41] 4774 3-8-12 45 ... KirstyMilczarek 9 57
(D W P Arbuthnot) *hld up: last over 5f out: gd prog 3f out: chsd ldrs but outpcd 2f out: hung lft but kpt on* **33/1**
-000 **5** *8* **Looping The Loop (USA)**[128] 2046 3-9-3 53 ... JamesDoyle 8 49
(J G Portman) *hld up in midfield: in tch over 3f out: rdn and wl outpcd fr over 2f out* **50/1**
0 **6** *2 ¼* **Tignello (IRE)**[19] 5463 3-9-3 0 ... TQuinn 7 45
(D R C Elsworth) *t.k.h early: hld up in midfield: in tch over 3f out: outpcd and wl btn 2f out* **16/1**
4-40 **7** *12* **Tamdiid (USA)**[7] 5803 3-8-12 60 ... NCallan 3 21
(C E Brittain) *prom: disp 2nd 3f out: wknd rapidly 2f out: virtually p.u fnl f* **8/1**[3]
05- **8** *¾* **Beauchamp Viking**[17] 2666 4-9-11 0 ... (t) JimCrowley 13 25
(S C Burrough) *plld hrd in midfield: wknd 3f out: sn wl bhd* **66/1**
6020 **9** *shd* **Royal Tender (IRE)**[14] 5602 4-9-6 45 ... (v) DavidKinsella 10 20
(H J Collingridge) *s.s and reluctant early: in tch in rr to over 3f out: sn btn* **40/1**
-244 **10** *3 ½* **Cherokee Star**[18] 3835 3-9-3 72 ... SamHitchcott 11 19
(C C Bealby) *hanging lft thrght: led: wd and hdd over 4f out: v wd bnd 3f out: sn wknd* **14/1**
P00 **11** *7* **Hungry For More**[62] 4123 4-9-8 0 ... KevinGhunowa(3) 6 8
(M R Hoad) *t.k.h early: hld up: wknd wl over 3f out: sn wl bhd* **100/1**
0000 **12** *½* **Starfinch**[14] 5607 3-8-12 34 ... RichardKingscote 1 2
(J J Bridger) *in tch in midfield on outer: wknd rapidly 3f out* **100/1**
0-00 **13** *1* **Newcastle Sam**[35] 4978 3-9-0 35 ... (p) MarcHalford(3) 2 6
(J J Bridger) *dwlt: many reminders and a in last trio* **100/1**

2m 32.87s (-1.63) **Going Correction** -0.10s/f (Stan)
WFA 3 from 4yo 8lb **13** Ran SP% **119.0**
Speed ratings (Par 101): **101,99,99,94,89 87,79,79,78,76 71,71,70**
toteswinger: 1&2 £3.60, 1&3 £1.40, 2&3 £5.10. CSF £19.42 TOTE £3.20: £1.80, £3.60, £1.02; EX 21.90.
Owner Lord Derby **Bred** Stanley Estate And Stud Co **Trained** Newmarket, Suffolk

FOCUS
A weak maiden and the market was headed by a couple of dodgepots. However, they did have the best form on offer and in the end one of them finally got his head in front. Not a race to be too positive about.
Tamdiid(USA) Official explanation: jockey said filly ran too free
Cherokee Star Official explanation: jockey said gelding hung left-handed throughout
Starfinch Official explanation: jockey said filly had no more to give

6019 DIGIBET H'CAP 1m 4f (P)
7:50 (7:51) (Class 6) (0-60,63) 3-Y-0+ **£2,047** (£604; £302) **Stalls** Centre

Form RPR
004 **1** **Oasis Sun (IRE)**[14] 5611 5-8-10 54 ... (b) AndreaAtzeni(7) 12 63
(J R Best) *trckd ldr to 5f out and again 3f out: rdn to ld over 1f out: styd on wl to assert ins fnl f* **20/1**
4535 **2** *1 ¾* **Just Intersky (USA)**[32] 5105 5-9-6 57 ... NCallan 11 63
(H J Collingridge) *hld up in 5th: wl plcd whn pce lifted over 3f out: effrt on inner 2f out: pressed wnr 1f out: one pce after* **11/1**
3501 **3** *1 ¼* **Formidable Guest**[7] 5802 4-9-7 58 6ex ... AdamKirby 9 62+
(J Pearce) *hld up in 7th: effrt 3f out but plenty to do w pce qckning: prog 2f out: styd on to take 3rd ins fnl f: no ch to chal* **13/2**[2]
4434 **4** *1* **Best Selection**[37] 4935 4-9-6 57 ... PaulDoe 3 60
(Mrs L J Mongan) *hld up in 6th: rdn over 3f out: tried to cl fr 2f out: kpt on but nt pce to chal* **15/2**[3]
3405 **5** *1 ½* **Spume (IRE)**[11] 5712 4-9-3 57 ... (tp) TolleyDean(3) 10 57
(S Parr) *rrd s: hld up in abt 10th and t.k.h early: effrt 3f out: styd on fnl 2f and nrst fin: no ch to be involved* **16/1**
321 **6** *nk* **Split The Wind (USA)**[41] 4774 4-9-2 53 ... EdwardCreighton 7 53
(Miss Sheena West) *led at modest pce: kicked on over 3f out and had most of rivals in trble: hdd & wknd over 1f out* **20/1**
6132 **7** *4 ½* **Tabulate**[8] 5787 5-9-9 60 ... IanMongan 4 53
(P Howling) *hld up in 8th: one of few stl gng wl enough whn pce lifted 3f out: shkn up and no rspnse over 2f out: btn after* **9/1**
0010 **8** *2 ¼* **Hallings Overture (USA)**[18] 5489 9-9-5 56 ... (p) RichardKingscote 1 45
(C A Horgan) *t.k.h and hld up in rr: allowed to stride past field to go 2nd 5f out to 3f out: sn wknd* **20/1**
4562 **9** *½* **Bienheureux**[6] 5833 7-9-6 57 ... (t) JamieSpencer 6 45
(Miss Gay Kelleway) *hld up in last pair in modestly run r: shuffled along and nt look keen over 2f out: nvr a factor* **5/1**[1]
0565 **10** *½* **Fateful Attraction**[7] 5802 5-9-8 59 ... (vt[1]) JamesDoyle 14 46
(I A Wood) *trckd ldng pair: rdn over 3f out: wknd on inner over 2f out* **12/1**
3063 **11** *1 ¼* **Garafena**[14] 5611 5-9-9 60 ... StephenDonohoe 5 45
(B G Powell) *chsd ldng trio: rdn over 3f out: wknd 2f out* **14/1**
5051 **12** *nk* **Shraayef**[7] 5803 3-9-4 63 6ex ... KirstyMilczarek 2 48
(M Botti) *t.k.h early: hld up in 9th: rdn over 3f out: no impact on ldrs on outer over 2f out: wknd* **5/1**[1]
2400 **13** *3* **Mix N Match**[7] 5802 4-9-3 54 ... TQuinn 13 34
(R M Stronge) *hld up in last pair in modestly run r: no ch after pce qcknd over 3f out* **22/1**
1-66 **14** *2 ¾* **Sir Haydn**[13] 5630 8-9-9 60 ... (v) MickyFenton 8 36
(J R Jenkins) *t.k.h: hld up in last trio in modestly run r: nvr a factor* **20/1**

2m 36.6s (2.10) **Going Correction** -0.10s/f (Stan)
WFA 3 from 4yo+ 8lb **14** Ran SP% **120.4**
Speed ratings (Par 101): **89,87,87,86,85 85,82,80,80,79 79,78,76,75**
toteswinger: 1&2 £66.00, 1&3 £36.50, 2&3 £13.40. CSF £209.50 CT £1605.61 TOTE £19.70: £6.60, £3.60, £2.50; EX 224.50.
Owner Mrs J Schabacker **Bred** Peter Jones And G G Jones **Trained** Hucking, Kent

FOCUS
An open-looking handicap, but it was run at a steady pace and in a time 3.73sec slower than the earlier maiden. It turned into something of a sprint and little got into it from the rear. Not form to be too positive about.
Hallings Overture(USA) Official explanation: jockey said gelding ran too free

6020 DIGIBET CASINO H'CAP 7f (P)
8:20 (8:20) (Class 5) (0-75,75) 3-Y-0+ **£2,590** (£770; £385; £192) **Stalls** High

Form RPR
4322 **1** **King's Wonder**[11] 5713 3-9-4 75 ... MartinDwyer 12 93
(W R Muir) *mde all: drew rt away fr over 2f out: maintained gallop fnl 2f: impressive* **8/1**[3]
0002 **2** *6* **Onenightinlisbon (IRE)**[4] 5915 4-9-0 68 ... PatCosgrave 13 71
(J R Boyle) *prom: chsd wnr 1/2-way: lft wl bhd fr over 2f out: jst hld on for 2nd* **8/1**[3]
0041 **3** *shd* **Lawton**[14] 5616 3-8-9 66 ... PaulFitzsimons 4 68
(Miss J R Tooth) *trckd ldrs on outer: effrt over 2f out: styd on fr over 1f out: nrly snatched 2nd* **16/1**
0304 **4** *½* **Blue Charm**[7] 5800 4-9-0 68 ... LPKeniry 6 69
(S Kirk) *hld up in midfield: effrt over 2f out: styd on fnl f to press plcd horses nr fin* **17/2**
2306 **5** *hd* **Scarlet Flyer (USA)**[14] 5600 5-9-1 69 ... (p) StephenCarson 10 70
(G L Moore) *hld up in rr: effrt on inner over 2f out: styd on to press for a pl fnl f* **16/1**
2124 **6** *1 ½* **Glenridding**[30] 5156 4-9-7 75 ... JimCrowley 7 72
(J G Given) *chsd wnr to 1/2-way: u.p after: outpcd but kpt on* **8/1**[3]
0003 **7** *nk* **Napoletano (GER)**[14] 5600 7-9-1 69 ... (p) NCallan 2 65
(S Dow) *dropped in fr wd draw and hld up: midfield 1/2-way: effrt over 2f out: plugged on but nvr really on terms* **16/1**
-22 **8** *1 ¼* **War And Peace (IRE)**[13] 5634 4-9-5 73 ... JamieSpencer 1 66
(Jane Chapple-Hyam) *dropped in fr wd draw and hld up in last trio: wd bnd 3f out: modest prog 2f out: nvr on terms* **11/2**[2]
1220 **9** *¾* **Greystoke Prince**[14] 5600 3-9-4 75 ... (p) AdamKirby 8 65
(W R Swinburn) *hld up bhd ldrs: gng bttr than most 3f out: rdn and no rspnse over 2f out: fdd* **8/1**[3]
0030 **10** *1 ½* **Shot To Fame (USA)**[25] 5267 9-9-1 69 ... RichardKingscote 11 56
(S Kirk) *hld up in midfield on inner: effrt over 2f out: no prog and wl btn whn n.m.r over 1f out* **12/1**
0030 **11** *3* **Jebel Tara**[25] 5273 3-9-3 74 ... (t) GregFairley 3 51
(C E Brittain) *chsd ldrs on outer: losing pl u.p 3f out: sn no ch* **18/1**
4561 **12** *¾* **Landucci**[23] 5345 7-9-2 73 ... (v) PatrickHills(3) 9 49
(J W Hills) *t.k.h early: hld up in rr: squeezed out bdly after 2f: nvr a factor after* **5/1**[1]
2-50 **13** *4* **Rydal (USA)**[18] 5492 7-8-11 65 ... TravisBlock 5 31
(Miss Jo Crowley) *s.i.s: nvr gng wl in rr: wd bnd 3f out: sn bhd* **14/1**

1m 24.43s (-1.57) **Going Correction** -0.10s/f (Stan)
WFA 3 from 4yo+ 3lb **13** Ran SP% **124.3**
Speed ratings (Par 103): **104,97,97,96,96 94,94,92,91,90 86,85,81**
toteswinger: 1&2 £11.10, 1&3 £39.70, 2&3 £10.60. CSF £73.66 CT £1057.30 TOTE £12.30: £3.80, £2.40, £5.50; EX 63.50.
Owner D G Clarke & C L A Edginton **Bred** Bearstone Stud **Trained** Lambourn, Berks
■ Stewards' Enquiry : L P Keniry three-day ban: careless riding (Oct 1,2,6)

FOCUS
They went a solid gallop here but again little got into it from the rear, the winner making all. He looks much improved.
Landucci Official explanation: jockey said gelding suffered interference in running

6021 ARCTIC DESERT MEMORIAL H'CAP 1m (P)
8:50 (8:51) (Class 4) (0-85,85) 3-Y-0 **£4,727** (£1,406; £702; £351) **Stalls** High

Form RPR
52 **1** **Priti Fabulous (IRE)**[54] 4377 3-8-9 76 ... JamieSpencer 10 87+
(W J Haggas) *covered up bhd ldrs: got thorugh on inner to ld wl over 1f out: sn sharp reminders: drew clr fnl f: in no real danger after* **5/2**[1]
-606 **2** *1* **Mujaadel (USA)**[32] 5104 3-8-13 80 ... MartinDwyer 11 88
(E A L Dunlop) *s.s and last tl 2f out: rapid prog over 1f out: wnt 2nd last 100yds and clsd on wnr but nvr able to chal* **9/1**
4314 **3** *2 ½* **Minus Fifteen (IRE)**[11] 5697 3-8-13 80 ... NCallan 2 82
(K A Ryan) *trckd ldng pair: reminder 3f out: drvn to chal 2f out: chsd wnr over 1f out: wl hld and lost 2nd last 100yds* **7/2**[2]
-101 **4** *1 ½* **Angel Rock (IRE)**[34] 5018 3-9-1 82 ... JimmyQuinn 4 81
(M Botti) *s.i.s: t.k.h early and hld up in rr: effrt over 2f out: kpt on one pce fr over 1f out* **4/1**[3]
0116 **5** *1 ¼* **Bluejain**[34] 5032 3-8-7 74 ... MickyFenton 1 70
(Miss Gay Kelleway) *t.k.h early and racd wd: in tch 2f out: sn outpcd and btn* **8/1**
5220 **6** *¾* **Taken (IRE)**[74] 3745 3-8-9 76 ... DarryllHolland 7 70
(Miss Gay Kelleway) *rn in snatches in midfield on inner: effrt whn short of room over 1f out: sn btn* **16/1**
600 **7** *2 ¼* **Gone Fast (USA)**[33] 5071 3-8-12 79 ... StephenDonohoe 6 68
(D M Simcock) *w ldr: led briefly 2f out: sn lost pl and grad wknd* **33/1**
4212 **8** *5* **Silent Master (USA)**[8] 5789 3-8-12 79 ... GregFairley 8 57
(M Johnston) *led to 2f out: wknd rapidly* **6/1**

1m 38.4s (-1.40) **Going Correction** -0.10s/f (Stan) **8** Ran SP% **115.0**
Speed ratings (Par 103): **103,102,99,98,96 96,93,88**
toteswinger: 1&2 £6.70, 1&3 £2.70, 2&3 £7.90. CSF £26.21 CT £78.89 TOTE £3.10: £1.20, £2.80, £2.00; EX 26.50.
Owner Kevin Murphy **Bred** Deln Ltd **Trained** Newmarket, Suffolk

FOCUS
Not a bad little handicap although it was not strongly run. The form seems sound enough though.

6022 KEMPTON.CO.UK H'CAP 2m (P)
9:20 (9:22) (Class 6) (0-65,65) 3-Y-0+ **£2,047** (£604; £302) **Stalls** High

Form RPR
3050 **1** **Miss Serena**[24] 5322 3-8-7 56 ow2 ... MickyFenton 3 64
(Mrs P Sly) *hld up in midifeld: prog to go 3rd 1/2-way: chsd ldr over 4f out: sustained chal fnl 2f to ld ins fnl f: hld on* **25/1**

-104 2 1/2 **The Composer**[18] 5489 6-9-2 **53**.......................... AdamKirby 9 60
(M Blanshard) *hld up towards rr: gd prog over 4f out to chse ldng pair over 3f out: drvn over 2f out: kpt on fnl f to take 2nd on line* **20/1**
2622 3 nse **Borrowdale**[11] 5698 3-9-1 **64**.......................... ShaneKelly 13 71
(J A Osborne) *led: stdd pce after 4f: tried to kick on again fr 4f out: edgd lft and hdd ins fnl f: lost 2nd on line* **5/2**[1]
/003 4 nk **Towerofcharlemagne (IRE)**[7] 5802 5-9-6 **57**..........(v) NCallan 7 64+
(Miss E C Lavelle) *hld up in rr: prog over 3f out: drvn and limited rspnse 2f out: grad clsd on ldrs fnl f but nvr got there* **10/1**
5204 5 2 1/2 **Capal Dubh Alainn (IRE)**[58] 4247 3-8-12 **61**..........(vt[1]) GregFairley 6 65
(T J Pitt) *a trcking ldrs: one pce u.p fnl 3f: nvr able to chal* **13/2**[3]
6011 6 1 1/4 **Mohawk Star (IRE)**[4] 5917 7-9-13 **64** 6ex..........(v) MartinDwyer 14 66+
(I A Wood) *hld up in last trio: prog on wd outside 4f out: chsd ldrs and rdn 2f out: no imp: fdd* **11/4**[2]
4002 7 2 1/2 **Good Effect (USA)**[28] 5183 4-9-11 **62**.......................... TQuinn 1 61
(C P Morlock) *mostly chsd ldr to over 4f out: steadily lost pl fnl 3f* **16/1**
333 8 nk **Adage**[6] 5833 5-9-1 **52**..........(t) SaleemGolam 8 51
(David Pinder) *settled in midfield: lost pl on inner 5f out: brief effrt again over 2f out: no threat to ldrs* **10/1**
0556 9 1 **Kalokairi (IRE)**[14] 5613 3-8-8 **57** ow1..........(b) JamieSpencer 2 55
(J L Dunlop) *hld up in last trio: prog on outside fr 4f out: no imp on ldrs 2f out: eased fnl f* **9/1**
000 10 nk **National Day (IRE)**[7] 5802 4-9-2 **56**.......................... MarcHalford(3) 10 53
(D R C Elsworth) *trckd ldrs: lost pl and rdn over 3f out: one pce and no prog after* **33/1**
5P/0 11 25 **Cosmic Messenger (FR)**[15] 5583 5-9-4 **55**..........(t) CatherineGannon 5 22
(L A Dace) *a in last trio: wknd over 3f out: t.o* **100/1**
6020 12 2 1/4 **Brave Boogie**[14] 5613 3-8-5 **54**.......................... JimmyQuinn 11 19
(H J L Dunlop) *trckd ldrs tl wknd 4f out: t.o* **25/1**
-046 13 nk **King Of The Beers (USA)**[87] 2482 4-9-8 **62**.....(p) KevinGhunowa(3) 12 26
(R A Harris) *t.k.h: cl up tl wknd wl over 3f out: t.o* **40/1**

3m 30.33s (0.23) **Going Correction** -0.10s/f (Stan)
WFA 3 from 4yo+ 12lb **13** Ran SP% **121.5**
Speed ratings (Par 101): **95,94,94,94,93 92,91,91,90,90 78,77,76**
toteswinger: 1&2 £70.10, 1&3 £13.00, 2&3 £7.70. CSF £434.10 CT £1706.97 TOTE £28.40: £6.20, £6.20, £1.30; EX 675.10 Place 6 £207.99, Place 5 £131.64 .
Owner Erik Amlie **Bred** Wood Hall Stud **Trained** Thorney, Cambs

FOCUS
A moderate staying handicap run at a steady gallop. The first three were the first three turning in and the form is rated around the second and third, with the winner a surprise improver up 5lb.
T/Plt: £303.00 to a £1 stake. Pool: £77,711.33. 187.20 winning tickets. T/Qpdt: £34.70 to a £1 stake. Pool: £7,142.50. 152.29 winning tickets. JN

5860 SANDOWN (R-H)
Wednesday, September 17

OFFICIAL GOING: Good (good to soft in places on sprint course)
Wind: Nil

6023 FLAKT WOODS NURSERY 5f 6y
2:20 (2:20) (Class 5) (0-75,77) 2-Y-O **£3,885** (£1,156; £577; £288) **Stalls** High

Form RPR
160 1 **Lesley's Choice**[12] 5680 2-9-7 **74**.......................... NCallan 3 76
(P A Blockley) *mde virtually all: rdn and asserted over 1f out: hld on wl u.p fnl f* **12/1**
0401 2 3/4 **Court Approval (IRE)**[4] 5904 2-9-10 **77** 6ex.......... StephenDonohoe 4 76
(T G Mills) *chsd ldrs: hrd rdn over 2f out: chsd wnr ins fnl 2f: styd on to cl ins fnl f but a hld* **7/1**
6621 3 1/2 **Jubilee Juggins (IRE)**[3] 5933 2-9-4 **71** 6ex.......... KirstyMilczarek 6 69
(N P Littmoden) *swtg: stdd towards rr but in tch: rdn and hdwy fr 2f out: styd on wl to cl on ldng duo ins fnl f but a hld* **15/8**[1]
5201 4 2 **Azwa**[12] 5680 2-9-6 **73**.......................... MartinDwyer 8 63
(E A L Dunlop) *chsd ldrs: rdn over 1f out: no imp whn edgd rt ins fnl f: wknd sn after* **6/1**[3]
2560 5 2 **Straitjacket**[20] 5432 2-9-1 **68**.......................... LPKeniry 5 51
(R Hannon) *in rr but in tch: rdn 2f out: sme prog fnl f but nvr in contention* **10/1**
660 6 3/4 **Place The Duchess**[17] 5530 2-8-2 **55**.......................... JimmyQuinn 9 36+
(D W P Arbuthnot) *t.k.h: chsd ldrs: rdn 2f out: sn one pce: hld whn n.m.r on rail ins fnl f* **12/1**
4026 7 1/2 **Song Of Praise**[13] 5647 2-9-1 **68**.......................... AdamKirby 7 47
(M Blanshard) *in rr but in tch: rdn and no imp on ldrs 2f out* **25/1**
304 8 2 1/2 **Eagles Call (USA)**[13] 5628 2-9-6 **73**.......................... JamieSpencer 2 43
(P W Chapple-Hyam) *lw: stdd in rr: rdn 2f out and no rspnse: eased whn no ch ins fnl f* **5/1**[2]
6230 9 nse **Sonhador**[41] 4768 2-9-3 **70**.......................... JimCrowley 10 39
(P Winkworth) *w wnr: rdn 1/2-way: wknd ins fnl 2f* **10/1**
2303 10 4 **Camelot Communion (IRE)**[76] 3639 2-9-5 **72**.......... DO'Donohoe 1 27
(Mrs A Duffield) *lw: s.i.s: rdn 1/2-way and no prog and sn wknd* **16/1**

62.02 secs (0.42) **Going Correction** +0.05s/f (Good) **10** Ran SP% **121.5**
Speed ratings (Par 95): **98,96,96,92,89 88,87,83,83,77**
toteswinger: 1&2 £19.20, 1&3 £7.00, 2&3 £2.80. CSF £97.32 CT £233.36 TOTE £17.00: £4.30, £3.00, £1.60; EX 103.10.
Owner B C Allen **Bred** B C Allen **Trained** Lambourn, Berks

FOCUS
The 5f course was at its full width and the time for this modest nursery was 1.5 seconds slower than standard, which suggests that the track was riding good. As has been the case in 5f races here at recent meetings, there seemed no draw bias. The form has been rated around the principals.

NOTEBOOK
Lesley's Choice had been unable to go the gallop on his Polytrack debut at Lingfield, a race won by Azwa, but he had shown plenty of pace on all his previous starts and this time he made just about all the running, shaking off the early attentions of Sonhador and keeping on well. Decent ground and 5f look to be his optimum requirements. (op 14-1)
Court Approval(IRE) was 3lb well in under the penalty for his all-the-way win at Great Leighs but connections were a little concerned about him carrying 9st 10lb as he is not that big. He ran a good race, unable to get to the front this time and one of the first to come under the shove, but keeping on well to the line. (op 8-1)
Jubilee Juggins(IRE), penalised for his Goodwood win on Sunday, looked a threat when beginning his run but never quite picked up as well as he had promised on this faster ground and was edging slightly to his right under a left-handed drive inside the last. (op 13-8 tchd 2-1 and 85-40 in a place)
Azwa, raised 3lb for her victory at Lingfield when she had today's winner back in seventh, appeared to be found out by this stiffer track in a truly-run race over this trip. (op 5-1 tchd 4-1)
Straitjacket, who was well supported on most of her previous runs, was without the blinkers for this drop back in trip. She could benefit from a return to 6f but is probably not one in which to place too much trust in. (op 17-2)
Place The Duchess was receiving at least 13lb from all her rivals on this nursery debut and was the subject of on-course support. She was held when slightly short of room against the rail early in the final furlong. (op 33-1)
Eagles Call(USA) was dropped in from stall 2 and found little when asked to improve, never looking likely to get into the race. (op 15-2 tchd 8-1)

6024 CONSTRUCTION NEWS CLAIMING STKS 5f 6y
2:55 (2:55) (Class 5) 3-Y-O+ **£3,885** (£1,156; £577; £288) **Stalls** High

Form RPR
0363 1 **Meridian Line (IRE)**[14] 5601 3-8-1 60..........(b) AdrianMcCarthy 4 61
(J G Portman) *pushed along and in tch: hdwy u.p over 1f out: styd on to ld fnl 75yds and hung rt: rdn out* **12/1**
5546 2 shd **Back In The Red (IRE)**[11] 5709 4-8-4 63.......... KevinGhunowa(3) 5 66
(R A Harris) *b: broke wl: sn outpcd towards rr: rdn 1/2-way: hdwy over 1f out: str run on outside ins fnl f: fin wl: jst failed* **4/1**[2]
-135 3 1/2 **Barbary Boy (FR)**[34] 5028 3-8-10 74.......................... JamieSpencer 7 68
(M L W Bell) *lw: led after 1f: hrd rdn whn chal appr fnl f and kpt slt advantage: edgd rt: hdd and no ex fnl 75yds* **15/8**[1]
0006 4 1/2 **The Name Is Frank**[9] 5748 3-8-6 60.......................... JamesDoyle 9 62
(J W Mullins) *chsd ldrs: styng on whn carried rt and one pce fnl 75yds* **25/1**
4514 5 nk **Our Acquaintance**[26] 5217 3-8-12 71..........(b) MartinDwyer 2 67
(W R Muir) *lw: chsd ldrs: rdn to chal 1f out and stl upside ins fnl f: edgd rt and one pce fnl 75yds* **5/1**[3]
3343 6 1 1/4 **Night Prospector**[13] 5645 8-8-9 61..........(p) JimCrowley 6 58
(R A Harris) *led 1f: styd chsng ldrs and rdn over 2f out: wknd ins fnl f* **5/1**[3]
1000 7 1/2 **Who's Winning (IRE)**[14] 5601 7-8-8 56 ow2..........(t) StephenDonohoe 3 56
(B G Powell) *in rr: rdn after 2f: stl plenty to do whn hdwy over 1f out: styd on ins fnl f but nvr in contention* **16/1**
2300 8 hd **Cape Of Storms**[19] 5474 5-8-13 48.......................... NCallan 10 60
(R Brotherton) *chsd ldrs: rdn 1/2-way: wknd fnl f* **16/1**
006 9 4 **Lauras Joy (IRE)**[17] 5533 5-7-10 40.......................... SophieDoyle(5) 8 34
(G P Enright) *a outpcd* **100/1**
0-00 10 7 **Here And How**[38] 4891 3-8-0 43.......................... JimmyQuinn 11 8
(M H Tompkins) *skowly into stride: racd alone far side to 1/2-way but a outpcd* **50/1**
0000 11 11 **The Real Guru**[13] 5626 3-8-10 49..........(b[1]) TravisBlock 1 —
(Miss Tor Sturgis) *in tch: rdn 1/2-way and sn wknd* **50/1**

61.86 secs (0.26) **Going Correction** +0.05s/f (Good)
WFA 3 from 4yo+ 1lb **11** Ran SP% **116.3**
Speed ratings (Par 103): **99,98,98,97,96 94,93,93,87,76 58**
toteswinger: 1&2 £7.40, 1&3 £5.00, 2&3 £3.00. CSF £58.04 TOTE £14.80: £3.00, £1.60, £1.40; EX 70.20.
Owner Berkeley Racing **Bred** George Darling **Trained** Compton, Berks
■ Stewards' Enquiry : Martin Dwyer caution: careless riding.
Adrian McCarthy three-day ban: careless riding (Oct 1,2,6)

FOCUS
An ordinary claimer run in a slightly faster time than the opening nursery. Most of the field headed towards the centre of the course, although the winner was one of several who edged back towards the far rail under pressure late on. Modest form with the proximity of the fourth raising doubts.

6025 COMBISAFE NOVICE STKS 7f 16y
3:30 (3:35) (Class 3) 2-Y-O
£8,100 (£2,425; £1,212; £607; £302; £152) **Stalls** High

Form RPR
1 1 **Wingwalker**[40] 4826 2-9-4 0.......................... TPQueally 6 106+
(H R A Cecil) *w'like: athletic: tall: lw: plld hrd: trckd ldrs on ins: no room fr over 2f out tl swtchd lft appr fnl f: qcknd smartly ins fnl f to ld fnl 100yds: impressive* **1/2**[1]
1620 2 1 1/2 **Rileyskeepingfaith**[24] 5330 2-9-4 99.......................... SamHitchcott 4 94
(M R Channon) *stdd in rr but in tch: rdn and hdwy fr over 2f out to chal fr over 1f out: stl upsides whn wnr swept ahd fnl 100yds: kpt on same pce* **8/1**[3]
313 3 nse **Touching (IRE)**[55] 4348 2-8-11 87.......................... JimCrowley 1 87
(R Hannon) *lw: chsd ldrs: chal 2f out: slt advantage wl over 1f out: hdd by impressive wnr fnl 100yds: one pce* **12/1**
1 4 4 **Parthenon**[8] 5777 2-9-4 0.......................... DarryllHolland 5 84
(M Johnston) *w'like: str: upsides tl def advantage wl over 2f out: hdd wl over 1f out: wknd fnl f* **11/2**[2]
3 5 2 **Confucius Captain (IRE)**[9] 5756 2-8-12 0.......................... PatCosgrave 7 73
(J R Boyle) *leggy: in rr but in tch: pushed along over 3f out: kpt on same pce fnl 2f* **33/1**
6 1 3/4 **Augusta Gold (USA)** 2-8-9 0.......................... MartinDwyer 3 66
(B J Meehan) *w'like: bit bkwd: slowly away: a in rr* **40/1**
50 7 1 **Ayrus (USA)**[19] 5462 2-8-12 0.......................... JamieSpencer 2 66
(B J Meehan) *slt advantage tl hdd wl over 2f out: wkng whn hmpd sn after* **25/1**

1m 29.26s (-0.24) **Going Correction** +0.05s/f (Good) **7** Ran SP% **110.1**
Speed ratings (Par 99): **103,101,101,96,94 92,91**
toteswinger: 1&2 £1.80, 1&3 £2.60, 2&3 £3.30. CSF £4.57 TOTE £1.60: £1.20, £2.70; EX 5.10.
Owner K Abdulla **Bred** Juddmonte Farms Ltd **Trained** Newmarket, Suffolk

FOCUS
A fascinating novice event which produced an impressive winner in Wingwalker who can rate a bit higher. The pace was nothing special.

NOTEBOOK
Wingwalker ◆, as on his debut at Newmarket, form that has worked out well, raced rather keenly behind the leaders. He was trapped in a pocket with no outlet from early in the home straight, but his chance came over a furlong out as Ayrus dropped back and Queally switched him left. The colt responded instantly when asked to quicken, cutting down the pair in front of him to score readily and by no means extended. He will need to settle better, and a truer gallop will help in that respect, but beat a rival rated 99 with something in hand here and is a colt with considerable potential. Connections are thinking in terms of the Dewhurst for him, and he may run before then in the Group 3 Somerville Tattersall Stakes, also at Newmarket. In the longer term his pedigree suggests he should have the stamina for 1m4f. (tchd 8-15 in places and 4-7 in a place)
Rileyskeepingfaith beat only one home behind Bushranger in the Prix Morny last time but that race was on easy ground and this surface suited him better. He looked set to be the principal benefiary of the favourite's predicament on the rail, going on as the leaders dropped away, but he had to fight to get the better of the third and in the end the pair of them were beaten comfortably by the winner. He seemed to stay this longer trip well enough. (op 6-1)
Touching(IRE), third in a Listed race against her own sex over course and distance last time, had every chance and, while no match for Wingwalker in the end, just missed out on second. She has the scope for a bit more improvement and is worth another try in Listed grade. (op 10-1 tchd 14-1)

Parthenon, a good-bodied colt who made a winning debut in heavy ground at Leicester, was perhaps the pick of the paddock. After helping cut out the pace he had no answers when headed, and this run might have come too soon. (op 7-1 tchd 15-2)
Confucius Captain(IRE) was never able to get into the action but this second outing should have taught him a bit more. (op 66-1)
Augusta Gold(USA), who was sold for £78,000 earlier this year, is a half-brother to numerous winners including the high-class Lear Spear. Never seen with a chance after an awkward start, he should do better in time (tchd 33-1 and 66-1)
Ayrus(USA), out of his depth in Listed company last time, matched strides with Parthenon but was beginning to struggle when he was slightly hampered. (op 33-1)

6026 VAILLANT EBF MAIDEN STKS — 1m 14y
4:05 (4:08) (Class 4) 2-Y-O — £5,180 (£1,541; £770; £384) Stalls High

Form — RPR
3 **1** **Four Winds**[26] 5246 2-9-3 0 .... JamieSpencer 7 87+
(M L W Bell) *lw: trckd ldrs tl qcknd to ld 2f out: shkn up and clr fnl f: readily* **6/4**[1]
4 **2** 2 **Ra Junior (USA)**[19] 5468 2-9-3 0 .... NCallan 2 80+
(B J Meehan) *leggy: chsd ldrs: rdn to chse wnr ins fnl 2f: kpt on but a readily hld fnl f* **7/4**[2]
3 2 **Red Junior** 2-9-0 0 .... PatrickHills(3) 9 74+
(B J Meehan) *w'like: leggy: bit bkwd: s.i.s: in rr and rdn over 3f out: gd hdwy fr 2f out: wnt 3rd ins fnl f: gng on cl home but nvr a threat to ldng duo* **50/1**
4 ¾ **Moresco** 2-9-3 0 .... AdamKirby 6 73+
(W R Swinburn) *w'like: scope: bit bkwd: in rr: hdwy over 3f out: drvn to chse ldrs 2f out: nvr on terms and styd on same pce appr fnl f* **9/1**
5 1¾ **Alanbrooke** 2-9-3 0 .... DarryllHolland 4 69+
(M Johnston) *w'like: str: s.i.s: in rr: pushed along and sme hdwy over 2f out: kpt on but nvr in contention after* **15/2**[3]
6 1 **Whisky Galore** 2-9-3 0 .... IanMongan 1 67
(C G Cox) *leggy: chsd ldrs early: rdn and outpcd over 3f out: kpt on again fnl f but nvr a threat* **66/1**
0 **7** nk **Cry For The Moon (USA)**[26] 5246 2-9-3 0 .... JimCrowley 10 66
(Mrs A J Perrett) *lw: led: rdn 3f out: hdd 2f out: wknd ins fnl f* **12/1**
00 **8** 3¾ **Foxtrot Charlie**[24] 5314 2-9-3 0 .... StephenCarson 5 58
(P Winkworth) *in rr tl styd on fnl 2f: nvr a threat* **66/1**
9 4½ **Akmal** 2-9-3 0 .... MartinDwyer 8 48
(J L Dunlop) *w'like: bit bkwd: in tch: rdn and bhd fr 1/2-way* **28/1**
05 **10** ¾ **Persian Buddy**[12] 5678 2-9-3 0 .... AmirQuinn 12 46
(Jamie Poulton) *plld hrd: chsd ldr: chal fr over 4f out tl 3f out: wknd qckly over 2f out* **100/1**
0 **11** ½ **Urban Space**[16] 5579 2-9-3 0 .... TQuinn 11 45+
(B G Powell) *s.i.s: rdn 4f out and a wl in rr* **100/1**

1m 44.12s (0.82) **Going Correction** +0.05s/f (Good) 11 Ran SP% **116.2**
Speed ratings (Par 97): **97,95,93,92,90 89,89,85,80,80 79**
toteswinger: 1&2 £1.80, 1&3 £19.00, 2&3 £14.30. CSF £4.11 TOTE £2.70: £1.10, £1.10, £9.70; EX 4.70.
Owner The Queen **Bred** The Queen **Trained** Newmarket, Suffolk

FOCUS
An informative maiden which should produce winners, with better to come from Four Winds. The form looks pretty strong.

NOTEBOOK
Four Winds ◆, who made a promising debut when third to Delegator over 7f at Newmarket, was always nicely placed and he quickened up well to strike the front, always comfortably holding the runner-up through the final furlong. Still not fully wound up for this, he is highly regarded by his jockey and looks a very nice prospect for next season, although he holds a Racing Post Trophy entry and could run again this term. (op 13-8 tchd 7-4 in places)
Ra Junior(USA), a promising fourth over 7f here on his debut, stepped up on that, chasing the winner through and not given too hard a time when held. He should soon go one better. (op 13-8 tchd 6-4 and 15-8, 2-1 in places)
Red Junior ◆, representing the connections of the runner-up and seemingly unfancied, made good late progress down the outside for third and, sure to come on for the experience, should have no problem landing an ordinary maiden.
Moresco, a half-brother to three decent winners for Mark Johnston out of a high-class filly in France, was another to make a promising debut. He should find his niche in middle-distance handicaps next season. (op 8-1 tchd 10-1)
Alanbrooke comes from a fine family, being a half-brother to a string of winners, most notably dual Champion Stakes scorer Alborada. He was keeping on nicely enough and is another with considerably more to offer. (op 10-1 tchd 7-1)
Whisky Galore has a sprinting pedigree but he stuck on well to suggest that this sort of trip is not a problem to him.
Cry For The Moon(USA), behind Four Winds on his debut, faded in the final furlong after making the running (op 14-1)
Foxtrot Charlie should step up on what he has shown so far now that he is qualified for nurseries. (tchd 100-1)
Persian Buddy Official explanation: jockey said gelding ran too free
Urban Space Official explanation: jockey said gelding suffered interference in running

6027 SPEEDY HIRE SAFETY FIRST FILLIES' H'CAP — 1m 14y
4:40 (4:40) (Class 4) (0-85,83) 3-Y-O — £6,476 (£1,927; £963; £481) Stalls High

Form — RPR
2221 **1** **Rhadegunda**[27] 5203 3-8-11 76 .... DarryllHolland 11 85+
(J H M Gosden) *lw: trckd ldrs: n.m.r over 1f out and swtchd rt to rail ins fnl f: str run to ld fnl 50yds: comf* **7/2**[1]
1244 **2** ½ **Diamond Yas (IRE)**[9] 5759 3-9-1 80 .... TPQueally 1 86
(H R A Cecil) *lw: t.k.h early: sn chsng ldr: slt advantage fr over 2f out but a clly attended: hdd and readily outpcd fnl 50yds* **8/1**
3426 **3** ¾ **Mekong Melody (IRE)**[18] 5506 3-9-1 80 .... AdamKirby 6 84
(C G Cox) *led tl narrowly hdd over 2f out but styd pressing ldr tl wknd fnl 100yds* **10/1**
5422 **4** 1¾ **Ainia**[43] 4708 3-8-11 76 .... StephenDonohoe 7 76
(D M Simcock) *in rr: rdn over 2f out: hdwy over 1f out and kpt on ins fnl f: nvr gng pce to rch ldrs* **14/1**
2103 **5** nse **Lee Miller (IRE)**[18] 5504 3-8-8 80 .... (v[1]) MJMurphy(7) 5 80
(L M Cumani) *hld up in tch: hdwy on outside over 2f out: kpt on fnl f but nvr in contention* **9/2**[2]
2554 **6** ¾ **Astrodonna**[16] 5580 3-8-9 74 .... JimmyQuinn 4 72
(M H Tompkins) *chsd ldrs: rdn 3f out: styd on same pce fr over 1f out* **10/1**
0221 **7** ¾ **Trumpet Lily**[39] 4872 3-9-4 83 .... JimCrowley 2 80
(J G Portman) *lw: stdd in rr after s: hdwy over 2f out: n.m.r over 1f out: wkng whn crossed ins fnl f* **7/1**
-066 **8** ½ **Miss Emma May (IRE)**[30] 5149 3-9-1 80 .... (v) TQuinn 8 76
(D R C Elsworth) *plld hrd: chsd ldrs: rdn over 2f out: styd on same pce fr over 1f out* **25/1**
1623 **9** nk **Badweia (USA)**[16] 5580 3-8-11 76 .... MartinDwyer 3 71
(J L Dunlop) *in rr: rdn 3f out: mod prog fnal 2f* **12/1**
0300 **10** 1¾ **Falcolnry (IRE)**[33] 5071 3-9-1 80 .... PatCosgrave 9 71
(J R Fanshawe) *in rr: rdn 3f out on ins: no prog and nvr in contention after* **25/1**
3113 **11** 9 **Snowdrop Princess**[33] 5075 3-8-11 76 .... (b) JamieSpencer 10 46
(W J Haggas) *s.i.s: in rr: sn in tch: rdn over 2f out: no imp on ldrs: eased whn no ch ins fnl f* **6/1**[3]

1m 43.36s (0.06) **Going Correction** +0.05s/f (Good) 11 Ran SP% **118.5**
Speed ratings (Par 100): **101,100,99,98,97 97,96,95,95,93 84**
toteswinger: 1&2 £7.10, 1&3 £6.80, 2&3 £14.30. CSF £32.06 CT £259.00 TOTE £4.30: £1.90, £3.00, £4.10; EX 23.20.
Owner A E Oppenheimer **Bred** Hascombe And Valiant Studs **Trained** Newmarket, Suffolk

FOCUS
This fillies' handicap was steadily run and not many got into it, with the first three always prominent. The placed fillies set the standard with the winner capable of better than the bare form.

6028 PKF H'CAP — 1m 2f 7y
5:10 (5:10) (Class 4) (0-80,78) 3-Y-O+ — £6,476 (£1,927; £963; £481) Stalls High

Form — RPR
1256 **1** **Gallego**[23] 5370 6-9-0 66 .... TPQueally 6 73
(R J Price) *stdd s: hld up in rr: stdy hdwy on outside fr 2f out: str run to ld fnl 110yds: kpt on wl* **20/1**
264 **2** ¾ **Roodolph**[18] 5512 4-9-7 73 .... StephenCarson 12 78
(Eve Johnson Houghton) *led 3f: styd chsng ldrs: rdn to ld again over 1f out: hdd and no ex fnl 110yds* **11/1**
406/ **3** ¾ **Wiggy Smith**[676] 2169 9-9-7 73 .... AdamKirby 10 77+
(H Candy) *hld up in rr: hdwy and n.m.r 2f out: n.m.r again and swtchd rt over 1f out: styd on and stl nt clr run ins fnl f: no ex cl home* **8/1**
0306 **4** 3 **Cape Of Luck (IRE)**[56] 4310 5-9-8 74 .... (p) IanMongan 9 72
(P M Phelan) *in rr: stl plenty to do whn rdn over 2f out: styd on fr over 1f out and gng on ins fnl f: nt rch ldrs* **25/1**
4030 **5** ¾ **Jo'Burg (USA)**[23] 5350 4-9-7 73 .... JimCrowley 3 69
(Mrs A J Perrett) *chsd ldrs: rdn over 2f out: wknd ins fnl f* **8/1**
0000 **6** 2 **Risque Heights**[27] 5209 4-9-3 69 .... PatCosgrave 4 61
(J R Boyle) *in tch: rdn and effrt to chse ldrs 2f out: nvr on terms: wknd fnl f* **20/1**
5446 **7** ½ **Palmerin**[19] 5472 3-9-6 78 .... JamieSpencer 8 69
(R Hannon) *sn chsng ldrs: rdn to ld over 2f out: hung rt sn after: hdd over 1f out: sn wknd* **5/1**[1]
1224 **8** 1½ **Houri (IRE)**[20] 5428 3-9-3 75 .... (p) RichardKingscote 7 63
(R M Beckett) *lw: in tch: rdn and effrt 3f out: nvr rchd ldrs: wknd ins fnl 2f* **6/1**[2]
1043 **9** shd **Benfleet Boy**[46] 4627 4-9-10 76 .... DarryllHolland 5 64+
(B G Powell) *led after 3f: hdd 5f out: styd chsng ldrs tl wknd and hmpd ins fnl 2f* **10/1**
001 **10** shd **Maybe I Will (IRE)**[14] 5602 3-9-0 72 .... NCallan 2 60
(S Dow) *in rr: sme prog whn nt clr run over 2f out: nvr in contention after* **12/1**
2064 **11** 2 **Danamight (IRE)**[19] 5472 3-8-5 63 .... MartinDwyer 1 47+
(J L Dunlop) *plld hrd: sn prom: led 5f out: rdn and hdd over 2f out: no ch whn hmpd sn after* **13/2**[3]
022 **12** 3 **Air Chief**[9] 5759 3-8-13 71 .... JimmyQuinn 11 49+
(H J L Dunlop) *prom early: bhd fnl 4f* **6/1**[2]

2m 9.98s (-0.52) **Going Correction** +0.05s/f (Good)
WFA 3 from 4yo+ 6lb 12 Ran SP% **119.3**
Speed ratings (Par 105): **104,103,102,100,99 98,97,96,96,96 94,92**
toteswinger: 1&2 £59.10, 1&3 £42.10, 2&3 £24.60. CSF £220.70 CT £1920.71 TOTE £24.00: £5.70, £4.40, £2.60; EX 293.90 Place 6 £ 49.59, Place 5 £ 25.44.
Owner My Left Foot Racing Syndicate **Bred** Mrs C C Regalado-Gonzalez **Trained** Ullingswick, H'fords
■ Stewards' Enquiry : Adam Kirby two-day ban: careless riding (Oct 1-2)

FOCUS
An ordinary handicap run at a steady pace, and things got a bit messy in the latter stages with a number finding trouble on the inside. The winner is rated up 3lb.
Palmerin Official explanation: jockey said colt ducked right-handed
Houri(IRE) Official explanation: jockey said filly was denied a clear run
Air Chief Official explanation: jockey said gelding was denied a clear clear
T/Plt: £99.10 to a £1 stake. Pool: £63,211.56. 465.58 winning tickets. T/Qpdt: £50.20 to a £1 stake. Pool: £4,020.49. 59.20 winning tickets. ST

6001 YARMOUTH (L-H)
Wednesday, September 17

OFFICIAL GOING: Good (7.7)
Wind: Light half-against Weather: Overcast

6029 E. B. F./FIRSTBET INSTANT DEBIT BETTING 0800 230 0800 MAIDEN STKS (DIV I) — 7f 3y
1:40 (1:43) (Class 4) 2-Y-O — £4,731 (£1,416; £708; £354; £176) Stalls High

Form — RPR
6 **1** **Marching Time**[48] 4570 2-9-3 0 .... RyanMoore 6 80+
(Sir Michael Stoute) *hld up: hdwy over 3f out: rdn and plenty to do over 1f out: edgd lft and r.o wl to ld nr fin* **2/1**[1]
00 **2** nk **Tamarah**[87] 3292 2-8-12 0 .... PhilipRobinson 2 73
(Miss D Mountain) *led: rdn over 1f out: hdd nr fin* **40/1**
2 **3** 2¼ **Rafaan (USA)**[16] 5579 2-9-3 0 .... RHills 1 72
(M Johnston) *chsd ldr: rdn over 1f out: styd on same pce ins fnl f* **3/1**[2]
00 **4** ¾ **Forte Dei Marmi**[21] 5404 2-9-3 0 .... DaneO'Neill 4 70+
(L M Cumani) *chsd ldrs: rdn over 1f out: styng on same pce whn nt clr run ins fnl f* **12/1**
5 1¼ **Thousand Miles (IRE)** 2-9-3 0 .... RichardMullen 10 67
(P W Chapple-Hyam) *chsd ldrs: rdn over 3f out: styd on same pce appr fnl f* **14/1**
6 nk **Emirates Roadshow (USA)** 2-9-3 0 .... LDettori 5 66+
(Saeed Bin Suroor) *hld up in tch: racd keenly: rdn over 1f out: styd on same pce* **7/2**[3]
7 4½ **Hi Fling** 2-9-3 0 .... JimmyFortune 7 55+
(B J Meehan) *hld up: outpcd over 3f out: hdwy 2f out: wknd fnl f* **12/1**
8 hd **Sofonisba** 2-8-12 0 .... HayleyTurner 3 50
(M L W Bell) *hld up: rdn over 3f out: wknd over 1f out* **40/1**
9 8 **Hilltop Artistry** 2-9-0 0 .... LukeMorris(3) 11 35
(S W James) *s.i.s: hld up: hdwy over 3f out: wknd over 2f out* **200/1**
10 nk **Braveheart Move (IRE)** 2-9-3 0 .... J-PGuillambert 12 34
(Sir Mark Prescott) *s.s: outpcd* **40/1**

The Form Book, Raceform Ltd, Compton, RG20 6NL

11 15 **Ausonius** 2-9-3 0 ChrisCatlin 9 —
(L M Cumani) *s.i.s: hld up: bhd fr 1/2-way* **33/1**

12 9 **Princess Janet** 2-8-12 0 AlanMunro 8 —
(A B Coogan) *s.s: outpcd: bhd fr 1/2-way* **50/1**

1m 26.42s (-0.18) **Going Correction** -0.225s/f (Firm) **12** Ran SP% **115.3**
Speed ratings (Par 97): **92,91,89,88,86 86,81,81,71,71 54,44**
toteswinger: 1&2 £18.80, 1&3 £2.00, 2&3 £23.10. CSF £101.72 TOTE £2.60: £1.20, £9.90, £1.40; EX 110.20 TRIFECTA Not won.
Owner K Abdulla **Bred** Juddmonte Farms Ltd **Trained** Newmarket, Suffolk

FOCUS
A fair maiden which saw the first pair come clear. The form is rated through the third and the winner should be up to handling a rise in grade.

NOTEBOOK
Marching Time found plenty of support to open his account and he duly obliged with a cosy success. He hit a flat spot around 2f out and took time to hit top gear when asked for maximum effort, but he ate up the ground inside the final furlong. He ultimately scored with something up his sleeve and left the impression he is now crying out for another furlong. He has entries in the Racing Post Trophy and Dewhurst and will need to come on plenty to justify inclusion in one of those, but he looks sure to learn again for the experience and the extra furlong of the RP Trophy would seem more logical. Rather surprisingly, being by Sadler's Wells, he does not possess a Derby entry and it may be that his trainer views him more as a 1m2f horse in the making for next year. (op 5-2 tchd 11-4)
Tamarah showed by far her best form on this return from an 87-day break and enjoyed the longer trip, as could have been expected. She only just got reeled in and, while her proximity limits the form, she did get very much the run of the race out in front. She was clear of the remainder and it will be interesting to see what mark she is now allotted for nurseries.
Rafaan(USA) proved easy to back, despite having been just held on his debut after running distinctly green. He showed a more professional attitude, but was one-paced at the business end and can have no excuse. (op 2-1)
Forte Dei Marmi raced more prominently and had his chance back over this shorter trip. This was his best effort to date and a return to 1m should enhance his chances further, especially as he now qualifies for an official mark. (op 14-1 tchd 16-1)
Thousand Miles(IRE) ◆, a half-brother to a triple sprint winner in Italy, was not given too hard a time on this racecourse debut and did his best work late on. The kindness should pay off next time and he has a future. (op 20-1)
Emirates Roadshow(USA), who cost $800,000, is clearly held in high regard by his leading connections as he holds numerous fancy entries. He was unable to quicken when the race became serious, however, and left the impression this initial experience was needed (op 4-1 tchd 10-3)

6030 EUROPEAN BREEDERS' FUND MAIDEN FILLIES' STKS 6f 3y
2:10 (2:12) (Class 4) 2-Y-O **£5,046** (£1,510; £755; £377; £188) **Stalls** High

Form RPR

22 1 **Bouvardia**[13] 5640 2-9-0 0 TedDurcan 6 80+
(H R A Cecil) *mde all: pushed along and drifted to stands' rail ins fnl f: kpt on strly* **8/11**[1]

23 2 ¾ **Never Lose**[28] 5184 2-9-0 0 KShea 12 78
(C E Brittain) *chsd ldrs: effrt 2f out: chsd wnr ins fnl f: r.o* **14/1**

44 3 1 **Fen Spirit (IRE)**[16] 5570 2-9-0 0 JimmyFortune 16 75
(J H M Gosden) *pressed wnr to ins fnl f: kpt on same pce u.p* **10/1**[3]

4 2 ½ **Tiger Eye (IRE)** 2-9-0 0 PhilipRobinson 15 68+
(M A Jarvis) *prom: rdn and rn green 2f out: edgd lft and kpt on same pce fnl f* **9/2**[2]

5 1 **Sley (FR)** 2-9-0 0 TPO'Shea 13 65+
(B J Meehan) *hld up: pushed along over 2f out: hdwy over 1f out: no imp fnl f* **150/1**

6 ½ **Rublevka Star (USA)** 2-9-0 0 ShaneKelly 5 63
(J Noseda) *cl up: rdn over 2f out: wknd appr fnl f* **10/1**[3]

7 nk **West With The Wind (USA)** 2-9-0 0 LDettori 14 62
(P W Chapple-Hyam) *hld up bhd ldng gp: pushed along over 2f out: sn no imp* **20/1**

8 ¾ **In The Mood (IRE)** 2-9-0 0 AlanMunro 8 60+
(W Jarvis) *hld up: shkn up and green over 2f out: hdwy over 1f out: nvr rchd ldrs* **100/1**

9 ½ **Awfeyaa** 2-9-0 0 RHills 10 58+
(W J Haggas) *t.k.h: hld up: shkn up 2f out: n.d* **40/1**

10 ¾ **Rumramah (USA)** 2-9-0 0 RichardMullen 9 56
(D M Simcock) *dwlt: hld up: pushed along over 2f out: sn btn* **80/1**

4 11 1 **Granny McPhee**[11] 5711 2-8-9 0 DavidProbert(5) 2 53
(A Bailey) *prom tl rdn and wknd over 2f out* **40/1**

12 3 ¾ **Arabian Mirage** 2-9-0 0 RyanMoore 7 42
(B J Meehan) *sn niggled along in midfield: lost pl over 2f out* **40/1**

40 13 hd **Spiritual Art**[16] 5572 2-9-0 0 DaneO'Neill 1 41
(S A Callaghan) *hld up: shortlived effrt over 2f out: sn btn* **66/1**

14 3 ¼ **Brushing** 2-8-7 0 AshleyMorgan(7) 11 32
(M H Tompkins) *s.v.s: nvr on terms* **125/1**

15 3 ¼ **La Gifted** 2-9-0 0 EdwardCreighton 4 22
(M R Channon) *sn pushed along in rr: struggling fr 1/2-way* **20/1**

16 13 **Pocket Queens** 2-9-0 0 SaleemGolam 3 —
(Miss D Mountain) *s.i.s: sn wl bhd: no ch fr 1/2-way* **150/1**

1m 12.69s (-1.71) **Going Correction** -0.225s/f (Firm) **16** Ran SP% **123.6**
Speed ratings (Par 94): **102,101,99,96,95 94,93,92,92,91 89,84,84,80,76 58**
toteswinger: 1&2 £4.10, 1&3 £4.00, 2&3 £12.10. CSF £12.41 TOTE £1.60: £1.02, £3.20, £3.00; EX 14.40 Trifecta £32.50 Pool: £279.34, 6.36 winning units.
Owner K Abdulla **Bred** Juddmonte Farms Ltd **Trained** Newmarket, Suffolk

FOCUS
A fair fillies' maiden although the winner was again below her debut form. The next two showed improvement.

NOTEBOOK
Bouvardia, second on her two previous outings, made just about all the running and opened her account with a fairly straightforward display. The positive ride over the shorter trip helped, but she does look a somewhat headstrong character as she ran freely early on and then drifted over to the stands' rail when asked to win the race. She looks short of Pattern class at this stage but deserves a crack at something better. (op Evens)
Never Lose had been placed on her two previous starts and met support at big odds, so her proximity gives the form a fair look. She will appreciate stepping back to another furlong and has more options now she is eligible for a mark. (op 33-1)
Fen Spirit(IRE) had disappointed over 1m on her All-Weather debut last time, but this was more like it and she finished closer to the winner than had been the case on her debut on softer ground last month. She is eligible for a mark and, best kept to this trip for the short term, evidently has a race in her this year. (op 9-1 tchd 14-1)
Tiger Eye(IRE) ◆ met good support on the morning exchanges, but was allowed to drift on course and she ran as though this initial outing was needed. Her pedigree suggests she will improve as she goes over further and there was a lot in this display to back that up. (op 3-1)
Sley(FR), related to winners over longer trips, caught the eye staying on when the race was all but over and seems sure to benefit a great deal for the debut experience.

La Gifted Official explanation: jockey said filly was slowly away

6031 E. B. F./FIRSTBET INSTANT DEBIT BETTING 0800 230 0800 MAIDEN STKS (DIV II) 7f 3y
2:45 (2:45) (Class 4) 2-Y-O **£4,731** (£1,416; £708; £354; £176) **Stalls** High

Form RPR

0 1 **Glass Harmonium (IRE)**[19] 5468 2-9-3 0 RyanMoore 10 80+
(Sir Michael Stoute) *chsd ldrs: led 2f out: shkn up and r.o wl* **8/15**[1]

0 2 4 **Burma Rock (IRE)**[41] 4792 2-9-3 0 DaneO'Neill 9 64+
(L M Cumani) *hld up: hdwy over 1f out: wnt 2nd ins fnl f: no ch w wnr* **66/1**

0 3 ½ **Navajo Nation (IRE)**[45] 4665 2-9-3 0 JimmyFortune 11 63
(B J Meehan) *mid-div: pushed along 1/2-way: hdwy over 2f out: rdn over 1f out: styd on same pce ins fnl f* **25/1**

4 2 ½ **Royal Diamond (IRE)** 2-9-3 0 J-PGuillambert 4 57
(Sir Mark Prescott) *hld up: outpcd over 2f out: styd on ins fnl f* **33/1**

5 ¾ **Gassin** 2-9-3 0 AlanMunro 5 55
(G Wragg) *chsd ldrs: rdn and ev ch over 1f out: wknd ins fnl f* **25/1**

6 2 **Markhesa** 2-8-12 0 TedDurcan 8 45
(C F Wall) *s.i.s: hld up: hdwy 1/2-way: wknd fnl f* **25/1**

0 7 ½ **Causeway King (USA)**[19] 5469 2-9-3 0 RoystonFfrench 7 48
(M Johnston) *sn led: rdn and hdd 2f out: wknd fnl f* **4/1**[2]

0 8 3 ½ **Take The Micky**[26] 5246 2-9-3 0 PaulDoe 2 40
(W J Knight) *s.i.s: hld up: rdn over 2f out: n.d* **15/2**[3]

5 9 nk **Seek The Fair Land**[7] 5798 2-9-3 0 LDettori 1 39
(J R Boyle) *s.i.s: sn prom: rdn over 1f out: wknd fnl f* **25/1**

00 10 hd **Sparkaway**[33] 5066 2-9-3 0 NeilPollard 3 38
(W J Musson) *hld up: rdn over 2f out: a in rr* **100/1**

11 9 **Topcroft** 2-9-3 0 TGMcLaughlin 6 16
(Mrs C A Dunnett) *chsd ldrs: rdn 1/2-way: wknd over 2f out* **80/1**

1m 26.1s (-0.50) **Going Correction** -0.225s/f (Firm) **11** Ran SP% **119.0**
Speed ratings (Par 97): **93,88,87,85,84 81,81,77,76,76 66**
toteswinger: 1&2 £16.00, 1&3 £6.70, 2&3 £93.30. CSF £76.19 TOTE £1.60: £1.02, £15.90, £6.20; EX 63.10 TRIFECTA Not won..
Owner Ballymacoll Stud **Bred** Ballymacoll Stud Farm Ltd **Trained** Newmarket, Suffolk

FOCUS
A fair maiden in which the winner did not need to improve much on his debut effort. He can do better.

NOTEBOOK
Glass Harmonium(IRE) had been green on his debut at Sandown, but did show plenty of ability before tiring into seventh. That race has already produced winners and he was backed as though defeat was out of the question. Always travelling well at the head of affairs, he powered clear over 2f from home and was never going to be caught. One gets the impression that he will develop into a nice sort with time, so if he achieves something good this season he will be one to follow next year. (op 4-6)
Burma Rock(IRE) was very green on his debut at this course over 6f well over a month ago, but he displayed much more professionalism in this. Held up early, he stayed on really well after meeting a little traffic as the tempo lifted and will no doubt do better with time. (op 80-1)
Navajo Nation(IRE), who caught the eye behind Marine Boy on his first start, had clearly made progress from his debut and kept on well after being pushed along at halfway. He was comfortably held by the winner and the runner-up (despite the narrow margin he was beaten by Burma Rock) but looks well up to landing a maiden. (op 16-1)
Royal Diamond(IRE), a half-brother to the Group 1-placed filly Mad About You, was not knocked about on his debut and looks capable of winning races this season, although he gives the impression he has some filling out to do. (op 25-1 tchd 20-1)
Causeway King(USA) found disappointingly little once headed and paid for running freely early on. (op 5-1 tchd 11-2)

6032 DANNY WRIGHT MEMORIAL (S) STKS 1m 2f 21y
3:20 (3:20) (Class 6) 3-4-Y-O **£1,942** (£578; £288; £144) **Stalls** Low

Form RPR

-400 1 **Blue Admiral**[30] 5163 3-8-5 62 (b[1]) AshleyMorgan(7) 4 64
(M H Tompkins) *dwlt: hld up: rdn 3f out: gd hdwy to ld ins fnl f: sn clr* **9/1**

0001 2 3 **Mick Is Back**[9] 5748 4-9-9 55 (p) RyanMoore 9 63
(G G Margarson) *t.k.h: prom: effrt over 2f out: kpt on fnl f: nt pce of wnr* **13/2**[3]

3053 3 nk **Fairly Honest**[8] 5787 4-8-13 50 WilliamCarson(5) 5 57
(P W Hiatt) *t.k.h: cl up: led over 2f out to ins fnl f: no ex* **9/2**[2]

0025 4 nk **Tank Commander**[6] 5813 3-8-12 60 RichardMullen 2 56
(W R Muir) *in tch: drvn 3f out: effrt over 1f out: one pce fnl f* **9/1**

002 5 ¾ **Well Informed**[11] 5710 3-8-7 57 ChrisCatlin 15 50
(E J O'Neill) *stdd in rr: hdwy over 2f out: drifted lft fr over 1f out: kpt on fnl f* **7/1**

6010 6 1 ¾ **Caltire (GER)**[18] 3845 3-9-3 63 (b) JerryO'Dwyer 3 56
(M G Quinlan) *hld up: drvn over 4f out: kpt on fnl f: no imp* **13/2**[3]

-000 7 2 **Aura**[34] 5019 3-8-7 52 HayleyTurner 8 42
(M L W Bell) *cl up: drvn over 2f out: wknd appr fnl f* **12/1**

5005 8 10 **General Tufto**[18] 4698 3-8-12 55 (v[1]) RobertWinston 1 27
(C Smith) *led to over 2f out: wknd over 1f out* **22/1**

0 9 ½ **Defectivedetective**[30] 5148 4-9-1 0 LukeMorris(3) 14 26
(Dr J D Scargill) *dwlt: t.k.h and sn in tch: rdn 3f out: sn wknd* **100/1**

0000 10 1 ¾ **Classy Affair**[34] 5020 4-8-13 42 TGMcLaughlin 13 18
(D Morris) *trckd ldrs tl rdn and wknd fr 2f out* **33/1**

600- 11 11 **Goldhill Fair**[18] 5302 3-8-7 42 JackDean(5) 6 1
(W G M Turner) *midfield: rdn and lost pl 1/2-way: sn btn* **66/1**

3000 12 1 ¼ **Scientific**[16] 5575 3-8-12 52 (b) SaleemGolam 11 —
(G Prodromou) *t.k.h: hld up: drvn over 3f out: sn wknd* **20/1**

6-44 13 11 **Beggars End (USA)**[64] 4066 3-8-12 64 DaneO'Neill 7 —
(E F Vaughan) *midfield on outside: rdn over 4f out: sn struggling* **4/1**[1]

2m 9.23s (-1.27) **Going Correction** -0.225s/f (Firm)
WFA 3 from 4yo 6lb **13** Ran SP% **119.6**
Speed ratings (Par 101): **96,93,93,93,92 91,89,81,81,79 70,69,61**
toteswinger: 1&2 £16.80, 1&3 £24.90, 2&3 £4.60. CSF £63.43 TOTE £11.80: £3.10, £1.80, £2.00; EX 72.10 Trifecta £165.20 Part won. Pool: £223.34, 0.50 winning units..Aura was claimed by Harry Dunlop for £5,000
Owner Roalco Limited **Bred** F Adams **Trained** Newmarket, Suffolk

FOCUS
This ordinary seller featured just three previous winners. The form makes sense.

Beggars End(USA) Official explanation: jockey said gelding moved poorly throughout; vet said gelding had been struck into

6033 BENNETTS ELECTRICAL H'CAP (FOR THE GOLDEN JUBILEE TROPHY) 1m 2f 21y

3:55 (3:55) (Class 3) (0-90,89) 3-Y-0+

£7,477 (£2,239; £1,119; £560; £279; £140) **Stalls** Low

Form	Pos	Dist	Horse / Trainer / Comment	RPR
031	**1**		**Novikov**[41] 4791 4-9-2 **86** ...(tp) Louis-PhilippeBeuzelin(5) 4 (J H M Gosden) *s.i.s: sn chsng ldrs: led over 8f out: rdn and hrd pressed fr over 1f out: styd on gamely* **10/1**	93
3321	**2**	*hd*	**Dark Prospect**[14] 5605 3-8-4 **75** ... HayleyTurner 1 (M A Jarvis) *trckd ldrs: rdn and ev ch fr over 1f out: edgd rt ins fnl f: styd on* **7/2**[2]	82
3611	**3**	*shd*	**Kingdom Of Fife**[19] 5472 3-8-10 **81** ... RyanMoore 6 (Sir Michael Stoute) *chsd ldrs: rdn over 1f out: r.o* **11/4**[1]	88+
F531	**4**	*2*	**Dragon Slayer (IRE)**[18] 5512 6-8-5 **75** oh2 ... DavidProbert(5) 2 (John A Harris) *hld up: racd keenly: hdwy over 2f out: nt rch ldrs* **10/1**	78
-500	**5**	*3 1/2*	**Points Of View**[12] 5682 3-8-13 **84** ... J-PGuillambert 7 (Sir Mark Prescott) *plld hrd and prom: outpcd over 2f out: styd on ins fnl f* **15/2**[3]	80
2102	**6**	*1*	**Wee Charlie Castle (IRE)**[18] 5512 5-8-5 **75** oh4 ... WilliamCarson(5) 10 (G C H Chung) *hld up: rdn and hung lft over 1f out: nt trble ldrs* **12/1**	69
4210	**7**	*1 3/4*	**Qui Moi (CAN)**[41] 4790 3-8-12 **83** ... RobertWinston 11 (J R Fanshawe) *hld up in tch: rdn and edgd lft over 1f out: wknd fnl f* **16/1**	73
5001	**8**	*3*	**Bahar Shumaal (IRE)**[16] 5569 6-9-7 **86** ... JimmyFortune 9 (C E Brittain) *sn led: hdd over 8f out: rdn and wknd over 1f out* **10/1**	70
3050	**9**	*shd*	**Kayak (SAF)**[16] 5569 6-9-3 **82** ... RichardMullen 5 (D M Simcock) *hld up: rdn over 2f out: a in rr* **20/1**	66
1000	**10**	*shd*	**Polish Power (GER)**[23] 5349 8-9-7 **89** ... LukeMorris(3) 3 (J S Moore) *hld up: rdn over 3f out: a in rr* **33/1**	73
1036	**11**	*1*	**Premier Danseur (IRE)**[12] 5675 3-8-11 **82** ...(b) RoystonFfrench 8 (M Johnston) *hld up: pushed along 7f out: rdn and wknd over 2f out* **12/1**	64

2m 8.14s (-2.36) **Going Correction** -0.225s/f (Firm)
WFA 3 from 4yo+ 6lb **11** Ran SP% **116.9**
Speed ratings (Par 107): **100,99,99,98,95 94,93,90,90,90 89**
toteswinger: 1&2 £10.60, 1&3 £8.10, 2&3 £2.10. CSF £44.66 CT £125.29 TOTE £16.30: £3.70, £1.60, £1.60; EX 55.40 Trifecta £164.00 Pool: £376.82, 1.70 winning units.
Owner George Strawbridge **Bred** The Duke Of Devonshire **Trained** Newmarket, Suffolk

FOCUS
A good handicap, run at an uneven pace and the first two were always to the fore. The first three came clear in a bobbing finish and the form makes sense at face value.

NOTEBOOK
Novikov had very much the run of the race, but obviously gets on well with this jockey and followed up his Sandown success 41 days previously from a 6lb higher mark. He was there to be shot at 2f out, but he kept responding for his rider's urgings and was always doing just enough. His season looks to be really taking off and there is no reason why he should not go close to bagging the hat-trick. (op 15-2 tchd 12-1)
Dark Prospect, 5lb higher for getting off the mark at Kempton a fortnight previously, was upside the winner throughout the final 2f and only just failed to follow up on this return to turf. He has obviously improved since being gelded and, while he will go up again for this, further progression looks on the cards. (op 5-1 tchd 10-3)
Kingdom Of Fife ◆ had to wait for his challenge nearing the 2f pole and basically found the first pair got first run on him. He was eating up the ground inside the final furlong and was only narrowly denied, so this represents another improved effort from a 5lb higher mark. It is fair to expect to see him back in the winner's enclosure when faced with a more truly run race. (op 7-2 tchd 5-2)
Dragon Slayer(IRE) had beaten Wee Charlie Castle at Sandown 18 days previously and, while unable to get to the first three, he confirmed that form on 2lb better terms. (op 9-1)
Points Of View met a little support and ran more encouragingly than has been the case on the all-weather of late. He left the impression he would have enjoyed a stronger early pace. (op 8-1)

6034 EBF ATTHERACES.COM BEST ODDS JOHN MUSKER FILLIES' STKS (LISTED RACE) 1m 2f 21y

4:30 (4:32) (Class 1) 3-Y-0+

£22,432 (£8,540; £4,276; £2,136; £1,068; £536) **Stalls** Low

Form	Pos	Dist	Horse / Trainer / Comment	RPR
6036	**1**		**Cape Amber (IRE)**[26] 5243 3-8-9 104 ... AlanMunro 4 (P W Chapple-Hyam) *t.k.h: mde all: sn clr: kpt on strly fnl 2f: unchal* **5/1**[1]	111
4131	**2**	*4*	**Moon Sister (IRE)**[17] 5536 3-8-9 85 ... HayleyTurner 12 (W Jarvis) *chsd (clr) wnr: effrt and clr of remainder over 2f out: edgd lft: one pce fnl f* **25/1**	103
11-	**3**	*7*	**Classic Legend**[319] 6652 3-8-9 93 ... TPO'Shea 13 (B J Meehan) *prom chsng gp: effrt over 3f out: no imp fnl 2f* **16/1**	89
3-06	**4**	*hd*	**Samira Gold (FR)**[48] 4549 4-9-1 103 ... DaneO'Neill 10 (L M Cumani) *hld up: hdwy and edgd lft 2f out: edgd rt and kpt on fnl f: nvr rchd ldrs* **5/1**[1]	89+
003	**5**	*2 1/4*	**Makaaseb (USA)**[54] 4395 3-8-9 99 ... RHills 6 (M A Jarvis) *hld up: hdwy over 2f out: sn rdn: no imp over 1f out* **8/1**[3]	84
1260	**6**	*3/4*	**Melodramatic (IRE)**[31] 5120 3-8-9 100 ... ChrisCatlin 1 (R Charlton) *hld up: effrt and rdn 3f out: btn over 1f out* **7/1**[2]	83
0544	**7**	*3/4*	**Farley Star**[24] 5311 4-9-1 90 ... JimmyFortune 3 (R Charlton) *hld up: pushed along and hdwy 2f out: nvr rchd ldrs* **8/1**[3]	81+
6230	**8**	*1/2*	**Nolas Lolly (IRE)**[31] 5120 4-9-1 96 ... LDettori 16 (M Botti) *stdd rr: drvn over 3f out: nvr able to chal* **28/1**	80
-030	**9**	*2 1/2*	**Maramba (USA)**[49] 4520 3-8-9 91 ... RyanMoore 2 (Sir Michael Stoute) *prom: pushed along over 3f out: btn 2f out* **16/1**	75
4-20	**10**	*1 1/2*	**Kotsi (IRE)**[97] 2975 3-8-9 99 ... RichardMullen 7 (E F Vaughan) *prom: drvn over 3f out: wknd over 2f out* **16/1**	72
2131	**11**	*1/2*	**La Sarrazine (FR)**[32] 5108 3-8-9 88 ... RobertWinston 9 (J R Fanshawe) *midfield: pushed along over 3f out: sn struggling* **20/1**	71
3-10	**12**	*4 1/2*	**Basque Beauty**[35] 4977 3-8-9 99 ... ShaneKelly 5 (W J Haggas) *dwlt: bhd: pushed along over 3f out: n.d* **9/1**	62
2613	**13**	*nk*	**Born Tobouggie (GER)**[20] 5425 3-8-9 89 ... TedDurcan 8 (H R A Cecil) *hld up towards rr: effrt over 2f out: btn over 1f out* **10/1**	62
2605	**14**	*6*	**Cruel Sea (USA)**[31] 5120 3-8-9 92 ... MichaelHills 11 (B W Hills) *plld hrd on outside: effrt over 3f out: edgd lft and wknd over 2f out* **20/1**	50
2013	**15**	*8*	**Mazaaya (USA)**[27] 5209 3-8-9 88 ... KShea 15 (D R Lanigan) *prom tl wknd over 2f out* **33/1**	34

2m 4.04s (-6.46) **Going Correction** -0.225s/f (Firm)
WFA 3 from 4yo 6lb **15** Ran SP% **124.6**
Speed ratings (Par 108): **116,112,107,107,105 104,104,103,101,100 100,96,96,91,85**
toteswinger: 1&2 £33.10, 1&3 £21.60, 2&3 £56.20. CSF £144.46 TOTE £6.70: £2.20, £5.40, £6.20; EX 183.90 Trifecta £214.30 Pool: £289.72, 1.00 winning units.
Owner Five Horses Ltd **Bred** Five Horses Ltd **Trained** Newmarket, Suffolk

FOCUS
A wide-open Listed contest for fillies and not the strongest of races for the class on paper, but the winner won well in a fast time. She has been rated up 8lb.

NOTEBOOK
Cape Amber(IRE), who has acquitted herself creditably in much better company this season, completed the task with a commanding performance. She took the race by the scruff of the neck on the home turn and it was clear entering the final furlong she had the race in safe keeping. She is up to success at Group 3 level and this does appear to be her optimum trip, but it was no doubt her easiest task since winning her maiden at two. (tchd 9-2 and 6-1)
Moon Sister(IRE) ran the race of her life in defeat and finished a clear second-best to the classier winner. She was suited by racing prominently and her official rating will shoot up now, but her potential paddock value will have been enhanced.
Classic Legend ◆ had been unbeaten in two outings as a juvenile and this was a belated return to the track. She kept to her task for pressure, suggesting a stiffer test will suit, and is entitled to improve a bundle for the run. (op 20-1)
Samira Gold(FR), whose previous success came in this event last year, had disappointed in two previous outings this term. She got behind here and was finishing all too late over this shorter trip, but this was more encouraging. (tchd 9-2)

6035 SEA-DEER H'CAP 1m 3y

5:00 (5:02) (Class 4) (0-85,84) 3-Y-0+ **£4,731** (£1,416; £708; £354; £176) **Stalls** High

Form	Pos	Dist	Horse / Trainer / Comment	RPR
4106	**1**		**Opus Maximus (IRE)**[11] 5697 3-9-1 **79** ... RoystonFfrench 9 (M Johnston) *mde all: rdn over 1f out: edgd rt: r.o* **11/1**	90
2100	**2**	*1 3/4*	**Timetable**[41] 4783 3-9-0 **78** ...(v) TedDurcan 1 (H R A Cecil) *hld up: hdwy over 2f out: rdn to chse wnr over 1f out: hung rt ins fnl f: styd on* **18/1**	85
4460	**3**	*2*	**Phluke**[11] 5697 7-9-5 **79** ...(v1) RichardMullen 13 (Eve Johnson Houghton) *chsd ldrs: rdn over 1f out: styd on same pce* **25/1**	81
P00	**4**	*nk*	**Bid For Glory**[13] 5635 4-9-3 **82** ... AshleyHamblett(5) 10 (H J Collingridge) *hld up: hdwy over 1f out: nt rch ldrs* **25/1**	84+
5630	**5**	*nk*	**Obezyana (USA)**[4] 5908 6-8-12 **77** ... DavidProbert(5) 4 (A Bailey) *chsd ldrs: rdn over 2f out: styd on same pce fnl f* **10/1**	78
0060	**6**	*1 1/4*	**Southandwest (IRE)**[19] 5470 4-9-5 **82** ... LukeMorris(3) 12 (J S Moore) *hld up: hdwy over 1f out: sn rdn: no imp ins fnl f* **40/1**	80
310	**7**	*1*	**Bustan (IRE)**[46] 4649 9-9-7 **81** ... RyanMoore 8 (G C Bravery) *chsd ldrs: rdn over 3f out: no ex fnl f* **14/1**	77
2013	**8**	*1*	**Nutkin**[35] 4970 4-9-7 **81** ... RobertWinston 11 (J R Fanshawe) *mid-div: rdn over 3f out: styd on same pce appr fnl f* **12/1**	75
6301	**9**	*shd*	**Grand Vizier (IRE)**[12] 5675 4-8-12 **75** ... JackMitchell(3) 16 (C F Wall) *chsd ldrs: rdn over 2f out: wknd ins fnl f* **7/2**[1]	68
5515	**10**	*2 1/2*	**Capucci**[65] 4017 3-9-3 **81** ...(t) JimmyFortune 15 (J H M Gosden) *hld up: plld hrd: rdn over 2f out: n.d* **7/2**[1]	69
0-00	**11**	*1 1/2*	**Kestrel Cross (IRE)**[82] 3461 6-9-3 **77** ... DaneO'Neill 7 (L M Cumani) *mid-div: rdn over 1f out: nvr trbld ldrs* **20/1**	61
3203	**12**	*3/4*	**Marvo**[5] 5863 4-8-8 **75** ...(b1) AshleyMorgan(7) 14 (M H Tompkins) *hld up in tch: racd keenly: rdn and wknd over 1f out* **9/1**[3]	57
0000	**13**	*2 3/4*	**Fool's Wildcat (USA)**[12] 5682 3-9-3 **81** ... AlanMunro 5 (B J Meehan) *mid-div: rdn and wknd over 2f out* **25/1**	57
4501	**14**	*3 1/2*	**Russian Epic**[38] 4895 4-9-4 **78** ...(t) PhilipRobinson 2 (M A Jarvis) *chsd ldrs: lost pl over 2f out: sn bhd* **6/1**[2]	46
2120	**15**	*1/2*	**Maslaha**[115] 2428 3-9-5 **83** ... ChrisCatlin 3 (R W Price) *hld up: hdwy over 3f out: rdn and wknd over 1f out* **40/1**	50

1m 37.75s (-2.85) **Going Correction** -0.225s/f (Firm)
WFA 3 from 4yo+ 4lb **15** Ran SP% **127.0**
Speed ratings (Par 105): **105,103,101,100,100 99,98,97,97,94 93,92,89,86,85**
toteswinger: 1&2 £20.50, 1&3 £28.90, 2&3 £22.60. CSF £186.06 CT £4887.76 TOTE £11.80: £3.00, £4.20, £4.90; EX 124.30 Trifecta £145.90 Pool: £197.28, 1.00 winning units.
Owner Jim McGrath And Reg Griffin **Bred** Mrs Anne Marie Burns **Trained** Middleham Moor, N Yorks

FOCUS
A fair handicap for the grade which produced another front-running winner, rated up 5lb.
Capucci Official explanation: jockey said colt ran too free
Maslaha Official explanation: jockey said filly had no more to give

6036 EASTERN DAILY PRESS H'CAP 7f 3y

5:30 (5:32) (Class 6) (0-60,62) 3-Y-0+ **£2,266** (£674; £337; £168) **Stalls** High

Form	Pos	Dist	Horse / Trainer / Comment	RPR
3003	**1**		**Poppets Sweetlove**[24] 5318 4-9-7 **59** ... RyanMoore 11 (A B Haynes) *hld up in tch: rdn to ld ins fnl f: edgd lft: r.o* **7/2**[1]	70
6000	**2**	*1 1/2*	**Morocchius (USA)**[49] 4524 3-9-4 **59** ...(p) RoystonFfrench 1 (Miss J A Camacho) *chsd ldrs: led over 2f out: rdn and hdd ins fnl f: unable qck* **33/1**	66
4035	**3**	*1*	**Astroangel**[14] 5604 4-8-9 **54** ... AshleyMorgan(7) 5 (M H Tompkins) *s.i.s: hld up: hdwy: nt clr run and swtchd lft over 1f out: styd on* **8/1**[3]	59
-000	**4**	*2*	**La Famiglia**[34] 5019 3-9-2 **57** ... DaneO'Neill 8 (H Candy) *led over 4f: rdn over 1f out: styd on same pce ins fnl f* **14/1**	57
-000	**5**	*1/2*	**Tarraburn (USA)**[30] 5161 4-9-0 **57** ... WilliamCarson(5) 2 (G C H Chung) *chsd ldrs: rdn over 1f out: no ex fnl f* **25/1**	56
3634	**6**	*shd*	**Al Rayanah**[24] 5318 5-9-1 **53** ...(p) SaleemGolam 7 (G Prodromou) *s.i.s: hld up: hrd rdn over 1f out: r.o ins fnl f: nvr trbld ldrs* **8/1**[3]	51
3605	**7**	*nk*	**Seasonal Cross**[14] 5616 3-9-4 **59** ... NickyMackay 6 (S Dow) *mid-div: hdwy 1/2-way: rdn over 1f out: no ex ins fnl f* **20/1**	57
00-4	**8**	*3 3/4*	**Felicia**[205] 700 3-9-3 **58** ... J-PGuillambert 3 (S C Williams) *chsd ldrs: rdn over 2f out: wknd fnl f* **12/1**	46
60	**9**	*2 3/4*	**Welcome Releaf**[38] 4910 5-9-0 **57** ... DavidProbert(5) 4 (P Leech) *mid-div: hdwy over 2f out: wknd fnl f* **14/1**	38
0066	**10**	*1 1/4*	**Loyal Knight (IRE)**[29] 5167 3-9-5 **60** ... JimmyFortune 15 (S Kirk) *prom: rdn over 2f out: edgd lft and wknd fnl f* **9/1**	38
4200	**11**	*1 1/2*	**Mganga**[29] 5167 3-8-10 **58** ... MatthewDavies(7) 10 (M R Channon) *mid-div: sn pushed along: wknd over 1f out* **16/1**	32
0100	**12**	*1 3/4*	**Valverde (IRE)**[5] 5871 5-9-1 **53** ...(v) ChrisCatlin 12 (George Baker) *hld up: rdn 1/2-way: wknd over 1f out* **16/1**	23
0041	**13**	*1/2*	**Hucking Harkness**[9] 5755 3-9-7 **62** 6ex ... TedDurcan 14 (J R Best) *prom: rdn over 2f out: wknd over 1f out* **7/1**[2]	31
0501	**14**	*1 1/4*	**Djalalabad (FR)**[4] 5916 4-9-4 **56** 6ex ...(tp) HayleyTurner 9 (Mrs C A Dunnett) *hld up: rdn over 2f out: sn edgd lft and wknd* **8/1**[3]	22
0000	**15**	*8*	**Siena**[7] 5803 3-9-0 **55** ... TGMcLaughlin 16 (Mrs C A Dunnett) *s.i.s: hdwy 1/2-way: rdn and wknd over 2f out* **66/1**	1

1m 25.29s (-1.31) **Going Correction** -0.225s/f (Firm)
WFA 3 from 4yo+ 3lb **15** Ran SP% **123.9**
Speed ratings (Par 101): **98,96,95,92,92 92,91,87,84,82 81,79,78,77,68**
toteswinger: 1&2 £39.10, 1&3 £9.90, 2&3 £55.80. CSF £147.63 CT £914.98 TOTE £4.10: £1.70, £11.70, £3.10; EX 180.40 TRIFECTA Not won. Place 6 £ 29.17, Place 5 £ 19.05.

Owner Graham Robinson **Bred** G And Mrs Robinson **Trained** Limpley Stoke, Bath

FOCUS

This was a weak handicap, but it could hardly have been more open. There was a good early pace on and the first three eventually pulled clear.

Loyal Knight(IRE) Official explanation: jockey said gelding lost its action

T/Plt: £22.50 to a £1 stake. Pool: £62,754.16. 2,032.69 winning tickets. T/Qpdt: £22.20 to a £1 stake. Pool: £2,878.08. 95.80 winning tickets. CR

5414 AYR (L-H)

Thursday, September 18

OFFICIAL GOING: Heavy (5.1)

Wind: Breezy, half against Weather: Cloudy

6037 SUPPORT THE AYRSHIRE HOSPICE 01292 291960 MAIDEN AUCTION STKS — 6f

2:20 (2:21) (Class 5) 2-Y-0 **£4,015** (£1,194; £597; £298) **Stalls** High

Form				RPR
3602	1		**Kyllachy Star**[28] 5200 2-8-11 77 ... PaulHanagan 2 (R A Fahey) *pressed ldr: led over 1f out: rdn clr* 15/8[1]	80+
20	2	5	**Frontline Girl (IRE)**[48] 4593 2-8-6 0 ... AndrewElliott 1 (K R Burke) *chsd ldrs: pushed along over 2f out: chsd wnr ins fnl f: no imp* 5/2[2]	60
	3	1 1/4	**Mohawk Ridge** 2-8-11 0 ... TonyHamilton 8 (M Dods) *rn green in rr: hdwy over 1f out: styd on steadily fnl f: bttr for r* 10/1	61
02	4	1	**Asserting**[27] 5219 2-8-4 0 ... AdrianTNicholls 4 (A G Foster) *dwlt: in tch: rdn over 2f out: kpt on fnl f: no imp* 14/1	51
3U	5	1 1/2	**Bees River (IRE)**[111] 2581 2-8-8 0 ... NCallan 9 (A P Jarvis) *led to over 1f out: wknd ins fnl f* 5/1[3]	51
02	6	11	**Liberty Trail (IRE)**[66] 4014 2-8-9 0 ... PaulMulrennan 10 (Miss L A Perratt) *prom: pushed along after 2f: wknd 2f out* 10/1	19
	7	8	**Murrays Magic (IRE)** 2-8-4 0 ... SilvestreDeSousa 5 (D Nicholls) *missed break: sn in tch: rdn 1/2-way: sn wknd* 16/1	—

1m 15.7s (2.10) **Going Correction** +0.35s/f (Good) **7** Ran SP% **110.8**

Speed ratings (Par 95): **100,93,91,90,88 73,63**

toteswinger: 1&2 £1.80, 1&3 £3.90, 2&3 £5.10. CSF £6.23 TOTE £2.40: £1.60, £2.20; EX 6.40.

Owner CBWS Partnership **Bred** John James **Trained** Musley Bank, N Yorks

FOCUS

An ordinary juvenile maiden. Kyllachy Star was a pretty emphatic winner but probably didn't need to improve.

NOTEBOOK

Kyllachy Star outclassed his rivals and came right away inside the final furlong to lose his maiden tag at the sixth attempt. He was the most experienced runner in this field and that told on the testing ground, which he handled without fuss. This was a deserved win and, with another furlong likely to suit before long, he will be high on confidence now. (op 13-8)

Frontline Girl(IRE), having her first outing for 48 days, kept on without ever threatening the winner and posted a more encouraging effort. She has no trouble with this sort of ground and, sure to appreciate a stiffer test in due course, now has more options as she becomes qualified for an official mark. (op 7-2)

Mohawk Ridge, whose stable took this with a debutant in 2006, was always playing catch-up after a sluggish start. He was doing some nice work towards the finish, however, and will be suited by a stiffer test. (op 20-1)

Asserting probably found this even softer ground against her and never got seriously involved. She is another who should find her feet now that she can enter nurseries. (op 16-1)

Bees River(IRE), making her debut for a new stable, showed up well on the rail until tiring right out of it from the furlong pole. This extra distance on such ground found her out, but she too now qualifies for a mark and is entitled to come on a deal for the run. (op 4-1)

Liberty Trail(IRE), a close second over course and distance 66 days previously, was easy to back and ran well below his previous level on this different ground. He is yet another who needed this for an official mark and should prove a different proposition again when returning a sounder surface. Official explanation: jockey said gelding was unsuited by the heavy ground (op 13-2)

6038 NEILSON BINNIE MCKENZIE E.B.F. NOVICE STKS — 1m

2:50 (2:50) (Class 4) 2-Y-0 **£5,828** (£1,734; £866; £432) **Stalls** Low

Form				RPR
0321	1		**Tale Of Silver (IRE)**[18] 5539 2-9-0 87 ... PJMcDonald 4 (G A Swinbank) *set stdy pce: mde all: rdn over 1f out: styd on strly* 9/2[3]	84
51	2	2	**Guestofthenation (USA)**[11] 5716 2-9-5 0 ... GregFairley 1 (M Johnston) *pressed wnr: ev ch 2f out: sn rdn: kpt on same pce fnl f* 2/1[2]	85
41	3	1 1/4	**Aahaykid (IRE)**[14] 5649 2-9-5 80 ... AndrewElliott 3 (K R Burke) *t.k.h: trckd ldrs: rdn over 2f out: hung lft over 1f out: sn no ex* 5/6[1]	78
0	4	22	**Romantic Interlude (IRE)**[34] 5048 2-8-8 0 ow1 ... DarrenWilliams 2 (A P Jarvis) *in tch: drvn over 3f out: wknd over 2f out: t.o* 50/1	15

1m 53.19s (9.39) **Going Correction** +1.10s/f (Soft) **4** Ran SP% **108.0**

Speed ratings (Par 97): **97,95,93,71**

CSF £13.49 TOTE £5.20; EX 8.50.

Owner Mrs I Gibson **Bred** Audrey Frances Stynes **Trained** Melsonby, N Yorks

FOCUS

There were three last-time-out winners in this little novice event and each of them looked potentially very useful. It was run at a fair pace and the race should work out. Aahaykid was below his Warwick form.

NOTEBOOK

Tale Of Silver(IRE), easily off the mark at Musselburgh, had raced only on sound surfaces previously and was faced with another furlong. He was given a very positive ride and, after being given an easy time on the lead, eventually made all in tidy fashion. Despite his sharp pedigree he is evidently a horse that stays well, is obviously versatile as regards underfoot conditions, and has now improved with each of his five career outings. His connections later indicated he may now be put away for the year and, with the best of him likely still to be seen, he rates a decent three-year-old prospect.

Guestofthenation(USA) arrived here on the back of a decisive win on testing ground at Thirsk and was representing a leading stable with a decent previous record in the race. He had every chance, but it was clear shortly after the furlong pole he was not going to get to the winner. He has a deal of scope and remains open to further progression. (op 6-4 tchd 11-8)

Aahaykid(IRE), a clear-cut winner on similar ground at Warwick a fortnight previously, proved all the rage in the betting to follow up over this extra furlong. He was the first of the principals in trouble, however, and did not look to be helping his rider when under pressure. It is too soon to be writing him off, but he has now a little to prove all the same. (op 5-4 tchd 11-8 in places)

Romantic Interlude(IRE), upped a furlong in trip for this turf debut, was well beaten, but will look more interesting when qualifying for a mark after her next outing. (tchd 40-1)

6039 BELL LAWRIE INVESTMENT MANAGEMENT H'CAP — 5f

3:20 (3:20) (Class 5) (0-70,68) 3-Y-0+ **£5,051** (£1,503; £751; £375) **Stalls** High

Form				RPR
0400	1		**Grimes Faith**[12] 5709 5-8-10 58 ... (p) NCallan 3 (K A Ryan) *in tch: drvn to ld over 1f out: kpt on wl fnl f* 12/1	69
0010	2	1 1/2	**Almost Married (IRE)**[22] 5392 4-8-10 58 ... DanielTudhope 4 (J S Goldie) *bhd: outpcd after 2f: gd hdwy over 1f out: chsd wnr ins fnl f: r.o* 6/1	64
5011	3	nk	**Lake Chini (IRE)**[9] 5775 6-9-4 66 6ex ... (b) DaleGibson 5 (M W Easterby) *dwlt: bhd: hdwy over 1f out: kpt on u.p fnl f* 11/2[3]	71
4451	4	1 1/2	**Witchry**[10] 5751 6-9-6 68 6ex ... PaulHanagan 11 (A G Newcombe) *chsd ldrs: rdn 2f out: one pce fnl f* 4/1[1]	67
0341	5	2	**Killer Class**[21] 5417 3-9-0 68 ... KellyHarrison(5) 7 (J S Goldie) *hld up: hdwy whn n.m.r briefly wl over 1f out: one pce fnl f* 8/1	60
00-0	6	2 1/2	**Jadan (IRE)**[20] 5452 7-8-5 53 oh2 ... (b) AdrianTNicholls 8 (E J Alston) *towards rr: drvn over 2f out: nvr able to chal* 16/1	36
4100	7	1 1/4	**Gleaming Spirit (IRE)**[34] 5046 4-9-2 64 ... DarrenWilliams 2 (A P Jarvis) *led to over 1f out: sn wknd* 20/1	42
0-00	8	1/2	**Sunley Sovereign**[9] 5770 4-8-5 53 oh8 ... (b) AndrewElliott 1 (Mrs R A Carr) *cl up on outside tl wknd fr 2f out* 100/1	30
1130	9	1/2	**Invincible Lad (IRE)**[8] 5796 4-9-5 67 ... PaulMulrennan 6 (E J Alston) *cl up: rdn over 2f out: wknd wl over 1f out* 5/1[2]	42
4061	10	8	**Wicked Wilma (IRE)**[9] 5770 4-8-7 60 6ex ow5 ... SladeO'Hara(5) 9 (A Berry) *cl up: ev ch whn sddle slipped and hung lft 2f out: nt rcvr* 5/1[2]	6+

61.42 secs (1.32) **Going Correction** +0.35s/f (Good)

WFA 3 from 4yo+ 1lb **10** Ran SP% **113.4**

Speed ratings (Par 103): **103,100,100,97,94 90,88,87,86,74**

toteswinger: 1&2 £9.80, 1&3 £7.90, 2&3 £7.50. CSF £80.03 CT £443.81 TOTE £14.60: £3.20, £2.30, £2.10; EX 128.50.

Owner Mrs Angie Bailey **Bred** John Grimes **Trained** Hambleton, N Yorks

■ Stewards' Enquiry : Darren Williams one-day ban: failed to ride to draw (Oct 2)

FOCUS

The ground was probably not as bad as on the round course. While this was a moderate sprint, there were still four last-time-out winners in attendance (three penalised). There was a decent pace on. The form looks sound enough.

Wicked Wilma(IRE) Official explanation: jockey said saddle slipped

6040 MACB (S) STKS — 1m 2f

3:50 (3:51) (Class 4) 3-Y-0+ **£6,476** (£1,927; £963; £481) **Stalls** Low

Form				RPR
0000	1		**Jim Martin**[18] 5544 3-8-10 57 ... PJMcDonald 10 (Miss L A Perratt) *cl up: led 3f out to over 1f out: rallied u.p to regain ld nr fin* 80/1	72
0643	2	hd	**Resonate (IRE)**[4] 5935 10-9-2 72 ... PaulHanagan 9 (A G Newcombe) *prom: chal over 2f out: kpt on u.p fnl f: jst hld* 9/2[2]	72
4501	3	hd	**She's Our Lass (IRE)**[9] 5773 7-9-0 75 ... NCallan 3 (K A Ryan) *dwlt: hld up: hdwy to ld over 1f out: kpt on: hdd nr fin* 2/5[1]	70
0006	4	6	**Distant Rock**[11] 5714 3-8-0 58 ... (t) KellyHarrison(5) 4 (D Carroll) *hld up: hdwy and in tch over 2f out: sn rdn and outpcd* 66/1	55
0440	5	12	**Carry On Cleo**[3] 5968 3-8-3 51 ow2 ... (b) KrishGundowry(7) 8 (A Berry) *led to 3f out: wknd 2f out* 50/1	36
2-05	6	3 1/4	**Pugnacity**[26] 5262 4-8-7 44 ow1 ... SladeO'Hara(5) 2 (A Berry) *bhd: drvn over 3f out: sn btn* 80/1	25
0506	7	1/2	**Hawkit (USA)**[36] 4972 7-9-2 63 ... PaulMulrennan 11 (P Monteith) *hld up: stdy hdwy on outside over 4f out: rdn and edgd lft over 2f out: sn wknd* 14/1	28
3432	8	6	**Our Blessing (IRE)**[14] 5629 4-9-2 60 ... DarrenWilliams 6 (A P Jarvis) *chsd ldrs tl rdn and wknd over 2f out* 12/1[3]	16
5555	9	6	**Rotuma (IRE)**[54] 4420 9-8-9 45 ... (b) JohnCavanagh(7) 7 (M Dods) *prom tl rdn and wknd over 3f out* 33/1	4
0026	U		**Ulysees (IRE)**[20] 5456 9-9-2 49 ... TonyHamilton 5 (Miss L A Perratt) *help up on ins: stmbld: hit rails and uns rdr 3f out* 28/1	—

2m 22.07s (10.07) **Going Correction** +1.10s/f (Soft)

WFA 3 from 4yo+ 6lb **10** Ran SP% **116.3**

Speed ratings (Par 105): **103,102,102,97,88 85,85,80,75,—**

toteswinger: 1&2 £19.70, 1&3 £14.30, 2&3 £1.30. CSF £402.15 TOTE £52.20: £19.80, £1.10, £1.10; EX 376.20.There was no bid for the winner. She's Our Lass was subject to a friendly claim.

Owner Ken McGarrity **Bred** Southill Stud **Trained** Carluke, S Lanarks

FOCUS

A fair seller but rather confusing form with a shock winner and a disappointing favourite. The form is far from solid.

Jim Martin Official explanation: trainer said, regarding the apparent improvement in form, that gelding was better suited by the step up in trip.

6041 MCEWAN'S ALES H'CAP (FOR THE KILKERRAN CUP) — 1m 2f

4:20 (4:20) (Class 2) (0-100,92) 3-Y-0+ **£12,952** (£3,854; £1,926; £962) **Stalls** Low

Form				RPR
432	1		**Allied Powers (IRE)**[7] 5830 3-9-3 92 ... MickyFenton 1 (M L W Bell) *cl up: led on bit wl over 2f out: pushed out fnl f* 1/1[1]	102+
5140	2	1 3/4	**Blue Spinnaker (IRE)**[24] 5360 9-8-13 82 ... PaulMulrennan 7 (M W Easterby) *prom: effrt over 2f out: chsd wnr 1f out: kpt on* 8/1[3]	88
1304	3	5	**Wigwam Willie (IRE)**[40] 4856 6-8-13 82 ... (p) NCallan 8 (K A Ryan) *prom: chal 3f out to over 1f out: no ex fnl f* 11/2[2]	78
1000	4	3 3/4	**Best Prospect (IRE)**[9] 5772 6-9-8 91 ... (t) PaulHanagan 2 (M Dods) *hld up: rdn over 2f out: nvr able to chal* 16/1	80
3016	5	1/2	**Charlie Tipple**[14] 5635 4-8-9 78 ... (p) TonyHamilton 5 (T D Easterby) *in tch: outpcd over 2f out: sn n.d* 12/1	66
3602	6	6	**Capable Guest (IRE)**[5] 5903 6-9-1 91 ... (v) MatthewDavies(7) 4 (M R Channon) *hld up: rdn 3f out: edgd lft: nvr on terms* 8/1[3]	67
1-00	7	17	**Bigfanofthat (IRE)**[6] 5863 3-8-3 78 ... AndrewElliott 6 (K R Burke) *cl up tl hung lft and wknd over 2f out: t.o* 16/1	20
4242	8	3 1/4	**Ella Woodcock (IRE)**[45] 4688 4-8-13 82 ... (p) AdrianTNicholls 3 (E J Alston) *led to wl over 2f out: sn wknd: t.o* 12/1	17

2m 22.06s (10.06) **Going Correction** +1.10s/f (Soft)

WFA 3 from 4yo+ 6lb **8** Ran SP% **114.8**

Speed ratings (Par 109): **103,101,97,94,94 89,75,73**

toteswinger: 1&2 £3.10, 1&3 £2.40, 2&3 £6.10. CSF £9.80 CT £30.86 TOTE £1.90: £1.10, £2.00, £1.60; EX 8.70.

Owner David Fish And Edward Ware **Bred** Saad Bin Mishrif **Trained** Newmarket, Suffolk

FOCUS

The time was almost identical to the seller and this is probably not form to be too positive about. A marginal persanal best from the winner.

NOTEBOOK

Allied Powers(IRE) came home to score readily and register his fourth win of the year. He raced a too freely through the first 2f, but found plenty when asked to win the race in between the final 2f and should be rated value for a bit further as he looked to idle somewhat late on. This ground evidently holds no fears for him and he has had an excellent time of things this season, remembering his first success came from a mark of 68. The November Handicap back over 1m4f looks a viable target for this tough performer and he appeals as the sort to progress even further as a four-year-old. (tchd 11-8)

Blue Spinnaker(IRE) emerged from out of the pack as the clear danger to the winner and eventually finished well clear in second. This was a lot better from him, but he is a little flattered by his proximity at the finish. (op 6-1)

Wigwam Willie(IRE) made a positive move three out, but he failed to sustain his effort when push really came to shove and was eventually well held by the first pair. (op 5-1)

Best Prospect(IRE) had finished second in this event in the last two years and was given his usual patient ride. He flattered briefly at the top of the home straight and looks in need of respite from the handicapper. (tchd 14-1)

Charlie Tipple failed to really convince he wants this longer distance and does look held by the handicapper. (op 16-1 tchd 11-1)

Capable Guest(IRE), second at Goodwood five days previously, had nowhere to go when going well out the back around 2f out, but his response when in the clear was laboured. (op 12-1)

Ella Woodcock(IRE) Official explanation: jockey said gelding was unsuited by the heavy ground

6042 TOTESUPER7 H'CAP — 1m
4:50 (4:51) (Class 5) (0-70,66) 3-Y-O — £4,533 (£1,348; £674; £336) Stalls Low

Form — RPR

1305 **1** **Grit (IRE)**[3] 5965 3-9-1 **63** ... PaulMulrennan 5 — 70
(M R Channon) *prom: drvn over 2f out: led over 1f out: r.o strly* **7/1**

0155 **2** 3 ½ **Red Skipper (IRE)**[19] 5504 3-8-9 **62** ... AshleyHamblett(5) 6 — 61
(N Wilson) *hld up: hdwy over 2f out: hung lft and chsd wnr over 1f out: r.o* **7/1**

044- **3** nk **Ibrox (IRE)**[316] 6723 3-9-3 **65** ... SilvestreDeSousa 9 — 63
(A D Brown) *s.i.s: bhd tl styd on fnl 2f: nrst fin* **16/1**

4124 **4** ½ **Tamasou (IRE)**[27] 5224 3-9-4 **66** ... DaleGibson 1 — 63
(Garry Moss) *midfield: drvn and outpcd over 2f out: kpt on same pce u.p fnl f* **5/1**[2]

0023 **5** 5 **Natural Rhythm (IRE)**[5] 5888 3-8-12 **60** ... (b) AndrewElliott 11 — 46
(Mrs R A Carr) *led: rdn over 3f out: hdd over 2f out: rallied: wknd fnl f* **9/2**[1]

0400 **6** 7 **Daring Dream (GER)**[20] 5458 3-9-4 **66** ... (v[1]) NCallan 10 — 36
(A P Jarvis) *cl up: led over 2f out to over 1f out: sn wknd* **8/1**

2226 **7** ½ **Willyn (IRE)**[18] 5544 3-8-1 **54** ... KellyHarrison(5) 2 — 22
(J S Goldie) *bhd: drvn over 3f out: n.d* **10/1**

3651 **8** 11 **Talon (IRE)**[18] 5544 3-8-8 **56** ... (tp) PaulQuinn 8 — —
(G A Swinbank) *cl up tl wknd qckly over 2f out* **7/1**

0560 **9** 7 **Kargan (IRE)**[27] 5224 3-8-10 **58** ... PaulHanagan 4 — —
(A G Foster) *in tch: effrt over 2f out: wknd wl over 1f out* **14/1**

4030 **10** 11 **Medici Time**[92] 3126 3-8-5 **56** ... (p) DuranFentiman(3) 3 — —
(T D Easterby) *towards rr: drvn over 3f out: sn struggling* **6/1**[3]

1m 51.69s (7.89) **Going Correction** +1.10s/f (Soft) — **10** Ran SP% **119.4**

Speed ratings (Par 101): **104,100,100,99,94 87,87,76,69,58**

toteswinger: 1&2 £14.80, 1&3 £21.30, 2&3 £14.00. CSF £56.69 CT £767.49 TOTE £7.90: £2.40, £3.10, £4.40; EX 55.10.

Owner M Channon **Bred** M G Masterson **Trained** West Ilsley, Berks

■ Stewards' Enquiry : Paul Mulrennan caution: used whip when clearly winning

FOCUS

This moderate handicap for three-year-olds was run at a solid early pace. The winner is rated up 6lb and the form is sound enough.

6043 UNICK ARCHITECTS H'CAP — 7f 50y
5:20 (5:20) (Class 5) (0-75,73) 3-Y-O+ — £4,533 (£1,348; £674; £336) Stalls Low

Form — RPR

0161 **1** **Keys Of Cyprus**[3] 5965 6-9-3 **69** 6ex ... AdrianTNicholls 1 — 83
(D Nicholls) *t.k.h early: chsd ldrs: rdn over 2f out: led over 1f out: styd on strly* **7/2**[1]

42 **2** 2 ¾ **Nok Twice (IRE)**[36] 4961 7-8-13 **65** ... NCallan 14 — 72
(K A Ryan) *s.i.s: bhd tl hdwy over 2f out: chsd wnr wl ins fnl f: r.o* **8/1**[3]

0500 **3** 1 **Blindspin**[22] 5397 3-9-3 **72** ... PJMcDonald 9 — 75
(M Dods) *hld up: hdwy over 2f out: kpt on same pce ins fnl f* **20/1**

2004 **4** 1 **Ninefineirishmen (IRE)**[22] 5390 3-9-3 **72** ... (p) DarrenWilliams 6 — 73
(K R Burke) *led to over 1f out: wknd ins fnl f* **15/2**[2]

-610 **5** nse **Eternal Legacy (IRE)**[9] 5779 6-8-7 **64** ... GaryBartley(5) 4 — 65
(E J Alston) *cl up tl rdn and wknd over 1f out* **11/1**

0510 **6** ¾ **Balakiref**[2] 5991 9-9-2 **73** ... KellyHarrison(5) 5 — 74+
(M Dods) *hld up: nt clr run fr over 2f out tl last 75yds: kpt on: no ch w ldrs* **9/1**

550- **7** ¾ **Betty Burke**[63] 4134 3-8-6 **61** ... (t) SilvestreDeSousa 10 — 57
(Liam McAteer, Ire) *midfield: drvn over 3f out: wknd 2f out* **25/1**

4223 **8** 1 **Ancient Cross**[22] 5390 4-9-2 **68** ... (b[1]) PaulMulrennan 2 — 63
(M W Easterby) *midfield: effrt ins over 2f out: wknd fnl f* **7/2**[1]

4603 **9** ¾ **Yorkshire Blue**[17] 5562 9-8-12 **64** ... DanielTudhope 8 — 57
(J S Goldie) *s.i.s: nvr on terms* **12/1**

0040 **10** 3 ¾ **Flying Bantam (IRE)**[16] 5594 7-9-4 **70** ... PaulHanagan 3 — 53
(R A Fahey) *cl up tl rdn and wknd fr 2f out* **20/1**

1402 **11** 2 ¼ **Celtic Lynn (IRE)**[40] 4875 3-9-3 **72** ... MickyFenton 13 — 47
(M Dods) *hld up: hdwy on outside over 2f out: wknd qckly wl over 1f out* **10/1**

0046 **12** 1 ½ **Cat Whistle**[26] 5273 3-9-3 **72** ... TonyHamilton 7 — 43
(R A Fahey) *t.k.h in midfield: wknd over 2f out* **16/1**

1m 40.06s (6.66) **Going Correction** +1.10s/f (Soft)

WFA 3 from 4yo+ 3lb — **12** Ran SP% **121.7**

Speed ratings (Par 103): **105,101,100,99,99 98,97,96,95,91 88,87**

toteswinger: 1&2 £6.10, 1&3 £28.00, 2&3 £34.30. CSF £31.69 CT £509.92 TOTE £4.00: £1.70, £2.60, £8.30; EX 38.30 Place 6: £183.42 Place 5: £145.77 .

Owner The Beasley Gees **Bred** Juddmonte Farms **Trained** Sessay, N Yorks

FOCUS

A modest handicap, run at a generous early pace. The winner improved by 10lb on his win earlier in the week, with the runner-up the best guide.

Balakiref Official explanation: jockey said gelding was denied a clear run

T/Plt: £191.60 to a £1 stake. Pool: £59,927.93. 228.28 winning tickets. T/Qpdt: £38.00 to a £1 stake. Pool: £4,119.09. 80.20 winning tickets. RY

5936 GREAT LEIGHS (A.W) (L-H)
Thursday, September 18

OFFICIAL GOING: Standard

Wind: virtually nil Weather: bright, dry

6044 NAZE H'CAP — 1m 6f (P)
6:50 (6:51) (Class 5) (0-70,70) 3-Y-O — £2,590 (£770; £385; £192) Stalls Low

Form — RPR

0042 **1** **Sunny Spells**[7] 5837 3-8-5 **52** ... SaleemGolam 7 — 65
(S C Williams) *a travelling wl: trckd ldrs: wnt 2nd over 7f out: led jst over 3f out: rdn clr wl over 1f out: easily* **4/1**[3]

0005 **2** 5 **Black Or Red (IRE)**[7] 5833 3-8-4 **51** ... (bt) CatherineGannon 6 — 57
(I A Wood) *t.k.h: hld up in tch: snatched up 8f out: hdwy 3f out: chsd wnr and hung lft fr over 1f out: styd on but no ch w wnr* **16/1**

-640 **3** 6 **Bet Noir (IRE)**[8] 5803 3-9-3 **64** ... AdamKirby 2 — 62
(W R Swinburn) *s.i.s: hld up bhd: hdwy over 3f out: chsd ldrs and rdn jst over 2f out: no ch w ldng pair but plugged on to go 3rd nr fin* **7/2**[2]

0054 **4** hd **West Lorne (USA)**[6] 5868 3-8-6 **53** ... ChrisCatlin 4 — 50
(E J O'Neill) *chsd ldrs: chsd ldr and rdn over 2f out: wl outpcd over 1f out: plugged on* **12/1**

-334 **5** ½ **Limelight (USA)**[18] 5537 3-8-4 **51** ... DO'Donohoe 11 — 48
(Sir Mark Prescott) *sn led: hdd over 8f out: pushed along over 7f out: reminder 6f out: rdn 4f out: wl outpcd 2f out: no ch fnl f* **11/4**[1]

5046 **6** ½ **Opera De Luna**[15] 5605 3-9-4 **65** ... GeorgeBaker 8 — 61
(D Shaw) *stdd s: hld up in rr: hdwy 3f out: rdn and no imp fr jst over 2f out* **8/1**

000 **7** shd **Our Nations**[45] 4689 3-7-13 **51** oh1 ... Louis-PhilippeBeuzelin(5) 1 — 47
(D Carroll) *stmbld s: towards rr: rdn and unable qck 3f out: no ch w ldrs last 2f* **22/1**

-540 **8** 11 **Dedicate**[36] 4985 3-9-9 **70** ... HayleyTurner 5 — 50
(R Charlton) *stdd s: t.k.h: hld up in rr: bustled along over 6f out: rdn and no prog 3f out: wl bhd fnl f* **8/1**

3546 **9** 2 ¾ **Kimbolton**[48] 4607 3-9-1 **62** ... TPQueally 3 — 39
(H R A Cecil) *t.k.h: hld up in midfield: hmpd 8f out: rdn wl over 2f out: sn wl btn* **8/1**

0000 **10** 5 **Tewin Green**[22] 5407 3-8-4 **51** oh1 ... (p) KirstyMilczarek 10 — 21
(M D Squance) *t.k.h: chsd ldr tl led over 8f out: rdn and hdd 3f out: wknd qckly: t.o* **50/1**

5006 **11** 37 **Etta Place**[18] 5537 3-8-9 **56** ... (t) MartinDwyer 9 — —
(P W Chapple-Hyam) *rn in snatches: racd in midfield on outer: rdn 5f out: wl bhd last 3f out: t.o and eased fr over 1f out* **20/1**

3m 3.53s (0.33) **Going Correction** +0.025s/f (Slow) — **11** Ran SP% **126.9**

Speed ratings (Par 101): **100,97,93,93,93 93,92,86,85,82 61**

toteswinger: 1&2 £8.50, 1&3 £8.50, 2&3 £4.10. CSF £70.05 CT £256.21 TOTE £3.90: £2.10, £6.10, £1.40; EX 62.30.

Owner W E Enticknap **Bred** Whitsbury Manor Stud **Trained** Newmarket, Suffolk

FOCUS

This looked a very modest event, as quite a few of these came into the race in not particularly good form and most of them were trying the trip for the first time. With all those elements combined, the form is probably weak, although the winner improved to the tune of 4lb.

6045 WEST PARK LODGE CLAIMING STKS — 5f (P)
7:20 (7:20) (Class 6) 3-Y-O+ — £2,590 (£770; £385; £192) Stalls Low

Form — RPR

1160 **1** **Desperate Dan**[6] 5861 7-8-5 73 ... (b) PNolan(7) 4 — 69
(A B Haynes) *taken down early: chsd ldrs: wnt 2nd over 2f out: edgd rt fnl f: r.o u.p to ld fnl stride* **7/1**[3]

3242 **2** shd **Harry Up**[28] 5206 7-9-4 84 ... (p) LDettori 1 — 75
(K A Ryan) *led: rdn over 1f out: kept on u.p fnl f tl hdd fnl stride* **8/13**[1]

0000 **3** ¾ **Mutamared (USA)**[24] 5347 8-9-8 92 ... TedDurcan 5 — 76
(K A Ryan) *stdd s: hld up bhd: hdwy on inner wl over 1f out: chsd ldng pair jst over 1f out: r.o but nvr quite getting to ldrs* **3/1**[2]

3503 **4** 2 ¼ **Sands Crooner (IRE)**[44] 4703 5-9-6 74 ... TPQueally 7 — 66
(J G Given) *stdd s: bhd: hdwy and nt clr run wl over 1f out: sn swtchd lft: r.o to chse ldng trio ins fnl f: nvr able to chal* **12/1**

046 **5** ¾ **Cranworth Blaze**[40] 4877 4-8-6 44 ... SaleemGolam 8 — 49?
(T J Etherington) *racd in midfield on outer: rdn 1/2-way: sn struggling: no ch fr over 1f out* **80/1**

0505 **6** 2 ½ **Mollyatti**[16] 5592 3-8-5 47 ... DominicFox(3) 12 — 43
(Miss V Haigh) *towards rr: effrt 1/2-way: no imp whn nt clr run over 1f out: no ch after* **66/1**

0600 **7** shd **Mambazo**[20] 5474 6-8-4 55 ... (p) WilliamCarson(5) 2 — 43
(S C Williams) *chsd ldrs: rdn 2f out: outpcd wl over 1f out: no ch fnl f* **16/1**

0305 **8** 1 **Joss Stick**[14] 5645 3-8-9 66 ... (p) EddieAhern 6 — 40
(P J Makin) *t.k.h: chsd ldr tl over 2f out: sn rdn: wknd over 1f out* **16/1**

60.12 secs (-0.08) **Going Correction** +0.025s/f (Slow)

WFA 3 from 4yo+ 1lb — **8** Ran SP% **121.6**

Speed ratings (Par 101): **101,100,99,96,94 90,90,89**

toteswinger: 1&2 £1.10, 1&3 £6.50, 2&3 £1.10. CSF £12.52 TOTE £6.80: £3.00, £1.02, £1.30; EX 20.40.

Owner Joe McCarthy **Bred** Sheikh Amin Dahlawi **Trained** Limpley Stoke, Bath

FOCUS

The field was cut by a third during the morning, but it still left a competitive-looking race. The form looks muddling though, with the principals not rated at their best.

6046 JASPER H'CAP — 6f (P)
7:50 (7:50) (Class 5) (0-70,70) 3-Y-O+ — £3,885 (£1,156; £577; £288) Stalls Low

Form — RPR

000 **1** **The Cayterers**[65] 4051 6-8-8 **63** ... MCGeran(5) 9 — 73
(A W Carroll) *s.i.s: bhd: hdwy over 1f out: str run to ld fnl 100yds: eased nr fin: readily* **17/2**

2622 **2** 1 **Towy Boy (IRE)**[27] 5217 3-8-12 **64** ... (t) CatherineGannon 13 — 71
(I A Wood) *t.k.h: hld up towards rr: hdwy to chse ldrs 4f out: rdn wl over 1f out: led ent fnl f: hdd fnl 100yds: nt pce of wnr* **12/1**

5264 **3** 2 ¼ **Louphole**[41] 4809 6-9-3 **67** ... EddieAhern 4 — 67
(P J Makin) *stdd s: t.k.h: hld up towards rr: hdwy over 3f out: swtchd lft over 1f out: ev ch ent fnl f: outpcd fnl 100yds* **9/2**[2]

3022 **4** nk **Norcroft**[17] 5582 6-8-13 **63** ... ChrisCatlin 5 — 65+
(Mrs C A Dunnett) *in tch: swtchd lft and nt clr run wl over 1f out: shuffled bk and swtchd rt jst over 1f out: r.o fnl f: nt able to chal* **9/2**[2]

0400 **5** *1* **Tamino (IRE)**[98] 2983 5-8-6 **56** oh2..............(t) KirstyMilczarek 1 52
(P Howling) *chsd ldrs on inner: drvn and ev ch ent fnl f: wknd ins fnl f* **12/1**

2355 **6** *¾* **Rosie Says No**[14] 5629 3-8-11 **63**.............. ShaneKelly 8 56
(R M H Cowell) *t.k.h: hld up in midfield on outer: rdn and effrt 2f out: kpt on same pce u.p fnl f* **10/1**

0012 **7** *½* **Spoof Master (IRE)**[9] 5775 4-9-3 **67**..............(p) LPKeniry 7 59
(C R Dore) *led: rdn 2f out: hdd ent fnl f: wknd ins fnl f* **4/1**[1]

0061 **8** *½* **Applesnap (IRE)**[14] 5629 3-9-4 **70**..............(b) DO'Donohoe 12 60
(Miss Amy Weaver) *w ldr: ev ch and nt qckn over 1f out: wknd ins fnl f* **7/1**[3]

6600 **9** *nse* **Muktasb (USA)**[15] 5610 7-9-0 **64**..............(v) AdamKirby 2 54
(D Shaw) *towards rr: rdn and effrt on inner over 2f out: nvr trbld ldrs* **16/1**

0000 **10** *1* **Brazilian Brush (IRE)**[22] 5401 3-8-13 **65**..............(t) JimmyFortune 6 52
(H Morrison) *hld up in midfield: rdn over 2f out: no prog fr wl over 1f out* **12/1**

0000 **11** *½* **Imperial Echo (USA)**[9] 5779 7-9-6 **70**.............. TGMcLaughlin 3 55
(P Howling) *s.i.s: a bhd:* **20/1**

1m 13.64s (-0.06) **Going Correction** +0.025s/f (Slow)
WFA 3 from 4yo+ 2lb **11 Ran SP% 122.2**
Speed ratings (Par 103): **101,99,96,96,94 93,93,92,92,91 90**
toteswinger: 1&2 £37.20, 1&3 £0.00, 2&3 £14.80. CSF £110.15 CT £537.23 TOTE £9.50: £2.40, £4.40, £1.60; EX 207.30.
Owner R D Willis and M C Watts **Bred** Acrum Lodge Stud **Trained** Cropthorne, Worcs

FOCUS
Even though this was a race for horses rated up to 70, the standard did not look that high on recent evidence, although the form looks sound enough. The winner went against the recent pattern here in coming from the rear.
Norcroft Official explanation: jockey said gelding was denied a clear run
Applesnap(IRE) Official explanation: jockey said filly hung left

6047 COWLINGE MAIDEN STKS — 1m (P)
8:20 (8:23) (Class 5) 3-Y-O+ £3,885 (£1,156; £577; £288) Stalls Centre

Form RPR

1 **Tactful (IRE)** 3-8-12 0.............. RichardKingscote 15 71+
(R M Beckett) *stdd s: hld up in midfield on outer: rdn and gd hdwy wd over 2f out: edgd lft but r.o to ld ent fnl f: pushed out* **20/1**

0-24 **2** *1¼* **Plavius (USA)**[47] 4620 3-9-3 76..............(v[1]) LDettori 9 73
(Saeed Bin Suroor) *chsd ldr for 1f and again 4f out: rdn to ld over 1f out: sn hung lft and hdd: one pce fnl f* **4/5**[1]

0-56 **3** *3¼* **Intabih (USA)**[6] 5864 3-9-3 0.............. EddieAhern 12 65
(C E Brittain) *hld up in midfield: hdwy over 2f out: rdn wl over 1f out: styd on to go 3rd nr fin: nvr trbld ldng pair* **12/1**

0- **4** *1* **Royal Manor**[373] 5306 3-8-12 0.............. KirstyMilczarek 13 58
(N J Vaughan) *in tch: rdn to chse ldng pair wl over 1f out: outpcd over 1f out: plugged on same pce: lost 3rd nr fin* **25/1**

5 *1¼* **Cara's Request (AUS)** 3-8-4 0.............. ChrisCatlin 4 55+
(L M Cumani) *t.k.h: hld up in midfield: effrt 2f out: kpt on same pce fr over 1f out* **14/1**

6 *¾* **Qeyaada (USA)** 3-8-12 0.............. TGMcLaughlin 8 54+
(E A L Dunlop) *hld up in midfield on inner: rdn over 2f out: shuffled bk over 2f out: swtchd rt off of rail over 1f out: kpt on but nvr trbld ldrs* **16/1**

56 **7** *nk* **Mutawahej (USA)**[26] 5278 4-9-7 0.............. MartinDwyer 10 58+
(J H M Gosden) *bmpd s: bhd: hdwy over 2f out: n.m.r briefly over 1f out: nvr trbld ldrs* **7/2**[2]

5263 **8** *1* **Reve Vert (FR)**[42] 4777 3-9-3 48.............. ShaneKelly 14 56?
(A W Carroll) *led and crossed to rail: rdn jst over 2f out: hdd over 1f out: fdd ins fnl f* **25/1**

0-0 **9** *3½* **Street Power (USA)**[54] 4431 3-9-3 0.............. LiamJones 11 47
(J R Gask) *lft at s: t.k.h: hld up towards rr: hdwy on wd outside 2f out: no imp fr over 1f out* **33/1**

10 *3¼* **Alqaffay (IRE)** 3-9-3 0.............. TedDurcan 2 40
(Saeed Bin Suroor) *s.i.s: sn in tch: rdn wl over 1f out: sn hung lft and btn: eased fnl f* **7/1**[3]

11 *4½* **Admiral Arry** 3-9-3 0.............. HayleyTurner 6 30
(G A Butler) *a bhd: rdn 4f out: wl bhd last 2f* **25/1**

6260 **12** *½* **Una Auroraborealis**[83] 3458 3-8-12 44.............. J-PGuillambert 3 24
(S W James) *t.k.h: chsd ldrs tl rdn and btn over 2f out* **80/1**

13 *2* **Alyseve** 3-8-7 0.............. AmyBaker(5) 7 19
(Mrs C A Dunnett) *t.k.h: hld up towards rr: snatched up over 4f out: rdn and lost tch over 3f out* **100/1**

26 **14** *3¼* **Classic Lass**[20] 5471 3-8-12 0.............. SaleemGolam 1 11
(Rae Guest) *chsd ldr after 1f tl 4f out: rdn and wknd qckly jst over 2f out* **11/1**

15 *15* **Miss Medusa** 3-8-12 0..............(t) TPQueally 5 —
(Mrs C A Dunnett) *sn bhd: rdn and struggling fr 1/2-way: wl t.o last 2f* **66/1**

1m 39.68s (-0.22) **Going Correction** +0.025s/f (Slow)
WFA 3 from 4yo 4lb **15 Ran SP% 141.8**
Speed ratings (Par 103): **102,100,97,96,95 94,94,93,89,86 81,81,79,76,61**
toteswinger: 1&2 £8.80, 1&3 £23.70, 2&3 £8.50. CSF £40.41 TOTE £28.70: £9.90, £1.40, £4.30; EX 146.50.
Owner Mrs David Aykroyd **Bred** London Thoroughbred Services Ltd **Trained** Whitsbury, Hants

FOCUS
Plenty of the top stables were represented in this, but this was probably only an ordinary maiden. That said, several shaped a bit better than the bare form and can rate higher. Those with experience looked to hold the advantage, but the race eventually went to a newcomer.

6048 HECTOR H'CAP — 1m (P)
8:50 (8:53) (Class 6) (0-65,70) 3-Y-O £2,590 (£770; £385; £192) Stalls Centre

Form RPR

3056 **1** **Ben Ami**[18] 5532 3-8-11 **65**.............. AndreaAtzeni(7) 13 75
(Miss J R Gibney) *in tch: hdwy over 2f out: drvn to ld over 1f out: forged ahd wl ins fnl f* **28/1**

3653 **2** *¾* **Siren Sound**[22] 5402 3-9-1 **62**.............. JimmyFortune 12 70
(H Morrison) *t.k.h: prom: upsides ldr gng wl over 2f out: rdn over 1f out: unable qck fnl f: no ex and btn wl ins fnl f* **8/1**

4444 **3** *hd* **Outside Edge (IRE)**[15] 5616 3-9-1 **62**.............. AdamKirby 2 70
(W R Swinburn) *hld up in tch: hdwy over 2f out: chsd ldrs 1f out: drvn and flashed tail ins fnl f: kpt on* **5/1**[2]

1005 **4** *2* **Themwerethedays**[14] 5639 3-9-4 **65**.............. LPKeniry 16 68
(S Kirk) *s.i.s: sn in midfield: effrt jst over 2f out: kpt on same pce u.p fnl f* **14/1**

4221 **5** *¾* **Jollyhockeysticks**[7] 5836 3-9-9 **70** 6ex.............. SamHitchcott 9 71
(M R Channon) *chsd ldr tl led over 3f out: sn rdn: hdd over 1f out: wknd fnl 100yds* **11/2**[3]

5310 **6** *hd* **Bramalea**[12] 5712 3-8-9 **63**.............. AmyScott(7) 11 64
(B W Duke) *s.i.s: hld up wl bhd: hdwy on outer over 3f out: rdn and styd on fr over 1f out: nvr rchd ldrs* **11/1**

0344 **7** *4½* **Poyle Dee Dee**[22] 5402 3-9-4 **65**.............. GeorgeBaker 8 56
(R M Beckett) *hld up in midfield: effrt 2f out: sn hung lft and no imp: wl hld fnl f* **11/2**[3]

1666 **8** *½* **Rio L'Oren (IRE)**[15] 5616 3-9-1 **62**..............(p) KirstyMilczarek 14 52
(N J Vaughan) *t.k.h: chsd ldrs: rdn 2f out: wknd ent fnl f* **20/1**

0450 **9** *2* **Milanollo**[43] 4727 3-8-12 **59**.............. HayleyTurner 1 44
(M L W Bell) *t.k.h: hld up towards rr: rdn and effrt 2f out: no imp over 1f out* **18/1**

6006 **10** *2* **Alzaroof (USA)**[41] 4825 3-9-2 **63**.............. MartinDwyer 3 43
(E A L Dunlop) *a towards rr: nvr trbld ldrs* **25/1**

5310 **11** *½* **Mr Fantozzi (IRE)**[23] 5378 3-9-1 **62**.............. JerryO'Dwyer 15 41
(M Botti) *sn led: hdd over 3f out: rdn and wknd over 2f out* **9/2**[1]

0-00 **12** *nk* **Usetheforce (IRE)**[215] 590 3-8-13 **60**.............. EddieAhern 10 38
(M J Wallace, Australia) *a towards rr: no ch fnl 2f* **8/1**

0626 **13** *1½* **Hasty Lady**[14] 5638 3-9-1 **62**..............(p) TedDurcan 5 37
(K A Ryan) *chsd ldrs tl over 3f out: sn struggling* **11/1**

4000 **14** *16* **Salt Of The Earth (IRE)**[15] 5617 3-9-4 **65**.............. ShaneKelly 6 —
(T G Mills) *t.k.h: a bhd: lost tch 2f out: eased fnl f: t.o* **20/1**

-640 **15** *6* **Bid To The Beat**[50] 4524 3-8-13 **60**.............. ChrisCatlin 7 —
(H J Collingridge) *a bhd: t.o fnl f* **33/1**

1m 40.31s (0.41) **Going Correction** +0.025s/f (Slow) **15 Ran SP% 136.2**
Speed ratings (Par 99): **98,97,97,95,94 94,89,89,87,85 84,84,82,66,60**
toteswinger: 1&2 £30.90, 1&3 £0.00, 2&3 £12.80. CSF £252.00 CT £1381.03 TOTE £41.60: £15.10, £3.00, £2.00; EX 643.80.
Owner Wood Hall Stud Limited **Bred** Wood Hall Stud **Trained** Shenley, Herts

FOCUS
A modest-looking race full of exposed sorts. The form is very ordinary, rated through the third.
Usetheforce(IRE) Official explanation: jockey said gelding lost a shoe

6049 LITTLE BENTLEY H'CAP — 1m 2f (P)
9:20 (9:21) (Class 5) (0-70,70) 3-Y-O £3,885 (£1,156; £577; £288) Stalls Low

Form RPR

4506 **1** **Andaman Sunset**[29] 5185 3-9-3 **69**..............(p) TedDurcan 6 77
(G Wragg) *stdd s: towards rr: rdn 5f out: drvn and hdwy over 3f out: chal ent fnl f: led ins fnl f: styd on* **16/1**

6336 **2** *nk* **Dusk**[8] 5803 3-8-12 **64**..............(b) EddieAhern 15 71
(J L Dunlop) *stdd s: hld up bhd: smooth hdwy over 3f out: rdn to chal ent fnl f: nt qckn towards fin* **5/2**[1]

6322 **3** *3½* **Azure Mist**[17] 5568 3-8-6 **65**.............. AshleyMorgan(7) 13 65
(M H Tompkins) *t.k.h: chsd ldrs: rdn and ev ch 2f out: sn led: hdd ins fnl f: sn fdd* **12/1**

2454 **4** *shd* **Saleima (IRE)**[16] 5595 3-9-4 **70**.............. TPQueally 2 70
(P W Chapple-Hyam) *v.s.a and early reminders: hdwy over 2f out: styd on u.p: nvr trbld ldrs* **6/1**[3]

01 **5** *¾* **Director's Chair**[59] 4260 3-8-13 **68**..............(b) RussellKennemore(3) 10 66
(Miss J Feilden) *awkward s: bmpd sn after: bhd: hdwy over 2f out: hung rt over 1f out: styd on but nvr trbld ldrs* **16/1**

3010 **6** *1* **Space Pirate**[7] 5815 3-8-4 **56**..............(p) DO'Donohoe 9 52
(J Pearce) *bhd: hdwy on outer over 2f out: styd on but nvr threatened ldrs* **33/1**

0000 **7** *¾* **Civitas Filius (USA)**[8] 5803 3-8-11 **63**.............. RichardMullen 1 58
(D M Simcock) *in tch: drvn to chse ldrs jst over 2f out: wknd u.p over 1f out* **20/1**

3040 **8** *4* **Classical Rhythm (IRE)**[56] 4344 3-9-1 **67**.............. MartinDwyer 4 54
(J R Boyle) *chsd ldr tl led jst over 2f out: sn rdn: hdd over 1f out: wknd qckly* **20/1**

0041 **9** *1¾* **Havanavich**[5] 5912 3-7-13 **56** 6ex.............. Louis-PhilippeBeuzelin(5) 11 39
(S Kirk) *s.i.s: hld up bhd: rdn and unable qck 3f out: nvr trbld ldrs* **8/1**

-003 **10** *¾* **Southern Mistral**[8] 5803 3-8-8 **60**.............. ShaneKelly 8 42
(M Wigham) *hld up towards rr: rdn and 3f out: no hdwy and wl btn last 2f* **16/1**

2112 **11** *11* **Circadian Rhythm**[14] 5631 3-8-7 **59**.............. SaleemGolam 14 19
(S C Williams) *t.k.h: hld up in tch on outer: rdn 3f out: sn struggling: wl bhd fnl f* **11/2**[2]

-000 **12** *1½* **Marchpane**[71] 3843 3-8-12 **64**..............(b) RichardKingscote 7 21
(R M Beckett) *led: rdn 3f out: hdd jst over 2f out: sn btn: eased fnl f* **33/1**

2106 **13** *2* **Emshabb**[15] 5602 3-9-1 **67**.............. LiamJones 5 20
(W J Haggas) *s.i.s: sn bustled up to chse ldrs: rdn 4f out: wl bhd last 2f: t.o* **16/1**

0-00 **14** *2¼* **Langham House**[116] 2429 3-8-8 **60**.............. ChrisCatlin 12 8
(J R Jenkins) *t.k.h: chsd ldrs tl rdn and wknd qckly over 3f out: t.o and eased fnl f* **28/1**

3-20 **15** *12* **Rahere (IRE)**[26] 5278 3-9-1 **67**.............. J-PGuillambert 3 —
(M Johnston) *stdd and rrd s: hld up in midfield: rdn and effrt on inner over 3f out: wknd over 2f out: sn wl bhd: eased fnl f: t.o* **13/2**

2m 7.76s (-0.84) **Going Correction** +0.025s/f (Slow) **15 Ran SP% 132.8**
Speed ratings (Par 101): **104,103,100,100,100 99,98,95,94,93 84,83,82,80,70**
toteswinger: 1&2 £30.90, 1&3 £0.00, 2&3 £37.10. CSF £57.66 CT £541.18 TOTE £16.10: £3.90, £1.70, £2.30; EX 83.10 Place 6: £110.15 Place 5: £46.00.
Owner J L C Pearce **Bred** J L C Pearce **Trained** Newmarket, Suffolk

FOCUS
An open-looking handicap, where any number of the runners looked to have a chance of winning. The winner was well in on his 2yo form and was just a little below his best.
Director's Chair Official explanation: jockey said gelding missed the break
Rahere(IRE) Official explanation: jockey said colt sulked wearing first-time net muzzle
T/Plt: £162.70 to a £1 stake. Pool: £81,086.92. 363.68 winning tickets. T/Qpdt: £70.60 to a £1 stake. Pool: £5,766.09. 60.40 winning tickets. SP

4739 PONTEFRACT (L-H)
Thursday, September 18

OFFICIAL GOING: Good to soft (good in places; 7.3)
Wind: Almost nil Weather: Fine

6050 PONTEFRACT APPRENTICE SERIES (ROUND 4) H'CAP — 1m 2f 6y
2:30 (2:31) (Class 5) (0-70,70) 3-Y-O+ £3,238 (£963; £481; £240) Stalls Low

Form RPR

0412 **1** **Princess Flame (GER)**[9] 5783 6-9-4 **63**.............. KylieManser 6 79
(B G Powell) *mid-div: hdwy to chse ldrs over 2f out: chal over 1f out: styd on to ld nr fin* **8/1**[3]

-501 **2** *nk* **Timocracy**[7] 5815 3-9-4 **69** 6ex.............. FrederikTylicki 8 84
(M Johnston) *w ldrs: led after 2f: hdd towards fin* **5/2**[1]

1000 **3** *7* **Trouble Mountain (USA)**[22] 5391 11-9-1 **65**.........(t) BradleyRoper(5) 12 66
(M W Easterby) *in rr: drvn over 3f out: styd on to take modest 3rd ins fnl f* **50/1**

1554 **4** *5* **Dan Tucker**[17] 5563 4-9-6 **65**.......................... AndreaAtzeni 9 56
(N Tinkler) *mid-div: hdwy over 2f out: one pce* **11/1**

5353 **5** *shd* **Coral Shores**[7] 5815 3-9-0 **65**..........................(v) BillyCray 10 56
(P W Hiatt) *w ldrs: t.k.h: one pce fnl 2f* **8/1**[3]

0300 **6** *2* **Chicken George (IRE)**[47] 4650 4-9-7 **66**.................. DavidProbert 11 53
(M F Harris) *mid-div: hdwy over 2f out: wknd over 1f out* **18/1**

14-6 **7** *1 1/4* **Paradise Walk**[25] 5305 4-9-11 **70** ow2.................. RyanMania 13 54
(E W Tuer) *trckd ldrs: t.k.h: wknd over 1f out* **33/1**

22-0 **8** *shd* **Can Can Star**[14] 5630 5-9-11 **70**.................. JemmaMarshall 3 54
(A W Carroll) *prom: wknd over 1f out* **20/1**

0-5 **9** *1 3/4* **Ergo (FR)**[137] 1822 4-8-12 **60**..........................(p) NSLawes(3) 14 41
(James Moffatt) *a towards rr* **50/1**

105- **10** *nk* **Top Tiger**[319] 6666 4-9-1 **65**.......................... MJMurphy(5) 5 45
(M H Tompkins) *chsd ldrs: wkng whn hmpd over 1f out* **12/1**

6000 **11** *3* **Byron Bay**[108] 2672 6-8-12 **60**.................. RichardRowe(3) 4 34
(R C Guest) *s.s: hld up in rr: nvr on terms* **33/1**

1161 **12** *1* **Kimono My House**[9] 5783 4-9-8 **67** 6ex.................. RosieJessop 16 39
(J G Given) *led 2f: w ldrs: wknd over 1f out* **6/1**[2]

2441 **13** *12* **Astrolibra**[25] 5321 4-8-13 **58**.................. AshleyMorgan 1 6
(M H Tompkins) *prom: lost pl over 2f out: sn bhd* **8/1**[3]

0204 **14** *9* **Saluscraggie**[18] 5543 6-9-0 **59**.................. BMcHugh 17 —
(R E Barr) *s.s: hdwy on wd outside over 4f out: sn wknd: t.o 2f out* **22/1**

40 **P** **Street Life (IRE)**[38] 4930 10-8-8 **56**.................. DebraEngland(3) 15 —
(W J Musson) *s.s: in rr-div whn broke hing leg and p.u over 2f out: dead* **12/1**

2m 15.95s (2.25) **Going Correction** +0.40s/f (Good)
WFA 3 from 4yo+ 6lb **15** Ran SP% **124.1**
Speed ratings (Par 103): **107,106,101,97,97 95,94,94,93,92 90,89,79,72,—**
toteswinger: 1&2 £3.80, 1&3 £70.20, 2&3 £28.30. CSF £26.88 CT £981.93 TOTE £8.40: £2.10, £1.40, £18.70; EX 23.40.
Owner B G Powell **Bred** V Kaufling **Trained** Upper Lambourn, Berks

■ Stewards' Enquiry : Kylie Manser caution: used whip with excessive frequency
Frederik Tylicki five-day ban: used whip with excessive frequency down shoulder in forehand position, without giving colt time to respond (Oct 2-4, 6-7)

FOCUS
A race restricted to apprentice riders who had not ridden more than ten winners. The first two, both 3lb ahead of the handicapper, pulled well clear and this is reasonable form for the level. The winning time was 0.54 seconds quicker than the later maiden.
Coral Shores Official explanation: jockey said filly ran too free
Astrolibra Official explanation: jockey said filly ran flat

6051 STRAWBERRY HILL MEDIAN AUCTION MAIDEN STKS 5f
3:00 (3:02) (Class 5) 2-Y-O **£3,885** (£1,156; £577; £288) **Stalls** Low

Form RPR

402 **1** **Red Rosanna**[36] 4965 2-8-12 71.................. GrahamGibbons 6 73
(R Hollinshead) *mde most: rdn along wl over 1f out: drvn ins fnl f and kpt on gamely* **9/4**[1]

2 *shd* **Gilt Edge Girl** 2-8-12 0.................. PhilipRobinson 10 73
(C G Cox) *trckd ldrs: hdwy 2f out: swtchd rt and rdn to chal ent fnl f: ev ch tl drvn and nt qckn nr line* **9/1**

3 *3 1/4* **Diamond Daisy (IRE)** 2-8-9 0.................. AndrewMullen(3) 1 61
(Mrs A Duffield) *in tch on inner: hdwy 2f out: rdn over 1f out: styd on ins fnl f: nrst fin* **10/1**

4 *nk* **Fesko** 2-8-12 0.................. JoeFanning 5 60+
(M Johnston) *s.i.s and bhd: hdwy wl over 1f out: styd on ins fnl f: nrst fin* **12/1**

0240 **5** *1 1/4* **Wotatomboy**[35] 5004 2-8-9 65.................. MichaelJStainton(3) 3 55
(R M Whitaker) *chsd ldrs: rdn along 2f out: drvn over 1f out and kpt on same pce* **12/1**

6 *nk* **Chocolicious (IRE)** 2-8-12 0.................. TomEaves 8 54+
(B Smart) *sn outpcd and bhd: swtchd wd and hdwy 2f out: styd on strly ins fnl f: nrst fin* **12/1**

00 **7** *1 1/2* **Igoyougo**[104] 2775 2-9-3 0.................. JamieMoriarty 15 54
(P T Midgley) *cl up: effrt 2f out and ev ch tl rdn and wknd appr fnl f* **33/1**

6 **8** *1/2* **May Need A Spell**[21] 5431 2-9-3 0.................. StephenDonohoe 7 52
(J G M O'Shea) *in tch: hdwy to chse ldrs 2f out: sn rdn and one pce* **16/1**

9 *1 1/4* **Cafe Fiore (IRE)** 2-8-12 0.................. DavidAllan 2 43
(T J Pitt) *nvr bttr then midfield* **33/1**

10 *nse* **Esprit De Midas** 2-9-3 0.................. RobertWinston 17 47
(K A Ryan) *chsd ldrs: rdn along 2f out and grad wknd* **15/2**[2]

530 **11** *nse* **Dotty's Brother**[22] 5394 2-9-0 65.................. JackMitchell(3) 13 47
(Mrs A Duffield) *towards rr: effrt on outer 2f out: sn rdn and hung lft over 1f out: n.d* **40/1**

40 **12** *2 3/4* **Dark Echoes**[26] 5277 2-9-3 0.................. TravisBlock 12 37
(Jedd O'Keeffe) *midfield: effrt 2f out and sn rdn: no imp whn hmpd over 1f out* **8/1**[3]

0 **13** *1 1/2* **No Quarter Given (IRE)**[14] 5633 2-9-3 0.................. TonyCulhane 11 32
(Mrs A Duffield) *towards rr: effrt whn n.m.r over 1f out: nvr a factor* **66/1**

5555 **14** *nk* **Miss Moloney (IRE)**[41] 4827 2-8-12 51.................. DaneO'Neill 9 26
(Mrs S Lamyman) *a towards rr* **20/1**

15 *1* **Aestival** 2-9-3 0.................. PatCosgrave 4 27
(Sir Mark Prescott) *s.i.s: a in rr* **20/1**

2650 **16** *2 3/4* **Meg Jicaro**[102] 2865 2-8-9 65.................. RussellKennemore(3) 16 12
(Mrs L Williamson) *in tch: rdn along and wkng whn hmpd over 1f out* **25/1**

0 **17** *6* **Eyesore**[19] 5500 2-8-12 0..........................(e) PAspell 14 —
(R C Guest) *chsd ldrs: rdn along 2f out: wkng whn hung rt over 1f out: eased* **100/1**

66.26 secs (2.96) **Going Correction** +0.40s/f (Good) **17** Ran SP% **125.9**
Speed ratings (Par 95): **92,91,86,86,84 83,81,80,78,78 78,73,71,71,69 65,56**
toteswinger: 1&2 £7.00, 1&3 £8.50, 2&3 £27.60. CSF £20.53 TOTE £3.10: £1.40, £3.70, £3.40; EX 25.90.
Owner Mrs Debbie Hodson **Bred** J R Mitchell **Trained** Upper Longdon, Staffs

FOCUS
The bare form is probably just ordinary, but plenty of these shaped nicely and the race should produce a few winners. Red Rosanna sets the standard as much as any.

NOTEBOOK
Red Rosanna just proved good enough to get off the mark at the fifth attempt, despite being on her toes and getting warm in the paddock. She showed bags of speed throughout, very much putting her experience to good use and, despite continually flashing her tail, she stuck on gamely to just get the better of a newcomer. Her natural pace should enable her to remain competitive when switching to handicaps, but she would be no sure thing to confirm form with one or two of those in behind in future. She is now being aimed at a nursery at Chester. (op 9-2)
Gilt Edge Girl, a 17,000gns daughter of Monsieur Bond, half-sister to among others high-class multiple sprint winner Godfrey Street, knew her job and very nearly made a winning debut. She showed good speed to chase the pace and threw down a big challenge in the straight, but was just held. She might not be open to as much bare improvement as some of those further back, but she still rates as a useful prospect. (op 6-1)
Diamond Daisy(IRE), a £16,000 daughter of Elnadim, came under pressure a fair way out but gradually got the hang of things and finished well, although it has to be noted she flashed her tail late on. (tchd 11-1)
Fesko ◆, a daughter of Shinko Forest, half-sister to 1m-1m2f winner Makai, out of a 1m1f scorer, was well out the back early on after falling out of the stalls, but she finished powerfully down the outside and was very much nearest at the finish. She will be a lot sharper and might have the speed for this trip, but her breeding suggests she will have little problem getting slightly further. Whatever, she appeals as worth a bet if turned out in similarly ordinary company next time. (tchd 11-1)
Wotatomboy might be better off in low-grade nurseries. (tchd 14-1)
Chocolicious(IRE) ◆, a 34,000gns daughter of Captain Rio, was another to catch the eye. She was well out the back and running green early on, so it was a surprise to see her so close at the finish. She can improve significantly for this experience. (op 10-1)
Esprit De Midas, a 100,000gns son of Namid, out of a 6f-1m winner, is quite a nice type but, after showing early speed, he was quickly in trouble when the race got serious and looked to need this mentally. (op 7-1 tchd 13-2)
Aestival, a son of Falbrav, half-brother to several winners, was never involved after starting slowly and is going to want further when switching to handicaps. (op 16-1)

6052 SUBSCRIBE TO RACING UK ONLINE AT RACINGUK.TV H'CAP 1m 4y
3:30 (3:31) (Class 4) (0-80,80) 3-Y-O+ **£6,476** (£1,927; £963; £481) **Stalls** Low

Form RPR

3614 **1** **Major Magpie (IRE)**[21] 5418 6-9-8 **80**.................. DarryllHolland 9 92
(M Dods) *in rr: hrd drvn over 2f out: styd on wl to go 2nd ins fnl f: led post* **7/1**[3]

1453 **2** *nse* **Ezdeyaad (USA)**[11] 5717 4-9-4 **76**.................. RobertWinston 6 88
(G A Swinbank) *trckd ldrs: led over 1f out: ct post* **6/1**[2]

0554 **3** *4* **Nevada Desert (IRE)**[9] 5772 8-9-1 **76**.................. MichaelJStainton(3) 3 79
(R M Whitaker) *chsd ldrs: kpt on same pce appr fnl f* **14/1**

4444 **4** *3/4* **Violent Velocity (IRE)**[11] 5717 5-8-13 **78**.................. JamieKyne(7) 7 81+
(J J Quinn) *mid-div: hdwy on ins whn nt clr run over 1f out: kpt on ins fnl f* **10/1**

2501 **5** *1/2* **Observatory Star (IRE)**[47] 4649 5-9-7 **79**..........................(p) DavidAllan 12 79
(T D Easterby) *in rr: styd on on outer 2f out: edgd lft: nt rch ldrs* **10/1**

5000 **6** *shd* **Bold Marc (IRE)**[14] 5635 6-8-9 **74**.................. DeclanCannon(7) 11 77+
(K R Burke) *in rr: nt clr run over 2f out: kpt on: nvr nr ldrs* **16/1**

3300 **7** *1* **My Paris**[21] 5418 7-9-5 **77**..........................(v[1]) JamieMoriarty 14 74
(Ollie Pears) *mid-div on outer: edgd rt over 1f out: kpt on: nvr trbld ldrs* **25/1**

3216 **8** *3 1/4* **Tartan Gigha (IRE)**[22] 5397 3-9-4 **80**.................. JoeFanning 4 70
(M Johnston) *w ldrs: wknd jst ins fnl f* **12/1**

5425 **9** *1* **Hartshead**[49] 4567 9-9-3 **75**.................. DeanMcKeown 15 63
(G A Swinbank) *dwlt: in rr: kpt on fnl 2f: nvr on terms* **18/1**

-604 **10** *4 1/2* **Princess Valerina**[9] 5789 4-8-13 **71**.................. TonyCulhane 5 48
(H R A Cecil) *mid-div: hdwy 4f out: lost pl over 2f out* **11/1**

1400 **11** *1 1/4* **Sunnyside Tom (IRE)**[47] 4627 4-8-11 **76**.................. BMcHugh(7) 8 50
(R A Fahey) *s.i.s: sn mid-div: hdwy on inner and edgd lft over 1f out: sn wknd* **14/1**

1460 **12** *hd* **Piper's Song (IRE)**[51] 4500 5-9-3 **75**.................. PatCosgrave 10 49
(B G Powell) *dwlt: in rr: rdn 3f out: nvr on terms* **28/1**

6-43 **13** *nk* **Young Bertie**[120] 2308 5-8-13 **71**..........................(v) TravisBlock 2 44
(H Morrison) *led tl hdd & wknd over 1f out* **5/1**[1]

5000 **14** *shd* **Bright Falcon**[6] 5858 3-8-11 **78**.................. DavidProbert(5) 13 51
(S Parr) *chsd ldrs on outside: lost pl over 1f out* **66/1**

4155 **15** *2 1/4* **Hula Ballew**[36] 4970 8-9-8 **80**.................. TomEaves 17 48
(M Dods) *chsd ldrs on outside: lost pl over 2f out* **20/1**

2600 **16** *16* **Wovoka (IRE)**[22] 5390 5-8-10 **73**.................. FrederikTylicki(5) 1 4
(D W Barker) *mid-div: lost pl over 2f out: eased whn bhd ins fnl f* **14/1**

1m 47.76s (1.86) **Going Correction** +0.40s/f (Good)
WFA 3 from 4yo+ 4lb **16** Ran SP% **122.4**
Speed ratings (Par 105): **106,105,101,101,100 100,99,96,95,90 89,89,89,89,86 70**
toteswinger: 1&2 £8.30, 1&3 £13.10, 2&3 £21.90. CSF £46.72 CT £587.54 TOTE £7.90: £2.20, £1.90, £3.70, £2.50; EX 56.30.
Owner Mrs Patsy Monk **Bred** J Hutchinson **Trained** Denton, Co Durham

FOCUS
A fair, competitive handicap run at a decent pace, which suited the winner who ran a personal best. The first two were clear.
Young Bertie Official explanation: trainer had no explanation for the poor form shown

6053 HIGHFIELD FARM FILLIES' H'CAP 6f
4:00 (4:04) (Class 3) (0-90,86) 3-Y-O+
£9,346 (£2,799; £1,399; £700; £349; £175) **Stalls** Low

Form RPR

3110 **1** **Persian Sea (UAE)**[26] 5273 3-9-5 **85**.................. PhilipRobinson 4 97
(M A Jarvis) *cl up on inner: led 1/2-way: rdn clr over 1f out: drvn and styd on strly ins fnl f* **11/4**[1]

5053 **2** *2 1/4* **Vital Statistics**[14] 5644 4-9-5 **83**.................. DaneO'Neill 11 88
(D R C Elsworth) *dwlt: sn in tch: hdwy 3f out: rdn along wl over 1f out: styd on u.p to chse wnr ins fnl f: sn no imp* **11/2**[3]

450 **3** *2* **Goodbye**[14] 5635 4-9-4 **82**.................. RobertWinston 6 81
(G A Swinbank) *hld up in tch: hdwy 2f out: sn rdn and styd on u.p ins fnl f* **6/1**

042 **4** *nse* **Mango Music**[9] 5781 5-9-5 **83**.................. FrancisNorton 5 81
(M Quinn) *narrow ld tl hdd 1/2-way: cl up and ev ch 2f out: sn rdn and wknd appr fnl f* **3/1**[2]

-605 **5** *2* **Dresden Doll (USA)**[45] 4696 3-8-0 **71**.................. DavidProbert(5) 10 63
(M L W Bell) *chsd ldng pair: rdn along 2f out: drvn over 1f out and grad wknd* **11/1**

0250 **6** *1/2* **Cristal Clear (IRE)**[8] 5795 3-9-6 **86**.................. DavidAllan 8 76
(T D Easterby) *hld up in rr: hdwy on inner whn nt clr run wl over 1f out: swtchd rt and rdn: styd on strly ins fnl f: nrst fin* **12/1**

0400 **7** *5* **Mey Blossom**[24] 5358 3-8-11 **80**.................. MichaelJStainton(3) 7 54
(R M Whitaker) *chsd ldrs: rdn along 1/2-way: sn wknd* **20/1**

300 **8** *4 1/2* **Coachhouse Lady (USA)**[26] 5273 3-8-10 **76**.................. JoeFanning 1 36
(K A Ryan) *chsd ldng pair: rdn along over 2f out: sn wknd* **8/1**

0100 **9** *22* **Dubai Power**[14] 5644 3-9-4 **84**.................. DarryllHolland 3 —
(C E Brittain) *a in rr* **20/1**

1m 18.41s (1.51) **Going Correction** +0.40s/f (Good)
WFA 3 from 4yo+ 2lb **9** Ran SP% **118.0**
Speed ratings (Par 104): **105,102,99,99,96 95,89,83,53**
toteswinger: 1&2 £3.50, 1&3 £4.40, 2&3 £6.50. CSF £18.78 CT £82.49 TOTE £3.20: £1.60, £1.70, £2.30; EX 19.50.

The Form Book, Raceform Ltd, Compton, RG20 6NL

Owner Sheikh Ahmed Al Maktoum **Bred** Darley **Trained** Newmarket, Suffolk

FOCUS

A decent, competitive handicap won by the only progressive filly in the race, rated up 8lb.

NOTEBOOK

Persian Sea(UAE) ◆ produced quite a taking effort. She was continually pressed for the lead by Mango Music, who ended up dropping back into fourth, but kept on really strongly once she had shaken off that rival and was always doing more than enough to keep Vital Statistics, the only horse to pose any sort of a threat, well at bay. This was her first run over a trip this short – her two wins to date had both been gained over 7f – and she showed improved form. She looks capable of progressing into quite a smart filly over this trip and should be up to gaining black type at some point. This is very much her sort of ground. (op 7-2 tchd 9-4)

Vital Statistics recovered from a slow start to have every chance. She had dropped to a career-low rating, but ran into a most progressive rival. Although not the force of old, and perhaps not one to place too much faith in, she should be able to exploit her current sort of mark in the right company. (op 9-2 tchd 7-1)

Goodbye stuck on for pressure but could not muster the pace to take some tight gaps and was never a serious threat. She will probably be happier back over 7f, but looks weight up to her best right now. (op 8-1)

Mango Music likes to dominate, but she was unable to do so this time and was not quite at her best. (tchd 11-4 and 7-2)

Dresden Doll(USA) probably found this company a bit hot and will be better off in a slightly lower grade, but she didn't run badly. (op 12-1)

6054 PONTEFRACT STAYERS CHAMPIONSHIP H'CAP (ROUND 6) 2m 1f 22y

4:30 (4:31) (Class 6) (0-75,75) 3-Y-0+ £3,885 (£1,156; £577; £288) Stalls Low

Form RPR

3411 **1** **Kiribati King (IRE)**[14] 5651 3-9-0 **73**........ TonyCulhane 7 84
(M R Channon) *hld up in rr: hdwy 6f out: sn chsng ldrs: rdn over 3f out: led over 1f out: hld on towards fin* **5/1**[1]

531/ **2** *nk* **Kanpai (IRE)**[629] 5201 6-8-11 **58**........ RobertWinston 1 68
(J G M O'Shea) *hld up in mid-div: hdwy on inner over 2f out: styd on wl fnl f: jst hld* **14/1**

3536 **3** *1 1/2* **Thewhirlingdervish (IRE)**[19] 5498 10-9-2 **63**........ DavidAllan 2 71
(T D Easterby) *chsd ldrs: chal over 1f out: styd on same pce* **13/2**[3]

-500 **4** *1 3/4* **Tribe**[101] 2888 6-9-4 **65**........(t) PatCosgrave 11 72+
(P R Webber) *hld up in rr: stdy hdwy over 2f out: nt clr run and swtchd rt over 1f out: styd on wl: nt rch ldrs* **12/1**

232 **5** *1* **Mr Crystal (FR)**[22] 5396 4-9-2 **68**........ FrederikTylicki(5) 10 73
(Micky Hammond) *trckd ldrs: styd on same pce fnl 2f* **6/1**[2]

031/ **6** *2 1/2* **Pseudonym (IRE)**[222] 2879 6-9-4 **65**........(t) FrancisNorton 6 67
(M F Harris) *hld up towards rr: hdwy and nt clr run over 2f out: kpt on: nvr rchd ldrs* **33/1**

0 **7** *1 1/4* **Rare Ruby (IRE)**[22] 5396 4-9-3 **64**........ PAspell 3 65
(Jennie Candlish) *in tch: effrt over 2f out: kpt on: nvr nr to chal* **40/1**

20/0 **8** *3/4* **Risk Runner (IRE)**[46] 4662 5-9-10 **71**........(b) TomEaves 17 71
(James Moffatt) *hld up in rr: hdwy on outer over 3f out: hung lft over 1f out: nvr rchd ldrs* **40/1**

-200 **9** *3* **Riguez Dancer**[33] 5092 4-9-4 **70**........(t) PatrickDonaghy(5) 4 66
(P C Haslam) *hld up in rr: kpt on fnl 2f: nvr nr ldrs* **20/1**

3630 **10** *hd* **Burnt Oak (UAE)**[6] 5853 6-9-7 **68**........ JoeFanning 12 64
(C W Fairhurst) *sn prom: chal over 2f out: one pce whn sltly hmpd 1f out* **12/1**

6020 **11** *1 3/4* **Irish Quest (IRE)**[23] 5376 4-10-0 **75**........(p) PhilipRobinson 8 69
(M A Jarvis) *chsd ldrs: led over 3f out: hdd over 1f out: sn wknd* **8/1**

16-4 **12** *1 1/4* **Kentucky Boy (IRE)**[23] 5385 4-8-11 **58**........ TravisBlock 5 50
(Jedd O'Keeffe) *chsd ldrs: drvn 6f out: lost pl over 1f out* **5/1**[1]

/030 **13** *9* **Stolen Light (IRE)**[67] 3296 7-8-9 **59** oh2 ow2..(b) MichaelJStainton(3) 16 40
(A Crook) *led: hung rt throught: hdd over 3f out: sn lost pl: bhd whn eased ins fnl f* **100/1**

5425 **14** *17* **Victory Quest (IRE)**[54] 4439 8-9-7 **68**........(v) DaneO'Neill 14 29
(Mrs S Lamyman) *chsd ldrs: chal over 2f out: sn wknd: bhd whn eased ins fnl f* **33/1**

0642 **15** *30* **Inchpast**[50] 4516 7-9-7 **75**........(b) AshleyMorgan(7) 13 —
(M H Tompkins) *s.i.s: in rr: effrt on outside over 3f out: sn wknd: bhd whn virtually p.u ins fnl f: t.o* **8/1**

3m 59.6s (8.00) **Going Correction** +0.40s/f (Good)

WFA 3 from 4yo+ 12lb **15 Ran SP% 121.7**

Speed ratings (Par 101): **97,96,96,95,94 93,93,92,91,91 90,89,85,77,63**

toteswinger: 1&2 £8.20, 1&3 £4.60, 2&3 £15.10. CSF £72.14 CT £469.98 TOTE £5.30: £2.40, £4.60, £2.30; EX 72.80.

Owner Box 41 **Bred** Noel Finnegan **Trained** West Ilsley, Berks

■ Stewards' Enquiry : Pat Cosgrave £80 fine: breach of Rule 149 (ii) (modified whip)

P Aspell £80 fine: breach of Rule 149 (ii) (modified whip)

FOCUS

A more competitive handicap than is often the case in staying events and they went a reasonable pace. Further improvement from Kiribati King, with the form making sense at face value.

6055 JACKIE CARR RETIRED, PUT OUT TO GRASS MAIDEN STKS 1m 2f 6y

5:00 (5:05) (Class 5) 3-Y-0+ £3,885 (£1,156; £577; £288) Stalls Low

Form RPR

-22 **1** **Duncan**[45] 4695 3-9-3 0........ PhilipRobinson 16 92+
(J L Dunlop) *t.k.h: in tch on outer: rapid hdwy 3f out: led wl over 1f out and sn clr: easily* **10/11**[1]

4 **2** *5* **Mubrook (USA)**[19] 5491 3-9-3 0........ DaneO'Neill 11 75
(L M Cumani) *hld up in tch: hdwy 3f out: rdn to chal 2f out: sn rdn and kpt on u.p: no ch w wnr* **8/1**[3]

3 *shd* **Mysterious Moon** 3-9-3 0........ RobertWinston 6 75
(Saeed Bin Suroor) *a.p: effrt 3f out: rdn2f out: drvn to chse wnr over 1f out: kpt on: no ch w wnr* **11/1**

340 **4** *1* **Onemoreandstay**[15] 5608 3-8-9 67........ JackMitchell(3) 4 68
(R W Price) *in tch: hdwy to chse ldrs 4f out: rdn along over 2f out: drvn and kpt on same pce appr fnl f* **18/1**

5 *1 1/4* **Surrealism** 3-8-12 0........ DavidKinsella 15 66+
(J H M Gosden) *hld up in rr: hdwy over 4f out: rdn to chse ldrs 2f out: sn rdn and kpt on same pce* **20/1**

45 **6** *6* **Garra Molly (IRE)**[63] 4116 3-8-12 0........ DavidAllan 13 54
(G A Swinbank) *in tch: pushed along and hdwy 3f out: rdn 2f out and sn no imp* **33/1**

7 *5* **Cape Tribulation**[166] 4-9-9 0........ TomEaves 17 49+
(J M Jefferson) *dwlt: hld up in rr tl styd on fnl 2f: nrst fin* **9/1**

04 **8** *nk* **Oscar Wild**[20] 5453 6-9-9 0........ PatrickMathers 5 48
(James Moffatt) *cl up: rdn along 3f out: drvn 2f out and sn wknd* **100/1**

9 *1* **Ibbetson (USA)** 3-9-3 0........ PatCosgrave 12 46
(W R Swinburn) *s.i.s: a in rr* **25/1**

35-3 **10** *4* **Pragmatism**[34] 5076 3-9-3 75........ JoeFanning 3 38
(M Johnston) *led: rdn along 3f out: drvn 2f out: sn hdd & wknd* **6/1**[2]

4 **11** *nk* **Turjuman (USA)**[19] 5505 3-9-3 75........ StephenDonohoe 14 37
(W J Musson) *a in rr* **18/1**

0 **12** *8* **Miss Ferney**[24] 5361 4-9-4 0........ PAspell 2 16
(A Kirtley) *chsd ldrs on inner: rdn along 3f out and sn wknd* **150/1**

0 **13** *nk* **Rimsky Korsakov (IRE)**[19] 5505 4-9-9 0........ TonyCulhane 1 21
(Micky Hammond) *hld up: a in rr* **100/1**

0 **14** *3 3/4* **Supremely Blessed**[89] 3282 4-9-1 0........ AndrewMullen(3) 8 8
(D W Thompson) *a towards rr* **200/1**

0- **15** *2* **Cashmere Jack**[338] 6255 3-8-12 0........ FrederikTylicki(5) 9 9
(K G Reveley) *a towards rr* **100/1**

00 **16** *1 1/2* **High Shanamara**[40] 4877 3-8-12 0........ JamieMoriarty 10 —
(P T Midgley) *a towards rr* **200/1**

00 **17** *10* **Won More Night**[10] 5750 6-9-4 0........ TravisBlock 7 —
(D J Wintle) *prom: rdn along over 3f out: sn wknd* **66/1**

2m 16.49s (2.79) **Going Correction** +0.40s/f (Good)

WFA 3 from 4yo+ 6lb **17 Ran SP% 124.3**

Speed ratings (Par 103): **104,100,99,99,98 93,89,89,88,85 84,78,78,75,73 72,64**

toteswinger: 1&2 £3.40, 1&3 £4.60, 2&3 £9.70. CSF £8.33 TOTE £2.00: £1.10, £2.20, £2.60; EX 11.30.

Owner Normandie Stud Ltd **Bred** Normandie Stud Ltd **Trained** Arundel, W Sussex

FOCUS

Although the bare form of this older-horse maiden is probably just ordinary, there were some big stables represented. The winning time was 0.54 seconds slower than the earlier handicap won by a mare rated 63, but they early pace was much steadier in this race. The winner was a cut above, rated up a stone on his debut with the fourth the best guide.

Ibbetson(USA) Official explanation: jockey said gelding was slowly away

6056 GO RACING AT CATTERICK ON SATURDAY H'CAP 1m 4y

5:30 (5:33) (Class 5) (0-70,70) 3-Y-0+ £3,238 (£963; £481; £240) Stalls Low

Form RPR

0321 **1** **Effigy**[14] 5639 4-9-7 **69**........ DaneO'Neill 3 80
(H Candy) *s.i.s: hdwy on outer over 2f out: swtchd lft and styd on wl to ld fnl 75yds* **7/2**[1]

015 **2** *1 1/2* **Ours (IRE)**[39] 4895 5-9-3 **65**........(p) StephenDonohoe 13 72
(John A Harris) *mid-div: hdwy to ld 1f out: hdd and no ex ins fnl f* **14/1**

312 **3** *shd* **Straight Sets (IRE)**[14] 5639 4-9-7 **69**........ TonyCulhane 4 76
(M R Channon) *chsd ldrs: effrt over 3f out: chal 1f out: styd on same pce last 75yds* **9/2**[2]

3203 **4** *1/2* **Drawn Gold**[50] 4532 4-9-3 **65**........ GrahamGibbons 1 71
(R Hollinshead) *mid-div: effrt on inner 2f out: sn chsng ldrs: styd on same pce fnl f* **10/1**

5050 **5** *2* **Packers Hill (IRE)**[60] 4219 4-9-3 **65**........ RobertWinston 17 66
(G A Swinbank) *hld up towards rr: effrt and hmpd over 2f out: styd on over outer fnl f: nt rch ldrs* **16/1**

6520 **6** *2 1/2* **Hits Only Cash**[10] 5755 6-9-3 **65**........(p) JoeFanning 14 61
(J Pearce) *in rr: sn pushed along: styd on fnl 2f: nt rch ldrs* **28/1**

2430 **7** *1 1/2* **Palmetto Point**[19] 5492 4-9-5 **67**........(tp) TravisBlock 5 59
(H Morrison) *chsd ldrs: hung lft and led over 1f out: hdd & wknd 1f out* **14/1**

0004 **8** *1 1/4* **Fort Amhurst (IRE)**[20] 5478 4-9-2 **64**........ DavidAllan 9 53
(M W Easterby) *in tch: effrt over 2f out: one pce* **16/1**

3265 **9** *nk* **Society Music (IRE)**[41] 4813 6-9-6 **68**........(p) TomEaves 2 56
(M Dods) *t.k.h: in tch: effrt over 2f out: wknd fnl f* **14/1**

1030 **10** *2 3/4* **Very Well Red**[19] 5492 5-9-0 **69**........ BillyCray(7) 7 51
(P W Hiatt) *trckd ldrs: wknd 1f out* **18/1**

0 **11** *1 1/2* **Smarty Socks (IRE)**[14] 5635 4-9-8 **70**........ JamieMoriarty 6 49
(P T Midgley) *s.s: nvr on terms* **80/1**

3311 **12** *1/2* **Shotley Mac**[14] 5638 4-9-3 **70**........(b) FrederikTylicki(5) 12 48
(N Bycroft) *led tl hdd & wknd over 1f out* **5/1**[3]

2251 **13** *1/2* **Nesno (USA)**[20] 5478 5-9-6 **68**........(p) PatCosgrave 15 44
(J D Bethell) *trckd ldrs: wknd fnl f* **12/1**

206 **14** *1 3/4* **Lordship (IRE)**[30] 5168 4-8-10 **65**........ BMcHugh(7) 8 37
(A W Carroll) *prom: effrt over 2f out: sn wknd* **22/1**

500- **15** *2 1/4* **Sea Storm (IRE)**[307] 5556 10-9-2 **64**........ PAspell 16 31
(James Moffatt) *mid-div: lost pl 3f out* **100/1**

-365 **16** *35* **San Silvestro (IRE)**[26] 5258 3-8-13 **68**........ AndrewMullen(3) 11 —
(Mrs A Duffield) *chsd ldrs on outer: rdn over 3f out: lost pl over 2f out: wl bhd whn virtually p.u ins fnl f: t.o* **16/1**

1m 47.8s (1.90) **Going Correction** +0.40s/f (Good)

WFA 3 from 4yo+ 4lb **16 Ran SP% 126.8**

Speed ratings (Par 103): **106,104,104,103,101 99,97,96,96,93 92,91,91,89,87 53**

toteswinger: 1&2 £12.70, 1&3 £3.60, 2&3 £12.90. CSF £55.37 CT £244.51 TOTE £4.60: £2.20, £2.80, £1.80, £2.90; EX 88.20 Place 6: £56.19 Place 5: £24.16 .

Owner The Earl Cadogan **Bred** The Earl Cadogan **Trained** Kingston Warren, Oxon

FOCUS

A modest but competitive handicap. Solid form. The winning time was only 0.04 seconds slower than the earlier handicap won by a horse rated 80.

T/Jkpt: £4,232.40 to a £1 stake. Pool: £318,921.97. 53.50 winning tickets. T/Plt: £29.30 to a £1 stake. Pool: £84,078.31. 2,094.23 winning tickets. T/Qpdt: £10.30 to a £1 stake. Pool: £3,480.33. 248.25 winning tickets. WG

6029 YARMOUTH (L-H)

Thursday, September 18

OFFICIAL GOING: Good (good to firm in places)

Wind: Light across Weather: Fine and sunny

6057 EUROPEAN BREEDERS' FUND MAIDEN STKS 1m 3y

2:10 (2:11) (Class 4) 2-Y-0 £5,046 (£1,510; £755; £377; £188) Stalls High

Form RPR

3 **1** **Alwaary (USA)**[13] 5672 2-9-3 0........ RHills 8 82+
(J H M Gosden) *hld up: hdwy over 1f out: edgd lft and led wl ins fnl f: readily* **9/4**[2]

03 **2** *1 1/2* **Cloudy Start**[47] 4625 2-9-3 0........ TPQueally 1 76
(H R A Cecil) *w ldrs: racd keenly: led over 3f out: rdn and hdd wl ins fnl f* **5/6**[1]

0 **3** *1 1/2* **Tilos Gem (IRE)**[55] 4360 2-9-3 0........ RoystonFfrench 4 73
(M Johnston) *wnt rt s: sn led: hdd over 3f out: rdn over 1f out: styd on* **66/1**

24 **4** *3* **Too Tall**[36] 4982 2-9-3 0........ JimmyFortune 7 66
(L M Cumani) *chsd ldrs: rdn over 1f out: no ex ins fnl f* **16/1**

5 **5** *3/4* **Land Hawk (IRE)**[14] 5649 2-9-3 0........ RichardMullen 6 64
(J Pearce) *prom: rdn over 2f out: no ex fnl f* **25/1**

6 *1 1/4* **Proper Holiday (USA)** 2-9-3 0........ AlanMunro 10 62
(P W Chapple-Hyam) *chsd ldrs: rdn over 2f out: wknd over 1f out* **40/1**

05 **7** ½ **Muhim**[13] 5672 2-9-3 0.. EddieAhern 9 61
(C E Brittain) *hld up: hdwy over 3f out: wknd over 1f out* **66/1**

3 **8** 4 **Omokoroa (IRE)**[43] 4747 2-9-3 0.. JimmyQuinn 3 52
(M H Tompkins) *hld up: effrt over 3f out: wknd 2f out* **20/1**

03 **9** 1½ **Worth A King'S**[22] 5404 2-9-3 0.. RyanMoore 5 49
(Sir Michael Stoute) *s.i.s and hmpd s: hld up: hdwy over 3f out: wknd wl over 1f out* **11/1[3]**

10 ¾ **Shakin John** 2-9-3 0.. ChrisCatlin 2 47
(E J O'Neill) *w ldr 3f: wknd 1/2-way* **33/1**

1m 39.99s (-0.61) **Going Correction** -0.275s/f (Firm) **10** Ran SP% **116.5**
Speed ratings (Par 97): **92,90,89,86,85 84,83,79,78,77**
toteswinger: 1&2 £1.30, 1&3 £18.80, 2&3 £12.20. CSF £4.14 TOTE £3.90: £1.40, £1.10, £14.40; EX 5.30 Trifecta £91.20 Pool: £622.46 - 5.05 winning units..
Owner Hamdan Al Maktoum **Bred** Shadwell Farm LLC **Trained** Newmarket, Suffolk

FOCUS
The ground was drying all the time on a hot, sunny day and the going stick reading had changed from 7.7 to 8.8. This looked a decent maiden with Alwaary value for more than the winning margin.

NOTEBOOK
Alwaary(USA), a most promising third on his recent debut at Kempton (green before staying on nicely for third), was always likely to have improved for that initial experience and travelled powerfully under Richard Hills. Asked to take closer order two out, he took a while to organise himself, but really strode out well inside the final furlong and was nicely on top close home. Entered in all the remaining major juvenile contests, he is from the family of the yard's 1,000 Guineas winner Lahan, and fully deserves his place in either the Royal Lodge or Racing Post Trophy, with the promise of better to come. (op 7-4 tchd 13-8 and 5-2)
Cloudy Start performed to a similarly useful level on each of his first two starts and was understandably made favourite. Expected to be suited by the extra furlong, he was prominent throughout (racing a shade keenly early on) and tried to kick on over two out. The winner always looked to have him covered though and he could never get away, being run down inside the final half furlong. An ordinary maiden should come his way on this evidence. (op 6-5 tchd 5-4)
Tilos Gem(IRE), a well-beaten last of six on his debut at Ascot (stable struggling for form at time) looked a different horse on this occasion and ran a massively improved race. He made a lot of the running and stayed on right the way to the line, suggesting he can win a maiden with further progress likely.
Too Tall did not have the form to match the front pair and he ran as well as could have been expected back in third. He is now qualified for nurseries. (op 20-1 tchd 22-1)
Land Hawk(IRE) confirmed the promise of his Warwick debut and will be of obvious interest once handicapping. (op 22-1)
Proper Holiday(USA), a half-brother to four winners in the US, made a satisfactory debut and should know more next time. (tchd 50-1)
Worth A King'S, a half-brother to four winners in the US, made a satisfactory debut and should know more next time. (op 10-1)

6058 ATTHERACES.COM NURSERY 1m 3y
2:40 (2:40) (Class 4) (0-85,82) 2-Y-O **£4,415** (£1,321; £660; £330; £164) **Stalls** High

Form RPR

150 **1** **Rafiqa (IRE)**[19] 5511 2-9-3 78.. EddieAhern 9 86+
(C F Wall) *hld up: hdwy over 2f out: rdn to ld ins fnl f: r.o wl* **10/1**

345 **2** 3 **Rumble Of Thunder (IRE)**[20] 5461 2-8-13 74.......... JimmyFortune 2 75
(D W P Arbuthnot) *sn led: rdn and hdd over 1f out: styd on same pce ins fnl f* **15/2**

610 **3** nk **Proclaim**[27] 5228 2-9-5 80.. RoystonFfrench 6 80
(M Johnston) *chsd ldr tl led over 1f out: rdn and hdd ins fnl f: styd on same pce* **7/1[3]**

6320 **4** 1½ **Andhaar**[30] 5165 2-9-2 77.. RHills 3 74
(E A L Dunlop) *chsd ldrs: rdn over 2f out: no ex fnl f* **15/2**

3351 **5** 1¼ **Woolston Ferry (IRE)**[21] 5432 2-9-3 78.................. EdwardCreighton 5 72
(M R Channon) *hld up: hdwy over 2f out: kpt on ins fnl f: nvr trbld ldrs* **11/1**

0404 **6** hd **Mymateeric**[9] 5785 2-8-12 73.. JimmyQuinn 8 67
(J Pearce) *chsd ldrs: lost pl 1/2-way: rallied over 1f out: no ex fnl f* **16/1**

4415 **7** nk **Stirling Castle**[26] 5274 2-9-7 82.. TedDurcan 4 75
(M J Wallace, Australia) *dwlt: hld up: hdwy over 3f out: rdn over 1f out: no ex fnl f* **9/4[1]**

2610 **8** 1¼ **Highland Storm**[5] 5895 2-9-3 78.. AlanMunro 1 68
(J G Given) *chsd ldrs: rdn over 2f out: wknd ins fnl f* **9/2[2]**

000 **9** 3¾ **Lake Kalamalka (IRE)**[27] 5240 2-8-5 66.................. RichardMullen 7 48
(J L Dunlop) *s.i.s: hld up: a in rr: hung lft ins fnl f* **18/1**

064 **10** 14 **Who Art Thou (USA)**[54] 4430 2-7-12 59 oh9.......... CatherineGannon 10 10
(P A Blockley) *hld up: rdn and wknd over 2f out* **80/1**

1m 38.32s (-2.28) **Going Correction** -0.275s/f (Firm) **10** Ran SP% **114.8**
Speed ratings (Par 97): **100,97,96,95,93 93,93,92,88,74**
toteswinger: 1&2 £15.00, 1&3 £13.10, 2&3 £6.40. CSF £81.50 CT £574.95 TOTE £11.10: £1.80, £2.60, £2.40; EX 84.50 TRIFECTA Not won..
Owner The Equema Partnership **Bred** Lady Juliet Tadgell **Trained** Newmarket, Suffolk

FOCUS
An ordinary nursery. The winner was much improved and the form sems pretty solid.

NOTEBOOK
Rafiqa(IRE), a 6f maiden winner on debut, had run disappointingly in two subsequent starts, especially last time at Sandown on her nursery debut, but she showed that running to be all wrong here and cleared right away inside the final furlong. She is probably in line for a hike up the weights following this and will need to improve to defy it. (op 17-2 tchd 8-1)
Rumble Of Thunder(IRE), up to 1m for the first time, shaped with promise on all three starts in maidens and he seemed more than happy bowling along in front. He kept battling away once headed, rallying back past Proclaim, and has a race in him off this sort of mark. (op 7-1)
Proclaim, ready winner of a 7f Chester maiden on his second start (made all) was unable to cope with the drop back to 6f at Newbury last time on his nursery debut and shaped better here. He was run out of second close home though and 7f may prove his optimum for the time being. (op 9-1)
Andhaar, below his best in soft ground at Brighton last time, ran respectably on this nursery debut, but is hardly progressing and will probably remain vulnerable to improvers. (tchd 9-1)
Woolston Ferry(IRE), narrow winner of a modest Lingfield nursery, had been raised 5lb and struggled in this better race. (op 7-1)
Mymateeric, up in trip, got closer to Woolston Ferry than he had at Lingfield two starts back, but is likely to continue to come up short off his current mark.
Stirling Castle was most disappointing. He looked to be crying out for a return to this distance when fifth at Newmarket last time, but started to come under pressure over three out and never picked up. This was not his form. Official explanation: jockey said colt hung right (op 7-2)
Highland Storm, who ran dreadfully at Doncaster last week, had nothing left to give inside the final furlong and faded right out. (op 5-1 tchd 4-1)

6059 EASTERN POWERS SYSTEMS (S) NURSERY 1m 3y
3:10 (3:12) (Class 6) (0-65,64) 2-Y-O **£1,942** (£578; £288; £144) **Stalls** High

Form RPR

0460 **1** **Balladiene (IRE)**[55] 4373 2-9-6 63.. JimmyQuinn 7 66
(M H Tompkins) *trckd ldrs: rdn over 1f out: edgd lft ins fnl f: r.o to ld post* **11/2[2]**

4200 **2** shd **Rockinit (IRE)**[5] 5914 2-9-7 64.. TPO'Shea 6 67
(M R Channon) *led: rdn and edgd rt 2f out: hdd post* **25/1**

2445 **3** 2¼ **Tarawa Atoll**[5] 5909 2-8-7 50.. EdwardCreighton 14 48
(M R Channon) *s.i.s: hld up: hdwy over 1f out: edgd lft ins fnl f: nt rch ldrs* **12/1**

030 **4** 2½ **Mistress Mary**[71] 3848 2-8-8 51..................(b[1]) AdrianMcCarthy 1 44
(G G Margarson) *chsd ldrs: rdn and ev ch over 1f out: no ex ins fnl f* **22/1**

0263 **5** ½ **Cherry Belle (IRE)**[10] 5747 2-8-12 55..................(v) RyanMoore 15 46
(P D Evans) *hld up: hdwy over 2f out: rdn and edgd lft fr over 1f out: no ex ins fnl f* **11/4[1]**

4060 **6** nk **Igneous**[14] 5632 2-8-8 51.. (b[1]) LiamJones 4 42
(K R Burke) *s.i.s: hld up: hdwy over 3f out: rdn and ev ch over 1f out: no ex ins fnl f* **16/1**

0502 **7** nk **Ba Globetrotter**[5] 5909 2-9-5 62.. SamHitchcott 3 52
(M R Channon) *chsd ldrs: rdn and ev ch over 1f out: no ex ins fnl f* **20/1**

6304 **8** 1 **Ashwinder (IRE)**[15] 5614 2-8-13 56.. JimmyFortune 10 44
(B J Meehan) *mid-div: outpcd over 2f out: styd on u.p ins fnl f* **6/1[3]**

0500 **9** ½ **Kneesy Earsy Nosey**[11] 5715 2-8-5 48.. KimTinkler 12 35
(N Tinkler) *s.i.s: sn pushed along in rr: n.d* **22/1**

0560 **10** ½ **Noworneva**[56] 4340 2-8-2 45.. CatherineGannon 11 31
(S Kirk) *hld up: pushed along 1/2-way: n.d* **18/1**

560 **11** 1¼ **Teneo Vestri**[43] 4720 2-8-12 55.. ChrisCatlin 2 38
(A B Haynes) *hld up: effrt over 2f out: wknd over 1f out* **40/1**

006 **12** 2¼ **Dancing Delta**[15] 5614 2-8-4 47.. HayleyTurner 16 25
(W R Muir) *hld up in tch: rdn and edgd lft over 2f out: wknd over 1f out* **28/1**

300 **13** 1½ **Loched Up**[34] 5041 2-8-11 54.. J-PGuillambert 8 29
(P A Blockley) *chsd ldrs: rdn 1/2-way: wknd 2f out* **11/1**

0160 **14** ½ **Missy Que (IRE)**[41] 4823 2-8-11 54..................(b) RichardMullen 13 28
(W R Muir) *chsd ldrs: rdn over 3f out: edgd lft and wknd 2f out* **28/1**

5020 **15** 1¼ **Kapowee**[41] 4827 2-8-6 49 ow1.. EddieAhern 9 20
(W J Musson) *hld up in tch: hmpd over 5f out: wknd 2f out* **10/1**

000 **16** 6 **Laraffelle (GR)**[17] 5570 2-8-12 55.. TGMcLaughlin 5 13
(E A L Dunlop) *s.i.s: hld up: rdn 1/2-way: hung lft and wknd over 2f out* **14/1**

1m 40.2s (-0.40) **Going Correction** -0.275s/f (Firm) **16** Ran SP% **125.9**
Speed ratings (Par 93): **91,90,88,86,85 85,85,84,83,83 81,79,78,77,76 70**
toteswinger: 1&2 £24.30, 1&3 £20.20, 2&3 £20.60. CSF £145.68 CT £1689.20 TOTE £5.80: £1.30, £5.10, £3.90, £3.90; EX 182.90 TRIFECTA Not won..The winner was bought in for 6,200gns. Rockinit was claimed by R. A. Harris for £5000.
Owner Churchview Syndicate **Bred** A Cunningham, A Grace & O Hegarty **Trained** Newmarket, Suffolk

FOCUS
A really competitive selling nursery but the form is obviously modest, the third helping limit the level.

NOTEBOOK
Balladiene(IRE), who beat only the one home on her nursery debut back in July, had been dropped 5lb and improved markedly for the extra furlong. Always nicely positioned just in behind the leaders, she was driven into contention over two out and found plenty for strong pressure. She may well stay further next season and could have more to offer. Connections bought her back in for 6,200gns. (tchd 5-1)
Rockinit(IRE), never involved on last week's nursery debut at Kempton, was dropped in grade and ran an improved race. Always on the speed, she looked the winner deep into the final furlong and can win off a similar mark. (op 28-1)
Tarawa Atoll, not beaten far in a 1m2f claimer at Great Leighs just the other day, stayed on strongly into third and would have been challenging the front pair in another furlong. She has a bit of size and will probably benefit from a return to further. (op 11-1)
Mistress Mary, making her nursery debut, showed improved form in the first-time blinkers and stayed on again close home to snatch fourth. (op 20-1)
Cherry Belle(IRE) ran as well as ever when third in a nursery at Bath earlier in the month and she held decent claims on this drop back in grade. She was under strong pressure from two out though and could only keep on at the one pace. Official explanation: jockey said filly wandered left and right (op 7-2 tchd 5-2)
Igneous improved on his initial effort in nurseries and this seems his level. (op 18-1 tchd 20-1)
Ba Globetrotter, ahead of stablemate Tarawa Atoll at Great Leighs, was up there early on, but could find no extra from over a furlong out. (op 16-1)
Ashwinder(IRE), fourth in a seller at Lingfield earlier in the month, could make no impact on this nursery debut and does not look the quickest. (op 8-1)

6060 FIRSTBET £50 MATCHED TELEPHONE BET 0800 230 0800 H'CAP 2m
3:40 (3:40) (Class 5) (0-70,70) 3-Y-O+
£3,115 (£933; £466; £233; £116; £58) **Stalls** Low

Form RPR

-123 **1** **That Look**[19] 4935 5-9-12 56.. ChrisCatlin 7 64
(D E Cantillon) *led after 1f: rdn over 1f out: styd on gamely* **10/1[3]**

P014 **2** 1 **Caffari (GER)**[53] 4457 3-9-6 62.. KShea 2 69
(K R Burke) *prom: lost pl over 4f out: hdwy 3f out: rdn over 1f out: styd on wl* **18/1**

3444 **3** nk **Capstan**[27] 5216 3-9-11 67.. RyanMoore 13 74
(L M Cumani) *a.p: rdn to chse wnr 2f out: styd on* **7/1[2]**

3423 **4** 1¾ **Silk Hall (UAE)**[26] 5269 3-9-13 69.. JimmyFortune 1 74
(D W P Arbuthnot) *hld up: hdwy over 2f out: rdn and edgd lft over 1f out: styd on same pce fnl f* **7/1[2]**

0664 **5** 4½ **No Rules**[40] 4859 3-9-0 56.. JimmyQuinn 12 55
(M H Tompkins) *prom: chsd wnr 13f out: tl rdn 2f out: wknd ins fnl f* **14/1**

2545 **6** 2½ **Flam**[21] 5428 3-10-0 70.. EddieAhern 10 66
(J R Fanshawe) *hld up: hdwy over 3f out: sn rdn: wknd over 1f out* **20/1**

2041 **7** hd **Kritzia**[7] 5833 3-9-6 62 6ex.. TedDurcan 6 58
(H R A Cecil) *trckd ldrs: rdn over 2f out: wknd over 1f out* **1/1[1]**

-523 **8** 2¾ **Suite Francaise**[27] 5223 3-9-0 56.. DO'Donohoe 8 49
(Sir Mark Prescott) *dwlt: hld up: hdwy u.p over 2f out: sn hung lft and wknd* **25/1**

400- **9** 1¾ **Lady Traill**[38] 4877 4-9-1 45..................(b) RichardMullen 4 36
(G L Moore) *s.i.s: hld up: effrt over 3f out: n.d* **25/1**

620 **10** 1¼ **Pairumani Pat (IRE)**[31] 5148 3-8-4 46.. AdrianMcCarthy 5 35
(J Pearce) *s.i.s and pushed along early: sn mid-div: rdn over 3f out: sn lost tch* **20/1**

0460 **11** 7 **Synonymy**[14] 5651 5-9-8 52..................(b) LiamJones 3 33
(M Blanshard) *led 1f: chsd ldrs tl rdn and wknd over 3f out* **33/1**

60 **12** 18 **Ashmolian (IRE)**[24] 5367 5-9-3 47.. SamHitchcott 11 6
(Miss Z C Davison) *s.i.s: hld up: hdwy 1/2-way: wknd over 3f out* **66/1**

The Form Book, Raceform Ltd, Compton, RG20 6NL

Anglezarke(IRE) was the big disappointment but she had a very tough task from stall 1 and she could simply never get into it in the second half of the contest. (op 15-8 tchd 9-4)

6069 JOHN SMITH'S AYR SILVER CUP H'CAP — 6f

4:40 (4:40) (Class 2) 3-Y-O+

£31,155 (£9,330; £4,665; £2,335; £1,165; £585) **Stalls** High

Form — RPR

45 **1** **Against The Grain**[75] 3758 5-9-0 **82** ... JoeFanning 7 — 98
(L Lungo) *cl up far side: led that gp over 1f out: styd on strly* **16/1**

1162 **2** 2 ¾ **Harrison George (IRE)**[9] 5795 3-9-4 **88** ... PaulHanagan 1 — 95
(R A Fahey) *midfield far side: effrt over 2f out: styd on wl fnl f: wnt 2nd nr fin: 2nd of 12 in gp* **10/1**[3]

4043 **3** nk **Joseph Henry**[8] 5831 6-9-6 **88** ... SilvestreDeSousa 25 — 94+
(D Nicholls) *cl up stands' side: led that gp over 1f out: edgd lft and kpt on strly fnl f: nt rch far side wnr: 1st of 15 in gp* **12/1**

121 **4** hd **Bel Cantor**[20] 5503 5-9-2 **89** 5ex ... (p) KellyHarrison(5) 3 — 94
(W J H Ratcliffe) *led far side to over 1f out: kpt on fnl f: no ex and lost two pls nr fin: 3rd of 12 in gp* **16/1**

3616 **5** 3 **Marvellous Value (IRE)**[34] 5102 3-9-8 **92** ... TonyHamilton 4 — 88
(M Dods) *hld up far side: hdwy over 2f out: kpt on fnl f: no imp: 4th of 12 in gp* **50/1**

-000 **6** nk **Protector (SAF)**[34] 5109 7-9-8 **90** ... (p) RobertWinston 27 — 85
(A G Foster) *in tch stands' side: drvn over 2f out: chsd (clr) stands' side ldr ins fnl f: r.o: 2nd of 15 in gp* **12/1**

0010 **7** ½ **Mister Hardy**[8] 5831 3-8-9 **84** ... FrederikTylicki(5) 5 — 77
(R A Fahey) *chsd far side ldrs: rdn over 2f out: one pce fnl f: 5th of 12 in gp* **33/1**

0500 **8** ¾ **Stevie Gee (IRE)**[8] 5831 4-9-6 **88** ... PJMcDonald 6 — 79
(G A Swinbank) *in tch far side: outpcd over 2f out: kpt on fnl f: no imp: 6th of 12 in gp* **22/1**

0005 **9** ½ **Dream Theme**[3] 5991 5-9-6 **88** ... MickyFenton 20 — 77
(D Nicholls) *dwlt: bhd stands' side tl hdwy over 2f out: r.o fnl f: nrst fin: 3rd of 15 in gp* **33/1**

0003 **10** ½ **Sunrise Safari (IRE)**[19] 5542 5-9-3 **92** ... BMcHugh(7) 10 — 80
(R A Fahey) *bhd far side tl hdwy over 1f out: n.d: 7th of 12 in gp* **40/1**

0020 **11** ¾ **The Nifty Fox**[8] 5831 4-8-12 **80** ... DavidAllan 15 — 65
(T D Easterby) *chsd stands' side ldrs tl rdn and no ex over 1f out: 4th of 15 in gp* **66/1**

5006 **12** nse **Dickie Le Davoir**[7] 5861 4-8-11 **79** ... AndrewElliott 23 — 64
(John A Harris) *bhd stands' side tl styd on fnl 2f: nrst fin: 5th of 15 in gp* **40/1**

4065 **13** ½ **Glasshoughton**[7] 5861 5-8-11 **79** ... DanielTudhope 19 — 62
(M Dods) *midfield stands' side: drvn over 2f out: nt pce to chal: 6th of 15 in gp* **40/1**

1460 **14** ½ **Geojimali**[19] 5542 6-9-1 **83** ... SaleemGolam 18 — 65
(J S Goldie) *bhd stands' side tl sme late hdwy: nrst fin: 7th of 15 in gp* **25/1**

0021 **15** ¾ **Green Park (IRE)**[6] 5886 5-9-1 **90** 5ex ... (b) ClGillies(7) 11 — 69
(R A Fahey) *prom far side tl wknd fr 2f out: 8th of 12 in gp* **25/1**

4621 **16** nk **Mullein**[39] 4928 3-9-0 **84** ... RichardKingscote 24 — 63
(R M Beckett) *led stands' side to over 1f out: sn no ex: 8th of 15 in gp* **6/1**[1]

5000 **17** nse **Northern Dare (IRE)**[8] 5831 4-9-6 **88** ... AdrianTNicholls 9 — 66
(D Nicholls) *chsd far side ldrs tl wknd over 1f out: 9th of 12 in gp* **16/1**

3522 **18** nse **Gift Horse**[8] 5831 8-8-8 **83** ... (p) LanceBetts(7) 14 — 61
(D Nicholls) *prom on outside of far side gp tl wknd fr 2f out: 10th of 12 in gp* **9/1**[2]

4063 **19** hd **Burning Incense (IRE)**[41] 4854 5-9-5 **87** ... PaulMulrennan 21 — 65
(M Dods) *bhd stands' side: drvn over 2f out: n.d: 9th of 15 in gp* **10/1**[3]

000- **20** ¾ **Trafalgar Bay (IRE)**[419] 3941 5-9-7 **89** ... DarrenWilliams 26 — 64
(K R Burke) *bhd stands' side: pushed along 1/2-way: nvr on terms: 10th of 15 in gp* **50/1**

023 **21** ¾ **Kaldoun Kingdom (IRE)**[41] 4842 3-9-7 **91** ... JamieMoriarty 17 — 64
(R A Fahey) *hld up stands' side: drvn over 2f out: sn btn: 11th of 15 in gp* **11/1**

203 **22** 2 ¼ **Methaaly (IRE)**[3] 5990 5-8-9 **84** ... (be) DeanHeslop(7) 2 — 50
(M Mullineaux) *bhd far side: no ch fr 1/2-way: 11th of 12 in gp* **40/1**

5006 **23** nk **He's A Humbug (IRE)**[9] 5796 4-8-11 **84** ... (p) PatrickDonaghy(5) 22 — 49
(K A Ryan) *cl up stands' side tl wknd over 1f out: 12th of 15 in gp* **33/1**

0000 **24** 3 ¼ **Luscivious**[8] 5831 4-9-0 **85** ... (b) TolleyDean(3) 13 — 38
(A J McCabe) *dwlt: bhd stands' side: drvn 1/2-way: nvr on terms: 13th of 15 in gp* **100/1**

0600 **25** 2 **Obe Gold**[8] 5831 6-9-7 **89** ... (v) FrancisNorton 16 — 35
(D Nicholls) *towards rr stands' side: drvn 1/2-way: sn wknd: 14th of 15 in gp* **50/1**

330 **26** ½ **Cha Cha Cha**[35] 5071 4-8-12 **80** ... NCallan 8 — 25
(K A Ryan) *midfield far side: drvn and lost pl over 2f out: last of 12 in gp* **25/1**

1543 **27** 7 **Thebes**[12] 5731 3-9-7 **91** ... RoystonFfrench 12 — 13
(M Johnston) *sn swtchd to r on outside of stands' side gp: hung lft and wknd over 2f out: last of 15 in gp* **14/1**

1m 15.67s (2.07) **Going Correction** +0.60s/f (Yiel)
WFA 3 from 4yo+ 2lb — **115** Ran SP% **133.3**
Speed ratings (Par 109): **110,106,105,105,101 101,100,99,98,98 97,97,96,95,94 94,94,94,94,93 92,89,88,83,81 80,71**
toteswinger: 1&2 £218.90, 1&3 £99.50, 2&3 £53.40. CSF £149.97 CT £2054.22 TOTE £19.70: £3.80, £4.10, £3.90, £4.80; EX 232.50 TRIFECTA Not won..
Owner Len Lungo Racing Limited **Bred** Mrs C F Van Straubeenzee And Miss A G **Trained** Carrutherstown, D'fries & G'way

FOCUS

Four of the first five horses home came from single-figure stalls and, Joseph Henry apart, the far side absolutely thrashed the group that kept stands' side. The relatively unexposed Against the Grain is rated up 8lb, with the second and fourth close to their pre-race marks.

NOTEBOOK

Against The Grain has been campaigned over longer trips than this so far, so his stamina proved the most important asset in the conditions. Already proven after layoffs, he came into this on the back of a 75-day break, and he did not handle quicker ground when last seen. These conditions clearly played to his strengths and, kept a couple of horse-widths away from that far rail by Joe Fanning, he stayed on strongly to lead inside the final furlong and win fairly emphatically. Connections reported afterwards that this had been the target for some time. (op 20-1)

Harrison George(IRE) is also proven in these conditions and although exposed from a handicapping point of view, he ran a blinder, finishing strongly to snatch second up the far side. (tchd 11-1)

Joseph Henry finished third from stall 25 and that stands out as particularly meritorious, but he also hung his way out into the centre of the track in the closing stages, forfeiting even more ground. Still, he did remarkably well to pull so far clear of the remainder on the stands' side and has run an absolute stormer.

Bel Cantor came into the race in cracking form. He took them along on the far side and was only collared in the dying strides by the second and third. (op 14-1)

Marvellous Value(IRE), less exposed than most, finished well on the far side without ever being able to land a blow on the principals.

Protector(SAF), sporting first-time cheekpieces, finished best of the stands' side group behind Joseph Henry (op 14-1 tchd 11-1)

Mister Hardy, proven in soft ground, stayed on well without being able to land a blow. (op 40-1)

Stevie Gee(IRE), without the blinkers this time, hit a flat spot before staying on again and he may just be better over the extra furlong now. (op 20-1)

Mullein, up 7lb for her Windsor victory, made much of the running on the stands' side and although she was drawn on the wrong flank as it turned out, the fact that she was ultimately well beaten on her side suggests she can have few excuses. Official explanation: jockey said filly was unable to obtain enough cover early stages (op 7-1)

Gift Horse Official explanation: jockey said gelding was unsuited by the heavy ground

Burning Incense(IRE) Official explanation: jockey said gelding was unsuited by the heavy ground

6070 BETFAIR SCOTTISH RACING FORTNIGHT H'CAP — 1m

5:15 (5:15) (Class 4) (0-85,84) 3-Y-O+ — **£6,476** (£1,927; £963; £481) **Stalls** Low

Form — RPR

1501 **1** **Medici Pearl**[15] 5635 4-9-5 **81** ... DavidAllan 8 — 92+
(T D Easterby) *trckd ldrs gng wl: nt clr run and swtchd rt over 2f out: qcknd to ld fnl 75yds: readily* **7/1**[3]

1402 **2** nk **Blue Spinnaker (IRE)**[1] 6041 9-9-6 **82** ... PaulMulrennan 3 — 91
(M W Easterby) *prom: led over 1f out: hdd and no ex wl ins fnl f* **13/2**[2]

5223 **3** 7 **Ink Spot**[22] 5419 3-8-13 **84** ... (v) FrederikTylicki(5) 2 — 78
(M L W Bell) *stdd s: hld up in rr: effrt on outside over 2f out: kpt on one pce appr fnl f* **10/3**[1]

0206 **4** 4 **The Osteopath (IRE)**[22] 5419 5-9-7 **83** ... RoystonFfrench 10 — 69
(M Dods) *hld up towards rr: kpt on fnl 2f: nvr nr ldrs* **12/1**

21- **5** ½ **Red And White (IRE)**[449] 3013 3-9-0 **80** ... JoeFanning 14 — 65
(M Johnston) *trckd ldr: t.k.h: drvn over 3f out: one pce fnl 2f* **12/1**

2203 **6** ½ **Billy Dane (IRE)**[10] 5772 4-9-5 **81** ... (p) PaulHanagan 4 — 65
(R A Fahey) *trckd ldrs: wnt 2nd over 3f out: hung lft and wknd over 1f out* **11/1**

0502 **7** ¾ **Moheebb (IRE)**[23] 5390 4-8-8 **70** ... (b) AndrewElliott 6 — 52
(Mrs R A Carr) *in rr: nt clr run and swtchd rt 2f out: styng on whn swtchd lft ins fnl f: nvr a factor* **7/1**[3]

1413 **8** 1 ¾ **Marning Star**[81] 3560 3-8-13 **79** ... AdrianTNicholls 1 — 58
(D Nicholls) *t.k.h: led tl hdd & wknd over 1f out* **11/1**

5242 **9** 2 ¼ **Jamieson Gold (IRE)**[22] 5418 5-9-0 **76** ... (b) TonyHamilton 13 — 50
(Miss L A Perratt) *chsd ldrs: drvn over 3f out: wknd appr fnl f* **12/1**

1142 **10** 2 ¾ **Esoterica (IRE)**[22] 5419 5-9-2 **78** ... (v) DanielTudhope 5 — 46
(J S Goldie) *hld up toward rr: effrt 3f out: wknd over 1f out* **15/2**

0300 **11** 5 **Minority Report**[25] 5360 8-9-4 **80** ... SilvestreDeSousa 9 — 38
(D Nicholls) *sn detached in rr: nvr on terms* **28/1**

03-2 **12** 20 **Elliwan**[91] 3227 3-9-0 **80** ... DaleGibson 11 — —
(M W Easterby) *chsd ldrs: drvn over 4f out: sn lost pl: bhd fnl 2f: t.o* **33/1**

1m 52.92s (9.12) **Going Correction** +1.275s/f (Soft)
WFA 3 from 4yo+ 4lb — **12** Ran SP% **119.3**
Speed ratings (Par 105): **105,104,97,93,93 92,91,90,87,85 80,60**
toteswinger: 1&2 £13.00, 1&3 £6.90, 2&3 £5.90. CSF £52.41 CT £184.72 TOTE £8.90: £2.80, £2.80, £1.70; EX 65.60.
Owner Ryedale Partners No 3 **Bred** Larkwood Stud **Trained** Great Habton, N Yorks

FOCUS

A good pace set by Marning Star, who could not see it out, but the finish was dominated by two bang in-form handicappers. Despite the gap back to the form this is probably not form to rate too positively, with the ground having a huge influence on the result.

Marning Star Official explanation: jockey said gelding ran too free and hung right-handed throughout

6071 ROBB FERGUSON C A H'CAP (FOR THE EGLINTON & WINTON CHALLENGE CUP) — 2m 1f 105y

5:45 (5:46) (Class 4) (0-80,78) 4-Y-O+ — **£6,476** (£1,927; £963; £481) **Stalls** Low

Form — RPR

4242 **1** **Sphinx (FR)**[12] 5718 10-9-7 **78** ... (b) PaulMulrennan 3 — 86
(E W Tuer) *t.k.h: hld up: smooth hdwy 5f out: led on bit over 2f out: shkn up and drew clr over 1f out* **5/2**[2]

6020 **2** 6 **Dr Sharp (IRE)**[12] 5718 8-9-4 **75** ... MickyFenton 7 — 77
(T P Tate) *led to over 2f out: kpt on: no ch w wnr* **11/4**[3]

3-02 **3** 24 **Los Nadis (GER)**[27] 4972 4-9-2 **73** ... PaulHanagan 9 — 68
(P Monteith) *t.k.h early: trckd ldrs: wnt 2nd over 5f out: effrt over 3f out: wknd 2f out* **6/4**[1]

5-50 **4** 20 **Act Sirius (IRE)**[72] 3832 4-8-2 **59** oh3 ... FrancisNorton 8 — 17
(A Crook) *prom tl rdn and wknd fr over 5f out* **12/1**

/0-0 **5** 1 **Propinquity**[61] 4225 6-9-4 **75** ... RobertWinston 4 — 32
(Liam McAteer, Ire) *t.k.h: hld up: hdwy over 5f out: wknd over 4f out* **16/1**

0044 **6** 42 **Stravonian**[22] 5415 8-8-3 **60** oh14 ow1 ... AndrewElliott 6 — —
(D A Nolan) *chsd ldr to over 5f out: sn wknd* **40/1**

/40- **7** 57 **Jardines Bazaar**[429] 3640 4-8-2 **59** oh11 ... (t) DaleGibson 1 — —
(Martin Brassil, Ire) *hld up: drvn over 6f out: sn struggling* **33/1**

4m 18.74s (18.24) **Going Correction** +1.275s/f (Soft) — **7** Ran SP% **114.2**
Speed ratings (Par 105): **108,105,93,84,84 64,37**
toteswinger: 1&2 £2.10, 1&3 £1.90, 2&3 £2.10. CSF £9.82 CT £12.70 TOTE £3.40: £1.90, £2.30; EX 11.40 Place 6: £213.60 Place 5: £84.49 .
Owner E Tuer **Bred** Martyn Arbib **Trained** Great Smeaton, N Yorks

FOCUS

Only three really counted here and they filled the places, although they were very well strung out in the testing ground. The form may be worth very little.

T/Jkpt: Not won. T/Plt: £465.10 to a £1 stake. Pool: £82,350.64. 129.25 winning tickets. T/Qpdt: £40.30 to a £1 stake. Pool: £6,231.86. 114.40 winning tickets. RY

5225 NEWBURY (L-H)

Friday, September 19

OFFICIAL GOING: Good (good to soft in places; 7.0)

Wind: Virtually nil Weather: Bright and sunny

6072 DUBAI DUTY FREE GOLF WORLD CUP MAIDEN STKS (DIV I) — 6f 8y

1:40 (1:43) (Class 4) 2-Y-O — **£5,504** (£1,637; £818; £408) **Stalls** Centre

Form — RPR

2 **1** **Huntdown (USA)**[27] 5271 2-9-3 0 ... LDettori 3 — 95+
(J H M Gosden) *trckd ldrs: ld ins fnl 2f: sn clr: v easily* **30/100**[1]

2 7 **All About You (IRE)** 2-9-3 0 ... SteveDrowne 13 — 69
(R Charlton) *leggy: bit bkwd: pressed ldr: slt ld 2f out: sn hdd and no ch w v easy wnr* **14/1**[3]

3 1 **Sharpened Edge** 2-8-12 0 CatherineGannon 5 61+
(B Palling) *bit bkwd: s.i.s: rr: pushed along 3f out: swtchd rt and hdwy over 1f out: styd on to take 3rd wl ins fnl f but nvr any ch* **33/1**

45 4 1 **Bartica (IRE)**[16] 5609 2-9-3 0 RyanMoore 9 63
(R Hannon) *in tch: pushed along and outpcd 1/2-way: kpt on again final f but nvr in contention* **14/1**[3]

5 1 1/4 **George Rex (USA)** 2-9-3 0 TPO'Shea 11 59
(B J Meehan) *w'like: strong: bit bkwd: chsd ldrs: rdn 2f out: one pce fr over 1f out* **28/1**

0 6 hd **Day In Dubai**[37] 4974 2-8-9 0 MarcHalford(3) 8 54
(J J Bridger) *sn led: rdn 1/2-way: hdd 2f out: wknd ins fnl f* **100/1**

06 7 hd **Ready For Battle (IRE)**[15] 5649 2-9-3 0 AdamKirby 7 58
(C G Cox) *w'like: scope: in tch: pushed along over 2f out: styd on ins fnl f but nvr in contention* **33/1**

8 1/2 **Rosco Flyer (IRE)** 2-9-3 0 TPQueally 2 57
(J R Boyle) *in tch: shkn up over 2f out: styd on ins fnl f but n.d* **80/1**

9 3 1/4 **Chapter And Verse (IRE)** 2-9-3 0 TonyCulhane 10 47
(B W Hills) *w'like: bit bkwd: s.i.s: a in rr* **16/1**

10 2 1/4 **Hekaaya (IRE)** 2-8-12 0 HayleyTurner 1 35+
(M P Tregoning) *scope: bit bkwd: sn rdn and green: aways in rr* **12/1**[2]

1m 14.81s (1.81) **Going Correction** +0.20s/f (Good) **10** Ran SP% **115.4**
Speed ratings (Par 97): **95,85,84,83,81 81,80,80,75,72**
toteswinger: 1&2 £3.10, 1&3 £10.60, 2&3 £81.80. CSF £5.24 TOTE £1.20: £1.02, £2.80, £7.20; EX 6.60.
Owner H R H Princess Haya Of Jordan **Bred** Darley **Trained** Newmarket, Suffolk

FOCUS

A dry night meant the ground had changed to good, good to soft in places. This looked an ordinary maiden by Newbury standards, but one could not fail to be impressed by Huntdown.

NOTEBOOK

Huntdown(USA) was the subject of strong support, suggesting that none of the newcomers was expected to put up any meaningful opposition to John Gosden's colt, who had run so well on his debut in a Newmarket maiden that is working out well. He duly landed the odds without much fuss, Dettori never having to get serious with him as he lengthened in style from a furlong out. He should have no trouble stepping up to 7f and he looks a very useful prospect, but while there were a few quotes flying around for the Guineas afterwards, it is much too early for that sort of talk. (op 4-9 tchd 1-2 in a place)

All About You(IRE), a 120,000gns brother to high-class sprinting two-year-old Always Hopeful, who finished third in the Prix Morny and Middle Park, is bred to be speedy. This was a promising debut as his stable's juveniles invariably come on for their debuts.

Sharpened Edge is from a successful sprinting family and her half-sister Edge Of Gold was first past the post on her juvenile debut here. This daughter of Exceed And Excel shaped encouragingly after a slow start and will not mind quicker ground.

Bartica(IRE) had shown only modest form in his previous two starts and probably ran close to that level this time. He is probably a fair guide to the level of the form and should find things easier himself in nursery company. (op 16-1)

George Rex(USA), a half-brother to four winners in the US, is already a gelding. He looked in need of the experience and should do better for this initial outing. (op 25-1)

Day In Dubai, a very cheap purchase, showed early speed before weakening.

Ready For Battle(IRE), who was dropping back in trip on his third run for a mark, was a bit keen and got blocked in his run approaching the furlong marker. He should do better in handicap company. (op 28-1)

6073 DUBAI DUTY FREE CUP (LISTED RACE) 7f (S)

2:10 (2:14) (Class 1) 3-Y-0+

£24,978 (£9,468; £4,738; £2,362; £1,183; £594) **Stalls** Centre

Form RPR

1411 1 **Kalahari Gold (IRE)**[41] 4869 3-8-13 102 LPKeniry 12 117+
(A M Balding) *trckd ldrs: drvn and qcknd over 1f out: led fnl 110yds: r.o strly* **9/2**[2]

0245 2 1 1/4 **Il Warrd (IRE)**[34] 5095 3-8-13 109 LDettori 13 113
(Saeed Bin Suroor) *trckd ldrs: led over 3f out: rdn over 1f out: hdd and outpcd fnl 110yds but hld on wl for clr 2nd* **6/1**[3]

521 3 2 1/2 **Ordnance Row**[36] 5025 5-9-5 109 DaneO'Neill 17 110+
(R Hannon) *prom early but sn towards rr: rdn and hdwy fr 2f out: kpt on ins fnl f but nvr gng pce to trble ldng duo* **10/1**

5460 4 1 **Majestic Roi (USA)**[48] 4623 4-8-11 110 TPO'Shea 5 100
(M R Channon) *t.k.h: towards rr: hdwy fr 2f out: kpt on fnl f but nvr gng pce to trble ldrs* **6/1**[3]

-313 5 3/4 **Easy Target (FR)**[54] 4459 3-8-13 101 TomEaves 11 102+
(B Smart) *swtg: t.k.h: trckd ldrs 2f: stdd mid-div: hrd rdn over 1f out: sme prog ins fnl f but nvr a threat* **25/1**

15-4 6 1 1/4 **Almajd (IRE)**[85] 3396 3-8-13 100 RyanMoore 10 98+
(Sir Michael Stoute) *swtg: towards rr: rdn and hdwy fr over 2f out: nvr gng pce to rch ldrs and sn one pce* **20/1**

2100 7 1/2 **Iguazu Falls (USA)**[40] 4912 3-8-13 103 GregFairley 1 97
(Saeed Bin Suroor) *chsd ldrs: rdn over 2f out: wknd fnl f* **16/1**

0033 8 nk **Beaver Patrol (IRE)**[17] 5586 6-9-2 105 (v) StephenCarson 16 97
(Eve Johnson Houghton) *t.k.h and pressed ldr 3f: rdn over 2f out: wknd over 1f out* **16/1**

212 9 nse **Royal Vintage (SAF)**[174] 1088 4-9-2 0 KShea 9 97
(M F De Kock, South Africa) *lw: chsd ldrs: rdn over 2f out: wknd ins fnl 2f* **7/2**[1]

10-1 10 nk **Sharp Nephew**[167] 1213 3-8-13 101 ShaneKelly 8 95
(B J Meehan) *in rr: rdn and sme prog over 2f out: sn n.m.r: nvr rchd ldrs* **16/1**

0405 11 4 1/2 **Captain Marvelous (IRE)**[8] 5840 4-9-2 104 (b[1]) TonyCulhane 6 84
(B W Hills) *chsd ldrs tl wknd qckly 2f out* **25/1**

6-43 12 3/4 **Lizard Island (USA)**[197] 812 3-8-13 113 JohnEgan 3 81
(Jane Chapple-Hyam) *lw: chsd ldrs: rdn over 2f out and sn wknd* **20/1**

0006 13 1/2 **Sonny Red (IRE)**[6] 5899 4-9-2 106 EddieAhern 14 81
(R Hannon) *lw: slt ld tl hdd over 3f out: wknd appr fnl 2f* **25/1**

0-00 14 1 **Hotel Du Cap**[35] 5070 5-9-2 98 SteveDrowne 2 78
(G Wragg) *nvr travelling and a bhd* **25/1**

450- 15 10 **Mac Love**[335] 6332 7-9-2 103 TPQueally 7 51
(Stef Liddiard) *bit bkwd: v.s.a and a in rr* **50/1**

1m 25.35s (-0.35) **Going Correction** +0.20s/f (Good)
WFA 3 from 4yo+ 3lb **15** Ran SP% **122.6**
Speed ratings (Par 111): **110,108,105,104,103 102,101,101,101,100 95,94,94,93,81**
toteswinger: 1&2 £4.00, 1&3 £8.80, 2&3 £13.90. CSF £28.75 TOTE £5.70: £2.30, £2.80, £3.10; EX 38.80.
Owner The Toucan Syndicate **Bred** Mick McGinn And James Waldron **Trained** Kingsclere, Hants

FOCUS

A pretty big field went to post for this Listed contest and it looked a competitive heat. The early pace was not that strong, though, and a few raced keenly enough. Kalahari Gold was maintaining his progress with another clear personal best, while Il Warrd was basically to his Jersey Stakes form.

NOTEBOOK

Kalahari Gold(IRE) only made his racecourse debut in June, but he has quickly shot up through the handicapping ranks and he proved himself a pattern-class performer with this effort. He has raced exclusively over 7f so far and, having only had five starts to date, could well be capable of even further improvement. The next logical step would appear to be the Group 2 Challenge Stakes at Newmarket on Champions Day. (op 5-1)

Il Warrd(IRE) was in the van throughout and travelling best of all when Dettori pressed the button inside the final two furlongs, but while he picked up well, he did not put the race to bed. He has had excuses since finishing a fine second in the Jersey, and this was a return to form. He beat the rest well enough, but the way he travelled through the race suggests he could be worth trying back over 6f. (op 15-2)

Ordnance Row ran a solid race under his 3lb penalty but his last four wins have come over 1m and he finds this trip a bit on the short side these days. (op 9-1)

Majestic Roi(USA), who won the Fred Darling over this course and distance earlier in her career, was the only filly in the line-up and had not run at this low a level or this short a trip since this time last year. Prepping for her defence of the Sun Chariot Stakes, the race served its purpose and quicker ground at Newmarket will be in her favour. (op 7-1)

Easy Target(FR) ran quite well considering he was keen in the early stages and got involved in a barging match with the winner and Royal Vintage at halfway. Having lost his place he ran on again late, leaving the impression he was a bit better than the bare form. (op 33-1)

Almajd(IRE), disappointing when beaten at odds-on at Great Leighs on his only previous start this term back in June, has clearly not been the easiest to train. This was more encouraging but he still has a way to go to live up to his initial promise from last year. (op 16-1)

Iguazu Falls(USA), the Godolphin second string, has struggled since winning a weak Listed race at Epsom in June, and he again weakened at the end of his race. (op 20-1)

Beaver Patrol(IRE), not disgraced in Group company on his last two starts, should have been suited by this better ground, but he was keen early and could have done with a stronger pace. (op 20-1)

Royal Vintage(SAF) looked a decent prospect in the spring when finishing second to Honour Devil on dirt in both the UAE 2000 Guineas and UAE Derby, but he was switching back to turf here following a 174-day absence and the drop back in trip was another negative. He was disappointing, but he holds a couple of Group 1 entries and perhaps this will have done its job in bringing him on. (op 11-4 tchd 4-1)

Sharp Nephew had been off the track since April. He has gone well fresh in the past but never threatened to land a blow. (op 20-1)

Mac Love Official explanation: jockey said gelding banged its head in the stalls

6074 DUBAI DUTY FREE ARC TRIAL (GROUP 3) 1m 3f 5y

2:45 (2:45) (Class 1) 3-Y-0+

£36,900 (£13,988; £7,000; £3,490; £1,748; £877) **Stalls** Low

Form RPR

0-20 1 **Blue Monday**[13] 5694 7-9-3 106 SteveDrowne 1 119
(R Charlton) *pushed along to go prom after s: rdn and dropped in rr over 5f out: hdwy fr 3f out: hung lft over 2f out: squeezed through 1f out to take slt ld fnl 110yds: hld on all out* **15/2**

6631 2 shd **Spanish Moon (USA)**[27] 5288 4-9-3 111 RyanMoore 7 118
(Sir Michael Stoute) *chsd ldrs: pushed along over 3f out: led over 1f out: hdd fnl 110yds: rallied u.p: jst failed* **13/2**[3]

014 3 4 1/2 **Multidimensional (IRE)**[12] 5732 5-9-6 118 TPQueally 8 114
(H R A Cecil) *trckd ldrs: slt ld appr fnl 3f: rdn 2f out: hdd over 1f out: wknd fnl 110yds* **6/4**[1]

4026 4 3/4 **Regime (IRE)**[26] 5335 4-9-6 112 HayleyTurner 4 113
(M L W Bell) *towards rr but in tch: hdwy to chse ldrs over 2f out: effrt over 1f out: nvr quite upsides: wknd fnl 110yds* **14/1**

-236 5 3 **Sushisan (AUS)**[174] 1091 6-9-3 0 ShaneKelly 2 104
(J M P Eustace) *swtg: sn trcking ldrs: rdn and effrt over 2f out: nvr on terms and wknd over 1f out* **16/1**

4112 6 3/4 **Staying On (IRE)**[92] 3156 3-8-10 108 AdamKirby 5 103
(W R Swinburn) *lw: sn led: hdd over 3f out: weaking on rails whn hmpd 2f out* **9/2**[2]

0002 7 4 1/2 **Illustrious Blue**[13] 5694 5-9-3 109 PaulDoe 6 96
(W J Knight) *in rr but in tch: rdn and effrt over 3f out: nvr gng pce to rch ldrs and btn over 2f out* **12/1**

40-5 8 nk **Numide (FR)**[133] 1944 5-9-3 105 GeorgeBaker 3 95
(G L Moore) *lw: s.i.s: rr: rdn and mod prog on outside over 3f out: nvr rchd ldrs and wknd over 2f out* **25/1**

0450 9 8 **Halicarnassus (IRE)**[13] 5694 4-9-3 110 SamHitchcott 9 81
(M R Channon) *lw: in tch: rdn and hdwy on outside over 3f out: nvr rchd ldrs and wknd over 2f out* **12/1**

2m 20.62s (-0.58) **Going Correction** +0.25s/f (Good)
WFA 3 from 4yo+ 7lb **9** Ran SP% **115.1**
Speed ratings (Par 113): **112,111,108,108,105 105,102,101,96**
toteswinger: 1&2 £3.00, 1&3 £3.30, 2&3 £3.20. CSF £55.17 TOTE £8.80: £2.70, £1.40, £1.40; EX 50.10.
Owner Mountgrange Stud **Bred** Darley **Trained** Beckhampton, Wilts
■ Stewards' Enquiry : Steve Drowne two-day ban: careless riding (Oct 6-7)

FOCUS

An Arc trial in name only, and the early pace was far from frantic, but the form looks solid enough. Blue Monday was back to his best, and Spanish Moon ran to the level of his reappearance at Ascot.

NOTEBOOK

Blue Monday, who won this race in 2006, did not look like repeating the trick for most of this race as he was rousted along early on after being sluggish out of the stalls and did not travel particularly well. He was also held in by Regime from two furlongs to a furlong out, but once he got a gap he stayed on strongly, just edging out Spanish Moon. It looks like he has returned to something like his best following a light campaign this term - he returned from Australia with chips in his joints - and his trainer will now be on the lookout for another Group 3 at around 1m4f. (op 12-1)

Spanish Moon(USA) has struggled somewhat since his Ascot win but has come back to form on his last two starts. Still lightly raced, he could be capable of further improvement next year over distances around 1m4f on decent ground. (op 11-2 tchd 5-1)

Multidimensional(IRE), whose second in the Hardwicke and fourth in the Irish Champion set a solid level for the rest to aim at, did not seem to get home. He does stay this trip, though, so it is likely that this was simply a below-par effort following some hard races. (op 5-4 tchd 2-1)

Regime(IRE), who ran poorly in Norway last time, had his chance but did not get home back up in distance. He is probably at his best over 1m2f. (op 16-1)

Sushisan(AUS)'s performances in the last two Sheema Classics gave him a sound chance at this level if at his best following a 174-day absence. During that time he had undergone surgery to remove a bone chip from his near-fore and had switched from being trained in South Africa to a new stable over here, though, so there was plenty that had to be taken on trust. Having sweated up beforehand, he ran as though the race would bring him on, and the St Simon Stakes back here next month, when hopefully he will get softer ground, is the plan. (op 12-1)

Staying On(IRE) had been given a mid-season break since finishing second in the Hampton Court Stakes at Royal Ascot, and as the only three-year-old and the least exposed horse in the line-up, he looked an interesting contender. However, his stamina, which was open to question, seemed to let him down on this step up in class. (op 7-1)

Illustrious Blue ran his best race of the campaign last time, but that was on Polytrack and he never really threatened back on turf. He could have done with a stronger pace. (tchd 14-1)

Numide(FR) also struggled. He was very slow out of the blocks on his first outing since May, and unless connections can find a good opportunity on proper soft ground he could be kept for hurdling. (tchd 20-1)

Halicarnassus(IRE), whose last win came in this race last year, could not repeat the trick on this slightly slower ground. (op 14-1 tchd 11-1)

6075 HAYNES, HANSON & CLARK CONDITIONS STKS 1m (S)

3:20 (3:20) (Class 2) 2-Y-O

£11,215 (£3,358; £1,679; £840; £419; £210) **Stalls** Centre

Form — RPR

1 **Taameer** 2-8-12 0 HayleyTurner 1 95+
(M P Tregoning) *unf: scope: in rr but in tch: shkn up: green and hdwy 2f out: swtchd lft and qcknd over 1f out: led ins fnl f: drvn and styd on strly cl home* **20/1**

221 2 ½ **Full Toss**[20] 5497 2-9-2 90 RyanMoore 7 98
(R Hannon) *in rr but in tch: drvn and qcknd to chse ldrs 2f out: str chal fr over 1f out: outpcd by wnr ins fnl f but hld on gamely for 2nd* **11/4**[2]

2 3 *shd* **Palavicini (USA)**[28] 5246 2-8-12 0 EddieAhern 4 94
(J L Dunlop) *lw: t.k.h early: chsd ldr: chal 2f out: sit ld sn after: hdd and nt pce of wnr ins fnl f but styd on wl to dispute cl 2nd* **10/11**[1]

01 4 5 **Aurorian (IRE)**[18] 5578 2-9-2 83 DaneO'Neill 2 87
(R Hannon) *led: rdn 2f out: narrowly hdd sn after: wknd ins fnl f* **12/1**

2 5 1 ¼ **Souter Point (USA)**[21] 5468 2-8-12 0 SteveDrowne 3 80
(R Charlton) *chsd ldrs: rdn 3f out: wknd 2f out* **9/2**[3]

6 29 **Lord Of The Flame** 2-8-12 0 PaulDoe 6 16
(W De Best-Turner) *w'like: bit bkwd: prom tl wknd qckly 1/2-way* **100/1**

1m 41.19s (1.49) **Going Correction** +0.20s/f (Good) **6 Ran SP% 110.7**
Speed ratings (Par 101): **100,99,99,94,93 64**
toteswinger: 1&2 £6.60, 1&3 £3.80, 2&3 £1.20. CSF £72.00 TOTE £16.30: £4.60, £2.10; EX 49.90.

Owner Hamdan Al Maktoum **Bred** Genesis Green Stud **Trained** Lambourn, Berks

FOCUS

A race with a proud history, having thrown up a number of Classic winners in the past.

NOTEBOOK

Taameer ◆ overcame inexperience to win. Anchored at the rear off the steady early pace, he was a little slow to get the message as to what was required, but once the penny dropped he quickened up well and burst between horses to hit the front inside the last. He was strongly challenged close home but was always holding off his more experienced rivals, and the way he was looking about on pulling up confirmed how green he still is, so he looks sure to have learned plenty from this. He was the trainer's fourth winner of the race in the last ten years, and he is now likely to take a similar path to his previous winners Elshadi and Nayef, and take in the Autumn Stakes at Ascot next. His pedigree suggests he should make up into a middle-distance performer next year, and he looks a smart prospect on this evidence. (op 16-1)

Full Toss, whose sire Nayef won this race in 2000, got off the mark at the third attempt at Chester last time and stepping up a furlong in trip promised to suit him. Giving 4lb to the winner, he could not quite make his experience tell, but he ran a sound race and helps set a level for the form. (op 5-2 tchd 3-1and 10-3 in places)

Palavicini(USA), who holds plenty of Group-race entries, was an eye-catcher on his debut, and stepping up a furlong in distance was also expected to suit him. Sent off a short price, he raced a bit keenly in the early stages, which would not have helped, and a stronger pace is likely to suit him in future as he has plenty of stamina in his pedigree. (op 6-5 tchd 5-4)

Aurorian(IRE), a stablemate of Full Toss, made all on the favoured stands' side at Lingfield last time. With no draw bias to take advantage of here he was easily brushed aside inside the last. (tchd 10-1)

Souter Point(USA) shaped with plenty of promise on his debut in a Sandown maiden that is working out well but he was one-paced under pressure here and this was a step backwards. (op 7-2)

6076 DUBAI DUTY FREE FULL OF SURPRISES E B F FILLIES' CONDITIONS STKS 7f (S)

3:55 (3:56) (Class 2) 2-Y-O

£11,215 (£3,358; £1,679; £840; £419; £210) **Stalls** Centre

Form — RPR

1 **Lassarina (IRE)** 2-8-12 SteveDrowne 9 84
(B W Hills) *w'like: leggy: s.i.s: rr: shkn up and qcknd fr 2f out: styd on to ld fnl 110yds: kpt on wl* **14/1**

0 2 ¾ **Super Sleuth (IRE)**[28] 5241 2-8-12 TPO'Shea 11 83
(B J Meehan) *lw: in tch: rdn and qcknd fr 2f out to chse ldrs 1f out: styd on wl thrght fnl f but a jst hld by wnr* **14/1**

1 3 ½ **Al Sabaheya**[31] 5165 2-8-12 HayleyTurner 3 81
(C E Brittain) *w'like: strong: chsd ldrs: rdn to chal ins fnl f: one pce u.p whn hung lft fnl 100yds* **9/2**[2]

231 4 ½ **Feeling Fab (FR)**[10] 5788 2-9-2 GregFairley 7 84
(M Johnston) *lw: led: rdn over 2f out: kpt slt advantage tl hdd and no ex fnl 110yds* **7/1**

01 5 *hd* **Silver Games (IRE)**[19] 5535 2-9-2 81 EdwardCreighton 2 84
(M R Channon) *hld up in rr: gd hdwy fr 2f out: styd on ins fnl f but nvr gng pce to press ldrs* **11/2**

2 6 ½ **Capitelli (IRE)**[28] 5240 2-8-12 DaneO'Neill 10 78+
(R Hannon) *lw: chsd ldrs: rdn and effrt over 1f out: nvr gng pce to chal* **5/1**[3]

7 ¾ **Phillipina** 2-8-12 RyanMoore 6 76+
(Sir Michael Stoute) *w'like: scope: lw: chsd ldrs: rdn over 2f out: wknd ins fnl f* **16/1**

3 8 2 **Suba (USA)**[34] 5097 2-8-12 LDettori 4 71
(Saeed Bin Suroor) *lw: chsd ldrs: rdn 1/2-way: no ch fnl 2f* **11/4**[1]

9 *hd* **Lady Drac (IRE)** 2-8-12 TonyCulhane 8 71
(B W Hills) *w'like: bit bkwd: hld up in rr: stdy hdwy fr 2f out but nvr gng pce to be competitive* **50/1**

5 10 3 ¼ **Mejala (IRE)**[15] 5643 2-8-12 EddieAhern 1 63
(J L Dunlop) *t.k.h: stdd rr after 2f: rdn over 2f out and nvr in contention after* **16/1**

11 17 **Pursuit Of Purpose** 2-8-12 TPQueally 5 20
(G L Moore) *unf: a in rr* **50/1**

1m 26.52s (0.82) **Going Correction** +0.20s/f (Good) **11 Ran SP% 118.4**
Speed ratings (Par 98): **103,102,101,101,100 100,99,97,96,93 73**
toteswinger: 1&2 £51.50, 1&3 £17.80, 2&3 £22.10. CSF £196.17 TOTE £20.80: £4.80, £4.10, £2.50; EX 366.50.

Owner J Hanson **Bred** Philip Brady **Trained** Lambourn, Berks

FOCUS

A race that hasn't really produced a top-class filly in recent seasons. Seven of the last ten winners had won their previous starts, while only one newcomer had been successful in that time. The pace looked solid enough, but there wasn't much covering the first seven at the line which suggests the form is all right without being outstanding.

NOTEBOOK

Lassarina(IRE), one of four newcomers in the field, was by no means the best away but she travelled powerfully off the pace and once switched to make her effort closest to the stands' rail, saw her race out in grand style. Although she is out of a half-sister to the top-class sprinter Continent, the way she won this suggests she has inherited stamina from her sire. She is likely to have one more run this term and she should come on for this, so she looks well worth a try in something rather better. (tchd 16-1)

Super Sleuth(IRE) ◆, an eye-catcher on her Newmarket debut, stepped up from that and had every chance. A Fillies' Mile entry, she gave the impression that she is still far from the finished article so a maiden should be a formality. (op 16-1)

Al Sabaheya, an easy debut winner of a Brighton maiden auction that has produced several placed horses, proved popular in the market. Tracking the pace throughout, she made her effort on the far side of the leader while the first two challenged on the opposite side, but she still kept on well enough. (op 8-1)

Feeling Fab(FR), the most experienced in the field and an easy winner on Polytrack the previous week, was sent straight to the front and set a decent gallop. She looked to have all her rivals in trouble passing the 2f pole, but she started to tire inside the last furlong and was swamped on either side in the last 100 yards. (op 6-1)

Silver Games(IRE), a half-sister to Nahoodh, had finished seven lengths behind Suba on her debut here before winning easily at Folkestone. She comprehensively turned the form around with her old rival here, though she never looked like winning. The Fillies' Mile may be aiming a bit high, but the way she stayed on under pressure does suggest that she needs 1m now. (op 6-1 tchd 5-1)

Capitelli(IRE), who acquitted herself very well when runner-up on her Newmarket debut, was close enough for most of the way but couldn't pick up sufficiently when asked and perhaps needs better ground. (op 4-1)

Phillipina, whose winning dam is a half-sister to Cesare and Nowhere To Exit, proved very weak in the market but didn't run badly. She was still in the mix entering the last furlong before tiring and starting to hang away to the far side, but Ryan Moore wasn't at all hard on her by then. She is bred to stay much further than this and looks one for next year. (op 10-1)

Suba(USA), a fine third in a decent maiden here on her debut, is bred to have appreciated this extra furlong so the way she faded late on was very disappointing. Something must have been amiss. (op 3-1 tchd 5-2 tchd 10-3 in a place)

Lady Drac(IRE) never figured on this debut.

Mejala(IRE) was another to disappoint in view of her promising debut. She wasn't going well from a long way out and is surely better than this. (tchd 14-1)

Pursuit Of Purpose was always at the back after missing the break, but this half-sister to three winners including one over hurdles is probably one for middle-distance handicaps in due course. (op 66-1)

6077 DUBAI DUTY FREE GOLF WORLD CUP MAIDEN STKS (DIV II) 6f 8y

4:30 (4:31) (Class 4) 2-Y-O

£5,504 (£1,637; £818; £408) **Stalls** Centre

Form — RPR

0 1 **Wave Aside**[88] 3323 2-9-3 0 LDettori 9 88+
(B J Meehan) *lw: in rr but in tch: drvn along over 2f out: gd prog over 1f out: rdn to ld fnl 100yds: sn in command: readily* **9/1**[3]

453 2 2 **Invincible Heart (GR)**[9] 5794 2-9-3 0 JohnEgan 10 82
(Jane Chapple-Hyam) *lw: chsd ldrs: rdn to chal ins fnl 2f: led over 1f out: hdd and outpcd fnl 100yds* **8/11**[1]

3 ½ **Bennelong** 2-9-3 0 GeorgeBaker 1 81
(R M Beckett) *w'like: lw: led: rdn whn chal ins fnl 2f: hdd over 1f out: outpcd ins fnl f* **12/1**

4 4 3 ¾ **Star Links (USA)**[11] 5754 2-9-3 0 RyanMoore 11 69
(R Hannon) *w'like: lw: in tch: rdn and styd on to chse ldrs over 2f out wknd over 1f out* **4/1**[2]

5 1 ¼ **Battle** 2-9-3 0 SteveDrowne 4 66
(H Morrison) *w'like: bit bkwd: towards rr: styng on whn hung lft ins fnl 2f: kpt on again fnl f wout ever looking a threat* **16/1**

6 2 ½ **The Happy Hammer (IRE)** 2-9-3 0 ShaneKelly 2 58
(T Keddy) *w'like: chsd ldrs: rdn over 2f out: wknd sn after* **66/1**

0 7 ½ **Rest By The River**[37] 4974 2-8-12 0 LPKeniry 3 52
(A G Newcombe) *in tch: pushed along and one pce over 2f out: mod prog ins fnl f* **100/1**

8 1 ½ **Castleburg** 2-8-12 0 TPQueally 7 47+
(G L Moore) *unf: scope: chsd ldrs: rdn and green whn n.m.r and wknd ins fnl 2f* **16/1**

9 1 **Chateauneuf (IRE)** 2-8-12 0 TonyCulhane 5 44
(B W Hills) *unf: scope: a towards rr* **25/1**

10 13 **Oisin's Boy** 2-9-3 0 KShea 8 10
(J R Boyle) *w'like: bit bkwd: a in rr* **50/1**

11 1 ¼ **Merry May** 2-8-12 0 DaneO'Neill 12 —
(R Hannon) *leggy: s.i.s: a towards rr* **33/1**

1m 13.92s (0.92) **Going Correction** +0.20s/f (Good) **11 Ran SP% 118.6**
Speed ratings (Par 97): **101,98,97,92,91 87,87,85,83,66 64**
toteswinger: 1&2 £2.90, 1&3 £13.70, 2&3 £3.70. CSF £15.75 TOTE £11.10: £2.90, £1.10, £3.90; EX 19.80.

Owner N Attenborough,Mrs L Mann,Mrs L Way **Bred** Rosyground Stud **Trained** Manton, Wilts

FOCUS

They went a fair pace here and the winning time was 0.89sec quicker than the first division.

NOTEBOOK

Wave Aside ◆, who was too green to do himself justice on his debut at Windsor back in June, had been given a little break since and, while he improved to win this time, he once again ran as though still learning his trade. There could be even better to come from him and he will have his chance in the Redcar Two-Year-Old Trophy. (op 8-1)

Invincible Heart(GR) had improved when third in a conditions race at Doncaster last time and an official rating of 95 suggested he had a fine chance back in maiden company, but he disappointed. The ground was really soft on Town Moor, and while his trainer expected this better surface to suit, it is now possible that he needs that sort of ground to show his best. (tchd 10-11 and 1-1 in a place)

Bennelong ◆ shaped encouragingly on his debut, showing plenty of speed and only finding a couple of rivals with more experience too good in the closing stages. He pulled clear of the rest and looks well up to winning his maiden. (op 11-1)

Star Links(USA) was beaten a fair way on his debut but shaped with some promise and this was a step up on that. Still showing signs of inexperience, he looks the type who will do better in handicap company after one more run. (op 11-2 tchd 6-1 in places)

Battle, whose dam was a dual 5f winner at two and is a half-sister to The Trader, looked in need of the experience and should be all the better for the run. (op 10-1)

The Happy Hammer(IRE), who is a half-brother to winning sprinters Genki and Hazelrigg, showed pace and did not run too badly on his debut. Being by Acclamation he might be suited by quicker ground. (tchd 80-1)

Castleburg ran green when the race got a bit more serious, but there was promise there and she is bred to stay further in time. (tchd 14-1)

6078 DUBAI DUTY FREE FINEST SURPRISE (H'CAP) 1m 2f 6y
5:05 (5:06) (Class 4) (0-85,85) 3-Y-0+ **£5,180** (£1,541; £770; £384) **Stalls** Low

Form RPR
3352 **1** **Dar Es Salaam**[8] [5843] 4-8-9 **70** .... TPQueally 1 84
(J S Goldie) *chsd ldrs: led over 1f out: styd on wl to go clr ins fnl f* **4/1**[1]
5021 **2** *3 1/4* **Cupid's Glory**[15] [5630] 6-9-1 **76** .... GeorgeBaker 16 84
(G L Moore) *rr: hdwy on ins fr 3f out: rdn and hung lft fr 2f out: chsd wnr ins fnl f but a readily hld* **5/1**[2]
4125 **3** *1 1/4* **Slip**[18] [5573] 3-8-11 **85** .... KatiaScallan(7) 5 90
(M P Tregoning) *hld up in rr: hdwy on rails fr 3f out: n.m.r and swtchd rt over 1f out: kpt on ins fnl f but nvr gng pce to trble ldng duo* **8/1**
1034 **4** *1/2* **Buddy Holly**[34] [5098] 3-8-13 **80** .... DaneO'Neill 14 84
(Pat Eddery) *lw: chsd ldrs: led appr fnl 2f: and sn rdn: hdd over 1f out: wknd ins fnl f* **11/2**[3]
3130 **5** *1* **Stow**[48] [4621] 3-8-10 **77** .... SteveDrowne 10 79
(H Morrison) *swtg: in rr: rdn over 3f out: hdwy on outside fr 2f out: styd on ins fnl f and gng on cl home but nvr a threat* **7/1**
0010 **6** *1 1/2* **Tri Nations (UAE)**[27] [5279] 3-9-3 **84** .... EddieAhern 11 83
(J W Hills) *hld up in rr: hdwy fr 3f out: styd on to chse ldrs ins fnl 2f: one pce appr fnl f* **12/1**
0660 **7** *nk* **Black Rain**[13] [5699] 3-8-6 **73** ow2 .... (v) JohnEgan 9 71
(P J McBride) *in rr: rdn and sme hdwy on outside 3f out: nvr in contention and wknd over 1f out* **16/1**
035/ **8** *1/2* **Power Elite (IRE)**[15] [5654] 8-9-8 **83** .... TonyCulhane 4 80
(K A Morgan) *chsd ldrs: pushed along over 3f out: styd wl there tl wknd over 1f out* **33/1**
0000 **9** *nk* **Jadalee (IRE)**[22] [5423] 5-9-5 **80** .... (t) HayleyTurner 6 77
(G A Butler) *in rr: pushed along 3f out: mod prog fnl 2f* **33/1**
64 **10** *1* **Baylini**[19] [5536] 4-9-4 **79** .... JamesDoyle 15 74
(Ms J S Doyle) *led: rdn 3f out: hdd appr fnl 2f: sn btn* **20/1**
6125 **11** *2 3/4* **Higgy's Boy (IRE)**[11] [5759] 3-9-2 **83** .... RyanMoore 3 72
(R Hannon) *lw: chsd ldrs: rdn 3f out: wknd 2f out* **6/1**
0-03 **12** *2 1/4* **Encircled**[111] [2593] 4-9-3 **78** .... LPKeniry 2 63
(D Haydn Jones) *nvr bttr than mid-div* **20/1**
5500 **13** *2 1/4* **Shake On It**[29] [5209] 4-9-2 **77** .... StephenCarson 13 57
(Eve Johnson Houghton) *chsd ldrs: rdn 3f out: wknd qckly 2f out* **25/1**
0 **14** *4 1/2* **Wild Desert (FR)**[35] [5070] 3-9-4 **85** .... StephenDonohoe 8 56
(Ian Williams) *lw: chsd ldrs over 5f* **18/1**
250- **15** *14* **Ravenna**[353] [5892] 4-9-0 **75** .... TPO'Shea 12 18
(J R Gask) *sn bhd* **40/1**

2m 9.24s (0.44) **Going Correction** +0.25s/f (Good)
WFA 3 from 4yo+ 6lb **15** Ran SP% **130.5**
Speed ratings (Par 105): **108,105,104,104,103 102,101,101,101,100 98,96,94,90,79**
toteswinger: 1&2 £3.40, 1&3 £10.60, 2&3 £12.70. CSF £23.12 CT £164.26 TOTE £4.00: £1.80, £2.70, £3.20; EX 19.10.
Owner John Macgregor **Bred** Cliveden Stud Ltd **Trained** Uplawmoor, E Renfrews

FOCUS
Sound form, with the well-treated winner reproducing his Sandown form and the second to his recent all-weather form. The third and fourth ran to their marks.

6079 DUBAI DUTY FREE FOUNDATION H'CAP 1m 4f 5y
5:35 (5:36) (Class 4) (0-85,85) 3-Y-0+ **£5,180** (£1,541; £770; £384) **Stalls** Low

Form RPR
4412 **1** **Times Vital (IRE)**[7] [5865] 3-8-10 **76** .... DeanMcKeown 18 91
(E J O'Neill) *lw: s.i.s: hld up in rr: gd hdwy on outside fr 3f out: drvn and qcknd to press ldr jst ins fnl f: led fnl 110yds: all out* **11/2**[2]
0133 **2** *1/2* **Howdigo**[8] [5843] 3-9-1 **81** .... LDettori 10 95
(J R Best) *in tch: rdn and hdwy fr 3f out: slt ld wl over 1f out: hdd and no ex fnl 110yds but stl wl clr of 3rd* **4/1**[1]
1-12 **3** *4 1/2* **The Carlton Cannes**[150] [1547] 4-9-12 **84** .... TPO'Shea 1 91
(G Wragg) *chsd ldrs: rdn along 3f out: styd on to go 3rd fnl f but nvr any ch w ldng duo* **14/1**
3416 **4** *1* **Miss Rochester (IRE)**[36] [5024] 3-8-12 **78** .... RyanMoore 3 83
(Sir Michael Stoute) *chsd ldrs: rdn 3f out: styd on same pce fnl 2f* **13/2**[3]
503 **5** *3/4* **Ballochroy (IRE)**[34] [5098] 3-9-2 **82** .... TonyCulhane 8 86
(B W Hills) *chsd ldrs: drvn along over 3f out: one pce fnl 2f* **16/1**
5313 **6** *nk* **Killcara Boy**[21] [5464] 3-9-2 **82** .... DaneO'Neill 16 86
(H Candy) *sn pressing ldr: led over 3f out: hdd 2f out and sn wknd* **8/1**
6-11 **7** *nk* **Force Group (IRE)**[142] [1732] 4-9-2 **74** .... JohnEgan 14 77
(M H Tompkins) *lw: in rr tl rdn and hdwy 3f out: no imp on ldrs fr 2f out and styd on same pce* **11/1**
061 **8** *1 1/2* **Look To This Day**[28] [5216] 3-8-12 **78** .... HayleyTurner 11 79
(R Charlton) *lw: in rr tl hdwy on outside fr 3f out: edgd lft u.p fr 2f out: kpt on but nvr in contention* **14/1**
350/ **9** *1/2* **Forthright**[44] [4611] 7-9-4 **83** .... (t) KylieManser(7) 5 83
(B G Powell) *lw: in rr: hdwy 3f out: nt clr run 2f out: swtchd rt sn after and styd on fnl f: nvr nr ldrs* **40/1**
613- **10** *1* **Esthlos (FR)**[336] [6302] 5-9-11 **83** .... GregFairley 12 81
(J Jay) *chsd ldrs: rdn and slt ld appr fnl 2f: hdd & wknd wl over 1f out* **20/1**
1022 **11** *1 1/4* **Sleepy Hollow**[34] [5100] 3-8-12 **78** .... SteveDrowne 2 74
(H Morrison) *in rr: sme hdwy on ins over 2f out but nvr in contention* **10/1**
1350 **12** *1 1/2* **Trachonitis (IRE)**[36] [5017] 4-9-6 **78** .... StephenDonohoe 4 72
(J R Jenkins) *in rr tl sme hdwy 3f out: n.d sn after* **33/1**
0150 **13** *4 1/2* **Sinbad The Sailor**[21] [5472] 3-8-8 **74** .... EddieAhern 13 66+
(J W Hills) *lw: in rr: rdn and styng on whn nt clr run over 2f out: nvr a factor after* **12/1**
026- **14** *4* **Shavansky**[126] [2402] 4-9-7 **79** .... StephenCarson 17 59
(C J Mann) *chsd ldrs: rdn 3f out: wknd over 2f out* **25/1**
1-20 **15** *6* **Nawow**[129] [2076] 8-9-5 **77** .... SimonWhitworth 9 48
(P D Cundell) *slt ld tl hdd over 3f out: grad wknd* **50/1**
2516 **16** *5* **Dalhaan (USA)**[57] [4351] 3-9-5 **85** .... TPQueally 15 48
(J L Dunlop) *in tch: chsd ldrs 4f out: wknd 3f out* **28/1**

2m 36.91s (1.41) **Going Correction** +0.25s/f (Good)
WFA 3 from 4yo+ 8lb **16** Ran SP% **123.6**
Speed ratings (Par 105): **105,104,101,101,100 100,100,99,98,98 97,96,93,90,86 83**
toteswinger: 1&2 £7.20, 1&3 £12.50, 2&3 £9.60. CSF £25.86 CT £304.20 TOTE £6.60: £2.40, £1.80, £2.90, £2.20; EX 37.10 Place 6: £56.23 Place 5: £46.42 .
Owner G A Lucas **Bred** Miss Louise Fitzgerald **Trained** Averham Park, Notts

FOCUS
A competitive handicap on paper, but the finish was totally dominated by two progressive three-year-olds who were officially well in at the weights. Solid form.
T/Plt: £75.40 to a £1 stake. Pool: £57,906.39. 560.50 winning tickets. T/Qpdt: £33.20 to a £1 stake. Pool: £3,007.69. 66.90 winning tickets. ST

5271
NEWMARKET (ROWLEY) (R-H)
Friday, September 19

OFFICIAL GOING: Good to firm (9.2)
There was a significant bias towards those drawn high in most races, despite them racing up the middle of the track throughout.
Wind: Almost nil Weather: Fine and sunny

6080 EXPRESS COFFEE CARS MEDIAN AUCTION MAIDEN STKS 6f
1:55 (1:58) (Class 4) 2-Y-O **£5,180** (£1,541; £770; £384) **Stalls** Centre

Form RPR
5 **1** **Archie Rice (USA)**[56] [4394] 2-9-3 0 .... AlanMunro 19 84
(W Jarvis) *unf: scope: led: hdd over 4f out: chsd ldrs tl led over 1f out: sn rdn: jst hld on* **4/1**[1]
2 *shd* **Winged Harriet (IRE)** 2-8-12 0 .... LiamJones 16 79+
(W J Haggas) *w'like: leggy: hld up: racd keenly: swtchd lft and hdwy over 1f out: r.o wl* **25/1**
3 *1 3/4* **Shabib (USA)** 2-9-3 0 .... RHills 20 78
(B W Hills) *strong: lw: trckd ldrs: rdn over 1f out: styd on* **7/1**
3 **4** *nk* **Bounty Box**[43] [4792] 2-8-9 0 .... JackMitchell(3) 8 73+
(C F Wall) *w'like: lw: trckd ldrs: racd keenly: led over 2f out: rdn and hdd over 1f out: styd on same pce ins fnl f* **5/1**[2]
5 *1 1/4* **Glowing Praise** 2-9-3 0 .... RichardMullen 15 74
(E S McMahon) *w'like: mid-div: hdwy over 2f out: rdn over 1f out: one pce fnl f* **14/1**
6 *2 1/2* **Quick Single (USA)** 2-9-3 0 .... TQuinn 17 66+
(D R C Elsworth) *w'like: bit bkwd: s.i.s: sn pushed along in rr: styd on ins fnl f: nvr nrr* **40/1**
53 **7** *nk* **Veroon (IRE)**[27] [5277] 2-9-3 0 .... PatCosgrave 13 65
(J G Given) *chsd ldrs: rdn over 2f out: wknd over 1f out* **9/1**
8 *nk* **Margarita (IRE)** 2-8-12 0 .... OscarUrbina 14 60+
(J R Fanshawe) *leggy: sn pushed along in rr: styd on ins fnl f: nvr nrr* **16/1**
3 **9** *shd* **Larkham (USA)**[34] [5099] 2-9-3 0 .... ChrisCatlin 5 64
(R M Beckett) *chsd ldrs: rdn over 2f out: wknd fnl f* **6/1**[3]
543 **10** *1* **Retro (IRE)**[16] [5609] 2-9-3 80 .... JimCrowley 2 61
(R Hannon) *swtg: hld up in tch: rdn over 1f out: sn edgd rt and wknd* **7/1**
11 *nse* **Border Maid** 2-8-12 0 .... NeilPollard 3 56
(E A L Dunlop) *w'like: scope: bit bkwd: prom: racd keenly: rdn over 2f out: wknd fnl f* **66/1**
60 **12** *1/2* **Spinning Belle (IRE)**[19] [5535] 2-8-12 0 .... MichaelHills 6 55
(J W Hills) *plld hrd and prom: wknd over 1f out* **25/1**
13 *1/2* **The Hague** 2-9-3 0 .... JimmyFortune 1 58
(J H M Gosden) *w'like: leggy: dwlt: hld up: a in rr* **14/1**
14 *1 1/2* **Full Blue** 2-8-12 0 .... AdrianMcCarthy 18 49
(S C Williams) *w'like: bit bkwd: mid-div: wknd wl over 1f out* **100/1**
15 *2 1/2* **Bishop Rock (USA)** 2-9-3 0 .... JimmyQuinn 10 46
(M H Tompkins) *leggy: unf: s.i.s: a in rr* **66/1**
0 **16** *1/2* **Red Horse (IRE)**[35] [5066] 2-9-3 0 .... JamieSpencer 4 45
(M L W Bell) *bit bkwd: s.s: outpcd* **40/1**
17 *3/4* **Northern Hero (IRE)** 2-9-3 0 .... TGMcLaughlin 7 42
(E A L Dunlop) *w'like: strong: bit bkwd: s.i.s: a in rr* **66/1**
05 **18** *1 1/2* **Billy Beetroot (USA)**[94] [3114] 2-8-12 0 .... WilliamCarson(5) 12 38
(S C Williams) *chsd ldrs: led over 4f out tl over 2f out: wknd over 1f out* **66/1**

1m 12.56s (0.36) **Going Correction** 0.0s/f (Good) **18** Ran SP% **124.7**
Speed ratings (Par 97): **97,96,94,94,92 89,88,88,88,86 86,86,85,83,80 79,78,76**
toteswinger: 1&2 £24.10, 1&3 £4.70, 2&3 £53.70. CSF £114.39 TOTE £5.20: £2.50, £6.30, £3.30; EX 165.20.
Owner Anthony Foster **Bred** Baltusrol Thoughbreds Llc Et Al **Trained** Newmarket, Suffolk

FOCUS
This looked an ordinary maiden by Newmarket's usual standards, but plenty of nice types lined up and the race should still produce a good few winners. They raced up the middle of the track and, although on the eye there did not seem to be any bias, the race was dominated by those drawn in double figures.

NOTEBOOK
Archie Rice(USA) ◆ was well backed and confirmed the promise he showed when fifth on his debut over 7f at York. He is sprint bred, so this drop in trip suited, and he stuck on well after showing good speed throughout, although he would have been passed in another stride. Although the form is probably nothing out of the ordinary, he has some size and scope and looks capable of progress. (op 13-2)

Winged Harriet(IRE), a 115,000gns daughter of Hawk Wing, half-sister to dual 6f-7f Listed winner Misu Bond, out of a 1m scorer, was out the back early after starting slowly, but she travelled kindly and, once switched nearside, she picked up from a good five or so lengths behind under hands-and-heels riding. The way she finished was actually reminiscent of her sire's effort in his 2,000 Guineas (although at a completely different level) and, like Hawk Wing, she carried her head just a touch proud. She is clearly talented; it just has to be hoped she goes the right way mentally.

Shabib(USA), a half-brother to a 1m winner, out of a dual 7f juvenile winner, was never too far away and kept on to the line. He should know more next time. (op 9-2)

Bounty Box confirmed the ability she showed when third on her debut at Yarmouth and might need rating even better than the bare form as she was the only horse in the first eight drawn in a single-figure stall. However, she may just have her own ideas as she was reluctant to go behind the stalls beforehand (her jockey had to get off and she was walked round) and, in the race itself, having shown good speed, she did not find quite as much as had looked likely. She has the ability to win races; it's probably just a question of which way she will go, but she is with the right trainer to fulfil her potential. (op 7-2)

Glowing Praise ◆, a 14,000gns son of Fantastic Light, out of a 1m winner, was backed at big prices and showed ability. He can do better when stepped up in trip and could be half decent next year. (op 25-1)

Quick Single(USA), a £24,000 brother to dual 6f-1m1f dirt winner Donerella, ran green early and was doing his best work at the finish. (op 33-1)

Veroon(IRE) showed speed but dropped out tamely and was below the form he showed when third in a weak sales race on the July course last time. He might prefer easier ground. (op 12-1)

Margarita(IRE), a sister to the stable's top-class miler Soviet Song, lacked the speed of some of these and ran green, but she was going on at the finish.

Larkham(USA), whose trainer won this last year, dropped out disappointingly and could not confirm the promise he showed when third in a maiden over this trip at the July course on his debut. (op 8-1)

Red Horse(IRE) Official explanation: jockey said gelding lost a shoe

6081 E B F ORIENTAL FOODS AND NORFOLK ICE-CREAM MAIDEN FILLIES' STKS — 1m

2:30 (2:32) (Class 4) 2-Y-O — **£6,476** (£1,927; £963; £481) **Stalls** Centre

Form — RPR

03 **1** **Midday**[28] 5241 2-9-0 0 .... TedDurcan 19 — 85
(H R A Cecil) *lw: w.w wl in tch: hdwy over 3f out: ev ch over 2f out: rdn 2f out: c clr w ldr over 1f out: styd on wl to ld wl ins fnl f* **10/11**[1]

22 **2** *shd* **Three Moons (IRE)**[15] 5643 2-9-0 0 .... RichardMullen 13 — 85
(H J L Dunlop) *chsd ldrs tl led 3f out: rdn over 2f out: c clr w wnr over 1f out: hdd and no ex wl ins fnl f* **11/2**[2]

3 **3** *3* **Featherweight (IRE)**[10] 5788 2-9-0 0 .... MichaelHills 15 — 78
(B W Hills) *w'like: t.k.h: chsd ldrs: rdn and unable qck 3f out: kpt on u.p fnl f: snatched 3rd last strides* **8/1**

64 **4** *hd* **Al Tamooh (IRE)**[15] 5640 2-9-0 0 .... RHills 16 — 78
(J L Dunlop) *lw: t.k.h: chsd ldr: ev ch 3f out: rdn over 2f out: outpcd wl over 1f out: kpt on same pce fnl f: lost 3rd last strides* **15/2**[3]

5 *5* **Aromatic** 2-9-0 0 .... JimmyFortune 4 — 67+
(J H M Gosden) *w'like: strong: bit bkwd: in tch: pushed along and hdwy over 3f out: ev ch and rdn wl over 2f out: wknd over 1f out* **16/1**

6 *3/4* **Inhibition** 2-8-9 0 .... DavidProbert(5) 11 — 65
(A M Balding) *unf: s.i.s: bhd: hdwy 5f out: chsd ldrs and rdn 3f out: wknd over 2f out: wl hld whn hung rt over 1f out* **33/1**

7 *2 1/4* **Take The Hint** 2-9-0 0 .... JimCrowley 6 — 60+
(J H M Gosden) *w'like: bit bkwd: bhd: styd on steadily last 3f: nvr trbld ldrs* **25/1**

8 *1 3/4* **Dulcie** 2-9-0 0 .... LiamJones 14 — 56
(M H Tompkins) *w'like: wnt rt and stdd s: hld up in midfield: pushed along and outpcd over 3f out: sltly short of room and swtchd rt wl over 1f out: styd on fnl f* **100/1**

43 **9** *hd* **Demeanour (USA)**[40] 4897 2-9-0 0 .... JamieSpencer 1 — 56+
(E A L Dunlop) *racd in pair towards stands' side tl 1/2-way: chsd ldrs: ev ch and rdn 3f out: wknd over 2f out* **16/1**

00 **10** *3 1/2* **Aula**[10] 5788 2-9-0 0 .... TGMcLaughlin 17 — 48
(E A L Dunlop) *s.i.s: hld up bhd: hdwy 1/2-way: drvn and no prog over 2f out: wl btn fnl f* **100/1**

0 **11** *1/2* **Highland Burn**[15] 5643 2-9-0 0 .... TQuinn 3 — 47+
(D R C Elsworth) *racd in pair towards stands' side tl 1/2-way: in tch: rdn and wknd 3f out: wl btn fnl 2f* **66/1**

12 *2 1/2* **Ela Gorrie Mou** 2-8-9 0 .... MCGeran(5) 18 — 42
(T T Clement) *w'like: led tl 3f out: sn rdn and wknd: wl btn last 2f* **100/1**

13 *2 1/2* **Blessing Belle (IRE)** 2-9-0 0 .... JimmyQuinn 7 — 36
(M H Tompkins) *w'like: leggy: stdd s: hld up bhd: shkn up over 3f out: sn outpcd and no ch* **66/1**

14 *4 1/2* **Peal Park** 2-8-11 0 .... PatrickHills(3) 10 — 26
(B J Meehan) *leggy: t.k.h: chsd ldrs tl rdn and wknd qckly over 3f out: wl bhd over 2f out* **66/1**

0 **15** *1 1/2* **Lily Of The Nile (UAE)**[26] 5314 2-9-0 0 .... PatCosgrave 8 — 23
(J G Portman) *t.k.h: chsd ldrs tl rdn and wknd qckly over 3f out: sn wl bhd* **66/1**

16 *shd* **Coka (IRE)** 2-9-0 0 .... KirstyMilczarek 5 — 23
(Miss D Mountain) *neat: hld up in tch in midfield: rdn and struggling over 3f out: wl bhd last 2f* **100/1**

00 **17** *4 1/2* **Sutania**[18] 5571 2-9-0 0 .... JerryO'Dwyer 9 — 13
(P F I Cole) *in tch tl 1/2-way: sn rdn and struggling: t.o fnl f* **100/1**

00 **18** *6* **Guilin (IRE)**[18] 5570 2-9-0 0 .... ChrisCatlin 2 — —
(P F I Cole) *stdd s: hld up bhd: rdn and lost tch over 3f out: t.o last 2f* **100/1**

1m 37.96s (-0.64) **Going Correction** 0.0s/f (Good) — **18** Ran SP% **121.1**
Speed ratings (Par 94): **103,102,99,99,94 93,91,89,89,86 85,83,80,76,74 74,70,64**
toteswinger: 1&2 £2.30, 1&3 £2.40, 2&3 £5.90. CSF £5.31 TOTE £2.00: £1.10, £2.00, £2.20; EX 6.90.
Owner K Abdulla **Bred** Juddmonte Farms Ltd **Trained** Newmarket, Suffolk

FOCUS
Often a good fillies' maiden and the race should produce some nice winners. They raced up the middle of the track, which you would think would make it a level-playing field but, just as in the first race, those in double-figure stalls dominated. The winning time was 0.74 seconds quicker than the later juvenile maiden contested by only colts and geldings.

NOTEBOOK
Midday ◆, whose trainer won this race in 2006 with subsequent Oaks winner Light Shift, repeated the trick with a filly who, like Henry Cecil's latest winner of this race, was having her third start and had previously finished third in a 7f maiden on the July course last time. Although Cecil was apparently keen to play down this one's prospects, Ted Durcan felt she was just running a little lazily, suggesting there is plenty more to come, and she rates as a very useful prospect. She may have one more run this year and is expected to stay 1m2f next season. (op 5-6 tchd Evens, 4-5 in a place)
Three Moons(IRE) ◆ travelled nicely and kept on well for pressure but, just as on her first two starts, she found one too good, although only just. This was a decent effort in defeat and she looks very useful. (op 9-2 tchd 4-1)
Featherweight(IRE), who finished well in a weaker maiden than this over 7f on Polytrack at Lingfield on her debut, kept on for third without ever posing a threat. She should stay 1m2f next year. (op 11-1)
Al Tamooh(IRE) raced with no cover and was too keen for her own good on this step up in trip. She is bred to stay even further, but will need to learn to settle better. (op 12-1)
Aromatic ◆, a sister to 1m3f winner Red Petal, is one to take from the race. She was not helped by racing more towards the near side than those who finished in front of her, but kept on really nicely and easily fared best of those from a single-figure stall. She rates as a very useful prospect. (op 10-1)
Inhibition ◆, by Nayef, half-sister to among others high-class miler Passing Glance, shaped nicely further back in the field and is open to a good deal of improvement. (tchd 28-1)
Take The Hint, like her stablemate in fourth, was not helped by a single-figure stall but this daughter of Montjeu, half-sister to among others smart 7f-1m performer Stronghold, showed ability and is open to improvement. (op 33-1 tchd 20-1)
Dulcie stayed on well enough further back in the field, despite meeting a bit of trouble, and should do better over further next year.
Demeanour(USA), beaten at short odds over 7f at Redcar on her previous start, is better than she showed as she was one of only two to race towards the near side early, well away from the others, and that was not the place to be. Official explanation: jockey said filly hung right and had no more to give

6082 EXPRESS CAFES NURSERY — 7f

3:05 (3:08) (Class 3) (0-95,94) 2-Y-O — **£9,066** (£2,697; £1,348; £673) **Stalls** Centre

Form — RPR

3214 **1** **Johnmanderville**[73] 3809 2-8-1 74 .... LiamJones 14 — 78
(K R Burke) *w'like: scope: led over 4f: rdn to ld ins fnl f: r.o* **16/1**

344 **2** *1/2* **Russian George (IRE)**[43] 4780 2-7-13 75 .... DominicFox(3) 13 — 77
(T P Tate) *neat: chsd ldrs: pushed along 1/2-way: led over 2f out: sn rdn: hdd ins fnl f: styd on* **14/1**

51 **3** *1/2* **Absent Pleasure (USA)**[27] 5271 2-9-1 88 .... JamieSpencer 3 — 91+
(B J Meehan) *hld up: plld hrd: hdwy over 1f out: hrd rdn and ev ch ins fnl f: unable qck towards fin* **5/4**[1]

5130 **4** *nk* **Cornish Rose (IRE)**[49] 4589 2-7-12 71 oh2 .... JimmyQuinn 7 — 71
(M H Tompkins) *hld up: hdwy over 1f out: sn rdn: styd on* **66/1**

101 **5** *hd* **Swingfire (USA)**[18] 5581 2-7-6 72 oh1 ow1 .... (p) AndreaAtzeni(7) 11 — 72
(R M H Cowell) *hld up: swtchd rt and hdwy over 1f out: sn rdn styd on* **16/1**

033 **6** *1* **Brooksby**[17] 5584 2-7-12 71 oh1 .... DavidKinsella 12 — 68+
(R Hannon) *chsd ldrs: rdn over 2f out: styd on same pce fnl f* **16/1**

6154 **7** *shd* **Agente Parmigiano (IRE)**[42] 4822 2-8-12 90 Louis-PhilippeBeuzelin(5) 6 — 87
(G A Butler) *chsd ldrs: rdn over 2f out: styd on same pce fnl f* **33/1**

6151 **8** *hd* **Swift Chap**[20] 5511 2-8-10 83 .... AlanMunro 9 — 80
(B R Millman) *chsd ldrs: rdn over 1f out: styd on same pce ins fnl f* **7/1**[3]

041 **9** *3/4* **Cyflymder (IRE)**[29] 5200 2-8-5 78 .... RichardMullen 1 — 73+
(J G Given) *w'like: s.i.s: hld up: hdwy 1/2-way: rdn over 2f out: styd on same pce fnl f* **20/1**

3012 **10** *nse* **Perfect Citizen (USA)**[27] 5274 2-8-13 86 .... JimCrowley 10 — 81+
(W R Swinburn) *s.i.s: hld up: rdn over 2f out: styd on ins fnl f: nt trble ldrs* **5/1**[2]

4314 **11** *1/2* **Senatorial**[81] 3553 2-8-7 80 ow1 .... MichaelHills 5 — 73
(B W Hills) *prom: outpcd 2f out: styd on ins fnl f* **25/1**

435 **12** *1 3/4* **Versaki (IRE)**[15] 5641 2-9-7 94 .... JimmyFortune 8 — 83
(R Hannon) *chsd ldrs: rdn over 2f out: hung rt over 1f out: wknd fnl f* **33/1**

6016 **13** *21* **Oriental Rose**[41] 4874 2-8-0 73 .... NickyMackay 4 — 9
(G M Moore) *hld up in tch: rdn over 2f out: sn wknd* **33/1**

12 **14** *1 1/2* **Kings Troop**[42] 4828 2-8-13 86 .... TedDurcan 2 — 19
(H R A Cecil) *s.i.s: hld up: hdwy 1/2-way: hung rt and wknd over 2f out: eased* **14/1**

1m 25.16s (-0.24) **Going Correction** 0.0s/f (Good) — **14** Ran SP% **123.5**
Speed ratings (Par 99): **101,100,99,99,99 98,98,97,96,96 96,94,70,68**
toteswinger: 1&2 £45.80, 1&3 £13.30, 2&3 £59.50. CSF £211.68 CT £500.63 TOTE £21.50: £4.70, £4.10, £1.50; EX 220.20.
Owner Jet Racing Partnership **Bred** Natton House Thoroughbreds & Mark Woodall **Trained** Middleham Moor, N Yorks
■ Stewards' Enquiry : Andrea Atzeni five-day ban: excessive use of the whip (Oct 3-4, 6-8)

FOCUS
All bar two of these had already won at least one race and this was a decent, competitive nursery. However, just as in the first two races there was a big draw bias, with those in double-figure stalls very much at an advantage.

NOTEBOOK
Johnmanderville ◆ looked to be found out in a half-decent nursery over 6f at Pontefract last time, but he had been off the track for over two months since then and improved for this step up to 7f on his return. He is a horse with plenty of size and also seems pretty tough, so he should make a nice handicapper next year. (op 20-1)
Russian George(IRE), gelded since he was last seen, was dropped in trip for his handicap debut. Having chased the winner throughout, he kept on strongly to the line and ran a good race.
Absent Pleasure(USA) ◆, a Dewhurst entry, did nothing wrong and this rates as a huge effort in defeat. Nothing had finished closer than fourth from a single-figure stall in the two previous races and, berthed in stall three, he looked to be at a big disadvantage held up more towards the near side than many of these. He did well to get so close, very nearly overcoming the bias, and losses will surely be recouped. (op 13-8 tchd 11-10)
Cornish Rose(IRE) ran a good race from 2lb out of the handicap, keeping on well from off the pace to take fourth.
Swingfire(USA) was effectively 8lb higher than when winning a 6f nursery on the turf at Lingfield, but he is a tough sort and kept on to finish close up.
Brooksby ◆ looked the type for a 7f nursery when third in a 6f maiden at Goodwood on her previous start, but this ground was probably too quick. She remains of interest and can win off her current sort of mark when there is some give underfoot. Official explanation: jockey said filly was unsuited by the good to firm ground (op 12-1)
Cyflymder(IRE), who narrowly beat a subsequent winner when landing his maiden at Chester last time, was not helped by the lowest stall of all and is better than he showed.
Versaki(IRE) Official explanation: jockey said colt was unsuited by the good to firm ground
Oriental Rose Official explanation: jockey said filly lost its action

6083 E B F WARRENS OF WARWICK MAIDEN STKS (DIV I) — 7f

3:40 (3:40) (Class 4) 2-Y-O — **£6,152** (£1,830; £914; £456) **Stalls** Centre

Form — RPR

1 **Nehaam** 2-9-3 0 .... RHills 14 — 80+
(J H M Gosden) *unf: scope: in tch: hdwy to chse ldng pair wl over 1f out: rdn and r.o wl to ld fnl 100yds: readily* **9/2**[2]

0 **2** *1 1/4* **Baariq**[34] 5099 2-9-3 0 .... AlanMunro 6 — 76
(P W Chapple-Hyam) *w'like: led tl 3f out: chsd ldr after: rdn and flashed tail over 1f out: ev ch ins fnl f: kpt on same pce fnl 100yds* **16/1**

22 **3** *hd* **Summers Target (USA)**[21] 5469 2-9-3 0 .... JamieSpencer 3 — 75+
(B J Meehan) *lw: taken down early: t.k.h: hld up in midfield tl c to r alone towards stands' rail after 1f: led 3f out: sn clr: drvn over 1f out: hdd fnl 100yds: no ex* **4/5**[1]

0 **4** *shd* **Call It On (IRE)**[60] 4256 2-9-3 0 .... JimmyQuinn 5 — 75+
(M H Tompkins) *leggy: unf: hld up in midfield: hdwy over 2f out: chsd ldng trio over 1f out: kpt on u.p ins fnl f* **66/1**

5 *4 1/2* **Twisted** 2-9-3 0 .... JimmyFortune 2 — 64+
(J H M Gosden) *w'like: scope: bit bkwd: s.i.s: hld up bhd: styd on steadily last 2f: nvr trbld ldrs* **12/1**

60 **6** *1 1/2* **Solar Graphite (IRE)**[36] 5021 2-9-3 0 .... TedDurcan 4 — 60
(J L Dunlop) *chsd ldr tl over 3f out: rdn and outpcd over 2f out: plugged on same pce after* **66/1**

00 **7** *1* **Taste The Wine (IRE)**[62] 4184 2-9-3 0 .... DO'Donohoe 8 — 58
(J R Best) *t.k.h: chsd ldrs: rdn wl over 2f out: wknd u.p 2f out* **66/1**

064 **8** *1/2* **Dalradian (IRE)**[16] 5615 2-9-3 78 .... RichardMullen 9 — 56
(W J Knight) *lw: t.k.h: hld up in tch in midfield: rdn and unable qck over 2f out: no ch fr wl over 1f out* **10/1**[3]

9 *1/2* **Theologist (IRE)** 2-9-3 0 .... JimCrowley 11 — 55
(Mrs A J Perrett) *unf: scope: in tch in midfield: rdn and struggling 3f out: no ch last 2f* **25/1**

10 *1 1/4* **Incendo** 2-9-3 0 .... OscarUrbina 1 — 52
(J R Fanshawe) *w'like: bit bkwd: s.i.s: hld up in tch in rr: shkn up 3f out: sn outpcd: wl btn fnl 2f* **50/1**

0 **11** *nk* **Bob Stock (IRE)**[100] 2951 2-9-3 0 .... NeilPollard 10 — 51
(W J Musson) *strong: stdd s: hld up in tch in rr: shkn up wl over 2f out: nvr trbld ldrs* **100/1**

12 *nse* **Devotion To Duty (IRE)** 2-9-3 0 ..... MichaelHills 13 51
(B W Hills) *w'like: s.i.s: hld up in tch in midfield: rdn and struggling 3f out: no ch last 2f* **10/1**[3]

13 *1 3/4* **Miss Perfectionist** 2-8-12 0 ..... KirstyMilczarek 12 42
(S A Callaghan) *strong: bit bkwd: t.k.h: hld up in tch in midfield: lost pl 3f out: no ch last 2f* **40/1**

1m 26.15s (0.75) **Going Correction** 0.0s/f (Good) **13** Ran SP% **119.2**
Speed ratings (Par 97): **95,93,93,93,88 86,85,84,84,82 82,82,80**
toteswinger: 1&2 £12.00, 1&3 £2.00, 2&3 £6.00. CSF £70.36 TOTE £5.10: £1.80, £3.70, £1.40; EX 126.30.
Owner Hamdan Al Maktoum **Bred** Pollards Stables **Trained** Newmarket, Suffolk

FOCUS
This maiden was probably nothing special but there were some nice types on show. The winning time was 0.99 seconds slower than the previous 0-95 nursery and 0.02 seconds quicker than the second division of this race.

NOTEBOOK
Nehaam ◆, a 200,000gns son of Nayef, half-brother to among others very useful 7f-1m6f winner Astrocharm, proved good enough to make a winning debut. It looked as though he might be held inside the final two furlongs, but he really found his stride coming out of the Dip and, after changing his legs in the final 100 yards or so, he lengthened well. There should be a good deal of improvement to come and his trainer mentioned that he's entered in a big sales race back here in October. He also has entries in the Royal Lodge and the Racing Post Trophy and should make a very decent sort over further next year. (op 4-1)
Baariq ◆ was in front up the middle from a long way out and could not quite sustain his effort after flashing his tail the first two times he was hit with the whip. This was a big improvement on the form he showed on his debut over 6f and he gives the impression he can progress significantly so the flashing of the tail does not look like anything to be worried about. (tchd 20-1)
Summers Target(USA) was taken to race on his own towards the near side of the track by Jamie Spencer. In the three earlier races, the only horse from a single-figure stall to get anywhere near winning was a colt with a Group 1 entry in the nursery, who was in fact ridden by Spencer, so punters who took the short price are entitled to feel a little aggrieved. However, he got warm beforehand and, having been taken down early, he immediately raced keenly in the race itself, so perhaps Spencer felt he would have a better chance of settling if taken away from his rivals. To be fair, although still free, the horse did seem to drop his head a little more once on his own. Whatever the case, the horse was basically no help to his rider and lost this as much by refusing to settle as he did by racing on a possibly unfavoured part of the track. Official explanation: jockey said colt ran too free (op 5-6 tchd 8-11, 10-11 in a place)
Call It On(IRE) stepped up significantly on the form he showed first time up at Yarmouth and was going on at the finish.
Twisted ◆, a 150,000gns son of Selkirk, did not handle the Dip that well but there was plenty to like about the way he kept on. He has a bit of size and should improve and a slightly easier surface may suit better. (op 10-1 tchd 14-1 in a place)
Solar Graphite(IRE) is now qualified for a handicap mark and should find his level.

6084 E B F WARRENS OF WARWICK MAIDEN STKS (DIV II) 7f
4:15 (4:16) (Class 4) 2-Y-O £6,152 (£1,830; £914; £456) **Stalls** Centre

Form RPR

1 **North East Corner (USA)** 2-9-3 0 ..... MichaelHills 14 81
(B W Hills) *unf: scope: chsd ldrs: led over 1f out: rdn out* **5/1**[3]

2 *1/2* **Alhaque (USA)** 2-9-3 0 ..... JamieSpencer 13 80
(P W Chapple-Hyam) *w'like: scope: chsd ldr: rdn and ev ch over 1f out: styd on* **4/1**[2]

3 *2 1/4* **Surrounded** 2-8-12 0 ..... TGMcLaughlin 11 69
(R W Price) *w'like: hld up: hdwy 1/2-way: rdn over 1f out: styd on same pce fnl f* **16/1**

06 4 *1/2* **Survivor's Song**[37] 4982 2-9-3 0 ..... AlanMunro 10 73
(D K Ivory) *led: rdn and hdd over 1f out: no ex ins fnl f* **33/1**

5 *3/4* **Jumaana (IRE)** 2-8-12 0 ..... DO'Donohoe 8 66+
(J L Dunlop) *s.i.s: hld up: hdwy over 1f out: no imp ins fnl f* **33/1**

6 *1* **Just Like Silk (USA)** 2-9-3 0 ..... PatCosgrave 1 69+
(G A Butler) *w'like: hld up: rdn over 2f out: r.o ins fnl f: nrst fin* **14/1**

7 *1/2* **Bravo Echo** 2-9-3 0 ..... JimmyFortune 12 69+
(J H M Gosden) *lengthy: scope: bit bkwd: hld up in tch: racd keenly: hung rt and lost pl over 2f out: n.d after* **5/2**[1]

8 *1* **Kansai Spirit (IRE)** 2-9-3 0 ..... PhilipRobinson 6 65+
(J H M Gosden) *w'like: s.i.s: hld up: shkn up over 2f out: nt trble ldrs* **12/1**

9 *hd* **Orbitor** 2-9-3 0 ..... JimCrowley 3 64+
(M L W Bell) *w'like: s.s: outpcd: styd on ins fnl f: nvr nrr* **14/1**

10 *1 1/4* **Dubai Echo (USA)** 2-9-3 0 ..... RichardMullen 7 61+
(Sir Michael Stoute) *w'like: strong: bit bkwd: sn pushed along in rr: n.d* **9/1**

11 *nk* **Kyleene** 2-8-12 0 ..... TedDurcan 4 55+
(J Noseda) *w'like: prom: rdn over 2f out: wknd over 1f out* **16/1**

12 *1/2* **Gavi** 2-9-3 0 ..... TQuinn 9 59
(W R Swinburn) *w'like: scope: chsd ldrs tl wknd over 1f out* **16/1**

13 *5* **Waheeba** 2-8-12 0 ..... RHills 2 42
(J L Dunlop) *w'like: scope: bit bkwd: mid-div: hdwy 3f out: hung rt and wknd over 1f out* **14/1**

0 14 *5* **Outland (IRE)**[32] 5158 2-9-3 0 ..... JimmyQuinn 5 34
(M H Tompkins) *w'like: hld up: hmpd: hung rt and wknd over 2f out* **40/1**

1m 26.17s (0.77) **Going Correction** 0.0s/f (Good) **14** Ran SP% **128.9**
Speed ratings (Par 97): **95,94,91,91,90 89,88,87,87,85 85,85,79,73**
toteswinger: 1&2 £5.90, 1&3 £32.80, 2&3 £26.90. CSF £26.88 TOTE £5.70: £2.10, £1.90, £5.50; EX 19.20.
Owner Thomas Barr **Bred** Earle I Mack **Trained** Lambourn, Berks

FOCUS
The bias towards those drawn high continued, with the first four emerging from double-figure stalls. The winning time was 1.01 seconds slower than the earlier 0-95 nursery and 0.02 seconds slower than the first division of this race.

NOTEBOOK
North East Corner(USA), a 375,000gns son of Giant's Causeway, first foal of a 7f juvenile winner who was later useful in the US, has been entered in the Dewhurst and produced a likeable effort. He was a touch keen under a positive ride, but was travelling really well within himself, and had plenty left at the business end, staying on well to record a decisive success. He can do even better in a stronger-run race. (tchd 4-1)
Alhaque(USA), a $600,000 son of Galileo, came under pressure before the winner but responded and showed ability in second. Entries in both the Dewhurst and Racing Post Trophy show the regard in which he is held. (tchd 5-1)
Surrounded, a 20,000gns daughter of Distant Music, was backed at big prices in the morning and shaped nicely in third. She travelled well in behind through the early stages and kept on nicely once switched, although she did display a bit of a knee action, suggesting easier ground may suit better. (op 14-1)
Survivor's Song had shown limited form on his first two starts, so his proximity does little for the form, but he is nicely bred and this was clearly an improved effort. He is now qualified for a handicap mark, but this run will not have done his prospective rating any favours.
Jumaana(IRE) ◆, by Selkirk out of a 1m2f winner, was the owner's second string. Having raced a little keenly out the back, she did not seem to handle the Dip all that well and her run just flattened out, but there was promise in this effort. Easier ground may suit. (op 40-1)
Just Like Silk(USA), a 120,000gns daughter of Elusive Quality, first foal of a high-class middle-distance performer, was doing his best work at the finish and should do better over a little further.
Bravo Echo ◆, a son of Oasis Dream, out of a 6f winner, was sent off favourite, but he seemed to become unbalanced when the race got serious and Jimmy Fortune, who never looked happy with him, was unable to get serious. He is much better than his finishing position suggests. Official explanation: jockey said, regarding running and riding, that his orders were to jump out and achieve the best possible placing, adding that the colt ran too keen to halfway, and from 3f out had no more to give. (op 6-1)
Kansai Spirit(IRE), by Sinndar, will know more next time. (tchd 11-1 and 14-1)
Orbitor ◆, a son of Galileo, was well out the back and struggling early but finished well when getting the hang of things late on.
Dubai Echo(USA), a son of Mr Greeley, ran green and was never involved. (op 15-2)
Kyleene gave the impression a flatter track might suit better.
Gavi seemed to need the experience and might be more of a handicap prospect. (tchd 14-1)

6085 MC SEAFOOD MEDIAN AUCTION MAIDEN STKS 1m
4:50 (4:51) (Class 4) 2-Y-O £5,180 (£1,541; £770; £384) **Stalls** Centre

Form RPR

445 1 **Tudor Key (IRE)**[69] 3968 2-9-3 86 ..... JimCrowley 8 88
(Mrs A J Perrett) *lw: t.k.h: hld up in tch: hdwy 3f out: rdn and ev ch over 1f out: led ins fnl f: styd on wl fnl 100yds* **8/1**

0 2 *3/4* **Charlie Tiger (USA)**[120] 2324 2-9-3 0 ..... OscarUrbina 6 86+
(C G Cox) *lw: racd off the pce in midfield: pushed along 1/2-way: hdwy over 2f out: chsd wnr ins fnl f: kpt on* **50/1**

3 *2* **Coiled Spring** 2-9-3 0 ..... PatCosgrave 13 82
(Mrs A J Perrett) *w'like: scope: hld up in midfield: hdwy 3f out: chsd ldrs and swtchd lft over 1f out: sn led: hdd ins fnl f: one pce fnl 100yds* **33/1**

0 4 *3 1/4* **Hula King (GER)**[27] 5271 2-9-3 0 ..... JimmyFortune 15 75
(B J Meehan) *lw: racd in midfield: rdn 1/2-way: hdwy u.p jst over 2f out: chsd ldrs over 1f out: wknd jst ins fnl f* **11/4**[1]

0 5 *1 1/2* **Orthology (IRE)**[14] 5672 2-9-3 0 ..... JimmyQuinn 11 72
(M H Tompkins) *towards rr: pushed along and unable qck 3f out: styd on fr over 1f out: nt trble ldrs* **100/1**

6 *1 1/4* **It's A Mans World** 2-9-3 0 ..... AlanMunro 9 69
(P W Chapple-Hyam) *w'like: bit bkwd: chsd clr ldr: clsd over 1f out: rdn and sn ev ch: wknd ent fnl f* **16/1**

236 7 *3/4* **Dreamwalk (IRE)**[43] 4788 2-9-3 83 ..... JamieSpencer 14 67
(R M Beckett) *chsd ldrs: rdn and lost pl 1/2-way: drvn over 2f out: swtchd rt over 1f out: no prog u.p fnl f* **4/1**[2]

8 *nk* **Darwin's Dragon** 2-9-3 0 ..... NelsonDeSouza 10 66
(P F I Cole) *w'like: bit bkwd: t.k.h: chsd ldrs: clsd over 1f out: rdn and ev ch briefly over 1f out: sn wknd* **66/1**

5 9 *2* **Harlestone Snake**[43] 4788 2-9-3 0 ..... RHills 16 62
(J L Dunlop) *s.i.s: hld up towards rr: hdwy 3f out: chsd ldrs over 1f out: sn shkn up and no prog* **16/1**

10 *2* **Opinion Poll (IRE)** 2-9-3 0 ..... PhilipRobinson 7 58+
(M A Jarvis) *w'like: sn bhd: detached last 1/2-way: sme late hdwy: n.d* **8/1**

64 11 *nk* **Shooting Party (IRE)**[25] 5344 2-9-3 0 ..... RichardMullen 1 57
(R Hannon) *towards rr: rdn 1/2-way: hdwy u.p 2f out: wknd over 1f out* **20/1**

0 12 *1/2* **Cornish Castle (USA)**[28] 5246 2-9-3 0 ..... TedDurcan 4 56
(H R A Cecil) *chsd ldrs: rdn over 3f out: wknd u.p 2f out: wl btn fnl f* **7/1**[3]

4 13 *3 1/2* **Omnium Duke (IRE)**[28] 5225 2-9-3 0 ..... MichaelHills 17 48
(J W Hills) *hld up in tch: effrt to chse ldrs over 1f out: sn rdn and wknd* **7/1**[3]

0 14 *1* **New Adventure**[78] 3645 2-9-3 0 ..... KirstyMilczarek 18 46
(P F I Cole) *chsd ldrs: rdn wl over 2f out: wknd 2f out: wl bhd fnl f* **28/1**

00 15 *1* **Highland River**[32] 5158 2-9-3 0 ..... TQuinn 3 44
(D R C Elsworth) *a bhd: struggling fr 1/2-way: wl bhd last 2f* **50/1**

16 *nse* **Daredevil Dan** 2-9-3 0 ..... AdrianMcCarthy 2 44
(M H Tompkins) *w'like: bit bkwd: bhd: struggling 3f out: wl bhd last 2f* **100/1**

500 17 *15* **Itshim**[11] 5753 2-8-12 0 ..... (t) WilliamCarson(5) 12 11
(S C Williams) *racd freely: led: wl clr 1/2-way: tired qckly and hdd over 1f out: sn dropped rt out: eased ins fnl f* **100/1**

1m 38.7s (0.10) **Going Correction** 0.0s/f (Good) **17** Ran SP% **125.2**
Speed ratings (Par 97): **99,98,96,93,91 90,89,89,87,85 84,84,80,79,78 78,63**
toteswinger: 1&2 £76.90, 1&3 £62.30, 2&3 £43.80. CSF £383.47 TOTE £11.80: £2.80, £10.30, £9.40; EX 519.70.
Owner Coombelands Racing Syndicate **Bred** Gainsborough Stud Management Ltd **Trained** Pulborough, W Sussex

FOCUS
An ordinary renewal of what is traditionally quite a good maiden, but there should still be a few winners among them. The winning time was 0.74 seconds slower than the earlier fillies' maiden. They raced up the middle of the track and, unlike in the earlier races, there seemed to be no bias towards those drawn high.

NOTEBOOK
Tudor Key(IRE) was a little keen on this step up to 1m, but he was basically just travelling really strongly and had enough left when asked. His fourth in the Chesham two starts back showed both the regard in which he held, and that he is capable of useful form, and he deserves a step back up in class. (op 7-1)
Charlie Tiger(USA), whose trainer won this with Dunelight in 2005, stepped up massively on the form he showed on his debut at Goodwood. There should be more to come again and he rates as a useful prospect. (tchd 66-1)
Coiled Spring, the first foal of a 1m winner, fared best of the newcomers and this was a pleasing start. He is open to improvement.
Hula King(GER) was beaten as favourite, but he still stepped up on the form he showed over 6f on his debut and is going the right way. (op 3-1 tchd 10-3)
Orthology(IRE) should do better over further once handicapped.
It's A Mans World, a 26,000gns son of Kyllachy, showed ability and might do better on easier ground. It was slightly surprising to see him start off over this trip considering his sire, but his dam was a 1m2f winner.
Dreamwalk(IRE) was below the form he showed on his first two starts at Sandown last time and this was another disappointing effort. He has something to prove now. (op 6-1)
Darwin's Dragon was a little keen but seemed to have his chance.
Harlestone Snake should do better over a lot further when handicapped, and easier ground may suit. (op 25-1)
Opinion Poll(IRE), a son of Halling, was never a threat and seemed to need the experience. Official explanation: jockey said colt stumbled shortly after start (op 15-2 tchd 9-1)
Cornish Castle(USA) did not improve on the form he showed on his debut over 7f at the July course. (op 8-1 tchd 17-2 in a place)

Omnium Duke(IRE) shaped well when fourth on his debut over 7f at Newbury, but this was disappointing. (op 9-2)
New Adventure Official explanation: jockey said colt hung left
Highland River Official explanation: jockey said colt became unbalanced in the dip

6086 TRADITIONAL PIE AND PASTY NURSERY 1m 1f
5:25 (5:26) (Class 4) (0-85,81) 2-Y-O **£6,476** (£1,927; £963; £481) **Stalls** Centre

Form | | | | RPR
003 **1** **Oasis Knight (IRE)**[77] 3682 2-9-3 **77** .... TedDurcan 2 81+
(M P Tregoning) *s.i.s: sn prom: hung rt fr over 2f out: sn rdn: styd on to ld wl ins fnl f* **5/1**[2]
0155 **2** *nk* **Fastnet Storm (IRE)**[36] 5006 2-8-12 **72** .... AlanMunro 7 75
(T P Tate) *led: rdn over 1f out: hdd wl ins fnl f* **5/1**[2]
040 **3** *4* **Rockfella**[28] 5213 2-9-0 **74** .... JamieSpencer 9 69
(D J Coakley) *hld up: swtchd rt and hdwy over 1f out: rdn and hung lft fr over 1f out: styd on same pce ins fnl f* **12/1**
1330 **4** *¾* **Jazacosta (USA)**[17] 5585 2-9-7 **81** .... JimCrowley 6 75
(Mrs A J Perrett) *chsd ldrs: rdn over 1f out: no ex ins fnl f* **3/1**[1]
016 **5** *1 ¼* **Dazinski**[21] 5460 2-8-12 **72** .... RichardMullen 10 64
(M H Tompkins) *hld up: hdwy over 3f out: rdn and edgd lft over 1f out: no ex fnl f* **11/2**[3]
6064 **6** *½* **Give (IRE)**[39] 4925 2-7-12 **58** .... JimmyQuinn 11 49+
(R Hannon) *prom: rdn over 2f out: nt clr run over 1f out: styd on same pce* **10/1**
3300 **7** *2* **Fong's Alibi**[27] 5294 2-8-10 **70** .... PhilipRobinson 5 57
(J S Moore) *chsd ldrs: rdn over 1f out: sn wknd* **14/1**
0361 **8** *3 ½* **One Cool Kitty**[15] 5632 2-8-8 **71** .... DominicFox(3) 3 51
(M G Quinlan) *awkward leaving stalls: hld up: rdn over 3f out: wknd over 1f out* **8/1**
0000 **9** *3 ¼* **Daily Planet (IRE)**[11] 5747 2-7-7 **60** .... AndreaAtzeni(7) 1 34
(B W Duke) *s.i.s: sn prom: rdn over 4f out: wknd 2f out* **100/1**
5543 **10** *9* **Russian Art**[6] 5914 2-7-13 **59** ....(t) AdrianMcCarthy 4 16
(R M Beckett) *prom: rdn over 2f out: wknd and eased wl over 1f out* **8/1**

1m 52.81s (2.21) **Going Correction** 0.0s/f (Good) **10 Ran SP% 120.4**
Speed ratings (Par 97): **90,89,86,85,84 83,82,79,76,68**
toteswinger: 1&2 £6.00, 1&3 £14.70, 2&3 £9.70. CSF £31.35 CT £298.23 TOTE £5.50: £2.30, £2.10, £3.40; EX 42.30 Place 6: £211.14 Place 5: £79.54 .
Owner Lady Tennant **Bred** Deerfield Farm **Trained** Lambourn, Berks

FOCUS
A reasonable nursery.

NOTEBOOK
Oasis Knight(IRE) improved on the form he showed in three runs in maiden company at up to 7f. The track did not look ideal, as he didn't seem to handle the Dip all that well, but he also very much needed his mind making up for him. In that sense he is not too dissimilar to his half-brother, High Accolade, who was talented but often wore headgear (as well as a tongue-tie on a couple of occasions). He gives the impression he is even better than he showed and should make a good three-year-old, but it might be that he will need headgear at some point as well. (op 7-2)
Fastnet Storm(IRE) ran a really game race from the front on his first run beyond an extended 7f, keeping on well all the way to the line. (op 6-1)
Rockfella was stepped up significantly in trip for his nursery debut and showed improved form. (tchd 11-1)
Jazacosta(USA) travelled well for much of the way but did not get home as well as the front three. (op 4-1)
Dazinski was well off the pace early and never posed a threat. He is stoutly bred, so a little better could have been expected on this step up in trip. (op 9-1)
Give(IRE) was keeping on when briefly stopped in her run around a furlong out. (op 11-1)
Russian Art's rider was looking down in the closing stages and something may have been amiss. Official explanation: jockey said colt lost its action (op 7-1)
T/Plt: £70.70 to a £1 stake. Pool: £51,449.19. 530.90 winning tickets. T/Qpdt: £27.70 to a £1 stake. Pool: £2,882.88. 77.00 winning tickets. CR

5866 WOLVERHAMPTON (A.W) (L-H)
Friday, September 19

OFFICIAL GOING: Standard
Wind: Nil Weather: Fine

6087 OPEN A HILLS ACCOUNT - 0800 44 40 40 NURSERY 7f 32y(P)
6:20 (6:20) (Class 5) (0-75,80) 2-Y-O **£4,209** (£1,252; £625; £312) **Stalls** High

Form | | | | RPR
520 **1** **Atabaas Allure (FR)**[23] 5387 2-9-7 **74** .... J-PGuillambert 2 79
(M Johnston) *led: pushed along 3f out: hdd and rdn wl over 1f out: led ins fnl f: r.o* **5/1**[2]
4401 **2** *nk* **Silent Hero**[17] 5591 2-9-3 **70** .... ChrisCatlin 9 74+
(M A Jarvis) *s.i.s: hld up in rr: hdwy over 2f out: swtchd lft over 1f out: rdn to take 2nd towards fin: r.o* **3/1**[1]
030 **3** *1* **Kersivay**[15] 5649 2-9-7 **74** .... AdamKirby 4 76
(W R Swinburn) *hld up in tch: led wl over 1f out: sn edgd rt and rdn: hdd ins fnl f: nt qckn* **7/1**[3]
5132 **4** *2 ¼* **Striding Edge (IRE)**[22] 5432 2-8-10 **68** .... DavidProbert(5) 7 64
(W R Muir) *hld up in mid-div: bmpd over 3f out: hdwy 2f out: rdn and one pce fnl f* **3/1**[1]
5500 **5** *2 ¾* **Jobekani (IRE)**[38] 4956 2-8-9 **65** .... RussellKennemore(3) 8 55+
(Mrs L Williamson) *hld up and bhd: hdwy on ins wl over 1f out: sn rdn and n.m.r: wknd ins fnl f* **50/1**
330 **6** *7* **Champagne Fizz (IRE)**[15] 5642 2-9-6 **73** .... TravisBlock 5 45
(Miss Jo Crowley) *w ldr over 1f: prom whn bmpd over 3f out: rdn and wknd 2f out* **14/1**
0465 **7** *shd* **Abhainn (IRE)**[32] 5153 2-9-4 **71** ....(v[1]) CatherineGannon 6 43
(B Palling) *prom: jnd wnr over 5f out: ev ch over 2f out: sn rdn: wknd qckly wl over 1f out* **25/1**
43 **8** *2 ½* **Imperial Skylight**[22] 5414 2-8-13 **66** .... SamHitchcott 10 32
(M R Channon) *hld up in mid-div: bmpd over 3f out: sn pushed along and bhd* **14/1**
5054 **9** *6* **Hum Cat (IRE)**[22] 5432 2-8-10 **66** ....(p) LukeMorris(3) 12 17
(J S Moore) *hld up and bhd: sme hdwy whn bmpd on outside over 3f out: wknd over 2f out* **7/1**[3]

1m 30.02s (0.42) **Going Correction** -0.075s/f (Stan) **9 Ran SP% 110.8**
Speed ratings (Par 95): **94,93,92,89,86 78,78,75,68**
toteswinger: 1&2 not won, 1&3 £3.90, 2&3 £3.90. CSF £19.08 CT £99.07 TOTE £6.90: £2.30, £1.10, £3.20; EX 25.00.
Owner Mrs R J Jacobs **Bred** Newsells Park Stud **Trained** Middleham Moor, N Yorks
■ Stewards' Enquiry : Chris Catlin one-day ban: careless riding (Oct 6)
Luke Morris two-day ban: careless riding (Oct 6-7)

FOCUS
This was quite a competitive nursery with a battle to the finish.

NOTEBOOK
Atabaas Allure(FR) broke smartly from her inside draw to take up the running on the rail, was angled out wider in the straight and dug deep to hold off the late challengers. She weakened at Ayr last time when the soft ground was against her, but Polytrack evidently suits, though connections felt this track was on the sharp side, and she will eventually appreciate further. (op 9-2 tchd 4-1 and 11-2)
Silent Hero had been slowly away when winning at Southwell last time, and from his wide draw the same tactics were tried again, but he was bumped on the home turn and could not find a gap until the home straight. He made significant late headway but had too much ground to make up. He can resume winning ways on a track that is more favourable for hold-up horses. (op 4-1)
Kersivay tracked the winner on the rail and challenged into the straight, only being run out of it close home. Having faded in the soft ground at Warwick last time, this was a more encouraging run in his first nursery. (op 5-1)
Striding Edge(IRE) was outpaced until making headway on the home turn. (op 7-2 tchd 11-4)

6088 GET A BONUS AT WILLIAMHILLCASINO.COM H'CAP 7f 32y(P)
6:50 (6:52) (Class 6) (0-65,65) 3-Y-O **£2,388** (£705; £352) **Stalls** High

Form | | | | RPR
6326 **1** **Romantic Verse**[65] 4083 3-9-2 **63** ....(b[1]) LiamJones 5 69
(W J Haggas) *racd keenly: chsd ldr: rdn to ld over 1f out: drvn out* **7/1**
6532 **2** *1 ½* **Plumage**[42] 4825 3-8-13 **60** .... AdamKirby 3 62
(M Blanshard) *a.p: swtchd rt over 1f out: rdn and wnt 2nd jst ins fnl f: nt qckn* **7/2**[1]
046 **3** *1* **Beetuna (IRE)**[4] 5965 3-9-4 **65** .... TomEaves 4 64
(B Smart) *hld up and bhd: pushed along and hdwy on ins over 2f out: rdn and one pce fnl f* **5/1**[2]
2050 **4** *¾* **Miss Phoebe (IRE)**[60] 4253 3-8-13 **65** .... DavidProbert(5) 6 62
(S Kirk) *hld up in tch: pushed along over 3f out: outpcd 2f out: rdn and kpt on ins fnl f* **11/1**
2350 **5** *2* **Wiseman's Diamond (USA)**[37] 4961 3-9-2 **63** .... FrankieMcDonald 8 55
(P T Midgley) *hld up in tch: rdn over 2f out: edgd lft over 1f out: no imp fnl f* **16/1**
5140 **6** *1* **Spent**[8] 5816 3-9-0 **61** .... ChrisCatlin 9 50
(Mouse Hamilton-Fairley) *hld up in mid-div: c wd st: sn wknd* **12/1**
4016 **7** *shd* **Lujano**[39] 4920 3-9-1 **65** .... DuranFentiman(3) 11 54
(Ollie Pears) *hld up in rr: rdn and sme prog fnl f: nvr nr ldrs* **22/1**
0460 **8** *1 ¼* **Semah Harold**[36] 5008 3-8-13 **60** ....(b) GrahamGibbons 2 46
(E S McMahon) *dwlt: towards rr: rdn and hdwy wl over 1f out: eased whn btn towards fin* **7/2**[1]
5400 **9** *hd* **Gainshare**[16] 5617 3-9-0 **61** .... J-PGuillambert 1 46
(T D Barron) *t.k.h: sn bhd* **6/1**[3]
6000 **10** *2 ¾* **Connor's Choice**[16] 5616 3-8-13 **60** ....(b[1]) AlanDaly 7 38
(Andrew Turnell) *led: rdn and hdd over 1f out: wknd fnl f* **22/1**
0106 **11** *15* **Bahamian Princess**[26] 5307 3-9-0 **64** .... RussellKennemore(3) 10 1
(R Hollinshead) *a bhd: lost tch wl over 1f out* **33/1**

1m 29.28s (-0.32) **Going Correction** -0.075s/f (Stan) **11 Ran SP% 121.4**
Speed ratings (Par 99): **98,96,95,94,92 90,90,89,89,85 68**
toteswinger: 1&2 £4.00, 1&3 £24.10, 2&3 £3.10. CSF £32.07 CT £138.30 TOTE £5.00: £1.70, £1.80, £1.20; EX 22.40.
Owner Romantic Verse Partnership **Bred** Cheveley Park Stud Ltd **Trained** Newmarket, Suffolk

FOCUS
Quite a strong early pace in this handicap but those that mattered at the finish were prominent throughout. The winner is rated up 7lb on her previous best with the second to her latest mark.

6089 ALL THE BALLS AT WILLIAMHILLBINGO.COM MEDIAN AUCTION MAIDEN FILLIES' STKS 5f 216y(P)
7:20 (7:21) (Class 5) 2-Y-O **£2,729** (£806; £403) **Stalls** Low

Form | | | | RPR
3 **1** **Via Mia**[43] 4763 2-9-0 **0** .... TomEaves 10 71
(P F I Cole) *led over 1f: w ldr: rdn wl over 1f out: led wl ins fnl f: r.o* **13/2**
30 **2** *1 ¼* **Albertine Rose**[17] 5584 2-9-0 **0** .... DO'Donohoe 2 67
(W R Muir) *a.p: led jst over 1f out: hrd rdn and hdd wl ins fnl f: nt qckn* **5/1**[2]
02 **3** *2 ½* **Dream Of Mine**[14] 5673 2-9-0 **0** .... ChrisCatlin 5 60
(Saeed Bin Suroor) *w ldr: led over 4f out: rdn and hdd jst over 1f out: no ex ins fnl f* **6/5**[1]
23 **4** *¾* **Whispering Spirit (IRE)**[24] 5384 2-8-11 **0** .... AndrewMullen(3) 4 58
(Mrs A Duffield) *hld up in tch: rdn wl over 1f out: one pce fnl f* **7/1**
5 *1 ¾* **Glimpse Of Light (IRE)** 2-8-9 **0** .... DavidProbert(5) 1 52
(A M Balding) *s.i.s: hld up and bhd: hdwy wl over 1f out: sn rdn: no further prog fnl f* **6/1**[3]
0 **6** *1 ½* **Swing It Ruby (IRE)**[7] 5857 2-8-11 **0** .... DuranFentiman(3) 6 48
(Miss V Haigh) *hld up in mid-div: pushed along over 2f out: no hdwy* **33/1**
0 **7** *nse* **Kutanga (USA)**[22] 5431 2-9-0 **0** .... LiamJones 3 48
(R M H Cowell) *hld up and bhd: rdn over 1f out: nvr nr ldrs* **40/1**
0 **8** *½* **Lady Lu**[46] 4692 2-9-0 **0** .... JerryO'Dwyer 13 46
(P F I Cole) *sn outpcd: sme prog on ins wl over 1f out: n.d* **33/1**
9 *¾* **Lupe Lamora** 2-9-0 **0** .... ShaneKelly 11 44
(J A Osborne) *s.i.s: hld up and bhd: hdwy on outside over 3f out: wknd over 1f out* **33/1**
10 *6* **Queen Of Destiny (IRE)** 2-9-0 **0** .... CatherineGannon 7 26
(B Palling) *chsd ldrs: rdn over 2f out: wknd wl over 1f out* **66/1**
11 *9* **Its Alice** 2-9-0 **0** .... AdamKirby 9 —
(Peter Grayson) *dwlt: outpcd* **66/1**
0 **12** *2 ¾* **Jessy Jones**[28] 5213 2-9-0 **0** .... J-PGuillambert 8 —
(R Brotherton) *mid-div: bhd fnl 3f* **100/1**

1m 15.1s (0.10) **Going Correction** -0.075s/f (Stan) **12 Ran SP% 117.5**
Speed ratings (Par 92): **96,94,91,90,87 85,85,84,83,75 63,60**
toteswinger: 1&2 £1.70, 1&3 £2.10, 2&3 £2.80. CSF £37.14 TOTE £8.30: £1.60, £2.10, £1.30; EX 56.00.
Owner A1 Partnerships 3 **Bred** Kirtlington Stud **Trained** Whatcombe, Oxon

FOCUS
Not much strength in depth in this maiden, and the three early pacesetters dominated the finish.

NOTEBOOK
Via Mia duelled for the lead on the outside and those early exertions looked like they may have taken their toll when she hit a bit of a flat spot round the turn before staying on strongly. Well backed when disappointing on her debut at Bath last month, she was a drifter here but looks like there will be more to come, and a step up in trip might suit. (op 9-2 tchd 7-1)
Albertine Rose was a little free tracking the leaders but kept up with the winner along the inside rail in the straight. She tired in the soft at Goodwood last time but showed no lasting effects of that effort here. (op 11-2 tchd 13-2)
Dream Of Mine was the most expensive purchase in the field, having cost £180,000, and after showing some form last time out at Kempton was a warm order to post her first win. She disputed the early pace but never looked happy, as could be seen from her flattened ears, and as soon as she was challenged in the straight she capitulated tamely. It may have just been an off day but this was still disappointing. (op 13-8)

Whispering Spirit(IRE) raced on the inside rail and was one-paced. Having been outpaced at 5f in her previous two races, she might need further still. (op 9-2 tchd 4-1)

6090 GET YOUR CHIPS AT WILLIAMHILLPOKER.COM H'CAP 1m 1f 103y(P)
7:50 (7:50) (Class 6) (0-65,65) 3-Y-O+ **£2,388** (£705; £352) **Stalls** Low

Form RPR

0621 **1** **Strike Force**[13] 5712 4-9-1 **62**........ JackMitchell(3) 1 70
(K F Clutterbuck) *hld up in rr: stdy prog 2f out: rdn to ld cl home* **15/2**[2]

3203 **2** 1 **My Mirasol**[18] 5577 4-9-4 **62**........(p) TGMcLaughlin 7 68
(D E Cantillon) *a.p: rdn over 2f out: led wl over 1f out: hdd cl home* **9/1**

2206 **3** ½ **It's A Dream (FR)**[39] 4934 5-9-7 **65**........(t) ChrisCatlin 3 70
(M W Easterby) *hld up in rr: c v wd st: hdwy on outside over 1f out: r.o ins fnl f* **17/2**[3]

05-0 **4** ½ **United Nations**[42] 4813 7-8-13 **62**........ AshleyHamblett(5) 6 66
(N Wilson) *hld up in mid-div: rdn and hdwy 2f out: nt qckn ins fnl f* **14/1**

4620 **5** ½ **Baltimore Jack (IRE)**[21] 5450 4-9-3 **61**........ AdamKirby 4 64
(M W Easterby) *a.p: rdn wl over 1f out: nt qckn ins fnl f* **10/1**

6560 **6** *shd* **Pelham Crescent (IRE)**[10] 5779 5-9-3 **61**........ CatherineGannon 10 64
(B Palling) *hld up in rr: rdn over 1f out: styd on ins fnl f: nrst fin* **40/1**

2435 **7** 2 **Bavarica**[20] 5512 6-9-2 **65**........ AmyBaker(5) 5 63
(Miss J Feilden) *hld up in mid-div: hdwy on outside over 2f out: rdn over 1f out: wknd ins fnl f* **10/1**

0001 **8** ½ **Tous Les Deux**[32] 5157 5-9-3 **61**........ J-PGuillambert 8 58
(G L Moore) *hld up towards rr: rdn over 1f out: swtchd rt to outside ins fnl f: n.d* **7/2**[1]

1000 **9** 3 ¾ **Moment Of Clarity**[54] 4458 6-9-4 **62**........(p) PAspell 2 52
(R C Guest) *hld up in rr: hdwy on ins whn nt clr run jst over 2f out: rdn and wknd wl over 1f out* **33/1**

41 **10** 1 ¼ **Old Romney**[22] 5429 4-9-3 **61**........(b) ShaneKelly 12 48
(M Wigham) *led: rdn and hdd wl over 1f out: eased whn btn ins fnl f* **7/2**[1]

260 **11** 1 **Uig**[69] 3944 7-9-2 **65**........ SophieDoyle(5) 9 50
(H S Howe) *hld up towards rr: hung rt and reminders over 3f out: sn struggling* **33/1**

-300 **12** 10 **Mafasina (USA)**[39] 4934 3-9-2 **65**........ TomEaves 11 29
(B Smart) *hld up in tch: rdn over 3f out: wknd 2f out* **40/1**

-060 **13** 1 ¼ **Montrose Man**[90] 3258 4-9-3 **64**........ PatrickHills(3) 13 25
(B J Meehan) *chsd ldr tl rdn over 2f out: wknd wl over 1f out* **33/1**

2m 0.21s (-1.49) **Going Correction** -0.075s/f (Stan) **13 Ran SP% 115.3**
WFA 3 from 4yo+ 5lb
Speed ratings (Par 101): **103,102,101,101,100 100,98,98,95,94 93,84,83**
toteswinger: 1&2 £4.90, 1&3 £21.00, 2&3 £33.60. CSF £67.28 CT £582.44 TOTE £10.00: £2.70, £2.20, £4.00; EX 30.30.
Owner Miss A L Hutchinson **Bred** Cheveley Park Stud Ltd **Trained** Exning, Suffolk
■ Stewards' Enquiry : Ashley Hamblett one-day ban: used whip down shoulder in forehand position (Oct 6)

FOCUS
A strong early pace produced a close finish in this handicap between a number of hold-up horses. The form looks sound.
Baltimore Jack(IRE) Official explanation: jockey said gelding hung left

6091 REAL TIME RADIO AT WILLIAMHILL.CO.UK MEDIAN AUCTION MAIDEN STKS 1m 141y(P)
8:20 (8:21) (Class 6) 3-5-Y-O **£2,388** (£705; £352) **Stalls** Low

Form RPR

0050 **1** **Forzarzi (IRE)**[19] 5538 4-9-4 50 ow1........(p) PBradley(5) 4 63
(H A McWilliams) *hld up towards rr: hdwy over 2f out: rdn and hung lft over 1f out: r.o u.p to ld nr fin* **66/1**

5340 **2** *nk* **Unbiased (IRE)**[15] 5652 3-9-3 67........(b) ShaneKelly 3 61
(J L Dunlop) *hld up in mid-div: nt clr run over 2f out: swtchd rt ent st: rdn and hdwy over 1f out: styd on towards fin* **14/1**

000 **3** *shd* **The Wily Woodcock**[38] 4946 4-9-8 60........ ChrisCatlin 13 61
(G Wragg) *hld up in tch: rdn over 1f out: r.o ins fnl f* **20/1**

3332 **4** ¾ **Seventh Cavalry (IRE)**[15] 5652 3-9-3 70........(b) JimmyQuinn 8 59
(H R A Cecil) *led: clr 2f out: hrd rdn 1f out: ct nr fin* **9/4**[2]

245 **5** 1 **Crafty Dealer (IRE)**[22] 5426 3-9-3 70........ JamesDoyle 11 57
(J W Hills) *hld up in mid-div: pushed along over 3f out: hdwy on outside to chse ldr jst over 2f out: rdn wl over 1f out: no ex wl ins fnl f* **13/2**[3]

0 **6** 8 **Actress Annie**[21] 5471 3-8-12 0........ AdamKirby 2 34
(Mike Murphy) *hld up in rr: short-lived effrt over 2f out* **66/1**

4-6 **7** 3 ¾ **Modern Practice (IRE)**[252] 130 3-9-3 0........ EdwardCreighton 10 30
(Miss V Haigh) *chsd ldr tl rdn jst over 2f out: sn wknd* **80/1**

8 9 **Enjoy The Mood** 5-9-0 0........ DuranFentiman(3) 1 —
(Ms N M Hugo) *rel to r: rdn 4f out: a in rr* **100/1**

2-2 **9** *nk* **Girl Of Pangaea (GER)**[10] 5790 3-8-12 0........ SteveDrowne 7 —
(E A L Dunlop) *prom: wnt 2nd briefly over 3f out: wknd qckly over 2f out* **10/11**[1]

4006 **10** 4 **St Michael's Mount**[27] 5268 3-9-3 60........ HayleyTurner 5 —
(M P Tregoning) *t.k.h in tch: rdn and wknd over 2f out* **20/1**

11 14 **Lucky Forteen** 5-9-3 0........ TGMcLaughlin 9 —
(P W Hiatt) *s.i.s: a in rr* **100/1**

1m 50.58s (0.08) **Going Correction** -0.075s/f (Stan)
WFA 3 from 4yo+ 5lb **11 Ran SP% 118.9**
Speed ratings (Par 101): **96,95,95,94,94 86,83,75,75,71 59**
toteswinger: 1&2 not won, 1&3 not won, 2&3 £24.00. CSF £772.24 TOTE £73.70: £14.30, £4.40, £2.60; EX 966.50.
Owner J D Riches **Bred** Primrose Cottage **Trained** Cockerham, Co Durham

FOCUS
With the two market leaders disappointing and the first five finishing in a heap, it might not be a race with that many clues for the future. Modest form, and none too solid.
Girl Of Pangaea(GER) Official explanation: trainer said filly finished distressed

6092 BET ONLINE AT WILLIAMHILL.CO.UK H'CAP 1m 4f 50y(P)
8:50 (8:51) (Class 5) (0-75,71) 3-Y-O **£3,238** (£963; £481; £240) **Stalls** Low

Form RPR

0615 **1** **Bushy Dell (IRE)**[16] 5605 3-8-13 **71**........ AmyBaker(5) 7 75
(Miss J Feilden) *chsd ldr: slt ld over 4f out: rdn over 1f out: r.o* **17/2**

0055 **2** ½ **Into The Light**[63] 4173 3-8-13 **66**........ GrahamGibbons 1 69
(E S McMahon) *a.p: rdn over 2f out: styd on u.p to take 2nd wl ins fnl f: kpt on* **7/1**[3]

5433 **3** 2 **The Last Bottle (IRE)**[7] 5868 3-8-8 **61**........ JamesDoyle 4 61
(W M Brisbourne) *hld up in tch: rdn over 2f out: styd on towards fin* **17/2**

053- **4** ½ **Hada Men (USA)**[347] 6051 3-9-3 **70**........ HayleyTurner 2 69
(M P Tregoning) *hld up and bhd: pushed along and struggling over 3f out: styd on wl ins fnl f: nrst fin* **9/2**[2]

6511 **5** *nk* **Astrodome**[37] 4972 3-8-13 **66**........(b) J-PGuillambert 8 65
(Sir Mark Prescott) *led: narrowly hdd over 4f out: rdn over 2f out: ev ch over 1f out: fdd towards fin* **1/1**[1]

006 **6** 1 ¾ **Enderby Light (FR)**[96] 3058 3-9-0 **67**........ TomEaves 5 63
(Ollie Pears) *hld up and bhd: pushed along and struggling over 3f out: sme late prog* **25/1**

-220 **7** 2 ¾ **Next Of Kin (IRE)**[41] 4859 3-9-1 **68**........ JimmyQuinn 3 60
(Jennie Candlish) *hld up: rdn and struggling 4f out: n.d after* **9/1**

2m 39.83s (-1.27) **Going Correction** -0.075s/f (Stan) **7 Ran SP% 115.6**
Speed ratings (Par 101): **101,100,99,99,98 97,95**
toteswinger: 1&2 £5.20, 1&3 £6.80, 2&3 £6.80. CSF £66.15 CT £524.38 TOTE £11.70: £3.60, £2.70; EX 59.70 Place 6 £1315.65, Place 5 £743.59..
Owner R J Creese **Bred** Don Commins **Trained** Exning, Suffolk

FOCUS
This modest three-year-old handicap was run at a strong pace. Ordinary form with the favourite disappointing back on Polytrack.
Enderby Light(FR) Official explanation: jockey said gelding hung left
T/Plt: £6,867.10 to a £1 stake. Pool: £76,667.52. 8.15 winning tickets. T/Qpdt: £304.90 to a £1 stake. Pool: £6,757.47. 16.40 winning tickets. KH

6100 - (Foreign Racing) - See Raceform Interactive

6065 AYR (L-H)
Saturday, September 20

OFFICIAL GOING: Heavy (5.3)
Wind: Breezy, half against Weather: Overcast

6101 NIGEL ANGUS MEMORIAL NURSERY 1m
1:45 (1:45) (Class 2) 2-Y-O
£16,574 (£4,963; £2,481; £1,242; £619; £311) **Stalls** Low

Form RPR

130 **1** **Rising Prospect**[7] 5895 2-9-2 **77**........ EddieAhern 3 82+
(G M Moore) *in tch: hdwy to ld over 2f out: sn clr: pushed out* **15/2**

2220 **2** 2 ¾ **Cosmic Sun**[7] 5895 2-9-2 **82**........ FrederikTylicki(5) 5 81
(R A Fahey) *bhd tl hdwy over 1f out: wnt 2nd towards fin: nt rch wnr* **3/1**[1]

0601 **3** ½ **Woteva**[11] 5774 2-8-9 **70**........(p) DavidAllan 9 68
(B Ellison) *chsd ldrs: effrt over 2f out: wnt 2nd over 1f out: sn no imp* **11/2**

2650 **4** 3 ¾ **Veronicas Boy**[16] 5632 2-8-8 **69**........ AndrewElliott 1 59
(G M Moore) *bhd: outpcd over 2f out: styd on fnl f: n.d* **20/1**

0502 **5** ½ **Victorian Tycoon (IRE)**[7] 5914 2-8-2 **63**........ ChrisCatlin 8 52
(E J O'Neill) *led to over 3f out: wknd wl over 1f out* **10/1**

6231 **6** 3 ¼ **Huxaar**[11] 5771 2-8-13 **74**........ TomEaves 2 56
(Mrs L Stubbs) *prom tl rdn and wknd over 2f out* **9/2**[2]

522 **7** ¾ **Mannlichen**[53] 4497 2-9-4 **79**........ RoystonFfrench 7 59
(M Johnston) *s.i.s: bhd: rdn and edgd lft over 2f out: sn btn* **5/1**[3]

3530 **8** 1 ½ **Becausewecan (USA)**[7] 5895 2-8-13 **74**........ NCallan 10 51
(M Johnston) *t.k.h: cl up: led over 3f out to over 2f out: sn wknd* **7/1**

1m 49.34s (5.54) **Going Correction** +0.70s/f (Yiel) **8 Ran SP% 113.4**
Speed ratings (Par 101): **100,97,96,93,92 89,88,87**
toteswinger: 1&2 £6.30, 1&3 £9.50, 2&3 £7.20. CSF £29.75 CT £135.16 TOTE £8.70: £2.60, £1.50, £2.20; EX 25.10.
Owner Geoff & Sandra Turnbull **Bred** Geoff & Sandra Turnbull **Trained** Middleham Moor, N Yorks

FOCUS
No further rain since the previous day, but testing conditions once more. The ground was described as 'gluey' by one rider in the first and 'nearly unraceable' by another. This was not a strong nursery for the money on offer but it produced an impressive winner.

NOTEBOOK
Rising Prospect travelled well before bounding clear once set alight. He had won his maiden at York in heavy ground but had not built on that in soft conditions and Cosmic Sun appeared to have his measure on their meeting at Doncaster. Well regarded and entered for the Derby, he was suited by the hold-up tactics here. (op 8-1 tchd 7-1)
Cosmic Sun was being shoved along early in the straight. He stayed on well in the end to grab second, getting the mile well enough, but was never a threat to the winner. He has now finished second on four of his last five starts. (op 5-1)
Woteva ran a respectable race off a 7lb higher mark than when winning in similar ground at Beverley. (op 5-1 tchd 9-2)
Veronicas Boy travelled quite well and made late headway, but had been left with too much to do in the circumstances. He handled the ground and rise in trip well enough. (op 16-1)
Victorian Tycoon(IRE), runner-up at Kempton last time, was taken on for the lead by Becausewecan and the exertions eventually told. (op 9-1)
Huxaar was a little disappointing after winning his maiden in heavy ground last time.

6102 LAUNDRY COTTAGE STUD FIRTH OF CLYDE STKS (GROUP 3) (FILLIES) 6f
2:20 (2:21) (Class 1) 2-Y-O
£45,416 (£17,216; £8,616; £4,296; £2,152; £1,080) **Stalls** High

Form RPR

3051 **1** **Aspen Darlin (IRE)**[22] 5448 2-8-12 98........(p) JimmyQuinn 12 109+
(A Bailey) *trckd stands' side ldrs: led over 1f out: styd on strly to go clr fnl f* **12/1**

3122 **2** 3 ¼ **Sneak Preview**[16] 5642 2-8-12 95........ RichardMullen 6 98
(E S McMahon) *led far side: rdn over 2f out: kpt on fnl f: nt rch stands' side wnr: 1st of 5 in gp* **5/1**[2]

1044 **3** ½ **Danehill Destiny**[8] 5852 2-8-12 102........ RobertWinston 2 97
(W J Haggas) *hld up in tch far side: hdwy 2f out: kpt on u.p fnl f: 2nd of 5 in gp* **3/1**[1]

1 **4** *nse* **Summer Fete (IRE)**[47] 4685 2-8-12 0........ TomEaves 1 97
(B Smart) *prom far side: effrt over 1f out: kpt on same pce fnl f: 3rd of 5 in gp* **7/1**

1663 **5** 3 **Ares Choix**[35] 5112 2-8-12 94........ RoystonFfrench 9 88
(P C Haslam) *led stands' side untl edgd lft and hdd over 1f out: kpt on same pce: 2nd of 9 in gp* **22/1**

5110 **6** ½ **Coconut Shy**[8] 5852 2-8-12 75........(t) AdrianMcCarthy 8 86
(G Prodromou) *cl up stands' side tl rdn and no ex over 1f out: 3rd of 9 in gp* **22/1**

0130 **7** ½ **Danidh Dubai (IRE)**[56] 4403 2-8-12 101........ TPO'Shea 15 85
(M R Channon) *towards rr stands' side: effrt u.p over 2f out: no imp over 1f out: 4th of 9 in gp* **13/2**[3]

2100 **8** *shd* **Spring Tale (USA)**[56] 4434 2-8-12 83........ StephenDonohoe 13 84
(M J Wallace, Australia) *bhd stands' side: drvn 1/2-way: hdwy over 1f out: nvr able to chal: 5th of 9 in gp* **50/1**

0144 **9** 1 **La Brigitte**[1] 6068 2-8-12 88........ EddieAhern 10 81
(A J McCabe) *bhd stands' side: rdn 1/2-way: no imp whn n.m.r ins fnl f: 6th of 9 in gp* **16/1**

The Form Book, Raceform Ltd, Compton, RG20 6NL

3012 **10** *shd* **Favourite Girl (IRE)**[26] 5359 2-8-12 93.............................. DavidAllan 5 81
(T D Easterby) *swtchd to r w stands' side gp sn after s: hld up: drvn 1/2-way: n.d: 7th of 9 in gp* **7/1**

022 **11** *3/4* **Minotaurious (IRE)**[63] 4202 2-8-12 79........................ AndrewElliott 7 79
(K R Burke) *toook t.k.h: cl up far side tl wknd over 1f out: 4th of 5 in gp* **50/1**

01 **12** *hd* **Top Town Girl**[9] 5838 2-8-12 0.. PaulHanagan 11 78
(R M Beckett) *midfield stands' side: drvn over 2f out: btn over 1f out: 8th of 9 in gp* **20/1**

13 **13** *3 1/4* **Riotista (IRE)**[36] 5055 2-8-12 0.................................... ChrisCatlin 14 68
(E J O'Neill) *in tch stands' side: drvn 1/2-way: btn over 1f out: last of 9 in gp* **14/1**

250 **14** *9* **Maggie Lou (IRE)**[28] 5272 2-8-12 87.. NCallan 3 41
(K A Ryan) *chsd far side ldrs tl wknd over 2f out: last of 5 in gp* **28/1**

1m 15.63s (2.03) **Going Correction** +0.40s/f (Good) **14** Ran SP% **121.1**
Speed ratings (Par 102): **102,97,97,96,92 92,91,91,90,90 89,88,84,72**
toteswinger: 1&2 £15.50, 1&3 £8.10, 2&3 £3.50. CSF £65.81 TOTE £14.00: £2.80, £2.30, £1.80; EX 98.10 Trifecta £129.60 Part won. Pool: £175.20, 0.30 winning units..
Owner Indian Haven Syndicate **Bred** Miss Annmarie Burke **Trained** Newmarket, Suffolk
■ Stewards' Enquiry : Royston Ffrench one-day ban: careless riding (Oct 6)

FOCUS
A fair renewal of what is not the strongest Group 3. Five of the runners elected to make the trek across to the far side rail in search of the supposedly better ground and although three made the frame the winner raced stands' side.

NOTEBOOK
Aspen Darlin(IRE) kept a straight course up the stands' rail and absolutely thrashed everything else on her side of the track. \n\x\x Having travelled well in behind the pacesetting Coconut Shy, she soon took control of the stands' group and began to draw clear and it was then simply a case of where she stood with the principals on the far side, and she proved far too strong for all concerned. She clearly handles easy ground well, as she showed when winning her maiden on soft on her debut, but the application of cheekpieces helped her produce a career-best at Chester last time and this was another step forward. Unfortunately she doesn't hold an entry in the Cheveley Park Stakes, unlike a few in here, but connections are eyeing a Group 3 race at The Curragh next. (op 10-1)
Sneak Preview did really well up the far side, taking that group along from an early stage and staying on strongly to hold off the challenges of the third and fourth. She continues to go the right way and she clearly possesses the right attitude. (op 6-1)
Danehill Destiny seemed to run her race again and proved she handles the ground. (op 7-2 tchd 9-4)
Summer Fete(IRE) is much less exposed than some of these but she is clearly very highly regarded and she ran extremely well to hold off Danehill Destiny who has already proved herself in some of the top fillies' Pattern races this season. (op 9-1 tchd 10-1)
Danidh Dubai(IRE), whose best previous form was on a sound suurface, looked to find this testing ground not playing to her strengths. (op 15-2)

6103 JOHN SMITH'S EXTRA SMOOTH AYRSHIRE H'CAP 1m
2:50 (2:50) (Class 2) (0-100,99) 3-Y-0+

£26,170 (£7,837; £3,918; £1,961; £978; £491) **Stalls** Low

Form RPR

-400 **1** **Bolodenka (IRE)**[9] 5830 6-9-1 90.. PaulHanagan 3 101
(R A Fahey) *chsd ldrs: styd on to ld 1f out: kpt on wl* **12/1**

5024 **2** *2 1/2* **The Snatcher (IRE)**[7] 5896 5-9-1 90.................................. EddieAhern 8 96
(R Hannon) *hld up towards rr: hdwy over 2f out: styd on fnl f: no real imp* **10/1**

6000 **3** *nse* **Benandonner (USA)**[21] 5508 5-9-0 94..................... FrederikTylicki(5) 2 99
(R A Fahey) *chsd ldrs: edgd rt fnl f: kpt on same pce* **8/1**

0002 **4** *1* **Fremen (USA)**[5] 5968 8-8-11 86.................................. AdrianTNicholls 6 89+
(D Nicholls) *dwlt: in rr: hdwy on outer over 2f out: styd on same pce fnl f* **12/1**

213 **5** *1/2* **Zero Tolerance (IRE)**[20] 5550 8-9-5 94................... GrahamGibbons 11 96
(T D Barron) *chsd ldrs: sn drvn along: kpt on fnl f* **15/8**[1]

1131 **6** *1 3/4* **Osteopathic Remedy (IRE)**[26] 5360 4-9-4 93........................ NCallan 1 91
(M Dods) *trckd ldrs: led 2f out: hdd 1f out: wkng whn hmpd and snatched up ins fnl f* **6/1**[2]

5006 **7** *3 3/4* **Lucky Dance (BRZ)**[26] 5360 6-8-9 84......................... RobertWinston 5 73
(A G Foster) *t.k.h in rr: styd on fnl 2f: nvr a factor* **14/1**

0003 **8** *2* **Fishforcompliments**[26] 5368 4-9-4 93............................ JamieMoriarty 7 78
(R A Fahey) *drvn to ld: hdd 2f out: sn wknd* **25/1**

0020 **9** *2* **Rio Riva**[7] 5896 6-9-8 97.. TomEaves 13 77
(Miss J A Camacho) *hld up toward rr: nvr a factor* **14/1**

-000 **10** *7* **Majuro (IRE)**[9] 5831 4-8-10 85.. ChrisCatlin 10 49
(M W Easterby) *hld up in mid-div: lost pl 3f out: sn bhd* **20/1**

2015 **11** *12* **Underworld**[21] 5495 3-9-6 99.. RoystonFfrench 12 35
(M Johnston) *w ldrs: wknd 2f out: sn bhd: eased ins fnl f* **13/2**[3]

1m 47.57s (3.77) **Going Correction** +0.70s/f (Yiel)
WFA 3 from 4yo+ 4lb **11** Ran SP% **119.9**
Speed ratings (Par 109): **109,106,106,105,104 103,99,97,95,88 76**
toteswinger: 1&2 £27.10, 1&3 £24.30, 2&3 £12.20. CSF £128.82 CT £1045.50 TOTE £16.40: £3.80, £2.20, £2.90; EX 109.60 Trifecta £316.70 Part won. Pool: £428.08, 0.10 winning units..
Owner Enda Hunston **Bred** Kildaragh Stud **Trained** Musley Bank, N Yorks
■ Stewards' Enquiry : Paul Hanagan caution: used whip down shoulder in forehand position
Frederik Tylicki three-day ban: careless riding (Oct 8-10)

FOCUS
A good handicap run at an even gallop and plenty in with a chance as the field grouped up well over two furlongs out. The form is rated through the runner-up with the winner assessed around recent efforts.

NOTEBOOK
Bolodenka(IRE) who had taken the shortest route, tight up the inside rail on the fresh ground, bounded to the front well over a furlong out and stayed on strongly to score in pretty decisive fashion. While he has proved himself effective on soft ground in the past, he had yet to win on anything easier than good so this cleared up any fears about his effectiveness in the conditions. Although he has not been discredited in his last couple of starts, this was a much stronger effort on the book and he was handicapped to do so having slipped 8lb below the mark of his last handicap victory in 2007. Connections have apparently been meaning to go jumping with him for a while now and it is likely that he will be seen over obstacles sooner rather than later. (op 14-1 tchd 11-1)
The Snatcher(IRE) is proven in the conditions but he was ridden with a lot more patience than is often the case, coming from well off the pace. He stayed on well up the inside without ever looking like landing a blow and is consistent sort in these conditions. (op 11-1)
Benandonner(USA), a stable companion of the winner, put behind him a couple of below-par efforts, keeping on well for pressure despite edging right in the closing stages. (op 16-1)
Fremen(USA), winner of this race 12 months ago, missed the break before plugging on well from off the pace but he is still to convince that ground this testing is ideal. (op 9-1)
Zero Tolerance(IRE), a confirmed mud-lover, didn't travel with any real fluency, having to be niggled along well over half a mile from home. Although he wasn't beaten far, this wasn't a convincing effort and he can definitely do better, especially on this sort of ground or some thing less sticky. (op 2-1 tchd 9-4 in a place)
Osteopathic Remedy(IRE) has been in good form of late and made a good fist of it on ground that is possibly softer than ideal, and his finishing position was not helped by being snatched up late on.
Rio Riva Official explanation: trainer's rep said gelding never travelled
Underworld, who is relatively inexperienced, clearly found his first encounter with this testing surface too much and was allowed to come home in his own time once beaten. (op 11-2)

6104 JOHN SMITH'S AYR GOLD CUP (HERITAGE H'CAP) 6f
3:30 (3:30) (Class 2) 3-Y-0+

£93,465 (£27,990; £13,995; £7,005; £3,495; £1,755) **Stalls** High

Form RPR

6130 **1** **Regal Parade**[50] 4587 4-8-10 99.............................. WilliamCarson(5) 20 112
(D Nicholls) *hld up stands' side: gd hdwy 2f out: led that gp ins fnl f: edgd lft: sn clr* **18/1**

3101 **2** *2 1/4* **Tajneed (IRE)**[35] 5109 5-8-12 96.................................. AdrianTNicholls 21 102
(D Nicholls) *prom stands' side: led that gp over 1f out to ins fnl f: kpt on u.p: 2nd of 13 in gp* **8/1**[2]

6005 **3** *nse* **Confuchias (IRE)**[35] 5109 4-9-2 100........................... JamieMoriarty 26 106
(K R Burke) *prom stands' side: drvn over 2f out: edgd lft ins fnl f: kpt on: 3rd of 13 in gp* **8/1**[2]

1600 **4** *nk* **Knot In Wood (IRE)**[7] 5891 6-9-4 102........................ PaulHanagan 11 107+
(R A Fahey) *in midfield far side: effrt 2f out: led that gp ins fnl f: kpt on: nt rch stands' side: 1st of 14 in gp* **20/1**

10 **5** *3/4* **Skhilling Spirit**[133] 1982 5-8-9 93................................ GrahamGibbons 24 95
(T D Barron) *missed break: bhd stands' side tl styd on wl fnl 2f: nrst fin: 4th of 13 in gp* **22/1**

-006 **6** *hd* **Patavellian (IRE)**[35] 5109 10-8-6 95.........(v[1]) Louis-PhilippeBeuzelin(5) 4 97
(R Charlton) *chsd far side ldrs: led that gp briefly ins fnl f: no ex towards fin: 2nd of 14 in gp* **28/1**

000 **7** *3/4* **Rising Shadow (IRE)**[35] 5109 7-8-10 94.......................... JimmyQuinn 10 93
(N Wilson) *dwlt: bhd far side: gd hdwy and ev ch that gp ins fnl f: no ex nr fin: 3rd of 14 in gp* **25/1**

1050 **8** *nk* **Aahayson**[48] 4660 4-9-9 107.. AndrewElliott 6 105
(K R Burke) *cl up far side: ev ch that gp over 1f out: kpt on same pce fnl f: 4th of 14 in gp* **25/1**

0030 **9** *nk* **Tamagin (USA)**[7] 5890 5-9-1 99..................................(p) RobertWinston 5 97
(K A Ryan) *led far side: edgd rt and hdd over 1f out: no ex fnl f: 5th of 14 in gp* **25/1**

0562 **10** *nk* **River Falcon**[7] 5890 8-8-3 92.. KellyHarrison(5) 2 89
(J S Goldie) *in midfield far side: effrt over 1f out: kpt on: nvr able to chal: 6th of 14 in gp* **12/1**[3]

5012 **11** *hd* **Valery Borzov (IRE)**[35] 5109 4-9-3 101......................... FrancisNorton 7 97
(D Nicholls) *trckd far side ldrs tl rdn and no ex over 1f out: 7th of 14 in gp* **8/1**[2]

11-6 **12** *1/2* **Fonthill Road (IRE)**[28] 5259 8-9-1 104....................... FrederikTylicki(5) 1 98
(R A Fahey) *prom far side: drvn over 2f out: no ex over 1f out: 8th of 14 in gp* **16/1**

5422 **13** *nk* **Advanced**[28] 5259 5-9-6 104.. NCallan 3 97
(K A Ryan) *cl up far side: led that gp over 1f out to ins fnl f: sn btn: 9th of 14 in gp* **15/2**[1]

0200 **14** *nk* **Dhaular Dhar (IRE)**[35] 5109 6-9-2 100........................... DanielTudhope 8 92
(J S Goldie) *bhd far side tl hdwy fnl f: n.d: 10th of 14 in gp* **28/1**

6000 **15** *1/2* **Dabbers Ridge (IRE)**[22] 5446 6-8-11 95................................ TPO'Shea 18 86
(B W Hills) *hld up stands' side: effrt over 2f out: hung lft and wknd over 1f out: 5th of 13 in gp* **28/1**

6500 **16** *nk* **Raptor (GER)**[26] 5360 5-8-12 96...............................(b[1]) RichardMullen 16 86
(K R Burke) *swtchd to r far side sn after s: in midfield: drvn over 2f out: no imp: 11th of 14 in gp* **33/1**

6401 **17** *nk* **Hogmaneigh (IRE)**[7] 5890 5-9-7 105 5ex........................ SaleemGolam 27 94
(S C Williams) *prom stands' side: effrt and ev ch that gp over 1f out: wknd ins fnl f: 6th of 13 in gp* **12/1**[3]

0430 **18** *3/4* **Evens And Odds (IRE)**[7] 5890 4-8-13 97.....................(b) ChrisCatlin 13 83
(K A Ryan) *prom stands' side tl rdn and no ex over 1f out: 7th of 13 in gp* **66/1**

0030 **19** *1 1/4* **Northern Fling**[7] 5890 4-9-2 100.. DavidAllan 23 82
(D Nicholls) *towards rr stands' side: drvn 1/2-way: nvr able to chal: 8th of 13 in gp* **40/1**

1114 **20** *2* **Shifting Star (IRE)**[26] 5347 3-8-13 99.............................. EddieAhern 22 75
(W R Swinburn) *hld up stands' side: drvn over 2f out: nt pce to chal: 9th of 13 in gp* **20/1**

5041 **21** *1 3/4* **Ishetoo**[20] 5542 4-8-13 97 5ex.. StephenDonohoe 19 67
(A Dickman) *bhd stands' side: rdn over 2f out: nvr on terms: 10th of 13 in gp* **28/1**

-614 **22** *1* **Turnkey**[140] 1796 6-8-2 93.. AdeleRothery(7) 12 60
(D Nicholls) *bhd far side: pushed along over 2f out: nvr on terms: 12th of 14 in gp* **22/1**

6000 **23** *1/2* **Indian Trail**[49] 4624 8-8-6 97... NSLawes(7) 25 63
(D Nicholls) *led stands' side to over 1f out: sn wknd: 11th of 13 in gp* **66/1**

1560 **24** *1/2* **Inter Vision (USA)**[7] 5890 8-8-13 97............................ RoystonFfrench 9 61
(A Dickman) *a bhd far side: 13th of 14 in gp* **80/1**

3444 **25** *1 3/4* **Appalachian Trail (IRE)**[18] 5586 7-9-5 108.......(b) PatrickDonaghy(5) 14 66
(Miss L A Perratt) *sn swtchd to far side gp: in tch tl wknd fr 2f out: last of 14 in gp* **40/1**

6220 **26** *3 1/4* **Baby Strange**[35] 5109 4-8-12 96.................................. DarrenWilliams 17 44
(D Shaw) *in midfield stands' side: rdn over 2f out: sn wknd: 12th of 13 in gp* **33/1**

2030 **27** *6* **Burnwynd Boy**[48] 4660 3-9-5 105.. TomEaves 15 34
(Miss L A Perratt) *a bhd stands' side: struggling fr over 2f out: last of 13 in gp* **50/1**

1m 15.48s (1.88) **Going Correction** +0.60s/f (Yiel)
WFA 3 from 4yo+ 2lb **27** Ran SP% **132.1**
Speed ratings (Par 109): **111,108,107,107,106 106,105,104,104,104 103,103,102,102,101 101,100,99,98,95 93,91,91,90,88 8**
toteswinger: 1&2 £31.20, 1&3 £45.20, 2&3 £14.80. CSF £124.78 CT £1285.85 TOTE £23.40: £4.70, £2.70, £2.90, £5.10; EX 237.90 Trifecta £3620.00 Pool: £33,754.77, 6.90 winning units.
Owner Dab Hand Racing **Bred** Highclere Stud And Harry Herbert **Trained** Sessay, N Yorks
■ Stewards' Enquiry : Louis-Philippe Beuzelin one-day ban: careless riding (Oct 6)

FOCUS
A strong renewal of this highly competitive sprint that featured the likes of Portland one-two Hogmaneigh and River Falcon, last year's winner Advanced, 2006 winner Fonthill Road and Great St Wilfrid one-two, stablemates Tajneed and Valery Borzov. Those drawn stands' side came out best and the placed horses are rated to this year's marks.

NOTEBOOK

Regal Parade plundered this valuable prize despite having never previously run over 6f. It was no surprise to see the field split in two, but from stall 20 Carson had little choice but to keep his mount stands' side and, held up towards the back of that group, possibly finding the pace on the brisk side, he still had plenty to do two furlongs out. However, as everything in front of him began to come under pressure, his superior staying power kicked in and he came to the fore just inside the final furlong before forging clear in the closing stages.He has been an absolute star for David Nicholls (who has now won five of the last nine runnings of this race) this term over 7f, winning the Buckingham Palace Stakes at Royal Ascot in June, but he had never previously proven himself on ground as testing as this. (op 20-1)

Tajneed(IRE) completing a one-two for his trainer. Proven in the conditions and coming here on the back of a win in the Great St Wilfrid handicap, he was far from handicapped out of this off just a 4lb higher mark and he ran at least as well, staying on strongly and only finding the stamina-laden winner too good. (op 17-2 tchd 9-1)

Confuchias(IRE) was unable to reverse Ripon placings with Tajneed on these 4lb better terms but he remains a well handicapped horse on old form and is a proven mud-lover, so it was no surprise to see him figure prominently. (op 17-2 tchd 9-1)

Knot In Wood(IRE) disappointed in this race last year but he fared much better this time, leading the group on the far side home and justifying Hanagan's decision to partner him rather than 2006 winner Fonthill Road. Not for the first time in his career has he been unfortunate on the draw front and he deserves to bag a big prize. (op 22-1)

Skhilling Spirit, like the winner, has also done most of his racing over longer trips and, after missing the break, he came from towards the back of the stands' side group to stay on gamely in the closing stages as the sprinters began to struggle. (op 28-1)

Patavellian(IRE), with a visor replacing the usual blinkers, led briefly on the far side in the final furlong before just succumbing to the stronger staying power of Knot In Wood. (op 33-1)

Rising Shadow(IRE), who went close in the Silver Cup two years ago, is well suited by these conditions so it was no surprise he left behind some very modest recent efforts.

River Falcon, who is well suited by soft ground, could never bustle up the leaders on the far side but was not far away.

Valery Borzov(IRE) could never find the extra gear he needed to mount a serious threat. (tchd 17-2)

Advanced had not won since taking this last season, but had put up some decent efforts in Group and Listed company and was 5lb lower. He appeared to have every chance, leading into the final furlong, but was then swamped late on. (op 7-1 tchd 8-1)

6105 CAMPBELL BROTHERS H'CAP — 7f 50y

4:05 (4:06) (Class 3) (0-95,91) 3-Y-O+

£11,091 (£3,321; £1,660; £831; £414; £208) Stalls Low

Form			Horse	RPR
3400	1		**Game Lad**[42] 4875 6-8-8 **78**....(t) DavidAllan 2 (T D Easterby) *hld up towards rr: hdwy and c outside over 2f out: styd on strly to ld last 75yds: v readily* **10/3**[2]	91
0031	2	1 ½	**Kings Point (IRE)**[13] 5717 7-9-7 **91**.... AdrianTNicholls 5 (D Nicholls) *led: kpt on gamely fnl 2f: hdd and no ex wl ins fnl f* **11/2**[3]	99
-065	3	1 ½	**College Scholar (GER)**[34] 5133 4-8-10 **80**....(t) RobertWinston 9 (Liam McAteer, Ire) *hld up towards rr: hdwy over 2f out: kpt on same pce fnl f* **12/1**	84
-000	4	3	**Broken Applause (IRE)**[10] 5795 3-8-10 **88**.... FrederikTylicki(5) 12 (R A Fahey) *w ldr: wknd fnl f* **12/1**	83
1005	5	shd	**Zomerlust**[21] 5503 6-9-5 **89**.... GrahamGibbons 8 (J J Quinn) *trckd ldrs: effrt over 2f out: fdd fnl f* **7/1**	84
4600	6	1 ¾	**Geojimali**[1] 6069 6-8-11 **81**.... SaleemGolam 1 (J S Goldie) *dwlt: hld up in last: nvr a factor* **14/1**	72
1241	7	nk	**Amicus Meus (IRE)**[23] 5419 4-8-12 **82**.... ChrisCatlin 11 (A Bailey) *sweating and v edgy stalls: sn trcking ldrs: effrt over 2f out: wknd over 1f out* **7/4**[1]	72
0001	8	21	**Obe Brave**[19] 5562 5-8-10 **80**.... PaulHanagan 10 (R A Fahey) *trckd ldrs: t.k.h: lost pl over 1f out: sn bhd and eased* **14/1**	13

1m 38.15s (4.75) **Going Correction** +0.90s/f (Soft)
WFA 3 from 4yo+ 3lb — **8** Ran SP% **116.0**
Speed ratings (Par 107): **108,106,104,101,101 99,98,74**
toteswinger: 1&2 £3.80, 1&3 £10.20, 2&3 £9.00. CSF £22.40 CT £195.99 TOTE £4.70: £1.70, £1.90, £3.30; EX 22.10.
Owner T D Easterby **Bred** M H Easterby **Trained** Great Habton, N Yorks

FOCUS

A decent handicap although it was weakened by five non-runners. The pace was just moderate and the form is rated around the placed horses.

NOTEBOOK

Game Lad relished the return to testing conditions. Held up, he had a bit to do when pulled out for a run but swept through to win readily in the end. He had fallen to a mark 3lb lower than when last successful at Newcastle in June 2007, also on heavy ground, and could supplement this before the end of the season. (op 9-2)

Kings Point(IRE) was unable to defy the 4lb rise for his win at Thirsk earlier in the month but made a good fist of it from the front, only giving best inside the last. (op 5-1)

College Scholar(GER), Irish-trained these days but formerly with Ed Dunlop, had run an improved race in heavy ground at Leopardstown last time. He made decent progress down the outside to go into second place but was run out of that position in the final furlong. (op 14-1 tchd 10-1)

Broken Applause(IRE), runner-up in the Firth Of Clyde on this card a year ago, had not shown much in a three-race campaign this term. After tracking the leader, her exertions told late on. (op 16-1)

Zomerlust, a heavy-ground winner at York in July, was plugging on again at the end and is worth persevering with over this trip. (op 6-1)

Amicus Meus(IRE) impressed plenty of observers with a course-and-distance win last month and his trainer was confident he would take all the beating, but he was 9lb higher in a better race and on even worse ground. Sweating up beforehand, and slowly away, he was close enough turning into the straight but failed to really pick up. Official explanation: trainer had no explanation for the poor form shown (op 2-1)

Obe Brave Official explanation: trainer said gelding was unsuited by the heavy ground

6106 ALPHABET SUPPLIES DOONSIDE CUP STKS (LISTED RACE) — 1m 2f

4:40 (4:40) (Class 1) 3-Y-O+

£34,062 (£12,912; £6,462; £3,222; £1,614; £810) Stalls Low

Form			Horse	RPR
5114	1		**Lady Deauville (FR)**[6] 5932 3-8-7 109.... FrancisNorton 9 (P A Blockley) *trckd ldrs: led over 2f out: styd on strly* **15/2**	110
210	2	1 ¾	**Mutajarred**[70] 3974 4-9-0 106.... PaulHanagan 6 (W J Haggas) *trckd ldrs: outpcd over 2f out: kpt on fnl f: nt rch wnr* **7/1**[3]	108
0011	3	1 ½	**Perks (IRE)**[10] 5792 3-8-8 110.... JimmyQuinn 4 (J L Dunlop) *hld up in tch: effrt over 2f out: edgd lft and one pce fnl f* **1/1**[1]	105
3630	4	nse	**Alfie Flits**[77] 3721 6-9-0 100.... RobertWinston 7 (G A Swinbank) *hld up: hdwy and ev ch over 2f out: one pce fnl f* **22/1**	104
1520	5	3 ¾	**Sweet Lilly**[27] 5332 4-8-13 108.... TPO'Shea 5 (M R Channon) *hld up: hdwy over 1f out: nvr able to chal* **16/1**	96
0205	6	1 ¾	**Dunaskin (IRE)**[70] 3974 8-9-0 95.... DavidAllan 8 (B Ellison) *led to over 2f out: sn rdn and wknd* **25/1**	93
112	7	hd	**Bushman**[78] 3683 4-9-0 105.... RichardMullen 2 (D M Simcock) *hld up: effrt and hdwy 3f out: wknd 2f out* **9/2**[2]	93
232	8	1 ¼	**Redolent (IRE)**[17] 5624 3-8-12 107....(p) EddieAhern 10 (R Hannon) *w ldr tl wknd over 2f out* **16/1**	95
1100	9	26	**Wise Dennis**[37] 5025 6-9-4 109.... DarrenWilliams 1 (A P Jarvis) *hld up: rdn over 3f out: lost tch over 2f out* **40/1**	43

2m 20.34s (8.34) **Going Correction** +1.10s/f (Soft)
WFA 3 from 4yo+ 6lb — **9** Ran SP% **114.8**
Speed ratings (Par 111): **110,108,107,107,104 102,102,101,81**
toteswinger: 1&2 £5.20, 1&3 £3.40, 2&3 £2.90. CSF £56.92 TOTE £7.80: £2.00, £2.20, £1.20; EX 57.40.
Owner P J Hughes Developments Ltd **Bred** Aerial Bloodstock Et Al **Trained** Lambourn, Berks
■ Stewards' Enquiry : Richard Mullen two-day ban: failed to ride out for 6th place (Oct 6-7)

FOCUS

A reasonable Listed race although the form may not prove that solid given the testing conditions and as a result has not been rated too positively.

NOTEBOOK

Lady Deauville(FR) is a force to be reckoned with in this grade, all five of her career victories, three this term, having come in Listed events with cut in the ground. In contrast she has yet to win in eight tries at Group level, with her trainer inclined to blame her latest defeat in a Group 3 at Goodwood on her being too fresh. She settled better here and was never going to be caught once striking the front. She could bid to break her Group-race duck at Gowran Park next weekend and longer term her trainer is eyeing the Group 1 Premio Lydia Tesio in Rome next month. (op 7-1 tchd 8-1)

Mutajarred had not been seen since flopping when favourite for the John Smith's Cup at York in July when the heavy ground ought not to have been a problem. He ran a decent race on this return from a break and first try in Listed company, rallying for second after being slightly outpaced when the race began in earnest. (op 10-1)

Perks(IRE) was upped in grade following comfortable wins in a handicap at Haydock and a three-horse conditions event at the St Leger meeting. He ran a reasonable race in this better company and remains at the head of the ante-post listings for the Cambridgeshire, for which he avoids a penalty. (op 5-4)

Alfie Flits, off since a couple of lacklustre efforts in the summer, showed more here but lacked a change of pace when one was required. (op 28-1 tchd 20-1)

Sweet Lilly, who split Lady Deauville and subsequent Listed winner Cape Amber at Salisbury last time, ran on from the rear without reaching a challenging position.

Dunaskin(IRE), last seen in July when fifth in the John Smith's Cup with Mutajarred behind, won the battle for the lead but had no answers when headed. (op 28-1)

Bushman, off the track since July, came with a promising run down the outside in the home straight before his effort fizzled out. This was only his fifth appearance and he should be given another chance. (op 3-1)

Redolent(IRE), runner-up in a German Group 3 last time, harried leader Dunaskin from his wide draw before fading going to the two pole as the race hotted up. Official explanation: jockey said colt was unsuited by the heavy ground (op 22-1)

6107 DOBBIE ELECTRICAL CONTRACTORS H'CAP — 1m 5f 13y

5:15 (5:15) (Class 3) (0-90,87) 3-Y-O+ £11,527 (£3,430; £1,714; £856) Stalls Low

Form			Horse	RPR
0103	1		**Tarkheena Prince (USA)**[24] 5391 3-9-3 **85**.... RobertWinston 3 (G A Swinbank) *hld up in tch: hdwy to ld over 2f out: edgd lft u.p: kpt on wl fnl f* **9/2**[2]	98
21	2	hd	**Torphichen**[11] 5780 3-8-12 **80**.... NCallan 1 (M A Jarvis) *cl up: rdn and ev ch fr over 2f out: leaned on ins fnl f: kpt on wl: jst hld* **5/4**[1]	93
5603	3	4 ½	**Red Wine**[5] 5967 9-8-9 **75**.... StacyRenwick(7) 6 (A J McCabe) *hld up: hdwy over 2f out: no imp fnl f* **14/1**	81
5222	4	¾	**Gordonsville**[19] 5563 5-9-2 **75**.... DanielTudhope 2 (J S Goldie) *hld up: effrt over 2f out: one pce over 1f out* **9/1**	80
5333	5	3 ¾	**Rosbay (IRE)**[45] 4742 4-10-0 **87**.... DavidAllan 7 (T D Easterby) *in tch: hdwy after 4f: ev ch over 2f out: sn rdn: wknd over 1f out* **15/2**	87
0331	6	4 ½	**Lady Sorcerer**[37] 5027 3-8-3 **71**.... AndrewElliott 8 (A P Jarvis) *led 2f: chsd ldrs tl wknd over 3f out* **20/1**	65
232	7	1 ¼	**Dubai Petal (IRE)**[29] 5216 3-8-4 **72**.... JimmyQuinn 9 (J S Moore) *cl up: led after 2f to over 2f out: sn wknd* **7/1**[3]	64
-000	8	8	**Lets Roll**[8] 5858 7-9-5 **78**.... SaleemGolam 5 (C W Thornton) *chsd ldrs tl wknd over 2f out* **10/1**	59

3m 14.94s (18.34) **Going Correction** +1.10s/f (Soft)
WFA 3 from 4yo+ 9lb — **8** Ran SP% **117.4**
Speed ratings (Par 107): **87,86,84,83,81 78,77,72**
toteswinger: 1&2 £2.80, 1&3 £10.70, 2&3 £5.10. CSF £10.84 CT £73.19 TOTE £6.00: £1.80, £1.30, £2.30; EX 13.40.
Owner G H Bell **Bred** Whitewood Stable Inc **Trained** Melsonby, N Yorks
■ Stewards' Enquiry : Robert Winston one-day ban: careless riding (Oct 6); two-day ban: used whip with excessive frequency (Oct 7-8)

FOCUS

A decent handicap in which the pace was only steady in the bad ground. It produced a cracking finish and the form is rated at face value.

NOTEBOOK

Tarkheena Prince(USA) just getting the better of fellow three-year-old Torphichen after a sustained duel. They came pretty close together and the result stood after an inquiry. A staying-on third over 1m2f here last month, he came here with a fairly progressive profile and he had no problem with the extra yardage, albeit off the modest gallop. He showed the right attitude too, sticking his neck out well in the drive to the line. (op 5-1)

Torphichen ◆, by far the least experienced runner in the line-up, was making his handicap debut on only his third run following a heavy-ground Leicester maiden win. His yard won this event 12 months ago with another three-year-old, Black Rock, and he came close to repeating the trick, never far away and going down fighting after being done no favours by the winner late on. He can gain compensation and there should be a nice handicap to be won with him at some stage. (tchd 6-4 in places)

Red Wine has been creeping back down the weights but was still 3lb above his last winning mark. He goes well for this apprentice and stayed on from the back of the field for third. (op 12-1)

Gordonsville, who arrived here with a hat-trick of seconds behind him, was 2lb higher. He dropped to the rear turning in but stuck on again. (op 8-1 tchd 10-1)

Rosbay(IRE) had his chance but does look in the Handicapper's control now. (op 7-1 tchd 8-1)

Lady Sorcerer raced keenly in the early stages when the reluctant leader and did not last long once into the home straight.

Lets Roll, who won this race in 2005 and 2006 and was a beaten favourite when fourth last year, was in trouble over 2f out. (tchd 9-1)

6108 SKED CONSTRUCTION - CONCRETE WHAT WE DO H'CAP 1m 2f

5:45 (5:46) (Class 5) (0-75,75) 3-Y-O+

£4,860 (£1,455; £727; £364; £181; £91) **Stalls** Low

Form					RPR
4113	1		**Wind Shuffle (GER)**[19] 5564 5-9-3 **75** GaryBartley(5) 7 (J S Goldie) *mde all: rdn over 2f out: hld on wl* **13/2**		82
0414	2	½	**Grandad Bill (IRE)**[23] 5420 5-8-3 **61** oh3 KellyHarrison(5) 4 (J S Goldie) *chsd ldrs: effrt and cl up over 2f out: sn drvn: chsd wnr ins fnl f: kpt on: hld towards fin* **6/1**[3]		67
0101	3	1¾	**Persian Peril**[23] 5418 4-9-3 **75** FrederikTylicki(5) 6 (G A Swinbank) *prom: effrt and ev ch over 2f out: one pce ins fnl f* **9/4**[1]		77
-504	4	6	**Freeloader (IRE)**[34] 1067 8-9-8 **75** PaulHanagan 3 (R A Fahey) *trckd ldrs tl rdn and no ex fr 2f out* **9/1**		65
10-	5	¾	**Nans Best (IRE)**[6] 5950 4-9-2 **69** RobertWinston 2 (Liam McAteer, Ire) *t.k.h: hld up in tch: rdn and edgd lft over 2f out: sn no imp* **4/1**[2]		58
6104	6	8	**Krugerrand (USA)**[11] 5783 9-9-1 **68** StephenDonohoe 5 (W J Musson) *hld up: shkn up over 2f out: sn btn* **10/1**		41
6106	7	2¾	**Shy Glance (USA)**[24] 5390 6-9-2 **69** EddieAhern 10 (P Monteith) *hld up: rdn over 2f out: sn wknd* **20/1**		36
4006	8	17	**Daring Dream (GER)**[2] 6042 3-8-7 **66** AndrewElliott 8 (A P Jarvis) *hld up: struggling 1/2-way: t.o* **20/1**		—

2m 22.23s (10.23) **Going Correction** +1.10s/f (Soft)
WFA 3 from 4yo+ 6lb **8 Ran SP% 107.0**
Speed ratings (Par 103): **103,102,101,96,95 89,87,73**
toteswinger: 1&2 £5.40, 1&3 £3.60, 2&3 £3.10. CSF £38.94 CT £96.68 TOTE £7.80: £2.10, £1.60, £1.50; EX 32.00 Place 6 £168.56, Place 5 £77.32..
Owner Mrs S E Bruce **Bred** Gestut Elsetal **Trained** Uplawmoor, E Renfrews

FOCUS
A modest handicap and in the conditions not a race to treat too positively.
Daring Dream(GER) Official explanation: jockey said colt ran flat
T/Jkpt: Not won. T/Plt: £415.70 to a £1 stake. Pool: £131,100.94. 230.21 winning tickets. T/Qpdt: £87.60 to a £1 stake. Pool: £7,363.46. 62.20 winning tickets. RY

5394 CATTERICK (L-H)

Saturday, September 20

OFFICIAL GOING: Good to soft (soft in places; 8.1)
Wind: Nil Weather: Sunny

6109 EUROPEAN BREEDERS' FUND MAIDEN STKS (DIV I) 5f 212y

1:25 (1:26) (Class 5) 2-Y-O **£3,561** (£1,059; £529; £264) **Stalls** Low

Form					RPR
5	1		**Darcey**[21] 5499 2-8-12 0 TonyHamilton 2 (R A Fahey) *cl up on inner: led over 2f out: rdn over 1f out and sn clr* **11/4**[1]		77+
5	2	8	**Chambers (IRE)**[7] 5905 2-9-3 0 JoeFanning 11 (M Johnston) *qckly away and sn led: rdn along and hdd over 2f out: drvn and one pce appr fnl f* **7/2**[3]		58
0	3	1	**Point Of Light**[7] 5905 2-9-3 0 J-PGuillambert 6 (Sir Mark Prescott) *in tch: hdwy 2f out and sn rdn: styd on ins fnl f: tk 3rd nr line* **10/3**[2]		55
60	4	hd	**Magic Haze**[45] 4734 2-9-3 0 MickyFenton 8 (Miss S E Hall) *chsd ldrs: rdn along 2f out: one pce fr wl over 1f out: edgd lft ins fnl f: lost 3rd nr line* **25/1**		54
00	5	nk	**Rising Kheleyf (IRE)**[7] 5882 2-9-3 0 PJMcDonald 10 (G A Swinbank) *towards rr: hdwy 2f out: rdn and styd on ins fnl f: nrst fin* **14/1**		53+
	6	2¾	**Kiama Bay (IRE)** 2-8-10 0 JamieKyne(7) 1 (J J Quinn) *dwlt and in rr: hdwy over 2f out: styd on ins fnl f: nrst fin* **10/1**		45
000	7	6	**Peckforton**[53] 4499 2-8-9 44 RussellKennemore(3) 9 (Mrs L Williamson) *chsd ldng pair: rdn along 3f out and sn wknd* **100/1**		22
00	8	6	**Willin Dillon (IRE)**[92] 3225 2-9-0 0 DominicFox(3) 4 (W Storey) *a towards rr* **150/1**		9
0003	9	½	**Pennine Rose**[51] 4557 2-8-6 44 ow1 KrishGundowry(7) 12 (A Berry) *chsd ldrs: rdn along 3f out: sn wknd* **33/1**		—
	10	2	**Benyw (IRE)** 2-8-5 0 RosieJessop(7) 3 (J G Given) *t.k.h on inner: a towards rr* **9/1**		—
	11	2¾	**Cause For Applause (IRE)** 2-8-12 0 PaulMulrennan 7 (B Smart) *dwlt: sn rdn along and outpcd in rr: bhd fr 1/2-way* **10/1**		—
	12	¾	**Broomfield Buddy** 2-8-12 0 PaulFessey 5 (D W Barker) *in midfield: rdn along 1/2-way: sn wknd* **28/1**		—

1m 15.71s (2.11) **Going Correction** +0.25s/f (Good) **12 Ran SP% 118.7**
Speed ratings (Par 95): **95,84,83,82,82 78,70,62,62,59 55,54**
toteswinger: 1&2 £3.10, 1&3 £3.50, 2&3 £4.10. CSF £11.89 TOTE £3.30: £1.20, £2.00, £1.80; EX 13.30.
Owner R Cowie **Bred** Raymond Cowie **Trained** Musley Bank, N Yorks
■ Stewards' Enquiry : J-P Guillambert two-day ban: careless riding (Oct 6-7)
Micky Fenton caution: careless riding

FOCUS
A modest maiden with only one of these having previously made the frame, and that was when a well-beaten third of four. They all came across to the stands' side off the home bend, as they usually do in soft ground here.

NOTEBOOK
Darcey was very well backed and, having raced close to the pace throughout, eventually stormed clear in a race where only two counted from a very long way out. She had been very green on her debut, but was much more the finished article here and she seemed to relish the ground. She is only small, but should still be able to hold her own in better company. (op 9-2)
Chambers(IRE), who drifted alarmingly in the market, broke well enough from his wide draw and made the early running, but when the filly ranged alongside he was very quickly left behind. He does not look anything special, though better ground or a return to sand might be what he needs. (op 6-4)
Point Of Light, another of those well backed, plugged on from off the pace to snatch third and he finished a bit closer to Chambers than he had on his Great Leighs debut. The best of him is likely to be seen in handicap company next year. (op 13-2)
Magic Haze was never far away, and plugged on in a way that suggested a return to further will suit him. He now qualifies for nurseries. (tchd 28-1)
Rising Kheleyf(IRE) stayed on over the last couple of furlongs and showed a bit more than in his two previous tries. He is another that now qualifies for nurseries. (op 16-1)
Kiama Bay(IRE) ◆ made a more promising debut than his finishing position might suggest, especially as he raced furthest from the stands' rail down the home straight and looked green. A half-brother to six winners including the useful Tritonix, he should come on from this and will appreciate further in time. (op 14-1 tchd 9-1)
Willin Dillon(IRE) Official explanation: jockey said gelding suffered interference
Benyw(IRE), another well-backed debutant, should not be judged too harshly on this as she was badly hampered against the inside rail approaching the turn out of the back straight. Official explanation: vet said filly had found to be lame left hind (op 12-1)
Cause For Applause(IRE) Official explanation: jockey said filly missed the break
Broomfield Buddy Official explanation: jockey said saddle slipped

6110 EUROPEAN BREEDERS' FUND MAIDEN STKS (DIV II) 5f 212y

1:55 (1:55) (Class 5) 2-Y-O **£3,561** (£1,059; £529; £264) **Stalls** Low

Form					RPR
0	1		**Hartley**[56] 4415 2-9-3 0 PaulFessey 3 (J D Bethell) *mde virtually all: styd on strly to forge clr fnl f: v readily* **20/1**		90+
2	2	7	**Enderby Spirit (GR)**[49] 4647 2-9-3 0 PaulMulrennan 11 (B Smart) *w wnr: effrt over 2f out: kpt on same pce* **5/4**[1]		69
53	3	1¼	**Intikama (IRE)**[9] 5838 2-8-5 0 AshleyMorgan(7) 10 (M H Tompkins) *towards rr: hdwy centre over 2f out: kpt on: nvr a threat* **3/1**[2]		60
	4	hd	**Blue Noodles** 2-9-3 0 TonyHamilton 1 (D W Barker) *chsd ldrs: styd on same pce fnl 2f* **20/1**		64
55B	5	1½	**Antigua Sunrise (IRE)**[7] 5882 2-8-5 0 BMcHugh(7) 9 (R A Fahey) *sn towards rr: hdwy over 2f out: styng on wl at fin* **12/1**		55+
6	6	shd	**Dreamonandon (IRE)**[13] 5716 2-9-3 0 PJMcDonald 4 (G A Swinbank) *sn detached in last: styd on wl fnl 2f: nt rch ldrs* **16/1**		60+
6	7	2¼	**Reel Bluff**[142] 1749 2-9-3 0 SilvestreDeSousa 2 (D W Barker) *chsd ldrs: kpt on one pce fnl 2f* **33/1**		53
54	8	6	**Lady Gem**[4] 5989 2-8-12 0 JoeFanning 7 (D H Brown) *chsd ldrs: wknd 2f out* **10/1**		30
	9	1½	**Alicante** 2-8-12 0 J-PGuillambert 5 (Sir Mark Prescott) *sn outpcd and in rr: nvr on terms* **17/2**[3]		25
6	10	2½	**Bun Penny**[61] 4237 2-8-12 0 MickyFenton 8 (G M Moore) *mid-div: outpcd over 4f out: bhd fnl 2f* **40/1**		18
0	11	8	**Bulella**[99] 3005 2-8-9 0 DuranFentiman(3) 12 (Garry Moss) *mid-div: lost pl over 2f out: sn bhd* **80/1**		—

1m 15.36s (1.76) **Going Correction** +0.25s/f (Good) **11 Ran SP% 118.8**
Speed ratings (Par 95): **98,88,87,86,84 84,81,73,71,68 57**
toteswinger: 1&2 £8.90, 1&3 £12.60, 2&3 £1.50. CSF £44.27 TOTE £31.40: £5.10, £1.50, £1.10; EX 64.00.
Owner Clarendon Thoroughbred Racing **Bred** Mrs R D Peacock **Trained** Middleham Moor, N Yorks
■ Stewards' Enquiry : Ashley Morgan caution: used whip above shoulder height.

FOCUS
Another modest maiden although a couple of these had already shown some ability. Again the runners came stands' side in the straight and the winning time was 0.35 seconds quicker than the first division.

NOTEBOOK
Hartley had not shown much on his Newcastle debut, but it was a totally different story this time. One of three disputing the lead around the home bend, he looked to be going very much least well of the trio at that point, but once he bagged the stands' rail in front in the home straight he fairly bounded clear of his rivals and his rider was able to ease him down late on. The different ground may have been a factor in the improvement and he may have one more run this season, but the very best of him is likely to be seen next year. (op 25-1)
Enderby Spirit(GR) travelled well enough early, but as soon as Hartley started to turn the screw he looked very unhappy. This was disappointing in view of his promising debut, and whilst this extra furlong should not have been a problem, perhaps the softer ground was. (op 11-8 tchd 6-4)
Intikama(IRE), back up in trip, stayed on late. She was never a threat to the winner, but she was probably not helped by being stuck out more towards the centre of the track in the straight and she may have more joy in nurseries now. (op 11-4)
Blue Noodles, a £38,000 two-year-old, was never far away and fared much the better of the two newcomers. There is plenty of stamina on the dam's side of his pedigree so he should progress as he goes up in trip. (op 12-1)
Antigua Sunrise(IRE), who was more experienced than most, stayed on late and needs a return to further. She now qualifies for a mark. (op 16-1)
Dreamonandon(IRE), who was backed at long odds, did make some late headway. He had looked in need of further when sixth over 1m on his debut, so this big drop in trip was unlikely to suit him and he is one to watch out for if stepped back up in trip, especially once he is handicapped. (op 28-1)

6111 GO RACING AT BEVERLEY NEXT TUESDAY (S) STKS 1m 5f 175y

2:25 (2:25) (Class 6) 3-Y-O **£2,047** (£604; £302) **Stalls** Low

Form					RPR
6520	1		**Miss Cruisecontrol**[28] 5269 3-8-7 45 ow2 PaulMulrennan 11 (J R Best) *trckd ldrs: hdwy 4f out: rdn to ld 2f out: drvn ent fnl f and kpt on* **9/4**[1]		54
05-6	2	4½	**Ras Laffan**[26] 4663 3-8-10 56 PAspell 5 (D McCain Jnr) *in tch: hdwy 4f out: rdn to chse ldrs 3f out: drvn to chse wnr ent fnl f: sn no imp* **10/1**		51
6404	3	¾	**Ask Nicely**[14] 5710 3-8-5 49 PaulFessey 3 (W R Muir) *t.k.h: trckd ldrs: hdwy and cl up over 5f out: rdn along over 2f out: ev ch tl drvn and one pce appr fnl f* **5/2**[2]		45
0230	4	2	**Hoar Frost**[9] 5833 3-8-11 49 SamHitchcott 9 (M R Channon) *hld up in rr: hdwy to trck ldrs over 5f out: effrt 3f out: rdn 2f out: sn drvn and one pce appr fnl f* **7/2**[3]		48
0060	5	1¾	**Kuriyama (IRE)**[21] 4564 3-8-3 49 (b[1]) AshleyMorgan(7) 8 (M H Tompkins) *dwlt: sn trcking ldrs: hdwy to ld after 4f: rdn along 4f out: hdd wl over 2f out: sn drvn and wknd* **8/1**		45
5060	6	13	**Lady In Chief**[81] 3580 3-8-2 46 (p) AndrewMullen(3) 7 (Miss J A Camacho) *trckd ldrs: hdwy and cl up 5f out: rdn along over 3f out: drvn and wknd over 2f out* **16/1**		22
666	7	23	**Mcheppie**[77] 3715 3-8-2 37 DominicFox(3) 4 (W Storey) *a in rr* **25/1**		—
0-0	8	11	**Fleetway (IRE)**[92] 3227 3-7-12 0 JamieKyne(7) 2 (F Watson) *in tch: rdn along and bhd fr 1/2-way* **40/1**		—
0-00	9	47	**Spooky**[41] 4901 3-8-10 40 MickyFenton 1 (W Storey) *led 4f: prom tl rdn along 1/2-way: sn lost pl and bhd* **33/1**		—

3m 9.32s (5.72) **Going Correction** +0.25s/f (Good) **9 Ran SP% 116.9**
Speed ratings (Par 99): **93,90,90,88,87 80,67,61,34**
toteswinger: 1&2 £9.10, 1&3 £1.40, 2&3 £4.80. CSF £25.56 TOTE £3.70: £1.20, £3.10, £1.40; EX 32.00.The winner was bought in for 4,800gns.
Owner Dave Standbridge **Bred** Bloomsbury Stud **Trained** Hucking, Kent
■ Stewards' Enquiry : Paul Fessey caution: careless riding

FOCUS
A very weak seller in which only one had previously won a race, so a contest that is unlikely to live very long in the memory. The form looks far from reliable.

6112 BOOK NOW FOR TOTESPORT SATURDAY 18TH OCTOBER NURSERY 7f
3:00 (3:06) (Class 4) (0-85,81) 2-Y-O **£3,885** (£1,156; £577; £288) **Stalls** Low

Form				RPR
056	**1**		**Sampower Rose (IRE)**[45] 4740 2-8-0 **60** .... PaulQuinn 1 (D Carroll) *prom on inner: hdwy to chse ldng pair over 2f out: rdn to chal ent fnl f: sn drvn and styd on to ld nr fin* **16/1**	62
5533	**2**	*nk*	**The Kyllachy Kid**[21] 5497 2-9-7 **81** .... MickyFenton 2 (T P Tate) *mde most: rdn 2f out: drvn ent fnl f: hdd and no ex nr fin* **7/1**	82
4510	**3**	*1*	**Richo**[28] 5274 2-9-4 **78** .... PaulMulrennan 12 (D H Brown) *trckd ldrs: hdwy on outer to chal 3f out: sn rdn and ev ch tl drvn and nt qckn ent fnl f* **6/1**[3]	77
5420	**4**	*1 1/2*	**Digger Derek (IRE)**[28] 5274 2-8-2 **65** .... AndrewMullen(3) 8 (R A Fahey) *hld up: hdwy wl over 2f out: rdn to chse ldrs over 1f out: kpt on ins fnl f: nrst fin* **9/2**[2]	60+
3150	**5**	*3 1/4*	**Beautiful Breeze (IRE)**[10] 5791 2-9-5 **79** .... JoeFanning 9 (M Johnston) *chsd ldrs: rdn along 3f out: drvn over 2f out and grad wknd* **11/1**	66
665	**6**	*1/2*	**Red Max (IRE)**[57] 4384 2-8-1 **64** .... DuranFentiman(3) 10 (T D Easterby) *in tch: rdn along over 2f out: drvn and kpt on same pce fnl 2f* **28/1**	49
3515	**7**	*1*	**Woolston Ferry (IRE)**[2] 6058 2-9-4 **78** .... SamHitchcott 6 (M R Channon) *dwlt: hdwy 3f out: rdn along over 2f out: sn no imp* **7/1**	61
004	**8**	*2 1/2*	**Jacobite Prince (IRE)**[38] 4960 2-8-5 **72** .... AshleyMorgan(7) 4 (M H Tompkins) *in tch: hdwy 3f out: rdn to chse ldrs 2f out: sn drvn and wknd over 1f out* **7/1**	49
223	**9**	*2 1/4*	**Dean Iarracht (IRE)**[23] 5416 2-8-13 **73** .... TonyHamilton 3 (M Dods) *hld up: a in rr* **4/1**[1]	44
040	**10**	*1*	**Sardan Dansar (IRE)**[28] 5256 2-7-8 **61** ow2 .... RosieJessop(7) 11 (Mrs A Duffield) *t.k.h: cl up: rdn along 3f out and sn wknd* **22/1**	30
604	**11**	*8*	**Shaker Style (USA)**[21] 5500 2-8-12 **72** .... (b) PaulFessey 5 (J D Bethell) *a in rr* **18/1**	21

1m 29.43s (2.43) **Going Correction** +0.25s/f (Good) **11** Ran SP% **117.2**
Speed ratings (Par 97): **96,95,94,92,89 88,87,84,81,80 71**
toteswinger: 1&2 £9.80, 1&3 £17.00, 2&3 £3.80. CSF £123.47 CT £773.88 TOTE £18.70: £4.00, £2.40, £2.30; EX 74.10.
Owner J F O'Sullivan **Bred** N Fagan **Trained** Sledmere, E Yorks

FOCUS
An open nursery, but very few ever got into it.

NOTEBOOK
Sampower Rose(IRE), who had run really well for a 100-1 shot here two starts ago, made the most of her modest mark on this nursery debut and responded well to pressure to wear down the two leaders after they had gone clear. This was her first try on soft ground and she clearly enjoyed it. Official explanation: trainer said, regarding the apparent improvement in form, that he had no explanation other than, as previously stated, the filly had moved poorly on her last run, and that this was its first in a nursery. (tchd 12-1)
The Kyllachy Kid tried to make just about every yard and only just failed to do so. This was a good effort, considering he was raised 4lb from his last start when only third at Chester and he deserves to break his duck on consistency alone. (op 11-2 tchd 5-1)
Richo went clear with the eventual runner-up starting up the home straight. Until now he has looked more suited by quicker ground. (op 13-2)
Digger Derek(IRE) appreciated this return to a slower surface and was doing all his best work late, but he probably needs a stiffer track or a step up to 1m now. (op 6-1)
Beautiful Breeze(IRE) ran better than at Doncaster, when he reportedly lost his action, but he was possibly not helped by being marooned out towards the centre of the track. (op 8-1 tchd 12-1)
Dean Iarracht(IRE) was very well backed beforehand, but he was soon out the back and never got into the race at all. (op 8-1)

6113 CONSTANT SECURITY SEPTEMBER STKS (H'CAP) 1m 3f 214y
3:35 (3:36) (Class 3) (0-90,88) 3-Y-O+ **£7,771** (£2,312; £1,155; £577) **Stalls** High

Form				RPR
-050	**1**		**Lost Soldier Three (IRE)**[7] 5894 7-9-10 **88** .... SilvestreDeSousa 7 (D Nicholls) *hld up: hdwy to trck ldrs 1/2-way: pushed along 3f out: rdn to ld 1 1/2f out: edgd lft and drvn ins fnl f: styd on wl* **13/2**	98
1	**2**	*1 1/2*	**Another Moment**[36] 5042 4-9-4 **82** .... PJMcDonald 3 (G A Swinbank) *hld up in tch: pushed along 1/2-way: rdn and outpcd over 4f out: rdn and hdwy 2f out: drvn to chse wnr ins fnl f: kpt on* **9/4**[1]	90+
6-04	**3**	*5*	**Luna Landing**[45] 4742 5-8-13 **77** .... PaulMulrennan 6 (Jedd O'Keeffe) *trckd ldrs: effrt 4f out: rdn along on inner to chse ldng pair over 2f out: swtchd rt and drvn over 1f out: kpt on same pce* **17/2**	77
21	**4**	*1 1/4*	**Woody Waller**[73] 3835 3-8-3 **75** .... PaulFessey 5 (J Howard Johnson) *in tch: pushed along 1/2-way: rdn: rn green and outpcd 4f out: styd on fnl 2f: nrst fin* **7/1**	73
2254	**5**	*hd*	**Inspector Clouseau (IRE)**[56] 4419 3-8-7 **79** ow1 .... MickyFenton 2 (T P Tate) *led: rdn along 3f out: drvn and hdd 1 1/2f out: wknd* **5/1**[3]	77
3212	**6**	*1 3/4*	**Shady Gloom (IRE)**[49] 4619 3-8-8 **80** .... JoeFanning 1 (K A Ryan) *chsd ldr: cl up 4f out: rdn over 2f out and ev ch tl drvn and wknd over 1f out* **4/1**[2]	75
0113	**7**	*1*	**Holiday Cocktail**[36] 5040 6-8-6 **77** .... (p) JamieKyne(7) 4 (J J Quinn) *a in rr* **8/1**	70

2m 38.63s (-0.27) **Going Correction** +0.25s/f (Good)
WFA 3 from 4yo+ 8lb **7** Ran SP% **114.9**
Speed ratings (Par 107): **110,109,105,104,104 103,102**
toteswinger: 1&2 £3.60, 1&3 £14.60, 2&3 £6.50. CSF £21.78 TOTE £8.00: £4.30, £2.20; EX 30.10.
Owner Eamon Maher **Bred** Darley **Trained** Sessay, N Yorks

FOCUS
A decent little handicap containing a couple of unexposed and progressive sorts, but difficult form to pin down with confidence. The early pace was only modest, which caused a couple to race keenly, and the tempo did not really pick up until around halfway. On this occasion the runners all stayed on the inside up the home straight. The winner was well in on old form and the runner-up unexposed and probably better than the bare form.

NOTEBOOK
Lost Soldier Three(IRE) had not been successful since winning a Listed race more than three years ago, but most of that time has been spent in Pattern events. He had not run well when dropped into handicap company at Doncaster last time either, but another 3lb drop in his mark did the trick. He saw plenty of daylight on the outside when up with the early pace and he was inclined to take a grip, but he was also in the ideal place to strike when the race started to develop. Sent for home passing the 2f pole, he soon established enough of an advantage to hold the late effort of the runner-up. (op 8-1 tchd 6-1)
Another Moment ◆, winner of an Aintree bumper and a course-and-distance maiden in his only previous try on the Flat proper, was well backed. He is the type that does not do much in front, so his rider seemed intent in producing him as late as possible, but he had a fair amount of ground to make up when the winner was committed and he could never quite get to him. A more truly run race is what he needs and there will be another day. (op 7-2)
Luna Landing, who is better handicapped now, was never far off the pace, but lacked a turn of foot when it mattered. This ground would have been more testing than he prefers though. (op 7-1 tchd 6-1)
Woody Waller, whose maiden win over further has not worked out at all, was out the back for most of the way before making some laboured late progress. He is still far from the finished article though, and he seems very likely to be seen over hurdles in due course. (tchd 8-1)
Inspector Clouseau(IRE), trying this trip for the first time, was not disgraced but he was able to dictate at a steady early pace and this did not really prove his stamina. (op 11-2 tchd 7-1)
Shady Gloom(IRE) was another to race keenly up with the pace early and he did not get home. This was his first try on soft ground and it may not have suited. (op 7-2)

6114 BOOK RACEDAY HOSPITALITY ON 01748 810165 MAIDEN STKS 7f
4:10 (4:11) (Class 5) 3-4-Y-O **£2,590** (£770; £385; £192) **Stalls** Low

Form				RPR
-52	**1**		**Eton Rifles (IRE)**[19] 5561 3-9-3 0 .... PaulMulrennan 6 (J Howard Johnson) *sn cl up: led 3f out: rdn clr wl over 1f out: easily* **7/2**[1]	84+
2-4	**2**	*8*	**Somerset Falls (UAE)**[57] 4379 3-8-12 0 .... JoeFanning 10 (M Johnston) *prom: cl up 1/2-way: rdn over 2f out: sn drvn and kpt on: no ch w wnr* **4/1**[2]	57
	3	*1 1/2*	**Business Class (BRZ)** 3-8-5 0 .... SilvestreDeSousa 4 (D Nicholls) *in tch: hdwy 3f out: rdn 2f out: kpt on same pce u.p appr fnl f* **8/1**	46
0	**4**	*1/2*	**My Mate Mal**[180] 991 4-9-6 0 .... TonyHamilton 13 (B Ellison) *hld up towards rr: hdwy 1/2-way: rdn to chse ldrs 2f out: drvn over 1f out: kpt on same pce* **66/1**	58
0-50	**5**	*1*	**Transmission (IRE)**[110] 2665 3-9-3 **69** .... PAspell 11 (B Smart) *chsd ldrs: effrt 3f out: sn rdn and kpt on same pce fnl 2f* **8/1**	54
03	**6**	*2*	**Cullybackey (IRE)**[16] 5636 3-8-12 0 .... PJMcDonald 15 (G A Swinbank) *in rr tl hdwy over 2f out: kpt on ins fnl f: nrst fin* **10/1**	44+
0	**7**	*3/4*	**Promise Maker (USA)**[156] 1417 3-9-0 0 .... DuranFentiman(3) 14 (T D Walford) *in midfield: rdn along over 2f out: sn no imp* **7/1**	47
	8	*2 3/4*	**Brave Optimist (IRE)** 3-8-12 0 .... PaulQuinn 9 (Paul Green) *s.i.s and bhd: sme hdwy whn bmpd wl over 1f out: nvr a factor* **40/1**	34
	9	*5*	**Rosies Dawn** 3-8-12 0 .... DNolan 3 (D Carroll) *a towards rr* **33/1**	21
	10	*3 1/4*	**Occasion** 3-8-12 0 .... PaulFessey 12 (G M Moore) *in tch: hdwy to chse ldrs over 2f out: sn rdn and btn* **50/1**	12
	11	*1 1/2*	**Take That** 3-9-0 0 .... MichaelJStainton(3) 7 (S P Griffiths) *chsd ldrs: rdn along 1/2-way and sn wknd* **66/1**	13
	12	*15*	**Fiveonthreeforjd** 3-9-0 0 .... AndrewMullen(3) 1 (W J H Ratcliffe) *s.i.s: a in rr* **33/1**	—
	13	*5*	**Foolish Optimist** 3-8-12 0 .... SamHitchcott 2 (Paul Green) *cl up on inner: led after 1f: rdn along and hdd 3f out: sn drvn and wknd* **33/1**	—
2	**14**	*1 3/4*	**Top Tribute**[26] 5361 3-9-3 0 .... MickyFenton 5 (T P Tate) *led 1f: cl up tl rdn along and wknd over 2f out: swtchd lft and eased wl over 1f out: virtually p.u ins fnl f* **5/1**[3]	—
	15	*30*	**Avatea (IRE)** 3-8-5 0 .... KrishGundowry(7) 8 (A Berry) *v.s.a: a wl bhd* **100/1**	—

1m 28.52s (1.52) **Going Correction** +0.25s/f (Good)
WFA 3 from 4yo 3lb **15** Ran SP% **119.9**
Speed ratings (Par 103): **101,91,90,89,88 86,85,82,76,72 71,53,48,46,11**
toteswinger: 1&2 £4.10, 1&3 £6.40, 2&3 £10.60. CSF £16.12 TOTE £3.40: £1.40, £2.20, £2.70; EX 19.00.
Owner Transcend Bloodstock LLP **Bred** Grangecon Stud **Trained** Billy Row, Co Durham

FOCUS
A big field, but only a handful could be given a realistic chance. The runners reverted to coming up the stands' rail in the home straight. The impressive winner looks a nice type, but the form behind him looks weak.
Cullybackey(IRE) Official explanation: jockey said, regarding running and riding, that his orders were to slot in from a wide draw and finish in the best possible position, adding that the early pace was very strong and he was unable to take up an early position and in latter stages worked his way through tired horses.
Top Tribute Official explanation: jockey said gelding lost its action but returned sound

6115 RICHMOND H'CAP 1m 7f 177y
4:45 (4:46) (Class 6) (0-65,62) 3-Y-O+ **£2,388** (£705; £352) **Stalls** Low

Form				RPR
2534	**1**		**Merrymaker**[40] 4935 8-9-7 **58** .... DuranFentiman(3) 8 (W M Brisbourne) *in rr: hdwy 6f out: hrd drvn over 3f out: styd on to ld last 75yds* **11/1**	68
4000	**2**	*1/2*	**Mt Desert**[18] 3399 6-9-13 **61** .... PaulMulrennan 12 (E W Tuer) *w ldr: led after 3f: hdd wl ins fnl f: no ex* **22/1**	70
6401	**3**	*1 3/4*	**Mister Pete (IRE)**[19] 5559 5-9-6 **57** .... DominicFox(3) 14 (W Storey) *trckd ldrs: chal over 1f out: kpt on same pce last 100yds* **13/2**[3]	64
3025	**4**	*7*	**Court Of Appeal**[24] 5396 11-9-3 **58** .... (tp) ClGillies(7) 6 (B Ellison) *chsd ldrs: wnt 2nd over 2f out: one pce* **8/1**	57
0626	**5**	*3 3/4*	**Sendali (FR)**[25] 5385 4-9-1 **49** .... PaulFessey 1 (J D Bethell) *mid-div: hdwy 6f out: kpt on same pce fnl 2f: nvr rchd ldrs* **3/1**[1]	43
00-0	**6**	*2*	**Jetta Joy (IRE)**[117] 2468 3-7-8 **47** ow1 .... RosieJessop(7) 3 (Mrs A Duffield) *hld up in rr: hdwy over 4f out: kpt on: nvr nr ldrs* **40/1**	39
5120	**7**	*2 1/4*	**Chiff Chaff**[7] 5917 4-9-7 **55** .... SamHitchcott 11 (C R Dore) *led 3f: chsd ldrs: wknd over 1f out* **8/1**	44
2460	**8**	*1 3/4*	**Toboggan Lady**[105] 2849 4-9-8 **59** .... AndrewMullen(3) 15 (Mrs A Duffield) *chsd ldrs: hrd drvn over 3f out: lost pl over 2f out* **9/2**[2]	46
40-5	**9**	*5*	**Karlani (IRE)**[20] 5543 5-9-13 **61** .... PJMcDonald 9 (G A Swinbank) *towards rr: drvn 7f out: nvr on terms* **8/1**	42
2506	**10**	*1 3/4*	**Coronado's Gold (USA)**[19] 5559 7-9-7 **55** .... PAspell 13 (B Ellison) *s.i.s: hld up in rr: sme hdwy 6f out: wknd over 2f out* **20/1**	34
6043	**11**	*21*	**Saturday Boy**[107] 2750 3-8-4 **50** .... PaulQuinn 5 (Paul Green) *in rr: reminders and lost pl over 6f out: sn bhd: eased 2f out: t.o* **11/1**	4

3/0- 12 dist **Northerner (IRE)**[564] 631 5-9-2 **50**........................ SilvestreDeSousa 10 —
(J O'Reilly) *chsd ldrs: drvn 8f out: sn lost pl: hopelessly t.o 6f out: virtually p.u* **25/1**

3m 34.88s (2.88) **Going Correction** +0.25s/f (Good)
WFA 3 from 4yo+ 12lb 12 Ran SP% **121.9**
Speed ratings (Par 101): **102,101,100,97,95 94,93,92,90,89 78,—**
toteswinger: 1&2 £21.50, 1&3 £12.30, 2&3 £10.30. CSF £238.60 CT £1713.70 TOTE £11.40: £3.20, £5.40, £2.20; EX 351.30.
Owner The Blacktoffee Partnership **Bred** Hascombe And Valiant Studs **Trained** Great Ness, Shropshire

FOCUS
A moderate staying handicap and a few of them were returning from layoffs. They went a decent pace, however, and that seemed to sort the men out from the boys.

6116 CATTERICKBRIDGE.CO.UK H'CAP 7f
5:20 (5:21) (Class 6) (0-60,60) 3-Y-O+ **£2,388** (£705; £352) **Stalls** Low

Form RPR
0100 **1** **Trans Sonic**[16] 5638 5-8-12 **58**........................(b) JamieKyne(7) 4 67
(A J Lockwood) *hld up: hdwy on inner 2f out: rdn and nt clr run ent fnl f: drvn and styd on to ld nr fin* **12/1**
6053 **2** *nk* **Bertie Vista**[42] 4877 3-9-0 **59**........................ DuranFentiman(3) 11 66
(T D Easterby) *chsd ldrs: hdwy and cl up 3f out: rdn 2f out: drvn to ld 1f out: edgd lft ins fnl f: hdd and no ex towards fin* **12/1**
0000 **3** ½ **Provost**[82] 3557 4-8-11 **57**........................ BradleyRoper(7) 9 64
(M W Easterby) *hld up towards rr: hdwy wl over 1f out: rdn ent fnl f: styd on wl towards fin* **22/1**
3425 **4** 1 ½ **Admirals Way**[9] 5836 3-9-4 **60**........................ MickyFenton 8 62
(C N Kellett) *led: rdn along over 2f out: sn drvn: hdd ent fnl f: wknd towards fin* **6/1**[2]
-060 **5** 1 **Zamalik (USA)**[5] 5965 5-9-4 **60**........................ AndrewMullen(3) 13 60
(Mrs A Duffield) *in tch: hdwy to chse ldrs 2f out: sn rdn: drvn and n.m.r over 1f out: kpt on same pce u.p ins fnl f* **14/1**
0236 **6** 2 ½ **The Salwick Flyer (IRE)**[24] 5389 5-9-5 **58**........................ PaulFessey 3 51
(Miss L A Perratt) *trckd ldrs: hdwy 2f out: rdn to chse ldrs whn nt clr run appr fnl f: sn drvn and wknd* **11/2**[1]
0030 **7** ¾ **Kirkby's Treasure**[20] 5538 10-9-2 **55**........................ JoeFanning 14 46
(A Berry) *s.i.s and bhd: rdn along and hdwy over 2f out: kpt on ins fnl f: nrst fin* **14/1**
0640 **8** ½ **Joshua's Gold (IRE)**[14] 5712 7-9-4 **57**........................(v) DNolan 10 47
(D Carroll) *prom: effrt 3f out: rdn along 2f out: drvn over 1f out and wknd ent fnl f* **8/1**
-000 **9** ½ **Mundo's Magic**[105] 2846 4-9-2 **55**........................ PJMcDonald 1 43
(M Dods) *chsd ldrs: rdn along wl over 2f out: drvn and wknd over 1f out* **7/1**[3]
1000 **10** ½ **Tri Chara (IRE)**[14] 5712 4-9-3 **56**........................(p) PAspell 5 43
(R Hollinshead) *hld up: hdwy 3f out: rdn to chse ldrs 2f out: sn drvn and wknd over 1f out* **16/1**
0100 **11** ½ **Umverti**[62] 4219 3-8-13 **58**........................ MichaelJStainton(3) 15 43
(N Bycroft) *a towards rr* **25/1**
1200 **12** 8 **Messiah Garvey**[40] 4919 4-9-4 **57**........................ SilvestreDeSousa 6 21
(D Nicholls) *a in rr* **11/2**[1]
1606 **13** 2 **Maison Dieu**[41] 4903 5-9-3 **56**........................ PaulMulrennan 12 15
(E J Alston) *a towards rr* **17/2**
3-65 **14** 3 ¾ **Eternal Optimist (IRE)**[30] 5203 3-9-4 **60**........................ PaulQuinn 7 8
(Paul Green) *chsd ldrs: rdn along 3f out: drvn over 2f out and sn wknd* **33/1**
6000 **15** 9 **Kabis Amigos**[45] 4736 6-9-3 **56**........................ TonyHamilton 2 —
(S T Mason) *cl up on inner: rdn along 3f out: sn drvn and wknd* **50/1**

1m 30.01s (3.01) **Going Correction** +0.25s/f (Good)
WFA 3 from 4yo+ 3lb 15 Ran SP% **126.9**
Speed ratings (Par 101): **92,91,91,89,88 85,84,83,83,82 82,73,70,66,56**
toteswinger: 1&2 £20.10, 1&3 £97.20, 2&3 £49.80. CSF £150.26 CT £3220.90 TOTE £19.40: £6.40, £3.30, £7.20; EX 138.80 Place 6 £16.96, Place 5 £13.72..
Owner Mrs Lynne Lumley **Bred** I A Balding **Trained** Brawby, N Yorks

FOCUS
Another moderate handicap to end the card, but competitive nonetheless and they went a decent early pace, though that may have told later on as the winning time was slower than both the older-horse maiden and the nursery. Again the runners came stands' side up the home Sound form, with a mix of prominent runners and hold-up horses fighting out the finish.
Messiah Garvey Official explanation: jockey said gelding was unsuited by the good to soft (soft in places) ground
Kabis Amigos Official explanation: jockey said gelding hung right-handed throughout
T/Plt: £18.20 to a £1 stake. Pool: £40,266.01. 1,608.20 winning tickets. T/Qpdt: £18.10 to a £1 stake. Pool: £1,620.99. 66.20 winning tickets. JR

6072 NEWBURY (L-H)
Saturday, September 20

OFFICIAL GOING: Good (good to soft in places; 6.8)
Wind: Nil. Weather: Sunny

6117 E B F DUBAI TENNIS CHAMPIONSHIPS MAIDEN STKS (DIV I) 7f (S)
1:35 (1:39) (Class 4) 2-Y-O **£5,504** (£1,637; £818; £408) **Stalls** Centre

Form RPR
6 **1** **Alazeyab (USA)**[22] 5468 2-9-3 0........................(t) PhilipRobinson 1 83+
(M A Jarvis) *trckd ldrs: drvn to ld jst ins fnl f: styd on strly cl home* **6/1**[2]
0 **2** 1 **King's Sabre**[17] 5615 2-9-3 0........................ DO'Donohoe 7 80+
(W R Muir) *led: shkn up 2f out: hdd jst ins fnl f: outpcd by wnr fnl 110yds but styd on strly for clr 2nd* **50/1**
40 **3** 3 ¼ **Holyrood**[49] 4625 2-9-3 0........................ RyanMoore 8 72
(Sir Michael Stoute) *chsd ldrs: rdn and styd on same pce fr over 1f out* **11/4**[1]
4 ¾ **Tactic** 2-9-3 0........................ DPMcDonogh 14 70+
(J L Dunlop) *in rr: drvn along over 2f out: green and swtchd rt over 1f out: rapid hdwy ins fnl f: fin strly* **18/1**
0 **5** *hd* **Block Party**[22] 5469 2-9-3 0........................ SteveDrowne 19 70+
(R Charlton) *towards rr early: hdwy 3f out: chsd ldrs 2f out: styd on same pce ins fnl f* **13/2**[3]
0 **6** ½ **Durgan**[22] 5468 2-9-3 0........................ IanMongan 3 68
(C G Cox) *chsd ldrs: rdn over 2f out: styd on same pce fr over 1f out* **33/1**
7 *nk* **Above Average (IRE)** 2-9-3 0........................ GeorgeBaker 16 68+
(B W Hills) *in rr: pushed along over 2f out: gd hdwy over 1f out: styd on strly ins fnl f: gng on cl home* **10/1**
8 1 **Legislate** 2-9-3 0........................ MichaelHills 13 65+
(B W Hills) *in rr: pushed along over 2f out: hdwy fr over 1f out: gng on ins fnl f and swtchd rt nr fin* **8/1**
9 ¾ **Netta (IRE)** 2-8-12 0........................ JimmyFortune 10 58
(P J Makin) *sn chsng ldrs: drvn along over 2f out: kpt on same pce fnl f* **33/1**
10 ¾ **Blue Tango (IRE)** 2-9-3 0........................ JimCrowley 4 61
(Mrs A J Perrett) *chsd ldrs: rdn along over 2f out: grad fdd fnl f* **33/1**
11 1 ¼ **Silverglas (IRE)** 2-9-3 0........................ RichardKingscote 2 58
(C A Horgan) *s.i.s: sn rcvrd and in tch 1/2-way: pushed along 2f out and sn dropped away* **80/1**
12 ¾ **Nicky Nutjob (GER)** 2-9-3 0........................ AlanMunro 5 56+
(P W Chapple-Hyam) *s.i.s: hdwy 1/2-way: kpt on fnl f but nvr in contention* **16/1**
0 **13** ½ **Dane's World (IRE)**[52] 4521 2-8-12 0........................ DaneO'Neill 17 50
(R Hannon) *in rr tl sme prog fnl 2f* **40/1**
14 4 ½ **Eastern Empire** 2-9-3 0........................ TQuinn 18 44+
(J W Hills) *chsd ldrs: rdn 1/2-way: wknd fr 2f out: no ch whn hmpd cl home* **50/1**
15 *nk* **Tarruji (IRE)** 2-9-3 0........................ LDettori 6 43+
(P W Chapple-Hyam) *chsd ldrs: rdn over 2f out: wknd fnl f and hld whn hmpd nr fin* **11/1**
16 2 **Pagan Flight (IRE)** 2-9-3 0........................ PaulEddery 12 38
(B J Meehan) *s.i.s: a towards rr* **40/1**
17 *hd* **Red Hot Pepper** 2-8-12 0........................ LPKeniry 15 33
(A M Balding) *s.i.s: a in rr* **33/1**
18 11 **Fire King** 2-9-3 0........................ StephenCarson 9 10
(J A Geake) *slowly away: a in rr* **66/1**

1m 27.51s (1.81) **Going Correction** +0.05s/f (Good) 18 Ran SP% **117.3**
Speed ratings (Par 97): **91,89,86,85,85 84,84,83,82,81 79,79,78,73,72 70,70,57**
toteswinger: 1&2 £53.70, 1&3 £4.00, 2&3 £31.80. CSF £249.25 TOTE £7.20: £2.60, £19.00, £1.50; EX 376.80.
Owner Hamdan Al Maktoum **Bred** Shadwell Farm LLC **Trained** Newmarket, Suffolk
■ Stewards' Enquiry : Michael Hills caution: careless riding.

FOCUS
The pace seemed reasonable, but the eventual runner-up was left alone up front and very few were ever seriously involved. They raced up the middle of the track early, but were edging across to the stands' side late on.

NOTEBOOK
Alazeyab(USA), who carried Hamdan Al Maktoum's second colours, had a tongue-tie on for the first time and improved on the form he showed when sixth in a good maiden over this trip at Sandown on his debut. He was always well placed towards the far side of the main group and, after coming off the bridle well over 2f out, stayed on best to run out a decisive winner. His dam, although by Green Desert, stayed 1m4f, and this one will soon want further than this 7f. He is entered in both the Dewhurst and Racing Trophy, so is clearly very well regarded, and deserves his chance in something better now. (op 9-2)
King's Sabre improved massively on the form he showed when beaten 15 lengths in a Polytrack maiden at 66-1 on his debut. However, while he clearly has plenty of ability, it must be noted that he was allowed a very easy lead. (tchd 40-1)
Holyrood ◆ has not progressed as expected since running fourth in a hot maiden at the July course on his debut. Having been a beaten favourite at Goodwood last time, he again ran below market expectations, plugging on at one pace after coming under pressure a fair way out. However, he can be expected to improve significantly when stepped up to middle-distances next year - he is by Falbrav, out of a Shirley Heights mare - and is now qualified for a handicap mark. (op 2-1 tchd 3-1)
Tactic ◆, by Sadler's Wells and a half-brother to a 1m winner out of a 1m2f winner, fared easily best of the newcomers and this was an eye-catching debut. He looked to be going nowhere for much of the race and dropped well out the back but finished strongly once switched towards the stands' rail late on. He holds an entry in the Racing Post Trophy and rates as a decent prospect when stepped up in trip. (op 22-1 tchd 16-1)
Block Party, whose trainer won this race with Trade Fair in 2002 and Proponent in 2006, travelled well to point, but did not really pick up. (op 8-1 tchd 9-1)
Durgan was only a length and a half behind today's winner at Sandown on his debut, but that one has clearly made more improvement. (tchd 40-1)
Above Average(IRE) ◆, a 70,000 euros son of High Chaparral, out of a 6f juvenile winner, made a pleasing debut. He was well off the pace for much of the way, but made some encouraging late headway without being given an unnecessarily hard time and should be a lot better for the run. He could live up to his name in time. (op 25-1)
Legislate needed a blanket for stalls entry and was reluctant to load. He was never seen with a chance but should learn from the whole experience. (op 10-1)
Eastern Empire Official explanation: jockey said colt suffered interference in running

6118 USK VALLEY STUD NURSERY 6f 8y
2:05 (2:10) (Class 2) 2-Y-O
£12,462 (£3,732; £1,866; £934; £466; £234) **Stalls** Centre

Form RPR
021 **1** **Nasri**[36] 5053 2-8-10 **83**........................ JamieSpencer 3 93
(B J Meehan) *squeezed out s: towards rr: swtchd lft and hdwy over 2f out: sn rdn: led ent fnl f: kpt on strly: rdn out* **3/1**[1]
521 **2** 1 **Definightly**[11] 5784 2-8-10 **83**........................ SteveDrowne 4 90
(R Charlton) *prom: rdn 2f out: led briefly ent fnl f: kpt on but nt pce of wnr* **4/1**[2]
2606 **3** ½ **Skid Solo (IRE)**[40] 4931 2-8-6 **79**........................ AlanMunro 5 85
(P W Chapple-Hyam) *prom: led over 3f out: rdn and hdd enetering fnl f: kpt on but no ex* **33/1**
01 **4** ½ **Cheviot (USA)**[19] 5572 2-8-7 **80**........................ PhilipRobinson 16 84
(M A Jarvis) *mid-div: smooth prog fr over 2f out: rdn and ev ch ent fnl f: edgd rt and nt qckn* **13/2**[3]
2314 **5** 2 ¾ **Timeteam (IRE)**[22] 5466 2-8-4 **77**........................ CatherineGannon 14 73
(S Kirk) *prom: rdn over 2f out: ev ch over 1f out: kpt on same pce fnl f* **14/1**
5200 **6** 3 ¼ **Saucy Brown (IRE)**[8] 5852 2-9-7 **94**........................ JimmyFortune 8 80
(R Hannon) *mid-div: effrt over 2f out: styd on same pce fr over 1f out* **14/1**
1206 **7** ¾ **Finnegan McCool**[49] 4626 2-8-13 **86**........................ RichardKingscote 6 70
(R M Beckett) *mid-div: rdn over 2f out: kpt on same pce* **16/1**
031 **8** ½ **Smokey Ryder**[20] 5530 2-8-3 **76**........................ DO'Donohoe 1 58
(G L Moore) *mid-div: rdn to chse ldrs 2f out: one pce fr over 1f out* **14/1**
3130 **9** *nse* **Evelyn May (IRE)**[29] 5244 2-8-9 **82**........................ MichaelHills 7 64
(B W Hills) *rdn 3f out: a mid-div* **16/1**
2160 **10** 3 ½ **Harriet's Girl**[25] 5381 2-8-5 **78**........................ LiamJones 15 50
(K R Burke) *a towards rr* **33/1**
5100 **11** ½ **Klynch**[14] 5693 2-9-2 **94**........................(b) GabrielHannon(5) 13 64
(B J Meehan) *rdn 3f out: nvr bttr than mid-div* **40/1**
0320 **12** ½ **Jeremiah (IRE)**[28] 5294 2-8-3 **76**........................ FrankieMcDonald 2 45
(J G Portman) *mid-div: effrt 3f out: wknd over 1f out* **25/1**

3106 **13** *1 ¾* **Tishtar**[22] 5466 2-8-12 **85**.. RyanMoore 12 48
(R Hannon) *led for over 2f: chsd ldrs and sn rdn: fdd fnl 2f* **10/1**

000 **14** *¾* **Polly's Choice (IRE)**[29] 5228 2-7-5 **71** oh5............... CharlesEddery(7) 9 32
(R Hannon) *mid-div: rdn 3f out: wknd 2f out* **66/1**

000 **15** *10* **Costa Lotta**[47] 4692 2-7-12 **71** oh8.................................. DavidKinsella 10 2
(E A L Dunlop) *s.i.s: a towards rr* **66/1**

3313 **16** *hd* **Carnaby Haggerston (IRE)**[50] 4594 2-8-9 **82**........... DPMcDonogh 11 13
(K A Ryan) *sn outpcd and bhd* **14/1**

1m 12.22s (-0.78) **Going Correction** +0.05s/f (Good) **16** Ran SP% **121.0**
Speed ratings (Par 101): **107,105,105,104,100 96,95,94,94,89 89,88,86,85,71 71**
toteswinger: 1&2 £2.50, 1&3 £25.10, 2&3 £28.10. CSF £13.08 CT £293.69 TOTE £3.40: £1.50, £1.60, £7.00, £1.80; EX 8.90 Trifecta £213.30 Part won. Pool: £288.30, 0.30 winning units..
Owner Saleh Al Homaizi & Imad Al Sagar **Bred** Lady Hardy **Trained** Manton, Wilts

FOCUS
A very good sprint nursery and the 'right' horses dominated. They went a good pace and this looks like decent form for the grade. They raced up the middle of the track pretty much as one, but those towards the far side just had the edge and the first three home were drawn low.

NOTEBOOK
Nasri ◆ recovered well from a slow start and stayed on strongest of all when switched towards the outer of the main group with his challenge. This was a very useful effort and he is progressing into a decent colt. Although by Kyllachy, he is out of a 1m2f winner and is likely to be stepped up to 7f next time. The Group 3 Somerville Tattersall Stakes at Newmarket is apparently being considered, but connections will wait and see what the handicapper does before making any decisions. (tchd 11-4 and 10-3 in places)
Definightly ◆, who beat little of note at Lingfield last time but still did the job impressively, ran his race in second but could not reverse earlier course form with Nasri, and his connections are entitled to feel a little hard done by that he had to reoppose that rival on the same terms. Having travelled really powerfully, he found plenty and this still rates as a decent effort in defeat.
Skid Solo(IRE) has not been progressing as one might have hoped and was well beaten in a Wolverhampton maiden on his latest start, but this was much more like it. Having gone off at a good pace, he kept on well for pressure and posted a decent effort behind a couple of well-handicapped rivals.
Cheviot(USA), off the mark in a Polytrack maiden over this trip at Kempton on his previous start, ran well to finish close up and his effort is all the more creditable considering he fared best of those in a double-figure stall. (op 9-2)
Timeteam(IRE) ran a solid race stepped back up in trip and should find slightly easier opportunities. (op 20-1)
Saucy Brown(IRE) was dropping significantly in class, but had no easy task under his big weight. This was a respectable effort, but he might not be the easiest to place, unless an ordinary novice event can be found.
Finnegan McCool looks on a stiff enough mark and was reported to have been unsuited by the ground. Official explanation: jockey said colt was unsuited by the good (good to soft places) ground

6119 DUBAI DUTY FREE MILL REEF STKS (GROUP 2) 6f 8y
2:35 (2:39) (Class 1) 2-Y-O

£45,416 (£17,216; £8,616; £4,296; £2,152; £1,080) **Stalls** Centre

Form RPR

3235 **1** **Lord Shanakill (USA)**[8] 5852 2-9-1 108........................... JimCrowley 5 117
(K R Burke) *chsd ldrs: rdn over 2f out: styd on to chal 1f out: r.o gamely u.p to ld fnl 110yds* **10/1**

6122 **2** *½* **Gallagher**[27] 5330 2-9-1 114... JimmyFortune 7 115
(B J Meehan) *hld up in rr but in tch: stdy hdwy over 2f out: rdn and styd on strly to chal 1f out: no ex cl home* **11/8**[1]

223 **3** *hd* **Sayif (IRE)**[52] 4517 2-9-1 107.................................... JamieSpencer 2 114
(P W Chapple-Hyam) *pressed ldr tl rdn to take slt ld over 1f out: hdd fnl 110yds: no ex cl home* **7/1**

142 **4** *1 ¾* **Damien (IRE)**[9] 5827 2-9-1 0.. MichaelHills 8 109
(B W Hills) *towards rr but in tch: hdwy fr 2f out: rdn and r.o wl fnl f but nt pce to rch ldng trio* **9/2**[2]

10 **5** *1 ¼* **Marine Boy (IRE)**[29] 5226 2-9-1 100.................... RichardKingscote 3 105
(Tom Dascombe) *slt advantage: rdn over 2f out: narrowly hdd over 1f out: styd pressing ldrs tl wknd fnl 110yds* **11/2**[3]

1104 **6** *4* **Khor Dubai (IRE)**[14] 5693 2-9-1 94..................................... LDettori 4 93
(Saeed Bin Suroor) *chsd ldrs: rdn over 2f out: wknd fnl f* **18/1**

1100 **7** *½* **Icesolator (IRE)**[53] 4507 2-9-1 100.................................. RyanMoore 1 92
(R Hannon) *chsd ldrs: rdn over 2f out: wknd appr fnl f* **25/1**

11 **8** *1 ¼* **Masamah (IRE)**[43] 4822 2-9-1 0...................................... DPMcDonogh 9 88
(E A L Dunlop) *rdn ins fnl 3f: a outpcd* **14/1**

2 **9** *9* **Sign Of Approval**[12] 5756 2-9-1 0................................... GeorgeBaker 6 61
(K R Burke) *s.i.s and wnt lft s: a bhd* **40/1**

1m 11.82s (-1.18) **Going Correction** +0.05s/f (Good) **9** Ran SP% **115.5**
Speed ratings (Par 107): **109,108,108,105,104 98,98,96,84**
toteswinger: 1&2 £4.80, 1&3 £13.50, 2&3 £3.80. CSF £24.17 TOTE £11.70: £2.40, £1.30, £2.00; EX 29.10 Trifecta £105.20 Pool: £625.60, 4.40 winning units.
Owner Mark T Gittins **Bred** Vimal Khosla, Gillian Khosla Et Al **Trained** Middleham Moor, N Yorks

FOCUS
There was not a single Group winner among the nine runners and this was an ordinary renewal of the Mill Reef. The winning time was only 0.40 seconds quicker than the earlier nursery, although that was a very hot race for the grade.

NOTEBOOK
Lord Shanakill(USA) came into this 0-4 in Group company but had been running most consistently in defeat - he had achieved an RPR of at least 100 on all of his starts since winning his maiden - and he deserved this. Having found 5f too sharp when fifth in the Flying Childers at Doncaster on his latest start, he appreciated the step back up in trip and reversed earlier Prix Morny form with Gallagher in determined fashion. The Dewhurst is a possibility, but he may not race again this year. Connections suggested he could be campaigned in the US at some point. (op 8-1 tchd 11-1 in a place)
Gallagher could not confirm Prix Morny form with today's winner, who was two and a half lengths behind when the pair met in France. He travelled enthusiastically and had his chance, but the winner was simply more determined. He deserves to take his chance in the Middle Park, but has now found one too good on all three of his starts in Group company. (op 6-4 tchd 13-8)
Sayif(IRE) ◆ had been off the track since finishing only a neck behind today's winner in the Vintage Stakes at Goodwood almost two months previously and had missed the opening maiden at Newmarket on Friday with a vet's certificate. He apparently had a dirty scope on the Monday before this race and also suffered from a touch of colic during the week. He was produced with his chance, but Jamie Spencer felt he blew up, which is understandable, and, all things considered, this was a highly creditable effort in defeat. He may now be given his chance in the Middle Park and must surely go close if things go smoothly in the build up. (op 8-1)
Damien(IRE), just touched off in a sales race over an extended 6f at Doncaster on his previous start, promised to be suited by this slight drop in trip but still had something to find and simply encountered three too good. (op 5-1)
Marine Boy(IRE) improved on the form he showed when disappointing in the rescheduled Gimcrack over course and distance on his previous start, keeping on much better this time when headed. He is still not quite living up to the promise of his impressive debut success, but may be ready for a step up to 7f now. (op 6-1 tchd 13-2)
Khor Dubai(IRE) is not quite up to this class, but he could still have been expected to finish slightly closer. (op 16-1 tchd 20-1)
Icesolator(IRE) has struggled since winning a 5f Listed race at Sandown in May and looks badly treated on a mark of 100. (tchd 16-1)
Masamah(IRE) won well in minor company on his first two starts and deserved a shot at something like this but was never going. Official explanation: trainer said colt was found to have tied up after the race (tchd 12-1)
Sign Of Approval, beaten a short-head into second in a four-runner novice event on his debut at Folkestone 12 days earlier, still looked very green. Official explanation: jockey said colt had no more to give (op 66-1)

6120 JOHN SMITH'S STKS (HERITAGE H'CAP) 1m 2f 6y
3:10 (3:10) (Class 2) (0-105,104) 3-Y-O+

£62,310 (£18,660; £9,330; £4,670; £2,330; £1,170) **Stalls** Low

Form RPR

5122 **1** **Presvis**[28] 5279 4-9-1 **92**.. RyanMoore 15 113
(L M Cumani) *mid-div: hmpd over 7f out: hdwy 4f out: rdn to ld over 1f out: forged clr: comf* **11/2**[2]

2-21 **2** *7* **Rose Street (IRE)**[25] 5382 4-9-1 **92** 5ex.................. PhilipRobinson 6 99
(M A Jarvis) *trckd ldr: led 3f out: sn rdn: hdd over 1f out: kpt on but sn no ch w wnr* **15/2**[3]

0315 **3** *½* **Indian Days**[6] 5932 3-9-1 **98**.. AlanMunro 9 104
(J G Given) *chsd ldr: rdn and ev ch 3f out: styd on same pce: regained 3rd ins fnl f* **14/1**

1141 **4** *1 ½* **Prince Kalamoun (IRE)**[22] 5449 3-8-10 **93** 5ex.......... JamieSpencer 20 96+
(G A Swinbank) *hld up towards rr: swtchd rt over 3f out: sn rdn and hung lft: styd on wl fnl f: nrst fin* **12/1**

0335 **5** *hd* **Samsons Son**[15] 5677 4-8-11 **88**.................................... LPKeniry 2 91
(J R Best) *chsd ldrs: rdn 3f out: kpt on same pce fnl 2f* **33/1**

1411 **6** *1 ¼* **Ask The Butler**[21] 5508 4-9-9 **100** 5ex......................... DaneO'Neill 17 105+
(L M Cumani) *squeezed out s: sn mid-div: sltly hmpd over 7f out: lost pl 4f out: sn rdn: nt clr run over 1f out: styd on: nvr able to mount chal* **7/2**[1]

3605 **7** *¾* **Monte Alto (IRE)**[53] 4504 4-9-7 **98**................................... LDettori 11 97
(L M Cumani) *mid-div: rdn over 2f out: no imp tl styd on fnl f* **10/1**

4054 **8** *¾* **Beauchamp Viceroy**[19] 5569 4-8-10 **87**.................. RichardKingscote 1 84
(G A Butler) *led tl 3f out: kpt chsng ldrs and sn rdn: one pce fr over 1f out* **33/1**

0004 **9** *nk* **Night Crescendo (USA)**[15] 5677 5-9-1 **92**................... JimCrowley 5 89
(Mrs A J Perrett) *trckd ldrs: rdn 3f out: one pce fnl 2f* **25/1**

0314 **10** *nse* **Tazeez (USA)**[21] 5508 4-9-10 **101**.............................. JimmyFortune 16 97
(J H M Gosden) *cl up: hmpd over 7f out: rdn 3f out: wknd fnl f* **14/1**

0021 **11** *nk* **Siberian Tiger (IRE)**[7] 5903 3-9-4 **101** 5ex............. EdwardCreighton 19 97
(M R Channon) *mid-div on outer: hdwy over 4f out: rdn over 2f out: one pce after* **12/1**

0 **12** *¾* **Tamimi's History**[42] 4845 4-9-1 **97**......................... RichardEvans(5) 12 91
(P D Evans) *rdn over 3f out: nvr bttr than mid-div* **50/1**

2105 **13** *¾* **Love Galore (IRE)**[13] 5741 3-9-5 **102**............................. MichaelHills 8 95
(M Johnston) *hld up bhd: gd hdwy on rails over 4f out: chsd ldrs over 2f out: sn rdn: wknd fnl f* **16/1**

2310 **14** *nk* **Nanton (USA)**[21] 5508 6-9-0 **91**.................................... GeorgeBaker 7 83
(J S Goldie) *hld up towards rr: hdwy into mid-div over 2f out: no further imp* **25/1**

-201 **15** *½* **Unshakable (IRE)**[28] 5279 9-9-5 **96**............................... PaulEddery 4 87
(Bob Jones) *nvr bttr than mid-div: wknd fnl f* **20/1**

1400 **16** *1 ¾* **Count Ceprano (IRE)**[15] 5675 4-8-8 **85**.............................. TQuinn 3 73
(M D I Usher) *squeezed up on rails over 7f out: a towards rr* **66/1**

5016 **17** *nk* **Kings Quay**[8] 5858 6-8-7 **84**..(t) LiamJones 14 71
(J J Quinn) *a towards rr* **25/1**

1605 **18** *¾* **Proponent (IRE)**[21] 5508 4-9-5 **96**............................ SteveDrowne 10 82
(R Charlton) *mid-div: rdn 3f out: sn btn* **14/1**

60 **19** *32* **Mount Hadley (USA)**[52] 4528 4-8-11 **88**................... StephenCarson 13 10
(G A Butler) *a bhd: eased whn btn fnl 2f* **66/1**

-504 **20** *2 ½* **Alexander Castle (USA)**[8] 5856 3-9-7 **104**................. DPMcDonogh 18 21
(K A Ryan) *mid-div whn bdly hmpd over 7f out: hung bdly lft fr over 4f out: sn btn and eased* **66/1**

2m 7.51s (-1.29) **Going Correction** +0.10s/f (Good)
WFA 3 from 4yo+ 6lb **20** Ran SP% **128.4**
Speed ratings (Par 109): **109,103,103,101,101 100,100,99,99,99 98,98,97,97,97 95,95,94,69,67**
toteswinger: 1&2 £8.50, 1&3 £9.40, 2&3 £35.20. CSF £43.13 CT £568.12 TOTE £7.00: £2.20, £2.10, £3.90, £2.50; EX 51.20 Trifecta £1082.90 Part won. Pool: £1,463.40, 0.90 winning units..
Owner L Marinopoulos **Bred** Mrs M Campbell-Andenaes **Trained** Newmarket, Suffolk

FOCUS
A really hot renewal of this valuable handicap, but the pace was steady and there was trouble in running. The highly progressive Presvis won in a style seldom seen in handicaps at this level and looks sure to be competing in Group company next year. Progressive sorts chased him home too, and a positive view has been taken of the form.

NOTEBOOK
Presvis ◆ was admittedly well placed considering the way the race was run, but it's still rare to see a horse quicken so well off a slow pace, especially in what looked such a competitive handicap and after being bumped in the trouble on the first bend. Though beaten twice since hacking up on his handicap debut, he looked unlucky on the second occasion and took this in the style of a Group horse in the making. He is in the Cambridgeshire, and with just a 4lb penalty the temptation may prove impossible to resist, although Luca Cumani regards him as a 1m4f horse in the making and has one eye on next year's Dubai carnival. (op 13-2)
Rose Street(IRE), 1lb well-in under the penalty she picked up for her Ripon success, ran well, especially considering she was the only filly in this big field. She was a touch keen towards the front end but avoided the trouble. Although keeping on well, she never looked likely to muster the pace to threaten the winner and would have preferred a stronger-run race. (op 6-1 tchd 8-1)
Indian Days, like the runner-up, avoided the trouble in behind and ran another decent race in third. He is holding his form really well and continues to thrive. (op 12-1)
Prince Kalamoun(IRE) ◆ was 3lb well-in under the penalty he picked up for his recent Chester success, but he did not have the race run to suit. He was held up well out the back, so the steady pace was totally against him, and he did really well to stay on down the outside and get so close. He is in the Cambridgeshire, which was won in 2006 by his trainer's third in this race, Formal Decree, but he is not certain to make the cut.
Samsons Son is more exposed than some of these, but this was a decent effort in defeat. He has won over 1m4f, so the steady pace cannot have been ideal.
Ask The Butler ◆, a stablemate of the winner, is better than he showed as he was held up off the slow pace and, after meeting a little bit of trouble on the first bend, did not get the best of runs when switched inside in the straight. It is probably worth just putting a line through this, and the bookmakers may have overreacted by easing him for the Cambridgeshire (he is out to 16-1 in places), as that is still the plan and he remains one of the likelier types. The stronger pace there will suit him much better. (op 4-1 tchd 9-2 in a place)
Monte Alto(IRE), 6lb higher than when winning this last year, could never threaten and is one of many who did not have the race run to suit. (op 9-1)

Beauchamp Viceroy, due to be dropped 1lb, was the horse responsible for all the slow fractions, so there can be no excuses for him. Official explanation: jockey said gelding had no more to give
Tazeez(USA) had no easy task conceding weight all round, but he was one of those hampered early on and is better than he showed. (tchd 16-1)
Siberian Tiger(IRE) was 4lb ahead of the handicapper under the penalty he picked up for last week's Goodwood success, but he was always out wide from his outside draw and never got involved this time. (op 16-1)
Love Galore(IRE) had 3lb in hand, but he was well out the back early and never threatened. (op 20-1)
Proponent(IRE) was short of room on the first bend and was never seen with a chance thereafter.
Alexander Castle(USA) , due to be eased 2lb, was another caught up in all the trouble and suffered more than most, but even allowing for that, his recent efforts leave him with plenty to prove. He was reported to have pulled the bit through his mouth. Official explanation: jockey said bit pulled through gelding's mouth on leaving stalls

6121 DUBAI DUTY FREE 25TH ANNIVERSARY WORLD TROPHY (GROUP 3) 5f 34y

3:45 (3:49) (Class 1) 3-Y-O+

£36,900 (£13,988; £7,000; £3,490; £1,748; £877) **Stalls** Centre

Form RPR
063 **1** **Moorhouse Lad**[10] 5793 5-9-0 109 JimCrowley 14 104
(B Smart) *pressed ldr tl slt advantage fr 2f out: hrd rdn and kpt on gamely whn chal thrght fnl f* **8/1**
4030 **2** *nk* **Wi Dud**[7] 5891 4-9-0 102 (b) AlanMunro 15 103
(K A Ryan) *sn pressing ldrs: hrd rdn and styd on thrght fnl f: tk 2nd cl home but nt rch wnr* **9/1**
0140 **3** *nk* **Toms Laughter**[7] 5890 4-9-0 95 (b) KevinGhunowa 16 102
(R A Harris) *t.k.h: in tch: hrd rdn 2f out: styd on u.p to press ldrs thrght fnl f: no ex cl home* **20/1**
6112 **4** *hd* **Look Busy (IRE)**[7] 5884 3-8-13 106 SladeO'Hara 6 101
(A Berry) *sn chsng ldrs and upsides fr 1/2-way: chal fr 2f out and ev ch thrght fnl f tl no ex cl home* **11/2**[1]
0005 **5** *nk* **Judd Street**[7] 5906 6-9-0 95 (b[1]) StephenCarson 9 100
(Eve Johnson Houghton) *t.k.h: sn chsng ldrs: hrd drvn to chal fr ins fnl 2f tl wknd cl home* **33/1**
0064 **6** *3/4* **Rowe Park**[39] 4957 5-9-0 104 (p) LPKeniry 5 97
(Mrs L C Jewell) *in tch: rdn fr 1/2-way: styd on u.p ins fnl f but nvr quite gng pce to chal* **14/1**
3501 **7** *hd* **Enticing (IRE)**[51] 4550 4-9-0 107 LiamJones 4 96
(W J Haggas) *in tch: rdn and hdwy fr 2f out to chse ldrs 1f out: one pce ins fnl f* **13/2**[2]
6311 **8** *nse* **Green Manalishi**[48] 4660 7-9-0 100 DPMcDonogh 12 96
(K A Ryan) *in tch: rdn and outpcd after 2f: styd on again u.p ins fnl f: gng on cl home* **14/1**
1406 **9** *3/4* **Misaro (GER)**[7] 5906 7-9-0 91 (b) DaneO'Neill 13 93
(R A Harris) *sn rdn and outpcd: rdn 1/2-way: hdwy fnl f: fin wl* **50/1**
5030 **10** *1/2* **Reverence**[7] 5891 7-9-0 103 JimmyFortune 2 92
(E J Alston) *in tch: rdn and sme prog fr 2f out: nvr gng pce to be competitive* **12/1**
0-02 **11** *1* **Loch Verdi**[10] 5793 5-8-11 97 LDettori 10 85
(A M Balding) *slt ld tl narrowly hdd 2f out: wknd appr fnl f* **7/1**[3]
2030 **12** *hd* **Fullandby (IRE)**[7] 5890 6-9-0 103 GregFairley 7 87
(T J Etherington) *a outpcd* **12/1**
4100 **13** *2* **Brave Prospector**[48] 4660 3-8-13 105 (t) JamieSpencer 3 80
(P W Chapple-Hyam) *in rr tl rdn and sme prog in bhd ldrs 2f out: wknd sn after* **12/1**
0401 **14** *shd* **Galeota (IRE)**[10] 5793 6-9-0 101 RyanMoore 8 80
(R Hannon) *chsd ldrs tl wknd over 1f out* **15/2**

60.67 secs (-0.73) **Going Correction** +0.05s/f (Good)
WFA 3 from 4yo+ 1lb **14** Ran SP% **120.2**
Speed ratings (Par 113): **107,106,106,105,105 104,103,103,102,101 100,99,96,96**
toteswinger: 1&2 £15.80, 1&3 £36.90, 2&3 £49.10. CSF £76.66 TOTE £9.30: £2.90, £3.30, £6.00; EX 97.60 TRIFECTA Not won..
Owner Ron Hull **Bred** Peter Onslow **Trained** Hambleton, N Yorks
■ Stewards' Enquiry : Alan Munro one-day ban: used whip with excessive frequency without giving colt time to respond (Oct 6)
Kevin Ghunowa one-day ban: used whip with excessive frequency (Oct 6)

FOCUS
A wide-open race on paper and plenty were still in with a chance going into the final furlong, with the field spread across the track, although all were under strong pressure. Muddling form, and the proximity of the third and the ninth is a concern.

NOTEBOOK
Moorhouse Lad stuck his neck out to post his best performance since bolting up in a Group 3 at Goodwood in August 2007. Although he hadn't won since then, he'd not fared at all badly on his last couple of starts and came into this in pretty good shape. Appreciating the drying ground, he was allowed to bowl along with the pace and, despite challengers on all sides entering the final furlong, battled on strongly. (tchd 15-2 and 7-1 in places)
Wi Dud hasn't won since September 2006 but has been ultra-consistent over this trip throughout his career, including when only a length and a half behind Look Busy at The Curragh last month. Having been outpaced mid race, he picked up strongly in the final furlong to get within a neck of the winner and overturn that form with the aforementioned Look Busy. (op 11-1 tchd 17-2)
Toms Laughter had a tough task on at these weights, so he ran an absolute blinder, quite possibly a career-best. Ron Harris felt that on quicker ground he might have won, but his handicap mark will obviously suffer. He might now go for the Listed Rous Stakes at Newmarket next month, ground permitting. (op 25-1)
Look Busy(IRE) has had a fantastic season and ran another blinder, looking the most likely winner until just running out of steam in the closing stages. She has been admirable this summer. (tchd 5-1 and 6-1)
Judd Street, who was third in this last year, had a similar chance to Toms Laughter on these terms and, despite being too free in the first-time blinkers early on, battled on well to post his best effort since running with credit in the Temple Stakes in May. He is likely to bid for a repeat win in the Listed Rous Stakes at Newmarket next.
Rowe Park , wearing first-time cheek pieces, was finally free of the Group-race penalty he incurred for winning this race last year but he couldn't repeat the feat. That said, he was not beaten at all far. (op 16-1)
Enticing(IRE) was best in here on official figures but the ground had not dried out enough for her. (tchd 7-1)
Fullandby(IRE) Official explanation: jockey said gelding missed the break

6122 E B F DUBAI TENNIS CHAMPIONSHIPS MAIDEN STKS (DIV II) 7f (S)

4:20 (4:25) (Class 4) 2-Y-O **£5,504** (£1,637; £818; £408) **Stalls** Centre

Form RPR
1 **Control Zone (IRE)** 2-9-3 0 JamieSpencer 1 87+
(B J Meehan) *s.i.s: towards rr: hdwy over 3f out: shkn up to ld ins fnl f: rn green and hung lft: r.o wl: readily* **9/1**
6 **2** *2 3/4* **History Lesson**[36] 5053 2-9-3 0 RyanMoore 12 77
(R Hannon) *led: hung lft u.p over 1f out: hdd ins fnl f: nt pce of ready wnr* **4/1**[1]
0 **3** *1* **Wilfred Pickles (IRE)**[27] 5314 2-9-3 0 JimCrowley 7 75
(Mrs A J Perrett) *chsd ldrs: rdn and ev ch over 1f out: sn hung lft: kpt on but no ex fnl f* **20/1**
4 *1* **Nora Mae (IRE)** 2-8-12 0 JamesDoyle 18 67
(S Kirk) *w'like: bit bkwd: slowly away: towards rr: nt clr run over 2f out: rdn and prog over 1f out: styd on wl ins fnl f: snatched 4th fnl strides* **50/1**
5 *nk* **Baron Otto (IRE)** 2-9-3 0 LiamJones 13 71
(W J Haggas) *hld up towards rr: hdwy 3f out: swtchd rt 2f out: sn rdn: styd on fnl f* **25/1**
6 *nk* **Al Marmoom (USA)** 2-9-3 0 LDettori 3 71
(Saeed Bin Suroor) *prom: rdn and ev ch fr 2f out: no ex fnl f* **9/2**[2]
7 *nk* **Splendorinthegrass (IRE)** 2-9-3 0 SteveDrowne 5 70+
(R Charlton) *w'like: bit bkwd: s.i.s: sn pushed along into midfield: rdn and abt to chal whn squeezed out over 1f out: no ch after* **7/1**[3]
8 *nk* **Gibb River (IRE)** 2-9-3 0 AlanMunro 15 69+
(P W Chapple-Hyam) *s.i.s: bhd: rdn and stdy prog fr 2f out: styd on fnl f: nvr trbld ldrs* **15/2**
9 *1 1/2* **Playful Asset (IRE)** 2-8-12 0 RichardKingscote 8 60
(R M Beckett) *wnt sligtly rt s: chsd ldrs: rdn over 2f out: wknd over 1f out* **28/1**
6 **10** *1/2* **Devil To Pay**[37] 5022 2-9-3 0 DaneO'Neill 9 64+
(J L Dunlop) *hmpd leaving stalls: sn mid-div: rdn 3f out: no imp fnl 2f* **20/1**
11 *5* **Marju King (IRE)** 2-9-3 0 TQuinn 10 52
(W S Kittow) *mid-div: rdn over 2f out: sn btn* **33/1**
06 **12** *1/2* **Makhaaleb (IRE)**[41] 4890 2-9-3 0 MichaelHills 14 50
(B W Hills) *mid-div tl lost pl 3f out: nvr got bk on terms* **9/2**[2]
0 **13** *2* **Kaiser Willie (IRE)**[63] 4187 2-8-10 0 AmyScott[(7)] 2 45
(B W Duke) *chsd ldrs: rdn over 2f out: sn wknd* **40/1**
14 *1/2* **Red Sabre** 2-9-3 0 (t) LPKeniry 4 44
(J S Moore) *chsd ldrs tl wknd 2f out* **66/1**
15 *1 1/2* **Silvador** 2-9-3 0 DO'Donohoe 6 40
(W R Muir) *chsd ldrs tl wknd 2f out* **14/1**
0 **16** *1/2* **Hypnotic Gaze (IRE)**[37] 5022 2-9-3 0 PhilipRobinson 17 39
(C G Cox) *chsd ldrs: rdn 3f out: wknd 2f out* **25/1**
17 *1 1/2* **Sky Gate (USA)** 2-9-3 0 JimmyFortune 16 35
(B J Meehan) *mid-div: rdn 3f out: sn wknd* **20/1**

1m 27.61s (1.91) **Going Correction** +0.05s/f (Good) **17** Ran SP% **131.6**
Speed ratings (Par 97): **91,87,86,85,85 84,84,84,82,81 76,75,73,72,71 70,68**
toteswinger: 1&2 £10.60, 1&3 £69.40, 2&3 £36.10. CSF £42.79 TOTE £15.50: £4.10, £2.10, £6.90; EX 68.50.
Owner Clipper Logistics **Bred** Ballyhane Stud **Trained** Manton, Wilts

FOCUS
This looked quite a decent maiden and the race should produce some nice winners. The winning time was 0.10sec slower than the first division, but they didn't look to go that quick.

NOTEBOOK
Control Zone(IRE) ◆, by Daggers Drawn, half-brother to useful dual 6f-7f winner Capt Chaos, out of a quite useful 1m winner, made an impressive racecourse debut. He was out the back early after starting slowly, but arrived on the scene going really well and found plenty when asked, although he did show his inexperience by wandering around once clear in front. This looks to be his trip and he deserves his chance in something better now. The Somerville Tattersall Stakes at Newmarket, or the Horris Hill back over this course and distance might suit. (tchd 17-2 and 10-1)
History Lesson improved significantly on the form he showed on his debut over 6f, but found one too good. He hung left late on and is still learning. (op 6-1)
Wilfred Pickles(IRE) is a nice big horse and this was a huge improvement on the form he showed first time up over 1m at Goodwood. He should do even better next year as he continues to strengthen up. (tchd 22-1)
Nora Mae(IRE) ◆, the first foal of a 1m winner, was one of only two fillies in the line up and made a very pleasing debut. She missed the break, but made some good late headway, despite meeting a little bit of trouble, and will know more next time. She should stay further.
Baron Otto(IRE) is bred to want further next year, but he was keeping on well and this was an encouraging start. (op 16-1)
Al Marmoom(USA), whose stable won a division of this race in 2004 and 2005, cost $250,000 and is by Medaglia D'Oro. He seemed to have his chance, but is entitled to improve. (op 4-1 tchd 7-2)
Splendorinthegrass(IRE), a 185,000gns son of Selkirk, is better than he showed as he was short of room when trying to stay on over a furlong out. (op 8-1)
Gibb River(IRE), a 170,000gns son of Mr Greeley, out of a 1m4f winner, is a very big horse and was entitled to need this. He stayed on well and is likely to do a good bit better over a little further next year. (op 11-1 tchd 7-1)
Makhaaleb(IRE) was below the form he showed on his debut at Leicester last time and this was another slightly disappointing effort. (op 4-1 tchd 5-1)
Kaiser Willie(IRE) finished up well beaten, but ran well to a point and looks to have ability. (op 50-1 tchd 33-1)

6123 JOHN SMITH'S CONDITIONS STKS 1m 1f

4:55 (4:56) (Class 3) 3-Y-O+

£7,477 (£2,239; £1,119; £560; £279; £140) **Stalls** Low

Form RPR
2132 **1** **Yaddree**[56] 4404 3-8-6 100 PhilipRobinson 2 110
(M A Jarvis) *w'like: trckd ldr: slt ld 2f out: narrowly hdd appr fnl f: rallied u.p to ld again ins fnl f: styd on strly* **2/1**[1]
6440 **2** *3/4* **Cat Junior (USA)**[28] 5276 3-8-6 115 JamieSpencer 5 108
(B J Meehan) *hld up in rr: hdwy fr 3f out: slt ld u.p appr fnl f: hdd ins fnl f: no ex nr fin* **5/1**[3]
1142 **3** *1 1/4* **With Interest**[10] 5792 5-8-11 107 LDettori 8 105
(Saeed Bin Suroor) *hld up towards rr: hdwy on outside fr 3f out: styd on to take 3rd 1f out but no imp on ldng duo* **9/2**[2]
1 **4** *1 1/4* **Acclaimed (IRE)**[40] 4929 3-8-8 0 RyanMoore 9 105+
(J Noseda) *chsd ldrs tl rdn and outpcd 3f out: styd on again fnl f but nvr gng pce to trble ldng trio* **5/1**[3]
1362 **5** *hd* **Igor Protti**[30] 5208 6-8-11 108 (v[1]) DO'Donohoe 7 104+
(Saeed Bin Suroor) *hld up towards rr: effrt on ins whn n.m.r: lost pl and swtchd rt ins fnl 2f: styd on ins fnl f but nvr a threat* **12/1**
0620 **6** *shd* **Alfathaa**[49] 4622 3-8-6 105 (b) LiamJones 3 102
(W J Haggas) *t.k.h: chsd ldrs: rdn over 2f out: sn one pce: wknd ins fnl f* **11/1**
4062 **7** *5* **Caldra (IRE)**[26] 5368 4-8-11 99 DPMcDonogh 4 91
(S Kirk) *chsd ldrs: rdn and effrt 3f out: wknd over 2f out* **16/1**
05 **8** *1/2* **Escape Route (USA)**[36] 5070 4-8-11 98 (b[1]) JimmyFortune 1 90
(J H M Gosden) *led tl hdd 2f out: sn wknd* **11/1**

510/ **9** *7* **Spectait**[223] 5675 6-8-11 100 .... DaneO'Neill 6 75
(Jonjo O'Neill) *wnt bdly lft s and slowly away: sn rcvrd in rr and t.k.h: rdn and no ch fnl 3f* **33/1**

1m 54.66s (-0.84) **Going Correction** +0.10s/f (Good)
WFA 3 from 4yo+ 5lb **9** Ran SP% **118.0**
Speed ratings (Par 107): **107,106,105,104,103 103,99,98,92**
toteswinger: 1&2 £3.50, 1&3 £2.20, 2&3 £4.80. CSF £12.38 TOTE £2.90: £1.30, £1.80, £2.00; EX 12.70.
Owner Sheikh Ahmed Al Maktoum **Bred** Darley **Trained** Newmarket, Suffolk

FOCUS
Not a bad conditions contest, although the early pace was just ordinary and most of them had questions to answer. Yaddree continues to progress, but Cat Junior was 8lb off his Group 1 form, although he had travelled into the race like a winner.

NOTEBOOK
Yaddree defied an absence of almost two months with a decisive success on his first run beyond 1m. He was always well placed considering the way the race was run and showed a really good attitude to get the better of a protracted duel with Cat Junior. Now his stamina for 1m1f is proven he is likely to take up his entry in the Cambridgeshire, for which he has picked up a 4lb penalty. He is progressing into a smart colt and deserves his chance. (op 7-2)
Cat Junior(USA), without the tongue-tie this time, was the best off at the weights and had no less than 15lb in hand over the winner, so this could be considered slightly disappointing. However, Jamie Spencer was of the opinion that he simply did not stay and it would be no surprise to see him dropped back to 1m or even 7f next time. (op 7-2 tchd 11-2)
With Interest has had some problems over the years, but he is still capable at this level and ran a respectable third. (op 10-3 tchd 3-1)
Acclaimed(IRE), impressive at Windsor on debut, had a stiff task and ran well. He is open to more improvement and should make a nice four-year-old, but the handicapper is unlikely to be kind (op 6-1 tchd 13-2)
Igor Protti did not get the best of runs through against the far rail and had to switch, so he is a little better than he showed. He also gave the impression a stronger pace would have suited better. (tchd 9-1)
Alfathaa, with the blinkers refitted, was far too keen for his own good early on, but he still finished clear of the remainder, who were well beaten. (op 14-1)
Escape Route(USA) Official explanation: jockey said gelding lost its action

6124 JOHN SMITH'S LONGLEVENS COMMUNITY ASSOCIATION H'CAP 7f (S)
5:25 (5:28) (Class 4) (0-80,80) 3-Y-O **£4,857** (£1,445; £722; £360) **Stalls** Centre

Form RPR
0150 **1** **Elysee Palace (IRE)**[59] 4300 3-9-3 79 .... DaneO'Neill 7 93
(M A Jarvis) *prom in centre: rdn to ld wl over 1f out: kpt on wl: rdn out* **12/1**
0305 **2** *¾* **Lodi (IRE)**[19] 5580 3-9-3 79 .... (t) IanMongan 12 91
(J Akehurst) *lw: chsd ldrs in centre: rdn to chse wnr over 1f out: kpt on but a jst hld* **20/1**
5613 **3** *3¾* **Willkandoo (USA)**[7] 5910 3-9-0 76 .... (p) DPMcDonogh 9 78
(K A Ryan) *overall ldr in centre: rdn and hdd wl over 1f out: kpt on* **9/1**
6124 **4** *1* **Tina's Best (IRE)**[78] 3679 3-9-1 77 .... RyanMoore 11 76
(R Hannon) *mid-div in centre: rdn over 2f out: styd on steadily: wnt 4th jst ins fnl f: nt pce to chal* **7/1**[3]
2522 **5** *¾* **Cape Rock**[11] 5786 3-8-10 72 .... TQuinn 3 69+
(C A Horgan) *lw: hld up towards rr of centre gp: swtchd lft and hdwy 2f out: sn rdn: styd on* **11/1**
1000 **6** *1¼* **Benedetto**[9] 5841 3-8-11 73 .... (p) JimCrowley 5 67
(Mrs A J Perrett) *chsd ldrs in centre: rdn over 2f out: styd on same pce* **20/1**
3143 **7** *2½* **Whiteoak Lady (IRE)**[13] 5714 3-8-6 73 ow1 .... JackDean(5) 4 60
(J L Spearing) *hld up towards rr of centre gp: rdn and hdwy 2f out: one pce fnl f* **20/1**
2011 **8** *nse* **Billberry**[15] 5684 3-8-2 67 .... (t) LukeMorris(3) 6 54
(S C Williams) *lw: mid-div in centre: rdn over 3f out: no imp fnl 2f* **11/4**[1]
0020 **9** *½* **Sir Kyffin's Folly**[51] 4572 3-8-6 68 .... RichardThomas 1 54
(J A Geake) *hld up towards rr of centre gp: rdn 2f out: sme late prog: nvr a threat* **25/1**
6056 **10** *½* **Amylee (IRE)**[19] 5580 3-8-10 72 .... (p) SteveDrowne 18 56
(C G Cox) *racd w one other on stands' side: chsd ldr: effrt and edgd lft 2f out: sn wknd* **16/1**
0105 **11** *3¼* **Divine Power**[31] 5185 3-9-3 79 .... RichardKingscote 15 55
(R M Beckett) *chsd ldrs in centre tl wknd 2f out* **16/1**
1000 **12** *¾* **Centenerola (USA)**[66] 4082 3-9-1 77 .... AlanMunro 2 51
(B W Hills) *racd in centre: prom: rdn 3f out: sn btn* **40/1**
0200 **13** *¾* **Mister New York (USA)**[9] 5841 3-8-13 75 .... StephenCarson 16 46
(Noel T Chance) *mid-div in centre tl wknd 2f out* **33/1**
3-06 **14** *¾* **Russian Reel**[15] 5681 3-9-4 80 .... (t) EdwardCreighton 19 49
(E J Creighton) *lw: sn swtchd to centre gp: hld up: hdwy over 3f out: sn rdn: wknd 2f out* **33/1**
1146 **15** *1¼* **Novellen Lad (IRE)**[41] 4900 3-9-2 78 .... JimmyFortune 10 44
(E J Alston) *mid-div in centre: rdn over 2f out: wknd over 1f out* **14/1**
3-11 **16** *1¾* **Manhattan Dream (USA)**[52] 4539 3-9-2 78 .... MichaelHills 17 39
(B W Hills) *racd w one other on stands' side: prom tl 2f out* **6/1**[2]

1m 25.46s (-0.24) **Going Correction** +0.05s/f (Good) **16** Ran SP% **124.4**
Speed ratings (Par 103): **103,102,97,96,95 94,91,91,90,90 86,85,84,84,82 80**
toteswinger: 1&2 £44.50, 1&3 £31.20, 2&3 £36.80. CSF £238.64 CT £2277.90 TOTE £16.70: £3.40, £5.70, £2.00, £1.50; EX 420.10 Place 6 £196.04, Place 5 £110.99..
Owner Sheikh Ahmed Al Maktoum **Bred** Darley **Trained** Newmarket, Suffolk

FOCUS
A good, competitive three-year-old handicap. Two raced towards the stands' side, but they were well beaten and the main action took place up the middle. It paid to be handy, for the pair who dominated the closing stages were always up there chasing the front-running third.
T/Plt: £66.80 to a £1 stake. Pool: £98,516.06. 1,075.82 winning tickets. T/Qpdt: £27.30 to a £1 stake. Pool: £4,618.63. 125.10 winning tickets. TM

6080 NEWMARKET (R-H)
Saturday, September 20

OFFICIAL GOING: Good to firm
Wind: Nil Weather: Fine and sunny

6125 MIKE DE KOCK INTERNATIONAL RACING H'CAP 6f
2:10 (2:11) (Class 4) (0-85,90) 3-Y-O+ **£6,476** (£1,927; £963; £481) **Stalls** Centre

Form RPR
0020 **1** **Fantasy Explorer**[10] 5796 5-9-3 82 .... PatCosgrave 5 91
(J J Quinn) *racd towards stands' side: chsd ldrs: swtchd rt over 2f out: led over 1f out: rdn out* **14/1**[3]
1605 **2** *½* **Resplendent Alpha**[23] 5433 4-8-7 72 .... TGMcLaughlin 10 79
(P Howling) *racd centre: dwlt: hld up: hdwy over 1f out: sn rdn: r.o* **25/1**
6040 **3** *½* **Wyatt Earp (IRE)**[9] 5831 7-9-1 80 .... (b) DaleGibson 19 85
(R A Fahey) *racd centre: chsd ldrs: rdn over 1f out: r.o* **16/1**
0350 **4** *nk* **Johannes (IRE)**[51] 4555 5-8-12 77 .... DeanMcKeown 2 81
(E J O'Neill) *s.s: hld up: plld hrd: sn swtchd centre: swtchd lft over 1f out: sn rdn and hung rght: r.o wl ins fnl f: nt rch ldrs* **14/1**[3]
5003 **5** *nk* **Mogok Ruby**[35] 5101 4-8-13 78 .... DarryllHolland 3 81
(L Montague Hall) *racd towards stands' side: hld up: edgd rt over 2f out: sn rdn: r.o wl ins fnl f: nrst fin* **20/1**
0000 **6** *½* **Forest Dane**[120] 2371 8-8-7 72 .... PaulDoe 12 74+
(Mrs N Smith) *racd centre: hld up: nt clr run over 1f out: r.o ins fnl f: nt rch ldrs* **66/1**
0020 **7** *shd* **Compton's Eleven**[7] 5897 7-8-11 83 .... MatthewDavies(7) 8 85
(M R Channon) *racd centre: hld up: r.o fnl f: nvr nrr* **16/1**
0636 **8** *hd* **Jake The Snake (IRE)**[33] 5144 7-8-10 75 .... KirstyMilczarek 13 76
(A W Carroll) *racd centre: chsd ldrs: rdn over 2f out: styd on* **10/1**[2]
0164 **9** *½* **Royal Island (IRE)**[16] 5635 6-8-8 73 .... TedDurcan 4 72
(M G Quinlan) *racd towards stands' side: prom: rdn and edgd rt 2f out: styd on* **20/1**
1215 **10** *hd* **Charlie Delta**[71] 3904 5-8-8 73 .... (b) KShea 7 72
(J G M O'Shea) *racd towards stands' side: chsd ldrs: hung rt over 2f out: sn rdn: styd on same pce fnl f* **16/1**
0410 **11** *¾* **Mandarin Spirit (IRE)**[11] 5789 8-8-6 71 .... (b) OscarUrbina 14 67
(G C H Chung) *racd centre: plld hrd and prom: led 4f out: rdn and hdd over 1f out: no ex ins fnl f* **20/1**
321 **12** *nk* **Without Prejudice (USA)**[49] 4638 3-8-7 74 .... TPQueally 17 69
(J Noseda) *racd centre: hld up in tch: rdn over 1f out: no ex ins fnl f* **6/4**[1]
1016 **13** *¾* **Registrar**[45] 4746 6-8-3 73 oh9 ow2 .... (p) MCGeran(5) 16 66
(Mrs C A Dunnett) *racd centre: mid-div: rdn and hung rt over 1f out: nvr trbld ldrs* **33/1**
6262 **14** *¾* **Rockfield Lodge (IRE)**[29] 5247 3-8-9 76 .... TonyCulhane 20 67
(M E Rimmer) *racd centre: hld up in tch: rdn over 1f out: no ex fnl f* **14/1**[3]
6600 **15** *hd* **Malcheek (IRE)**[47] 4687 6-9-0 79 .... JohnEgan 11 69
(T D Easterby) *racd centre: hld up: rdn over 1f out: nvr trbld ldrs* **16/1**
0001 **16** *hd* **Elhamri**[7] 5906 4-9-4 90 .... MatthewBirch(7) 18 79
(S Kirk) *led centre: 2f: chsd ldrs: rdn over 2f out: wknd ins fnl f* **16/1**
1200 **17** *4½* **Millfields Dreams**[50] 4601 9-8-4 72 .... (p) MarcHalford(3) 6 47
(P Leech) *racd towards stands' side: led that gp: rdn and edgd rt over 2f out: wknd over 1f out* **50/1**
530 **18** *hd* **Romany Nights (IRE)**[16] 5639 8-7-13 71 oh5 .... (bt) AndreaAtzeni(7) 15 45
(Miss Gay Kelleway) *racd centre: chsd ldrs: rdn over 2f out: wknd over 1f out* **33/1**
2000 **19** *7* **Hessian (IRE)**[11] 5789 4-8-6 71 oh3 .... HayleyTurner 9 23
(M D Squance) *racd centre: mid-div: rdn over 2f out: wknd over 1f out* **50/1**

1m 12.72s (0.52) **Going Correction** +0.05s/f (Good)
WFA 3 from 4yo+ 2lb **19** Ran SP% **127.9**
Speed ratings (Par 105): **98,97,96,96,95 95,95,94,94,93 92,92,91,90,90 89,83,83,74**
toteswinger: 1&2 £72.40, 1&3 £54.20, 2&3 £89.30. CSF £341.72 CT £5702.21 TOTE £21.80: £3.90, £6.00, £3.80, £4.00; EX 355.70.
Owner The Fantasy Fellowship E **Bred** Sexton Enterprises **Trained** Settrington, N Yorks

FOCUS
A big field of mostly exposed sprinters. Slightly messy form, but the principals were all close to their current marks and the race could have been rated a tad higher.
Jake The Snake(IRE) Official explanation: jockey said gelding was struck into
Royal Island(IRE) Official explanation: jockey said gelding hung right
Charlie Delta Official explanation: jockey said gelding hung right

6126 RACING ASSOCIATION SA & SIR PETER O'SULLEVAN MAIDEN STKS 1m 4f
2:40 (2:45) (Class 4) 3-4-Y-O **£5,180** (£1,541; £770; £384) **Stalls** Centre

Form RPR
1 **Mango Lady** 3-8-12 0 .... HayleyTurner 2 79+
(C F Wall) *prom: swtchd lft over 2f out: led over 1f out: edgd rt and styd on wl fnl f* **13/2**[3]
043 **2** *4½* **Hammer**[18] 5587 3-9-3 68 .... DaleGibson 6 75
(M P Tregoning) *chsd ldrs: rdn over 4f out: led over 2f out: hdd over 1f out* **10/1**
256 **3** *5* **West With The Wind**[79] 3633 3-9-3 81 .... TonyCulhane 1 67
(T P Tate) *s.i.s: rcvrd to ld over 10f out: rdn and hdd over 2f out: styd on same pce appr fnl f* **4/6**[1]
2300 **4** *4½* **Stormy View (USA)**[33] 5155 3-8-12 70 .... DarryllHolland 4 55
(J H M Gosden) *led: hdd over 10f out: chsd ldr: rdn and ev ch over 2f out: wknd over 1f out*
5 *28* **The Little Master (IRE)**[208] 4-9-8 0 .... MarcHalford(3) 5 15
(D R C Elsworth) *s.i.s: hld up: wknd over 3f out* **25/1**
00 **6** *53* **Percyslavenderblue**[9] 5814 3-8-12 0 .... TPQueally 7 —
(J Gallagher) *hld up: rdn 1/2-way: sn lost tch* **66/1**

2m 31.1s (-2.40) **Going Correction** -0.075s/f (Good)
WFA 3 from 4yo 8lb **6** Ran SP% **110.8**
Speed ratings (Par 105): **105,102,98,95,77 41**
toteswinger: 1&2 £3.30, 1&3 £1.70, 2&3 £2.20. CSF £61.80 TOTE £7.10: £2.10, £3.20; EX 27.70.
Owner Ms Aida Fustoq **Bred** Deerfield Farm **Trained** Newmarket, Suffolk

FOCUS
An ordinary maiden, typical for the time of year, but while the favourite was clearly not at his best the time was good and it might have been underrated. A nice start from the winner and seeming improved form from the second.

6127 RACING SOUTH AFRICA E B F FILLIES' H'CAP 1m 4f
3:15 (3:19) (Class 3) (0-95,90) 3-Y-O+ **£9,714** (£2,890; £1,444; £721) **Stalls** Centre

Form RPR
1335 **1** **Storyland (USA)**[22] 5472 3-8-7 76 .... KirstyMilczarek 3 89+
(W J Haggas) *hld up: hdwy over 2f out: led 1f out: styd on wl* **8/1**
4-21 **2** *2½* **Montbretia**[64] 4166 3-9-6 89 .... TedDurcan 6 98
(H R A Cecil) *hld up in tch: lost pl over 5f out: hdwy over 2f out: led over 1f out: sn rdn and hdd: styd on same pce ins fnl f* **11/2**[3]
1212 **3** *4½* **Inchwood (IRE)**[35] 5111 3-9-7 90 .... DarryllHolland 7 91
(M A Jarvis) *chsd ldrs: rdn over 2f out: nt clr run over 1f out: styd on same pce* **9/2**[2]
2102 **4** *nk* **Rio Guru (IRE)**[15] 5683 3-8-9 78 .... TonyCulhane 10 79
(M R Channon) *hld up: hdwy over 3f out: rdn over 2f out: styd on same pce appr fnl f* **20/1**
211 **5** *¾* **Starfala**[19] 5573 3-9-2 85 .... KShea 11 88+
(P F I Cole) *hld up: hdwy 7f out: nt clr run and lost pl over 2f out: n.d after* **4/1**[1]

112- **6** ½ **Kahara**[330] 6473 4-9-12 **87** PatCosgrave 9 86
(L M Cumani) *hld up: rdn over 2f out: nvr trbld ldrs* **7/1**
1124 **7** 1 ¾ **Cosmea**[22] 5464 3-8-10 **79** TPQueally 5 75
(A King) *hld up: hdwy over 7f out: chsd ldr 3f out: rdn and ev ch over 1f out: wknd ins fnl f* **8/1**
5231 **8** ½ **Dramatic Solo**[57] 4382 3-8-3 **72** (b) DaleGibson 2 67
(K R Burke) *led: rdn and hdd over 1f out: wknd fnl f* **14/1**
4141 **9** 3 ½ **Mount Lavinia (IRE)**[56] 4432 3-8-6 **75** HayleyTurner 4 65
(R M Beckett) *chsd ldr 10f out tl rdn 3f out: wknd 2f out* **9/1**
4225 **10** 16 **Ornella**[30] 5209 4-8-11 **72** TravisBlock 1 36
(H Morrison) *hld up: plld hrd: hdwy 1/2-way: rdn over 2f out: wknd and eased over 1f out* **12/1**

2m 32.24s (-1.26) **Going Correction** -0.075s/f (Good)
WFA 3 from 4yo+ 8lb **10** Ran SP% **117.4**
Speed ratings (Par 104): **101,99,96,96,95 95,94,93,91,80**
toteswinger: 1&2 £9.40, 1&3 £9.10, 2&3 £4.40. CSF £51.97 CT £225.38 TOTE £10.30: £2.60, £1.70, £2.00; EX 65.00.
Owner Mr & Mrs R Scott **Bred** Arthur B Hancock III & James H Stone **Trained** Newmarket, Suffolk
■ Stewards' Enquiry : Kirsty Milczarek one-day ban triggerring deferred four-day ban: careless riding (Oct 6-10)

FOCUS
A pretty decent handicap featuring a number of progressive fillies. Decent form from the first two.

NOTEBOOK
Storyland(USA), who was held up in the early stages, appreciated the quick ground and the step up to 1m4f for the first time and came through smoothly to show marked improvement. Getting her settled off the pace is probably the key to her. (op 11-1)
Montbretia had been off the track for two months, but her maiden form from the spring, coupled with her pedigree, appeared to give her a leading chance over this longer trip. She ran well, coming there going well on the outside two furlongs out, only to find the winner travelling even better. Having pulled clear of the rest in the closing stages she is now going to be put up a fair amount by the handicapper, but she has had only four starts to date and can progress again. (op 5-1 tchd 9-2)
Inchwood(IRE) had not run on ground this fast since her debut, but she seemed to handle it well enough. She simply ran into a couple of better-handicapped rivals. (op 4-1 tchd 5-1)
Rio Guru(IRE) was another who had little previous experience of running on fast ground. She certainly got the trip well, but she is vulnerable to improvers off her current mark. (tchd 16-1)
Starfala, chasing a hat-trick following recent successes on the Polytrack, enjoyed a far from clear run and would surely have finished third with more luck. Official explanation: jockey said filly was denied a clear run (op 9-2 tchd 6-1)
Kahara, who was making a belated seasonal reappearance and dropping back in distance, was outpaced when the principals quickened up, but she stayed on. She should benefit from the outing and a return to 1m6f plus. (op 8-1 tchd 13-2)
Cosmea enjoyed a successful summer but her form appears to have plateaued now. (op 9-1)
Ornella would not settle and gave herself little chance of getting home. Official explanation: jockey said filly ran too free

6128 INVESTEC H'CAP 1m 2f
3:50 (3:52) (Class 2) (0-100,92) 3-Y-O **£12,952** (£3,854; £1,926; £962) **Stalls** Centre

Form RPR
2636 **1** **Midships (USA)**[19] 5573 3-9-4 **92** DarryllHolland 7 102
(Mrs A J Perrett) *mde all: rdn over 1f out: edgd rt ins fnl f: unchal* **11/4**[2]
21 **2** 1 ½ **Electrolyser (IRE)**[227] 454 3-8-13 **87** TedDurcan 9 94
(C G Cox) *prom: rdn and hung rt over 1f out: sn chsng wnr: styd on same pce ins fnl f* **9/1**
2101 **3** 1 ¼ **Soft Shoe Shuffle (IRE)**[41] 4906 3-9-0 **88** AdamKirby 5 93
(W R Swinburn) *hld up: hdwy over 1f out: sn rdn: one pce ins fnl f* **6/1**
3111 **4** 3 ½ **Grande Annee (USA)**[28] 5290 3-9-1 **89** TPQueally 2 87
(J Noseda) *hld up: hdwy u.p over 1f out: no ex ins fnl f* **9/4**[1]
5521 **5** 2 ¾ **Spell Caster**[52] 4520 3-8-10 **84** KirstyMilczarek 8 76
(R M Beckett) *chsd wnr tl rdn over 1f out: wknd fnl f* **4/1**[3]
0000 **6** 4 **Latin Lad**[51] 4552 3-8-12 **89** PatrickHills(3) 4 73
(R Hannon) *hld up: hdwy over 2f out: rdn and wknd over 1f out* **16/1**
0003 **7** 5 **Mystery Star (IRE)**[15] 5682 3-8-9 **83** PaulDoe 3 57
(M H Tompkins) *hld up: rdn and wknd over 1f out* **14/1**

2m 2.41s (-3.39) **Going Correction** -0.075s/f (Good) **7** Ran SP% **114.3**
Speed ratings (Par 107): **110,108,107,105,102 99,95**
toteswinger: 1&2 £6.70, 1&3 £3.70, 2&3 £7.30. CSF £27.03 CT £136.61 TOTE £3.80: £2.30, £3.10; EX 39.20 Trifecta £160.80 Part won. Pool: £217.34, 0.50 winning units..
Owner K Abdulla **Bred** Juddmonte Farms Inc **Trained** Pulborough, W Sussex

FOCUS
An interesting little handicap run in a decent time. The winner was given a fine front-running ride and probably had only to match his good early-season form, with neither the second nor the third well treated.

NOTEBOOK
Midships(USA) was granted an uncontested lead and made every yard. He did not see out 1m4f at Kempton last time, but back over his ideal trip and on ground that suits, he was quickly into his stride and set sensible early fractions, meaning that he had enough in reserve to hold off his pursuers on the climb to the line. It was a fine front-running ride. The Cambridgeshire, for which he picks up a 4lb penalty, could well be next, but he is unlikely to get such an easy time of it out in front in that race. (op 9-2 tchd 5-1)
Electrolyser(IRE) ◆ was running on turf for the first time having won his maiden on Polytrack on his last start back in February. He came out of the pack to get nearest to the front-running winner, but his chase was in vain. This was still a promising effort on his handicap debut, though, and it suggests that there is a race to be won with him off his current mark, either on turf or back on the all-weather. (op 11-1 tchd 12-1)
Soft Shoe Shuffle(IRE) can race keenly so she has to be held up in her races. That put her at a disadvantage here as it was a tactical affair, and she was unable to make up the ground gifted to the leader early on. She still looks progressive, though, and will be seen to better effect in a stronger-run race. (tchd 11-2 and 7-1)
Grande Annee(USA) also looked to be given a lot to do, but she looked a non-stayer, too. She travelled well out the back and came through to challenge for the places but just did not see the trip out as well as the runner-up or third. A return to a mile looks in order. (op 15-8 tchd 7-4)
Spell Caster led the chase for much of the way but she may have needed this first outing since Glorious Goodwood as she dropped out of things exiting the Dip. Official explanation: trainer's rep said filly failed to stay the 1m 2f trip (tchd 7-2)
Latin Lad has dropped 11lb in the handicap since the beginning of the season, but looks to need further mercy. (op 14-1 tchd 20-1)

6129 BLOODSTOCK SOUTH AFRICA "PREMIER" CLAIMING STKS 1m 4f
4:25 (4:26) (Class 4) 3-5-Y-O **£6,476** (£1,927; £963; £481) **Stalls** Centre

Form RPR
6305 **1** **Apache Fort**[19] 5576 5-8-13 60 (b[1]) TonyCulhane 3 75
(T Keddy) *hld up: hdwy over 2f out: rdn over 1f out: styd on u.p to ld post* **12/1**
-300 **2** nk **Agente Romano (USA)**[127] 2151 3-8-3 71 (t) HayleyTurner 6 72
(G A Butler) *chsd ldrs: led over 3f out: rdn over 1f out: hdd post* **16/1**
4050 **3** 1 ½ **Jeer (IRE)**[19] 5569 4-9-9 86 TedDurcan 4 82
(E A L Dunlop) *hld up: hdwy 1/2-way: rdn over 1f out: styd on* **7/2**[2]
5346 **4** ½ **Know The Law**[7] 5910 4-9-4 76 (b) MarcHalford(3) 2 79
(D R C Elsworth) *s.i.s: hld up: hdwy over 1f out: kpt on* **7/1**[3]
0602 **5** 1 ¾ **Calzaghe (IRE)**[92] 3198 4-8-8 66 (v) DeclanCannon(7) 11 70
(K R Burke) *chsd ldrs: chal over 3f out: rdn over 1f out: no ex ins fnl f* **14/1**
4331 **6** nk **Aypeeyes (IRE)**[35] 5092 4-9-7 83 (b[1]) TravisBlock 1 76
(A King) *hld up: hdwy over 3f out: rdn over 1f out: no ex ins fnl f* **3/1**[1]
0102 **7** 5 **Bella Medici**[44] 4796 3-8-4 65 PaulDoe 7 59
(M H Tompkins) *hld up: rdn over 4f out: n.d* **14/1**
4061 **8** 5 **Animator**[33] 5146 3-9-6 71 KShea 10 67
(P F I Cole) *hld up: racd keenly: rdn over 2f out: wknd over 1f out* **14/1**
5424 **9** ¾ **Dancing Dik**[10] 5803 3-8-10 63 DarryllHolland 5 56
(Mrs A J Perrett) *chsd ldrs: wnt centre over 8f out: hung rt and wknd over 2f out* **7/1**[3]
0030 **10** ½ **Petrosian**[7] 5917 4-8-6 45 NicolPolli(5) 8 48
(T T Clement) *w ldr: plld hrd: wnt centre over 8f out: hung rt and wknd over 2f out* **100/1**
1002 **11** 6 **North Parade**[29] 5230 3-9-1 82 (bt[1]) TPQueally 9 50
(B J Meehan) *led: rdn and hdd over 3f out: wknd over 2f out* **15/2**

2m 33.81s (0.31) **Going Correction** -0.075s/f (Good)
WFA 3 from 4yo+ 8lb **11** Ran SP% **118.6**
Speed ratings (Par 105): **95,94,93,93,92 92,88,85,84,84 80**
toteswinger: 1&2 £38.90, 1&3 £17.90, 2&3 £16.30. CSF £189.94 TOTE £18.60: £4.20, £5.90, £2.00; EX 401.20.
Owner Andrew Duffield **Bred** Juddmonte Farms Ltd **Trained** Newmarket, Suffolk

FOCUS
A fair claimer, although a couple of the better fancied runners failed to perform.
Animator Official explanation: jockey said gelding ran too free

6130 PHUMELELA GOLD ENTERPRISES H'CAP 1m
5:00 (5:02) (Class 3) (0-90,90) 3-Y-O+ **£9,066** (£2,697; £1,348; £673) **Stalls** Centre

Form RPR
6211 **1** **Oat Cuisine**[15] 5683 4-8-11 **79** HayleyTurner 7 90+
(M L W Bell) *a.p: rdn to chse ldr over 1f out: led ins fnl f: r.o* **8/1**
3220 **2** ¾ **Den's Gift (IRE)**[53] 4509 4-8-13 **81** (b) AdamKirby 2 90
(C G Cox) *led: rdn over 1f out: hdd ins fnl f: styd on* **8/1**
1406 **3** 1 ¼ **Princess Taylor**[27] 5311 4-9-0 **82** (t) JohnEgan 11 88
(M Botti) *chsd ldrs: pushed along 1/2-way: rdn over 1f out: styd on* **12/1**
0600 **4** 1 ¾ **Daaweitza**[22] 5446 5-9-1 **83** TGMcLaughlin 14 85+
(B Ellison) *hld up: rdn over 1f out: r.o ins fnl f: nt trble ldrs* **33/1**
0315 **5** shd **The Which Doctor**[37] 5033 3-8-13 **85** TPQueally 1 87
(J Noseda) *s.i.s: hld up: rdn and hung rt fr 2f out: r.o ins fnl f: nvr trbld ldrs* **8/1**
3110 **6** nse **Light From Mars**[44] 4790 3-8-12 **84** DarryllHolland 5 86
(B R Millman) *chsd ldrs: rdn over 2f out: edgd rt over 1f out: no ex ins fnl f* **15/2**[3]
5211 **7** nk **Red Somerset (USA)**[40] 4927 5-9-2 **89** MCGeran(5) 10 90
(R J Hodges) *mid-div: hdwy over 3f out: rdn over 1f out: no ex ins fnl f* **12/1**
6050 **8** 1 ½ **Vainglory (USA)**[11] 5772 4-8-10 **85** AndreaAtzeni(7) 12 83
(D M Simcock) *hld up: plld hrd: hdwy over 2f out: rdn over 1f out: wknd ins fnl f* **11/1**
4540 **9** nk **Sonny Parkin**[12] 5759 6-8-8 **76** oh2 (v) DavidKinsella 13 73
(J Pearce) *s.i.s: hld up: styd on ins fnl f: nvr nrr* **25/1**
3164 **10** nk **Wikaala (USA)**[27] 5309 3-8-5 **77** DaleGibson 9 73
(M P Tregoning) *hld up: rdn over 2f out: wknd fnl f* **13/2**[2]
105 **11** 1 ½ **Axiom**[53] 4509 4-9-5 **87** PatCosgrave 6 80
(L M Cumani) *mid-div: hdwy over 3f out: rdn and wknd over 1f out* **8/1**
0440 **12** ½ **Prince Of Thebes (IRE)**[22] 5470 7-8-8 **76** KirstyMilczarek 8 68
(M J Attwater) *chsd ldr tl rdn and wknd over 1f out* **16/1**
-432 **13** 1 ¾ **Webbow (IRE)**[26] 5360 6-9-8 **90** TedDurcan 4 78
(T D Easterby) *hld up: rdn over 2f out: sn wknd* **9/2**[1]

1m 37.43s (-1.17) **Going Correction** +0.05s/f (Good)
WFA 3 from 4yo+ 4lb **13** Ran SP% **124.1**
Speed ratings (Par 107): **107,106,105,103,103 103,102,101,101,100 99,98,96**
toteswinger: 1&2 £14.50, 1&3 £20.30, 2&3 £25.50. CSF £73.55 CT £808.64 TOTE £6.30: £2.30, £2.70, £4.80; EX 96.30.
Owner Mrs G Rowland-Clark **Bred** Glebe Stud & J F Dean **Trained** Newmarket, Suffolk

FOCUS
They went a decent pace in this competitive handicap and the winner can rate higher again.

NOTEBOOK
Oat Cuisine appreciated the good gallop back over 1m and ran on strongly to wear down the leader inside the last and notch the hat-trick. A progressive filly, she clearly relishes fast ground, and could well be capable of defying a further rise in the weights. (tchd 15-2)
Den's Gift(IRE), who was well backed, likes to be ridden positively and set a good gallop. He took plenty of catching and was perhaps unlucky to bump into an improving filly. The way he is ridden, though, means he holds no secrets from the handicapper, and things will not get any easier for him if put up a pound or two for this. (op 16-1)
Princess Taylor, who did not run badly from out of the weights in a 1m2f Listed handicap at Goodwood last time, came under pressure some way out but kept responding and was staying on well at the finish. She could be worth another try over a bit further. (op 14-1)
Daaweitza has been out of sorts lately and this track and trip would not have appeared a combination likely to elicit a return to form. However, he was back down to his last winning mark and ran on in the closing stages to just edge the photo for fourth.
The Which Doctor did not help his chances by hanging right under pressure. It is not the first time he has done that and, while he did not have a happy experience on his previous visit, Kempton appeals as a suitable track for him. (op 10-1 tchd 12-1)
Light From Mars was never too far off the pace and seemed to have every chance. Official explanation: jockey said colt lost its action in the dip (op 10-1)
Axiom had never run on ground faster than good before, so perhaps conditions were just too quick for him. (op 9-1 tchd 15-2)
Prince Of Thebes(IRE) Official explanation: jockey said gelding stopped quickly
Webbow(IRE) is a consistent sort who goes on any ground, and this looked too bad to be true. Official explanation: jockey said gelding never travelled (op 7-2)

6131 KENILWORTH QUARANTINE STATION H'CAP 5f
5:35 (5:35) (Class 5) (0-75,74) 3-Y-O+ **£3,885** (£1,156; £577; £288) **Stalls** Centre

Form RPR
5200 **1** **Namir (IRE)**[29] 5250 6-9-6 **74** (vt) TedDurcan 12 83
(D Shaw) *racd centre: hld up: swtchd rt and gd hdwy over 1f out: r.o to ld post* **14/1**
2321 **2** nk **Matterofact (IRE)**[9] 5817 5-8-13 **67** TGMcLaughlin 3 75
(M S Saunders) *racd towards stands' side: rdn: swvd rt and led over 1f out: hdd post* **17/2**[3]

2446 **3** ¾ **Brandywell Boy (IRE)**[30] 5206 5-8-4 **65** .... BillyCray(7) 4 70+
(D J S Ffrench Davis) *racd towards stands' side: hung rt 1/2-way: rdn over 1f out: r.o* **20/1**

1120 **4** ½ **Speedy Senorita (IRE)**[21] 5490 3-8-11 **73** .... DeclanCannon(7) 17 76
(K R Burke) *led centre: rdn and hdd over 1f out: styd on* **16/1**

/3-4 **5** nk **Gold Express**[22] 5467 5-9-0 **68** .... OscarUrbina 16 70
(P J O'Gorman) *racd centre: trckd ldrs: rdn and swtchd lft over 1f out: styd on* **3/1**[1]

0502 **6** hd **Pic Up Sticks**[22] 5467 9-8-7 **61** .... HayleyTurner 6 63
(B G Powell) *s.i.s: racd centre: hld up: hdwy over 1f out: r.o* **11/1**

2160 **7** 1 ¾ **Nusoor (IRE)**[29] 5250 5-8-13 **67** ....(v) KirstyMilczarek 14 62
(Peter Grayson) *racd centre: chsd ldrs: rdn over 1f out: no ex ins fnl f* **16/1**

3020 **8** 1 **Malapropism**[10] 5796 8-9-3 **71** .... DarryllHolland 8 63
(M R Channon) *racd centre: chsd ldr: rdn 1/2-way: outpcd 2f out: styd on ins fnl f* **8/1**[2]

0005 **9** hd **Multahab**[24] 5401 9-8-6 **60** oh3 ....(t) SimonWhitworth 11 51
(M Wigham) *racd centre: prom: rdn over 1f out: styd on same pce* **33/1**

46-6 **10** hd **Joyeaux**[11] 5775 6-8-10 **64** .... DavidKinsella 15 54
(L R James) *racd centre: chsd ldrs: rdn and nt clr run over 1f out: wknd ins fnl f* **33/1**

5046 **11** ¾ **Bertie Southstreet**[22] 5467 5-8-5 **66** ....(b) JemmaMarshall(7) 1 54
(J R Best) *racd towards stands' side: hld up: rdn and edgd rt over 1f out: n.d* **16/1**

4330 **12** 1 **Kings College Boy**[28] 5260 8-8-10 **64** ....(b) DaleGibson 10 48
(R A Fahey) *s.i.s: racd centre: hld up: rdn over 1f out: n.d* **12/1**

4330 **13** ½ **Cosmic Destiny (IRE)**[4] 6006 6-8-8 **69** .... AndreaAtzeni(7) 5 51
(E F Vaughan) *stdd s: racd centre: hld up: plld hrd: rdn over 1f out: n.d* **16/1**

2023 **14** 1 **Don Pele (IRE)**[8] 5861 6-9-5 **73** ....(b) AdamKirby 2 52
(R A Harris) *racd towards stands' side: hld up: rdn 1/2-way: edgd rt over 1f out: n.d* **12/1**

0502 **15** ½ **Magical Speedfit (IRE)**[20] 5531 3-9-5 **74** .... JohnEgan 13 51
(G G Margarson) *racd centre: prom: rdn over 1f out: wknd ins fnl f* **20/1**

-300 **16** 1 ½ **Fabuleux Cherie**[26] 5346 3-8-4 **62** .... MarcHalford(3) 7 33
(W R Muir) *racd centre: mid-div: rdn 1/2-way: sn lost pl* **50/1**

1034 **17** 2 **Diane's Choice**[4] 6006 5-9-4 **72** ....(v[1]) KShea 18 36
(Miss Gay Kelleway) *racd centre: hld up: rdn over 1f out: sn wknd* **10/1**

513 **18** 2 ¼ **Enodoc**[20] 5531 3-8-13 **68** .... TonyCulhane 9 24
(W R Muir) *racd centre: prom: rdn 1/2-way: wknd over 1f out* **25/1**

59.22 secs (0.12) **Going Correction** +0.05s/f (Good)
WFA 3 from 5yo+ 1lb **18 Ran SP% 130.9**
Speed ratings (Par 103): **101,100,99,98,98 97,94,93,93,92 91,89,89,87,86 84,81,77**
toteswinger: 1&2 £21.70, 1&3 £80.40, 2&3 £59.90. CSF £125.56 CT £2494.24 TOTE £18.20: £3.10, £2.40, £4.50; EX 208.90.
Owner ownaracehorse.co.uk (Shakespeare) **Bred** B Kennedy **Trained** Danethorpe, Notts
■ Stewards' Enquiry : T G McLaughlin three-day ban: careless riding (Oct 6-8)

FOCUS
An ordinary sprint handicap, but solid form, with the winner to his best and the runner-up running a slight personal best.
Matterofact(IRE) Official explanation: jockey said mare hung right
Gold Express Official explanation: jockey said gelding lost its action
Magical Speedfit(IRE) Official explanation: jockey said gelding lost its action
T/Plt: £11,731.60 to a £1 stake. Pool: £66,693.58. 4.15 winning tickets. T/Qpdt: £457.60 to a £1 stake. Pool: £5,132.58. 8.30 winning tickets. CR

6087 WOLVERHAMPTON (A.W) (L-H)
Saturday, September 20

OFFICIAL GOING: Standard
Wind: Nil Weather: Fine

6132 OPEN A HILLS ACCOUNT - 0800 44 40 40 H'CAP 7f 32y(P)
6:20 (6:20) (Class 6) (0-65,65) 3-Y-0+ **£2,388** (£705; £352) **Stalls** High

Form RPR

5230 **1** **A Big Sky Brewing (USA)**[24] 5389 4-8-13 **64** ....(b) DeanHeslop(7) 11 75
(T D Barron) *sn prom: rdn and wnt 2nd wl over 1f out: led wl ins fnl f: r.o* **7/1**[2]

4360 **2** ¾ **Dancing Deano (IRE)**[22] 5478 6-9-0 **61** .... RussellKennemore(3) 10 70
(R Hollinshead) *sn chsng ldr: led 3f out: rdn over 1f out: hdd wl ins fnl f: nt qckn* **11/1**

000 **3** hd **Valentino Swing (IRE)**[11] 5779 5-9-1 **62** .... TolleyDean(3) 9 70
(Miss T Spearing) *dwlt: hld up in rr: rdn and hdwy over 1f out: kpt on ins fnl f* **25/1**

0054 **4** 1 ½ **Vanadium**[12] 5755 6-9-4 **62** .... GeorgeBaker 7 66
(G L Moore) *hld up and bhd: sme prog on outside over 2f out: c wd st: rdn over 1f out: kpt on ins fnl f: nt trble ldrs* **7/2**[1]

3436 **5** ¾ **Sheriff's Silk**[17] 5610 4-9-4 **62** ....(v[1]) PaulEddery 2 64
(G D Blake) *hld up in mid-div: swtchd rt 3f out: rdn and hdwy 2f out: no ex wl ins fnl f* **11/1**

1400 **6** ½ **Sovereignty (JPN)**[16] 5629 6-9-4 **65** .... JackMitchell(3) 5 66
(D K Ivory) *hld up in mid-div: rdn and no hdwy fnl 2f* **9/1**

5050 **7** 1 ¾ **Hunt The Bottle (IRE)**[44] 4782 3-8-13 **63** .... PatrickHills(3) 4 59
(B W Hills) *hld up and bhd: rdn wl over 2f out: nvr nr ldrs* **15/2**[3]

0330 **8** ¾ **Sedge (USA)**[26] 5345 8-9-5 **63** ....(b) FrankieMcDonald 1 57
(P T Midgley) *led early: prom: n.m.r on ins over 2f out: sn wknd* **9/1**

2042 **9** 2 ¾ **Ghafeer (USA)**[49] 4629 4-8-8 **59** ....(p) LanceBetts(7) 3 45
(B Ellison) *prom: rdn over 2f out: wknd qckly ins fnl f* **11/1**

2502 **10** 7 **H Harrison (IRE)**[17] 5600 8-8-11 **62** .... BMcHugh(7) 6 30
(I W McInnes) *sn led: hdd 3f out: rdn over 2f out: wknd over 1f out* **15/2**[3]

4320 **11** 10 **Bentley**[17] 5610 4-9-4 **62** .... J-PGuillambert 12 3
(J G Given) *hld up in mid-div: bhd fnl 3f: eased whn no ch wl over 1f out* **9/1**

1m 28.12s (-1.48) **Going Correction** -0.15s/f (Stan)
WFA 3 from 4yo+ 3lb **11 Ran SP% 117.1**
Speed ratings (Par 101): **102,101,100,99,98 97,95,94,91,83 72**
toteswinger: 1&2 £0, 1&3 £0, 2&3 £14.60. CSF £81.17 CT £1226.90 TOTE £9.90: £2.90, £3.60, £4.40; EX 105.90.
Owner Trevor Boanas **Bred** Braeburn Farm Corp **Trained** Maunby, N Yorks

FOCUS
A modest handicap, run at a fair pace. Sound form, the winner building on his good record over course and distance.
Bentley Official explanation: jockey said gelding never travelled

6133 GET A BONUS AT WILLIAMHILLCASINO.COM (S) STKS 7f 32y(P)
6:50 (6:52) (Class 6) 2-Y-0 **£2,047** (£604; £302) **Stalls** High

Form RPR

0256 **1** **Gassal**[7] 5909 2-8-6 **67** ....(b) GregFairley 4 58
(J R Boyle) *bmpd s: mde all: rdn and edgd rt ins fnl f: jst hld on* **3/1**[3]

3136 **2** hd **Meydan Groove**[43] 4828 2-8-12 **67** .... TravisBlock 3 64+
(P F I Cole) *wnt rt and bmpd s: hld up in rr: hdwy over 2f out: hrd rdn wl over 1f out: r.o ins fnl f: jst failed* **13/8**[1]

006 **3** nk **Abuelito John (IRE)**[5] 5966 2-8-11 0 ....(v) J-PGuillambert 1 62
(D Carroll) *hld up in tch: chsd wnr over 3f out: rdn 2f out: ev ch fnl f: kpt on* **12/1**

00 **4** 7 **Star Of Sophia (IRE)**[18] 5590 2-8-6 0 ....(v[1]) PaulEddery 2 39
(Mrs A Duffield) *bmpd s: hld up in tch: outpcd over 3f out: n.d after* **40/1**

60 **5** 1 ¾ **Cwmni**[8] 5866 2-8-6 0 .... CatherineGannon 8 35
(B Palling) *prom: rdn over 3f out: wknd 2f out* **66/1**

52 **6** 1 ¼ **Glan Lady (IRE)**[13] 5715 2-8-1 0 .... SophieDoyle(5) 10 32
(J L Spearing) *sn in mid-div: hdwy on ins over 2f out: rdn and wknd over 1f out* **5/2**[2]

0 **7** 6 **Lastbustowoodstock (IRE)**[59] 4304 2-8-11 0 .... PaulFitzsimons 5 22
(J A Osborne) *s.i.s: hdwy over 5f out: wknd over 2f out* **28/1**

06 **8** 7 **Erris Lady**[34] 5116 2-8-8 0 ow5 .... RussellKennemore(3) 6 4
(Mrs L Williamson) *chsd wnr tl rdn over 3f out: sn wknd* **66/1**

0 **9** 4 **Badtanman**[49] 4634 2-8-11 0 .... LPKeniry 7 —
(Peter Grayson) *n.m.r s: hdwy over 5f out: wknd 4f out* **66/1**

3 **10** 2 ¼ **Jaubertie**[11] 5782 2-7-13 0 .... CharlesEddery(7) 12 —
(W G M Turner) *a in rr* **16/1**

00 **11** 8 **Dicksons Delight (USA)**[29] 5225 2-8-8 0 .... JackMitchell(3) 11 —
(D K Ivory) *outpcd* **66/1**

1m 29.79s (0.19) **Going Correction** -0.15s/f (Stan) **11 Ran SP% 117.1**
Speed ratings (Par 93): **92,91,91,83,81 80,73,65,60,58 48**
toteswinger: 1&2 £2.20, 1&3 £6.10, 2&3 £1.10. CSF £8.00 TOTE £4.40: £1.10, £1.30, £3.40; EX 10.40.There was no bid for the winner. Meydan Groove was claimed by Robert Johnson for £6,000
Owner M Khan X2 **Bred** N Poole And A Franklin **Trained** Epsom, Surrey
■ Stewards' Enquiry : Travis Block four-day ban: used whip with excessive frequency (Oct 6-9)

FOCUS
A weak juvenile event and the only pair with official ratings filled the first two places.

NOTEBOOK
Gassal, best-in at the weights, opened her account at the seventh time of asking with a gutsy effort from the front. She set off at a decent pace and was there to be shot at in the home straight, but kept responding to her rider's urgings and just held on. Having failed to last home over 1m2f under similar tactics on turf last time, the drop back to this trip proved ideal and she has evidently found her level. (tchd 7-2)
Meydan Groove ◆, identically rated to the winner on a mark of 67, was eating into her rival's lead inside the final furlong but just failed. A more positive ride may well have brought success and compensation in this sort of grade should not be far off. (op 6-4)
Abuelito John(IRE) showed by far his most worthwhile form and was clear of the rest in third. He looked likely to get the better of the winner passing the furlong pole but seemed to be worried out of it close home and it is not hard to see why he wears headgear. (op 18-1 tchd 10-1)
Star Of Sophia(IRE), dropping back in trip and making her All-Weather debut, posted her most worthwhile effort for the drop in class. The first-time visor also helped. (op 33-1)
Glan Lady(IRE) was another having her first run in such company and on an artificial surface. She had to race wide from an unfavourable draw and could muster only one pace down the home straight. A drop back to 6f in this grade could get her get closer again. (op 7-2)

6134 NUSS IS 40 CELEBRATION H'CAP 1m 141y(P)
7:20 (7:20) (Class 5) (0-70,70) 3-Y-0+ **£3,885** (£1,156; £577; £288) **Stalls** Low

Form RPR

P106 **1** **Alfie Tupper (IRE)**[30] 5209 5-9-5 **66** .... PatCosgrave 5 77
(J R Boyle) *hld up: sn in mid-div: hdwy on ins over 3f out: rdn whn carried lft and led wl ins fnl f: r.o* **8/1**

2104 **2** nk **Sabre Light**[9] 5836 3-9-1 **70** ....(p) JackMitchell(3) 7 80
(A Bailey) *hld up in tch: led over 2f out: rdn over 1f out: edgd rt and hdd wl ins fnl f* **14/1**

0556 **3** 7 **Ahlawy (IRE)**[61] 4244 5-9-6 **67** ....(b[1]) LPKeniry 2 61
(M W Easterby) *chsd ldr tl over 6f out: prom: ev ch over 2f out: rdn over 1f out: wknd ins fnl f* **14/1**

6000 **4** nk **Sir Billy Nick**[36] 5052 3-8-11 **70** .... CharlesEddery(7) 6 64
(J Noseda) *hld up in mid-div: hdwy over 2f out: sn pushed along: one pce* **33/1**

0642 **5** 5 **Lunar River (FR)**[22] 5478 5-9-5 **66** ....(t) GeorgeBaker 4 48
(David Pinder) *hld up in rr: nt clr run and swtchd rt jst over 2f out: hdwy wl over 1f out: nvr nr ldrs* **5/1**[2]

3055 **6** ½ **Hucking Heat (IRE)**[11] 5783 4-9-5 **66** ....(p) DO'Donohoe 3 47
(R Hollinshead) *hld up towards rr: hdwy on ins whn nt clr run jst over 2f out: no further prog* **20/1**

/05 **7** 1 ¼ **Pugilist**[36] 5069 6-9-6 **70** .... PatrickHills(3) 13 48
(B J Meehan) *hld up in tch: pushed along over 3f out: wknd 2f out* **8/1**

621- **8** ¾ **King's Majesty (IRE)**[17] 7189 6-9-9 **70** .... VinceSlattery 9 46
(T J Pitt) *hld up towards rr: pushed along over 2f out: rdn and swtchd rt wl over 1f out: n.d* **33/1**

1606 **9** 4 **Harare**[8] 5863 7-8-12 **66** ....(b) AshleyMorgan(7) 11 33
(R J Price) *hld up in mid-div: shortlived effrt over 3f out* **20/1**

3561 **10** 4 ½ **Valdan (IRE)**[9] 5837 4-9-2 **63** .... DeanMcKeown 10 20
(P D Evans) *prom: chsd clr ldr over 6f out: wknd over 2f out* **6/1**[3]

0340 **11** nk **Wing Play (IRE)**[38] 4984 3-9-2 **68** ....(t) TravisBlock 8 24
(H Morrison) *hld up in rr: hdwy on outside over 3f out: rdn over 2f out: sn wknd* **9/2**[1]

1440 **12** ¾ **Machinate (USA)**[30] 5198 6-9-6 **67** .... LiamJones 12 21
(W M Brisbourne) *a bhd* **22/1**

0040 **13** 11 **Fort Amhurst (IRE)**[2] 6056 4-9-3 **64** .... J-PGuillambert 1 —
(M W Easterby) *led: clr over 6f out: rdn and hdd over 2f out: sn wknd: eased wl over 1f out* **9/2**[1]

1m 48.27s (-2.23) **Going Correction** -0.15s/f (Stan)
WFA 3 from 4yo+ 5lb **13 Ran SP% 122.6**
Speed ratings (Par 103): **103,102,96,96,91 91,90,89,86,82 81,81,71**
toteswinger: Not won CSF £108.26 CT £1552.57 TOTE £16.80: £4.50, £3.30, £3.30; EX 181.60.
Owner Epsom Equine Spa Partnership **Bred** Stone Ridge Farm **Trained** Epsom, Surrey
■ Stewards' Enquiry : Dean McKeown two-day ban: careless riding (Oct 6-7)

FOCUS
A modest handicap which saw the first pair come well clear. The form of the principals seems sound enough.
Lunar River(FR) Official explanation: jockey said mare was denied a clear run

Fort Amhurst(IRE) Official explanation: jockey said gelding ran too free

6135 E B F GET YOUR CHIPS WITH WILLIAMHILLPOKER.COM MAIDEN STKS 1m 141y(P)
7:50 (7:51) (Class 5) 2-Y-O **£3,885** (£1,156; £577; £288) **Stalls** Low

Form RPR

2222 **1** **Fullback (IRE)**[14] 5711 2-9-3 86 LPKeniry 5 81
(J S Moore) *a.p: led wl over 1f out: sn rdn: hung rt 1f out: flashed tail whn hit w whip: r.o* **2/1**[1]

46 **2** ¾ **Doncosaque (IRE)**[24] 5404 2-9-3 0 TPQueally 10 79
(H R A Cecil) *hld up in tch: rdn to chse wnr whn hung lft 1f out: nt qckn towards fin* **8/1**

53 **3** 5 **Ascendant**[9] 5811 2-9-3 0 J-PGuillambert 13 69
(Sir Mark Prescott) *a.p: disp ld over 2f out: rdn over 1f out: wknd ins fnl f* **9/4**[2]

02 **4** ½ **Excelsior Academy**[24] 5404 2-9-0 0 (b[1]) PatrickHills(3) 11 68
(B J Meehan) *w ldr: led over 3f out: rdn and hdd wl over 1f out: wknd ins fnl f* **5/1**[3]

00 **5** 2½ **Recession Proof (FR)**[9] 5842 2-8-10 0 HollyHall(7) 7 63+
(S A Callaghan) *hld up and bhd: sme hdwy on outside over 2f out: no imp whn hung lft over 1f out* **50/1**

6 10 **Calling Birds (IRE)** 2-8-12 0 LiamJones 3 37
(J A Osborne) *in rr: impr into mid-div over 5f out: pushed along over 3f out: no ch whn carried lft jst over 1f out* **28/1**

7 3½ **Captain Cavendish (IRE)** 2-9-0 0 JackMitchell(3) 1 34
(A Bailey) *in rr: pushed along 3f out: no rspnse* **33/1**

340 **8** ¾ **Superstitious Me (IRE)**[17] 5606 2-8-12 57 CatherineGannon 2 28
(B Palling) *led: hdd over 3f out: rdn and wknd 2f out* **40/1**

000 **9** 4 **Coral Point (IRE)**[37] 5022 2-9-3 55 PaulFitzsimons 4 24
(S Kirk) *a in rr* **100/1**

00 **10** nk **Accumulation (UAE)**[13] 5716 2-8-5 0 LanceBetts(7) 6 19
(M W Easterby) *s.i.s: a in rr* **100/1**

0 **11** 13 **Welsh Passion**[9] 5812 2-8-12 0 PatrickMathers 12 —
(D Flood) *hld up in tch: rdn over 3f out: sn wknd* **66/1**

12 nk **Grey Ghost** 2-9-3 0 GeorgeBaker 8 —
(E F Vaughan) *s.s: a in rr* **8/1**

1m 49.61s (-0.89) **Going Correction** -0.15s/f (Stan) **12** Ran SP% **117.3**
Speed ratings (Par 95): **97,96,91,91,89 80,77,76,73,72 61,60**
toteswinger: 1&2 £22.50, 1&3 £3.60, 2&3 £17.30. CSF £17.99 TOTE £3.10: £1.10, £2.50, £1.70; EX 19.10.
Owner A J Speyer & R J Lilley **Bred** S Couldrige **Trained** Upper Lambourn, Berks

FOCUS
This race was won last year by subsequent St Leger winner Conduit and, while it is highly unlikely to throw up another performer of that one's class, it could still prove to be an okay maiden

NOTEBOOK
Fullback(IRE), runner-up on his previous four outings, set the standard with an official mark of 86 and ran out a deserving winner. Although he has bumped into decent performers, some observers would have questioned his attitude with a string of seconds, but he really dispelled of any temperament theories and will be high on confidence after this. However, while he is useful and has scope, he may not prove that simple to place. (op 7-4 tchd 13-8)
Doncosaque(IRE) travelled every bit as well as the winner into the home straight and was the only one to make that rival work. He is coming good and should not be long in finding a race, but his prospective handicap mark will have suffered as a result of this. He should enjoy stepping up in trip next year. (op 6-1 tchd 9-1)
Ascendant attracted support on this return from turf and had his chance over the longer trip. He paid for spending energy in getting across early from his outside stall and should not be written off now he is eligible for nurseries. (op 11-4)
Excelsior Academy, in first-time blinkers, was again ridden positively, yet proved unable to gain a clear lead. He proved one-paced and failed to confirm Great Leighs form with the runner-up, so while he now qualifies for a nursery mark, his fancy entries look totally unjustified. (op 9-2 tchd 11-2)
Recession Proof(FR) was making his All-Weather debut and stayed on without posing a threat. This was his best form and there are more options now he can enter nurseries (op 100-1)

6136 REAL TIME RADIO AT WILLIAMHILL.CO.UK H'CAP 1m 4f 50y(P)
8:20 (8:20) (Class 6) (0-60,62) 3-Y-O+ **£2,388** (£705; £352) **Stalls** Low

Form RPR

0401 **1** **Zalkani (IRE)**[8] 5869 8-9-3 54 JerryO'Dwyer 10 59
(J Pearce) *dropped out s: hld up towards rr: smooth hdwy on outside 3f out: rdn to ld and edgd lft jst over 1f out: rdn out* **9/2**[3]

3464 **2** 1¾ **Thorny Mandate**[22] 5450 6-9-4 55 PatCosgrave 5 57
(W M Brisbourne) *hld up and bhd: stdy hdwy over 3f out: rdn and swtchd rt over 1f out: kpt on same pce ins fnl f* **10/3**[1]

-006 **3** 1 **Corrib (IRE)**[14] 5712 5-9-5 56 CatherineGannon 3 57
(B Palling) *hld up towards rr: rdn and hdwy on outside over 1f out: edgd lft ins fnl f: nt qckn* **16/1**

005 **4** 1 **Sleepy Mountain**[17] 5612 4-9-4 62 ow2 HarryPoulton(7) 1 61
(A Middleton) *plld hrd: chsd ldr: led wl over 2f out: rdn and hdd jst over 1f out: one pce* **33/1**

4030 **5** ½ **Garibaldi (GER)**[41] 4898 6-8-11 53 (t) AshleyHamblett(5) 8 51
(N Wilson) *a.p: rdn over 2f out: one pce* **8/1**

-000 **6** 3¼ **Royal Indulgence**[23] 5427 8-9-5 56 (e[1]) LiamJones 2 49
(W M Brisbourne) *hld up towards rr: sme hdwy over 2f out: rdn wl over 1f out: sn btn* **16/1**

120/ **7** ¾ **Rahy's Crown (USA)**[748] 4448 5-9-5 56 GeorgeBaker 7 48
(G L Moore) *hld up in mid-div: hdwy on ins 4f out: chsd ldr 2f out tl over 1f out: sn wknd* **4/1**[2]

2050 **8** ½ **Bailieborough (IRE)**[92] 3229 9-8-11 55 LanceBetts(7) 4 46
(B Ellison) *wnt rt s: hld up in mid-div: rdn over 2f out: sn bhd* **14/1**

0350 **9** nse **Rudry World (IRE)**[19] 5559 5-9-2 60 DeanHeslop(7) 11 53+
(M Mullineaux) *hld up in rr: rdn over 1f out: no ch whn nt clr run on ins ins fnl f* **10/1**

5166 **10** 2¼ **Shandelight (IRE)**[66] 4075 4-9-4 55 (p) DO'Donohoe 9 42
(Mrs A Duffield) *hld up in tch: wknd 3f out* **11/1**

3 **11** 2½ **Allez Frank (GER)**[21] 4932 7-9-9 60 TravisBlock 12 43
(A E Jones) *led: rdn and hdd wl over 2f out: sn wknd* **12/1**

2m 40.18s (-0.92) **Going Correction** -0.15s/f (Stan) **11** Ran SP% **118.9**
Speed ratings (Par 101): **97,95,95,94,94 92,91,91,89 87**
toteswinger: 1&2 £7.20, 1&3 £16.60, 2&3 £16.60. CSF £20.11 CT £223.88 TOTE £4.30: £2.30, £1.90, £4.20; EX 12.30.
Owner Mrs Lisa Matthews **Bred** His Highness The Aga Khan's Studs S C **Trained** Newmarket, Suffolk
■ Stewards' Enquiry : Pat Cosgrave three-day ban: used whip with excessive force (Oct 6-8)

FOCUS
A moderate handicap which was steadily run. The form is rated through the first two.

6137 ALL BALLS AT WILLIAMHILLBINGO.COM H'CAP 5f 216y(P)
8:50 (8:50) (Class 5) (0-75,75) 3-Y-O+ **£2,729** (£806; £403) **Stalls** Low

Form RPR

6000 **1** **Yungaburra (IRE)**[10] 5796 4-9-1 72 (t) TolleyDean(3) 2 81+
(S Parr) *hld up and bhd: hdwy wl over 1f out: sn rdn and swtchd rt: led ins fnl f: drvn out* **17/2**

4611 **2** 1½ **Royal Challenge**[8] 5867 7-9-4 72 PatrickMathers 5 77
(I W McInnes) *hld up: sn in mid-div: c wd st: rdn and hdwy on outside over 1f out: kpt on to take 2nd cl home* **10/3**[1]

6640 **3** ½ **Vigano (IRE)**[14] 5713 3-9-0 70 LPKeniry 1 73
(S Kirk) *hld up in tch: rdn to ld over 1f out: hdd and no ex ins fnl f* **8/1**

0562 **4** 2¾ **Bishopbriggs (USA)**[18] 5592 3-8-11 70 RussellKennemore(3) 8 64
(S Parr) *led: rdn and hdd over 1f out: fdd wl ins fnl f* **5/1**[2]

4625 **5** 1½ **Whitbarrow (IRE)**[54] 4478 9-9-2 73 (b) JamesMillman(3) 11 62
(B R Millman) *w ldrs: c wd st: wknd fnl f* **6/1**[3]

265- **6** 5 **Showtime Ice**[285] 7095 3-8-12 73 RichardEvans(5) 10 46
(Ms Deborah J Evans) *s.i.s: hld up and bhd: rdn whn swtchd rt over 1f out: nvr nr ldrs* **50/1**

0553 **7** ¾ **Buy On The Red**[23] 5433 7-9-6 74 (p) DO'Donohoe 9 45
(W R Muir) *prom: rdn over 1f out: wknd fnl f* **7/1**

6320 **8** 2½ **Double Bill (USA)**[126] 2205 4-9-1 69 GregFairley 4 32
(P F I Cole) *s.i.s: a in rr* **7/1**

2050 **9** 1½ **La Chicaluna**[13] 5714 3-9-2 72 TPQueally 6 30
(J G Given) *w ldr: ev ch 2f out: wknd over 1f out* **12/1**

10-0 **10** hd **No Page (IRE)**[16] 5648 3-8-12 75 BillyCray(7) 3 33
(B P J Baugh) *hld up in tch: rdn and wknd wl over 1f out* **40/1**

1-20 **11** 15 **Seta Pura**[29] 5222 3-8-10 66 PatCosgrave 12 —
(Mrs A Duffield) *s.i.s: a in rr* **16/1**

1m 14.18s (-0.82) **Going Correction** -0.15s/f (Stan)
WFA 3 from 4yo+ 2lb **11** Ran SP% **118.6**
Speed ratings (Par 103): **99,97,96,92,90 84,83,79,77,77 57**
toteswinger: 1&2 £0, 1&3 £6.50, 2&3 £0. CSF £37.27 CT £241.78 TOTE £9.70: £3.80, £1.20, £3.00; EX 60.10 Place 6 £ 238.41, Place 5 £ 34.42.
Owner Willie McKay **Bred** Newlands House Stud **Trained** Bawtry, S Yorks

FOCUS
This modest sprint was run at a solid pace and it suited those coming from behind. The form is sound enough with the winner taking advantage of a good mark.
T/Plt: £288.30 to a £1 stake. Pool: £73,533.28. 186.19 winning tickets. T/Qpdt: £25.80 to a £1 stake. Pool: £7,835.37. 224.59 winning tickets. KH

6146 - 6157a (Foreign Racing) - See Raceform Interactive

5952

LONGCHAMP (R-H)
Saturday, September 20

OFFICIAL GOING: Good

6147a PRIX DES CHENES (GROUP 3) (C&G) 1m
3:00 (3:00) 2-Y-O **£29,412** (£11,765; £8,824; £5,882; £2,941)

RPR

1 **Calvados Blues (FR)**[19] 2-9-2 IMendizabal 2 104
(P Demercastel, France) *racd in 3rd: chal over 1 1/2f out: rdn to ld fnl f: styd on wl* **114/10**

2 ½ **Naval Officer (USA)**[32] 2-9-2 C-PLemaire 1 103
(J-C Rouget, France) *hld up in 4th: disputing 4th st: rdn and r.o over 1f out: chal 100yds out: nrest at fin* **13/10**[1]

3 1 **Canwinn (IRE)**[28] 5300 2-9-2 OPeslier 5 101
(M R Channon) *led 2f: pushed along to ld again 1 1/2f out: sn rdn: hdd fnl f: styd on* **28/10**[2]

4 2½ **Topclas (FR)**[24] 2-9-2 SPasquier 3 95
(P Demercastel, France) *hld up in last: drvn over 1f out and styd on: wnt 4th 100yds out* **84/10**

5 3 **Temple Lord (FR)**[34] 5139 2-9-2 CSoumillon 6 89
(Y De Nicolay, France) *led after 2f: hdd 1 1/2f out: sn rdn and one pce* **66/10**

6 1½ **Vesuve (IRE)**[24] 2-9-2 ACrastus 4 85
(E Lellouche, France) *hld up in 5th: disputing 4th st: sn pushed along: unable qck u.p* **57/10**[3]

1m 43.3s (4.50) **6** Ran SP% **116.6**
PARI-MUTUEL: WIN 12.40; PL 3.50, 1.70; SF 34.10.
Owner M Parrish **Bred** T, Mme D & A De La Heronniere **Trained** France

NOTEBOOK
Calvados Blues(FR) who was a maiden going into the race, was given a really professional ride. Third early on and coming in to the straight, he made progress to take the lead at the furlong marker and then hung on well to fend off the runner up. This was an astute supplementary entry by the trainer and this colt, who was the outsider of six, looks to have further improvement in him and could go for the Criterium International, although owner feels he should be retired for the season.
Naval Officer(USA), a big long-striding horse, still had plenty to do coming into the straight. He did not really engage top gear until one and a half out and then finished well but may not have acted at this track but is a possible for the longer Prix du Conde and may even be sent to Santa Anita for one of the Breeders' Cup Juvenile events. He can only improve further.
Canwinn(IRE), a consistent colt, once again put up a decent performance. Tucked in behind the leader early on, he went to the head of affairs halfway up the straight and was passed by the winner at the furlong marker. He kept on one paced and did not give up second until well inside the final furlong.
Topclas(FR), behind for much of the race, did make some late progress and was probably unsuited by a lack of early pace.

6148a PRIX DU PRINCE D'ORANGE (GROUP 3) 1m 2f
4:10 (4:12) 3-Y-O **£29,412** (£11,765; £8,824; £5,882; £2,941)

RPR

1 **Never On Sunday (FR)**[51] 4577 3-8-12 (b) C-PLemaire 5 113
(J-C Rouget, France) *hld up: 6th on outside st: r.o to ld over 1f out: rdn and fnd more fnl f: drvn out* **51/10**[3]

2 nk **Russian Cross (IRE)**[28] 5302 3-9-2 SPasquier 1 116
(A Fabre, France) *prom: 3rd 1/2-way: 2nd st: led over 1 1/2f out to 1f out: rdn and r.o to press wnr ins fnl f: r.o* **11/10**[1]

3 4 **Trincot (FR)**[69] 4010 3-9-0 IMendizabal 3 106
(P Demercastel, France) *hld up: last st: styd on fr over 1f out: nrest at fin* **83/10**

4 4 **Ashantee (GER)**[27] 5329 3-8-11 .... DPorcu 6 95
(M Rulec, Germany) *mid-div: 5th st: rdn and disputing 3rd 1f out: no ex clsng stages* **72/1**

5 ¾ **Belle Et Celebre (FR)**[104] 2877 3-9-1 .... CSoumillon 4 98
(A De Royer-Dupre, France) *hld up: 7th st: n.d* **11/1**

6 5 **Akiem (IRE)**[34] 5137 3-8-12 .... ASuborics 2 85
(Andreas Lowe, Germany) *prom: 3rd st: rdn 1 1/2f out: one pce fr appr fnl f* **24/1**

7 15 **Assafair (FR)**[17] 3-8-12 .... ELacaille 7 55
(Mme C Dufreche, France) *prom: 2nd 1/2-way: 4th and wkng on outside st: sn btn* **43/1**

P **River Proud (USA)**[28] 5302 3-8-12 .... OPeslier 8 —
(P F I Cole) *led: hdd over 1 1/2f out: sn wknd: p.u: heart attack: dead* **27/10[2]**

2m 6.30s (-0.60) **8** Ran SP% **117.8**
PARI-MUTUEL: WIN 6.10; PL 1.40, 1.10, 1.70; DF 5.20.
Owner D-Y Treves **Bred** Scea Des Prairies **Trained** Pau, France

NOTEBOOK
Never On Sunday(FR) refused to have blinkers put on him in the paddock so finally ran without them. Held up early, he had plenty to do coming into the straight but came with a sweeping late run, to hit the front inside the last furlong then had to battle to hold on. There are no plans for this colt as he is entered in the Arqana Arc de Triomphe sale but is not entered in the race itself and everything depends on if he is sold. He could become a possible for the Emirates Champion Stakes.
Russian Cross(IRE) was ruled out of the Arc de Triomphe immediately after the race this colt as connections felt that 1m2f is now his maximum distance. He is a fine-looking individual and was given every possible chance and only lost out narrowly to a rival to whom he was coceding weight. Connections have now decided to supplement him into the Champion Stakes at Newmarket.
Trincot(FR), who was held up, did make some late progress but never looked like troubling the winner and is not up to this level.
Ashantee(GER) was mid-division early on but was not a factor in the straight.
River Proud(USA) set a strong early pace and still seemed to be going well before the straight. Soon after the colt began wobble and his jockey jumped off him as the poor horse fell to the ground. Sadly he ruptured his aorta valve and collapsed and died at the furlong marker.

5559 HAMILTON (R-H)
Sunday, September 21

OFFICIAL GOING: Soft (heavy in places; 6.4)
Wind: Breezy, half-behind Weather: Cloudy, bright

6149 TOTEPLACEPOT NURSERY — 6f 5y
2:10 (2:11) (Class 3) (0-85,83) 2-Y-O **£7,123** (£2,119; £1,059; £529) **Stalls** Low

Form RPR

6031 1 **Count Paris (USA)**[12] 5785 2-8-10 **72** .... JoeFanning 3 73
(M Johnston) *w ldrs: led 1/2-way: kpt on wl u.p fnl f* **6/4[1]**

3011 2 ½ **Scenic Pass**[20] 5560 2-8-13 **75** .... PaulHanagan 5 74
(E S McMahon) *t.k.h: cl up: effrt and disp ld over 1f out to wl ins fnl f: no ex nr fin* **7/2[3]**

453 3 ¾ **Doric Echo**[56] 4456 2-8-10 **72** .... TomEaves 6 69
(B Smart) *wnt rt s: sn outpcd: hdwy over 1f out: r.o wl fnl f: nrst fin* **8/1**

12 4 6 **Noodles Blue Boy**[26] 5375 2-9-7 **83** .... FrancisNorton 1 62
(Ollie Pears) *trckd ldrs: drvn and edgd rt over 2f out: hung rt and wknd over 1f out* **9/1**

211 5 3 ¾ **Bold Account (IRE)**[24] 5414 2-8-7 **69** .... AndrewElliott 2 37
(K R Burke) *slt ld to 1/2-way: wknd over 1f out: fin lame* **11/4[2]**

1m 15.58s (3.38) **Going Correction** +0.675s/f (Yiel) **5** Ran SP% **110.0**
Speed ratings (Par 99): **104,103,102,94,89**
toteswinger: 1&2 £8.10. CSF £7.02 TOTE £2.40: £1.50, £1.60; EX 8.10.
Owner Sheikh Hamdan Bin Mohammed Al Maktoum **Bred** Darley **Trained** Middleham Moor, N Yorks
■ Stewards' Enquiry : Paul Hanagan caution: used whip with excessive frequency

FOCUS
Just the five runners, but a tight little nursery nonetheless and they seemed to go a decent pace.

NOTEBOOK
Count Paris(USA) ◆, who had been raised 5lb for his victory in similarly testing conditions over an extra furlong at Lingfield last time, would have been suited by the decent pace. Always up with the pace, it looked as though the runner-up might get the better of him entering the last 2f, but the stiff finish and testing ground brought his stamina into play and he was well on top at the line. He looks the type that can continue to progress, especially back over further. (op 7-4 tchd 15-8 & 2-1 in places)
Scenic Pass, bidding for a hat-trick after winning a Redcar seller and a claimer here, found herself off a 10lb higher mark than when last in a nursery as a result. After racing keenly on the outside of the leaders, she came to win her race, but her stamina just appeared to give out in the run to the line. (op 4-1 tchd 9-2)
Doric Echo, the only maiden in the field and racing on much softer ground than he had encountered before, ran a remarkable race on this nursery debut. After swerving away to his right exiting the stalls, he was soon in a detached last and apparently going nowhere, but he really found his stride on reaching the rising ground and was still catching the front pair at the line. He gives the impression he is still learning the game and, on this evidence, a step up to 7f may be in order.
Noodles Blue Boy, the least exposed in the field and making his nursery debut, struggled to go the early pace and, although he managed to get himself back in touch with the leaders, he tended to hang about up the final climb and may not want conditions as testing as this. (op 8-1 tchd 15-2)
Bold Account(IRE), proven in soft ground but a whopping 18lb higher in this bid for a hat-trick, tried to make all against the stands' rail, but he had nothing left when collared passing the 2f pole. It transpired that he finished lame. Official explanation: vet said colt returned lame on its right-fore (op 5-2)

6150 TOTESWINGER H'CAP — 6f 5y
2:40 (2:44) (Class 5) (0-70,70) 3-Y-O **£3,885** (£1,156; £577; £288) **Stalls** Low

Form RPR

51 1 **Chosen One (IRE)**[25] 5395 3-8-11 **63** .... TomEaves 11 68
(B Smart) *t.k.h: cl up on outside: drvn and outpcd 2f out: edgd rt and styd on wl fnl f: led nr fin* **7/2[1]**

0060 2 ½ **Baronovici (IRE)**[25] 5397 3-8-4 **56** oh1 .... (v[1]) PaulHanagan 10 59
(D W Barker) *led: rdn and edgd rt over 1f out: kpt on: hdd nr fin* **13/2**

6603 3 ¾ **Night Premiere (IRE)**[18] 5617 3-8-4 **56** .... HayleyTurner 2 57
(R Hannon) *trckd ldrs: effrt and ev ch ins fnl f: kpt on same pce* **5/1[3]**

0500 4 1 ½ **Planet Queen**[25] 5389 3-7-11 **56** oh6 .... (b[1]) DeclanCannon(7) 1 52
(K R Burke) *towards rr: pushed along 1/2-way: kpt on fnl f: nrst fin* **25/1**

4346 5 ½ **Kinout (IRE)**[19] 5592 3-9-1 **67** .... SilvestreDeSousa 9 61
(K A Ryan) *cl up tl rdn and no ex over 1f out* **7/2[1]**

02-2 6 1 **Tito (IRE)**[17] 5636 3-9-3 **69** .... PaulFessey 7 60
(T D Barron) *bhd and sn pushed along: hdwy over 1f out: kpt on: nvr able to chal* **4/1[2]**

6120 7 nk **Andrasta**[14] 5714 3-8-0 **59** .... DanielleMooney(7) 8 49
(A Berry) *in midifeld on outside: drvn and outpcd over 2f out: no imp* **14/1**

5000 8 ½ **Rascasse**[43] 4850 3-8-4 **56** oh8 .... RoystonFfrench 6 44
(Bruce Hellier) *bhd and sn outpcd: sme late hdwy: nvr on terms* **50/1**

3510 9 1 ¾ **Mandelieu (IRE)**[25] 5400 3-9-4 **70** .... FrancisNorton 4 53
(Ollie Pears) *prom tl rdn and wknd over 1f out* **10/1**

005- 10 30 **Jazz Stick (IRE)**[318] 6729 3-8-4 **56** oh11 .... (bt) AndrewElliott 3 —
(D A Nolan) *prom 2f: sn struggling* **150/1**

1m 16.84s (4.64) **Going Correction** +0.675s/f (Yiel) **10** Ran SP% **116.7**
Speed ratings (Par 101): **96,95,94,92,91 90,89,89,86,46**
toteswinger: 1&2 £6.30, 1&3 £4.90, 2&3 £9.20. CSF £26.52 CT £116.44 TOTE £5.00: £1.80, £2.00, £2.30; EX 32.60.
Owner Ceffyl Racing **Bred** Carl Holt **Trained** Hambleton, N Yorks

FOCUS
A modest handicap in which four of the ten runners were out of the handicap, though there were a couple of lightly raced and unexposed sorts in the field. They went a serious early pace, perhaps too fast as the winning time was 1.26sec slower than the nursery and the form is moderate and best rated around the placed horses.

6151 ALWAYS TRYING EBF MAIDEN STKS — 1m 65y
3:10 (3:10) (Class 5) 2-Y-O **£3,885** (£1,156; £577; £288) **Stalls** High

Form RPR

1 **Quai D'Orsay** 2-9-3 0 .... GregFairley 8 79+
(M Johnston) *mde all: rdn over 2f out: drew clr fr wl over 1f out* **3/1[2]**

4 2 3 ¾ **Forty Thirty (IRE)**[17] 5641 2-9-3 0 .... TonyCulhane 9 69
(M R Channon) *t.k.h: cl up: effrt and rdn 3f out: kpt on fnl f: nt rch wnr* **13/8[1]**

6 3 2 ½ **Hard Luck Story**[25] 5387 2-9-3 0 .... PaulMulrennan 7 64
(Miss L A Perratt) *prom: drvn over 3f out: outpcd 2f out: r.o fnl f* **9/1**

3 4 1 ½ **Miss Cracklinrosie**[12] 5771 2-8-12 0 .... PJMcDonald 2 56
(J R Weymes) *hld up: hdwy over 3f out: edgd rt u.p over 1f out: wknd ins fnl f* **10/1**

50 5 4 ½ **New Tricks**[25] 5387 2-9-3 0 .... RoystonFfrench 4 51
(Miss L A Perratt) *in tch tl rdn and wknd over 2f out* **14/1**

6 1 ¾ **Quick Gourmet** 2-8-12 0 .... PaulHanagan 3 42
(A G Foster) *prom tl rdn and wknd over 3f out* **40/1**

7 2 ½ **Gesseem (IRE)** 2-9-3 0 .... JoeFanning 1 42
(M Johnston) *hld up: shkn up over 3f out: sn no imp* **6/1[3]**

8 6 **Radegund Abbey** 2-9-3 0 .... TomEaves 6 30
(B Smart) *s.i.s: rdn in rr 4f out: sn btn* **8/1**

1m 54.69s (6.29) **Going Correction** +0.675s/f (Yiel) **8** Ran SP% **116.7**
Speed ratings (Par 95): **95,91,88,87,82 81,78,72**
toteswinger: 1&2 £2.40, 1&3 £5.80, 2&3 £4.50. CSF £8.48 TOTE £4.80: £1.50, £1.30, £2.70; EX 9.20.
Owner Sheikh Hamdan Bin Mohammed Al Maktoum **Bred** Miss K Rausing **Trained** Middleham Moor, N Yorks

FOCUS
An interesting maiden featuring a couple that had shown ability on their debuts and some well-bred newcomers. The pace was a fair one, but very few ever got into it and the order hardly changed throughout the contest.

NOTEBOOK
Quai D'Orsay ◆, a 50,000gns half-brother to four winning stayers including the smart Foreign Affairs, seems to have inherited plenty of stamina himself judged on this impressive debut. Sent straight to the front, he kept on galloping and basically ran his rivals into the ground. He can go on from here and looks a very interesting staying prospect for next season. (op 10-3 tchd 7-2)
Forty Thirty(IRE), who showed plenty of promise when just behind a subsequent winner in a Salisbury novice event on his debut, was always in about the same place and, although he tried to get on terms with the winner, he could never do so. He probably ran into an above-average sort here and there is an ordinary maiden waiting for him. (op 7-4 tchd 11-8)
Hard Luck Story, who showed ability despite going off at 66-1 in an Ayr maiden that has produced a couple of subsequent winners, stayed on again after seeming to get outpaced. He still appeared in need of the experience and looks capable of better. (tchd 8-1 & 10-1 ih places)
Miss Cracklinrosie, who showed some ability in similarly testing conditions in a Beverley maiden on debut, looked a possible danger when arriving from off the pace entering the last 2f, but she was unable to maintain her effort. There was a doubt over her Beverley performance as the horse one place behind her was rated just 35, but this suggests that she does have the ability to win a race. (tchd 11-1)
New Tricks was a springer in the market despite having finished behind his stable companion Hard Luck Story at Ayr last time, but he never figured. (op 40-1)
Gesseem(IRE), a 200,000gns half-brother to a winner at up to 1m1f, proved too green to do himself justice on this debut and is surely capable of better. (op 13-2 tchd 8-1)
Radegund Abbey, an 85,000gns half-brother to four winners over distances ranging from 6f to 1m6f, was also very green and trailed throughout after starting very slowly. (op 7-1)

6152 BET TOTEPOOL ON ALL UK RACING PREMIER CLAIMING STKS — 1m 1f 36y
3:40 (3:40) (Class 4) 3-5-Y-O **£5,180** (£1,541; £770; £384) **Stalls** High

Form RPR

2411 1 **Talk Of Saafend (IRE)**[5] 6001 3-8-8 **75** .... HayleyTurner 2 79
(R Hannon) *hld up in tch: smooth hdwy 3f out: led on bit over 1f out: pushed clr* **15/8[1]**

6010 2 6 **Moody Tunes**[17] 5635 5-9-4 **75** .... DarrenWilliams 7 71
(K R Burke) *pressed ldr: led after 3f to over 1f out: no ch w wnr* **3/1[3]**

56 3 ¾ **Getrah**[42] 4899 4-8-13 **55** .... (p) PaulHanagan 3 65
(C Grant) *dwlt: hld up in tch: hdwy 3f out: kpt on same pce fnl f* **33/1**

6110 4 4 ½ **King Of The Moors (USA)**[12] 5773 5-8-13 **72** .... (p) PaulFessey 6 55
(T D Barron) *led 3f: cl up: c alone to stands' rail over 4f out: no imp fnl 2f* **11/4[2]**

6-25 5 2 **Top Jaro (FR)**[172] 1160 5-8-13 **60** .... TonyHamilton 1 51
(D W Barker) *trckd ldrs tl wknd over 2f out* **6/1**

1030 6 1 ¼ **Grethel (IRE)**[20] 5564 4-8-8 **61** .... SladeO'Hara(5) 4 49
(A Berry) *prom tl edgd lft and wknd over 2f out* **11/1**

0U0- 7 26 **Recoil (IRE)**[354] 5896 3-8-8 **60** .... TomEaves 5 —
(R Johnson) *bhd: lost tch fr 4f out* **50/1**

2m 4.32s (4.62) **Going Correction** +0.675s/f (Yiel)
WFA 3 from 4yo+ 5lb **7** Ran SP% **114.0**
Speed ratings (Par 105): **106,100,100,96,94 93,70**
toteswinger: 1&2 £1.80, 1&3 £8.00, 2&3 £14.10. CSF £7.73 TOTE £2.60: £1.70, £2.20; EX 8.50.Talk of Saafend was claimed by Mr P. Monteith for £25,000.
Owner J B R Leisure Ltd **Bred** Michael Dalton **Trained** East Everleigh, Wilts

FOCUS
A reasonable claimer, but they went no pace early and although the winner is the best guide and rated to form, she may not have had to run to her mark in the circumstances. Most of the runners stayed far side on reaching the home straight, but King Of The Moors was switched to race alone up the stands' rail.

6153 TOTEPOOL CONDITIONS STKS 6f 5y
4:10 (4:11) (Class 2) 3-Y-0+

£12,462 (£3,732; £1,866; £934; £466; £234) Stalls Low

Form RPR
6004 1 **Knot In Wood (IRE)**[1] 6104 6-8-9 102 PaulHanagan 2 107
(R A Fahey) *cl up: led over 1f out: pushed clr* **10/11**[1]
5635 2 5 **Cake (IRE)**[22] 5509 3-8-2 92 HayleyTurner 7 86
(R Hannon) *t.k.h: led to over 1f out: no ch w wnr* **4/1**[2]
0300 3 2 1/4 **Burnwynd Boy**[1] 6104 3-8-7 105 TomEaves 5 84
(Miss L A Perratt) *hld up towards rr: rdn over 2f out: kpt on fnl f: no imp* **5/1**[3]
2500 4 shd **Pawan (IRE)**[8] 5897 8-8-9 90 (b) AnnStokell 3 83
(Miss A Stokell) *bhd and outpcd: hung rt over 2f out: kpt on fnl f: no imp* **7/1**
201- 5 2 1/4 **Ponty Rossa (IRE)**[455] 2914 4-8-4 0 RoystonFfrench 8 71
(T D Easterby) *wnt rt s: hld up: effrt over 2f out: btn fnl f* **8/1**
0250 6 7 **Fern House (IRE)**[44] 4813 6-8-9 48 PaulMulrennan 6 54
(Bruce Hellier) *prom tl rdn and wknd over 2f out* **100/1**
6440 7 6 **Howards Prince**[23] 5452 5-8-9 43 AndrewElliott 1 35
(D A Nolan) *prom tl rdn and wknd over 2f out* **200/1**
4550 8 15 **Seafield Towers**[23] 5452 8-8-9 42 (p) FrederikTylicki 4 —
(D A Nolan) *cl up tl rdn and wknd over 2f out* **200/1**

1m 14.78s (2.58) **Going Correction** +0.675s/f (Yiel)
WFA 3 from 4yo+ 2lb 8 Ran SP% **114.6**
Speed ratings (Par 109): **109,102,99,99,96 86,78,58**
toteswinger: 1&2 £2.00, 1&3 £2.00, 2&3 £3.40. CSF £4.92 TOTE £2.00: £1.10, £1.70, £1.90; EX 5.50.
Owner Rhodes, Kenyon & Gill **Bred** Rathbarry Stud **Trained** Musley Bank, N Yorks

FOCUS
This was effectively a five-horse race as the other three had no chance and were merely making up the numbers. A fascinating contest nonetheless, featuring two horses that ran in the Ayr Gold Cup 24 hours earlier. The winning time was predictably much faster than the earlier handicap and nursery and the winner sets the level.

NOTEBOOK
Knot In Wood(IRE) 'won' the race on his side of the track in the previous day's Ayr Gold Cup, but was only fourth overall. His bid for quick compensation was never really in doubt as he was always travelling well behind the leaders and, when asked to go and pick up the pacemaker, he found more than enough. (tchd Evens)
Cake(IRE) had a bit to prove with regards to trip and ground and also had 5lb to find with the favourite on these terms. Despite the doubts, she was given a positive ride from the start, but there was nothing she could do when the winner was unleashed, though she did keep on for second. (op 5-1)
Burnwynd Boy, who finished last of the 27 runners in the previous day's Ayr Gold Cup, ran much better this time having held every chance out towards the centre of the track, but the feeling is that he is still flattered by his third in a Group 3 at Newcastle in June and that he will remain hard to place. (op 11-2)
Pawan(IRE), having his 17th start of the year, attracted market support even though he had quite a bit to find with a few of these at the weights. Back in trip after four outings at around 7f, he was completely taken off his feet early before plugging on to reach his final position. On this evidence he needs a return to further, even though he is yet to really convince over it. (op 10-1)
Ponty Rossa(IRE), who stays further than this, was always stuck out in the centre of the track and could never get involved, but she was returning from 15 months off so should at least come on for it. (op 7-1)

6154 TOTESUPER7 BUTTONHOOK H'CAP 1m 5f 9y
4:40 (4:42) (Class 3) (0-95,94) 3-Y-0+

£10,592 (£3,172; £1,586; £793; £396; £198) Stalls High

Form RPR
0633 1 **Always Bold (IRE)**[7] 5940 3-8-11 86 JoeFanning 3 94
(M Johnston) *cl up: led over 2f out: hld on gamely fnl f* **4/1**[2]
-333 2 1/2 **Acropolis (IRE)**[92] 3253 7-9-9 94 (v) FrederikTylicki(5) 4 101
(Miss L A Perratt) *cl up: effrt over 1f out: kpt on fnl f but a hld* **9/1**
2511 3 1 1/2 **Hurlingham**[20] 5563 4-8-12 78 PaulMulrennan 2 83
(M W Easterby) *hld up: hdwy to chse ldrs over 1f out: rdn and no ex ins fnl f* **11/2**[3]
3201 4 3 3/4 **Merchant Of Dubai**[6] 5967 3-8-3 78 6ex RoystonFfrench 7 77+
(G A Swinbank) *racd keenly: chsd ldrs: nt clr run and lost pl over 2f out: kpt on fnl f: nt rch ldrs* **11/8**[1]
1016 5 2 1/2 **Lochiel**[25] 5391 4-8-11 77 PJMcDonald 1 73
(Mrs S C Bradburne) *hld up in tch: hdwy over 3f out: edgd rt and no ex over 1f out* **7/1**
015- 6 3 3/4 **Mirjan (IRE)**[190] 6181 12-9-9 89 (b) PaulHanagan 8 79
(L Lungo) *hld up in tch: drvn and outpcd over 3f out: n.d after* **16/1**
015/ 7 1 1/2 **Zeitgeist (IRE)**[565] 4478 7-9-10 90 (b[1]) TomEaves 5 78
(Miss L A Perratt) *hld up: rdn over 3f out: sn btn* **33/1**
1233 8 3/4 **Channel Crossing**[20] 5563 6-8-2 75 oh7 DeanHeslop(7) 6 62
(S Wynne) *led to over 2f out: sn rdn and wknd* **16/1**

2m 59.78s (5.88) **Going Correction** +0.675s/f (Yiel)
WFA 3 from 4yo+ 9lb 8 Ran SP% **114.7**
Speed ratings (Par 107): **108,107,106,104,102 100,99,99**
toteswinger: 1&2 £6.80, 1&3 £4.70, 2&3 £6.00. CSF £39.40 CT £198.01 TOTE £5.50: £1.40, £2.10, £2.00; EX 39.40 Trifecta £157.70 Pool: £234.53 - 1.10 winning units..
Owner Always Trying Partnership V **Bred** R N Auld **Trained** Middleham Moor, N Yorks

FOCUS
A decent handicap which would have been quite a test of stamina in the ground, and they finished well spread out even though the early pace did not look that strong. It proved something of a rough race, too but the form looks sound rated around the first three.

NOTEBOOK
Always Bold(IRE), back on turf after a couple of fair efforts on Polytrack, had never encountered ground this testing before. Always in a decent position to attack, once in front he showed all the tenacity you come to expect from a Johnston runner in a driving finish. He now goes for the Cesarewitch for which a 4lb penalty will help his chances of getting in. (tchd 9-2)
Acropolis(IRE), without a win in four years, was never far away and battled on all the way to the line, but the winner proved too tough. The ground did not seem to be a problem to him. (op 11-1 tchd 12-1)
Hurlingham, up 3lb in his bid for a hat-trick and taking another step up in trip, was held up out the back as usual. Gradually weaving his way through runners up the home straight, he was close enough approaching the last furlong and, although again demonstrating a high head-carriage and not having much room to play with between the front pair entering the last furlong, it did not cost him his chance. (op 6-1 tchd 5-1)
Merchant Of Dubai, carrying a 6lb penalty for his win in testing ground at Musselburgh six days earlier, was still in with a chance when getting murdered against the inside rail passing the 2f pole. Although ultimately well held, the incident would not have done him any good and he is worth another chance to show this running to be all wrong. Official explanation: jockey said colt was denied a clear run (op 6-4 tchd 13-8 & 7-4 in places)
Lochiel, proven in the ground, was attempting his longest trip yet on the level. He had every chance down the outside entering the last 2f, but did not get home. (tchd 13-2 and 15-2)
Mirjan(IRE), last seen over hurdles and reappearing from six months off, has not raced over a trip this short for some time. He was on and off the bridle at various stages before getting left behind. (op 11-1)

6155 NEILSLAND AND EARNOCK H'CAP 1m 3f 16y
5:10 (5:10) (Class 5) (0-70,73) 3-Y-0 £3,238 (£963; £481; £240) Stalls High

Form RPR
5231 1 **Offshore Anna (IRE)**[8] 5888 3-9-2 73 FrederikTylicki(5) 2 86+
(J J Quinn) *chsd ldr: led over 3f out: styd on wl u.p* **2/1**[1]
4102 2 1/2 **China Pink**[13] 5758 3-8-5 57 (b) DO'Donohoe 5 65
(Sir Mark Prescott) *t.k.h: led to over 3f out: outpcd and hung rt over 2f out: rallied fnl f* **7/2**[3]
0015 3 3 1/2 **Prince Rhyddarch**[23] 5456 3-8-10 62 TomEaves 7 64
(Miss L A Perratt) *prom: effrt over 3f out: one pce over 1f out* **6/1**
-253 4 1 1/2 **Bollin Greta**[25] 5388 3-8-8 60 PaulMulrennan 1 60
(T D Easterby) *t.k.h: prom: rdn over 3f out: one pce fnl 2f* **10/1**
2011 5 1/2 **Casino Night**[20] 5565 3-8-8 67 DeanHeslop(7) 6 66
(R Johnson) *prom: drvn and outpcd over 3f out: rallied appr fnl f: no imp ins fnl f* **9/1**
0621 6 9 **Shaylee**[27] 5362 3-8-6 58 SilvestreDeSousa 4 42
(T D Walford) *chsd ldrs: lost pl 1/2-way: short-lived effrt 3f out: sn wknd* **10/3**[2]

2m 34.03s (8.43) **Going Correction** +0.675s/f (Yiel) **6** Ran SP% **112.0**
Speed ratings (Par 101): **96,95,93,92,91 85**
toteswinger: 1&2 £2.00, 1&3 £1.80, 2&3 £3.00. CSF £9.17 TOTE £3.00: £1.30, £2.10; EX 8.80 Place 6 £12.52, Place 5 £7.76..
Owner Colm McEvoy **Bred** Conor Murphy **Trained** Settrington, N Yorks
■ Stewards' Enquiry : D O'Donohoe three-day ban: used whip with excessive frequency (Oct 6-8)
Paul Mulrennan
Frederik Tylicki four-day ban: used whip with excessive frequency (Oct 11-14)

FOCUS
An ordinary handicap with one gelding taking on five fillies, though half the field did come into this off the back of a win. The pace was just a fair one, but this proved quite a test of stamina for these three-year-olds in the ground and the finish was in slow motion. The runner-up sets the standard.
T/Plt: £21.10 to a £1 stake. Pool: £58,452.94. 2,020.42 winning tickets. T/Qpdt: £5.40 to a £1 stake. Pool: £3,100.55. 422.29 winning tickets. RY

4233 FRANKFURT (L-H)
Sunday, September 21

OFFICIAL GOING: Good

6156a EURO-CUP DER MEHL MULHENS-STIFTUNG (GROUP 3) 1m 2f
3:55 (3:58) 3-Y-0+ £23,529 (£7,353; £3,676; £2,206)

RPR
1 **Zaungast (IRE)**[14] 4-9-2 EFrank 5 105
(W Hickst, Germany) *in tch: disputing 3rd: 3rd st: r.o to ld fnl f: styd on wl: pushed out* **43/10**[2]
2 3 1/2 **Fair Breeze (GER)**[28] 5332 5-9-2 AHelfenbein 6 98
(Mario Hofer, Germany) *racd in cl 2nd: led 1 1/2f out to 1f out: nt pce of wnr* **3/5**[1]
3 nse **Lindner (GER)**[21] 5554 3-8-8 ASuborics 4 96
(W Hickst, Germany) *settled in 5th: pushed along st: styd on wl fnl f: nrest at fin* **108/10**
4 1 1/2 **Lord Hill (GER)**[22] 5528 4-9-2 WMongil 8 95
(C Zeitz) *led: rdn ent st: hdd 1 1/2f out: one pce* **62/10**
5 shd **Lucidor (GER)**[14] 5-9-2 MSuerland 3 95
(Frau E Mader, Germany) *hld up in 6th: pushed along appr st: styd on fr over 1f out: nrest at fin* **28/1**
6 6 **Integral (GER)**[389] 4958 4-9-2 NRichter 2 83
(P Rau, Germany) *first to show: in tch disputing 3rd: 4th st: sn no ex* **127/10**
7 3 1/2 **Dawn Dew (GER)**[28] 5329 3-8-4 FilipMinarik 7 70
(P Schiergen, Germany) *racd in last: pushed along appr st: nvr a threat* **44/10**[3]

2m 7.40s (-1.17)
WFA 3 from 4yo+ 6lb 7 Ran SP% **133.0**
(Including 10 Euros stake): WIN 53; PL 11, 10, 12; SF 128.
Owner J Erhardt **Bred** J Erhardt **Trained** Germany

6149 HAMILTON (R-H)

Monday, September 22

OFFICIAL GOING: Soft (heavy in places)

Wind: Breezy, half behind Weather: Sunny

6158 EUROPEAN BREEDERS' FUND MEDIAN AUCTION MAIDEN STKS 6f 5y

2:10 (2:10) (Class 5) 2-Y-O **£3,885** (£1,156; £577; £288) **Stalls** Centre

Form				RPR
6	1		**Hit The Switch**[12] 5798 2-9-3 0 ... TonyHamilton 2	70
			(R A Fahey) *chsd ldrs: rdn over 2f out: led 1f out: drvn out* 9/2[3]	
	2	*nk*	**Box Office** 2-9-3 0 ... RoystonFfrench 3	70
			(M Johnston) *dwlt: bhd and pushed along: hdwy over 2f out: effrt and rn green appr fnl f: kpt on fnl f: jst hld: bttr for r* 9/4[1]	
5	3	1 1/4	**My Best Bet**[18] 5650 2-8-12 0 ... TonyCulhane 8	61
			(M R Channon) *t.k.h: cl up: rdn to chal appr fnl f: no ex wl ins fnl f* 4/1[2]	
50	4	1 1/4	**Lost In Paris (IRE)**[7] 5959 2-9-3 0 ... DavidAllan 7	62
			(T D Easterby) *hld up in tch: effrt over 2f out: kpt on fnl f: no imp* 6/1	
6500	5	5	**Meg Jicaro**[4] 6051 2-8-9 65 ... RussellKennemore(3) 1	42
			(Mrs L Williamson) *led to 1f out: hung rt and sn btn* 22/1	
	6	1 1/2	**Barbeito** 2-8-8 0 ow1 ... FrederikTylicki(5) 5	39
			(D J S Ffrench Davis) *dwlt: hdwy 1/2-way: sn rdn and wknd* 12/1	
	7	11	**Lady Vivien** 2-8-12 0 ... PaulMulrennan 4	5
			(D H Brown) *trckd ldrs tl rdn and wknd over 2f out* 11/2	

1m 17.62s (5.42) **Going Correction** +0.625s/f (Yiel) 7 Ran SP% 110.7

Speed ratings (Par 95): **88,87,85,84,77 75,60**

toteswinger: 1&2 £2.80, 1&3 £2.60, 2&3 £2.70. CSF £14.05 TOTE £6.50: £3.10, £1.50; EX 17.80.

Owner Rob Lloyd Racing Limited **Bred** Mrs M T Dawson **Trained** Musley Bank, N Yorks

FOCUS

A modest maiden with the winner improving from his debut.

NOTEBOOK

Hit The Switch was not disgraced on his debut in a better heat at Kempton 12 days previously and the drop to this trip on the more demanding surface proved much to his liking. No doubt his experience won him the day, but he is in good hands. It will be interesting to see how the Handicapper assesses him for nurseries. (op 8-1)

Box Office, whose dam was a 1m winner at three, fell out of the gates and it took an age for the penny to drop with him. He made up ground to join the leaders around 2f out, but proved distinctly green when put under maximum pressure. He just lost out, but there was more than enough in this display to suggest he can go one better now he has this under his belt. He may also be happier on a sounder surface. (op 2-1 tchd 11-4)

My Best Bet broke a lot better than she had done on her Warwick debut last time and showed a more professional attitude, though she failed to get home like the first pair despite this being a sharper test. She probably needs more time, but will be eligible for nurseries after her next race. (op 11-4 tchd 5-2)

Lost In Paris(IRE) was always in the same sort of place and simply lacked a change of gear. He has some scope and ought to find his feet now he is qualified for a nursery mark.

6159 BETXTRA AT TOTESPORT 0800 221 221 H'CAP 5f 4y

2:40 (2:41) (Class 6) (0-65,58) 3-Y-O+ **£2,590** (£770; £385; £192) **Stalls** Centre

Form				RPR
-000	1		**Sunley Sovereign**[4] 6039 4-8-6 45 ...(b) AndrewElliott 1	56
			(Mrs R A Carr) *chsd ldrs: effrt over 2f out: kpt on to ld wl ins fnl f: r.o* 50/1	
5245	2	1 1/4	**Gelert (IRE)**[13] 5770 3-8-5 45 ...(b) PatrickMathers 3	51
			(Peter Grayson) *led: rdn over 2f out: hdd wl ins fnl f: kpt on same pce* 10/1	
0102	3	*shd*	**Almost Married (IRE)**[4] 6039 4-9-5 58 ... DanielTudhope 9	64
			(J S Goldie) *hld up: hdwy over 2f out: rdn and r.o fnl f: nrst fin* 15/8[1]	
5400	4	1 1/2	**Howards Tipple**[40] 4971 4-9-3 56 ...(p) TomEaves 14	57+
			(Miss L A Perratt) *hld up centre: effrt 2f out: kpt on same pce fnl f* 12/1	
1000	5	*hd*	**Guto**[26] 5398 5-8-10 54 ... KellyHarrison(5) 5	54
			(W J H Ratcliffe) *prom: effrt over 1f out: one pce fnl f* 9/1	
2015	6	3/4	**Obe One**[5] 6011 8-8-10 54 ... SladeO'Hara(5) 4	51+
			(A Berry) *in tch: drvn over 2f out: edgd rt and one pce over 1f out* 8/1[3]	
2602	7	3/4	**Swallow Forest**[27] 5457 3-9-1 55 ...(b) PaulFessey 11	49
			(T D Barron) *bhd and outpcd: hdwy fnl f: nrst fin* 14/1	
044	8	3/4	**Foreign Rhythm (IRE)**[23] 5501 3-8-12 52 ...(v) KimTinkler 10	44
			(N Tinkler) *bhd and outpcd: hrd rdn and hung lft over 1f out: kpt on: nrst fin* 16/1	
3304	9	1/2	**Oeuf A La Neige**[22] 5538 8-9-1 54 ... PaulMulrennan 12	44
			(Miss L A Perratt) *bhd: hdwy on outside over 2f out: no imp over 1f out* 12/1	
2624	10	*nk*	**Rainbow Bay**[11] 5817 5-8-10 54 ...(v) FrederikTylicki(5) 7	43
			(Miss Tracy Waggott) *cl up tl rdn and wknd over 1f out* 11/2[2]	
603	11	1 1/2	**Distant Vision (IRE)**[24] 5452 5-8-6 45 ... RoystonFfrench 8	29
			(H A McWilliams) *midfield: drvn and outpcd over 2f out: sn n.d* 20/1	
0340	12	3 1/2	**Never Without Me**[30] 5260 8-9-4 57 ... MickyFenton 13	28
			(J F Coupland) *towards rr: struggling 1/2-way: nvr on terms* 16/1	
0000	13	23	**Mister Marmaduke**[31] 5220 7-8-3 45 ...(t) DuranFentiman(3) 2	—
			(D A Nolan) *missed break: a struggling* 200/1	

62.90 secs (2.90) **Going Correction** +0.625s/f (Yiel)

WFA 3 from 4yo+ 1lb 13 Ran SP% 121.4

Speed ratings (Par 101): **101,99,98,96,96 94,93,92,91,91 88,83,46**

toteswinger: 1&2 £69.10, 1&3 £17.20, 2&3 £6.80. CSF £498.76 CT £1490.85 TOTE £115.80: £19.60, £2.70, £1.50; EX 783.10.

Owner David W Chapman **Bred** John B Sunley **Trained** Stillington, N Yorks

FOCUS

A weak sprint in which it paid to be drawn low. The placed horses help set the level.

Sunley Sovereign Official explanation: trainer said, regarding apparent improvement in form, compared with its previous run, that the gelding was better suited by the stiffer track.

6160 EBF TOTESPORT FLOWER OF SCOTLAND FILLIES' H'CAP 6f 5y

3:10 (3:10) (Class 3) (0-95,92) 3-Y-O+ **£11,009** (£3,275; £1,637; £817) **Stalls** Centre

Form				RPR
011	1		**Prescription**[6] 5998 3-8-4 73 ... DO'Donohoe 7	84+
			(Sir Mark Prescott) *t.k.h: cl up: led over 3f out: rdn out fnl f* 8/13[1]	
6250	2	1 3/4	**Feisty Royale**[8] 5936 3-8-2 71 ...(b) RoystonFfrench 8	76
			(M Johnston) *trckd ldrs: ev ch over 2f out: sn rdn: kpt on same pce fnl f* 12/1	
2101	3	1	**Artistic License (IRE)**[8] 5936 3-8-9 78 6ex ... TonyCulhane 2	80
			(M R Channon) *prom: effrt over 1f out: edgd rt and nt qckn ins fnl f* 7/1[3]	
3403	4	2	**Ingleby Princess**[24] 5455 4-8-4 71 oh4 ... PaulFessey 6	66
			(T D Barron) *dwlt: hld up: hdwy over 2f out: rdn and no ex fnl f* 16/1	
5520	5	1/2	**Linda Green**[19] 5610 7-8-4 71 oh4 ... PatrickMathers 5	65
			(M R Channon) *bhd: rdn 1/2-way: kpt on fnl f: n.d* 18/1	
2205	6	3	**Sudden Impact (IRE)**[30] 5259 3-9-6 92 ... RussellKennemore(3) 1	76
			(Paul Green) *t.k.h: led to over 3f out: edgd rt and wknd over 2f out* 14/1	
3020	7	2 3/4	**Swift Princess (IRE)**[11] 5831 4-9-4 85 ...(v) AndrewElliott 4	60
			(K R Burke) *t.k.h: in tch tl hung rt and wknd fr 2f out* 5/1[2]	

1m 15.58s (3.38) **Going Correction** +0.625s/f (Yiel)

WFA 3 from 4yo+ 2lb 7 Ran SP% 116.6

Speed ratings (Par 104): **102,99,98,95,95 91,87**

toteswinger: 1&2 £3.70, 1&3 £2.20, 2&3 £8.20. CSF £10.21 CT £31.75 TOTE £1.80: £1.10, £6.80; EX 9.20.

Owner Cheveley Park Stud **Bred** Cheveley Park Stud Ltd **Trained** Newmarket, Suffolk

FOCUS

A fair fillies' handicap. Prescription confirmed she remains ahead of the Handicapper wuith the placed horses setting the standard.

NOTEBOOK

Prescription made it three wins from four career starts with a straightforward display on this return to turf. She went unpenalised for her success in an apprentice handicap at Lingfield six days previously, but probably did not have to improve on that effort to win this and had little trouble with the demanding surface. This highly progressive filly will get another furlong without much fuss and is likely to be out under a penalty in her quest for the four-timer. (tchd 4-6)

Feisty Royale posted a more encouraging effort in blinkers and reversed previous all-weather form with Artistic License on 6lb better terms. She looks reasonably handicapped, but is just struggling to find her optimum trip. (op 20-1)

Artistic License(IRE), a winner of two of her last three outings on Polytrack, was a little below her recent level and probably would have enjoyed a stronger early pace. This ground was also probably softer than she cares for. (op 5-1)

Ingleby Princess saves her best for this venue but found things too hot from 4lb out of the weights and ideally needs a sounder surface. (tchd 20-1)

Sudden Impact(IRE) Official explanation: jockey said filly hung right

6161 BETXTRA AT TOTESPORT.COM APPRENTICE SERIES H'CAP (FINAL OF HAMILTON PARK APPRENTICE SERIES) 1m 3f 16y

3:40 (3:40) (Class 6) (0-65,63) 3-Y-O+ **£2,590** (£770; £385; £192) **Stalls** High

Form				RPR
66-0	1		**Surprise Pension (IRE)**[64] 4219 4-8-13 53 ... JamieKyne(3) 9	63+
			(J J Quinn) *racd keenly: hld up: smooth hdwy to ld 3f out: rdn and hung lft ins fnl f: r.o wl* 9/1	
1510	2	1 1/4	**Jenny Soba**[13] 5776 5-9-2 58 ... MrJPFeatherstone(5) 3	63
			(Lucinda Featherstone) *led 3f: cl up: effrt over 2f out: chsd wnr ins fnl f: r.o* 10/1	
0220	3	1 1/2	**Primo Way**[21] 5564 7-9-12 63 ... PatrickDonaghy 8	65
			(Miss L A Perratt) *hld up: hdwy to chse wnr 2f out: hung rt and no ex ins fnl f* 12/1	
6423	4	2 1/2	**Always Brave**[7] 5971 3-9-5 63 ... CIGillies 1	61
			(M Johnston) *prom: drvn and ev ch 3f out: no ex over 1f out* 2/1[1]	
1-03	5	4 1/2	**Mayadeen (IRE)**[24] 5456 6-9-0 51 ...(v) FrederikTylicki 4	42
			(R A Fahey) *bhd: drvn along 1/2-way: effrt u.p 3f out: sn no imp* 3/1[2]	
0-40	6	3 1/2	**Rawaabet (IRE)**[12] 1025 6-8-12 49 oh4 ...(t) DeanHeslop 6	34
			(Tim Vaughan) *led after 3f to 3f out: sn rdn and wknd* 4/1[3]	
0404	7	25	**Jordan's Light (USA)**[28] 3954 5-9-4 58 ow4 ... RyanMania(3) 5	—
			(P Monteith) *hld up in tch: rdn over 3f out: sn wknd* 14/1	
5-00	8	8	**Catherines Cafe (IRE)**[25] 5415 5-8-9 49 oh4 ...(p) NSLawes(3) 10	—
			(A C Whillans) *cl up tl wknd fr 5f out* 40/1	

2m 32.31s (6.71) **Going Correction** +0.625s/f (Yiel)

WFA 3 from 4yo+ 7lb 8 Ran SP% 114.2

Speed ratings (Par 101): **100,99,98,96,92 90,72,66**

toteswinger: 1&2 £10.00, 1&3 £8.50, 2&3 £11.80. CSF £92.91 CT £1081.58 TOTE £16.00: £3.20, £3.30, £2.80; EX 107.00.

Owner Mrs S Quinn **Bred** Gabriel Bell **Trained** Settrington, N Yorks

FOCUS

This moderate handicap for apprentice riders was run at a modest early pace before Rawaabet went on and increased the tempo nearing the turn for home. The form is rated through the placed horses.

6162 TOTESPORT BETXTRA WIN ONLY H'CAP 1m 1f 36y

4:10 (4:10) (Class 5) (0-70,70) 3-Y-O+ **£3,238** (£963; £481; £240) **Stalls** High

Form				RPR
5020	1		**Moheebb (IRE)**[3] 6070 4-9-7 70 ...(b) AndrewElliott 13	81
			(Mrs R A Carr) *prom: hdwy to ld 1f out: sn clr* 7/2[1]	
6220	2	4	**Thornaby Green**[42] 4936 7-8-0 56 oh3 ... DeanHeslop(7) 6	58
			(T D Barron) *trckd ldrs: led over 2f out to 1f out: kpt on: nt pce of wnr* 12/1	
06	3	3/4	**Solis (GER)**[25] 5418 5-9-7 70 ... PaulMulrennan 12	71
			(P Monteith) *hld up: rdn over 3f out: hdwy over 1f out: kpt on fin* 40/1	
1460	4	1/2	**Sarraaf (IRE)**[22] 5538 12-8-2 56 oh3 ... PatrickDonaghy(5) 14	56
			(Miss L A Perratt) *hld up ins: hdwy and prom 2f out: one pce fnl f* 20/1	
4244	5	*shd*	**Mystical Ayr (IRE)**[21] 5564 6-8-7 56 oh1 ... RoystonFfrench 9	56
			(Miss L A Perratt) *prom: drvn over 2f out: one pce over 1f out* 7/1	
6500	6	3/4	**Brandane (IRE)**[69] 4044 3-7-13 56 oh5 ... AndrewMullen(3) 8	54
			(R A Fahey) *hld up: swtchd lft and hdwy over 2f out: no imp over 1f out* 10/1	
5001	7	2 1/2	**Superior Star**[24] 5454 5-9-1 64 ...(b) JamieMoriarty 1	57
			(N Wilson) *hld up: pushed along over 3f out: nvr rchd ldrs* 9/1	
3051	8	3 1/4	**Grit (IRE)**[4] 6042 3-9-1 69 6ex ... TonyCulhane 11	55
			(M R Channon) *t.k.h: led after 2f: hdd 2f out: edgd lft and wknd ins fnl f* 9/2[3]	
3400	9	2 1/4	**Boppys Pride**[45] 4813 5-8-7 56 oh9 ...(p) PaulFessey 7	37
			(P T Midgley) *hld up: rdn over 3f out: n.d* 28/1	
3452	10	2 3/4	**Doon Haymer (IRE)**[31] 5224 3-9-2 70 ...(v) TomEaves 10	45
			(Miss L A Perratt) *hld up: pushed along 3f out: sn btn* 4/1[2]	
2506	11	3 1/2	**Autumn Charm**[26] 5407 3-8-2 56 oh2 ... PatrickMathers 3	24
			(Lucinda Featherstone) *chsd ldrs tl rdn and wknd fr 3f out* 33/1	
600	12	2 1/2	**Defi (IRE)**[109] 2749 6-8-10 59 oh1 ow3 ...(bt) MickyFenton 5	22
			(D A Nolan) *led 2f: w ldr to over 2f out: wknd over 1f out* 50/1	
-006	13	11	**Apache Point (IRE)**[29] 5303 11-8-7 56 oh10 ... KimTinkler 4	—
			(N Tinkler) *towards rr: struggling over 3f out: sn btn* 28/1	

2m 4.02s (4.32) **Going Correction** +0.625s/f (Yiel)

WFA 3 from 4yo+ 5lb 13 Ran SP% 118.7

Speed ratings (Par 103): **105,101,100,100,100 99,97,94,92,90 86,84,74**

toteswinger: 1&2 £14.40, 1&3 £29.50, 2&3 £46.60. CSF £42.32 CT £1448.96 TOTE £4.90: £1.70, £3.80, £5.40; EX 68.20.

Owner Michael Hill **Bred** Hascombe And Valiant Studs **Trained** Stillington, N Yorks

FOCUS
There were eight running from out of the handicap proper in this moderate handicap. The runner-up sets the level backed up by the fourth and sixth.

6163 TIMEFORM MAIDEN STKS — 1m 1f 36y
4:40 (4:43) (Class 5) 3-4-Y-O — **£2,914** (£867; £433; £216) **Stalls** High

Form — RPR

242 **1** — **Expresso Star (USA)**[23] 5491 3-9-3 82 ... RobertHavlin 2 — 88+
(J H M Gosden) *mde all: drew wl clr fr 3f out: v easily* — **4/9**[1]

2 *18* **Lilly Grove** 3-8-12 0 ... TomEaves 3 — 45
(A G Foster) *in tch: rdn over 3f out: rallied to take 2nd ins fnl f: no ch w wnr* — **33/1**

3500 **3** *4* **Admiralcollingwood**[29] 5303 3-9-3 48 ... TonyHamilton 7 — 42
(C Grant) *chsd ldrs: drvn and hung lft over 2f out: sn no imp* — **25/1**[3]

0005 **4** *6* **Take To The Skies (IRE)**[27] 5380 4-9-3 45 ...(p) FrederikTylicki(5) 8 — 29
(Miss Tracy Waggott) *prom: effrt and chsd wnr over 4f out: wknd over 1f out* — **28/1**

43 **5** *13* **Proficiency**[28] 5361 3-8-9 0 ... DuranFentiman(3) 1 — —
(T D Walford) *cl up tl rdn and wknd over 3f out* — **8/1**[2]

6 *23* **Sunset Resort (IRE)** 3-8-12 0 ... SladeO'Hara(5) 4 — —
(A Berry) *missed break: a bhd* — **80/1**

-606 **7** *2 1/2* **Sheik'N'Knotsterd**[68] 4076 3-9-3 54 ... MickyFenton 6 — —
(J F Coupland) *towards rr: struggling fr 1/2-way* — **33/1**

2m 2.49s (2.79) **Going Correction** +0.625s/f (Yiel)
WFA 3 from 4yo 5lb — **7 Ran** SP% **94.8**
Speed ratings (Par 103): **112,96,92,87,75 55,52**
toteswinger: 1&2 £3.40, 1&3 £2.20, 2&3 £6.20. CSF £13.06 TOTE £1.20: £1.10, £5.80; EX 10.90.
Owner Stoneside Stable Llc **Bred** Stoneside Stable **Trained** Newmarket, Suffolk

FOCUS
Expresso Star proved in a different league to his rivals and did the job with the minimum of fuss. Tthere was nothing solid among the oppostion.
Sunset Resort(IRE) Official explanation: jockey said gelding hung badly left

6164 TOTESPORT BETXTRA SHOW ONLY H'CAP — 5f 4y
5:10 (5:11) (Class 4) (0-80,75) 3-Y-O+ — **£6,476** (£1,927; £963; £481) **Stalls** Centre

Form — RPR

0140 **1** — **Haajes**[12] 5796 4-9-1 73 ...(t) FrederikTylicki(5) 11 — 85
(S Parr) *prom on outside: led over 1f out: kpt on strly fnl f* — **13/2**[3]

2066 **2** *2* **Digital**[14] 5751 11-9-6 73 ...(v) TonyCulhane 12 — 81+
(M R Channon) *hld up: effrt whn nt clr run and swtchd rt appr fnl f: kpt on wl to take 2nd nr fin: nt rch wnr* — **14/1**

1114 **3** *hd* **Highland Warrior**[3] 6066 9-9-8 75 ... MickyFenton 6 — 79
(P T Midgley) *hld up in tch: effrt and chsd wnr ins fnl f: lost 2nd nr fin* **6/1**[2]

6050 **4** *1 1/4* **Curtail (IRE)**[22] 5542 5-9-8 75 ... TonyHamilton 13 — 75
(Miss L A Perratt) *hld up: hdwy over 1f out: kpt on fnl f: no imp* — **16/1**

0120 **5** *1/2* **By The Edge (IRE)**[5] 6011 4-8-6 66 ... DeanHeslop(7) 5 — 64
(T D Barron) *checked sn after s: bhd tl styd on wl fnl f: nrst fin* — **14/1**

0340 **6** *3/4* **Steel City Boy (IRE)**[8] 5930 5-9-1 73 ... AnnStokell(5) 8 — 68
(Miss A Stokell) *w ldr tl wknd ins fnl f* — **16/1**

3331 **7** *hd* **Bid For Gold**[24] 5455 4-9-0 67 ... AndrewElliott 9 — 61
(Jedd O'Keeffe) *prom: rdn over 2f out: no ex over 1f out* — **7/1**

0505 **8** *hd* **Elkhorn**[18] 5634 6-9-0 67 ...(b) TomEaves 7 — 61
(Miss J A Camacho) *hld up: rdn over 2f out: sme late hdwy: nvr on terms* — **8/1**

3510 **9** *nse* **Rothesay Dancer**[22] 5542 5-9-1 73 ... KellyHarrison(5) 10 — 66
(J S Goldie) *hld up in tch: effrt over 1f out: sn no imp* — **12/1**

0303 **10** *1 1/4* **The Bear**[3] 6066 5-8-12 70 ... PatrickDonaghy(5) 4 — 59
(R Johnson) *led to over 1f out: sn rdn and wknd* — **9/2**[1]

1000 **11** *nse* **Inspainagain (USA)**[10] 5861 4-9-4 71 ... PaulFessey 2 — 60
(T D Barron) *cl up tl rdn and wknd fr 2f out* — **12/1**

1605 **12** *2 1/4* **Opal Noir**[67] 4117 4-8-12 65 ...(v[1]) PaulMulrennan 1 — 46
(Miss L A Perratt) *chsd ldrs tl wknd over 1f out* — **28/1**

15 **13** *3 1/4* **Miacarla**[21] 5566 5-8-7 60 ...(t) RoystonFfrench 3 — 29
(H A McWilliams) *in tch: rdn 2f out: sn wknd* — **22/1**

62.38 secs (2.38) **Going Correction** +0.625s/f (Yiel) — **13 Ran** SP% **117.7**
Speed ratings (Par 105): **105,101,101,99,98 97,97,96,96,94 94,91,85**
toteswinger: 1&2 £29.00, 1&3 £8.00, 2&3 £12.10. CSF £92.86 CT £597.52 TOTE £8.50: £2.60, £2.90, £2.50; EX 91.80 Place 6: £71.19 Place 5: £46.03.
Owner Willie McKay **Bred** Irish National Stud **Trained** Bawtry, S Yorks

FOCUS
A competitive sprint run at a strong pace. The field tended to come to the near side early on, but the main action developed more down the middle of the track and the form is sound.
T/Plt: £287.70 to a £1 stake. Pool: £53,116.31. 134.75 winning tickets. T/Qpdt: £57.00 to a £1 stake. Pool: £3,850.35. 49.90 winning tickets. RY

6016 KEMPTON (A.W) (R-H)
Monday, September 22

OFFICIAL GOING: Standard
Wind: Across, moderate Races 1-4, strong remainder Weather: Fine but cloudy, rain between races 3-4

6165 SPARKS EBF MAIDEN STKS — 1m (P)
2:30 (2:33) (Class 4) 2-Y-O — **£5,342** (£1,589; £794; £396) **Stalls** High

Form — RPR

1 — **Red Spider** 2-9-3 0 ... JimmyFortune 1 — 81+
(J H M Gosden) *led over 6f out: mde rest: drew clr 2f out: comf* — **8/13**[1]

00 **2** *3 1/4* **Celtic Commitment**[67] 4126 2-9-3 0 ... RyanMoore 7 — 69
(R Hannon) *led 1f: chsd ldrs: rdn over 2f out: styd on to take 2nd jst ins fnl f: no ch w wnr* — **33/1**

06 **3** *3/4* **Mons Calpe (IRE)**[80] 3682 2-9-3 0 ... ChrisCatlin 5 — 67+
(P F I Cole) *detached in last trio tl sme prog 1/2-way: outpcd and hanging over 2f out: r.o u.str.p to take 3rd nr fin* — **11/1**[3]

0 **4** *3/4* **Merton Lad**[14] 5754 2-9-3 0 ... MichaelHills 9 — 65
(T G Mills) *pushed up to ld briefly after 1f: sn restrained bhd ldrs: outpcd 2f out: styd on wl over 1f out: kpt on one pce* — **16/1**

5 *nk* **Leulahleulahlay** 2-9-3 0 ... GregFairley 6 — 65
(M Johnston) *in tch: outpcd over 2f out: tried to cl on plcd horses 1f out: one pce* — **11/1**[3]

6 **6** *3* **Cut And Thrust (IRE)**[17] 5672 2-9-3 0 ... PhilipRobinson 4 — 58
(M A Jarvis) *cl up: trckd wnr after 2f: outpcd fr 2f out: wknd and lost pls fnl f* — **7/2**[2]

06 **7** *7* **Anaasheed**[21] 5570 2-8-12 0 ... TPQueally 2 — 38
(J L Dunlop) *detached in last trio: brief effrt on wd outside over 2f out: sn wknd* — **16/1**

00 **8** *13* **Bertie Smalls**[17] 5678 2-9-3 0 ... JimmyQuinn 8 — 14
(M H Tompkins) *sn pushed along: a detached in last pair: t.o* — **25/1**

1m 39.3s (-0.50) **Going Correction** 0.0s/f (Stan) — **8 Ran** SP% **119.4**
Speed ratings (Par 97): **102,98,98,97,96 93,86,73**
toteswinger: 1&2 £5.50, 1&3 £3.30, 2&3 £19.20. CSF £30.58 TOTE £1.80: £1.10, £4.80, £2.50; EX 24.50.
Owner H R H Princess Haya Of Jordan **Bred** Darley **Trained** Newmarket, Suffolk

FOCUS
An ordinary maiden that did not look like taking much winning. The winner was different class to the rest but the form is not totally convincing.

NOTEBOOK
Red Spider, a newcomer by Red Ransom out of a half-sister to multiple 7f-1m winner Egyptian, holds no big race entries, but he was very well backed and had clearly being showing a bit at home. Free to post, he was also keen to get on with things in the race itself and, despite being drawn in stall one, was in front at the end of the back straight. He easily stretched clear in the straight and his rider, who was looking around from a furlong out, just nudged him out gently to the line. He looks a useful prospect, but the opposition did not amount to much and his next start will tell us a lot more. (op 10-11)
Celtic Commitment had shown speed but dropped out to finish well beaten in his previous two starts over sprint distances, but on this return from a two-month break he was stepping up to 1m for the first time, and his pedigree suggested it might help. He ran his best race so far, and is now eligible for a handicap mark.
Mons Calpe(IRE), another for whom handicaps now become an option, broke well enough but struggled to go the early pace. As at Sandown last time, he hung right in the straight, but he ran on well in the closing stages to take third, appreciating every yard of this longer trip. (op 10-1 tchd 9-1)
Merton Lad, slowly away and green on his debut, had to be rousted along leaving the stalls to gain a prominent early pitch. He could only plug on one-paced in the straight, but is the type to do better in handicaps over middle distances next year. (op 20-1)
Leulahleulahlay, whose dam won three times at up to 1m2f in France, ran a reasonable race on his debut and can be expected to improve for it. (op 15-2 tchd 7-1)
Cut And Thrust(IRE) once again failed to get home, and a drop back to 7f looks in order. (op 4-1 tchd 11-2)

6166 AVANTA EBF MAIDEN FILLIES' STKS (DIV I) — 7f (P)
3:00 (3:05) (Class 4) 2-Y-O — **£4,695** (£1,397; £698; £348) **Stalls** High

Form — RPR

4 **1** — **Ave**[18] 5643 2-9-0 0 ... RyanMoore 12 — 84+
(Sir Michael Stoute) *mde all: stretched clr over 2f out: pushed along and unchal after* — **5/6**[1]

2 **2** *3 1/4* **Say No Now (IRE)**[17] 5674 2-9-0 0 ... TedDurcan 1 — 76
(D R Lanigan) *mostly chsd wnr: nt qckn over 2f out and fighting losing battle after: kpt on but no imp* — **7/2**[2]

3 *nk* **Ghanaati (USA)** 2-9-0 0 ... MichaelHills 4 — 75+
(B W Hills) *dwlt: rcvrd to trck ldrs over 4f out: prog to go 3rd over 2f out: shkn up and styd on to press runner-up nr fin* — **7/2**[2]

4 *3 1/2* **Mootriba** 2-8-11 0 ...(b[1]) GilmarPereira(3) 10 — 66+
(W J Haggas) *wl in rr: prog over 2f out but already wl outpcd: styd on to take modest 4th fnl f* — **50/1**

5 *2 3/4* **Quiquillo (USA)** 2-9-0 0 ... TPQueally 7 — 60
(H R A Cecil) *towards rr on outer: pushed along 1/2-way: sme prog over 2f out but outpcd by ldrs: kpt on fnl f* — **33/1**

6 *hd* **Clinging Vine (USA)** 2-9-0 0 ... DaneO'Neill 13 — 59+
(R Hannon) *dwlt: rousted along in last: prog and swtchd ins 2f out: no ch but kpt on* — **40/1**

0 **7** *3/4* **Caught On Camera**[35] 5147 2-9-0 0 ... JamieSpencer 14 — 57
(M L W Bell) *disp 2nd to 3f out: sn outpcd: wknd over 1f out* — **33/1**

8 *1 1/2* **Tottie** 2-9-0 0 ... JimCrowley 6 — 53
(Mrs A J Perrett) *sn wl in rr: outpcd fr 3f out: sme prog 2f out: nvr on terms* — **66/1**

9 *shd* **Commendation** 2-9-0 0 ... JimmyFortune 3 — 53
(J H M Gosden) *a in midfield: outpcd and shkn up over 2f out: no ch after* — **25/1**

0 **10** *1 3/4* **Molly The Witch (IRE)**[38] 5048 2-9-0 0 ... RichardMullen 11 — 49
(M P Tregoning) *hld up in midfield: outpcd and rdn over 2f out: wknd fnl f* — **20/1**[3]

11 *4 1/2* **Litenup (IRE)** 2-9-0 0 ... WandersonD'Avila 8 — 38
(A J Lidderdale) *chsd ldrs: wkng whn n.m.r on inner over 2f out: sn bhd* — **125/1**

12 *7* **Harley Fern** 2-9-0 0 ... AdamKirby 9 — 20
(P J McBride) *a wl in rr: lost tch over 2f out: t.o* — **100/1**

0 **13** *3/4* **Aine's Delight (IRE)**[31] 5214 2-9-0 0 ... AlanDaly 5 — 18
(Andrew Turnell) *nvr beyond midfield: wknd wl over 2f out: t.o* — **150/1**

0 **14** *hd* **Champion Girl (IRE)**[35] 5147 2-9-0 0 ... SteveDrowne 2 — 18+
(D Haydn Jones) *dwlt: racd wd in midfield: hanging bdly and almost off the crse bnd 4f out to 3f out: t.o after* — **66/1**

1m 25.79s (-0.21) **Going Correction** 0.0s/f (Stan) — **14 Ran** SP% **123.3**
Speed ratings (Par 94): **101,97,96,92,89 89,88,87,86,84 79,71,70,70**
toteswinger: 1&2 £2.40, 1&3 £2.30, 2&3 £3.40. CSF £3.69 TOTE £1.90: £1.80, £1.40, £1.40; EX 5.30.
Owner Plantation Stud **Bred** Plantation Stud **Trained** Newmarket, Suffolk

FOCUS
The punters wanted to know about only three in this maiden and they came home in market order. The runner-up is the only real guide and the form could be out either way.

NOTEBOOK
Ave had run with promise after being slowly away in what was a decent event at Salisbury on her debut, and she looked sure to have benefited greatly from that initial experience. Strong market support suggested that was the case and, well drawn, she was able to gain a prominent early position easily enough and was always going to be tough to catch once they swung into the straight. She was a comfortable winner in the end and it is possible that her connections may try to have a pop at gaining some black type with her before the season is out. (op 4-5 tchd 4-6 and evens in places)
Say No Now(IRE) had finished second in a small-field conditions event here on her debut and that form looked good enough to see her go close in this company, but she had the worst of the draw and, although she showed good early speed to cross over and race close to the favourite, she was a bit keen, and in the end that may have told. She was not given a hard race to hold on to second place, and this Fillies' Mile entry should be able to go one better soon. (op 3-1 tchd 11-4)
Ghanaati(USA), who carried her owner's first colours, was representing a stable that had won a division of this race in each of the previous two years. By Giant's Causeway out of a mare who went unbeaten in two starts over 7f at two, she was another burdened with a low draw. Unable to cross over towards the rail, she ended up racing wide throughout and in the circumstances it was a very good effort. She should be able to win a similar race. (op 5-1 tchd 11-2)

Mootriba, whose dam won over a mile and is a half-sister to 1000 Guineas winner Lahan, was wearing blinkers on her debut, which was a worrying sign, but she ran quite well and is entitled to improve for the outing.
Quiquillo(USA), a late foal bred to be effective on dirt, has plenty of speed in her pedigree and might eventually prove to be at her best over shorter.
Clinging Vine(USA), a half-sister to Lovers Knot and Foodbroker Founder, was staying on late. She comes from a stable whose juveniles invariably improve for their debuts, and looks one for handicaps next year. (op 50-1)
Champion Girl(IRE) Official explanation: jockey said he was unable to steer filly round the bend

6167 AVANTA EBF MAIDEN FILLIES' STKS (DIV II) 7f (P)
3:30 (3:37) (Class 4) 2-Y-O **£4,695** (£1,397; £698; £348) **Stalls** High

Form RPR
1 **Splashdown** 2-9-0 0 DaneO'Neill 13 75+
(L M Cumani) *reluctant to enter stalls: dwlt: t.k.h early and sn in tch: effrt and green over 2f out: prog over 1f out: r.o to ld fnl 50yds: wl on top at fin* **5/1**[3]
2 2 ¾ **Speedy Cleaners (IRE)**[21] 5571 2-9-0 0 RyanMoore 11 73
(R Hannon) *trckd ldr: led jst over 2f out: kpt on fr over 1f out: hdd last 50yds* **15/2**
5 3 ½ **Mayaalah**[38] 5048 2-9-0 0 JimmyFortune 6 72
(J H M Gosden) *trckd ldrs: effrt over 2f out: chsd ldr over 1f out: kpt on but lost 2nd ins fnl f* **7/2**[1]
0 4 ¾ **Badiat Alzaman (IRE)**[31] 5241 2-9-0 0 RichardMullen 7 70
(D M Simcock) *hld up in midfield: shkn up over 2f out: prog wl over 1f out: styd on fnl f: gaining at fin* **7/2**[1]
0 5 2 ¼ **Act Green**[31] 5241 2-9-0 0 TPQueally 10 64
(M L W Bell) *trckd ldrs: effrt to dispute 3rd over 2f out: hanging and nt qckn: no imp over 1f out: one pce* **66/1**
40 6 ¾ **Evening Sunset (GER)**[55] 4513 2-9-0 0 EdwardCreighton 5 62
(M R Channon) *wl in rr: shkn up over 2f out: styd on fr over 1f out: nrst fin* **20/1**
7 2 **Obvious** 2-9-0 0 MichaelHills 14 57
(B W Hills) *led to jst over 2f out: wknd jst over 1f out* **10/1**
8 ½ **Hold The Star** 2-9-0 0 JamieSpencer 9 56
(E F Vaughan) *mostly in midfield: hanging and struggling wl over 2f out: picked up and sme prog over 1f out: one pce fnl f* **20/1**
9 2 ½ **Veiled** 2-9-0 0 J-PGuillambert 8 50
(Sir Mark Prescott) *dwlt: mostly in last and rn green: late prog but nvr a factor* **33/1**
5 10 nk **Lonely Star (IRE)**[24] 5468 2-9-0 0 TedDurcan 1 49+
(D R Lanigan) *wl in rr: sme prog on outer 2f out: reminder and hanging over 1f out: fdd and eased* **9/2**[2]
11 ½ **Highland Starlight (USA)** 2-9-0 0 PhilipRobinson 2 48
(C G Cox) *awkward s: racd wd in midfield: lost pl on bnd 4f out to 3f out: steadily fdd* **25/1**
0 12 hd **Praise Of Folly**[22] 5534 2-9-0 0 JimCrowley 4 47
(P Winkworth) *wl in tch on outer tl steadily wknd fr jst over 2f out* **66/1**
04 13 ½ **Wanted (GER)**[18] 5650 2-9-0 0 TGMcLaughlin 12 46
(B R Millman) *trckd ldrs tl wknd rapidly on inner jst over 2f out* **66/1**
14 ¾ **On Cue (IRE)** 2-9-0 0 JimmyQuinn 3 44
(J M P Eustace) *dwlt: a towards rr: no prog over 2f out: fdd* **66/1**

1m 26.81s (0.81) **Going Correction** 0.0s/f (Stan) **83 Ran SP% 121.9**
Speed ratings (Par 94): **95,94,93,92,90 89,87,86,83,83 82,82,81,81**
toteswinger: 1&2 £5.20, 1&3 £4.40, 2&3 £3.20. CSF £39.65 TOTE £4.30: £1.80, £2.40, £1.70; EX 22.20.
Owner Fittocks Stud **Bred** Fittocks Stud Ltd **Trained** Newmarket, Suffolk

FOCUS
The slower of the two divisions by 1.02sec but a pleasing debut by the winner with the next three home setting the level.

NOTEBOOK
Splashdown had been popular in the betting in the morning but the pre-race market did not want to know her and she was shunted out to as big as 7-1 on the exchanges. She was reluctant to go into the stalls but did not do a lot wrong in the race, chasing the pace on the rail from her good high draw and then, once switched off it in the straight, stretching her legs and staying on stoutly to get up close home. A daughter of Falbrav and half-sister to Cosmodrome, a smart middle-distance filly who also won on her debut on Polytrack, being able to win over this trip at two is a bonus as she really ought not to come into her own until tackling middle distances next year. (op 9-4)
Speedy Cleaners(IRE) shaped with plenty of promise on her debut over this course and distance and again she had fared well with the draw. Up there throughout, she had no excuse and simply met one too good. (op 5-1)
Mayaalah, who is closely related to 1000 Guineas winner Lahan, had clearly learnt plenty from her debut here last month as she was far more professional this time. She did, however, race three wide most of the way, which would not have helped. (op 5-1)
Badiat Alzaman(IRE), who has a Fillies' Mile entry, made some of the running on her debut at Newmarket, but she was ridden with more restraint this time. However, she did not help her cause by racing very keenly in the early stages. (op 5-1)
Act Green, who briefly looked dangerous early in the straight, showed more than on her debut and looks to be progressing along the right lines. The best will not be seen of her until next year, though.
Evening Sunset(GER), who was taken over to Ireland for a maiden at Galway last time out, was never really a threat, but she has now had the three runs required for a mark. (op 33-1)
Lonely Star(IRE) had the worst of the draw and could not build on her promising debut at Sandown. (op 7-1 tchd 15-2)

6168 KENMORE PROPERTY GROUP MAIDEN FILLIES' STKS 1m 4f (P)
4:00 (4:02) (Class 4) 3-4-Y-O **£4,727** (£1,406; £702; £351) **Stalls** Centre

Form RPR
1 **Critical Acclaim** 3-8-12 0 JimmyFortune 4 78+
(J H M Gosden) *hld up in 5th: prog 1/2-way: effrt to ld 2f out: styd on wl and clr fnl f* **4/1**[2]
3400 2 3 ¾ **Lush (IRE)**[50] 4669 3-8-12 71 (p) DaneO'Neill 5 72
(R Hannon) *trckd ldrs: poised to chal gng easily over 2f out: v limited rspnse whn asked for effrt sn after: vain pursuit of wnr over 1f out* **4/1**[2]
64 3 4 **Alvee (IRE)**[14] 5750 3-8-12 0 JamieSpencer 1 66+
(J R Fanshawe) *s.i.s: mostly last tl effrt over 4f out: reminder over 3f out: plugged on to take 3rd 1f out: no ch* **9/2**[3]
533 4 2 ¾ **Cheeky Download (IRE)**[33] 5182 3-8-12 74 RyanMoore 2 61
(E A L Dunlop) *led after 2f: drvn and hdd 2f out: sn wknd* **11/4**[1]
3250 5 4 **Ethereal Flame**[28] 5369 3-8-12 71 TPQueally 7 55
(H R A Cecil) *led 2f: chsd ldr to over 2f out: immediately wknd* **4/1**[2]
-000 6 39 **Great Future**[101] 2989 3-8-12 43 SteveDrowne 3 —
(J R Holt) *chsd ldng pair to 1/2-way: wknd over 4f out: wl t.o over 2f out* **66/1**
/00- 7 1 ¾ **Fancy Woman**[465] 2620 4-9-6 45 JimmyQuinn 6 —
(C N Kellett) *in tch in rr to over 4f out: wl t.o over 2f out* **100/1**

2m 34.43s (-0.07) **Going Correction** 0.0s/f (Stan)
WFA 3 from 4yo 8lb **7 Ran SP% 107.3**
Speed ratings (Par 102): **100,97,94,93,90 64,63**
toteswinger: 1&2 £3.00, 1&3 £4.20, 2&3 £3.70. CSF £17.71 TOTE £3.40: £2.00, £2.90; EX 25.10.
Owner K Abdulla **Bred** Juddmonte Farms Ltd **Trained** Newmarket, Suffolk

FOCUS
An ordinary maiden with doubts over the form horses and the level somewhat fluid.

6169 AVANTA H'CAP 6f (P)
4:30 (4:31) (Class 4) (0-85,85) 3-Y-O **£4,727** (£1,406; £702; £351) **Stalls** High

Form RPR
0000 1 **Vhujon (IRE)**[25] 5424 3-9-3 84 TGMcLaughlin 9 90+
(P D Evans) *t.k.h early: hld up in 5th: nt clr run wl over 1f out and swtchd lft: drvn and r.o fnl f to ld fnl 50yds* **5/1**[3]
2500 2 ½ **Peter's Storm (USA)**[15] 5714 3-8-7 74 TedDurcan 10 78
(K A Ryan) *led to 2f out: drvn to ld again on inner over 1f out: collared last 50yds* **16/1**
5232 3 1 ¼ **Asian Power (IRE)**[135] 1995 3-8-9 76 OscarUrbina 1 76
(P J O'Gorman) *trckd ldrs: rdn and nt qckn wl over 1f out: one pce after* **9/1**
2066 4 nk **Sophie's Girl**[26] 5403 3-9-4 85 JimmyQuinn 5 84
(C A Dwyer) *pressed ldr: led 2f out to over 1f out: nt qckn after: wknd fnl 100yds* **25/1**
0140 5 hd **Light Hearted**[52] 4591 3-9-2 83 RyanMoore 11 83+
(J Noseda) *trckd ldng pair: trapped on inner w n.m.r fr 2f out: nvr able to land a blow* **3/1**[1]
0406 6 1 ¾ **Requisite**[23] 5490 3-8-13 80 WilliamBuick 7 73
(I A Wood) *t.k.h early: hld up in last trio: last and struggling over 2f out: modest prog 1f out: nvr on terms* **12/1**
3554 7 nk **Baunagain (IRE)**[20] 5594 3-8-12 79 JamieSpencer 6 71
(M J Wallace, Australia) *plld hrd and sn restrained to last: effrt over 2f out: no real prog* **7/2**[2]
-310 8 shd **Danish Art (IRE)**[66] 4158 3-8-9 76 DarryllHolland 8 68
(J A R Toller) *t.k.h early: hld up in last trio: effrt jst over 2f out: one pce and no prog* **7/1**
U000 9 nk **Lytton**[59] 4375 3-9-4 85 AdamKirby 3 76
(W R Swinburn) *mostly in 6th: effrt over 2f out: but hanging and fnd nil: wl btn over 1f out* **12/1**

1m 13.45s (0.35) **Going Correction** 0.0s/f (Stan) **9 Ran SP% 111.5**
Speed ratings (Par 103): **97,96,94,94,94 91,91,91,90**
toteswinger: 1&2 £9.60, 1&3 £6.60, 2&3 £5.80. CSF £76.20 CT £685.76 TOTE £5.60: £1.70, £4.70, £2.40; EX 71.10.
Owner Nick Shutts **Bred** Robert Berns **Trained** Pandy, Monmouths

FOCUS
An open-looking handicap. The winner is rated back to his early season form with the third to his recent best.
Lytton Official explanation: jockey said gelding hung right

6170 PARAGON H'CAP 1m (P)
5:00 (5:01) (Class 4) (0-85,85) 3-Y-O+ **£4,727** (£1,406; £702; £351) **Stalls** High

Form RPR
21-0 1 **Multakka (IRE)**[55] 4509 5-8-13 75 RichardMullen 3 85
(M P Tregoning) *hld up in rr: prog over 2f out: swtchd to inner over 1f out: drvn and r.o to ld fnl 75yds* **8/1**
1232 2 ½ **Arabian Spirit**[21] 5580 3-9-5 85 JimmyFortune 1 94
(E A L Dunlop) *trckd ldr: clsd easily to ld wl over 1f out: sn hrd pressed and drvn: hdd fnl 75yds* **6/1**[3]
145 3 nk **Summerstrand (IRE)**[29] 5309 3-8-12 78 PhilipRobinson 2 86
(M A Jarvis) *dwlt and rdr lost iron briefly: sn in tch on outer: prog over 2f out: tried to chal over 1f out: styd on fnl f but a hld* **11/2**[2]
020- 4 1 **Magic Rush**[70] 1121 6-8-10 72 EdwardCreighton 5 78
(Norma Twomey) *t.k.h early and hld up in last trio: gd prog jst over 2f out to press ldrs 1f out: pushed along and kpt on same pce* **33/1**
0006 5 2 **El Dececy (USA)**[11] 5831 4-9-5 84 (t) TolleyDean(3) 4 85
(S Parr) *hld up in midfield: effrt over 2f out: kpt on fr over 1f out: nt pce to rch ldrs* **20/1**
0200 6 nk **Gallantry**[9] 5908 6-9-8 84 JimmyQuinn 13 85
(P Howling) *prom: chsd ldng pair 1/2-way: clsd to chal over 1f out: wknd last 150yds* **11/1**
5506 7 nk **Nice To Know (FR)**[16] 5695 4-9-4 80 RyanMoore 9 80
(G L Moore) *dwlt: hld up in last trio: pushed along and no prog over 2f out: rdn and styd on on fnl f: no ch* **2/1**[1]
54/- 8 4 ½ **Remember Ramon (USA)**[547] 6205 5-9-2 78 ChrisCatlin 6 68
(J R Gask) *t.k.h early and sn restrained in last: shkn up and no prog over 2f out* **33/1**
-003 9 ½ **Hopeful Purchase (IRE)**[13] 5789 5-9-3 79 (b) JamieSpencer 8 68
(J R Gask) *blasted off in ld at str pce: hdd wl over 1f out: wknd rapidly fnl f* **12/1**
-166 10 4 ½ **Who's This (IRE)**[9] 5908 4-9-5 81 AdamKirby 7 59
(W R Swinburn) *hld up in midfield: lost pl fr 3f out: last pair and pushed along over 1f out: wknd* **14/1**
6040 11 2 ¾ **Tiger Dream**[30] 5257 3-8-13 79 DarryllHolland 14 51
(K A Ryan) *chsd ldrs 5f: wknd rapidly* **13/2**

1m 38.13s (-1.67) **Going Correction** 0.0s/f (Stan)
WFA 3 from 4yo+ 4lb **11 Ran SP% 120.8**
Speed ratings (Par 105): **108,107,107,106,104 103,103,99,98,94 91**
toteswinger: 1&2 £8.40, 1&3 £8.20, 2&3 £4.00. CSF £55.83 CT £239.25 TOTE £11.40: £2.80, £2.00, £2.00; EX 67.00.
Owner Hamdan Al Maktoum **Bred** Shadwell Estate Company Limited **Trained** Lambourn, Berks

FOCUS
A decent handicap and there was a good pace on thanks to Hopeful Purchase, who took them to the two-furlong marker before blowing up. The placed horses set the standard.
Tiger Dream Official explanation: jockey said gelding lost its action

6171 ROOKS RIDER REAL ESTATE H'CAP 1m 4f (P)
5:30 (5:30) (Class 3) (0-95,100) 3-Y-O+
£7,477 (£2,239; £1,119; £560; £279; £140) **Stalls** Centre

Form RPR
-101 1 **Armure**[16] 5699 3-8-9 85 PhilipRobinson 10 94
(M A Jarvis) *trckd ldr 2f: wnt 2nd again 2f out: drvn on inner to ld ent fnl f: asserted fnl 100yds* **13/2**[3]

6102 **2** ½ **Inventor (IRE)**[21] 5573 3-9-5 **95** .... JimmyFortune 1 103
(B J Meehan) *trckd ldr after 2f: hrd rdn and nt qckn 2f out and lost 2nd: styd on again fnl f to regain 2nd nr fin* **4/1**[2]

13-3 **3** nk **Walking Talking**[9] 5894 4-9-9 **91** .... JimmyQuinn 5 99
(H R A Cecil) *hld up bhd ldrs: effrt over 2f out: styd on fnl f to take 3rd last strides but nvr quite able to chal* **7/2**[1]

2201 **4** ½ **Detonator (IRE)**[8] 5938 3-9-10 **100** 6ex........ GregFairley 6 107
(M Johnston) *led at stdy pce: kicked on over 2f out: hdd ent fnl f: fading nr fin* **7/2**[1]

1110 **5** 1¼ **Hatton Flight**[57] 4444 4-9-5 **87** ....(b) WilliamBuick 4 92+
(A M Balding) *hld up in midfield: rdn over 2f out: styd on fr over 1f out: nt rch ldrs* **12/1**

0003 **6** hd **Olympic City (BRZ)**[21] 5569 5-9-10 **92** .... KShea 7 96
(M F De Kock, South Africa) *hld up bhd ldrs: effrt over 2f out: kpt on same pce and nvr able to chal* **16/1**

1110 **7** 1¼ **Art Man**[80] 3684 5-9-7 **89** .... RyanMoore 11 91
(G L Moore) *hld up in midfield: sme prog on inner over 1f out: nt qckn and no imp fnl f* **15/2**

0105 **8** shd **Boz**[25] 5423 4-9-4 **86** ....(v) JamieSpencer 2 88
(L M Cumani) *hld up in midfield: awkward off bnd wl over 2f out: styd on same pce fnl 2f and nvr rchd ldrs* **16/1**

0503 **9** nk **Royal Jet**[17] 5677 6-9-8 **90** .... DarryllHolland 9 92
(M R Channon) *hld up in last pair: rdn over 2f out: kpt on one pce and no real imp on ldrs* **10/1**

0346 **10** 10 **Prime Number (IRE)**[23] 5512 6-8-10 **78** oh1........ TPQueally 8 64
(J Akehurst) *t.k.h in last pair: rdn 4f out and immediately struggling* **40/1**

2m 33.08s (-1.42) **Going Correction** 0.0s/f (Stan)
WFA 3 from 4yo+ 8lb **10** Ran SP% **120.5**
Speed ratings (Par 107): **104,103,103,103,102 102,101,101,101,94**
toteswinger: 1&2 £6.30, 1&3 £5.00, 2&3 £5.70. CSF £33.90 CT £108.54 TOTE £8.00: £2.50, £2.20, £1.10; EX 31.00 Place 6: £58.74 Place 5: £38.57.
Owner Sarah J Leigh and Robin S Leigh **Bred** Sarah J Leigh And Robin S Leigh **Trained** Newmarket, Suffolk

FOCUS
A decent handicap featuring a number of useful, in-form horses. Nothing got into the race from the rear and those in the frame behind the winner are the best guides.

NOTEBOOK
Armure enjoyed the run of the race, tracking the leader on the rail, then nipping through on the inside at the point of the intersection. A progressive filly with a willing attitude, she defied a 6lb higher mark to take her record on the all-weather to three from three. (op 5-1 tchd 7-1)
Inventor(IRE), who raced on the leader's shoulder throughout, was only 1lb higher for finishing second over the course and distance last time. He again found one too good, but is a consistent performer and clearly handles this surface well. (op 5-1)
Walking Talking looked a candidate to bounce after a fine reappearance at Doncaster just nine days earlier, but in the event he ran a blinder as he gave away ground the whole way round racing wide, and one would have to suspect that, had he enjoyed the run of the race on the inside like the filly, he may well have won. (op 4-1 tchd 3-1)
Detonator(IRE) looked well in at the weights under his 6lb penalty for winning easily over 1m6f at Great Leighs eight days earlier. Soon in front, he dictated a fairly steady gallop and appeared to be in prime position entering the straight, but he could not quicken away from his rivals and, as he is essentially a stayer, perhaps he would have been better off setting a stronger pace. (op 4-1 tchd 5-1)
Hatton Flight, returning from a two-month break and making his debut on the all-weather, was 6lb higher than when last successful. A stronger pace would have suited him as he was staying on all too late. (op 14-1)
Olympic City(BRZ), was keen in the early stages, did not totally convince at the trip, even in this fairly steadily run affair. (tchd 20-1)
Art Man, another stepping up to 1m4f for the first time, never got competitive on his return from a summer's break. (tchd 7-1)
T/Plt: £44.50 to a £1 stake. Pool: £52,104.17. 853.13 winning tickets. T/Qpdt: £27.70 to a £1 stake. Pool: £3,549.65. 94.80 winning tickets. JN

5959 LEICESTER (R-H)
Monday, September 22

OFFICIAL GOING: Good (good to firm in places)
Wind: Light across Weather: Raining

6172 TODAY'S GROUP INDEPENDENTS' PARTY FILLIES' NURSERY 5f 218y
2:20 (2:27) (Class 4) (0-85,85) 2-Y-O **£3,885** (£1,156; £577; £288) **Stalls** Low

Form RPR

602 **1** **Caledonia Princess**[14] 5746 2-8-0 **64** ow1........ FrancisNorton 17 74+
(P A Blockley) *a.p: led over 1f out: rdn and hung lft ins fnl f: sn clr: eased nr fin* **25/1**

0620 **2** 2¾ **Norfolk Broads (IRE)**[10] 5855 2-8-5 **69** .... JoeFanning 10 71+
(M Johnston) *led: hdd over 3f out: rdn and ev ch over 1f out: styd on same pce ins fnl f* **16/1**

332 **3** 2½ **Blue Arctic**[56] 4488 2-8-8 **75** .... LukeMorris(3) 18 69
(J M P Eustace) *hld up: hdwy over 2f out: rdn and edgd lft over 1f out: no ex fnl f* **18/1**

4530 **4** ½ **Deyas Dream**[10] 5855 2-8-7 **71** .... LPKeniry 15 64
(A M Balding) *hld up: hdwy over 1f out: rdn and edgd lft ins fnl f: nt rch ldrs* **20/1**

51 **5** hd **Riolina (IRE)**[46] 4763 2-9-0 **85** .... MatthewDavies(7) 12 77
(J G Portman) *w ldr: led over 3f out: rdn and hdd over 1f out: wknd ins fnl f* **11/1**[3]

1400 **6** hd **Oasis Breeze**[18] 5642 2-9-4 **82** .... PaulEddery 2 74
(G D Blake) *mid-div: hdwy over 3f out: rdn over 2f out: wknd fnl f no ex fnl f* **33/1**

2214 **7** ¾ **Acquiesced (IRE)**[24] 5448 2-9-3 **81** .... TPO'Shea 9 70+
(R Hannon) *prom: rdn over 2f out: wknd fnl f* **11/1**[3]

303 **8** ¾ **Queen Sally (IRE)**[36] 5116 2-8-9 **76** .... TolleyDean(3) 6 63+
(J L Spearing) *hld up: rdn over 2f out: styd on ins fnl f: nvr nrr* **33/1**

1060 **9** nk **Barbee (IRE)**[32] 5204 2-8-12 **76** .... HayleyTurner 1 62
(E A L Dunlop) *dwlt: hld up: rdn over 2f out: nvr nrr* **33/1**

5600 **10** 1¼ **Calypso Girl (IRE)**[8] 5937 2-8-13 **77** .... JohnEgan 7 59
(P D Evans) *chsd ldrs: rdn over 2f out: wknd fnl f* **28/1**

4326 **11** 1¼ **Green Poppy**[42] 4925 2-8-5 **69** .... AdrianTNicholls 16 48
(Eve Johnson Houghton) *hld up: effrt over 2f out: n.d* **50/1**

3202 **12** ½ **Night Seed (IRE)**[10] 5866 2-8-12 **76** .... PatCosgrave 14 53
(R Hannon) *chsd ldrs: rdn over 2f out: wknd over 1f out* **16/1**

5222 **13** 3¼ **My Sweet Georgia (IRE)**[13] 5785 2-9-0 **78** .... AlanMunro 4 51+
(B W Hills) *mid-div: hdwy over 3f out: rdn over 2f out: hung rt and wknd over 1f out* **15/2**[2]

410 **14** 3 **Carina Nebula (USA)**[58] 4403 2-8-10 **74** .... StephenDonohoe 5 32
(T G Mills) *mid-div: rdn 1/2-way: sn wknd* **14/1**

21 **15** 2¾ **Raedah (USA)**[57] 4456 2-9-5 **83** .... NCallan 11 33
(M A Jarvis) *dwlt: sn prom: rdn and hung rt over 2f out: wknd over 1f out* **9/2**[1]

21 **16** 2 **Moonlight Affair (IRE)**[52] 4593 2-9-5 **83** .... GrahamGibbons 3 27
(E S McMahon) *mid-div: hdwy over 3f out: rdn and wknd over 2f out* **14/1**

0602 **17** 1¾ **Amosite**[24] 5461 2-8-12 **76** .... PaulHanagan 8 15
(J R Jenkins) *plld hrd and prom: wknd 2f out* **33/1**

1m 13.33s (0.33) **Going Correction** +0.15s/f (Good) **17** Ran SP% **102.8**
Speed ratings (Par 94): **103,99,96,95,95 94,93,92,92,90 89,88,84,80,76 73,71**
toteswinger: 1&2 £51.80, 1&3 £49.50, 2&3 £29.40. CSF £254.09 CT £4661.15 TOTE £27.60: £4.00, £3.20, £5.20, £5.00; EX 312.10 TRIFECTA Not won..
Owner Isla & Colin Cage **Bred** Mrs I M Cage And Mr C J Cage **Trained** Lambourn, Berks

FOCUS
There was a bit of a delay to this after one of the major contenders Key Signature broke through the stalls and got loose. Any number looked in with a chance in what was a wide-open nursery and those drawn in double-figure stalls dominated. The placed horses set the level.

NOTEBOOK
Caledonia Princess, whose rider was putting up 1lb overweight, looked a different horse when finishing second at 50-1 on her most recent outing. Ridden to improve under three furlongs out, she responded and was always in control once hitting the front, seeing out the extra furlong extremely well. (op 20-1)
Norfolk Broads(IRE), a progressive sort in maidens, made no impression on her recent nursery debut at Doncaster (testing ground possibly not ideal) and the combination of a more positive ride on this faster going seemed to suit. She is only modest, but can win a small race. (op 14-1)
Blue Arctic, off since finishing second in a 7f Yarmouth maiden in July, was not helped by this drop in trip and could only find the one pace under pressure. A step back up in trip will help. (op 20-1)
Deyas Dream disappointed in the same Doncaster nursery as Norfolk Broads and she too bounced back to form on this faster surface. She is beginning to look exposed, but may be worth another try at 7f. (tchd 18-1)
Rioliina(IRE), easy winner of a 6f Bath maiden in August, was handed a stiff mark as a result, and, having travelled well until over two furlongs out, could find no more inside the final furlong. (op 10-1)
Oasis Breeze, a winner on debut, has since struggled in decent company and this was more promising on her nursery debut. A step up to 7f may not go amiss on this evidence. (op 28-1)
Queen Sally(IRE), making her handicap debut off a stiff mark, was going on close home and, as her breeding suggests, is going to be helped by a seventh furlong.
My Sweet Georgia(IRE), raised 4lb having just been denied by a subsequent scorer at Lingfield last time, emptied out inside the final quarter mile and was most disappointing. (op 17-2 tchd 7-1)
Raedah(USA), all-the-way winner of a 5f Pontefract maiden in the summer, was expected to be suited by the extra furlong on this nursery debut, but she was slowly into stride and never looked like winning, coming under strong pressure before two out. Official explanation: trainer's rep said, regarding running, that the filly was unsuited by the good (good to firm places) ground (op 4-1 tchd 5-1)
Amosite Official explanation: jockey said filly hung right throughout

6173 CLEAN 'N FRESH (S) STKS 7f 9y
2:50 (2:55) (Class 6) 3-Y-O **£1,942** (£578; £288; £144) **Stalls** Low

Form RPR

3225 **1** **All In The Red (IRE)**[11] 5841 3-9-2 70........(p) NCallan 11 66
(Miss Gay Kelleway) *hld up: hdwy u.p over 2f out: styd on to ld wl ins fnl f* **5/4**[1]

54 **2** 1 **Charlie Allnut**[49] 4683 3-8-11 56........(b) DarrenWilliams 14 58
(K R Burke) *prom: led 4f out: rdn over 1f out: hdd wl ins fnl f* **6/1**[2]

030 **3** 1¾ **Gower Belle**[35] 5141 3-8-6 55........ HayleyTurner 13 48
(W R Muir) *a.p: chsd ldr over 2f out: sn rdn: styd on same pce fnl f* **11/1**[3]

0100 **4** 1 **Deal Flipper**[15] 5601 3-8-11 60........ StephenCarson 15 51
(P Winkworth) *s.i.s: hld up: hdwy u.p over 1f out: nt rch ldrs* **33/1**

0005 **5** nk **Wooden King (IRE)**[35] 5162 3-8-11 45........ JohnEgan 6 50
(P D Evans) *hld up: racd keenly: rdn and hung rt fr over 2f out: hdwy over 1f out: nt trble ldrs* **33/1**

0600 **6** 4½ **The Hoofer (IRE)**[12] 5799 3-8-11 52........(b) PaulHanagan 17 38
(I A Wood) *chsd ldrs: rdn and wknd 2f out* **33/1**

0654 **7** 4½ **Jal Music**[34] 5166 3-8-13 57........ KevinGhunowa(3) 4 30
(R A Harris) *stmbld s: sn prom: rdn and edgd rt over 2f out: sn wknd* **12/1**

0000 **8** ½ **Cool Fashion (IRE)**[23] 5501 3-8-6 43........(b) FrancisNorton 2 19
(Ollie Pears) *chsd ldrs: hung rt fr over 4f out: wknd 2f out* **66/1**

4516 **9** ½ **Redsensor**[6] 6001 3-9-2 60........ PatCosgrave 3 28
(M Quinn) *prom: rdn 1/2-way: wknd over 2f out* **14/1**

0155 **10** ¾ **Klarity**[45] 4808 3-8-6 50........(e) LiamJones 5 16
(J Pearce) *hld up: pushed along 1/2-way: rdn and hung rt over 1f out: n.d* **20/1**

0004 **11** ½ **Jimmy Dean**[54] 4531 3-8-11 45........(tp) PaulFitzsimons 18 19
(M Wellings) *mid-div: sn pushed along: wknd over 2f out* **28/1**

0000 **12** 3½ **Tapas Lad (IRE)**[27] 5378 3-8-9 53........(v) StacyRenwick(7) 8 15
(G J Smith) *s.i.s: hdwy 1/2-way: sn rdn: wknd over 2f out* **50/1**

3500 **13** 6 **Veni Bidi Vici**[26] 5407 3-8-6 52........(b[1]) LPKeniry 1 —
(A M Balding) *led 2f: sn rdn: wknd wl over 2f out* **16/1**

0040 **14** 3¾ **Townkab (IRE)**[69] 4053 3-9-2 54........(p) JamesDoyle 7 —
(N P Littmoden) *hld up: rdn and wknd 3f out* **12/1**

5-44 **15** 10 **Silver Deal**[228] 467 3-8-6 45........ JoeFanning 9 —
(J A Pickering) *chsd ldrs: rdn 1/2-way: hung rt and wknd over 2f out* **66/1**

6-04 **16** ¾ **Lechero (IRE)**[228] 462 3-8-11 48........(p) AlanMunro 10 —
(John A Harris) *bhd fnl 5f* **66/1**

1m 27.0s (0.80) **Going Correction** +0.15s/f (Good) **16** Ran SP% **118.5**
Speed ratings (Par 99): **101,99,97,96,96 91,86,85,84,84 83,79,72,68,56 56**
toteswinger: 1&2 £3.30, 1&3 £5.90, 2&3 £9.60. CSF £6.79 TOTE £2.10: £1.30, £2.10, £2.60; EX 10.20 Trifecta £36.60 Pool: £273.29 - 5.52 winning units..The winner was bought in for 5,500gns. Charlie Allnut was subject to a friendly claim.
Owner Countrywide Classics Limited **Bred** John McEnery **Trained** Exning, Suffolk

FOCUS
A fair seller, for all that it wasn't competitive, and the runner-up is the best guide to the form.
Cool Fashion(IRE) Official explanation: jockey said filly ran too freely
Klarity Official explanation: jockey said filly hung right
Lechero(IRE) Official explanation: jockey said gelding slipped leaving stalls

6174 WEATHERBYS PRINTING H'CAP 5f 2y
3:20 (3:22) (Class 4) (0-85,87) 3-Y-O+ **£4,857** (£1,445; £722; £360) **Stalls** Low

Form RPR

3540 **1** **Tony The Tap**[32] 5206 7-9-1 **80** .... HayleyTurner 9 91
(W R Muir) *hld up: pushed along 1/2-way: hdwy over 1f out: r.o to ld wl ins fnl f* **7/1**

4342 **2** 1¼ **Best One**[10] 5861 4-8-11 **79**..............................(b) KevinGhunowa(3) 7 85
(R A Harris) *outpcd: hdwy over 1f out: rdn to ld ins fnl f: sn edgd rt and hdd: unable qckn* **15/2**

4030 **3** 1¾ **Gallery Girl (IRE)**[23] 5503 5-9-0 **79**.............................. JohnEgan 8 79
(T D Easterby) *mid-div: hdwy u.p over 1f out: styd on same pce ins fnl f* **16/1**

1310 **4** *hd* **Arabian Art (USA)**[52] 4595 3-8-12 **78**.............................. IanMongan 3 77
(H R A Cecil) *chsd ldrs: outpcd 1/2-way: r.o ins fnl f* **8/1**

6501 **5** ½ **The Jobber (IRE)**[6] 6006 7-9-8 **87** 6ex.............................. PaulHanagan 6 84
(M Blanshard) *hld up: hdwy over 1f out: styd on towards fin: nt rch ldrs* **6/1**[3]

6145 **6** 1¼ **Woodcote (IRE)**[9] 5886 6-9-2 **81**..............................(vt) FrancisNorton 10 74
(P R Chamings) *chsd ldrs: rdn over 1f out: no ex fnl f* **14/1**

1133 **7** 1 **Equuleus Pictor**[6] 6006 4-8-11 **81**.............................. JackDean(5) 2 70
(J L Spearing) *chsd ldr: rdn 1/2-way: wknd fnl f* **9/2**[1]

0260 **8** *nk* **Ocean Blaze**[31] 5250 4-9-1 **80**.............................. AlanMunro 11 68
(B R Millman) *led: hung rt: hdd & wknd ins fnl f* **10/1**

02-0 **9** 4½ **Blue Eyed Miss (IRE)**[143] 1764 3-9-5 **85**.............................. GrahamGibbons 5 57
(P A Blockley) *s.i.s: hld up: rdn and wknd 2f out* **25/1**

4504 **10** 2¼ **Cape Royal**[10] 5861 8-8-11 **76**..............................(bt) PatCosgrave 1 40
(J M Bradley) *s.i.s: outpcd* **16/1**

1102 **11** *nk* **Rasaman (IRE)**[12] 5796 4-9-1 **80**..............................(p) NCallan 4 43
(K A Ryan) *chsd ldrs: rdn 1/2-way: wknd wl over 1f out: eased fnl f* **11/2**[2]

60.11 secs (0.11) **Going Correction** +0.15s/f (Good)
WFA 3 from 4yo+ 1lb **11 Ran SP% 114.6**
Speed ratings (Par 105): **105,103,100,99,99 97,95,95,87,84 83**
toteswinger: 1&2 £15.80, 1&3 £5.90, 2&3 £24.90. CSF £57.11 CT £809.06 TOTE £9.10: £2.90, £2.60, £5.60; EX 69.10 TRIFECTA Not won..
Owner K J Mercer & Mrs S Mercer **Bred** K J Mercer **Trained** Lambourn, Berks

FOCUS
A competitive sprint handicap and the first two are rated as having improved 3lb on this year's form.
Ocean Blaze Official explanation: jockey said filly hung right

6175 GALLO FAMILY VINEYARDS CLAIMING STKS 1m 1f 218y
3:50 (3:51) (Class 6) 3-4-Y-0 **£1,942** (£578; £288; £144) **Stalls** High

Form RPR

0320 **1** **Red Current**[29] 5312 4-8-9 61.............................. KevinGhunowa(3) 4 67+
(R A Harris) *hld up: hdwy to chse ldr over 2f out: sn edgd rt: led over 1f out: styd on wl* **3/1**[2]

6050 **2** 2¾ **Threestoneburn (USA)**[77] 3780 3-7-8 52.............................. AndreaAtzeni(7) 3 53
(J R Boyle) *hld up: hdwy over 3f out: rdn over 1f out: styd on: no ch w wnr* **20/1**

0652 **3** 1½ **No To Trident**[7] 5961 3-8-6 73..............................(v) RichardEvans(5) 2 60
(P D Evans) *led: hdd 7f out: led again 5f out: clr over 3f out: lost action wl over 1f out: sn rdn: hung lft and hdd: no ex* **11/8**[1]

0604 **4** *shd* **Fantastic Lass**[26] 5388 3-8-4 52.............................. PaulHanagan 11 53
(R A Fahey) *chsd ldrs: lost pl over 3f out: sn rdn: rallied over 1f out: styd on* **11/2**[3]

1610 **5** 1 **Haydens Mark**[54] 4528 3-9-3 80.............................. LiamJones 1 64
(D G Bridgwater) *plld hrd and prom: rdn over 2f out: no ex fnl f* **12/1**

6050 **6** 2½ **Sleeping**[11] 5837 3-8-1 47.............................. AshleyMorgan(7) 12 50
(M H Tompkins) *hld up: racd keenly: rdn and hung rt fr over 2f out: nt trble ldrs* **16/1**

00-0 **7** 1 **El Dottore**[131] 2100 4-9-2 50.............................. LukeMorris(3) 9 53
(A W Carroll) *s.s: hld up: hdwy over 3f out: wknd over 1f out* **40/1**

00-0 **8** 13 **Tinted View (USA)**[9] 5912 4-8-10 48.............................. LPKeniry 7 18
(W S Kittow) *hld up in tch: plld hrd: rdn over 2f out: wknd wl over 1f out* **22/1**

60-U **9** 6 **Captain Jack Black**[13] 5787 3-7-12 30.............................. GemmaElford(7) 8 7
(M R Bosley) *s.i.s: sn prom: wknd over 3f out* **80/1**

0000 **10** 7 **Alright Chuck**[25] 5427 4-8-12 34 ow1.............................. DarrenWilliams 10 —
(P W Hiatt) *hld up: racd keenly: wknd 3f out* **100/1**

000 **11** 8 **On The Map**[61] 4294 4-7-13 36.............................. SoniaEaton(7) 5 —
(Joss Saville) *w ldr: plld hrd: led 7f out: hdd 5f out: wknd 3f out* **66/1**

2m 10.14s (2.24) **Going Correction** +0.15s/f (Good)
WFA 3 from 4yo 6lb **11 Ran SP% 111.3**
Speed ratings (Par 101): **97,94,93,93,92 90,89,79,74,69 62**
CSF £64.33 TOTE £3.60: £1.50, £5.60, £1.20; EX 67.90 Trifecta £146.20 Pool: £264.83 - 1.34 winning units..
Owner Ridge House Stables Ltd **Bred** Wretham Stud **Trained** Earlswood, Monmouths

FOCUS
This was a weak contest and the early pace was very steady. The form is best rated around the first two backed up by the fourth.

6176 EBF TERRY ALBONE "LIFETIME IN RACING" NOVICE STKS 7f 9y
4:20 (4:20) (Class 4) 2-Y-0 **£5,180** (£1,541; £770; £384) **Stalls** Low

Form RPR

3236 **1** **Crackdown (IRE)**[11] 5825 2-8-12 88.............................. JoeFanning 3 88+
(M Johnston) *racd keenly: mde all: shkn up over 1f out: r.o wl* **13/8**[2]

0 **2** 2¼ **Indian Tonic (IRE)**[25] 5431 2-8-7 0.............................. AlanMunro 5 77
(W Jarvis) *chsd wnr: rdn over 1f out: styd on same pce* **8/1**

123 **3** 1 **Laahig**[35] 5143 2-9-2 92.............................. RobertWinston 4 84
(G A Butler) *hld up: hdwy over 2f out: sn rdn: styd on same pce fnl f* **6/4**[1]

0120 **4** ¾ **Keeptheboatafloat (USA)**[16] 5693 2-9-5 92.............................. DarrenWilliams 2 85
(K R Burke) *chsd ldrs: rdn over 2f out: styd on same pce fnl f* **5/1**[3]

0 **5** 5 **Magical Night**[149] 1627 2-8-8 0 ow1.............................. GrahamGibbons 6 62
(T D Walford) *prom: rdn over 2f out: sn wknd* **28/1**

1m 28.52s (2.32) **Going Correction** +0.15s/f (Good) **5 Ran SP% 109.3**
Speed ratings (Par 97): **92,89,88,87,81**
toteswinger: 1&2 £6.90. CSF £13.79 TOTE £2.20: £1.20, £3.20; EX 8.80 TRIFECTA Not won..
Owner Sheikh Hamdan Bin Mohammed Al Maktoum **Bred** Rancho San Peasea S A **Trained** Middleham Moor, N Yorks

FOCUS
Just an ordinary novice stakes and the form is rated around the winner.

NOTEBOOK
Crackdown(IRE) led throughout for a comfortable victory. He had disappointed on his last two starts in soft ground, having earlier displayed useful form on a faster surface, and the going here was much more to his liking. Always travelling kindly, he was asked to stretch over a furlong out and found plenty, suggesting a step up to 1m would not go amiss. Fast ground is imperative to the son of Refuse To Bend and he is expected to improve for getting a lead in future. (op 11-8)
Indian Tonic(IRE), who came home well having been outpaced over 6f on her Lingfield debut, was always likely to improve for the extra furlong/switch to turf and she kept plugging away for second. This was a big improvement and she should be able to win a maiden. (op 12-1)
Laahig had shown useful form on all three previous starts, but as was the case at Lingfield last time, he was found wanting for a change of pace. He has a rather high official rating for what he has achieved. (op 2-1)
Keeptheboatafloat(USA), outclassed in a Group 3 at Kempton earlier in the month, could not quicken when asked and came up short under the penalty. He faced a stiff task giving 7lb to the winner. (op 7-2)
Magical Night was always going to struggle and has yet to beat a rival in two starts. (op 40-1)

6177 WKD H'CAP 1m 60y
4:50 (4:50) (Class 5) (0-75,75) 3-Y-0+ **£2,590** (£770; £385; £192) **Stalls** High

Form RPR

03-0 **1** **Ghost Dancer**[23] 5492 4-9-3 70.............................. PatCosgrave 7 80
(L M Cumani) *hld up: hdwy over 3f out: rdn over 1f out: r.o to ld wl ins fnl f* **20/1**

-031 **2** ½ **Spate River**[16] 5713 3-9-3 74.............................. GeorgeBaker 12 83
(C F Wall) *chsd ldrs: led over 1f out: rdn and hdd wl ins fnl f* **4/1**[2]

-163 **3** 1¼ **Cool Ebony**[67] 4104 5-9-8 75.............................. NCallan 11 81+
(P J Makin) *chsd ldrs: rdn over 2f out: nt clr run over 1f out: styd on* **3/1**[1]

0300 **4** ¾ **Man Of Gwent (UAE)**[12] 5800 4-9-0 72.............................. RichardEvans(5) 9 76
(P D Evans) *hld up: hdwy over 1f out: r.o: nt rch ldrs* **16/1**

0600 **5** 1¼ **Summer Dancer (IRE)**[13] 5789 4-9-4 71.............................. TQuinn 8 73
(D R C Elsworth) *sn led: rdn and hdd over 1f out: no ex ins fnl f* **17/2**

2145 **6** *nk* **Bold Cross (IRE)**[10] 5863 5-9-1 68.............................. PaulFitzsimons 1 69
(E G Bevan) *hld up: hdwy over 3f out: rdn over 1f out: no ex ins fnl f* **13/2**[3]

2360 **7** ½ **Bobski (IRE)**[21] 5569 6-9-1 75.............................. KylieManser(7) 3 75+
(Miss Gay Kelleway) *s.s: hld up: hdwy over 3f out: nt clr run over 1f out: hmpd and swtchd lft ins fnl f: nvr able to chal* **14/1**

1342 **8** *hd* **Castano**[13] 5779 4-9-0 70..............................(p) JamesMillman(3) 6 69
(B R Millman) *hld up: rdn and hung rt fr over 2f out: styd on ins fnl f: nvr trbld ldrs* **7/1**

6000 **9** *nk* **Lord Theo**[19] 5600 4-9-3 70.............................. JamesDoyle 10 69
(N P Littmoden) *prom: rdn over 3f out: styd on same pce appr fnl f* **14/1**

026 **10** 1 **Green Diamond**[20] 5595 3-8-12 69.............................. JoeFanning 14 65
(M Johnston) *hld up: plld hrd: lost pl 4f out: nt clr run over 2f out: n.d after* **9/1**

0 **11** 1¼ **Querido (GER)**[40] 4978 4-8-11 64.............................. VinceSlattery 5 57
(M Bradstock) *hld up: a in rr* **33/1**

0060 **12** 4½ **Rock Anthem (IRE)**[28] 5350 4-9-0 67.............................. RobertWinston 2 50
(Mike Murphy) *chsd ldrs: rdn over 2f out: wknd fnl f* **22/1**

1m 45.64s (0.54) **Going Correction** +0.15s/f (Good)
WFA 3 from 4yo+ 4lb **12 Ran SP% 122.6**
Speed ratings (Par 103): **103,102,101,100,99 98,98,98,97,96 95,91**
toteswinger: 1&2 £17.40, 1&3 £13.20, 2&3 £4.70. CSF £99.79 CT £325.63 TOTE £12.80: £4.50, £1.80, £1.50; EX 66.30 TRIFECTA Not won..
Owner Kevin Bailey & Philip Booth **Bred** Floors Farming **Trained** Newmarket, Suffolk
■ Stewards' Enquiry : T Quinn two-day ban: careless riding (Oct 6-7)

FOCUS
A decent handicap in which the front pair are less exposed than the rest and the third sets the level.

6178 PERTEMPS PEOPLE DEVELOPMENT "HANDS AND HEELS" APPRENTICE SERIES H'CAP 7f 9y
5:20 (5:20) (Class 5) (0-70,70) 3-Y-0+ **£3,238** (£963; £481; £240) **Stalls** Low

Form RPR

6600 **1** **Prince Golan (IRE)**[44] 4858 4-8-6 60.............................. AlexEdwards(5) 18 66
(J W Unett) *mid-div: hdwy over 2f out: edgd lft fr over 1f out: led ins fnl f: r.o* **22/1**

4014 **2** ½ **Glencal**[46] 4770 4-8-13 67.............................. RyanClark(5) 7 72
(H Morrison) *hld up: hdwy and edgd rt over 4f out: chsd ldr over 1f out: r.o* **14/1**

0405 **3** *nse* **Flying Flute**[13] 5786 3-8-4 56.............................. AmyScott 4 60
(H Candy) *chsd ldrs: led 1/2-way: hdd ins fnl f: r.o* **14/1**

4600 **4** 1 **I Confess**[16] 5697 3-9-4 70..............................(b) RichardEvans 15 71
(P D Evans) *prom: rdn 1/2-way: n.m.r fr over 1f out: styd on* **16/1**

6032 **5** *nk* **Outer Hebrides**[40] 4979 7-7-8 56 oh4..............................(v) RosieJessop 11 57
(J M Bradley) *a.p: pushed along and n.m.r ins fnl f: styd on* **14/1**

2060 **6** 2 **Lordship (IRE)**[4] 6056 4-8-11 65.............................. JakePayne(5) 13 61
(A W Carroll) *hld up: plld hrd: r.o ins fnl f: nrst fin* **28/1**

-000 **7** 1 **Sweet Gale (IRE)**[16] 5697 4-9-4 70.............................. MJMurphy(3) 16 63
(Mike Murphy) *hld up: hdwy over 2f out: no ex ins fnl f* **7/1**[2]

0400 **8** 1¼ **Gee Ceffyl Bach**[29] 5318 4-8-4 56 oh7..............................(p) TobyAtkinson(3) 14 46
(John A Harris) *hld up: hdwy over 1f out: nt trble ldrs* **33/1**

0323 **9** 2¼ **Star Strider**[18] 5639 4-8-12 61.............................. AndreaAtzeni 5 45
(Miss Gay Kelleway) *s.s: outpcd: nvr nrr* **7/1**[2]

3316 **10** *nse* **Micky Mac (IRE)**[63] 4245 4-8-12 61.............................. MatthewDavies 12 45
(T D Walford) *led: hdd over 4f out: wknd over 1f out* **4/1**[1]

2200 **11** 3¼ **Follow The Flag (IRE)**[18] 5635 4-9-7 70.............................. BillyCray 2 45
(A J McCabe) *sn pushed along in rr: n.d* **14/1**

B035 **12** 3¼ **Imperium**[12] 5801 7-8-9 61 ow3..............................(v) DebraEngland(3) 6 27
(Jean-Rene Auvray) *dwlt: a in rr* **25/1**

-112 **13** 1½ **Sea Salt**[18] 5638 5-9-6 69.............................. DeclanCannon 3 31
(A J McCabe) *chsd ldrs: shkn up and hung lft over 2f out: sn wknd* **17/2**[3]

0005 **14** 1 **Sion Hill (IRE)**[16] 5709 7-8-8 57..............................(p) AshleyMorgan 9 16
(John A Harris) *chsd ldrs: hung rt and wknd over 2f out* **20/1**

50 **15** ¾ **Double Carpet (IRE)**[43] 4903 5-8-7 56 oh1.............................. RossAtkinson 17 13
(G Woodward) *chsd ldrs: led over 4f out: hdd 1/2-way: wknd over 1f out* **20/1**

6P3 **16** 5 **Torquemada (IRE)**[34] 5170 7-8-11 60..............................(t) BMcHugh 1 4
(M J Attwater) *hld up: hdwy 1/2-way: wknd over 2f out: sn hung rt* **16/1**

0000 **17** *nse* **Gilded Youth**[16] 5708 4-8-7 56 oh1.............................. StacyRenwick 8 —
(G F Bridgwater) *prom: lost pl 4f out: bhd fnl 3f* **33/1**

1m 27.74s (1.54) **Going Correction** +0.15s/f (Good)
WFA 3 from 4yo+ 3lb **17 Ran SP% 121.0**
Speed ratings (Par 103): **97,96,96,95,94 92,91,90,87,87 83,79,78,77,76 70,70**
toteswinger: 1&2 £49.50, 1&3 £56.10, 2&3 £17.70. CSF £279.10 CT £4567.76 TOTE £31.80: £6.20, £3.90, £3.10, £4.70; EX 476.50 Place 6: £117.23 Place 5: £25.78 .
Owner M E Hughes **Bred** K Molloy **Trained** Preston, Shropshire
■ Stewards' Enquiry : Alex Edwards three-day ban: careless riding (Oct 6-8)

FOCUS
This looked anyone's on paper and it was something of a slow-motion finish. The runner-up looks the best guide to the form.
T/Jkpt: Not won. T/Plt: £382.80 to a £1 stake. Pool: £74,364.77. 141.79 winning tickets. T/Qpdt: £19.40 to a £1 stake. Pool: £5,665.38. 215.90 winning tickets. CR

6179 - 6182a (Foreign Racing) - See Raceform Interactive

6008

BEVERLEY (R-H)

Tuesday, September 23

OFFICIAL GOING: Soft (good to soft in places)

Wind: Fresh across Weather: Sunny periods

6183 CHRISTMAS PARTIES AT BEVERLEY RACECOURSE NOVICE STKS 5f

2:00 (2:02) (Class 4) 2-Y-O **£3,885** (£1,156; £577; £288) **Stalls** High

Form RPR

21 1 **Blades Princess**[28] 5384 2-8-11 85 GrahamGibbons 7 91+
(E S McMahon) *trckd ldng pair: smooth hdwy to ld over 1f out: easily* **8/13**[1]

130 2 2 3/4 **Glamorous Spirit (IRE)**[97] 3123 2-9-0 88 JamieSpencer 2 78
(J Noseda) *led: rdn along wl over 1f out: sn hdd and kpt on same pce* **9/4**[2]

3610 3 1 1/2 **Love You Louis**[66] 4190 2-8-11 84 FrederikTylicki(5) 5 75
(J R Jenkins) *trckd ldr: swtchd lft and effrt over 1f out: sn rdn and no imp* **13/2**[3]

00 4 6 **Wrens Hope**[7] 5989 2-8-7 0 JimmyQuinn 4 44
(N Bycroft) *in tch: rdn along and outpcd fr 1/2-way* **66/1**

5 15 **Cindy Incidentally** 2-7-10 0 RosieJessop(7) 6 —
(Miss Gay Kelleway) *s.i.s: a bhd* **50/1**

65.39 secs (1.89) **Going Correction** +0.30s/f (Good) 5 Ran SP% **109.5**

Speed ratings (Par 97): **96,91,89,79,55**

toteswinger: 1&2 £2.20. CSF £2.20 TOTE £1.60: £1.10, £1.40; EX 2.10.

Owner R L Bedding **Bred** Mrs J McMahon **Trained** Lichfield, Staffs

FOCUS

This wasn't as competitive a novice event as it might have been with the withdrawal of the likely favourite Amour Propre, and in the end things worked out very much the way the market suggested that they would. The winner was in a different league and the fourth anchors the form.

NOTEBOOK

Blades Princess, representing last-year's winning stable, had been successful in a Ripon maiden last month that had not really worked out, but it did prove that she could handle soft ground. Always close to the pace, her rider was looking around for dangers well over a furlong from home and when he asked her to stretch she did it nicely. She should continue to do well when conditions are in her favour, though she may be put away for the season now. (op 8-11 tchd 4-7 and 5-6 in a place early)

Glamorous Spirit(IRE), who had not been seen since finishing out the back in the Queen Mary, was tackling soft ground for the first time. Soon taken over to bag the early lead against the inside rail which had proved a major advantage at this track the previous week, she was quite keen in front and it was obvious from some way out that the favourite was running all over her. She should have derived some benefit from this, but probably needs the ground to dry out if she is going to find another opportunity this season. (tchd 2-1 and 5-2)

Love You Louis, not seen since finishing last in the Weatherbys Super Sprint, was proven in soft ground and he had every chance here, but he had 6lb to find with the front pair on these terms so probably ran close to form. (op 7-1 tchd 8-1)

Wrens Hope predictably found this company too hot, but she does at least now qualify for a mark.

Cindy Incidentally, who is bred for speed, was soon struggling following a slow start, but the market suggested that not much was expected of her in the face of this stiff task. (op 22-1)

6184 VIOLET AND EDDIE SMITH MEMORIAL CONDITIONS STKS 5f

2:30 (2:30) (Class 3) 3-Y-O+

£7,477 (£2,239; £1,119; £560; £279; £140) **Stalls** High

Form RPR

0300 1 **Fullandby (IRE)**[3] 6121 6-8-9 102 GregFairley 7 103
(T J Etherington) *chsd ldr: rdn along wl over 1f out: drvn ent fnl f: kpt on wl u.p to ld on line* **7/2**[3]

2210 2 nse **Strike Up The Band**[10] 5890 5-8-9 99 AdrianTNicholls 9 103
(D Nicholls) *led: rdn along wl over 1f out: drvn ins fnl f: hdd on line* **10/3**[2]

5054 3 shd **Oldjoesaid**[10] 5890 4-8-9 104 DaneO'Neill 3 103
(H Candy) *stdd s and hld up towards rr: hdwy to trck ldrs 1/2-way: rdn along and sltly outpcd wl over 1f out: drvn ent fnl f: kpt on wl towards fin* **6/4**[1]

5503 4 1 1/4 **Manzila (FR)**[10] 5884 5-8-4 97 SilvestreDeSousa 5 93
(D Nicholls) *sn pushed along in rr: hdwy 2f out: rdn over 1f out: styd on wl fnl f: nrst fin* **11/2**

5004 5 1/2 **Pawan (IRE)**[2] 6153 8-8-5 88 ow1 (b) AnnStokell(5) 8 97
(Miss A Stokell) *dwlt: sn chsng ldrs: rdn along wl over 1f out and kpt on same pce* **18/1**

2000 6 9 **Tabaret**[10] 5906 5-8-9 92 (p) DeanMcKeown 1 64
(R M Whitaker) *in tch: pushed along 1/2-way: sn rdn and outpcd* **33/1**

2550 7 2 1/4 **Fire Up The Band**[10] 5886 9-8-2 62 DanielleMooney(7) 6 56
(A Berry) *a outpcd in rr* **150/1**

63.91 secs (0.41) **Going Correction** +0.30s/f (Good) 7 Ran SP% **109.6**

Speed ratings (Par 107): **108,107,107,105,104 90,86**

toteswinger: 1&2 £2.40, 1&3 £1.90, 2&3 £1.90. CSF £14.19 TOTE £3.80: £2.00, £2.30; EX 15.00.

Owner Miss M Greenwood **Bred** Mrs A Haskell Ellis **Trained** Norton, N Yorks

■ Stewards' Enquiry : Greg Fairley caution: used whip down the shoulder in the forehand position

FOCUS

A decent conditions sprint in which the pace was good without being breakneck and it resulted in a thrilling finish. The runner-up and fifth set the level.

NOTEBOOK

Fullandby(IRE), without a win since last year's Portland, showed no ill-effects from his modest effort in a Group 3 at Newbury three days earlier. Appreciating the softening ground, this stiff track suited him ideally and he battled on very gamely between horses to snatch the race on the line. He may now be allowed to take his chance in the Prix de l'Abbaye. (op 4-1 tchd 9-2)

Strike Up The Band, who had finished behind Oldjoesaid but ahead of Fullandby in the Portland, had a bit to find with that pair on these terms but he did have the plum draw and his rider tried to make the most of it. He set a fair pace, but tried to keep just enough in reserve to see him home and all but succeeded. He had a few pounds to find with his two main rivals at the weights, so this was a fine effort. (op 11-4)

Oldjoesaid, a fine fourth in the Portland, was best in at the weights and like the winner he would have been well suited by the easing in the conditions. He travelled well enough behind the leaders, but when asked for his effort he took too long to respond and by the time he did he was just too late. (op 13-8 tchd 5-4)

Manzila(FR), a stable-companion of the runner-up, was down in class but soon found herself outpaced on this drop back to 5f and, though she put in some strong late work down the wide outside, she was never getting there in time. (tchd 13-2 in a place)

Pawan(IRE), reappearing just two days after getting outpaced over 6f at Hamilton, missed the break and was then vigorously ridden in order to avoid a repeat. He was close enough this time, but could not pick up sufficiently under pressure late on. This was still a decent effort at the weights, however. (op 20-1 tchd 22-1)

Tabaret, who had the worst of the draw, would not have appreciated the easing ground and was always struggling having been trapped out wide throughout. Official explanation: jockey said gelding was unsuited by the soft, good to soft in places ground (tchd 40-1)

6185 EXORS. OF SIBYL DUDDY (S) STKS 1m 4f 16y

3:00 (3:01) (Class 5) 3-4-Y-O **£2,590** (£770; £385; £192) **Stalls** High

Form RPR

0420 1 **Pondapie (IRE)**[44] 4902 3-8-8 70 (p) TomEaves 11 65
(R M Whitaker) *bmpd s: sn trcking ldrs: hdwy 3f out: swtchd lft and rdn to chal wl over 1f out: led appr fnl f and sn clr* **9/2**[2]

0053 2 9 **Run Free**[17] 5710 4-8-11 52 FrederikTylicki(5) 5 50
(N Wilson) *led: rdn along 2f out: drvn and hdd over 1f out: kpt on same pce* **15/2**

-004 3 nk **Valentine Blue**[12] 5813 3-8-8 47 (tp) JimmyQuinn 3 50
(A B Haynes) *hld up towards rr: hdwy 3f out: rdn to chse ldrs 2f out: drvn and kpt on ins fnl f: nrst fin* **20/1**

6300 4 1 3/4 **Lady Killer Queen**[19] 5637 4-8-11 50 (v) DavidAllan 12 42
(D Carroll) *hld up in midfield: hdwy 3f out: rdn to chse ldrs 2f out: sn drvn and kpt on same pce* **11/2**

31 5 2 3/4 **Sorrento Moon (IRE)**[28] 5380 4-9-2 48 PJMcDonald 6 43
(G M Moore) *in tch: pushed along over 4f out: rdn along to chse ldrs 3f out: drvn and edgd rt 2f out: sn no imp* **5/1**[3]

4304 6 1 1/2 **Jane Of Arc (FR)**[8] 5968 4-8-11 45 (p) DanielTudhope 1 35
(J S Goldie) *trckd ldr: rdn along 3f out: drvn and hung lft wl over 1f out: sn wknd* **3/1**[1]

-056 7 hd **Pugnacity**[5] 6040 4-8-9 44 ow3 SladeO'Hara(5) 7 38
(A Berry) *chsd ldng pair: rdn along 3f out: drvn 2f out and sn wknd* **33/1**

5000 8 2 1/4 **Foxxy**[75] 3863 4-8-11 37 (v) PaulMulrennan 2 31
(J R Norton) *a towards rr* **33/1**

0-40 9 9 **Still Calm**[104] 2949 4-8-13 55 (be[1]) LukeMorris(3) 8 22
(N J Vaughan) *wnt bdly rt s: a in rr* **8/1**

0050 10 11 **General Tufto**[6] 6032 3-8-9 55 ow1 (v) RobertWinston 10 5
(C Smith) *bmpd s: chsd ldrs: rdn along over 3f out and sn wknd* **16/1**

0050 11 110 **Babieca (USA)**[66] 4181 4-9-2 45 (t) DaneO'Neill 9 —
(A B Haynes) *s.i.s: a in rr: t.o fnl 4f* **25/1**

2m 46.71s (5.81) **Going Correction** +0.55s/f (Yiel)

WFA 3 from 4yo 8lb 11 Ran SP% **118.5**

Speed ratings (Par 103): **102,96,95,94,92 91,91,90,84,76** —

toteswinger: 1&2 £6.50, 1&3 £12.60, 2&3 £15.90. CSF £36.64 TOTE £5.60: £1.60, £3.00, £5.00; EX 45.60.The winner was bought in for 6,200gns.

Owner Clipper Logistics **Bred** Haras De St Pair Du Mont **Trained** Scarcroft, W Yorks

FOCUS

A moderate seller in which only one of these had managed to win a race so far this season and so the form is rated negatively. The pace was a fair one in the conditions and they finished very well spread out.

Pondapie(IRE) Official explanation: trainer said, regarding the apparent improvement of form, gelding is unreliable, but appeared to concentrate better with the application of first-time cheekpieces

6186 ORGANS FOR LIFE H'CAP 7f 100y

3:30 (3:30) (Class 5) (0-75,75) 3-Y-O+ **£3,238** (£963; £481; £240) **Stalls** High

Form RPR

0532 1 **Jonny Lesters Hair (IRE)**[27] 5397 3-8-13 **70** DavidAllan 11 81
(T D Easterby) *trckd ldr: effrt 2f out: rdn to ld over 1f out: drvn ins fnl f and kpt on* **6/1**[2]

0605 2 3/4 **We'Re Delighted**[8] 5964 3-8-11 **68** GrahamGibbons 3 77
(T D Walford) *trckd ldrs on inner: hdwy over 2f out: swtchd lft and rdn over 1f out: drvn to chse wnr ins fnl f: kpt on* **14/1**

0204 3 2 3/4 **Nuit Sombre (IRE)**[50] 4688 8-9-3 **71** (p) SilvestreDeSousa 6 74
(G A Harker) *led: rdn along over 2f out: drvn and hdd over 1f out: kpt on same pce* **12/1**

2045 4 1 **Paraguay (USA)**[53] 4603 5-9-5 **73** EdwardCreighton 13 73+
(Miss V Haigh) *hld up in rr: hdwy 2f out: swtchd lft over 1f out: styd on ins fnl f: nrst fin* **10/1**

4013 5 nk **West End Lad**[14] 5779 5-8-9 **63** (b) JimmyQuinn 14 62
(S R Bowring) *trckd ldrs: hdwy 3f out: rdn along over 2f out: sn drvn and kpt on same pce* **9/2**[1]

2521 6 3 3/4 **Handsome Falcon**[27] 5390 4-9-2 **75** FrederikTylicki(5) 2 64
(R A Fahey) *trckd ldrs: effrt on outer 3f out: rdn along over 2f out: sn drvn: edgd rt and wknd* **6/1**[2]

6320 7 1 3/4 **King Of Rhythm (IRE)**[44] 4895 5-9-7 **75** DNolan 1 59
(D Carroll) *midfield: effrt 3f out: sn rdn along and no hdwy* **22/1**

0053 8 nk **Champain Sands (IRE)**[48] 4744 9-8-7 **64** AndrewMullen(3) 8 47
(E J Alston) *hld up: a towards rr* **16/1**

6300 9 2 1/2 **Passion Fruit**[19] 5635 7-9-7 **75** DeanMcKeown 9 52
(C W Fairhurst) *hld up and bhd: nvr a factor* **20/1**

300 10 hd **Shadowtime**[10] 5915 3-8-9 **66** ow1 PaulMulrennan 4 41
(Miss Tracy Waggott) *chsd ldrs: rdn along 3f out and sn wknd* **40/1**

22 11 5 **Nok Twice (IRE)**[5] 6043 7-8-11 **65** RobertWinston 12 28
(K A Ryan) *hld up towards rr: effrt on inner 3f out: rdn over 2f out and no hdwy* **9/2**[1]

0021 12 10 **Mr Toshiwonka**[31] 5258 4-8-12 **66** AdrianTNicholls 10 2
(D Nicholls) *sn pushed along: a in rr* **13/2**[3]

1m 36.58s (2.78) **Going Correction** +0.55s/f (Yiel)

WFA 3 from 4yo+ 3lb 12 Ran SP% **119.1**

Speed ratings (Par 103): **106,105,102,100,100 96,94,93,91,90 85,73**

toteswinger: 1&2 £17.00, 1&3 £15.50, 2&3 £38.80. CSF £85.13 CT £997.67 TOTE £6.70: £2.10, £5.00, £3.60; EX 120.70.

Owner Habtons Baggie Rams **Bred** Gary O'Reilly **Trained** Great Habton, N Yorks

FOCUS

An ordinary handicap, but a competitive one and they went a decent pace in the conditions. Despite that, the first three home were handy throughout and the third is the best guide to the form.

Nok Twice(IRE) Official explanation: jockey said gelding ran flat

Mr Toshiwonka Official explanation: jockey said gelding was unsuited by the soft, good to soft in places ground

6187 E B F HAPPY BIRTHDAY MUM FOR THE WEEKEND MEDIAN AUCTION MAIDEN STKS 7f 100y

4:00 (4:01) (Class 6) 2-Y-O **£2,077** (£2,077; £473) **Stalls** High

Form RPR

34 1 **Kudu Country (IRE)**[59] 4415 2-9-3 0 MickyFenton 7 77
(T P Tate) *a.p: effrt to chal 2f out: sn rdn and led ent fnl f: sn drvn and jnd on line* **3/1**[2]

3 1 dht **Hunterview**[14] 5777 2-9-3 0 PhilipRobinson 14 77
(M A Jarvis) *led: jnd and rdn along 2f out: hdd ent fnl f: drvn and rallied to join ldr on line* **1/1**[1]

0 **3** *4* **Eddie Boy**[32] 5227 2-9-3 0 .... JamieSpencer 5 68+
(M L W Bell) *sn chsng ldrs: effrt 3f out: swtchd lft and rdn 2f out: sn drvn and no imp* **6/1**[3]

04 **4** *1 1/2* **Yeoman Of England (IRE)**[23] 5539 2-9-3 0 .... TomEaves 2 64
(B Smart) *trckd ldrs: hdwy 3f out: rdn along over 2f out: sn drvn and kpt on same pce* **66/1**

5 *2 1/2* **Trumpstoo (USA)** 2-9-3 0 .... TonyHamilton 11 58+
(R A Fahey) *dwlt: sn in tch: hdwy 3f out: rdn along 2f out: sn drvn and kpt on same pce* **28/1**

6 **6** *3 1/2* **Upton Seas**[21] 5590 2-8-12 0 .... PJMcDonald 1 45
(R D E Woodhouse) *midfield: hdwy 3f out: rdn along over 2f out and sn no imp* **66/1**

7 *7* **Rock Relief (IRE)** 2-9-3 0 .... J-PGuillambert 6 34
(Sir Mark Prescott) *dwlt and in rr tl sme late hdwy* **14/1**

6 **8** *3/4* **Age Of Couture**[23] 5535 2-8-12 0 .... RobertWinston 3 27
(W Jarvis) *in tch: effrt on outer wl over 2f out: sn rdn and btn* **17/2**

9 *2 3/4* **Irish Saint (IRE)** 2-9-3 0 .... GregFairley 9 25
(T J Pitt) *a towards rr* **66/1**

00 **10** *4* **Coniston Reload**[43] 4921 2-9-3 0 .... PaulMulrennan 4 16
(M W Easterby) *a in rr* **125/1**

11 *hd* **Transporter (IRE)** 2-9-0 0 .... DuranFentiman(3) 12 15
(T D Easterby) *a in rr* **100/1**

12 *3* **Indigo Belle (IRE)** 2-8-9 0 .... AndrewMullen(3) 10 —
(Mrs A Duffield) *a bhd* **66/1**

0 **13** *nk* **Kabougg**[60] 4387 2-8-5 0 .... ManavNem(7) 13 —
(P A Blockley) *chsd ldng pair: rdn along 1/2-way and sn wknd* **66/1**

00 **14** *1 1/2* **Dance Society**[6] 6014 2-9-3 0 .... DavidAllan 8 —
(T D Easterby) *in tch: rdn along 3f out: wknd over 2f out* **80/1**

1m 38.48s (4.68) **Going Correction** +0.55s/f (Yiel) **14** Ran SP% **120.4**
Speed ratings (Par 93): **95,95,90,88,85 81,73,73,69,65 65,61,61,59**WIN: Hunterview £1.00, Kudu Country £3.60; PL: H £1.10, KC £1.50; EX: H/KC £3.60, KC/H £3.00, CSF: H/KC £1.88, KC.H £3.90. toteswinger: Hunterview & Kudu Country £2.00, Hunterview & Eddie Boy: £2.90; Kudu Country & Eddie Boy: £3.40., £2.00.
Owner The Ivy Syndicate/Sh.Ahmed Al Maktoum **Bred** RogerARyan/Darley **Trained**Tadcaster/Newmarket

FOCUS
Basically a modest maiden and those that raced handily dominated. The front pair, who couldn't be separated at the line, pulled clear of the others and a few of these are entitled to improve. The third and sixth help set the level.

NOTEBOOK
Kudu Country(IRE), who had run well in two maidens that have both produced winners, was well backed and raced close to the pace throughout. The race looked his when he hit the front, but although he did little wrong he could not shake the favourite off and was forced to share the prize. He looks a real stayer in the making and will be much more the finished article next year, possibly even a hurdler in the longer term. (op 4-1 tchd 9-2)
Hunterview, a close third in a five-runner Leicester maiden on debut, shaped then as though he would appreciate a decent test of stamina and he was duly given a positive ride here. It looked as though he would have to settle for the runner-up spot when his rival headed him, but he fought back in great style to share the spoils on the line. He will appreciate even further than this. (op 4-1 tchd 9-2)
Eddie Boy, very green on his Newbury debut, was never far away and kept staying on, but he still showed signs of greenness and may well come on again for it. (op 11-2 tchd 5-1)
Yeoman Of England(IRE) was another to race handily and though he could only plug on at one pace late, this was a fair effort given his price. He now qualifies for nurseries which will open up more opportunities. (op 80-1)
Trumpstoo(USA) was far from disgraced and fared the best of the newcomers. He should come on for the run. (op 33-1)
Upton Seas again showed some ability and is likely to show even more once handicapped. (op 100-1)
Rock Relief(IRE), who attracted some market support, was not given at all a hard time on this debut. A 200,000 euros colt out of a half-sister to Oath, he is likely to improve a good deal on this in due course. (op 20-1)
Age Of Couture was a springer in the market, but she could not pick up under pressure down the wide outside. The jockey reported that Age Of Couture was unsuited by the ground. Official explanation: jockey said filly was unsuited by the soft, good to soft in places ground (op 20-1)

6188 IAN WOOLFITT 65TH BIRTHDAY H'CAP — 1m 100y
4:30 (4:30) (Class 5) (0-75,75) 3-Y-O — **£3,238** (£963; £481; £240) **Stalls** High

Form — RPR

4454 **1** **Shaloo Diamond**[24] 5504 3-9-0 74 .... MichaelJStainton(3) 16 83
(R M Whitaker) *sn led: qcknd clr wl over 2f out: rdn over 1f out: drvn ins fnl f and kpt on* **11/4**[1]

5003 **2** *3/4* **Blindspin**[5] 6043 3-9-1 72 .... TonyHamilton 7 79
(M Dods) *in tch: hdwy on inner 3f out and sn chsng wnr: rdn wl over 1f out: drvn ins fnl f: styd on wl towards fin* **5/1**[3]

0304 **3** *6* **Dancing Maite**[27] 5397 3-8-7 64 .... JimmyQuinn 6 57
(S R Bowring) *in tch on outer: effrt whn pushed wd home turn: rdn to chse ldng pair over 2f out: sn edgd rt and kpt on same pce* **8/1**

4000 **4** *2* **King's Icon (IRE)**[21] 5595 3-8-3 67 .... TobyAtkinson(7) 13 56
(M Wigham) *hld up in rr: hdwy over 3f out: rdn along 2f out: kpt on appr fnl f: nrst fin* **33/1**

6305 **5** *5* **King Kenny**[17] 5713 3-9-4 75 .... TonyCulhane 5 52
(S Parr) *t.k.h: hld up in rr: hdwy over 3f out: rdn to chse ldrs over 2f out: sn one pce* **11/1**

5005 **6** *3* **Thunderstruck**[10] 5888 3-8-12 69 .... (b) PaulMulrennan 10 39
(K A Ryan) *t.k.h: hld up in rr: effrt and hdwy 3f out: rdn over 2f out and sn wknd* **14/1**

513 **7** *6* **Metal Madness (IRE)**[49] 4715 3-8-13 70 .... GrahamGibbons 11 26
(M G Quinlan) *in tch on inner: pushed along 1/2-way: rdn wl over 2f out and sn wknd* **7/2**[2]

14-0 **8** *19* **Salingers Star (IRE)**[16] 5717 3-9-3 74 .... PJMcDonald 8 —
(G A Swinbank) *t.k.h: in tch: pushed along over 3f out: sn rdn and wknd* **20/1**

2620 **9** *2 1/2* **Grey Command (USA)**[25] 5449 3-8-12 69 .... DavidAllan 9 —
(M Brittain) *prom: rdn along 3f out: sn wknd* **15/2**

4-00 **10** *22* **Emerald Crystal (IRE)**[111] 2714 3-9-1 72 .... (b) JamieSpencer 14 —
(B J Meehan) *racd wd: cl up tl rdn along 3f out and sn wknd* **16/1**

1m 52.0s (4.40) **Going Correction** +0.55s/f (Yiel) **10** Ran SP% **117.0**
Speed ratings (Par 101): **100,99,93,91,86 83,77,58,55,33**
toteswinger: 1&2 £3.40, 1&3 £6.30, 2&3 £8.50. CSF £16.65 CT £100.46 TOTE £3.80: £1.90, £1.80, £2.90; EX 21.20.
Owner G B Bedford **Bred** Hellwood Stud Farm **Trained** Scarcroft, W Yorks

FOCUS
Another modest handicap, but still quite competitive despite all the non-runners. The winner made sure it was run at a true pace, they finished very well spread out, and the front pair pulled well clear. The runner-up is rated back to near his best.
Thunderstruck Official explanation: jockey said gelding missed the break
Metal Madness(IRE) Official explanation: vet said colt was lame behind when pulled up
Grey Command(USA) Official explanation: jockey said gelding lost its action

6189 BRIAN AND JASON MERRINGTON MEMORIAL AMATEUR RIDERS' H'CAP — 1m 1f 207y
5:00 (5:00) (Class 6) (0-60,60) 3-Y-O+ — **£2,498** (£774; £387; £193) **Stalls** High

Form — RPR

0406 **1** **Kingsholm**[11] 5871 6-11-1 54 .... MissARyan 2 67+
(K A Ryan) *dwlt: swtchd rt after s to inner rail: in tch after 3f: hdwy 3f out: swtchd lft and effrt to chal 2f out: sn led: rdn clr ent fnl f: eased towards fin* **11/2**[3]

-640 **2** *1 1/2* **Stravita**[21] 5593 4-10-9 53 .... (p) MrStephenHarrison(5) 1 61
(R Hollinshead) *hld up towards rr: stdy hdwy 4f out: effrt 2f out: rdn to chse wnr ins fnl f: kpt on: nrst fin* **12/1**

5320 **3** *6* **Emperor's Well**[40] 5008 9-11-3 59 .... (b) MissJCoward(3) 15 55
(M W Easterby) *cl up on inner: led 1/2-way: rdn along wl over 2f out: hdd wl over 1f out: sn one pce* **9/2**[2]

4000 **4** *1* **Bed Fellow (IRE)**[22] 5559 4-10-10 56 .... MissJKWilson(7) 6 50
(Paul Murphy) *in tch: hdwy to chse ldrs 1/2-way: rdn along 3f out: kpt on same pce fnl 2f* **50/1**

0000 **5** *2* **Hurricane Thomas (IRE)**[22] 5559 4-11-0 60 .... MissPhillipaTutty(7) 12 50
(R E Barr) *chsd ldrs: rdn along 3f out: one pce fnl 2f* **25/1**

0200 **6** *1 1/2* **Tizzy May (FR)**[40] 5008 8-11-3 56 .... MissLEllison 7 43
(B Ellison) *hld up towards rr: hdwy 3f out: rdn 2f out and nvr rch ldrs* **11/2**[3]

5500 **7** *1 1/4* **Fenners (USA)**[25] 5476 5-10-13 57 .... MissJoannaMason(5) 4 42
(M W Easterby) *hld up in rr: hdwy 3f out: rdn over 1f out: sn no imp* **14/1**

0065 **8** *3 1/2* **Kirstys Lad**[11] 5871 6-10-9 53 .... MissMMullineaux(5) 5 31
(M Mullineaux) *hld up: hdwy and wd st: sn rdn and edgd rt 2f out: nvr a factor* **16/1**

6 **9** *5* **Jonquille (IRE)**[33] 5203 3-10-9 59 .... MrHarryChalloner(5) 11 27
(R Ford) *midfield: effrt on inner over 3f out: sn rdn along and wknd* **28/1**

2040 **10** *7* **Saluscraggie**[5] 6050 6-10-13 59 .... (p) MissVBarr(7) 10 13
(R E Barr) *s.i.s: a bhd* **16/1**

0600 **11** *10* **Paparaazi (IRE)**[14] 5776 6-10-10 54 .... MissKSharp(5) 13 —
(I W McInnes) *prom: rdn along 3f out: sn wknd* **16/1**

1020 **12** *18* **Faraday (IRE)**[35] 4704 5-10-13 52 .... MissNCarberry 8 —
(N P Mulholland) *in tch: effrt and hdwy to chse ldrs whn carried wd home turn: sn rdn and btn over 2f out* **7/2**[1]

1040 **13** *6* **High Five Society**[14] 5779 4-10-8 54 .... (bt) MrKApark(7) 14 —
(S R Bowring) *led: hdd 1/2-way: sn rdn along: wknd qckly and bhd* **13/2**

2m 15.66s (8.66) **Going Correction** +0.55s/f (Yiel)
WFA 3 from 4yo+ 6lb **13** Ran SP% **125.8**
Speed ratings (Par 101): **87,85,81,80,78 77,76,73,69,64 56,41,36**
toteswinger: 1&2 £12.60, 1&3 £5.20, 2&3 £11.80. CSF £72.80 CT £332.59 TOTE £6.40: £1.90, £4.10, £1.50; EX 88.70 Place 6: £59.31 Place 5: £48.76.
Owner Riverside Racing **Bred** J C , J R And S R Hitchins **Trained** Hambleton, N Yorks

FOCUS
A moderate amateur riders' event to end the card. The pace looked a fair one and these riders used the full width of the track once into the home straight. The winner is value for more than the official margin with the runner-up rated close to recent form.
Faraday(IRE) Official explanation: jockey said gelding was unsuited by the soft, good to soft in places ground
T/Plt: £55.60 to a £1 stake. Pool: £56,965.73. 747.04 winning tickets. T/Qpdt: £18.20 to a £1 stake. Pool: £3,995.12. 162.20 winning tickets. JR

5753 FOLKESTONE (R-H)
Tuesday, September 23

OFFICIAL GOING: Good to soft (good in places) changing to good to soft after race 2 (2.50) changing to soft after race 3 (3.20)
Wind: medium across Weather: raining

6190 LIPSCOMB.CO.UK H'CAP — 5f
2:20 (2:20) (Class 6) (0-60,60) 3-Y-O+ — **£2,590** (£770; £385; £192) **Stalls** Low

Form — RPR

246 **1** **Azygous**[19] 5645 5-9-5 60 .... (b[1]) AlanMunro 3 69
(J Akehurst) *racd stands' side: sn pushed along and struggling to go pce: hdwy and swtchd rt over 1f out: styd on to ld wl ins fnl f* **9/1**

003 **2** *1* **Bookiesindex Boy**[34] 5187 4-9-5 60 .... (v) JimmyFortune 2 65
(J R Jenkins) *racd stands' side: chsd overall ldr tl led over 1f out: rdn ins fnl f: hdd and no ex wl ins fnl f: 2nd of 6 in gp* **11/1**

0262 **3** *1/2* **Overstayed (IRE)**[5] 6063 5-9-1 56 .... (t) RichardMullen 1 60
(P J McBride) *racd stands' side: sn pushed along and outpcd: hdwy u.p and hmpd over 1f out: swtchd rt jst ins fnl f: r.o: nt quite rch ldrs: 3rd of 6 in gp* **4/1**[2]

5522 **4** *nk* **Fast Freddie**[11] 5867 4-9-3 58 .... (t) JohnEgan 8 61
(S Parr) *racd stands' side: overall ldr tl over 1f out: one pce fnl 100yds: 4th of 6 in gp* **5/2**[1]

5105 **5** *3* **Jayanjay**[12] 5817 9-9-0 55 .... AdamKirby 12 47
(B R Johnson) *racd far side: in tch: led far side gp over 1f out: kpt on but no ch w stands' side: 1st of 6 in gp* **11/1**

3213 **6** *1/2* **Penrice Castle**[22] 5582 3-8-11 53 .... RichardHughes 6 43
(R Hannon) *racd stands' side: t.k.h early: chsd ldng pair: effrt and rdn 2f out: wknd jst over 1f out: 5th of 6 in gp* **12/1**

2660 **7** *2 1/2* **Black Moma (IRE)**[35] 5171 4-9-4 59 .... RyanMoore 9 40
(A B Haynes) *racd far side: in tch: hdwy to chse far side ldr over 1f out: no imp: 2nd of 6 in gp* **7/1**[3]

0006 **8** *hd* **Swindon Town Flyer (IRE)**[27] 5393 3-8-9 58 .... (b) PNolan(7) 4 38
(A B Haynes) *racd stands' side: wnt bdly rt s and v.s.a.: a wl bhd: 6th of 6 in gp* **33/1**

006 **9** *3 1/4* **Bluebok**[27] 5401 7-9-2 60 .... (bt) KevinGhunowa(3) 14 29
(J M Bradley) *racd far side: led far side gp tl over 1f out: wknd: 3rd of 6 in gp* **20/1**

5000 **10** *7* **Spanish Ace**[86] 3520 7-9-2 57 .... TedDurcan 10 —
(J M Bradley) *racd far side: a bhd: 4th of 6 in gp* **25/1**

4366 **11** *2 3/4* **Wynberg (IRE)**[28] 5374 3-9-4 60 .... (b[1]) WilliamBuick 11 —
(S A Callaghan) *racd far side: prom tl hung lft and wknd fr 1/2-way: eased fnl f: 5th of 6 in gp* **14/1**

5000 **12** *1/2* **Affirmatively**[20] 5617 3-9-4 60 .... ShaneKelly 13 —
(A W Carroll) *racd far side: t.k.h: chsd ldr tl wknd qckly 2f out: eased fnl f: 6th of 6 in gp* **16/1**

61.58 secs (1.58) **Going Correction** +0.375s/f (Good)
WFA 3 from 4yo+ 1lb **12** Ran SP% **119.5**
Speed ratings (Par 101): **102,100,99,99,94 93,89,89,84,72 68,67**
toteswinger: 1&2 £19.80, 1&3 £8.90, 2&3 £6.60. CSF £102.34 CT £369.97 TOTE £10.30: £4.20, £4.00, £1.90; EX 121.10 Trifecta £236.70 Part won. Pool: £319.95 - 0.10 winning units..

The Form Book, Raceform Ltd, Compton, RG20 6NL

Owner The Grass Is Greener Partnership V **Bred** Mrs R D Peacock **Trained** Epsom, Surrey
■ Stewards' Enquiry : Alan Munro two-day ban: careless riding (Oct 7-8)

FOCUS
A modest sprint handicap. They split into two even groups, but the first four home racing stands' side. They probably went off a little too quickly on the near side and that set the race up for the closers. The form is rated around the placed horses and could be rated a fraction higher.

6191 GARDEN OF ENGLAND NURSERY 5f
2:50 (2:50) (Class 6) (0-65,69) 2-Y-O **£2,914** (£867; £433; £216) **Stalls** Low

Form RPR
5235 **1** **Key To Love (IRE)**[18] 5671 2-9-7 **64**........................ RichardHughes 7 69
(H J L Dunlop) *in tch: hdwy over 2f out: led over 1f out: r.o wl: eased nr fin* **3/1**[2]
054 **2** *2 1/4* **Itainteasybeingme**[38] 5089 2-9-2 **59**........................ PatCosgrave 5 56
(J R Boyle) *pressed ldr tl led 2f out: sn rdn: hdd over 1f out: nt pce of wnr but battled on to hold 2nd* **14/1**
300 **3** *1* **Sorrel Ridge (IRE)**[19] 5628 2-8-7 **50**........................ AlanMunro 6 43
(M G Quinlan) *chsd ldrs: ev ch and rdn over 1f out: kpt on same pce fnl f* **12/1**
6021 **4** *shd* **Caledonia Princess**[1] 6172 2-9-9 **69** 6ex................ KevinGhunowa(3) 8 62
(P A Blockley) *dwlt: in tch: pushed along and hdwy 3f out: ev ch over 1f out: one pce u.p fnl f* **2/1**[1]
0004 **5** *1* **Silver Salsa**[23] 5530 2-9-3 **60**........................ ChrisCatlin 4 49
(J R Jenkins) *hld up bhd: effrt 2f out: keeping on same pce whn nt clr run and hit by rivals whip ins fnl f: nvr trbld ldrs* **20/1**
4325 **6** *1/2* **Turn To Dreams**[12] 5834 2-8-7 **55**........................ RichardEvans(5) 2 43
(P D Evans) *hld up on stands' rail: rdn and struggling over 2f out: plugging on but no ch whn swtchd rt wl ins fnl f* **4/1**[3]
6066 **7** *1* **Rapanui Belle**[15] 5746 2-8-8 **51** ow2........................ RyanMoore 3 35
(G L Moore) *racd keenly: led tl 2f out: rdn and wknd over 1f out* **7/1**
0040 **8** *2* **Goodenough Magic**[29] 5363 2-8-4 **47**........................ HayleyTurner 9 24
(Andrew Turnell) *a bhd: no ch fr over 1f out* **16/1**

62.30 secs (2.30) **Going Correction** +0.375s/f (Good) **8 Ran SP% 115.8**
Speed ratings (Par 93): **96,92,90,90,89 88,86,83**
toteswinger: 1&2 £10.20, 1&3 £11.20, 2&3 £34.00. CSF £44.05 CT £443.69 TOTE £3.60: £1.50, £4.30, £4.00; EX 42.90 Trifecta £234.40 Pool: £380.18 - 1.20 winning units..
Owner Anamoine Ltd **Bred** Windflower Overseas Holdings Inc **Trained** Lambourn, Berks

FOCUS
This was a moderate nursery and they all stayed stands' side, but the rail was no advantage. The form is rated around the winner and third.

NOTEBOOK
Key To Love(IRE) had already had a few chances, but her third at Chester two starts back was a much better effort than it looked at the time, as the runner-up subsequently won by five lengths, and she was not beaten far in a better race than this at Kempton on her latest outing. She showed good speed throughout, a few horse widths off the near rail, and stayed on well to get off the mark at the sixth attempt. A rise in the weights will force her up in class and that should be enough to stop her following up. (op 10-3 tchd 5-2)
Itainteasybeingme showed plenty of speed and was suited by this drop in trip on his nursery debut. He has the natural pace to take a race over this trip. (op 16-1)
Sorrel Ridge(IRE) was always well placed, but he didn't really pick up and gave the impression a flatter track may suit better. (op 14-1 tchd 16-1 and 9-1)
Caledonia Princess, carrying a penalty for her success in a similar race over 6f at Leicester the previous day, loomed up about 2f out after being outpaced early, but she quickly came back off the bridle and her run flattened out. This probably came too soon and she should also appreciate a step back up in trip. Official explanation: jockey said filly ran flat (op 13-8 tchd 11-4)
Silver Salsa would have finished around a length closer had she not been slightly impeded and hit by a rival jockey's whip inside the final furlong. She gave the impression this undulating track was not ideal. (op 16-1)
Rapanui Belle Official explanation: jockey said filly was unbalanced on ground that did not suit

6192 ROMNEY MARSH MAIDEN STKS 6f
3:20 (3:21) (Class 5) 3-Y-O+ **£2,914** (£867; £433; £216) **Stalls** Low

Form RPR
0-43 **1** **Perfect Silence**[39] 5057 3-8-12 64........................ AdamKirby 9 78
(C G Cox) *chsd ldr tl led wl over 1f out: rdn over 1f out: clr ins fnl f: comf* **6/1**[2]
42-2 **2** *3 1/4* **Anne Of Kiev (IRE)**[33] 5205 3-8-12 74........................ JimmyFortune 3 68
(J H M Gosden) *hld up in tch: chsd wnr wl over 1f out: hit on nose by rival's whip ent fnl f: wl hld after* **8/15**[1]
3354 **3** *1 1/2* **Chelsea Girl**[15] 5749 3-8-12 63........................ IanMongan 13 63
(C G Cox) *chsd ldrs: wnt 3rd over 1f out: kpt on same pce fnl f* **14/1**
-045 **4** *nse* **Kenton Street**[64] 4258 3-9-3 63........................ RobertHavlin 6 68
(J A R Toller) *hld up in midfield: hdwy over 2f out: chsd ldng trio 1f out: kpt on but nvr able to chal* **16/1**
4 **5** *4 1/2* **Motivated Choice**[33] 5205 3-8-12 0........................ RyanMoore 2 48
(L M Cumani) *hld up towards rr: outpcd 3f out: styd on steadily fr over 1f out: nvr trbld ldrs* **16/1**
00 **6** *2 1/2* **Faintly Hopeful**[14] 5786 3-9-3 0........................ PaulEddery 7 45
(R A Teal) *s.i.s: bhd: modest late hdwy: nvr trbld ldrs* **100/1**
0000 **7** *1 1/4* **Solemn**[26] 5421 3-9-3 48........................(b[1]) ChrisCatlin 8 41
(J M Bradley) *led tl wl over 1f out: wknd qckly over 1f out* **100/1**
00- **8** *1* **Chinese Profit**[326] 6616 3-9-3 0........................ JoeFanning 11 38
(G C Bravery) *bhd: sme hdwy 1/2-way: rdn and no prog wl over 1f out: wl btn fnl f* **50/1**
0300 **9** *3* **Milldown Bay**[63] 4277 3-8-12 60........................(b[1]) TGMcLaughlin 1 23
(B R Millman) *s.i.s: a bhd* **66/1**
6 **10** *13* **Pappoose**[7] 6003 3-8-12 0........................ FrankieMcDonald 5 —
(H Candy) *chsd ldrs tl 1/2-way: sn wknd: t.o* **20/1**
4400 **11** *15* **Heroic Fool**[7] 6003 3-9-3 47........................ SamHitchcott 12 —
(Miss Z C Davison) *s.i.s: bhd: brief effrt 1/2-way: t.o fnl f* **100/1**
6265 **12** *1/2* **Warden Fizz**[41] 4989 3-9-3 70........................ HayleyTurner 4 —
(D R C Elsworth) *a bhd: t.o wl over 1f out* **12/1**[3]

1m 14.81s (2.11) **Going Correction** +0.375s/f (Good)
WFA 3 from 4yo 2lb **12 Ran SP% 116.8**
Speed ratings (Par 103): **100,95,93,93,87 84,82,81,77,59 39,39**
toteswinger: 1&2 £1.80, 1&3 £6.10, 2&3 £3.20. CSF £9.17 TOTE £7.40: £2.00, £1.02, £3.60; EX 14.60 Trifecta £44.20 Pool: £446.16 - 7.46 winning units..
Owner Wild Beef Racing (Mr & Mrs R J Vines) **Bred** R J Vines **Trained** Lambourn, Berks

FOCUS
A modest sprint maiden in which they all raced stands' side. The form looks fluid with a couple disappointing.

6193 STONE OF FOLCA NOVICE STKS 6f
3:50 (3:51) (Class 4) 2-Y-O **£3,885** (£1,156; £577; £288) **Stalls** Low

Form RPR
0363 **1** **Daddy's Gift (IRE)**[14] 5785 2-8-9 74........................ RyanMoore 3 81
(R Hannon) *mde all: sn crossed to stands rail: rdn 2f out: styd on gamely u.p fnl f* **5/2**[2]
134 **2** *1/2* **Ginobili (IRE)**[24] 5487 2-9-5 94........................ RichardHughes 6 90
(R Hannon) *plld hrd: trckd ldrs: rdn and unable qck and edgd lft over 1f out: hdwy and swtchd rt lins fnl f: chsd wnr wl ins fnl f: r.o but nvr quite getting to wnr* **11/4**[3]
4003 **3** *1 1/4* **Effort**[24] 5496 2-9-5 95........................ JoeFanning 7 86
(M Johnston) *chsd ldr: ev ch wl over 1f out: rdn over 1f out: wknd wl ins fnl f* **9/4**[1]
11 **4** *9* **Portugese Caddy (IRE)**[15] 5756 2-9-9 0........................ JimCrowley 2 63
(P Winkworth) *in tch: rdn 1/2-way: drvn and btn wl over 1f out* **11/2**
6 **5** *3 1/2* **Big Stormy (USA)**[46] 4822 2-8-12 0........................(t) MartinDwyer 5 41
(C E Brittain) *s.i.s: t.k.h: hld up in last pair: hdwy to chse ldrs over 2f out: wknd over 1f out* **16/1**
6 *1/2* **Flavour** 2-8-3 0........................ ChrisCatlin 1 31
(A W Carroll) *s.i.s: bhd: hdwy and in tch 1/2-way: wknd wl over 1f out* **50/1**

1m 15.3s (2.60) **Going Correction** +0.375s/f (Good) **6 Ran SP% 109.2**
Speed ratings (Par 97): **97,96,94,82,78 77**
toteswinger: 1&2 £1.10 1&3 £1.50, 2&3 £1.30. CSF £9.22 TOTE £3.60: £1.40, £2.30; EX 6.70.
Owner Charlee & Hollie Allan **Bred** Vincent Dunne **Trained** East Everleigh, Wilts

FOCUS
An ordinary novice event and something of a tactical affair. The runner-up is rated close to form but with the third disappointing it is form to treat with caution.

NOTEBOOK
Daddy's Gift(IRE) was wrong at the weights with both Ginobili and Effort, but she soon bagged the stands' rail. Although kept honest up front by the eventual third, she was allowed the run of things and stayed on strongly to hold off her stablemate, who raced too keenly. It would probably be unwise to take this form at face value and her official mark is going to suffer. (op 9-2)
Ginobili(IRE) did not help his chance by pulling hard early on and, having been inclined to edge left, knuckled down too late once switched off the rail inside the final furlong. He was below his official mark of 94. Official explanation: jockey said colt hung badly to the left (op 7-2 tchd 5-2)
Effort pressed Daddy's Gift for much of the way and looked the winner about 2f out, but he appeared to throw this away. It might be that he wants quicker ground and a less undulating track, but his attitude appears suspect. (op 5-4)
Portugese Caddy(IRE) had no easy task conceding weight all round as his two wins (including over course and distance last time) had been gained in ordinary company. He was trapped towards the inside and probably would have preferred a stronger pace, but he was still well beaten. (op 6-1 tchd 9-2)
Big Stormy(USA) finished up out the back, but he showed ability and should be capable of better in time, possibly on a quicker surface. (op 22-1)

6194 HYTHE H'CAP 7f (S)
4:20 (4:22) (Class 4) (0-85,83) 3-Y-O+ **£5,046** (£1,510; £755; £377; £188) **Stalls** Low

Form RPR
2123 **1** **Rum Jungle**[21] 5588 4-9-4 **78**........................ FrankieMcDonald 13 87
(H Candy) *mde all: crossed to stands' rail: rdn 2f out: hrd pressed ent fnl f: styd on gamely and holding rivals fnl f* **11/4**[2]
0620 **2** *1 1/2* **Almoutaz (USA)**[66] 4206 3-9-6 **83**........................ MartinDwyer 4 87
(B W Hills) *chsd wnr tl over 1f out: unable qckn ent fnl f: rallied u.p to go 2nd again fnl stride: no pce to chal wnr* **8/1**
5656 **3** *shd* **Always Ready**[26] 5425 3-9-1 **78**........................(v[1]) TedDurcan 1 82
(C E Brittain) *trckd ldrs on stands' rail: chsd wnr and rdn over 1f out: ev ch ent fnl f: no ex fnl 100yds: lost 2nd last stride* **9/1**
0405 **4** *1* **Purus (IRE)**[21] 5589 6-9-6 **80**........................ ChrisCatlin 3 82
(R A Teal) *s.i.s: hld up in tch: hdwy over 2f out: chsd ldrs over 1f out: one pce fnl f* **14/1**
2103 **5** *hd* **Credit Swap**[8] 5962 3-9-3 **80**........................ RyanMoore 12 80
(L M Cumani) *s.i.s: bhd and crossed to stands' rail: hdwy over 2f out: drvn over 1f out: no real prog* **5/2**[1]
2010 **6** *1 1/2* **Carlitos Spirit (IRE)**[25] 5470 4-9-7 **81**........................ AlanMunro 6 78
(B R Millman) *hung rt thrght: chsd ldrs: outpcd 2f out: plugged on same pce fnl f* **5/1**[3]
4336 **7** *13* **Cativo Cavallino**[14] 5789 5-8-8 **73**........................ NataliaGemelova(5) 10 35
(J E Long) *towards rr on outer: rdn over 2f out: wknd 2f out: wl btn and eased ins fnl f* **14/1**
1150 **8** *29* **Onceaponatime (IRE)**[27] 5403 3-9-6 **83**........................ JimmyFortune 7 —
(E A L Dunlop) *stdd and dropped in after s: hld up bhd: lost tch over 2f out: virtually p.u ins fnl f: t.o* **16/1**

1m 29.33s (2.03) **Going Correction** +0.375s/f (Good)
WFA 3 from 4yo+ 3lb **8 Ran SP% 112.2**
Speed ratings (Par 105): **103,101,101,100,99 98,83,50**
toteswinger: 1&2 £5.80, 1&3 £7.50, 2&3 £8.90. CSF £23.94 CT £171.79 TOTE £3.10: £1.30, £2.80, £3.40; EX 27.00 Trifecta £78.40 Pool: £421.07 - 3.97 winning units..
Owner The Earl Cadogan **Bred** The Earl Cadogan **Trained** Kingston Warren, Oxon

FOCUS
Not as strong a race as this might have been, with six non-runners, but Rum Jungle was a decent winner. They all raced stands' side and the form appears sound enough.
Carlitos Spirit(IRE) Official explanation: jockey said gelding hung right
Onceaponatime(IRE) Official explanation: jockey said gelding was unsuited by the soft going

6195 RYE H'CAP 1m 4f
4:50 (4:50) (Class 3) (0-95,92) 3-Y-O **£8,100** (£2,425; £1,212; £607) **Stalls** Low

Form RPR
1315 **1** **Any Given Day (IRE)**[32] 5249 3-8-9 **80**........................ RichardMullen 4 87
(D M Simcock) *chsd ldr tl pushed into ld 5f out: rdn 2f out: hld on gamely fnl f* **7/2**[3]
5012 **2** *hd* **Timocracy**[5] 6050 3-8-2 **73** oh1........................ WilliamBuick 3 79
(M Johnston) *led at stdy gallop tl hdd 5f out: chsd wnr after: rdn over 2f out: ev ch fnl f: jst hld* **11/10**[1]
1105 **3** *2 1/2* **Goodwood Starlight (IRE)**[22] 5569 3-9-7 **92**........................ JimmyFortune 5 94
(J L Dunlop) *t.k.h: hld up in 3rd pl: rdn and effrt between horses over 1f out: outpcd ins fnl f: eased whn btn towards fin* **13/2**
3315 **4** *2* **Belotto (IRE)**[18] 5683 3-8-6 **77**........................ HayleyTurner 1 76
(R Charlton) *stdd s: t.k.h: hld up in last pl: rdn and effrt wl over 1f out: no prog ent fnl f* **10/3**[2]

2m 51.42s (10.52) **Going Correction** +0.375s/f (Good) **4 Ran SP% 106.3**
Speed ratings (Par 105): **79,78,77,75**
CSF £7.62 TOTE £5.00; EX 7.50.

Owner Malcolm Martin Partnership **Bred** Ralph And Helen O'Brien **Trained** Newmarket, Suffolk

FOCUS

Only four runners, and they went steady for much of the way, but this was still a good three-year-old handicap. The third sets the standard.

NOTEBOOK

Any Given Day(IRE) ◆ was given a fine ride by Mullen, who made a race-winning move when sending his mount to the front well before the straight. He is very much a stayer in the making, so a sprint finish on such a tight track would not have suited, and his rider did the right thing by putting his stamina to good use. He was being closed down at the finish, but this was a better effort than the bare result suggests and there should be more to come, particularly over further. (op 3-1)

Timocracy ◆, 1lb out of the handicap, enjoyed the run of the race for much of the way, but crucially he lost the lead down the back straight when Any Given Day was sent to the front and he could never peg that rival back. He kept on for pressure in the straight and was closing at the line, but he was unable to regain the lead. This was the longest trip he has tried to date and he is progressing well. (op 5-4 tchd Evens)

Goodwood Starlight(IRE) ruined his chance by refusing to settle pretty much all the way round and would have preferred a stronger pace. (op 5-1)

Belotto(IRE) raced a little keenly in last place and was never involved. She is another who did not have the race run to suit. (op 7-2 tchd 4-1 and 3-1)

6196 GARDEN COAST H'CAP — 1m 1f 149y

5:20 (5:20) (Class 3) (0-90,90) 3-Y-O+

£8,100 (£2,425; £1,212; £607; £302; £152) Stalls Centre

Form / RPR

-310 **1** **Sortita (GER)**[18] 5682 3-9-0 **86** .... MartinDwyer 9 — 95+
(M A Jarvis) *chsd ldr tl led 7f out: mde rest: rdn 2f out: clr ins fnl f: styd on and a holding on* **7/2**[2]

2215 **2** ½ **King Supreme (IRE)**[17] 5699 3-8-6 **78** .... (b) TPO'Shea 1 — 86+
(R Hannon) *hld up in last: rdn over 2f out: hdwy and hung rt over 1f out: r.o to go 2nd wl ins fnl f: nvr quite getting to wnr* **17/2**

0231 **3** 2¼ **Celt**[34] 5182 3-8-11 **83** .... RyanMoore 6 — 86
(L M Cumani) *hld up in last pair: hdwy over 2f out: chsd wnr 2f out: sn drvn: btn jst ins fnl f: lost 2nd wl ins fnl f* **10/11**[1]

2556 **4** 3¾ **E Major**[39] 5047 3-7-13 **76** oh2 .... Louis-PhilippeBeuzelin(5) 12 — 71
(Sir Michael Stoute) *s.i.s: sn chsng ldrs: swtchd lft and rdn 2f out: wknd over 1f out* **16/1**

1145 **5** 12 **Press The Button (GER)**[29] 5349 5-9-3 **83** .... PatCosgrave 2 — 53
(J R Boyle) *led tl 7f out: chsd wnr after tl wl 2f out: sn wknd: eased fnl f* **5/1**[3]

4040 **6** 1¼ **Paveroc**[31] 5279 3-9-0 **86** .... (p) JohnEgan 3 — 54
(Jane Chapple-Hyam) *in tch in midfield: rdn 4f out: rdr dropped whip and wknd 2f out: eased fnl f* **20/1**

2m 6.80s (1.90) **Going Correction** +0.375s/f (Good)
WFA 3 from 4yo+ 6lb — **6** Ran SP% **112.4**
Speed ratings (Par 107): **107,106,104,101,92 91**
toteswinger: 1&2 £3.60, 1&3 £2.00, 2&3 £1.80. CSF £31.37 CT £46.41 TOTE £5.30: £2.10, £2.00; EX 26.70 Trifecta £51.30 Pool: £311.69 - 4.49 winning units. Place 6: £173.85 Place 5: £63.09.

Owner Hamdan Al Maktoum **Bred** Gestut Karlshof **Trained** Newmarket, Suffolk

FOCUS

A decent handicap run at a fair pace with the winner looking progressive.

NOTEBOOK

Sortita(GER) disappointed when a beaten favourite on the Polytrack at Lingfield last time, but she was able to dominate this time, just as when winning her maiden at Doncaster, and that made all the difference. She looked to have gone off plenty quick enough but is clearly at her best when out in front and she stayed on strongly. (tchd 10-3 and 4-1)

King Supreme(IRE), dropped slightly in trip, stayed on well from out the back but never looked like getting to the winner. (op 8-1 tchd 9-1)

Celt finally came good in a weak course-and-distance maiden last time, but the suspicion remains that he is not straightforward and he didn't really see his race out in this stronger company. (op 11-10 tchd 5-4)

E Major never posed a threat and is not progressing. (op 9-1)

Press The Button(GER) ran no sort of race on ground softer than ideal. (op 6-1 tchd 4-1)

Paveroc Official explanation: jockey said colt had no more to give

T/Jkpt: Not won. T/Plt: £461.30 to a £1 stake. Pool: £66,679.64. 105.50 winning tickets. T/Qpdt: £53.00 to a £1 stake. Pool: £4,502.31. 62.80 winning tickets. SP

5929 GOODWOOD (R-H)

Wednesday, September 24

OFFICIAL GOING: Good to firm

Dolling out added around 15yds to advertised distances on the round course.
Wind: Strong, across Weather: Light rain

6197 ELECTROLUX PROFESSIONAL MEDIAN AUCTION MAIDEN STKS (DIV I) — 7f

2:00 (2:02) (Class 5) 2-Y-O

£2,914 (£867; £433; £216) Stalls High

Form / RPR

002 **1** **Appraisal**[13] 5811 2-9-3 **78** .... RichardHughes 8 — 76+
(R Hannon) *led after 1f: mde rest: shkn up to qckn pce over 2f out: r.o wl: readily* **3/1**[2]

0 **2** 2½ **Roman Glory (IRE)**[26] 5468 2-9-3 0 .... LDettori 9 — 70
(B J Meehan) *led for 1f: restrained bhd ldrs: rdn and nt qckn over 2f out: kpt on ins fnl f: wnt 2nd towards fin: nt pce of wnr* **4/5**[1]

46 **3** shd **Importer (IRE)**[45] 4905 2-9-3 0 .... DO'Donohoe 11 — 70
(W R Muir) *t.k.h in tch: hdwy over 2f out: sn rdn to dispute 2nd: kpt on same pce fnl f* **33/1**

53 **4** ½ **Tarzan (IRE)**[31] 5316 2-9-3 0 .... GregFairley 6 — 68+
(M Johnston) *trckd ldrs: edgd lft and rdn 2f out: chsd wnr ent fnl f: hung rt and lost 2nd towards fin* **10/1**

0 **5** shd **Sairaam (IRE)**[46] 4870 2-8-12 0 .... MartinDwyer 3 — 63+
(J L Dunlop) *hld up towards rr: hdwy whn short of room briefly over 2f out: sn rdn: kpt on same pce fnl f* **8/1**[3]

06 **6** 1 **Herschel (IRE)**[13] 5812 2-9-3 0 .... GeorgeBaker 4 — 66
(G L Moore) *hld up and bhd: hdwy over 2f out: sn rdn and edgd rt: kpt on same pce fnl f* **33/1**

7 1¾ **Golden Flight (IRE)** 2-9-3 0 .... RyanMoore 5 — 61+
(J W Hills) *s.i.s: towards rr: sme late prog: nvr a danger* **50/1**

00 **8** 2¼ **Sunshine Ellie**[20] 5643 2-8-12 0 .... AdamKirby 10 — 51
(C G Cox) *mid-div: rdn over 2f out: wknd over 1f out* **80/1**

00 **9** 2½ **Diamond Heist**[117] 2562 2-9-3 0 .... PatDobbs 12 — 49
(M P Tregoning) *s.i.s: towards rr: rdn and sme hdwy over 2f out: wknd over 1f out* **40/1**

0 **10** 1 **Venture Capitalist**[33] 5227 2-9-3 0 .... DaneO'Neill 2 — 47
(L M Cumani) *w wnr after 1f: rdn over 2f out: sn wknd* **25/1**

0 **11** 5 **Dazzel**[24] 5534 2-8-12 0 .... TedDurcan 7 — 29
(D R Lanigan) *a towards rr* **33/1**

12 8 **Trusted Venture (USA)** 2-9-3 0 .... LPKeniry 1 — 14
(J R Best) *in tch: effrt 3f out: wknd 2f out* **66/1**

1m 28.55s (1.15) **Going Correction** 0.0s/f (Good) — **12** Ran SP% **120.6**
Speed ratings (Par 95): **93,90,90,89,89 88,86,83,80,79 73,64**
toteswinger: 1&2 £2.00, 1&3 £16.20, 2&3 £10.80. CSF £5.47 TOTE £4.10: £1.50, £1.20, £6.80; EX 6.40.

Owner The Waney Racing Group Inc **Bred** Messinger Stud Ltd **Trained** East Everleigh, Wilts

FOCUS

No more than a fair juvenile maiden with the decisive winner the best guide.

NOTEBOOK

Appraisal was very much allowed the run of the race at a steady pace. He looks flattered by the manner of this success, as everything went his way, but he has improved with every run so far is progressing into a fair type. (op 9-4 tchd 2-1)

Roman Glory(IRE) was all the rage beforehand having looked unlucky not to finish a lot closer than ninth in a good maiden at Sandown on his debut, but he ran below expectations. He was well enough placed considering the steady pace, but dropped back when hitting a flat spot at the top of the straight and found his stride far too late, only staying on near the line to take a modest second. He would have preferred a stronger-run race, but this was still a disappointing. (op 11-10 tchd 5-4 and 11-8 in places)

Importer(IRE) got warm beforehand and did not help his chance by racing keenly off the steady pace, but he kept on in the straight. He can do better in a stronger-run race and is now qualified for a handicap mark. (tchd 40-1)

Tarzan(IRE) carried his head awkwardly under pressure and gave the impression he might not have been totally comfortable on this track. (op 9-1 tchd 17-2)

Sairaam(IRE) showed ability on her debut over this trip on soft ground at the July course, but she was very easy to back this time. Like so many of these, she did not have the race run to suit and was never competitive. (op 9-1 tchd 10-1)

Herschel(IRE) did not help his chance by continually edging right in the straight and appeared unsuited by the track. He is now qualified for a handicap and can do better on a more conventional course, possibly over further. (op 25-1)

6198 ELECTROLUX PROFESSIONAL MEDIAN AUCTION MAIDEN STKS (DIV II) — 7f

2:35 (2:36) (Class 5) 2-Y-O

£2,914 (£867; £433; £216) Stalls High

Form / RPR

50 **1** **Master Fong (IRE)**[53] 4625 2-9-3 0 .... MichaelHills 8 — 81
(B W Hills) *cl up: swtchd lft 2f out: sn rdn and edgd lft: r.o to ld jst ins fnl f: drifted rt: rdn clr* **20/1**

3232 **2** 1½ **Zebrano**[16] 5753 2-9-3 **78** .... AlanMunro 11 — 77
(Miss E C Lavelle) *led: rdn 2f out: hdd jst ins fnl f: no ex* **2/1**[1]

6533 **3** 1 **Admiral Sandhoe (USA)**[26] 5459 2-9-3 **78** .... JimCrowley 5 — 75
(Mrs A J Perrett) *s.i.s: sn mid-div: rdn over 2f out: styd on fnl f: wnt 3rd nr fin* **4/1**[2]

0 **4** ½ **Sworn (USA)**[33] 5240 2-8-12 0 .... ShaneKelly 7 — 68
(J Noseda) *w ldr: rdn and ev ch over 1f out: kpt on same pce* **10/1**

5 ¾ **Midnight In May (IRE)** 2-9-3 0 .... MartinDwyer 4 — 71+
(W R Muir) *s.i.s: sn outpcd and bhd: latched on to rr of gp 4f out: styd on fr over 1f out: nvr nrr* **25/1**

0 **6** shd **Manolito Montoya (IRE)**[26] 5468 2-9-3 0 .... (p) LiamJones 3 — 71
(J W Hills) *t.k.h: hld up: swtchd lft 2f out: sn rdn: styd on ins fnl f: nrst fin* **50/1**

56 **7** 2½ **Ailsa Craig (IRE)**[7] 6013 2-8-12 0 .... RichardHughes 6 — 60
(R Hannon) *trckd ldrs: rdn over 2f out: wknd fnl f* **8/1**

02 **8** 2 **Flute Magic**[95] 3267 2-9-3 0 .... RyanMoore 9 — 60
(W S Kittow) *cl up: rdn for effrt 3f out: wknd over 1f out* **9/2**[3]

30 **9** 1¼ **Spinning Waters**[26] 5468 2-9-3 0 .... StephenCarson 2 — 57
(Eve Johnson Houghton) *mid-div early: bhd fnl 3f* **40/1**

04 **10** 2¼ **Squad**[20] 5649 2-9-3 0 .... TedDurcan 12 — 51
(Pat Eddery) *s.i.s: sn shoved along in mid-div: wknd 1f out* **15/2**

1m 27.88s (0.48) **Going Correction** 0.0s/f (Good) — **10** Ran SP% **116.5**
Speed ratings (Par 95): **97,95,94,93,92 92,89,87,86,83**
toteswinger: 1&2 £5.80, 1&3 £6.30, 2&3 £2.60. CSF £58.66 TOTE £16.70: £2.70, £1.30, £1.80; EX 74.80.

Owner Mrs Barbara James **Bred** Keatly Overseas Ltd **Trained** Lambourn, Berks

FOCUS

Again just a fair two-year-old maiden but the placed horses already have official marks and set the level.

NOTEBOOK

Master Fong(IRE) was making hard work of this for much of the straight, but he finally decided to run on inside the final couple of furlongs and produced a sustained burst, despite being inclined to edge right, to ultimately take this in decisive fashion. He had shown promise first-time up at Lingfield before running down the field in a good maiden here at the Glorious meeting, but his connections were of the opinion that last run might have come too soon, and he has been helped by a near two-month break. Considering the runner-up came into this rated 78 he will probably get a mark in the mid-to-low 80s, which will make things tougher, but there should be more to come when he steps up in trip. The plan now is apparently a 1m nursery. Official explanation: trainer said, regarding apparent improvement in form, that the previous race had come too soon and that the colt had strengthened up since. (op 16-1)

Zebrano set a good, even pace in front and had his chance. He displayed a bit of a knee action, so a return to easier ground should help, and he also gave the impression he is worth a try at 1m. (op 3-1)

Admiral Sandhoe(USA) travelled quite well, but he could only keep on at the one pace and seemed to run slightly below his official mark of 78. (tchd 7-2 and 9-2)

Sworn(USA) was well enough placed if good enough and improved on the form she showed on her debut. She might be more of a three-year-old prospect. (tchd 9-1 and 12-1)

Midnight In May(IRE), a 14,500gns son of Mull Of Kintyre, missed the break and ran green early, but kept on well close home without being given an unnecessarily hard time and can improve significantly next time. (op 40-1)

Manolito Montoya(IRE), with cheekpieces replacing blinkers, also finished well and this was an improvement on the form he showed on his debut at Sandown. (op 66-1)

Ailsa Craig(IRE) did not look the easiest of rides as she was keen early, then swerved right when switched towards the inside after a couple of furlongs. She shaped well on her debut over 6f at this course, but has not progressed since. (op 7-1)

Flute Magic was looked after once it became apparent he was not picking up. (op 4-1 tchd 6-1)

6199 E.B.F. / R. H. HALL MAIDEN STKS 1m 1f
3:10 (3:11) (Class 4) 2-Y-O **£4,695** (£1,397; £698; £348) **Stalls** High

Form RPR
4040 **1** **Heliodor (USA)**[13] 5827 2-9-3 78 RichardHughes 11 79
(R Hannon) *cl up: wnt 2nd over 1f out: swtchd lft ent fnl f: shkn up to ld fnl 100yds: r.o strly: readily* **6/1**[3]
3 **2** *2 1/4* **Headline Act**[12] 5859 2-9-3 0 JimmyFortune 13 75
(J H M Gosden) *s.i.s: sn led: 2l clr 2f out: rdn 1f out: edgd lft and hdd fnl 100yds: sn hld* **4/6**[1]
04 **3** *1/2* **King Of Wands**[13] 5842 2-9-3 0 DaneO'Neill 12 74
(J L Dunlop) *trckd ldrs: rdn to chse wnr over 2f out tl over 1f out: kpt on same pce* **9/2**[2]
0455 **4** *3 3/4* **Supernoverre (IRE)**[26] 5460 2-9-3 71 JimCrowley 10 66
(Mrs A J Perrett) *prom: rdn over 3f out: hung rt over 1f out: kpt on same pce* **12/1**
0 **5** *1/2* **Some Time Good (IRE)**[23] 5578 2-9-3 0 TPO'Shea 6 65+
(M R Channon) *mid-div: rdn over 3f out: hdwy over 2f out: styd on but nvr able to get on terms w ldrs* **50/1**
05 **6** *1 3/4* **Sherman McCoy**[53] 4636 2-9-0 0 JamesMillman(3) 7 62
(B R Millman) *trckd ldrs: rdn over 3f out: one pce fnl 2f* **100/1**
7 *2 3/4* **Lava Steps (USA)** 2-9-3 0 JohnEgan 3 56
(P F I Cole) *hld up towards rr: swtchd lft ent st: sn rdn and hdwy: styd on: nvr trbld ldrs* **25/1**
40 **8** *1* **Money Money Money**[24] 5535 2-8-12 0 LiamJones 1 49
(P Winkworth) *plld hrd: restrained in last: swtchd lft over 2f out: sn rdn: sme late prog: nvr a danger* **50/1**
54 **9** *nse* **Security Joan (IRE)**[19] 5674 2-8-12 0 RyanMoore 4 49
(R Hannon) *sn nudged along towards rr: swtchd lft 3f out: sn rdn: sme late prog: nvr a factor* **25/1**
10 *1* **Ermyn Lodge** 2-9-3 0 IanMongan 5 52
(P M Phelan) *towards rr of mid-div: rdn over 3f out: no imp* **100/1**
05 **11** *3 1/4* **Royal Toerag**[11] 5901 2-9-3 0 PaulDoe 15 45
(W J Knight) *in tch: rdn over 3f out: wkng whn hmpd 2f out* **20/1**
0 **12** *1 1/4* **Doran's Lodge (IRE)**[19] 5678 2-9-3 0 SamHitchcott 8 43
(M R Channon) *mid-div: rdn over 3f out: wknd 2f out* **100/1**
13 *1/2* **Ritano (IRE)** 2-8-12 0 DavidProbert(5) 2 42
(B I Case) *a towards rr* **100/1**
50 **14** *3 1/4* **Mr Deal**[26] 5469 2-9-3 0 StephenCarson 9 35
(Eve Johnson Houghton) *mid-div tl wknd 2f out* **100/1**
15 *22* **Six Of Clubs** 2-8-12 0 JackDean(5) 16 —
(W G M Turner) *s.i.s: a towards rr* **100/1**

1m 57.42s (1.12) **Going Correction** 0.0s/f (Good) **15** Ran SP% **122.5**
Speed ratings (Par 97): **95,93,92,89,88 87,84,83,83,82 80,78,78,75,56**
toteswinger: 1&2 £2.90, 1&3 £3.60, 2&3 £2.10. CSF £9.91 TOTE £7.50: £2.10, £1.10, £1.80; EX 13.10.
Owner Mrs J Wood **Bred** Kim Nardelli Et Al **Trained** East Everleigh, Wilts

FOCUS
Just an ordinary maiden with the winner repeating recent course form.

NOTEBOOK
Heliodor(USA), having his ninth start, looked vulnerable to some lightly raced rivals beforehand, but he was actually unexposed over this sort trip and had run well on his only previous try beyond 6f when fourth in a course nursery over 1m two starts back. His stamina was put to the test, but he travelled well throughout and stayed on best in the straight. He could find a nursery over this trip or 1m2f if kept on the go this season. (op 5-1 tchd 13-2)
Headline Act, a promising third on his debut over 1m on soft ground at Doncaster, looked all over the winner when noticeably quickening from the front halfway up the straight, but he didn't draw away as expected after that slight burst of acceleration and was picked off late on. He seemed to handle the quicker ground, and his pedigree is all stamina, so the trip should have suited, but he did look to go off plenty quick enough. He also got warm beforehand. (tchd 8-13, 5-6 in places, 4-5 in places and 8-11 in places)
King Of Wands had offered encouragement on his first two starts and this was another respectable effort. He should come into his own over 1m4f plus next year, probably on a more galloping track when there is some give underfoot. (op 7-1)
Supernoverre(IRE) chased the strong pace and was outstayed in the straight after hanging right. A flatter track, as well as both a shorter trip and easier ground should suit better. (op 14-1)
Some Time Good(IRE) could not muster the pace to get seriously involved and is still learning. (op 33-1)
Money Money Money Official explanation: jockey said filly ran too free and stumbled

6200 3663 FIRST FOR FOODSERVICE STKS (H'CAP) 6f
3:45 (3:46) (Class 4) (0-80,81) 3-Y-O+ **£4,857** (£1,445; £722; £360) **Stalls** Low

Form RPR
3220 **1** **Peter Island (FR)**[27] 5424 5-9-1 75 (v) ChrisCatlin 9 84
(J Gallagher) *slt advantage tl narrowly hdd 3f out: styd pressing ldr and sn hrd drvn: led again fnl 50yds: styd on strly* **10/1**[3]
3221 **2** *1/2* **King's Wonder**[7] 6020 3-9-5 81 6ex MartinDwyer 8 88
(W R Muir) *bmpd s: pressed ldrs tl slt advantage 3f out: rdn 2f out: hdd and no ex fnl 50yds* **10/3**[1]
2203 **3** *nk* **Memphis Man**[8] 5991 5-8-8 73 RichardEvans(5) 14 79
(P D Evans) *in tch: rdn and hdwy 3f out: pressed ldrs fr 2f out: styd on ins fnl f but nt pce of ldng duo nr fin* **14/1**
4100 **4** *2* **Mandarin Spirit (IRE)**[4] 6125 8-8-6 71 (b) WilliamCarson(5) 10 71
(G C H Chung) *sn in tch: rdn: hdwy and swtchd rt 2f out: styd on ins fnl f but nvr gng pce to be competitive* **11/1**
0230 **5** *2* **Don Pele (IRE)**[4] 6131 6-8-10 73 (b) KevinGhunowa(3) 16 67
(R A Harris) *pressed ldrs: rdn over 2f out: wknd ins fnl f* **10/1**[3]
1000 **6** *3/4* **Lunces Lad (IRE)**[39] 5101 4-9-1 75 DarryllHolland 19 66
(M R Channon) *sn pressing for ld: rdn 1/2-way: wknd 1f out* **16/1**
0000 **7** *1/2* **Dazed And Amazed**[33] 5233 4-8-12 72 RichardHughes 5 62
(R Hannon) *bmpd s: towards rr: rdn and sme prog fr 2f out: nvr gng pce to be competitive* **14/1**
000- **8** *shd* **Avening**[364] 5722 8-8-3 66 oh7 LukeMorris(3) 15 55
(Eve Johnson Houghton) *towards rr: rdn over 2f out and sme prog fr over 1f out but nvr gng pce to be competitive* **33/1**
0530 **9** *nk* **Fleuret**[95] 3272 4-9-6 80 RichardKingscote 1 68
(M D Squance) *reluctant to post: in rr: stl plenty to do 2f out: styd on fnl f but nt trble ldrs* **20/1**
1106 **10** *shd* **Stand In Flames**[13] 5841 3-9-3 79 LDettori 11 67
(Pat Eddery) *broke wl: stdd in tch: sme prog fr over 1f out: nvr in contention* **14/1**
2020 **11** *1 1/2* **North South Divide (IRE)**[20] 5648 4-9-1 75 (p) DaneO'Neill 12 58
(R A Teal) *w ldrs: ev ch 2f out: wknd qckly 1f out* **17/2**[2]
1121 **12** *3 1/4* **Patavium Prince (IRE)**[39] 5091 5-9-0 74 TravisBlock 17 47
(Miss Jo Crowley) *pressed ldrs to 2f out: wknd over 1f out* **11/1**
0005 **13** *1 1/2* **Tudor Prince (IRE)**[16] 5751 4-8-4 69 (v[1]) MCGeran(5) 18 37
(A W Carroll) *in tch to 1/2-way: sn rdn and outpcd* **14/1**
0022 **14** *3 1/2* **Charles Darwin (IRE)**[8] 5991 5-9-5 79 LPKeniry 3 36
(M Blanshard) *bmpd s: sn in tch: wknd 2f out* **12/1**
2310 **15** *5* **Even Bolder**[8] 6006 5-9-6 80 StephenCarson 2 21
(E A Wheeler) *spd 3f* **12/1**

1m 10.85s (-1.35) **Going Correction** -0.10s/f (Good)
WFA 3 from 4yo+ 2lb **15** Ran SP% **124.1**
Speed ratings (Par 105): **105,104,103,101,98 97,96,96,96,96 94,89,87,83,76**
toteswinger: 1&2 £9.20, 1&3 £17.50, 2&3 £12.20. CSF £44.07 CT £489.82 TOTE £14.50: £3.70, £1.80, £4.50; EX 57.20.
Owner C R Marks (banbury) **Bred** E A R L Elevage De La Source **Trained** Moreton-in-Marsh, Gloucs

FOCUS
A fair handicap in which the field split into two groups with some up the stands' side and the remainder in the centre. The third was close to his recent best.
North South Divide(IRE) Official explanation: jockey said gelding lost a shoe
Even Bolder Official explanation: trainer said gelding was unsuited by the good to firm ground

6201 FOUNDATION STKS (LISTED RACE) 1m 1f 192y
4:20 (4:20) (Class 1) 3-Y-O+
£15,658 (£15,658; £4,308; £2,148; £1,076; £540) **Stalls** High

Form RPR
3630 **1** **Hearthstead Maison (IRE)**[18] 5743 4-9-0 114 RyanMoore 5 117
(M Johnston) *disp 2nd chsng clr ldr: rdn 2f out: clsd on ldr over 1f out: fin strly: jnd ldr on line* **9/1**
2125 **1** *dht* **Tranquil Tiger**[54] 4585 4-9-0 114 (b) TPQueally 2 117
(H R A Cecil) *led and sn clr: 11 l ahd over 4f out: rdn over 1f out: 3l clr ent fnl f: jnd on line* **6/1**
2114 **3** *7* **Many Volumes (USA)**[18] 5694 4-9-0 112 TedDurcan 4 103
(H R A Cecil) *disp 2nd chsng clr ldr: rdn 3f out: one pce fnl 2f* **9/4**[1]
3026 **4** *1 1/4* **Pinpoint (IRE)**[25] 5508 6-9-0 108 AdamKirby 6 101
(W R Swinburn) *disp 4th: rdn 3f out: one pce fnl 2f* **5/1**[3]
162- **5** *1/2* **Purple Moon (IRE)**[323] 6712 5-9-0 0 JamieSpencer 3 100
(L M Cumani) *disp 4th: rdn and sltly outpcd 3f out: styd on ins fnl f* **13/2**
3115 **6** *9* **Meydan City (USA)**[32] 5263 3-8-8 103 LDettori 7 82+
(Saeed Bin Suroor) *hld up in last pair: rdn 3f out: sn btn* **9/2**[2]
2010 **7** *28* **Mr Aviator (USA)**[57] 4504 4-9-0 107 RichardHughes 1 26+
(R Hannon) *hld up last: rdn 3f out: wknd 2f out: eased fnl f* **11/1**

2m 5.19s (-2.81) **Going Correction** 0.0s/f (Good)
WFA 3 from 4yo+ 6lb **7** Ran SP% **111.6**
Speed ratings (Par 111): **111,111,105,104,104 96,74**
WIN: Hearthstead Maison £5.40, Tranquil Tiger £4.10. PL: HM £4.40, TT £2.90. EX: HM/TT £21.00, TT/HM £25.00. CSF: HM/TT £28.89, TT/HM £26.91. TRIFECTA toteswinger: HM/TT £8.80, HM/MV £4.70, TT/MV/ £2.90..
Owner Hearthstead Homes Ltd **Bred** Tetsu Nakata **Trained** Middleham Moor, N Yorks
Owner K Abdulla **Bred** Juddmonte Farms Ltd **Trained** Newmarket, Suffolk

FOCUS
A good Listed race on paper and the time was decent with the first two setting the level.

NOTEBOOK
Hearthstead Maison(IRE) returned to his best after running no sort of race on sand in Turkey last time. This was a decent effort as none of the others was able to get anywhere near Tranquil Tiger. (tchd 11-1)
Tranquil Tiger often goes off in front, but he was dropping back to his shortest trip since June 2007, so Queally was obviously particularly keen to make it a decent test, and he did a fine job. Having travelled well out in front, he understandably got tired when coming under pressure in the straight, and his stride shortened noticeably in the last furlong, but he just hung on to gain a much-deserved share of the spoils. This was his fourth Listed-race success, and his third of the season. (tchd 11-1)
Many Volumes(USA) probably failed to see out 1m4f in the September Stakes on his previous start, so this drop in trip was in his favour, but he could not land a telling blow and was not quite at his best. Although the ground was quick, his connections felt it was a little loose on top, which didn't suit. (tchd 2-1 and 5-2 in places)
Pinpoint(IRE) was never quite getting there, but he kept on and this was a decent effort in defeat. (op 6-1)
Purple Moon(IRE) was given a long break after last season's second in the Melbourne Cup, then suffered a small injury in June, so this was a belated return and he was expected to need it. The trip was too short for him as well, but he offered plenty of encouragement as he was keeping on nicely in the closing stages after getting outpaced and he should come on for this. Australia is off the agenda this year, but connections are looking at a Group 1 in Milan, before considering options in Hong Kong and Dubai. (tchd 15-2)
Meydan City(USA) was dropped in trip after running like a non-stayer in the rescheduled Great Voltigeur here last time, but he ran no sort of race and has something to prove now. Perhaps he might appreciate a return to easier ground. (tchd 5-1 in places)
Mr Aviator(USA) ran as though something was amiss. (op 10-1)

6202 COORS BREWERS CELEBRATING JOHN SPIERS RETIREMENT STKS (H'CAP) 1m 3f
4:55 (4:55) (Class 4) (0-85,85) 3-Y-O **£4,857** (£1,445; £722; £360) **Stalls** Low

Form RPR
0333 **1** **Greylami (IRE)**[16] 5759 3-9-0 81 MichaelHills 3 92+
(T G Mills) *hld up: hdwy and nt clr run over 2f out: stl travelling wl whn swtchd rt and nt clr run over 1f out: qcknd up wl whn gap appeared: led ent fnl f: styd on strly* **5/1**[3]
3031 **2** *1 1/4* **Red Merlin (IRE)**[13] 5814 3-8-4 71 (v) RichardMullen 11 78
(C G Cox) *t.k.h in midfield: hdwy and nt clr run briefly over 2f out: sn rdn: styd on wl fnl f: wnt 2nd nr fin* **11/1**
-600 **3** *nk* **Safari Sunup (IRE)**[23] 5573 3-9-4 85 StephenCarson 10 91
(P Winkworth) *disp ld: rdn into def advantage over 1f out: hdd ent fnl f: no ex: lost 2nd nr fin* **20/1**
2066 **4** *4 1/2* **Celtic Dragon**[10] 5938 3-8-9 76 JimCrowley 4 75
(Mrs A J Perrett) *in tch: rdn over 2f out: no imp tl styd on fnl f* **16/1**
0242 **5** *3/4* **Tomintoul Flyer**[7] 6012 3-9-1 82 (v) TPQueally 7 80
(H R A Cecil) *racd freely: disp ld tl rdn wl over 1f out: fdd fnl f* **7/2**[2]
5441 **6** *1* **Isle Of Capri**[58] 4485 3-8-7 74 ow1 RyanMoore 6 70
(R Hannon) *s.i.s: sn mid-div: rdn over 2f out: sn one pce* **7/1**
0121 **7** *3/4* **Thumbs Up**[10] 5935 3-9-0 81 6ex JamieSpencer 2 76
(L M Cumani) *trckd ldrs: rdn wl over 2f out: sn one pce* **11/4**[1]
0044 **8** *nk* **Hawaana (IRE)**[12] 5863 3-8-4 74 LukeMorris(3) 5 68
(Eve Johnson Houghton) *hld up in rr: rdn over 2f out: no imp* **14/1**
2014 **9** *1/2* **Latin Scholar (IRE)**[38] 5118 3-8-9 76 TravisBlock 8 69
(A King) *t.k.h trcking ldrs: rdn over 2f out: wknd fnl f* **20/1**

1035 **10** *26* **Never Ending Tale**[26] 5449 3-9-1 **82** .... AlanMunro 1 31
(W Jarvis) *towards rr on outer: nudged along over 5f out: wknd over 2f out: sn eased* **10/1**

2m 26.09s (-2.21) **Going Correction** 0.0s/f (Good) **10** Ran SP% **117.6**
Speed ratings (Par 103): **108,107,106,103,103 102,101,101,101,82**
toteswinger: 1&2 £10.20, 1&3 £28.40, 2&3 £34.50. CSF £59.28 CT £998.81 TOTE £8.00: £2.00, £3.00, £6.30; EX 69.00.
Owner J Daniels **Bred** Barouche Stud Ireland Ltd **Trained** Headley, Surrey

FOCUS
A good, competitive three-year-old handicap run at a good pace in which the runner-up recorded a slight personal best and is the guide to the form.

6203 MERBURY CATERING CONSULTANTS STKS (H'CAP) 1m 4f
5:30 (5:30) (Class 4) (0-80,80) 3-Y-O+ **£4,857** (£1,445; £722; £360) **Stalls** Low

Form RPR
1466 **1** **Shimoni**[11] 5900 4-9-6 **74** ....(v) GeorgeBaker 6 87
(G L Moore) *hld up: hdwy over 3f out: sn rdn: edgd lft over 1f out: led ent fnl f: drew clr: readily* **8/1**
3433 **2** *5* **Penang Cinta**[38] 5118 5-8-12 **66** ....(p) StephenDonohoe 12 71
(P D Evans) *chsd ldrs: rdn over 2f out: ev ch ent fnl f: kpt on but sn hld by wnr* **12/1**
6234 **3** *½* **Spirit Of Adjisa (IRE)**[15] 5773 4-9-8 **76** ....(b) ShaneKelly 11 80
(Pat Eddery) *led: sn 10l clr: rdn over 2f out: hung rt and hdd ent fnl f: no ex* **11/1**
642 **4** *1* **Roodolph**[7] 6028 4-9-5 **73** .... StephenCarson 10 76
(Eve Johnson Houghton) *chsd ldrs tl outpcd 3f out: styd on again fnl f* **9/1**
3514 **5** *2 ¼* **Adorabella (IRE)**[26] 5476 5-9-2 **70** .... TravisBlock 2 69
(A King) *hld up: rdn and hdwy fr 3f out: no further imp ins fnl f* **10/1**
5115 **6** *2 ¼* **Constant Cheers (IRE)**[70] 4078 5-9-5 **78** .... DavidProbert(5) 9 73
(W R Swinburn) *mid-div: rdn 3f out: kpt on same pce fnl 2f* **11/2**[2]
5002 **7** *1 ½* **Mustajed**[11] 5913 7-9-4 **75** ....(b) JamesMillman(3) 5 68
(B R Millman) *chsd clr ldr: rdn 3f out: fdd fnl f* **14/1**
0060 **8** *1 ¼* **William's Way**[11] 5900 6-9-9 **77** .... TedDurcan 7 68
(I A Wood) *s.i.s: a towards rr* **14/1**
3341 **9** *2 ¼* **Moville (IRE)**[22] 5587 3-9-4 **80** .... MichaelHills 3 67
(B W Hills) *mid-div tl lost pl on outer over 5f out: rdn 3f out: sn hung lft and nvr able to get bk on terms* **7/1**[3]
0/0- **10** *1 ¾* **Hills Of Aran**[194] 4576 6-8-12 **66** oh6 .... KirstyMilczarek 8 51
(W K Goldsworthy) *s.i.s: a towards rr* **11/1**
3224 **11** *24* **Riverscape (IRE)**[42] 4985 3-9-0 **76** .... JimCrowley 4 22
(Mrs A J Perrett) *chsd clr ldr tl rdn over 3f out: sn btn: eased fnl 2f* **7/2**[1]
0010 **12** *9* **Snowed Under**[30] 5370 7-9-12 **80** .... DarrylHolland 1 12
(J D Bethell) *chsd clr ldr tl over 3f out: eased whn btn fnl 2f* **20/1**

2m 36.97s (-1.43) **Going Correction** 0.0s/f (Good)
WFA 3 from 4yo+ 8lb **12** Ran SP% **122.8**
Speed ratings (Par 105): **104,100,100,99,98 96,95,94,93,92 76,70**
toteswinger: 1&2 £26.60, 1&3 £23.50, 2&3 £16.30. CSF £103.97 CT £1075.78 TOTE £10.20: £2.60, £4.00, £4.00; EX 132.50.
Owner The Welldiggers Partnership **Bred** Lakin Bloodstock And H And W Thornton **Trained** Woodingdean, E Sussex

FOCUS
A fair handicap and the form is solid rated around the placed horses.
Moville(IRE) Official explanation: jockey said gelding hung left
Riverscape(IRE) Official explanation: trainer had no explanation for the poor form shown
Snowed Under Official explanation: jockey said gelding lost a shoe

6204 MERBURY 18TH ANNIVERSARY APPRENTICE STKS (H'CAP) 5f
6:00 (6:01) (Class 5) (0-70,68) 3-Y-O+ **£3,238** (£963; £481; £240) **Stalls** Low

Form RPR
130 **1** **Enodoc**[4] 6131 3-9-2 **68** ....(t) DavidProbert(3) 15 76
(W R Muir) *trckd ldrs: chal ins fnl 2f: led over 1f out: pushed out ins fnl f: readily* **8/1**
-000 **2** *½* **Calabaza**[47] 4809 6-8-7 **55** .... TolleyDean 14 62
(M J Attwater) *chsd ldrs: rdn over 2f out: kpt on to chse wnr ins fnl f but a hld* **16/1**
5462 **3** *nk* **Back In The Red (IRE)**[7] 6024 4-9-1 **63** .... TravisBlock 11 69
(R A Harris) *chsd ldrs: drvn along fr 1/2-way: styd on ins fnl f but nvr gng pce to chal* **4/1**[1]
30 **4** *½* **Sofinella (IRE)**[82] 3695 5-8-8 **56** .... LukeMorris 16 60
(A W Carroll) *slt advantage: rdn over 2f out: hdd over 1f out: kpt on same pce u.p ins fnl f* **16/1**
343 **5** *½* **Compton Rose**[11] 5902 3-8-13 **67** .... AmyScott(5) 9 69
(H Candy) *towards rr and pushed along 3f out: hdwy over 1f out: kpt on ins fnl f but nvr gng pce to be competitive* **5/1**[2]
1405 **6** *¾* **Arfinnit (IRE)**[21] 5610 7-8-3 **54** oh2 ....(v) MCGeran(3) 12 53
(Mrs A L M King) *chsd ldrs: rdn 1/2-way: one pce ins fnl f* **14/1**
0500 **7** *½* **Diademas (USA)**[8] 6004 3-7-12 **54** oh2 ....(p) RichardRowe(7) 10 52
(M J Gingell) *sn pushed along in rr: hdwy over 1f out: styd on fnl f but nvr any danger* **40/1**
3436 **8** *nse* **Night Prospector**[7] 6024 8-8-8 **61** ....(p) RichardEvans(5) 8 58
(R A Harris) *trckd ldrs: pushed along 2f out: no further prog* **15/2**[3]
1044 **9** *1 ½* **Mr Funshine**[22] 5592 3-8-8 **57** .... JackMitchell 6 49
(Mrs P N Dutfield) *chsd ldrs: rdn 3f out: wknd fnl f* **22/1**
041 **10** *hd* **Blessed Place**[12] 5861 8-9-1 **68** .... BillyCray(5) 5 59
(D J S Ffrench Davis) *pressed ldr and sn rdn: wknd over 1f out* **15/2**[3]
00/ **11** *1 ¾* **Great Fox (IRE)**[747] 5148 7-8-9 **62** .... WilliamCarson(5) 7 47
(S C Williams) *towards rr: pushed along 1/2-way and nvr gng pce to be competitive* **12/1**
0045 **12** *nse* **Seven Royals (IRE)**[67] 4194 3-8-10 **64** .... JemmaMarshall(5) 4 49
(Miss A M Newton-Smith) *outpcd most of way* **20/1**
3000 **13** *nk* **Fabuleux Cherie**[4] 6131 3-8-13 **62** .... MarcHalford 1 46
(W R Muir) *a outpcd* **20/1**
5560 **14** *¾* **Dancing Mystery**[69] 4107 14-8-1 **54** oh3 ....(b) SophieDoyle(5) 3 35
(E A Wheeler) *sn outpcd* **25/1**
6005 **15** *9* **Wavertree Princess (IRE)**[24] 5531 3-9-2 **65** .... KirstyMilczarek 13 14
(N P Littmoden) *v.s.a and a trailing* **11/1**

58.43 secs (0.03) **Going Correction** -0.10s/f (Good)
WFA 3 from 4yo+ 1lb **15** Ran SP% **125.9**
Speed ratings (Par 103): **95,94,93,92,92 90,90,90,87,87 84,84,83,82,68**
toteswinger: 1&2 £38.50, 1&3 £7.80, 2&3 £20.40. CSF £124.44 CT £601.75 TOTE £8.90: £3.30, £4.90, £1.90; EX 181.30 Place 6 £129.70, Place 5 £106.17.
Owner Mrs D Edginton **Bred** Fonthill Stud **Trained** Lambourn, Berks

FOCUS
A modest but competitive sprint handicap restricted to apprentices. The form seems sound enough with the third to his recent best.
Enodoc Official explanation: trainer said, regarding apparent improvement in form, that the tongue strap was reapplied.
Fabuleux Cherie Official explanation: jockey said filly reared up in stalls
T/Plt: £153.90 to a £1 stake. Pool: £64,766.40. 307.19 winning tickets. T/Qpdt: £86.00 to stake. Pool: £3,525.40. 30.30 winning tickets. TM

6165 KEMPTON (A.W) (R-H)
Wednesday, September 24

OFFICIAL GOING: Standard
Wind: Modest, across Weather: Dry

6205 KEMPTON.CO.UK MEDIAN AUCTION MAIDEN FILLIES' STKS 1m (P)
6:20 (6:25) (Class 6) 2-Y-O **£2,047** (£604; £302) **Stalls** High

Form RPR
20 **1** **Latin Tinge (USA)**[13] 5828 2-9-0 0 .... ChrisCatlin 5 84+
(P F I Cole) *hld up in midfield: plld out and hdwy over 1f out: qcknd to ld 1f out: sn clr: v easily* **10/11**[1]
6 **2** *4 ½* **Attainable**[16] 5753 2-9-0 0 .... MartinDwyer 9 68
(Mrs A J Perrett) *s.i.s: sn pressing ldr: rdn over 2f out: chsd wnr vainly fnl f but kpt on to hold 2nd* **20/1**
02 **3** *½* **Timpanist**[13] 5812 2-9-0 0 .... PatCosgrave 3 67
(P W Chapple-Hyam) *chsd ldng pair: rdn over 2f out: disp 2nd fnl f: kpt on: no ch w wnr* **11/1**
0 **4** *4* **Heart Of Tuscany**[20] 5643 2-9-0 0 .... PaulDoe 11 58
(W J Knight) *t.k.h: prom: stdd to trck ldrs after 2f: rdn and effrt over 2f out: wknd ent fnl f* **16/1**
5 *½* **Hometown** 2-9-0 0 .... JimmyFortune 13 57
(J H M Gosden) *sn led: rdn over 2f out: hdd 1f out: sn wknd* **10/3**[2]
02 **6** *3* **Chalk Hill Blue**[30] 5364 2-9-0 0 .... WilliamBuick 12 51
(Eve Johnson Houghton) *in tch: rdn and effrt on inner jst over 2f out: wknd over 1f out* **10/1**[3]
7 *½* **Salybia Bay** 2-9-0 0 .... RichardHughes 10 49
(R Hannon) *hld up in midfield: pushed along wl over 3f out: chsd ldrs and rdn over 2f out: wknd qckly over 1f out* **25/1**
8 *1 ¾* **Midsummer Madness (IRE)** 2-9-0 0 .... DaneO'Neill 4 46
(David Pinder) *s.i.s: bhd: nvr trbld ldrs* **66/1**
0 **9** *¾* **Ma Patrice**[23] 5578 2-9-0 0 .... RobertHavlin 8 44
(T D McCarthy) *t.k.h: hld up in tch in midfield: rdn over 3f out: wknd wl over 2f out* **100/1**
10 *hd* **Flowerwood (IRE)** 2-8-9 0 .... NicolPolli(5) 1 43
(M G Quinlan) *hld up towards rr: rdn and struggling 3f out: n.d* **100/1**
0 **11** *nk* **Ravine Rose**[47] 4823 2-9-0 0 ....(t) JamesDoyle 14 43
(B I Case) *s.i.s: bhd: effrt u.p on inner over 2f out: nvr trbld ldrs* **100/1**
12 *nk* **Seeking Faith (USA)** 2-9-0 0 .... AdamKirby 6 42
(C G Cox) *a bhd: rdn wl over 3f out: nvr a factor* **16/1**
0 **13** *12* **Miss Jodarah (USA)**[35] 5184 2-9-0 0 .... LPKeniry 2 16
(J R Best) *broke wl and prom briefly: bhd fr 1/2-way: t.o* **100/1**
14 *9* **Kaijai (IRE)** 2-9-0 0 .... JerryO'Dwyer 7 —
(Mrs L C Jewell) *s.i.s: sn toiling in last: t.o* **150/1**

1m 39.93s (0.13) **Going Correction** -0.10s/f (Stan) **14** Ran SP% **119.4**
Speed ratings (Par 90): **95,90,90,86,85 82,82,80,79,79 79,78,66,57**
toteswinger: 1&2 £5.30, 1&3 £4.30, 2&3 £25.60. CSF £28.02 TOTE £1.70: £1.20, £4.60, £2.80; EX 26.10.
Owner Frank Stella **Bred** Delahanty Stock Farm **Trained** Whatcombe, Oxon

FOCUS
A fair maiden but hard form to pin down behind the easy winner.

NOTEBOOK
Latin Tinge(USA) ran with plenty of promise on her debut in a Newbury maiden, and although last of seven in the May Hill Stakes last time, she still looked the one to beat back down to this grade. She had been keen in her previous two starts so was ridden more patiently this time, and that helped her as she settled matters quickly once switched to challenge in the straight. A middle-distance filly for next year, she looks a useful prospect, and it would not be a surprise if connections were keen to have another crack at a Pattern race before the season is out. (op 11-10 tchd 6-5 in places)
Attainable, well beaten in soft ground on her debut, found this surface far more to her liking and, with that initial experience under her belt, posted an improved effort, really keeping the third at bay in the final stages. There is plenty of stamina in her pedigree and she has the makings of nice middle-distance handicapper next season. (op 25-1)
Timpanist, who finished a long way behind Latin Tinge on her debut but improved to finish second at Brighton next time, got a bit closer to her old rival on this third outing, but handicaps should see her in a better light. (op 10-1)
Heart Of Tuscany, who made her debut in a decent Salisbury maiden, was never far off the pace and kept on.
Hometown was well drawn and made full use of that advantage, but she lacked the pace of the first three in the closing stages. She is by Storming Home and is a half-sister to Nadia, who won the 1m2f Group 1 Prix Saint-Alary, and therefore bred to come into her own over further next season. (op 5-2 tchd 7-2)
Chalk Hill Blue did not look to have many excuses, but she is another now eligible for handicaps, and may find things easier in that sphere. (op 9-1)

6206 DAY TIME, NIGHT TIME, GREAT TIME MEDIAN AUCTION MAIDEN STKS 1m (P)
6:50 (6:57) (Class 6) 3-5-Y-O **£2,047** (£604; £302) **Stalls** High

Form RPR
-322 **1** **Mille Feuille (IRE)**[40] 5049 3-8-12 **71** .... RyanMoore 6 68
(R M Beckett) *chsd ldr: led over 2f out: clr over 1f out: r.o wl* **1/1**[1]
323 **2** *2 ½* **Mazaris (IRE)**[15] 5790 3-9-3 **72** .... DaneO'Neill 8 67
(L M Cumani) *hld up in tch: hdwy over 2f out: chsd wnr 2f out: r.o but no imp on wnr after* **5/2**[2]
000 **3** *7* **Frosty's Gift**[97] 3177 4-9-2 **45** .... LPKeniry 10 46
(J C Fox) *chsd ldrs on inner: rdn over 2f out: wl outpcd by ldng pair wl over 1f out: hld on for 3rd* **50/1**
0 **4** *hd* **Otis May (IRE)**[25] 5491 4-9-7 0 .... VinceSlattery 9 51
(A W Carroll) *bhd: hdwy over 2f out: swtchd rt over 1f out: kpt on and nrly snatched 3rd: nvr trbld ldrs* **66/1**
0- **5** *½* **First In Show**[327] 6617 3-8-12 0 .... WilliamBuick 4 45+
(A M Balding) *towards rr: pushed along 1/2-way: rdn and sme hdwy jst over 2f out: kpt on but nvr trbld ldrs* **14/1**
6 *2 ¼* **Captain Sirus (FR)**[158] 761 5-9-7 0 ....(t) AdamKirby 7 44
(P Butler) *bhd: rdn and lost tch 3f out: no ch after: modest late hdwy* **100/1**
06 **7** *nk* **One Oi**[88] 3484 3-9-3 0 .... SimonWhitworth 2 44
(D W P Arbuthnot) *hld up bhd: c wd bnd 3f out: sn outpcd: and no ch after* **18/1**

24 **8** *4 1/2* **Miss Carlotta**[46] 4860 3-8-12 0.. MartinDwyer 5 28
(M P Tregoning) *chsd ldrs: hung lft bnd 3f out: rdn over 2f out: sn btn* **5/1**[3]

-500 **9** *8* **Teadancer (IRE)**[96] 3206 3-8-12 50................................ JamesDoyle 11 10
(J G Portman) *led tl over 2f out: wknd qckly 2f out: eased ins fnl f* **40/1**

0660 **10** *7* **Illusionary**[47] 4807 3-9-3 37..(b[1]) PatCosgrave 1 —
(J G Portman) *rel to r and rdn along early: hdwy into midfield 5f out: drvn and wknd over 3f out: hung rt and wl bhd over 2f out: t.o and eased fnl f* **66/1**

1m 39.48s (-0.32) **Going Correction** -0.10s/f (Stan)
WFA 3 from 4yo+ 4lb **10** Ran SP% **115.5**
Speed ratings (Par 101): **97,94,87,87,86 84,84,79,71,64**
toteswinger: 1&2 £1.60, 1&3 £16.10, 2&3 £20.20. CSF £3.45 TOTE £2.10: £1.10, £1.30, £13.00; EX 4.30.
Owner P K Gardner **Bred** Lisieux Stud **Trained** Whitsbury, Hants

FOCUS
A pretty uncompetitive contest, and the winning time was slightly slower than that of the earlier two-year-old maiden. The time was moderate and the form looks shaky.

6207 DIGIBET.COM NURSERY 7f (P)
7:20 (7:24) (Class 6) (0-65,65) 2-Y-O **£2,047** (£604; £302) **Stalls** High

Form RPR

3352 **1** **Aladdin's Lamp (IRE)**[9] 5960 2-9-3 **62**........................ RoystonFfrench 6 69
(M Johnston) *chsd ldr: clr w ldr 2f out: led over 1f out: clr fnl f: rdn out* **15/8**[1]

315 **2** *4* **Hip Hip Hooray**[33] 5228 2-9-5 **64**.............................. CatherineGannon 1 61
(L A Dace) *dropped in after s: bhd: swtchd lft and hdwy over 2f out: edgd rt fr over 1f out: chsd ldng pair 1f out: r.o to snatch 2nd on post: nvr nr wnr* **14/1**

4066 **3** *nse* **Misty Glade**[10] 5937 2-9-3 **62**...(b) MartinDwyer 2 59
(B J Meehan) *led: rdn and clr w wnr 2f out: hdd over 1f out: no ch w wnr fnl f: lost 2nd on post* **16/1**

0210 **4** *1 1/2* **Sienna Lake (IRE)**[26] 5460 2-9-3 **62**.................................. RyanMoore 3 55
(R Hannon) *hld up bhd: hdwy and edging rt over 2f out: r.o fnl f: nvr rchd ldrs* **15/2**[2]

3663 **5** *shd* **Herring Senior (IRE)**[26] 5473 2-9-5 **64**.............................. ShaneKelly 4 57
(P F I Cole) *chsd ldrs: 3rd and drvn over 2f out: sn nt qckn and btn: lost 3rd 1f out* **10/1**

000 **6** *shd* **Sapphire Rose**[22] 5584 2-9-2 **61**.. JamesDoyle 8 54
(J G Portman) *bhd: sltly hmpd bnd 4f out: hdwy and edging to inner 2f out: r.o fnl f: nvr rchd ldrs* **10/1**

4400 **7** *nk* **Minder**[25] 5511 2-9-6 **65**.. PatCosgrave 7 57
(J G Portman) *v.s.a: detached last and reminders early: hdwy over 2f out: r.o but nvr trbld ldrs* **40/1**

5604 **8** *1 1/2* **Sharav**[7] 6017 2-9-3 **62**...(b[1]) WilliamBuick 9 50
(Eve Johnson Houghton) *s.i.s: rdn over 3f out: c wd 3f out: styd on but n.d* **16/1**

5540 **9** *3 1/4* **Daily Double**[7] 6017 2-9-4 **63**................................... RichardHughes 12 43+
(R Hannon) *t.k.h: chsd ldrs tl hmpd and lost pl 4f out: nvr a threat after* **15/2**[2]

6660 **10** *1/2* **Welcome Applause (IRE)**[15] 5774 2-9-3 **62**............... JerryO'Dwyer 10 41
(M G Quinlan) *in tch: rdn over 3f out: outpcd over 2f out: no ch last 2f* **17/2**[3]

0050 **11** *2* **Spring Quartet**[33] 5213 2-9-3 **62**................................ JimmyFortune 11 36+
(Pat Eddery) *s.i.s: bhd: sltly hmpd bnd 4f out: nvr a factor* **20/1**

064 **12** *1 3/4* **Primo Dilettante**[13] 5812 2-9-3 **62**.. PaulDoe 13 32
(W J Knight) *t.k.h: hld up towards rr: effrt towards inner over 2f out: nvr trbld ldrs* **12/1**

0045 **13** *8* **Call Me Courageous (IRE)**[23] 5581 2-9-6 **65**.................... JohnEgan 5 15
(A B Haynes) *in tch in midfield: v wd bnd 3f out: sn struggling and bhd* **66/1**

0054 **14** *12* **Hatchet Man**[25] 5488 2-9-6 **65**..................................(p) StephenCarson 14 —
(P Winkworth) *chsd ldrs tl hung lft and nt handle bnd 4f out: lost pl over 3f out: t.o fnl f* **40/1**

1m 26.44s (0.44) **Going Correction** -0.10s/f (Stan) **14** Ran SP% **124.3**
Speed ratings (Par 93): **93,88,88,86,86 86,86,84,80,80 77,75,66,52**
toteswinger: 1&2 £7.90, 1&3 £15.10, 2&3 £32.20. CSF £31.21 CT £351.38 TOTE £2.40: £1.70, £5.00, £6.10; EX 30.50.
Owner Sheikh Hamdan Bin Mohammed Al Maktoum **Bred** Keatly Overseas Ltd **Trained** Middleham Moor, N Yorks
■ Stewards' Enquiry : Jerry O'Dwyer one-day ban: used whip with excessive force (Oct 8)

FOCUS
Only two previous winners lined up in this modest nursery, and one of them had only scored in a seller. Apart from the winner this does not look a race to dwell on.

NOTEBOOK
Aladdin's Lamp(IRE), who was always well placed towards the front end, ran out a comfortable winner. He had run well to finish second on his nursery debut at Leicester last time and he got to race off the same mark here, making him look well in at the weights, so he was perfectly entitled to score. There could be better to come from him and 1m should not bother him in time. (op 9-4 tchd 5-2)
Hip Hip Hooray had the worst of the draw and ended up racing very wide into the first turn. She finished well once in line for home but the damage had been done. Better than the bare form suggests, she is open to some improvement at this trip. (op 12-1)
Misty Glade was drawn poorly in stall two, but her rider got her out quickly and by the time they got to the first turn he had secured a position in front and had edged towards the rail. That tactical advantage saw her post an improved effort but she would be no good thing to repeat it. (op 14-1)
Sienna Lake(IRE), who was a beaten favourite on her handicap debut last time, was another burdened with a low draw. Settled towards the rear, she tended to hang right as she ran on in the straight, but did not shape too badly in the circumstances. (op 7-1 tchd 8-1)
Herring Senior(IRE) got himself into a fair position early considering his low draw and seemed to have every chance. (op 9-1)
Sapphire Rose, running in a handicap for the first time, is a half-sister to five winners out of a mare who won at up to 1m4f. She was staying on at the finish and another furlong will not hurt her on this evidence. (op 20-1)
Daily Double had hampered his chances by being slowly away in recent starts. This time he jumped with the field and tried to make use of his high draw, but he was keen and his rider tried to get him to settle in behind Hatchet Man on the rail. That one stumbled on the turn, though, and hampered him, causing him to lose his place. (op 6-1 tchd 11-2)
Hatchet Man Official explanation: jocket said gelding had steering problems

6208 DIGIBET.COM H'CAP 7f (P)
7:50 (7:58) (Class 6) (0-50,50) 3-Y-O+ **£2,047** (£604; £302) **Stalls** High

Form RPR

5002 **1** **Mulberry Lad (IRE)**[14] 5797 6-9-0 **50**................................ JamesDoyle 13 60
(S Curran) *hld up towards rr: plld out wl over 1f out: str run on outer to ld fnl 100yds: hld on: all out* **7/1**

0536 **2** *nse* **Takitwo**[20] 5639 5-9-0 **50**...(b[1]) SimonWhitworth 7 60
(P D Cundell) *in tch: effrt and rdn jst over 2f out: ev ch ins fnl f: jst hld* **9/2**[2]

0203 **3** *1 1/2* **Monda**[11] 5916 6-8-9 **50**.. AmyBaker[(5)] 4 56
(M Hill) *led: rdn 2f out: kpt on wl tl hdd and no ex fnl 100yds* **8/1**

6000 **4** *1 1/4* **Turkish Sultan (IRE)**[16] 5755 5-9-0 **50**.......................(p) DaneO'Neill 12 53
(J M Bradley) *hld up in midfield: hdwy on inner jst over 2f out: r.o to go 4th wl ins fnl f: nvr rchd ldrs* **22/1**

-004 **5** *nk* **Lights Of Vegas**[11] 5916 4-9-0 **50**...................................... RyanMoore 6 52
(S Kirk) *chsd ldng trio: hdwy to chse ldr wl over 1f out: wknd u.p ins fnl f* **4/1**[1]

0-00 **6** *3/4* **Hurricane Coast**[12] 5871 9-9-0 **50**...........................(b) RichardHughes 10 50
(D Flood) *hld up in midfield: rdn and effrt 2f out: plugged on same pce* **16/1**

5020 **7** *1 3/4* **Dancing Duo**[12] 5871 4-9-0 **50**...(v) SaleemGolam 14 45
(D Shaw) *bhd: pushed along over 3f out: hdwy on inner jst over 2f out: kpt on same pce u.p fnl f* **14/1**

065 **8** *1 1/4* **Moverra (IRE)**[14] 5797 4-8-6 **49**.....................................(v) HollyHall[(7)] 1 41
(M J Gingell) *t.k.h: prom tl rdn 2f out: wknd qckly jst over 1f out* **28/1**

0403 **9** *1/2* **Vogarth**[16] 5749 4-8-11 **50**... JamesMillman[(3)] 11 40
(B R Millman) *bhd: effrt on inner and hanging rt over 2f out: n.d* **8/1**

2630 **10** *1/2* **Ugenius**[40] 5045 4-8-13 **49**.. JohnEgan 3 38
(Mrs C A Dunnett) *bolted and overshot s: in tch on outer: rdn over 2f out: wknd 2f out* **14/1**

3630 **11** *3/4* **Autograph Hunter**[47] 4824 4-9-0 **50**...................................... LPKeniry 9 37
(Peter Grayson) *bhd: drvn and effrt over 2f out: no prog* **20/1**

000/ **12** *nk* **Jiggy Spriggy (IRE)**[760] 4806 5-8-12 **48**........................ JerryO'Dwyer 8 34
(H J Collingridge) *squeezed out after s: a bhd: hanging rt fr over 2f out* **40/1**

0422 **13** *1/2* **Ten To The Dozen**[24] 5533 5-9-0 **50**...................................... ChrisCatlin 2 35
(P W Hiatt) *t.k.h: w ldr tl wknd qckly wl over 1f out* **5/1**[3]

1m 25.7s (-0.30) **Going Correction** -0.10s/f (Stan) **13** Ran SP% **123.8**
Speed ratings (Par 101): **97,96,95,93,93 92,90,89,88,88 87,86,86**
toteswinger: 1&2 £8.60, 1&3 £14.20, 2&3 £12.20. CSF £38.21 CT £275.46 TOTE £9.70: £2.50, £2.00, £3.30; EX 46.10.
Owner Grey Fox Racing **Bred** Mountarmstrong Stud **Trained** Hatford, Oxon
■ Stewards' Enquiry : Simon Whitworth two-day ban: used whip with excessive frequency (Oct 8-9)

FOCUS
A moderate but competitive handicap run at a good gallop and the form looks sound rated through the third.

6209 DIGIBET CASINO H'CAP 6f (P)
8:20 (8:28) (Class 6) (0-65,64) 3-Y-O+ **£2,047** (£604; £302) **Stalls** High

Form RPR

4440 **1** **Rondeau (GR)**[21] 5616 3-9-3 **63**... JimCrowley 6 77
(P R Chamings) *chsd ldr: upsides ldr over 2f out: rdn to ld over 1f out: forged ahd fnl 100yds* **12/1**

0001 **2** *1 3/4* **Edie Superstar (USA)**[37] 5141 3-9-4 **64**......................(v) RyanMoore 1 72
(M A Magnusson) *led and sn crossed to rail: rdn and clr w wnr 2f out: hdd over 1f out: ev ch tl no ex fnl 100yads* **14/1**

0224 **3** *1 3/4* **Norcroft**[6] 6046 6-9-5 **63**.. JohnEgan 3 65
(Mrs C A Dunnett) *racd in midfield: rdn over 2f out: kpt on u.p fnl f: wnt 3rd nr fin: nvr pce to trble ldng pair* **4/1**[1]

6254 **4** *nk* **Morse (IRE)**[18] 5709 7-9-0 **58**..(p) ShaneKelly 5 59
(J A Osborne) *chsd ldng air: rdn and unable qckn over 2f out: kpt on same pce: lost 3rd nr fin* **9/2**[2]

0025 **5** *1/2* **Dualagi**[31] 5315 4-9-5 **63**.. GeorgeBaker 8 63
(M R Bosley) *stdd after s: hld up in rr: hdwy and swtchd lft over 1f out: kpt on: nvr trbld ldrs* **5/1**[3]

0300 **6** *1 1/2* **Thabaat**[38] 5121 4-9-1 **59**...(b) DaneO'Neill 12 54
(J M Bradley) *t.k.h: hld up in midfield: rdn 3f out: no prog* **25/1**

3000 **7** *1 1/2* **Corlough Mountain**[26] 5458 4-9-3 **61**........................(tp) WilliamBuick 7 51
(P Butler) *s.i.s: bhd: rdn 1/2-way: nvr a factor* **12/1**

14-0 **8** *1* **Bronte's Hope**[11] 5915 4-9-5 **63**...................................... MartinDwyer 4 50
(M P Tregoning) *s.i.s: bhd: rdn and no rspnse wl over 2f out* **8/1**

6000 **9** *3/4* **Muktasb (USA)**[6] 6046 7-9-6 **64**...................................(v) AdamKirby 10 49
(D Shaw) *s.i.s: a bhd* **10/1**

063 **10** *1 1/4* **Garstang**[18] 5709 5-9-4 **62**... PatrickMathers 11 43
(Peter Grayson) *t.k.h: hld up in tch: rdn over 2f out: wknd 2f out* **11/2**

1m 12.02s (-1.08) **Going Correction** -0.10s/f (Stan)
WFA 3 from 4yo+ 2lb **10** Ran SP% **116.3**
Speed ratings (Par 101): **103,100,98,97,97 95,93,91,90,89**
toteswinger: 1&2 £14.60, 1&3 £9.60, 2&3 £8.00. CSF £166.51 CT £795.54 TOTE £14.90: £4.70, £2.70, £1.60; EX 216.80.
Owner Mrs Ann Jenkins **Bred** Ippotour Stud **Trained** Baughurst, Hants

FOCUS
An open handicap on paper, but very few got into it and it was the two three-year-olds who fought out the finish. The next three home set the level and the form looks reasonable.
Garstang Official explanation: jockey said gelding pulled very hard

6210 TFM NETWORKS H'CAP 1m 4f (P)
8:50 (8:55) (Class 5) (0-75,75) 3-Y-O+ **£2,590** (£770; £385; £192) **Stalls** Centre

Form RPR

2412 **1** **Mixing**[14] 5802 6-8-5 **61** oh2.. DavidProbert[(5)] 10 65
(M J Attwater) *hld up in midfield: hdwy over 2f out: chsd ldrs over 1f out: styd on to ld fnl 100yds: in command towards fin* **6/1**[3]

0-03 **2** *3/4* **Wait For The Light**[11] 5913 4-9-6 **71**................................ SteveDrowne 7 74
(Mrs S Leech) *chsd ldr: rdn and ev ch over 1f out tl no ex fnl 100yds* **25/1**

3061 **3** *1/2* **Paddy Rielly (IRE)**[22] 5593 3-8-3 **62**.................................... ChrisCatlin 6 64
(P D Evans) *hld up in midfield: rdn and hdwy jst over 2f out: kpt on wl ins fnl f: nvr quite getting to ldng pair* **14/1**

5001 **4** *shd* **Wind Flow**[11] 5913 4-9-8 **73**..................................(b) CatherineGannon 13 75
(C A Dwyer) *led: rdn over 2f out: kpt on wl tl hdd fnl 100yds: lost 2 pls towards fin* **16/1**

6255 **5** *shd* **Alfie Noakes**[29] 5376 6-9-4 **69**..(v[1]) JimCrowley 2 71
(Mrs A J Perrett) *racd in midfield: rdn and chsd ldrs 2f out: kpt on u.p but nvr pce to get to ldrs* **8/1**

1633 **6** *1 1/2* **Resplendent Ace (IRE)**[8] 5999 4-9-9 **74**........................ JimmyQuinn 14 76+
(P Howling) *trckd ldrs: effrt and swtchd rt jst over 2f out: nt clr run and swtchd lft over 1f out: nt clr run after tl one pce fnl 100yds* **9/2**[2]

6504 **7** *3/4* **Sahrati**[11] 5910 4-9-8 **73**..(b) RyanMoore 12 71
(C E Brittain) *sn pushed along: bhd: rdn and effrt on inner over 3f out: swtchd lft over 2f out: kpt on but nvr trbld ldrs* **3/1**[1]

4300 **8** *1* **Clovis**[27] 5428 3-8-9 **68**..(b) ShaneKelly 11 65
(N P Mulholland) *stdd s: hld up in last pair: hdwy towards inner over 2f out: keeping on same pce whn hung rt ent fnl f* **66/1**

6000 **9** 1 1/2 **Tilapia (IRE)**[19] 5675 4-9-3 **75** KylieManser(7) 8 69
(Miss Gay Kelleway) *stdd s: hld up bhd: rdn over 2f out: nvr trbld ldrs* **33/1**

0004 **10** 3/4 **Always Certain (USA)**[20] 5630 3-8-4 **63** RoystonFfrench 4 56
(M Johnston) *chsd ldrs tl 3f out: sn rdn and wknd* **12/1**

6040 **11** 1 **Royal Jasra**[96] 3220 4-9-7 **72** JimmyFortune 5 63
(E A L Dunlop) *stdd after s: hld up bhd: brief effrt over 2f out: nvr trbld ldrs* **20/1**

/23- **12** 6 **Counting House (IRE)**[195] 7151 5-9-5 **70** RichardHughes 3 52
(J A B Old) *hld up towards rr: rdn 4f out: sn struggling: no ch fr 3f out* **6/1**[3]

2000 **13** 2 1/2 **Our Kes (IRE)**[30] 5350 6-9-5 **70** PaulDoe 9 48
(P Howling) *t.k.h: chsd ldrs tl over 3f out: sn wknd* **50/1**

2m 32.61s (-1.89) **Going Correction** -0.10s/f (Stan)
WFA 3 from 4yo+ 8lb **13** Ran SP% **118.1**
Speed ratings (Par 103): **102,101,101,101,101 100,99,98,97,97 96,92,91**
toteswinger: 1&2 £27.40, 1&3 £11.20, 2&3 £69.30. CSF £154.75 CT £2012.31 TOTE £6.90: £1.60, £8.10, £3.50; EX 191.00.
Owner Canisbay Bloodstock **Bred** Juddmonte Farms **Trained** Epsom, Surrey

FOCUS
A competitive handicap run at a solid gallop and the form is ordinary but sound.

6211 BARRETTSTOWN STUD H'CAP 1m (P)
9:20 (9:27) (Class 6) (0-65,65) 3-Y-0+ **£2,047** (£604; £302) **Stalls** High

Form RPR

5166 **1** **Grey Boy (GER)**[11] 5915 7-9-3 **64** LukeMorris(3) 10 79+
(A W Carroll) *hld up in midfield: hdwy on inner over 2f out: trcking ldrs and gng wl whn nt clr run wl over 1f out: stdd and swtchd lft jst over 1f out: qcknd to ld fnl 75yds: pushed out: comf* **12/1**

31 **2** 1 3/4 **Myfrenchconnection (IRE)**[53] 4650 4-9-5 **63** MickyFenton 7 72
(P T Midgley) *hld up in midfield: hdwy over 2f out: rdn 2f out: led over 1f out: hdd and nt pce of wnr fnl 75yds* **5/1**[2]

4130 **3** 3 **April Fool**[61] 4390 4-9-5 **63** (v) DaneO'Neill 11 65
(J A Geake) *sn led: hdd 5f out: styd pressing ldr: ev ch and rdn wl over 1f out: outpcd ins fnl f* **6/1**[3]

5513 **4** 2 **Le Chiffre (IRE)**[14] 5799 6-9-0 **63** (p) DavidProbert(5) 1 61
(Miss Sheena West) *w ldrs tl led 5f out: rdn over 2f out: hdd over 1f out: wknd ins fnl f* **13/2**

0054 **5** 1 **Themwerethedays**[6] 6048 3-9-3 **65** RichardHughes 9 60
(S Kirk) *in tch: swtchd sharply lft over 2f out: kpt on same pce last 2f* **4/1**[1]

0000 **6** 1 **Smokin Joe**[11] 5915 7-9-6 **64** (b) SteveDrowne 4 57
(J R Best) *s.i.s: bhd: effrt and hanging rt over 2f out: styd on fnl f: nvr trbld ldrs* **25/1**

0023 **7** hd **Feasible**[21] 5616 3-9-2 **64** (b) JamesDoyle 6 56
(J G Portman) *w ldrs: rdn over 2f out: wknd qckly wl over 1f out* **9/1**

3003 **8** 1/2 **Affrettando (IRE)**[16] 5755 4-9-4 **62** RobertHavlin 5 53
(J A R Toller) *s.i.s: towards rr: rdn wl over 3f out: nvr trbld ldrs* **7/1**

0520 **9** hd **Ryedale Ovation (IRE)**[25] 4785 5-9-5 **63** TravisBlock 12 54
(M Hill) *trckd ldrs: effrt on inner over 2f out: sn rdn: wknd qckly over 1f out* **16/1**

0534 **10** hd **Sofia's Star**[22] 5589 3-9-3 **65** (p) StephenCarson 8 55
(P Winkworth) *hld up bhd: effrt on inner jst over 2f out: nvr trbld ldrs* **14/1**

4123 **11** 3 3/4 **Leptis Magna**[34] 5198 4-9-0 **61** MarcHalford(3) 14 43
(R H York) *s.i.s: hld up bhd: n.d* **12/1**

0120 **12** 3 1/2 **Time To Regret**[21] 5604 8-9-5 **63** (p) PatrickMathers 3 37
(I W McInnes) *racd in midfield on outer: rdn over 3f out: wl bhd last 2f* **25/1**

0040 **13** 1 3/4 **Fantasy Parkes**[20] 5639 4-9-4 **62** (t) ChrisCatlin 13 32
(K Bishop) *nvr gng wl: bhd: swtchd to outer 5f out: wl bhd fr 1/2-way* **33/1**

1m 37.96s (-1.84) **Going Correction** -0.10s/f (Stan)
WFA 3 from 4yo+ 4lb **13** Ran SP% **125.4**
Speed ratings (Par 101): **105,103,100,98,97 96,96,95,95,95 91,87,86**
toteswinger: 1&2 £12.30, 1&3 £18.60, 2&3 £4.60. CSF £73.17 CT £412.17 TOTE £15.90: £5.00, £2.40, £2.90; EX 104.30 Place 6 £164.98, Place 5 £99.89.
Owner Paul Downing **Bred** J Potempa **Trained** Cropthorne, Worcs

FOCUS
A modest handicap run at a decent pace and the form looks worth being positive about.
Themwerethedays Official explanation: jockey said gelding pulled too hard
Leptis Magna Official explanation: jockey said gelding was unsuited by the all-weather surface
T/Plt: £52.60 to a £1 stake. Pool: £69,233.61. 959.67 winning tickets. T/Qpdt: £19.80 to a £1 stake. Pool: £5,308.20. 198.20 winning tickets. SP

5632 REDCAR (L-H)
Wednesday, September 24

OFFICIAL GOING: Good to soft (good in places; 8.2)
Wind: Moderate, half-against Weather: overcast

6212 EUROPEAN BREEDERS' FUND MAIDEN STKS (DIV I) 7f
1:45 (1:45) (Class 5) 2-Y-0 **£3,561** (£1,059; £529; £264) **Stalls** High

Form RPR

56 **1** **Floor Show**[26] 5461 2-9-3 0 NCallan 9 73+
(E S McMahon) *trckd ldrs: smooth hdwy 2f out: hmpd and swtchd lft over 1f out: qcknd to ld jst ins fnl f: comf* **4/1**[3]

04 **2** 1 3/4 **Spinners End (IRE)**[25] 5499 2-9-3 0 AndrewElliott 7 67
(K R Burke) *cl up: led 1/2-way: rdn and edgd rt over 1f out: drvn and hdd jst ins fnl f: kpt on same pce* **2/1**[1]

5 **3** 2 **Kellies Rocket (IRE)**[51] 4681 2-8-12 0 PJMcDonald 2 57
(G A Swinbank) *in tch: hdwy 3f out: rdn to chal wl over 1f out and ev ch tl drvn and one pce ent fnl f* **14/1**

0 **4** 1 3/4 **Hawkleaf Flier (IRE)**[7] 6013 2-8-12 0 DavidAllan 1 52
(T D Easterby) *in tch on outer: hdwy 3f out: rdn and ev ch 2f out: drvn and wknd appr fnl f* **16/1**

5 1 1/4 **Minturno (USA)** 2-9-0 0 AndrewMullen(3) 8 54
(Mrs A Duffield) *dwlt: sn in tch: hdwy and cl up 1/2-way: rdn to chal on inner 2f out and ev ch tl drvn and hld whn n.m.r over 1f out* **14/1**

0 **6** 3 1/4 **Who's Shirl**[45] 4897 2-8-12 0 DeanMcKeown 3 41
(C W Fairhurst) *s.i.s and bhd tl styd on fnl 2f* **200/1**

7 nk **Green Agenda** 2-9-3 0 JoeFanning 4 45
(M Johnston) *dwlt and towards rr: pushed along 1/2-way: kpt on fnl 2f: n.d* **10/3**[2]

0 **8** 7 **Rebel Radio (USA)**[25] 5499 2-9-3 0 TomEaves 10 28
(J Howard Johnson) *cl up: rdn along 1/2-way: sn wknd* **16/1**

0 **9** 7 **Steer**[56] 4536 2-9-3 0 AdrianTNicholls 6 10
(M Brittain) *midfield: rdn along 1/2-way: nvr a factor* **40/1**

60 **10** 24 **Reel Bluff**[4] 6110 2-9-3 0 TonyHamilton 5 —
(D W Barker) *sn led: pushed along and hdd 1/2-way: sn rdn and lost pl: bhd fnl 2f* **25/1**

02 **11** 23 **Mimicker**[106] 2910 2-8-12 0 PaulMulrennan 11 —
(M W Easterby) *sn outpcd in rr and wl bhd fr 1/2-way* **12/1**

1m 27.42s (2.92) **Going Correction** +0.20s/f (Good) **11** Ran SP% **116.0**
Speed ratings (Par 95): **91,89,86,84,83 79,79,71,63,35 9**
toteswinger: 1&2 £2.00, 1&3 £10.60, 2&3 £5.10. CSF £12.03 TOTE £4.20: £1.20, £1.50, £3.90; EX 13.90.
Owner J C Fretwell **Bred** Wyck Hall Stud Ltd **Trained** Lichfield, Staffs

FOCUS
The ground had dried out a little overnight. This was just a fair maiden, but the pace was reasonable and the time was 1.4 seconds quicker than the second division. The form is a little guessy.

NOTEBOOK
Floor Show, who showed clear signs of greenness on his first two outings, was stepped up a furlong in trip and tackling an easier surface. He had trouble getting a run going to the furlong pole but, once switched into the clear, soon settled the issue. A nice, big sort, there should be further improvement to come from him. (op 5-1 tchd 7-2)
Spinners End(IRE) set a reasonable standard on the form of his first two runs, the second of which came in a Ripon maiden which has been working out well. He was always to the fore on this first run over 7f but could not match the winner for speed late on. (op 5-2 tchd 15-8 and 11-4 in a place)
Kellies Rocket(IRE), stepping up two furlongs in trip, showed a lot more than she had first time and was in there fighting inside the last. A little race should come her way. (op 12-1)
Hawkleaf Flier(IRE), who raced on the outside of the pack from her low draw, was supported on the exchanges and ran a better race than she had on her debut. She looks a handicap type.
Minturno(USA)'s pedigree sends mixed messages as he is a half-brother to a number of dirt sprinters in the USA by a stallion who stayed 1m4f well. This was a pleasing debut and he could be interesting if allowed to tackle an artificial surface. (tchd 12-1)
Who's Shirl was sent off at a huge price following an inauspicious debut and soon trailed the field, but she was getting the hang of things late on. (op 150-1)
Green Agenda, a half-brother to a couple of useful winners out of a mare who was fourth in the 1000 Guineas, was badly in need of the experience and considerably better can be expected in time. (op 11-4 tchd 7-2 and 4-1 in a place)

6213 EUROPEAN BREEDERS' FUND MAIDEN STKS (DIV II) 7f
2:15 (2:16) (Class 5) 2-Y-0 **£3,561** (£1,059; £529; £264) **Stalls** High

Form RPR

1 **Regal Lyric (IRE)** 2-9-3 0 TonyCulhane 4 71+
(T P Tate) *hdwy to trck ldrs after 2f: led over 1f out: jst hld on* **20/1**

3 **2** shd **High Office**[28] 5387 2-9-3 0 PaulHanagan 9 71+
(R A Fahey) *led 1f: w ldrs: hung lft thrght: styd on ins fnl f: jst hld* **5/1**[2]

3 2 1/4 **Tiger Reigns** 2-9-3 0 TonyHamilton 3 65
(M Dods) *s.i.s: hld up in rr: hdwy and hung bdly lft 2f out: kpt on wl fnl f* **33/1**

22 **4** nse **Master Rooney (IRE)**[68] 4164 2-9-3 0 TomEaves 8 65
(B Smart) *trckd ldrs: t.k.h: rdn over 1f out: kpt on same pce* **40/85**[1]

00 **5** 3 1/4 **Nut Hand (IRE)**[7] 6008 2-9-3 0 DavidAllan 5 57+
(T D Easterby) *w ldrs: led 3f out tl over 1f out: wknd last 100yds* **100/1**

6 2 1/4 **Ateeb** 2-9-3 0 JoeFanning 7 52
(M Johnston) *w ldr: led after 1f tl 3f out: wknd over 1f out* **7/1**[3]

7 3 **Speed Dating** 2-9-3 0 J-PGuillambert 11 44
(Sir Mark Prescott) *slowly away: sn drvn along: sme hdwy 4f out: wknd fnl 2f* **20/1**

8 1/2 **Northside Prince (IRE)** 2-9-3 0 PJMcDonald 6 43
(G A Swinbank) *hld up in midfield: wknd over 1f out* **33/1**

9 1 **Suprise Gift** 2-8-12 0 GrahamGibbons 1 35
(J J Quinn) *a towards rr* **40/1**

10 2 1/2 **Pattern Mark** 2-9-3 0 PaulMulrennan 2 34
(Ollie Pears) *sn w ldrs: lost pl over 1f out* **50/1**

1m 28.82s (4.32) **Going Correction** +0.20s/f (Good) **10** Ran SP% **117.9**
Speed ratings (Par 95): **83,82,80,80,76 73,70,69,68,65**
toteswinger: 1&2 £9.00, 1&3 £53.30, 2&3 £16.70. CSF £111.82 TOTE £31.60: £4.90, £1.20, £8.10; EX 229.60.
Owner JMH Lifestyle Ltd **Bred** P Kavanagh, Roalso Ltd & R Raucher **Trained** Tadcaster, N Yorks

FOCUS
This looked the better of the two divisions on paper, but the pace was only steady and the time was 1.4 seconds slower than division one. The favourite disappointed and it was one of the seven newcomers who prevailed but the level looks fairly fluid.

NOTEBOOK
Regal Lyric(IRE), out of a smart half-sister to Great Voltigeur winner Bonny Scot, travelled up well on the outside and, after showing ahead, just held the runner-up's late flourish. His rider did not go for everything and there should be more to come from him. (op 16-1)
High Office ◆, a promising third to subsequent Listed winner Zafisio on his debut at Ayr, was rather free going to post. Racing nearest the stands' rail, he showed a tendency to hang but knuckled down well late on and nearly caught the winner. He is still learning and should quickly make amends. (tchd 9-2)
Tiger Reigns hung right over into the centre of the track, but still finished well to grab third. He will have learned from this and should make the grade. (op 25-1)
Master Rooney(IRE), well regarded and already runner-up in a couple of 6f maidens, hardened in the on-course market but let down his supporters. He was again rather keen off the steady early pace and he failed to pick up once coming under pressure. He is better than this but his Group 1 entries do not look realistic. Official explanation: jockey said colt ran too free early stages (op 4-5 tchd 4-9)
Nut Hand(IRE) ran a satisfactory race and can now ply his trade in handicaps.
Ateeb, out of a Listed-placed mare from a top family, needed this debut and will come on for the outing. (op 6-1)
Speed Dating is a half-brother to prolific 6f-1m2f winner Secret Liaison out of a useful winner over similar trips. A scopey sort, he proved very keen both on the way to post and in the race and will need time before he begins to fulfil his potential. (op 14-1)

6214 PERTEMPS EMPLOYMENT ALLIANCE NURSERY 1m
2:50 (2:51) (Class 6) (0-65,65) 2-Y-0 **£2,266** (£674; £337; £168) **Stalls** High

Form RPR

002 **1** **Bounty Reef**[15] 5778 2-8-10 **54** TGMcLaughlin 13 56
(P D Evans) *hld up in midfield: swtchd outside and hdwy over 2f out: rdn over 1f out: styd on to ld ins fnl f: kpt on wl* **16/1**

0040 **2** 2 **Aven Mac (IRE)**[7] 6014 2-8-6 **50** (p) FrancisNorton 9 48
(N Bycroft) *dwlt and towards rr: hdwy on outer 2f out: sn rdn and styd on wl u.p fnl f* **50/1**

3643 **3** hd **Dispol Diva**[15] 5774 2-8-10 **54** (v) JamieMoriarty 3 51
(P T Midgley) *in tch on outer: hdwy 1/2-way: chsd ldrs 3f out: rdn to ld over 1f out: drvn and hdd ins fnl f: kpt on same pce* **14/1**

The Form Book, Raceform Ltd, Compton, RG20 6NL

500 **4** *1 1/4* **Andean Margin (IRE)**[13] 5842 2-9-4 **62**.......................... HayleyTurner 1 56
(S A Callaghan) *hld up towards rr: hdwy on outer over 3f out: chsd ldrs 2f out: sn rdn and one pce ent fnl f* **15/2**[2]

U035 **5** *2 3/4* **Just Five (IRE)**[9] 5966 2-8-6 **50**.......................... PaulFessey 6 38
(M Dods) *trckd ldrs: hdwy to ld 3f out: rdn along and hdd over 1f out: sn drvn and wknd ent fnl f* **18/1**

006 **6** *1/2* **Acclaben (IRE)**[25] 5499 2-9-5 **63**.......................... PJMcDonald 4 50
(G A Swinbank) *chsd ldrs: hdwy and cl up 1/2-way: rdn along over 2f out and sn one pce* **16/1**

0504 **7** *nk* **Royal Max (IRE)**[15] 5774 2-8-10 **54**..........................(v[1]) PaulHanagan 19 41
(R A Fahey) *chsd ldrs: rdn along 3f out: drvn 2f out and grad wknd* **8/1**[3]

0441 **8** *2 1/2* **Hollow Green (IRE)**[15] 5778 2-9-2 **60**.......................... RobertWinston 15 41
(P D Evans) *in rr and rdn along 1/2-way: hdwy over 3f out: kpt on u.p fnl 2f: nvr nr ldrs* **15/2**[2]

5205 **9** *1 1/2* **Yokozuna**[22] 5591 2-9-2 **65**..........................(b) KellyHarrison(5) 2 43
(Mrs R A Carr) *in tch: hdwy 3f out: rdn over 2f out and sn no imp* **25/1**

500 **10** *2 1/4* **Royal Salsa (IRE)**[25] 5500 2-8-9 **53**.......................... TonyHamilton 11 26
(R A Fahey) *towards rr: effrt and sme hdwy 3f out: sn rdn and no imp fnl 2f* **16/1**

3034 **11** *1/2* **Little Tokyo (USA)**[9] 5966 2-9-0 **63**.......................... FrederikTylicki(5) 7 35
(J Howard Johnson) *in tch: effrt to chse ldrs over 3f out: rdn along over 2f out and sn wknd* **16/1**

5000 **12** *4* **Monsieur Jourdain (IRE)**[49] 4733 2-8-13 **57**.......................... DavidAllan 14 20
(T D Easterby) *towards rr and rdn along 1/2-way: nvr a factor* **25/1**

5000 **13** *1* **Isabella Romee (IRE)**[22] 5591 2-9-6 **64**.......................... FrankieMcDonald 12 25
(Jane Chapple-Hyam) *led 1f: cl up tl rdn along 3f out and grad wknd* **18/1**

600 **14** *2 3/4* **Well Of Echoes**[69] 4109 2-8-11 **62**.......................... BMcHugh(7) 5 17
(A J McCabe) *cl up: led after 1f: pushed along 1/2-way: hdd 3f out and sn wknd* **20/1**

604 **15** *1 1/2* **King's Counsel (IRE)**[31] 5304 2-9-0 **58**..........................(v[1]) TomEaves 20 9
(B Smart) *in tch: hdwy on stands' rail 3f out: rdn over 2f out and sn wknd* **16/1**

5602 **16** *nse* **Shifting Gold (IRE)**[15] 5774 2-9-1 **59**.......................... NCallan 8 10
(K A Ryan) *prom: rdn along after 3f: drvn 1/2-way: sn lost pl and bhd* **13/2**[1]

046 **17** *3/4* **Feeling Stylish (IRE)**[29] 5384 2-8-11 **55**.......................... KimTinkler 16 5
(N Tinkler) *hld up towards rr: effrt over 3f out: sn rdn along and nvr a factor* **16/1**

4655 **18** *1* **Kingaroo (IRE)**[15] 5771 2-8-11 **55**.......................... DaleGibson 17 2
(Garry Moss) *towards rr: sme hdwy over 3f out: sn rdn and wknd over 2f out* **25/1**

0304 **19** *1 3/4* **Mistress Mary**[6] 6059 2-8-7 **51**..........................(b) AdrianMcCarthy 10 —
(G G Margarson) *in tch: rdn along 1/2-way: sn wknd* **40/1**

066 **20** *8* **Shadows Lengthen**[58] 4474 2-9-2 **60**.......................... PaulMulrennan 18 —
(M W Easterby) *s.i.s: a bhd* **20/1**

1m 41.25s (3.25) **Going Correction** +0.20s/f (Good) **20** Ran SP% **127.0**
Speed ratings (Par 93): **91,89,88,87,84 84,84,81,80,77 77,73,72,69,68 67,67,66,64,56**
toteswinger: 1&2 £190.60, 1&3 £74.50, 2&3 £250.20. CSF £697.28 CT £11122.29 TOTE £28.00: £6.00, £14.00, £4.30, £2.70; EX 1095.90.
Owner Mrs I M Folkes **Bred** Terry Minahan **Trained** Pandy, Monmouths
■ Stewards' Enquiry : Paul Hanagan three-day ban: used whip with excessive frequency (Oct 8-10)

FOCUS
This big-field nursery had a definite back-end feel to it. It was run at a strong pace and presented quite a stamina test for these moderate juveniles. Most of the principals came from the rear and they set the standard.

NOTEBOOK
Bounty Reef turned around Leicester selling form with stablemate Hollow Green on these 6lb better terms. Switched to the outer for her run, she stayed on strongly once hitting the front and is on the upgrade at a lowly level. (op 14-1)
Aven Mac(IRE) found herself at the back after being hampered leaving the stalls. She stayed on to grab second on the line on this nursery debut, the first-time cheekpieces bringing about improvement.
Dispol Diva, fully exposed, was the only one of the first four to race up with the pace. She is running well in the visor at present. (op 16-1)
Andean Margin(IRE) had not shown a whole lot in three maidens, but he cost 250,000gns as a yearling and was the subject of a big morning gamble down from 14-1 on this nursery debut. Well drawn as the race panned out, with the main action developing up the centre of the track, he improved from the rear to have his chance but could not quicken up when required. (op 6-1)
Just Five(IRE) ran a respectable race, up with the speed throughout, but he is exposed as very moderate. (op 16-1 tchd 20-1)
Acclaben(IRE) was another nursery debutant to acquit himself well. (op 14-1)
Royal Max(IRE) ran a decent race in the first-time visor, never far away on the stands' side and keeping on to suggest that he will get further. (op 12-1)
Hollow Green(IRE) raced at the back of the field in company with her winning stablemate, whom she had beaten on 6lb better terms last time. She made some progress without getting into the race. Official explanation: jockey said filly never travelled (op 17-2)
Shifting Gold(IRE) disappointed after his improved effort last time. Official explanation: trainer had no explanation for the poor form shown (op 11-2)
Shadows Lengthen Official explanation: jockey said colt had no more to give

6215 BODDINGTONS REDCAR STRAIGHT-MILE CHAMPIONSHIP (QUALIFIER) (PREMIER CLAIMING STKS) 1m
3:25 (3:26) (Class 4) 3-Y-O+ £4,857 (£1,445; £722; £360) Stalls High

Form RPR

006 **1** **Middlemarch (IRE)**[9] 5968 8-9-1 65..........................(b) GaryBartley(5) 3 79
(J S Goldie) *in rr: gd hdwy over 1f out: fin fast to ld last 50yds* **18/1**

2102 **2** *2* **Efidium**[31] 5303 10-8-9 65 ow3.......................... FrederikTylicki(5) 4 68
(N Bycroft) *hld up in midfield: hdwy over 2f out: styd on to ld jst ins fnl f: hdd and no ex wl ins fnl f* **4/1**[1]

6450 **3** *1* **Royal Applord**[31] 5303 3-8-11 66..........................(p) NCallan 8 67
(K A Ryan) *w ldrs: led over 3f out: hung bdly lft: hdd jst ins fnl f: kpt on same pce* **25/1**

6002 **4** *1/2* **Crocodile Bay (IRE)**[55] 4559 5-9-3 80.......................... TonyHamilton 6 68
(D W Barker) *led tl over 3f out: carried lft over 1f out: kpt on same pce* **9/1**

1-05 **5** *1* **Maryqueenofscots (IRE)**[40] 5075 3-9-2 76.......................... HayleyTurner 9 69
(M L W Bell) *chsd ldrs: outpcd over 2f out: styd on wl ins fnl f* **14/1**

3013 **6** *2 3/4* **Inside Story (IRE)**[42] 4969 6-9-1 70..........................(b) DaleGibson 1 57
(M W Easterby) *mid-div: drvn 3f out: kpt on: nvr nr ldrs* **11/1**

000 **7** *shd* **Aussie Blue (IRE)**[46] 4878 4-9-3 60.......................... DeanMcKeown 17 59
(R M Whitaker) *in rr: sn drvn along: kpt on fnl 2f: nvr nr ldrs* **16/1**

4144 **8** *2 3/4* **Boundless Prospect (USA)**[9] 5961 9-8-11 68.......................... PaulHanagan 19 47
(Ollie Pears) *in rr: drvn 3f out: nvr on terms* **6/1**[3]

0306 **9** *1* **Grethel (IRE)**[3] 6152 4-8-13 61.......................... SladeO'Hara(5) 2 51
(A Berry) *mid-div: drvn over 2f out: nvr rchd ldrs* **28/1**

0005 **10** *7* **Dry Speedfit (IRE)**[8] 6001 3-8-11 65..........................(b) J-PGuillambert 7 32
(G G Margarson) *s.i.s: hld up sn in midfield: effrt over 2f out: sn wknd* **20/1**

4020 **11** *3* **Cecina Marina**[31] 5308 5-8-2 43.......................... KellyHarrison(5) 5 17
(Mrs K Walton) *chsd ldrs: lost pl 3f out* **100/1**

00 **12** *nk* **Pennybid (IRE)**[46] 4878 6-8-13 0.......................... PAspell 11 23
(C R Wilson) *mid-div: sn drvn along: nvr a threat* **200/1**

5003 **13** *1/2* **Admiralcollingwood**[2] 6163 3-8-9 48 ow2.......................... PaulMulrennan 20 22
(C Grant) *w ldrs: lost pl over 2f out* **33/1**

0630 **14** *1/2* **Kaymich Perfecto**[56] 4540 8-8-8 56..........................(v) MichaelJStainton(3) 14 18
(R M Whitaker) *in rr: sn drvn along: nvr on terms* **33/1**

00-0 **15** *6* **Fortunate Isle (USA)**[186] 958 6-9-4 87.......................... BMcHugh(7) 10 19
(R A Fahey) *in rr: drvn 3f out: nvr on terms* **10/1**

000- **16** *10* **Bravely (IRE)**[90] 3424 4-9-11 80.......................... DavidAllan 12 —
(T D Easterby) *chsd ldrs: lost pl over 2f out: eased whn bhd ins fnl f* **14/1**

000 **17** *1 3/4* **Geordie Girl**[49] 4741 3-8-8 58..........................(p) PaulFessey 13 —
(R C Guest) *chsd ldrs: lost pl 3f out* **100/1**

5300 **18** *33* **Very Wise**[57] 4509 6-9-11 83.......................... JoeFanning 15 —
(W J Haggas) *s.v.s: a wl t.o in last* **5/1**[2]

1m 39.06s (1.06) **Going Correction** +0.20s/f (Good)
WFA 3 from 4yo+ 4lb **18** Ran SP% **123.3**
Speed ratings (Par 105): **102,100,99,98,97 94,94,91,90,83 80,80,80,79,73 63,61,28**
.Crocodile Bay was claimed by John A. Harris for £12,000.\n\x\x
Owner W M Johnstone **Bred** Swettenham Stud And Hugo Lascelles **Trained** Uplawmoor, E Renfrews

FOCUS
A reasonable claimer. Not many got into it and again it seemed a disadvantage to race up the stands' side. The placed horses are the best guides to the level.

6216 PERTEMPS PEOPLE DEVELOPMENT GROUP H'CAP 1m 2f
4:00 (4:00) (Class 5) (0-70,68) 3-Y-O+ £2,590 (£770; £385; £192) Stalls Low

Form RPR

0646 **1** **Bavarian Nordic (USA)**[11] 5888 3-8-13 **66**.......................... AndrewMullen(3) 13 73
(Mrs A Duffield) *hld up: stdy hdwy on outer 3f out: rdn to chal over 1f out: drvn to ld ins fnl f: kpt on gamely* **8/1**

1002 **2** *1/2* **Moonstreaker**[23] 5564 5-9-3 **64**.......................... MichaelJStainton(3) 9 70+
(R M Whitaker) *hld up: gd hdwy over 3f out: n.m.r over 2f out: swtchd rt and rdn over 1f out: styd on strly ins fnl f* **10/3**[1]

3010 **3** *shd* **Emirate Isle**[41] 5008 4-9-10 **68**..........................(p) RobertWinston 8 74
(C Grant) *trckd ldrs: hdwy 3f out: rdn to dispute ld wl over 1f out: drvn and ev ch ins fnl f: edgd consistently lft and no ex towards fin* **14/1**

6440 **4** *2* **Island Music (IRE)**[49] 4741 3-9-3 **67**.......................... PaulHanagan 2 69
(J J Quinn) *in tch on inner: hdwy 3f out: rdn over 2f out: drvn appr fnl f: kpt on same pce* **15/2**

635- **5** *shd* **Cripsey Brook**[193] 6561 10-9-8 **66**.......................... TomEaves 4 68
(K G Reveley) *towards rr: hdwy 4f out: effrt whn n.m.r wl over 1f out: sn swtchd rt and rdn: styd on ins fnl f: nrst fin* **22/1**

-062 **6** *nse* **Madison Heights (IRE)**[59] 4455 3-8-11 **61**.......................... PaulMulrennan 7 63
(J Howard Johnson) *chsd ldr: rdn along 3f out: drvn over 1f out and kpt on same pce* **12/1**

1440 **7** *1 1/4* **Eijaaz (IRE)**[9] 5971 7-9-3 **61**.......................... TonyHamilton 6 63+
(G A Harker) *hld up in rr: hdwy on inner 3f out: nt clr run wl over 1f out and again ent fnl f: kpt on: nrst fin* **18/1**

202 **8** *shd* **Evelith Regent (IRE)**[46] 4878 5-9-6 **64**.......................... PJMcDonald 5 63
(G A Swinbank) *led: rdn along 3f out: drvn 2f out: hdd over 1f out: wknd* **7/1**[3]

6313 **9** *3/4* **Boy Dancer (IRE)**[46] 4850 5-9-3 **61**.......................... JamieMoriarty 1 58
(J J Quinn) *chsd ldrs: rdn along 3f out: drvn whn n.m.r 2f out: sn wknd* **11/2**[2]

5004 **10** *3/4* **Neon Blue**[46] 4849 7-9-1 **59**.......................... DeanMcKeown 11 55
(R M Whitaker) *a towards rr* **20/1**

0502 **11** *1* **Plenilune (IRE)**[30] 5362 3-9-2 **66**.......................... AdrianTNicholls 10 60
(M Brittain) *a towards rr* **14/1**

5544 **12** *1/2* **Dan Tucker**[2] 6050 4-9-7 **65**.......................... KimTinkler 14 58
(N Tinkler) *a in rr* **12/1**

2004 **13** *22* **John Potts**[26] 5477 3-8-6 **56**.......................... AndrewElliott 12 5
(B P J Baugh) *chsd ldrs: rdn along 4f out: sn wknd* **50/1**

2m 8.27s (1.17) **Going Correction** +0.20s/f (Good)
WFA 3 from 4yo+ 6lb **13** Ran SP% **118.9**
Speed ratings (Par 103): **103,102,102,100,100 100,99,99,99,98 97,97,79**
toteswinger: 1&2 £8.40, 1&3 £23.40, 2&3 £16.10. CSF £33.74 CT £377.27 TOTE £10.00: £2.40, £1.70, £3.90; EX 38.00.
Owner Six Iron Partnership **Bred** Gainsborough Farm Llc **Trained** Constable Burton, N Yorks
■ Stewards' Enquiry : Andrew Mullen four-day ban: used whip with excessive frequency (Oct 8-11)

FOCUS
A modest handicap run at a sound gallop but the time was 0.39secs slower than the following seller. the third and fourth set the standard but the form is somewhat muddling.
Emirate Isle Official explanation: jockey said gelding hung left shortly before winning post and he had to drop hands for fear of colliding with the rail

6217 WEDDINGS AT REDCAR (S) STKS 1m 2f
4:35 (4:36) (Class 6) 3-5-Y-O £2,047 (£604; £302) Stalls Low

Form RPR

-255 **1** **Top Jaro (FR)**[3] 6152 5-9-1 60.......................... TonyHamilton 6 66
(D W Barker) *trckd ldrs: led over 3f out: drvn clr 1f out: kpt on* **7/2**[1]

3250 **2** *1 3/4* **Lady Valentino**[15] 5776 4-8-10 52.......................... TomEaves 11 58
(M Dods) *hld up in mid-div: hdwy 3f out: styd on to take 2nd nr fin* **8/1**

0064 **3** *nk* **Distant Rock**[6] 6040 3-7-13 55..........................(t) KellyHarrison(5) 3 57
(D Carroll) *hld up in midfield: wnt 2nd over 2f out: styd on same pce fnl f* **12/1**

3200 **4** *3 3/4* **Just Sam (IRE)**[24] 5544 3-8-4 51.......................... PaulFessey 7 49
(D W Barker) *chsd ldrs: wknd fnl f* **20/1**

0012 **5** *shd* **Mick Is Back**[7] 6032 4-9-7 55..........................(p) NCallan 14 60
(G G Margarson) *mid-div: hdwy 3f out: hung lft: kpt on: nvr rchd ldrs* **13/2**[3]

0500 **6** *3/4* **Predictable (IRE)**[7] 6015 3-8-4 48.......................... DaleGibson 9 48
(M W Easterby) *s.s: hdwy over 2f out: styd on fnl f: nt rch ldrs* **66/1**

0000 **7** *1 1/4* **The Flying Cowboy (IRE)**[39] 5087 4-9-1 58.......................... TGMcLaughlin 5 50
(Jane Chapple-Hyam) *in rr: hdwy 3f out: hung lft: nvr nr ldrs* **11/2**[2]

3613 **8** *8* **Intersky Melody (USA)**[29] 5380 3-9-1 57.......................... DeanMcKeown 12 40
(R M Whitaker) *prom: drvn over 3f out: wknd 2f out* **13/2**[3]

563 **9** *2 1/2* **Getrah**[3] 6152 4-9-1 55..........................(p) PaulHanagan 8 29
(C Grant) *s.s: sme hdwy over 2f out: nvr on terms* **8/1**

00 **10** hd **Seven Stars**[102] 3043 3-8-9 0 PAspell 15 29
(M E Sowersby) *a towards rr* **40/1**

F205 **11** shd **Lizzie Wiggins**[28] 5399 3-8-10 55 PaulMulrennan 4 30
(Mrs Marjorie Fife) *led: hdd over 3f out: lost pl over 2f out* **9/1**

306 **12** nk **Roman History (IRE)**[56] 4541 5-9-1 52 (p) SilvestreDeSousa 10 28
(Miss Tracy Waggott) *mid-div: wkng whn n.m.r on inner 3f out* **14/1**

2000 **13** 4 **Lewis Lloyd (IRE)**[22] 4217 5-9-4 52 MichaelJStainton(3) 13 26
(R E Barr) *s.i.s: a in rr* **66/1**

00 **14** 6 **Supremely Blessed**[6] 6055 4-8-10 0 AndrewElliott 2 3
(D W Thompson) *chsd ldrs: wknd over 2f out* **150/1**

60 **15** 27 **Amy's Mercdes**[61] 4378 4-8-7 0 DuranFentiman(3) 1 —
(N Bycroft) *towards rr: hung bdly lft 7f out: sn bhd and c stands' side: virtually p.u: t.o* **125/1**

2m 7.88s (0.78) **Going Correction** +0.20s/f (Good)
WFA 3 from 4yo+ 6lb **15** Ran SP% **122.5**
Speed ratings (Par 101): **104,102,102,99,99 98,97,91,89,89 89,88,85,80,59**
toteswinger: 1&2 £7.70, 1&3 £14.10, 2&3 £20.40. CSF £31.10 TOTE £4.30: £1.80, £3.40, £3.90; EX 37.40.The winner was sold to D W Chapman for 5,800gns.
Owner D W Barker **Bred** Jean Biraben And Robert Labeyrie **Trained** Scorton, N Yorks

FOCUS
The time for this seller was 0.39 seconds quicker than the preceding handicap, and this might be decent form for the grade with the first five close to recent marks.
Mick Is Back Official explanation: jockey said gelding hung left from 3f out
Amy's Mercdes Official explanation: jockey said filly hung right-handed

6218 ROTARY WATCHES AT MARKET CROSS JEWELLERS H'CAP 5f
5:10 (5:10) (Class 5) (0-70,70) 3-Y-0+ **£2,590** (£770; £385; £192) **Stalls** High

Form RPR
-060 **1** **Ingleby Star (IRE)**[28] 5393 3-8-8 60 (b) PaulFessey 11 69
(T D Barron) *chsd ldrs: hdwy 2f out: rdn to ld over 1f out: drvn and edgd lft ins fnl f: jst hld on* **66/1**

0610 **2** nk **Wicked Wilma (IRE)**[6] 6039 4-8-5 56 oh1 FrancisNorton 2 64
(A Berry) *wnt rt s: chsd ldrs: hdwy 2f out: rdn over 1f out: swtchd rt and drvn ins fnl f: kpt on strly: jst hld* **10/1**

3026 **3** hd **The Little Fizzer (IRE)**[27] 5421 3-8-1 56 oh3 AndrewMullen(3) 7 63
(P D Evans) *midfield: rdn along 1/2-way: hdwy wl over 1f out: styd on u.p ins fnl f* **12/1**

0320 **4** nse **Feelin Foxy**[28] 5401 4-8-12 70 RosieJessop(7) 8 77
(J G Given) *led: rdn and hdd over 1f out: drvn and edgd lft ins fnl f: rallied towards fin* **9/1**

6031 **5** 2 1/4 **Pride Of Northcare (IRE)**[19] 5679 4-8-11 62 DarrenWilliams 15 61
(D Shaw) *hmpd s and towards rr: hdwy wl over 1f out: rdn and styd on ins fnl f: nrst fin* **11/1**

0000 **6** nk **Jilly Why (IRE)**[11] 5886 7-8-11 67 (b) FrederikTylicki(5) 3 65
(Paul Green) *chsd ldrs: rdn along 2f out: drvn and one pce appr fnl f* **15/2**[2]

6300 **6** dht **Tangerine Trees**[53] 4615 3-8-13 65 TomEaves 10 63
(B Smart) *cl up: rdn along 2f out: drvn and one pce appr fnl f* **25/1**

404 **8** 2 **Ursus**[15] 5775 3-8-4 56 oh1 SilvestreDeSousa 6 47
(C R Wilson) *hld up towards rr: hdwy 2f out: swtchd outside and rdn over 1f out: no imp ins fnl f* **12/1**

1000 **9** nk **Toy Top (USA)**[28] 5398 5-8-9 60 (b) PaulMulrennan 9 50
(M Dods) *prom: rdn 2f out: drvn and wknd appr fnl f* **33/1**

4501 **10** shd **First Swallow**[32] 5261 3-8-13 65 PaulHanagan 16 54
(R A Fahey) *hmpd s: towards rr tl styd on fnl 2f* **12/1**

2210 **11** shd **Grudge**[14] 5796 3-9-4 70 TonyHamilton 17 59
(D W Barker) *wnt lft s: cl up tl rdn along 2f out and grad wknd appr fnl f* **12/1**

3102 **12** 1/2 **Baybshambles (IRE)**[17] 5719 4-8-10 68 BMcHugh(7) 5 55
(R E Barr) *a in rr* **8/1**[3]

4162 **13** nk **Cheshire Rose**[11] 5902 3-8-10 69 DeanHeslop(7) 14 55
(T D Barron) *hmpd s: nvr bttr than midfield* **20/1**

-005 **14** 1 **Northern Chorus (IRE)**[50] 4703 5-8-5 56 oh5 (v) AndrewElliott 12 38
(J O'Reilly) *hmpd s: a towards rr* **28/1**

6000 **15** 3 3/4 **Prigsnov Dancer (IRE)**[99] 3111 3-8-13 65 TGMcLaughlin 4 34
(J O'Reilly) *a in rr* **50/1**

0000 **16** 3/4 **Making Music**[32] 5260 5-8-2 56 oh1 (bt) DuranFentiman(3) 19 22
(T D Easterby) *in tch: rdn along and lost pl 1/2-way: sn in rr* **40/1**

4433 **17** 2 **Coleorton Dancer**[20] 5634 6-9-1 66 (b) NCallan 1 25
(K A Ryan) *in tch: rdn along over 2f out and sn wknd* **5/1**[1]

064 **18** 1/2 **Windjammer**[9] 5970 4-8-10 61 (b) DavidAllan 18 18
(T D Easterby) *in tch: rdn along 2f out and sn wknd* **11/1**

58.60 secs **Going Correction** +0.20s/f (Good)
WFA 3 from 4yo+ 1lb **18** Ran SP% **127.0**
Speed ratings (Par 103): **108,107,107,107,103 103,103,99,99,99 99,98,97,96,90 88,85,84**
toteswinger: 1&2 £75.00, 1&3 £195.80, 2&3 £31.30. CSF £633.17 CT £8491.35 TOTE £81.00: £15.50, £2.40, £3.20, £2.70; EX 1877.40.
Owner Dave Scott **Bred** Pat Cosgrove **Trained** Maunby, N Yorks
■ Stewards' Enquiry : Silvestre De Sousa two-day ban: careless riding (Oct 8-9)

FOCUS
An ordinary handicap run at a furious gallop, and it resulted in a blanket finish. The form is solid for the grade rated around those in the frame behind the winner.
Coleorton Dancer Official explanation: jockey said gelding never travelled

6219 SUBSCRIBE TO RACING UK H'CAP 6f
5:40 (5:40) (Class 6) (0-65,65) 3-Y-0+ **£2,388** (£705; £352) **Stalls** High

Form RPR
0050 **1** **Apollo Shark (IRE)**[28] 5400 3-9-4 65 RobertWinston 12 77
(J Howard Johnson) *mde virtually all towards centre: hld on wl towards fin* **22/1**

0224 **2** 1/2 **Imperial Sword**[28] 5392 5-8-6 58 (b) DeanHeslop(7) 18 68
(T D Barron) *in rr stands' side: hung lft fr over 3f out and ended up on far side: upsides 1f out: no ex nr fin* **8/1**[3]

0062 **3** 3/4 **Avontuur (FR)**[28] 5392 6-8-9 57 MichaelJStainton(3) 15 65
(Mrs R A Carr) *mid-div towards centre: hdwy 2f out: hrd rdn and edgd lft 1f out: styd on same pce ins fnl f* **13/2**[2]

0140 **4** nk **Feeling Fresh (IRE)**[34] 5198 3-9-3 64 PaulQuinn 10 71
(Paul Green) *in rr in centre: hdwy and swtchd lft over 1f out: no ex ins fnl f* **14/1**

6225 **5** 1 1/2 **Soto**[15] 5775 5-9-5 64 PaulMulrennan 20 66
(M W Easterby) *in tch stands' side: effrt over 1f out: kpt on same pce ins fnl f* **12/1**

2005 **6** hd **Royal Composer (IRE)**[32] 5260 5-8-10 58 (b) DuranFentiman(3) 17 60+
(T D Easterby) *in rr towards centre: styd on fnl 2f: nt rch ldrs* **16/1**

4000 **7** 1 **Royal Acclamation (IRE)**[20] 5634 3-9-3 64 SilvestreDeSousa 5 64+
(G A Harker) *hld up in mid-div towards far side: hdwy 2f out: n.m.r and eased ins fnl f* **22/1**

450- **8** nk **Bourbon Balistic**[338] 6384 3-8-8 58 AndrewMullen(3) 3 55
(Mrs A Duffield) *w ldrs towards far side: keeping on same pce whn hmpd jst ins fnl f* **40/1**

4452 **9** nk **Lake Sabina**[28] 5402 3-9-4 65 GrahamGibbons 19 61
(E S McMahon) *chsd ldrs stands' side: kpt on same pce appr fnl f* **14/1**

0040 **10** 1 **Paris Bell**[7] 6011 6-9-5 64 DavidAllan 8 57+
(T D Easterby) *dwlt: hdwy in centre whn nt clr run over 1f out: nvr trbld ldrs* **6/1**[1]

6050 **11** nse **Lady Benjamin**[40] 5045 3-8-5 57 (b) PatrickDonaghy(5) 9 50
(P C Haslam) *w ldrs towards far side: wknd whn hmpd jst ins fnl f* **18/1**

0-00 **12** 3/4 **Top Bid**[83] 3626 4-9-4 63 DanielTudhope 4 53
(T D Easterby) *mid-div towards far side: hdwy to chse ldrs 2f out: wkng whn n.m.r and eased jst ins fnl f* **40/1**

0505 **13** 2 1/2 **Everything**[17] 5714 3-9-1 62 JamieMoriarty 13 44
(P T Midgley) *a towards rr in centre* **20/1**

3000 **14** 1 1/4 **Maia**[109] 2846 4-9-1 60 PaulHanagan 6 38
(Ollie Pears) *s.i.s: hung rt 2f out and racd stands' side: nvr a threat* **18/1**

010 **15** 3 3/4 **Actabou**[56] 4542 3-9-2 63 TomEaves 1 29
(M Dods) *w ldrs far side: wknd over 1f out* **16/1**

3610 **16** nk **Uace Mac**[20] 5634 4-9-1 65 FrederikTylicki(5) 16 30
(N Bycroft) *chsd ldrs stands' side: wknd 2f out* **11/1**

0045 **17** 1/2 **Dakota Rain (IRE)**[15] 5779 6-9-4 63 (p) HayleyTurner 2 27
(Jennie Candlish) *w ldrs far side: wknd 2f out* **8/1**[3]

2000 **18** 1 3/4 **Dolly No Hair**[81] 3717 3-9-1 62 TonyHamilton 14 20
(D W Barker) *chsd ldrs in centre: lost pl over 1f out* **33/1**

1m 12.6s (0.80) **Going Correction** +0.20s/f (Good)
WFA 3 from 4yo+ 2lb **18** Ran SP% **122.8**
Speed ratings (Par 101): **102,101,100,99,97 97,96,95,95,94 94,93,89,88,83 82,82,79**
toteswinger: 1&2 £52.80, 1&3 £41.60, 2&3 £7.20. CSF £176.77 CT £1296.42 TOTE £28.60: £7.40, £1.50, £2.40, £4.40; EX 397.90 Place 6 £781.39, Place 5 £490.12.
Owner Transcend Bloodstock LLP **Bred** Churchtown House Stud **Trained** Billy Row, Co Durham
■ Stewards' Enquiry : Michael J Stainton two-day ban: careless riding (Oct 8-9)

FOCUS
Just a moderate handicap, but it was certainly competitive and the form looks sound enough rated around the placed horses.
Royal Acclamation(IRE) Official explanation: jockey said, regarding running and riding, he had received no orders other than to win if he could as he had ridden the gelding on previous occasions, adding that he was denied a clear run in the early stages and when the gap did finally appear inside the final furlong he suffered interference and it lost its action; vet said gelding finished lame.
Paris Bell Official explanation: jockey said gelding was denied a clear run
Lady Benjamin Official explanation: vet said filly had been struck into
Maia Official explanation: jockey said filly hung right-handed
T/Jkpt: Not won. T/Plt: £1,259.90 to a £1 stake. Pool: £55,232.32. 32.00 winning tickets. T/Qpdt: £127.40 to a £1 stake. Pool: £4,752.10. 27.60 winning tickets. JR

6220 - 6222a (Foreign Racing) - See Raceform Interactive

6044 GREAT LEIGHS (A.W) (L-H)
Thursday, September 25

OFFICIAL GOING: Standard
Wind: fresh against Weather: bright and dry

6223 NAYLAND NURSERY 6f (P)
6:50 (6:51) (Class 5) (0-70,70) 2-Y-0 **£4,079** (£1,214; £606; £303) **Stalls** Low

Form RPR
010 **1** **Brierty (IRE)**[10] 5960 2-9-7 70 DNolan 11 75+
(D Carroll) *in tch: squeezed between horses to ld over 1f out: rdn clr and flashed tail: eased towards fin* **20/1**

0620 **2** 1 3/4 **West Leake (IRE)**[44] 4956 2-8-11 60 MichaelHills 1 58
(B W Hills) *racd in midfield: pushed along over 3f out: hdwy 2f out: chsd wnr ent fnl f: kpt on* **12/1**

0531 **3** 3/4 **Ray Of Joy**[8] 6017 2-9-2 70 6ex DavidProbert(5) 2 71+
(J R Jenkins) *s.i.s: sn pushed up to trck ldrs: effrt on inner and ev ch whn bdly hmpd over 1f out: rallied u.p to chse ldng pair ins fnl f: kpt on* **6/4**[1]

0462 **4** nk **On The Feather**[9] 5997 2-9-5 68 JimCrowley 10 63
(P Winkworth) *bhd and sn pushed along: hdwy 2f out: swtchd rt jst ins fnl f: kpt on but nvr trbld wnr* **7/2**[2]

0100 **5** 3 **Flawless Diamond (IRE)**[24] 5581 2-8-12 61 (b) LPKeniry 6 47
(J S Moore) *chsd ldrs: rdn over 2f out: outpcd over 1f out: kpt on same pce fnl f* **33/1**

0004 **6** shd **Madison Belle**[11] 5937 2-8-9 58 RichardKingscote 5 44
(K R Burke) *pressed ldrs: rdn over 2f out: wknd over 1f out* **12/1**

0450 **7** nk **Al Mukaala (IRE)**[20] 5671 2-9-5 68 PaulDoe 4 53
(C E Brittain) *s.i.s: sn pushed up to chse ldr: ev ch wl over 1f out: wknd over 1f out* **12/1**

0643 **8** 1/2 **Calley Ho**[20] 5671 2-9-6 69 DarryllHolland 12 52
(Mrs L Stubbs) *towards rr on outer: rdn jst over 2f out: no prog and kpt on same pce* **10/1**[3]

000 **9** 1/2 **Kyle Of Bute**[20] 5671 2-9-1 64 (b[1]) AdamKirby 13 46
(J L Dunlop) *sn outpcd in rr: nvr trbld ldrs* **33/1**

064 **10** shd **Arrogance**[22] 5609 2-9-7 70 GeorgeBaker 9 51
(G L Moore) *a outpcd in rr: rdn jst over 2f out: n.d* **12/1**

030 **11** 1 1/4 **Lois Darlin (IRE)**[150] 1680 2-8-12 61 (b[1]) MartinDwyer 7 39
(J S Moore) *sn pushed along in rr: n.d* **40/1**

454 **12** 1 3/4 **Chatterszaha**[14] 5835 2-9-5 68 (v[1]) RobertHavlin 3 40
(C Drew) *led: rdn 2f out: hung lft and barging match w rival over 1f out: wl btn after* **16/1**

1m 13.94s (0.24) **Going Correction** -0.025s/f (Stan) **12** Ran SP% **121.0**
Speed ratings (Par 95): **97,94,93,93,89 89,88,88,87,87 85,83**
toteswinger: 1&2 £25.80, 1&3 £16.10, 2&3 £1.80. CSF £238.68 CT £592.89 TOTE £33.20: £7.70, £3.30, £1.10; EX 942.40.
Owner G P Clarke **Bred** Fortbarrington Stud **Trained** Sledmere, E Yorks

FOCUS
A modest sprint nursery run at a good pace but featuring a few interesting types.

NOTEBOOK
Brierty(IRE) offered little on her return from a break over 7f on soft ground at Leicester last time, but proved suited by both the drop in trip and switch to a better surface and returned to the sort of form she showed when winning a maiden at Warwick in May, despite flashing her tail under pressure. She is lightly raced and open to more improvement, but a rise in the weights will force her up in class. (tchd 25-1)
West Leake(IRE) ran much better than on his nursery debut on soft ground at Nottingham and this rates as a career best, but he was still no match for the winner. (op 10-1)

Ray Of Joy, well-in under the penalty she picked up for her recent Kempton success, was hampered at the top of the straight by Chatterszaha when that one edged left. Having held a decent position just in behind the speed early on, a nice opening appeared on the inside rail early in the straight, but she did not pick up immediately, hence the reason she was unable to take the gap. To be fair, she did well to recover her momentum, but it is doubtful whether she would have troubled the winner whatever the case. (tchd 15-8, 2-1 in places)
On The Feather was never in this, but she is a little better than she showed as she was slow to find her stride after possibly being a little bit short of room at the start, and then had to switch in the straight after getting caught behind the trouble on the rail. (op 4-1)
Madison Belle showed speed, but she was caught wide and weakened in the straight.
Chatterszaha Official explanation: jockey said filly hung left

6224 BRADWELL-ON-SEA MEDIAN AUCTION MAIDEN STKS — 5f (P)
7:20 (7:22) (Class 6) 3-5-Y-O — **£2,590** (£770; £385; £192) **Stalls** Low

Form — RPR
2262 **1** **Wreningham**[21] 5627 3-9-3 59 ShaneKelly 6 64
(T Keddy) *mde all: rdn clr over 1f out: in n.d fnl f: easily* **10/3**[1]
465 **2** 4 **Cranworth Blaze**[7] 6045 4-8-13 44 SaleemGolam 4 45
(T J Etherington) *racd in midfield: rdn 1/2-way: hdwy u.p over 1f out: chsd wnr ins fnl f: nvr a threat* **11/1**
0600 **3** ½ **Fantasy Fighter (IRE)**[51] 4702 3-9-3 40 JimmyQuinn 10 48
(J J Quinn) *v.s.a: swtchd rt and hdwy wl over 1f out: flashed tail and edgd lft u.p after: wnt 3rd wl ins fnl f: nvr nr wnr* **18/1**
5062 **4** 2½ **Mystickhill (IRE)**[54] 4615 3-8-7 58 MCGeran(5) 11 34
(J Balding) *chsd wnr: rdn 2f out: outpcd by wnr over 1f out: wl btn fnl f: lost 2 pls ins fnl f* **8/1**[3]
3053 **5** 1¼ **Shatter Resistant (IRE)**[20] 5679 3-9-3 50 (e) KirstyMilczarek 3 35
(M D Squance) *chsd ldrs: rdn wl over 1f out: wknd qckly ent fnl f* **9/1**
3000 **6** 1 **Rose De Rita**[17] 5749 3-8-12 31 VinceSlattery 12 26
(L P Grassick) *dropped in after s: modest hdwy over 1f out: swtchd rt ins fnl f: n.d* **100/1**
02 **7** ½ **Green Velvet**[20] 5679 3-8-12 0 RichardSmith 2 24
(P J Makin) *chsd ldrs: rdn 1/2-way: wknd wl over 1f out* **6/1**[2]
0000 **8** 2¾ **Groundhog Day**[42] 5007 4-8-10 35 (p) RussellKennemore(3) 1 14
(J Balding) *v.s.a: bhd: sme hdwy over 3f out: n.d* **66/1**
0000 **9** hd **Lovely Lilling**[40] 5110 3-8-12 35 (p) FrankieMcDonald 7 13
(P T Midgley) *s.i.s: sn in midfield: rdn 1/2-way: nvr trbld ldrs* **100/1**
0006 **10** 1½ **Hucking Harmony (IRE)**[20] 5679 3-8-12 45 LPKeniry 9 8
(J R Best) *chsd ldrs over 2f out: wknd wl over 1f out* **18/1**
000 **11** 1¼ **Tycoon's Buddy**[71] 4076 3-9-3 44 ChrisCatlin 8 9
(E J O'Neill) *s.i.s: a struggling in rr* **33/1**

60.16 secs (-0.04) **Going Correction** -0.025s/f (Stan)
WFA 3 from 4yo 1lb — **11** Ran SP% **83.7**
Speed ratings (Par 101): **99,92,91,87,85 84,83,79,78,76 74**
toteswinger: 1&2 £19.50, 1&3 £19.50, 2&3 £0. CSF £19.58 TOTE £2.50: £1.10, £2.70, £6.00; EX 25.60.
Owner Mervyn Ayers **Bred** Executive Bloodlines Ltd **Trained** Newmarket, Suffolk
■ Stewards' Enquiry : Kirsty Milczarek two-day ban: careless riding (Oct 11-12)
Frankie McDonald two-day ban: careless riding (Oct 9-10)

FOCUS
A very moderate, uncompetitive older-horse sprint maiden with the form limited by the proximity of the placed horses.

6225 FLACKS H'CAP — 6f (P)
7:50 (7:53) (Class 5) (0-75,79) 3-Y-O+ — **£4,209** (£1,252; £625; £312) **Stalls** Low

Form — RPR
011 **1** **Al Gillani (IRE)**[15] 5801 3-9-0 70 GeorgeBaker 7 85+
(J R Boyle) *pressed ldrs on outer: rdn 2f out: led over 1f out: edgd rt but styd on wl fnl f* **5/2**[2]
2042 **2** 1½ **Doubtful Sound (USA)**[19] 5708 4-8-12 69 (p) KevinGhunowa(3) 4 79
(R A Harris) *led narrowly tl rdn and hdd wl over 1f out: kpt on same pce u.p fnl f* **14/1**[3]
0111 **3** ¾ **Prescription**[3] 6160 3-9-9 79 6ex J-PGuillambert 6 87
(Sir Mark Prescott) *pressed ldrs: rdn and unable qckn wl over 1f out: kpt on again wl ins fnl f* **4/7**[1]
1630 **4** 1 **Danzili Bay**[40] 5091 6-8-9 63 ShaneKelly 1 67
(A W Carroll) *w ldr on inner: rdn 2f out: wknd jst ins fnl f* **28/1**
0400 **5** 4½ **Corridor Creeper (FR)**[9] 6006 11-9-1 74 (p) DavidProbert(5) 3 64
(J M Bradley) *broke wl: w ldrs for 2f: sn outpcd: n.d after* **25/1**
/0-0 **6** 6 **Beau Jazz**[28] 5433 7-7-13 60 oh15 GemmaElford(7) 2 31
(W De Best-Turner) *w ldrs for 2f: sn outpcd and struggling* **100/1**

1m 13.54s (-0.16) **Going Correction** -0.025s/f (Stan)
WFA 3 from 4yo+ 2lb — **6** Ran SP% **107.2**
Speed ratings (Par 103): **100,98,97,95,89 81**
toteswinger: 1&2 £1.90, 1&3 £1.02, 2&3 £2.70. CSF £27.57 TOTE £3.20: £1.10, £3.10; EX 18.10.
Owner The Paddock Space Partnership **Bred** Sean Finnegan **Trained** Epsom, Surrey

FOCUS
A good sprint handicap for the grade, but a smaller field than one would expect and many trainers were no doubt running scared of the well-in Prescription. The runner-up is rated to recent claiming-race form.

6226 TOLLESHUNT MAIDEN STKS — 1m 6f (P)
8:20 (8:20) (Class 5) 3-Y-O+ — **£3,238** (£963; £481; £240) **Stalls** Low

Form — RPR
-433 **1** **Houghton (IRE)**[10] 5963 3-9-2 72 RichardMullen 9 76
(Sir Michael Stoute) *sn bustled along: racd in midfield: rdn to chse ldrs over 3f out: chsd ldr over 2f out: led ent fnl f: styd on* **11/4**[1]
3443 **2** 1¾ **Mushtaaq (USA)**[29] 5406 3-9-2 73 (p) MartinDwyer 10 74
(M A Jarvis) *chsd ldr tl led after 2f: rdn over 2f out: hdd ent fnl f: one pce after* **3/1**[2]
0303 **3** 1¼ **Pure Song**[38] 5155 3-8-11 72 EddieAhern 1 67
(J L Dunlop) *hld up wl in tch: chsd ldng pair and rdn 2f out: swtchd rt over 1f out: kpt on same pce fnl f* **9/2**
5456 **4** 3¾ **Flam**[7] 6060 3-8-11 70 (p) AdamKirby 12 62
(J R Fanshawe) *chsd ldrs: wnt 2nd 4f out tl over 2f out: wknd u.p over 1f out* **7/2**[3]
0 **5** 6 **Lagavulin (IRE)**[35] 4821 4-9-7 0 DavidProbert(5) 2 59
(Miss E C Lavelle) *hld up in rr: hdwy over 4f out: rdn to chse ldng quartet over 2f out: no imp and hung lft over 1f out* **20/1**
060 **6** 3¼ **Bonzo**[103] 3035 3-9-2 53 TGMcLaughlin 7 54
(P Howling) *hld up in midfield: rdn 4f out: sn outpcd by ldrs: no ch fr over 2f out* **100/1**
4 **7** 2¼ **Scania Classic**[16] 5780 7-9-7 0 JackDean(5) 6 51
(M J Scudamore) *s.i.s: hld up bhd: rdn over 5f out: modest hdwy fr 3f out: nvr a factor* **50/1**
603 **8** 4 **Mary Athena (FR)**[22] 5612 3-8-6 58 NicolPolli(5) 13 40
(M G Quinlan) *hld up towards rr: effrt 5f out: sn rdn: no prog: wl btn last 3f* **12/1**
9 10 **Generous Star**[35] 5-9-12 0 JimmyQuinn 14 31
(J Pearce) *s.i.s: hld up in rr: hdwy on outer 6f out: no prog over 3f out: wl btn after* **33/1**
5005 **10** 15 **Valart**[178] 1109 5-9-7 39 (t) GeorgeBaker 8 5
(M R Bosley) *led for 2f: chsd ldr after tl 4f out: wknd qckly u.p over 2f out: eased fnl f: t.o* **28/1**
0 **11** 14 **Prophet's Star**[10] 5963 3-9-2 0 (bt[1]) JimCrowley 3 —
(H J L Dunlop) *hld up towards rr: hdwy 8f out: rdn and struggling over 5f out: t.o and eased fr over 1f out* **40/1**
000 **12** 2¼ **Bertie Boo**[26] 5505 3-9-2 50 TomEaves 11 —
(B Smart) *racd in midfield: rdn 8f out: bhd last 4f: t.o and eased fr over 1f out* **66/1**
0 **13** 5 **Frankly Fantastic**[39] 5117 4-9-12 0 (bt) StephenCarson 15 —
(Jean-Rene Auvray) *chsd ldrs tl rdn and lost pl qckly 6f out: t.o last 3f* **100/1**

3m 1.21s (-1.99) **Going Correction** -0.025s/f (Stan)
WFA 3 from 4yo+ 10lb — **13** Ran SP% **118.8**
Speed ratings (Par 103): **104,103,102,100,96 94,93,91,85,77 69,67,64**
toteswinger: 1&2 £3.80, 1&3 £6.10, 2&3 £3.60 CSF £10.37 TOTE £4.10: £2.00, £1.10, £3.20; EX 11.80.
Owner M Tabor, D Smith & Mrs J Magnier **Bred** Tullamaine Castle Stud And Partners **Trained** Newmarket, Suffolk

FOCUS
This staying maiden was full of disappointing sorts and is not a race to dwell on. The pace was steady early but the overall time was reasonable.
Valart Official explanation: jockey said mare had no more to give

6227 HONEY TYE H'CAP — 1m 2f (P)
8:50 (8:51) (Class 6) (0-60,60) 3-Y-O — **£3,043** (£905; £452; £226) **Stalls** Low

Form — RPR
6234 **1** **Carmela Maria**[17] 5758 3-9-2 58 IanMongan 5 68
(C F Wall) *sn pushed up to ld: mde rest: pushed clr 4f out: wl clr and rdn jst over 2f out: kpt on and nvr gng to be ct after* **5/1**[1]
5000 **2** 1½ **Princess India (IRE)**[15] 5803 3-9-4 60 StephenCarson 4 67
(P Winkworth) *hld up in midfield: n.m.r jst over 3f out: hdwy to chse wnr over 1f out: hung lft fr over 1f out: r.o but nvr rchd wnr* **10/1**
006 **3** 1¼ **American Madness (USA)**[36] 5182 3-9-4 60 ShaneKelly 1 65
(M G Quinlan) *hld up in midfield: rdn to chse ldng pair over 1f out: kpt on u.p: nvr chal wnr* **25/1**
1120 **4** 1¼ **Circadian Rhythm**[7] 6049 3-9-3 59 J-PGuillambert 12 61
(S C Williams) *towards rr: niggled along over 7f out: hdwy 2f out: kpt on fnl f: nvr able to rch ldrs* **5/1**[1]
0000 **5** nk **Silky Steps (IRE)**[37] 5167 3-9-3 59 EddieAhern 6 60
(P J Makin) *stdd s: t.k.h: hld up bhd: c wd and hdwy wl over 1f out: r.o fnl f: nvr trbld ldrs* **11/1**
630 **6** 2 **Jemiliah**[22] 5602 3-9-2 58 PatCosgrave 2 55
(B G Powell) *hld up towards rr: hdwy and rdn on inner jst over 2f out: kpt on fnl f but nvr nr wnr* **20/1**
0002 **7** 4½ **Yes Eighteen (IRE)**[15] 5799 3-9-4 60 MichaelHills 13 48
(J W Hills) *hld up towards rr: rdn 3f out: sme modest late hdwy: nvr a factor* **7/1**[2]
2306 **8** 2 **Italian Goddess**[40] 5108 3-9-4 60 HayleyTurner 14 44
(M L W Bell) *stdd s: t.k.h: hld up in rr: rdn 3f out: nvr a factor* **12/1**
0100 **9** ¾ **Ricci De Mare**[23] 5593 3-8-13 60 DavidProbert(5) 7 43
(A B Haynes) *chsd wnr: rdn and unable qckn wl over 3f out: lost 2nd over 1f out: wknd* **14/1**
-400 **10** 1¼ **Tamdiid (USA)**[8] 6018 3-9-2 58 LiamJones 15 38
(C E Brittain) *hld up towards rr: nvr a factor* **25/1**
055 **11** 8 **Oops Another Act**[46] 4909 3-9-2 58 AdamKirby 8 22
(W R Swinburn) *t.k.h: chsd ldrs: rdn 3f out: wknd qckly 2f out* **7/1**[2]
6104 **12** 2¾ **Whaston (IRE)**[30] 5378 3-9-2 58 (v) JimmyQuinn 10 17
(J D Bethell) *hld up in midfield on outer: rdn over 3f out: wl btn last 2f* **15/2**[3]
4600 **13** 6 **Little Firecracker**[22] 5602 3-9-1 57 LPKeniry 3 4
(Miss M E Rowland) *chsd ldrs: rdn over 4f out: sn struggling: t.o last 2f* **33/1**
10 **14** 22 **Blue Savannah (FR)**[32] 5318 3-9-1 60 KevinGhunowa(3) 16 —
(G J Smith) *nvr gng wl: racd in midfield on outer: drvn and wknd over 4f out: t.o and virtually p.u last 2f* **20/1**

2m 7.55s (-1.05) **Going Correction** -0.025s/f (Stan) — **14** Ran SP% **122.0**
Speed ratings (Par 99): **103,101,100,99,99 97,94,92,92,91 84,82,77,60**
toteswinger: 1&2 £7.90, 1&3 £0, 2&3 £0. CSF £51.57 CT £1162.65 TOTE £6.70: £1.70, £2.90, £7.20; EX 63.10.
Owner O Pointing **Bred** O Pointing **Trained** Newmarket, Suffolk

FOCUS
A moderate three-year-old handicap and very few were ever involved, despite them going a good pace. The winning time was 0.69 seconds quicker than the following 46-50 handicap for three-year-olds and upwards and the runner-up is rated close to this year's best with the fifth close to recent efforts.
Ricci De Mare Official explanation: jockey said filly hung right throughout
Blue Savannah(FR) Official explanation: jockey said filly never travelled

6228 STOCK H'CAP — 1m 2f (P)
9:20 (9:22) (Class 6) (0-50,50) 3-Y-O+ — **£2,590** (£770; £385; £192) **Stalls** Low

Form — RPR
4304 **1** **Personify**[13] 5869 6-8-11 48 (p) TolleyDean(3) 11 57
(J L Flint) *hld up bhd: hdwy on outer jst over 2f out: rdn to ld wl ins fnl f: r.o* **8/1**[2]
2150 **2** ¾ **Classic Blue (IRE)**[103] 3025 4-9-1 49 StephenDonohoe 4 56
(Ian Williams) *hld up in midfield: hdwy over 2f out: rdn to ld over 1f out: hdd and no ex wl ins fnl f* **8/1**[2]
000 **3** nse **Sagunt (GER)**[111] 2782 5-8-7 48 RossAtkinson(7) 13 55
(S Curran) *bhd: rdn over 4f out: c wd and hdwy u.p jst over 1f out: r.o: nt quite rch ldrs* **8/1**[2]
0540 **4** 1¼ **Mango Masher (IRE)**[225] 544 4-9-0 48 (p) AdamKirby 14 52
(J L Flint) *towards rr: reminders over 7f out: rdn 4f out: hdwy u.p over 1f out: chsd ldrs ins fnl f: one pce last 100yds* **20/1**
3050 **5** nse **Hatch A Plan (IRE)**[22] 5611 7-8-11 50 DavidProbert(5) 15 54
(Mouse Hamilton-Fairley) *hld up in midfield: plld out and hdwy wl over 1f out: edgd lft over 1f out: chsd ldrs ins fnl f: one pce last 100yds* **7/1**[1]
5000 **6** 1¾ **Hawkstar Express (IRE)**[9] 5994 3-8-9 49 ow1 (t) PatCosgrave 7 50
(J R Boyle) *bhd: rdn 4f out: hdwy u.p over 1f out: kpt on fnl f: nt rch ldrs* **50/1**

04 **7** 2 1/2 **Margot Mine (IRE)**[14] 5832 3-8-9 **49**........................(bt[1]) MartinDwyer 16 45
(J S Moore) *sn led: hdd over 8f out: led again over 3f out: rdn over 2f out: hdd over 1f out: wknd ins fnl f* **16/1**

3030 **8** 1 1/4 **The Grey One (IRE)**[12] 5912 5-8-11 **48**...............(p) KevinGhunowa(3) 10 41
(J M Bradley) *t.k.h: in tch: hmpd and swtchd rt 8f out: chsd ldr 6f out: drvn 2f out: wknd jst ins fnl f* **11/1**

6033 **9** nk **Piverina (IRE)**[32] 5308 3-8-10 **50**.. TomEaves 2 43
(Miss J A Camacho) *hld up in midfield: rdn and unable qck 4f out: kpt on same pce u.p fr over 2f out* **7/1**[1]

0000 **10** 1/2 **King After**[29] 5407 6-9-2 **50**..(v) LPKeniry 12 45+
(J R Best) *t.k.h: hld up in tch: rdn and nt qckn over 1f out: short of room and swtchd rt 1f out: no hdwy fnl f* **25/1**

0000 **11** 1 **Tewin Green**[7] 6044 3-8-10 **50**..........................(p) KirstyMilczarek 5 40
(M D Squance) *t.k.h: chsd ldrs: rdn wl over 2f out: wknd over 1f out* **40/1**

4015 **12** 1 1/4 **Itsy Bitsy**[55] 4599 6-9-1 **49**...(p) EddieAhern 6 36
(W J Musson) *s.i.s: hld up bhd: nvr a factor* **16/1**

460/ **13** 1/2 **Samson Quest**[768] 4585 6-9-1 **49**.. JimCrowley 8 35
(J Gallagher) *t.k.h: hld up in midfield: hdwy to chse ldr over 2f out: ev ch and drvn 2f out: wknd qckly over 1f out* **25/1**

221 **14** 1 3/4 **The Gaikwar (IRE)**[22] 5604 9-9-2 **50**......................(b) RichardKingscote 1 33
(R A Harris) *t.k.h: chsd ldrs: rdn over 2f out: wknd 2f out* **7/1**[1]

0556 **15** 6 **Danish Monarch**[16] 5787 7-9-0 **48**...................................... HayleyTurner 3 19
(David Pinder) *chsd ldr tl led over 8f out: rdn and hdd over 3f out: wknd over 2f out: wl btn and eased fnl f* **18/1**

4004 **16** 8 **Kadouchski (FR)**[12] 5912 4-9-0 **48**.......................................(p) TPO'Shea 9 3
(John Berry) *hld up in tch in midfield: rdn and struggling over 2f out: wl bhd and eased fnl f* **9/1**[3]

2m 8.24s (-0.36) **Going Correction** -0.025s/f (Stan)
WFA 3 from 4yo+ 6lb **16** Ran SP% **123.0**
Speed ratings (Par 101): **100,99,99,98,98 96,94,93,93,93 92,91,91,89,84 78**
toteswinger: 1&2 £41.40, 1&3 £45.60, 2&3 £0. CSF £67.04 CT £542.08 TOTE £10.60: £2.60, £1.60, £3.20, £4.70; EX 97.40 Place 6 £ 164.36, Place 5 £ 80.17.
Owner J L Flint **Bred** Darley **Trained** Kenfig Hill, Bridgend

FOCUS
A very moderate handicap, but they went 7-1 the field and it was wide open. The pace, however, was steady early and the winning time was 0.69 seconds slower than the previous 46-60 handicap for three-year-olds. the form is a little fluid but makes sense rated around the first two.
Mango Masher(IRE) Official explanation: jockey said gelding hung badly left
The Grey One(IRE) Official explanation: jockey said gelding raced keenly
King After Official explanation: jockey said gelding was denied a clear run
The Gaikwar(IRE) Official explanation: jockey said gelding was denied a clear run
Kadouchski(FR) Official explanation: jockey said gelding hung right from halfway
T/Jkpt: Part won. £113,601.90 to a £1 stake. Pool: £160,002.78. 0.50 winning tickets. T/Plt: £97.70 to a £1 stake. Pool: £110,272.09. 823.60 winning tickets. T/Qpdt: £40.20 to a £1 stake. Pool: £6,491.36. 119.40 winning tickets. SP

6050 PONTEFRACT (L-H)
Thursday, September 25

OFFICIAL GOING: Good to firm (good in places; 8.4)
Wind: Slight against Weather: Fair and bright

6229 EUROPEAN BREEDERS' FUND POPPIN LANE MAIDEN STKS (DIV I) 6f
2:30 (2:30) (Class 4) 2-Y-O **£4,857** (£1,445; £722; £360) **Stalls** Low

Form RPR

4 **1** **Big Apple Boy (IRE)**[69] 4169 2-9-3 0.............................. AndrewElliott 4 81+
(Jedd O'Keeffe) *cl up: effrt 2f out: rdn to ld over 1f out: styd on wl* **11/2**[2]

2 2 3/4 **Goliaths Boy (IRE)** 2-9-3 0.. PaulHanagan 12 73+
(R A Fahey) *in tch on outer: pushed along and edgd lft over 2f out: rdn over 1f out: styd on to chse wnr ins fnl f: no imp towards fin* **10/1**[3]

65 **3** 4 **Final Salute**[61] 4438 2-9-3 0..(v[1]) TedDurcan 10 61
(B Smart) *led: rdn along 2f out: drvn and hdd over 1f out: sn one pce* **28/1**

222 **4** 2 1/4 **Imaam**[24] 5578 2-9-3 79.. RHills 9 54
(J L Dunlop) *dwlt: sn chsng ldrs: pushed along 1/2-way: rdn over 2f out: sn drvn and btn* **2/5**[1]

5 **5** 1/2 **Embsay Crag**[26] 5500 2-9-3 0.............................. PaulMulrennan 3 53
(Mrs K Walton) *chsd ldrs on inner: effrt over 2f out: sn rdn along and grad wknd appr fnl f* **20/1**

0 **6** 1/2 **Georgie Bee**[8] 6010 2-8-12 0.. TonyCulhane 2 46
(D Carroll) *towards rr: hdwy wl over 1f out: kpt on ins fnl f: nrst fin* **66/1**

00 **7** 1 1/2 **Oneofthesedayz (IRE)**[10] 5959 2-8-12 0................. EdwardCreighton 7 42
(Miss V Haigh) *chsd ldrs: rdn along over 2f out: drvn wl over 1f out and sn wknd* **100/1**

60 **8** 2 **Hettie Hubble**[46] 4896 2-8-12 0.. DavidAllan 8 36
(T D Easterby) *s.i.s and bhd: hdwy 2f out: kpt on ins fnl f: n.d* **33/1**

9 9 **Melkatant** 2-8-9 0... DuranFentiman(3) 1 9
(N Bycroft) *in tch: rdn along 1/2-way: sn wknd* **80/1**

50 **10** 3 **Distinctive Spirit (IRE)**[10] 5959 2-9-3 0.............................. NCallan 5 —
(K A Ryan) *midfield: rdn along 2f over 2f out and sn wknd* **10/1**[3]

0 **11** 7 **Bill On The Hill**[9] 5989 2-9-3 0.. DaleGibson 6 —
(M W Easterby) *a towards rr* **100/1**

0 **12** 14 **Kannie Annie**[131] 2206 2-8-12 0.. TomEaves 13 —
(T J Pitt) *a in rr* **100/1**

1m 16.83s (-0.07) **Going Correction** -0.025s/f (Good) **12** Ran SP% **121.8**
Speed ratings (Par 97): **99,95,90,87,86 85,83,81,69,65 55,37**
toteswinger: 1&2 £4.30, 1&3 £12.80, 2&3 £17.70. CSF £56.38 TOTE £5.90: £1.50, £2.40, £7.40; EX 60.50.
Owner Highbeck Racing **Bred** Thomas Keane **Trained** Middleham Moor, N Yorks

FOCUS
An ordinary maiden in which very few had shown much in the way of ability, but one that had was the winner. the form looks rather guessy and is best rated around the winner and third.

NOTEBOOK
Big Apple Boy(IRE) ◆, who finished a promising fourth on his debut over course and distance in July and had been given a break since then, travelled powerfully behind the leaders before being delivered with his effort soon after straightening up for home. Once in front, he did edge over towards the far rail but he also found a decent turn of foot to pull clear. A big colt, he looks the type to improve as he strengthens and could be a nice sort for next year. (op 7-1)
Goliaths Boy(IRE) ◆, an already gelded half-brother to a winning chaser whose sales price leapt from 4,600euros as a foal to 44,000gns as a yearling, took quite a grip on the outside of the field, but despite that he stayed on very strongly up the final hill to finish a clear second best. There are certainly races to be won with him. (op 15-2)
Final Salute, who had not beaten a rival in his two previous starts, had the visor on for the first time and it made quite a difference, as he set the pace and although eventually swamped by the front pair, he kept on to hold on to the minor berth. If the headgear continues to work, he could have a future in nurseries. (op 25-1)
Imaam was a massive disappointment after finishing runner-up in all three of his previous starts in 7f maidens, including twice as a short-priced favourite, and he suffered the same ignominy here. Not best away, he was close enough if good enough for most of the journey, but he never looked happy and was a tired horse up the final hill. His official rating of 79 cannot be used as a benchmark to this form as he has run miles below that, and is one to have serious reservations about now. (op 4-9 tchd 1-2)
Embsay Crag ran another fair race, but is bred to appreciate much further so there is probably more to come from him when presented with a stiffer test.
Georgie Bee, well beaten from a bad draw on her Beverley debut, made a little late progress over this extra furlong and will probably come into her own once handicapped. (op 50-1)
Distinctive Spirit(IRE) Official explanation: jockey said gelding lost its action

6230 EUROPEAN BREEDERS' FUND POPPIN LANE MAIDEN STKS (DIV II) 6f
3:00 (3:03) (Class 4) 2-Y-O **£4,857** (£1,445; £722; £360) **Stalls** Low

Form RPR

5 **1** **Calligrapher (USA)**[24] 5578 2-9-3 0.............................. PhilipRobinson 11 84+
(M A Jarvis) *cl up: led over 2f out: jnd and rdn over 1f out: drvn ins fnl f and hld on wl* **4/1**[1]

2 hd **Film Set (USA)** 2-9-3 0.. LDettori 3 84+
(Saeed Bin Suroor) *hld up in midfield: gd hdwy on inner 2f out: chal over 1f out: sn rdn and ev ch: drvn ins fnl f and kpt on towards fin: jst hld* **9/2**[2]

4 **3** 7 **Striker Torres (IRE)**[74] 3997 2-9-3 0.................................. TomEaves 9 67+
(B Smart) *in tch: hdwy 2f out: sn rdn and styd on ins fnl f* **11/2**

550 **4** 1 1/2 **Soviet Rhythm**[45] 4923 2-8-12 68.............................. PJMcDonald 14 53
(G M Moore) *prom: effrt 2f out: rdn wl over 1f out: sn one pce* **11/1**

5 hd **Mary West (IRE)** 2-8-12 0.. PaulHanagan 13 52
(R A Fahey) *t.k.h: chsd ldrs: rdn along 2f out: kpt on same pce appr fnl f* **25/1**

6 1/2 **Puzzlemaster** 2-9-3 0.. RyanMoore 8 56
(G G Margarson) *towards rr: hdwy wl over 1f out: kpt on ins fnl f: nrst fin* **20/1**

7 hd **City Bank (USA)** 2-9-3 0.. JoeFanning 12 55
(M Johnston) *dwlt: green in rr tl styd on on outer fnl 2f: nrst fin* **11/1**

8 2 3/4 **Solis** 2-9-3 0.. GrahamGibbons 5 47+
(J J Quinn) *nvr nr ldrs* **25/1**

00F **9** nse **Nayessence**[12] 5882 2-9-3 0.. PaulMulrennan 7 47
(M W Easterby) *wnt bdly rt s: nvr bttr than midfield* **100/1**

0 **10** 2 1/2 **Residency (IRE)**[24] 5572 2-9-3 0.. TedDurcan 4 39+
(M J Wallace, Australia) *chsd ldrs: rdn along over 2f out: grad wknd and eased fnl f* **16/1**

0 **11** 1 **Melange (USA)**[34] 5227 2-9-3 0.. NCallan 2 36
(P F I Cole) *led: rdn along 1/2-way: hdd over 2f out and sn wknd* **5/1**[3]

0 **12** nse **Cafe Fiore (IRE)**[7] 6051 2-8-12 0.............................. WilliamBuick 10 31
(T J Pitt) *a in rr* **66/1**

13 hd **Avitus** 2-9-3 0.. TonyCulhane 1 36
(Micky Hammond) *a towards rr* **50/1**

14 3/4 **Legal Legacy** 2-9-3 0.. TonyHamilton 6 33
(M Dods) *dwlt: a in rr* **10/1**

1m 18.11s (1.21) **Going Correction** -0.025s/f (Good) **14** Ran SP% **118.8**
Speed ratings (Par 97): **90,89,80,78,78 77,77,73,73,70 68,68,68,67**
toteswinger: 1&2 £5.40, 1&3 £5.00, 2&3 £4.90. CSF £19.84 TOTE £5.40: £2.20, £2.10, £1.80; EX 21.80.
Owner Sheikh Ahmed Al Maktoum **Bred** Darley **Trained** Newmarket, Suffolk

FOCUS
Less previous form to go on than in the first division and despite what looked a decent pace the winning time was 1.28 seconds slower. The first two came clear of the remainder.

NOTEBOOK
Calligrapher(USA), green on debut when well behind the disappointing favourite in the previous division Imaam, proved rather awkward to load but once under way he helped force the pace alongside Melange. After seeing off that rival, he then faced a stern challenge up his inside from the runner-up all the way up the home straight, but showed real grit to keep on going and just gain the day. (op 7-2 tchd 9-2)
Film Set(USA) ◆, whose price rose from $40,000 as a yearling to 370,000gns as a two-year-old, is by Johar, who dead-heated with High Chaparral in the 2003 Breeders' Cup turf. Well backed earlier in the day for this debut, he enjoyed a dream run up the inside rail rounding the home turn and looked likely to prevail, but the more-experienced winner kept on finding a bit more and just managed to hold him at bay. He should not take long in going one better. (op 4-1)
Striker Torres(IRE), green on his Haydock debut in July though he did show some ability, was on very different ground this time and he was having to be niggled along to go the pace from a long way out. He kept on to win the separate race for third and shapes as though an extra furlong will suit him now. (op 5-1 tchd 9-2)
Soviet Rhythm, racing beyond the minimum trip for the first time in her fourth outing, was never far off the pace and kept on to the line. Already rated 68, she may be better off in nurseries. (op 10-1)
Mary West(IRE) ◆, out of half-sister to four winning sprinters, did well considering she took quite a grip behind the leaders early and there should be much better to come. (op 40-1)
Puzzlemaster ◆, who has a middle-distance pedigree despite being a half-brother to the winning sprinter Norcroft, showed some ability on this debut and should progress with experience as he goes up in trip. (op 25-1)
City Bank(USA), a half-brother to the 7f winner Profitability, proved very green on this debut but made a little late headway down the wide outside and should be capable of better. (tchd 12-1)
Residency(IRE) Official explanation: jockey said colt was unsuited by the good to firm (good in places) ground
Legal Legacy was a major springer in the market, but after missing the break he showed nothing. (op 50-1)

6231 BEST HORSE RACING SKY CHANNEL 432 FILLIES' NURSERY 1m 4y
3:30 (3:31) (Class 4) (0-85,84) 2-Y-O **£4,533** (£1,348; £674; £336) **Stalls** Low

Form RPR

616 **1** **Zaaqya**[34] 5242 2-8-10 **73**.. RHills 7 76
(J L Dunlop) *hld up in rr: pushed along over 2f out: hdwy on outer whn checked jst over 1f out: sn rdn and styd on wl to ld nr fin* **4/1**[1]

452 **2** 1 **Caster Sugar (USA)**[25] 5534 2-8-4 **67**.............................. HayleyTurner 8 68
(L M Cumani) *in tch: hdwy wl over 1f out: rdn to ld ins fnl f: hdd and nt qckn nr fin* **9/2**[2]

432 **3** hd **Chilly Filly (IRE)**[16] 5771 2-8-9 **72**.............................. RoystonFfrench 1 72+
(M Johnston) *prom: hdwy to ld 2f out: rdn: hung bdly rt and hdd jst over 1f out: kpt on u.p ins fnl f* **4/1**[1]

3412 **4** 3/4 **Musical Maze**[17] 5747 2-8-1 **67**.............................. DuranFentiman(3) 4 66
(W M Brisbourne) *dwlt: hdwy 1/2-way: chsd ldrs over 2f out: rdn and led jst over 1f out: drvn and hdd ins fnl f: one pce* **8/1**[3]

3166 **5** ½ **Maid For Music (IRE)**[27] 5462 2-9-7 **84**.......................... RichardMullen 2 82
(E S McMahon) *led: rdn along and hdd 2f out: c lose up whn bmpd jst over 1f out: sn drvn and one pce* **8/1**[3]

300 **6** 1¼ **Triple Cee (IRE)**[34] 5241 2-8-11 **74**.......................... TonyCulhane 6 69
(M R Channon) *hld up towards rr: hdwy over 2f out: sn rdn and no imp appr last* **9/1**

0205 **7** 1¼ **Very Distinguished**[12] 5895 2-8-3 **66**.......................... LiamJones 5 58
(M G Quinlan) *hld up in tch: hdwy on inner 2f out: rdn to chse ldrs over 1f out: wknd ins fnl f* **9/2**[2]

5605 **8** 19 **Straitjacket**[8] 6023 2-8-5 **68**.......................... WilliamBuick 3 18
(R Hannon) *t.k.h: chsd ldrs: rdn along over 2f out and sn wknd* **16/1**

1m 45.67s (-0.23) **Going Correction** -0.125s/f (Firm) **8** Ran SP% **114.5**
Speed ratings (Par 94): **96,95,94,94,93 92,91,72**
toteswinger: 1&2 £5.20, 1&3 £2.90, 2&3 £3.00. CSF £22.12 CT £76.18 TOTE £5.00: £1.90, £1.50, £1.90; EX 22.60.

Owner Hamdan Al Maktoum **Bred** Launceston Stud **Trained** Arundel, W Sussex

FOCUS
Quite a decent little fillies' nursery, but they went no pace early and there were six fillies in a line across the track passing the furlong pole. The form is messy but still looks fairly reliable.

NOTEBOOK
Zaaqya, down 2lb after a fair effort in a Newmarket nursery that has already produced three subsequent winners, was well backed earlier in the day but she did not look the most likely winner on the home bend as she was stone last and being ridden along. However, once she was switched to the wide outside her stamina came in to play and she swept past her rivals to lead well inside the last furlong and in the end won a shade cosily. She still has a bit of scope and obviously stays well. (op 6-1)
Caster Sugar(USA), bred to be suited by this extra furlong on this nursery debut, travelled well off the pace and was brought with her effort between horses in plenty of time, but the winner produced a better turn of foot. She may have appreciated a more solid pace and her first win cannot be too far off. (op 7-2)
Chilly Filly(IRE), beaten at odds of 2-5 last time, was on much faster ground than she had encountered before on this nursery debut. She had every chance, but was inclined to hang about once into the home straight and, though she plugged on she was never doing enough. She may be worth another chance on genuinely good ground. (op 9-2 tchd 7-2)
Musical Maze, the most-experienced filly in the field who has been running well on much softer ground recently, missed the break but with the early pace so modest she was soon back in touch. Produced with her effort passing the furlong pole, she briefly hit the front but could not match the finishing speed of the principals. (tchd 17-2)
Maid For Music(IRE), highly tried in Listed company since winning a Salisbury maiden, was responsible for the modest pace on this nursery debut, but she already looked to be getting the worst of it when hampered by the errant Chilly Filly passing the furlong pole. (tchd 9-1 in a place)
Triple Cee(IRE), disappointing in two outings since a promising debut, was up in trip for this nursery debut but she never seemed to be travelling that well and merely plugged on to reach her final position. (op 10-1 tchd 12-1)
Very Distinguished, far from disgraced in a much stronger nursery at Doncaster last time, had her chance against the inside rail up the home straight but she then looked one-paced and is another that would probably have appreciated a stronger early gallop. (op 4-1 tchd 5-1 in a place)

6232 RIFLES CUP H'CAP 5f
4:00 (4:00) (Class 5) (0-75,81) 3-Y-O+ **£3,885** (£1,156; £577; £288) **Stalls** Low

Form RPR

2033 **1** **Mr Wolf**[26] 5493 7-9-1 **71**.......................... (p) TonyHamilton 5 79
(D W Barker) *mde all: rdn over 1f out: drvn ins fnl f and hld on gamely* **9/2**[2]

3245 **2** nk **Make My Dream**[15] 5796 5-9-0 **70**.......................... TPO'Shea 4 77
(J Gallagher) *in tch: hdwy on inner wl over 1f out: swtchd rt and rdn to chse wnr ins fnl f: kpt on* **11/2**[3]

5001 **3** ½ **Hotham**[6] 6066 5-9-11 **81** 6ex.......................... JamieMoriarty 2 86
(N Wilson) *s.i.s and rr: gd hdwy on inner 2f out: swtchd rt and rdn ent fnl f: styd on wl* **11/2**[3]

5020 **4** ¾ **Magical Speedfit (IRE)**[5] 6131 3-9-3 **74**.......................... RyanMoore 1 77
(G G Margarson) *hld up in rr on inner: hdwy and swtchd to wd outside over 1f out: rdn and styd on strly ins fnl f* **14/1**

1033 **5** ¾ **Angle Of Attack (IRE)**[12] 5886 3-9-4 **75**.......................... SilvestreDeSousa 3 75
(A D Brown) *chsd wnr: effrt 2f out: sn rdn and ch tl drvn and one pce ent fnl f* **12/1**

-411 **6** nk **Arganil (USA)**[8] 6011 3-9-7 **78** 6ex.......................... NCallan 15 77+
(K A Ryan) *stmbld and wnt rt s: sn chsng ldrs on outer: rdn wl over 1f out: drvn: edgd lft and one pce ins fnl f* **11/4**[1]

6156 **7** hd **Comptonspirit**[13] 5867 4-8-11 **67**.......................... DavidAllan 9 65
(B P J Baugh) *chsd ldrs: hdwy 2f out: sn rdn and kpt on same pce appr fnl f* **7/1**

6-60 **8** 1½ **Joyeaux**[5] 6131 6-8-5 **64**.......................... DuranFentiman(3) 8 57
(L R James) *in tch: rdn and hdwy to chse ldrs over 1f out: sn drvn and no imp ins fnl f* **25/1**

6004 **9** ½ **Weet A Surprise**[8] 6011 3-8-13 **70**.......................... HayleyTurner 10 61
(R Hollinshead) *dwlt: towards rr tl sme late hdwy* **20/1**

6006 **10** 2½ **Yorke's Folly (USA)**[60] 4462 7-8-0 **61** oh16..........(v) KellyHarrison(5) 7 43
(C W Fairhurst) *a in rr* **100/1**

0-50 **11** 3¾ **Chookie Heiton (IRE)**[62] 4393 10-8-11 **67**.......................... TomEaves 14 46
(Miss L A Perratt) *in tch: rdn along 2f out and sn wknd* **33/1**

0600 **12** 1¾ **Jonny Ebeneezer**[10] 5970 9-8-5 **61** oh4..........(b) WilliamBuick 6 34
(D Flood) *midfield: rdn along 1/2-way: nvr a factor* **33/1**

4514 **13** 2¼ **Barraland**[12] 5902 3-9-4 **75**.......................... TonyCulhane 11 40
(M R Channon) *chsd ldrs: effrt and cl up 1/2-way: rdn 2f out and wknd qckly over 1f out* **25/1**

62.73 secs (-0.57) **Going Correction** -0.025s/f (Good)
WFA 3 from 4yo+ 1lb **13** Ran SP% **121.8**
Speed ratings (Par 103): **103,102,101,100,99 98,98,96,95,91 90,87,83**
toteswinger: 1&2 £6.00, 1&3 £4.60, 2&3 £7.60. CSF £27.77 CT £127.95 TOTE £5.30: £2.10, £2.30, £2.40; EX 24.30 Trifecta £100.40 Pool: £760.46 - 5.60 winning units..

Owner Andrew Turton & David Barker **Bred** P Asquith **Trained** Scorton, N Yorks

FOCUS
An ordinary if competitive sprint handicap and this race was arguably won and lost at the start. The form is pretty ordinary but sound rated around the third and fourth.
Arganil(USA) Official explanation: jockey said gelding stumbled at start

6233 DALBY SCREW-DRIVER H'CAP 1m 2f 6y
4:30 (4:30) (Class 2) (0-100,99) 3-Y-O+
£12,462 (£3,732; £1,866; £934; £466; £234) **Stalls** Low

Form RPR

024 **1** **Fragrancy (IRE)**[54] 4644 4-9-4 **93**.......................... PhilipRobinson 8 106
(M A Jarvis) *hld up in rr: hdwy 3f out: rdn to ld over 1f out: drvn ins fnl f and styd on strly* **7/2**[2]

3040 **2** 2¾ **Heaven Knows**[75] 3974 5-9-5 **94**.......................... RHills 5 101
(W J Haggas) *hld up in rr: hdwy 2f out: rdn to chse wnr ins fnl f: sn drvn and no imp* **7/2**[2]

0603 **3** ¾ **Kinsya**[12] 5903 5-9-0 **89**.......................... NCallan 6 95
(M H Tompkins) *trckd ldrs: hdwy to ld over 2f out: rdn and hdd over 1f out: sn drvn and kpt on same pce ins fnl f* **7/1**

02 **4** 3¾ **Granston (IRE)**[54] 4618 7-8-10 **85** oh1.......................... GrahamGibbons 2 83
(J D Bethell) *trckd ldng pair: hdwy on inner 2f out: rdn and ev ch over 1f out: sn drvn and wknd ins fnl f* **9/2**[3]

1300 **5** 5 **Luberon**[26] 5508 5-9-4 **93**.......................... JoeFanning 4 81
(M Johnston) *led: rdn along 3f out: hdd over 2f out and sn wknd* **11/4**[1]

2210 **6** 12 **Demolition**[13] 5858 4-8-10 **85** oh3.......................... JamieMoriarty 7 49
(N Wilson) *chsd ldr: rdn along 3f out: sn wknd* **9/1**

2m 9.97s (-3.73) **Going Correction** -0.125s/f (Firm)
WFA 3 from 4yo+ 6lb **6** Ran SP% **111.8**
Speed ratings (Par 109): **109,106,106,103,99 89**
toteswinger: 1&2 £2.80, 1&3 £6.40, 2&3 £3.90. CSF £15.88 CT £77.75 TOTE £4.10: £2.00, £1.90; EX 13.40.

Owner Mohammed Al Nabouda **Bred** Darley **Trained** Newmarket, Suffolk

FOCUS
A decent handicap, though the race lost some of its competitiveness with the withdrawal of the likely favourite Ascot Lime. The early pace set by Luberon did not appear that strong, though the final time was good and the form is best rated through the runner-up to previous fast-ground form. The runners were inclined to come off the rail and race up the centre of the track in the home straight.

NOTEBOOK
Fragrancy(IRE), runner-up in this year's Zetland Gold Cup in her only previous try over this trip, was held up right out the back before being delivered with her effort around the outside on the home bend. Once in front, had there been any doubts over her stamina then this stiff track would have exposed them, but as it was she kept on finding enough and ran out a clear-cut winner. (tchd 9-2 in a place)
Heaven Knows, not at his best lately and still 6lb above his last winning mark, was returning from a short break and was without the visor this time. Another to be switched off out the back, he stayed on to chase the filly up the straight, but could never get on terms with her. (op 3-1)
Kinsya, whose best form has been on softer ground, is yet to truly prove himself over this far but he was brought to hold every chance starting up the final climb and, although he could not hold off the front pair, it would be harsh to blame lack of stamina for this defeat. (op 13-2 tchd 6-1)
Granston(IRE) enjoyed a lovely run up the inside on the home turn, but patently failed to get home and almost certainly found this stiff track testing his stamina beyond its limits. (op 6-1)
Luberon, a confirmed front-runner, had an easy time of it out in front so it was disappointing that he folded so tamely after getting swamped on the home bend. (op 3-1)
Demolition, 3lb out of the handicap which meant that he was 8lb higher than when winning at Ripon last month, got warm beforehand and despite racing prominently for a long way he faded out of it very disappointingly. Official explanation: jockey said gelding suffered interference in running (op 10-1)

6234 EUROPEAN BREEDERS' FUND FRIER WOOD MAIDEN STKS 1m 4y
5:00 (5:00) (Class 4) 2-Y-O **£5,180** (£1,541; £770; £384) **Stalls** Low

Form RPR

05 **1** **Takaatuf (IRE)**[14] 5842 2-9-3 0.......................... RHills 5 81+
(M Johnston) *mde all: rdn over 1f out: clr ins fnl f: styd on* **15/8**[2]

62 **2** 3½ **Custody (IRE)**[20] 5672 2-9-3 0.......................... RyanMoore 8 73
(Sir Michael Stoute) *cl up: effrt over 2f out and sn rdn: drvn over 1f out and sn one pce* **4/6**[1]

0 **3** 9 **Saffron's Son (IRE)**[18] 5716 2-9-3 0.......................... MickyFenton 4 54
(P T Midgley) *towards rr: hdwy 3f out: snr idden along: styd on fnl 2f: n.d* **50/1**

4 3¾ **Rebel Prince (IRE)** 2-9-3 0.......................... EdwardCreighton 7 45+
(M G Quinlan) *s.i.s: hdwy 1/2-way: rdn 3f out and n.d* **16/1**[3]

00 **5** nk **Urban Space**[8] 6026 2-9-3 0.......................... DaleGibson 1 45
(B G Powell) *in tch: rdn along and outpcd 3f out: kpt on u.p fnl 2f: nvr a factor* **50/1**

6 nk **Dalesway** 2-9-3 0.......................... TPQueally 6 44
(J G Given) *chsd ldng pair: rdn along 3f out: drvn and wknd 2f out* **25/1**

0 **7** 9 **Duratwill**[8] 6013 2-8-12 0.......................... PaulMulrennan 3 19
(M W Easterby) *chsd ldrs: rdn along 1/2-way: outpcd fnl 3f* **80/1**

8 2 **Challenging (UAE)** 2-8-12 0.......................... PJMcDonald 2 15
(R D E Woodhouse) *hld up: a in rr* **50/1**

1m 46.35s (0.45) **Going Correction** -0.125s/f (Firm) **8** Ran SP% **111.6**
Speed ratings (Par 97): **92,88,79,75,75 75,66,64**
toteswinger: 1&2 £1.20, 1&3 £7.10, 2&3 £6.70. CSF £3.23 TOTE £2.60: £1.10, £1.10, £5.20; EX 3.60.

Owner Hamdan Al Maktoum **Bred** Ballyreddin Stud **Trained** Middleham Moor, N Yorks

FOCUS
A very uncompetitive maiden and a two-horse race according to the market. That is how it turned out as the pair dominated from the start, but they did not finish in the order most would have expected and this is not form to get carried away with. The winning time was 0.68 seconds slower than the earlier fillies' nursery.

NOTEBOOK
Takaatuf(IRE), bred for stamina on the dam's side of his pedigree, stepped up from his Sandown effort and seemed to appreciate this stiff track. He was going better than his only rival rounding the home turn and it was soon clear that the race was his. He can continue to improve and should make a three-year-old, but he will need to if he is to recoup his 100,000gns price tag. (tchd 2-1)
Custody(IRE), just in front of a subsequent winner over this trip on the Kempton Polytrack earlier this month, could not match his rival up the final climb and looked ill at ease on this quick ground. He may be worth another chance on an easier surface or back on sand, especially as he can now be handicapped, but he is obviously nothing special. (tchd 8-13 and 8-11 in places)
Saffron's Son(IRE), well beaten on soft ground on his debut but not unsupported at monster prices here, looked more likely to finish last starting the turn for home, but he plugged on to win the separate race for third and may not be a total lost cause. (op 100-1)
Rebel Prince(IRE), a brother to a winner over 7f, can be given a little extra credit as he went up in the air as the stalls opened and lost quite a bit of ground. Official explanation: jockey said gelding missed the break (op 20-1)
Urban Space, who missed the break in his first two starts, did not this time and ran his best race yet though that is not saying much. (op 80-1)

6235 PONTEFRACT APPRENTICE SERIES H'CAP (FINAL ROUND) 1m 2f 6y
5:30 (5:30) (Class 5) (0-75,74) 3-Y-O+ **£3,238** (£963; £481; £240) **Stalls** Low

Form RPR

4121 **1** **Princess Flame (GER)**[7] 6050 6-9-9 **72** 6ex.......................... KylieManser 7 78
(B G Powell) *trckd ldrs: hdwy on inner 2f out: rdn over 1f out: styd on to ld ins fnl f* **2/1**[1]

00 **2** 1 **Celtic Strand (IRE)**[58] 4500 3-9-5 **74**.......................... DeanHeslop 6 78
(T P Tate) *led: rdn along 2f out: drvn over 1f out: hdd ins fnl f: kpt on* **14/1**

3535 **3** 3/4 **Coral Shores**[7] 6050 3-8-9 **64**..............................(v) BillyCray 2 66
(P W Hiatt) *hld up towards rr: hdwy 2f out: swtchd lft and rdn over 1f out: styd on u.p ins fnl f: nrst fin* **5/1**[3]

1620 **4** 1/2 **New Star (UAE)**[54] 4633 4-9-11 **74**.............................. MatthewDavies 3 75
(W M Brisbourne) *hld up: hdwy 3f out: rdn to chse ldrs wl over 1f out: sn drvn and one pce ent fnl f* **7/1**

4000 **5** 2 3/4 **Boppys Pride**[3] 6162 5-8-8 **60** oh13.............................. JamesRogers(3) 4 56
(P T Midgley) *trckd ldng pair: hdwy 3f out: rdn to chse ldr 2f out: drvn appr fnl f and grad wknd* **14/1**

4-60 **6** 3/4 **Paradise Walk**[7] 6050 4-9-5 **68**.............................. JamieKyne 1 62
(E W Tuer) *chsd ldrs: effrt 3f out: rdn 2f out: sn drvn and wknd appr fnl f* **13/2**

6120 **7** 2 1/4 **Smarterthanuthink (USA)**[63] 4331 3-8-13 **68**..............(p) BMcHugh 5 58
(R A Fahey) *trckd ldr: effrt 3f out: sn rdn and lost pl over 2f out* **4/1**[2]

000 **8** 1 1/2 **Byron Bay**[7] 6050 6-8-11 **60**.............................. StacyRenwick 9 47
(R C Guest) *a in rr* **20/1**

2m 13.53s (-0.17) **Going Correction** -0.125s/f (Firm)
WFA 3 from 4yo+ 6lb **8 Ran SP% 113.9**
Speed ratings (Par 103): **95,94,93,93,91 90,88,87**
toteswinger: 1&2 £5.50, 1&3 £2.70, 2&3 £8.60. CSF £32.24 CT £123.90 TOTE £2.40: £1.10, £5.00, £1.20; EX 25.80 Place 6: £40.23 Place 5: £8.67.
Owner B G Powell **Bred** V Kaufling **Trained** Upper Lambourn, Berks

FOCUS
A modest apprentice handicap containing four horses who contested an identical event here seven days earlier. The early pace was modest, causing a few to take a grip, and the winning time was 3.56 seconds slower than the earlier handicap. the close-up fifth racing from well out of the handicap raises doubts about the form.
Smarterthanuthink(USA) Official explanation: vet said gelding lost a front shoe
T/Plt: £77.90 to a £1 stake. Pool: £59,544.58. 557.52 winning tickets. T/Qpdt: £6.60 to a £1 stake. Pool: £5,273.15. 582.60 winning tickets. JR

4471 MAISONS-LAFFITTE (R-H)
Thursday, September 25

OFFICIAL GOING: Good to soft

6237a LA COUPE DE MAISONS-LAFFITTE (GROUP 3) (STRAIGHT COURSE) 1m 2f (S)
2:50 (2:56) 3-Y-O+ **£29,412** (£11,765; £8,824; £5,882; £2,941)

RPR

1 **Pallodio (IRE)**[34] 3-8-8 .... DBonilla 2 103
(J E Hammond, France) *cl up: rdn to ld over 1 1/2f out: drvn out* **176/10**

2 3/4 **Full Of Gold (FR)**[11] 5953 3-9-0 ....(p) DBoeuf 6 107
(Mme C Head-Maarek, France) *prom tl hrd rdn to ld over 2 1/2f out: hdd over 1 1/2f out: kpt on* **9/1**

3 hd **Chinchon (IRE)**[33] 5302 3-8-8 .... CSoumillon 5 101
(C Laffon-Parias, France) *hld up in 7th bhd slow pce: rdn and styd on down outside fr over 2f out: tk 3rd over 1f out: kpt on* **18/10**[1]

4 2 **Terra Incognita**[40] 5114 4-8-10 .... IMendizabal 7 93
(Y De Nicolay, France) *midfield: smooth hdwy to go 3rd over 2f out: hrd rdn and lost 3rd over 1f out: one pce* **21/1**

5 1 1/2 **Candy Gift (ARG)**[25] 5557 5-9-0 .... JAuge 9 94
(A Fabre, France) *in rr: brief effrt against stands' rail over 2f out: nvr a factor* **66/10**

6 1 **Stubbs Art (IRE)**[100] 3102 3-8-8 .... C-PLemaire 8 92
(D R C Elsworth) *reluctant ldr at slow pce racing freely: hdd over 2 1/2f out: wknd* **37/10**[2]

7 1/2 **Indian Choice (USA)**[14] 5851 4-9-0 ....(p) SPasquier 1 91
(P Bary, France) *racd in 2nd tl wknd over 2f out* **4/1**[3]

8 2 **Bucintoro (IRE)**[90] 4-9-0 .... TGillet 4 87
(J E Hammond, France) *a in rr* **12/1**

2m 4.70s (2.30)
WFA 3 from 4yo+ 6lb **8 Ran SP% 117.8**
PARI-MUTUEL: WIN 18.60; PL 3.30, 2.50, 1.50; DF 60.40.
Owner Mme A-M Springer **Bred** Millinium Partnership **Trained** France

NOTEBOOK
Pallodio(IRE), held up behind the leaders on the rail, travelled well throughout in what was a slowly run race. He quickened well when asked one and a half furlongs out and galloped on strongly to the line. A very consistent colt, he is due to go through the sales ring at the Arc sale on October 4th.
Full Of Gold(FR) put up a much better effort. He sat closer to the pace on this occasion and was the first to take the initiative one and a half furlongs out, hitting the front and looking all the over winner, but he could not quite go through with his effort. Clearly this straight course suited him and his trainer confirmed his dislike of going right handed. He has an entry in the Champion Stakes at Newmarket.
Chinchon(IRE), held up at the back, gradually progressed through the field when the tempo quickened, but was under pressure and looked one-paced until finding a second wind in the dying stages to just miss second place on the line. His trainer reported that he was probably in need of a rest after a busy campaign
Terra Incognita, always well placed, tried to respond when things quickened up but found the first three too good and she could only stay on one pace to the line.
Stubbs Art(IRE) was disappointing, though this was his first racecourse appearance since Royal Ascot. Just behind the leaders on the outside early, he was sent to the front after 2f and tried to make the best of his way home, but when things eventually quickened up he faded tamely away.

4840 ASCOT (R-H)
Friday, September 26

OFFICIAL GOING: Good to firm (good in places on round course) changing to good after race 1 (2.10)

6238 EBF RATCLIFFES SYNDICATION CLASSIFIED STKS 1m 2f
2:10 (2:10) (Class 3) 3-Y-O+
£11,215 (£3,358; £1,679; £840; £419; £210) **Stalls High**

Form RPR

1602 **1** **Amanjena**[89] 3527 3-8-7 87.............................. WilliamBuick 5 96
(A M Balding) *in tch: effrt and rdn 2f out: chal 1f out: led ins fnl f: hld on wl towards fin* **10/1**

4110 **2** shd **Australia Day (IRE)**[27] 5508 5-9-2 90.............................. MartinDwyer 4 99
(P R Webber) *led: rdn over 2f out: battled on gamely tl hdd ins fnl f: rallied towards fin* **9/2**[1]

1151 **3** 4 1/2 **Fair Gale**[28] 5464 3-8-10 89.............................. RyanMoore 9 90
(S Kirk) *chsd ldr for 1f: chsd ldng pair after tl wnt 2nd again 2f out: sn ev ch: wknd ins fnl f* **8/1**

3355 **4** 3 **Samsons Son**[6] 6120 4-9-2 88.............................. LPKeniry 7 84
(J R Best) *w.w in midfield: rdn 3f out: kpt on to chsd ldng trio ins fnl f: nvr threatened ldrs* **7/1**[3]

0161 **5** 2 1/4 **Amanda Carter**[62] 4419 4-8-8 86.............................. FrederikTylicki(5) 8 76
(R A Fahey) *t.k.h: chsd ldr after 1f: rdn over 2f out: lost 2nd 2f out: sn wknd* **5/1**[2]

2265 **6** 1/2 **Trans Siberian**[36] 5207 4-9-2 86.............................. NCallan 6 78
(P F I Cole) *stdd and awkward s: plld hrd: hld up bhd: rdn 3f out: no imp* **9/1**

13B6 **7** 6 **Cheshire Prince**[13] 5885 4-9-2 87.............................. EddieAhern 2 66
(W M Brisbourne) *stdd and dropped in after s: hld up in last trio: clipped heels and hmpd over 5f out: rdn and effrt 3f out: sn no hdwy and wl btn* **20/1**

5424 **8** 7 **Bandama (IRE)**[55] 4642 5-9-2 89.............................. JimCrowley 10 52
(Mrs A J Perrett) *hld up in midfield: pushed along 5f out: rdn 3f out: no prog: wl btn last 2f* **9/2**[1]

302 **9** 21 **Hustle (IRE)**[21] 5682 3-8-10 89.............................. RichardHughes 1 10
(R Hannon) *nvr travelling wl in rr: reminders 5f out: rdn and lost tch wl over 2f out: eased fnl f: t.o* **7/1**[3]

2m 7.78s (-2.02) **Going Correction** 0.0s/f (Good)
WFA 3 from 4yo+ 6lb **9 Ran SP% 113.0**
Speed ratings (Par 107): **108,107,104,101,100 99,94,89,72**
toteswinger: 1&2 £7.50, 1&3 £11.70, 2&3 £5.10. CSF £53.36 TOTE £12.60: £3.10, £1.80, £2.40; EX 65.90 Trifecta £258.60 Pool: £905.37 - 2.59 winning units..
Owner Mrs M E Wates **Bred** M E Wates **Trained** Kingsclere, Hants

FOCUS
The ground had been advertised as good to firm with good patches, but was officially amended to good all round after this opener. This was a decent classified event and a typically tight race of its type, with just 4lb separating the nine runners on official adjusted figures. Nothing got involved from the rear which prevents the race being rated higher.

NOTEBOOK
Amanjena , who had been off the track for three months after finishing second in a Windsor handicap, turned for home in fourth and came with a sustained run to collar the front-running Australia Day in the last half-furlong. She will not run again this year but will stay in training, with the prospect of further improvement to come. (op 8-1)
Australia Day(IRE) adopted the same tactics which had brought him success in summer handicaps at Windsor and Sandown. He fought off one challenge, that of Fair Gale, but could not quite repel the filly despite battling on most willingly. He did not show much in a light campaign over hurdles last winter, tending to pull too hard, but would be an interesting novice hurdling prospect this season if he could transfer some of his Flat improvement across. (op 7-2)
Fair Gale is a front-runner but he was unable to lead this time and had to be content with tracking the pace. He delivered a strong challenge to Australia Day but could not get past and weakened inside the last.
Samsons Son, fifth in a warm handicap at Newbury on Saturday, ran another creditable race but was never really in the hunt in a race not run to suit. (op 10-1)
Amanda Carter, successful at Newcastle when last in action two months ago, helped force the pace before fading under pressure in the straight. (tchd 9-2)
Trans Siberian was much too keen through the early stages and could never get involved, although he did stay on a bit. (op 12-1)
Bandama(IRE), who had been running consistently in handicaps, could not get into it off a fairly steady pace and was below par. (op 4-1)
Hustle(IRE) had returned to form when runner-up on Polytrack three weeks ago but never appeared to be travelling towards the back of the field and was eased when well beaten. Official explanation: jockey said colt was unsuited by the good to firm (good in places) ground (op 8-1)

6239 JEAN BRYANT MEMORIAL H'CAP 6f
2:45 (2:45) (Class 2) (0-100,100) 3-Y-O
£12,462 (£3,732; £1,866; £934; £466; £234) **Stalls Centre**

Form RPR

13 **1** **Laddies Poker Two (IRE)**[42] 5071 3-8-9 **91**.............................. TPQueally 9 107+
(J Noseda) *hld up in midfield travelling wl: hdwy over 2f out: led over 1f out: pushed clr and in command fnl f: comf* **9/2**[1]

1300 **2** 1 3/4 **Van Bossed (CAN)**[13] 5890 3-8-12 **94**.............................. AdrianTNicholls 16 101
(D Nicholls) *chsd ldrs: led over 2f out: sn rdn and edgd lft: hdd over 1f out: no ch w wnr fnl f: kpt on* **20/1**

1040 **3** nk **Great Charm (IRE)**[15] 5831 3-8-5 **87**.............................. JohnEgan 18 93
(M L W Bell) *hld up in midfield: hdwy 1/2-way: pressed ldrs and rdn over 1f out: nt pce of wnr after: kpt on u.p fnl f* **14/1**

0512 **4** 2 1/2 **Masada (IRE)**[67] 4252 3-8-5 **87**.............................. MartinDwyer 14 85+
(B J Meehan) *taken down early: s.i.s and hmpd s: bhd: swtchd to far rail and hdwy over 2f out: r.o wl but nvr trbld ldrs* **12/1**

5506 **5** 3/4 **Berbice (IRE)**[34] 5270 3-8-6 **88** ow1..............................(t) RichardHughes 7 84
(R Hannon) *racd keenly led for 1f: styd prom: rdn and hanging rt 2f out: kpt on one pce fr over 1f out* **16/1**

-630 **6** 1 **Striking Spirit**[104] 3047 3-8-7 **89**.............................. SteveDrowne 6 81
(B W Hills) *sn pushed along in midfield: lost pl after 2f: rallied u.p over 1f out: styd on fnl f but nvr trbld ldrs* **9/1**[2]

5405 **7** 1/2 **Aye Aye Digby (IRE)**[13] 5897 3-8-5 **87**.............................. RichardMullen 10 78
(H Candy) *chsd ldrs: rdn and outpcd over 2f out: kpt on again u.p fnl f* **9/1**[2]

4010 **8** 1 **Film Maker (IRE)**[21] 5681 3-8-11 **93**..............................(b[1]) TPO'Shea 3 81
(B J Meehan) *taken down early: chsd ldrs tl led after 1f: hdd over 2f out: wknd wl over 1f out* **20/1**

5010 **9** 1 **Hadaf (IRE)**[36] 5206 3-8-6 **88**.............................. RHills 11 72
(M P Tregoning) *stdd after s: hld up bhd: hdwy and rdn jst over 2f out: no imp fr over 1f out* **16/1**

2115 **10** 3 **Pretty Bonnie**[10] 6006 3-7-13 **86** oh5.............................. NataliaGemelova(5) 4 61
(A E Price) *racd in midfield: rdn and struggling 1/2-way: n.d after* **33/1**

6120 **11** 1 **Silver Wind**[41] 5096 3-8-4 **86** oh2..............................(v) ChrisCatlin 8 58
(P D Evans) *hld up in midfield: rdn and no prog over 2f out: wl btn after* **16/1**

6601 **12** 1/2 **Speedy Dollar (USA)**[10] 6005 3-8-11 **93** 6ex.............................. PhilipRobinson 17 63
(M A Jarvis) *s.i.s: hdwy into midfield after 2f: brief effrt over 2f out: sn btn* **9/2**[1]

1135 **13** 1 1/4 **Pavershooz**[47] 4900 3-8-4 **86** oh3.............................. JimmyQuinn 2 52
(N Wilson) *hld up in midfield: rdn and struggling 1/2-way: no ch after* **16/1**

000 **14** 3 **Spirit Of Sharjah (IRE)**[55] 4617 3-9-4 **100**..............................(v[1]) RyanMoore 15 56
(Miss J Feilden) *wnt lft s: t.k.h: hld up bhd: brief effrt and rdn over 2f out: wl btn and hung rt over 1f out* **28/1**

-440 **15** ½ **Exhibition (IRE)**[41] 5102 3-8-11 **93**..............(b[1]) PatDobbs 5 48
(S A Callaghan) *s.i.s: hld up bhd: struggling wl over 2f out: wl btn last 2f* **40/1**

-400 **16** 1 **Nacho Libre**[48] 4869 3-9-1 **97**.............. WilliamBuick 13 49
(B W Hills) *in midfield for 2f: bhd and rdn 1/2-way: sn wl bhd* **20/1**

5-00 **17** 3 ¾ **Mount Pleasure (USA)**[13] 5897 3-8-8 **90**..............(b[1]) RichardThomas 1 30
(Christian Wroe) *s.i.s: nvr gng wl: bhd fr 1/2-way* **40/1**

2314 **18** 1 ¼ **Spanish Bounty**[48] 4842 3-9-0 **96**.............. PatCosgrave 12 32
(J G Portman) *pressed ldrs: ev ch and rdn wl over 2f out: wknd qckly jst over 2f out* **10/1**[3]

1m 13.1s (-1.30) **Going Correction** 0.0s/f (Good) **18** Ran SP% **128.9**
Speed ratings (Par 107): **108,105,105,101,100 99,98,97,96,92 90,90,88,84,83 82,77,75**
toteswinger: 1&2 £28.20, 1&3 £25.90, 2&3 £97.00. CSF £104.46 CT £1241.65 TOTE £5.70: £1.70, £5.70, £3.90, £2.80; EX 128.40 TRIFECTA Not won..
Owner Ladbrokes International Ltd **Bred** Jerry O'Sullivan **Trained** Newmarket, Suffolk

FOCUS
A competitive sprint handicap, in which the field raced down the centre of the course initially before tending to migrate more towards the far side, without quite getting over to the rail. the winner looks Listed class while the third ran close to form.

NOTEBOOK
Laddies Poker Two(IRE) ◆, who had been off the track for seven months following her winning debut prior to finishing third on her handicap debut six weeks ago at Newmarket, where she needed the run, was a taking winner. Tracking the leaders going well, and gradually steered by her rider towards the far side of the track, she quickened up smartly to assert. She had no problem with the drop down from 7f and clocked a time 0.7 seconds faster than standard, and there looks to be plenty more to come from her. She should be capable of holding her own in Listed company. (op 4-1)
Van Bossed(CAN), sharper for his recent return to action and favourably drawn as things turned out, showed something of a return to form. He kept on after striking the front. (op 25-1)
Great Charm(IRE) could not quicken up with the winner but stuck on pleasingly for third. This was a good effort on ground that was perhaps faster than he'd ideally like. (op 16-1)
Masada(IRE) ◆ was slow to break then hampered soon after, finding herself at the back of the field. She ended up making good headway nearest the inside rail and looks ready to strike soon, with this first run for two months likely to bring her on.
Berbice(IRE) has dropped no less than 19lb in the weights this year after some uninspiring efforts and this was better as he showed bright pace and was only run out of the frame inside the last. He does give the impression that he might benefit from some headgear though.
Striking Spirit was supported on-course on this first run since June and made pleasing late progress after losing his pitch. (op 14-1)
Aye Aye Digby(IRE) ran well over a trip that is on the sharp side for him these days. (op 12-1)
Film Maker(IRE) showed plenty of early pace in the first-time blinkers before fading. (op 25-1)
Hadaf(IRE) travelled quite well in the pack but again gave the impression that 5f is his trip.
Speedy Dollar(USA) was 3lb well-in under the penalty for his Yarmouth victory but never figured following a slow start. Official explanation: jockey said gelding was unsuited by the good ground (op 4-1)

6240 WATERSHIP DOWN STUD SALES RACE 6f 110y
3:20 (3:26) (Class 2) 2-Y-O

£136,837 (£54,746; £27,373; £13,672; £6,836; £6,836) **Stalls** Centre

Form RPR

1202 **1** **Penny's Gift**[34] 5272 2-8-6 101 ow1.............. RichardHughes 7 84
(R Hannon) *hld up towards rr nr side: prog over 2f out: drvn to hd gp narrowly jst ins fnl f: edgd rt u.p: r.o to ld overall nr fin* **15/8**[1]

1 **2** nk **Rosy Mantle**[15] 5835 2-8-5 0.............. DO'Donohoe 19 82
(W R Muir) *prom on outer of nr side: led gp over 1f out: narrowly hdd jst ins fnl f: r.o and pressed wnr to fin* **12/1**[3]

5123 **3** hd **Golden Destiny (IRE)**[22] 5647 2-8-0 0.............. WilliamBuick 21 77
(P J Makin) *prom far side: led gp 3f out: in command 2f out and overall ldr: edgd lft fnl f: hdd nr fin* **16/1**

1501 **4** 1 **Rafiqa (IRE)**[8] 6058 2-8-6 0.............. AlanMunro 14 80+
(C F Wall) *racd on outer of nr side gp: trckd ldrs: nt clr run wl over 2f out: nt pce to hold pl after: drvn and r.o fnl f: nrst fin* **9/1**[2]

5240 **5** 1 **Bouggie Daize**[27] 5511 2-7-12 0.............. SilvestreDeSousa 15 69
(C G Cox) *prom on outer of nr side gp: hrd rdn to chal 2f out: one pce fr jst over 1f out* **33/1**

130 **6** nse **Foundation Room (IRE)**[15] 5827 2-8-3 0.............. MartinDwyer 1 74
(A M Balding) *trckd nr side ldrs: nt qckn 2f out: styd on wl fnl f: unable to chal* **14/1**

234 **7** nse **Poyle Meg**[28] 5461 2-8-8 0..............(p) RichardKingscote 28 79
(R M Beckett) *racd far side: prom: chsd ldr 2f out: edgd lft fnl f: kpt on* **25/1**

4324 **8** ½ **Amber Sunset**[25] 5567 2-7-12 63.............. LukeMorris 13 67
(J Jay) *wnt lft s: wl plcd in nr side: outpcd fr over 2f out: kpt on fnl f* **100/1**

5361 **9** 2 ¾ **Gower Valentine**[58] 4521 2-8-5 66.............. AdrianTNicholls 3 67
(D Nicholls) *w ldr nr side: led gp 1/2-way to over 1f out: wknd fnl f* **12/1**[3]

001 **10** 3 ¾ **Red Kyte**[43] 5004 2-8-13 0.............. NCallan 4 65
(K A Ryan) *led nr side to 1/2-way: wknd wl over 1f out* **50/1**

31 **11** 1 **Accede**[118] 2618 2-8-6 78.............. AdrianMcCarthy 22 55
(J G Portman) *prom far side: wl outpcd by ldng pair fnl 2f* **25/1**

2361 **12** hd **Gal Aloud (USA)**[34] 5274 2-8-10 82..............(v[1]) RyanMoore 11 58
(R Hannon) *trckd ldrs nr side: wl outpcd fr over 2f out: plugged on* **14/1**

43 **13** ¾ **Multiplication**[22] 5643 2-9-0 0.............. SteveDrowne 12 60+
(R Charlton) *dwlt and hmpd s: racd on outer of nr side gp: nvr on terms w ldrs: outpcd fnl 2f* **20/1**

23 **14** hd **Positivity**[59] 4499 2-8-1 0 ow1.............. RoystonFfrench 17 47
(B Smart) *dwlt: racd on outer of nr side gp: in tch tl wknd 2f out* **40/1**

2031 **15** 1 ¾ **Shiva Adiva**[40] 5116 2-7-12 75.............. JimmyQuinn 23 39
(Tom Dascombe) *racd far side: chsd ldrs: wl outpcd fr over 2f out* **33/1**

13 **16** nk **Leadenhall Lass (IRE)**[31] 5375 2-8-3 0.............. ChrisCatlin 9 43
(P M Phelan) *prom nr side: hanging over 2f out: wknd rapidly over 1f out* **50/1**

3 **17** 2 ½ **Prowl**[122] 2479 2-8-8 0.............. HayleyTurner 10 41+
(E A L Dunlop) *dwlt and hmpd s: hld up in rr nr side: no prog over 2f out: sn btn* **12/1**[3]

3252 **18** hd **Today's The Day**[38] 5165 2-8-8 0..............(p) PhilipRobinson 6 41
(M A Jarvis) *trckd nr side ldrs: wknd 2f out* **33/1**

1411 **19** ½ **Crystal Moments**[39] 5153 2-8-11 0.............. EddieAhern 16 42
(E A L Dunlop) *trckd ldrs on outer of nr side gp: hmpd 3f out: nt rcvr and sn btn* **12/1**[3]

440 **20** 1 ½ **Russian Rave**[57] 4554 2-8-8 0.............. JamesDoyle 5 35
(J G Portman) *chsd nr side ldrs: wknd u.p over 2f out* **100/1**

0000 **21** ¾ **Damassin**[13] 5904 2-8-2 0.............. LiamJones 29 27
(Eve Johnson Houghton) *led far side gp after 2f to 3f out: wknd rapidly fnl 2f* **100/1**

600 **22** 1 ¼ **Order Order**[57] 4554 2-8-0 0.............. CatherineGannon 27 22
(H J L Dunlop) *racd far side: struggling fr 3f out: sn bhd* **100/1**

064 **23** ¾ **Jewelled Reef (IRE)**[26] 5534 2-8-8 0.............. RichardMullen 20 28
(Eve Johnson Houghton) *dwlt: racd far side: bhd fnl 2f* **100/1**

05 **24** 2 ½ **Impressionist Art (USA)**[26] 5534 2-8-10 0.............. TPO'Shea 18 23
(B J Meehan) *racd outer of nr side gp: a in rr: wknd over 2f out* **66/1**

00 **25** 2 **Broughtons Paradis (IRE)**[15] 5835 2-8-8 0.............. StephenDonohoe 8 15
(W J Musson) *racd nr side: a toiling in rr* **100/1**

00 **26** 5 **Inis Boffin**[22] 5640 2-8-10 0.............. LPKeniry 26 3
(S Kirk) *dwlt: swtchd fr far side to r nr side: a bhd* **100/1**

055 **27** 3 ¾ **Lady Angelica**[31] 5375 2-8-2 0 ow4.............. RichardThomas 25 —
(Dr J D Scargill) *led far side gp 2f: sn lost pl and bhd* **100/1**

4010 **28** 23 **Princess Hannah**[10] 5997 2-8-11 0.............. TedDurcan 2 —
(R Hannon) *dwlt: a in rr: virtually p.u whn no ch fnl 2f* **66/1**

1m 21.15s (0.45) **Going Correction** 0.0s/f (Good) **28** Ran SP% **133.3**
Speed ratings (Par 101): **97,96,96,95,94 94,94,93,90,86 84,84,83,83,81 81,78,78,77,75 75,73,72,69,67 61,57,31**
toteswinger: 1&2 £9.00, 1&3 £7.40, 2&3 £146.90. CSF £21.40 TOTE £2.60: £1.60, £4.30, £6.20; EX 30.20 Trifecta £149.40 Pool: £1474.67 - 7.30 winning units..
Owner Malcolm Brown & Mrs Penny Brown **Bred** Capt A L Smith-Maxwell **Trained** East Everleigh, Wilts

FOCUS
A sales race worth around £23,000 more to the winner than the Group 1 Fillies' Mile. The field split into two groups, with 20 going stands' side and eight taking the far-side option. The race produced a track record, although this intermediate distance is only rarely used and the winner was below for while the third, fifth and eighth suggest the form is otherwise solid.

NOTEBOOK
Penny's Gift, for whom this looked a straightforward opportunity as she was 18lb clear on RPRs, won but only just and she was clearly below her best in doing so. She boasted much the best form coming into this, second to Cuis Ghaire in the Albany Stakes at the royal meeting and an unlucky seventh in the Weatherbys Super Sprint before being beaten a nose by stablemate Infamous Angel in the Lowther at Newmarket. Racing in the much larger group, she was switched to the stands' flank of that bunch and made good progress to show ahead on her side, but it was only late on that she caught Golden Destiny who had raced in the far-side group. Her jockey, who put up a pound overweight, reported that she raced lazily and was hardly ever on the bit. She is better than this, and may take her chance in the Cheveley Park Stakes, a race Richard Hannon's Indian Ink won after taking this prize two years ago. (tchd 7-4 and 9-4 in a palce)
Rosy Mantle ◆ made her move at about the same time as the winner, on the opoosite side of the main bunch, and had every chance. This was a fine performance from a filly who had run just once before, when taking a Polytrack maiden a fortnight ago. (op 10-1 tchd 8-1)
Golden Destiny(IRE) was in front in her group a long way out and soon had nothing to race with. She edged over to the centre of the track when the pressure was on (she also strayed off a true line on her two previous starts in Warwick nurseries) and was only caught well inside the final furlong. This was a good effort.
Rafiqa(IRE) made useful late progress over a trip on the short side for her now, her Yarmouth nursery win having come over 1m. (op 14-1)
Bouggie Daize, who was always prominent on the outside of the much larger group, had shown just a modest level of ability in her previous outings and her proximity does not do much for the form.
Foundation Room(IRE) showed the benefit of a return from a break at Doncaster, keeping on stoutly near the stands' rail on the fastest ground she has encountered. (op 16-1)
Poyle Meg ran a decent race in the cheekpieces, finishing second of the eight to take the far-side option. Official explanation: jockey said filly hung left (op 20-1)
Amber Sunset, who is still a maiden, was lightly weighted and was another to finish well.
Gower Valentine, a winner of a Glorious Goodwood maiden when last seen two months back, raced up with the pace before fading. (op 16-1)
Prowl, off the track since finishing third on her debut to subsequent Cherry Hinton winner Please Sing back on May, having hurt herself when slipping after the race, was always struggling after an awkward start. She probably requires 7f. (op 10-1 tchd 9-1)
Crystal Moments Official explanation: jockey said filly lost its action
Inis Boffin Official explanation: jockey said filly hung badly left

6241 PRINCESS ROYAL EBF PRICEWATERHOUSECOOPERS STKS (LISTED RACE) 1m 4f
3:55 (3:56) (Class 1) 3-Y-O+

£24,978 (£9,468; £4,738; £2,362; £1,183; £594) **Stalls** High

Form RPR

2111 **1** **Crystal Capella**[33] 5311 3-8-12 98.............. RyanMoore 4 107
(Sir Michael Stoute) *s.i.s: sn chsng ldrs: rdn 3f out: rdn to ld 2f out: edgd rt jst ins fnl f: styd on wl u.p and a holding runner up* **9/4**[1]

2006 **2** ½ **Under The Rainbow**[15] 5826 5-9-3 95..............(p) NCallan 9 103
(B W Hills) *stdd after s: hld up towards rr: hdwy 3f out: chsd wnr over 1f out: ch ins fnl f: nt qckn and hld fnl 100yds* **16/1**

1022 **3** 2 ½ **Ronaldsay**[34] 5288 4-9-6 105..............(v[1]) RichardHughes 8 105+
(R Hannon) *hld up in midfield: hdwy and nt clr run on inner over 2f out tl swtchd lft over 1f out: squeezed through jst ins fnl f: r.o to go 3rd fnl 100yds: nt rch ldng pair* **13/2**[3]

3246 **4** ¾ **Susie May**[34] 5264 4-9-3 90.............. GeorgeBaker 1 98
(G L Moore) *stdd and swtchd rt after s: racd in last pair: hdwy and rdn 3f out: swtchd lft over 1f out: styd on fnl f but nvr pce to trble ldrs* **20/1**

5156 **5** 2 ¾ **Elmaleeha**[54] 4667 3-8-9 97.............. RHills 7 93
(J L Dunlop) *chsd ldr tl jnd ldr 6f out: led wl over 2f out: sn rdn: hdd 2f out: wknd ent fnl f* **14/1**

11-3 **6** ½ **Classic Legend**[9] 6034 3-8-9 93.............. TPO'Shea 12 93
(B J Meehan) *t.k.h: hld up in midfield: rdn and effrt to chse ldrs 2f out: wknd jst over 1f out* **8/1**

2-1 **7** 1 ¾ **Island Vista**[53] 4695 3-8-9 82.............. PhilipRobinson 15 90
(M A Jarvis) *t.k.h: chsd ldrs: rdn wl over 2f out: wknd over 1f out: btn whn short of room jst ins fnl f* **13/2**[3]

-334 **8** 6 **Hobby**[33] 5329 3-8-9 101.............. LDettori 13 80
(R M Beckett) *led: stdd gallop and jnd 6f out: rdn 3f out: sn hdd: wknd 2f out: sn wl btn* **5/1**[2]

3-00 **9** nk **Silver Mitzva (IRE)**[33] 5329 4-9-3 94..............(b) JohnEgan 10 80
(M Botti) *hld up in midfield on outer: rdn 3f out: no prog and wl btn last 2f* **33/1**

3232 **10** 5 **Time Control**[28] 5445 3-8-9 77..............(b[1]) MartinDwyer 5 72
(L M Cumani) *rn in snatches: stdd s: bhd: rdn over 3f out: sn btn: wl bhd last 2f* **25/1**

1306 **11** 1 ¼ **Wood Chorus**[44] 4977 3-8-9 100.............. HayleyTurner 14 70
(M L W Bell) *hld up in tch in midfield: rdn 3f out: sn struggling: wl btn last 2f* **25/1**

2011 **12** 3 ¾ **Ragdollianna**[32] 5369 4-9-3 82.............. LPKeniry 11 64
(Norma Twomey) *hld up in rr: rdn and no prog 3f out: wl btn after* **20/1**

1246 **13** *11* **Amicable Terms**[26] 5536 3-8-9 79 ChrisCatlin 6 46
(Rae Guest) *hld up towards rr: rdn and btn 3f out: t.o* **66/1**

2m 31.5s (-4.00) **Going Correction** 0.0s/f (Good)
WFA 3 from 4yo+ 8lb **13** Ran SP% **119.4**
Speed ratings (Par 111): **113,112,111,110,108 108,107,103,102,99 98,96,88**
toteswinger: 1&2 £11.70, 1&3 £4.20, 2&3 £26.30. CSF £38.53 TOTE £3.00: £1.60, £5.60, £2.00; EX 42.40 Trifecta £220.60 Pool: £1073.34 - 3.60 winning units..
Owner Sir Evelyn De Rothschild **Bred** Southcourt Stud **Trained** Newmarket, Suffolk

FOCUS
No stars here, but a strong-enough field by Listed race standards. The pace was steadied at halfway though, and it developed into a bit of a sprint, which mitigated against fillies who were held up. The form looks solid with the fourth and sixth to their marks.

NOTEBOOK
Crystal Capella went to post with the most progressive of profiles, but she was stepping up from handicap company and she had her stamina to prove over an extra 2f. In that respect, the steadying of the pace was to her advantage and she got the trip fine, for she was always holding the runner-up through the final furlong, having gone to the front sooner than Moore had intended. She may have to step up in grade again. (op 2-1 tchd 5-2 in places)
Under The Rainbow was third in the corresponding race a year ago and is more than able, but she has not won for nearly three years. This was one of her better efforts, but while she was clear of the rest she was never going to get by the winner. (op 25-1)
Ronaldsay is a grand filly whose latest second at Windsor had been well advertised, but she was not seen to best advantage here. Tried in a visor for the first time, she travelled well in a handy position but was trapped on the rail from over 2f out until approaching the final furlong, by which time the first two had gone beyond recall. She was not exactly flying at the finish, but she was closing all the way to the line and connections regard the experiment with headgear a success. (op 9-2 tchd 7-1 in a place)
Susie May is vastly improved this year, and another good effort from off the pace in a steadily run race suggests she has not been unduly flattered lately and may yet have more to offer, as she had a lot on her plate here and was hardly favoured by the way the race was run.
Elmaleeha, who had every chance, having taken the lead straightening up, faded in the last furlong.
Classic Legend, for whom this may have come plenty quick enough, as she only made her reappearance the previous week and was below par. (op 11-1 tchd 12-1)
Island Vista was much too keen and paid the penalty in the closing stages. (tchd 7-1)
Hobby was well placed to dictate, but she came under pressure as soon as they straightened for home and she gradually weakened. This was disappointing. Official explanation: jockey said filly had no more to give (op 15-2)
Silver Mitzva(IRE) was not helped by being stuck out wide most of the way.
Time Control, may have had the blinkers to blame for a poor effort as she was never really going.

6242 DJP INTERNATIONAL H'CAP 1m (S)
4:30 (4:30) (Class 4) (0-85,85) 3-Y-O **£6,476** (£1,927; £963; £481) **Stalls** Centre

Form RPR
21 **1** **Mawatheeq (USA)**[34] 5278 3-9-4 85 RHills 1 104+
(M P Tregoning) *hld up in tch: hdwy to trck ldr jst over 2f out: led over 1f out: sn pushed clr: impressive* **11/8**[1]
5146 **2** *6* **Dunn'o (IRE)**[16] 5795 3-9-4 85 PhilipRobinson 8 89
(C G Cox) *in tch: hdwy to press ldrs 3f out: led jst over 2f out: sn rdn and hdd: no ch w wnr fnl f: kpt on* **16/1**
2351 **3** *1/2* **Thunder Gorge (USA)**[24] 5588 3-8-6 73 RoystonFfrench 12 76
(Mouse Hamilton-Fairley) *hld up in midfield: hdwy 3f out: chsd ldng pair over 1f out: no ch w wnr fnl f but kpt on* **33/1**
4035 **4** *1 1/2* **Oceana Blue**[42] 5071 3-8-8 75 (t) WilliamBuick 11 74
(A M Balding) *hld up towards rr: hdwy over 2f out: chsd ldrs and rdn over 1f out: kpt on same pce fnl f* **20/1**
1152 **5** *1/2* **Admiral Dundas (IRE)**[14] 5862 3-9-3 84 AlanMunro 6 82
(W Jarvis) *in tch in midfield: rdn and lost pl 1/2-way: hdwy u.p over 2f out: hung rt over 1f out: kpt on but nvr a threat* **6/1**[2]
1350 **6** *2* **Autumn Blades (IRE)**[20] 5697 3-8-8 75 TQuinn 5 68
(J W Hills) *stdd s: hld up bhd: hdwy over 2f out: swtchd lft over 1f out: kpt on fnl f: nvr trbld ldrs* **33/1**
0313 **7** *nk* **Gross Prophet**[33] 5309 3-8-8 75 RichardKingscote 13 68
(Tom Dascombe) *chsd ldrs: ev ch and rdn over 2f out: wknd over 1f out: no ch fnl f* **14/1**
1-0 **8** *shd* **Amazing Star (IRE)**[27] 5516 3-9-4 85 NCallan 4 77
(M Halford, Ire) *hld up in tch: effrt to chse ldrs over 2f out: drvn 2f out: btn over 1f out* **25/1**
3221 **9** *3 1/2* **Victoria Reel**[62] 4433 3-9-4 85 RichardHughes 9 69
(R Hannon) *hld up in midfield: rdn over 2f out: no prog and wl btn last 2f* **12/1**[3]
1400 **10** *1/2* **Burnbrake**[41] 5104 3-8-4 71 oh1 HayleyTurner 10 54
(J A R Toller) *racd in midfield: rdn 1/2-way: sn struggling:* **40/1**
1306 **11** *1* **Last Three Minutes (IRE)**[14] 5862 3-9-3 84 LDettori 2 64
(E A L Dunlop) *hld up towards rr: rdn and effrt over 2f out: sn hung rt and no prog* **12/1**[3]
-000 **12** *4* **Messias Da Silva (USA)**[17] 5789 3-8-8 75 ShaneKelly 16 46
(J Noseda) *led: rdn and hdd 2f out: hung rt and wknd over 1f out* **66/1**
0004 **13** *4 1/2* **Eastern Gift**[15] 5841 3-9-2 83 RyanMoore 3 43
(R Hannon) *a towards rr: nvr a factor* **16/1**
0144 **14** *2 3/4* **Monashee Rock (IRE)**[24] 5588 3-8-8 75 JimmyQuinn 15 28
(M Salaman) *nvr travelling in rr: rdn and struggling fr 1/2-way* **33/1**
4-51 **15** *8* **Cigalas**[32] 5366 3-9-4 85 ChrisCatlin 14 19
(B W Hills) *racd freely: chsd ldr tl 3f out: sn wknd: t.o* **12/1**[3]
2135 **16** *9* **Totally Focussed (IRE)**[20] 5695 3-8-13 80 IanMongan 7 —
(S Dow) *stdd s: hld up in rr: struggling 3f out: wl btn after: t.o and eased fnl f* **16/1**

1m 39.38s (-1.22) **Going Correction** 0.0s/f (Good) **16** Ran SP% **125.1**
Speed ratings (Par 103): **106,100,99,98,97 95,95,95,91,91 90,86,81,78,70 61**
toteswinger: 1&2 £8.80, 1&3 £16.60, 2&3 £95.00. CSF £24.71 CT £580.57 TOTE £2.30: £1.30, £3.70, £5.20, £4.30; EX 30.40 Trifecta £771.50 Pool: £1042.62 - 1.00 winning units..
Owner Hamdan Al Maktoum **Bred** Shadwell Farm LLC **Trained** Lambourn, Berks

FOCUS
A decent handicap which was turned into a rout by the lightly raced Mawatheeq. The form looks solid rated around those in the frame behind the winner.
Totally Focussed(IRE) Official explanation: jockey said gelding was unsuited by the good ground

6243 BOLLINGER CHAMPAGNE CHALLENGE SERIES FINAL H'CAP (FOR GENTLEMAN AMATEUR RIDERS) 1m 4f
5:05 (5:05) (Class 4) (0-80,77) 4-Y-O+
£6,002 (£1,875; £937; £469; £234; £118) **Stalls** High

Form RPR
503- **1** **Alsadaa (USA)**[175] 4355 5-10-5 63 oh1 MrBJToomey(5) 12 77
(Mrs L J Mongan) *trckd ldr: led 4f out: drew at least 8l clr 2f out: unchal after* **10/1**
0042 **2** *3 1/2* **Overrule (USA)**[10] 6007 4-10-8 66 MrDaleSwift(5) 9 74+
(B Ellison) *hld up towards rr: effrt whn rn into wall of trble over 2f out: gd prog to take 2nd over 1f out: clsd on wnr fnl f but no ch* **5/1**[2]
2-14 **3** *4* **Oldrik (GER)**[41] 5092 5-10-13 71 (p) MrIPopham(5) 3 73
(P J Hobbs) *dwlt: hld up wl in rr: gng v easily over 3f out: prog after but wnr already flown: carried lft 2f out: styd on to take 3rd fnl f* **12/1**
2002 **4** *3/4* **Optimus (USA)**[24] 5583 6-11-0 70 MrPCollington(3) 11 70
(B G Powell) *hld up in midfield: effrt whn nt clr run over 2f out: prog over 1f out: styd on fnl f* **20/1**
3032 **5** *5* **Potentiale (IRE)**[10] 5999 4-11-2 72 (p) MrBenBrisbourne(3) 14 64
(J W Hills) *dwlt: hld up in last trio: modest prog 3f out: urged along and styd on past btn rivals fnl 2f: no ch* **6/1**[3]
0510 **6** *nk* **Fort Churchill (IRE)**[13] 5900 7-11-1 75 (bt) MrOJMurphy(7) 19 67
(B Ellison) *hld up bhd ldrs: prog to go 3rd over 3f out: hung bdly lft over 2f out: btn after* **33/1**
1300 **7** *1/2* **Double Spectre (IRE)**[50] 4771 6-10-10 70 MrHGMiller(7) 15 61
(Jean-Rene Auvray) *dwlt: hld up in last pair: stl there whn rdn over 2f out: nt clr run sn after: plugged on* **33/1**
6600 **8** *1* **Calculating (IRE)**[53] 4691 4-11-5 72 MrLeeNewnes 18 62
(M D I Usher) *trckd ldrs on inner: rdn and struggling over 3f out: effrt again over 2f out: sn btn* **20/1**
0020 **9** *1/2* **Kalasam**[10] 5993 4-10-7 67 MrJakeGreenall(7) 2 56
(M W Easterby) *dwlt: racd wd in midfield: effrt over 3f out: one pce whn carried lft 2f out* **20/1**
2532 **10** *1/2* **Sporting Gesture**[61] 4457 11-11-0 70 MrOGreenall(3) 16 58
(M W Easterby) *a in midfield: effrt but outpcd over 2f out: no hdwy after* **16/1**
0/4 **11** *3/4* **Meneur (FR)**[28] 5465 6-10-10 68 MrJoshuaMoore(5) 5 55
(G L Moore) *t.k.h early: hld up bhd ldrs: gng wl enough 3f out: already outpcd whn carried lft 2f out: wknd* **4/1**[1]
26-0 **12** *3/4* **Ameeq (USA)**[13] 5900 6-11-5 77 SamHanson(5) 10 63
(G L Moore) *hld up in midfield: outpcd fr 3f out: no ch after* **20/1**
5314 **13** *1/2* **Dragon Slayer (IRE)**[9] 6033 6-11-6 73 MrSDobson 7 58
(John A Harris) *prom: chsd wnr over 3f out: sn lft bhd: wknd over 1f out* **12/1**
0564 **14** *8* **Bell Island**[10] 5999 4-11-8 75 MrSWalker 1 47
(Lady Herries) *chsd ldrs: wknd u.p 3f out* **7/1**
/4-6 **15** *4* **Neutrino**[19] 4691 6-10-9 65 (p) MrMJJSmith(3) 13 31
(D G Bridgwater) *nvr beyond midfield: struggling in rr 4f out* **33/1**
0300 **16** *4 1/2* **Turner's Touch**[13] 5913 6-10-8 66 (b) MrJAkehurst(5) 8 24
(G L Moore) *dwlt: hld up in rr: sme prog on outer fr 5f out: wknd u.p 3f out* **40/1**
4000 **17** *3 1/2* **Rapid City**[13] 5910 5-11-3 75 MrRBirkett(5) 4 28
(Miss J Feilden) *led to 4f out: wknd rapidly* **40/1**

2m 35.02s (-0.48) **Going Correction** 0.0s/f (Good) **17** Ran SP% **126.6**
Speed ratings (Par 105): **101,98,96,95,92 91,91,90,90,90 89,89,88,83,80 77,75**
toteswinger: 1&2 £13.30, 1&3 £30.20, 2&3 £15.30. CSF £53.33 CT £628.35 TOTE £16.40: £3.30, £1.80, £2.80, £3.60; EX 110.50 TRIFECTA Not won. Place 6: £97.47 Place 6: £34.77.
Owner Mrs P J Sheen **Bred** Shadwell Farm LLC **Trained** Epsom, Surrey
■ Stewards' Enquiry : Mr O J Murphy three-day ban: careless riding (Oct 14, Nov 7,10)
Mr I Popham two-day ban: careless riding (Oct 14, Nov 7)

FOCUS
A competitive amateurs' handicap on paper, but it produced a clear-cut winner and the form looks sound rated around the placed horses.
T/Jkpt: £6,723.20 to a £1 stake. Pool: £118,366.55. 12.50 winning tickets. T/Plt: £67.30 to a £1 stake. Pool: £121,416.33. 1,315.17 winning tickets. T/Qpdt: £9.80 to a £1 stake. Pool: £7,332.60. 552.25 winning tickets. SP

5988 HAYDOCK (L-H)
Friday, September 26

OFFICIAL GOING: Good to firm (good in places; 8.9)
Rail realignment on the home turn added 10yds to advertised distances of races 6 & 7 and on far turn reduced the distance of race 5 by about 22 yds.
Wind: light half across Weather: dry and sunny

6244 VALE UK MAIDEN FILLIES' STKS (DIV I) 6f
2:00 (2:02) (Class 5) 2-Y-O **£2,914** (£867; £433; £216) **Stalls** Centre

Form RPR
0 **1** **Shamwari Lodge (IRE)**[41] 5097 2-9-0 0 JimmyFortune 9 80+
(R Hannon) *trckd ldrs stands' side: swtchd lft and hdwy 2f out: rdn to ld 1f out: drvn out* **2/1**[1]
2 *1* **Damaniyat Girl (USA)** 2-8-10 0 MichaelHills 5 74+
(W J Haggas) *hld up far side: gd hdwy over 2f out: led that gp wl over 1f out: rdn and ev ch ent fnl f: nt qckn towards fin: 1st of 8 in gp* **3/1**[2]
4 **3** *2* **Fesko**[8] 6051 2-9-0 0 GregFairley 10 71
(M Johnston) *cl up stands' side: effrt to ld that gp and overall ldr 2f out: rdn and hdd 1f out: kpt on same pce: 2ndof 4 in gp* **4/1**[3]
06 **4** *4 1/2* **Nimmy's Special**[63] 4384 2-9-0 0 TomEaves 12 58
(B Smart) *trckd ldr stands' side: rdn along over 2f out: sn one pce: 4th of 4 in gp* **40/1**
04 **5** *1/2* **Assent (IRE)**[24] 5584 2-9-0 0 TGMcLaughlin 7 56
(B R Millman) *s.i.s and in rr far side: hdwy over 2f out: rdn over 1f out: kpt on ins fnl f: 2nd of 8 in gp* **15/2**
0 **6** *1 1/4* **Alicante**[6] 6110 2-9-0 0 J-PGuillambert 11 52
(Sir Mark Prescott) *led stands' side gp: rdn along over 2f out: sn hdd and grad wknd: 3rd of 4 in gp* **40/1**
06 **7** *3 1/2* **Winterbourne**[14] 5860 2-9-0 0 FrancisNorton 3 42
(M Blanshard) *t.k.h: cl up far side: rdn along over 2f out and grad wknd: 3rd of 8 in gp* **20/1**
0 **8** *1 1/4* **Saving Grace**[26] 5539 2-9-0 0 DavidAllan 6 38
(E J Alston) *trckd ldrs far side: effrt over 2f out: sn rdn and wknd: 4th of 8 in gp* **50/1**
9 *6* **In Her Shoes** 2-8-10 0 DarryllHolland 4 16
(B J Meehan) *a towards rr far side: 5th of 8 in gp* **8/1**
00 **10** *3/4* **Varsa (IRE)**[35] 5241 2-9-0 0 DarrenWilliams 1 18
(K R Burke) *led far side gp and overall ldr to 1/2-way: continued to ld far side gp tl hdd & wknd wl over 1f out: 6th of 8 in gp* **66/1**
0600 **11** *5* **Neo's Mate (IRE)**[32] 5363 2-9-0 49 PaulQuinn 8 —
(Paul Green) *t.k.h: prom far side: rdn along over 2f out and sn wknd: 7th of 8 in gp* **100/1**

00 **12** *3* **Following Wind**[31] 5384 2-9-0 0..............................(b[1]) PaulMulrennan 2 —
(K A Ryan) *a in rr far side: 8th of 8 in gp* **66/1**
1m 12.77s (-1.23) **Going Correction** -0.25s/f (Firm) **12** Ran SP% **116.8**
Speed ratings (Par 92): **98,96,94,88,87 85,81,79,71,70 63,59**
toteswinger: 1&2 £3.10, 1&3 £3.30, 2&3 £3.90. CSF £7.42 TOTE £3.40: £1.30, £1.90, £1.40; EX 10.80.
Owner Andrew Russell **Bred** Pier House Stud **Trained** East Everleigh, Wilts

FOCUS
The field for the first division of the fillies' maiden split into two groups and, while just four came over to the near rail, they went off at a sounder pace than those who stayed far side. The form appears nothing special and is slightly messy.

NOTEBOOK
Shamwari Lodge(IRE), despite taking time to settle, eventually ran out a ready winner on the nearside. She still looked green when pulled out for her challenge nearing the final furlong, but she came right away from her rivals on that side and did not have any trouble with the faster ground. While her pedigree has a lot of speed, she looks like getting another furlong in time and should learn again for this experience. (op 15-8 tchd 9-4)
Damaniyat Girl(USA) ◆, whose stable's two previous runners in this event were both placed, proved popular in the betting ring and only just missed out. She ran out a clear winner on the far side, looking suited by the ground, and should not be long in finding compensation. (tchd 11-4 and 10-3)
Fesko broke better than had been the case at Pontefract on her debut eight days earlier. There was more than enough in this display to suggest she will benefit from another furlong. (op 3-1)
Nimmy's Special was returning from a 63-day break and having her first run over the extra furlong. She left the impression she would come on for the run and now has the option of nurseries. (op 50-1 tchd 66-1)

6245 VALE UK MAIDEN FILLIES' STKS (DIV II) 6f
2:35 (2:35) (Class 5) 2-Y-O **£2,914** (£867; £433; £216) **Stalls** Centre

Form RPR
1 **Cashleen (USA)** 2-8-10 0.............................. PaulMulrennan 3 68+
(K A Ryan) *s.i.s and rr far side: stdy hdwy 1/2-way: rdn to ld ent fnl f: drvn and kpt on wl towards fin* **12/1**
2 *½* **Bea Menace (USA)** 2-8-10 0.............................. JoeFanning 1 67+
(P F I Cole) *in tch far side: pushed along and sltly outpcd 2f out: swtchd rt and rdn over 1f out: styd on wl fnl f: 2nd in gp* **14/1**
2 **3** *½* **Keep Dancing (IRE)**[17] 5784 2-8-9 0.............................. DavidProbert[(5)] 8 69
(A M Balding) *cl up stands' side: hdwy over 2f out: rdn to ld that gp 1 1/2f out and ev ch tl drvn and nt qckn ins fnl f: 1st of 5 in gp* **13/8[1]**
60 **4** *½* **Miss Fritton (IRE)**[91] 3456 2-9-0 0.............................. JimmyFortune 4 68
(R Hannon) *trckd ldrs far side: hdwy to ld that gp after 2f and overall ldr 2f out: rdn and hdd ent fnl f: wknd: 3rd of 6 in gp* **4/1[3]**
0 **5** *1* **Petella**[43] 5004 2-9-0 0.............................. TGMcLaughlin 6 65
(C W Thornton) *in rr far side tl styd on appr last: nrst fin: 4th of 6 in gp* **100/1**
0 **6** *2 ¼* **Dillenda**[9] 6013 2-9-0 0.............................. DavidAllan 7 58
(T D Easterby) *dwlt: in tch stands' side: rdn along over 2f out: kpt on same pce: 2nd of 5 in gp* **20/1**
6 **7** *nk* **Chocolicious (IRE)**[8] 6051 2-9-0 0.............................. TomEaves 11 57
(B Smart) *led stands' side gp: pushed along over 2f out: sn rdn: hdd 1 1/2f out and grad wknd: 3rd of 5 in gp* **7/2[2]**
00 **8** *1 ½* **Noble Heart (IRE)**[46] 4921 2-9-0 0.............................. GrahamGibbons 5 52
(T D Barron) *cl up far side: led and overall elader 1/2-way: pushed along and hdd 2f out: sn drvn and wknd: 5th of 6 in gp* **16/1**
0506 **9** *8* **That Boy Ronaldo**[10] 5988 2-8-9 53.............................. SladeO'Hara[(5)] 10 28
(A Berry) *chsd ldng pair stands' side: rdn along over 2f out and sn wknd: 4th of 5 in gp* **50/1**
10 *4 ½* **Prima Laurea (IRE)** 2-8-10 0.............................. PaulHanagan 9 11
(J G Given) *s.i.s: a in rr stands' side: 5th of 5 in gp* **16/1**
00 **11** *11* **Tallulah's Secret**[38] 5165 2-9-0 0.............................. RobertWinston 2 —
(J Gallagher) *overall ldr far side: hdd 1/2-way: sn wknd: 6th of 6 in gp* **100/1**

1m 13.51s (-0.49) **Going Correction** -0.25s/f (Firm) **45** Ran SP% **115.1**
Speed ratings (Par 92): **93,92,91,91,89 86,86,84,73,67 52**
toteswinger: 1&2 £12.20, 1&3 £5.20, 2&3 £3.80. CSF £159.17 TOTE £13.70: £3.40, £2.60, £1.20; EX 102.70.
Owner L Rutherford Mrs R G Hillen Mrs J Ryan **Bred** Dell Ridge Farm **Trained** Hambleton, N Yorks

FOCUS
The second division of the fillies' maiden and again the field split into two groups, with the riders keen to avoid the middle of the track. It was the slower of the pair and the form is ordinary, but this time it was those on the far side who came out on top.

NOTEBOOK
Cashleen(USA), a half-sister to four winners from 6-12f, got her career off to a perfect start with a ready success. She lost ground with a tardy start and then ran green through the first two furlongs, but picked up most positively when asked for an effort. She was always holding off her pursuers at the business end and, considering her slow start, rates value for a little better than the bare margin. She ought to appreciate stepping up in distance as she matures, and looks a nice prospect for next term. (op 14-1)
Bea Menace(USA), a $50,000 May foal, showed plenty of promise and, as her pedigree would suggest, looks set to relish another furlong before the season ends. It is fair to expect her to go close next time. (op 11-1)
Keep Dancing(IRE) came clear of her rivals on the near side and probably ran very close to the level of her debut second on soft ground 17 days earlier. She deserves another chance. (op 2-1)
Miss Fritton(IRE) was always on the pace on the far side and did nothing wrong. She helps to set the level of this form and has more options now she is eligible for a nursery mark. (tchd 7-2)
Petella improved nicely on her debut effort over 5f last month and looks sure to progress again as she steps up in distance. She will be qualified for a mark after her next assignment and is one to keep an eye on. (op 80-1)

6246 KING'S REGIMENT CUP MAIDEN STKS (C&G) 6f
3:10 (3:11) (Class 5) 2-Y-O **£3,885** (£1,156; £577; £288) **Stalls** Centre

Form RPR
0 **1** **Alyarf (USA)**[77] 3895 2-9-0 0.............................. MichaelHills 8 96+
(B W Hills) *cl up: led on bit 2f out: clr appr fnl f: easily* **11/4[2]**
004 **2** *8* **All Spin (IRE)**[34] 5286 2-9-0 75.............................. DaneO'Neill 6 69
(A P Jarvis) *led: rdn along and hdd 2f out: sn drvn and kpt on: no ch w wnr* **8/1[3]**
3 *1* **Apache Ridge (IRE)** 2-9-0 0.............................. PaulHanagan 9 66
(K A Ryan) *towards rr: hdwy over 2f out: rdn over 1f out: kpt on ins fnl f: nrst fin* **12/1**
4 *¾* **Barbarian** 2-9-0 0.............................. DarryllHolland 3 64
(B W Hills) *in tch on inner: pushed along and green over 2f out: swtchd rt and rdn over 1f out: styd on ins fnl f: nrst fin* **11/1**
4 **5** *4* **Sunniva Duke (IRE)**[12] 5929 2-9-0 0.............................. JimmyFortune 1 52
(R Hannon) *trckd ldng pair: pushed along 1/2-way: rdn 2f out and sn btn* **7/4[1]**
0 **6** *nse* **Winning Band (IRE)**[8] 6062 2-9-0 0.............................. JamieSpencer 7 52
(B J Meehan) *chsd ldrs: rdn along over 2f out: grad wknd* **12/1**
7 *6* **Oasis On Island** 2-9-0 0.............................. TomEaves 2 43+
(B Smart) *dwlt: rn green and a outpcd in rr* **10/1**
06 **8** *19* **Piccolo Express**[27] 5497 2-9-0 0.............................. J-PGuillambert 4 —
(B P J Baugh) *a towards rr: bhd fr 1/2-way* **125/1**
9 *6* **Short Sharp Shock** 2-9-0 0.............................. RobertWinston 5 —
(J Mackie) *in tch: pushed along 1/2-way: sn wknd and bhd* **50/1**
10 *32* **Secret Star (IRE)** 2-9-0 0.............................. PaulMulrennan 10 —
(R Bastiman) *s.i.s and a wl bhd* **66/1**

1m 12.62s (-1.38) **Going Correction** -0.25s/f (Firm) **10** Ran SP% **111.2**
Speed ratings (Par 95): **99,88,87,86,80 80,72,47,39,—**
toteswinger: 1&2 £4.90, 1&3 £6.80, 2&3 £10.30. CSF £23.59 TOTE £3.70: £1.30, £2.30, £2.80; EX 21.00.
Owner Hamdan Al Maktoum **Bred** Shadwell Farm LLC **Trained** Lambourn, Berks

FOCUS
The field went to the far side in this maiden and it was the quickest winning time of the four races on the card over course and distance. The runner-up sets the standard.

NOTEBOOK
Alyarf(USA) ◆ showed he has improved a bundle for his time off the track and could hardly have done the job more impressively. As was the case last time, he ran freely early on, but he bounced off the quicker ground and could have been called the winner two furlongs out. He was eased in the closing stages and rates value for a good bit further than his already wide-winning margin. While this may have been only a modest heat, the runner-up has an official rating of 75 and the well-related winner does look potentially very useful, so it will be very interesting to see where connections pitch him in next. (tchd 9-4 and 3-1 in places)
All Spin(IRE) had finished behind Alyarf at Ascot on his penultimate start but has improved since then, yet he was beaten a lot further by his rival here. He probably ran close enough to his official rating, thus helping to put the form into some perspective, and he could be worth stepping up to another furlong. (op 17-2 tchd 9-1)
Apache Ridge(IRE), who cost 140,000 euros, was easy to back for this debut and ultimately proved too green to do himself justice. He was keeping on nicely towards the finish, however, and should prove much sharper for the run. (tchd 11-1 and 14-1)
Barbarian was slow to break and never seriously got into the race. He was keeping on steadily late on, though, and it is fair to expect him to prove a lot wiser with the benefit of this debut experience. (op 12-1 tchd 9-1)
Sunniva Duke(IRE) proved very disappointing and ran well below the level of his debut fourth at Goodwood. It may have been the quicker ground that found him out, but he does now have something to prove. (op 11-8 tchd 15-8 and 2-1 in places)
Short Sharp Shock Official explanation: jockey said colt was unsuited by the good to firm (good in places) ground and lost its action.

6247 VALE UK NURSERY 6f
3:45 (3:45) (Class 4) (0-80,77) 2-Y-O **£6,476** (£1,927; £963; £481) **Stalls** Centre

Form RPR
5440 **1** **Mabait**[22] 5632 2-9-0 **70**.............................. DaneO'Neill 4 74+
(L M Cumani) *in tch far side: hdwy over 2f out: rdn to ld appr fnl f: sn drvn and kpt on wl* **5/1[2]**
351 **2** *½* **Dark Lane**[34] 5277 2-9-6 **76**.............................. JamieSpencer 13 78+
(T D Barron) *cl up stands' side gp: hdwy to ld that gp over 2f out: sn rdn and hung bdly lft: drvn and ev ch ins fnl f: no ex towards fin: 1st of 6 in gp* **7/2[1]**
6046 **3** *3 ¼* **Rio Cobolo (IRE)**[32] 5363 2-7-12 **54** oh1..............................(v[1]) PaulQuinn 6 46
(Paul Green) *prom far side: effrt over 2f out: rdn to ld wl over 1f out: hdd appr fnl f: sn drvn and kpt on same pce: 2nd of 7 in gp* **40/1**
3520 **4** *¾* **River Rye (IRE)**[14] 5855 2-9-5 **75**.............................. JimmyFortune 10 65
(R Hannon) *chsd ldrs stands' side: rdn along 2f out: drvn and edgd lft over 1f out: kpt on ins fnl f nrst fin: 2nd of 6 in gp* **12/1**
6330 **5** *¾* **Abbey Steps (IRE)**[31] 5381 2-8-1 **60**..............................(b[1]) DuranFentiman[(3)] 2 48
(T D Easterby) *chsd ldrs far side: rdn along over 2f out: grad wknd appr last: 3rd of 7 in gp* **33/1**
042 **6** *shd* **Equinine (IRE)**[24] 5584 2-9-1 **71**.............................. MichaelHills 5 58
(B W Hills) *s.i.s and sn rdn along and outpcd in rr: hdwy 2f out: kpt on u.p ins fnl f: nrst fin: 4th of 7 in gp* **5/1[2]**
3235 **7** *3 ¼* **Jimwil (IRE)**[65] 4292 2-9-1 **71**.............................. TomEaves 3 49
(M Dods) *dwlt: towards rr far side: swtchd rt and rdn over 1f out: nvr a factor: 5th of 7 in gp* **14/1**
013 **8** *3 ½* **Toledo Gold (IRE)**[28] 5451 2-9-7 **77**.............................. DavidAllan 7 44
(E J Alston) *overall ldr far side: rdn along and hdd 2f out: sn wknd: 6th of 7 in gp* **14/1**
3004 **9** *nse* **Custard Cream Kid (IRE)**[28] 5447 2-8-8 **64**.............................. PaulHanagan 11 31
(R A Fahey) *in tch stands' side: rdn along 1/2-way: sn wknd: 4th of 6 in gp* **6/1[3]**
540 **10** *6* **Kings Ace (IRE)**[28] 5461 2-8-9 **65**..............................(v[1]) DarrenWilliams 1 14
(A P Jarvis) *clsd up far side: led that gp and overall ldr 2f out: sn rdn and hdd wl over 1f out: wknd qckly: 7th of 7 in gp* **33/1**
1330 **11** *1 ½* **Lisburn (IRE)**[14] 5855 2-9-1 **71**.............................. JoeFanning 12 16
(M Brittain) *cl up stands' side: effrt over 2f out: sn rdn and wknd: 4th of 6 in gp* **7/1**
040 **12** *1 ½* **Especially For You (IRE)**[137] 2048 2-8-2 **58**.............................. FrancisNorton 9 —
(E J O'Neill) *in tch stands' side: rdn along over 2f out and sn wknd: 5th of 6 in gp* **25/1**
5535 **13** *11* **Amorachy**[55] 4628 2-8-12 **68**.............................. RobertWinston 8 —
(K A Ryan) *led stands' side: gp: rdn along 1/2-way: sn hdd & wknd: 6th of 6 in gp* **33/1**

1m 13.4s (-0.60) **Going Correction** -0.25s/f (Firm) **13** Ran SP% **118.5**
Speed ratings (Par 97): **94,93,89,88,87 86,82,77,77,69 67,65,51**
toteswinger: 1&2 £3.20, 1&3 £44.80, 2&3 £35.00. CSF £21.39 CT £654.98 TOTE £6.20: £2.10, £1.60, £17.80; EX 20.80.
Owner Sheikh Mohammed Obaid Al Maktoum **Bred** L A C Ashby Newhall Estate Farm **Trained** Newmarket, Suffolk

FOCUS
A modest nursery in which the field split into two groups, but again the main action developed on the far side. The winner was back to form and the runner-up is on the upgrade.

NOTEBOOK
Mabait had flopped on his nursery debut 22 days earlier, but he confirmed that effort to be all wrong and got off the mark at the fifth time of asking. He was slowly into his stride, but soon recovered and travelled nicely into contention. He then showed a willing attitude under pressure, proving suited by the return to quicker ground, and is best kept to this trip for the short term. Official explanation: trainer's rep said, regarding apparent improvement in form, that the colt was better suited to 6f and the faster ground. (op 8-1 tchd 9-2)
Dark Lane proved popular to follow up his Newmarket win on this drop in class. He very nearly rewarded his supporters, but lost the race by hanging right over from the stands' rail to join those on the far side. He may not have enjoyed the quicker ground, but he clearly has an engine and has begun life in nurseries on a good mark. (tchd 10-3, 4-1 and 9-2 in places)

Rio Cobolo(IRE) had shown very little of late, but this was much his best effort in the first-time visor. He got the trip well enough on the quicker ground and connections will presumably try to get him out before the Hhandicapper can raise him. But one will have to be wary of the headgear holding a similarly positive effect next time. (op 66-1)
River Rye(IRE) came from behind on the near side and posted a better effort on this return to a sounder surface, helping to set the level of the form. (op 11-1)
Equinine(IRE) disappointed on this much quicker going. (op 7-2 tchd 10-3 and 11-2 in places)
Amorachy Official explanation: jockey said gelding hung left

6248 VALE UK (S) STKS — 1m 6f

4:20 (4:20) (Class 4) 3-4-Y-0 — **£6,476** (£1,927; £963; £481) **Stalls** Low

Form	Pos	Btn	Runner	RPR
0065	**1**		**Blue Jet (USA)**[22] 5637 4-9-7 46 ... TomEaves 1 (R M Whitaker) *trckd ldrs on inner: hdwy 4f out: rdn to ld over 2f out: drvn and styd on strly fnl f* **7/1**[3]	61
025	**2**	*4½*	**Well Informed**[9] 6032 3-8-6 57 ... DeanMcKeown 2 (E J O'Neill) *hld up and bhd: hdwy on inner over 3f out: swtchd outside and effrt 2f out: sn rdn and chsd wnr ins fnl f: drvn and no imp* **14/1**	50
4205	**3**	*1*	**Cossack Prince**[38] 5169 3-8-11 62 ... JamieSpencer 11 (B J Meehan) *trckd ldr: hdwy to ld over 3f out: rdn and hdd over 2f out: sn drvn and kpt on same pce appr fnl f* **4/1**[2]	54
6440	**4**	*6*	**Fever**[11] 5971 4-9-7 61 ... PaulMulrennan 8 (M W Easterby) *trckd ldrs: hdwy over 3f out: rdn over 2f out: sn drvn and kpt on same pce* **8/1**	45
0206	**5**	*5*	**Bond Casino**[15] 5833 4-9-2 47 ... PJMcDonald 6 (G R Oldroyd) *led: rdn along 4f out: hdd over 3f out and grad wknd* **16/1**	33
00	**6**	*1¾*	**Alkyoni (IRE)**[102] 3094 3-8-6 0 ...(p) FrankieMcDonald 10 (Jane Chapple-Hyam) *in midfield: sme hdwy 4f out: rdn along 3f out and no imp* **66/1**	31
3200	**7**	*2½*	**Loveofmylife**[43] 5027 3-8-1 50 ...(t) DavidProbert(5) 5 (R M Beckett) *in midfield: effrt over 3f out: sn rdn and no hdwy* **8/1**	27
5060	**8**	*2¾*	**Montevetro**[48] 4859 3-8-11 53 ... JimmyFortune 3 (R Hannon) *hld up: a towards rr* **11/1**	28
-000	**9**	*8*	**Sweet Seville (FR)**[24] 5593 4-8-13 45 ... MichaelJStainton(3) 7 (Mrs G S Rees) *a in rr* **50/1**	12
2200	**10**	*14*	**Bocciani (GER)**[13] 5887 3-8-11 58 ... PaulHanagan 9 (A Berry) *in tch: rdn along 5f out: sn wknd* **20/1**	—
334P	**11**	*18*	**Stringsofmyheart**[62] 4426 4-9-6 75 ... DarryllHolland 4 (Miss Gay Kelleway) *trckd ldng pair on inner: pushed along 4f out: rdn 3f out and sn wknd* **13/8**[1]	—

2m 58.89s (-5.41) **Going Correction** -0.325s/f (Firm) course record
WFA 3 from 4yo 10lb — **11** Ran SP% **121.9**
Speed ratings (Par 105): **102,99,98,95,92 91,90,88,84,76 65**
toteswinger: 1&2 £14.00, 1&3 £5.90, 2&3 £9.30. CSF £102.23 TOTE £9.00: £2.60, £3.50, £1.90; EX 130.70.The winner was bought in for £9,000.
Owner Country Lane Partnership **Bred** Latitude 27, Llc **Trained** Scarcroft, W Yorks

FOCUS
This seller was run at a fair gallop and the field came home strung out behind the decisive winner. The front pair are rated to form.
Stringsofmyheart Official explanation: jockey said filly was unsuited by the good to firm (good in places) ground

6249 GRIFFITHS & ARMOUR H'CAP — 1m 30y

4:55 (4:56) (Class 3) (0-95,94) 3-Y-0+ — **£9,346** (£2,799; £1,399; £700; £349; £175) **Stalls** Low

Form	Pos	Btn	Runner	RPR
2430	**1**		**Kal Barg**[29] 5425 3-9-2 **92** ... J-PGuillambert 14 (M A Jarvis) *sn cl up: rdn to ld wl over 1f out: drvn ins fnl f and hld on gamely* **6/1**[2]	101
3030	**2**	*½*	**Suits Me**[14] 5858 5-8-13 **85** ... MickyFenton 12 (T P Tate) *hld up on outer in midfield: hdwy 3f out: rdn to chal over 1f out and ev ch tl no ex towards fin* **12/1**	93
2501	**3**	*1¼*	**Rainbow Mirage (IRE)**[17] 5772 4-9-1 **87** ... GrahamGibbons 10 (E S McMahon) *trckd ldrs: hdwy on inner over 2f out: rdn wl over 1f out and ev ch tl drvn and no ex ins fnl f* **13/2**[3]	92
0506	**4**	*¾*	**Scartozz**[25] 5569 6-8-12 **91** ...(b) AndreaAtzeni(7) 3 (M Botti) *hld up in rr: hdwy on wd outside over 2f out: sn rdn and kpt on ins fnl f: nrst fin* **16/1**	94
0353	**5**	*¾*	**Silver Rime (FR)**[14] 5862 3-8-11 **87** ... DaneO'Neill 4 (R Hannon) *in tch on inner: hdwy over 2f out: sn rdn and kpt on u.p ins fnl f: nrst fin* **9/2**[1]	89
1061	**6**	*½*	**Opus Maximus (IRE)**[9] 6035 3-8-9 **85** 6ex ... GregFairley 13 (M Johnston) *led: rdn along 3f out: hdd wl over 1f out and grad wknd* **7/1**	85
512	**7**	*2*	**Brasingaman Hifive**[22] 5635 3-8-4 **80** ... DaleGibson 6 (Mrs G S Rees) *in midfield: effrt and sme hdwy 3f out: sn rdn along and no imp fnl 2f* **9/1**	76
1105	**8**	*nk*	**Gala Casino Star (IRE)**[13] 5907 3-8-12 **88** ... PaulHanagan 8 (R A Fahey) *chsd ldrs: effrt 3f out: rdn over 2f out: drvn over 1f out and grad wknd* **25/1**	83
1206	**9**	*7*	**Goodbye Mr Bond**[54] 4661 8-8-13 **85** ... DavidAllan 1 (E J Alston) *hld up: a in rr* **12/1**	64
2563	**10**	*nk*	**Kay Gee Be (IRE)**[48] 4845 4-9-8 **94** ... JamieSpencer 2 (M J Wallace, Australia) *hld up in rr: swtchd rt and sme hdwy over 2f out: sn rdn and btn* **7/1**	72
6204	**11**	*3¼*	**Mujood**[10] 6005 5-9-5 **91** ...(v) StephenCarson 7 (Eve Johnson Houghton) *chsd ldng pair: rdn along 3f out: sn wknd* **33/1**	62
6141	**12**	*1¾*	**Major Magpie (IRE)**[8] 6052 6-9-0 **86** 6ex ... DarryllHolland 11 (M Dods) *hld up in rr: effrt and sme hdwy 3f out: sn rdn and nvr a factor* **10/1**	53

1m 41.36s (-2.44) **Going Correction** -0.325s/f (Firm)
WFA 3 from 4yo+ 4lb — **12** Ran SP% **117.9**
Speed ratings (Par 107): **99,98,97,96,95 95,93,92,85,85 82,80**
toteswinger: 1&2 £16.00, 1&3 £9.40, 2&3 £17.20. CSF £75.68 CT £487.08 TOTE £5.20: £2.00, £3.60, £3.00; EX 69.60.
Owner Sheikh Ahmed Al Maktoum **Bred** Mrs C G Gardiner **Trained** Newmarket, Suffolk

FOCUS
A very open handicap, run at a solid pace, and the form looks sound enough rated around those in the frame behind the winner.

NOTEBOOK
Kal Barg showed his lifeless display at Great Leighs 29 days earlier to be totally wrong and came home to score in game fashion. Handy from the off, he displayed a willing attitude under maximum pressure and proved at home on the sound surface. This was his first win of the season and he looks the sort who can progress a little further as a four-year-old. (op 11-2 tchd 5-1)
Suits Me was ridden with much more restraint than is often the case and he emerged with every chance two furlongs out. He just lacked the resolution of the winner at the business end, but ran right up to his best. (op 14-1)
Rainbow Mirage(IRE) had been upped 4lb for winning on heavy ground 17 days earlier and he did nothing wrong on this contrasting surface. He probably needs a stiffer test on this sort of ground and remains capable of further success. (op 15-2 tchd 8-1)
Scartozz was doing his best work at the finish under a much more patient ride, but he did not convince with his head carriage and is not easy to catch right. (op 14-1)
Major Magpie(IRE) Official explanation: trainer had no explanation for the poor form shown

6250 VALE UK H'CAP — 1m 30y

5:25 (5:25) (Class 4) (0-80,79) 3-Y-0+ — **£5,504** (£1,637; £818; £408) **Stalls** Low

Form	Pos	Btn	Runner	RPR
0200	**1**		**Just Bond (IRE)**[13] 5908 6-9-8 **79** ... PJMcDonald 13 (G R Oldroyd) *hld up in rr: gd hdwy on outer 2f out: rdn over 1f out: styd on strly ins fnl f to ld nr line* **16/1**	88
1412	**2**	*shd*	**Isphahan**[28] 5470 5-9-2 **78** ... DavidProbert(5) 5 (A M Balding) *prom: effrt over 2f out: rdn to ld 1f out: drvn ins fnl f: hdd and nt qckn nr line* **9/4**[1]	87
4240	**3**	*1¼*	**Vicious Warrior**[15] 5843 9-9-2 **73** ... DeanMcKeown 2 (R M Whitaker) *led: rdn along 3f out: drvn and hdd 1f out: kpt on u.p ins fnl f* **10/1**	79
0056	**4**	*1*	**Thunderstruck**[3] 6188 3-8-8 **69** ...(b) PaulMulrennan 9 (K A Ryan) *hld up in rr: gd hdwy 2f out: nt clr run over 1f out: swtchd rt and rdn ins fnl f: styd on wl: nrst fin* **40/1**	74+
0-05	**5**	*hd*	**Harvest Warrior**[17] 5773 6-9-2 **73** ... DavidAllan 12 (T D Easterby) *s.i.s and rr: rdn along wl over 2f out: swtchd rt and gd hdwy on outer over 1f out: fin strly* **9/1**	76
2443	**6**	*hd*	**Pitbull**[49] 4813 5-8-8 **65** oh2 ...(p) GrahamGibbons 7 (Mrs G S Rees) *s.i.s: hdwy on inner over 3f out: rdn to chse ldrs over 1f out: sn drvn and one pce ent fnl f* **14/1**	68
6251	**7**	*nk*	**Sotik Star (IRE)**[27] 5492 5-9-3 **74** ... DarryllHolland 11 (P J Makin) *in tch: hdwy on outer 3f out: rdn to chse ldrs 2f out: drvn and edgd lft ent fnl f: one pce* **15/2**[3]	76
0433	**8**	*2¼*	**Resounding Glory (USA)**[17] 5773 3-9-1 **76** ... PaulHanagan 4 (R A Fahey) *chsd ldrs: rdn along over 2f out: drvn and grad wknd over 1f out* **16/1**	73
6105	**9**	*hd*	**Eternal Legacy (IRE)**[8] 6043 6-8-8 **65** oh1 ... FrancisNorton 6 (E J Alston) *hld up in midfield: hdwy over 2f out: sn rdn to chse ldrs and swtchd lft over 1f out: drvn and one pce ins fnl f* **25/1**	61
5006	**10**	*1¾*	**Full Victory (IRE)**[46] 4927 6-8-13 **70** ... DaneO'Neill 14 (R A Farrant) *nvr bttr than midfield* **14/1**	62
0530	**11**	*4½*	**Champain Sands (IRE)**[3] 6186 9-8-8 **65** oh1 ... JamieSpencer 3 (E J Alston) *dwlt: hld up: a in rr* **7/1**[2]	47
0430	**12**	*1¼*	**Benfleet Boy**[9] 6028 4-9-4 **75** ... MichaelHills 10 (B G Powell) *prom: rdn along over 3f out and sn wknd* **14/1**	54
4603	**13**	*6*	**Phluke**[9] 6035 7-9-8 **79** ...(v) StephenCarson 8 (Eve Johnson Houghton) *in tch: rdn along 3f out: sn wknd* **16/1**	44

1m 42.12s (-1.68) **Going Correction** -0.325s/f (Firm)
WFA 3 from 4yo+ 4lb — **13** Ran SP% **118.1**
Speed ratings (Par 105): **95,94,93,92,92 92,91,89,89,87 83,82,76**
toteswinger: 1&2 £12.80, 1&3 £40.30, 2&3 £6.80. CSF £51.22 CT £408.94 TOTE £20.50: £5.00, £1.50, £3.60; EX 78.40 Place 6: £66.28 Place 5: £55.69.
Owner R C Bond **Bred** Schwindibode Ag **Trained** Brawby, N Yorks

FOCUS
A modest handicap, but it was run at a decent pace and the form looks fair and solid enough for the grade.
Thunderstruck Official explanation: jockey said gelding was denied a clear run
Champain Sands(IRE) Official explanation: jockey said gelding was denied a clear run
Benfleet Boy Official explanation: jockey said gelding was unsuited by the good to firm (good in places) ground
T/Plt: £133.10 to a £1 stake. Pool: £58,398.09. 320.25 winning tickets. T/Qpdt: £59.70 to a £1 stake. Pool: £3,332.28. 41.30 winning tickets. JR

6132 WOLVERHAMPTON (A.W) (L-H)

Friday, September 26

OFFICIAL GOING: Standard to fast
Wind: Almost nil Weather: Bright and dry

6251 OPEN A HILLS ACCOUNT - 0800 44 40 40 H'CAP — 5f 216y(P)

6:20 (6:20) (Class 6) (0-55,55) 3-Y-0+ — **£2,388** (£705; £352) **Stalls** Low

Form	Pos	Btn	Runner	RPR
43	**1**		**Casela Park (IRE)**[22] 5627 3-9-3 **55** ... TPQueally 10 (S Kirk) *wnt lft s: hdwy on outside 2f out: sustained run u.p to ld cl home* **11/2**[2]	68
6202	**2**	*hd*	**Elusive Dreams (USA)**[14] 5871 4-9-5 **55** ...(v) TGMcLaughlin 8 (P Howling) *hmpd and bmpd s: in rr: hdwy 2f out: edgd lft bef le3d 1f out: hdd cl home* **4/1**[1]	67
6240	**3**	*3*	**Rainbow Bay**[4] 6159 5-9-4 **54** ...(v) RobertWinston 3 (Miss Tracy Waggott) *chsd ldrs: rdn to ld over 1f out: hdd 1f out: one pce* **6/1**[3]	56
0636	**4**	*2¼*	**Musical Script (USA)**[15] 5817 5-9-4 **54** ...(b) RobertHavlin 1 (Mouse Hamilton-Fairley) *in rr: hdwy and effrt over 1f out: fdd ins fnl f* **11/2**[2]	49
0551	**5**	*1¾*	**Welcome Approach**[39] 5152 5-9-5 **55** ... JamieMoriarty 13 (J R Weymes) *sn bhd: rdn 3f out: nvr on terms* **16/1**	45
3300	**6**	*1¼*	**Jun Fan (USA)**[52] 4703 6-9-4 **54** ... TomEaves 2 (B Ellison) *hld up in tch: rdn over 1f out: sn btn* **8/1**	40
5034	**7**	*1¼*	**Out Of India**[43] 5007 6-9-2 **52** ... JerryO'Dwyer 9 (P T Dalton) *trckd ldrs: rdn over 1f out: wknd 1f out* **16/1**	34
0465	**8**	*½*	**Tugalu (IRE)**[30] 5395 3-9-3 **55** ...(p) AndrewElliott 4 (K A Ryan) *broke wl: chsd ldrs: wknd over 1f out* **11/1**	35
0320	**9**	*2½*	**Pasta Prayer**[25] 5574 3-8-10 **55** ...(v1) HollyHall(7) 7 (S A Callaghan) *wnt rt s: sn w ldrs: ev ch over 1f out: wknd fnl f* **20/1**	27
4020	**10**	*4½*	**Hollywood George**[48] 4863 4-9-2 **52** ...(p) PatrickMathers 11 (Miss M E Rowland) *prom rdn over 2f out: wknd over 1f out* **10/1**	10
50-0	**11**	*3*	**Tarkamara (IRE)**[23] 5604 4-9-5 **55** ...(b1) JoeFanning 6 (P F I Cole) *sn led: hdd over 1f out: wknd rapidly* **18/1**	3

1m 14.07s (-0.93) **Going Correction** -0.075s/f (Stan)
WFA 3 from 4yo+ 2lb — **11** Ran SP% **115.4**
Speed ratings (Par 101): **103,102,98,95,93 91,90,89,86,80 76**
toteswinger: 1&2 £4.50, 1&3 £9.00, 2&3 £14.00. CSF £27.18 CT £139.00 TOTE £6.10: £1.70, £1.10, £3.10; EX 31.50.
Owner Norman Ormiston **Bred** Airlie Stud **Trained** Upper Lambourn, Berks

The Form Book, Raceform Ltd, Compton, RG20 6NL

FOCUS
The race was littered with infrequent winners but a number of contenders were in fair form. The first two fought out an exciting finish and pulled clear of the rest. The placed horses set the level and the form looks fairly solid.

6252 GET A BONUS AT WILLIAMHILLCASINO.COM H'CAP 1m 5f 194y(P)
6:50 (6:50) (Class 5) (0-75,74) 3-Y-0+ £3,238 (£963; £481; £240) Stalls Low

Form				RPR
3445	1		**Right Option (IRE)**[32] 5367 4-9-11 **67**........ TolleyDean(3) 5	74
			(J L Flint) *hld up: rdn and hdwy over 2f out: led appr fnl f: rdn out* **9/2**[2]	
2021	2	½	**River Kent**[14] 5868 3-8-8 **57**........ CatherineGannon 8	63
			(Mrs A Duffield) *t.k.h: trckd ldrs: wnt 2nd over 1f out and ev ch tl no imp towards fin* **10/3**[1]	
/0-6	3	1 ¾	**Cash On (IRE)**[28] 5476 6-10-0 **67**........(p) JerryO'Dwyer 6	71
			(Karen George) *slowly away: in rr: hdwy 2f out: ev ch ent fnl f: nt qckn ins fnl f* **14/1**	
0021	4	3	**Bundle Up**[51] 4722 5-8-11 **50**........ TGMcLaughlin 3	50+
			(P D Evans) *hld up: hdwy whn checked 2f out: hdwy on ins over 1f out: kpt on one pce fnl f* **5/1**[3]	
1323	5	¾	**Blue Hills**[147] 1779 7-10-0 **67**........(b) DarrenWilliams 4	66
			(P W Hiatt) *led: rdn clr over 2f out: hdd appr fnl f and sn wknd* **9/1**	
4600	6	1 ¾	**Synonymy**[8] 6060 5-8-9 **48**........(b) JamesDoyle 10	44
			(M Blanshard) *in tch tl rdn and wknd over 2f out* **8/1**	
0065	7	4	**Peas 'n Beans (IRE)**[33] 5321 5-8-2 **48** oh3........(t) RosieJessop(7) 9	39
			(T Keddy) *towards rr: rdn over 3f out: sn lost pl* **22/1**	
64-1	8	7	**Crispian (IRE)**[226] 545 4-9-11 **64**........ LiamJones 2	45
			(Jamie Snowden) *mid-div: rdn to go 2nd 3f out: wknd over 1f out* **5/1**[3]	
0000	9	6	**Bright Falcon**[8] 6052 3-9-11 **74**........(t1) JoeFanning 1	46
			(S Parr) *trckd ldrs tl rdn and wknd over 2f out* **20/1**	

3m 5.02s (-0.98) **Going Correction** -0.075s/f (Stan)
WFA 3 from 4yo+ 10lb **9 Ran SP% 111.5**
Speed ratings (Par 103): **99,98,97,96,95 94,92,88,84**
toteswinger: 1&2 £4.60, 1&3 £11.10, 2&3 £5.30. CSF £18.86 CT £185.74 TOTE £5.90: £2.10, £1.10, £5.40; EX 20.30.
Owner Roy Mathias **Bred** Paul Monaghan, R Berns And P Sexton **Trained** Kenfig Hill, Bridgend

FOCUS
The going was changed from standard to fast after the first race, but the change was not reflected in the time of this fairly competitive handicap which was run at a steady pace and turned into a bit of a sprint. The first three home all came from behind, despite the muddling gallop. The form makes sense although the third is a slight doubt.

6253 ALL THE BALLS AT WILLIAMHILLBINGO.COM MAIDEN STKS 7f 32y(P)
7:20 (7:20) (Class 5) 2-Y-0 £3,070 (£906; £453) Stalls High

Form				RPR
0	1		**Braveheart Move (IRE)**[9] 6029 2-9-3 0........ J-PGuillambert 8	77+
			(Sir Mark Prescott) *hld up towards rr: hdwy over 1f out: shkn up and r.o strly to ld nr fin* **66/1**	
3	2	hd	**Officer In Command (USA)**[48] 4861 2-9-3 0........ LPKeniry 10	71
			(J S Moore) *mid-div: hdwy on outside over 1f out: hung lft but r.o to go 2nd nr fin* **9/1**[3]	
3	3	½	**Caerus (USA)**[25] 5572 2-9-3 0........ PaulDoe 1	70
			(W J Knight) *led: rdn over 1f out: hdd and lost 2nd nr fin* **5/2**[2]	
4	4	1	**Standpoint**[20] 5696 2-9-3 0........ JamieSpencer 9	68
			(Sir Michael Stoute) *trckd ldr: rdn over 1f out: wknd ins fnl f* **8/11**[1]	
0	5	¾	**Darwin's Dragon**[7] 6085 2-9-3 0........ JoeFanning 11	66
			(P F I Cole) *prom: rdn over 2f out: styd on one pce fnl f* **28/1**	
0	6	1 ½	**Valkyrie (IRE)**[34] 5271 2-8-12 0........ KirstyMilczarek 4	57
			(N P Littmoden) *outpcd in rr: mde sme late hdwy on outside* **80/1**	
	7	2 ½	**Prince Andjo (USA)** 2-9-3 0........ PatrickMathers 5	56
			(I W McInnes) *v.s.a: nvr on terms* **125/1**	
	8	½	**Liteup My World (USA)** 2-9-3 0........ TomEaves 7	54
			(B Ellison) *mid-div: rdn 1/2-way: wknd appr fnl f* **14/1**	
	9	2	**Statute Book (IRE)** 2-9-3 0........ AdamKirby 2	49
			(S Kirk) *in rr: effrt over 2f out: wkng whn hmpd and swtchd rt over 1f out* **66/1**	
0	10	nk	**Sampower Quin (IRE)**[14] 5870 2-9-3 0........ DNolan 6	49
			(D Carroll) *trckd ldrs tl rdn and lost pl sn after 1/2-way* **150/1**	

1m 29.85s (0.25) **Going Correction** -0.075s/f (Stan) **10 Ran SP% 112.3**
Speed ratings (Par 95): **95,94,94,93,92 90,87,87,84,84**
toteswinger: 1&2 £27.50, 1&3 £27.50, 2&3 £28.00. CSF £540.61 TOTE £37.20: £8.60, £2.30, £1.30; EX 381.70.
Owner Moyglare Stud Farm Ltd **Bred** Moyglare Stud Farm Ltd **Trained** Newmarket, Suffolk

FOCUS
An interesting event, the market leaders seemed to have the race between them from some way out but were overhauled by two fast finishers. The race is rated slightly negatively around the third and fourth.

NOTEBOOK
Braveheart Move(IRE) was a shock 66-1 winner for Sir Mark Prescott. He was always outpaced over this trip on his debut, but motored from well off the pace to get up close home on this all-weather debut. This was really good performance considering the amount of stamina he has on the dam's side of his pedigree and he could be very progressive, particularly when faced with a stiffer test.
Officer In Command(USA) also deserves plenty of credit for finding a strong finishing burst from well off the pace, has probably stepped up considerably on his debut effort and will be suited by a return to 1m. (op 11-1 tchd 14-1)
Caerus(USA) had solid form claims and ran well under an aggressive ride, but was mugged close home. He may have done a bit too much in front and should have no trouble in winning a maiden. (op 9-4 tchd 2-1)
Standpoint was always well positioned just behind the leader and showed a long, fluent action but his response to pressure was slightly disappointing. It is possible that a sustained dual with the leader early in the straight may have blunted his finishing weapons, and he may be worth another chance next time. (op 5-6 tchd 10-11)
Darwin's Dragon ran his second promising race in the last week and could be one to note when qualified for nurseries. (op 33-1)

6254 GET YOUR CHIPS AT WILLIAMHILLPOKER.COM MEDIAN AUCTION MAIDEN STKS 7f 32y(P)
7:50 (7:54) (Class 6) 3-5-Y-0 £2,388 (£705; £352) Stalls High

Form				RPR
0202	1		**Bahamian Kid**[83] 3731 3-9-3 70........ DO'Donohoe 4	75
			(R Hollinshead) *in tch in mid-div: hdwy 3f out: wnt 2nd over 2f out: led over 1f out: r.o wl* **5/2**[2]	
45	2	2 ¾	**Ishiadancer**[25] 5561 3-8-12 0........ JohnEgan 5	63
			(E J Alston) *led tl rdn and hdd over 1f out: nt pce of wnr* **16/1**	
-206	3	2 ¾	**Red Tarn**[83] 3731 3-9-3 67........(t) TomEaves 1	60
			(B Smart) *chsd ldrs: rdn over 2f out: kpt on one pce* **11/1**	
0420	4	¾	**Billy Bowmore**[48] 4877 3-9-3 63........ TonyHamilton 10	58
			(M Dods) *s.i.s: rdn 2f out: kpt on one pce after* **10/1**	
00-5	5	1 ½	**Moscow Oznick**[242] 343 3-9-3 64........ ChrisCatlin 3	54
			(N J Vaughan) *s.i.s: in rr: mde sme late hdwy* **14/1**	
	6	2 ½	**Dashing Daniel** 3-9-0 0........ LukeMorris(3) 8	47
			(N J Vaughan) *s.i.s: sn mid-div: rdn over 2f out: hung rt over 1f out and wknd* **6/1**	
3320	7	2 ¼	**El Fuser**[50] 4777 3-9-3 67........ TravisBlock 6	41
			(P J Makin) *trckd ldr to over 2f out: wknd over 1f out* **4/1**[3]	
0	8	1 ½	**Little Pandora**[137] 2038 4-9-1 0........ CatherineGannon 9	32
			(G P Kelly) *a towards rr* **100/1**	
00	9	2 ¼	**Interchoice Star**[22] 5627 3-9-3 0........ DeanMcKeown 11	31
			(K G Wingrove) *hld up: rdn over 2f out: no hdwy after* **16/1**	
43	10	1 ¾	**Reine De Violette**[151] 1669 3-8-12 0........ TPQueally 12	21
			(H R A Cecil) *slowly away: sn in tch on outside: rdn over 1f out and hung bdly rt into st: wknd qckly: fin lame* **2/1**[1]	
0	11	17	**Rare Old Bird**[21] 5679 3-8-12 0........ SaleemGolam 7	—
			(J F Panvert) *chsd ldrs: rdn 1/2-way: sn btn* **100/1**	

1m 28.45s (-1.15) **Going Correction** -0.075s/f (Stan)
WFA 3 from 4yo 3lb **11 Ran SP% 134.0**
Speed ratings (Par 101): **103,99,96,95,94 91,88,87,84,82 63**
toteswinger: 1&2 £18.80, 1&3 £13.50, 2&3 £18.80. CSF £50.15 TOTE £4.20: £1.70, £3.60, £4.70; EX 67.10.
Owner Exors Of The Late J D Graham **Bred** J D Graham **Trained** Upper Longdon, Staffs

FOCUS
A fair event, but several who had a chance on form were reasonably exposed. They went a steady pace and the first three were fairly prominent throughout. The winner looks the best guide.
Ishiadancer Official explanation: jockey said filly hung left
Reine De Violette Official explanation: jockey said filly hung left; vet said filly returned lame

6255 REAL TIME RADIO AT WILLIAMHILL.CO.UK H'CAP 1m 141y(P)
8:20 (8:20) (Class 6) (0-55,60) 3-Y-0+ £2,388 (£705; £352) Stalls Low

Form				RPR
4061	1		**Kingsholm**[3] 6189 6-9-9 **60** 6ex........ JamieSpencer 1	69
			(K A Ryan) *s.i.s: hld up in mid-div: hdwy on ins to ld over 1f out: kpt up to work but r.o* **2/1**[1]	
6346	2	¾	**Al Rayanah**[9] 6036 5-9-2 **53**........(p) SaleemGolam 9	60
			(G Prodromou) *s.i.s: in rr: hdwy on ins whn carried lft over 1f out: r.o to go 2nd ins fnl f* **10/1**	
060	3	nk	**Roman History (IRE)**[2] 6217 5-9-1 **52**........(p) SilvestreDeSousa 5	58
			(Miss Tracy Waggott) *mid-div: rdn and hdwy on ins over 1f out: r.o: nvr nrr* **40/1**	
2500	4	1	**Mystic Roll**[55] 4635 5-9-2 **53**........ JohnEgan 3	57
			(Jane Chapple-Hyam) *trckd ldrs: rdn over 3f out: ev ch appr fnl f: one pce after* **14/1**	
0004	5	2 ½	**Summer Recluse (USA)**[14] 5871 9-8-12 **52**........(t) KevinGhunowa(3) 12	50
			(J M Bradley) *trckd ldrs: rdn 3f out: kpt on one pce fr over 1f out* **33/1**	
-465	6	½	**Semi Detached (IRE)**[92] 3422 5-8-11 **55**........ AlexEdwards(7) 7	52
			(J W Unett) *t.k.h: hld up: hdwy and squeezed throug over 1f out: no ex fnl f* **22/1**	
0300	7	shd	**Very Well Red**[8] 6056 5-9-4 **55**........ DarrenWilliams 4	52
			(P W Hiatt) *led after 1f: rdn and hdd over 1f out: wknd* **10/1**	
0325	8	½	**Outer Hebrides**[4] 6178 7-9-1 **52**........(v) KirstyMilczarek 8	48
			(J M Bradley) *led for 1f: rdn 2f out: sn wknd* **12/1**	
-003	9	2	**Confide In Me**[39] 5157 4-9-2 **53**........(t) RobertWinston 10	44
			(G A Butler) *mid-div on outside: rdn over 2f out: wknd over 1f out* **3/1**[2]	
0002	10	shd	**Franksalot (IRE)**[23] 5604 8-9-1 **52**........(p) PatrickMathers 6	43
			(I W McInnes) *in rr: rdn 3f out and no hdwy after* **16/1**	
3533	11	nk	**Ready To Crown (USA)**[15] 5837 4-9-2 **53**........ ChrisCatlin 13	43
			(Andrew Turnell) *hld up: hdwy over 4f out: rdn and wknd over 1f out* **9/1**[3]	
2660	12	hd	**Just Oscar (GER)**[62] 4428 4-9-1 **52**........ TGMcLaughlin 11	42
			(W M Brisbourne) *a in rr* **25/1**	

1m 49.4s (-1.10) **Going Correction** -0.075s/f (Stan) **12 Ran SP% 120.3**
Speed ratings (Par 101): **101,100,100,99,96 96,96,95,94,94 93,93**
toteswinger: 1&2 £5.30, 1&3 £23.20, 2&3 £23.20. CSF £22.66 CT £638.88 TOTE £2.60: £1.10, £4.70, £8.30; EX 29.40.
Owner Riverside Racing **Bred** J C , J R And S R Hitchins **Trained** Hambleton, N Yorks

FOCUS
A moderate handicap, but they went a reasonable pace and the form looks sound.

6256 BET ONLINE AT WILLIAMHILL.CO.UK H'CAP 1m 1f 103y(P)
8:50 (8:50) (Class 5) (0-75,75) 3-Y-0 £3,238 (£963; £481; £240) Stalls Low

Form				RPR
3135	1		**St Trinians**[24] 5595 3-9-2 **73**........ LPKeniry 6	83
			(E F Vaughan) *mde all: qcknd pce 2f out: rdn out* **14/1**	
001	2	1	**Lady Brora**[29] 5426 3-9-1 **72**........ FrancisNorton 10	80
			(A M Balding) *s.i.s: trckd wnr after 2f: kpt on but no imp fr over 1f out* **6/1**[3]	
5402	3	1 ¼	**Barliffey (IRE)**[57] 4571 3-9-2 **73**........(v) TPO'Shea 4	78+
			(D J Coakley) *slowly away: hdwy whn nt clr run and swtchd rt over 1f out: r.o: nvr nrr* **9/1**	
3055	4	¾	**King Kenny**[3] 6188 3-9-4 **75**........ JohnEgan 7	78
			(S Parr) *a in tch: rdn over 2f out: kpt on one pce fnl f* **8/1**	
0622	5	nk	**Title Role**[23] 5605 3-8-10 **74**........ AshleyMorgan(7) 2	77
			(P F I Cole) *mid-div: hdwy 4f out: wknd ent fnl f* **3/1**[1]	
66	6	hd	**Paint The Town Red**[33] 5309 3-9-1 **75**........ JackMitchell(3) 9	77+
			(H J Collingridge) *in rr: mde sme late hdwy* **14/1**	
5400	7	1 ¼	**House Of Lords (USA)**[28] 5472 3-9-4 **75**........(v1) JamieSpencer 5	75
			(M L W Bell) *t.k.h in mid-div: rdn over 2f out: wknd over 1f out* **5/1**[2]	
0053	8	nk	**Rockfield Tiger (IRE)**[20] 5713 3-9-2 **73**........ ShaneKelly 3	72
			(J A Osborne) *in rr: brief effrt over 1f out but nvr on terms* **6/1**[3]	
-051	9	10	**Colour Trooper (IRE)**[17] 5790 3-9-4 **75**........ StephenCarson 1	53
			(P Winkworth) *trckd ldrs tl rdn and wknd 2f out* **10/1**	
6-12	10	11	**Tevez**[239] 376 3-9-4 **75**........ JerryO'Dwyer 11	30
			(Miss Amy Weaver) *stdd s: a bhd* **16/1**	

2m 1.16s (-0.54) **Going Correction** -0.075s/f (Stan) **10 Ran SP% 119.7**
Speed ratings (Par 101): **99,98,97,96,96 95,94,94,85,75**
toteswinger: 1&2 £21.70, 1&3 £21.70, 2&3 £21.70. CSF £98.14 CT £814.93 TOTE £16.70: £4.40, £2.20, £3.20; EX 173.90 Place 6: £229.70 Place 5: £144.46.
Owner Hungerford Park Stud **Bred** Mrs E L Hunter **Trained** Newmarket, Suffolk

FOCUS
A competitive handicap but it was run at a dawdling pace and nothing got into it from behind. The race has been rated negatively.
T/Plt: £157.30 to a £1 stake. Pool: £83848.12. 388.98 winning tickets. T/Qpdt: £76.10 to a £1 stake. Pool: £6544.36. 63.60 winning tickets. JS

6257 - 6260a (Foreign Racing) - See Raceform Interactive

6138 DUNDALK (A.W) (L-H)

Friday, September 26

OFFICIAL GOING: Standard

6261a DIAMOND STKS LISTED RACE 1m 2f 150y

8:40 (8:40) 3-Y-O+ £23,933 (£7,022; £3,345; £1,139)

RPR

1 **Muhannak (IRE)**[32] 5349 4-9-7 PJSmullen 12 101
(R M Beckett) *mid-div: clsd into 4th under 2f out: r.o wl u.p to ld wl ins fnl f* **7/1**

2 *nk* **Mr Medici (IRE)**[19] 5729 3-9-1 101 CDHayes 5 101
(Kevin Prendergast, Ire) *chsd ldrs: travelling wl in 3rd into st: rdn and narrowly in front under 2f out: kpt on wl: hdd wl ins fnl f* **5/1**[3]

3 *shd* **Fiery Lad (IRE)**[19] 5726 3-9-1 107 KLatham 11 101
(G M Lyons, Ire) *towards rr: travelling wl and hdwy on inner over 1f out: sn 3rd: rdn ins fnl f: kpt on wout rching 1st 2* **9/2**[2]

4 *1 3/4* **Northgate (IRE)**[27] 5517 3-9-1 91 KJManning 7 97
(Joseph G Murphy, Ire) *chsd ldrs: rdn in 5th under 2f out: no imp and kpt on fnl f* **25/1**

5 *1/2* **Green Tobasco**[7] 6100 5-9-7 90 CO'Donoghue 10 96+
(M J P O'Brien, Ire) *towards rr: hdwy into 6th under 2f out: no imp and kpt on u.p fr 1f out* **10/1**

6 *hd* **Arch Rebel (USA)**[13] 5921 7-9-7 106 (p) FMBerry 8 95+
(Noel Meade, Ire) *towards rr: kpt on wl u.p on outer wout threatening fr over 1f out* **10/1**

7 *shd* **Kevkat (IRE)**[7] 6100 7-9-7 91 RPCleary 4 95+
(Eoin Griffin, Ire) *mid-div: clsd into 7th travelling wl fr 2f out: kpt on same pce u.p fr 1f out* **20/1**

8 *3/4* **Zulu Chief (USA)**[12] 5944 3-9-1 105 JMurtagh 14 95+
(A P O'Brien, Ire) *towards rr: sme hdwy and rdn under 2f out: no imp and kpt on same pce fr over 1f out* **5/2**[1]

9 *3 1/2* **Cassique Lady (IRE)**[73] 4068 3-8-12 95 WMLordan 3 85
(T Stack, Ire) *chsd ldrs: 6th over 4f out: kpt on same pce u.p fr under 2f out* **7/1**

10 *1 1/2* **King Of Westphalia (USA)**[12] 5944 3-9-1 93 JAHeffernan 6 85
(A P O'Brien, Ire) *led: hdd under 2f out: sn no ex* **20/1**

11 *3/4* **Superius (IRE)**[19] 5729 3-9-1 98 WJLee 1 84
(T Stack, Ire) *trckd ldr in 2nd: no ex u.p fr under 2f out* **16/1**

12 *nk* **Rinterval (IRE)**[92] 3415 3-8-12 NGMcCullagh 2 80
(David Wachman, Ire) *mid-div: 10th over 4f out: no imp u.p fr under 2f out* **20/1**

13 *1 1/4* **Joshua's Princess**[29] 5441 4-9-4 92 MJKinane 13 77
(John M Oxx, Ire) *chsd ldrs: 5th over 4f out: rdn bef st: sn no ex* **14/1**

14 *3* **Dollar Chick (IRE)**[11] 5983 4-9-4 91 (b) NPMadden 9 71
(Noel Meade, Ire) *trckd ldrs in 3rd: 4th into st: sn no ex u.p* **25/1**

2m 11.63s (131.63)
WFA 3 from 4yo+ 7lb **14 Ran SP% 141.1**
CSF £46.12 TOTE £11.90: £2.80, £2.10, £1.80; DF 97.70.
Owner R A Pegum **Bred** Mount Coote Stud **Trained** Whitsbury, Hants

FOCUS
An ordinary Listed race rated around the runner-up.

NOTEBOOK
Muhannak(IRE) notched his sixth win, and the most important yet. He challenged on the outside in the straight and ran on well under pressure, despite edging left, to get on top well inside the final furlong.

6262 - 6265a (Foreign Racing) - See Raceform Interactive

6238 ASCOT (R-H)

Saturday, September 27

OFFICIAL GOING: Good (8.6, str 9.2, rnd 8.3)
Wind: Virtually nil Weather: Sunny

6266 FASIG-TIPTON ROSEMARY STKS (H'CAP) (LISTED RACE) (F&M) 1m (R)

1:55 (1:57) (Class 1) (0-110,100) 3-Y-O+
£24,978 (£9,468; £4,738; £2,362; £1,183; £594) **Stalls High**

Form RPR

0225 1 **Eva's Request (IRE)**[28] 5506 3-9-6 **99** EdwardCreighton 13 107
(M R Channon) *mid-div: hdwy fr 2f out: led ent fnl f: r.o wl: rdn out* **12/1**

4263 2 *1* **Mekong Melody (IRE)**[10] 6027 3-8-3 **82** oh2 WilliamBuick 9 88
(C G Cox) *trckd ldrs: rdn whn nt clr run over 1f out: ev ch ent fnl f: kpt on but nt pce of wnr* **12/1**

1653 3 *shd* **Ghaidaa (IRE)**[28] 5506 3-9-6 **99** RHills 4 105
(M A Jarvis) *lw: hld up towards rr: hdwy over 2f out: sn rdn: r.o ent fnl f: fin wl* **11/2**[1]

3400 4 *3/4* **Don't Forget Faith (USA)**[34] 5311 3-8-12 **91** AdamKirby 14 95
(C G Cox) *trckd ldrs: rdn over 2f out: ev ch ent fnl f: kpt on same pce* **25/1**

2111 5 *hd* **Oat Cuisine**[7] 6130 4-8-9 **84** HayleyTurner 2 88
(M L W Bell) *lw: chsd ldrs: rdn 3f out: edgd lft over 1f out: kpt on* **13/2**[3]

1216 6 *1* **Maghya (IRE)**[70] 4189 3-8-11 **90** MartinDwyer 5 91
(W J Haggas) *mid-div: rdn over 2f out: prog over 1f out: kpt on fnl f* **10/1**

2110 7 *1 1/4* **Lindelaan (USA)**[28] 5506 3-9-3 **96** (v) SteveDrowne 12 94
(Sir Michael Stoute) *mid-div: rdn over 3f out: hdwy over 1f out: kpt on* **12/1**

1000 8 *1* **Raymi Coya (CAN)**[28] 5506 3-9-7 **100** DarryllHolland 11 96
(M Botti) *chsd ldrs: rdn over 2f out: ev ch jst over 1f out: fdd fnl f* **20/1**

5000 9 *1/2* **Try Me (UAE)**[56] 4618 3-8-9 **88** LiamJones 3 83
(C E Brittain) *swtg: mid-div: effrt over 2f out: kpt on same pce* **50/1**

1505 10 *1 1/4* **Jamboretta (IRE)**[93] 3415 4-9-4 **93** RyanMoore 16 85
(Sir Michael Stoute) *lw: hld up towards rr: weaved way through field over 2f out: sn rdn: one pce fnl f* **6/1**[2]

-100 11 *nk* **Basque Beauty**[10] 6034 3-9-1 **94** JMurtagh 7 85
(W J Haggas) *swtg: hld up bhd: rdn 3f out: swtchd rt over 1f out: sme late prog* **8/1**

0510 12 *2* **Rosaleen (IRE)**[28] 5506 3-9-6 **99** LDettori 15 86
(B J Meehan) *lw: led: rdn and hdd ent fnl f: fdd* **12/1**

3003 13 *2 1/2* **Tender The Great (IRE)**[14] 5908 5-8-7 **82** oh13 AlanMunro 8 63
(H J Collingridge) *a towards rr* **50/1**

0500 14 *3/4* **Nijoom Dubai**[16] 5829 3-9-7 **100** TPO'Shea 1 79
(M R Channon) *hld up towards rr: rdn and hdwy over 2f out: wknd over 1f out* **28/1**

-200 15 *2* **Kotsi (IRE)**[10] 6034 3-9-3 **96** (p) JimmyFortune 17 71
(E F Vaughan) *mid-div: rdn 3f out: wknd over 1f out* **25/1**

60-6 16 *nse* **Lady Jane Digby**[41] 5120 3-9-2 **95** RoystonFfrench 6 70
(M Johnston) *a towards rr* **25/1**

0230 17 *14* **Annie Skates (USA)**[84] 3807 3-9-5 **98** JohnEgan 10 40
(Jane Chapple-Hyam) *s.i.s: sn mid-div: wknd over 2f out* **16/1**

1m 41.09s (0.29) **Going Correction** +0.20s/f (Good)
WFA 3 from 4yo+ 4lb **17 Ran SP% 123.5**
Speed ratings (Par 111): **106,105,104,104,103 102,101,100,100,98 98,96,94,93,91 91,77**
toteswinger: 1&2 £34.60, 1&3 £18.70, 2&3 £16.70. CSF £138.10 CT £922.93 TOTE £14.90: £3.00, £3.00, £1.90, £8.20; EX 200.20 TRIFECTA Not won..
Owner Liam Mulryan **Bred** Ballylinch Stud **Trained** West Ilsley, Berks

FOCUS
This looked a really competitive fillies' Listed handicap, but it was won in decisive fashion by Eva's Request. The form looks solid enough.

NOTEBOOK
Eva's Request(IRE) had been struggling somewhat this year, but her Bath second to Lady Deauville two starts back was a very good effort. The big field and turning track made for a bit of traffic congestion but, having been handily paced throughout, she got the split when required and quickened up well.

Mekong Melody(IRE) raced even handier than the winner and had her chance. She is much improved, but her mark has been rising, and she was 2lb out of the handicap. This was another cracking effort, and she deserves another win before the end of the season.

Ghaidaa(IRE) ◆ did well, as she was drawn low and had to come from towards the rear on the outside. She was hemmed in by Nijoom Dubai starting up the straight, but was in the clear two furlongs out and stayed on well to all but snatch second. This trip seems to suit her well. (op 15-2 tchd 5-1 in a place)

Don't Forget Faith(USA), a stablemate of the second, chased the pace from the start and showed signs of a return to form. (op 28-1)

Oat Cuisine has had a fantastic season, but the first of four wins came off 65 and she is now on 84. That and her outside draw made it tough for her, but she was far from disgraced. (op 6-1)

Maghya(IRE), carrying her owner's second colours, was keeping on in the closing stages. (tchd 11-1)

Lindelaan(USA) left a disappointing effort at Sandown behind her, but she still did not have the pace to get in a blow.

Jamboretta(IRE) never got competitive and faded in the final furlong after making a bit of headway starting up the straight. She had been off three months and could be better for the race. (op 11-2 tchd 5-1)

Basque Beauty Official explanation: jockey said filly missed the break

Kotsi(IRE) Official explanation: jockey said filly stopped quickly

Annie Skates(USA) Official explanation: jockey said filly never travelled and hung right

6267 JUDDMONTE ROYAL LODGE STKS (GROUP 2) (C&G) 1m (R)

2:30 (2:30) (Class 1) 2-Y-O
£76,037 (£28,823; £14,425; £7,192; £3,602; £1,808) **Stalls High**

Form RPR

143 1 **Jukebox Jury (IRE)**[20] 5739 2-8-12 0 RoystonFfrench 9 114+
(M Johnston) *s.i.s: hld up last: hdwy over 2f out: sn rdn: swtchd lft over 1f out: r.o strly: led fnl 30yds: won gng away* **8/1**

21 2 *3/4* **Cityscape**[23] 5641 2-8-12 106 SteveDrowne 6 112
(R Charlton) *lw: t.k.h: cl up: rdn 2f out: led over 1f out: edgd lft ins fnl f: no ex whn hdd fnl 30yds* **15/8**[1]

312 3 *3 1/2* **On Our Way**[29] 5462 2-8-12 100 TPQueally 7 104
(H R A Cecil) *lw: prom: led over 2f out: sn rdn: hdd over 1f out: nt pce of ldng pair* **5/1**[3]

151 4 *2* **Orizaba (IRE)**[59] 4517 2-9-1 111 LDettori 5 103+
(M R Channon) *hld up: swtchd wd after 1f tl jnd main gp again 4f out: rdn 3f out: styng on at the same pce whn sltly hmpd over 1f out* **11/4**[2]

41 5 *1* **Almiqdaad**[43] 5068 2-8-12 90 RHills 10 98
(M A Jarvis) *w'like: scope: str: trckd ldrs: rdn over 2f out: one pce fnl f* **8/1**

13 6 *9* **Patrician's Glory (USA)**[28] 5507 2-8-12 108 JohnEgan 3 78+
(Jane Chapple-Hyam) *plld hrd: trckd ldrs: rdn 3f out: btn whn short of room sn after* **12/1**

2153 7 *2* **Measurement (IRE)**[14] 5898 2-8-12 95 RichardHughes 2 74
(R Hannon) *racd wd of main gp: prom: rdn 3f out: sn btn* **25/1**

3110 8 *shd* **Firth Of Fifth (IRE)**[59] 4517 2-9-1 108 RichardKingscote 4 76
(Tom Dascombe) *led: rdn and hdd over 2f out: sn btn* **20/1**

1m 40.59s (-0.21) **Going Correction** +0.20s/f (Good) 2y crse rec **8 Ran SP% 116.6**
Speed ratings (Par 107): **109,108,104,102,101 92,90,90**
toteswinger: 1&2 £3.70, 1&3 £8.00, 2&3 £2.80. CSF £23.97 TOTE £10.00: £2.10, £1.80, £2.70; EX 29.00 Trifecta £389.20 Pool: £2,348.81 - 9.38 winning units..
Owner A D Spence **Bred** Paul Nataf **Trained** Middleham Moor, N Yorks

FOCUS
The 2003 Royal Lodge was won by subsequent Guineas runner-up Snow Ridge, with the following year's St Leger winner Rule Of Law third, but more recent renewals have had little impact on the Classics. The bare form of this year's race does not look anything special on paper, but they went a good, even gallop, and the winning time, a new juvenile course record, was 0.50 seconds quicker than the opening fillies & mares Listed contest for three-year-olds and upwards, and 0.23 seconds faster than the time recorded by Rainbow View in the Fillies' Mile. All that suggests the form, although not outstanding, is strong and solid. The winner was impressive in overcoming traffic problems, and there was improvement too from the second and third.

NOTEBOOK
Jukebox Jury(IRE), although his form prior to this was well short of Group 2 level, his recent third in France represented his best effort to date and he progressed significantly again, with both the step up to 1m, and the return to quick ground very much in his favour. He was last early after starting rather awkwardly, but they went a fair clip up front and he was able to ease into contention. Although he had to wait for a split early in the straight, he picked up well when switched slightly left over a furlong out and produced a sustained burst to deny the favourite. Mark Johnston said afterwards that the colt did not really face the whip at Deauville two starts back, but he was given a few cracks by Royston Ffrench this time and responded in the desired manner. He is now guaranteed a run in the Breeders' Cup Juvenile Turf, but still needs to be supplemented – he's also in the Dewhurst and the Racing Post Trophy. He's clearly very smart, and he should be capable of even better over a little further next year, provided he continues to go the right way mentally. (op 11-1)

Cityscape ◆ earned a shot in a race like this when a nine-length winner of a novice event at Salisbury on his second start and, although failing to justify favouritism, he still created a good impression in defeat. The ground was probably the quickest he has encountered to date, and he probably would have preferred a bit more give underfoot judging by the time he took to get past On Our Way. He briefly looked the winner, but he was unable to go clear and was picked off late on. He remains an exciting prospect on easier ground and should make a smart three-year-old. (op 2-1 tchd 9-4 in places)

On Our Way travelled really strongly into the straight, but he might have been in front too soon, Firth Of Fifth probably having dropped away sooner than Tom Queally would have liked. This was a decent effort, but like the runner-up, he might appreciate slightly easier ground in future. (op 6-1)

Orizaba(IRE)'s Vintage Stakes success has worked out well and he could have been expected to fare a little better, even allowing for his 3lb penalty. He looked in trouble early in the straight, having been brought wide, and was only keeping on at the one pace when slightly bumped by the eventual winner over a furlong out. He might not have been suited by this step up to 1m, but he looked beaten before stamina was an issue. (op 5-2 tchd 3-1 & 100-30 in places)

Almiqdaad had the benefit of a previous run when beating Cityscape in a maiden at the July course earlier in the season and that one has made the more progression since then. To be fair, he lost a shoe, so might be a little better than this run suggests. Official explanation: jockey said colt lost a shoe

Patrician's Glory(USA) looked worth a try at this trip when third in what had appeared to be a decent renewal of the Solario Stakes on his previous start, but he was beaten before the straight. (tchd 11-1)

Measurement(IRE) is not up to this level., (tchd 33-1)

Firth Of Fifth(IRE), returning from two months off, was well below the form he showed when winning the Superlative Stakes earlier in the season. (op 16-1)

6268 MEON VALLEY STUD FILLIES' MILE (GROUP 1) 1m (R)

3:05 (3:07) (Class 1) 2-Y-O

£113,540 (£43,040; £21,540; £10,740; £5,380; £2,700) **Stalls** High

Form RPR

111 **1** **Rainbow View (USA)**[16] [5828] 2-8-12 0 JimmyFortune 4 117+
(J H M Gosden) *swtg: edgy: racd in cl 5th: prog 2f out: qcknd up wl to ld jst ins fnl f: r.o wl: rdn clr* **4/7**[1]

11 **2** 2 ½ **Fantasia**[35] [5266] 2-8-12 0 LDettori 7 111
(L M Cumani) *lw: trckd ldr: rdn to ld over 1f out: drifted lft and hdd jst ins fnl f: nt pce of wnr* **7/2**[2]

1 **3** 3 ¼ **Dreamtheimpossible (USA)**[14] [5924] 2-8-12 0 JMurtagh 1 104
(David Wachman, Ire) *w'like: scope: tall: cl up: rdn to chal 2f out: kpt on same pce fnl f: jst hung on for 3rd* **8/1**[3]

0420 **4** shd **Beat Seven**[49] [4868] 2-8-12 96 RichardHughes 3 104
(Miss Gay Kelleway) *hld up last: hdwy over 2f out: swtchd lft and rdn over 1f out: styd on: jst failed to snatch 3rd* **66/1**

1 **5** 4 ½ **Golden Stream (IRE)**[36] [5241] 2-8-12 0 RyanMoore 8 94
(Sir Michael Stoute) *lw: led: rdn and hdd over 1f out: fdd fnl f* **8/1**[3]

232 **6** 3 ¾ **Never Lose**[10] [6030] 2-8-12 0 LiamJones 2 85
(C E Brittain) *t.k.h: trckd ldrs: rdn over 2f out: wknd over 1f out* **50/1**

015 **7** 1 **Silver Games (IRE)**[8] [6076] 2-8-12 81 EdwardCreighton 6 83
(M R Channon) *s.i.s: hld up: effrt whn hung rt over 2f out: wknd over 1f out* **33/1**

301 **8** 2 **Brief Candle**[29] [5469] 2-8-12 88 (t) AdamKirby 5 79
(W R Swinburn) *in tch: outpcd whn hmpd on rails over 2f out: nvr bk on terms* **33/1**

1m 40.82s (0.02) **Going Correction** +0.20s/f (Good) **8** Ran SP% **117.4**

Speed ratings (Par 106): **107,104,101,101,96 92,91,89**

toteswinger: 1&2 £1.40, 1&3 £2.10, 2&3 £2.60. CSF £2.90 TOTE £1.70: £1.10, £1.40, £1.70; EX 3.10 Trifecta £8.60 Pool: £9,847.61 - 837.83 winning units..

Owner George Strawbridge **Bred** Augustin Stable **Trained** Newmarket, Suffolk

■ Stewards' Enquiry : Edward Creighton three-day ban: careless riding (Oct 11-13)

FOCUS

A very strong renewal of the Fillies' Mile, featuring three unbeaten fillies, including the John Gosden-trained Rainbow View, who was already a hot favourite for the 1000 Guineas after three highly impressive wins, and had been described earlier in the week by Luca Cumani, who saddled main rival Fantasia, as the best two-year-old filly he had seen during his career as a trainer. Another very impressive performance from Rainbow View, who has already shown form of a level high enough to win an average 1000 Guineas. A good effort too from Fantasia, who looks sure to do better again.

NOTEBOOK

Rainbow View(USA) had looked very special in her first three starts, working her way up from a maiden to a Group 2, and she confirmed it here by beating Fantasia comfortably, despite having threatened to boil over in the preliminaries. Her demeanour in the parade ring was a real concern, but she had relaxed by the time she got to the start and settled well in the race, as she has done every time. Though only fifth into the straight, she was clearly going well, and having moved up smoothly to challenge Fantasia, she then quickened readily clear to win in a time 0.23 slower than Jukebox Jury's in the Royal Lodge, which looked to be run at a faster pace. She is unquestionably an outstanding juvenile, and she may well have enough in hand to win the Guineas without any improvement, but it's seven months away and she does not have the scope for progress through the winter that some of her rivals there will have. What's more, she is with a trainer who is not one to push his fillies hard in the spring, preferring instead to let them come in their own time. At current cramped odds it can pay to wait and see how she winters and what sort of spring we have. As for the Oaks, let's wait and see what happens at Newmarket first. In the meantime, she may even run at the Breeders' Cup, which might be construed as an indication that Gosden wants to make the most of her at two. (op 1-2 after 4-9 in places tchd 8-13 in a place)

Fantasia won the same Newmarket maiden as her trainer's 2001 winner of this race, Gossamer, and like that one, came into this having landed the Prestige Stakes at Goodwood. Luca Cumani reckoned she would have been good enough to win this race nine years out of ten, but having been handy on the inner throughout and driven to the front with more than a furlong to go, she had no answer to the winner's change of pace and was inclined to drift left under pressure. She still finished well clear of the rest, and despite her comprehensive beating, she, too, was cut for the Guineas. She looks sure to make a three-year-old, but although she is by Sadler's Wells, her granddam, Blue Duster, won the Queen Mary and the Cheveley Park, so the Guineas is more likely to be her race than the Oaks. (op 6-1)

Dreamtheimpossible(USA) created a good impression when landing a decent Listed race over this trip but on testing ground at the Curragh on her previous start. She seemed to have her chance, and the quicker surface was not a problem, but she still looked inexperienced. She should make up into a lovely three-year-old. (op 10-1)

Beat Seven started the season held in high regard but had begun to look exposed. She ran well, though, and the extra furlong was a big help, as was the opportunity to race on a sound surface again. (tchd 50-1)

Golden Stream(IRE) had made the right impression on her debut at Newmarket, but her pedigree is very much that of a middle-distance three-year-old. She should be a different proposition in 2009, but it was still a bit disappointing to see her brushed aside so readily after making the running. (tchd 15-2)

Never Lose, second in a 6f maiden last time, had a very stiff task, but she was much too keen in any case and gave herself little chance of doing herself justice. (tchd 33-1)

Silver Games(IRE), making a quick reappearance after Newbury last week, got into a bumping match with Brief Candle, but she had a very stiff task in any case and looked to be struggling at the time. (tchd 40-1)

Brief Candle had plenty to find and looked in trouble when hampered by Silver Games over two furlongs out. Official explanation: jockey said filly suffered interference in running (op 40-1)

6269 TOTESPORT.COM CHALLENGE CUP (HERITAGE H'CAP) 7f

3:40 (3:41) (Class 2) 3-Y-O+

£93,465 (£27,990; £13,995; £7,005; £3,495; £1,755) **Stalls** Centre

Form RPR

-361 **1** **Furnace (IRE)**[28] [5495] 4-8-11 89 HayleyTurner 22 100
(M L W Bell) *racd far side: in tch: swtchd lft and bmpd rival over 1f out: rdn to ld far side jst ins fnl f: overall ldr ins fnl f: hld on wl* **12/1**[3]

3312 **2** hd **Relative Order**[14] [5907] 3-9-0 95 SteveDrowne 25 104
(J R Best) *lw: racd far side: hld up in tch: hdwy and rdn over 2f out: swtchd rt over 1f out: led far side 1f out: sn hdd: pressed wnr fnl f: a jst hld: 2nd of 14 in gp* **9/1**[1]

0236 **3** ¾ **We'll Come**[49] [4853] 4-9-0 92 (p) DarryllHolland 17 100
(M A Jarvis) *lw: racd far side: hld up in rr: hdwy over 2f out: chsd ldrs ldrs and hanging lft ins fnl f: swtchd lft nr fin: nt rch ldng pair: 3rd of 14 in gp* **16/1**

2000 **4** nk **Dhaular Dhar (IRE)**[7] [6104] 6-9-7 99 OPeslier 28 106
(J S Goldie) *racd far side: hld up towards rr: swtchd rt and hdwy 2f out: chsd ldrs ins fnl f: r.o: 4th of 14 in gp* **16/1**

310 **5** nk **Golden Desert (IRE)**[31] [5405] 4-8-11 89 JohnEgan 2 95
(T G Mills) *lw: racd stands' side: in tch: rdn over 2f out: chsd ldrs ent fnl f: led stands' side ins fnl f: kpt on but hld by far side last 75yds: 1st of 15 in gp* **20/1**

4001 **6** 1 **Bolodenka (IRE)**[7] [6103] 6-8-13 96 FrederikTylicki(5) 24 100
(R A Fahey) *racd far side: racd in midfield: rdn and effrt over 2f out: kpt on u.p fnl f: nt pce to rch ldrs: 5th of 14 in gp* **20/1**

053 **7** ¾ **Giganticus (USA)**[63] [4405] 5-9-6 98 MichaelHills 1 100
(B W Hills) *lw: racd stands' side: chsd ldrs: rdn to ld stands' side over 1f out tl ins fnl f: no ex fnl 100yds: 2nd of 15 in gp* **12/1**[3]

0300 **8** 1 **Tamagin (USA)**[7] [6104] 5-9-6 98 (p) AlanMunro 23 97
(K A Ryan) *racd far side: led far side tl rdn and hdd 1f out: wknd ins fnl f: 6th of 14 in gp* **40/1**

4213 **9** shd **Signor Peltro**[14] [5897] 5-8-12 90 DaneO'Neill 15 89
(H Candy) *racd stands' side: stdd s and hld up towards rr: swtchd rt and hdwy jst over 2f out: chsd ldrs ins fnl f: kpt on same pce fnl 100yds: 3rd of 15 in gp* **16/1**

2051 **10** ½ **South Cape**[14] [5897] 5-8-12 90 TPO'Shea 16 87
(M R Channon) *racd far side: in tch: rdn over 2f out: keeping on same pce whn hmpd over 1f out: kpt on same pce fnl f: 7th of 14 in gp* **33/1**

3100 **11** ¾ **Zaahid (IRE)**[63] [4405] 4-9-5 97 RHills 8 92
(B W Hills) *lw: racd stands' side: bhd: hdwy: n.m.r over 1f out: edgd out rt ent fnl f: r.o wl but nvr threatened ldrs: 4th of 15 in gp* **11/1**[2]

0542 **12** ½ **Vanderlin**[28] [5495] 9-8-13 96 DavidProbert(5) 4 90
(A M Balding) *racd stands' side: chsd overall ldr stands' side: rdn jst over 2f out: kpt on same pce u.p: 5th of 15 in gp* **33/1**

1402 **13** hd **Cape Hawk (IRE)**[21] [5695] 4-8-13 91 RichardHughes 6 84
(R Hannon) *lw: racd stands' side: in tch: rdn and effrt jst over 2f out: chsd ldrs over 1f out: no prog fnl f: 6th of 15 in gp* **16/1**

6604 **14** shd **Flipando (IRE)**[14] [5897] 7-8-12 90 JimmyFortune 5 83
(T D Barron) *racd stands' side: s.i.s: bhd: hdwy into midfield and drvn 3f out: styd on u.p fnl f: nvr trbld ldrs: 7th of 15 in gp* **16/1**

6016 **15** 1 ½ **Pearly Wey**[35] [5275] 5-9-7 99 AdamKirby 3 88
(C G Cox) *racd stands' side: hld up in midfield: rdn and effrt 2f out: hrd rdn and btn ent fnl f: 8th of 15 in gp* **50/1**

0150 **16** nk **Underworld**[7] [6103] 3-9-4 99 RoystonFfrench 29 86
(M Johnston) *racd far side: chsd ldr: rdn and ev ch 2f out tl ent fnl f: fdd fnl f: 8th of 14 in gp* **25/1**

1154 **17** nse **Markab**[22] [5681] 5-9-1 93 PatCosgrave 12 81
(K A Morgan) *racd stands' side: overall ldr tl rdn and hdd over 1f out: wknd fnl f: 9th of 15 in gp* **25/1**

0014 **18** 1 **Conquest (IRE)**[42] [5109] 4-9-8 100 ShaneKelly 13 85
(W J Haggas) *racd stands' side: stdd s: t.k.h: hld up in rr: hdwy over 2f out: hanging rt wl over 1f out: keeping on but hld whn nt clr run jst over 1f out: no ch and eased after: 10th of 15 in gp* **28/1**

00 **19** ¾ **Hitchens (IRE)**[56] [4624] 3-9-10 105 RyanMoore 20 87
(G L Moore) *racd far side: hld up in midfield: rdn and effrt 2f out: kpt on same pce and nvr able to chal: 9th of 14 in gp* **33/1**

0042 **20** nse **Big Noise**[31] [5405] 4-8-12 90 RichardThomas 18 73
(Dr J D Scargill) *racd far side: hld up towards rr: pushed along over 3f out: rdn over 2f out: no hdwy: 10th of 14 in gp* **20/1**

0043 **21** 5 **Extraterrestrial**[28] [5495] 4-8-13 91 (p) JamieMoriarty 11 61
(R A Fahey) *racd on stands' side: racd in midfield: rdn over 2f out: wl btn over 1f out: 11th of 15 in gp* **25/1**

05 **22** nk **Skhilling Spirit**[7] [6104] 5-9-1 93 JimmyQuinn 27 62
(T D Barron) *racd far side: stdd s hld up in rr: nvr a factor: 11th of 14 in gp* **33/1**

1050 **23** shd **Phantom Whisper**[14] [5897] 5-8-12 93 (p) JamesMillman(3) 10 62
(B R Millman) *racd stands' side: bhd: rdn and effrt towards centre over 2f out: nvr on terms: 12th of 15 gp* **66/1**

0620 **24** hd **Caldra (IRE)**[7] [6123] 4-9-3 95 RichardKingscote 21 63
(S Kirk) *racd far side: bhd: rdn and struggling 1/2-way: no ch last 2f: 12th of 14 in gp* **50/1**

5200 **25** nk **Al Muheer (IRE)**[28] [5495] 3-9-3 98 LiamJones 7 64
(C E Brittain) *racd stands stands' side: a bhd: 14th of 15 in gp* **50/1**

5000 **26** 1 **Celtic Sultan (IRE)**[28] [5495] 4-9-6 98 MickyFenton 9 63
(T P Tate) *racd stands' side: chsd ldrs tl wknd u.p over 1f out: 14th of 15 in gp* **40/1**

1125 **27** 1 **Atlantic Story (USA)**[16] [5831] 6-8-12 90 (bt) TPQueally 26 52
(M W Easterby) *racd far side: in midfield tl rdn and btn over 2f out: 13th of 14 in gp* **20/1**

1-10 **28** 4 **Military Cross**[57] [4587] 5-9-9 101 LDettori 14 52
(L M Cumani) *racd stands' side: a bhd: rdn and no reponse 3f out: 15th of 15 in gp* **14/1**

2403 **29** 26 **Mastership (IRE)**[33] [5347] 4-9-4 96 (b) JMurtagh 19 —
(J J Quinn) *warm: edgy: racd far side: bhd: rdn over 2f out: no prog: wl btn and virtually p.u ins fnl f: 14th of 14 in gp* **11/1**[2]

1m 26.64s (-1.36) **Going Correction** +0.10s/f (Good)

WFA 3 from 4yo+ 3lb **29** Ran SP% **136.2**

Speed ratings (Par 109): **111,110,109,109,109 108,107,106,105,105 104,103,103,103,101 101,101,100,99,99 93,93,93,93,92**

toteswinger: 1&2 £10.60, 1&3 £73.00, 2&3 £50.30. CSF £93.94 CT £1806.26 TOTE £15.30: £3.40, £2.40, £5.70, £3.60; EX 48.60 Trifecta £1971.60 Pool: £7,762.29 - 4.60 winning units..

Owner Highclere Thoroughbred Racing XXXV **Bred** Barouche Stud Ireland Ltd **Trained** Newmarket, Suffolk

■ Stewards' Enquiry : John Egan two-day ban: careless riding (Oct 11-12)

Hayley TurnerM three-day ban: careless riding (Oct 11-13)

FOCUS

A typically competitive renewal of this valuable handicap. They split into two groups and, although there wasn't much in it, the far side just had the edge, providing the first four home, so a high draw was an advantage. For some reason the stands' side group tended to edge off the rail and ended up more towards the middle of the track, which can't have helped their chances. The form looks solid rated around the third and fourth.

NOTEBOOK

Furnace(IRE) tracked the pacesetting Tamagin in a good position pretty much throughout. He did have to be switched when the early leader began to tire about a furlong and a half out, and slightly bumped South Cape, but he found plenty and just got the better of Relative Order in a driving finish. He had only been raised 3lb for his recent Chester success over half a furlong further, a race in which he had five of today's rivals behind, and he progressed again to follow up. He may now head to the Horses In Training Sale at Newmarket next week and will surely be popular, particularly among those with one eye on the Dubai Carnival. (op 14-1)

Relative Order was produced with every chance and probably just got first run on the eventual winner, as that one had to switch, but he was just held at bay. He had been raised a further 2lb for his recent second over 1m on Polytrack at Great Leighs and this was clearly a career best. (op 12-1)

We'll Come emerges with plenty of credit as he was drawn in the middle and was dropped in behind towards the far side. He stayed on well to fare best of those held up, despite having to be switched, and is clearly very talented, but it is most frustrating that he has just a maiden success to his name. (op 18-1 tchd 20-1)

Dhaular Dhar(IRE) is well suited to this course and distance, as he showed when second in both the Buckingham Palace and the Totesport International earlier in the season, and he was fifth in this last year. This was another cracking effort, and he looks just type who could do well at the Dubai Carnival.

Golden Desert(IRE), 6lb higher than when winning a valuable Ladies' race over course and distance on King George day, fared best of those in the stands' side group, and this was probably a career best.

Bolodenka(IRE), raised 6lb for his recent Ayr success, was well drawn and seemed to have his chance. (op 25-1)

Giganticus(USA), returning from a two-month break, was drawn in stall one, but ended up racing up the middle of the track and was possibly both edged and intimidated by Golden Desert. This was a good effort in the circumstances.

Tamagin(USA) has struggled for consistency this season, but he kept on once headed, and this was a respectable effort. (op 50-1)

Signor Peltro had a poor draw in 15, but he ran with credit to fare third best in the near-side group.

South Cape was already in trouble when bumped by the eventual winner over a furlong out.

Zaahid(IRE) was never seen with a chance, he was noted to be keeping on nicely enough at the finish once switched towards the centre of the track. He might be ready for a return to 1m. (tchd 12-1)

Cape Hawk(IRE) was worth a try at this trip, but he failed to pick up as one might have hoped.

Pearly Wey is a little better than he showed, as he was short of room inside the final furlong, although he had not found ad much as had looked likely.

Markab led the nearside group, but he had got warm beforehand and was soon beaten.

Conquest(IRE) was another short of room late on, but he was well held at the time.

Skhilling Spirit Official explanation: jockey said gelding was slowly away

Caldra(IRE) Official explanation: jockey said gelding ran too freely to post

Al Muheer(IRE) Official explanation: jockey said colt suffered interference in running

Celtic Sultan(IRE) could not dominate and ran no sort of race. (op 50-1)

Atlantic Story(USA) should do better back on sand this winter. (op 16-1)

Military Cross Official explanation: jockey said gelding lost its action

Mastership(IRE) lost his race when getting very warm at the start. Official explanation: jockey said gelding boiled over at start. (tchd 10-1)

6270 QUEEN ELIZABETH II STKS (SPONSORED BY SONY) (GROUP 1) 1m (R)

4:15 (4:18) (Class 1) 3-Y-O+

£151,859 (£57,566; £28,809; £14,364; £7,195; £3,611) **Stalls** High

Form RPR

2221 **1** **Raven's Pass (USA)**[35] 5265 3-8-13 122 .... JimmyFortune 1 131
(J H M Gosden) *lw: broke wl: hld up bhd ldng quartet: smooth prog fr over 2f out: led jst over 1f out: kpt on gamely: rdn out* **3/1**[3]

1115 **2** *1* **Henrythenavigator (USA)**[20] 5740 3-8-13 0 .... JMurtagh 5 128
(A P O'Brien, Ire) *warm: hld up in last trio: trckd wnr through fr over 2f out: rdn and 1l down ent fnl f: kpt on but a jst hld* **11/8**[1]

-115 **3** *4 1/2* **Sabana Perdida (IRE)**[55] 4674 5-9-0 0 .... (t) C-PLemaire 7 114
(A De Royer-Dupre, France) *lw: hld up last: hdwy 2f out: sn rdn: styd on: wnt 3rd ins fnl f: nt pce of ldng pair* **14/1**

1011 **4** *3* **Tamayuz**[41] 5138 3-8-13 0 .... DBonilla 2 110
(F Head, France) *w'like: str: swtg: chsd clr ldrs: rdn to ld briefly over 1f out: no ex fnl f* **9/4**[2]

-040 **5** *7* **Winker Watson**[35] 5275 3-8-13 115 .... RyanMoore 4 94
(P W Chapple-Hyam) *hld up: nudged along 4f out: effrt 2f out: wknd fnl f* **20/1**

0000 **6** *25* **Honoured Guest (IRE)**[20] 5740 4-9-3 0 .... CO'Donoghue 3 37
(A P O'Brien, Ire) *w ldr: led after 3f: hdd over 1f out: sn wknd: eased whn btn* **150/1**

-010 **7** *1 1/4* **Racinger (FR)**[41] 5138 5-9-3 0 .... OPeslier 6 34
(F Head, France) *led at gd pce: hdd after 3f: chsd ldr tl wknd over 2f out: eased whn btn* **66/1**

1m 38.94s (-1.86) **Going Correction** +0.20s/f (Good)
WFA 3 from 4yo+ 4lb **7** Ran SP% **111.5**
Speed ratings (Par 117): **117,116,111,108,101 76,75**
toteswinger: 1&2 £1.50, 1&3 £3.80, 2&3 £3.40. CSF £7.12 TOTE £4.90: £2.60, £1.80; EX 12.00.
Owner H R H Princess Haya Of Jordan **Bred** Stonerside Stable **Trained** Newmarket, Suffolk

FOCUS

A compelling clash between three outstanding three-year-old milers. Although it was the first time that all three had met in the same race, there was plenty of interlinking form, yet there were still enough variables in play here for solid cases to be made for any of the three. The pacemakers, Honoured Guest and Racinger, set a fierce gallop, soon racing some six lengths or so clear, and the winning time was only 0.24 seconds slower than Henrythenavigator's St James's Palace course record. Raven's Pass is entitled to move past Henrythenavigator to the top of the pecking order among three-year-old milers, as from four clashes now this looks the most solid form, with the pair clear and the third seeming to run her race.

NOTEBOOK

Raven's Pass(USA) was ridden handier in the chasing pack than he had been in previous meetings with Henrythenavigator, and most significantly of all, was always in front of him this time. The telling point came when the pair began their moves in the straight, for while Raven's Pass closed smoothly without serious effort, Henrythenavigator soon had to be chased along vigorously. The winner hit the front over a furlong out and was holding his old rival by a length or so. He had been getting closer with every meeting, and a first Group 1 win has seldom been more deserved. John Gosden has long had the Breeders' Cup on the agenda for the winner's final start, but it remains to be seen if he runs in the Mile or the Classic. His worry with the Mile is that it is run around two turns and can be a bit of a lottery. The Classic, however, is another two furlongs, and on a synthetic surface, both of which are unknown quantities. (op 7-2)

Henrythenavigator(USA), like the winner, now has the option of either the Breeders' Cup Mile, or Classic. He had looked a superstar in running up his sequence of four Group 1 wins, and while the bubble had been burst behind Goldikova at Longchamp, it was possible to excuse that on account of the softish ground. Although it clearly was not soft here, conditions may still have been a partial excuse, for he loves it really firm and it was still loose on top following Thursday's watering and two heavy dews. The other factors that need taking into account are his late arrival at the track owing to fog, for he had little time to settle in and was warm in the preliminaries, and a suggestion from experienced paddock judges that he did not look as hard fit as had done earlier in the season. That said, he was a long way clear of the others and it is conceivable he ran to his best and was simply beaten by a rival who has been closing on him all year and has now simply overtaken him. (tchd 6-4 & 13-8 in places)

Sabana Perdida(IRE), the only mare in the race, has had very few opportunities at this level, but she had won both her previous starts over here and was not a no-hoper. She stayed on for a clear third, having been held up in last until into the straight, and she plainly loves a sound surface, which is why she is seen to best advantage over here. (op 20-1)

Tamayuz, beaten previously only from a poor draw in the French 2000 Guineas, was hugely disappointing, leading only briefly in the straight and quickly being left behind by the principals. He had taken the notable scalp of 1000 Guineas winner Natagora at Deauville after beating Raven's Pass (given plenty to do) in the Prix Jean Prat, but he just didn't run his race this time. Connections were mystified, although Freddie Head did point out he got very warm in the preliminaries. That may have been a factor, and he was also effectively making his own running until the rider of stablemate Racinger realised the pacemakers were too far clear of the pack and took a bit of a pull. (op 2-1 tchd 15-8 & 5-2 in a place)

Winker Watson was up against it, and he has not looked the horse he was at two, but his stamina looked suspect once again. His best opportunities look to be at shorter. (op 33-1)

Honoured Guest(IRE) went flat to the boards to ensure a very strong pace.

Racinger(FR) is a good horse in his own right, but he was only in this to help ensure a strong pace for his stablemate. (op 100-1)

6271 MILES & MORRISON OCTOBER STKS (LISTED RACE) (F&M) 7f

4:50 (4:58) (Class 1) 3-Y-O+

£24,978 (£9,468; £4,738; £2,362; £1,183; £594) **Stalls** Centre

Form RPR

2302 **1** **Meydan Princess (IRE)**[63] 4424 3-8-10 93 .... ShaneKelly 16 107
(J Noseda) *lw: s.i.s: sn mid-div: nt clr run and swtchd rt 2f out: qcknd up wl to ld ent fnl f: r.o strly: rdn out* **9/1**

261 **2** *3* **Medicea Sidera**[63] 4424 4-8-13 92 .... TPQueally 12 99
(E F Vaughan) *led: rdn and hdd ent fnl f: drifted lft and no ex* **16/1**

1-03 **3** *hd* **Francesca D'Gorgio (USA)**[11] 6005 3-8-10 100 .... (v) LDettori 11 98
(J Noseda) *chsd ldr: rdn 2f out: kpt on fnl f* **12/1**

3466 **4** *3/4* **Crystany (IRE)**[14] 5884 3-8-10 92 .... RyanMoore 14 96
(E A L Dunlop) *hld up towards rr: rdn and hdwy over 2f out: kpt on fnl f* **16/1**

0532 **5** *1* **Vital Statistics**[9] 6053 4-8-13 83 .... DaneO'Neill 2 93
(D R C Elsworth) *swtg: s.i.s: bhd: pushed along over 4f out: rdn over 2f out: r.o ins fnl f: nrst fin* **25/1**

4604 **6** *shd* **Majestic Roi (USA)**[8] 6073 4-8-13 110 .... DarryllHolland 6 93
(M R Channon) *lw: in tch: swtchd rt u.p 2f out: kpt on same pce* **5/2**[1]

511 **7** *3/4* **Ethaara**[21] 5697 3-8-10 81 .... RHills 8 91
(W J Haggas) *lw: mid-div: hdwy 2f out: sn rdn: kpt on same pce fnl f* **7/1**[2]

0230 **8** *1/2* **Illusion**[57] 4590 3-8-10 96 .... JimmyFortune 13 90
(J H M Gosden) *chsd ldrs: rdn over 2f out: one pce fnl f* **7/1**[2]

5006 **9** *2 3/4* **Steam Cuisine**[14] 5896 4-8-13 89 .... AlanMunro 1 82
(M G Quinlan) *nvr bttr than mid-div* **25/1**

1404 **10** *2 1/4* **Salsa Steps (USA)**[35] 5275 4-8-13 98 .... (t) SteveDrowne 5 76
(H Morrison) *mid-div: rdn over 2f out: hung rt over 1f out: wknd fnl f* **8/1**[3]

0/0 **11** *5* **Ghostmilk (IRE)**[30] 5441 4-8-13 .... RichardHughes 10 63
(P D Deegan, Ire) *w'like: leggy: hld up towards rr: sme hdwy into midfield over 2f out: sn rdn: wknd fnl f* **33/1**

-004 **12** *nk* **Monaazalah (IRE)**[14] 5899 3-8-10 92 .... JimmyQuinn 3 62
(Rae Guest) *a towards rr* **40/1**

0 **13** *2 3/4* **Indian Diva (IRE)**[133] 2196 3-8-10 84 .... RoystonFfrench 15 54
(P A Blockley) *wnt rt s: mainly towards rr* **50/1**

1430 **14** *shd* **Candle Sahara (IRE)**[16] 5829 3-8-10 90 .... TPO'Shea 7 54
(M R Channon) *chsd ldrs tl wknd 2f out* **50/1**

0005 **15** *3 1/4* **Spinning Lucy (IRE)**[16] 5829 3-8-10 95 .... MichaelHills 9 45
(B W Hills) *chsd ldrs for 3f: wknd over 2f out* **10/1**

3306 **16** *1 1/2* **Kylayne**[16] 5829 3-8-10 97 .... JohnEgan 4 41
(P W D'Arcy) *a towards rr: lame* **16/1**

1m 27.69s (-0.31) **Going Correction** +0.10s/f (Good)
WFA 3 from 4yo 3lb **16** Ran SP% **126.1**
Speed ratings (Par 111): **105,101,101,100,99 99,98,97,94,92 86,86,82,82,79 77**
toteswinger: 1&2 £35.80, 1&3 £14.60, 2&3 £40.90. CSF £141.01 TOTE £11.90: £3.40, £6.10, £3.20; EX 142.60 Trifecta £919.20 Pool: £1,1614.94 - 1.30 winning units..
Owner Franconson Partners **Bred** J Costello **Trained** Newmarket, Suffolk

FOCUS

Plenty of runners, but this was a weak fillies and mares' Listed contest. They raced up the middle early, but edged over towards the far side in the closing stages and the first four emerged from double-figure stalls. The runner-up is generally progressive and the third is rated to her juvenile best.

NOTEBOOK

Meydan Princess(IRE), although slightly missing the break, still got away quicker than is usually the case and travelled better than anything throughout. She looked the winner a fair way out and, although her rider was probably reluctant to let her go too soon, she found plenty when switched towards the favoured far side of the track. She had finished half a length behind Medicea Sidera at the July course last time, and was 2lb worse off with that rival today, but she reversed placings in no uncertain terms. She's always looked a filly with plenty of talent and this was a career best.

Medicea Sidera could not confirm earlier Newmarket form with Meydan Princess, but she kept on well when headed on her return from two months off to pick up some valuable black type.

Francesca D'Gorgio(USA) was having just her second start since returning from a break, and was more settled than has been the case in the past. She kept on without ever looking likely to winm and may ultimately prove best back over 6f. (op 10-1)

Crystany(IRE) had her chance towards the far rail late on. This was her first run over 7f and the trip probably stretched her. (op 22-1)

Vital Statistics fared best of those from a low stall and emerges with plenty of credit. However, having just dropped down to a favourable mark, she may now be due a slight rise.

Majestic Roi(USA) was not helped by a low draw, but she was still well below her best and is struggling for form. (op 7-2 tchd 4-1)

Ethaara had been progressing nicely, but she was never a threat on this rise in class. (op 9-2)

Illusion was well after two months off. (op 11-1)

Salsa Steps(USA) ran below form having been reluctant to load. (op 15-2)

Kylayne Official explanation: trainer said filly was lame behind

6272 BROADWAY GORDON CARTER STKS H'CAP 2m
5:25 (5:27) (Class 2) (0-100,95) 3-Y-O+ **£10,361** (£3,083; £1,540; £769) **Stalls** High

Form RPR

0251 **1** **Ascalon**[42] 5100 4-10-0 **95** AlanMunro 3 107
(Pat Eddery) *lw: trckd ldr: led wl over 2f out: sn rdn and hrd pressed: battled on u.str.p thrght fnl f: all out* **11/2**[2]

1643 **2** *hd* **Downhiller (IRE)**[13] 5938 3-8-13 **92** JimmyFortune 5 103
(J L Dunlop) *trckd ldr: rdn to chal fr wl over 2f out: battled on and ev ch thrght fnl f: narrowly hld* **8/1**

0030 **3** *2 ¾* **Grande Caiman (IRE)**[43] 5054 4-9-5 **86** (b[1]) RichardHughes 2 94
(R Hannon) *in tch: hdwy 3f out: sn rdn to chse ldng pair: kpt on same pce* **20/1**

4-00 **4** *3* **Minkowski**[36] 5229 5-9-9 **90** ShaneKelly 7 94
(J Noseda) *lw: mid-div: hdwy 3f out: sn rdn: styd on to go 4th ins fnl f* **11/2**[2]

3105 **5** *1* **Victoria Montoya**[13] 5938 3-7-9 **79** (p) DavidProbert(5) 15 82
(A M Balding) *lw: in tch: rdn 3f out: kpt on same pce fnl 2f* **5/1**[1]

1062 **6** *2 ¾* **Desert Sea (IRE)**[13] 5940 5-9-10 **91** RoystonFfrench 8 91
(D W P Arbuthnot) *mid-div: rdn and hdwy over 2f out: kpt on same pce fr over 1f out* **11/1**

0410 **7** *1 ½* **Missoula (IRE)**[91] 3490 5-9-7 **88** SamHitchcott 13 86
(Miss Suzy Smith) *mid-div: rdn 3f out: sn one pce* **16/1**

-254 **8** *2* **Whenever**[49] 4866 4-9-1 **82** SteveDrowne 1 78
(R T Phillips) *hld up towards rr: sme late prog u.p: nvr a danger* **7/1**[3]

0404 **9** *1 ½* **Kasthari (IRE)**[20] 5718 9-8-13 **80** (v) DarryllHolland 10 74
(J D Bethell) *sn led: 5 l clr 1/2-way: rdn and hdd wl over 2f out: sn one pce: fdd fnl f* **20/1**

1030 **10** *21* **Crossbow Creek**[26] 5569 10-9-4 **85** AdamKirby 14 54
(M G Rimell) *a towards rr* **40/1**

3211 **11** *18* **Greenwich Village**[44] 5017 5-8-10 **77** oh2 PaulDoe 12 24
(W J Knight) *chsd ldrs tl wknd over 3f out: eased whn btn* **14/1**

0121 **12** *4 ½* **Four Miracles**[63] 4439 4-9-4 **85** MichaelHills 6 27
(M H Tompkins) *a towards rr: eased whn btn fnl 2f* **7/1**[3]

00-P **P** **Full House (IRE)**[28] 1916 9-9-8 **89** MickyFenton 4 —
(P R Webber) *a bhd: t.o fr over 5f out: p.u ins fnl f: dismntd* **14/1**

3m 28.07s (-4.53) **Going Correction** +0.10s/f (Good)
WFA 3 from 4yo+ 12lb **13** Ran SP% **123.1**
Speed ratings (Par 109): **115,114,113,112,111 110,109,108,107,97 88,85,—**
toteswinger: 1&2 £11.370, 1&3 £24.30, 2&3 £23.30. CSF £49.50 CT £840.22 TOTE £6.60: £2.60, £3.40, £5.70; EX 53.80 Trifecta £966.10 Pool: £1,305.55 - 1.00 winning units. Place 6 £78.77, Place 5 £26.41.

Owner P J J Eddery, Mrs John Magnier, M Tabor **Bred** Patrick Eddery Ltd **Trained** Nether Winchendon, Bucks

FOCUS
A decent staying handicap dominated by a couple of progressive types. They went a fair pace and the form looks solid rated around the third, fourth and fifth.

NOTEBOOK
Ascalon was hammered by the handicapper for a ten-length win over 1m4f on the July course last time, being put up 13lb, but he was able to defy the rise having improved again for this step up to 2m. He showed a good attitude to come out on top in a terrific battle with Downhiller, and his trainer is hopeful he can make up into a Group horse next year, as he is from a family that gets better with age. (op 8-1)
Downhiller(IRE)'s recent third over 1m6f at Great Leighs looked a career best at the time, but this was even better off a 3lb higher mark. He improved again for this first attempt at 2m and looks a decent stayer in the making. (op 9-1 tchd 10-1)
Grande Caiman(IRE) returned to form behind a couple of progressive types, and the blinkers (replacing cheekpieces) clearly helped. (op 16-1)
Minkowski kept on from off the pace, but he could not muster the speed to land a telling blow. This was his best effort yet since returning to the Flat. (tchd 6-1 in places)
Victoria Montoya had plenty of use made of her, which should have suited as she is simply just a galloper, but she still struggled to match the pace of some of her rivals rounding the final bend. She might have been closer had she been able to hold her position and take a gap just before the straight, but one suspects she is not really applying herself, and some stronger headgear may be in order unless she starts to get her act together. There is little doubt she has the ability to make a useful stayer if she puts her mind to it. (tchd 9-2 and 11-2 and 6-1 in a place)
Desert Sea(IRE) looked to be going well before the turn in, but he never really got involved. (op 12-1)
Full House(IRE) Official explanation: jockey said gelding never travelled
T/Jkpt: Not won. T/Plt: £145.40 to a £1 stake. Pool: £171,699.55. 861.53 winning tickets. T/Qpdt: £18.10 to a £1 stake. Pool: £7,916.59. 322.80 winning tickets. TM

5882 CHESTER (L-H)
Saturday, September 27

OFFICIAL GOING: Good to firm (good in places)
Wind: Light, across Weather: Sunny

6273 PREMIER ESTATES LTD 10TH ANNIVERSARY MAIDEN FILLIES' STKS 7f 2y
2:15 (2:16) (Class 4) 2-Y-O **£4,533** (£1,348; £674; £336) **Stalls** Low

Form RPR

542 **1** **Purple Sage (IRE)**[18] 5788 2-9-0 **76** ChrisCatlin 1 82+
(B W Hills) *flashed tail several times: racd keenly: prom: stdd over 5f out: n.m.r and lost grnd over 4f out: rallied 3f out: prog to chal over 1f out: r.o to ld 100yds out: kpt on wl under hand ride* **5/4**[1]

40 **2** *nse* **Granny McPhee**[10] 6030 2-8-9 **0** NicolPolli(5) 9 82+
(A Bailey) *in midfield: hdwy 3f out: led over 1f out: sn hrd pressed: hdd 100yds out: battled gamely to the line* **20/1**

3 *3 ½* **Do The Deal (IRE)** 2-9-0 **0** GrahamGibbons 7 73
(J J Quinn) *towards rr: hdwy whn nt clr run over 2f out: chsd ldng pair 1f out but nt pce to threaten* **12/1**

03 **4** *1 ½* **Persian Memories (IRE)**[58] 4554 2-9-0 **0** RichardMullen 6 69
(J L Dunlop) *trckd ldrs: effrt whn nt clr run wl over 1f out: kpt on same pce ins fnl f* **11/4**[2]

0 **5** *2 ¼* **Hindford Oak Sioux**[10] 6013 2-8-11 **0** RussellKennemore(3) 11 64
(Mrs L Williamson) *stdd s: hld up: pushed along over 2f out: hdwy on outside over 1f out: one pce ins fnl f* **100/1**

6 **6** *2* **Lindy Hop (IRE)**[18] 5788 2-9-0 **0** SaleemGolam 3 59
(W R Swinburn) *trckd ldrs: rdn over 1f out: sn outpcd* **7/1**

5 **7** *5* **Diamond Surprise**[10] 6013 2-9-0 **0** FrancisNorton 4 46
(P A Blockley) *hung rt most of way and t.k.h: w ldr: led over 5f out: rdn and hdd over 1f out: wknd ins fnl f* **5/1**[3]

06 **8** *4 ½* **Miss Mojito (IRE)**[129] 2306 2-9-0 **0** JamesDoyle 10 35
(J W Hills) *trckd ldrs: wnt cl 2nd over 5f out: sn upsides: rdn and wknd over 1f out* **25/1**

0 **9** *13* **Haafhds Delight (IRE)**[75] 4027 2-9-0 **0** TGMcLaughlin 12 3
(W M Brisbourne) *sn pushed along in rr: nvr on terms* **100/1**

00 **10** *9* **Avonlini**[127] 2357 2-9-0 **0** DaleGibson 2 —
(B P J Baugh) *led: hdd over 5f out: lost pl over 4f out: n.d after* **150/1**

00 **11** *13* **Welsh Passion**[7] 6135 2-9-0 **0** (b[1]) LPKeniry 8 —
(D Flood) *sn rdn along in rr: nvr on terms* **66/1**

1m 27.48s (0.98) **Going Correction** +0.05s/f (Good) **11** Ran SP% **120.7**
Speed ratings (Par 94): **96,95,91,90,87 85,79,74,59,49 34**
toteswinger: 1&2 £9.00, 1&3 £5.30, 2&3 £29.30. CSF £35.11 TOTE £2.20: £1.30, £3.70, £3.10; EX 28.10.

Owner Lady Bamford **Bred** Swordlestown Stud **Trained** Lambourn, Berks

FOCUS
An average juvenile fillies' maiden run at a fair pace and the first two came clear. Solid enough form.

NOTEBOOK
Purple Sage(IRE) just did enough to reward her backers, but made hard work of doing so and her rider deserves the plaudits. A filly with talent, she is also clearly temperamental, as her rider was intent on not picking up his stick inside the final furlong and she also flashed her tail more than once. It will be interesting to see how she fares in nurseries, as she should not go up in the handicap for this effort. (op 6-4)
Granny McPhee swung around rivals into the home straight and was the only one to give the winner a serious race. She lost out narrowly and this was by far her best effort, but her prospective handicap mark will suffer as a result. (tchd 25-1)
Do The Deal(IRE) cost 90,000 euros and is the first foal of 2003 Rockfel winner Cairns. She was given time to find her feet through the first half of the race and kept on steadily without threatening. She will know more next time. (op 14-1 tchd 10-1)
Persian Memories(IRE) proved one paced when push came to shove and failed to improve on the level of her Goodwood third. She now qualifies for nurseries and should do better as she matures. (op 5-2 tchd 10-3)
Diamond Surprise Official explanation: jockey said filly hung right throughout
Avonlini Official explanation: jockey said filly hung right throughout

6274 LEGAT OWEN NURSERY 5f 16y
2:50 (2:52) (Class 4) 2-Y-O **£6,476** (£1,927; £963; £481) **Stalls** Low

Form RPR

12 **1** **Aldermoor (USA)**[54] 4685 2-9-7 **90** SaleemGolam 1 96+
(S C Williams) *racd keenly: in tch: rdn to ld ins fnl f: r.o* **15/8**[1]

2410 **2** *½* **Doughnut**[70] 4190 2-9-6 **89** PatDobbs 2 93
(R Hannon) *w ldrs: led over 1f out: sn rdn: hdd ins fnl f: nt qckn towards fin* **9/2**[2]

3441 **3** *3 ¾* **Just The Lady**[10] 6009 2-8-8 **77** AdrianTNicholls 6 68
(D Nicholls) *led: rdn and hdd over 1f out: no ex ins fnl f* **14/1**

1440 **4** *1* **Red Rossini (IRE)**[29] 5466 2-8-8 **77** LPKeniry 3 64
(R Hannon) *n.m.r sn after s: chsd ldrs: rdn over 1f out: styd on same pce ins fnl f* **8/1**[3]

2334 **5** *nk* **Titus Andronicus (IRE)**[33] 5363 2-8-0 **74** Louis-PhilippeBeuzelin(5) 8 60
(K A Ryan) *in midfield: swtchd lft to r on rail wl over 1f out: styd on ins fnl f: nt pce to chal ldrs* **12/1**

210 **6** *nk* **Global City (IRE)**[60] 4507 2-9-6 **89** (t) FrancisNorton 10 74+
(Saeed Bin Suroor) *hld up: shkn up over 1f out: r.o and prog ins fnl f: nrst fin* **10/1**

021 **7** *½* **Red Rosanna**[9] 6051 2-8-6 **75** GrahamGibbons 13 58+
(R Hollinshead) *missed break: sn swtchd lft to r in midfield: rdn over 1f out: no imp on ldrs: no ex ins fnl f* **28/1**

541 **8** *1* **Lucky Art (USA)**[56] 4647 2-9-4 **87** RobertWinston 9 67
(J Howard Johnson) *w ldr: rdn and hung rt wl over 1f out: wknd fnl f* **10/1**

3214 **9** *nk* **Captain Scooby**[23] 5647 2-8-6 **78** ow2 MichaelJStainton(3) 12 56+
(R M Whitaker) *sn outpcd and hung rt: nt clr run ent fnl f: sme late prog: nt pce to threaten* **16/1**

0431 **10** *¾* **Lucky Numbers (IRE)**[47] 4923 2-8-8 **77** StephenDonohoe 7 53
(Paul Green) *a towards rr: nvr on terms* **22/1**

601 **11** *1 ¼* **Lesley's Choice**[10] 6023 2-8-11 **80** J-PGuillambert 5 51+
(P A Blockley) *n.m.r sn after s: chsd ldrs tl rdn and wknd wl over 1f out* **8/1**[3]

4616 **12** *½* **Transcentral**[64] 4389 2-7-12 **70** DuranFentiman(3) 11 39+
(W M Brisbourne) *sn pushed along and outpcd: nvr on terms* **66/1**

4125 **13** *4 ½* **Bahamian Ceilidh**[63] 4434 2-8-10 **79** TGMcLaughlin 4 32
(B R Millman) *n.m.r sn after s: chsd ldrs tl wknd 2f out* **20/1**

60.95 secs (-0.05) **Going Correction** +0.05s/f (Good) **13** Ran SP% **127.7**
Speed ratings (Par 97): **102,101,95,93,93 92,91,90,89,88 86,85,78**
toteswinger: 1&2 £2.40, 1&3 £9.00, 2&3 £8.60. CSF £9.88 CT £100.93 TOTE £3.60: £1.90, £1.60, £2.30; EX 11.60.

Owner Phil & Frances Kendall **Bred** Gulf Coast Farms LLC **Trained** Newmarket, Suffolk

FOCUS
This was a competitive nursery with five last-time-out winners. It was run at a decent early pace and the form looks straightforward enough.

NOTEBOOK
Aldermoor(USA) made it two wins from three outings with a dogged display under top weight on this nursery debut. He had the ideal draw, but evidently prefers to come from off the pace and he had ground to make on the eventual runner-up at the top of the home straight. He responded positively to pressure and was always getting there. This confirms his versatility as regards underfoot conditions and he remains one to follow. (tchd 5-2)
Doughnut was not disgraced in the Super Sprint last time and had beaten subsequent Listed and Group 2 winner Madame Trop Vite over course and distance on her penultimate outing. She, too, had a great draw and took advantage, travelling best of all into the home straight. She was worn down late on, but this was another solid effort and her turn does not look far off again. (op 7-2 tchd 3-1)
Just The Lady, raised a stone for registering a third win of the year at Beverley ten days earlier, showed decent early speed and only tired in the closing stages. She goes on any ground, but looks held by the Handicapper.
Red Rossini(IRE) did not have a lot go right at Sandown on his previous outing and was well supported. He was handy from the off and had his chance, but his fate was apparent shortly after the home turn. (op 14-1)
Lucky Art(USA) Official explanation: jockey said colt was unsuited by the track

6275 M&S MONEY MAIDEN FILLIES' STKS 1m 2f 75y
3:20 (3:21) (Class 4) 3-Y-O+ **£5,828** (£1,734; £866; £432) **Stalls** High

Form RPR

5641 **1** **Hamalka (IRE)**[29] 5445 3-8-12 **68** ChrisCatlin 8 68
(B W Hills) *mde all: rdn over 1f out: sn hrd pressed: hld on gamely fnl strides* **5/1**[3]

-420 **2** *hd* **Filigree Lace (USA)**[80] 3849 3-8-7 74........... Louis-PhilippeBeuzelin(5) 9 68
(Sir Michael Stoute) *in tch: wnt 2nd over 1f out: sn upsides and str chal: r.o* **11/2**

5 **3** *½* **Surrealism**[9] 6055 3-8-12 0.. PatDobbs 1 67+
(J H M Gosden) *in midfield: rdn and hdwy over 1f out: wnt 3rd ins fnl f: clsng on ldng pair whn n.m.r post* **6/4**[1]

62 **4** *3 ½* **Turfwolke (GER)**[29] 5471 3-8-12 0................................ JamesDoyle 10 60
(J W Hills) *racd keenly: prom: rdn to chal 2f out: wknd fnl 75yds* **16/1**

0-4 **5** *1 ¼* **Royal Manor**[9] 6047 3-8-12 0.. LPKeniry 11 57
(N J Vaughan) *in midfield: hdwy 5f out: rdn and hung rt over 2f out: sn lost grnd: kpt on wout threatening ldrs fnl f* **14/1**

00 **6** *1 ¾* **Miss Ferney**[9] 6055 4-9-4 0.. FrancisNorton 4 54
(A Kirtley) *racd keenly: prom tl wknd over 1f out* **100/1**

243 **7** *1* **Emirates Lady (USA)**[44] 5031 3-8-12 66....................... RichardMullen 6 52
(Saeed Bin Suroor) *in midfield: hung rt over 2f out: sn wknd* **7/2**[2]

0-50 **8** *2* **Elusive Deal (USA)**[88] 3580 3-8-9 51.................. RussellKennemore(3) 2 48
(Mrs L Williamson) *racd keenly: chsd ldrs: lost pl 5f out: no imp after* **33/1**

0 **9** *10* **Enjoy The Mood**[8] 6091 5-9-1 0............................... DuranFentiman(3) 7 28
(Ms N M Hugo) *a bhd* **100/1**

R000 **10** *3 ¾* **Tot Hill**[37] 5203 5-8-11 45.. RossAtkinson(7) 3 20
(C N Kellett) *missed break: a bhd* **150/1**

036 **11** *2 ¼* **Cullybackey (IRE)**[7] 6114 3-8-12 0........................... RobertWinston 12 16
(G A Swinbank) *a bhd: eased whn n.d over 1f out* **11/1**

2m 12.79s (0.59) **Going Correction** +0.05s/f (Good)
WFA 3 from 4yo+ 6lb 11 Ran SP% **120.7**
Speed ratings (Par 102): **99,98,98,95,94 93,92,90,82,79 78**
toteswinger: 1&2 £3.20, 1&3 £1.70, 2&3 £3.70. CSF £33.55 TOTE £4.60: £1.50, £2.10, £1.40; EX 21.10.
Owner E D Kessly **Bred** Mrs C F Van Straubenzee And Partners **Trained** Lambourn, Berks

FOCUS
A modest fillies' maiden. The first three came clear in a tight finish and the winner is the best guide to the level.
Cullybackey(IRE) Official explanation: jockey said filly was unsuited by the good to firm (good in places) ground

6276 BETDAQ THE BETTING EXCHANGE H'CAP 1m 2f 75y
3:50 (3:51) (Class 2) (0-100,97) 3-Y-O
£21,185 (£6,344; £3,172; £1,587; £792; £397) **Stalls** High

Form RPR

0525 **1** **Albaqaa**[15] 5858 3-8-5 84.. PaulHanagan 7 92
(R A Fahey) *sweating: racd keenly: chsd ldr over 8f out: rdn to ld over 1f out: r.o ins fnl f: in command towards fin* **10/1**

1005 **2** *1 ¾* **Upton Grey (IRE)**[14] 5903 3-8-10 89................................ PatDobbs 8 94
(J H M Gosden) *led: rdn and hdd over 1f out: no ex towards fin* **15/2**

2130 **3** *5* **Bowder Stone (IRE)**[15] 5858 3-8-4 83 oh2.................. RichardMullen 4 78
(M H Tompkins) *trckd ldrs: rdn wl over 1f out: outpcd by front pair fnl f* **14/1**

2101 **4** *1 ¼* **Deep Winter**[31] 5391 3-8-1 83 oh2............................ DuranFentiman(3) 1 75
(R A Fahey) *broke wl: sn stdd into midfield: rdn and hdwy over 3f out: one pce fr over 1f out* **8/1**

0603 **5** *1 ¾* **Ramona Chase**[13] 5942 3-9-1 94................................... JamesDoyle 5 83
(S Kirk) *in rr: rdn over 1f out: sn lugged lft: kpt on steadily fnl f: nvr able to chal* **7/1**[3]

1205 **6** *6* **Decameron (USA)**[14] 5908 3-8-4 88............. Louis-PhilippeBeuzelin(5) 3 65
(Sir Michael Stoute) *in midfield: rdn and wknd 2f out* **7/2**[2]

1164 **7** *hd* **My Aunt Fanny**[35] 5257 3-8-8 87.. LPKeniry 6 63
(A M Balding) *in midfield: hung rt fr 6f out: rdn over 4f out: wknd 3f out* **11/4**[1]

0222 **8** *½* **Nightjar (USA)**[29] 5449 3-8-5 84.................................. AdrianTNicholls 9 59
(M Johnston) *trckd ldrs: rdn over 3f out: wknd over 2f out* **8/1**

45-1 **9** *1* **Bazergan (IRE)**[29] 5463 3-9-4 97...(tp) ChrisCatlin 2 70
(C E Brittain) *in rr: niggled along over 4f out: nvr on terms* **14/1**

2m 10.89s (-1.31) **Going Correction** +0.05s/f (Good) 9 Ran SP% **117.8**
Speed ratings (Par 107): **107,105,101,100,99 94,94,93,93**
toteswinger: 1&2 £11.70, 1&3 £45.70, 2&3 £16.10. CSF £84.03 CT £1060.03 TOTE £16.10: £3.80, £2.80, £4.90; EX 123.70 Trifecta £259.90 Pool: £526.89 - 1.50 winning units..
Owner Mrs Josephine Tattersall **Bred** C Eddington And Partners **Trained** Musley Bank, N Yorks

FOCUS
This was not a bad three-year-old handicap by any means, but it was run at a modest early pace and the first two had it to themselves in the home straight. The first two set the standard.

NOTEBOOK
Albaqaa got warm beforehand and took a walk in the market, but he produced a career-best effort to score on the fastest ground he would probably have encountered. It was also his first outing at this turning track and it proved right up his street as he gained his third win of the year. He looks capable of climbing further up the handicap ladder as a four-year-old. (op 15-2)
Upton Grey(IRE) won the battle for the early lead and has to rate as somewhat unfortunate, as he finished a clear second best. He enjoyed the quicker ground and deserves to win again, but he will likely go back up a few pounds. (op 8-1)
Bowder Stone(IRE), 2lb out of the handicap, took time to settle through the early parts, but was travelling well nearing the home turn and kept on to post a much more encouraging effort. (op 12-1)
Deep Winter, another 5lb higher, was chasing a fifth win from her last six starts and simply looked to find things too hot from 2lb out of the weights. (op 7-1 tchd 13-2)
Decameron(USA) looked a potential improver for the step up in trip, but he posted a tame effort from off the pace and was beaten turning for home. He was later reported to have been struck into. Official explanation: trainer's rep said colt had been struck into (op 9-2)
My Aunt Fanny was bidding to make it three from three over course and distance, but she refused to settle and was the first off the bridle. Something may have been amiss with her. Official explanation: jockey said filly never travelled (op 7-2)

6277 INNOSPEC H'CAP 7f 2y
4:25 (4:26) (Class 3) (0-95,93) 3-Y-O+ **£9,714** (£2,890; £1,444; £721) **Stalls** Low

Form RPR

2350 **1** **Guilded Warrior**[34] 5313 5-8-7 86................ Louis-PhilippeBeuzelin(5) 4 94
(W S Kittow) *a.p: rdn to ld over 1f out: jst hld on cl home* **9/2**[2]

3003 **2** *nk* **Fathsta (IRE)**[17] 5795 3-9-0 91.. LPKeniry 3 97
(S Kirk) *dwlt: racd keenly: trckd ldrs: outpcd over 2f out: rdn over 1f out: r.o ins fnl f: gaining at fin* **6/1**[3]

6662 **3** *nse* **Kay Es Jay (FR)**[23] 5644 3-8-12 89................................ ChrisCatlin 10 95
(B W Hills) *trckd ldrs: rdn and outpcd by ldrs over 1f out: r.o and gaing at fin* **14/1**

2130 **4** *½* **Brassini**[15] 5862 3-8-13 90.. TGMcLaughlin 6 95
(B R Millman) *trckd ldrs: rdn 5f out: outpcd 2f out: r.o and clsd ins fnl f* **14/1**

0312 **5** *hd* **Kings Point (IRE)**[7] 6105 7-9-5 93................................ AdrianTNicholls 1 98
(D Nicholls) *led: rdn and hdd over 1f out: remained chalng ins fnl f: no ex towards fin* **4/1**[1]

1206 **6** *½* **Lindoro**[48] 4893 3-8-13 90...(t) SaleemGolam 8 93
(W R Swinburn) *hld up: hdwy over 1f out: styng on whn nt clr run towards fin: nt quite pce to chal* **25/1**

0000 **7** *hd* **Hinton Admiral**[28] 5495 4-8-13 87................................ PaulHanagan 9 90
(R A Fahey) *in midfield: lost pl 5f out: swtchd lft and hdwy ent fnl f: fin wl* **16/1**

4040 **8** *nk* **Barons Spy (IRE)**[14] 5897 7-9-0 88................................ JamesDoyle 11 90
(R J Price) *in rr: rdn and hdwy ent fnl f: kpt on towards fin: nt quite pce to shake up ldrs* **33/1**

0055 **9** *2 ¾* **Zomerlust**[7] 6105 6-8-13 87.. GrahamGibbons 12 82
(J J Quinn) *stdd s: sn swtchd lft: in rr: rdn 1f out: nvr able to chal* **20/1**

2414 **10** *shd* **The Kiddykid (IRE)**[29] 5446 8-8-11 85.......................... StephenDonohoe 7 80
(P D Evans) *in midfield: pushed along and lost pl over 2f out: n.d after* **11/1**

5040 **11** *4 ½* **Captain Jacksparra (IRE)**[31] 5405 4-8-9 83................ RichardMullen 5 79
(K A Ryan) *in midfield: lost pl 3f out: nt clr run over 1f out: eased whn btn ins fnl f* **10/1**

2102 **12** *2 ¼* **Heywood**[29] 5446 4-9-4 92...(p) FrancisNorton 2 69
(D Nicholls) *racd keenly: prom tl wknd 2f out* **4/1**[1]

1m 26.49s (-0.01) **Going Correction** +0.05s/f (Good)
WFA 3 from 4yo+ 3lb 12 Ran SP% **120.7**
Speed ratings (Par 107): **102,101,101,101,100 100,100,99,96,96 91,88**
toteswinger: 1&2 £6.40, 1&3 £14.60, 2&3 £12.40. CSF £31.56 CT £362.01 TOTE £5.80: £1.80, £2.50, £3.10; EX 34.80.
Owner The Racing Guild **Bred** Manor Farm Packers Ltd **Trained** Blackborough, Devon

■ Stewards' Enquiry : Adrian T Nicholls two-day ban: used whip down shoulder in forehand position (Oct 11-12)

FOCUS
A good handicap run at a generous early pace. There was a very tight finish but the form looks sound with the first six close to recent marks.

NOTEBOOK
Guilded Warrior was soon handy from a favourable draw and, getting the better of his duel with Kings Point in the home straight, proved game to fend off the closers. This was his first win since July last year and his consistency since meant he was still racing from a 2lb higher mark than when last successful. He is obviously capable of holding his form and will no doubt continue to pay his way after a rise in the handicap. (op 11-2)
Fathsta(IRE) had not convinced on his two previous outings at the track, but he did nothing wrong here and remains in great heart despite a very busy time this year. He helps to set the standard of this form. (op 5-1)
Kay Es Jay(FR) ◆ just held at Salisbury on softer ground 23 days earlier, picked up nicely when asked for maximum effort in the home straight and posted another solid effort from a 2lb higher mark. She also deserves extra credit, as she was drawn poorly and her turn looks to be nearing again (op 12-1)
Brassini hit a flat spot before staying on again and left the impression a return to 1m on similar ground is what he needs. (op 12-1)
Kings Point(IRE) paid the price for his early exertions at the business end, but was still not beaten far.
Lindoro Official explanation: jockey said gelding was denied a clear run
Heywood, another who enjoys this track, refused to settle early on and was disappointingly beaten well before his 4lb higher mark came into play. This was certainly not his true form. (op 5-1)

6278 ADVANCED INSULATION PLC H'CAP 6f 18y
5:00 (5:01) (Class 4) (0-85,85) 3-Y-O+ **£6,476** (£1,927; £963; £481) **Stalls** Low

Form RPR

0403 **1** **Wyatt Earp (IRE)**[7] 6125 7-9-1 80.................................(b) PaulHanagan 2 95
(R A Fahey) *trckd ldrs: led over 1f out: sn dashed away: r.o wl and in command fnl f* **5/2**[1]

5431 **2** *3 ¾* **Makshoof (IRE)**[11] 5991 4-9-2 81.................................(p) ChrisCatlin 5 84
(K A Ryan) *in midfield: rdn over 1f out: hdwy ent fnl f: r.o to take 2nd post: n.d to wnr* **5/1**[2]

030 **3** *shd* **Methaaly (IRE)**[8] 6069 5-8-12 84................................ DeanHeslop(7) 1 87
(M Mullineaux) *in tch: rdn over 1f out: chsd wnr in vain ins fnl f: lost 2nd post* **9/1**

3030 **4** *nk* **River Thames**[27] 5542 5-8-10 75.. PatDobbs 7 77+
(K A Ryan) *in rr: hdwy on outside ent fnl f: fin wl* **12/1**

2001 **5** *1 ¼* **Namir (IRE)**[7] 6131 6-8-9 77.................................(vt) DuranFentiman(3) 9 75+
(D Shaw) *towards rr: hdwy ent fnl f: styd on towards fin: nvr nrr* **14/1**

600 **6** *½* **Not My Choice (IRE)**[16] 5831 3-9-2 83........................(t) FrancisNorton 4 79
(S Parr) *in midfield: nt clr run 2f out: rdn and hdwy ent fnl f: one pce fnl 75yds* **7/1**[3]

1110 **7** *nk* **Earlsmedic**[16] 5831 3-8-10 82.................................(v) WilliamCarson(5) 12 77+
(S C Williams) *in rr: rdn on outside over 1f out: styd on fnl f: nt pce to chal* **12/1**

4423 **8** *1 ½* **Sparton Duke (IRE)**[31] 5403 3-8-12 79........................(p) RichardMullen 6 70
(K A Ryan) *s.i.s: in rr: rdn over 1f out: n.m.r and hmpd ins fnl f: kpt on wout troubling ldrs* **12/1**

2360 **9** *nk* **Cornus**[36] 5247 6-8-11 76...(be) JamesDoyle 8 66
(A J McCabe) *led: rdn and hdd over 1f out: wknd ins fnl f* **16/1**

100 **10** *1* **My Gacho (IRE)**[28] 5503 6-9-4 83................................(b) J-PGuillambert 13 70
(M Johnston) *w ldr: rdn and rn wd ent st over 1f out: wknd ins fnl f* **25/1**

0250 **11** *1* **Pacific Pride**[36] 5247 5-8-12 77...(p) LPKeniry 3 60
(J J Quinn) *in tch: n.m.r 2f out: rdn over 1f out: wknd ins fnl f* **16/1**

0044 **12** *1 ¾* **Topflightcoolracer**[14] 5884 4-9-1 80................................ DaleGibson 16 58
(Mrs G S Rees) *towards rr: rdn whn bdly hmpd over 1f out: nvr on terms* **25/1**

0050 **13** *3 ½* **Dream Theme**[8] 6069 5-9-6 85................................ AdrianTNicholls 14 52
(D Nicholls) *completely missed break: a bhd* **14/1**

0000 **14** *2 ½* **Dig Deep (IRE)**[47] 4928 6-8-11 76................................ GrahamGibbons 11 35
(J J Quinn) *trckd ldrs: rdn and wknd over 1f out: eased ins fnl f* **18/1**

1m 13.93s (0.13) **Going Correction** +0.05s/f (Good)
WFA 3 from 4yo+ 2lb 14 Ran SP% **128.9**
Speed ratings (Par 105): **101,96,95,95,93 93,92,90,90,89 87,85,80,77**
toteswinger: 1&2 £2.30, 1&3 £8.30, 2&3 £7.00. CSF £14.79 CT £98.53 TOTE £2.80: £1.60, £2.20, £3.10; EX 13.50.
Owner Los Bandidos Racing **Bred** J W Parker And Keith Wills **Trained** Musley Bank, N Yorks

FOCUS
This looked an open sprint on paper, but it produced a most decisive winner. The form is rated around the placed horses.

6279 MORSON INTERNATIONAL H'CAP — 1m 5f 89y
5:35 (5:35) (Class 4) (0-80,79) 3-Y-0+ £6,476 (£1,927; £963; £481) Stalls Low

Form — RPR

0211 **1** **Blimey O'Riley (IRE)**[42] 5111 3-9-7 79 .... RichardMullen 1 — 92+
(M H Tompkins) *trckd ldrs: led over 1f out: sn clr: eased down towards fin* — **11/8**[1]

4642 **2** 4 ½ **Thorny Mandate**[7] 6136 6-8-9 58 oh1 .... ChrisCatlin 3 — 63
(W M Brisbourne) *hld up: hdwy 3f out: rdn to take 2nd 1f out: no ch w wnr fnl f* — **9/1**

3051 **3** 1 **Apache Fort**[7] 6129 5-9-7 70 .... (b) TonyCulhane 2 — 73
(T Keddy) *in midfield: n.m.r wl over 7f out: hdwy 6f out: rdn to chse ldrs wl over 1f out: styd on same pce ins fnl f* — **7/1**[3]

2033 **4** nk **York Cliff**[25] 5583 10-8-6 58 oh1 .... DuranFentiman(3) 10 — 61
(W M Brisbourne) *hld up: hdwy over 1f out: kpt on ins fnl f to chal for pls* — **25/1**

5264 **5** ½ **Mae Cigan (FR)**[14] 5900 5-9-3 66 .... FrancisNorton 11 — 68
(M Blanshard) *in midfield: effrt over 3f out: lost pl 2f out: styd on to chal for pls 1f out: one pce fnl 75yds* — **8/1**

1003 **6** 2 ½ **Abstract Folly (IRE)**[31] 5396 6-9-4 67 .... GrahamGibbons 9 — 65
(J D Bethell) *s.i.s: in midfield: rdn over 2f out: swtchd rt 1f out: one pce* — **11/1**

1100 **7** 2 **Puy D'Arnac (FR)**[147] 1798 5-10-0 77 .... PaulHanagan 5 — 72
(G A Swinbank) *racd keenly: trckd ldrs: led over 2f out: rdn and hdd over 1f out: wknd ins fnl f* — **13/2**[2]

3150 **8** 1 ½ **Monfils Monfils (USA)**[15] 5858 6-9-9 77 .... Louis-PhilippeBeuzelin(5) 7 — 70
(A J McCabe) *prom: led narrowly 3f out: hdd over 2f out: wknd over 1f out* — **12/1**

3532 **9** 3 ½ **Sir Sandicliffe (IRE)**[14] 5887 4-8-4 60 .... (v[1]) DeanHeslop(7) 13 — 48
(W M Brisbourne) *hld up: toiling wl over 2f out* — **14/1**

0006 **10** 1 **Turfshuffle (GER)**[11] 5992 5-10-0 77 .... StephenDonohoe 4 — 63
(Ian Williams) *led: rdn and hdd 3f out: wknd wl over 1f out* — **33/1**

2600 **11** 21 **Prelude**[29] 5450 7-9-7 70 .... TGMcLaughlin 12 — 25
(W M Brisbourne) *trckd ldrs: lost pl 7f out: pushed along 5f out: n.d after* — **20/1**

2m 55.66s (-0.04) **Going Correction** +0.05s/f (Good)
WFA 3 from 4yo+ 9lb — **11** Ran SP% **123.3**
Speed ratings (Par 105): **102,99,98,98,98 96,95,94,92,91 78**
toteswinger: 1&2 £4.20, 1&3 £2.80, 2&3 £9.00. CSF £15.17 CT £72.22 TOTE £2.20: £1.30, £2.80, £1.90; EX 17.50 Place 6 £150.93, Place 5 £73.90.
Owner Trevor Benton **Bred** Mrs Ann Kennedy **Trained** Newmarket, Suffolk

FOCUS
A modest staying handicap. The winner remains highly progressive and the next three home help set the level.
T/Plt: £62.70 to a £1 stake. Pool: £74,241.55. 863.27 winning tickets. T/Qpdt: £39.40 to a £1 stake. Pool: £3,028.80. 56.80 winning tickets. DO

6223

GREAT LEIGHS (A.W) (L-H)
Saturday, September 27

OFFICIAL GOING: Standard
Wind: Virtually nil Weather: bright and sunny

6280 NEW HOLLAND LIBERTY MAIDEN STKS — 1m 2f (P)
5:50 (5:53) (Class 4) 3-Y-0+ £6,476 (£1,927; £963; £481) Stalls Low

Form — RPR

0-2 **1** **Distinctive Image (USA)**[18] 5780 3-9-3 0 .... KShea 4 — 83
(R Hollinshead) *t.k.h: hld up towards rr: hdwy and carried rt wl over 1f out: led ent fnl f: pushed clr: readily* — **11/1**

6 **2** 2 ¾ **Streets Apart (USA)**[29] 5463 3-8-12 0 .... MartinDwyer 10 — 72
(W R Swinburn) *led: rdn: rn green and hdd over 2f out: hung rt and led again over 1f out: hdd ent fnl f: no ch w wnr* — **14/1**

22 **3** 6 **Vine Street (IRE)**[24] 5612 3-8-12 0 .... WilliamBuick 2 — 60
(M A Jarvis) *trckd ldrs: rdn over 2f out: fnd little and sn btn: wnt modest 3rd over 1f out* — **11/4**[2]

4 **4** 12 **Time To Play**[30] 5426 3-9-3 0 .... KirstyMilczarek 1 — 41
(T T Clement) *hld up in tch: rdn 4f out: wknd over 2f out: plodded on into modest 4th nr fin* — **20/1**

5 shd **Scarab (IRE)** 3-9-3 0 .... GregFairley 6 — 41
(M Johnston) *chsd ldr tl led on inner over 2f out: sn rdn: hdd over 1f out: immediately btn and wknd qckly* — **6/1**[3]

6 3 **Stormy Summer** 3-9-3 0 .... (t) EdwardCreighton 9 — 35
(R W Price) *sn bustled along: bhd tl hdwy into midfield over 7f out: lost pl 5f out: wl btn last 2f* — **50/1**

33 **7** 10 **Wellington Square**[29] 5463 3-9-3 0 .... TravisBlock 3 — 15
(H Morrison) *t.k.h: hld up in tch: rdn 3f out: sn btn and wl bhd: t.o* — **5/6**[1]

0 **8** 8 **Prairie Hawk (USA)**[11] 5995 3-9-3 0 .... MHNaughton 8 — —
(Tim Vaughan) *a bhd: rdn over 5f out: t.o fr over 2f out* — **66/1**

P **Wild By Nature** 3-8-12 0 .... DeanMcKeown 7 — —
(P Leech) *s.i.s: plld hrd: hdwy and clipped heels over 7f out: sn plld to outer: sddle slipped and p.u 6f out* — **100/1**

2m 6.33s (-2.27) **Going Correction** -0.10s/f (Stan)
WFA 3 from 4yo 6lb — **9** Ran SP% **119.7**
Speed ratings (Par 105): **105,102,98,88,88 85,77,71,—**
toteswinger: 1&2 £18.30, 1&3 £6.30, 2&3 £8.70. CSF £145.56 TOTE £15.00: £2.40, £2.80, £1.50; EX 82.30.
Owner Stevenson Leadbeater & Hollinshead **Bred** Juddmonte Farms Inc **Trained** Upper Longdon, Staffs

FOCUS
An inauspicious start to a good quality evening's racing and a race in which did not take as much winning as seemed likely as both market leaders ran below expectations. The form is difficult to pin down.
Wellington Square Official explanation: jockey said gelding ran flat
Wild By Nature Official explanation: jockey said filly had steering problems

6281 NEW HOLLAND MIDAS CLAIMING STKS — 6f (P)
6:20 (6:20) (Class 4) 2-Y-0 £6,476 (£1,927; £963; £481) Stalls Low

Form — RPR

3431 **1** **Desert Falls**[14] 5905 2-9-5 83 .... DeanMcKeown 8 — 86
(R M Whitaker) *broke wl: mde all: rdn over 1f out: styd on wl* — **15/2**

3521 **2** 1 ¼ **Gone Hunting**[15] 5866 2-8-9 84 .... JackDean(5) 1 — 77
(W G M Turner) *chsd ldrs: wnt 2nd over 1f out: kpt on same pce u.p fnl f* — **5/1**[2]

133 **3** nk **Leftontheshelf (IRE)**[28] 5487 2-8-8 87 .... TolleyDean(3) 9 — 73
(J L Spearing) *t.k.h: hld up in tch: rdn and hdwy on outer over 2f out: chsd ldng pair ins fnl f: one pce fnl 100yds* — **9/2**[1]

1000 **4** 1 ½ **Klynch**[7] 6118 2-9-5 93 .... (b) MartinDwyer 6 — 77
(B J Meehan) *chsd ldr tl over 1f out: kpt on same pce u.p fnl f* — **5/1**[2]

0 **5** ½ **Trigger McCann**[109] 2916 2-8-12 0 .... PatCosgrave 2 — 68
(J S Moore) *s.i.s: sn in tch: rdn 2f out: no imp fr over 1f* — **20/1**

1011 **6** ½ **The Magic Of Rio**[37] 5204 2-8-10 89 .... LiamJones 13 — 65
(W J Haggas) *towards rr: rdn and hdwy on outer wl over 1f out: no hdwy fnl f* — **9/2**[1]

3000 **7** 4 ½ **Duke Of Aquitaine (USA)**[29] 5460 2-8-13 67 .... WilliamBuick 10 — 54
(P F I Cole) *sn outpcd: reminder over 4f out: edgd lft and plugged on fnl f: n.d* — **33/1**

4012 **8** hd **Court Approval (IRE)**[10] 6023 2-8-11 80 .... JackMitchell(3) 7 — 55
(T G Mills) *sn rdn to chse ldrs: rdn over 2f out: struggling 2f out: wl hld fnl f* — **6/1**[3]

6516 **9** 1 ¾ **Courageous Nature (IRE)**[11] 5997 2-8-11 68 .... HayleyTurner 5 — 47
(A J McCabe) *t.k.h: hld up in tch: rdn over 2f out: wknd over 1f out* — **20/1**

0110 **10** 2 ¾ **Mythical Blue (IRE)**[12] 5969 2-8-7 78 .... (t) MCGeran(5) 3 — 39
(S C Williams) *rrd s and v.s.a: n.d* — **8/1**

040 **11** nk **Home Before Dark**[10] 6010 2-8-13 52 .... KShea 11 — 39
(R M Whitaker) *racd in midfield on outer tl hung rt and lost pl 4f out: wl bhd last 2f* — **50/1**

1m 13.7s **Going Correction** -0.10s/f (Stan) — **11** Ran SP% **121.3**
Speed ratings (Par 97): **96,94,93,91,91 90,84,84,82,78 77**
toteswinger: 1&2 £5.00, 1&3 Not won, 2&3 £22.10. CSF £44.38 TOTE £11.60: £3.60, £1.50, £2.30; EX 43.00.
Owner J Barry Pemberton **Bred** Hellwood Farm And J B Pemberton **Trained** Scarcroft, W Yorks

FOCUS
A fair race of its type and one in which the pace was sound. The form is rated at face value through the runner-up.

NOTEBOOK
Desert Falls, who has reportedly had wind problems, looked to have a bit to find conceding weight nearly all round but he took two lengths out of the field at the start and that made the difference between defeat and victory. He's a much better horse on Polytrack than on turf and is a fair sort for this grade but he is going to find life tougher after reassessment if the handicap option is taken up. (op 8-1 tchd 10-1)
Gone Hunting had shown improved form on his two previous starts and ran creditably after enjoying the run of the race from his low draw. He'll continue to give a good account. (op 6-1 tchd 13-2 in a place)
Leftontheshelf(IRE) had a decent chance at the weights and ran creditably after racing wide throughout, in the process proving her effectiveness over this trip. (op 7-2 tchd 5-1)
Klynch is an exposed sort who ran a solid race in defeat but he'll surely struggle to win a nursery from his current mark. (op 7-1)
Trigger McCann ◆ again shaped with plenty of promise against more experienced rivals and, although his proximity to some fair sorts isn't going to have done his prospective mark much good, he's one to keep an eye on, especially if upped in distance. (op 40-1)
The Magic Of Rio looked the pick of the weights but was found out from the widest stall over this trip in a race where the leaders weren't stopping. She was not disgraced but her current mark of 89 offers little margin for error when she goes back into handicaps. (op 10-3)
Duke Of Aquitaine(USA), an inconsistent maiden, had a stiff task at the weights and didn't look an easy ride but shaped as though a return to further would suit.
Mythical Blue(IRE) Official explanation: jockey said colt missed the break
Home Before Dark Official explanation: jockey said colt hung right throughout

6282 NEW HOLLAND SPRINGBOARD MAIDEN STKS — 1m (P)
6:50 (6:53) (Class 4) 2-Y-0 £6,476 (£1,927; £963; £481) Stalls Centre

Form — RPR

1 **Nawaadi (USA)** 2-9-3 0 .... MartinDwyer 12 — 73+
(J H M Gosden) *hld up in midfield on outer: hdwy to chse ldrs 3f out: shkn up to ld over 1f out: rn green ent fnl f: rdn out* — **5/4**[1]

00 **2** 1 ½ **Chadwell Spring (IRE)**[43] 5066 2-8-9 0 .... JackMitchell(3) 2 — 62
(Miss J Feilden) *in tch: hdwy on inner over 2f out: ev ch and hung bdly rt over 1f out: kpt on same pce fnl 100yds* — **33/1**

60 **3** 2 ½ **Give Us A Song (USA)**[56] 4616 2-9-3 0 .... HayleyTurner 6 — 61
(J S Moore) *hld up in midfield: hdwy over 2f out: chsd ldng pair and sltly hmpd ent fnl f: edgd lft and kpt on same pce after* — **33/1**

06 **4** 2 ¼ **Rawaaj**[26] 5579 2-9-3 0 .... WilliamBuick 8 — 56
(Sir Michael Stoute) *s.i.s: bhd: hdwy 3f out: chsd ldrs and hung rt over 1f out: swtchd lft ent fnl f: kpt on same pce after* — **7/1**[3]

3 **5** 1 ½ **Fin Vin De Leu (GER)**[15] 5870 2-9-3 0 .... GregFairley 3 — 53
(M Johnston) *led for 1f: pressed ldr tl led again over 3f out: rdn and hdd over 1f out: wknd ent fnl f* — **2/1**[2]

5 **6** 2 ¼ **Loulou (USA)**[26] 5570 2-8-12 0 .... PatCosgrave 5 — 43
(S A Callaghan) *sn rdn along: towards rr and drvn over 3f out: nvr trbld ldrs* — **8/1**

0 **7** ½ **Canmoss (USA)**[33] 5365 2-9-3 0 .... DeanMcKeown 9 — 47+
(E J O'Neill) *dwlt: sn in midfield: shkn up and outpcd over 2f out: no ch after* — **16/1**

0 **8** ½ **Hayley's Girl**[92] 3456 2-8-12 0 .... TravisBlock 10 — 41
(S W James) *a bhd: drvn and effrt on inner over 2f out: nvr trbld ldrs* — **100/1**

0 **9** 1 **Winterbrook King**[17] 5798 2-9-3 0 .... RichardKingscote 7 — 44
(J R Best) *bhd: reminders 5f out: nvr trbld ldrs* — **25/1**

000 **10** 1 **Tightrope (IRE)**[13] 5929 2-9-3 45 .... KirstyMilczarek 11 — 41
(T D McCarthy) *chsd ldrs: rdn over 2f out: hung lft and wknd wl over 1f out* — **100/1**

00 **11** 2 ½ **My Les**[27] 5535 2-8-5 0 .... JemmaMarshall(7) 1 — 31
(J R Best) *sn wl bhd: nvr a factor* — **100/1**

0 **12** 13 **Major Potential (USA)**[33] 5364 2-9-3 0 .... LiamJones 4 — 7
(R M H Cowell) *chsd ldr tl led after 1f: hung lft fr 4f out: hdd over 3f out: wknd qckly 2f out: eased fnl f* — **33/1**

1m 41.16s (1.26) **Going Correction** -0.10s/f (Stan) — **12** Ran SP% **122.9**
Speed ratings (Par 97): **89,87,85,82,81 79,78,78,77,76 73,60**
toteswinger: 1&2 £18.60, 1&3 £17.40, 2&3 £27.90. CSF £59.87 TOTE £3.10: £1.50, £10.60, £3.50; EX 115.20.
Owner Hamdan Al Maktoum **Bred** John R Penn & Frank Penn **Trained** Newmarket, Suffolk
■ Stewards' Enquiry : Jack Mitchell two-day ban: careless riding (Oct 11-12)

FOCUS
Another maiden on the card lacking strength in depth and the proximity of the placed horses confirms this bare form is modest. The pace was soon sound but the winner is the type to progress with experience.

NOTEBOOK

Nawaadi(USA) ◆, a $575,000 yearling who holds optimistic-looking entries in the Dewhurst and Racing Post Trophy, overcame his inexperience and the widest draw to beat some ordinary rivals in workmanlike fashion. However, he can only improve for this debut run and is sure to win more races. (op Evens tchd 6-4, 13-8 in a place)

Chadwell Spring(IRE) had hinted at ability on her debut on turf but turned in an improved effort on this all-weather debut, despite edging off a true line in the closing stages. Her stable does well with its runners on sand and she may progress in handicaps.

Give Us A Song(USA) had shown only poor form in two previous starts over 6f but shaped much better over this longer trip returned to Polytrack. He should also fare better in ordinary handicaps. (tchd 40-1)

Rawaaj, who is an unexposed sort from a top yard, did not look the easiest of rides once asked for an effort but he showed enough on this third and qualifying run for a mark to suggest he'll be of interest when upped to 1m2f in handicaps. (op 10-1)

Fin Vin De Leu(GER) had shaped with promise on his debut at Wolverhampton but failed to confirm that after being asked to race close to the strong pace. He is in good hands and would not be one to write off yet. (op 9-4 tchd 5-2)

Loulou(USA) was off the bridle at an early stage and probably ran to a similar level as on her debut. She is likely to remain vulnerable in this type of event. (op 10-1)

Winterbrook King Official explanation: jockey said colt ran green

Tightrope(IRE) Official explanation: jockey said colt hung left throughout

Major Potential(USA) Official explanation: jockey said colt hung left

6283 NEW HOLLAND PROVIDENCE H'CAP — 1m (P)

7:20 (7:23) (Class 2) (0-100,96) 3-Y-O

£15,577 (£4,665; £2,332; £1,167; £582; £292) **Stalls** Centre

Form				RPR
-322	**1**		**Roaring Forte (IRE)**^{34} 5309 3-8-8 **86** ... LiamJones 4	106+
			(W J Haggas) *mde all: rdn and drew clr over 2f out: in n.d last 2f: easily* **4/1^{2}**	
0011	**2**	*6*	**Storm Sir (USA)**^{14} 5908 3-8-7 **85** ...(t) MartinDwyer 2	90
			(B J Meehan) *chsd ldrs: rdn to chse wnr over 2f out: no imp on wnr but kpt on to hold 2nd* **8/1**	
3441	**3**	*1*	**Opera Prince**^{15} 5863 3-8-6 **84** ... HayleyTurner 7	87
			(S Kirk) *in tch: rdn to go 3rd over 2f out: drvn and hung lft over 1f out: kpt on same pce* **10/1**	
4-4	**4**	*1¼*	**Slam Dunk (USA)**^{7} 6141 3-8-12 **90** ... KLatham 9	90
			(G M Lyons, Ire) *hld up in midfield: rdn 4f out: chsd ldng trio over 1f out: no imp* **7/1**	
3014	**5**	*2*	**Hilbre Court (USA)**^{24} 5607 3-8-4 **82** oh2... WilliamBuick 5	77
			(B J Meehan) *hld up bhd: rdn and no hdwy 3f out: kpt on fnl f: nvr on terms* **18/1**	
-113	**6**	*nk*	**Aromatherapy**^{35} 5273 3-8-11 **89** ... TPQueally 6	83
			(H R A Cecil) *t.k.h: hld up towards rr on outer: rdn and no prog 2f out* **7/2^{1}**	
1200	**7**	*shd*	**Commander Cave (USA)**^{34} 5313 3-9-4 **96** ... RyanMoore 8	90
			(R Hannon) *chsd ldrs early: sn lost pl: bhd and rdn 4f out: n.d after* **15/2**	
0041	**8**	*½*	**Fervent Prince**^{29} 5470 3-9-3 **95** ... TravisBlock 3	88
			(H Morrison) *hld up in last trio: effrt on inner over 2f out: plugged on but no ch* **11/2^{3}**	
4060	**9**	*hd*	**Dubai Dynamo**^{14} 5907 3-8-12 **90** ... JohnEgan 1	83
			(P F I Cole) *hld up in midfield: rdn over 3f out: no imp last 2f* **14/1**	
0001	**10**	*4½*	**Red Rumour (IRE)**^{15} 5862 3-8-12 **90** ... RichardKingscote 10	72
			(R M Beckett) *chsd wnr tl over 2f out: sn wknd* **14/1**	

1m 37.16s (-2.74) **Going Correction** -0.10s/f (Stan) **10** Ran SP% **120.7**

Speed ratings (Par 107): **109,103,102,100,98 98,98,97,97,93**

toteswinger: 1&2 £3.60, 1&3 £2.20, 2&3 £10.10. CSF £37.55 CT £313.01 TOTE £5.60: £1.90, £3.10, £4.20; EX 31.50.

Owner Flying Tiger Partnership **Bred** Grangecon Stud **Trained** Newmarket, Suffolk

FOCUS

A valuable and competitive handicap with six of the ten having won on either of their previous two starts. Despite a pace that was only fair early on, this was the quickest time to date over 1m at Great Leighs and those held up failed to land a blow. The placed horses set the level backed up by the fourth.

NOTEBOOK

Roaring Forte(IRE) took this in impressive fashion returned to Polytrack. He'll face a hefty rise in the weights for winning a competitive handicap with so much in hand but he is only relatively lightly raced and may well have more to offer on artificial surfaces. (op 11-2)

Storm Sir(USA) came into the race at the top of his game and ran creditably but could never really get to grips with the ready winner. However, he probably was not far off his best and looks a good guide to the worth of this form. (op 6-1)

Opera Princes two wins have been on turf but he ran creditably, despite edging off a true line in the closing stages, from this career high mark. He may be ideally suited by more give in the ground back on turf. (op 8-1 tchd 11-1)

Slam Dunk(USA) was not disgraced returned to 1m considering he came from just off the pace. He's a fairly consistent sort but this showed he has little margin for error from his current mark. (op 10-1)

Hilbre Court(USA) was not at his best in claiming company on his previous start but was not disgraced in a race that did not suit the hold up horses back in a handicap. He is worth another try over 1m2f but is high enough in the weights at present. (tchd 20-1)

Aromatherapy looked to have a valid excuse for his previous turf run but he proved disappointing, even allowing for the fact this race suited the prominent racers. He is lightly raced enough to be open to further improvement but is going to have to settle better if he is to progress. (tchd 3-1 and 4-1)

Fervent Prince came into this race after a career best on turf but proved a disappointment on only this second Polytrack start. He will be worth another chance back on turf. (tchd 5-1 and 6-1)

6284 NEW HOLLAND THOROUGHBRED OPEN JUVENILE (CONDITIONS STKS) — 1m (P)

7:50 (7:51) (Class 2) 2-Y-O

£24,924 (£7,464; £3,732; £1,868; £932; £468) **Stalls** Centre

Form				RPR
0010	**1**		**Shampagne**^{36} 5244 2-9-0 101... MartinDwyer 1	100
			(P F I Cole) *t.k.h: hld up bhd ldng pair: effrt to chal wl over 1f out: led 1f out: hung lft but r.o wl fnl f* **15/2^{3}**	
2221	**2**	*1¾*	**Fullback (IRE)**^{7} 6135 2-9-0 86... HayleyTurner 8	96
			(J S Moore) *chsd ldr: chal 2f out: led over 1f out: sn hdd: nt pce of wnr ins fnl f* **16/1**	
1545	**3**	*2¾*	**Talking Hands**^{16} 5827 2-9-0 106... JamieSpencer 7	90
			(S Kirk) *bhd: pushed along 5f out: rdn and swtchd rt 3f out: drvn and edgd lft over 1f out: wnt 3rd ins fnl f: nvr threatened ldrs* **3/1^{2}**	
411	**4**	*nk*	**Poster (IRE)**^{21} 5711 2-9-0 100... DaneO'Neill 4	89
			(L M Cumani) *hld up in last pair: rdn and unable qck over 2f out: edgd lft u.p over 1f out: no imp* **4/5^{1}**	
2312	**5**	*2*	**Thunderball**^{14} 5895 2-9-0 80... PatCosgrave 2	85
			(A J McCabe) *led: rdn and qcknd over 2f out: hdd over 1f out: wknd ent fnl f* **11/1**	
1150	**6**	*1*	**Doctor Crane (USA)**^{29} 5462 2-9-0 92... LDettori 5	83+
			(J H M Gosden) *racd in midfield tl hung rt and rn wd and lost pl bnd over 3f out: bhd and rdn wl over 1f out: nvr trbld ldrs* **9/1**	

1m 39.24s (-0.66) **Going Correction** -0.10s/f (Stan) **6** Ran SP% **116.5**

Speed ratings (Par 101): **99,97,94,94,92 91**

toteswinger: 1&2 £13.00, 1&3 £2.30, 2&3 £11.00. CSF £105.38 TOTE £7.80: £2.60, £4.60; EX 78.30.

Owner Sisters Syndicate **Bred** Stringston Farm **Trained** Whatcombe, Oxon

■ Stewards' Enquiry : Martin Dwyer two-day ban: careless riding (Oct 11-12)

FOCUS

The first of the "Breeders Cup Trials" but not an overly strong race for the money and a steadily run contest in which the two market leaders disappointed and this bare form does not look entirely reliable. The winner is rated to form.

NOTEBOOK

Shampagne may not be the most straightforward as he tends to race with the choke out and he drifted to his left under pressure but he maintained his unbeaten record on artificial surfaces and in the process confirmed himself a useful performer up to 1m. He's a versatile sort too but he's fairly exposed and will have to take a further step forward if he is to hold his own in stronger company. (op 7-1 tchd 8-1)

Fullback(IRE) looked to have a stiff task but turned in a career best after enjoying the run of the race (despite being carried left by the winner late on), in the process comfortably reversing recent Wolverhampton placings with Poster on these less-favourable terms. He pulled clear of the remainder but this improved effort means life is going to be considerably tougher in handicaps after reassessment. (tchd 20-1)

Talking Hands, a smart sort on turf and all-weather, was not seen to best effect back on sand after being dropped out in a race run at just a modest early gallop. A more end-to-end gallop would have seen him in a better light and he is worth another chance in similar company when there looks like being more pace on. (tchd 10-3 and 7-2 in places)

Poster(IRE), who was ridden less prominently than when impressively beating Fullback at Wolverhampton, was well backed but proved a disappointment after racing keenly and tending to edge off a true line under pressure. He had looked a progressive sort up to this point, though, and may do better granted a stiffer test. (op Evens)

Thunderball had a stiff task at the weights and ran as well as could be expected after being allowed his own way in front. He will be seen to better effect returned to handicaps (op 17-2 tchd 12-1)

Doctor Crane(USA) , making his all-weather debut, disappointed for the third successive time and he looks one to tread carefully with at present. Official explanation: jockey said colt hung right (op 10-1)

6285 NEW HOLLAND THOROUGHBRED OPEN SPRINT (CONDITIONS STKS) — 6f (P)

8:20 (8:20) (Class 2) 3-Y-O+

£24,924 (£7,464; £3,732; £1,868; £932; £468) **Stalls** Low

Form				RPR
2101	**1**		**Ceremonial Jade (UAE)**^{74} 4059 5-9-2 107...(t) JohnEgan 2	112
			(M Botti) *hld up in bhd ldrs: plld out off rail 2f out: rdn and qcknd to ld over 1f out: clr ins fnl f: r.o strly: readily* **5/1^{2}**	
25-2	**2**	*2¼*	**Asset (IRE)**^{14} 5899 5-9-2 109...(v^{1}) LDettori 9	105
			(Saeed Bin Suroor) *hld up towards rr: plld out and rdn jst over 1f out: r.o to chse wnr last 100yds: no ch w wnr* **9/4^{1}**	
4043	**3**	*1¼*	**Matsunosuke**^{14} 5906 6-9-2 94... AlanMunro 11	101
			(A B Coogan) *pressed ldrs: rdn wl over 1f out: outpcd jst over 1f out: kpt on: edgd lft wl ins fnl f* **20/1**	
0006	**4**	*½*	**Tabaret**^{4} 6184 5-9-2 90...(p) KShea 5	99
			(R M Whitaker) *led: rdn wl over 1f out: hdd jst over 1f out: sn no ch w wnr: lost 2 pls last 100yds* **33/1**	
0100	**5**	*¾*	**Racer Forever (USA)**^{60} 4506 5-9-2 108...(b) JimmyFortune 7	99+
			(J H M Gosden) *t.k.h: hld up wl in tch in midfield: rdn and unable to qckn over 1f out: swtchd lft 1f out: keeping on but no ch whn nt clr run wl ins fnl f* **5/1^{2}**	
6254	**6**	*shd*	**Damika (IRE)**^{16} 5840 5-9-2 103... DeanMcKeown 4	97+
			(R M Whitaker) *in tch: rdn 2f out: outpcd over 1f out: kpt on same pce fnl f: n.m.r wl ins fnl f* **9/1**	
6405	**7**	*shd*	**Excusez Moi (USA)**^{25} 5586 6-9-2 106... LiamJones 8	96
			(C E Brittain) *s.i.s: t.k.h: hld up towards rr: n.m.r over 1f out: sn swtchd rt: kpt on u.p but nvr trbld ldrs* **12/1**	
1050	**8**	*shd*	**Orpsie Boy (IRE)**^{56} 4624 5-9-2 102... KirstyMilczarek 12	96
			(N P Littmoden) *in tch on outer: rdn 2f out: outpcd over 1f out: plugged on same pce fnl f* **20/1**	
0006	**9**	*nk*	**Capricorn Run (USA)**^{56} 4617 5-9-2 98...(v) PatCosgrave 3	95
			(A J McCabe) *v.s.a: bhd: rdn over 2f out: styd on fnl f: n.d* **33/1**	
0-40	**10**	*nk*	**Finicius (USA)**^{126} 2417 4-9-2 0... JamieSpencer 13	94
			(Eoin Griffin, Ire) *dropped in after s: hld up bhd: plld out and drvn wl over 1f out: no hdwy fnl f* **12/1**	
2340	**11**	*4*	**Bonus (IRE)**^{147} 1809 8-9-2 107...(b) HayleyTurner 6	81
			(G A Butler) *stdd s: hld up bhd: effrt and rdn 2f out: no prog: wl hld fnl f* **15/2^{3}**	
4010	**12**	*4*	**Galeota (IRE)**^{7} 6121 6-9-2 101... RyanMoore 10	68
			(R Hannon) *chsd ldr tl 2f out: sn wknd: eased ins fnl f* **12/1**	

1m 11.63s (-2.07) **Going Correction** -0.10s/f (Stan) **12** Ran SP% **124.4**

Speed ratings (Par 109): **109,106,104,103,102 102,102,102,101,101 96,90**

toteswinger: 1&2 £1.50, 1&3 £56.80, 2&3 £31.70. CSF £16.68 TOTE £5.20: £1.50, £1.50, £8.30; EX 18.80.

Owner Giuliano Manfredini **Bred** Darley **Trained** Newmarket, Suffolk

FOCUS

Several smart sorts on show in a race run at a sound pace throughout and this form should stand up at a similar level.

NOTEBOOK

Ceremonial Jade(UAE) was ridden more prominently than is usually the case and he bounded clear after travelling really strongly to register a career best. He has thrived on Polytrack in the last 12 months and is a reliable sort but is going to need another big step forward to trouble the best US sprinters around at the Breeders Cup and his best chance of overseas success in the near future could be on dirt at next year's Dubai Racing Carnival. (op 7-2)

Asset(IRE) ◆ looks better than the bare form after faring the best of the hold-up horses on this second start for Godolphin. Fitted with a first time visor, he did well on only this second all-weather start given the winner was allowed first run and he remains capable of winning in at least a similar grade either on turf or on artificial surfaces for this yard. (op 7-2)

Matsunosuke had plenty to find at the weights but ran a blinder upped in distance, especially as he failed to settle early on and raced much more prominently than is usually the case. Life is going to be much tougher after reassessment back in handicap company, though.

Tabaret, from a yard among the winners, also had plenty to prove at these weights but ran well against the inside rail from his decent draw. However, consistency has not been his strongest suit and it remains to be seen whether this will be reproduced either on turf or sand next time. (op 40-1 tchd 50-1)

Racer Forever(USA) looked to have decent claims on only this third all-weather start but did not really look suited by the step back to this trip. The return to 7f should suit but he's the type that needs everything to drop just right. (op 6-1)
Damika(IRE), a model of consistency on turf, ran creditably on this first start on artificial surfaces without suggesting that he'd improved for the switch to it. Official explanation: jockey said gelding was denied a clear run (op 8-1)
Excusez Moi(USA), who failed to settle, is not the most reliable around and failed to land a blow back on Polytrack. (tchd 14-1)

6286 NEW HOLLAND THOROUGHBRED OPEN MARATHON (CONDITIONS STKS) 1m 5f 66y(P)

8:50 (8:50) (Class 2) 3-Y-O+

£24,924 (£7,464; £3,732; £1,868; £932; £468) **Stalls** Low

Form RPR
4531 **1** **Red Gala**[28] 5494 5-9-7 113 RyanMoore 8 112+
(Sir Michael Stoute) *hld up wl in tch: chal 2f out: sn led and hung rt: clr and hung lft u.p ins fnl f: rdn out* **6/5**[1]
6054 **2** *4 1/2* **Big Robert**[14] 5926 4-9-7 96 MartinDwyer 3 105
(W R Muir) *s.i.s: hld up in last: hdwy 3f out: rdn and effrt on outer 2f out: swtchd lft 1f out: kpt on to go 2nd towards fin: no ch w wnr* **25/1**
0665 **3** *nk* **Dansili Dancer**[23] 5646 6-9-7 99 AdamKirby 4 105
(C G Cox) *hld up in last pair: hdwy 3f out: rdn 2f out: chsd wnr ent fnl f: no imp: lost 2nd towards fin* **20/1**
0031 **4** *4 1/2* **Hattan (IRE)**[21] 5694 6-9-7 113 (v) NCallan 2 98
(C E Brittain) *trckd ldrs: rdn and nt qckn 2f out: wknd qckly ent fnl f* **5/2**[2]
226 **5** *2 1/2* **Tempelstern (GER)**[20] 5736 4-9-7 114 (b) TPQueally 1 94
(H R A Cecil) *t.k.h: chsd ldr tl led over 2f out: hdd over 1f out: wknd qckly 1f out: wl btn after* **5/1**[3]
0615 **6** *7* **Judgethemoment (USA)**[65] 4351 3-8-12 88 JohnEgan 5 84
(Jane Chapple-Hyam) *led: rdn over 3f out: hdd over 2f out: sn wknd: wl bhd fnl f* **25/1**
040 **7** *14* **Supersonic Dave (USA)**[21] 5694 4-9-7 101 (v[1]) JamieSpencer 6 63
(B J Meehan) *hld up in last trio: rdn over 3f out: sn struggling: wl btn fr over 1f out: eased fnl f* **11/1**

2m 48.87s (-4.73) **Going Correction** -0.10s/f (Stan)
WFA 3 from 4yo+ 9lb 7 Ran SP% **111.5**
Speed ratings (Par 109): **110,107,107,104,102 98,89**
toteswinger: 1&2 £3.20, 1&3 £4.00, 2&3 £13.00. CSF £35.89 TOTE £2.80: £1.60, £4.90; EX 29.80.
Owner Cheveley Park Stud **Bred** Cheveley Park Stud Ltd **Trained** Newmarket, Suffolk

FOCUS
A couple of smart sorts but, with Hattan and Templestern disappointing in this muddling contest, this proved a straightforward task for the winner. The form is rated around the placed horses to this year's best.

NOTEBOOK
Red Gala ◆ translated the pick of his turf form to Polytrack and won with plenty in hand after his main rivals disappointed. He's a reliable sort who is well worth a try over further than 1m6f and looks more than capable of picking up a minor Group win. (op 11-8 tchd 6-4 and 13-8 in places)
Big Robert had something to find at the weights but he ran respectably, especially as he was dropped out in a race run at less than a true gallop. However, he has only won a three-runner conditions event since landing his maiden and is likely to remain difficult to place either in this type of event or from his current mark in handicaps. (tchd 20-1)
Dansili Dancer was not disgraced after hanging left on only this second all-weather start but, although he may be suited by a more truly run race over 1m4f, he is likely to remain vulnerable in this grade and has little margin for error from his current mark. (op 16-1)
Hattan(IRE) was unpenalised for this year's Group 3 victories in the Winter Derby and in a muddling event at Kempton on his previous start and he proved disappointing after meeting trouble over this longer trip in a race that was not a true test of stamina. This was clearly not his running and he will be of more interest back over shorter. (tchd 9-4 and 11-4)
Tempelstern(GER) looked to have fine claims at these weights, despite a poor run in Group 1 company on his previous start but he dropped out very tamely on this all-weather debut after enjoying the run of the race. He looks one to have reservations about at present. (op 3-1)
Judgethemoment(USA) is an improved performer around this trip this year but, although he enjoyed the run of the race, he had a stiff task at the weights and had his limitations firmly exposed. (tchd 33-1)

6287 NEW HOLLAND THOROUGHBRED OPEN CLASSIC (CONDITIONS STKS) 1m 1f 46y(P)

9:20 (9:20) (Class 2) 3-Y-O+

£24,924 (£7,464; £3,732; £1,868; £932; £468) **Stalls** Low

Form RPR
1136 **1** **Lucky Find (SAF)**[182] 1092 5-9-5 0 RyanMoore 1 113
(M F De Kock, South Africa) *t.k.h: trckd ldrs: swtchd rt wl over 1f out: sn ev ch: led over 1f out: r.o wl* **6/1**[3]
0105 **2** *1* **Re Barolo (IRE)**[13] 5941 5-9-5 105 (t) JohnEgan 10 111+
(M Botti) *stdd s: hld up in rr: c wd and hdwy 2f out: chsd ldng pair over 1f out: wnt 2nd ins fnl f: r.o but nvr getting to wnr* **25/1**
2123 **3** *1 1/2* **Familiar Territory**[21] 5743 5-9-5 110 LDettori 7 108
(Saeed Bin Suroor) *led: rdn 2f out: hdd over 1f out: one pce fnl f: lost 2nd ins fnl f* **4/1**[2]
2120 **4** *2 3/4* **Royal Vintage (SAF)**[8] 6073 4-9-8 0 KShea 6 104
(M F De Kock, South Africa) *hmpd s: hld up towards rr: hdwy on outer over 2f out: hung rt u.p over 1f out: nvr able to chal* **9/4**[1]
3165 **5** *nk* **Mia's Boy**[14] 5896 4-9-5 104 JimmyQuinn 2 101
(C A Dwyer) *hld up in midfield on inner: rdn 2f out: no imp ent fnl f: kpt on* **13/2**
4334 **6** *5* **Dubai's Touch**[35] 5265 4-9-5 104 GregFairley 5 90
(M Johnston) *hld up in tch in midfield: rdn over 3f out: wl btn fr wl over 1f out* **8/1**
0046 **7** *3/4* **Happy Boy (BRZ)**[21] 5743 5-9-8 112 (v[1]) TedDurcan 4 91
(Saeed Bin Suroor) *chsd ldr tl 5f out: chsd ldr again over 2f out tl over 1f out: wknd qckly ent fnl f* **11/1**
1244 **8** *5* **Tamasou (IRE)**[9] 6042 3-9-0 66 AdamKirby 3 77?
(Garry Moss) *racd in last pair: rdn jst over 2f out: sn wl btn* **100/1**
322 **9** *3/4* **Yarqus**[14] 5908 5-9-5 94 (bt) NCallan 11 75
(C E Brittain) *hld up in tch in midfield: rdn jst over 2f out: wknd wl over 1f out* **16/1**
0453 **10** *9* **Jack Junior (USA)**[13] 5941 4-9-5 95 JamieSpencer 9 56
(B J Meehan) *racd in midfield on outer: hdwy to chse ldrs over 6f out: wnt 2nd 5f out tl over 2f out: sn btn* **16/1**

1m 54.08s (114.08)
WFA 3 from 4yo+ 5lb 10 Ran SP% **116.5**
toteswinger: 1&2 £28.70, 1&3 £8.80, 2&3 £12.40. CSF £96.51 TOTE £8.20: £2.40, £7.10, £1.20; EX 108.10 Place 6 £994.01, Place 5 £303.67..
Owner Sh Ahmed bin Mohd bin Khalifa Al Maktoum **Bred** Oldlands Stud **Trained** South Africa

FOCUS
The feature event on a cracking evening's racing but a race run at just a fair gallop. The form is a bit muddling with the runner-up the best guide.

NOTEBOOK
Lucky Find(SAF) showed he retained all his ability on this Polytrack debut and first run since finishing down the field in this year's Dubai World Cup. Plans are reportedly fluid at present but it won't be a surprise to see him back in Dubai early next year and, while he falls short of top class, he appeals as the type to win more races around this trip. (tchd 11-2)
Re Barolo(IRE) ◆ had not been at his best on his last couple of starts but turned in his best effort yet and he deserves extra credit as he fared easily the best of those to make ground from off the pace. A more strongly run race would have suited and he's capable of winning a similar event on this evidence. (op 14-1)
Familiar Territory, a progressive sort in Dubai earlier this year, had the run of the race and bettered his latest all-weather run (after a break) in Turkey. He pulled clear of the remainder and should continue to give a good account in this type of event. (op 9-2)
Royal Vintage(SAF), for the second time in succession, failed to reproduce the pick of his dirt form at Nad Al Sheba returned to an artificial surface and was the disappointment of the race. He looked anything but an easy ride once pressure was applied and he will have to show a fair bit more before he can be backed at skinny odds again. (tchd 15-8)
Mia's Boy was far from disgraced but failed to improve for the return to this trip back on Polytrack. A more strongly run race over 1m may be more to his liking but his improvement seems to have levelled out and he may well continue to look vulnerable to the better types in this grade. (op 7-1 tchd 11-2)
Dubai's Touch failed to improve for the return to Polytrack and the return to this trip. (tchd 10-1)
Happy Boy(BRZ), who was fitted with a first-time visor, again disappointed and he looks one to have reservations about at present. Official explanation: jockey said horse had no more to give (op 10-1 tchd 12-1)
T/Plt: £408.20 to a £1 stake. Pool: £71,578.76. 128.00 winning tickets. T/Qpdt: £56.40 to a £1 stake. Pool: £7,945.50. 104.10 winning tickets. SP

6244 HAYDOCK (L-H)

Saturday, September 27

OFFICIAL GOING: Good to firm (9.3)
Rail realignment around the far turn reduced the distance of race 1 by about 22yds and on home turn added 10yards to distances of races 4, 5, & 6.
Wind: Virtually nil Weather: Warm and sunny

6288 BETFRED LADIES' POKER TOUR H'CAP 1m 6f

2:25 (2:25) (Class 3) (0-105,93) 3-Y-O+

£31,155 (£9,330; £4,665; £2,335; £1,165; £585) **Stalls** Low

Form RPR
1205 **1** **Meshtri (IRE)**[14] 5894 3-8-10 **89** PhilipRobinson 2 100
(M A Jarvis) *led 6f: cl up tl led again 6f out: rdn along 3f out: drvn over 1f out: styd on gamely u.p ins fnl f* **11/4**[1]
2221 **2** *1* **Buddhist Monk**[10] 6018 3-8-4 **83** DO'Donohoe 16 92
(Sir Mark Prescott) *dwlt: hld up in rr: gd hdwy on outer 3f out: rdn to chal and hung bdly lft wl over 1f out: sn drvn and ev ch tl flashed tail: carried hd high and no ex ins fnl f* **7/1**[3]
0315 **3** *3/4* **Jagger**[9] 6061 8-9-0 **86** (p) LukeMorris[(3)] 3 94
(G A Butler) *trckd ldrs: rdn along and outpcd 4f out: hdwy over 2f out: sn rdn: styd on wl u.p ins fnl f* **11/1**
3340 **4** *3* **Pass The Port**[36] 5249 7-8-4 **78** KellyHarrison[(5)] 15 82
(D Haydn Jones) *hld up in rr: stdy hdwy 3f out: chsd ldrs whn n.m.r wl over 1f out: sn rdn and kpt on same pce appr fnl f* **25/1**
0515 **5** *hd* **Dzesmin (POL)**[15] 5853 6-9-1 **84** PaulHanagan 7 88
(R A Fahey) *trckd ldrs: hdwy over 3f out: rdn over 2f out and ev ch tl drvn and one pce fr over 1f out* **15/2**
4000 **6** *3 3/4* **Double Banded (IRE)**[9] 6061 4-9-6 **89** (p) EddieAhern 10 87
(J L Dunlop) *trckd ldrs: hdwy 4f out: cl up whn hmpd 2f out: sn rdn and n.m.r over 1f out: wknd* **8/1**
6331 **7** *1* **Always Bold (IRE)**[6] 6154 3-8-12 **91** 6ex JoeFanning 4 88
(M Johnston) *prom: rdn along over 3f out: drvn whn n.m.r 2f out: grad wknd* **13/2**[2]
2066 **8** *1* **Greenwich Meantime**[13] 5940 8-9-5 **88** TonyHamilton 14 84
(R A Fahey) *hld up in rr: hdwy 3f out: sn rdn along and no imp fr wl over 1f out* **16/1**
0020 **9** *1 1/4* **Bajan Parkes**[15] 5858 5-9-2 **85** DavidAllan 17 79
(E J Alston) *chsd ldrs on outer: rdn along 4f out: grad wknd* **50/1**
4/24 **10** *3* **Souffleur**[11] 5992 5-8-12 **81** JimCrowley 12 71
(P Bowen) *hld up in rr: sme hdwy on inner over 3f out: sn rdn along and nvr nr ldrs* **10/1**
400- **11** *hd* **Hernando Royal**[217] 6014 5-9-3 **86** TomEaves 8 75
(Dr R D P Newland) *cl up on outer: led after 6f tl 6f out: rdn along over 3f out and sn wknd* **33/1**
51/0 **12** *6* **Mikado**[15] 5853 7-9-7 **90** (p) GeorgeBaker 9 71
(Jonjo O'Neill) *a towards rr: rdn along 4f out: nvr a factor* **33/1**
10 **13** *6* **Ozone Trustee (NZ)**[15] 5858 4-8-11 **84** ow1 PJMcDonald 1 53
(G A Swinbank) *trckd ldrs on inner: rdn along over 4f out: wknd 3f out* **11/1**

2m 58.46s (-5.84) **Going Correction** -0.225s/f (Firm) course record
WFA 3 from 4yo+ 10lb 13 Ran SP% **118.7**
Speed ratings (Par 107): **107,106,106,104,104 102,101,100,100,98 98,94,91**
toteswinger: 1&2 £5.60, 1&3 £8.10, 2&3 £13.30. CSF £20.27 CT £186.90 TOTE £3.60: £1.80, £2.40, £3.20; EX 21.80 Trifecta £157.20 Part won. Pool: £212.46 - 0.30 winning units..
Owner Sheikh Ahmed Al Maktoum **Bred** Round Hill Stud **Trained** Newmarket, Suffolk

FOCUS
A good, competitive staying handicap with just 10lb separating the whole field on official ratings. This race often goes to an improving type and did so again plus the track record was broken. The form looks sound.

NOTEBOOK
Meshtri(IRE) put up a game performance under a typically astute Robinson ride. This lightly-raced course winner, whose only previous try at this trip was on soft ground, got it well enough and battled on too strongly for the somewhat reluctant second. He looks to have more to offer. (op 3-1 tchd 7-2 in places)
Buddhist Monk was settled in the rear before being produced with a run down the outside in the straight, tactics that worked so well at Kempton on his previous start. However, he ducked left under pressure and, carrying his head high, looked less than willing in the closing stages. He may not have quite got home over this longer trip but it would be no surprise if some form of headgear was employed before long. (op 8-1)
Jagger has been in reasonable form of late and, on his favourite sound surface with cheekpieces back on, he ran a creditable race, staying on as if he would not mind a return to 2m. (op 14-1)
Pass The Port was held up out the back as usual and, back on a flat track, put a couple of below-par efforts behind him to just get the better of Dzesmin for a place in the frame. (op 20-1)

Dzesmin(POL) ran another decent race but is arguably best at 1m4f on a turning track and was 6lb higher than his last winning mark. (op 8-1 tchd 7-1)
Double Banded(IRE) moved up looking a big threat early in the straight but was beginning to tread water when the runner-up hung across him. (op 12-1)
Always Bold(IRE) raced close to the leaders throughout but was unable to respond as the pace quickened early in the straight before staying on again in the closing stages. (op 7-1)
Ozone Trustee(NZ), who beat Buddhist Monk on his seasonal debut, was far too keen early on this big step up in trip. (op 12-1)

6289 BETFRED.COM H'CAP 6f
3:00 (3:03) (Class 2) (0-100,100) 3-Y-O+ £12,952 (£3,854; £1,926; £962) Stalls Centre

Form				RPR
1260	1		**Chief Editor**[14] 5890 4-9-3 97 ... PhilipRobinson 11 (M A Jarvis) *hld up in tch stands' side: smooth hdwy over 2f out: rdn and edgd lft over 1f out: rdn and qcknd wl to ld ent fnl f: rdn clr* **8/1**[3]	112
0400	2	4 1/2	**Barney McGrew (IRE)**[28] 5503 5-8-12 92 ... TomEaves 9 (M Dods) *in tch far side: hdwy 2f out and sn rdn: styd on ins fnl f: no ch w wnr: 1st of 7 in gp* **16/1**	93
2050	3	1 1/2	**Lipocco**[14] 5890 4-9-6 100 ...(p) GeorgeBaker 5 (R M Beckett) *overall ldr far side: rdn wl over 1f out: hdd ent fnl f and kpt on same pce: 2nd of 7 in gp* **10/1**	96
4060	4	shd	**Misaro (GER)**[7] 6121 7-8-12 92 ...(b) JoeFanning 14 (R A Harris) *prom stands' side: rdn along over 2f out: sn drvn and kpt on same pce: 2nd of 7 in gp* **25/1**	88
2000	5	1/2	**Cute Ass (IRE)**[14] 5890 3-8-13 95 ... AndrewElliott 8 (K R Burke) *chsd ldrs far side: hdwy 2f out: sn rdn and one pce appr last: 3rd of 7 in gp* **18/1**	89
0630	6	3/4	**Burning Incense (IRE)**[8] 6069 5-8-3 86 ...(p) AndrewMullen(3) 1 (M Dods) *s.i.s and bhd far side tl styd on fnl 2f: nrst fin: 4th of 7 in gp* **12/1**	78
005	7	1/2	**Blue Tomato**[27] 5542 7-8-6 86 oh1 ... DO'Donohoe 16 (D Nicholls) *s.i.s and in rr stands' side tl sme late hdwy: 3rd of 7 in gp* **16/1**	76
1214	8	1 1/2	**Bel Cantor**[8] 6069 5-8-5 90 ...(p) KellyHarrison(5) 12 (W J H Ratcliffe) *led stands' side gp: rdn along 2f out: sn edgd lft: drvn and wknd over 1f out: 4th of 7 in gp* **10/1**	75
6140	9	1/2	**Turnkey**[7] 6104 6-8-6 93 ... AdeleRothery(7) 17 (D Nicholls) *s.i.s and a in rr stands' side: 5th of 7 in gp* **25/1**	77
-110	10	1/2	**Musaalem (USA)**[63] 4405 4-9-0 94 ... TonyCulhane 3 (W J Haggas) *trckd ldrs far side: effrt over 2f out: sn rdn and btn: 5th of 7 in gp* **4/1**[1]	76
0560	11	nse	**Mac Gille Eoin**[33] 5347 4-9-3 97 ... JimCrowley 6 (J Gallagher) *cl up far side: rdn along over 2f out: sn wknd: 6th of 7 in gp* **17/2**	79
0433	12	3 1/4	**Joseph Henry**[8] 6069 6-8-9 89 ... SilvestreDeSousa 13 (D Nicholls) *chsd ldrs stands' side: rdn along 2f out: sn wknd: 6th of 7 in gp* **9/2**[2]	61
3100	13	1 1/4	**Total Impact**[16] 5831 5-8-6 86 oh1 ... TonyHamilton 7 (R A Fahey) *s.i.s and a in rr far side: 7th of 7 in gp* **16/1**	54
4106	14	shd	**Everymanforhimself (IRE)**[30] 5424 4-8-12 92 ... NCallan 10 (K A Ryan) *chsd ldrs stands' side: rdn along over 2f out: sn wknd: 7th of 7 in gp* **14/1**	59

1m 11.63s (-2.37) **Going Correction** -0.15s/f (Firm)
WFA 3 from 4yo+ 2lb 14 Ran SP% **123.0**
Speed ratings (Par 109): **109,103,101,100,100 99,98,96,95,95 95,90,89,89**
toteswinger: 1&2 £41.60, 1&3 £19.20, 2&3 £48.80. CSF £132.60 CT £1331.08 TOTE £10.40: £3.30, £7.10, £3.10; EX 200.50 TRIFECTA Not won..
Owner Mrs P Good **Bred** J R And Mrs P Good **Trained** Newmarket, Suffolk

FOCUS
A decent sprint handicap that has gone to improvers in two of its three previous runnings but featuring mostly exposed performers. The form is rated around the third and fifth but probably not the strongest race for the grade.

NOTEBOOK
Chief Editor ◆, who was trying the full 6f for the first time on his debut for Michael Jarvis. He travelled extremely well in the stands'-side group and was still pulling at the quarter-mile pole. Although he ended up in the unfavoured centre of the track, the result was never in doubt once he was asked for his effort. He looks to have more to offer and could make up into a Listed or Group-race performer next season. (op 7-1 tchd 10-1)
Barney McGrew(IRE) once again proved difficult to load despite the aid of a blanket, but with the ground in his favour he did nothing wrong in the race. He finished best of those racing on the far side of the track, despite having no chance with the winner. (op 14-1)
Lipocco has not scored since May 2007 and is still 9lb above his last winning mark. Fitted with first-time cheekpieces, he made the running and kept on well enough, although he had nothing in reserve when the winner swept past. (op 11-1)
Misaro(GER) had been in good form in midsummer (winning four from five) and the sunny weather and fast ground helped him to stage something of a revival. That said, he still appears in the Handicapper's grip. (tchd 28-1)
Cute Ass(IRE), who was Group placed as a juvenile, has been struggling for form this season but had dropped 10lb in handicap since her return to action and this was more encouraging. (tchd 16-1)
Burning Incense(IRE), a stable companion of the runner-up, would have preferred more cut in the ground but, having not won for over two years, at last looks to be back on a competitive mark and the reapplied cheekpieces seemed to help. Official explanation: jockey said gelding was unsuited by the good to firm ground
Bel Cantor Official explanation: jockey said horse hung left-handed
Musaalem(USA), having his first run since July, got a good tow from Lipocco but found very little under pressure. (tchd 9-2)
Joseph Henry Official explanation: jockey said gelding hung left-handed

6290 BETFRED LESTER PIGGOTT "START TO FINISH" H'CAP 5f
3:35 (3:36) (Class 2) (0-100,97) 3-Y-O+ £19,428 (£5,781; £2,889; £1,443) Stalls Centre

Form				RPR
0055	1		**Judd Street**[7] 6121 6-9-4 96 ...(b) StephenCarson 1 (Eve Johnson Houghton) *trckd ldrs far side: hdwy and cl up 2f out: rdn to ld jst ins fnl f: kpt on strly* **8/1**	109
0201	2	2	**Fantasy Explorer**[7] 6125 5-8-0 85 ... JamieKyne(7) 9 (J J Quinn) *prom stands' side: hdwy to ld thatr gp wl over 1f out: sn rdn and ev ch tl drvn and nt qckn ins fnl f: 1st of 8 in gp* **7/1**[3]	91
1005	3	3/4	**Quiet Elegance**[14] 5884 3-8-10 89 ... DavidAllan 12 (E J Alston) *s.i.s and towards rr stands' side: hdwy over 2f out: rdn and edgd lft over 1f out: kpt on ins fnl f: nrst fin: 2nd of 8 in gp* **18/1**	92
552	4	hd	**Secret Asset (IRE)**[14] 5906 3-8-13 92 ... EddieAhern 4 (W M Brisbourne) *overall ldr far side: rdn along and jnd 2f out: drvn and hdd jst ins fnl f: one pce: 2nd of 6 in gp* **16/1**	95
1403	5	shd	**Toms Laughter**[7] 6121 4-9-2 97 ...(b) KevinGhunowa(3) 6 (R A Harris) *cl up far side: rdn along 2f out: sn drvn and kpt on same pce appr fnl f: 3rd of 6 in gp* **4/1**[1]	99
-100	6	1/2	**Royalist (IRE)**[17] 5795 3-8-6 85 ow1 ... PhilipRobinson 11 (M A Jarvis) *led stands' side gp: rdn along over 2f out: hdd wl over 1f out and grad wknd: 3rd of 8 in gp* **6/1**[2]	85
0452	7	1/2	**Invincible Force (IRE)**[11] 5990 4-8-11 89 ...(b) JimCrowley 10 (Paul Green) *dwlt and towards rr stands' side: hdwy 2f out: sn rdn and kpt on same pce fnl f: 4th of 8 in gp* **7/1**[3]	88
600	8	shd	**Fyodor (IRE)**[28] 5509 7-9-0 92 ...(b[1]) TonyCulhane 3 (W J Haggas) *hld up in tch far side: hdwy 2f out: sn rdn and no imp: 4th of 6 in gp* **11/1**	90
0250	9	3/4	**Prior Warning**[30] 5424 4-9-0 92 ...(t) PaulEddery 14 (Miss D Mountain) *in rr stands' side: hdwy 2f out: sn rdn and edgd lft over 1f out: kpt on ins fnl f: nt rch ldrs: 5th of 8 in gp* **33/1**	88
0556	10	1 3/4	**Fol Hollow (IRE)**[27] 5542 3-8-2 88 ... AdeleRothery(7) 16 (D Nicholls) *chsd ldrs stands' side: rdn along 1/2-way: sn wknd: 6th of 8 in gp* **14/1**	77
3510	11	1 3/4	**Regal Royale**[8] 6066 5-8-5 83 oh10 ...(v) PatrickMathers 13 (Peter Grayson) *chsd ldrs stands' side: rdn along 1/2-way: sn wknd: 8th of 8 in gp* **50/1**	66
0260	12	1/2	**Aegean Dancer**[62] 4445 6-9-3 95 ... TomEaves 2 (B Smart) *chsd ldrs far side: rdn along 1/2-way: sn wknd: 5th of 6 in gp* **16/1**	76
124	13	1 1/2	**Hypnosis**[17] 5793 5-8-6 84 oh3 ow1 ... TonyHamilton 7 (D W Barker) *sn cl up far side: rdn along over 2f out and sn wknd: 6th of 6 in gp* **20/1**	60
0000	14	3/4	**Northern Empire (IRE)**[62] 4445 5-8-10 88 ow1 ... NCallan 15 (K A Ryan) *chsd ldrs stands' side: rdn along 1/2-way: sn wknd: 8th of 8 in gp* **14/1**	61

59.55 secs (-0.95) **Going Correction** -0.15s/f (Firm)
WFA 3 from 4yo+ 1lb 14 Ran SP% **118.8**
Speed ratings (Par 109): **101,97,96,96,96 95,94,94,93,90 87,86,84,83**
toteswinger: 1&2 £13.50, 1&3 £43.90, 2&3 £35.30. CSF £61.01 CT £1016.65 TOTE £8.30: £3.10, £2.90, £5.40; EX 72.40 Trifecta £494.10 Part won. Pool: £667.78 - 0.50 winning units..
Owner R F Johnson Houghton **Bred** R F Johnson Houghton **Trained** Blewbury, Oxon

FOCUS
This good 5f sprint that has fallen to improvers on the last three runnings but this time it went to an established sprinter. The form looks reasonable rated around the runner-up and fourth.

NOTEBOOK
Judd Street likes this track and the only time he finished out of the frame here was in the Group 2 Temple Stakes. He got a good lead into the race and, once the gap opened next to the far rail, he burst through and soon had the race won, reversing Newbury form with Toms Laughter at the same time. (op 15-2 tchd 7-1)
Fantasy Explorer, who was 3lb higher for his win over 6f last week, was made plenty of use of at the head of the stands'-side group and kept on well. Fast ground suits and he will need it to remain dry if he is to add to his score. (op 13-2)
Quiet Elegance has struggled in Group and Listed company since winning a conditions race on her seasonal debut, but she showed much more on this handicap debut and kept going despite the fact she was somewhat isolated in the centre of the track. She handled this fast ground pretty well considering she is a half-sister to the soft ground-loving Reverence, and she should have a handicap in her if the assessor does not punish her for this. (op 28-1)
Secret Asset(IRE), a course and distance winner who is best at 5f on fast ground, ran a fine race from the front and, having returned from a break in good heart, looks capable of scoring again before long.
Toms Laughter, a progressive sprinter who started the year rated just 58 but who has won six times and was third in a Group 3 last time, is now rated 97 and, 8lb above last winning mark, looks as if the Handicapper has finally caught up with him. (op 6-1)
Royalist(IRE), a lightly raced colt who was dropping back from 7f, is keen sort but did not quite have the pace to lead against these specialist sprinters and, although staying on, never looked likely to win. He may be better at 6f with a little cut in the ground. (tchd 11-2)
Invincible Force(IRE) goes well on heavy ground but handles faster and, although he has not won since coming from Ireland, is now 5lb below his last winning mark so should prove competitive at a slightly lower level. (op 8-1 tchd 13-2)
Fyodor(IRE), whose only win in last two and a half years was over course and distance, was off the same mark as for that last success and had blinkers for the first time, having worn a visor when last successful. He was too keen under restraint early and had nothing left for the closing stages. (op 15-2)

6291 ERIC BENTHAM 80TH BIRTHDAY EBF MAIDEN FILLIES' STKS 1m 30y
4:05 (4:05) (Class 5) 2-Y-O £4,533 (£1,348; £674; £336) Stalls Low

Form				RPR
53	1		**Fallen In Love**[23] 5640 2-9-0 0 ... EddieAhern 9 (J L Dunlop) *prom: hdwy 3f out: rdn 2f out and sn led: drvn ins fnl f and hld on gamely* **11/8**[1]	73+
34	2	3/4	**Polly's Mark (IRE)**[36] 5227 2-9-0 0 ... PhilipRobinson 2 (C G Cox) *cl up: led after 3f: rdn along over 2f out: hdd wl over 1f out: rallied and ev ch ins fnl f tl no ex last 50yds* **4/1**[2]	71+
6	3	shd	**Holamo (IRE)**[26] 5571 2-9-0 0 ... TedDurcan 3 (M Botti) *in tch on inner: effrt and swtchd rt 2f out: rdn and n.m.r over 1f out and ins fnl f: swtchd rt and kpt on towards fin* **12/1**	71+
	4	1/2	**Bessie Lou (IRE)** 2-9-0 0 ... NCallan 8 (K A Ryan) *in tch: hdwy 3f out: rdn 2f out: drvn and ch ent fnl f: kpt on same pce* **11/1**	70+
	5	3/4	**Valletta** 2-9-0 0 ... RobertHavlin 13 (J H M Gosden) *stdd and swtchd lft s: hld up towards rr tl hdwy 3f out: swtchd outside and rdn to chse ldrs wl over 1f out: one pce ins fnl f* **8/1**	68+
05	6	1/2	**Lilly Blue (IRE)**[14] 5898 2-9-0 0 ... TonyCulhane 7 (M R Channon) *chsd ldrs: rdn along over 2f out: drvn and edgd lft over 1f out and ins fnl f: wknd* **11/2**[3]	67
50	7	3/4	**Shanavaz**[50] 4815 2-9-0 0 ... AndrewElliott 11 (Mrs G S Rees) *hld up towards rr: hdwy over 2f out: sn rdn and kpt on same pce* **100/1**	65+
46	8	3/4	**Diesis Of Cloyne (USA)**[35] 5256 2-9-0 0 ... DarrenWilliams 1 (K R Burke) *chsd ldrs: rdn along 3f out: sn wknd* **25/1**	64+
005	9	2 1/4	**Kilsyth (IRE)**[36] 5219 2-9-0 0 ... DO'Donohoe 4 (S Parr) *t.k.h: a towards rr* **66/1**	58
	10	4	**Suitably Accoutred (IRE)** 2-8-11 0 ... AndrewMullen(3) 10 (Mrs A Duffield) *a towards rr* **40/1**	49
0	11	1 1/4	**Step Fast (USA)**[22] 5672 2-9-0 0 ... JoeFanning 5 (M Johnston) *led 3f: cl up tl rdn along 3f out and sn wknd* **25/1**	46

1m 46.47s (2.67) **Going Correction** -0.225s/f (Firm) 11 Ran SP% **117.2**
Speed ratings (Par 92): **77,76,76,75,74 74,73,72,70,66 65**
toteswinger: 1&2 £2.20, 1&3 £4.80, 2&3 £5.80. CSF £6.34 TOTE £1.90: £1.40, £1.60, £3.20; EX 7.80.
Owner Normandie Stud Ltd **Bred** Normandie Stud Ltd **Trained** Arundel, W Sussex

FOCUS
Just a fair fillies' maiden and something of a bunched finish, and although the principals ran close to their form some of those in behind look flattered.

NOTEBOOK
Fallen In Love, who made a promising debut behind Filles' Mile winner Rainbow View at Newmarket (first three all won since) and, despite being a one-paced third over 7f next time, had possibly the best form on offer. She went on a fair way from home but pricked her ears and was not doing much in the final furlong. Being by Galileo she may get a little further, although her dam and her half-brother were best around a mile. She looks to have more to offer and is clearly held in high regard as she is entered in both the Irish 1000 Guineas and Irish Oaks. (op 13-8 tchd 7-4 in places)
Polly's Mark(IRE) had put up a couple of fair efforts in Newbury maidens over 7f on soft ground and she handles this surface well enough, but could not respond when the winner went past. (op 9-2)
Holamo(IRE) had shown some ability on her debut in a 1m Polytrack maiden and built on that despite still showing signs of inexperience. This 110,000gns yearling looks capable of winning races but may have to improve a fair amount to justify her purchase price. (op 9-1)
Bessie Lou(IRE), another expensive purchase, did best of the newcomers, moving up to challenge early in the straight and sticking to her task. Her breeding suggests she will appreciate middle distances next season. (op 14-1)
Valletta, a half-sister to Veracity out of a mare who stayed 1m4f plus, also put up a promising effort and should do better next season. (op 14-1)
Lilly Blue(IRE), an Irish Oaks entry, finished last of five in Listed race last time but was the only non-winner and only filly in the field so did not do badly. However, the time for that race was moderate and she may have been flattered, as she failed to make much impression this time. (op 4-1)

6292 STEPHEN HEAPS 50TH BIRTHDAY E B F MAIDEN STKS (C&G) 1m 30y
4:40 (4:41) (Class 5) 2-Y-O £4,533 (£1,348; £674; £336) Stalls Low

Form RPR
2 **1** **Imposing**[18] 5777 2-9-0 0 RobertWinston 5 80+
(Sir Michael Stoute) *in tch: hdwy 3f out: effrt 2f out: rdn over 1f out: styd on to ld last 100yds: drvn out* **5/2**[1]
2 ½ **Big Bound (USA)** 2-9-0 0 RobertHavlin 2 79+
(J H M Gosden) *t.k.h: prom: effrt whn carried rt over 1f out: sn rdn and hit in face by rival's whip 1f out: drvn: hung lft and styd on to ld briefly wl ins fnl f: edgd lft again and sn hdd: no ex last 30yds* **7/2**[3]
22 **3** 1 ¾ **Union Island (IRE)**[15] 5859 2-9-0 0 NCallan 6 75
(K A Ryan) *led: rdn along over 2f out: sn hung bdly rt: drvn over 1f out: hdd ins fnl f: one pce* **11/4**[2]
25 **4** 3 ¼ **Bandanaman (IRE)**[10] 6014 2-9-0 0 PJMcDonald 4 68
(G A Swinbank) *prom: effrt 3f out: rdn over 2f out: drvn and one pce appr fnl f* **14/1**
5 5 **Naheell** 2-9-0 0 PhilipRobinson 10 57+
(M A Jarvis) *hld up: hdwy over 2f out: swtchd lft and rdn to chse ldrs over 1f out: sn drvn and wknd ent fnl f* **9/1**
00 **6** 1 ½ **Brad's Luck (IRE)**[36] 5225 2-9-0 0 JimCrowley 8 54
(M Blanshard) *hld up: a towards rr* **25/1**
65 **7** ¾ **Howard**[71] 4150 2-9-0 0 EddieAhern 3 52+
(J L Dunlop) *in tch: hdwy on inner over 3f out: rdn to chse ldrs 2f out: sn drvn and wknd appr fnl f* **8/1**
8 2 ¾ **Kiwi Moon** 2-9-0 0 TomEaves 1 46
(B Smart) *s.i.s: a in rr* **12/1**
000 **9** 10 **Susurrayshaan**[25] 5590 2-9-0 20 (p) AndrewElliott 7 24
(Mrs G S Rees) *chsd ldrs: rdn along 3f out: drvn over 2f out and sn wknd* **100/1**

1m 45.07s (1.27) **Going Correction** -0.225s/f (Firm) 9 Ran SP% **117.8**
Speed ratings (Par 95): **84,83,81,78,73 72,71,68,58**
toteswinger: 1&2 £3.20, 1&3 £2.30, 2&3 £3.30. CSF £11.83 TOTE £2.80: £1.30, £1.80, £1.50; EX 12.00.
Owner D Smith, Mrs J Magnier, M Tabor **Bred** N P Bloodstock And Morton Bloodstock **Trained** Newmarket, Suffolk
■ Stewards' Enquiry : N Callan two-day ban: careless riding (Oct 11-12)

FOCUS
A reasonable maiden for colts run 1.4 seconds faster than the preceding race for fillies. There were some nice types from major stables in the line-up and the first three in the betting dominated the finish. The third is rated 5lb below his soft-ground form.

NOTEBOOK
Imposing, a Derby entry who cost 170,000gns, is bred to appreciate further next season. He had shown promise on his debut over 7f on heavy ground but he took a long time to settle things on this much faster going. In some ways he got the run of the race as the third took the runner-up across the track and left the winner a big gap, but he is the sort who will come into his own over middle distances, especially back on a more forgiving surface. (op 9-4 tchd 3-1)
Big Bound(USA) ◆, a half-brother to three winners including Pampas Cat, was really unlucky on this debut. He travelled well close to the pace but when moving up to challenge got carried right across the track by the third and was also hit across the face. Despite showing signs of inexperience he eventually got past and made sure the winner did not have an easy time of it. He is in the Racing Post Trophy and, although that may come a bit soon, he looks sure to win races and should fill out into an imposing individual next season. (op 4-1 tchd 9-2)
Union Island(IRE), a 70,000euros son of Rock Of Gibraltar, had been runner-up on both his starts over 1m on soft ground. He made the running in an attempt to put his proven stamina and experience to good use. However, under pressure he appeared to be feeling this fast surface and wandered right across the track, taking the runner-up with him and effectively handing the race to the favourite, earning his rider a ban in the process. He should be capable of winning races on easier ground and now qualifies for a handicap mark. (op 7-2)
Bandanaman(IRE) had been touched off on his debut over 7f on soft ground but was never going next time. He put that effort behind him with a decent effort and should be able to win races as he also now qualified for a handicap mark. (op 12-1 tchd 11-1)
Naheell was relatively unfancied on this racecourse debut for his in-form yard and did not have the pace to go with the front four in the last quarter-mile. (op 8-1)
Howard Official explanation: jockey said colt was unsuited by the good to firm ground
Kiwi Moon, a 175,000gns half-brother to a couple of juvenile winners, looked in need of the outing, missed the break on this debut and never got involved. (op 14-1)

6293 EUROPEAN BREEDERS' FUND "REPROCOLOR" FILLIES' H'CAP 1m 2f 120y
5:15 (5:15) (Class 3) (0-90,88) 3-Y-O+ £11,656 (£3,468; £1,733; £865) Stalls Centre

Form RPR
4063 **1** **Princess Taylor**[7] 6130 4-9-3 82 (t) NCallan 8 93
(M Botti) *stdd s: t.k.h in rr tl hdwy to trck ldng pair after 3f: effrt over 2f out: rdn to ld 1 1/2f out: drvn ins fnl f and styd on wl* **5/2**[1]
-030 **2** 1 ¾ **Encircled**[8] 6078 4-8-11 76 RobertHavlin 4 84
(D Haydn Jones) *stdd s and hld up in rr: gd hdwy on outer over 2f out: rdn to chse ldr and hung lft ent fnl f: sn drvn to chal and ev ch tl no ex last 100yds* **11/1**
15-5 **3** 1 ½ **Turban Heights (IRE)**[44] 5017 4-8-9 74 EddieAhern 3 79
(E J O'Neill) *s.i.s: reminders: t.k.h and sn led: rdn along 3f out and sn hdd: cl up tl drvn over 1f out and kpt on same pce* **16/1**
0115 **4** ½ **Quirina**[34] 5311 3-9-2 88 TedDurcan 1 92
(J H M Gosden) *trckd ldrs: effrt 3f out: rdn to chse ldrs 2f out: sn drvn and kpt on same pce* **3/1**[2]
21-5 **5** 1 ¼ **Red And White (IRE)**[8] 6070 3-8-7 79 JoeFanning 9 81
(M Johnston) *chsd ldrs on inner: effrt 3f out: sn rdn along and no imp fr wl over 1f out* **6/1**[3]
0130 **6** 4 **Mazaaya (USA)**[10] 6034 3-9-2 88 DO'Donohoe 10 83
(D R Lanigan) *trckd ldr: hdwy to ld wl over 2f out: sn rdn and hdd 1 1/2f out: grad wknd* **12/1**
462 **7** hd **Magic Echo**[15] 5858 4-9-9 88 TomEaves 6 82
(M Dods) *hld up: stdy hdwy on outer 3f out: chsd ldrs over 2f out: sn rdn and wknd* **6/1**[3]
0-10 **8** 1 ½ **Honorable Love**[31] 5391 4-8-12 77 TonyHamilton 2 69
(M Dods) *a towards rr* **8/1**

2m 12.8s (-3.90) **Going Correction** -0.225s/f (Firm)
WFA 3 from 4yo 7lb 8 Ran SP% **115.2**
Speed ratings (Par 104): **105,103,102,102,101 98,98,97**
toteswinger: 1&2 £4.30, 1&3 £9.70, 2&3 £20.60. CSF £31.06 CT £364.34 TOTE £3.20: £1.40, £2.80, £3.90; EX 25.20 Place 6 £121.37, Place 5 £63.27.
Owner Rothmere Racing Limited **Bred** Blenheim Bloodstock **Trained** Newmarket, Suffolk

FOCUS
A decent fillies' handicap run at a sound gallop and the form looks solid enough.

NOTEBOOK
Princess Taylor justified favouritism on this step back up in trip. Both her wins had been over 1m on firm ground and she travelled well throughout on this going. She hung left and did the third no favours when going to the front, but once on the rail she found plenty for pressure and scored decisively. (op 7-2)
Encircled, who is proven at this trip, was 5lb above her last winning mark but has dropped 5lb from a high of 81. She showed the benefit of her recent return from a break by sweeping down the outside and got almost upsides the winner, only for that rival to find extra when challenged. She is relatively fresh for the time of year and connections may be able to get a win out of her either on turf or Polytrack before long. (op 14-1)
Turban Heights(IRE) missed the break and had to be rousted to take the lead. She was taken on early in the straight but rallied and kept going pretty well despite the winner going across her bows at one point. Her recent return to action had been over 1m6f and she was clearly more at home at this trip.
Quirina, a winner at 1m and 1m2f on good ground, set the standard but she did not look that happy on this fast surface and, in trouble early in the straight, only stayed on when the race was over. (tchd 11-4 and 10-3)
Red And White(IRE) is relatively inexperienced and had only raced on soft ground prior to this but appeared to handle the surface and showed no sign of the bounce factor, having only recently returned from 15 months off. (tchd 7-1)
Magic Echo was held up and had her chance over two furlongs from home. She goes well on soft and looks less effective on this sort of going plus she is 8lb above her last winning mark and probably held by the Handicapper. (op 5-1 tchd 9-2)
T/Plt: £163.70 to a £1 stake. Pool: £95,600.29. 426.19 winning tickets. T/Qpdt: £11.40 to a £1 stake. Pool: £3,751.10. 242.20 winning tickets. JR

6294 - 6297a (Foreign Racing) - See Raceform Interactive

4993
GOWRAN PARK (R-H)
Saturday, September 27

OFFICIAL GOING: Good (yielding in places)

6298a DENNY CORDELL LAVARACK & LANWADES STUD FILLIES STKS (GROUP 3) 1m 1f 100y
4:30 (4:31) 3-Y-O+ £47,794 (£13,970; £6,617; £2,205)

RPR
1 **Shreyas (IRE)**[45] 4997 3-8-11 100 KJManning 7 103
(J S Bolger, Ire) *chsd ldrs: rdn along 3f out: cl 5th on inner 2f out: swtchd to outer and styd on wl fnl f: narrowly led cl home* **10/1**
2 hd **She's Our Mark**[20] 5732 4-9-2 108 DMGrant 6 103
(Patrick J Flynn, Ire) *hld up: rdn in 6th under 2f out: styd on strly fnl f: wnt 2nd last strides: jst failed* **7/1**
3 nk **Soft Morning**[56] 4623 4-9-2 DPMcDonogh 12 102
(Sir Mark Prescott) *broke wl and led: jnd and rdn 2 1/2f out: hdd ins fnl f: dropped to 3rd last strides* **5/1**[3]
4 nk **Jalmira (IRE)**[14] 5920 7-9-2 107 WJLee 11 101
(C F Swan, Ire) *mid-div: rdn in 5th 2 1/2f out: kpt on wl fnl f* **16/1**
5 hd **Beach Bunny (IRE)**[14] 5920 3-8-11 108 CDHayes 13 101
(Kevin Prendergast, Ire) *prom: disp ld fr 2 1/2f out: hdd cl home: dropped to 5th last strides* **4/1**[2]
6 1 ¼ **Varsity**[27] 5547 5-9-2 89 (t) MCHussey 9 99
(C F Swan, Ire) *dwlt sltly and in rr: pushed along briefly 1/2-way: rdn in 5th under 2f out: kpt on fnl f* **33/1**
7 1 ¼ **Mystical Lady (IRE)**[13] 5944 3-8-11 99 JAHeffernan 14 96
(A P O'Brien, Ire) *mid-div: no imp fr 2 1/2f out* **9/1**
8 1 **Navajo Moon (IRE)**[14] 5920 4-9-2 106 WMLordan 2 94
(David Wachman, Ire) *in rr of mid-div: no imp fr 3f out* **14/1**
9 1 ¼ **Carribean Sunset (IRE)**[20] 5730 3-9-2 113 PJSmullen 5 97
(D K Weld, Ire) *mid-div: prog into 4th 2 1/2f out: sn rdn: no ex over 1f out* **7/2**[1]
10 2 ½ **Sail (IRE)**[14] 5920 3-8-11 100 SMLevey 4 87
(A P O'Brien, Ire) *in rr: no imp st* **20/1**
11 ½ **Deauville Vision (IRE)**[14] 5920 5-9-2 100 (p) RPCleary 3 86
(M Halford, Ire) *mid-div on outer: no imp fr 2 1/2f out* **25/1**
12 hd **Magic Carpet (IRE)**[50] 4832 4-9-2 103 FMBerry 10 85
(David Wachman, Ire) *in rr: no imp st* **12/1**
13 8 **Teacht An Earraig (USA)**[24] 5620 3-8-11 104 DJMoran 8 69
(J S Bolger, Ire) *prom: rdn in 3rd 2 1/2f out: sn wknd* **16/1**
14 1 ¾ **Dane Blue (IRE)**[27] 5550 6-9-2 91 NGMcCullagh 1 66
(S J Treacy, Ire) *chsd ldrs: 3rd ent st: sn rdn and wknd* **33/1**
15 1 **Simawa (IRE)**[45] 4997 3-8-11 98 (b[1]) MJKinane 15 64
(John M Oxx, Ire) *chsd ldrs: wknd fr 3f out: eased fnl f* **14/1**

2m 0.16s (-6.84)
WFA 3 from 4yo+ 5lb 15 Ran SP% **137.8**
CSF £86.17 TOTE £16.80: £5.20, £2.30, £1.50; DF 159.60.
Owner Miss A H Marshall **Bred** Frank Dunne **Trained** Coolcullen, Co Carlow

FOCUS
An average Group 3 race rated around the runner-up, third, fifth and seventh.

NOTEBOOK
Shreyas(IRE), a half-sister to Youmzain and Creachadoir, probably found the ground too testing when only sixth in a Listed contest here last time, but she showed she remains on the upgrade by taking this Group 3 race. Unexposed, she could be capable of better, especially next year, as her half-brothers both improved with age.
Soft Morning, outclassed in the Nassau Stakes last time, was more at home in this company and ran a solid race. (op 4/1 tchd 11/2)

6299 - 6301a (Foreign Racing) - See Raceform Interactive

6266 ASCOT (R-H)
Sunday, September 28

OFFICIAL GOING: Good
Wind: Almost nil Weather: Sunny and warm

6302 MARCHPOLE H'CAP — 1m 4f
2:05 (2:06) (Class 2) (0-105,102) 3-Y-0+
£17,446 (£5,224; £2,612; £1,307; £652; £327) **Stalls** High

Form — RPR

0040 **1** **Night Crescendo (USA)**[8] 6120 5-8-10 **88**..................(p) JimCrowley 10 96
(Mrs A J Perrett) *trckd ldng pair: drvn to ld wl over 1f out: wnt one l up ins fnl f: hld on despite being ct nr fin* **9/1**

2250 **2** *hd* **Young Mick**[22] 5694 6-9-10 **102**..................(v) RobertWinston 4 111+
(G G Margarson) *hld up towards rr: effrt and nt clr run 2f out: swtchd rt to ins rail over 1f out: r.o wl fnl f: clsng on wnr at fin* **4/1**[1]

3210 **3** *½* **Drill Sergeant**[17] 5830 3-9-2 **102**.................. GregFairley 2 109
(M Johnston) *led tl 7f out: led again over 3f out tl wl over 1f out: kpt on u.p* **12/1**

0404 **4** *½* **Pevensey (IRE)**[37] 5229 6-9-2 **94**..................(p) GrahamGibbons 3 100
(J J Quinn) *towards rr: rdn 3f out: styd on wl fnl 2f: nrst fin* **10/1**

0200 **5** *1 ¼* **Ladies Best**[15] 5894 4-9-4 **96**.................. JamieSpencer 6 100
(L M Cumani) *hld up in midfield: hdwy over 2f out: rdn to chse ldng pair jst over 1f out: one pce fnl f* **10/1**

0400 **6** *nk* **Players Please (USA)**[15] 5894 4-8-11 **89**.................. LDettori 1 93
(M Johnston) *hld up in rr: hdwy on outer fr 4f out: rdn and no imp fnl 2f* **8/1**

5040 **7** *1 ½* **Sahrati**[4] 6210 4-8-10 **88**..................(v[1]) HayleyTurner 8 90
(C E Brittain) *chsd ldrs: rdn 3f out: no ex jst over 1f out* **25/1**

1105 **8** *shd* **Hatton Flight**[6] 6171 4-8-10 **88** oh1..................(b) WilliamBuick 12 89
(A M Balding) *towards rr: rdn and outpcd in last ent st: modest hdwy over 1f out: nt rch ldrs* **8/1**

1020 **9** *nse* **Birkside**[37] 5249 5-8-10 **88** oh1.................. NCallan 5 89
(K A Ryan) *in tch: eased outside and effrt 2f out: wknd over 1f out* **12/1**

0354 **10** *½* **Rayhani (USA)**[36] 5279 5-8-13 **91**.................. RHills 9 91
(M P Tregoning) *t.k.h in midfield: outpcd and losing pl ent st: n.d after* **7/1**[3]

-10 **11** *8* **Kensington Oval**[101] 3156 3-8-7 **93** ow1.................. RyanMoore 11 81
(Sir Michael Stoute) *sluggish leaving stalls and rdn in rr early: drvn over 3f out: no rspnse* **6/1**[2]

6100 **12** *2* **Profit's Reality (IRE)**[43] 4844 6-9-1 **93**.................. IanMongan 7 77
(M J Attwater) *racd wd of others: chsd ldr: led 7f out tl over 3f out: wknd over 2f out* **33/1**

2m 32.29s (-3.21) **Going Correction** -0.025s/f (Good)
WFA 3 from 4yo+ 8lb **12** Ran SP% **119.4**
Speed ratings (Par 109): **109,108,108,108,107 107,106,106,106,105 100,99**
toteswinger: 1&2 £10.70, 1&3 £28.60, 2&3 £13.10. CSF £45.16 CT £445.05 TOTE £11.10: £3.00, £1.60, £4.40; EX 54.00 TRIFECTA Not won..
Owner John Connolly **Bred** Audley Farm Inc **Trained** Pulborough, W Sussex

FOCUS
A quality handicap, although not the race it once was. The pace was not strong, which contributed to several of these racing too keenly. The fourth looks a sound guide to the form.

NOTEBOOK
Night Crescendo(USA), 10lb lower than at the start of the season and wearing cheekpieces for the first time, had been backed from big prices in the morning and justified the support with a narrow first win in nearly a year. However, he was lucky, as Young Mick would have beaten him decisively with any luck in running. Having got away on terms, which is not always the case, the winner was handy from the start and took over from Drill Sergeant well over a furlong out. He saw the finish out well, and Crowley was convinced the headgear had made all the difference. (op 12-1)
Young Mick has a fantastic record at Ascot and was successful four times over the course and distance two years ago, including in the Group 3 Cumberland Lodge on this same card. That was his last win, but another good second here in July gave him every chance, and he would have been a clear winner but for getting held up in traffic going to two furlongs out when full of running. Switched to the rail, he ran on strongly, but was never quite getting there. George Margarson, who blamed himself for giving the wrong instructions, having expected a stronger pace, wants to bring him back for an even more valuable handicap here next month, but he is now praying the Handicapper does not raise him any higher than that race's 105 ceiling. Official explanation: jockey said gelding was denied a clear run (tchd 9-2 in places)
Drill Sergeant, back up in trip, ran much better than at Doncaster last time, but he had the run of the race in front, for even though he was headed by the ultimately well-beaten Profit's Reality before halfway, that one raced wide and was not really taking him on. (op 16-1)
Pevensey(IRE) is a course specialist, like Young Mick, and he stayed on well when the race was over, having been hard at work starting up the straight. His course wins have been on soft ground, so that wouldn't be a worry if conditions changed, assuming he returns here next month. (op 8-1 tchd 11-1)
Ladies Best, second in this race last year, was not disgraced, but he has yet to win for his new connections and is looking expensive. (tchd 12-1)
Players Please(USA) had the sound surface he prefers, but having been held up in rear he never quite got competitive.
Sahrati sweated up badly in the first-time headgear and was a bit below form. (tchd 28-1)
Kensington Oval again started slowly and needed chasing along from the word go. His winning debut at Sandown promised much, and connections are unlikely to give up on him in a hurry, but he is one to have reservations about now. (op 5-1)

6303 GROSVENOR CASINOS CUMBERLAND LODGE STKS (GROUP 3) — 1m 4f
2:40 (2:43) (Class 1) 3-Y-0+ **£36,900** (£13,988; £7,000; £3,490; £1,748) **Stalls** High

Form — RPR

1011 **1** **Sixties Icon**[43] 5094 5-9-3 117.................. LDettori 5 117+
(J Noseda) *stood in stalls and missed break: hld up in last pl and in tch after 2f: smooth hdwy to ld jst over 1f out: rdn clr* **11/10**[1]

1310 **2** *2 ¼* **Sugar Ray (IRE)**[63] 4444 4-9-0 104..................(vt[1]) JimmyFortune 3 110
(Sir Michael Stoute) *led: set modest pce tl increased tempo appr st: hdd jst over 1f out: nt pce of wnr* **10/1**

2-01 **3** *1 ¼* **Ajhar (USA)**[23] 5677 4-9-0 100.................. RHills 2 108
(M P Tregoning) *mainly 3rd or 4th tl rdn and dropped to last over 2f out: kpt on again u.p fnl f: nt trble first 2* **13/2**[3]

3026 **4** *1 ¼* **Galactic Star**[22] 5694 5-9-0 111.................. RyanMoore 1 106
(Sir Michael Stoute) *cl up bhd ldng pair: rdn 3f out: one pce fnl 2f* **11/4**[2]

4305 **5** *hd* **Lion Sands**[22] 5694 4-9-0 110.................. DaneO'Neill 4 106
(L M Cumani) *trckd ldr: rdn ent st: outpcd fnl 2f* **13/2**[3]

2m 33.68s (-1.82) **Going Correction** -0.025s/f (Good) **5** Ran SP% **110.0**
Speed ratings (Par 113): **105,103,102,101,101**
CSF £12.53 TOTE £1.90: £1.30, £2.30; EX 8.90.
Owner Mrs Susan Roy **Bred** Lordship Stud **Trained** Newmarket, Suffolk

FOCUS
Only the five runners for what looked an ordinary race by Group 3 standards but the form looks solid with the first three close to their marks.

NOTEBOOK
Sixties Icon, who was the clear form pick, despite conceding 3lb all round, recorded his fourth success from six starts this season. However, there was a real scare for his supporters when he stood still as the stalls opened and lost around five or six lengths. The sluggish start caught his rider by surprise and Dettori suggested afterwards the horse is getting a little wiser as he gets older. His attitude in the race itself could not be faulted, though, and he actually ended up racing a touch keenly by the time he made up the lost ground, certainly showing more enthusiasm that he did at the start. He was still cruising as the field entered the straight and found plenty when asked to eventually draw away, looking a real class act at this level. He will apparently now be aimed at the Breeders' Cup meeting and then head to the Far East for either the Japan Cup or the Hong Kong Cup, before being retired to stud. His connections are not ruling out the Turf at Santa Anita if the race looks like cutting up, but the new $500,000 Marathon contest over 1m4f on a surface not too dissimilar to Polytrack is the more likely option at this stage. He will need to break a lot quicker, but Jeremy Noseda, who has a terrific international record, is unlikely to leave much to chance. (tchd 5-4 and 11-8 in places)
Sugar Ray(IRE), returning from two months off, got a soft lead (just like when winning the Duke of Edinburgh at the royal meeting) in a first-time visor and ran his race, but he was no match for the classy winner. He is probably flattered a touch by the bare result and might not be the easiest to place from now on. His owner has been known to send horses to the US, and this one might find more opportunities out there. (op 9-1 tchd 8-1)
Ajhar(USA) earned a shot at a race like this when breaking the 1m3f course record on the Polytrack at Kempton last time, and his trainer had won four of the last seven renewals, but he came up short. He could only produce the one pace when asked, and undoubtedly would have preferred a better gallop, but it remains to be seen whether he is quite up to this level. (op 11-2 tchd 5-1)
Galactic Star again disappointed and appears to be going the wrong way. (tchd 3-1)
Lion Sands was as disappointing as Galactic Star and is another to have reservations about now. (op 9-1)

6304 JOHN GUEST DIADEM STKS (GROUP 2) — 6f
3:15 (3:17) (Class 1) 3-Y-0+
£56,770 (£21,520; £10,770; £5,370; £2,690; £1,350) **Stalls** Centre

Form — RPR

3020 **1** **King's Apostle (IRE)**[36] 5275 4-9-0 106..................(v[1]) LiamJones 10 116
(W J Haggas) *t.k.h: chsd ldrs: led jst over 1f out: drvn to hold on fnl f* **12/1**

0650 **2** *nk* **Diabolical (USA)**[15] 5891 5-9-0 114.................. LDettori 7 115
(Saeed Bin Suroor) *hld up in midfield: short of room over 2f out: hdwy over 1f out: r.o to press wnr fnl 100yds: jst hld* **11/2**[1]

1330 **3** *nk* **Sir Gerry (USA)**[79] 3922 3-8-12 114.................. JamieSpencer 1 114
(J R Fanshawe) *dwlt: hld up in rr: gd hdwy to chse ldrs over 1f out: r.o* **13/2**[2]

0005 **4** *nk* **Prime Defender**[15] 5891 4-9-0 111.................. WilliamBuick 4 113
(B W Hills) *led at ordinary pce: qcknd tempo over 2f out: rdn and hdd jst over 1f out: kpt on* **12/1**

5430 **5** *hd* **Strike The Deal (USA)**[15] 5891 3-8-12 106..................(v) PhilipRobinson 3 112
(J Noseda) *dwlt: t.k.h and stdd in midfield on stands' side of main gp: rdn to chse ldrs over 1f out: kpt on fnl f* **12/1**

1211 **6** *hd* **Lesson In Humility (IRE)**[15] 5899 3-8-9 103.................. AndrewElliott 14 109
(K R Burke) *led far side pair matching ldrs in main gp: rdn over 1f out: flashed tail: kpt on* **12/1**

0002 **7** *1 ½* **Assertive**[15] 5891 5-9-4 111..................(b) RyanMoore 6 111
(R Hannon) *hld up in rr: rdn and r.o wl fr over 1f out: nrst fin* **15/2**[3]

0104 **8** *shd* **Intrepid Jack**[28] 5553 6-9-0 113.................. GeorgeBaker 5 107
(H Morrison) *in rr of mid-div: effrt and in tch over 1f out: no imp fnl f* **14/1**

5004 **9** *shd* **Dark Missile**[50] 4840 5-8-11 98..................(t) HayleyTurner 13 103
(A M Balding) *trckd ldr in far side pair and gng wl: shkn up over 1f out: one pce* **12/1**

3020 **10** *1 ¾* **Balthazaar's Gift (IRE)**[15] 5891 5-9-0 110..................(p) DaneO'Neill 8 101
(L M Cumani) *towards rr: rdn 2f out: nvr able to chal* **12/1**

0501 **11** *1 ¾* **Edge Closer**[36] 5275 4-9-0 112..................(t) JimmyFortune 2 95
(R Hannon) *w ldr tl wknd wl over 1f out* **9/1**

5020 **12** *¾* **Zidane**[79] 3922 6-9-0 108.................. RobertWinston 9 93
(J R Fanshawe) *hld up in rr: plld way into prom position 1/2-way: wknd over 1f out* **18/1**

0004 **13** *¾* **Dhaular Dhar (IRE)**[1] 6269 6-9-0 100.................. JimCrowley 11 90
(J S Goldie) *mid-div: rdn along and struggling to hold pl whn hmpd ent fnl 2f: n.d after* **25/1**

4220 **14** *1 ½* **Advanced**[8] 6104 5-9-0 104.................. NCallan 12 86
(K A Ryan) *prom to 1/2-way: sn rdn and lost pl* **25/1**

0631 **15** *31* **Elletelle (IRE)**[63] 4467 3-8-9 0.................. KLatham 15 —
(G M Lyons, Ire) *last into stalls but restless ins and rrd bdly: a wl bhd: eased* **16/1**

1m 14.2s (-0.20) **Going Correction** -0.025s/f (Good)
WFA 3 from 4yo+ 2lb **15** Ran SP% **122.1**
Speed ratings (Par 115): **100,99,99,98,98 98,96,96,96,93 91,90,89,87,46**
toteswinger: 1&2 £15.90, 1&3 £16.50, 2&3 £6.80. CSF £77.09 TOTE £15.10: £3.90, £2.60, £2.80; EX 93.20 Trifecta £1093.90 Pool: £1,921.87 - 1.30 winning tickets..
Owner Bernard Kantor **Bred** Wentworth Racing **Trained** Newmarket, Suffolk

FOCUS
In terms of its make-up, this looked well up to its usual standard, but the pace was unusually steady for a sprint. Inevitably there was some congestion, followed by a blanket finish, and if the race was run ten times there might be ten different winners. Not form to put too much faith in, therefore, though the runner-up and fourth have been rated close to their marks in the July Cup, which is arguably the best guide.

NOTEBOOK
King's Apostle(IRE) deserved a decent prize. Making his Group race debut, he tracked Prime Defender, going well, and got first run on Diabolical, who was closing all the way to the line. Maureen Haggas felt the first-time visor helped, as hanging had arguably cost him the race at Goodwood. (op 14-1)
Diabolical(USA) has excellent sprint form on dirt in the States and Dubai, but he is pretty effective on turf, too - some say Ascot's relaid surface suits all-weather horses - and he might have won but for being short of room going to the two-furlong pole. Saeed Bin Suroor said he has never had him better, so we will definitely be seeing more of him. (op 8-1)

Sir Gerry(USA) seems to run his best races away from Newmarket, and he arguably did well to replicate his Golden Jubilee placing having been held up in a steadily run race. He is going in his coat, but has not had much racing this year and he will be back for another sprint here next month. (op 5-1)
Prime Defender was ridden unusually prominently, which turned out a good move the way the race was run. A reproduction of either his July Cup or his Doncaster Sprint Cup running would have given him a great chance here, though, and he continues to frustrate. (op 11-1 tchd 14-1)
Strike The Deal(USA) is finding it tough at three, like so many good sprinting two-year-olds, and this was a fair effort in fifth. (op 16-1)
Lesson In Humility(IRE) led Dark Missile towards the far side in a split away from the main pack, and she kept on despite flashing her tail vigorously.
Assertive, with blinkers back on, was not seeing a lot of daylight near the back of the field, but he ran on well in the closing stages. (op 8-1)
Dark Missile travelled strongly but did not find a lot when she was popped the question.
Balthazaar's Gift(IRE) would have been suited by a stronger pace. (op 11-1)
Zidane needed a stronger pace and pulled his way into contention much too soon. (op 16-1)
Elletelle(IRE) Official explanation: jockey said filly reared and struck him in face as stalls opened

6305 JNB ASSOCIATES NURSERY 7f
3:50 (3:54) (Class 3) 2-Y-O

£6,854 (£2,052; £1,026; £513; £256; £128) **Stalls** Centre

Form RPR
31 **1** **Liberation (IRE)**[17] 5811 2-8-8 **82** RHills 3 104+
(M Johnston) *hld up in tch and a full of running: led wl over 1f out: bolted clr: easily* **10/3**[2]
1 **2** *5* **Secrecy**[17] 5825 2-9-7 **95** PhilipRobinson 9 104+
(M A Jarvis) *stdd s: plld v hrd early and hdwy into midfield after 3f: r.o to go 2nd over 1f out: no ch w wnr* **15/8**[1]
21 **3** *5* **Good Again**[65] 4359 2-8-9 **83** HayleyTurner 11 78
(G A Butler) *mid-div: effrt over 2f out: no imp tl kpt on past btn horses to take 3rd nr fin* **12/1**
3225 **4** *nk* **River Dee (IRE)**[24] 5632 2-7-13 **73** JimmyQuinn 7 67
(Miss Amy Weaver) *bhd: styd on u.p fr over 1f out to dispute modest 3rd ins fnl f* **10/1**
2141 **5** *1* **Johnmanderville**[9] 6082 2-8-4 **78** AndrewElliott 2 70
(K R Burke) *led: set modest pce tl increased tempo after 3f: hdd over 2f out: wknd over 1f out* **14/1**
6032 **6** *2 ¾* **Mister Dee Bee (IRE)**[18] 5791 2-8-7 **81** WilliamBuick 6 66
(B W Hills) *mid-div: rdn along over 4f out: struggling towards rr fr 1/2-way: kpt on past btn horses fnl f* **8/1**
030 **7** *1* **Sweet Possession (USA)**[50] 4868 2-8-3 **77** RichardThomas 10 59
(A P Jarvis) *trckd ldrs: hrd rdn over 2f out: wknd over 1f out* **50/1**
0313 **8** *½* **Cook's Endeavour (USA)**[18] 5791 2-8-5 **79** DO'Donohoe 8 60
(K A Ryan) *prom tl 1/2-way: sn rdn and btn* **6/1**[3]
6420 **9** *nk* **Granski (IRE)**[29] 5511 2-7-12 **72** FrankieMcDonald 13 52
(R Hannon) *stdd s: plld hrd in rr early: sme hdwy u.p over 2f out: sn wknd* **33/1**
001 **10** *nk* **My Kingdom (IRE)**[25] 5599 2-8-4 **78** (t) GregFairley 12 58
(H Morrison) *prom: led over 2f out tl wl over 1f out: sn wknd* **16/1**
0514 **11** *4 ½* **Imperial Guest**[20] 5756 2-9-0 **88** RyanMoore 4 56
(G G Margarson) *sn towards rr: n.d fnl 3f* **33/1**
524 **12** *½* **Layer Cake**[29] 5497 2-8-1 **75** LiamJones 1 42
(J W Hills) *prom 3f: sn lost pl: no ch whn hung rt fnl 2f* **33/1**

1m 27.81s (-0.19) **Going Correction** -0.025s/f (Good) **12** Ran SP% **123.4**
Speed ratings (Par 99): **100,94,88,88,87 83,82,82,81,81 76,75**
toteswinger: 1&2 £2.90, 1&3 £7.50, 2&3 £5.80. CSF £10.13 CT £71.14 TOTE £4.60: £1.80, £1.80, £3.20; EX 12.30 Trifecta £114.30 Pool: £1,272.24 - 8.23 winning tickets..
Owner Sheikh Hamdan Bin Mohammed Al Maktoum **Bred** Epona Bloodstock Ltd **Trained** Middleham Moor, N Yorks

FOCUS
This nursery has been won by some good horses in recent years, including Horris Hill winner Rapscallion, subsequent dual Listed scorer Wise Dennis, and most notably last year by Ibn Khaldun, who went on to land the Group 1 Racing Post Trophy. This looked another really strong race, and the way the first two pulled clear off just an ordinary early gallop suggests they are both pretty smart. They raced up the middle of the track.

NOTEBOOK
Liberation(IRE), whose recent Brighton maiden success was boosted when the runner-up won next time at Goodwood, made a mockery of his official mark of 82 on this switch to nursery company with a taking display, pulling right away from the well-regarded Secrecy, who was in turn well clear of quite a decent-looking field. It has to be noted that he carried his head high in the closing stages, and he also got a little bit warm, but it was probably just immaturity. Whatever the case, he is clearly seriously talented, and the plan now is the Tattersalls Timeform Million at Newmarket on the October 4. In the longer term, it would be no surprise to see him in Godolphin's colours next year. (op 6-1)
Secrecy, who is already a gelding, had to shoulder top weight having been given a mark of 95 after bolting up in a conditions race on soft ground at Doncaster first time up. He was far too keen early on, with the steady early pace very much against him, and he proved no match for Liberation, who was clearly thrown in off 82, but he still came clear of the remainder. There should be more to come provided he settles better in future and time may show this was a very smart effort trying to concede 13lb to the winner. (op 2-1 tchd 9-4)
Good Again, one of only two fillies in the line-up, had been off since winning a course maiden over 6f two months previously, and was well held on her return here, but she will not always run into such decent types. (op 8-1)
River Dee(IRE) is a tough sort and ran an honest race off his light weight. (op 14-1 tchd 16-1)
Johnmanderville could not defy a 4lb rise for his recent Newmarket success, but he remains a decent three-year-old prospect. (tchd 16-1)
Mister Dee Bee(IRE) was below the form he showed when second on his nursery debut at Doncaster, but he confirmed form with the disappointing Cook's Endeavour. (op 13-2)
Cook's Endeavour(USA), a scopey son of Gone West who is entered in the Racing Post Trophy, was one of the first beaten and was well below the form. He got a bit worked up in the stalls and may have lost his race at the start. (tchd 11-2)
Layer Cake Official explanation: jockey said colt hung right

6306 SIS LIVE FENWOLF STKS (LISTED RACE) 2m
4:25 (4:25) (Class 1) 3-Y-O+

£24,978 (£9,468; £4,738; £2,362; £1,183; £594) **Stalls** High

Form RPR
6-31 **1** **Metaphoric (IRE)**[78] 3942 4-9-3 106 (vt) JamieSpencer 3 115+
(M L W Bell) *in tch: outpcd 3f out: rallying whn crowded and nowhere to go wl ins fnl 2f: swtchd to gap on rail over 1f out: qckd through to ld ins fnl f* **4/1**[2]
6032 **2** *1 ¼* **Balkan Knight**[16] 5854 8-9-3 110 GeorgeBaker 5 113
(D R C Elsworth) *hld up in rr: gd hdwy on outer whn hung rt fr over 1f out: led briefly ent fnl f: nt pce of wnr* **13/2**
5536 **3** *¾* **Sagara (USA)**[16] 5854 4-9-3 109 (v[1]) LDettori 2 112
(Saeed Bin Suroor) *chsd ldrs: led over 2f out: edgd rt over 1f out: hdd ent fnl f: one pce* **7/1**
3414 **4** *1 ½* **Sanbuch**[36] 5264 4-9-3 109 (b) DaneO'Neill 6 112+
(L M Cumani) *hld up in 6th: drvn to press ldrs over 2f out: hung rt over 1f out: disputing 3rd and hld whn squeezed for room ins fnl f* **9/2**[3]
3214 **5** *2* **Distinction (IRE)**[59] 4551 9-9-6 112 RyanMoore 7 111
(Sir Michael Stoute) *chsd ldr tl 5f out: disputing 4th and rdn whn carried rt and hmpd over 1f out: snatched up: no ex* **11/4**[1]
0362 **6** *2 ¼* **Petara Bay (IRE)**[36] 5264 4-9-3 108 JimmyFortune 4 105
(T G Mills) *hld up towards rr: effrt over 2f out: disputing fair 5th whn bdly squeezed over 1f out: n.d after* **8/1**
60-6 **7** *4* **Land 'n Stars**[24] 5646 8-9-3 95 PaulDoe 1 100
(Jamie Poulton) *chsd ldng pair: led 3f out tl over 2f out: sn hrd rdn and wknd* **50/1**
3215 **8** *36* **Tungsten Strike (USA)**[14] 5956 7-9-6 111 (p) JimCrowley 8 60
(Mrs A J Perrett) *led: set gd pce: hdd 3f out: sn wknd* **8/1**

3m 26.9s (-5.70) **Going Correction** -0.025s/f (Good) **8** Ran SP% **114.9**
Speed ratings (Par 111): **111,110,110,109,108 107,105,87**
toteswinger: 1&2 £5.60, 1&3 £6.30, 2&3 £9.00. CSF £30.17 TOTE £5.50: £1.80, £2.30, £2.10; EX 28.70 Trifecta £169.10 Pool: £1,024.23 - 4.48 winning tickets..
Owner The Royal Ascot Racing Club **Bred** Gerrardstown House Stud **Trained** Newmarket, Suffolk
■ Stewards' Enquiry : George Baker one-day ban: careless riding (Oct 12); two-day ban: careless riding (Oct 13-14)
Dane O'Neill three-day ban: careless riding (Oct 12-14)

FOCUS
A fairly competitive Listed contest, but it was a rather messy race. The pace was good for much of the way thanks to Tungsten Strike, but that one was beaten before the final turn, and as a result the field bunched up at the top of the straight. The form is rated around the winner and third.

NOTEBOOK
Metaphoric(IRE), although trapped towards the inside early in the straight, was only around three lengths off the lead as the field bunched up, and his rider excelled in forcing his mount through some tight gaps. He was ultimately a clever winner and has returned from a spell hurdling last winter as good as ever, with this success a follow-up from his course-and-distance handicap victory gained off a mark of 100 in July. (op 5-1 tchd 11-2)
Balkan Knight was kidded into contention down the outside in the straight despite looking far from keen. However, he continually edged right and had no answer when the winner burst through. (op 15-2 tchd 8-1)
Sagara(USA) was produced with every chance in a first-time visor, but he did very little once in front and did not impress with his attitude. (op 8-1)
Sanbuch had every chance out wide early in the straight, but he edged right and could only plug on at the one pace. Still, he might have been third had he not been squeezed up inside the final furlong. (op 5-1)
Distinction(IRE) was the chief sufferer when the field bunched at the top of the straight as he was stuck in the middle of the pack and had nowhere to go just as Moore looked anxious to make use of the horse's stamina. He was still trying to keep on when short of room over a furlong out, and it was game over from that point. (op 3-1)
Petara Bay(IRE) was hampered around a furlong and a half out when trying to stay on and is better than he showed. (op 7-1)
Land 'n Stars tried to get away turning for home, but he basically wasn't good enough. (op 33-1)

6307 BRUNSWICK H'CAP 1m (S)
5:00 (5:01) (Class 2) (0-100,99) 3-Y-O+

£12,462 (£3,732; £1,866; £934; £466; £234) **Stalls** Centre

Form RPR
4122 **1** **Isphahan**[2] 6250 5-8-3 **85** oh7 DavidProbert[(5)] 8 96
(A M Balding) *prom in chsng gp: clsd on clr ldr and disp ld over 2f out: led ent fnl f: rdn out* **4/1**[2]
1401 **2** *1 ¾* **Curzon Prince (IRE)**[45] 5033 4-8-12 **92** JackMitchell[(3)] 4 99
(C F Wall) *swtg: hld up in 4th: hdwy to dispute ld over 2f out: outpcd by wnr fnl f* **4/1**[2]
142 **3** *4 ½* **Gold Sovereign (IRE)**[15] 5896 4-9-8 **99** LDettori 7 95
(Saeed Bin Suroor) *hld up in midfield: effrt over 2f out: one pce* **9/4**[1]
0430 **4** *½* **Extraterrestrial**[1] 6269 4-9-0 **91** (p) RobertWinston 3 86
(R A Fahey) *hld up in rr: hdwy on bit 3f out: rdn 2f out: little rspnse* **11/2**[3]
0004 **5** *½* **Danehillsundance (IRE)**[30] 5470 4-8-8 **85** oh2 WilliamBuick 6 79
(S Parr) *prom in chsng gp: wnt 10 l 2nd after 3f: clsd on ldr over 2f out: sn outpcd* **10/1**
606 **6** *6* **Ivory Lace**[23] 5683 7-8-8 **85** oh12 JimCrowley 9 65
(S Woodman) *hld up in rr: sme hdwy 3f out: sn rdn and no imp* **25/1**
7 *4* **Zebra Crossing (SAF)**[232] 7-9-5 **96** JamesDoyle 5 67
(N L Bruss) *dwlt: bhd: rdn and n.d fnl 3f* **25/1**
2026 **8** *2 ½* **Mesbaah (IRE)**[32] 5405 4-8-8 **85** oh1 (b) JamieMoriarty 1 50
(R A Fahey) *swtg: led: sn 10l clr: c bk to others and hdd over 2f out: sn bhd* **16/1**
0510 **9** *21* **Mut'Ab (USA)**[15] 5907 3-8-11 **92** RyanMoore 2 9
(C E Brittain) *chsd clr ldr 3f: grad lost pl: bhd fnl 3f* **14/1**

1m 41.46s (0.86) **Going Correction** -0.025s/f (Good)
WFA 3 from 4yo+ 4lb **9** Ran SP% **115.5**
Speed ratings (Par 109): **94,92,87,87,86 80,76,74,53**
toteswinger: 1&2 £3.30, 1&3 £2.20, 2&3 £3.00. CSF £20.42 CT £43.12 TOTE £5.20: £1.70, £1.80, £1.50; EX 19.90 Trifecta £35.80 Pool: £1,134.43 - 23.41 winning tickets. Place 6 £35.13, Place 5 £12.50..
Owner Mohamad Rafique **Bred** J H Wall **Trained** Kingsclere, Hants

FOCUS
This looked like a weak handicap for the grade and it was won by a horse who, although in form and progressive, was out of the handicap. They went a very strong pace up the middle of the track, with Mesbaah, who was on his toes and got warm, tearing off into a clear lead before finishing tired. The form has been taken at face value, but it remains to be seen how it works out.

NOTEBOOK
Isphahan, although 7lb out of the weights, was no doubt due for a rise following his short-head second at Haydock two days earlier. He continued his terrific run of form with a decisive success, but this was a soft race for the level and things will be a lot harder once he is reassessed. (op 9-2)
Curzon Prince(IRE) pulled clear of the remainder, despite getting warm beforehand and racing over a trip probably short of his best on ground plenty quick enough. There should be more to come when he is stepped back up in trip, and more give underfoot or Polytrack should also help. (op 11-2)
Gold Sovereign(IRE) was a bit disappointing and has something to prove now. (op 11-4)
Extraterrestrial, down the field in the big 7f handicap here the day before, had the race teed up for him by his stablemate, but he did not look to go through with his effort. (op 9-2)
Danehillsundance(IRE) was on a good mark, even from 2lb out of the handicap, but he could not take advantage. (op 17-2 tchd 8-1)
T/Jkpt: Not won. T/Plt: £84.50 to a £1 stake. Pool: £133,947.55. 1,156.10 winning tickets.
T/Qpdt: £19.80 to a £1 stake. Pool: £6,585.80. 245.70 winning tickets. LM

5965

MUSSELBURGH (R-H)

Sunday, September 28

OFFICIAL GOING: Good (good to soft in places on straight course)

Wind: Light, against Weather: Sunny periods

6308 ROYAL SCOTS CUP H'CAP 5f

2:30 (2:31) (Class 6) (0-65,66) 3-Y-O **£2,590** (£770; £385; £192) **Stalls** Low

Form RPR

6001 **1** **Todber**[15] 5911 3-9-5 **60**.....................(v) RichardMullen 13 68
(M P Tregoning) *qckly away and sn led: rdn wl over 1f out: drvn ins fnl f: edgd rt towards fin: hld on gamely* **9/2**[1]

6034 **2** *nse* **Tanley**[15] 5911 3-8-9 **50**.....................(p) PJMcDonald 7 58
(J F Coupland) *in midfield: gd hdwy 2f out: rdn to chse wnr and hung lft ent fnl f: sn drvn and ev ch: nt qckn nr fin* **12/1**

-602 **3** *2* **Royal Degree**[36] 5261 3-9-8 **63**.....................(t) TomEaves 5 64
(B Smart) *towards rr: hdwy 1/2-way: effrt and n.m.r over 1f out: swtchd rt and rdn ent fnl f: kpt on* **9/2**[1]

4232 **4** *2 1/4* **Forrest Star**[57] 4632 3-9-3 **58**..................... TonyHamilton 4 51
(Miss L A Perratt) *prom: effrt over 1f out: sn rdn and kpt on same pce* **8/1**[3]

1200 **5** *3/4* **Andrasta**[7] 6150 3-8-13 **59**..................... SladeO'Hara(5) 11 49
(A Berry) *towards rr: hdwy on outer 2f out: sn rdn and kpt on same pce appr fnl f* **14/1**

230 **6** *nse* **Stoneacre Chris (USA)**[23] 5679 3-8-4 **50**..................... KellyHarrison(5) 1 40
(Peter Grayson) *dwlt: hdwy 1/2-way: n.m.r and swtchd rt over 1f out: kpt on ins fnl f* **11/1**

4165 **7** *shd* **Dalarossie**[32] 5393 3-9-9 **64**..................... DavidAllan 3 54
(E J Alston) *chsd ldrs: rdn along 2f out: no hdwy* **8/1**[3]

0601 **8** *4 1/2* **Ingleby Star (IRE)**[4] 6218 3-9-11 **66** 6ex.....................(b) PaulFessey 12 39
(T D Barron) *sn cl up: effrt and ev ch 2f out: sn rdn and wknd over 1f out* **5/1**[2]

0000 **9** *1 1/2* **Rascasse**[7] 6150 3-8-4 **48**..................... AndrewMullen(3) 8 16
(Bruce Hellier) *s.i.s: a in rr* **66/1**

2003 **10** *1/2* **Handsinthemist (IRE)**[15] 5911 3-8-9 **50**.....................(p) PaulHanagan 9 16
(P T Midgley) *cl up: rdn along wl over 2f out: sn wknd* **20/1**

0624 **11** *22* **Mystickhill (IRE)**[3] 6224 3-9-0 **58**..................... TolleyDean(3) 10 —
(J Balding) *cl up: rdn 2f out: sn wknd* **9/1**

61.28 secs (0.88) **Going Correction** +0.10s/f (Good) **11 Ran SP% 114.2**

Speed ratings (Par 99): **96,95,92,89,87 87,87,80,78,77 42**

toteswinger: 1&2 £17.10, 1&3 £4.60, 2&3 £14.00. CSF £57.02 CT £259.04 TOTE £4.50: £2.30, £3.80, £2.00; EX 59.30.

Owner Major & Mrs R B Kennard And Partner **Bred** Stowell Hill Ltd & Major & Mrs R B Kennard **Trained** Lambourn, Berks

FOCUS

Rain the previous day but a bright fine day and the ground rode just on the easy side of good. A low-grade sprint handicap and the form looks sound rated around the placed horses.

Mystickhill(IRE) Official explanation: jockey said filly ran flat

6309 NVT GROUP (S) STKS 1m 4f

3:05 (3:05) (Class 6) 3-Y-O+ **£1,942** (£578; £288; £144) **Stalls** High

Form RPR

3046 **1** **Jane Of Arc (FR)**[5] 6185 4-8-8 50.....................(p) KellyHarrison(5) 9 57
(J S Goldie) *a.p: effrt to ld over 2f out: sn rdn: clr appr fnl f: styd on* **3/1**[1]

0254 **2** *4* **Court Of Appeal**[8] 6115 11-9-3 56.....................(tp) LanceBetts(7) 3 62
(B Ellison) *a.p: hdwy to ld 3f out: rdn and hdd over 2f out: sn drvn and kpt on same pce* **3/1**[1]

0065 **3** *3* **Rehearsal**[43] 4075 7-9-4 65..................... PaulHanagan 7 51
(L Lungo) *in tch on inner: hdwy 3f out: rdn to chse ldng pair over 2f out: sn no imp* **7/2**[2]

00-0 **4** *1 1/4* **Shekan Star**[24] 5637 6-8-13 46..................... TomEaves 12 44
(K G Reveley) *hld up in rr: hdwy on inner 3f out: rdn 2f out: kpt on appr fnl f: nrst fin* **10/1**

3004 **5** *4 1/2* **Lady Killer Queen**[5] 6185 4-8-13 50.....................(v) DavidAllan 8 37
(D Carroll) *in tch: hdwy 4f out: rdn along to chse ldrs 3f out: drvn and no imp fnl 2f* **9/2**[3]

10 **6** *1* **Spiders Star**[33] 5385 5-9-5 45..................... MHNaughton 6 41
(Miss Kate Milligan) *hld up: hdwy 1/2-way: chsd ldrs over 3f out: sn rdn and wknd fnl 2f* **33/1**

0446 **7** *nse* **Stravonian**[9] 6071 8-8-13 32..................... GaryBartley(5) 1 40
(D A Nolan) *s.i.s and in rr: hdwy on outer over 2f out: sn rdn and no imp* **50/1**

0 **8** *shd* **Treetops Hotel (IRE)**[87] 3642 9-9-4 47..................... TonyHamilton 5 40
(L R James) *a in rr* **20/1**

00 **9** *1 3/4* **Karaburan (GER)**[158] 1305 4-9-1 45..................... NeilBrown(3) 2 37
(P Monteith) *in tch: pushed along and lost pl 1/2-way: sn bhd* **80/1**

0550 **10** *2 1/2* **Notnowrosie (IRE)**[24] 5637 3-8-2 45..................... AndrewMullen(3) 11 28
(A G Foster) *led: rdn along 4f out: hdd 3f out and sn wknd* **33/1**

0560 **11** *1/2* **Pugnacity**[5] 6185 4-8-9 44 ow1..................... SladeO'Hara(5) 10 28
(A Berry) *prom: rdn along 4f out: sn wknd* **33/1**

2m 38.24s (-1.46) **Going Correction** +0.05s/f (Good)

WFA 3 from 4yo+ 8lb **11 Ran SP% 116.3**

Speed ratings (Par 101): **106,103,101,100,97 96,96,96,95,93 93**

toteswinger: 1&2 £3.40, 1&3 £3.80, 2&3 £2.60. CSF £11.16 TOTE £4.30: £1.60, £1.40, £1.80; EX 11.70.There was no bid for the winner.

Owner C P F Racing **Bred** Paul-Henry Locke & Jill Locke **Trained** Uplawmoor, E Renfrews

FOCUS

A non-handicap seller run at a sound pace and not a race to be positive about despite the first two running to this year's form.

Jane Of Arc(FR) Official explanation: trainer said, regarding apparent improvement in form, that the filly was better suited by the faster ground.

6310 RSP CONSULTING ENGINEERS H'CAP 5f

3:35 (3:36) (Class 6) (0-65,65) 4-Y-O+ **£2,590** (£770; £385; £192) **Stalls** Low

Form RPR

0600 **1** **Spirit Of Coniston**[67] 4293 5-8-1 **51** oh2..................... DuranFentiman(3) 9 63
(P T Midgley) *cl up: rdn to ld 1f out: drvn ins fnl f and kpt on wl towards fin* **16/1**

0250 **2** *1* **Raccoon (IRE)**[13] 5970 8-9-0 **61**..................... PJMcDonald 4 69
(Mrs R A Carr) *trckd ldng pair: effrt and n.m.r wl over 1f out: swtchd rt and rdn to chal ins fnl f: ev ch tl drvn and nt qckn towards fin* **6/1**[2]

4001 **3** *1/2* **Grimes Faith**[10] 6039 5-8-11 **63** ow1.....................(p) FrederikTylicki(5) 1 69
(K A Ryan) *trckd ldrs: effrt whn n.m.r over 1f out: swtchd rt and rdn ent fnl f: styd on wl* **10/3**[1]

2502 **4** *nk* **Lambency (IRE)**[13] 5970 5-8-3 **55**..................... KellyHarrison(5) 6 60
(J S Goldie) *wnt lft s: sn outpcd and pushed along in rr: hdwy 2f out: rdn and n.m.r over 1f out: kpt on u.p ins fnl f* **8/1**

0543 **5** *1/2* **Botham (USA)**[13] 5970 4-8-4 **51** oh1..................... JoeFanning 7 54
(J S Goldie) *hmpd s: in midfield: hdwy 2f out: rdn and n.m.r over 1f out: kpt on u.p ins fnl f* **7/1**[3]

3400 **6** *1 1/4* **Never Without Me**[6] 6159 8-8-8 **58** ow1..................... NeilBrown(3) 8 57
(J F Coupland) *chsd ldrs: hdwy and ch 2f out tl rdn and wknd appr fnl f* **14/1**

0-06 **7** *hd* **Jadan (IRE)**[10] 6039 7-8-4 **51** oh3.....................(p) AdrianTNicholls 5 49
(E J Alston) *sn led: rdn along wl over 1f out: drvn and hdd 1f out: wknd ins fnl f* **14/1**

2506 **8** *nk* **Fern House (IRE)**[7] 6153 6-8-1 **51** oh3..................... AndrewMullen(3) 3 48
(Bruce Hellier) *s.i.s and in rr: hdwy to chse ldrs after 1 1/2f: rdn wl over 1f out and sn wknd* **12/1**

0001 **9** *5* **Yungaburra (IRE)**[8] 6137 4-9-1 **65**.....................(t) TolleyDean(3) 10 44
(S Parr) *hld up: effrt over 2f out: sn rdn: edgd lft and wknd* **7/1**[3]

4400 **10** *1* **Howards Prince**[7] 6153 5-8-6 **53** oh6 ow2..................... PatrickMathers 13 28
(D A Nolan) *a in rr* **50/1**

1600 **11** *1* **Optical Illusion (USA)**[30] 5455 4-8-11 **58**.....................(p) PaulHanagan 14 30
(R A Fahey) *in tch on outer: rdn along 2f out and sn wknd* **8/1**

/050 **12** *1 1/4* **She Who Dares Wins**[87] 3638 8-7-11 **51** oh6..................... JamieKyne(7) 11 18
(L R James) *cl up: rdn 2f out: sn wknd* **50/1**

5500 **13** *nk* **Seafield Towers**[7] 6153 8-8-4 **58** oh6 ow7..................... LanceBetts(7) 12 24
(D A Nolan) *chsd ldrs: rdn along 1/2-way: sn wknd* **66/1**

60.87 secs (0.47) **Going Correction** +0.10s/f (Good) **13 Ran SP% 116.9**

Speed ratings (Par 101): **100,98,97,97,96 94,94,93,85,83 82,80,79**

toteswinger: 1&2 £16.70, 1&3 £20.80, 2&3 £6.60. CSF £106.38 CT £417.49 TOTE £19.90: £5.70, £2.10, £1.80; EX 129.90.

Owner P O'Gara & N Kelly **Bred** Green Square Racing **Trained** Westow, N Yorks

FOCUS

Another low-grade sprint handicap run in a slightly quicker time than the opener and sound form with the three in the frame behind the winner close to their marks. Seven of the 13 runners had to carry more than their correct handicap mark.

Spirit Of Coniston Official explanation: trainer said, regarding apparent improvement in form, gelding had returned in better form after a two-month break

6311 EBF/TOM AND LESLEY MCGREGOR FILLIES' H'CAP 1m

4:10 (4:10) (Class 3) (0-95,81) 3-Y-O+ **£10,592** (£3,172; £1,586; £793; £396) **Stalls** High

Form RPR

0002 **1** **Debonnaire**[35] 5317 3-9-2 **76**..................... JoeFanning 3 79
(M Johnston) *led: rdn along over 2f out: hdd over 1f out: drvn whn n.m.r and bmpd ins fnl f: rallied wl to ld last 75yds* **13/2**

361 **2** *nk* **Hall Hee (IRE)**[29] 5491 3-9-4 **78**..................... RichardMullen 2 80
(M P Tregoning) *t.k.h: sn prom: effrt to chal wl over 2f out: rdn to ld over 1f out: drvn and edgd rt ins fnl f: hdd and no ex last 75yds* **1/1**[1]

4111 **3** *hd* **Talk Of Saafend (IRE)**[7] 6152 3-9-4 **81** 6ex..................... NeilBrown(3) 4 83
(P Monteith) *hld up in rr: hdwy 2f out: swtchd lft and rdn over 1f out: styd on strly ins fnl f* **4/1**[2]

1550 **4** *3 1/4* **Hula Ballew**[10] 6052 8-9-8 **78**..................... TomEaves 5 72
(M Dods) *trckd ldrs on inner: effrt over 2f out: rdn along wl over 1f out: sn one pce* **10/1**

4503 **5** *1 1/4* **Goodbye**[10] 6053 4-9-11 **81**..................... PJMcDonald 1 73
(G A Swinbank) *t.k.h: chsd ldng pair: effrt over 2f out: sn rdn and edgd rt over 1f out: wknd* **9/2**[3]

1m 42.86s (1.66) **Going Correction** +0.05s/f (Good)

WFA 3 from 4yo+ 4lb **5 Ran SP% 110.6**

Speed ratings (Par 104): **93,92,92,89,88**

CSF £13.76 TOTE £10.20: £1.70, £1.40; EX 17.40.

Owner Ali Saeed **Bred** Gainsborough Stud Management Ltd **Trained** Middleham Moor, N Yorks

FOCUS

A valuable fillies-only handicap but the top weight's rating was a stone below the race ceiling. The form is unconvincing despite the placed horses running close to their marks.

NOTEBOOK

Debonnaire, back to form when narrowly denied at Yarmouth last time, benefited from a typically inspired Fanning front-running ride. She slowed the pace in front until kicking for home three furlongs out. After her measure had looked to be taken she came out best in a bumping match and forced her head back in front where is really mattered. (op 5-1 tchd 7-1)

Hall Hee(IRE), off the mark at the third attempt on decent ground at Bath, took a keen hold due to the lack of pace on her handicap debut. She travelled supremely well and looked nailed on when going half a length up over a furlong out. Her inexperience showed and she edged in on the winner on her inside, the pair making contact. Just missing out in the end, this will have taught her plenty and she should gain compensation. (op 6-4)

Talk Of Saafend(IRE), winner of four claiming races this year, shouldered a 6lb penalty for her success at Hamilton after which she was claimed for £25,000. She did not settle quite as well as usual and, after being caught flat footed, came with a late dash and would have got there with a bit further to go. Even at this early stage she looks a shrewd claim. She has been schooled over hurdles and may make her debut in that sphere at Kelso on Sunday. (tchd 7-2)

Hula Ballew, slightly off the boil at present, would have appreciated a much stronger gallop and quicker ground. (op 7-1)

Goodbye, drawn wide, saw a lot of daylight and would not settle. When called on for an effort she hung in behind and a strongly-run seven is more her cup of tea. (tchd 11-2)

6312 MUSSELBURGH NEWS CLAIMING STKS 1m 1f

4:45 (4:46) (Class 4) 4-Y-O+ **£5,180** (£1,541; £770; £384) **Stalls** High

Form RPR

2551 **1** **Top Jaro (FR)**[4] 6217 5-8-0 60..................... DuranFentiman(3) 2 66
(Mrs R A Carr) *mde all: set stdy pce: qcknd 3f out: rdn wl over 1f out: drvn ins fnl f and kpt on gamely* **7/1**[3]

1520 **2** *1/2* **Abbondanza (IRE)**[13] 5968 5-9-5 85.....................(p) TomEaves 8 81
(Miss L A Perratt) *plld hrd: trckd wnr: effrt to chal 2f out and sn rdn: drvn ins fnl f: ev ch: nt qckn towards fin* **7/1**[3]

0024 **3** *hd* **Fremen (USA)**[8] 6103 8-9-8 85..................... AdrianTNicholls 11 84
(D Nicholls) *stdd s and hld up in rr: hdwy 3f out: chsd ldrs 2f out: sn rdn and styd on wl fnl furlong: nrst fin* **11/8**[1]

5305 **4** *3/4* **Peruvian Prince (USA)**[12] 5994 6-8-11 75..................... PaulHanagan 9 71
(R A Fahey) *chsd ldrs on inner: effrt over 2f out: rdn wl over 1f out: drvn ent fnl f: n.m.r and kpt on same pce* **11/2**[2]

04/3 **5** *1* **Desert Destiny**[13] 5968 8-8-12 75.....................(p) TonyHamilton 3 70
(C Grant) *hld up: hdwy on outer 3f out: rdn along 2f out: drvn and kpt on same pce ins fnl f* **20/1**

220 **6** *nk* **Nok Twice (IRE)**[5] 6186 7-8-7 65..................... SilvestreDeSousa 4 64
(K A Ryan) *t.k.h: trckd ldrs: effrt 3f out: rdn 2f out: drvn and one pce appr fnl f* **12/1**

0-35 **7** ¾ **Grand Art (IRE)**[121] 2577 4-8-11 70 ow4.................. FrederikTylicki[5] 1 71
(J Howard Johnson) *hld up: hdwy 3f out: rdn to chse ldrs 2f out: sn drvn and wknd over 1f out* **12/1**

3115 **8** *nk* **Lucayan Dancer**[12] 5994 8-8-8 73.................. AdeleRothery[7] 10 70
(D Nicholls) *in tch on inner: hdwy 3f out: rdn 2f out: grad wknd* **10/1**

0505 **9** *nk* **Packers Hill (IRE)**[10] 6056 4-9-3 64.................. PJMcDonald 7 71
(G A Swinbank) *trckd ldrs: pushed along wl over 2f out: grad wknd* **16/1**

1m 53.36s (-1.34) **Going Correction** +0.05s/f (Good) 9 Ran SP% **117.6**
Speed ratings (Par 105): **107,106,106,105,104 104,103,103,103**
toteswinger: 1&2 £5.40, 1&3 £2.80, 2&3 £3.70. CSF £56.12 TOTE £8.00: £2.50, £2.50, £1.20; EX 51.20.
Owner David W Chapman **Bred** Jean Biraben And Robert Labeyrie **Trained** Stillington, N Yorks

FOCUS
A fair claimer run at a sound pace with the winner close to this year's form and the seventh and ninth setting the standard.
Lucayan Dancer Official explanation: jockey said gelding was denied a clear run

6313 EAST LOTHIAN NEWS H'CAP 1m 6f
5:20 (5:20) (Class 4) (0-80,77) 3-Y-0+ **£5,828** (£1,734; £866; £432) **Stalls** High

Form RPR

3331 **1** **Wells Lyrical (IRE)**[73] 4116 3-9-4 77.................. TomEaves 4 85
(B Smart) *trckd ldrs: hdwy 3f out: chal over 2f out: rdn to ld wl over 1f out: drvn ins fnl f and styd on gamely* **3/1**[2]

2224 **2** *nk* **Gordonsville**[8] 6107 5-9-7 73.................. NeilBrown[3] 3 81
(J S Goldie) *hld up in rr: hdwy on outer over 2f out: chal wl over 1f out and sn rdn: drvn ins fnl f and fnd no ex* **5/2**[1]

405 **3** 3 ¼ **Cotton Eyed Joe (IRE)**[53] 4742 7-10-0 77.................. PJMcDonald 7 80
(G A Swinbank) *trckd ldrs: effrt 3f out: rdn over 2f out: drvn and kpt on same pce appr fnl f* **8/1**

1111 **4** *hd* **Let It Be**[32] 5396 7-9-12 75.................. PaulHanagan 5 78
(K G Reveley) *trckd ldr: hdwy over 3f out: rdn over 2f out: drvn and one pce appr fnl f* **13/2**

4316 **5** *nse* **Danzatrice**[13] 5967 6-9-1 69.................. FrederikTylicki[5] 8 72
(C W Thornton) *hld up in rr: hdwy over 2f out: sn rdn and no imp appr fnl f* **9/2**[3]

5134 **6** 2 ¾ **Kyber**[13] 5967 7-8-8 62.................. GaryBartley[5] 6 61
(J S Goldie) *trckd ldr: effrt 3f out: rdn 2f out and sn btn* **11/1**

5602 **7** 3 ¾ **Its Moon (IRE)**[13] 5967 4-8-8 60..................(b) DuranFentiman[3] 1 54
(T D Walford) *led: rdn along 3f out: drvn and hdd wl over 1f out: sn wknd* **8/1**

3m 6.87s (1.57) **Going Correction** +0.05s/f (Good)
WFA 3 from 4yo+ 10lb 7 Ran SP% **115.6**
Speed ratings (Par 105): **97,96,94,94,94 93,91**
toteswinger: 1&2 £2.50, 1&3 £4.60, 2&3 £5.20. CSF £11.24 CT £53.00 TOTE £4.50: £2.10, £2.10; EX 11.80.
Owner M Barber **Bred** Brittas House Stud **Trained** Hambleton, N Yorks

FOCUS
A fair handicap run at a modest pace but sound enough with the four immediately behind the winner close to form.
Kyber Official explanation: jockey said gelding hung left throughout

6314 SCOTTISH RACING YOUR BETTER BET H'CAP 7f 30y
5:50 (5:50) (Class 4) (0-80,80) 3-Y-0+ **£5,180** (£1,541; £770; £384) **Stalls** High

Form RPR

3000 **1** **Minority Report**[9] 6070 8-8-11 77.................. NSLawes[7] 4 85
(D Nicholls) *stdd s: hld up and bhd: hdwy over 2f out: rdn over 1f out: drvn and styd on strly ins fnl f to ld on line* **33/1**

2215 **2** *nse* **Gap Princess (IRE)**[76] 4016 4-8-9 68.................. PaulHanagan 8 76
(R A Fahey) *trckd ldrs on inner: hdwy over 2f out: rdn to chal over 1f out: drvn to ld wl ins fnl f: hdd on line* **16/1**

3414 **3** ½ **Zabeel Tower**[31] 5419 5-9-0 73..................(p) TonyHamilton 7 80
(R Allan) *cl up: effrt 3f out: rdn to ld wl over 1f out: drvn and hdd last 100yds: no ex nr fin* **5/1**[2]

2231 **4** ¾ **Turn Me On (IRE)**[32] 5400 5-8-10 72.................. DuranFentiman[3] 2 77
(T D Walford) *hld up: hdwy on wd outside 2f out: rdn wl over 1f out: styd on strly ins fnl f: nrst fin* **8/1**

0255 **5** *nk* **White Deer (USA)**[21] 5717 4-9-4 77..................(b) AdrianTNicholls 3 81
(D Nicholls) *chsd ldrs on inner: hdwy over 2f out: rdn wl over 1f out: drvn and kpt on same pce ins fnl f* **10/1**

3210 **6** *nk* **Alexander Hurricane (IRE)**[32] 5390 4-9-3 76......... SilvestreDeSousa 11 79
(K A Ryan) *s.i.s and bhd: hdwy 3f out: rdn to chse ldrs over 1f out: kpt on u.p ins fnl f: nrst fin* **11/2**[3]

6350 **7** 1 ¾ **San Jose City (IRE)**[55] 4682 3-9-2 78.................. DNolan 12 76
(D Carroll) *in midfield: effrt over 2f out: sn rdn and kpt on same pce appr fnl f* **16/1**

5020 **8** 1 ¼ **H Harrison (IRE)**[8] 6132 8-9-0 73.................. PatrickMathers 1 68
(I W McInnes) *chsd ldrs: hdwy over 2f out: rdn wl over 1f out and grad wknd* **16/1**

033 **9** 1 ½ **Flores Sea (USA)**[47] 4951 4-8-8 70.................. NeilBrown[3] 14 61
(T D Barron) *sn led: ruidden along wl over 2f out: drvn and hdd over 1f out: sn wknd* **7/2**[1]

6000 **10** *shd* **Malcheek (IRE)**[8] 6125 6-9-2 75.................. DavidAllan 6 66
(T D Easterby) *cl up: rdn along wl over 2f out: sn wknd* **10/1**

3133 **11** *1* **Dream Express (IRE)**[32] 5397 3-9-0 76.................. PJMcDonald 10 64
(M Dods) *trckd ldrs on inner: hdwy 3f out: rdn over 2f out and sn wknd* **10/1**

25-0 **12** 3 ¼ **Call For Liberty (IRE)**[198] 3-9-3 79.................. TomEaves 5 58
(B Smart) *a in rr* **33/1**

2120 **13** *20* **Silent Master (USA)**[11] 6021 3-9-4 80.................. JoeFanning 13 5
(M Johnston) *a towards rr* **14/1**

1m 28.99s (-1.31) **Going Correction** +0.05s/f (Good)
WFA 3 from 4yo+ 3lb 13 Ran SP% **122.9**
Speed ratings (Par 105): **109,108,108,107,107 106,104,103,101,101 100,96,73**
toteswinger: 1&2 £66.00, 1&3 £49.80, 2&3 £13.50. CSF £502.50 CT £3088.31 TOTE £29.50: £8.10, £4.80, £2.90; EX 831.00 Place 6 £7.41, Place 5 £3.85..
Owner Dandy Nicholls Racing Club **Bred** Fittocks Stud **Trained** Sessay, N Yorks

FOCUS
A fair handicap and a fast and furious gallop with a large blanket covering the first six home at the line. The form is sound with the placed horses close to their marks.
Minority Report Official explanation: trainer had no explanation for the apparent improvement in form.
Flores Sea(USA) Official explanation: jockey said gelding hung right-handed throughout
T/Plt: £24.50 to a £1 stake. Pool: £59,149.79. 1,756.42 winning tickets. T/Qpdt: £12.00 to a £1 stake. Pool: £3,171.50. 195.10 winning tickets. JR

5943 CURRAGH (R-H)
Sunday, September 28

OFFICIAL GOING: Yielding

6315a WATERFORD TESTIMONIAL STKS (LISTED RACE) 6f
1:50 (1:52) 3-Y-0+ **£23,933** (£7,022; £3,345; £1,139)

RPR

1 **Le Cadre Noir (IRE)**[70] 4223 4-9-3 107..................(b[1]) PJSmullen 11 102
(D K Weld, Ire) *dwlt: hld up in tch: prog into 4th 1/2-way: led 1 1/2f out: kpt on wl ins fnl f: comf* **7/1**[2]

2 ¾ **Snaefell (IRE)**[15] 5922 4-9-8 108.................. RPCleary 2 105
(M Halford, Ire) *hld up towards rr: hdwy on outer 1 1/2f out: 3rd under 1f out: kpt on u.p* **8/1**[3]

3 *shd* **Benbaun (IRE)**[18] 5793 7-9-3..................(b) FMBerry 6 100+
(M J Wallace, Australia) *prom on stands' rail: 2nd 1/2-way: disp ld 2f out: hdd 1 1/2f out: kpt on u.p ins fnl f* **7/2**[1]

4 ½ **Gist (IRE)**[9] 6095 5-9-0 77..................(b) NGMcCullagh 8 95
(W J Martin, Ire) *hld up in rr: hdwy on outer over 1f out: 4th and r.o wl fnl 100yds: nvr nrr* **66/1**

5 1 ¾ **Aleagueoftheirown (IRE)**[15] 5922 4-9-0 104..................(p) JAHeffernan 12 90
(David Wachman, Ire) *chsd ldrs: 6th 1/2-way: 4th and rdn under 2f out: no imp fr over 1f out* **16/1**

6 ½ **Senor Benny (USA)**[15] 5922 9-9-3 103.................. DPMcDonogh 7 91
(M McDonagh, Ire) *chsd ldrs: 5th 1/2-way: no imp fr under 2f out: kpt on same pce* **16/1**

7 *shd* **Impossible Dream (IRE)**[21] 5731 4-9-3 94.................. RMBurke 9 91
(A Kinsella, Ire) *mid-div: 8th and drvn along bef 1/2-way: kpt on same pce fr 2f out* **16/1**

8 *2* **Miranda's Girl (IRE)**[14] 5950 3-8-12 85..................(p) MCHussey 5 82
(Thomas Cleary, Ire) *chsd ldrs: rdn and no imp fr 2f out: 8th and no ex whn short of room and eased ins fnl f* **33/1**

9 ½ **Three Rocks (IRE)**[29] 5514 3-9-1.................. KJManning 10 84
(J S Bolger, Ire) *prom: 2nd appr 1/2-way: wknd fr 2f out* **9/1**

10 1 ¼ **Aine (IRE)**[91] 3532 3-8-12 100.................. WMLordan 1 77
(T Stack, Ire) *towards rr: no ex fr under 2f out* **8/1**[3]

11 1 ¾ **Domingues**[331] 6631 3-9-1 108.................. CDHayes 13 75
(Edward Lynam, Ire) *led: jnd after 1/2-way: hdd & wknd 2f out* **20/1**

12 1 ¾ **Bett's Spirit (IRE)**[8] 6141 3-8-12 95.................. MJKinane 3 66
(M J Grassick, Ire) *trckd ldrs on stands' rail: 4th bef 1/2-way: no ex fr over 2f out* **25/1**

U **Dohasa (IRE)**[44] 5081 3-9-1 111.................. JMurtagh 4 —
(G M Lyons, Ire) *fly j. and uns rdr leaving stalls* **7/2**[1]

1m 13.9s (-0.60) **Going Correction** +0.125s/f (Good)
WFA 3 from 4yo+ 2lb 13 Ran SP% **119.9**
Speed ratings: **109,108,107,107,104 104,104,101,100,99 96,94,—**
CSF £59.87 TOTE £9.10: £2.80, £3.70, £1.70; DF 65.10.
Owner Riccardo Angioli **Bred** Deni Srl **Trained** The Curragh, Co Kildare

FOCUS
Not reliable form, with the 77-rated Gist finishing close up in fourth.

NOTEBOOK
Le Cadre Noir(IRE), a former Italian-trained Group 3 winner, was blinkered for the first time in his career and it contributed to him registering his seventh career win and his first since arriving in Ireland. His trainer admitted afterwards the ease in the ground was another significant plus after the four-year-old crept closer to seize the initiative a furlong and a half from home and kept on well under pressure. (op 8/1)
Snaefell(IRE) had shown plenty of ability in testing ground notably when taking a Group 3 contest at Leopardstown last month. This ground was officially yielding with some riders describing it as dead but to his credit, despite not having underfoot conditions in his favour, he kept on under pressure to snatch second. (op 7/1)
Benbaun(IRE) was fancied to record his first win this year back on his favourite track. The six-time winner at this course, five of those in Group races, had no penalty for his Group 1 win in last year's Abbaye but he struggled in this ground after making headway up the near rail when asked for more. (op 3/1)
Dohasa(IRE) Official explanation: jockey said gelding jumped high, lost his balance and unseated him just after stalls opened

6316a JUDDMONTE BERESFORD STKS (GROUP 2) 1m
2:20 (2:20) 2-Y-O **£59,742** (£17,463; £8,272; £2,757)

RPR

1 **Sea The Stars (IRE)**[42] 5129 2-9-1.................. MJKinane 5 106
(John M Oxx, Ire) *trckd ldrs: 4th 1/2-way: 3rd and hdwy under 1 1/2f out: sn chal: led under 1f out: kpt on wl u.p* **7/4**[2]

2 ½ **Mourayan (IRE)**[74] 4096 2-9-1.................. FMBerry 1 105
(John M Oxx, Ire) *settled 2nd: chal st: led over 2f out: hdd under 1f out: kpt on u.p* **10/1**

3 *shd* **Masterofthehorse (IRE)**[54] 4714 2-9-1.................. JMurtagh 3 105
(A P O'Brien, Ire) *hld up in rr: 5th and prog on outer over 2f out: cl 4th 1f out: kpt on u.p* **11/8**[1]

4 *nk* **Recharge (IRE)**[29] 5523 2-9-1.................. CDHayes 2 104
(Kevin Prendergast, Ire) *trckd ldrs: 3rd 1/2-way: 4th early st: rdn 2f out: cl 3rd and chal 1f out: kpt on same pce* **12/1**

5 *3* **Hail Caesar (IRE)**[70] 4228 2-9-1.................. JAHeffernan 6 97
(A P O'Brien, Ire) *hld up towards rr: last early st: no imp fr under 2f out: one pce* **7/1**[3]

6 3 ½ **Sawtooth Mountain (USA)**[36] 5296 2-9-1 101.................. PJSmullen 4 93+
(A P O'Brien, Ire) *led: rdn and strly pressed ent st: hdd over 2f out: sn wknd* **20/1**

1m 42.3s (0.40) **Going Correction** +0.125s/f (Good) 6 Ran SP% **112.5**
Speed ratings: **103,102,102,102,99 95**
CSF £18.93 TOTE £3.10: £1.30, £3.50; DF 13.30.
Owner Christopher Tsui **Bred** Sunderland Holdings **Trained** Currabeg, Co Kildare

FOCUS
Aside from Jessica Harrington's intervention last season, Aidan O'Brien and John Oxx have monopolised this race over the past decade. Not surprisingly, O'Brien has been dominant, but Oxx got one back here with Sea The Stars following the path taken by Alamshar in 2002 and Azamour the following year. For good measure, the stable also provided the runner-up.

NOTEBOOK
Sea The Stars(IRE) got on top through the final furlong to win in the style of a smart colt. This was certainly not an extravagant victory, but Oxx is not in the habit of rushing his horses, and there is good reason to believe that the son of Cape Cross will mature into a very smart middle-distance performer. As a half-brother to Galileo, there is a great deal to look forward to, and it was no surprise to learn that he is now finished for the season. (op 7/4 tchd 2/1)

Mourayan(IRE) has evidently done well since his winning debut in a Leopardstown that got a further boost later on when Gan Amhras took second place behind Soul City. He is out of a mare that graduated from handicap company to win the Prix Royallieu, and is another potentially top-class prospect for next season.

Masterofthehorse(IRE) had won his maiden at prohibitive odds, and this was a big step up in the circumstances. The stable's powerful record in this race was probably the main factor in ensuring that he was sent off favourite. After being held up in a race in which one of his stablemates supplied the pace, he started to improve his position on the outside from over two furlongs out, and stuck to his task without picking up as well might have been expected. To be fair, his status as a brother to Alexandrova indicates that he may already need further than this, outweighing the significance of his relationship to speedy juvenile Magical Romance. (op 11/8 tchd 6/4)

Recharge(IRE), the odd-man-out in the context of the Oxx/O'Brien battle, ran a terrific race for Kevin Prendergast. He is bred to be smart (his dam Rebelline won at the Curragh in every category through from Listed to Group 1) and though there may be a temptation to use his proximity to question the form on the basis that his maiden was achieved in fairly modest company at Killarney, he could prove a very capable sort. (op 14/1)

Hail Caesar(IRE) did not show more dash here, never threatening to get seriously involved. (op 6/1)

Sawtooth Mountain(USA) dropped away after making the running.

6317a PARKNASILLA HOTEL GOFFS (C & G) MILLION — 7f

2:55 (2:57) 2-Y-O

£724,264 (£209,558; £99,264; £47,794; £22,794; £6,617)

RPR

1 — **Soul City (IRE)**[21] 5739 2-9-0 .... RichardHughes 17 — 102
(R Hannon) *mde virtually all: strly pressed fr 1 1/2f out: kpt on wl u.p ins fnl f* **5/2**[1]

2 ½ **Gan Amhras (IRE)**[67] 4317 2-9-0 .... KJManning 5 — 101
(J S Bolger, Ire) *a.p: 4th appr 1/2-way: 2nd 2f out: sn chal: ev ch 1f out: kpt on u.p* **7/2**[2]

3 1 **Intense Focus (USA)**[14] 5946 2-9-0 106.......... (bt) DJMoran 6 — 98
(J S Bolger, Ire) *trckd ldrs: 5th 1/2-way: 4th under 2f out: kpt on fnl f* **20/1**

4 nk **Drumbeat (IRE)**[14] 5946 2-9-0 100.......... JMurtagh 9 — 98
(A P O'Brien, Ire) *hld up: hdwy 2f out: 8th over 1f out: r.o wl cl home* **12/1**

5 shd **The Bull Hayes (IRE)**[42] 5129 2-9-0 .... FMBerry 15 — 97
(Mrs John Harrington, Ire) *dwlt sltly s: sn chsd ldrs on far rail: 6th 1/2-way: sn rdn: 7th 1f out: kpt on u.p* **8/1**

6 nk **Awinnersgame (IRE)**[17] 5827 2-9-0 .... MJKinane 3 — 97
(J Noseda) *trckd ldrs on stands' side: 7th after 1/2-way: 3rd and rdn under 2f out: no ex fnl f* **5/1**[3]

7 ¾ **Gluteus Maximus (IRE)**[28] 5546 2-9-0 98.......... JAHeffernan 18 — 95
(A P O'Brien, Ire) *hld up in tch: prog into 7th 1 1/2f out: kpt on same pce ins fnl f* **25/1**

8 ½ **Cruikadyke**[64] 4438 2-9-0 .... JohnEgan 2 — 93
(P F I Cole) *hld up: prog on outer 2f out: 9th 1 1/2f out: no imp fnl f* **16/1**

9 2 **Double Ex (IRE)**[44] 5080 2-9-0 82.......... (tp) WJLee 11 — 88
(T Stack, Ire) *towards rr: kpt on wout threatening fr 1 1/2f out* **80/1**

10 ½ **Akrisrun (IRE)**[21] 5734 2-9-0 .... (b[1]) PShanahan 19 — 87
(D K Weld, Ire) *prom on far rail: cl 2nd 1/2-way: wknd fr under 2f out* **50/1**

11 1 ¼ **Piazza San Pietro**[19] 5777 2-9-0 .... WMLordan 1 — 84
(C G Cox) *hld up: no imp fr over 2f out* **50/1**

12 ½ **Alhaban (IRE)**[63] 4465 2-9-0 107.......... DPMcDonogh 8 — 83
(Kevin Prendergast, Ire) *in rr of mid-div: rdn over 2f out: no imp: one pce* **12/1**

13 ½ **Three Way Stretch (IRE)**[28] 5546 2-9-0 92.......... DMGrant 13 — 82
(J T Gorman, Ire) *nvr a factor* **33/1**

14 ½ **Gaelic Chief (IRE)**[21] 5734 2-9-0 .... NGMcCullagh 10 — 80
(A P O'Brien, Ire) *in rr of mid-div: rdn and no imp fr 2 1/2f out* **50/1**

15 nk **Born To Rock (IRE)**[21] 5734 2-9-0 80.......... CDHayes 14 — 80
(J T Gorman, Ire) *a towards rr* **66/1**

16 1 ¼ **Mt Kintyre (IRE)**[15] 5901 2-9-0 .... MichaelHills 16 — 76
(M H Tompkins) *nvr a factor* **50/1**

17 shd **Good Operator (USA)**[28] 5552 2-9-0 .... PJSmullen 7 — 76
(D K Weld, Ire) *prom: 2nd early: 4th u.p over 2f out: sn wknd* **12/1**

18 7 **Anfield Star (IRE)**[14] 5943 2-9-0 .... EJMcNamara 4 — 59
(G M Lyons, Ire) *a bhd* **100/1**

1m 27.1s **Going Correction** +0.125s/f (Good) — **19** Ran SP% **130.6**
Speed ratings: **105,104,103,102,102 102,101,101,98,98 96,96,95,95,94 93,93,85**
CSF £10.62 TOTE £3.40: £1.40, £1.50, £6.60, £3.30; DF 10.60.
Owner Patrick J Fahey **Bred** Peter Thome **Trained** East Everleigh, Wilts
■ Stewards' Enquiry : K J Manning caution: excessive use of the whip
J A Heffernan one-day ban: careless riding (Oct 12)
D J Moran two-day ban: used whip with excessive force and frequency (Oct 12-13)

FOCUS

This looked a strong renewal of the third running of this valuable contest.

NOTEBOOK

Soul City(IRE) underlined his class with an authoritive front-running victory. He set the standard following his impressive Group 3 win at Longchamp in the Prix la Rochette after previously running fourth behind some useful sorts in the Group 2 Vintage Stakes. Always in the front rank with the benefit of the far running rail, he set a sensible clip in this dead ground before gradually quickening the tempo and shrugging off all challengers. The time of 1m27.15s was slower than last year's winning time of 1m 23.3s set by Luck Money on good to firm ground and the winner earned quotes of between 25/1 and 33/1 for next year's 2000 Guineas. The possibility of seeing the winner again in the Dewhurst wasn't ruled out, and we should learn more about the Elusive City colt there, but he looked a smart type on this evidence, doing things again in his now customary front-running fashion. (op 5/2 tchd 11/4)

Gan Amhras(IRE) looked the best of the domestic challenge on paper and so it proved. He emerged as a likely threat after passing the 2f pole but was unable to get the better of his market rival despite every call from the saddle. (op 4/1)

Intense Focus(USA) appreciated this better ground compared to his previous start in the National Stakes and ran creditably for a share of the spoils. (op 16/1)

Drumbeat(IRE) stayed on under pressure in the final furlong and looked like he'll appreciate further.

Awinnersgame(IRE), sixth in the Coventry, was seeking a hat-trick following wins at Newmarket and Doncaster. This looked a tougher task for the son of Kyllachy but this tacky ground probably did him no favours in the closing stages. (op 5/1 tchd 11/2)

Gluteus Maximus(IRE) helps set the level of the form.

Cruikadyke crept closer after halfway but couldn't maintain that momentum.

Piazza San Pietro, who had shown form on varying ground in maiden company, found this beyond him.

Alhaban(IRE), who was narrowly denied in the Railway Stakes before running below par behind Mastercraftsman in the Phoenix, never got in a blow on this holding surface.

Mt Kintyre(IRE) is well thought-of by connections but has shown only fair ability on the track.

6318a C.L. WELD PARK STKS (GROUP 3) (FILLIES) — 7f

3:40 (3:40) 2-Y-O — **£38,294** (£11,235; £5,352; £1,823)

RPR

1 — **Chintz (IRE)**[74] 4095 2-8-12 100.......... JAHeffernan 6 — 106+
(David Wachman, Ire) *a.p: 2nd 1/2-way: chal and led 2f out: rdn and qcknd clr over 1f out: kpt on wl: easily* **6/1**[3]

2 1 ¾ **Lahaleeb (IRE)**[17] 5828 2-8-12 .... SamHitchcott 1 — 102
(M R Channon) *trckd ldrs on stands' side: 5th 1/2-way: 3rd 1 1 /2f out: 2nd whn edgd lft u.p 1f out: kpt on cl home* **7/1**

3 2 **Hallie's Comet (IRE)**[9] 6099 2-8-12 .... RMBurke 11 — 97
(A Kinsella, Ire) *trckd ldrs on far side: rdn over 2f out: 4th 1 1/2f out: mod 3rd and kpt on fnl f* **50/1**

4 nk **What's Up Pussycat (IRE)**[14] 5947 2-8-12 93.......... FMBerry 8 — 96
(David Wachman, Ire) *hld up on far side: prog 2f out: 5th 1 1/2f out: mod 4th whn checked ins fnl f: kpt on* **12/1**

5 1 **Smart Coco (USA)**[54] 4711 2-8-12 .... WMLordan 13 — 93
(T Stack, Ire) *hld up on far side: effrt and no imp over 2f out: kpt on wout threatening fnl f* **9/2**[1]

6 1 ½ **Rare Ransom**[28] 5549 2-8-12 99.......... PJSmullen 9 — 90
(D K Weld, Ire) *in rr: hdwy under 2f out: mod 7th 1f out: kpt on* **12/1**

7 ½ **Roof Fiddle (USA)**[14] 5947 2-8-12 .... DPMcDonogh 2 — 88
(Kevin Prendergast, Ire) *towards rr: prog on stands' side over 2f out: no imp fr under 1 1/2f out* **14/1**

8 1 **Choose Me (IRE)**[21] 5722 2-8-12 95.......... CDHayes 7 — 86
(Kevin Prendergast, Ire) *towards rr: kpt on same pce fr 1f out* **10/1**

9 shd **Blas Ceoil (USA)**[137] 2112 2-8-12 102.......... KJManning 12 — 86
(J S Bolger, Ire) *chsd ldrs: 7th and rdn over 2f out: no imp* **11/2**[2]

10 1 ¾ **Baliyana (IRE)**[21] 5728 2-8-12 95.......... MJKinane 4 — 81+
(John M Oxx, Ire) *led: rdn and hdd 2f out: sn no ex and wknd* **9/2**[1]

11 6 **Beauthea (IRE)**[28] 5549 2-8-12 91.......... JohnEgan 10 — 66
(H Rogers, Ire) *prom: cl 3rd 1/2-way: rdn over 2f out: sn wknd* **33/1**

12 hd **Perfect Truth (IRE)**[15] 5924 2-8-12 93.......... JMurtagh 5 — 66
(A P O'Brien, Ire) *mid-div: rdn and no imp fr over 2f out* **14/1**

13 5 **Spira (IRE)**[42] 5132 2-8-12 .... NGMcCullagh 3 — 53
(A P O'Brien, Ire) *settled in 2nd: wknd fr 2 1/2f out* **40/1**

1m 25.8s (-1.30) **Going Correction** +0.125s/f (Good) — **13** Ran SP% **123.7**
Speed ratings: **112,110,107,107,106 104,103,102,102,100 93,93,87**
CSF £49.01 TOTE £7.60: £2.60, £2.20, £6.50; DF 41.90.
Owner Mrs Elaine Slattery **Bred** Loughtown Stud **Trained** Goolds Cross, Co Tipperary

FOCUS

Sound enough form for the level.

NOTEBOOK

Chintz(IRE), runner-up at Listed and Group 3 level since her debut win over this trip at Leopardstown in June, was returning from a break here and she ran out a comfortable winner after racing prominently and going to the front two furlongs out. Ridden clear over a furlong out, she ran on well and appeared to win with a nice bit in hand. Her trainer David Wachman said that the ground was a bit too quick for her at Leopardstown last time and that she is a fine big filly who should do well at a mile or a mile and a quarter next year.

Lahaleeb(IRE), runner-up to 1,000 Guineas favourite Rainbow View in the May Hill Stakes at Doncaster on her previous start, raced on the outside of the field and closed from 2f out. She had just gone second when she began to drift left under pressure entering the final furlong before staying on without worrying the winner. (op 8/1)

Hallie's Comet(IRE), beaten half a length in a 1m maiden at Dundalk on her second start, ran a big race. She chased the leaders and after being ridden along over 2f out, she kept on inside the final furlong.

What's Up Pussycat(IRE) has held her form well all season. She achieved her second win in a 6f Listed event on heavy ground here two weeks previously. She made headway from the back of the field over the last 2f and kept on, meeting some slight interference inside the final furlong.

Smart Coco(USA), a two-length winner over the trip on her debut at Gowran Park last month, made a forward move over 2f out. Unable to make much impression one and a half furlongs out, she kept on in the closing stages. (op 11/2)

Baliyana(IRE), a three-length maiden winner over the trip on her third start, was back in Pattern company and, after making the running to 2f out, she dropped out quickly. (op 11/2)

6319a PARKNASILLA HOTEL GOFFS FILLIES MILLION — 7f

4:15 (4:17) 2-Y-O

£724,264 (£209,558; £99,264; £47,794; £22,794; £6,617)

RPR

1 — **Minor Vamp (IRE)**[50] 4868 2-9-0 .... MJKinane 1 — 97+
(R Hannon) *mid-div: hdwy on stands' side over 2f out: chal over 1f out: sn led: r.o wl* **10/1**

2 2 **Baileys Cacao (IRE)**[28] 5549 2-9-0 .... RichardHughes 20 — 92+
(R Hannon) *hld up: 14th and prog 1 1/2f out: r.o strly fnl f: nvr nrr* **9/1**

3 ½ **Samba School (IRE)**[78] 3979 2-9-0 .... (b[1]) CDHayes 5 — 91
(Kevin Prendergast, Ire) *trckd ldrs on stands' side: 5th appr 1/2-way: chal under 2f out: cl 3rd over 1f out: kpt on* **66/1**

4 1 ¼ **Luminous Eyes (IRE)**[74] 4095 2-9-0 105.......... PJSmullen 25 — 88
(D K Weld, Ire) *trckd ldrs on far side: 6th after 1/2-way: rdn to dispute ld briefly over 1f out: 4th and no ex wl ins fnl f* **11/4**[1]

5 ½ **Oui Say Oui (IRE)**[42] 5132 2-9-0 .... WMLordan 11 — 86
(T Stack, Ire) *in tch: rdn and no imp 2f out: 8th 1f out: styd on cl home* **7/2**[2]

6 ¾ **High Heeled (IRE)**[27] 5571 2-9-0 .... MichaelHills 6 — 85
(B W Hills) *prom on stands' side: 4th after 1/2-way: rdn 2f out: kpt on u.p fr over 1f out*

7 1 **Maybe Grace (IRE)**[42] 5131 2-9-0 .... FMBerry 22 — 82
(Mrs John Harrington, Ire) *hld up: kpt on fr over 1 1/2f out* **33/1**

8 ½ **Miss Puss (IRE)**[70] 4228 2-9-0 .... (tp) JMurtagh 21 — 81
(David Wachman, Ire) *hld up: r.o fr under 1 1/2f out* **8/1**[3]

9 shd **Carefree Smile (IRE)**[21] 5728 2-9-0 .... PShanahan 17 — 81
(D K Weld, Ire) *in tch: 8th over 2f out: kpt on same pce fnl f* **20/1**

10 1 ¼ **Fanditha (IRE)**[24] 5640 2-9-0 .... PatDobbs 19 — 77
(R Hannon) *prom: led over 2f out: strly pressed 1 1/2f out: hdd and no ex over 1f out* **16/1**

11 shd **Ceist Eile (IRE)**[25] 5619 2-9-0 70.......... (t) DJMoran 7 — 77
(J S Bolger, Ire) *mid-div: kpt on same pce fr 2f out* **50/1**

12 1 **Estephe (IRE)** 2-9-0 .... WJLee 12 — 75
(T Stack, Ire) *towards rr: kpt on wout threatening fr under 2f out* **50/1**

13 shd **Cnocan Gold (IRE)**[42] 5131 2-9-0 76.......... (b[1]) SMGorey 13 — 74
(D K Weld, Ire) *nvr bttr than mid-div* **33/1**

14 nk **Law Of The Jungle (IRE)** 2-9-0 .... DMGrant 9 — 74
(David Wachman, Ire) *towards rr: sme late prog on stands' side* **50/1**

15 ¾ **Best Bidder (USA)**[15] 5882 2-9-0 .... MCHussey 2 — 72
(R A Fahey) *towards rr: drvn along 1/2-way: sme late prog* **66/1**

16 1 **Marina Of Venice (IRE)**[28] 5549 2-9-0 93..........(p) KJManning 8 69
(J S Bolger, Ire) *prom: 3rd after 1/2-way: rdn to chal over 2f out: sn no ex* **14/1**
17 shd **Royal Arruhan**[67] 4316 2-9-0 .... JohnEgan 18 69
(M Halford, Ire) *nvr a factor* **66/1**
18 hd **In The Mood (IRE)**[11] 6030 2-9-0 .... AlanMunro 23 69
(W Jarvis) *nvr a factor* **66/1**
19 1/2 **Apt (IRE)**[36] 5297 2-9-0 .... JAHeffernan 24 67
(David Wachman, Ire) *led: hdd & wknd over 2f out* **20/1**
20 hd **Light It Up (IRE)**[15] 5918 2-9-0 70.......... RPCleary 3 67
(M Halford, Ire) *a towards rr* **66/1**
21 nk **Stan's Cool Cat (IRE)**[45] 5016 2-9-0 .... ChrisCatlin 14 66
(P F I Cole) *a towards rr* **25/1**
22 nk **Mambo Light (USA)**[23] 5686 2-9-0 .... DPMcDonogh 10 72+
(A Wohler, Germany) *prom to over 2f out: sn no ex: sltly hmpd whn eased over 1f out* **25/1**
23 9 **Aahaygirl (IRE)**[9] 6068 2-9-0 .... SamHitchcott 15 43
(K R Burke) *prom: 4th and rdn over 2 1/2f out: sn wknd* **33/1**
24 3/4 **Midnight Manhattan (USA)** 2-9-0 .... SFoley 16 41
(M Halford, Ire) *a bhd* **50/1**

1m 27.2s (0.10) **Going Correction** +0.125s/f (Good) **25** Ran SP% **142.1**
Speed ratings: **104,101,101,99,99 98,97,96,96,95 94,93,93,93,92 91,91,90,90,90 89,89,79,78**
CSF £96.06 TOTE £20.50: £4.40, £2.40, £19.20, £1.50; DF 148.90.
Owner Michael Pescod & Justin Dowley **Bred** Mrs Joan Murphy **Trained** East Everleigh, Wilts

FOCUS
Another boost, if indeed she needed it, for the 1,000 Guineas favourite and Fillies' Mile winner Rainbow View, with Minor Vamp, who had finished just over six lengths behind the Gosden filly in a Group 3 at Newmarket last month, landing this valuable prize.

NOTEBOOK
Minor Vamp(IRE) began to close from mid-division over 2f out and hit the front entering the final furlong before being ridden clear. She ran on well and while connections feared her number 1 draw would be a disadvantage, it did not turn out that way. She apparently loved the ground and the Rockfel Stakes might be her next target.
Baileys Cacao(IRE), a stablemate of the winner and sixth behind Again in the Group 1 Moyglare Stud Stakes over the course and trip last month, found herself having to come from a long way back. Still in mid-division under 2f out, she stayed on quite strongly and with better luck in running would have run the winner close. (op 10/1)
Samba School(IRE), who had finished in rear behind Oui Say Oui (fifth here) on her debut over 6f here in July, was clearly suited by the fitting of blinkers. Always close up, she challenged from 2f out and was third entering the final furlong. She could not find enough but kept on nonetheless.
Luminous Eyes(IRE), a Group 3 winner over the trip at Leopardstown in July and returning from a break, tracked the leaders on the far rail and arrived with every chance over 1f out before finding no extra inside the final furlong. (op 7/2 tchd 5/2)
Oui Say Oui(IRE), runner-up to subsequent Group 1 winner Again in the Group 2 Debutante Stakes on heavy ground at Leopardstown last month, chased the leaders but was getting nowhere one and a half furlongs out before staying on in the closing stages. (op 3/1 tchd 4/1)
High Heeled(IRE), winner of 1m maiden on the all-weather at Kempton, raced prominently but failed to raise her effort 2f out before keeping on inside the final furlong. (op 12/1)
Fanditha(IRE), who beat two subsequent winners when scoring over this trip at Salisbury, showed up well for a long way but was run out of it in the last furlong.
Best Bidder(USA), who showed only minor promise on her debut, found this competitive contest beyond her at this stage of her career.
In The Mood(IRE) was another who faced a big task for one so inexperienced.
Stan's Cool Cat(IRE), who has some fair form on a sound surface, may not have handled the ground.
Aahaygirl(IRE) had form on soft ground but did not appear to get home over this longer trip.

6320a GOFFS SPORTSMAN'S CHALLENGE 6f
4:50 (4:54) 2-Y-0
£43,382 (£13,970; £6,617; £2,941; £1,470; £735)

RPR
1 **Pasar Silbano (IRE)**[63] 4463 2-8-12 99.......... JMurtagh 29 90+
(G M Lyons, Ire) *prom on far side: led fr over 2f out: styd on wl fr over 1f out: comf* **9/2[2]**
2 2 1/2 **City Dancer (IRE)**[36] 5292 2-8-12 .... MCHussey 16 80
(Miss S Collins, Ire) *in tch: prog in centre after 1/2-way: 3rd under 2f out: sn rdn: 2nd and kpt on ins fnl f* **50/1**
3 1/2 **Connie Mac (IRE)**[102] 3123 2-8-12 .... CDHayes 17 79
(Andrew Oliver, Ire) *prom in centre: 2nd 2f out: sn rdn to chal: 3rd ins fnl f: kpt on* **4/1[1]**
4 3 **Cristal Island (IRE)**[14] 5947 2-8-12 94.......... DMGrant 10 70
(Thomas Mullins, Ire) *hld up: 11th and prog over 1f out: kpt on* **8/1**
5 nk **The Tooth Fairy (IRE)**[9] 6093 2-9-3 61.......... GFCarroll 18 74
(Michael Mulvany, Ire) *mid-div: rdn under 2f out: mod 5th and kpt on ins fnl f* **50/1**
6 1/2 **Kardyls Hope (IRE)**[13] 5979 2-8-12 .... WJLee 23 68
(Jarlath P Fahey, Ire) *prom on far side: 3rd u.p 2f out: kpt on same pce* **33/1**
7 1/2 **Eurosmart Lady (IRE)** 2-8-12 .... MACleere 26 66
(John C McConnell, Ire) *chsd ldrs on far side: kpt on fr 1 1/2f out* **50/1**
8 1 1/4 **Streetline (IRE)**[14] 5948 2-8-12 77.......... PShanahan 15 62
(Miss S Collins, Ire) *chsd ldrs in centre: 6th under 2f out: kpt on same pce* **9/1**
9 1/2 **Lista Lightning (IRE)**[13] 5980 2-9-3 76.......... DPMcDonogh 19 66
(Kevin Prendergast, Ire) *hld up: r.o fr over 1f out* **16/1**
10 nk **Whiteball Wonder (IRE)**[21] 5721 2-9-3 .... RPCleary 21 65
(M Halford, Ire) *hld up: kpt on fr 1 1/2f out* **50/1**
11 1/2 **Luckydolly (IRE)**[31] 5442 2-8-12 50.......... BACurtis 22 58
(F Costello, Ire) *chsd ldrs far side: one pce fr 2f out* **66/1**
12 3/4 **Mr Magician (IRE)**[14] 5943 2-9-3 ....(b[1]) JAHeffernan 20 61
(W M Roper, Ire) *mid-div: kpt on same pce fr under 2f out* **50/1**
13 1 3/4 **Mac Jack (IRE)**[14] 5943 2-9-3 .... DJMoran 24 56
(Niall Moran, Ire) *chsd ldrs on far side: rdn and one pce fr over 2f out* **50/1**
14 1 3/4 **Moss Likely (IRE)**[64] 4403 2-8-12 .... SamHitchcott 13 46
(M R Channon) *prom on stands' side: 5th 1 1/2f out: no ex fr over 1f out* **6/1[3]**
15 1 1/4 **Chanthea (IRE)**[31] 5434 2-8-12 66..........(t) JohnEgan 12 42
(H Rogers, Ire) *mid-div: no imp fr 2f out* **33/1**
16 1 1/4 **Areutherepeg (IRE)**[9] 6099 2-8-12 ....(t) SFoley 14 38
(H Rogers, Ire) *nvr bttr than mid-div* **33/1**
17 1 **Vera Lilley (IRE)**[15] 5918 2-8-12 .... MJKinane 1 35
(M J Grassick, Ire) *led on stands' rail: hdd over 2f out: sn no ex and wknd* **12/1**
18 3/4 **Sharp Spartan (IRE)**[15] 5918 2-9-3 .... CPGeoghegan 25 38
(R J Osborne, Ire) *slowly away and nvr a factor* **66/1**
19 3/4 **Queens Fair (IRE)**[15] 5918 2-8-12 65.......... SMGorey 28 31
(Thomas Mullins, Ire) *mid-div on far side: rdn and no imp fr over 2f out* **40/1**
20 nk **Native Dame (IRE)**[15] 5918 2-8-12 .... ChrisCatlin 6 30
(P D Deegan, Ire) *a bhd* **66/1**
21 1 1/4 **Lovers Quest (IRE)**[21] 5722 2-8-12 79.......... EJMcNamara 27 26
(G M Lyons, Ire) *hld up on far side: no ex fr over 2f out* **20/1**
22 nk **River Captain (IRE)**[15] 5895 2-9-3 .... PJSmullen 11 30
(S Kirk) *nvr a factor* **10/1**
23 4 1/2 **Call The Law (IRE)**[9] 6093 2-8-12 73.......... FMBerry 4 —
(David Marnane, Ire) *nvr a factor* **16/1**
24 2 **Ice Bound (IRE)**[162] 1494 2-9-3 .... WMLordan 3 —
(J C Hayden, Ire) *a bhd* **33/1**
25 1 **Roos Abu (IRE)**[62] 4492 2-9-3 50..........(b[1]) MHarley 9 —
(John Joseph Hanlon, Ire) *towards rr thrght* **50/1**
26 1 **Spectagula (IRE)**[14] 5943 2-8-12 50.......... RMBurke 2 —
(Thomas Cleary, Ire) *a bhd* **50/1**
27 1/2 **Liberty To Rock (IRE)**[31] 5442 2-9-3 .... KJManning 7 —
(J T Gorman, Ire) *a towards rr* **16/1**
28 3 **Quelle Surprise (IRE)**[13] 5979 2-8-12 .... PBBeggy 8 —
(Tracey Collins, Ire) *bhd fr 1/2-way* **50/1**
29 23 **Drusus (IRE)**[13] 5980 2-9-3 .... AlanMunro 5 —
(John C McConnell, Ire) *sn trailing in rr: t.o fr over 2f out* **50/1**

1m 14.2s (-0.30) **Going Correction** +0.125s/f (Good) **29** Ran SP% **151.1**
Speed ratings: **107,103,103,99,98 97,97,95,94,94 93,92,90,88,86 84,83,82,81,81 79,79,73,70,69 67,67,63,32**
CSF £251.76 TOTE £4.60: £1.60, £14.90, £1.80, £3.60; DF 983.40.
Owner Mrs Lynne Lyons **Bred** Denis J Redden **Trained** Dunsany, Co. Meath

NOTEBOOK
Moss Likely(IRE), last seen running seventh in the Princess Margaret Stakes, was disappointing in this lesser company. (op 7/1)
River Captain(IRE) was taking on better opposition and never landed a blow back down in distance.

6321 - (Foreign Racing) - See Raceform Interactive

5137 COLOGNE (R-H)
Sunday, September 28

OFFICIAL GOING: Soft

6322a GROSSE EUROPA MEILE (GROUP 2) 1m
2:35 (2:46) 3-Y-0+ **£29,412** (£11,029; £4,412; £2,941)

RPR
1 **Precious Boy (GER)**[139] 2066 3-8-12 .... ADeVries 7 118
(W Hickst, Germany) *racd in 5th on outside: rdn to ld jst over 1f out: r.o strly* **21/10[1]**
2 1 1/4 **Laa Rayb (USA)**[15] 5893 4-9-1 .... RoystonFfrench 3 114
(M Johnston) *unruly ent stalls: cl up: 4th st: sltly outpcd 1 1/2f out: styd on wl to take 2nd last 150yds: nt pce of wnr* **34/10[2]**
3 3/4 **Forthe Millionkiss (GER)**[21] 5740 4-9-4 .... THellier 1 115
(Uwe Ostmann, Germany) *led: hld on gamely whn pressed over 2f out: hdd over 1f out: kpt on wl u.p fnl f* **13/2**
4 3/4 **Runaway**[42] 5138 6-9-1 .... TJarnet 8 110
(R Pritchard-Gordon, France) *hld up: effrt whn nt clr run on ins 1f out: styd on wl clsng stages* **22/1**
5 1 1/4 **In Chambers**[21] 5742 3-8-9 .... C-PLemaire 2 105
(M Delzangles, France) *racd in 3rd: rdn and led briefly over 1f out: sn wknd* **106/10**
6 3/4 **Turning For Home (FR)**[35] 5331 3-8-9 .... JVictoire 5 104
(H-A Pantall, France) *hld up: kpt on steadily fnl 2f* **35/2**
7 1/2 **Konig Concorde (GER)**[49] 4916 3-8-9 .... AStarke 11 103
(C Sprengel, Germany) *hld up: styd on at same pce fnl 2f* **76/10**
8 1/2 **Sehrezad (IRE)**[26] 5596 3-8-9 .... JiriPalik 9 101
(Andreas Lowe, Germany) *a towards rr* **13/1**
9 1/2 **El Vettorio (GER)**[43] 5113 5-9-1 .... LennartHammer-Hansen 6 102
(C Sprengel, Germany) *last st: a in rr* **39/1**
10 nse **Mharadono (GER)**[92] 3515 5-9-1 .... AHelfenbein 10 102
(P Hirschberger, Germany) *racd in 2nd: rdn over 2f out: sn btn* **33/1**
11 1 1/2 **Idolino (GER)**[28] 5554 3-8-9 .... EPedroza 4 97
(J Hirschberger, Germany) *midfield: rdn and btn over 1 1/2f out* **42/10[3]**

1m 37.46s (-0.93)
WFA 3 from 4yo+ 4lb **11** Ran SP% **130.1**
(including ten euro stakes): WIN 31; PL 14, 19, 19; SF 113.
Owner Gestut Park Wiedingen **Bred** Gestut Park Wiedingen **Trained** Germany

NOTEBOOK
Laa Rayb(USA) left behind him a disappointing effort at Doncaster last time and bounced back to the level which saw him win a Group 3 in France previously, only finding the German 2000 Guineas winner too strong.

6323a PREIS DER SPIELBANK BAD NEUENAHR (LISTED RACE) (F&M) 1m
3:40 (3:54) 3-Y-0+ **£9,559** (£2,941; £1,471; £735)

RPR
1 **Manipura (GER)**[25] 3-8-7 .... MCadeddu 4 97
(H Steguweit, Germany) **353/10**
2 1 **Emirates Girl (USA)**[25] 5622 3-8-13 .... JVictoire 2 100
(H-A Pantall, France) **29/10[1]**
3 nk **Waky Love (GER)**[26] 5596 4-9-0 .... ADeVries 6 97
(Frau Jutta Mayer, Germany) **42/10[2]**
4 3/4 **Alexa (GER)**[14] 4-8-12 .... TMundry 3 93
(H J Groschel, Germany) **21/1**
5 nk **Desert Chill (USA)**[45] 5038 3-8-11 .... TedDurcan 1 95
(Saeed Bin Suroor) *led 1f then trckd ldr on ins: 3rd st: sn wnt 2nd: hrd rdn 2f out: lost 2nd 150yds out: wknd and lost 4th cl home* **52/10[3]**
6 1/2 **Masako (IRE)**[14] 3-8-7 .... ASuborics 15 90
(W Hickst, Germany) **16/1**
7 3/4 **Cocopalm (FR)**[61] 3-8-13 .... C-PLemaire 8 94
(M Delzangles, France) **104/10**
8 3 **Now Forever (GER)**[63] 3-8-9 .... AStarke 16 83
(P Schiergen, Germany) **11/1**
9 2 1/2 **Zaya (GER)**[35] 5334 3-8-11 .... EPedroza 13 80
(A Wohler, Germany) **72/10**

10 1/2 **Rioka (IRE)**[36] 3-8-13 .... MaximeFoulon 10 80
(R Gibson, France) **29/1**
11 3/4 **Manita (IRE)** 3-8-7 ....(b) AHelfenbein 5 73
(Mario Hofer, Germany) **35/1**
12 3/4 **Hashbrown (GER)**[35] 4-9-0 .... LennartHammer-Hansen 14 74
(C Sprengel, Germany) **18/1**
13 nk **La Blue Hill**[50] 4-9-3 .... DBonilla 11 76
(J De Roualle, France) **50/1**
14 3/4 **Mouette (GER)**[385] 3-8-7 .... J-PCarvalho 7 69
(Mario Hofer, Germany) **35/1**
15 2 1/2 **Muthabaie (FR)**[112] 4-9-5 .... TJarnet 12 71
(R Pritchard-Gordon, France) **103/10**
16 8 **Giocita (GER)**[119] 2655 3-8-7 .... ASchikora 17 44
(Andreas Lowe, Germany) **65/1**

1m 36.14s (-2.25)
WFA 3 from 4yo 4lb — 16 Ran SP% **130.0**
WIN 363; PL 66, 19, 19; SF 857.
Owner Stall Dagobert **Bred** Stiftung Gestut Fahrhof **Trained** Germany

NOTEBOOK
Desert Chill(USA), who has an official mark of 86, was continuing in her quest for black type. She was prominent for a long way before dropping out of the places inside the last.

6324a IVG PREIS VON EUROPA (GROUP 1) — 1m 4f
4:15 (4:36) 3-Y-0+ — £73,529 (£24,265; £11,029; £5,147)

RPR

1 **Baila Me (GER)**[14] 5952 3-8-6 .... DBoeuf 1 110
(W Baltromei, Germany) *racd in 7th: rapid hdwy to ld over 2f out: strly pressed fnl 1 1/2f: hld on wl u.str.p: all out* **56/10**
2 shd **Poseidon Adventure (IRE)**[28] 5557 5-9-6 ....(b) ASuborics 6 116
(W Figge, Germany) *racd in 6th: wnt 2nd 2f out: pressed wnr thrght fnl 1 1/2f: jst failed* **64/10**
3 3 **King Of Rome (IRE)**[14] 5953 3-8-10 .... CO'Donoghue 7 109
(A P O'Brien, Ire) *racd in 5th: wnt 3rd 2f out: sn rdn and kpt on but outpcd by first two* **38/10**[3]
4 2 **Dickens (GER)**[21] 5741 5-9-6 .... JVictoire 2 108
(H Blume, Germany) *hld up in last: styd on fnl 2f but nvr nr ldrs* **72/10**
5 1/2 **Ostland (GER)**[21] 5736 3-8-10 .... AStarke 5 105
(P Schiergen, Germany) *racd in 4th: 3rd st: ev ch briefly over 2f out: sn one pce* **27/10**[1]
6 2 1/2 **Appel Au Maitre (FR)**[14] 5958 4-9-6 .... EPedroza 9 103
(Wido Neuroth, Norway) *hld up in 8th: hmpd on bnd under 4f out: nvr a factor: fin lame* **34/10**[2]
7 3/4 **Avanti Polonia (GER)**[14] 5954 4-9-2 .... DBonilla 10 98
(F Head, France) *hld up in 9th: a in rr* **24/1**
8 3/4 **Hindu Kush (IRE)**[15] 5892 3-8-10 .... SMLevey 8 99
(A P O'Brien, Ire) *racd in 3rd tl wnt 2nd after 3f: wknd 2f out* **18/1**
9 12 **Bashkirov**[15] 5892 3-8-10 .... DavidMcCabe 4 80
(A P O'Brien, Ire) *2nd early: 3rd after 3f: wknd over 2f out* **40/1**
10 5 **Satier (FR)**[25] 5624 3-8-10 ....(b) C-PLemaire 3 72
(Mario Hofer, Germany) *led to over 2f out: wknd qckly* **13/1**

2m 32.1s (-0.80)
WFA 3 from 4yo+ 8lb — 10 Ran SP% **130.3**
WIN 66; PL 29, 24, 22; SF 344.
Owner Gestut Karlshof **Bred** Gestut Karlshof **Trained** Germany

3308 SAN SIRO (R-H)
Sunday, September 28

OFFICIAL GOING: Good

6325a PREMIO FEDERICO TESIO (GROUP 3) — 1m 3f
4:10 (4:15) 3-Y-0+ — £26,801 (£11,793; £6,432; £3,216)

RPR

1 **Voila Ici (IRE)**[105] 3075 3-8-5 .... MDemuro 3 114
(V Caruso, Italy) *racd in 4th to st: hdwy in middle 2f out: drvn to ld 100yds out: pushed out and r.o wl (1.32/1F)* **13/10**[1]
2 nk **Basaltico (IRE)** 4-8-12 .... URispoli 1 113
(A & G Botti, Italy) *hld up: 7th st: hdwy 3f out: drvn and ev ch 100yds out: r.o same pce* **52/10**
3 2 1/4 **Storm Mountain (IRE)**[43] 5-8-12 .... DVargiu 8 110
(B Grizzetti, Italy) *5th st: r.o fnl 2f on outside to take 3rd last strides* **4/1**[3]
4 hd **Gimmy (IRE)**[14] 4-8-12 .... SUrru 6 109
(B Grizzetti, Italy) *led: qcknd into clr ld 1/2-way: c towards middle in st: hdd 100yds out: one pce* **28/10**[2]
5 2 1/2 **Estejo (GER)**[98] 3306 4-8-12 .... DPorcu 2 105
(R Rohne, Germany) *trckd ldr to st: styd on rails: hrd rdn 2f out: wknd fr dist* **133/10**
6 7 **Anton Chekhov**[70] 4232 4-8-12 .... GBietolini 5 93
(W Hickst, Germany) *racd in 3rd to st: btn wl over 2f out* **82/10**
7 1/2 **Sopran Promo (IRE)**[14] 4-8-12 .... PConvertino 7 92
(B Grizzetti, Italy) *6th st on ins: 5th 2f out: n.d* **16/1**
7 dht **Subitodopo**[140] 2027 4-8-12 .... NMurru 4 92
(M Gasparini, Italy) *last st: a bhd* **22/1**

2m 15.4s (-3.20)
WFA 3 from 4yo+ 7lb — 8 Ran SP% **134.0**
WIN 2.32; PL 1.33, 1.85, 1.76; DF 6.74.
Owner Scuderia Incolinx **Bred** Soc Finanza Locale Consulting **Trained** Italy

5746 BATH (L-H)
Monday, September 29

OFFICIAL GOING: Good to firm
Wind: Moderate against Weather: Fine

6327 JOHN SISK 150TH ANNIVERSARY MAIDEN STKS — 5f 161y
2:10 (2:13) (Class 5) 2-Y-O — £3,238 (£963; £481; £240) Stalls Centre

Form — RPR

32 **1** **Brief Encounter (IRE)**[25] 5628 2-9-3 0 .... LPKeniry 7 81
(A M Balding) *chsd ldrs: pushed along 4f out: led and hung lft ins fnl f: r.o wl* **11/4**[2]
2 3 1/2 **La Verte Rue (USA)** 2-8-12 0 .... ShaneKelly 4 65+
(J A Osborne) *hld up towards rr: hdwy 2f out: r.o ins fnl f: tk 2nd last strides: nt trble wnr* **40/1**
3 nk **Fulham Broadway (IRE)** 2-9-3 0 .... JamieSpencer 1 70+
(E F Vaughan) *hld up in mid-div: hdwy on ins 3f out: swtchd rt over 2f out: led wl over 1f out: sn rdn: hdd ins fnl f: sn hmpd: lost 2nd last strides* **9/4**[1]
5625 **4** 2 3/4 **Barnezet (GR)**[53] 4786 2-8-12 73 .... PatDobbs 5 55
(R Hannon) *led over 1f: w ldr tl rdn over 1f out: fdd ins fnl f* **9/1**
5 3/4 **Pressing Matters (IRE)** 2-9-3 0 .... RichardMullen 12 58+
(E S McMahon) *hld up in mid-div: hdwy over 1f out: nvr trbld ldrs* **12/1**
6 2 **Private Passion (IRE)** 2-9-3 0 .... PaulEddery 13 52
(Pat Eddery) *bhd tl hdwy jst over 1f out: no real prog fnl f* **25/1**
5 **7** 3/4 **Silky Way (GR)**[67] 4321 2-8-12 0 .... MickyFenton 8 44
(P R Chamings) *w ldr: led 4f out tl wl over 1f out: wknd fnl f: nt knocked abt* **40/1**
8 3/4 **Morning Queen (IRE)** 2-8-12 0 .... PhilipRobinson 2 42
(C G Cox) *chsd ldrs: swtchd rt over 2f out: wknd over 1f out* **16/1**
9 1 3/4 **Taste Of Honey (IRE)** 2-8-12 0 .... SaleemGolam 11 36
(D W P Arbuthnot) *hld up towards rr: pushed along whn hung lft 3f out: rdn over 1f out: n.d* **100/1**
4 **10** 1 1/2 **Majestic Lady (IRE)**[17] 5860 2-8-12 0 .... MichaelHills 6 40+
(B W Hills) *s.i.s: bhd: nt clr run on ins over 2f out: sme hdwy over 1f out: n.d* **4/1**[3]
11 1/2 **Miskin Flyer** 2-8-12 0 .... CatherineGannon 3 30
(B Palling) *outpcd* **66/1**
0 **12** 1 1/4 **Final Rhapsody**[38] 5214 2-8-12 0 .... RichardThomas 9 26
(J A Geake) *chsd ldrs tl wknd 2f out* **33/1**
13 35 **Captain Carey** 2-9-0 0 .... TolleyDean[(3)] 15 —
(M S Saunders) *wnt rt and stmbld s: sn wl in rr: eased over 1f out* **33/1**
0 **14** 1 3/4 **Boundless Applause**[31] 5459 2-8-12 0 .... JamesDoyle 16 —
(I A Wood) *w ldrs tl wknd over 2f out: t.o* **100/1**

1m 11.3s (0.10) **Going Correction** -0.125s/f (Firm) — 14 Ran SP% **119.1**
Speed ratings (Par 95): **94,89,88,85,84 81,80,79,77,75 74,72,26,23**
toteswinger: 1&2 £19.90, 1&3 £2.60, 2&3 £24.30. CSF £121.33 TOTE £3.70: £1.50, £13.60, £1.50; EX 142.20.
Owner Thurloe Thoroughbreds XXII **Bred** Ballyhane Stud **Trained** Kingsclere, Hants

FOCUS
A modest maiden, and, despite the big field, only a handful looked in with a chance. The winner has been rated as improving 7lb.

NOTEBOOK
Brief Encounter(IRE) set a decent standard, having twice placed in 5f maidens at Sandown and Great Leighs, and he stayed on too strongly for the gambled-on newcomer Fulham Broadway. He had to be ridden to maintain his early position but responded well to pressure and the interference he caused the favourite over half a furlong out made no difference to the result. He may well have more to offer in 6f nurseries. (op 5-2 tchd 3-1)
La Verte Rue(USA) stayed on well inside the final furlong to grab second. A half-sister to multiple sprint winners in the US, she travelled quite nicely through the race and was given a very sympathetic ride. Her stable have had a pretty poor year, but she looks more than capable of winning a maiden. (op 50-1)
Fulham Broadway(IRE), a half-brother to numerous winners who went for £85,000 at the breeze-ups, was heavily backed throughout the day and travelled beautifully into the race. He was driven to lead two out but could not shake off the winner and was beaten when getting hampered. It may have cost him second, though, and connections will be hopeful he can win back over a bare 5f. (op 10-3 tchd 4-1)
Barnezet(GR) was up there throughout and had every chance. She is likely to continue to come up short in maidens. (op 10-1)
Pressing Matters(IRE) ◆ cost 38,000gns as a yearling and he made a pleasing debut, staying on having been a bit short of room at halfway. He should learn from this and will be helped by 6f. (op 16-1)
Private Passion(IRE), a half-brother to useful handicapper Master Robbie, stayed on well from an unpromising position, and, like most juveniles from this yard, he should know a lot more next time.
Silky Way(GR) Official explanation: jockey said filly was unsuited by the good to firm ground
Majestic Lady(IRE) was not that well away and little went right for her. She had shaped really well on her debut at Sandown and deserves another chance to build on that promise. Official explanation: jockey said filly was unsuited by the track (op 3-1)
Captain Carey Official explanation: jockey said gelding stumbled on leaving stalls

6328 STONE KING SEWELL CLAIMING STKS — 5f 11y
2:40 (2:43) (Class 6) 3-Y-O+ — £2,266 (£674; £337; £168) Stalls Centre

Form — RPR

0000 **1** **Dazed And Amazed**[5] 6200 4-9-7 72 .... PatDobbs 14 86
(R Hannon) *hld up towards rr: hdwy 2f out: sn rdn: led 1f out: pushed out* **9/2**[2]
1601 **2** 3/4 **Desperate Dan**[11] 6045 7-8-6 70 ....(b) PNolan[(7)] 9 75
(A B Haynes) *carried rt s: sn hmpd: hld up in mid-div: hdwy over 2f out: chal gng wl over 1f out: rdn and nt qckn ins fnl f* **9/2**[2]
5040 **3** 4 1/2 **Cape Royal**[7] 6174 8-9-1 76 ....(bt) JamieSpencer 10 61
(J M Bradley) *hung lft sn after s: led after 1f to 1f out: wknd ins fnl f* **5/1**[3]
-040 **4** 1 1/2 **Doctor Hilary**[15] 5936 6-9-7 82 ....(v) ShaneKelly 7 62
(A B Haynes) *wnt rt s: sn hmpd and bhd: carried hd high: rdn and r.o ins fnl f: nvr nrr* **10/3**[1]
5145 **5** 3/4 **Our Acquaintance**[12] 6024 3-8-12 67 ....(b) RichardMullen 11 51
(W R Muir) *hld up in tch: rdn over 1f out: wknd ins fnl f* **15/2**
-000 **6** 3 **Talcen Gwyn (IRE)**[59] 4580 6-8-9 49 ....(vt) LPKeniry 4 36
(M F Harris) *chsd ldrs: rdn over 3f out: wknd over 1f out* **40/1**
0304 **7** 1 **Smirfys Gold (IRE)**[34] 5374 4-8-8 48 ....(v) StephenDonohoe 12 32
(E S McMahon) *s.i.s: sn in mid-div: hdwy over 2f out: sn rdn: wknd over 1f out* **14/1**
0000 **8** 1 **Spanish Ace**[6] 6190 7-8-10 57 ....(p) TolleyDean[(3)] 2 33
(J M Bradley) *hld up in tch: rdn and wknd over 2f out* **33/1**
0000 **9** nse **Rich Harvest (USA)**[11] 6063 3-8-4 52 .... DominicFox[(3)] 6 28
(P D Evans) *led 1f: prom tl rdn and wknd over 2f out* **14/1**
0446 **10** nk **Indian Lady (IRE)**[52] 4812 5-8-1 41 ....(b) CatherineGannon 13 20
(Mrs A L M King) *sn chsng ldr: wknd over 1f out* **20/1**
-060 **11** 7 **Iamagrey (IRE)**[59] 4580 3-8-4 48 ow2 ....(bt[1]) SaleemGolam 1 —
(C J Down) *outpcd and hmpd sn after s: a in rr* **80/1**
-000 **12** 1 1/4 **Amber Bamber**[21] 5749 3-8-9 43 .... RichardThomas 5 —
(D Haydn Jones) *hmpd sn after s: a in rr* **100/1**

61.70 secs (-0.80) **Going Correction** -0.125s/f (Firm)
WFA 3 from 4yo+ 1lb — 12 Ran SP% **113.6**
Speed ratings (Par 101): **101,99,92,90,89 84,82,81,80,80 69,67**
toteswinger: 1&2 £6.70, 1&3 £7.00, 2&3 £2.30. CSF £22.91 TOTE £5.90: £2.30, £1.80, £1.90; EX 24.10.Cape Royal was the subject of a friendly claim
Owner Mrs R Ablett **Bred** Whitsbury Manor Stud & Pigeon House Stud **Trained** East Everleigh, Wilts

FOCUS
A fair claimer in which the form horses came to the fore.
Cape Royal Official explanation: jockey said gelding jumped left on leaving stalls

6329 TARMAC SOUTH WEST H'CAP 2m 1f 34y
3:10 (3:14) (Class 5) (0-75,74) 3-Y-O+ £3,238 (£963; £481; £240) Stalls Low

Form				RPR
31/6	1		**Pseudonym (IRE)**[11] 6054 6-9-4 64 (t) LPKeniry 2 (M F Harris) *hld up towards rr: hdwy on ins over 4f out: rdn to ld 1f out: drvn out: jst hld on* **9/1**	72
4220	2	shd	**Callisto Moon**[34] 5376 4-9-8 68 (p) StephenDonohoe 4 (Ian Williams) *hld up in mid-div: hdwy over 7f out: swtchd rt over 1f out: nt clr run and lost action briefly ins fnl f: rdn and r.o wl: jst failed: unlucky* **15/2**	77+
4302	3	1 1/4	**Tobago Bay**[37] 5269 3-7-9 56 oh1 (b) DominicFox(3) 6 (Miss Sheena West) *w ldr: led over 5f out: rdn and hdd over 2f out: ev ch ins fnl f: nt qckn cl home* **9/2**[2]	63
1042	4	1/2	**The Composer**[12] 6022 6-8-9 55 oh1 SteveDrowne 14 (M Blanshard) *hld up in mid-div: hdwy over 7f out: rdn over 2f out: edgd lft ins fnl f: nt qckn* **9/1**	61
6210	5	2	**Benhego**[15] 5938 3-8-11 69 SaleemGolam 9 (S C Williams) *hld up in tch: rdn to ld over 2f out: hdd 1f out: fdd towards fin* **11/2**[3]	73
5004	6	1/2	**Tribe**[11] 6054 6-9-5 65 (t) JamieSpencer 1 (P R Webber) *hld up in rr: hdwy 2f out: hld whn hmpd ins fnl f* **4/1**[1]	69+
5030	7	hd	**Brief Goodbye**[44] 5092 8-9-11 71 MickyFenton 3 (John Berry) *hld up towards rr: rdn and styd on fnl 2f: nvr trbld ldrs* **18/1**	74
6420	8	6	**Inchpast**[11] 6054 7-9-6 73 (b) AshleyMorgan(7) 13 (M H Tompkins) *hld up in mid-div: hdwy 8f out: lost pl over 4f out: rdn and bhd fnl 3f* **12/1**	69
5545	9	5	**Go On Ahead (IRE)**[24] 5676 8-8-12 58 CatherineGannon 7 (M J Coombe) *hld up in tch: lost pl 7f out: bhd fnl 4f* **40/1**	48
5636	10	3	**Abstract Colours (IRE)**[21] 5752 3-8-4 62 RichardThomas 5 (A M Balding) *led: hdd over 5f out: hung lft 3f out: wknd wl over 1f out* **11/2**[3]	48

3m 50.37s (-1.53) **Going Correction** +0.075s/f (Good)
WFA 3 from 4yo+ 12lb **10 Ran SP% 116.1**
Speed ratings (Par 103): **106,105,105,105,104 103,103,101,98,97**
toteswinger: 1&2 £9.80, 1&3 £11.40, 2&3 £9.40. CSF £74.43 CT £346.69 TOTE £11.10: £3.70, £2.30, £2.20; EX 81.00.
Owner Mrs D J Brown **Bred** Ballymacoll Stud Farm Ltd **Trained** Edgcote, Northants

FOCUS
This was a competitive staying handicap run at a fair gallop. The form looks sound rated through the runner-up, third and fourth.
Tribe Official explanation: jockey said gelding hung right-handed

6330 NORWEST HOLST CONSTRUCTION MAIDEN STKS 1m 2f 46y
3:40 (3:46) (Class 5) 2-Y-O £3,238 (£963; £481; £240) Stalls Low

Form				RPR
044	1		**Blue Dynasty (USA)**[33] 5404 2-9-3 70 ShaneKelly 2 (Mrs A J Perrett) *a.p: led 3f out tl over 1f out: sn rdn: led wl ins fnl f: r.o* **11/4**[2]	69
024	2	shd	**Excelsior Academy**[9] 6135 2-9-3 70 JamieSpencer 3 (B J Meehan) *led: pushed along whn awkward bnd over 4f out: hdd 3f out: led over 1f out: sn hrd rdn: hdd wl ins fnl f* **15/8**[1]	69
540	3	2	**Security Joan (IRE)**[5] 6199 2-8-12 0 LPKeniry 4 (R Hannon) *hld up in tch: rdn over 1f out: kpt on same pce fnl f* **9/1**	60
0	4	hd	**Darley Sun (IRE)**[17] 5857 2-9-3 0 RichardMullen 6 (D M Simcock) *sn chsng ldrs: nt clr run on ins over 2f out: rdn over 1f out: kpt on one pce fnl f* **4/1**[3]	66+
00	5	1 1/2	**Corredor Sun (USA)**[53] 4788 2-9-3 0 SteveDrowne 1 (Carl Llewellyn) *hld up in tch: effrt over 2f out: one pce fnl f* **20/1**	62
000	6	4	**Diamond Heist**[5] 6197 2-9-3 0 MichaelHills 9 (M P Tregoning) *hld up and bhd: pushed along over 2f out: rdn over 1f out: n.d* **12/1**	55
043	7	1	**Hassadin**[16] 5909 2-8-10 66 (p) PNolan(7) 11 (A B Haynes) *hld up towards rr: pushed along over 2f out: nvr nr ldrs* **11/1**	53
5600	8	1 3/4	**Rio Del Oro (USA)**[16] 5914 2-9-3 55 (b[1]) PatDobbs 7 (R Hannon) *prom: rdn 2f out: wknd over 1f out* **33/1**	50
00	9	3	**Braishfield Lass**[28] 5570 2-8-7 0 GabrielHannon(5) 8 (B G Powell) *a bhd* **100/1**	40
64	10	52	**Graysland**[85] 3760 2-8-7 0 JackDean(5) 12 (W G M Turner) *a bhd: eased whn no ch fnl 2f* **100/1**	—

2m 13.03s (2.03) **Going Correction** +0.075s/f (Good) **10 Ran SP% 117.2**
Speed ratings (Par 95): **94,93,92,92,90 87,86,85,83,41**
toteswinger: 1&2 £1.80, 1&3 £4.30, 2&3 £2.10. CSF £8.15 TOTE £3.90: £1.50, £1.50, £2.00; EX 8.90.
Owner The Green Dot Partnership **Bred** B P Walden & H Sexton **Trained** Pulborough, W Sussex

FOCUS
A good test of stamina for these juveniles and it produced a cracking finish. Solid form for this modest level.

NOTEBOOK
Blue Dynasty(USA) looked to be crying out for this trip when a keeping-on fourth at Great Leighs last month and he kept finding for Jim Crowley, just getting up close home having had the advantage of the rail to race against. He holds a Derby entry, but that is pie in the sky, and something similar to this beckons. (op 3-1 tchd 7-2)

Excelsior Academy, going without the blinkers this time, was again made plenty of use of, but he looked uneasy in front and Spencer was niggling away at him for most of the journey. He kept finding and briefly looked to be holding the winner, but in the end just lost out. He has his quirks, as many by Montjeu do, and would not be one to take too short a price about, but has shown more than enough to win a small maiden. (op 2-1 tchd 7-4)

Security Joan(IRE) has gone up in trip with each start and she kept on for third. She had been a bit disappointing since her debut, but this was more promising and it will be interesting to see how she fares in nurseries. (op 15-2 tchd 7-1)

Darley Sun(IRE), unable to land a blow in a good maiden on his debut at Doncaster, was up in trip and faced with faster ground, so it was no surprise to see him improve. He got stopped in his run just as the tempo was increasing and connections have a good handicapping prospect for next season. (op 11-2)

Corredor Sun(USA) ran a really promising race back in fifth. This was his third start in maiden company and there may be more improvement to come at this distance in nurseries. (op 18-1 tchd 16-1)

6331 E.B.F./ THORN BAKER RECRUITMENT MAIDEN FILLIES' STKS 1m 2f 46y
4:10 (4:13) (Class 5) 3-Y-O+ £3,885 (£1,156; £577; £288) Stalls Low

Form				RPR
3054	1		**Basanti (USA)**[18] 5814 3-8-12 68 MichaelHills 5 (B W Hills) *w ldr: led over 4f out: clr whn rdn over 1f out: easily* **9/2**[3]	75
64	2	6	**Orange River (IRE)**[64] 4447 3-8-12 0 SteveDrowne 1 (J H M Gosden) *s.i.s: hld up and bhd: hdwy on outside 2f out: wnt 2nd and edgd lft ins fnl f: no ch w wnr* **11/4**[2]	63
34	3	2 1/4	**Beauchamp Wonder**[97] 3350 3-8-12 0 ShaneKelly 6 (G A Butler) *a.p: chsd wnr over 2f out: rdn wl over 1f out: no imp: lost 2nd ins fnl f* **13/2**	58
3230	4	5	**Suede**[46] 5019 3-8-12 67 PaulEddery 3 (Pat Eddery) *hld up in tch: pushed along and lost pl bnd over 4f out: rdn and rallied over 2f out: wknd 1f out* **5/1**	48
36	5	1 1/2	**Madam President**[56] 4695 3-8-12 0 RichardMullen 9 (W R Swinburn) *hld up in mid-div: hdwy over 3f out: wknd over 1f out* **9/4**[1]	45
U400	6	shd	**Dawn Wind**[36] 5318 3-8-12 43 CatherineGannon 2 (I A Wood) *rdn leaving stalls: sn prom: rdn 3f out: wknd wl over 1f out* **50/1**	45
0-03	7	5	**Ochenvay**[40] 3359 3-8-9 52 TolleyDean(3) 7 (C J Down) *s.i.s: a bhd* **33/1**	35
-000	8	6	**Les Allues (IRE)**[21] 5748 3-8-12 40 MickyFenton 10 (H S Howe) *plld hrd: led: hdd over 4f out: wknd wl over 1f out* **100/1**	23

2m 10.54s (-0.46) **Going Correction** +0.075s/f (Good) **8 Ran SP% 111.5**
Speed ratings (Par 100): **104,99,97,93,92 92,88,83**
toteswinger: 1&2 £3.30, 1&3 £4.80, 2&3 £5.10. CSF £16.36 TOTE £4.90: £1.60, £1.30, £2.00; EX 16.20.
Owner Lady Bamford **Bred** Gainsborough Farm Llc **Trained** Lambourn, Berks

FOCUS
They went just a steady gallop in what was a moderate maiden. The winner has been rated as improving 9lb from his previous best.
Madam President Official explanation: jockey said filly got upset at the start

6332 PERTEMPS PEOPLE DEVELOPMENT "HANDS AND HEELS" APPRENTICE SERIES H'CAP 1m 5y
4:40 (4:43) (Class 5) (0-70,69) 3-Y-O £2,914 (£867; £433; £216) Stalls Low

Form				RPR
6005	1		**Cinerama (IRE)**[88] 3636 3-8-7 60 KatiaScallan(3) 9 (M P Tregoning) *t.k.h: sn prom: led wl over 1f out tl ins fnl f: led nr fin* **10/1**	65
3223	2	nk	**Azure Mist**[11] 6049 3-9-1 65 AshleyMorgan 1 (M H Tompkins) *t.k.h: sn prom: sltly hmpd over 4f out: led ins fnl f: hdd nr fin* **4/1**[1]	69
2215	3	3 1/4	**Jollyhockeysticks**[11] 6048 3-9-3 67 MatthewDavies 4 (M R Channon) *hld up towards rr: pushed along and hdwy over 2f out: one pce fnl f* **4/1**[1]	64
4524	4	3	**Nikolaievich (IRE)**[26] 5603 3-8-9 59 (b) DTDaSilva 5 (P F I Cole) *s.i.s: in rr: no real prog fnl f* **11/2**[2]	49
665	5	1/2	**Tampopo (IRE)**[21] 5748 3-8-5 55 oh5 BillyCray 3 (D J S Ffrench Davis) *led: pushed along and hdd wl over 1f out: wknd ins fnl f* **10/1**	43
0106	6	2 1/2	**Lancaster Lad (IRE)**[54] 4724 3-8-11 61 (p) PNolan 6 (A B Haynes) *plld hrd: sn prom: ev ch wl over 1f out: sn wknd* **14/1**	44
0630	7	nk	**Jay Gee Wigmo**[24] 5684 3-8-5 55 oh5 AndreaAtzeni 7 (A W Carroll) *sn stdd towards rr: carried wd by loose horse bnd over 4f out: n.d after* **25/1**	37
3106	U		**Bramalea**[11] 6048 3-8-12 62 AmyScott 2 (B W Duke) *t.k.h: prom: cl 4th whn hmpd and uns rdr bnd over 4f out* **4/1**[1]	—

1m 42.11s (1.31) **Going Correction** +0.075s/f (Good) **8 Ran SP% 115.2**
Speed ratings (Par 101): **96,95,92,89,88 86,86,—**
toteswinger: 1&2 £6.40, 1&3 £5.80, 2&3 £2.10. CSF £40.88 CT £140.36 TOTE £11.70: £2.60, £1.60, £1.20; EX 53.60 Place 6 £ 33.72, Place 5 £ 21.41.
Owner Mrs Hugo Morris **Bred** Hascombe And Valiant Studs **Trained** Lambourn, Berks

FOCUS
This was a fairly weak handicap, run at a muddling pace. It has been rated through the fifth to his best maiden form.
Cinerama(IRE) Official explanation: trainer's rep said, regarding running, that the filly was better suited by a drop in class, a step up in trip and the track.
T/Plt: £25.80 to a £1 stake. Pool: £56,604.34. 1,598.52 winning tickets. T/Qpdt: £10.70 to a £1 stake. Pool: £3,760.00. 259.50 winning tickets. KH

5811 BRIGHTON (L-H)
Monday, September 29
OFFICIAL GOING: Good to firm (8.6)
Wind: Moderate, half behind Weather: Fine

6333 BRIGHTON MEDIAN AUCTION MAIDEN STKS 6f 209y
2:20 (2:22) (Class 6) 2-Y-O £2,396 (£712; £356; £177) Stalls Low

Form				RPR
4353	1		**Super Fourteen**[14] 5960 2-9-3 64 TedDurcan 3 (R Hannon) *in tch: hdwy over 2f out: rdn to ld over 1f out: r.o: hld on wl whn chal wl ins fnl f: drvn out* **11/10**[1]	63
0	2	shd	**Parc Des Princes (USA)**[54] 4728 2-9-3 0 WilliamBuick 2 (A M Balding) *hld up: struggling over 3f out: hdwy u.p over 1f out: r.o to chal wl ins fnl f: jst hld* **11/4**[2]	63
000	3	4	**Tobizzy**[50] 4907 2-8-12 50 NeilPollard 6 (J R Jenkins) *chsd ldr: rdn to ld over 2f out: hdd over 1f out: kpt on same pce* **25/1**	48
6400	4	1 1/4	**Captain Kallis (IRE)**[18] 5834 2-9-3 43 TQuinn 1 (D J S Ffrench Davis) *racd keenly: hld up: rdn and hdwy over 2f out: kpt on but nt pce to chal* **20/1**	49
0	5	2 1/4	**Echo Forest**[13] 6000 2-9-3 0 DaneO'Neill 8 (J R Best) *chsd ldrs: rdn and ev ch over 2f out: kpt on same pce* **16/1**	44
	6	3 1/2	**Molnaya (IRE)** 2-9-3 0 GeorgeBaker 5 (G L Moore) *in tch: rdn over 3f out: kpt on same pce fnl 2f* **6/1**[3]	35
	7	3 3/4	**Viking Rock (IRE)** 2-9-3 0 TGMcLaughlin 9 (M Salaman) *s.i.s: towards rr: nvr pce to chal* **11/1**	25
00	8	21	**Definite Honey**[38] 5214 2-8-12 0 TPQueally 7 (A B Haynes) *hld up: rdn over 3f out: wknd over 2f out* **80/1**	—+

0 **9** *nse* **Chicory Cottage**[20] 5784 2-9-3 0 J-PGuillambert 4 —
(G L Moore) *led: rdn and hdd over 2f out: sn wknd* **50/1**

1m 24.56s (1.46) **Going Correction** 0.0s/f (Good) **9** Ran SP% **114.6**
Speed ratings (Par 93): **91,90,86,84,82 78,74,50,49**
toteswinger: 1&2 £1.80, 1&3 £8.90, 2&3 £12.30. CSF £3.90 TOTE £2.10: £1.10, £1.20, £5.40; EX 4.20.
Owner White Paw **Bred** R F And S D Knipe **Trained** East Everleigh, Wilts

FOCUS
An ordinary maiden run at a fair pace, with the first two finishing clear of the rest.

NOTEBOOK
Super Fourteen had run well off a mark of 64 on his previous start and seemed to have a relatively straightforward task. He looked like he might score comfortably having taken control in the last two furlongs but idled a bit and just hung on in the closing stages. His mark should not be affected by this win and he should remain competitive in nurseries, but he may find it hard to cope with less exposed and more progressive rivals. (op 6-4)
Parc Des Princes(USA), a US-bred colt from the family of the stable's smart performer Vanderlin, was well backed on his debut but blew his chance at the start. It was almost a similar story here but he knuckled down really well from an unpromising position and just failed to reel in the leader. This represents a significant step forward and he should be able to win a similar event, particularly on a more galloping track. (op 9-2)
Tobizzy had not shown much on her last two starts but seemed to appreciate the return to fast ground and probably ran near her debut form. (tchd 18-1)
Captain Kallis(IRE) probably ran near his best too but is only rated 43, so puts the form in perspective. Official explanation: jockey said colt ran too freely and did not handle the track (op 25-1)
Molnaya(IRE) drifted markedly on his debut and never got into contention. (op 5-2)
Definite Honey Official explanation: jockey said filly was unsuited by the track
Chicory Cottage Official explanation: jockey said colt ran too freely

6334 BRAKES FRESH IDEAS H'CAP 5f 213y
2:50 (2:52) (Class 6) (0-58,58) 3-Y-O+ **£2,331** (£693; £346; £173) **Stalls** Low

Form RPR
4160 **1** **Conjecture**[68] 4293 6-9-3 **57** PatCosgrave 10 70
(R Bastiman) *chsd ldr: led 2f out: sn rdn and edgd lft: kpt on wl fnl f: rdn out* **9/1**
0041 **2** *1 3/4* **Kyllachy Storm**[36] 5315 4-8-10 **55** WilliamCarson(5) 2 62
(R J Hodges) *chsd ldrs: rdn over 2f out: ev ch over 1f out: kpt on ins fnl f: wnt 2nd nr fin* **7/1**[3]
6422 **3** *shd* **Rhapsilian**[19] 5801 4-9-4 **58** IanMongan 6 65
(J A Geake) *chsd ldrs: rdn over 2f out: kpt on ins fnl f* **6/1**[2]
604 **4** *1/2* **Nordic Light (USA)**[52] 4808 4-8-11 **51** (b) TravisBlock 3 56
(J M Bradley) *chsd ldrs: rdn 3f out: ev ch ent fnl f: no ex* **33/1**
63-0 **5** *1 1/4* **Whiskey Creek**[16] 5911 3-8-12 **54** TGMcLaughlin 11 55
(C A Dwyer) *mid-div: hdwy 4f out: sn rdn: kpt on ins fnl f* **50/1**
4622 **6** *1 1/2* **Gioacchino (IRE)**[21] 5749 3-8-12 **57** (p) KevinGhunowa(3) 12 53
(R A Harris) *hld up towards rr: rdn and hdwy over 1f out: r.o fnl f: nvr nrr* **12/1**
0004 **7** *3/4* **La Famiglia**[12] 6036 3-8-13 **55** DaneO'Neill 7 49+
(H Candy) *chsd ldrs: hung lft and rdn fr over 2f out: hld whn nt clr run ins fnl f* **11/2**[1]
0000 **8** *nk* **Who's Winning (IRE)**[12] 6024 7-9-1 **55** (t) TQuinn 4 48
(B G Powell) *hmpd leaving stalls: hld up towards rr: rdn 3f out: sme late prog: nvr a danger* **12/1**
6032 **9** *nse* **Billy Red**[25] 5626 4-9-1 **55** (b) DO'Donohoe 5 48
(J R Jenkins) *t.k.h in mid-div: rdn and hdwy over 2f out: fdd fnl f* **8/1**
0040 **10** *nk* **All You Need (IRE)**[23] 5709 4-8-12 **55** (b[1]) RussellKennemore(3) 8 47
(R Hollinshead) *led: rdn and hdd 2f out: one pce after* **16/1**
3035 **11** *1 1/2* **Namu**[11] 6063 5-8-10 **55** SophieDoyle(5) 13 42+
(Miss T Spearing) *towards rr: styng on whn hmpd ins fnl f: no ch after but nvr threatened* **14/1**
-652 **12** *nk* **Melt (IRE)**[28] 5574 3-9-1 **57** TPQueally 9 43+
(R Hannon) *s.i.s: nt clr run over 1f out: nvr bttr than mid-div* **14/1**
4024 **13** *10* **Miss Poppy**[46] 5026 3-9-2 **58** GeorgeBaker 1 12
(P R Chamings) *mid-div: rdn over 2f out: wknd over 1f out* **10/1**
0063 **14** *hd* **Briannsta (IRE)**[11] 6063 6-8-7 **52** NataliaGemelova(5) 16 5
(J E Long) *mid-div: rdn 3f out: sn btn* **16/1**
5004 **15** *1 1/2* **Charmel's Lad**[32] 5421 3-9-1 **57** TedDurcan 14 6
(W R Swinburn) *s.i.s: a towards rr* **33/1**

1m 10.01s (-0.19) **Going Correction** 0.0s/f (Good)
WFA 3 from 4yo+ 2lb **15** Ran SP% **120.7**
Speed ratings (Par 101): **101,98,98,97,96 94,93,92,92,92 90,89,76,76,74**
toteswinger: 1&2 £23.80, 1&3 £15.50, 2&3 £8.40. CSF £69.47 CT £426.67 TOTE £12.80: £4.20, £3.20, £2.40; EX 103.90.
Owner The McMaster Springford Partnership **Bred** Darley **Trained** Cowthorpe, N Yorks
■ Stewards' Enquiry : Sophie Doyle two-day ban: careless riding (Oct 13-14)

FOCUS
A competitive event run at a fast pace. Several were in trouble at an early stage and not many got into it from behind. The form is solid rated through the second and third.
Who's Winning(IRE) Official explanation: jockey said gelding hung right
Billy Red Official explanation: jockey said gelding hung right
Briannsta(IRE) Official explanation: trainer said gelding was found to have bled internally following a scope

6335 BLAKES BUTCHERS CLAIMING STKS 6f 209y
3:20 (3:24) (Class 6) 4-Y-O+ **£1,942** (£578; £288; £144) **Stalls** Low

Form RPR
0010 **1** **Obe Brave**[9] 6105 5-9-3 78 JamieMoriarty 1 73
(R A Fahey) *chsd ldrs: led over 2f out: hld on wl whn strly chal fnl f* **13/8**[1]
4220 **2** *hd* **Ten To The Dozen**[5] 6208 5-8-11 60 TonyCulhane 15 66
(P W Hiatt) *prom: wnt 2nd 2f out: drvn nrly level fnl f: narrowly hld* **7/1**[3]
0045 **3** *2* **Summer Recluse (USA)**[3] 6255 9-8-13 52 (t) TQuinn 2 63
(J M Bradley) *hld up towards rr: rdn and hdwy over 2f out: chsd ldng pair fnl f: nvr quite able to chal* **16/1**
4105 **4** *2 1/2* **Seneschal**[21] 5755 7-9-1 64 TPQueally 5 58
(A B Haynes) *chsd ldrs: swtchd rt and rdn over 2f out: one pce appr fnl f* **10/1**
0300 **5** *1 3/4* **Stargazy**[19] 5797 4-8-13 48 LiamJones 12 51
(W G M Turner) *led tl over 2f out: sn outpcd* **66/1**
1505 **6** *1 3/4* **Majestical (IRE)**[44] 5090 6-8-9 53 (p) TravisBlock 3 42
(R A Harris) *bhd: rdn and hdwy 2f out: no imp fnl f* **20/1**
4040 **7** *nk* **Punching**[52] 4809 4-8-13 66 DaneO'Neill 7 46
(Miss Gay Kelleway) *mid-div: rdn over 2f out: nt pce to chal* **5/1**[2]
1000 **8** *3/4* **Balerno**[90] 3588 9-8-13 52 IanMongan 16 44
(Mrs L J Mongan) *mid-div: rdn and outpcd 3f out: n.d after* **50/1**
0600 **9** *3/4* **Coup D'Etat**[32] 5429 6-8-6 47 (e[1]) KevinGhunowa(3) 8 38
(R A Harris) *prom over 4f* **33/1**
0004 **10** *1 1/4* **Turkish Sultan (IRE)**[5] 6208 5-8-13 50 (p) TGMcLaughlin 9 38
(J M Bradley) *t.k.h in midfield: rdn 3f out: outpcd fnl 2f* **33/1**
-000 **11** *1 1/2* **Chalentina**[52] 4825 5-7-13 45 NataliaGemelova(5) 13 25
(J E Long) *chsd ldrs on outside tl hrd rdn and wknd over 2f out* **66/1**
0546 **12** *1 3/4* **Rosie Cross (IRE)**[19] 5797 4-8-10 46 J-PGuillambert 4 26
(Eve Johnson Houghton) *bhd: rdn 3f out: nvr nr ldrs* **20/1**
6 **13** *4 1/2* **Sticky Tape**[111] 2917 4-7-9 0 Louis-PhilippeBeuzelin(5) 6 4
(J A Osborne) *dwlt: a towards rr* **8/1**
0044 **14** *5* **Border Artist**[29] 5533 9-8-9 50 (p) JerryO'Dwyer 14 —
(J Pearce) *bhd and wd: rdn 3f out: nvr a factor* **16/1**
500- **15** *6* **Mine The Balance (IRE)**[337] 4416 5-8-0 47 SophieDoyle(5) 10 —
(H J Manners) *chsd ldrs 2f: sn rdn and struggling to hold pl: n.d fnl 2f* **100/1**

1m 22.39s (-0.71) **Going Correction** 0.0s/f (Good) **15** Ran SP% **120.6**
Speed ratings (Par 101): **104,103,101,98,96 94,94,93,92,91 89,87,82,76,69**
toteswinger: 1&2 £5.20, 1&3 £9.90, 2&3 £11.80. CSF £11.63 TOTE £2.70: £1.30, £2.30, £3.90; EX 16.30.
Owner Mrs J Penman **Bred** Helshaw Grange Stud, E Kent & Mrs E Connelly **Trained** Musley Bank, N Yorks
■ Stewards' Enquiry : Jamie Moriarty two-day ban: used whip down shoulder with excessive force in forehand position (Oct 13-14)

FOCUS
A modest claimer rated through the runner-up and third.
Coup D'Etat Official explanation: jockey said gelding lost a front shoe
Chalentina Official explanation: trainer said mare bled from the nose

6336 HORSEMART.CO.UK H'CAP 7f 214y
3:50 (3:53) (Class 5) (0-70,70) 3-Y-O+ **£2,978** (£886; £442; £221) **Stalls** Low

Form RPR
4443 **1** **Outside Edge (IRE)**[11] 6048 3-8-13 **65** TedDurcan 11 73
(W R Swinburn) *mid-div: hdwy on rail to ld 2f out: hld on wl despite swishing tail fnl f* **10/1**
0364 **2** *1/2* **Wrighty Almighty (IRE)**[16] 5915 6-9-4 **66** TQuinn 6 73
(P R Chamings) *bhd: drvn along and gd hdwy over 1f out: hung lft: chsd wnr ins fnl f: kpt on: hld nr fin* **7/1**[3]
2000 **3** *1 3/4* **Haasem (USA)**[31] 5458 5-9-4 **66** DO'Donohoe 13 69
(J R Jenkins) *bhd: hdwy and hung lft fr 2f out: styd on u.p* **16/1**
3222 **4** *nse* **Valento**[13] 6001 3-9-0 **66** J-PGuillambert 12 69
(Eve Johnson Houghton) *towards rr: hrd rdn over 2f out: tk a long time to pick up but styd on strly fr over 1f out* **10/1**
4332 **5** *3/4* **Gulch's Rose (USA)**[26] 5616 3-9-0 **66** TPQueally 7 67
(J Noseda) *in tch: drvn to chal 2f out: no ex 1f out* **6/1**[2]
600 **5** *dht* **Carpe Diem**[76] 4044 3-8-5 **57** LiamJones 9 58
(W J Haggas) *in tch on outer: carried rt 3f out: effrt and edgd lft over 1f out: styd on same pce* **7/2**[1]
0030 **7** *1/2* **Napoletano (GER)**[12] 6020 7-9-7 **69** (p) IanMongan 14 71+
(S Dow) *hld up in rr of midfield: hdwy over 2f out: disputing 4th and hld whn squeezed out ins fnl f* **12/1**
0200 **8** *2 1/4* **Garden Party**[48] 4946 4-9-6 **68** TGMcLaughlin 5 63+
(Jane Chapple-Hyam) *sn towards rr: rdn and hdwy 2f out: disputing 4th whn short of room over 1f out: wl hld after* **25/1**
2210 **9** *1 1/2* **The Gaikwar (IRE)**[4] 6228 9-8-8 **59** (b) KevinGhunowa(3) 10 51
(R A Harris) *prom: drvn along over 2f out: sn wknd and hung lft* **16/1**
3230 **10** *3/4* **Star Strider**[7] 6178 4-8-13 **61** DaneO'Neill 15 51
(Miss Gay Kelleway) *towards rr: promising hdwy whn nt clr run over 2f out tl wl over 1f out: swtchd lft: nvr able to chal* **10/1**
3000 **11** *1 1/2* **Atheer Dubai (IRE)**[69] 4284 3-9-4 **70** PatCosgrave 1 56
(E F Vaughan) *prom: rdn over 2f out: disputing 4th and btn whn short of room on rail ins fnl f: qckly lost pl* **33/1**
0600 **12** *3 1/2* **Free Tussy (ARG)**[16] 5908 4-9-8 **70** (b[1]) GeorgeBaker 2 48
(G L Moore) *led tl 2f out: wknd over 1f out* **50/1**
-430 **13** *8* **Young Bertie**[11] 6052 5-9-8 **70** (v) TravisBlock 3 30
(H Morrison) *prom: hrd rdn 3f out: sn wknd* **8/1**
3000 **14** *4 1/2* **Very Well Red**[3] 6255 5-9-1 **68** WilliamCarson(5) 4 18
(P W Hiatt) *prom: hung rt 3f out: wknd 2f out: btn whn short of room over 1f out: eased* **20/1**
0420 **15** *2* **Magroom**[19] 5800 4-9-1 **68** MCGeran(5) 8 13
(R J Hodges) *in tch tl wknd over 2f out* **16/1**

1m 34.53s (-1.47) **Going Correction** 0.0s/f (Good)
WFA 3 from 4yo+ 4lb **15** Ran SP% **126.2**
Speed ratings (Par 103): **107,106,104,104,103 103,103,101,99,98 97,93,85,81,79**
toteswinger: 1&2 £12.90, 1&3 £49.70, 2&3 £28.00. CSF £78.74 CT £1171.10 TOTE £13.40: £3.40, £2.30, £7.80; EX 85.00.
Owner Crickceters Club Racing Group **Bred** Tally-Ho Stud **Trained** Aldbury, Herts
■ Stewards' Enquiry : T Quinn two-day ban: used whip with excessive frequency without giving gelding time to respond (Oct 13-14)

FOCUS
Another tight handicap. They went a reasonable pace and the field were spread across the track in the straight. The runners who stayed near the far rail seemed to have an advantage. Sound form rated through the second and third.
Wrighty Almighty(IRE) Official explanation: jockey said gelding hung left in final furlong

6337 HARINO.COM - VIRTUAL RACING, REAL EXCITEMENT APPRENTICE H'CAP 1m 1f 209y
4:20 (4:24) (Class 6) (0-65,64) 3-Y-O **£2,331** (£693; £346; £173) **Stalls** High

Form RPR
6000 **1** **Contrada**[75] 4086 3-8-9 **57** WilliamCarson(3) 12 70+
(R Charlton) *hld up in tch: led 2f out: hrd rdn over 1f out: styd on strly to get wl on top fnl f* **10/1**
5452 **2** *4* **Citron Presse (USA)**[26] 5611 3-9-3 **62** (p) Louis-PhilippeBeuzelin 5 67
(J H M Gosden) *towards rr: hmpd on rail over 4f out: hdwy over 2f out: drvn to go 2nd 1f out: styd on same pce but unable to match wnr* **3/1**[1]
0600 **3** *4 1/2* **Rosy Dawn**[25] 5631 3-8-2 **50** oh5 RossAtkinson(3) 10 46
(J J Bridger) *disp ld: reminders 5f out: hdd 2f out: hrd rdn and wknd over 1f out* **50/1**
246 **4** *shd* **Locum**[65] 4427 3-9-0 **64** ThomasBubb(5) 6 60
(M H Tompkins) *trckd ldrs: outpcd 3f out: rallied and edgd lft over 1f out: no ex* **4/1**[2]
0002 **5** *hd* **Cwm Rhondda (USA)**[18] 5815 3-9-2 **61** (t) AshleyHamblett 4 56
(P W Chapple-Hyam) *chsd ldrs: hrd rdn over 2f out: hung lft and wknd over 1f out* **9/2**[3]
3206 **6** *shd* **Pinnacle Point**[41] 5169 3-8-8 **56** JemmaMarshall(3) 11 51
(G L Moore) *disp ld tl hrd rdn and edgd rt 2f out: wknd over 1f out* **7/1**
0000 **7** *3/4* **Ubiquitous**[29] 5537 3-8-2 **50** oh5 SophieDoyle(3) 2 44
(S Dow) *stdd s: hld up in detached last: mod effrt on outside 3f out: edgd lft over 1f out: n.d* **50/1**

3400 **8** ¾ **Wing Play (IRE)**[9] 6134 3-9-5 **64**....................(t) MCGeran 9 56
(H Morrison) *hld up in midfield: hdwy to trck ldrs 4f out: rdn and hanging bdly on outside fr 2f out: sn wknd* **7/1**

6230 **9** 2½ **Be Free**[17] 5868 3-8-8 **58**.................... RosieJessop(5) 1 45
(Sir Mark Prescott) *hld up in rr: hdwy to chse ldrs 1/2-way: lost pl 3f out: sme hdwy on ins rail over 1f out: sn wknd* **14/1**

60-0 **10** 15 **Stateside (CAN)**[18] 5837 3-8-5 **50**.................... NicolPolli 7 7
(R A Fahey) *mid-div: lost pl 6f out: sn drvn along and bhd* **25/1**

0000 **11** 4½ **Super Al**[12] 6015 3-8-1 **51** oh5 ow1.................... TobyAtkinson(5) 8 —
(M Wigham) *dwlt: hld up in midfield: wknd over 4f out: sn bhd* **100/1**

050 **12** 14 **Katy Kitten (UAE)**[16] 5912 3-8-5 **53** oh2 ow3..........(b1) JPHamblett(3) 3 —
(G L Moore) *t.k.h: prom tl hrd rdn and wknd qckly 3f out: eased whn no ch fnl 2f* **14/1**

2m 4.29s (0.69) **Going Correction** 0.0s/f (Good) **12** Ran SP% **119.4**
Speed ratings (Par 99): **97,93,90,90,89 89,89,88,86,74 71,59**
toteswinger: 1&2 £10.20, 1&3 £86.00, 2&3 £19.10. CSF £39.76 CT £1471.93 TOTE £13.90: £3.30, £1.80, £9.80; EX 50.90.
Owner Mountgrange Stud **Bred** Minster Enterprises Ltd **Trained** Beckhampton, Wilts

FOCUS
A moderate apprentice handicap rated around the runner-up.
Contrada Official explanation: trainer said, regarding running, that the colt had a wind operation after its last run.
Cwm Rhondda(USA) Official explanation: trainer's rep said filly was unsuited by the good to firm ground

6338 HARDINGS BAR & CATERING SERVICES H'CAP 6f 209y
4:50 (4:54) (Class 6) (0-65,65) 3-Y-0+ **£2,331** (£693; £346; £173) **Stalls** Low

Form RPR

600 **1** **Eleonora (FR)**[37] 5278 3-9-7 **62**....................(p) LiamJones 3 68+
(W J Haggas) *hld up in tch: rdn to press ldrs whn n.m.r ins fnl 2f: late burst u.p to ld nr fin* **10/1**

0012 **2** ½ **Palais Polaire**[21] 5755 6-9-2 **54**....................(p) TQuinn 10 60
(J A Geake) *prom: drvn to chal over 1f out: nt qckn nr fin* **7/1**[3]

6000 **3** hd **Cinnamon Hill**[51] 4862 4-9-9 **64**.................... RussellKennemore(3) 1 69
(Eve Johnson Houghton) *led: hrd rdn 2f out: hld on gamely tl worn down nr fin* **33/1**

0211 **4** nk **Singleb (IRE)**[29] 5533 4-9-10 **62**.................... GeorgeBaker 12 67
(G L Moore) *mid-div on outer: hdwy over 2f out: drvn to press ldrs ins fnl f: kpt on* **5/2**[1]

-431 **5** ½ **Inquisitress**[61] 4529 4-8-9 **50**.................... MarcHalford(3) 9 53
(J J Bridger) *hld up towards rr: rdn and hdwy 2f out: pressed ldrs ins fnl f: kpt on* **9/1**

4300 **6** 1 **Palmetto Point**[11] 6056 4-9-13 **65**....................(p) TravisBlock 11 66
(H Morrison) *chsd ldrs: rdn and lost pl after 2f: rallying whn boxed in over 1f out: nt pick up whn clr* **6/1**[2]

5300 **7** ½ **Royal Encore**[11] 6063 4-9-3 **55**.................... PatCosgrave 16 54
(J R Fanshawe) *dropped in at rr fr wd draw: rdn 4f out: styd on u.p fnl 2f: nvr nrr* **16/1**

6040 **8** 2¼ **Last Of The Line**[17] 5867 3-9-4 **59**....................(v) TPQueally 7 55+
(H J L Dunlop) *hld up in midfield: shkn up over 2f out: effrt and hrd rdn whn nt clr run over 1f out: wl hld after* **16/1**

5300 **9** 1¾ **Romany Nights (IRE)**[9] 6125 8-9-6 **65**....................(b) KylieManser(7) 6 53
(Miss Gay Kelleway) *s.s: sn chsng ldrs on rail: outpcd 3f out: rallied and n.m.r 2f out: wknd over 1f out* **20/1**

3460 **10** 1 **Interactive (IRE)**[25] 5639 5-9-4 **63**.................... RossAtkinson(7) 2 49
(Andrew Turnell) *t.k.h: w ldrs: hrd rdn 2f out: wknd over 1f out* **16/1**

0320 **11** 2¾ **Crataegus**[21] 5755 3-9-9 **64**....................(v1) DaneO'Neill 8 41
(H Candy) *sn pushed along in rr: drvn along and n.d fnl 3f* **8/1**

030 **12** 38 **Telephonist**[44] 5086 3-8-11 **52**.................... TedDurcan 13 —
(J R Best) *mid-div on outer: wknd over 3f out: sn bhd* **20/1**

1m 23.37s (0.27) **Going Correction** 0.0s/f (Good)
WFA 3 from 4yo+ 3lb **12** Ran SP% **121.6**
Speed ratings (Par 101): **98,97,97,96,96 95,94,92,90,88 85,42**
toteswinger: 1&2 £14.10, 1&3 £47.10, 2&3 £38.90. CSF £74.33 CT £2250.81 TOTE £11.40: £3.70, £1.70, £9.80; EX 79.50.
Owner D I Scott **Bred** M Desmond Scott **Trained** Newmarket, Suffolk

FOCUS
A tight handicap run at a steady pace that produced a bunch finish, which casts some doubt over the form.
Eleonora(FR) Official explanation: trainer's rep said, regarding running, that the filly had benefited from a drop in class.

6339 FRIDAY-AD.CO.UK H'CAP 5f 59y
5:20 (5:22) (Class 6) (0-65,66) 3-Y-0+ **£2,396** (£712; £356; £177) **Stalls** Low

Form RPR

050 **1** **Multahab**[9] 6131 9-8-8 **55**....................(t) MarcHalford(3) 7 68
(M Wigham) *bhd: brought alone to stands' rail 2f out: gd hdwy to ld ins fnl f: drvn ahd: in command at fin* **12/1**

5026 **2** 2¼ **Pic Up Sticks**[9] 6131 9-9-2 **60**.................... GeorgeBaker 12 65
(B G Powell) *hld up in midfield: rdn and hdwy over 1f out: r.o to take 2nd nr fin* **11/2**[1]

5206 **3** 1 **Bilboa**[16] 5911 3-8-6 **51**....................(p) LiamJones 1 52
(J M Bradley) *chsd ldrs: led on far rail 2f out: sn kicked 2 l ahd: hdd and no ex ins fnl f* **20/1**

320 **4** 1 **This Ones For Eddy**[48] 4952 3-9-5 **64**.................... TedDurcan 5 62
(S Parr) *dwlt: bhd: edgd rt 2f out: gd late hdwy* **14/1**

0002 **5** nse **Metal Guru**[33] 5398 4-8-13 **60**....................(p) RussellKennemore(3) 8 58
(R Hollinshead) *fast away: sn lost pl in midfield: drvn to chse ldrs over 1f out: one pce fnl f* **8/1**[2]

4360 **6** ¾ **Night Prospector**[5] 6204 8-8-13 **60**....................(b) KevinGhunowa(3) 2 55
(R A Harris) *w ldrs: hrd rdn over 1f out: sn wknd* **8/1**[2]

1530 **7** ½ **Miss Firefly**[13] 5998 3-8-13 **63**.................... MCGeran(5) 15 56
(R J Hodges) *mid-div on outer: hrd rdn and hung lft 2f out: kpt on fnl f: nt pce to chal* **25/1**

0633 **8** nse **Bollin Franny**[52] 4824 4-8-2 **51**.................... NataliaGemelova(5) 3 44
(J E Long) *led tl 2f out: hrd rdn and wknd jst over 1f out* **9/1**[3]

5224 **9** nse **Fast Freddie**[6] 6190 4-9-0 **58**.................... TonyCulhane 14 51
(S Parr) *prom and wd: hrd rdn and grad fdd fnl 2f* **11/2**[1]

-530 **10** ½ **Smiddy Hill**[36] 5319 6-8-3 **54** oh2 ow5.................... RossAtkinson(7) 6 45
(R Bastiman) *hld up and bhd: sme hdwy whn nt clr run over 2f out: nvr able to chal* **16/1**

2461 **11** ½ **Azygous**[6] 6190 5-9-8 **66** 6ex....................(b) DaneO'Neill 16 55
(J Akehurst) *towards rr and v wd: hrd rdn and struggling in last pl over 2f out: edgd lft over 1f out: r.o fnl f* **9/1**[3]

060 **12** 1¼ **Fly Time**[15] 5941 4-8-0 **49** oh4.................... NicolPolli(5) 11 34
(T T Clement) *dwlt: bhd: gd hdwy on rail 2f out: hrd rdn and wknd over 1f out* **66/1**

060 **13** 1¾ **Bluebok**[6] 6190 7-9-2 **60**....................(bt) TGMcLaughlin 13 38
(J M Bradley) *prom to 1/2-way* **20/1**

104 **14** 7 **Croeso Bach**[41] 5171 4-8-13 **62**.................... SophieDoyle(5) 4 15
(J L Spearing) *in tch: shkn up over 2f out: wknd over 1f out: eased whn btn fnl f* **8/1**[2]

00 **15** nk **One Way Ticket**[66] 4370 8-8-9 **53**....................(p) TQuinn 10 5
(J M Bradley) *prom to 1/2-way: bhd whn eased fnl f* **25/1**

6500 **16** 7 **Hawaii Prince**[33] 5398 4-8-4 **53**.................... WilliamCarson(5) 9 —
(S T Mason) *prom to 1/2-way: wl bhd whn eased fnl f* **25/1**

62.06 secs (-0.24) **Going Correction** 0.0s/f (Good)
WFA 3 from 4yo+ 1lb **16** Ran SP% **126.9**
Speed ratings (Par 101): **101,97,95,94,94 92,92,92,91,91 90,88,85,74,73 62**
toteswinger: 1&2 £21.70, 1&3 £54.40, 2&3 £29.10. CSF £72.94 CT £1404.10 TOTE £14.70: £4.20, £2.00, £4.40, £3.10; EX 102.50 Place 6 £ 232.98, Place 5 £ 175.78.
Owner P J Burke and Dave Anderson **Bred** Shadwell Estate Company Limited **Trained** Newmarket, Suffolk

FOCUS
The early pace was not particularly fast, but it gradually increased and the winner was given an enterprising ride to win decisively against the stands' rail. The form has been rated around the runner-up.
Metal Guru Official explanation: jockey said filly hung left
Azygous Official explanation: jockey said gelding hung left
Croeso Bach Official explanation: jockey said filly missed the break and never travelled
T/Jkpt: Not won. T/Plt: £323.00 to a £1 stake. Pool: £70,680.93. 159.72 winning tickets. T/Qpdt: £58.30 to a £1 stake. Pool: £3,502.70. 44.45 winning tickets. LM

5286 WINDSOR (R-H)
Monday, September 29
OFFICIAL GOING: Good to firm (good in places; 8.4)
Wind: Moderate, behind Weather: Fine becoming cloudy

6340 GET ON WITH WILLIAM HILL - 0800 444040 H'CAP 6f
2:30 (2:31) (Class 5) (0-75,81) 3-Y-0+ **£2,729** (£806; £403) **Stalls** High

Form RPR

2033 **1** **Memphis Man**[5] 6200 5-9-1 **75**.................... RichardEvans(5) 4 88
(P D Evans) *taken down early: dwlt: wl in rr: prog fr 1/2-way: drvn to chse ldr fnl f: styd on wl to ld last 50yds* **18/1**

401 **2** ½ **Haajes**[7] 6164 4-9-5 **79** 6ex....................(t) FrederikTylicki(5) 3 90
(S Parr) *w ldrs: overall ldr on outer over 1f out: styd on but collared last 50yds* **13/2**[3]

2452 **3** 1¼ **Make My Dream**[4] 6232 5-9-1 **70**.................... TPO'Shea 14 77
(J Gallagher) *mde most but only narrowly: drvn fr 1/2-way: hdd over 1f out: edgd lft but kpt on* **11/2**[2]

0400 **4** 2 **Harlech Castle**[30] 5490 3-9-2 **73**....................(b) JimmyFortune 8 74
(P F I Cole) *sn chsd ldrs: effrt u.p over 2f out: kpt on one pce* **10/1**

-611 **5** ¾ **Tubby Isaacs**[26] 5610 4-9-3 **72**.................... EddieAhern 11 71+
(P J Makin) *taken down early: s.s: wl in rr: rdn over 2f out: sme prog over 1f out: nt clr run ent fnl f: styd on but w little enthusiasm* **7/2**[1]

2-16 **6** ½ **Luminous Gold**[14] 5962 3-9-4 **75**.................... AlanMunro 1 72
(C F Wall) *chsd ldrs on wd outside: rdn to try to chal 2f out: fdd over 1f out* **20/1**

2220 **7** nk **Alfresco**[23] 5695 4-9-4 **73**.................... RichardHughes 10 69
(I A Wood) *stdd s: hld up wl in rr: sme prog over 1f out: nt clr run sn after: kpt on: nvr nrr* **12/1**

2060 **8** ½ **Adantino**[17] 5867 9-8-11 **69**....................(b) JamesMillman(3) 5 63+
(B R Millman) *wl in rr: no prog tl jst over 1f out: nt clr run and swtchd rt ent fnl f: kpt on: nvr nrr* **20/1**

2201 **9** nse **Peter Island (FR)**[5] 6200 5-9-12 **81** 6ex....................(v) ChrisCatlin 12 75
(J Gallagher) *w ldr to 2f out: steadily fdd* **15/2**

000 **10** nse **Leading Edge (IRE)**[30] 5490 3-9-1 **72**.................... SamHitchcott 13 66
(M R Channon) *dwlt but sn chsd ldrs: no imp 2f out: sn fdd* **66/1**

-220 **11** 2¾ **War And Peace (IRE)**[12] 6020 4-9-4 **73**.................... FrankieMcDonald 6 58
(Jane Chapple-Hyam) *taken down early: s.i.s: mostly in last trio: hanging v bdly and reluctant whn asked for effrt fr 2f out: nvr on terms* **12/1**

0000 **12** 1 **Brunelleschi**[26] 5600 5-9-1 **70**....................(b) AdamKirby 16 52
(P L Gilligan) *early reminders: chsd ldrs: struggling over 2f out: eased fnl f* **25/1**

5404 **13** 1¼ **Maryolini**[13] 5998 3-9-1 **72**....................(v1) KirstyMilczarek 9 50
(N J Vaughan) *w ldrs to jst over 2f out: wknd over 1f out* **33/1**

0522 **14** 1 **Anosti**[13] 5998 3-9-4 **75**....................(p) NCallan 2 50
(K A Ryan) *cl up on outer: u.p fr 1/2-way: wknd over 1f out* **16/1**

100 **15** ¾ **Candela Bay (IRE)**[23] 5713 3-9-2 **73**.................... RyanMoore 7 46
(W J Haggas) *a in last trio: wl btn fnl 2f* **14/1**

0600 **16** 17 **We Have A Dream**[14] 5962 3-9-4 **75**.................... MartinDwyer 15 —
(W R Muir) *w ldrs 2f: sn lost pl u.p: t.o* **25/1**

1m 10.8s (-2.20) **Going Correction** -0.375s/f (Firm)
WFA 3 from 4yo+ 2lb **16** Ran SP% **126.6**
Speed ratings (Par 103): **99,98,96,94,93 92,91,91,91,91 87,86,84,83,82 59**
toteswinger: 1&2 £23.50, 1&3 £33.10, 2&3 £10.20. CSF £125.25 CT £782.33 TOTE £23.70: £4.00, £1.90, £1.30, £2.80; EX 155.30 Trifecta £194.40 Part won. Pool: £262.74, 0.10 winning units..
Owner M D Jones **Bred** R T And Mrs Watson **Trained** Pandy, Monmouths

FOCUS
While this was a modest sprint, it was still competitive enough and was run at a decent pace. The field came more towards the stands' side, but the main action developed down the middle of the track. Sound form rated around the third and fourth.
Harlech Castle Official explanation: jockey said colt hung left

6341 GET A BONUS AT WILLIAMHILLCASINO.COM EBF MAIDEN STKS (DIV I) 6f
3:00 (3:01) (Class 5) 2-Y-0 **£3,561** (£1,059; £529; £264) **Stalls** High

Form RPR

6424 **1** **Flintlock (IRE)**[13] 6002 2-9-3 73....................(b) JimmyFortune 2 71+
(J H M Gosden) *fast away fr poor draw: sn led and crossed to nr side: rdn and in command fr over 1f out: drvn out* **13/8**[1]

0 **2** 1¾ **Megasecret**[15] 5929 2-9-3 0.................... RichardHughes 9 65
(R Hannon) *wl plcd: prog 1/2-way and gng wl: chsd wnr over 1f out: sn rdn and no imp* **8/1**

2000 **3** ¾ **Whisky Jack**[14] 5960 2-9-3 63....................(b1) MartinDwyer 16 63
(W R Muir) *s.s: wl in rr and nt gng wl: effrt 1/2-way: prog and swtchd lft 2f out: tried to cl over 1f out: one pce* **7/1**[3]

0 **4** *nk* **Hawk's Eye**[15] 5929 2-9-3 0 TPO'Shea 15 62+
(E F Vaughan) *hld up wl in rr: gng wl 1/2-way: pushed along fr 2f out: carried hd high but styd on wl: nrst fin* **14/1**
5 *nk* **Ponting (IRE)** 2-9-3 0 RichardKingscote 14 61+
(R M Beckett) *chsd wnr to 1/2-way: one pce u.p fnl 2f* **13/2**[2]
6 *2 ¾* **Merry Diva** 2-8-9 0 JackMitchell(3) 10 47+
(C F Wall) *wl in rr: effrt and taken towards outer 2f out: urged along and kpt on: n.d* **12/1**
7 *3 ¼* **Royal Collection (IRE)** 2-9-3 0 HayleyTurner 3 43
(J Pearce) *dwlt: sn prom: chsd wnr 1/2-way: rn green and edgd lft 2f out: fdd over 1f out* **12/1**
0 **8** *1* **Brown Lentic (IRE)**[17] 5860 2-9-3 0 RyanMoore 6 40+
(G L Moore) *stdd s: t.k.h early and hld up towards rr: sme prog over 2f out: pushed along briefly over 1f out: nvr nr ldrs* **14/1**
0 **9** *1* **Oisin's Boy**[10] 6077 2-9-3 0 AlanMunro 8 37
(J R Boyle) *nvr beyond midfield: lft bhd fr 2f out* **100/1**
0 **10** *½* **Merry May**[10] 6077 2-8-9 0 PatrickHills(3) 12 30
(R Hannon) *a towards rr: no prog 2f out* **66/1**
11 *1 ½* **Fly By Nelly** 2-8-12 0 ChrisCatlin 11 26
(H Morrison) *racd wd and nvr beyond midfield: wknd 2f out* **25/1**
50 **12** *1* **Ready To Prime**[140] 2042 2-8-12 0 JimCrowley 13 23+
(D K Ivory) *prom to 1/2-way: floundering and btn over 2f out: sn eased* **100/1**
00 **13** *4 ½* **Buckle Up**[161] 1523 2-9-3 0 AdrianMcCarthy 4 14
(D K Ivory) *chsd ldrs on wd outside: pushed along bef 1/2-way: wknd 2f out* **100/1**
55 **14** *2 ½* **Rio Pomba (IRE)**[12] 6010 2-8-12 0 DNolan 5 2
(D Carroll) *prom to 1/2-way: wknd* **22/1**
0 **15** *3* **Night Dancer (IRE)**[17] 5860 2-8-12 0 NCallan 1 —+
(B W Hills) *free to post: wnt bdly lft s: a wl in rr* **40/1**

1m 12.27s (-0.73) **Going Correction** -0.375s/f (Firm) **15** Ran SP% **118.9**
Speed ratings (Par 95): **89,86,85,85,84 81,76,75,74,73 71,70,64,60,56**
toteswinger: 1&2 £4.50, 1&3 £3.20, 2&3 £9.70. CSF £13.53 TOTE £2.30: £1.10, £3.10, £2.20; EX 14.70 Trifecta £81.70 Pool: £164.60, 1.49 winning units.
Owner H R H Princess Haya Of Jordan **Bred** Dermot Brennan & Associates Ltd **Trained** Newmarket, Suffolk

FOCUS
This was probably just an ordinary first division of the juvenile maiden which again saw the field ignore the far side of the track. The form looks straightforward enough.

NOTEBOOK
Flintlock(IRE), who went off too fast over 7f at Yarmouth 13 days previously, put his early dash to great effect and was quick to bag the stands' rail. He eventually did the job comfortably from the front and the drop back to this trip worked the oracle. He should have a little more to offer back in nurseries over this trip now his confidence is high. (op 7-4 tchd 15-8)
Megasecret showed the clear benefit of his debut experience at Goodwood and improved significantly for this quicker surface. He should not remain a maiden for long and a stiffer test will suit him in due course. (op 10-1)
Whisky Jack, back in trip, was switched mid-track with his effort and posted a much better performance for the fitting of first-time blinkers. He probably needs a stiffer track over this distance and has a race in him, but whether the headgear has the same sort of effect next time remains to be seen. (op 8-1 tchd 13-2)
Hawk's Eye stayed on nicely from off the pace and stepped up a good deal on the level of his debut form at Goodwood, but could still not confirm that form with the runner-up. He ought to fare even better when qualifying for an official rating after his next run. (tchd 16-1)
Ponting(IRE) showed enough to suggest he will prove a deal sharper with this initial experience under his belt. (op 5-1 tchd 7-1)
Merry Diva, a sister to Paradise Isle and related to numerous sprint winners, took a while to get the hang of things but ran on from the rear in the closing stages. (tchd 10-1)
Ready To Prime Official explanation: jockey said filly hung left
Buckle Up Official explanation: jockey said colt hung left

6342 GET A BONUS AT WILLIAMHILLCASINO.COM EBF MAIDEN STKS (DIV II) 6f
3:30 (3:31) (Class 5) 2-Y-O **£3,561** (£1,059; £529; £264) **Stalls** High

Form RPR
1 **Enact** 2-8-12 0 RyanMoore 1 72+
(Sir Michael Stoute) *w.w in midfield: prog 2f out: clsd to ld 1f out: shkn up briefly: styd on wl: comf* **11/2**[3]
60 **2** *1 ¼* **Piccolo Mondo**[47] 4980 2-9-3 0 JimCrowley 6 73
(P Winkworth) *trckd ldrs: effrt to chal jst over 1f out: chsd wnr fnl f: styd on but readily hld* **20/1**
3 *2 ½* **Jordaura** 2-9-3 0 AdamKirby 2 66+
(W R Swinburn) *dwlt: wl in rr: prog on outer 2f out: reminder over 1f out: styd on wl but no threat to ldng pair* **16/1**
0 **4** *½* **Lujeanie**[47] 4980 2-9-0 0 JackMitchell(3) 5 64
(D K Ivory) *pressed ldrs: stl cl up jst over 1f out: fdd fnl f* **66/1**
445 **5** *1 ¾* **Party Cat (IRE)**[80] 3895 2-9-0 76 PatrickHills(3) 3 59
(R Hannon) *racd on wd outside: wl in tch: effrt and on terms 2f out: edgd lft and fdd 1f out* **9/2**[1]
6 *shd* **Diamond Twister (USA)** 2-9-3 0 HayleyTurner 15 59
(J R Best) *pressed ldr: led wl over 1f out: hdd & wknd rapidly 1f out* **12/1**
06 **7** *2 ½* **Pure Rhythm**[16] 5905 2-8-12 0 AdrianMcCarthy 4 46
(S C Williams) *hld up and wl in rr: sme prog fr 2f out: pushed along and kpt on: nvr on terms* **66/1**
8 *½* **Bold Tie** 2-9-3 0 RichardHughes 12 56+
(R Hannon) *sn trckd ldrs: cl up whn nt clr run briefly wl over 1f out: sn wknd and eased* **5/1**[2]
0 **9** *shd* **Everaard (USA)**[11] 6062 2-9-3 0 AlanMunro 10 49
(D R C Elsworth) *dwlt: a towards rr: shuffled along and modest late prog* **20/1**
00 **10** *1* **Ruby Best**[24] 5673 2-8-9 0 DuranFentiman(3) 7 41
(D K Ivory) *sn struggling and wl in rr: modest late prog* **66/1**
00 **11** *¾* **Law And Order**[16] 5905 2-9-3 0 PaulFitzsimons 16 44
(Miss J R Tooth) *mde most against nr side rail to wl over 1f out: wknd rapidly* **25/1**
0 **12** *dht* **The Hague**[10] 6080 2-9-3 0 JimmyFortune 13 44
(J H M Gosden) *chsd ldrs to 1/2-way: lost pl and struggling 2f out* **9/2**[1]
13 *4 ½* **Mr Prolific** 2-9-3 0 NCallan 9 31
(B W Hills) *dwlt: sn rdn and wl off the pce: nvr a factor* **6/1**
60 **14** *2 ¼* **Overbright (IRE)**[28] 5572 2-9-3 0 StephenCarson 8 24
(G L Moore) *bdly outpcd: t.o after 2f: kpt on fnl f* **28/1**
0 **15** *1* **Mezzoforte (IRE)**[52] 4826 2-9-3 0 (t) MartinDwyer 11 21
(J S Moore) *a towards rr: wknd 2f out* **40/1**

1m 11.9s (-1.10) **Going Correction** -0.375s/f (Firm) **15** Ran SP% **120.0**
Speed ratings (Par 95): **92,90,87,86,84 83,80,79,79,78 77,77,71,68,67**
toteswinger: 1&2 £22.10, 1&3 £17.20, 2&3 £48.20. CSF £116.15 TOTE £5.10: £1.90, £5.50, £6.20; EX 124.20 Trifecta £106.40 Part won. Pool: £143.81, 0.50 winning units..
Owner Cheveley Park Stud **Bred** Cheveley Park Stud Ltd **Trained** Newmarket, Suffolk

FOCUS
The second division of this maiden was an open heat and, while it was the quickest of the two, the form looks just ordinary rated around the fifth and seventh.

NOTEBOOK
Enact, the third foal of a 1m winner, proved easy to back on this racecourse bow yet got her career off to a perfect start with a professional display from the outside stall. She took time to warm up, but was always doing enough inside the final furlong and looked suited by the ground. She is open to improvement, appears best kept to this trip at the moment, and no doubt has a future. (op 4-1 tchd 6-1)
Piccolo Mondo, having his first outing for 47 days, emerged to have every chance and was the only one to give the winner a serious time at the business end. He enjoyed the extra furlong and it was a clear personal-best effort, so it will be interesting to see how he is now assessed for nurseries. (op 25-1)
Jordaura made a slow start and it took time for the penny to drop. He caught the eye staying on promisingly when the race was effectively over and looks set to come on plenty for the debut experience. (op 20-1 tchd 25-1)
Lujeanie showed a good deal more than was the case on his debut 47 days previously, when behind the runner-up, and will look more interesting when eligible for a nursery mark after his next assignment. (tchd 100-1)
Party Cat(IRE) set the standard with an official rating of 76 and was returning from an 80-day break. He ran below that mark, however, and did not help his rider by tending to hang left under pressure. He now has to prove he is not regressing. (op 4-1)

6343 BUGLER HOMES (S) STKS 1m 67y
4:00 (4:00) (Class 6) 2-Y-O **£2,047** (£604; £302) **Stalls** High

Form RPR
0063 **1** **Abuelito John (IRE)**[9] 6133 2-8-12 63 (v) DNolan 13 62
(D Carroll) *settled in rr: prog over 2f out: drvn to ld jst over 1f out: styd on wl* **7/1**[3]
2635 **2** *2 ¼* **Cherry Belle (IRE)**[11] 6059 2-8-13 56 RichardHughes 12 58
(P D Evans) *dwlt: wl in rr: pushed along 3f out: prog and swtchd lft over 1f out: chsd wnr fnl f: kpt on but no imp* **9/2**[1]
3650 **3** *1 ¾* **Aegean Warning**[17] 5870 2-8-12 58 (p) NCallan 6 53
(K A Ryan) *led and t.k.h: hung lft on bnd over 5f out: hrd rdn over 2f out: edgd lft over 1f out: sn hdd and outpcd* **7/1**[3]
0300 **4** *2 ½* **Lois Darlin (IRE)**[4] 6223 2-8-7 61 (b) TPO'Shea 10 43
(J S Moore) *prom: drvn 3f out: nt qckn after: wl outpcd over 1f out* **20/1**
506 **5** *1* **Virginia's Choice**[25] 5640 2-8-7 68 FrankieMcDonald 4 41
(Jane Chapple-Hyam) *towards rr: hrd rdn and effrt over 3f out: nvr really on terms* **9/2**[1]
1005 **6** *nk* **Flawless Diamond (IRE)**[4] 6223 2-8-13 61 (b) MartinDwyer 11 46
(J S Moore) *wl plcd: prog to trck ldr over 3f out gng easily: rdn and fnd nil over 2f out: stl ch over 1f out: wknd tamely* **9/1**
3040 **7** *½* **Ashwinder (IRE)**[11] 6059 2-8-12 55 EddieAhern 14 44
(B J Meehan) *hld up in midfield: brief effrt 2f out: sn nt qckn and no prog* **11/2**[2]
5020 **8** *½* **Ba Globetrotter**[11] 6059 2-8-12 54 ChrisCatlin 9 43
(M R Channon) *mostly chsd ldr to over 3f out: steadily lost pl* **16/1**
0060 **9** *1 ¾* **Lucky Punt**[16] 5914 2-8-12 56 RyanMoore 5 41+
(B G Powell) *awkward s: hld up in last: effrt on wd outside over 2f out: sn no prog: wknd over 1f out* **10/1**
00 **10** *4* **Dontforgeturshovel**[21] 5754 2-8-12 0 AdamKirby 8 30
(J Pearce) *plld hrd: hld up towards rr: no prog over 2f out* **33/1**
060 **11** *26* **Catenaccio (IRE)**[31] 5461 2-8-12 55 StephenCarson 3 —
(P Winkworth) *plld frntically: already wd bnd over 5f out whn almost carried off the crse: t.o after* **22/1**
5560 **U** **Old Father Zieten**[68] 4292 2-8-12 64 RichardKingscote 2 —
(Tom Dascombe) *t.k.h and prom: hung bdly lft bnd over 5f out: continued to hang and crashed into far rail over 4f out and uns rdr* **16/1**

1m 42.86s (-1.84) **Going Correction** -0.375s/f (Firm) 2y crse rec **12** Ran SP% **119.7**
Speed ratings (Par 93): **94,91,90,87,86 86,85,85,83,79 53,—**
toteswinger: 1&2 £6.70, 1&3 £7.00, 2&3 £2.30. CSF £37.91 TOTE £8.60: £2.70, £2.20, £2.70; EX 33.60 Trifecta £123.90 Part won. Pool: £167.46, 0.79 winning units..The winner was sold to Claes Bjorling for £11,200
Owner We-Know Partnership **Bred** B Kennedy **Trained** Sledmere, E Yorks
■ Stewards' Enquiry : D Nolan two-day ban: used whip with excessive frequency (Oct 13-14)

FOCUS
A typically moderate juvenile event for the class. It was run at a sound pace and the form looks straightforward enough rated through the runner-up.

NOTEBOOK
Abuelito John(IRE) had not looked the easiest of rides when third in this grade at Wolverhampton nine days previously, but he proved much happier over this longer distance and completed the task in fair style. This was his first win at the fifth attempt and there is little reason why he cannot score again in such company. (op 9-1)
Cherry Belle(IRE), one of two previous winners in attendance, stayed on from off the pace without threatening the winner and ran very close to her recent level. (op 15-2 tchd 8-1)
Aegean Warning got a positive ride on this first outing in a seller and showed up more encouragingly for the drop in grade, but he is evidently not straightforward. He hung off the bend into the home straight and caused interference to others. (op 8-1 tchd 6-1)
Lois Darlin(IRE) was another to improve for the drop into this class, but failed to see out the longer trip as well as the principals.
Dontforgeturshovel Official explanation: jockey said colt ran too free
Catenaccio(IRE) Official explanation: jockey said colt ran too free and suffered interference
Old Father Zieten was keen in the race but was hampered by Aegean Warning, which caused him to hang right over to the far side, taking the free-going Catenaccio with him and he eventually ran into the rail and unseated his rider.

6344 GET YOUR CHIPS AT WILLIAMHILLPOKER.COM NURSERY 1m 67y
4:30 (4:32) (Class 4) (0-85,80) 2-Y-O **£3,885** (£1,156; £577; £288) **Stalls** High

Form RPR
004 **1** **Sequillo**[24] 5678 2-8-11 **70** RichardHughes 3 72
(R Hannon) *trckd ldng trio: rdn over 2f out: got through to chal over 1f out: led ins fnl f: drvn out* **2/1**[1]
01 **2** *nk* **Hurakan (IRE)**[24] 5678 2-9-4 **77** JimCrowley 8 78
(Mrs A J Perrett) *led at mod pce: drvn and upped tempo over 2f out: kpt on against nr side rail but hdd ins fnl f: hld after* **8/1**
0221 **3** *¾* **Brazilian Art**[21] 5753 2-9-7 **80** AlanMunro 6 79
(P W Chapple-Hyam) *trckd ldr: rdn to chal over 2f out: upsides over 1f out: nt qckn fnl f* **4/1**[2]
31 **4** *2 ¾* **Lady Rusty (IRE)**[27] 5584 2-9-2 **75** StephenCarson 7 68
(P Winkworth) *t.k.h early and hld up in 5th: dropped to last 2f out but cl up: effrt on outer over 1f out but hanging lft: no imp* **10/1**
3035 **5** *nk* **Reaction**[17] 5870 2-9-2 **75** JimmyFortune 1 68
(M R Channon) *trckd ldng trio: effrt to chal 2f out: wknd jst over 1f out* **20/1**

0404 **6** 1 1/4 **Hambledon Hill**[14] 5960 2-9-1 **74**........................ RyanMoore 5 65+
(R Hannon) *hld up in 6th: effrt on outer over 2f out: tried to chal wl over 1f out: wknd sn after* **5/1**[3]

616 **7** 1 1/2 **Sultans Way (IRE)**[37] 5274 2-8-9 **68**........................ ChrisCatlin 2 57+
(P F I Cole) *hld up in last: awkward bnd 6f out to over 4f out and detached: prog on wd outside over 2f out: in tch over 1f out: wknd* **4/1**[2]

1m 42.78s (-1.92) **Going Correction** -0.375s/f (Firm) 2y crse rec **7** Ran SP% **115.0**
Speed ratings (Par 97): **94,93,92,90,89 88,87**
toteswinger: 1&2 £3.40, 1&3 £3.40, 2&3 £4.20. CSF £19.23 CT £58.79 TOTE £2.60: £1.70, £2.90; EX 15.00 Trifecta £111.50 Pool: £728.09, 4.83 winning units.
Owner White Beech Farm **Bred** Redmyre Bloodstock And S Hillen **Trained** East Everleigh, Wilts

FOCUS
This was not a bad nursery, with four previous winners lining up, and none of the runners looking that exposed. It was run at a fair early pace and each of the seven runners held a chance inside the final furlong. It has been rated around the runner-up and third.

NOTEBOOK
Sequillo had shaped better than the bare form of his fourth behind Hurakan at Lingfield 24 days previously and, racing on 6lb better terms with that rival, opened his account at the fourth attempt. He acted well on the quick ground and looked better the further he went, so looks a potentially decent middle-distance prospect for next year. (op 7-4 tchd 13-8)
Hurakan(IRE) had proved most game in winning narrowly on Polytrack last time and, under a positive ride, did not go down without a fight against the stands' rail on this nursery bow. He is developing into a very likeable sort and is another who will enjoy stepping up in distance next term. (op 7-1 tchd 9-1)
Brazilian Art, off the mark at Folkestone 21 days previously, was given every chance yet simply failed to stay the longer trip like the first pair. He is a consistent performer, goes on any ground, and has another race in him from this mark. (op 7-2 tchd 5-1)
Lady Rusty(IRE) was another who had her chance over the longer trip yet rather hung fire when put under maximum pressure. This was the fastest surface she had encountered to date and a move back to easier ground can see her in a better light. (tchd 9-1)
Reaction Official explanation: jockey said colt ran around

6345 REAL TIME RADIO AT WILLIAMHILL.CO.UK MAIDEN STKS 1m 67y
5:00 (5:00) (Class 5) 3-Y-0+ **£2,729** (£806; £403) **Stalls** High

Form RPR

2-55 **1** **Majeen**[107] 3031 3-9-3 73........................ RyanMoore 5 76
(W J Haggas) *mde all: hung lft bnd over 5f out: drew 3 l clr over 3f out: drvn over 1f out: hrd pressed fnl f: hld on wl* **9/2**[3]

2324 **2** nk **Special Reserve (IRE)**[31] 5463 3-9-3 77........................ RichardHughes 6 75
(R Hannon) *hld up in midfield: smooth prog fr 3f out: chsd wnr jst ins fnl f: nt qckn nr fin* **9/4**[2]

0 **3** 1 **Desert Kiss**[37] 5278 3-8-12 0........................ AdamKirby 12 68
(W R Swinburn) *hld up towards rr: clsd on ldrs fr over 2f out: plld out over 1f out: styd on: nrst fin* **28/1**

4 2 1/4 **Manere Bay** 3-8-12 0........................ EddieAhern 4 63+
(J L Dunlop) *hld up wl in rr: gd prog on outer fr 3f out: clsd on ldrs looking dangerous over 1f out: rn green and hung lft after* **33/1**

02 **5** 1/2 **Blessing (USA)**[37] 5278 3-8-12 0........................ LDettori 11 61
(J Noseda) *trckd ldrs: rdn over 2f out: wnt 2nd wl over 1f out: sn no imp on wnr: wknd ins fnl f* **10/11**[1]

0 **6** 2 3/4 **King's Colour**[68] 4302 3-9-0 0........................ JackMitchell(3) 10 60
(B R Johnson) *hld up wl in rr: pushed along and sme prog over 2f out: nt clr run briefly wl over 1f out: kpt on* **66/1**

40 **7** hd **Scania Classic**[4] 6226 7-9-7 0........................ KirstyMilczarek 3 60?
(M J Scudamore) *chsd ldng pair: wnt 2nd over 2f out to wl over 1f out: grad wknd* **100/1**

8 nk **Moandei** 4-9-2 0........................ NCallan 2 54
(R Ingram) *hld up wl in rr: pushed along 3f out: clsd on ldrs fr 2f out: one pce fr over 1f out* **66/1**

00 **9** 12 **Giadiniera**[131] 2307 3-8-12 0........................ AlanMunro 7 26
(C F Wall) *a towards rr: lost tch fr 3f out* **66/1**

0 **10** 1 **Colonel Sherman (USA)**[25] 5636 3-9-3 0........................ FrankieMcDonald 1 29
(Jane Chapple-Hyam) *plld hrd in rr: u.p and struggling over 3f out: sn wl bhd* **100/1**

-00 **11** 9 **Danse De Sioux (IRE)**[115] 2772 3-8-12 0........................ AdrianMcCarthy 14 —
(M Madgwick) *mostly chsd wnr to over 2f out: sn lost pl and eased* **100/1**

00 **12** 2 1/4 **Young Ollie**[126] 2449 3-8-12 0........................ StephenCarson 9 —
(E A Wheeler) *stdd s: hld up and a detached in last* **100/1**

42-0 **P** **Fastella (IRE)**[191] 965 3-8-12 70........................(t) HayleyTurner 13 —
(G A Butler) *chsd ldrs: 6th whn broke down over 2f out and p.u* **20/1**

1m 41.3s (-3.40) **Going Correction** -0.375s/f (Firm)
WFA 3 from 4yo+ 4lb **13** Ran SP% **120.9**
Speed ratings (Par 103): **102,101,100,98,97 95,95,94,82,81 72,70,—**
toteswinger: 1&2 £1.70, 1&3 £9.90, 2&3 £10.90. CSF £14.67 TOTE £5.20: £1.40, £1.30, £3.90; EX 12.20 Trifecta £332.70 Part won. Pool: £449.65, 0.79 winning units..
Owner Abdulla Al Khalifa **Bred** Sheikh Abdullah Bin Isa Al-Khalifa **Trained** Newmarket, Suffolk

FOCUS
An ordinary maiden and doubtful that the first two ran to their official marks.
Danse De Sioux(IRE) Official explanation: jockey said filly hung right

6346 FAST TRACK H'CAP 1m 2f 7y
5:30 (5:31) (Class 4) (0-85,82) 3-Y-0+ **£5,375** (£1,599; £799; £399) **Stalls** Low

Form RPR

1250 **1** **Higgy's Boy (IRE)**[10] 6078 3-9-6 **82**........................(b[1]) RichardHughes 6 96
(R Hannon) *hld up bhd ldrs: stdy prog jst over 2f out: trckd ldr over 1f out: rdn to ld ins fnl f: styd on wl* **8/1**[2]

640 **2** 1/2 **Baylini**[10] 6078 4-9-8 **78**........................ JamesDoyle 2 91
(Ms J S Doyle) *hld up in midfield: prog fr 3f out: led 2f out and kicked on: hdd and one pce ins fnl f* **20/1**

1103 **3** 5 **Supercast (IRE)**[32] 5418 5-9-3 **73**........................ SamHitchcott 3 76
(N J Vaughan) *prom: drvn and effrt over 2f out: chsd ldrs over 1f out: sn outpcd* **16/1**

5402 **4** 1/2 **Danetime Panther (IRE)**[24] 5675 4-9-4 **74**........................ LDettori 10 76
(P F I Cole) *dwlt: hld up in last quartet: prog on wd outside fr 3f out: no imp on ldrs over 1f out: kpt on* **9/1**[3]

0155 **5** 1 1/4 **Murrin (IRE)**[19] 5800 4-9-1 **74**........................ JackMitchell(3) 8 74
(T G Mills) *hld up in midfield: effrt over 2f out: kpt on but nvr rchd ldrs* **10/1**

0-00 **6** 1 1/4 **Gremlin**[18] 5843 4-9-6 **76**........................(b[1]) EddieAhern 4 73
(A King) *mostly trckd ldr to over 2f out: hanging lft and fdd* **12/1**

06/3 **7** 2 **Wiggy Smith**[12] 6028 9-9-4 **74**........................ FrankieMcDonald 11 67
(H Candy) *pressed ldrs: lost pl u.p 2f out: fdd* **8/1**[2]

2-23 **8** 1 1/4 **Two Left Feet**[191] 974 3-9-1 **77**........................ AdamKirby 1 68
(W R Swinburn) *hld up towards rr: no real prog fr 2f out* **18/1**

5-00 **9** nk **Monreale (GER)**[18] 5843 4-9-10 **80**........................ VinceSlattery 12 70
(G Brown) *stdd s: hld up in last quartet: effrt on outer over 2f out: nvr on terms* **100/1**

000 **10** nk **Shake On It**[10] 6078 4-9-4 **74**........................ StephenCarson 15 63
(Eve Johnson Houghton) *dwlt: hld up wl in rr: struggling over 2f out: n.d after* **20/1**

2100 **11** 3/4 **Qui Moi (CAN)**[12] 6033 3-9-6 **82**........................ RobertWinston 14 70
(J R Fanshawe) *prom tl wknd u.p 2f out* **14/1**

40-0 **12** hd **Woolfall Blue (IRE)**[44] 5115 5-9-10 **80**........................ AdrianMcCarthy 5 67
(G G Margarson) *led to 2f out: wknd* **33/1**

1-60 **13** 3/4 **Fr Dominic (USA)**[76] 4060 3-9-6 **82**........................ WilliamBuick 9 68
(R M Beckett) *hld up in rr: rdn and no prog wl over 2f out* **16/1**

0212 **14** 1/2 **Cupid's Glory**[10] 6078 6-9-10 **80**........................ RyanMoore 13 65
(G L Moore) *hld up in last quartet: sme prog on outer over 2f out: sn no hdwy and btn over 1f out: wknd* **2/1**[1]

0606 **15** 3 1/4 **Southandwest (IRE)**[12] 6035 4-9-10 **80**........................ MartinDwyer 16 58
(J S Moore) *plld hrd: trckd ldng pair to 3f out: sn wknd* **25/1**

-103 **16** 1 **Red Birr (IRE)**[26] 5033 7-9-9 **79**........................ JimmyFortune 7 55
(P R Webber) *hld up towards rr: no prog on outer over 2f out: heavily eased over 1f out* **12/1**

2m 3.34s (-5.36) **Going Correction** -0.375s/f (Firm)
WFA 3 from 4yo+ 6lb **16** Ran SP% **131.0**
Speed ratings (Par 105): **106,105,101,101,100 99,97,96,96,96 95,95,94,94,91 90**
toteswinger: 1&2 £48.90, 1&3 £31.90, 2&3 £85.60. CSF £173.27 CT £2548.33 TOTE £10.40: £2.70, £4.80, £3.30, £1.90; EX 217.50 TRIFECTA Not won. Place 6 £ 243.52, Place 5 £ 90.58.
Owner I Higginson **Bred** M Henochsberg **Trained** East Everleigh, Wilts

FOCUS
This was a fair handicap for the class and the first pair came well clear. It has been rated around the runner-up to last year's turf best.
Higgy's Boy(IRE) Official explanation: trainer said, regarding apparent improvement in form, that the colt appeared to benefit from the first-time blinkers.
Monreale(GER) Official explanation: jockey said gelding had a breathing problem
Red Birr(IRE) Official explanation: jockey said gelding moved poorly
T/Plt: £284.30 to a £1 stake. Pool: £69,772.61. 179.15 winning tickets. T/Qpdt: £78.80 to a £1 stake. Pool: £3,346.24. 31.40 winning tickets. JN

5590 SOUTHWELL (L-H)
Tuesday, September 30

OFFICIAL GOING: Standard
Wind: Fresh, behind Weather: Overcast and showers

6350 TOTEPLACEPOT NURSERY 5f (F)
2:20 (2:20) (Class 5) (0-70,70) 2-Y-O **£2,797** (£826; £413) **Stalls** High

Form RPR

304 **1** **The Cuckoo**[17] 5904 2-9-7 **70**........................ PatCosgrave 11 74
(M J Wallace, Australia) *chsd ldrs: hdwy to ld wl over 1f out: sn rdn: drvn ins fnl f: jst hld on* **15/2**

414 **2** nse **Dispol Grand (IRE)**[37] 5306 2-9-2 **65**........................ PaulFessey 6 69
(P T Midgley) *cl up: rdn wl over 1f out: drvn and ev ch ins fnl f: jst hld* **12/1**

2353 **3** 3 **You've Been Mowed**[14] 5997 2-9-2 **70**........................ FrederikTylicki(5) 1 63
(D K Ivory) *in tch: hdwy 1/2-way: rdn 2f out and sn ev ch tl drvn and one pce ent fnl f* **5/1**[1]

3040 **4** 1 3/4 **Marbled Cat (USA)**[14] 5997 2-9-7 **70**........................ GregFairley 4 57
(M Johnston) *midfield: hdwy 1/2-way: sn rdn and kpt on fnl f: nrst fin* **6/1**[2]

5502 **5** 1 **Sale Or Return (IRE)**[13] 6009 2-8-7 **56** ow1........................(b) DavidAllan 3 39
(T D Easterby) *in tch: rdn along and hdwy 1/2-way: drvn over 1f out and sn no imp* **10/1**

6541 **6** 1 3/4 **Compton Ford**[30] 5541 2-8-12 **61**........................ TonyHamilton 10 38
(M Dods) *led: rdn along 1/2-way: drvn and hdd wl over 1f out: grad wknd* **14/1**

605 **7** 1 3/4 **Ruasgreyasme (USA)**[53] 4823 2-8-7 **56**........................ RichardMullen 13 27
(W R Muir) *in tch: rdn along 1/2-way: no hdwy* **20/1**

0000 **8** 3/4 **Eilean Eeve**[21] 5774 2-8-6 **55** ow1........................(p) JamesDoyle 14 23
(A J McCabe) *chsd ldrs: rdn along 2f out: sn wknd* **40/1**

1353 **9** 3/4 **Silent Treatment (IRE)**[16] 5933 2-8-11 **60**........................(tp) ChrisCatlin 9 25
(Miss Gay Kelleway) *cl up: rdn along over 2f out and sn wknd* **5/1**[1]

000 **10** 2 **Mousy Mousy (IRE)**[50] 4923 2-8-0 **52**........................ DuranFentiman(3) 8 10
(T D Easterby) *s.i.s: a towards rr* **33/1**

414 **11** 7 **Alphabeth**[18] 5866 2-8-11 **65**........................ MCGeran(5) 7 —
(M R Channon) *sn outpcd and bhd* **7/1**[3]

4156 **12** nk **Adozen Dreams**[19] 5834 2-8-13 **62**........................ PJMcDonald 5 —
(G R Oldroyd) *midfield: rdn along 1/2-way and sn wknd* **14/1**

5346 **13** 3 **What A Fella**[37] 5306 2-9-1 **64**........................(b[1]) TPQueally 12 —
(Mrs A Duffield) *s.i.s: a bhd* **33/1**

59.86 secs (0.16) **Going Correction** -0.05s/f (Stan) **13** Ran SP% **115.1**
Speed ratings (Par 95): **96,95,91,88,86 83,81,79,78,75 64,63,59**
toteswinger: 1&2 £18.30, 1&3 £6.70, 2&3 £12.30. CSF £86.81 CT £510.60 TOTE £8.30: £2.50, £2.70, £2.40; EX 119.50 TRIFECTA Not won..
Owner Sefton Lodge Partners **Bred** Perle O'Rourke **Trained** Australia

FOCUS
A modest sprint nursery, but the form looks sound rated around the front pair, who came clear.

NOTEBOOK
The Cuckoo stepped up on the form he showed in three runs in maiden company to defy a mark of 70 on his nursery debut, although he had absolutely nothing in hand. He is lightly raced, and could progress again, but this was a weak race. (tchd 7-1 and 8-1)
Dispol Grand(IRE), trying sand for the first time, showed good speed throughout and stuck on to the line. The surface clearly suited. (op 10-1)
You've Been Mowed, having her first start on Fibresand, was stuck out wide of the main pack from stall one and could never get in a telling blow. She has had a few chances now. (op 9-2)
Marbled Cat(USA) had not been getting home over 6f, but he just lacked the speed of some of these on this drop in trip after taking time to find his stride. He kept on but this basically looks as good as he is. (tchd 7-1)
Sale Or Return(IRE) should find things easier back in sellers, and he may also get 6f. (op 12-1)
Eilean Eeve Official explanation: jockey said filly hung right
Alphabeth did not look to face the kickback once getting outpaced and will appreciate a switch of surfaces. Official explanation: jockey said filly hung right

6351 RACINGFIXTURES.CO.UK MAIDEN AUCTION STKS 6f (F)
2:50 (2:50) (Class 5) 2-Y-O **£2,797** (£826; £413) **Stalls** Low

Form RPR

20 **1** **Plotting**[39] 5241 2-8-8 0 ow1........................ NCallan 6 67+
(K A Ryan) *mde virtually all: rdn clr over 1f out: kpt on* **15/8**[2]

00 **2** *2* **Ditto Ditto**[27] 5609 2-8-10 0 TPQueally 5 65+
(D R Lanigan) *hmpd s: in rr whn pushed wd bnd after 2f: hdwy on outer wl over 1f out: rdn and styd on ins fnl f: nt rch wnr* **28/1**
3 *½* **Risky Capital** 2-8-12 0 RichardHughes 4 64
(S A Callaghan) *cl up: rdn along and edgd rt 2f out: drvn and edgd lft over 1f out: kpt on same pce* **9/1**[3]
000 **4** *1 ½* **Valdemar**[13] 6010 2-8-10 25 (p) DavidAllan 1 59+
(A D Brown) *trckd ldrs on inner: effrt 2f out: rdn and styng on whn nt clr run over 1f out: swtchd rt and drvn ent fnl f: kpt on* **100/1**
22 **5** *nk* **Silent Wonder**[14] 5988 2-8-9 0 ShaneKelly 9 55+
(R M H Cowell) *prom on outer whn rn wd bnd after 2f: effrt and ch 2f out: sn rdn and wknd over 1f out* **11/8**[1]
60 **6** *½* **Princess Rebecca**[19] 5835 2-8-7 0 RichardMullen 7 52
(E F Vaughan) *in tch: hdwy to chse ldrs 2f out: sn rdn and one pce appr fnl f* **18/1**
0064 **7** *6* **Accomplishment (IRE)**[64] 4486 2-8-8 62 RichardThomas 2 35
(A P Jarvis) *a towards rr* **14/1**
0400 **8** *1 ¼* **Especially For You (IRE)**[4] 6247 2-8-7 58 ChrisCatlin 3 30
(E J O'Neill) *wnt rt s: in rr whn hung rt bnd after 2f: nvr a factor* **25/1**
9 *2 ½* **La Capriosa** 2-8-7 0 NeilPollard 8 22
(A J McCabe) *cl up: rdn over 2f out and sn wknd* **11/1**

1m 19.86s (3.36) **Going Correction** +0.125s/f (Slow) **9** Ran SP% **115.4**
Speed ratings (Par 95): **82,79,78,76,76 75,67,65,62**
toteswinger: 1&2 £9.50, 1&3 £3.00, 2&3 £10.30. CSF £55.95 TOTE £2.40: £1.10, £4.70, £2.00; EX 54.40 Trifecta £325.40 Part won. Pool: £439.83 - 0.80 winning units..
Owner Ms Charlotte Musgrave **Bred** Broughton Bloodstock **Trained** Hambleton, N Yorks

FOCUS
A weak juvenile maiden and dubious form with the runner-up and fourth apparently putting up improved efforts.

NOTEBOOK
Plotting failed to build on the promise she made first time up at Doncaster when down the field at Newmarket last time, but this was by far the weakest race she has contested to date and she found this a straightforward opportunity to get off the mark. The form is not worth a great deal, particularly with the favourite failing to run his race, but she should get a reasonable mark when switching to handicaps. (op 9-4 tchd 5-2 in a place)
Ditto Ditto was bumped at the start by Especially For You, and was kept wide by that rival, but he was doing his best work at the finish. This was an improvement on his first two starts, but it has to be noted he continually edged left under pressure and had to be straightened up on a couple of occasions. He has the ability to win a small nursery/handicap, but might not be straightforward. (op 25-1)
Risky Capital, a 16,000gns gelded son of Tobougg, showed speed before becoming outpaced rounding the final bend, but he was keeping on again at the finish. He should appreciate a step up in trip. (op 8-1)
Valdemar, tried in cheekpieces for the first time, would have finished quite a bit closer had he not been hampered rounding the final bend and again two out.
Silent Wonder had shown plenty of ability when runner-up on his first two starts, both over 5f on easy ground, but this was very disappointing and his attitude looked suspect. He was stuck out wide early on having proved hard to steer around the bends, and then wandered around when asked to pick up in the straight. It might be that he simply hated the surface, but this effort still leaves him with plenty to prove. Official explanation: jockey said colt hung both ways (op 5-4 tchd 6-4 tchd 13-8 in places)

6352 TOTESWINGER H'CAP 1m (F)
3:20 (3:20) (Class 4) (0-85,84) 3-Y-0+ £5,180 (£1,541; £770; £384) **Stalls** Low

Form RPR
0000 **1** **Majuro (IRE)**[10] 6103 4-9-4 80 GrahamGibbons 6 93
(M W Easterby) *trckd ldrs: smooth hdwy 3f out: rdn to ld wl over 1f out: styd on* **12/1**
0454 **2** *3 ¼* **Paraguay (USA)**[7] 6186 5-8-11 73 EdwardCreighton 2 78
(Miss V Haigh) *s.i.s: hdwy 1/2-way: effrt 2f out: rdn to chse wnr ent fnl f: sn drvn and no imp* **8/1**
3143 **3** *½* **Minus Fifteen (IRE)**[13] 6021 3-9-0 80 NCallan 5 84
(K A Ryan) *led: hdd after 2f: cl up tl rdn to ld briefly 2f out: sn hdd: drvn and one pce appr fnl f* **4/1**[2]
0500 **4** *½* **Vainglory (USA)**[10] 6130 4-9-6 82 RichardMullen 8 85
(D M Simcock) *towards rr: rdn along 1/2-way: swtchd outside and hdwy 2f out: sn drvn and kpt on appr fnl f: nrst fin* **7/2**[1]
0000 **5** *nse* **Always A Rock (IRE)**[26] 5635 3-9-2 82 (b[1]) GregFairley 9 85
(M Johnston) *in rr and rdn along 1/2-way: hdwy 2f out: kpt on u.p appr fnl f: nrrst fin* **11/1**
5405 **6** *8* **Intersky Charm (USA)**[17] 5910 4-8-6 71 (v[1]) MichaelJStainton(3) 1 55
(R M Whitaker) *s.i.s: hdwy on inner to ld after 2f: rdn along and hdd 2f out: grad wknd* **9/2**[3]
3200 **7** *19* **August Gale (USA)**[15] 5968 3-9-2 82 DaleGibson 7 23
(G P Kelly) *sn rdn along and a in rr* **50/1**
0065 **8** *shd* **El Dececy (USA)**[8] 6170 4-9-5 84 TolleyDean(3) 10 24
(S Parr) *chsd ldrs: rdn along over 2f out and grad wknd* **9/1**
5300 **9** *18* **Sign Of The Cross**[51] 4894 4-9-4 80 RobertWinston 3 —
(J R Fanshawe) *trckd ldrs: effrt over 3f out: sn rdn and wknd over 2f out: sn eased* **10/1**
0-00 **10** *2 ¼* **Captain Royale (IRE)**[19] 5841 3-8-9 75 ShaneKelly 4 —
(J Noseda) *prom: rdn along 3f out: sn wknd* **14/1**

1m 44.51s (0.81) **Going Correction** +0.125s/f (Slow)
WFA 3 from 4yo+ 4lb **10** Ran SP% **115.3**
Speed ratings (Par 105): **100,96,96,95,95 87,68,68,50,48**
toteswinger: 1&2 £16.40, 1&3 £15.00, 2&3 £3.70. CSF £103.12 CT £456.09 TOTE £15.30: £4.00, £1.80, £1.30; EX 222.00 TRIFECTA Not won..
Owner Woodford Group Plc **Bred** Tally-Ho Stud **Trained** Sheriff Hutton, N Yorks

FOCUS
A good handicap run at a decent pace. The winning time was 0.82 seconds quicker than the following 46-60 handicap. The form looks solid rated around the third.
Sign Of The Cross Official explanation: jockey said gelding was unsuited by the surface and lost its action

6353 RACINGFIXTURES.CO.UK H'CAP 1m (F)
3:50 (3:50) (Class 6) (0-60,60) 3-Y-0+ £2,388 (£705; £352) **Stalls** Low

Form RPR
4530 **1** **Josr's Magic (IRE)**[20] 5802 4-9-2 54 JimmyQuinn 12 72
(H J Collingridge) *hld up in rr: smooth hdwy on inner 2f out: rdn to ld ent fnl f: styd on wl* **17/2**
000 **2** *2 ½* **Having A Ball**[26] 5653 4-9-5 57 ShaneKelly 5 69
(P D Cundell) *cl up: rdn to ld 2f out: drvn and hdd ent fnl f: kpt on same pce* **16/1**
0000 **3** *4 ½* **Aussie Blue (IRE)**[6] 6215 4-9-5 60 MichaelJStainton(3) 13 62
(R M Whitaker) *hld up and bhd: hdwy on inner wl over 1f out: sn rdn and kpt on ins fnl f: nrst fin* **10/1**
0506 **4** *¾* **Dasheena**[32] 5474 5-9-6 58 (be) JamesDoyle 8 58
(A J McCabe) *midfield: hdwy on outer 2f out: sn rdn and kpt on appr fnl f: nt rch ldrs* **12/1**
0001 **5** *1 ½* **It's Josr**[39] 5218 3-9-2 58 (b) CatherineGannon 2 54
(I A Wood) *s.i.s and towards rr: hdwy 3f out: swtchd rt and rdn 2f out: sn drvn and hung lft wl over 1f out: no imp after* **16/1**
3100 **6** *6* **Mr Fantozzi (IRE)**[12] 6048 3-9-4 60 (b) NCallan 4 43
(M Botti) *t.k.h: sn led: rdn along 3f out: drvn and hdd 2f out: sn wknd* **9/2**[1]
5322 **7** *1 ¾* **Plumage**[11] 6088 3-9-4 60 SteveDrowne 11 39
(M Blanshard) *in tch on outer: rdn along wl over 2f out and sn wknd* **8/1**[3]
00 **8** *2 ¾* **Welcome Releaf**[13] 6036 5-8-12 55 PatrickDonaghy(5) 3 27
(P Leech) *cl up: rdn along 3f out: wknd over 2f out* **20/1**
3005 **9** *5* **Young Gladiator (IRE)**[26] 5638 3-9-3 59 TomEaves 1 20
(Miss J A Camacho) *chsd ldrs: rdn along 3f out: no imp whn hmpd over 1f out and no ch after* **20/1**
6112 **10** *8* **Rowan Lodge (IRE)**[24] 5712 6-9-6 58 (b) JamieMoriarty 14 —
(Ollie Pears) *stdd and swtchd lft s: hld up: a in rr* **13/2**[2]
3250 **11** *3 ¼* **The Geester**[38] 5260 4-9-5 57 (b) RobertWinston 7 —
(S R Bowring) *s.i.s: plld hrd and sn chsng ldrs: rdn 3f out and sn wknd* **10/1**
0050 **12** *½* **Komreyev Star**[24] 5712 6-9-4 56 ChrisCatlin 6 —
(R E Peacock) *chsd ldrs: rdn along 3f out: sn drvn and wknd* **8/1**[3]
466 **13** *8* **Khazina (USA)**[45] 5088 3-9-4 60 (v[1]) RichardHughes 9 —
(C E Brittain) *midfield: rdn along on outer 3f out: sn outpcd* **10/1**

1m 45.33s (1.63) **Going Correction** +0.125s/f (Slow)
WFA 3 from 4yo+ 4lb **13** Ran SP% **120.5**
Speed ratings (Par 101): **96,93,89,88,86 80,79,76,71,63 60,59,51**
toteswinger: 1&2 £59.60, 1&3 £34.60, 2&3 £52.10. CSF £138.35 CT £1420.88 TOTE £12.10: £3.50, £7.60, £4.00; EX 374.60 TRIFECTA Not won..
Owner Ken Tyre & Lee Tyre **Bred** Bryan Ryan **Trained** Exning, Suffolk

FOCUS
A moderate handicap run at a good pace. The winning time was 0.82 slower than the previous 71-85. Sound form rated around the third.
It's Josr Official explanation: jockey said gelding missed the break
The Geester Official explanation: jockey said gelding ran too free
Komreyev Star Official explanation: vet said gelding had bled from the nose
Khazina(USA) Official explanation: jockey said filly moved poorly throughout

6354 TOTEEXACTA H'CAP 5f (F)
4:20 (4:21) (Class 3) (0-90,88) 3-Y-0+ £9,066 (£2,697; £1,348; £673) **Stalls** High

Form RPR
2100 **1** **Captain Dunne (IRE)**[20] 5796 3-8-13 83 DavidAllan 9 101+
(T D Easterby) *wnt sltly lft s: qckly into stride and mde all: clr 2f out: comf* **20/1**
0045 **2** *3 ¼* **Pawan (IRE)**[7] 6184 8-8-9 83 (b) AnnStokell(5) 2 87
(Miss A Stokell) *dwlt and hmpd s: hdwy on wd outside over 1f out: kpt on u.p ins fnl f: no ch w wnr* **8/1**[3]
0210 **3** *¾* **Green Park (IRE)**[11] 6069 5-9-0 88 (b) FrederikTylicki(5) 6 89
(R A Fahey) *prom: rdn along wl over 1f out: drvn and kpt on same pce ins fnl f* **7/1**[2]
4600 **4** *¾* **Efistorm**[17] 5906 7-9-1 84 LiamJones 13 83
(C R Dore) *chsd ldrs: rdn along 2f out: sn drvn and kpt on same pce appr fnl f* **12/1**
3121 **5** *¾* **Judge 'n Jury**[20] 5796 4-8-13 85 (t) KevinGhunowa(3) 11 81
(R A Harris) *chsd ldrs: effrt 2f out: sn rdn and no imp* **6/1**[1]
-510 **6** *1 ½* **Kay Two (IRE)**[71] 4240 6-8-12 81 (p) JimmyQuinn 14 72
(R J Price) *chsd ldrs: rdn along 2f out: wknd over 1f out* **14/1**
0006 **7** *½* **Xpres Maite**[23] 5717 5-9-4 87 (v) RobertWinston 12 76
(S R Bowring) *bhd tl sme late hdwy* **16/1**
0000 **8** *1 ½* **Luscivious**[11] 6069 4-9-3 86 PatCosgrave 1 69
(A J McCabe) *chsd ldrs: rdn over 2f out: drvn and wknd wl over 1f out* **10/1**
0000 **9** *shd* **Northern Empire (IRE)**[3] 6290 5-9-4 87 NCallan 4 70
(K A Ryan) *dwlt and towards rr: hdwy and in tch 2f out: sn rdn and wknd over 1f out* **6/1**[1]
0000 **10** *2 ¼* **Canadian Danehill (IRE)**[40] 5206 6-9-4 87 (p) ChrisCatlin 5 62
(R M H Cowell) *sn outpcd and bhd* **8/1**[3]
0210 **11** *4* **Lord Of The Reins (IRE)**[20] 5796 4-9-2 85 TPQueally 10 45
(J G Given) *s.i.s: a bhd* **16/1**
000 **12** *hd* **Chartist**[16] 5930 3-9-2 86 RichardHughes 8 46
(R Hannon) *slt bump s: prom: rdn along 2f out and sn wknd* **8/1**[3]
0400 **13** *3 ½* **Lady Avenger (IRE)**[17] 5906 3-9-1 85 (b[1]) SteveDrowne 7 32
(J M P Eustace) *dwlt: a in rr* **40/1**
00-0 **14** *10* **Obstructive**[17] 5906 4-9-2 85 (p) EdwardCreighton 3 —
(E J Creighton) *a towards rr* **50/1**

58.61 secs (-1.09) **Going Correction** -0.05s/f (Stan)
WFA 3 from 4yo+ 1lb **14** Ran SP% **118.8**
Speed ratings (Par 107): **106,100,99,98,97 94,94,91,91,87 81,81,75,59**
toteswinger: 1&2 £33.80, 1&3 £38.30, 2&3 £12.10. CSF £168.12 CT £1281.52 TOTE £28.00: £6.90, £2.70, £2.50; EX 331.50 TRIFECTA Not won..
Owner Middleham Park Racing Xv **Bred** Ballybrennan Stud Ltd **Trained** Great Habton, N Yorks

FOCUS
A good, competitive sprint handicap rated around the runner-up to last winter's course and distance form.

NOTEBOOK
Captain Dunne(IRE) ◆ failed to beat a rival in a 20-runner handicap at Doncaster on his previous start, but he returned to form in no uncertain terms on this first try on Fibresand. He was clearly well suited by the surface and had what looked a tricky sprint in the bag from some way out. There are several decent prizes over this course and distance through the course of the winter and he will have to be a candidate for some of them if kept on the go. (op 22-1 tchd 25-1)
Pawan(IRE), back on Fibresand, recovered from a slow start and kept on well for second. (op 15-2 tchd 7-1 and 17-2)
Green Park(IRE) is not easy to win with these days, but this was his first try on Fibresand and he ran well in defeat. (op 8-1)
Efistorm is on a reasonable mark and he didn't seem to have too many excuses. (op 16-1)
Judge 'n Jury is a progressive sprinter, but he could not defy a 2lb rise for his recent Doncaster success on this first try on Fibresand. He is probably better suited by easy ground on turf and Polytrack. Official explanation: jockey said gelding was unsuited by the surface (tchd 7-1)
Kay Two(IRE) is entitled to be sharper for this first run in over two months off. (tchd 12-1)
Northern Empire(IRE) was below his best turned out just three days after failing to beat a rival at Haydock. (tchd 13-2)

Lord Of The Reins(IRE) Official explanation: jockey said gelding was slowly away

6355 TOTESUPER7 H'CAP — 1m 4f (F)

4:50 (4:50) (Class 4) (0-85,85) 3-Y-O — £5,180 (£1,541; £770; £384) Stalls Low

Form — RPR

2014 **1** **Merchant Of Dubai**[9] 6154 3-8-13 **85** .... FrederikTylicki(5) 6 — 99
(G A Swinbank) *prom: led 4f out: rdn clr 2f out: styd on strly* — 11/2[3]

2333 **2** 3 **Mezzanisi (IRE)**[31] 5502 3-8-13 **80** .... HayleyTurner 3 — 89
(M L W Bell) *hld up in rr: hdwy over 4f out: effrt 3f out: rdn and edgd lft 2f out: chsd wnr over 1f out: drvn ins fnl f and no imp* — 13/2

1051 **3** 3 3/4 **Precision Break (USA)**[24] 5698 3-8-12 **79** .... NCallan 1 — 82
(P F I Cole) *prom: effrt over 3f out: rdn to chse wnr over 2f out tl drvn and wknd over 1f out* — 11/1

223 **4** 8 **Reclamation (IRE)**[29] 5573 3-8-13 **80** .... PatCosgrave 4 — 70
(Sir Mark Prescott) *sn led: rdn along and hdd 4f out: drvn over 2f out: sn wknd* — 7/2[1]

2001 **5** 1 3/4 **Taikoo**[17] 5900 3-8-12 **79** ....(p) TravisBlock 7 — 66
(H Morrison) *chsd ldrs: rdn along over 4f out: outpcd 3f out* — 12/1

3344 **6** 21 **Sweet Lightning**[16] 5938 3-9-4 **85** .... RichardMullen 8 — 39
(W R Muir) *hld up: effrt over 4f out: sn rdn and nvr a factor* — 5/1[2]

120 **7** 1 **Cape Colony**[61] 4573 3-8-10 **77** .... RichardHughes 9 — 29
(R Hannon) *chsd ldrs: reminders 1/2-way: rdn along over 4f out and sn wknd* — 8/1

4204 **8** 2 1/2 **Black Dahlia**[18] 5858 3-8-12 **79** .... JamesDoyle 5 — 27
(A J McCabe) *a in rr* — 33/1

3155 **9** 2 1/4 **Deadly Silence (USA)**[65] 4448 3-9-3 **84** .... SteveDrowne 2 — 29
(Dr J D Scargill) *in tch: rdn along and lost pl 1/2-way: sn bhd* — 6/1

2m 38.71s (-2.29) **Going Correction** +0.125s/f (Slow) — 9 Ran SP% **112.0**
Speed ratings (Par 103): **112,110,107,102,101 87,86,84,83**
toteswinger: 1&2 £8.10, 1&3 £11.50, 2&3 £8.10. CSF £39.29 CT £374.38 TOTE £6.50: £2.10, £2.00, £2.90; EX 32.00 Trifecta £338.30 Part won Pool: £457.19 - 0.40 winning units..
Owner Highland Racing 2 **Bred** A Smith **Trained** Melsonby, N Yorks

FOCUS
A good three-year-old handicap run at a sound pace, and the form is best rated around the runner-up and third.
Sweet Lightning Official explanation: jockey said gelding never travelled
Cape Colony Official explanation: jockey said colt lost its action

6356 DAVE MORGAN MEMORIAL H'CAP — 7f (F)

5:20 (5:21) (Class 5) (0-75,72) 3-Y-O+ — £3,070 (£906; £453) Stalls Low

Form — RPR

2324 **1** **Dan Chillingworth (IRE)**[24] 5713 3-9-4 **72** ....(v[1]) RobertWinston 13 — 84
(J R Fanshawe) *in tch: smooth hdwy to chse ldrs over 2f out: rdn to ld appr fnl f: sn drvn and kpt on* — 7/2[1]

1000 **2** 3/4 **Fools Gold**[57] 4696 3-9-4 **72** .... PaulEddery 4 — 82
(G D Blake) *trckd ldrs on inner: hdwy over 2f out: rdn to ld 1 1/2f out: hdd appr fnl f: sn drvn and no ex last 100yds* — 20/1

320 **3** 3 3/4 **Orpenella**[165] 1452 3-8-10 **64** .... NCallan 5 — 64
(K A Ryan) *cl up: rdn to ld over 2f out: drvn and hdd 1 1/2f out: kpt on same pce* — 12/1

0100 **4** 2 1/4 **Cool Sands (IRE)**[24] 5709 6-8-11 **62** ....(v) TPQueally 1 — 57
(J G Given) *midfield: hdwy 3f out: rdn to chse ldrs wl over 1f out: swtchd rt and drvn appr fnl f: no imp* — 12/1

041/ **5** 1 1/2 **Keel (IRE)**[72] 4229 5-9-5 **70** .... LiamJones 6 — 61
(C R Dore) *s.i.s and bhd: rdn along 1/2-way: hdwy 3f out: styd on u.p appr fnl f: nrst fin* — 40/1

1230 **6** 2 1/2 **Elusive Warrior (USA)**[71] 4245 5-9-2 **67** ....(p) NeilPollard 14 — 51
(A J McCabe) *chsd ldrs on outer: effrt over 2f out and sn rdn: drvn wl over 1f out and sn one pce* — 17/2

0050 **7** 3 **Prime Factor**[24] 5697 3-9-3 **71** ....(b) ChrisCatlin 10 — 46
(B W Hills) *cl up: rdn along 3f out: drvn and wknd 2f out* — 6/1[2]

/000 **8** 1 **Fitzwarren**[26] 5634 7-8-0 **58** oh13...................................(p) JamesRogers(7) 2 — 31
(A D Brown) *s.i.s: hdwy into midfield 1/2-way: swtchd outside and rdn over 2f out: nvr nr ldrs* — 125/1

3-36 **9** 1 **Rub Of The Relic (IRE)**[164] 1479 3-8-7 **61** .... MickyFenton 11 — 31
(P T Midgley) *nvr nr ldrs* — 16/1

035 **10** 3 **Aegean Pride**[27] 5608 3-8-10 **64** .... RichardHughes 12 — 26
(R Hannon) *chsd ldrs: rdn along 3f out and sn wknd* — 15/2[3]

0500 **11** 3 1/4 **La Chicaluna**[10] 6137 3-9-2 **70** ....(b[1]) PatCosgrave 3 — 23
(J G Given) *led: rdn along 3f out: hdd over 2f out and sn wknd* — 25/1

0000 **12** 2 1/4 **Sun Catcher (IRE)**[20] 5799 5-9-3 **68** ....(p) SteveDrowne 7 — 16
(P G Murphy) *a towards rr* — 12/1

5334 **13** 3/4 **Fly Kiss**[27] 5600 3-9-0 **68** ....(b) HayleyTurner 8 — 13
(C E Brittain) *a towards rr* — 9/1

1006 **14** 33 **Chjimes (IRE)**[16] 5936 4-9-7 **72** .... TomEaves 9 — —
(C R Dore) *midfield: rdn along and wknd qckly over 3f out: sn virtually p.u* — 8/1

1m 31.9s (1.60) **Going Correction** +0.125s/f (Slow)
WFA 3 from 4yo+ 3lb — 14 Ran SP% **120.7**
Speed ratings (Par 103): **95,94,89,87,85 82,79,78,77,73 69,67,66,28**
toteswinger: 1&2 £15.80, 1&3 £5.40, 2&3 £33.00. CSF £82.02 CT £794.77 TOTE £3.30: £1.40, £8.40, £2.80; EX 78.80 TRIFECTA Not won. Place 6 £892.53, Place 5 £323.24..
Owner R C Thompson **Bred** Ballylinch Stud **Trained** Newmarket, Suffolk
■ Stewards' Enquiry : Pat Cosgrave one-day ban: careless riding (Nov 2)

FOCUS
A modest handicap rated around the third to her maiden form.
T/Jkpt: Not won. T/Plt: £1,031.70 to a £1 stake. Pool: £65,933.44. 46.65 winning tickets. T/Qpdt: £195.10 to a £1 stake. Pool: £4,008.66. 15.20 winning tickets. JR

5647 WARWICK (L-H)

Tuesday, September 30

OFFICIAL GOING: Good
Wind: Fresh, behind Weather: Light showers

6357 WARWICKRACECOURSE.CO.UK H'CAP — 6f

1:40 (1:41) (Class 6) (0-65,65) 3-Y-O+ — £2,047 (£604; £302) Stalls Centre

Form — RPR

0414 **1** **Music Box Express**[27] 5601 4-8-8 **60** ....(t) MatthewDavies(7) 12 — 76
(George Baker) *mde all: clr whn c towards stands' side over 2f out: rdn over 1f out: unchal* — 11/1

4463 **2** 2 1/2 **Brandywell Boy (IRE)**[10] 6131 5-9-6 **65** .... RyanMoore 15 — 73
(D J S Ffrench Davis) *mid-div: rdn over 2f out: hdwy over 1f out: r.o: nt rch wnr* — 13/2[2]

0010 **3** 3/4 **Yungaburra (IRE)**[2] 6310 4-9-6 **65** ....(t) WilliamBuick 2 — 71
(S Parr) *stmbld s: sn mid-div: hdwy over 2f out: rdn over 1f out: styd on same pce fnl f* — 17/2[3]

0350 **4** 1 1/4 **Namu**[1] 6334 5-8-5 **55** .... SophieDoyle(5) 13 — 57
(Miss T Spearing) *hld up: rdn over 2f out: r.o ins fnl f: nrst fin* — 12/1

0000 **5** 1 1/4 **Royal Acclamation (IRE)**[6] 6219 3-9-3 **64** .... SilvestreDeSousa 14 — 62
(G A Harker) *hld up: hdwy over 1f out: styd on: nvr nrr* — 12/1

6-00 **6** 1 **Inka Dancer (IRE)**[18] 5871 6-8-11 **61** .... WilliamCarson(5) 3 — 56
(B Palling) *hmpd s: sn chsng ldrs: rdn over 2f out: wknd fnl f* — 16/1

0100 **7** 1 3/4 **Avoncreek**[58] 4327 4-8-6 **56** .... KellyHarrison(5) 16 — 45
(B P J Baugh) *hld up: last 2f out: r.o towards fin: nvr nrr* — 40/1

-560 **8** 1/2 **Gambling Jack**[27] 5610 3-8-10 **57** .... MartinDwyer 5 — 45
(A W Carroll) *chsd ldrs: rdn over 2f out: wknd fnl f* — 10/1

6050 **9** hd **Seasonal Cross**[13] 6036 3-8-9 **56** .... TQuinn 7 — 43
(S Dow) *hld up: n.d* — 14/1

4623 **10** nk **Back In The Red (IRE)**[6] 6204 4-9-1 **63** .... KevinGhunowa(3) 10 — 49
(R A Harris) *chsd ldrs: rdn over 3f out: wknd over 1f out* — 6/1[1]

4034 **11** 1 1/4 **Irving Place**[65] 4450 3-9-2 **63** ....(p) PaulHanagan 6 — 45
(R A Fahey) *chsd ldrs: rdn over 2f out: wknd over 1f out* — 13/2[2]

1066 **12** nk **Boldinor**[20] 5801 5-8-13 **58** ....(t) JimCrowley 8 — 39
(M R Bosley) *prom: rdn over 3f out: wknd over 1f out* — 14/1

000 **13** nse **Loyal Royal (IRE)**[35] 5374 5-8-12 **57** ....(p) DaneO'Neill 9 — 38
(J M Bradley) *dwlt: hld up: rdn 1/2-way: n.d* — 25/1

3100 **14** hd **Triumphant Welcome**[18] 5861 3-8-11 **65** .... StacyRenwick(7) 11 — 45
(G F Bridgwater) *hld up: n.d* — 16/1

66-0 **15** shd **Saratee**[65] 4447 3-8-10 **57** .... EddieAhern 4 — 37
(C E Brittain) *s.i.s and hmpd s: n.d* — 20/1

3600 **16** 12 **Rowaad**[14] 6003 3-8-13 **65** .... NataliaGemelova(5) 17 — 7
(A E Price) *s.i.s: rdn and hung lft 2f out: a in rr* — 66/1

1m 10.65s (-1.15) **Going Correction** -0.10s/f (Good) course record
WFA 3 from 4yo+ 2lb — 16 Ran SP% **121.9**
Speed ratings (Par 101): **103,99,98,97,95 94,91,91,90,90 88,88,88,87,87 71**
toteswinger: 1&2 £16.80, 1&3 £12.50, 2&3 £9.70. CSF £77.92 CT £678.50 TOTE £8.40: £1.60, £2.20, £2.40, £3.00; EX 92.30.
Owner The Betfair Radioheads **Bred** Dachel Stud **Trained** Moreton Morrell, Warwicks

FOCUS
A competitive handicap on paper but very few got into it. It has been rated around the runner-up and third.
Yungaburra(IRE) Official explanation: jockey said gelding stumbled leaving stalls
Rowaad Official explanation: jockey said colt suffered interference leaving stalls

6358 EUROPEAN BREEDERS' FUND MAIDEN FILLIES' STKS (DIV I) — 7f 26y

2:10 (2:15) (Class 5) 2-Y-O — £3,412 (£1,007; £504) Stalls Low

Form — RPR

4 **1** **Nora Mae (IRE)**[10] 6122 2-9-0 0 .... RyanMoore 3 — 82+
(S Kirk) *mde all: rdn over 1f out: r.o wl* — 7/4[1]

2 3 1/4 **Aroundthebay** 2-9-0 0 .... DaneO'Neill 14 — 74+
(H J L Dunlop) *wnt rt s fr outside stall: hld up in tch: chsd wnr wl over 1f out: sn rdn: no imp* — 100/1

0 **3** 4 **Naizak**[58] 4665 2-9-0 0 .... RHills 5 — 64+
(J L Dunlop) *wnt lft s: hld up in mid-div: hdwy on ins 2f out: rdn over 1f out: one pce fnl f* — 33/1

4 2 1/4 **King's Siren (IRE)** 2-9-0 0 .... WilliamBuick 1 — 58+
(A M Balding) *s.i.s: pushed along in rr: styd on fnl f: nvr nrr: bttr for r* 11/1

02 **5** 1 1/4 **Peace Concluded**[82] 3869 2-8-11 0 .... JamesMillman(3) 8 — 55
(B R Millman) *w wnr tl rdn wl over 1f out: wknd fnl f* — 4/1[2]

0 **6** 3/4 **Chateauneuf (IRE)**[11] 6077 2-9-0 0 .... MichaelHills 2 — 53
(B W Hills) *hld up in tch: pushed along over 3f out: wknd over 1f out* 8/1[3]

0 **7** 1 **Arlene Phillips**[26] 5643 2-9-0 0 .... PatDobbs 13 — 51
(R Hannon) *hld up in mid-div: pushed along over 2f out: wknd 1f out* 50/1

8 1 1/4 **Tomintoul Star** 2-9-0 0 .... TedDurcan 4 — 48
(H R A Cecil) *s.i.s and bmpd: hld up in rr: hung lft 2f out: n.d* — 8/1[3]

62 **9** nse **Fongoli**[21] 5782 2-9-0 0 .... TQuinn 11 — 48
(B G Powell) *towards rr: pushed along over 4f out: rdn 2f out: no rspnse* — 12/1

0 **10** 1 1/4 **Call Me Naan (IRE)**[34] 5394 2-9-0 0 .... DarrenWilliams 7 — 44+
(K R Burke) *t.k.h early: hld up in tch: rdn whn n.m.r 2f out: wknd over 1f out* — 66/1

0 **11** 10 **Clodoline**[25] 5673 2-9-0 0 .... JoeFanning 9 — 19
(P F I Cole) *hld up in tch: hung lft 2f out: sn wknd* — 40/1

1m 24.03s (-0.57) **Going Correction** -0.10s/f (Good) — 11 Ran SP% **104.4**
Speed ratings (Par 92): **99,95,90,88,86 85,84,83,83,81 70**
toteswinger: 1&2 £18.10, 1&3 £9.70, 2&3 £94.60. CSF £198.21 TOTE £2.30: £1.10, £15.10, £6.90; EX 85.40.
Owner Mrs Anne Gaffney **Bred** Churchtown House Stud **Trained** Upper Lambourn, Berks

FOCUS
This was a modest fillies' maiden but it has been rated positively. As in the first race, not many got into it and it was a pretty straightforward success for favourite Nora Mae.

NOTEBOOK
Nora Mae(IRE), a promising fourth at Newbury on her debut (kept on well having been denied a clear run), had clearly learned from that and was bounced out in front. She settled nicely, and, having been asked to quicken by Moore, was in control from over a furlong out. She won with a bit in hand and remains capable of better. (op 15-8 tchd 2-1)
Aroundthebay, a cheap purchase readily dismissed in the betting, seemed to know her job but was forced to race widest of all from stall 14. She closed in on the winner two out, but could not quicken and was forced to settle for second. She was nicely clear of the third and natural progress should see her capable of winning a standard maiden.
Naizak, a 110,000gns purchase who offered little encouragement on debut, had clearly learned from that and appreciated the extra furlong, staying on to take third. She will have no trouble getting a mile. (tchd 25-1 and 40-1)
King's Siren(IRE) ◆, a half-sister to the yard's formerly smart juvenile sprinter Speed Cop, was slowly into stride and seemed unsure of what was required. Still last turning in, the penny finally dropped in she stayed on to take fourth. This was a pleasing start and she should know a lot more next time. (op 12-1 tchd 16-1)
Peace Concluded, runner-up in a soft-ground Folkestone maiden back in July, was having her first start since, and, having showed early speed, began to tire from a furlong and a half out. She is now qualified for a handicap mark. (op 9-2 tchd 7-2)
Chateauneuf(IRE), never involved on her recent Newbury debut, was under pressure from halfway and could only keep on at the one pace in the straight. (op 17-2)

6359 ENTERTAIN CLIENTS AT WARWICK RACECOURSE MAIDEN STKS — 7f 26y

2:40 (2:44) (Class 5) 2-Y-O — £3,412 (£1,007; £504) Stalls Low

Form — RPR

02 **1** **Baariq**[11] 6083 2-9-0 0 .... JimmyFortune 2 — 79
(P W Chapple-Hyam) *mde virtually all: rdn and hung rt fr over 1f out: r.o* — 2/1[1]

03 **2** *1 ½* **Wilfred Pickles (IRE)**[10] 6122 2-9-0 0 .... JimCrowley 3 75
(Mrs A J Perrett) *a.p: chsd wnr 2f out: sn rdn and edgd lft: hung rt ins fnl f: styd on same pce* **11/4**[2]

30 **3** *nk* **Larkham (USA)**[11] 6080 2-9-0 0 .... WilliamBuick 8 75
(R M Beckett) *hld up in tch: rdn over 2f out: styd on* **10/1**

0 **4** *1 ¼* **Dr Valentine (FR)**[20] 5798 2-9-0 0 .... PatDobbs 5 71
(S Kirk) *s.s: hld up: hdwy over 1f out: sn rdn: styd on same pce ins fnl f* **66/1**

0 **5** *2 ¼* **Belated Silver (IRE)**[60] 4579 2-9-0 0 .... RichardKingscote 10 66
(Tom Dascombe) *prom: rdn over 2f out: styd on same pce appr fnl f* **20/1**

4 **6** *shd* **Royal Diamond (IRE)**[13] 6031 2-9-0 0 .... DO'Donohoe 1 66+
(Sir Mark Prescott) *chsd ldrs: rdn over 2f out: styd on same pce appr fnl f* **8/1**

7 *1* **Play It Sam** 2-9-0 0 .... AdamKirby 7 63+
(W R Swinburn) *s.i.s: hld up: outpcd over 2f out: styd on ins fnl f* **33/1**

0 **8** *1* **Moon Lightning (IRE)**[94] 3492 2-9-0 0 .... SaleemGolam 13 61+
(M H Tompkins) *broke wl: stdd and lost pl after 1f: n.d after* **33/1**

6 **9** *shd* **King's Chorister**[14] 5996 2-9-0 0 .... RyanMoore 4 60
(Sir Michael Stoute) *chsd wnr tl rdn and edgd rt 2f out: wknd fnl f* **5/1**[3]

0 **10** *½* **Night Knight (IRE)**[59] 4616 2-9-0 0 .... AndrewElliott 6 59
(M L W Bell) *chsd ldrs: rdn over 2f out: wknd over 1f out* **66/1**

04 **11** *3 ¼* **Amazing Blue Sky**[28] 5590 2-9-0 0 .... DaneO'Neill 9 51
(E J O'Neill) *hld up: rdn and wknd over 2f out* **50/1**

12 *nk* **Restless Knight** 2-9-0 0 .... LPKeniry 14 50
(W S Kittow) *sn pushed along: a in rr* **66/1**

0 **13** *23* **Remaah (IRE)**[29] 5578 2-9-0 0 .... (b[1]) RHills 11 —
(W J Haggas) *mid-div: rdn and wknd 1/2-way* **22/1**

1m 24.88s (0.28) **Going Correction** -0.10s/f (Good) **13 Ran SP% 118.3**
Speed ratings (Par 95): **94,92,91,90,87 87,86,85,85,84 81,80,54**
toteswinger: 1&2 £2.10, 1&3 £5.40, 2&3 £6.30. CSF £6.63 TOTE £3.00: £1.30, £1.50, £2.60; EX 7.80.
Owner Ziad A Galadari **Bred** Mrs A M Jenkins **Trained** Newmarket, Suffolk
■ Stewards' Enquiry : Jimmy Fortune one-day ban: used whip with excessive force (Oct 14)

FOCUS
A fair maiden and once again the early leader never came back. The time was slower than the first division of the fillies' maiden. It has been rated around the first two.

NOTEBOOK
Baariq, run out of it late on at Newmarket last time, was again made plenty of use of, and, despite hanging over to the stands' rail in the straight, always looked to be doing enough. He has a bit of size and may develop into a useful handicapper next season. (op 5-4 tchd 9-4 in places)
Wilfred Pickles(IRE), one place ahead of the winner of the previous race at Newbury last time, is another with some scope and he travelled strongly into the straight. He could not quicken under pressure though, and in the end just held second. We have yet to see the best of him and he is another likely to do well in handicaps next season. (op 10-3 tchd 5-2)
Larkham(USA), having his third run, showed improved form and seemed well suited by the extra furlong. He would have been second in a few more strides and this run sees him qualified for nurseries. (tchd 8-1 and 12-1)
Dr Valentine(FR) improved markedly on his debut effort, keeping on well up the straight and just missing out on the places. He is very much a handicap type.
Belated Silver(IRE), well backed only to run a shocker on his debut at Bath, was tackling an extra furlong here and ran much better, sticking on at the one pace having come more towards the stands' side. (tchd 22-1)
Royal Diamond(IRE) was a little disappointing, although his rider was anything but hard on him and it is likely he will do better once handicapping over 1m plus. (op 14-1 tchd 16-1)
Play It Sam, a 70,000euros son of Bahamian Bounty, kept on without being punished and will know a lot more next time.
King's Chorister could not improve on his modest debut showing and faded right out in the straight. (op 7-1)

6360 EUROPEAN BREEDERS' FUND MAIDEN FILLIES' STKS (DIV II) 7f 26y
3:10 (3:15) (Class 5) 2-Y-O £3,412 (£1,007; £504) Stalls Low

Form RPR

0 **1** **Lyra's Daemon**[26] 5640 2-9-0 0 .... MartinDwyer 4 71
(W R Muir) *led: edgd rt bnd over 2f out: rdn and hdd jst over 1f out: led nr fin* **40/1**

6 **2** *nk* **Good For Her**[25] 5673 2-9-0 0 .... EddieAhern 3 70
(J L Dunlop) *hld up in tch: hrd rdn to ld jst over 1f out: hdd nr fin* **20/1**

0 **3** *hd* **Honours Stride (IRE)**[21] 5788 2-9-0 0 .... RyanMoore 1 69
(Sir Michael Stoute) *a.p: rdn and ev ch fr over 1f out: kpt on* **7/1**

0 **4** *1* **Awfeyaa**[13] 6030 2-9-0 0 .... RHills 7 67
(W J Haggas) *hld up towards rr: hdwy 3f out: rdn wl over 1f out: styd on ins fnl f* **11/2**[3]

0 **5** *¾* **Dahama**[59] 4643 2-9-0 0 .... PhilipRobinson 2 65
(C E Brittain) *s.i.s: sn hld up in mid-div: hdwy 2f out: rdn over 1f out: nt qckn towards fin* **7/2**[2]

43 **6** *1 ½* **Wabi Sabi (IRE)**[14] 6000 2-9-0 0 .... MichaelHills 11 61+
(B W Hills) *a.p: forced wd ent st: sn nt clr run: one pce fnl 2f* **8/1**

2 **7** *2 ½* **Furious Belle (IRE)**[12] 6062 2-9-0 0 .... JimmyFortune 14 60+
(P W Chapple-Hyam) *broke wl: stdd into mid-div after 1f: lost pl over 3f out: no hdwy fnl 2f* **6/5**[1]

40 **8** *4 ½* **Second To Nun (IRE)**[13] 6016 2-9-0 0 .... StephenCarson 5 51+
(Jean-Rene Auvray) *chsd wnr to 2f out: sn hung rt: eased whn btn fnl f* **33/1**

9 *2 ¼* **Equinity** 2-9-0 0 .... JerryO'Dwyer 10 38
(J Pearce) *a in rr* **100/1**

6 **10** *6* **Flavour**[7] 6193 2-9-0 0 .... DarrylHolland 8 23
(A W Carroll) *hld up in tch: pushed along over 3f out: wknd over 2f out* **50/1**

11 *1 ½* **Cativo** 2-8-11 0 .... JamesMillman(3) 12 19
(B R Millman) *outpcd: a in rr* **40/1**

12 *23* **Music In The Glen** 2-9-0 0 .... DO'Donohoe 6 —
(P Leech) *s.i.s: t.k.h: a in rr* **66/1**

1m 25.35s (0.75) **Going Correction** -0.10s/f (Good) **12 Ran SP% 123.7**
Speed ratings (Par 92): **91,90,90,89,88 86,83,78,76,69 67,41**
toteswinger: 1&2 £59.10, 1&3 £65.00, 2&3 £14.50. CSF £659.08 TOTE £70.90: £8.80, £3.70, £2.20; EX 749.40.
Owner M J Caddy **Bred** Horizon Bloodstock Limited **Trained** Lambourn, Berks

FOCUS
This was run in a time over a second slower than the first division and it looks a race to be against overall.

NOTEBOOK
Lyra's Daemon led more or less throughout and battled on well having been brought towards the stands' side in the straight. She had beaten just two home on her debut at Sandown, but had clearly improved a lot from that initial experience and showed a good attitude. Her future depends on how the handicapper rates this performance. (op 33-1)
Good For Her, a keeping-on sixth on her debut at Kempton, was always likely to improve for the extra furlong and looked the winner when edging on inside the final furlong, but Lyra's Daemon proved too determined. She clearly has the ability to win a maiden. (tchd 25-1)
Honours Stride(IRE), too green to do herself justice on her debut when managing to beat just two home at Lingfield, looked a different horse here and stayed on right the way to the line, but she was always just coming off worst. (op 9-1 tchd 10-1)
Awfeyaa improved on her debut effort and was helped by the extra furlong, staying on well for pressure. She is related to a couple of useful winners and will be helped by another furlong before too long. (op 5-1 tchd 13-2)
Dahama, who shaped with a good deal of promise on her debut at Newmarket, took a while to pick up, but was not beaten far and will do better once handicapping. (op 9-2)
Wabi Sabi(IRE) is now eligible for a handicap mark and should fare better in that sphere. Official explanation: jockey said filly suffered interference in home straight (tchd 9-1)
Furious Belle(IRE) was a huge disappointment. A good second on her debut at Yarmouth, she looked the one to beat (despite a wide draw) but was forced to drop in and never looked like winning. This was not her form. (op 11-10 tchd 5-4 and 11-8 in places)
Second To Nun(IRE) Official explanation: jockey said filly hung right

6361 WARWICKRACECOURSE.CO.UK H'CAP 1m 6f 213y
3:40 (3:42) (Class 4) (0-85,83) 3-Y-O+ £5,180 (£1,541; £770; £384) Stalls Low

Form RPR

4232 **1** **Fregate Island (IRE)**[33] 5423 5-9-12 **81** .... DaneO'Neill 8 90
(A G Newcombe) *chsd ldrs: led over 2f out: rdn and edgd rt over 1f out: styd on: eased nr fin* **6/1**[3]

6463 **2** *1 ¾* **Haarth Sovereign (IRE)**[14] 5992 4-9-7 **76** .... AdamKirby 5 83
(W R Swinburn) *hld up: hdwy over 4f out: rdn to chse wnr 1f out: sn edgd rt: rdr dropped reins wl ins fnl f: kpt on* **6/1**[3]

6333 **3** *nk* **Mith Hill**[23] 5718 7-9-2 **71** .... (p) StephenDonohoe 10 77
(Ian Williams) *hld up in tch: lost pl over 4f out: r.o u.p ins fnl f* **9/1**

3164 **4** *¾* **Swingkeel (IRE)**[24] 5698 3-8-13 **79** .... EddieAhern 1 84
(J L Dunlop) *hld up: hdwy over 6f out: rdn over 2f out: styd on* **9/2**[1]

3133 **5** *nk* **Hawridge King**[31] 5498 6-9-8 **80** .... JamesMillman(3) 11 85
(W S Kittow) *hld up: hdwy over 4f out: rdn and nt clr run ins fnl f: styd on* **7/1**

30/5 **6** *hd* **Absolut Power (GER)**[16] 5940 7-9-11 **80** .... (v) LPKeniry 2 85
(J A Geake) *chsd ldrs: outpcd 3f out: styd on u.p fnl f* **40/1**

0200 **7** *2 ¾* **Irish Quest (IRE)**[12] 6054 4-9-3 **72** .... (p) PhilipRobinson 7 73
(M A Jarvis) *led 1f: chsd ldrs: led over 3f out: rdn and hdd 2f out: wknd ins fnl f* **5/1**[2]

2006 **8** *shd* **Horseford Hill**[24] 5699 4-10-0 **83** .... MartinDwyer 6 84
(D R C Elsworth) *hld up: rdn over 2f out: n.d* **9/1**

9 *50* **Tora Bora (GER)**[143] 6-9-11 **80** .... (p) TQuinn 3 16
(B G Powell) *s.i.s: sn drvn along to ld after 1f: rdn over 6f out: hdd over 3f out: sn wknd and eased* **20/1**

4-44 **10** *½* **Trew Style**[16] 5934 6-8-12 **67** .... (e) SaleemGolam 9 —
(M H Tompkins) *s.i.s: hdwy to chse ldr 12f out: rdn over 7f out: wknd over 3f out* **12/1**

/500 **P** **Toldo (IRE)**[23] 5718 6-9-8 **77** .... PaulHanagan 4 —
(G M Moore) *hld up in tch: lost pl 12f out: hmpd over 3f out: wl bhd whn p.u sn after* **12/1**

3m 16.3s (-2.70) **Going Correction** -0.10s/f (Good)
WFA 3 from 4yo+ 11lb **11 Ran SP% 118.5**
Speed ratings (Par 105): **103,102,101,101,101 101,99,99,73,72** —
toteswinger: 1&2 £7.90, 1&3 £8.60, 2&3 £12.20. CSF £42.27 CT £326.61 TOTE £5.00: £1.90, £2.50, £2.70; EX 45.30.
Owner Paul Moulton **Bred** G And Mrs Middlebrook **Trained** Yarnscombe, Devon

FOCUS
A decent staying handicap rated around the third and fifth to their recent marks.

6362 RACING UK NURSERY 7f 26y
4:10 (4:14) (Class 5) (0-75,75) 2-Y-O £3,753 (£1,108; £554) Stalls Low

Form RPR

4012 **1** **Silent Hero**[11] 6087 2-9-4 **72** .... PhilipRobinson 10 78+
(M A Jarvis) *hld up towards rr: c wd st: sn rdn: hdwy over 1f out: led jst ins fnl f: rdn out* **3/1**[1]

541 **2** *1 ¾* **Perfect Friend**[22] 5746 2-8-7 **66** .... Louis-PhilippeBeuzelin(5) 6 67
(S Kirk) *hld up in tch: rdn over 1f out: ev ch ins fnl f: kpt on* **17/2**

1405 **3** *½* **Ykikamoocow**[59] 4648 2-8-13 **67** .... SilvestreDeSousa 4 66
(G A Harker) *hld up in tch: rdn 2f out: ev ch 1f out: kpt on* **20/1**

6205 **4** *hd* **Deal Clincher**[42] 5165 2-8-12 **66** .... StephenCarson 9 65+
(P Winkworth) *in rr: hdwy whn swtchd rt ins fnl f: r.o wl: nrst fin* **20/1**

3462 **5** *½* **Sparkling Crystal (IRE)**[25] 5671 2-9-3 **71** .... MichaelHills 3 69
(B W Hills) *w ldr: led over 3f out: rdn and hdd jst ins fnl f: no ex towards fin* **8/1**[3]

620 **6** *1 ½* **Peninsula Girl (IRE)**[43] 5147 2-9-1 **69** .... DarryllHolland 11 63
(M R Channon) *hld up in mid-div: hdwy over 1f out: one pce fnl f* **13/2**[2]

036 **7** *½* **Peter Grimes (IRE)**[37] 5314 2-8-13 **67** .... DaneO'Neill 8 60
(H J L Dunlop) *prom: rdn and hung lft 2f out: wknd ins fnl f* **8/1**[3]

4046 **8** *2* **Mymateeric**[12] 6058 2-9-0 **68** .... (v[1]) JerryO'Dwyer 1 56+
(J Pearce) *hld up towards rr: hrd rdn over 2f out: nt clr run over 1f out: no hdwy* **16/1**

1015 **9** *3 ½* **Swingfire (USA)**[11] 6082 2-8-11 **72** .... (p) AndreaAtzeni(7) 12 51
(R M H Cowell) *hld up in rr: pushed along over 3f out: nvr nr ldrs* **13/2**[2]

4300 **10** *2 ¼* **Night Lily (IRE)**[14] 6002 2-9-6 **74** .... RichardKingscote 13 48
(J Jay) *led: hdd over 3f out: rdn and ev ch over 1f out: sn wknd* **20/1**

242 **11** *3 ½* **Dakota Hills**[17] 5904 2-9-7 **75** .... LPKeniry 2 40
(J R Best) *prom: bmpd 2f out: sn rdn and wknd* **14/1**

2010 **12** *20* **Cavendish Road (IRE)**[31] 5511 2-9-6 **74** .... MartinDwyer 14 —
(W R Muir) *in rr: rn wd bnd over 3f out: eased whn no ch over 1f out* **25/1**

234 **13** *17* **Whispering Spirit (IRE)**[11] 6089 2-9-0 **68** .... DO'Donohoe 5 —
(Mrs A Duffield) *a in rr: t.o fnl 4f* **20/1**

1m 24.56s (-0.04) **Going Correction** -0.10s/f (Good) **13 Ran SP% 119.9**
Speed ratings (Par 95): **96,94,93,93,92 90,90,88,84,81 77,54,35**
toteswinger: 1&2 £4.30, 1&3 £19.10, 2&3 £25.60. CSF £25.50 CT £443.57 TOTE £3.60: £1.30, £3.00, £6.50; EX 24.20.
Owner Mrs P Good **Bred** Mrs P Good **Trained** Newmarket, Suffolk

FOCUS
They went a decent gallop early and, in contrast to previous races over this trip earlier on the card, the principals came from off the pace. Solid nursery form rated around the second and third.

NOTEBOOK
Silent Hero has raced keenly in the past and once again he took a bit of settling, but the way this race was run suited him down to the ground and he came through once bagging the stands' side rail in the straight. A half-brother to those smart handicappers Tadeo and Attache, who both won plenty of races, he looks the type to keep improving as he gets older. (op 7-2)
Perfect Friend, whose previous three starts had come on a softish surface, showed she can be equally effective on fast ground. She challenged up the centre of the track and got the longer trip well. (op 11-2)

Ykikamoocow had been dropped 4lb since her last start, and that, coupled with the step up to 7f for the first time, brought about an improved show. She was another who appreciated the decent gallop. (op 18-1)
Deal Clincher, unlucky in running at Brighton last time, finished well and almost took third on the line. She looks likely to get a mile on this evidence. (op 16-1)
Sparkling Crystal(IRE) did best of those who raced up with the pace throughout. It is possible that she did not stay, but likelier that she simply helped set too strong a gallop. (op 10-1)
Peninsula Girl(IRE), running in a handicap for the first time, had her chance and proved a shade disappointing. (op 6-1 tchd 7-1)
Dakota Hills raced too freely in the early stages and although he looked to be travelling better than anything entering the straight, he soon hit the wall. (op 12-1 tchd 11-1)
Cavendish Road(IRE) Official explanation: jockey said colt was unsuited by the good ground

6363 TURFTV H'CAP — 1m 22y
4:40 (4:41) (Class 5) (0-75,75) 3-Y-O+ — £3,412 (£1,007; £504) Stalls Low

Form — RPR
-046 **1** **Jawaab (IRE)**74 4162 4-9-1 **69** ... MartinDwyer 6 78+
(W R Muir) *hld up: swtchd rt and hdwy over 1f out: rdn to ld and edgd lft ins fnl f: readily* **6/1**2
6225 **2** 1 1/4 **Navene (IRE)**43 5161 4-8-10 **64** ... TedDurcan 11 70
(C F Wall) *trckd ldrs: hmpd wl over 1f out: rdn and ev ch ins fnl f: edgd rt and unable qck* **8/1**
0002 **3** 1 3/4 **Eastern Emperor**18 5863 4-9-7 **75** ...(t) AdamKirby 9 77
(W R Swinburn) *hld up: nt clr run over 2f out: hdwy over 1f out: rdn and edgd lft ins fnl f: r.o: nvr able to chal* **9/2**1
4006 **4** nk **Daniel Thomas (IRE)**20 5800 6-9-6 **74** ... JimCrowley 3 75
(Mrs A L M King) *hld up: hdwy over 2f out: led over 1f out: rdn and hdd ins fnl f: styd on same pce* **12/1**
3440 **5** 3/4 **Poyle Dee Dee**12 6048 3-8-12 **70** ... RichardKingscote 1 70
(R M Beckett) *sn pushed along and prom: rdn 1/2-way: styd on same pce fnl f* **16/1**
5452 **6** 1 1/2 **Indy Driver**28 5595 3-9-2 **74** ... EddieAhern 17 70+
(J R Fanshawe) *hld up: hdwy over 2f out: nt clr run sn after: hmpd over 1f out: styd on same pce* **17/2**
1633 **7** 1 **Cool Ebony**8 6177 5-9-7 **75** ... DarryllHolland 16 69
(P J Makin) *chsd ldrs: rdn over 3f out: edgd rt over 1f out: wknd ins fnl f* **7/1**3
5600 **8** 2 **Lord Sandicliffe (IRE)**15 5962 3-9-0 **72** ...(p) MichaelHills 14 61
(B W Hills) *sn led: rdn over 2f out: sn edgd rt: hdd over 1f out: wknd ins fnl f* **16/1**
3005 **9** 3 1/2 **Wusuul**55 4724 3-8-8 **66** ... WilliamBuick 10 47
(C E Brittain) *s.i.s: sn pushed along in rr: n.d* **33/1**
1456 **10** 4 1/2 **Bold Cross (IRE)**8 6177 5-9-0 **68** ... PaulFitzsimons 13 39
(E G Bevan) *hld up: rdn over 1f out: n.d* **12/1**
4000 **11** 1/2 **Sunnyside Tom (IRE)**12 6052 4-9-6 **74** ... PaulHanagan 7 44
(R A Fahey) *broke wl: plld hrd: stdd and lost pl after 1f: rdn and wknd 2f out* **8/1**
1622 **12** 10 **Libre**43 5161 8-8-9 **63** ... LPKeniry 2 10
(F Jordan) *trckd ldrs tl rdn and wknd over 1f out* **17/2**
-400 **13** 1/2 **Zafonical Storm (USA)**146 1365 4-9-7 **75** ...(t) DO'Donohoe 15 21
(B W Duke) *chsd ldr: rdn over 2f out: wknd over 1f out* **40/1**

1m 39.76s (-1.24) **Going Correction** -0.10s/f (Good)
WFA 3 from 4yo+ 4lb — **13** Ran SP% **120.8**
Speed ratings (Par 103): **102,100,99,98,97 96,95,93,89,85 84,74,74**
toteswinger: 1&2 £12.00, 1&3 £6.50, 2&3 £9.30. CSF £54.12 CT £241.04 TOTE £7.80: £2.50, £3.20, £1.90; EX 70.20.
Owner C C Buckley **Bred** Hascombe And Valiant Studs **Trained** Lambourn, Berks

FOCUS
A competitive handicap rated around the runner-up and fifth.
Indy Driver Official explanation: jockey said colt was denied a clear run

6364 WARWICK AMATEUR RIDERS' H'CAP — 1m 2f 188y
5:10 (5:11) (Class 6) (0-60,66) 3-Y-O+ — £1,977 (£608; £304) Stalls Low

Form — RPR
1630 **1** **Opera Writer (IRE)**32 5450 5-11-1 **59** ...(p) MrStephenHarrison(5) 5 70
(R Hollinshead) *hld up in tch: carried hd high and led wl over 1f out: rdn out* **17/2**
5333 **2** 2 **Under Fire (IRE)**21 5783 5-10-13 **57** ... MrMWall(5) 8 64
(A W Carroll) *hld up in mid-div: hdwy over 4f out: rdn over 1f out: wnt 2nd ins fnl f: kpt on one pce* **15/2**3
06P5 **3** 2 1/2 **Saloon (USA)**27 5611 4-11-0 **53** ... MissFayeBramley 3 56
(S Curran) *t.k.h: prom: led over 5f out: rdn and hdd wl over 1f out: one pce fnl f* **8/1**
3330 **4** 1/2 **King Of Connacht**54 4785 5-11-0 **53** ...(p) MrSWalker 14 55
(M Wellings) *hld up in mid-div: hdwy over 4f out: rdn over 1f out: one pce fnl f* **7/1**2
4410 **5** shd **Astrolibra**12 6050 4-11-0 **58** ... MrJAkehurst(5) 6 60+
(M H Tompkins) *hld up towards rr: swtchd lft and hdwy 2f out: sn hrd rdn: one pce fnl f* **14/1**
0611 **6** 3/4 **Kingsholm**4 6255 6-11-13 **66** 12ex ... MissARyan 1 67+
(K A Ryan) *stdd s: hld up in rr: stdy prog over 3f out: rdn wl over 1f out: swtchd lft ins fnl f: nt rch ldrs* **2/1**1
060 **7** 1 1/4 **Dushstorm (IRE)**55 4748 7-10-9 **53** ... MrMPrice(5) 2 52
(R J Price) *hld up in rr: plld out and c wd st: hdwy over 1f out: no further prog fnl f* **16/1**
0006 **8** 3 1/2 **Terminate (GER)**33 5429 6-10-10 **56** ... MrJRavenall(7) 11 49
(Ian Williams) *s.i.s: hld up in rr: hdwy over 4f out: rdn wl over 1f out: sn wknd* **11/1**
0200 **9** 12 **Stark Contrast (USA)**32 5478 4-11-7 **60** ... MrLeeNewnes 9 32
(M D I Usher) *hld up towards rr: hdwy over 4f out: wknd 2f out* **25/1**
452- **10** 1 **Intensifier (IRE)**337 6534 4-10-13 **57** ... MissSallyRandell(5) 7 28
(D L Williams) *hld up in mid-div: lost pl over 5f out: bhd fnl 4f* **16/1**
5064 **11** 3/4 **Winning Show**30 4820 4-10-13 **57** ... MrBJToomey(5) 15 26
(C Gordon) *prom tl rdn and wknd over 2f out* **14/1**
-004 **12** 1/2 **Surprise Act**19 5816 4-10-12 **56** ... MrNdeBoinville(5) 10 24
(P R Chamings) *prom: lost pl 4f out: sn bhd* **25/1**
3-00 **13** 6 **Airman (IRE)**27 4409 5-11-0 **58** ...(p) MissAWallace(5) 4 16
(B P J Baugh) *hld up in tch: wknd 3f out* **66/1**
0000 **14** 64 **Gilded Youth**8 6178 4-10-9 **55** ... MrSeanKerr(7) 13 —
(G F Bridgwater) *t.k.h: led: hdd over 5f out: wknd qckly 4f out: t.o* **66/1**

2m 21.67s (0.57) **Going Correction** -0.10s/f (Good) — **14** Ran SP% **123.3**
Speed ratings (Par 101): **93,91,89,89,89 88,87,85,76,75 75,74,70,24**
toteswinger: 1&2 £15.30, 1&3 £14.60, 2&3 £13.80. CSF £70.93 CT £541.21 TOTE £11.30: £2.80, £2.20, £2.70; EX 87.40 Place 6 £497.74, Place 5 £157.32.
Owner John L Marriott **Bred** J Davison **Trained** Upper Longdon, Staffs

FOCUS
A low-quality handicap rated around the runner-up to his summer form and the third to his latest all-weather effort.
T/Plt: £605.50 to a £1 stake. Pool: £52,811.54. 63.66 winning tickets. T/Qpdt: £363.10 to a £1 stake. Pool: £3,287.90. 6.70 winning tickets. KH

6365 - (Foreign Racing) - See Raceform Interactive

6315 CURRAGH (R-H)
Tuesday, September 30

OFFICIAL GOING: Soft

6366a PETER KEATLEY CURRAGH EQUINE GROUNDCARE H'CAP — 6f
2:15 (2:19) (50-70,70) 3-Y-O+ — £5,334 (£1,243; £548; £316)

RPR
1 **Toasted Special (USA)**11 6095 3-9-12 70 ... MCHussey 30 80+
(W McCreery, Ire) *mid-div: hdwy to 5th 2f out: rdn to chal 1f out: led last 150yds: kpt on wl* **25/1**
2 3/4 **Harriers Call (IRE)**11 6095 3-9-5 68 ... PTownend(5) 16 75+
(J C Hayden, Ire) *chsd ldrs: 7th 2f out: rdn into 5th 1f out: kpt on fnl f* **14/1**
3 3/4 **Willoughby Bay (IRE)**15 5981 3-9-3 68 ...(b) CO'Farrell(7) 25 73
(P J Prendergast, Ire) *chsd ldrs: rdn to ld over 1f out: hdd last 150yds: no ex and kpt on same pce* **20/1**
4 2 1/2 **Napoleon Dynamite (IRE)**72 4222 4-9-9 65 ...(t) WJLee 20 63
(Miss Susan A Finn, Ire) *chsd ldrs: rdn in 8th 2f out: 6th 1f out: kpt on same pce fnl f* **16/1**
5 3 **Dafaroun (IRE)**19 5844 7-9-10 66 ... WMLordan 28 55
(M A Molloy, Ire) *mid-div: rdn into 8th 1f out: kpt on same pce fnl f* **12/1**3
6 nk **Mt Weather (IRE)**10 6138 5-10-0 70 ... DPMcDonogh 26 58
(R Donohoe, Ire) *chsd ldrs: rdn into 7th 1f out: kpt on same pce fnl f* **11/1**2
7 1 1/4 **Patrickswell (IRE)**3 6295 4-9-9 68 ... CPGeoghegan(3) 27 52
(Marcus Callaghan, Ire) *led: rdn and hdd over 1f out: kpt on same pce fnl f* **14/1**
8 1 **Rock Of Tarik (IRE)**19 5849 4-9-7 63 ... FMBerry 17 44
(M J Grassick, Ire) *rr of mid-div: hdwy to 12th over 1f out: kpt on same pce* **20/1**
9 shd **Hazelwood Ridge (IRE)**17 5919 5-9-6 65 ... SMGorey(3) 22 46
(James Bernard McCabe, Ire) *chsd ldrs: rdn in 6th 2f out: no ex and kpt on same pce fr over 1f out* **25/1**
10 1 1/4 **Juicy Couture (IRE)**421 4242 3-9-3 68 ... GFCarroll(7) 24 45
(Charles O'Brien, Ire) *chsd ldrs: rdn in 3rd 2f out: no ex in 4th 1f out: sn wknd* **20/1**
10 dht **Confide (IRE)**117 2768 6-9-2 63 ... MACleere(5) 19 40
(John C McConnell, Ire) *rr of mid-div: rdn and kpt on one pce fr over 2f out* **40/1**
12 nk **Littleton Telchar (USA)**18 5873 8-9-8 64 ...(p) CDHayes 10 40+
(S W Hall) *towards rr: sme late hdwy: nvr a factor* **25/1**
13 2 1/2 **Cihangir (IRE)**15 5981 3-9-9 67 ... PJSmullen 15 35+
(D K Weld, Ire) *prom: rdn in 6th 2f out: sn no ex* **11/1**2
14 nk **Gandolfini (IRE)**19 5844 5-9-10 66 ...(p) PShanahan 11 34+
(H Rogers, Ire) *rr of mid-div: rdn and no imp 2f out: kpt on one pce* **16/1**
15 nk **Promise Of Love**16 5949 3-9-7 70 ... EJMcNamara(5) 3 37+
(M J Grassick, Ire) *towards rr for most: sme late hdwy: nvr a factor* **20/1**
16 1/2 **Richelieu**19 5848 6-9-8 64 ... CO'Donoghue 9 29+
(J J Lambe, Ire) *chsd ldrs: rdn and no imp over 2f out* **11/1**2
17 1/2 **Parc Aux Boules**10 6138 7-9-9 70 ... SFoley(5) 4 34+
(John C McConnell, Ire) *nvr a factor* **20/1**
18 1 1/4 **Rookwith (IRE)**19 5846 8-9-3 66 ...(b) AmyKathleenParsons(7) 12 26+
(T G McCourt, Ire) *nvr a factor* **14/1**
19 shd **Over The Tylery (IRE)**33 5437 4-9-13 69 ...(b) JAHeffernan 5 29+
(Eamon Tyrrell, Ire) *chsd ldrs: rdn and wknd over 2f out* **20/1**
20 2 1/2 **Fandango Boy**34 5411 7-8-12 61 ... JPFahy(7) 7 13+
(J P Broderick, Ire) *towards rr for most* **16/1**
21 1 1/2 **If Paradise**19 5848 5-9-7 63 ...(b) NGMcCullagh 6 11+
(M Halford, Ire) *nvr a factor* **25/1**
22 nk **Desert Ben (IRE)**72 4231 5-9-8 64 ...(b) KJManning 14 11+
(Peter Casey, Ire) *chsd ldrs: wknd over 2f out* **10/1**1
23 3/4 **Bobby Jane**3 6294 3-9-5 70 ... APThornton(7) 23 14
(Mark L Fagan, Ire) *prom: rdn and wknd over 2f out* **25/1**
24 1 1/2 **Rebel Aclaim (IRE)**64 4494 3-9-2 67 ... BACurtis(7) 1 7+
(P F Cashman, Ire) *a towards rr* **14/1**
25 1 1/4 **Trotting Weasel (IRE)**33 5444 5-9-8 64 ...(t) RPCleary 2 —+
(M Halford, Ire) *nvr a factor* **20/1**
26 4 **Venelina (IRE)**354 6162 3-9-5 68 ...(t) MHarley(5) 18 —
(J S Bolger, Ire) *mid-div best: rdn and wknd over 2f out* **20/1**
27 nk **Adriatic**10 6138 8-9-9 68 ...(b) DJMoran(3) 8 —+
(Michael Mulvany, Ire) *mid-div: rdn and wknd over 2f out* **16/1**
28 1 1/2 **Be Fantastic (IRE)**31 5516 3-9-9 67 ...(p) JMurtagh 29 —
(G M Lyons, Ire) *nvr a factor* **11/1**2
29 7 **Lovely Dream (IRE)**15 5981 3-9-3 64 ... PBBeggy(3) 13 —+
(Patrick Morris, Ire) *nvr a factor: eased fnl f* **33/1**

1m 14.26s (-0.24) **Going Correction** +0.15s/f (Good)
WFA 3 from 4yo+ 2lb — **29** Ran SP% **163.0**
Speed ratings: **108,107,106,102,98 98,96,95,95,93 93,93,89,89,88 88,87,85,85,82 80,80,79,77,75 70,69,67,58**
CSF £347.87 CT £7128.31 TOTE £91.40: £13.70, £4.40, £5.40, £6.50; DF 443.20.
Owner Iona Equine Syndicate **Bred** Cho Llc **Trained** Maynooth, Co.Kildare

NOTEBOOK
Littleton Telchar(USA) got going too late from off the pace and ran well below his mark.

5745 BELMONT PARK (L-H)
Saturday, September 27

OFFICIAL GOING: Dirt - sloppy; turf - yielding

6373a JOCKEY CLUB GOLD CUP (GRADE 1) (DIRT) — 1m 2f (D)
10:52 (10:55) 3-Y-O+
£226,131 (£75,377; £37,688; £18,844; £11,307; £1,884)

RPR
1 **Curlin (USA)**28 5558 4-9-0 ... RAlbarado 4 123+
(Steven Asmussen, U.S.A) **2/5**1

2 3/4 **Wanderin Boy (USA)**[28] 5558 7-9-0 .... AGarcia 3 121
(Nicholas Zito, U.S.A) **74/10**[3]
3 3 3/4 **Merchant Marine (USA)**[20] 4-9-0 .... CVelasquez 2 114
(H Allen Jerkens, U.S.A) **168/10**
4 7 1/4 **Mambo In Seattle (USA)**[35] 3-8-10 .... EPrado 8 101
(Neil J Howard, U.S.A) **43/10**[2]
5 4 **Ravel (USA)**[259] 4-9-0 .... RBejarano 1 91
(Todd Pletcher, U.S.A) **32/1**
6 2 1/2 **Stones River (USA)**[26] 3-8-10 .... GSaez 7 88
(J Larry Jones, U.S.A) **28/1**
7 14 **A P Arrow (USA)**[28] 5558 6-9-0 .... RADominguez 6 58
(Todd Pletcher, U.S.A) **23/1**
8 21 **Angliana (USA)**[49] 6-9-0 .... RMaragh 5 16
(Gary Contessa, U.S.A) **63/1**

2m 1.93s (1.31)
WFA 3 from 4yo+ 6lb **8 Ran SP% 120.0**
PARI-MUTUEL: WIN 2.80; PL (1-2) 2.10, 4.20; SHOW (1-2-3) 2.10, 3.70, 5.70; SF 9.40.
Owner Stonestreet Stables LLC & Midnight Cry Stables **Bred** Fares Farm Inc **Trained** USA

NOTEBOOK
Curlin(USA) became the biggest prizemoney earner in North American racing when surpassing Cigar's record and going through the $10m barrier at the same time. He was not that impressive in repeating last year's success in this race but will now be shipped to California to see if he handles the all-weather surface at Santa Anita before taking his place in the Breeders' Cup Classic in a bid to repeat last year's success. The Japan Cup Dirt is a possible alternative.

6205 KEMPTON (A.W) (R-H)
Wednesday, October 1

OFFICIAL GOING: Standard
Wind: Moderate, across Weather: Fine

6374 PANORAMIC BAR & RESTAURANT CLASSIFIED STKS 1m 3f (P)
6:20 (6:23) (Class 6) 3-Y-O+ **£2,047** (£604; £302) **Stalls** High

Form RPR
0035 1 **Catholic Hill (USA)**[19] 5868 3-9-0 51 .... TPO'Shea 4 66+
(B J Meehan) *t.k.h: hld up bhd ldrs: cruised through to ld jst over 2f out: idled fr over 1f out but stl unchal* **4/1**[1]
404 2 1 **Colleoni (IRE)**[60] 4646 3-9-0 54 .... (b[1]) ShaneKelly 11 64
(G A Butler) *hld up towards rr: stdy prog over 3f out: rdn to chse wnr over 1f out: hung bdly rt and ref to exert himself* **6/1**[3]
5504 3 2 3/4 **Stand Guard**[20] 5837 4-9-6 53 .... IanMongan 14 59
(P Howling) *trckd ldrs: prog over 3f out: rdn to chal over 2f out: chsd wnr to over 1f out: one pce u.p* **6/1**[3]
0410 4 10 **Havanavich**[13] 6049 3-9-0 55 .... RobertHavlin 2 42
(S Kirk) *trckd ldrs: clsd over 3f out: led wl over 2f out to jst over 2f out: wknd* **5/1**[2]
5005 5 2 **High Coincidence**[20] 5837 3-8-7 52 .... RossAtkinson(7) 6 39
(Andrew Turnell) *settled wl in rr: sme prog to rch bk of main gp wl over 2f out: sn easily outpcd* **8/1**
-000 6 2 1/4 **Aston Boy**[27] 5653 3-9-0 50 .... JimmyQuinn 12 35
(M Blanshard) *rousted along early in midfield: in tch: n.m.r on inner wl over 2f out: sn bdly outpcd* **25/1**
6041 7 2 3/4 **Linby (IRE)**[64] 4498 3-9-0 55 .... DaneO'Neill 10 31
(Miss Tor Sturgis) *stdd s: hld up in rr: prog 4f out: jst in tch at bk of ldrs over 2f out: sn wknd* **8/1**
00-5 8 12 **Champagne Dancer**[16] 5961 3-9-0 50 .... StephenCarson 7 10
(P D Evans) *detached in last to 1/2-way: nvr on terms: t.o 3f out* **16/1**
-000 9 3/4 **Govenor Eliott (IRE)**[21] 5802 3-9-0 55 .... (b[1]) GregFairley 5 9
(M Johnston) *stmbld after 1f: trckd ldr: led briefly 3f out: sn wknd: t.o* **20/1**
0-00 10 4 1/2 **Ice Bellini**[149] 1876 3-9-0 48 .... JerryO'Dwyer 13 —
(Miss Gay Kelleway) *a in rr: rdn and struggling sn after 1/2-way: t.o* **50/1**
000 11 11 **Silver Willow**[121] 2668 3-9-0 55 .... RichardThomas 3 —
(J E Long) *a in rr: rdn and struggling bef 1/2-way: t.o* **66/1**
00-2 12 4 1/2 **King Canute (IRE)**[48] 5020 4-9-6 51 .... GeorgeBaker 1 —
(E F Vaughan) *fast away fr wd draw: led and set gd pce: hdd & wknd rapidly 3f out: t.o* **15/2**
00-0 13 11 **Goldhill Fair**[14] 6032 3-8-9 42 .... (b[1]) JackDean(5) 8 —
(W G M Turner) *t.k.h early: trckd ldng pair to over 5f out: wknd: t.o* **100/1**

2m 22.63s (0.73) **Going Correction** +0.175s/f (Slow)
WFA 3 from 4yo 6lb **13 Ran SP% 118.2**
Speed ratings (Par 101): **104,103,101,94,92 90,88,80,79,76 68,65,57**
toteswinger: 1&2 £7.20, 1&3 £4.00, 2&3 £9.70. CSF £26.17 TOTE £4.00: £1.50, £1.90, £2.30; EX 19.30.
Owner Mrs E O'Leary **Bred** Center Hills Farm **Trained** Manton, Wilts

FOCUS
A weak event featuring only two previous winners. The track had been harrowed a couple of times earlier in the day although the harrowing was apparently not deep, and the winning time suggested it was riding pretty normal.

6375 KEMPTON.CO.UK MAIDEN AUCTION STKS 7f (P)
6:50 (6:54) (Class 5) 2-Y-O **£3,885** (£1,156; £577; £288) **Stalls** High

Form RPR
0 1 **Tobond (IRE)**[37] 5344 2-8-3 0 .... AndreaAtzeni(7) 9 77+
(M Botti) *trckd ldrs: smooth prog to ld 2f out: shkn up and drew clr over 1f out: pushed out* **14/1**
2 4 **Farleigh** 2-8-5 0 .... GregFairley 5 62
(A M Balding) *pressed ldr: led briefly jst over 2f out: outpcd by wnr over 1f out but clr of rest* **14/1**
02 3 2 **Charlie Smirke (USA)**[15] 6000 2-9-0 0 .... GeorgeBaker 10 66
(G L Moore) *trckd ldrs: rdn and nt qckn over 2f out: wl outpcd over 1f out: jst hld on for 3rd* **9/4**[1]
5 4 hd **Ocean's Minstrel**[95] 3495 2-9-0 0 .... JerryO'Dwyer 8 66+
(J Ryan) *t.k.h early: hld up in midfield: shkn up over 2f out: styd on fnl f to press for 3rd nr fin* **6/1**[3]
5 nse **Absinthe (IRE)** 2-9-1 0 .... IanMongan 13 66
(W R Swinburn) *mostly in midfield: shkn up over 2f out: styd on same pce fnl f to press for 3rd nr fin* **7/1**
6 6 hd **Strathcal**[37] 5365 2-8-13 0 .... RobertHavlin 12 64+
(H Morrison) *dwlt: hld up in rr: sme prog 2f out but already outpcd: rdn and styd on fnl f to press for 3rd nr fin* **25/1**
0 7 1/2 **Co Dependent (USA)**[113] 2916 2-9-0 0 .... ShaneKelly 4 64+
(J A Osborne) *t.k.h early: hmpd and stmbld bdly after 1f: wd in midfield and forced wdr bnd 3f out: no ch after: styd on fnl f* **16/1**
8 1 1/2 **Alternative Choice (USA)** 2-9-2 0 .... KirstyMilczarek 14 62
(N P Littmoden) *dwlt: towards rr on inner: prog over 2f out: no imp on ldrs over 1f out: one pce after* **25/1**
9 1 3/4 **Thaumatology (USA)** 2-8-8 0 .... JimmyQuinn 11 50
(M Botti) *hld up in rr: sme prog on inner 2f out: hanging sn after: reminder jst ins fnl f: fdd* **10/1**
10 2 3/4 **Mister Standfast** 2-9-2 0 .... DaneO'Neill 1 51
(J M P Eustace) *dwlt: hld up in rr: shkn up and no prog over 2f out* **40/1**
35 11 2 3/4 **Confucius Captain (IRE)**[14] 6025 2-9-0 0 .... PatCosgrave 7 42
(J R Boyle) *wayward in early stages: cl up: hanging lft bnd 3f out: wknd sn after* **9/2**[2]
12 1 1/2 **Timbaa (USA)** 2-8-9 0 .... ChrisCatlin 2 33
(Rae Guest) *dwlt: a struggling in rr* **50/1**
0 13 nk **Nala (USA)**[55] 4778 2-8-10 0 ow2 .... SteveDrowne 6 33
(J R Best) *led to over 2f out: wknd rapidly* **50/1**

1m 28.39s (2.39) **Going Correction** +0.175s/f (Slow) **13 Ran SP% 118.1**
Speed ratings (Par 95): **93,88,86,85,85 85,85,83,81,78 75,73,73**
toteswinger: 1&2 £42.90, 1&3 £9.30, 2&3 £6.60. CSF £183.91 TOTE £21.70: £8.00, £5.40, £1.20; EX 140.70.
Owner Giuliano Manfredini **Bred** David John Brown **Trained** Newmarket, Suffolk

FOCUS
A modest maiden rated conservatively through the third and fourth.

NOTEBOOK
Tobond(IRE), whose trainer boasts a good record with his runners at this track, must have derived plenty from his debut here in August because he looked far more professional this time, always travelling quite kindly in behind the pace before being sent on two furlongs out. Shaken up, he came nicely clear, and while it is probably the case that he beat little, he does look to have a fair level of ability, clearly likes this surface, and could be capable of further improvement in handicap company. (tchd 12-1 and 16-1)
Farleigh did well to overcome her low draw and race prominently. She briefly threatened to give the eventual winner a race before having to settle for second, and she looks sure to come on for this initial experience. A half-sister to among others Missoula, who won this year's Ascot Stakes, she will clearly stay a lot further next year. (op 16-1)
Charlie Smirke(USA), whose Lingfield second seemed to give him every chance in this company, got a good early position tracking the leader on the rail, but he proved disappointing in the closing stages, just holding on for third place on the line. He does now have the option of handicaps, though. (op 15-8 tchd 7-4)
Ocean's Minstrel, second in the bunch finish for third, took a bit of stoking but was running on late. He should get further as he gets older (op 10-1)
Absinthe(IRE), a half-brother to a couple of winners, did not run too badly on his debut and should be better for the experience. (op 8-1)
Co Dependent(USA), who was well backed on his debut 113 days earlier but showed little, shaped a bit better than his finishing position suggests this time. He was hampered and stumbled in the early stages and raced widest of all around the bend into the straight. Keeping on at the finish, he can fulfil his potential in handicap company after one more run. (tchd 25-1)
Confucius Captain(IRE) Official explanation: jockey said gelding was struck into behind

6376 DIGIBET NURSERY 1m (P)
7:20 (7:21) (Class 4) (0-85,81) 2-Y-O **£3,885** (£1,156; £577; £288) **Stalls** High

Form RPR
51 1 **Stevie Junior**[19] 5870 2-9-7 81 .... AlanMunro 4 88+
(P W Chapple-Hyam) *t.k.h early: hld up in cl tch: smooth prog to ld jst over 2f out: reminder over 1f out: pushed along vigorously and steadily drew clr* **4/7**[1]
432 2 2 3/4 **Silver Print (USA)**[18] 5901 2-9-1 75 .... IanMongan 6 76+
(W R Swinburn) *hld up in last pair: prog on wd outside fr over 3f out: rdn and styd on to take 2nd jst ins fnl f: no imp on wnr* **11/2**[2]
005 3 3/4 **First Queen**[22] 5788 2-8-9 69 .... DaneO'Neill 2 68+
(L M Cumani) *hld up towards rr: prog 3f out: rdn to chse wnr over 1f out to jst ins fnl f: kpt on* **14/1**
340 4 2 **Aathaar**[32] 5499 2-9-5 79 .... RHills 7 74
(Sir Michael Stoute) *trckd ldng pair: rdn and nt qckn over 2f out: styd on same pce after* **8/1**[3]
050 5 nk **In Transit (IRE)**[23] 5747 2-8-12 72 .... (v[1]) DarryllHolland 9 66
(M R Channon) *hld up in rr: effrt on inner over 2f out: kpt on fr over 1f out: nt pce to threaten* **25/1**
6216 6 1/2 **Bright Enough**[23] 5747 2-9-3 77 .... ChrisCatlin 3 70
(E J O'Neill) *led to jst over 2f out: steadily outpcd fnl 2f* **14/1**
0403 7 5 **Rockfella**[12] 6086 2-8-12 72 .... TPO'Shea 1 54
(D J Coakley) *chsd ldr to wl over 2f out: hanging and losing pl whn short of room sn after: sn wknd* **25/1**
050 8 hd **Flashgun (USA)**[20] 5842 2-8-8 68 .... ShaneKelly 8 49
(M G Quinlan) *hld up: a in last pair: lost tch 2f out* **25/1**
564 9 1/2 **Fisher Hill (USA)**[44] 5143 2-8-7 67 .... JimmyQuinn 5 47
(K A Ryan) *settled in midfield: lost pl over 2f out: sn wknd* **25/1**

1m 41.18s (1.38) **Going Correction** +0.175s/f (Slow) **9 Ran SP% 118.9**
Speed ratings (Par 97): **100,97,96,94,94 93,88,88,88**
toteswinger: 1&2 £2.10, 1&3 £2.70, 2&3 £6.90. CSF £3.91 CT £19.70 TOTE £1.80: £1.30, £1.30, £2.70; EX 4.70.
Owner S Harris **Bred** Manor Farm Stud (rutland) **Trained** Newmarket, Suffolk

FOCUS
Not a bad nursery, and it was dominated both in the market and the race itself by Stevie Junior. Both the second and third look capable of winning races, too.

NOTEBOOK
Stevie Junior, solidly backed in from odds-against in the morning, had won his maiden over an extended mile at Wolverhampton last time and looked potentially well treated off a mark of 81 on his handicap debut. Ridden with plenty of confidence, he cruised up to the front approaching the two-furlong marker and then picked up well under pressure. He had things well in control at the finish, although greenness meant that he was kept up to his work, and he looked to win comfortably. Further success looks assured. (op 4-6 tchd 8-11 in places)
Silver Print(USA), whose pedigree suggested the switch to the all-weather might well suit him on his handicap debut, swung widest into the straight and kept on stoutly for second. He probably just bumped into a well-handicapped rival and it would not be a surprise to see him go one better in similar company. (op 5-1)
First Queen promised to be suited by the step up to 1m on her first outing in handicap company. She kept on well for the minor position, and like the runner-up she would appear to have the ability to win a race of this nature. (op 12-1)
Aathaar, who had shaped well in his first two starts before running poorly at Ripon last time, was again a little disappointing as he was in the box seat entering the straight but could not pick up like the principals. He looks on a stiff enough mark for what he has achieved. (tchd 9-1)
In Transit(IRE), the most exposed runner in the line-up, has yet to convince over this distance. (op 28-1 tchd 33-1)

Bright Enough was returning to the track where he bolted up on his handicap debut last month, but he was 14lb higher this time and taking on stiffer opposition. (op 12-1)

6377 DIGIBET.COM H'CAP 6f (P)
7:50 (7:51) (Class 6) (0-60,66) 3-Y-O+ £2,047 (£604; £302) Stalls High

Form RPR
0010 1 **Tous Les Deux**[12] 6090 5-9-4 60 GeorgeBaker 11 71
(G L Moore) *stdd s: hld up in last: stdy prog over 2f out: produced to ld fnl 150yds: sn rdn clr* 10/3[2]
2544 2 1 3/4 **Morse (IRE)**[7] 6209 7-9-2 58 (p) ShaneKelly 9 63
(J A Osborne) *wl plcd: rdn to chse ldr on inner jst over 1f out: chal ent fnl f: r.o fnl 100yds once wnr had flown by* 5/1[3]
6640 3 2 **Acquifer**[28] 5616 3-9-3 60 (b[1]) TedDurcan 5 59
(J L Dunlop) *rdn fr s to stay in tch: effrt over 2f out: kpt on wl fnl f to take 3rd nr fin* 16/1
0151 4 nk **Game Lady**[13] 6063 4-9-2 58 AlanMunro 2 56
(I A Wood) *prom fr wd draw: wnt 2nd 1/2-way: clsd to ld over 1f out: hdd & wknd last 150yds* 9/1
0660 5 nk **Boldinor**[1] 6357 5-9-2 58 DaneO'Neill 6 55
(M R Bosley) *rn wout tongue-strap: sn midfield: rdn wl over 2f out: grad clsd u.p over 1f out: sn outpcd* 8/1
630 6 1/2 **Hamaasy**[25] 5709 7-9-0 59 KevinGhunowa[(3)] 8 54
(R A Harris) *wl in tch: effrt over 2f out: hrd rdn to press ldrs over 1f out: nt qckn after* 14/1
00-0 7 3 1/2 **Avening**[7] 6200 8-9-3 59 StephenCarson 12 43
(Eve Johnson Houghton) *nvr bttr than midfield: effrt u.p over 2f out: sn no prog and btn* 14/1
1250 8 2 1/4 **Copperbottomed (IRE)**[65] 4476 3-9-3 60 (e) SteveDrowne 3 37
(P G Murphy) *hld up in last trio: rdn and no prog in last 2f out: plugged on fr over 1f out* 33/1
4141 9 3/4 **Music Box Express**[1] 6357 4-9-3 66 6ex (t) MatthewDavies[(7)] 7 40
(George Baker) *blasted off in front and sn 3 l clr: stdd 1/2-way: rdn and no rspnse 2f out: hdd & wknd rapidly over 1f out* 9/4[1]
0456 10 1 1/2 **Bold Diva**[55] 4766 3-8-12 60 (v) DavidProbert[(5)] 1 29
(A W Carroll) *s.i.s: a in last trio: u.p and struggling 1/2-way* 33/1
000 11 7 **Street Diva (USA)**[15] 5998 3-9-3 60 GregFairley 4 7
(P A Blockley) *chsd ldr to 1/2-way: wknd* 20/1

1m 14.71s (1.61) **Going Correction** +0.175s/f (Slow)
WFA 3 from 4yo+ 1lb 11 Ran SP% 121.5
Speed ratings (Par 101): **96,93,91,90,90 89,84,81,80,78 69**
toteswinger: 1&2 £5.40, 1&3 £13.40, 2&3 £18.10. CSF £20.81 CT £241.14 TOTE £4.90: £2.00, £1.80, £5.00; EX 23.20.
Owner A Grinter **Bred** G And Mrs Middlebrook **Trained** Woodingdean, E Sussex
■ Stewards' Enquiry : Kevin Ghunowa caution: used whip from above shoulder height

FOCUS
A strongly run sprint handicap and straightforward form to rate despite the favourite blowing out, with the second and third running close to their recent marks.

6378 DIGIBET MEDIAN AUCTION MAIDEN STKS 1m 4f (P)
8:20 (8:23) (Class 5) 3-5-Y-O £2,590 (£770; £385; £192) Stalls Low

Form RPR
0004 1 **Bluebell Ridge (IRE)**[14] 6018 3-8-12 51 KirstyMilczarek 11 60+
(D W P Arbuthnot) *hld up in rr: tried for effrt on inner and nowhere to go wl over 2f out: prog 2f out: swtchd lft 1f out: r.o wl to ld nr fin* 12/1
0600 2 1/2 **Silver Surprise**[26] 5676 4-9-0 40 DavidProbert[(5)] 7 57
(J J Bridger) *hld up in rr: stdy prog over 2f out: chsd ldr over 1f out: rdn to ld fnl 150yds: hdd nr fin* 66/1
3362 3 1 1/2 **Dusk**[13] 6049 3-9-3 69 (b) JimmyQuinn 9 60
(J L Dunlop) *hld up in rr: stdy prog 3f out: chsd wnr wl over 1f out: rdn and finding little whn n.m.r ent fnl f: sn btn* 15/8[1]
3223 4 shd **Brexca (IRE)**[14] 6018 3-9-3 74 (v) TedDurcan 6 60
(C G Cox) *trckd ldrs: moved up gng easily 3f out: led over 2f out: drvn and fnd little in front: hdd fnl 150yds: immediately btn* 4/1[3]
50 5 3 3/4 **Lazeyma**[44] 5155 3-8-12 0 DaneO'Neill 10 49
(M A Jarvis) *t.k.h early: led 1f: stdd to trck ldrs: lost pl steadily fr 4f out: shkn up over 2f out: kpt on same pce* 14/1
6 2 3/4 **Warrior Conquest** 3-9-3 0 PaulEddery 8 49
(C A Horgan) *s.s: hld up in last: outpcd over 2f out: pushed along and styd on encouragingly fr over 1f out* 33/1
0004 7 3 1/2 **Mtoto Girl**[30] 5577 4-9-2 40 MarcHalford[(3)] 2 39
(J J Bridger) *t.k.h early: prom: wknd rapidly over 2f out* 100/1
6054 8 8 **La Troupe (IRE)**[62] 4572 3-8-12 67 SteveDrowne 5 26
(J H M Gosden) *racd wd: in tch in rr: wknd rapidly over 2f out* 10/3[2]
3323 9 nk **Hawk House**[22] 5780 3-9-3 66 RHills 3 30
(B W Hills) *pressed ldr after 1f: led over 4f out: hdd & wknd over 2f out* 5/1
0 10 38 **Admiral Arry**[13] 6047 3-9-3 0 ShaneKelly 1 —
(G A Butler) *dwlt: rcvrd to ld after 1f: hdd over 4f out: wkng whn barged into wl over 2f out: eased: t.o* 66/1

2m 37.51s (3.01) **Going Correction** +0.175s/f (Slow)
WFA 3 from 4yo 7lb 10 Ran SP% 115.8
Speed ratings (Par 103): **96,95,94,94,92 90,87,82,82,57**
toteswinger: 1&2 £143.50, 1&3 £8.80, 2&3 £33.40. CSF £584.67 TOTE £16.60: £3.80, £15.90, £1.10; EX 367.50.
Owner The Bluebell Ridge Partnership **Bred** Yeomanstown Stud **Trained** Compton, Berks

FOCUS
A poor maiden featuring a number of disappointing sorts. The form is very dubious.

6379 TFM NETWORKS H'CAP 1m 4f (P)
8:50 (8:51) (Class 5) (0-75,75) 3-Y-O £3,238 (£963; £481; £240) Stalls Low

Form RPR
-053 1 **Falcativ**[33] 5472 3-9-2 73 DaneO'Neill 7 81+
(L M Cumani) *t.k.h early: hld up in midfield: prog over 2f out: led wl over 1f out: pressed ent fnl f: drvn and styd on stoutly* 7/4[1]
2011 2 1 1/4 **Soundbyte**[43] 5169 3-8-10 67 ChrisCatlin 9 73
(J Gallagher) *settled in last trio: pushed along 5f out: prog on wd outside over 2f out: drvn to press wnr jst over 1f out: no ex fnl f* 7/1[3]
3002 3 1 **Agente Romano (USA)**[11] 6129 3-8-11 68 (t) ShaneKelly 4 72
(G A Butler) *sn last and nt gng that wl: fnlly picked up and gd prog on inner over 2f out: looked a threat over 1f out: nt qckn after* 14/1
1 4 3 1/4 **Rotative**[30] 5568 3-9-4 75 TedDurcan 1 74
(W R Swinburn) *dwlt and immediately swtchd to inner: nt gng wl in last trio fr 1/2-way: effrt u.p over 2f out: wnt 4th ins fnl f: no imp* 8/1
06 5 1 3/4 **Totoman**[32] 5502 3-9-0 71 AlanMunro 3 67
(G G Margarson) *trckd ldrs: poised to chal gng strly over 2f out: sn upsides: wknd tamely over 1f out* 25/1
3022 6 1 3/4 **Mista Rossa**[63] 4527 3-9-0 71 TravisBlock 8 65
(H Morrison) *rn in snatches in midfield: effrt u.p over 2f out: fdd over 1f out* 7/2[2]
015 7 2 **Director's Chair**[13] 6049 3-8-8 68 RussellKennemore[(3)] 6 58
(Miss J Feilden) *led 1f: styd cl up: effrt on inner over 2f out: chalng sn after: wknd over 1f out* 16/1
2240 8 8 **Houri (IRE)**[14] 6028 3-9-3 74 (p) GeorgeBaker 5 52
(R M Beckett) *trckd ldr after 3f: led 3f out: sn drvn and fnd little: hdd & wknd wl over 1f out* 8/1
6200 9 12 **Heart Of Dubai (USA)**[69] 4344 3-8-9 66 (p) DarryllHolland 2 24
(C E Brittain) *led after 1f: hdd 3f out: sn wknd: t.o* 33/1

2m 35.61s (1.11) **Going Correction** +0.175s/f (Slow) 9 Ran SP% 112.6
Speed ratings (Par 101): **103,102,101,99,98 97,95,90,82**
toteswinger: 1&2 £4.40, 1&3 £4.60, 2&3 £12.70. CSF £14.06 CT £126.49 TOTE £2.50: £1.40, £2.30, £2.60; EX 15.50.
Owner Scuderia Rencati Srl **Bred** Az Agr Francesca **Trained** Newmarket, Suffolk

FOCUS
There was a good pace on here and that suited those who were held up early. The form looks sound rated around the runner-up and third.

6380 BARRETTSTOWN STUD H'CAP 7f (P)
9:20 (9:21) (Class 5) (0-70,70) 3-Y-O+ £3,238 (£963; £481; £240) Stalls High

Form RPR
3431 1 **Gazboolou**[18] 5915 4-9-5 69 ChrisCatlin 14 78
(David Pinder) *trckd ldrs: had to wait briefly for a run over 2f out: prog to chse ldr jst over 1f out: drvn and clsd to ld fnl 100yds: styd on wl* 4/1[2]
6504 2 hd **Carmenero (GER)**[37] 5345 5-9-6 70 ShaneKelly 8 78
(W R Muir) *hld up in midfield: nt clr run briefly over 2f out: prog over 1f out: r.o to chse wnr last 75yds: pressed nr fin: jst hld* 6/1[3]
0460 3 1 1/4 **Cat Whistle**[13] 6043 3-9-3 69 JimmyQuinn 9 74+
(R A Fahey) *hld up wl in rr: no clr run over 2f out: prog and weaved through over 1f out: clsd on ldrs ins fnl f: styng on but hld whn out of room nr fin* 10/1
0066 4 nk **Trafalgar Square**[29] 5588 6-9-6 70 PaulDoe 3 74
(M J Attwater) *dwlt: fierce hold early and hld up: stl in last trio over 2f out: gd prog over 1f out on wd outside: r.o fnl f: nrst fin* 16/1
260 5 1/2 **Green Diamond**[9] 6177 3-9-3 69 GregFairley 11 71
(M Johnston) *sn trckd ldr: led 2f out and kicked at least 2 l clr: hdd and folded fnl 100yds* 8/1
0436 6 nk **Sweet Kiss (USA)**[88] 3727 3-8-8 65 DavidProbert[(5)] 13 66
(M J Attwater) *hld up towards rr: gd prog on inner over 2f out: disp 2nd over 1f out: one pce fnl f* 16/1
044 7 7 **Blue Charm**[14] 6020 4-9-3 67 GeorgeBaker 10 50
(S Kirk) *trckd ldrs: effrt over 2f out: wknd wl over 1f out* 10/3[1]
0460 8 3/4 **Ten Pole Tudor**[68] 4369 3-9-0 69 KevinGhunowa[(3)] 2 49
(R A Harris) *wl in rr: u.p on outer wl over 2f out: brief effrt sn after: wknd over 1f out* 40/1
6-00 9 3 1/4 **Ambrosiano**[15] 5994 4-9-6 70 AlanMunro 5 42
(Miss E C Lavelle) *t.k.h early: hld up in midfield on outer: rdn and nt look keen over 2f out: sn btn* 25/1
0231 10 1 **Deira Dubai**[63] 4538 3-9-4 70 RHills 6 39
(B W Hills) *s.s: hld up in rr: effrt whn nowhere to go over 2f out: no ch after* 8/1
2506 11 3/4 **Ever Cheerful**[53] 4862 7-9-2 66 (p) SteveDrowne 12 34
(A B Haynes) *led at brisk pce: hdd & wknd rapidly 2f out* 20/1
0000 12 1 1/2 **Baby Princess (BRZ)**[39] 5291 4-9-4 68 TedDurcan 1 32
(J W Hills) *detached in last and in trble after 2f: nvr a factor* 66/1
0300 13 1 **Shot To Fame (USA)**[14] 6020 9-9-3 67 DaneO'Neill 7 28
(S Kirk) *prom: rdn over 2f out: sn wknd rapidly* 20/1
0022 14 1 **Onenightinlisbon (IRE)**[14] 6020 4-9-6 70 PatCosgrave 4 28
(J R Boyle) *trckd ldrs: rdn over 2f out: sn wknd rapidly* 12/1

1m 26.84s (0.84) **Going Correction** +0.175s/f (Slow)
WFA 3 from 4yo+ 2lb 14 Ran SP% 125.4
Speed ratings (Par 103): **102,101,100,100,99 99,91,90,86,85 84,82,81,80**
toteswinger: 1&2 £10.50, 1&3 £17.60, 2&3 £14.20. CSF £27.79 CT £240.89 TOTE £5.90: £2.40, £2.80, £4.50; EX 37.00 Place 6: £26.28 Place 5: £15.16.
Owner Mrs Angela Pinder **Bred** Cheveley Park Stud Ltd **Trained** Kingston Lisle, Oxon
■ Stewards' Enquiry : Chris Catlin two-day ban: careless riding (Oct 15-16)
Kevin Ghunowa three-day ban: careless riding (Oct 15-17)

FOCUS
A competitive but modest handicap which is straightforward to rate through the third.
T/Plt: £45.00 to a £1 stake. Pool: £71,995.95. 1,167.41 winning tickets. T/Qpdt: £14.10 to a £1 stake. Pool: £6,653.99. 347.70 winning tickets. JN

4733 NEWCASTLE (L-H)
Wednesday, October 1

OFFICIAL GOING: Heavy (soft in places and in last 3f)
Wind: Fresh, half against Weather: Cloudy, bright

6381 JAMES FLETCHER MARQUEE AND PAVILION HIRE MAIDEN AUCTION STKS 7f
2:10 (2:10) (Class 6) 2-Y-O £2,315 (£688; £344; £171) Stalls High

Form RPR
203 1 **Yorksters Girl (IRE)**[20] 5825 2-8-4 86 PaulHanagan 2 83
(M G Quinlan) *cl up far side: led that gp after 3f: drew clr fr 2f out: 1st of 7 in gp* 4/5[1]
2 7 **Allformary** 2-8-7 0 ow3 TomEaves 6 63
(B Smart) *stdd far side: hdwy over 2f out: chsd wnr ins fnl f: no imp: 2nd of 7 in gp* 33/1
4 3 1/2 **Hector's House**[14] 6008 2-8-9 0 TonyHamilton 15 66
(M Dods) *in tch stands' side: led that gp over 1f out: styd on wl: nt rch far side: 1st of 5 in gp* 8/1[3]
33 4 1 **Denton Diva**[31] 5539 2-8-4 0 DaleGibson 5 59
(M Dods) *tk keen early: cl up far side: chsd wnr over 2f out to ins fnl f: no ex: 3rd of 7 in gp* 12/1
002 5 7 **What A Day**[14] 6014 2-8-12 74 GrahamGibbons 13 49
(J J Quinn) *cl up stands' side: led over 2f to 1f out: sn no ex: 2nd of 5 in gp* 9/2[2]
04 6 7 **Hawkleaf Flier (IRE)**[7] 6212 2-8-10 0 DavidAllan 1 30
(T D Easterby) *prom far side: outpcd 1/2-way: plugged on fnl f: no imp: 4th of 7 in gp* 20/1
7 1 1/2 **High Tensile** 2-8-4 0 PaulFessey 16 20
(J G Given) *in tch stands' side: rdn over 2f out: sn no imp: 3rd of 5 in gp* 33/1

8 3 **Markadam** 2-8-9 0 ... MichaelJStainton(3) 10 21
(Miss S E Hall) *dwlt: sn prom stands' side: rdn over 2f out: sn btn: 4th of 5 in gp* **33/1**

0 9 1 1/2 **Transporter (IRE)**[8] 6187 2-8-12 0 ... DuranFentiman(3) 7 20
(T D Easterby) *cl up far side tl wknd wl over 2f out: 5th of 7 in gp* **100/1**

10 10 **Mythical Thrill** 2-8-12 0 ... RobertWinston 8 —
(J G Given) *bhd far side: struggling 3f out: sn btn: 6th of 7 in gp* **25/1**

0 11 1/2 **Cavitie**[18] 5904 2-8-12 0 ... EdwardCreighton 9 —
(E J Creighton) *led 3f far side: rdn and wknd fr 3f out: last of 7 in gp* **100/1**

024 12 28 **Asserting**[13] 6037 2-8-4 56 ... AdrianTNicholls 11 —
(A G Foster) *led stands' side to over 2f out: wknd qckly: last of 5 in gp* **20/1**

U **Liberty Estelle (IRE)** 2-8-7 0 ... PJMcDonald 3 —
(G A Swinbank) *hld up far side: clipped heels and uns rdr after 2f* **20/1**

1m 35.92s (8.52) **Going Correction** +1.00s/f (Soft) 13 Ran SP% **121.5**
Speed ratings (Par 93): **91,83,82,81,73 65,63,60,58,47 46,14,—**
toteswinger: 1&2 £7.80, 1&3 £3.40, 2&3 £17.50. CSF £46.95 TOTE £1.80: £1.10, £8.30, £2.70; EX 32.40 Trifecta £111.80 Part won. Pool: £151.19 - 0.89 winning units..
Owner B P York **Bred** Airlie Stud **Trained** Newmarket, Suffolk

FOCUS
This moderate juvenile maiden saw the field split into two groups, with five staying towards the near rail. There appeared no obvious draw bias.

NOTEBOOK
Yorksters Girl(IRE) set a clear standard on the form of her three previous runs and she could hardly have done the job any easier on this return to maiden company. She had showed when third to Secrecy at Doncaster last time that she handles soft ground and this deeper surface proved no problem as she came right away from her rivals in between the final two furlongs. She would have likely scored no matter what side of the track she raced on and ought to be high on confidence now, but she was very much entitled to take this. (tchd 10-11and tchd evens places)
Allformary, whose stable had won this event with two of its three previous runners in the past ten years, stayed on, on the far side to post a respectable debut effort and won the race for second. She found the winner in a different league, but looks sure to come on for this initial experience and will probably enjoy a slightly sounder surface over the trip. (op 25-1)
Hector's House, who did his best work at the finish on his debut at Beverley a fortnight previously, ran out a clear-cut winner on the near side and posted an improved effort. He evidently goes well on a deep surface and fully deserves to find an opening now. (op 9-1)
Denton Diva turned in a slightly improved effort for the return to a softer surface and now becomes eligible for a nursery mark. (op 14-1)
Asserting Official explanation: jockey said filly hung left-handed throughout

6382 WAVERLEY TBS H'CAP 5f
2:40 (2:41) (Class 6) (0-65,63) 3-Y-0+ **£2,266** (£674; £337; £168) **Stalls** High

Form RPR

0005 1 **Guto**[9] 6159 5-8-4 **54** ... KellyHarrison(5) 16 63
(W J H Ratcliffe) *cl up stands' side: led that gp wl ins fnl f: r.o: 1st of 6 in gp* **16/1**

3300 2 nk **Kings College Boy**[11] 6131 8-8-13 **63** ... (b) FrederikTylicki(5) 17 71
(R A Fahey) *led stands' side tl wl ins fnl f: r.o: 2nd of 6 in gp* **14/1**

4322 3 1 1/4 **Select Committee**[14] 6011 3-8-9 **61** ... (v) JamieKyne(7) 13 64
(J J Quinn) *in tch stands' side: drvn and outpcd 2f out: hung lft and rallied fnl f: 3rd of 6 in gp* **14/1**

4040 4 1/2 **Ursus**[7] 6218 3-8-10 **55** ... SilvestreDeSousa 5 57
(C R Wilson) *hld up far side: hdwy over 1f out: led that gp wl ins fnl f: hld by stands' side ldrs: 1st of 9 in gp* **10/1**[3]

5150 5 shd **Nabeeda**[33] 5455 3-8-12 **57** ... DavidAllan 15 58
(M Brittain) *trckd stands' side ldrs: effrt over 2f out: one pce fnl f: 4th of 6 in gp* **20/1**

0001 6 hd **Sunley Sovereign**[9] 6159 4-8-6 **51** 6ex ... (b) AndrewElliott 7 52
(Mrs R A Carr) *cl up far side: ev ch that gp ins fnl f: kpt on: 2nd of 9 in gp* **14/1**

0422 7 1 **Whozart (IRE)**[22] 5770 5-8-5 **50** ... DO'Donohoe 9 47
(A Dickman) *hld up far side: hdwy over 1f out: r.o fnl f: 3rd of 9 in gp* **10/1**[3]

0013 8 hd **Grimes Faith**[3] 6310 5-9-3 **62** ... (p) RobertWinston 4 58
(K A Ryan) *cl up far side: led that gp 2f out to wl ins fnl f: no ex: 4th of 9 in gp* **4/1**[1]

2623 9 nk **Overstayed (IRE)**[8] 6190 5-8-11 **56** ... (t) MartinDwyer 10 51
(P J McBride) *in tch far side: effrt over 1f out: one pce fnl f: 5th of 9 in gp* **13/2**[2]

0450 10 3/4 **Dakota Rain (IRE)**[7] 6219 6-9-4 **63** ... (v[1]) HayleyTurner 8 55
(Jennie Candlish) *led far side to 2f out: rallied: wknd ins fnl f: 6th of 9 in gp* **16/1**

0003 11 nk **Morristown Music (IRE)**[22] 5770 4-8-4 **49** ... (v) RoystonFfrench 1 40
(J S Wainwright) *sn outpcd far side: hdwy fnl f: r.o: 7th of 9 in gp* **10/1**[3]

3000 12 3/4 **Dark Champion**[57] 4703 8-8-9 **54** ... TomEaves 11 43
(R E Barr) *hld up in tch stands' side: drvn 1/2-way: no imp: 5th of 6 in gp* **33/1**

0602 13 hd **Baronovici (IRE)**[10] 6150 3-8-10 **55** ... (v) PaulHanagan 12 43
(D W Barker) *trckd stands' side ldrs: rdn over 2f out: no ex over 1f out: last of 6 in gp* **10/1**[3]

-060 14 4 1/2 **Jadan (IRE)**[3] 6310 7-8-4 **49** oh1 ... (p) AdrianTNicholls 6 21
(E J Alston) *bhd far side: drvn 1/2-way: btn over 1f out: 8th of 9 in gp* **20/1**

4300 15 4 **Mormeatmic**[22] 5770 5-8-4 **49** oh1 ... DaleGibson 3 6
(M W Easterby) *prom far side to 1/2-way: sn rdn and wknd: last of 9 in gp* **20/1**

65.59 secs (4.89) **Going Correction** +1.00s/f (Soft) 15 Ran SP% **120.6**
Speed ratings (Par 101): **100,99,97,96,96 96,94,94,93,92 92,90,90,83,77**
toteswinger: 1&2 £41.20, 1&3 £45.70, 2&3 £44.80. CSF £217.27 CT £1898.94 TOTE £19.60: £7.40, £5.00, £2.70; EX 215.90 TRIFECTA Not won..
Owner W J H Ratcliffe **Bred** H B Hughes **Trained** Wensley, N Yorks
■ Stewards' Enquiry : Kelly Harrison one-day ban: careless riding (Oct 15)

FOCUS
The field again split into two groups for this ordinary sprint handicap and this time the first two emerged on the near side. There is a chance that the far side is worthy of being rated a length better than the bare form.
Overstayed(IRE) Official explanation: trainer said gelding lost its off-fore shoe

6383 SALTWELL SIGNS / EBF MAIDEN STKS 6f
3:10 (3:10) (Class 4) 2-Y-0 **£5,180** (£1,541; £770; £384) **Stalls** High

Form RPR

2230 1 **Prime Mood (IRE)**[20] 5827 2-9-3 83 ... TomEaves 2 87+
(B Smart) *mde all far side: drew clr fr 2f out: easily: 1st of 6 in gp* **11/10**[1]

3 2 9 **York Key Bar**[14] 6010 2-9-3 0 ... DavidAllan 11 60
(B Ellison) *prom stands' side: hdwy to ld that gp 1f out: kpt on fnl f: no ch w far side wnr: 1st of 6 in gp* **5/1**[2]

3 3 1/2 **Starla Dancer (GER)** 2-8-12 0 ... PaulHanagan 10 45
(R A Fahey) *prom stands' side: effrt over 1f out: edgd lft: kpt on same pce fnl f: 2nd of 6 in gp* **5/1**[2]

4 nk **Mister Tinktastic (IRE)** 2-9-3 0 ... TonyHamilton 9 49
(M Dods) *chsd wnr far side: effrt over 2f out: sn one pce: 2nd of 6 in gp* **20/1**

55 5 1/2 **Embsay Crag**[6] 6229 2-9-3 0 ... JamieMoriarty 14 47
(Mrs K Walton) *cl up stands' side: led that gp over 2f out to 1f out: no ex: 3rd of 6 in gp* **25/1**

66 6 1 **Dreamonandon (IRE)**[11] 6110 2-9-3 0 ... PJMcDonald 8 44
(G A Swinbank) *sn drvn bhd far side ldrs: no imp fnl 2f: 3rd of 6 in gp* **20/1**

3 7 1 **Mohawk Ridge**[13] 6037 2-9-0 0 ... NeilBrown(3) 3 41
(M Dods) *hld up far side: shkn up over 2f out: nvr rchd ldrs: 4th of 6 in gp* **8/1**[3]

0 8 1 1/4 **Speed Dating**[7] 6213 2-9-3 0 ... DO'Donohoe 12 37
(Sir Mark Prescott) *dwlt: bhd stands' side: shkn up over 2f out: nvr nr ldrs: 4th of 6 in gp* **16/1**

9 3 1/2 **Northern Flyer (GER)** 2-9-3 0 ... GrahamGibbons 4 27
(J J Quinn) *chsd far side ldrs tl wknd over 2f out: 5th of 6 in gp* **25/1**

0 10 8 **Lady Zena**[32] 5500 2-8-12 0 ... DaleGibson 15 —
(M W Easterby) *led stands' side to over 2f out: sn wknd: 5th of 6 in gp* **100/1**

0 11 35 **Gibson Square (USA)**[13] 6062 2-9-3 0 ... PaulFessey 13 —
(S C Williams) *bhd and pushed along stands' side: lost tch fr 1/2-way: last of 6 in gp* **40/1**

12 18 **Freddie Bolt** 2-9-3 0 ... AdrianTNicholls 1 —
(F Watson) *slowly away: sn t.o far side: last of 6 in gp* **50/1**

1m 21.22s (6.02) **Going Correction** +1.00s/f (Soft) 12 Ran SP% **120.6**
Speed ratings (Par 97): **99,87,82,81,81 79,78,76,72,61 14,—**
toteswinger: 1&2 3.40, 1&3 £3.40, 2&3 £6.80. CSF £6.07 TOTE £1.80: £1.10, £1.70, £2.00; EX 9.20 Trifecta £21.50 Pool: £169.87 - 5.84 winning units..
Owner Prime Equestrian **Bred** Peter McCutcheon **Trained** Hambleton, N Yorks

FOCUS
An ordinary maiden, in which there was no draw bias, and the winner, who could be rated 10lb higher, scored as he was entitled to.

NOTEBOOK
Prime Mood(IRE) relished the drop in grade and got off the mark at the fifth attempt with an easy success. His previous form, most notably last time out in a valuable sales race, entitled him to score, and he had shown on his debut back in July that he could handle testing ground. While he is bred for speed, on this showing he should have no trouble with a seventh furlong next season and this will do his confidence a power of good. The Redcar Two-Year-Old Trophy on Saturday could be his next port of call, but that would be ground dependant. (op 13-8 tchd 7-4 in places)
York Key Bar fared best of those to race on the stands' side and appreciated the step up to this trip. He likes cut underfoot and will be eligible for an official mark after his next assignment. (op 11-2)
Starla Dancer(GER) met support and, running green, was not disgraced on the near side. She is entitled to improve a deal for the experience and should appreciate a stiffer test before long. (op 4-1)
Mister Tinktastic(IRE), a 50,000gns purchase whose dam was a 5f winner at three, was treading water inside the final furlong and a drop back to the minimum may prove best for him in the short term. He looks a three-year-old prospect in the making, however. (tchd 25-1 in places)

6384 PHOENIX SECURITY / EBF MAIDEN STKS 1m (R)
3:45 (3:45) (Class 4) 2-Y-0 **£5,180** (£1,541; £770; £384)

Form RPR

2 1 **Montaff**[20] 5842 2-9-3 0 ... EdwardCreighton 6 71+
(M R Channon) *hld up in tch: stdy hdwy over 2f out: led and hrd pressed over 1f out: pushed out fnl f* **2/5**[1]

63 2 3/4 **Hard Luck Story**[10] 6151 2-9-3 0 ... TonyHamilton 11 69
(Miss L A Perratt) *cl up: ev ch fr over 2f out: no ex wl ins fnl f* **7/1**[3]

0 3 2 1/4 **Radegund Abbey**[10] 6151 2-9-3 0 ... TomEaves 9 64
(B Smart) *led to over 1f out: no ex ins fnl f* **40/1**

06 4 1 1/4 **Royal Trooper (IRE)**[19] 5859 2-9-3 0 ... RobertWinston 5 62
(J G Given) *prom: pushed along over 2f out: no imp fnl f* **10/1**

40 5 5 **Graycliffe (IRE)**[18] 5882 2-9-3 0 ... PaulHanagan 3 51
(R A Fahey) *t.k.h: cl up: effrt over 2f out: wknd ins fnl f* **20/1**

0 6 21 **Akmal**[14] 6026 2-9-3 0 ... MartinDwyer 7 4
(J L Dunlop) *hld up: pushed along 1/2-way: sn struggling* **13/2**[2]

1m 56.3s (12.60) **Going Correction** +1.45s/f (Soft) 6 Ran SP% **113.6**
Speed ratings (Par 97): **95,94,92,90,85 64**
toteswinger: 1&2 £1.30, 1&3 £12.30, 2&3 £3.10. CSF £4.05 TOTE £1.40: £1.10, £2.20; EX 2.80 Trifecta £21.20 Pool: £352.13 - 12.26 winning units..
Owner Barry Walters Catering **Bred** B Walters **Trained** West Ilsley, Berks

FOCUS
The first pair came clear in this ordinary maiden, which had a flip start.

NOTEBOOK
Montaff was made to pull out all the stops by the runner-up. He travelled like a winner for most of the way and it looked a case of 'how far' passing the two-furlong pole, but he did not find as much as looked likely when asked to win the race. He was always doing just enough to hold the runner-up and perhaps this more testing ground was not really to his liking, but this was not an improvement on his initial effort. The form of his debut run at Sandown has worked out nicely so far, however, and he should come on for the experience, but on this evidence his Group 1 entry is fanciful. (op 4-7)
Hard Luck Story was the only one to give the winner a serious race and confirmed his last-time-out Hamilton form with the third. No doubt he can be placed to go one better this year and he now has the option of nurseries. (op 5-1 tchd 15-2)
Radegund Abbey, who fell out of the gates at Hamilton ten days previously, was able to race a lot more positively without the starting stalls in operation and, while unable to reverse debut form with the second, posted a much more encouraging display. He will enjoy stepping up in trip as he matures, and he looks a three-year-old in the making. (op 33-1)
Royal Trooper(IRE) did little wrong in defeat and has now improved with each of his three outings. He should fare even better now he is eligible for an official mark. (op 9-1 tchd 12-1)

6385 BRANDLING HOUSE CHRISTMAS PARTIES H'CAP 1m 3y(S)
4:15 (4:16) (Class 5) (0-70,75) 3-Y-0+ **£3,238** (£963; £481; £240) **Stalls** High

Form RPR

0-04 1 **Barkass (UAE)**[30] 5561 4-9-0 **63** ... DavidAllan 12 75
(B Ellison) *hld up: hdwy over 2f out: led appr fnl f: rdn out* **13/2**[3]

6000 2 1 1/4 **Wovoka (IRE)**[13] 6052 5-9-5 **68** ... TonyHamilton 2 77
(D W Barker) *hld up: smooth hdwy over 2f out: weaved through to chse wnr ins fnl f: r.o* **16/1**

0201 3 1 1/2 **Moheebb (IRE)**[9] 6162 4-9-12 **75** 6ex ... (b) AndrewElliott 5 81
(Mrs R A Carr) *hld up: hdwy over 2f out: cl up and effrt over 1f out: r.o same pce fnl f* **11/4**[2]

0004 **4** *2* **Lap Of Honour (IRE)**[15] 5991 4-9-7 **70**........(p) AdrianTNicholls 11 71
(Jennie Candlish) *led to appr fnl f: kpt on same pce* **16/1**

40-0 **5** *2* **Effingham (IRE)**[156] 1685 3-9-2 **68**........ HayleyTurner 9 64
(N J Vaughan) *midfield: pushed along 1/2-way: rallied 2f out: outpcd fnl f* **22/1**

3206 **6** *5* **Dechiper (IRE)**[30] 5564 6-8-11 **65**........ PatrickDonaghy(5) 7 50
(R Johnson) *chsd ldrs tl rdn and wknd over 1f out* **11/1**

0010 **7** *10* **Superior Star**[9] 6162 5-9-1 **64**........(b) JamieMoriarty 8 26
(N Wilson) *hld up: rdn over 2f out: sn btn* **14/1**

6052 **8** *16* **We'Re Delighted**[8] 6186 3-9-2 **68**........ GrahamGibbons 6 —
(T D Walford) *pressed ldr: rdn over 3f out: wknd over 2f out* **2/1**[1]

0000 **9** *nk* **Brother Barry (USA)**[69] 4329 3-8-12 **64**........ PJMcDonald 3 —
(G A Swinbank) *prom tl rdn and wknd over 2f out* **9/1**

4/0- **10** *69* **Skylarker (USA)**[462] 2987 10-8-13 **62**........ DaleGibson 1 —
(T A K Cuthbert) *sn towards rr on outside: rdn and lost tch fr 1/2-way* **80/1**

1m 50.24s (6.84) **Going Correction** +1.00s/f (Soft)
WFA 3 from 4yo+ 3lb **10** Ran SP% **115.7**
Speed ratings (Par 103): **105,103,102,100,98 93,83,67,66,—**
toteswinger: 1&2 £13.40, 1&3 £3.40, 2&3 £12.00. CSF £103.41 CT £362.54 TOTE £5.60: £2.10, £4.10, £1.50; EX 64.50 TRIFECTA Not won..

Owner Jelly Fish **Bred** Darley **Trained** Norton, N Yorks

■ Stewards' Enquiry : P J McDonald two-day ban: careless riding (Oct 15-16)

FOCUS
A modest handicap which was run at an ordinary early pace, and the runners all migrated over to the stands' side. Fair form for the grade rated around the runner-up, third and fourth.

6386 PARKLANDS GOLFCOURSE ANNUAL MEMBERSHIP H'CAP 2m 19y
4:50 (4:50) (Class 5) (0-70,63) 3-Y-O **£3,238** (£963; £481; £240) **Stalls** Low

Form RPR

004 **1** **Goldrenched (IRE)**[134] 2291 3-9-7 **63**........ HayleyTurner 5 68+
(M L W Bell) *trckd ldrs: effrt 3f out: led over 1f out: hld on wl fnl f* **7/1**

0000 **2** *nk* **Unawatuna**[27] 5637 3-8-3 **50**........ KellyHarrison(5) 2 55
(Mrs K Walton) *hld up: hdwy over 6f out: chsng ldrs over 3f out: effrt and wnt 2nd appr fnl f: kpt on but a hld* **28/1**

3031 **3** *2 1/4* **Bouggler**[56] 4735 3-9-3 **59**........ RoystonFfrench 1 61
(Miss J A Camacho) *cl up: led 1/2-way to over 1f out: one pce fnl f* **9/4**[1]

6645 **4** *24* **No Rules**[13] 6060 3-8-12 **54**........ MartinDwyer 7 28
(M H Tompkins) *hld up: drvn and outpcd over 5f out: plugged on but no imp fnl 3f* **11/4**[2]

6540 **5** *10* **Circus Clown (IRE)**[53] 4859 3-8-13 **55**........(v[1]) TomEaves 4 17
(Miss L A Perratt) *early reminders in rr: hdwy over 6f out: wknd over 4f out* **14/1**

5230 **6** *52* **Suite Francaise**[13] 6060 3-8-11 **53**........(t) DO'Donohoe 8 —
(Sir Mark Prescott) *prom: rdn after 4f: wknd over 6f out* **15/2**

0040 **7** *2* **Eddie Dowling**[39] 5269 3-8-11 **53**........ EdwardCreighton 6 —
(M R Channon) *cl up tl wknd over 4f out* **5/1**[3]

0506 **8** *22* **Rye Rocket**[62] 4564 3-8-3 **45**........ AndrewElliott 3 —
(K R Burke) *led to 1/2-way: lost tch fr 6f out* **11/1**

3m 57.87s (21.67) **Going Correction** +1.45s/f (Soft) **8** Ran SP% **116.8**
Speed ratings (Par 101): **103,102,101,89,84 58,57,46**
toteswinger: 1&2 £17.80, 1&3 £3.30, 2&3 £10.00. CSF £169.90 CT £580.21 TOTE £6.40: £2.00, £5.90, £1.20; EX 150.30 Trifecta £447.10 Pool: £604.31 - 1.00 winning units..

Owner Tsega Horses **Bred** Tsega Breeding Limited **Trained** Newmarket, Suffolk

■ Stewards' Enquiry : Kelly Harrison eight-day ban: used whip with excessive frequency (Oct 16-23)

FOCUS
There was another flip start here. The race was just a moderate event for the class, and it has been rated around the third.

Eddie Dowling Official explanation: jockey said gelding was unsuited by the heavy, soft in places ground

6387 EUROPEAN BREEDERS FUND FILLIES' H'CAP 7f
5:20 (5:24) (Class 5) (0-75,74) 3-Y-O+ **£3,238** (£963; £481; £240) **Stalls** High

Form RPR

6230 **1** **Badweia (USA)**[14] 6027 3-9-6 **74**........(b[1]) MartinDwyer 9 80
(J L Dunlop) *cl up: rdn to ld over 1f out: r.o fnl f* **7/2**[2]

0440 **2** *3/4* **Savannah Poppy (IRE)**[25] 5713 3-9-4 **72**........ HayleyTurner 6 76
(M L W Bell) *t.k.h: hld up: hdwy over 2f out: effrt over 1f out: kpt on fnl f* **9/2**[3]

1050 **3** *shd* **Eternal Legacy (IRE)**[5] 6250 6-8-11 **63**........ DavidAllan 4 67
(E J Alston) *led to over 1f out: kpt on same pce fnl f* **11/4**[1]

0115 **4** *2 3/4* **Casino Night**[10] 6155 3-8-6 **67**........ DeanHeslop(7) 7 63
(R Johnson) *prom: drvn over 2f out: one pce over 1f out* **8/1**

-425 **5** *5* **Orchestrion**[41] 5205 3-8-8 **62**........ PaulHanagan 10 45
(Miss T Jackson) *unruly leaving paddock: stdd s: hld up: effrt over 2f out: rdn and wknd over 1f out* **16/1**

1425 **6** *18* **Little Knickers**[15] 5998 3-8-13 **67** ow3........(b) AlanCreighton(3) 3 1
(E J Creighton) *cl up tl rdn and wknd over 2f out: t.o* **12/1**

3030 **7** *7* **Silca Destination**[102] 3266 3-8-9 **63**........ EdwardCreighton 1 —
(M R Channon) *swtchd to r alone far side: rdn 1/2-way: sn struggling: t.o* **18/1**

1m 36.23s (8.83) **Going Correction** +1.00s/f (Soft)
WFA 3 from 4yo+ 2lb **7** Ran SP% **97.0**
Speed ratings (Par 100): **89,88,88,84,79 58,50**
CSF £13.73 CT £27.84 TOTE £3.40: £1.80, £2.30; EX 14.80 Trifecta £24.80 Pool: £160.30 - 4.78 winning units. Place 6: £84.21 Place 5: £58.09.

Owner Hamdan Al Maktoum **Bred** Shadwell Farm LLC **Trained** Arundel, W Sussex

FOCUS
This modest fillies' handicap was weakened by the late withdrawal of Feisty Royale. All bar one of the runners came to the stands' side. It has been rated around the front two.

Little Knickers Official explanation: jockey said filly lost action in last 2 1/2f

T/Jkpt: £20,343.10 to a £1 stake. Pool: £57,304.64. 2.00 winning tickets. T/Plt: £41.20 to a £1 stake. Pool: £68,861.47. 1,218.73 winning tickets. T/Qpdt: £5.50 to a £1 stake. Pool: £4,244.59. 564.59 winning tickets. RY

5072 NOTTINGHAM (L-H)
Wednesday, October 1

OFFICIAL GOING: Good to soft (good in places on straight course) changing to soft (good to soft in places) after race 4 (3.20)
The first time the inner course has been used since the spring. The first race was delayed for an hour as one of the medical officers did not arrive in time.
Wind: Fresh against Weather: Showery

6388 LANSON CHAMPAGNE H'CAP 5f 13y
1:50 (2:51) (Class 5) (0-75,74) 3-Y-O+ **£2,590** (£770; £385; £192) **Stalls** High

Form RPR

0062 **1** **Rocker**[20] 5817 4-8-10 **66**........ RyanMoore 10 77+
(G L Moore) *trckd ldrs stands' side: hdwy over 1f out: swtchd rt and rdn ent fnl f: led fnl 100yds* **13/2**[3]

3212 **2** *1 1/4* **Matterofact (IRE)**[11] 6131 5-8-13 **69**........ TGMcLaughlin 6 75
(M S Saunders) *prom centre: rdn to ld over 1f out: drvn ins fnl f: hdd and nt qckn fnl 100yds* **6/1**[2]

3-45 **3** *nk* **Gold Express**[11] 6131 5-8-12 **68**........ AlanMunro 7 73
(P J O'Gorman) *trckd ldrs towards centre: hdwy 2f out: rdn to chal and ev ch ent fnl f: kpt on same pce* **11/2**[1]

-605 **4** *1/2* **Nickel Silver**[68] 4397 3-8-10 **66**........ PhilipRobinson 4 69+
(B Smart) *chsd ldrs far side: hdwy and cl up 2f out: sn rdn and edgd rt over 1f out: ev ch tl drvn and one pce ins fnl f* **14/1**

0255 **5** *1 1/2* **Charles Parnell (IRE)**[12] 6066 5-9-4 **74**........ RichardMullen 9 72
(M Dods) *in tch towards stands' side: hdwy 2f out: sn rdn and kpt on same pce fnl f* **8/1**

1560 **6** *1/2* **Comptonspirit**[6] 6232 4-8-11 **67**........ JimCrowley 11 63+
(B P J Baugh) *chsd ldrs stands' side: rdn along whn n.m.r over 1f out: grad wknd* **12/1**

0316 **7** *hd* **King Of Swords (IRE)**[14] 6011 4-8-8 **71**........ AndreaAtzeni(7) 13 66
(N Tinkler) *cl up stands' side: rdn along 2f out: grad wknd* **11/1**

066P **8** *2* **Rough Rock (IRE)**[71] 4271 3-8-7 **63**........ LiamJones 15 51
(G Prodromou) *stmbld s: a towards rr stands' side* **66/1**

301 **9** *nse* **Enodoc**[7] 6204 3-8-5 **66**........(t) DavidProbert(5) 16 54
(W R Muir) *cl up stands' side: rdn along 2f out and sn wknd* **7/1**

3204 **10** *1/2* **Feelin Foxy**[7] 6218 4-9-0 **70**........ TPQueally 1 56
(J G Given) *overall ldr far side: rdn along 2f out: sn edgd rt: hdd & wknd appr fnl f* **9/1**

0200 **11** *1/2* **Malapropism**[11] 6131 8-9-0 **70**........(v) TonyCulhane 12 54
(M R Channon) *led stands' side: gp: rdn along 2f out: sn hdd & wknd* **14/1**

6400 **12** *5* **Wibbadune (IRE)**[21] 5796 4-9-0 **70**........ NCallan 5 36
(D Shaw) *stmbld s: sn chsng ldrs far side: rdn along over 2f out and sn wknd* **22/1**

0303 **13** *1 1/2* **Kalligal**[20] 5817 3-8-8 **64** ow1........ RobertHavlin 2 25
(R Ingram) *chsd ldr far side: rdn along 1/2-way: sn wknd* **28/1**

410 **14** *1 1/4* **Blessed Place**[7] 6204 8-8-12 **68**........ JamesDoyle 3 24
(D J S Ffrench Davis) *chsd ldrs far side: rdn along over 2f out and sn wknd* **28/1**

62.02 secs (1.32) **Going Correction** -0.125s/f (Firm) **14** Ran SP% **118.7**
Speed ratings (Par 103): **84,82,81,80,78 77,77,74,73,73 72,64,61,59**
toteswinger: 1&2 £4.20, 1&3 £4.90, 2&3 £4.30. CSF £42.90 CT £232.24 TOTE £6.60: £2.10, £1.90, £2.20; EX 36.90.

Owner Sir Eric Parker **Bred** Sir Eric Parker **Trained** Woodingdean, E Sussex

FOCUS
A modest sprint handicap. They split into three groups early on, with the majority near side, two up the middle, and five far side, but nearly all of them ended up near the stands' rail late on. The form looks ordinary rated through the runner-up.

Comptonspirit Official explanation: jockey said filly was denied a clear run
Rough Rock(IRE) Official explanation: jockey said gelding stumbled leaving gates and was never travelling thereafter
Feelin Foxy Official explanation: jockey said filly hung badly right

6389 SARREGO MEMORIAL EBF MAIDEN STKS 5f 13y
2:20 (3:20) (Class 5) 2-Y-O **£3,885** (£1,156; £577; £288) **Stalls** High

Form RPR

22 **1** **Enderby Spirit (GR)**[11] 6110 2-9-3 0........ RichardMullen 3 85+
(B Smart) *mde all: rdn clr fnl f* **3/1**[1]

04 **2** *4 1/2* **Ben's Dream (IRE)**[15] 5988 2-9-3 0........ WilliamBuick 8 68
(A M Balding) *hld up: hdwy over 1f out: wnt 2nd ins fnl f: no ch w wnr* **5/1**[2]

05 **3** *2 1/4* **Arachnophobia (IRE)**[22] 5784 2-9-3 0........ PaulEddery 9 60+
(Pat Eddery) *s.i.s: sn pushed along: r.o wl ins fnl f: nt rch ldrs* **33/1**

62 **4** *shd* **Master Lightfoot**[34] 5430 2-9-3 0........ TedDurcan 6 60+
(W R Swinburn) *s.i.s: racd keenly and sn trcking ldrs: rdn over 1f out: wknd ins fnl f* **3/1**[1]

0 **5** *1/2* **Esprit De Midas**[13] 6051 2-9-3 0........ NCallan 4 58+
(K A Ryan) *chsd ldrs: hung lft thrght: rdn and wknd over 1f out* **8/1**

000 **6** *nk* **Excitable (IRE)**[16] 5959 2-8-9 50........ DominicFox(3) 7 52
(Miss V Haigh) *chsd wnr tl rdn 2f out: wknd ins fnl f* **100/1**

43 **7** *1 1/4* **Boho Chic**[15] 5988 2-8-12 0........ JimCrowley 11 48
(R M Beckett) *prom: swtchd lft 1/2-way: wknd over 1f out* **6/1**[3]

00 **8** *1/2* **Bulella**[11] 6110 2-8-12 0........ MickyFenton 14 46
(Garry Moss) *s.i.s: outpcd: hung lft fr over 1f out: nvr nrr* **150/1**

60 **9** *1 3/4* **Celtic Rebel (IRE)**[18] 5905 2-9-3 0........ PatCosgrave 12 44+
(S A Callaghan) *hld up: shkn up over 1f out: nvr nr to chal* **40/1**

65 **10** *2 1/2* **Perfect Class**[19] 5860 2-8-12 0........ PhilipRobinson 10 30
(C G Cox) *chsd ldrs: rdn 1/2-way: wknd over 1f out* **6/1**[3]

P **11** *8* **Wicklewood**[18] 5905 2-9-3 0........ TGMcLaughlin 5 —
(Mrs C A Dunnett) *mid-div: lost pl over 3f out: sn bhd* **150/1**

12 *nk* **Dynamo Dane (IRE)** 2-9-3 0........ TPQueally 2 —
(J G Given) *dwlt: outpcd* **22/1**

60.17 secs (-0.53) **Going Correction** -0.125s/f (Firm) **12** Ran SP% **118.4**
Speed ratings (Par 95): **99,91,88,88,87 86,84,83,81,77 64,63**
toteswinger: 1&2 £4.80, 1&3 £13.50, 2&3 £10.20. CSF £17.65 TOTE £3.60: £1.90, £1.60, £5.10; EX 16.90.

Owner John Walsh & Reuben Glynn **Bred** Stavloi Th Nanou S A **Trained** Hambleton, N Yorks

FOCUS
A fair juvenile sprint maiden and a few in behind the impressive winner suggested they can win races at some point. The time was really good, 1.85 seconds quicker than the previous handicap won by Rocker, who carried 7lb less than Enderby Spirit. They all raced stands' side. The race has been rated positively.

NOTEBOOK

Enderby Spirit(GR) ◆, who was runner-up on his debut for Declan Carroll before filling the same position on his first start for this yard, made no mistake this time, gradually drawing clear for a convincing success, having shown good speed throughout. The winning time suggests he is decent and his connections had been considering the Group 1 Middle Park, but felt he was still too immature and chose to win a maiden instead. He is expected to make a nice three-year-old and is all speed. (tchd 11-4 and 10-3)

Ben's Dream(IRE) ◆ got shuffled back early, but he moved well and finished nicely once switched out wide, despite still looking green. He will not always run into such a decent type and looks up to winning an ordinary maiden, but he now has the option of nurseries/handicaps. (op 15-2 tchd 8-1)

Arachnophobia(IRE) ◆ caught the eye running on late when fifth over 6f at Lingfield last time and this was an even more taking effort on this drop in trip. He was still green, but gradually responded to pressure and finished well to take third near the line once switched out wide. He will have gone into a few notebooks following this effort (if he wasn't already in them from last time), so he might not be a fancy price when taking the handicap route, but he can surely win races at the right level, as he should not be too harshly treated. He shapes as though a step back up in trip might help, but should have the speed for 5f when he gets the idea.

Master Lightfoot raced keenly early, despite being fitted with a cross-noseband. He did not see his race out and will probably be happier back on Polytrack, when the emphasis is firmly on speed. (op 5-2)

Esprit De Midas ◆ did not show much on his debut at Pontefract when the occasion seemed to get to him, but he is a nice-looking individual and this was more promising. He was caught wide early and was not given a hard time once his chance had gone after being switched inside, but he kept on. He still looks immature, but should progress into a useful type in time. (op 11-1 tchd 12-1)

Excitable(IRE)'s proximity does little for the form as she came into this rated 50, but this looked an improved performance.

Boho Chic was below form, but she was never really in the clear and is a little better than she showed. She is now eligible for a handicap mark. (op 5-1)

Celtic Rebel(IRE) gave the impression he will be capable of a lot better in time, possibly on quicker ground.

Perfect Class was well below form, but she is now eligible for a handicap mark. (op 7-1 tchd 15-2)

6390 GOOSEFAIR H'CAP — 2m 9y

2:50 (3:53) (Class 4) (0-85,79) 3-Y-O — £7,123 (£2,119; £1,059; £529) Stalls Low

Form	Pos	Dist	Horse	Jockey	RPR
1410	1		**Neve Lieve (IRE)**[17] 5938 3-9-0 72	AlanMunro 3	77
			(M Botti) *trckd ldr on inner: hdwy to ld 4f out: rdn along over 2f out: drvn ins fnl f and styd on wl*	**11/1**	
5331	2	1	**Hendersyde (USA)**[49] 4985 3-9-7 79	(t) TedDurcan 6	83
			(W R Swinburn) *hld up in rr: hdwy 5f out and sn pushed along: rdn to chse ldrs over 2f out: drvn and kpt on ins fnl f: tk 2nd nr fin*	**9/2**[2]	
4111	3	nk	**Kiribati King (IRE)**[13] 6054 3-9-4 76	TonyCulhane 5	79
			(M R Channon) *hld up: hdwy to trck ldrs 7f out: effrt over 4f out: chal over 3f out: rdn and hung lft over 2f out: sn drvn and one pce fnl f: lost 2nd nr line*	**3/1**[1]	
0466	4	¾	**Opera De Luna**[13] 6044 3-8-4 62	LiamJones 4	65
			(D Shaw) *hld up in rr: hdwy over 3f out: rdn along over 2f out: drvn over 1f out: kpt on wl u.p ins fnl f: nrst fin*	**33/1**	
4416	5	3 ¾	**Broken Moon**[25] 5698 3-9-3 75	PatCosgrave 2	73
			(J R Fanshawe) *trckd ldrs: hdwy over 4f out: chsd ldng pair whn n.m.r on inner over 2f out: sn rdn and one pce*	**15/2**	
0121	6	27	**Okafranca (IRE)**[18] 5887 3-9-0 72	RichardMullen 1	38
			(W R Muir) *prom: pushed along on inner over 4f out: rdn over 3f out and sn wknd*	**3/1**[1]	
4-53	7	5	**Keenes Day (FR)**[25] 5698 3-9-7 79	JoeFanning 7	39
			(M Johnston) *trckd ldrs: hdwy to chse ldr 1/2-way: rdn along 4f out and sn wknd*	**7/1**[3]	
454	8	36	**Purely By Chance**[27] 5651 3-8-2 60	(v) WilliamBuick 8	—
			(R M Beckett) *led: rdn along 5f out: hdd 4f out: wknd qckly*	**12/1**	

3m 36.01s (2.41) **Going Correction** +0.30s/f (Good) 8 Ran SP% **111.4**

Speed ratings (Par 103): **105,104,104,103,102 88,86,68**

toteswinger: 1&2 £7.60, 1&3 £5.60, 2&3 £2.70. CSF £56.67 CT £183.11 TOTE £14.30: £2.80, £1.60, £1.90; EX 75.40.

Owner The Great Partnership **Bred** Darley **Trained** Newmarket, Suffolk

■ Stewards' Enquiry : Tony Culhane caution: careless riding

FOCUS

Recent winners of this include Bulwark and Juniper Girl, but this looked just a fair race. They went a good pace and the form has been rated around the winner to his Yarmouth success.

Okafranca(IRE) Official explanation: jockey said gelding was never travelling

6391 EUROPEAN BREEDERS' FUND MAIDEN FILLIES' STKS (DIV I) — 1m 75y

3:20 (4:25) (Class 5) 2-Y-O — £3,561 (£1,059; £529; £264) Stalls Low

Form	Pos	Dist	Horse	Jockey	RPR
	1		**Enticement** 2-9-0 0	RyanMoore 7	74+
			(Sir Michael Stoute) *hld up in tch: shkn up 1/2-way: rdn and hung lft over 1f out: styd on to ld towards fin*	**11/4**[1]	
023	2	½	**Miss Sophisticat**[29] 5585 2-9-0 75	PaulDoe 11	73
			(W J Knight) *chsd ldrs: led over 2f out: rdn and edgd lft ins fnl f: hdd towards fin*	**3/1**[2]	
50	3	¾	**Phoenix Enforcer**[34] 5430 2-8-9 0	DavidProbert(5) 8	71
			(George Baker) *led: hdd over 6f out: led again 1/2-way: rdn: edgd lft and hdd over 2f out: no ex towards fin*	**50/1**	
0	4	hd	**Tottie**[9] 6166 2-9-0 0	JimCrowley 6	71+
			(Mrs A J Perrett) *unruly bhd stalls: s.s: hld up: hung lft and r.o wl ins fnl f: nt rch ldrs*	**14/1**	
43	5	1 ¼	**Perception (IRE)**[31] 5535 2-9-0 0	LiamJones 15	68
			(R Charlton) *hld up: rdn and nt clr run over 2f out: hdwy over 1f out: no imp ins fnl f*	**4/1**[3]	
0	6	3 ½	**Lyric Art (USA)**[54] 4815 2-9-0 0	TedDurcan 13	60+
			(B Smart) *hld up: hdwy over 3f out: rdn and edgd lft over 2f out: wknd ins fnl f*	**16/1**	
	7	hd	**Natural Flair (USA)** 2-9-0 0	AlanMunro 9	60
			(P W Chapple-Hyam) *mid-div: lost pl 1/2-way: n.d after*	**12/1**	
	8	2	**Marjury Daw (IRE)** 2-8-7 0	RosieJessop(7) 3	56
			(J G Given) *chsd ldrs: pushed along 5f out: wknd over 1f out*	**50/1**	
0	9	1	**Always Rocking (FR)**[30] 5571 2-9-0 0	PaulEddery 12	53
			(G D Blake) *chsd ldrs: rdn over 3f out: wknd over 1f out*	**66/1**	
	10	2 ¼	**Arcola (IRE)** 2-9-0 0	RichardMullen 14	48+
			(D M Simcock) *hld up: hdwy over 4f out: rdn over 2f out: wknd fnl f*	**33/1**	
	11	7	**Chanrossa (IRE)** 2-9-0 0	JimmyFortune 1	33
			(E A L Dunlop) *hld up in tch: pushed along and wknd over 2f out*	**12/1**	
0	12	9	**Desert Fairy**[77] 4080 2-9-0 0	MickyFenton 4	13
			(P W D'Arcy) *sn pushed along and prom: led over 6f out: hdd 1/2-way: wknd over 2f out*	**50/1**	
0	13	¾	**Blessing Belle (IRE)**[12] 6081 2-8-7 0	AshleyMorgan(7) 2	12
			(M H Tompkins) *sn pushed along: a in rr: wknd over 2f out*	**100/1**	
	14	nk	**Za Za** 2-9-0 0	TPQueally 5	11
			(H R A Cecil) *s.s: a bhd*	**9/1**	

1m 48.41s (3.01) **Going Correction** +0.30s/f (Good) 14 Ran SP% **120.9**

Speed ratings (Par 92): **96,95,94,94,93 89,89,87,86,84 77,68,67,67**

toteswinger: 1&2 £3.30 1&3 £45.50, 2&3 £42.50. CSF £10.70 TOTE £3.30: £1.60, £1.70, £13.90; EX 14.70.

Owner The Queen **Bred** Ecoutila Partnership **Trained** Newmarket, Suffolk

FOCUS

The ground was changed to soft, good to soft in places after this race. Probably just an ordinary juvenile fillies' maiden and some of the more interesting runners look longer-term prospects. The winning time was 0.11 seconds quicker than the second division. The form has been rated through the runner-up and fifth.

NOTEBOOK

Enticement, a 310,000gns daughter of Montjeu, got off the mark at the first attempt without being given too hard a time. The bare form is no more than fair, as the runner-up came into this rated 75, but Ryan Moore only went for his whip twice and she gave the impression she can improve significantly over middle distances next year. (tchd 5-2 and 3-1)

Miss Sophisticat gave the impression she would be suited by a galloping track when third off a mark of 73 on her nursery debut at Goodwood last time and this was a respectable effort. (op 4-1)

Phoenix Enforcer had not shown much on her first two starts at up to 6f, but this was a much-improved effort. Her dam stayed 1m3f and she was clearly well suited by this step up in trip, although this will not have helped her prospective handicap mark.

Tottie played up before the start, but she showed plenty of ability in the race, staying on nicely in the closing stages towards the outside having been well off the pace early. (op 11-1 tchd 10-1)

Perception(IRE) was not at her best and may not have been suited by easy ground. She is now eligible for a handicap mark. (op 9-2)

Lyric Art(USA) was noted going well towards the outside early in the straight, but she floundered under pressure. She has ability and should do better next year, when quicker ground should be a help. (op 20-1)

Natural Flair(USA), a $230,000 Giant's Causeway filly, showed some ability and will know more next time. Quicker ground may suit better. (op 11-1)

Arcola(IRE) ◆, a 60,000gns daughter of Nayef who has been entered in the Irish Oaks, travelled well for a long way before getting tired. She has plenty of ability and should leave this form behind over middle distances next year.

6392 EUROPEAN BREEDERS' FUND MAIDEN FILLIES' STKS (DIV II) — 1m 75y

3:55 (4:59) (Class 5) 2-Y-O — £3,561 (£1,059; £529; £264) Stalls Low

Form	Pos	Dist	Horse	Jockey	RPR
5	1		**Sampi**[14] 6016 2-9-0 0	JimCrowley 12	78+
			(Mrs A J Perrett) *in tch: n.m.r 2 1/2f out: swtchd rt to outside wl over 1f out: rdn and styd on to ld ins fnl f*	**11/2**[2]	
	2	1 ¾	**Tricky Situation** 2-9-0 0	TPQueally 13	72
			(J G Given) *midfield: gd hdwy on outer 3f out: chal wl over 1f out: sn rdn and ev ch tl drvn nt qckn ins fnl f*	**22/1**	
50	3	½	**Lonely Star (IRE)**[9] 6167 2-9-0 0	NCallan 7	71
			(D R Lanigan) *in tch: hdwy whn nt clr run wl over 1f out: swtchd rt and rdn appr fnl f: kpt on wl: nrst fin*	**7/1**[3]	
	4	1 ¾	**Welsh Anthem** 2-8-9 0	DavidProbert(5) 14	67
			(W R Muir) *a.p: hdwy to ld wl over 1f out and sn rdn: drvn and hdd ins fnl f: wknd*	**16/1**	
02	5	2	**Damini (USA)**[31] 5535 2-9-0 0	RyanMoore 1	63
			(Sir Michael Stoute) *trckd ldrs: hdwy 3f out: rdn to chal 2f out and ev ch tl drvn and wknd ent fnl f*	**1/1**[1]	
	6	1 ¼	**Charlotte Point (USA)** 2-9-0 0	JoeFanning 5	60
			(P F I Cole) *led: rdn along wl over 2f out: hdd wl over 1f out: sn drvn and grad wknd appr fnl f*	**25/1**	
	7	nk	**Spirit Of Dubai (IRE)** 2-9-0 0	RichardMullen 2	59+
			(D M Simcock) *dwlt: sn in tch on inner: effrt to chse ldrs 3f out: rdn along over 2f out and kpt on same pce appr fnl f*	**22/1**	
	8	1	**Penzena** 2-9-0 0	PaulDoe 8	57
			(W J Knight) *dwlt and bhd tl styd on fnl 2f*	**25/1**	
	9	1	**My Chestnut Girl (USA)** 2-9-0 0	TedDurcan 4	55
			(H R A Cecil) *dwlt and towards rr: hdwy on inner 3f out: in tch over 2f out: sn rdn and wknd*	**16/1**	
43	10	nk	**Paqueretta (FR)**[18] 5882 2-9-0 0	LDettori 10	54
			(D H Brown) *awkward s: a towards rr*	**8/1**	
	11	5	**New Beginning (FR)** 2-9-0 0	JamesDoyle 3	43
			(H J L Dunlop) *midfield: rdn along over 3f out: sn outpcd*	**40/1**	
0	12	½	**Baby Is Here (IRE)**[149] 1866 2-9-0 0	SamHitchcott 6	42
			(D J S Ffrench Davis) *clsd up: rdn along 3f out: drvn 2f out and sn wknd*	**100/1**	
	13	4 ½	**Astrobrava** 2-8-7 0	AshleyMorgan(7) 11	32
			(M H Tompkins) *s.i.s: a bhd*	**100/1**	
06	14	12	**Good Queen Best**[63] 4534 2-9-0 0	WilliamBuick 9	6
			(B De Haan) *chsd ldng pair: rdn along over 2f out: sn drvn and edgd lft wl over 1f out: wknd*	**100/1**	

1m 48.52s (3.12) **Going Correction** +0.30s/f (Good) 66 Ran SP% **122.6**

Speed ratings (Par 92): **96,94,93,92,90 88,88,87,86,86 81,80,76,64**

toteswinger: 1&2 £22.20, 1&3 £7.50, 2&3 £23.30. CSF £126.76 TOTE £6.90: £2.50, £6.50, £1.90; EX 106.00.

Owner K Abdulla **Bred** Juddmonte Farms Ltd **Trained** Pulborough, W Sussex

FOCUS

A reasonable juvenile fillies' maiden. The winning time was 0.11 seconds slower than the first division.

NOTEBOOK

Sampi stepped up significantly on the form she showed when fifth on her debut over this trip on the Polytrack at Kempton. She raced enthusiastically off the pace early, and if anything was a little keen, but she found plenty in the straight to win in decisive fashion. She should be effective at around 1m-1m2f next year and rates as a nice prospect. (op 9-1)

Tricky Situation ◆, a 26,000gns half-sister to the stable's smart middle-distance/stayer Trick Or Treat, made a pleasing debut. Like the winner she was well off the pace early, but she kept on pleasingly, despite looking green. She rates as a useful prospect when stepped up in trip next year. (op 16-1)

Lonely Star(IRE) ◆ could not confirm her debut promise from a bad draw at Kempton last time, but this was better, despite the ground probably being softer than ideal. She will be of interest if returned to a quicker surface when switching to nursery/handicap company. Official explanation: jockey said filly became unbalanced (op 13-2 tchd 8-1)

Welsh Anthem, a daughter of Singspiel, half-sister to among others high-class 7f-1m winner Trans Island, was backed at big prices and ran well. She travelled nicely for a long way and looked the one to beat inside the final two furlongs, but her effort flattened out. She should last a lot longer next time and looks up to winning a similar race. (op 25-1)

Damini(USA) was produced with every chance, but she could not sustain her challenge and did not look at home on the easy ground late on. She was below the form she showed when second at Folkestone last time and may do better back on a quicker surface. (op 11-10 tchd 5-4)

Charlotte Point(USA), a $170,000 half-sister to smart triple-winning US miler Rugula, is a little better than her finishing position suggests, as she was taken on for the lead by Baby Is Here and was too keen for her own good. (op 20-1)

Spirit Of Dubai(IRE) ◆, an 85,000gns daughter of Cape Cross, is well regarded and has entries in the Irish Guineas and Oaks. She ran a very similar race to her stablemate in the first division, travelling well early and showing signs of ability before finding little when asked. She should be capable of much better in time. (op 20-1 tchd 25-1)

My Chestnut Girl(USA), a half-sister to Big Brown, showed little, but she is very much regarded as a three-year-old prospect and quicker ground will probably help as well. (op 12-1)

6393 LANSON CHAMPAGNE MAIDEN STKS — 1m 75y

4:25 (5:31) (Class 5) 3-Y-O+ — £3,238 (£963; £481; £240) Stalls Low

Form — RPR

6-2 **1** **Otaared**[168] 1403 3-9-3 0 ... PhilipRobinson 4 — 82+
(M A Jarvis) *chsd ldrs: led 2f out: rdn out* **11/8**[1]

5 **2** 1 ½ **Cara's Request (AUS)**[13] 6047 3-8-5 0 ... LiamJones 14 — 75
(L M Cumani) *hld up in tch: racd keenly: rdn to chse wnr over 1f out: styd on same pce ins fnl f* **16/1**

3 shd **Red Jade** 3-9-3 0 ... JimmyFortune 12 — 81+
(J H M Gosden) *hld up: hdwy over 2f out: nt clr run wl over 1f out: swtchd lft: r.o wl ins fnl f: eased fnl strides* **16/1**

4 ½ **Lease Of Life (USA)** 3-9-3 0 ... MichaelHills 11 — 77+
(B W Hills) *dwlt: hld up: hdwy over 1f out: edgd lft: r.o: nt trble ldrs* **7/1**[3]

5 ¾ **Taqdeyr** 3-9-3 0 ... NCallan 1 — 77+
(M A Jarvis) *s.s: hld up: hdwy over 2f out: styd on same pce whn eased nr fin* **10/1**

5-0 **6** 1 ½ **Danse The Blues**[163] 1526 3-8-12 0 ... RyanMoore 10 — 67
(E A L Dunlop) *hld up: hdwy over 1f out: no ex ins fnl f* **20/1**

6 **7** 2 ¾ **Qeyaada (USA)**[13] 6047 3-8-12 0 ... TGMcLaughlin 16 — 61
(E A L Dunlop) *s.i.s: hld up: rdn over 2f out: hung lft fr over 1f out: r.o ins fnl f: nvr nrr* **25/1**

8 8 **Antillia** 3-8-12 0 ... JimCrowley 6 — 42
(C F Wall) *hld up: sme hdwy over 3f out: wknd over 2f out* **66/1**

0 **9** 1 ¼ **Golondrina**[85] 3823 3-8-12 0 ... CatherineGannon 9 — 39
(T J Fitzgerald) *hld up: last but one and detached over 4f out: nvr nrr* **100/1**

30- **10** 1 **Quick Off The Mark**[425] 4125 3-8-12 0 ... TPQueally 5 — 37
(J G Given) *prom: chsd ldr 4f out: rdn over 2f out: wknd over 1f out* **40/1**

20 **11** 3 ¾ **Top Tribute**[11] 6114 3-9-3 0 ... MickyFenton 7 — 33
(T P Tate) *led: rdn and hdd 2f out: sn wknd* **40/1**

12 2 ¾ **Planetary Motion (USA)** 3-9-3 0 ... JoeFanning 15 — 27
(M Johnston) *hld up: hdwy over 3f out: wkng whn hmpd over 2f out* **25/1**

6 **13** 1 **Act Of Diplomacy (USA)**[56] 4730 3-9-3 0 ... LDettori 8 — 25
(Saeed Bin Suroor) *prom: rdn over 3f out: wkng whn hmpd over 2f out* **9/4**[2]

0 **14** ¾ **Alyseve**[13] 6047 3-8-7 0 ... AmyBaker(5) 3 — 18
(Mrs C A Dunnett) *prom: rdn 1/2-way: wknd over 2f out* **150/1**

0 **15** 7 **Miss Medusa**[13] 6047 3-8-12 0 ... (t) SamHitchcott 2 — —
(Mrs C A Dunnett) *chsd ldr to 1/2-way: wknd 3f out* **150/1**

0 **16** 7 **Kiss Me Hardy**[60] 4651 3-8-12 0 ... TonyCulhane 13 — —
(J D Bethell) *s.i.s: sn outpcd and bhd: t.o fnl 6f* **100/1**

1m 47.71s (2.31) **Going Correction** +0.30s/f (Good) — **16** Ran SP% **128.4**
Speed ratings (Par 103): **100,98,98,97,97 95,92,84,83,82 78,76,75,74,67 60**
toteswinger: 1&2 £11.50, 1&3 £5.50, 2&3 £21.40. CSF £27.65 TOTE £2.00: £1.50, £4.10, £3.30; EX 29.20.
Owner Sheikh Ahmed Al Maktoum **Bred** Darley **Trained** Newmarket, Suffolk
■ Stewards' Enquiry : Jimmy Fortune ten-day ban: failed to ride out second place (Oct 15-24)
N Callan 19-day ban (takes into account previous offences; four days deferred): careless riding (Oct 31-Nov 15)

FOCUS
Plenty of big stables represented here and this was quite a good older-horse maiden for the time of year. The form should work out.

Taqdeyr ◆ Official explanation: jockey said colt hung and was difficult to steer

6394 SHOWSEC NURSERY — 1m 2f 50y

5:00 (6:01) (Class 5) (0-75,74) 2-Y-O — £3,238 (£963; £481; £240) Stalls Low

Form — RPR

0041 **1** **Lethal Glaze (IRE)**[29] 5585 2-9-3 **70** ... RyanMoore 11 — 77+
(R Hannon) *hld up towards rr: stdy hdwy 3f out: rdn to chse ldrs whn edgd lft over 1f out: drvn to ld ins fnl f: edgd lft and hdd fnl 50yds: kpt on u.p to ld on line* **13/8**[1]

0461 **2** nse **Dubai Crest**[18] 5914 2-9-2 **69** ... JimCrowley 3 — 76+
(Mrs A J Perrett) *trckd ldrs on inner: hdwy over 2f out: rdn to ld wl over 1f out: drvn and hdd ins fnl f: rallied to ld fnl 50yds: hdd on line* **6/1**[2]

6433 **3** 3 ½ **Dispol Diva**[7] 6214 2-8-1 **54** ... (v) FrankieMcDonald 9 — 54
(P T Midgley) *sn led: rdn along 3f out: drvn over 2f out: hdd wl over 1f out: kpt on u.p fnl f* **11/1**

5600 **4** 2 **Noworneva**[13] 6059 2-7-9 **51** oh6 ... DominicFox(3) 13 — 47
(S Kirk) *cl up: rdn along 3f out: drvn 2f out: hld in 3rd whn bmpd over 1f out: kpt on same pce after* **80/1**

5066 **5** nk **Flying Lady (IRE)**[16] 5960 2-9-2 **69** ... TonyCulhane 15 — 65
(M R Channon) *in rr: hdwy over 2f out: rdn along over 1f out: kpt on ins fnl f: nrst fin* **14/1**

000 **6** 4 **D'Artagnans Dream**[26] 5672 2-9-3 **70** ... OscarUrbina 12 — 58
(G D Blake) *chsd ldrs: rdn along over 2f out: drvn and wknd over 1f out* **66/1**

4601 **7** ¾ **Balladiene (IRE)**[13] 6059 2-8-7 **67** ... AshleyMorgan(7) 8 — 54
(M H Tompkins) *in rr tl styd on fnl 2f: nrst fin* **12/1**

0064 **8** ½ **Strikemaster (IRE)**[18] 5909 2-8-4 **57** ... LiamJones 2 — 43
(J W Hills) *in tch on inner: hdwyt 3f out: rdn over 2f out and grad wknd* **66/1**

0540 **9** 6 **Siciliando**[40] 5242 2-9-1 **68** ... TPQueally 10 — 43
(M L W Bell) *s.i.s and a in rr* **33/1**

000 **10** 2 ½ **Hesketh (IRE)**[26] 5672 2-8-2 **55** ... WilliamBuick 6 — 26
(R M Beckett) *a towards rr* **20/1**

510 **11** ¾ **Sergeant Pink (IRE)**[18] 5895 2-9-7 **74** ... MickyFenton 7 — 43
(S Gollings) *in midfield: rdn along over 3f out: sn wknd* **9/1**[3]

4450 **12** 2 ¼ **Tae Kwon Do (USA)**[18] 5914 2-8-7 **60** ... TGMcLaughlin 16 — 25
(E A L Dunlop) *in tch on wd outside: rdn along over 3f out: sn wknd* **18/1**

5004 **13** 4 ½ **Andean Margin (IRE)**[7] 6214 2-8-9 **62** ... RichardMullen 4 — 19
(S A Callaghan) *chsd ldrs: rdn along 3f out: sn wknd* **9/1**[3]

050 **14** 13 **Muhim**[13] 6057 2-9-1 **68** ... NCallan 14 — —
(C E Brittain) *chsd ldrs: rdn along over 2f out: drvn and edgd lft wl over 1f out: sn wknd* **16/1**

006 **15** 17 **Noble Artist**[22] 5771 2-7-10 **56** oh1 ow5 ... AdeleRothery(7) 5 — —
(D H Brown) *a in rr* **125/1**

2m 16.66s (4.16) **Going Correction** +0.30s/f (Good) — **15** Ran SP% **118.9**
Speed ratings (Par 95): **95,94,92,90,90 87,86,86,81,79 78,76,73,62,49**
toteswinger: 1&2 £5.90, 1&3 £7.40, 2&3 £13.00. CSF £9.85 CT £83.85 TOTE £2.80: £1.40, £2.80, £2.20; EX 14.50.
Owner Nigel Morris **Bred** B Kennedy **Trained** East Everleigh, Wilts

FOCUS
They went an ordinary pace early, but 1m2f on soft ground understandably still proved a good test for these two-year-olds. The form looks decent for the grade.

NOTEBOOK
Lethal Glaze(IRE) looked a thorough stayer when winning over 1m on his nursery debut at Goodwood and he improved again for this step up in trip to defy a 2lb rise, although he very nearly threw this away by continually hanging left. He was determined enough under strong pressure to come out on top in a battling finish, despite his waywardness, and looked more the finished article than the runner-up, but he will need to stay straight in future to compete at a higher level. (op 6-4 tchd 7-4)
Dubai Crest, just as when winning off a 4lb lower mark at Kempton last time, looked immature and did not knuckle down quite as well as Lethal Glaze, which allowed the winner to stay in the contest despite hanging. He eventually just lost out, but has the size and scope to do better as a three-year-old. (op 5-1 tchd 13-2)
Dispol Diva was 1lb lower than in future and she ran well behind a couple of progressive types. Official explanation: jockey said filly lost action (op 14-1)
Noworneva was down the field in a seller over 1m at Yarmouth last time, but he ran surprisingly well from 8lb out of the handicap and the step up in trip clearly suited. (op 100-1)
Flying Lady(IRE), upped three furlongs in trip, followed the eventual winner through in the straight but her run soon flattened out. (tchd 12-1 and 16-1)
Sergeant Pink(IRE) looked a nice prospect when winning his maiden at Beverley, but he completely blew out in a 1m nursery at Doncaster last time. He was again well beaten, but can be excused this to an extent as he seemed to lose his action a little after being squeezed up when trying to stay on over three furlongs out. (tchd 17-2)
Andean Margin(IRE) Official explanation: jockey said colt was unsuited by the soft, good to soft in places ground

6395 AMATEUR JOCKEYS ASSOCIATION H'CAP (FOR GENTLEMAN AMATEUR RIDERS) — 1m 2f 50y

5:30 (6:25) (Class 5) (0-70,70) 3-Y-O+ — £2,637 (£811; £405) Stalls Low

Form — RPR

0556 **1** **Hucking Heat (IRE)**[11] 6134 4-10-7 **56** oh1 ... (p) MrLeeNewnes 14 — 65
(R Hollinshead) *a.p: led 1f out: pushed out* **14/1**

0100 **2** ½ **Serious Choice (IRE)**[17] 5935 3-11-0 **68** ... MrSWalker 2 — 76
(J R Boyle) *chsd ldrs: rdn over 1f out: styd on* **16/1**

6600 **3** 2 ¼ **Black Rain**[12] 6078 3-10-13 **70** ... (v) MrPCollington(3) 10 — 74
(P J McBride) *led: rdn over 2f out: hdd 1f out: styd on same pce* **8/1**

0200 **4** ¾ **Kalasam**[5] 6243 4-11-0 **66** ... MrOGreenall(3) 3 — 68
(M W Easterby) *s.i.s: hdwy over 7f out: rdn and hung lft over 1f out: nt clr run ins fnl f: styd on same pce* **13/2**[2]

4350 **5** ½ **Bavarica**[12] 6090 6-10-8 **62** ... MrRBirkett(5) 11 — 63
(Miss J Feilden) *prom: rdn over 2f out: styd on same pce fnl f* **11/1**

0235 **6** 2 ½ **Kangrina**[33] 5478 6-10-12 **61** ... MrWBiddick 6 — 57
(George Baker) *hld up: hdwy over 2f out: rdn and wknd over 1f out* **8/1**

6402 **7** ½ **Stravita**[8] 6189 4-10-2 **56** oh3 ... (p) MrStephenHarrison(5) 16 — 51+
(R Hollinshead) *s.i.s: hld up: rdn over 2f out: hung rt and styd on fr over 1f out: nvr nrr* **15/2**[3]

0630 **8** 4 **Garafena**[14] 6019 5-10-4 **58** ... MrBJToomey(5) 4 — 45
(B G Powell) *hld up in tch: rdn and wknd over 2f out* **16/1**

35-5 **9** 1 ¼ **Cripsey Brook**[7] 6216 10-10-10 **66** ... MrCMcCormack(7) 15 — 51
(K G Reveley) *hld up: disputing last pl 4f out: nvr nrr* **12/1**

2312 **10** ½ **Everyman**[18] 5912 4-10-8 **60** ... MrMJJSmith(3) 8 — 44
(A W Carroll) *mid-div: rdn and wknd over 2f out* **11/1**

342 **11** hd **Malinsa Blue (IRE)**[60] 4633 6-10-2 **56** ... MrDaleSwift(5) 12 — 39
(B Ellison) *plld hrd: trckd ldr: rdn over 2f out: edgd lft and wknd over 1f out* **10/1**

2561 **12** 4 **Gallego**[14] 6028 6-11-1 **69** ... MrMPrice(5) 7 — 44
(R J Price) *hld up: a in rr* **6/1**[1]

-005 **13** 3 ¼ **Mansii**[47] 5049 3-10-8 **69** ... MrSMcBride(7) 13 — 37
(P J McBride) *hld up: disputing last pl 4f out: a bhd* **33/1**

5- **14** 1 ¾ **Tamreen (IRE)**[374] 693 7-11-2 **70** ... MrRHodges(5) 9 — 34
(R J Price) *hld up: rdn and wknd over 3f out* **16/1**

2m 19.08s (6.58) **Going Correction** +0.30s/f (Good)
WFA 3 from 4yo+ 5lb — **14** Ran SP% **122.3**
Speed ratings (Par 103): **85,84,82,82,81 79,79,76,75,74 74,71,68,67**
toteswinger: 1&2 £35.30, 1&3 £59.50, 2&3 £38.50. CSF £224.48 CT £1928.75 TOTE £17.80: £7.50, £4.40, £2.90; EX 307.80 Place 6: £49.06 Place 5: £27.56 .
Owner Ed Weetman (haulage & Storage) Ltd **Bred** Thomas J Reid **Trained** Upper Longdon, Staffs

FOCUS
A modest amateur riders' handicap and not form to dwell on. The first three were ridden handily. The form has been rated around the third.
T/Plt: £69.50 to a £1 stake. Pool: £62,785.73. 658.85 winning tickets. T/Qpdt: £28.90 to a £1 stake. Pool: £3,123.49. 79.90 winning tickets. JR

5639 SALISBURY (R-H)

Wednesday, October 1

OFFICIAL GOING: Good (good to firm in places) changing to good after race 2 (2.00)
Wind: strong against Weather: dry, heavy shower after Race 6

6396 BATHWICK TYRES LADY RIDERS SERIES H'CAP — 1m

1:30 (1:31) (Class 6) (0-65,65) 3-Y-O+ — £2,810 (£871; £435; £217) Stalls High

Form — RPR

3464 **1** **Moves Goodenough**[55] 4772 5-10-0 **58** ... (b) MissEJJones 6 — 73
(Andrew Turnell) *t.k.h: hld up: gd hdwy on bit over 3f out: bmpd 2f out: led over 1f out: shkn up and r.o strly: comf* **5/1**[2]

0010 **2** 6 **Batchworth Blaise**[28] 5604 5-9-4 **55** ... MissCNosworthy(7) 7 — 56
(E A Wheeler) *s.i.s: detached in rr: stdy prog but hung rt fr over 3f out: swtchd lft over 2f out: styd on wl fnl f: wnt 2nd towards fin: no ch w wnr* **14/1**

0430 **3** ½ **Island Treasure**[23] 5755 3-9-8 **60** ... MissVCartmel(5) 12 — 60
(H Morrison) *led tl over 2f out: sn rdn and hung lft: styd on to regain 2nd ins fnl f but no ch w wnr: lost 2nd towards fin* **9/1**

0000 **4** 3 ¼ **Corlough Mountain**[7] 6209 4-10-0 **65** ow4 ... MissMBryant(7) 14 — 58
(P Butler) *hld up towards rr: hdwy over 2f out: styd on fnl f* **33/1**

4004 **5** *nk* **Shaded Edge**[33] 5458 4-9-11 **55**................(v[1]) MissGDGracey-Davison 8 47
(D W P Arbuthnot) *hld up: hdwy over 3f out: led over 2f out: rdn and hdd over 1f out: no ex fnl f* **7/1**[3]

500 **6** *1 3/4* **Tinnarinka**[82] 3903 4-9-11 **60**.................................. MissHGrissell(5) 1 48
(R Hannon) *hld up in mid-div: hdwy wl over 2f out: sn rdn: kpt on same pce fr over 1f out* **25/1**

4063 **7** *2 1/2* **Mountain Pass (USA)**[21] 5799 6-9-9 **58**.....(p) MissIsabelTompsett(5) 10 40
(B J Llewellyn) *s.i.s: sn in mid-div: effrt 2f out: one pce fnl f* **9/1**

0150 **8** *1 1/2* **Barathea Dreams (IRE)**[27] 5639 7-10-7 **65**..................... MrsSMoore 2 44
(J S Moore) *s.i.s: sn prom: rdn over 2f out: fdd ent fnl f* **11/1**

0400 **9** *2 1/4* **Dubai Samurai**[21] 5803 3-9-11 **61**.....................(v[1]) MissMSowerby(3) 11 34
(J W Hills) *trckd ldrs: rdn over 2f out: wknd ent fnl f* **12/1**

0400 **10** *shd* **Sheer Bluff (IRE)**[20] 5836 3-9-10 **64**.......................... MissOMaylam(7) 13 37
(D R C Elsworth) *chsd ldrs tl wknd over 2f out* **16/1**

0004 **11** *1/2* **Bed Fellow (IRE)**[8] 6189 4-9-5 **56**.......................... MissJKWilson(7) 16 28
(Paul Murphy) *mid-div tl wknd 2f out* **25/1**

1406 **12** *13* **Spent**[12] 6088 3-9-13 **60**.. MissFayeBramley 15 2
(Mouse Hamilton-Fairley) *mid-div early: bhd fnl 3f* **14/1**

2012 **13** *14* **Uhuru Peak**[33] 5458 7-9-11 **55**.................................(bt) MissSBrotherton 9 —
(M W Easterby) *chsd ldrs tl wknd over 2f out* **9/2**[1]

4-10 **14** *3 1/4* **Crispian (IRE)**[5] 6252 4-9-13 **64**.......................... MissALMurphy(7) 5 —
(Jamie Snowden) *prom: rdn 3f out: sn btn* **18/1**

3000 **15** *3* **Milldown Bay**[8] 6192 3-9-13 **60**.................................. MissCHannaford 3 —
(B R Millman) *s.i.s: a bhd* **66/1**

1m 47.59s (4.09) **Going Correction** +0.35s/f (Good)
WFA 3 from 4yo+ 3lb **15** Ran SP% **120.0**
Speed ratings (Par 101): **93,87,86,83,82 81,78,77,74,74 74,61,47,44,41**
toteswinger: 1&2 £10.10, 1&3 £9.70, 2&3 £26.70. CSF £69.98 CT £637.20 TOTE £6.30: £2.20, £5.10, £3.10; EX 87.90.

Owner D Goodenough Removals & Transport **Bred** G Foster **Trained** Broad Hinton, Wilts

FOCUS
A moderate-looking event, and the form is unlikely to be that reliable. The early pace was not that quick and there was a strong headwind that seemed to affect the runners all afternoon.

Uhuru Peak Official explanation: jockey was unable to explain the poor form shown

Milldown Bay Official explanation: jockey said filly missed the break

6397 E.B.F./ ALLIED IRISH BANK (GB) SOUTHAMPTON MAIDEN STKS (DIV I) 1m

2:00 (2:00) (Class 4) 2-Y-O **£4,371** (£1,300; £650; £324) **Stalls** High

Form RPR

1 **State Banquet (USA)** 2-9-3 0.. TravisBlock 2 78+
(H Morrison) *wnt sltly lft s: hld up in last trio: hdwy over 2f out: swtchd rt ent fnl f: r.o wl: led nr fin: rdn out* **14/1**

032 **2** *nk* **Sandor**[15] 5996 2-9-3 82.. EddieAhern 5 75
(P J Makin) *cl up: jnd ldrs 3f out: rdn to take narrow advantage over 1f out: hdd nr fin* **5/2**[2]

0 **3** *nk* **Decision**[47] 5053 2-9-3 0... IanMongan 6 74
(C G Cox) *trckd ldr: led 3f out: sn rdn: narrowly hdd over 1f out: ev ch thrght fnl f: no ex cl home* **11/1**

4 *3/4* **Clowance House** 2-9-3 0.. SteveDrowne 8 73+
(R Charlton) *mid-div: nt clr run on rails and lost pl 3f out: sn swtchd lft and rdn: kpt on wl ins fnl f: wnt 4th fnl stride* **8/1**

5 *hd* **Simon Gray** 2-9-3 0.. RichardHughes 1 72+
(R Hannon) *wnt lft s: hld up last: rdn and stdy prog fr over 2f out: kpt on ins fnl f* **12/1**

3 **6** *1/2* **Princability (IRE)**[18] 5901 2-9-3 0.............................. DarryllHolland 10 72+
(M R Channon) *trckd ldrs: rdn whn bmpd 2f out: nt clrest of runs after: kpt on: no ex fnl 50yds* **9/4**[1]

7 *1 1/4* **Perfect Affair (USA)** 2-9-3 0... GeorgeBaker 4 68+
(R M Beckett) *mid-div: hdwy over 3f out: rdn and ev ch fr over 2f out: sn hung lft: one pce fnl f* **7/2**[3]

0 **8** *3 3/4* **Saborido (USA)**[15] 5996 2-9-3 0.. PatDobbs 9 60
(Mrs A J Perrett) *cl up: effrt whn bmpd 3f out: wknd fnl f* **50/1**

9 *3 1/4* **Oke Bay** 2-8-12 0.. RichardKingscote 3 48
(R M Beckett) *wnt rt s: hld up in last trio: wknd 3f out* **25/1**

00 **10** *8* **Clear Hand**[15] 5996 2-9-0 0.. JamesMillman(3) 7 35
(B R Millman) *racd keenly: led tl 3f out: sn wknd* **100/1**

1m 47.4s (3.90) **Going Correction** +0.35s/f (Good) **10** Ran SP% **122.2**
Speed ratings (Par 97): **94,93,93,92,92 91,90,86,83,75**
toteswinger: 1&2 £10.20, 1&3 £32.50, 2&3 £6.90. CSF £51.26 TOTE £23.10: £3.90, £1.40, £3.10; EX 81.70.

Owner De La Warr Racing **Bred** Shell Bloodstock **Trained** East Ilsley, Berks

FOCUS
Both divisions of this race last year went to decent sorts. Huzzah has made a very nice handicapper this season, while Look Here went on to win the Epsom Oaks before finishing third in the St Leger. The pace in this event was very moderate in the early stages. It has been rated around the winner, runner-up and sixth.

NOTEBOOK
State Banquet(USA), whose dam is a half-sister to some top-class horses, cost a lot at the sales and took a while to fully get going during the race. However, he started to motor inside the final furlong and won with a bit in hand. There is a chance he may be seen again this year but connections have made no firm plans. Whatever happens, he is one to keep an eye on next season. (op 20-1 tchd 22-1)

Sandor was trying turf for the first time after showing plenty of ability on Polytrack. Stepped up to a mile again, he kept on in game style after sitting close to the pace and was narrowly denied. A similar contest is well within his scope. (op 10-3 tchd 7-2)

Decision sat just behind the early leader and had every chance inside the final furlong before being passed late on. His trainer has not really hit the mark with his juveniles this year but this one can win soon. (op 14-1 tchd 16-1)

Clowance House, whose dam was a half-sister to the very useful Si Seductor, did not have the clearest of runs when needed and took a while to get out in the clear. However, it was a decent start to his racing career and this athletic-looking sort can only get better. (tchd 17-2)

Simon Gray, a half-brother to Sahaadi, was held up in the last and faced an impossible task to get to the leaders when moved into the strong headwind to make his effort. Much like Clowance House, he will be better for the experience. (op 9-1)

Princability(IRE), who shaped with promise on his debut, did not have the clearest of runs in the latter stages but managed to get out in time to make an effort. He is probably a bit better than the bare result suggests. (op 2-1 tchd 5-2)

Perfect Affair(USA), a half-brother to smart turf performer No Place Like It, is a big sort who should do better in time. He travelled well when the pace was not that strong but struggled once the tempo increased. One would imagine that middle-distances will be his optimum trip next year from the way he shaped in this. Official explanation: jockey said colt hung left handed (op 5-1 tchd 10-3)

6398 E.B.F./ ALLIED IRISH BANK (GB) SOUTHAMPTON MAIDEN STKS (DIV II) 1m

2:30 (2:34) (Class 4) 2-Y-O **£4,371** (£1,300; £650; £324) **Stalls** High

Form RPR

0 **1** **Ouster (GER)**[19] 5857 2-9-3 0.. GeorgeBaker 1 92+
(D R C Elsworth) *broke wl: t.k.h: retsrained in last pair after 2f: smooth hdwy over 2f out: shkn up to ld ent fnl f: qcknd clr: easily* **9/4**[1]

44 **2** *5* **Star Links (USA)**[12] 6077 2-9-3 0.................................... RichardHughes 8 76
(R Hannon) *trckd ldrs: led over 2f out: rdn and hdd ent fnl f: nt pce of easy wnr* **9/2**[3]

00 **3** *1 1/2* **Cry For The Moon (USA)**[14] 6026 2-9-3 0..................... DarryllHolland 6 72+
(Mrs A J Perrett) *hld up in last pair: struggling 4f out: stdy prog fr 3f out: hung rt and styd on fnl 2f: wnt 3rd ins fnl f* **5/1**

05 **4** *1* **Davids Matador**[49] 4973 2-9-3 0.................................. StephenCarson 10 70
(Eve Johnson Houghton) *trckd ldrs: rdn over 2f out: kpt on same pce* **10/1**

5 *2* **Pointillist (IRE)** 2-8-12 0.. RichardKingscote 5 61
(R M Beckett) *prom: led 3f out: rdn and hdd over 2f out: sn one pce* **8/1**

03 **6** *6* **Admirable Duque (IRE)**[30] 5579 2-9-3 0................................ TQuinn 2 52
(D J S Ffrench Davis) *hld up in last pair early: hdwy 6f out: effrt 3f out: wknd 2f out* **4/1**[2]

7 *nse* **Mountain Forest (GER)** 2-9-3 0.................................... SteveDrowne 4 52
(H Morrison) *s.i.s: sn in tch: rdn over 3f out: no imp after* **20/1**

0 **8** *43* **Fire King**[11] 6117 2-9-3 0.. TravisBlock 9 —
(J A Geake) *led tl 3f out: sn hung rt and wknd: t.o* **66/1**

1m 46.2s (2.70) **Going Correction** +0.35s/f (Good) **49** Ran SP% **112.1**
Speed ratings (Par 97): **100,95,93,92,90 84,84,41**
toteswinger: 1&2 £2.60, 1&3 £3.70, 2&3 £4.40. CSF £11.96 TOTE £3.20: £1.30, £1.50, £1.90; EX 11.60.

Owner Raymond Tooth **Bred** Newsells Park Stud Ltd **Trained** Newmarket, Suffolk

FOCUS
The going was officially changed to good before this contest. There was little strength in depth to this, although the time was over a second quicker than the first division. The form looks solid and the winner a nice type for next year.

NOTEBOOK
Ouster(GER) ◆, strongly backed to improve David Elsworth's already fine course record with juveniles, had finished down the field in a good Doncaster maiden on debut and was always likely to know a lot more this time. He raced keenly through the early stages but it did not affect his finishing effort and, having come there on the bit two out, he strode away inside the final furlong to win comfortably. Still showing distinct signs of greenness when asked to go clear, this fine, big sort has plenty of scope for improvement and may well progress into a Pattern performer next season. (op 9-2)

Star Links(USA), up in trip having been a bit disappointing over 6f at Newbury last time, was asked for his effort over two furlongs out and stayed on, but the winner was in a different league. He has now qualified for a handicap mark and should fare better in that sphere. (op 9-4 tchd 5-1)

Cry For The Moon(USA) needed this to qualify for a handicap mark and he kept on into third without being given an overly hard time. His yard has not had the best of seasons, but he can win a small race. (op 9-2 tchd 4-1)

Davids Matador, who is bred to be suited by this trip, came under strong pressure over two out and could only find the one pace. He has now qualified for a handicap mark. (op 33-1)

Pointillist(IRE), a half-sister to numerous winners, seemed to know her job and went on three out, but was soon left trailing by the winner and was run out of the places. She should learn from this and will stay further in time. (op 11-1 tchd 7-1)

Admirable Duque(IRE) Official explanation: trainer said colt ran flat

6399 E.B.F./ COORS BREWERS NOVICE STKS 6f 212y

3:00 (3:02) (Class 4) 2-Y-O **£4,695** (£1,397; £698) **Stalls** High

Form RPR

6202 **1** **Rileyskeepingfaith**[14] 6025 2-9-5 97............................. DarryllHolland 2 96+
(M R Channon) *travelled wl bhd ldng pair: qcknd to ld whe gap appeared over 1f out: sn clr: easily* **10/11**[1]

1060 **2** *7* **Instalment**[32] 5507 2-9-5 102.. RichardHughes 4 76
(R Hannon) *led after 1f: rdn and edgd sltly lft off rails 2f out: sn hdd: kpt on for 2nd but no ch w wnr* **Evs**[2]

00 **3** *nk* **Countess Zara (IRE)**[14] 6016 2-8-7 0............................... FrancisNorton 1 63
(A M Balding) *led for 1f: w ldr: rdn over 2f out: kpt pressing for 2nd but no ch w wnr* **25/1**[3]

1m 31.91s (2.91) **Going Correction** +0.35s/f (Good) **3** Ran SP% **106.2**
Speed ratings (Par 97): **97,89,88**
CSF £2.12 TOTE £1.90; EX 2.30.

Owner Jolly Roger Racing **Bred** M Barrett **Trained** West Ilsley, Berks

FOCUS
This race has a history of small fields but, over the years, the winners have often gone on to be decent. However, none of the three remaining runners, after Second To Nun came out, had a particularly progressive profile coming into race, and it might have been a weak renewal.

NOTEBOOK
Rileyskeepingfaith bumped into the potentially smart Wingwalker at Sandown last time and was unsurprisingly not good enough to hold that rival once it had found room. He was given a good ride in the pocket behind the leader early in this and threaded his way up the inside rail to win easily. However, the form is worth very little and he will need to improve again to follow up. (op Evens)

Instalment finished seventh in the Group 3 Solario Stakes last time (form of that race is not working out particularly well), and did all the work out in front here. He more or less set the race up for the winner and could not accelerate when faced with the headwind after being joined. It is probably worth ignoring this effort as a guide to his true ability. (tchd 10-11, 21-20 in a place)

Countess Zara(IRE), a grand-daughter of Lochsong, showed nothing to suggest she was good enough to make any impact against the other two on previous form but was only just behind the second as they passed the line. She has probably improved again but her proximity to the runner-up is not a true reflection of her ability. (op 18-1 tchd 16-1)

6400 BEGBIES TRAYNOR CLAIMING STKS 1m 1f 198y

3:35 (3:35) (Class 5) 3-4-Y-O **£3,238** (£963; £481; £240) **Stalls** High

Form RPR

0540 **1** **Afram Blue**[15] 5994 3-8-5 59..................(t) Louis-PhilippeBeuzelin(5) 10 70
(W J Knight) *mid-div: rdn and hdwy fr 3f out: swtchd lft 2f out: styd on to ld jst ins fnl f: a doing enough: pushed out* **10/1**

1523 **2** *1/2* **Auntie Mame**[33] 5476 4-9-0 67... TPO'Shea 2 68
(D J Coakley) *in tch: hdwy over 3f out: rdn to ld over 1f out: hdd jst ins fnl f: kpt on* **13/2**[3]

0610 **3** *1* **Animator**[11] 6129 3-9-5 71.. DarryllHolland 7 76
(P F I Cole) *hld up bhd: hdwy 3f out: rdn over 2f out: wnt 3rd ent fnl f: styd on same pce* **11/1**

0610 **4** *hd* **Zuwaar**[67] 4419 3-9-1 71 (t) StephenDonohoe 1 72
(Ian Williams) *hld up bhd: last u.p over 2f out: weaved way through field and gd hdwy over 1f out: styd on wl* **14/1**

4400 **5** *1 1/4* **Stage Acclaim (IRE)**[16] 5961 3-8-11 69 ChrisCatlin 14 65
(B R Millman) *mid-div tl lost pl 4f out: weaved way through field fr over 1f out: styd on wout getting bk on terms* **33/1**

020 **6** *1 1/4* **North Parade**[11] 6129 3-8-13 80 (t) RichardHughes 8 65
(B J Meehan) *mid-div: rdn 3f out: sltly hmpd 2f out: styd on fnl f* **9/2**[1]

332 **7** *1 1/4* **Street Crime**[33] 5477 3-9-0 67 FrancisNorton 13 63
(A M Balding) *plld hrd: led: rdn 3f out: veered lft 2f out: sn hdd: one pce fnl f* **14/1**

6523 **8** *1 1/2* **No To Trident**[9] 6175 3-8-5 73 (p) RichardEvans(5) 9 56
(P D Evans) *hld up towards rr: hdwy 4f out: rdn 2f out: sn btn* **5/1**[2]

3201 **9** *hd* **Red Current**[9] 6175 4-8-7 61 KevinGhunowa(3) 3 51
(R A Harris) *trckd ldrs: rdn 3f out: wknd fnl f* **8/1**

2030 **10** *1 1/4* **Marvo**[14] 6035 4-9-7 74 (v1) SaleemGolam 11 59
(M H Tompkins) *chsd ldrs: rdn 3f out: wknd fnl f* **12/1**

5 **11** *1 3/4* **The Little Master (IRE)**[11] 6126 4-9-2 0 MarcHalford(3) 12 54
(D R C Elsworth) *mid-div tl lost pl over 4f out: nt a threat after* **28/1**

3-05 **12** *2 3/4* **Stalking Tiger (IRE)**[33] 5476 4-9-1 66 SteveDrowne 6 44
(R Charlton) *prom: rdn over 2f out: sn btn* **7/1**

6150 **13** *nk* **Colorado Blue (IRE)**[8] 5199 3-8-12 79 (b) EddieAhern 4 46
(C E Longsdon) *wnt lft s: towards rr: gd hdwy on outer of bnd over 6f out to trck ldrs: rdn 3f out: sn wknd* **12/1**

2m 12.29s (2.39) **Going Correction** -0.025s/f (Good)
WFA 3 from 4yo 5lb **13** Ran SP% **124.3**
Speed ratings (Par 103): **89,88,87,87,86 85,84,83,83,82 80,78,78**
toteswinger: 1&2 £22.00, 1&3 £37.30, 2&3 £7.30. CSF £76.73 TOTE £18.90: £4.60, £2.50, £3.40; EX 123.10.
Owner Mr & Mrs I H Bendelow **Bred** Mrs Jenny Willment **Trained** Patching, W Sussex
■ Stewards' Enquiry : Louis-Philippe Beuzelin two-day ban: careless riding (Oct 15-16)

FOCUS
An ordinary-looking claimer that probably took little winning. It has been rated around the runner-up.
Animator Official explanation: jockey said gelding hung right-handed
Street Crime Official explanation: jockey said gelding hung left-handed

6401 WINTERTHUR LIFE CONDITIONS STKS 6f
4:05 (4:08) (Class 2) 2-Y-O **£9,034** (£2,705; £1,352; £677; £337) **Stalls High**

Form RPR

2104 **1** **Ouqba**[18] 5889 2-9-1 108 RHills 4 102+
(B W Hills) *trckd ldr: led over 1f out: r.o wl: pushed out* **15/8**[1]

2210 **2** *2* **Qalahari (IRE)**[39] 5266 2-8-7 92 TPO'Shea 5 88+
(D J Coakley) *trckd ldng pair: sltly outpcd wl over 1f out: kpt on ins fnl f: snatched 2nd fnl stride* **11/4**[2]

1342 **3** *nse* **Ginobili (IRE)**[8] 6193 2-9-1 94 PatDobbs 6 96
(R Hannon) *racd keenly: led: rdn and hdd over 1f out: kpt on but sn hld by wnr: lost 2nd fnl stride* **15/2**

1 **4** *3 1/4* **Mamlakati (IRE)**[72] 4251 2-8-10 0 RichardHughes 2 81+
(R Hannon) *rrd bdly leaving stalls: last of 5 but cl enough: nt clr run briefly wl over 1f out: sn swtchd lft and rdn: nt qckn: wnt 4th nr fin* **7/2**[3]

1143 **5** *3/4* **Wildcat Wizard (USA)**[33] 5486 2-9-4 101 ChrisCatlin 3 87
(P F I Cole) *unsettled waiting in stalls: t.k.h: racd in cl 4th: effrt 2f out: fdd fnl f* **11/2**

1m 18.22s (3.42) **Going Correction** +0.35s/f (Good) **5** Ran SP% **110.8**
Speed ratings (Par 101): **91,88,88,83,82**
toteswinger: 1&2 £5.70. CSF £7.34 TOTE £2.70: £1.40, £1.60; EX 7.20.
Owner Hamdan Al Maktoum **Bred** Highclere Stud **Trained** Lambourn, Berks

FOCUS
This looked a decent little conditions race, but they went an unsatisfactory gallop and it turned into a sprint for the line. The winner is much better than this grade and the race has been rated through the second and third.

NOTEBOOK
Ouqba, dropping markedly in grade having contested the Group 2 Champagne Stakes at Doncaster last time, was well positioned to counter the lack of pace and was always doing enough inside the final furlong. His best form before this had come with some give in the ground, but good going is clearly fine and he is likely to step back up in grade now. (op 7-4 tchd 2-1)
Qalahari(IRE), an impressive Bath maiden winner who seemed to find 7f beyond her in a Group 3 at Goodwood last time, was ridden with more restraint than usual and it probably counted against her. She kept on having been outpaced by the winner, just snatching second, and can be rated a shade better than the bare form. (op 7-2 tchd 5-2)
Ginobili(IRE) recorded a personal best when second at Folkestone last time and he again ran well, for all that he had the run of the race off the front end. He is not an easy one to place. (op 7-1 tchd 8-1)
Mamlakati(IRE), off since winning on her debut at Windsor in July, is a fine-looking filly and it was interesting that Hughes chose her over the more proven Ginobili. However, she reared badly leaving the stalls and, although making the ground up quickly due to the lack of pace, it could not have helped. She deserves another chance. (tchd 4-1)
Wildcat Wizard(USA), conceding weight all round, finished third in a Listed contest at Deauville last time and needed to have improved to match the favourite. He was produced to have every chance, but could not quicken. (op 6-1 tchd 7-2)

6402 WOOD BMW H'CAP 6f
4:40 (4:42) (Class 4) (0-85,83) 3-Y-O+ **£5,180** (£1,541; £770; £384) **Stalls High**

Form RPR

0450 **1** **Kelamon**[27] 5648 4-8-8 71 TQuinn 13 83
(M D I Usher) *hld up towards rr: rdn and no imp 3f out: hdwy over 1f out: swtchd lft ent fnl f: fin strly: led fnl 25yds* **20/1**

1414 **2** *nk* **Filligree (IRE)**[32] 5510 3-8-11 80 WilliamCarson(5) 12 91+
(Rae Guest) *chsd ldr: led over 2f out: sn rdn: no ex whn ct fnl 25yds* **10/1**

2150 **3** *2 1/4* **Charlie Delta**[11] 6125 5-8-6 72 (b) LukeMorris(3) 9 76
(J G M O'Shea) *mid-div: hdwy over 2f out: sn rdn: wnt 2nd ent fnl f: no ex fnl 40yds* **16/1**

0006 **4** *shd* **Forest Dane**[11] 6125 8-8-4 72 SophieDoyle(5) 8 76
(Mrs N Smith) *hld up bhd: smooth prog fr over 2f out: shkn up and r.o fnl f: nrst fin* **16/1**

4321 **5** *3/4* **Ivory Silk**[35] 5402 3-8-6 70 ChrisCatlin 4 71
(D K Ivory) *chsd ldrs: rdn and ev ch over 2f out: kpt on same pce fnl f* **14/1**

2204 **6** *1/2* **Blue Jack**[17] 5936 3-9-0 78 FrancisNorton 11 78
(W R Muir) *t.k.h in midfield: rdn and hdwy 2f out: kpt on same pce fnl f* **17/2**[3]

1000 **7** *nk* **Piscean (USA)**[32] 5510 3-9-0 78 SteveDrowne 1 77
(T Keddy) *dwlt and wnt bdly rt s: detached in rr: hdwy fr 2f out: chsd ldrs ent fnl f: no ex fnl 75yds* **20/1**

0035 **8** *nk* **Mogok Ruby**[11] 6125 4-9-1 78 PatDobbs 10 76
(L Montague Hall) *hld up towards rr: rdn over 2f out: styd on fnl f: nvr nrr* **12/1**

0006 **9** *1* **Golden Dixie (USA)**[15] 6006 9-9-1 78 EddieAhern 2 72
(R A Harris) *nvr bttr than mid-div* **10/1**

0000 **10** *1 3/4* **Bazroy (IRE)**[18] 5906 4-9-0 82 (b) RichardEvans(5) 14 71
(P D Evans) *chsd ldrs: rdn over 2f out: wknd fnl f* **6/1**[1]

5124 **11** *3/4* **Superduper**[20] 5839 3-9-4 82 RichardHughes 3 68
(R Hannon) *a towards rr* **11/1**

4040 **12** *1 1/2* **Rash Judgement**[21] 5795 3-9-0 83 Louis-PhilippeBeuzelin(5) 5 65
(W S Kittow) *in tch: sn pumped along: hung rt 2f out: sn btn* **7/1**[2]

0332 **13** *1/2* **Tadalavil**[16] 5962 3-8-12 76 DarryllHolland 7 56
(M R Channon) *chsd ldrs: rdn 4f out: wknd 2f out* **9/1**

3313 **14** *2* **Polar Annie**[32] 5490 3-8-11 78 TolleyDean(3) 15 52
(M S Saunders) *led tl over 2f out: sn wknd* **17/2**[3]

2305 **15** *2* **Don Pele (IRE)**[7] 6200 6-8-6 72 (p) KevinGhunowa(3) 6 39
(R A Harris) *chsd ldrs tl wknd over 2f out* **14/1**

1m 16.09s (1.29) **Going Correction** +0.35s/f (Good)
WFA 3 from 4yo+ 1lb **15** Ran SP% **126.7**
Speed ratings (Par 105): **105,104,101,101,100 99,99,99,97,95 94,92,91,89,86**
toteswinger: 1&2 £72.50, 1&3 £116.40, 2&3 £40.70. CSF £216.99 CT £3288.60 TOTE £31.50: £9.00, £4.50, £5.90; EX 317.00.
Owner Mr & Mrs Richard Hames And Friends **Bred** R And Mrs Hames **Trained** Upper Lambourn, Berks

FOCUS
An interesting contest between three-year-olds and the older generation. There were good reasons for thinking quite a few of them had a chance, so the form ought to be sound for the level, especially with the third a reliable guide.
Kelamon Official explanation: trainer said, regarding the improved form, that gelding was better suited by being held up today
Piscean(USA) Official explanation: jockey said colt missed the break

6403 "SEE YOU 3RD MAY 2009" H'CAP 1m 6f 21y
5:10 (5:11) (Class 5) (0-75,75) 3-Y-O+ **£3,238** (£963; £481; £240)

Form RPR

1410 **1** **Mount Lavinia (IRE)**[11] 6127 3-9-4 74 RichardKingscote 9 86
(R M Beckett) *middiv: hdwy in centre of trck fr 3f out: led and hung rt 2f out: drifted rt across to far rail but a in command: rdn out* **7/2**[1]

53-4 **2** *1 3/4* **Hada Men (USA)**[12] 6092 3-9-0 70 PatDobbs 12 80
(M P Tregoning) *mid-div: hdwy 4f out: sn rdn: styd on to go 2nd ins fnl f but a hld by wnr* **7/1**[3]

6435 **3** *2 1/2* **Wester Ross (IRE)**[17] 5934 4-8-13 63 LukeMorris(3) 5 69
(J M P Eustace) *mid-div: hdwy 4f out: rdn to chse wnr over 1f out tl ins fnl f: kpt on same pce* **8/1**

6213 **4** *4* **Moonshine Creek**[15] 6007 6-9-0 61 DarrenWilliams 1 61
(P W Hiatt) *trckd ldrs: led 4f out: rdn and drifted lft whn hdd 2f out: sn one pce* **11/1**

0050 **5** *1 1/2* **Forget It**[54] 4829 3-8-5 64 PatrickHills(3) 4 62
(R Hannon) *trckd ldrs: rdn 3f out: sn drifted lft: wknd over 1f out* **16/1**

2531 **6** *1/2* **Colonel Flay**[33] 5465 4-9-7 71 JackMitchell(3) 13 69
(Mrs P N Dutfield) *settled in rr: hdwy over 2f out: sn rdn to chse ldrs: wknd over 1f out* **4/1**[2]

005R **7** *2 1/2* **Lisathedaddy**[26] 5683 6-9-7 75 (p) KylieManser(7) 7 69
(B G Powell) *v.s.a: bhd: hdwy over 3f out: sn rdn: wknd over 1f out* **33/1**

4320 **8** *1* **Hadron Collider (FR)**[25] 5698 3-8-13 69 RichardHughes 14 62
(R Hannon) *mid-div: rdn and hdwy over 3f out: drifted rt fr 2f out: wknd over 1f out* **7/1**[3]

3000 **9** *7* **Clovis**[7] 6210 3-8-12 68 EddieAhern 2 51
(N P Mulholland) *hld up towards rr: hdwy over 3f out: sn rdn: wknd over 1f out* **40/1**

2555 **10** *9* **Alfie Noakes**[7] 6210 6-9-8 69 (v) DarryllHolland 10 39
(Mrs A J Perrett) *led tl 4f out: sn rdn: wknd 2f out* **7/1**[3]

11 *9* **Fredo (IRE)**[186] 4-9-1 62 StephenDonohoe 11 20
(Ian Williams) *trckd ldrs: rdn 4f out: sn wknd: eased fnl f* **14/1**

/50- **12** *26* **Jockser (IRE)**[167] 5820 7-8-11 58 FrancisNorton 6 —
(J W Mullins) *a towards rr: lost tch over 3f out* **50/1**

1020 **R** **Bella Medici**[11] 6129 3-8-7 63 SaleemGolam 3 —
(M H Tompkins) *ref to r: tk no part* **25/1**

3m 5.69s (-1.71) **Going Correction** -0.025s/f (Good)
WFA 3 from 4yo+ 9lb **13** Ran SP% **122.9**
Speed ratings (Par 103): **103,102,100,98,97 97,95,95,91,86 80,66,—**
toteswinger: 1&2 £8.50, 1&3 £10.30, 2&3 £14.50. CSF £28.18 CT £190.29 TOTE £5.90: £2.00, £2.30, £2.40; EX 37.20 Place 6: £102.32 Place 5: £34.74.
Owner Thurloe Thoroughbreds XX **Bred** Knocklong House Stud **Trained** Whitsbury, Hants

FOCUS
A wide range of abilities were on show in this staying handicap and, on balance, it looked a modest affair. Colonel Flay and Lisathedaddy had handlers at the start to help ensure they jumped off but it was Bella Medici who caught everyone off guard and refused point blank to start. The form looks sound rated around the third.
Moonshine Creek Official explanation: jockey said gelding hung left handed
Jockser(IRE) Official explanation: jockey said gelding was never travelling
T/Plt: £145.70 to a £1 stake. Pool: £47,995.39. 240.34 winning tickets. T/Qpdt: £15.50 to a £1 stake. Pool: £3,829.70. 182.70 winning tickets. TM

6404 - (Foreign Racing) - See Raceform Interactive

6101 AYR (L-H)
Thursday, October 2

OFFICIAL GOING: Heavy
Wind: Breezy, half against Weather: Overcast, raining

6405 KIDZPLAY H'CAP 5f
2:20 (2:22) (Class 6) (0-58,56) 3-Y-O+ **£2,729** (£806; £403) **Stalls Low**

Form RPR

0000 **1** **Note Perfect**[39] 5307 3-8-5 45 (b) DaleGibson 13 55
(M W Easterby) *trckd ldrs: rdn over 1f out: led ins fnl f: styd on wl* **40/1**

0000 **2** *1 1/2* **Jakeini (IRE)**[36] 5398 5-8-11 51 (v1) GrahamGibbons 11 56
(E S McMahon) *hld up in tch: stdy hdwy 2f out: effrt and edgd lft ins fnl f: kpt on: nt rch wnr* **7/1**[3]

6102 **3** *1 1/2* **Wicked Wilma (IRE)**[8] 6218 4-8-10 55 SladeO'Hara(5) 8 55
(A Berry) *led to ins fnl f: kpt on same pce* **9/2**[1]

306 **4** *2 1/2* **Stoneacre Chris (USA)**[4] 6308 3-8-5 50 KellyHarrison(5) 10 41
(Peter Grayson) *hld up: hdwy over 1f out: nvr rchd ldrs* **14/1**

0263 **5** *1* **The Little Fizzer (IRE)**[8] 6218 3-8-10 53 AndrewMullen(3) 6 40
(P D Evans) *prom: drvn 1/2-way: rallied over 1f out: sn no ex* **5/1**[2]

0030 **6** ½ **Morristown Music (IRE)**[1] 6382 4-8-9 **49**....................(v) PJMcDonald 1 34
(J S Wainwright) *midfield: rdn 1/2-way: no imp over 1f out* **8/1**

0603 **7** ¾ **She's Our Beauty (IRE)**[31] 5566 5-8-6 **46**.........(v) SilvestreDeSousa 12 29
(S T Mason) *trckd ldrs tl rdn and wknd wl over 1f out* **12/1**

0506 **8** ¾ **Polish Star**[35] 5420 4-7-12 **45**.. SFeeney(7) 4 25
(Miss L A Perratt) *s.s: wl bhd tl sme late hdwy: nvr on terms* **25/1**

2452 **9** 2 ¾ **Gelert (IRE)**[10] 6159 3-8-5 **45**......................................(b) PatrickMathers 7 15
(Peter Grayson) *trckd ldrs tl rdn and wknd over 1f out* **7/1**[3]

4004 **10** 3 ½ **Howards Tipple**[10] 6159 4-9-2 **56**..(p) TomEaves 3 13
(Miss L A Perratt) *sn drvn in rr: no imp fr 1/2-way* **8/1**

6010 **11** 1 ¾ **Dubai To Barnsley**[23] 5770 3-8-6 **49**.......................... DuranFentiman(3) 2 —
(Garry Moss) *in tch: outpcd 1/2-way: sn wknd* **16/1**

0254 **12** 10 **Missus Molly Brown**[23] 5770 4-8-5 **45**........................ AndrewElliott 14 —
(R A Fahey) *s.i.s: a struggling* **9/1**

63.72 secs (3.62) **Going Correction** +0.75s/f (Yiel) **12** Ran SP% **118.6**
Speed ratings (Par 101): **101,98,96,92,90 89,88,87,83,77 74,58**
toteswinger: 1&2 £80.50, 1&3 £43.30, 2&3 £8.80. CSF £301.53 CT £1534.21 TOTE £34.70: £9.20, £2.50, £1.70; EX 297.40.
Owner Mrs Jean Turpin **Bred** Mrs Jean Turpin **Trained** Sheriff Hutton, N Yorks

FOCUS
A modest handicap which produced a shock winner. The first three raced near the middle of the track and the field finished strung out. The time was over five seconds above standard. Probably not form to take literally given the bad ground.
Note Perfect Official explanation: trainer's rep said, regarding apparent improvement in form, that the filly appreciated the break of five weeks and the heavy ground.
Polish Star Official explanation: jockey said gelding missed the break
Gelert(IRE) Official explanation: jockey said colt was unsuited by the heavy ground
Missus Molly Brown Official explanation: jockey said filly missed the break; vet said filly finished distressed

6406 COLTART CONTRACTS NURSERY 6f
2:55 (2:55) (Class 5) (0-75,72) 2-Y-O £2,914 (£867; £433; £216) Stalls Low

Form RPR

4533 **1** **Doric Echo**[11] 6149 2-9-7 **72**.. TomEaves 3 78
(B Smart) *trckd ldrs: effrt 2f out: led ins fnl f: styd on wl* **5/2**[2]

0112 **2** 2 ¾ **Scenic Pass**[11] 6149 2-9-7 **72**.. GrahamGibbons 7 70
(E S McMahon) *led to ins fnl f: kpt on same pce* **11/8**[1]

2060 **3** 1 **Identity**[17] 5966 2-8-11 **62**.. PaulMulrennan 2 57
(E J O'Neill) *dwlt: bhd tl hdwy over 1f out: kpt on fnl f* **10/1**

460 **4** 5 **Artesium**[71] 4289 2-8-2 **53**.. DaleGibson 8 33
(R A Fahey) *in tch: drvn and outpcd over 2f out: styd on past btn horses ins fnl f: no imp* **5/1**[3]

060 **5** hd **Scarlets**[47] 5097 2-8-2 **56**.. AndrewMullen(3) 1 35
(P D Evans) *prom tl rdn and wknd 2f out* **18/1**

506 **6** nk **Danderdandan**[25] 5715 2-7-10 **50** oh4 ow1.............. DuranFentiman(3) 9 29
(P T Midgley) *prom tl edgd lft and wknd over 1f out* **14/1**

0000 **7** 4 ½ **Peckforton**[12] 6109 2-7-5 **49** oh4.................................. JamieKyne(7) 4 14
(Mrs L Williamson) *pressed ldr tl wknd fr 2f out* **33/1**

1m 19.0s (5.40) **Going Correction** +0.75s/f (Yiel) **7** Ran SP% **111.3**
Speed ratings (Par 95): **94,90,89,82,82 81,75**
toteswinger: 1&2 £1.20, 1&3 £4.70, 2&3 £3.70. CSF £5.94 CT £24.35 TOTE £3.60: £2.10, £1.10; EX 5.40.
Owner Doric Dream Partnership **Bred** A L Cohen **Trained** Hambleton, N Yorks
■ Stewards' Enquiry : Graham Gibbons one-day ban: failed to ride to draw (Oct 16)

FOCUS
There did not seem to be much strength in depth in this nursery. The main interest centred around Scenic Pass and Doric Echo who were closely matched on latest Hamilton form. They went a careful pace in the early stages and the form has been rated on the conservative side.

NOTEBOOK
Doric Echo sweated before the race and was weak in the market but travelled more enthusiastically than he had last time and emphatically reversed that form with Scenic Pass. He did still look inexperienced when pressure was applied and carried his head a bit high but stayed on strongly and gave the impression that a step up to 7f would suit. (op 15-8 tchd 7-4)
Scenic Pass dictated the pace and seemed to be travelling sweetly but did not find as much as expected and was brushed aside in the closing stages. She does seem to have plenty of speed and could be worth trying at 5f, but this was her 12th race for two different yards since June and it is possible that the busy campaign may be taking its toll. (op 6-4 tchd 13-8 in places)
Identity was never travelling when favourite for a 7f seller on soft ground last time, but stayed on steadily from some way off the pace and gave the impression she is worth another try over an extra furlong. (tchd 11-1)
Artesium was one of the first in trouble and put in a laboured effort on his nursery debut for a new yard, with a tongue tie removed. (op 6-1 tchd 13-2)
Danderdandan was supported at big prices but had no reply when the pace quickened. (op 33-1)
Peckforton Official explanation: jockey said filly was unsuited by the heavy ground

6407 GILTECH LTD MEDIAN AUCTION MAIDEN STKS 6f
3:30 (3:31) (Class 5) 2-Y-O £2,914 (£867; £433; £216) Stalls Low

Form RPR

5332 **1** **The Kyllachy Kid**[12] 6112 2-9-3 84.................................... MickyFenton 6 79+
(T P Tate) *trckd ldrs: rdn over 2f out: led over 1f out: styd on wl* **6/4**[1]

52 **2** 3 ¼ **Liberty Diamond**[16] 5989 2-8-12 0.............................. AndrewElliott 5 64+
(K R Burke) *prom: effrt 2f out: chsd wnr ent fnl f: kpt on: no imp* **5/2**[2]

2 **3** 4 **Box Office**[10] 6158 2-9-3 0.. JoeFanning 2 57+
(M Johnston) *cl up: rdn over 2f out: no ex over 1f out* **10/3**[3]

60 **4** 2 **Grissom (IRE)**[16] 5988 2-8-12 0..............................(t) SladeO'Hara(5) 1 51
(A Berry) *led to over 1f out: sn btn* **125/1**

5 1 ¾ **Zegna (IRE)** 2-9-3 0.. TomEaves 4 46+
(B Smart) *s.i.s: green in rr: effrt over 2f out: wknd over 1f out* **13/2**

0 **6** 6 **Aestival**[14] 6051 2-9-3 0.. PaulMulrennan 3 28
(Sir Mark Prescott) *in tch: struggling 1/2-way: sn wknd* **20/1**

1m 19.24s (5.64) **Going Correction** +0.75s/f (Yiel) **6** Ran SP% **110.5**
Speed ratings (Par 95): **92,87,82,79,77 69**
toteswinger: 1&2 £1.50, 1&3 £1.50, 2&3 £1.50. CSF £5.31 TOTE £2.10: £1.20, £2.10; EX 4.60.
Owner P J MArtin **Bred** Conor J C Parsons & Brian M Parsons **Trained** Tadcaster, N Yorks

FOCUS
An ordinary maiden in which the market leaders filled the first three positions. It was run at a pedestrian gallop in the conditions and athough The Kyllachy Kid won decisively this is probably not form to take at face value.

NOTEBOOK
The Kyllachy Kid, ridden more patiently than he has been, swept into the lead at the one furlong pole and was the only runner to find a change of gear on the taxing ground. He had a solid form chance, so his mark should not change too much for this stylish success, and the likeable sort should continue to be a force when switched back to nurseries. (op 7-4 tchd 15-8 and 2-1 in places)
Liberty Diamond ran well but was no match for the winner. She probably ran below the form of her latest effort on heavy at Haydock, and is probably going to need to find a bit of improvement to make a major impact when switched to nurseries. (op 7-2)
Box Office had looked very inexperienced when narrowly beaten as favourite on soft ground on his debut. There was no sign of market confidence here and he did not find a great deal, but he may not have handled the heavy ground and it would be no surprise to see him do much better in time, particularly when faced with a stiffer test next year. (op 2-1)
Grissom(IRE) had shown little on his two previous starts, was sent off at an astronomical price and seems to have found some improvement, but did dictate the steady pace and may flattered by the form. (op 100-1)
Zegna(IRE) started very slowly and ran green on his debut. (op 8-1)
Aestival was badly outpaced at the halfway stage. (op 18-1 tchd 16-1)

6408 HAPPY RETIREMENT CAROL WALKER H'CAP 1m
4:05 (4:05) (Class 6) (0-65,65) 3-Y-O+ £2,729 (£806; £403) Stalls Low

Form RPR

4520 **1** **Apache Nation (IRE)**[32] 5538 5-8-12 **55**..................(b) PaulMulrennan 5 63
(M Dods) *in tch: rdn to ld 1f out: styd on strly* **6/1**[3]

-505 **2** 1 ½ **Transmission (IRE)**[12] 6114 3-9-5 **65**.................................. TomEaves 4 70
(B Smart) *t.k.h: cl up: led wl over 1f out to 1f out: kpt on same pce* **15/2**

0005 **3** ½ **Boppys Pride**[7] 6235 5-8-0 **50** oh3.............................. JamesRogers(7) 7 53
(P T Midgley) *in midfield: effrt over 2f out: kpt on fnl f* **12/1**

5115 **4** hd **Wednesdays Boy (IRE)**[34] 5454 5-8-12 **58**...............(p) NeilBrown(3) 3 61
(P D Niven) *stdd in rr: hdwy over 2f out: rdn and kpt on ins fnl f* **3/1**[1]

3142 **5** ¾ **Silly Gilly (IRE)**[32] 5538 4-9-0 **57**................................ AndrewElliott 13 58
(R E Barr) *led to wl over 1f out: kpt on same pce* **13/2**

0152 **6** 3 ¾ **Tanforan**[42] 5198 6-9-3 **60**.. DavidAllan 6 53
(B P J Baugh) *hld up: rdn 1/2-way: hdwy over 1f out: nvr rchd ldrs* **15/2**

2445 **7** ½ **Mystical Ayr (IRE)**[10] 6162 6-8-9 **55**.......................... AndrewMullen(3) 11 46
(Miss L A Perratt) *prom tl rdn and wknd over 1f out* **11/2**[2]

0300 **8** 10 **Kirkby's Treasure**[12] 6116 10-8-11 **54**................................ JoeFanning 8 22
(A Berry) *chsd ldrs: outpcd over 3f out: n.d after* **22/1**

5064 **9** 7 **Pequeno Dinero (IRE)**[31] 5565 3-7-13 **50** oh5........(v) KellyHarrison(5) 9 —
(C W Fairhurst) *bhd: struggling over 3f out: sn btn* **22/1**

-056 **10** 22 **Beck**[45] 5157 4-8-4 **50** oh2.. DuranFentiman(3) 14 —
(W M Brisbourne) *hld up in midfield: rdn 3f out: sn wknd* **16/1**

1m 53.7s (9.90) **Going Correction** +1.275s/f (Soft)
WFA 3 from 4yo+ 3lb **10** Ran SP% **113.8**
Speed ratings (Par 101): **101,99,99,98,98 94,93,83,76,54**
toteswinger: 1&2 £8.60, 1&3 £16.10, 2&3 £19.60. CSF £49.16 CT £516.83 TOTE £6.50: £2.50, £2.30, £3.30; EX 64.40.
Owner Doug Graham **Bred** Crone Stud Farms Ltd **Trained** Denton, Co Durham

FOCUS
An ordinary event and very modest form, the winner rated to this year's best. They went a very steady pace, moved towards the centre of the track in the straight and finished in a bit of a bunch.
Apache Nation(IRE) Official explanation: trainer's rep said, regarding apparent improvement in form, that the gelding was better suited by the heavy ground.

6409 FLOWERS@7 H'CAP 7f 50y
4:40 (4:40) (Class 6) (0-60,59) 3-Y-O+ £2,729 (£806; £403) Stalls Low

Form RPR

0003 **1** **Provost**[12] 6116 4-9-6 **59**.. PaulMulrennan 7 66
(M W Easterby) *prom: smooth hdwy to ld over 1f out: sn rdn: hld on wl fnl f* **3/1**[1]

0013 **2** shd **Distant Pleasure**[35] 5420 4-9-4 **57**.................................... TomEaves 9 63
(M Dods) *hld up: hdwy over 2f out: rdn and ev ch ins fnl f: kpt on: jst hld* **10/3**[2]

4604 **3** ½ **Sarraaf (IRE)**[10] 6162 12-8-9 **53**.............................. PatrickDonaghy(5) 10 58
(Miss L A Perratt) *hld up: smooth hdwy over 2f out: rdn over 1f out: kpt on ins fnl f* **16/1**

5435 **4** 3 ¾ **Botham (USA)**[4] 6310 4-8-11 **50**....................................... JoeFanning 14 45
(J S Goldie) *prom: effrt over 2f out: outpcd fnl f* **4/1**[3]

3461 **5** ¾ **Many Welcomes**[34] 5457 3-8-9 **50**................................. AndrewElliott 3 43
(B P J Baugh) *midfield: effrt and hdwy 2f out: no ex fnl f* **10/1**

3200 **6** 2 ¼ **Hansomis (IRE)**[54] 4851 4-9-1 **54**..................................... DaleGibson 8 41
(B Mactaggart) *t.k.h: chsd ldr: led 3f out to over 1f out: wknd ins fnl f* **16/1**

0200 **7** 10 **Ensign's Trick**[14] 6063 4-8-8 **50**............................... DuranFentiman(3) 5 11
(W M Brisbourne) *prom tl rdn and wknd over 1f out* **18/1**

3040 **8** 4 **Oeuf A La Neige**[10] 6159 8-9-1 **54**....................................... PaulFessey 6 5
(Miss L A Perratt) *hld up: rdn over 2f out: n.d* **15/2**

5000 **9** 4 ½ **Kool Katie**[59] 4684 3-8-9 **50**.. GrahamGibbons 11 —
(Mrs G S Rees) *midfield: effrt over 2f out: sn wknd* **25/1**

5004 **10** 1 ½ **Planet Queen**[11] 6150 3-8-2 **50**.........................(b) DeclanCannon(7) 2 —
(K R Burke) *led: hung rt to r alone stands rail and hdd 3f out: sn wknd* **12/1**

1m 41.72s (8.32) **Going Correction** +1.275s/f (Soft)
WFA 3 from 4yo+ 2lb **10** Ran SP% **117.5**
Speed ratings (Par 101): **103,102,102,98,97 94,83,78,73,71**
toteswinger: 1&2 £3.90, 1&3 £10.60, 2&3 £13.90. CSF £13.13 CT £137.00 TOTE £5.10: £1.50, £1.50, £3.70; EX 13.10.
Owner A G Black **Bred** Charlie Wyatt **Trained** Sheriff Hutton, N Yorks
■ Stewards' Enquiry : Paul Mulrennan one-day ban: used whip with excessive frequency (Oct 16)

FOCUS
The hard-puller Planet Queen led the field at a decent pace and moved to the near rail in the straight, while the rest raced towards the centre to far side. The first three were involved in an exciting finish and were clear of the rest. The form is fairly sound.

6410 GLAISNOCK TRYST 30 YEAR H'CAP 1m 5f 13y
5:15 (5:15) (Class 3) (0-95,90) 3-Y-O+ £7,771 (£2,312; £1,155; £577) Stalls Low

Form RPR

2221 **1** **Hits Only Vic (USA)**[16] 5992 4-10-0 **90**................................ DavidAllan 2 100+
(D Carroll) *in tch: smooth hdwy to ld over 1f out: shkn up and sn clr* **4/5**[1]

/3-5 **2** 2 ½ **First Look (FR)**[151] 1824 8-8-10 **72**................................... PaulFessey 5 75
(P Monteith) *prom: effrt over 2f out: chsd wnr over 1f out: hung lft ins fnl f: kpt on: no imp* **7/1**[3]

5113 **3** 2 ¼ **Hurlingham**[11] 6154 4-9-2 **78**....................................... PaulMulrennan 7 77
(M W Easterby) *hld up: hdwy over 3f out: rdn over 1f out: sn no ex* **10/3**[2]

35/0 **4** nk **Power Elite (IRE)**[13] 6078 8-9-4 **80**.......................... GrahamGibbons 4 79
(K A Morgan) *cl up: led 6f out to over 1f out: sn no ex* **10/1**

15/0 **5** 26 **Zeitgeist (IRE)**[11] 6154 7-10-0 **90**.....................................(b) TomEaves 1 50
(Miss L A Perratt) *cl up tl rdn and wknd over 2f out* **25/1**

00-0 **6** 22 **Monolith**[151] 1824 10-8-12 **77**.. NeilBrown(3) 3 4
(L Lungo) *led to 6f out: wknd over 4f out* **16/1**

3m 19.43s (22.83) **Going Correction** +1.275s/f (Soft) **6** Ran SP% **110.0**
Speed ratings (Par 107): **80,78,77,76,60 47**
toteswinger: 1&2 £1.80, 1&3 £1.30, 2&3 £1.90. CSF £6.75 TOTE £1.60: £1.20, £2.80; EX 6.20.
Owner Kell-Stone & Watson **Bred** Peter E Blum **Trained** Sledmere, E Yorks
■ Stewards' Enquiry : Paul Fessey caution: used whip down the shoulder in the forehand position

FOCUS
This race was weakened by the withdrawal of the progressive Another Moment, but it did still involve two in-form four-year-olds and some potentially well treated older rivals. Hits Only Vic impressed again. The time was 32 seconds above standard.

NOTEBOOK
Hits Only Vic(USA) travelled stylishly, coasted to the lead and was value for more than the winning margin. This success was his fifth win of the season and was off a 26lb higher mark than when opening his account in June. He is tactically versatile, handles any ground and has a good cruising speed over staying trips. The next target is likely to be the Cesarewitch. He still has to prove he stays beyond 2m but could be potentially well treated carrying a 7lb penalty for his two wins this month. (op 11-10 tchd 6-5 in a place)
First Look(FR) has shown decent winning form in the mud over hurdles and fences, and ran really well on his second Flat run of the year back from five months off. He could not cope with the progressive winner but showed a fighting spirit, would benefit from a stronger pace at this trip and could be able to win a similar event. Official explanation: caution: used whip with excessive frequency (op 11-2 tchd 9-2)
Hurlingham looked the main rival to the favourite but wasted valuable energy by taking a strong grip in the early stages, was tapped for speed when the pace quickened and had no more to offer in the closing stages. (op 3-1 tchd 7-2)
Power Elite(IRE) moved well for a long way but folded up tamely. He was useful on the Flat and over hurdles for Noel Meade in his youth but his finishing effort does look questionable these days. (op 11-1 tchd 12-1)

6411 RACING UK SETANTA SPORTS H'CAP 6f
5:50 (5:50) (Class 5) (0-70,68) 3-Y-O+ **£2,914** (£867; £433; £216) **Stalls** Low

Form				RPR
0623	**1**		**Avontuur (FR)**[8] 6219 6-8-9 **57** ... AndrewElliott 10 (Mrs R A Carr) *cl up: led over 2f out: hdd briefly ins fnl f: hld on wl* **6/1**[3]	67
0050	**2**	*1*	**Lambrini Lace (IRE)**[17] 5970 3-8-5 **54** ... JoeFanning 12 (Mrs L Williamson) *trckd ldrs: effrt 2f out: led briefly ins fnl f: hld nr fin* **33/1**	60
3331	**3**	*¾*	**Strawberry Moon (IRE)**[28] 5636 3-9-4 **67** ... TomEaves 6 (B Smart) *trckd ldrs: effrt over 2f out: kpt on same pce ins fnl f* **8/1**	71
6030	**4**	*1 ½*	**Yorkshire Blue**[14] 6043 9-8-10 **63** ... GaryBartley(5) 3 (J S Goldie) *hld up: pushed along over 2f out: kpt on fnl f: nvr rchd ldrs* **14/1**	62
2242	**5**	*shd*	**Imperial Sword**[8] 6219 5-8-7 **58** ... (b) NeilBrown(3) 1 (T D Barron) *in tch: rdn over 1f out: edgd lft: no ex fnl f* **4/1**[2]	57
1023	**6**	*2 ½*	**Almost Married (IRE)**[10] 6159 4-8-5 **58** ... PatrickDonaghy(5) 8 (J S Goldie) *prom: effrt over 2f out: btn fnl f* **7/2**[1]	49
0400	**7**	*5*	**Paris Bell**[8] 6219 6-9-1 **63** ... DavidAllan 7 (T D Easterby) *t.k.h: stdd rr: hdwy over 2f out: btn fnl f* **7/2**[1]	38
4400	**8**	*1*	**Obe Royal**[42] 5198 4-8-12 **63** ... (b) AndrewMullen(3) 4 (P D Evans) *dwlt: bhd: rdn over 3f out: nvr rchd ldrs* **16/1**	35
0-06	**9**	*1 ½*	**Ugly Betty**[54] 4849 3-7-11 **53** oh8 ... JamieKyne(7) 9 (Bruce Hellier) *bhd: rdn and hung lft over 2f out: sn btn* **66/1**	20
-000	**10**	*1 ¼*	**The Thrifty Bear**[64] 4542 5-8-5 **53** oh8 ... PaulFessey 2 (C W Fairhurst) *led to over 2f out: sn rdn and wknd* **80/1**	16
2354	**11**	*9*	**Capone (IRE)**[25] 5714 3-9-2 **68** ... (b[1]) DuranFentiman(3) 11 (Garry Moss) *dwlt: hld up: rdn over 2f out: sn wknd* **9/1**	2

1m 17.37s (3.77) **Going Correction** +0.75s/f (Yiel)
WFA 3 from 4yo+ 1lb **11 Ran SP% 118.1**
Speed ratings (Par 103): **104,102,101,99,99 96,89,88,86,84 72**
toteswinger: 1&2 £29.90, 1&3 £7.50, 2&3 £20.00. CSF £183.80 CT £1632.66 TOTE £6.10: £2.30, £11.90, £2.70; EX 130.40 Place 6: £23.26 Place 5: £8.35 .
Owner J M Chapman **Bred** Haras D'Etreham **Trained** Stillington, N Yorks

FOCUS
A modest handicap run at a decent pace. Sound form. They raced down the middle of the track and those who raced prominently seemed to have an advantage.
T/Plt: £54.30 to a £1 stake. Pool: £54,533.66. 732.28 winning tickets. T/Qpdt: £17.00 to a £1 stake. Pool: £3,192.68. 138.30 winning tickets. RY

6197 GOODWOOD (R-H)
Thursday, October 2

OFFICIAL GOING: Good to firm
Wind: Moderate, across Weather: Fine

6412 EUROPEAN BREEDERS' FUND MEDIAN AUCTION MAIDEN STKS 7f
2:10 (2:11) (Class 5) 2-Y-O **£3,238** (£963; £481; £240) **Stalls** High

Form				RPR
6	**1**		**Truism**[41] 5225 2-9-3 0 ... JimCrowley 12 (Mrs A J Perrett) *hld up bhd ldrs on inner: fnd way through fr over 1f out: rdn and r.o to ld fnl 100yds: readily* **7/1**[2]	79+
0	**2**	*½*	**Chapter And Verse (IRE)**[13] 6072 2-9-3 0 ... RobertWinston 3 (B W Hills) *dwlt: sn prom: chsd ldr 1/2-way: rdn over 2f out: clsd to chal ent fnl f: outpcd fnl 100yds* **33/1**	78
2	**3**	*1*	**Noverre To Go (IRE)**[61] 4616 2-9-3 0 ... (t) RichardKingscote 1 (Tom Dascombe) *t.k.h and sn led: rdn wl over 1f out: hdd and nt qckn fnl 100yds* **6/5**[1]	75
0	**4**	*¾*	**La Tizona (IRE)**[16] 6000 2-9-3 0 ... HayleyTurner 8 (R Charlton) *hld up in last trio: covered up and stl gng wl 2f out: nudged along and styd on takingly fnl f: do bttr* **25/1**	74+
5	**5**	*1 ¾*	**Mabuya (UAE)**[41] 5225 2-9-3 0 ... NCallan 2 (P J Makin) *t.k.h early: hld up in tch: effrt over 2f out: chsd ldrs over 1f out: one pce after* **9/1**	69+
6	**6**	*hd*	**Curacao**[16] 6000 2-9-3 0 ... EddieAhern 5 (Mrs A J Perrett) *racd on outer in midfield: rdn over 2f out: no prog tl kpt on fnl f: n.d* **14/1**	69+
463	**7**	*½*	**Importer (IRE)**[8] 6197 2-8-12 0 ... DavidProbert(5) 6 (W R Muir) *chsd ldr to 1/2-way: styd cl up tl fdd over 1f out* **8/1**[3]	67
00	**8**	*3*	**Banda Sea (IRE)**[16] 6000 2-9-3 0 ... TravisBlock 13 (P J Makin) *sn last: rdn 3f out: no prog tl kpt on fnl f* **66/1**	60+
3	**9**	*½*	**Beat Up**[31] 5579 2-9-3 0 ... GeorgeBaker 10 (P R Chamings) *hld up towards rr: shkn up and no real imp 2f out: btn whn hung rt ins fnl f* **10/1**	62+
5	**10**	*2*	**Royal Society**[13] 6065 2-9-3 0 ... RoystonFfrench 7 (M Johnston) *dwlt: sn rdn in rr: a struggling* **14/1**	54+
3044	**11**	*2 ¼*	**Arushore (IRE)**[24] 5747 2-9-3 66 ... TedDurcan 4 (R Hannon) *prom to 1/2-way: sn lost pl and btn* **17/2**	48

1m 27.49s (0.09) **Going Correction** -0.075s/f (Good) **11 Ran SP% 120.3**
Speed ratings (Par 95): **96,95,94,93,91 91,90,87,86,84 81**
toteswinger: 1&2 £42.20, 1&3 £3.20, 2&3 £12.00. CSF £220.36 TOTE £6.60: £2.10, £7.70, £1.20; EX 242.60.
Owner K Abdulla **Bred** Juddmonte Farms Ltd **Trained** Pulborough, W Sussex

FOCUS
A fair juvenile maiden, run at an average pace. The form seems sound enough and there is better to come from the winner.

NOTEBOOK
Truism stepped up markedly on the level of his Newbury debut and opened his account in good style. He can be rated value for further than the bare margin as he had to wait for his challenge around 2f out, and showed a willing attitude when asked to win the race. His pedigree suggests that he will relish further as he matures and he looks a useful prospect. (op 8-1 tchd 6-1)
Chapter And Verse(IRE) ran a little freely through the early parts, but showed the clear benefit of his debut experience at Newbury and turned in a much-improved effort. The extra furlong was to his liking and he should not remain a maiden for too long. (tchd 40-1)
Noverre To Go(IRE) set the standard on his debut second at Doncaster and met plenty of support to go one better. He did not help his chances of staying the longer trip by racing keenly early on, however, and was a sitting duck inside the final furlong. He should learn again for the experience and can be placed to strike in the coming weeks, but his Group 1 entry does look very ambitious. (op 15-8 tchd 2-1 in places)
La Tizona(IRE) ◆, who ran distinctly green on his debut on Lingfield's Polytrack 16 days previously, was doing some decent late work and posted a much more encouraging display. This well-related colt left the impression he would come on again nicely for the run and looks sure to appreciate a stiffer test in due course. (op 22-1)
Mabuya(UAE) took a little time to settle and performed close enough to his debut form, helping to set the standard. He needs one more run for a mark and is another who should appreciate stepping up in trip as a three-year-old. (op 15-2)

6413 BOXGROVE PRIORY MAIDEN STKS 1m 6f
2:45 (2:46) (Class 5) 3-Y-O+ **£3,238** (£963; £481; £240) **Stalls** Low

Form				RPR
	1		**Viper**[74] 6-9-10 0 ... HayleyTurner 3 (R Hollinshead) *dwlt: rcvrd to go 2nd after 2f: led after 5f: drew clr fr 5f out: galloped on relentlessly fnl 3f* **12/1**	86
3033	**2**	*8*	**Pure Song**[7] 6226 3-8-10 72 ... EddieAhern 5 (J L Dunlop) *led 5f: chsd wnr after: rdn and one pce fnl 3f* **11/2**[3]	70
2542	**3**	*1*	**Shy**[24] 5750 3-8-10 70 ... JimCrowley 1 (P Winkworth) *trckd ldr 2f: mostly in 3rd after: one pce u.p fnl 3f* **7/2**[2]	69
	4	*1 ½*	**Dayia (IRE)**[162] 4-9-5 0 ... JerryO'Dwyer 4 (J Pearce) *s.s: wl in rr: rn wd bnd 5f out: struggling 4f out: kpt on u.p fr over 2f out* **10/1**	67
-230	**5**	*6*	**Guardian Of Truth (IRE)**[27] 5677 4-9-10 74 ... (p) GeorgeBaker 8 (G L Moore) *hld up and sn last: rdn wl over 2f out: no ch* **8/1**	63
05	**6**	*6*	**Lagavulin (IRE)**[7] 6226 4-9-5 0 ... DavidProbert(5) 6 (Miss E C Lavelle) *a towards rr: rdn 3f out: sn lft wl bhd: lame* **33/1**	55
323	**7**	*½*	**Star Rocker**[21] 5814 3-9-1 78 ... TedDurcan 2 (J H M Gosden) *trckd ldrs: disp 3rd 4f out: no prog u.p 3f out: wknd over 2f out* **2/1**[1]	54
4565	**8**	*7*	**Dubai's Wonder (IRE)**[17] 5963 3-9-1 66 ... NCallan 7 (B W Hills) *mostly in midfield: u.p over 3f out: wknd over 2f out* **7/1**	44

3m 1.52s (-2.08) **Going Correction** -0.075s/f (Good)
WFA 3 from 4yo+ 9lb **8 Ran SP% 114.3**
Speed ratings (Par 103): **102,97,96,96,92 89,88,84**
toteswinger: 1&2 £12.20, 1&3 £3.80, 2&3 £5.50. CSF £75.93 TOTE £11.50: £1.90, £1.70, £1.60; EX 106.40.
Owner Geoff Lloyd **Bred** R Hollinshead **Trained** Upper Longdon, Staffs

FOCUS
A modest maiden which has been rated around the placed horses. The impressive winner could be rated higher, but there are doubts over the opposition.
Lagavulin(IRE) Official explanation: vet said gelding finished lame
Star Rocker Official explanation: jockey said colt had no more to give

6414 CENTRELINE AIR PRIVATE JET NURSERY (H'CAP) 6f
3:20 (3:20) (Class 4) (0-80,80) 2-Y-O **£3,885** (£1,156; £577; £288) **Stalls** Low

Form				RPR
6202	**1**		**Norfolk Broads (IRE)**[10] 6172 2-8-13 **69** ... RoystonFfrench 13 (M Johnston) *w ldrs: narrow ld 2f out: drvn and edgd rt fnl f: hld on wl* **7/2**[1]	74
3140	**2**	*nk*	**Senatorial**[13] 6082 2-9-7 **77** ... NCallan 9 (B W Hills) *trckd ldrs: rdn wl over 1f out: prog u.p ent fnl f: gaining on wnr nr fin: jst hld* **11/2**[3]	81
3631	**3**	*1*	**Daddy's Gift (IRE)**[9] 6193 2-9-10 **80** 6ex ... PatDobbs 14 (R Hannon) *prom: upsides 2f out: pressed wnr after: no ex fnl 100yds* **9/2**[2]	81
2413	**4**	*¾*	**Ruby Tallulah**[47] 5103 2-9-5 **75** ... KirstyMilczarek 2 (N P Littmoden) *trckd ldrs: effrt 2f out: cl enough over 1f out: one pce after* **13/2**	74
2505	**5**	*1 ¼*	**Flyit (IRE)**[16] 5997 2-9-0 **70** ... TPO'Shea 10 (M R Channon) *wl in rr: rdn and prog fr 2f out: kpt on one pce fnl f: nvr able to chal* **16/1**	65
4650	**6**	*¾*	**Skruton (IRE)**[16] 5997 2-8-12 **68** ... TedDurcan 3 (M G Quinlan) *towards rr: rdn over 2f out: kpt on fnl f: nvr threatened ldrs* **14/1**	61
2304	**7**	*¾*	**My Best Man**[16] 5997 2-9-0 **70** ... JimCrowley 5 (B R Millman) *w ldr: stl upsides 2f out: fdd jst over 1f out* **16/1**	61
0003	**8**	*nse*	**Clerical (USA)**[21] 5834 2-7-8 **57** oh4 ow3 ... (p) AndreaAtzeni(7) 8 (M J Gingell) *mostly in midfield: n.m.r 1/2-way: no prog fnl 2f* **33/1**	47
1020	**9**	*nk*	**Anacaona (IRE)**[31] 5581 2-8-4 **60** ... HayleyTurner 6 (R Hannon) *wl in tch: lost pl steadily and pushed along fr 2f out: n.d fnl f* **16/1**	50
6355	**10**	*shd*	**Spit And Polish**[17] 5959 2-9-4 **74** ... (b) EddieAhern 12 (J L Dunlop) *wnt lft s: trckd ldrs: poised to chal gng easily 2f out: rdn and no rspnse over 1f out: wknd tamely* **14/1**	63
036	**11**	*¾*	**Lady Mulligan**[23] 5784 2-8-10 **66** ... JamesDoyle 4 (M Blanshard) *towards rr: rdn 2f out: no real prog* **50/1**	53
025	**12**	*½*	**Handful Of Magic**[57] 4747 2-7-13 **62** ow2 ... RossAtkinson(7) 11 (Tom Dascombe) *bmpd s: a wl in rr: struggling over 2f out* **14/1**	48
0455	**13**	*1 ¼*	**Elusive Ronnie (IRE)**[18] 5933 2-7-7 **54** ... (b[1]) DavidProbert(5) 1 (R A Teal) *mde most to 2f out: racd awkwardly and wknd over 1f out* **16/1**	36
636	**14**	*5*	**Fortune In Faith (USA)**[19] 5904 2-8-11 **67** ... IanMongan 7 (C G Cox) *w ldrs to over 2f out: wknd v rapidly* **20/1**	34

1m 12.6s (0.40) **Going Correction** +0.15s/f (Good) **14 Ran SP% 122.3**
Speed ratings (Par 97): **103,102,101,100,98 97,96,96,96,96 95,94,92,86**
toteswinger: 1&2 £6.50, 1&3 £5.00, 2&3 £5.60. CSF £21.90 CT £91.14 TOTE £5.00: £1.90, £2.50, £2.00; EX 27.70.
Owner Sheikh Hamdan Bin Mohammed Al Maktoum **Bred** Darley **Trained** Middleham Moor, N Yorks

FOCUS
An open nursery and the form looks solid. The winner is progressive.

NOTEBOOK

Norfolk Broads(IRE), second off this mark against her own sex at Leicester ten days previously, deservedly shed her maiden tag at the sixth attempt and completed the task in tenacious fashion. She was always on the pace, proving well suited by the quick ground, and dug deep to repel the runner-up. A step up to 7f should prove within her range in due course, but she looks best kept to this trip in the short term and should remain competitive. (op 4-1 tchd 5-1 in places)

Senatorial tracked the winner through the first half of the race and, after taking time to hit top gear, only just missed out. On this showing an easy 7f is what he ideally needs at present and he looks capable of adding to his tally before the season's end. (op 7-1)

Daddy's Gift(IRE) was far from disgraced on this return to quicker ground under top weight and helps to give the form a good look. She is probably happiest on easier ground, but is already due to race from a 5lb higher mark in the future. (op 5-1 tchd 11-2)

Ruby Tallulah moved sweetly through the race, but did not see out the extra furlong as well as the principals. She remains in good form. (op 11-2 tchd 5-1)

Spit And Polish found nothing and looks one to be wary of. (op 12-1 tchd 16-1)

6415 SPINAL RESEARCH FILLIES' STKS (H'CAP) 1m 4f

3:55 (3:55) (Class 3) (0-95,92) 3-Y-0+ £9,714 (£2,890; £1,444; £721) Stalls Low

Form RPR

3351 **1** **Storyland (USA)**[12] 6127 3-9-2 85 KirstyMilczarek 7 93+
(W J Haggas) *hld up in last: stdy prog over 3f out: nt clr run briefly over 2f out: eased out to trck ldr: led 1f out: pushed out: readily* **9/2**[2]

2115 **2** *1* **Starfala**[12] 6127 3-9-2 85 NCallan 8 89+
(P F I Cole) *trckd ldrs: rdn and nt qckn over 2f out: rallied u.p over 1f out: styd on to take 2nd fnl strides* **7/2**[1]

-212 **3** *nk* **Montbretia**[12] 6127 3-9-9 92 TedDurcan 10 96
(H R A Cecil) *mostly trckd ldr: led over 2f out and gng strly: rdn and hdd 1f out: one pce and lost 2nd last strides* **7/2**[1]

41 **4** *1 3/4* **Interchange (IRE)**[54] 4871 3-8-13 82 JimCrowley 6 83
(J R Fanshawe) *prom: rdn to dispute cl 3rd 2f out: one pce fr jst over 1f out* **12/1**

5120 **5** *3* **Sea Chorus**[41] 5249 3-8-8 77 (t) HayleyTurner 3 73
(M L W Bell) *led at mod pce: tried to kick on 4f out: hdd over 2f out: sn outpcd: fdd fnl f* **16/1**

4164 **6** *7* **Miss Rochester (IRE)**[13] 6079 3-8-3 77 Louis-PhilippeBeuzelin(5) 9 62
(Sir Michael Stoute) *in tch: dropped to last u.p 3f out: n.d after* **9/2**[2]

-356 **7** *3* **Lady Friend**[51] 4945 6-8-10 75 PatrickHills(3) 2 55
(J W Hills) *s.i.s: t.k.h early and hld up in last trio: sme prog on inner 4f out: wknd over 2f out* **33/1**

4661 **8** *shd* **Shimoni**[8] 6203 4-9-4 80 6ex (v) GeorgeBaker 1 60
(G L Moore) *hld up in last trio: effrt on outer 4f out: wknd over 2f out* **7/1**[3]

1024 **9** *8* **Rio Guru (IRE)**[12] 6127 3-8-7 76 TonyCulhane 4 43
(M R Channon) *hld up in midfield: wd bnd 5f out: prog on outer 4f out: wknd wl over 2f out* **20/1**

2m 38.75s (0.35) **Going Correction** -0.075s/f (Good)
WFA 3 from 4yo+ 7lb **9 Ran SP% 114.6**
Speed ratings (Par 104): **95,94,94,92,90 86,84,84,78**
toteswinger: 1&2 £3.80, 1&3 £3.50, 2&3 £3.90. CSF £20.46 CT £60.65 TOTE £4.90: £1.40, £2.10, £1.70; EX 20.80.
Owner Mr & Mrs R Scott **Bred** Arthur B Hancock III & James H Stone **Trained** Newmarket, Suffolk
■ Stewards' Enquiry : Ted Durcan caution: careless riding

FOCUS

A decent fillies' handicap. The winner won cosily and the form makes sense, with the first three reopposing from Newmarket. The winner is rated up another 4lb.

NOTEBOOK

Storyland(USA) ◆ maintained her progression and followed up her Newmarket win 12 days previously from a 9lb higher mark. She confirmed last-time-out form with the placed horses without her rider resorting to the whip and is now two from two over this distance. She looks worth a chance in better grade. (op 6-1)

Starfala looked to have decent claims of reversing form with the winner as she met that rival on 9lb better terms and had no luck at Newmarket. She managed to reverse form with Montbretia on 3lb better terms, but while she was closing at the finish she is somewhat flattered by her proximity. No doubt she remains progressive, however, and looks well worth a try over a longer trip. (op 4-1 tchd 10-3)

Montbretia, 6lb better off with the winner, took it up in the home straight and held every chance. She could be worth dropping back in trip and there will be other days for her. (op 9-2 tchd 10-3)

Interchange(IRE) had her chance on this handicap bow and was certainly not disgraced. This was an improved effort and she may have even more to offer as she matures further (op 10-1)

Sea Chorus had very much the run of the race out in front and turned in a much better effort on this drop back in trip, but still looks held by the handicapper.

Miss Rochester(IRE) disappointed, with no real excuse. Official explanation: jockey said filly suffered interference in running (op 5-1)

Shimoni Official explanation: jockey said filly hung left under pressure

6416 RACING WELFARE STKS (H'CAP) 1m 3f

4:30 (4:30) (Class 4) (0-80,80) 3-Y-0 £6,476 (£1,927; £963; £481) Stalls Low

Form RPR

010 **1** **Colourways (IRE)**[60] 4667 3-9-4 80 JimCrowley 7 92
(Mrs A J Perrett) *sn last: nt gng wl 1/2-way: detached and edging out wd over 4f out: gd prog fr 3f out: surged into ld over 1f out: sn in command* **8/1**

2042 **2** *2 3/4* **Hawk Flight (IRE)**[21] 5814 3-8-1 68 DavidProbert(5) 9 75
(W R Muir) *hld up in last pair: prog to go 3rd 3f out: clsd smoothly after: produced to chal over 1f out but surprised by wnr: hung lft and easily outpcd* **6/1**[3]

0122 **3** *5* **Timocracy**[9] 6195 3-8-12 74 RoystonFfrench 6 73+
(M Johnston) *trckd ldr: led 6f out: sn pressed: sustained dual w chalr tl beat him off over 2f out: hdd & wknd over 1f out* **13/8**[1]

2214 **4** *7* **Pediment**[26] 5699 3-9-4 80 RobertWinston 5 67
(J R Fanshawe) *hld up towards rr: rdn and struggling 3f out: hanging rt 2f out: nvr on terms w ldrs* **4/1**[2]

0440 **5** *1 1/2* **Hawaana (IRE)**[8] 6202 3-8-12 74 PaulDoe 4 58
(Eve Johnson Houghton) *prom: trckd ldr over 5f out and sn pressing: upsides over 4f out to over 2f out: btn and hanging rt after: wknd over 1f out* **16/1**

5010 **6** *1 1/2* **Flying Applause**[34] 5472 3-9-0 76 TravisBlock 1 58
(A King) *led at str pce to 6f out: sn dropped to 3rd and nt keen u.p: fdd over 2f out* **16/1**

1500 **7** *11* **Sinbad The Sailor**[13] 6079 3-8-10 72 TQuinn 3 35
(J W Hills) *hld up in rr: rdn and struggling 3f out: t.o* **8/1**

4000 **8** *2 1/4* **Mon Plaisir (USA)**[16] 5999 3-8-8 70 (b) EddieAhern 8 29
(J L Dunlop) *mostly midfield tl wknd over 3f out: t.o* **14/1**

2m 24.82s (-3.48) **Going Correction** -0.075s/f (Good) **8 Ran SP% 113.0**
Speed ratings (Par 103): **109,107,103,98,97 96,88,86**
toteswinger: 1&2 £5.90, 1&3 £4.50, 2&3 £2.80. CSF £53.62 CT £115.58 TOTE £11.00: £2.50, £1.60, £1.20; EX 53.60.
Owner Lady Clague **Bred** Newberry Stud Company **Trained** Pulborough, W Sussex

FOCUS

A fair handicap which was run at a generous early pace with several quickly off the bridle. The winner is up 12lb and the second 3lb, but there are doubts over how reliable the bare form is.

6417 MYSPINE.ORG STKS (H'CAP) 1m

5:05 (5:06) (Class 5) (0-75,74) 3-Y-0 £3,238 (£963; £481; £240) Stalls High

Form RPR

0312 **1** **Spate River**[10] 6177 3-9-4 74 GeorgeBaker 1 85
(C F Wall) *wl away fr wd draw and trckd ldng pair: led jst over 2f out: rdn clr fnl f* **4/1**[1]

665 **2** *3 1/2* **Candy Rose**[23] 5790 3-7-11 60 KatiaScallan(7) 7 63
(M P Tregoning) *hld up in last trio: c wdst of all in st: prog on outer 3f out: chsd wnr wl over 1f out: one pce fnl f* **14/1**

3643 **3** *nk* **Sir Ike (IRE)**[21] 5836 3-8-1 62 (t) Louis-PhilippeBeuzelin(5) 3 64
(W S Kittow) *settled in midfield: rdn wl over 2f out: prog and hung rt over 1f out: styd on fnl f to take 3rd last strides* **8/1**

5546 **4** *nk* **Astrodonna**[15] 6027 3-9-2 72 NCallan 10 73
(M H Tompkins) *trckd ldrs: effrt and clr path to dispute 2nd wl over 1f out: kpt on same pce and no ch w wnr: lost 3rd last strides* **6/1**[3]

1165 **5** *3/4* **Bluejain**[15] 6021 3-9-3 73 HayleyTurner 13 73+
(Miss Gay Kelleway) *s.s: detached in last: nt gng wl and stl last 3f out: prog on outer 2f out: styd on: no ch of rching ldrs* **8/1**

0006 **6** *1/2* **Benedetto**[12] 6124 3-9-1 71 (p) JimCrowley 14 69+
(Mrs A J Perrett) *trckd ldrs on inner: trapped bhd rivals fr 3f out w no ch of getting out: r.o fnl 150yds: no ch* **7/1**

4335 **7** *nk* **Timber Creek**[21] 5816 3-8-7 63 FrankieMcDonald 9 61+
(H Candy) *hld up in midfield: trapped bhd rivals fr 3f out: eased out 2f out and effrt: hmpd over 1f out and no ch after: styd on* **16/1**

2640 **8** *2 1/2* **Rankayo Hitam (USA)**[26] 5708 3-8-9 65 (b) RobertWinston 12 57
(P F I Cole) *plld hrd: hld up cl bhd ldrs: nowhere to go 3f out to 2f out: effrt wl over 1f out: no rspnse* **20/1**

6205 **9** *3/4* **Bauhaus Bourbon (USA)**[19] 5915 3-8-7 63 NelsonDeSouza 8 53
(P F I Cole) *led to jst over 2f out: wknd over 1f out* **16/1**

4600 **10** *1 3/4* **My Shadow**[22] 5800 3-9-1 71 IanMongan 11 57
(S Dow) *hld up in rr: effrt on outer whn bmpd and squeezed wl over 2f out: no prog after* **25/1**

6-06 **11** *5* **Sayedati Elhasna (IRE)**[54] 4872 3-8-10 66 EddieAhern 15 41
(J L Dunlop) *trckd ldrs: cl up but nowhere to go fr 3f out: wknd jst over 1f out* **25/1**

4131 **12** *3* **Oriental Girl**[56] 4766 3-8-11 67 (p) TQuinn 5 35
(J A Geake) *pressed ldr: chal and upsides 3f out to jst over 2f out: wknd rapidly over 1f out* **5/1**[2]

0300 **13** *3 3/4* **Silca Destination**[1] 6387 3-8-7 63 TPO'Shea 2 22+
(M R Channon) *hld up in rr: effrt towards outer whn bdly hmpd and nrly fell wl over 2f out: nt rcvr* **50/1**

334 **14** *22* **Gang Show (IRE)**[16] 6001 3-8-10 66 TedDurcan 6 —
(W J Musson) *hld up in midfield towards outer: gng wl enough whn barged into fr bhd wl over 2f out: sn wknd and eased: t.o* **20/1**

1m 39.43s (-0.47) **Going Correction** -0.075s/f (Good) **14 Ran SP% 123.3**
Speed ratings (Par 101): **99,95,95,94,94 93,93,90,90,88 83,80,76,54**
toteswinger: 1&2 £11.70, 1&3 £9.80, 2&3 £13.50. CSF £58.70 CT £442.34 TOTE £5.00: £1.90, £3.40, £3.30; EX 79.10.
Owner Firman Webster Racing **Bred** Firman And Webster Bloodstock **Trained** Newmarket, Suffolk
■ Stewards' Enquiry : Katia Scallan four-day ban: careless riding (Oct 16-17,19-20)

FOCUS

A modest handicap for three-year-olds. The winner won well from the outside stall, but there were some hard-luck stories in behind. The winner ran basically to form, the second is up 12lb, and the next two ran to their latest.

Benedetto Official explanation: jockey said colt was denied a clear run

Rankayo Hitam(USA) Official explanation: jockey said colt hung left

Oriental Girl Official explanation: jockey said filly lost its action after interference

Silca Destination Official explanation: jockey said filly suffered interference

Gang Show(IRE) Official explanation: jockey said gelding suffered interference twice

6418 BETFAIR APPRENTICE TRAINING SERIES STKS (H'CAP) 5f

5:40 (5:44) (Class 5) (0-70,67) 3-Y-0+ £3,561 (£1,059; £529; £264) Stalls Low

Form RPR

0600 **1** **Bluebok**[3] 6339 7-8-12 60 (bt) JackDean 13 67
(J M Bradley) *racd centre and wl in tch: chsd clr ldr over 2f out: clsd u.p fnl f: led fnl 75yds: jst hld on* **16/1**

2212 **2** *shd* **Shakespeare's Son**[26] 5709 3-9-5 67 DavidProbert 3 74
(H J Evans) *hld up in rr: prog wl over 1f out: styd on fnl f to press wnr nr fin: jst failed* **3/1**[1]

0400 **3** *nk* **Punching**[3] 6335 4-9-4 66 (b) KylieManser 11 72
(Miss Gay Kelleway) *wl away: led: clr 1/2-way: rdn over 1f out: hdd and no ex fnl 75yds* **8/1**[3]

5000 **4** *1* **Diademas (USA)**[8] 6204 3-8-0 53 oh3 (v) RichardRowe(5) 6 55
(M J Gingell) *s.s: mostly in last pair tl styd on wl fr over 1f out: gaining at fin* **50/1**

0060 **5** *1/2* **Sand Cat**[20] 5861 5-9-1 66 (b) JemmaMarshall(3) 7 66
(G L Moore) *wl in rr and off the pce: effrt 1/2-way: styd on fr over 1f out: nrst fin* **12/1**

0030 **6** *1 1/2* **Lithaam (IRE)**[36] 5401 4-8-0 53 oh2 (p) PietroRomeo(5) 2 48
(J M Bradley) *in tch in chsng gp: urged along furiously and clsd over 1f out: fdd ins fnl f* **20/1**

2136 **7** *1/2* **Penrice Castle**[9] 6190 3-8-0 53 CharlesEddery(5) 12 46
(R Hannon) *racd in centre: early spd and wl in tch: wknd over 1f out* **16/1**

435 **8** *1/2* **Compton Rose**[8] 6204 3-9-2 67 BillyCray(3) 9 58
(H Candy) *in tch in chsng gp: urged along and lost pl 2f out: sn btn* **13/2**[2]

600 **9** *nk* **Coconut Moon**[19] 5884 6-9-2 67 RobbieEgan(3) 4 57
(D Flood) *in tch in chsng gp: lost pl 2f out: btn after* **12/1**

650 **10** *1* **Moverra (IRE)**[8] 6208 4-8-5 53 oh4 (v) AmyBaker 5 39
(M J Gingell) *in tch in chsng gp tl wknd wl over 1f out* **33/1**

304 **11** *8* **Sofinella (IRE)**[8] 6204 5-8-8 56 MCGeran 1 14
(A W Carroll) *racd against nr side rail: chsd ldr to 1/2-way: wknd rapidly: t.o* **12/1**

59.55 secs (1.15) **Going Correction** +0.15s/f (Good) **11 Ran SP% 93.9**
Speed ratings (Par 103): **96,95,95,93,92 90,89,88,88,86 74**
toteswinger: 1&2 £9.30, 1&3 £16.40, 2&3 £7.30. CSF £39.10 CT £190.57 TOTE £16.00: £3.80, £1.40, £2.40; EX 58.30 Place 6: £20.26 Place 5: £13.28.
Owner E A Hayward **Bred** E A Duggan And D Churchman **Trained** Sedbury, Gloucs
■ Bertie Southstreet was withdrawn (3/1 JF, unruly in stalls). R4 applies, deduct 25p in the £.

FOCUS

A modest sprint. The first three came clear and the form is best rated around the runner-up.
T/Jkpt: Not won. T/Plt: £22.90 to a £1 stake. Pool: £67,066.12. 2,132.57 winning tickets. T/Qpdt: £4.90 to a £1 stake. Pool: £4,089.88. 612.25 winning tickets. JN

6280 GREAT LEIGHS (A.W) (L-H)

Thursday, October 2

OFFICIAL GOING: Standard

Wind: Modest, across Weather: dry

6419 WEST PARK LODGE H'CAP 6f (P)

6:50 (6:51) (Class 6) (0-52,56) 3-Y-0+ £2,590 (£770; £385; £192) Stalls Low

Form RPR

0602 1 **Willhewiz**45 5152 8-9-0 52 (v) TGMcLaughlin 3 59
(W M Brisbourne) *chsd ldr: rdn and pressed ldr over 1f out: kpt on u.p to ld towards fin* 5/1[1]

0000 2 nk **George The Second**21 5817 5-9-0 52 RichardKingscote 6 58
(Miss Tor Sturgis) *led: rdn over 1f out: kpt on tl hdd and no ex towards fin* 16/1

6006 3 1 **The Hoofer (IRE)**10 6173 3-8-13 52 (t) DarryllHolland 12 55
(I A Wood) *towards rr on outer: rdn and hdwy wl over 1f out: styd on wl fnl f: wnt 3rd wl ins fnl f: nt rch ldng pair* 28/1

4-00 4 nk **Comrade Cotton**34 5474 4-9-0 52 (p) JerryO'Dwyer 11 54
(J Ryan) *racd wd in midfield: drvn over 3f out: styd on u.p fnl f: nt rch ldrs* 8/1[3]

0340 5 1 **Out Of India**6 6251 6-9-0 52 DaneO'Neill 13 51
(P T Dalton) *hld up in rr on outer: rdn wl over 1f out: kpt on fnl f but nvr pce to rch ldrs* 8/1[3]

1343 6 nk **City For Conquest (IRE)**49 5007 5-9-0 52 StephenDonohoe 10 50
(John A Harris) *in tch: rdn and unable qck 2f out: kpt on u.p fnl f* 9/1

-600 7 nk **Kindallachan**55 4825 5-8-11 52 (b[1]) JackMitchell(3) 7 49
(G C Bravery) *hld up in tch: hdwy to chse ldng pair and rdn jst over 2f out: drvn and unable qck wl over 1f out: wknd ins fnl f* 12/1

0200 8 nk **Hollywood George**6 6251 4-9-0 52 (p) ChrisCatlin 5 48
(Miss M E Rowland) *s.i.s: hld up in midfield: n.m.r briefly over 2f out: hdwy u.p over 1f out: kpt on same pce fnl f* 10/1

3546 9 1 1/4 **Easy Wonder (GER)**45 5162 3-8-13 52 (p) CatherineGannon 1 44
(I A Wood) *bhd: hdwy over 2f out: rdn and effrt on inner wl over 1f out: sn hung lft and no imp* 16/1

4056 10 1 1/4 **Arfinnit (IRE)**8 6204 7-9-0 52 (p) LiamJones 9 40
(Mrs A L M King) *s.i.s: sn pushed along: nvr trbld ldrs* 9/1

0021 11 3 1/2 **Mulberry Lad (IRE)**8 6208 6-9-4 56 6ex (p) JamesDoyle 2 33
(S Curran) *awkward s and v.s.a: a bhd* 6/1[2]

0016 12 3 1/4 **Slip Star**84 3866 5-9-0 52 GregFairley 4 18
(T J Etherington) *chsd ldrs: rdn 1/2-way: sn struggling: wl bhd fnl f* 12/1

2500 13 17 **Honest Value (IRE)**19 5911 3-8-13 52 RichardThomas 8 —
(Mrs L C Jewell) *chsd ldrs tl wl over 2f out: sn wknd: wl bhd and eased fnl f* 40/1

1m 13.6s (-0.10) **Going Correction** -0.05s/f (Stan)
WFA 3 from 4yo+ 1lb 13 Ran SP% 115.3
Speed ratings (Par 101): **98,97,96,95,94 94,93,93,91,90 85,81,58**
toteswinger: 1&2 £12.20, 1&3 £12.20, 2&3 £20.60. CSF £82.89 CT £2076.93 TOTE £6.30: £1.30, £5.10, £9.80; EX 81.80.
Owner Stephen Jones **Bred** L T And M Foster **Trained** Great Ness, Shropshire

FOCUS
A modest but competitive-looking sprint where it paid to be at the head of affairs. Pretty weak form.
Mulberry Lad(IRE) Official explanation: jockey said gelding missed the break because it tried to get under stalls
Honest Value(IRE) Official explanation: jockey said gelding lost its action; vet said gelding had been struck into

6420 HECTOR H'CAP 6f (P)

7:20 (7:20) (Class 4) (0-80,80) 3-Y-0+ £4,857 (£1,445; £722; £360) Stalls Low

Form RPR

6202 1 **Beat The Bell**49 5028 3-8-4 70 NicolPolli(5) 4 81
(A Bailey) *dwlt: sn in tch: hdwy to chse ldrs 1/2-way: led wl over 1f out: styd on wl fnl f and a holding runner up* 15/2

3500 2 1 **San Jose City (IRE)**4 6314 3-9-3 78 DarryllHolland 1 86
(D Carroll) *stdd s: hld up towards rr: hdwy 1/2-way: chsd ldrs 2f out: swtchd rt over 1f out: sn chsng wnr: kpt on wl but a hld fnl f* 11/2[2]

6550 3 4 1/2 **Dvinsky (USA)**23 5789 7-9-4 78 (b) JimmyQuinn 5 72
(P Howling) *t.k.h: hld up in tch: pushed along 1/2-way: chsd ldng pair and rdn over 1f out: sn no prog: kpt on* 6/1[3]

6403 4 1 **Vigano (IRE)**12 6137 3-8-9 70 RichardHughes 8 60
(S Kirk) *racd in midfield on outer: rdn and lost pl over 3f out: kpt on u.p fnl f but no ch w ldrs* 5/1[1]

6255 5 1/2 **Whitbarrow (IRE)**12 6137 9-8-9 72 (b) JamesMillman(3) 2 61
(B R Millman) *w ldrs tl led after 1f: hdd over 2f out: ev ch and rdn 2f out: wknd ent fnl f* 8/1

4066 6 shd **Requisite**10 6169 3-9-5 80 AlanMunro 9 68
(I A Wood) *s.i.s: hld up and bhd: hdwy jst over 2f out: swtchd rt and rdn over 1f out: sn no imp* 14/1

6563 7 1 3/4 **Always Ready**9 6194 3-9-3 78 (v) LiamJones 3 61
(C E Brittain) *chsd ldr tl led over 2f out: rdn and hdd over 1f out: wknd ent fnl f* 5/1[1]

2266 8 6 **Lieutenant Pigeon**84 3890 3-9-0 75 PaulEddery 6 39
(G D Blake) *sn pushed up to ld: hdd after 1f: rdn and wknd over 2f out: wl btn and eased ins fnl f* 11/1

2323 9 nk **Asian Power (IRE)**10 6169 3-9-1 76 OscarUrbina 7 39
(P J O'Gorman) *hld up in last trio: rdn and no rspnse wl over 1f out: wl btn and eased ins fnl f* 7/1

1m 11.9s (-1.80) **Going Correction** -0.05s/f (Stan)
WFA 3 from 7yo+ 1lb 9 Ran SP% 113.4
Speed ratings (Par 105): **110,108,102,101,100 100,98,90,89**
toteswinger: 1&2 £28.10, 1&3 £28.10, 2&3 £7.00. CSF £47.41 CT £264.83 TOTE £7.60: £3.20, £2.80, £1.60; EX 84.70.
Owner D J P Turner **Bred** D J P Turner **Trained** Newmarket, Suffolk

FOCUS
Only a small turnout but a decent contest of its type. It was not surprising the market had a really open look to it. The first pair came clear with the winner up 6lb.

6421 HATFIELD PEVEREL H'CAP 2m (P)

7:50 (7:50) (Class 6) (0-65,65) 3-Y-0+ £2,590 (£770; £385; £192) Stalls Centre

Form RPR

0501 1 **Miss Serena**15 6022 3-9-2 58 MickyFenton 14 72
(Mrs P Sly) *chsd ldrs tl chsd clr ldr 8f out: pushed along and clsd 4f out: rdn to ld over 2f out: forged clr over 1f out: styd on wl* 13/2[3]

0651 2 7 **Blue Jet (USA)**6 6248 4-9-8 53 6ex J-PGuillambert 6 59
(R M Whitaker) *hld up in rr: hdwy 6f out: trckd ldng pair 3f out: chsd wnr 2f out: sn rdn: btn over 1f out* 11/2[2]

0064 3 3/4 **Whaxaar (IRE)**19 5917 4-9-11 56 RobertHavlin 9 61
(R Ingram) *hld up towards rr: hdwy over 6f out: chsd ldrs and rdn over 2f out: wnt 3rd over 1f out: kpt on same pce fnl f* 9/1

000 4 3 3/4 **Tapaellya (IRE)**16 6007 4-9-5 50 RichardThomas 7 51
(J E Long) *chsd ldrs: rdn and lost pl over 4f out: rallied u.p over 1f out: kpt on to snatch 4th nr fin* 50/1

634 5 3/4 **Compton Falcon**21 5833 4-9-11 59 LukeMorris(3) 10 59
(G A Butler) *hld up towards rr: hdwy 7f out: chsd ldrs and rdn over 2f out: wnt 3rd briefly over 1f out: sn no imp* 11/1

3330 6 5 **Adage**15 6022 5-9-4 49 (t) DaneO'Neill 3 43
(David Pinder) *hld up in midfield: effrt and rdn on outer 4f out: plugged on u.p fr 2f out: nvr trbld ldrs* 7/1

6223 7 3/4 **Borrowdale**15 6022 3-9-9 65 ShaneKelly 15 58
(J A Osborne) *led: clr after 4f: rdn over 4f out: hdd over 2f out: wknd wl over 1f out: wl btn and eased fnl f* 9/2[1]

0006 8 3/4 **Pearl (IRE)**7 5802 4-9-4 49 (v) StephenDonohoe 5 41
(I A Wood) *hld up in midfield: rdn wl over 3f out: sn struggling: no ch last 2f* 22/1

0005 9 5 **Looping The Loop (USA)**15 6018 3-8-11 53 JamesDoyle 2 39
(J G Portman) *hld up in midfield: rdn over 4f out: sn btn: no ch fr over 2f out* 50/1

2600 10 17 **Prince Of Medina**21 5833 5-9-4 49 SteveDrowne 16 15
(J R Best) *hld up in rr: nt clr run briefly over 4f out: sn lost tch: wl btn last 2f: t.o* 16/1

0000 11 10 **Our Nations**14 6044 3-8-5 47 (v[1]) JimmyQuinn 12 1
(D Carroll) *in tch: chsd ldrs and rdn 4f out: wknd over 3f out: wl btn after: t.o* 16/1

6004 12 6 **Tenement (IRE)**23 5787 4-9-8 53 AmirQuinn 11 —
(Jamie Poulton) *hld up in rr: hdwy on outer 6f out: no hdwy 4f out: wl bhd last 3f: t.o* 33/1

5-00 13 13 **Massams Lane**68 4409 4-9-8 53 AlanMunro 4 —
(G C Bravery) *t.k.h: hld up wl in tch: wknd over 5f out: wl t.o last 2f* 33/1

3000 14 92 **Muharjam**20 5868 3-9-6 62 (v[1]) LiamJones 8 —
(C E Brittain) *t.k.h: chsd ldr tl 8f out: sn rdn and steadily lost pl: wl t.o and virtually p.u last 2f* 40/1

0606 R **Chapter (IRE)**34 5450 6-9-5 50 (v[1]) KirstyMilczarek 1 —
(Mrs A L M King) *ref to r* 20/1

0214 P **Bundle Up**6 6252 5-9-5 50 RichardHughes 13 —
(P D Evans) *hld up in rr: hdwy on outer 6f out: drvn and btn over 3f out: sn hung bdly rt: eased and p.u over 1f out* 11/2[2]

3m 29.94s (-0.06) **Going Correction** -0.05s/f (Stan)
WFA 3 from 4yo+ 11lb 16 Ran SP% 126.2
Speed ratings (Par 101): **98,94,94,92,91 89,89,88,86,77 72,69,63,17,— —**
toteswinger: 1&2 £7.50, 1&3 £34.40, 2&3 £2.90. CSF £40.74 CT £334.15 TOTE £7.80: £1.80, £2.10, £2.40, £6.90; EX 44.60.
Owner Erik Amlie **Bred** Wood Hall Stud **Trained** Thorney, Cambs

FOCUS
This was probably only a moderate staying event, but it was not that pleasing on the eye to see them strung out like 3m chasers up the home straight. Indeed, at least three of them were being pulled up in the latter stages. The form looks solid for the grade though, with the progressive Miss Serena up another 8lb.
Borrowdale Official explanation: jockey said gelding hung left
Chapter(IRE) Official explanation: jockey said gelding refused to race
Bundle Up Official explanation: trainer said mare hung badly right

6422 NAZE H'CAP 1m (P)

8:20 (8:24) (Class 5) (0-70,70) 3-Y-0+ £2,590 (£770; £385; £192) Stalls Centre

Form RPR

5134 1 **Le Chiffre (IRE)**8 6211 6-9-0 63 (p) StephenDonohoe 10 72
(Miss Sheena West) *mde all: hrd pressed and rdn wl over 1f out: hld on gamely fnl f* 12/1

0561 2 nk **Ben Ami**14 6048 3-8-11 70 AndreaAtzeni(7) 14 78
(Miss J R Gibney) *hld up in tch: hdwy to chal wnr wl over 1f out: unable qck u.p fnl f* 6/1[1]

-563 3 1 1/4 **Intabih (USA)**14 6047 3-9-1 67 EddieAhern 2 74+
(C E Brittain) *hld up in midfield: hdwy on rail 2f out: wnt 3rd ent fnl f: nt clr run thrght fnl f: eased towards fin* 10/1

0603 4 1 1/4 **Convivial Spirit**26 5712 4-8-11 60 (t) JamieSpencer 4 63
(E F Vaughan) *hld up in midfield: hdwy jst over 2f out: edgd out rt and hrd rdn over 1f out: one pce fnl f* 7/1[2]

6/0- 5 1/2 **Keep Your Distance**626 139 4-8-7 56 oh1 JimmyQuinn 3 57
(P J McBride) *stdd s: hld up towards rr: hdwy on inner 2f out: kpt on fnl f: nvr pce to threaten ldrs* 66/1

6425 6 nk **Lunar River (FR)**12 6134 5-9-2 65 (t) DaneO'Neill 16 66
(David Pinder) *hld up in last pair: c wd and hdwy wl over 1f out: r.o fnl f: nt rch ldrs* 12/1

0230 7 hd **Speyside (IRE)**19 5915 3-9-0 69 (v) PatrickHills(3) 6 69
(J W Hills) *s.i.s: sn in tch in midfield: rdn and unable qck over 2f out: kpt on u.p fnl f* 14/1

004 8 3/4 **Triple Dream**16 5995 3-9-3 69 TedDurcan 12 68
(J L Dunlop) *dwlt: hld up in rr: rdn over 3f out: styd on u.p ins fnl f: nvr trbld ldrs* 10/1

000 9 hd **Samahir (USA)**11 4282 4-8-7 56 oh9 AlanMunro 8 54
(T T Clement) *t.k.h: hld up in rr: hdwy over 1f out: kpt on u.p fnl f but nvr pce to trble ldrs* 33/1

0004 10 nk **Sir Billy Nick**12 6134 3-8-7 66 CharlesEddery(7) 1 63
(J Noseda) *bhd: rdn 3f out: sme hdwy fnl f: nvr trbld ldrs* 16/1

6134 11 1/2 **Moon Crystal**146 1959 3-9-2 68 (t) RichardHughes 7 64
(E A L Dunlop) *t.k.h: hld up in midfield: rdn and effrt wl over 1f out: no prog* 8/1[3]

0405 12 1 **Cape Roberto (IRE)**37 5378 3-8-7 59 ow1 RobertHavlin 5 53
(Jamie Poulton) *chsd wnr tl wl over 1f out: sn drvn: wknd fnl f* 16/1

3210 13 1 1/4 **Luck Will Come (IRE)**32 5536 4-9-4 70 JackMitchell(3) 9 61
(H J Collingridge) *chsd ldrs: drvn and hung rt over 1f out: wknd ent fnl f* 8/1[3]

5103 14 6 **Dinner Date**126 2533 6-9-2 65 J-PGuillambert 11 42
(T Keddy) *racd in midfield: rdn and struggling 3f out: wl btn and eased ins fnl f* 11/1

2413 **15** *8* **Dawson Creek (IRE)**[19] 5915 4-9-3 **66**............................ ChrisCatlin 15 25
(B Gubby) *awkward leaving stalls: t.k.h: sn chsng ldrs: rdn and wknd over 2f out: wl bhd and eased fnl f* **9/1**

1m 39.35s (-0.55) **Going Correction** -0.05s/f (Stan)
WFA 3 from 4yo+ 3lb **15** Ran SP% **123.8**
Speed ratings (Par 103): **100,99,98,97,96 96,96,95,95,94 94,93,92,86,78**
toteswinger: 1&2 £41.00, 1&3 £25.90, 2&3 £27.30. CSF £83.96 CT £784.82 TOTE £15.00: £5.80, £3.00, £3.10; EX 98.50.
Owner Michael Moriarty **Bred** Agricola Del Parco **Trained** Falmer, E Sussex

FOCUS
A competitive event in which once again it paid to stay handy with the winner getting a good ride from the front. He is rated to this year's best. The third was perhas unlucky and the ninth limits the form.
Intabih(USA) Official explanation: jockey said colt was denied a clear run

6423 LITTLE BENTLEY MAIDEN STKS 1m (P)
8:50 (8:52) (Class 4) 2-Y-O **£4,857** (£1,445; £722; £360) **Stalls** Centre

Form RPR
04 **1** **Hula King (GER)**[13] 6085 2-9-3 0............................ JamieSpencer 6 86+
(B J Meehan) *mde all: rdn clr over 1f out: in n.d after: easily* **3/1**[2]
4 **2** *6* **Noordhoek Kid**[22] 5798 2-9-3 0............................ SteveDrowne 1 73+
(C R Egerton) *s.i.s: hld up in midfield: rdn over 2f out: edgd lft fr over 1f out: wnt 2nd last 100yds: no ch w wnr* **25/1**
52 **3** *½* **Free Thinker**[27] 5678 2-9-3 0............................ EddieAhern 2 72+
(P W D'Arcy) *s.i.s: sn rcvrd and chsd wnr tl 6f out: rdn to chse wnr again wl over 1f out: sn outpcd: lost 2nd last 100yds* **15/8**[1]
06 **4** *2* **Gtaab**[21] 5842 2-9-3 0............................ RHills 4 67
(E A L Dunlop) *s.i.s: sn pushed along in rr: hdwy into midfield over 3f out: wnt modest 4th 1f out: kpt on but n.d* **25/1**
00 **5** *2 ¾* **Causeway King (USA)**[15] 6031 2-9-3 0............................ GregFairley 3 61
(M Johnston) *in tch in midfield: rdn over 2f out: sn outpcd: no ch last 2f* **16/1**[3]
6 *3 ½* **Alpha Tauri (USA)** 2-9-3 0............................ TPQueally 9 53+
(H R A Cecil) *racd keenly: chsd ldr after 2f: rdn jst over 2f out: wknd over 1f out: wl btn fnl f* **15/8**[1]
0 **7** *1* **Veiled**[10] 6167 2-8-12 0............................ DO'Donohoe 7 46
(Sir Mark Prescott) *a towards rr: rdn and outpcd 3f out: no ch last 2f* **33/1**
8 *8* **Sham Sheer** 2-9-3 0............................ DaneO'Neill 8 33+
(L M Cumani) *s.i.s: sn bustled along and rn green in last pair: lost tch 3f out* **20/1**
0 **9** *2* **Cooper Island Kid (USA)**[18] 5939 2-9-3 0............................ ChrisCatlin 5 29
(P W D'Arcy) *a bhd: rdn and lost tch over 3f out: wl btn after* **50/1**

1m 39.31s (-0.59) **Going Correction** -0.05s/f (Stan) **9** Ran SP% **117.8**
Speed ratings (Par 97): **100,94,93,91,88 85,84,76,74**
toteswinger: 1&2 £19.40, 1&3 £2.50, 2&3 £16.30. CSF £77.09 TOTE £4.20: £1.40, £3.90, £1.10; EX 50.80.
Owner Atlantic Crossing **Bred** Newsells Park Stud Ltd **Trained** Manton, Wilts

FOCUS
A small field but this had the look of a decent little contest. Much improved form from Hula King, another on the night to make all. The form is rated around the next three home.

NOTEBOOK
Hula King(GER) shaped nicely in two Newmarket maidens and put his experience to good use by making every yard of the running, which had been a positive on the night. He does not hold any fancy entries, so it remains to be seen whether he is a handicap type or capable of holding his own in a higher grade. His jockey definitely liked him and expects him to be at his best on Polytrack. (op 10-3 tchd 5-2)
Noordhoek Kid looked green in the early stages of his debut but started to work out what was required at the end. He travelled much more kindly in this but could never get on terms after being outpaced off the final bend. His pedigree and the way he shaped in this suggests he may well be best at around 1m2f next year.
Free Thinker had shown plenty of ability already and was proven on the surface after a good effort over 1m at Lingfield last time. He was always well positioned during the race but, like the runner-up, lacked the pace to make any impact on Hula King. (op 3-1 tchd 10-3)
Gtaab had not set the world alight in two previous runs but kept on quite well when the race was all but over. He definitely shapes like a staying type for next year.
Causeway King(USA) was disappointing again but evidently not as disappointing as the other joint-favourite. (op 18-1 tchd 20-1)
Alpha Tauri(USA) does not possess a really flashy pedigree but was certainly expected to go close in this. He travelled well for a long way before looking woefully one-paced under pressure. It is too early to write him off but he will need to improve a great deal from this effort to fulfil his hype. (op 5-4 tchd 6-5)
Sham Sheer, who went through the sales ring twice for a lot of money, was always towards the rear and showed nothing to suggest he was a bargain. (op 25-1 tchd 16-1)

6424 JASPER H'CAP 1m 2f (P)
9:20 (9:23) (Class 4) (0-85,85) 3-Y-O+ **£4,857** (£1,445; £722; £360) **Stalls** Low

Form RPR
1612 **1** **Mahadee (IRE)**[21] 5836 3-8-10 **77**............................(b) JamieSpencer 13 85
(C E Brittain) *sn led: mde rest: rdn wl over 1f out: hld on wl u.p fnl f* **10/1**
3212 **2** *nk* **Dark Prospect**[15] 6033 3-8-10 **77**............................ PhilipRobinson 6 84
(M A Jarvis) *chsd wnr tl 5f out: swtchd lft and chsd wnr again wl over 1f out: ev ch ins fnl f: unable qck last 100yds* **6/4**[1]
4120 **3** *nk* **Suzi Spends (IRE)**[17] 5964 3-8-5 **72**............................ JimmyQuinn 2 78+
(H J Collingridge) *hld up towards rr: hdwy and nt clr run over 2f out: rdn wl over 1f out: swtchd rt ent fnl f: r.o wl last 100yds: nt quite rch ldng pair* **20/1**
0000 **4** *nk* **Jadalee (IRE)**[13] 6078 5-9-0 **76**............................(t) HayleyTurner 3 82+
(G A Butler) *stdd s: t.k.h: hld up and bhd: hdwy over 2f out: plld out and rdn over 1f out: r.o wl ins fnl f: nt quite rch ldrs* **20/1**
0300 **5** *1* **Prince Of Light (IRE)**[20] 5858 5-9-7 **83**............................ EddieAhern 4 87
(M Johnston) *hld up in tch: rdn and effrt on inner wl over 1f out: chsd ldng pair and drvn ent fnl f: no imp last 100yds: eased nr fin* **10/1**
000 **6** *1 ½* **Folio (IRE)**[19] 5910 8-8-13 **75**............................ StephenDonohoe 10 76
(W J Musson) *hld up in midfield: rdn and hdwy over 2f out: swtchd rt ent fnl f: kpt on same pce u.p fnl f* **14/1**
1042 **7** *nk* **Sabre Light**[12] 6134 3-8-7 **74**............................(p) MickyFenton 12 74
(A Bailey) *in tch: rdn over 3f out: hdwy u.p to chse ldrs jst over 2f out: hung lft over 1f out: one pce fnl f* **12/1**
023 **8** *3 ¼* **Sky Dive**[126] 2532 3-9-3 **84**............................ DaneO'Neill 5 78
(L M Cumani) *hld up in tch: rdn 2f out: keeping on same pce whn n.m.r ent fnl f: wl hld fnl f* **7/1**[2]
100 **9** *nk* **Bustan (IRE)**[15] 6035 9-9-4 **80**............................ AlanMunro 1 73
(G C Bravery) *t.k.h: hld up in midfield: rdn and effrt wl over 1f out: no prog* **25/1**
6062 **10** *hd* **Mujaadel (USA)**[15] 6021 3-9-4 **85**............................ RHills 7 78
(E A L Dunlop) *t.k.h: chsd ldrs: wnt 2nd 5f out tl wl over 1f out: wknd ent fnl f* **8/1**
1014 **11** *nk* **Angel Rock (IRE)**[15] 6021 3-9-1 **82**............................ DarryllHolland 8 74
(M Botti) *hld up towards rr: shkn up 4f out: rdn and hdwy on outer wl over 2f out: wknd jst over 1f out* **15/2**[3]
0300 **12** *22* **Petrosian**[12] 6129 4-8-7 **69** oh24............................ DO'Donohoe 9 17
(T T Clement) *s.i.s: hld up and bhd on outer: rdn and lost tch 3f out: t.o* **100/1**

2m 6.13s (-2.47) **Going Correction** -0.05s/f (Stan)
WFA 3 from 4yo+ 5lb **12** Ran SP% **122.3**
Speed ratings (Par 105): **107,106,106,106,105 104,104,101,101,101 100,83**
toteswinger: 1&2 £2.50, 1&3 £49.90, 2&3 £6.00. CSF £25.10 CT £319.60 TOTE £11.10: £2.90, £1.20, £4.30; EX 37.10 Place 6 £272.39, Place 5 £70.45 .
Owner Saeed Manana **Bred** Darley **Trained** Newmarket, Suffolk

FOCUS
This was possibly the best and most competitive race of the night. A few of these were far from exposed while others set a very decent level of form to aim at. However, it seemed almost unbelievable, considering earlier results, that the winner was allowed an unchallenged lead. The form looks sound.
T/Plt: £187.20 to a £1 stake. Pool: £94,179.16. 367.15 winning tickets. T/Qpdt: £18.30 to a £1 stake. Pool: £7,921.97. 319.60 winning tickets. SP

6125 NEWMARKET (ROWLEY) (R-H)
Thursday, October 2

OFFICIAL GOING: Good to firm
Wind: Fresh behind Weather: Overcast

6425 EUROPEAN BREEDERS' FUND MAIDEN STKS (C&G) 1m
2:00 (2:07) (Class 4) 2-Y-O **£6,476** (£1,927; £963; £481) **Stalls** Low

Form RPR
1 **Redwood** 2-9-0 0............................ RHills 5 88+
(B W Hills) *w'like: bit bkwd: dwlt: hld up: hdwy and swtchd rt over 1f out: hung lft and r.o to ld wl ins fnl f* **22/1**
2 **2** *¾* **Alhaque (USA)**[13] 6084 2-9-0 0............................ JamieSpencer 12 83
(P W Chapple-Hyam) *lw: chsd ldr tl led over 3f out: rdn over 2f out: hdd wl ins fnl f* **11/8**[1]
02 **3** *1 ¾* **Roman Glory (IRE)**[8] 6197 2-9-0 0............................ RichardHughes 1 79
(B J Meehan) *lw: chsd ldrs: rdn over 2f out: nt clr run ins fnl f: styd on same pce* **10/1**
0 **4** *½* **Kansai Spirit (IRE)**[13] 6084 2-9-0 0............................ RichardMullen 7 78+
(J H M Gosden) *lw: a.p: rdn over 2f out: styng on same pce whn hmpd ins fnl f* **20/1**
0 **5** *1 ¾* **Above Average (IRE)**[12] 6117 2-9-0 0............................ MichaelHills 3 74
(B W Hills) *lw: n.m.r s: hld up: hdwy over 3f out: rdn and edgd rt over 1f out: no ex fnl f* **17/2**[3]
6 *3* **Favours Brave** 2-9-0 0............................ SteveDrowne 14 67+
(J H M Gosden) *w'like: leggy: leggy: prom: rdn over 1f out: wknd fnl f* **16/1**
7 *¾* **Aspro Mavro (IRE)** 2-9-0 0............................ RobertHavlin 10 65+
(J H M Gosden) *str: gd bodied: bit bkwd: s.i.s: sn prom: rdn over 2f out: wknd fnl f* **33/1**
0 **8** *1 ½* **Double Rubble (USA)**[20] 5859 2-9-0 0............................ ShaneKelly 4 62
(J Noseda) *w'like: leggy: prom: rdn over 3f out: wknd over 1f out* **33/1**
0 **9** *¾* **Play To Win (IRE)**[20] 5859 2-9-0 0............................ DaneO'Neill 17 60
(D R C Elsworth) *lw: hld up in tch: rdn over 2f out: wknd over 1f out* **66/1**
10 *¾* **Jedi** 2-9-0 0............................ RyanMoore 6 59+
(Sir Michael Stoute) *w'like: athletic: dwlt: sn pushed into mid-div: lost pl 1/2-way: n.d after* **9/1**
11 *nk* **Shemoli** 2-9-0 0............................ PhilipRobinson 15 58+
(M A Jarvis) *lwggy: scope: bit bkwd: edgy: chsd ldrs: rdn over 2f out: wknd over 1f out* **16/1**
12 *shd* **Ruler Of All (IRE)** 2-9-0 0............................ WilliamBuick 18 58+
(B W Hills) *w'like: scope: hld up: pushed along 1/2-way: n.d* **40/1**
13 *3 ¼* **Prohibition (IRE)** 2-9-0 0............................ JMurtagh 8 50+
(W J Haggas) *leggy: bit bkwd: s.s: effrt over 3f out: wknd 2f out* **13/2**[2]
14 *1* **Strong Storm (USA)** 2-9-0 0............................ TPQueally 13 48+
(J Noseda) *str: gd bodied: bit bkwd: s.i.s: hdwy 1/2-way: wknd over 2f out* **25/1**
15 *1 ½* **Galucci (IRE)**[137] 2222 2-9-0 0............................(b[1]) PaulEddery 11 44
(Miss D Mountain) *bit bkwd led: hdd over 3f out: wknd over 2f out* **20/1**
16 *½* **Captain Flack** 2-9-0 0............................ OscarUrbina 9 43
(J A R Toller) *tall: lengthy: bit bkwd: hld up: pushed along over 4f out: sn wknd* **100/1**
17 *31* **Supa Seeker (USA)** 2-9-0 0............................ DarryllHolland 16 —
(A W Carroll) *leggy: bit bkwd: angular: s.i.s: outpcd* **100/1**

1m 36.42s (-2.18) **Going Correction** -0.20s/f (Firm) 2y crse rec **17** Ran SP% **126.3**
Speed ratings (Par 97): **102,101,99,99,97 94,93,92,91,90 90,90,86,85,84 83,52**
toteswinger: 1&2 £11.40, 1&3 £35.90, 2&3 £4.20. CSF £50.44 TOTE £30.20: £6.80, £1.40, £2.90; EX 83.30.
Owner K Abdulla **Bred** Juddmonte Farms Ltd **Trained** Lambourn, Berks

FOCUS
Often a good maiden and this looked another decent renewal, with useful types at the head of affairs - none more so than than the impressive winner, who looks an exciting prospect - and plenty of promising sorts further back. The level is set through the runner-up's debut form. They raced towards the stands' side and the main action took place close to the rail.

NOTEBOOK
Redwood ◆, by High Chaparral, first foal of a 1m-1m1f winner in France, created a really good impression in a race his owner won last year with Twice Over. He was soon out the back after taking time to find his stride, but travelled quite well for much of the way and picked up in pleasing fashion under mainly just hands and heels riding. He should be all the better for this experience and rates as a very useful prospect. His connections are considering the Horris Hill if they decide to run him again this year. (op 25-1)
Alhaque(USA), runner-up in a course maiden over 7f on his debut, had his chance but again found one too good. A host of big-race entries show the regard in which he is held, and he clearly has plenty of ability, but he has now had two reasonably tough races without winning. (op 13-8 tchd 7-4)
Roman Glory(IRE) was unsuited by a slow pace when failing to justify strong market support over 7f at Goodwood on his previous start, but this was better. He again hit a bit of a flat spot and still seems to be learning. There will be more options for him now he is qualified for a handicap mark. (op 17-2)
Kansai Spirit(IRE) moved really nicely for a lot of the way before his effort just flattened out a little late on. This was an improvement on the form he showed when seventh (behind Alhaque) over 7f here on his debut and he should progress again.

Above Average(IRE) ◆, a stablemate of the winner, caught the eye on his debut over 7f at Newbury and this was another pleasing effort. He should do better over further next year. (op 6-1 tchd 9-1)
Favours Brave ◆, by Galileo, half-brother to among others smart 1m2f winner Tuning Fork, out of a smart 1m6f winner, fared best of those to race away from the stands' side out wide and can do better. He rates as a nice middle-distance prospect for next season. (op 14-1)
Aspro Mavro(IRE), a 40,000gns son of Spartacus, closely related to Deauville Vision, a multiple 1m winner who loves the mud, showed ability but was ultimately well held. He will be one to look out for when switched to soft ground.
Double Rubble(USA) was again well held and probably needs more time. (op 28-1)
Play To Win(IRE) showed ability out wide and should come into his own in handicaps over further next year.
Jedi attracted support on course but seemed to need the experience. (op 16-1)
Prohibition(IRE) had Johnny Murtagh booked for his debut, but was never seen with a chance. (op 5-1)

6426 £250000 TATTERSALLS OCTOBER AUCTION STKS 6f

2:35 (2:41) (Class 2) 2-Y-O

£147,055 (£58,834; £29,387; £17,650; £11,736; £5,883) **Stalls** Low

Form				RPR
3232	**1**		**Kingship Spirit (IRE)**[15] 6010 2-8-13 0 ... JMurtagh 11 *(J Noseda) racd stands' side: a.p: rdn over 1f out: r.o to ld wl ins fnl f* **8/1**[2]	94
210	**2**	½	**Pyrrha**[68] 4403 2-8-2 84 ... MartinDwyer 3 *(C F Wall) lw: w ldr stands' side tl led overall over 1f out: hdd wl ins fnl f* **8/1**[2]	82
5140	**3**	½	**Imperial Guest**[4] 6305 2-8-11 86 ... TPQueally 13 *(G G Margarson) lw: racd centre: prom: hung lft and led that gp over 1f out: rdn and ev ch ins fnl f: unable qck* **66/1**	89
0010	**4**	2	**Red Kyte**[6] 6240 2-8-10 0 ... DarryllHolland 16 *(K A Ryan) led centre tl rdn and hdd over 1f out: edgd lft: styd on same pce* **66/1**	82
010	**5**	hd	**Ballyalla**[28] 5642 2-8-10 85 ... RyanMoore 20 *(R Hannon) racd centre: chsd ldrs: rdn over 2f out: styd on* **16/1**	81
3145	**6**	½	**Timeteam (IRE)**[12] 6118 2-8-7 74 ... JamieSpencer 21 *(S Kirk) racd centre: hld up: swtchd rt over 2f out: hdwy over 1f out: styd on* **25/1**	77
2421	**7**	¾	**Magaling (IRE)**[14] 6062 2-9-1 0 ... DaneO'Neill 18 *(L M Cumani) lw: racd centre: hld up in tch: rdn over 2f out: no ex towards fin* **16/1**	83
0021	**8**	¾	**Appraisal**[8] 6197 2-8-13 0 ... RichardHughes 15 *(R Hannon) lw: racd centre: chsd ldrs: rdn over 2f out: no ex fnl f* **11/1**[3]	78
6021	**9**	½	**Kyllachy Star**[14] 6037 2-8-7 0 ... PaulHanagan 2 *(R A Fahey) racd stands' side: prom: outpcd 2f out: nt clr run and swtchd rt ins fnl f: styd on* **25/1**	71
1332	**10**	nse	**Excellerator (IRE)**[34] 5448 2-8-2 78 ... DO'Donohoe 1 *(George Baker) overall ldr stands' side: rdn and hdd over 1f out: wknd ins fnl f* **11/4**[1]	66
214	**11**	shd	**Diddums**[40] 5274 2-8-7 0 ... LiamJones 24 *(W J Haggas) lw: racd far side: hld up: hdwy 2f out: led that gp 1f out: r.o: no ch w stands' side* **11/1**[3]	70+
0054	**12**	1	**Fathey (IRE)**[13] 6067 2-8-11 79 ... JamieMoriarty 7 *(R A Fahey) racd stands' side: prom: rdn over 2f out: wknd over 1f out* **100/1**	71
42	**13**	nk	**Park Lane**[18] 5929 2-8-13 0 ... MichaelHills 10 *(B W Hills) lw: stmbld s: racd stands' side: hld up: rdn and hung rt over 2f out: nt trble ldrs* **11/1**[3]	73
1003	**14**	nk	**Fault**[34] 5466 2-9-1 86 ... SteveDrowne 25 *(R Charlton) lw: racd far side: prom: led that gp over 2f out: rdn and hdd 1f out: no ex* **40/1**	74+
0222	**15**	½	**Hi Shinko**[17] 5959 2-8-7 0 ... TGMcLaughlin 22 *(B R Millman) racd far side: trckd ldrs: racd keenly: rdn over 2f out: wkng whn hung lft ins fnl f* **100/1**	64+
0033	**16**	shd	**Effort**[9] 6193 2-9-1 99 ... GregFairley 23 *(M Johnston) on toes: racd far side: chsd ldrs: rdn and ev ch 1f out: wknd towards fin f* **16/1**	72+
100	**17**	nk	**Queen Of Thebes (IRE)**[28] 5642 2-8-4 0 ow2 ... RichardMullen 27 *(G L Moore) racd far side: chsd ldrs: rdn over 2f out: styd on same pce appr fnl f* **25/1**	60+
0235	**18**	nk	**Peper Harow (IRE)**[24] 5746 2-8-0 0 ... FrancisNorton 8 *(M D I Usher) racd stands' side: prom: rdn over 2f out: wknd over 1f out* **80/1**	55
3323	**19**	½	**Blue Arctic**[10] 6172 2-8-0 0 ... LukeMorris 6 *(J M P Eustace) on toes: racd s side: hld up: hdwy u.p over 2f out: wknd over 1f out* **66/1**	54
4016	**20**	½	**Grand Honour (IRE)**[68] 4402 2-8-9 88 ... JimmyQuinn 14 *(P Howling) swtg: racd centre: hld up: rdn over 2f out: n.d* **100/1**	61
2	**21**	shd	**Master Of Disguise**[141] 2098 2-8-7 0 ... PhilipRobinson 4 *(C G Cox) racd stands' side: prom: rdn: hung rt and wknd 2f out* **28/1**	59
042	**22**	½	**Spinners End (IRE)**[8] 6212 2-8-13 0 ... PatCosgrave 30 *(K R Burke) racd far side: chsd ldrs: rdn over 2f out: wknd fnl f* **50/1**	63+
2100	**23**	½	**Smokey Storm**[62] 4588 2-9-3 96 ... (b[1]) AlanMunro 29 *(W Jarvis) led far side over 3f: sn rdn: wknd fnl f* **33/1**	66+
1300	**24**	4	**Mister Laurel**[21] 5827 2-8-13 84 ... TonyHamilton 5 *(R A Fahey) racd stands' side: mid-div: rdn and wknd over 2f out* **66/1**	50
5	**25**	½	**Seek N' Destroy (IRE)**[18] 5929 2-8-13 0 ... WilliamBuick 26 *(B W Hills) lw: racd far side: prom: rdn over 2f out: wknd over 1f out* **25/1**	48+
101	**26**	nk	**Cool Art (IRE)**[16] 5997 2-9-1 75 ... LDettori 17 *(S A Callaghan) racd centre: hld up: rdn over 2f out: wknd over 1f out* **33/1**	49+
04	**27**	1 ¼	**Turkish Lokum**[17] 5959 2-8-2 0 ... ChrisCatlin 9 *(J M P Eustace) on toes: racd stands' side: hld up: rdn and wknd over 2f out* **100/1**	33
02	**28**	37	**Jatman**[35] 5416 2-8-7 0 ... ShaneKelly 28 *(Mrs L Stubbs) racd far side: s.i.s: outpcd* **66/1**	—

69.96 secs (-2.24) **Going Correction** -0.20s/f (Firm) **28** Ran SP% **133.3**
Speed ratings (Par 101): **106,105,104,102,101 101,100,99,98,98 98,96,96,96,95 95,94,94,93,93 93,92,91,86,85 85,83,34**
toteswinger: 1&2 £42.50, 1&3 £46.70, 2&3 £191.50. CSF £63.33 TOTE £9.60: £3.20, £3.40, £57.30; EX 105.30.
Owner Saeed Suhail **Bred** Gary O'Reilly **Trained** Newmarket, Suffolk

FOCUS
An ordinary renewal of this valuable sales race, rather short on quality this year. They split into three groups early, with nine going far side, eight up the middle, and 11 on the stands' side. As it turned out, the near side was the place to be, and those far side were at a big disadvantage, with the nearest horse from that group finishing 11th. The form is rock solid but limited.

NOTEBOOK
Kingship Spirit(IRE) had been noted carrying his head high on three of his four starts to date, and had been a beaten favourite on all of his runs prior to this, including when second at odds of 2-5 in a 5f maiden at Beverley last time. However, he had the assistance of the brilliant Johnny Murtagh, who was in the saddle on the one previous occasion the horse really seemed to knuckle down and race (at the July course two starts back), and there was nothing wrong with his attitude this time. Despite the big field, he was out in the open for long enough if he was going to shirk it, but he responded well to pressure to reel in Pyrrha, who had looked the winner when sent to the front, and this was a very useful effort conceding 11lb to that rival. There are no plans for him - this was the plan - but he is expected to stay 7f. He is in the Horses In Training Sales. (op 10-1)
Pyrrha's last run in a Group 3 at Ascot could be excused as she was badly hampered just as she tried to make a move, and she confirmed the potential she showed when an impressive winner of a Newbury maiden earlier in the season with a gallant effort in defeat. She was in front on the stands' side fully two furlongs out, and it is understandable they would want to make use of her stamina, as she should stay 7f, but she got tired late on having been off the track for two months. A good-looking filly, she has the size and scope to make a nice three-year-old. (op 5-1 tchd 9-1, 10-1 in places)
Imperial Guest, dropped a furlong in trip, fared best of those to race up the middle of the track early, although he did edge over to the stands' side late on.
Red Kyte was second best of those who raced up the middle and this was an improvement on the form she showed when only tenth in the Watership Down Stud Sales race.
Ballyalla, down the field in a Listed race at Salisbury last time, ran a solid race in defeat to fare third best of those up the middle. (op 20-1)
Timeteam(IRE) had his chance once switched and this was a respectable effort (op 33-1)
Magaling(IRE) found this tougher than the Yarmouth maiden he won and had a big weight. (op 14-1)
Appraisal had the run of the race when winning a 7f maiden at Goodwood on his previous start and was well held this time. (tchd 10-1, 12-1 in places)
Kyllachy Star bolted up in testing ground at Ayr last time and probably found conditions a little quicker than ideal.
Excellerator(IRE) was well below form and was almost certainly unsuited by the quick surface. She was easily best in on official figures and appeared the one to beat off such a light weight, but she was in trouble two out and did not look comfortable on the ground, the quickest she has encountered to date. She should do better back over 5f on easy ground, but it remains to be seen which way she will go now (op 7-2 tchd 5-2, 4-1 in places)
Diddums fared best of those on the far side, yet finished only 11th overall. (op 12-1 tchd 10-1)
Park Lane was below the form he showed when second at Goodwood last time, but stumbled at the start and can be given another chance. (op 10-1 tchd 17-2)
Fault was second best on the stands' side, but he is well exposed now.
Hi Shinko might do better over 5f on easier ground. (op 66-1)
Master Of Disguise had been off the track since running second at Bath in May and he ruined his chance by continually hanging. Official explanation: jockey said colt hung right throughout (tchd 33-1)

6427 NOEL MURLESS STKS (LISTED RACE) 1m 6f

3:10 (3:17) (Class 1) 3-Y-O

£22,708 (£8,608; £4,308; £2,148; £1,076; £540) **Stalls** Centre

Form				RPR
1622	**1**		**Savarain**[64] 4519 3-9-0 104 ... LDettori 5 *(L M Cumani) hld up: hdwy over 3f out: rdn to chse ldr over 1f out: led ins fnl f: styd on wl* **10/11**[1]	113+
2001	**2**	1 ¾	**Fiulin**[14] 6061 3-9-0 95 ... RyanMoore 2 *(M Botti) lw: led after 1f: rdn over 1f out: hdd and unable qckn ins fnl f* **7/2**[2]	108
0311	**3**	11	**The Betchworth Kid**[20] 5853 3-9-0 100 ... JamieSpencer 4 *(M L W Bell) hld up: hdwy over 3f out: rdn and hung rt over 2f out: wknd over 1f out* **9/2**[3]	92
1144	**4**	3	**Resplendent Light**[19] 5927 3-9-0 97 ... MartinDwyer 1 *(W R Muir) prom: rdn over 2f out: wknd over 1f out* **10/1**	88
6560	**5**	1 ¾	**Silk Affair (IRE)**[81] 4006 3-8-9 94 ... EdwardCreighton 6 *(M G Quinlan) prom: chsd ldr over 10f out: rdn and wknd over 2f out* **25/1**	81
0421	**6**	28	**Lough Diver (IRE)**[18] 5931 3-9-0 83 ... MichaelHills 7 *(M H Tompkins) led 1f: chsd ldrs tl rdn and wknd over 3f out* **33/1**	46

2m 51.83s (-6.67) **Going Correction** -0.20s/f (Firm) course record **6** Ran SP% **108.7**
Speed ratings (Par 109): **111,110,103,102,101 85**
toteswinger: 1&2 £1.40, 1&3 £1.70, 2&3 £1.90. CSF £3.97 TOTE £1.80: £1.20, £2.20; EX 4.10.
Owner Ronchalon Racing (UK) Ltd **Bred** Fittocks Stud **Trained** Newmarket, Suffolk

FOCUS
Several progressive handicappers lined up for this Listed contest. They went a good pace and the first two finished clear. Savarain has been rated to form, with Fiulin up 6lb.

NOTEBOOK
Savarain ◆, runner-up off marks of 96 and 99 respectively over 1m4f at Royal Ascot and Glorious Goodwood, posted a classy performance on this step up in trip. Despite being held up on this occasion (usually ridden prominently), and allowing Fiulin to poach a lead, he was well on top at the line. He got a nice run against the far rail with half a mile to run, and, despite not picking up immediately, began to close once Dettori got serious, it being clear from a furlong out he was going to win. He is a fine-looking individual and any further progress over the winter will see him challenging for Group honours next season. Luca Cumani feels he will stay 2m and as a result he may develop into a cup horse. (tchd 5-4 in places)
Fiulin recorded a career-best when winning off a mark of a mark of 89 over this trip at Yarmouth last time and it was no surprise to see Moore send him off in front. He gradually wound it up and briefly looked to have the winner in trouble, but was eventually worn down. There may well be more to come from this progressive son of Galileo. (tchd 4-1 in places)
The Betchworth Kid's recent improvement has coincided with racing on soft ground, his impressive Doncaster victory seeing him put up 10lb to a mark of 100, so he held every chance at the weights, but this faster surface would not have been to his liking. He moved through to have every chance just over three out, but seemed reluctant to fully let himself down. This run should not be held against him and the ground is sure to come in his favour again before long. (op 4-1)
Resplendent Light, a dual handicap winner in June, has twice finished fourth in minor French Listed races and he needed to find improvement from somewhere to trouble the principals in this. He could find no more from well over a furlong out and may not be the easiest to place now. (op 7-1)
Silk Affair(IRE), outclassed in the Irish Oaks latest, has never run on fast ground before and she was beaten some way out. (tchd 20-1)
Lough Diver(IRE) made hard enough work of winning a weak maiden at Goodwood last time and it was no surprise to see him struggle. (op 25-1)

6428 SOMERVILLE TATTERSALL STKS (GROUP 3) (C&G) 7f

3:45 (3:48) (Class 1) 2-Y-O

£34,062 (£12,912; £6,462; £3,222; £1,614; £810) **Stalls** Low

Form				RPR
12	**1**		**Ashram (IRE)**[26] 5696 2-8-12 0 ... RyanMoore 1 *(J W Hills) lw: hld up: hdwy over 2f out: led over 1f out: edgd lft: rdn clr* **14/1**	113+

1 **2** 4 ½ **Control Zone (IRE)**[12] 6122 2-8-12 0............................ JamieSpencer 2 101
(B J Meehan) *lw: stdd s: hld up: hdwy over 3f out: led and edgd lft over 2f out: rdn and hdd over 1f out: no ex* **4/1**[2]
413 **3** 1 ¾ **Derbaas (USA)**[34] 5462 2-8-12 100.. RHills 9 97
(E A L Dunlop) *prom: chsd ldr 4f out: rdn and ev ch over 2f out: edgd lft: styd on same pce fnl f* **6/1**[3]
631 **4** nk **Akhenaten**[19] 5882 2-8-12 84.. SamHitchcott 4 96
(M R Channon) *chsd ldrs: outpcd over 2f out: styd on ins fnl f* **33/1**
11 **5** 2 ¼ **Wingwalker**[15] 6025 2-8-12 107... TPQueally 6 91+
(H R A Cecil) *lw: racd keenly: trckd ldr 3f: remained handy: stmbld wl over 1f out: sn wknd* **10/11**[1]
0300 **6** 13 **Dabbers Chief (USA)**[21] 5827 2-8-12 93......................... WilliamBuick 3 58
(B W Hills) *prom: rdn 1/2-way: wknd over 2f out* **33/1**
1 **7** 2 **North East Corner (USA)**[13] 6084 2-8-12 0.................. MichaelHills 7 53+
(B W Hills) *led: rdn and hdd over 2f out: wknd and eased over 1f out* **13/2**

1m 22.39s (-3.01) **Going Correction** -0.20s/f (Firm) 2y crse rec **7** Ran SP% **112.6**
Speed ratings (Par 105): **109,103,101,101,98 84,81**
toteswinger: 1&2 £5.40, 1&3 £5.80, 2&3 £2.80. CSF £66.48 TOTE £15.80: £4.40, £2.40; EX 62.80.
Owner Mountgrange Stud **Bred** Waterford Hall Stud **Trained** Upper Lambourn, Berks

FOCUS
Some good horses have won this over the years, Where Or When and Milk It Mick being the pick of them, and outsider Ashram scored in the style of a very smart performer, rated the joint best winner of this in the past decade. The fourth is probably the long-term key to the form. Wingwalker was very disappointing, 16lb off his best.

NOTEBOOK
Ashram(IRE) ◆'s task was made easier with the below-par running of Wingwalker, but given the manner of his victory, he would probably have won regardless of whether that one ran his race. A taking winner on debut before suffering some interference when beaten in a conditions race at Kempton, he was a bit slow into stride but seemed happy enough out the back and settled nicely. Moved wide to challenge, he quickened well to lead over a furlong out, and, despite still showing signs of immaturity, strode clear to win impressively. John Hills reportedly has nothing that can go with him at home and his next race will be the Dewhurst. Things will obviously be tougher there, but his acceleration will stand him in good stead, assuming the ground is decent, and it is not hard to see him running a big race. (tchd 12-1)
Control Zone(IRE), a cosy winner of a fair Newbury maiden on his debut, comes from a yard whose juveniles often benefit greatly from their initial run and he took a big step forward in finishing second. Sent on plenty soon enough, he came onto the rail and briefly looked the winner, but Ashram was soon at his quarters and he was ultimately left trailing. He too still looked green and further improvement is likely. (op 11-2 tchd 7-2)
Derbaas(USA) had finished third in a decent Listed contest at Salisbury last time (both the winner and second placed in Group 2 company next time) and he was well positioned if good enough, but was found wanting for pace on this drop in trip. He will be helped by a return to further but probably is not up to this level. (op 8-1 tchd 9-1)
Akhenaten, rated just 84, is well regarded by connections and got off the mark at the third attempt when scoring tidily at Chester last month. This represented a big step up and he was dismissed in the betting, but it did not prevent him from running a good race. He has plenty of size and should make a better three-year-old at trips of 1m and further. (tchd 40-1)
Wingwalker, who won despite pulling hard at Sandown last time, again compromised his chance by pulling to post and racing freely in the race itself. He found the way blocked when trying to make a move and was already beaten when stumbling around two out. He plugged on, looking rather ungainly in the process, and, although this was the fastest ground he has tackled, he has a fair bit to prove now. Official explanation: jockey said colt stumbled 2f out (op 4-6 tchd Evens)
North East Corner(USA) had won a course maiden on debut, beating the runner-up in today's opener, looked fitter this time and he looked one of the more interesting ones. Soon in front, he came under pressure well over two furlongs out and quickly surrendered the lead. There may well have been something amiss. Official explanation: jockey said colt stopped quickly (op 17-2 tchd 9-1)

6429 G4S ROUS STKS (LISTED RACE) 5f
4:20 (4:22) (Class 1) 3-Y-0+
£24,978 (£9,468; £4,738; £2,362; £1,183; £594) **Stalls** Low

Form RPR
6114 **1** **Peace Offering (IRE)**[40] 5259 8-8-12 108.................. AdrianTNicholls 6 105
(D Nicholls) *chsd ldr: rdn 1/2-way: led ins fnl f: r.o* **8/1**
3003 **2** ½ **Siren's Gift**[19] 5890 4-8-7 95...(b) WilliamBuick 13 99
(A M Balding) *chsd ldrs: rdn and ev ch ins fnl f: r.o* **13/2**[3]
4320 **3** 1 **Princess Ellis**[22] 5793 4-8-7 87.................................. JimmyQuinn 3 95
(E J Alston) *led: rdn over 1f out: hdd and unable qck ins fnl f* **40/1**
0433 **4** hd **Matsunosuke**[5] 6285 6-8-12 94.. AlanMunro 9 99
(A B Coogan) *s.i.s: hld up: r.o ins fnl f: nt rch ldrs* **16/1**
0551 **5** ¾ **Judd Street**[5] 6290 6-8-12 96.......................................(b) StephenCarson 1 97
(Eve Johnson Houghton) *lw: chsd ldrs: rdn over 1f out: styd on same pce ins fnl f* **9/2**[2]
0500 **6** ½ **Orpsie Boy (IRE)**[5] 6285 5-8-12 94.............................. LukeMorris 8 95
(N P Littmoden) *mid-div: rdn over 1f out: r.o ins fnl f: nt trble ldrs* **40/1**
0523 **7** hd **Crimson Fern (IRE)**[19] 5899 4-8-7 96.......................... TGMcLaughlin 4 89
(M S Saunders) *on toes: s.i.s: hld up: r.o ins fnl f: nvr trbld ldrs* **10/1**
000 **8** ¾ **Day By Day**[40] 5275 4-8-7 91...(b) MartinDwyer 5 86
(B J Meehan) *chsd ldrs: rdn over 1f out: no ex fnl f* **66/1**
3602 **9** nk **Hoh Mike (IRE)**[16] 6005 4-8-12 106............................ JamieSpencer 12 90
(M L W Bell) *lw: sn pushed along in rr: nvr nrr* **9/1**
0646 **10** ¾ **Rowe Park**[12] 6121 5-8-12 104...(p) DaneO'Neill 10 88
(Mrs L C Jewell) *s.i.s: a in rr* **11/1**
1131 **11** nk **Main Aim**[21] 5831 3-8-12 100....................................... RyanMoore 11 87
(Sir Michael Stoute) *hld up: effrt over 1f out: n.d* **5/2**[1]
-343 **P** **Starlit Sands**[32] 5553 3-8-7 102..................................... DO'Donohoe 7 —
(Sir Mark Prescott) *p.u fnl 4f* **10/1**

56.87 secs (-2.23) **Going Correction** -0.20s/f (Firm) **12** Ran SP% **120.0**
Speed ratings (Par 111): **109,108,106,106,105 104,103,102,102,101 100,—**
toteswinger: 1&2 £11.60, 1&3 £23.90, 2&3 £43.50. CSF £59.53 TOTE £7.70: £2.40, £2.50, £9.70; EX 54.80.
Owner Lady O'Reilly **Bred** Chevington Stud **Trained** Sessay, N Yorks

FOCUS
A weak Listed sprint and it paid to race handy. They raced stands' side.

NOTEBOOK
Peace Offering(IRE) has been around a while now, but he has looked as good as ever on occasions this year. He was unable to dominate, as he often likes to, but got a good lead off Princess Ellis through the early stages and battled on gamely when strongly challenged to narrowly gain his third win from five starts this season. He may now be aimed at a race at Dundalk. (op 6-1)
Siren's Gift was produced with her chance but simply found one too strong. She has a modest strike-rate for a horse of her ability, but she didn't seem to do too much wrong. (op 8-1)
Princess Ellis took then along early tight against the near-side rail and had her chance.
Matsunosuke has struggled for winning opportunities this season, but this was a solid effort in defeat as he fared best of those to race off the pace.
Judd Street, struggled to pick up when it mattered and if anything looked a little intimidated by Princess Ellis, who he had tracked throughout. (op 11-2 tchd 6-1)
Orpsie Boy(IRE) basically wasn't good enough, but he was going on at the finish and should do better back at 6f. (op 50-1)
Crimson Fern(IRE) travelled well off the pace, but the leaders didn't come back. (op 14-1)
Main Aim, successful off 90 in a 6f handicap at Doncaster on his previous start, was stuck out wide on his first try over 5f and failed to run his race. He should appreciate a return to further and looks the type to make a better four-year-old. Official explanation: jockey said colt had no more to give (tchd 11-4, 3-1 in places)
Starlit Sands was pulled up as if something was amiss. Official explanation: jockey said filly felt wrong behind (op 11-1)

6430 EUROPEAN BREEDERS' FUND FILLIES' H'CAP 6f
4:55 (4:55) (Class 2) (0-100,97) 3-Y-0+
£12,462 (£3,732; £1,866; £934; £466; £234) **Stalls** Low

Form RPR
5124 **1** **Masada (IRE)**[6] 6239 3-8-8 87.. MartinDwyer 8 93
(B J Meehan) *b: lw: chsd ldrs: rdn and edgd lft fr over 1f out: led 1f out: r.o* **7/2**[2]
10-3 **2** hd **Bastakiya (IRE)**[97] 3460 3-8-12 91.................................. RyanMoore 1 97
(J H M Gosden) *lw: on toes: chsd ldrs: nt clr run over 1f out: rdn and hmpd sn after: r.o* **4/1**[3]
0511 **3** 2 ¾ **Angus Newz**[19] 5884 5-8-12 90.. FrancisNorton 6 87
(M Quinn) *led: rdn and edgd lft over 1f out: sn hdd and hmpd: no ex ins fnl f* **3/1**[1]
5034 **4** 4 **Manzila (FR)**[9] 6184 5-9-5 97.................................... AdrianTNicholls 4 81
(D Nicholls) *prom: lost pl over 4f out: n.d after* **9/1**
036 **5** ¾ **Temple Of Thebes (IRE)**[39] 5310 3-8-8 87............... RichardHughes 3 69
(E A L Dunlop) *w ldr: rdn and ev ch over 1f out: n.m.r sn after: eased* **4/1**[3]
600 **6** 22 **Cape**[54] 4854 5-8-13 91... JamieSpencer 7 2
(P Howling) *lw sn outpcd* **7/1**

1m 10.0s (-2.20) **Going Correction** -0.20s/f (Firm) course record
WFA 3 from 4yo+ 1lb **6** Ran SP% **109.7**
Speed ratings (Par 96): **106,105,102,96,95 66**
toteswinger: 1&2 £3.00, 1&3 £2.70, 2&3 £3.00. CSF £16.81 CT £41.51 TOTE £4.50: £2.40, £2.50; EX 13.40 Trifecta £90.40 Pool: £389.79 - 3.19 winning units..
Owner Ballymacoll Stud **Bred** Ballymacoll Stud Farm Ltd **Trained** Manton, Wilts
■ Stewards' Enquiry : Ryan Moore caution: careless riding

FOCUS
There was quite a rough finish to this decent fillies' handicap, with the front three getting very close from a furlong out. Just ordinary form for the grade.

NOTEBOOK
Masada(IRE), a slightly unlucky fourth at Ascot the previous weekend (slowly away and hampered before running on), was off the same mark and showed a gritty attitude to score. She has been keen in the past and it was pleasing to see her stick it out so well. (op 10-3)
Bastakiya(IRE) returned from over a year off to finish third in a conditions race at the July course this summer, but had been absent again since. Moore tried to force his way through over a furlong out, and she did not shirk the issue, but she was never quite getting there. She could not be called unlucky as she had enough time to pass, although the bumping could hardly have helped. (op 5-1)
Angus Newz is an admirable performer and looked as good as ever when winning a Listed contest at Chester last time. She was not able to get things her own way though, with Temple Of Thebes racing alongside for much of the way, and she was already looking booked for third when hampered inside the final furlong. Her best efforts have come on a slower surface. (op 11-4 tchd 10-3, 7-2 in places)
Manzila(FR) was under pressure early and kept plodding away to take fourth. (op 6-1)
Temple Of Thebes(IRE), who ran well below form in soft ground at Goodwood last time, showed speed for a long way but was already beaten when tightened up on the rail. Official explanation: jockey said filly hung badly left (op 5-1)
Cape Official explanation: trainer said mare was unsuited by the good to firm ground

6431 NGK SPARK PLUGS / TATAMI H'CAP 1m
5:30 (5:30) (Class 3) (0-95,95) 3-Y-0+
£9,346 (£2,799; £1,399; £700; £349; £175) **Stalls** Low

Form RPR
2120 **1** **Willow Dancer (IRE)**[26] 5695 4-8-11 85.........................(p) SteveDrowne 10 95
(W R Swinburn) *chsd ldr tl led over 3f out: drvn out* **9/2**[2]
2224 **2** ¾ **Ace Of Hearts**[19] 5903 9-9-4 95................................. JackMitchell(3) 8 103
(C F Wall) *a.p: chsd wnr over 2f out: rdn over 1f out: styd on* **7/2**[1]
6004 **3** 2 ¼ **Daaweitza**[12] 6130 5-8-8 82.. TGMcLaughlin 4 85
(B Ellison) *hld up: rdn over 2f out: hdwy over 1f out: nt rch ldrs* **10/1**
6410 **4** hd **Habshan (USA)**[65] 4509 8-8-13 87................................. MartinDwyer 2 89+
(C F Wall) *hld up: swtchd rt over 2f out: r.o ins fnl f: nrst fin* **8/1**
5533 **5** nse **Formation (USA)**[26] 5695 3-8-8 85............................. RichardHughes 3 87
(E A L Dunlop) *chsd ldrs: rdn and flashed tail fr over 1f out: no ex* **11/2**[3]
6 9 **Don Julio A (ARG)**[152] 4-9-7 95... KShea 5 77
(M F De Kock, South Africa) *s.i.s: hld up: hdwy 1/2-way: rdn and wknd over 1f out* **20/1**
213- **7** 7 **Direct Debit (IRE)**[426] 4134 5-8-7 81.......................... JamieSpencer 1 46
(M L W Bell) *hld up: racd keenly: wknd wl over 1f out: eased* **9/2**[2]
1014 **8** 3 ¼ **Summer Gold (IRE)**[54] 4841 4-8-8 82............................ PatCosgrave 11 40
(E J Alston) *sn led: hdd over 3f out: rdn and wknd 2f out* **8/1**
-213 **9** 2 ½ **Ramaad**[96] 3475 3-8-7 84.. PaulEddery 6 36
(Miss D Mountain) *prom: rdn over 3f out: wknd over 2f out* **25/1**

1m 36.0s (-2.60) **Going Correction** -0.20s/f (Firm)
WFA 3 from 4yo+ 3lb **9** Ran SP% **113.9**
Speed ratings (Par 107): **105,104,102,101,101 92,85,82,80**
toteswinger: 1&2 £4.50, 1&3 £12.30, 2&3 £9.00. CSF £20.32 CT £148.03 TOTE £5.40: £1.80, £1.50, £3.60; EX 21.90 Place 6: £298.99 Place 5: £163.20 .
Owner Mrs G Godfrey & Mrs A Horner **Bred** Exors Of The Late R E Sangster **Trained** Aldbury, Herts

FOCUS
A fair handicap. Sound form, the winner up 3lb.

NOTEBOOK
Willow Dancer(IRE), who was well supported beforehand, bounced back from a below-par effort behind Premio Loco at Kempton last time. Always travelling strongly, he went on over three out and was moved onto the rail by Drowne. He looked like winning comfortably a furlong and a half out, but it got tough and in the end he was all out to score. Forgetting his last run, he has been progressing all season and there is no reason why he should not continue to pay his way. (op 7-1)
Ace Of Hearts, below form on soft ground at Goodwood last time, had earlier been running extremely well in defeat and this was another good effort. He is currently 5lb higher than when last winning, but the veteran could find a similar race if continuing to hold his form. (op 4-1)
Daaweitza, who got going too late over course and distance last time, was once again putting in his best work at the finish, just getting there for third. He is weighted to win again. (op 8-1 tchd 15-2)
Habshan(USA), 4lb higher than when winning at the July course two starts back, did not seem overly happy around Goodwood last time and this was little better. He ran on having been given a little too much to do and can be rated a tad better than the bare form. (op 9-1 tchd 10-1)

The Form Book, Raceform Ltd, Compton, RG20 6NL

Formation(USA) has his quirks but has been running well and finished ahead of the winner at Kempton last time. He was unable to reverse the form but would probably have been third had Hughes been a bit more vigorous inside the final furlong. (op 8-1)
Don Julio A(ARG), not beaten far in Group 1 company in Argentina last season, was ultimately well held on this British debut, but ran well to a point and should strip fitter next time. (op 10-1)
Direct Debit(IRE) was keen on this return from an absence of 14 months and seemed pretty tired inside the final furlong. (op 4-1 tchd 7-2)
T/Plt: £375.60 to a £1 stake. Pool: £88,721.52. 172.41 winning tickets. T/Qpdt: £105.80 to a £1 stake. Pool: £4,418.98. 30.90 winning tickets. CR

5994 LINGFIELD (L-H)

Friday, October 3

OFFICIAL GOING: Standard
Wind: Moderate, against Weather: Fine but cloudy

6432 MARSH GREEN MAIDEN AUCTION FILLIES' STKS — 1m (P)
2:30 (2:30) (Class 6) 2-Y-O — **£2,266** (£674; £337; £168) **Stalls** High

Form — RPR
25 **1** **Uvinza**[22] 5828 2-8-8 0 .... PaulDoe 11 71+
(W J Knight) *nt that wl away: sn prom on outer: wnt 2nd 3f out: led wl over 1f out: rdn ent fnl f: sn in command* **1/2**[1]
3420 **2** *1* **Young Dottie**[53] 4925 2-8-6 70 .... CatherineGannon 5 67
(P M Phelan) *t.k.h early: hld up in rr: prog over 3f out: rdn to chse wnr over 1f out: tried to chal but readily hld after* **9/1**[3]
00 **3** *¾* **Nesayem (IRE)**[16] 6016 2-8-10 0 .... RichardMullen 4 69
(D M Simcock) *trckd ldrs: pushed along over 3f out: prog over 2f out: styd on fr over 1f out: nvr able to chal* **66/1**
02 **4** *hd* **It's Dubai Dolly**[29] 5650 2-8-6 0 .... WandersonD'Avila 2 69+
(A J Lidderdale) *prom: pushed along on inner and nt qckn over 2f out: n.m.r and swtchd rt jst over 1f out: styd on again fnl f* **8/1**[2]
6400 **5** *nk* **The Saucy Snipe**[32] 5567 2-8-8 55 .... StephenCarson 12 66
(P Winkworth) *in tch in midfield: outpcd and rdn over 3f out: styd on wl again fr over 1f out: nrst fin* **50/1**
0 **6** *2¾* **Diktalina**[29] 5643 2-8-10 0 .... MartinDwyer 8 66+
(W R Muir) *last of main gp and pushed along after 3f: detached 3f out: styd on fr over 1f out: nrst fin* **25/1**
0004 **7** *5* **Caressing**[25] 5746 2-8-12 59 .... PatDobbs 3 53
(R Hannon) *wl in rr: outpcd fr 3f out: no ch after: modest late prog* **14/1**
00 **8** *shd* **Deckchair**[16] 6016 2-8-8 0 ....(v[1]) FrancisNorton 10 49
(H J Collingridge) *led to wl over 1f out: wknd rapidly fnl f* **66/1**
0 **9** *2¾* **Miss Jabba (IRE)**[19] 5939 2-8-8 0 .... SaleemGolam 7 43
(Miss J Feilden) *mostly chsd ldr to 3f out: wknd rapidly over 1f out* **66/1**
0000 **10** *3¾* **Fleur De'Lion (IRE)**[39] 5364 2-9-0 52 .... LPKeniry 1 46+
(S Kirk) *snatched up in midfield 5f out: dropped to last trio after: no ch fnl 3f* **33/1**
11 *2½* **Regal Wave** 2-8-10 0 .... ChrisCatlin 6 31
(P F I Cole) *s.i.s: sn t.o in last* **11/1**
00 **12** *2½* **Kutanga (USA)**[14] 6089 2-8-12 0 .... TPQueally 9 27
(R M H Cowell) *t.k.h early: hld up bhd ldrs: rdn on wd outside 3f out: wknd rapidly* **50/1**

1m 37.52s (-0.68) **Going Correction** -0.175s/f (Stan) — **12** Ran SP% **118.0**
Speed ratings (Par 90): **96,95,94,94,93 91,86,85,83,79 76,74**
toteswinger: 1&2 £2.50, 1&3 £22.00, 2&3 £69.70. CSF £5.23 TOTE £1.40: £1.10, £1.80, £17.70; EX 6.80 Trifecta £82.90 Pool: £555.07 - 4.95 winning units..
Owner Mrs Alison Ruggles **Bred** Mrs A Ruggles **Trained** Patching, W Sussex

FOCUS
Modest previous form except for the odds-on winner, and she was probably not at her best. The runner-up is rated to her recent mark.

NOTEBOOK
Uvinza second-last out of the stalls but soon recovering, had to be kept up to her work but she was idling in front and can improve on this as she gains experience. Her trainer rates her highly and will probably put her away for the winter to contest a decent race early next year. (op 2-5)
Young Dottie, who ran a solid race despite having to be switched wide, stayed the mile well. Though probably flattered to finish so close, she is worth another try in nursery company over this longer distance. (op 10-1 tchd 11-1)
Nesayem(IRE) ran her best race to date and seems to be coming to hand just in time for the switch to handicaps.
It's Dubai Dolly was trapped in a pocket off the home turn and lost momentum by having to be pulled wide. She was recovering well at the finish and looks capable of finding a race. (op 7-1 tchd 13-2)
The Saucy Snipe stayed this longer trip well, but lack of early pace was again her undoing.
Diktalina is taking time to mature, but she seems to need at least a mile and was not knocked about. (op 33-1)
Caressing got too far back early on, and only began to recover too late, with Dobbs reporting that she would not face the kickback. Official explanation: jockey said filly did not face the kickback (tchd 16-1)
Deckchair, true to her name, folded up quickly in the straight despite the first-time visor. (op 50-1)

6433 THREE BRIDGES (S) STKS — 7f (P)
3:00 (3:00) (Class 6) 3-Y-O — **£1,978** (£584; £292) **Stalls** Low

Form — RPR
6004 **1** **I Confess**[11] 6178 3-8-7 70 ....(b) RichardEvans(5) 10 66
(P D Evans) *mde virtually all: asserted over runner-up over 1f out: rdn out* **3/1**[1]
0003 **2** *1½* **Blues Minor (IRE)**[91] 3675 3-8-12 69 .... PatDobbs 11 62
(R Hannon) *w wnr to wl over 1f out: nt qckn after but in n.d of losing 2nd pl* **11/2**[2]
1004 **3** *2¼* **Deal Flipper**[11] 6173 3-8-13 63 .... StephenCarson 4 57
(P Winkworth) *taken down early: hld up in midfield: effrt over 2f out: prog and swtchd ins jst over 1f out: kpt on to take 3rd fnl 100yds: no imp on ldng pair* **11/1**
0000 **4** *shd* **Brazilian Brush (IRE)**[15] 6046 3-9-4 61 ....(t) TravisBlock 3 62
(H Morrison) *trckd ldrs: effrt over 2f out: kpt on one pce fr over 1f out* **9/1**
0-20 **5** *hd* **Royal Sovereign (IRE)**[44] 5186 3-8-12 60 .... OscarUrbina 8 55
(G C H Chung) *taken down early: trckd ldng pair: rdn and nt qckn wl over 1f out: one pce after* **8/1**[3]
0 **6** *1¾* **Tropical Tradition (IRE)**[17] 5995 3-8-12 0 .... MartinDwyer 2 50
(D W P Arbuthnot) *dwlt: pushed along towards rr after 3f: sme prog on inner 2f out: pushed along again and one pce over 1f out* **33/1**
2251 **7** *1½* **All In The Red (IRE)**[11] 6173 3-8-11 70 ....(p) KylieManser(7) 1 52
(Miss Gay Kelleway) *dwlt: struggling in rr over 4f out: modest late prog u.p* **3/1**[1]
2650 **8** *4½* **Warden Fizz**[10] 6192 3-8-9 70 .... MarcHalford(3) 14 34
(D R C Elsworth) *prom on outer: disputing 3rd whn rn wd bnd 2f out: wknd* **20/1**
4050 **9** *4½* **Jalons Bridewell**[46] 5141 3-8-12 56 .... TPQueally 7 22
(M Quinn) *trckd ldrs: lost pl and rdn 3f out: grad wknd* **16/1**
00 **10** *5* **Sidestreet**[202] 897 3-8-12 0 ....(v[1]) ChrisCatlin 12 9
(K McAuliffe) *t.k.h early: hld up in tch and racd wd: wknd over 2f out* **50/1**
00 **11** *14* **Stoneacre Paddy (IRE)**[28] 5679 3-8-12 0 .... LPKeniry 9 —
(Peter Grayson) *sn scrubbed along in rr: nvr a factor: t.o* **25/1**
0-00 **12** *2* **Art Value**[17] 6004 3-8-12 65 .... FrancisNorton 6 —
(M Wigham) *sn last and struggling: t.o* **14/1**
46 **13** *1¾* **Pas De Roland**[24] 5780 3-8-12 0 .... SaleemGolam 5 —
(S W Hall) *dwlt: keen and hld up in last pair: wl bhd 1/2-way: rdn and no rspnse 3f out: t.o* **66/1**

1m 23.72s (-1.08) **Going Correction** -0.175s/f (Stan) — **13** Ran SP% **122.4**
Speed ratings (Par 99): **99,97,94,94,94 92,90,85,80,74 58,56,54**
.The winner was bought in for 7,200gns. Blues Minor was claimed by M Mullineaux for £6000.
\n\x\x
Owner Jim Ennis **Bred** Gestut Sohrenhof **Trained** Pandy, Monmouths
■ Stewards' Enquiry : Oscar Urbina caution: used whip without giving gelding time to respond

FOCUS
Dominated by front-runners, with nothing coming from behind in this routine seller. The runner-up and fourth are rated to their recent marks.
All In The Red(IRE) Official explanation: jockey said, regarding running and riding, instructions were to jump out and be as handy as possible, adding that gelding jumped well enough but was slowly into stride and she had pushed all the way and gelding had never been travelling; trainer added she was disappointed with the gelding's run but it had its problems

6434 FOREST ROW MEDIAN AUCTION MAIDEN STKS — 5f (P)
3:35 (3:35) (Class 6) 2-Y-O — **£2,266** (£674; £337; £168) **Stalls** High

Form — RPR
5 **1** **Moscow Eight (IRE)**[41] 5286 2-9-3 0 .... ChrisCatlin 1 79+
(E J O'Neill) *led 100yds: v keen and restrained bhd ldr: moved comf into the ld over 1f out: rdn out* **7/4**[1]
03 **2** *2* **Satwa Street (IRE)**[19] 5939 2-9-3 0 .... RichardMullen 9 71
(D M Simcock) *led after 100yds: rdn and hdd over 1f out: kpt on but no real ch w wnr after* **9/2**[3]
2 **3** *1½* **Corton Charlemagne (IRE)**[19] 5939 2-8-12 0 .... SaleemGolam 2 60
(Rae Guest) *a disputing 3rd: no imp on ldng pair fr 2f out: pushed along firmly to hold off rival* **9/4**[2]
30 **4** *hd* **Five Star Junior (USA)**[57] 4778 2-9-3 0 .... OscarUrbina 3 65
(S A Callaghan) *a disputing 3rd: rdn and no imp on ldng pair 2f out: kpt on same pce* **20/1**
0 **5** *1* **Desert Strike**[20] 5904 2-9-3 0 .... IanMongan 6 61+
(P F I Cole) *a in same pl: outpcd and green fr 2f out: kpt on* **9/1**
6 *3¾* **Hanta Yo (IRE)** 2-9-3 0 .... TPQueally 5 48+
(J R Gask) *dwlt: t.k.h early and hld up in 7th: effrt and rdn 2f out: sn wknd* **12/1**
7 *15* **Yes She Can Can** 2-8-12 0 .... LPKeniry 10 —
(Peter Grayson) *s.s: a in last trio: wknd 1/2-way: t.o* **50/1**
8 *11* **Sparks Alive** 2-8-9 0 .... MarcHalford(3) 8 —
(D R C Elsworth) *lft in stalls: a t.o* **20/1**

59.26 secs (0.46) **Going Correction** -0.175s/f (Stan) — **8** Ran SP% **114.5**
Speed ratings (Par 93): **89,85,83,83,81 75,51,33**
toteswinger: 1&2 £1.80, 1&3 £1.50, 2&3 £2.40. CSF £9.82 TOTE £2.90: £1.50, £1.50, £1.10; EX 9.90 Trifecta £15.70 Pool: £771.03 - 36.20 winning units..
Owner Red Army Partnership **Bred** Stephanie Hanly **Trained** Averham Park, Notts

FOCUS
Front runners held sway, with few changes in the order thoughout. The form could be rated higher but the moderate time limits things.

NOTEBOOK
Moscow Eight(IRE) confirmed the promise of his debut, which had been on turf over 6f. At least as well suited by this turning 5f, he settled the issue in a matter of strides and looks the sort to find even more as long he is kept to a realistic level. (op 2-1 tchd 9-4)
Satwa Street(IRE), dropping to 5f, made a good fist of it out in front. Though no match for the winner, he has done well enough in his last two races to suggest that his turn will come. (op 7-2 tchd 10-3 and 5-1)
Corton Charlemagne(IRE) has shown ability in her two maidens, though a return to 6f would probably be in her favour. (tchd 2-1 and 5-2)
Five Star Junior(USA) made a fair Polytrack debut, but essentially looks a modest handicapper in the making. (tchd 16-1)
Desert Strike never managed to land a blow but battled away in a manner which suggested that 6f would suit. (op 14-1)
Hanta Yo(IRE), a 105,000gns yearling by Alhaarth out of a mare who stayed a mile, was too green to get involved but looks capable of better given time and a longer trip. (op 16-1 tchd 20-1)

6435 TOTESUPER7 H'CAP — 6f (P)
4:10 (4:12) (Class 5) (0-75,75) 3-Y-0+ — **£2,590** (£770; £385; £192) **Stalls** Low

Form — RPR
2643 **1** **Louphole**[15] 6046 6-8-8 **65** .... TravisBlock 5 72
(P J Makin) *dwlt and hmpd s: hld up in last pair: prog over 1f out: rdn and got between rivals fnl f to ld fnl 100yds* **10/3**[2]
-060 **2** *½* **Russian Reel**[13] 6124 3-9-0 **75** ....(t) AlanCreighton(3) 3 80
(E J Creighton) *awkward s: trckd ldng pair: lft in 2nd bnd wl over 1f out: rdn to ld 1f out: hdd and nt qckn fnl 100yds* **16/1**
5530 **3** *1½* **Buy On The Red**[13] 6137 7-9-2 **73** ....(p) MartinDwyer 4 73
(W R Muir) *trckd ldrs: nt qckn and wd bnd 2f out: kpt on fnl f to take 3rd last strides* **10/3**[2]
11-5 **4** *nk* **For Life (IRE)**[164] 1537 6-8-13 **75** .... NataliaGemelova(5) 8 75+
(J E Long) *taken down early: unruly bef ent stalls: led and racd freely: hdd 1f out: sn btn: eased fnl strides* **8/1**
01 **5** *hd* **Princess Rose Anne (IRE)**[120] 2757 3-9-3 **75** .... LPKeniry 2 74
(E F Vaughan) *chsd ldr tl hung rt bnd wl over 1f out: nt qckn and btn after* **6/1**[3]
6033 **6** *shd* **Night Premiere (IRE)**[12] 6150 3-8-3 **61** oh5 .... ChrisCatlin 6 59
(R Hannon) *trckd ldrs: rdn 2f out: nt qckn over 1f out: no prog after* **14/1**
-315 **7** *6* **Kingsgate Castle**[240] 457 3-8-11 **69** .... TPQueally 7 48
(J R Best) *racd wd: wl in tch: lost grnd over 2f out: sn wknd* **12/1**
-231 **8** *1¼* **Silvanus (IRE)**[65] 4523 3-9-3 **75** .... TonyCulhane 1 50
(W J Haggas) *plld hrd: hld up in last pair: rdn and no rspnse 2f out* **3/1**[1]

1m 11.15s (-0.75) **Going Correction** -0.175s/f (Stan)
WFA 3 from 6yo+ 1lb — **8** Ran SP% **116.8**
Speed ratings (Par 103): **98,97,95,94,94 94,86,84**
toteswinger: 1&2 £11.00, 1&3 £3.00, 2&3 £12.30. CSF £54.79 CT £192.51 TOTE £3.60: £1.50, £4.50, £1.60; EX 65.40 Trifecta £573.30 Part won. Pool: £774.78 - 0.80 winning units..
Owner Ten Of Hearts **Bred** Mrs P Harford **Trained** Ogbourne Maisey, Wilts

■ Stewards' Enquiry : Natalia Gemelova ten-day ban: breach of Rule 156 (eased up towards line and lost 4th) (Oct 17-27)

FOCUS
A competitive sprint, if slightly lacking in numbers, and a good gallop which set the race up for the hold-up winner. The form is limited by the proximity of the sixth racing from out of the handicap.

For Life(IRE) Official explanation: vet said gelding was found to have an irregular heatbeat after the race

Princess Rose Anne(IRE) Official explanation: jockey said filly hung right

6436 ASHURST WOOD H'CAP — 1m 4f (P)
4:45 (4:46) (Class 6) (0-60,60) 3-Y-O — £1,942 (£578; £288; £144) Stalls Low

Form — RPR

4504 **1** **Graylyn Ruby (FR)**[73] 4281 3-8-13 **58** .... LukeMorris(3) 1 — 71
(J Jay) *dwlt: hld up in 5th: prog 3f out: rdn to chse ldr over 1f out: led fnl 150yds: powered clr* **10/1**

0005 **2** *4* **Silky Steps (IRE)**[8] 6227 3-9-3 **59** .... RichardSmith 4 — 66
(P J Makin) *trckd ldrs: wnt 2nd over 3f out: led over 2f out and tried to kick on: hdd and easily outpcd fnl 150yds* **8/1[3]**

0001 **3** *3* **Contrada**[4] 6337 3-8-10 **57** .... WilliamCarson(5) 8 — 59
(R Charlton) *hld up in rr gp and off the pce: prog on wd outside fr 3f out: drvn and hanging over 1f out but sn kpt on to take 3rd* **7/4[1]**

0035 **4** *1¾* **Trinkila (USA)**[23] 5803 3-9-4 **60** .... ChrisCatlin 2 — 59
(P F I Cole) *trckd ldr 1f: styd prom: outpcd and rdn over 3f out: plugged on again fr over 1f out to take 4th nr fin* **7/1[2]**

-004 **5** *hd* **Crimsonwing (IRE)**[56] 4810 3-8-7 **54** .... NicolPolli(5) 16 — 53
(A M Hales) *awkward s: hld up off the pce in 6th: lost position on inner 3f out but stl gng wl: rdn over 1f out: plugged on: hopeless task* **20/1**

006 **6** *¾* **Water Violet**[30] 5612 3-9-1 **57** .... MartinDwyer 5 — 55
(J R Fanshawe) *dwlt: hld up in rr gp and wl off the pce: shkn up 3f out: pushed along and kpt on fr over 1f out: nvr nr ldrs* **12/1**

5560 **7** *½* **Kalokairi (IRE)**[16] 6022 3-8-13 **55** ....(b) DarrylHolland 15 — 52
(J L Dunlop) *trckd ldr after 1f: led 4f out: hdd & wknd over 2f out* **7/1[2]**

5016 **8** *4½* **Siryena**[18] 5961 3-9-2 **58** ....(tp) GeorgeBaker 7 — 48
(B I Case) *s.s: hld up in rr gp and off the pce: prog fr 3f out: disp 4th over 2f out: wknd over 1f out* **8/1[3]**

5543 **9** *6* **Orbital Orchid**[30] 4978 3-8-11 **53** ....(v) SimonWhitworth 11 — 33
(W S Kittow) *dwlt: hld up in last and wl off the pce: rdn over 3f out: nvr on terms* **10/1**

0000 **10** *nse* **Funseeker (UAE)**[15] 6060 3-8-10 **52** .... FrancisNorton 10 — 32
(Jamie Poulton) *nvr gng wl: a in rr and off the pce* **40/1**

2600 **11** *4* **Highly Regal (IRE)**[30] 5611 3-9-1 **57** .... StephenCarson 14 — 31
(R A Teal) *hld up in rr gp and off the pce: rdn 4f out: fnd nil and btn wl over 2f out* **33/1**

0600 **12** *6* **Squire Boldwood (IRE)**[32] 5574 3-8-8 **53** ....(b) MarcHalford(3) 12 — 17
(D R C Elsworth) *led and racd freely: hdd & wknd 4f out: t.o* **25/1**

2m 30.66s (-2.34) **Going Correction** -0.175s/f (Stan) — **12** Ran SP% **123.4**
Speed ratings (Par 99): **100,97,95,94,94 93,93,90,86,86 83,79**
toteswinger: 1&2 £14.20, 1&3 £6.10, 2&3 £4.90. CSF £87.68 CT £210.78 TOTE £12.80: £3.40, £3.20, £1.40; EX 117.70 Trifecta £192.00 Part won. Pool: £259.55 - 0.10 winning units..
Owner Graham & Lynn Knight **Bred** Jonathan Jay **Trained** Newmarket, Suffolk
■ Stewards' Enquiry : Marc Halford one-day ban: failed to ride to draw (Oct 17)

FOCUS
A run-of-the-mill race, but the winner looks progressive on this surface. They went an ordinary gallop, but the field were soon strung out and the first two were always handy. The fourth and fifth are rated close to their recent best.

6437 HARTFIELD H'CAP — 1m 2f (P)
5:20 (5:23) (Class 6) (0-65,65) 3-Y-O — £1,942 (£578; £288; £144) Stalls Low

Form — RPR

065 **1** **Miss Pelling (IRE)**[42] 5231 3-9-2 **63** .... MartinDwyer 13 — 69
(B J Meehan) *cl up: pressed ldr over 3f out: clr of rest over 1f out: maintained chal u.p and led post* **14/1**

4000 **2** *nse* **Bookiebasher Babe (IRE)**[22] 5836 3-9-2 **63** .... FrancisNorton 2 — 69
(M Quinn) *cl up: trckd ldr 5f out: led over 3f out: hrd pressed sn after: kpt on u.p: hdd fnl stride* **16/1**

464 **3** *1* **Locum**[4] 6337 3-9-3 **64** .... TPQueally 3 — 72+
(M H Tompkins) *trckd ldrs: lost pl and bdly outpcd fr 3f out: hrd rdn and rallied over 1f out on inner: styd on wl to take 3rd nr fin* **11/2[2]**

0002 **4** *nk* **Princess India (IRE)**[8] 6227 3-8-13 **60** .... StephenCarson 11 — 63
(P Winkworth) *prom and racd wd: pressed ldng pair 3f out: drvn and nt qckn wl over 1f out: kpt on again fnl 100yds but lost 3rd nr fin* **4/1[1]**

5556 **5** *½* **Kashmina**[111] 3023 3-9-1 **62** .... DarrylHolland 12 — 64
(Miss Sheena West) *hld up wl in rr: rdn and struggling on outer 3f out: styd on fr 2f out: hanging over 1f out: nt rch ldrs* **10/1**

0400 **6** *3* **Classical Rhythm (IRE)**[15] 6049 3-9-3 **64** .... GeorgeBaker 7 — 60
(J R Boyle) *hld up in midfield: rdn wl over 3f out: sn outpcd and struggling: modest prog 2f out: nvr on terms* **11/2[2]**

000 **7** *1½* **James Pollard (IRE)**[17] 5995 3-8-10 **60** .... MarcHalford(3) 6 — 53+
(D R C Elsworth) *t.k.h early: hld up in rr: gng easily but trapped bhd rivals over 3f out to over 1f out: rn into trble again on inner ins fnl f and snatched up: fin full of running* **10/1**

3666 **8** *2* **Pharaohs Queen (IRE)**[22] 5815 3-9-2 **63** .... TGMcLaughlin 8 — 52
(E A L Dunlop) *dwlt: hld up and sn in midfield: cl enough 3f out: sn u.p and btn* **28/1**

3004 **9** *5* **Stormy View (USA)**[13] 6126 3-9-4 **65** ....(p) RichardMullen 5 — 44
(J H M Gosden) *pressed ldr to 5f out: wknd u.p 4f out: sn bhd* **13/2[3]**

000 **10** *2¼* **Mayfair's Future**[24] 5790 3-8-13 **60** .... ChrisCatlin 14 — 35
(J R Jenkins) *a in rr: rdn and struggling over 4f out* **40/1**

600 **11** *1½* **Plum Asset (USA)**[36] 5426 3-8-10 **57** .... NelsonDeSouza 10 — 29
(R M Beckett) *s.s: a in last pair: rdn and struggling over 4f out* **28/1**

-263 **12** *12* **Grand Value (USA)**[64] 4560 3-8-7 **59** ow1 .... WilliamCarson(5) 1 — 7
(R Ford) *led to over 3f out: wknd rapidly: t.o* **16/1**

2m 5.35s (-1.25) **Going Correction** -0.175s/f (Stan) — **12** Ran SP% **110.1**
Speed ratings (Par 99): **98,97,97,96,96 94,92,91,87,85 84,74**
toteswinger: 1&2 £36.20, 1&3 £11.30, 2&3 £17.60. CSF £180.36 CT £1031.08 TOTE £13.50: £2.80, £5.10, £1.90; EX 201.00 TRIFECTA Not won. Place 6: £34.94 Place 5: £27.58.
Owner Kennet Valley Thoroughbreds Iii **Bred** Epona Bloodstock Ltd **Trained** Manton, Wilts
■ Stewards' Enquiry : T G McLaughlin caution: careless riding

FOCUS
A medium gallop at best, and the first two home were always well placed. The runner-up is rated back to his best with the winner up 4lb on maiden form.

Miss Pelling(IRE) Official explanation: trainer's rep said, regarding the apparent improvement in form, filly had been weak and was more suited by her first run on the all-weather

T/Plt: £46.60 to a £1 stake. Pool: £49,308.26. 771.27 winning tickets. T/Qpdt: £18.70 to a £1 stake. Pool: £2,736.28. 107.90 winning tickets. JN

6425 **NEWMARKET (ROWLEY)** (R-H)
Friday, October 3

OFFICIAL GOING: Good to firm
Wind: Fresh behind Weather: Overcast

6438 NUNNERY STUD EBF MAIDEN STKS (DIV I) — 7f
1:00 (1:01) (Class 4) 2-Y-O — £6,152 (£1,830; £914; £456) Stalls High

Form — RPR

3 **1** **Evasive**[23] 5798 2-9-3 0 .... RyanMoore 4 — 81+
(Sir Michael Stoute) *w'like: scope: lw: sn led: shkn up over 1f out: r.o wl* **8/11[1]**

2 *2¼* **Makaamen** 2-9-3 0 .... RHills 10 — 75+
(B W Hills) *str: gd bodied: s.s: hld up: hdwy over 2f out: r.o wl to take 2nd on line: nt rch wnr* **7/1[2]**

3 *shd* **Infiraad** 2-9-3 0 .... MichaelHills 3 — 75+
(B W Hills) *str: athletic: bit bkwd: dwlt: hdwy over 5f out: rdn over 1f out: r.o* **11/1[3]**

5 **4** *2¼* **George Rex (USA)**[14] 6072 2-9-3 0 .... EddieAhern 12 — 69
(B J Meehan) *chsd wnr: rdn over 1f out: edgd lft and no ex ins fnl f* **12/1**

5 *1¾* **Stoic (IRE)** 2-9-3 0 .... ShaneKelly 9 — 65+
(J Noseda) *w'like: athletic: hld up: r.o wl ins fnl f: nvr nrr* **12/1**

55 **6** *nse* **Land Hawk (IRE)**[15] 6057 2-9-3 0 .... JimmyQuinn 11 — 65+
(J Pearce) *w'like; chsd ldrs: rdn over 2f out: styd on same pce appr fnl f* **25/1**

0 **7** *2½* **Royal Willy (IRE)**[25] 5754 2-9-3 0 .... AlanMunro 13 — 58
(W Jarvis) *w'like: hld up: racd keenly: rdn over 1f out: n.d* **25/1**

8 *¾* **Halfway House** 2-9-3 0 .... HayleyTurner 14 — 56
(M L W Bell) *leggy: gd bodied: chsd ldrs tl rdn and wknd over 1f out* **16/1**

0 **9** *5* **Hilltop Artistry**[16] 6029 2-9-3 0 .... AdamKirby 7 — 44
(S W James) *w'like: chsd ldrs: rdn over 2f out: sn wknd* **100/1**

10 *nse* **Wahan (USA)** 2-9-3 0 .... NCallan 2 — 44
(C E Brittain) *leggy: unf: chsd ldrs: rdn 1/2-way: wknd over 2f out* **25/1**

0 **11** *½* **Ela Gorrie Mou**[14] 6081 2-8-12 0 .... RobertWinston 1 — 38
(T T Clement) *s.i.s: a in rr: wknd over 2f out* **200/1**

00 **12** *5* **Come On Toby**[74] 4256 2-9-3 0 .... MickyFenton 15 — 30
(Miss Amy Weaver) *leggy: s.i.s: hld up: rdn 1/2-way: wknd over 2f out* **100/1**

13 *nk* **Cake Stand** 2-9-3 0 .... RobertHavlin 8 — 29
(J A R Toller) *hld up: a in rr: nt clr run over 2f out: sn wknd* **33/1**

1m 25.34s (-0.06) **Going Correction** -0.225s/f (Firm) — **13** Ran SP% **117.0**
Speed ratings (Par 97): **91,88,88,85,83 83,80,79,74,74 73,67,67**
toteswinger: 1&2 £2.20, 1&3 £3.40, 2&3 £4.90. CSF £5.22 TOTE £1.70: £1.10, £2.00, £2.80; EX 6.40.
Owner Cheveley Park Stud **Bred** Cheveley Park Stud Ltd **Trained** Newmarket, Suffolk

FOCUS
3mm of rain in the morning would not have had much affect on the ground, which remained on the fast side. There was also a pretty strong tailwind. A decent enough maiden that should throw up its fair share of winners, but the early pace was very steady and the winner is rated to his Kempton debut form.

NOTEBOOK
Evasive gave trouble at the start on his debut at Kempton but ran an encouraging race despite showing signs of greenness, and he had clearly learnt plenty from that and knew what was required this time. Smartly away, he had little trouble getting to the front and, in a steadily run race, dominated throughout. He only had to be pushed out to score comfortably, and is clearly held in some regard as he holds a Dewhurst entry. That race could now be on his agenda, although his trainer also mentioned the Horris Hill as a possibility. Wherever he goes it is likely that fast ground will continue to see him at his best. (op 5-6)
Makaamen, whose dam is a half-sister to five winners, including Etlaala, who won the Champagne Stakes for these connections, was the stable's first string on jockey bookings, but it was only close to the line that he finally got the better of stablemate Infiraad. He showed signs of inexperience and will have derived plenty from this. (op 11-2)
Infiraad, whose dam is a sister to three-time 6f-7f Group 3 winner Desert Style, kept battling away on his debut, and could well find a similar maiden before the season is out. (op 9-1)
George Rex(USA), like the winner, showed the benefit of a previous run as he was quickly away and was prominent throughout. He was suited by the way the race was run, especially with the tailwind to help. (op 14-1 tchd 16-1)
Stoic(IRE), bred to be effective at around this trip, hails from a stable fully capable of getting them ready first time up, but he was keen early on off the steady gallop. Running on at the finish, he looks capable of better off a stronger pace. Official explanation: jockey said colt ran too keen early on (op 10-1)
Land Hawk(IRE) has now had the three runs required for a mark and will be of more interest in handicap company.
Royal Willy(IRE) could be expected to appreciate this quicker ground, but he was another who was keen enough in the early stages and would have appreciated a better pace.
Halfway House, a half-brother to that smart middle-distancer Spice Route, is bred to do better next year over further.

6439 SAKHEE OH SO SHARP STKS (GROUP 3) (FILLIES) — 7f
1:30 (1:36) (Class 1) 2-Y-O
£28,385 (£10,760; £5,385; £2,685; £1,345; £675) Stalls High

Form — RPR

0154 **1** **Souter's Sister (IRE)**[29] 5642 2-8-12 93 .... JimmyFortune 11 — 105
(R Hannon) *towards rr far side: hdwy over 2f out: r.o wl to ld fnl 50yds* **25/1**

61 **2** *½* **Moonlife (IRE)**[28] 5674 2-8-12 0 .... LDettori 2 — 104
(Saeed Bin Suroor) *led centre: kpt on wl fnl f: hdd and no ex towards fin* **20/1**

0145 **3** *1* **Nashmiah (IRE)**[34] 5507 2-8-12 103 .... NCallan 13 — 101
(C E Brittain) *chsd ldrs towards far side: chal appr fnl f: styd on same pce ins fnl f* **16/1**

410 **4** *½* **Pachattack (USA)**[41] 5266 2-8-12 90 .... HayleyTurner 9 — 100
(G A Butler) *chsd ldrs centre: outpcd over 1f out: styd on wl ins fnl f* **20/1**

02 **5** *nk* **Super Sleuth (IRE)**[14] 6076 2-8-12 0 .... EddieAhern 14 — 99
(B J Meehan) *chsd ldrs towards far side: upsides over 1f out: kpt on same pce ins fnl f* **12/1**

3133 **6** *2½* **Touching (IRE)**[16] 6025 2-8-12 90 .... RichardHughes 10 — 93
(R Hannon) *mid-div towards centre: hdwy over 2f out: sn chsng ldrs: wknd fnl 75yds* **11/1**

0212 **7** *1¼* **Misdaqeya**[55] 4868 2-8-12 96 .... RHills 6 — 90
(B W Hills) *trckd ldrs centre: effrt 2f out: kpt on same pce* **6/1[3]**

1421 **8** *¾* **Starlarks (IRE)**[19] 5937 2-8-12 90 .... ShaneKelly 7 — 88+
(W J Knight) *gave problems in stalls sand re-loaded: in rr centre: nvr a factor* **33/1**

41 **9** *1 1/4* **Ave**[11] 6166 2-8-12 0 .... RyanMoore 3 85
(Sir Michael Stoute) *on toes: trckd ldrs centre: effrt over 2f out: wknd appr fnl f* **11/2**[2]

101 **10** *1* **Ballantrae (IRE)**[23] 5791 2-8-12 90 .... JamieSpencer 5 82
(M L W Bell) *stdd s: hld up in rr centre: effrt 3f out: sn btn* **8/1**

21 **11** *1 3/4* **Intense**[29] 5643 2-8-12 87 .... MichaelHills 4 78
(B W Hills) *lw: mid-div: effrt centre over 2f out: sn wknd* **6/1**[3]

3112 **12** *15* **Snoqualmie Girl (IRE)**[22] 5828 2-8-12 99 .... TQuinn 8 41+
(D R C Elsworth) *edgy: nvr gng wl in rr centre: bhd and eased over 1f out* **9/2**[1]

1300 **13** *37* **Danidh Dubai (IRE)**[13] 6102 2-8-12 98 .... AlanMunro 1 —
(M R Channon) *lw: in rr centre: dropped rt out over 3f out: t.o and virtually p.u* **14/1**

1m 22.47s (-2.93) **Going Correction** -0.225s/f (Firm) 2y crse rec **13** Ran SP% **118.1**
Speed ratings (Par 102): **107,106,105,104,104 101,100,99,97,96 94,77,35**
toteswinger: 1&2 £62.20, 1&3 £57.60, 2&3 £58.10. CSF £434.13 TOTE £33.10: £6.80, £4.60, £4.90; EX 591.00 TRIFECTA Not won..
Owner P D Merritt **Bred** John Cullinan **Trained** East Everleigh, Wilts

FOCUS
An interesting Group 3 in which a number had been victims of the prepotent Rainbow View or her Ascot victim Fantasia. An open betting heat but those at the head of the market were ultimately well beaten. The time was decent but the form is only fair for th grade.

NOTEBOOK
Souter's Sister(IRE) had already proved effective on fast ground, having scored on it twice, and her only previous try over 7f was on easy ground behind Fantasia at Goodwood. She broke well but was settled in behind before making good progress going into the Dip and finding enough to peg back the runner-up. Winning at this trip and acquiring black type will increase her potential value when she appears at the sales, which is reportedly on the cards now. (op 28-1 tchd 33-1)
Moonlife(IRE) soon showed in front and brought the field up the centre of the track. She stuck on really well up the hill but the more experienced Souter's Sister had too much for her. Having won her maiden on Polytrack the ground was an unknown but she handled it really well and is progressing. (op 16-1)
Nashmiah(IRE) had a bit to find with Misdaqeya on previous running but had won over the trip and on the ground. She showed up throughout and this was a creditable effort.
Pachattack(USA) ran a strange race. Close up from the start, she was being pushed along vigorously over 2f out and lost her place but then rallied really well up the hill to finish on the heels of the placed horses. She put a disappointing effort at Goodwood behind her back on this faster surface and looks in need of a step up in trip. (tchd 25-1)
Super Sleuth(IRE), a maiden coming into this, had already shown her ability to handle the trip and a sound surface and was another to run well having been in the leading group throughout. She should have little difficulty winning races on this evidence. (op 14-1)
Touching(IRE) has already been placed in Listed company and appeared to run her race, just having nothing in reserve on the climb to the line. (op 16-1)
Misdaqeya appeared to have her chance but faded in the closing stages and should have finished ahead of Nashmiah on previous form, although that was on easy ground, so perhaps she found this surface too quick. (op 11-2 tchd 7-1 in places)
Starlarks(IRE) did not run badly considering she compromised her chance by playing up in the stalls and going down on her hindquarters beforehand. (tchd 40-1)
Ave was well fancied to build on her Polytrack success last time but was struggling a fair way from home. (tchd 6-1 in places)
Ballantrae(IRE) had gained both her successes on soft ground and had disappointed on faster in between so perhaps it was not the biggest surprise to see her fail to shine. (tchd 15-2 and 17-2)
Intense was another who was never really going on this fast ground. (op 11-2)
Snoqualmie Girl(IRE), whose best efforts had been on a softer surface and who had hung when scoring on fast going at Salisbury. It has to be assumed the either quick ground did not suit or she is over the top now. Official explanation: jockey said filly never travelled (tchd 5-1 in places)
Danidh Dubai(IRE) Official explanation: jockey said filly lost its action

6440 NAYEF JOEL STKS (GROUP 3) 1m
2:05 (2:09) (Class 1) 3-Y-O+

£36,900 (£13,988; £7,000; £3,490; £1,748; £877) **Stalls** High

Form RPR

212- **1** **Eagle Mountain**[349] 6334 4-9-0 0 .... KShea 10 115
(M F De Kock, South Africa) *b.hind: chsd ldrs: outpcd over 1f out: rallied to ld post* **5/1**[2]

5222 **2** *hd* **Bankable (IRE)**[19] 5932 4-9-0 117 .... DaneO'Neill 1 114
(L M Cumani) *lw: hld up: hdwy u.p and hung rt over 1f out: r.o* **2/1**[1]

213 **3** *hd* **Ordnance Row**[14] 6073 5-9-3 109 .... RichardHughes 7 117
(R Hannon) *chsd ldrs: led over 3f out: rdn over 1f out: edgd lft and hdd post* **20/1**

1-10 **4** *1/2* **General Eliott (IRE)**[145] 2032 3-8-11 104 .... ShaneKelly 3 113
(P F I Cole) *hld up: hdwy over 4f out: chsd ldr 2f out: sn rdn: ev ch ins fnl f: unable qckn towards fin* **40/1**

366 **5** *3* **Stubbs Art (IRE)**[8] 6237 3-8-11 112 .... JimmyFortune 11 106
(D R C Elsworth) *s.i.s: sn chsng ldrs: rdn over 1f out: wknd towards fin* **12/1**

1010 **6** *3/4* **Calming Influence (IRE)**[33] 5555 3-8-11 107 ....(t) TedDurcan 4 104
(Saeed Bin Suroor) *s.i.s and hmpd s: hdwy over 6f out: rdn and hung rt fr over 2f out: wknd ins fnl f* **20/1**

3-31 **7** *1 1/4* **Eddie Jock (IRE)**[19] 5941 4-9-0 110 .... LDettori 15 101
(Saeed Bin Suroor) *chsd ldrs: rdn over 2f out: wknd fnl f* **8/1**

1126 **8** *nk* **Staying On (IRE)**[14] 6074 3-8-11 108 .... AdamKirby 5 101
(W R Swinburn) *slowly into stide and hmpd s: hdwy to ld over 6f out: hdd over 4f out: outpcd over 2f out: sn hung rt: styd on ins fnl f* **14/1**

3531 **9** *shd* **Shabiba (USA)**[34] 5506 3-8-8 103 .... RHills 2 97
(M P Tregoning) *hld up: racd keenly: hdwy over 1f out: no imp fnl f* **16/1**

1-60 **10** *1 1/4* **Moynahan (USA)**[106] 3156 3-8-11 104 .... NCallan 8 98
(P F I Cole) *hld up: rdn over 2f out: nt trble ldrs* **50/1**

-016 **11** *4 1/2* **Perfect Stride**[62] 4622 3-8-11 102 .... RyanMoore 9 87
(Sir Michael Stoute) *lw: hld up: hung rt fr 1/2-way: n.d* **7/1**[3]

5042 **12** *1 1/4* **Moyenne Corniche**[21] 5856 3-8-11 109 ....(b[1]) AlanMunro 12 84
(G Wragg) *led: hdd over 6f out: led again over 4f out: hdd 3f out: rdn and wknd over 1f out* **20/1**

0-10 **13** *4 1/2* **Sharp Nephew**[14] 6073 3-8-11 99 .... JamieSpencer 14 74
(B J Meehan) *hld up: rdn and wknd over 2f out* **33/1**

15 **14** *1* **Fanjura (IRE)**[141] 2121 3-8-11 102 .... JMurtagh 6 72
(J Noseda) *wnt lft s: hld up: a in rr* **16/1**

15 *2 3/4* **Bestofthem (USA)**[101] 3-8-11 84 .... PaulEddery 13 65
(Miss D Mountain) *hld up: wknd over 3f out* **200/1**

1m 34.07s (-4.53) **Going Correction** -0.225s/f (Firm) course record
WFA 3 from 4yo+ 3lb **15** Ran SP% **121.9**
Speed ratings (Par 113): **113,112,112,112,109 108,107,106,106,105 100,99,95,94,91**
toteswinger: 1&2 £4.00, 1&3 £16.80, 2&3 £10.20. CSF £14.18 TOTE £5.20: £2.10, £1.70, £4.70; EX 13.30 Trifecta £434.70 Pool: £ 763.70 - 1.30 winning units..
Owner Sheikh Mohammed Bin Khalifa Al Maktoum **Bred** London Thoroughbred Services Ltd **Trained** South Africa

■ Stewards' Enquiry : Richard Hughes one-day ban, plus three deferred; careless riding (Oct 17, 19-21)

FOCUS
A good, competitive Group 3 race run at a decent gallop, and the tailwind contributed to a course record. The penalised third looks the key to the form, and the first two, who are better class, have been rated 9lb off their best.

NOTEBOOK
Eagle Mountain had been off the track since finishing second in the Champion Stakes here last autumn as a result of fracturing his pelvis in Dubai over the winter. Having his first outing for Mike de Kock, this former Derby runner-up was initially weak in the betting but in the minutes leading up to the race came in for good support, suggesting he was fit enough. The strong pace suited over a trip which is almost certainly on the short side for him, but he has plenty of class and, once switched out to challenge, he really found his stride when they hit the rising ground, and he stayed on very strongly. De Kock had been considering the Breeders' Cup for him if he ran well here, but Kevin Shea's first reaction was to suggest that it would be better to go for the Group 3 Darley Stakes next and then prepare him for Hong Kong, where the Vase is likely to be his race. (op 6-1 tchd 7-1)
Bankable(IRE) is threatening to become a bit of a disappointing horse, despite once again putting up a fine effort in defeat. It is arguable that he did not do a lot wrong, especially as he was drawn in stall one and raced away from the main action, but in fact he came to have every chance and, not for the first time, was seemingly outbattled by the winner. The number of excuses for him is beginning to mount, but the Darley Stakes over a furlong further here on the Friday of the Champions meeting might provide him with an opportunity to put the record straight. Like the winner, Hong Kong could also be on his agenda later in the year. (op 9-4 tchd 5-2)
Ordnance Row ran a fine race under his penalty, especially as softer ground suits him ideally, and at the weights he emerges the best horse in the race. Up with the pace throughout, he took a deal of passing and confirmed himself reliable at this level. (op 16-1)
General Eliott(IRE) ◆ did best of the three-year-olds, finishing clear of the rest in fourth. He had looked a promising type earlier in the year but was injured in the French 2,000 Guineas and had not run since. He ran a fine race and, if as expected he comes on for this outing, he could well win a Pattern race before the season is out. (op 50-1)
Stubbs Art(IRE), third in the 2000 Guineas over this course and distance, is a keen-going type who appreciates a decent gallop to run off. He saw more daylight than ideal here and was a shade disappointing, but the fact remains that he has only won one race in a 12-race career, a handicap off 72, and he is clearly not that straightforward. (tchd 14-1)
Calming Influence(IRE), whose stable had won the last two renewals of this race, came with a threatening run down the outside two furlongs out but, not for the first time, did not see his race out.
Eddie Jock(IRE), who impressed on the Polytrack at Great Leighs last time, was a bit disappointing back on turf and may have bounced. Official explanation: jockey said gelding lost its action and hung right (op 15-2 tchd 7-1)
Staying On(IRE) should have been suited by the drop back to a mile on fast ground, but he would have liked to have his own way in front and that was never going to be likely with other confirmed pacesetters in the race. (op 16-1)
Shabiba(USA), the only filly in the field, was a bit keen in the early stages and found taking on the boys in this better grade a bit too much. She will be more at home back against her own sex. (tchd 20-1 in places)
Moynahan(USA) looked a promising type last year but not a lot has gone right for him this season as he has suffered a number of problems. He could be the type to fulfil his potential at four.
Perfect Stride, whose poor effort at Goodwood last time was put down to him not acting on the ground or the track, was again disappointing. He hung from halfway and possibly all was not well. (op 13-2 tchd 6-1)

6441 32RED.COM CHEVELEY PARK STKS (GROUP 1) (FILLIES) 6f
2:40 (2:45) (Class 1) 2-Y-O

£134,970 (£51,163; £25,605; £12,767; £6,395; £3,209) **Stalls** High

Form RPR

11 **1** **Serious Attitude (IRE)**[29] 5642 2-8-12 105 .... JimmyFortune 11 110
(Rae Guest) *lw: trckd ldrs far side: hrd rdn to ld fnl 100yds: hld on gamely* **4/1**[1]

0511 **2** *1/2* **Aspen Darlin (IRE)**[13] 6102 2-8-12 107 ....(p) JimmyQuinn 13 109
(A Bailey) *sn w ldrs far side: chal over 1f out: no ex towards fin* **12/1**

3 *3/4* **Pursuit Of Glory (IRE)**[18] 5979 2-8-12 0 .... JMurtagh 6 106+
(David Wachman, Ire) *w'like: lw: prom centre: hdwy 2f out: styd on strly ins fnl f* **5/1**[2]

41 **4** *3/4* **Adorn**[28] 5673 2-8-12 86 .... RyanMoore 5 104
(J Noseda) *w'like: str: lw: trckd ldrs centre: qcknd to ld over 1f out: edgd rt: hdd ins fnl f* **10/1**

04 **5** *2 1/2* **Heart Shaped (USA)**[86] 3851 2-8-12 0 .... JamieSpencer 3 97+
(A P O'Brien, Ire) *tall: lengthy: lw: dwlt: in rr centre: hdwy 2f out: styd on fnl f: nt rch ldrs* **33/1**

162 **6** *nk* **Faraway Flower (USA)**[23] 5794 2-8-12 0 .... MichaelHills 14 96
(B W Hills) *lw: mid-div towards far side: effrt over 2f out: kpt on fnl f* **12/1**

6121 **7** *3/4* **Infamous Angel**[41] 5272 2-8-12 106 .... RichardHughes 10 93
(R Hannon) *chsd ldrs: styd on same pce appr fnl f* **8/1**[3]

1112 **8** *shd* **Rosabee (IRE)**[69] 4403 2-8-12 102 .... EdwardCreighton 9 93
(Miss V Haigh) *on toes: towards rr: hdwy 2f out: kpt on wl fnl f* **33/1**

3 **9** *3/4* **Beyond Our Reach (IRE)**[33] 5549 2-8-12 0 .... KJManning 7 91+
(T Stack, Ire) *tall: unf: mid-div: effrt over 2f out: n.m.r: nvr rchd ldrs* **16/1**

55 **10** *hd* **Sugar Free (IRE)**[33] 5549 2-8-12 0 .... WMLordan 8 90
(T Stack, Ire) *trckd ldrs on outer: effrt over 2f out: fdd over 1f out* **16/1**

1213 **11** *nk* **Langs Lash (IRE)**[41] 5272 2-8-12 108 .... AlanMunro 12 89
(M G Quinlan) *ponied to post: led 2 over 2f out: wknd appr fnl f* **8/1**[3]

0250 **12** *2* **Art Princess (USA)**[22] 5827 2-8-12 99 .... HayleyTurner 15 83
(B W Hills) *b.hind: lw: chse ldrs far side: wknd over 1f out* **66/1**

3113 **13** *3/4* **Jargelle (IRE)**[66] 4507 2-8-12 102 .... LiamJones 4 81
(W J Haggas) *towards rr in centre: nvr a factor* **16/1**

13 **14** *3 1/2* **Mythical Border (USA)**[21] 5852 2-8-12 0 .... LDettori 2 71+
(J Noseda) *in rr centre: bhd fnl 2f* **9/1**

0443 **15** *1 3/4* **Danehill Destiny**[13] 6102 2-8-12 102 ....(b[1]) RobertWinston 16 65+
(W J Haggas) *towards rr far side: nvr on terms* **20/1**

01 **16** *nk* **Especially Special (IRE)**[29] 5628 2-8-12 79 .... EddieAhern 1 64+
(S Kirk) *lw: chsd ldr centre: led over 2f out: hdd & wknd qckly over 1f out* **66/1**

69.94 secs (-2.26) **Going Correction** -0.225s/f (Firm) **16** Ran SP% **124.6**
Speed ratings (Par 106): **106,105,104,103,100 99,98,98,97,97 96,94,93,88,86 85**
toteswinger: 1&2 £11.10, 1&3 £5.80, 2&3 £14.70. CSF £51.52 TOTE £3.40: £1.60, £3.90, £2.00; EX 59.30 Trifecta £92.20 Pool: £5260.80 - 42.18 winning units..
Owner Derek J Willis & Rae Guest **Bred** Paddy Twomey **Trained** Newmarket, Suffolk

FOCUS
One of the three most important juvenile fillies' races of the season and it has experienced a revival in the last couple of seasons with last year's winner Natagora going on to win the 1000 Guineas and the previous year's scorer Indian Ink subsequently taking the Coronation Stakes. This year's line-up did not appear to include any outstanding fillies, although the Queen Mary and Lowther winners were present, backed up by the runners-up in the Cherry Hinton and Princess Margaret. The pace was strong, helped by the tail wind, and the time was just a third of a second outside Oasis Dream's track record. This was only an average renewal but the form looks sound enough.

NOTEBOOK

Serious Attitude(IRE), supplemented for £15,000, maintained her unbeaten record with a determined display on the fastest ground she has so far encountered. Backed into favouritism, she got plenty of cover early, was given a good tow into the race by the runner-up, then galloped on just the stronger with the rail to help. Her dam was a winner over a mile and, although there are several sprinters in her pedigree, she is by the top-class middle-distance performer Mtoto, so should have little trouble getting a mile. She has already given a fantastic return for her owners' outlay of 7,500gns and must not be underestimated when she returns here for the 1000 Guineas. (op 9-2 tchd 5-1)

Aspen Darlin(IRE), another bargain buy, having cost 10,000euros, is consistent and progressive and, the second highest-rated filly in the race, is probably the best guide to the form as she made the winner work really hard. She acts on any ground, has improved for the fitting of cheekpieces, and is a credit to connections. She is likely to be put away for the season and, as she is not a forward juvenile on looks, she may be able to go on again next season. (tchd 14-1)

Pursuit Of Glory(IRE) ◆, whose dam Sophisticat was runner-up in this race, was also held up and got outpaced for a few strides going into the Dip before running on in good style late on. Having only previously run on Polytrack, winning the second of two starts at Dundalk, she handled this surface well and looks sure to make up into a high-class three-year-old. (op 13-2 tchd 9-2)

Adorn, who built on the promise of her debut when scoring by 6l over 6f on Polytrack at Kempton next time, ran well but, having gone for home running into the Dip, she had nothing left for the climb to the finish and was run out the placings close home. Her breeding suggests she will struggle to get the Guineas mile and may be best at sprint trips, although she may last 7f. (op 12-1)

Heart Shaped(USA) had not run since finishing fourth in Cherry Hinton (behind Art Princess), but put up a fair effort from the rear on ground that suits and may be best at trips short of a mile next season.

Faraway Flower(USA), who had been well held by Fantasia in the Prestige Stakes over 7f on her only previous try in Group company, ran reasonably but may be better on easier ground. (op 16-1 tchd 20-1)

Infamous Angel, a narrow winner of the Lowther from Penny's Gift and Langs Lash, with Danehill Destiny behind, had no excuses on account of the ground but did get involved in some scrimmaging just after the halfway stage. (op 13-2)

Rosabee(IRE), runner-up in the Princess Margaret, had been off since that race in July but handled the fast ground and was doing her best work in the latter stages.

Beyond Our Reach(IRE) had been third in the Moyglare Stud Stakes last time but the drop back from 7f on this much faster ground and not getting much room well over 2f out did not help her cause. (tchd 20-1)

Langs Lash(IRE), the Queen Mary winner, was ponied to the start in an effort to settle her but she showed plenty of early pace and probably did too much too soon. (op 9-1)

Danehill Destiny, who was fitted with first-time blinkers, was never really involved. Official explanation: jockey said filly was unsuited by the good to firm ground (op 25-1)

Especially Special(IRE), who improved on her debut when scoring over 5f on Polytrack last month, was supported in the market and showed blistering speed in the early stages before dropping away quickly on meeting the rising ground.

6442 SHADWELL MIDDLE PARK STKS (GROUP 1) (ENTIRE COLTS) 6f

3:10 (3:15) (Class 1) 2-Y-O

£111,893 (£42,415; £21,227; £10,584; £5,301; £2,660) **Stalls** High

Form				RPR
2131	**1**		**Bushranger (IRE)**[40] 5330 2-8-12 0 .... JMurtagh 1 (David Wachman, Ire) *lw: racd centre: chsd ldr: edgd rt over 2f out: rdn to ld ins fnl f: r.o* **15/8**[1]	120
2233	**2**	1 ¼	**Sayif (IRE)**[13] 6119 2-8-12 110 .... JamieSpencer 2 (P W Chapple-Hyam) *on toes: led centre: overall ldr 1/2-way: edgd rt sn after: rdn over 1f out: hdd and unable qckn ins fnl f* **5/1**[3]	116
21	**3**	2 ½	**Huntdown (USA)**[14] 6072 2-8-12 100 .... LDettori 5 (J H M Gosden) *lw: hld up: racd far side: hdwy u.p over 1f out: edgd rt: styd on same pce ins fnl f* **9/2**[2]	109+
1222	**4**	1 ¼	**Gallagher**[13] 6119 2-8-12 114 .... JimmyFortune 4 (B J Meehan) *racd far side: hld up: hdwy over 2f out: sn rdn: styd on same pce ins fnl f* **13/2**	105
1110	**5**	½	**Classic Blade (IRE)**[40] 5330 2-8-12 108 .... RichardKingscote 9 (Tom Dascombe) *racd far side: overall ldr to 1/2-way: rdn over 1f out: wknd ins fnl f* **25/1**	104
2331	**6**	shd	**Prolific (IRE)**[63] 4588 2-8-12 107 .... RichardHughes 6 (R Hannon) *lw: stmbld s: racd far side: chsd ldrs: shkn up over 2f out: edgd rt: nt clr run and lost pl over 1f out: styd on towards fin* **11/1**	105+
31	**7**	shd	**Galpin Junior (USA)**[57] 4778 2-8-12 87 .... TedDurcan 3 (B J Meehan) *athletic: hld up: outpcd over 2f out: styd on towards fin* **40/1**	103
313	**8**	shd	**Jobe (USA)**[42] 5226 2-8-12 103 .... NCallan 7 (K A Ryan) *lw: racd far side: chsd ldr: rdn over 1f out: wknd ins fnl f* **14/1**	103
121	**9**	2	**Finjaan**[66] 4507 2-8-12 110 .... RHills 8 (M P Tregoning) *lw: free to post: stdd s: hld up: racd keenly: racd far side: nt clr run fr over 2f out: hmpd ins fnl f: nvr any ch* **7/1**	105+

69.56 secs (-2.64) **Going Correction** -0.225s/f (Firm) 2y crse rec **9** Ran SP% **116.7**

Speed ratings (Par 109): **108,106,103,101,100 100,100,100,97**

toteswinger: 1&2 £3.70, 1&3 £3.00, 2&3 £4.30. CSF £11.44 TOTE £2.30: £1.10, £2.90, £1.60; EX 19.50 Trifecta £86.70 Pool: £5298.27 - 86.70 winning units..

Owner D Smith, Mrs J Magnier, M Tabor **Bred** Tally-Ho Stud **Trained** Goolds Cross, Co Tipperary

FOCUS

A juvenile Group 1 race which tends to highlight future sprinting stars rather than Guineas candidates these days, and this year's renewal looks no exception. They raced in two groups to begin with, with the winner and second, together with Galpin Junior, racing apart from the rest, until edging over towards the bigger group at halfway. Helped by a tailwind, the winning time was a course record and the form looks solid; it could go a shade higher too in time.

NOTEBOOK

Bushranger(IRE) had beaten Gallagher a shade comfortably in the Prix Morny last time out, and that piece of form, coupled with his previous success in the Phoenix Stakes over subsequent Champagne Stakes winner Westphalia, made him the one to beat on paper. The worry was the faster ground as his only two defeats to date had come on ground officially described as good to firm. He coped with conditions well, though, saw the trip out strongly and confirmed himself a leading sprinting juvenile. A speedy type and not the biggest, he might get 7f, but a mile is likely to stretch him, and a top quote of 20-1 for the Guineas from Blue Square makes little appeal. It would not be a surprise to see him out again before the season ends, and the Dewhurst and Breeders' Cup are possibilities, but his stamina will face a sterner test in those contests. (op 2-1 tchd 9-4)

Sayif(IRE) must be the best juvenile maiden in training as he came into the race having recorded three placed efforts in Group 2 company in his last three starts and this effort added a Group 1 placing to his CV. Given that he had excuses the last twice (pulled too hard and did not get home over 7f at Goodwood, and had a bout of colic prior to finishing second at Newbury) it was easy to see why people were prepared to give him another chance. He deserves to get his head in front, but that is probably it for the season now, and he will apparently be brought back early in the spring with the intention of winning a maiden on the Polytrack before taking in a Guineas trial. (op 8-1)

Huntdown(USA) ◆ won a maiden in impressive style at Newbury, and although he was taking on proven Group-race horses and that form left him with plenty to find, market confidence suggested that he would not be disgraced. He ran really well in third and will be suited by a step up to 7f. He could well return for the Dewhurst. (op 11-2)

Gallagher, runner-up in the Richmond, Morny and Mill Reef, was a shade disappointing considering that he had finished close behind Bushranger in France. He is a smart juvenile, a sprinter pure and simple, but appears to have his limitations. (op 15-2)

Classic Blade(IRE) made every yard to win the July Stakes two starts back, but he was well beaten in the Morny and the stable has been bang out of form since the middle of August. In the circumstances it was not a bad effort.

Prolific(IRE), who won the Richmond Stakes last time, had ground conditions to suit, but he stumbled leaving the stalls and did not get the clearest of runs from two furlongs out. He shaped a bit better than the bare form suggests. (op 8-1)

Galpin Junior(USA), a good walker who took a modest Folkestone maiden last time out, was always likely to struggle, upped significantly in class. (op 33-1)

Jobe(USA) was representing the stable that sent out Amadeus Wolf to win this race three years ago, but his Gimcrack third left him with a bit to find with the market principals. A little keen early on, he hung right as he tired in the closing stages, something he has done before. (op 16-1)

Finjaan, the Molecomb winner, was stepping up to 6f for the first time. A progressive type who relishes fast ground, he ruined his chance by being free to post and racing keenly in the race itself. Stuck on the rail and surrounded by horses, he had nowhere to go inside the final two furlongs and was eased down after being hampered. He is capable of a lot better. Official explanation: jockey said colt was denied a clear run (op 9-2)

6443 NUNNERY STUD EBF MAIDEN STKS (DIV II) 7f

3:45 (3:46) (Class 4) 2-Y-O **£6,152** (£1,830; £914; £456) **Stalls** High

Form				RPR
42	**1**		**Ra Junior (USA)**[16] 6026 2-9-3 0 .... JamieSpencer 12 (B J Meehan) *lw: w ldrs: led 3f out: edgd lft: drvn clr fnl f: readily* **7/4**[1]	89+
6	**2**	5	**Emirates Roadshow (USA)**[16] 6029 2-9-3 0 .... LDettori 5 (Saeed Bin Suroor) *str: lw: led tl 3f out: sn intimidated: kpt on same pce appr fnl f: no ch w wnr* **5/1**[3]	75
	3	3	**Getcarter** 2-9-3 0 .... RichardHughes 8 (R Hannon) *angular: athletic: green: t.k.h: sn trcking ldrs: kpt on same pce appr fnl f* **14/1**	67+
	4	½	**Wajaha (IRE)** 2-8-12 0 .... RHills 10 (J H M Gosden) *neat: athletic: lw: sn trcking ldrs: kpt on same pce fnl 2f: will improve* **11/4**[2]	61+
	5	½	**Just Mustard (USA)** 2-9-3 0 .... HayleyTurner 2 (G A Butler) *w'like: bit bkwd: trckd ldrs: outpcd over 2f out: kpt on fnl f* **25/1**	65
	6	hd	**Altimatum (USA)** 2-9-3 0 .... NCallan 14 (P F I Cole) *w'like: green: sn chsng ldrs: outpcd over 2f out: kpt on wl ins fnl f* **20/1**	64+
	7	¾	**Captain Dancer (IRE)** 2-9-3 0 .... MichaelHills 3 (B W Hills) *dwlt: hdwy to chse ldrs over 3f out: fdd appr fnl f* **8/1**	62+
05	**8**	2 ½	**Clerk's Choice (IRE)**[36] 5431 2-9-3 0 .... AlanMunro 13 (W Jarvis) *chsd ldrs: outpcd over 2f out: wknd over 1f out* **50/1**	56
0	**9**	1	**Theologist (IRE)**[14] 6083 2-9-3 0 .... JimCrowley 4 (Mrs A J Perrett) *mid-div: sn drvn along: lost pl over 2f out* **20/1**	53
	10	1	**Mid Wicket (USA)** 2-9-3 0 .... WilliamBuick 9 (B W Hills) *str: lw: bit bkwd: s.i.s: in rr: outpcd over 2f out: sn lost pl* **25/1**	51
0	**11**	30	**Princess Janet**[16] 6029 2-8-12 0 .... KShea 7 (A B Coogan) *leggy: bit bkwd: trckd ldrs: lost pl over 3f out: sn wl bhd: hopelessly t.o and virtually p.u* **200/1**	—

1m 24.2s (-1.20) **Going Correction** -0.225s/f (Firm) **11** Ran SP% **117.1**

Speed ratings (Par 97): **97,91,87,87,86 86,85,82,81,80 46**

toteswinger: 1&2 £3.00, 1&3 £6.60, 2&3 £6.70. CSF £9.76 TOTE £2.50: £1.20, £2.00, £2.30; EX 10.00.

Owner Roldvale Limited **Bred** Darley **Trained** Manton, Wilts

FOCUS

This second division of the maiden was run 1.14secs faster than the first leg but 1.73secs slower than the earlier fillies' Group 3 and featured several who ran with promise on their debuts behind the more experienced winner. Nothing got into the race from off the pace but several in behind should improve for the outing.

NOTEBOOK

Ra Junior(USA) stepped up on his Sandown debut when runner-up over 1m of the same track and his RPR of 80 set the standard. He travelled well throughout and, despite edging left when asked to go about his business, was well in command in the final furlong. He is in the Dewhurst but, as he needs fast ground, his next race depends on getting suitable ground. (op 9-4)

Emirates Roadshow(USA) dictated the early gallop but was no match for the winner, although that rival did rather cut across him when taking the advantage. He cost $800,000 as a yearling and is clearly held in high regard by connections as he holds several fancy entries including the Derby, and this was a big step up on his debut effort at Yarmouth. (op 11-2 tchd 6-1)

Getcarter ◆ cost less (10,000gns) at the breeze-ups than as a foal but put up an encouraging debut. He was keen racing up with the pace early but, despite getting tired in the closing stages, he kept on well enough to hold on to third behind two more experienced rivals. From a stable with a plethora of juvenile talent, he looks sure to come on for the run providing he learns to settle.

Wajaha(IRE), closely related to 1000 Guineas winner Lahan and a half-sister to several other winners at around 1m, was quite keen under restraint but was keeping on steadily up the hill under a sympathetic ride. She should come on for the experience. (op 7-4 tchd 3-1)

Just Mustard(USA), a $150,000 first foal of a mare from the family of Lady Capulet and El Prado, also ran a nice race on this debut and should be sharper next time. (op 33-1)

Altimatum(USA), a $260,000 half-brother to a couple of multiple US winners out of a top-class mare on dirt, was close enough at halfway before getting outpaced but then stayed on again after meeting the rising ground. This Derby entry is likely to come into his own over middle distances and, with his pedigree, will be interesting if tried on Polytrack. (op 16-1)

Captain Dancer(IRE), a 175,000euros son of an unraced half-sister to Dr Devious and Archway, was slowly away on this debut and did a lot of running to get onto the heels of the leaders at one point, but not surprisingly faded in the closing stages. (op 12-1)

6444 HAAFHD GODOLPHIN STKS (LISTED RACE) 1m 4f

4:20 (4:23) (Class 1) 3-Y-O+

£24,978 (£9,468; £4,738; £2,362; £1,183; £594) **Stalls** Centre

Form				RPR
4514	**1**		**Buccellati**[26] 5741 4-9-0 108 ....(v) WilliamBuick 7 (A M Balding) *chsd ldrs: rdn to ld 1f out: hung lft towards fin: r.o* **5/1**[2]	113
0040	**2**	1 ¼	**Classic Punch (IRE)**[83] 3942 5-9-0 100 .... TQuinn 8 (D R C Elsworth) *lw: led: rdn and hdd 1f out: styng on same pce whn edgd lft ins fnl f* **33/1**	111
345B	**3**	1 ½	**Speed Gifted**[34] 5494 4-9-0 109 .... DaneO'Neill 10 (L M Cumani) *a.p: rdn over 1f out: r.o* **5/1**[2]	109+
1035	**4**	2	**Ezdiyaad (IRE)**[55] 4856 4-9-0 102 .... RHills 11 (M P Tregoning) *chsd ldr tl rdn 2f out: no ex fnl f* **17/2**	105

4026 **5** *nk* **Gravitas**[26] 5741 5-9-0 107 .... TedDurcan 9 105+
(Saeed Bin Suroor) *hld up: nt clr run over 2f out: hdwy over 1f out: r.o: nt trble ldrs* **16/1**

-221 **6** *1 1/4* **Duncan**[15] 6055 3-8-7 90 .... PhilipRobinson 3 103
(J L Dunlop) *lw: hld up: hdwy and hung rt 2f out: no ex ins fnl f* **13/2**[3]

1050 **7** *4* **Love Galore (IRE)**[13] 6120 3-8-7 102 .... JamieSpencer 6 97
(M Johnston) *hld up: hdwy over 2f out: wknd ins fnl f* **15/2**

3651 **8** *10* **Regal Flush**[29] 5646 4-9-0 109 .... LDettori 4 81
(Saeed Bin Suroor) *chsd ldrs: hung rt fr over 4f out: rdr dropped whip 3f out: wknd wl over 1f out* **5/2**[1]

0123 **9** *18* **Strategic Mount**[20] 5885 5-9-0 103 .... NCallan 2 52
(P F I Cole) *hld up: rdn over 2f out: hmpd and wknd sn after* **16/1**

-240 **10** *12* **Whistledownwind**[20] 5892 3-8-8 104 ow1 .... RichardHughes 1 34
(J Noseda) *hld up in tch: rdn over 3f out: hung rt and wknd over 2f out* **12/1**

2050 **11** *48* **New Beginning (IRE)**[24] 5773 4-9-0 76 .... JimmyQuinn 5 —
(Mrs S Lamyman) *hld up: wknd over 3f out* **150/1**

2m 28.28s (-5.22) **Going Correction** -0.225s/f (Firm)
WFA 3 from 4yo+ 7lb **11** Ran SP% **120.6**
Speed ratings (Par 111): **108,107,106,104,104 103,101,94,82,74 42**
toteswinger: 1&2 £34.40, 1&3 £6.30, 2&3 £34.40. CSF £157.68 TOTE £6.30: £1.90, £7.50, £2.10; EX 209.20.
Owner Mr & Mrs P McMahon & Mr & Mrs R Gorell **Bred** Burton Agnes Stud Co Ltd **Trained** Kingsclere, Hants

FOCUS
An ordinary Listed contest and something of a tactical affair. The fourth sets the level judged on his handicap form.

NOTEBOOK
Buccellati, who had the visor back on, had travelled well through the race and two furlongs out it looked a question of 'how far?', but he was made to pull out all the stops in the end. A progressive sort, he finished fourth in a Turkish Group 2 last time out, two places in front of Gravitas, and he confirmed that form with the Godolphin horse. He could go for a Group 1 race in Italy before the end of the season, and next year his trainer plans on sending him down under for the Caulfield Cup. (op 11-2)
Classic Punch(IRE) was allowed to take them along at a steady gallop. At his best when fresh, he was coming back from an 83-day break and dropping back to a more suitable trip having failed to get home over 2m last time. He battled on well to the line, but was just beaten off by Buccellati close home.
Speed Gifted's efforts in Group company earlier in the campaign gave him every chance in this company, but he had to prove his unfortunate experience at Chester last time had not affected him mentally. He did that, but the way he was staying on at the finish suggests that he could have done with a stronger all-round pace. (tchd 6-1)
Ezdiyaad(IRE), for whom the fast ground was a worry, raced close to the pace throughout and that counted for plenty the way things unfolded. (op 12-1 tchd 8-1)
Gravitas, who had finished behind the winner in Turkey last time, was unsuited by the way the race was run and was caught out when the leaders quickened. He was staying on well close home and will be suited by a better pace in future. (op 12-1)
Duncan, who had shown promise in three maidens, winning easily at Pontefract last time, was taking a big step up in class, but he is a half-brother to Listed winner Samuel and the longer trip looked sure to suit. Being held up right at the back of the field was never going to be ideal given the steady early gallop, though, and he was finishing all too late in the end while still showing signs of inexperience. Given his pedigree, he should progress as he gets older and steps up further in distance. (op 7-1 tchd 6-1)
Love Galore(IRE) made some progress from the rear but did not look that keen in the closing stages and perhaps the ground was a bit quick for him. (op 9-1 tchd 7-1)
Regal Flush was one of the highest rated in the field, but the drop back in distance was a concern as he is essentially a stayer, and the lack of early pace made it a double whammy. Official explanation: jockey said colt hung right and was unsuited by the good to firm ground (op 11-4 tchd 3-1)
Strategic Mount Official explanation: jockey said gelding ran flat
Whistledownwind, down the field in the St Leger last time, was keen enough in the early stages and as a result, despite appearing to travel well to half a mile out, he soon dropped away once put under pressure. Official explanation: jockey said colt stumbled in the dip (op 14-1)
New Beginning(IRE) Official explanation: vet said gelding finished distressed

6445 STANDING FOR SUCCESS H'CAP 1m 2f
4:55 (4:56) (Class 2) (0-100,96) 3-Y-O
£18,693 (£5,598; £2,799; £1,401; £699; £351) **Stalls** High

Form RPR

4105 **1** **Swinging Sixties (IRE)**[22] 5830 3-9-1 93 .... PhilipRobinson 11 105+
(M A Jarvis) *trckd ldrs: chal 2f out: led appr fnl f: edgd lft: styd on strly* **9/4**[1]

6361 **2** *1 3/4* **Midships (USA)**[13] 6128 3-9-4 96 .... JimCrowley 7 104
(Mrs A J Perrett) *lw: drvn to ld: stdd 6f out: hdd appr fnl f: edgd lft and styd on same pce ins fnl f* **3/1**[2]

4311 **3** *2 1/4* **Closertobelieving**[21] 5858 3-9-1 93 .... TQuinn 6 97
(D R C Elsworth) *lw: racd in last: pushed along 6f out: hdwy and hung rt over 3f out: styd on to take 3rd wl ins fnl f* **15/2**

1210 **4** *3/4* **Laterly (IRE)**[21] 5853 3-9-4 96 .... MickyFenton 2 98
(T P Tate) *racd wd: chsd ldr: rdn and edgd lft over 2f out: rallied 1f out: styd on same pce* **10/1**

2135 **5** *1 1/2* **Tanto Faz (IRE)**[19] 5942 3-8-7 85 .... LiamJones 1 84
(W J Haggas) *trckd ldrs: drvn over 4f out: hung rt: one pce* **5/1**[3]

2110 **6** *4* **Tajweed (IRE)**[118] 2825 3-8-6 84 .... RHills 9 75
(M Johnston) *hld up towards rr: sme hdwy over 3f out: wknd over 1f out* **7/1**

3013 **7** *7* **Slam**[20] 5907 3-9-3 95 .... MichaelHills 3 72
(B W Hills) *hld up towards rr: effrt over 3f out: rdn and wknd 2f out* **12/1**

2m 1.26s (-4.54) **Going Correction** -0.225s/f (Firm) **7** Ran SP% **113.5**
Speed ratings (Par 107): **109,107,105,105,104 100,95**
toteswinger: 1&2 £2.20, 1&3 £4.60, 2&3 £4.70. CSF £8.99 CT £40.96 TOTE £3.40: £2.00, £2.30; EX 11.70.
Owner Sheikh Ahmed Al Maktoum **Bred** Darley **Trained** Newmarket, Suffolk

FOCUS
A good three-year-old handicap with 12lb covering the entire field judged on official ratings and with several front-runners in the line-up it promised to be run at a good gallop. That was the case early on but the leaders dropped anchor at around halfway before kicking on again from the bushes and it proved difficult to get involved from off the pace. Nevertheless, the form looks sound rated around the placed horses.

NOTEBOOK
Swinging Sixties(IRE) ◆, a course-and-distance winner here on his debut in the spring, had not had things go his way since winning at Windsor in June, but the return to faster ground and drop back to this trip made the difference. Backed into favouritism, he got a good lead from the winner in the early stages but appeared to be going best some way from home. However, he had to work hard to get past the runner-up but was well on top at the finish. He is quite talented and looks sure to make up into an even better four-year-old. (op 11-4 tchd 3-1 and 10-3 in places)
Midships(USA), raised 4lb for his recent course-and-distance success, was deposed as favourite by the winner then missed the break and had to be ridden along to get the lead. His rider got a breather into him at around the halfway mark and he battled really well when challenged, only to find the winner too strong. (tchd 7-2)
Closertobelieving has been in good form of late, having won his last two over this trip, but had been raised 15lb as a result. Held up as usual, he did best of those adopting similar tactics but never looked likely to get involved in the finish. Things did not pan out for him on this occasion but he is not one to give up on. (op 7-1 tchd 13-2)
Laterly(IRE) did not have things fall right, as he is most effective when making the running and was unable to do so with the runner-up in the race. He raced wide of the rest in the early stages in an attempt to overcome that but had tacked across to join the others by the halfway mark. However, he was in trouble some way from home and will be better back at 1m4f when getting an uncontested lead, possibly on a flatter track. (tchd 8-1)
Tanto Faz(IRE) got a good lead from the front-runners but was pretty keen under restraint and then tended to carry his head awkwardly under pressure. This was his first try on fast ground and possibly it did not suit, although he has carried his head high in the past.
Tajweed(IRE), a dual winner on soft ground in the spring, had not run since June and never really figured. A return to an easier surface should help. (op 15-2 tchd 8-1)
Slam, a dual winner over 1m at Great Leighs, had to prove himself over the trip and on the ground. However, the manner in which he dropped away in the closing stages suggested that he failed to get home over this longer distance. (op 10-1)

6446 NEWMARKET CHALLENGE WHIP (H'CAP) 1m 2f
5:30 (5:31) (Class 6) (0-85,84) 3-Y-O+ **£0Stalls** High

Form RPR

5100 **1** **Bencoolen (IRE)**[28] 5682 3-9-1 84 .... SteveDrowne 4 92
(R Charlton) *mde all: rdn over 1f out: styd on gamely* **6/1**[3]

1305 **2** *hd* **Stow**[14] 6078 3-8-8 77 .... RichardHughes 7 85
(H Morrison) *lw: a.p: chsd wnr over 4f out: rdn and ev ch fr over 1f out: styd on* **6/4**[1]

5465 **3** *9* **Free Offer**[33] 5536 4-9-4 82 .... EddieAhern 6 72
(J L Dunlop) *prom: rdn over 2f out: wknd fnl f* **11/4**[2]

5400 **4** *1/2* **Sonny Parkin**[13] 6130 6-8-9 73 .... (v) JimmyQuinn 5 62
(J Pearce) *hld up: plld hrd: hdwy 2f out: sn rdn: wknd fnl f* **8/1**

0660 **5** *8* **Miss Emma May (IRE)**[16] 6027 3-8-8 77 .... (v) TQuinn 8 50
(D R C Elsworth) *hld up: plld hrd: hdwy over 6f out: rdn and wknd over 2f out* **12/1**

4-05 **6** *3* **Debdene Bank (IRE)**[17] 5995 5-8-1 65 .... HayleyTurner 9 32
(Mrs Mary Hambro) *trckd ldr: plld hrd: stdd and lost pl after 1f: hdwy over 3f out: rdn and wknd over 1f out* **8/1**

0000 **7** *8* **Marchpane**[15] 6049 3-7-7 69 oh7 ow2 .... (b) RichardFelton(7) 2 20
(R M Beckett) *chsd ldr over 8f out: pushed along 4f out: wknd over 2f out* **40/1**

2m 2.40s (-3.40) **Going Correction** -0.225s/f (Firm)
WFA 3 from 4yo+ 5lb **7** Ran SP% **113.3**
Speed ratings (Par 101): **104,103,96,96,89 87,81**
toteswinger: 1&2 £2.50, 1&3 £3.30, 2&3 £2.30. CSF £15.19 CT £29.87 TOTE £8.30: £3.50, £1.50; EX 14.90 Place 6: £124.78 Place 5: £107.42.
Owner Lord De La Warr **Bred** Darley **Trained** Beckhampton, Wilts
■ No prize money for this historic race.

FOCUS
Very few got involved because far too many of the runners would not settle off the steady early gallop. The gap to the third is probably exaggerated but the first two are rated slight improvers.
T/Jkpt: Not won. T/Plt: £221.50 to a £1 stake. Pool: £107,838.44. 355.37 winning tickets. T/Qpdt: £4.70 to a £1 stake. Pool: £10,405.08. 1,632.65 winning tickets. CR

6251 WOLVERHAMPTON (A.W) (L-H)
Friday, October 3

OFFICIAL GOING: Standard
Wind: Almost nil Weather: Fine

6447 BETFAIR APPRENTICE TRAINING SERIES H'CAP 1m 5f 194y(P)
6:50 (6:51) (Class 6) (0-65,65) 3-Y-O **£2,388** (£705; £352) **Stalls** Low

Form RPR

0040 **1** **Eventide**[27] 5698 3-9-10 65 .... DavidProbert 1 71
(W J Knight) *hld up in tch: chal wl over 1f out: rdn to ld ins fnl f: r.o* **4/1**[3]

4333 **2** *1 1/2* **The Last Bottle (IRE)**[14] 6092 3-9-5 60 .... JackDean 9 64
(W M Brisbourne) *a.p: wnt 2nd over 5f out: led 2f out: rdn and hdd ins fnl f: nt qckn* **17/2**

6200 **3** *1 1/2* **Pairumani Pat (IRE)**[15] 6060 3-8-5 46 oh1 .... AmyBaker 2 48
(J Pearce) *hld up in rr: rdn over 3f out: hdwy over 1f out: styd on ins fnl f* **7/1**

5603 **4** *2* **Fleurs De Censier**[22] 5813 3-8-4 50 .... JosephineBruning(5) 8 49
(D M Simcock) *hld up in rr: hdwy wl over 1f out: one pce fnl f* **20/1**

3345 **5** *2 3/4* **Limelight (USA)**[15] 6044 3-8-5 49 .... (b[1]) RosieJessop(3) 4 44
(Sir Mark Prescott) *t.k.h: sn led: clr to 7f out: hdd 2f out: wknd ins fnl f* **7/2**[2]

0613 **6** *1 3/4* **Paddy Rielly (IRE)**[9] 6210 3-9-6 61 .... (p) RichardEvans 7 54
(P D Evans) *hld up: hdwy over 3f out: rdn over 1f out: wknd fnl f* **2/1**[1]

0000 **7** *14* **Super Al**[4] 6337 3-8-1 47 oh1 ow1 .... TobyAtkinson(5) 3 20
(M Wigham) *hld up towards rr: no ch fnl 3f* **66/1**

4403 **8** *3 3/4* **Sparkling Montjeu (IRE)**[40] 5320 3-8-12 53 .... MatthewDavies 5 21
(George Baker) *led early: chsd ldr tl over 5f out: rdn over 4f out: wknd over 3f out* **9/1**

3m 8.22s (2.22) **Going Correction** +0.05s/f (Slow) **8** Ran SP% **114.8**
Speed ratings (Par 99): **95,94,93,92,90 89,81,79**
toteswinger: 1&2 £6.30, 1&3 £42.70, 2&3 £42.70. CSF £37.63 CT £230.21 TOTE £5.60: £1.60, £2.20, £2.60; EX 35.90.
Owner Mrs Alison Ruggles **Bred** Mrs A R Ruggles **Trained** Patching, W Sussex

FOCUS
This was a typically moderate staying handicap for apprentice riders, which was run at a sound gallop thanks to the free-going Limelight. The form is rated through the runner-up.

6448 SPONSOR A RACE BY CALLING 01902 390009 CLAIMING STKS 5f 216y(P)
7:20 (7:21) (Class 6) 3-Y-O+ **£2,388** (£705; £352) **Stalls** Low

Form RPR

0422 **1** **Doubtful Sound (USA)**[8] 6225 4-9-2 69 .... (p) KevinGhunowa(3) 13 78
(R A Harris) *hld up in mid-div: hdwy on outside over 2f out: led ins fnl f: drvn out* **7/1**[3]

0000 **2** *1/2* **Monsieur Reynard**[17] 5991 3-9-0 69 .... AdrianTNicholls 9 72
(D Nicholls) *t.k.h: sn in mid-div: hdwy on ins whn nt clr run wl over 1f out: sn rdn: carried hd high whn swtchd rt 1f out: sn chal: nt qckn towards fin* **16/1**

0050 **3** 4½ **What Katie Did (IRE)**[81] [4028] 3-8-1 70....................(p) DavidProbert(5) 5 50
(George Baker) *led: rdn wl over 1f out: hdd ins fnl f: fdd* **5/1**[2]
1040 **4** ¾ **Another Genepi (USA)**[31] [5594] 5-9-0 75..............(p) EdwardCreighton 3 55
(E J Creighton) *s.i.s: in rr: rdn over 2f out: c wd st: hdwy 1f out: edgd lft: kpt on* **16/1**
4520 **5** 2½ **Lake Sabina**[9] [6219] 3-8-9 65.. GrahamGibbons 8 43
(E S McMahon) *prom: rdn over 1f out: wknd ins fnl f* **8/1**
2005 **6** ¾ **Westport**[37] [5400] 5-9-9 71...(p) PaulMulrennan 7 53
(K A Ryan) *outpcd: nt clr run jst over 1f out: nvr nrr* **10/1**
0000 **7** 3 **Bertbrand**[16] [6011] 3-9-1 67... RobbieEgan(7) 10 44
(D Flood) *hld up in mid-div: rdn over 3f out: nt clr run briefly 2f out: no hdwy* **50/1**
5100 **8** nse **Mandelieu (IRE)**[12] [6150] 3-9-4 65...................................... TonyHamilton 2 39
(Ollie Pears) *prom: rdn over 2f out: wknd fnl f* **40/1**
0101 **9** 1½ **Obe Brave**[4] [6335] 5-9-5 78... PaulHanagan 6 35
(R A Fahey) *prom: rdn over 2f out: sn wknd* **7/4**[1]
1313 **10** ¾ **Bazguy**[39] [5346] 3-9-0 70...(b) PatCosgrave 11 28
(P D Evans) *prom on outside: wknd over 3f out* **8/1**
4005 **11** ¾ **Corridor Creeper (FR)**[8] [6225] 11-9-5 71.......................(b) GregFairley 1 30
(J M Bradley) *bhd: short-lived effrt on ins over 1f out* **28/1**
6050 **12** 1½ **Opal Noir**[11] [6164] 4-9-1 65.. TomEaves 4 21
(Miss L A Perratt) *prom: rdn and wknd wl over 1f out* **20/1**

1m 15.35s (0.35) **Going Correction** +0.05s/f (Slow)
WFA 3 from 4yo+ 1lb **12** Ran SP% **121.2**
Speed ratings (Par 101): **99,98,92,91,88 87,83,82,80,79 78,76**
toteswinger: 1&2 £26.40, 1&3 £6.40, 2&3 £22.30. CSF £110.68 TOTE £6.60: £1.90, £5.60, £2.80; EX 116.40.Monsieur Reynard was claimed by Milton Bradley for £8,000; What Katie Did was claimed by Milton Bradley for £4,000
Owner The Govin Partnership **Bred** Millsec, Ltd **Trained** Earlswood, Monmouths

FOCUS
Not a bad claimer and it was a competitive heat. The winner is rated to his best and the form could be rated higher.
Obe Brave Official explanation: jockey said gelding had a breathing problem

6449 PWM GROUP H'CAP 5f 20y(P)
7:50 (7:50) (Class 4) (0-85,86) 3-Y-0+ **£5,180** (£1,541; £770; £384) **Stalls** Low

Form RPR
5401 **1** **Tony The Tap**[11] [6174] 7-9-0 **86** 6ex................................ DavidProbert(5) 3 95
(W R Muir) *outpcd: hdwy whn swtchd rt ins fnl f: str run to ld last strides* **10/3**[2]
0013 **2** ½ **Hotham**[8] [6232] 5-8-11 **78**... JamieMoriarty 2 85
(N Wilson) *chsd ldrs: rdn to ld jst over 1f out: hdd last strides* **3/1**[1]
6612 **3** ½ **Supermassive Muse (IRE)**[20] [5886] 3-9-4 **85**......(p) GrahamGibbons 10 90
(E S McMahon) *mid-div: pushed along over 3f out: hdwy 2f out: rdn over 1f out: nt qckn towards fin* **10/1**
1600 **4** ¾ **First Trim (IRE)**[49] [5056] 3-8-9 **76**................................. TPO'Shea 6 78
(B J Meehan) *wnt rt s: hld up: hdwy over 1f out: squeezed through ins fnl f: no ex towards fin* **16/1**
4310 **5** 3 **First Order**[33] [5542] 7-9-2 **83**..(v) TomEaves 4 75
(Miss L A Perratt) *prom: rdn and outpcd over 2f out: n.d after* **9/1**
1114 **6** 2¼ **Le Toreador**[57] [4787] 3-8-12 **79**....................................(t) JamieSpencer 1 62+
(K A Ryan) *chsd ldr: rdn over 1f out: nt qckn whn hmpd ins fnl f* **7/2**[3]
6023 **7** 1¾ **Northern Bolt**[23] [5796] 3-8-13 **80**................................ AdrianTNicholls 8 57
(D Nicholls) *hmpd s: bhd: rdn over 3f out: sn struggling: eased ins fnl f* **11/2**
000 **8** hd **Classic Encounter (IRE)**[60] [4693] 5-8-12 **79**.......... StephenDonohoe 11 55
(D M Simcock) *t.k.h: led: rdn and hdd jst over 1f out: wknd ins fnl f* **22/1**

62.13 secs (-0.17) **Going Correction** +0.05s/f (Slow) **8** Ran SP% **115.0**
Speed ratings (Par 105): **103,102,101,100,95 91,89,88**
toteswinger: 1&2 £21.60, 1&3 £4.50, 2&3 £3.50. CSF £13.89 CT £89.27 TOTE £4.70: £1.90, £1.20, £1.70; EX 16.10.
Owner K J Mercer & Mrs S Mercer **Bred** K J Mercer **Trained** Lambourn, Berks
■ Stewards' Enquiry : Jamie Moriarty two-day ban: used whip with excessive frequency with an element of force (Oct 17,19)

FOCUS
This was a fair sprint handicap, run at a generous pace, and the first four were fairly closely covered at the finish. The form is sound, the winner rated to his best.
Le Toreador Official explanation: jockey said gelding was unsuited by being unable to dominate
Northern Bolt Official explanation: jockey said colt hung right-handed throughout

6450 CARLSBERG PROBABLY THE BEST H'CAP 1m 1f 103y(P)
8:20 (8:20) (Class 5) (0-75,75) 3-Y-0+ **£3,238** (£963; £481; £240) **Stalls** Low

Form RPR
6204 **1** **New Star (UAE)**[8] [6235] 4-9-6 **74**.................................... GrahamGibbons 7 85
(W M Brisbourne) *a.p: led over 2f out: rdn over 1f out: hld on wl* **28/1**
1163 **2** hd **Royal Amnesty**[27] [5699] 5-9-5 **73**...................................(b) TomEaves 9 84
(Miss L A Perratt) *s.i.s: sn hld up in tch: wnt 2nd 2f out: rdn over 1f out: chal ins fnl f: kpt on* **5/1**[2]
5563 **3** hd **Ahlawy (IRE)**[13] [6134] 5-8-11 **65**..............................(b) PaulMulrennan 1 76
(M W Easterby) *hld up towards rr: hdwy on ins whn n.m.r over 2f out: sn rdn: wandered ins fnl f: r.o wl cl home* **10/1**
20-4 **4** 7 **Magic Rush**[11] [6170] 6-9-4 **72**..................................... EdwardCreighton 12 69
(Norma Twomey) *hld up towards rr: styd on fnl f: n.d* **16/1**
3002 **5** nk **Ballora (FR)**[20] [5888] 3-9-3 **75**.. JamieSpencer 3 71
(S Kirk) *led early: hld up in mid-div: hdwy 3f out: sn rdn: wknd wl over 1f out* **9/1**[3]
-400 **6** ¾ **Hyde Lea Flyer**[112] [3004] 3-8-10 **68**.................................. PaulHanagan 13 63
(E S McMahon) *t.k.h in mid-div: lost pl over 2f out: edgd lft over 1f out* **25/1**
3446 **7** nse **Given A Choice (IRE)**[20] [5913] 6-9-5 **73**......................(p) JerryO'Dwyer 8 67
(J Pearce) *s.i.s and reminders: nvr nr ldrs* **18/1**
31- **8** 3¾ **Phoenix Flight (IRE)**[459] [3171] 3-9-3 **75**.......................... J-PGuillambert 4 62
(Sir Mark Prescott) *t.k.h: sn led: hdd after 1f: prom: rdn over 2f out: wknd over 1f out* **7/4**[1]
5-04 **9** 1¼ **United Nations**[14] [6090] 7-8-8 **62**..................................... AndrewElliott 2 46
(N Wilson) *s.i.s: a in rr* **12/1**
6610 **10** ¾ **Mont Cervin**[43] [5202] 3-9-3 **75**...................................... StephenDonohoe 5 58
(Ian Williams) *a towards rr* **40/1**
3130 **11** ½ **Western Roots**[34] [5512] 7-8-11 **70**................................ DavidProbert(5) 10 52
(A M Balding) *led after 1f: rdn and hdd over 2f out: wknd over 1f out* **5/1**[2]
050 **12** 26 **Pugilist**[13] [6134] 6-8-11 **68**.. PatrickHills(3) 11 —
(B J Meehan) *prom: rdn 4f out: wknd 3f out: t.o* **20/1**

2m 0.64s (-1.06) **Going Correction** +0.05s/f (Slow)
WFA 3 from 4yo+ 4lb **12** Ran SP% **122.1**
Speed ratings (Par 103): **106,105,105,99,99 98,98,95,94,93 92,69**
toteswinger: 1&2 £40.20, 1&3 £40.20, 2&3 £23.60. CSF £162.42 CT £1542.46 TOTE £43.40: £11.80, £1.10, £4.30; EX 74.20.
Owner Shropshire Wolves **Bred** Darley **Trained** Great Ness, Shropshire
■ Stewards' Enquiry : Tom Eaves three-day ban: used whip with excessive force (Oct 17, 19-20)
Graham Gibbons three-day ban: used whip with excessive frequency without giving gelding time to respond (Oct 17, 19-20)

FOCUS
There was a cracking three-way finish to this modest handicap. The pace was good and the form is solid, with the first three finishing clear. A personal best (by 6lb) from the winner.
Given A Choice(IRE) Official explanation: jockey said gelding never travelled

6451 CARLSBERG UK MAIDEN AUCTION STKS 1m 141y(P)
8:50 (8:51) (Class 6) 2-Y-O **£2,729** (£806; £403) **Stalls** Low

Form RPR
1 **Eloquently** 2-8-6 0.. JamieSpencer 5 76+
(E F Vaughan) *sltly hmpd s: hld up and bhd: smooth prog on outside 3f out: led jst over 1f out: clr ins fnl f: easily* **7/4**[1]
5 **2** 5 **Cool Strike (UAE)**[25] [5754] 2-8-11 0.. LPKeniry 4 65+
(A M Balding) *hld up in tch: rdn over 2f out: kpt on to take 2nd towards fin: no ch w wnr* **6/1**[2]
5 **3** nk **Norwegian Dancer (UAE)**[53] [4921] 2-8-13 0............. GrahamGibbons 7 66
(E S McMahon) *chsd ldr: rdn and ev ch over 1f out: one pce: lost 2nd towards fin* **7/4**[1]
6 **4** 1 **Carter**[108] [3107] 2-8-9 0.. PatCosgrave 1 60+
(W M Brisbourne) *hld up towards rr: swtchd rt and hdwy wl over 1f out: sn rdn: kpt on to take 4th nr fin* **33/1**
0 **5** ½ **Candilejas**[28] [5678] 2-8-8 0... TPO'Shea 10 58
(D J Coakley) *hld up in mid-div: hdwy on outside over 3f out: rdn over 2f out: one pce fnl f* **12/1**[3]
4 **6** 5 **Kristopher James (IRE)**[61] [4658] 2-8-9 0............................... ShaneKelly 6 48
(W M Brisbourne) *led: rdn over 2f out: wknd over 1f out* **14/1**
7 7 **Longboat Key** 2-8-11 0.. GregFairley 9 36
(M Johnston) *s.i.s: bhd: no ch fnl 2f* **16/1**
00 **8** nk **Cabo Polonio (IRE)**[44] [5184] 2-8-9 0................................... JamesDoyle 13 33
(S Kirk) *s.i.s: in rr: no ch fnl 2f* **50/1**
04 **9** ½ **Lomica**[26] [5716] 2-8-6 0.. PaulHanagan 8 29
(Miss J A Camacho) *hld up in tch: rdn and wknd over 2f out* **14/1**
0 **10** 24 **Perfect Honour (IRE)**[38] [5384] 2-8-2 0.................... DuranFentiman(3) 3 —
(Joss Saville) *prom: wkng whn hmpd on ins wl over 1f out: eased fnl f* **100/1**

1m 51.13s (0.63) **Going Correction** +0.05s/f (Slow) **10** Ran SP% **119.8**
Speed ratings (Par 93): **99,94,94,93,92 88,82,82,81,60**
toteswinger: 1&2 £7.20, 1&3 £6.30, 2&3 £2.20. CSF £13.75 TOTE £2.90: £1.40, £1.70, £1.20; EX 20.10.
Owner The Eloquently Partnership **Bred** Mrs S F Dibben **Trained** Newmarket, Suffolk

FOCUS
A modest maiden won very easily by Eloquently, who was value for 8l and is a nice type for the grade. The form could turn out to be better than it has been initially rated.

NOTEBOOK
Eloquently, a cheap purchase related to 1m winners, was very well backed to get her career off to the perfect start and she duly obliged with an easy success. She was given time to find her stride after a sluggish start, but once asked to make up her ground nearing the turn for home, it was clear she was the one to be on. She put the race to bed at the furlong pole, coming right away from her rivals, and rates value for a good bit further than her already wide winning margin. This was just a moderate affair, but she evidently stays well and certainly has a future. (op 13-8 tchd 15-8)
Cool Strike(UAE), fifth on testing ground on his debut at Folkestone last month, hit a flat spot in the home straight before staying on again and may not be all that straightforward. He should improve again for the experience though and will be eligible for a mark after his next run. (op 4-1)
Norwegian Dancer(UAE) was made to look pedestrian when the winner asserted for home and eventually just lost out on second place. This step up from 7f really looked beyond him at this stage. (op 7-2)
Carter, up in trip, was doing some fair work late in the day and should benefit for this first run since June. He will look more interesting when becoming eligible for a mark after his next assignment. (op 28-1)
Candilejas, whose Lingfield debut form has worked out well, failed to improve on her initial effort over this slightly longer trip and looks to need more time. (tchd 9-1)

6452 PERCY MILLS H'CAP 1m 141y(P)
9:20 (9:21) (Class 4) (0-80,80) 3-Y-0+ **£5,180** (£1,541; £770; £384) **Stalls** Low

Form RPR
0331 **1** **Internationaldebut (IRE)**[72] [4301] 3-9-0 **77**..................... TolleyDean(3) 9 86
(S Parr) *s.s: hld up in rr: hdwy wl over 1f out: weaved through ins fnl f: led last strides* **12/1**
2302 **2** hd **Prince Noel**[46] [5156] 4-8-9 **72**... BMcHugh(7) 8 81
(N Wilson) *hld up towards rr: hdwy on ins 2f out: rdn to ld jst ins fnl f: hdd last strides* **8/1**
0400 **3** 1½ **Fort Amhurst (IRE)**[13] [6134] 4-8-6 **62**..............................(p) DaleGibson 6 68
(M W Easterby) *t.k.h in mid-div: hdwy on ins whn nt clr run over 2f out: wandered u.p ins fnl f: nt qckn* **28/1**
1061 **4** 2 **Alfie Tupper (IRE)**[13] [6134] 5-9-2 **72**................................. PatCosgrave 2 73+
(J R Boyle) *a.p: wnt 2nd over 2f out: edgd rt over 1f out: ev ch ins fnl f: one pce* **3/1**[1]
1246 **5** 3½ **Glenridding**[16] [6020] 4-9-4 **74**... PaulHanagan 1 67
(J G Given) *led: rdn and hdd jst over 1f out: wknd fnl f* **6/1**[3]
0432 **6** 1 **Blow Hole (USA)**[23] [5800] 3-8-13 **73**................................... ShaneKelly 5 64
(J Noseda) *hld up in tch: pushed along and wknd 2f out* **10/3**[2]
2-42 **7** ½ **Somerset Falls (UAE)**[13] [6114] 3-8-4 **64**.............................. GregFairley 4 53
(M Johnston) *chsd ldr tl over 2f out: wknd over 1f out* **17/2**
-000 **8** 1¼ **Roman Maze**[20] [5908] 8-9-3 **73**... JamesDoyle 11 60
(W M Brisbourne) *hld up towards rr: pushed along over 3f out: no rspnse* **33/1**
0145 **9** nse **Hilbre Court (USA)**[6] [6283] 3-9-3 **80**............................. PatrickHills(3) 13 66
(B J Meehan) *hld up in mid-div: lost pl and c wd st* **10/1**
0000 **10** hd **Ninth House (USA)**[86] [3840] 6-9-5 **75**.............................. AndrewElliott 10 61
(Mrs R A Carr) *a towards rr* **14/1**
2510 **11** 1½ **Nesno (USA)**[15] [6056] 5-8-11 **67**..........................(p) GrahamGibbons 12 50
(J D Bethell) *sn prom: wknd wl over 1f out* **9/1**

1m 50.26s (-0.24) **Going Correction** +0.05s/f (Slow)
WFA 3 from 4yo+ 4lb **11** Ran SP% **123.8**
Speed ratings (Par 105): **103,102,101,99,96 95,95,94,94,93 92**
toteswinger: 1&2 £17.10, 1&3 £29.10, 2&3 £37.30. CSF £110.17 CT £2662.56 TOTE £12.30: £3.80, £3.80, £6.40.
Owner W McKay, J Barton **Bred** Ennistown Stud **Trained** Bawtry, S Yorks

FOCUS
A fair handicap run at a strong pace, and the first pair came from the rear. The winner built on his maiden win, with the next two close to form.
T/Plt: £380.80 to a £1 stake. Pool: £103,005.16. 197.45 winning tickets. T/Qpdt: £20.60 to a £1 stake. Pool: £9,267.45. 332.40 winning tickets. KH

HOPPEGARTEN (R-H)
Friday, October 3

OFFICIAL GOING: Soft

6461a PREIS DER DEUTSCHEN EINHEIT (GROUP 3) 1m 2f
3:30 (3:50) 3-Y-0+ **£23,529** (£7,253; £3,676; £2,206)

RPR

1 **Prince Flori (GER)**[34] 5528 5-9-4 .... TMundry 10 109
(S Smrczek, Germany) *in tch: 4th st: chalng 1 1/2f out: led ins fnl f: pushed out* **19/10**[1]

2 1 1/2 **Zaungast (IRE)**[12] 6156 4-9-4 .... WPanov 3 106
(W Hickst, Germany) *cl 2nd: led 1 1/2f out: hdd ins fnl f: nt pce of wnr* **21/10**[2]

3 1 1/2 **Walzertraum (USA)**[30] 5624 3-8-11 .... FJohansson 2 101
(J Hirschberger, Germany) *hld up: 6th st on ins: styd on fr over 1f out: nrst fin* **96/10**

4 1 1/2 **White Lightning (GER)**[180] 1237 6-9-4 .... APietsch 9 100
(U Stech, Norway) *led: hdd 1 1/2f out: kpt on same pce* **149/10**

5 1/2 **Duellant (IRE)**[30] 5624 3-8-11 .... FilipMinarik 4 97
(P Schiergen, Germany) *a in midfield* **104/10**

6 nk **Dwilano (GER)**[34] 5528 5-9-4 .... VSchulepov 7 98
(T Satra, Czech Republic) *hld up in last: drvn 2f out: styd on fr over 1f out* **28/1**

6 dht **Il Divo (GER)**[89] 3773 3-8-11 .... MMonteriso 8 96
(A Wohler, Germany) *in tch: cl 5th st: rdn to chse ldrs 1 1/2f out: no ex fnl f* **165/10**

8 2 1/2 **Blue Coral (IRE)**[482] 4-9-4 .... JChaloupka 5 93
(J Vana Jr, Czech Republic) *hld up: nvr able to chal* **27/1**

9 3/4 **Schutzenjunker (GER)**[26] 3-8-11 .... THellier 6 90
(U Ostmann, Germany) *in tch: 3rd st: sn btn* **39/10**[3]

10 2 **Proud Boris (GER)**[370] 5821 4-9-4 .... RJuracek 1 88
(J Hanacek, Czech Republic) *n.d* **189/10**

2m 9.20s (2.50)
WFA 3 from 4yo+ 5lb **10 Ran SP% 129.4**
(including 10 Euro stake): WIN 29; PL 16, 14, 21; SF 81.
Owner Stall Reni **Bred** H A Wacek **Trained** Germany

6462 - 6465a (Foreign Racing) - See Raceform Interactive

6374 **KEMPTON (A.W)** (R-H)
Saturday, October 4

OFFICIAL GOING: Standard
Wind: Strong, behind Weather: Overcast

6466 GET VALUE AT ODDSCHECKER.COM CONDITIONS STKS 1m (P)
2:05 (2:10) (Class 3) 2-Y-O
£6,854 (£2,052; £1,026; £513; £256; £128) **Stalls** High

Form RPR

1 **Serva Jugum (USA)** 2-8-8 0.......................... StephenDonohoe 1 86+
(P F I Cole) *hld up in 4th: prog on outer over 2f out: edgd lft but led over 1f out: rdn clr* **11/2**

014 2 2 **Aurorian (IRE)**[15] 6075 2-9-0 83.......................... FrancisNorton 2 87
(R Hannon) *trckd ldr: rdn to chal and upsides 2f out: styd on fnl f but readily outpcd by wnr* **7/1**

1 3 1 1/2 **Something Perfect (USA)**[17] 6016 2-8-7 0 ow1.......... PatCosgrave 6 77
(H R A Cecil) *nvr gng that sweetly: hld up in 5th: urged along and effrt over 2f out: kpt on same pce fr over 1f out w tail swishing* **5/2**[2]

136 4 1 **Jazz Police**[21] 5889 2-9-0 92.......................... PatDobbs 4 82
(R Hannon) *led: edgd lft whn rdn 2f out: hdd over 1f out: wknd* **2/1**[1]

105 5 3/4 **Parisian Art (IRE)**[24] 5794 2-9-0 93.......................(b) AdamKirby 7 80
(J Noseda) *trckd ldng pair: rdn and nt qckn over 2f out: wknd tamely over 1f out* **7/2**[3]

5 6 17 **Bigalo's Star (IRE)**[23] 5825 2-8-6 0.......................... NataliaGemelova(5) 5 40
(L A Mullaney) *dwlt: a last: rdn 1/2-way: sn lost tch: t.o* **50/1**

1m 42.31s (2.51) **Going Correction** +0.175s/f (Slow) **6 Ran SP% 114.0**
Speed ratings (Par 99): **94,92,90,89,88 71**
toteswinger: 1&2 £5.10, 1&3 £1.70, 2&3 £2.00 CSF £42.27 TOTE £7.60: £3.10, £2.70; EX 61.70.

Owner Mrs Fitri Hay **Bred** B Wayne Hughes **Trained** Whatcombe, Oxon

FOCUS
An ordinary juvenile conditions contest and they didn't go that quick early on, resulting in a slow time.

NOTEBOOK
Serva Jugum(USA) ◆, a $250,000 son of Fusaichi Pegasus out of Coronation Stakes winner Shake The Yoke, was an impressive winner on this debut. Having travelled kindly just off the lead, he came three wide into the straight and gradually pulled away when asked for his effort. He is likely to run again this year and his connections think there is improvement to come. In the longer term he looks the type to make a nice three-year-old and could be smart in time, although it remains to be seen whether he will be as effective on turf. (op 9-2 tchd 7-1 after 7-2 in a place)
Aurorian(IRE) came into the race rated just 83 and looks a good guide to the strength of the form. He was carried slightly left by his stablemate Jazz Police in the straight, but had every chance. (op 8-1 tchd 13-2)
Something Perfect(USA) was a course-and-distance winner on her debut, but she was noted to have flashed her tail and has apparently not been the easiest to deal with at home. This was tougher and she again showed signs of temperament, proving reluctant to load (needed a blanket for stalls entry), and again flashing her tail. (op 2-1 tchd 15-8)
Jazz Police got a soft enough lead but he was well below his official mark of 92 on this first try over 1m. (op 9-4 tchd 5-2)
Parisian Art(IRE) almost certainly failed to see out the trip and will be better back over 7f, or even 6f. (op 13-2)

6467 ODDSCHECKER.COM CASINO & POKER ROOM H'CAP 1m (P)
2:35 (2:37) (Class 3) (0-90,90) 3-Y-O
£7,477 (£2,239; £1,119; £560; £279; £140) **Stalls** High

Form RPR

2322 1 **Arabian Spirit**[12] 6170 3-9-1 87.......................... TGMcLaughlin 9 96
(E A L Dunlop) *settled in midfield: prog in centre over 2f out: drvn to ld ins fnl f: styd on* **8/1**

1013 2 3/4 **Soft Shoe Shuffle (IRE)**[14] 6128 3-9-1 87.......................... AdamKirby 6 96+
(W R Swinburn) *hld up in midfield: effrt whn carried lft jst over 2f out: prog over 1f out: carried lft and tightened up ins fnl f: rallied to snatch 2nd last strides* **4/1**[1]

3315 3 nk **Border Owl (IRE)**[49] 5098 3-8-7 79.......................... PatDobbs 7 85
(R Hannon) *trckd ldrs: wnt 2nd over 2f out and carried lft: led over 1f out: hung lft after: hdd and no ex ins fnl f: lost 2nd last strides* **12/1**

1002 4 1/2 **Timetable**[17] 6035 3-8-8 80.......................(v) PatCosgrave 10 85
(H R A Cecil) *nt that wl away: hld up in rr: rdn 3f out: carried hd high over 2f out and carried lft sn after: tried to cl on ldrs and carried lft 1f out: nt qckn* **8/1**

2326 5 nk **Ellemujie**[21] 5907 3-9-1 87.......................... RichardKingscote 8 91
(D K Ivory) *hld up in last trio: rdn wl over 2f out: stl last wl over 1f out: gd prog ent fnl f: nt rch ldrs* **7/1**[3]

1350 6 1 **Totally Focussed (IRE)**[8] 6242 3-8-3 80.......................... WilliamCarson(5) 12 82
(S Dow) *dwlt: hld up in last: rdn and prog over 2f out: kpt on but nvr quite on terms w ldrs* **10/1**

21-0 7 2 1/4 **Hold The Gold (IRE)**[105] 3251 3-8-4 81.......................... MCGeran(5) 13 78
(E J O'Neill) *dwlt: towards rr: rdn over 2f out: kpt on fr over 1f out: nvr on terms w ldrs* **25/1**

311 8 2 3/4 **Stalking Shadow (USA)**[52] 4976 3-9-4 90.......................... TonyCulhane 3 81
(Saeed Bin Suroor) *led briefly over 6f out: chsd ldr untl over 2f out: nt qckn u.p: sn fdd* **6/1**[2]

0050 9 1 1/2 **Pha Mai Blue**[75] 4252 3-8-1 78.......................... DavidProbert(5) 4 65
(W J Knight) *led to over 6f out: prom tl wknd u.p 2f out* **33/1**

-150 10 3/4 **Regal Best (IRE)**[22] 5862 3-8-11 83.......................... JamesDoyle 5 68
(Mrs A J Perrett) *hld up in midfield: rdn over 2f out: wknd over 1f out* **14/1**

1453 11 nk **Summerstrand (IRE)**[12] 6170 3-8-7 79.......................... StephenDonohoe 11 64
(M A Jarvis) *dwlt: hld up in rr but nvr really gng wl: rdn over 2f out: sn no prog: wknd over 1f out* **6/1**[2]

1313 12 7 **Cave Lion (USA)**[29] 5675 3-8-10 87.......... Louis-PhilippeBeuzelin(5) 2 56
(J H M Gosden) *led after 2f: racd freely and 3 l clr 3f out: hung lft over 2f out: hdd & wknd rapidly over 1f out* **6/1**[2]

1m 40.05s (0.25) **Going Correction** +0.175s/f (Slow) **12 Ran SP% 127.8**
Speed ratings (Par 105): **105,104,103,103,103 102,99,97,95,94 94,87**
toteswinger: 1&2 £8.80, 1&3 £7.60, 2&3 £24.90. CSF £43.28 CT £403.41 TOTE £9.00: £3.50, £2.00, £2.80; EX 52.40 TRIFECTA Not won..
Owner P A Deal A L Deal & G Holland-Bosworth **Bred** Malih Lahij Al Basti **Trained** Newmarket, Suffolk
■ Stewards' Enquiry : Pat Dobbs three-day ban: careless riding (Oct 19-21)

FOCUS
A good, competitive three-year-old handicap with some good formlines represented. However, it was quite a rough race and they were all over the place in the straight after long-time leader Cave Lion continually edged left when coming back to the field. The winner is rated up a length but the runner-up has been rated as finishing upsides.

NOTEBOOK
Arabian Spirit made his move after Cave Lion had begun to wander, so he avoided the trouble, and took full advantage. This rates as a career best, and he is clearly a tough sort, but he does not appeal as one to back to follow up off a higher mark. (op 7-1)
Soft Shoe Shuffle(IRE) looked a slightly unlucky loser, as she endured a troubled run in the straight, firstly having to wait for a gap over two out, and then being bumped over a furlong out before being squeezed up inside the distance, all the time being forced left towards the stands' rail. (op 5-1 tchd 11-2)
Border Owl(IRE) was another who ended up more towards the stands' side in the closing stages, and he was inclined to keep edging in that direction late on, but he had his chance. (op 16-1 tchd 20-1)
Timetable is probably not the most straightforward, and he had to be driven along for a few strides soon after the start, but this was not a bad run.
Ellemujie got going too late and is proving tricky to win with. He was inclined to stick his tongue out and may do better with it tied down. (op 11-1)
Hold The Gold(IRE) Official explanation: jockey said colt hung left
Stalking Shadow(USA), chasing a hat-trick on his return from nearly two months off, proved disappointing on this first try on Polytrack. He did not look the most convincing under pressure, although that's harsh on a horse who has a 50 per cent strike-rate. (op 8-1 tchd 5-1)
Pha Mai Blue Official explanation: jockey said gelding hung left
Summerstrand(IRE) was slowly away and simply never involved. This was disappointing. Official explanation: jockey said filly missed the break and never travelled (op 4-1)
Cave Lion(USA) was far too free and hung badly left in the straight. Official explanation: jockey said colt hung left (tchd 11-2 and 13-2)

6468 ODDSCHECKER.COM STKS (HERITAGE H'CAP) 6f (P)
3:10 (3:11) (Class 2) (0-105,103) 3-Y-O+
£24,924 (£7,464; £3,732; £1,868; £932; £468) **Stalls** High

Form RPR

0041 1 **Knot In Wood (IRE)**[13] 6153 6-9-2 102.......................... BMcHugh(7) 2 114
(R A Fahey) *hld up in midfield on outer: prog over 2f out: rdn to ld over 1f out: styd on strly fnl f* **7/1**[3]

300 2 1 1/2 **Artimino**[70] 4405 4-9-1 99.......................... Louis-PhilippeBeuzelin(5) 5 106
(J R Fanshawe) *dwlt: hld up in last: gd prog on outer 2f out: pressed wnr jst over 1f out: styd on but no imp fnl f* **6/1**[2]

3002 3 3/4 **Ebraam (USA)**[40] 5347 5-9-7 100.......................... IanMongan 11 105
(P Howling) *dwlt: sn trckd ldrs on inner: effrt over 2f out: nt clrest of runs and swtchd lft over 1f out: styd on wl but nvr able to chal* **6/1**[2]

3001 4 nk **Fullandby (IRE)**[11] 6184 6-9-9 102.......................... SaleemGolam 8 106
(T J Etherington) *trckd ldrs: rdn 2f out: kpt on u.p but nvr able to chal* **7/1**[3]

0300 5 1/2 **Reverence**[14] 6121 7-9-9 102.......................... AdrianTNicholls 12 104
(E J Alston) *t.k.h early: hld up in rr on inner: prog over 2f out: drvn to try to cl on ldrs over 1f out: one pce after* **8/1**

0160 6 2 1/2 **Pearly Wey**[7] 6269 5-9-5 98.......................... TonyCulhane 7 92
(C G Cox) *hld up in rr: urged along fr 2f out: nt pce to threaten* **8/1**

3006 7 2 1/2 **Bertoliver**[69] 4445 4-9-1 94.......................... RichardKingscote 10 80
(Tom Dascombe) *w ldrs: led over 2f out: hung rt and hdd over 1f out: immediately wknd* **9/1**

2200 8 1 1/4 **Baby Strange**[14] 6104 4-9-2 95.......................... DarrenWilliams 4 77
(D Shaw) *dwlt: t.k.h early: hld up towards rr: gng wl enough over 2f out: sn rdn and no rspnse* **14/1**

0500 9 1/2 **Aahayson**[14] 6104 4-9-7 100.......................... PatCosgrave 3 81
(K R Burke) *w ldr to over 2f out: wknd over 1f out* **8/1**

3010 10 7 **Stoneacre Lad (IRE)**[56] 4840 5-9-5 103..................(b) PatrickDonaghy(5) 6 61
(Peter Grayson) *racd wd: pressed ldrs: losing pl 1/2-way: wknd 2f out: sn bhd* **25/1**

1040 **11** *4* **Viking Spirit**[49] 5109 6-9-7 **100**.................................(t) AdamKirby 9 46
(W R Swinburn) *mde most to over 2f out: wknd rapidly* **4/1**[1]

1m 12.71s (-0.39) **Going Correction** +0.175s/f (Slow)
WFA 3 from 4yo+ 1lb **11** Ran SP% **127.4**
Speed ratings (Par 109): **109,107,106,105,104 101,98,96,95,86 81**
toteswinger: 1&2 £11.50, 1&3 £8.50, 2&3 £10.00. CSF £53.03 CT £282.77 TOTE £4.90: £2.50, £2.70, £2.00; EX 67.90 TRIFECTA Not won..
Owner Rhodes, Kenyon & Gill **Bred** Rathbarry Stud **Trained** Musley Bank, N Yorks
■ Stewards' Enquiry : Ian Mongan one-day ban: careless riding (Oct 19)

FOCUS
A decent, competitive sprint handicap in which Knot In Wood ran a personal best under his claiming jockey. Sound form.

NOTEBOOK
Knot In Wood(IRE) produced an even better performance than the bare result suggests, as he was drawn in stall two and raced at least three wide throughout. He will be worth his place in Listed or Group 3 company while in this form. (op 5-1)

Artimino, dropped back to 6f for the first time since his debut and trying Polytrack for the first time, was last two furlongs out but produced a sustained effort on the outside in the straight. He had his chance if good enough. (op 12-1)

Ebraam(USA), raised 2lb for his recent course-and-distance second, was switched to challenge over a furlong out but was not unlucky. (op 11-2)

Fullandby(IRE) travelled strongly for a long way, but his effort flattened out when he got a run inside the final two furlongs. He should be suited by a return to 5f. (op 11-2)

Reverence went for a run up the inside rail in the straight and, although there was not that much room, he seemed to have his chance. (op 10-1)

Bertoliver weakened after showing early speed on his debut for the Tom Dascombe yard. He is entitled to come on for this first run in over two months and will be worth a second look if dropped back to 5f next time. (op 12-1)

Baby Strange found very little after travelling well. (op 16-1 tchd 12-1)

Viking Spirit carried his head slightly to one side in the straight, seemingly hanging, and weakened quickly. Something looked amiss. (op 11-2)

6469 BET ON THE ARC AT ODDSCHECKER.COM NURSERY 5f (P)
3:45 (3:46) (Class 4) (0-85,84) 2-Y-O £3,885 (£1,156; £577; £288) Stalls High

Form RPR

41 **1** **Happy Forever (FR)**[43] 5214 2-8-13 **76**.................................. OscarUrbina 11 79+
(M Botti) *trckd ldrs: got through gap 1f out: rdn to ld last 75yds: a holding off rivals fin* **7/4**[1]

1300 **2** *nk* **Evelyn May (IRE)**[14] 6118 2-9-3 **80**.................................. IanMongan 6 82
(B W Hills) *t.k.h early: hld up in midfield: effrt over 1f out: r.o ins fnl f to take 2nd nr fin: hld by wnr* **8/1**

5136 **3** *nk* **Agnes Love**[20] 5933 2-7-8 **62**.................................. DavidProbert(5) 1 63+
(J Akehurst) *forced wdst of all bnd after 1f: rcvrd to chse ldng pair: rdn to chal 1f out: upsides ins fnl f: jst outpcd* **20/1**

0040 **4** *½* **Piste**[18] 5997 2-8-7 **70**.................................. RichardKingscote 3 69+
(B J Meehan) *forced wd bnd after 1f: towards rr after: rdn and styd on fr over 1f out: nt quite able to chal* **20/1**

115 **5** *nk* **Fangfoss Girls**[29] 5680 2-8-8 **71**.................................. StephenDonohoe 10 69
(D M Simcock) *racd on inner and sn led as rest wnt wd bnd after 1f: drvn over 1f out: hdd last 75yds: swamped by rivals nr fin* **16/1**

4103 **6** *nse* **Mazzola**[22] 5866 2-9-6 **83**.................................. TonyCulhane 12 81
(M R Channon) *v awkward s: last tl effrt against rail over 1f out: styd on ins fnl f: nrst fin* **16/1**

4404 **7** *nse* **Red Rossini (IRE)**[7] 6274 2-8-12 **75**.................................. PatDobbs 4 74+
(R Hannon) *dwlt: hld up wl in rr: nt clr run fr over 1f out tl fnl 100yds: styd on wl: nt rcvr* **11/1**

230 **8** *hd* **Mister Green (FR)**[43] 5244 2-9-0 **84**.................................. RobbieEgan(7) 9 82+
(D Flood) *nt as wl away as most: towards rr: swtchd lft over 1f out and nt clr run after: styd on last 75yds: nrst fin* **16/1**

0310 **9** *shd* **Smokey Ryder**[14] 6118 2-8-11 **74**.................................. AdamKirby 2 71
(G L Moore) *forced wd bnd after 1f: towards rr after: rdn 2f out: styd on fnl f: nrst fin* **7/1**[3]

012 **10** *1* **Lady Master**[36] 5466 2-8-12 **75**.................................. FrankieMcDonald 8 68
(H Candy) *sltly awkward bnd after 1f: mostly chsd ldr: rdn to chal over 1f out: nt qckn: wknd ins fnl f* **3/1**[2]

3041 **11** *2¾* **The Cuckoo**[4] 6350 2-8-13 **76** 6ex.................................. PatCosgrave 7 59
(M J Wallace, Australia) *chsd ldrs: lost pl 1f out: no ch whn hmpd nr fin* **15/2**

6000 **12** *4* **Calypso Girl (IRE)**[12] 6172 2-8-8 **74**.................................. LukeMorris(3) 5 43
(P D Evans) *forced wd bnd after 1f: wl in rr after: struggling 1/2-way* **25/1**

61.33 secs (0.83) **Going Correction** +0.175s/f (Slow) **12** Ran SP% **136.1**
Speed ratings (Par 97): **100,99,99,98,97 97,97,97,97,95 91,84**
toteswinger: 1&2 £7.80, 1&3 £14.00, 2&3 £37.20. CSF £19.57 CT £250.89 TOTE £2.70: £1.50, £2.70, £4.80; EX 24.60.
Owner Mrs R J Jacobs **Bred** Newsells Park Stud **Trained** Newmarket, Suffolk

FOCUS
The first ten finished in a heap and the form does not look reliable. They looked to go too fast into the first bend (a particularly tight turn), with about six disputing the early lead, and a host of them ended up out very wide.

NOTEBOOK
Happy Forever(FR) got a bit worked up before the start, but she was one of the few who handled the first bend having got a lead and stayed on best in the straight to follow up her Bath maiden victory. While it is hard to enthuse about the form, and one would like to see her stay calmer before her races in future, she is quite well regarded. She is likely to be put away for the year. (op 9-4 tchd 6-4 & 5-2 in a place)

Evelyn May(IRE) was not one of those who disputed the frantic early pace, but she still failed to handle the first bend. She did well to recover and was not beaten far, confirming herself suited by Polytrack. (op 10-1)

Agnes Love was stuck out deepest of all from stall one, at least eight horse widths off the inside rail, and she ran a remarkable race to finish so close. (op 16-1)

Piste was another to take the first bend very wide, but she kept on to post a respectable effort. (tchd 22-1)

Fangfoss Girls, unlike so many of her rivals, railed like a greyhound and can have no excuses. (op 14-1)

Mazzola was doing his best work at the finish having started rather awkwardly. (op 14-1)

Red Rossini(IRE) was stopped in his run when beginning to pick up inside the final furlong. (op 9-1 tchd 12-1)

Mister Green(FR) endured a nightmare passage, firstly being squeezed up on the turn into the straight, then continually being blocked inside the final two furlongs. (tchd 18-1)

Lady Master was another who was not great on the first turn, but she still gave away less ground than most. However, she was still below form, failing to gain compensation for an unlucky defeat at Sandown. (op 11-2)

6470 COMPARE POKER & CASINO AT ODDSCHECKER.COM MAIDEN STKS 1m 2f (P)
4:20 (4:27) (Class 5) 3-Y-O £3,885 (£1,156; £577; £288) Stalls High

Form RPR

4 **1** **Empowered (IRE)**[184] 1172 3-9-3 0.................................. SaleemGolam 1 85+
(W J Haggas) *dwlt: hld up in 7th: prog but hanging lft bnd 3f out: hdwy to ld over 1f out: sn clr: comf* **2/1**[1]

5253 **2** *3* **Crusoe's Return**[35] 5505 3-9-3 **76**.................................. PatCosgrave 5 79
(L M Cumani) *trckd ldrs in 5th: prog over 2f out: styd on wl to take 2nd fnl f: no imp on wnr* **4/1**[2]

0 **3** *1½* **Alqaffay (IRE)**[16] 6047 3-9-3 0.................................. TonyCulhane 13 76+
(Saeed Bin Suroor) *sltly awkward s: hld up in 8th: effrt over 2f out: hanging over 1f out: styd on to take 3rd ins fnl f: no threat to ldng pair* **14/1**

0 **4** *1½* **Confederate**[170] 1417 3-9-3 0.................................. RichardKingscote 9 73
(R Charlton) *hld up in 6th: outpcd fr 2f out: swtchd lft and styd on same pce fnl f* **15/2**

6234 **5** *nse* **Cheney Manor**[33] 5568 3-9-3 **69**.................................. PatDobbs 6 73
(B W Hills) *led: tried to kick on 2f out: hdd over 1f out: folded tamely* **7/1**[3]

6 *5* **Icy Cool (IRE)** 3-9-3 0.................................. FrancisNorton 8 63+
(J Noseda) *s.i.s and rousted along: mostly in last pair: modest late prog: no ch* **9/1**

50 **7** *4½* **Sea Swell (USA)**[18] 5995 3-8-12 0.................................. PaulDoe 4 49
(G A Butler) *trckd ldng pair: wnt 2nd wl over 2f out to wl over 1f out: wknd rapidly* **20/1**

0040 **8** *3½* **First Tracks (IRE)**[26] 5748 3-9-3 **52**.................................. SimonWhitworth 7 47
(J W Hills) *hld up in last pair: nvr a factor* **80/1**

05 **9** *5* **Deer Lake (IRE)**[32] 5587 3-9-3 0.................................. AdamKirby 3 37
(J Noseda) *chsd ldr to over 2f out: wknd rapidly* **33/1**

0 **10** *5* **Seconditis**[19] 5963 3-9-3 0.................................. StephenDonohoe 12 27
(Mrs N S Evans) *chsd ldng trio tl wknd over 3f out* **100/1**

2m 8.29s (0.29) **Going Correction** +0.175s/f (Slow) **10** Ran SP% **104.2**
Speed ratings (Par 101): **105,102,101,100,100 96,92,89,85,81**
toteswinger: 1&2 £2.20, 1&3 £6.70, 2&3 £8.80. CSF £7.28 TOTE £2.60: £1.50, £1.50, £3.10; EX 9.10.
Owner Cheveley Park Stud **Bred** Marengo Investments & Knighton House Ltd & M Kina **Trained** Newmarket, Suffolk

FOCUS
A fair maiden, solidly run, and the form should prove more reliable than most late-season races of its type. The winner looks sure to do better.

6471 ODDSCHECKER - THE ODDS COMPARISON SITE H'CAP 7f (P)
4:55 (4:56) (Class 4) (0-85,88) 3-Y-O+ £6,476 (£1,927; £963; £481) Stalls High

Form RPR

31 **1** **Noble Citizen (USA)**[33] 5580 3-9-2 **83**.................................. StephenDonohoe 8 96+
(D M Simcock) *mde all: mod pce to 1/2-way: rdn and styd on strly fnl 2f* **11/2**[3]

0032 **2** *1¾* **Woodcote Place**[28] 5697 5-9-2 **81**.................................. FrancisNorton 5 89
(P R Chamings) *t.k.h early: prom on outer: chsd wnr over 2f out: no imp fr over 1f out: jst hld on for 2nd* **5/1**[2]

51 **3** *shd* **Hallingdal (UAE)**[24] 5800 3-8-11 **78**.................................. JamesDoyle 3 85
(Ms J S Doyle) *stdd s and swtchd fr wd draw to inner: hld up in last: prog over 2f out: styd on wl fnl f: jst failed to snatch 2nd* **8/1**

4000 **4** *2¼* **Mey Blossom**[16] 6053 3-8-7 **77**.................................. RussellKennemore(3) 11 78
(R M Whitaker) *chsd ldrs: rdn 1/2-way: kpt on u.p but nvr pce to threaten* **50/1**

0001 **5** *2¼* **Vhujon (IRE)**[12] 6169 3-9-4 **88**.................................. LukeMorris(3) 9 83
(P D Evans) *awkward s: hld up wl in rr: rdn and prog over 2f out: chsd ldrs over 1f out but nowhere nr on terms: one pce after* **12/1**

1021 **6** *nse* **Portodora (USA)**[45] 5185 3-9-4 **85**.................................. IanMongan 14 79
(H R A Cecil) *trckd ldrs: effrt over 2f out: nt qckn wl over 1f out: fdd* **7/2**[1]

5321 **7** *¾* **Jonny Lesters Hair (IRE)**[11] 6186 3-8-9 **76**.................................. PatDobbs 12 68
(T D Easterby) *plld hrd early: prom on inner: hmpd wl over 2f out: tried to rally wl over 1f out: sn btn* **5/1**[2]

120 **8** *½* **Naughty Frida (IRE)**[50] 5071 3-9-1 **82**.................................. KirstyMilczarek 13 73
(M Botti) *hld up in midfield: effrt u.p over 2f out: sn no prog and btn* **9/1**

-030 **9** *shd* **Hip**[87] 3852 3-9-3 **84**.................................. TGMcLaughlin 10 75
(E A L Dunlop) *hld up wl in rr: shkn up over 2f out: no real prog* **16/1**

5501 **10** *1¾* **Buxton**[31] 5600 4-9-6 **85**.................................(t) RobertHavlin 4 72
(R Ingram) *hld up wl in rr: rdn over 2f out: no prog* **16/1**

6106 **11** *nse* **Twilight Star (IRE)**[97] 3529 4-9-0 **79**.................................(t) PatCosgrave 6 66
(R A Teal) *plld hrd and hld up in rr: rdn and no prog over 2f out* **20/1**

034 **12** *1½* **Titan Triumph**[29] 5675 4-8-9 **74**.................................(t) PaulDoe 2 57
(W J Knight) *t.k.h early and racd wd: nvr on terms w ldrs: struggling over 2f out* **10/1**

314- **13** *1* **Barnaby Rudge (IRE)**[305] 7027 3-9-1 **82**.................................. FrankieMcDonald 7 61
(Jane Chapple-Hyam) *chsd wnr to over 2f out: wknd rapidly* **33/1**

1m 25.95s (-0.05) **Going Correction** +0.175s/f (Slow)
WFA 3 from 4yo+ 2lb **13** Ran SP% **130.3**
Speed ratings (Par 105): **107,105,104,102,99 99,98,98,98,96 96,94,93**
toteswinger: 1&2 £7.20, 1&3 £5.60, 2&3 £12.50. CSF £35.85 CT £233.14 TOTE £8.20: £2.30, £2.00, £3.00; EX 34.40.
Owner Khalifa Dasmal **Bred** Don M Robinson **Trained** Newmarket, Suffolk

FOCUS
A fair handicap, although Noble Citizen was able to set just an ordinary pace and not many got involved from behind. The form looks sound.
Jonny Lesters Hair(IRE) Official explanation: jockey said gelding ran too free

6472 ODDSCHECKER.COM APPRENTICE DERBY H'CAP 1m 4f (P)
5:30 (5:30) (Class 4) (0-85,82) 3-Y-O+ £6,476 (£1,927; £963; £481) Stalls Centre

Form RPR

0110 **1** **Dance The Star (USA)**[33] 5573 3-9-4 **81**.................................. MarcHalford 3 92+
(D M Simcock) *hld up towards rr: rdn over 3f out: prog u.p over 2f out: led over 1f out: edgd rt but stormed clr* **11/8**[1]

32-0 **2** *3½* **Gabier**[147] 1984 5-9-5 **80**.................................. JemmaMarshall(5) 5 82
(G L Moore) *hld up in rr: rdn and nt qckn over 2f out: styd on wl fr over 1f out to take 2nd ins fnl f* **16/1**

2300 **3** *½* **Celticello (IRE)**[21] 5900 6-9-3 **73**.................................. KirstyMilczarek 2 74
(P D Evans) *hld up in last pair: rdn and prog 2f out: styd on fnl f to take 3rd last strides* **12/1**

50/0 **4** *nk* **Forthright**[15] 6079 7-9-5 **80**.................................. KylieManser(5) 4 81
(B G Powell) *prom: rdn to ld over 2f out: hdd and outpcd over 1f out* **8/1**

1026 **5** ½ **Wee Charlie Castle (IRE)**[17] 6033 5-8-10 **71**.......... WilliamCarson(5) 6 71
(G C H Chung) *prom: wnt 2nd 1/2-way: led over 3f out to over 2f out: edgd rt jst over 1f out: one pce* **10/1**
0300 **6** 1¼ **Crossbow Creek**[7] 6272 10-9-12 **82**.......................... LukeMorris 7 80
(M G Rimell) *led 1f: trckd ldr to 1/2-way: rdn 3f out: stl cl up 2f out: one pce* **25/1**
210 **7** 2¼ **Blakfrankisch (IRE)**[49] 5092 5-8-12 **73**.................... RossAtkinson(5) 9 69+
(Tom Dascombe) *hld up in midfield: prog over 2f out: one pce and wl btn whn squeezed out 1f out* **9/1**
0014 **8** 14 **Wind Flow**[10] 6210 4-9-0 **73**..........................(b) Louis-PhilippeBeuzelin(3) 1 45
(C A Dwyer) *rrd s: rcvrd to ld after 1f: hdd over 3f out: wknd rapidly over 2f out: t.o* **5/1**[3]
1211 **9** 2¾ **Swords**[36] 5476 6-8-7 **68**................................ AshleyMorgan(5) 8 36
(R E Peacock) *rrd s: a in last pair: lost tch over 2f out: t.o* **9/2**[2]

2m 36.76s (2.26) **Going Correction** +0.175s/f (Slow)
WFA 3 from 4yo+ 7lb **9** Ran SP% **124.6**
Speed ratings (Par 105): **99,96,96,96,95 94,93,84,82**
toteswinger: 1&2 £7.70, 1&3 £7.00, 2&3 £22.30. CSF £30.56 CT £213.47 TOTE £3.00: £1.70, £4.40, £3.10; EX 34.60 Place 6 £407.13, Place 5 £49.26..
Owner Sultan Ali **Bred** B M Kelley And B P Walden **Trained** Newmarket, Suffolk

FOCUS
Just an ordinary apprentice handicap. There was no pace through the first furlong, but Wind Flow, who reared as the stalls opened and had to be driven along for a few strides, soon took over. Muddling form, the winner rated up 4lb but some doubt over the opposition.
Celticello(IRE) Official explanation: jockey said gelding suffered interference in running
T/Plt: £356.80 to a £1 stake. Pool: £64,722.53. 132.41 winning tickets. T/Qpdt: £9.50 to a £1 stake. Pool: £3,562.96. 277.40 winning tickets. JN

6438
NEWMARKET (ROWLEY) (R-H)
Saturday, October 4

OFFICIAL GOING: Good to firm (firm in places)
Wind: Fresh across Weather: Overcast

6473 TATTERSALLS TIMEFORM FILLIES' 800 7f
2:10 (2:10) (Class 2) 2-Y-O

£433,360 (£177,280; £78,880; £29,520; £29,520; £7,840) **Stalls** High

Form RPR
4 **1** **Tiger Eye (IRE)**[17] 6030 2-9-0 0........................ PhilipRobinson 11 98+
(M A Jarvis) *w'like: scope: lw: mde all: rdn clr fr over 1f out* **5/1**[2]
21 **2** 2¾ **Vitoria (IRE)**[71] 4380 2-9-0 0............................ EddieAhern 16 91
(M J Wallace, Australia) *lw: a.p: rdn to chse wnr over 1f out: edgd lft: styd on* **7/1**
01 **3** 1½ **The Miniver Rose (IRE)**[22] 5859 2-9-0 0.......... RichardHughes 5 87
(R Hannon) *hld up: swtchd lft over 2f out: hdwy over 1f out: r.o* **12/1**
2 **4** 3 **Winged Harriet (IRE)**[15] 6080 2-9-0 0..................... LiamJones 6 80
(W J Haggas) *lw: s.i.s: hld up: hdwy over 1f out: nrst fin* **6/1**
34 **4** dht **Moneycantbuymelove (IRE)**[42] 5256 2-9-0 0.......... JamieSpencer 17 80
(M L W Bell) *chsd wnr tl rdn over 2f out: no ex fnl f* **16/1**
5130 **6** nk **Ahla Wasahl**[56] 4868 2-9-0 **98**.............................. DarryllHolland 10 79
(D M Simcock) *hld up: rdn over 2f out: hdwy over 1f out: nvr nrr* **14/1**
025 **7** nk **Dubai Legend**[29] 5673 2-9-0 0............................ RichardMullen 15 78
(D M Simcock) *hld up: hdwy 1/2-way: rdn over 2f out: wknd over 1f out* **50/1**
3 **8** ½ **Lady Francesca**[40] 5365 2-9-0 0.......................... MartinDwyer 8 77
(W R Muir) *w'like: leggy: hld up in tch: rdn over 2f out: wknd fnl f* **33/1**
9 1¾ **Oasis Sunset (IRE)**[15] 6098 2-9-0 0........................(v[1]) WMLordan 1 73
(David Wachman, Ire) *hld up: hdwy 1/2-way: rdn: edgd lft and wknd over 1f out* **16/1**
105 **10** nk **Kissing The Camera**[56] 4868 2-9-0 0......................... MJKinane 13 73+
(J Noseda) *plld hrd and prom: rdn over 2f out: wkng whn hmpd over 1f out* **9/2**[1]
51 **11** 1¼ **My Superstar**[34] 5534 2-9-0 0.............................. RyanMoore 2 70+
(Sir Michael Stoute) *str: lw: hld up: hdwy 1/2-way: wkng whn hmpd over 1f out* **11/2**[3]
02 **12** ¾ **Indian Tonic (IRE)**[12] 6176 2-9-0 0......................... AlanMunro 4 67
(W Jarvis) *hld up: n.d* **33/1**
6 **13** 1¾ **King's Starlet**[43] 5241 2-9-0 0........................... RobertHavlin 18 63
(H Morrison) *on toes: hld up: hdwy 1/2-way: rdn and wknd over 1f out* **11/1**
14 7 **Forgotten Dreams (IRE)** 2-9-0 0......................... SteveDrowne 12 45
(H J L Dunlop) *w'like: s.i.s: hld up: a in rr* **50/1**
000 **15** 12 **Suakin Dancer (IRE)**[25] 5788 2-9-0 0.......................... DaneO'Neill 9 15
(H Morrison) *s.i.s: a in rr* **100/1**
03 **16** 2 **Mekong Miss**[17] 6014 2-9-0 0................................ ChrisCatlin 7 10
(J Jay) *leggy: attr: chsd ldrs: rdn and lost pl 1/2-way: sn bhd* **100/1**

1m 23.76s (-1.64) **Going Correction** -0.025s/f (Good) **16** Ran SP% **123.3**
Speed ratings (Par 98): **108,104,103,99,99 99,99,98,96,96 94,93,91,83,70 67**
toteswinger: 1&2 £11.80, 1&3 £14.30, 2&3 £15.40. CSF £39.20 TOTE £6.70: £2.30, £2.60, £3.70; EX 51.10 Trifecta £247.30 Part won..
Owner Highclere Thoroughbred Racing (VC2) **Bred** J M Beever **Trained** Newmarket, Suffolk
■ The first running of this very valuable event. Prizemoney went down to tenth place.

FOCUS
The tailwind that been a feature of the two preceding days had veered around and was blowing from right to left across the track and the official going was changed to good to firm, firm in placed beforehand. This sales race for fillies featured a wide range of abilities amongst the runners, although many were short on experience and it was one of those who dominated. The field raced in one group up the centre of the track.

NOTEBOOK
Tiger Eye(IRE) ◆, who nearly doubled her original sale price when re-sold for 82,000gns, gave her connections a big return on their investment by making all the running. She had clearly come on for her debut over 6f at Yarmouth and the result was not in doubt from over a furlong out. She was given quotes of 33-1 for the 1000 Guineas, but there are no definite plans as yet. (op 9-2)
Vitoria(IRE) had built on her promising debut on Polytrack by scoring over 7f on fast ground at Thirsk. The runner-up and third had won since and it was no surprise that she was well backed. She tracked the winner throughout and was travelling well at the bushes, but she could not respond when the winner set sail for home, although she held off the rest comfortably enough. She will not run again this season and, as her trainer is going to Australia soon, she will have a new handler and it would not be the biggest surprise if she races under the Godolphin banner next year. (op 9-1)
The Miniver Rose(IRE) did best of those held up off the pace, making good headway from the top of the hill despite edging right, but her effort flattened out on meeting the rising ground. She will be put away now and will probably appreciate a longer trip next season. (op 10-1)
Winged Harriet(IRE) was another to come from the back, and this 115,000gns half-sister to dual 6f-7f Listed winner Misu Bond built on her promising debut on this step up in trip. She was clear of the rest and should be winning before long. (op 13-2)
Moneycantbuymelove(IRE) had shown only modest form on good and soft ground and, although her proximity tends to limit the form, she appeared to run an improved race on this faster surface. (op 13-2)
Ahla Wasahl, whose third in Cherry Hinton set the standard, had only previously encountered easy ground on turf but ran on late over this longer trip on this quicker surface. (op 16-1)
Dubai Legend was having only her second run on turf and also handled the different conditions.
Lady Francesca stepped up on her debut on much softer ground.
Oasis Sunset(IRE), who has already shown form at a mile, did not improve for the fitting of a visor.
Kissing The Camera, was dropping in grade having been held in Group company since her winning debut, but she was one of the first beaten. Official explanation: jockey said filly hung left (op 5-1 tchd 11-2 and 6-1 in places)
My Superstar travelled well enough behind the leading group but was beginning to feel the pinch when hampered in the dip. (op 5-1 tchd 6-1 in places)

6474 TATTERSALLS TIMEFORM MILLION 7f
2:45 (2:49) (Class 2) 2-Y-O

£541,700 (£221,600; £98,600; £49,200; £24,600; £9,800) **Stalls** High

Form RPR
4201 **1** **Donativum**[41] 5316 2-9-3 **87**.................................... MartinDwyer 2 101
(J H M Gosden) *swtchd rt s: hld up in mid-div: hdwy over 2f out: styd on strly to ld nr fin* **33/1**
01 **2** ½ **Crowded House**[29] 5672 2-9-3 0................................ MJKinane 8 100+
(B J Meehan) *lw: w ldrs: styd on to ld fnl 50yds: hdd fnl strides* **12/1**
0211 **3** 1 **Nasri**[14] 6118 2-9-3 0.. JamieSpencer 24 97
(B J Meehan) *trckd ldrs gng wl: edgd lft over 1f out: led jst ins fnl f: hdd and ex last 50yds* **7/1**[3]
311 **4** hd **Liberation (IRE)**[6] 6305 2-9-3 0............................ GregFairley 23 97
(M Johnston) *dwlt: sn trcking ldrs: led and edgd lft 2f out: hdd jst ins fnl f: no ex* **2/1**[1]
1 **5** ½ **Mafaaz**[24] 5798 2-9-3 0.. RHills 15 95
(J H M Gosden) *trckd ldrs: chal 1f out: no ex ins fnl f* **16/1**
3 **6** 1¼ **Monitor Closely (IRE)**[22] 5857 2-9-3 0...................... AlanMunro 17 92
(P W Chapple-Hyam) *w ldrs: kpt on same pce appr fnl f* **14/1**
16 **7** nk **Prince Siegfried (FR)**[35] 5507 2-9-3 0.................. WilliamBuick 20 91
(A M Balding) *in tch: outpcd over 2f out: kpt on wl fnl f* **20/1**
11 **8** ½ **Sri Putra**[35] 5507 2-9-3 0................................... PhilipRobinson 22 92+
(M A Jarvis) *lw: led: hdd 2f out: one pce whn hmpd over 1f out* **9/2**[2]
1144 **9** nk **Sohcahtoa (IRE)**[21] 5898 2-9-3 **83**............................ DaneO'Neill 1 89
(R Hannon) *trckd ldrs: kpt on same pce fnl 2f* **40/1**
212 **10** nk **Weald Park (USA)**[85] 3920 2-9-3 **105**...................... RichardHughes 4 89
(R Hannon) *in tch: effrt over 2f out: kpt on one pce* **8/1**
1226 **11** nk **High Alert**[24] 5791 2-9-3 0...(b) ShaneKelly 16 88
(J Noseda) *trckd ldrs: effrt over 2f out: one pce whn n.m.r over 1f out* **66/1**
41 **12** 1½ **Gyr (IRE)**[67] 4510 2-9-3 0.................................... RichardMullen 14 84
(J L Dunlop) *lw: swtchd rt after s: sn trcking ldrs: effrt 2f out: kpt on one pce* **20/1**
01 **13** ½ **Felday**[43] 5225 2-9-3 0.. SteveDrowne 19 83
(H Morrison) *on toes: chsd ldrs: wkng whn hmpd over 1f out* **66/1**
21 **14** nse **Imposing**[7] 6292 2-9-3 0.. RyanMoore 12 83+
(Sir Michael Stoute) *sn outpcd towards rr: kpt on fnl 2f: nvr a factor* **25/1**
20 **15** 1½ **Sign Of Approval**[14] 6119 2-9-3 0.............................. CDHayes 7 79
(K R Burke) *s.s: sme hdwy over 2f out: nvr a factor* **100/1**
110 **16** 2¾ **Cry Of Freedom (USA)**[35] 5507 2-9-3 0.................. DarryllHolland 18 72
(M Johnston) *w ldrs: hmpd over 2f out: wknd over 1f out* **20/1**
17 2¼ **Laurie Grove (IRE)** 2-9-3 0.................................... MichaelHills 13 67
(T G Mills) *tall: on toes: reminders after s: nvr a factor* **100/1**
314 **18** nk **Satwa Laird**[24] 5791 2-9-3 0...................................... ChrisCatlin 10 66
(E A L Dunlop) *mid-div: lost pl 2f out* **80/1**
6100 **19** 1½ **Highland Storm**[16] 6058 2-9-3 0..................................(b[1]) JimCrowley 9 62
(J G Given) *hld up in rr: effrt over 2f out: sn wknd* **100/1**
220 **20** hd **Seminole (IRE)**[56] 4861 2-9-3 0..............................(b) RobertHavlin 5 62
(J H M Gosden) *w ldrs: wknd over 2f out* **100/1**
02 **21** 2 **King's Sabre**[14] 6117 2-9-3 0................................... DO'Donohoe 3 57
(W R Muir) *chsd ldrs: wknd over 2f out* **80/1**
0 **22** 17 **Green Agenda**[10] 6212 2-9-3 0............................ J-PGuillambert 6 14
(M Johnston) *w'like: in rr: wl bhd fnl 3f: t.o* **100/1**
23 2¼ **Happy Day (IRE)** 2-9-3 0.. WMLordan 21 8
(David Wachman, Ire) *w'like: gd bodied: lw: in rr: sn drvn along: bhd fnl 3f: t.o* **40/1**
P **Dark Humour (IRE)**[27] 5721 2-9-3 0............................(v[1]) EddieAhern 11 —
(D K Weld, Ire) *sn detached in last: wl t.o whn p.u 4f out: dismntd* **40/1**

1m 24.22s (-1.18) **Going Correction** -0.025s/f (Good) **24** Ran SP% **134.2**
Speed ratings (Par 101): **105,104,103,103,102 101,100,100,99,99 99,97,96,96,95 91,89,89,87,87 84,65,62,—**
toteswinger: 1&2 £0.00, 1&3 £55.70, 2&3 £19.70. CSF £379.05 TOTE £70.70: £14.50, £4.60, £2.60; EX 969.80 TRIFECTA Not won..
Owner H R H Princess Haya Of Jordan **Bred** Stratford Place Stud **Trained** Newmarket, Suffolk
■ Stewards' Enquiry : Greg Fairley four-day ban: careless riding (Oct 19-22)
M J Kinane caution: used whip in incorrect place.

FOCUS
The inaugural running of this incredibly valuable sales race, with almost £500,000 going to the winner and prize-money going all the way down to tenth place. The winner's prize was more than double the 1000 and 2000 Guineas combined. They raced in two groups middle to far side to begin with but the principals drifted left towards the stands' side in the closing stages and the first two, who had raced more towards the centre for much of the race, challenged up the stands' rail in the end. They finished in a bit of a heap and the winning time was 0.46sec slower than that recorded by the fillies in the earlier sales race.

NOTEBOOK
Donativum did not always look the most straightforward earlier in the season, but he was gelded before winning his maiden at Yarmouth last time and improved on that form to take this race. Having edged left under pressure from a furlong out, it helped that he had the stands' rail to race next to in the closing stages, and he stayed on strongly up the stands' rail to just get up close home, the extra furlong clearly suiting him. That is likely to be it for the season now.
Crowded House, who is considered a Group horse in the making by his trainer, built on the promise of his maiden win at Kempton with a fine display. Always towards the fore, he travelled strongly throughout and kept on well from the Dip. Only denied close home, he has the pedigree to make up into a middle-distance horse next season and one would imagine that he can only progress from two to three. (tchd 11-1)
Nasri, who raced towards the far side for much of the race but edged left under pressure, got the longer trip well enough and remains progressive, but a bit of juice in the ground would have probably helped his cause. (op 9-1 tchd 10-1 in places)
Liberation(IRE), an impressive winner in a fast time of an Ascot nursery just six days earlier, had not run on ground this quick before and he hung left from two furlongs out. He ran well but it is possible that the race still came a bit too soon. (op 9-4 tchd 5-2)

Mafaaz, who made a winning debut in a Kempton maiden, had seen that form boosted when the third Evasive easily won a maiden here the previous day. He ran a perfectly sound race considering his relative lack of experience.

Monitor Closely(IRE), a well-bred colt who made a promising debut in a decent looking Doncaster maiden on his debut, might not have been suited by the drop back in trip as he was slightly outpaced before running on from the Dip. (op 16-1 tchd 18-1)

Prince Siegfried(FR), only sixth behind Sri Putra in the Solario Stakes last time, turned that form around, although he was fortunate to do so as the latter was hampered. (tchd 22-1)

Sri Putra, successful in the Group 3 Solario Stakes last time, made the running, but was looking beaten when hampered just inside the final two furlongs and had his momentum badly checked. (op 4-1 tchd 5-1 in places)

Sohcahtoa(IRE), held in Listed company on his last two starts and one of the more exposed horses in the line-up, probably gives the best guide to the level of the form.

Weald Park(USA) looked a leading contender on the form he showed when runner-up in the Superlative Stakes at the July meeting, but it was slightly worrying that he had been off the track since then, and this performance was well short of the form he showed in that Group 2 race. (tchd 15-2)

High Alert, who had done all his previous racing on turf on soft ground, ran a sound race considering these very different conditions, although he missed out on prizemoney by one place.

Gyr(IRE), not seen since winning his maiden at Goodwood in July, did not look very happy on the quick ground and this son of Pivotal will appreciate more give in future. (op 28-1)

Imposing, who only won his maiden a week earlier, struggled to go the early pace but passed a few beaten horses in the closing stages. He was another not suited by the drop back from a mile and can do better back over a longer trip. (op 20-1)

6475 KINGDOM OF BAHRAIN SUN CHARIOT STKS (GROUP 1) (F&M) 1m

3:15 (3:25) (Class 1) 3-Y-O+

£120,920 (£45,837; £22,940; £11,438; £5,729; £2,875) **Stalls** High

Form RPR

3113 **1** **Halfway To Heaven (IRE)**[27] 5730 3-8-13 0 .... JAHeffernan 6 118
(A P O'Brien, Ire) *mde all: rdn over 1f out: styd on gamely* **8/1**

2222 **2** *1/2* **Darjina (FR)**[27] 5740 4-9-2 0 .... RichardHughes 1 117
(A De Royer-Dupre, France) *lw: a.p: chsd wnr 3f out: rdn and edgd lft over 1f out: sn ev ch: styd on* **11/10**[1]

0-21 **3** *1* **Visit**[64] 4590 3-8-13 108 .... AlanMunro 3 114
(Sir Michael Stoute) *a.p: rdn over 2f out: swtchd rt over 1f out: r.o* **20/1**

-241 **4** *3 3/4* **Spacious**[22] 5856 3-8-13 112 .... RobertWinston 2 106+
(J R Fanshawe) *s.i.s: hld up: hdwy and nt clr run over 1f out: r.o ins fnl f: nt rch ldrs* **20/1**

1234 **5** *3/4* **Heaven Sent**[63] 4623 5-9-2 111 .... RyanMoore 9 104
(Sir Michael Stoute) *lw: prom: rdn over 2f out: wknd ins fnl f* **15/2**

2264 **6** *1 1/2* **Barshiba (IRE)**[35] 5506 4-9-2 108 .... TQuinn 5 101
(D R C Elsworth) *chsd wnr tl rdn 3f out: wer 1f out* **33/1**

6142 **7** *4 1/2* **Nahoodh (IRE)**[27] 5730 3-8-13 115 .... MJKinane 7 90
(M Johnston) *prom: rdn over 2f out: wknd over 1f out* **6/1**[3]

5-20 **8** *5* **Harvest Queen (IRE)**[108] 3120 5-9-2 106 .... EddieAhern 10 79
(P J Makin) *hld up: rdn over 2f out: sn wknd* **50/1**

53-3 **9** *3 1/4* **Festoso (IRE)**[23] 5829 3-8-13 105 .... SteveDrowne 4 71
(H J L Dunlop) *hld up: wknd over 2f out* **50/1**

21-5 **10** *2 1/4* **Listen (IRE)**[27] 5730 3-8-13 0 .... JamieSpencer 11 66
(A P O'Brien, Ire) *hld up: wknd 2f out* **5/1**[2]

1m 35.41s (-3.19) **Going Correction** -0.025s/f (Good)
WFA 3 from 4yo+ 3lb **10** Ran SP% **117.8**
Speed ratings (Par 117): **114,113,112,108,108 106,102,97,93,91**
toteswinger: 1&2 £3.30, 1&3 £12.80, 2&3 £6.80. CSF £16.63 TOTE £8.60: £2.40, £1.02, £7.30; EX 17.20 Trifecta £274.20 Pool: £11860.18 - 32 winning units..
Owner M Tabor, D Smith & Mrs John Magnier **Bred** T Stewart **Trained** Ballydoyle, Co Tipperary
■ Stewards' Enquiry : Alan Munro one-day ban: careless riding (Oct 19)

FOCUS

A top-class contest that has thrown up a couple of surprise winners in the last two seasons, but this looked a decent renewal beforehand, with two Classic winners and a Classic runner-up, and two more Group 1 winners in the field. The Classic winners dominated and it was a satisfactory result from a form point of view, although there is a slight doubt how much Halfway To Heaven improved (rated up 4lb). Darjina was 5lb off this year's best and Visit another improver, with the rest probably below par.

NOTEBOOK

Halfway To Heaven(IRE) made all and, despite carrying her head rather high, battled on gamely to give Aidan O'Brien his 21st Group 1 winner of the season. The winner of the Irish 1000 Guineas and Nassau Stakes is well suited by fast ground and put her stamina to good use to hold off the well-backed favourite. She could now go to the Breeders' Cup meeting and will have a choice of the Mile or the Filly And Mare Turf. With the ground likely to be on the fast side she must have a sound chance in whichever contest is chosen for her. (op 7-1 tchd 9-1, 10-1 in places)

Darjina(FR) had every chance but, even with the rail to race against, was unable to get past the winner. She has now been runner-up in all six starts this season (all Group 1s), including the Moulin, Queen Anne and Dubai Duty Free, and this consistent sort once again appeared to do nothing wrong. She will now be retired to stud. (op 6-4 tchd 13-8 in places)

Visit is a dual Group 3 winner but was well beaten on her only previous try at this level. Loaded with the aid of a blanket, she tracked the leaders before keeping on in good fashion to finish on the heels of the principals. If kept in training she may be able to score at this level, although she could be switched to race in the USA. (op 14-1)

Spacious, runner-up to Natagora in the 1000 Guineas and fourth in the Coronation Stakes, had been a narrow winner on her return from a break and ran quite well considering she was stopped in her run when the third went across her going into the dip. She gave the impression on this occasion that she would get a little further. (op 16-1)

Heaven Sent, who wore the first colours of Cheveley Park Stud, is a Group 3 winner and Group 2 placed but showed again that she is not up to this level. (op 8-1 tchd 13-2)

Barshiba(IRE) kept the winner company in the early stages before losing her place and then staying on late, and is another who is not up to Group 1 class.

Nahoodh(IRE), winner of the Falmouth Stakes and runner-up in the Matron Stakes with Halfway To Heaven behind, acts best on good and easy ground and was less effective on this faster surface. (op 13-2 tchd 11-2)

Listen(IRE), the winner's stable companion, was a well-backed second favourite on the strength of her good fifth in Matron Stakes on her belated seasonal return, but ran a disappointing race. She may not have handled the fast ground but also she may have bounced. (tchd 9-2 and 11-2)

6476 TOTESPORT.COM CAMBRIDGESHIRE (HERITAGE H'CAP) 1m 1f

3:50 (3:58) (Class 2) 3-Y-O+

£99,696 (£29,856; £14,928; £7,472; £3,728; £1,872) **Stalls** High

Form RPR

3140 **1** **Tazeez (USA)**[14] 6120 4-9-2 **102** .... RHills 21 113+
(J H M Gosden) *w ldrs centre: edgd lft over 2f out: styd on to ld fnl 75yds* **25/1**

3100 **2** *1* **Nanton (USA)**[14] 6120 6-7-13 **90** .... KellyHarrison(5) 1 99
(J S Goldie) *chsd ldrs: led overall on stands' side 2f out: hdd and no ex wl ins fnl f* **66/1**

2123 **3** *1 1/4* **Swop (IRE)**[35] 5508 5-8-12 **98** .... RichardHughes 2 104+
(L M Cumani) *hld up in rr stands' side: gd hdwy over 2f out: kpt on wl fnl f* **7/1**[1]

1132 **4** *3 3/4* **Little White Lie (IRE)**[41] 5313 4-9-4 **104** .... MJKinane 9 102
(J R Jenkins) *chsd ldrs stands' side: led overall 3f out: hdd 2f out: one pce appr fnl f* **25/1**

1321 **5** *1 1/4* **Yaddree**[14] 6123 3-9-0 **104** 4ex .... PhilipRobinson 22 100+
(M A Jarvis) *lw: chsd ldrs centre: styd on same pce fnl 2f* **9/1**

-011 **6** *hd* **Premio Loco (USA)**[28] 5695 4-9-3 **103** 4ex .... GeorgeBaker 18 98+
(C F Wall) *lw: hld up towards rr: hdwy 3f out: kpt on same pce fnl f* **8/1**[2]

1-36 **7** *1 1/4* **Caravel (IRE)**[67] 4504 4-8-5 **91** .... J-PGuillambert 10 83
(Sir Mark Prescott) *lw: chsd ldrs stands' side: styd on same pce fnl 2f* **12/1**

4116 **8** *hd* **Ask The Butler**[14] 6120 4-9-4 **104** .... DaneO'Neill 7 96
(L M Cumani) *lw: dwlt: hld up towards rr stands' side: kpt on fnl 2f: nvr nr ldrs* **10/1**

1206 **9** *3/4* **Dream Lodge (IRE)**[20] 5941 4-9-0 **100** .... TQuinn 26 90
(J G Given) *in rr stands' side: styd on fnl 2f: nvr nr ldrs* **100/1**

3153 **10** *1/2* **Indian Days**[14] 6120 3-8-8 **98** .... JimCrowley 27 87+
(J G Given) *chsd ldrs on outer: kpt on same pce fnl 2f* **16/1**

5030 **11** *1/2* **Watamu (IRE)**[35] 5508 7-9-5 **105** .... (v) EddieAhern 8 93
(P J Makin) *trckd ldrs stands' side: effrt over 2f out: wknd over 1f out* **66/1**

653 **12** *1 1/2* **Huzzah (IRE)**[21] 5896 3-8-9 **99** .... MichaelHills 11 84
(B W Hills) *lw: led stands' side gp tl 3f out: wknd over 1f out* **33/1**

2-15 **13** *nk* **Charlie Farnsbarns (IRE)**[128] 2543 4-9-4 **107** .... PatrickHills(3) 17 92
(B J Meehan) *swtchd lft after s: mid-div: effrt over 2f out: wknd over 1f out* **28/1**

4004 **14** *1 1/4* **Feared In Flight (IRE)**[23] 5830 3-8-9 **99** .... ChrisCatlin 31 81+
(B W Hills) *chsd ldrs on outer: wknd 2f out* **28/1**

3346 **15** *hd* **Dubai's Touch**[7] 6287 4-9-4 **104** .... GregFairley 28 86+
(M Johnston) *prom on outer: rdn over 2f out: sn btn* **50/1**

-142 **16** *hd* **Ada River**[35] 5506 3-8-10 **100** .... WilliamBuick 30 81+
(A M Balding) *in tch on outer: effrt over 2f out: sn fdd* **20/1**

2010 **17** *nk* **Unshakable (IRE)**[14] 6120 9-8-10 **96** .... PaulEddery 12 76
(Bob Jones) *b.hind: in rr: nvr on terms* **66/1**

0002 **18** *2 1/4* **Lang Shining (IRE)**[35] 5508 4-9-4 **104** .... RyanMoore 35 80
(Sir Michael Stoute) *hld up towards rr: sme hdwy over 2f out: sn btn* **16/1**

1124 **19** *1 1/4* **Military Power**[20] 5942 3-8-3 **93** .... LiamJones 15 66
(J W Hills) *chsd ldrs stands' side: wknd wl over 2f out* **11/1**

1224 **20** *1 1/4* **Don't Panic (IRE)**[120] 2788 4-9-5 **105** .... AlanMunro 14 76
(P W Chapple-Hyam) *mid-div: lost pl over 2f out* **25/1**

4046 **21** *2 1/2* **Alan Devonshire**[67] 4505 3-8-10 **100** .... TPO'Shea 33 65
(M H Tompkins) *mde most centre tl hdd & wknd 3f out* **50/1**

1414 **22** *1/2* **Prince Kalamoun (IRE)**[14] 6120 3-8-6 **96** .... JamieSpencer 19 60+
(G A Swinbank) *hld up: in rr centre: drvn and sme hdwy 3f out: nvr a factor: eased over 1f* **17/2**[3]

1655 **23** *3 1/4* **Mia's Boy**[7] 6287 4-9-4 **104** .... JimmyQuinn 29 61
(C A Dwyer) *in rr: effrt over 2f out: sn wknd* **20/1**

0210 **24** *3/4* **Siberian Tiger (IRE)**[14] 6120 3-8-10 **100** 4ex .... EdwardCreighton 16 56
(M R Channon) *a in rr* **50/1**

1510 **25** *1/2* **Fifteen Love (USA)**[27] 5742 3-9-3 **107** .... (p) SteveDrowne 23 62
(R Charlton) *in rr div: bhd fnl 2f* **14/1**

2052 **26** *2 1/2* **Docofthebay (IRE)**[20] 5941 4-9-7 **107** .... ShaneKelly 34 57
(J A Osborne) *dwlt: nvr on terms* **20/1**

0030 **27** *1/2* **Fishforcompliments**[14] 6103 4-8-8 **94** ow1 .... RobertWinston 24 42
(R A Fahey) *prom centre: rdn over 2f out: sn lost pl* **50/1**

5000 **28** *nk* **Raptor (GER)**[14] 6104 5-8-7 **93** .... CDHayes 20 41
(K R Burke) *a in rr* **66/1**

1m 47.66s (-2.94) **Going Correction** -0.025s/f (Good)
WFA 3 from 4yo+ 4lb **35** Ran SP% **138.2**
Speed ratings (Par 109): **112,111,110,106,105 105,104,104,103,102 102,101,100,99,99 99,99,97,96,94 92,92,89,88,88 86,85**
toteswinger: 1&2 £0.00, 1&3 £264.10, 2&3 £819.00. CSF £1188.32 CT £12156.17 TOTE £35.80: £8.00, £13.30, £3.30, £4.70; EX 5716.70 TRIFECTA Not won..
Owner Hamdan Al Maktoum **Bred** Clovelly Farms **Trained** Newmarket, Suffolk

FOCUS

A very open Cambridgeshire in which they raced in two groups to begin with before joining up at around halfway and edging towards the stands' side. While only one horse had defied a single-figure draw in the last ten years, races earlier on the card suggested that those racing on the stands' side would be at an advantage this time around. That proved to be the case and therefore there is a slight doubt over the overall form. Improved efforts from the winner (up 8lb) and runner-up. There were seven non-runners on the day including topweight Smokey Oakey (9-10) and Mutajarred, from whom Richard Hills switched to replace Martin Dwyer on Tazeez.

NOTEBOOK

Tazeez(USA) ◆ deserves extra credit for overcoming stall 21. Hampered at Newbury last time, his previous fourth to Ask The Butler, Lang Shining and Swop in a Sandown handicap arguably gave him a better chance than the market suggested. A gelding who apparently does not like to be crowded, he was up with the pace from the start in the group racing up the centre, edged left from two furlongs out and ran on well to cosily see off Nanton and Swop, who had both enjoyed the benefit of racing on the stands' side throughout. Now beginning to fulfil the potential he shows at home, he was winning here off a mark of 102 and will have to step up into Pattern company next. He might well enjoy dominating small-field Listed races, though, so could make his mark in that grade next year. (op 33-1)

Nanton(USA) looked up against it off a 5lb higher mark than when last successful, but as it turned out he was drawn best of all and he made full use of it, seeing the trip out strongly. Another rise in the handicap will make things even more difficult for him future, though.

Swop(IRE), a lightly raced five-year-old who had been targeted by Luca Cumani at this race for some time, had finished one place in front of Tazeez at Sandown in August. Held up right at the back of the stands'-side group, he was given a lot to do, but with a furlong and a half to go he looked to be coming with an irresistible run up the stands' rail, only to find the one pace inside the last. Perhaps a mile run at a strong gallop is his best trip. (op 15-2 tchd 8-1 in places)

Little White Lie(IRE) was another who raced towards the stands' side and he ran well over this longer trip considering the ground was faster than ideal. There was talk that he might go hurdling at some point this winter.

Yaddree, who was 5lb well-in under his penalty following his win in a conditions event over this trip at Newbury a fortnight earlier, was never too far off the pace on the far side, but unlike the winner he did not drift over towards the stands' side but stayed more towards the centre. It was a good effort in the circumstances, better than the bare form suggests, and he remains a progressive three-year-old. (tchd 10-1 in places)

Premio Loco(USA) was another well-in at the weights, in his case by 6lb, but he had his stamina to prove over this longer trip. He is, however, a brother to a four-time winner between 1m2f and 1m4f and he seemed to stay well enough, although his draw and where he raced did him no great favours. Official explanation: jockey said gelding lost a front shoe (tchd 9-1 in places)

Caravel(IRE), who completed a five-timer last term, has not really gone on this time around. He had every chance towards the stands' side and the assumption must be that the Handicapper has his measure at the moment. (op 14-1 tchd 16-1 in places)

Ask The Butler did not have much go right for him at Newbury last time, but he had previously looked an ideal candidate for this race when winning at Sandown in August. Although favourably drawn, he was being shoved along from some way out, and this drop back in trip looked to find him out. He does, after all, stay 1m4f. (op 11-1 tchd 14-1 in a place)
Dream Lodge(IRE) often races up with the pace but he was ridden more patiently this time. He kept on without ever threatening the principals and continues to look held off his current mark Official explanation: jockey said colt hung left throughout
Indian Days, officially 2lb well-in, deserves rating better than the bare form as he was poorly drawn and raced wide throughout.
Watamu(IRE), who can race freely, appreciated the decent gallop, but he remains on a stiff mark and ran about as well as could be expected.
Huzzah(IRE) had stamina to prove and, after taking them along on the stands' side, he dropped out over two furlongs from home.
Charlie Farnsbarns(IRE), who has had his fair share of problems, was returning from another layoff and faced a stiff task off top weight. (op 33-1 tchd 25-1)
Ada River was the only filly in the field and, having only had two starts in maidens and two in Listed company, she came into this highly competitive handicap short on experience. Being drawn wide and racing towards the outside probably did not help her cause. (op 16-1)
Lang Shining(IRE), drawn on the wide outside, never really got competitive. Possibly the ground was fast enough for him.
Military Power, who sneaked in at the bottom of the weights and was well backed, was disappointing, dropping out of contention a long way from home. (op 10-1 tchd 12-1, 14-1 in places)
Prince Kalamoun(IRE) was another to run below expectations. He looked to have conditions to suit, but never got involved and was eased when beaten. Perhaps something was amiss. Official explanation: jockey said gelding lost its action (op 9-1 tchd 10-1)
Mia's Boy Official explanation: jockey said colt stumbled on leaving stalls

6477 EUROPEAN BREEDERS' FUND JERSEY LILY FILLIES' NURSERY 7f
4:25 (4:31) (Class 2) 2-Y-0

£18,693 (£5,598; £2,799; £1,401; £699; £351) **Stalls** High

Form				RPR
2314	**1**		**Feeling Fab (FR)**^{15} 6076 2-9-7 **87** ... GregFairley 6 (M Johnston) *lw: plld hrd: and prom: swtchd to r stands' side after 1f: led that gp over 5f out: overall ldr over 2f out: sn rdn: styd on gamely* **9/1**	91
0101	**2**	*hd*	**Brierty (IRE)**^{9} 6223 2-8-13 **79** ... DNolan 7 (D Carroll) *w ldr far side: swtchd to stands' side over 4f out: rdn and ev ch fr over 1f out: styd on* **20/1**	82
3610	**3**	*1/2*	**Gal Aloud (USA)**^{8} 6240 2-9-0 **80** ... RyanMoore 4 (R Hannon) *swtchd to r stands' side after 1f: hld up: hdwy over 1f out: r.o* **6/1**	82
5431	**4**	*1 1/4*	**Dream In Waiting**^{22} 5855 2-9-3 **83** ... JamieSpencer 11 (P F I Cole) *racd far side: chsd ldrs far side: swtchd to stands' side over 4f out: rdn over 2f out: styd on same pce fnl f* **11/2**^{3}	82
2140	**5**	*1/2*	**Acquiesced (IRE)**^{12} 6172 2-9-1 **81** ... RichardHughes 1 (R Hannon) *s.s: hld up: swtchd to stands' side after 1f: r.o ins fnl f: nt rch ldrs* **14/1**	79
0410	**6**	*1/2*	**Bobbie Soxer (IRE)**^{42} 5274 2-8-9 **75** ... JimmyQuinn 2 (J L Dunlop) *lw: swtchd to r stands' side after 1f: hld up in tch: rdn over 1f out: edgd rt and no ex ins fnl f* **9/2**^{1}	71
6141	**7**	*nk*	**Calahonda**^{18} 6002 2-8-12 **78** ... EddieAhern 5 (P W D'Arcy) *swtchd to r stands' side after 1f: led that gp to over 5f out: remained handy: rdn over 1f out: no ex ins fnl f* **5/1**^{2}	74
016	**8**	*1 1/2*	**Punch Drunk**^{21} 5895 2-7-11 **70** ... RosieJessop$^{(7)}$ 3 (J G Given) *swtchd to r stands' side after 1f: prom: rdn over 3f out: wknd over 1f out* **12/1**	62
011	**9**	*nk*	**Athania (IRE)**^{37} 5422 2-8-12 **78** ... JimCrowley 12 (A P Jarvis) *overall ldr far side: swtchd to r stands' side over 4f out: hdd over 2f out: sn rdn: wknd ins fnl f* **16/1**	69
615	**10**	*1*	**It's Toast (IRE)**^{22} 5855 2-8-2 **68** ... WilliamBuick 8 (R M Beckett) *prom far side: swtchd to r stands' side over 4f out: rdn and wknd over 1f out* **8/1**	57
043	**11**	*5*	**Dream Date (IRE)**^{23} 5835 2-8-0 **66** ... LiamJones 9 (W J Haggas) *racd far side: hld up: swtchd to r stands' side over 4f out: rdn over 2f out: sn wknd* **9/1**	42
0600	**12**	*hd*	**Barbee (IRE)**^{12} 6172 2-8-7 **73** ... RichardMullen 10 (E A L Dunlop) *racd far side: hld up: swtchd to r stands' side over 4f out: rdn over 2f out: sn wknd* **33/1**	49

1m 25.83s (0.43) **Going Correction** -0.025s/f (Good) **12** Ran SP% **123.6**
Speed ratings (Par 98): **96,95,95,93,93 92,92,90,90,89 83,83**
toteswinger: 1&2 £34.90, 1&3 £11.90, 2&3 £34.30. CSF £182.32 CT £1183.00 TOTE £11.60: £3.20, £7.00, £2.50; EX 244.10.
Owner A D Spence **Bred** Alain Decrion & Sunland Holdings Ltd **Trained** Middleham Moor, N Yorks

FOCUS
A decent prize for this fillies' nursery and, although the field originally split into two groups, with the wind to help they converged on the stands' side before halfway.

NOTEBOOK
Feeling Fab(FR) was runner-up to Vitoria on her debut at Thirsk and the form was advertised when that filly finished second in the sales race earlier in the day. Since then she has run consistently and she put up a game performance to defy top weight here. Keen early, once in front on the rail she showed the tenacity that is a notable attribute of horses from the Johnston yard and stuck her head out to hold off the runner-up. She may run again this season providing she gets the fast ground that is important to her. (op 8-1 tchd 10-1)
Brierty(IRE) was stepping back up in trip having scored over 6f on Polytrack last time, and proved that she stays by making the winner pull out all the stops to hold on. Well suited by a sound surface, she will now be put away as she is expected to make up into a decent three-year-old. (op 25-1)
Gal Aloud(USA), without the visor she wore on her previous start, ran best of those held up, making significant headway from the quarter-mile pole and staying on strongly to the line. She is basically progressive and looks capable of scoring again, probably over a little further. (op 8-1)
Dream In Waiting had finished 2 3/4 lengths behind the winner at Thirsk but was 4lb better off and ran close to that form despite the fact she was inconvenienced by having deliver her challenge wide of where the main action took place. She continues to be progressive and a softer surface holds no fears for her. (op 5-1 tchd 6-1 in places)
Acquiesced(IRE) was slowly away and swerved left leaving the stalls, and after being held up ran on steadily from the rear, although not as strongly as her stable companion. (op 16-1)
Bobbie Soxer(IRE) was a well-backed favourite and moved up looking a big threat running into the dip, only for her effort to peter out once she met the rising ground. (op 7-1)
Calahonda eased out from favouritism in the face of support for Bobbie Soxer, but had a good pitch just behind the leaders for most of the race. However, she failed to find an extra gear when pressure was applied and it may be that she is less effective on genuinely fast ground and possibly happiest on a flatter track. (op 4-1)
Punch Drunk got a good tow from the winner up the rail but failed to pick up and was another who may not have handled the fast ground. (op 16-1)
Athania(IRE), a winner on good to soft, cut out the running at the head of the far-side group and remained in contention until weakening running into the dip. (op 10-1)

6478 TOTESWINGER H'CAP 7f
5:00 (5:00) (Class 2) (0-100,96) 3-Y-0+

£12,462 (£3,732; £1,866; £934; £466; £234) **Stalls** High

Form				RPR
1000	**1**		**Plum Pudding (IRE)**^{70} 4405 5-9-6 **96** ... RyanMoore 11 (R Hannon) *overall ldr in centre to 1/2-way: hung lft and led over 1f out: drvn out* **8/1**^{3}	107
0042	**2**	*1*	**Masai Moon**^{20} 5930 4-9-0 **93** ... JamesMillman$^{(3)}$ 16 (B R Millman) *lw: chsd ldrs in centre: rdn over 2f out: edgd lft ins fnl f: styd on* **9/1**	101
6040	**3**	*nk*	**Flipando (IRE)**^{7} 6269 7-8-12 **88** ... PaulFessey 12 (T D Barron) *hld up: swtchd to r stands' side over 5f out: nt clr run over 1f out: r.o ins fnl f: nt rch ldrs* **13/2**^{2}	95+
0200	**4**	*1/2*	**Orchard Supreme**^{21} 5903 5-8-10 **86** ... RichardHughes 7 (R Hannon) *chsd ldr stands' side: rdn over 2f out: styd on same pce ins fnl f* **12/1**	92
3520	**5**	*1*	**Countdown**^{37} 5419 6-8-6 **82** ... RichardMullen 4 (M D Squance) *racd stands' side: prom: rdn over 2f out: styd on same pce ins fnl f* **25/1**	85
	6	*3/4*	**Wasp (AUS)**^{283} 6-8-9 **85** ... AlanMunro 13 (W Jarvis) *racd centre: chsd ldrs: rdn over 2f out: no ex fnl f* **33/1**	86
5430	**7**	*shd*	**Thebes**^{15} 6069 3-8-13 **91** ... GregFairley 5 (M Johnston) *led stands' side: overall ldr 1/2-way: rdn and hdd over 1f out: no ex ins fnl f* **10/1**	92
105	**8**	*2 1/2*	**Golden Desert (IRE)**^{7} 6269 4-8-13 **89** ... SteveDrowne 10 (T G Mills) *racd stands' side: s.i.s sn prom: rdn over 1f out: eased whn btn ins fnl f* **7/2**^{1}	83
0001	**9**	*shd*	**Slugger O'Toole**^{24} 5795 3-9-2 **94** ... ChrisCatlin 14 (B W Hills) *lw: racd centre: chsd ldrs: outpcd over 2f out: styd on ins fnl f* **7/2**^{1}	88
0010	**10**	*1 1/4*	**Sir Xaar (IRE)**^{36} 5446 5-8-12 **88** ... (v) JimCrowley 3 (B Smart) *racd stands' side: prom: rdn 1/2-way: wknd over 1f out* **12/1**	78
3052	**11**	*2 1/4*	**Lodi (IRE)**^{14} 6124 3-8-1 **84** ... (t) KellyHarrison$^{(5)}$ 8 (J Akehurst) *racd centre: chsd wnr tl swtchd to r stands' side over 5f out: remained handy tl rdn and wknd over 1f out* **12/1**	68
5140	**12**	*20*	**Kafuu (IRE)**^{36} 5446 4-8-10 **86** ... JamieSpencer 6 (S A Callaghan) *s.s: racd stands' side: a bhd: eased fnl 2f* **14/1**	16

1m 24.22s (-1.18) **Going Correction** -0.025s/f (Good)
WFA 3 from 4yo+ 2lb **12** Ran SP% **124.5**
Speed ratings (Par 109): **105,103,103,102,101 100,100,97,97,96 93,71**
toteswinger: 1&2 £11.30, 1&3 £13.40, 2&3 £11.60. CSF £82.25 CT £509.36 TOTE £7.40: £2.40, £2.60, £2.80; EX 54.30.
Owner Hyde Sporting Promotions Limited **Bred** Tom Deane **Trained** East Everleigh, Wilts

FOCUS
A decent handicap run in an identical time to that recorded by the two-year-old Donativum in the earlier sales race. Course specialist Plum Pudding ran to form, with a slight step up from the second.

NOTEBOOK
Plum Pudding(IRE) comes alive at this track, and he notched his fifth career success here under a fine ride from Moore, leading a group up the centre of the track but gradually working his way over to the favoured stands'-side rail and seeing the trip out strongly, as one would expect of a three-time winner over a mile. He will again be worth bearing in mind if he returns here for a similar race in the spring.
Masai Moon, racing off a career-high mark, is versatile with regard to ground conditions and appreciated the return to 7f. He ran well from his wide draw but another rise in the weights will not make things any easier. (op 10-1)
Flipando(IRE) has not been in the best of form this season but as a result he got to race here off an 8lb lower mark than he began the season off. Starting off in the group up the centre, his rider decided he was in the wrong company and soon switched him to join the stands'-side group. Coming through from off the pace, he kept finding his path blocked, and had he got a clearer run he would surely have given the winner more of a race. He will be suited by a return to a mile. Official explanation: jockey said gelding was denied a clear run (tchd 6-1 and 7-1)
Orchard Supreme looked well handicapped on his best form from earlier in the year, but he is an in-an-out performer and his last two efforts had been very disappointing. This was better, but he will be of more interest when switched back onto his favoured Polytrack. (tchd 14-1)
Countdown, who ran without headgear on his first start for his new trainer, has never won on a surface quicker than good so this was a decent effort on ground plenty quick enough. (tchd 33-1)
Wasp(AUS), previously trained in Hong Kong, was making his debut for his new trainer and having his first outing since December. Fully entitled to need the run, he shaped encouragingly and will surely come on for this. Perhaps he can be found an opening on the Polytrack in the coming weeks. (tchd 40-1)
Thebes had the run of the race on the favoured stands' side rail but did not get home. His best trip is probably 6f, which is the distance he won at on the July course in August. (op 12-1)
Golden Desert(IRE), who won on the 'wrong' side in the totesport.com Challenge Cup at Ascot a week earlier, got to race off the same mark in this less competitive affair and appeared to hold sound claims. He was disappointing, though, and perhaps the race came too soon. (tchd 4-1 and 9-2 in places)
Slugger O'Toole won in soft ground at Doncaster last time but, off a 6lb higher mark on a quicker surface he could not repeat that form. (op 4-1 tchd 9-2)
Kafuu(IRE) Official explanation: jockey said colt missed the break

6479 SUFFOLK INSULATION AND RENOVATION SERVICES H'CAP 1m 4f
5:35 (5:35) (Class 3) (0-95,95) 3-Y-0+

£9,346 (£2,799; £1,399; £700; £349; £175) **Stalls** Centre

Form				RPR
P006	**1**		**The Last Drop (IRE)**^{22} 5853 5-9-1 **85** ... MichaelHills 6 (B W Hills) *swtg: chsd ldrs: rdn to ld 1f out: styd on* **15/2**	95
4006	**2**	*nk*	**Players Please (USA)**^{6} 6302 4-9-5 **89** ... GregFairley 10 (M Johnston) *chsd ldr tl led 3f out: rdn and hdd 1f out: hung rt: styd on* **6/1**^{2}	99
3144	**3**	*1 3/4*	**Tifernati**^{16} 6061 4-9-2 **86** ... LiamJones 5 (W J Haggas) *hld up: hdwy over 2f out: rdn over 1f out: swtchd rt ins fnl f: styd on* **9/4**^{1}	93
5540	**4**	*4*	**Prince Sabaah (IRE)**^{59} 4742 4-8-13 **83** ... RichardHughes 8 (R Hannon) *chsd ldrs: rdn and ev ch over 2f out: wknd ins fnl f* **10/1**	84
0106	**5**	*1/2*	**Bee Sting**^{23} 5843 4-9-3 **87** ... (p) ShaneKelly 12 (W R Swinburn) *prom: reminders 1/2-way: outpcd 3f out: swtchd rt over 1f out: styd on ins fnl f* **17/2**	87
2152	**6**	*nk*	**King Supreme (IRE)**^{11} 6196 3-8-4 **81** oh2 ... (b) TPO'Shea 14 (R Hannon) *hld up: rdn over 2f out: styd on ins fnl f: nvr nrr* **7/1**^{3}	81
4240	**7**	*1 3/4*	**Bandama (IRE)**^{8} 6238 5-9-3 **87** ... (p) JimCrowley 7 (Mrs A J Perrett) *lw: hld up in tch: rdn over 2f out: wknd fnl f* **15/2**	84

1046 **8** 3 ½ **Coyote Creek**[16] 6061 4-8-12 **82**......................................(p) EddieAhern 9 73
(E F Vaughan) *lw: led: hdd 3f out: wknd over 1f out* **14/1**
-000 **9** *nse* **Veenwouden**[42] 5264 4-9-8 **95**.. JamesMillman(3) 3 86
(E F Vaughan) *hld up: sme hdwy over 1f out: sn wknd* **28/1**
5400 **10** 6 **Smart Instinct (USA)**[43] 5229 4-9-6 **90**........................... MartinDwyer 15 71
(R A Fahey) *hld up: hdwy over 2f out: sn rdn and wknd* **10/1**
6202 **11** 4 ½ **Quince (IRE)**[28] 5699 5-8-12 **82**...................................(v) JimmyQuinn 16 56
(J Pearce) *lw: hld up: rdn over 3f out: wknd over 2f out* **10/1**

2m 30.93s (-2.57) **Going Correction** -0.025s/f (Good)
WFA 3 from 4yo+ 7lb **11** Ran SP% **129.0**
Speed ratings (Par 107): **107,106,105,102,102 102,101,98,98,94 91**
toteswinger: 1&2 £10.40, 1&3 £7.30, 2&3 £6.10. CSF £57.41 CT £140.18 TOTE £11.80: £3.00, £3.10, £1.80; EX 67.50 Place 6: £2834.75 Place 5: £931.40.
Owner J Hanson, Cavendish Inv Ltd, A Patrick **Bred** Sunderland Holdings **Trained** Lambourn, Berks

FOCUS
A good handicap that often falls to an improving type, but six withdrawals reduced the field by more than a third. As in the races on the straight course it appeared an advantage to race close to the pace, although the time was relatively modest. The form is sound.

NOTEBOOK
The Last Drop(IRE) looked really well beforehand, was always on the premises and found what was required to get the better of Players Please up the hill. He has had his problems and had not won since April 2006, during which time he has been pulled up twice having lost his action. However, he is best on a sound surface and has dropped 17lb since the start of the year, and that enabled him to rediscover his form. His trainer reported he has never had him better and the November Handicap is a possibility, while he is also in the sales at the end of the year. (op 7-1)
Players Please(USA) had not scored for over a year but had conditions to suit and was back to his last winning mark. He took over from the long-time leader Coyote Creek going into the dip and, despite running about under pressure, kept on all the way to the line. (tchd 15-2)
Tifernati, the well-backed favourite, was settled out the back but moved onto the heels of the leaders looking a big threat before he could find nothing extra. He is 4lb above his last winning mark and looks held by the Handicapper. (op 7-2 tchd 4-1 in places)
Prince Sabaah(IRE) had the cheekpieces left off this time and ran well enough following a break. A return to the all-weather, where he gained his only previous success, looks on the cards. (op 11-1 tchd 12-1)
Bee Sting ◆ having his first try at this trip and with cheekpieces replacing the visor, tracked the leaders on the rail but was switched rather extravagantly to the outside before finishing to some effect. He looks one to bear in mind now he has proven he gets this far as he appears to handle most ground. (op 8-1)
King Supreme(IRE) was held up out the back and did not really start to run on until the race was over. He is generally consistent and would have been closer given a more positive ride. (op 8-1)
Bandama(IRE) stays this trip but has been running over shorter of late and, although he had not won since June 2006, is still 2lb above his last winning mark. He ran quite well in the first-time cheekpieces, only fading on meeting the rising ground. (op 6-1)
Veenwouden, who was dropping back in distance, is another to have fallen in the handicap but she also was unsuited by being held up in a race where it paid to be near the front. (op 33-1 tchd 25-1)
Quince(IRE) Official explanation: jockey said gelding had no more to give
T/Jkpt: Not won. T/Plt: £3,768.70 to a £1 stake. Pool: £191,327.62. 37.06 winning tickets. T/Qpdt: £134.30 to a £1 stake. Pool: £11,111.10. 61.20 winning tickets. CR

6212 REDCAR (L-H)
Saturday, October 4

OFFICIAL GOING: Good (good to firm in places; 8.6)
Wind: Strong, half behind Weather: Overcast and blustery

6480 EBF O'GRADY'S HOTEL AT REDCAR MAIDEN STKS (DIV I) 7f
1:25 (1:26) (Class 4) 2-Y-O **£5,536** (£1,647; £823; £411) **Stalls** Centre

Form RPR
032 **1** **Cloudy Start**[16] 6057 2-9-3 86.. TPQueally 2 90+
(H R A Cecil) *prom on outer: led 3f out: pushed clr wl over 1f out: easily* **8/11**[1]
020 **2** 6 **Threestepstoheaven**[22] 5857 2-9-3 73...................................... NCallan 6 73
(B W Hills) *cl up: pushed along 3f out: rdn over 2f out: kpt on u.p appr fnl f: no ch w wnr* **15/2**[3]
3 1 ¾ **Petsas Pleasure** 2-9-0 0.. DuranFentiman(3) 5 69
(L R James) *a.p: led briefly 1/2-way: rdn and hdd 3f out: drvn 2f out and kpt on same pce appr fnl f* **33/1**
3323 **4** 1 ½ **Taazur**[18] 6002 2-9-3 81.. JoeFanning 12 65
(M Johnston) *dwlt: sn trcking ldrs on outer: hdwy 1/2-way: rdn wl over 2f out: sn drvn and one pce wl over 1f out* **9/2**[2]
4 **5** 1 ½ **Battle Royal (IRE)**[52] 4968 2-9-3 0.................................... TedDurcan 3 61+
(B Smart) *chsd ldrs: rdn along 3f out: sn one pce* **10/1**
4 **6** 2 ¾ **Blue Noodles**[14] 6110 2-9-3 0.................................... TonyHamilton 14 54
(D W Barker) *chsd ldrs: rdn along 3f out: wknd 2f out* **33/1**
400 **7** *shd* **Millway Beach (IRE)**[36] 5459 2-9-3 0..........................(p) HayleyTurner 13 54
(Pat Eddery) *led: pushed along and hdd 1/2-way: sn rdn and wknd* **25/1**
8 2 ½ **Duke Of Normandy (IRE)** 2-9-3 0................................ AndrewElliott 7 48
(M Johnston) *cl up: rdn along 1/2-way: sn wknd* **16/1**
9 1 ¾ **Vita Mia** 2-8-12 0.. LeeEnstone 4 38
(P C Haslam) *a towards rr* **100/1**
10 1 **Stanstill (IRE)** 2-9-3 0.. PJMcDonald 11 41
(G A Swinbank) *dwlt: a in rr* **50/1**
0 **11** *shd* **Cause For Applause (IRE)**[14] 6109 2-8-12 0.................. TomEaves 10 36
(B Smart) *a in rr* **100/1**
60 **12** 16 **Hill Cross (IRE)**[100] 3411 2-9-0 0.............................. AndrewMullen(3) 15 1
(Mrs A Duffield) *a in rr: bhd fnl 3f* **100/1**

1m 23.59s (-0.91) **Going Correction** -0.125s/f (Firm) **12** Ran SP% **117.5**
Speed ratings (Par 97): **100,93,91,89,87 84,84,81,79,78 78,60**
toteswinger: 1&2 £2.70, 1&3 £9.60, 2&3 £31.90. CSF £6.37 TOTE £1.60: £1.10, £2.00, £8.60; EX 6.90.
Owner K Abdulla **Bred** Juddmonte Farms Ltd **Trained** Newmarket, Suffolk

FOCUS
After a dry night, the ground remained good. There there was a strong wind more or less behind them. This was the first of two maidens that lacked much depth.

NOTEBOOK
Cloudy Start, not beaten far by Royal Lodge winner Jukebox Jury on his second start, had shown more than enough to win a race of this nature and was backed as though defeat was not an option. He strode easily clear of his rivals in the final stages and will surely be upped in grade next time. (op 5-6)
Threestepstoheavendid not look to handle soft last time but shaped better on this quick ground. He will find his level in handicaps. (op 7-1 tchd 8-1)
Petsas Pleasure, who was already gelded, ran a massive race on his debut and only time will tell if it was a fluke or not. He certainly looked clued up for his first run.
Taazur was returning to maiden company after trying his luck in nurseries but once again found something too good form him. (op 4-1)
Battle Royal(IRE), a half-brother to Grey Swallow among many other winners, did not show much in soft ground on his debut but does hold a Racing Post Trophy entry. He broke much better this time and tracked the winner early, but did not look to be given a really hard ride inside the final furlong once his chance was gone. One would imagine that he is better than he showed in this. (op 11-1)

6481 EBF O'GRADY'S HOTEL AT REDCAR MAIDEN STKS (DIV II) 7f
1:55 (1:56) (Class 4) 2-Y-O **£5,536** (£1,647; £823; £411) **Stalls** Centre

Form RPR
433 **1** **Hail Promenader (IRE)**[22] 5860 2-9-3 79................................ NCallan 13 78+
(B W Hills) *cl up: led over 2f out: rdn clr over 1f out: hung lft ins fnl f: kpt on u.p* **9/4**[1]
43 **2** ¾ **Striker Torres (IRE)**[9] 6230 2-9-3 0.................................... TomEaves 6 76+
(B Smart) *in midfield: hdwy and in tch 1/2-way: effrt over 2f out and sn pushed along: rdn wl over 1f out: styd on strly ins fnl f* **5/2**[2]
56 **3** 1 ½ **Senor Berti**[49] 5106 2-9-3 0.. PaulMulrennan 5 72
(B Smart) *led: rdn along 3f out: hdd over 2f out: sn drvn and kpt on same pce appr fnl f* **18/1**
4 4 **Caress The Soul (IRE)** 2-8-12 0................................ JamieMoriarty 4 57+
(P T Midgley) *towards rr: pushed along and hdwy whn rn green over 2f out: swtchd rt and n.m.r 2f out: styd on ins fnl f: nrst fin* **50/1**
05 **5** ½ **Mister Bombastic (IRE)**[38] 5387 2-9-0 0.......................... NeilBrown(3) 7 61
(M Dods) *cl up: pushed along 3f out: rdn over 2f out and grad wknd* **14/1**
30 **6** 1 **Le Reve Royal**[23] 5835 2-8-12 0.. PJMcDonald 9 54
(G R Oldroyd) *in midfield: hdwy over 2f out: sn rdn and hung lft 2f out: kpt on same pce* **16/1**
7 1 ½ **Bollin Judith** 2-8-12 0.. DavidAllan 11 50
(T D Easterby) *s.i.s and bhd: effrt and rdn along over 2f out: kpt on appr fnl f: nrst fin* **28/1**
8 1 **Miss Cameo (USA)** 2-8-12 0.. DeanMcKeown 10 47
(R M Whitaker) *s.i.s and bhd: hdwy wl over 2f out: sn rdn and no imp appr fnl f* **28/1**
0 **9** 1 ¾ **Strevelyn**[127] 2569 2-9-0 0.. AndrewMullen(3) 3 48
(Mrs A Duffield) *t.k.h: hld up in rr: sme late hdwy* **66/1**
06 **10** ½ **Citizenship**[62] 4658 2-9-3 0.......................................(b[1]) TedDurcan 1 47
(Pat Eddery) *chsd ldrs on outer: rdn along over 3f out: sn wknd* **13/2**[3]
11 3 ½ **Sydney Cove (IRE)** 2-9-3 0.. JoeFanning 15 38
(M Johnston) *chsd ldrs: rdn along 1/2-way: sn wknd* **9/1**
12 *nk* **Alacity (IRE)** 2-8-9 0.. DuranFentiman(3) 8 32
(N Bycroft) *a in rr* **28/1**
13 1 ½ **Ask Dan (IRE)** 2-9-3 0.. PAspell 2 34
(B Smart) *prom: pushed along 3f out: sn rdn and wknd* **12/1**

1m 24.2s (-0.30) **Going Correction** -0.125s/f (Firm) **13** Ran SP% **122.0**
Speed ratings (Par 97): **96,95,93,88,88 87,85,84,82,81 77,77,75**
toteswinger: 1&2 £2.90, 1&3 £11.40, 2&3 £11.20. CSF £7.64 TOTE £3.60: £1.30, £1.50, £6.30; EX 8.00.
Owner N Browne,J Clarke,P McNamara,S Richards **Bred** Rathbarry Stud **Trained** Lambourn, Berks

FOCUS
As the betting suggested, this was the more open of the two divisions of this race but it resulted in an unsatisfactory finish. The winning time was slower that the preceding event.

NOTEBOOK
Hail Promenader(IRE) had no problem with the step up in trip and won in good style once in the front. Already officially rated 79 coming into this race, he may find it hard to make an impact in nurseries this season. (op 5-2 tchd 85-40)
Striker Torres(IRE) was far from disgraced last time and surely would have won this had he not been chopped for room when the tempo increased. He ought to score next time. (op 4-1)
Senor Berti, stepping up a furlong in trip, was always thereabouts but weakened inside the final furlong. (op 14-1)
Caress The Soul(IRE) did not have much idea what was going on early but really started to motor inside the final furlong. She can make his presence felt in a lesser maiden. (op 40-1)
Mister Bombastic(IRE) probably ran up to the form he showed last time and will be one for handicaps. (op 12-1)
Bollin Judith finished really well after being clueless early. She will be better with time and experience. (op 33-1 tchd 25-1)
Citizenship, wearing blinkers for the first time, was hard at work at the halfway point and never looked like playing a part in the finish. (op 4-1)

6482 BODDINGTONS REDCAR STRAIGHT-MILE CHAMPIONSHIP FINAL (H'CAP) 1m
2:25 (2:26) (Class 2) 3-Y-O+
£18,693 (£5,598; £2,799; £1,401; £699; £351) **Stalls** High

Form RPR
0165 **1** **Charlie Tipple**[16] 6041 4-8-9 **78**..............................(b[1]) PaulMulrennan 9 87
(T D Easterby) *a.p: cl up 1/2-way: led over 2f out: rdn over 1f out: edgd lft ent fnl f: sn drvn and hld on gamely towards fin* **22/1**
2064 **2** *nse* **The Osteopath (IRE)**[15] 6070 5-8-13 **82**.......................... TonyHamilton 7 91
(M Dods) *hld up in tch: hdwy wl over 2f out: rdn to chse ldrs wl over 1f out: drvn and styd on wl fnl f: jst failed* **25/1**
5011 **3** 1 ¼ **Medici Pearl**[15] 6070 4-9-4 **87**.. DavidAllan 13 93
(T D Easterby) *trckd ldrs: hdwy 3f out: rdn and ev ch whn nt clr run and swtchd rtg ent fnl f: sn drvn and kpt on wl* **8/1**[2]
0616 **4** ½ **Opus Maximus (IRE)**[8] 6249 3-8-13 **85**.......................... JoeFanning 6 90
(M Johnston) *cl up: rdn along 2f out: sn drvn and ev ch tl edgd rt ent fnl f and kpt on same pce* **14/1**
2013 **5** 2 ¾ **Moheebb (IRE)**[3] 6385 4-8-7 **76**..................................(b) AndrewElliott 15 75
(Mrs R A Carr) *hld up towards rr: hdwy over 2f out: sn rdn and styd on appr fnl f: nrst fin* **16/1**
3110 **6** 2 ½ **Shotley Mac**[16] 6056 4-7-12 **70**................................(b) DuranFentiman(3) 14 63
(N Bycroft) *in tch: hdwy to chse ldrs over 2f out and sn rdn: drvn and one pce fr over 1f out* **20/1**
2315 **7** 1 ¾ **Reel Buddy Star**[25] 5772 3-8-4 **76**.................................. HayleyTurner 4 65
(G M Moore) *in tch: hdwy to chse ldrs 2f out: sn rdn and one pce fr over 1f out* **18/1**
1005 **8** 1 ¼ **Spinning**[38] 5390 5-8-7 **79**..(b) NeilBrown(3) 5 65
(T D Barron) *hld up: gd hdwy on wd outside over 2f out: rdn to chse ldrs wl over 1f out: drvn and wknd appr fnl f* **16/1**
4202 **9** 1 ¼ **Exit Smiling**[25] 5772 6-9-6 **89**.. MickyFenton 12 72
(P T Midgley) *in midfield: hdwy and in tch over 2f out: sn rdn and no imp* **18/1**
2001 **10** *nse* **Just Bond (IRE)**[8] 6250 6-9-0 **83**.................................... PJMcDonald 11 66
(G R Oldroyd) *in midfield: hdwy wl over 2f out: sn rdn and no imp fr wl over 1f out* **14/1**
4250 **11** ¾ **Hartshead**[16] 6052 9-8-4 **73**.. SilvestreDeSousa 2 54
(G A Swinbank) *in midfield: effrt and hdwy 3f out: rdn over 2f out and sn no imp* **16/1**

1316 **12** *nse* **Osteopathic Remedy (IRE)**[14] 6103 4-9-10 **93**................. TomEaves 3 74
(M Dods) *cl up: led 3f out: rdn and hdd over 2f out: sn drvn and grad wknd* **12/1**

4416 **12** *dht* **King Fingal (IRE)**[66] 4539 3-7-11 **76**............................. JamieKyne(7) 22 57
(J J Quinn) *towards rr: hdwy over 2f out: sn rdn and kpt on appr fnl f: nt rch ldrs* **33/1**

4444 **14** *½* **Violent Velocity (IRE)**[16] 6052 5-8-8 **77**.................. GrahamGibbons 19 57
(J J Quinn) *a in midfield* **11/1**[3]

5120 **15** *nk* **Brasingaman Hifive**[8] 6249 3-8-8 **80**............................ DaleGibson 24 59
(Mrs G S Rees) *in midfield: effrt and in tch 3f out: sn rdn and wknd over 2f out* **25/1**

0061 **16** *hd* **Middlemarch (IRE)**[10] 6215 8-8-7 **76**............................(b) TPQueally 17 55
(J S Goldie) *in midfield: effrt and sme hdwy 3f out: sn rdn along and wknd* **16/1**

0002 **17** *1½* **Wovoka (IRE)**[3] 6385 5-7-13 **68**................................ CatherineGannon 8 43
(D W Barker) *a towards rr* **14/1**

1050 **18** *3* **Gala Casino Star (IRE)**[8] 6249 3-9-0 **86**.................... JamieMoriarty 10 55
(R A Fahey) *towards rr: rdn along 1/2-way: nvr a factor* **33/1**

0024 **19** *1¼* **Crocodile Bay (IRE)**[10] 6215 5-8-8 **77** ow1..................... TedDurcan 20 43
(John A Harris) *in tch: rdn along over 2f out and sn wknd* **33/1**

1022 **20** *6* **Efidium**[10] 6215 10-7-12 **67** oh1.................................. NickyMackay 25 19
(N Bycroft) *a towards rr* **28/1**

0100 **21** *8* **Superior Star**[3] 6385 5-7-12 **67** oh3................................(b) PaulQuinn 21 —
(N Wilson) *a towards rr* **66/1**

4532 **22** *3* **Ezdeyaad (USA)**[16] 6052 4-8-11 **80**.................................. NCallan 1 7
(G A Swinbank) *led: rdn along and hdd 3f out: sn drvn and wknd* **6/1**[1]

P004 **23** *12* **Bid For Glory**[17] 6035 4-8-11 **80**.............................. JerryO'Dwyer 23 —
(H J Collingridge) *a in rr* **12/1**

1m 35.18s (-2.82) **Going Correction** -0.125s/f (Firm)
WFA 3 from 4yo+ 3lb **40** Ran SP% **133.7**
Speed ratings (Par 109): **109,108,107,107,104 101,100,98,97,97 96,96,96,96,96 95,94,91,90,84 76,73,61**
toteswinger: 1&2 £67.20, 1&3 £22.40, 2&3 Not won. CSF £485.35 CT £4755.01 TOTE £29.80: £5.40, £5.10, £2.30, £4.40; EX 1151.80 TRIFECTA Not won..
Owner Norman Jackson **Bred** Paul Wyatt Ranby Hall **Trained** Great Habton, N Yorks

FOCUS
A massive field of handicappers chasing a decent prize after running in the qualifiers, so finding the winner was always going to be particularly difficult. The pace was good, as one would expect, they finished well strung out and the form is solid rated around those in the frame behind the winner.

NOTEBOOK
Charlie Tipple, wearing blinkers for the first time, just got the better of a really tight finish. Although he has won on decent ground, much of his best form has come on an easier surface, so he was not an easy one to pick out. The trainer feels he is at his best in with an end-to-end gallop. (op 25-1)
The Osteopath(IRE) had not been running well coming into this race but only just lost out in a tight finish. Much like the winner, he was another who had shown most of his best form on softer ground. (op 28-1)
Medici Pearl, chasing her fifth win of the year, came into this in great heart and ran a blinder off such a high handicap mark. She may struggle a little now, but only because she has kept her form so well. (tchd 15-2)
Opus Maximus(IRE) was a little bit disappointing last time but ran much better in this. One would imagine that he will contest a lot of the better handicaps next season for his astute handler. (op 12-1)
Moheebb(IRE), who ran only three days previously, kept on well but was too far off the leaders to make an impact. However, it was still a good effort.
Shotley Mac was bang there until the final furlong but weakened close to home.
Osteopathic Remedy(IRE) Official explanation: jockey said gelding ran too free
Ezdeyaad(USA) won one the qualifiers for this race back in June and had held his form well since. Drawn one, he was prominent early but dropped out quickly under pressure. Official explanation: jockey said gelding ran flat; trainer said gelding was found to have a twisted pelvis on returning home (op 7-1)
Bid For Glory Official explanation: jockey said colt had bled from the nose

6483 TOTESCOOP6 TWO-YEAR-OLD TROPHY (LISTED RACE) 6f
3:00 (3:03) (Class 1) 2-Y-O

£113,540 (£43,040; £21,540; £10,740; £5,380; £2,700) **Stalls** Centre

Form RPR

6152 **1** **Total Gallery (IRE)**[15] 6068 2-8-9 105.................................. LPKeniry 7 101
(J S Moore) *trckd ldrs: hdwy 2f out: squeezed through wl over 1f out: rdn to ld wl ins fnl f: drvn edgd rt and hld on wl towards fin* **11/2**[2]

0120 **2** *nse* **Favourite Girl (IRE)**[14] 6102 2-8-11 93............................ DavidAllan 23 103
(T D Easterby) *clsd up: led over 2f out and sn rdn: drvn and hung bdly lft ins fnl f: hdd last 100yds: jst hld* **33/1**

01 **3** *hd* **Wave Aside**[15] 6077 2-8-9 0.. TravisBlock 6 100+
(B J Meehan) *trckd ldrs: hdwy 2f out: rdn and ev ch whn n.m.r wl ins fnl f: drvn and styng on whn n.m.r nr line* **12/1**

1046 **4** *hd* **Khor Dubai (IRE)**[14] 6119 2-8-9 103.............................. TedDurcan 10 100
(Saeed Bin Suroor) *trckd ldrs: hdwy over 2f out: rdn over 1f out and sn ev ch: drvn and n.m.r ins fnl f: nt qckn towards fin* **16/1**

5136 **5** *2¼* **Caranbola**[24] 5794 2-8-1 92.. DaleGibson 19 85
(M Brittain) *chsd ldrs: rdn along 2f out: drvn and kpt on same pce ent fnl f* **22/1**

331 **6** *1½* **Frognal (IRE)**[31] 5609 2-8-9 95..................................... TPQueally 22 89
(B J Meehan) *trckd ldrs: effrt and hdwy over 2f out: rdn wl over 1f out: no imp ent fnl f* **10/1**

1416 **7** *nk* **Viva Ronaldo (IRE)**[23] 5827 2-8-12 99........................ TonyHamilton 13 91
(R A Fahey) *towards rr: rdn along and sme hdwy 2f out: swtchd rt over 1f out: drvn ent fnl f and styd on wl towards fin* **8/1**[3]

1032 **8** *1¼* **Polish Pride**[15] 6067 2-8-7 85....................................... MickyFenton 14 82
(M Brittain) *in midfield: effrt and rdn along over 2f out: styd on ins fnl f: nrst fin* **10/1**

0600 **9** *1* **Harwalla (IRE)**[23] 5827 2-8-9 96.................................... JoeFanning 16 81
(M Johnston) *in rr: rdn along 1/2-way: styd on fnl 2f: nrst fin* **33/1**

0323 **9** *dht* **Brae Hill (IRE)**[23] 5827 2-8-6 91................................... HayleyTurner 12 78
(M L W Bell) *prom: rdn along over 2f out: sn drvn and kpt on same pce* **8/1**[3]

1520 **11** *2¼* **Deadly Secret (USA)**[23] 5827 2-9-2 97........................ PaulMulrennan 8 81
(R A Fahey) *cl up: rdn along over 2f out: grad wknd* **33/1**

012 **12** *½* **Olynard (IRE)**[29] 5680 2-9-2 87................................... PJMcDonald 15 80
(R M Beckett) *in rr: rdn along 1/2-way: sme late hdwy* **33/1**

2043 **13** *2* **Salsa Star (USA)**[15] 6068 2-8-11 86............................ JamieMoriarty 9 69
(R A Fahey) *cl up: rdn along over 2f out: grad wknd* **25/1**

0260 **14** *¾* **White Shift (IRE)**[28] 5693 2-8-7 91.............................. RichardEvans 20 62
(P D Evans) *in midfield: rdn along wl over 2f out and sn btn* **80/1**

222 **15** *1¼* **Captain Ellis (USA)**[26] 5754 2-8-9 0............................ AndrewElliott 17 61
(K R Burke) *towards rr: rdn along over 2f out: sme late hdwy* **33/1**

2301 **16** *1¾* **Prime Mood (IRE)**[3] 6383 2-8-12 78.................................. TomEaves 18 58
(B Smart) *a in rr* **12/1**

521 **17** *1¼* **Quanah Parker (IRE)**[35] 5499 2-8-9 82......................... DeanMcKeown 1 52
(R M Whitaker) *led: pushed along and hdd over 2f out: sn wknd* **9/1**

311 **18** *1¼* **Zuzu (IRE)**[49] 5107 2-8-11 93.. NCallan 5 50+
(M A Jarvis) *cl up: rdn along over 2f out: wkng whn bmpd wl over 1f out: eased* **5/1**[1]

6301 **19** *1¼* **Cerito**[19] 5969 2-8-12 88.. SamHitchcott 3 47
(M R Channon) *a towards rr* **28/1**

2320 **20** *nk* **Olympic Dream**[43] 5244 2-9-0 83.............................. SilvestreDeSousa 4 48
(R A Fahey) *cl up: rdn along appr 1/2-way and sn wknd* **80/1**

0105 **21** *½* **Burning Flute**[35] 5496 2-8-9 88.................................... NickyMackay 2 42
(B J Meehan) *a towards rr* **100/1**

1405 **22** *2¾* **She's A Shaw Thing**[84] 3978 2-8-1 81........................ AndrewMullen 11 25
(P D Evans) *a towards rr* **100/1**

1m 10.22s (-1.58) **Going Correction** -0.125s/f (Firm) **22** Ran SP% **134.5**
Speed ratings (Par 103): **105,104,104,104,101 99,99,97,96,96 93,92,89,88,87 84,83,81,79,79 78,74**
toteswinger: 1&2 £3.30, 1&3 £23.90, 2&3 £69.30. CSF £196.83 TOTE £6.90: £2.60, £10.00, £4.90; EX 268.20 TRIFECTA Not won..
Owner Coleman Bloodstock Limited **Bred** Michael Woodlock And Seamus Kennedy **Trained** Upper Lambourn, Berks

■ Stewards' Enquiry : David Allan one-day ban: careless riding (Oct 19)
L P Keniry one-day ban: careless riding (Oct 19); three-day ban: careless riding (Oct 20-22)

FOCUS
This race has produced plenty of decent performers in the past, such as Pipalong, Captain Rio, Peak To Creek and more recently Misu Bond. However, on the flip side, the last two winners have not managed a win between them in plenty subsequent starts. Quite how this renewal will rate in years to come is open to question, as plenty of them had already met in various sales races and Pattern events.

NOTEBOOK
Total Gallery(IRE) looked nicely treated on his form at a higher level and just about hung on close to the line. Representing last year's winning trainer, he could be spotted going well at halfway and, luckily for him, the gaps opened when he needed room. Interestingly, his trainer believes he will be a proper 5f horse next season. (op 9-2)
Favourite Girl(IRE), well beaten in the Group 3 Firth Of Clyde Stakes last time, came within inches of landing the big pot despite hanging in the closing stages. She may not be the easiest to place next season.
Wave Aside came back after a break to land a fair-looking Newbury event last time. Lacking experience and a bit of room at times, he ran a belter and may emerge the best horse from the race. (op 8-1)
Khor Dubai(IRE) had been running in better company than this and appreciated the drop in class. It will be interesting to see what Godolphin do with him, but one would expect to see him at the Dubai Carnival next year if they keep hold of him.
Caranbola has been a grand servant to her connections this season and once again did herself proud after struggling to go the early gallop. Official explanation: jockey said filly suffered interference at start (tchd 25-1)
Frognal(IRE) came through to have every chance but wandered under pressure late on. (op 8-1)
Viva Ronaldo(IRE) wasable to go the pace early but finished quite strongly when back on an even keel. (op 16-1)
Harwalla(IRE) Official explanation: jockey said colt suffered interference at start (op 10-1)
Brae Hill(IRE) showed plenty of early toe and hung in quite well once passed. (op 10-1)
Captain Ellis(USA) Official explanation: jockey said colt suffered interference at start
Quanah Parker(IRE), the winner of a maiden that has worked out very well, was prominent early but dropped away under pressure. She is worth another chance. (op 11-1)
Zuzu(IRE) landed the Horn Blower Stakes at Ripon last time (that race has not worked out that well) but dropped away quickly once under strong pressure. Official explanation: jockey said filly suffered interference 2f out. (tchd 6-1 in a place)
Olympic Dream Official explanation: jockey said colt suffered interference in running

6484 GUISBOROUGH STKS (LISTED RACE) 7f
3:35 (3:35) (Class 1) 3-Y-O+

£22,708 (£8,608; £4,308; £2,148; £1,076; £540) **Stalls** Centre

Form RPR

2452 **1** **Il Warrd (IRE)**[15] 6073 3-9-1 109.................................... TedDurcan 10 114
(Saeed Bin Suroor) *mde all: hrd pressed fr 2f out: edgd lft u.p ins fnl f: hld on wl* **11/4**[1]

-102 **2** *nk* **Tombi (USA)**[70] 4437 4-9-0 104............................... PaulMulrennan 14 110
(J Howard Johnson) *t.k.h early: hld up in tch: hdwy to chal over 1f out: kpt on: jst hld* **12/1**

1-13 **3** *hd* **Icelandic**[23] 5840 6-9-0 102...(t) MDemuro 11 109+
(Frank Sheridan) *hld up: swtchd lft and hdwy over 2f out: ev ch ins fnl f: hld towards fin* **10/1**

2546 **4** *2* **Damika (IRE)**[7] 6285 5-9-0 103................................ MichaelJStainton 1 104
(R M Whitaker) *hld up: hdwy and in tch over 1f out: kpt on same pce fnl f* **10/1**

0001 **5** *¾* **Bond City (IRE)**[18] 5990 6-9-0 91............................... PJMcDonald 13 102
(G R Oldroyd) *cl up: rdn over 2f out: kpt on ins fnl f* **50/1**

3135 **6** *hd* **Easy Target (FR)**[15] 6073 3-8-12 101............................... TomEaves 6 100
(B Smart) *prom: rdn over 2f out: kpt on same pce fnl f* **12/1**

0006 **7** *1¼* **Protector (SAF)**[15] 6069 7-9-0 89.................................(t) NeilBrown 8 98
(A G Foster) *stdd in midfield: effrt and swtchd rt 2f out: kpt on fnl f: no imp* **40/1**

3060 **8** *2* **Aeroplane**[49] 5095 5-9-0 95.. JoeFanning 4 93
(S A Callaghan) *hld up: hdwy and prom over 2f out: no ex over 1f out* **22/1**

2506 **9** *nk* **Cristal Clear (IRE)**[16] 6053 3-8-7 84............................(p) DavidAllan 15 86
(T D Easterby) *hld up: rdn over 2f out: nt pce to chal* **80/1**

-111 **10** *1* **Scuffle**[84] 3971 3-8-8 100 ow1...................................... NCallan 9 84
(R Charlton) *trckd ldrs tl rdn and wknd over 2f out* **11/4**[1]

15 **11** *1¼* **Russian Empress (IRE)**[27] 5731 4-8-9 0...................... SamHitchcott 3 81
(David P Myerscough, Ire) *dwlt: hld up: rdn over 2f out: n.d* **28/1**

000 **12** *shd* **Rising Shadow (IRE)**[14] 6104 7-9-0 93........................ AndrewElliott 2 86
(N Wilson) *trckd ldrs tl wknd over 2f out* **33/1**

-033 **13** *1½* **Francesca D'Gorgio (USA)**[7] 6271 3-8-7 95..............(v) HayleyTurner 7 77
(J Noseda) *cl up tl wknd over 2f out* **8/1**[3]

2212 **14** *3½* **Dijeerr (USA)**[23] 5840 4-9-0 109..(v) TPQueally 16 72
(Saeed Bin Suroor) *racd w one other stands' side: rdn after 3f: sn no imp* **7/1**[2]

3000 **15** *¾* **Passion Fruit**[11] 6186 7-8-9 75..........................(p) DeanMcKeown 12 65
(C W Fairhurst) *hld up: rdn over 2f out: sn wknd* **100/1**

3003 **16** *17* **Burnwynd Boy**[13] 6153 3-8-12 103............................(p) JamieMoriarty 17 24
(Miss L A Perratt) *racd w one other stands' side: sn rdn along: wknd fr 1/2-way* **50/1**

1m 22.97s (-1.53) **Going Correction** -0.125s/f (Firm)
WFA 3 from 4yo+ 2lb **16** Ran SP% **129.8**
Speed ratings (Par 111): **103,102,102,100,99 97,97,95,95,93 92,92,90,86,85 66**
toteswinger: 1&2 £9.50, 1&3 £11.10, 2&3 £28.10. CSF £40.73 TOTE £3.80: £1.40, £3.60, £2.60; EX 47.20.
Owner Godolphin **Bred** Castleton Group **Trained** Newmarket, Suffolk

FOCUS
This was a fair contest for the grade, with a handful of unexposed sorts taking on several more established performers.\n\x\x They went a reasonable gallop early, with two runners, Dijeerr and Burnwynd Boy, racing alone near the stands' side rail and the rest of the field converging towards the centre of the track. The two nearside runners were soon under pressure and their runs are probably best forgotten. The form is a bit muddling but sound enough amongst the principals.

NOTEBOOK
Il Warrd(IRE), who was carrying a 3lb penalty for winning a Listed contest on the all-weather in the spring when trained by Marcus Tregoning, was briefly headed at the furlong pole by the eventual runner-up, but fought back gamely to hold off the challengers on either side in a driving finish. He did well to defy his penalty and there may be more to come from him. He has won over a mile, but he would appear best over 6 or 7f. (op 10-3 tchd 7-2 in a place)
Tombi(USA) has mainly been running over sprint trips but he appeared to see out this extra furlong well. He was returning from a 70-day break but that was of no great concern as he has an excellent record when fresh. He may be put away for the season now, but is certainly one to watch out for early next year as he has won on his seasonal debut for the last two years. (op 10-1)
Icelandic, the winner of a Group 3 in Italy at the end of last season, had finished just behind Dijeerr when third at Sandown on his latest start and he ran a fine race in defeat once again. He was forced to race widest of all despite being drawn in the middle and responded gamely to pressure all the way to the line. He looks capable of picking up a similar prize, perhaps over slightly further. (op 9-1)
Damika(IRE), who looked well beforehand, is probably best over 6f but he is a tough sort and he responded well to pressure. (op 11-1)
Bond City(IRE), who is rated 18lb below Il Warrd, had a lot to find on these terms but he ran as well as could be expected. Connections should be able to find another sprint handicap for him before the season is out.
Easy Target(FR) raced prominently but was never travelling with any great fluency and gradually faded from about two out, although he did finish about the same distance behind the winner as he had done at Newbury previously. (op 16-1)
Protector(SAF), who ran a solid race in the Ayr Silver Cup on his previous outing, came under strong pressure two out but he finished to good effect despite wandering around. (op 50-1)
Scuffle, the least exposed runner coming into this race, may have been unsuited by the rain-softened ground and deserves to be given another chance, perhaps over slightly further. (op 7-2)

6485 ROTARY WATCHES AT MARKET CROSS JEWELLERS (S) STKS 1m 2f
4:10 (4:11) (Class 5) 3-5-Y-0 **£3,885** (£1,156; £577; £288) **Stalls** Low

Form RPR
5050 **1** **Packers Hill (IRE)**[6] 6312 4-9-0 64.................................. PJMcDonald 5 69
(G A Swinbank) *in midfield: smooth hdwy on inner 3f out: swtchd rt and effrt to chal over 2f out: led wl over 1f out: rdn ent fnl f and kpt on* **9/2**[2]
020 **2** *1 1/4* **Evelith Regent (IRE)**[10] 6216 5-9-0 62.............................. NCallan 6 66
(G A Swinbank) *in midfield: hdwy 3f out: rdn over 1f out: chsd wnr ins fnl f: kpt on* **13/2**
5340 **3** *1 1/4* **Mister Fizzbomb (IRE)**[19] 5971 5-9-0 62...............(v) GrahamGibbons 9 64
(J S Wainwright) *led: rdn along 3f out: drvn and hdd wl over 1f out: kpt on u.p ins fnl f* **6/1**[3]
2502 **4** *1/2* **Lady Valentino**[10] 6217 4-8-9 52.. TomEaves 11 58
(M Dods) *hld up in rr: hdwy wl over 2f out: swtchd outside and rdn over 1f out: kpt on ins fnl f: nrst fin* **10/1**
0016 **5** *nk* **Jafra (IRE)**[61] 4688 3-9-1 63..(p) PaulQuinn 4 68
(R M Whitaker) *trckd ldrs on inner: hdwy 3f out: rdn wl over 1f out: sn drvn and kpt on same pce appr fnl f* **9/1**
2063 **6** *1 1/4* **It's A Dream (FR)**[15] 6090 5-9-6 68.............................(t) HayleyTurner 1 65
(M W Easterby) *hld up towards rr: hdwy on inner whn n.m.r wl over 2f out: rdn and n.m.r over 1f out: kpt on same pce ins fnl f* **7/2**[1]
1104 **7** *9* **King Of The Moors (USA)**[13] 6152 5-9-3 70............(p) NeilBrown(3) 12 47
(T D Barron) *prom: rdn along 3f out: drvn and wknd 2f out* **6/1**[3]
0603 **8** *9* **Roman History (IRE)**[8] 6255 5-9-0 52.................(p) SilvestreDeSousa 3 23
(Miss Tracy Waggott) *prom: chsd ldr 1/2-way: rdn along 3f out and sn wknd* **22/1**
0643 **9** *3/4* **Distant Rock**[10] 6217 3-8-1 52.................................(t) DuranFentiman(3) 13 17
(D Carroll) *hld up: sme hdwy on outer 3f out: rdn along over 2f out and sn btn* **20/1**
0066 **10** *1/2* **Enderby Light (FR)**[15] 6092 3-8-9 65.......................... JamieMoriarty 14 21
(Ollie Pears) *in tch: rdn along over 3f out: sn wknd* **25/1**
0000 **11** *1 1/2* **Kayflaa (IRE)**[17] 6015 3-8-4 50.. JoeFanning 8 13
(T D Walford) *trckd ldrs: effrt over 3f out: sn rdn along and wknd* **33/1**
0160 **12** *15* **Lujano**[15] 6088 3-9-1 63... PaulMulrennan 7 —
(Ollie Pears) *hld up in midfield: effrt 4f out: sn rdn along and wknd* **25/1**
U0-0 **13** *13* **Recoil (IRE)**[13] 6152 3-8-9 55.. TonyHamilton 15 —
(R Johnson) *a bhd* **100/1**

2m 8.73s (1.63) **Going Correction** +0.25s/f (Good)
WFA 3 from 4yo+ 5lb **13** Ran SP% **122.1**
Speed ratings (Par 103): **103,102,101,100,100 99,92,84,84,83 82,70,60**
toteswinger: 1&2 £8.50, 1&3 £7.80, 2&3 £8.70. CSF £31.66 TOTE £6.90: £2.20, £2.50, £3.10; EX 42.30.There was no bid for the winner.
Owner B Valentine **Bred** G J King **Trained** Melsonby, N Yorks

FOCUS
Plenty of these came into this seller with some sort of chance, so the form could be more reliable than most events run at this level, although it has to be said that a couple of them looked to have quirks under pressure. The form is limited by the proximity of the fourth and fifth.

6486 SHEPHERD CONSTRUCTION H'CAP 5f
4:45 (4:46) (Class 5) (0-75,79) 3-Y-O+ **£3,238** (£963; £481; £240) **Stalls** Centre

Form RPR
012 **1** **Haajes**[5] 6340 4-9-5 79..(t) TolleyDean(3) 11 93
(S Parr) *in tch: hdwy to ld 1f out: edgd lft: r.o strly* **10/3**[1]
2502 **2** *1 1/2* **Raccoon (IRE)**[6] 6310 8-8-4 61.................................... AndrewElliott 3 70
(Mrs R A Carr) *racd far side: led to 1f out: kpt on u.p* **9/1**[2]
3006 **3** *1* **Tangerine Trees**[10] 6218 3-8-8 65 ow2........................ TomEaves 10 70
(B Smart) *trckd ldrs: effrt and ch over 1f out: kpt on fnl f* **20/1**
4116 **4** *hd* **Miss Daawe**[52] 4971 4-8-4 68.. LanceBetts(7) 14 72
(B Ellison) *in tch towards stands' side: hdwy over 1f out: r.o fnl f: nrst fin* **10/1**[3]
3160 **5** *1 1/4* **King Of Swords (IRE)**[3] 6388 4-9-0 71.......................... KimTinkler 15 71
(N Tinkler) *towards rr: rdn over 2f out: kpt on fnl f: nrst fin* **22/1**
0113 **6** *nk* **Lake Chini (IRE)**[16] 6039 6-8-9 66.............................(b) PaulMulrennan 9 65
(M W Easterby) *trckd ldrs tl rdn and nt qckn appr fnl f* **10/1**[3]
0640 **7** *1 3/4* **Windjammer**[10] 6218 4-8-4 61 oh1..........................(b) SilvestreDeSousa 18 53
(T D Easterby) *in midfield towards stands' side: hdwy over 1f out: nt pce to chal* **16/1**
50-0 **7** *dht* **Cayman Fox**[18] 5991 3-8-11 68.. PJMcDonald 5 60
(James Moffatt) *chsd ldr tl edgd rt and wknd over 1f out* **50/1**
5140 **9** *1/2* **Barraland**[9] 6232 3-9-2 73.. SamHitchcott 13 64
(M R Channon) *hld up: hdwy over 2f out: rdn and no imp over 1f out: eased whn btn ins fnl f* **33/1**
4340 **10** *1/2* **Sandwith**[15] 6066 5-8-13 73.. NeilBrown(3) 19 62
(R Johnson) *bhd stands' side: rdn 1/2-way: sme late hdwy: nvr on terms* **12/1**
503 **11** *nk* **Tartatartufata**[144] 2082 6-9-1 72..................................(v) TPQueally 4 60
(J G Given) *in tch far side: drvn and outpcd 1/2-way: no imp after* **16/1**
2200 **12** *nse* **Bahamian Ballet**[18] 6006 6-9-3 74................................ GrahamGibbons 7 62
(E S McMahon) *hld up: rdn 1/2-way: no imp fr wl over 1f out: eased whn btn ins fnl f* **10/1**[3]
2335 **13** *hd* **Rio Sands**[37] 5417 3-8-9 69..................................... MichaelJStainton(3) 12 56
(R M Whitaker) *dwlt: sn rdn towards rr: n.d* **16/1**
3030 **14** *1 1/2* **The Bear**[12] 6164 5-8-13 70.. JamieMoriarty 17 51
(R Johnson) *dwlt: a bhd towards stands' side* **16/1**
1230 **15** *nse* **Mission Impossible**[19] 5962 3-9-3 74............................(p) LeeEnstone 6 55
(P C Haslam) *dwlt: sn in midfield: effrt u.p over 2f out: btn over 1f out* **28/1**
1204 **16** *1 1/4* **Speedy Senorita (IRE)**[14] 6131 3-8-9 73................. DeclanCannon(7) 8 50
(K R Burke) *prom tl rdn and wknd over 1f out* **12/1**
-000 **17** *nk* **Top Bid**[10] 6219 4-8-1 61 oh2................................ DuranFentiman(3) 16 37
(T D Easterby) *bhd and sn outpcd towards stands' side: nvr on terms* **28/1**
0060 **18** *1 1/4* **Dickie Le Davoir**[15] 6069 4-9-4 75.................................... MickyFenton 1 46
(John A Harris) *s.i.s: sn wl bhd far side: nvr on terms* **16/1**
0-00 **19** *4* **Fish Called Johnny**[257] 255 4-8-5 62.............................. JoeFanning 2 19
(A Berry) *in tch: sn drvn along: wknd fr 1/2-way* **50/1**

57.78 secs (-0.82) **Going Correction** -0.125s/f (Firm) **19** Ran SP% **128.0**
Speed ratings (Par 103): **101,98,97,96,94 94,91,91,90,89 89,89,88,86,86 84,83,81,75**
toteswinger: 1&2 £5.80, 1&3 £20.60, 2&3 £42.20. CSF £29.33 CT £560.43 TOTE £3.20: £1.40, £2.00, £4.60, £3.10; EX 38.60.
Owner Willie McKay **Bred** Irish National Stud **Trained** Bawtry, S Yorks

FOCUS
This looked an ordinary sprint handicap on paper with plenty of these runners looking out of form or in the grip of the assessor. The form looks sound rated around the first four.
Sandwith Official explanation: jockey said gelding hung left-handed throughout

6487 RACING HERE FRIDAY 17TH OCTOBER H'CAP 1m 2f
5:20 (5:21) (Class 5) (0-75,75) 3-Y-O+ **£3,238** (£963; £481; £240) **Stalls** Low

Form RPR
2210 **1** **Maria Di Scozia**[84] 3962 3-9-4 75....................................(t) TedDurcan 14 83
(P W Chapple-Hyam) *in tch: hdwy to ld over 1f out: drvn and hld on wl fnl f* **5/1**[2]
0624 **2** *nk* **Applaude**[21] 5888 3-9-1 72.. NCallan 5 80
(G A Swinbank) *prom: swtchd rt and ev ch over 1f out: rdn and hung to stands' side: kpt on towards fin* **5/1**[2]
6416 **3** *3/4* **Karmest**[131] 2453 4-9-1 67.................................(b) SilvestreDeSousa 3 73
(A D Brown) *hld up: hdwy over 2f out: drifted to stands' rail fr over 1f out: r.o fin* **25/1**
1214 **4** *10* **Highland Love**[35] 5502 3-9-0 71...................................... TonyHamilton 9 57
(Jedd O'Keeffe) *cl up: led over 2f to 1f out: sn outpcd* **6/1**[3]
3123 **5** *1 1/2* **Straight Sets (IRE)**[16] 6056 4-9-4 70............................ SamHitchcott 11 53
(M R Channon) *in midfield on outside: drvn fr 4f out: outpcd fr over 2f out* **7/2**[1]
3000 **6** *3/4* **My Paris**[16] 6052 7-9-9 75..(v) JamieMoriarty 1 57
(Ollie Pears) *in midfield: drvn over 3f out: no imp fnl 2f* **16/1**
204- **7** *2 1/2* **Prince Evelith (GER)**[431] 4039 5-9-9 75...................... GrahamGibbons 8 52
(J J Quinn) *in midfield: rdn over 3f out: nvr able to chal* **12/1**
-305 **8** *5* **Tsaroxy (IRE)**[33] 5563 6-9-5 71.............................(b) PaulMulrennan 7 38
(J Howard Johnson) *missed break: bhd: rdn 4f out: nvr on terms* **14/1**
0022 **9** *1 3/4* **Moonstreaker**[10] 6216 5-8-11 66............................ MichaelJStainton(3) 12 29
(R M Whitaker) *missed break: sn prom: edgd lft and wknd over 2f out* **15/2**
2420 **10** *hd* **Jamieson Gold (IRE)**[15] 6070 5-9-9 75..........................(p) TomEaves 4 38
(Miss L A Perratt) *hld up: rdn over 3f out: sn wknd* **12/1**
400- **11** *2 3/4* **Isent She Rich (IRE)**[22] 5877 3-8-12 69..................(b[1]) AndrewElliott 10 26
(David P Myerscough, Ire) *chsd clr ldr tl wknd wl over 2f out* **22/1**
6355 **12** *1 3/4* **Elk Trail (IRE)**[36] 5450 3-9-2 73.................................(b[1]) MickyFenton 13 27
(T P Tate) *t.k.h: led and clr: hdd over 2f out: sn btn: eased whn no ch* **14/1**
13 *5* **Masterofceremonies**[395] 5147 5-9-5 71.............................(p) PAspell 2 15
(James Moffatt) *missed break: a bhd* **20/1**

2m 8.79s (1.69) **Going Correction** +0.25s/f (Good)
WFA 3 from 4yo+ 5lb **13** Ran SP% **129.2**
Speed ratings (Par 103): **103,102,102,94,92 92,90,86,84,84 82,81,77**
toteswinger: 1&2 £6.40, 1&3 £29.50, 2&3 £33.60. CSF £32.08 CT £603.16 TOTE £8.00: £2.60, £2.00, £7.00; EX 32.90 Place 6 £220.28, Place 5 £157.80. .
Owner Miss K Rausing **Bred** Miss K Rausing **Trained** Newmarket, Suffolk
■ Stewards' Enquiry : N Callan two-day ban: careless riding (Oct 19-20)

FOCUS
A difficult handicap to finish the meeting. It saw a few hardened campaigners take on a couple of interesting, unexposed sorts. The pace looked sound and the form, rated through the third, should be fairly reliable for Class 5 company with the first trio clear.
Tsaroxy(IRE) Official explanation: jockey said gelding missed the break
Elk Trail(IRE) Official explanation: jockey said gelding ran too free

T/Plt: £288.20 to a £1 stake. Pool: £67,114.83. 169.98 winning tickets. T/Qpdt: £125.20 to a £1 stake. Pool: £3,369.18. 19.90 winning tickets. JR

6447 **WOLVERHAMPTON (A.W)** (L-H)

Saturday, October 4

OFFICIAL GOING: Standard

Wind: Moderate, half-behind. Weather: Light rain.

6488 FREE CASINO CHIPS @ FREEBETS.CO.UK MEDIAN AUCTION MAIDEN STKS 5f 216y(P)

6:50 (6:51) (Class 5) 2-Y-O **£3,070** (£906; £453) **Stalls** Low

Form RPR

1 **Hermione's Magic** 2-8-12 0 PatrickMathers 3 71+
(P J McBride) *s.i.s: in rr: plld out 2f out: hdwy on outside wl over 1f out: sn rdn and hung lft: r.o to ld cl home* **28/1**

5233 2 *hd* **Forward Feline (IRE)**[20] 5929 2-8-12 74 CatherineGannon 7 70
(B Palling) *chsd ldr: led 2f out: sn rdn: hdd cl home* **9/4**[1]

5 3 *1 3/4* **Glimpse Of Light (IRE)**[15] 6089 2-8-7 0 DavidProbert(5) 10 65
(A M Balding) *t.k.h to post: prom: rdn 2f out: wnt 2nd ins fnl f: nt qckn* **3/1**[3]

5 4 *5* **Kinigi (IRE)**[25] 5777 2-8-12 0 JerryO'Dwyer 1 50+
(S A Callaghan) *bhd: hdwy over 1f out: swtchd lft ins fnl f: nvr trbld ldrs* **11/1**

00 5 *nse* **Cafe Fiore (IRE)**[9] 6230 2-8-12 0 VinceSlattery 9 50
(T J Pitt) *hld up in tch: no hdwy fnl 2f* **66/1**

0 6 *3/4* **Shirley High**[20] 5939 2-8-12 0 DNolan 2 47
(P Howling) *hld up in mid-div: no real prog fnl 2f* **22/1**

023 7 *2 1/4* **Dream Of Mine**[15] 6089 2-8-12 70 DO'Donohoe 8 41
(Saeed Bin Suroor) *led: hdd 2f out: sn rdn: wknd fnl f* **11/4**[2]

0 8 *2 3/4* **Rock Relief (IRE)**[11] 6187 2-9-3 0 J-PGuillambert 13 37
(Sir Mark Prescott) *hung rt and rn wd bnd over 3f out: a bhd* **11/1**

0 9 *10* **Top Flight Splash**[18] 5989 2-8-12 0 DaleGibson 5 —
(Mrs G S Rees) *prom over 3f: eased whn no ch fnl f* **50/1**

60 10 *10* **May Need A Spell**[16] 6051 2-9-0 0 KevinGhunowa(3) 11 —
(J G M O'Shea) *a in rr: eased whn no ch fnl f* **33/1**

11 *13* **Jung (USA)** 2-9-3 0 AdrianTNicholls 12 —
(J R Gask) *a in rr: t.o* **16/1**

1m 16.58s (1.58) **Going Correction** +0.10s/f (Slow) **11** Ran SP% **119.2**

Speed ratings (Par 95): **93,92,90,83,83 82,79,76,62,49 32**

toteswinger: 1&2 £23.40, 1&3 £23.40, 2&3 £4.90. CSF £89.53 TOTE £36.30: £5.30, £1.20, £1.40; EX 691.30.

Owner Peter Charter **Bred** East Burrow Farm **Trained** Newmarket, Suffolk

FOCUS

An ordinary maiden in which the gallop was soon sound and the runner-up looks a good guide to the form.

NOTEBOOK

Hermione's Magic, whose dam is from the family of high-class middle distance performer Sally Brown, overcame inexperience on her debut to score with a bit more in hand than the bare margin suggests. She will be suited by the step up to 7f and is entitled to improve for this initial outing. (op 25-1 tchd 33-1)

Forward Feline(IRE), a reliable sort on turf, had the run of the race and seemed to reproduce the pick of her form on this all-weather debut. While vulnerable to progressive sorts in this grade, she is more than capable of picking up a minor event away from progressive sorts over this trip. (op 5-2 tchd 3-1)

Glimpse Of Light(IRE) again attracted support and bettered the form of her racecourse debut. She should have no problems with 7f and may do better once handicapped. (op 9-2)

Kinigi(IRE), who ran well for a long way in heavy ground in a fair Leicester maiden on her debut. The filly will be suited by the return to 7f and beyond and should improve in handicaps. (op 10-1 tchd 12-1)

Cafe Fiore(IRE) had shown precious little on turf but shaped much better on this all-weather debut. Run-of-the-mill handicaps over further will be the way forward with her. (tchd 50-1)

Shirley High, who bettered her debut effort, is another who will probably make her mark once handicapped. (tchd 25-1)

Dream Of Mine was the disappointment of the race as he dropped out tamely after leading and looks one to have reservations about. (op 5-2 tchd 3-1)

6489 FREE BETTING @ FREEBETS.CO.UK (S) STKS 5f 20y(P)

7:20 (7:20) (Class 6) 2-Y-O **£2,047** (£604; £302) **Stalls** Low

Form RPR

3664 1 **Tillers Satisfied (IRE)**[44] 5200 2-8-1 56 DavidProbert(5) 4 60+
(R Hollinshead) *hld up in tch: rdn to ld over 1f out: r.o* **7/2**[1]

00 2 *1* **Autumn Morning (IRE)**[51] 5022 2-8-3 0 KevinGhunowa(3) 2 55
(Eve Johnson Houghton) *s.i.s: in rr: swtchd lft and hdwy over 1f out: wnt 2nd and kpt on u.p ins fnl f* **25/1**

4650 3 *1 3/4* **Abhainn (IRE)**[16] 6087 2-8-11 67 CatherineGannon 3 54
(B Palling) *led: hdd over 3f out: prom: rdn wl over 1f out: one pce fnl f* **9/2**[2]

5160 4 *1 1/2* **Courageous Nature (IRE)**[7] 6281 2-9-2 68 DO'Donohoe 11 54
(A J McCabe) *hld up in tch: wnt 2nd briefly 2f out: rdn over 1f out: no ex ins fnl f* **5/1**[3]

00 5 *2* **No Quarter Given (IRE)**[16] 6051 2-8-11 0 TonyCulhane 8 42
(Mrs A Duffield) *w ldrs: led over 3f out: rdn and hdd over 1f out: wknd wl ins fnl f* **9/2**[2]

0535 6 *1 3/4* **Franchesca's Gold**[17] 6009 2-8-8 52 ow2 RobertHavlin 9 32
(B R Millman) *hld up in tch: rdn and wknd wl over 1f out* **15/2**

6465 7 *3/4* **Wee Bizzom**[34] 5541 2-8-6 46 FrancisNorton 6 28
(A Berry) *prom: n.m.r and lost pl 3f out: wknd over 1f out* **28/1**

3256 8 *1 1/4* **Turn To Dreams**[11] 6191 2-8-1 53 SophieDoyle(5) 13 23
(P D Evans) *s.i.s: in rr: sltly hmpd over 1f out: n.d* **10/1**

0040 9 *nk* **Carmanjoe**[17] 6009 2-8-11 62 (p) DaleGibson 10 27
(M W Easterby) *prom tl rdn and wknd wl over 1f out* **14/1**

3033 10 *shd* **Dazzling Dust (IRE)**[95] 3570 2-8-6 52 (tp) JackDean(5) 7 27
(W G M Turner) *bhd: pushed along over 3f out: no rspnse* **16/1**

00 11 *1/2* **Badtanman**[14] 6133 2-8-11 0 JerryO'Dwyer 5 25
(Peter Grayson) *hung lft over 1f out: a bhd* **66/1**

0 12 *9* **Its Alice**[15] 6089 2-8-6 0 PatrickMathers 1 —
(Peter Grayson) *prom on ins: lost pl over 3f out: bhd fnl 2f* **50/1**

63.55 secs (1.25) **Going Correction** +0.10s/f (Slow) **12** Ran SP% **119.4**

Speed ratings (Par 93): **94,92,89,87,84 81,80,78,77,77 76,62**

toteswinger: 1&2 £15.80, 1&3 £3.10, 2&3 £9.80. CSF £99.92 TOTE £3.60: £1.70, £4.70, £2.30; EX 134.40.There was no bid for the winner. Autumn Morning was claimed by P. D. Evans for £6,000.

Owner Dean Wootton **Bred** R Honniball **Trained** Upper Longdon, Staffs

FOCUS

A weak event but another race in which the pace was sound. Winner and second raced against the inside rail in the straight.

NOTEBOOK

Tillers Satisfied(IRE), from a yard in good form, had been disappointing but appreciated the decent gallop and turned in her best effort since her debut on this all-weather bow. She should prove equally effective over 6f and, although this was not much of a race, she may be capable of a little better on sand. (op 6-1)

Autumn Morning(IRE) had shown little in turf maidens but fared better dropped in grade. There should be a small handicap in her on artificial surfaces this winter. (tchd 22-1)

Abhainn(IRE), dropped in trip, fared the best of those to race up with the strong pace but he is an inconsistent maiden who is likely to struggle in handicaps from his current mark. (op 5-1 tchd 11-2)

Courageous Nature(IRE), the only winner in the field, may be a bit better than the bare form after racing four deep from his wide draw. The return to 6f will be in his favour and he is capable of winning a similar event granted a more favourable stall.

No Quarter Given(IRE) had been soundly beaten at big prices in maidens on easy ground and showed his first worthwhile form down in grade on this all-weather debut. He may improve. Official explanation: jockey said gelding ran too free (op 5-1 tchd 4-1)

Franchesca's Gold looked to have fair claims in this company returned to Polytrack but again had her limitations exposed. (op 11-2)

Wee Bizzom Official explanation: jockey said filly hung left

Badtanman Official explanation: jockey said colt hung left

6490 FREE POKER CHIPS @ FREEBETS.CO.UK CLAIMING STKS 7f 32y(P)

7:50 (7:50) (Class 5) 3-Y-0+ **£3,238** (£963; £481; £240) **Stalls** High

Form RPR

0000 1 **Final Verse**[61] 4687 5-9-10 88 AlanMunro 6 88
(Jane Chapple-Hyam) *hld up in mid-div: hdwy on outside wl over 1f out: rdn and r.o wl to ld last stride* **10/1**

5220 2 *hd* **Gift Horse**[15] 6069 8-9-8 88 (p) StephenDonohoe 3 85
(D Nicholls) *hld up towards rr: rdn and hdwy over 1f out: led wl ins fnl f: hdd last stride* **5/2**[2]

2555 3 *1 1/2* **White Deer (USA)**[6] 6314 4-9-10 77 (b) AdrianTNicholls 1 83
(D Nicholls) *sn led: rdn over 2f out: hdd and no ex wl ins fnl f* **7/1**[3]

4503 4 *1 3/4* **Royal Applord**[10] 6215 3-8-10 75 (p) ChrisCatlin 5 66
(K A Ryan) *led early: prom: rdn to chse ldr wl over 1f out: lost 2nd and no ex wl ins fnl f* **25/1**

0405 5 *1/2* **Teasing**[24] 5799 4-9-0 67 (p) RobertHavlin 12 67
(J Pearce) *s.i.s: hld up in rr: pushed along over 2f out: styd on u.p ins fnl f: nt rch ldrs* **28/1**

440 6 *shd* **Blue Charm**[3] 6380 4-8-11 67 LPKeniry 10 64
(S Kirk) *hld up and bhd: rdn and kpt on fnl f: nvr trbld ldrs* **14/1**

0000 7 *1 1/4* **Imperial Echo (USA)**[16] 6046 7-8-12 65 TGMcLaughlin 2 61
(P Howling) *hld up in tch: rdn wl over 1f out: wknd ins fnl f* **66/1**

5610 8 *1 3/4* **Landucci**[17] 6020 7-9-1 73 (v) PatrickHills(3) 8 63
(J W Hills) *prom: rdn over 1f out: wknd fnl f* **14/1**

0044 9 *2 1/4* **Ninefineirishmen (IRE)**[16] 6043 3-9-0 70 (p) DarrenWilliams 7 54
(K R Burke) *prom: rdn and chal over 2f out: wknd wl over 1f out* **22/1**

0005 10 *hd* **Incline (IRE)**[19] 5968 9-8-8 0 FrankieMcDonald 9 46
(R McGlinchey, Ire) *prom tl rdn and wknd 2f out* **6/4**[1]

0030 11 *1 1/4* **Hopeful Purchase (IRE)**[12] 6170 5-9-1 78 (b) DavidProbert(5) 11 55
(J R Gask) *s.i.s: a in rr* **20/1**

265- 12 *46* **Gifted Gamble**[567] 699 6-9-2 75 PatrickMathers 4 —
(Peter Grayson) *s.i.s: a in rr: rdn over 3f out: t.o fnl 2f* **40/1**

1m 29.86s (0.26) **Going Correction** +0.10s/f (Slow)

WFA 3 from 4yo+ 2lb **12** Ran SP% **123.8**

Speed ratings (Par 103): **102,101,100,98,97 97,95,93,91,91 89,37**

toteswinger: 1&2 £49.00, 1&3 £49.00, 2&3 £3.10. CSF £34.35 TOTE £17.70: £3.40, £1.90, £2.40; EX 67.90.Final Verse was claimed by Mr M. Salaman for £20,000. Incline was claimed by Horses First Racing Limited for £4,000.

Owner Mrs Fitri Hay **Bred** A Christodoulou **Trained** Lambourn, Berks

■ Stewards' Enquiry : Alan Munro caution: used whip without giving gelding time to respond.

FOCUS

Few regular winners but a fair race for the grade. The pace was reasonable and the winner raced in the centre, while runner-up ended up against the inside rail. The third and fourth looks the best guides to the form.

Incline(IRE) Official explanation: jockey said gelding had no more to give

Gifted Gamble Official explanation: jockey said gelding had no more to give

6491 FREEBETS.CO.UK H'CAP 1m 141y(P)

8:20 (8:21) (Class 5) (0-75,78) 3-Y-0+ **£3,238** (£963; £481; £240) **Stalls** Low

Form RPR

1351 1 **St Trinians**[8] 6256 3-9-8 **78** LPKeniry 4 93+
(E F Vaughan) *prom: wnt 2nd 7f out: led on bit over 2f out: clr wl over 1f out: rdn ins fnl f: eased towards fin* **10/3**[1]

R335 2 *4 1/2* **Claret And Amber**[28] 5708 6-8-10 **62** ChrisCatlin 8 64
(W K Goldsworthy) *hld up in mid-div: tk 2nd last strides: no ch w wnr* **10/1**

3340 3 *nse* **Atabaas Pride**[38] 5390 3-9-4 **74** J-PGuillambert 13 76
(M Johnston) *a.p: rdn 2f out: kpt on same pce fnl f* **16/1**

2250 4 *nk* **Spanish Diva**[36] 5450 4-8-6 **63** (p) DavidProbert(5) 9 64
(S C Williams) *hld up in rr: hdwy fnl f: nrst fin* **8/1**[3]

1003 5 *nk* **Millfield (IRE)**[24] 5800 5-9-8 **74** AlanMunro 10 75
(P R Chamings) *hld up in rr: hdwy whn swtchd rt jst over 1f out: nvr nrr* **8/1**[3]

4122 6 *1* **Mr Lu**[19] 5965 3-8-7 **66** DuranFentiman(3) 1 64
(Miss L A Perratt) *led early: prom: rdn and chsd wnr 2f out: lost 2nd and fdd towards fin* **5/1**[2]

0501 7 *2 1/4* **Forzarzi (IRE)**[15] 6091 4-9-1 **67** (p) StephenDonohoe 6 60
(H A McWilliams) *hld up in rr: short-lived effrt over 1f out* **20/1**

3650 8 *1* **San Silvestro (IRE)**[16] 6056 3-8-9 **68** AndrewMullen(3) 2 59
(Mrs A Duffield) *hld up in mid-div: rdn and hdwy on ins wl over 1f out: wknd fnl f* **33/1**

0136 9 *2 1/4* **Inside Story (IRE)**[10] 6215 6-9-2 **68** (b) DaleGibson 7 54
(M W Easterby) *s.i.s: rdn over 2f out: a towards rr* **14/1**

60-0 10 *1 1/4* **Writ (IRE)**[19] 5968 6-9-3 **69** PJMcDonald 3 52
(Miss L A Perratt) *sn led: rdn and hdd over 2f out: wknd wl over 1f out* **10/1**

1640 11 *3 1/4* **Royal Island (IRE)**[14] 6125 6-9-6 **72** VinceSlattery 11 47
(M G Quinlan) *t.k.h in rr: hdwy on outside over 3f out: wknd over 2f out* **14/1**

310 12 *4* **Shindy (FR)**[23] 5841 3-9-2 **72** KirstyMilczarek 5 38
(J A R Toller) *hld up in tch: rdn and wknd qckly over 1f out* **9/1**

4400 **13** *6* **Machinate (USA)**[14] 6134 6-9-0 66 TGMcLaughlin 12 18
(W M Brisbourne) *hld up in mid-div: stdy hdwy over 5f out: wknd over 2f out* **33/1**

1m 50.28s (-0.22) **Going Correction** +0.10s/f (Slow)
WFA 3 from 4yo+ 4lb **13** Ran SP% **120.0**
Speed ratings (Par 103): **104,100,99,99,99 98,96,95,93,92 89,86,80**
toteswinger: 1&2 £4.00, 1&3 £31.90, 2&3 Not won. CSF £36.49 CT £484.86 TOTE £5.00: £1.40, £4.90, £5.70; EX 47.20.

Owner Hungerford Park Stud **Bred** Mrs E L Hunter **Trained** Newmarket, Suffolk

FOCUS
What looked a fairly open handicap was turned into a procession by the progressive winner who is rated value for six lengths.

Millfield(IRE) Official explanation: jockey said gelding ran very keenly

Shindy(FR) Official explanation: jockey said filly ran flat

6492 FREE SPORTS BETS H'CAP — 1m 1f 103y(P)
8:50 (8:50) (Class 6) (0-55,55) 3-Y-O — £2,388 (£705; £352) Stalls Low

Form — RPR

400 **1** **Star Choice**[165] 1535 3-8-9 53 LukeMorris(3) 4 64+
(M L W Bell) *hld up in mid-div: rdn and hdwy over 2f out: r.o to ld wl ins fnl f* **4/1**[1]

-230 **2** *1/2* **Just Mossie**[27] 432 3-8-7 53 (p) JackDean(5) 9 63
(W G M Turner) *hld up in tch: wnt 2nd over 2f out: rdn to ld 1f out: hdd and no ex wl ins fnl f* **22/1**

6620 **3** *3 1/4* **Ceili Mor (IRE)**[49] 5087 3-8-12 53 J-PGuillambert 13 57
(M Johnston) *prom: chsd ldr 7f out: led 3f out: rdn and hdd 1f out: fdd towards fin* **16/1**

2353 **4** *1 3/4* **Peas In A Pod**[58] 4793 3-8-9 53 JackMitchell(3) 6 53
(J R Best) *hld up towards rr: hdwy over 2f out: rdn over 1f out: one pce* **4/1**[1]

-640 **5** *3 1/4* **Augmentation**[106] 3221 3-8-13 54 (p) AlanMunro 3 47
(P W D'Arcy) *t.k.h in rr: sme hdwy on ins over 1f out: n.d* **7/1**[2]

520 **6** *1/2* **Sendefaa (IRE)**[30] 5653 3-8-12 53 ChrisCatlin 10 45
(S Lycett) *hld up in mid-div: no hdwy fnl 2f* **10/1**

11 **7** *4* **Flashy Max**[79] 4115 3-8-9 53 AndrewMullen(3) 8 37
(Jedd O'Keeffe) *led 1f: prom tl wknd over 2f out* **4/1**[1]

0001 **8** *1 1/4* **Jelly Mo**[25] 5787 3-8-10 54 (p) PatrickHills(3) 1 35
(J W Hills) *a in rr* **17/2**[3]

0106 **9** *3 1/4* **Space Pirate**[16] 6049 3-9-0 55 (p) RobertHavlin 7 29
(J Pearce) *hld up in rr: rdn 3f out: no rspnse* **12/1**

0000 **10** *15* **Marino Prince (FR)**[168] 1479 3-8-12 53 LPKeniry 11 —
(T Wall) *hld up in tch: pushed along over 3f out: wknd wl over 2f out* **33/1**

-400 **11** *3/4* **Sunshine Lady (IRE)**[125] 2639 3-9-0 55 (v1) FrancisNorton 12 —
(D Haydn Jones) *led after 1f: hdd 3f out: sn rdn: wknd 2f out* **20/1**

2m 2.39s (0.69) **Going Correction** +0.10s/f (Slow) **11** Ran SP% **117.7**
Speed ratings (Par 99): **100,99,96,95,92 91,88,87,84,70 70**
toteswinger: 1&2 £27.40, 1&3 £21.50, 2&3 £23.20. CSF £102.44 CT £1280.11 TOTE £6.40: £3.10, £7.80, £6.10; EX 215.90.

Owner B J Warren **Bred** B J Warren **Trained** Newmarket, Suffolk

FOCUS
A modest handicap run at a decent gallop. The winner raced against the inside rail in the straight. The placed horses are rated slight improvers but the form could go either way.

6493 FREE BETS @ FREEBETS.CO.UK H'CAP — 1m 4f 50y(P)
9:20 (9:20) (Class 5) (0-70,70) 3-Y-O+ — £3,238 (£963; £481; £240) Stalls Low

Form — RPR

335 **1** **Summer Lodge**[19] 5971 5-8-13 59 DavidProbert(5) 3 74
(A J McCabe) *chsd ldr: disp ld 6f out: led over 3f out: clr whn rdn 2f out: styd on* **5/1**[3]

6025 **2** *2 1/2* **Calzaghe (IRE)**[14] 6129 4-9-11 66 (v) DarrenWilliams 10 77
(K R Burke) *hld up in mid-div: hdwy on outside 3f out: wnt 2nd 2f out: sn rdn: styd on ins fnl f: nt trble wnr* **10/1**

4332 **3** *9* **Penang Cinta**[10] 6203 5-9-10 65 StephenDonohoe 9 62+
(P D Evans) *hld up in rr: hdwy on wd outside over 2f out: rdn and edgd lft over 1f out: no imp* **9/2**[2]

0212 **4** *hd* **River Kent**[8] 6252 3-9-0 62 CatherineGannon 2 58+
(Mrs A Duffield) *t.k.h in tch: stdd and lost pl 7f out: outpcd over 2f out: styng on whn edgd lft over 1f out: n.d* **7/2**[1]

6422 **5** *3* **Thorny Mandate**[7] 6279 6-9-4 59 ChrisCatlin 1 50
(W M Brisbourne) *hld up towards rr: sme hdwy 2f out: nvr nr ldrs* **7/1**

550 **6** *4 1/2* **Ryan's Future (IRE)**[25] 5783 8-9-6 61 GregFairley 4 45
(J S Moore) *dwlt: t.k.h: a in rr* **12/1**

001 **7** *nk* **Jim Martin**[16] 6040 3-9-8 70 PJMcDonald 7 54
(Miss L A Perratt) *awkward leaving stalls: plld hrd: sn in tch: wknd 2f out* **12/1**

1004 **8** *3* **Rare Coincidence**[138] 2252 7-9-10 65 DNolan 6 44
(R F Fisher) *led: hdd over 3f out: wknd 2f out* **25/1**

5000 **9** *3 1/4* **Fenners (USA)**[11] 6189 5-9-4 59 DaleGibson 5 33
(M W Easterby) *hld up in tch: wknd over 2f out* **12/1**

4011 **10** *18* **Zalkani (IRE)**[14] 6136 8-9-5 60 JerryO'Dwyer 8 —
(J Pearce) *hld up towards rr: sme prog on outside 4f out: rdn 3f out: sn struggling* **6/1**

2m 41.48s (0.38) **Going Correction** +0.10s/f (Slow)
WFA 3 from 4yo+ 7lb **10** Ran SP% **119.9**
Speed ratings (Par 103): **102,100,94,94,92 89,89,87,84,72**
toteswinger: 1&2 £6.30, 1&3 £2.50, 2&3 £5.50. CSF £55.78 CT £245.14 TOTE £7.40: £2.80, £3.60, £2.30; EX 72.20 Place 6 £130.70, Place 5 £75.83..

Owner Paul J Dixon **Bred** Seymour Cohn **Trained** Babworth, Notts

FOCUS
A run-of-the-mill handicap in which the pace was just fair and those held up were not seen to best advantage. The race is rated at face value with the runner-up to form.

Ryan's Future(IRE) Official explanation: jockey said horse ran too free

T/Plt: £618.40 to a £1 stake. Pool: £87,175.44. 102.90 winning tickets. T/Qpdt: £179.70 to a £1 stake. Pool: £7,286.07. 30.00 winning tickets. KH

6147 LONGCHAMP (R-H)
Saturday, October 4

OFFICIAL GOING: Good

6494a QATAR PRIX CHAUDENAY (GROUP 2) — 1m 7f
12:45 (12:45) 3-Y-O — £54,485 (£21,029; £10,037; £6,691; £3,346)

RPR

1 **Watar (IRE)**[29] 5685 3-9-2 DBonilla 5 115
(F Head, France) *s.i.s: hld up in rr: last st: gd hdwy on outside 2f out: edgd rt and qcknd to ld over 1f out: easily* **33/10**[3]

2 *5* **Shemima**[29] 5685 3-8-13 CSoumillon 2 106
(A De Royer-Dupre, France) *hld up: 6th st: hdwy on ins 2f out: swtchd out over 1f out: kpt on one pce* **9/10**[1]

3 *1/2* **Centennial (IRE)**[20] 5953 3-9-2 (b) OPeslier 4 108
(J H M Gosden) *led after 2f: set gd pce: hdd over 1f out: kpt on* **31/10**[2]

4 *2* **Enroller (IRE)**[21] 5892 3-9-2 C-PLemaire 6 106
(W R Muir) *racd in 4th: rdn 2f out: kpt on one pce* **38/1**

5 *2* **Hindu Kush (IRE)**[6] 6324 3-9-2 PJSmullen 7 104
(A P O'Brien, Ire) *sn led: hdd after 2f: trckd ldr to over 1f out: no ex* **11/1**

6 *1 1/2* **Tsar De Russie (IRE)**[29] 5685 3-9-2 (b) ACrastus 3 102
(E Lellouche, France) *racd in 5th to st: rdn 2f out: nvr a factor* **21/1**

7 *8* **Hold Me Love Me (IRE)**[23] 5826 3-8-13 JMurtagh 8 89
(A P O'Brien, Ire) *racd in 3rd to st: rdn and btn 2f out* **11/1**

8 *20* **Speedy Silver (FR)**[21] 5927 3-9-2 JVictoire 1 68
(H-A Pantall, France) *first to show: settled in 6th: pushed along 1/2-way: 7th st: sn bhd: t.o* **52/1**

3m 10.7s (-5.30) **8** Ran SP% **125.9**
PARI-MUTUEL (Including 1 Euro stake): WIN 4.30; PL 1.10, 1.10, 1.10; DF 2.80.

Owner Hamdan Al Maktoum **Bred** Haras Du Mezeray **Trained** France

NOTEBOOK
Watar(IRE) ◆, produced an extraordinary turn of foot halfway up the straight and had this this race won in a couple of strides. He may well turn out for the Prix Royal-Oak and will be aimed at cup events next year. He has not been very lucky this season but is certainly one for the notebook.

Shemima, the odds-on favourite, could do nothing when the winner sped past her halfway up the straight. She was given every possible chance but had to settle for second place, although she did battle on well to the end.

Centennial(IRE) took on the pacemaker from the very start and set a pretty fast gallop. He came into the straight with a decent advantage but had nothing in reserve when passed by the winner and runner-up, although he battled on gamely during the closing stages.

Enroller(IRE) was thereabouts for much of the 1m7f but never looked like finishing in the first three. He is another who will be trained for cup events next year.

6495a QATAR PRIX DE ROYALLIEU (GROUP 2) (F&M) — 1m 4f 110y
1:15 (1:16) 3-Y-O+ — £54,485 (£21,029; £10,037; £6,691; £3,346)

RPR

1 **Balladeuse (FR)**[32] 5597 3-8-7 OPeslier 9 113
(A Fabre, France) *hld up: 10th st: hdwy on outside over 2f out: led over 1f out: drvn out* **332/10**

2 *1/2* **Tres Rapide (IRE)**[32] 5597 3-8-7 DBoeuf 10 113
(H-A Pantall, France) *hld up: last st: hdwy on outside over 2f out: ev ch appr fnl f: r.o same pce* **48/1**

3 *1 1/2* **Dar Re Mi**[20] 5952 3-8-7 C-PLemaire 3 110
(J H M Gosden) *a cl up: 5th st: led briefly 1 1/2f out: one pce* **1/1**[1]

4 *3/4* **Astrologie (FR)**[32] 5597 3-8-7 JVictoire 12 109
(A Fabre, France) *in rr to st: edgd to outside 2f out: r.o to rch 4th 1f out: one pce* **69/10**

5 *3/4* **Leo's Starlet (IRE)**[97] 3543 3-8-7 CSoumillon 2 108
(A De Royer-Dupre, France) *9th st: hdwy 2f out: 4th appr fnl f: one pce* **39/10**[2]

6 *3* **La Boum (GER)**[73] 4320 5-9-1 IMendizabal 5 103
(Robert Collet, France) *a in tch: cl 8th st: 5th over 1f out: one pce* **37/1**

7 *3* **Ezima (IRE)**[57] 4833 4-9-1 KJManning 1 98
(J S Bolger, Ire) *a in tch: hdwy and 2nd st: led wl over 2f out to 1 1/2f out: sn wknd* **27/1**

8 *1/2* **Alix Road (FR)**[31] 5623 5-9-1 AlexisBadel 4 97
(Mme M Bollack-Badel, France) *hdwy on ins and 7th st on ins whn n.m.r and bmpd 2f out: one pce* **37/1**

9 *1/2* **Gagnoa (IRE)**[20] 5952 3-8-7 SPasquier 13 97
(A Fabre, France) *6th st: nvr able to chal* **9/2**[3]

10 *4* **Ice Queen (IRE)**[20] 5952 3-8-7 PaulHanagan 7 90
(A P O'Brien, Ire) *last at 1/2-way: nvr a factor* **9/2**[3]

11 *3* **Honoria (IRE)**[20] 5952 3-8-7 PJSmullen 6 85
(A P O'Brien, Ire) *led to wl over 2f out* **9/2**[3]

12 *8* **Adored (IRE)**[20] 5952 3-8-11 ow2 JMurtagh 11 77
(A P O'Brien, Ire) *racd in 3rd: pushed along st: sn rdn and btn* **9/2**[3]

13 *6* **Mimetico (IRE)**[24] 4-9-1 (b) DVargiu 8 63
(B Grizzetti, Italy) *trckd ldr to over 3f out: 4th st: sn btn* **55/1**

2m 38.3s (-1.60) **Going Correction** +0.275s/f (Good)
WFA 3 from 4yo+ 7lb **13** Ran SP% **171.4**
Speed ratings: **115,114,113,113,112 111,109,108,108,106 104,99,95**
PARI-MUTUEL: WIN 34.20; PL 5.20, 6.00, 1.30; DF 159.90.

Owner Wertheimer Et Frere **Bred** Wertheimer Et Frere **Trained** Chantilly, France

NOTEBOOK
Balladeuse(FR) ran much better over this longer trip. She was held up towards the tail of the field in the early stages before coming with a sweeping late run and finally won with something in hand. An improving filly, for whom there are no specific plans for the rest of the season, she will be kept in training as a four-year-old.

Tres Rapide(IRE), on whom waiting tactics were also employed, did not appear on the scene until way up the straight. She finished well but could not peg back the winner.

Dar Re Mi was given every possible chance but ran rather free in the early part of the race. She hit the front a furlong and a half out but then failed to produce any extra as the principals challenged late on her outside. She might have been a little tired after a strenuous season but connections have decided to keep her in training as a four-year-old.

Astrologie(FR), well behind from the start and with plenty to do in the straight, did not really engage top gear until the race was over and she only took fourth place well inside the final furlong.

6496a TOTAL PRIX DE LA FORET (GROUP 1) 7f

2:20 (2:21) 3-Y-0+ **£105,037** (£42,022; £21,011; £10,496; £5,257)

RPR

1 **Paco Boy (IRE)**[27] 5740 3-9-0 .... CSoumillon 6 127+
(R Hannon) *hld up: 7th st: hdwy to ld wl over 1f out: rdn clr: r.o wl* **6/4**[1]

2 3 **Natagora (FR)**[27] 5740 3-8-11 .... C-PLemaire 9 116
(P Bary, France) *a cl up: 2nd st: led 2f out to wl over 1f out: one pce* **53/10**[3]

3 2 1/2 **US Ranger (USA)**[21] 5891 4-9-2 .... (b) JMurtagh 7 112+
(A P O'Brien, Ire) *hld up in rr: last st: rdn over 2f out: styd on to take 3rd last strides* **20/1**

4 snk **Captain's Lover (SAF)**[27] 5738 4-8-13 .... OPeslier 3 109
(A Fabre, France) *sn cl up: 4th st: rdn wl over 1f out: styd on same pce* **54/10**

5 snk **Welsh Emperor (IRE)**[21] 5893 9-9-2 .... (b) IMendizabal 1 111
(T P Tate) *3rd st on ins: 5th 2f out: disp 4th ins fnl f: one pce* **18/1**

6 1 1/2 **Utmost Respect**[21] 5891 4-9-2 .... PaulHanagan 2 107
(R A Fahey) *6th st: nvr able to chal* **15/1**

7 3/4 **African Rose**[21] 5891 3-8-11 .... SPasquier 8 102
(Mme C Head-Maarek, France) *sn cl up: 5th st: 2nd briefly 2f out: sn wknd* **28/10**[2]

8 3 **Duff (IRE)**[57] 4832 5-9-2 .... FMBerry 4 97
(Edward Lynam, Ire) *led to 2f out* **38/1**

1m 19.8s (-1.10) **Going Correction** +0.275s/f (Good)
WFA 3 from 4yo+ 2lb 8 Ran SP% **116.7**
Speed ratings: **117,113,110,110,110 108,107,104**
PARI-MUTUEL: WIN 2.50; PL 1.30, 1.80, 3.40; DF 7.40.
Owner The Calvera Partnership No 2 **Bred** Mrs Joan Browne **Trained** East Everleigh, Wilts

FOCUS
With so few opportunities at Group 1 level over 7f this usually attracts a decent field, and this latest running looked well up to scratch. With Natagora running to her mark and the fourth and fifth to their best level of 2008 this was yet another clear personal best for the progressive Paco Boy.

NOTEBOOK
Paco Boy(IRE) gained his first Group 1 success impressively, and in a time bettered only by Poplar Bluff and Dedication in the last 15 years. Few would have had him down as a future top notcher when he signed off last year with a conditions race defeat of older horses in a modest 6f event at Newmarket in November, but he has now won all his five races at 7f, his only defeats coming at 1m in the French 2000 Guineas and the Prix du Moulin. His third to Goldikova in the latter race was decent enough, but the combination of 7f and easy ground seem to be what brings out the best in him. Held up, he was still towards the rear as they straightened up but picked up impressively on the wide outside, and having arrived on the scene just as Natagora was taking over from Duff, he quickly took her measure and was in charge through the final furlong. He stays in training, and with so few top 7f races to go for, connections will be forced to go back up to 1m or drop him to 6f, or the extended 6f of a race like the Prix Maurice de Gheest. The sprint option might prove attractive, as competition at the shorter trips is seldom as hot, and he clearly isn't short of speed.
Natagora(FR) has not won since the 1000 Guineas, but she has had some tough tasks, including when third over 1m2f in the Prix du Jockey-Club. She was three lengths behind Paco Boy when sixth in the Moulin, and it was the same story here after she had tracked the leader and then been in front only briefly in the straight. Connections had considered campaigning her in the Far East, but that is in the balance, as she has had a hardish season at the top level.
US Ranger(USA), who once promised so much, has been bitterly frustrating, hence the blinkers that were deployed for the first time here. His July Cup second gave him outstanding claims, but he had to be chased along in the first 50 yards to take up a position even at the back of the field and he was still last turning in. When he came under pressure straightening up, he could make only laboured headway in the winner's wake, and he may have run out of excuses.
Captain's Lover(SAF), formerly trained in South Africa, had made the right sort of impression over course and distance on her French debut, but this was two grades up and she was beaten fair and square.
Welsh Emperor(IRE) had been second here for the last two years, but he has not been quite as good this year and Duff denied him the lead.
Utmost Respect was never going quite well enough and Hanagan reported he ran flat. Softer ground would have helped too.
African Rose, the Sprint Cup winer, was the disappointment of the race. The extra furlong was not the problem and her trainer was puzzled, although she did say afterwards that she was not sure the filly had been moving right. That will be it for 2008, but she is expected to stay in training.
Duff(IRE) has never won out of Listed company and was biting off a bit more than he could chew.

6497a QATAR PRIX DU CADRAN (GROUP 1) 2m 4f

2:55 (2:55) 4-Y-0+ **£105,037** (£42,022; £21,011; £10,496; £5,257)

RPR

1 **Bannaby (FR)**[20] 5956 5-9-2 .... CSoumillon 3 115
(M Delcher Sanchez, Spain) *racd in 4th: running on st: chal 2f out: led 1 1/2f out: drvn appr fnl f: styd on wl* **97/10**

2 hd **Incanto Dream**[20] 5956 4-9-2 .... YLerner 1 115
(C Lerner, France) *hld up: disputing 7th 1/2-way: 5th st: rdn and gd hdwy down outside 1 1/2f out: wnt 2nd fnl f: styd on wl: nrst fin* **9/1**[3]

3 1/2 **Orion Star (FR)**[82] 4041 6-9-2 .... JVictoire 2 115
(H-A Pantall, France) *sn racing in 2nd: led appr st: rdn and r.o 2f out: hdd 1 1/2f out: styd on u.p* **38/1**

4 3/4 **Kasbah Bliss (FR)**[20] 5956 6-9-2 .... TThulliez 5 114
(F Doumen, France) *in tch: 5th 1/2-way: pushed along over 2f out: rdn and 4th 1 1/2f out: kpt on steadily* **7/2**[2]

5 4 **Yeats (IRE)**[65] 4551 7-9-2 .... JMurtagh 8 111
(A P O'Brien, Ire) *prom: 3rd 1/2-way: 2nd and pushed along st: sn rdn: no imp* **7/10**[1]

6 2 **Le Miracle (GER)**[107] 3154 7-9-2 .... DBoeuf 9 108
(W Baltromei, Germany) *hld up in 10th: disputing 9th st: n.d* **20/1**

7 1 1/2 **Ponte Tresa (FR)**[41] 5333 5-8-13 .... OPeslier 11 103
(Y De Nicolay, France) *hld up: 9th 1/2-way: disputing 7th st: n.d* **16/1**

8 2 1/2 **Harbore (FR)**[20] 5956 4-9-2 .... ACrastus 10 104
(E Lellouche, France) *racd in last: nvr a factor* **73/1**

9 1 1/2 **Caudillo (GER)**[41] 5333 5-9-2 .... ADeVries 4 102
(Dr A Bolte, Germany) *mid-div: 6th 1/2-way: rdn and disputing 7th st: sn btn* **94/1**

10 15 **Green Tango (FR)**[41] 5333 5-9-2 .... RonanThomas 7 87
(P Van De Poele, France) *towards rr: disputing 7th 1/2-way: disputing 9th st: nvr a factor* **55/1**

11 10 **Noble Prince (GER)**[20] 5956 4-9-2 .... PJSmullen 6 77
(A Fabre, France) *led: drvn over 3f out: hdd and 3rd appr st: sn wknd* **7/10**[1]

4m 22.2s (-1.60) **Going Correction** +0.275s/f (Good) 11 Ran SP% **176.6**
Speed ratings: **114,113,113,113,111 111,110,109,108,102 98**
PARI-MUTUEL: WIN 10.70; PL 2.80, 2.90, 6.20; DF 23.30.
Owner Cuadra Miranda SL **Bred** Eight International Racing Ltd **Trained** Spain

FOCUS
The form is rated through the second and fourth with the disappointing Yeats running to the same figure as when third in this a year ago.

NOTEBOOK
Bannaby(FR), a Spanish-trained five-year-old, put up a fine effort. Settled in fourth place next to Yeats, he made his way to the head of affairs halfway up the straight and then held on bravely when driven to the line with his jockey earning a four-day ban for his use of the whip. Still progressing, he could go for the Prix Royal-Oak and will be aimed at the Ascot Gold Cup next year.
Incanto Dream, who was very unlucky and nearly fell in his previous race, nearly made amends on this occasion. In mid-division at the entrance to the straight, he was brought with a sweeping late run up the centre of the track and only just failed. He is another marked down for the Prix Royal-Oak at the end of the month.
Orion Star(FR), well placed throughout, was in second place until well inside the final furlong. He is a genuine gelding who always runs his heart out and is another for the Prix Royal-Oak.
Kasbah Bliss(FR) was unsuited by the cut in the ground, although it was officially good. As usual he was held up for a late run but did not have the zip he had when winning the trial for this race last month. His trainer immediately blamed the going and was disappointed.
Yeats(IRE), who had warmed up for last year's Cadran with a victory in the Irish St Leger, was running this time off the back of a fair absence, having not raced since July when he won the Goodwood Cup. The way he ran suggested he may have benefited from a more recent outing, though it has to be said that he has never won outside Britain or Ireland and his record from September onwards reads 2-8, whereas earlier in the year he is 11-13. All looked to be going swimmingly until the false straight, but he found disappointingly little on ground that shouldn't have inconvenienced him.

6498a QATAR PRIX DANIEL WILDENSTEIN (GROUP 2) 1m

3:30 (3:37) 3-Y-0+ **£54,485** (£21,029; £10,037; £6,691; £3,346)

RPR

1 **Spirito Del Vento (FR)**[27] 5738 5-9-0 .... OPeslier 5 119
(J-M Beguigne, France) *settled in 6th: 5th and pushed along st: rdn to chse ldng pair 1 1/2f out: qcknd to ld fnl strides* **29/10**[3]

2 3/4 **Sageburg (IRE)**[27] 5740 4-9-5 .... CSoumillon 1 122
(A De Royer-Dupre, France) *racd in 2nd: pushed along to chse ldr 2f out: chal over 1f out: rdn to ld 150yds out: hdd fnl strides* **21/10**[2]

3 1 1/2 **Famous Name**[27] 5729 3-8-11 .... (v) PJSmullen 3 114
(D K Weld, Ire) *led and set gd pce: pushed along 1 1/2f out: hdd 150yds out: no ex u.p cl home* **17/10**[1]

4 1/2 **Belle Allure (IRE)**[41] 5331 3-8-8 .... DBonilla 2 109
(R Pritchard-Gordon, France) *hld up in 7th: pushed along 2f out: rdn and styd on in centre 1 1/2f out: wnt 4th 100yds out* **26/1**

5 1 1/2 **Blythe Knight (IRE)**[21] 5896 8-9-1 .... SPasquier 8 110
(J J Quinn) *disp 4th: 4th 1/2-way: pushed along and disputing 3rd st: 4th and u.p 1 1/2f out: no ex fnl f* **15/1**

6 2 1/2 **Foundry Condor (JPN)**[69] 5-9-0 .... YTake 6 103
(S Takahashi, Japan) *racd in 3rd: disputing 3rd st: rdn over 1 1/2f out: sn one pce* **41/1**

7 4 **Altamira**[23] 5851 4-8-11 .... ACrastus 7 91
(E Lellouche, France) *hld up in last: nvr on terms* **17/1**

8 3/4 **Holocene (USA)**[34] 5555 4-9-0 .... C-PLemaire 4 92
(P Bary, France) *disp 4th: 6th st: sn btn* **25/1**

1m 39.1s (0.30) **Going Correction** +0.275s/f (Good)
WFA 3 from 4yo+ 3lb 8 Ran SP% **116.7**
Speed ratings: **109,108,106,106,104 102,98,97**
PARI-MUTUEL: WIN 3.90; PL 1.20, 1.20, 1.30; DF 3.70.
Owner L Ciampi **Bred** Haras Des Sablonnets **Trained** France

NOTEBOOK
Spirito Del Vento(FR) was landing back to back victories in this mile and once again did it in style, having benefited from the strong pace set by Famous Name. The usual waiting tactics were employed, and when his jockey, who knows him so well, pressed the button at the furlong marker he quickened impressively to take the lead inside the last 50 yards. He goes to Hong Kong for the Mile race next time out.
Sageburg(IRE) was supplemented into this race and, giving 2kg to the winner, ran a decent race. He was very well behaved in the preliminaries and looked in great shape as he cantered to the post. Second for much of the time, he took over one out but could not hold the late surge of the winner. There are no specific plans but a trip abroad is likely next time out.
Famous Name, another supplementary entry and blinkered for the first time, had no option but to make the running, otherwise the race would have gone off at a crawl. He did a good job until the furlong marker but at that point he was outpaced, although he did stay on well to the line.
Belle Allure(IRE), another supplementary entry, still had plenty to do coming into the straight. He slipped into top gear halfway up the straight and kept on well inside the final furlong.
Blythe Knight(IRE), settled in mid-division for most of the race, but proved one paced in the straight.

6499a QATAR PRIX DOLLAR (GROUP 2) 1m 1f 165y

4:00 (4:05) 3-Y-0+ **£54,485** (£21,029; £10,037; £6,691; £3,346)

RPR

1 **Trincot (FR)**[14] 6148 3-8-9 .... IMendizabal 1 113
(P Demercastel, France) *racd in 3rd: 4th st: qcknd to chal 2f out: led over 1f out: rdn and hld on wl cl home* **58/10**

2 hd **Loup Breton (IRE)**[34] 5557 4-9-5 .... ACrastus 4 118
(E Lellouche, France) *hld up in 5th: disputing 7th st: hdwy on ins fr 2f out: rdn to chal fnl f: ev ch cl home: jst failed* **54/10**

3 2 **The Bogberry (USA)**[27] 5729 3-8-9 .... CSoumillon 8 109
(A De Royer-Dupre, France) *settled in 6th: 5th st: rdn 1 1/2f out: styd on: tk 3rd on line* **47/10**[3]

4 hd **Boris De Deauville (IRE)**[49] 5114 5-9-0 .... DBoeuf 5 109
(S Wattel, France) *racd in 2nd: led 1/2-way: rdn and hdd over 1f out: lost 3rd on line* **4/1**[2]

5 2 **Liang Kay (GER)**[31] 5624 3-9-0 .... THellier 3 110
(U Ostmann, Germany) *hld up disputing last: disputing 7th st: effrt on outside 1 1/2f out to go 5th: nvr nrr* **21/10**[1]

6 1 1/2 **Drumfire (IRE)**[20] 5932 4-9-0 .... JMurtagh 6 102
(M Johnston) *racd in 4th: 2nd st: rdn to chse ldr 2 1/2f out: sn one pce* **21/1**

7 1 **Hapsburg (FR)**[41] 5332 4-8-10 .... OPeslier 2 96
(E Libaud, France) *hld up disputing last: last st: effrt 2f out: n.d* **10/1**

8 3/4 **Gloria De Campeao (BRZ)**[49] 5115 5-9-0 .... C-PLemaire 7 98
(P Bary, France) *led to 1/2-way: 3rd st: wknd fr 1 1/2f out* **24/1**

2m 3.50s (0.60) **Going Correction** +0.275s/f (Good)
WFA 3 from 4yo+ 5lb 8 Ran SP% **117.8**
Speed ratings: **108,107,106,106,104 103,102,101**
PARI-MUTUEL: WIN 6.80; PL 2.00, 2.00, 2.10; DF 15.00.
Owner S C E A Ecurie Bader **Bred** Scea Ecurie Bader **Trained** France

NOTEBOOK

Trincot(FR) had luck was on his side on this occasion, which had not been the case earlier in the season. He had come on considerably since his previous race and was given an excellent ride. Tucked in just behind the leaders, he went into the lead at the furlong marker and then had to hold off the late challenge of the runner-up, who made his effort up the far rail. Was very brave to the end and may now have earnt a tilt at the Hollywood Derby.

Loup Breton(IRE) saves his best efforts for this track and is particularly effective when there is cut in the ground. Held up early on, he came with a late run up the far rail but could not quite get to the winner. He may well return for a Group 2 later in the month.

The Bogberry(USA), running for the first time for his new French owner after leaving Aidan O'Brien, put up a promising effort. Fifth into the straight, he ran on best of all to take third place inside the final furlong and should definitely make it at this level with his new trainer later in his career.

Boris De Deauville(IRE), quickly into his stride, he went into the lead before the straight before his stride shortened at the furlong marker. He was run out of third place in the dying stages.

Drumfire(IRE) was well up until the straight then dropped out of contention.

6373 BELMONT PARK (L-H)

Saturday, October 4

OFFICIAL GOING: Turf - good; dirt - fast

6500a FRIZETTE STKS (GRADE 1) (FILLIES) (DIRT) — 1m

9:43 (9:45) 2-Y-O **£120,603** (£40,201; £20,101; £10,050; £6,030)

				RPR
1		**Sky Diva (USA)**[25] 2-8-8 (Steven B Klesaris, U.S.A) **56/10**[3]	RADominguez 1	112
2	3 ¾	**Persistently (USA)**[21] 2-8-8 (Claude McGaughey III, U.S.A) **11/10**[1]	AGarcia 5	104
3	2	**Gemswick Park (USA)** 2-8-8 (Thomas Albertrani, U.S.A) **73/20**[2]	CDeCarlo 10	100
4	¾	**War Echo (USA)** 2-8-8 (Steven Asmussen, U.S.A) **18/1**	CHill 3	99
5	3 ¾	**Coffee In Bed (USA)** 2-8-8 (Kelly Breen, U.S.A) **64/1**	ECastro 8	91
6	½	**Heavenly Vision (USA)**[21] 2-8-8 (Bob Baffert, U.S.A) **12/1**	(b) VEspinoza 9	90
7	29	**Winning Brew (USA)**[34] 2-8-8 (Francis J Vitale, U.S.A) **90/1**	(b) JLEspinoza 7	32
8	5 ¼	**Collegiate (USA)**[34] 2-8-8 (Mark Hennig, U.S.A) **10/1**	(b) EPrado 6	22
9	11 ¼	**Miss Ocean City (USA)**[21] 2-8-8 (Nicholas Zito, U.S.A) **15/1**	RMaragh 4	—
10	8 ½	**Royal Ballade (USA)** 2-8-8 (Thomas Albertrani, U.S.A) **19/1**	ECoa 2	—

1m 37.4s (97.40) **10** Ran SP% **120.2**

PARI-MUTUEL (including $2 stakes): WIN 13.20; PL (1-2) 4.70, 2.90;SHOW (1-2-3) 3.30, 2.40, 3.10; SF 37.00.

Owner Puglisi Racing **Bred** John D Murphy **Trained** USA

6501a CHAMPAGNE STKS (GRADE 1) (DIRT) — 1m

10:15 (10:19) 2-Y-O **£120,603** (£40,201; £20,101; £10,050; £6,030)

				RPR
1		**Vineyard Haven (USA)**[33] 2-8-10 (Robert Frankel, U.S.A) **42/10**[2]	(b) EPrado 3	116
2	5 ¾	**Munnings (USA)**[33] 2-8-10 (Todd Pletcher, U.S.A) **61/10**	CDeCarlo 10	104
3	¾	**Cribnote (USA)**[33] 2-8-10 (Richard Violette Jr, U.S.A) **69/20**[1]	RMaragh 2	103
4	1 ¾	**Gone Astray (USA)**[21] 2-8-10 (Claude McGaughey III, U.S.A) **15/1**	RADominguez 9	99
5	1 ¼	**Hello Broadway (USA)** 2-8-10 (Barclay Tagg, U.S.A) **17/2**	ECoa 4	97
6	1 ¼	**Girolamo (USA)**[21] 2-8-10 (Kiaran McLaughlin, U.S.A) **15/2**	AGarcia 5	94
7	3 ¼	**Brave Victory (USA)** 2-8-10 (Nicholas Zito, U.S.A) **89/10**	JASanchez 8	88
8	2 ¼	**Break Water Edison (USA)**[33] 2-8-10 (John C Kimmel, U.S.A) **16/1**	RMigliore 1	83
9	9 ½	**A P Cardinal (USA)** 2-8-10 (Cam Gambolati, U.S.A) **39/1**	CHill 6	64
10	16 ½	**Ventana (USA)** 2-8-10 (Bob Baffert, U.S.A) **48/10**[3]	(b) VEspinoza 7	31

1m 36.06s (96.06) **10** Ran SP% **120.1**

PARI-MUTUEL: WIN 10.40; PL (1-2) 6.20, 6.60; SHOW (1-2-3) 3.90, 5.00,3.70; SF 87.00.

Owner R J Frankel **Bred** Lynne M Scace **Trained** USA

6462 KEENELAND (L-H)

Saturday, October 4

OFFICIAL GOING: Turf - firm; polytrack - fast

6502a INVASOR (ALLOWANCE) (POLYTRACK) — 7f

7:46 (7:47) 2-Y-O **£16,201** (£5,226; £2,613; £1,307; £784)

				RPR
1		**Casey's On Call (USA)** 2-8-8 (Wayne Catalano, U.S.A) **42/10**[3]	EBaird 12	—
2	nse	**Troy G (USA)** 2-8-10 (Kenneth McPeek, U.S.A) **6/4**[1]	RAlbarado 9	—
3	nse	**Beethoven (USA)** 2-8-6 (John T Ward Jr, U.S.A) **31/10**[2]	RBejarano 5	—
4	6	**General Quarters (USA)**[91] 2-8-6 (Thomas R McCarthy, U.S.A) **49/1**	(b) WTroilo 1	—
5	2 ¼	**Tamborim (USA)** 2-8-8 (William Mott, U.S.A) **23/2**	RRDouglas 11	—
6	3 ¾	**Crown The Chief (USA)** 2-8-6 (Helen Pitts, U.S.A) **8/1**	CHBorel 6	—
7	3 ½	**Hongkong Superstar (USA)** 2-8-6 (Jeffrey D Thornbury, U.S.A) **71/10**	(b) HJTheriotII 3	—
8	hd	**Mesa Gold (USA)** 2-8-6 (David E Pate, U.S.A) **24/1**	BHernandezJr 4	—
9	1 ¼	**Classy Wonder (USA)** 2-8-6 (Larry Lay, U.S.A) **54/1**	(b) PWOuzts 7	—
10	1 ¾	**Elegant Cad (CAN)**[35] 5496 2-8-6 (J R Best) *always outpaced* **16/1**	JRLeparoux 8	—
11	1 ¾	**Ivan Ivan (USA)** 2-8-6 (Megan Morrison, U.S.A) **93/1**	CChavez 10	—
12	¾	**Promise Me Merlot (USA)** 2-8-7 ow2 (W Cesare, U.S.A) **56/1**	DRodriguez(5) 2	—

1m 22.79s (82.79) **12** Ran SP% **131.6**

PARI-MUTUEL: WIN 10.40; PL (1-2) 5.60, 4.20; SHOW (1-2-3) 3.60, 3.20,3.20; SF 42.80.

Owner Frank C Calabrese **Bred** Cheryl A Curtin **Trained** USA

NOTEBOOK

Elegant Cad(CAN), last of six in a conditions race at Chester last time out but previously a winner of a Polytrack maiden, never figured on his US debut.

6503a LANE'S END BREEDERS' FUTURITY (GRADE 1) (POLYTRACK) — 1m 110y

9:22 (9:22) 2-Y-O **£155,779** (£50,251; £25,125; £12,563; £7,538)

				RPR
1		**Square Eddie (CAN)**[28] 5693 2-8-9 (J R Best) *raced in 3rd, 2nd straight, soon led & went clear, easily* **91/10**	RBejarano 8	115+
2	4 ¾	**Terrain (USA)**[21] 2-8-9 (Albert Stall Jr, U.S.A) **48/10**[3]	HJTheriotII 9	105
3	3 ¼	**Pioneerof The Nile (USA)**[40] 2-8-9 (William Mott, U.S.A) **46/10**[2]	KDesormeaux 5	99
4	½	**Deposer (IRE)**[28] 5693 2-8-9 (J R Best) *always in touch, 6th on outside straight, soon ridden & kept on same pace* **29/1**	CVelasquez 10	98
5	¾	**Majestic Blue (USA)** 2-8-9 (Kiaran McLaughlin, U.S.A) **11/2**	RAlbarado 6	96
6	½	**His Greatness (USA)**[21] 2-8-9 (Marco P Salazar, U.S.A) **18/1**	MMena 4	95
7	1 ½	**Zion (USA)**[21] 2-8-9 (Steven Asmussen, U.S.A) **15/1**	CLanerie 7	92
8	hd	**Flashmans Papers**[28] 5693 2-8-9 (J R Best) **61/1**	JLCastanon 1	92
9	1 ¼	**Advice (USA)**[21] 2-8-9 (Todd Pletcher, U.S.A) **39/10**[1]	RRDouglas 11	89
10	3 ½	**Reynaldothewizard (USA)**[51] 2-8-9 (Eoin Harty, U.S.A) **53/10**	JRLeparoux 2	82
11	3 ½	**Notonthesamepage (USA)**[33] 2-8-9 (Wesley A Ward, U.S.A) **10/1**	(b) EBaird 3	75

1m 43.04s (103.04) **11** Ran SP% **122.2**

PARI-MUTUEL: WIN 20.20; PL (1-2) 9.60, 5.40; SHOW (1-2-3) 6.20, 4.00,4.00; SF 117.80.

Owner J Paul Reddam **Bred** Kinghaven Farms Limited **Trained** Hucking, Kent

NOTEBOOK

Square Eddie(CAN), runner-up in the Sirenia Stakes last time out, came to the front off the home bend and ran away with this Grade 1 contest in the straight. He will now go for the Breeders' Cup Juvenile, but as he has been sold he will be trained by Doug O'Neill for that race.

Deposer(IRE), sixth in the Sirenia, was far from disgraced in fourth and will surely be able to find a decent race on this surface.

Flashmans Papers did not stay and will be happier back over sprint distances.

6504a SHADWELL TURF MILE STKS (GRADE 1) — 1m

9:55 (9:55) 3-Y-O+ **£186,935** (£60,302; £30,151; £15,075; £9,045)

				RPR
1		**Thorn Song (USA)**[42] 5-9-0 (Dale Romans, U.S.A) **32/10**[1]	(b) RAlbarado 3	116
2	1 ¼	**Shakis (IRE)**[21] 5928 8-9-0 (Kiaran McLaughlin, U.S.A) **42/10**[3]	RBejarano 1	113
3	nse	**War Monger (USA)**[42] 4-9-0 (William Mott, U.S.A) **38/10**[2]	KDesormeaux 6	113
4	hd	**Lord Admiral (USA)**[27] 5732 7-9-0 (Charles O'Brien, Ire) *headway into mid-division half-way, 6th straight, not much room & bumped distance, driven to reach 3rd well inside final f, lost 3rd last strides* **135/10**	(b) HJTheriotII 5	112
5	1	**Karelian (USA)**[70] 6-9-0 (George R Arnold II, U.S.A) **21/1**	MMena 11	110
6	¾	**Rahy's Attorney (CAN)**[27] 4-9-0 (Ian Black, Canada) **68/10**	(b) SCallaghan 12	108
7	¾	**French Beret (CAN)**[27] 5-9-0 (Mark Frostad, Canada) **34/1**	(b) JRLeparoux 10	107
8	nk	**Elusive Fort (SAF)**[42] 6-9-0 (Raja Malek, U.S.A) **36/1**	RRDouglas 4	106
9	nse	**Lovelace**[27] 5740 4-9-0 (M Johnston) *mid-division, 6th after 3f, 7th on outside straight, ridden & edged in bumping Lord Admiral, hard ridden & one pace* **17/2**	RoystonFfrench 8	106
10	½	**Buffalo Man (CAN)**[35] 4-9-0 (Cam Gambolati, U.S.A) **18/1**	CHMarquezJr 7	105
11	¾	**Kingship (USA)**[21] 5-9-0 (Charles Dickey, U.S.A) **162/10**	CVelasquez 2	103
12	5 ¾	**Society's Chairman (CAN)**[33] 5-9-0 (Roger L Attfield, Canada) **22/1**	JCJones 9	90

1m 34.97s (94.97) **12** Ran SP% **119.6**

PARI-MUTUEL: WIN 8.40; PL (1-2) 4.60, 5.20; SHOW (1-2-3) 2.80, 3.40,3.40; SF 36.20.

Owner Zayat Stables LLC **Bred** Pinnacle Racing LLC & Taylor Made Farm Inc **Trained** USA

NOTEBOOK

Thorn Song(USA) made all to hold the fast-finishing runner-up.

Lovelace, outclassed in the Moulin last time, could never land a blow on his first start in the US.

2472 WOODBINE (L-H)

Saturday, October 4

OFFICIAL GOING: Firm

6505a E P TAYLOR STKS (GRADE 1) (F&M) (TURF) — 1m 2f (T)

10:16 (10:16) 3-Y-O+ **£306,122** (£102,041; £56,122; £30,612; £15,306)

				RPR
1		**Folk Opera (IRE)**[20] 5952 4-8-11 (Saeed Bin Suroor) *made all, ridden under 1 1/2f out, ridden out, ran on strongly* **31/20**[1]	LDettori 4	113

2 1 3/4 **Callwood Dancer (IRE)**27 4-8-11 .... ERosaDaSilva 7 109
(Roger L Attfield, Canada) **127/10**

3 hd **Sealy Hill (CAN)**27 4-8-11 .... (b) PHusbands 1 109
(Mark Casse, Canada) **113/10**

4 1/2 **J'Ray (USA)**27 5-8-11 .... JBravo 2 108
(Todd Pletcher, U.S.A) **44/10**3

5 3 **Toque De Queda**56 4888 4-8-11 .... GKGomez 5 102
(M Delzangles, France) **9/2**

6 2 **Royal Pleasure (USA)**21 5-8-11 .... RosemaryHomeister 8 98
(Jonathan Sheppard, U.S.A) **31/1**

7 1 3/4 **Hostess (USA)**33 5-8-11 .... JJCastellano 9 94
(H J Bond, U.S.A) **37/10**2

8 3 3/4 **Green Lyons (IRE)**43 4-8-11 .... JimmyFortune 6 87
(Neil Drysdale, U.S.A) **28/1**

9 2 1/4 **Classy Landlady (CAN)**13 4-8-11 .... TPizarro 3 82
(Michael J Doyle, Canada) **62/1**

2m 3.70s (-0.32) **9** Ran SP% **120.8**
PARI-MUTUEL (including $2 stake): WIN 5.10; PL (1-2) 3.80, 9.20;SHOW (1-2-3) 2.70, 6.10, 5.70; SF 51.90.
Owner Godolphin **Bred** Abbeville And Meadow Court Partners **Trained** Newmarket, Suffolk

NOTEBOOK
Folk Opera(IRE) was given a fine front-running ride by Dettori. She was allowed to do her own thing out in front, setting a steady enough early pace before quickening turning into the straight. She is now likely to be aimed at the Breeders' Cup Filly And Mare Turf.

6506a PATTISON CANADIAN INTERNATIONAL (GRADE 1) (TURF) 1m 4f (T)
10:48 (10:50) 3-Y-O+ **£612,245** (£204,081; £112,245; £61,224; £30,612)

RPR

1 **Marsh Side (USA)**27 5-9-0 .... JJCastellano 6 117
(Neil Drysdale, U.S.A) **296/10**

2 1 3/4 **Spice Route**27 4-9-0 .... (b) JMcAleney 10 114
(Roger L Attfield, Canada)

3 nk **Champs Elysees**27 5-9-0 .... GKGomez 5 114
(Robert Frankel, U.S.A) **4/1**2

4 1 1/2 **Seaside Retreat (USA)**27 5-9-0 .... PHusbands 8 111
(Mark Casse, Canada) **119/10**

5 1/2 **Doctor Dino (FR)**34 5557 6-9-0 .... LDettori 3 110
(R Gibson, France) **14/10**1

6 nk **Mourilyan (IRE)**28 5694 4-9-0 .... JohnEgan 1 110
(H J Brown, South Africa) **26/1**

8 1 1/4 **Lauro (GER)**552 882 5-9-0 .... EPedroza 7 107
(A Wohler, Germany) **79/10**3

8 nk **Lucarno (USA)**27 5736 4-9-0 .... JimmyFortune 9 107
(J H M Gosden) *led 4f, remained pressing leader on inside til led again over 3f out, headed over 1 1/2f out, one pace* **79/10**3

9 2 3/4 **Quijano (GER)**27 6-9-0 .... AStarke 4 103
(P Schiergen, Germany) **4/1**2

10 6 1/2 **Marlang (CAN)**34 3-8-7 .... RDosRamos 2 93
(Deborah England, Canada) **117/10**

2m 28.73s (-0.87)
WFA 3 from 4yo+ 7lb **10** Ran SP% **129.2**
PARI-MUTUEL: WIN 61.10; PL (1-2) 23.00, 35.50; SHOW (1-2-3) 15.60,15.50, 4.50; SF 1062.20.

Owner Robert S Evans **Bred** Robert S Evans **Trained** USA

NOTEBOOK
Marsh Side(USA), last of 12 in this a year ago and without a win since December 2006, forged clear for a shock victory.
Spice Route ran his best race since leaving Michael Bell.
Doctor Dino(FR), usually so consistent, had his ground but ran below par, flattering only briefly in the straight.
Lucarno(USA), who has lost his form since winning the Princess of Wales's Stakes in July, made the running, taken on by Marlang, but dropped out tamely from a furlong and a half out.
Quijano(GER), beaten a nose by Champs Elysees over course and distance last time, was disappointing.

6453 DUNDALK (A.W) (L-H)
Sunday, October 5

OFFICIAL GOING: Standard

6507a BOYNE RACE 5f
2:05 (2:09) 2-Y-O **£9,573** (£2,808; £1,338; £455)

RPR

1 **City Dancer (IRE)**7 6320 2-8-9 .... MCHussey 1 86+
(Miss S Collins, Ire) *trckd ldr on rail: short of room under 2f out: swtchd 1 1/2f out: 3rd 1f out: r.o wl to ld last 100yds* **1/1**1

2 1/2 **Rain Delayed (IRE)**9 6257 2-9-0 .... (t) KLatham 2 89
(G M Lyons, Ire) *hld up in rr: hdwy in 3rd 1 1/2f: rdn to ld over 1f out: hdd last 100yds and no ex* **7/1**3

3 3 **Arfajah (IRE)**9 6258 2-9-1 89 .... DPMcDonogh 6 79
(Kevin Prendergast, Ire) *trckd ldr: 2nd 2f out: impr to dispute and led briefly 1 1/2f out: hdd over 1f out: no ex fnl f* **3/1**2

4 5 **First Choice (IRE)**24 5834 2-8-12 .... PaulMulrennan 3 58
(K A Ryan) *led: rdn and hdd 1 1/2f out: sn no ex and wknd* **3/1**2

59.42 secs (59.42) **4** Ran SP% **112.5**
CSF £7.89 TOTE £1.80; DF 6.50.
Owner JNSQ Partnership **Bred** John Quigley **Trained** the Curragh, Co Kildare

NOTEBOOK
First Choice(IRE) went off too fast for her own good and was a sitting duck nearing the furlong pole.

6510a TALLANSTOWN H'CAP 7f
3:45 (3:46) (60-100,94) 3-Y-O+ **£11,966** (£3,511; £1,672; £569)

RPR

1 **Phoenix Ice (IRE)**35 5550 4-9-2 87 .... PTownend(5) 3 93+
(M J P O'Brien, Ire) *towards rr: hdwy in 7th 3f out: impr to 4th 1 1/2f out: chal ins fnl f and led cl home* **6/1**2

2 shd **Leandros (FR)**51 5081 3-9-9 91 .... KLatham 6 97+
(G M Lyons, Ire) *chsd ldrs: 4th 1/2-way: hdwy in 3rd 1 1/2f out: impr to ld 1f out: strly pressed fnl f and hdd cl home* **10/1**

3 1 1/4 **Funatfuntasia**15 6141 4-9-1 81 .... CDHayes 11 84
(Ms Joanna Morgan, Ire) *chsd ldr: 2nd 1/2-way: impr to ld 2f out: hdd 1f out: no ex and kpt on same pce* **13/2**3

4 shd **Electric Warrior (IRE)**29 5695 5-9-10 90 .... DPMcDonogh 12 92
(K R Burke) *chsd ldrs: 5th 1/2-way: hdwy to 3rd under 2f out: rdn to chal 1f out: no ex fnl f and kpt on same pce* **13/2**3

5 1 1/2 **Regaleya (IRE)**8 6301 5-8-11 82 .... (bt) MHarley(5) 2 80
(H Rogers, Ire) *chsd ldrs: 6th 1/2-way: rdn into 5th 2f out: kpt on same pce* **10/1**

6 nk **Killinan (IRE)**16 6095 4-8-11 82 .... EJMcNamara(5) 8 79
(G M Lyons, Ire) *mid-div: rdn ent st: 7th 1f out: kpt on same pce fnl f* **10/3**1

7 1 1/2 **Baggio (IRE)**28 5731 7-10-0 94 .... NGMcCullagh 5 87
(Charles O'Brien, Ire) *towards rr: sme late hdwy in 7th over 1f out: kpt on same pce fnl f* **8/1**

8 nk **Arc Bleu (GER)**69 4493 7-9-9 92 .... RCColgan(3) 7 85
(A J Martin, Ire) *dwlt and towards rr: sme late hdwy in 8th 1f out: kpt on same pce fnl f* **10/1**

9 3 **Colombard (IRE)**112 3068 3-8-5 80 .... JamesPSullivan(7) 4 65
(J G Burns, Ire) *towards rr for most: sme late hdwy fr over 1f out: nvr a factor* **20/1**

10 1 **Finsburra (USA)**100 3468 3-7-13 74 .... DEMullins(7) 10 56
(Eoin Griffin, Ire) *led: rdn and hdd 2f out: sn no ex and wknd* **20/1**

11 3/4 **Johar Jamal (IRE)**16 6095 3-8-9 80 .... PBBeggy(3) 1 60
(P D Deegan, Ire) *chsd ldrs: 3rd 1/2-way: rdn in 5th and no ex 1 1/2f out: sn wknd* **8/1**

12 1 3/4 **Miranda's Girl (IRE)**7 6315 3-9-3 85 .... (p) RPCleary 13 60
(Thomas Cleary, Ire) *chsd ldrs: 7th 1/2-way: rdn and wknd ent st* **7/1**

13 4 **Pinkabout (IRE)**352 6300 4-8-9 80 .... MACleere(5) 9 44
(N Nevin, Ire) *mid-div: rdn 3f out: sn no ex and wknd* **20/1**

14 3/4 **Grey Rhythm (IRE)**15 6138 4-8-11 77 .... MCHussey 14 39
(Timothy Doyle, Ire) *rr of mid-div: rdn and wknd 3f out* **25/1**

1m 25.24s (85.24)
WFA 3 from 4yo+ 2lb **14** Ran SP% **144.2**
CSF £74.80 CT £444.75 TOTE £8.60: £3.70, £3.10, £1.30; DF 234.70.
Owner Mrs Noeleen McCreevy **Bred** Durlacher Ltd **Trained** Naas, Co Kildare

NOTEBOOK
Phoenix Ice(IRE) Official explanation: trainer's rep said, regarding the apparent improvement in form, the ground was soft last time and gelding hit a bad patch of ground, faded and was eased once his chance had gone
Electric Warrior(IRE), better for his run at Kempton last month, won over 1m here in the spring so was proven at the track. He had every chance but that longer trip probably suits him better these days. (op 6/1)

6511a KILSARAN H'CAP 1m
4:15 (4:16) (60-80,80) 3-Y-O+ **£6,351** (£1,479; £652; £376)

RPR

1 **Willkandoo (USA)**15 6124 3-9-7 76 .... PaulMulrennan 9 81
(K A Ryan) *trckd ldr: travelled wl to ld 2f out: rdn and kpt on wl fnl f: jinked last 50yds* **7/2**1

2 1 3/4 **Monthly Medal**16 6097 5-9-6 79 .... (t) DEMullins(7) 4 80
(Anthony Mullins, Ire) *towards rr: hdwy to 5th 1 1/2f out: 4th 1f out: chal on outer fnl f and drifted sltly rt: nt rch wnr* **7/1**

3 1/2 **Desert Mile (IRE)**20 5983 5-9-6 77 .... SFoley(5) 5 77
(Edward Lynam, Ire) *towards rr: hdwy in 8th 2f out: 3rd 1 1/2f out: rdn into 2nd 1f out: no ex fnl f and kpt on same pce* **13/2**3

4 4 1/2 **Lidana (IRE)**28 5726 3-9-11 80 .... NGMcCullagh 12 70
(John M Oxx, Ire) *trckd ldrs: 6th 1/2-way: hdwy to 4th 2f out: rdn in 5th and no ex 1f out: kpt on same pce* **9/2**2

5 shd **Maximo (GER)**24 5847 5-9-1 74 .... (b1) AmyKathleenParsons(7) 7 63
(T G McCourt, Ire) *chsd ldrs: 4th 1/2-way: hdwy to 2nd under 2f out: rdn and no ex over 1f out: kpt on same pce fnl f* **8/1**

6 1 1/2 **Lucies Pride (IRE)**5 6371 3-9-4 73 .... (p) RPCleary 6 59
(M Halford, Ire) *mid-div: hdwy in 7th 2f out: rdn into 6th 1f out: kpt on same pce fnl f* **10/1**

7 1 1/2 **Herbert Crescent**8 6295 3-9-7 76 .... CDHayes 2 59
(Edward Lynam, Ire) *rr of mid-div: hdwy to 8th 1 1/2f out: rdn into mod 7th 1f out: kpt on same pce* **10/1**

8 nk **Inwood (IRE)**8 6301 5-9-11 77 .... (bt) KLatham 11 59
(Paul Magnier, Ire) *towards rr: hdwy to 7th 1 1/2f out: rdn in 9th and no ex 1f out: kpt on one pce* **20/1**

9 3/4 **Kalinka Malinka (IRE)**130 2516 3-9-6 78 .... SMGorey(3) 1 58
(D K Weld, Ire) *leapt leaving stalls: sn mid-div: rdn in 6th 2f out: no ex fr 1 1/2f out* **10/1**

10 4 **So Serene**80 4136 3-9-1 70 .... DPMcDonogh 10 41
(Charles O'Brien, Ire) *towards rr for most: nvr a factor* **9/1**

11 3/4 **Keen Look (IRE)**24 5846 9-9-1 72 .... (p) MHarley(5) 13 41
(Gerard Keane, Ire) *mid-div: rdn and no imp 3f out* **12/1**

12 5 **Privet (IRE)**120 2852 3-9-7 76 .... MCHussey 8 34
(W McCreery, Ire) *chsd ldrs: 3rd 1/2-way: rdn in 5th 2f out: no ex and wknd* **16/1**

13 2 **Treeko (IRE)**347 6442 3-9-0 72 .... PBBeggy(3) 14 25
(Francis Ennis, Ire) *chsd ldrs: 5th 1/2-way: rdn and wknd 3f out* **20/1**

14 1 1/4 **Orpen's Art (IRE)**43 5260 3-9-4 73 .... PShanahan 3 23
(R McGlinchey, Ire) *led: rdn and hdd 2f out: sn wknd* **10/1**

1m 37.85s (97.85)
WFA 3 from 5yo+ 3lb **14** Ran SP% **146.8**
CSF £35.02 CT £171.95 TOTE £2.50: £1.10, £4.70, £3.40; DF 43.90.
Owner M Forsyth,J Turner And M F Logistics Ltd **Bred** Craig Singer **Trained** Hambleton, N Yorks

NOTEBOOK
Willkandoo(USA), prominent throughout, stuck to the rail in the straight and ran on well. A progressive sort, he won without the cheekpieces he had worn on his previous three starts. (op 5/2)

6512 - 6513a (Foreign Racing) - See Raceform Interactive

5437 TIPPERARY (L-H)

Sunday, October 5

OFFICIAL GOING: Heavy

6514a LONGFIELD STABLES ABERGWAUN STKS (LISTED RACE) 5f

2:15 (2:16) 2-Y-O+ £26,327 (£7,724; £3,680; £1,253)

RPR

1 **Senor Benny (USA)**[7] 6315 9-9-11 103 CPGeoghegan 1 102
(M McDonagh, Ire) *cl up: rdn to ld 2f out: kpt on wl fnl f* **5/1**[3]

2 2 **Aine (IRE)**[7] 6315 3-9-8 100 WJLee 4 92
(T Stack, Ire) *chsd ldrs: rdn fr 2f out: disputing 2nd over 1f out: lost 2nd last strides* **5/1**[3]

3 shd **Hogmaneigh (IRE)**[15] 6104 5-9-11 SaleemGolam 7 94
(S C Williams) *chsd ldrs: 3rd 2f out: rdn and disputing 2nd over 1f out: wnt 2nd last strides* **6/4**[1]

4 2 1/2 **Tornadodancer (IRE)**[22] 5919 5-9-11 85 BACurtis 3 85
(T G McCourt, Ire) *hld up: rdn in 4th over 1f out: kpt on same pce* **20/1**

5 3 **Nubar Lady (IRE)**[38] 5438 2-8-4 97 WMLordan 6 73
(T Stack, Ire) *led: rdn and hdd 2f out: sn no ex* **4/1**[2]

6 8 **Shining Armour (IRE)**[38] 5437 3-9-11 88 (b) PJSmullen 2 46
(D K Weld, Ire) *hld up: rdn and no imp fr 2f out* **12/1**

7 4 **Domingues**[7] 6315 3-9-11 108 EddieAhern 5 31
(Edward Lynam, Ire) *s.i.s: sn in tch in rr: rdn and no imp fr 2f out* **7/1**

62.94 secs (3.94) 7 Ran SP% **118.3**
CSF £31.36 TOTE £6.30: £2.90, £3.60; DF 39.90.
Owner M McDonagh **Bred** Landon Knight **Trained** Turloughmore, Co Galway

NOTEBOOK
Senor Benny(USA) returned to form in a major way to win this contest for the second straight year. He's a decent horse given the right conditions and everything just worked out a treat for the old boy here. (op 9/2)
Hogmaneigh(IRE) looked to have the right credentials for this particular contest but was somewhat disappointing, although maybe his recent efforts in very competitive handicaps across the water have just taken the edge off him. He had a good position tucked in behind the leaders to halfway but soon came off the bridle and didn't look likely from that point. (op 7/4 tchd 2/1)

6516a COOLMORE STUD HOME OF CHAMPIONS CONCORDE STKS (GROUP 3) 7f 100y

3:20 (3:20) 3-Y-O+ £38,235 (£11,176; £5,294; £1,764)

RPR

1 **Psalm (IRE)**[28] 5730 3-8-12 109 SMLevey 3 114+
(A P O'Brien, Ire) *in tch in rr: mod 5th 3f out: prog on outer ent st: rdn to ld 1f out: styd on strly: easily* **15/8**[1]

2 8 **Jumbajukiba**[21] 5944 5-9-8 114 (b) ADLeigh 6 102+
(Mrs John Harrington, Ire) *led after 1f: clr 3f out: rdn and strly pressed 1 1/2f out: hdd 1f out: no imp* **3/1**[2]

3 1 **Hard Rock City (USA)**[5] 6370 8-9-3 96 EddieAhern 4 93
(M J Grassick, Ire) *chsd ldr in mod 2nd: rdn along 3f out: no ex and rdn along in mod 3rd over 1f out: wnt 3rd cl home* **10/1**

4 nk **Rock Of Rochelle (USA)**[22] 5922 3-9-4 108 RMBurke 2 95
(A Kinsella, Ire) *prom early: rdn in mod 4th 3f out: disp mod 3rd over 1f out: lost 3rd cl home* **8/1**

5 10 **Tian Shan (IRE)**[147] 2026 4-9-3 107 (b) PJSmullen 8 68
(D K Weld, Ire) *in rr: rdn and no imp fr 3f out* **7/2**[3]

6 3 **Three Rocks (IRE)**[7] 6315 3-9-1 DJMoran 1 61
(J S Bolger, Ire) *chsd ldrs: rdn in mod 3rd 3f out: no imp st* **14/1**

7 1 1/4 **Dane Blue (IRE)**[8] 6298 6-9-0 91 WMLordan 7 55
(S J Treacy, Ire) *chsd ldrs: wknd fr 1/2-way* **16/1**

8 3 1/2 **Crooked Throw (IRE)**[19] 4512 9-9-3 103 WJLee 5 50
(C F Swan, Ire) *s.i.s and a bhd* **16/1**

1m 39.48s (99.48)
WFA 3 from 4yo+ 2lb 8 Ran SP% **120.6**
CSF £8.15 TOTE £2.80: £1.10, £1.60, £1.80; DF 7.90.
Owner Mrs John Magnier **Bred** Mrs A M O'Brien **Trained** Ballydoyle, Co Tipperary

NOTEBOOK
Psalm(IRE) once again showed her liking for this venue as she registered an impressive victory in this testing ground. It was a fine patient ride too by Sean Levey, as he switched the filly off and held her up well off a pace that was almost guaranteed to be strong. She made good progress from the top of the straight and kept up the momentum to go right away inside the final furlong. Obviously, given the conditions, the face value of the form is questionable, but this filly has finally come good after a disappointing start to the season and, if staying in training, there's no reason why she shouldn't be able to step up in grade next season. (op 9/4 tchd 5/2)
Jumbajukiba probably ran as good a race as he ever has away from the Curragh. As usual, he bounced out in front and attempted to burn off his rivals in similar fashion to his win at headquarters last time in similar ground conditions. He did manage to open up a six-length lead entering the straight before completely running out of steam inside the final furlong. (op 3/1 tchd 7/2)

6515 - 6516a (Foreign Racing) - See Raceform Interactive

3306 DORTMUND (R-H)

Sunday, October 5

OFFICIAL GOING: Soft

6517a GROSSER PREIS VON DSW21 DEUTSCHES ST LEGER (GROUP 3) 1m 6f

4:25 (4:41) 3-Y-O+ £23,529 (£9,559; £4,779; £2,574)

RPR

1 **Valdino (GER)**[32] 5625 3-8-11 ow1 THellier 7 114
(U Ostmann, Germany) *racd in 3rd to st: led over 2f out: sn clr: easily* **1/1**[1]

2 6 **Peppertree Lane (IRE)**[50] 5094 5-9-6 JoeFanning 2 106
(M Johnston) *trckd ldr: clsd up 4f out: 2nd st: ev ch 2f out: one pce* **9/2**[2]

3 3/4 **Court Canibal**[127] 2636 3-8-10 J-PCarvalho 4 104
(M Delzangles, France) *hld up: 5th st: styd on at same pce* **5/1**[3]

4 3/4 **Brisant (GER)**[32] 5625 6-9-6 DPorcu 6 104
(M Trybuhl, Germany) *hld up: 6th st: styd on at one pce fnl 2f* **11/1**

5 20 **Alma Mater**[314] 6953 5-9-2 J-PGuillambert 1 74
(Sir Mark Prescott) *led to over 2f out: sn wknd* **6/1**

6 7 **Flamingo Fantasy (GER)** 3-8-11 ow1 ADeVries 3 69
(W Hickst, Germany) *disp 3rd: 4th st: sn btn: eased* **12/1**

7 4 **Waldvogel (IRE)**[32] 5625 4-9-6 (b) EPedroza 8 64
(A Wohler, Germany) *racd in 5th: last st: sn wl bhd* **12/1**

3m 9.06s (3.56)
WFA 3 from 4yo+ 9lb 7 Ran SP% **122.9**
(including 10 Euro stake): WIN 17; PL 11, 13, 14; SF 41.
Owner Frau H Endres **Bred** Gestut Auenquelle **Trained** Germany

NOTEBOOK
Valdino(GER) is a progressive young stayer and especially effective in testing conditions. He was second to the subsequent Deutsches Derby runner-up Ostland on his debut in April but is undefeated in five appearances since.
Peppertree Lane(IRE) pressed the leader and closed up onto her shoulder starting the final turn. He looked as if he might take over early in the straight but had no answer as soon as the winner joined in.
Alma Mater was running for the first time this year and should improve for the outing. She had won on soft going last November but stopped rapidly once headed here. It was an ambitious spot to start her off in.

6494 LONGCHAMP (R-H)

Sunday, October 5

OFFICIAL GOING: Good to soft

6518a QATAR PRIX DE L'ABBAYE DE LONGCHAMP (GROUP 1) 5f (S)

1:15 (5:58) 2-Y-O+ £105,037 (£42,022; £21,011; £10,496; £5,257)

RPR

1 **Marchand D'Or (FR)**[56] 4915 5-9-11 DBonilla 20 121+
(F Head, France) *in midfield on outside: hdwy over 2f out: led over 1f out: drvn out* **2/1**[1]

2 1 1/2 **Moorhouse Lad**[15] 6121 5-9-11 JimCrowley 6 116
(B Smart) *pressed ldrs on ins rail: led 1/2-way to over 1f out: r.o* **25/1**

3 1 **Borderlescott**[44] 5245 6-9-11 PatCosgrave 9 112
(R Bastiman) *chsd ldrs: drvn 1/2-way rchd 3rd over 1f out: r.o* **11/2**[3]

4 1/2 **Strike Up The Band**[12] 6184 5-9-11 AdrianTNicholls 13 110
(D Nicholls) *cl up after 2f: styd on fnl f: nrest at fin* **50/1**

5 hd **Fleeting Spirit (IRE)**[110] 3101 3-9-7 RyanMoore 17 106
(J Noseda) *a in tch: outpcd 2f out: gd hdwy appr fnl f: jst missed 4th* **7/2**[2]

6 hd **Rock Harmonie (FR)**[21] 5955 3-9-7 C-PLemaire 1 106
(Mme C Head-Maarek, France) *in rr early: hdwy fr 1/2-way: nrst fin* **66/1**

7 1 1/2 **Tiza (SAF)**[35] 5556 6-9-11 CSoumillon 11 103
(A De Royer-Dupre, France) *outpcd tl styd on fnl 2f: nrst fin* **25/1**

8 3/4 **Black Mambazo (IRE)**[14] 3-9-11 DVargiu 10 101
(L Riccardi, Italy) *pressed ldr: 2nd wl over 1f out: one pce* **100/1**

9 hd **Equiano (FR)**[44] 5245 3-9-11 SPasquier 18 100
(B W Hills) *reluctant to load: pressed ldrs on outside tl wknd fr over 1f out* **10/1**

10 1 1/2 **National Colour (SAF)**[44] 5245 6-9-7 KShea 4 92
(S Tarry, South Africa) *in midfield on ins rail: nvr in position to chal* **11/2**[3]

11 snk **Enticing (IRE)**[15] 6121 4-9-7 LiamJones 3 91
(W J Haggas) *a outpcd* **25/1**

12 hd **Dandy Man (IRE)**[44] 5245 5-9-11 LDettori 8 93
(Saeed Bin Suroor) *a in midfield* **20/1**

13 1 1/2 **Green Manalishi**[15] 6121 7-9-11 (b) IMendizabal 14 88
(K A Ryan) *prom 3f* **66/1**

14 1 **Mariol (FR)**[28] 5738 5-9-11 DBoeuf 2 84
(Robert Collet, France) *a towards rr* **50/1**

15 1 **Captain Gerrard (IRE)**[44] 5245 3-9-11 TomEaves 12 81
(B Smart) *led to 1/2-way: wkng whn hmpd wl over 1f out: dropped out qckly* **14/1**

16 snk **Wi Dud**[15] 6121 4-9-11 (b) NCallan 7 80
(K A Ryan) *a outpcd* **33/1**

17 1 1/2 **Abraham Lincoln (IRE)**[22] 5891 4-9-11 JMurtagh 19 75
(A P O'Brien, Ire) *a in rr* **66/1**

54.40 secs (-2.30) **Going Correction** -0.025s/f (Good) 17 Ran SP% **130.7**
Speed ratings: **117,114,113,112,111 111,109,107,107,105 105,104,102,100,99 98,96**
PARI-MUTUEL: WIN 2.40; PL 1.50, 8.70, 2.20; DF 66.00.
Owner Mme J-L Giral **Bred** Mme C Giral **Trained** France

FOCUS
A strong renewal of this top-class sprint that is traditionally a benefit for British-trained sprinters. However, everything was thrown into chaos when Fleeting Spirit's stall failed to open and a false start was called. The unbeaten Hungarian challenger Overdose 'won' the race that wasn't, chased home by Strike Up The Band and Desert Lord, but most of the other jockeys saw the flag and either pulled up or eased their mounts. Not surprisingly Overdose and Desert Lord, along with Only Answer, were not asked to race again just over four and a half hours later (off 5.58 UK time) but that still left a good-sized field and in the end produced a satisfactory result. The runner-up and fourth set the standard.

NOTEBOOK
Marchand D'Or(FR), who went to post early for the original running but late for the second try, captured the European champion sprinter title with an authoritative success in recording his third Group 1 win of the season. A horse who does not like to be crowded, he broke well from his outside stall but was settled just off the pace. Picking up really well when asked for his effort, he swept past his rivals and collared the runner-up inside the last to score with something in hand. He is a consistent and versatile performer and a credit to connections. If he runs again, it will be in the Hong Kong Sprint, and as he is a gelding he will remain in training next year.
Moorhouse Lad has come back to form of late and was well suited by this flat track. He made the running, travelling well, and looked like he might hold on until the winner loomed up on his outside. His run was all the more meritorious as he was one of those who completed the 'race' earlier, albeit not totally flat out, and he looks capable of winning more good races at the minimum trip.
Borderlescott, the Nunthorpe winner, ran his usual fine race but was one of the first under pressure and probably found this flat five sharper than ideal. He could go for the Hong Kong Sprint, but might not travel if Marchand d'Or is in the field.
Strike Up The Band, who finished second in the original running, put up a remarkable effort, especially considering he looked outclassed on all known form. The track clearly suits him and it would be no surprise if next season he was trained with this race in mind.
Fleeting Spirit(IRE), whose stall didn't open in the original running, was not surprisingly well backed this time, but her trainer agonised over running her as she had hit her head on the stalls and then twisted off a plate on the way back to the stands. She tracked the leaders before running on quite well in the closing stages and hopefully she will stay in training, having had quite a light season this time.
Rock Harmonie(FR) had smart form at Group 3 level but appeared to have something to find to figure here. Another who was held up before staying on nicely in the closing stages, she seems to be progressing.
Tiza(SAF), who was sixth in this last year, raced in company with Fleeting Spirit but could not pick up in quite the same manner.

Black Mambazo(IRE), an Italian challenger, showed plenty of pace before tiring in the final furlong.
Equiano(FR), who proved difficult to load on both occasions despite being fitted with a blanket, also showed plenty of pace before tiring in the final furlong.
National Colour(SAF) did not exhibit the same pace that she had shown in previous runs but that may have been down to a combination of the rain-softened ground and her earlier exertions.
Enticing(IRE) is also best on fast ground and has now been well held on all three tries at this level.
Dandy Man(IRE) failed to fire following his earlier exertions and needs a faster surface.
Green Manalishi, in first-time blinkers, showed the same initial pace as he had earlier in the day before fading.
Captain Gerrard(IRE) travelled strongly early on ground that suits before dropping right away.
Wi Dud was always struggling to go the pace.

6519a TOTAL PRIX MARCEL BOUSSAC (GROUP 1) (FILLIES) 1m

1:50 (2:02) 2-Y-O **£126,044** (£50,426; £25,213; £12,596; £6,309)

RPR

1 **Proportional**[24] 2-8-11 .... SPasquier 11 114+
(Mme C Head-Maarek, France) *a cl up: 3rd st: rdn to ld over 1f out: drvn out* **20/1**
2 *3* **Elusive Wave (IRE)**[43] 5301 2-8-11 .... C-PLemaire 7 107
(J-C Rouget, France) *a cl up: 5th st: hdwy over 2f out: rdn over 1f out: kpt on to take 2nd last 50yds* **7/1[3]**
3 *3/4* **Copperbeech (IRE)**[21] 2-8-11 .... LDettori 2 107+
(A Fabre, France) *in midfield: 8th st: rdn wl over 1f out: kpt on at one pce fnl f* **11/4[1]**
4 *nse* **Plumania**[30] 2-8-11 .... OPeslier 1 107+
(A Fabre, France) *in midfield: 9th st: hdwy on outside wl over 1f out: hrd drvn and r.o: jst missed 3rd* **12/1**
5 *1/2* **Marquesa (USA)**[35] 5549 2-8-11 .... JAHeffernan 6 105
(David Wachman, Ire) *led to over 1f out: kpt on and only lost 2nd in last 50yds* **100/1**
6 *4* **Go Lovely Rose (IRE)**[56] 2-8-11 .... DBoeuf 5 96
(Robert Collet, France) *a.p: 2nd st: 3rd 1f out: grad wknd* **12/1**
7 *1/2* **Rose Diamond (IRE)**[24] 5828 2-8-11 .... RichardHughes 12 95
(R Charlton) *hld up in rr: styd on fnl 2f: nvr nr to chal* **28/1**
8 *nk* **Ana Americana (FR)**[20] 5987 2-8-11 .... IMendizabal 4 94
(P Demercastel, France) *trckd ldrs: 4th st: wknd 1 1/2f out* **25/1**
9 *4* **Palme Royale (IRE)**[28] 2-8-11 .... ACrastus 10 85
(E Lellouche, France) *a in midfield* **12/1**
10 *nk* **Denomination (USA)**[20] 5987 2-8-11 .... TGillet 14 85+
(Mme C Head-Maarek, France) *last tl appr st: effrt on ins over 2f out: btn over 1f out* **25/1**
11 *3* **Please Sing**[43] 5272 2-8-11 .... DarryllHolland 3 78
(M R Channon) *prom: 7th st: wknd over 1f out* **33/1**
12 *1 1/2* **African Skies**[43] 5272 2-8-11 .... NCallan 9 75
(K A Ryan) *6th st: wknd wl over 1f out* **33/1**
13 *6* **Paidrin (USA)**[42] 5327 2-8-11 .... MJKinane 8 61
(J S Bolger, Ire) *nvr nrr than midfield* **33/1**
14 *6* **Again (IRE)**[35] 5549 2-8-11 .... JMurtagh 17 48
(David Wachman, Ire) *a in rr* **10/3[2]**
15 *1 1/2* **Pill (IRE)**[15] 2-8-11 .... CSoumillon 16 45
(A De Royer-Dupre, France) *in midfield: 10th st on outside: btn 2f out* **10/1**
16 *hd* **Maoineach (USA)**[35] 5546 2-8-11 .... KJManning 13 44
(J S Bolger, Ire) *a in rr: last fr over 2f out* **10/1**

1m 36.0s (-2.80) **Going Correction** -0.125s/f (Firm) **16** Ran SP% **129.2**
Speed ratings: **109,106,105,105,104 100,100,99,95,95 92,91,85,79,77 77**
PARI-MUTUEL: WIN 28.80; PL 5.10, 2.40, 1.80; DF 82.30.
Owner K Abdulla **Bred** Juddmonte Farms Ltd **Trained** Chantilly, France
■ Stewards' Enquiry : J A Heffernan €200 fine: whip abuse

FOCUS
This is a race that boasts an illustrious roll of honour in recent years, Six Perfections, Divine Proportions, Finsceal Beo, and most recently Zarkava winning. They went a fast pace, courtesy of pacemaker Marquesa, and very few got into it, favourite Again being one of many to get behind early and never feature. Those drawn very wide were at a disadvantage but the winner was impressive and the form is solid, if unspectacular.

NOTEBOOK
Proportional ◆, coming from stall 11, secured a good early sit and was always well placed to strike. A beaten favourite behind Copperbeech on her debut, a defeat her trainer put down to greenness, she overcame the drop to 7f when winning at Chantilly last time and this return to a stiffer test was always likely to see her in a much better light, especially off such a strong gallop. She used up a bit of early speed, but settled nicely into the race and picked up immediately when asked to go for home two furlongs out. In front before the furlong pole, she stayed on strongly to win with plenty in hand and earned immediate an quote from sponsors Stan James of 8-1 for next season's 1000 Guineas (as low as 6-1 in places). Her trainer, who has won the Guineas with Ma Biche, Ravinella and Hatoof, very much has that race in mind and there is every hope that this strapping daughter of Beat Hollow will improve further over the winter.
Elusive Wave(IRE), bought out of the Richard Hannon yard having made a winning debut at Goodwood, has improved since joining current connections and made it three from three when winning a Group 3 over this trip at Deauville last time. This run elevated her form to a new level and she seemed to improve again for a further step up in trip, staying on into second without ever looking likely to catch the winner. She may do better again on a sound surface, and she has been marked down for next year's Poule d'Essai des Pouliches.
Copperbeech(IRE), ready winner of a minor contest over course and distance last time, had a few of these behind when winning on debut and was viewed as being the best of the 'home' team. Held up in midfield, she ran on nicely when switched out in the straight and just held third, but was never looked like winning. Perhaps a more positive ride will help in future.
Plumania ◆ is one to take from the race from among beaten horses. A half-sister to Saturday's Prix de Royallieu winner Balladeuse, she won over course and distance last month and may well have been second here but for getting so far back. It took her a while to hit top gear but she stayed on takingly down the outside and just failed to snatch third. Needless to say she is going to appreciate a further rise in distance next season and she already looks an obvious one for the Prix de Diane.
Marquesa(USA), who acted as a pacemaker for Again in the Moyglare, set off in front and set what appeared to be a really decent gallop. She tried to kick again off the home bend and was still in front with under two to run, but in the end those early exertions took their toll. This was a cracking effort.
Go Lovely Rose(IRE), who split Copperbeech and Pill on her debut in August, chased the early leader for much of the way but was beaten with two to run and weakened steadily inside the final furlong.
Rose Diamond(IRE) fared best of the English runners, staying on well from an unpromising position.
Please Sing was well enough positioned straightening up, but was not good enough to make an impact at this level over this longer trip.
African Skies, stepping up 2f in trip, was not good enough to figure at this level.
Again(IRE) has progressed rapidly since finishing eighth on her debut at Roscommon and supplemented her ready Group 2 victory at Leopardstown with a gritty display in the Group 1 Moyglare Stakes at the Curragh in August. Already proven in soft ground, she set a high standard, with the step up to 1m not expected to present a problem, but her draw had her beaten before the race got going, for she could not obtain a good position and found herself towards the rear and trapped wide. That said, she never even made a forward move and was toiling as they straightened for home. This was clearly not her running and she has the size to make a high-class three-year-old.
Pill(IRE) reportedly severed a tendon, and her future hangs in the balance.
Maoineach(USA), whose yard took this with Finsceal Beo in 2006, won a 6f Group 3 on her debut, but she was a little slowly into stride here and was another that never got out of the rear, being last turning in and staying there.

6520a PRIX JEAN-LUC LAGARDERE (GRAND CRITERIUM) (GROUP 1) (C&F) 7f

2:25 (2:34) 2-Y-O **£147,051** (£58,831; £29,415; £14,695; £7,360)

RPR

1 **Naaqoos**[21] 2-9-0 .... DBonilla 7 119
(F Head, France) *led after 1 1/2f: mde rest: rdn wl over 1f out: hld on wl whn pressed clsng stages* **9/2[2]**
2 *nk* **Milanais (FR)**[28] 5739 2-9-0 .... TJarnet 2 118
(B De Watrigant, France) *hld up in rr: 6th st on ins: swtchd off rail 2 1/2f out: wnt 2nd 1f out: styd on wl but hld by wnr last 50yds* **10/1[3]**
3 *2* **Intense Focus (USA)**[7] 6317 2-9-0 ....(b) KJManning 4 113
(J S Bolger, Ire) *hld up on outside: 5th st: rdn over 2f out: pressing for 2nd on outside over 1 1/2f out: one pce fnl f* **16/1**
4 *nk* **Mastercraftsman (IRE)**[21] 5946 2-9-0 .... JMurtagh 3 113
(A P O'Brien, Ire) *s.i.s: sn rcvrd: wnt 2nd 1/2-way: rdn to press wnr over 2f out: lost 2nd over 1f out: one pce* **4/9[1]**
5 *6* **Desert Phantom (USA)**[41] 5359 2-9-0 .... LDettori 1 98
(D M Simcock) *led 1 1/2f then racd in 2nd on ins: relegated to 4th 1/2-way: 3rd st: outpcd fr over 1 1/2f out* **12/1**
6 *1* **Higha (FR)**[37] 5486 2-8-11 .... SPasquier 5 92
(P Demercastel, France) *hld up in last: a in rr* **33/1**
7 *dist* **Sea Of Marmara (USA)**[21] 5946 2-9-0 .... JAHeffernan 6 —
(A P O'Brien, Ire) *immediately pushed along on outside but unable to get to ld: 4th st: sn wknd and eased* **150/1**

1m 18.4s (-2.50) **Going Correction** -0.125s/f (Firm) **7** Ran SP% **113.7**
Speed ratings: **109,108,106,106,99 98,—**
PARI-MUTUEL: WIN 5.00; PL 2.80, 3.00; SF 17.80.
Owner Hamdan Al Maktoum **Bred** S Boucheron **Trained** France
■ Stewards' Enquiry : K J Manning €100 fine: whip abuse

FOCUS
A smallish field for this major race for juvenile colts. Aidan O'Brien had been responsible for six of the last nine winners of this contest and saddled the odds-on favourite, who was 6lb off his National Stakes mark in a lack-lustre fourth behind the potentially top-class winner. Otherwise the form looks reasonable, and the winner looks capable of better, as he was always very comfortable on the lead.

NOTEBOOK
Naaqoos ◆ improved on his previous appearance in a Group 1, when fifth behind Bushranger in the Prix Morny. The winner of lesser contests either side of that race, he showed good early pace to take the lead, was travelling noticeably well in front before kicking on early in the straight and having enough in hand to hold off the late surge of the runner-up. A big, strapping colt with an exuberant action, this Oasis Dream half-brother to a 1m2f winner should have no difficulty staying the mile and, with improvement likely, looks set to be a major player in either the 2000 Guineas or the Poulains next season.
Milanais(FR), a Listed winner over 6f, had finished just ahead of Naaqoos in the Morny and made a bold bid to catch his old rival in the last furlong but never quite looked as if he would get there. Having run pretty close to collateral form with Intense Focus on a line through Soul City, he looks a good guide to the level. Next season he is likely to be aimed at the Poule d'Essai des Poulains.
Intense Focus(USA) had twice finished behind Mastercraftsman in Ireland this season but ran pretty close to his mark relative to the runner-up, which suggests the favourite was below par and the overall form does not look particularly strong. He could go to the Dewhurst next.
Mastercraftsman(IRE) came into this unbeaten in four starts including the Phoenix Stakes and National Stakes (both Group 1s) and was also proven over the trip and on the ground. Things did not go right for him as, along with his pacemaker Sea Of Marmara, he missed the break slightly and, although he was soon close to the pace, Murtagh was niggling soon after straightening for home and he failed to pick up. This has to go down as disappointing but connections felt this was a race too many and that a gruelling battle on heavy ground last time had left its mark.
Desert Phantom(USA), the winner of all three starts at 6f on good to soft and heavy ground, was taking a big step up in grade and raced up with the pace early before settling. He was close enough turning in but had nothing extra to give from that point. The fact that the runner-up in the Listed race he won last time was touched off in Redcar's sales race the day before is another reason to believe this was not the strongest renewal of this contest.
Higha(FR), the only filly in the race, is no better than Listed class on earlier evidence and was always at the back of the field.

6521a QATAR PETROLEUM PRIX DE L'OPERA (GROUP 1) (F&M) 1m 2f

3:00 (3:08) 3-Y-O+ **£105,037** (£42,022; £21,011; £10,496; £5,257)

RPR

1 **Lady Marian (GER)**[42] 5331 3-8-11 .... DBoeuf 11 123
(W Baltromei, Germany) *relcutant to load: hld up: 8th st: swtchd outside 1 1/2f out: r.o to ld 120yds out: rdn out* **16/1**
2 *1 1/2* **Lush Lashes**[28] 5730 3-8-11 .... KJManning 3 120
(J S Bolger, Ire) *a in tch: 5th st on ins: squeezed through against rail 1 1/2f out: drvn to ld 1f out: hdd 120yds out: r.o* **2/1[1]**
3 *1 1/2* **Katiyra (IRE)**[22] 5920 3-8-11 .... MJKinane 7 117
(John M Oxx, Ire) *hld up towards rr: hdwy on outside fr over 2f out: r.o to take 3rd cl home* **9/2[2]**
4 *3/4* **Treat Gently**[21] 5952 3-8-11 .... SPasquier 10 116
(A Fabre, France) *led after 1f to 8f out: trckd ldr: 3rd st: styd on at one pce fr over 1f out* **11/2[3]**
5 *3/4* **Lady Gloria**[21] 5932 4-9-2 .... TPQueally 8 113
(J G Given) *led after 2f: 3l clr 1/2-way: hdd 1f out: kpt on at one pce* **28/1**
6 *1* **Light Green (BRZ)**[21] 5954 4-9-2 .... CSoumillon 6 111
(A De Royer-Dupre, France) *a.p: 7th st: rdn wl over 1f out: kpt on same pce* **20/1**
7 *shd* **Proviso**[22] 5925 3-8-11 .... LDettori 12 112
(A Fabre, France) *prom: wnt 2nd over 4f out: 2nd st: stl 3rd 1f out: no ex* **16/1**
8 *nk* **You'resothrilling (USA)**[28] 5730 3-8-11 .... JMurtagh 16 111
(A P O'Brien, Ire) *6th st: rdn 2f out: one pce* **7/1**
9 *1 1/2* **Alamanni (USA)**[21] 4-9-2 .... ASanna 2 107
(E Borromeo, Italy) *dwlt: towards rr to st: sme late hdwy: nvr a factor* **150/1**

10 *1 1/2* **Rosenreihe (IRE)**63 [4675] 3-8-11 .... AStarke 4 105
(P Schiergen, Germany) *last to st: a bhd* **20/1**

11 *3/4* **Turfrose (GER)**21 [5952] 4-9-2 .... YTake 5 103
(A Fabre, France) *led 1f: restrained bhd ldrs: 4th st: wknd wl over 1f out* **33/1**

12 *nk* **Moonstone**84 [4006] 3-8-11 .... JAHeffernan 13 103
(A P O'Brien, Ire) *a in rr* **10/1**

13 *nk* **Lady Deauville (FR)**15 [6106] 3-8-11 .... FrancisNorton 1 103
(P A Blockley) *in midfield: 9th st: sme hdwy on ins 2f out: nvr nrr than midfield* **28/1**

14 *20* **Fair Breeze (GER)**14 [6156] 5-9-2 .... JVictoire 14 62
(Mario Hofer, Germany) *prom early: restrained after 2f: wl bhd fnl 2f* **25/1**

2m 3.80s (-3.10) **Going Correction** +0.15s/f (Good)
WFA 3 from 4yo+ 5lb **14** Ran SP% **124.1**
Speed ratings: **118,116,115,115,114 113,113,113,112,110 110,110,109,93**
PARI-MUTUEL: WIN 12.90; PL 2.70, 1.70, 1.30; DF 21.50.
Owner Rennstall Gestut Hachtsee **Bred** Count & Countess Von Stauffenberg **Trained** Germany

FOCUS

A cracking contest that certainly looked stronger than the previous year's renewal. The race is rated around the fourth and fifth, with the progressive first and third both recording personal bests.

NOTEBOOK

Lady Marian(GER) ◆, a German raider, upset a couple of the better-fancied runners. Unplaced in a handicap earlier in the season, she has improved no end since winning a Group 3 at Hamburg in July, finishing second in the German Oaks and then beating Treat Gently in another Group 3 at Deauville in August. This required a major step forward, but she was more than up to it and came with a strong late run to win cosily, despite edging right under pressure. She got shuffled back early, but made smooth headway and was still full of running two out, quickening well once a gap opened. The daughter of Nayef beat some of the best fillies around and there is no reason why she cannot progress further. She could be targeted at the Breeders' Cup Filly & Mare Turf next, and she will go through the Tattersalls Sales ring at Newmarket in December.

Lush Lashes, who has had a long, hard season, showed no signs of wilting and produced yet another cracking effort. Bidding for a fifth Group 1 victory of the season and back up to what is probably her optimum trip, she started to look for a run over two out and Manning opted to try his luck against the rail. Things got pretty tight but she squeezed through and briefly looked the winner. However, Lady Marian possessed a superior change of pace on the slow ground and she was forced to settle for second. She may have lost some momentum when coming through against the fence but the best horse seemed to win on the day. However, it was later reported that she came out of the race with a cut, and if she recovers well, she could be off to Hong Kong for the Hong Kong Cup in December.

Katiyra(IRE) still appears to be learning and this represented another improved effort. Third and fifth in the Epsom and Irish Oaks respectively, she has really come to herself in the past couple of months and headed into this in search of a hat-trick, having readily scored in Group 2 company at the Curragh last month. Held up early, she was widest of all straightening for home and lacked the winner's acceleration when asked to pick up, but came home strongly for third. She will be capable of winning over 1m4f as she strengthens further and is going to make an even better four-year-old.

Treat Gently was probably unlucky not to beat the winner at Deauville two starts back and had since finished third to Zarkava in the Vermeille. She was ideally placed and came to have every chance two out but was found wanting for speed. The drop in trip clearly counted against her.

Lady Gloria continues to get better and better. Not far behind Lush Lashes in the Matron Stakes, she beat Bankable in a Group 3 at Goodwood last time and ran a stormer off the front-end here. Connections had planned to hold her up, but the early pace was slow and Queally brought her through to lead. She hung in there a long way and it was only in the final half furlong that she started to tire.

Proviso has run many good races in defeat this season and gained a deserved win at Bordeaux last time. She came through to dispute it with Lady Gloria straightening up but could find no more from a furlong out.

You'resothrilling(USA) had been restricted to just one previous run this season, a fine fourth behind Lush Lashes in the Matron Stakes, but she used up too much gas from her wide draw.

Alamanni(USA) was cut up by Lush Lashes leaving the stalls and ran well considering.

Moonstone, the Irish Oaks winner, had been off since and Johnny Murtagh partnered You'resothrilling. She had a bit to prove on this drop in trip too and never left the rear.

Lady Deauville(FR) came into this in form but found this company too hot to handle.

6522a QATAR PRIX DE L'ARC DE TRIOMPHE (GROUP 1) (C&F) 1m 4f

3:40 (3:53) 3-Y-O+ **£1,680,588** (£672,353; £252,059; £252,059; £84,118)

RPR

1 **Zarkava (IRE)**21 [5952] 3-8-8 .... CSoumillon 1 129+
(A De Royer-Dupre, France) *broke on terms: hld up towards rr on ins: 10th st: hdwy over 2f out: angled out 1 1/2f out: quickened to ld 150yds out: impressive* **13/8**[1]

2 *2* **Youmzain (IRE)**71 [4406] 5-9-5 .... RHills 3 128
(M R Channon) *in tch on ins: 4th st: no room on ins trcking ldrs whn swtchd lft 1f out: fin wl* **12/1**

3 *1/2* **Soldier Of Fortune (IRE)**98 [3542] 4-9-5 .... JAHeffernan 9 126
(A P O'Brien, Ire) *cl up: 3rd st on outside: sn pressing ldr: styd on but could nvr get past* **9/2**[3]

3 *dht* **It's Gino (GER)**28 [5736] 5-9-5 .... TThulliez 2 126
(P Vovcenko, Germany) *racd in 3rd: hdwy on ins to ld narrowly ent st: hld on wl u.p tl hdd 150yds out: kpt on* **150/1**

5 *1* **Vision D'Etat (FR)**21 [5953] 3-8-11 .... IMendizabal 8 124
(E Libaud, France) *in midfield: 9th st: hdwy to dispute 5th jst over 1 1/2f out: styd on at same pce* **7/1**

6 *nk* **Ask**71 [4406] 5-9-5 .... RyanMoore 15 124+
(Sir Michael Stoute) *in rr: 13th st: hdwy and 10th jst over 1 1/2f out: styd on wl fnl f: nrst fin* **33/1**

7 *hd* **Duke Of Marmalade (IRE)**43 [5276] 4-9-5 .... JMurtagh 14 124+
(A P O'Brien, Ire) *in midfield on outside: 8th st: rdn over 1 1/2f out: styd on at same pce* **4/1**[2]

8 *1* **Getaway (GER)**35 [5557] 5-9-5 .... OPeslier 7 122+
(A Fabre, France) *dropped out in last: 15th 1 1/2f out: styd on wl fnl f* **11/1**

9 *1* **Cima De Triomphe (IRE)**18 3-8-11 .... DVargiu 16 119
(B Grizzetti, Italy) *towards rr on outside: 11th st: one pce fnl 2f* **150/1**

10 *shd* **Meisho Samson (JPN)**98 5-9-5 .... YTake 4 120
(S Takahashi, Japan) *in tch: 6th on ins st: sn rdn and nt qckn* **25/1**

11 *2 1/2* **Kamsin (GER)**28 [5736] 3-8-11 .... JVictoire 12 116
(P Schiergen, Germany) *towards rr: 12th st: nvr a factor* **25/1**

12 *1 1/2* **Papal Bull**49 [5137] 5-9-5 .... JimmyFortune 5 114
(Sir Michael Stoute) *dropped out in rr: 14th st: nvr a factor* **16/1**

13 *4* **Schiaparelli (GER)**21 [5954] 5-9-5 .... LDettori 10 108
(Saeed Bin Suroor) *chsd clr ldr in 2nd: disp ld briefly ent st: sn wknd* **33/1**

14 *3* **Blue Bresil (FR)**43 [5302] 3-8-11 .... WMongil 6 103+
(L Larrigade, France) *in midfield on ins: 7th st: wnt for ambitious gap and bdly hmpd 2f out: nt rcvr* **250/1**

15 *10* **Zambezi Sun**21 [5954] 4-9-5 ....(b) SPasquier 11 87
(P Bary, France) *prom on outside: 5th and wknd st* **50/1**

16 *dist* **Red Rock Canyon (IRE)**28 [5732] 4-9-5 .... CO'Donoghue 13 —
(A P O'Brien, Ire) *led and sn clr: taken wd and hdd 2 1/2f out: eased* **250/1**

2m 28.8s (-2.40) **Going Correction** +0.15s/f (Good)
WFA 3 from 4yo+ 7lb **16** Ran SP% **128.3**
Speed ratings: **114,112,112,112,111 111,111,110,110,109 108,107,104,102,95** —
PARI-MUTUEL: WIN 2.00; PL 1.50, 2.50, 2.50 (Soldier of Fortune),3.90 (It's Gino); DF 10.10.
Owner H H Aga Khan **Bred** His Highness The Aga Khan's Studs S C **Trained** Chantilly, France

■ Zarkava was the first filly to win the Arc since 1993 and first Vermeille winner to win the same year since Three Troikas in 1979.

FOCUS

This looked a quality Arc beforehand and it went to a very special winner. No horse had won from stall one since 1964, but it is interesting to note three of the first four home were drawn in the bottom three boxes, and only two winners (Sakhee and Dalakhani) since 1994 have been berthed higher than seven. A field of 16 was the largest since 2004, and there was undoubtedly the quality to match the quantity, with an unbeaten dual Classic-winning filly heading the market, a colt chasing a sixth Group 1 in a row, an unbeaten French Derby/Prix Niel winner, last year's runner-up, this year's German Derby hero, and a contender from Japan to name but a few. Zarkava came from an unpromising position to score in great style from Youmzain and the deadheaters Soldier Of Fortune and It's Gino. Value for a bit more, she has been rated the best filly or mare of the last decade, with Youmzain and Soldier Of Fortune both very close to their marks in the Grand Prix de Saint-Cloud and the much improved It's Gino possibly flattered a little from the front.

NOTEBOOK

Zarkava(IRE) was bidding to become the first filly to win this great race since Urban Sea in 1993 and the first three-year-old of her sex since 1982 and had really captured the imagination in the build-up. She did not disappoint, and in extending her unbeaten record to seven races, five of the last six of them at the top level, she marked herself down as one of the greatest fillies of all time and earned comparisons with the brilliant Allez France, who won this in 1974 as a four-year-old. Having first came to prominence when landing the Marcel Boussac on this card last year, she had confirmed herself an outstanding filly this season, winning both the French Guineas and Oaks, as well as her prep for this, the Vermeille, on her first try over 1m4f. Although ultimately an impressive winner there, she gave real cause for concern when starting very slowly, so her connections were taking no chances this time and had someone placed to give her a slap on the backside as the stalls opened. It worked to a point, as she broke on her terms. However, she seemed to lose her balance after a couple of strides when looking as if she might go through the tapes and take a short cut back to the paddock and her jockey could easily have come off. As a result, she dropped to the rear early on, and was trapped towards the inside, but they went a good, even gallop. She had a wall of horses in front of her early in the straight, but a nice gap appeared when she was switched slightly left with 300m to go and she produced her trademark turn of foot to seal matters impressively inside the final furlong. There had been concerns on the morning of the race that heavy rain would scupper her chances, but Longchamp missed most of the bad weather and conditions were absolutely fine. The Breeders' Cup was quickly ruled out and though it's not impossible she will stay in training at four, connections are understandably keen to see her retired her to the paddocks unbeaten.

Youmzain(IRE), arguably unlucky not to get last year's Arc in the stewards' room, ran another terrific race to fill the same position once again. Having travelled like a dream for much of the way, he looked full of running early in the straight, but was continually denied a clear run and got going too late when finally in the clear. However, Richard Hills was of the opinion that he was not unlucky, and it is doubtful that he would have troubled the brilliant winner whatever. He will stay in training as a six-year-old.

Soldier Of Fortune(IRE), fifth last year, was trained specifically for the race but he had every chance and was unable to reverse Grand Prix de Saint-Cloud placings with Youmzain. This looks as good as he is. The Breeders' Cup Turf will surely come into consideration, but he has yet to race on ground with 'firm' in the description.

It's Gino(GER) was always well placed close up against the seemingly favoured inside rail and he kept on willingly in the straight to post a huge effort in defeat. Interestingly his trainer was convinced the judge had called the result incorrectly and that he was a clear third. Unfortunately he picked up a slight injury and so a crack at the Japan Cup, where he was expected to appreciate the likely fast ground, has been ruled out.

Vision D'Etat(FR), successful since the Prix du Jockey-Club and the Prix Niel, which had produced the winner of this race seven times in the last ten years, was bidding to become the first horse trained in the French Provinces to take this race. He came up short, but ran well and would apparently have preferred more give in the ground. He will not race again this season and a decision on 2009 has yet to be made.

Ask was soon out the back after starting slowly and Moore was of the opinion he would have been closer had he been able to get him handier. The jockey also felt even softer ground would have been more beneficial.

Duke Of Marmalade(IRE)'s terrific winning sequence came to an end, and he was not at his best. Although Aidan O'Brien was not using the ground as an excuse, it can't have been ideal, especially over this trip. Regardless of the conditions, though, it is debatable whether he is at his best over 1m4f, as the King George form (his only previous try over the trip) is highly suspect. It might be that he has simply had enough, but he is with a master trainer and it would be no surprise to see him turn up at the Breeders' Cup. If he does make it to Santa Anita, the Classic is surely the race to go for.

Getaway(GER), last year's fourth, was given far too much to do and was also taken very wide into the straight. He did well to run on and finish so close, and surely such a strong stayer would have been seen to better advantage racing handier.

Cima De Triomphe(IRE) displayed an action that suggests he will be happier back on quicker ground.

Meisho Samson(JPN), the Japanese raider who won his country's Derby in 2006, could not muster the pace in the straight to land a telling blow.

Kamsin(GER), a supplementary entry, was slightly short of room at the top of the straight, but he basically failed to fire on the day.

Papal Bull was well below the form he showed when a close second to Duke Of Marmalade in the King George and Fortune simply felt he ran flat.

Schiaparelli(GER) ran well to be second in the Prix Foy on his debut for Godolphin, but this was his second run back after a long break and he failed to run a race.

Blue Bresil(FR) was short of room turning in and badly hampered 400m out which ended what chance he may have had.

Zambezi Sun, who beat Schiaparelli in the Foy, ran a stinker in first-time blinkers.

6502 KEENELAND (L-H)

Sunday, October 5

OFFICIAL GOING: Turf - firm; polytrack - fast

6523a JUDDMONTE SPINSTER STKS (GRADE 1) (F&M) (POLYTRACK) 1m 1f

10:10 (10:14) 3-Y-O+ **£155,779** (£50,251; £25,126; £12,563; £7,538)

RPR

1 **Carriage Trail (USA)**45 5-8-11 .... KDesormeaux 3 113
(Claude McGaughey III, U.S.A) **36/10**[2]

2 *7 3/4* **Model (USA)**38 4-8-11 ....(b) CHBorel 2 98
(Neil Drysdale, U.S.A) **87/10**

3 1 1/4 **Rosinka (IRE)**[57] [4888] 5-8-11 .... JRose 10 96
(H Graham Motion, U.S.A) **119/10**
4 1/2 **Little Belle (USA)**[29] 3-8-8 .... RMaragh 5 96
(Saeed Bin Suroor) **17/2**
5 1/2 **Wake Up Maggie (IRE)**[38] 5-8-11 ....(b) JRLeparoux 1 94
(Julio C Canani, U.S.A) **66/10**
6 2 1/2 **Say You Will (IRE)**[22] 4-8-11 .... MMena 9 89
(Saeed Bin Suroor) **239/10**
7 nk **Jibboom (USA)**[42] 4-8-11 .... EPrado 6 88
(Robert Frankel, U.S.A) **38/10**[3]
8 3/4 **Sharp Susan (USA)**[45] 4-8-11 ....(b) RRDouglas 4 87
(William Mott, U.S.A) **233/10**
9 1 **Unbridled Belle (USA)**[44] 5-8-11 ....(b) JRVelazquez 8 85
(Todd Pletcher, U.S.A) **28/10**[1]
10 2 1/4 **Rolling Sea (USA)**[42] 5-8-11 .... SXBridgmohan 7 81
(Steven Asmussen, U.S.A) **67/1**

1m 46.77s (106.77)
WFA 3 from 4yo+ 4lb **10** Ran SP% **120.2**
PARI-MUTUEL (Including $2 stake): WIN 9.20; PL (1-2) 5.00, 9.20; SHOW (1-2-3) 3.40, 6.00, 7.80; SF 83.20.
Owner Stuart S Janney III & Phipps Stable **Bred** Stuart S Janney III & Phipps Stable **Trained** USA

[6229] PONTEFRACT (L-H)
Monday, October 6

OFFICIAL GOING: Good (good to soft in places)
Wind: Light, across Weather: Sunny periods

6524 EBF SATURDAY RACING AT SANTA ROSA MAIDEN STKS 1m 2f 6y
2:10 (2:11) (Class 4) 2-Y-O **£5,180** (£1,541; £770; £384) **Stalls** Low

Form RPR
52 **1** **Madamlily (IRE)**[19] [6013] 2-8-12 0........ GrahamGibbons 4 75
(J J Quinn) *hld up in midfield: smooth hdwy 3f out: trckd ldrs 2f out: rdn to ld over 1f out: drvn ins fnl f and kpt on wl* **15/2**
05 **2** *hd* **Orthology (IRE)**[17] [6085] 2-9-3 0........ PaulMulrennan 2 80
(M H Tompkins) *hld up in rr: smooth hdwy on inner over 3f out: chsd ldng pair when n.m.r on inner and swtchd rt over 1f out: rdn to chal ins fnl f: sn drvn and kpt on wl towards fin* **14/1**
402 **3** *2 1/2* **Perfect Shot (IRE)**[43] [5314] 2-9-3 81........ JimmyQuinn 1 75
(J L Dunlop) *prom on inner: hdwy to ld 3f out: rdn along 2f out: drvn and hdd over 1f out: kpt on same pce ins fnl f* **2/1**[1]
0 **4** *7* **Nicky Nutjob (GER)**[16] [6117] 2-9-3 0........ JimmyFortune 8 63
(P W Chapple-Hyam) *hld up towards rr: hdwy on wd outside 4f out: rdn wl over 1f out: kpt on ins fnl f: nrst fin* **10/1**
462 **5** *1 1/4* **Doncosaque (IRE)**[16] [6135] 2-9-3 80........ TPQueally 10 60
(H R A Cecil) *midfield: hdwy over 4f out: effrt to chse ldrs over 2f out: sn rdn and kpt on same pce* **4/1**[2]
0400 **6** *1 3/4* **Ay Tay Tate (IRE)**[23] [5895] 2-9-3 68........ PatrickMathers 9 57
(I W McInnes) *hld up: hdwy on outer over 4f out: rdn to chse ldrs 2f out: drvn over 1f out and sn no imp* **25/1**
60 **7** *1 1/4* **State General (IRE)**[52] [5068] 2-9-0 0........ RussellKennemore(3) 6 55
(Miss J Feilden) *midfield: hdwy to chse ldrs 1/2-way: rdn along over 3f out: drvn 2f out and sn one pce* **100/1**
66 **8** *15* **Upton Seas**[13] [6187] 2-8-12 0........ PJMcDonald 3 23
(R D E Woodhouse) *sn led: rdn along and hdd over 4f out: grad wknd* **100/1**
03 **9** *1 1/4* **Saffron's Son (IRE)**[11] [6234] 2-9-3 0........ JamieMoriarty 5 26
(P T Midgley) *chsd ldrs: rdn along over 4f out: grad wknd* **100/1**
0402 **10** *3 1/4* **Aven Mac (IRE)**[12] [6214] 2-8-7 52........(p) KellyHarrison(5) 7 15
(N Bycroft) *midfield: rdn along over 4f out and sn wknd* **50/1**
42 **11** *nk* **Forty Thirty (IRE)**[15] [6151] 2-9-3 0........ TonyCulhane 13 19
(M R Channon) *chsd ldrs: rdn along 4f out: drvn over 2f out and sn wknd* **5/1**[3]
254 **12** *1 1/2* **Bandanaman (IRE)**[9] [6292] 2-9-3 78........ JamieSpencer 14 17
(G A Swinbank) *chsd ldrs: rdn along over 4f out: sn wknd* **7/1**
00 **13** *7* **Super Flight**[23] [5882] 2-9-3 0........ JoeFanning 12 4
(P W Chapple-Hyam) *cl up: led over 4f out: rdn along and hdd 3f out: sn drvn and wknd over 2f out* **22/1**
06 **14** *nk* **Who's Shirl**[12] [6212] 2-8-12 0........ TomEaves 11 —
(C W Fairhurst) *dwlt: a bhd* **100/1**

2m 19.59s (5.89) **Going Correction** +0.425s/f (Yiel) **14** Ran SP% **124.1**
Speed ratings (Par 97): **93,92,90,85,84 82,81,69,68,66 66,64,59,58**
toteswinger: 1&2 £14.40, 1&3 £4.20, 2&3 £12.10. CSF £107.12 TOTE £8.40: £2.30, £3.90, £1.40; EX 115.00.
Owner Bob McMillan **Bred** Dermot Brennan And Associates Ltd **Trained** Settrington, N Yorks
■ Stewards' Enquiry : Paul Mulrennan one-day ban: used whip with excessive frequency (Oct 20)

FOCUS
A modest maiden that provided a good test of stamina for these juveniles. The form is solid with the first three clear.

NOTEBOOK
Madamlily(IRE) had stepped up markedly on her debut when second over an extended 7f at Beverley last time and this rise in distance was right up her alley. She came through to lead over a furlong out and stuck on well to hold the runner-up. Her dam was an unraced half-sister to dual Chester Cup winner Rainbow High and she is expected to stay further next season. (op 8-1)
Orthology(IRE) ran a promising race at Newmarket last time and was only going to improve for the step up in trip. He was ridden patiently and made ground against the rail, but had to be switched just inside the furlong pole and could not get there in time. He has scope to improve again and is now qualified for a handicap mark. (op 16-1 tchd 12-1)
Perfect Shot(IRE), narrowly denied at Goodwood last time, was not that quick away and had to be ridden to take a prominent position. He moved through to lead leaving the back straight and had every chance, but could find no extra in the final half-furlong. (op 5-2 tchd 11-4 in places)
Nicky Nutjob(GER) got a bit behind early and had to make his effort wide, in the end staying on for fourth. This was an improvement on his first run. (op 20-1)
Doncosaque(IRE), second over 1m1/2f at Wolverhampton last time, appeared not to stay the extra distance and was beaten over a furlong out. (op 10-3)
Ay Tay Tate(IRE) ran better than his finishing position suggests and has a small race in him, probably back in handicaps. (op 18-1)
Forty Thirty(IRE) dropped away tamely in the straight and was the main disappointment. (op 11-2 tchd 4-1 and 6-1 in places)

6525 SOCA WARRIORS NURSERY 6f
2:40 (2:40) (Class 5) (0-85,84) 2-Y-O **£3,238** (£963; £481; £240) **Stalls** Low

Form RPR
410 **1** **Go Go Green (IRE)**[26] [5791] 2-8-12 **75**........ TonyCulhane 10 82
(S Parr) *mde all: rdn wl over 1f out: edgd lft ent fnl f: sn drvn and kpt on wl* **12/1**
500 **2** *nk* **Whatyouwoodwishfor (USA)**[114] [3049] 2-8-3 **66**........ DaleGibson 5 72
(R A Fahey) *towards rr: pushed along and gd hdwy on inner 2f out: rdn to chse ldng pair and hung lft over 1f out: swtchd rt and chal ins fnl f: edgd lft and kpt on* **25/1**
41 **3** *3* **Big Apple Boy (IRE)**[11] [6229] 2-9-7 **84**........ AndrewElliott 4 81
(Jedd O'Keeffe) *cl up: rdn to chal 2f out and ev ch: drvn and n.m.r on inner ent fnl f: sn one pce* **3/1**[1]
005 **4** *2* **Rising Kheleyf (IRE)**[16] [6109] 2-7-12 **61**........ SilvestreDeSousa 7 52
(G A Swinbank) *in rr: hdwy over 2f out: rdn over 1f out: kpt on ins fnl f: nrst fin* **25/1**
524 **5** *3/4* **Zelloof (IRE)**[31] [5672] 2-8-7 **70**........ TPQueally 15 59
(Saeed Bin Suroor) *dwlt and towards rr: hdwy and n.m.r over 2f out and again over 1f out: kpt on ins fnl f: nrst fin* **9/1**
U263 **6** *2 3/4* **Verinco**[58] [4874] 2-9-1 **78**........ TomEaves 11 59
(B Smart) *chsd ldrs: rdn along 2f out: sn drvn and one pce* **16/1**
0232 **7** *2 1/4* **Ishe Mac**[58] [4874] 2-9-3 **80**........ JimmyQuinn 1 54
(N Bycroft) *in tch on inner: hdwy to chse ldrs 3f out: rdn along 2f out and grad wknd* **12/1**
442 **8** *1/2* **Eldorado Days (IRE)**[98] [3547] 2-9-1 **78**........ DarrenWilliams 13 50
(K R Burke) *in tch: rdn along over 2f out: sn no imp* **40/1**
0410 **9** *nk* **Cyflymder (IRE)**[17] [6082] 2-9-1 **78**........ JamieSpencer 12 49
(J G Given) *chsd ldrs on outer: rdn along over 2f out: drvn and wknd wl over 1f out* **7/1**[3]
61 **10** *1 1/4* **Hit The Switch**[14] [6158] 2-8-9 **72**........ TonyHamilton 8 40
(R A Fahey) *a towards rr* **14/1**
3521 **11** *11* **Aladdin's Lamp (IRE)**[12] [6207] 2-8-9 **72**........ JoeFanning 14 —
(M Johnston) *prom: rdn along over 2f out: sn drvn and wknd* **5/1**[2]
2123 **12** *14* **Countrywide City (IRE)**[87] [3908] 2-9-5 **82**........ JimmyFortune 6 —
(P W Chapple-Hyam) *chsd ldrs: rdn along over 2f out: sn drvn and wknd* **7/1**[3]
124 **13** *17* **Noodles Blue Boy**[15] [6149] 2-9-2 **79**........ PaulMulrennan 9 —
(Ollie Pears) *chsd ldrs: rdn along wl over 2f out: sn wknd* **16/1**

1m 20.53s (3.63) **Going Correction** +0.425s/f (Yiel) **13** Ran SP% **120.6**
Speed ratings (Par 95): **92,91,87,84,83 80,77,76,76,74 59,41,18**
toteswinger: 1&2 £74.50, 1&3 £34.40, 2&3 £22.20. CSF £286.59 CT £1172.56 TOTE £19.80: £4.70, £6.70, £1.50; EX 659.30.
Owner S Bolland P Holling **Bred** Edmond And Richard Kent **Trained** Bawtry, S Yorks

FOCUS
This was a fairly ordinary nursery. The time and principals set the level.

NOTEBOOK
Go Go Green(IRE) was well supported beforehand. Just 2lb higher than when winning at Hamilton in August, the step up to 7f did not work in his favour at Doncaster last time and he showed plenty of pace on this drop in trip. He raced clear with Big Apple Boy turning in, and, despite getting a little tired late on, just did enough to hold the runner-up's late challenge. This trip is as far as he wants to go. (op 25-1)
Whatyouwoodwishfor(USA), unplaced in three 6f York maidens earlier in the year, has clearly improved for a break and he may well have won in a few more strides. There is a race in him off a similar mark and he should have little trouble staying 7f. (op 33-1)
Big Apple Boy(IRE), a cosy winner over course and distance last month, looked on a relatively stiff mark for this nursery debut and he could find no extra inside the final furlong. He is related to numerous winners over much further than this, but shows plenty of speed and will fare better on a faster surface. (op 11-4 tchd 5-2)
Rising Kheleyf(IRE), a promising fifth over 6f at Catterick on last month's qualifying run for a mark, stayed on all too late and again suggested a return to 7f would help. There is a small race in him. (op 33-1)
Zelloof(IRE) had little go right for her. Fourth behind a couple of smart performers at Kempton last time, she was expected to prove well suited by this drop in trip, but had to be dropped out from her wide draw and got no run when trying to make a move early in the straight. She can be rated better than the bare form. She was later reported to have been unsuited by the ground. Official explanation: jockey said filly was unsuited by the good (good to soft places) ground (op 10-1 tchd 17-2)
Aladdin's Lamp(IRE), a cosy winner over 7f at Kempton last month, was 10lb higher for this return to turf and had to use up too much gas from his wide draw.
Countrywide City(IRE) was reported to have been unsuited by the going. Official explanation: jockey said colt was unsuited by the good (good to soft places) ground (op 9-1 tchd 10-1)
Noodles Blue Boy Official explanation: jockey said gelding ran flat

6526 TRINIDAD & TOBAGO H'CAP 1m 4y
3:10 (3:10) (Class 3) (0-95,90) 3-Y-O
£9,346 (£2,799; £1,399; £700; £349; £175) **Stalls** Low

Form RPR
2310 **1** **Mangham (IRE)**[42] [5360] 3-8-11 **83**........ PaulMulrennan 1 98
(D H Brown) *cl up on inner tl led after 1f: rdn along wl over 1f out: drvn and kpt on wl fnl f* **11/1**
411- **2** *1* **Jack Dawkins (USA)**[346] [6471] 3-9-3 **89**........ TPQueally 5 101
(H R A Cecil) *hld up in midfield: hdwy over 2f out: rdn to chse wnr and hung lft 1f out: drvn and kpt on ins fnl f* **5/1**[2]
0200 **3** *2 3/4* **Unbreak My Heart (IRE)**[26] [5795] 3-9-4 **90**........ TomEaves 2 96
(R Charlton) *hld up towards rr: hdwy 3f out: rdn to chse ldrs 2f out: kpt on same pce u.p fnl f* **16/1**
214 **4** *2* **Once A Gulch (USA)**[39] [5425] 3-8-13 **85**........ ShaneKelly 11 86
(J Noseda) *in tch: hdwy to chse ldrs over 2f out and sn rdn: drvn over 1f out and kpt on same pce* **7/1**[3]
1165 **5** *6* **Topazes**[24] [5862] 3-9-2 **88**........ JamieSpencer 10 76
(M L W Bell) *in rr: hdwy on outer 3f out: rdn over 2f out: kpt on u.p ins fnl f* **9/1**
1525 **6** *3/4* **Admiral Dundas (IRE)**[10] [6242] 3-8-12 **84**........ TonyCulhane 8 70
(W Jarvis) *chsd ldrs: rdn along over 2f out: drvn and wknd wl over 1f out* **7/1**[3]
164 **7** *2 1/2* **City Of The Kings (IRE)**[72] [4417] 3-9-4 **90**........ SilvestreDeSousa 3 70
(G A Harker) *trckd ldrs: hdwy on inner 3f out: rdn wl over 1f out and sn btn* **14/1**
2220 **8** *hd* **Nightjar (USA)**[9] [6276] 3-8-9 **81**........ JoeFanning 9 61
(M Johnston) *prom whn carried rt bnd after 1f: chsd ldrs tl rdn along 3f out and sn wknd* **16/1**
210 **9** *4 1/2* **Rochefort (IRE)**[30] [5695] 3-9-4 **90**........ JimmyFortune 4 59
(J H M Gosden) *in rr: sme hdwy 3f out: drvn 2f out and nvr a factor* **3/1**[1]

5300 **10** *5* **By Command**[24] 5862 3-8-13 **85**....(b) JimmyQuinn 7 43
(J L Dunlop) *dwlt: a in rr* **16/1**

050 **11** *14* **Navajo Joe (IRE)**[24] 5862 3-8-13 **85**.... LDettori 6 11
(B J Meehan) *led tl hung rt and hdd bnd after 1f: cl up and hanging rt thrght: rdn over 2f out: wkng whn edgd rt home bnd: sn eased and bhd* **11/1**

1m 48.17s (2.27) **Going Correction** +0.425s/f (Yiel) **11** Ran SP% **117.6**
Speed ratings (Par 105): **105,104,101,99,93 92,90,89,85,80 66**
toteswinger: 1&2 £16.60, 1&3 £23.80, 2&3 £20.80. CSF £65.26 CT £892.16 TOTE £12.50: £4.20, £2.30, £4.10; EX 101.60.

Owner Ron Hull **Bred** Dr Dean Harron **Trained** Tickhill, S Yorks

■ Stewards' Enquiry : Jimmy Fortune one-day ban: careless riding (Oct 27)

FOCUS
This was a decent handicap. The winner improved by 7lb with a nice return from the runner-up.

NOTEBOOK
Mangham(IRE), 3lb higher than when making all at Haydock in August, had since run poorly at Ripon, but he came right back to his best here. Presented with the lead after Navajo Joe ran wide at the first bend, he was the last one off the bridle and, despite displaying his customary awkward head carriage, always looked to be doing enough. Effective from 1m-1m2f, he acts on any ground and may well progress further. Connections are likely to aim him at next season's Lincoln. (tchd 12-1)

Jack Dawkins(USA), two from two in nurseries towards the end of last season, was returning from nearly a year off and had a 7lb higher mark to contend with but he seems to have progressed further and did his best to reel in the winner. This run should shake any rust and he remains open to further improvement, with a step up to 1m4f unlikely to present a problem. (op 4-1)

Unbreak My Heart(IRE), second to Mangham at Haydock in August, was 4lb better off this time but could not be fancied as his two subsequent efforts had been abysmal. He ran well here, travelling up strongly leaving the back and keeping on down the straight. Consistency is clearly not his strong point. (op 14-1)

Once A Gulch(USA), 1lb lower than when flopping on his handicap debut at Great Leighs, was having his first taste of turf and ran well, coming wide into the straight and keeping on for pressure. He needs to improve to win off his current mark, but that is possible.

Topazes has already had a profitable season and he was unable to get any closer to the winner than he did at Haydock. The handicapper looks in control right now. (tchd 8-1 and 10-1 in places)

Rochefort(IRE), 8lb higher than when winning an ordinary handicap on the Newmarket July course on his penultimate outing, ran a lifeless race at Kempton last time and it was much the same here. He was under pressure early and never picked up. Official explanation: jockey said colt never travelled (op 5-1)

Navajo Joe(IRE) Official explanation: jockey said colt hung right

6527 PHIL BULL TROPHY CONDITIONS STKS 2m 1f 216y
3:40 (3:40) (Class 3) 3-Y-O+
£9,346 (£2,799; £1,399; £700; £349; £175) **Stalls** Low

Form RPR

25-5 **1** **Veracity**[23] 5885 4-9-3 108.... LDettori 5 102
(Saeed Bin Suroor) *chsd clr ldr: hdwy 3f out: rdn to chal over 1f out and sn led: kpt on wl u.p fnl f* **7/4**[1]

3320 **2** *1 1/4* **Bogside Theatre (IRE)**[24] 5853 4-8-12 92.... PJMcDonald 3 96
(G M Moore) *led and sn clr: pushed along over 2f out: rdn wl over 1f out: sn drvn and hdd over 1f out: kpt on u.p fnl f* **6/1**[3]

1031 **3** *10* **Tarkheena Prince (USA)**[16] 6107 3-8-6 91 ow1.... JamieSpencer 4 91
(G A Swinbank) *hld up towards rr: hdwy to trck ldrs after 6f: effrt over 3f out and sn rdn: drvn 2f out and plugged on same pce* **9/2**[2]

0010 **4** *5* **Baddam**[24] 5854 6-9-3 92.... JimmyFortune 13 85
(Ian Williams) *chsd ldng pair: rdn along 4f out: drvn and outpcd 3f out: plugged on u.p fnl 2f* **14/1**

2102 **5** *1 3/4* **Dolly Penrose**[58] 4866 3-8-0 80.... JimmyQuinn 8 78
(M R Channon) *hld up towards rr: hdwy 6f out: effrt to chse ldrs over 3f out and sn rdn: drvn 2f out and sn wknd* **15/2**

6 *9* **Tazbar (IRE)**[165] 6-9-3 0.... TomEaves 10 73+
(K G Reveley) *hld up in rr: sme hdwy over 4f out: rdn along over 3f out: nvr nr ldrs* **6/1**[3]

2421 **7** *3 1/2* **Sphinx (FR)**[17] 6071 10-9-3 83.... (b) PaulMulrennan 7 69
(E W Tuer) *hld up: sme hdwy over 4f out: rdn along over 3f out: nvr a factor* **16/1**

4250 **8** *2* **Victory Quest (IRE)**[18] 6054 8-9-3 65.... (v) PAspell 1 67
(Mrs S Lyman) *in tch: rdn along over 4f out and sn outpcd* **100/1**

1114 **9** *2* **Let It Be**[8] 6313 7-8-12 75.... TonyCulhane 12 59
(K G Reveley) *hld up: sme hdwy over 4f out: sn rdn along and nvr a factor* **33/1**

3-00 **10** *15* **Mceldowney**[21] 5961 6-9-0 67.... LeeVickers[(3)] 9 48
(M C Chapman) *chsd ldrs: rdn along 5f out: sn wknd* **100/1**

4m 9.37s (5.47) **Going Correction** +0.425s/f (Yiel)
WFA 3 from 4yo+ 12lb **10** Ran SP% **112.4**
Speed ratings (Par 107): **104,103,99,96,96 92,90,89,88,82**
toteswinger: 1&2 £3.40, 1&3 £3.20, 2&3 £7.50. CSF £11.82 TOTE £2.40: £1.30, £2.20, £1.70; EX 13.30.

Owner Godolphin **Bred** Darley **Trained** Newmarket, Suffolk

■ Stewards' Enquiry : Jimmy Quinn two-day ban: careless riding (Oct 20-21)

FOCUS
A good staying event but not a race to read much into and the form is pretty muddling, with the first two given a pretty easy time of it up front.

NOTEBOOK
Veracity, second in last season's Goodwood Cup and fifth in the St Leger, finished a well-beaten fifth over an inadequate trip on his seasonal reappearance at Chester, but had the benefit of that run under his belt and was always likely to fare better returned to this kind of trip. He raced clear with the runner-up down the back straight and, despite being the first of the pair off the bridle, he came strong in the straight, leading over a furlong out and staying on well. This was still some way below his best form but at least he is back on track. (op 5-2 tchd 11-4 in places)

Bogside Theatre(IRE) is one tough filly. She has run so many gutsy races in defeat this season, her front-running style often leaving her vulnerable late on in races, and she was once again unable to hold on. This was a good effort against the winner at the weights and she now heads for the Cesarewitch. (op 8-1)

Tarkheena Prince(USA), a progressive handicapper stepping up five furlongs in trip, was left behind leaving the back straight but stayed on again to reclaim third. (op 10-3)

Baddam stays all day and kept plodding away for fourth. He could have done with a quicker surface. (tchd 12-1)

Dolly Penrose, another progressive type, seemed to find 2m stretching her at Newmarket last time and she failed to get home over this even longer trip. (op 6-1)

Tazbar(IRE) was making a belated Flat debut. A general 20-1 shot for next year's World Hurdle, he was soon in rear and came under strong pressure down the far side. It would have been nice to see him show a little more, but he kept on in his own time and is expected to improve for the outing. (op 7-1 tchd 15-2)

6528 BUCCOO REEF "PREMIER" CLAIMING STKS 1m 4y
4:10 (4:10) (Class 4) 3-Y-O **£6,476** (£1,927; £963; £481) **Stalls** Low

Form RPR

102 **1** **Ogre (USA)**[20] 5994 3-7-13 74.... JimmyQuinn 2 81
(P D Evans) *trckd ldrs: smooth hdwy on inner 2f out: swtchd rt and effrt over 1f out: rdn to ld appr fnl f and sn clr* **7/1**[3]

3130 **2** *5* **Gross Prophet**[10] 6242 3-8-4 75.... SilvestreDeSousa 7 74
(Tom Dascombe) *cl up: rdn to ld briefly 1 1/2f out: sn drvn and hdd appr fnl f: kpt on u.p: no ch w wnr* **7/2**[2]

2326 **3** *3 1/4* **Welcome Return (IRE)**[61] 4741 3-7-10 65....(b) DuranFentiman[(3)] 9 62
(T D Easterby) *led: rdn along over 2f out: drvn and hdd wl over 1f out: kpt on same pce* **25/1**

1046 **4** *1/2* **Indian Skipper (IRE)**[24] 5865 3-9-0 77.... PaulMulrennan 12 76+
(M H Tompkins) *stdd s and hld up in rr: hdwy over 2f out: hung lft wl over 1f out: sn rdn and styd on ins fnl f: nrst fin* **12/1**

2156 **5** *1* **Sacrilege**[27] 5773 3-9-2 76.... MarcHalford[(3)] 10 79
(D R C Elsworth) *hld up in tch: hdwy 3f out: rdn along 2f out: sn drvn and no imp* **7/1**[3]

0000 **6** *4 1/2* **Fool's Wildcat (USA)**[19] 6035 3-8-9 78....(b) TomEaves 8 58
(B J Meehan) *hld up: hdwy over 3f out: rdn along over 2f out: sn drvn and no imp fr wl over 1f out* **22/1**

2206 **7** *4* **Taken (IRE)**[19] 6021 3-8-10 74....(p) TonyCulhane 1 50+
(Miss Gay Kelleway) *hld up towards rr: pushed along on inner whn n.m.r and hmpd wl over 1f out: nvr a factor* **33/1**

2442 **8** *1/2* **Diamond Yas (IRE)**[19] 6027 3-8-7 81.... TPQueally 11 46
(H R A Cecil) *hld up in tch: hdwy 3f out: rdn to chse ldrs 2f out: sn drvn and wknd* **6/4**[1]

345 **9** *6* **Joinedupwriting**[42] 5362 3-7-13 64.... KellyHarrison[(5)] 4 29
(R M Whitaker) *cl up: rdn along 3f out: drvn over 2f out and sn wknd* **16/1**

2-00 **10** *55* **Louis Seffens (USA)**[149] 2008 3-8-9 66....(t) PJMcDonald 5 —
(G A Swinbank) *in tch: rdn along 3f out: wknd qckly and sn bhd: eased over 1f out* **40/1**

1m 48.13s (2.23) **Going Correction** +0.425s/f (Yiel) **10** Ran SP% **114.4**
Speed ratings (Par 103): **105,100,96,96,95 90,86,86,80,25**
toteswinger: 1&2 £3.90, 1&3 £13.10, 2&3 £16.00. CSF £29.83 TOTE £7.30: £2.00, £1.80, £5.00; EX 33.40.

Owner Diamond Racing Ltd **Bred** Gulf Coast Farms LLC **Trained** Pandy, Monmouths

■ Stewards' Enquiry : Marc Halford two-day ban: careless riding (Oct 20-21)
Paul Mulrennan caution: careless riding.

FOCUS
This was a decent claimer and the time was the best of the three races over the trip. The form looks sound, the winner up 8lb.

Sacrilege Official explanation: jockey said gelding was unsuited by the good (good to soft places) ground

Taken(IRE) Official explanation: jockey said gelding suffered interference

Louis Seffens(USA) Official explanation: jockey said colt suffered a breathing problem

6529 DEM WINDOW SOLUTIONS H'CAP 1m 4f 8y
4:40 (4:42) (Class 5) (0-70,70) 3-Y-O **£3,885** (£1,156; £577; £288) **Stalls** Low

Form RPR

2534 **1** **Bollin Greta**[15] 6155 3-8-7 **59**.... DavidAllan 7 67+
(T D Easterby) *midfield: hdwy 3f out: pushed along and n.m.r 2f out: rdn and styd on to chse ldr ent fnl f: sn led: kpt on wl towards fin* **14/1**

6312 **2** *1/2* **Hawk Mountain (UAE)**[32] 5637 3-8-13 **65**.... GrahamGibbons 8 72+
(J J Quinn) *towards rr: pushed along on inner after 4f: rdn along 1/2-way: swtchd rt 3f out: rdn and n.m.r wl over 1f out: swtchd outside and drvn ent fnl f: styd on strly towards fin* **5/2**[1]

456 **3** *1 3/4* **Garra Molly (IRE)**[18] 6055 3-8-13 **65**.... JamieSpencer 11 70+
(G A Swinbank) *hld up towards rr: stdy hdwy on outer 3f out: rdn to chse ldrs and edgd lft over 1f out: sn drvn and kpt on fnl f* **11/1**

2436 **4** *2 1/4* **Red Lily (IRE)**[20] 6007 3-9-1 **67**.... TPQueally 13 68
(J R Fanshawe) *trckd ldrs: hdwy to ld 3f out: rdn clr wl over 1f out: drvn and wandered ent fnl f: sn hdd and one pce* **10/1**

5206 **5** *1 1/4* **Berry Baby (IRE)**[51] 5105 3-8-8 **60**.... AndrewElliott 2 59
(G A Butler) *trckd ldrs: rdn along and lost pl 4f out: sn in rr: hdwy wl over 1f out: styd on ins fnl f: nrst fin* **9/1**

44-3 **6** *nk* **Ibrox (IRE)**[18] 6042 3-8-13 **65**.... SilvestreDeSousa 12 64
(A D Brown) *hld up towards rr: hdwy 3f out: rdn to chse ldrs wl over 1f out: sn drvn and one pce ent fnl f* **16/1**

6044 **7** *1 1/4* **Fantastic Lass**[14] 6175 3-8-4 **56** oh3.... DaleGibson 5 53
(R A Fahey) *prom: effrt 3f out: rdn to chse ldr 2f out: sn drvn and wknd appr fnl f* **20/1**

320 **8** *2 1/4* **Dubai Petal (IRE)**[16] 6107 3-9-4 **70**.... JimmyQuinn 1 63
(J S Moore) *chsd ldrs: rdn along over 2f out: grad wknd fr wl over 1f out* **9/2**[2]

6403 **9** *1 3/4* **Bet Noir (IRE)**[18] 6044 3-8-10 **62**.... ShaneKelly 10 52
(W R Swinburn) *trckd ldrs: hdwy over 3f out: rdn along and ev ch 2f out: sn drvn and wknd over 1f out* **9/1**

6216 **10** *3 1/4* **Shaylee**[15] 6155 3-8-5 **57**.... JoeFanning 6 42
(T D Walford) *chsd ldr: hdwy and cl up 3f out: ev ch tl rdn 2f out and grad wknd* **25/1**

4201 **11** *3/4* **Pondapie (IRE)**[13] 6185 3-9-4 **70**....(p) TomEaves 9 54
(R M Whitaker) *hld up in rr: stdy hdwy on outer 3f out: rdn to chse ldrs 2f out: sn drvn and wknd* **8/1**[3]

-500 **12** *53* **Elusive Deal (USA)**[9] 6275 3-8-4 **56** oh3.... PaulQuinn 3 —
(Mrs L Williamson) *led: rdn along 4f out: hdd 3f out: wknd qckly and sn bhd* **66/1**

2m 46.35s (5.55) **Going Correction** +0.425s/f (Yiel) **12** Ran SP% **117.9**
Speed ratings (Par 101): **98,97,96,95,94 93,93,91,90,88 87,52**
toteswinger: 1&2 £10.40, 1&3 £14.90, 2&3 £5.90. CSF £47.86 CT £416.15 TOTE £17.50: £3.80, £1.60, £2.80; EX 41.30.

Owner Sir Neil Westbrook **Bred** Sir Neil & Exors Of Late Lady Westbrook **Trained** Great Habton, N Yorks

FOCUS
A modest handicap but potentially fair form for the grade with the first three all looking capable of better. The form is rated through the fourth and sixth with the winner up 6lb.

6530 MARACAS BAY MAIDEN STKS — 1m 4y
5:10 (5:10) (Class 5) 3-Y-O — £3,238 (£963; £481; £240) Stalls Low

Form — RPR

6- **1** **Jaadull**[451] 3479 3-9-3 0 .... JoeFanning 1 — 84+
(M Johnston) *cl up: led over 2f out: rdn clr wl over 1f out: drvn ins fnl f: kpt on wl* **9/4**[2]

0- **2** ½ **Etosha (IRE)**[353] 6295 3-9-3 0 .... ShaneKelly 16 — 83+
(Saeed Bin Suroor) *hld up towards rr: hdwy on outer 2f out: rdn over 1f out: styd on strly ins fnl f* **5/1**

6 **3** ¾ **Shamali**[27] 5786 3-9-3 0 .... TonyCulhane 2 — 81+
(W J Haggas) *hld up towards rr: gd hdwy 2f out: rdn to chse ldrs and rn green appr fnl f: styd on wl towards fin* **16/1**

4522 **4** 7 **Totem Flower (IRE)**[21] 5964 3-8-12 74 .... PaulMulrennan 14 — 60
(R Charlton) *trckd ldrs: hdwy on outer 3f out: ev ch 2f out: sn rdn and wknd over 1f out* **2/1**[1]

2530 **5** 1¼ **Dream Of Olwyn (IRE)**[25] 5836 3-8-12 62 .... TPQueally 5 — 57
(J G Given) *in tch: hdwy to chse ldrs over 2f out: sn rdn and ev ch tl drvn wl over 1f out and sn wknd* **16/1**

24 **6** 4½ **Alsace Lorraine (IRE)**[80] 4161 3-8-12 0 .... JamieSpencer 4 — 47
(J R Fanshawe) *hld up in midfield: hdwy 3f out: rdn to chse ldrs wl over 1f out: sn drvn and no imp* **9/2**[3]

0000 **7** 7 **Carlton Mac**[41] 5380 3-9-3 41 .... JimmyQuinn 13 — 36
(N Bycroft) *a towards rr* **100/1**

00 **8** 1¾ **Promise Maker (USA)**[16] 6114 3-9-3 0 .... GrahamGibbons 15 — 32
(T D Walford) *hld up: a in rr* **40/1**

0064 **9** 9 **Amyann (IRE)**[38] 5471 3-8-12 47 .... TomEaves 11 — 6
(J R Holt) *cl up: led 1/2-way: rdn along and hdd over 2f out: sn wknd* **100/1**

0000 **10** 2 **Amber Ridge**[38] 5457 3-9-3 42 ....(t) DarrenWilliams 9 — 6
(B P J Baugh) *chsd ldrs: rdn along 3f out: drvn and wknd over 2f out* **100/1**

11 1¾ **Oskari** 3-9-3 0 .... JamieMoriarty 12 — 2
(P T Midgley) *s.i.s: a in rr* **100/1**

00 **12** 3½ **Distant Rainbow (IRE)**[58] 4877 3-9-3 0 .... DavidAllan 8 — —
(M Brittain) *a in rr* **150/1**

0-00 **13** 11 **Tiegan An Josh**[37] 5505 3-8-7 16 .... KellyHarrison(5) 7 — —
(A Crook) *chsd ldrs: rdn along 3f out and sn wknd* **200/1**

0 **14** 26 **Occasion**[16] 6114 3-8-12 0 .... PJMcDonald 10 — —
(G M Moore) *led to 1/2-way: sn rdn along and wknd 3f out* **100/1**

1m 48.93s (3.03) **Going Correction** +0.425s/f (Yiel) — **14 Ran SP% 119.3**
Speed ratings (Par 101): **101,100,99,92,91 87,80,78,69,67 65,62,51,25**
toteswinger: 1&2 £3.70, 1&3 £8.40, 2&3 £9.10. CSF £14.00 TOTE £4.00: £1.70, £1.60, £2.90; EX 18.20 Place 6 £179.41, Place 5 £81.12.
Owner Sheikh Ahmed Al Maktoum **Bred** Darley **Trained** Middleham Moor, N Yorks

FOCUS
Not a bad little maiden.
T/Plt: £195.70 to a £1 stake. Pool: £64,325.77. 239.90 winning tickets. T/Qpdt: £61.10 to a £1 stake. Pool: £4,141.08. 50.10 winning tickets. JR

6357 WARWICK (L-H)
Monday, October 6

OFFICIAL GOING: Good to soft (soft in places) changing to soft after race 1 (1.50)
The ground had been fast at declaration time and there were 21 non-runners due to the conditions.
Wind: Almost nil Weather: Some drizzle

6531 RACING UK MAIDEN STKS — 6f
1:50 (1:53) (Class 5) 2-Y-O — £3,885 (£1,156; £577; £288) Stalls Centre

Form — RPR

1 **Purissima (USA)** 2-8-12 0 .... RyanMoore 12 — 81+
(Sir Michael Stoute) *trckd ldr: racd keenly: led over 1f out: qcknd clr* **7/1**[3]

2 4½ **Nemorosa** 2-8-12 0 .... LiamJones 15 — 65+
(W J Haggas) *hld up: hdwy over 2f out: styd on to go 2nd nr fin: no ch w wnr* **15/2**

5 **3** hd **Battle**[17] 6077 2-9-3 0 .... DarrylHolland 1 — 69
(H Morrison) *chsd ldrs: shkn up over 2f out: edgd lft over 1f out: styd on same pce* **11/4**[2]

46 **4** 1½ **Albaseet (IRE)**[22] 5929 2-9-3 0 .... RHills 8 — 65
(M P Tregoning) *led: rdn and hdd over 1f out: wknd ins fnl f* **13/8**[1]

5 nk **Diapason (IRE)** 2-8-12 0 .... RichardKingscote 6 — 59
(Tom Dascombe) *chsd ldrs: rdn 1/2-way: styd on same pce fnl 2f* **16/1**

000 **6** 1¼ **Hellbender (IRE)**[64] 4665 2-9-3 48 .... GeorgeBaker 10 — 60
(S Kirk) *hld up in tch: rdn over 2f out: styd on same pce* **50/1**

00 **7** nk **Bob Stock (IRE)**[17] 6083 2-9-3 0 .... StephenDonohoe 13 — 59+
(W J Musson) *s.i.s: hld up: rdn over 2f out: nvr nrr* **66/1**

65 **8** 3¼ **Tricky Trev (USA)**[39] 5430 2-9-3 0 .... PaulDoe 11 — 49+
(S Curran) *prom: rdn over 2f out: wkng whn hung lft over 1f out* **16/1**

9 1¼ **Drum Dragon** 2-8-12 0 .... WilliamBuick 17 — 41
(M H Tompkins) *dwlt: hld up: a in rr* **33/1**

10 ½ **Princess Soraya** 2-8-7 0 .... WilliamCarson(5) 4 — 39
(R Dickin) *dwlt: a in rr* **66/1**

0 **11** ½ **Exopuntia**[19] 6010 2-8-9 0 .... MichaelJStainton(3) 9 — 38
(R M Whitaker) *s.i.s: rdn 1/2-way: a in rr* **66/1**

12 28 **Pepin (IRE)** 2-9-3 0 .... PaulHanagan 7 — —
(D Haydn Jones) *s.s: a in rr* **40/1**

1m 14.41s (2.61) **Going Correction** +0.35s/f (Good) — **12 Ran SP% 112.6**
Speed ratings (Par 95): **96,90,89,87,87 85,85,80,79,78 77,40**
toteswinger: 1&2 £5.70, 1&3 £4.30, 2&3 £7.10. CSF £53.26 TOTE £5.30: £2.00, £2.60, £1.30; EX 45.60.
Owner K Abdulla **Bred** Juddmonte Farms Inc **Trained** Newmarket, Suffolk

FOCUS
The ground was changed to soft (from good to soft, soft in places) after this race, but some of the jockeys felt it was only riding on the easy side of good. Just a modest juvenile sprint maiden from the front pair should certainly progress.

NOTEBOOK
Purissima(USA), a daughter of Fusaichi Pegasus, is a half-sister to top-class multiple 7f-1m winner Etoile Montante. She was fitted with a cross noseband and was inclined to race a little keenly close up through the early stages, but she was still full of running early in the straight. Just pushed out with hands and heels, she came well clear for an impressive success. She looks a very useful filly in the making and should do even better when able to get a lead in a stronger-run race, with quicker ground possibly also likely to suit. However, she will need to learn to settle better, especially if she is going to stay further. (op 7-2 tchd 15-2)
Nemorosa, a daughter of Pivotal, out of a 6f juvenile winner, made a pleasing debut. She was no match for the winner, but showed plenty of ability and looked as though she will improve for the run. (op 9-1 tchd 11-1)
Battle showed ability on his debut at Newbury and this was another respectable effort. He might find a sprint maiden, but will also have the option of handicaps after one more run. (op 4-1 tchd 9-4)
Albaseet(IRE) had every chance from the front but basically wasn't good enough, although he did race more towards the far side (usually a disadvantage on soft ground at Warwick) than most of these. He is now qualified for a handicap mark and might do better on quicker ground. (op 7-4)
Diapason(IRE) made a respectable introduction and gave the impression she will be all the better of this experience. (op 12-1 tchd 10-1)
Tricky Trev(USA) was keeping on when squeezed up against the stands' rail by Hellbender and might do better now he is qualified for a handicap mark. Official explanation: jockey said colt suffered slight interference in running (op 18-1)

6532 WARWICKRACECOURSE.CO.UK H'CAP — 6f
2:20 (2:21) (Class 4) (0-85,85) 3-Y-O+ — £5,180 (£1,541; £770; £384) Stalls Centre

Form — RPR

6210 **1** **Mullein**[17] 6069 3-9-5 85 .... GeorgeBaker 2 — 97+
(R M Beckett) *a.p: led wl over 1f out: rdn and hung rt fnl f: r.o wl* **11/2**[2]

0440 **2** 1¾ **Topflightcoolracer**[9] 6278 4-9-1 80 .... LiamJones 17 — 86
(Mrs G S Rees) *reluctant to leave paddock and mounted on crse: led: rdn and hdd wl over 1f out: hld on for 2nd* **18/1**

3320 **3** hd **Tadalavil**[5] 6402 3-8-10 76 .... DarryllHolland 10 — 81
(M R Channon) *swtchd rt sn after s: a.p: kpt on ins fnl f* **10/1**

0650 **4** nk **Glasshoughton**[17] 6069 5-8-7 75 .... NeilBrown(3) 13 — 79+
(M Dods) *stdd s: hld up in rr: swtchd lft and hdwy over 1f out: rdn fnl f: kpt on* **8/1**[3]

3000 **5** hd **Quest For Success (IRE)**[93] 3723 3-8-11 77 .... PaulHanagan 9 — 81
(R A Fahey) *hld up in tch: rdn over 1f out: kpt on ins fnl f* **16/1**

022 **6** 1¼ **Jeninsky (USA)**[25] 5841 3-8-13 84 .... DavidProbert(5) 8 — 88+
(Rae Guest) *plld hrd in mid-div: rdn and hdwy on stands' rail over 1f out: nt clr run ins fnl f: n.d after* **7/2**[1]

0060 **7** nk **Bonnie Prince Blue**[25] 5831 5-8-13 78 ....(b) RyanMoore 4 — 77
(B W Hills) *prom: rdn wl over 1f out: fdd ins fnl f* **8/1**[3]

1135 **8** hd **Muftarres (IRE)**[37] 5510 3-8-11 77 .... RHills 1 — 75
(Sir Michael Stoute) *mid-div: rdn and hdwy over 1f out: wknd wl ins fnl f* **11/2**[2]

0340 **9** 1½ **Ice Planet**[17] 6066 7-8-4 76 .... AdeleRothery(7) 3 — 69
(D Nicholls) *hld up towards rr: rdn wl over 1f out: no rspnse* **12/1**

-100 **10** ½ **Restless Genius (IRE)**[52] 5067 3-8-11 77 ....(t) WilliamBuick 7 — 69
(A M Balding) *n.m.r s: hld up in tch: rdn and wknd 2f out* **14/1**

6000 **11** 3½ **Obe Gold**[17] 6069 6-9-0 84 .... IDaCosta(5) 15 — 65
(D Nicholls) *uns rdr leaving paddock and bolted to s: sltly hmpd after s: hld up and bhd: rdn 2f out: no rspnse* **33/1**

1010 **12** 1½ **Crying Aloud (USA)**[20] 5990 3-9-5 85 ....(b[1]) GregFairley 5 — 61
(P A Blockley) *a in rr* **25/1**

1m 13.09s (1.29) **Going Correction** +0.35s/f (Good)
WFA 3 from 4yo+ 1lb — **12 Ran SP% 116.6**
Speed ratings (Par 105): **105,102,102,102,101 100,99,99,97,96 92,90**
toteswinger: 1&2 £26.20, 1&3 £13.10, 2&3 £36.90. CSF £98.42 CT £979.65 TOTE £6.60: £2.20, £5.90, £3.20; EX 178.20.
Owner Landmark Racing Limited **Bred** C D S Bryce And Mrs M Bryce **Trained** Whitsbury, Hants

FOCUS
A fair, competitive sprint handicap, but they finished in a bit of a heap behind the decisive winner. They raced middle to stands' side in the straight and front runners seemed at an advantage. The form looks pretty sound.

6533 WEATHERBYS BANK NURSERY — 6f
2:50 (2:52) (Class 3) (0-95,88) 2-Y-O — £7,771 (£2,312; £1,155; £577) Stalls Centre

Form — RPR

3361 **1** **Noble Storm (USA)**[32] 5647 2-9-1 82 .... StephenDonohoe 3 — 87
(E S McMahon) *mde virtually all: rdn and edgd rt over 1f out: styd on* **5/1**[3]

1340 **2** 2 **Dove Mews**[24] 5855 2-9-0 81 .... HayleyTurner 7 — 80
(M L W Bell) *chsd wnr: rdn and edgd rt over 1f out: styd on* **16/1**

0311 **3** hd **Count Paris (USA)**[15] 6149 2-8-9 76 .... GregFairley 8 — 74
(M Johnston) *prom: rdn over 2f out: lost pl whn nt clr run over 1f out: rallied and hung lft ins fnl f: r.o* **10/3**[2]

5621 **4** nk **Kingswinford (IRE)**[45] 5228 2-8-6 73 .... JamesDoyle 4 — 71
(P D Evans) *chsd ldrs: rdn 1/2-way: hung rt over 1f out: styd on same pce fnl f* **11/1**

51 **5** ¾ **Darcey**[16] 6109 2-8-10 77 .... PaulHanagan 1 — 72
(R A Fahey) *chsd ldrs: rdn 1/2-way: no ex fnl f* **14/1**

1440 **6** ½ **La Brigitte**[16] 6102 2-9-4 88 .... TolleyDean(3) 5 — 82
(A J McCabe) *hld up: rdn over 1f out: nt trble ldrs* **16/1**

221 **7** nk **Bouvardia**[19] 6030 2-9-2 83 .... TedDurcan 9 — 76
(H R A Cecil) *hld up: racd keenly: sme hdwy over 1f out: sn rdn: no ex ins fnl f* **6/4**[1]

0004 **8** 7 **Klynch**[9] 6281 2-9-4 85 ....(b) DaneO'Neill 2 — 57
(B J Meehan) *hld up: rdn 1/2-way: wknd over 1f out* **25/1**

1m 13.2s (1.40) **Going Correction** +0.35s/f (Good) — **8 Ran SP% 110.4**
Speed ratings (Par 99): **104,101,101,100,99 99,98,89**
toteswinger: 1&2 £17.00, 1&3 £3.40, 2&3 £8.90. CSF £72.80 CT £287.35 TOTE £6.00: £1.90, £4.10, £1.70; EX 94.50.
Owner R L Bedding **Bred** Brereton C Jones **Trained** Lichfield, Staffs

FOCUS
This looked a decent enough nursery, but the first two home filled those positions pretty much throughout and few were ever involved. The winning time was good, only 0.11sec slower than the previous race won by a three-year-old rated 85, and 1.21sec faster than the opening juvenile maiden. They raced stands' side in the straight.

NOTEBOOK
Noble Storm(USA), just as when successful over an extended 5f here on his nursery debut, was able to dominate and he ran on strongly to defy an 8lb rise, despite having got warm beforehand. He is progressing into a very useful type and is well suited by easy ground, but he is unlikely to run again this year. (op 9-2 tchd 4-1)
Dove Mews has struggled a little since winning on her debut at Newmarket, but this was a respectable effort and she can have few excuses. (tchd 18-1)
Count Paris(USA) was chasing a hat-trick, but he could not defy a 4lb rise for his recent Hamilton success. He is probably better suited by a stiffer 6f, or an easy 7f. (op 11-2)

Kingswinford(IRE) had not been seen since winning a Newbury nursery off a 5lb lower mark 45 days earlier and he was comfortably held. (op 9-1)
Darcey seemingly found this tougher than the Catterick maiden she won. (op 15-2 tchd 7-1)
Bouvardia was a major disappointment. She made all at Yarmouth on her previous start, but could not dominate this time and failed to pick up. Official explanation: jockey said filly was unsuited by the soft ground (op 7-4 tchd 15-8)

6534 TURFTV MAIDEN AUCTION STKS (DIV I) 7f 26y
3:20 (3:22) (Class 5) 2-Y-O £2,914 (£867; £433; £216) Stalls Low

Form RPR
5 1 **Glowing Praise**[17] 6080 2-8-11 0 TedDurcan 4 71+
(E S McMahon) *t.k.h: a.p: rdn fnl f: r.o wl to ld cl home* **5/4**[1]
233 2 *nk* **Dr Jameson (IRE)**[20] 5989 2-8-12 75 PaulHanagan 12 71
(R A Fahey) *a.p: rdn over 1f out: led ins fnl f: edgd lft and hdd cl home* **2/1**[2]
2 3 *1 1/2* **Bea Menace (USA)**[10] 6245 2-8-8 0 DarryllHolland 9 63
(P F I Cole) *w ldr: led over 4f out: pushed along over 1f out: hdd ins fnl f: no ex towards fin* **7/2**[3]
4 *2* **Emeebee** 2-8-10 0 StephenDonohoe 2 60+
(W J Musson) *s.i.s: hld up in rr: swtchd rt jst over 1f out: r.o ins fnl f: nrst fin* **20/1**
0 5 *2 1/2* **On Cue (IRE)**[14] 6167 2-8-5 0 HayleyTurner 5 49
(J M P Eustace) *n.m.r s: hld up towards rr: sme prog over 1f out: n.d* **28/1**
0000 6 *3/4* **Susurrayshaan**[9] 6292 2-8-10 30 (v[1]) LiamJones 8 52?
(Mrs G S Rees) *hld up in tch: rdn 2f out: wkng whn hung lft over 1f out* **66/1**
60 7 *nse* **River Style (IRE)**[28] 5746 2-8-5 0 GregFairley 3 47
(A P Jarvis) *led: hdd over 4f out: chsd ldr tl over 2f out: rdn over 1f out: wknd ins fnl f* **66/1**
00 8 *6* **Jessy Jones**[17] 6089 2-7-13 0 DavidProbert(5) 10 31
(R Brotherton) *hld up: sn mid-div: rdn over 2f out: sn hung lft and wknd* **100/1**
00 9 *3 1/4* **Julie Mill (IRE)**[53] 5022 2-8-4 0 WilliamBuick 11 23
(P G Murphy) *s.i.s: a in rr* **100/1**
605 10 *nk* **Tax Dodger (IRE)**[42] 5365 2-8-7 58 TolleyDean(3) 1 28
(J L Spearing) *hld up in mid-div: rdn 3f out: sn bhd* **14/1**

1m 29.07s (4.47) **Going Correction** +0.35s/f (Good) **10 Ran SP% 119.8**
Speed ratings (Par 95): **88,87,85,83,80 79,79,73,69,68**
toteswinger: 1&2 £1.70, 1&3 £2.50, 2&3 £2.70. CSF £3.94 TOTE £2.00: £1.40, £1.10, £1.50; EX 5.70.
Owner J C Fretwell **Bred** Wyck Hall Stud Ltd **Trained** Lichfield, Staffs
■ Stewards' Enquiry : Paul Hanagan two-day ban: used whip with excessive frequency (Oct 20-21)

FOCUS
An ordinary juvenile maiden and the early pace was just steady, resulting in a time 2.08sec slower than the second division. The main action took place up the middle of the track. The form has been rated conservatively around the first three.

NOTEBOOK
Glowing Praise confirmed the promise he showed when fifth in a 6f maiden at Newmarket on his debut. Although he only got on top close home, he gave the impression he did this a shade cleverly. He is unlikely to run again this year, but could be useful at around 1m-1m2f next year, and his connections think he will be even better suited by quicker ground. (op 5-2 tchd 6-5)
Dr Jameson(IRE) had his chance on this step back up in trip but was just held. He should find a similar race at some point, and also has the option of handicaps. (tchd 7-4 and 5-2)
Bea Menace(USA) did not look to go too hard in front, but she was swamped late on. She was runner-up on quick ground first time out and conditions might have been soft enough for her. (op 11-4 tchd 9-2)
Emeebee, a gelded son of Medicean, kept on towards the stands' rail without ever getting close enough to land a telling blow. This was a pleasing introduction. (op 14-1)
On Cue(IRE) is probably more of a handicap prospect. (op 33-1 tchd 25-1)
River Style(IRE) could well find a race when going handicapping. She did not last home, but travelled well for a long way and will be of interest in moderate company over a sprint trip.

6535 TURFTV MAIDEN AUCTION STKS (DIV II) 7f 26y
3:50 (3:52) (Class 5) 2-Y-O £2,914 (£867; £433; £216) Stalls Low

Form RPR
3240 1 **Amber Sunset**[10] 6240 2-8-4 72 PaulHanagan 12 73
(J Jay) *mde all: rdn clr fnl f* **8/1**[3]
06 2 *7* **Oriental Cavalier**[19] 6014 2-8-10 0 TedDurcan 8 62
(R Hollinshead) *dwlt: hld up: hdwy over 2f out: hung rt over 1f out: r.o wl towards fin: no ch w wnr* **14/1**
0003 3 *nk* **Whisky Jack**[7] 6341 2-8-12 63 (b) RyanMoore 1 63
(W R Muir) *chsd wnr: rdn over 2f out: styd on same pce appr fnl f* **7/2**[2]
5 4 *2 1/4* **Baron Otto (IRE)**[16] 6122 2-8-12 0 LiamJones 7 57
(W J Haggas) *chsd ldrs: rdn over 2f out: wknd fnl f* **1/1**[1]
5 *shd* **Kingshill Prince** 2-8-9 0 StephenDonohoe 2 54+
(W J Musson) *s.s: hld up: shkn up over 1f out: r.o ins fnl f: nvr nr to chal* **66/1**
40 6 *1* **Seaquel**[23] 5901 2-8-0 0 DavidProbert(5) 11 47
(A B Haynes) *chsd ldrs: rdn 1/2-way: wknd 2f out* **28/1**
7 *1* **Akbabend** 2-8-11 0 GregFairley 4 51+
(M Johnston) *sn pushed along in rr: nvr nrr* **12/1**
000 8 *1* **Cabo Polonio (IRE)**[3] 6451 2-8-7 0 RichardKingscote 10 44
(S Kirk) *in rr and rdn 1/2-way: n.d* **100/1**
00 9 *3/4* **Ravine Rose**[12] 6205 2-8-4 0 (t) WilliamBuick 3 40
(B I Case) *prom: rdn 1/2-way: wknd over 2f out* **100/1**
3030 10 *nse* **Queen Sally (IRE)**[14] 6172 2-8-4 71 TolleyDean(3) 6 42
(J L Spearing) *hld up: plld hrd: hdwy 1/2-way: wknd over 2f out* **11/1**
5005 11 *4* **Indian Blade (IRE)**[70] 4475 2-8-10 53 HayleyTurner 9 35
(M D I Usher) *mid-div: rdn 1/2-way: wknd over 2f out* **80/1**

1m 26.99s (2.39) **Going Correction** +0.35s/f (Good) **11 Ran SP% 114.2**
Speed ratings (Par 95): **100,92,91,89,88 87,86,85,84,84 80**
toteswinger: 1&2 £10.40, 1&3 £3.70, 2&3 £7.50. CSF £105.60 TOTE £8.10: £1.50, £3.00, £1.70; EX 117.40.
Owner David J Orchard **Bred** Southill Stud **Trained** Newmarket, Suffolk

FOCUS
Another ordinary two-year-old maiden. The winning time was 2.08sec quicker than the first division, although that race was slowly run. Few of these were ever involved and the winner did not need to improve much to thrash this opposition. They raced middle to stands' side in the straight.

NOTEBOOK
Amber Sunset, trying 7f for the first time, was left alone up front and ran on strongly to get off the mark at the eighth attempt in decisive fashion. Although she could have more to offer over this trip, she looks flattered by the bare result and things are likely to be a lot tougher from now on. (op 6-1)
Oriental Cavalier very much caught the eye running on when the race was as good as over, making up several positions to take second near the line. He might be able to find a race in modest handicap company. (op 10-1)
Whisky Jack was well backed against the favourite, but he could only plug on at the one pace. He might do better back over shorter. (op 6-1 tchd 10-3)
Baron Otto(IRE) failed to pick up in the straight after racing a little keenly and could not confirm the promise he showed when fifth on his debut at Newbury. (tchd 11-10 in places)
Kingshill Prince, a gelded son of Mark Of Esteem, kept on from quite a way back under a considerate ride and could be one to look out for when handicapped. The stewards held an enquiry into his running and riding and noted explanations from connections. Official explanation: jockey said, regarding running and riding, instructions were to settle gelding as it was its first run and creep into race and make effort in home straight; he added gelding ran very free on way to post and lost rhythm in home straight. He therefore delayed his effort until approaching final furlong when gelding ran on past tired horses; trainer said gelding was found to be lame following day (op 50-1)
Akbabend was keeping on in the closing stages and will know a lot more next time. (tchd 18-1)
Cabo Polonio(IRE) Official explanation: jockey said filly lost a shoe
Queen Sally(IRE) Official explanation: jockey said the filly ran too free

6536 WEATHERBYS BLOODSTOCK INSURANCE H'CAP 1m 2f 188y
4:20 (4:20) (Class 3) (0-95,93) 3-Y-O+ £9,714 (£2,890; £1,444; £721) Stalls Low

Form RPR
3223 1 **First Avenue**[46] 5199 3-8-9 86 (p) WilliamBuick 1 96
(M A Jarvis) *led after 1f: rdn and wandered fr over 1f out: carried hd high ins fnl f: drvn out* **6/4**[1]
610 2 *3/4* **Voice Coach (IRE)**[58] 4867 3-8-10 87 RyanMoore 5 96
(Sir Michael Stoute) *hld up in tch: lost pl 5f out: hdwy on ins 3f out: rdn and chsd wnr over 1f out: nt qckn towards fin* **7/1**[3]
6026 3 *4 1/2* **Capable Guest (IRE)**[18] 6041 6-9-0 90 (v) MCGeran(5) 2 91
(M R Channon) *hld up towards rr: rdn over 2f out: styd on fr over 1f out: tk 3rd cl home* **16/1**
1455 4 *hd* **Press The Button (GER)**[13] 6196 5-8-9 83 JackMitchell(3) 6 84
(J R Boyle) *led 1f: w wnr: rdn 3f out: lost 2nd over 1f out: wknd ins fnl f* **25/1**
2654 5 *1 1/4* **Eglevski (IRE)**[25] 5843 4-8-12 83 (b) DaneO'Neill 7 82
(J L Dunlop) *t.k.h in mid-div: hdwy 5f out: rdn wl over 1f out: wknd fnl f* **11/2**[2]
0060 6 *2* **Lucky Dance (BRZ)**[16] 6103 6-8-8 82 NeilBrown(3) 8 77
(A G Foster) *prom: rdn 2f out: hung lft 1f out: wknd ins fnl f* **10/1**
0004 7 *1* **Best Prospect (IRE)**[18] 6041 6-9-2 87 (t) PaulHanagan 4 80
(M Dods) *hld up in rr: pushed along 5f out: nvr nr ldrs* **10/1**
3B60 8 *3* **Cheshire Prince**[10] 6238 4-9-0 85 LiamJones 10 73
(W M Brisbourne) *hld up in tch: rdn over 3f out: wknd wl over 1f out* **33/1**
0036 9 *13* **Olympic City (BRZ)**[14] 6171 5-9-7 92 TedDurcan 12 58
(M F De Kock, South Africa) *hld up in mid-div: bhd fnl 3f* **9/1**
10/0 10 *2 3/4* **Spectait**[16] 6123 6-9-5 90 GeorgeBaker 11 52
(Jonjo O'Neill) *stdd s: hld up wl in rr: effrt on ins 2f out: sn hung lft and wknd* **40/1**
1000 11 *10* **Profit's Reality (IRE)**[8] 6302 6-9-8 93 (p) DarryllHolland 13 38
(M J Attwater) *hld up towards rr: hdwy over 6f out: wknd 4f out: eased whn no ch over 2f out* **20/1**

2m 22.03s (0.93) **Going Correction** +0.35s/f (Good)
WFA 3 from 4yo+ 6lb **11 Ran SP% 115.9**
Speed ratings (Par 107): **110,109,106,106,105 103,102,100,91,89 82**
toteswinger: 1&2 £3.10, 1&3 £8.00, 2&3 £17.80. CSF £11.20 CT £121.81 TOTE £2.30: £1.10, £2.70, £4.40; EX 13.20.
Owner Michael Tabor **Bred** The National Stud Never Say Die Club Ltd **Trained** Newmarket, Suffolk

FOCUS
A fair handicap but the early pace was not frantic with the winner not given a hard time in front. It is doubtful he had to improve on his mildly progressive previous form.

NOTEBOOK
First Avenue, who has shown steadily improving form this season while also looking far from the most straightforward, was able to dominate almost throughout in first-time cheekpieces. The head did go up in the air as his rider asked for the maximum in the closing stages but to his credit he did find a bit extra when challenged by Voice Coach, and was nicely on top at the finish. He could yet progress further if the headgear continues to have a positive effect and a race like the November Handicap could be a suitable target. (op 5-2)
Voice Coach(IRE) was disappointing at Newmarket last time, albeit that form had been given a boost when the winner won the Cambridgeshire, and this was far more encouraging. A stronger pace would have probably suited him, though. (op 9-2 tchd 4-1)
Capable Guest(IRE) is hard to predict but he was back down to a mark 1lb lower than when successful in the Zetland Gold Cup in May, and he ran on well from off the pace to just edge the photo for third. (op 20-1)
Press The Button(GER) had the benefit of racing prominently in a race not run at a strong gallop, but he is a fast-ground horse and got quite tired in these conditions. (op 18-1)
Eglevski(IRE) had conditions to suit but he did not help his chances by racing keenly. (op 6-1)
Lucky Dance(BRZ) did not appear to see this longer trip out. (op 12-1)
Best Prospect(IRE) is a confirmed hold-up horse who needs a decent gallop to be seen at his best. This race just was not run to suit him. (op 9-1 tchd 8-1)
Olympic City(BRZ) Official explanation: jockey said mare was unsuited by the soft ground
Profit's Reality(IRE) Official explanation: jockey said gelding moved poorly

6537 WARWICK RACECOURSE FOR CONFERENCES H'CAP 1m 22y
4:50 (4:53) (Class 5) (0-75,75) 3-Y-O+ £3,885 (£1,156; £577; £288) Stalls Low

Form RPR
504 1 **Starlight Gazer**[27] 5779 5-8-6 65 (vt[1]) DavidProbert(5) 1 73
(J A Geake) *dwlt: sn chsng ldrs: edgd lft: led and hmpd over 1f out: sn hung rt: rdn out* **4/1**[3]
4436 2 *1 1/2* **Pitbull**[10] 6250 5-8-9 63 (p) LiamJones 10 68
(Mrs G S Rees) *hld up: racd keenly: hdwy 1/2-way: rdn and ev ch whn hung lft ins fnl f: no ex* **15/2**
1-45 3 *2 1/2* **Spring Goddess (IRE)**[198] 969 7-9-6 74 GregFairley 16 73
(A P Jarvis) *s.s: hld up: racd keenly: hdwy over 2f out: rdn 1f out: wknd towards fin* **20/1**
5061 4 *nk* **Andaman Sunset**[18] 6049 3-9-4 75 (b[1]) TedDurcan 11 74
(G Wragg) *sn pushed along and prom: outpcd over 4f out: styd on u.p fnl f* **15/2**
540- 5 *3/4* **Carson's Spirit (USA)**[305] 1920 4-9-6 74 RyanMoore 7 71
(W S Kittow) *trckd ldrs: racd keenly: lost pl over 3f out: styd on ins fnl f* **10/1**
1611 6 *hd* **Keys Of Cyprus**[18] 6043 6-9-0 75 NSLawes(7) 17 71
(D Nicholls) *led 1f: chsd ldr tl led again 3f out: sn rdn and hung lft: hdd over 1f out: sn wknd* **3/1**[1]
0224 7 *13* **Bikini**[44] 5291 3-9-1 72 DaneO'Neill 8 38
(H Candy) *led 7f out: hdd 3f out: sn rdn: hmpd and wknd over 1f out* **7/2**[2]

3602 **8** *hd* **Street Devil (USA)**[51] 4920 3-9-1 **72**.............................. DarryllHolland 5 38
(P A Blockley) *chsd ldrs: rdn over 3f out: wkng whn hung lft over 2f out* **10/1**

1m 44.41s (3.41) **Going Correction** +0.35s/f (Good)
WFA 3 from 4yo+ 3lb 8 Ran SP% **113.7**
Speed ratings (Par 103): **96,94,92,91,90 90,77,77**
toteswinger: 1&2 £7.40, 1&3 £11.20, 2&3 £8.40. CSF £33.33 CT £533.51 TOTE £5.70: £2.10, £2.30, £3.80; EX 40.90.
Owner The Burning Stars **Bred** Dr J M Leigh **Trained** Kimpton, Hants

FOCUS
Nine non-runners left a rather depleted field and this was just a modest handicap. They did not appar to go very quick but the front runners did not get home. The winner is rated close to this year's best.
Spring Goddess(IRE) Official explanation: jockey said mare missed the break

6538 JUMP SEASON NEXT H'CAP 1m 4f 134y
5:20 (5:21) (Class 6) (0-65,65) 3-Y-O+ **£2,729** (£806; £403) **Stalls** Low

Form RPR
6301 **1** **Opera Writer (IRE)**[6] 6364 5-9-4 **65** 6ex...................(p) DavidProbert(5) 1 71
(R Hollinshead) *hld up in tch: led over 4f out: rdn over 1f out: r.o* **3/1**[1]
5102 **2** *nk* **Jenny Soba**[14] 6161 5-8-13 **62** ow3..................... MrJPFeatherstone(7) 2 68
(Lucinda Featherstone) *hld up towards rr: hdwy over 4f out: chsd wnr 2f out: sn rdn: styd on towards fin* **8/1**
0063 **3** *8* **Corrib (IRE)**[16] 6136 5-9-4 **60**.............................. CatherineGannon 3 53
(B Palling) *hld up in rr: hdwy on ins over 3f out: rdn and outpcd 2f out: tk 3rd wl ins fnl f* **20/1**
0020 **4** *nk* **Good Effect (USA)**[19] 6022 4-9-4 **60**............................... GeorgeBaker 7 53
(C P Morlock) *led 2f: prom: disp ld over 4f out: rdn whn hung rt 2f out: sn wknd* **7/2**[2]
00-0 **5** *5* **Prima Ballerina**[28] 5750 4-9-2 **58**............................ RichardKingscote 6 43
(J G Portman) *prom tl wknd over 3f out* **25/1**
0054 **6** *½* **Sleepy Mountain**[16] 6136 4-8-13 **60**..................... WilliamCarson(5) 12 44
(A Middleton) *t.k.h: led after 2f tl over 4f out: wknd 3f out* **12/1**
0223 **7** *¾* **Leyte Gulf (USA)**[96] 3613 5-9-4 **60**................................ DaneO'Neill 4 43
(C C Bealby) *hld up in mid-div: hmpd and lost pl over 4f out: sn bhd* **4/1**[3]
1524 **8** *7* **Desert Hawk**[34] 5583 7-9-3 **59**.......................................(b) LiamJones 11 31
(W M Brisbourne) *ducked whn stalls opened: wnt lft and s.s: hld up in rr: rdn and hdwy 3f out: wknd 2f out* **12/1**
2500 **9** *39* **Fantasy Ride**[20] 6007 6-9-4 **60**.................................. DarryllHolland 13 —
(J Pearce) *sn prom: wknd over 4f out: eased whn no ch over 2f out* **7/1**

2m 50.49s (5.89) **Going Correction** +0.35s/f (Good) 9 Ran SP% **114.8**
Speed ratings (Par 101): **95,94,89,89,86 86,85,81,57**
toteswinger: 1&2 £5.80, 1&3 £6.30, 2&3 £12.10. CSF £27.44 CT £404.81 TOTE £3.80: £1.50, £1.80, £2.70; EX 24.50 Place 6 £60.98, Place 5 £35.63.
Owner John L Marriott **Bred** J Davison **Trained** Upper Longdon, Staffs
■ Stewards' Enquiry : Mr J P Featherstone two-day ban: used whip with excessive force (Oct 20-21)

FOCUS
A moderate handicap in which the first two finished clear, although neither really needed to improve.
Desert Hawk Official explanation: jockey said gelding stumbled when leaving the stalls
T/Plt: £97.10 to a £1 stake. Pool: £53,019.57. 398.31 winning tickets. T/Qpdt: £10.00 to a £1 stake. Pool: £3,925.54. 289.16 winning tickets. KH

6340 WINDSOR (R-H)
Monday, October 6

OFFICIAL GOING: Good to soft (6.8)
Wind: Almost nil Weather: Overcast

6539 EUROPEAN BREEDERS' FUND MAIDEN STKS 1m 67y
2:30 (2:33) (Class 4) 2-Y-O **£5,018** (£1,493; £746; £372) **Stalls** High

Form RPR
04 **1** **Call It On (IRE)**[17] 6083 2-9-3 0............................. SaleemGolam 12 81+
(M H Tompkins) *prom: led over 2f out: rdn 2 l clr over 1f out: kpt on wl: slipped up after fin* **12/1**
4 **2** *1* **Antinori (IRE)**[20] 5996 2-9-3 0.. AdamKirby 14 78+
(W R Swinburn) *hld up towards rr: prog 3f out: rdn to chse ldng pair over 1f out: styd on fnl f to snatch 2nd last strides* **7/1**[3]
32 **3** *hd* **Popiel**[33] 5599 2-9-3 0.. EddieAhern 9 77
(Saeed Bin Suroor) *trckd ldrs: prog 4f out: chsd wnr 2f out: kpt on but nvr really able to chal: lost 2nd last strides* **9/1**
03 **4** *5* **La Diosa (IRE)**[43] 5314 2-8-12 0.................................. MichaelHills 13 61
(W J Haggas) *hld up towards rr: prog on outer over 2f out: hanging over 1f out: kpt on fnl f: n.d* **5/1**[2]
04 **5** *nk* **Mitra Jaan (IRE)**[35] 5571 2-8-12 0..........................(t) EdwardCreighton 3 61+
(W R Swinburn) *in tch: trckd ldrs over 4f out: outpcd over 2f out: plugged on* **40/1**
3 **6** *2¼* **Coiled Spring**[17] 6085 2-9-3 0...................................... JimCrowley 7 61
(Mrs A J Perrett) *prom: chsd ldr over 5f out tl lost pl u.p over 3f out: struggling after* **13/8**[1]
66 **7** *3¾* **Cut And Thrust (IRE)**[14] 6165 2-9-3 0.......................... PhilipRobinson 10 53
(M A Jarvis) *led 1f: led over 5f out to over 2f out: wknd* **25/1**
8 *1* **Lennie Briscoe (IRE)** 2-9-3 0..................................... RichardHughes 1 50
(S Kirk) *hld up in last trio: pushed along and sme prog 3f out: no hdwy 2f out: wknd over 1f out* **33/1**
42 **9** *¾* **Sgt Roberts (IRE)**[19] 6008 2-9-3 0............................... SimonWhitworth 6 49
(J S Moore) *hld up in tch: prog and prom over 3f out: wknd over 2f out* **12/1**
60 **10** *4½* **Now**[88] 3869 2-8-12 0.. StephenCarson 2 34
(P Winkworth) *hld up in rr: gng wl enough 1/2-way: rdn 3f out: sn fdd* **100/1**
6 **11** *1* **Proper Holiday (USA)**[18] 6057 2-9-3 0............................ RobertHavlin 8 37
(P W Chapple-Hyam) *prom 2f: reminders over 4f out: lost pl sn after: struggling over 2f out* **16/1**
0 **12** *2¾* **City Bank (USA)**[11] 6230 2-9-3 0..................................... IanMongan 11 31
(M Johnston) *nvr gng wl: urged along in rr after 2f: nvr a factor* **10/1**
0 **13** *10* **Kessraa (IRE)**[42] 5344 2-9-3 0.. SamHitchcott 4 9
(M R Channon) *a struggling in last trio: wl bhd 3f out* **100/1**
0 **14** *19* **Red Dagger (IRE)**[20] 6000 2-9-3 0...................................... RichardThomas 5 —
(T D McCarthy) *led after 1f tl wd bnd over 5f out: sn lost pl and bhd: t.o* **100/1**

1m 46.66s (1.96) **Going Correction** +0.275s/f (Good) 14 Ran SP% **119.8**
Speed ratings (Par 97): **101,100,99,94,94 92,88,87,86,82 81,78,68,49**
toteswinger: 1&2 £13.60, 1&3 £16.80, 2&3 £14.30. CSF £90.46 TOTE £14.00: £4.30, £2.70, £2.10; EX 108.40 TRIFECTA Not won..
Owner GPD Investments (UK) Ltd **Bred** Martyn J McEnery **Trained** Newmarket, Suffolk

FOCUS
An average maiden which was run at a sound early pace and the runners elected to go over to the far side in the home straight. The form looks straightforward enough with the first three coming clear.

NOTEBOOK
Call It On(IRE) had shown much-improved form on his second outing 17 days previously and stepped up again as might have been expected over this longer distance. He was also racing on an easy surface for the first time, which helped his cause, and he responded most positively when asked to win the race from the furlong pole. He slipped up after passing the post, but was soon up on his feet and appeared to be fine. While his future lies with the Handicapper, he is open to more improvement over this sort of trip and, although his pedigree boasts a deal of speed, he obviously stays well. (op 10-1)
Antinori(IRE) ◆ stayed on stoutly on this switch to turf and turned in an improved effort for the step up in distance. He has scope and looks well up to shedding his maiden tag before the year is out (op 13-2 tchd 8-1)
Popiel showed a much more professional attitude on this first outing beyond 7f and turned in his best effort to date. He is the best guide to this form and now qualifies for a nursery mark. (op 8-1)
La Diosa(IRE) was keen in the preliminaries on this return from a 43-day break. She stayed on without threatening and performed a little below her previous level, but does now have the option of nurseries. (tchd 7-1)
Mitra Jaan(IRE) was racing in a first-time tongue tie and seemed to appreciate being ridden with greater restraint on the easier ground. She now qualifies for a mark.
Coiled Spring was in trouble shortly after turning in and still looked a bit green, but it was most likely the softer surface which acted against him. (op 9-4 tchd 11-8)

6540 THEATRE ROYAL "RUN FOR YOUR WIFE" NURSERY 5f 10y
3:00 (3:03) (Class 4) (0-95,91) 2-Y-O **£5,180** (£1,541; £770; £384) **Stalls** High

Form RPR
10 **1** **Cut The Cackle (IRE)**[32] 5642 2-8-12 **82**......................... JimCrowley 4 84+
(P Winkworth) *chsd ldrs: nt qckn whn tightened up jst over 1f out: rallied wl fnl f: r.o to ld last 50yds* **11/1**
0116 **2** *hd* **The Magic Of Rio**[9] 6281 2-8-11 **88**........................ AshleyMorgan(7) 11 88
(W J Haggas) *sltly outpcd in 6th: effrt on outer over 1f out: r.o to dispute ld last 50yds: jst pipped* **14/1**
0030 **3** *1½* **Fault**[4] 6426 2-9-3 **87**.. RichardHughes 5 82
(R Charlton) *w ldr: led after 2f: hdd over 1f out: rallied to press ldr ins fnl f: wknd last 50yds* **7/2**[2]
014 **4** *nse* **Cheviot (USA)**[16] 6118 2-8-13 **83**................................ PhilipRobinson 6 78
(M A Jarvis) *bmpd s: outpcd in last: prog on outer 1/2-way: led over 1f out: pushed along vigorously and edgd lft: wknd and hdd last 50yds* **8/11**[1]
6254 **5** *1¼* **Barnezet (GR)**[7] 6327 2-8-3 **73**... TPO'Shea 9 63
(R Hannon) *wnt lft s: in tch but hanging lft thrght: effrt over 1f out: nt qckn* **25/1**
103 **6** *¾* **To The Point**[99] 3528 2-8-10 **87**............................... MatthewDavies(7) 12 77+
(E S McMahon) *racd v freely bhd ldng pair: nt qckn whn squeezed out over 1f out: no imp after* **8/1**[3]
0004 **7** *6* **Louie's Lad**[22] 5933 2-8-2 **72** oh19 ow4....................(p) RichardThomas 1 38
(J A Geake) *led at str pce for 2f: losing pl whn hmpd against rail over 1f out: wknd* **100/1**

62.29 secs (1.99) **Going Correction** +0.275s/f (Good) 7 Ran SP% **111.1**
Speed ratings (Par 97): **95,94,92,92,90 89,79**
toteswinger: 1&2 £14.80, 1&3 £3.40, 2&3 £5.60. CSF £134.71 CT £630.46 TOTE £11.80: £4.10, £4.60; EX 85.10 Trifecta £368.90 Part won. Pool: £498.53 - 0.59 winning tickets..
Owner P Winkworth **Bred** Mountarmstrong Stud **Trained** Chiddingfold, Surrey

FOCUS
This nursery was weakened by five non-runners. There was a fair pace on and the runners again went over to the far side down the home straight. The winner is value for further.

NOTEBOOK
Cut The Cackle(IRE) was found out in Listed company early last month, but the drop back to the minimum trip and a switch to nurseries worked the oracle as she just did enough to make it two wins from her three career starts. She rates value for a good bit further than her narrow winning margin as she was squeezed up inside the final furlong and her rider momentarily had to stop riding. She found a ready turn of foot when getting reorganised, however, and obviously enjoys some cut underfoot. (op 14-1)
The Magic Of Rio, beaten in a claimer last time, proved a big market drifter on this return to turf, but ran a blinder and only just lost out. She is a game filly, who goes on any ground, and this is no doubt her best trip. (op 9-1 tchd 16-1)
Fault, back down in trip, had every chance against the far rail and fared best of those to force the early pace. This was a fair effort just four days after his creditable seventh on quicker ground in a valuable heat at Newmarket. (op 9-2 tchd 5-1 and 10-3)
Cheviot(USA), whose stable had Ancient Regime turned over in this event last year, proved all the rage in the betting ring for this first run over 5f. He did little right through the race, however, as he was not the best away and got a little squeezed at the start. He then used up energy in making his move around the furlong pole, but did show a turn of foot to hit the front, before edging left late on and doing the winner no favours in the process. It may be that he prefers a stiffer test and he certainly has ability, but has now hung on his last two outings and will probably not come into his own until next term. Official explanation: jockey said colt hung left and slipped on leaving stalls (op 10-11 tchd 4-6)
To The Point did little to help her cause on this first run since June by running very freely early on and was beaten before being tightened for room approaching the furlong marker. Her pedigree suggests she ought to benefit from a stiffer test. (op 6-1)

6541 FANTASTIC FIREWORKS (S) STKS 1m 2f 7y
3:30 (3:31) (Class 6) 3-Y-O **£2,047** (£604; £302) **Stalls** Low

Form RPR
6050 **1** **Highland Homestead**[28] 5748 3-8-11 **55**............... JamesMillman(3) 13 58
(B R Millman) *s.i.s: wl in rr: stdy prog over 3f out on outer: led wl over 1f out: clr fnl f: rdn out* **6/1**[2]
0300 **2** *2½* **Alfredtheordinary**[41] 5378 3-9-0 **58**................................ SamHitchcott 9 53
(M R Channon) *t.k.h early: hld up in tch: n.m.r 3f out and lost pl: styd on again over 1f out: tk 2nd post* **20/1**
0254 **3** *nse* **Tank Commander**[19] 6032 3-9-0 **55**............................ RichardHughes 3 53
(W R Muir) *hld up in rr: prog and rdn 3f out: racd against far rail fnl 2f: chsd wnr over 1f out: no imp: lost 2nd post* **6/1**[2]
2300 **4** *½* **Rowan Dancer**[41] 5378 3-8-9 **53**..................................... RobertHavlin 6 47
(J R Boyle) *trckd ldrs: on terms 4f out: led jst over 2f out to wl over 1f out: one pce* **9/1**
2304 **5** *nk* **Hoar Frost**[16] 6111 3-9-1 **47**.. TPO'Shea 16 52
(M R Channon) *hld up in rr: n.m.r over 3f out: rdn and prog after: swtchd rt over 1f out: kpt on but nt time to rch ldrs* **10/1**
0106 **6** *1¾* **Caltire (GER)**[19] 6032 3-9-6 **60**.. AdamKirby 8 54
(M G Quinlan) *hld up wl in rr: rdn and prog over 3f out: chsd ldrs 2f out: no imp over 1f out* **7/1**[3]

2400 **7** ½ **The Willowy Wigeon**[48] 5167 3-8-9 58.................(b[1]) StephenCarson 10 42
(P Winkworth) *w ldr: led 4f out: hdd jst over 2f out: fnd nil and sn btn* **8/1**

0050 **8** 1 **Dry Speedfit (IRE)**[12] 6215 3-9-0 58.................. EddieAhern 15 45
(G G Margarson) *s.v.s: rcvrd to midfield after 3f: prog to join ldrs 4f out: hung lft 3f out: wknd over 1f out* **9/2**[1]

0502 **9** 5 **Threestoneburn (USA)**[14] 6175 3-8-2 52.................. RosieJessop[(7)] 1 30
(J R Boyle) *w ldrs: n.m.r and lost pl 3f out: tried to rally 2f out: sn wknd* **10/1**

0605 **10** 2 ¼ **Kuriyama (IRE)**[16] 6111 3-8-7 45..........................(b) AshleyMorgan[(7)] 5 30
(M H Tompkins) *hld up in midfield: prog and on terms w ldrs over 3f out: wknd 2f out* **20/1**

6003 **11** 12 **Rosy Dawn**[7] 6337 3-9-1 42.................................. JimCrowley 14 7
(J J Bridger) *wl plcd: on terms w ldrs over 3f out: wknd rapidly 2f out: t.o* **20/1**

0600 **12** 1 ½ **Xaravella (IRE)**[33] 5215 3-8-9 44..........................(p) EdwardCreighton 2 —
(J G M O'Shea) *mde most to 4f out: wknd: t.o* **66/1**

0500 **13** 6 **Fly In Johnny (IRE)**[31] 5684 3-9-0 49.......................... IanMongan 7 —
(M R Hoad) *prom tl wknd 3f out: t.o* **33/1**

0000 **14** 4 **House Of Tudor**[28] 5748 3-9-0 45..........................(b) SaleemGolam 12 —
(David Pinder) *wl in rr whn snatched up after 3f: drvn and struggling over 4f out: t.o* **40/1**

000 **15** nse **Daarth**[11] 3362 3-8-9 31..........................(bt[1]) GabrielHannon[(5)] 11 —
(B W Duke) *a bhd in last pair: t.o 4f out* **100/1**

16 2 **Marikova** 3-8-2 0.. PNolan[(7)] 4 —
(A B Haynes) *rel to r: a bhd in last pair: t.o 4f out* **66/1**

2m 12.88s (4.18) **Going Correction** +0.275s/f (Good) **16** Ran SP% **122.2**
Speed ratings (Par 99): **94,92,91,91,91 89,89,88,84,82 73,72,67,64,64 62**
toteswinger: 1&2 £20.60, 1&3 £13.80, 2&3 £12.00. CSF £127.49 TOTE £9.10: £2.70, £7.90, £2.80; EX 159.20 Trifecta £87.80 Part won. Pool: £118.67 - 0.30 winning tickets..The winner was sold to M Hoad for £3,000. Dry Speedfit was claimed by M Hammond for £6,000.
Owner Mrs G J Rowe **Bred** Rowcliffe Stud **Trained** Kentisbeare, Devon

FOCUS
A typically weak affair of its type and once more the runners migrated more towards the far side in the home straight. The form is rated through the winner and fifth.
Caltire(GER) Official explanation: jockey said gelding never travelled
Dry Speedfit(IRE) Official explanation: jockey said gelding missed the break

6542 MORELLI GROUP H'CAP — 1m 3f 135y
4:00 (4:01) (Class 4) (0-85,88) 3-Y-O — **£5,698** (£1,695; £847; £423) **Stalls** Low

Form RPR

035 **1** **Ballochroy (IRE)**[17] 6079 3-8-12 **79**.......................... MichaelHills 4 88
(B W Hills) *hld up: rapid prog to trck ldr 7f out: rdn to ld wl over 2f out: kpt on wl u.p fnl f* **7/1**

0220 **2** ½ **Sleepy Hollow**[17] 6079 3-8-10 **77**.......................... RobertHavlin 10 85
(H Morrison) *hld up in midfield: prog 3f out: drvn over 2f out: chsd ldng pair and edgd lft over 1f out: plld rt ins fnl f: r.o to take 2nd nr fin and gaining on wnr* **10/1**

2501 **3** ¾ **Higgy's Boy (IRE)**[7] 6346 3-9-7 **88** 6ex..........................(b) RichardHughes 9 95
(R Hannon) *stdd s: hld up in rr: stdy prog over 3f out: hrd rdn to chse wnr over 1f out: hld ins fnl f: lost 2nd nr fin* **7/1**

2313 **4** 3 ¼ **Celt**[13] 6196 3-9-0 **81**.................................. JimCrowley 2 82
(L M Cumani) *hld up wl in rr: prog and rdn 3f out: chsng ldrs 2f out: no imp over 1f out* **13/2**[3]

20 **5** nk **Air Chief**[19] 6028 3-8-5 **72**.................................. NickyMackay 7 73
(H J L Dunlop) *mde most to wl over 2f out: steadily fdd fr over 1f out* **16/1**

030 **6** ½ **Dauberval (IRE)**[22] 5938 3-9-3 **84**.......................... AdamKirby 5 84
(S Kirk) *mostly in midfield: u.p over 3f out: plugged on one pce* **16/1**

3602 **7** 1 ½ **Top Ticket (IRE)**[27] 5773 3-8-9 **76**.......................... StephenCarson 1 74
(D M Simcock) *prom: snatched up after 2f: lost pl rapidly after and last 7f out: u.p sn after: rallied on outer 3f out: no imp fnl 2f* **10/1**

3520 **8** 1 **French Riviera**[32] 5630 3-8-8 **75**.......................... TPO'Shea 12 71
(Sir Michael Stoute) *wl plcd: cl up and drvn over 2f out: wknd wl over 1f out* **12/1**

6613 **9** 5 **Star Of Gibraltar**[23] 5900 3-8-13 **80**.......................... EddieAhern 8 67
(J L Dunlop) *trckd ldrs: rdn 3f out: steadily wknd fr over 2f out* **11/2**[2]

0006 **10** ½ **Latin Lad**[16] 6128 3-9-4 **85**.................................. PatDobbs 3 72
(R Hannon) *hld up in rr: rdn 3f out: no prog and btn after* **16/1**

2060 **11** ¾ **King Columbo (IRE)**[46] 5209 3-8-9 **76**.......................... JerryO'Dwyer 6 61
(Miss J Feilden) *prom early: drvn in rr 5f out: sn struggling* **33/1**

1023 **12** 43 **Albarouche**[31] 5683 3-8-13 **80**..........................(tp) PhilipRobinson 11 —
(M A Jarvis) *trckd ldrs: wknd rapidly 3f out and eased: t.o* **4/1**[1]

2m 31.41s (1.91) **Going Correction** +0.275s/f (Good) **12** Ran SP% **120.2**
Speed ratings (Par 103): **104,103,103,101,100 100,99,98,95,95 94,65**
toteswinger: 1&2 £23.20, 1&3 £7.80, 2&3 £18.40. CSF £76.35 CT £516.30 TOTE £6.60: £2.70, £3.70, £2.30; EX 109.70 Trifecta £202.60 Part won. Pool: £273.88 - 0.77 winning tickets..
Owner The Mystic Mogg Partnership **Bred** Manister House Stud **Trained** Lambourn, Berks

FOCUS
A fair three-year-old handicap which saw the first three come clear. Sound form with the winner up 3lb.
Albarouche Official explanation: jockey said filly had a breathing problem

6543 AT THE RACES MAIDEN STKS — 6f
4:30 (4:31) (Class 5) 3-Y-O+ — **£2,729** (£806; £403) **Stalls** High

Form RPR

45 **1** **Motivated Choice**[13] 6192 3-8-12 0.......................... RichardHughes 14 67+
(L M Cumani) *t.k.h early: pressed ldrs and racd on outer: effrt 2f out: edgd lft over 1f out: drvn to ld last 100yds: a holding on* **20/1**

5225 **2** ½ **Cape Rock**[16] 6124 3-9-3 71.................................. PaulEddery 1 71
(C A Horgan) *hld up in midfield: prog 1/2-way: led wl over 1f out: hrd rdn and hdd last 100yds: a jst hld* **3/1**[1]

0454 **3** ½ **Kenton Street**[13] 6192 3-9-3 63.......................... RobertHavlin 3 69
(J A R Toller) *w ldrs: chalng 2f out: upsides ins fnl f: no ex last 100yds* **10/1**

2-26 **4** 1 ¼ **Tito (IRE)**[15] 6150 3-9-3 67.................................. PaulFessey 12 65+
(T D Barron) *hld up in rr: prog over 2f out: hanging lft after: drvn to go 4th ins fnl f: unable to chal* **7/1**[3]

60 **5** 1 ¾ **Gold Again (USA)**[20] 5995 3-8-12 0.......................... AdamKirby 9 54+
(W R Swinburn) *hld up in midfield: prog to trck ldrs over 2f out: n.m.r over 1f out: jst pushed along whn hld fnl f* **6/1**[2]

-0 **6** nk **Enlightened**[20] 6003 3-8-12 0.......................... JimCrowley 10 53
(J H M Gosden) *hld up in rr: prog towards far rail over 2f out: hrd rdn over 1f out: no imp after: fdd ins fnl f* **8/1**

7 2 **Irish Bay (IRE)**[715] 6114 5-9-4 0.......................... JerryO'Dwyer 13 52+
(Luke Comer, Ire) *dwlt: wl in rr and struggling to go the pce: styd on fr over 1f out: nrst fin* **50/1**

420- **8** ½ **Far Gone**[384] 5496 3-8-5 68.......................... LanceBetts[(7)] 8 45
(M L W Bell) *chsd ldrs: nt qckn over 2f out: fdd over 1f out* **12/1**

9 1 ¾ **Towy Valley** 3-8-12 0.................................. PhilipRobinson 15 40
(C G Cox) *dwlt: rcvrd and in tch on outer: effrt 2f out: no hdwy over 1f out: wknd* **16/1**

60 **10** ½ **Pappoose**[13] 6192 3-8-12 0.......................... SimonWhitworth 16 38
(H Candy) *a in rr and struggling to go the pce: n.d fnl 2f* **40/1**

4302 **11** hd **Baby Rock**[20] 6003 3-9-3 66.......................... EddieAhern 5 43
(C F Wall) *s.i.s: sn rcvrd: led over 3f out to wl over 1f out: n.m.r sn after: wknd* **3/1**[1]

0-00 **12** shd **Kaystar Ridge**[267] 146 3-9-3 62.......................... PatDobbs 11 42
(D K Ivory) *in tch in rr: rdn and no prog over 2f out: fdd* **66/1**

-0 **13** 16 **Tophorsnopedigree**[20] 6003 3-9-3 0.......................... EdwardCreighton 6 —
(E J Creighton) *led to over 3f out: wknd rapidly over 2f out: t.o* **100/1**

1m 15.59s (2.59) **Going Correction** +0.275s/f (Good)
WFA 3 from 5yo 1lb **13** Ran SP% **122.2**
Speed ratings (Par 103): **93,92,91,90,87 87,84,83,81,80 80,80,59**
toteswinger: 1&2 £13.30, 1&3 £20.80, 2&3 £7.90. CSF £79.70 TOTE £13.60: £3.80, £1.70, £2.50; EX 84.20 TRIFECTA Not won..
Owner Allevamento Gialloblu **Bred** Biddestone Stud **Trained** Newmarket, Suffolk

FOCUS
A typically modest sprint maiden for the time of year. A big step up from the winner to reverse Folkestone form with the third.
Baby Rock Official explanation: jockey said gelding had been unsuited by the good to soft ground

6544 WINDSOR FIREWORKS EXTRAVAGANZA SATURDAY 1ST NOVEMBER H'CAP — 1m 67y
5:00 (5:00) (Class 5) (0-70,70) 3-Y-O+ — **£2,729** (£806; £403) **Stalls** Low

Form RPR

5340 **1** **Sofia's Star**[12] 6211 3-8-11 **63**.................................. JimCrowley 8 72
(P Winkworth) *hld up in midfield: gd prog to ld wl over 1f out: edgd lft but sn drvn clr: in n.d fnl f* **12/1**

1303 **2** 2 ¾ **April Fool**[12] 6211 4-9-0 **63**..........................(v) RichardThomas 6 65
(J A Geake) *trckd ldrs: rdn 4f out: nt qckn over 2f out: kpt on to take 2nd 1f out: no ch w wnr* **10/1**

3566 **3** ½ **Dancing Storm**[22] 5935 5-8-12 **61**.......................... TPO'Shea 10 62
(W S Kittow) *trckd ldrs: rdn over 3f out: kpt on u.p to go 3rd fnl f* **5/1**[2]

2224 **4** ½ **Valento**[7] 6336 3-9-0 **66**.................................. StephenCarson 2 66
(Eve Johnson Houghton) *hld up in last trio: rdn wl over 2f out: prog u.p over 1f out: nt pce to trble ldrs* **8/1**[3]

0006 **5** nk **Risque Heights**[19] 6028 4-9-2 **65**.......................... IanMongan 1 64
(J R Boyle) *hld up in midfield: pushed along over 3f out: no imp on ldrs wl over 1f out: plugged on u.p* **14/1**

0060 **6** 3 **Full Victory (IRE)**[10] 6250 6-9-5 **68**.......................... EddieAhern 12 63
(R A Farrant) *sn pressed ldr: led 4f out: gng easily 3f out: rdn and no rspnse over 2f out: hdd wl over 1f out: eased whn btn last 100yds* **5/1**[2]

0054 **7** ¾ **Challow Hills (USA)**[21] 5964 3-8-13 **65**.......................... MichaelHills 4 56
(B W Hills) *w ldrs to 1/2-way: steadily fdd fnl 2f* **9/1**

1230 **8** ½ **Leptis Magna**[12] 6211 4-8-12 **61**.......................... SimonWhitworth 14 51
(R H York) *dwlt: t.k.h early: hld up in last pair: effrt over 3f out: sn no prog and btn* **10/1**

040 **9** ¾ **Pop Music (IRE)**[26] 5799 5-8-6 **60**..........................(v) SophieDoyle[(5)] 5 52
(Ms J S Doyle) *led to 1/2-way: hung lft intersection sn after: btn over 2f out: eased whn nov ch last 100yds* **20/1**

5206 **10** 3 ¼ **Hits Only Cash**[18] 6056 6-9-0 **63**..........................(p) RobertHavlin 7 43
(J Pearce) *dwlt: hld up in last pair: rdn and no prog 3f out* **10/1**

0031 **11** 4 ½ **Poppets Sweetlove**[19] 6036 4-9-1 **64**.......................... RichardHughes 3 34
(A B Haynes) *trckd ldrs: rdn and lost pl over 2f out: eased whn no ch fnl f* **4/1**[1]

1m 46.21s (1.51) **Going Correction** +0.275s/f (Good)
WFA 3 from 4yo+ 3lb **11** Ran SP% **120.8**
Speed ratings (Par 103): **103,100,99,99,98 95,95,94,93,90 86**
toteswinger: 1&2 £26.80, 1&3 £11.90, 2&3 £13.20. CSF £129.78 CT £689.71 TOTE £20.40: £4.70, £3.20, £2.00; EX 174.90 TRIFECTA Not won. Place 6 £9,609.75, Place 5 £2,454.16.
Owner David Holden **Bred** Bearstone Stud **Trained** Chiddingfold, Surrey

FOCUS
A modest handicap, run at a decent early pace. The winner had slipped a long way in the weights and the second and third were close to their latest form.
Poppets Sweetlove Official explanation: jockey said filly lost her action
T/Jkpt: Not won. T/Plt: £12,246.70 to a £1 stake. Pool: £81,365.60. 4.85 winning tickets. T/Qpdt: £104.10 to a £1 stake. Pool: £7,255.50. 51.55 winning tickets. JN

6109 CATTERICK (L-H)
Tuesday, October 7

OFFICIAL GOING: Good (good to soft in places; 8.2)
Wind: fresh 1/2 behind Weather: wet and windy 1st 2 races, then overcast, rain race 7

6545 18TH OCTOBER IS TOTESPORT SATURDAY MAIDEN STKS (DIV I) — 5f
2:00 (2:00) (Class 5) 2-Y-O — **£2,266** (£674; £337; £168) **Stalls** Low

Form RPR

43 **1** **Fesko**[11] 6244 2-8-12 0.................................. GregFairley 1 80+
(M Johnston) *chsd ldrs: sn pushed along: styd on to ld ins fnl f: r.o* **9/4**[2]

3223 **2** 1 **Majuba (USA)**[22] 5969 2-9-3 82.......................... PaulMulrennan 8 81
(K A Ryan) *led: rdr dropped whip 1f out: hdd and no ex ins fnl f* **10/11**[1]

3 7 **Breakevie (IRE)** 2-8-12 0.......................... PaulHanagan 3 51
(R A Fahey) *dwlt: sn mid-div: outpcd after 2f: hdwy 2f out: kpt on: no ch w 1st 2* **22/1**

605 **4** 2 **Miss Thippawan (USA)**[24] 5904 2-8-12 52.......................... MickyFenton 9 44
(P T Midgley) *chsd ldrs: edgd rt and wknd over 1f out* **66/1**

2230 **5** 1 **Dean Iarracht (IRE)**[17] 6112 2-9-3 71.......................... TonyHamilton 7 45
(M Dods) *sn outpcd and in rr: kpt on fnl f: nvr nr ldrs* **10/1**[3]

53 **6** nk **Kellies Rocket (IRE)**[13] 6212 2-8-12 0.......................... PJMcDonald 2 39
(G A Swinbank) *mid-div: outpcd after 2f: kpt on fnl f* **16/1**

0 **7** 3 **Wunder Strike (USA)**[20] 6010 2-9-3 0.......................... TomEaves 6 34
(M J Wallace, Australia) *sn outpcd and in rr: nvr on terms* **40/1**

6 **8** ¾ **Kiama Bay (IRE)**[17] 6109 2-9-3 0.......................... GrahamGibbons 4 31
(J J Quinn) *s.s: a bhd* **14/1**

9 4 ½ **Fifth Amendment** 2-8-12 0.......................... SladeO'Hara[(5)] 11 15
(A Berry) *swvd rt s: sn outpcd and bhd* **100/1**

59.30 secs (-0.50) **Going Correction** -0.075s/f (Good) **9** Ran SP% **114.1**
Speed ratings (Par 95): **101,99,88,85,83 82,78,76,69**
toteswinger: 1&2 £1.30, 1&3 £6.90, 2&3 £6.10. CSF £4.43 TOTE £2.70: £1.10, £1.02, £5.40; EX 4.50.

Owner C H Greensit & W A Greensit **Bred** C H And W A Greensit **Trained** Middleham Moor, N Yorks

FOCUS

A modest juvenile sprint maiden and very few ever got into it. A group of three were soon in a clear lead and they included the first two home, who finished clear in the end. The form is sound with the winner up another 9lb.

NOTEBOOK

Fesko, who had shown plenty of ability in her first two starts, was back over the minimum trip. She responded well to pressure to get the better of the front-running favourite inside the last furlong and was well on top at the line. This was not a very competitive race, but she is progressing and should have a future in nurseries. (op 2-1 tchd 15-8)

Majuba(USA), who has been knocking at the door in all six of his previous starts, tried to make all but was comfortably picked off and his rider dropping his whip probably made little difference. This was the fourth time he has finished runner-up and he did pull well clear of the rest, but he is running out of excuses. (op 11-10 tchd 6-5 in a place)

Breakevie(IRE), a half-sister to a winner over 7f out of a half-sister to Fayr Jag, did best of those that raced adrift of the clear leaders early and even though she was a long way behind the front pair at the line, she is entitled to come on for this. (op 20-1 tchd 25-1)

Miss Thippawan(USA) was the other to go clear early, but she did not get home. Rated just 52, she may be worth switching to moderate nurseries or dropping in class. (op 100-1)

Dean Iarracht(IRE), disappointing when well backed for a nursery here last month, was done few favours by the drop to the minimum trip for the first time and found everything happening too quickly. (op 11-1 tchd 12-1)

Kiama Bay(IRE) failed to build on his promising debut here last month after missing the break, though the drop in trip may not have helped.

6546 BETTER SAFE THAN SORRY AMATEUR RIDERS' H'CAP — 5f

2:30 (2:30) (Class 6) (0-55,59) 3-Y-0+ — **£2,307** (£709; £354) **Stalls** Low

Form — RPR

4220 **1** — **Whozart (IRE)**[6] 6382 5-11-3 **50** .... MrSDobson 3 — 63
(A Dickman) *mde all: kpt on fnl f: hld on towards fin* — **4/1**[1]

6001 **2** *nk* **Spirit Of Coniston**[9] 6310 5-11-3 **55** 6ex........ MissWGibson(5) 10 — 67
(P T Midgley) *chsd wnr: kpt on wl fnl f: jst hld* — **9/1**[3]

0306 **3** *4 1/2* **Lithaam (IRE)**[5] 6418 4-11-1 **51**........(p) MrOGreenall(3) 9 — 47
(J M Bradley) *rr-div: hdwy 2f out: kpt on ins fnl f* — **16/1**

2063 **4** *2 3/4* **Bilboa**[8] 6339 3-10-11 **51**........(p) MissHDavies(7) 13 — 37
(J M Bradley) *chsd ldrs: kpt on same pce fnl 2f* — **14/1**

0051 **5** *1 1/4* **Guto**[6] 6382 5-11-12 **59** 6ex........ MrSWalker 4 — 40
(W J H Ratcliffe) *prom: sn drvn along: outpcd over 2f out: kpt on fnl f* **4/1**[1]

1066 **6** *hd* **Town House**[53] 5074 6-10-12 **50**........ MissAWallace(5) 1 — 31
(B P J Baugh) *chsd ldrs: fdd over 1f out* — **22/1**

0066 **7** *1 1/4* **Strensall**[76] 4294 11-10-12 **52**........ MissVBarr(7) 5 — 28
(R E Barr) *prom: one pce fnl 2f* — **28/1**

0156 **8** *hd* **Obe One**[15] 6159 8-11-6 **53**........ MrsCBartley 6 — 28
(A Berry) *sn outpcd in rr: hdwy over 1f out: nvr nrr* — **12/1**

0050 **9** *1/2* **Northern Chorus (IRE)**[13] 6218 5-11-4 **51**........(v) MissADeniel 2 — 25
(J O'Reilly) *chsd ldrs: wknd over 1f out* — **12/1**

0000 **10** *nk* **Dark Champion**[6] 6382 8-11-0 **54**........(v) MrGRSmith(7) 7 — 27
(R E Barr) *sn outpcd in rr: kpt on fnl f: nvr a factor* — **14/1**

3006 **11** *1/2* **Jun Fan (USA)**[11] 6251 6-11-0 **52**........ MrDaleSwift(5) 8 — 23
(B Ellison) *chsd ldrs: sn drvn along: outpcd over 2f out: sn wknd* — **10/1**

5406 **12** *2 1/2* **Beaumont Boy**[33] 5636 4-10-11 **51**........(p) MrMEnnis(7) 14 — 13
(A G Foster) *chsd ldrs on outer: wknd over 1f out* — **25/1**

0016 **13** *1/2* **Sunley Sovereign**[6] 6382 4-10-13 **49**........(b) MrBenBrisbourne(3) 11 — 9
(Mrs R A Carr) *in rr: edgd lft over 1f out: nvr a factor* — **8/1**[2]

0000 **14** *9* **Gilded Youth**[7] 6364 4-10-12 **52**........(t) MrSeanKerr(7) 15 — —
(G F Bridgwater) *dwlt: a towards rr: bhd fnl 2f* — **100/1**

60.91 secs (1.11) **Going Correction** -0.075s/f (Good) — **14** Ran SP% **117.4**

Speed ratings (Par 101): **88,87,80,75,73 73,71,71,70,70 69,65,64,50**

toteswinger: 1&2 £8.20, 1&3 £16.70, 2&3 £27.80. CSF £37.13 CT £537.01 TOTE £4.50: £2.30, £2.30, £4.30; EX 45.60.

Owner The Marooned Crew **Bred** Mrs E Mulhern, Sonarc Bloodstock & Tower Bloodsto **Trained** Sandhutton, N Yorks

FOCUS

A modest amateur riders' sprint handicap. The whole field race centre to far side and those drawn low appeared to hold an advantage. As in the first race, very few ever got into it. The winner's two previous best runs also came over this course and distance.

Guto Official explanation: trainer had no explanation for the poor form shown

6547 SUBSCRIBE TO RACING UK ON 08700 506947 NURSERY — 5f 212y

3:00 (3:02) (Class 6) (0-65,65) 2-Y-0 — **£2,388** (£705; £352) **Stalls** Low

Form — RPR

0663 **1** — **Misty Glade**[13] 6207 2-9-2 **63**........(b) NickyMackay 4 — 70+
(B J Meehan) *chsd ldrs: led over 2f out: clr over 1f out: pushed out* — **5/1**[1]

4440 **2** *5* **Rossett Rose (IRE)**[33] 5632 2-9-3 **64**........ MickyFenton 1 — 56
(M Brittain) *s.i.s: rapid hdwy to ld after 100yds: hdd over 2f out: kpt on: no ch w wnr* — **6/1**[2]

430 **3** *3/4* **Imperial Skylight**[18] 6087 2-9-2 **63**........ TonyCulhane 9 — 53+
(M R Channon) *in rr: hdwy over 2f out: styd on same pce* — **8/1**

0U46 **4** *1 1/4* **Chantilly Dancer (IRE)**[20] 6008 2-9-3 **64**........ PaulHanagan 2 — 50+
(M J Wallace, Australia) *mid-div: styd on fnl 2f: nvr trbld ldrs* — **8/1**

3054 **5** *1/2* **Secret City (IRE)**[59] 4874 2-9-4 **65**........(b) PaulMulrennan 10 — 50
(R Bastiman) *chsd ldrs: rn wd bnd over 2f out: kpt on fnl f* — **12/1**

0030 **6** *1 3/4* **Chipolini (IRE)**[20] 6014 2-9-3 **64**........ DNolan 3 — 43
(D Carroll) *chsd ldrs: one pce fnl 2f* — **16/1**

3302 **7** *shd* **Raise All In (IRE)**[34] 5614 2-9-4 **65**........ PJMcDonald 7 — 44+
(N Wilson) *s.i.s: in rr: kpt on fnl 2f: nvr on terms* — **6/1**[2]

5504 **8** *nk* **Soviet Rhythm**[12] 6230 2-9-4 **65**........ TomEaves 12 — 43
(G M Moore) *led 100yds: chsd ldrs: c stands' side over 2f out: kpt on ins fnl f* — **7/1**[3]

600 **9** *1 3/4* **Reel Bluff**[13] 6212 2-9-3 **64**........ TonyHamilton 5 — 37
(D W Barker) *in tch: c stands' side over 2f out: nvr a threat* — **50/1**

2240 **10** *3/4* **Madame Jourdain (IRE)**[42] 5381 2-8-11 **65**........ DeanHeslop(7) 6 — 36
(N Wilson) *mid-div: c stands' side over 2f out: nvr a factor* — **12/1**

0440 **11** *24* **Bubbly Baby**[25] 5855 2-9-3 **64**........ DavidAllan 11 — —
(T D Easterby) *sn drvn along and outpcd on outer: c stands' side over 2f out: bhd whn virtually p.u over 1f out: t.o* — **12/1**

3030 **P** — **Camelot Communion (IRE)**[20] 6023 2-9-1 **65**....(v[1]) AndrewMullen(3) 8 — —
(Mrs A Duffield) *is.i.s: in rr whn p.u over 4f out: broke leg: dead* — **16/1**

1m 16.88s (3.28) **Going Correction** +0.425s/f (Yiel) — **12** Ran SP% **116.8**

Speed ratings (Par 93): **95,88,87,85,85 82,82,82,79,78 46,—**

toteswinger: 1&2 £9.30, 1&3 £9.60, 2&3 £8.80. CSF £33.44 CT £240.85 TOTE £5.50: £1.90, £2.60, £2.70; EX 35.70.

Owner F C T Wilson **Bred** Mrs C R Philipson & Mrs H G Lascelles **Trained** Manton, Wilts

FOCUS

A modest nursery in which only one of these had previously been successful, and that was in a seller. The form has been rated negatively. This was more like a classified event as just 2lb covered the 12 runners and again very few ever got into it. This was the first race on the card to be run on the round course and there was a difference of opinion as to where the best ground was. Four jockeys decided to come over to the stands' rail turning in, but it did them few favours as they were the last four to finish.

NOTEBOOK

Misty Glade had looked better over further on Polytrack up until now, but she benefited from racing handily in a race where it was crucial to do so and, after grabbing the initiative from the leader on the home bend, just pulled further and further clear. She can expect a hefty rise for this so may be best turned out quickly under a penalty. (op 6-1)

Rossett Rose(IRE), who did not seem to see out the extra furlong at Redcar last time, did not break too well but she was quickly rushed up the inside rail to take the lead. She lost the advantage to the eventual winner when not appearing to take the bend into the straight too well, but she did keep on for second and may be able to find a similar event. (op 15-2 tchd 8-1)

Imperial Skylight, who attracted market support despite being more exposed than most, stayed on in the latter stages but was never doing quite enough. (op 12-1 tchd 15-2)

Chantilly Dancer(IRE), making her nursery debut after showing a little ability in maidens, was another to plug on late and may need a return to 7f on better ground. (tchd 9-1)

Secret City(IRE), dropped 4lb from his nursery debut, was prominent early but after looking as though he was going to be brought over to the stands' side turning in, his rider seemed to change his mind and he rather ended up in no man's land. He may be worth another chance. (op 11-1)

6548 18TH OCTOBER IS TOTESPORT SATURDAY MAIDEN STKS (DIV II) — 5f

3:30 (3:30) (Class 5) 2-Y-0 — **£2,266** (£674; £337; £168) **Stalls** Low

Form — RPR

3345 **1** — **Titus Andronicus (IRE)**[10] 6274 2-9-3 72........ PaulMulrennan 6 — 73
(K A Ryan) *led tl narrowly hdd jst ins fnl f: stuck on gamely to regain ld fnl 75yds* — **9/4**[1]

62 **2** *1/2* **Kheleyf's Silver (IRE)**[41] 5394 2-8-12 0........ TomEaves 8 — 66
(B Smart) *trckd ldrs: slt ld jst ins fnl f: hdd and no ex* — **3/1**[2]

4 **3** *3* **Premier Lad**[20] 6010 2-9-0 0........ NeilBrown(3) 10 — 60
(T D Barron) *chsd ldrs: outpcd over 2f out: kpt on fnl f* — **4/1**[3]

5 **4** *4* **Mary West (IRE)**[12] 6230 2-8-12 0........ PaulHanagan 2 — 41
(R A Fahey) *chsd ldrs: outpcd over 2f out: kpt on fnl f* — **6/1**

000 **5** *hd* **Igoyougo**[19] 6051 2-9-3 60........ MickyFenton 1 — 45
(P T Midgley) *w wnr: wknd over 1f out* — **20/1**

3 **6** *3 3/4* **Diamond Daisy (IRE)**[19] 6051 2-8-9 0........ AndrewMullen(3) 5 — 27
(Mrs A Duffield) *sn outpcd and in rr: kpt on fnl f: nvr a factor* — **11/2**

7 *1 1/2* **Rafta (IRE)** 2-8-9 0........ DuranFentiman(3) 4 — 21
(W G Harrison) *dwlt: nvr on terms* — **66/1**

0 **8** *3/4* **Shining Times (IRE)**[33] 5633 2-8-12 0........ TonyHamilton 7 — 19
(D W Barker) *s.i.s: a in rr* — **100/1**

9 *6* **Gore Hill (IRE)** 2-9-3 0........ AndrewElliott 9 — —
(K R Burke) *s.i.s: kpt on fnl 2f: nvr on terms* — **16/1**

0030 **10** *3 1/2* **Pennine Rose**[17] 6109 2-8-9 44 ow2........ SladeO'Hara(5) 3 — —
(A Berry) *sn drvn along and wl outpcd: sn bhd* — **150/1**

60.01 secs (0.21) **Going Correction** -0.075s/f (Good) — **10** Ran SP% **119.2**

Speed ratings (Par 95): **95,94,89,83,82 76,74,73,63,57**

toteswinger: 1&2 £4.00, 1&3 £2.80, 2&3 £3.80. CSF £9.25 TOTE £3.00: £1.20, £1.80, £1.40; EX 10.10.

Owner John Browne & Paddy McGinty **Bred** Tally-Ho Stud **Trained** Hambleton, N Yorks

FOCUS

Another modest maiden and another race in which those that raced handily dominated throughout. Solid but limited form.

NOTEBOOK

Titus Andronicus(IRE) was by far the most experienced in the field, but he had shown enough to suggest he could win a race like this. Helping to force the pace from the off, he looked likely to be collared by the runner-up but showed admirable battling qualities to get off the mark at the eighth attempt. Currently rated 72, he may be able to find a nursery off this sort of mark now that he has got his head in front. (op 11-4)

Kheleyf's Silver(IRE), narrowly beaten over course and distance in her most recent start, had every chance but she found the winner in a very determined mood. The way she kept on suggests a return to 6f may help her and nurseries now become an option. (op 5-2 tchd 9-4 and 4-1 in a place, tchd 7-2 in places)

Premier Lad ◆, a promising fourth on his Beverley debut in which the previous week's big sales race-winner Kingship Spirit was second, did not fare badly once again as he started from the widest stall and tried to come from further back than the front pair. A return to a stiffer track or an extra furlong may be what he needs now. (op 11-2)

Mary West(IRE), down a furlong from her promising Pontefract debut, lacked the speed to go with the leaders in the last furlong or so. She still showed signs of greenness so there is probably more to come from her back over further. (op 8-1 tchd 9-1)

Igoyougo ran his best race so far, but probably benefited from a positive ride in a race where the pacesetters dominated. Currently rated 60, he may need a drop in grade or a switch to nurseries. (op 16-1)

6549 TURFTV.CO.UK NURSERY — 7f

4:00 (4:00) (Class 4) (0-85,85) 2-Y-0 — **£3,885** (£1,156; £577; £288) **Stalls** Low

Form — RPR

4204 **1** — **Digger Derek (IRE)**[17] 6112 2-7-13 **63**........ PaulHanagan 2 — 71
(R A Fahey) *led 1f: chsd ldrs: swtchd rt over 2f out: led over 1f out: styd on wl* — **11/2**[2]

3362 **2** *2 1/4* **Lakeman (IRE)**[24] 5883 2-8-8 **79**........ LanceBetts(7) 12 — 81+
(B Ellison) *chsd ldrs: hmpd over 2f out: styd on same pce fnl f: no real imp* — **15/2**

0031 **3** *2* **Pride Of Kings**[76] 4292 2-8-10 **74**........ GregFairley 10 — 71
(M Johnston) *led after 1f: hdd 4f out: led 2f out: sn hdd and no ex* — **11/2**[2]

141 **4** *1 1/2* **Firebet (IRE)**[24] 5883 2-9-4 **85**........ AndrewMullen(3) 6 — 78+
(Mrs A Duffield) *mid-div: rdn over 2f out: styd on fnl f* — **4/1**[1]

5150 **5** *1 1/2* **Woolston Ferry (IRE)**[17] 6112 2-8-12 **76**........ TonyCulhane 8 — 66+
(M R Channon) *sn drvn along and detached in rr: hdwy 3f out: one pce fnl f* — **18/1**

2210 **6** *3/4* **Inheritor (IRE)**[27] 5791 2-9-4 **82**........ TomEaves 9 — 70
(B Smart) *chsd ldrs: rdn and outpcd over 2f out: kpt on fnl f* — **12/1**

6656 **7** *nk* **Red Max (IRE)**[17] 6112 2-7-9 **62** oh2........ DuranFentiman(3) 3 — 49
(T D Easterby) *drvn to chse ldrs: led 4f out tl 2f out: one pce* — **22/1**

5103 **8** *1/2* **Richo**[17] 6112 2-9-1 **79**........ PaulMulrennan 11 — 65
(D H Brown) *reluctant to go to post: mid-div: one pce fnl 2f* — **8/1**

2050 **9** *3/4* **Yokozuna**[13] 6214 2-7-11 **68** oh1 ow6........(b) AdeleRothery(7) 7 — 52
(Mrs R A Carr) *s.i.s: styd on fnl 2f: nvr nr ldrs* — **50/1**

0211 **10** *4 1/2* **Nchike**[22] 5966 2-8-2 **66**........(v) SilvestreDeSousa 5 — 39+
(D Nicholls) *prom: drvn and lost pl over 3f out: bhd whn eased ins fnl f* — **12/1**

2144 **11** *2 1/2* **Fitzolini**[24] 5883 2-8-10 **74**....................(p) AndrewElliott 1 40+
(A D Brown) *hld up in rr: bhd whn eased ins fnl f* **22/1**

31 **12** *5* **Ubi Ace**[20] 6008 2-8-12 **76**.................... GrahamGibbons 4 30+
(T D Walford) *in rr: drvn and lost pl 4f out: beheind whn eased ins fnl f* **7/1**[3]

1m 29.48s (2.48) **Going Correction** +0.425s/f (Yiel) **12** Ran SP% **117.4**
Speed ratings (Par 97): **102,99,97,95,93 92,92,91,91,85 83,77**
toteswinger: 1&2 £9.10, 1&3 £6.20, 2&3 £10.70. CSF £44.97 CT £242.84 TOTE £7.60: £2.10, £2.30, £3.00; EX 58.80.
Owner Dr W D Ashworth **Bred** Airlie Stud **Trained** Musley Bank, N Yorks
■ Stewards' Enquiry : Paul Hanagan two-day ban: careless riding (Oct 22-23)

FOCUS
A much better nursery than the earlier one and this time there was plenty of previous winning form on show. The winner stepped forward with the runner-up setting the level. The early gallop seemed generous with a few battling for the advantage, but yet again it was crucial to race up with the pace from the start.

NOTEBOOK
Digger Derek(IRE), closely matched with a few of these on their meeting here last month, had looked as though in need of a greater test of stamina, so the decent pace was probably a help. Never far away, he responded well to pressure to get on top and connections believe he will be suited by around 1m2f next year. (op 7-1)
Lakeman(IRE), 1lb better off with Firebet for a head defeat at Chester last month, had the best of the draw then but the worst of it here. Nonetheless, he was able to take a handy position from the off and had every chance, but found the winner much too good. (op 7-1 tchd 8-1)
Pride Of Kings, 6lb higher than when winning a nursery over course and distance in July that has worked out well, was one of those responsible for the strong early pace and on a day when speed was holding up so well, he kept on to gain a place in the frame. He still has a bit of scope and there will be another day. (op 4-1 tchd 6-1)
Firebet(IRE), winner of two of his three previous starts and closely matched with Lakeman on their meeting at Chester last month, was in touch early but he became outpaced rounding the home turn and there was no way he was ever going to recover the lost ground. Despite this defeat, he remains a nice prospect. Official explanation: jockey said colt was unsuited by the track (op 5-1 tchd 7-2)
Woolston Ferry(IRE) deserves credit for finishing where he did given the way the race panned out, as he was right out the back early. His victory came in his only attempt on Polytrack, so he would be of obvious interest if returned to that surface. (op 16-1)
Inheritor(IRE), progressive until well beaten in soft ground on his nursery debut at Doncaster last month, was close enough until dropping away up the home straight and could probably have done without the rain. (op 10-1)
Richo Official explanation: jockey said gelding was unsuited by the good (good to soft places) ground
Ubi Ace, the least exposed in the field, had made all when winning at Beverley last time but he barely went a yard here and this was far too bad to be true. Official explanation: jockey said gelding was unsuited by the track (op 17-2 tchd 9-1 and 11-1 in a place)

6550 SKYRAM H'CAP — 1m 7f 177y
4:30 (4:30) (Class 6) (0-60,60) 3-Y-0+ **£2,388** (£705; £352) **Stalls** Low

Form RPR

2045 **1** **Capal Dubh Alainn (IRE)**[20] 6022 3-9-4 **60**....................(vt) GregFairley 10 71
(T J Pitt) *chsd ldrs: led over 3f out: hld on wl towards fin* **11/2**[2]

5060 **2** *3/4* **Coronado's Gold (USA)**[17] 6115 7-8-12 **50**.................... LanceBetts(7) 6 60
(B Ellison) *hld up in rr: hdwy 5f out: chal over 1f out: no ex wl ins fnl f* **20/1**

5320 **3** *5* **Sir Sandicliffe (IRE)**[10] 6279 4-9-6 **58**.................... DeanHeslop(7) 9 62
(W M Brisbourne) *mid-div: lost pl over 5f out: hdwy over 2f out: kpt on same pce* **7/1**

03-4 **4** *2* **Aston Lad**[154] 1892 7-9-2 **47**.................... PaulHanagan 3 49
(Micky Hammond) *hld up in rr: hdwy over 4f out: kpt on same pce fnl 2f* **10/1**

0620 **5** *2* **Simple Jim (FR)**[223] 720 4-9-12 **57**.................... SilvestreDeSousa 5 57
(A D Brown) *hld up in rr: gd hdwy 3f out: kpt on same pce: nvr nr ldrs* **20/1**

0065 **6** *2 1/2* **Marieschi (USA)**[76] 4295 4-9-5 **50**.................... TomEaves 15 47
(R F Fisher) *t.k.h in midfield: hdwy 6f out: sn chsng ldrs: wknd 1f out* **16/1**

0342 **7** *4 1/2* **Wulimaster (USA)**[25] 5869 5-9-8 **53**.................... TonyHamilton 7 44
(D W Barker) *hld up in midfield: sme hdwy 3f out: nvr nr ldrs* **9/2**[1]

024- **8** *1 3/4* **Admiral Savannah (IRE)**[249] 4821 4-9-3 **48**....................(b) DavidAllan 8 37
(T D Easterby) *in tch: one pce fnl 3f* **14/1**

106 **9** *15* **Spiders Star**[9] 6309 5-9-2 **47** ow2.................... MHNaughton 4 18
(Miss Kate Milligan) *dwlt: hdwy to chse ldrs after 6f: rn wd and lost pl over 2f out: in rr whn eased fnl f* **33/1**

0350 **10** *hd* **Restart (IRE)**[24] 5917 7-9-4 **49**....................(p) DNolan 11 20
(Lucinda Featherstone) *chsd ldr: led after 3f: qcknd over 7f out: hdd over 3f out: sn lost pl* **17/2**

11 *3 3/4* **Leopold (SLO)**[207] 7-9-0 **50**.................... PatrickDonaghy(5) 14 16
(D W Thompson) *hld up in mid-div: drvn over 4f out: sn bhd* **66/1**

650/ **12** *3* **Boing Boing (IRE)**[212] 1295 8-9-4 **49**.................... PaulMulrennan 13 12
(G A Harker) *chsd ldrs: lost pl over 4f out* **9/1**

0-50 **13** *3/4* **Karlani (IRE)**[17] 6115 5-9-12 **57**....................(tp) PJMcDonald 1 19
(G A Swinbank) *drvn to ld for 3f: reminders over 7f out: lost pl over 5f out* **13/2**[3]

502- **14** *11* **Doonigan (IRE)**[37] 6060 4-9-6 **51**....................(p) JohnEgan 12 —
(Tim Vaughan) *in rr: sn drvn along: bhd fnl 6f: t.o over 3f out* **20/1**

3m 41.98s (9.98) **Going Correction** +0.425s/f (Yiel)
WFA 3 from 4yo+ 11lb **14** Ran SP% **120.3**
Speed ratings (Par 101): **92,91,89,88,87 85,83,82,75,75 73,71,71,65**
toteswinger: 1&2 £31.20, 1&3 £11.20, 2&3 £36.90. CSF £118.23 CT £790.08 TOTE £6.50: £2.40, £6.30, £2.20; EX 119.20.
Owner Burke, Daly, Boyle, Prosser, McConnon **Bred** J Burke **Trained** Norton, N Yorks

FOCUS
A moderate staying handicap in which several were returning from lengthy layoffs, a few of which were presumably having a spin before a jumping campaign. The early pace looked decent which made this a proper test of stamina. The form seems to make sense.

6551 BOOK ON-LINE AT CATTERICKBRIDGE.CO.UK H'CAP — 1m 3f 214y
5:00 (5:00) (Class 5) (0-75,75) 3-Y-0+ **£2,590** (£770; £385; £192) **Stalls** High

Form RPR

4550 **1** **Giant Love (USA)**[24] 5900 3-8-11 **70**.................... GregFairley 5 83
(M Johnston) *wore net muzzle: chsd ldrs: led over 1f out: styd on strly to forge clr ins fnl f* **11/1**

4400 **2** *5* **Eijaaz (IRE)**[13] 6216 7-8-9 **61** oh2.................... DavidAllan 3 66
(G A Harker) *hld up in rr: c wd and hdwy over 2f out: kpt on to take 2nd towards fin* **14/1**

2126 **3** *1/2* **Elite Land**[22] 5971 5-8-10 **65**.................... NeilBrown(3) 9 69
(K A Ryan) *hld up in rr: gd hdwy 7f out: sn trcking ldrs: hung lft and led over 2f out: hdd over 1f out: kpt on same pce* **4/1**[1]

0220 **4** *5* **Edas**[22] 5971 6-8-8 **63**.................... DuranFentiman(3) 12 59
(J J Quinn) *t.k.h: hdwy to trck ldrs over 7f out: upsides over 2f out: wknd over 1f out* **12/1**

2220 **5** *1 1/4* **Maha Dubai (USA)**[21] 6007 3-8-10 **69**.................... TomEaves 4 63
(M Johnston) *prom: one pce fnl 3f* **13/2**[3]

0626 **6** *nk* **Madison Heights (IRE)**[13] 6216 3-7-13 **61** oh1.................... AndrewMullen(3) 2 55
(J Howard Johnson) *led 1f: chsd ldrs: one pce fnl 3f* **16/1**

2150 **7** *1 1/2* **Gulf Coast**[14] 4966 3-8-7 **66** ow2.................... GrahamGibbons 8 57
(T D Walford) *chsd ldrs: drvn over 4f out: outpcd 3f out: kpt on fnl 2f* **8/1**

2343 **8** *3 1/4* **Spirit Of Adjisa (IRE)**[13] 6203 4-9-8 **74**....................(b) JohnEgan 15 60
(Pat Eddery) *racd wd 1st 3f: led after 1f: hdd over 2f out: sn wknd* **9/2**[2]

0/00 **9** *3/4* **Risk Runner (IRE)**[19] 6054 5-9-2 **68**....................(b) PJMcDonald 13 53
(James Moffatt) *sn chsng ldrs: wknd 2f out* **33/1**

5320 **10** *2 1/4* **Sporting Gesture**[11] 6243 11-8-9 **68**.................... BradleyRoper(7) 1 49
(M W Easterby) *mid-div: drvn 5f out: nvr a factor* **20/1**

3-46 **11** *9* **Smugglers Bay (IRE)**[156] 1824 4-9-5 **71**.................... PaulMulrennan 10 38
(T D Easterby) *in rr: hdwy over 3f out: c wd over 2f out: sn wknd* **8/1**

4/35 **12** *17* **Desert Destiny**[9] 6312 8-9-9 **75**....................(p) TonyHamilton 7 15
(C Grant) *in rr: sme hdwy 4f out: c wd over 2f out: sn lost pl: bhd whn eased ins fnl f* **22/1**

0-50 **13** *13* **Ergo (FR)**[19] 6050 4-8-9 **61** oh4....................(v) MickyFenton 11 —
(James Moffatt) *in rr: bhd fnl 4f: t.o* **50/1**

2m 43.52s (4.62) **Going Correction** +0.425s/f (Yiel)
WFA 3 from 4yo+ 7lb **13** Ran SP% **116.3**
Speed ratings (Par 103): **101,97,97,94,93 92,91,89,89,87 81,70,61**
toteswinger: 1&2 £23.10, 1&3 £9.00, 2&3 £17.70. CSF £144.82 CT £725.64 TOTE £15.00: £4.90, £3.60, £1.90; EX 226.80 Place 6: £55.17 Place 5: £46.14.
Owner Crone Stud Farms Ltd **Bred** Swettenham Stud **Trained** Middleham Moor, N Yorks

FOCUS
An ordinary handicap, but they went a decent early pace. The runners fanned right out across the track on reaching the home straight, but it still seemed an advantage to stay towards the inside. The first two are rated back to their best old form.
Giant Love(USA) Official explanation: trainer's rep had no explanation for the apparent improvement in form
Spirit Of Adjisa(IRE) Official explanation: jockey said gelding was unsuited by the good (good to soft places) ground
T/Jkpt: Not won. T/Plt: £67.30 to a £1 stake. Pool: £62,528.43. 677.40 winning tickets. T/Qpdt: £22.60 to a £1 stake. Pool: £3,581.60. 117.00 winning tickets. WG

6190 FOLKESTONE (R-H)
Tuesday, October 7

OFFICIAL GOING: Soft
Wind: blustery across Weather: overcast, showers threatening

6552 STONE OF FOLCA MAIDEN STKS (DIV I) — 7f (S)
2:20 (2:22) (Class 5) 2-Y-0 **£2,590** (£770; £385; £192) **Stalls** Low

Form RPR

0 **1** **Saturn Way (GR)**[27] 5798 2-9-3 0.................... LPKeniry 4 72
(P R Chamings) *hld up in tch: swtchd rt and hdwy over 1f out: ev ch and edgd rt ins fnl f: led fnl 50yds* **16/1**

00 **2** *hd* **Champion Girl (IRE)**[15] 6166 2-8-12 0.................... RobertHavlin 5 66
(D Haydn Jones) *racd stands' side: w ldr tl led 1/2-way: rdn over 1f out: kpt on gamely tl tl hdd and no ex last 50yds: 2nd of 6 in gp* **50/1**

0 **3** *1 1/4* **Incendo**[18] 6083 2-9-3 0.................... WilliamBuick 6 68
(J R Fanshawe) *racd stands' side: hld up in tch: swtchd rt and effrt over 1f out: edging lft fnl f: ev ch ins fnl f tl no ex fnl 50yds: 3rd of 6 in gp* **16/1**

0 **4** *1 1/4* **Blue Tango (IRE)**[17] 6117 2-9-3 0.................... JimCrowley 1 65
(Mrs A J Perrett) *racd stands' side: led tl 1/2-way: sn rdn: kpt on same pce fnl f: 4th of 6 in gp* **10/3**[2]

43 **5** *8* **Surprise Party**[75] 4328 2-8-9 0.................... JackMitchell(3) 11 50+
(C F Wall) *racd far side: hld up in tch: hdwy to ld far side 2f out: sn in command of that gp but no ch w stands' side: 1st of 7 in gp* **11/4**[1]

6 **6** *1 1/4* **Puzzlemaster**[12] 6230 2-9-3 0.................... TPQueally 10 52+
(G G Margarson) *racd far side: hld up in tch: rdn over 2f out: chsd far side ldr over 1f out: no ch w stands' side gp: 2nd of 7 in gp* **7/1**[3]

0 **7** *2 1/4* **Ausonius**[20] 6029 2-9-3 0.................... DaneO'Neill 7 46+
(L M Cumani) *racd far side: hld up in tch: rdn and effrt over 2f out: nvr a ch w stands' side gp: 3rd of 7 in gp* **22/1**

0 **8** *2 3/4* **Gesseem (IRE)**[16] 6151 2-9-3 0.................... JoeFanning 12 39+
(M Johnston) *racd far side: w ldr tl led far side gp 1/2-way tl 2f out: sn wl btn: 4th of 7 in gp* **14/1**

9 *shd* **Sircozy (IRE)** 2-8-12 0.................... WilliamCarson(5) 2 29
(S C Williams) *racd stands' side: s.i.s: a bhd: 5th of 6 in gp* **33/1**

10 *10* **Castlemaine** 2-8-12 0.................... RichardHughes 13 —+
(R Hannon) *racd far side: in tch tl 1/2-way: sn wl btn: 5th of 7 in gp* **10/1**

3 **11** *2 3/4* **Do Be Brave (IRE)**[62] 4728 2-9-3 0.................... PaulEddery 9 —+
(G D Blake) *racd far side: t.k.h: led far side tl 1/2-way: wl bhd last 2f: 6th of 7 in gp* **8/1**

12 *3 1/2* **Raffys Rock (IRE)** 2-9-3 0.................... SaleemGolam 3 —
(S C Williams) *racd stands' side: s.i.s: t.k.h: sn in tch: rdn and struggling 1/2-way: 6th of 6 in gp* **40/1**

13 *8* **Derringbay (IRE)** 2-9-3 0.................... GeorgeBaker 8 —
(M H Tompkins) *racd far side: v.s.a: a bhd: t.o last 2f: 7th of 7 in gp* **22/1**

1m 31.5s (4.20) **Going Correction** +0.50s/f (Yiel) **13** Ran SP% **116.9**
Speed ratings (Par 95): **96,95,94,92,83 82,79,76,76,65 61,57,48**
toteswinger: 1&2 £142.30, 1&3 £68.50, 2&3 £134.20. CSF £661.75 TOTE £21.80: £5.30, £13.30, £5.20; EX 767.90 TRIFECTA Not won..
Owner Mrs Alexandra J Chandris **Bred** Queensway S A **Trained** Baughurst, Hants

FOCUS
The ground was riding pretty much as described. They split into two groups for this opening contest and it was the stands' side that came out well on top, being responsible for the first four with the other side effectively having no chance. Guessy form with little strength in depth.

NOTEBOOK
Saturn Way(GR), who failed to get home having raced keenly on his debut at Kempton, was ridden with more restraint on this occasion and emerged as a big threat when switching off the rail under two out. He had to battle to get past outsider Champion Girl, but was in front at the half-furlong pole and just did enough. His dam was a 1m2f winner, so he should have little trouble getting a bit further, and the soft ground was clearly of no inconvenience. (op 20-1)
Champion Girl(IRE) had shown little in two previous attempts and was understandably dismissed in the market. She showed good speed for a long way and clearly improved for this softer ground but could not repel the winner's challenge. She is now qualified for a handicap mark and should prove just as effective back at 6f. (op 66-1 tchd 40-1)
Incendo had every chance and ran well, improving markedly on his debut effort. He will stay further than this, being a half-brother to useful stayer Numero Due, and should improve again. (op 22-1 tchd 25-1)

Blue Tango(IRE), down the field on his Newbury debut, bagged the usually favoured stands' rail but was being ridden at halfway and could only keep on at the one pace. A faster surface may be more to his liking. (op 4-1 tchd 3-1)

Surprise Party, who shaped with some promise on slow ground when fourth at Nottingham on debut, did best of those on the far side but found herself well adrift in the stands' group. She is now qualified for a handicap mark. (op 10-3 tchd 7-2 and 5-2)

Puzzlemaster is more of a long-term prospect and he found this longer trip still on the sharp side. He will have a future in middle-distance handicaps next season. (op 10-1)

Derringbay(IRE) Official explanation: jockey said gelding ran green

6553 STONE OF FOLCA MAIDEN STKS (DIV II) 7f (S)

2:50 (2:52) (Class 5) 2-Y-O **£2,590** (£770; £385; £192) **Stalls** Low

Form RPR

1 **Saint Arch (CAN)** 2-9-3 0 ... JoeFanning 7 82+
(M Johnston) *chsd ldr tl led 3f out: drew clr 2f out: r.o strly and in n.d after: rdn out* **10/1**

02 2 6 **Burma Rock (IRE)**[20] 6031 2-9-3 0 ... DaneO'Neill 4 67
(L M Cumani) *in tch: chsd ldng pair 1/2-way: chsd wnr over 1f out: kpt on but no imp* **3/1**[2]

4 3 ½ **Calaloo (IRE)**[136] 2411 2-9-3 0 ... RobertHavlin 5 66
(C R Egerton) *s.i.s: hld up in midfield: outpcd 1/2-way: hdwy 2f out: kpt on fnl f: no ch w wnr* **6/1**[3]

5 4 1 **Emirates World (IRE)**[52] 5099 2-9-3 0 ... MartinDwyer 3 64+
(Saeed Bin Suroor) *led tl 3f out: sn rdn: no ch w wnr last 2f: plugged on same pce fnl f* **2/1**[1]

40 5 1 **Omnium Duke (IRE)**[18] 6085 2-9-3 0 ... JamesDoyle 13 61
(J W Hills) *stdd s and dropped in towards rr: rdn and sme hdwy over 2f out: plugged on fnl f: nvr nr wnr* **14/1**

0 6 4 **Rosco Flyer (IRE)**[18] 6072 2-9-3 0 ... TPQueally 9 51
(J R Boyle) *chsd ldrs: rdn 3f out: sn struggling: no ch last 2f* **14/1**

00 7 1 **Almazar**[21] 5996 2-9-3 0 ... JimCrowley 2 48
(J L Dunlop) *in tch: rdn 1/2-way: sn outpcd: no ch last 2f* **16/1**

60 8 1 ¾ **Eager To Bow (IRE)**[23] 5929 2-9-3 0 ... LPKeniry 12 44
(P R Chamings) *a towards rr: rdn and toiling fr 1/2-way* **33/1**

00 9 2 **Winterbrook King**[10] 6282 2-9-0 0 ... MarcHalford(3) 1 39
(J R Best) *chsd ldrs tl lost pl and rdn 1/2-way: no ch after* **50/1**

00 10 2 ¾ **Outland (IRE)**[18] 6084 2-9-3 0 ... GeorgeBaker 11 32
(M H Tompkins) *s.i.s: a bhd* **33/1**

00 11 10 **Demand**[37] 5534 2-8-12 0 ... LiamJones 10 —+
(W J Haggas) *racd alone on far side: nvr competitive: hung lft last 2f* **16/1**

12 7 **Just Josie** 2-8-12 0 ... PatDobbs 6 —
(G L Moore) *v.s.a: a bhd: t.o* **33/1**

13 5 **Straboe (USA)** 2-9-3 0 ... SaleemGolam 8 —
(S C Williams) *s.i.s: a bhd: t.o* **66/1**

1m 31.0s (3.70) **Going Correction** +0.50s/f (Yiel) 13 Ran SP% **119.1**

Speed ratings (Par 95): **98,91,90,89,88 83,82,80,78,75 63,55,50**

toteswinger: 1&2 £6.40, 1&3 £11.10, 2&3 £4.70. CSF £38.67 TOTE £8.80: £3.00, £1.50, £2.10; EX 34.20 Trifecta £165.90 Pool: £282.51 - 1.26 winning units..

Owner Sheikh Hamdan Bin Mohammed Al Maktoum **Bred** Ascot Thoroughbreds **Trained** Middleham Moor, N Yorks

FOCUS

This looked the stronger of the two divisions, and, unlike in the first race, all bar one raced on the stands' side. The winner won decisively and his form could be rated higher.

NOTEBOOK

Saint Arch(CAN) went on inside the final quarter-mile and cleared right away. An 82,000gns half-brother to numerous winners in the US, he has plenty of size and scope and coped better than expected with the soft ground. He knew his job, and, with the promise of better to come as he goes up to 1m on a sounder surface, looks a horse to keep on side as he goes into handicaps. (op 8-1 tchd 12-1)

Burma Rock(IRE), second to a promising sort at Yarmouth last time, is bred to handle this soft ground and he kept on best of the rest for second. He is now qualified for a mark and will stay further. (tchd 11-4)

Calaloo(IRE), last of four at Newmarket on his debut back in May, was very well backed on this first run since and ran a lot better. He kept plugging away for pressure and should stay further. (op 14-1)

Emirates World(IRE), fifth at Newmarket on debut, was soon in front on the rail but came under pressure just under three out and was readily brushed aside. This softer ground looked to be against him. (op 11-4)

Omnium Duke(IRE) ran better than he had done at Newmarket last time and is now qualified for a mark. He should fare better in that sphere. (op 10-1 tchd 9-1)

Demand, the only one to go far side, needed this to qualify for handicaps and should improve back on faster going. (op 14-1)

6554 GARDEN OF ENGLAND H'CAP 7f (S)

3:20 (3:21) (Class 5) (0-75,75) 3-Y-O+ **£2,914** (£867; £433; £216) **Stalls** Low

Form RPR

4441 1 **Granary**[28] 5779 4-9-1 **72** ... DaneO'Neill 9 85
(H Candy) *in tch: hdwy to ld 2f out: sn rdn clr: in n.d fnl f: easily* **9/2**[1]

6010 2 5 **Kinnego Bay (IRE)**[31] 5713 3-8-11 **70** ... RichardHughes 1 69
(B W Hills) *hld up in tch: swtchd rt and hdwy over 1f out: chsd wnr ins fnl f: no ch* **5/1**[2]

0000 3 2 **Westwood**[22] 5962 3-8-13 **72** ... RobertHavlin 11 65
(D Haydn Jones) *taken down early: led after 1f: hdd 2f out: sn no ch w wnr: lost 2nd ins fnl f* **33/1**

5005 4 ¾ **My Learned Friend (IRE)**[34] 5600 4-9-4 **75** ... WilliamBuick 7 67
(A M Balding) *chsd ldrs tl short of room and lost pl 4f out: rallied u.p 2f out: kpt on same pce fnl f* **6/1**[3]

6036 5 2 ½ **Kensington (IRE)**[28] 5779 7-8-12 **69** ... JamesDoyle 2 54
(P D Evans) *towards rr: outpcd 1/2-way: plugged on past btn horses fr over 1f out: n.d* **12/1**

0010 6 4 **Shamrock Lady (IRE)**[34] 5600 3-9-1 **74** ... TPO'Shea 12 48
(J Gallagher) *chsd ldrs: wnt 2nd briefly 1/2-way: sn rdn and struggling: no ch last 2f* **20/1**

0066 7 ¾ **Benedetto**[5] 6417 3-8-12 **71** ... (p) JimCrowley 13 43
(Mrs A J Perrett) *hld up towards rr: hdwy over 3f out: rdn and btn over 2f out* **8/1**

5426 8 10 **Bere Davis (FR)**[38] 5492 3-9-0 **73** ... (p) DarryllHolland 10 18
(P D Evans) *dwlt and hmpd s: a bhd: rdn 1/2-way: wl bhd last 2f* **6/1**[3]

1100 9 4 **Elusive Hawk (IRE)**[21] 5991 4-9-0 **71** ... TPQueally 4 6
(A P Stringer) *s.i.s: sn rcvrd and in tch: losing pl and hmpd over 3f out: wl bhd last 2f: t.o and eased ins fnl f* **12/1**

0410 10 3 ¼ **Hucking Harkness**[20] 6036 3-8-3 **62** ... MartinDwyer 8 —
(J R Best) *led for 1f: chsd ldr after tl 1/2-way sn drvn and wknd: t.o and eased ins fnl f* **15/2**

0600 11 10 **Liberty Belle (IRE)**[50] 5151 3-8-7 **66** ... LPKeniry 6 —
(J R Best) *chsd ldrs tl 1/2-way: sn lost pl: t.o and eased fnl f* **20/1**

1m 30.19s (2.89) **Going Correction** +0.50s/f (Yiel)

WFA 3 from 4yo+ 2lb 11 Ran SP% **114.1**

Speed ratings (Par 103): **103,97,95,94,91 86,85,74,69,66 54**

toteswinger: 1&2 £2.60, 1&3 £25.70, 2&3 £18.00. CSF £24.97 CT £667.32 TOTE £4.80: £1.80, £1.70, £4.40; EX 21.20 Trifecta £175.60 Part won. Pool: £237.35 - 0.59 winning..

Owner Major M G Wyatt **Bred** W And R Barnett Ltd **Trained** Kingston Warren, Oxon

FOCUS

This was just an ordinary handicap. Improvement from Granary, but there seems no fluke, with the next two close to this year's form.

Bere Davis(FR) Official explanation: jockey said gelding suffered interference leaving stalls

6555 HYTHE MAIDEN FILLIES' STKS 6f

3:50 (3:51) (Class 5) 2-Y-O **£2,914** (£867; £433; £216) **Stalls** Low

Form RPR

1 **Miss Eze** 2-9-0 0 ... DarryllHolland 8 70+
(G Wragg) *hld up in tch: edgd out rt over 2f out: led over 1f out: edgd lft: pushed clr and in command ins fnl f: eased nr fin* **6/1**[3]

00 2 1 **Midnight Fantasy**[46] 5214 2-9-0 0 ... SaleemGolam 9 64+
(Rae Guest) *chsd ldr tl 3f out: rdn over 2f out: swtchd rt ent fnl f: chsd wnr fnl 100yds: styd on* **33/1**

3 1 **Dareh (IRE)** 2-9-0 0 ... MartinDwyer 5 61+
(Saeed Bin Suroor) *s.i.s: bhd: hdwy and edgd out rt over 2f out: pushed along and styd on steadily to go 3rd nr fin: nt rch ldrs* **15/2**

305 4 1 **Sharpener (IRE)**[66] 4634 2-9-0 **67** ... RichardHughes 10 58
(R Hannon) *led tl 2f out: chsd wnr again ent fnl f: no imp: wknd and lost 2 pls fnl 100yds* **11/2**[2]

0000 5 1 **Missou Maiden**[33] 5632 2-9-0 **56** ... (b[1]) JoeFanning 11 55
(M H Tompkins) *sn pushed up to chse ldrs: wnt 2nd 3f out: led 2f out: hdd over 1f out: wknd ins fnl f* **33/1**

5 6 5 **Sley (FR)**[20] 6030 2-9-0 0 ... TPO'Shea 7 40
(B J Meehan) *dwlt: sn in tch in midfield: rdn over 3f out: struggling over 2f out: wl hld last 2f* **11/4**[1]

7 3 ¼ **Freepressionist** 2-9-0 0 ... JimCrowley 13 30
(R A Teal) *s.i.s: sn swtchd lft: bhd: sme late hdwy: n.d* **22/1**

06 8 nk **Alicante**[11] 6244 2-9-0 0 ... TPQueally 4 29
(Sir Mark Prescott) *nvr bttr than midfield: struggling 3f out: wl btn last 2f* **12/1**

350 9 5 **Black Nun**[46] 5241 2-9-0 **65** ... PatDobbs 12 14
(R Hannon) *a bhd: rdn and toiling 1/2-way* **17/2**

040 10 ¾ **Amatara (IRE)**[20] 6016 2-8-9 **40** ... GabrielHannon(5) 1 12
(B G Powell) *chsd ldrs tl 1/2-way: sn wknd: wl btn last 2f* **66/1**

0 11 1 **Border Maid**[18] 6080 2-9-0 0 ... DaneO'Neill 14 9
(E A L Dunlop) *wnt rt s: a wl bhd: lost tch 1/2-way* **13/2**

12 nk **Sarasota Sunshine** 2-9-0 0 ... JamesDoyle 2 8
(N P Littmoden) *racd in midfield: rdn and struggling 1/2-way: wl bhd last 2f* **33/1**

1m 16.7s (4.00) **Going Correction** +0.50s/f (Yiel) 12 Ran SP% **114.3**

Speed ratings (Par 92): **93,91,90,89,87 81,76,76,69,68 67,66**

toteswinger: 1&2 £30.00, 1&3 £8.90, 2&3 £28.30. CSF £194.19 TOTE £8.30: £2.20, £9.20, £2.30; EX 227.20 TRIFECTA Not won..

Owner J L C Pearce **Bred** J L C Pearce **Trained** Newmarket, Suffolk

FOCUS

This was a weak maiden overall but it saw a decisive winner in Miss Eze.

NOTEBOOK

Miss Eze, a half-sister to the stable's useful Moyenne Corniche, is bred to handle this ground and she moved up nicely to lead a furlong and a half out. She won with more in hand than the official margin suggests, being eased close home, and it will be fascinating to see what mark she is given. She was in the Lowther Stakes until the penultimate forfeit stage and is clearly well thought of, so don't be surprised if she is tried at Listed/Group3 level at some stage. (op 13-2 tchd 11-2)

Midnight Fantasy seemed to improve for this step up to 6f and is now qualified for nurseries. She kept on all the way to the line and evidently has the ability to win races. (op 50-1)

Dareh(IRE) made a promising debut. A daughter of Invincible Spirit, she is clearly no star to be making her debut at this venue, but stayed on nicely into third and looks good enough to land a similar contest. (op 6-1)

Sharpener(IRE) put her experience to use and came across to bag the stands' rail, but she is not really progressing and was readily brushed aside by the winner. (op 9-2 tchd 4-1)

Missou Maiden, unplaced in four previous attempts, showed a lot more in the first-time blinkers and could find a minor contest if the headgear continues to have a positive effect.

Sley(FR), a pleasing fifth on her Yarmouth debut, was under strong pressure at halfway and failed to improve. She looks ready for further now. (op 3-1 tchd 10-3)

Alicante was not disgraced on this third start and is sure to do better once contesting handicaps over further. (op 16-1)

6556 SELLINGE H'CAP 6f

4:20 (4:20) (Class 4) (0-80,78) 3-Y-O+ **£5,046** (£1,510; £755; £377; £188) **Stalls** Low

Form RPR

6040 1 **Princess Valerina**[19] 6052 4-8-9 **69** ... TPQueally 8 76
(H R A Cecil) *chsd ldrs: wnt 2nd over 2f out: led 2f out: hung lft u.p after: fnd ex whn pressed nr fin* **6/1**

5044 2 ¾ **Artsu**[22] 5962 3-8-8 **74** ... JackDean(5) 5 79
(M L W Bell) *awkward s: hld up bhd: swtchd sharply rt and effrt over 1f out: sn drvn: pressed wnr wl ins fnl f: hld nr fin* **9/2**[2]

1004 3 1 **Mandarin Spirit (IRE)**[13] 6200 8-8-5 **70** ... (b) WilliamCarson(5) 3 71
(G C H Chung) *hld up in tch: swtchd rt over 1f out: drvn and chsd wnr ins fnl f: one pce and lost 2nd fnl 100yds* **7/1**

0220 4 nse **Charles Darwin (IRE)**[13] 6200 5-9-4 **78** ... LPKeniry 2 79
(M Blanshard) *hld up wl in tch: rdn and nt qckn 2f out: keeping on same pce whn short of room and swtchd rt ins fnl f: kpt on* **6/1**

0305 5 5 **Really Really Wish**[26] 5839 3-8-4 **65** ... MartinDwyer 1 50
(J R Best) *w ldr tl over 2f out: sn drvn: wknd u.p ent fnl f* **9/1**

0200 6 2 **North South Divide (IRE)**[13] 6200 4-9-0 **74** ... (p) DaneO'Neill 4 53
(R A Teal) *taken down early: dwlt: sn pushed up to ld: hdd 2f out: sn rdn: wknd over 1f out* **5/1**[3]

000 7 5 **Leading Edge (IRE)**[8] 6340 3-8-11 **72** ... DarryllHolland 6 35
(M R Channon) *nvr gng wl: sn pushed along and a bhd: struggling fr 1/2-way* **16/1**

4514 8 2 **Witchry**[19] 6039 6-8-7 **67** ... SamHitchcott 7 23
(A G Newcombe) *in tch: lost pl and rdn after 2f: hdwy 3f out: rdn and struggling whn stmbld over 2f out: wl hld whn hmpd over 1f out* **4/1**[1]

1m 16.8s (4.10) **Going Correction** +0.50s/f (Yiel)

WFA 3 from 4yo+ 1lb 8 Ran SP% **111.8**

Speed ratings (Par 105): **92,91,89,89,82 80,73,70**

toteswinger: 1&2 £6.70, 1&3 £11.00, 2&3 £5.80. CSF £31.54 CT £191.26 TOTE £7.30: £3.30, £1.20, £2.20; EX 49.90 Trifecta £197.10 Part won. Pool: £266.42 - 0.49 winning units..

Owner G J Hicks **Bred** George Joseph Hicks **Trained** Newmarket, Suffolk

FOCUS
Unusually for here, they raced more towards the middle of the track for this 6f handicap. Pretty ordinary form.
Witchry Official explanation: jockey said gelding never travelled

6557 WESTENHANGER H'CAP — 5f
4:50 (4:50) (Class 3) (0-90,86) 3-Y-O+
£7,477 (£2,239; £1,119; £560; £279; £140) **Stalls** Low

Form | | | | RPR
121 **1** **Haajes**[3] 6486 4-9-0 **85** 6ex..........(t) TolleyDean(3) 2 101
(S Parr) *chsd ldr tl led 2f out: rdn over 1f out: r.o wl and drew clr ins fnl f* **6/5**[1]
5015 **2** *2 1/2* **The Jobber (IRE)**[15] 6174 7-9-4 **86**.......... DaneO'Neill 1 93
(M Blanshard) *hld up in tch: hdwy to chse wnr over 1f out: rdn and tried to chal 1f out: btn fnl 100yds* **7/1**
424 **3** *8* **Mango Music**[19] 6053 5-9-0 **82**.......... TPQueally 6 60
(M Quinn) *chsd ldrs: rdn 1/2-way: wknd ent fnl f* **4/1**[2]
5100 **4** *hd* **Regal Royale**[10] 6290 5-8-5 **73**..........(v) PatrickMathers 4 50
(Peter Grayson) *sn drvn in rr: sme hdwy u.p fnl f: nvr nr ldrs* **9/2**[3]
0000 **5** *1/2* **Chartist**[7] 6354 3-9-4 **86**.......... RichardHughes 3 62
(R Hannon) *stdd s: hld up in rr: hdwy over 2f out: rdn: hld hd high and hung rt 2f out: nt run on and immediately btn* **8/1**
1000 **6** *26* **Godfrey Street**[65] 4668 5-8-12 **80**..........(b) LPKeniry 5 —
(A G Newcombe) *led tl 2f out: sn wknd: eased ins fnl f: t.o* **16/1**
61.58 secs (1.58) **Going Correction** +0.50s/f (Yiel) **6 Ran SP% 113.1**
Speed ratings (Par 107): **107,103,90,89,89 47**
toteswinger: 1&2 £2.00, 1&3 £2.00, 2&3 £2.40. CSF £10.53 TOTE £2.00: £1.10, £2.20; EX 8.60.
Owner Willie McKay **Bred** Irish National Stud **Trained** Bawtry, S Yorks

FOCUS
Two drew well clear in what was a modest sprint handicap, and only they showed their form. Another improved effort from Haajes.

NOTEBOOK
Haajes has been in really good form this autumn and was bidding for a quick follow-up, having scored at Redcar the previous Saturday. Shouldering a 6lb penalty, he raced into the lead inside the final quarter-mile and drew clear of the persistent runner-up close home. He is effective from 5f-6f, acts on any ground, and may well win again whilst in this sort of form, even though things are only going to get tougher. (tchd 11-10 and 5-4)
The Jobber(IRE) ran a really good race in defeat and was the only one who could go with the winner. He was always being held but has found his form again and should continue to pay his way. (op 6-1 tchd 15-2)
Mango Music just held on for third. She has been running well but does not look up to winning off her current rating. (op 9-2)
Regal Royale, successful in two of his four previous course visits, received a few early reminders (never travels that well) and failed to get into the race. (op 6-1)
Chartist has not progressed as expected and he failed to get home having pulled early on. (op 9-1)

6558 ROMNEY MARSH H'CAP — 1m 4f
5:20 (5:20) (Class 5) (0-70,70) 3-Y-O+ **£2,914** (£867; £433; £216) **Stalls** Low

Form | | | | RPR
0216 **1** **Pocketwood**[58] 4892 6-9-11 **69**.......... JimCrowley 10 77
(Jean-Rene Auvray) *mde all: rdn over 2f out: styd on wl and clr ins fnl f: eased nr fin* **4/1**[2]
5150 **2** *2 1/4* **Xtravaganza (IRE)**[53] 5058 3-8-13 **64**.......... JamesDoyle 9 68
(J W Hills) *hld up in tch: hdwy u.p wl over 1f out: chsd wnr fnl 100yds: no imp* **12/1**
0220 **3** *1/2* **Act Three**[23] 5934 4-9-8 **66**.......... WilliamBuick 7 69
(Mouse Hamilton-Fairley) *chsd wnr for 2f: wnt 2nd again 2f out: rdn and hld hd high over 1f out: nt qckn and btn ent fnl f: lost 2nd fnl 100yds* **11/4**[1]
6165 **4** *7* **Love And Glory (FR)**[98] 3586 3-9-0 **65**.......... PatDobbs 8 57
(G L Moore) *hld up in tch: rdn and effrt over 2f out: carried bdly lft fr 2f out: no imp over 1f out: wl hld fnl f* **9/2**[3]
-663 **5** *2 3/4* **Desert Thistle (IRE)**[29] 5758 3-9-3 **68**..........(v[1]) IanMongan 4 56
(J L Dunlop) *t.k.h: chsd ldrs: rdn 3f out: wknd ent fnl f* **5/1**
6360 **6** *3 1/4* **Abstract Colours (IRE)**[8] 6329 3-8-11 **62**..........(p) MartinDwyer 11 44
(A M Balding) *chsd wnr after 2f: hung lft fr 3f out: lost 2nd and hung bdly lft fr 2f out: no ch after* **4/1**[2]
-110 **7** *28* **Me Fein**[21] 5992 4-9-9 **67**.......... TPQueally 3 5
(A P Stringer) *hld up in last pl: lost tch: 3f out: t.o and eased fnl f* **16/1**
2m 49.14s (8.24) **Going Correction** +0.775s/f (Yiel)
WFA 3 from 4yo+ 7lb **7 Ran SP% 115.1**
Speed ratings (Par 103): **103,101,101,96,94 92,73**
toteswinger: 1&2 £5.70, 1&3 £1.90, 2&3 £6.90. CSF £49.11 CT £152.86 TOTE £5.20: £3.50, £3.70; EX 40.80 Trifecta £78.40 Pool: £219.56 - 2.07 winning units. Place 6: £827.32 Place 5: £61.14.
Owner Jean-Rene Auvray **Bred** M J Lewin **Trained** Upper Lambourn, Berks

FOCUS
Nearly half the field defected from this moderate handicap. Pocketwood got the run of things and is rated to his best form in the past two years.
Abstract Colours(IRE) Official explanation: jockey said gelding hung left
T/Plt: £1,344.80 to a £1 stake. Pool: £52,227.95. 28.35 winning tickets. T/Qpdt: £12.10 to a £1 stake. Pool: £6,047.54. 369.36 winning tickets. SP

6172 LEICESTER (R-H)
Tuesday, October 7

OFFICIAL GOING: Soft (good to soft in places)
Wind: Fresh behind Weather: Raining

6559 EBF LADBROKES.COM MAIDEN FILLIES' STKS (DIV I) — 7f 9y
2:10 (2:13) (Class 4) 2-Y-O **£4,857** (£1,445; £722; £360) **Stalls** Low

Form | | | | RPR
1 **Burgundy Ice (USA)** 2-9-0 0.......... LDettori 7 82+
(Saeed Bin Suroor) *chsd ldrs: rdn to chal over 1f out: led ins fnl f: r.o* **9/2**[3]
2 *1/2* **Hukba (IRE)** 2-9-0 0.......... AdamKirby 10 81+
(E A L Dunlop) *trckd ldrs: led narrowly 2f out: rdn and hdd ins fnl f: hld cl home* **20/1**
0 **3** *2 1/4* **West With The Wind (USA)**[20] 6030 2-9-0 0.......... MichaelHills 15 75
(P W Chapple-Hyam) *a.p: rdn to chal 2f out tl kpt on same pce ins fnl f* **3/1**[1]
4 *shd* **Piquante** 2-9-0 0.......... JamieSpencer 11 75+
(M L W Bell) *racd keenly: led: hdd 4f out: rdn to regain ld briefly over 2f out: continued to chal tl no ex fnl 75yds* **10/3**[2]
5 *2 3/4* **Aswaaq (IRE)** 2-9-0 0.......... TedDurcan 5 71+
(J L Dunlop) *missed break: hld up: pushed along over 2f out and rn green: prog and edgd rt over 1f out: styd on wout troubling ldrs* **14/1**
60 **6** *1* **Dance Club (IRE)**[40] 5430 2-9-0 0.......... ShaneKelly 8 66
(W Jarvis) *cl up: rdn 2f out: one pce fr over 1f out* **25/1**
00 **7** *8* **Hayley's Girl**[10] 6282 2-8-9 0.......... DavidProbert(5) 12 46
(S W James) *prom: led 4f out: rdn 3f out: hdd over 2f out: wknd over 1f out* **66/1**
8 *1* **Fleurissimo** 2-9-0 0.......... EddieAhern 2 43
(J L Dunlop) *hld up: hdwy into midfield 1/2-way: rdn 2f out: sn outpcd: wl btn fnl f* **16/1**
9 *1 3/4* **Admiring Glances** 2-9-0 0.......... JimmyQuinn 9 39
(J Pearce) *missed break: in rr: pushed along 2f out: nvr on terms* **50/1**
10 *2 3/4* **Alimarr (IRE)** 2-9-0 0.......... NCallan 14 32
(B J Meehan) *missed break: in tch: pushed along and wknd over 2f out* **14/1**
11 *3/4* **Pinkalicious (IRE)** 2-9-0 0.......... HayleyTurner 16 30
(M L W Bell) *midfield: pushed along 1/2-way: wknd 2f out* **14/1**
00 **12** *1 1/4* **Xaaroon (IRE)**[65] 4665 2-9-0 0.......... ChrisCatlin 3 27
(Rae Guest) *towards rr: u.p over 2f out: nvr on terms* **66/1**
0 **13** *nk* **Waheeba**[18] 6084 2-9-0 0.......... RHills 1 26
(J L Dunlop) *in tch: rdn and wknd over 2f out* **8/1**
14 *20* **Canucatcher (IRE)** 2-9-0 0.......... JamieMoriarty 4 —
(T D Walford) *a bhd: sn rdn along: lost tch 3f out* **100/1**
1m 26.53s (0.33) **Going Correction** +0.15s/f (Good) **14 Ran SP% 117.8**
Speed ratings (Par 94): **104,103,100,100,97 96,87,86,84,81 80,78,78,55**
toteswinger: 1&2 £19.50, 1&3 £4.70, 2&3 £19.70. CSF £99.19 TOTE £5.80: £2.30, £4.50, £1.50; EX 133.40.
Owner Godolphin **Bred** Darley **Trained** Newmarket, Suffolk

FOCUS
This first division of the fillies' maiden was made up of largely well-related juveniles who should come into their own next year. The runners were spread across the track and there was no obvious bias with the draw. Not easy to rate with little previous form on the board, but the first two look nice recruits.

NOTEBOOK
Burgundy Ice(USA), whose dam was top-class at around 1m in the US, is a sister to the high-class Ile De France and half-sister to the outstanding Bernadini. She got her career off to a winning start with a fairly ready display, looking better the further she went, and went through the easy ground without much fuss. She is entitled to come on for the experience and could prove very useful next year. (op 4-1 tchd 13-2)
Hukba(IRE) ◆, bred to make her mark at around 1m2f as a three-year-old, posted a very pleasing debut effort and finished a clear second best. She will learn plenty for this and ought to be going one better before long. (op 33-1)
West With The Wind(USA) showed the benefit of her debut outing over 6f at Yarmouth 20 days previously and raced more prominently. She hit a flat spot before staying on again, if anything shaping as though she already needs 1m. (tchd 5-2 and 10-3)
Piquante is related to winners at around 1m and showed up promisingly on her racecourse bow. She only felt the pinch inside the final furlong and would have no doubt finished third had her rider been more vigorous on her close home, so should be placed to strike now she has this run under her belt. (op 11-4 tchd 7-2)
Aswaaq(IRE), whose choicely-bred dam was a 1m winner at three, made a sluggish start and it took a long time for the penny to drop with her. She should prove a lot sharper next time out. (op 18-1 tchd 12-1)
Dance Club(IRE), whose stable won a division of this event last year with a similar type, raced prominently before being outstayed on this further step up in trip. Now qualified for a nursery mark, she is one to keep on side when returning to a sounder surface.

6560 ARTHUR GADSBY APPRENTICE H'CAP — 7f 9y
2:40 (2:42) (Class 5) (0-70,69) 3-Y-O+ **£2,590** (£770; £385; £192) **Stalls** Low

Form | | | | RPR
0024 **1** **Ken's Girl**[63] 4708 4-9-2 **64**.......... Louis-PhilippeBeuzelin 15 69
(W S Kittow) *mde virtually all: clr 2f out: rdn out* **5/1**[1]
0005 **2** *1 1/4* **Bidable**[74] 4368 4-8-7 **55** oh8.......... MCGeran 13 57
(B Palling) *chsd wnr: rdn over 1f out: styd on* **22/1**
002 **3** *2* **Having A Ball**[7] 6353 4-8-4 **55** oh2.......... AmyBaker(3) 3 51+
(P D Cundell) *mid-div: rdn 1/2-way: outpcd over 2f out: rallied and hung rt fr over 1f out: styd on* **10/1**[3]
006 **4** *2* **Charlie Bear**[44] 5318 7-8-4 **55** oh7.......... RossAtkinson(3) 9 46
(Miss Z C Davison) *hld up: hdwy over 1f out: nt trble ldrs* **25/1**
4053 **5** *1 1/2* **Flying Flute**[15] 6178 3-8-3 **58**.......... RosieJessop(5) 14 45
(H Candy) *prom: racd keenly: rdn over 2f out: wknd ins fnl f* **5/1**[1]
6001 **6** *2* **Prince Golan (IRE)**[15] 6178 4-9-1 **63**.......... RichardEvans 12 44
(J W Unett) *chsd ldrs: rdn 1/2-way: wknd fnl f* **5/1**[1]
0606 **7** *2* **Lordship (IRE)**[15] 6178 4-8-9 **60**.......... BMcHugh(3) 4 36
(A W Carroll) *hld up: hdwy 1/2-way: rdn over 2f out: sn wknd* **5/1**[1]
5060 **8** *3/4* **Autumn Charm**[15] 6162 3-8-2 **55** oh5.......... RobbieEgan(3) 10 29
(Lucinda Featherstone) *chsd ldrs: rdn 1/2-way: wknd over 2f out* **25/1**
5362 **9** *1* **Takitwo**[13] 6208 5-8-2 **55** oh2..........(b) TobyAtkinson(5) 6 26
(P D Cundell) *hld up: rdn 1/2-way: a in rr* **15/2**[2]
0450 **10** *3 1/4* **Seven Royals (IRE)**[13] 6204 3-8-9 **62**.......... JemmaMarshall(3) 8 24
(Miss A M Newton-Smith) *hld up: rdn over 2f out: a in rr* **16/1**
00-0 **11** *3 3/4* **Allahor**[185] 1216 3-8-9 **62**.......... BillyCray(3) 1 14
(D J S Ffrench Davis) *mid-div: pushed along over 4f out: sn lost pl* **33/1**
106 **12** *2 1/4* **Nice Matin (USA)**[61] 4795 3-9-0 **67**.......... AshleyMorgan(3) 5 13
(J A R Toller) *dwlt: hld up: a in rr* **20/1**
0000 **13** *3/4* **Dolly No Hair**[13] 6219 3-8-9 **59**.......... KellyHarrison 2 3
(D W Barker) *hld up: rdn: hung rt and wknd over 2f out* **33/1**
1m 26.62s (0.42) **Going Correction** +0.15s/f (Good)
WFA 3 from 4yo+ 2lb **13 Ran SP% 116.1**
Speed ratings (Par 103): **103,101,99,97,95 93,90,89,88,85 80,78,77**
toteswinger: 1&2 £29.80, 1&3 £9.90, 2&3 £30.00. CSF £121.88 CT £1081.91 TOTE £3.70: £1.20, £6.80, £4.10; EX 168.30.
Owner Midd Shire Racing **Bred** D R Tucker **Trained** Blackborough, Devon

FOCUS
A moderate handicap, confined to apprentice riders, in which five raced from out of the handicap. The main action developed down the centre of the track and the form should be treated with a degree of caution, with the first pair always to the fore.
Prince Golan(IRE) Official explanation: jockey said gelding was unsuited by the soft (good to soft places) ground

Seven Royals(IRE) Official explanation: jockey said gelding was unsuited by the soft (good to soft places) ground

6561 LADBROKES.COM SQUIRREL CONDITIONS STKS 1m 1f 218y
3:10 (3:10) (Class 3) 2-Y-O **£6,854** (£2,052; £1,026; £513) **Stalls** High

Form RPR
1 **1** **Alcalde**[26] 5812 2-8-13 80 RoystonFfrench 5 83+
(M Johnston) *mde all: shkn up 3f out: sn hrd pressd: rdn and hung lft fr wl over 1f out: styd on gamely towards fin* **8/13**[1]
0401 **2** ½ **Heliodor (USA)**[13] 6199 2-9-1 83 RyanMoore 2 84
(R Hannon) *trckd ldrs: rdn wl over 1f out: styd on to take 2nd and hung lft ins fnl f: sn pressed wnr: hld cl home* **3/1**[2]
001 **3** 2 ½ **Le Grand Amour (IRE)**[28] 5782 2-8-10 75 MichaelHills 3 75
(B W Hills) *trckd wnr: chal 3f out: upsides fr over 2f out tl rdn over 1f out: lost 2nd ins fnl f: no ex fnl 150yds* **6/1**[3]
021 **4** 14 **Bounty Reef**[13] 6214 2-8-6 60 HayleyTurner 4 54+
(P D Evans) *plld hrd: dropped to rr after 2f: u.p 2f out: lost tch w front trio 1f out: sn eased whn wl btn* **16/1**
2m 13.38s (5.48) **Going Correction** +0.50s/f (Yiel) **4** Ran SP% **107.1**
Speed ratings (Par 99): **98,97,95,84**
toteswinger: 1&2 £2.20. CSF £2.66 TOTE £1.80; EX 2.20.
Owner Sheikh Hamdan Bin Mohammed Al Maktoum **Bred** Miss K Rausing And Mrs S Rogers **Trained** Middleham Moor, N Yorks

FOCUS
A tight conditions event which proved a real stamina test for the juveniles. Solid form, the winner rated to his mark.

NOTEBOOK
Alcalde was allowed his own way out in front early on and responded when pressed from 3f out, but harmed his cause by drifting right over to the near side inside the final furlong. That allowed his rivals a chance, but when he met the stands' rail he picked up again and was always doing enough. From a prolific staying family, this trip not surprisingly proved well within his compass, and he looks sure to appreciate 1m4f and beyond next term. The stable's previous runner of this race, Philanthropy, contested the Zetland Stakes next time, so that event in November could be on the agenda for this imposing son of Hernando. (op 4-6 tchd 8-11 in places)
Heliodor(USA) had officially been raised 5lb for belatedly getting off the mark at Goodwood 13 days previously. He came through to make the winner work inside the final furlong, but is a little flattered by his proximity as that rival lost ground by hanging. This rates a personal-best effort in defeat, he got the longer trip, and time may tell he faced an impossible task in conceding 2lb. (op 11-4 tchd 5-2 and 10-3)
Le Grand Amour(IRE), off the mark over 1m on a taxing surface at the track last month, tried to put it up to the winner from 3f out but her stamina gave way in the end. This was no disgrace and a move into nurseries now looks her best option. (tchd 7-1)
Bounty Reef had been upped 6lb for winning a 1m nursery 13 days previously. She spoilt her chance of getting home over the extra 2f by refusing to settle under early restraint, but found things all too hot in any case. Official explanation: jockey said filly had no more to give

6562 LADBROKES.COM STOAT (S) STKS 1m 1f 218y
3:40 (3:41) (Class 6) 3-Y-O **£1,942** (£578; £288; £144) **Stalls** High

Form RPR
-4 **1** **Dazzling Begum**[21] 6004 3-8-6 0 JimmyQuinn 2 51
(J Pearce) *chsd ldrs: lost pl over 6f out: rdn over 4f out: hdwy and hung rt over 1f out: styd on to ld wl ins fnl f* **4/1**[2]
1000 **2** ½ **Ricci De Mare**[12] 6227 3-8-6 57 DavidProbert(5) 4 55
(A B Haynes) *chsd ldr: led over 7f out: hdd over 6f out: rdn to ld 1f out: hdd wl ins fnl f* **14/1**
0002 **3** ½ **Oronsay**[26] 5813 3-8-6 47 (t) ChrisCatlin 8 49
(B R Millman) *s.i.s: hld up: racd keenly: hdwy over 2f out: rdn and ev ch ins fnl f: unable qck nr fin* **20/1**
5030 **4** 2 ¾ **Mill Beattie**[28] 5783 3-8-6 53 FrancisNorton 1 44
(G M Moore) *s.i.s: sn rcvrd to ld: hdd over 7f out: rdn over 3f out: styd on same pce fnl f* **7/1**
3036 **5** ½ **Balais Folly (FR)**[31] 5710 3-8-6 42 MCGeran(5) 3 48
(B Palling) *prom: lost pl over 6f out: rdn over 3f out: hdwy over 1f out: no ex ins fnl f* **16/1**
0006 **6** 1 ¾ **Veronicas Way**[38] 5501 3-8-1 43 KellyHarrison(5) 12 39
(G M Moore) *chsd ldrs: led over 6f out: rdn and hdd 1f out: sn wknd* **28/1**
2004 **7** 7 **Just Sam (IRE)**[13] 6217 3-8-6 47 RoystonFfrench 9 25
(D W Barker) *prom: hmpd and lost pl after 1f: hdwy 6f out: rdn and ev ch over 1f out: wknd fnl f* **9/1**
2002 **8** 3 ¾ **Near The Front**[20] 6015 3-8-11 56 (v) NCallan 6 23
(Miss Gay Kelleway) *hld up: hdwy 1/2-way: rdn and wknd over 1f out* **7/2**[1]
0000 **9** ¾ **Dancing Marabout (IRE)**[52] 4485 3-8-11 60 RyanMoore 13 21
(C R Egerton) *s.i.s: hld up: rdn over 4f out: a in rr* **9/2**[3]
0500 **10** 2 **General Tufto**[14] 6185 3-8-8 49 RussellKennemore(3) 10 17
(C Smith) *s.i.s: a in rr* **40/1**
0506 **11** 1 ¼ **Sleeping**[15] 6175 3-8-0 50 ow1 (b[1]) AshleyMorgan(7) 5 11
(M H Tompkins) *prom: rdn over 2f out: sn wknd* **12/1**
0055 **P** **Wooden King (IRE)**[15] 6173 3-8-11 50 StephenDonohoe 7 —
(P D Evans) *plld hrd and prom: sddle slipped sn after s: wknd over 4f out: sn p.u* **16/1**
2m 12.94s (5.04) **Going Correction** +0.50s/f (Yiel) **12** Ran SP% **119.7**
Speed ratings (Par 99): **99,98,98,96,95 94,88,85,85,83 82,—**
toteswinger: 1&2 £15.00, 1&3 £15.10, 2&3 £52.70. CSF £58.28 TOTE £5.10: £2.90, £8.20, £3.40; EX 89.90.The winner was bought in for 4,800gns.
Owner Macniler Racing Partnership **Bred** Ian Bryant **Trained** Newmarket, Suffolk

FOCUS
A typically weak seller. The winner was less exposed than most and is rated up 3lb on her debut effort.
Balais Folly(FR) Official explanation: jockey said gelding ran too freely early stages
Wooden King(IRE) Official explanation: jockey said saddle slipped

6563 LADBROKES.COM QUORN H'CAP 1m 3f 183y
4:10 (4:13) (Class 2) (0-100,92) 3-Y-O
£11,215 (£3,358; £1,679; £840; £419; £210) **Stalls** High

Form RPR
212 **1** **Electrolyser (IRE)**[17] 6128 3-9-0 88 AdamKirby 3 99+
(C G Cox) *in tch: effrt to ld under 2f out: r.o ins fnl f: drvn out* **13/2**[3]
3332 **2** ¾ **Mezzanisi (IRE)**[7] 6355 3-8-6 80 HayleyTurner 11 90+
(M L W Bell) *hld up: hdwy on inner over 3f out: nt clr run 2f out: rdn and swtchd lft over 1f out: r.o strly to take 2nd fnl 100yds: gaining at finsh* **9/1**
6113 **3** 1 ¾ **Kingdom Of Fife**[20] 6033 3-8-9 83 RyanMoore 12 90
(Sir Michael Stoute) *midfield: hdwy 3f out: rdn to chse ldrs over 1f out: styd on same pce ins fnl f* **10/1**
212 **4** hd **Torphichen**[17] 6107 3-8-11 85 PhilipRobinson 4 92
(M A Jarvis) *trckd ldrs: effrt to ld 2f out: sn hdd: no ex fnl 100yds* **3/1**[1]
4321 **5** nk **King O'The Gypsies (IRE)**[51] 5117 3-9-2 90 LDettori 9 96
(R Charlton) *trckd ldrs: nt clr run 2f out: rdn over 1f out: kpt on ins fnl f: nt quite pce to chal* **7/1**
106 **6** 1 ¾ **Secret Dancer (IRE)**[26] 5830 3-8-10 89 Louis-PhilippeBeuzelin(5) 10 93
(J R Fanshawe) *hld up: rdn and hdwy into midfield 2f out: no real imp on ldrs whn carried lft over 1f out: one pce ins fnl f* **20/1**
121 **7** 3 ½ **Times Vital (IRE)**[18] 6079 3-8-9 83 ChrisCatlin 8 81
(E J O'Neill) *hld up in rr: rdn 2f out: kpt steadily ins fnl f: nvr able to chal* **9/2**[2]
144 **8** 1 ¾ **Manyriverstocross (IRE)**[53] 5054 3-8-13 87 ShaneKelly 5 82
(A King) *prom: w ldr 1/2-way: led over 2f out: sn rdn and hdd: wknd 1f out* **10/1**
5213 **9** 10 **Kossack**[19] 6061 3-9-4 92 JamieSpencer 6 71
(L M Cumani) *in rr: rdn and hung rt wl over 2f out: eased whn btn 1f out* **15/2**
1053 **10** 12 **Goodwood Starlight (IRE)**[14] 6195 3-9-4 92 EddieAhern 7 52
(J L Dunlop) *sn led: hdd over 2f out: wknd wl over 1f out: eased whn btn ins fnl f* **33/1**
2130 **11** 11 **Moonquake (USA)**[24] 5894 3-9-4 92 JimmyFortune 2 34
(J H M Gosden) *midfield: dropped away qckly 2f out* **33/1**
120 **12** 20 **Le Brocquy**[23] 5938 3-8-10 84 ow1 NCallan 1 —
(M G Quinlan) *midfield: pushed along 4f out: wknd 2f out* **66/1**
2m 36.4s (2.50) **Going Correction** +0.50s/f (Yiel) **12** Ran SP% **121.1**
Speed ratings (Par 107): **111,110,109,109,109 107,105,104,97,89 82,69**
toteswinger: 1&2 £18.60, 1&3 £16.30, 2&3 £11.80. CSF £62.99 CT £591.15 TOTE £7.20: £2.90, £3.20, £2.80; EX 85.70.
Owner Mr And Mrs P Hargreaves **Bred** Darley **Trained** Lambourn, Berks
■ Stewards' Enquiry : Hayley Turner one-day ban: careless riding (Oct 21)

FOCUS
This decent handicap attracted a good field with a number of unexposed and progressive performers. The unexposed winner is up 4lb and the second improved too with the next pair and the sixth close to their solid recent form.

NOTEBOOK
Electrolyser(IRE) ◆, a progressive colt, ran out a decisive winner on his fourth start. Having raced only at 1m2f on a sound surface and Polytrack, there had to be a doubt beforehand about him getting the trip on this softer surface, but he was ridden confidently and if anything improved for the extra distance. He will now be aimed at the November Handicap and looks a really nice prospect for next season. (op 8-1)
Mezzanisi(IRE) had no questions to answer regarding trip and ground and did best of those held up at the back. Having done Secret Dancer no favours when switching for a run, he stayed on nicely and is probably a fair guide to the level of the form. (op 12-1)
Kingdom Of Fife, a dual winner over 1m2f at Sandown, travelled into the race going well but his effort flattened out as if he did not quite get home on his first try over the trip. (op 8-1)
Torphichen travelled well just off the pace and looked the likely winner early in the straight, but when taken on by the winner he had nothing in reserve. The 5lb rise for finishing second at Ayr may have anchored him but he travelled so well until coming off the bridle that he might be worth dropping back to 1m2f. (op 7-2)
King O'The Gypsies(IRE), an easy winner of a moderate contest over just short of this trip last time, had been raised 6lb for that. He was stuck in a pocket when his jockey wanted to make his move but, once he got an opening, he did not really find that much. (op 8-1)
Times Vital(IRE), a well-backed second favourite, was restrained early and failed to reach a challenging position. In view of his previously progressive profile this was somewhat disappointing but he may have had enough for the season. (op 5-1 tchd 11-2)
Moonquake(USA) Official explanation: jockey said colt stopped very quickly

6564 LADBROKESCASINO.COM FILLIES' H'CAP 5f 218y
4:40 (4:44) (Class 5) (0-70,67) 3-Y-O+ **£3,238** (£963; £481; £240) **Stalls** Low

Form RPR
114 **1** **Hurricane Harriet**[44] 5319 3-9-2 65 OscarUrbina 13 77+
(R M H Cowell) *chsd ldr tl led over 1f out: rdn and edgd lft ins fnl f: r.o: eased nr fin* **11/2**[2]
5650 **2** 1 ½ **Diminuto**[34] 5610 4-8-3 56 DavidProbert(5) 8 63
(M D I Usher) *led: rdn and hdd over 1f out: styd on same pce ins fnl f* **18/1**
0501 **3** 1 ¾ **Doric Lady**[21] 6003 3-9-2 65 EddieAhern 1 67
(J A R Toller) *chsd ldrs: rdn 1/2-way: no ex ins fnl f* **8/1**[3]
0336 **4** hd **Night Premiere (IRE)**[4] 6435 3-8-7 56 JimmyQuinn 12 57
(R Hannon) *chsd ldrs: rdn over 2f out: no ex ins fnl f* **17/2**
3556 **5** 1 ½ **Rosie Says No**[19] 6046 3-8-10 59 ShaneKelly 16 55
(R M H Cowell) *chsd ldrs: rdn 1/2-way: sn outpcdr.o ins fnl f* **14/1**
4034 **6** ½ **Ingleby Princess**[15] 6160 4-9-5 67 JamieSpencer 6 62+
(T D Barron) *hld up: swtchd rt over 2f out: hdwy over 1f out: sn rdn: no imp fnl f* **10/1**
5205 **7** ¾ **Linda Green**[15] 6160 7-9-4 66 EdwardCreighton 15 58
(M R Channon) *mid-div: rdn 1/2-way: no ch whn hmpd wl over 1f out* **14/1**
-600 **8** 1 ¼ **Joyeaux**[12] 6232 6-8-12 60 RoystonFfrench 2 48
(L R James) *s.i.s: hld up: sme hdwy over 2f out: sn edgd rt: nvr trbld ldrs* **11/1**
0255 **9** nse **Dualagi**[13] 6209 4-9-0 62 HayleyTurner 4 50
(M R Bosley) *hld up: rdn over 2f out: n.d* **9/1**
501 **10** hd **Belle Bellino (FR)**[29] 5749 3-8-11 60 RyanMoore 5 47
(R M Beckett) *s.i.s: hld up: rdn over 2f out: n.d* **5/1**[1]
6520 **11** 3 ¼ **Melt (IRE)**[8] 6334 3-8-8 57 FrancisNorton 3 34
(R Hannon) *hld up: rdn 1/2-way: a in rr* **10/1**
1550 **12** 2 ¼ **Tilsworth Charlie**[27] 5801 5-9-1 63 (b) StephenDonohoe 11 33
(R J Jenkins) *hld up: a in rr* **50/1**
3631 **13** 3 ¼ **Meridian Line (IRE)**[20] 6024 3-8-11 60 (b) AdrianMcCarthy 10 19
(J G Portman) *s.s: hdwy over 4f out: rdn and wknd wl over 1f out* **16/1**
1m 13.46s (0.46) **Going Correction** +0.15s/f (Good)
WFA 3 from 4yo+ 1lb **13** Ran SP% **116.6**
Speed ratings (Par 100): **102,100,97,97,95 94,93,92,92,91 87,84,80**
toteswinger: 1&2 £28.80, 1&3 £8.80, 2&3 £40.50. CSF £98.07 CT £815.52 TOTE £5.90: £2.40, £6.50, £3.90; EX 140.90.
Owner Mr & Mrs R Foulkes & Mrs Eugenie Abel Smith **Bred** Mrs K E Collie **Trained** Six Mile Bottom, Cambs

FOCUS
This was a wide-open fillies' handicap. The field again came down the middle of the track and few managed to get into it from off the pace, despite there being a sound early pace on. Ordinary form, but there could be more to come from the winner.

Dualagi Official explanation: jockey said filly hung right

6565 EBF LADBROKES.COM MAIDEN FILLIES' STKS (DIV II) 7f 9y

5:10 (5:13) (Class 4) 2-Y-O £4,857 (£1,445; £722; £360) Stalls Low

Form RPR

1 **July Jasmine (USA)** 2-9-0 0 .... RyanMoore 14 80+
(Sir Michael Stoute) *midfield: hdwy 3f out: rdn to chal over 1f out: r.o to ld towards fin* **11/2**[3]

2 ½ **Mezenah** 2-9-0 0 .... LDettori 12 79+
(Saeed Bin Suroor) *a.p: led over 2f out: rdn 1f out: r.o u.p: hdd towards fin* **13/2**

3 1 **Spring Adventure** 2-9-0 0 .... JimmyFortune 10 76+
(E A L Dunlop) *hld up: hdwy over 2f out: chsd ldrs over 1f out: chal ins fnl f: nt qckn towards fin* **33/1**

4 4 1 ¼ **Bessie Lou (IRE)**[10] 6291 2-9-0 0 .... NCallan 15 73
(K A Ryan) *led: hdd over 2f out: sn rdn: kpt on u.p tl no ex cl home* **15/2**

5 3 **Kasaa Ed** 2-9-0 0 .... RoystonFfrench 11 66+
(M Johnston) *prom: chal over 2f out: sn rdn: no ex fnl 100yds* **14/1**

6 1 **Brilliana** 2-9-0 0 .... TedDurcan 9 63+
(D R Lanigan) *midfield: pushed along over 2f out: styd on ins fnl f: nvr able to chal ldrs* **33/1**

00 7 2 ¼ **Ja One (IRE)**[33] 5640 2-9-0 0 .... MichaelHills 5 57+
(B W Hills) *midfield: effrt over 2f out: sn chsd ldrs: wknd fnl f* **16/1**

0 8 nse **In Her Shoes**[11] 6244 2-9-0 0 .... ChrisCatlin 2 57
(B J Meehan) *midfield: rdn 2f out: sn outpcd: n.d after* **50/1**

04 9 ¾ **Golden Games (IRE)**[37] 5535 2-9-0 0 .... JimmyQuinn 1 55+
(J L Dunlop) *hld up: pushed along 2f out: nvr on terms* **33/1**

5 10 1 ¾ **Mooteeah (IRE)**[46] 5240 2-9-0 0 .... RHills 6 51
(M A Jarvis) *chsd ldrs: rdn and hung lft whn wknd over 2f out* **9/4**[1]

11 ½ **Moggy (IRE)** 2-9-0 0 .... JamieSpencer 8 50+
(M L W Bell) *in rr: pushed along 2f out: rn green: eased whn n.d ins fnl f* **25/1**

06 12 1 ¾ **Congenial**[29] 5754 2-9-0 0 .... EddieAhern 7 45
(J R Fanshawe) *dwlt: hld up: pushed along 2f out: nvr on terms* **33/1**

5 13 1 ¼ **Jumaana (IRE)**[18] 6084 2-9-0 0 .... PhilipRobinson 16 42
(J L Dunlop) *chsd ldrs tl rdn and wknd over 2f out* **9/2**[2]

0 14 15 **Harley Fern**[15] 6166 2-9-0 0 .... StephenDonohoe 13 5
(P J McBride) *w ldr to 1/2-way: sn wknd* **100/1**

1m 27.65s (1.45) **Going Correction** +0.15s/f (Good) 14 Ran SP% 120.5
Speed ratings (Par 94): **97,96,95,93,90 89,86,86,85,83 83,81,79,62**
toteswinger: 1&2 £8.50, 1&3 £37.50, 2&3 £34.50. CSF £38.90 TOTE £6.60: £2.70, £3.10, £9.40; EX 40.90.
Owner K Abdulla **Bred** Juddmonte Farms Inc **Trained** Newmarket, Suffolk

FOCUS
The second division of the fillies' maiden and, like the first, the field was largely made up of 3yo prospects. It was the slower of the pair, but still looks a good heat.

NOTEBOOK
July Jasmine(USA), from the stable that took the first division of this last year, proved easy to back on this racecourse bow. She was given time to find her feet through the first half of the race, but responded most positively to pressure from 2f out and was always going to get there in the closing stages. This half-sister to Rob Roy – who also won on his debut over this trip at two – may prove happier on a sounder surface and looks to have a bright future. (op 13-2 tchd 7-1)
Mezenah, whose connections took the first division earlier on the card, almost did enough to make a winning debut but was collared near the line. She looked well served by this easy surface and really ought to be placed to open her account before the season's end. (op 11-2 tchd 5-1)
Spring Adventure ◆ is more precociously bred than most of these, but her dam only managed to enter the winner's enclosure at the age of four. She turned in a promising debut, doing her best work from halfway, and is another who should not remain a maiden for long. (op 28-1)
Bessie Lou(IRE) helped to force the early pace and did not go down without a fight. She had finished a creditable fourth on her debut at Haydock ten days previously and sets the standard of this form. She is likely to move back up a furlong next time on this showing. (op 7-1 tchd 8-1)
Kasaa Ed left the impression that a drop to 6f is what she wants at present and this was a pleasing debut. (op 20-1)
Mooteeah(IRE) was in trouble passing the 2f pole and ran miles below the level of her Newmarket debut on this softer surface. (op 11-4)

6566 LADBROKES.COM DORMOUSE MAIDEN STKS 7f 9y

5:40 (5:43) (Class 5) 3-Y-O £2,590 (£770; £385; £192) Stalls Low

Form RPR

1 **Sirocco Breeze** 3-9-3 0 .... LDettori 13 94+
(Saeed Bin Suroor) *led: hdd 5f out: led over 2f out: shkn up over 1f out: sn clr: edgd lft ins fnl f* **3/1**[2]

0560 2 4 **Amylee (IRE)**[17] 6124 3-8-12 69 .... PhilipRobinson 9 73
(C G Cox) *chsd wnr tl led 5f out: hdd 1/2-way: sn rdn: outpcd fr over 1f out* **4/1**[3]

342 3 ¾ **Pivka**[34] 5608 3-8-12 70 .... RyanMoore 11 71
(Sir Michael Stoute) *chsd ldrs: led 1/2-way: rdn and hdd over 2f out: edgd rt over 1f out: sn outpcd* **11/4**[1]

323 4 8 **Shakedown**[21] 6003 3-9-3 69 .... StephenDonohoe 4 54
(E S McMahon) *plld hrd and prom: rdn over 2f out: wknd over 1f out* **9/2**

60 5 hd **Second Opinion (IRE)**[90] 3833 3-8-12 58 .... HayleyTurner 1 49
(J M P Eustace) *prom: rdn 1/2-way: wknd 2f out* **33/1**

40-5 6 1 ¼ **Kinlochard**[53] 5057 3-8-12 53 .... StephenCarson 7 45
(Eve Johnson Houghton) *mid-div: rdn and outpcd 1/2-way: n.d after* **50/1**

6000 7 3 ¼ **Rowaad**[7] 6357 3-9-3 65 .... JimmyQuinn 14 42
(A E Price) *mid-div: hdwy over 4f out: rdn and wknd over 2f out* **66/1**

8 hd **Cotswolds** 3-9-3 0 .... RoystonFfrench 6 41
(M Johnston) *mid-div: hdwy over 4f out: hmpd sn after: rdn and wknd over 2f out* **9/1**

0 9 nse **Melia (GR)**[66] 4651 3-8-12 0 .... ChrisCatlin 3 36
(Jane Chapple-Hyam) *hld up: plld hrd: wknd over 2f out* **50/1**

6 10 16 **Historical Giant (USA)**[43] 5366 3-9-3 0 .... JamieSpencer 8 —
(E F Vaughan) *s.i.s: a bhd* **16/1**

11 10 **Alabaster Flatley (IRE)** 3-8-12 0 .... DavidProbert(5) 15 —
(J R Jenkins) *dwlt: outpcd* **66/1**

12 54 **Amazing Toto** 3-9-3 0 .... PaulQuinn 12 —
(Miss Diana Weeden) *s.i.s: outpcd* **100/1**

1m 27.39s (1.19) **Going Correction** +0.15s/f (Good) 12 Ran SP% 116.6
Speed ratings (Par 101): **99,94,93,84,84 82,79,78,78,60 49,—**
toteswinger: 1&2 £4.20, 1&3 £2.70, 2&3 £4.40. CSF £14.76 TOTE £3.60: £1.80, £1.80, £1.50; EX 17.60 Place 6: £356.55 Place 5: £175.29.
Owner Godolphin **Bred** Gainsborough Stud Management Ltd **Trained** Newmarket, Suffolk

FOCUS
No more than a modest maiden for 3yos. It was run at an average pace and, with the runners coming more towards the stands' side, few got involved from off the pace. The form looks straightforward with a big gap to the fourth.

T/Plt: £489.80 to a £1 stake. Pool: £60,303.15. 89.87 winning tickets. T/Qpdt: £72.30 to a £1 stake. Pool: £4,172.18. 42.70 winning tickets. CR

6064 CHANTILLY (R-H)

Tuesday, October 7

OFFICIAL GOING: Soft

6567a PRIX CHARLES LAFFITTE (LISTED) (FILLIES) 1m 2f

2:50 (2:55) 3-Y-O £20,221 (£8,088; £6,066; £4,044; £2,022)

RPR

1 **Kareemah (IRE)**[54] 5039 3-8-12 .... TGillet 6 105
(J E Hammond, France)

2 nse **Sanjida (IRE)**[24] 5925 3-9-2 .... MGuyon 8 109
(A Fabre, France)

3 1 **Changing Skies (IRE)**[44] 5331 3-9-2 .... DBonilla 2 107
(B J Meehan) *led: pushed along ent st: qcknd 2f out: rdn and hdd appr fnl f: no ex nr fin* **17/10**[1]

4 ½ **Montagne Lointaine (IRE)**[72] 3-8-12 .... ACrastus 1 102
(E Lellouche, France)

5 2 **Rainbow Dancing**[70] 3-8-12 .... DBoeuf 3 98
(Mlle H Van Zuylen, France)

6 1 **Sea Sex Sun**[142] 2231 3-9-2 .... JVictoire 7 100
(A Fabre, France)

7 ¾ **Virana (IRE)**[24] 5925 3-8-12 .... CSoumillon 5 95
(A De Royer-Dupre, France)

8 hd **Lune Rose**[85] 4040 3-8-12 .... C-PLemaire 4 94
(P Bary, France)

2m 10.7s (5.90) 8 Ran SP% 37.0
PARI-MUTUEL: WIN 6.10; PL 1.80, 1.60, 1.30; DF 17.50.
Owner Hamdan Al Maktoum **Bred** Shadwell Estate Company Ltd **Trained** France

NOTEBOOK
Changing Skies(IRE), who was touched off by Top Toss in the Prix de Psyche and then behind Prix de L'Opera winner Lady Marian in two visits to France in August, made the running as usual and quickened early in the straight. However, she stuck to her task when headed and was only run out of it close home. She deserves to pick up a race at this level.

6568a PRIX DE BONNEVAL (LISTED) 5f 110y

3:20 (3:23) 3-Y-O+ £19,118 (£7,647; £5,735; £3,824; £1,912)

RPR

1 **Masta Plasta (IRE)**[37] 5551 5-9-2 .... AdrianTNicholls 4 109
(D Nicholls) *led or disp ld: 2nd 1/2-way: drvn and dropped to 3rd over 1 1/2f out: rdn to chal fnl f: styd on to ld 100yds out* **2/1**[1]

2 nk **Sarissa (BRZ)**[30] 5740 5-8-8 .... C-PLemaire 5 100
(P Bary, France)

3 ½ **Mood Music**[16] 4-9-2 .... DBoeuf 10 106
(Mario Hofer, Germany)

4 ¾ **Derison (USA)**[12] 6-9-2 ....(b) TJarnet 9 104
(P Van De Poele, France)

5 shd **Quaroma**[19] 6064 3-8-8 .... PaulDoe 1 97
(Jane Chapple-Hyam) *cl up on rail: 3rd 1/2-way: ev ch 2f out: rdn and styd in front rnk tl no ex fnl 50yds* **10/1**[2]

6 6 **Brass Damask (USA)**[14] 3-8-8 .... JVictoire 3 77
(A Fabre, France)

7 6 **Delvita (FR)**[45] 4-8-8 .... GBenoist 7 56
(J-V Toux, France)

8 6 **Regence (IRE)**[53] 4-8-10 ow1 .... THuet 2 38
(Stal Darnal, France)

9 5 **Calbuco (FR)**[23] 5955 4-9-2 .... OPlacais 6 28
(Mme E Holmey, France)

65.10 secs (0.60) 9 Ran SP% 42.4
PARI-MUTUEL: WIN 3.00; PL 1.40, 3.80, 2.30; DF 37.40.
Owner Lady O'Reilly **Bred** Shane Doyle **Trained** Sessay, N Yorks

NOTEBOOK
Masta Plasta(IRE) who has travelled abroad regularly this season, added to a couple of wins in valuable handicaps by scoring his first win at this grade, although he won the Norfolk Stakes as a juvenile back in 2005. It was also compensation for being caught on the post over 5f here in June. This consistent sort seems well suited to travelling and, able to handle most ground, it gives connections plenty of options.
Quaroma, a dual 6f winning on a sound surface, ran her second successive good race at this track on the softest ground she has yet encountered. She looks capable of earning black type on this evidence.

6466 KEMPTON (A.W) (R-H)

Wednesday, October 8

OFFICIAL GOING: Standard
Wind: virtually nil Weather: dry

6570 KEMPTON.CO.UK H'CAP 1m 1f (P)

5:50 (5:51) (Class 6) (0-50,50) 3-Y-O+ £2,047 (£604; £302) Stalls High

Form RPR

1502 1 **Classic Blue (IRE)**[13] 6228 4-8-12 50 .... StephenDonohoe 8 59+
(Ian Williams) *hld up in midfield: plld out and hdwy over 1f out: swtchd lft ent fnl f: str run to ld fnl 100yds: sn in command* **7/2**[1]

0040 2 1 ¾ **Turkish Sultan (IRE)**[9] 6335 5-8-6 49 ....(p) McGeran(5) 1 54
(J M Bradley) *stdd and dropped in after s: bhd: hdwy and rdn over 2f out: r.o wl to go 2nd wl ins fnl f: nt rch wnr* **40/1**

6003 3 hd **Joe Jo Star**[25] 5912 6-8-11 49 .... JamesDoyle 14 54
(B P J Baugh) *t.k.h: chsd ldrs: rdn and effrt on inner 2f out: kpt on wl but nt pce of wnr fnl 100yds* **6/1**[2]

-006 4 ¾ **Hurricane Coast**[14] 6208 9-8-12 50 ....(b) TonyCulhane 10 53
(D Flood) *s.i.s: hld up in last trio: hdwy on outer over 2f out: sltly hmpd ent fnl f: r.o wl but nvr rchd ldrs* **12/1**

0045 5 ½ **Lights Of Vegas**[14] 6208 4-8-11 49 .... RichardHughes 9 51
(S Kirk) *led tl 7f out: w ldr tl led again 3f out: drvn 2f out: hdd fnl 100yds: lost 3 pls towards fin* **8/1**

4405 6 1 **Floodlight Fantasy**[8] 5710 5-8-12 50 ....(v) HayleyTurner 5 50
(Dr R D P Newland) *chsd ldr tl led 7f out: hdd 3f out: drvn jst over 2f out: wknd jst ins fnl f* **7/1**[3]

0006 **7** *shd* **Bold Phoenix (IRE)**[37] 5577 7-8-12 50..........(t) J-PGuillambert 2 52+
(Miss Amy Weaver) *hld up in last trio: hdwy 2f out: hmpd and swtchd lft ent fnl f: r.o but nvr nr ldrs* **20/1**

0300 **8** *1* **Anduril**[38] 5538 7-8-9 50..........(b) LukeMorris(3) 11 47
(I W McInnes) *s.i.s: hld up towards rr: styd on u.p fnl f: n.d* **16/1**

0505 **9** *1* **Hatch A Plan (IRE)**[13] 6228 7-8-11 49.......... WilliamBuick 3 44+
(Mouse Hamilton-Fairley) *s.i.s: racd in midfield on outer: hdwy to chse ldr 4f out: sn drvn: keeping on same pce and wl hld whn hmpd ent fnl f* **7/1**[3]

605- **10** *½* **Palanoverre (IRE)**[370] 5945 4-8-12 50.......... DarryllHolland 7 44
(D J S Ffrench Davis) *in tch: rdn over 2f out: wknd over 1f out* **14/1**

2100 **11** *1¼* **The Gaikwar (IRE)**[9] 6336 9-8-8 49..........(b) KevinGhunowa(3) 13 40
(R A Harris) *s.i.s: sn drvn up into midfield: rdn and struggling over 2f out: no ch fr over 1f out* **14/1**

00-0 **12** *1* **Major League (USA)**[186] 1207 6-8-12 50.......... NCallan 12 39
(W S Kittow) *chsd ldrs: rdn 2f out: keeping on same pce and edging rt whn hmpd ent fnl f: wl btn after* **10/1**

6000 **13** *3¼* **Jarvo**[28] 5802 7-8-8 49..........(v) PatrickHills(3) 6 31
(I W McInnes) *s.i.s: a towards rr: drvn 3f out: wl bhd last 2f* **20/1**

6600 **14** *3¾* **Just Oscar (GER)**[12] 6255 4-8-11 49.......... ShaneKelly 4 23
(W M Brisbourne) *chsd ldng pair tl lost pl 4f out: wl bhd last 2f* **16/1**

1m 56.19s (116.19) **14** Ran SP% **126.5**
toteswinger: 1&2 £44.80, 1&3 £1.90, 2&3 £67.20. CSF £184.04 CT £876.25 TOTE £4.60: £1.70, £19.70, £1.50; EX 197.30.
Owner Boston R S Ian Bennett **Bred** Michael Conlon **Trained** Portway, Worcs
■ Stewards' Enquiry : Stephen Donohoe three-day ban: careless riding (Oct 22-24)

FOCUS
A modest event, all 14 runners rated within 1lb of each other. It was run at a decent pace and three of the first four home came from some way off the pace. The form is very modest and a bit muddling.
Bold Phoenix(IRE) Official explanation: jockey said gelding suffered interference in running

6571 RACING UK MEDIAN AUCTION MAIDEN STKS 1m (P)
6:20 (6:21) (Class 6) 3-5-Y-O **£2,047** (£604; £302) **Stalls** High

Form RPR

22-3 **1** **Izzibizzi**[29] 5786 3-8-12 75.......... RichardHughes 13 63
(E A L Dunlop) *hld up in midfield: edgd out lft over 2f out: hdwy and rdn over 1f out: led ins fnl f: hld on wl nr fin* **5/2**[2]

3402 **2** *shd* **Unbiased (IRE)**[19] 6091 3-9-3 66..........(b) ShaneKelly 12 68
(J L Dunlop) *hld up wl in tch: hdwy over 2f out: rdn to ld over 1f out: hdd ins fnl f: rallied gamely towards fin: jst hld* **7/1**[3]

-203 **3** *1¼* **Dark Camellia**[125] 2756 3-8-12 70..........(t) JamesDoyle 2 60
(H J L Dunlop) *hld up in tch: swtchd rt and gd hdwy wl over 1f out: ev ch 1f out: tl wknd fnl 50yds* **9/1**

0/ **4** *½* **Silaah**[750] 5454 4-9-6 0.......... NeilPollard 10 64
(E A L Dunlop) *s.i.s: sn in midfield: hdwy on outer over 2f out: carried wdr 2f out: r.o wl fnl f: snatched 4th nr fin* **10/1**

4526 **5** *nk* **Indy Driver**[8] 6363 3-9-3 74.......... JamieSpencer 11 66+
(J R Fanshawe) *hld up towards rr: hdwy over 2f out: swtchd rt 2f jst over 2f out: nt clr run and swtchd lft wl over 1f out: keeping on same pce whn nt clr run nr fin* **2/1**[1]

06 **6** *1* **Tignello (IRE)**[21] 6018 3-9-3 0.......... TQuinn 8 61
(D R C Elsworth) *chsd ldrs: wnt 2nd over 4f out: led over 2f out: hung rt and hdd over 1f out: wknd ins fnl f* **20/1**

0-5 **7** *3¼* **First In Show**[14] 6206 3-8-12 0.......... WilliamBuick 7 49+
(A M Balding) *bhd: shkn up 3f out: kpt on past btn horses fr over 1f out: nvr nr ldrs* **25/1**

7 *dht* **Lady Hestia (USA)** 3-8-12 0.......... MartinDwyer 6 49
(M P Tregoning) *rn green: in midfield tl lost pl over 4f out: bhd 3f out: kpt on past btn horses over 1f out: n.d* **17/2**

00-0 **9** *5* **Up The Chimney**[27] 5837 4-9-6 52.......... DarrenWilliams 5 42
(A P Jarvis) *s.i.s: hld up towards rr: gd hdwy on outer 4f out: chal and rdn jst over 2f out: hung lft 2f out: sn btn: wknd qckly* **66/1**

04 **10** *1* **Otis May (IRE)**[14] 6206 4-9-6 0.......... VinceSlattery 1 40
(A W Carroll) *hld up bhd: wd bnd 3f out: n.d* **50/1**

06 **11** *shd* **Actress Annie**[19] 6091 3-8-12 0.......... TonyCulhane 4 34
(Mike Murphy) *dropped in after s: wl bhd: nvr a factor* **80/1**

0506 **12** *7* **Follow The Band**[29] 5790 3-9-0 55.......... PatrickHills(3) 14 23
(R Hannon) *chsd ldr tl over 4f out: wknd qckly jst over 2f out* **33/1**

0560 **13** *25* **Santa Clara**[3] 5186 3-8-12 43..........(tp) RobertHavlin 9 —
(P Leech) *led tl over 2f out: sn wknd: t.o and eased fnl f* **100/1**

1m 40.13s (0.33) **Going Correction** -0.025s/f (Stan)
WFA 3 from 4yo 3lb **13** Ran SP% **121.2**
Speed ratings (Par 101): **97,96,95,95,94 93,90,90,85,84 84,77,52**
toteswinger: 1&2 £4.00, 1&3 £10.40, 2&3 £14.70. CSF £19.78 TOTE £3.20: £1.20, £2.10, £3.80; EX 18.20.
Owner J Weatherby, Champneys **Bred** Broughton Bloodstock **Trained** Newmarket, Suffolk
■ A triumph for the Dunlop family, who sent out the first four home.
■ Stewards' Enquiry : James Doyle two-day ban: careless riding (Oct 22-23)

FOCUS
Indy Driver and Izzibizzi both had marks in the mid 70s, and they set the standard. The winner was a stone+ off his 2yo form. There did not seem to be much strength in depth, but the pace was a bit muddling and they finished in a bunch. Not form to be too positive about.
First In Show Official explanation: jockey said filly suffered interference early on

6572 DIGIBET NURSERY (DIV I) 6f (P)
6:50 (6:50) (Class 6) (0-60,60) 2-Y-O **£1,706** (£503; £252) **Stalls** High

Form RPR

065 **1** **Bold Ring**[40] 5475 2-9-0 53.......... WilliamBuick 12 58+
(D W P Arbuthnot) *t.k.h: hld up in midfield: plld out wl over 1f out: drvn to ld fnl 100yds: r.o wl and clr nr fin* **7/2**[2]

0542 **2** *2* **Itainteasybeingme**[15] 6191 2-9-7 60.......... MartinDwyer 9 58
(J R Boyle) *led: narrowly hdd and rdn jst over 2f out: led again 1f out: hung lft u.p fnl f: hdd fnl 100yds: nt pce of wnr* **5/1**[3]

000 **3** *1½* **Baby Josr**[23] 5959 2-9-7 60..........(vt[1]) NCallan 11 54
(I A Wood) *squeezed and hmpd sn after s: reminders early: hdwy and rdn over 2f out: edgd out lft over 1f out: r.o to snatch 3rd nr fin: nvr threatened ldng pair* **33/1**

2560 **4** *nk* **Turn To Dreams**[4] 6489 2-8-9 53.......... RichardEvans(5) 2 46
(P D Evans) *chsd ldrs: rdn 2f out: kpt on same pce fnl f: lost 3rd nr finsh* **20/1**

4550 **5** *hd* **Elusive Ronnie (IRE)**[6] 6414 2-9-1 54..........(p) DarryllHolland 10 46
(R A Teal) *pressed ldrs on inner: rdn and unable qck over 1f out: kpt on same pce ins fnl f* **9/1**

0056 **6** *shd* **Flawless Diamond (IRE)**[9] 6343 2-9-5 58..........(b) LPKeniry 3 50
(J S Moore) *w ldr: led narrowly jst over 2f out: rdn 2f out: hdd 1f out: wknd fnl 100yds: btn whn n.m.r towards fin* **12/1**

50 **7** *nk* **Kayceebee**[59] 4905 2-9-2 55.......... GeorgeBaker 7 47+
(R M Beckett) *chsd ldrs: rdn wl over 2f out: keeping on same pce whn nt clr run over 1f out: no imp fnl f* **11/4**[1]

000 **8** *2¼* **Dark Ranger**[30] 5753 2-9-1 54.......... RobertHavlin 1 38
(T J Pitt) *carried rt s: a in rr* **16/1**

0200 **9** *1* **Anacaona (IRE)**[6] 6414 2-9-7 60.......... RichardHughes 6 41
(R Hannon) *racd in midfield: rdn along 1/2-way: effrt and edgd rt wl over 1f out: wknd ent fnl f* **8/1**

0000 **10** *shd* **Red Robert**[25] 5914 2-9-3 56.......... ShaneKelly 5 37
(J L Dunlop) *hld up towards rr on outer: rdn and no imp wl over 2f out* **16/1**

000 **11** *3* **Ain't Talkin'**[81] 4184 2-9-5 58.......... PaulDoe 4 30
(M J Attwater) *dwlt: detached in last pl and rdn 1/2-way: nvr a factor* **66/1**

3500 **12** *nk* **Cash In The Attic**[37] 5567 2-9-5 58.......... EdwardCreighton 8 29
(M R Channon) *dwlt: a towards rr: rdn and no prog 3f out* **10/1**

1m 14.35s (1.25) **Going Correction** -0.025s/f (Stan) **12** Ran SP% **124.4**
Speed ratings (Par 93): **90,87,85,84,84 84,84,81,79,79 75,75**
toteswinger: 1&2 £7.00, 1&3 £42.20, 2&3 £26.30. CSF £22.32 CT £428.88 TOTE £5.90: £1.50, £1.70, £7.50; EX 32.30.
Owner Bonusprint **Bred** J A Pickering & T Pears **Trained** Compton, Berks
■ Stewards' Enquiry : William Buick one-day ban: careless riding (Oct 22)

FOCUS
A modest nursery in which the runners had managed just two wins between them in 60 starts. The first two are going the right way.

NOTEBOOK
Bold Ring had looked to still be getting the hang of things in three previous runs and was beaten in a 5f seller from a tough draw last time, but she appreciated the step up in trip on her nursery debut and put in a much more polished performance.She travelled enthusiastically, quickened up well and won in really good style. Further progress looks likely and she should be capable of scoring again. Official explanation: trainer said, regarding the apparent improvement in form, that in the filly's previous start she was badly drawn. (op 5-1)
Itainteasybeingme raced up with the pace and looked in serious trouble as the finishers began to swoop, but he then stuck on really well and showed a commendable fighting spirit. (op 7-2)
Baby Josr received an early reminder and looked a bit short of tactical pace at a crucial stage, but he stayed on strongly in his first-time visor and gave the impression that an extra furlong would suit.
Turn To Dreams has struggled for speed over 5f recently, but she looked much more competitive stepped back up to 6f.
Elusive Ronnie(IRE) was a bit short of room against the far rail, but he eventually plugged on well and ran a reasonable race with cheekpieces reapplied. He is, however, fairly exposed and yet to win in nine starts now. (op 12-1)
Kayceebee, returning from a break, was staying on when a bit short of room in the latter stages. (op 3-1 tchd 7-2)

6573 DIGIBET NURSERY (DIV II) 6f (P)
7:20 (7:21) (Class 6) (0-60,60) 2-Y-O **£1,706** (£503; £252) **Stalls** High

Form RPR

5342 **1** **Chicken Momo**[38] 5541 2-9-0 53.......... DarrenWilliams 12 67+
(K R Burke) *racd keenly: mde all: gng best over 2f out: rdn clr 2f out: in n.d fnl f: rdn out* **10/1**

000 **2** *6* **Highland River**[19] 6085 2-9-3 56.......... TQuinn 9 52
(D R C Elsworth) *wnt rt s: chsd ldng pair: rdn to chse wnr 2f out: sn wl outpcd: kpt on to hold 2nd* **8/1**

4604 **3** *nk* **Artesium**[6] 6406 2-9-0 53.......... TonyHamilton 11 48
(R A Fahey) *wnt lft s: racd in midfield: rdn and effrt over 2f out: wnt 3rd over 1f out: no ch w wnr* **7/1**[3]

0001 **4** *1½* **Barcode**[39] 5488 2-9-4 57.......... RichardHughes 2 49+
(R Hannon) *bhd: drvn 3f out: styd on fnl f: wnt 4th towards fin: nvr nr ldrs* **6/1**[2]

0060 **5** *½* **Join Up**[37] 5581 2-9-5 58..........(v[1]) GeorgeBaker 4 47
(W R Swinburn) *chsd wnr tl 2f out: sn outpcd: wl btn fnl f* **11/2**[1]

0250 **6** *nse* **Handful Of Magic**[6] 6414 2-9-7 60.......... RichardKingscote 10 49
(Tom Dascombe) *sn after s: bhd: effrt u.p on inner 2f out: kpt on but n.d* **7/1**[3]

0130 **7** *1½* **Nun Today (USA)**[36] 5591 2-9-3 59..........(b) LukeMorris(3) 5 43
(J S Moore) *racd in midfield: drvn over 2f out: wl hld fr wl over 1f out* **6/1**[2]

010 **8** *1¼* **All Angel**[61] 4827 2-9-5 58..........(t) MickyFenton 7 39
(Miss Amy Weaver) *towards rr: rdn on outer 3f out: nvr nr ldrs* **16/1**

0400 **9** *1½* **Home Before Dark**[11] 6281 2-8-13 52.......... DeanMcKeown 6 28
(R M Whitaker) *chsd ldrs: rdn 3f out: wknd ent fnl2f* **7/1**[3]

0356 **10** *2* **Gemini Jive (IRE)**[37] 5567 2-9-7 60.......... RichardMullen 1 30
(M G Quinlan) *s.i.s: t.k.h: hld up in rr: a bhd* **16/1**

0000 **11** *shd* **Eilean Eeve**[8] 6350 2-9-1 54..........(p) StephenDonohoe 8 24
(A J McCabe) *t.k.h: hld up in midfield: rdn and struggling over 2f out: no ch after* **33/1**

4556 **12** *10* **Wigan Pier**[69] 4558 2-9-2 55.......... AdamKirby 3 —
(M D Squance) *racd in midfield on outer: rdn 3f out: wknd 2f out: wl btn and eased ins fnl f* **25/1**

1m 13.36s (0.26) **Going Correction** -0.025s/f (Stan) **61** Ran SP% **120.2**
Speed ratings (Par 93): **97,89,88,86,85 85,83,82,80,77 77,64**
toteswinger: 1&2 £17.00, 1&3 £9.20, 2&3 £15.80. CSF £89.01 CT £451.58 TOTE £12.50: £2.90, £2.80, £4.00; EX 84.80.
Owner Mrs Lorraine Charge **Bred** J A And Mrs Duffy **Trained** Middleham Moor, N Yorks

FOCUS
A weak nursery but the winner did it well, showing big improvement. The winning time was significantly faster than that of the winner of the first division.

NOTEBOOK
Chicken Momo ◆ took a strong grip, but grabbed the early lead from stall 12, was always in control and absolutely hammered the opposition on his all-weather debut and first try at 6f. This clearly represents a significant leap forward and the time was almost a second quicker than the earlier division of this nursery. He will be hit hard by the handicapper for this wide-margin success, but he should have a very strong chance of striking again if turned out quickly under a penalty. (op 8-1)
Highland River had three noughts next to his name, but he was reported to have been unbalanced at Newmarket last time, and showed a hint of promise on his nursery debut. (op 10-1)
Artesium did best of the hold-up horses, but he never really got into it. (op 8-1)
Barcode pounced late to win a 5f Bath claimer last time but never got competitive here. (op 9-2)
Join Up was well backed and had to use up some energy to get into a prominent position from a difficult draw, but he had no answer when the winner made his decisive move, and it was a bit disappointing how quickly his effort petered out with a first-time visor tried. (op 9-1)

All Angel Official explanation: jockey said filly had breathing problems

6574 DIGIBET CASINO CLAIMING STKS 7f (P)
7:50 (7:51) (Class 6) 2-Y-O £2,047 (£604; £302) Stalls High

Form RPR

0 **1** **Jonah's Cruising (IRE)**[27] 5835 2-8-9 0 ChrisCatlin 14 60
(M J Wallace, Australia) *racd in midfield: rdn over 2f out: wnt 3rd over 1f out: kpt on u.str.p to ld fnl 100yds: hld on* **6/1**[3]

2 *nse* **Swiss Art (IRE)** 2-8-7 0 WilliamBuick 11 58
(R M Beckett) *t.k.h: hld up in midfield: shkn up: rn green and lost pl wl over 2f out: hdwy over 1f out: str run to press wnr fnl 100yds: jst hld* **8/1**

0110 **3** *1 1/4* **Shadow Bay (IRE)**[47] 5242 2-9-5 76 RichardKingscote 7 67+
(Tom Dascombe) *chsd ldr tl led over 4f out: sn hdd: chsd ldr after: drvn to ld again jst ins fnl f: hdd and no ex fnl 100yds* **9/4**[1]

0 **4** *3 3/4* **Statute Book (IRE)**[12] 6253 2-8-12 0 AdamKirby 6 51+
(S Kirk) *stdd and dropped in after s: hld up towards rr: hdwy 2f out: plugged on to go 4th ins fnl f: nvr pce to threaten ldrs* **20/1**

1604 **5** *1* **Courageous Nature (IRE)**[4] 6489 2-8-13 68 (b[1]) StephenDonohoe 1 49+
(A J McCabe) *chsd ldrs tl led 4f out: clr 3f out: rdn 2f out: wknd and hdd jst ins fnl f: fdd* **10/1**

0000 **6** *1 1/4* **Duke Of Aquitaine (USA)**[11] 6281 2-9-0 67 (b[1]) MartinDwyer 4 47
(P F I Cole) *bhd: rdn and no hdwy 3f out: no ch after* **11/2**[2]

555 **7** *hd* **Fajita**[21] 6008 2-9-5 70 RichardMullen 8 51
(M G Quinlan) *in tch: chsd ldrs and drvn over 2f out: wknd 2f out* **7/1**

6 **8** *shd* **Barbeito**[16] 6158 2-8-5 0 CatherineGannon 13 37
(D J S Ffrench Davis) *s.i.s: a towards rr: sme late hdwy: nvr on terms* **25/1**

05 **9** *1 1/2* **My Dixie Darling (USA)**[68] 4579 2-8-11 0 RichardHughes 12 39
(R Hannon) *led tl over 4f out: chsd ldrs after: rdn over 2f out: sn wknd: wl btn after* **8/1**

00 **10** *5* **Spiritual Bond**[76] 4321 2-8-3 0 ow1 KevinGhunowa(3) 10 22
(R A Harris) *in tch: rdn 4f out: wknd wl over 2f out* **100/1**

4 **11** *nk* **Hartshead Flyer (IRE)**[187] 1183 2-8-12 0 JamieSpencer 5 27
(M J Wallace, Australia) *stdd s: wl bhd and styd wd tl 1/2-way: nvr a factor* **20/1**

6 **12** *6* **Fruitful Job (IRE)**[39] 5488 2-9-0 0 NCallan 2 14
(A G Newcombe) *s.i.s: a struggling in rr: wl bhd last 3f* **50/1**

0 **13** *6* **Restless Knight**[8] 6359 2-8-9 0 ShaneKelly 9 —
(W S Kittow) *chsd ldrs tl 1/2-way: wl bhd last 2f: t.o* **33/1**

1m 27.35s (1.35) **Going Correction** -0.025s/f (Stan) **13** Ran SP% **123.5**
Speed ratings (Par 93): **91,90,89,85,84 82,82,82,80,74 74,67,60**Jonah's Cruising was claimed by M Khan for £10000. Swiss Art was claimed by M Quinn for £3000..Jonah's Cruising was claimed by M Khan for £10000. Swiss Art was claimed by M Quinn for £3000.
Owner M J Wallace **Bred** Wellsummers Stud **Trained** Australia

FOCUS
Four of the runners had an official rating between 67 and 76 in this claimer, but this is just modest form. The strong pace set the race up for late finishers.

NOTEBOOK
Jonah's Cruising(IRE) was always behind on her debut and it looked like it was going to be a similar scenario here. She was matched at 999-1 on the exchanges but picked up really well in the straight, and swooped into the lead close home. Whether she can reproduce this in a race not run at such a searing pace is open to question but she does have a fair amount of ability and is open to improvement and should stay a bit further. (op 7-1)
Swiss Art(IRE) was retained for just 3,000gns last year, a tenth of his sales price as a foal, but ran a really promising race and was only narrowly beaten by another fast finisher on his debut. This will have been a valuable learning experience and he was subject to 25 claims, before eventually being sold to Micky Quinn. (op 7-1)
Shadow Bay(IRE) dominated a seller, and a nursery off a mark of 68, during the summer and had strong form claims. He probably paid the price for having a sustained battle with the leader in the straight and was a sitting duck for the late marauders. This was still a creditable effort, particularly considering the stable he represents has been quiet since going down with a viral infection. (op 11-4)
Statute Book(IRE) had not shown much on his debut but shaped with some promise, staying on late.

6575 DIGIBET.COM NOVICE STKS 6f (P)
8:20 (8:22) (Class 5) 2-Y-O £3,885 (£1,156; £577; £288) Stalls High

Form RPR

1060 **1** **Tishtar**[18] 6118 2-9-5 81 RichardHughes 5 82
(R Hannon) *hld up towards rr: smooth hdwy on inner jst over 2f out: rdn 1f out: hung lft ins fnl f: drvn to ld fnl strides* **14/1**

2 *nk* **Pat's Legacy (USA)** 2-8-11 0 ow3 DarrenWilliams 7 73
(D Shaw) *bdly hmpd s: t.k.h: hld up in midfield: swtchd to inner and gd hdwy jst over 2f out: chsd ldr ent fnl f: rdn to ld ins fnl f: edgd lft after: hdd fnl strides* **66/1**

23 **3** *1 1/4* **Bajan Tryst (USA)**[20] 6062 2-8-12 0 NCallan 11 70
(K A Ryan) *chsd ldng pair: wnt 2nd over 2f out: drvn to ld over 1f out: hdd and ins fnl f: one pce fnl 100yds* **5/1**[3]

4311 **4** *2 3/4* **Desert Falls**[11] 6281 2-9-5 95 DeanMcKeown 10 69
(R M Whitaker) *led: rdn 2f out: hdd over 1f out: sn edgd lft: wknd fnl f* **7/2**[2]

210 **5** *3/4* **Raedah (USA)**[16] 6172 2-9-0 83 MartinDwyer 6 62
(M A Jarvis) *wnt rt s: racd in midfield on outer: rdn over 3f out: hung lft fr 2f out: kpt on fnl f: nt trble ldrs* **7/1**

0 **6** *hd* **Art Fund (USA)**[34] 5628 2-8-12 0 PatDobbs 2 59
(G L Moore) *v awkward s and slowly away: bhd: hdwy and hung lft fr 2f out: styd on but nvr trbld ldrs* **50/1**

0 **7** *shd* **Castleburg**[19] 6077 2-8-7 0 RichardMullen 4 54
(G L Moore) *stdd s: t.k.h: hld up bhd: swtchd rt and hdwy jst over 2f out: no imprssion fnl f* **50/1**

3230 **8** *1* **Missile Dodger (USA)**[32] 5693 2-9-0 92 (v) RichardKingscote 1 58
(R M Beckett) *chsd ldr tl over 2f out: sn hrd rdn: wknd wl over 1f out* **9/1**

2300 **9** *2 3/4* **Mister Green (FR)**[4] 6469 2-9-2 84 TonyCulhane 9 52
(D Flood) *chsd ldrs: rdn over 3f out: edgd lft and wknd 2f out* **10/1**

10 *3 1/2* **Action That (IRE)**[63] 4760 2-8-12 0 CatherineGannon 8 37
(C A Dwyer) *s.i.s: a struggling in rr* **100/1**

223 **11** *nk* **Summers Target (USA)**[19] 6083 2-8-12 88 JamieSpencer 3 36
(B J Meehan) *t.k.h: chsd ldrs: wd bnd 3f out: wknd over 2f out* **6/4**[1]

1m 12.89s (-0.21) **Going Correction** -0.025s/f (Stan) **11** Ran SP% **123.6**
Speed ratings (Par 95): **100,99,97,94,93 93,92,91,87,83 82**
toteswinger: 1&2 £63.10, 1&3 £25.70, 2&3 £35.20. CSF £702.05 TOTE £21.30: £4.90, £5.00, £2.00; EX 2050.90.
Owner The Waney Racing Group Inc **Bred** Waney Racing Group Inc **Trained** East Everleigh, Wilts

FOCUS
A decent event run at a strong pace, but the two main form contenders both disappointed. The winner is rated back to his best on this sand debut but the time and the poor tenth limit the form.

NOTEBOOK
Tishtar faced a difficult task at the weights and had a bit to prove after three modest efforts since winning a 5f Salisbury maiden in May, but bounded back to form on his All-Weather debut. The switch to patient tactics seemed to do the trick and he travelled smoothly and showed a strong will to get up close home. He should be able to go on from this, is clearly well suited by the Polytrack and probably needs fast ground to show his best form on turf. (op 16-1)
Pat's Legacy(USA) cost $87,000 and is a gelded half-brother to the quite useful Striving Storm, a 1m winner at two. He was unfancied and had to recover from being hampered at the start, but hit the front at the furlong pole and was just picked off close home. This was an admirable effort in a tough race on his debut, and he should improve for the experience.
Bajan Tryst(USA) raced near the pace and put in a solid effort on his Polytrack debut. He has shown consistent form in three starts and should be able to make an impact when switched to handicaps off a mark that is likely to be in the low 80s. (op 7-1 tchd 15-2)
Desert Falls had looked progressive dominating two 6f events at Great Leighs on his last two starts and had strong form claims. He got to his favoured front-running position, but it was disappointing how easily he was brushed aside. Official explanation: jockey said colt hung left up the straight (op 3-1)
Action That(IRE) Official explanation: jockey said colt jumped awkwardly
Summers Target(USA) raced keenly and dropped away quickly a long way out. Official explanation: jockey said colt hung left and boiled over at start (tchd 7-4 and 15-8 in a place)

6576 TFM NETWORKS H'CAP 7f (P)
8:50 (8:52) (Class 3) (0-95,95) 3-Y-O+
£7,477 (£2,239; £1,119; £560; £279; £140) Stalls High

Form RPR

0410 **1** **Russki (IRE)**[32] 5695 4-9-6 95 (b) RichardMullen 12 109+
(D M Simcock) *dwlt: sn rdn up to chse ldrs: wnt 2nd over 2f out: led 2f out: sn rdn clr: in n.d fnl f: eased wl ins fnl f* **5/2**[1]

2210 **2** *2 3/4* **Victoria Reel**[12] 6242 3-8-8 85 RichardHughes 4 90
(R Hannon) *stdd and dropped in after s: stdy hdwy into midfield 1/2-way: rdn over 2f out: kpt on to chse wnr fnl 100yds: nvr a threat* **16/1**

2066 **3** *3/4* **Lindoro**[11] 6277 3-8-13 90 (t) AdamKirby 3 93
(W R Swinburn) *stdd s and dropped in bhd: hdwy u.p wl over 1f out: styd on to snatch 3rd on post: no ch w wnr* **16/1**

000 **4** *shd* **My Gacho (IRE)**[11] 6278 6-8-6 81 (b) J-PGuillambert 13 84
(M Johnston) *led: drvn and hdd 2f out: no ch w wnr after: lost 2 pls ins fnl f* **16/1**

0510 **5** *1/2* **South Cape**[11] 6269 5-9-1 90 TPO'Shea 11 91
(M R Channon) *chsd ldrs: rdn and effrt over 2f out: plugged on but no ch w wnr fr over 1f out* **6/1**[3]

0000 **6** *1* **Pride Of Nation (IRE)**[25] 5896 6-9-3 92 EddieAhern 1 91
(J W Hills) *stdd s and dropped in bhd: hdwy on inner over 2f out: edging out lft fnl f: nvr trbld ldrs* **33/1**

0300 **7** *1/2* **Presumptive (IRE)**[45] 5313 8-9-3 92 RichardKingscote 10 89
(R Charlton) *in tch: rdn over 3f out: wknd u.p jst over 2f out* **7/1**

4020 **8** *1 1/2* **Halsion Chancer**[24] 5936 4-8-10 85 SteveDrowne 5 78
(J R Best) *stdd s: t.k.h: hld up towards rr: bhd and rdn 3f out: n.d after* **25/1**

0032 **9** *nk* **Fathsta (IRE)**[11] 6277 3-9-1 92 LPKeniry 2 84
(S Kirk) *stdd and dropped in after s: t.k.h: hld up in rr: nvr trbld ldrs* **12/1**

-430 **10** *2 3/4* **Lizard Island (USA)**[19] 6073 3-9-4 95 JohnEgan 8 80
(Jane Chapple-Hyam) *hld up towards rr: drvn wl over 2f out: no prog* **12/1**

2212 **11** *1 1/2* **King's Wonder**[14] 6200 3-8-8 85 MartinDwyer 6 66
(W R Muir) *chsd ldr: rdn jst over 2f out: wknd qckly over 1f out* **4/1**[2]

1405 **12** *2* **Irony (IRE)**[46] 5290 9-8-1 81 oh2 DavidProbert(5) 9 57
(A M Balding) *in tch tl lost pl over 3f out: wl bhd last 2f* **12/1**

0050 **13** *1* **Silver Hotspur**[25] 5908 4-8-9 84 LiamJones 7 57
(C R Dore) *t.k.h: hld up towards rr: rdn and struggling over 2f out: no ch last 2f* **66/1**

1m 24.18s (-1.82) **Going Correction** -0.025s/f (Stan)
WFA 3 from 4yo+ 2lb **13** Ran SP% **124.4**
Speed ratings (Par 107): **109,105,105,104,104 103,102,100,100,97 95,93,92**
toteswinger: 1&2 £11.70, 1&3 £17.70, 2&3 £54.50. CSF £48.38 CT £579.24 TOTE £3.90: £1.50, £4.30, £5.90; EX 71.10.
Owner DXB Bloodstock Ltd **Bred** Mark Commins **Trained** Newmarket, Suffolk

FOCUS
A competitive handicap, run at a searching early pace, and that resulted in a decent winning time for the grade. The winner recorded a career best, with the next two close to form.

NOTEBOOK
Russki(IRE) had a rating right on the ceiling for this 0-95 handicap and was heavily backed. Things did not look too promising after he missed the break and had to be ridden with more restraint than usual, but he gradually moved into contention, seemed to come back on the bridle at the two-furlong pole and showed a useful turn of foot to shoot clear and register a time 0.62 seconds faster than standard. This win will possibly take his mark above 100 but he seems to be developing more speed and potent weapons as he progresses and looks one to follow. His next target could be a Listed event here next month and after that he may head to the Dubai Carnival. (op 4-1)
Victoria Reel lost a little momentum when switched against the far rail in the straight but stayed on steadily to run a decent race on her all-weather debut behind a very impressive winner. She is relatively lightly raced, should have some more scope for improvement and may be able to add to her decisive Salisbury win off 8lb lower in July. (op 20-1)
Lindoro stayed on well from some way back and probably ran near his best turf form on this first effort on sand. (op 14-1)
My Gacho(IRE) has done all his winning at 6f, but ran really well over a trip further than ideal, particularly considering the strong pace he dictated in the early stages.
South Cape did quite well to plug on after racing near the damaging pace. (op 9-1)
Lizard Island(USA) Official explanation: jockey said colt hung left

6577 BARRETTSTOWN STUD H'CAP 1m 4f (P)
9:20 (9:23) (Class 6) (0-65,65) 3-Y-O+ £2,047 (£604; £302) Stalls Centre

Form RPR

46- **1** **Kerayasi (FR)**[363] 5093 6-9-3 60 GeorgeBaker 8 67+
(G L Moore) *stdd and dropped in bhd after s: hld up in rr: hdwy over 2f out: jnd ldrs travelling wl over 1f out: led ins fnl f: a comf holding runner up* **10/1**

6336 **2** *1/2* **Ommadawn (IRE)**[22] 5999 4-9-7 64 JamieSpencer 3 70
(J R Fanshawe) *hld up in rr: swtchd sharply lft and hdwy over 2f out: sn drvn: chsd wnr ins fnl f: kpt on u.str.p but a readily hld* **4/1**[2]

6345 **3** *1* **Ghufa (IRE)**[22] 6007 4-9-3 60 MartinDwyer 12 65
(E A L Dunlop) *chsd ldr: rdn over 3f out: drvn to ld wl over 1f out: hdd ins fnl f: one pce* **7/2**[1]

4506 **4** *1 1/4* **Generous Lad (IRE)**[37] 5576 5-9-2 59 (p) SteveDrowne 10 62
(A B Haynes) *hld up in rr: hdwy 4f out: rdn 3f out: hdwy to chse ldrs over 1f out: kpt on same pce u.p fnl f* **16/1**

5610 **5** *3/4* **Valdan (IRE)**[18] 6134 4-9-5 62 DeanMcKeown 5 63
(P D Evans) *hld up towards rr: hdwy over 3f out: keeping on same pce whn hung rt over 1f out: kpt on* **14/1**

4/00 **6** *nk* **Cover Drive (USA)**[34] 5639 5-9-3 **60**........................[1] EdwardCreighton 6 61
(Christian Wroe) *t.k.h: hld up towards rr: hdwy on outer over 3f out: hmpd over 2f out: edging rt fr over 1f out: styd on wl fnl f: nt rch ldrs* **33/1**

0000 **7** *5* **Lord Theo**[16] 6177 4-9-7 **64**........................ JamesDoyle 14 57
(N P Littmoden) *sn led: rdn jst over 2f out: hdd wl over 1f out: wknd qckly* **12/1**

064 **8** *½* **Cape Of Luck (IRE)**[21] 6028 5-9-6 **63**........................ IanMongan 11 55
(P M Phelan) *hld up in midfield: rdn over 3f out: sme hdwy and swtchd lft 2f out: sn wknd* **8/1**[3]

0210 **9** *1¼* **Papradon**[61] 4819 4-9-7 **64**........................(v) LPKeniry 9 54
(J R Best) *chsd ldrs: rdn to chse ldng pair wl over 2f out: wknd ent fnl 2f* **8/1**[3]

4221 **10** *3¾* **Little Richard (IRE)**[194] 1062 9-9-5 **62**........................(p) AdamKirby 13 46
(M Wellings) *chsd ldrs: rdn and hung rt wl over 2f out: sn wknd* **14/1**

4121 **11** *2½* **Mixing**[14] 6210 6-9-3 **65**........................ DavidProbert(5) 2 45
(M J Attwater) *hld up in midfield: rdn and lost pl over 3f out: wl bhd last 2f* **4/1**[2]

006 **12** *¾* **Kylkenny**[78] 4267 13-8-12 **62**........................(t) RyanClark(7) 1 41
(H Morrison) *racd in midfield: hdwy over 4f out: wknd 3f out* **33/1**

23-5 **13** *17* **Sovereign Spirit (IRE)**[126] 14 6-9-4 **61**........................ ChrisCatlin 4 13
(C Gordon) *chsd ldrs tl lost pl 4f out: t.o fnl f* **16/1**

2m 34.74s (0.24) **Going Correction** -0.025s/f (Stan) **13** Ran SP% **132.2**
Speed ratings (Par 101): **98,97,97,96,95 95,92,91,90,88 86,86,74**
toteswinger: 1&2 £7.80, 1&3 £18.20, 2&3 £6.60. CSF £55.17 CT £178.19 TOTE £11.80: £2.60, £2.00, £2.30; EX 66.60 Place 6: £358.23 Place 5: £162.53 .
Owner Jack Brown, Brian Spiby **Bred** Mme Bernard Jeffroy Et Al **Trained** Woodingdean, E Sussex

FOCUS
A moderate handicap, run at a steady early pace although the first two came from the rear. The form looks sound overall with the winner rated close to last year's turf level.
Valdan(IRE) Official explanation: jockey said gelding hung right inside final furlong
Little Richard(IRE) Official explanation: jockey said gelding hung badly right
T/Plt: £196.70 to a £1 stake. Pool: £73,920.00. 274.33 winning tickets. T/Qpdt: £105.30 to a £1 stake. Pool: £7,598.68. 53.40 winning tickets. SP

6388 NOTTINGHAM (L-H)
Wednesday, October 8

OFFICIAL GOING: Soft (6.3)
Wind: light 1/2 against Weather: fine and sunny

6578 EUROPEAN BREEDERS' FUND MAIDEN STKS 5f 13y
1:40 (1:40) (Class 4) 2-Y-O **£5,180** (£1,541; £770; £384) **Stalls** High

Form RPR

23 **1** **Joe Caster**[78] 4279 2-9-0 0........................ LukeMorris(3) 6 75
(J M P Eustace) *chsd ldrs: effrt and hdwy 2f out: sn rdn: edgd rt ent fnl f: styd on to ld fnl 100yds* **4/1**[3]

3U5 **2** *2¼* **Bees River (IRE)**[20] 6037 2-8-12 0........................ DaneO'Neill 10 62
(A P Jarvis) *led: pushed along 2f out: rdn over 1f out: drvn: edgd lft and hdd ins fnl f: kpt on same pce* **9/4**[1]

4 **3** *hd* **Rare Art**[55] 5016 2-9-3 0........................ HayleyTurner 2 66
(S A Callaghan) *trckd ldr: hdwy 2f out: rdn to chal over 1f out and ev ch tl drvn: edgd lft and one pce ins fnl f* **7/2**[2]

05 **4** *3* **Belated Silver (IRE)**[8] 6359 2-9-3 0........................ RichardKingscote 3 55+
(Tom Dascombe) *chsd ldrs: rdn along and outpcd 2f out: kpt on u.p ins fnl f* **11/2**

5 *hd* **Makaykla** 2-8-12 0........................ DavidAllan 4 50
(E J Alston) *chsd ldrs: rdn along and outpcd 2f out: kpt on u.p ins fnl f* **17/2**

00 **6** *2* **Iachimo**[26] 5860 2-9-3 0........................ JimCrowley 8 47+
(K R Burke) *dwlt: t.k.h: sn chsng ldng pair: rdn 2f out: wknd appr fnl f* **12/1**

0 **7** *2½* **Prima Laurea (IRE)**[12] 6245 2-8-12 0........................ TPQueally 7 33
(J G Given) *dwlt: a in rr* **40/1**

8 *nk* **Dawn Wee** 2-8-12 0........................ PJMcDonald 1 32
(G R Oldroyd) *wnt lft s: sn outpcd and a bhd* **28/1**

61.59 secs (0.89) **Going Correction** +0.125s/f (Good) **8** Ran SP% **112.5**
Speed ratings (Par 97): **97,93,93,88,87 84,80,80**
toteswinger: 1&2 £1.50, 1&3 £2.20, 2&3 £3.60. CSF £12.96 TOTE £4.90: £1.20, £1.10, £1.80; EX 12.10.
Owner The Greek Myths **Bred** Ms G P Walker **Trained** Newmarket, Suffolk
■ Stewards' Enquiry : Luke Morris one-day ban: used whip with arm above shoulder height (Oct 22)

FOCUS
An uncompetitive juvenile maiden and probably just fair form. The winning time was 0.72 seconds quicker than the following 0-65 nursery. They raced towards the stands' side, but the winner ended up making his move up the middle.

NOTEBOOK
Joe Caster was well held on quick ground at Yarmouth when last seen over two months previously, but he had shown loads of ability on a soft surface on his debut when second to subsequent Coventry winner Art Connoisseur at Leicester, and ran out a ready winner with conditions clearly in his favour. He was niggled along with three to run, but responded well and eventually came clear for a convincing success. He is clearly a fair horse when there is give underfoot. (op 3-1)
Bees River(IRE), unlike the winner, raced against the stands' rail and showed early speed. She will have more options now she is qualified for a handicap mark. (op 5-2 tchd 11-4)
Rare Art had to be rushed up early and he still looks to be learning. He is probably more of a handicap type. (op 11-4)
Belated Silver(IRE) is now qualified for a handicap mark and may do better back over further. (op 9-1 tchd 5-1)
Makaykla, sprint bred, showed ability and will know more next time. (op 14-1)

6579 CALYX SOFTWARE NURSERY 5f 13y
2:10 (2:11) (Class 6) (0-65,65) 2-Y-O **£2,729** (£806; £403) **Stalls** High

Form RPR

0052 **1** **Cocktail Party (IRE)**[24] 5933 2-8-13 **57**........................ EddieAhern 5 62
(J W Hills) *trckd ldrs: styd on to ld jst ins fnl f: edgd rt and swished tail: styd on* **7/1**[2]

400 **2** *1¼* **Spiritual Art**[21] 6030 2-8-13 **57**........................ HayleyTurner 2 58
(S A Callaghan) *hld up in midfield: effrt over 2f out: sn chsng ldrs: styd on same pce ins fnl f* **9/2**[1]

142 **3** *hd* **Dispol Grand (IRE)**[8] 6350 2-9-7 **65**........................ PaulFessey 10 66+
(P T Midgley) *chsd ldrs: keeping on same pce whn intimidated wl ins fnl f* **9/2**[1]

045 **4** *hd* **Assent (IRE)**[12] 6244 2-9-7 **65**........................ JimCrowley 14 64
(B R Millman) *dwlt: in rr on inner: swtchd outside over 2f out: hrd rdn and dived lft jst ins fnl f: kpt on* **8/1**[3]

3662 **5** *1½* **Imaginary Diva**[40] 5475 2-8-12 **56**........................ TPQueally 3 50
(G G Margarson) *led tl hdd jst ins fnl f: sn fdd* **8/1**[3]

5400 **6** *nk* **Kings Ace (IRE)**[12] 6247 2-9-2 **60**........................(v) DaneO'Neill 9 53
(A P Jarvis) *swvd lft s: in rr: hdwy on outside over 2f out: kpt on same pce appr fnl f* **25/1**

0000 **7** *hd* **Mousy Mousy (IRE)**[8] 6350 2-8-5 **52**........................ DuranFentiman(3) 11 44
(T D Easterby) *in rr: kpt on fnl 2f: nvr trbld ldrs* **50/1**

5025 **8** *hd* **Sale Or Return (IRE)**[8] 6350 2-8-11 **55**........................(b) DavidAllan 4 46
(T D Easterby) *chsd ldrs: fdd appr fnl f* **14/1**

0006 **9** *nse* **Excitable (IRE)**[7] 6389 2-8-3 **50**........................ DominicFox(3) 12 41
(Miss V Haigh) *in rr and sn drvn along: kpt on fnl 2f: nvr a factor* **9/1**

3003 **10** *5* **Sorrel Ridge (IRE)**[15] 6191 2-7-13 **48**........................ NicolPolli(5) 6 21
(M G Quinlan) *hmpd s: sn chsng ldrs: rdn over 2f out: wknd over 1f out* **14/1**

5005 **11** *nk* **Meg Jicaro**[16] 6158 2-8-11 **58**........................ RussellKennemore(3) 13 30
(Mrs L Williamson) *prom: lost pl after 2f: bhd fnl 2f* **40/1**

5416 **12** *¾* **Compton Ford**[8] 6350 2-9-3 **61**........................ PaulMulrennan 1 30
(M Dods) *unruly and led rdrless to post: swvd lft s: mid-div: effrt over 2f out: sn wknd* **20/1**

6430 **13** *¾* **Weet In Nerja**[36] 5591 2-9-2 **60**........................ GrahamGibbons 8 26
(R Hollinshead) *hmpd s: a in rr: hung lft and bhd fnl 2f* **12/1**

62.31 secs (1.61) **Going Correction** +0.125s/f (Good) **13** Ran SP% **115.1**
Speed ratings (Par 93): **92,90,89,89,86 86,86,85,85,77 77,76,74**
toteswinger: 1&2 £8.50, 1&3 £3.60, 2&3 £5.80. CSF £35.50 CT £162.94 TOTE £8.70: £2.50, £1.90, £1.80; EX 43.20.
Owner Christopher Wright & Mrs J A Wright **Bred** Rathbarry Stud **Trained** Upper Lambourn, Berks

FOCUS
A moderate nursery run in a time 0.72 seconds slower than the previous maiden. The form is solid with the winner an improver and the third setting the level. They raced stands' side early, and that's where the winner was positioned throughout, but a few of these ended up more towards the middle late on.

NOTEBOOK
Cocktail Party(IRE) raced a little keenly just in behind the leaders early on, but she still had plenty left at the business end and found plenty when pulled out with two to run. Although she flashed her tail slightly late on, she certainly responded well to pressure. She displays plenty of knee action and is obviously well suited by soft ground. (tchd 8-1)
Spiritual Art was quite well backed on her nursery debut/first try over the minimum trip, but she was always stuck towards the outer of the main group from stall two and ended up challenging up the middle of the track. (op 7-1 tchd 4-1)
Dispol Grand(IRE) showed speed and looked to have his chance, but he could not take advantage of a mark 5lb lower than in future. (op 3-1)
Assent(IRE) travelled nicely out the back after missing the kick, but she had to switch out very wide, and then lugged even further left when in the clear. She has ability, but might not be totally straightforward. (op 6-1)
Excitable(IRE) was 5lb lower than in future following what had appeared to be an improved effort over course and distance the previous week, but she was never really travelling. (op 12-1)
Weet In Nerja Official explanation: jockey said gelding hung left-handed throughout

6580 RACING UK CHANNEL 432 MAIDEN STKS (DIV I) 1m 75y
2:40 (2:41) (Class 5) 2-Y-O **£2,914** (£867; £433; £216) **Stalls** Low

Form RPR

5 **1** **Alanbrooke**[21] 6026 2-9-3 0........................ RoystonFfrench 11 67+
(M Johnston) *chsd ldrs: effrt on outer and pushed along over 2f out: rdn over 1f out: styd on strly ins fnl f to ld fnl 50yds* **2/1**[1]

5 **2** *nk* **Thousand Miles (IRE)**[21] 6029 2-9-3 0........................ RichardMullen 2 66
(P W Chapple-Hyam) *trckd ldrs: gd hdwy on inner over 3f out: rdn to ld wl over 1f out: drvn ins fnl f: hdd and no ex last 50yds* **5/2**[2]

3 *2¾* **Horsley Warrior** 2-9-3 0........................ GrahamGibbons 6 60+
(E S McMahon) *dwlt: hdwy and in tch 1/2-way: effrt over 2f out: rdn over 1f out: kpt on ins fnl f: nrst fin* **33/1**

3 **4** *nse* **Surrounded**[19] 6084 2-8-12 0........................ EdwardCreighton 1 55
(R W Price) *led: rdn along 3f out: drvn 2f out: sn hdd & wknd ent fnl f* **6/1**

5 *1* **Martha's Girl (USA)** 2-8-12 0........................ DNolan 13 53
(D Carroll) *cl up: effrt 3f out: rdn 2f out and ev ch tl drvn and wknd ent fnl f* **66/1**

6 *1* **Advisor (FR)** 2-9-3 0........................ JamieSpencer 10 60+
(M L W Bell) *trckd ldrs on inner: swtchd rt and pushed along 4f out: n.m.r and wandered over 2f out: swtchd outside over 1f out: kpt on ins fnl f: nrst fin* **3/1**[3]

7 *shd* **Lend A Light** 2-9-3 0........................ PatrickMathers 5 55
(I W McInnes) *s.i.s and bhd: hdwy over 2f out: sn rdn and styd on ins fnl f: nrst fin* **100/1**

00 **8** *3* **Strongarm**[45] 5316 2-9-3 0........................ MickyFenton 7 49
(A Bailey) *in tch on outer: rdn along 3f out: wknd over 2f out* **100/1**

6 **9** *nk* **Dalesway**[13] 6234 2-9-3 0........................ TPQueally 4 48
(J G Given) *trckd ldrs: effrt 3f out: sn rdn along and wknd 2f out* **100/1**

00 **10** *½* **Saving Grace**[12] 6244 2-8-12 0........................ DavidAllan 3 42
(E J Alston) *in rr: hdwy inner 3f out: rdn wl over 1f out and sn no imp* **100/1**

00 **11** *hd* **Tinkerbelle (IRE)**[38] 5534 2-8-12 0........................ EddieAhern 9 42
(J L Dunlop) *cl up: rdn along over 2f out: grad wknd and eased ins fnl f* **66/1**

1m 49.78s (4.38) **Going Correction** +0.275s/f (Good) **11** Ran SP% **111.1**
Speed ratings (Par 95): **89,88,85,85,84 83,83,80,80,80 79**
toteswinger: 1&2 £2.10, 1&3 £8.20, 2&3 £8.10. CSF £6.62 TOTE £2.80: £1.50, £1.10, £2.90; EX 8.20.
Owner Sheikh Hamdan Bin Mohammed Al Maktoum **Bred** Miss K Rausing **Trained** Middleham Moor, N Yorks

FOCUS
Just a fair maiden, but the race should produce some winners. The winning time was 0.83 seconds slower than the second division and there were some moderate types rather too close for comfort, so the level of the form is very modest, but the first four are capable of considerably better.

NOTEBOOK
Alanbrooke made hard work of this, but he's very much a stayer in the making. He got a little worked up in the stalls, and didn't really travel in the race itself, but he was given a fine ride by Royston Ffrench, who managed to keep the well-fancied Advisor hemmed in when getting serious with his mount fully half a mile out. To the horse's credit, he responded well to pressure and managed to reel in Thousand Miles, who had travelled the better of the pair. He is going to want 1m4f at the very least next year and it would be no surprise if he progressed into a Queen's Vase horse. (op 6-4)
Thousand Miles(IRE) confirmed the promise of his debut effort over 7f at Yarmouth and was just denied. He was settled a fair way off the pace early, but got a good run through in the straight and had every chance. He seemed well suited by the ground. (op 11-4)

Horsley Warrior ◆, a son of Alhaarth, missed the kick but travelled well for a long way and showed plenty of ability. He looks quite a nice type in the making.
Surrounded, just as when third on her debut on quick ground over 7f at Newmarket, displayed a significant knee action, so the underfoot conditions should have suited, but she failed to build on that initial effort. She looks worth another go on easy ground, but will probably do better back over 7f. (tchd 13-2 in a place)
Martha's Girl(USA), 27,000euros daughter of E Dubai, showed up well for a long way and has ability. A quicker surface might suit even better. (op 80-1)
Advisor(FR), a 120,000euros brother to Anamilina, who was placed over 1m at three in France, is better than he showed as he was continually kept in a pocket by the eventual winner when looking to angle out inside the final half-mile. (op 10-3 tchd 7-2)
Lend A Light completely blew the start, but he obviously has some ability.

6581 RACING UK CHANNEL 432 MAIDEN STKS (DIV II) 1m 75y
3:10 (3:10) (Class 5) 2-Y-O **£2,914** (£867; £433; £216) **Stalls** Low

Form RPR
1 **Mastery** 2-9-3 0 JoeFanning 2 83+
(M Johnston) *set modest pce: qcknd up 3f out: shkn up and wnt clr over 1f out: eased towards fin* **15/2[3]**
2 4½ **Kings Destiny** 2-9-3 0 PhilipRobinson 6 69+
(M A Jarvis) *t.k.h: trckd ldrs: wnt 2nd over 1f out: no ch w wnr* **9/2[2]**
3 ¾ **Bin End** 2-9-3 0 JamieSpencer 8 67+
(M L W Bell) *in rr: hdwy over 3f out: kpt on wl fnl f* **8/1**
0 4 1½ **Dubai Echo (USA)**[19] 6084 2-9-3 0 RyanMoore 4 64
(Sir Michael Stoute) *chsd ldrs: drvn over 3f out: one pce fnl 2f* **11/8[1]**
0 5 ½ **Musigny (USA)**[20] 6062 2-9-3 0 MichaelHills 1 65+
(W Jarvis) *chsd ldrs: nt clr run 2f out: kpt on steadily* **33/1**
6 3 **Gitano Hernando** 2-9-0 0 JackMitchell(3) 5 56
(M Botti) *mid-div: effrt over 3f out: lost pl over 2f out* **8/1**
0 7 3¼ **Aziz (IRE)**[47] 5246 2-9-3 0 PaulEddery 11 49
(Miss D Mountain) *sn chsng ldrs: chal over 3f out: wknd over 1f out* **100/1**
0 8 ¾ **Shakin John**[20] 6057 2-9-3 0 (b[1]) ChrisCatlin 10 48
(E J O'Neill) *stdd s: rapid hdwy to trck ldrs after 1f: wknd 2f out* **40/1**
9 ½ **Bansha (IRE)**[31] 5721 2-9-3 0 MickyFenton 7 47
(A Bailey) *t.k.h: a towards rr* **66/1**
0 10 3 **Anotherbottleteddy**[45] 5304 2-8-12 0 PatrickMathers 9 35
(I W McInnes) *s.i.s: nvr on terms* **100/1**
11 1 **Kazbow (IRE)** 2-9-3 0 DaneO'Neill 3 38
(L M Cumani) *sn pushed along in rr: bhd fnl 2f* **15/2[3]**
0 12 4½ **Ditzy Diva**[63] 4728 2-8-7 0 SophieDoyle(5) 12 24
(Jean-Rene Auvray) *s.i.s: in rr: bhd fnl 3f* **100/1**

1m 48.95s (3.55) **Going Correction** +0.275s/f (Good) 12 Ran SP% **115.9**
Speed ratings (Par 95): **93,88,87,86,85 82,79,78,78,75 74,69**
toteswinger: 1&2 £5.70, 1&3 £5.50, 2&3 £7.20. CSF £39.59 TOTE £8.70: £3.10, £2.00, £2.60; EX 36.20.
Owner Sheikh Hamdan Bin Mohammed Al Maktoum **Bred** Darley **Trained** Middleham Moor, N Yorks

FOCUS
A reasonable maiden. The time was 0.83 seconds faster than the first division and Mastery, who won well, can go on to better things.

NOTEBOOK
Mastery ◆, a son of Sulamani, half-brother to high-class triple 7f-1m2f winner Kirklees, out of a 1m1f winner in France, was allowed to dictate at just an ordinary pace, but a winning time 0.83 seconds quicker than the first division suggests he is no way flattered by this. He had his rivals in trouble when still travelling strongly approaching the two-furlong marker and drew clear when coming under pressure to post a very impressive introduction. He could be pretty smart, although it remains to be seen whether he will be as effective on quicker ground. (op 7-1 tchd 6-1)
Kings Destiny, a Dubai Destination colt, out of a middle-distance winner, showed ability but was no match whatsoever for the above-average winner. He was just a touch keen early and will know more next time. (op 4-1 tchd 5-1)
Bin End is bred to want at least 1m4f next year, so this was a respectable introduction. (op 10-1 tchd 12-1)
Dubai Echo(USA) was well backed to improve on the form he showed on his debut over 7f at Newmarket, but he was in trouble four furlongs out. (op Evens tchd 6-4 in places)
Musigny(USA), down the field on his debut over 6f at Yarmouth, was stopped in his run when briefly looking threatening two furlongs out and the race was as good as over by the time he recovered his momentum. He has plenty of ability and both his action and his US pedigree suggests he can do better on a quicker surface.

6582 BEST RACECOURSES ON TURFTV H'CAP 1m 2f 50y
3:40 (3:41) (Class 4) (0-85,85) 3-Y-0+ **£6,476** (£1,927; £963; £481) **Stalls** Low

Form RPR
2421 1 **Expresso Star (USA)**[16] 6163 3-8-13 **82** JimmyFortune 15 103+
(J H M Gosden) *trckd ldrs gng wl: smooth hdwy to ld over 2f out: rdn clr over 1f out: easily* **5/2[1]**
2402 2 5 **St Jean Cap Ferrat**[39] 5502 3-9-0 **83** (v) TPO'Shea 4 92
(G Wragg) *hld up towards rr: gd hdwy on inner 3f out: swtchd rt and rdn whn n.m.r wl over 1f out: styd on to chse wnr appr last: sn no imp* **9/1[3]**
0503 3 6 **Jeer (IRE)**[18] 6129 4-9-4 **82** RyanMoore 11 79
(E A L Dunlop) *towards rr: hdwy on wd outside over 2f out: sn rdn and styd on ins fnl f: nrst fin* **12/1**
1131 4 1¼ **Wind Shuffle (GER)**[18] 6108 5-8-9 **78** GaryBartley(5) 14 72
(J S Goldie) *cl up: led 1after 3f: rdn along 3f out: hdd over 2f out: sn drvn and grad wknd* **14/1**
4405 5 ½ **Ellmau**[21] 6012 3-8-13 **82** ChrisCatlin 13 75
(E J O'Neill) *chsd ldrs: effrt 3f out: rdn along 2f out: sn drvn and one pce* **20/1**
2656 6 1½ **Trans Siberian**[12] 6238 4-9-7 **85** JoeFanning 12 75
(P F I Cole) *hld up towards rr: stdy hdwy 1/2-way: effrt to chse ldrs 2f out: sn rdn and no imp* **14/1**
1210 7 1 **Thumbs Up**[14] 6202 3-8-13 **82** DaneO'Neill 1 70
(L M Cumani) *in tch: hdwy to chse ldrs 4f out: rdn along 3f out: drvn over 2f out and sn btn* **12/1**
2403 8 1¼ **Vicious Warrior**[12] 6250 9-8-9 **73** JimCrowley 5 59
(R M Whitaker) *led 3f: cl up tl rdn along 3f out and grad wknd* **16/1**
0135 9 1½ **Moheebb (IRE)**[4] 6482 4-8-12 **76** (b) AndrewElliott 7 59
(Mrs R A Carr) *towards rr: effrt and sme hdwy over 2f out: sn rdn and nvr a facfor* **12/1**
2425 10 8 **Tomintoul Flyer**[14] 6202 3-9-1 **84** (v) TPQueally 9 51
(H R A Cecil) *trckd ldrs: effrt 3f out: rdn over 2f out: sn drvn and wknd* **10/1**
031- 11 6 **Russian Invader (IRE)**[249] 6061 4-8-12 **76** EddieAhern 10 31
(A King) *nvr nr ldrs* **22/1**
3004 12 9 **Man Of Gwent (UAE)**[16] 6177 4-8-8 **72** RichardMullen 16 9
(P D Evans) *cl up: rdn along over 3f out and sn wknd* **20/1**
0-00 13 ½ **Fortunate Isle (USA)**[14] 6215 6-8-6 **77** BMcHugh(7) 6 13
(R A Fahey) *midfield: rdn along over 3f out and sn wknd* **66/1**
005- 14 1¾ **Along The Nile**[200] 5748 6-8-12 **76** TomEaves 8 8
(K G Reveley) *s.i.s: a in rr* **50/1**
313 P **King Olav (UAE)**[26] 5858 3-9-1 **84** PhilipRobinson 2 —
(M A Jarvis) *trckd ldrs on inner: wknd qckly and lost pl 4f out: lost action and bhd whn p.u 2f out: lame* **5/1[2]**

2m 12.53s (0.03) **Going Correction** +0.275s/f (Good)
WFA 3 from 4yo+ 5lb 15 Ran SP% **123.9**
Speed ratings (Par 105): **110,106,101,100,99 98,97,96,95,89 84,77,76,75,—**
toteswinger: 1&2 £7.00, 1&3 £5.00, 2&3 £12.80. CSF £23.77 CT £240.94 TOTE £3.20: £1.70, £4.00, £3.30; EX 32.30.
Owner H R H Princess Haya Of Jordan **Bred** Stonerside Stable **Trained** Newmarket, Suffolk

FOCUS
This fair handicap was run at a sound early pace and the field eventually trailed home behind the ultra-impressive Expresso Star who looks likely to prove better than a handicapper. The form is rated around the placed horses.
King Olav(UAE) Official explanation: vet said gelding finished lame on its right-fore

6583 RACINGUK.TV MAIDEN STKS (DIV I) 1m 2f 50y
4:10 (4:12) (Class 5) 3-Y-0+ **£2,914** (£867; £433; £216) **Stalls** Low

Form RPR
3 1 **Red Jade**[7] 6393 3-9-3 0 JimmyFortune 1 79+
(J H M Gosden) *trckd ldrs: pushed along over 3f out: led over 2f out: styd on wl fnl f: readily* **8/13[1]**
5 2 3½ **Scarab (IRE)**[11] 6280 3-9-3 0 GregFairley 2 72+
(M Johnston) *chsd ldrs: hung lft over 2f out: upsides over 1f out: kpt on same pce ins fnl f* **12/1**
2255 3 1¼ **Eqbaal**[62] 4790 3-9-3 81 (b) RHills 9 70
(J L Dunlop) *chsd ldrs: kpt on same pce fnl 2f* **10/3[2]**
4 4 nk **Lyceana**[54] 5057 3-8-12 0 PhilipRobinson 8 64
(M A Jarvis) *led: hdd over 2f out: kpt on same pce* **9/1[3]**
5 1½ **Blushing Heart**[494] 4-9-3 0 AndrewElliott 10 61
(G M Moore) *in rr div: hdwy 4f out: outpcd over 2f out: kpt on fnl f* **200/1**
0 6 ½ **Ibbetson (USA)**[20] 6055 3-9-3 0 AdamKirby 7 65
(W R Swinburn) *trckd ldrs: outpcd over 2f out: kpt on steadily fnl f* **14/1**
0- 7 2¼ **Solid Silver**[177] 2253 7-9-8 0 PaulMulrennan 11 61
(K G Reveley) *chsd ldrs: outpcd over 2f out: no threat after* **80/1**
8 nk **Indiana Fox**[163] 5-9-3 0 MichaelHills 4 55
(B G Powell) *hld up in rr: hdwy 4f out: outpcd over 2f out: no ch after* **66/1**
002 9 3 **Baileys Benchmark**[43] 5380 3-8-12 47 TomEaves 5 49
(M E Sowersby) *mid-div: outpcd over 3f out: lost pl over 2f out* **66/1**
2600 10 1¾ **Una Auroraborealis**[20] 6047 3-8-12 44 ChrisCatlin 3 45
(S W James) *stdd sn after s: hld up in rr: nvr a factor* **200/1**
0/00 11 8 **Out Of This Way**[72] 4479 5-9-8 49 CatherineGannon 6 34
(Mrs N S Evans) *in rr: bhd fnl 3f* **200/1**

2m 16.1s (3.60) **Going Correction** +0.275s/f (Good)
WFA 3 from 4yo+ 5lb 11 Ran SP% **115.1**
Speed ratings (Par 103): **96,93,92,91,90 90,88,88,85,84 78**
toteswinger: 1&2 £2.90, 1&3 £1.70, 2&3 £4.10. CSF £9.96 TOTE £1.70: £1.20, £2.10, £1.10; EX 10.60.
Owner H R H Princess Haya Of Jordan **Bred** Darley **Trained** Newmarket, Suffolk

FOCUS
An uncompetitive older-horse maiden. The winning time was 1.82 seconds slower than the second division. They raced up the middle of the track. The form is muddling due to the steady pace, with the bare form limited and rated around the winner and fourth.

6584 RACINGUK.TV MAIDEN STKS (DIV II) 1m 2f 50y
4:40 (4:40) (Class 5) 3-Y-0+ **£2,914** (£867; £433; £216) **Stalls** Low

Form RPR
0 1 **Cape Tribulation**[20] 6055 4-9-8 0 TomEaves 9 83+
(J M Jefferson) *trckd ldrs: hdwy 3f out: rdn to chse ldr over 1f out: drvn ins fnl f and styd on strly to ld nr line* **7/2[2]**
42 2 hd **Mubrook (USA)**[20] 6055 3-9-3 0 DaneO'Neill 4 83+
(L M Cumani) *trckd ldrs: hdwy 4f out: rdn to ld wl over 1f out: drvn ins fnl f: hdd and no ex nr fin* **2/1[1]**
3444 3 6 **Almonafis (IRE)**[49] 5182 3-9-3 72 RHills 7 71
(Sir Michael Stoute) *sn led: rdn along 3f out: drvn over 2f out: hdd wl over 1f out: kpt on same pce* **7/2[2]**
63 4 nse **Yetholm (USA)**[26] 5864 3-9-3 0 EddieAhern 10 71
(J R Fanshawe) *trckd ldrs: hdwy 4f out: rdn and ev ch wl over 2f out: sn drvn and one pce* **11/2[3]**
45 5 ½ **Gifted Leader (USA)**[92] 3810 3-9-3 0 JimCrowley 6 70
(Pat Eddery) *hld up towards rr: hdwy 1/2-way: chsd ldrs 3f out: rdn wl over 2f out: kpt on same pce* **8/1**
4043 6 7 **Ba Dreamflight**[38] 5537 3-9-3 46 FrancisNorton 8 56
(H Morrison) *cl up: rdn along over 3f out: sn drvn and wknd* **25/1**
00 7 1 **Nyumba (IRE)**[39] 5491 3-8-7 0 DavidProbert(5) 11 49
(P R Chamings) *hld up: hdwy and in tch 4f out: rdn along over 3f out and sn wknd* **66/1**
6 8 12 **Stormy Summer**[11] 6280 3-9-0 0 (t) JackMitchell(3) 5 30
(R W Price) *hld up: a towards rr* **50/1**
-040 9 14 **Lechero (IRE)**[16] 6173 3-9-3 45 GregFairley 2 —
(John A Harris) *chsd ldrs: rdn along 4f out: sn wknd* **80/1**
00-0 10 10 **Fancy Woman**[16] 6168 4-8-10 40 RossAtkinson(7) 1 —
(C N Kellett) *a towards rr* **100/1**

2m 14.28s (1.78) **Going Correction** +0.275s/f (Good)
WFA 3 from 4yo 5lb **41** Ran SP% **113.8**
Speed ratings (Par 103): **103,102,98,98,97 92,91,81,70,62**
toteswinger: 1&2 £3.20, 1&3 £3.70, 2&3 £1.90. CSF £10.43 TOTE £6.30: £1.70, £1.50, £1.40; EX 11.50.
Owner J David Abell **Bred** Taker Bloodstock **Trained** Norton, N Yorks

FOCUS
Just a fair older-horse maiden, but the first two look to have decent enough futures. The sixth limitd the bare form and the third, fourth and fifth were also below par. The winning time was 1.82 seconds quicker than the first division. They raced up the middle of the track in the straight.
Cape Tribulation Official explanation: trainer said, regarding the improved form shown, last time out gelding was drawn wide and jumped away slowly, got blocked twice on its passage and then ran on, adding that today's soft ground may have helped

6585 COLWICK PARK APPRENTICE H'CAP 1m 75y
5:10 (5:11) (Class 5) (0-70,68) 3-Y-0+ **£3,238** (£963; £481; £240) **Stalls** Low

Form RPR
4641 1 **Moves Goodenough**[7] 6396 5-9-6 **64** 6ex (b) DavidProbert 3 74
(Andrew Turnell) *dwlt: stmbld after 50yds: hdwy on ins over 3f out: led 1f out: hld on towards fin* **3/1[1]**

45 **2** ½ **Sirvino**[39] 5505 3-8-12 **62** DeanHeslop(3) 4 71
(T D Barron) *mid-div: hdwy to ld over 1f out: sn hdd: styd on towards fin* **10/1**

1526 **3** 1¼ **Tanforan**[6] 6408 6-8-13 **60** BillyCray(3) 6 66
(B P J Baugh) *chsd ldrs: styd on same pce ins fnl f* **12/1**

0152 **4** 1 **Ours (IRE)**[20] 6056 5-9-5 **66** (p) StacyRenwick(3) 7 70+
(John A Harris) *hld up in rr: hdwy over 3f out: chsng ldrs 2f out: kpt on wl fnl f* **8/1**[3]

0053 **5** 1¾ **Boppys Pride**[6] 6408 5-8-3 **52** oh2 JamesRogers(5) 13 52
(P T Midgley) *mid-div: hdwy over 3f out: sn chsng ldrs: kpt on same pce appr fnl f* **12/1**

3331 **6** 2¼ **Rossini's Dancer**[21] 6015 3-8-7 **57** (p) BMcHugh(3) 5 52
(R A Fahey) *in rr: sn pushed along: hdwy over 3f out: kpt on: nvr a threat* **8/1**[3]

0110 **7** ½ **Billberry**[18] 6124 3-9-3 **67** (t) WilliamCarson(3) 14 60
(S C Williams) *hld up in rr: hdwy on ins over 3f out: c wd 2f out: kpt on: nvr rchd ldrs* **6/1**[2]

5511 **8** nk **Top Jaro (FR)**[10] 6312 5-9-10 **68** 6ex KellyHarrison 11 61
(Mrs R A Carr) *led 2f: chsd ldr: led over 3f out: hdd over 1f out: one pce* **8/1**[3]

1001 **9** 1¼ **Trans Sonic**[18] 6116 5-9-2 **63** (b) AshleyMorgan(3) 9 53
(A J Lockwood) *chsd ldr: led after 2f: hdd over 3f out: wknd over 1f out* **16/1**

3505 **10** 1 **Wiseman's Diamond (USA)**[19] 6088 3-8-8 **60** PaulPickard(5) 10 47
(P T Midgley) *sn chsng ldrs: wknd 2f out* **40/1**

6060 **11** 6 **Lordship (IRE)**[1] 6560 4-8-11 **60** RosieJessop(5) 1 34
(A W Carroll) *trckd ldrs: t.k.h: lost pl over 1f out* **12/1**

0003 **12** 1¼ **The Wily Woodcock**[19] 6091 4-9-7 **65** GaryBartley 8 36
(G Wragg) *mid-div: t.k.h: c wd and lost pl 4f out: sn bhd* **14/1**

0000 **13** 21 **Strictly Elsie (IRE)**[83] 4112 3-8-2 **52** oh7 (v1) LanceBetts(3) 12 —
(J R Norton) *s.i.s: sn chsng ldrs: lost pl over 3f out: sn wl bhd* **100/1**

1m 47.76s (2.36) **Going Correction** +0.275s/f (Good)
WFA 3 from 4yo+ 3lb **13 Ran SP% 120.8**
Speed ratings (Par 103): **99,98,97,96,94 92,91,91,90,89 83,81,60**
toteswinger: 1&2 £12.30, 1&3 £9.30, 2&3 £19.30. CSF £34.05 CT £268.27 TOTE £3.70: £1.60, £5.20, £4.10; EX 49.20 Place 6: £11.19 Place 5: £8.89.
Owner D Goodenough Removals & Transport **Bred** G Foster **Trained** Broad Hinton, Wilts

FOCUS
A moderate but competitive handicap restricted to apprentices who had not ridden more than 25 winners. Straightforward form which looks solid.
The Wily Woodcock Official explanation: jockey said gelding was unsuited by the soft ground
T/Plt: £15.60 to a £1 stake. Pool: £46,756.37. 2,175.71 winning tickets. T/Qpdt: £8.30 to a £1 stake. Pool: £2,643.64. 234.88 winning tickets. JR

6419 GREAT LEIGHS (A.W) (L-H)
Thursday, October 9

OFFICIAL GOING: Standard
Wind: Virtually nil Weather: Dry

6594 ROMAN WAYS (S) STKS — 1m 5f 66y(P)
6:50 (6:50) (Class 6) 3-Y-0+ — **£2,266** (£674; £337; £168) **Stalls** Low

Form RPR

1-0 **1** **Veloso (FR)**[23] 5999 6-9-2 70 PaulMulrennan 6 72
(Ollie Pears) *hld up in midfield: hdwy gng wl over 4f out: chsd ldr wl over 3f out: rdn over 2f out: led jst ins fnl f: kpt on wl* **10/3**[2]

2053 **2** 1¾ **Cossack Prince**[13] 6248 3-8-8 65 JamieSpencer 5 70
(B J Meehan) *led: rdn and clr w wnr over 2f out: hdd jst ins fnl f: one pce after* **11/4**[1]

006- **3** 1 **Tender Falcon**[458] 3385 8-9-2 64 GeorgeBaker 13 68
(R J Hodges) *hld up towards rr: hdwy 4f out: chsd clr ldng pair over 2f out: kpt on wl u.p: nt rch ldng pair* **12/1**

4400 **4** 10 **Love Empire (USA)**[37] 5593 3-8-8 52 (b) GregFairley 2 54
(M Johnston) *s.i.s: sn bustled along: in tch towards rr: hdwy over 4f out: wnt modest 4th over 2f out: no imp* **11/1**

0000 **5** 9 **Arabian Sun**[26] 5917 4-9-8 44 (b) IanMongan 12 48
(M J Attwater) *chsd ldrs: rdn 6f out: wl outpcd over 3f out: no ch last 2f* **33/1**

022- **6** nk **Flying Spirit (IRE)**[32] 2055 9-9-2 65 (b) JimmyQuinn 14 41
(G L Moore) *chsd ldr tl wl over 3f out: sn outpcd u.p: no ch last 2f* **6/1**[3]

4362 **7** 2¼ **Vincenzio (IRE)**[16] 4075 4-9-2 60 (t) ShaneKelly 8 38
(C R Egerton) *hld up in midfield: rdn wl over 3f out: sn struggling: wl btn last 3f* **6/1**[3]

0-50 **8** 1¾ **Champagne Dancer**[8] 6374 3-8-8 50 DeanMcKeown 10 36
(P D Evans) *chsd ldrs: rdn and struggling 4f out: sn wl btn* **33/1**

0350 **9** ¾ **Summer Bounty**[99] 3606 12-9-2 47 LPKeniry 1 34
(F Jordan) *stdd s: hld up in rr: nvr a factor* **40/1**

060- **10** hd **Leonardo's Friend**[14] 4451 5-9-2 48 (p) PatDobbs 9 34
(B G Powell) *hld up in tch: rdn and btn wl over 3f out* **33/1**

5404 **11** 10 **Mango Masher (IRE)**[14] 6228 4-9-2 48 (p) AdamKirby 11 20
(J L Flint) *in tch: rdn 6f out: wl bhd last 3f: t.o* **9/1**

0000 **12** 4½ **Kennyboy**[26] 5913 3-8-8 50 (p) RichardThomas 7 14
(P G Murphy) *a bhd: rdn 8f out: t.o last 2f* **100/1**

5550 **13** 18 **Pie O My (IRE)**[18] 2552 3-8-8 52 ChrisCatlin 3 —
(J Jay) *stdd s: t.k.h: hld up in rr: lost tch over 4f out: t.o and eased fnl f* **50/1**

2m 51.34s (-2.26) **Going Correction** -0.025s/f (Stan)
WFA 3 from 4yo+ 8lb **13 Ran SP% 118.6**
Speed ratings (Par 101): **105,103,103,97,91 91,90,88,88,88 82,79,68**
toteswinger: 1&2 £15.00, 1&3 £15.00, 2&3 £15.00. CSF £12.16 TOTE £4.60: £1.80, £1.40, £4.70; EX 13.10.The winner was sold to A. J. McCabe for 8,500gns. Cossack Prince was claimed by Mrs L. J. Mongan for £5,000.
Owner Ollie Pears **Bred** Jean Louis Pariente **Trained** Norton, N Yorks

FOCUS
A mixed bag comprising mainly exposed and disappointing sorts but a fair gallop and the first three pulled clear. The form is best rated around the runner-up.
Pie O My(IRE) Official explanation: jockey said colt had no more to give

6595 BRENTWOOD H'CAP — 5f (P)
7:20 (7:21) (Class 6) (0-50,50) 3-Y-0+ — **£2,266** (£674; £337; £168) **Stalls** Low

Form RPR

0342 **1** **Tanley**[11] 6308 3-8-12 **50** (p) ChrisCatlin 10 57
(J F Coupland) *racd in midfield on outer: rdn 1/2-way: gd hdwy jst over 1f out: edgd lft fnl f: r.o wl to ld towards fin* **5/1**[2]

0400 **2** hd **Reigning Monarch (USA)**[21] 6063 5-8-12 **50** SamHitchcott 3 56
(Miss Z C Davison) *chsd ldrs: wnt 2nd 2f out: rdn to ld over 1f out: kpt on wl u.p tl hdd and no ex towards fin* **7/1**

6006 **3** 1 **Scots W'Hae**[41] 5457 3-8-9 **47** JamieMoriarty 1 51+
(Miss L A Perratt) *s.i.s: sn in midfield: effrt 2f out: chsd ldrs and swtchd rt 1f out: kpt on fnl f* **7/1**

1030 **4** ½ **Taboor (IRE)**[35] 5626 10-8-12 **50** EddieAhern 2 51
(R M H Cowell) *squeezed and short of room sn after s: bhd: hdwy on inner over 1f out: kpt on fnl f: nt rch ldrs* **6/1**[3]

0100 **5** ¾ **Dubai To Barnsley**[7] 6405 3-8-12 **50** ow1 AdamKirby 6 48
(Garry Moss) *chsd ldr tl 2f out: ev ch and drvn over 1f out: edgd rt ent fnl f: one pce fnl 100yds* **14/1**

0040 **6** nk **Young Ivanhoe**[34] 5684 3-8-12 **50** (b) CatherineGannon 9 47
(C A Dwyer) *chsd ldrs: drvn wl over 1f out: wknd ins fnl f* **33/1**

0234 **7** ½ **Rann Na Cille (IRE)**[35] 5626 4-8-12 **50** TPQueally 7 45
(P T Midgley) *hld up in midfield: rdn and effrt over 1f out: no imp fnl f* **9/2**[1]

652 **8** nk **Cranworth Blaze**[14] 6224 4-8-11 **49** GregFairley 8 43
(T J Etherington) *sn rdn and outpcd in rr: wl bhd 1/2-way: kpt on u.p fnl f: nvr trbld ldrs* **10/1**

0630 **9** nse **Linnet Park**[42] 5421 3-8-4 **49** RosieJessop(7) 4 43
(J G Given) *led: rdn jst over 2f out: hdd over 1f out: wknd ins fnl f* **7/1**

4004 **10** 10 **Tittle**[34] 5679 3-8-12 **50** DaneO'Neill 5 8
(H Candy) *s.i.s: nvr gng in rr: lost tch 1/2-way: wl btn and eased ins fnl f* **8/1**

60.66 secs (0.46) **Going Correction** -0.025s/f (Stan) **10 Ran SP% 116.4**
Speed ratings (Par 101): **95,94,93,92,91 90,89,89,89,73**
toteswinger: 1&2 £22.50, 1&3 £22.50, 2&3 £22.50. CSF £39.88 CT £251.49 TOTE £5.80: £1.20, £3.00, £4.20; EX 42.00.
Owner J F Coupland **Bred** Mrs J A Moffatt And Brian T Clark **Trained** East Ravendale, Lincs
■ Stewards' Enquiry : Sam Hitchcott caution: careless riding

FOCUS
This was run at a strong pace throughout and the form is straightforward with the first three close to their marks.

6596 MUCH HADHAM MAIDEN STKS — 1m 5f 66y(P)
7:50 (7:50) (Class 5) 3-Y-0+ — **£2,914** (£867; £433; £216) **Stalls** Low

Form RPR

002 **1** **Drum Major (IRE)**[25] 5931 3-9-3 70 RyanMoore 5 58
(G L Moore) *chsd ldrs: wnt 2nd over 6f out: led over 2f out: hrd rdn over 1f out: hld on wl u.p: all out* **8/1**

0302 **2** ½ **Eureka Moment**[29] 5803 3-8-12 66 EddieAhern 13 52
(E A L Dunlop) *hld up in tch: swtchd rt and effrt wl over 1f out: hung lft ent fnl f: kpt on u.p to go 2nd towards fin: nt quite rch wnr* **8/1**

4 **3** shd **Dayia (IRE)**[7] 6413 4-9-6 0 JimmyQuinn 10 52+
(J Pearce) *s.i.s: t.k.h: hld up in last pl: hdwy on outer over 4f out: chsng ldrs and running on whn nt clr run ent fnl f: sn swtchd sharply lft: r.o but nvr quite getting to wnr* **7/2**[3]

0432 **4** ½ **Hammer**[19] 6126 3-9-3 70 PatDobbs 3 56
(M P Tregoning) *chsd ldr tl over 6f out: rdn over 2f out: ev ch ent fnl f: unable qckn fnl f: lost 2 pls towards fin* **3/1**[2]

-004 **5** 3 **Fleur De Montjeu (IRE)**[44] 5379 3-8-12 48 AdamKirby 11 47
(W R Swinburn) *in rr: pushed along 8f out: hdwy u.p over 3f out: kpt on but nvr trbld ldrs* **33/1**

6223 **6** 1¼ **Sphere (IRE)**[35] 5651 3-8-12 72 JamieSpencer 12 46
(J R Fanshawe) *led tl over 2f out: hrd drvn wl over 1f out: wknd fnl f* **15/8**[1]

300- **7** 2¾ **Covert Mission**[307] 7060 5-9-6 50 PatCosgrave 9 42
(P D Evans) *hld up towards rr: hdwy over 4f out: rdn over 2f out: wknd u.p over 1f out* **33/1**

0650 **8** ¾ **Peas 'n Beans (IRE)**[13] 6252 5-9-6 42 (t) NicolPolli(5) 7 46
(T Keddy) *towards rr: struggling u.p 3f out: no imp last 2f* **100/1**

0 **9** nk **Generous Star**[14] 6226 5-9-11 0 JerryO'Dwyer 6 45
(J Pearce) *s.i.s: hld up in rr: rdn over 4f out: lost tch 3f out* **66/1**

6-20 **10** nk **Stealth Project**[153] 1962 3-9-3 62 HayleyTurner 8 45
(A M Hales) *racd in midfield on outer: rdn over 3f out: wknd wl over 1f out* **25/1**

11 16 **Jethro Wheeler**[163] 5-9-11 0 EdwardCreighton 1 22
(E J Creighton) *hld up in midfield: lost pl and rdn over 4f out: wl bhd fr over 2f out: t.o* **100/1**

2m 56.21s (2.61) **Going Correction** -0.025s/f (Stan)
WFA 3 from 4yo+ 8lb **11 Ran SP% 117.4**
Speed ratings (Par 103): **90,89,89,89,87 86,85,84,84,84 74**
toteswinger: 1&2 £5.50, 1&3 £24.20, 2&3 £11.00. CSF £65.98 TOTE £12.10: £3.00, £2.10, £1.10; EX 29.50.
Owner R A Green **Bred** The Queen **Trained** Woodingdean, E Sussex

FOCUS
A run-of-the-mill maiden and a steady early pace means this bare form is not entirely reliable. The first four finished in a heap and the proximity of the 48-rated fifth holds down the form.
Eureka Moment Official explanation: jockey said filly hung left in straight
Stealth Project Official explanation: jockey said gelding hung right throughout

6597 CLACTON MAIDEN STKS — 1m (P)
8:20 (8:21) (Class 4) 2-Y-0 — **£4,533** (£1,348; £674; £336) **Stalls** Centre

Form RPR

1 **Close Alliance (USA)** 2-9-3 0 JimmyFortune 3 82+
(J H M Gosden) *pushed along briefly early: in tch: hdwy 2f out: sn ev ch: led ent fnl f: r.o wl: in command nr fin* **15/2**[3]

0 **2** ½ **Redding Colliery (USA)**[76] 4360 2-9-3 0 (b1) JohnEgan 4 80
(Jane Chapple-Hyam) *t.k.h: sn trcking ldrs: plld out off rail and hdwy wl over 1f out: sn led: hdd ent fnl f: r.o but hld by wnr nr fin* **16/1**

32 **3** 3¼ **Officer In Command (USA)**[13] 6253 2-9-3 0 LPKeniry 11 73
(J S Moore) *in tch: rdn and effrt jst over 2f out: chsd ldng pair u.p 1f out: kpt on same pce* **10/1**

4 1 **Neuchatel (GER)** 2-9-3 0 GregFairley 8 71
(M Johnston) *dwlt: sn in midfield: rdn and effrt wl over 1f out: kpt on u.p fnl f: no ch w ldng pair* **20/1**

3 **5** 1¼ **Red Junior**[22] 6026 2-9-3 0 JamieSpencer 12 68
(B J Meehan) *hld up towards rr: hdwy on outer over 2f out: drvn over 1f out: no imp fnl f* **13/8**[1]

5 **6** 2¼ **Gassin**[22] 6031 2-9-3 0 AlanMunro 1 63
(G Wragg) *led: rdn and hdd over 1f out: wknd ent fnl f* **10/1**

500 **7** 1½ **Ayrus (USA)**[22] 6025 2-9-3 75 EddieAhern 10 60
(B J Meehan) *chsd ldr tl wl over 1f out: wknd u.p jst over 1f out* **20/1**

0 **8** ½ **Ritano (IRE)**[15] 6199 2-8-12 0 DavidProbert(5) 13 59+
(B I Case) *racd on outer: nvr bttr than midfield: rdn over 3f out: nvr trbld ldrs* **66/1**

6 **9** *hd* **Just Like Silk (USA)**[20] 6084 2-9-3 0........................ RobertWinston 6 58+
(G A Butler) *hld up in midfield: hdwy on inner 2f out: sn shkn up: wknd ent fnl f* **11/4**[2]

00 **10** *nk* **Sampower Quin (IRE)**[13] 6253 2-9-3 0........................ DNolan 5 58
(D Carroll) *in tch in midfield: rdn over 3f out: struggling 2f out: n.d after* **100/1**

11 *¾* **Sams Spirit** 2-9-0 0........................ JackMitchell(3) 7 56
(P J McBride) *s.i.s: a in rr: rdn and no hdwy 3f out* **80/1**

00 **12** *nk* **Pure Crystal**[37] 5590 2-8-12 0........................ JerryO'Dwyer 14 50
(M E Rimmer) *stdd and dropped in bhd after s: nvr a factor* **100/1**

06 **13** *¾* **Beaubrav**[38] 5578 2-9-3 0........................ ShaneKelly 2 54
(P W D'Arcy) *t.k.h: pressed ldrs: rdn wl over 1f out: wknd qckly over 1f out* **66/1**

56 **14** *nk* **Loulou (USA)**[12] 6282 2-8-12 0........................ TPQueally 9 48
(S A Callaghan) *a towards rr: rdn 3f out: nvr trbld ldrs* **50/1**

1m 41.08s (1.18) **Going Correction** -0.025s/f (Stan) **14** Ran SP% **118.3**
Speed ratings (Par 97): **93,92,89,88,87 84,83,82,82,82 81,81,80,80**
toteswinger: 1&2 £21.40, 1&3 £23.50, 2&3 £23.50. CSF £110.63 TOTE £8.80: £2.80, £8.30, £1.60; EX 147.30.

Owner K Abdulla **Bred** Juddmonte Farms Inc **Trained** Newmarket, Suffolk

FOCUS
This looked a fair maiden but with the two market leaders disappointing, it did not take as much winning as seemed likely. The gallop was ordinary and those held up were at a disadvantage.

NOTEBOOK
Close Alliance(USA) ◆, a well-bred sort who holds an entry in the Racing Post Trophy, was easy to back but created a favourable impression on this debut. He's a decent sort with plenty of physical scope and is sure to win more races. (op 6-1)

Redding Colliery(USA) was well beaten on his debut at Ascot in July but fared a good deal better on this all-weather debut in first-time blinkers. He had the run of the race but can pick up a similar event. (op 11-1)

Officer In Command(USA), who had shown ability on Polytrack, again gave it his best shot and looks a good guide to this form. He will be of more interest away from progressive sorts in handicaps. (op 8-1)

Neuchatel(GER) ◆, a half-brother to 1m2f Polytrack winner Man Of Vision, is from a yard going really well and showed ability after missing the break on this debut. He is entitled to improve for this experience and is sure to win a race. (op 16-1)

Red Junior caught the eye in a decent Sandown maiden on his debut but was unable to build on that from his wide draw on this all-weather debut in a race that suited the prominent racers. He will be worth another chance back on grass in due course. (op 6-4 tchd 15-8)

Gassin looked to have something to find and had his limitations exposed on this all-weather debut. He did not look the most straightforward (raced keenly and carried head high) but may do better once handicapped. (op 16-1)

Just Like Silk(USA) was well supported but also failed to confirm the promise of his turf debut over a trip he should have appreciated. However, he was not knocked about and would not be one to write off yet. (op 9-2)

6598 INGATESTONE H'CAP — 1m (P)
8:50 (8:51) (Class 4) (0-80,80) 3-Y-0+ **£5,180** (£1,541; £770; £384) **Stalls** Centre

Form RPR

1-01 **1** **Multakka (IRE)**[17] 6170 5-9-6 **79**........................ RHills 6 89+
(M P Tregoning) *dwlt: towards rr: hdwy into midfield over 3f out: looking for gap and bmpd wl over 1f out: chsng ldrs and swtchd rt jst ins fnl f: qcknd wl to ld towards fin* **7/2**[1]

1341 **2** *½* **Le Chiffre (IRE)**[7] 6422 6-8-3 **67** 6ex........................(p) DavidProbert(5) 2 76
(Miss Sheena West) *led: rdn over 2f out: r.o wl tl hdd and no ex towards fin* **14/1**

3211 **3** *1 ¾* **Effigy**[21] 6056 4-9-2 **75**........................ DaneO'Neill 3 80+
(H Candy) *hld up bhd: hdwy over 1f out: swtchd rt ins fnl f: r.o to go 3rd nr fin: nt rch ldrs* **5/1**[2]

2160 **4** *nk* **Tartan Gigha (IRE)**[21] 6052 3-9-2 **78**........................ JoeFanning 12 82
(M Johnston) *hld up towards rr: hdwy over 1f out: keeping on whn hmpd ent fnl f: rn to go 4th nr fin: nt rch ldrs* **10/1**

0552 **5** *hd* **Heroes**[37] 5588 4-9-7 **80**........................(v[1]) AlanMunro 1 84
(C F Wall) *chsd ldrs on inner: drvn and effrt 2f out: kpt on same pce u.p fnl f* **13/2**

4400 **6** *½* **Prince Of Thebes (IRE)**[19] 6130 7-8-13 **72**........................ PaulDoe 8 74
(M J Attwater) *chsd ldr: rdn and unable qckn over 2f out: kpt on tl lost 2nd ins fnl f: wknd last 100yds* **20/1**

2036 **7** *2 ½* **Billy Dane (IRE)**[20] 6070 4-9-0 **80**........................(p) BMcHugh(7) 14 77
(R A Fahey) *hld up towards rr on outer: rdn and effrt 3f out: no imp u.p fr over 1f out* **20/1**

3-01 **8** *nse* **Ghost Dancer**[17] 6177 4-9-1 **74**........................ PatCosgrave 11 71
(L M Cumani) *hld up in midfield: bmpd wl over 1f out: sn drvn: no imp u.p fnl f* **6/1**[3]

0564 **9** *¾* **Rubacuori (BRZ)**[26] 5908 4-9-1 **77**........................(b[1]) LukeMorris(3) 5 72
(J M P Eustace) *dwlt: sn pushed along in midfield: drvn and nt qckn over 2f out: wknd over 1f out* **16/1**

6140 **10** *1 ¾* **Dream Of Fortune (IRE)**[122] 2897 4-8-12 **71**........................(t) TPQueally 7 62
(M G Quinlan) *in tch: rdn over 2f out: edgd rt and wknd ins fnl f: eased towards fin* **25/1**

600 **11** *2 ½* **Mount Hadley (USA)**[19] 6120 4-9-7 **80**........................(b[1]) HayleyTurner 4 65
(G A Butler) *stdd after s: hld up in last pl: n.d* **33/1**

3200 **12** *1* **King Of Rhythm (IRE)**[16] 6186 5-9-1 **74**........................ DNolan 10 57
(D Carroll) *in tch: rdn over 2f out: wkng whn hmpd jst ins fnl f* **22/1**

2332 **13** *10* **Moonlight Man**[45] 5350 7-9-7 **80**........................(t) RobertWinston 9 40
(C R Dore) *chsd ldrs: rdn and struggling over 3f out: wl bhd fr over 1f out* **16/1**

1300 **14** *1* **Avertis**[64] 4731 3-9-2 **78**........................ JohnEgan 13 35
(M Botti) *racd on outer in midfield: rdn over 3f out: sn struggling: wl bhd fnl f* **28/1**

1m 39.71s (-0.19) **Going Correction** -0.025s/f (Stan)
WFA 3 from 4yo+ 3lb **14** Ran SP% **118.1**
Speed ratings (Par 105): **99,98,96,96,96 95,93,93,92,90 88,87,77,76**
toteswinger: 1&2 £4.80, 1&3 £3.90, 2&3 £13.90. CSF £47.15 CT £248.19 TOTE £4.90: £1.90, £3.50, £2.60; EX 58.90.

Owner Hamdan Al Maktoum **Bred** Shadwell Estate Company Limited **Trained** Lambourn, Berks

FOCUS
A fair handicap and one run at just an ordinary gallop but sound form rated around the third and fourth.

Avertis Official explanation: jockey said gelding had a breathing problem

6599 BIRCH H'CAP — 1m 2f (P)
9:20 (9:25) (Class 4) (0-80,80) 3-Y-0+ **£5,180** (£1,541; £770; £384) **Stalls** Low

Form RPR

5612 **1** **Ben Ami**[7] 6422 3-8-1 **70**........................ AndreaAtzeni(7) 6 79
(Miss J R Gibney) *hld up towards rr: gd hdwy on outer 3f out: led 2f out: clr 1f out: nvr gng to get ct but all out nr fin* **5/1**[1]

2120 **2** *hd* **Cupid's Glory**[10] 6346 6-9-9 **80**........................ GeorgeBaker 4 89+
(G L Moore) *stdd and dropped in bhd after s: hld up in last pair: hdwy and nt clr run 2f out: swtchd lft over 1f out: chsd wnr ins fnl f: clsng wl towards fin: jst hld* **5/1**[1]

5241 **3** *1 ½* **Golden Bishop**[46] 5320 3-8-4 **66**........................ JoeFanning 5 72
(R A Fahey) *hld up in last trio: gd hdwy on inner over 1f out: chsd ldng pair ins fnl f: kpt on* **14/1**

6000 **4** *1 ¼* **Master Pegasus**[45] 5349 5-8-9 **66**........................ PatCosgrave 7 69
(J R Boyle) *t.k.h: hld up in tch: rdn to chse wnr wl over 1f out: unable qckn u.p: lost 2nd ins fnl f* **33/1**

4/-0 **5** *1 ¼* **Remember Ramon (USA)**[17] 6170 5-9-3 **74**........................ ChrisCatlin 9 75
(J R Gask) *t.k.h: hld up in last: hdwy on outer 2f out: styd on steadily fnl f: nvr pce to threaten ldrs* **66/1**

0232 **6** *¾* **Del Mar Sunset**[49] 5209 9-9-3 **74**........................ LiamJones 3 73
(W J Haggas) *t.k.h: hld up in midfield: edgd out over 2f out: rdn wl over 1f out: kpt on same pce u.p fr over 1f out* **15/2**[3]

1653 **7** *1* **Emperor Court (IRE)**[101] 3561 4-9-9 **80**........................ EddieAhern 2 77
(P J Makin) *t.k.h: hld up in midfield: rdn and effrt jst over 2f out: one pce fr over 1f out* **12/1**

436 **8** *¾* **Bois Joli (IRE)**[24] 5964 3-8-12 **74**........................ JohnEgan 11 70
(M Botti) *towards rr: rdn and struggling over 3f out: rallied u.p over 1f out: plugged on same pce fnl f* **16/1**

6620 **9** *1 ½* **Fitzroy Crossing (USA)**[26] 5910 3-9-1 **77**........................ GregFairley 12 70
(M Johnston) *led tl 2f out: sn drvn: wknd qckly ent fnl f* **20/1**

322 **10** *1 ½* **Fantasy Princess (USA)**[26] 5910 3-9-3 **79**........................ HayleyTurner 10 69
(G A Butler) *t.k.h: chsd ldrs: rdn over 2f out: wknd wl over 1f out: btn whn short of room over 1f out* **7/1**[2]

6105 **11** *7* **Valdan (IRE)**[1] 6577 4-8-9 **66** oh4........................ DeanMcKeown 14 42
(P D Evans) *t.k.h: chsd ldr tl 2f out: sn wknd* **16/1**

560 **12** *8* **Mutawahej (USA)**[21] 6047 4-8-9 **66**........................(t) RHills 1 26
(J H M Gosden) *sn pushed up to chse ldng pair: rdn over 3f out: wknd over 2f out: wl btn and eased ins fnl f* **5/1**[1]

2m 6.96s (-1.64) **Going Correction** -0.025s/f (Stan)
WFA 3 from 4yo+ 5lb **12** Ran SP% **109.6**
Speed ratings (Par 105): **105,104,103,102,101 101,100,99,98,97 91,85**
toteswinger: 1&2 £10.20, 1&3 £5.50, 2&3 £57.20. CSF £23.54 CT £243.23 TOTE £6.30: £2.00, £2.00, £3.80; EX 26.90 Place 6 £179.40, Place 5 £104.52.

Owner Wood Hall Stud Limited **Bred** Wood Hall Stud **Trained** Shenley, Herts

■ Filigree Lace was withdrawn (6/1, ref to enter stalls). R4 applies, deduct 10p in the £.
■ Stewards' Enquiry : Greg Fairley three-day ban: careless riding (Oct 23, 24 & 27)

FOCUS
Another fair handicap but, although the pace was not overly strong, the hold-up horses came to the fore in the straight. The form looks sound rated around the third and fourth.

Emperor Court(IRE) Official explanation: vet said colt was lame

T/Plt: £225.80 to a £1 stake. Pool: £99,450.67. 321.48 winning tickets. T/Qpdt: £27.00 to a £1 stake. Pool: £8,292.26. 227.00 winning tickets. SP

6117 NEWBURY (L-H)
Thursday, October 9

OFFICIAL GOING: Good to soft (soft in places; 6.2)
Wind: Nil

6600 VODAFONE EBF MAIDEN STKS (DIV I) — 6f 110y
1:40 (1:40) (Class 4) 2-Y-0 **£5,504** (£1,637; £818; £408) **Stalls** High

Form RPR

1 **Club Tahiti** 2-8-12 0........................ SteveDrowne 8 87+
(R Charlton) *w'like: scope: s.i.s: in rr: pushed along and hdwy over 2f out: wnt 2nd 1f out: styd on to ld fnl 110yds: sn forged clr* **16/1**

2 *4* **Sakhee's Pearl** 2-8-12 0........................ MickyFenton 9 75+
(Miss Gay Kelleway) *leggy: bit bkwd: s.i.s: sn rcvrd and led after 1f: rdn 2f out: hdd fnl 110yds and no ch w wnr but styd on wl for clr 2nd* **66/1**

3 *3 ¼* **Dunes Queen (USA)** 2-8-12 0........................ EdwardCreighton 5 66+
(M R Channon) *lengthy: scope: lw: in tch: hdwy and edgd lft 3f out: styd on to go 3rd over 1f out but no imp on ldng duo* **8/13**[1]

0 **4** *4* **Tarruji (IRE)**[19] 6117 2-9-3 0........................ AlanMunro 3 60+
(P W Chapple-Hyam) *pressed ldrs: rdn over 2f out: wknd over 1f out* **10/1**

5 *5* **Compton Blue** 2-9-3 0........................ RichardHughes 7 46+
(R Hannon) *str: bit bkwd: s.i.s: sn chsng ldrs: wkng whn hmpd 2f out* **6/1**[2]

06 **6** *nk* **Winning Band (IRE)**[13] 6246 2-9-3 0........................ JamieSpencer 10 45
(B J Meehan) *unf: w ldrs 2f: styd prom tl fdd fr 2f out* **15/2**[3]

0 **7** *nk* **Dicey Affair**[39] 5535 2-8-12 0........................ RyanMoore 1 40+
(G L Moore) *w'like: bit bkwd: in tch whn rdn 1/2-way: nvr gng pce to be competitive* **33/1**

8 *¾* **Al Sayed** 2-9-3 0........................ PhilipRobinson 11 43+
(Miss D Mountain) *tall: lengthy: s.i.s: plld hrd and sn chsng ldrs: wknd 2f out* **25/1**

9 *2 ¼* **Freedom Fire (IRE)** 2-9-0 0........................ LukeMorris(3) 4 36
(J M P Eustace) *str: unf: chsd ldrs over 3f* **50/1**

50 **10** *1 ¼* **Katie Higgins**[31] 5754 2-8-9 0........................ TolleyDean(3) 6 28+
(J L Spearing) *leggy: led 1f: losing position whn hmpd 3f out* **66/1**

0 **11** *nk* **Hekaaya (IRE)**[20] 6072 2-8-12 0........................ MartinDwyer 2 27
(M P Tregoning) *s.i.s: a in rr* **25/1**

1m 24.37s (5.07) **Going Correction** +0.625s/f (Yiel) **11** Ran SP% **118.5**
Speed ratings (Par 97): **96,91,87,83,77 77,76,75,73,71 71**
toteswinger: 1&2 £69.00, 1&3 £3.60, 2&3 £20.00. CSF £781.43 TOTE £19.90: £3.50, £14.30, £1.10; EX 337.60.

Owner Seasons Holidays **Bred** B Hurley **Trained** Beckhampton, Wilts

FOCUS
The winning time was 0.51 seconds slower than the second division and this looked just an ordinary maiden. They raced stands' side, and the rail looked an advantage.

The Form Book, Raceform Ltd, Compton, RG20 6NL

NOTEBOOK

Club Tahiti, a daughter of Hernando and a half-sister to Oaks fourth Clowance, won in good style on her racecourse debut. She tracked Dunes Queen early on, but was switched inside when it became clear that one wasn't going anywhere, and she picked up well under hands-and-heels riding. She was visually impressive and rates as a decent prospect, particularly as she is bred to improve over further next year. However, it might be unwise to get carried away at this stage, as it remains to be seen what she beat given the favourite failed to give her running, and the winning time was slower than the second division. Her aim now is the Listed Radley Stakes back here over 7f, and that will tell us more.

Sakhee's Pearl, the first foal of a 6f-7f winner, recovered from a slow start to lead and enjoyed the run of the race against the possibly favoured stands' rail. She clearly has ability and should find a similar race.

Dunes Queen(USA), a daughter of top-class two-year-old Queen's Logic, was really well backed to make a winning debut, but she did not enjoy the best of trips and it was clear from some way out she wasn't picking up. She might not have been helped by ending up away from the stands' rail, but she was just too green to do herself justice, and her jockey felt she would come on a lot. Creighton also felt the filly just got tired in the quite testing ground, so perhaps a better surface will suit, and she might be worth another chance. (op 10-11 tchd evens in places)

Tarruji(IRE) was well held, but this was still an improvement on the form he showed first-time up and his effort was all the more creditable considering he was stuck out wide of the near rail for much of the way. (tchd 14-1)

Compton Blue was in trouble when hampered two out, but he kept on again without being given an unnecessarily hard time. (op 9-2)

Winning Band(IRE) Official explanation: jockey said colt hung left

Dicey Affair should do better when eligible for handicaps after one more run.

Al Sayed Official explanation: jockey said colt hung badly left

6601 VODAFONE EBF MAIDEN STKS (DIV II) 6f 110y

2:10 (2:10) (Class 4) 2-Y-O **£5,504** (£1,637; £818; £408) **Stalls** High

Form RPR

2 **1** **Film Set (USA)**[14] 6230 2-9-3 0 LDettori 7 89
(Saeed Bin Suroor) *str: lw: led: rdn and hdd over 1f out: edgd rt and rallied to ld ins fnl f: r.o wl* **11/4**[2]

23 **2** *2 ¾* **Noverre To Go (IRE)**[7] 6412 2-9-3 0 (t) RichardKingscote 4 81
(Tom Dascombe) *cmpt: sn trcking wnr: rdn to ld and hung rt over 1f out: hdd and unable qckn ins fnl f* **9/2**[3]

3 **3** *½* **Shabib (USA)**[20] 6080 2-9-3 0 RHills 10 80+
(B W Hills) *lw: hld up: hdwy 1/2-way: rdn and hung lft over 2f out: styd on same pce fnl f* **11/8**[1]

4 **4** *4* **King's Siren (IRE)**[9] 6358 2-8-12 0 WilliamBuick 9 64
(A M Balding) *unf: scope: chsd ldrs: outpcd 1/2-way: hung rt and styd on ins fnl f* **12/1**

5 *4 ½* **Fantastic Dubai (USA)** 2-9-3 0 SamHitchcott 1 56
(M R Channon) *tall: lengthy: lw: wnt lft s: sn chsng ldrs: rdn over 2f out: wkng whn hung rt fnl f* **6/1**

6 *nse* **Feet Of Fury** 2-8-12 0 ShaneKelly 2 51
(W M Brisbourne) *w'like: swtg: mid-div: rdn and hung lft 1/2-way: sn wknd* **100/1**

0 **7** *28* **Allexes (IRE)**[27] 5860 2-8-12 0 PatCosgrave 6 —
(J R Boyle) *sn pushed along in rr: wknd 1/2-way* **100/1**

00 **8** *1 ¼* **Mezzoforte (IRE)**[10] 6342 2-8-10 0 (t) MarieLequarre(7) 8 —
(J S Moore) *prom: lost pl 5f out: sn bhd* **100/1**

1m 23.86s (4.56) **Going Correction** +0.625s/f (Yiel) **41** Ran SP% **111.9**

Speed ratings (Par 97): **98,94,94,89,84 84,52,51**

toteswinger: 1&2 £2.10, 1&3 £1.40, 2&3 £2.10. CSF £14.80 TOTE £3.40: £1.60, £1.50, £1.10; EX 13.70.

Owner Godolphin **Bred** Christopher Grosso **Trained** Newmarket, Suffolk

FOCUS

The runners were inclined to race further away from the stands' rail early than they did in the opener, though a couple did edge over to it late on. Despite the smaller field and the presence of some massive outsiders, the winning time was over half a second quicker than division one, and those with proven ability dominated.

NOTEBOOK

Film Set(USA), just beaten by a rival with previous experience on his Pontefract debut, showed the benefit of that under a positive ride in these testing conditions, despite being weak in the market. He showed a decent attitude when the runner-up got to him and he was going away again at the line. A step up in class now looks to be in order (op 13-8 tchd 3-1 and 6-4 in places)

Noverre To Go(IRE), who has shown ability in both of his previous starts but who raced too keenly in the first-time tongue tie at Goodwood last time, was produced to win his race in plenty of time, but he hung over to the stands' rail under pressure and didn't get home. He may have got there too soon, but he may also be worth another slight drop in trip and nurseries now become an option. (op 5-1 tchd 11-2)

Shabib(USA), a promising third in a Newmarket maiden on his debut last month from which the fifth horse has since been successful, was well backed to go two-better, but he became outpaced at halfway just as the principals went for home and, although he gradually clawed back some of the deficit, he was never doing it quickly enough. He looks in need of another step up in trip and has a fast-ground action. (op 5-2)

King's Siren(IRE), despite plenty of speed on the dam's side of her pedigree, seemed to need all of the 7f on her debut and it was a similar story over this slightly shorter trip, as she came off the bridle at halfway and could only plug on after that. (op 14-1)

Fantastic Dubai(USA), a $400,000 half-brother to three winners, including the stable's high-class miler Zafeen, showed up for a while but he showed signs of greenness and gradually dropped away. He may need better ground and is entitled to come on for this, but he will need to. (op 5-1)

Feet Of Fury, a 7,000gns filly out of a winner in the US, wasn't at all disgraced at this level considering her price. She will find easier opportunities than this and her breeding suggests she may be worth a try on sand at some stage. Official explanation: jockey said filly hung left (tchd 80-1)

6602 HARINO.COM - VIRTUAL RACING, REAL EXCITEMENT MAIDEN STKS (DIV I) 1m (S)

2:40 (2:44) (Class 4) 2-Y-O **£5,504** (£1,637; £818; £408) **Stalls** High

Form RPR

23 **1** **Palavicini (USA)**[20] 6075 2-9-3 0 EddieAhern 6 84+
(J L Dunlop) *lw: trckd ldrs: led over 3f out: pushed along and styd on strly thrght fnl f* **5/6**[1]

2 *1* **Lasso The Moon** 2-9-3 0 TPO'Shea 5 82+
(M R Channon) *lengthy: scope: lw: towards rr: hdwy over 2f out: chsd wnr ins fnl f and kpt on wl but a hld* **20/1**

3 *3 ¼* **Border Patrol** 2-9-3 0 SteveDrowne 18 75+
(R Charlton) *tall: unf: s.i.s: in rr tl hdwy 1/2-way: rdn and styd on fnl 2f but outpcd by ldng duo fnl f* **9/1**[3]

0 **4** *hd* **Directorship**[28] 5842 2-9-3 0 JimmyQuinn 4 74+
(P R Chamings) *lw: sn chsng ldrs: rdn to go 2nd ins fnl 2f: nvr rchd wnr and styd on same pce fnl f* **66/1**

64 **5** *7* **Holberg (UAE)**[27] 5859 2-9-3 0 RoystonFfrench 16 59
(M Johnston) *sn w ldrs: rdn 3f out: wknd ins fnl 2f* **5/1**[2]

6 *1 ½* **Zulu Moon** 2-9-3 0 WilliamBuick 10 56
(A M Balding) *w'like: chsd ldrs: rdn over 3f out: wknd 2f out* **14/1**

00 **7** *1 ¾* **Saborido (USA)**[8] 6397 2-9-3 0 JimCrowley 11 52
(Mrs A J Perrett) *chsd ldrs: rdn over 3f out: wknd qckly 2f out* **40/1**

8 *2* **Canton Road** 2-9-3 0 AlanMunro 7 47
(P F I Cole) *w'like: tall: chsd ldrs: rdn over 3f out: wknd over 2f out* **28/1**

9 *3 ½* **Mystic Prince** 2-9-3 0 JamieSpencer 8 40
(B J Meehan) *neat: bit bkwd: nvr bttr than mid-div: bhd fr 1/2-way* **20/1**

0 **10** *¾* **Pagan Flight (IRE)**[19] 6117 2-9-3 0 RyanMoore 3 38
(B J Meehan) *slt ld towards centre crse tl hdd over 3f out: sn wknd* **33/1**

11 *9* **Great Western (USA)** 2-9-3 0 StephenDonohoe 17 18
(P F I Cole) *leggy: s.i.s: a in rr* **33/1**

12 *6* **Sermons Mount (USA)** 2-9-3 0 LPKeniry 2 5
(Mouse Hamilton-Fairley) *w'like: str: bit bkwd: in tch tl rdn and wknd 1/2-way* **100/1**

0 **13** *7* **Spinning Joy**[23] 5996 2-8-12 0 PatCosgrave 9 —
(J R Boyle) *sn bhd* **100/1**

14 *11* **Conclusive** 2-9-3 0 GeorgeBaker 12 —
(R M Beckett) *w'like: str: bit bkwd: pressed ldrs to 1/2-way* **10/1**

1m 44.84s (5.14) **Going Correction** +0.625s/f (Yiel) **77** Ran SP% **121.7**

Speed ratings (Par 97): **99,98,94,94,87 86,84,82,78,78 69,63,56,45**

toteswinger: 1&2 £7.20, 1&3 £3.10, 2&3 £16.20. CSF £26.82 TOTE £1.70: £1.30, £3.30, £2.50; EX 23.20.

Owner Windflower Overseas Holdings Inc **Bred** Windflower Overseas Holdings Inc **Trained** Arundel, W Sussex

FOCUS

A decent maiden, but they finished strung out. The winning time was 1.14 seconds quicker than the second division, although that race was steadily run. They split into two groups early, but merged late on and the main action took place up the middle of the track.

NOTEBOOK

Palavicini(USA), second on his debut at Newmarket before running third in the Haynes, Hanson & Clark over this course and distance, made hard enough work of landing the odds, but is better than the bare result suggests. Ahern said he was in front much sooner than he would have liked, as he would have preferred to get a lead until the two pole, and he also felt the ground was softer than ideal. He rates as very useful prospect for next year, when he should stay at least 1m2f. (op 11-10)

Lasso The Moon ◆, a 180,000gns son of Sadler's Wells and half-brother to Fillies' Mile and Falmouth Stakes winner Simply Perfect, made a pleasing debut in second. He was always just being held by the above-average winner, but was well clear of the remainder and rates as a very decent prospect. His connections felt he needed the run and were of the opinion the result might be different if they were to meet the winner again. (op 16-1)

Border Patrol ◆, a half-brother to six winners, including very useful sprinter Eisteddfod, fared best of those in a double-figure stall and this was a pleasing debut. (op 8-1)

Directorship built on the promise of his debut effort at Sandown with a respectable fourth. He is evidently reasonably well regarded and should continue to go the right way.

Holberg(UAE) dropped away rather tamely late on, but a high draw might not have been a help and he will have more options now he is qualified for a handicap mark. (op 4-1 tchd 11-2 in places)

Zulu Moon, on his toes in the paddock, showed ability and should do better in time. (op 22-1 tchd 25-1)

Great Western(USA) is a close-coupled colt. (op 25-1)

6603 SIR GERALD WHENT MEMORIAL NURSERY 6f 8y

3:15 (3:15) (Class 4) (0-85,85) 2-Y-O **£6,476** (£1,927; £963; £481) **Stalls** High

Form RPR

6214 **1** **Kingswinford (IRE)**[3] 6533 2-8-9 73 RobertWinston 5 79
(P D Evans) *a.p: rdn to ld over 1f out: edgd wl ins fnl f: styd on gamely* **8/1**

1456 **2** *hd* **Timeteam (IRE)**[7] 6426 2-8-11 75 JamieSpencer 7 80
(S Kirk) *stdd s: hld up: hdwy over 1f out: rdn and ev ch ins fnl f: r.o* **9/2**[2]

010 **3** *2 ¼* **Top Town Girl**[19] 6102 2-9-7 85 GeorgeBaker 11 84
(R M Beckett) *hld up: hdwy over 1f out: sn rdn: eased whn hld nr fin* **14/1**

504 **4** *2 ¼* **Lost In Paris (IRE)**[17] 6158 2-8-3 67 HayleyTurner 4 59
(T D Easterby) *chsd ldrs: outpcd over 3f out: styd on fnl f* **25/1**

2332 **5** *hd* **Forward Feline (IRE)**[5] 6488 2-8-10 74 DarryllHolland 9 65
(B Palling) *lw: prom: rdn 1/2-way: styng on same pce whn hung lft ins fnl f* **17/2**

0010 **6** *1 ¼* **Bermondsey Bob (IRE)**[23] 6002 2-8-9 76 TolleyDean(3) 3 64
(J L Spearing) *led: rdn over 2f out: hdd over 1f out: no ex fnl f* **50/1**

1233 **7** *1 ¾* **Golden Destiny (IRE)**[13] 6240 2-9-2 80 RyanMoore 12 62
(P J Makin) *hld up: rdn whn hmpd 2f out: nt clr run ins fnl f: n.d* **7/2**[1]

01 **8** *1* **Dustry (IRE)**[24] 5959 2-9-1 79 RichardHughes 2 58
(R Hannon) *lw: chsd ldrs: rdn over 2f out: wknd over 1f out* **9/1**

6063 **9** *3* **Skid Solo (IRE)**[19] 6118 2-9-5 83 AlanMunro 6 53
(P W Chapple-Hyam) *lw: chsd ldrs: rdn over 2f out: wknd over 1f out* **5/1**[3]

1 **10** *1 ½* **Regal Lyric (IRE)**[15] 6213 2-9-4 82 TonyCulhane 8 48
(T P Tate) *lw: s.i.s: hld up: rdn over 3f out: n.d* **16/1**

0004 **11** *2 ½* **Sweet Applause (IRE)**[34] 5680 2-8-11 75 DaneO'Neill 14 33
(A P Jarvis) *lw: hld up: hdwy 1/2-way: sn rdn: wknd 2f out* **33/1**

6213 **12** *nse* **Jubilee Juggins (IRE)**[22] 6023 2-8-6 73 LukeMorris(3) 13 31+
(N P Littmoden) *hld up: hdwy 1/2-way: rdn and wknd 2f out* **12/1**

303 **13** *6* **Imperial Skylight**[2] 6547 2-7-13 63 CatherineGannon 15 —
(M R Channon) *racd alone on stands' side: hld up: hdwy 1/2-way: rdn and wknd over 2f out* **33/1**

1m 16.97s (3.97) **Going Correction** +0.625s/f (Yiel) **13** Ran SP% **120.6**

Speed ratings (Par 97): **98,97,94,91,91 89,87,86,82,80 76,76,68**

toteswinger: 1&2 £9.80, 1&3 £23.00, 2&3 £23.80. CSF £42.98 CT £509.33 TOTE £10.50: £3.40, £2.40, £5.20; EX 58.70.

Owner Nick Shutts **Bred** J Costello **Trained** Pandy, Monmouths

FOCUS

A competitive nursery and the pace looked solid. The field came down the centre of the track, except for Imperial Skylight who did a solo down the stands' rail.

NOTEBOOK

Kingswinford(IRE), 5lb higher than when winning a course-and-distance nursery in August, probably needed his return from a short break at Warwick three days earlier. Close to the pace early, once he had taken over in front it did look as though he was going to be nailed by the runner-up, but he responded very well to pressure to hold him off. This was his 14th outing which doesn't suggest he has much in the way of scope, but he is well suited to these conditions. He is likely to be kept to similar events and may find another opportunity before the season is out. (op 7-1)

Timeteam(IRE) was given a waiting ride before smoothly travelling into contention and he looked the most likely winner when produced with his effort towards the far side, but the winner kept pulling out a bit more. He remains in good form, but he is already due to go up 3lb after his good sixth in a valuable sales race at Newmarket last week, so he will still need to find a bit more improvement if he is to get his head in front again. (op 11-2 tchd 6-1 and 13-2 in places)

Top Town Girl, out of her depth in Group 3 company last time, had previous won well in testing conditions at Sandown. She stayed on well over the last quarter-mile and looked as though she might poke her nose between the front pair inside the last furlong, but she had little left after that. She is less exposed than the two that beat her and other opportunities can be found. (op 12-1)
Lost In Paris(IRE), making his nursery debut after showing his first sign of ability in a Hamilton maiden last time, came off the bridle at halfway but was staying on nicely in the latter stages. With further progress likely he should be able to make his mark, possibly over further. (op 28-1 tchd 33-1)
Forward Feline(IRE) was another to stay on late after getting outpaced. Placed in six of her eight previous starts and making her nursery debut, she is yet to win but was another to shape as though another furlong might suit. (op 10-1)
Bermondsey Bob(IRE), well beaten off a 2lb higher mark on his nursery debut last time, showed up for a long way and this effort suggests that his 150-1 victory in a Salisbury maiden two outings ago may not have been that much of a fluke. However, he did not look great in his coat.
Golden Destiny(IRE), a fine third in the Watership Down Sales Race at Ascot last time, found herself off an 8lb higher mark than when beaten in a nursery before that. She was already making hard work of it when running into trouble passing the 2f pole and there was no way back from there. It does appear that she is badly handicapped now. (op 4-1 tchd 9-2 in places)
Skid Solo(IRE), raised 4lb for finishing third in a hot nursery here last month, showed to the fore early but came off the bridle entering the last quarter-mile and folded rather tamely. Official explanation: jockey said colt ran too free (op 11-2 tchd 9-2)

6604 HARINO.COM - VIRTUAL RACING, REAL EXCITEMENT MAIDEN STKS (DIV II) 1m (S)

3:50 (3:50) (Class 4) 2-Y-O **£5,504** (£1,637; £818; £408) **Stalls** High

Form RPR

1 **Skanky Biscuit** 2-9-3 0 RichardHughes 6 82+
(B J Meehan) *w'like: scope: athletic: lw: in tch: drvn and qcknd to chse ldr 1f out: upsides ins fnl f: led fnl 50yds: kpt on strly* **5/1[3]**

2 *hd* **Bothy** 2-9-3 0 GeorgeBaker 1 82+
(R M Beckett) *leggy: attractive: bit bkwd: in rr: stl last over 2f out: sn swtchd rt to stands' side and rapid hdwy over 1f out to take slt ld fnl 110yds: hdd fnl 50yds but kpt on* **25/1**

4 **3** *2 1/2* **Tactic**[19] 6117 2-9-3 0 RHills 18 76
(J L Dunlop) *lw: trckd ldrs: led 2f out: sn rdn: hdd fnl 110yds: wknd cl home* **7/2[2]**

4 *2 3/4* **Mehendi (IRE)** 2-9-3 0 MartinDwyer 4 70+
(B J Meehan) *w'like: athletic: lw: in rr: pushed along 3f out: hdwy fr 2f out: kpt on fnl f but nvr gng pce to rch ldrs* **50/1**

5 *nk* **Final Victory** 2-9-3 0 WilliamBuick 5 69+
(A M Balding) *lengthy: unf: bit bkwd: in tch: pushed along 3f out: kpt on fr over 1f out but nvr gng pce to be competitive* **50/1**

6 **6** *3/4* **Whisky Galore**[22] 6026 2-9-3 0 AdamKirby 7 68
(C G Cox) *pressed ldrs: rdn over 2f out: wknd fnl f* **11/1**

7 *1/2* **Roman Republic (FR)** 2-9-3 0 RoystonFfrench 12 67
(M Johnston) *w'like: unf: bit bkwd: chsd ldrs: rdn to chal ins fnl 2f: wknd appr fnl f* **11/8[1]**

8 *hd* **Eastern Warrior** 2-9-3 0 EddieAhern 11 66+
(J W Hills) *str: bit bkwd: towards rr but in tch: hdwy fr 3f out: styd on same pce fr over 1f out* **66/1**

9 *nk* **Brunston** 2-9-3 0 RichardKingscote 2 66+
(R Charlton) *w'like: tall: bit bkwd: in rr tl styd on fr over 2f out: kpt on fnl f but nvr in contention* **40/1**

10 *3* **Going For Gold** 2-8-12 0 SteveDrowne 14 54
(R Charlton) *tall: in rr: sme prog whn bmpd appr fnl 2f: mod prog again ins fnl f* **25/1**

0 **11** *1 1/4* **Lava Steps (USA)**[15] 6199 2-9-3 0 ShaneKelly 10 56
(P F I Cole) *led tl hdd 2f out: sn wknd* **40/1**

12 *1* **Rowan Tiger** 2-9-3 0 PatCosgrave 8 54
(J R Boyle) *chsd ldrs: rdn 3f out: wknd ins fnl 2f* **66/1**

13 *3* **Decorum (USA)** 2-9-3 0 JimmyFortune 3 47
(J H M Gosden) *w'like: attractive: bit bkwd: in tch: pushed along 3f out: sn wknd* **6/1**

14 *9* **Cousin Charlie** 2-9-3 0 LPKeniry 9 28
(S Kirk) *unf: s.i.s: sn rcvrd to chse ldrs: wknd over 2f out* **66/1**

15 *4* **Hope Junior (USA)** 2-9-3 0 HayleyTurner 17 19
(B J Meehan) *str: bit bkwd: s.i.s: a in rr* **25/1**

1m 45.98s (6.28) **Going Correction** +0.625s/f (Yiel) **15** Ran SP% **128.4**
Speed ratings (Par 97): **93,92,90,87,87 86,86,85,85,82 81,80,77,68,64**
toteswinger: 1&2 £34.00, 1&3 £5.00, 2&3 £18.30. CSF £131.96 TOTE £7.50: £2.70, £5.90, £2.00; EX 248.70.
Owner Iraj Parvizi **Bred** Mr & Mrs G Middlebrook **Trained** Manton, Wilts
■ Stewards' Enquiry : George Baker one-day ban: careless riding (Oct 23)

FOCUS
A good maiden, but they went steady for much of the way and the winning time was 1.14 seconds slower than the first division. They raced up the middle early, but the principals ended up towards the stands' rail.

NOTEBOOK
Skanky Biscuit, a half-brother to eight-time winner Blushing Name, and five-timer winner Sweet Brush, out of a Group 3-winning juvenile, looks well bought at 30,000gns judged on this likeable debut effort. He had to be withdrawn on his intended debut here last month after refusing to enter the stalls, but went in this time and was fine in the race itself. Although he had to be niggled along inside the final three furlongs, he gradually got the idea and picked up well, before battling on gamely to record a narrow success. He is entered in the Racing Post Trophy. (op 7-2)
Bothy, a son of Pivotal, half-brother to Villa Sonata and Shela House, both 1m2f winners, out of a multiple middle-distance scorer, was just held. He was drawn in stall one, but after racing in the rear early he ended up switching right the way across to the stands' rail and picked up in fine style, ultimately finding only one too good. He rates as a useful prospect. (op 33-1)
Tactic, who shaped as though he would be suited by a step up in trip when fourth on his debut over 7f here, had every chance and his proximity helps give the form a very solid look, despite the slow winning time. (op 4-1 tchd 9-2)
Mehendi(IRE), an already gelded son of Indian Danehill, out of a 1m4f winner, made a pleasing introduction. He should come on for this and ought to stay further next year.
Final Victory, by Generous, showed ability and can be expected to get further in time.
Whisky Galore was stuck towards the far side of the main group, but he showed ability and should make a fair handicapper a little bit further down the line. (op 16-1 tchd 10-1)
Roman Republic(FR), a 200,000gns son of Cape Cross and half-brother to 1m winner Hurricane Mist, out of a high-class dual 1m1f scorer, has entries in the Dewhurst and Racing Post Trophy and was all the rage beforehand, but he produced a rather tame effort. He found disappointingly little when the pace increased, but is presumably thought capable of better. (op 6-4 tchd 15-8)
Eastern Warrior, a gelded son of Barathea, showed ability on debut. He has plenty of size and could be alright in time.
Brunston, a son of High Chaparral, kept on quite nicely in the closing stages and should do better over further next year. (op 50-1)
Going For Gold, a half-sister to dual 7f winner Firestreak, was slightly on her toes beforehand.
Decorum(USA), a son of Dynaformer, is another with loads of size so, although he didn't show much this time, he might be more of a longer-term prospect. (op 8-1 tchd 9-1)

6605 VODAFONE FILLIES' H'CAP 1m 2f 6y

4:25 (4:25) (Class 4) (0-85,85) 3-Y-O+ **£4,857** (£1,445; £722; £360) **Stalls** Low

Form RPR

3154 **1** **Belotto (IRE)**[16] 6195 3-8-9 **76** RichardKingscote 8 87
(R Charlton) *hld up: hdwy over 4f out: rdn and edgd lft over 1f out: sn chsng ldr: styd on to ld nr fin* **12/1**

2211 **2** *nk* **Rhadegunda**[22] 6027 3-8-13 **80** JimmyFortune 6 90
(J H M Gosden) *lw: led 2f: chsd ldrs: swtchd rt 3f out: led wl over 1f out: sn rdn and edgd lft: hdd nr fin* **11/4[1]**

1 **3** *2 1/4* **Summer's Lease**[55] 5076 3-8-13 **80** HayleyTurner 12 86
(M L W Bell) *w'like: str: lw: swtchd lft sn after s: hld up: hdwy over 1f out: nt rch ldrs* **9/2[2]**

0012 **4** *nk* **Lady Brora**[13] 6256 3-8-7 **74** FrancisNorton 13 79
(A M Balding) *lw: a.p: chsd ldr 1/2-way: rdn and ev ch 2f out: no ex ins fnl f* **12/1**

4224 **5** *1/2* **Ainia**[22] 6027 3-8-8 **75** RichardMullen 2 79
(D M Simcock) *hld up: hdwy over 2f out: sn rdn: styd on* **17/2**

0025 **6** *2 3/4* **Ballora (FR)**[6] 6450 3-8-8 **75** RichardHughes 1 74
(S Kirk) *trckd ldrs: racd keenly: rdn over 1f out: wknd fnl f* **25/1**

1035 **7** *1/2* **Lee Miller (IRE)**[22] 6027 3-8-12 **79** DaneO'Neill 4 77
(L M Cumani) *chsd ldrs: rdn and hung lft over 2f out: styd on same pce appr fnl f* **8/1[3]**

450 **8** *1* **Folly Lodge**[84] 4110 4-9-7 **83** SteveDrowne 14 79
(G Wragg) *s.i.s: hld up: rdn over 2f out: hung lft over 1f out: nt trble ldrs* **28/1**

2210 **9** *1/2* **Trumpet Lily**[22] 6027 3-9-1 **82** JimCrowley 10 77
(J G Portman) *hld up: hdwy over 2f out: wknd over 1f out* **20/1**

6210 **10** *3 1/2* **Censored**[27] 5865 3-8-11 **78** (v[1]) RyanMoore 9 66
(Sir Michael Stoute) *chsd ldr: led 8f out: rdn and hdd wl over 1f out: wknd fnl f* **12/1**

0302 **11** *1/2* **Encircled**[12] 6293 4-9-1 **77** RobertHavlin 5 64
(D Haydn Jones) *hld up: effrt over 2f out: sn wknd* **16/1**

2600 **12** *10* **Uig**[20] 6090 7-8-7 **69** oh2 AlanMunro 3 36
(H S Howe) *hld up in tch: rdn and wknd over 3f out* **80/1**

02 **13** *6* **Baylini**[10] 6346 4-9-2 **78** JamesDoyle 11 33
(Ms J S Doyle) *hld up: hdwy 1/2-way: rdn and wknd over 1f out: eased* **10/1**

0000 **14** *2 3/4* **Try Me (UAE)**[12] 6266 3-9-4 **85** TedDurcan 7 34
(C E Brittain) *chsd ldrs: rdn over 3f out: wknd over 2f out* **33/1**

2m 13.86s (5.06) **Going Correction** +0.625s/f (Yiel)
WFA 3 from 4yo+ 5lb **14** Ran SP% **120.8**
Speed ratings (Par 102): **104,103,101,101,101 99,98,97,97,94 94,86,81,79**
toteswinger: 1&2 £12.70, 1&3 £17.50, 2&3 £2.60. CSF £42.74 CT £179.51 TOTE £17.20: £4.60, £1.40, £2.00; EX 65.10.
Owner Lady Rothschild **Bred** The Rt Hon Lord Rothschild **Trained** Beckhampton, Wilts

FOCUS
A fair fillies' handicap, but they went no pace early, so the form may not be totally reliable. The winner is rated up 4lb, the second up 3lb.
Baylini Official explanation: jockey said filly had no more to give

6606 VODAFONE H'CAP 2m

4:55 (4:55) (Class 5) (0-75,75) 3-Y-O+ **£2,590** (£770; £385; £192) **Stalls** High

Form RPR

1343 **1** **Kokkokila**[36] 5613 4-9-0 **61** RichardHughes 1 72
(Lady Herries) *hld up in tch: hdwy 3f out: drvn to ld appr fnl f: hld on wl* **6/1[2]**

0423 **2** *3/4* **Featherlight**[180] 1337 4-9-3 **64** RobertHavlin 3 74
(Jamie Poulton) *in tch: hdwy over 3f out: led over 2f out: hdd appr fnl f: styd on same pce ins fnl f* **25/1**

6300 **3** *1* **Burnt Oak (UAE)**[21] 6054 6-9-4 **65** TedDurcan 10 74
(C W Fairhurst) *in rr: hdwy fr 4f out: styd on to chse ldrs fr 2f out: kpt on fnl f but nvr quite gng pce to chal* **10/1**

2645 **4** *1 3/4* **Mae Cigan (FR)**[12] 6279 5-9-4 **65** SteveDrowne 12 72
(M Blanshard) *in rr tl hdwy 3f out: styd on fr over 1f out but nvr gng pce to rch ldrs* **9/1**

2-50 **5** *2 1/4* **Tritonville Lodge (IRE)**[45] 3104 6-10-0 **75** AlanMunro 2 79
(Miss E C Lavelle) *chsd ldrs: rdn 3f out: wknd appr fnl f* **33/1**

0465 **6** *5* **Squirtle (IRE)**[26] 5887 5-9-1 **65** LukeMorris[(3)] 8 63
(W M Brisbourne) *chsd ldrs: rdn 3f out: wknd fr 2f out* **25/1**

6000 **7** *1* **Calculating (IRE)**[13] 6243 4-9-8 **69** HayleyTurner 5 66
(M D I Usher) *in rr: hdwy and n.m.r 3f out: sn rdn: nvr gng pce to be competitive* **16/1**

-360 **8** *1 3/4* **Ned Ludd (IRE)**[117] 3044 5-10-0 **75** PatCosgrave 14 70
(J G Portman) *chsd ldrs: led over 3f out: hdd over 2f out: sn wknd* **12/1**

/0-0 **9** *1/2* **Hills Of Aran**[15] 6203 6-8-7 **59** DavidProbert[(5)] 16 53
(W K Goldsworthy) *chsd ldrs: rdn 3f out: sn lost position and n.d after* **9/1**

31/2 **10** *1* **Kanpai (IRE)**[21] 6054 6-8-13 **60** RobertWinston 6 53
(J G M O'Shea) *in rr: sme prog over 3f out: sn rdn and nvr in contention after* **11/2[1]**

0/0 **11** *3 1/4* **Corso Palladio (IRE)**[23] 5993 6-9-6 **67** (t) J-PGuillambert 15 56
(B P J Baugh) *in tch: rdn and effrt over 3f out: nvr in contention and sn bhd* **66/1**

0202 **12** *1 1/2* **Dr Sharp (IRE)**[20] 6071 8-9-12 **73** MickyFenton 9 60
(T P Tate) *led: hdd over 3f out: sn wknd* **7/1[3]**

0052 **13** *1/2* **Rock 'N' Roller (FR)**[25] 5934 4-9-13 **74** RichardMullen 4 61
(W R Muir) *in rr: sme hdwy 3f out: sn wknd* **6/1[2]**

6-34 **14** *5* **Gallileo Figaro (USA)**[194] 1080 5-9-12 **73** JerryO'Dwyer 7 54
(N B King) *bit bkwd: in tch: rdn and effrt 3f out: sn wknd* **25/1**

0 **15** *30* **Axinit (GER)**[39] 4935 8-8-13 **60** (tp) EdwardCreighton 11 5
(E J Creighton) *chsd ldr to 5f out: sn rdn and wknd* **66/1**

0-63 **16** *55* **Cash On (IRE)**[13] 6252 6-9-8 **69** (p) DarryllHolland 13 —
(Karen George) *sn t.o* **40/1**

3m 43.04s (6.14) **Going Correction** +0.625s/f (Yiel) **16** Ran SP% **119.0**
Speed ratings (Par 103): **109,108,108,107,106 103,103,102,102,101 99,99,98,96,81 53**
toteswinger: 1&2 £19.90, 1&3 £14.10, 2&3 £64.40. CSF £154.14 CT £1477.43 TOTE £7.80: £1.90, £5.10, £3.00, £2.70; EX 205.60.
Owner Lady Mary Mumford J Woodcock & J Cowdrey **Bred** Lady Mary & Group Captain A Mumford **Trained** Patching, W Sussex

FOCUS
A modest staying handicap run at a strong pace. The main action took place up the middle of the track in the straight. The form is sound, with the winner rated up 4lb.
Rock 'N' Roller(FR) Official explanation: jockey said gelding was never travelling

Cash On(IRE) Official explanation: jockey said gelding was reluctant to race

6607 EVENTS BAR MANAGEMENT APPRENTICE H'CAP 1m 3f 5y
5:30 (5:30) (Class 5) (0-75,75) 3-Y-O+ **£2,590** (£770; £385; £192) **Stalls** Low

Form RPR

5435 **1** **Mistress Eva**[31] 5758 3-8-7 **67** .... WilliamCarson(5) 1 76+
(P Winkworth) *prom: racd keenly: lost pl over 9f out: hdwy over 3f out: rdn and swtchd rt over 1f out: styd on u.p to ld post* **14/1**

5563 **2** *nse* **It's A Date**[22] 6012 3-9-1 **75** .... ByronMoorcroft(5) 5 82
(A King) *lw: hld up in tch: nt clr run and lost pl over 4f out: hdwy 3f out: rdn over 1f out: edgd lft and styd on: jst denied* **4/1**[1]

0121 **3** *hd* **Nawamees (IRE)**[24] 5961 10-9-7 **73** .... RichardEvans(3) 12 80
(P D Evans) *chsd ldrs: led 9f out: hdd over 2f out: rdn to ld over 1f out: hdd post* **17/2**[3]

-110 **4** *1 1/4* **Force Group (IRE)**[20] 6079 4-9-5 **73** .... AshleyMorgan(5) 17 78+
(M H Tompkins) *hld up in tch: outpcd 3f out: rallied over 1f out: styd on* **4/1**[1]

1002 **5** *1 3/4* **Serious Choice (IRE)**[8] 6395 3-8-13 **68** .... JackMitchell 10 70
(J R Boyle) *lw: a.p: rdn over 2f out: styd on same pce fnl f* **9/1**

1220 **6** *1* **Outlandish**[26] 5900 5-9-7 **73** .... DavidProbert(3) 11 73
(Andrew Turnell) *trckd ldrs: led over 2f out: rdn: edgd lft and hdd over 1f out: hung lft and no ex ins fnl f* **10/1**

2541 **7** *1* **Mr Napoleon (IRE)**[38] 5576 6-9-3 **71** .... JemmaMarshall(5) 18 69
(G L Moore) *lw: hld up: hung lft and styd on u.p fr over 1f out: nt trble ldrs* **16/1**

200 **8** *1 1/4* **Night Orbit**[23] 6007 4-9-3 **66** ....(v[1]) RussellKennemore 9 62
(Miss J Feilden) *chsd ldrs: rdn over 2f out: wknd over 1f out* **25/1**

-520 **9** *5* **Awatuki (IRE)**[106] 3375 5-9-9 **72** .... DNolan 8 60
(J R Boyle) *hld up: hdwy over 3f out: wkng whn hung lft over 1f out* **40/1**

5-53 **10** *1 1/4* **Turban Heights (IRE)**[12] 6293 4-9-11 **74** .... WilliamBuick 7 59
(E J O'Neill) *sn led: hdd 9f out: chsd ldr tl rdn and wknd over 1f out* **8/1**[2]

3000 **11** *1 1/2* **Double Spectre (IRE)**[13] 6243 6-9-2 **68** ..... Louis-PhilippeBeuzelin(3) 16 51
(Jean-Rene Auvray) *hld up: hdwy over 3f out: sn rdn: wknd 2f out* **22/1**

2-00 **12** *1* **Can Can Star**[21] 6050 5-9-4 **67** .... LukeMorris 6 48
(A W Carroll) *s.i.s: hld up: rdn and wknd over 2f out* **33/1**

4120 **13** *1/2* **Captain Mainwaring**[35] 5651 3-8-9 **64** .... TolleyDean 4 44
(N P Littmoden) *hld up: plld hrd: rdn over 3f out: wknd over 2f out* **20/1**

0024 **14** *2 1/2* **Optimus (USA)**[13] 6243 6-9-1 **69** .... KylieManser(5) 15 45
(B G Powell) *s.i.s: hld up: rdn and wknd over 2f out* **14/1**

0000 **15** *3/4* **Tilapia (IRE)**[15] 6210 4-9-4 **72** .... AmyBaker(5) 13 47
(Miss Gay Kelleway) *s.i.s: hld up: rdn over 3f out: a bhd* **50/1**

2216 **16** *7* **Olimpo (FR)**[45] 5369 7-9-9 **72** .... JamesMillman 2 35
(B R Millman) *prom: rdn over 3f out: sn wknd* **14/1**

2m 30.57s (9.37) **Going Correction** +0.625s/f (Yiel)
WFA 3 from 4yo+ 6lb **16** Ran **SP% 126.9**
Speed ratings (Par 103): **90,89,89,88,87 86,86,85,81,80 79,78,78,76,76 71**
toteswinger: 1&2 £18.90, 1&3 £25.40, 2&3 £10.30. CSF £66.85 CT £531.95 TOTE £18.00: £3.40, £1.40, £2.00, £2.00; EX 98.90 Place 6 £26.85, Place 5 £18.48.
Owner Mrs F A Veasey **Bred** Mrs F A Veasey **Trained** Chiddingfold, Surrey
■ Stewards' Enquiry : Richard Evans four-day ban: used whip with excessive frequency (Oct 23-24, 27-28)

FOCUS
A modest apprentice handicap, but still very competitive. They didn't go much of a pace, however, and it developed into a bit of a sprint. The form is a bit muddling, rated through the second and third.
Outlandish Official explanation: jockey said gelding was unsuited byu the good to soft, soft in places going
Olimpo(FR) Official explanation: jockey said gelding had no more to give
T/Jkpt: £54,352.70 to a £1 stake. Pool: £114,829.79. 1.50 winning tickets. T/Plt: £52.70 to a £1 stake. Pool: £62,118.36. 860.04 winning tickets. T/Qpdt: £27.40 to a £1 stake. Pool: £3,414.44. 92.00 winning tickets. ST

6608 - 6611a (Foreign Racing) - See Raceform Interactive

5925 BORDEAUX LE BOUSCAT (R-H)
Thursday, October 9

OFFICIAL GOING: Soft

6612a PRIX ANDRE BABOIN (GRAND PRIX DES PROVINCES) (GROUP 3) 1m 1f 110y
2:20 (2:27) 3-Y-O+ **£29,412** (£11,765; £8,824; £5,882; £2,941)

RPR

1 **Chopastair (FR)**[17] 7-9-1 .... J-BEyquem 8 111
(T Lemer, France) *5th early: cl 3rd st: r.o to chal 1 1/2f out: pushed along to ld appr fnl f: qcknd clr fnl stages: easily* **36/10**[2]

2 *3* **Anabaa's Creation (IRE)**[28] 5851 4-8-8 .... CSoumillon 6 98
(A De Royer-Dupre, France) *racd in cl 2nd: led st: rdn and r.o 1 1/2f out: hdd appr fnl f: jst hld 2nd cl home* **5/4**[1]

3 *hd* **Indian Daffodil (IRE)**[82] 4212 3-9-1 .... IMendizabal 5 109
(J-C Rouget, France) *hld up: disputing 5th st: drvn to chse ldrs 1 1/2f out: styd on fnl f: jst missed 3rd* **4/1**[3]

4 *snk* **Rento (FR)**[26] 5926 5-8-11 .... F-XBertras 1 100
(W Walton, France) *mid-div: disputing 5th st: rdn 1 1/2f out: kpt on at one pce* **17/2**

5 *4* **Blue Ridge View (FR)** 4-8-8 .... EDelbarba 2 89
(C Delcher Sanchez, Spain) *mid-div: 7th st: nvr in chalng position* **54/1**

6 *hd* **Elasos (FR)**[54] 5114 6-8-11 .... DBonilla 7 92
(D Sepulchre, France) *hld up: last st: drvn 1 1/2f out: no imp* **12/1**

7 *1 1/2* **Corconte (FR)**[28] 3-8-8 .... PSogorb 4 91
(R Avial Lopez, Spain) *in tch: 4th st: drvn over 1 1/2f out: unable qck* **24/1**

8 *2 1/2* **Claire Et Bleu (FR)**[133] 2553 4-8-11 .... AlexisBadel 3 84
(Mme M Bollack-Badel, France) *led to st: u.p over 1 1/2f out: sn rdn and wknd* **15/1**

2m 2.94s (122.94)
WFA 3 from 4yo+ 4lb **8** Ran **SP% 116.5**
PARI-MUTUEL (Including 1 Euro stake): WIN 4.60; PL 1.30, 1.10, 1.30; DF 4.60.
Owner Mlle G Ivoula & P Blazy **Bred** Alain Chopard & Mme Maryse Delteil **Trained** France

NOTEBOOK
Chopastair(FR) put up an impressive display and never looked like being beaten. Dropped in behind the leaders before moving smoothly into the lead a furlong and a half out, he then drew clear and won with plenty in hand. He was carrying joint top-weight and will now try and land back-to-back wins in the Group 3 Prix Perth at Saint-Cloud.
Anabaa's Creation(IRE), who got a little warm in the preliminaries, was settled in second place early on. Still going well round the final turn, she went to the head of affairs early in the straight but could do nothing when the favourite swept past her. She battled on well throughout the final furlong.
Indian Daffodil(IRE) put up a decent performance considering that he is a three-year-old and was carrying joint top-weight. Dropped out in the early stages, he still had plenty to do in the straight, and although he ran on well he could not quicken inside the final furlong.
Rento(FR), given a waiting race, did not really engage top gear until halfway up the straight. He was putting in his best work at the finish.

6523 KEENELAND (L-H)
Wednesday, October 8

OFFICIAL GOING: Fast

6613a MAIDEN (FILLIES) (POLYTRACK) 1m 110y
8:10 (8:12) 2-Y-O **£15,691** (£5,025; £2,513; £1,256; £641)

RPR

1 **Bluegrass Princess (USA)** 2-8-6 .... KDesormeaux 3 —
(Kiaran McLaughlin, U.S.A) **56/10**[2]

2 *4* **True Bliss (USA)** 2-8-6 .... JRLeparoux 9 —
(John C Kimmel, U.S.A) **8/1**

3 *1* **Nala's Pride (USA)** 2-8-6 .... RRDouglas 8 —
(Hugh Robertson, U.S.A) **7/1**[3]

4 *1* **The Best Day Ever (USA)** 2-8-6 .... CHBorel 4 —
(Kenneth McPeek, U.S.A) **73/10**

5 *hd* **Pearl Of Valor (USA)**[108] 2-8-6 .... HJTheriotII 1 —
(Dallas Stewart, U.S.A) **97/10**

6 *3* **Verdant (USA)** 2-8-6 .... JLCastanon 5 —
(George R Arnold II, U.S.A) **10/1**

7 *3* **Ashapoo (USA)** 2-8-6 .... BHernandezJr 10 —
(Anthony Mitchell, U.S.A) **342/10**

8 *1 1/2* **Lustful (USA)** 2-8-6 .... JMJohnson 7 —
(Gary G Hartlage, U.S.A) **118/10**

9 *1/2* **Graphite Halo (USA)** 2-8-1 .... DRodriguez(5) 6 —
(Charles Simon, U.S.A) **62/1**

10 *3/4* **Acting Lady (USA)**[49] 5184 2-8-6 .... MMena 2 —
(J R Best) *always towards rear SP 84-10* **84/10**

11 *4 3/4* **State Treasure (USA)**[52] 2-8-6 .... RAlbarado 11 —
(Neil J Howard, U.S.A) **28/10**[1]

12 *16 1/2* **With Touch (USA)** 2-8-6 .... JEnriquez 12 —
(Luis E Seglin, U.S.A) **84/1**

1m 44.29s (104.29) **12** Ran **SP% 119.6**
PARI-MUTUEL (Including $2 stake): WIN 13.20; PL (1-2) 6.80, 9.00; SHOW (1-2-3) 5.60, 5.80, 7.00; SF 128.00.
Owner Dell Ridge Farm **Bred** Highclere **Trained** USA

NOTEBOOK
Acting Lady(USA), sixth of 14 in a Folkestone maiden on her debut, never got competitive on her first start in the US.

6405 AYR (L-H)
Friday, October 10

6614 Meeting Abandoned - waterlogged

6432 LINGFIELD (L-H)
Friday, October 10

OFFICIAL GOING: Standard
Wind: Moderate to strong, behind Weather: Fine

6620 GSE GROUP MAIDEN STKS (DIV I) 7f (P)
1:45 (1:46) (Class 4) 2-Y-O **£3,561** (£1,059; £529; £264) **Stalls** Low

Form RPR

1 **Bab Al Salam (USA)** 2-9-3 0 .... LDettori 5 78+
(Saeed Bin Suroor) *trckd ldng pair: wnt 2nd over 2f out: rdn to ld over 1f out: grad asserted fnl f* **4/1**[2]

0 **2** *1 1/4* **Ucantmissme**[26] 5939 2-9-3 0 .... WilliamBuick 10 75
(D W P Arbuthnot) *mde most: rdn and hdd over 1f out: kpt on fnl f to hold on for 2nd* **20/1**

6 **3** *nk* **Charlotte Point (USA)**[9] 6392 2-8-12 0 .... NCallan 7 69
(P F I Cole) *awkward s: sn rchd midfield: rdn 2f out: prog over 1f out: styd on wl to snatch 3rd last strides* **10/1**

6 **4** *hd* **Brenthurst (USA)**[55] 5099 2-9-3 0 .... RyanMoore 3 74
(J Noseda) *prom: rdn to chse ldng pair over 1f out: no real imp: lost 3rd last strides* **9/4**[1]

6 **5** *1 1/2* **Quick Single (USA)**[21] 6080 2-9-3 0 .... TQuinn 1 70
(D R C Elsworth) *cl up: rdn 2f out: stuck on wl enough but nvr able to chal* **5/1**

0 **6** *nk* **Ariadnes Filly (IRE)**[36] 5640 2-8-12 0 .... JimCrowley 8 64
(Mrs A J Perrett) *hld up in midfield: effrt on outer over 2f out: chsd ldrs over 1f out: one pce* **11/1**

7 *nk* **Tafaool (IRE)** 2-8-12 0 .... RHills 2 65+
(M P Tregoning) *s.s: hld up in abt 8th: pushed along 2f out: no prog tl styd on steadily fnl f: nrst fin* **9/2**[3]

0 **8** *1 1/4* **Manero**[153] 1987 2-9-3 0 .... ShaneKelly 9 66+
(J A Osborne) *chsd ldr to over 2f out: styd chsng tl wknd fnl f* **33/1**

0 **9** *3* **Sky Gate (USA)**[20] 6122 2-9-3 0 .... MartinDwyer 12 58
(B J Meehan) *towards rr: rousted along and effrt on outer 1/2-way: no prog over 2f out* **66/1**

0 **10** *3/4* **Golden Flight (IRE)**[16] 6197 2-9-3 0 .... EddieAhern 4 56+
(J W Hills) *dwlt: wl in rr: rdn and no prog over 2f out: n.d after* **25/1**

00 **11** *nk* **Rainbow Seeker**[24] 6000 2-9-3 0 .... TonyCulhane 11 55+
(W J Haggas) *dwlt: a struggling in last pair: plugged on fnl f* **33/1**

00 **12** *1/2* **Speed Dating**[9] 6383 2-9-3 0 .... DO'Donohoe 6 54+
(Sir Mark Prescott) *dwlt: detached in last and green: nvr a factor: plugged on fnl f* **66/1**

1m 24.7s (-0.10) **Going Correction** -0.10s/f (Stan) **12** Ran **SP% 120.5**
Speed ratings (Par 97): **96,94,94,94,92 91,91,90,86,85 85,84**
toteswinger: 1&2 £27.80, 1&3 £7.20, 2&3 £34.00. CSF £88.22 TOTE £3.40: £2.20, £3.10, £3.00; EX 102.90 TRIFECTA Not won..

Owner Godolphin **Bred** Darley **Trained** Newmarket, Suffolk

FOCUS

A fair maiden and the time was only 0.07sec slower than the second division.

NOTEBOOK

Bab Al Salam(USA), by Seeking The Gold and a half-brother to two winners including on the dirt in the US, was always well positioned close to the lead and looked the winner from the top of the straight. He found plenty when asked and ultimately won in tidy fashion. His connections will look for something better. (op 5-2 tchd 9-2)

Ucantmissme built on the promise he showed when running very green on his debut over 6f at Great Leighs. Ridden much handier this time, he was given every chance and kept on for pressure in the straight, but he was simply beaten by a better one on the day. In the longer term he might prove better over 5f-6f, and he should make a fair handicapper. (op 16-1)

Charlotte Point(USA), too keen for her own good over 1m on debut at Nottingham, was ridden with patience this time. She stayed on well after getting outpaced turning in and did best of those to race away from the lead. There should be an ordinary maiden to be won with her, and she also has the option of switching to fillies' races. (tchd 11-1)

Brenthurst(USA), held on his debut on the July course, was well enough placed if good enough, but he did not see his race out after nearly two months off. He might do better back over shorter. (op 3-1 tchd 10-3 in a place)

Quick Single(USA) did not build on the form he showed on his debut in a reasonable maiden at Newmarket and might be best watched until switched to handicaps. (op 6-1)

Ariadnes Filly(IRE), although ultimately well held, travelled well to a point and looks to have ability. She might have the speed for 6f. (tchd 14-1)

Tafaool(IRE), a daughter of Green Desert, half-sister to a 1m winner, out of a 1m2f scorer, did not have the clearest of runs when trying to make ground from off the pace turning in, but she kept on at one pace late on. She should be a lot sharper next time. (op 7-1)

Speed Dating offered very little, but he should do better over slightly further and it might be unwise to underestimate him now he is qualified for a handicap mark.

6621 GSE GROUP MAIDEN STKS (DIV II) 7f (P)
2:15 (2:16) (Class 4) 2-Y-O £3,561 (£1,059; £529; £264) Stalls Low

Form				RPR
2	1		**Musleh (USA)**[37] 5615 2-9-3 0 LDettori 12 *(Saeed Bin Suroor) racd wd early and t.k.h: led after 1f: mde rest: in command fr over 1f out but had to be drvn out* **8/13**[1]	78+
	2	1	**Pedasus (USA)** 2-9-3 0 TonyCulhane 4 *(T Keddy) towards rr early: prog on inner fr 1/2-way: rdn in 4th over 2f out: styd on wl fnl f to take 2nd last stride* **66/1**	76
023	3	shd	**Ysing Yi**[38] 5590 2-9-3 72 NCallan 2 *(K A Ryan) led 1f: chsd wnr: rdn and no imp fr 2f out: kpt on but lost 2nd last stride* **14/1**	75
3	4	shd	**The Fonz**[70] 4598 2-9-3 0 RyanMoore 5 *(Sir Michael Stoute) chsd ldrs: outpcd fr 3f out: rdn in 5th over 2f out: styd on wl fnl f: jst failed to snatch 3rd* **9/2**[2]	75
	5	2 1/4	**Test Match (IRE)** 2-9-3 0 MartinDwyer 1 *(M P Tregoning) s.s: pushed along and rcvrd to chse ldrs: cl 3rd and rdn over 2f out: stl cl up whn hanging and green over 1f out: wknd* **11/2**[3]	69
6	6	2 3/4	**Ateeb**[16] 6213 2-9-3 0 RHills 10 *(M Johnston) dwlt: in tch in midfield on outer: outpcd fr wl over 2f out: nvr on terms after* **16/1**	63+
0	7	3 3/4	**Eastern Empire**[20] 6117 2-9-3 0 EddieAhern 7 *(J W Hills) settled in midfield: lost grnd on ldrs fr over 2f out: eased w rdr looking down over 1f out* **66/1**	53+
46	8	2 1/2	**Royal Diamond (IRE)**[10] 6359 2-9-3 0 DO'Donohoe 9 *(Sir Mark Prescott) sn struggling in last pair and detached: nvr a factor* **33/1**	47
00	9	7	**Lady Lu**[21] 6089 2-8-12 0 JoeFanning 6 *(P F I Cole) nvr bttr than midfield: wknd over 2f out* **100/1**	24
0	10	34	**Music In The Glen**[10] 6360 2-8-12 0 RobertWinston 3 *(P Leech) s.s: a wl bhd: t.o* **100/1**	—

1m 24.63s (-0.17) **Going Correction** -0.10s/f (Stan) **10** Ran SP% **115.9**

Speed ratings (Par 97): **96,94,94,94,92 88,84,81,73,34**

toteswinger: 1&2 £4.70, 1&3 £1.70, 2&3 £47.70. CSF £77.01 TOTE £1.70: £1.10, £15.30, £3.10; EX 72.20 TRIFECTA Not won..

Owner Godolphin **Bred** Nesco II Limited **Trained** Newmarket, Suffolk

FOCUS

The second division of the juvenile maiden was run at just an average pace and the first four came clear. It was a marginally quicker winning time than the first.

NOTEBOOK

Musleh(USA) was second in a novice over course and distance on his debut 37 days earlier and the form had been advertised by the winner Playfellow finishing third in the Group 2 Champagne Stakes. Quickly away from his outside draw, he was allowed to stride on through the early stages and dictated the pace. He was always doing enough when asked to win the race at the furlong pole, but did not show an immediate turn of foot and did get very much the run of the race. He is well regarded and is likely to step up in grade, but on this evidence his Group 1 entries are somewhat ambitious. However, he does have the scope to make up into a useful sort next year. (op 4-7 tchd 4-6)

Pedasus(USA) ◆, whose unraced dam is a half-sister to Fasliyev, was motoring inside the final furlong and made a very pleasing start to his career. He should learn plenty for the experience and looks to have a good deal of ability.

Ysing Yi had been placed on his last two runs and he had his chance from a good draw. The return to this sounder surface proved more in his favour and with an official mark of 72 he sets the level, but it would be little surprise to see him back over 1m next time. (op 16-1)

The Fonz, third on his debut in a fair maiden over 6f at Newmarket 70 days earlier, got outpaced before staying on again with some purpose and only just lost out on third place. He looks more of a three-year-old in the making and needs one more run for a mark. (op 4-1)

Test Match(IRE) attracted some support on this debut, but paid the price for running freely through the early stages and looked very green. He is entitled to come on for the run and perhaps a drop to 6f would suit in the short term. (op 7-1)

Eastern Empire did not look to be given a hard time from off the pace and is one to keep an eye on. His rider reported that the colt did not face the kickback and coughed post-race. Official explanation: jockey said colt did not face the kickback and returned coughing

6622 MARK BAUSOLA MAIDEN FILLIES' STKS 1m (P)
2:45 (2:46) (Class 4) 2-Y-O £3,885 (£1,156; £577; £288) Stalls High

Form				RPR
	1		**Hazy Dancer** 2-9-0 0 MartinDwyer 11 *(M P Tregoning) pressed ldr in modly run r: rdn to ld over 1f out: 1 l clr fnl f: jst hld on* **11/1**	71+
3	2	shd	**Applause (IRE)**[35] 5674 2-9-0 0 ShaneKelly 10 *(J Noseda) t.k.h early: hld up bhd ldrs: shkn up over 2f out: no prog tl styd on wl fr jst over 1f out: fin strly: jst failed* **6/4**[1]	71+
3	3	nse	**Greenisland (IRE)**[49] 5240 2-9-0 0 RobertHavlin 7 *(H Morrison) hld up bhd ldrs: effrt and cl up 2f out: hanging over 1f out: styd on wl fnl f: jst lost out* **5/2**[2]	71+
	4	1/2	**Special Bond** 2-9-0 0 SamHitchcott 8 *(J A Osborne) s.i.s: hld up in last in modly run contest: prog over 2f out: clsd on ldrs ins fnl f: no ex nr fin* **66/1**	70+
0	5	1 1/4	**Highland Starlight (USA)**[18] 6167 2-9-0 0 PhilipRobinson 5 *(C G Cox) led at mod pce: rdn and hdd over 1f out: swamped for pls wl ins fnl f* **25/1**	67
	6	hd	**Queen Eleanor** 2-9-0 0 JimmyFortune 6 *(J H M Gosden) dwlt: settled in rr: pushed along and no prog 2f out: styd on ins fnl f: nrst fin* **9/2**[3]	67+
00	7	hd	**Highland Burn**[21] 6081 2-9-0 0 TQuinn 1 *(D R C Elsworth) hld up in tch: effrt and cl up 2f out: nt qckn over 1f out: fdd ins fnl f* **66/1**	66
60	8	3/4	**Water Hen (IRE)**[36] 5640 2-9-0 0 WilliamBuick 4 *(R Charlton) settled towards rr: nt qckn over 2f out: shkn up and one pce after: nvr on terms* **25/1**	65
0	9	hd	**Kiyari**[36] 5650 2-8-7 0 AndreaAtzeni(7) 2 *(M Botti) hld up in midfield: effrt on inner over 2f out: chsng ldrs and in tch jst over 1f out: wknd ins fnl f* **20/1**	64
	10	nk	**Precocious Air (IRE)** 2-9-0 0 EddieAhern 12 *(J A Osborne) pressed ldng pair: wd and green bnd 2f out: wknd* **50/1**	63
00	11	3	**Veiled**[8] 6423 2-9-0 0 DO'Donohoe 9 *(Sir Mark Prescott) a in rr: shkn up and no prog over 2f out* **66/1**	57
	12	34	**Carita Mia** 2-9-0 0 RyanMoore 3 *(G L Moore) dwlt: taken wd and rapid prog to join ldrs after 3f: v green and wknd rapidly 3f out: t.o* **10/1**	—

1m 40.87s (2.67) **Going Correction** -0.10s/f (Stan) **12** Ran SP% **123.1**

Speed ratings (Par 94): **82,81,81,81,80 79,79,78,78,78 75,41**

toteswinger: 1&2 £16.80, 1&3 £21.90, 2&3 £1.10. CSF £27.78 TOTE £16.90: £3.10, £1.30, £1.20; EX 40.10 Trifecta £128.70 Pool: £328.86 - 1.89 winning tickets..

Owner Minster Stud & Mrs Hugh Dalgety **Bred** Minster Stud And Mrs H Dalgety **Trained** Lambourn, Berks

FOCUS

They finished in a bit of a bunch after going steady early and this looked like an ordinary fillies' maiden.

NOTEBOOK

Hazy Dancer ◆, a daughter of Oasis Dream out of Oaks third Shadow Dancing, showed a fair amount of ability to make a winning debut. There was not much pace on early, so she was able to get across from stall 11, and she raced in the front rank. Well placed when the race turned into something of a sprint at the top of the straight, she found just enough but was being closed down near the line and would have been passed in another few strides. Everything went her way, but her trainer considers her more of a longer term prospect, which is understandable considering her breeding, and it was encouraging she could win first time up. (op 16-1 tchd 20-1)

Applause(IRE) did not build on the form she showed when third of four in a conditions race at Kempton first time up, and she still looked in need of the experience. Having been keen to post, and keen in the race, she took a while to respond when coming under pressure before just getting going too late. She does not look anything special at this stage, but was still green and can leave this form behind at some stage, maybe next year. (op 15-8 tchd 2-1)

Greenisland(IRE) was well placed and had every chance, but did not improve a great deal on her debut third at Newmarket nearly two months earlier. She is entitled to come on again for this outing and will probably prefer a stronger-run race. (op 11-4 tchd 3-1)

Special Bond, a half-sister to triple middle-distance winner Formidable Guest out of a winning sprinter, stayed on from well off the pace. Having been last early, she was slightly short of room when trying to make ground turning in, but picked up in the straight, despite having to be switched off the rail over a furlong out, before her effort just flattened out a touch late on. She has plenty of ability and might have the speed for 7f.

Highland Starlight(USA) had her chance from the front and improved on the form she showed on her debut over 7f at Kempton.

Queen Eleanor ◆, the first foal of a 7f winner, made an eyecatching debut. Out the back for much of the way, she ran green when coming under pressure but gradually got the idea and finished very nicely out wide. She should improve enough to go very close in similar company next time. (tchd 5-1)

Highland Burn did not convince with her head carriage under pressure, but she is now qualified for a handicap mark. Official explanation: jockey said filly did not handle the bend

Water Hen(IRE) is now eligible for an official rating and should do better. (op 16-1)

Veiled was never competitive but should do a lot better next year when stepped up significantly in trip and sent handicapping. Official explanation: jockey said, regarding the running and riding, his orders were to jump out and get cover, adding that filly was unsuited by the slow early pace, which quickened af 3f marker where filly could not go the pace; trainer's rep added that filly would be suited by another year and stays

Carita Mia Official explanation: jockey said filly hung badly right throughout

6623 PHILIP HALL MEMORIAL H'CAP 5f (P)
3:20 (3:20) (Class 4) (0-80,80) 3-Y-O+ £6,308 (£1,888; £944; £472; £235) Stalls High

Form				RPR
0000	1		**Piscean (USA)**[9] 6402 3-9-2 78 TonyCulhane 5 *(T Keddy) hld up in midfield: prog over 1f out: rdn and r.o to ld last 100yds: readily* **11/2**[3]	87
3006	2	1	**Mambo Spirit (IRE)**[41] 5493 4-9-2 78 JimCrowley 1 *(J G Given) nt wl away but sn in midfield: smooth prog 2f out: trckd ldng pair over 1f out but nowhere to go: got through and r.o to take 2nd nr fin but wnr already home* **15/2**	87+
3422	3	3/4	**Best One**[18] 6174 4-8-11 76 (b) KevinGhunowa(3) 2 *(R A Harris) mde most: hrd pressed over 1f out: hdd and outpcd last 100yds* **11/4**[1]	78
0060	4	nse	**He's A Humbug (IRE)**[21] 6069 4-9-4 80 (p) NCallan 3 *(K A Ryan) pressed ldr after 1f: drvn and upsides over 1f out: nt qckn ins fnl f and sn outpcd* **4/1**[2]	82
005	5	nk	**Loose Caboose (IRE)**[44] 5403 3-8-9 76 (b[1]) DavidProbert(5) 8 *(A J McCabe) racd wd: pressed ldrs: nt qckn 2f out and lost grnd bnd sn after: styd on again last 150yds* **14/1**	77
1456	6	nk	**Woodcote (IRE)**[18] 6174 6-9-3 79 (vt) GeorgeBaker 4 *(P R Chamings) pressed ldrs: nt qckn and lost pl wl over 1f out: plugged on again last 100yds* **6/1**	79
666	7	2 1/4	**Requisite**[8] 6420 3-9-3 79 RyanMoore 10 *(I A Wood) a in rr: brief effrt on inner over 1f out: sn no prog* **20/1**	71
3556	8	1 1/4	**Hereford Boy**[53] 5151 4-9-0 76 RobertHavlin 6 *(D K Ivory) a struggling to go the pce in rr: nvr on terms* **11/1**	63
1166	9	3	**Heaven**[41] 5510 3-9-2 78 DarryllHolland 9 *(P J Makin) s.i.s: racd wd in rr: bhd fnl 2f* **14/1**	55

57.72 secs (-1.08) **Going Correction** -0.10s/f (Stan) **9** Ran SP% **114.5**

Speed ratings (Par 105): **104,102,101,101,100 100,96,94,89**

toteswinger: 1&2 £29.50, 1&3 £5.20, 2&3 £8.00. CSF £45.77 CT £137.59 TOTE £6.90: £2.20, £3.20, £1.70; EX 74.70 TRIFECTA Not won..

Owner Andrew Duffield **Bred** Connie And John Iacuone **Trained** Newmarket, Suffolk

The Form Book, Raceform Ltd, Compton, RG20 6NL

FOCUS
This was a tight sprint handicap with just 4lb covering the field and it was run at a generous pace. The winner has been rated to the best view of this season's form, but the runner-up was unlucky. The next two add doubts to the form as they had not shown their best previously on sand.
Mambo Spirit(IRE) ◆ Official explanation: jockey said gelding was denied a clear run

6624 KENT LAND RECLAMATION H'CAP — 6f (P)
3:50 (3:52) (Class 3) (0-90,90) 3-Y-0+
£8,100 (£2,425; £1,212; £607; £302; £152) **Stalls** Low

Form RPR
3243 **1** **Safari Mischief**[41] 5509 5-9-2 **90** LukeMorris(3) 11 96
(P Winkworth) *t.k.h early: pressed ldng pair: effrt over 1f out: drvn ahd ins fnl f: kpt on wl* **15/2**
2215 **2** *nk* **Vintage (IRE)**[26] 5936 4-8-7 **78** EddieAhern 1 87+
(J Akehurst) *hld up in 7th: gng easily but trapped bhd rivals fr wl over 1f out: no room tl barged through ins fnl f: r.o wl nr fin* **7/1**
0002 **3** *¾* **Lone Wolfe**[34] 5697 4-9-2 **87** AlanMunro 7 90
(Jane Chapple-Hyam) *led: mod pce 1st 2f: drvn and hrd pressed 2f out: hdd and one pce ins fnl f* **15/2**
0003 **4** *nk* **Mutamared (USA)**[22] 6045 8-9-2 **87** NCallan 10 89
(K A Ryan) *nt wl away: swtchd fr outside draw and sn in midfield: effrt 2f out: styng on but hld whn bmpd 50yds out: kpt on nr fin* **25/1**
1006 **5** *nk* **Royalist (IRE)**[13] 6290 3-8-12 **84** PhilipRobinson 9 85
(M A Jarvis) *t.k.h early: pressed ldr: stl travelling strly 2f out: rdn and fnd nil 1f out* **5/1**[3]
3362 **6** *1* **Orpenindeed (IRE)**[43] 5424 5-8-12 **90** (t) AndreaAtzeni(7) 3 88
(M Botti) *trckd ldrs: cl up bhd ldng pair 1f out: nt that much room but nt qckn and lost pls nr fin* **3/1**[1]
3230 **7** *nse* **Asian Power (IRE)**[8] 6420 3-8-4 **76** SaleemGolam 2 74
(P J O'Gorman) *trckd ldrs: cl up on inner fr 2f out: nt qckn fnl f and lost pl nr fin* **50/1**
0005 **8** *½* **Ashdown Express (IRE)**[27] 5899 9-9-5 **90** RyanMoore 4 86
(W J Knight) *settled in rr: struggling for pce fr 1/2-way: kpt on fnl f but nvr on terms* **9/2**[2]
1200 **9** *2 ¼* **Silver Wind**[14] 6239 3-8-11 **83** (v) RobertWinston 5 72
(P D Evans) *a in rr: u.p and struggling fr 1/2-way* **28/1**
0-24 **10** *1 ¼* **Johnstown Lad (IRE)**[33] 5720 4-9-2 **87** (t) ShaneKelly 8 72
(Niall Moran, Ire) *a in rr: rdn and no prog over 2f out* **16/1**
4031 **11** *nse* **Wyatt Earp (IRE)**[13] 6278 7-9-4 **89** (b) JamieMoriarty 6 74
(R A Fahey) *sn struggling in last: nvr gng wl* **11/1**

1m 10.04s (-1.86) **Going Correction** -0.10s/f (Stan) course record
WFA 3 from 4yo+ 1lb **11** Ran SP% **119.3**
Speed ratings (Par 107): **108,107,106,106,105 104,104,103,100,99 99**
toteswinger: 1&2 £11.20, 1&3 £31.50, 2&3 £12.90. CSF £59.07 CT £420.55 TOTE £9.20: £1.70, £1.50, £2.60; EX 66.50 TRIFECTA Not won..
Owner Foxtrot Racing Partnership **Bred** Bearstone Stud **Trained** Chiddingfold, Surrey
■ Stewards' Enquiry : Eddie AhernM five-day ban: careless riding (Oct 24-29)

FOCUS
A fair and competitive sprint handicap, although the early pace was not strong. The runner-up was an unlucky loser, rated a length winner. The form has been rated around Safari Mischief and the third.

NOTEBOOK
Safari Mischief avoided any trouble and took full advantage with a narrow success off a career-high mark. He was obviously a fortunate winner, but is now 2-4 on the Lingfield Polytrack (tchd 8-1)
Vintage(IRE) ◆ looked a desperately unlucky loser. Settled off the lead from stall one, he was stuck towards the inside with nowhere to go for much of the straight and only got in the clear well inside the final furlong. He would have been a convincing winner had he been able to get out sooner and is clearly a fair bit better than his current mark suggests. (op 10-1 tchd 6-1)
Lone Wolfe ran a good race from the front off a mark 2lb higher than when second over 7f at Kempton on his previous start. He is winless since landing a Kempton maiden on his debut in January 2007, but has yet to be out of the places in three runs on Polytrack. (op 10-1 tchd 11-1)
Mutamared(USA) was forced to race about four wide throughout and was held when hampered by the eventual runner-up near the line. (op 16-1)
Royalist(IRE), trying Polytrack for the first time, did well to finish close up considering he raced freely. He can make his mark in this sort of company provided he learns to settle. (op 4-1)
Orpenindeed(IRE) did not pick up quite as well as one might have hoped and is proving hard to win with in Britain. (op 4-1)

6625 PML GROUP - CHANGE MANAGEMENT H'CAP — 1m (P)
4:20 (4:22) (Class 3) (0-95,92) 3-Y-0+
£8,100 (£2,425; £1,212; £607; £302; £152) **Stalls** High

Form RPR
3155 **1** **The Which Doctor**[20] 6130 3-8-9 **84** RyanMoore 2 91
(J Noseda) *hld up in midfield: prog over 2f out: drvn to chal ins fnl f: styd on wl to ld last strides* **11/2**[2]
1501 **2** *hd* **Elysee Palace (IRE)**[20] 6124 3-8-11 **86** PhilipRobinson 6 92
(M A Jarvis) *trckd ldrs: wnt 2nd over 2f out: rdn to ld ent fnl f: worn down nr fin* **8/1**
5-10 **3** *1* **Bazergan (IRE)**[13] 6276 3-9-3 **92** (tp) NCallan 1 96
(C E Brittain) *s.i.s: pushed up into midfield on inner: rdn and effrt over 2f out: prog to chal ent fnl f: nt qckn and edgd rt nr fin* **25/1**
1-00 **4** *1 ¼* **Amazing Star (IRE)**[14] 6242 3-8-10 **85** ShaneKelly 5 86
(M Halford, Ire) *hld up in rr and racd wd: effrt over 2f out: prog over 1f out: styd on fnl f: nt pce to trble ldrs* **14/1**
0500 **5** *1 ¼* **Kayak (SAF)**[23] 6033 6-9-4 **90** (b) DarryllHolland 12 88
(D M Simcock) *pressed ldr: led over 3f out: drvn 2f out: hdd & wknd ent fnl f* **25/1**
5335 **6** *¾* **Formation (USA)**[8] 6431 3-8-10 **85** EddieAhern 9 81
(E A L Dunlop) *hld up wl in rr: n.m.r over 2f out: pushed along and kpt on fr over 1f out w occasional tail flash* **15/2**[3]
3010 **7** *3 ¼* **Grand Vizier (IRE)**[23] 6035 4-9-0 **86** AlanMunro 3 75
(C F Wall) *a towards rr: u.p 3f out: nvr on terms* **11/2**[2]
12 **8** *1 ¾* **Charm School**[168] 1598 3-9-0 **89** JimmyFortune 4 85+
(J H M Gosden) *dwlt: plld hrd and hld up in rr: pushed along and trying to make prog whn rn into trble jst over 1f out: no ch after and eased* **2/1**[1]
4032 **9** *1* **Salient**[27] 5897 4-9-0 **86** PaulDoe 10 69
(M J Attwater) *led to over 3f out: wknd u.p fr 2f out* **16/1**
5- **10** *2* **Saltagioo (ITY)**[65] 4-8-9 **88** (t) AndreaAtzeni(7) 7 66
(M Botti) *chsd ldrs: u.p and losing pl fr 3f out: sn btn* **33/1**
2200 **11** *4* **Alfresco**[11] 6340 4-8-11 **88** (v) DavidProbert(5) 8 57
(I A Wood) *sn trckd ldrs: wknd rapidly over 2f out* **14/1**

1m 35.51s (-2.69) **Going Correction** -0.10s/f (Stan) course record
WFA 3 from 4yo+ 3lb **11** Ran SP% **116.8**
Speed ratings (Par 107): **109,108,107,106,105 104,101,99,98,96 92**
toteswinger: 1&2 £8.90, 1&3 £47.40, 2&3 £9.90. CSF £47.58 CT £1032.08 TOTE £5.70: £2.10, £2.40, £6.00; EX 49.90 TRIFECTA Not won..
Owner G C Stevens **Bred** Limestone And Tara Studs **Trained** Newmarket, Suffolk

FOCUS
A decent handicap, run at a fair pace and three-year-olds filled the first four places. The form looks pretty sound, rated through the runner-up and fourth.

NOTEBOOK
The Which Doctor was having his first start at the track since winning his maiden on this card last year and eventually got his head back in front with a game effort. He dug deep when asked for everything nearing the furlong pole and was always just getting there in the closing stages. This was his best effort, he evidently likes this track, and he could just have a bit more to offer over a stiffer test, as he is bred to get a little further. (op 8-1)
Elysee Palace(IRE), 7lb higher than when successful at Newbury 20 days earlier, had pretty much the run of the race just off the early pace and was perfectly positioned to strike turning in. She did nothing wrong in defeat and only just lost out, so still looks capable of adding to her tally before the season is over.
Bazergan(IRE) showed his previous effort at Chester to be all wrong. He can be counted as somewhat unfortunate, as he lost more ground with a sluggish start than he was beaten, and it is likely the best of him has still to be seen.
Amazing Star(IRE), an Irish raider, did best of those to be given waiting rides and ran very close to his recent level, helping to set the standard of the form. (op 12-1 tchd 10-1)
Kayak(SAF) was given a positive ride and shaped more encouragingly, but looks to need respite from the handicapper. (op 33-1)
Formation(USA) ran his usual sort of race and is another who helps to set the level. (op 12-1)
Grand Vizier(IRE) proved disappointingly one-paced on this return to his favoured surface. (op 7-1 tchd 9-2)
Charm School was having his first outing since finishing second in a good heat at Sandown in April and had been allotted what looked a potentially lenient mark of 89 for this handicap debut. After a tardy start, he refused to settle under early restraint, but was coming with his effort before being switched to the inside and squeezed at the furlong marker. He was quickly eased off soon afterwards and while this was obviously disappointing, he is worth another chance to prove his worth. Official explanation: jockey said gelding was denied a clear run (op 7-4 tchd 5-2 and 13-8 in a place)

6626 GSE BUILDING & CIVIL ENGINEERING H'CAP — 1m 4f (P)
4:55 (4:55) (Class 4) (0-80,78) 3-Y-0+ **£6,308** (£1,888; £944; £472; £235) **Stalls** Low

Form RPR
5564 **1** **E Major**[17] 6196 3-8-11 **70** (v[1]) RyanMoore 3 79
(Sir Michael Stoute) *led 1f: trckd ldr: led wl over 2f out and dashed clr: drvn and hung rt fr over 1f out: a lasting home* **9/1**[3]
6001 **2** *½* **War Of The Roses (IRE)**[24] 5999 5-9-11 **77** J-PGuillambert 6 85
(R Brotherton) *hld up in rr: stl there over 2f out: drvn and prog after: wnt 2nd 1f out: edgd rt but clsd on wnr: nvr gng to get there* **11/2**[2]
0604 **3** *½* **Rationale (IRE)**[26] 5940 5-9-10 **76** (t) NCallan 8 83
(S C Williams) *hld up in midfield: prog fr 4f out: rdn to chse wnr over 2f out: no imp and lost 2nd 1f out: kpt on* **11/2**[2]
6000 **4** *nk* **Fongs Gazelle**[55] 5092 4-9-8 **74** JoeFanning 2 81
(M Johnston) *hld up: snatched up after 3f on inner: last 3f out: drvn and prog over 1f out: styd on wl fnl f: nrst fin* **16/1**
00-2 **5** *½* **Limbo King**[26] 5935 4-9-7 **73** RobertWinston 7 79
(J R Fanshawe) *hld up in last trio: prog 2f out: drvn and styd on fnl f: nrst fin* **11/1**
0513 **6** *½* **Apache Fort**[13] 6279 5-9-4 **70** (b) TonyCulhane 9 75
(T Keddy) *hld up in last trio: prog over 2f out: chsd ldrs 1f out: hanging and nt qckn after* **14/1**
4316 **7** *5* **Dr Brass**[32] 5759 3-9-3 **76** (b) EddieAhern 10 73
(H J L Dunlop) *dwlt: sn prom: drvn on inner over 2f out: wknd over 1f out* **16/1**
1 **8** *3* **Mango Lady**[20] 6126 3-9-5 **78** AlanMunro 1 70
(C F Wall) *trckd ldrs: rdn and nt qckn whn pce lifted wl over 2f out: steadily lost pl* **9/4**[1]
1500 **9** *¾* **Monfils Monfils (USA)**[13] 6279 6-9-5 **76** DavidProbert(5) 11 67
(A J McCabe) *trckd ldrs: lost pl over 3f out: wknd over 2f out* **25/1**
335 **10** *7* **Erdeli (IRE)**[90] 3947 4-9-6 **72** MartinDwyer 5 52
(P R Webber) *t.k.h early: hld up in midfield: outpcd and lost pl over 2f out: sn bhd* **10/1**
0600 **11** *½* **William's Way**[16] 6203 6-9-8 **74** JimCrowley 12 53
(I A Wood) *dwlt: led after 1f to wl over 2f out: sn wknd* **20/1**
6105 **12** *¾* **Haydens Mark**[18] 6175 3-9-2 **75** TGMcLaughlin 4 53
(D G Bridgwater) *mostly in midfield: n.m.r on inner over 5f out to over 3f out: wknd and sn bhd* **66/1**

2m 29.74s (-3.26) **Going Correction** -0.10s/f (Stan)
WFA 3 from 4yo+ 7lb **12** Ran SP% **117.5**
Speed ratings (Par 105): **106,105,105,105,104 104,101,99,98,93 93,93**
toteswinger: 1&2 £14.80, 1&3 £6.10, 2&3 £9.10. CSF £56.24 CT £302.68 TOTE £9.80: £2.90, £2.20, £2.20; EX 80.60 Trifecta £162.90 Pool: £372.19 - 1.69 winning tickets..
Owner Sir Evelyn De Rothschild **Bred** Southcourt Stud **Trained** Newmarket, Suffolk

FOCUS
A fair handicap run at a decent gallop. The form looks solid with the fourth and fifth running to their marks. The winner was up 4lb on his early-season form.

6627 ADVANCE SCREEDING H'CAP — 7f (P)
5:25 (5:25) (Class 4) (0-80,80) 3-Y-0+ **£6,308** (£1,888; £944; £472; £235) **Stalls** Low

Form RPR
0106 **1** **Shamrock Lady (IRE)**[3] 6554 3-8-13 **74** TPO'Shea 4 81
(J Gallagher) *trckd ldrs: rdn to ld over 1f out: styd on wl fnl f* **25/1**
066 **2** *¾* **Ivory Lace**[12] 6307 7-9-0 **73** JimCrowley 6 79
(S Woodman) *hld up in last quartet: drvn and prog over 1f out: styd on wl to take 2nd nr fin: nvr able to chal* **11/1**
6611 **3** *½* **Fiefdom (IRE)**[31] 5789 6-9-2 **75** PatrickMathers 1 80
(I W McInnes) *hld up bhd ldrs: prog over 2f out: chsd wnr jst over 1f out: no real imp: lost 2nd nr fin* **7/1**
513 **4** *½* **Hallingdal (UAE)**[6] 6471 3-9-3 **78** JamesDoyle 5 84+
(Ms J S Doyle) *dwlt: sn in midfield: effrt 2f out: clsng whn squeezed out and snatched up 1f out: r.o nr fin: nt rcvr* **3/1**[1]
4150 **5** *1 ¼* **Liberation Spirit (USA)**[49] 5247 3-9-5 **80** (v) ShaneKelly 10 79
(J Noseda) *led at str pce: edgd rt and hdd over 1f out: fdd* **4/1**[2]
405 **6** *hd* **Perfect Treasure (IRE)**[31] 5789 5-9-1 **74** RyanMoore 3 73
(J A R Toller) *trckd ldrs: nt qckn and lost pl wl over 1f out: plugged on* **9/2**[3]

4230 **7** 1½ **Sparton Duke (IRE)**[13] 6278 3-9-4 **79**........................(p) RichardMullen 8 73
(K A Ryan) *sn rdn in rr: struggling thrght: styd on fnl f: nrst fin* **7/1**

6050 **8** hd **Divertimenti (IRE)**[34] 5697 4-8-13 **72**...................(p) RobertWinston 11 67
(C R Dore) *hld up in last quartet: gng wl on inner over 2f out: prog over 1f out: shkn up and fnd nil sn after* **12/1**

2000 **9** 1 **Mister New York (USA)**[20] 6124 3-9-5 **80**..................... SamHitchcott 7 71
(Noel T Chance) *wl in rr: rdn 4f out: struggling after: trying to stay on but no ch whn out of room jst ins fnl f* **25/1**

0000 **10** 2¼ **Super Frank (IRE)**[133] 2556 5-9-6 **79**........................ J-PGuillambert 12 65
(J Akehurst) *sn trckd ldng pair: wknd wl over 1f out* **16/1**

-506 **11** 4 **Incomparable**[128] 2732 3-9-0 **75**.. NCallan 2 49
(A J McCabe) *plld hrd: hld up bhd ldrs: wknd wl over 1f out* **33/1**

1m 23.73s (-1.07) **Going Correction** -0.10s/f (Stan)
WFA 3 from 4yo+ 2lb **11** Ran SP% **120.7**
Speed ratings (Par 105): **102,101,100,100,98 98,96,96,95,92 88**
toteswinger: 1&2 £33.30, 1&3 £14.00, 2&3 £6.90. CSF £278.82 CT £2188.38 TOTE £42.40: £7.70, £2.80, £2.10; EX 205.90 TRIFECTA Not won. Place 6 £151.31, Place 5 £44.60.
Owner Mrs Irene Clifford **Bred** Mrs Irene Clifford **Trained** Moreton-in-Marsh, Gloucs

FOCUS
This was an open handicap run at a solid pace. A career-best from the winner, with the third close to his recent form, but the fourth was another unlucky loser on this card.
Fiefdom(IRE) Official explanation: jockey said gelding hung right in straight
Hallingdal(UAE) ◆ Official explanation: jockey said filly suffered interference in running
T/Plt: £121.40 to a £1 stake. Pool: £66,252.31. 398.13 winning tickets. T/Qpdt: £31.60 to a £1 stake. Pool: £6,136.50. 143.68 winning tickets. JN

6488 WOLVERHAMPTON (A.W) (L-H)
Friday, October 10

OFFICIAL GOING: Standard
Wind: Moderate, behind Weather: Fine

6628 PARADE RESTAURANT H'CAP (DIV I) 7f 32y(P)
6:20 (6:20) (Class 6) (0-65,65) 3-Y-0+ **£2,388** (£705; £352) **Stalls** High

Form RPR

3365 **1** **Imperial Lucky (IRE)**[64] 4770 5-9-3 **62**........................... PatCosgrave 7 72
(M J Wallace, Australia) *hld up in mid-div: hdwy 2f out: squeezed through 1f out: led ins fnl f: drvn out* **11/1**

10 **2** 1½ **Chosen Forever**[62] 4875 3-9-3 **64**...................................... PJMcDonald 9 69
(G R Oldroyd) *hld up in mid-div: hdwy on outside over 3f out: hung rt bnd over 2f out: rdn wl over 1f out: kpt on to take 2nd nr fin: nt trble wnr* **14/1**

4163 **3** ¾ **Grand Diamond (IRE)**[25] 5965 4-9-5 **64**..................(p) DanielTudhope 1 68
(J S Goldie) *chsd ldr over 1f: prom: led wl over 1f out: sn rdn and edgd rt: hdd ins fnl f: no ex* **11/4**[1]

6205 **4** ¾ **Baltimore Jack (IRE)**[21] 6090 4-9-1 **60**..................(b) PaulMulrennan 8 61
(M W Easterby) *led: hdd wl over 1f out: sn rdn and edgd lft: one pce fnl f* **4/1**[2]

3300 **5** ¾ **Sedge (USA)**[20] 6132 8-9-1 **60**..(p) MickyFenton 5 59
(P T Midgley) *hld up in tch: pressed ldrs gng wl over 1f out: rdn ins fnl f: one pce* **7/1**

0003 **6** 2½ **Valentino Swing (IRE)**[20] 6132 5-9-3 **65**............... TolleyDean[(3)] 3 58
(Miss T Spearing) *s.i.s: hld up in rr: swtchd rt jst over 1f out: late prog: nvr trbld ldrs* **5/1**[3]

355 **7** 1 **Mr Burton**[31] 5780 4-8-13 **65**.................................... DeanHeslop[(7)] 6 55
(M Mullineaux) *s.i.s: hld up towards rr: rdn wl over 1f out: n.d* **33/1**

3006 **8** ½ **Nordic Commander (IRE)**[58] 4991 3-8-13 **60**............. HayleyTurner 11 48
(E A L Dunlop) *s.i.s: sn swtchd lft: hld up in rr: rdn wl over 1f out: edgd lft ins fnl f: n.d* **12/1**

2500 **9** ½ **Copperbottomed (IRE)**[9] 6377 3-8-13 **60**..................(e) SteveDrowne 4 46
(P G Murphy) *hld up in tch: pushed along and wknd wl over 1f out* **33/1**

2010 **10** 8 **Party In The Park**[30] 5799 3-9-4 **65**...........................(p) TomEaves 2 30
(Miss J A Camacho) *t.k.h: chsd ldr over 5f out tl over 2f out: sn wknd* **11/1**

1m 30.56s (0.96) **Going Correction** +0.15s/f (Slow)
WFA 3 from 4yo+ 2lb **10** Ran SP% **112.7**
Speed ratings (Par 101): **100,98,97,96,95 92,91,91,90,81**
toteswinger: 1&2 £23.70, 1&3 £10.70, 2&3 £3.80. CSF £148.68 CT £551.50 TOTE £9.60: £5.30, £7.70, £1.60; EX 84.40.
Owner David Cohen **Bred** Holborn Trust Co **Trained** Australia

FOCUS
An ordinary handicap but the quicker of the two divisions. The form looks pretty sound.

6629 HOTEL & CONFERENCING AT WOLVERHAMPTON H'CAP 1m 1f 103y(P)
6:50 (6:50) (Class 5) (0-70,68) 3-Y-0+ **£3,238** (£963; £481; £240) **Stalls** Low

Form RPR

0062 **1** **Mick's Dancer**[24] 6004 3-8-13 **65**..................................... SteveDrowne 6 73
(W R Muir) *hld up in mid-div: hdwy over 3f out: hrd rdn and edgd lft wl ins fnl f: led last strides* **28/1**

5633 **2** shd **Ahlawy (IRE)**[7] 6450 5-9-3 **65**.......................................(b) PaulMulrennan 7 73
(M W Easterby) *led after 1f: rdn and edgd lft ins fnl f: hdd last strides* **7/2**[1]

0564 **3** ½ **Thunderstruck**[14] 6250 3-9-2 **68**..................................(b) FrancisNorton 11 75
(K A Ryan) *hld up towards rr: rdn and hdwy 2f out: styd on wl towards fin* **12/1**

12 **4** 1½ **Myfrenchconnection (IRE)**[16] 6211 4-9-3 **65**................. MickyFenton 1 69+
(P T Midgley) *hld up in mid-div: hdwy on ins over 2f out: rdn and kpt on same pce fnl f* **9/2**[2]

500 **5** 1¾ **Mischief Lady**[29] 5836 3-8-13 **65**... AdamKirby 2 65
(E A L Dunlop) *a.p: rdn and wnt 2nd wl over 1f out: wknd wl ins fnl f* **8/1**

1- **6** ½ **Coral Creek (IRE)**[42] 5480 4-9-3 **65**................................... HayleyTurner 3 64
(M J Grassick, Ire) *led 1f: prom: rdn and wknd ins fnl f* **12/1**

6211 **7** 1½ **Strike Force**[21] 6090 4-9-1 **66**....................................... JackMitchell[(3)] 12 62+
(K F Clutterbuck) *hld up in rr: c v wd bnd over 2f out: rdn over 1f out: nvr nr ldrs* **8/1**

2504 **8** 1 **Spanish Diva**[6] 6491 4-8-10 **63**...........................(p) WilliamCarson[(5)] 5 57
(S C Williams) *s.i.s: hld up in rr: rdn over 1f out: n.d* **6/1**[3]

3352 **9** 1½ **Claret And Amber**[6] 6491 6-9-0 **62**............................... ChrisCatlin 13 53
(W K Goldsworthy) *hld up in tch: wknd 2f out* **17/2**

0000 **10** 6 **Our Kes (IRE)**[16] 6210 6-9-4 **66**...................................... JimmyQuinn 9 44
(P Howling) *hld up towards rr: pushed along 3f out: no rspnse* **50/1**

2511 **11** ½ **Kings Topic (USA)**[44] 5407 8-8-13 **68**........................(p) PNolan[(7)] 8 45
(A B Haynes) *sn prom: chsd ldr over 6f out tl over 3f out: hung rt bnd over 2f out: wknd wl over 1f out* **12/1**

0004 **12** 8 **King's Icon (IRE)**[17] 6188 3-8-6 **65**............................ TobyAtkinson[(7)] 4 25
(M Wigham) *a towards rr* **28/1**

100 **13** 9 **Portrush Storm**[31] 5773 3-9-1 **67**.. DNolan 10 8
(D Carroll) *s.i.s: t.k.h: sn in tch: rdn over 3f out: sn wknd* **40/1**

2m 3.00s (1.30) **Going Correction** +0.15s/f (Slow)
WFA 3 from 4yo+ 4lb **13** Ran SP% **121.8**
Speed ratings (Par 103): **100,99,99,98,96 94,93,92,87 86,79,71**
toteswinger: 1&2 £48.20, 1&3 £116.70, 2&3 £13.00. CSF £123.92 CT £1293.63 TOTE £36.30: £10.80, £1.80, £4.30; EX 226.40.
Owner Perspicacious Punters Racing Club **Bred** Cheveley Park Stud Ltd **Trained** Lambourn, Berks

FOCUS
A modest handicap run at a fairly steady early pace. The winner is clearly much better on sand than on turf, and the next two were close to their latest form.

6630 WOLVERHAMPTON-RACECOURSE.CO.UK H'CAP 1m 5f 194y(P)
7:20 (7:21) (Class 4) (0-85,82) 3-Y-0+ **£5,180** (£1,541; £770; £384) **Stalls** Low

Form RPR

2431 **1** **Factotum**[25] 5963 4-10-0 **82**.. DaneO'Neill 6 97
(L M Cumani) *chsd ldr: led over 2f out: rdn wl over 1f out: drvn out* **3/1**[2]

2 ½ **Laurel Creek (IRE)**[41] 5520 3-8-0 **63**............................ WilliamBuick 4 77
(M J Grassick, Ire) *hld up: hdwy over 3f out: chal 2f out: hrd rdn and hung lft fr over 1f out: nt qckn ins fnl f* **16/1**

1101 **3** 5 **Dance The Star (USA)**[6] 6472 3-9-1 **81**....................... MarcHalford[(3)] 8 88
(D M Simcock) *hld up in rr: rdn and hdwy on outside 3f out: sn ev ch: hung lft and wknd over 1f out* **2/1**[1]

6402 **4** 2½ **My Mate Max**[102] 3555 3-8-12 **75**...........................(p) GrahamGibbons 7 79
(R Hollinshead) *prom tl rdn and wknd wl over 1f out* **8/1**

3404 **5** 2 **Pass The Port**[13] 6288 7-9-4 **77**.............................. KellyHarrison[(5)] 3 78
(D Haydn Jones) *hld up in rr: hdwy over 2f out: wknd wl over 1f out* **12/1**

4331 **6** 5 **Houghton (IRE)**[15] 6226 3-8-13 **76**..................................(v) TedDurcan 2 70
(Sir Michael Stoute) *led: rdn and hdd over 2f out: wknd wl over 1f out* **7/2**[3]

610 **7** 18 **Look To This Day**[21] 6079 3-9-0 **77**................................. HayleyTurner 1 46
(R Charlton) *hld up: pushed along over 3f out: sn bhd* **12/1**

3m 6.19s (0.19) **Going Correction** +0.15s/f (Slow)
WFA 3 from 4yo+ 9lb **7** Ran SP% **112.9**
Speed ratings (Par 105): **105,104,101,100,99 96,86**
toteswinger: 1&2 £7.50, 1&3 £1.80, 2&3 £4.80. CSF £45.55 CT £115.37 TOTE £4.00: £1.90, £5.60; EX 43.70.
Owner Scuderia Rencati Srl & Mrs John Magnier **Bred** Azienda Agricola Francesca **Trained** Newmarket, Suffolk

FOCUS
Quite an interesting little handicap. Good efforts from the front pair to pull clear although the favourite was disappointing.

6631 PARADE RESTAURANT H'CAP (DIV II) 7f 32y(P)
7:50 (7:51) (Class 6) (0-65,65) 3-Y-0+ **£2,388** (£705; £352) **Stalls** High

Form RPR

6532 **1** **Siren Sound**[22] 6048 3-9-5 **65**...................................... SteveDrowne 8 76
(H Morrison) *chsd ldr: led over 2f out: rdn over 1f out: drvn out* **7/1**[3]

001 **2** 1¼ **Sendreni (FR)**[28] 5871 4-9-6 **64**...................................... ChrisCatlin 3 72
(M Wigham) *a.p: rdn and kpt on ins fnl f* **6/4**[1]

6650 **3** ¾ **Fine Ruler (IRE)**[174] 1491 4-9-5 **63**.............................. VinceSlattery 4 69
(M R Bosley) *t.k.h towards rr: rdn and hdwy over 1f out: kpt on ins fnl f* **40/1**

2022 **4** ½ **Elusive Dreams (USA)**[14] 6251 4-9-1 **59**......................(v) JimmyQuinn 1 64
(P Howling) *s.i.s: hld up in rr: hdwy on ins 2f out: hrd rdn over 1f out: nt qckn ins fnl f* **6/1**[2]

1000 **5** ½ **Zaarmit (IRE)**[53] 5162 3-8-13 **62**........................(b) MarcHalford[(3)] 6 65
(D M Simcock) *hld up in tch: rdn wl over 1f out: one pce whn hung lft ins fnl f* **40/1**

0150 **6** ¾ **Finsbury**[25] 5965 5-9-3 **61**... DanielTudhope 7 65+
(J S Goldie) *hld up towards rr: pushed along over 2f out: styng on whn hmpd wl ins fnl f* **8/1**

31 **7** ½ **Casela Park (IRE)**[14] 6251 3-9-0 **60**................................... LPKeniry 12 60
(S Kirk) *plld hrd: sn mid-div: carried hd high whn rdn and no real prog fnl f* **7/1**[3]

6000 **8** 2½ **Optical Illusion (USA)**[12] 6310 4-9-0 **58**........................ TonyHamilton 5 51
(R A Fahey) *led: hdd over 2f out: rdn wl over 1f out: wknd ins fnl f* **28/1**

4006 **9** nk **Sovereignty (JPN)**[20] 6132 6-9-5 **63**.............................. DaneO'Neill 11 55
(D K Ivory) *prom tl wknd over 2f out* **20/1**

0101 **10** 2½ **Tous Les Deux**[9] 6377 5-9-7 **65** 6ex.............................. GeorgeBaker 10 51
(G L Moore) *t.k.h in rr: hdwy on outside 5f out: c wd st: wknd wl over 1f out* **6/1**[2]

1m 30.94s (1.34) **Going Correction** +0.15s/f (Slow)
WFA 3 from 4yo+ 2lb **10** Ran SP% **117.8**
Speed ratings (Par 101): **98,96,95,95,94 93,93,90,89,87**
toteswinger: 1&2 £5.10, 1&3 £37.50, 2&3 £12.80. CSF £17.49 CT £405.32 TOTE £7.90: £2.10, £1.10, £7.50; EX 27.90.
Owner Helena Springfield Ltd **Bred** Meon Valley Stud **Trained** East Ilsley, Berks

FOCUS
The early pace was not strong and the winning time was the slower of the two divisions by 0.38sec. It was arguably a better race though with the winner's Great Leighs form working out well. He is rated up 6lb with the form pretty sound.
Casela Park(IRE) Official explanation: jockey said gelding ran too freely

6632 BOOK TICKETS ONLINE NURSERY 1m 141y(P)
8:20 (8:20) (Class 6) (0-65,65) 2-Y-0 **£2,729** (£806; £403) **Stalls** Low

Form RPR

005 **1** **Recession Proof (FR)**[20] 6135 2-9-6 **64**........................ GeorgeBaker 11 80+
(S A Callaghan) *hld up and bhd: hdwy over 3f out: led and edgd lft jst over 1f out: rdn clr ins fnl f: eased towards fin* **4/1**[2]

5025 **2** 6 **Victorian Tycoon (IRE)**[20] 6101 2-9-4 **62**......................... ChrisCatlin 12 62
(E J O'Neill) *chsd ldr: led over 3f out: rdn and hdd jst over 1f out: one pce: jst hld on for 2nd* **11/2**[3]

5005 **3** nse **Jobekani (IRE)**[21] 6087 2-8-13 **60**................... RussellKennemore[(3)] 5 60
(Mrs L Williamson) *hld up towards rr: hdwy 3f out: rdn wl over 1f out: kpt on same pce fnl f: jst failed to take 2nd* **40/1**

0600 **4** 3¾ **Dream Huntress**[37] 5606 2-9-2 **60**.................................... DaneO'Neill 2 52
(B J Meehan) *s.i.s: in rr: rdn and hdwy wl over 1f out: edgd lft ins fnl f: nvr nrr* **20/1**

003 **5** 1¼ **Crystallize**[29] 5812 2-9-2 **60**... RobertHavlin 6 50
(A B Haynes) *hld up in tch: rdn over 1f out: wknd ins fnl f* **16/1**

005 **6** 2¼ **Hawkeyethenoo (IRE)**[24] 5989 2-9-2 **60**...................... PaulMulrennan 9 45
(M W Easterby) *s.i.s: hdwy over 6f out: chsd ldr over 3f out tl over 2f out: wknd over 1f out* **6/1**

030 **7** ¾ **Game Roseanna**[48] 5256 2-9-6 **64**...................................... LiamJones 10 47
(W M Brisbourne) *hld up in tch: rdn over 4f out: wknd wl over 2f out* **33/1**

4500 **8** *3 1/4* **Tae Kwon Do (USA)**[9] 6394 2-9-2 60 TPQueally 13 37
(E A L Dunlop) *hld up towards rr: pushed along over 3f out: struggling over 2f out* **15/2**
060 **9** *1* **Save The Day**[39] 5570 2-9-2 60 GregFairley 7 35
(M Johnston) *prom tl wknd over 3f out* **7/2**[1]
4410 **10** *13* **Hollow Green (IRE)**[16] 6214 2-8-11 60 RichardEvans(5) 4 7
(P D Evans) *bhd fnl 5f* **8/1**
6020 **11** *1/2* **Shifting Gold (IRE)**[16] 6214 2-9-1 59 (p) TedDurcan 3 5
(K A Ryan) *pushed along 7f out: a in rr* **14/1**
3220 **12** *28* **Come On Buckers (IRE)**[48] 5294 2-9-2 65 (v) ShaneCreighton(5) 8 —
(E J Creighton) *led: clr over 6f out: hdd over 3f out: wknd wl over 2f out* **33/1**

1m 51.86s (1.36) **Going Correction** +0.15s/f (Slow) **12** Ran SP% **120.4**
Speed ratings (Par 93): **99,93,93,90,89 87,86,83,82,71 70,45**
toteswinger: 1&2 £5.40, 1&3 £14.70, 2&3 £26.80. CSF £25.74 CT £793.21 TOTE £5.60: £2.00, £1.90, £14.40; EX 27.70.
Owner N A Callaghan **Bred** N P Bloodstock Ltd & Morton Bloodstock **Trained** Newmarket, Suffolk

FOCUS
A modest nursery, but they went a good gallop over this extended mile, and stamina came to the fore. The winner produced a useful performance.

NOTEBOOK
Recession Proof(FR), on whom George Baker was taking over in the saddle from a 7lb claimer, is a half-brother to five winners out of a mare who is a half-sister to high-class middle-distance performers Sun Princess and Saddlers' Hall. Dropping in class on his handicap debut, he appreciated every yard of this trip and drew clear inside the last to win easily. Clearly well ahead of the handicapper, his connections will no doubt be keen to get him out quickly under a penalty now. Official explanation: trainer's rep said, regarding the improved form shown, colt had been very green in its previous races, whereas here it had got into its stride and this race was a drop in class (op 7-2)
Victorian Tycoon(IRE), who led the chasing pack for much of the way, kept battling away under pressure and is another who clearly gets the trip well. He was unlucky to bump into a very well-handicapped rival here, but given the way the race was run he did well to stick around having raced prominently. He has shown enough to suggest he can win a race off his current rating. (op 4-1)
Jobekani(IRE) was not sure to appreciate the step up in distance, but his dam is from the family of Irish Derby winner Old Vic, and he plugged on well to take third.
Dream Huntress was slowly away and had to be roused along in the early stages. Towards the rear for much of the contest, she kept on late, benefiting from the strong early gallop. (op 28-1 tchd 33-1)
Crystallize, running in a handicap for the first time, came to have his chance at the top of the straight but did not see it out. He might do better back over 7f. (tchd 20-1)
Hawkeyethenoo(IRE), making his handicap debut and upped in trip, had too much use made of him early and gave away ground racing wide. (op 12-1)
Save The Day was being pushed along some way out and proved disappointing. Perhaps Polytrack just does not suit her. (op 5-1 tchd 11-2)
Shifting Gold(IRE) Official explanation: jockey said gelding had no more to give

6633 SPONSOR A RACE BY CALLING 01902 390009 MAIDEN STKS 5f 20y(P)
8:50 (8:50) (Class 5) 3-Y-0+ **£3,070** (£906; £453) **Stalls** Low

Form RPR
2-22 **1** **Anne Of Kiev (IRE)**[17] 6192 3-8-12 72 JimmyFortune 8 79
(J H M Gosden) *chsd ldr: led over 1f out: sn hung rt: drvn clr ins fnl f* **2/5**[1]
2 *7* **Titus Gent** 3-9-3 0 MickyFenton 2 59
(J Ryan) *hld up in mid-div: hdwy on ins wl over 1f out: kpt on to take 2nd nr fin: no ch w wnr* **25/1**
0 **3** *hd* **Promise Of Love**[10] 6366 3-8-12 0 (b) WilliamBuick 6 53
(M J Grassick, Ire) *chsd ldrs: rdn over 1f out: hung lft ins fnl f: one pce* **9/2**[2]
2054 **4** *hd* **Rathmolyon**[103] 3526 3-8-12 61 RobertHavlin 7 52
(D Haydn Jones) *led: rdn and hdd over 1f out: sn btn: edgd lft and lost 2nd nr fin* **7/1**[3]
00- **5** *1 1/2* **Rightcar Lewis**[363] 6177 3-8-12 0 LPKeniry 3 47
(Peter Grayson) *chsd ldrs: rdn wl over 1f out: wkng whn hmpd wl ins fnl f* **40/1**
0 **6** *3 1/4* **Rosies Dawn**[20] 6114 3-8-12 0 DNolan 11 35
(D Carroll) *prom tl rdn and wknd wl over 2f out* **50/1**
7 *2 1/2* **Rindless** 3-8-5 0 RobbieEgan(7) 9 26
(J F Panvert) *s.s: outpcd: nvr nr ldrs* **50/1**
-550 **8** *nk* **Firewalker**[147] 2159 3-8-12 60 DaneO'Neill 13 25
(P T Dalton) *mid-div: wknd over 2f out* **16/1**
00 **9** *3* **Rare Old Bird**[14] 6254 3-8-12 0 VinceSlattery 10 14
(J F Panvert) *sn outpcd* **66/1**
10 *1 3/4* **Slim Jim Phantom** 3-9-3 0 TPQueally 4 13
(J G Given) *s.i.s: hung lft over 1f out: a towards rr* **10/1**

62.71 secs (0.41) **Going Correction** +0.15s/f (Slow) **10** Ran SP% **128.8**
Speed ratings (Par 103): **102,90,90,90,87 82,78,78,73,70**
toteswinger: 1&2 £10.10, 1&3 £3.00, 2&3 £12.60. CSF £24.01 TOTE £1.50: £1.02, £7.50, £1.60; EX 14.40.
Owner H R H Princess Haya Of Jordan **Bred** Deerfield Farm **Trained** Newmarket, Suffolk

FOCUS
A weak maiden which Anne Of Kiev was entitled to win easily. The form was not solid behind.

6634 RINGSIDE SUITE CONFERENCE CENTRE H'CAP 5f 216y(P)
9:20 (9:21) (Class 5) (0-75,76) 3-Y-0+ **£3,238** (£963; £481; £240) **Stalls** Low

Form RPR
2021 **1** **Beat The Bell**[8] 6420 3-9-0 76 6ex NicolPolli(5) 9 95
(A Bailey) *chsd ldr: led over 1f out: rdn clr ins fnl f: r.o wl* **5/1**[2]
6112 **2** *4 1/2* **Royal Challenge**[20] 6137 7-9-3 73 PatrickMathers 3 77
(I W McInnes) *hld up in tch: rdn wl over 1f out: kpt on to take 2nd last strides: no ch w wnr* **13/2**[3]
0331 **3** *hd* **Mr Wolf**[15] 6232 7-9-3 73 (p) TonyHamilton 7 77
(D W Barker) *led: rdn and hdd over 1f out: one pce: lost 2nd last strides* **7/1**
2021 **4** *nk* **Bahamian Kid**[14] 6254 3-9-2 73 (p) DO'Donohoe 12 76+
(R Hollinshead) *t.k.h towards rr: hdwy wl over 1f out: rdn and kpt on ins fnl f* **9/1**
4221 **5** *1 1/4* **Doubtful Sound (USA)**[7] 6448 4-9-2 75 6ex (p) KevinGhunowa(3) 1 74
(R A Harris) *hld up in tch: swtchd rt ent st: rdn over 1f out: kpt on one pce fnl f* **4/1**[1]
0500 **6** *1/2* **Gwilym (GER)**[49] 5250 5-8-5 66 KellyHarrison(5) 2 63
(D Haydn Jones) *t.k.h: prom: rdn over 1f out: wknd ins fnl f* **20/1**
5000 **7** *nse* **Royal Envoy (IRE)**[26] 5936 5-9-4 74 JimmyQuinn 6 71
(P Howling) *swtchd rt ins fnl f: nvr nrr* **16/1**
0610 **8** *nk* **Applesnap (IRE)**[22] 6046 3-8-13 70 HayleyTurner 4 66
(Miss Amy Weaver) *hld up towards rr: hdwy on ins wl over 1f out: rdn and wknd ins fnl f* **16/1**
0000 **9** *1* **Bertbrand**[7] 6448 3-8-4 68 ow1 RobbieEgan(7) 8 61
(D Flood) *t.k.h towards rr: c wd ent st: rdn over 1f out: n.d* **50/1**
2000 **10** *1/2* **Follow The Flag (IRE)**[18] 6178 4-8-11 67 PatCosgrave 11 58
(A J McCabe) *s.i.s: a bhd* **20/1**
0360 **11** *1/2* **Rabbit Fighter (IRE)**[28] 5861 4-8-13 69 (v) DarrenWilliams 13 58
(D Shaw) *broke wl: sn stdd and lost pl: a in rr* **17/2**
3406 **12** *nk* **Steel City Boy (IRE)**[18] 6164 5-8-10 71 AnnStokell(5) 5 60+
(Miss A Stokell) *rrd s: plld hrd: sn mid-div: rdn and wknd wl over 1f out* **10/1**
1603 **13** *3 1/4* **Mafaheem**[28] 5867 6-9-0 70 (b) DaneO'Neill 10 48
(A B Haynes) *hld up in mid-div: wknd wl over 1f out* **10/1**

1m 14.61s (-0.39) **Going Correction** +0.15s/f (Slow)
WFA 3 from 4yo+ 1lb **13** Ran SP% **125.2**
Speed ratings (Par 103): **108,102,101,101,99 99,98,98,97,96 95,95,91**
toteswinger: 1&2 £11.20, 1&3 £15.10, 2&3 £4.00. CSF £38.66 CT £243.78 TOTE £7.50: £2.30, £3.50, £2.30; EX 26.60 Place 6 £108.26, Place 5 £47.54.
Owner D J P Turner **Bred** D J P Turner **Trained** Newmarket, Suffolk
■ Stewards' Enquiry : Tony Hamilton three-day ban: careless riding (Oct 24,27-28)

FOCUS
Habitual front-runner Mr Wolf ensured a sound gallop in this competitive sprint handicap, but very few got into it. Another step up from Beat The Bell, up 12lb, with the runner-up close to his latest.
Steel City Boy(IRE) Official explanation: jockey said gelding reared leaving stalls and hung right-handed in final 2f
T/Plt: £203.30 to a £1 stake. Pool: £97,191.80. 348.87 winning tickets. T/Qpdt: £19.20 to a £1 stake. Pool: £8,527.75. 327.10 winning tickets. KH

6635 - 6636a (Foreign Racing) - See Raceform Interactive

6507 DUNDALK (A.W) (L-H)
Friday, October 10

OFFICIAL GOING: Standard

6637a IRISH STALLION FARMS EUROPEAN BREEDERS FUND STAR APPEAL STKS (LISTED RACE) 7f
7:40 (7:44) 2-Y-O **£33,507** (£9,830; £4,683; £1,595)

RPR
1 **Captain Ramius (IRE)**[34] 5696 2-9-1 JamieSpencer 4 98+
(M J Wallace, Australia) *mde all: rdn fr 1 1/2f out: kpt on wl u.p fnl f: edgd sltly rt cl home* **7/4**[1]
2 *3/4* **Excelente (IRE)**[14] 6259 2-8-12 79 (p) FMBerry 5 93
(Mrs John Harrington, Ire) *settled in mid-div: 7th 3f out: hdwy into 4th 1f out: kpt on into 2nd fnl f wout rching wnr* **12/1**
3 *nk* **Gluteus Maximus (IRE)**[12] 6317 2-9-1 98 JAHeffernan 3 95
(A P O'Brien, Ire) *mid-div: 5th on inner 1/2-way: 3rd and u.p 1 1/2f out: kpt on one pce* **6/1**[3]
4 *nk* **Blas Ceoil (USA)**[12] 6318 2-8-12 100 KJManning 6 92
(J S Bolger, Ire) *trckd ldrs: 4th 3f out: 2nd and chal under 2f out: no ex and dropped to 4th fnl f* **4/1**[2]
5 *1 1/2* **Ohiyesa (IRE)**[26] 5947 2-8-12 90 KLatham 9 88+
(G M Lyons, Ire) *settled in rr: sme hdwy ent st: short of room fr 2f out: 5th 1f out: no imp ins fnl f* **12/1**
6 *3* **Vilasol (IRE)**[48] 5296 2-9-1 100 DPMcDonogh 8 83
(Kevin Prendergast, Ire) *mid-div on outer: 6th over 2f out: no ex fr over 1 1/2f out* **10/1**
7 *shd* **Haaf Ok**[27] 5924 2-8-12 90 RPCleary 10 80
(M Halford, Ire) *settled in rr on outer: 8th 3f out: no ex and kpt on fr 1 1/2f out* **20/1**
8 *1 1/4* **Cristal Island (IRE)**[12] 6320 2-8-12 93 PJSmullen 7 77
(Thomas Mullins, Ire) *trckd ldr: 2nd 3f out: no ex and wknd fr under 2f out* **10/1**
9 *1* **Miss Puss (IRE)**[12] 6319 2-8-12 88 (t) WMLordan 2 75
(David Wachman, Ire) *trckd ldrs: 3rd 1/2-way: wknd fr 2f out* **8/1**
10 *12* **Island Breeze (IRE)**[11] 6347 2-8-12 72 (b1) CDHayes 1 45
(Andrew Oliver, Ire) *in rr and sn rdn: no imp fr over 2f out* **50/1**

1m 25.68s (85.68) **10** Ran SP% **122.0**
CSF £26.92 TOTE £2.00: £2.00, £2.50, £1.90; DF 16.20.
Owner Mrs Clodagh McStay **Bred** P G Lyons **Trained** Australia

NOTEBOOK
Captain Ramius(IRE) maintained his unbeaten record, following up his two wins over the trip on a similar surface at Kempton by making all. Asked to raise his effort in the straight, he responded well and kept on well under pressure, edging right close home. (op 15/8 tchd 13/8)
Excelente(IRE) had won a maiden over the course and distance two weeks previously. She showed improvement here and, after being seventh into the straight, warmed well to her task from a furlong and a half out and went second inside the final furlong, staying on well without quite getting to the winner.
Gluteus Maximus(IRE), seventh in the Goffs Million on his previous start, was soon tracking the leaders on the inside and closed from two furlongs out. Third over a furlong out, he kept on under pressure. (op 5/1)

6638 - 6641a (Foreign Racing) - See Raceform Interactive

6464 SAINT-CLOUD (L-H)
Friday, October 10

OFFICIAL GOING: Good to soft

6642a PRIX THOMAS BRYON (GROUP 3) 1m
1:50 (1:49) 2-Y-O **£29,412** (£11,765; £8,824; £5,882; £2,941)

RPR
1 **Silver Frost (IRE)**[47] 5330 2-9-1 OPeslier 4 108
(Y De Nicolay, France) *a in tch: 5th st: hdwy on outside fr over 2f out: reminder 1 1/2f out: led 1f out: pushed clr: r.o wl* **46/10**[3]
2 *2* **Fuisse (FR)**[35] 2-8-12 TGillet 6 101
(Mme C Head-Maarek, France) *restrained in 5th early: wnt up to trck ldr over 5f out: 2nd st: led 2 1/2f out: rdn over 1f out: hdd 1f out: one pce* **1/1**[1]
3 *1/2* **Topclas (FR)**[20] 6147 2-8-12 IMendizabal 3 100
(P Demercastel, France) *hld up in rr: last and pushed along st: hdwy on outside fr wl over 1f out: 3rd appr fnl f: styd on same pce* **18/1**
4 *2 1/2* **Rolling Bag (FR)**[21] 6157 2-8-12 CSoumillon 7 94
(M Roussel, France) *racd in 4th: 3rd st: no ex fr over 1 1/2f out* **38/10**[2]
5 *3* **Sokar (FR)**[48] 5300 2-8-12 MAndrouin 5 87
(J Boisnard, France) *trckd ldr early: 4th st: wknd wl over 1f out* **10/1**

6 1 1/2 **Stormy Weather (FR)**[33] 2-8-12 .... YLerner 1 84
(J-L Pelletan, France) *6th st: nvr a factor* **23/1**

7 8 **Baby Wood (FR)**[29] 2-8-12 .... SPasquier 2 67
(S Loeuillet, France) *led to 2 1/2f out: sn wknd* **9/1**

1m 41.7s (-5.80) **7** Ran SP% **117.2**
PARI-MUTUEL: WIN 5.60; PL 2.20, 1.50; SF 17.70.
Owner J D Cotton **Bred** Skymarc Farm **Trained** France

NOTEBOOK
Silver Frost(IRE), who finished in midfield in the Morny last time out, was given a patient and intelligent ride towards the tail of the field early on, hit the front just outside the final furlong and never looked like tasting defeat from that point on. Improving with every race, he was winning his second Group 3 race of the season. His trainer will probably bring him back here for the Criterium International next month.
Fuisse(FR), in second place rounding the final turn, took the lead a furlong and a half out but could not accelerate with the winner when passed at the furlong marker. He still galloped on well to hold second place but is not quite up to this level.
Topclas(FR), held up early on, was first seen with a chance halfway up the straight. He finished well but never really looked like taking a better place.
Rolling Bag(FR), racing at a major Paris track for the first time after two wins in the provinces, was virtually in mid-division throughout and one-paced when the race warmed up early in the straight.

6302 ASCOT (R-H)
Saturday, October 11

OFFICIAL GOING: Good to soft (straight course - good in places; round course - soft in places)
Wind: Virtually nil Weather: Sunny and bright

6644 WILLMOTT DIXON CORNWALLIS STKS (GROUP 3) 5f
1:10 (1:12) (Class 1) 2-Y-O

£28,385 (£10,760; £5,385; £2,685; £1,345; £675) **Stalls** Centre

Form RPR

011 **1** **Amour Propre**[79] 4323 2-9-0 110 .... DaneO'Neill 1 108
(H Candy) *racd in stands' side pair: mde virtually all: rdn wl over 1f out: edgd rt briefly ins fnl f: hld on gamely* **10/1**

1052 **2** nk **Waffle (IRE)**[56] 5103 2-9-0 90 .... LDettori 2 107
(J Noseda) *racd in stands' side pair: trckd wnr: plld out and rdn jst over 1f out: r.o wl: nt quite rch wnr* **12/1**

2101 **3** 1 3/4 **Mrs Kipling (IRE)**[27] 5951 2-8-11 98 .... JamieSpencer 11 98
(S A Callaghan) *hld up in rr: gd hdwy and edgd rt 2f out: chsd ldng pair ent fnl f: kpt on same pce fnl f* **12/1**

1625 **4** 1 3/4 **Anglezarke (IRE)**[22] 6068 2-8-11 104 .... EddieAhern 14 91+
(T D Easterby) *chsd ldrs: rdn 2f out: unable qck over 1f out: kpt on same pce* **9/1**[3]

0430 **5** 1/2 **Bahamian Babe**[29] 5852 2-8-11 93 .... PhilipRobinson 6 90
(M L W Bell) *led main gp tl ent fnl f: no ex u.p* **25/1**

51 **6** 1/2 **Archie Rice (USA)**[22] 6080 2-9-0 87 .... AlanMunro 16 91
(W Jarvis) *hld up in tch: hdwy 2f out: pressed ldrs ent fnl f: hung rt and no ex fnl f* **25/1**

4102 **7** nk **Doughnut**[14] 6274 2-8-11 96 .... RichardHughes 4 87
(R Hannon) *chsd ldrs: drvn wl over 1f out: wknd ent fnl f* **16/1**

2500 **8** 1 **Art Princess (USA)**[8] 6441 2-8-11 96 .... MichaelHills 17 83
(B W Hills) *towards rr: hdwy over 1f out: kpt on u.p fnl f: nvr trbld ldrs* **25/1**

1350 **9** hd **Able Master (IRE)**[30] 5827 2-9-0 97 .... JimCrowley 13 85
(B Smart) *taken down early: towards rr: rdn over 2f out: nvr trbld ldrs* **33/1**

211 **10** 1/2 **Magic Cat**[22] 6068 2-9-0 107 .... AndrewElliott 19 84
(K R Burke) *prom: rdn 2f out: wknd u.p over 1f out* **3/1**[1]

3423 **11** 1 1/4 **Ginobili (IRE)**[10] 6401 2-9-0 94 .... RyanMoore 10 79
(R Hannon) *chsd ldrs: rdn 2f out: sn wknd* **14/1**

1016 **12** 1 **Light The Fire (IRE)**[48] 5330 2-9-0 102 .... JimmyFortune 20 75
(B J Meehan) *prom: ev ch over 1f out: sn drvn: wknd qckly fnl f* **10/1**

211 **13** shd **Blades Princess**[18] 6183 2-8-11 92 .... GrahamGibbons 5 72
(E S McMahon) *chsd ldrs: rdn over 2f out: wknd wl over 1f out* **8/1**[2]

1250 **14** hd **Spin Cycle (IRE)**[50] 5226 2-9-0 105 .... RichardMullen 12 74
(B Smart) *towards rr: short of room and lost pl jst over 2f out: no ch after* **16/1**

01 **15** hd **Spiritofthewest (IRE)**[24] 6010 2-9-0 89 .... WilliamBuick 18 74
(S Parr) *in tch: rdn 2f out: wknd over 1f out* **33/1**

100 **16** nk **Matwan (FR)**[30] 5850 2-8-11 0 .... MickaelForest 7 70
(C Boutin, France) *hld up in midfield: rdn and no imp 2f out: no ch fnl f* **100/1**

51 **17** 3 1/2 **Moscow Eight (IRE)**[8] 6434 2-9-0 0 .... ChrisCatlin 3 60
(E J O'Neill) *s.i.s: t.k.h and hld up in tch: rdn and btn jst over 2f out* **20/1**

1106 **18** 1 1/2 **Coconut Shy**[21] 6102 2-8-11 93 ....(t) LPKeniry 15 52
(G Prodromou) *chsd ldrs: rdn 2f out: wknd qckly jst over 1f out* **66/1**

2110 **19** 10 **Russet Reward**[99] 3681 2-9-0 89 .... DarryllHolland 9 19
(Mrs L Stubbs) *w ldrs tl 1/2-way: sn wknd: eased ins fnl f* **100/1**

61.39 secs (0.89) **Going Correction** +0.35s/f (Good) **19** Ran SP% **123.8**
Speed ratings (Par 105): **106,105,102,99,99 98,97,96,95,95 93,91,91,91,90 90,84,82,66**
toteswinger: 1&2 £21.10, 1&3 £18.10, 2&3 £24.40. CSF £112.71 TOTE £10.00: £3.40, £3.90, £3.80; EX 125.30 Trifecta £645.20 Part won. Pool £871.99 - 0.10 winning units..
Owner Simon Broke And Partners **Bred** Mrs Sheila Oakes **Trained** Kingston Warren, Oxon

FOCUS
A big field of the season's speedier juveniles assembled, but they had a distinctly autumnal look about them, with several going in their coats and getting warm and edgy, among them the fancied Magic Cat and Waffle. There was very little incident, despite the number of runners, but it proved an unsatisfactory race, as there appeared to be a significant track bias, with the two runners who raced apart from the rest up the stands' rail finishing first and second.

NOTEBOOK
Amour Propre ◆ had broken the juvenile track record when winning at Warwick and Bath in the summer and has blistering speed, but firm ground was considered essential for him to show his best. He coped with this easier surface, however, showing terrific speed again, and even allowing for him being favoured by his track position, this has to go down as a smart effort. Henry Candy said the winner has made unbelievable physical progress in the last year and sees no reason why he shouldn't train on in 2009, when he sees him as a 5f horse, pure and simple. He is from the family of the stable's other good sprinter Corrybrough, and Candy reckons he is fully entitled to be mentioned in the same breath as the likes of Kyllachy and Airwave, who he also had. (op 7-1 tchd 11-1)
Waffle(IRE) was on edge in the preliminaries but showed improved form, albeit with the proviso that racing up the rail may well have flattered him somewhat. He looked up against it, but 5f suits him. He is in the sales, so his future is uncertain. (op 14-1)
Mrs Kipling(IRE) came from off the pace to lead the main pack going into the final furlong, but she could not get to grips with the first two. She is another who seems best at 5f, and one could argue that she was the moral winner. (tchd 14-1 in places)
Anglezarke(IRE), second in the Flying Childers before a disappointing run behind Magic Cat at Ayr, ran better again, racing up the middle of the track. (op 11-1 tchd 12-1)
Bahamian Babe showed a deal of speed and looked back to nearer her spring form. (op 33-1)
Archie Rice(USA) was up in class and back in trip but emerged best of those racing towards the far side, showing improved form despite hanging right in the closing stages.
Doughnut keeps her form and enthusiasm extremely well and showed up well again.
Art Princess(USA), another filly who has been busy, was keeping on towards the far side on this drop back in trip. (op 40-1)
Magic Cat had highly progressive form but looked as if he might just be past his best. He faded in the final furlong after showing good speed. (tchd 100-30 and 7-2 in places)
Light The Fire(IRE), back down in trip, faded late on after racing up with the pace. (op 17-2 tchd 8-1)
Spin Cycle(IRE) would have preferred faster ground, and he was short of room just after halfway. (tchd 20-1)
Russet Reward Official explanation: jockey said gelding moved poorly

6645 WILLMOTT DIXON BENGOUGH MEMORIAL STKS (GROUP 3) 6f
1:45 (1:45) (Class 1) 3-Y-O+

£36,900 (£13,988; £7,000; £3,490; £1,748; £877) **Stalls** Centre

Form RPR

0140 **1** **Conquest (IRE)**[14] 6269 4-9-1 100 .... JimmyFortune 5 114
(W J Haggas) *t.k.h: chsd ldrs tl stdd towards rr over 4f out: hdwy between horses to chse ldr ent fnl f: hrd rdn to ld wl ins fnl f* **16/1**

0200 **2** 3/4 **Zidane**[13] 6304 6-9-1 108 .... LDettori 2 112
(J R Fanshawe) *stdd s: hld up in rr: hdwy jst over 2f out: led over 1f out: edgd rt ins fnl f: hdd and no ex wl ins fnl f* **8/1**

3303 **3** 1 1/4 **Sir Gerry (USA)**[13] 6304 3-9-0 114 .... JamieSpencer 13 108+
(J R Fanshawe) *hld up towards rr: hdwy 2f out: rdn and hung rt over 1f out: chsd ldng pair jst ins fnl f: one pce* **7/2**[1]

1301 **4** 1 1/2 **Regal Parade**[21] 6104 4-9-1 106 .... WilliamCarson 11 103+
(D Nicholls) *in tch: rdn 2f out: n.m.r sn after: kpt on fnl f* **10/1**

010- **5** 1 1/4 **Major Eazy (IRE)**[364] 6182 3-9-0 0 .... EddieAhern 10 99
(B J Meehan) *led tl over 1f out: wknd u.p fnl f* **66/1**

0054 **6** hd **Prime Defender**[13] 6304 4-9-1 110 .... MichaelHills 6 98
(B W Hills) *chsd ldrs: rdn and unable qck over 1f out: one pce after* **5/1**[2]

0200 **7** 1 **Balthazaar's Gift (IRE)**[13] 6304 5-9-1 110 ....(v) DaneO'Neill 9 95
(L M Cumani) *awkward s and slowly away: a towards rr: nvr trbld ldrs* **10/1**

0020 **8** 1 1/4 **Assertive**[13] 6304 5-9-7 111 ....(v) RyanMoore 7 97
(R Hannon) *s.i.s: a in rr: rdn 2f out: plugging on same pce whn swtchd lft ins fnl f* **15/2**[3]

0-11 **9** hd **Perfect Polly**[133] 2606 3-8-11 104 .... ShaneKelly 4 87
(J Noseda) *chsd ldrs: rdn jst over 2f out: struggling whn n.m.r over 1f out: wl hld whn sltly hmpd ins fnl f* **8/1**

1040 **10** 6 **Intrepid Jack**[13] 6304 6-9-5 113 .... GeorgeBaker 3 75
(H Morrison) *chsd ldrs: rdn over 2f out: wknd over 1f out: eased ins fnl f* **12/1**

0040 **11** 1 1/2 **Dark Missile**[13] 6304 5-8-12 98 ....(t) WilliamBuick 8 63
(A M Balding) *in tch: effrt and rdn 2f out: ev ch over 1f out: wknd 1f out: eased whn btn ins fnl f* **11/1**

0100 **12** 6 **Galeota (IRE)**[14] 6285 6-9-1 101 .... RichardHughes 12 47
(R Hannon) *chsd ldr tl wl over 1f out: sn wknd: eased ins fnl f* **40/1**

1m 14.74s (0.34) **Going Correction** +0.35s/f (Good)
WFA 3 from 4yo+ 1lb **12** Ran SP% **116.9**
Speed ratings (Par 113): **111,110,108,106,104 104,103,101,101,93 91,83**
toteswinger: 1&2 £20.30, 1&3 £13.10, 2&3 £6.20. CSF £136.69 TOTE £19.90: £4.90, £2.60, £2.00; EX 219.10 Trifecta £935.80 Part won. Pool £1,264.61 - 0.70 winning units..
Owner Highclere Thoroughbred Racing XXXVIII **Bred** Gerrardstown House Stud **Trained** Newmarket, Suffolk
■ The first running of this event, which replaces the discontinued Bentinck Stakes at Newmarket in the Pattern.

FOCUS
A decent field for this Group 3 sprint, with most of these having raced in a higher grade this year. The effects of the draw were not as pronounced as they had been in the opener, but the first two did race near to the stands' side. The pace was sound. The winner was back to the pick of his 2yo form, with the runner-up the best guide. Judd Strret (25/1) was withdrawn at the start on vet's advice.

NOTEBOOK
Conquest(IRE), a Group 2 winner as a juvenile who has contested mainly handicaps this season, came with a sustained run from the back of the field to lead inside the last furlong, despite displaying his usual high head carriage. His Stewards' Cup-winning form has been boosted by the exploits of the runner-up King's Apostle (his stablemate), who beat seven of these in the Diadem over course and distance at the last meeting, and of the third Borderlescott, who went on to win the Nunthorpe. He ran respectably in the Great St Wilfrid next time but became worked up before his latest run here and tried to get out from under the stalls. He is in the Horses in Training sales, so his future is in the balance. (op 20-1)
Zidane finished last of the septet who ran in the Diadem but he had what appeared the best of the draw from stall two here, with Judd Street, the only horse berthed on his inside, withdrawn at the start. He ran an improved race, but was in front plenty soon enough and was cut down late on. He could run in the Listed Wentworth Stakes at Doncaster on the final day of the turf season. (op 10-1)
Sir Gerry(USA), in contrast to his stablemate Zidane, was unfavourably drawn in 13, otherwise he might well have finished a good deal closer. After tracking the pace out wide, he angled quite sharply across to his left when making ground and could not get to the front two inside the last furlong. He likes this track and had been third in the Golden Jubilee and the Diadem over course and distance this year. (op 4-1)
Regal Parade, the Ayr Gold Cup winner whose rider was unable to claim his usual 5lb allowance, was slightly inconvenienced by Sir Gerry's shift left but was staying on well inside the last, as befits a horse who won the Buckingham Palace Handicap over 7f at the royal meeting here. This was a commendable effort on his first try in Group company. (op 8-1 tchd 11-1)
Major Eazy(IRE) was a very useful juvenile, although found wanting in this sort of grade, and he showed good pace to lead for more than three furlongs on this first start for a year before fading late on. (op 100-1)
Prime Defender showed pace too, but has now failed to win in 13 tries at Group level despite some smart efforts. The ground had probably not dried out quite enough for him (op 13-2 tchd 7-1 in places)
Balthazaar's Gift(IRE) had his ground, but could never get involved after a slow start (op 12-1)
Assertive was always being held, despite the return of the visor in which he had run his best race of the season when second to African Rose in the Sprint Cup at Doncaster. The penalty for his Group 2 win at York in May did not help. (op 8-1 tchd 7-1)
Perfect Polly, off the track since winning a fillies' Listed event at Haydock in May, tends to get stirred up at the start but did so more markedly than usual here. She was already in trouble when meeting with traffic problems late on. (tchd 10-1 in places)
Intrepid Jack was found out under his Group 3 penalty despite a decent draw. (tchd 11-1)

Dark Missile ran creditably for a long way, but was beaten when tightened up slightly going to the furlong pole and was soon eased off by her rider, possibly with something amiss. (tchd 12-1)
Galeota(IRE) weakened right out of it after showing pace from his high draw. (op 33-1)

6646 LADBROKES.COM STKS (HERITAGE H'CAP) 1m 4f

2:20 (2:23) (Class 2) (0-105,105) 3-Y-O+

£46,732 (£13,995; £6,997; £3,502; £1,747; £877) **Stalls** High

Form RPR

0401 **1** **Night Crescendo (USA)**^{13} 6302 5-8-11 **92**................(p) JimCrowley 15 97
(Mrs A J Perrett) *trckd ldng pair: rdn over 2f out: drvn over 1f out: burst between horses to ld nr fin* **20/1**

4044 **2** *nk* **Pevensey (IRE)**^{13} 6302 6-9-0 **95**...............................(p) GrahamGibbons 4 100
(J J Quinn) *hld up in tch: rdn and effrt over 2f out: kpt on u.p ins fnl f: wnt 2nd last strides* **12/1**

2103 **3** *hd* **Drill Sergeant**^{13} 6302 3-9-2 **104**............................... JoeFanning 16 109
(M Johnston) *led tl 8f out: styd pressing ldr: drvn over 2f out: led again narrowly ins fnl f: hdd and lost 2 pls towards fin* **22/1**

1022 **4** *nk* **Inventor (IRE)**^{19} 6171 3-8-10 **98**............................... JimmyFortune 19 102
(B J Meehan) *w ldr tl led 8f out: drvn over 2f out: battled on wl tl hdd ins fnl f: unable qck last 100yds* **12/1**

6653 **5** *hd* **Dansili Dancer**^{14} 6286 6-9-4 **99**............................... AdamKirby 3 103
(C G Cox) *hld up in midfield: hdwy over 2f out: kpt on wl u.p fnl f: nvr quite getting to ldrs* **25/1**

2330 **6** *nk* **Cool Judgement (IRE)**^{29} 5853 3-8-9 **97**.................. PhilipRobinson 8 100
(M A Jarvis) *t.k.h: chsd ldrs: rdn over 2f out: unable qck u.p fnl f* **9/1**

01-1 **7** *½* **Magicalmysterytour (IRE)**^{28} 5894 5-9-5 **100**................ EddieAhern 5 103+
(W J Musson) *hld up in midfield on outer: plld out and rdn over 2f out: kpt on but nvr quite pce to chal ldrs* **7/1**^{2}

232 **8** *nse* **Tastahil (IRE)**^{28} 5894 4-9-0 **95**............................... RHills 14 98+
(B W Hills) *trckd ldrs on inner: rdn and effrt 2f out: n.m.r and edging out lft over 1f out: kpt on same pce u.p fnl f* **9/1**

3554 **9** *½* **Samsons Son**^{15} 6238 4-8-7 **88**............................... LPKeniry 6 90
(J R Best) *hld up in tch: rdn and unable qck wl over 2f out: hdwy u.p over 1f out: keeping on whn swtchd rt nr fin: nt pce to chal ldrs* **33/1**

2502 **10** *nk* **Young Mick**^{13} 6302 6-9-10 **105**...............................(v) RyanMoore 7 106+
(G G Margarson) *hld up towards rr: plld out and rdn over 2f out: sn edging rt: kpt on fnl f: nvr pce to chal ldrs* **9/2**^{1}

4321 **11** *½* **Allied Powers (IRE)**^{23} 6041 3-8-10 **98**.................. JamieSpencer 13 98
(M L W Bell) *chsd ldrs: rdn 3f out: unable qck u.p 2f out: btn whn n.m.r wl ins fnl f* **8/1**^{3}

5251 **12** *½* **Albaqaa**^{14} 6276 3-8-3 **91**............................... WilliamBuick 12 92+
(R A Fahey) *t.k.h: hld up towards rr: effrt on inner over 2f out: swtchd lft 1f out: styng on whn nt clr run ins fnl f: eased after* **25/1**

3310 **13** *nse* **Always Bold (IRE)**^{14} 6288 3-8-3 **91**............................... GregFairley 2 91
(M Johnston) *hld up towards rr on outer: rdn and effrt over 2f out: unable qck u.p over 1f out: kpt on* **28/1**

4260 **14** *¾* **Candle**^{44} 5423 5-8-10 **91**............................... DaneO'Neill 9 89
(H Candy) *hld up in midfield: lost pls and towards rr 8f out: rdn over 2f out: kpt on but nvr gng pce to trble ldrs* **33/1**

2122 **15** *nse* **Spring Dream (IRE)**^{65} 4771 5-7-8 **80**............................... SophieDoyle(5) 1 78
(A King) *stdd and dropped in bhd after s: t.k.h: hld up in last pl: rdn over 2f out: nvr threatened ldrs* **25/1**

0-50 **16** *½* **Group Captain**^{28} 5894 6-9-4 **99**............................... RichardHughes 10 96
(H J Collingridge) *stdd s: hld up in rr: rdn over 2f out: kpt on but nvr pce to threaten ldrs* **40/1**

2212 **17** *½* **Buddhist Monk**^{14} 6288 3-7-12 **86**............................... DO'Donohoe 11 83
(Sir Mark Prescott) *stdd s: hld up in rr: plld out and rdn over 2f out: nvr threatened ldrs* **12/1**

0244 **18** *2 ¾* **Mull Of Dubai**^{29} 5853 5-8-12 **93**............................... TonyCulhane 18 85
(T P Tate) *hld up in midfield: rdn over 2f out: unable qck u.p 2f out: btn 1f out* **16/1**

0542 **19** *15* **Crete (IRE)**^{23} 6061 6-8-11 **92**...............................(v1) MichaelHills 17 60
(W J Haggas) *stmbld sn after s: t.k.h: hld up in rr: rdn over 2f out: btn and eased fnl f* **14/1**

2m 35.34s (-0.16) **Going Correction** +0.225s/f (Good)
WFA 3 from 4yo+ 7lb **19** Ran SP% **129.8**
Speed ratings (Par 109): **109,108,108,108,108 108,107,107,107,107 106,106,106,106,106 105,105,103,93**
toteswinger: 1&2 £101.90, 1&3 £89.00, 2&3 £81.90. CSF £230.59 CT £5304.56 TOTE £26.70: £5.00, £3.00, £4.60, £3.00; EX 297.50 Trifecta £6014.90 Pool £65,839.09 - 8.10 winning units..
Owner John Connolly **Bred** Audley Farm Inc **Trained** Pulborough, W Sussex

FOCUS
What should have been a thoroughly competitive handicap was rendered a thoroughly unsatisfactory one owing to the steady pace at which it was run. Horses racing handily were massively favoured, and it proved virtually impossible to come from off the pace, so the running of most of those who raced towards the rear can effectively be ignored. At the finish all except the last two were within five lengths of the winner. The winner was closely matched with the second and third on his latest course-and-distance win.

NOTEBOOK
Night Crescendo(USA) likes Ascot, and having raced on the heels of the leaders, hugging the inner, he squeezed between rivals inside the final furlong for a narrow win. He has been transformed by the recent application of cheekpieces, which help him get away on terms, and he will have to go on the shortlist for the November Handicap, in which he should be on a similar mark to last year, when he was third.
Pevensey(IRE), another course specialist, was never worse than about fifth or sixth. He ran his usual good race, but was another favoured by the way the race was run. (op 14-1)
Drill Sergeant shared pacemaking duties and was therefore favoured in such a steadily run affair. (op 20-1)
Inventor(IRE), runner-up on the Kempton Polytrack the last twice, shared pacemaking duties which was an advantage the way the race was run. (op 11-1)
Dansili Dancer deserves plenty of credit, as he passed quite a few horses to take his close fifth place. (op 33-1)
Cool Judgement(IRE) was in the same sort of place throughout. (op 11-1 tchd 12-1)
Magicalmysterytour(IRE) tried to make his effort towards the outer from mid-division, but they had not gone fast enough for him. He had impressed at Doncaster on his reappearance when beating Tastahil, and confirmed those placings on worse terms. He could be a different proposition off a stronger gallop back at Doncaster in the November Handicap, which looks the obvious target for him. (op 15-2 tchd 8-1)
Tastahil(IRE) Official explanation: jockey said colt was denied a clear run
Samsons Son Official explanation: jockey said gelding was denied a clear run
Young Mick did not have the race run to suit and is one of the many who can be forgiven. (op 11-2 tchd 6-1 in places)
Albaqaa was making ground under pressure up the rail when he ran out of room and had to be switched. He never saw any daylight in the final furlong and finished with plenty in the tank. He remains one to keep an eye on. (op 33-1)
Spring Dream(IRE) finished strongly, albeit well down the field, and the Stewards looked into her running and riding. Official explanation: jockey said, regarding the running and riding, her orders were to drop in and pick her way through runners, adding that mare was slow to pick up in straight but ran on well when the gaps came; trainer's rep added that mare was returning from a short break and was in good form at home, and it was decided to leave the blinkers off here; vet said mare finished lame and was coughing post-race (tchd 33-1)
Crete(IRE) needed a stronger pace but appeared to resent the first-time visor. Official explanation: jockey said gelding stumbled after start (op 16-1)

6647 ROYAL ASCOT RACING CLUB ANNIVERSARY HYPERION CONDITIONS STKS 7f

2:50 (2:52) (Class 2) 2-Y-O **£8,411** (£2,519; £945; £945) **Stalls** Centre

Form RPR

2021 **1** **Rileyskeepingfaith**^{10} 6399 2-9-0 97............................... DarryllHolland 5 98+
(M R Channon) *t.k.h: hld up in tch: plld out over 1f out: nt clr run 1f out tl squeezed between horses to ld wl ins fnl f: r.o wl* **10/3**^{3}

2120 **2** *½* **Weald Park (USA)**^{7} 6474 2-9-0 105............................... RichardHughes 3 93
(R Hannon) *led: hrd pressed and rdn jst over 2f out: hdd over 1f out: rallied u.p last 100yds to snatch 2nd last stride* **11/8**^{1}

61 **3** *shd* **Alazeyab (USA)**^{21} 6117 2-9-0 88...............................(t) RHills 1 93
(M A Jarvis) *chsd ldr: upsides and rdn jst over 2f out: led narrowly over 1f out: hdd and no ex wl ins fnl f* **2/1**^{2}

413 **3** *dht* **Aahaykid (IRE)**^{23} 6038 2-9-0 83............................... JimCrowley 2 93
(K R Burke) *stdd s: hld up in tch: hdwy to chal over 1f out: ev ch tl unable qck wl ins fnl f* **7/1**

1m 30.3s (2.30) **Going Correction** +0.35s/f (Good) **4** Ran SP% **111.0**
Speed ratings (Par 101): **100,99,99,99**
CSF £8.57 TOTE £3.10; EX 4.40.
Owner Jolly Roger Racing **Bred** M Barrett **Trained** West Ilsley, Berks
■ Stewards' Enquiry : Darryll Holland four-day ban: careless riding (Oct 27-30)

FOCUS
An interesting conditions event despite the small field. The pace was fairly steady, and things became tight in the latter stages as the winner looked for room - the result standing following a stewards' inquiry. There was just over half a length between the four runners at the line and the form should not be taken too literally, although there is no doubt the best horse won.

NOTEBOOK
Rileyskeepingfaith settled disputing third after taking a keen hold in the early stages, was hemmed in by Aahaykid on his outer on the heels of the leading pair when the pace quickened with around two furlongs to run. Darryll Holland had to sit and suffer until eventually driving his mount through a fairly tight gap between Aahaykid and Alazeyab, with the colt quickening up to win readily in the end. He was following up his win in a three-runner race at Salisbury, after proving no match for Wingwalker at Sandown, and is a tough and useful performer at this sort of level but has been found wanting when upped in grade. He has to be held up and connections think he will improve next year. (op 9-4 tchd 2-1)
Weald Park(USA) was the form pick on his second to Firth Of Fifth in the Group 2 Superlative Stakes at Newmarket, but had been disappointing in a valuable sales race last time following a break. After bringing the field over to the stands' rails and setting just a steady gallop, he could not counter immediately when tackled and seemed set for last place, but was staying on well at the line. He should get a bit further at three. (op 7-4 tchd 15-8 in places and 2-1 in a place)
Aahaykid(IRE) was disappointing in heavy ground at Ayr last time after a taking Warwick maiden win. This was more like it and he had every chance, but he was momentarily unbalanced when bumped by the winner as that horse burst through and he could not counter. (op 6-1)
Alazeyab(USA) tracked the leader on his outer and had his chance with no real excuse. He won a Newbury maiden from King's Sabre, who was well behind Weald Park at Newmarket last time, and he had something to find at the weights, so this was a sound effort. (op 6-1)

6648 DELOITTE AUTUMN STKS (GROUP 3) 1m (R)

3:30 (3:31) (Class 1) 2-Y-O

£28,385 (£10,760; £5,385; £2,685; £1,345; £675) **Stalls** High

Form RPR

21 **1** **Kite Wood (IRE)**^{29} 5857 2-9-0 92............................... PhilipRobinson 8 108+
(M A Jarvis) *mde all: rdn and qcknd over 1f out: r.o wl* **9/4**^{1}

1 **2** *1 ½* **Taameer**^{22} 6075 2-9-0 0............................... RHills 9 105+
(M P Tregoning) *hld up wl in tch: nt clr run over 2f out: swtchd lft 2f out: chsd wnr over 1f out: wandered u.p ins fnl f: kpt on but no imp on wnr* **11/4**^{2}

31 **3** *2 ¼* **Four Winds**^{24} 6026 2-9-0 91............................... JamieSpencer 6 100+
(M L W Bell) *hld up wl in tch: unable qck and short of room over 2f out: shuffled towards rr: swtchd rt and rallied over 1f out: styd on to go 3rd ins fnl f: nt pce to threaten ldng pair* **4/1**^{3}

314 **4** *1 ¼* **Whispering Angel**^{56} 5093 2-9-0 90............................... JimmyFortune 7 97+
(B J Meehan) *dwlt and short of room sn after s: hld up in last trio: nt clr run and hmpd over 2f out: sn swtchd ins: sn rdn: edgd lft and no imp ins fnl f* **18/1**

6314 **5** *1 ½* **Akhenaten**^{9} 6428 2-9-0 84............................... SamHitchcott 1 94
(M R Channon) *stdd after s: hld up in last trio: hdwy on outer 3f out: rdn jst over 2f out: wknd over 1f out* **25/1**

5453 **6** *2 ½* **Talking Hands**^{14} 6284 2-9-0 103............................... RichardHughes 3 88
(S Kirk) *stdd s: hld up in last pl: hdwy and nt clr run over 2f out: no ch w ldrs after* **14/1**

12 **7** *2* **Anmar (USA)**^{28} 5898 2-9-0 100............................... LDettori 2 84
(Saeed Bin Suroor) *t.k.h early: chsd ldrs: rdn to chse wnr over 2f out tl over 1f out: sn wknd* **11/2**

1 **8** *5* **Quai D'Orsay**^{20} 6151 2-9-0 0............................... GregFairley 4 73
(M Johnston) *w wnr tl over 2f out: wknd u.p wl over 1f out* **11/1**

1m 42.42s (1.62) **Going Correction** +0.225s/f (Good) **8** Ran SP% **116.9**
Speed ratings (Par 105): **100,98,96,95,93 91,89,84**
toteswinger: 1&2 £2.30, 1&3 £2.80, 2&3 £3.00. CSF £8.85 TOTE £3.10: £1.30, £1.40, £1.90; EX 9.10 Trifecta £31.90 Pool £1,641.75 - 38.04 winning units..
Owner Thomas Barr **Bred** Elsdon Farms **Trained** Newmarket, Suffolk

FOCUS
This looked a good renewal of a race with a strong tradition, because it attracted a good-looking field of prospective middle-distance stars from leading stables, all eight of them winners and two of them unbeaten. Winners of this race have not all gone on to great things, but they include Nashwan in 1988, Nayef in 2000 and the subsequent Racing Post Trophy winner Ibn Khaldun a year ago.

NOTEBOOK
Kite Wood(IRE) was taking a big step up in grade after winning a Doncaster maiden, but it was the same for most of his rivals. He got a bit warm in the preliminaries, but Philip Robinson said that is just the Galileo in him and he was relaxed in the race, when he jumped off in front on the rail and made all the running. One or two of those behind got into a bit of trouble, but he was a worthy winner and had them reasonably well strung out at the finish. Michael Jarvis sees the winner very much as a 1m2f to 1m4f prospect and he is a 20-1 chance with Ladbrokes and Boylesports for the Derby (generally shorter). (op 5-2 tchd 11-4)

Taameer tracked the winner on the rail but needed to be switched left for his effort. He never quite looked like getting there and wandered a bit in the final furlong, but he stuck on well enough for a clear second without having too hard a time, and connections were not disappointed. Marcus Tregoning anticipates significant improvement from him and he still has a bright future over further next year. (tchd 100-30)

Four Winds, whose Sandown win is working out, got spooked in the paddock. He can be rated better than the bare form, as he was hemmed in by Akhenaten when Jamie Spencer wanted to make his move. The colt did not get the run of the race by any means but kept on well and is still held in high regard. He is sure to improve again when stepped up to middle distances. (op 9-2 tchd 7-2)

Whispering Angel was badly hampered approaching the two-furlong marker. He was rather one-paced when switched to the rail and could not make an impression, but it might have been a different story without the interference. (op 20-1 tchd 16-1)

Akhenaten had form at this level, having been fourth in the previous week's Somerville Tattersalls Stakes. He gives the form a solid look. (tchd 33-1)

Talking Hands, a dual winner here on the straight course, was held up as usual and did not get the clearest of runs, although he wasn't going conspicuously well anyway. (op 16-1)

Anmar(USA) made the right impression when winning at Sandown on his debut, but he has not looked so good in better company since. That could be down to softer ground, but it is hard to be sure. (tchd 6-1 and 13-2 in places)

Quai D'Orsay, who had won in testing conditions at Hamilton, was outpaced here after pressing the leader. He was a bit on edge and got spooked in the paddock, but he was not alone, as it happened to Four Winds at the same point. (op 10-1 tchd 9-1)

6649 DAVID & TONI EYLES H'CAP — 1m 2f

4:05 (4:05) (Class 2) (0-105,102) 3-Y-O+

£11,215 (£3,358; £1,679; £840; £419; £210) **Stalls** High

Form				RPR
0402	1		**Heaven Knows**[16] 6233 5-9-1 **94** .... RHills 10	101
		(W J Haggas) *chsd ldrs: plld out off rail over 2f out: sn chsng ldr 2f out: rdn to ld over 1f out: r.o wl* **5/1**[2]
6035	2	1 1/4	**Ramona Chase**[14] 6276 3-8-9 **93** .... RichardHughes 8	98
		(S Kirk) *t.k.h: hld up towards rr: hdwy over 2f out: nt clr run and swtchd lft jst over 1f out: chsd wnr last 100yds: no imp* **12/1**
6456	3	3/4	**Prince Forever (IRE)**[49] 5279 4-9-1 **94** .... PhilipRobinson 4	97
		(M A Jarvis) *led after 2f: rdn over 2f out: hdd over 1f out: one pce fnl f and lost 2nd last 100yds* **6/1**[3]
2100	4	1 1/4	**Siberian Tiger (IRE)**[7] 6476 3-9-4 **102** .... TonyCulhane 3	103
		(M R Channon) *hld up in midfield: rdn and unable qck 3f out: rallied u.p over 1f out: kpt on* **20/1**
4000	5	1/2	**Whitcombe Minister (USA)**[27] 5941 3-8-11 **95** .... RobertHavlin 7	95
		(Jamie Poulton) *hld up in rr: hdwy on outer over 2f out: rdn and no imp fr over 1f out* **25/1**
212	6	1/2	**Ascot Lime**[36] 5677 3-8-7 **91** ow2 .... RyanMoore 5	90
		(Sir Michael Stoute) *chsd ldrs: rdn and effrt over 2f out: edgd rt and wknd fnl f* **15/8**[1]
5360	7	3	**King Charles**[42] 5508 4-9-5 **98** .... JimmyFortune 2	91
		(E A L Dunlop) *hld up towards rr on outer: hdwy 7f out: rdn over 2f out: wknd ent fnl f* **7/1**
2005	8	3 1/4	**Ladies Best**[13] 6302 4-9-2 **95** .... DaneO'Neill 6	81
		(L M Cumani) *hld up towards rr: plld out and rdn over 2f out: no hdwy: wl hld last 2f* **8/1**
0-50	9	1	**Allanit (GER)**[42] 5528 4-9-7 **100** .... ShaneKelly 9	84
		(A P Stringer) *hld up in last pair: shkn up and effrt over 2f out: no real hdwy* **50/1**
135	10	1	**Zero Tolerance (IRE)**[21] 6103 8-9-1 **94** .... JamieSpencer 11	80
		(T D Barron) *led for 2f: chsd ldr after tl 2f out: wknd over 1f out: eased ins fnl f* **8/1**

2m 11.0s (1.20) **Going Correction** +0.225s/f (Good)
WFA 3 from 4yo+ 5lb — **10** Ran SP% **118.7**
Speed ratings (Par 109): **104,103,102,101,101 100,98,95,94,94**
toteswinger: 1&2 £10.70, 1&3 £7.20, 2&3 £13.60. CSF £62.66 CT £372.49 TOTE £5.70: £1.90, £3.30, £2.30; EX 75.20 Trifecta £1089.40 Part won. Pool £1,472.19 - 0.80 winning units..
Owner Hamdan Al Maktoum **Bred** Southcourt Stud **Trained** Newmarket, Suffolk

FOCUS
A decent race, but a good number of these arrived looking held by the handicapper. The pace was only modest and it is doubtful if the winner had to improve. The form is rated around the placed horses.

NOTEBOOK
Heaven Knows, whose latest win had come off a 6lb lower mark a year ago, was chased along early after being tightened up leaving the stalls but was soon well placed. In front going to the last furlong, he found plenty. Connections were pleased with his second at Pontefract last time, as they thought he'd need the run after a break, and they may look for another race for him this season, although he is entered in the sales (op 9-2 tchd 11-2)

Ramona Chase was held up racing keenly, if not taking quite so much of a tug as he often does. He had to be switched around the leading pair for his run, and could not get to the winner. He has generally run well all season, but has been unable to add to his one win, which came in a novice event 13 months ago (op 16-1)

Prince Forever(IRE) is normally held up but there was a change of tactics and he soon got over to lead and set just an ordinary pace. He could not counter when tackled and remains without a win since his debut two seasons ago, but he has dropped steadily in the weights this year and is 12lb lower than at the start of the season. (op 8-1)

Siberian Tiger(IRE) was one of the first under pressure and was staying on quite well for fourth, but he is another of whom the handicapper looks in control. (op 16-1)

Whitcombe Minister(USA) was last turning in and ran on well down the outer without threatening the placed horses. This was more encouraging.

Ascot Lime had a more progressive look than most of these, but he was 5lb higher than when second on the Kempton Polytrack and his rider put up 2lb overweight. He improved to look a threat going to the furlong pole, but his effort flattened out. (op 2-1 tchd 9-4)

King Charles, third in the Duke of Edinburgh over 1m4f here at the royal meeting, continues in the handicapper's grip. (op 15-2 tchd 8-1)

Ladies Best came in for support but was never able to land a blow, and remains a bit disappointing. (tchd 15-2 and 9-1 in places)

Allanit(GER) won in Listed company in Germany this summer, ridden by Shane Kelly, who partnered him here, but he was never a factor on this debut for the yard and probably needs to come down a few pounds in the weights. (op 66-1 tchd 40-1)

Zero Tolerance(IRE) lost the early tussle for the lead. He was still in second place at the two-furlong pole before dropping away. (tchd 7-1 and 9-1 in places)

6650 SODHEXO APPRENTICE H'CAP — 5f

4:40 (4:42) (Class 4) (0-85,93) 3-Y-O+

£6,231 (£1,866; £933; £467; £233; £117) **Stalls** Centre

Form				RPR
1215	1		**Judge 'n Jury**[11] 6354 4-9-0 **85** ....(t) AndreaAtzeni(5) 16	104
		(R A Harris) *a travelling wl: chsd ldrs: led over 2f out: clr over 1f out: r.o strly: easily* **8/1**[3]
6410	2	4 1/2	**Bosun Breese**[71] 4591 3-9-2 **85** ....(t) Louis-PhilippeBeuzelin(3) 9	88
		(P W D'Arcy) *taken down early: led tl over 3f out: outpcd by wnr wl over 1f out: no ch w wnr fnl f: edgd lft but kpt on to go 2nd wl ins fnl f* **16/1**
5060	3	3/4	**The Tatling (IRE)**[25] 6006 11-8-8 **77** .... JackDean(3) 8	77
		(J M Bradley) *slowly away: bhd: hdwy 1/2-way: chalng for 2nd fnl f: kpt on same pce: no ch w wnr* **25/1**
0063	4	1	**Peopleton Brook**[30] 5832 6-8-0 **71** oh24 ....(t) RossAtkinson(5) 13	67
		(B G Powell) *stdd s: hld up towards rr: hdwy and rdn 1/2-way: chalng for 2nd ins fnl f: one pce last 100yds: no ch w wnr* **100/1**
1-02	5	nk	**Lochstar**[27] 5936 4-9-1 **81** .... WilliamBuick 14	76
		(A M Balding) *chsd ldr tl led over 3f out: rdn and hdd over 2f out: no ch w wnr fr over 1f out: lost 2nd wl ins fnl f: short of room nr fin* **7/2**[1]
4005	6	3/4	**Zowington**[33] 5757 6-8-9 **80** ....(v) WilliamCarson(5) 10	73
		(C F Wall) *racd in midfield: rdn 1/2-way: hld hd awkwardly and hanging rt u.p: styd on fnl f: nvr nr wnr* **16/1**
1211	7	1/2	**Haajes**[4] 6557 4-9-13 **93** 6ex ....(t) TolleyDean 11	84
		(S Parr) *nvr travelling: chsd ldrs and sn bustled along: outpcd 1/2-way: no ch last 2f* **4/1**[2]
322	8	1/2	**Valatrix (IRE)**[42] 5510 3-8-8 **79** .... JPHamblett(5) 6	68
		(C F Wall) *hld up towards rr: hdwy and n.m.r over 2f out: sn rdn and edging lft: kpt on u.p fnl f: nvr nr wnr* **10/1**
0340	9	3/4	**Diane's Choice**[21] 6131 5-8-5 **71** ....(b) MarcHalford 17	57
		(Miss Gay Kelleway) *awkward s and s.i.s: bhd: hdwy and rdn 1/2-way: hung rt last 2f: nvr able to chal* **33/1**
0006	10	1/2	**Lunces Lad (IRE)**[17] 6200 4-8-1 **72** ....(v) MatthewDavies(5) 12	57
		(M R Channon) *chsd ldrs: rdn 1/2-way: sn struggling: wknd 2f out* **28/1**
6004	11	3/4	**Efistorm**[11] 6354 7-9-3 **83** .... LukeMorris 3	65
		(C R Dore) *wnt rt s: towards rr: rdn 1/2-way: nvr trbld ldrs: no ch whn swtchd rt ins fnl f* **8/1**[3]
1552	12	1 1/2	**Billion Dollar Kid**[30] 5839 3-9-3 **83** ....(t) TravisBlock 2	59
		(R A Harris) *racd in midfield: rdn and struggling 1/2-way: no ch last 2f* **14/1**
0303	13	nk	**Gallery Girl (IRE)**[19] 6174 5-8-9 **78** .... MCGeran(3) 5	53
		(T D Easterby) *racd in midfield: struggling whn edgd rt u.p over 2f out: n.d after* **16/1**
-453	14	hd	**Gold Express**[10] 6388 5-8-0 **71** oh3 .... AshleyMorgan(5) 7	46
		(P J O'Gorman) *s.i.s: a bhd: nvr a factor* **8/1**[3]
5410	15	1	**Angel Voices (IRE)**[43] 5455 5-8-0 **71** oh4 ....(p) DeclanCannon(5) 4	42
		(K R Burke) *hmpd s: nvr trbld ldrs* **33/1**
2100	16	3 3/4	**Lord Of The Reins (IRE)**[11] 6354 4-8-13 **84** .... RosieJessop(5) 1	42
		(J G Given) *s.i.s: a towards rr: no ch last 2f* **16/1**

61.25 secs (0.75) **Going Correction** +0.35s/f (Good) — **16** Ran SP% **129.0**
Speed ratings (Par 105): **108,100,99,98,97 96,95,94,93,92 91,89,88,88,86 80**
toteswinger: 1&2 £36.00, 1&3 £41.80, 2&3 £72.40. CSF £131.48 CT £3215.32 TOTE £9.10: £2.20, £3.10, £3.20, £10.80; EX 195.30 TRIFECTA Not won. Place 6 £685.93 Place 5 £158.53..
Owner Mrs Ruth M Serrell **Bred** C A Cyzer **Trained** Earlswood, Monmouths

FOCUS
Just a fair apprentice handicap. The field raced down the centre of the track, with those racing on the far side of the group showing much more prominently than those on the stands' side flank. The progressive Judge N' Jury is rated up 10lb and the form seems sound, despite the presence of the fourth from 24lb out of the weights.

Lord Of The Reins(IRE) Official explanation: jockey said gelding finished lame behind

T/Jkpt: Not won. T/Plt: £1,122.70 to a £1 stake. Pool: £141,270.45. 91.85 winning tickets. T/Qpdt: £72.40 to a £1 stake. Pool: £8,943.86. 91.30 winning tickets. SP

6308 MUSSELBURGH (R-H)

Saturday, October 11

OFFICIAL GOING: Good to soft (soft in places)

Fixture transferred from York.

Wind: Fresh half against Weather: Sunny periods

6651 NATIONAL EXPRESS RESERVE H'CAP (CONSOLATION RACE FOR 3.15) — 5f

2:10 (2:12) (Class 2) 3-Y-O+

£12,462 (£3,732; £1,866; £934; £466; £234) **Stalls** Low

Form				RPR
0132	1		**Hotham**[8] 6449 5-9-1 **81** .... DanielTudhope 9	90
		(N Wilson) *in tch: hdwy 2f out: rdn over 1f out: styd on strly ent fnl f: led last 75yds* **7/1**
4400	2	1/2	**Foxy Music**[42] 5493 4-8-12 **78** .... DeanMcKeown 13	85
		(E J Alston) *racd wd: led: rdn and hung rt over 1f out: drvn ins fnl f: hdd and no ex last 75yds* **28/1**
5560	3	3/4	**Fol Hollow (IRE)**[14] 6290 3-8-13 **86** .... AdeleRothery(7) 3	90
		(D Nicholls) *in tch: hdwy 2f out: sn rdn and styd on ins fnl f: nrst fin* **16/1**
5106	4	3/4	**Kay Two (IRE)**[11] 6354 6-9-4 **85** ....(p) SaleemGolam 4	86
		(R J Price) *cl up: rdn over 1f out and ev ch tl drvn and nt qckn ins fnl f* **10/1**
3430	5	1/2	**How's She Cuttin' (IRE)**[82] 4240 5-9-3 **83** ....(v) PJMcDonald 5	83
		(T D Barron) *bmpd s and in rr: hdwy 2f out: swtchd rt and rdn over 1f out: styd on ins fnl f: nrst fin* **5/1**[2]
2103	6	1 1/4	**Green Park (IRE)**[11] 6354 5-9-8 **88** ....(b) PaulHanagan 14	83
		(R A Fahey) *chsd ldrs: hdwy 2f out: rdn over 1f out and kpt on same pce ent fnl f* **16/1**
6006	7	1/2	**Geojimali**[21] 6105 6-8-9 **80** .... GaryBartley(5) 1	74
		(J S Goldie) *outpcd and bhd tl hdwy wl over 1f out: styd on ins fnl f: nt rch ldrs* **18/1**
1020	8	1/2	**Rasaman (IRE)**[19] 6174 4-8-11 **80** ....(tp) NeilBrown(3) 11	72
		(K A Ryan) *prom: rdn along 2f out: grad wknd* **12/1**
0053	9	hd	**Quiet Elegance**[14] 6290 3-9-9 **89** .... MickyFenton 7	80
		(E J Alston) *wnt lft and sltly bmpd s: midfield: rdn along 2f out: sn drvn and no imp appr fnl f* **6/1**[3]
5400	10	3/4	**Avertuoso**[59] 4962 4-8-12 **78** ....(vt) TomEaves 12	66
		(B Smart) *prom: rdn along 2f out: sn drvn and grad wknd* **16/1**

3203 **11** ½ **Princess Ellis**[9] 6429 4-9-10 **87** JimmyQuinn 2 76
(E J Alston) *prom stands' rail: rdn along 2f out: drvn and wknd ent fnl f* **4/1**[1]

0620 **12** 1¼ **Irish Pearl (IRE)**[26] 5962 3-9-4 **84** RobertWinston 8 66
(K R Burke) *prom: rdn along 2f out: sn drvn and wknd* **20/1**

3105 **13** 1 **First Order**[8] 6449 7-8-9 **83** (v) BMcHugh(7) 10 60
(Miss L A Perratt) *a towards rr* **50/1**

0000 **14** 2 **Northern Empire (IRE)**[11] 6354 5-9-4 **85** (t) PaulMulrennan 16 55
(K A Ryan) *stdd and swtchd lft s: a in rr* **50/1**

240 **15** 5 **Hypnosis**[14] 6290 5-9-0 **80** TonyHamilton 15 33
(D W Barker) *prom on outer: rdn along 2f out: sn wknd* **16/1**

63.73 secs (3.33) **Going Correction** +0.625s/f (Yiel) **15** Ran SP% **121.2**
Speed ratings (Par 109): **98,97,96,94,94 92,91,90,90,88 88,86,84,81,73**
toteswinger: 1&2 £42.30, 1&3 £25.30, 2&3 £74.50. CSF £199.28 CT £3076.10 TOTE £9.20: £2.60, £6.30, £5.30; EX 292.60 TRIFECTA Not won..

Owner Far 2 Many Sues **Bred** Capt J H Wilson **Trained** Flaxton, N Yorks

FOCUS

A consolation race for the heritage handicap later on the card, but a competitive enough race in its own right. The runner-up backed up by the third, look the best guides to the form.

NOTEBOOK

Hotham copes well with cut in the ground, has been in terrific form of late and loves to have something to chase. He found a way through the main pack and, once in front of them, edged over to chase down Foxy Music, who raced apart from the rest towards the centre of the track. The winner's recent second at Wolverhampton suggests he should be just as effective on the sand if connections decide to keep him on the go over the winter. (op 15-2 tchd 8-1)

Foxy Music, whose ideal conditions are a sharp 5f on easy ground, showed blinding early speed and, racing wide of the main bunch up the centre of the track, kept on well to hold off all bar Hotham. He still only has one win from 21 career starts, but this was a fine effort from his draw in stall 13. (op 33-1)

Fol Hollow(IRE), who had a good draw and is well handicapped on his best form from earlier in the season, is an inconsistent type. He ran one of his better races here, although he was never a real threat. (tchd 14-1)

Kay Two(IRE), back on the mark he won off three starts back at Newmarket in July, looked to have conditions to suit and had been handed a favourable draw. He showed up well for a long way, but seemed to go for home a bit too soon and did not quite see it out. (op 9-1)

How's She Cuttin'(IRE) had previous form figures of 11121 over this course and distance, but she was slowly away and bumped as the stalls opened and, although she made up some late ground, she was perhaps a little ring-rusty having been off the track since July.

Green Park(IRE) had a difficult draw to overcome and did not run too badly in the circumstances. (op 12-1)

Geojimali needs further than the bare minimum these days, evidenced by this effort where he got tailed-off before running on late. Official explanation: jockey said, regarding the running and riding, his orders were to jump out and not be too foreceful on gelding early on as it resents this, adding that he was squeezing gelding along from 4f out and it ran on final 2f, doing its best work at the end; trainer said gelding is probably suited by a longer trip these days and it was outpaced early on over 5f, adding that it always comes with a strong late run and needs everything to go right for it (tchd 16-1 and 20-1)

Princess Ellis looked well in off a mark of 90 following her third in a Listed race at Newmarket last time, and a record of three wins at this track was encouraging. The softer ground was a concern, though, and having failed to dominate as she likes, she dropped right out in the end. (op 7-2)

6652 PLAY SCOTBETPOKER.COM H'CAP 1m 6f
2:40 (2:40) (Class 2) (0-100,98) 3-Y-0+

£15,577 (£4,665; £2,332; £1,167; £582; £292) **Stalls** High

Form RPR

0141 **1** **Merchant Of Dubai**[11] 6355 3-8-11 **90** PJMcDonald 6 98
(G A Swinbank) *mde all: qcknd 5f out: qcknd 3f out: rdn wl over 1f out: drvn ins fnl f and styd on wl* **7/4**[1]

2242 **2** ¾ **Gordonsville**[13] 6313 5-8-4 **84** oh1 KellyHarrison(5) 3 86
(J S Goldie) *hld up in rr: pushed along over 3f out: rdn 2f out: drvn ins fnl f: kpt on wl towards fin* **13/2**

0006 **3** nk **Double Banded (IRE)**[14] 6288 4-9-3 **87** (p) JimmyQuinn 7 94
(J L Dunlop) *trckd ldrs: hdwy over 3f out: rdn wl over 1f out: drvn and ev ch ent fnl f: sn hung rt and no ex towards fin* **4/1**[2]

0501 **4** 4 **Lost Soldier Three (IRE)**[21] 6113 7-9-11 **95** SilvestreDeSousa 8 96
(D Nicholls) *trckd wnr: effrt 3f out: rdn along and ev ch wl over 1f out: sn drvn and btn* **6/1**

2050 **5** 2¼ **Record Breaker (IRE)**[29] 5853 4-9-8 **92** RoystonFfrench 1 90
(M Johnston) *trckd ldrs: rdn along 5f out: drvn 3f out and sn outpcd* **9/2**[3]

3332 **6** 34 **Acropolis (IRE)**[20] 6154 7-10-0 **98** (v) TomEaves 4 48
(Miss L A Perratt) *hld up: hdwy 4f out: rdn along wl over 2f out and sn btn* **11/1**

7 50 **Francesco (FR)**[217] 4-8-10 **80** PaulMulrennan 5 —
(Mrs L B Normile) *chsd ldng pair: rdn along 5f out: sn wknd* **50/1**

3m 9.16s (3.86) **Going Correction** +0.25s/f (Good)
WFA 3 from 4yo+ 9lb **7** Ran SP% **112.5**
Speed ratings (Par 109): **98,97,97,95,93 74,45**
toteswinger: 1&2 £2.80, 1&3 £2.10, 2&3 £4.20. CSF £13.33 CT £38.94 TOTE £2.90: £1.80, £2.90; EX 15.30 Trifecta £38.40 Part won. Pool £51.90 - 0.50 winning units..

Owner Highland Racing 2 **Bred** A Smith **Trained** Melsonby, N Yorks

■ Stewards' Enquiry : Jimmy Quinn two-day ban: careless riding (Oct 27-28)

FOCUS

Not a bad little handicap, and it was dominated throughout by the improving three-year-old Merchant Of Dubai. The form seems sound enough rated around the third and fourth.

NOTEBOOK

Merchant Of Dubai, in a change of tactics, was sent to the front early and set no more than an ordinary gallop before winding it up rounding the bend out of the back straight. He stays well and responded well to pressure, galloping on strongly to the line, and one would imagine that he will make a nice hurdler in time. However, right now he is developing into a very useful Flat performer, and the November Handicap is likely to be his next target. (op 9-4)

Gordonsville, effectively running off a 6lb higher mark than when runner-up over the course and distance 13 days earlier, is a frustrating type and once again he ran on late to take his familiar finishing position. This was the tenth time he has finished runner-up in a 20-race career. (op 7-1 tchd 8-1)

Double Banded(IRE) ran a better race than of late, but he hung right, in behind the eventual winner, when having his chance inside the final furlong.

Lost Soldier Three(IRE), who took advantage of having been dropped 20lb since the beginning of the season when winning at Catterick last time, was 7lb higher here. Having chased the leader into the straight he was seen off with a furlong to run, and this has to go down as a shade disappointing. (op 9-2 tchd 13-2)

Record Breaker(IRE) has shown before that he is far more effective in a small field than with lots of runners in the race, but on this occasion the ground appeared too soft for him to show his best. (op 5-1)

Acropolis(IRE) looked far from enthusiastic when pressure was applied. (op 8-1 tchd 15-2)

6653 NATIONAL EXPRESS YORK SPRINT CUP (HERITAGE H'CAP) 5f
3:15 (3:18) (Class 2) (0-105,104) 3-Y-0+

£37,386 (£11,196; £5,598; £2,802; £1,398; £702) **Stalls** Low

Form RPR

2100 **1** **Hamish McGonagall**[28] 5890 3-9-1 **95** DavidAllan 7 105
(T D Easterby) *chsd ldrs: rdn over 1f out: drvn ins fnl f and styd on wl to ld nr line* **11/1**

1115 **2** nk **Cheveton**[28] 5890 4-8-13 **93** SaleemGolam 17 102
(R J Price) *cl up on outer: effrt over 1f out: rdn to ld ent fnl f: sn drvn: hdd and no ex nr line* **9/1**[3]

1001 **3** hd **Captain Dunne (IRE)**[11] 6354 3-8-12 **95** DuranFentiman(3) 5 103
(T D Easterby) *qckly away and led: rdn along wl over 1f out: drvn and hdd ent fnl f: kpt on gamely* **20/1**

0103 **4** ½ **Hogmaneigh (IRE)**[6] 6514 5-9-5 **104** KellyHarrison(5) 2 110
(S C Williams) *outpcd and towards rr: hdwy 2f out: swtchd rt and rdn over 1f out: styd on strly ins fnl f: nrst fin* **8/1**[2]

5620 **5** ¾ **River Falcon**[21] 6104 8-9-1 **95** DanielTudhope 16 98
(J S Goldie) *midfield hdwy on outer 2f out: rdn and styd on to chse ldrs ent fnl f: drvn and one pce towards fin* **14/1**

1022 **6** ½ **Tombi (USA)**[7] 6484 4-9-10 **104** PaulMulrennan 11 106
(J Howard Johnson) *sltly hmpd s: midfield: rdn along and hdwy 2f out: drvn and ev ch ent fnl f: kpt on same pce* **16/1**

0410 **7** 1¼ **Ishetoo**[21] 6104 4-9-3 **97** SilvestreDeSousa 3 94
(A Dickman) *midfield: rdn along 2f out: sn drvn and kpt on ins fnl f: nrst fin* **9/1**[3]

0014 **8** 1 **Fullandby (IRE)**[7] 6468 6-9-8 **102** RoystonFfrench 6 95
(T J Etherington) *towards rr: hdwy 2f out: sn rdn and kpt on ins fnl f: nt rch ldrs* **10/1**

3005 **9** 1 **Reverence**[7] 6468 7-9-7 **101** JimmyQuinn 10 91
(E J Alston) *wnt rt s: sn cl up: rdn along 2f out: drvn and ch over 1f out: grad wknd* **9/1**[3]

4300 **10** hd **Evens And Odds (IRE)**[21] 6104 4-9-0 **94** (b) TonyHamilton 13 83
(K A Ryan) *hmpd s and in rr: swtchd wd and hdwy 2f out: sn rdn and kpt on ins fnl f: nt rch ldrs* **28/1**

0032 **10** dht **Siren's Gift**[9] 6429 4-8-10 **95** (b) DavidProbert(5) 15 84
(A M Balding) *trckd ldrs: hdwy and ev ch 2f out: sn rdn and wknd appr fnl f* **4/1**[1]

0000 **12** 1½ **Indian Trail**[21] 6104 8-8-6 **93** NSLawes(7) 4 77
(D Nicholls) *a towards rr* **25/1**

2600 **13** ½ **Aegean Dancer**[14] 6290 6-8-12 **92** TomEaves 14 74
(B Smart) *slt hmpd s: sn chsng ldrs: rdn along over 2f out and sn wknd* **25/1**

0005 **14** 1½ **Cute Ass (IRE)**[14] 6289 3-8-13 **93** (v1) TedDurcan 8 69
(K R Burke) *cl up: rdn along 2f out: drvn and wknd over 1f out* **25/1**

5246 **15** hd **Fathom Five (IRE)**[28] 5890 4-9-5 **99** RobertWinston 12 75
(B Smart) *hmpd s: a in rr* **10/1**

0100 **16** 4½ **Stoneacre Lad (IRE)**[7] 6468 5-9-1 **95** (b) PaulHanagan 1 55
(Peter Grayson) *a towards rr* **33/1**

62.32 secs (1.92) **Going Correction** +0.625s/f (Yiel) **16** Ran SP% **122.9**
Speed ratings (Par 109): **109,108,108,107,106 105,103,101,100,99 99,97,96,94,93 86**
toteswinger: 1&2 £23.20, 1&3 £66.70, 2&3 £51.00. CSF £97.43 CT £2053.98 TOTE £13.90: £2.60, £2.50, £4.20, £2.80; EX 138.10 Trifecta £140.00 Pool £946.10 - 5.00 winning units.

Owner Reality Racing Syndicate No 1 **Bred** J P Coggan And Whitsbury Manor Stud **Trained** Great Habton, N Yorks

■ This race is usually run at York.

FOCUS

A good, competitive sprint handicap, run in a time 1.41sec quicker than the consolation handicap earlier on the card. The form is solid with the first two slight improvers and the fourth the best guide.

NOTEBOOK

Hamish McGonagall did not get home after showing plenty of speed in the Portland, but that trip on that track was always going to stretch his stamina, whereas this sharp 5f promised to suit him ideally. He had been aimed at this race for some time, and the plan came off, although it took plenty of work from the saddle to pull it off. Official explanation: trainer's rep said, regarding the improved form shown, gelding had been suited by the drop back to 5f (op 16-1)

Cheveton ran very well from the widest draw. Fifth in the Portland last time and previously unbeaten in five starts over the bare 5f, he showed good speed throughout and was only worn down close home. He looks to be still improving. (tchd 8-1)

Captain Dunne(IRE), a stablemate of the winner, had made all in impressive style at Southwell last time, but he had paid the price with a 12lb hike in the weights. From a good draw here, he took them along towards the stands' side and justified the Handicapper's decision with a fine effort in third. All ground seems to come alike to him. (op 16-1)

Hogmaneigh(IRE), who did not have the race run to suit in Ireland last time, bounced back to something like his Portland-winning form and would have gone close to landing this with a clear run. His style of running means that he will sometimes not find a way through from off the pace, and that was the case this time as he was forced to follow the winner through and never really got clear daylight at any stage. (op 17-2)

River Falcon, who narrowly failed to catch Hogmaneigh in the Portland, had a 1lb pull in the weights with that rival, but he again finished one place behind him. Like the runner-up, he had a wide draw to contend with, though, and did not run badly in the circumstances. (tchd 16-1)

Tombi(USA) coped pretty well with the drop back to 5f, but one would imagine that he would have been happier over further. Official explanation: jockey said gelding suffered interference after leaving stalls (op 14-1)

Ishetoo ran a better race than he did in the Ayr Gold Cup, but it just looks like he is in the grip of the Handicapper now. (op 12-1)

Fullandby(IRE) was always likely to find this 5f at this track on the sharp side. (op 17-2)

Siren's Gift should have been at home around here, but she raced a bit too keenly out wide and did not get home. (op 9-2 tchd 7-2)

Evens And Odds(IRE) Official explanation: jockey said gelding suffered interference on leaving stalls (op 9-2 tchd 7-2)

Fathom Five(IRE) Official explanation: jockey said gelding suffered interference on leaving stalls

6654 SCOTBET.COM CONDITIONS STKS 1m 1f
3:45 (3:46) (Class 3) 3-Y-0+ **£7,771** (£2,312; £1,155; £577) **Stalls** High

Form RPR

1423 **1** **With Interest**[21] 6123 5-9-2 105 TedDurcan 7 95
(Saeed Bin Suroor) *hld up: hdwy on outer wl over 2f out: rdn wl over 1f out: drvn to chse ldr and hung rt ins fnl f: kpt on u.p to ld nr line* **5/6**[1]

2006 **2** shd **Jewelled Dagger (IRE)**[70] 4618 4-9-2 88 (b) LeeEnstone 6 95
(Miss L A Perratt) *led and sn clr: pushed along 3f out: rdn wl over 1f out: drvn ins fnl f: hdd and no ex nr line* **18/1**

0016 **3** 2¼ **Bolodenka (IRE)**[14] 6269 6-9-2 96 PaulHanagan 2 90
(R A Fahey) *hld up in tch: hdwy on inner 3f out: rdn wl over 1f out: drvn and kpt on same pce ins fnl f* **5/2**[2]

0606 **4** *nk* **Lucky Dance (BRZ)**[5] 6536 6-9-2 82 RobertWinston 3 89
(A G Foster) *chsd clr ldr: rdn along 3f out: drvn wl over 1f out: kpt on same pce ent fnl f* **28/1**

1002 **5** *shd* **Nanton (USA)**[7] 6476 6-8-11 89 KellyHarrison(5) 8 89
(J S Goldie) *hld up: effrt and pushed along 3f out: hdwy 2f out: swtchd lft and drvn over 1f out: kpt on ins fnl f: nrst fin* **11/2**[3]

2060 **6** *11* **Goodbye Mr Bond**[15] 6249 8-9-2 83 DavidAllan 4 65
(E J Alston) *hld up: hdwy 3f out: rdn over 2f out and nvr nr ldrs* **20/1**

4405 **7** *10* **Carry On Cleo**[23] 6040 3-8-0 48 (v) DanielleMooney(7) 1 38
(A Berry) *a in rr: sddle slipped and bhd fr 1/2-way* **200/1**

000 **8** *4* **Ignition**[26] 5968 6-8-4 46 (p) DeanHeslop(7) 5 29
(A Kirtley) *chsd ldng pair: rdn along 3f out: sn wknd* **200/1**

1m 56.95s (2.25) **Going Correction** +0.25s/f (Good)
WFA 3 from 4yo+ 4lb 8 Ran SP% **113.0**
Speed ratings (Par 107): **100,99,97,97,97 87,78,75**
toteswinger: 1&2 £4.20, 1&3 £1.50, 2&3 £4.30. CSF £18.08 TOTE £1.90: £1.02, £3.20, £1.40; EX 21.20 Trifecta £39.90 Pool £205.30 - 3.80 winning units.
Owner Godolphin **Bred** George Strawbridge **Trained** Newmarket, Suffolk
■ Stewards' Enquiry : Lee Enstone one-day ban: used whip without allowing time to respond (Oct 27)

FOCUS
An ordinary conditions race in which Jewelled Dagger almost took advantage of being granted an easy lead. The form is muddling with the runner-up the best guide backed up by the fourth.

NOTEBOOK
With Interest had 7lb in hand of his nearest rival on official ratings and looked to have a clear chance in this ordinary conditions race, but he made hard work of landing the odds, having let Jewelled Dagger, rated 15lb his inferior, enjoy the run of the race and quicken off the front. He had a good time of it out in Dubai last winter, and it would be a surprise if he is not once again a fixture at the carnival next year. (tchd 4-5, evens in a place)
Jewelled Dagger(IRE) would have ideally preferred better ground, but he was allowed to build up a substantial lead and he had them all on the stretch early in the straight. Keeping on well for pressure, he only narrowly failed to hold off the favourite's late challenge, but it was still a good ride from Enstone. (op 16-1 tchd 20-1)
Bolodenka(IRE) was a bit disappointing as he looked the main danger to the favourite on the figures and had been in fair form lately. A stronger pace might have suited him. (tchd 9-4 and 11-4)
Lucky Dance(BRZ), who went in pursuit of the leader in the straight, did not run badly. This trip was far more suitable than the 1m3f he ran over at Warwick last time. (op 33-1)
Nanton(USA), who was probably flattered in the Cambridgeshire as he had the best of the draw that day, may well have found this race coming plenty soon enough after that hard race. (op 15-2)
Goodbye Mr Bond had work to do at the weights, and he has not been at his best since finishing second at Haydock in June.
Carry On Cleo Official explanation: jockey said saddle slipped

6655 NATIONAL EXPRESS / EBF MAIDEN STKS 7f 30y
4:20 (4:22) (Class 5) 2-Y-O £3,885 (£1,156; £577; £288) Stalls High

Form RPR

0 **1** **Anthology**[29] 5857 2-9-3 0 TedDurcan 4 82
(B Smart) *a.p: effrt to chse ldr 3f out: rdn to chal 2f out: drvn to ld and edgd rt ins fnl f: hld on wl* **20/1**

32 **2** *nse* **Henderson Park**[45] 5387 2-9-3 0 PJMcDonald 11 82
(A G Foster) *led: pushed along 3f out: jnd and rdn 2f out: drvn: hdd and n.m.r ins fnl f: rallied wl towards fin* **2/1**[1]

2 **3** *3 1/2* **Goliaths Boy (IRE)**[16] 6229 2-9-3 0 TonyHamilton 9 75+
(R A Fahey) *trckd ldrs: effrt and n.m.r over 2f out: nt clr run over 1f out: rdn and kpt on ins fnl f: tk 3rd nr fin* **9/2**[3]

2202 **4** *hd* **Cosmic Sun**[21] 6101 2-9-3 82 PaulHanagan 14 75+
(R A Fahey) *trckd ldrs on inner: n.m.r on bnd over 3f out: effrt and n.m.r over 2f out: rdn and nt clr run whn swtchd lft over 1f out: sn drvn and kpt on same pce ent fnl f* **5/2**[2]

003 **5** *1 1/4* **Countess Zara (IRE)**[10] 6399 2-8-7 73 DavidProbert(5) 13 65+
(A M Balding) *trckd ldrs on inner: effrt over 2f out and sn nt clr run: swtchd lft and rdn over 1f out: kpt on same pce* **18/1**

6 *3 1/2* **Love Pegasus (USA)** 2-9-3 0 JimmyQuinn 2 61+
(M Johnston) *in tch whn n.m.r bnd over 3f out: rdn over 2f out: sn one pce* **16/1**

04 **7** *1 1/4* **Lock 'N' Load (IRE)**[78] 4380 2-8-12 0 TomEaves 8 53+
(B Smart) *in tch whn n.m.r and pushed wd on bnd over 3f out: rdn along over 2f and sn no hdwy* **28/1**

0 **8** *1 1/4* **Northside Prince (IRE)**[17] 6213 2-9-3 0 RobertWinston 10 55+
(G A Swinbank) *in tch whn nt clr run and hmpd on bnd over 3f out: rdn over 2f out and sn no imp* **50/1**

9 *shd* **Matraash (USA)** 2-9-3 0 RoystonFfrench 1 55
(M Johnston) *prom: effrt 3f out: rdn and ev ch over 2f out: sn drvn and wknd wl over 1f out* **13/2**

10 *3* **Paint Splash** 2-8-5 0 DeanHeslop(7) 3 42+
(T D Barron) *s.i.s and bhd: hdwy on outer whn carried wd on bnd over 3f out: sn outpcd after* **66/1**

11 *2 1/4* **Safari Song (IRE)** 2-9-3 0 PaulMulrennan 7 42
(B Smart) *s.i.s: a bhd* **33/1**

50 **12** *2 1/2* **Lady Dunhill (IRE)**[45] 5387 2-8-9 0 ow2 GaryBartley(5) 6 33
(J S Goldie) *a towards rr* **66/1**

13 *3/4* **Teddy West (IRE)** 2-9-0 0 RussellKennemore(3) 12 34
(Mrs L Williamson) *s.i.s: a bhd* **100/1**

1m 32.67s (2.37) **Going Correction** +0.25s/f (Good) 13 Ran SP% **121.7**
Speed ratings (Par 95): **96,95,91,91,90 86,84,83,83,79 77,74,73**
toteswinger: 1&2 £12.60, 1&3 £22.20, 2&3 £3.30. CSF £59.55 TOTE £25.60: £6.10, £1.50, £1.70; EX 74.20.
Owner H E Sheikh Rashid Bin Mohammed **Bred** Usk Valley Stud **Trained** Hambleton, N Yorks
■ Stewards' Enquiry : David Probert four-day ban: careless riding (Oct 27-30)

FOCUS
A fair maiden.

NOTEBOOK
Anthology continued Bryan Smart's good record with his two-year-olds at this track this season. Far too green to do himself justice on his debut, this 100,000gns son of Haafhd and half-brother to a mare who was placed in Graded company in the US, showed the benefit of that outing and just got the better of a final-furlong duel with the more experienced favourite. He has the pedigree to improve from two to three, and looks a useful prospect.
Henderson Park did not do a lot wrong in defeat, although he struggled a bit to handle these tight turns. Handicaps are now an option for him, although he has shown enough in his three starts to date to suggest he can win an ordinary maiden. (op 9-4 tchd 15-8, 5-2 in places)
Goliaths Boy(IRE), a promising second over 6f on his debut, looked likely to be suited by the extra furlong this time. Squeezed for room on more than one occasion inside the final two furlongs, he shaped a bit better than his finishing position suggests. (op 8-1)
Cosmic Sun was not really suited by the drop back to 7f on this sharp track. Switched off the rail when things got a bit tight two furlongs out, he stayed on well, but his overall profile makes him look pretty exposed now. (tchd 9-4)
Countess Zara(IRE) did not look particularly happy on the ground, and a quicker surface is likely to suit her in handicap company. (op 14-1)
Love Pegasus(USA), who cost $85,000 and is out of top-class mare who won three times in Grade 1 company on dirt in the US, showed signs of inexperience, but also ability, and he will be much more the finished article next season. (op 14-1)
Matraash(USA) threatened to get into the argument early in the straight, but he hung right through greenness and is another who will benefit from this debut outing. A half-brother to four winners, including smart performers Ajhar and Mutasallil, he is another who is likely to appreciate a quicker surface. (op 7-1 tchd 6-1)

6656 E.B.F./PLAY SCOTBETCASINO.COM NURSERY 5f
4:55 (4:55) (Class 4) (0-85,85) 2-Y-O £6,476 (£1,927; £963; £481) Stalls Low

Form RPR

0113 **1** **Visterre (IRE)**[48] 5306 2-9-1 79 TomEaves 2 83
(B Smart) *mde all: rdn along over 1f out: drvn ins fnl f and styd on gamely* **9/2**[3]

6236 **2** *3/4* **Musical Bridge**[25] 5989 2-8-10 77 RussellKennemore(3) 4 78
(Mrs L Williamson) *in tch: hdwy on outer over 1f out: sn rdn and styd on strly ins fnl f* **16/1**

5202 **3** *nk* **Fivefootnumberone (IRE)**[26] 5969 2-9-6 84 (v) RobertWinston 8 84
(J J Quinn) *cl up: rdn over 1f out and ev ch tl drvn and kpt on same pce ins fnl f* **4/1**[2]

604 **4** *hd* **Grissom (IRE)**[9] 6407 2-7-7 62 oh1 (t) DavidProbert(5) 9 62
(A Berry) *trckd ldrs: hdwy over 1f out: rdn and ev ch ent fnl f tl drvn and no ex last 100yds* **25/1**

2021 **5** *2 1/4* **Norfolk Broads (IRE)**[9] 6414 2-8-11 75 RoystonFfrench 3 66
(M Johnston) *cl up: rdn along 2f out: drvn and one pce appr fnl f* **3/1**[1]

0304 **6** *3/4* **Cutting Comments**[37] 5632 2-8-8 72 ow1 PaulMulrennan 6 61
(M Dods) *in tch: rdn along 1/2-way: sn btn* **4/1**[2]

3106 **7** *1* **Secret Venue**[26] 5969 2-8-9 73 TonyHamilton 5 58
(Jedd O'Keeffe) *cl up: rdn along 2f out: drvn and wknd over 1f out* **7/1**

6130 **8** *3/4* **Dispol Kylie (IRE)**[22] 6068 2-9-7 85 PaulFessey 1 67
(P T Midgley) *s.i.s: a in rr* **10/1**

63.80 secs (3.40) **Going Correction** +0.625s/f (Yiel) 8 Ran SP% **114.5**
Speed ratings (Par 97): **97,95,95,95,91 90,88,87**
toteswinger: 1&2 £14.70, 1&3 £3.50, 2&3 £10.90. CSF £70.95 CT £311.87 TOTE £5.00: £1.30, £5.10, £1.90; EX 94.10.
Owner Prime Equestrian **Bred** Miss Eileen Farrelly **Trained** Hambleton, N Yorks

FOCUS
A competitive little nursery on paper.

NOTEBOOK
Visterre(IRE), who had won her previous two starts at this track, bounced back to winning form. Showing speed from the gate and, with the rail to help throughout, she was always just in control. The winner did not get home over 5f at Beverley last time, but this sharper track suits her better, and confirmed that she can handle cut with no problem. (op 3-1)
Musical Bridge is still a maiden, but he has shown on more than one occasion that he has the ability to win a race of this sort. All the better for his return from a three-month break at Haydock last time, he saw his race out well once switched out wide. (op 20-1)
Fivefootnumberone(IRE), who improved for the fitting of a visor last time, confirmed his liking for cut in the ground with another solid effort. Things will not get any easier if he goes up another pound or two for this, though. (tchd 7-2)
Grissom(IRE), who had the widest draw to overcome, looks to be improving with racing, and this was another step in the right direction 1lb out of the handicap. His pedigree suggests he should get a bit further in time.
Norfolk Broads(IRE) was not suited by the drop back in trip, and as a daughter of Noverre it is unlikely that the ground was in her favour either. (op 7-2)
Cutting Comments, whose rider put up 1lb overweight, ran over 7f last time, and unsurprisingly he was taken off his feat over this sharp 5f. (op 5-1)

6657 NATIONAL EXPRESS H'CAP 1m 4f
5:25 (5:26) (Class 4) (0-80,79) 3-Y-O+ £6,476 (£1,927; £963; £481) Stalls High

Form RPR

4142 **1** **Grandad Bill (IRE)**[21] 6108 5-8-7 63 KellyHarrison(5) 2 73
(J S Goldie) *trckd ldrs: hdwy 3f out: led wl over 1f out: rdn clr ent fnl f: sn drvn and kpt on gamely towards fin* **7/1**[3]

0000 **2** *1/2* **Lets Roll**[21] 6107 7-9-9 74 DanielTudhope 8 83
(C W Thornton) *hld up towards rr: hdwy on outer over 2f out: rdn over 1f out: drvn to chse wnr ins fnl f: kpt on towards fin* **16/1**

2421 **3** *5* **Chookie Hamilton**[26] 5971 4-8-12 63 TomEaves 9 64
(Miss L A Perratt) *hld up and bhd: hdwy 3f out: swtchd outside and rdn to chse ldrs wl over 1f out: drvn and edgd rt ent fnl f: kpt on towards fin* **7/1**[3]

0501 **4** *1/2* **Packers Hill (IRE)**[7] 6485 4-9-0 65 PJMcDonald 6 65
(G A Swinbank) *midfield: smooth hdwy on outer to join ldrs 1/2-way: led wl over 2f out: rdn and hdd wl over 1f out: sn drvn and kpt on same pce* **8/1**

1223 **5** *1/2* **Timocracy**[9] 6416 3-9-4 76 RoystonFfrench 10 75
(M Johnston) *cl up: rdn along 3f out and ev ch tl drvn wl over 1f out and sn one pce* **5/2**[1]

3521 **6** *5* **Dar Es Salaam**[22] 6078 4-10-0 79 JimmyQuinn 11 70
(J S Goldie) *hld up in midfield: hdwy 3f out: rdn along 2f out: sn drvn and no imp* **5/1**[2]

/1-0 **7** *hd* **Ifatfirst (IRE)**[41] 5543 5-8-9 60 oh2 SaleemGolam 12 51
(J S Goldie) *chsd ldrs: rdn along on inner 3f out: wknd over 2f out* **14/1**

043 **8** *1/2* **Luna Landing**[21] 6113 5-9-11 76 PaulMulrennan 14 66
(Jedd O'Keeffe) *led: rdn along 4f out: drvn and hdd over 2f out: grad wknd* **9/1**

-404 **9** *nk* **Sin City**[85] 4146 5-9-8 73 PaulHanagan 13 63
(R A Fahey) *hld up: a towards rr* **9/1**

010 **10** *1/2* **Jim Martin**[7] 6493 3-8-7 68 NeilBrown(3) 1 57
(Miss L A Perratt) *midfield: hdwy on outer over 3f out: rdn along wl over 2f out and sn wknd* **25/1**

0500 **11** *3 1/4* **Baillieborough (IRE)**[21] 6136 9-8-11 62 (b) DavidAllan 5 46
(B Ellison) *a in rr* **40/1**

1- **12** *15* **Commit To Memory**[34] 5735 3-9-4 76 TedDurcan 3 36
(Andrew Oliver, Ire) *chsd ldrs: rdn along 3f out: sn wknd* **25/1**

2m 41.2s (1.50) **Going Correction** +0.25s/f (Good)
WFA 3 from 4yo+ 7lb 12 Ran SP% **124.0**
Speed ratings (Par 105): **105,104,101,101,100 97,97,96,96,96 94,84**
toteswinger: 1&2 £25.60, 1&3 £7.70, 2&3 £26.50. CSF £116.12 CT £830.13 TOTE £6.80: £3.00, £3.90, £1.90; EX 100.50 Place 6 £214.78, Place 5 £33.31..
Owner Tough Construction Ltd **Bred** M Hosokawa **Trained** Uplawmoor, E Renfrews

FOCUS
They went a good gallop here, and the form looks solid for the grade rated around the third and fourth.
Ifatfirst(IRE) Official explanation: jockey said gelding was unsuited by the good to soft (soft in places) ground

Luna Landing Official explanation: jockey said gelding was unsuited by the good to soft (soft in places) ground
T/Plt: £75.80 to a £1 stake. Pool: £73,334.01. 705.41 winning tickets. T/Qpdt: £10.60 to a £1 stake. Pool: £4,202.80. 292.24 winning tickets. JR

6628 **WOLVERHAMPTON (A.W)** (L-H)
Saturday, October 11

OFFICIAL GOING: Standard
Wind: Light behind Weather: Rain clearing

6658 FREE CASINO CHIPS @ FREEBETS.CO.UK H'CAP 5f 20y(P)
6:50 (6:50) (Class 5) (0-70,70) 3-Y-0+ £3,238 (£963; £481; £240) Stalls Low

Form RPR
3543 1 **Chelsea Girl**[18] 6192 3-8-8 **60** .... SteveDrowne 11 75
(C G Cox) *hld up: pushed along 1/2-way: hdwy over 1f out: rdn and hung lft ins fnl f: r.o to ld nr fin* **12/1**
4000 2 ½ **Wibbadune (IRE)**[10] 6388 4-9-2 **68** .... AdamKirby 2 81
(D Shaw) *chsd ldrs: led 1f out: sn rdn: hdd nr fin* **16/1**
030 3 2½ **Another Socket**[24] 6011 3-9-2 **68** .... GrahamGibbons 7 72
(E S McMahon) *dwlt: hdwy over 3f out: led over 1f out: sn rdn and hdd: no ex ins fnl f* **8/1**
606 4 1½ **Comptonspirit**[10] 6388 4-9-0 **66** .... J-PGuillambert 12 65
(B P J Baugh) *s.i.s: hld up: hdwy over 1f out: r.o: nrst fin* **10/1**
2635 5 1½ **The Little Fizzer (IRE)**[9] 6405 3-8-4 **56** .... LiamJones 13 49+
(P D Evans) *prom: lost pl 4f out: nt clr run wl over 1f out: styd on ins fnl f* **14/1**
2122 6 1 **Matterofact (IRE)**[10] 6388 5-9-4 **70** .... TGMcLaughlin 8 60
(M S Saunders) *chsd ldr tl led 2f out: sn rdn and hdd: wknd ins fnl f* **7/1**[3]
-260 7 ¾ **Blakeshall Diamond**[61] 4922 3-9-4 **70** .... JerryO'Dwyer 3 57
(K G Wingrove) *hld up: hdwy over 1f out: wknd ins fnl f* **40/1**
1350 8 3¾ **Grand Palace (IRE)**[95] 3819 5-8-13 **65** ....(v) DarrenWilliams 6 39
(D Shaw) *prom: lost pl over 2f out: wkng whn edgd lft over 1f out* **28/1**
0012 9 ½ **Edie Superstar (USA)**[17] 6209 3-8-13 **65** ....(v) DaneO'Neill 4 37
(M A Magnusson) *led 3f: sn rdn: wknd fnl f* **7/2**[1]
5624 10 ½ **Bishopbriggs (USA)**[21] 6137 3-9-4 **70** .... TonyCulhane 5 40
(S Parr) *chsd ldrs: pushed along 1/2-way: sn wknd* **4/1**[2]
3465 11 1¼ **Kinout (IRE)**[20] 6150 3-8-13 **65** ....(b[1]) ChrisCatlin 9 31
(K A Ryan) *chsd ldrs: rdn and wknd over 1f out* **9/1**
040 12 8 **Sofinella (IRE)**[9] 6418 5-8-4 **56** oh2 .... CatherineGannon 1 —
(A W Carroll) *chsd ldrs: lost pl 1/2-way: wknd 2f out* **22/1**

61.91 secs (-0.39) **Going Correction** 0.0s/f (Stan) **12** Ran SP% **115.4**
Speed ratings (Par 103): **103,102,98,95,93 91,90,84,83,83 81,68**
toteswinger: 1&2 £1.70, 1&3 £0, 2&3 £17.90. CSF £180.30 CT £1650.98 TOTE £14.70: £3.00, £7.30, £3.30; EX 110.80.
Owner A D Spence **Bred** Hedsor Stud **Trained** Lambourn, Berks

FOCUS
A wet day meant the surface had become more compact and therefore riding slightly faster than normal, though the time of this was just outside standard, despite the ferocious early pace. This looked fairly competitive for the grade with 5lb covering the top nine runners, many of whom came into this in fair form. The speed horses dropped away in the straight as the closers took over and the form is best rated around the placed horses.
The Little Fizzer(IRE) Official explanation: jockey said filly was denied a clear run
Sofinella(IRE) Official explanation: jockey said mare hung left

6659 FREE BETTING @ FREEBETS.CO.UK CLAIMING STKS 1m 1f 103y(P)
7:20 (7:23) (Class 5) 3-Y-0+ £3,238 (£963; £481; £240) Stalls Low

Form RPR
0014 1 **Blacktoft (USA)**[25] 5994 5-9-8 71 .... J-PGuillambert 6 83
(S C Williams) *hld up: plld hrd: hdwy over 2f out: led over 1f out: sn rdn and hung rt: styd on* **13/2**
1450 2 1¼ **Hilbre Court (USA)**[8] 6452 3-8-12 77 .... NickyMackay 3 75
(B J Meehan) *chsd ldrs: rdn over 2f out: styd on same pce ins fnl f* **10/3**[1]
5050 3 ¾ **Gold Prospect**[35] 5699 4-9-7 76 .... TPQueally 7 78
(M L W Bell) *hld up: hdwy over 3f out: ev ch over 1f out: sn rdn: hung lft ins fnl f: nt run on* **5/1**[3]
0000 4 ½ **Rapid City**[15] 6243 5-9-0 76 .... JerryO'Dwyer 8 70
(Miss J Feilden) *chsd ldr tl led over 2f out: rdn and hdd over 1f out: no ex ins fnl f* **15/2**
21-0 5 4 **King's Majesty (IRE)**[21] 6134 6-8-5 69 .... LanceBetts(7) 4 59
(T J Pitt) *hld up in tch: rdn over 2f out: wknd ins fnl f* **10/1**
3-20 6 11 **Elliwan**[22] 6070 3-9-3 78 .... DaleGibson 2 46
(M W Easterby) *hld up: nvr nrr* **16/1**
0061 7 nk **Saviour Sand (IRE)**[88] 4066 4-9-12 70 ....(b) RobertHavlin 11 50
(D R C Elsworth) *sn led: hdd over 2f out: sn rdn: wknd over 1f out* **16/1**
2000 8 2¼ **August Gale (USA)**[11] 6352 3-8-7 77 .... BradleyRoper(7) 9 38
(G P Kelly) *chsd ldrs: rdn 1/2-way: wknd 3f out* **66/1**
3054 9 3½ **Peruvian Prince (USA)**[13] 6312 6-9-4 72 .... JamieMoriarty 1 30
(R A Fahey) *chsd ldrs: rdn over 3f out: wknd over 2f out* **7/2**[2]
1/40 10 12 **Permanent Way (IRE)**[61] 1076 5-9-4 85 ....(t) SteveDrowne 10 4
(R Lee) *hld up: rdn over 4f out: sn lost tch* **25/1**
00- 11 69 **Quorn Master**[355] 6385 6-8-12 0 .... PaulFitzsimons 12 —
(Mrs P Ford) *bolted bef s: hld up: racd keenly: rdn over 5f out: sn wknd* **200/1**
00 12 3¾ **Prophet's Star**[16] 6226 3-8-8 0 ....(bt) ChrisCatlin 13 —
(H J L Dunlop) *hld up: a bhd: lost tch fr 1/2-way* **66/1**

2m 0.16s (-1.54) **Going Correction** 0.0s/f (Stan)
WFA 3 from 4yo+ 4lb **12** Ran SP% **115.2**
Speed ratings (Par 103): **106,104,104,103,100 90,90,88,85,74 13,9**
toteswinger: 1&2 £7.20, 1&3 £8.00, 2&3 £2.90. CSF £27.24 TOTE £6.50: £2.50, £2.30, £2.40; EX 39.80.Hilbre Court was claimed by B. P. J. Baugh for £10,000; King's Majesty was claimed by Gary P. Martin for £6,000; Rapid City was claimed by A. J. McCabe for £8,000
Owner Chris Watkins And David N Reynolds **Bred** Paradigm Thoroughbreds Inc **Trained** Newmarket, Suffolk

FOCUS
Quite a competitive claimer in which they again went a fairly strong pace throughout and the form looks reasonable for the grade rated around the first three. Once again the jockeys elected to come down the middle of the track in the straight, suggesting the inside is not the place to be right now.

Prophet's Star Official explanation: jockey said gelding had a breathing problem

6660 FREE POKER CHIPS @ FREEBETS.CO.UK MEDIAN AUCTION MAIDEN STKS 7f 32y(P)
7:50 (7:52) (Class 6) 3-5-Y-0 £2,729 (£806; £403) Stalls High

Form RPR
0345 1 **Duty Doctor**[50] 5218 3-8-12 67 .... WilliamBuick 6 67+
(S Kirk) *chsd ldrs: outpcd 1/2-way: hdwy over 1f out: hung lft ins fnl f: str run to ld post* **4/1**[2]
3232 2 *nse* **Mazaris (IRE)**[17] 6206 3-9-3 72 .... DaneO'Neill 11 72
(L M Cumani) *chsd ldr over 5f out tl led and hung lft over 1f out: sn rdn: hdd post* **7/4**[1]
30- 3 1½ **Red Expresso (IRE)**[523] 1540 3-9-3 0 .... J-PGuillambert 10 68
(M L W Bell) *chsd ldrs: rdn 1/2-way: outpcd over 1f out: hung lft and styd on u.p ins fnl f* **8/1**
3324 4 ¾ **Seventh Cavalry (IRE)**[22] 6091 3-9-3 70 ....(b) TPQueally 12 66
(H R A Cecil) *sn led: rdn and hdd over 1f out: hmpd sn after: no ex wl ins fnl f* **4/1**[2]
04 5 1½ **My Mate Mal**[21] 6114 4-8-12 0 .... LanceBetts(7) 3 62
(B Ellison) *prom: rdn over 2f out: styd on same pce fnl f* **20/1**
2260 6 2½ **Great Knight (IRE)**[38] 5616 3-9-3 62 .... TonyCulhane 9 55
(W J Haggas) *chsd ldrs: rdn over 2f out: wknd fnl f* **15/2**[3]
6 7 6 **Dashing Daniel**[15] 6254 3-9-0 0 .... LukeMorris(3) 8 39
(N J Vaughan) *s.i.s: hdwy 1/2-way: rdn and hung rt over 2f out: wknd over 1f out* **25/1**
8 1 **Mr Skipiton (IRE)** 3-9-3 0 .... JerryO'Dwyer 4 36
(B J McMath) *dwlt: outpcd* **25/1**
4000 9 2½ **Sunshine Lady (IRE)**[7] 6492 3-8-12 50 ....(v) RobertHavlin 2 24
(D Haydn Jones) *s.s: outpcd: effrt on outer over 2f out: sn wknd* **50/1**
00 10 1½ **Dancing Rhythm**[58] 5023 3-9-3 0 .... TGMcLaughlin 7 25
(M S Saunders) *s.i.s: a in rr* **150/1**
0 11 8 **Arikinui**[47] 5361 3-8-12 0 .... DarrenWilliams 1 —
(K R Burke) *dwlt: outpcd: bhd fr 1/2-way* **40/1**

1m 29.86s (0.26) **Going Correction** 0.0s/f (Stan)
WFA 3 from 4yo 2lb **11** Ran SP% **116.8**
Speed ratings (Par 101): **98,97,96,95,93 90,83,82,79,78 69**
toteswinger: 1&2 £1.20, 1&3 £7.30, 2&3 £3.60. CSF £10.58 TOTE £4.90: £1.50, £1.30, £2.80; EX 10.90.
Owner J C Smith **Bred** Littleton Stud **Trained** Upper Lambourn, Berks

FOCUS
Not a strong maiden by any means but a few of these had achieved a fair level of form and the principals set the level.
Dashing Daniel Official explanation: jockey said gelding hung right throughout

6661 FREEBETS.CO.UK MAIDEN AUCTION STKS 5f 216y(P)
8:20 (8:22) (Class 5) 2-Y-0 £3,885 (£1,156; £577; £288) Stalls Low

Form RPR
002 1 **Ditto Ditto**[11] 6351 2-8-10 67 .... TPQueally 4 69
(D R Lanigan) *chsd ldr tl led over 4f out: hrd rdn and hung rt ins fnl f: all out* **7/1**[3]
05 2 *shd* **Trigger McCann**[14] 6281 2-8-9 0 .... PatCosgrave 10 68
(J S Moore) *led: hdd over 4f out: chsd wnr: hrd rdn and ev ch ins fnl f: styd on* **11/8**[1]
4242 3 *hd* **Black N Brew (USA)**[66] 4729 2-8-11 71 .... DaneO'Neill 5 69
(J R Best) *chsd ldrs: rdn over 2f out: r.o towards fin* **15/8**[2]
000 4 2¾ **Venetian Lady**[32] 5771 2-8-8 35 .... TPO'Shea 3 58
(Mrs A Duffield) *hld up: plld hrd: hdwy over 2f out: rdn and hung lft fnl f: styd on* **80/1**
06 5 1 **Shirley High**[7] 6488 2-8-4 0 .... LiamJones 2 51
(P Howling) *prom: rdn over 1f out: no ex ins fnl f* **8/1**
0 6 ¾ **Trusted Venture (USA)**[17] 6197 2-8-3 0 .... AndreaAtzeni(7) 9 55
(J R Best) *trckd ldrs: plld hrd: stdd and lost pl over 4f out: hung lft and styd on fr over 1f out* **25/1**
00 7 10 **Nala (USA)**[10] 6375 2-8-8 0 .... SteveDrowne 7 23
(J R Best) *sn pushed along in rr: bhd fr 1/2-way* **33/1**
8 1¾ **Kathanikki Girl (IRE)** 2-8-5 0 .... CatherineGannon 6 14
(Mrs L Williamson) *s.s: outpcd* **40/1**
5350 9 ¾ **Amorachy**[15] 6247 2-9-0 63 ....(p) ChrisCatlin 8 21
(K A Ryan) *hld up in tch: rdn and wknd over 2f out* **14/1**

1m 15.72s (0.72) **Going Correction** 0.0s/f (Stan) **9** Ran SP% **117.6**
Speed ratings (Par 95): **95,94,94,90,89 88,75,72,71**
toteswinger: 1&2 £7.40, 1&3 £2.60, 2&3 £2.90. CSF £17.12 TOTE £5.00: £1.70, £1.20, £1.10; EX 28.30.
Owner J J May **Bred** J J May, Esterdale Stud **Trained** Newmarket, Suffolk
■ Stewards' Enquiry : Pat Cosgrave three-day ban: used whip with excessive frequency and in the incorrect place (Oct 27-29)

FOCUS
No strength in depth here and the absence of morning favourite Dakota Hills detracted further from the quality of this contest.

NOTEBOOK
Ditto Ditto stepped up on his recent Southwell effort here, on this fourth start, to battle on gamely for a first success. Always on the sharp end, he looked in trouble as Trigger McCann loomed large on the turn for home but he responded really well to pressure to see off that rival and the late finish of Black N Brew, despite being rated 4lb inferior to the latter. (op 6-1)
Trigger McCann did little wrong, forcing the winner to pull out all the stops and, with the strong possibility of more to come, he will find a race soon. (op 7-4)
Black N Brew(USA) looked to be making good headway in the final furlong but he couldn't reel in the front two. Another furlong would suit him ideally. (op 7-4 tchd 2-1)
Venetian Lady, trying Polytrack for the first time, shaped with much more encouragement than in her three previous starts, finishing her race in eyecatching style. (op 66-1)
Shirley High did not run badly and arguably this was her best effort so far. She now qualifies for a handicap mark. (op 10-1 tchd 11-1)
Trusted Venture(USA) dropping in trip on only this second start and all-weather debut, was too keen early before running on late.

6662 FREE SPORTS BETS @ FREEBETS.CO.UK H'CAP 1m 4f 50y(P)
8:50 (8:50) (Class 5) (0-75,74) 3-Y-0+ £3,238 (£963; £481; £240) Stalls Low

Form RPR
30-0 1 **Five Two**[30] 5846 5-9-0 **63** ....(t) TPO'Shea 12 72
(Gavin Patrick Cromwell, Ire) *s.i.s: hld up: hdwy over 1f out: hung lft and r.o u.p to ld wl ins fnl f* **33/1**
0020 2 1¼ **Mustajed**[17] 6203 7-9-8 **74** .... JamesMillman(3) 7 81
(B R Millman) *chsd ldrs: rdn over 3f out: led 1f out: hdd wl ins fnl f* **7/1**
3351 3 2¼ **Summer Lodge**[7] 6493 5-9-3 **66** .... PatCosgrave 8 69
(A J McCabe) *chsd ldrs: led over 2f out: rdn and hdd over 1f out: styd on same pce* **9/2**[2]

0100 **4** *1* **Inch Lodge**[95] 3824 6-9-8 **71**..(t) PaulEddery 1 72
(Miss D Mountain) *chsd ldr over 3f: remained handy: led over 1f out: sn rdn and hdd: no ex ins fnl f* **20/1**

3005 **5** *3/4* **Silver Blue (IRE)**[34] 4791 5-9-4 **67**............................ CatherineGannon 2 67
(W K Goldsworthy) *hld up: hdwy u.p over 3f out: styd on same pce appr fnl f* **22/1**

330 **6** *1/2* **Jackie Kiely**[32] 5783 7-9-8 **71**.....................................(t) J-PGuillambert 5 70
(R Brotherton) *hld up: hdwy over 1f out: nt trble ldrs* **14/1**

0-32 **7** *nk* **Babilu**[54] 5155 3-9-3 **73**.. DaneO'Neill 6 72
(A G Newcombe) *hld up: hdwy over 4f out: rdn over 1f out: edgd lft and styd on same pce* **13/2**

0610 **8** *4* **Three Boars**[200] 1017 6-9-8 **71**....................................(b) ChrisCatlin 4 64
(S Gollings) *hld up: sme hdwy 2f out: wknd fnl f* **25/1**

-032 **9** *2 3/4* **Wait For The Light**[17] 6210 4-9-9 **72**........................ SteveDrowne 3 60
(Mrs S Leech) *led: rdn and hdd over 2f out: wknd fnl f* **5/1**[3]

520- **10** *2 1/4* **Calatagan (IRE)**[178] 6802 9-9-3 **66**........................... JamieMoriarty 11 51
(J M Jefferson) *prom: chsd ldr over 8f out: rdn and wknd over 2f out* **33/1**

0241 **P** **Lindy Lou**[25] 6007 4-9-4 **67**.. GeorgeBaker 9 —
(C F Wall) *hld up: hdwy 4f out: sn rdn: wknd 2f out: p.u and dismntd fnl f* **9/4**[1]

2m 40.24s (-0.86) **Going Correction** 0.0s/f (Stan)
WFA 3 from 4yo+ 7lb 11 Ran SP% **117.0**
Speed ratings (Par 103): **102,101,99,99,98 98,97,95,93,91** —
toteswinger: 1&2 £0, 1&3 £27.20, 2&3 £15.10. CSF £234.77 CT £1253.68 TOTE £18.20: £4.50, £2.00, £1.90; EX 527.90.
Owner W T Racing Syndicate **Bred** Darley **Trained** Balrath, Co. Meath

FOCUS
A turn-up here but otherwise the form is fairly straightforward rated through the third.
Lindy Lou Official explanation: jockey said filly finished distressed

6663 FREE BETS @ FREEBETS.CO.UK H'CAP 1m 141y(P)
9:20 (9:21) (Class 4) (0-80,88) 3-Y-0+ **£5,180** (£1,541; £770; £384) **Stalls** Low

Form RPR

2106 **1** **Alexander Huricane (IRE)**[13] 6314 4-9-3 **75**.................... ChrisCatlin 5 84+
(K A Ryan) *hld up: racd keenly: nt clr run over 2f out: hdwy over 1f out: rdn to ld ins fnl f: r.o* **9/1**[3]

0104 **2** *nk* **Wisdom's Kiss**[26] 5965 4-9-2 **74**.............................(b) GrahamGibbons 12 82
(J D Bethell) *hld up: rdn over 3f out: hdwy u.p over 1f out: ev ch ins fnl f: r.o* **12/1**

3511 **3** *1/2* **St Trinians**[7] 6491 3-9-12 **88**.. LPKeniry 9 95
(E F Vaughan) *chsd ldrs: led 2f out: sn rdn: hdd and unable qckn ins fnl f* **4/1**[2]

3520 **4** *1/2* **Claret And Amber**[1] 6629 6-8-8 **66** oh4.................... CatherineGannon 2 72
(W K Goldsworthy) *hld up: hdwy over 1f out: edgd lft: r.o* **12/1**

6/01 **5** *3 1/4* **What's Up Doc (IRE)**[40] 5577 7-9-3 **75**........................ WilliamBuick 4 74
(Mrs T J Hill) *chsd ldrs: led and hung lft fr over 5f out: rdn and hdd over 1f out: wknd fnl f* **16/1**

3311 **6** *2* **Internationaldebut (IRE)**[8] 6452 3-9-6 **82**..................... TonyCulhane 1 76
(S Parr) *trckd ldrs: rdn over 2f out: wknd fnl f* **9/4**[1]

3121 **7** *nk* **Spate River**[9] 6417 3-9-6 **82**.. GeorgeBaker 11 76
(C F Wall) *prom: pushed along over 3f out: wknd over 1f out* **4/1**[2]

41/5 **8** *1 1/4* **Keel (IRE)**[11] 6356 5-8-10 **68**.. LiamJones 10 59
(C R Dore) *hld up: rdn over 3f out: a in rr* **40/1**

6100 **9** *2 1/2* **Mont Cervin**[8] 6450 3-8-10 **72**.....................................(t) PaulEddery 7 57
(Ian Williams) *s.i.s: a in rr* **33/1**

6400 **10** *nk* **Royal Island (IRE)**[7] 6491 6-8-12 **70**..........................(b[1]) VinceSlattery 6 55
(M G Quinlan) *hld up: rdn over 2f out: a in rr* **22/1**

3403 **11** *18* **Atabaas Pride**[7] 6491 3-8-12 **74**................................ J-PGuillambert 3 19
(M Johnston) *led: hdd over 5f out: chsd ldr tl rdn over 2f out: sn wknd* **9/1**[3]

5000 **12** *2 1/2* **Jord (IRE)**[39] 5594 4-8-12 **70**...................................... PatCosgrave 8 10
(A J McCabe) *chsd ldr to over 5f out: rdn over 3f out: wknd over 2f out* **50/1**

1m 49.34s (-1.16) **Going Correction** 0.0s/f (Stan)
WFA 3 from 4yo+ 4lb 12 Ran SP% **123.7**
Speed ratings (Par 105): **105,104,104,103,100 99,98,97,95,95 79,77**
toteswinger: 1&2 £48.20, 1&3 £4.60, 2&3 £11.20. CSF £112.97 CT £515.66 TOTE £11.10: £4.00, £3.80, £2.40; EX 110.50 Place 6 £160.82, Place 5 £ 26.36.
Owner N O'Callaghan, R Fagan & R O'Callaghan **Bred** Mrs M Fox **Trained** Hambleton, N Yorks

FOCUS
A fair handicap and a finish dominated by horses that came from off the pace. The solid runner-up is the best guide to the level.
T/Plt: £230.10 to a £1 stake. Pool: £91,186.43. 289.26 winning tickets. T/Qpdt: £14.70 to a £1 stake. Pool: £8,586.17. 430.78 winning tickets. CR

6236 MAISONS-LAFFITTE (R-H)
Saturday, October 11

OFFICIAL GOING: Soft

6664a PRIX LE FABULEUX (LISTED RACE) (STRAIGHT) 1m 1f
3:30 (3:32) 3-Y-O **£20,221** (£8,088; £6,066; £4,044; £2,022)

RPR

1 **Virtual**[28] 5896 3-8-12 .... CSoumillon 1 102
(J H M Gosden) *prom early: shuffled bk towards rr on ins: hdwy 1 1/2f out: 4th whn no room briefly on rail 100yds out: led cl home: cosily* **10/1**[1]

2 *nk* **Lady Deauville (FR)**[6] 6521 3-8-13 .... FrancisNorton 7 103
(P A Blockley) *sn pressing ldr: led over 2f out: sn hrd rdn: hdd and no ex cl home* **14/1**[2]

3 *shd* **Birbone (FR)**[59] 5001 3-8-12 .... OPeslier 10 101
(J-M Beguigne, France)

4 *1 1/2* **Trois Rois (FR)**[132] 2654 3-9-2 .... DBonilla 6 102
(F Head, France)

5 *snk* **Lindner (GER)**[20] 6156 3-9-2 .... ASuborics 4 102
(W Hickst, Germany)

6 *hd* **Jamindar (IRE)**[39] 3-8-12 .... SPasquier 3 98
(A Lyon, France)

7 *shd* **Starlish (IRE)**[49] 5302 3-9-2 .... ACrastus 2 101
(E Lellouche, France)

8 *1 1/2* **Taverny**[50] 3-8-12 .... TJarnet 11 94
(S Wattel, France)

9 *hd* **Koenigsberg (USA)**[109] 3-8-12 .... TThulliez 12 94
(N Clement, France)

10 *6* **Ballerina Blue (IRE)**[21] 3-8-8 .... MGuyon 5 77
(Y De Nicolay, France)

0 **Iolith (GER)**[39] 3-8-12 .... JVictoire 9 —
(A Fabre, France)

0 **Ottomax (GER)**[21] 3-8-12 .... DBoeuf 8 —
(Andreas Lowe, Germany)

1m 51.3s (-3.40) **12** Ran SP% **15.8**
PARI-MUTUEL: WIN 11.20; PL 3.80, 4.50, 4.60; DF 71.90.
Owner Cheveley Park Stud **Bred** Cheveley Park Stud Ltd **Trained** Newmarket, Suffolk
■ Stewards' Enquiry : Francis Norton €200 fine: whip abuse

NOTEBOOK
Virtual, held up for much of the way, had nowhere to go at the furlong and a half marker. A gap finally appeared on the rail and he burst through to just hold off the eventual second. He will apparently not run again this season, but remains in training as a four-year-old.
Lady Deauville(FR), quickly out of the gates, sat just behind the leader until the furlong and a half marker. She looked to have nothing left in reserve at that point but rallied throughout the final furlong and galloped on strongly, ultimately just be pipped by the fast-finishing winner. This was her second race in a week and she could now go for the Premio Lydio Tesio in Rome on October 26.

6327 BATH (L-H)
Sunday, October 12

OFFICIAL GOING: Good to soft (good in places) changing to good (good to soft in places) after race 2 (2.45)
Wind: Gentle breeze Weather: Sunny

6665 TOTEPLACEPOT NOVICE STKS 1m 5y
2:10 (2:11) (Class 5) 2-Y-O **£3,756** (£1,117; £558; £278) **Stalls** Low

Form RPR

01 **1** **Classic Vintage (USA)**[31] 5842 2-9-5 83........................ JimCrowley 8 87
(Mrs A J Perrett) *towards rr: hdwy over 2f out: shkn up to ld jst ins fnl f: styd on wl: pushed out* **3/1**[2]

2106 **2** *1 1/2* **Wilbury Star (IRE)**[44] 5447 2-9-2 81............................. RyanMoore 1 81
(R Hannon) *led: rdn over 2f out: hdd jst ins fnl f: kpt on but sn hld by wnr* **9/2**[3]

232 **3** *1 1/2* **Miss Sophisticat**[11] 6391 2-8-7 76.................................. PaulDoe 6 68
(W J Knight) *prom: rdn over 2f out: ev ch and hung rt over 1f out: kpt on same pce fnl f* **7/4**[1]

6210 **4** *1* **Blazing Buck**[32] 5791 2-9-2 76...................................... JimmyQuinn 9 75
(H J L Dunlop) *chsd ldrs: rdn over 2f out: kpt on same pce fnl f* **6/1**

5 *3 3/4* **Midnight Bay** 2-8-8 0.. TonyCulhane 7 59
(M R Channon) *towards rr: rdn 3f out: styd on fnl f: nvr a danger* **12/1**

0 **6** *3/4* **Bishop Rock (USA)**[23] 6080 2-8-12 0............................. PaulMulrennan 10 61
(M H Tompkins) *in tch: rdn 3f out: one pce fnl 2f* **16/1**

0 **7** *7* **Viking Rock (IRE)**[13] 6333 2-8-12 0............................... FrancisNorton 5 46
(M Salaman) *t.k.h: a towards rr* **40/1**

00 **8** *2 3/4* **Haafhds Delight (IRE)**[15] 6273 2-8-7 0.......................... LiamJones 2 35
(W M Brisbourne) *chsd ldrs: rdn over 2f out: wknd over 1f out* **100/1**

9 *10* **Aligned** 2-8-0 0.. LukeMorris[(3)] 3 9
(A W Carroll) *sn struggling: a in rr* **33/1**

0 **10** *3/4* **Hart House**[26] 5989 2-8-5 0 ow1...................................... KevinGhunowa[(3)] 4 12
(C J Gray) *in tch tl wknd 3f out* **100/1**

1m 42.68s (1.88) **Going Correction** +0.15s/f (Good) **10** Ran SP% **114.8**
Speed ratings (Par 95): **96,94,93,92,88 87,80,77,67,67**
toteswinger: 1&2 £2.70, 1&3 £1.90, 2&3 £3.00. CSF £16.44 TOTE £3.90: £1.70, £1.80, £1.10; EX 23.80 Trifecta £59.90 Pool: £242.14 - 2.99 winning units..
Owner R & P Scott A & J Powell Gallagher Stud **Bred** Gallagher's Stud **Trained** Pulborough, W Sussex

FOCUS
No strength in depth here. The winner is progressive and the form is best rated around those in the frame behind the winner.

NOTEBOOK
Classic Vintage(USA) responded to pressure and stayed on strongly inside the final furlong to get well on top. Both of his victories have come with a little give underfoot, and it will be interesting to see if this Derby entry can progress again. He is bred to stay 1m2f and should be even better as a three-year-old. (op 5-2)
Wilbury Star(IRE), twice well held off a mark of 83 since going handicapping, was made plenty of use of on this step up to 1m, and he saw the trip out well enough without being able to fend off Classic Vintage. He is not the easiest to place right now. (op 5-1)
Miss Sophisticat, twice a runner-up in maidens and placed off a mark of 73 in a nursery, looked a big player in receipt of 12lb from Classic Vintage, and she had every chance, but could find no extra inside the final furlong. A modest maiden should come her way at some point, although she is likely to remain vulnerable to improvers. (op 2-1)
Blazing Buck, a Warwick maiden winner, made no show on his recent handicap debut, but showed that running to be all wrong with a creditable fourth. He seemed to improve for the extra furlong. (op 13-2 tchd 5-1)

6666 BET TOTEPOOL ON ALL UK RACING NURSERY 5f 11y
2:45 (2:46) (Class 5) (0-75,81) 2-Y-O **£3,885** (£1,156; £577; £288) **Stalls** Centre

Form RPR

4101 **1** **Go Go Green (IRE)**[6] 6525 2-9-13 **81** 6ex...................... TonyCulhane 10 85+
(S Parr) *mde all: rdn over 1f out: r.o wl: readily* **6/1**[3]

0200 **2** *1 1/4* **Val De Flores**[25] 6017 2-8-8 **62**.. LPKeniry 9 62
(E F Vaughan) *prom: rdn over 3f out: kpt on but nt pce to chal wnr* **16/1**

0136 **3** *1/2* **Asian Tale (IRE)**[51] 5228 2-9-7 **75**................................ JimmyQuinn 1 73
(A B Haynes) *mid-div: rdn over 3f out: hdwy over 2f out: kpt on fnl f* **16/1**

6160 **4** *nk* **Transcentral**[15] 6274 2-9-1 **69**...................................... LiamJones 2 66
(W M Brisbourne) *chsd ldrs: rdn over 3f out: battled on: no ex ins fnl f* **33/1**

4040 **5** *nse* **Red Rossini (IRE)**[8] 6469 2-9-7 **75**............................... RyanMoore 11 72
(R Hannon) *chsd ldrs: rdn over 3f out: kpt on same pce fr 2f out: nt pce to mount chal* **3/1**[2]

0330 **6** *hd* **Handcuff**[25] 6017 2-8-8 **62**.. FrancisNorton 8 58
(J Gallagher) *hld up: rdn and hdwy 2f out: styd on fnl f* **50/1**

6606 **7** *1 1/2* **Place The Duchess**[25] 6023 2-7-9 **52** oh3........................ DominicFox[(3)] 6 43
(D W P Arbuthnot) *chsd ldrs: rdn over 3f out: one pce fnl 2f* **28/1**

1250 **8** *1/2* **Bahamian Ceilidh**[15] 6274 2-9-4 **75**.............................. JamesMillman[(3)] 5 64
(B R Millman) *towards rr: rdn and hdwy over 2f out: one pce fnl f* **16/1**

4241 **9** *shd* **Flintlock (IRE)**[13] 6341 2-9-5 **73**.................................(b) LDettori 3 61
(J H M Gosden) *hld up: rdn 3f out: hdwy over 1f out: hld whn short of room ins fnl f* **7/4**[1]

3100 **10** *2 1/2* **Smokey Ryder**[8] 6469 2-9-6 **74**...................................... JimCrowley 12 53
(G L Moore) *in tch: rdn over 3f out: wknd fnl f* **8/1**

6330 **11** *4* **Ridgeway Silver**[28] 5937 2-8-11 **65** JamesDoyle 7 30
(M D I Usher) *mid-div: rdn over 3f out: wknd 2f out* **50/1**

0310 **12** *3 1/4* **Shiva Adiva**[16] 6240 2-8-10 **71** RossAtkinson(7) 4 24
(Tom Dascombe) *s.i.s: a towards rr* **12/1**

0304 **13** *2 1/2* **Bold Rose**[95] 3846 2-8-4 **58** PaulHanagan 14 2
(M D I Usher) *a outpcd in rr* **33/1**

62.50 secs **Going Correction** -0.075s/f (Good) **13** Ran SP% **125.4**
Speed ratings (Par 95): **97,95,94,93,93 93,90,90,89,85 79,74,70**
toteswinger: 1&2 £18.90, 1&3 £25.50, 2&3 £61.40. CSF £97.92 CT £1521.40 TOTE £7.30: £2.90, £6.00, £5.10; EX 163.30 TRIFECTA Not won..
Owner S Bolland P Holling **Bred** Edmond And Richard Kent **Trained** Bawtry, S Yorks

FOCUS
A modest nursery which is rated around the runner-up.

NOTEBOOK
Go Go Green(IRE) looked worth another try at this distance when just lasting home over 6f at Pontefract earlier in the week and he made light of the 6lb penalty. With speed to burn, this progressive son of Acclamation remains capable of better, for all that things will be tougher in future as he climbs the weights. (tchd 13-2)
Val De Flores has not gone on as expected, but she was off the same mark as when finishing second at Kempton three starts back and the return 5f on turf seemed to suit. She was soon up there pressing the winner, and can find a small race if going forward. (op 14-1)
Asian Tale(IRE) really came home strongly. A easy winner of a claimer earlier in the season, she has twice run well subsequently and was found out here by the drop to 5f, getting outpaced at a crucial stage. Her yard are hardly in the best of form and it was her first start since August, so it is reasonable to expect further progress when she goes back up to 6f. (op 18-1 tchd 20-1)
Transcentral bagged the rails position and was soon up with the speed. She had every chance if good enough, but could find no extra inside the final furlong and was run out of the places. Official explanation: vet said filly lost a right-fore shoe
Flintlock(IRE) was most disappointing. He seemed helped by the drop from 7f when winning over 6f at Windsor last time, but found things happening all too quickly here over the minimum distance and never threatened to get involved. (op 2-1)
Bold Rose Official explanation: jockey said filly hung right-handed throughout

6667 TOTESUPER7 H'CAP 1m 2f 46y
3:20 (3:20) (Class 3) (0-90,90) 3-Y-0+ **£7,771** (£2,312; £1,155; £577) **Stalls** Low

Form RPR

6003 **1** **Safari Sunup (IRE)**[18] 6202 3-9-0 **86** StephenCarson 3 95
(P Winkworth) *chsd ldrs: rdn over 2f out: swtchd rt over 1f out: r.o wl: led fnl 40yds* **5/1[2]**

/30- **2** *3/4* **Cold Quest (USA)**[438] 4059 4-9-9 **90** LDettori 12 97
(J H M Gosden) *led after 1f: rdn and narrowly hdd over 1f out: rallied and remained w ev ch thrght fnl f: no ex fnl 40yds* **8/1[3]**

1014 **3** *hd* **Deep Winter**[15] 6276 3-8-9 **81** PaulHanagan 7 88
(R A Fahey) *led for over 1f: trckd ldr: rdn to take narrow advantage over 1f out: no ex whn hdd fnl 40yds* **8/1[3]**

6033 **4** *4* **Kinsya**[17] 6233 5-9-7 **88** PaulMulrennan 11 87+
(M H Tompkins) *racd keenly: hld up: rdn 3f out: styd on same pce fnl 2f: wnt 4th ins fnl f* **8/1[3]**

1253 **5** *3/4* **Slip**[23] 6078 3-9-1 **87** (p) RyanMoore 9 84
(M P Tregoning) *hld up: rdn and hdwy over 2f out: one pce fr over 1f out: lost 4th ins fnl f* **11/4[1]**

1000 **6** *shd* **Throne Of Power (USA)**[29] 5907 3-9-4 **90** AlanMunro 1 87
(M A Magnusson) *t.k.h in tch: rdn over 3f out: kpt on the same pce fnl 2f* **12/1**

4101 **7** *1* **Dr Livingstone (IRE)**[30] 5865 3-8-12 **84** LiamJones 10 79+
(C R Egerton) *hld up: rdn over 2f out: swtchd rt wl over 1f out: sme late prog: nvr a factor* **8/1[3]**

2110 **8** *1/2* **Red Somerset (USA)**[22] 6130 5-9-2 **88** MCGeran(5) 4 82
(R J Hodges) *mid-div: rdn and hdwy over 2f out: wknd ent fnl f* **16/1**

000- **9** *1/2* **Norman The Great**[166] 6439 4-8-9 **76** oh6 JimmyQuinn 5 69
(A King) *hld up: effrt 3f out: wknd over 1f out* **16/1**

0160 **10** *1* **Kings Quay**[22] 6120 6-9-1 **82** (t) GrahamGibbons 8 73
(J J Quinn) *t.k.h: hld up: rdn 3f out: no imp* **8/1[3]**

6000 **11** *1 3/4* **Uig**[3] 6605 7-8-6 **76** oh9 LukeMorris(3) 6 63
(H S Howe) *chsd ldrs: rdn 3f out: wknd over 1f out* **66/1**

2m 12.27s (1.27) **Going Correction** +0.15s/f (Good)
WFA 3 from 4yo+ 5lb **11** Ran SP% **119.8**
Speed ratings (Par 107): **100,99,99,96,95 95,94,94,93,92 91**
toteswinger: 1&2 £17.10, 1&3 £7.30, 2&3 £18.90. CSF £45.77 CT £321.01 TOTE £7.80: £2.50, £3.00, £2.70; EX 46.20 TRIFECTA Not won..
Owner P Winkworth **Bred** Lars Pearson **Trained** Chiddingfold, Surrey

FOCUS
This good handicap was run at just a modest early pace and the first three are rated close to their marks.

NOTEBOOK
Safari Sunup(IRE) came right back to form when finishing third at Goodwood last time and this drop to 1m2f looked in his favour. The ground would have been ideal, and, having held a prominent sit throughout, he stayed on strongly inside the final furlong to get up close home. He could be the type to make a hurdler and will now head for the Horses In Training sales. (op 11-2 tchd 6-1)
Cold Quest(USA), returning from a 14-month absence, has been gelded during that period, and it looked significant connections were persevering with the lightly raced four-year-old. He bossed things under Dettori and did not go down without a fight, rallying back past Deep Winter for second, but could do nothing about the winner. It is hoped he goes the right way from this.
Deep Winter has had a cracking first season, winning four times already, and she looked likely to make it five when going on inside the final quarter mile. She was unable to get away, though, and in the end got run out of it. The rating she ran off was 22lb higher than when first winning, but she may well progress again over the winter.
Kinsya has found some form again, and he fared best of the hold-up horses, keeping on despite having been a bit free early on. He remains a few pounds higher than when last winning. (op 11-2)
Slip, although 15lb higher than when last winning, was well supported at the head of the market and clearly expected to improve for the fitting of cheekpieces. The race was not run to suit, though, and he never threatened to play a part in the finish. (op 4-1)
Dr Livingstone(IRE) Official explanation: jockey said gelding hung left-handed

6668 TOTETRIFECTA H'CAP 1m 5f 22y
3:55 (3:55) (Class 6) (0-60,60) 3-Y-0+ **£2,590** (£770; £385; £192) **Stalls** High

Form RPR

6060 **1** **Bold Bobby Be (IRE)**[63] 4902 4-9-7 **57** (v1) JimmyQuinn 11 67
(J L Dunlop) *trckd ldrs: rdn over 2f out: led ins fnl f: styd on wl: drvn out* **8/1**

6P53 **2** *1* **Saloon (USA)**[12] 6364 4-9-2 **52** (t) PaulDoe 6 60
(S Curran) *sltly hmpd leaving stalls: towards rr: hdwy fr 6f out: led wl over 2f out: sn rdn: hdd ins fnl f: kpt on but sn hld* **5/1[2]**

01/5 **3** *2* **Accompanist**[16] 6263 5-9-0 **57** (v) AmyKathleenParsons(7) 12 62
(T G McCourt, Ire) *hld up towards rr: drvn and hdwy fr 3f out: styd on fnl f* **13/2**

4250 **4** *2* **Compton Charlie**[32] 5802 4-9-6 **56** JimCrowley 8 58
(J G Portman) *mid-div: hdwy over 3f out: rdn to chal over 2f out: ev ch over 1f out: kpt on same pce* **12/1**

5555 **5** *1/2* **Abounding**[76] 4029 4-9-9 **59** RyanMoore 3 60
(M J Attwater) *mid-div: rdn over 3f out: styd on fr over 1f out* **12/1**

2000 **6** *hd* **Check Up (IRE)**[29] 5917 7-9-1 **54** (p) KevinGhunowa(3) 13 55
(J L Flint) *racd keenly: led for 1f: trckd ldr: rdn over 3f out: one pce fnl 2f* **12/1**

3235 **7** *2 1/4* **Blue Hills**[16] 6252 7-9-7 **57** (b) DarrenWilliams 14 55
(P W Hiatt) *led after 1f: rdn and hdd wl over 2f out: sn one pce* **12/1**

52-0 **8** *1/2* **Intensifier (IRE)**[12] 6364 4-9-5 **55** GrahamGibbons 7 52
(D L Williams) *t.k.h: in tch: hdwy over 4f out: effrt over 2f out: wknd fnl f* **20/1**

5630 **9** *1/2* **Bold Adventure**[44] 5476 4-9-10 **60** TonyCulhane 5 56
(W J Musson) *hld up towards rr: rdn and hdwy over 2f out: wknd ent fnl f* **6/1[3]**

5002 **10** *3/4* **Bob's Your Uncle**[43] 5489 5-9-8 **58** AlanMunro 2 53
(J G Portman) *mid-div tl lost pl 4f out: nvr bk on terms* **4/1[1]**

1030 **11** *shd* **Soviet Sceptre (IRE)**[4] 5802 7-9-6 **56** (tp) LPKeniry 4 51
(Tim Vaughan) *a towards rr* **12/1**

00-4 **12** *17* **Dawn At Sea**[51] 5232 6-8-13 **52** LeeVickers(3) 9 21
(Mrs K Waldron) *a towards rr* **33/1**

0-00 **13** *16* **El Dottore**[20] 6175 10-9-0 **53** LukeMorris(3) 1 —
(A W Carroll) *a towards rr* **66/1**

2m 57.61s (5.61) **Going Correction** +0.15s/f (Good) **13** Ran SP% **123.1**
Speed ratings (Par 101): **88,87,86,84,84 84,83,82,82,82 81,71,61**
toteswinger: 1&2 £9.80, 1&3 £26.90, 2&3 £15.40. CSF £48.45 CT £284.93 TOTE £9.80: £3.20, £2.60, £2.80; EX 50.60 TRIFECTA Not won..
Owner Windflower Overseas Holdings Inc **Bred** Windflower Overseas Holdings Inc **Trained** Arundel, W Sussex
■ Stewards' Enquiry : Amy Kathleen Parsons two-day ban: used whip with excessive frequency and without giving gelding time to respond (Oct 27 -28)

FOCUS
This was a moderate handicap with the winner back to early-season form and the third to Irish form.
Check Up(IRE) Official explanation: jockey said gelding suffered interference in running
Intensifier(IRE) Official explanation: jockey said gelding hung left-handed in the last 3f

6669 TOTESWINGER H'CAP 5f 11y
4:30 (4:32) (Class 3) (0-95,94) 3-Y-0 **£7,569** (£2,265; £1,132; £566; £282) **Stalls** Centre

Form RPR

4210 **1** **Osiris Way**[28] 5930 6-9-0 **90** JimCrowley 5 99
(P R Chamings) *w ldr: led over 1f out: sn rdn: r.o wl* **3/1[1]**

524 **2** *3/4* **Secret Asset (IRE)**[15] 6290 3-9-2 **92** LiamJones 4 98
(W M Brisbourne) *hld up: travelling wl whn nt clr run 3f out: sn rdn and stdy prog: chsd wnr ent fnl f: edgd lft: kpt on* **9/1**

0604 **3** *3 3/4* **Misaro (GER)**[15] 6289 7-9-1 **91** (b) LPKeniry 7 84
(R A Harris) *prom: rdn over 3f out: kpt on same pce fnl f* **9/1**

0060 **4** *shd* **Bertoliver**[8] 6468 4-8-9 **92** RossAtkinson(7) 2 84
(Tom Dascombe) *led: rdn and hdd over 1f out: one pce after* **4/1[2]**

4334 **5** *1 1/4* **Matsunosuke**[10] 6429 6-9-4 **94** AlanMunro 6 82
(A B Coogan) *chsd ldrs: rdn to chal over 2f out: fdd ent fnl f* **9/2[3]**

2500 **6** *nk* **Prior Warning**[15] 6290 4-8-10 **91** (t) MCGeran(5) 3 78
(Miss D Mountain) *s.i.s: nvr able to get on terms* **11/1**

0010 **7** *1 1/4* **Elhamri**[22] 6125 4-9-0 **90** RyanMoore 8 72
(S Kirk) *hld up: drvn over 2f out: swtchd rt over 1f out: no imp* **6/1**

6064 **8** *1* **Little Edward**[29] 5906 10-9-0 **90** FrancisNorton 1 68
(R J Hodges) *chsd ldrs: rdn 3f out: wknd ent fnl f* **17/2**

61.41 secs (-1.09) **Going Correction** -0.075s/f (Good) **8** Ran SP% **116.3**
Speed ratings (Par 107): **105,103,97,97,95 95,93,91**
toteswinger: 1&2 £5.40, 1&3 £6.60, 2&3 £11.20. CSF £31.31 CT £219.38 TOTE £3.90: £1.70, £3.10, £3.40; EX 43.50 Trifecta £331.90 Part won. Pool: £448.64 - 0.80 winning units..
Owner Mrs Alexandra J Chandris **Bred** Whitsbury Manor Stud **Trained** Baughurst, Hants

FOCUS
A wide-open handicap. The first pair came clear and the form could be underrated.

NOTEBOOK
Osiris Way, a winner over this trip earlier in the season, scored over 6f at Goodwood two starts back and was just 3lb higher here. The winner disappointed last time when the soft ground was deemed unsuitable, but showed plenty of pace and stayed on strongly having gone on over a furlong out. (op 9-2)
Secret Asset(IRE) has come right back to his best since returning from a break, and he followed his Great Leighs second with a fine fourth at Haydock last time. He was off the same mark here, and, although unable to lead, got a nice tow through and finished a creditable second. An easier 5f is preferable. (op 8-1 tchd 15-2)
Misaro(GER) came out best of the rest in third, but he was well held and remains 8lb higher than when last winning. (op 8-1)
Bertoliver has yet to find his best form for new connections and failed to get home. He will soon be back on a good mark, though, and is not one to lose faith in. (op 5-1 tchd 11-2)

6670 TOTEEXACTA CONDITIONS STKS 1m 5y
5:05 (5:05) (Class 3) 3-Y-0+ **£7,569** (£2,265; £1,132; £566; £282) **Stalls** Low

Form RPR

0203 **1** **Alexandros**[30] 5856 3-8-12 106 LDettori 3 112+
(Saeed Bin Suroor) *mde all: pushed clr ent fnl f: comf* **11/8[1]**

150 **2** *3 3/4* **Charlie Farnsbarns (IRE)**[8] 6476 4-9-7 107 NickyMackay 9 109
(B J Meehan) *in tch: hdwy to trck wnr after 2f: rdn over 2f out: kpt on but no ch w wnr fnl f* **4/1[3]**

-600 **3** *2 1/4* **Moynahan (USA)**[9] 6440 3-8-12 104 AlanMunro 5 98
(P F I Cole) *hld up: rdn and hdwy over 2f out: styd on same pce fr over 1f out* **6/1**

0-43 **4** *2* **Banknote**[106] 3503 6-9-1 103 FrancisNorton 7 94
(A M Balding) *chsd ldrs: rdn over 2f out: fdd ent fnl f* **3/1[2]**

0400 **5** *1/2* **Barons Spy (IRE)**[15] 6277 7-9-1 86 JamesDoyle 1 92
(R J Price) *hld up: rdn over 2f out: sme late prog: nvr trbld ldrs* **40/1**

2004 **6** *1/2* **Orchard Supreme**[8] 6478 5-9-1 86 RyanMoore 2 91
(R Hannon) *chsd ldrs: rdn over 2f out: fdd fnl f* **20/1**

0460 **7** *1* **Alan Devonshire**[8] 6476 3-8-12 100 PaulMulrennan 8 96+
(M H Tompkins) *hld up: rdn over 2f out: styng on but no ch whn short of room on rails ins fnl f: nt rcvr* **18/1**

1m 40.6s (-0.20) **Going Correction** +0.15s/f (Good)
WFA 3 from 4yo+ 3lb **7** Ran SP% **113.9**
Speed ratings (Par 107): **107,103,101,99,98 98,97**
toteswinger: 1&2 £2.20, 1&3 £2.00, 2&3 £4.70. CSF £7.17 TOTE £2.10: £1.40, £2.70; EX 8.40 Trifecta £65.20 Pool: £403.00 - 4.57 winning units.
Owner Godolphin **Bred** Darley **Trained** Newmarket, Suffolk

FOCUS
A good conditions event, with four of the seven runners officially rated 100 or better. The form is rated through the runner-up backed up by the third.

NOTEBOOK
Alexandros, officially the highest-rated runner in the field, has contested some really good races this season and even the conditions race he was dropped into last time ended up being won by Spacious. The winner set the standard here in receipt of weight from his elders and was always going to take some beating once Dettori bagged an uncontested lead. He gradually wound it up and responded when asked to go on and win his race a furlong and a half out, ultimately winning with tons in hand. This was a deserved first victory of the season. (op 6-4 tchd 6-5)
Charlie Farnsbarns(IRE), well held in last weekend's Cambridgeshire, was not going to find life easy with a 6lb penalty to carry, but he would not have beaten Alexandros whether he had it or not. He was never far from the lead and kept on to hold a comfy second, but is going to remain difficult to place. (op 11-2 tchd 7-1)
Moynahan(USA), who kicked off his season by finishing sixth in the Guineas, was not beaten far on last week's return from a break, and he stayed on to take third. He raced too keenly on his previous try at 1m2f, but shapes as though well worth another go at it. (op 8-1)
Banknote, off since finishing third in a Listed contest at Windsor in June, picked up a Group 3 abroad last season and looked a major threat if at his best, but he failed to pick up and was ultimately well held. This was not his true form and he should strip fitter next time. (op 11-4 tchd 5-2)
Alan Devonshire Official explanation: jockey said colt ran too freely and hung left throughout

6671 TOTESPORT HOME OF POOL BETTING H'CAP — 1m 5y
5:35 (5:37) (Class 5) (0-70,70) 3-Y-O+ — £3,238 (£963; £481; £240) Stalls Low

Form — RPR

5060 **1** **Support Fund (IRE)**[39] [5600] 4-9-5 **68** ... StephenCarson 11 — 77
(Eve Johnson Houghton) *hld up towards rr: hdwy over 2f out: sn rdn: drifted lft but r.o wl fnl f: led towards fin* **16/1**

0240 **2** 1 1/4 **Idesia (IRE)**[58] [5069] 4-9-3 **66** ... (t) RyanMoore 5 — 72
(W R Swinburn) *chsd ldr: rdn to ld over 1f out: hdd towards fnl f: no ex* **4/1**[1]

1661 **3** 1 1/4 **Grey Boy (GER)**[18] [6211] 7-9-4 **70** ... LukeMorris(3) 7 — 76+
(A W Carroll) *mid-div: hdwy over 2f out: sn rdn: styng on in cl 3rd whn squeezed out ins fnl f: no ch after* **7/1**

1524 **4** hd **Ours (IRE)**[4] [6585] 5-9-3 **66** ... (p) PaulHanagan 12 — 69+
(John A Harris) *hld up towards rr: rdn 3f out: hdwy 2f out: styd on wl fnl f: nrst fin* **6/1**[3]

0000 **5** nk **Very Well Red**[13] [6336] 5-9-2 **65** ... DarrenWilliams 13 — 67
(P W Hiatt) *led after 1f: rdn 3f out: hdd over 1f out: kpt on* **20/1**

6220 **6** 1/2 **Libre**[12] [6363] 8-8-13 **62** ... PaulFitzsimons 16 — 63
(F Jordan) *hld up towards rr: rdn and hdwy over 2f out: hld whn hmpd ins fnl f* **20/1**

5060 **7** 2 **Flying Goose (IRE)**[55] [5144] 4-9-4 **70** ... KevinGhunowa(3) 9 — 66
(R A Harris) *hld up towards rr: rdn and stdy prog fr 3f out: one pce whn hung lft ins fnl f* **16/1**

40-5 **8** 3/4 **Cantabilly (IRE)**[186] [1267] 5-9-2 **70** ... MCGeran(5) 1 — 65+
(R J Hodges) *mid-div: rdn over 3f out: hld whn nt clr run ent fnl f* **20/1**

060 **9** nk **Madame Hoi (IRE)**[39] [5600] 3-9-2 **68** ... TonyCulhane 6 — 62
(M R Channon) *a towards rr* **25/1**

-000 **10** 3/4 **Invention (USA)**[130] [2153] 5-9-6 **69** ... AlanMunro 3 — 61
(Miss E C Lavelle) *chsd ldrs: rdn over 3f out: wknd over 1f out* **25/1**

3642 **11** 1 1/4 **Wrighty Almighty (IRE)**[13] [6336] 6-9-6 **69** ... JimCrowley 2 — 58
(P R Chamings) *mid-div: rdn whn bdly hmpd over 1f out: wknd* **5/1**[2]

1054 **12** 4 1/2 **Seneschal**[13] [6335] 7-8-6 **62** ... PNolan(7) 4 — 41
(A B Haynes) *chsd ldrs: rdn 3f out: wknd over 1f out* **16/1**

5610 **13** 1/2 **Gallego**[11] [6395] 6-9-5 **68** ... LiamJones 14 — 46
(R J Price) *s.i.s: a towards rr* **14/1**

010 **14** 1 1/4 **Make Amends (IRE)**[56] [5119] 3-9-1 **67** ... FrancisNorton 15 — 42
(R J Hodges) *mid-div: rdn whn short of room over 1f out: nvr trbld ldrs* **12/1**

1460 **15** hd **Scarlet Oak**[40] [5588] 4-9-0 **63** ... LPKeniry 8 — 37
(D J S Ffrench Davis) *s.i.s: towards rr: hdwy over 2f out: sn rdn: wkng whn hmpd jst ins fnl f* **33/1**

624 **16** 12 **Turfwolke (GER)**[15] [6275] 3-8-12 **64** ... JamesDoyle 10 — 11
(J W Hills) *led for 1f: chsd ldrs: rdn over 3f out: wknd 2f out* **14/1**

1m 42.09s (1.29) **Going Correction** +0.15s/f (Good)
WFA 3 from 4yo+ 3lb — **16 Ran SP% 127.0**
Speed ratings (Par 103): **99,97,96,96,96 95,93,92,92,91 90,85,85,84,84 72**
toteswinger: 1&2 £20.90, 1&3 £20.60, 2&3 £6.90. CSF £74.23 CT £515.22 TOTE £18.20: £4.50, £1.50, £2.20, £1.90; EX 107.00 Trifecta £232.80 Part won. Pool £314.69. 0.10 winning units. Place 6 £145.83 Place 5 £122.16..
Owner Betfair Club ROA **Bred** W Maxwell Ervine **Trained** Blewbury, Oxon

FOCUS
A low-grade handicap, but it was certainly competitive and the form looks solid for the class. The winner is rated back to soemthing like her best.
Grey Boy(GER) Official explanation: jockey said gelding was denied a clear run close to home
Cantabilly(IRE) Official explanation: jockey said gelding was denied a clear run
Wrighty Almighty(IRE) Official explanation: jockey said gelding suffered interference in running
Gallego Official explanation: jockey said gelding was never travelling
T/Jkpt: £12,901.40 to a £1 stake. Pool: £18,171.03. 0.50 winning tickets. T/Plt: £439.40 to a £1 stake. Pool: £71,593.38. 118.92 winning tickets. T/Qpdt: £54.30 to a £1 stake. Pool: £5,524.39. 75.20 winning tickets. TM

6412 GOODWOOD (R-H)
Sunday, October 12

OFFICIAL GOING: Good to soft
A gloriously, bright sunny day meant the good to soft (going stick 7.8) ground had become tacky and gluey and it looked pretty hard work.
Wind: Light, across Weather: Perfect

6672 UCELLO II AND UBU III TROPHY (H'CAP) (FOR NATIONAL HUNT JOCKEYS) — 2m
2:00 (2:01) (Class 5) (0-70,70) 4-Y-O+ — £3,238 (£963; £481; £240) Stalls Low

Form — RPR

0642 **1** **Munlochy Bay**[34] [5752] 4-10-11 **55** ... PJBrennan 10 — 64
(W S Kittow) *hld up off the pce towards rr: stdy prog fr 5f out: wnt 2nd over 2f out: rdn to ld over 1f out: styd on wl* **9/1**

056/ **2** 2 1/2 **Kawagino (IRE)**[143] [3405] 8-11-12 **70** ... ChristianWilliams 3 — 76
(J W Mullins) *swtg: hld up in midfield: prog 6f out: trckd ldrs gng strly 3f out: plld out over 1f out: r.o to take 2nd last strides* **12/1**

226- **3** 1/2 **To Arms**[314] [7008] 6-10-11 **55** ... WTKennedy 6 — 60
(K J Burke) *prom: gng strly in bhd ldrs 3f out: plld out and effrt over 2f out: rdn to chal wl over 1f out: one pce* **18/1**

3013 **4** nk **At The Money**[125] [2888] 5-11-10 **68** ... RichardHughes 7 — 73
(J M P Eustace) *fast away: led 2f: trckd ldr: led again over 6f out: drvn and hdd over 1f out: lost 2 pls nr fin* **5/1**[2]

0651 **5** 9 **Wyeth**[21] [5752] 4-11-2 **60** ... (p) JamieMoore 15 — 54
(G L Moore) *hld up wl in rr and off the pce: sme prog 4f out: kpt on u.p fr 3f out: nvr on terms* **7/1**[3]

00 **6** 1 3/4 **Rare Ruby (IRE)**[24] [6054] 4-11-3 **61** ... LiamTreadwell 13 — 53
(Jennie Candlish) *mostly in midfield: prog to chse ldrs 4f out: no imp over 2f out: wknd* **25/1**

5104 **7** hd **Salute (IRE)**[61] [4955] 9-11-11 **69** ... ColinBolger 5 — 61
(P G Murphy) *w ldrs: u.p 3f out: wknd 2f out* **20/1**

3165 **8** 7 **Danzatrice**[14] [6313] 6-11-11 **69** ... AndrewThornton 9 — 52
(C W Thornton) *s.s: wl off the pce in last: effrt 4f out: laboured prog u.p fr 3f out: no ch* **16/1**

1120 **9** 1/2 **Bugsy's Boy**[150] [2135] 4-11-12 **70** ... AndrewTinkler 12 — 53
(George Baker) *prom: chsd ldr 5f out to over 2f out: wknd* **16/1**

5330 **10** 6 **Lapina (IRE)**[44] [5465] 4-10-13 **57** ... (b) JasonMaguire 11 — 33
(Pat Eddery) *swtg: a wl in rr: lost tch w ldng gp fr 4f out: bhd after* **12/1**

4341 **11** shd **Go Amwell**[28] [5934] 5-11-4 **62** ... TimmyMurphy 4 — 38
(J R Jenkins) *lw: dwlt: hld up wl in rr and off the pce: effrt 5f out: u.p and no prog over 3f out* **4/1**[1]

0116 **12** 2 1/2 **Mohawk Star (IRE)**[25] [6022] 7-11-8 **66** ... (v) MarcusFoley 1 — 39
(I A Wood) *in tch in midfield: chsng ldrs 4f out: sn rdn: wknd and wandered fr wl over 2f out* **16/1**

1553 **13** hd **Trigger's Friend**[28] [5934] 4-10-11 **55** ... MattieBatchelor 14 — 27
(Jamie Poulton) *a towards rr: struggling 4f out: bhd after: fin lame* **8/1**

4200 **14** 8 **Mister Completely (IRE)**[37] [5676] 7-10-12 **56** ... (v) SeanCurran 8 — 19
(Ms J S Doyle) *dwlt: hld up wl in rr: no prog over 4f out: t.o* **25/1**

3300 **15** 10 **Is It Me (USA)**[19] [5917] 5-11-2 **60** ... PaulMoloney 2 — 11
(A W Carroll) *led after 2f to over 6f out: wknd over 4f out: t.o* **33/1**

0310 **16** 16 **Zeloso**[38] [5651] 10-10-8 **52** ... (v) DaveCrosse 16 — —
(M F Harris) *a in rr: dropped to last over 6f out: sn t.o* **33/1**

3m 36.2s (3.00) **Going Correction** +0.275s/f (Good) — **16 Ran SP% 126.9**
Speed ratings (Par 103): **103,101,101,101,96 95,95,92,92,89 89,87,87,83,78 70**
toteswinger: 1&2 £17.80, 1&3 £41.30, 2&3 £54.30. CSF £109.82 CT £1927.73 TOTE £10.70: £2.50, £3.00, £4.30, £1.80; EX 152.50.
Owner John & Val Urquhart **Bred** John Urquhart **Trained** Blackborough, Devon

FOCUS
The field were strung out from an early stage as Is It Me wrestled the early advantage from At The Money to ensure a solid gallop, and not a great deal got into it from off the pace. The front four pulled a long way clear and the form looks sound, with the fourth probably the best guide.
Trigger's Friend Official explanation: trainer said filly was lame in front

6673 E.B.F. RUK NURSERY — 7f
2:35 (2:39) (Class 4) (0-85,84) 2-Y-O — £5,504 (£1,637; £818; £408) Stalls High

Form — RPR

0355 **1** **Reaction**[13] [6344] 2-8-9 **72** ... DarryllHolland 9 — 75
(M R Channon) *t.k.h early: trckd ldrs: u.p fr 3f out: hrd rdn over 1f out: hung rt and nt look keen: chal fnl f: forced ahd on line* **16/1**

1410 **2** nse **Calahonda**[8] [6477] 2-9-1 **78** ... PhilipRobinson 7 — 81
(P W D'Arcy) *w ldrs: led 3f out: sn hrd pressed: kpt on wl fnl f: hdd post* **11/2**[2]

545 **3** 1 **Mr Udagawa**[26] [5996] 2-8-6 **69** ... EddieAhern 6 — 70
(R M Beckett) *dwlt: hld up in rr: prog 2f out: styd on to take 3rd nr fin: nvr able to chal* **33/1**

212 **4** 1/2 **Key Signature**[43] [5511] 2-9-7 **84** ... ShaneKelly 13 — 83
(Pat Eddery) *lw: w ldrs: chal fr over 2f out: upsides ent fnl f: nt qckn* **13/2**[3]

066 **5** nk **Herschel (IRE)**[18] [6197] 2-8-5 **68** ... TPO'Shea 4 — 67
(G L Moore) *lw: hld up in rr and racd wd: rdn fr 3f out: kpt on fnl 2f but nvr looked like rching ldrs* **10/1**

0120 **6** shd **Perfect Citizen (USA)**[23] [6082] 2-9-7 **84** ... AdamKirby 11 — 82+
(W R Swinburn) *hld up in tch: rdn over 2f out: tried to cl on ldrs 1f out: one pce after* **17/2**

4455 **7** 1/2 **Party Cat (IRE)**[13] [6342] 2-8-11 **74** ... PatDobbs 8 — 71+
(R Hannon) *dwlt: t.k.h and swtchd to inner: hld up in tch: nt clr run over 2f out to over 1f out: no rspnse whn in the clr* **33/1**

2254 **7** dht **River Dee (IRE)**[14] [6305] 2-8-2 **70** ... KellyHarrison(5) 5 — 67
(Miss Amy Weaver) *hld up and racd wd: urged along fr 3f out: plugged on one pce and nvr threatened* **7/1**

22 **9** 1 1/4 **Campbeltown Trader (IRE)**[94] [3882] 2-8-13 **76**(v1) RichardKingscote 12 — 70
(Tom Dascombe) *led to 3f out: steadily wknd fr 2f out* **16/1**

412 **10** 1 **Perfect Friend**[12] [6362] 2-7-13 **67** ... Louis-PhilippeBeuzelin(5) 14 — 58
(S Kirk) *cl up: trapped bhd ldrs over 2f out: wknd tamely over 1f out* **8/1**

305 **11** 3 **Edgeworth (IRE)**[26] [6000] 2-7-13 **62** ... DO'Donohoe 3 — 46
(B G Powell) *taken down early: racd wd in rr: rdn 3f out: no prog* **50/1**

0210 **12** 6 **Appraisal**[10] [6426] 2-9-2 **79** ... RichardHughes 10 — 48+
(R Hannon) *hld up in tch: lost pl over 2f out: btn after: eased whn no ch* **3/1**[1]

1m 30.15s (2.75) **Going Correction** +0.275s/f (Good) — **12 Ran SP% 116.6**
Speed ratings (Par 97): **95,94,93,93,92 92,92,92,90,89 86,79**
toteswinger: 1&2 £17.70, 1&3 £41.60, 2&3 £32.70. CSF £98.85 CT £2877.72 TOTE £21.60: £4.80, £2.30, £7.30; EX 131.50.
Owner Highclere Thoroughbred Racing (St Simon) **Bred** Mrs Brid Cosgrove **Trained** West Ilsley, Berks

FOCUS
A competitive nursery with plenty of in-form and improving runners, but the pace was only steady and things got a bit messy for a couple of the runners who tried to make headway up the inside. It paid to be handy and the form might not turn out to be too reliable.

NOTEBOOK
Reaction was very big odds considering he was top rated on RPRs, but he hadn't looked to be progressing over slightly longer trips recently. The combination of the drop back to 7f and a 3lb ease by the assessor allowed him to record that elusive first success, though he needed every single yard of this 7f to score, staying on strongly to collar Calahonda on the line. He once again didn't convince with the way he carried his head under pressure but connections will be delighted he has got off the mark and it may be that easy ground is the key to him for he had only raced on a sound surface prior to this. (op 20-1)
Calahonda, who pressed on three furlongs out as Robinson decided the pace wasn't strong enough, battled on bravely and lost little in defeat, though she looks vulnerable from a handicapping point of view. (op 7-1)
Mr Udagawa finished his race much better than he had been doing in his qualifying maiden runs. He stayed on steadily having managed to avoid any of the trouble in behind and this was a definite step in the right direction. (tchd 25-1)

Key Signature had been given a break since breaking out of the stalls at Leicester but she proved that incident hadn't affected her confidence but she is 19lb higher than when scoring at Kempton in August, and that looks to be enough for now. (op 5-1 tchd 7-1)
Herschel(IRE) stayed on steadily down the outside once switched to get a clear run. (op 12-1 tchd 9-1)
Perfect Citizen(USA) ran another sound enough race in defeat, though he never really looked like bustling up the principles. (op 11-1 tchd 8-1)
Party Cat(IRE) ◆ was shuffled back early up the inside and had his headway blocked in the straight. He stayed on well once getting clear and would probably have finished a fair bit closer with a trouble free passage.
Perfect Friend was another who didn't have a clear passage and he too can be forgiven this. Official explanation: jockey said filly was denied a clear run (op 10-1)
Appraisal Official explanation: jockey said colt suffered interference in running

6674 E.B.F. TURFTV MAIDEN STKS — 1m 1f

3:10 (3:14) (Class 4) 2-Y-O — £5,180 (£1,541; £770; £384) Stalls High

Form — RPR

0 **1** **Dulcie**[23] 6081 2-8-12 0 .... SaleemGolam 4 75
(M H Tompkins) *settled in midfield: shkn up 3f out: prog 2f out: got through and rdn to ld ins fnl f: styd on* **33/1**

2 ¾ **Dome Rocket** 2-9-3 0 .... ShaneKelly 3 78+
(W J Knight) *w'like: scope: tall: wl in rr and wd early: pushed along and green 4f out: prog over 2f out: nt clr run briefly over 1f out: stl green but r.o wl fnl f to take 2nd nr fin* **50/1**

36 **3** 1 **Princability (IRE)**[11] 6397 2-9-3 0 .... DarryllHolland 12 76
(M R Channon) *lw: pressed ldrs: urged along fr 1/2-way: rdn to chal over 3f out: led wl over 2f out: hrd rdn and hdd ins fnl f: one pce and lost 2nd nr fin* **11/2**

6 **4** 1 **Penang Princess**[37] 5678 2-8-12 0 .... RichardKingscote 9 69
(R M Beckett) *wl in rr and green early: limited prog fr over 3f out: stl only 10th over 1f out: styd on wl after: nrst fin* **12/1**

33 **5** ½ **Featherweight (IRE)**[23] 6081 2-8-12 0 .... MichaelHills 13 68
(B W Hills) *hld up bhd ldrs: n.m.r jst over 3f out: prog to chal 2f out: nt qckn over 1f out: wknd ins fnl f* **7/2**[2]

26 **6** 3 **Capitelli (IRE)**[23] 6076 2-8-12 0 .... RichardHughes 11 62
(R Hannon) *lw: trckd ldrs: prog on outer to chal 3f out: nt qckn over 2f out: wknd jst over 1f out* **11/4**[1]

3 **7** 2 **Sixties Swinger (USA)**[92] 3939 2-9-3 0 .... PhilipRobinson 6 63+
(M A Jarvis) *lw: hld up in midfield: effrt on outer 3f out: nt qckn 2f out: wknd and hung rt fr over 1f out* **5/1**[3]

503 **8** hd **Lonely Star (IRE)**[11] 6392 2-8-12 80 .... PatDobbs 5 58
(D R Lanigan) *swtg: w ldrs: led 4f out: hdd wl over 2f out: wknd fnl 2f* **8/1**

9 2 **Guga (IRE)** 2-9-3 0 .... DO'Donohoe 8 59
(George Baker) *w'like: leggy: green to post: s.i.s: green and pushed along early: effrt to rch midfield 3f out: no imp on ldrs 2f out: wknd fnl f* **14/1**

0 **10** 1¼ **Ermyn Lodge**[18] 6199 2-9-3 0 .... TPO'Shea 14 56
(P M Phelan) *sn last and v green: virtually t.o 4f out: hanging all over the pl but styd on fr over 2f out: nrst fin* **66/1**

4554 **11** 2¾ **Supernoverre (IRE)**[18] 6199 2-9-3 71 ....(b[1]) JimmyFortune 10 51
(Mrs A J Perrett) *mde most to 4f out: wkng on inner whn hmpd over 2f out* **14/1**

06 **12** 12 **Manolito Montoya (IRE)**[18] 6198 2-9-3 0 .... EddieAhern 2 27
(J W Hills) *racd wd in midfield: wknd 3f out: t.o* **16/1**

0 **13** 7 **Mountain Forest (GER)**[11] 6398 2-9-3 0 .... SteveDrowne 1 13
(H Morrison) *racd wd in midfield: dropped to rr 4f out: sn wknd t.o* **50/1**

14 3¾ **Wolverton (IRE)** 2-9-3 0 .... JoeFanning 7 5
(N P Littmoden) *w'like: s.i.s: rn green and pushed along: a in rr: t.o over 3f out* **66/1**

2m 0.11s (3.81) **Going Correction** +0.275s/f (Good) **14** Ran SP% **128.8**
Speed ratings (Par 97): **94,93,92,91,91 88,86,86,84,83 81,70,64,60**
toteswinger: 1&2 £135.30, 1&3 £37.80, 2&3 £68.30. CSF £1191.39 TOTE £47.10: £8.90, £11.30, £2.50; EX 2541.50.
Owner Indian Racing **Bred** Dullingham Park **Trained** Newmarket, Suffolk

FOCUS
The more experienced horses, who had already shown a fair degree of ability, were largely disappointing and the finish was dominated by lightly raced types.

NOTEBOOK
Dulcie was always going to appreciate this longer trip both on breeding and the way she finished on debut over 1m1f at Newmarket and, despite having around ten lengths to find with Featherwight, she managed to turn the form around fairly emphatically. Clearly she has come on plenty for that first run and the way she saw this out, looking stronger the further they went and relishing the ease in the ground, the step up to 1m2f looks inevitable. (op 40-1 tchd 50-1)
Dome Rocket ◆ shaped with an enormous amount of encouragement in second. Coltish beforehand and very green in the race itself, he was a fair way back at the top of the straight but the further they went the he responded to his rider's urgings and stormed home in the final furlong. He will need to channel his energies in a more economical manner, but he appears to have the raw talent and is one to keep a close eye on next time, with a stiffer test no problem on breeding. Official explanation: jockey said colt suffered interference in running (op 66-1)
Princability(IRE) was again ridden prominently but despite being in the firing line at the distance, he didn't really see his race out and it's hard to know whether he is progressing. (op 10-1)
Penang Princess ◆ was the other big eyecatcher. Edgy beforehand and green in the race itself, she made significant headway from the back of the field and this was a definite step forward on her Lingfield debut. She clearly has ability and any further progress should be enough to see her off the mark in similar company, though it may be that will not be until next season now. (op 14-1)
Featherweight(IRE) travelled well in behind the pace and although she was blocked initially as she went for a gap, she had plenty of time to throw down a challenge once in the clear and it was slightly disappointing she couldn't do so. However, she has quite a whippy action, suggestion she might be better suited by a sound surface, so she could be worth another chance back on good ground or faster. (op 4-1 tchd 9-2)
Capitelli(IRE) was well below the form she showed in two runs over 7f and was seemingly unsuited by the step up in trip. (op 4-1)
Sixties Swinger(USA) was another who seemed unsuited by a step up in trip from 7f. (op 3-1)
Lonely Star(IRE) might want better ground. (tchd 10-1)
Mountain Forest(GER) Official explanation: jockey said colt stopped quickly

6675 KEN WILKIE BIRTHDAY H'CAP — 1m

3:45 (3:48) (Class 4) (0-85,85) 3-Y-O+ — £5,180 (£1,541; £770; £384) Stalls High

Form — RPR

1324 **1** **The Fifth Member (IRE)**[36] 5695 4-9-5 81 .... PatCosgrave 10 95
(J R Boyle) *lw: trckd ldrs: smooth prog to ld jst over 2f out: wl in command over 1f out: styd on strly* **5/1**[1]

0300 **2** 3¼ **Marvo**[11] 6400 4-8-8 70 .... SaleemGolam 6 76
(M H Tompkins) *stdd s: hld up wl in rr: gd prog fr 3f out: drvn to chse wnr over 1f out: styd on but no imp* **25/1**

5150 **3** 1 **Capucci**[25] 6035 3-9-1 80 ....(t) JimmyFortune 13 84
(J H M Gosden) *lw: hld up towards rr: stdy prog over 3f out: rdn 2f out: styd on same pce after* **8/1**[3]

3153 **4** ¾ **Border Owl (IRE)**[8] 6467 3-9-0 79 .... RichardHughes 9 74
(R Hannon) *lw: stdd s: hld up in last: sme prog fr 3f out: nowhere nr ldrs 2f out: kpt on but n.d* **8/1**[3]

1606 **5** nk **Mountain Pride (IRE)**[29] 5903 3-9-6 85 .... SteveDrowne 11 79
(J L Dunlop) *trckd ldrs on inner: prog to chal over 2f out: sn btn: wknd over 1f out* **12/1**

0030 **6** 4½ **St Petersburg**[29] 5915 8-8-10 72 .... EddieAhern 12 55
(J R Boyle) *hld up towards rr: sme prog 3f out: nt on terms and hanging rt 2f out: wknd over 1f out* **14/1**

2202 **7** ½ **Den's Gift (IRE)**[22] 6130 4-9-7 83 ....(b) PhilipRobinson 1 65
(C G Cox) *lw: fast away fr wd draw: led at str pce: hdd & wknd jst over 2f out* **11/2**[2]

3513 **8** 4 **Thunder Gorge (USA)**[16] 6242 3-8-9 74 .... JoeFanning 4 46
(Mouse Hamilton-Fairley) *prom: u.p over 3f out: reluctant and sn btn* **8/1**[3]

5-21 **9** ½ **Pippbrook Gold**[128] 2772 3-8-8 78 .... Louis-PhilippeBeuzelin(5) 3 49
(J R Boyle) *racd wd in midfield: struggling fr 3f out: sn wl btn* **16/1**

4300 **10** 1¾ **Benfleet Boy**[16] 6250 4-8-11 73 .... MichaelHills 14 40
(B G Powell) *chsd ldrs: rdn and struggling over 3f out: wknd* **16/1**

1244 **11** 2 **Tina's Best (IRE)**[22] 6124 3-8-11 76 .... PatDobbs 8 38
(R Hannon) *in tch in midfield tl wekaened fr 3f out: sn bhd* **22/1**

0106 **12** ¾ **Carlitos Spirit (IRE)**[19] 6194 4-9-4 80 .... DarryllHolland 5 40
(B R Millman) *wl away fr wd draw and chsd ldr: rdn over 3f out: sn wknd* **14/1**

1501 **13** 2¾ **Shanzu**[27] 5964 3-8-12 77 .... AdamKirby 2 31
(H Candy) *chsd ldrs: u.p and losing pl 3f out: sn bhd* **14/1**

340 **14** 11 **Titan Triumph**[8] 6471 4-8-10 72 ....(t) RichardKingscote 7 —
(W J Knight) *racd wd in midfield: wknd over 3f out: t.o* **8/1**[3]

1m 40.24s (0.34) **Going Correction** +0.275s/f (Good)
WFA 3 from 4yo+ 3lb **14** Ran SP% **124.1**
Speed ratings (Par 105): **109,105,104,101,100 96,95,91,91,89 87,86,83,72**
toteswinger: 1&2 £36.00, 1&3 £12.40, 2&3 £63.20. CSF £135.44 CT £1033.84 TOTE £6.80: £2.30, £6.80, £2.70; EX 161.60.
Owner Chris Simpson, Miss Elizabeth Ross **Bred** Ms Amy Mulligan **Trained** Epsom, Surrey

FOCUS
A fair handicap run at a sound pace. A personal best from the winner, with the runner-up to form.
Titan Triumph Official explanation: jockey said colt was unsuited by the good to soft ground

6676 IDLE POWER STKS (H'CAP) — 6f

4:20 (4:20) (Class 3) (0-95,95) 3-Y-O+ — £7,771 (£2,312; £1,155; £577) Stalls Low

Form — RPR

0500 **1** **Phantom Whisper**[15] 6269 5-9-2 91 .... DarryllHolland 8 100
(B R Millman) *lw: chsd ldrs: pushed along fr 1/2-way: clsng whn nt clr run 1f out: got through ins fnl f: hrd rdn and r.o to ld nr fin* **11/2**[3]

1304 **2** nk **Brassini**[15] 6277 3-9-0 90 .... JimmyFortune 5 98
(B R Millman) *sweating: w ldrs: led over 2f out: hrd pressed after: kpt on fnl f: hdd nr fin* **7/1**

1413 **3** 1½ **Maimoona (IRE)**[49] 5310 3-8-13 89 .... MichaelHills 10 92
(W J Haggas) *lw: wl in tch on outer: effrt over 2f out: rdn and nt qckn 2f out: kpt on same pce after and a hld* **7/2**[1]

5615 **4** hd **Baldemar**[28] 5930 3-8-12 88 .... AndrewElliott 7 90
(K R Burke) *b.hind: chsd ldrs: rdn over 2f out: stl pressing 1f out: one pce* **9/1**

1550 **5** shd **Idle Power (IRE)**[50] 5270 10-8-7 82 .... EddieAhern 3 84
(J R Boyle) *racd against nr side rail: led after 1f to 3f out: hrd rdn over 2f out: plugged on fnl f* **9/1**

0066 **6** ½ **Patavellian (IRE)**[22] 6104 10-9-0 94 ....(v) Louis-PhilippeBeuzelin(5) 6 94
(R Charlton) *lw: taken down early: dwlt: chsd ldrs: lost pl after 2f: rdn over 2f out: plld out wd ent fnl f: kpt on but nt pce to chal* **4/1**[2]

0200 **7** ½ **Compton's Eleven**[22] 6125 7-8-7 82 .... TPO'Shea 9 81
(M R Channon) *bdly outpcd in last: clsd over 2f out: no real imp on ldrs after: kpt on* **12/1**

-240 **8** nse **Johnstown Lad (IRE)**[2] 6624 4-8-8 83 ....(t) ShaneKelly 4 82
(Niall Moran, Ire) *str: swtg: led 1f: pressed ldr: led 3f out to over 2f out: hanging rt after but stl chalng: wknd ins fnl f* **14/1**

06 **9** 4 **Sir Edwin Landseer (USA)**[28] 5930 8-8-13 88 ......(p) RichardThomas 1 74
(Christian Wroe) *taken down early: chsd ldrs to 1/2-way: sn lost tch* **25/1**

5020 **10** 16 **Royal Intruder**[32] 5795 3-9-5 95 .... RichardHughes 2 30
(R Hannon) *s.s: t.k.h and sn trckd ldrs: wknd rapidly 2f out: eased: t.o* **10/1**

1m 13.13s (0.93) **Going Correction** +0.275s/f (Good)
WFA 3 from 4yo+ 1lb **10** Ran SP% **117.4**
Speed ratings (Par 107): **104,103,101,101,101 100,99,99,94,73**
toteswinger: 1&2 £8.70, 1&3 £5.70, 2&3 £4.80. CSF £44.12 CT £158.89 TOTE £7.50: £2.40, £2.60, £1.90; EX 43.80.
Owner Mrs Tina Ann Dormer **Bred** Robin Lawson **Trained** Kentisbeare, Devon

FOCUS
A competitive sprint handicap and not surprisingly there were many chances entering the final furlong. Sound, if ordinary, form.

NOTEBOOK
Phantom Whisper burst through down the middle of the track to lead home a 1-2 for trainer Rod Millman. Back down to the same mark as when scoring on soft ground at Chepstow in July, he appreciated the slightly easier company than at Ascot last time, where he wore cheekpieces, storming home having been held up off the pace. Official explanation: trainer said, regarding the improved form shown, gelding was dropped in class here (op 7-1 tchd 15-2)
Brassini, who was always close to the pace, made a bold effort despite looking a shade vulnerable off his current mark, and he seems equally effective over 6f and 7f. (op 8-1 tchd 17-2)
Maimoona(IRE) was once again drawn widest of all and she kept straight and true down the middle, but she didn't have the pace to sustain her challenge in the closing stages. Official explanation: jockey said filly hung right (tchd 3-1 and 4-1)
Baldemar fared slightly better than when a solid fifth here last time. (op 10-1)
Idle Power(IRE), running in a race named in his honour, was unable to make an impact having raced on the speed early. His finishing effort was just one paced. (tchd 17-2)
Patavellian(IRE) was a touch disappointing given how well he had run in the Ayr Gold Cup last time. Running off his lowest mark in three years, he appeared to have a solid chance but he was always being pestered in behind the leaders and he never really had a clear run until switched wide late in the day. (op 7-2 tchd 9-2 in a place)
Johnstown Lad(IRE) ran well given how little he showed at Lingfield two days earlier. He was up there throughout until weakening in the closing stages but he ideally wants ground a touch quicker than this.

Royal Intruder Official explanation: jockey said colt finished distressed

6677 TURFTV FOR BETTING SHOPS MEDIAN AUCTION MAIDEN STKS 6f
4:55 (4:56) (Class 5) 2-Y-O £3,238 (£963; £481; £240) Stalls Low

Form RPR
4 1 **Son Of The Cat (USA)**[26] 6000 2-9-3 0 .... MichaelHills 4 83
(B Gubby) *swtg: mde virtually all: rdn whn runner-up chal ins fnl f: edgd rt but styd on wl* 10/1
5340 2 nk **Piazza San Pietro**[14] 6317 2-9-3 87 .... PhilipRobinson 8 82
(C G Cox) *lw: hld up: prog 2f out: urged along to press wnr last 100yds: a jst hld* 10/3[2]
3 3 ½ **Bennelong**[23] 6077 2-9-3 0 .... JimmyFortune 6 80
(R M Beckett) *lw: pressed wnr: hrd rdn over 1f out: hld ins fnl f and sn lost 2nd* 8/11[1]
5430 4 2 ¾ **Retro (IRE)**[23] 6080 2-9-3 77 .... RichardHughes 7 72
(R Hannon) *lw: pressed ldng pair to 2f out: steadily fdd* 8/1[3]
5 4 ½ **Yellow Printer** 2-9-3 0 .... RichardKingscote 1 59
(Tom Dascombe) *w'like: leggy: rousted along early and green: in tch: hung rt over 2f out: sn btn* 16/1
6 5 **Downstream** 2-8-12 0 .... DarryllHolland 3 39
(D M Simcock) *bit bkwd: struggling in rr by 1/2-way: sn no ch* 18/1
7 ¾ **Ethics Girl (IRE)** 2-8-12 0 .... TPO'Shea 2 36
(John Berry) *w'like: bit bkwd: chsd ldrs: hrd rdn over 2f out: wknd* 50/1
00 8 1 ¾ **Brown Lentic (IRE)**[13] 6341 2-9-3 0 .... AdamKirby 5 36
(G L Moore) *lw: plld hrd early: hld up and sn last: shkn up and no rspnse 2f out: wknd* 50/1

1m 13.85s (1.65) **Going Correction** +0.275s/f (Good) 8 Ran SP% 116.3
Speed ratings (Par 95): **100,99,98,95,89 82,81,79**
toteswinger: 1&2 £4.30, 1&3 £3.40, 2&3 £1.20. CSF £44.14 TOTE £10.10: £2.20, £1.30, £1.10; EX 44.40.
Owner Brian Gubby **Bred** Andover Stable Llc **Trained** Bagshot, Surrey
■ Stewards' Enquiry : Jimmy Fortune two-day ban: used whip with excessive force and in an incorrect place (Oct 28-29)

FOCUS
A fair sprint maiden.

NOTEBOOK
Son Of The Cat(USA) got the job done a shade more comfortably than the bare result suggests and clearly came on plenty for his first start. Appreciating the drop back to 6f, he travelled strongly throughout and was the last to come off the bridle, recording a time only marginally slower than that of the 0-95 handicap 35 minutes earlier. Michael Hills didn't get overly serious with him and this was a fair effort given the runner-up's official rating of 87, although whether that is an accurate reflection of his ability is debatable. Either way, the winner is clearly going the right way and he looks well suited by this trip. (tchd 11-1)
Piazza San Pietro had run very well in a valuable sales race at the Curragh last month and he set a fair benchmark. Responding gamely to pressure he did little wrong, just bumping into a less exposed rival, and there is clearly a similar event in him. (op 2-1)
Bennelong, who shaped with so much promise on debut, was strongly supported to make it second time lucky, and his effort can't really be crabbed given he battled on well once coming under pressure and was attacked from both sides. He too will not be long in winning his maiden. (op 11-10 tchd 6-5 in places)
Retro(IRE) was once again disappointing and has regressed on his last two starts. (tchd 9-1)
Yellow Printer fared best of the newcomers but he only showed minor promise. (op 25-1)

6678 VALETE STKS (H'CAP) 1m 4f
5:25 (5:28) (Class 5) (0-75,75) 3-Y-O £3,238 (£963; £481; £240) Stalls Low

Form RPR
0312 1 **Red Merlin (IRE)**[18] 6202 3-9-1 **72** .... (v) PhilipRobinson 8 79
(C G Cox) *hld up in 6th: crept clsr fr 3f out: nudged along and hanging rt 2f out: effrt to ld jst ins fnl f: hung lft but styd on wl* 5/4[1]
0644 2 2 **Blue Citadel (USA)**[46] 5406 3-8-9 **66** .... DarryllHolland 1 70
(Mrs A J Perrett) *lw: trckd ldr: quick move to ld 6f out and kicked on: rdn and hrd pressed fr 3f out: battled on wl: hdd and outpcd jst ins fnl f* 7/1[3]
205 3 ¾ **Air Chief**[6] 6542 3-9-1 **72** .... SteveDrowne 5 75
(H J L Dunlop) *swtg: trckd ldng pair: moved up to chal 3f out: w ldr 2f out: nt qckn and hld jst over 1f out: one pce* 7/1[3]
1-40 4 ½ **Ragamuffin Man (IRE)**[149] 2151 3-9-4 **75** .... ShaneKelly 6 77
(W J Knight) *lw: led to 1/2-way: n.m.r and snatched up sn after: tried to chal again 3f out: nt qckn and hld 2f out: hanging but kpt on nr fin* 3/1[2]
0016 5 3 ¾ **World Time**[111] 3327 3-9-2 **73** .... JimmyFortune 4 69
(J H M Gosden) *s.s: hld up in last: tried to cl fr 3f out: rdn and no real imp over 2f out* 7/1[3]
6350 6 3 **Amwell House**[58] 5077 3-7-13 **61** oh16 .... Louis-PhilippeBeuzelin[(5)] 7 52?
(J R Jenkins) *t.k.h: hld up in 4th: effrt over 3f out: edgd rt 2f out: wknd over 1f out* 25/1
4002 7 52 **Lush (IRE)**[20] 6168 3-9-0 **71** .... RichardHughes 2 —
(R Hannon) *hld up in 5th: wknd 3f out: sn wl bhd: t.o* 14/1

2m 43.64s (5.24) **Going Correction** +0.275s/f (Good) 7 Ran SP% 117.5
Speed ratings (Par 101): **93,91,91,90,88 86,51**
toteswinger: 1&2 £3.50, 1&3 £2.40, 2&3 £8.10. CSF £11.53 CT £46.11 TOTE £2.60: £1.50, £3.70; EX 13.20 Place 6 £685.57 Place 5 £214.11..
Owner Reid's Allstars **Bred** Keatly Overseas Ltd **Trained** Lambourn, Berks
■ Stewards' Enquiry : Darryll Holland three-day ban: careless riding (Oct 31, Nov 1-2)

FOCUS
A modest handicap but straightfoward form at face value with the first four within a pound of recent marks. The sixth casts some doubt though.
T/Plt: £3,085.70 to a £1 stake. Pool: £76,932.71. 18.20 winning tickets. T/Qpdt: £63.60 to a £1 stake. Pool: £6,001.50. 69.75 winning tickets. JN

6594 GREAT LEIGHS (A.W) (L-H)
Sunday, October 12

OFFICIAL GOING: Standard
Wind: Nil Weather: Sunny and warm

6679 CLARE LOUISE MEMORIAL H'CAP (DIV I) 6f (P)
1:50 (1:50) (Class 6) (0-55,56) 3-Y-O+ £2,388 (£705; £352) Stalls Low

Form RPR
-004 1 **Milne Bay (IRE)**[41] 5574 3-9-0 **53** .... (t) RichardMullen 9 64+
(D M Simcock) *hld up in tch: nt clr run fr over 1f out: swtchd rt jst ins fnl f: rdn and qcknd to ld wl ins fnl f* 13/2[3]
2440 2 ¾ **Grizedale (IRE)**[57] 5088 9-9-2 **54** .... (tp) IanMongan 3 60
(M J Attwater) *hld up in midfield: hdwy and nt clr run over 1f out: burst between horses ent fnl f: ev ch ins fnl f: no ex nr fin* 9/1
3-05 3 1 **Whiskey Creek**[13] 6334 3-9-0 **53** .... TedDurcan 1 56
(C A Dwyer) *hld up in tch: hdwy on inner 2f out: rdn to ld ent fnl f: hdd and one pce wl ins fnl f* 7/1
0060 4 shd **River Kirov (IRE)**[39] 5601 5-8-13 **51** .... SimonWhitworth 12 54
(M Wigham) *hld up in tch: rdn and hdwy wl over 1f out: ev ch 1f out: uanble to qckn fnl 100yds* 10/1
350 5 ¾ **Charming Tale (USA)**[41] 5574 3-9-1 **54** .... (b) JamieSpencer 2 54
(B J Meehan) *dwlt: towards rr: nt clr run over 1f out tl swtchd lft ins fnl f: kpt on: nvr able to chal* 13/2[3]
5515 6 nse **Welcome Approach**[16] 6251 5-9-3 **55** .... JamieMoriarty 8 55
(J R Weymes) *dwlt: towards rr: rdn over 3f out: swtchd rt over 1f out: kpt on u.p fnl f: nvr rchd ldrs* 6/1[2]
0000 7 nk **Brigadore**[72] 4609 9-8-13 **51** .... TPQueally 5 50
(J G Given) *slowly itno stride: towards rr: rdn and effrt on outer 1/2-way: kpt on but nvr pce to threaten ldrs* 10/1
3305 8 1 ¾ **Nawaaff**[29] 5911 3-8-13 **52** .... (v) SamHitchcott 11 46
(M R Channon) *dwlt: sn pushed up to press ldrs: ev ch and rdn wl over 1f out: looked reluctant u.p: wknd fnl f* 9/1
6021 9 4 **Willhewiz**[10] 6419 8-9-4 **56** .... (v) TGMcLaughlin 7 37
(W M Brisbourne) *w ldrs: led over 2f out: hrd rdn over 1f out: hdd ent fnl f: wknd qckly fnl f* 9/2[1]
0000 10 3 ¼ **Affirmatively**[19] 6190 3-8-11 **55** .... DavidProbert[(5)] 6 25
(A W Carroll) *led tl over 2f out: sn rdn: wknd qckly ent fnl f* 16/1
5400 11 13 **El Potro**[33] 5775 6-8-12 **50** .... (b[1]) JerryO'Dwyer 4 —
(J R Holt) *v.s.a: a toiling in rr: rdn and no rspnse over 3f out: eased fnl f: t.o* 16/1

1m 14.12s (0.42) **Going Correction** +0.10s/f (Slow)
WFA 3 from 5yo+ 1lb 11 Ran SP% 121.6
Speed ratings (Par 101): **101,100,98,98,97 97,97,94,89,85 67**
toteswinger: 1&2 £15.40, 1&3 £12.30, 2&3 £7.00. CSF £66.15 CT £438.03 TOTE £9.70: £2.20, £2.50, £2.00; EX 72.80.
Owner DXB Bloodstock Ltd **Bred** Michael Boland **Trained** Newmarket, Suffolk

FOCUS
A moderate sprint handicap with the top weight rated just 56 and the lead changed a few times down the home straight. The race is rated through the third with the winner better than the bare form.
Charming Tale(USA) Official explanation: jockey said filly was denied a clear run
El Potro Official explanation: jockey said gelding was slowly away

6680 RIVER CROUCH CLAIMING STKS 6f (P)
2:25 (2:26) (Class 6) 3-Y-O+ £2,590 (£770; £385; £96) Stalls Low

Form RPR
0004 1 **Brazilian Brush (IRE)**[9] 6433 3-8-8 61 .... (t) TravisBlock 14 71
(H Morrison) *mde all: sn crossed to rail: clr over 1f out: kpt on u.p fnl f* 14/1
4320 2 1 **Our Blessing (IRE)**[24] 6040 4-9-1 60 .... RichardMullen 6 74
(A P Jarvis) *chsd ldng pair tl rdn to chse wnr over 1f out: sn edgd lft: kpt on u.p but nvr gng to rch wnr* 16/1
0050 3 1 ¼ **Blue Tomato**[15] 6289 7-8-10 84 .... WilliamCarson[(5)] 2 70
(D Nicholls) *chsd wnr tl over 1f out: sn swtchd rt: kpt on one pce fnl f* 9/2[3]
3215 4 ½ **Ivory Silk**[11] 6402 3-8-8 75 .... DavidProbert[(5)] 3 67+
(D K Ivory) *hld up towards rr: rdn and effrt wl over 1f out: kpt on steadily fnl f: nvr rchd ldrs* 11/4[2]
2202 4 dht **Gift Horse**[8] 6490 8-9-4 85 .... (p) TedDurcan 12 71+
(D Nicholls) *towards rr: hdwy over 2f out: swtchd rt 2f out: kpt on steadily fnl f: nvr rchd ldrs* 9/4[1]
2243 6 2 ½ **Norcroft**[18] 6209 6-8-13 62 .... TGMcLaughlin 4 58
(Mrs C A Dunnett) *in tch in midfield: rdn and struggling over 2f out: no ch fr over 1f out* 10/1
1550 7 7 **Klarity**[20] 6173 3-8-4 48 .... (e) FrankieMcDonald 8 28
(J Pearce) *taken down early: awkward leaving stalls and v.s.a: sn swtchd lft: a bhd* 66/1
0406 8 nk **Young Ivanhoe**[3] 6595 3-8-7 50 .... (b) CatherineGannon 7 30
(C A Dwyer) *stdd s: t.k.h: hld up in last pair: wd 3f out: n.d* 40/1
3000 9 nk **Attacca**[61] 4951 7-8-9 46 .... WilliamBuick 5 30
(J R Weymes) *towards rr: rdn and struggling over 3f out: no ch last 2f* 40/1
4006 10 1 **Never Without Me**[14] 6310 8-8-3 54 .... AndreaAtzeni[(7)] 11 28
(J F Coupland) *racd in midfield: rdn and struggling fr 1/2-way: no ch fr wl over 1f out* 33/1
0404 11 17 **Doctor Hilary**[13] 6328 6-9-7 78 .... (v) JamieSpencer 1 —
(A B Haynes) *dwlt: sn rdn along to chse ldrs: rdn and struggling over 2f out: wl btn over 1f out: virtually p.u ins fnl f* 11/2

1m 12.8s (-0.90) **Going Correction** +0.10s/f (Slow)
WFA 3 from 4yo+ 1lb 11 Ran SP% 122.0
Speed ratings (Par 101): **109,107,106,105,105 102,92,92,91,90 67**
toteswinger: 1&2 £14.40, 1&3 £11.60, 2&3 £17.80. CSF £216.64 TOTE £19.60: £7.40, £3.10, £1.40; EX 535.60.Brazilian Brush was claimed by J. M. Bradley for £6,000. Ivory Silk was claimed by J. R. Gask for £16,000.
Owner Betfair Club ROA **Bred** Mrs T Mahon **Trained** East Ilsley, Berks

FOCUS
An ordinary claimer in which only a few appeared to have a realistic chance at the weights. It was also a race where very few ever got into it and the first three home basically held those positions throughout. A strong pace meant that the winning time was 1.32 seconds quicker than the opener. The form is tricky to pin down but best rated through the first two.
Klarity Official explanation: jockey said filly run right
Doctor Hilary Official explanation: jockey said gelding moved badly

6681 CLARE LOUISE MEMORIAL H'CAP (DIV II) 6f (P)
3:00 (3:00) (Class 6) (0-55,55) 3-Y-O+ £2,388 (£705; £352) Stalls Low

Form RPR
0206 1 **Scruffy Skip (IRE)**[24] 6063 3-9-0 **53** .... TGMcLaughlin 3 58
(Mrs C A Dunnett) *sn rdn along towards rr: drvn 1/2-way: hdwy u.p over 1f out: r.o fnl f to ld last strides* 10/1
0000 2 shd **Who's Winning (IRE)**[13] 6334 7-8-12 **55** .... GabrielHannon[(5)] 4 60
(B G Powell) *wl bhd: rdn over 1f out: swtchd rt ent fnl f: r.o wl to chal wl ins fnl f: jst hld* 7/1
6000 3 hd **Kindallachan**[10] 6419 5-8-12 **50** .... (p) TPQueally 9 54
(G C Bravery) *chsd ldrs: effrt on inner 2f out: drvn over 1f out: led narrowly ins fnl f: hdd and lost 2 pls last strides* 12/1
-205 4 nk **Eleanor Eloise (USA)**[220] 806 4-8-10 **55** .... (p) AndreaAtzeni[(7)] 14 58
(J R Gask) *chsd ldrs: rdn and hung rt over 1f out: edgd lft and hdwy 1f out: ev ch ins fnl f: no ex last strides* 12/1
0000 5 2 ¼ **Bountiful Bay**[59] 5026 3-8-12 **51** .... (t) JamieSpencer 7 47
(B J Meehan) *chsd ldng pair: rdn over 2f out: drvn to ld over 1f out: hdd ins fnl f: fdd wl ins fnl f* 11/1

The Form Book, Raceform Ltd, Compton, RG20 6NL

2464 **6** 2 ¾ **Marmooq**^{106} [3501] 5-9-1 **53** .... IanMongan 2 40
(M J Attwater) *sn wl bhd: hdwy on inner 2f out: kpt on fnl f: nvr rchd ldrs* **13/2**^{3}

0000 **7** ¾ **Mundo's Magic**^{22} [6116] 4-9-1 **53** .... (b^{1}) JamieMoriarty 11 38
(M Dods) *s.i.s: wl bhd: rdn over 3f out: sme late hdwy: nvr trbld ldrs* **17/2**

0002 **8** ¾ **George The Second**^{10} [6419] 5-9-3 **55** .... RobertHavlin 1 37+
(Miss Tor Sturgis) *chsd ldr: led on inner over 2f out: rdn wl over 1f out: hdd ent fnl f: wknd fnl f* **4/1**^{1}

0000 **9** 1 ¾ **Connor's Choice**^{23} [6088] 3-9-2 **55** .... (b) WilliamBuick 8 32+
(Andrew Turnell) *led at fast pce: hdd over 2f out: hung lft u.p wl over 1f out: sn wknd* **8/1**

0063 **10** *nk* **The Hoofer (IRE)**^{10} [6419] 3-8-8 **52** .... (t) DavidProbert$^{(5)}$ 6 28
(I A Wood) *s.i.s: wl bhd: rdn over 3f out: c wd 2f out: nvr trbld ldrs* **5/1**^{2}

0060 **11** 9 **Battling Lil (IRE)**^{98} [3757] 4-8-9 **52** .... JackDean$^{(5)}$ 5 —
(J L Spearing) *dwlt: sn rdn along in rr: nvr a factor: wl btn and eased fnl f* **16/1**

0-42 **12** 8 **East Coast Girl (IRE)**^{236} [614] 3-9-0 **53** .... JerryO'Dwyer 10 —
(S W Hall) *stdd s: a bhd: rdn over 3f out: no hdwy: wl btn over 1f out* **16/1**

1m 14.78s (1.08) **Going Correction** +0.10s/f (Slow)
WFA 3 from 4yo+ 1lb **12** Ran SP% **128.7**
Speed ratings (Par 101): **96,95,95,95,92 88,87,86,84,83 71,61**
toteswinger: 1&2 £10.90, 1&3 £54.00, 2&3 £32.20. CSF £85.27 CT £891.81 TOTE £10.50: £4.30, £3.10, £3.70; EX 162.80.
Owner M Bringloe, D Cooper & R Clarke **Bred** Darley **Trained** Hingham, Norfolk

FOCUS
Another moderate handicap with the top weight rated 55. This was another race run at a strong early pace, but this time they went off far too quick and the pair responsible for the blistering gallop eventually paid the penalty. The form may not prove reliable. The winning time was 0.66 seconds slower than the first division and nearly two seconds slower than the claimer.
The Hoofer(IRE) Official explanation: jockey said filly missed the break

6682 DYNES MAIDEN FILLIES' STKS 1m (P)
3:35 (3:36) (Class 4) 2-Y-O **£5,180** (£1,541; £770; £384) **Stalls** Centre

Form RPR

05 **1** **Act Green**^{20} [6167] 2-9-0 0 .... JamieSpencer 10 79+
(M L W Bell) *mde all: swtchd to r centre wl over 1f out: sn rdn clr: wandered but in n.d fnl f: comf* **7/2**^{2}

23 **2** 2 ¾ **Wake Me Now (IRE)**^{25} [6016] 2-9-0 0 .... WilliamBuick 11 71
(R M Beckett) *in tch: hdwy to chse ldng pair 2f out: sn rdn: no ch w wnr fnl f: wnt 2nd fnl 100yds* **5/2**^{1}

0 **3** ½ **Breadstick**^{38} [5640] 2-9-0 0 .... TravisBlock 12 70
(H Morrison) *chsd wnr: rdn 2f out: outpcd by wnr over 1f out: wl hld after: lost 2nd fnl 100yds* **8/1**

4 1 ½ **Catamarca (USA)** 2-9-0 0 .... RobertHavlin 8 67+
(J H M Gosden) *dwlt: hld up in tch in midfield: hdwy to chse ldrs over 2f out: rdn 2f out: kpt on same pce fr over 1f out* **5/1**^{3}

0 **5** 1 ¼ **Peal Park**^{23} [6081] 2-8-11 0 .... PatrickHills$^{(3)}$ 6 64
(B J Meehan) *hld up towards rr: outpcd over 3f out: kpt on steadily fnl f: nvr trbld ldrs* **25/1**

056 **6** *nse* **Lilly Blue (IRE)**^{15} [6291] 2-9-0 77 .... TedDurcan 13 64
(M R Channon) *hld up in midfield on outer: hdwy over 2f out: rdn and no imp over 1f out: btn whn swtchd lft ins fnl f* **13/2**

04 **7** 2 **Romantic Interlude (IRE)**^{24} [6038] 2-9-0 .... RichardMullen 9 59
(A P Jarvis) *in tch in midfield: rdn 4f out: wknd u.p over 2f out* **50/1**

0 **8** 5 **Midsummer Madness (IRE)**^{18} [6205] 2-8-9 0 .... DavidProbert$^{(5)}$ 4 48
(David Pinder) *racd in midfield: rdn and struggling over 2f out: wl btn fr wl over 1f out* **16/1**

00 **9** ½ **Caught On Camera**^{20} [6166] 2-9-0 0 .... J-PGuillambert 3 47
(M L W Bell) *chsd ldng pair: rdn over 3f out: wknd over 1f out* **8/1**

00 **10** 1 **Desert Fairy**^{11} [6391] 2-9-0 0 .... IanMongan 2 45
(P W D'Arcy) *racd in midfield: rdn 4f out: struggling 3f out: no ch last 2f* **50/1**

11 7 **Aigle De Mer (IRE)** 2-8-9 0 .... GabrielHannon$^{(5)}$ 7 30
(B J Meehan) *awkward leaving stalls and s.i.s: a in last pair: lost tch wl over 2f out: t.o* **14/1**

12 16 **Ascot Fayre** 2-9-0 0 .... TGMcLaughlin 1 —
(Miss Gay Kelleway) *awkward leaving stalls and s.i.s: a in last pair: lost tch over 2f out: t.o and eased fnl f* **33/1**

1m 42.28s (2.38) **Going Correction** +0.10s/f (Slow) **12** Ran SP% **126.3**
Speed ratings (Par 94): **92,89,88,87,86 85,83,78,78,77 70,54**
toteswinger: 1&2 £2.30, 1&3 £10.60, 2&3 £8.10. CSF £13.27 TOTE £5.20: £1.90, £1.60, £2.80; EX 17.00.
Owner W J Gredley **Bred** Stetchworth Park Stud Ltd **Trained** Newmarket, Suffolk

FOCUS
An ordinary fillies' maiden in which they went a sensible pace, but not that many got into it.

NOTEBOOK
Act Green, whose most recent outing was an improvement from her debut, progressed once again and benefited from a well-judged front-running ride by Spencer. The only moment of concern came when she hung away to her right off the home bend, but once straightened she proved much too good for these rivals. She is improving with racing, but is still not the finished article and she should be a nice filly at around 1m2f next season. (op 4-1 tchd 100-30)
Wake Me Now(IRE), placed in her first two outings, was never far away and ended up widest coming up the straight. She kept on and now qualifies for a mark which will widen her options. (op 11-4)
Breadstick, who showed nothing on her debut, ran much better this time and was another to race handily throughout. She may come into her own once handicapped after one more run.
Catamarca(USA), a half-sister to winning miler Northern Spy, travelled well into the race but did not find as much off the bridle as had looked likely. She still fared much the best of the newcomers and is likely to improve. (op 9-2 tchd 6-1)
Peal Park, beaten a very long way on her Newmarket debut, made a little late headway and may show more when qualifying for a mark after one more run.
Lilly Blue(IRE), the most experienced in the field and highly tried in her short career, was close enough turning in but failed to pick up adequately for pressure. She is already rated 77 and may not be the easiest to place from now on. (op 7-1 tchd 6-1)
Caught On Camera, well beaten in both starts so far, attracted market support and ran well for a long way. She is bred to stay further and needed this for a mark. (op 10-1 tchd 7-1)

6683 HARLOW H'CAP 1m (P)
4:10 (4:12) (Class 5) (0-75,75) 3-Y-O **£3,238** (£963; £481; £240) **Stalls** Centre

Form RPR

443 **1** **Pension Policy (USA)**^{26} [5995] 3-8-10 **67** .... KShea 9 75+
(R Charlton) *hld up wl in tch: hdwy 2f out: rdn to ld jst over 1f out: r.o wl: in command and eased nr fin* **13/2**^{3}

1640 **2** 2 **Wikaala (USA)**^{22} [6130] 3-9-4 **75** .... RHills 2 78
(M P Tregoning) *hld up in tch: plld out off rail wl over 2f out: rdn and ev ch over 1f out: chsd wnr fnl f: nt pce of wnr fnl 100yds* **5/2**^{1}

6000 **3** 1 ¼ **My Shadow**^{10} [6417] 3-9-0 **71** .... IanMongan 11 71
(S Dow) *towards rr: hdwy and rdn over 2f out: chsd ldrs ent fnl f: kpt on same pce fnl f* **20/1**

3221 **4** ¾ **Mille Feuille (IRE)**^{18} [6206] 3-9-0 **71** .... WilliamBuick 13 69
(R M Beckett) *w ldr: ev ch and rdn wl over 1f out: wknd jst ins fnl f* **9/2**^{2}

16 **5** ¾ **Wallonia (IRE)**^{47} [5378] 3-8-8 **65** .... RichardMullen 4 62
(K A Ryan) *led narrowly: rdn wl over 1f out: hdd jst over 1f out: wknd jst ins fnl f* **10/1**

0103 **6** ½ **Addwaitya**^{59} [5032] 3-9-0 **71** .... TedDurcan 5 69+
(C F Wall) *sn bustled along in midfield: effrt on inner jst over 2f out: chsd ldrs over 1f out: wknd 1f out: wl hld whn nt clr run and swtchd rt towards fin* **7/1**

2153 **7** *nse* **Jollyhockeysticks**^{13} [6332] 3-8-10 **67** .... SamHitchcott 7 62
(M R Channon) *t.k.h: hld up in tch in midfield: rdn and unable qck over 2f out: kpt on same pce u.p fr over 1f out* **8/1**

3140 **8** 3 **Penchesco (IRE)**^{30} [5863] 3-9-3 **74** .... PaulEddery 8 63
(Pat Eddery) *hld up in tch: rdn and unable qck over 2f out: no imp fr over 1f out* **14/1**

3000 **9** *nk* **Silca Destination**^{10} [6417] 3-8-2 **66** .... MatthewDavies$^{(7)}$ 15 54
(M R Channon) *hld up towards rr: rdn over 2f out: no hdwy: wl btn over 1f out* **50/1**

-120 **10** 4 **Tevez**^{16} [6256] 3-9-1 **72** .... (v^{1}) TPQueally 6 51
(Miss Amy Weaver) *awkward leaving stalls and s.i.s: a bhd: n.d* **20/1**

6U05 **11** *nk* **Dynamo Dave (USA)**^{121} [2988] 3-7-13 **61** oh2 .... DavidProbert$^{(5)}$ 12 39
(M D I Usher) *chsd ldrs: rdn and struggling over 3f out: wl bhd last 2f* **66/1**

0000 **12** *shd* **Street Diva (USA)**^{11} [6377] 3-8-4 **61** oh4 .... CatherineGannon 14 39
(P A Blockley) *a towards rr: rdn 3f out: no ch last 2f* **40/1**

-055 **13** 8 **Maryqueenofscots (IRE)**^{18} [6215] 3-8-13 **70** .... JamieSpencer 3 29
(M L W Bell) *stdd s: hld up in rr: rdn and effrt over 2f out: no hdwy wl over 1f out: wl btn and eased fnl f* **12/1**

1m 40.7s (0.80) **Going Correction** +0.10s/f (Slow) **13** Ran SP% **122.6**
Speed ratings (Par 101): **100,98,96,96,95 94,94,91,91,87 87,87,79**
toteswinger: 1&2 £5.30, 1&3 £31.10, 2&3 £16.70. CSF £22.50 CT £333.22 TOTE £6.20: £2.50, £1.60, £7.60; EX 26.10.
Owner Bridgewater Equine Ltd **Bred** Claiborne Farm **Trained** Beckhampton, Wilts

FOCUS
An ordinary handicap in which the pace was honest. Fair form for the grade, the winner up 8lb, and sound too.
Maryqueenofscots(IRE) Official explanation: jockey said filly had no more to give

6684 BANQUETING AT GREAT LEIGHS FILLIES' H'CAP 1m (P)
4:45 (4:46) (Class 4) (0-85,83) 3-Y-O+ **£5,180** (£1,541; £770; £384) **Stalls** Centre

Form RPR

1 **1** **Tactful (IRE)**^{24} [6047] 3-8-10 **74** .... WilliamBuick 2 89+
(R M Beckett) *t.k.h: in tch: hdwy to chse ldr gng wl 2f out: led and edgd rt ent fnl f: sn pushed clr: easily* **9/4**^{2}

0354 **2** 3 ¾ **Oceana Blue**^{16} [6242] 3-8-6 **75** .... (t) DavidProbert$^{(5)}$ 1 81
(A M Balding) *w ldr tl led 3f out: rdn over 2f out: hdd ent fnl f: outpcd by wnr but hld on wl for 2nd* **9/2**^{3}

200 **3** *hd* **Secret Night**^{36} [5697] 5-9-5 **80** .... (p) IanMongan 5 86
(C G Cox) *hld up in last pair: rdn and effrt wl over 1f out: chsd ldrs ent fnl f: kpt on same pce after* **17/2**

21 **4** 1 ¼ **Priti Fabulous (IRE)**^{25} [6021] 3-9-5 **83** .... JamieSpencer 3 86
(W J Haggas) *stdd s: hld up in last pair: rdn and effrt 2f out: chsd ldrs over 1f out: one pce fnl f* **13/8**^{1}

0030 **5** ¾ **Tender The Great (IRE)**^{15} [6266] 5-9-7 **82** .... JerryO'Dwyer 4 83
(H J Collingridge) *hld up wl in tch: rdn over 2f out: ev ch and drvn over 1f out: wknd ins fnl f* **9/1**

0 **6** 18 **Indian Diva (IRE)**^{15} [6271] 3-9-4 **82** .... J-PGuillambert 6 42
(P A Blockley) *led tl hdd and rdn 3f out: wknd 2f out: wl bhd fnl f* **20/1**

1m 39.77s (-0.13) **Going Correction** +0.10s/f (Slow)
WFA 3 from 5yo 3lb **6** Ran SP% **112.3**
Speed ratings (Par 102): **104,100,100,98,98 80**
toteswinger: 1&2 £1.80, 1&3 £4.00, 2&3 £4.30. CSF £12.72 TOTE £3.40: £1.80, £2.50; EX 12.60.
Owner Mrs David Aykroyd **Bred** London Thoroughbred Services Ltd **Trained** Whitsbury, Hants

FOCUS
A fair little fillies' handicap run at a solid pace and the winning time was 0.93 seconds faster than the preceding handicap. Tactful was a big improver on the bare form of her maiden win, with a career best too from the second under a claimer.
Priti Fabulous(IRE) Official explanation: jockey said filly broke awkardly

6685 GREAT YELDHAM APPRENTICE H'CAP 1m 2f (P)
5:15 (5:16) (Class 6) (0-60,60) 3-Y-O **£2,590** (£770; £385; £192) **Stalls** Low

Form RPR

0020 **1** **Yes Eighteen (IRE)**^{17} [6227] 3-9-5 **60** .... LanceBetts 10 69
(J W Hills) *bhd: hdwy and rdn 3f out: styd on to ld over 1f out: kpt on wl fnl f* **14/1**

3002 **2** ¾ **Alfredtheordinary**^{6} [6541] 3-9-3 **58** .... MatthewDavies 15 65
(M R Channon) *bhd: rdn and hdwy on outer 3f out: hrd rdn and carried rt wl over 1f out: chsd ldr jst over 1f out: kpt on u.p* **10/1**^{3}

4001 **3** 2 **Star Choice**^{8} [6492] 3-8-13 **59** .... CharlesEddery$^{(5)}$ 8 62
(M L W Bell) *hld up in midfield: hdwy on inner 3f out: swtchd rt over 1f out: chsd ldrs ent fnl f: nudged along and kpt on steadily fnl f* **3/1**^{1}

0-40 **4** 1 ½ **Felicia**^{25} [6036] 3-9-1 **56** .... WilliamCarson 11 56
(S C Williams) *racd keenly: chsd ldr: rdn 3f out: ev ch over 1f out: no ex ins fnl f* **10/1**^{3}

3000 **5** 6 **Bobal Girl**^{31} [5837] 3-8-11 **52** .... JPHamblett 9 40
(E F Vaughan) *racd in midfield on outer: wl off the pce: rdn over 3f out: plugged on fnl f: nvr trbld ldrs* **16/1**

4254 **6** 3 ½ **Admirals Way**^{22} [6116] 3-9-1 **56** .... SophieDoyle 16 37
(C N Kellett) *chsd ldrs: rdn over 3f out: wknd over 2f out* **11/2**^{2}

0000 **7** 2 **Civitas Filius (USA)**^{24} [6049] 3-9-5 **60** .... (b^{1}) DeanHeslop 1 37
(D M Simcock) *racd keenly: led: clr 6f out: rdn over 2f out: hung rt and hdd wl over 1f out: wknd qckly over 1f out* **14/1**

0055 **8** 2 ½ **High Coincidence**^{11} [6374] 3-8-9 **50** .... (b^{1}) BillyCray 3 22
(Andrew Turnell) *a bhd: rdn along 8f out: past btn horses fr over 1f out: n.d* **20/1**

3342 **9** 8 **Complete Frontline (GER)**^{41} [5575] 3-9-1 **56** .... (p) DeclanCannon 4 12
(K R Burke) *t.k.h: chsd ldrs: rdn 3f out: sn wknd* **11/2**^{2}

0060 **10** 1 ¼ **Lightning Squall (USA)**^{89} [4061] 3-9-2 **60** .... AndreaAtzeni$^{(3)}$ 2 14
(M Botti) *dwlt: t.k.h: sn chsng ldrs: rdn over 3f out: wknd qckly over 2f out* **18/1**

0030 **11** 1 ¾ **Southern Mistral**^{24} [6049] 3-9-0 **60** .... TobyAtkinson$^{(5)}$ 13 10
(M Wigham) *a bhd: nvr a factor* **16/1**

6005 **12** *1* **Can Can Dancer**^{25} [6015] 3-8-8 **52**.................... RosieJessop$^{(3)}$ 7 —
(J G Given) *racd wl off the pce in midfield: rdn and toiling over 3f out* **20/1**
2050 **13** *7* **Lizzie Wiggins**^{18} [6217] 3-8-12 **58**..........(p) JohnCavanagh$^{(5)}$ 6 —
(Mrs Marjorie Fife) *t.k.h: hld up in tch: rdn and wknd qckly 4f out: t.o fnl f* **18/1**

2m 9.21s (0.61) **Going Correction** +0.10s/f (Slow) **13** Ran SP% **119.1**
Speed ratings (Par 99): **101,100,98,97,92 90,88,86,80,79 77,76,71**
toteswinger: 1&2 £24.90, 1&3 £12.60, 2&3 £7.10. CSF £132.64 CT £407.34 TOTE £18.70: £4.20, £3.10, £1.80; EX 122.70 Place 6 £433.94, Place 5 £144.97..
Owner Yes Eighteen **Bred** David F Byrne **Trained** Upper Lambourn, Berks
■ Augmentation was withdrawn (9/1, unruly in stalls). R4 applies, deduct 10p in the £.
■ Stewards' Enquiry : Andrea Atzeni three-day ban: careless riding (Oct 27-29)

FOCUS
A very modest apprentice handicap to end the card and only four of these had ever previously won a race. The form just about makes sense though. The early pace was very strong and that played into the hands of the hold-up horses. They finished spread out all over Essex.
Admirals Way Official explanation: jockey said gelding was never travelling
T/Plt: £662.10 to a £1 stake. Pool: £52,881.02. 58.30 winning tickets. T/Qpdt: £59.30 to a £1 stake. Pool: £4,404.48. 54.90 winning tickets. SP

6686 - 6690a (Foreign Racing) - See Raceform Interactive

4882 NAAS (L-H)
Sunday, October 12

OFFICIAL GOING: Soft (soft to heavy in places)

6689a CASTLEMARTIN STUD EUROPEAN BREEDERS FUND GARNET STKS (LISTED RACE) (F&M) 1m
5:00 (5:02) 3-Y-0+ **£35,900** (£10,533; £5,018; £1,709)

RPR
1 **Mad About You (IRE)**^{91} [4006] 3-8-12 114..........(b^{1}) PJSmullen 1 104+
(D K Weld, Ire) *trckd ldrs: impr to ld under 3f out: clr 1 1/2f out: kpt on strly: easily* **7/4^{1}**
2 *3 1/2* **Kalidaha (IRE)**^{140} [2436] 3-8-12 96.................... FMBerry 20 93
(John M Oxx, Ire) *trckd ldrs: 8th 1/2-way: hdwy in 5th ent st and racd on stands' rail: 2nd over 2f out: rdn and no imp on ldr 1 1/2f out: kpt on same pce* **8/1^{3}**
3 *shd* **Patio**^{20} [6180] 3-8-12 93.................... RPCleary 2 93
(David Marnane, Ire) *chsd ldrs: 4th 1/2-way: rdn 2f out: no ex in 3rd over 1f out: kpt on same pce* **16/1**
4 *4 1/2* **Solas Na Greine (IRE)**^{175} [1509] 3-8-12 90.................... MHarley 17 82
(J S Bolger, Ire) *chsd ldrs: 7th 1/2-way: rdn in 5th 2f out: kpt on same pce fr over 1f out* **40/1**
5 *hd* **Mystical Lady (IRE)**^{15} [6298] 3-9-1 99.................... SMLevey 6 85
(A P O'Brien, Ire) *towards rr: hdwy ent st: 7th 2f out: rdn into mod 4th 1f out: kpt on same pce fnl f* **12/1**
6 *1 3/4* **Tis Mighty (IRE)**^{42} [5550] 5-9-1 97.................... KLatham 12 78
(P J Prendergast, Ire) *mid-div: rdn in 11th 2f out: mod 7th 1f out: kpt on same pce* **9/1**
7 *1 1/4* **Customary Chorus (IRE)**^{60} [4998] 3-8-12.................... SMGorey 7 75
(D K Weld, Ire) *led: hdd under 3f out: rdn and no ex in 6th 2f out: kpt on one pce* **33/1**
8 *nk* **Mooretown Lady (IRE)**^{29} [5922] 5-9-1 99..........(p) WJLee 10 74
(H Rogers, Ire) *towards rr: sme hdwy in 12th 2f out: mod 9th 1f out: kpt on one pce* **16/1**
9 *nk* **Galistic (IRE)**^{50} [5293] 5-9-1 100.................... DMGrant 11 74
(Patrick J Flynn, Ire) *towards rr: sme late hdwy fr over 1f out: nvr a factor* **20/1**
10 *6* **Rinterval (IRE)**^{16} [6261] 3-8-12 86.................... WMLordan 4 60
(David Wachman, Ire) *in rr of mid-div: hdwy ent st: rdn in 8th 2f out: sn no ex and kpt on one pce* **33/1**
11 *hd* **Dimenticata (IRE)**^{77} [4467] 4-9-4 103.................... CDHayes 18 62
(Kevin Prendergast, Ire) *mid-div: rdn in 9th 2f out: no imp and kpt on one pce* **12/1**
12 *nk* **Queen Jock (USA)**^{102} [3619] 3-8-12 85.................... PShanahan 13 59
(Tracey Collins, Ire) *chsd ldrs early: 9th 1/2-way: rdn and no imp over 2f out* **40/1**
13 *3* **Gist (IRE)**^{14} [6315] 5-9-1 95..........(b) NGMcCullagh 16 52
(W J Martin, Ire) *nvr a factor* **33/1**
14 *1/2* **Clever Millie (USA)**^{15} [6294] 4-9-1 78.................... PTownend 9 51
(John E Kiely, Ire) *mid-div: rdn and wknd over 2f out* **66/1**
15 *1/2* **Sharleez (IRE)**^{45} [5441] 3-8-12 103.................... MJKinane 3 49
(John M Oxx, Ire) *trckd ldrs: hdwy into 4th ent st: rdn in 3rd 2f out: 6th and no ex 1f out: eased* **3/1^{2}**
16 *2 1/2* **Cheyenne Star (IRE)**^{35} [5730] 5-9-6 107.................... DPMcDonogh 14 49
(Ms F M Crowley, Ire) *a towards rr* **10/1**
17 *hd* **Ard Fheis (IRE)**^{42} [5550] 3-8-12 90.................... KJManning 15 43
(J S Bolger, Ire) *chsd ldrs: 6th 1/2-way: rdn and wknd over 2f out* **20/1**
18 *10* **Dollar Chick (IRE)**^{16} [6261] 4-9-1 91.................... MCHussey 19 20
(Noel Meade, Ire) *chsd ldr: 2nd 1/2-way: rdn in 6th early st: sn wknd* **33/1**

1m 44.5s (4.50)
WFA 3 from 4yo+ 3lb **20** Ran SP% **146.4**
CSF £18.60 TOTE £1.70: £1.20, £2.90, £7.50, £6.50; DF 21.10.
Owner Moyglare Stud Farm **Bred** Moyglare Stud Farm Ltd **Trained** The Curragh, Co Kildare

NOTEBOOK
Mad About You(IRE) stood out on form and duly obliged, running out an easy winner. Placed four times at Group 1 level, she failed to stay in the Irish Oaks and was having her first race since, with blinkers on for the first time. Well suited by ease, she tracked the leaders and once she went to the front over 2f out the contest was as good as over. She may bow out for the season in the Breeders' Cup Filly And Mare Turf, depending on how she recovers from this race, and will be kept in training next year. (op 2/1 tchd 9/4)
Kalidaha(IRE), rated 18lb below the winner, had won her only start last year and had not run since scoring on her reappearance at the Curragh in May. This was her first attempt on soft ground and she acquitted herself well, challenging towards the stands' side all the way up the straight and keeping on quite well without troubling the winner.
Patio had run well in the same grade at Tipperary two runs before winning a lesser contest at Ballinrobe last month. She gave a good account here and stuck to her task over the last 2f after being fourth into the straight.
Solas Na Greine(IRE), whose only win was over 7f at Dundalk last year, had not run since finishing an eased-down last of seven in a 1m2f Group 3 event at Leopardstown in April. Considering her lengthy absence, she ran a decent race and will be worth considering when she next appears.
Mystical Lady(IRE) is much better suited by quicker ground, and after making headway from halfway to go fourth over 1f out, was unable to make any further impression.

Sharleez(IRE) had finished second, beaten in a photo finish both times, at this level on her two previous starts. Held up, she made a forward move turning for home and went third under 2f out before weakening up the hill and being eased when any chance of her figuring in the money had gone. (op 3/1 tchd 7/2)

5334 DUSSELDORF (R-H)
Sunday, October 12

OFFICIAL GOING: Soft

6691a RACEBETS.COM - EBF STUTENPREIS (GROUP 3) (F&M) 1m 3f
2:35 (2:37) 3-Y-0+ **£23,529** (£9,559; £4,779; £2,574)

RPR
1 **Goathemala (GER)**^{49} [5329] 3-8-10.................... AStarke 7 103
(P Schiergen, Germany) *led after 1f: rdn out and r.o wl* **19/10^{1}**
2 *3/4* **Stella Di Quattro**^{31} [5851] 4-9-4.................... THellier 1 104
(U Ostmann, Germany) *led 1f: settled in cl 3rd to st: penned on rail bhd wnr fr jst over 2f out to over 1f out: r.o but could nvr worry wnr* **39/10^{2}**
3 *3* **Salve Germania (IRE)**^{40} [5597] 3-8-10.................... ASuborics 8 97
(W Hickst, Germany) *sn trcking wnr: 2nd st: one pce fr over 1f out* **44/10^{3}**
4 *1 1/2* **Themelie Island (IRE)**^{35} [5737] 3-8-10.................... SPasquier 4 94
(A Trybuhl, Germany) *hld up: 8th st: kpt on fnl 2f: tk 4th on line* **13/2**
5 *nse* **Bittersweetsymfony (GER)**^{35} [5737] 3-8-10.................... WMongil 5 94
(Frau E Mader, Germany) *racd in 4th to st: one pce fr over 1f out: lost 4th on line* **10/1**
6 **Foreign Music (FR)**^{39} [5625] 4-9-4.................... VSchulepov 9 96
(H J Groschel, Germany) *hld up: last to st: nvr a factor* **27/1**
7 *nk* **Every Day (GER)**^{28} 3-8-10.................... AHelfenbein 2 94
(Mario Hofer, Germany) *cl up: 5th st: btn over 1f out* **20/1**
8 *2 1/2* **Counterclaim**^{49} [5329] 3-8-10.................... JVictoire 6 90
(H-A Pantall, France) *mid-div: 6th st: btn over 1f out: eased* **67/10**
9 *10* **Dancing Abbie (USA)**^{49} [5336] 3-8-10.................... MickyFenton 3 73
(M L W Bell) *hld up in rr: 8th st: sn btn* **11/2**

2m 21.71s (141.71)
WFA 3 from 4yo 6lb **9** Ran SP% **132.5**
(including 10 Euro stake): WIN 29; PL 13, 14, 15; SF 86.
Owner Stiftung Gestut Fahrhof **Bred** Gestut Erlenhof **Trained** Germany

NOTEBOOK
Dancing Abbie(USA), winner of a Listed race in Norway on her previous start, was unable to get involved on this occasion. This was not her form and something may have been amiss.

6692a GROSSER PREIS DER LANDESHAUPTSTADT DUSSELDORF (GROUP 3) 1m 110y
3:50 (3:52) 3-Y-0+ **£23,529** (£9,559; £4,779; £2,574)

RPR
1 **Apollo Star (GER)**^{29} 6-9-2.................... SPasquier 9 117
(Lenka Horakova, Czech Republic) *prom: led ent st: sn clr: unchal* **38/10^{3}**
2 *11* **Wiesenpfad (FR)**^{43} [5528] 5-9-4.................... ASuborics 4 97
(W Hickst, Germany) *prom: 3rd st: styd on to go 2nd: no ch w wnr* **16/10^{1}**
3 *3/4* **Lord Hill (GER)**^{21} [6156] 4-9-2.................... VSchulepov 8 93
(C Zeitz) *in tch: styd on steadily fr 2f out* **11/1**
4 *1/2* **Lucidor (GER)**^{21} [6156] 5-9-2..........(b) WMongil 5 92
(Frau E Mader, Germany) *in tch: 4th and pushed along st: styd on at one pce* **28/1**
5 *1* **Mharadono (GER)**^{14} [6322] 5-9-2.................... AHelfenbein 2 90
(P Hirschberger, Germany) *hld up in last: drvn 2f out: styd on but n.d* **7/1**
6 *5* **Waky Love (GER)**^{14} [6323] 4-8-12.................... AStarke 1 76
(Frau Jutta Mayer, Germany) *led to st: 2nd st: sn no ex* **74/10**
7 *9* **Forthe Millionkiss (GER)**^{14} [6322] 4-9-6.................... THellier 3 66
(Uwe Ostmann, Germany) *mid-div: nvr a threat* **26/10^{2}**
8 *3/4* **Sutra (GER)**^{35} 3-8-6.................... J-PCarvalho 6 55
(Mario Hofer, Germany) *mid-div: nvr a threat* **17/1**
9 *22* **Integral (GER)**^{21} [6156] 4-9-2.................... TMundry 7 17
(P Rau, Germany) *mid-div: pushed along appr st: nvr able to chal* **22/1**

1m 43.22s (-4.36)
WFA 3 from 4yo+ 3lb **9** Ran SP% **133.2**
WIN 48; PL 22, 15, 25; SF 225.
Owner Mrs Erika Krajnikova **Bred** H Gerwin **Trained** Czechoslavakia

6570 **KEMPTON (A.W)** (R-H)

Monday, October 13

OFFICIAL GOING: Standard

Wind: Moderate, across Weather: Overcast

6693 BET PREMIER LEAGUE FOOTBALL - BETDAQ H'CAP 1m (P)

2:10 (2:11) (Class 6) (0-52,52) 3-Y-0+ £2,047 (£604; £302) Stalls Centre

Form RPR

5006 1 **Brandane (IRE)**[21] 6162 3-8-11 52 PaulHanagan 14 58
(R A Fahey) *mde virtually all: drvn over 2f out: narrow ld and hrd pressed fr over 1f out: hld on: all out* 7/1[1]

0203 2 nse **Fun In The Sun**[35] 5748 4-9-0 52 JamieSpencer 4 58
(A B Haynes) *hld up in rr and racd wd: prog over 2f out: drvn and making hrd work of it over 1f out: clsd fnl f: wnt 2nd last strides and jst failed* 7/1[1]

-004 3 shd **Comrade Cotton**[11] 6419 4-9-0 52 (p) JerryO'Dwyer 3 58
(J Ryan) *prom: rdn to chse wnr wl over 2f out: chal over 1f out: edgd clsr fnl f but lost 2nd last strides* 12/1[3]

3250 4 nk **Outer Hebrides**[17] 6255 7-8-9 52 (v) MCGeran(5) 7 57
(J M Bradley) *trckd ldrs: rdn over 2f out: tried to cl fr over 1f out: kpt on but nvr quite able to chal* 12/1[3]

0064 5 ½ **Hurricane Coast**[5] 6570 9-8-12 50 (b) TonyCulhane 8 54
(D Flood) *taken down early: stdd s: hld up wl in rr: prog over 2f out: hanging whn trying to cl over 1f out: styd on ins fnl f: gaining at fin* 8/1[2]

3000 6 ¾ **Anduril**[5] 6570 7-8-12 50 (b) PatrickMathers 11 52
(I W McInnes) *chsd ldrs: rdn over 2f out: tried to cl fr over 1f out: one pce u.p* 16/1

0000 7 1 **Balerno**[14] 6335 9-8-12 50 IanMongan 6 50
(Mrs L J Mongan) *hld up in midfield on inner: prog over 2f out: chsd ldrs over 1f out: fdd ins fnl f* 20/1

4550 8 ½ **The Graig**[49] 4597 4-8-12 50 (b[1]) GregFairley 9 49
(J R Holt) *chsd wnr to wl over 2f out: styd chsng ldrs and wl in tch: wknd ins fnl f* 12/1[3]

5040 9 ½ **Goose Green (IRE)**[31] 5871 4-8-12 50 JimmyQuinn 1 48
(R J Hodges) *hld up in last pair fr wd draw: effrt on outer over 2f out: plugged on fr over 1f out: nvr rchd ldrs* 16/1

0020 10 5 **Franksalot (IRE)**[17] 6255 8-9-0 52 (p) RoystonFfrench 2 38
(I W McInnes) *towards rr: rdn over 2f out: no prog after: wl btn over 1f out* 16/1

0560 11 6 **Beck**[11] 6408 4-8-12 50 ShaneKelly 12 22
(W M Brisbourne) *prom: rdn on inner over 2f out: no imp over 1f out: wknd rapidly fnl f* 12/1[3]

0060 12 10 **Bold Phoenix (IRE)**[5] 6570 7-8-12 50 (t) J-PGuillambert 13 —
(Miss Amy Weaver) *nvr gng that wl and a in rr: lost tch over 2f out: eased fnl f* 8/1[2]

-000 13 6 **Great Man (FR)**[39] 5651 7-8-12 50 (t) JohnEgan 5 —
(K M Prendergast) *nt wl away and rousted along on outer: wknd u.p 3f out: sn bhd: t.o* 16/1

0453 P **Summer Recluse (USA)**[14] 6335 9-9-0 52 (t) LPKeniry 10 —
(J M Bradley) *dropped out suddenly bef 1/2-way: p.u 3f out: collapsed* 8/1[2]

1m 40.14s (0.34) **Going Correction** +0.05s/f (Slow)
WFA 3 from 4yo+ 3lb 14 Ran SP% 117.4
Speed ratings (Par 101): **100,99,99,99,99 98,97,96,96,91 85,75,69,—**
toteswinger: 1&2 £9.50, 1&3 £24.10, 2&3 £8.70. CSF £52.12 CT £598.45 TOTE £6.80: £2.00, £2.30, £5.80; EX 52.40.
Owner R A Fahey **Bred** King Bloodstock **Trained** Musley Bank, N Yorks
■ Stewards' Enquiry : Paul Hanagan four-day ban: used whip with excessive frequency (Oct 27-30)

FOCUS
Some old favourites on show here but not a strong race by any means and most of these find winning difficult nowadays. The winner is a bit less exposed than most and the form is sound.
Franksalot(IRE) Official explanation: jockey said gelding never travelled

6694 BET CHAMPIONS LEAGUE FOOTBALL - BETDAQ CLAIMING STKS 1m (P)

2:40 (2:43) (Class 5) 2-Y-0 £2,590 (£770; £385; £192) Stalls Centre

Form RPR

0540 1 **Hum Cat (IRE)**[24] 6087 2-8-13 63 LPKeniry 3 67+
(J S Moore) *trckd ldrs: rdn and prog fr over 2f out: hung rt but sustained effrt to ld jst over 1f out: drvn out* 16/1

6000 2 ¾ **Protiva**[38] 5671 2-8-10 60 (v[1]) JimmyQuinn 8 62
(A P Jarvis) *led after 1f: drvn over 2f out: hdd jst over 1f out: already hld whn tightened up by wnr 150yds out: kpt on* 14/1

0505 3 2 ¼ **In Transit (IRE)**[12] 6376 2-8-13 70 DarryllHolland 2 60
(M R Channon) *trckd ldrs: wnt 2nd over 2f out to over 1f out: one pce u.p* 5/1[1]

6635 4 2 ¾ **Herring Senior (IRE)**[19] 6207 2-9-1 64 (b[1]) ShaneKelly 5 56
(P F I Cole) *led 1f: chsd ldr to over 2f out: grad outpcd u.p after* 6/1[2]

4666 5 1 ¾ **Reel Ale**[26] 6017 2-8-8 61 SaleemGolam 1 46+
(P Winkworth) *rrd bdly s and lost at least 6 l: rcvrd to rch 7th 1/2-way: outpcd over 2f out: plugged on* 5/1[1]

6352 6 ¾ **Cherry Belle (IRE)**[14] 6343 2-8-6 60 (v) JohnEgan 10 42
(P D Evans) *trckd ldng pair: rdn 3f out: steadily fdd fnl 2f* 5/1[1]

00 7 1 ½ **Santoriney (IRE)**[26] 6014 2-8-3 0 (b[1]) RobbieEgan(7) 12 43
(D Flood) *rdn in rr after 3f: struggling after: bhd 3f out: modest late prog* 100/1

0040 8 1 ½ **Caressing**[10] 6432 2-8-9 59 ow1 PatDobbs 4 38
(R Hannon) *chsd ldrs: rdn over 3f out: wknd over 2f out* 11/1

0006 9 1 ½ **Diamond Heist**[14] 6330 2-8-8 59 MartinDwyer 7 34
(M P Tregoning) *struggling towards rr fr 1/2-way: bhd over 2f out* 8/1[3]

560U 10 nse **Old Father Zieten**[14] 6343 2-8-4 58 (p) RossAtkinson(7) 11 37
(Tom Dascombe) *plld hrd: hld up in rr: prog to 8th 3f out and in tch: wknd over 2f out* 25/1

0 11 2 **Grey Ghost**[23] 6135 2-8-11 0 LiamJones 9 32
(E F Vaughan) *drvn in rr bef 1/2-way: sn wl btn* 16/1

050 12 6 **My Dixie Darling (USA)**[5] 6574 2-7-13 0 CharlesEddery(7) 6 14
(R Hannon) *hld up: struggling in rr fr 1/2-way: sn bhd* 20/1

00 13 6 **Going Going Gone**[51] 5277 2-8-13 0 (vt[1]) StephenCarson 14 8
(Tom Dascombe) *dismntd and walked to s: nvr gng wl: last and wl bhd 1/2-way* 20/1

1m 41.5s (1.70) **Going Correction** +0.05s/f (Slow) 13 Ran SP% 116.5
Speed ratings (Par 95): **93,92,90,87,85 84,83,81,80,80 78,72,66**
toteswinger: 1&2 £30.90, 1&3 £9.10, 2&3 £14.50. CSF £207.68 TOTE £17.20: £4.90, £4.90, £1.90; EX 236.00.
Owner Coleman Bloodstock Limited **Bred** Michael Woodlock & Seamus Kennedy **Trained** Upper Lambourn, Berks
■ Stewards' Enquiry : L P Keniry one-day ban: careless riding (Oct 27)

FOCUS
A weak claimer but run at a decent pace and they were pretty well strung out up the straight, although the time was slightly slower than the previous handicap.

NOTEBOOK
Hum Cat(IRE) hadn't made much of an impact in nurseries over shorter trips this summer and, although this represented a drop in class, the extra furlong was not sure to suit. However, he travelled eye-catchingly well off the pace and, having made smooth headway to join the leaders approaching the home turn, he stayed on strongly up the straight to lead inside the final furlong and win fairly comfortably. If the third-placed horse is a reliable yardstick, then Hum Cat ran above his mark here and he might be able to go on from this.
Protiva, another with stamina to prove over this trip, made a bold bid from the front, kicking a couple of lengths clear 2f out and staying on well to finish clear of everything but the winner. The first-time visor had a positive effect and she might be able to go one better back over 7f, providing the headgear continues to work.
In Transit(IRE) has had a fairly tough first season, this being his 13th run, but he just doesn't seem to be progressing. Although he ran okay, it was slightly disappointing he couldn't make a better fist of this given he is rated 7lb higher than the winner and was meeting him on equal terms. (tchd 9-2)
Herring Senior(IRE) is bred to be better suited by 6f/7f and did not see out this trip. (op 9-1)
Reel Ale lost all chance at the start, where he lost several lengths. He ran well in the circumstances because he made ground up quickly and kept on well in the closing stages, tackling this trip for the first time. From a stable bang in form, he looks worth persevering with. Official explanation: jockey said colt reared on leaving stalls (op 4-1 tchd 6-1)
Cherry Belle(IRE) had the visor back on, but she could not build on her recent Windsor second. (tchd 9-2)

6695 BETDAQ THE BETTING EXCHANGE H'CAP 7f (P)

3:10 (3:12) (Class 5) (0-75,75) 3-Y-0+ £2,590 (£770; £385; £192) Stalls High

Form RPR

3210 1 **Without Prejudice (USA)**[23] 6125 3-9-3 74 ShaneKelly 11 85+
(J Noseda) *hld up in abt 5th: decisive move and got through to ld 1f out: immediately in command: r.o wl* 11/2[2]

31 2 1 ½ **Lake Windermere (IRE)**[86] 4195 3-9-1 72 JimmyFortune 10 79+
(J H M Gosden) *trckd ldr: tried to chal fr 2f out: swept aside by wnr 1f out: chsd him after but no imp* 7/2[1]

5042 3 1 **Carmenero (GER)**[12] 6380 5-9-3 72 MartinDwyer 9 76
(W R Muir) *hld up towards rr: prog fr 2f out but had to weave through: r.o to take 3rd nr fin but no ch w wnr* 11/2[2]

-631 4 ¾ **Provence**[83] 4277 3-9-3 74 RHills 1 76
(B W Hills) *tk keen early: hld up in last trio: effrt on outer over 2f out: r.o fnl f: nrst fin* 11/1

3100 5 nk **Danish Art (IRE)**[21] 6169 3-9-4 75 DarryllHolland 13 76
(J A R Toller) *trckd ldng pair: drvn 2f out: readily outpcd fr 1f out: eased fnl strides* 33/1

3360 6 ½ **Cativo Cavallino**[20] 6194 5-8-11 71 NataliaGemelova(5) 2 71
(J E Long) *trckd ldrs: drvn to chal 2f out: nt qckn over 1f out: one pce fnl f and lost pls* 20/1

-166 7 hd **Luminous Gold**[14] 6340 3-8-13 73 JackMitchell(3) 12 72
(C F Wall) *sn led: drvn and pressed 2f out: hdd and fdd 1f out* 16/1

0664 8 ½ **Trafalgar Square**[12] 6380 6-9-0 69 PaulDoe 4 70+
(M J Attwater) *hld up in last pair: nt clr run jst over 2f out: prog whn rn into trble again ent fnl f: stl fin w flourish last 75yds* 14/1

2660 9 ½ **Lieutenant Pigeon**[11] 6420 3-9-1 72 PaulEddery 3 69
(G D Blake) *nvr bttr than midfield: no prog whn rdn over 2f out: plugged on* 33/1

0040 10 ½ **Eastern Gift**[17] 6242 3-9-2 73 PatDobbs 14 68
(R Hannon) *hld up in midfield on inner: prog and cl up over 1f out: wknd fnl f* 14/1

3506 10 dht **Autumn Blades (IRE)**[17] 6242 3-9-3 74 JamieSpencer 8 79+
(J W Hills) *s.i.s: swtchd to inner and hld up in last trio: prog 2f out: nt clr run over 1f out: rn into trble ins fnl f: no ch but appeared to fin w plenty lft* 9/1

4600 12 nse **Bahiano (IRE)**[68] 4744 7-9-6 75 LiamJones 7 70+
(C E Brittain) *settled midfield: effrt over 2f out: chsng ldrs but no imp over 1f out: wl hld whn short of room ent fnl f and fdd* 20/1

5000 13 1 **Dancer's Legacy**[59] 5052 3-9-2 73 (t) PatCosgrave 5 65
(E A L Dunlop) *settled midfield: rdn 3f out: struggling sn after: fdd fnl 2f* 66/1

6360 14 3 ½ **Jake The Snake (IRE)**[23] 6125 7-9-5 74 TonyCulhane 6 57+
(A W Carroll) *tk keen early: hld up in rr: effrt over 2f out: trying to stay on but no realistic ch whn squeezed out 1f out: eased* 7/1[3]

1m 26.24s (0.24) **Going Correction** +0.05s/f (Slow)
WFA 3 from 5yo+ 2lb 14 Ran SP% 119.9
Speed ratings (Par 103): **100,98,97,96,95 95,95,94,94,93 93,93,92,88**
toteswinger: 1&2 £5.40, 1&3 £6.10, 2&3 £5.00. CSF £23.32 CT £113.73 TOTE £4.70: £2.70, £2.00, £1.70; EX 28.50.
Owner Michael Tabor **Bred** Skymarc Farm And Castlemartin Stud **Trained** Newmarket, Suffolk
■ Stewards' Enquiry : Martin Dwyer one-day ban: careless riding (Oct 27)

FOCUS
Plenty of well-handicapped horses on show and the finish was dominated by a couple of unexposed 3yos. Things got very messy in behind with several meeting trouble. The form is rated around the third.
Autumn Blades(IRE) Official explanation: jockey said gelding was denied a clear run
Bahiano(IRE) Official explanation: jockey said gelding suffered interference in running
Jake The Snake(IRE) Official explanation: jockey said felding suffered interference in running

6696 BETDAQPOKER.CO.UK MAIDEN FILLIES' STKS (DIV I) 6f (P)

3:40 (3:43) (Class 4) 2-Y-0 £3,561 (£1,059; £529; £264) Stalls High

Form RPR

2 1 **Damaniyat Girl (USA)**[17] 6244 2-9-0 0 RHills 7 79+
(W J Haggas) *trckd ldr: clsd to ld jst over 1f out: pushed out: readily* 8/11[1]

443 2 1 ¼ **Fen Spirit (IRE)**[26] 6030 2-9-0 77 JimmyFortune 5 75
(J H M Gosden) *trckd ldng trio: rdn to cl 2f out: kpt on to take 2nd ins fnl f: no real ch w wnr* 5/1[3]

2340 3 ½ **Poyle Meg**[17] 6240 2-9-0 83 (p) MartinDwyer 10 74
(R M Beckett) *late on to crse: prom: rdn and cl up 2f out: pressed for 2nd fnl f: kpt on* 9/2[2]

0040 4 1 ¼ **Sweet Applause (IRE)**[4] 6603 2-9-0 75 PaulHanagan 8 70
(A P Jarvis) *led to jst over 1f out: fdd ins fnl f* 40/1

0 5 1 ¾ **Kyleene**[24] 6084 2-9-0 0 JamieSpencer 4 65+
(J Noseda) *dwlt: towards rr: shkn up and outpcd 2f out: pushed along and kpt on fnl f* 33/1

00 6 1 ¼ **Final Rhapsody**[14] 6327 2-9-0 0 LPKeniry 9 61
(J A Geake) *chsd ldrs: rdn 2f out: no imp over 1f out: wknd fnl f* 66/1

2 7 1 1/4 **La Verte Rue (USA)**[14] 6327 2-9-0 0 ShaneKelly 12 57
(J A Osborne) *mostly in midfield on inner: effrt 2f out: sn lft bhd by ldrs* **10/1**

8 1 1/2 **Pumpkin** 2-8-9 0 Louis-PhilippeBeuzelin(5) 2 53
(Sir Michael Stoute) *dwlt: rn green and sn firmly pushed along: a in rr: kpt on fnl f* **25/1**

9 hd **Thegirlsgonewild (USA)** 2-9-0 0 JimmyQuinn 11 52
(H J L Dunlop) *dwlt: wl in rr: brief effrt on inner 2f out: sn no prog and btn* **50/1**

5640 10 6 **Anjuna (USA)**[29] 5937 2-9-0 52 DarryllHolland 1 34
(J H M Gosden) *dwlt: a wl in rr: hd high and losing tch wl over 2f out* **50/1**

00 11 4 1/2 **Baby Is Here (IRE)**[12] 6392 2-9-0 0 SamHitchcott 3 21
(D J S Ffrench Davis) *racd wd: rdn towards rr 1/2-way: sn wknd* **66/1**

1m 13.55s (0.45) **Going Correction** +0.05s/f (Slow) 11 Ran SP% **118.0**
Speed ratings (Par 94): **99,97,96,95,92 91,89,87,87,79 73**
toteswinger: 1&2 £1.80, 1&3 £1.70, 2&3 £2.90. CSF £4.40 TOTE £1.70: £1.10, £1.40, £1.40; EX 5.30.

Owner Mohamed Obaida **Bred** Gainsborough Farm Llc **Trained** Newmarket, Suffolk

FOCUS
Not a bad maiden for the track, and certainly stronger than the second division, with Poyle Meg setting a fair standard on her Ascot sales-race effort last time and a handful of these having shown plenty of promise from limited opportunities. The pace was solid, set by Sweet Applause, and the form should be worth following.

NOTEBOOK
Damaniyat Girl(USA), a promising second on debut at Haydock, was strongly backed throughout the morning to go one better and she justified the support in pretty commanding style, putting her seal on the race when given a tap over a furlong out, though still displaying signs of greenness. She lengthened well in the closing stages and, given how smartly she is bred (dam was second in a 1,000 Guineas), she could possess the class to step up into Pattern company next term, with trips up to a mile within range. (op 4-6 tchd 4-5 in places)

Fen Spirit(IRE) improved for the drop back to this trip last time and she again ran very well in defeat, finishing just ahead of a rival rated 6lb her superior. She will be unlucky to bump into a rival as classy as Damaniyat Girl in future and a similar event is well within her grasp. (op 4-1)

Poyle Meg, officially rated 83, is a good guide to the strength of this form. She was slightly tapped for speed early in the straight as the pace quickened, but she stayed on well through the final furlong and she will be seen to better effect back up to 7f, where she would be a certainty for most fillies' maidens. (op 5-1)

Sweet Applause(IRE) was always going to be vulnerable back in maiden company but she set good fractions and arguably ran somewhere near her best in keeping on for fourth. (op 25-1)

Kyleene's finishing effort from midfield caught the eye, though she couldn't get into it. This was a step forward from her first start and, despite clearly still being green, she looks to be going the right way.

6697 BETDAQPOKER.CO.UK MAIDEN FILLIES' STKS (DIV II) 6f (P)
4:10 (4:12) (Class 4) 2-Y-0 **£3,561** (£1,059; £529; £264) **Stalls** High

Form RPR

00 1 **It's A Game (USA)**[72] 4643 2-9-0 0 JimmyFortune 2 72+
(J H M Gosden) *trckd ldrs: effrt to ld jst over 1f out: shkn up and sn in command: styd on wl nr fin* **10/1**

5 2 3/4 **Minute Limit (IRE)**[32] 5835 2-9-0 0 ShaneKelly 4 68
(J A Osborne) *dwlt: hld up wl in rr: gd prog fr 2f out: wnt 2nd last 100yds: tried to cl but readily hld nr fin* **5/1**[1]

0 3 1 3/4 **Beautiful Filly**[32] 5835 2-9-0 0 MartinDwyer 1 62
(D M Simcock) *dwlt: steadily rcvrd and midfield 3f out: prog after to chse ldrs over 1f out: wnt 2nd briefly ins fnl f: outpcd last 100yds* **11/2**[2]

0 4 3/4 **Equinity**[13] 6360 2-9-0 0 JerryO'Dwyer 11 60
(J Pearce) *led to jst over 1f out: readily outpcd fnl f* **33/1**

650 5 3/4 **Ageebah**[39] 5640 2-9-0 65 DarryllHolland 10 58
(C E Brittain) *settled in midfield: effrt on inner and shkn up over 2f out: chsd ldrs over 1f out: outpcd fnl f* **7/1**[3]

600 6 nk **Spinning Belle (IRE)**[24] 6080 2-9-0 66 RHills 6 58+
(J W Hills) *t.k.h early: hld up in midfield: pushed along and sme prog wl over 1f out: styd on ins fnl f* **8/1**

300 7 1 **True Britannia**[96] 3837 2-9-0 51 LPKeniry 9 54
(S Kirk) *trckd ldng pair: effrt on inner and nrly upsides 2f out: wknd 1f out* **33/1**

04 8 hd **Iliketoboogie**[101] 3689 2-9-0 0 PatCosgrave 8 53
(A J McCabe) *hld up wl in rr: pushed along over 2f out: nvr on terms w ldrs but kpt on fnl f* **16/1**

9 shd **Diamond Til (IRE)** 2-9-0 0 AdamKirby 7 53
(G L Moore) *hld up wl in rr: outpcd 2f out: plugged on ins fnl f* **9/1**

0 10 3/4 **Morning Queen (IRE)**[14] 6327 2-9-0 0 PhilipRobinson 5 51
(C G Cox) *t.k.h early: pressed ldr tl wknd tamely wl over 1f out* **8/1**

11 5 **Rag And Bone (CAN)** 2-9-0 0 JamieSpencer 3 36
(B J Meehan) *hld up in midfield: shkn up over 2f out: wknd rapidly sn after* **11/2**[2]

12 shd **Che Castagna** 2-8-7 0 RossAtkinson(7) 12 36
(Tom Dascombe) *awkward s and slowly away: rn green and a in last pair: bhd fnl 3f* **9/1**

1m 14.64s (1.54) **Going Correction** +0.05s/f (Slow) 12 Ran SP% **123.0**
Speed ratings (Par 94): **91,90,87,86,85 85,83,83,83,82 75,75**
toteswinger: 1&2 £12.20, 1&3 £13.20, 2&3 £6.80. CSF £61.69 TOTE £10.60: £3.50, £1.60, £2.00; EX 58.50.

Owner George Strawbridge **Bred** Augustin Stable **Trained** Newmarket, Suffolk

FOCUS
This had the look of a modest affair, with those that had run not setting too high a standard, and the time was slower than the first division.

NOTEBOOK
It's A Game(USA) showed little on her first two starts but, returning from a 72-day absence, she left those efforts behind. She travelled strongly behind the pace and quickened up to lead over a furlong out, staying on strongly. Clearly she has improved considerably during her break, and it may be that she is much better suited by this surface, but she might not have beaten a great deal.

Minute Limit(IRE) built on the promise she showed on her first start and finished well. She is going the right way. (op 13-2)

Beautiful Filly was another to step up on her debut running and also finished well. (op 5-1)

Equinity had shown very little on debut and stepped up a fair amount on that to plug on for fourth. (op 40-1)

Spinning Belle(IRE) Official explanation: jockey said filly ran too free

Diamond Til(IRE) makes some appeal as a future winner as she stayed on fairly well in the closing stages, from well off the pace, and Gary Moore's runners tend not to be anywhere near fully tuned up for debut. (op 16-1)

6698 BETDAQ.CO.UK H'CAP 1m 4f (P)
4:40 (4:41) (Class 3) (0-90,90) 3-Y-0+
£7,477 (£2,239; £1,119; £560; £279; £140) **Stalls** High

Form RPR

1050 1 **Boz**[21] 6171 4-9-6 85 JamieSpencer 3 99
(L M Cumani) *hld up in 8th: prog on inner to chse ldr over 2f out: edgd lft over 1f out but clsd: drvn ahd last 100yds: hld on wl* **14/1**

-123 2 nk **The Carlton Cannes**[24] 6079 4-9-5 84 DarryllHolland 7 98+
(G Wragg) *hld up in 9th: plenty to do whn nt clr run jst over 2f out and swtchd lft: gd prog over 1f out: styd on to take 2nd last 75yds and cl on wnr: nvr gng to get there* **3/1**[1]

1065 3 1 3/4 **Bee Sting**[9] 6479 4-9-6 85 (p) AdamKirby 12 96
(W R Swinburn) *led: kicked on 3f out: worn down last 100yds and sn lost 2nd* **14/1**

2560 4 hd **William Blake**[38] 5677 3-8-11 83 GregFairley 2 93
(M Johnston) *racd wd: hld up in midfield: prog 3f out: drvn to go 3rd 2f out and edging lft: nt qckn over 1f out: kpt on* **14/1**

0200 5 5 **Birkside**[15] 6302 5-9-11 90 (p) PaulHanagan 1 92
(K A Ryan) *s.i.s: hld up in last trio: shkn up and prog on inner over 2f out: no imp on ldrs over 1f out: wknd* **12/1**

-302 6 1 1/4 **King's Event (USA)**[42] 5569 4-9-7 86 JimmyFortune 9 86
(Sir Michael Stoute) *trckd ldrs: wnt 2nd briefly wl over 2f out: u.p and nt qckn after: wknd over 1f out* **9/2**[2]

-124 7 1 **Pacifism (UAE)**[171] 1600 3-9-4 90 PhilipRobinson 4 89
(M A Jarvis) *t.k.h early: trckd ldr after 1f tl after 3f: styd handy: pushed along and nt qckn over 2f out: wknd* **5/1**[3]

3460 8 8 **Prime Number (IRE)**[21] 6171 6-8-11 76 oh1 J-PGuillambert 6 62
(J Akehurst) *hld up in last: pushed along and steadily lost grnd fr over 2f out* **50/1**

2545 9 1 **Inspector Clouseau (IRE)**[23] 6113 3-8-4 76 JimmyQuinn 10 60
(T P Tate) *t.k.h early: chsd ldr 1f: styd wl in tch tl wknd u.p over 2f out* **16/1**

3540 10 2 1/2 **Rayhani (USA)**[15] 6302 5-9-11 90 MartinDwyer 5 70
(M P Tregoning) *s.s: lit up after 1f and rapid prog to press ldr after 3f: wknd rapidly wl over 2f out* **11/2**

5/04 11 7 **Power Elite (IRE)**[11] 6410 8-9-0 79 TonyCulhane 11 48
(K A Morgan) *hld up in last pair: rdn 3f out: sn wknd and lost tch* **40/1**

00 12 19 **Agapanthus (GER)**[99] 3773 3-9-3 89 ShaneKelly 8 28
(A P Stringer) *wl in tch in midfield tl wknd over 3f out: eased whn no ch: t.o* **66/1**

2m 32.05s (-2.45) **Going Correction** +0.05s/f (Slow)
WFA 3 from 4yo+ 7lb 12 Ran SP% **114.7**
Speed ratings (Par 107): **110,109,108,108,105 104,103,98,97,96 91,78**
toteswinger: 1&2 £10.30, 1&3 £23.80, 2&3 £10.20. CSF £53.65 CT £612.22 TOTE £14.70: £4.30, £1.50, £3.00; EX 67.00.

Owner Aston House Stud **Bred** Aston House Stud **Trained** Newmarket, Suffolk

FOCUS
A quick time, a second under standard, and so it was no surprise that the finish was contested by two horses that have stamina for further than this. The first four finished clear and the form is rated positively around the fourth, the winner up 9lb.

NOTEBOOK
Boz settled well in midfield and found the gaps opening up for him along the inside in the straight. Despite being hard ridden, he stayed on strongly up the straight to pick off long-time leader Bee Sting and hold off the fast-finishing The Carlton Cannes. This can be rated as a career-best effort, winning off a mark 6lb higher than when scoring at Doncaster in July, but the key to him is a strong pace over this trip, and he has now won seven of his 13 starts on Polytrack. He is still only a 4yo and Jamie Spencer is inclined to think there could be even more to come next year.

The Carlton Cannes ran a blinder in defeat, storming home down the wide outside and running the winner mighty close. He was arguably denied victory by having to come wide, whereas the winner was saving ground up the inside. He is clearly still progressing and, still very lightly raced, he'll be winning plenty more races. (op 7-2)

Bee Sting deserves credit for setting such a strong pace and only succumbing in the final furlong. This was his first try on Polytrack and he clearly handled it well. (op 16-1)

William Blake ran well, given he was trapped wide throughout, and this was easily his best effort for some time. Now only 3lb higher than when last winning, he might be able to build on this.

Birkside kept on well from a long way off the pace to run another solid race.

Pacifism(UAE) was quite keen in the early stages, returning from a 171-day absence, and he didn't see out his race. (op 9-2 tchd 4-1)

6699 BACK OR LAY AT BETDAQ H'CAP 6f (P)
5:10 (5:10) (Class 4) (0-85,85) 3-Y-0+ **£5,180** (£1,541; £770; £384) **Stalls** High

Form RPR

5503 1 **Dvinsky (USA)**[11] 6420 7-8-11 77 (b) JimmyQuinn 4 86
(P Howling) *bustled along early to chse clr ldr: clsd u.p over 1f out: led last 150yds: kpt on* **6/1**[2]

2010 2 1 **Peter Island (FR)**[14] 6340 5-8-11 77 (v) JamieSpencer 6 83
(J Gallagher) *led at str pce: 3 l clr 3f out: rdr looking rnd 2f out: drvn and hdd last 150yds: no ex* **5/1**[1]

0001 3 3/4 **Dazed And Amazed**[14] 6328 4-9-4 84 PatDobbs 3 87
(R Hannon) *mostly in abt 7th and wl off the pce: prog over 1f out: edgd rt but styd on to take 3rd ins fnl f: nvr able to chal ldng pair* **6/1**[2]

0350 4 hd **Mogok Ruby**[12] 6402 4-8-11 77 DarryllHolland 10 80
(L Montague Hall) *hld up in last trio: sn outpcd: shkn up and no prog over 2f out: gd hdwy fnl f: clsng at fin* **13/2**[3]

4030 5 nk **Tia Mia**[30] 5906 3-8-11 85 AndreaAtzeni(7) 5 87
(M Botti) *chsd ldng trio: wnt 3rd over 1f out tl ins fnl f: kpt on but nvr able to chal* **8/1**

1405 6 nse **Light Hearted**[21] 6169 3-9-2 83 ShaneKelly 1 85
(J Noseda) *trckd ldng pair: rdn 2f out: nt qckn and no imp: one pce after* **8/1**

2120 7 1 **Farthermost (IRE)**[79] 4408 3-8-9 79 PatrickHills(3) 8 77
(R Hannon) *mostly abt same pl: off the pce tl effrt 2f out: no real imp* **10/1**

1013 8 1 **Artistic License (IRE)**[21] 6160 3-9-2 83 TonyCulhane 7 78
(M R Channon) *sn outpcd in last trio: nvr able to rch ldrs: plugged on* **7/1**

256 9 3 **Playful**[71] 4668 5-8-13 79 MartinDwyer 2 65
(R M Beckett) *trckd ldrs in 5th: rdn and fnd nil over 2f out: sn btn* **10/1**

21/- 10 1 1/4 **Stanley Goodspeed**[751] 5534 5-9-5 85 JamesDoyle 11 67
(J W Hills) *a last and wl off the pce* **12/1**

1m 12.46s (-0.64) **Going Correction** +0.05s/f (Slow)
WFA 3 from 4yo+ 1lb 10 Ran SP% **119.2**
Speed ratings (Par 105): **106,104,103,103,103 102,101,100,96,94**
toteswinger: 1&2 £8.40, 1&3 £10.80, 2&3 £8.70. CSF £36.97 CT £191.41 TOTE £7.90: £2.30, £1.80, £3.70; EX 38.00 Place 6 £ 45.53, Place 5 £ 16.68.

The Form Book, Raceform Ltd, Compton, RG20 6NL

Owner Richard Berenson **Bred** Eclipse Bloodstock & Tipperary Bloodstock **Trained** Newmarket, Suffolk

FOCUS
A fair sprint handicap in which the runner-up set a good pace. The form seems sound enough.
Farthermost(IRE) Official explanation: jockey said colt hung left-handed
T/Plt: £24.00 to a £1 stake. Pool: £58,496.02. 1,776.91 winning tickets. T/Qpdt: £6.00 to a £1 stake. Pool: £3,925.80. 476.80 winning tickets. JN

6539 WINDSOR (R-H)

Monday, October 13

OFFICIAL GOING: Good (7.8)
Wind: Moderate across Weather: Dull

6700 AT THE RACES NURSERY — 1m 67y

2:30 (2:30) (Class 5) (0-75,74) 2-Y-O — **£2,729** (£806; £403) **Stalls** High

Form — RPR

640 **1** **Shooting Party (IRE)**[24] 6085 2-9-3 **70** ... RichardHughes 11 — 75
(R Hannon) *sn led: hdd over 3f out: styd chsng ldr and led again appr fnl f: drvn out* **18/1**

1324 **2** 1 1/4 **Striding Edge (IRE)**[24] 6087 2-8-13 **66** ... DO'Donohoe 14 — 68
(W R Muir) *t.k.h: chsd ldrs: rdn over 2f out: styd on fnl f to take 2nd cl home but no ch w wnr* **16/1**

4612 **3** nk **Dubai Crest**[12] 6394 2-9-7 **74** ... JimCrowley 10 — 76
(Mrs A J Perrett) *pressed ldrs: led over 3f out: rdn over 2f out: hdd appr fnl f: wknd and lost 2nd cl home* **7/2**[1]

1304 **4** 1 1/2 **Cornish Rose (IRE)**[24] 6082 2-9-4 **71** ... RichardMullen 5 — 70+
(M H Tompkins) *mid-div: rdn and hdwy over 2f out: styd on ins fnl f but nvr gng pce to be competitive* **12/1**

030 **5** 1 1/2 **Lucky Score (IRE)**[52] 5227 2-8-10 **68** ... DavidProbert(5) 9 — 63
(Mouse Hamilton-Fairley) *pressed ldrs: rdn fr 3f out: wknd fnl f* **20/1**

0336 **6** hd **Brooksby**[24] 6082 2-9-2 **69** ... RyanMoore 1 — 64
(R Hannon) *stdd in mid-div after 1f: hdwy 3f out: rdn and hung rt fr 2f out: n.d after but kpt on* **11/2**[2]

036 **7** nk **Admirable Duque (IRE)**[12] 6398 2-9-6 **73** ... StephenDonohoe 6 — 67+
(D J S Ffrench Davis) *in rr: rdn 3f out: sme prog fnl 2f: nvr in contention* **40/1**

000 **8** nk **Taste The Wine (IRE)**[24] 6083 2-9-0 **67** ... SteveDrowne 13 — 61+
(J R Best) *plld hrd: stdd towards rr after 2f: rdn over 2f out and styd on: gng on ins fnl f but nvr in contention* **16/1**

4522 **9** 3/4 **Caster Sugar (USA)**[18] 6231 2-9-2 **69** ... LDettori 4 — 61
(L M Cumani) *pressed ldrs: rdn over 2f out: wknd over 1f out* **7/2**[1]

0242 **10** 1 1/4 **Excelsior Academy**[14] 6330 2-9-3 **70** ... EddieAhern 8 — 60
(B J Meehan) *in tch: rdn 3f out: wknd fr 2f out* **7/1**[3]

3610 **11** 1 1/2 **One Cool Kitty**[24] 6086 2-9-0 **70** ... DominicFox(3) 12 — 56
(M G Quinlan) *rrd stalls: a towards rr* **20/1**

0030 **12** hd **Sicilian Pink**[61] 4975 2-8-13 **66** ... TedDurcan 2 — 52
(J L Dunlop) *sn towards rr: nvr in contention* **33/1**

063 **13** 3 3/4 **Mons Calpe (IRE)**[21] 6165 2-9-1 **68** ... WilliamBuick 7 — 46
(P F I Cole) *s.i.s: a in rr* **16/1**

023 **14** 2 1/2 **Timpanist**[19] 6205 2-9-7 **74** ... AlanMunro 3 — 47
(P W Chapple-Hyam) *in rr: sme prog 3f out: rdn and wknd over 2f out* **16/1**

1m 47.4s (2.70) **Going Correction** +0.175s/f (Good) — **14** Ran SP% **123.7**
Speed ratings (Par 95): **93,91,91,89,88 88,87,87,86,85 84,83,80,77**
toteswinger: 1&2 £62.90, 1&3 £16.90, 2&3 £14.60. CSF £274.73 CT £930.47 TOTE £21.30: £5.60, £5.40, £1.80; EX 377.10 TRIFECTA Not won..
Owner Mrs R Ablett **Bred** Harron Eakin Farms **Trained** East Everleigh, Wilts

FOCUS
This was a modest nursery, but it had an open look about it with half of the runners making their handicap debuts. It was run at a solid early pace, but few got seriously involved from off the pace.

NOTEBOOK
Shooting Party(IRE) showed his true colours over this slightly stiffer test and, aggressively ridden, opened his account at the fourth time of asking. He has the scope to progress in this sphere and should do better as a three-year-old. (op 20-1 tchd 22-1)
Striding Edge(IRE), rated 2lb higher on the all-weather, kept on gamely to register his best effort to date on turf and got the longer trip well. He looks up to adding to his tally before the season's end.
Dubai Crest was given every chance and performed with credit from a 5lb higher mark. He probably ideally prefers easier ground, but remains in good heart and rates the benchmark for the form. (tchd 3-1)
Cornish Rose(IRE) performed close to her previous level and stayed the longer distance without much fuss, but just looks held by the handicapper. (tchd 10-1)
Caster Sugar(USA) was in trouble soon after passing the two-furlong pole and was beaten before her 2lb higher mark came into play. She now has something to prove. (op 10-3)

6701 EUROPEAN BREEDERS' FUND MAIDEN STKS (DIV I) — 6f

3:00 (3:02) (Class 5) 2-Y-O — **£3,561** (£1,059; £529; £264) **Stalls** High

Form — RPR

0 **1** **Bold Tie**[14] 6342 2-9-3 0 ... RichardHughes 2 — 77
(R Hannon) *broke wl and sn led main gp on far side: c lft towards far side over 2f out and chsd wnr over 1f out: drvn and qcknd to ld cl home* **8/1**

44 **2** hd **Standpoint**[17] 6253 2-9-3 0 ... RyanMoore 6 — 76
(Sir Michael Stoute) *chsd ldrs nr side tl edgd lft to far side over 2f out: led wl over 1f out: hrd drvn ins fnl f: hdd cl home* **2/1**[1]

04 **3** 2 1/4 **Fortunate Bid (IRE)**[34] 5784 2-9-3 0 ... WilliamBuick 12 — 70
(B W Hills) *chsd ldrs stands' side: edging to centre whn pushed rt 2f out and outpcd: kpt on again ins fnl f* **14/1**

0 **4** 1 **Fly By Nelly**[14] 6341 2-8-12 0 ... TravisBlock 7 — 62
(H Morrison) *wnt rt s: sn chsng ldrs stands' side: swtchd lft to far side over 2f out: styd on same pce ins fnl f* **66/1**

52 **5** shd **Chambers (IRE)**[23] 6109 2-9-3 0 ... LDettori 1 — 66
(M Johnston) *racd along far side and sn def ldr: edgd rt over 2f out and hdd wl over 1f out: wknd fnl f* **3/1**[2]

00 **6** 1 1/2 **Oisin's Boy**[14] 6341 2-9-3 0 ... AlanMunro 3 — 62
(J R Boyle) *chsd ldrs stands' side: edgd towards far side over 2f out: wknd fnl f* **100/1**

0 **7** hd **Double Act**[42] 5578 2-9-3 0 ... TedDurcan 9 — 61
(J Noseda) *bmpd s: t.k.h in mid-div stands' side: c to centre of crse and outpcd over 2f out: kpt on again ins fnl f* **16/1**

8 3 1/4 **Integria** 2-9-0 0 ... LukeMorris(3) 4 — 52
(J M P Eustace) *s.i.s: rdn and bhd fr 1/2-way* **16/1**

000 **9** 5 **Emerald Lass**[52] 5214 2-8-12 42 ... TPO'Shea 10 — 32
(D J Coakley) *t.k.h: in tch to 1/2-way* **100/1**

03 **10** 3/4 **Point Of Light**[23] 6109 2-9-3 0 ... DO'Donohoe 11 — 34
(Sir Mark Prescott) *a in rr* **16/1**

6 **11** 3/4 **Private Passion (IRE)**[14] 6327 2-9-3 0 ... JimCrowley 5 — 32
(Pat Eddery) *unruly stals: s.i.s: a towards rr* **9/2**[3]

12 4 **Jonnie Skull (IRE)** 2-9-0 0 ... MarcHalford(3) 8 — 20
(D R C Elsworth) *wnt rt s: sn rdn and outpcd* **40/1**

1m 13.6s (0.60) **Going Correction** +0.075s/f (Good) — **12** Ran SP% **117.9**
Speed ratings (Par 95): **99,98,95,94,94 92,92,87,81,80 79,73**
toteswinger: 1&2 £4.50, 1&3 £12.40, 2&3 £6.60. CSF £24.07 TOTE £9.70: £2.60, £1.20, £2.90; EX 35.40 Trifecta £249.20 Pool: £464.80, 1.38 winning units.
Owner Lady Whent **Bred** Raffin Bloodstock **Trained** East Everleigh, Wilts

FOCUS
The first division of the juvenile maiden saw all bar one of the runners stay on the stands' side through the early parts of the race.

NOTEBOOK
Bold Tie had met support on his debut over course and distance a fortnight previously only to show moderate ability, but he has obviously come on a bundle for that experience and just did enough to edge this. He looked well suited by racing on the pace and showed a determined attitude to fend off the runner-up at the business end. Now likely to be put away for the year, he should come into his own with a winter on his back and could be a useful sprinter in the making. (op 12-1 tchd 14-1)
Standpoint enjoyed the drop back in trip on this switch to the turf and was the only one to give the winner a serious race late on. He now becomes eligible for a handicap mark and, while he may be one of his leading stable's lesser lights, the best of him has likely yet to be seen. (op 7-4, tchd 9-4 in places)
Fortunate Bid(IRE) stayed on for his most encouraging display to date and did more than enough to suggest he will relish another furlong. He also now has the option of nurseries. (op 12-1)
Fly By Nelly showed the clear benefit of her initial outing over course and distance a fortnight previously and posted a greatly improved effort in defeat. She ought to come on again for the run and is obviously going the right way.
Chambers(IRE) was taken to the far rail from the start and established a clear lead coming into the home straight, but he was there to be shot at from 2f out. He did not help his cause by getting warm beforehand and may need more time, but should look of greater interest now he is eligible for a handicap rating. (op 11-4)

6702 EUROPEAN BREEDERS' FUND MAIDEN STKS (DIV II) — 6f

3:30 (3:31) (Class 5) 2-Y-O — **£3,561** (£1,059; £529; £264) **Stalls** High

Form — RPR

2 **1** **All About You (IRE)**[24] 6072 2-9-3 0 ... SteveDrowne 12 — 86+
(R Charlton) *pressed ldrs tl led over 1f out: styd on strly ins fnl f* **10/11**[1]

2 1 1/4 **Desert Creek (IRE)** 2-9-3 0 ... RyanMoore 3 — 81+
(Sir Michael Stoute) *sn drvn along in rr: rapid hdwy over 1f out: fin strly to chse wnr ins fnl f but a hld* **4/1**[2]

5 **3** 2 1/4 **Pressing Matters (IRE)**[14] 6327 2-9-3 0 ... RichardMullen 8 — 74
(E S McMahon) *s.i.s: sn chsng ldrs: hung lft over 2f out: kpt on same pce fr over 1f out* **13/2**[3]

5 **4** 1 **Diapason (IRE)**[7] 6531 2-8-12 0 ... RichardKingscote 1 — 66
(Tom Dascombe) *pressed ldrs: led ins fnl 2f: hdd over 1f out: wknd ins fnl f* **11/1**

40 **5** 5 **Majestic Lady (IRE)**[14] 6327 2-8-12 0 ... WilliamBuick 11 — 51
(B W Hills) *slt ld tl hdd ins fnl 2f: wknd fnl f* **14/1**

6 3 1/2 **Kuanyao (IRE)** 2-9-3 0 ... EddieAhern 5 — 47+
(P J Makin) *s.i.s: sn drvn along: a outpcd* **14/1**

7 3/4 **Newlyn Art** 2-9-3 0 ... RobertHavlin 2 — 43
(D R C Elsworth) *s.i.s: sn rdn in rr: mod late prog* **66/1**

8 shd **Improper (USA)** 2-8-12 0 ... DavidProbert(5) 10 — 42
(Mouse Hamilton-Fairley) *pressed ldrs tl wknd over 2f out* **66/1**

00 **9** 14 **Mojeerr**[27] 6000 2-9-3 0 ... TedDurcan 7 — —
(M P Tregoning) *in rr whn hmpd over 2f out* **50/1**

F **Geneva Geyser (GER)** 2-9-0 0 ... LukeMorris(3) 9 — —
(J M P Eustace) *in rr: sn rdn: no ch whn veered bdly lft, clipped heels and fell over 2f out* **25/1**

1m 13.3s (0.30) **Going Correction** +0.075s/f (Good) — **10** Ran SP% **116.2**
Speed ratings (Par 95): **101,99,96,95,88 83,82,82,63,—**
toteswinger: 1&2 £2.10, 1&3 £3.60, 2&3 £4.60. CSF £4.42 TOTE £1.80: £1.10, £1.30, £1.90; EX 5.10 Trifecta £22.60 Pool: £291.25, 9.50 winning units.
Owner Mountgrange Stud **Bred** Ballylinch Stud **Trained** Beckhampton, Wilts

FOCUS
This second division of the maiden again saw the runners go more towards the far side in the home straight and could prove to be the stronger of the pair. It was also a quicker winning time than the first.

NOTEBOOK
All About You(IRE) set the standard on his debut second to Huntdown at Newbury 24 days previously and did not have to improve obviously on that level to take this. Always on the pace, he put the race to bed at the furlong pole and rates value for a little further than the bare margin. He may get a bit further in time, but he is best kept to this trip for the short term and he looks the type to rate higher as he gains further experience. (op 5-6 tchd 4-5 and 6-5)
Desert Creek(IRE) ◆ registered a promising debut display and was motoring home down the middle of the track inside the final furlong, having been markedly outpaced early on. He looks to need a stiffer test, something his pedigree backs up, and should not remain a maiden for long. (op 9-2 tchd 7-2)
Pressing Matters(IRE), fifth on debut at Bath a fortnight previously, raced more handily this time and had his chance. This was a definite step in the right direction and he is another who may enjoy a stiffer test before long. (op 9-1 tchd 10-1 and 6-1)
Diapason(IRE) ran a similar race to that on her debut at Warwick a week earlier, but this was a slightly improved effort and she should find her feet when qualifying for an official mark after her next outing. (op 10-1 tchd 12-1)
Improper(USA) Official explanation: jockey said saddle slipped

6703 NORTH STAR IVER CANCER RESEARCH FUNDRAISING H'CAP — 1m 3f 135y

4:00 (4:01) (Class 5) (0-70,70) 3-Y-O — **£2,729** (£806; £403) **Stalls** Low

Form — RPR

6003 **1** **Black Rain**[12] 6395 3-9-4 **70** ... RichardMullen 11 — 78
(P J McBride) *chsd ldrs: led over 1f out: hld on wl thrght fnl f* **8/1**[3]

052 **2** nk **Plaisterer**[54] 5182 3-9-2 **68** ... AlanMunro 16 — 75
(C F Wall) *chsd ldrs: led over 7f out: rdn and hdd over 1f out: styd pressing wnr but continually swished tail ins fnl f: no ex cl home* **7/1**[1]

6543 **3** 2 1/2 **Politeia (USA)**[46] 5428 3-9-4 **70** ... (v) RichardHughes 3 — 73
(R Hannon) *in tch: hdwy over 4f out: outpcd over 2f out: kpt on again over 1f out: no imp on ldng duo ins fnl f* **15/2**[2]

-060 **4** 1/2 **Cozy Tiger (USA)**[28] 5964 3-9-2 **68** ... EddieAhern 1 — 70
(W J Musson) *in rr: hdwy fr 4f out: styd on fnl 2f and fin strly ins fnl f: nt rch ldng trio* **9/1**

0000 **5** 1 3/4 **Prince Desire (IRE)**[89] 4081 3-9-1 **67** ... (p) RichardKingscote 2 — 66
(Tom Dascombe) *in tch: hdwy over 3f out: chsd ldrs 2f out: sn one pce* **20/1**

2104 **6** 2 1/2 **Bosamcliff (IRE)**[32] 5815 3-8-13 **65** ... RyanMoore 12 — 60
(A B Haynes) *chsd ldrs: rdn over 3f out: wknd fr 2f out* **12/1**

4240 **7** 2½ **Dancing Dik**[23] 6129 3-8-10 62....................(p) JimCrowley 15 53
(Mrs A J Perrett) *chsd ldrs: wnt 2nd over 3f out: sn rdn: wknd 2f out* **8/1**[3]
065 **8** 3½ **Totoman**[12] 6379 3-8-11 68.................... DavidProbert(5) 5 53
(G G Margarson) *in tch: hdwy on outside to chse ldrs over 3f out: wknd ins fnl 2f* **16/1**
6104 **9** 4½ **Zuwaar**[12] 6400 3-9-3 69....................(t) StephenDonohoe 8 46
(Ian Williams) *bhd most of way* **10/1**
1060 **10** 3¼ **Sweet Sara**[27] 5999 3-9-4 70.................... LDettori 14 42
(C E Brittain) *led tl hdd over 7f out: wknd over 2f out* **12/1**
0013 **11** ¾ **Contrada**[10] 6436 3-8-12 64.................... SteveDrowne 9 34
(R Charlton) *in rr: hdwy 5f out: rdn and wknd qckly over 3f out* **10/1**
034 **12** 3¼ **Shayera**[29] 5931 3-9-4 70.................... RobertHavlin 6 35
(B R Johnson) *nvr bttr than in mid-div: bhd fr 1/2-way* **40/1**
3100 **13** 2¼ **Beautiful Lady (IRE)**[47] 5406 3-9-4 70.................... WilliamBuick 4 31
(P F I Cole) *chsd ldrs: rdn 4f out: wknd 3f out* **12/1**
4030 **14** 2¾ **Bet Noir (IRE)**[7] 6529 3-8-10 62.................... TedDurcan 10 18
(W R Swinburn) *slowly into stride: a bhd* **14/1**
40 **15** 14 **Turjuman (USA)**[25] 6055 3-9-2 68.................... KShea 13 —
(W J Musson) *a towards rr* **16/1**
0002 **P** **Zia Zabel (IRE)**[79] 4410 3-8-12 64.................... TPO'Shea 7 —
(M G Quinlan) *a in rr: t.o whn p.u over 2f out: lame* **20/1**

2m 32.36s (2.86) **Going Correction** +0.175s/f (Good) **16** Ran SP% **128.1**
Speed ratings (Par 101): **97,96,95,94,93 91,90,87,84,82 82,80,78,76,67** —
toteswinger: 1&2 £17.20, 1&3 £10.80, 2&3 £12.90. CSF £64.69 CT £454.98 TOTE £8.70: £2.70, £2.10, £2.10, £3.60; EX 92.20 TRIFECTA Not won..
Owner PMRacing **Bred** Kirtlington Stud And Gilridge Bloodstock **Trained** Newmarket, Suffolk

FOCUS
An ordinary three-year-old handicap. The form makes sense, rated through the third and third.
Sweet Sara Official explanation: jockey said filly lost its action
Zia Zabel(IRE) Official explanation: jockey said filly pulled up lame

6704 READING FC H'CAP 1m 2f 7y
4:30 (4:31) (Class 4) (0-85,85) 3-Y-O **£5,375** (£1,599; £799; £399) **Stalls** Low

Form RPR
4413 **1** **Opera Prince**[16] 6283 3-9-3 84.................... RichardHughes 2 93+
(S Kirk) *hld up in rr: stdy hdwy fr 3f out: quicking to chal whn bdly hmpd ins fnl 2f: rallied and squeezed through fnl f: led fnl 50yds: r.o gamely* **10/1**
1-55 **2** *nse* **Red And White (IRE)**[16] 6293 3-8-10 77.................... RoystonFfrench 8 84
(M Johnston) *s.i.s: in rr: rdn over 3f out: styd on wl fnl 2f: str run ins fnl f: fin wl: nt quite get up* **14/1**
3356 **3** ¾ **Formation (USA)**[3] 6625 3-9-4 85.................... RyanMoore 7 91
(E A L Dunlop) *in tch: hdwy over 2f out: styd on u.p to take narrow ld ins fnl f: hdd and one pce fnl 50yds* **9/2**[2]
6121 **4** 2 **Mahadee (IRE)**[11] 6424 3-8-13 80....................(b) EddieAhern 4 82
(C E Brittain) *chsd ldrs: led over 2f out: hung bdly lft u.p sn after: hdd appr fnl f: eased whn hld ins fnl f* **16/1**
4022 **5** 1 **St Jean Cap Ferrat**[5] 6582 3-9-2 83....................(v) TPO'Shea 6 87+
(G Wragg) *in tch: hdwy on ins over 2f out: ev ch whn hmpd over 1f out and ins fnl f: nt rcvr and eased cl home* **11/4**[1]
1303 **6** ¾ **Bowder Stone (IRE)**[16] 6276 3-9-0 81.................... RichardMullen 10 79
(M H Tompkins) *t.k.h: chsd ldrs: rdn fr 3f out: one pce fnl 2f* **12/1**
416- **7** ½ **Silver Regent (USA)**[353] 6471 3-9-1 82.................... JimCrowley 1 79
(Mrs A J Perrett) *chsd ldrs: chal ins fnl 2f: slt ld 1f out: sn hdd: hung lft and n.m.r on rail ins fnl f: sn eased whn hld* **9/1**
6225 **8** 1¼ **Title Role**[17] 6256 3-8-7 74 ow1.................... SteveDrowne 3 69
(P F I Cole) *led tl hdd over 2f out: wknd over 1f out* **12/1**
3410 **9** 4½ **Moville (IRE)**[19] 6203 3-8-11 78.................... WilliamBuick 9 64
(B W Hills) *chsd ldr to 3f out: sn rdn: wknd over 2f out* **16/1**
114 **10** 5 **Addikt (IRE)**[52] 5230 3-9-0 81.................... SaleemGolam 11 57
(J R Turner) *in tch: rdn 4f out: wknd fr 3f out* **25/1**
4342 **11** ½ **Arts Guild (USA)**[60] 5032 3-8-9 76.................... KShea 14 51
(W J Musson) *slowly away: a towards rr* **15/2**[3]
1-40 **12** 22 **Benhavis**[50] 5309 3-8-12 79....................(t) TedDurcan 12 10
(J L Dunlop) *a in rr* **40/1**

2m 9.14s (0.44) **Going Correction** +0.175s/f (Good) **12** Ran SP% **115.8**
Speed ratings (Par 103): **105,104,104,102,101 101,100,99,96,92 91,74**
toteswinger: 1&2 £22.50, 1&3 £8.60, 2&3 £13.30. CSF £138.79 CT £720.34 TOTE £10.60: £3.90, £3.80, £2.20; EX 132.10 Trifecta £207.60 Part won. Pool: £280.57, 0.40 winning units..
Owner J C Smith **Bred** Littleton Stud **Trained** Upper Lambourn, Berks
■ Stewards' Enquiry : Jim Crowley caution: careless riding.

FOCUS
This was a decent handicap for three-year-olds, run at a sound pace. The race is best rated around the exposed third. There should be more to come from the winner.
St Jean Cap Ferrat Official explanation: jockey said colt was denied a clear run

6705 WINDSOR FIREWORKS SPECTACULAR SATURDAY 1ST NOVEMBER MAIDEN STKS 1m 67y
5:00 (5:03) (Class 5) 3-Y-O+ **£2,729** (£806; £403) **Stalls** High

Form RPR
4 **1** **Lease Of Life (USA)**[12] 6393 3-9-3 0.................... WilliamBuick 2 94+
(B W Hills) *sn trcking ldrs: slt ld 5f out: shkn up to go clr fr 2f out: eased whn wl clr fnl f* **5/2**[2]
03 **2** 7 **Desert Kiss**[14] 6345 3-8-12 0.................... TedDurcan 5 70
(W R Swinburn) *chsd ldrs: wnt 2nd over 1f out but nvr any ch w eased down wnr* **12/1**
0-2 **3** 3½ **Etosha (IRE)**[7] 6530 3-9-3 0.................... LDettori 1 67
(Saeed Bin Suroor) *pressed ldrs: chsd wnr ins fnl 3f but nvr any ch: fnd no ex and wknd fr 2f out* **11/8**[1]
4 **4** ¾ **Manere Bay**[14] 6345 3-8-12 0.................... EddieAhern 6 61
(J L Dunlop) *s.i.s: sn chsng ldrs: wknd and hung lft fr 2f out* **16/1**
0 **5** 3¼ **Antillia**[12] 6393 3-8-12 0.................... AlanMunro 4 53
(C F Wall) *in rr: styd on fr 2f out but nvr in contention* **100/1**
0 **6** *hd* **Sharki**[86] 4194 3-8-12 0.................... RobertHavlin 9 53+
(J H M Gosden) *in tch whn hmpd and lost position after 2f: nvr in contention after* **12/1**
06 **7** *nk* **King's Colour**[14] 6345 3-9-0 0.................... JackMitchell(3) 11 57
(B R Johnson) *chsd ldrs: rdn 3f out: wknd 2f out* **50/1**
03- **8** 1¼ **Lemon N Sugar (USA)**[391] 5498 3-8-12 0.................... RyanMoore 7 49
(J Noseda) *chsd ldrs: rdn 3f out: wknd over 2f out* **11/2**[3]
0 **9** ½ **Moandei**[14] 6345 4-9-1 0.................... SteveDrowne 14 48
(R Ingram) *a towards rr* **100/1**
05 **10** ½ **Watercolours (IRE)**[35] 5750 3-8-12 0.................... RichardMullen 12 47
(G L Moore) *rdn 3f out: alway towards rr* **66/1**
11 *hd* **Sestet** 3-8-12 0.................... NickyMackay 10 46
(S Dow) *in rr: effrt 4f out: sn wknd* **100/1**
0 **12** 1¼ **Irish Bay (IRE)**[7] 6543 5-9-1 0.................... AmyBaker(5) 3 49
(Luke Comer, Ire) *in tch and rdn 1/2-way: wknd 3f out* **100/1**
50 **13** 1½ **Al Asayl Rose (USA)**[35] 5750 3-8-12 0.................... RichardHughes 8 40
(H J L Dunlop) *led tl hdd 5f out: styd w wnr tl rdn 3f out and sn wknd* **20/1**
14 *nk* **Roleplay (IRE)** 3-8-9 0.................... LukeMorris(3) 13 39
(J M P Eustace) *slowly away: a bhd* **66/1**

1m 45.11s (0.41) **Going Correction** +0.175s/f (Good)
WFA 3 from 4yo+ 3lb **14** Ran SP% **121.0**
Speed ratings (Par 103): **104,97,93,92,89 89,89,87,87,86 86,85,83,83**
toteswinger: 1&2 £6.80, 1&3 £1.70, 2&3 £4.50. CSF £31.89 TOTE £3.60: £1.30, £2.00, £1.40; EX 35.80 Trifecta £77.80 Pool: £513.45, 4.88 winning units.
Owner K Abdulla **Bred** Juddmonte Farms Inc **Trained** Lambourn, Berks

FOCUS
Not much strength in depth, but the form horses set a good standard for this late in the season. It is difficult to know exactly what the winner achieved, with the favourite below par, but he looks well above average.

6706 ADANTINO 100 NOT OUT H'CAP 6f
5:30 (5:32) (Class 5) (0-70,69) 3-Y-O+ **£2,729** (£806; £403) **Stalls** High

Form RPR
-431 **1** **Perfect Silence**[20] 6192 3-9-3 68.................... EddieAhern 8 81+
(C G Cox) *chsd ldrs: led 1f out: kpt on strly* **5/2**[1]
4600 **2** 1 **Interactive (IRE)**[14] 6338 5-8-8 58.................... AlanDaly 12 68
(Andrew Turnell) *s.i.s: in rr: hdwy 2f out: qcknd to chal 1f out: drvn and hung lft sn after: no ex nr fin* **40/1**
504 **3** 1¾ **Cheap Street**[52] 5233 4-9-3 67.................... RyanMoore 4 71
(J G Portman) *in tch: rdn and hdwy 2f out: led over 1f out: sn hdd: one pce ins fnl f* **8/1**[3]
4401 **4** *nk* **Rondeau (GR)**[19] 6209 3-9-4 69.................... JimCrowley 5 72
(P R Chamings) *chsd ldrs: rdn to chal ins fnl 2f: no ex ins fnl f* **8/1**[3]
2122 **5** 1½ **Shakespeare's Son**[11] 6418 3-8-13 69.................... DavidProbert(5) 13 67
(H J Evans) *chsd ldrs: rdn and hung lft over 1f out and sn wknd* **9/2**[2]
5050 **6** *nk* **Elkhorn**[21] 6164 6-9-2 66....................(b) SteveDrowne 3 63
(Miss J A Camacho) *in rr tl hdwy over 2f out: drvn to chse ldrs over 1f out: wknd ins fnl f* **16/1**
2050 **7** *hd* **Linda Green**[6] 6564 7-9-2 66.................... TPO'Shea 2 63
(M R Channon) *in rr: sme prog over 2f out: nvr gng pce to be competitive* **16/1**
0600 **8** 1 **Adantino**[14] 6340 9-9-0 67....................(b) JamesMillman(3) 10 60
(B R Millman) *in rr tl sme prog fnl f* **14/1**
3150 **9** ½ **Kingsgate Castle**[10] 6435 3-9-1 66....................(b[1]) TedDurcan 1 58
(J R Best) *racd along far side over 3f and pressing for ld and slt advantage 2f out: hdd & wknd appr fnl f* **25/1**
6020 **10** 6 **Realt Na Mara (IRE)**[31] 5867 5-9-3 67.................... TravisBlock 7 40
(H Morrison) *chsd ldrs: rdn over 2f out: sn wknd* **10/1**
001 **11** 2¼ **The Cayterers**[25] 6046 6-9-0 69.................... MCGeran(5) 9 34+
(A W Carroll) *bmpd s and s.i.s: stl in rr whn hmpd over 1f out* **11/1**
350 **12** ½ **Compton Rose**[11] 6418 3-9-0 65.................... FrankieMcDonald 11 29
(H Candy) *in tch over 3f* **33/1**
0064 **13** 1¼ **The Name Is Frank**[26] 6024 3-8-9 60.................... WilliamBuick 6 20
(J W Mullins) *pressed ldrs tl wknd 2f out: no ch whn hung lft over 1f out* **33/1**
1000 **14** 2¾ **Triumphant Welcome**[13] 6357 3-8-11 62.................... RichardHughes 16 13
(G F Bridgwater) *slt ld tl hdd 2f out: sn wknd* **16/1**

1m 12.94s (-0.06) **Going Correction** +0.075s/f (Good)
WFA 3 from 4yo+ 1lb **14** Ran SP% **122.9**
Speed ratings (Par 103): **103,101,99,98,96 96,96,94,94,86 83,82,80,77**
toteswinger: 1&2 £29.40, 1&3 £7.40, 2&3 £68.50. CSF £134.13 CT £759.60 TOTE £3.60: £1.70, £13.40, £4.10; EX 138.70 TRIFECTA Not won. Place 6 £ 50.93, Place 5 £ 15.99.
Owner Wild Beef Racing (Mr & Mrs R J Vines) **Bred** R J Vines **Trained** Lambourn, Berks

FOCUS
A modest sprint, rated through the runner-up. The winner remains progressive but this form is tricky to pin down as the second's best form is on sand.
Triumphant Welcome Official explanation: jockey said gelding moved poorly and hung left
T/Jkpt: Not won. T/Plt: £63.70 to a £1 stake. Pool: £81,022.94. 927.95 winning tickets. T/Qpdt: £10.60 to a £1 stake. Pool: £4,704.02. 328.00 winning tickets. ST

6658 WOLVERHAMPTON (A.W) (L-H)
Monday, October 13

OFFICIAL GOING: Standard to fast
Wind: Light behind Weather: Fine

6707 WOLVERHAMPTON HOLIDAY INN MEDIAN AUCTION MAIDEN STKS 5f 216y(P)
2:20 (2:22) (Class 6) 3-Y-O **£3,070** (£906; £453) **Stalls** Low

Form RPR
0063 **1** **Tangerine Trees**[9] 6486 3-9-3 65.................... TomEaves 12 65
(B Smart) *led: rdn wl over 1f out: hdd wl ins fnl f: led last strides* **9/2**[3]
3043 **2** *shd* **Dancing Maite**[20] 6188 3-9-3 61.................... ChrisCatlin 3 65
(S R Bowring) *a.p: rdn over 1f out: led wl ins fnl f: hdd last strides* **11/4**[2]
0326 **3** 1¼ **Spic 'n Span**[35] 5749 3-9-0 55....................(p) KevinGhunowa(3) 10 61
(R A Harris) *hld up in mid-div: hdwy on outside 3f out: rdn and kpt on towards fin* **9/1**
0535 **4** 1¾ **Shatter Resistant (IRE)**[18] 6224 3-8-10 48.................... HollyHall(7) 1 55
(M D Squance) *t.k.h in mid-div: hdwy and swtchd lft wl over 1f out: sn rdn: no ex ins fnl f* **33/1**
6222 **5** ½ **Towy Boy (IRE)**[25] 6046 3-9-3 65....................(t) NCallan 6 54
(I A Wood) *t.k.h: a.p: one pce fnl f* **5/2**[1]
4204 **6** 2½ **Billy Bowmore**[17] 6254 3-9-3 60.................... TonyHamilton 7 46+
(M Dods) *hld up towards rr: hung lft wl over 1f out: swtchd rt ent fnl f: nvr nrr* **8/1**
0005 **7** 1 **Johnny McGurk**[27] 6004 3-9-3 54....................(b) NeilPollard 5 43
(M E Rimmer) *nvr trbld ldrs* **50/1**
00 **8** 1¼ **Curly Brown**[34] 5786 3-9-3 0.................... MickyFenton 2 39
(A Bailey) *s.i.s: nvr nr ldrs* **66/1**
65-6 **9** 1¼ **Showtime Ice**[23] 6137 3-8-7 70.................... RichardEvans(5) 13 30
(Ms Deborah J Evans) *sn prom: rdn wl over 1f out: wknd fnl f* **16/1**
-606 **10** *shd* **Kiwi Princess**[105] 3549 3-8-12 50.................... DavidAllan 13 29
(M Brittain) *w ldr: rdn over 2f out: wknd wl over 1f out* **40/1**
504 **11** 2¼ **Bahamian Ballad**[72] 4615 3-8-12 52....................(v) FrancisNorton 8 22
(J D Bethell) *prom 4f* **20/1**
12 *shd* **Arch Event** 3-8-7 0....................(p) JackDean(5) 4 22
(J M Bradley) *s.i.s: outpcd* **100/1**

30 13 1¼ **Flying Free**[56] 5160 3-9-3 0 RobertWinston 9 23
(J R Fanshawe) *hld up and bhd: c wd st: sn rdn: no rspnse* **20/1**
1m 15.0s **Going Correction** -0.075s/f (Stan) **13** Ran SP% **119.8**
Speed ratings (Par 99): **97,96,95,92,92 88,87,85,84,84 81,80,79**
toteswinger: 1&2 £1.50, 1&3 £7.30, 2&3 £10.90. CSF £16.24 TOTE £5.40: £1.80, £1.40, £3.50; EX 20.90.
Owner Tangerine Trees Partnership **Bred** Mrs B A Matthews **Trained** Hambleton, N Yorks
■ Stewards' Enquiry : Holly Hall two-day ban: used whip with excessive frequency (Oct 27-28)

FOCUS
They went a modest pace in this ordinary event. The field was tightly grouped in the early stages and few got into it from off the pace. The third and fourth are the best guide to this modest form.

6708 BET TOTEPOOL ON ALL UK RACING H'CAP 1m 5f 194y(P)
2:50 (2:51) (Class 5) (0-70,68) 3-Y-0+ **£3,238** (£963; £481; £240) **Stalls** Low

Form RPR
4234 1 **Silk Hall (UAE)**[25] 6060 3-9-5 **68** KirstyMilczarek 3 82+
(D W P Arbuthnot) *s.i.s: hld up towards rr: gd hdwy 3f out: led over 1f out: pushed clr fnl f: comf: uns rdr after fin* **5/4**[1]
0552 2 8 **Into The Light**[24] 6092 3-9-5 **68** GrahamGibbons 8 69
(E S McMahon) *prom: wnt 2nd 9f out: led 3f out: sn rdn: hdd over 1f out: sn btn* **3/1**[2]
6060 3 1½ **Amir Pasha (UAE)**[43] 5537 3-8-10 **59** JoeFanning 7 58
(W R Swinburn) *t.k.h: led 1f: 2nd tl 9f out: chsd ldr over 2f out tl wl over 1f out: sn hung lft and btn* **11/1**
5341 4 6 **Merrymaker**[23] 6115 8-9-6 **63** DuranFentiman(3) 9 54
(W M Brisbourne) *s.i.s: in rr: pushed along over 4f out: styd on to take 4th wl ins fnl f: n.d* **6/1**[3]
400 5 1 **Scania Classic**[14] 6345 7-9-6 **65** JackDean(5) 2 54
(M J Scudamore) *s.i.s: hld up towards rr: rdn over 2f out: nvr nr ldrs* **22/1**
4000 6 1 **Vanishing Dancer (SWI)**[189] 1246 11-8-9 **49** oh4 DeanMcKeown 6 37
(Mrs D Thomas) *prom: pushed along and lost pl over 3f out* **50/1**
0040 7 6 **Rare Coincidence**[9] 6493 7-9-9 **63** (p) ChrisCatlin 12 42
(R F Fisher) *led after 1f to 3f out: sn wknd* **14/1**
10-5 8 7 **Foursquare Flyer (IRE)**[237] 617 6-10-0 **68** (t) TomEaves 13 38
(T J Pitt) *s.i.s: a in rr: no ch fnl 3f* **20/1**
0/0 9 7 **Aura Of Calm (IRE)**[19] 6220 6-9-0 **54** TonyHamilton 10 14
(Ronald O'Leary, Ire) *hld up in tch: rdn over 2f out: wknd wl over 1f out* **8/1**
650- 10 27 **Malibu (IRE)**[4] 3927 7-8-9 **49** oh4 (p) CatherineGannon 11 —
(A W Carroll) *sn stdd into mid-div: rdn over 3f out: sn struggling: t.o* **66/1**
3m 3.24s (-2.76) **Going Correction** -0.075s/f (Stan)
WFA 3 from 4yo+ 9lb **10** Ran SP% **122.4**
Speed ratings (Par 103): **104,99,98,95,94 94,90,86,82,67**
toteswinger: 1&2 £2.50, 1&3 £4.60, 2&3 £9.90. CSF £5.07 CT £29.76 TOTE £2.30: £1.10, £1.50, £3.40; EX 6.20.
Owner Bonusprint **Bred** Darley **Trained** Compton, Berks

FOCUS
A moderate handicap. Silk Hall was impressive but probably didn't have to improve that much to win. The next two ran to form.

6709 WOLVERHAMPTON-RACECOURSE.CO.UK (S) STKS 7f 32y(P)
3:20 (3:24) (Class 6) 2-Y-0 **£2,047** (£604; £302) **Stalls** High

Form RPR
0 1 **Captain Cavendish (IRE)**[23] 6135 2-8-11 0 (b[1]) MickyFenton 3 54
(A Bailey) *s.i.s: hld up in mid-div: swtchd lft over 2f out: rdn and hdwy over 1f out: r.o u.p to ld cl home* **12/1**
4003 2 hd **Svindal (IRE)**[28] 5966 2-8-11 58 (p) NCallan 12 54
(K A Ryan) *s.i.s: sn prom: rdn and hung bdly rt 1f out: led ins fnl f: hdd cl home* **5/1**[3]
3 nse **Wickedly Fast (USA)** 2-7-13 0 (t) MatthewDavies(7) 1 49
(George Baker) *s.i.s: sn in tch: rdn over 1f out: hung rt ins fnl f: r.o* **16/1**
064 4 nk **Nimmy's Special**[17] 6244 2-8-6 63 TomEaves 11 48
(B Smart) *s.i.s: bhd: swtchd rt jst over 1f out: rdn and r.o wl towards fin* **9/4**[1]
000 5 ¾ **Spiritual Bond**[5] 6574 2-8-5 0 ow2 KevinGhunowa(3) 5 48
(R A Harris) *prom: nt clr run on ins and swtchd rt jst over 1f out: rdn and kpt on ins fnl f* **66/1**
000 6 hd **Deckchair**[10] 6432 2-8-6 60 (v) FrancisNorton 2 46
(H J Collingridge) *led: rdn and edgd lft over 1f out: hdd and no ex ins fnl f* **11/2**
1300 7 1½ **Nun Today (USA)**[5] 6573 2-8-12 59 (b) RobertWinston 9 48
(J S Moore) *mid-div: rdn and lost pl over 2f out: n.d after* **4/1**[2]
8 ¾ **Woodland Violet** 2-8-6 0 CatherineGannon 7 40
(I A Wood) *hld up towards rr: hdwy on ins wl over 1f out: hmpd jst over 1f out: no imp* **40/1**
00 9 8 **Proper Tool (IRE)**[157] 1955 2-8-11 0 JoeFanning 4 26
(R A Harris) *s.i.s: t.k.h: sn prom: rdn and wknd over 1f out* **8/1**
50 10 14 **May Boy**[34] 5778 2-8-11 0 TGMcLaughlin 10 —
(R J Hodges) *s.i.s: a bhd: eased whn no ch ins fnl f* **66/1**
00 11 41 **Buddha O' Neil**[32] 5812 2-8-11 0 ChrisCatlin 8 —
(M R Channon) *s.i.s: sn t.o* **25/1**
00 12 68 **Maisie Mouse**[34] 5788 2-8-6 0 AdrianTNicholls 6 —
(S C Williams) *s.i.s: sn t.o: lame* **50/1**
1m 31.94s (2.34) **Going Correction** -0.075s/f (Stan) **12** Ran SP% **118.7**
Speed ratings (Par 93): **83,82,82,82,81 81,79,78,69,53 6,—**
toteswinger: 1&2 £12.90, 1&3 £43.30, 2&3 £4.80. CSF £69.29 TOTE £14.90: £2.90, £2.10, £5.90; EX 80.60.There was no bid for the winner
Owner The Glenbuccaneers **Bred** William Madden & Michael O'Riordan **Trained** Newmarket, Suffolk
■ Stewards' Enquiry : Francis Norton caution: careless riding.

FOCUS
The pace was only steady and they finished in a bunch, with the time four seconds above standard. The form looks dubious.

NOTEBOOK
Captain Cavendish(IRE) was in trouble a long way out on his debut last month but seemed to be galvanised by the application of blinkers on his All-Weather debut. He kept grinding away from some way off the pace and eventually prevailed close home. The form is modest but there should be more to come and his style suggests he should stay a bit further. (op 16-1)
Svindal(IRE), with cheekpieces replacing blinkers, had to use up some energy to get into a prominent position from stall 12, but he still found a fair amount for pressure, although he hung badly right in the closing stages. (op 11-2 tchd 9-2)
Wickedly Fast(USA) looked very inexperienced and was forced wide in the straight but stayed on resolutely to run a promising race on her debut. (op 14-1 tchd 18-1)
Nimmy's Special had to be switched several times but eventually found a good finishing burst. She would have probably reeled in the leaders in a few more strides and is worth another chance in a similar event next time. (op 11-4)
Spiritual Bond's proximity casts a cloud over the form. She had shown very little at big prices in three previous starts but it is possible that she is a slow learner who may be starting to get the hang of things. (op 50-1)
Maisie Mouse Official explanation: jockey said filly finished lame

6710 TOTESUPER7 H'CAP 7f 32y(P)
3:50 (3:53) (Class 4) (0-85,85) 3-Y-0+ **£6,476** (£1,927; £963; £481) **Stalls** High

Form RPR
6 1 **Wasp (AUS)**[9] 6478 6-9-4 **83** JoeFanning 2 92
(W Jarvis) *led 1f: a.p: rdn fnl f: led towards fin* **7/1**[3]
2006 2 ¾ **Gallantry**[21] 6170 6-9-3 **82** TGMcLaughlin 7 89
(P Howling) *hld up: sn towards rr: hdwy over 1f out: rdn whn swtchd lft wl ins fnl f: r.o* **8/1**
0440 3 hd **Kiwi Bay**[58] 5104 3-9-1 **82** TonyHamilton 9 88
(M Dods) *hld up towards rr: c wd st: rdn and hdwy fnl f: r.o* **20/1**
3134 4 shd **Councellor (FR)**[122] 2995 6-9-5 **84** (t) MickyFenton 5 90
(Stef Liddiard) *prom: n.m.r and lost pl after 1f: hdwy over 1f out: rdn and r.o ins fnl f* **8/1**
1331 5 ½ **Willkandoo (USA)**[8] 6511 3-9-1 **82** 6ex NCallan 8 86
(K A Ryan) *a.p: led 2f out: rdn and hung lft over 1f out: hdd and no ex towards fin* **9/2**[2]
2106 6 ½ **Prince Hamlet (IRE)**[70] 4682 3-9-2 **83** (v[1]) TomEaves 10 86
(B Smart) *sn prom: rdn and hung lft ins fnl f: nt qckn* **12/1**
4140 7 nse **The Kiddykid (IRE)**[16] 6277 8-9-0 **84** RichardEvans(5) 3 87
(P D Evans) *hld up in mid-div: rdn whn nt clr run jst over 1f out: carried lft ins fnl f: kpt on* **8/1**
0045 8 1 **Danehillsundance (IRE)**[15] 6307 4-9-3 **82** FrancisNorton 1 85+
(S Parr) *dwlt: in rr: hdwy on ins 1f out: styng on whn nt clr run towards fin* **4/1**[1]
6306 9 1 **Burning Incense (IRE)**[16] 6289 5-9-6 **85** (p) PaulMulrennan 12 82
(M Dods) *hld up towards rr: nt clr run briefly over 1f out: nvr trbld ldrs* **12/1**
0060 10 1¾ **Xpres Maite**[13] 6354 5-9-6 **85** (v) RobertWinston 6 78
(S R Bowring) *led after 1f: hdd 2f out: nt clr run on ins over 1f out: wkng whn hmpd ins fnl f* **9/1**
0000 11 1 **Lytton**[21] 6169 3-8-10 **80** KevinGhunowa(3) 4 70
(W R Swinburn) *prom tl wknd wl over 1f out* **33/1**
1523 12 1 **Will He Wish**[247] 502 12-9-4 **83** (b) ChrisCatlin 11 70
(S Gollings) *s.i.s: a in rr* **16/1**
1m 28.87s (-0.73) **Going Correction** -0.075s/f (Stan)
WFA 3 from 4yo+ 2lb **12** Ran SP% **123.0**
Speed ratings (Par 105): **101,100,99,99,99 98,98,97,96,94 93,92**
toteswinger: 1&2 £18.70, 1&3 £39.00, 2&3 £27.90. CSF £64.55 CT £1107.90 TOTE £10.00: £3.50, £1.90, £7.50; EX 84.90.
Owner Dr J Walker **Bred** Woodlands Stud NSW **Trained** Newmarket, Suffolk

FOCUS
A decent handicap which produced a bunch finish off a fairly ordinary pace and there were a few hard-luck stories. The winner is up 6lb on his British debut, with the next two close to their summer form.
Danehillsundance(IRE) Official explanation: jockey said colt was denied a clear run
Lytton Official explanation: jockey said gelding hung right throughout

6711 TOTESWINGER H'CAP 5f 20y(P)
4:20 (4:22) (Class 6) (0-62,62) 3-Y-0+ **£2,388** (£705; £352) **Stalls** Low

Form RPR
0315 1 **Pride Of Northcare (IRE)**[19] 6218 4-9-1 **62** DarrenWilliams 5 74+
(D Shaw) *n.m.r briefly sn after s: mid-div: hdwy on ins 2f out: led 1f out: rdn out* **11/2**[2]
0025 2 ½ **Metal Guru**[14] 6339 4-8-10 **60** (p) RussellKennemore(3) 3 70+
(R Hollinshead) *hmpd sn after s: towards rr: nt clr run over 2f out: hdwy wl over 1f out: r.o wl towards fin: nt rch wnr* **13/2**[3]
6400 3 1½ **Windjammer**[9] 6486 4-8-12 **59** (b) DavidAllan 2 64
(T D Easterby) *a.p: wnt 2nd briefly wl over 1f out: nt qckn ins fnl f* **7/2**[1]
3041 4 ¾ **Pegasus Dancer (FR)**[48] 5374 4-9-0 **61** (p) NCallan 6 63
(K A Ryan) *led: rdn and hdd 1f out: no ex ins fnl f* **11/2**[2]
2006 5 2½ **Admiral Bond (IRE)**[47] 5395 3-9-1 **62** (b) PJMcDonald 11 55
(G R Oldroyd) *dwlt: bhd tl hdwy over 1f out: hung lft ins fnl f: nvr trbld ldrs* **33/1**
6505 6 ½ **Just Joey**[76] 4502 4-9-0 **61** (b) ChrisCatlin 4 53
(J R Weymes) *chsd ldrs: no hdwy fnl 2f* **14/1**
6230 7 1½ **Back In The Red (IRE)**[13] 6357 4-8-12 **62** (p) KevinGhunowa(3) 12 48
(R A Harris) *mid-div: pushed along and lost pl over 3f out: c wd st: n.d* **15/2**
3000 8 nk **Cape Of Storms**[26] 6024 5-8-13 **60** (p) PaulMulrennan 1 45
(R Brotherton) *mid-div: shortlived effrt on ins over 1f out* **8/1**
3606 9 ¾ **Night Prospector**[14] 6339 8-8-6 **58** (b) RichardEvans(5) 9 40
(R A Harris) *mid-div: rdn and wknd wl over 1f out* **12/1**
0000 10 nse **Fabuleux Cherie**[19] 6204 3-8-13 **60** FrancisNorton 8 42
(W R Muir) *chsd ldrs: n.m.r ent st: sn wknd* **14/1**
5300 11 hd **Miss Firefly**[14] 6339 3-9-0 **61** MickyFenton 10 42
(R J Hodges) *w ldr tl rdn wl over 1f out: sn wknd* **25/1**
63 12 6 **Lady Bahia (IRE)**[82] 4308 7-8-6 **58** KellyHarrison(5) 7 18
(Peter Grayson) *s.i.s: hung lft jst over 1f out: a in rr* **25/1**
0534 13 4 **Triskaidekaphobia**[200] 1037 5-9-1 **62** (t) PaulFitzsimons 13 7
(Miss J R Tooth) *w ldrs tl rdn and wknd 2f out* **20/1**
61.45 secs (-0.85) **Going Correction** -0.075s/f (Stan) **13** Ran SP% **125.6**
Speed ratings (Par 101): **103,102,99,98,94 93,91,90,89,89 89,79,73**
toteswinger: 1&2 £7.80, 1&3 £6.50, 2&3 £7.20. CSF £41.47 CT £135.51 TOTE £6.00: £2.10, £3.10, £2.00; EX 27.80.
Owner George Houghton **Bred** Mrs L Miller **Trained** Danethorpe, Notts

FOCUS
A modest handicap but the time was good for the grade. The winner is progressing and the form is rated through the third.

6712 TOTETRIFECTA H'CAP 1m 1f 103y(P)
4:50 (4:51) (Class 5) (0-70,70) 3-Y-0 **£3,238** (£963; £481; £240) **Stalls** Low

Form RPR
5633 1 **Intabih (USA)**[11] 6422 3-9-1 **67** NCallan 7 86+
(C E Brittain) *a.p: led over 1f out: rdn and r.o wl* **5/2**[1]
4006 2 3 **Hyde Lea Flyer**[10] 6450 3-8-13 **65** GrahamGibbons 1 74
(E S McMahon) *hld up in mid-div: hdwy over 2f out: ev ch over 1f out: sn rdn: nt qckn ins fnl f* **10/1**
0545 3 3½ **Themwerethedays**[19] 6211 3-8-12 **64** MickyFenton 12 66
(S Kirk) *hld up in rr: swtchd rt over 2f out: c wd st: hdwy and edgd lft fnl f: nvr nrr* **10/1**

463 **4** ¾ **Beetuna (IRE)**[24] 6088 3-8-11 **63** .... TomEaves 5 63
(B Smart) *hld up in mid-div: hdwy 3f out: rdn and wknd over 1f out* **7/1**[3]
3650 **5** ½ **Game Park (USA)**[33] 5800 3-9-4 **70** .... RobertWinston 4 69+
(J R Fanshawe) *hld up towards rr: nt clr run over 2f out: hdwy on ins whn swtchd rt jst over 1f out: nvr nr to chal* **6/1**[2]
2232 **6** 2 ¼ **Azure Mist**[14] 6332 3-9-2 **68** .... PaulMulrennan 11 63
(M H Tompkins) *t.k.h: prom: led briefly wl over 1f out: sn rdn: wknd ins fnl f* **9/1**
2000 **7** ¾ **Mganga**[26] 6036 3-8-4 **56** .... CatherineGannon 10 49
(M R Channon) *hld up in rr: sme hdwy wl over 1f out: sn rdn: no further prog fnl f* **33/1**
0040 **8** 6 **Always Certain (USA)**[19] 6210 3-8-8 **60** .... JoeFanning 8 40
(M Johnston) *hld up and bhd: pushed along over 2f out: no rspnse* **11/1**
0002 **9** 5 **Bookiebasher Babe (IRE)**[10] 6437 3-8-13 **65** .... FrancisNorton 6 35
(M Quinn) *led: hdd wl over 1f out: sn wknd* **8/1**
150 **10** ½ **Director's Chair**[12] 6379 3-8-12 **67** .... RussellKennemore(3) 3 36
(Miss J Feilden) *reminders sn after s: w ldr: reminder and lost 2nd over 3f out: wknd wl over 1f out: sn hung rt* **14/1**
0540 **11** ¾ **La Troupe (IRE)**[12] 6378 3-8-13 **65** .... ChrisCatlin 2 32
(J H M Gosden) *hld up in tch: wknd over 2f out* **14/1**
0460 **12** *26* **Hellfire Bay**[95] 3886 3-8-6 **58** ow1 .... (p) AdrianTNicholls 13 —
(J Mackie) *t.k.h: a towards rr: lost tch 2f out: t.o* **33/1**

1m 59.59s (-2.11) **Going Correction** -0.075s/f (Stan) **12 Ran SP% 122.2**
Speed ratings (Par 101): **106,103,100,99,99 97,96,91,86,86 85,62**
toteswinger: 1&2 £6.70, 1&3 £9.60, 2&3 £18.20. CSF £29.60 CT £220.16 TOTE £3.40: £1.80, £2.60, £4.40; EX 32.10 TRIFECTA Not won. Place 6 £ 143.80, Place 5 £ 73.01.
Owner Saeed Manana **Bred** Dr George S Stefanis **Trained** Newmarket, Suffolk

FOCUS
An ordinary handicap run in a good time for the grade. The winner is progressing and was value for a bit extra, with the second rated to this year's form.
Director's Chair Official explanation: jockey said gelding never travelled
T/Plt: £215.00 to a £1 stake. Pool: £56,464.28. 191.70 winning tickets. T/Qpdt: £65.10 to a £1 stake. Pool: £3,141.22. 35.70 winning tickets. KH

6567 CHANTILLY (R-H)
Monday, October 13

OFFICIAL GOING: Good to soft

6713a PRIX ECLIPSE (GROUP 3) 6f
2:05 (2:05) 2-Y-O **£29,412** (£11,765; £8,824; £5,882; £2,941)

RPR
1 **Smooth Operator (GER)**[41] 2-8-11 .... AHelfenbein 5 106
(Mario Hofer, Germany) *hld up: 7th 1/2-way: drvn and hdwy 1 1/2f out: rdn to chal over 1f out: led fnl f: rdn out* **269/10**
2 ¾ **Saxford**[52] 5226 2-8-11 .... TPQueally 3 104
(Mrs L Stubbs) *led after 1f: pushed along and r.o 2f out: rdn 1 1/2f out: hdd fnl f: kpt on u.p to hold on for 2nd cl home* **16/1**
3 *nse* **Bonnie Charlie**[33] 5794 2-8-11 .... CSoumillon 7 104
(R Hannon) *in tch: 5th 1/2-way: rdn and r.o 1 1/2f out to press ldrs: ev ch 100yds out: styd on* **16/10**[1]
4 *snk* **Treasure (FR)**[32] 5850 2-8-8 .... DBoeuf 2 101
(Mme C Head-Maarek, France) *prom: 4th on rail 1/2-way: pushed along 2f out: rdn to chal over 1f out: led briefly ins fnl f: styd on* **29/10**[2]
5 1 **Doncaster Rover (USA)**[31] 5852 2-8-11 .... TolleyDean 9 101
(S Parr) *prom: 3rd and pushed along 1/2-way: sn wnt 2nd: drvn 1 1/2f out: no ex fnl 150yds* **61/10**
6 1 ½ **Queen America (FR)**[28] 5987 2-8-8 .... OPeslier 4 93
(Robert Collet, France) *towards rr: 8th 1/2-way: rdn to chse ldrs 1 1/2f out: nvr able to chal* **12/1**
7 5 **Damien (IRE)**[23] 6119 2-8-11 .... MichaelHills 8 81
(B W Hills) *mid-div: 6th 1/2-way: n.d* **51/10**[3]
8 ¾ **Giordana (IRE)**[44] 2-8-8 .... FilipMinarik 1 76
(P Vovcenko, Germany) *racd in last: nvr in contention* **16/1**
9 4 **Ladouce (FR)**[32] 5850 2-8-8 .... IMendizabal 6 64
(Robert Collet, France) *led 1f: 2nd 1/2-way: sn lost pl: n.d after* **12/1**

1m 13.0s (1.60) **9 Ran SP% 125.3**
PARI-MUTUEL: WIN 27.90; PL 5.20, 3.50, 1.40; DF 158.90.
Owner Stall Jenny **Bred** Mario Hofer **Trained** Germany
■ Stewards' Enquiry : T P Queally €100 fine: whip abuse

NOTEBOOK
Smooth Operator(GER), held up towards the back of the field for much of the way, took time to get into top gear and then had to wait for a gap to appear. He showed good acceleration once in the open and galloped on strongly to the line to win a shade cosily. His trainer reported that he could go for the Criterium de Maisons-Laffitte on November 4th.
Saxford, quickly at the head of affairs, looked all over the winner a furlong and a half out but then seemed to hit a flat spot, before rallying. He could go next for the Horris Hill Stakes.
Bonnie Charlie raced prominently on the outside for much of the race but took time to find top gear when the pace quickened. He finished well showing late acceleration and was just pipped for second.
Treasure(FR), held up on the rail behind the long-time leader, made late progress and finished best of all to beaten just over a length by the winner.
Doncaster Rover(USA), quickly out of the gates, raced up with the leaders on the outside and battled all the way to the line, but he just lacked acceleration at a crucial stage of the race.
Damien(IRE), on the wide outside, took time to settle and could not quicken when the pace was increased.

6742a PRIX DE LA COYE LA FORET (CLAIMER) (FILLIES) 1m 1f
1:05 (1:07) 3-Y-O **£7,721** (£3,088; £2,316; £1,544; £772)

RPR
1 **Rava (IRE)**[40] 3-8-9 .... OPeslier 69
(S Wattel, France)
2 1 ½ **Equinoreva (FR)**[12] 3-8-8 .... JeremyDaSilva(8) 73
(J-P Pelat, France)
3 1 ½ **Fligane (FR)**[45] 3-9-2 .... TJarnet 70
(Mlle S-V Tarrou, France)
4 *nk* **Vaccaria (GER)** 3-8-12 65
(W Hickst, Germany)
5 1 ½ **Shalamara (FR)**[12] 3-9-11 75
(P Demercastel, France)
6 ¾ **Swing And Rock (IRE)** 3-9-2 65
(A Trybuhl, Germany)
7 *8* **Diagora (FR)**[76] 3-8-12 44
(Robert Collet, France)
8 ½ **Rain Esteem**[76] 3-8-12 43
(H-A Pantall, France)
9 ½ **Cottage Club (IRE)**[116] 3-9-2 46
(N Clement, France)
10 1 ½ **Champion's Time (GER)**[14] 3-8-9 36
(M Rulec, Germany)
0 **Chaminka (FR)**[219] 3-8-9 .... —
(Mme N Rossio, France)
0 **Martingrange Lass (IRE)**[52] 5223 3-8-9 .... TolleyDean —
(S Parr) *hld up: 14th st: sn rdn and btn* **121/1**[1]
0 **Salamandra (FR)**[320] 3-8-12 .... —
(C Laffon-Parias, France)
0 **Maid For Sucess (FR)**[40] 3-8-12 .... —
(Robert Collet, France)
0 **Gold Cup One (FR)**[41] 3-8-9 .... —
(Mme N Rossio, France)
0 **Maraoute Gaugain (FR)**[40] 3-8-9 .... —
(Ron Caget, France)
0 **Miss Varreville (FR)**[25] 3-8-9 .... —
(Ron Caget, France)
0 **Generous Gift (FR)**[25] 3-8-9 .... (b) —
(Mme M Bollack-Badel, France)
0 **Fly Me To The Moon (FR)** 3-9-2 .... —
(C Boutin, France)

1m 52.5s (1.40) **19 Ran SP% 0.8**
PARI-MUTUEL (Including 1 Euro stake): WIN 6.60; PL 2.70, 3.20, 5.10;DF 33.20.
Owner Mme J Adamian **Bred** Cranford Stud **Trained** France

NOTEBOOK
Martingrange Lass(IRE) tried to accelerate on the turn into the straight but could not go through with his effort.

6743a PRIX DU PLESSIS LUZARCHES 6f
2:35 (2:36) 3-Y-O **£10,662** (£4,265; £3,199; £2,132; £1,066)

RPR
1 **Dunkerque (FR)**[68] 3-9-4 .... WMongil 104
(Mme C Head-Maarek, France)
2 1 ½ **White Spire (FR)**[54] 3-8-8 .... SPasquier 90
(F Rohaut, France)
3 2 ½ **Dam D'Augy (FR)**[25] 6064 3-9-1 .... TJarnet 89
(Mlle S-V Tarrou, France)
4 1 ½ **Not My Choice (IRE)**[16] 6278 3-9-4 .... OPeslier 88
(S Parr) *prom on ins: 3rd and ev ch 1f out: styd on* **15/1**[1]
5 1 ½ **Galaktea (IRE)**[25] 6064 3-8-8 73
(C Laffon-Parias, France)
6 3 **Vassinella (FR)**[96] 3-8-8 64
(Mme C Head-Maarek, France)
7 ¾ **Topkapi Diamond (IRE)**[20] 3-9-1 69
(E Kurdu, Germany)
8 *hd* **Laokoon (GER)**[54] 3-9-4 .... (b) 71
(Mario Hofer, Germany)
9 1 ½ **Zia Sofi (FR)**[213] 3-8-8 57
(Mme M Bollack-Badel, France)
10 *nse* **Jane Blue (FR)**[25] 6064 3-9-4 67
(C Ferland, France)
0 **Niska (USA)**[51] 3-8-8 .... —
(A Fabre, France)

1m 12.4s (1.00) **11 Ran SP% 6.3**
PARI-MUTUEL: WIN 3.10 (coupled with Vassinella); PL 1.20, 1.40, 1.40;DF 6.00.
Owner Alec Head **Bred** A & Mme A Head **Trained** Chantilly, France

NOTEBOOK
Not My Choice(IRE), quickly at the head of affairs, raced up the stands' rail but could not follow the winner's burst of speed in the final furlong.

6744a PRIX DU PORTAIL (APPRENTICES) 1m
3:35 (3:38) 3-Y-O **£8,088** (£3,235; £2,426; £1,618; £809)

RPR
1 **Rockette (FR)**[115] 3-9-5 .... JBensimon 94
(Y De Nicolay, France)
2 3 **Ballpoint (IRE)**[155] 3-8-13 .... JCabre 81
(E Libaud, France)
3 *nk* **Deacon Blue (FR)**[62] 3-9-2 .... YLerner 83
(F Rohaut, France)
4 2 ½ **King Kenny**[17] 6256 3-9-0 .... StephaneBreux 75
(S Parr) *trckd ldrs: styd on fr over 1 1/2f out: wnt 4th ins fnl f* **18/1**[1]
5 1 ½ **Haadeej (USA)**[51] 3-9-4 76
(C Boutin, France)
6 2 **Zania (FR)**[78] 4471 3-8-10 63
(M Delzangles, France)
7 3 **Atlantic Racer (GER)** 3-9-0 60
(M Rulec, Germany)
8 5 **Avant Premiere (USA)**[54] 3-9-1 50
(C Boutin, France)
9 *nk* **Fairybook (USA)**[157] 3-9-1 49
(H-A Pantall, France)
10 *10* **Premiere Dan (FR)**[42] 3-8-8 19
(D Allard, France)

1m 37.1s (-0.70) **10 Ran SP% 5.3**
PARI-MUTUEL: WIN 10.10; PL 2.00, 4.40, 1.20; DF 110.30.
Owner Mme H Devin **Bred** Mme H Devin **Trained** France

NOTEBOOK
King Kenny, held up in midfield for much of the race, was brought with his run up the straight on the outside and finished well.

[6559]LEICESTER (R-H)

Tuesday, October 14

OFFICIAL GOING: Good (good to soft in places)

Wind: Light, behind Weather: Overcast

6714 EBF REFERENCE POINT MAIDEN STKS (C&G) (DIV I) 7f 9y

1:40 (1:42) (Class 4) 2-Y-O **£4,857** (£1,445; £722; £360) **Stalls** Low

Form RPR

0 **1** **Bravo Echo**[25] 6084 2-9-0 0................................ RichardMullen 14 85+
(J H M Gosden) *trckd ldr: racd keenly: shkn up 2f out: rdn to ld wl ins fnl f* **2/1**[1]

62 **2** *¾* **Emirates Roadshow (USA)**[11] 6443 2-9-0 0.................. LDettori 11 83+
(Saeed Bin Suroor) *led: rdn over 1f out: edgd rt and hdd wl ins fnl f* **5/2**[2]

3 *6* **Takeover Bid (USA)** 2-9-0 0................................ JoeFanning 7 68
(M Johnston) *hld up: hdwy 1/2-way: rdn over 1f out: edgd lft and wknd ins fnl f* **16/1**

0 **4** *½* **Prohibition (IRE)**[12] 6425 2-9-0 0.......................... DarryllHolland 3 67+
(W J Haggas) *s.i.s: hld up: hdwy 1/2-way: rdn and edgd rt fr over 2f out: wknd ins fnl f* **11/2**[3]

0 **5** *1 ¼* **Kiwi Moon**[17] 6292 2-9-0 0.................................. TedDurcan 13 64+
(B Smart) *chsd ldrs: rdn over 2f out: wknd fnl f* **33/1**

6 **6** *½* **Alpha Tauri (USA)**[12] 6423 2-9-0 0.......................... TPQueally 6 63+
(H R A Cecil) *hld up in tch: plld hrd: nt clr run over 2f out: rdn and edgd rt over 1f out: styd on same pce* **8/1**

4 **7** *½* **Barbarian**[18] 6246 2-9-0 0.................................. MichaelHills 2 61
(B W Hills) *hld up in tch: rdn over 2f out: edgd rt and wknd over 1f out* **20/1**

0 **8** *shd* **King Of Defence**[62] 4982 2-9-0 0.......................... PhilipRobinson 9 61
(M A Jarvis) *chsd ldrs: rdn over 2f out: wknd over 1f out* **50/1**

60 **9** *shd* **Devil To Pay**[24] 6122 2-9-0 0.............................. EddieAhern 10 61+
(J L Dunlop) *hld up: nvr trbld ldrs* **33/1**

0 **10** *1 ½* **Billy Smart (IRE)**[48] 5404 2-9-0 0.......................... LPKeniry 12 57
(D J S Ffrench Davis) *plld hrd and prom: rdn over 2f out: sn wknd* **200/1**

11 *2 ¼* **Dancourt (IRE)** 2-9-0 0...................................... RyanMoore 1 51
(Sir Michael Stoute) *dwlt: hld up: rdn and hung rt over 1f out: a in rr* **14/1**

12 *hd* **Shy Prophet** 2-8-9 0.. DavidProbert(5) 8 51
(A J McCabe) *s.i.s: outpcd* **100/1**

00 **13** *4 ½* **Night Knight (IRE)**[14] 6359 2-9-0 0.......................... HayleyTurner 4 40
(M L W Bell) *hld up: rdn over 2f out: a in rr* **100/1**

0 **14** *nse* **Timbaa (USA)**[13] 6375 2-9-0 0.............................. ChrisCatlin 5 40
(Rae Guest) *sn outpcd* **200/1**

1m 24.95s (-1.25) **Going Correction** -0.225s/f (Firm) **14** Ran SP% **116.5**
Speed ratings (Par 97): **98,97,90,89,88 87,87,87,86,85 82,82,77,77**
toteswinger: 1&2 £2.20, 1&3 £10.80, 2&3 £12.10. CSF £6.29 TOTE £3.00: £1.50, £1.10, £5.70; EX 7.50.

Owner K Abdulla **Bred** Juddmonte Farms Ltd **Trained** Newmarket, Suffolk

FOCUS

This looked a fair juvenile maiden and the first pair came clear. Both look useful performers in the making.

NOTEBOOK

Bravo Echo, well backed, rewarded his supporters at the second time of asking and completed the task in game fashion on this suitably easier surface. He was always well placed and dug deep when asked to reel in the eventual runner-up from the furlong pole. This more galloping track was in his favour and he looked better the further he went, suggesting a longer trip will be required for him as a 3yo. He has the size and scope to progress next year and is one to follow. (op 7-2)

Emirates Roadshow(USA) again had his own way out in front, but he seemed to pay late in the day for running freely in the early stages. He pulled well clear of the remainder and is certainly up to winning a maiden before the season is out. (op 15-8)

Takeover Bid(USA) ◆, whose dam was a Listed winner over this trip at two, took time to get the hang of things on this racecourse bow and was doing some pleasing late work. He looks sure to prove a lot sharper next time out and has a future. (op 14-1 tchd 18-1)

Prohibition(IRE) was expected to step up on the form of his Newmarket debut 12 days earlier and duly did so, but still looked inexperienced. The return to 1m will be more in his favour and he should not be too long in finding a winning turn. (op 4-1)

Kiwi Moon showed the benefit of his initial experience at Haydock and ran respectably without threatening. He should come into his own next year.

Alpha Tauri(USA) was dropping down a furlong for this turf debut and did not help his chance by refusing to settle, but still showed ability. (op 12-1 tchd 15-2)

6715 EBF REFERENCE POINT MAIDEN STKS (C&G) (DIV II) 7f 9y

2:10 (2:11) (Class 4) 2-Y-O **£4,857** (£1,445; £722; £360) **Stalls** Low

Form RPR

23 **1** **Box Office**[12] 6407 2-9-0 0.................................. RoystonFfrench 6 81+
(M Johnston) *sn led: hdd over 4f out: led again over 2f out: rdn out* **7/1**[2]

6 **2** *2 ¼* **Al Marmoom (USA)**[24] 6122 2-9-0 0.......................... LDettori 11 74+
(Saeed Bin Suroor) *chsd ldrs: rdn and ev ch over 1f out: edgd lft ins fnl f: eased whn btn towards fin* **4/6**[1]

0 **3** *4 ½* **Silvador**[24] 6122 2-9-0 0.................................... MartinDwyer 8 62+
(W R Muir) *hld up: hdwy over 2f out: sn rdn: styd on same pce appr fnl f* **12/1**

0 **4** *2 ¼* **Ask Dan (IRE)**[10] 6481 2-9-0 0.............................. RichardMullen 10 57
(B Smart) *chsd ldrs: rdn and ev ch 2f out: wknd fnl f* **80/1**

5 *¾* **King's Song (IRE)** 2-9-0 0.................................. RyanMoore 7 55+
(Sir Michael Stoute) *dwlt: hdwy over 4f out: rdn and wknd over 1f out* **7/1**[2]

6 *1 ¼* **Troubletimestwo (FR)** 2-9-0 0................................ EddieAhern 14 52
(H J L Dunlop) *chsd ldrs: rdn over 2f out: wknd over 1f out* **33/1**

0 **7** *¾* **Play It Sam**[14] 6359 2-9-0 0................................ AdamKirby 12 50
(W R Swinburn) *hld up: hdwy 1/2-way: wknd over 1f out* **10/1**[3]

0 **8** *1 ¾* **Mr Prolific**[15] 6342 2-9-0 0................................ MichaelHills 13 45
(B W Hills) *hld up: nvr trbld ldrs* **33/1**

0 **9** *hd* **Mister Standfast**[13] 6375 2-8-11 0.......................... LukeMorris(3) 4 45
(J M P Eustace) *prom: rdn over 2f out: wknd wl over 1f out* **100/1**

00 **10** *1 ½* **Kaiser Willie (IRE)**[24] 6122 2-8-11 0........................ KevinGhunowa(3) 9 41
(B W Duke) *prom: lost pl 4f out: n.d after* **100/1**

0 **11** *1 ½* **Short Sharp Shock**[18] 6246 2-9-0 0.......................... AdrianTNicholls 3 37
(J Mackie) *plld hrd: w ldrs tl led over 4f out: rdn: edgd lft and hdd over 2f out: sn wknd* **200/1**

0 **12** *shd* **Marju King (IRE)**[24] 6122 2-9-0 0.......................... SteveDrowne 5 37
(W S Kittow) *hld up: rdn 1/2-way: a in rr* **40/1**

13 *½* **Notker (IRE)** 2-9-0 0.. RobertHavlin 2 36
(R T Phillips) *dwlt: hdwy 4f out: rdn and wknd over 2f out* **100/1**

14 *1* **Big Nige (IRE)** 2-9-0 0...................................... JerryO'Dwyer 1 33
(J Pearce) *s.s: hld up: plld hrd: rdn 1/2-way: sn wknd* **100/1**

1m 25.21s (-0.99) **Going Correction** -0.225s/f (Firm) **14** Ran SP% **115.8**
Speed ratings (Par 97): **96,93,88,85,84 83,82,80,80,78 76,76,76,75**
toteswinger: 1&2 £3.00, 1&3 £13.90, 2&3 £4.30. CSF £11.32 TOTE £7.70: £1.60, £1.20, £2.60; EX 14.80.

Owner Sheikh Hamdan Bin Mohammed Al Maktoum **Bred** Gainsborough Stud Management Ltd **Trained** Middleham Moor, N Yorks

FOCUS

This second division of the maiden looked the weaker of the pair and the runners went more towards the far side of the track. It was also run at a slower early pace, but as in the first division the first pair came well clear and the form should work out.

NOTEBOOK

Box Office came good at the third time of asking and seemed to relish the extra distance. The switch to a sounder surface also proved right up his street and there was a lot to like in the way he knuckled down under pressure. He will have no trouble getting a mile at least next season and looks the type his trainer excels with, presuming he does not join Godolphin during the off season. (op 11-2 tchd 8-1 in places)

Al Marmoom(USA), sixth on debut at Newbury 24 days earlier, proved all the rage in the betting ring and was given every chance. He had no answer when the winner hit top gear late on, but was a clear second-best and it would be surprising if he could not be placed to go one better soon. (op 10-11)

Silvador, a half-brother to useful middle-distance stayers Bauer and Boz, had some support and posted a much-improved effort, finishing a good deal closer to the runner-up than had been the case on debut last time. This 160,000gns purchase seems sure to appreciate a stiffer test in time and is going the right way. (op 16-1)

Ask Dan(IRE) had finished last on his debut at Redcar ten days earlier, but had clearly come on a bundle for the experience and shaped a lot more encouragingly. (op 100-1)

King's Song(IRE), a 600,000 euros half-brother to Allegretto among others, proved easy to back on this racecourse bow and ran very much as though the run was needed. He would probably appreciate stepping up a furlong already and should know more next time. (op 9-2)

6716 WHISSENDINE (S) STKS 7f 9y

2:40 (2:40) (Class 6) 3-4-Y-O **£1,942** (£578; £288; £144) **Stalls** Low

Form RPR

2114 **1** **Singleb (IRE)**[15] 6338 4-9-3 62.............................. RyanMoore 16 72
(G L Moore) *trckd ldrs: led over 2f out: rdn and edgd lft ins fnl f: r.o* **15/8**[1]

4406 **2** *2 ½* **Blue Charm**[10] 6490 4-8-12 64..........................(t) RichardHughes 18 60
(S Kirk) *a.p: chsd wnr over 1f out: rdn and hung lft ins fnl f: styd on same pce* **5/1**[2]

2003 **3** *hd* **Yakama (IRE)**[28] 6001 3-8-10 55.......................(b) DO'Donohoe 4 58
(Mrs C A Dunnett) *s.s: hdwy u.p over 1f out: nt rch ldrs* **50/1**

4600 **4** *3 ½* **Semah Harold**[25] 6088 3-8-10 57.......................(b) DarryllHolland 2 49
(E S McMahon) *chsd ldrs: rdn over 2f out: hung rt over 1f out: wknd fnl f* **20/1**

6540 **5** *hd* **Jal Music**[22] 6173 3-8-12 55.............................. KevinGhunowa(3) 7 53
(R A Harris) *led: rdn and hdd over 2f out: wknd fnl f* **40/1**

303 **6** *shd* **Gower Belle**[22] 6173 3-8-5 52.............................. MartinDwyer 8 43
(W R Muir) *prom: rdn and hung rt 2f out: wknd fnl f* **18/1**

0000 **7** *shd* **Cracking Nick (IRE)**[41] 5601 3-8-11 51 ow1...............(t) AdamKirby 11 49
(W R Swinburn) *hld up: hdwy u.p and hung rt over 1f out: nvr trbld ldrs* **25/1**

0000 **8** *1 ½* **Asmodea**[135] 2639 3-8-5 52.................................. JoeFanning 12 43+
(D J Coakley) *plld hrd and prom: hmpd 2f out: sn wknd* **50/1**

0400 **9** *1 ¼* **High Five Society**[21] 6189 4-9-3 54.....................(bt) RoystonFfrench 17 47
(S R Bowring) *chsd ldrs: rdn over 2f out: wknd over 1f out* **28/1**

3530 **10** *½* **Just Jimmy (IRE)**[46] 5474 3-9-1 57.......................... PatCosgrave 9 44
(P D Evans) *hld up in tch: rdn 1/2-way: sn lost pl: n.d after* **16/1**

000 **11** *1 ½* **Usetheforce (IRE)**[26] 6048 3-8-10 60...................(v[1]) EddieAhern 3 35
(M J Wallace, Australia) *hld up: wknd over 2f out* **16/1**

2510 **12** *hd* **All In The Red (IRE)**[11] 6433 3-9-1 70...................(v[1]) NCallan 10 40
(Miss Gay Kelleway) *s.s: hdwy 5f out: rdn whn hmpd 2f out: eased whn btn* **11/2**[3]

0000 **13** *nk* **Maia**[20] 6219 4-8-7 56.. HayleyTurner 15 30
(Ollie Pears) *s.s: a in rr* **20/1**

050 **14** *1* **Diktat Tempo**[34] 5799 3-8-0 50.......................(p) DavidProbert(5) 6 26
(I A Wood) *chsd ldrs: rdn 1/2-way: hung rt and wknd over 2f out* **80/1**

4150 **15** *nk* **Montemayorprincess (IRE)**[106] 3569 4-8-12 53.........(p) TedDurcan 13 31
(D Haydn Jones) *prom: rdn and wknd over 2f out* **28/1**

14-0 **16** *7* **Barnaby Rudge (IRE)**[10] 6471 3-9-1 80.....................(t) JohnEgan 1 16
(Jane Chapple-Hyam) *mid-div: hung rt thrght: rdn and wknd over 2f out* **12/1**

-000 **17** *9* **Art Value**[11] 6433 3-8-10 58................................ FrancisNorton 5 —
(M Wigham) *sn outpcd* **66/1**

1m 24.72s (-1.48) **Going Correction** -0.225s/f (Firm)
WFA 3 from 4yo 2lb **17** Ran SP% **120.9**
Speed ratings (Par 101): **99,96,95,91,91 91,91,89,88,87 86,85,85,84,83 75,65**
toteswinger: 1&2 £3.50, 1&3 £28.40, 2&3 £21.50. CSF £8.63 TOTE £3.30: £1.30, £2.50, £6.90; EX 11.50.The winner was bought in for 10,000gns. All In The Red was claimed by B. Pollock for £6,000.

Owner R A Green **Bred** Spratstown Stud Gm **Trained** Woodingdean, E Sussex

FOCUS

An ordinary seller. The winner showed improved form and the race could be rated higher, bur few of these came here with a solid profile.

All In The Red(IRE) Official explanation: jockey said gelding suffered interference in running

6717 IVECO STRALIS CONDITIONS STKS 7f 9y

3:10 (3:10) (Class 3) 2-Y-O **£6,938** (£2,076; £1,038; £519; £258) **Stalls** Low

Form RPR

2260 **1** **High Alert**[10] 6474 2-8-13 85..............................(b) LDettori 4 89
(J Noseda) *trckd ldrs: rdn over 2f out: r.o u.p to ld ins fnl f: eased nr fin* **11/4**[2]

3000 **2** *1* **Indian Art (IRE)**[33] 5827 2-8-13 83.......................... RyanMoore 6 87
(R Hannon) *w ldr: rdn and ev ch ins fnl f: styd on same pce* **11/1**

3130 **3** *1 ½* **Carnaby Haggerston (IRE)**[24] 6118 2-8-13 82..............(p) NCallan 7 83
(K A Ryan) *led: rdn over 1f out: hdd and no ex ins fnl f* **28/1**

3145 **4** *¾* **Akhenaten**[3] 6648 2-9-2 99.................................. SamHitchcott 1 84
(M R Channon) *hld up: hdwy over 2f out: rdn over 1f out: edgd rt: styd on same pce ins fnl f* **4/1**[3]

410 **5** *½* **Gyr (IRE)**[10] 6474 2-9-2 85.................................. RichardMullen 3 83
(J L Dunlop) *hld up: rdn over 2f out: nvr trbld ldrs* **6/1**

513 **6** *1 ¼* **Absent Pleasure (USA)**[25] 6082 2-9-2 95.................. MartinDwyer 5 80
(B J Meehan) *hld up: plld hrd: rdn over 1f out: wknd towards fin* **7/4**[1]

350 **7** *¾* **Versaki (IRE)**[25] 6082 2-9-2 92.............................. RichardHughes 2 78
(R Hannon) *hld up: rdn over 2f out: n.d* **12/1**

350 **8** *nk* **Confucius Captain (IRE)**[13] 6375 2-8-13 70................. PatCosgrave 8 74
(J R Boyle) *s.i.s: sn chsng ldrs: rdn over 2f out: styd on same pce* **100/1**

1m 24.75s (-1.45) **Going Correction** -0.225s/f (Firm) **8** Ran SP% **117.8**
Speed ratings (Par 99): **99,97,96,95,94 93,92,92**
toteswinger: 1&2 £9.10, 1&3 £9.30, 2&3 £42.90. CSF £33.82 TOTE £3.30: £1.10, £4.40, £8.10; EX 38.00.
Owner Mrs Susan Roy and Mountgrange Stud **Bred** Cyril Humphris **Trained** Newmarket, Suffolk

FOCUS
An interesting juvenile conditions race in which three stood out on official ratings but, in a race where the pace was not strong and it seemed an advantage to race close to the pace, none of them finished in the first three.

NOTEBOOK
High Alert had been pretty consistent on varying ground and had been slightly unlucky in a sales race on faster ground early in the month. He was well supported and travelled well in the slipstream of the leaders, but when asked for his effort he took a while to get to the front before settling the issue in the last half-furlong. He has already been held off lower marks in nurseries, so will need to improve to score in handicap company, but he did win on Polytrack on his debut and may have more to offer on that surface. (op 5-1)
Indian Art(IRE) had the visor he wore last time left off and seemed to run better under a positive ride, having every chance until finding the winner too strong late on. (op 14-1 tchd 16-1)
Carnaby Haggerston(IRE), who was stepping up in trip and was fitted with cheekpieces for the first time, made much of the running but did not quite get home. (tchd 25-1)
Akhenaten, who was making a quick reappearance having run in a Group 3 at the weekend, may have found the drying ground against him, although he was staying on quite well towards the end. (op 7-2)
Gyr(IRE), who had a bit to find with the winner on their running in the sales race at Newmarket, was held up and never got in a blow. (tchd 9-2)
Absent Pleasure(USA) was keen under restraint early in a steadily run race and had nothing left for the closing stages. Official explanation: jockey said colt ran too freely (op 6-4 tchd 2-1 and 9-4 in places)
Versaki(IRE) seems to have gone off the boil in recent races. (op 11-1 tchd 16-1)
Confucius Captain(IRE) was outclassed at this level.

6718 IVECO EUROCARGO FILLIES' CONDITIONS STKS — 1m 60y
3:40 (3:40) (Class 3) 3-Y-O — £7,569 (£2,265; £1,132; £566; £282) Stalls High

Form RPR
6130 **1** **Born Tobougie (GER)**[27] 6034 3-9-1 88.................. TPQueally 3 100
(H R A Cecil) *hld up in tch: racd keenly: rdn over 1f out: hung lft: led wl ins fnl f: r.o* **6/1**[2]

2040 **2** *1 1/4* **Dream Day**[33] 5829 3-8-12 98.................. RichardHughes 4 94
(R Hannon) *chsd ldr: led over 1f out: sn rdn: hung lft and hdd wl ins fnl f* **8/1**[3]

6533 **3** *1 1/2* **Ghaidaa (IRE)**[17] 6266 3-9-1 101.................. RHills 5 94
(M A Jarvis) *trckd ldrs: racd keenly: nt clr run 2f out: sn rdn: styd on: nvr able to chal* **4/9**[1]

3060 **4** *1/2* **Kylayne**[17] 6271 3-8-12 94.................. PhilipRobinson 6 89
(P W D'Arcy) *led: qcknd over 3f out: rdn and hdd over 1f out: no ex ins fnl f* **16/1**

1154 **5** *8* **Casino Night**[13] 6387 3-8-5 66.................. AndreaAtzeni[(7)] 2 71
(R Johnson) *chsd ldrs: rdn over 2f out: sn wknd* **100/1**

2300 **6** *9* **Annie Skates (USA)**[17] 6266 3-8-12 95.................. JohnEgan 1 50
(Jane Chapple-Hyam) *hld up: rdn and wknd over 2f out* **11/1**

1m 44.59s (-0.51) **Going Correction** +0.025s/f (Good) **6** Ran SP% **109.9**
Speed ratings (Par 102): **103,101,100,99,91 82**
toteswinger: 1&2 £2.80, 1&3 £1.10, 2&3 £1.30. CSF £47.59 TOTE £7.70: £2.50, £3.50; EX 36.50.
Owner The Sticky Wicket Syndicate **Bred** Graf Und Grafin Von Stauffenberg **Trained** Newmarket, Suffolk

FOCUS
This decent 3yo fillies' conditions event was run at an uneven pace and the form is muddling. The favourite disappointed and the race is rated around the first two.

NOTEBOOK
Born Tobougie(GER), despite being outclassed in Listed company last time, has been well placed this season and landed her third career success in game fashion. She had a stiff-looking task under her penalty on official figures and was not certain to have enjoyed a tactical affair, but she dug deep when asked for maximum effort, unlike some of her rivals. In beating the runner-up, who is officially rated 10lb her superior and was getting 3lb, this rates by far her best effort to date and, while the form may be suspect, she could have more to offer if kept in training as a 4yo. (op 8-1)
Dream Day bounced back from a lifeless effort in a Listed race and showed her true colours in this less taxing company. She was travelling best of all at the furlong pole and should have beaten the winner at these weights, so could be deemed somewhat disappointing. (op 15-2 tchd 17-2)
Ghaidaa(IRE) had run respectably in Listed events the last twice at Sandown and Ascot and looked the clear pick at the weights. She did not enjoy the uneven pace and had to wait for her challenge passing 2f out, but still ran some way below her recent level. This leaves her with plenty to prove, despite the race not being run to suit. Official explanation: jockey said filly ran flat (op 4-7)
Kylayne had finished a long way in front of today's runner-up at Doncaster on her penultimate outing, but was a flop at Ascot last time. She returned to some form for being allowed to dictate here, but she is flattered to have had the run of the race and is not easy to place successfully. (op 12-1)
Annie Skates(USA), who ran no sort of race, although she finished a similar distance behind Ghaidaa at Ascot last time. She seems to have some sort of problem. Official explanation: jockey said filly lost its action (op 8-1)

6719 IVECO DAILY LADY RIDERS' CLAIMING STKS — 1m 3f 183y
4:10 (4:11) (Class 6) 3-4-Y-O — £2,498 (£774; £387; £193) Stalls High

Form RPR
4020 **1** **Stravita**[13] 6395 4-9-9 56..................(p) MissRKneller[(5)] 8 60
(R Hollinshead) *s.i.s: hdwy 10f out: rdn to chse ldr 1f out: edgd rt and styd on to ld nr fin* **5/1**[1]

5020 **2** *hd* **Corking (IRE)**[32] 5868 3-9-0 52.................. MissAWallace[(5)] 11 58
(J L Flint) *led: rdn over 1f out: edgd rt: hdd nr fin* **25/1**

2225 **3** *1* **Ambrose Princess (IRE)**[45] 5489 3-9-7 57............ MissFayeBramley 4 58
(R A Harris) *chsd ldrs: rdn and hung rt over 1f out: styd on* **5/1**[1]

0330 **4** *1/2* **Piverina (IRE)**[19] 6228 3-9-5 50.................. MissSBrotherton 5 55
(Miss J A Camacho) *hld up: hdwy over 3f out: rdn and edgd rt ins fnl f: styd on* **8/1**[3]

3044 **5** *3/4* **Giddywell**[35] 5776 4-9-7 51.................. MissStefaniaGandola[(7)] 10 56
(R Hollinshead) *chsd ldr tl rdn over 1f out: no ex ins fnl f* **6/1**[2]

2010 **6** *2 1/4* **Red Current**[13] 6400 4-9-12 62 ow3.................. MissHDavies[(7)] 7 57
(R A Harris) *hld up: hdwy over 3f out: rdn and hung rt: styd on same pce* **6/1**[2]

4030 **7** *1 3/4* **Sparkling Montjeu (IRE)**[11] 6447 3-9-3 50... MissGDGracey-Davison 6 46
(George Baker) *prom: rdn over 3f out: styd on same pce fnl 2f* **10/1**

5401 **8** *4* **Afram Blue**[13] 6400 3-9-10 67..................(t) MrsEJJKnight[(7)] 1 53+
(W J Knight) *s.s: a bhd: mod late prog: no ch whn nt clr run ins fnl f* **9/1**

0533 **9** *3/4* **Fairly Honest**[27] 6032 4-10-0 53.................. MrsMarieKing 12 42
(P W Hiatt) *chsd ldrs: rdn and edgd lft over 2f out: sn wknd* **10/1**

605 **10** *8* **Enderby Princess (IRE)**[97] 3835 3-9-0 53............(t) MissVCoates[(7)] 9 29
(Ollie Pears) *s.s: a in rr: bhd fnl 5f* **28/1**

0004 **11** *nk* **Corlough Mountain**[13] 6396 4-10-0 58.................. MissMBryant[(7)] 2 36
(P Butler) *a bhd* **25/1**

60-0 **12** *11* **Hawk Gold (IRE)**[19] 1563 4-10-2 40.................. MissZoeLilly[(5)] 3 18
(P Butler) *mid-div: lost pl over 9f out: bhd fnl 5f* **150/1**

2m 36.1s (2.20) **Going Correction** +0.025s/f (Good)
WFA 3 from 4yo 7lb **12** Ran SP% **113.0**
Speed ratings (Par 101): **93,92,92,91,91 89,88,86,85,80 80,72**
toteswinger: 1&2 £31.40, 1&3 £8.00, 2&3 £23.40. CSF £131.72 TOTE £6.60: £2.30, £6.40, £1.80; EX 123.60.
Owner E Bennion **Bred** Eric Bennion And Miss Sarah Hollinshead **Trained** Upper Longdon, Staffs

FOCUS
A weak claimer, confined to lady amateur riders, this was run at a moderate tempo and few got into it from off the pace. The form seems sound enough at face value.
Afram Blue Official explanation: jockey said gelding jinked leaving stalls

6720 EBF SOAR MAIDEN STKS — 1m 60y
4:40 (4:41) (Class 4) 2-Y-O — £5,180 (£1,541; £770; £384) Stalls High

Form RPR
0 **1** **Opinion Poll (IRE)**[25] 6085 2-9-3 0.................. PhilipRobinson 9 83
(M A Jarvis) *chsd ldr over 6f out: led over 2f out: rdn over 1f out: r.o* **16/1**

222 **2** *1* **Three Moons (IRE)**[25] 6081 2-8-12 85.................. RichardHughes 2 76+
(H J L Dunlop) *chsd ldrs: rdn over 1f out: r.o* **13/8**[1]

3 *2* **Lord Chancellor (IRE)** 2-9-3 0.................. JoeFanning 8 77+
(M Johnston) *sn led: rdn and hdd over 2f out: styd on same pce ins fnl f* **22/1**

04 **4** *1/2* **La Tizona (IRE)**[12] 6412 2-9-3 0.................. SteveDrowne 12 76+
(R Charlton) *hld up: hdwy over 1f out: r.o wl ins fnl f: nt rch ldrs* **10/1**[3]

03 **5** *1/2* **Decision**[13] 6397 2-9-3 0.................. IanMongan 6 75
(C G Cox) *chsd ldrs: rdn over 1f out: styd on same pce* **18/1**

4 **6** *1* **Moresco**[27] 6026 2-9-3 0.................. AdamKirby 13 73
(W R Swinburn) *hld up in tch: rdn over 2f out: styd on same pce fnl f* **7/4**[2]

7 *3/4* **All Guns Firing (IRE)** 2-9-3 0.................. NCallan 11 71
(M A Jarvis) *hld up in tch: shkn up over 2f out: no ex fnl f* **40/1**

0 **8** *nk* **Royal Collection (IRE)**[15] 6341 2-9-3 0.................. HayleyTurner 14 70
(J Pearce) *plld hrd and prom: rdn over 1f out: edgd rt and no ex fnl f* **80/1**

9 *2* **Class Is Class (IRE)** 2-9-3 0.................. RyanMoore 1 66
(Sir Michael Stoute) *hld up: hdwy over 3f out: wknd over 1f out* **12/1**

10 *3/4* **Bruton Street (USA)** 2-9-3 0.................. RobertHavlin 7 65
(J H M Gosden) *dwlt: hld up: nt clr run over 2f out: n.d* **25/1**

50 **11** *2* **Harlestone Snake**[25] 6085 2-9-3 0.................. TedDurcan 4 60
(J L Dunlop) *s.i.s: hld up: effrt over 2f out: n.d* **66/1**

6205 **12** *1 3/4* **Josiah Bartlett (IRE)**[41] 5606 2-9-3 57.................. MichaelHills 10 57
(J W Hills) *s.i.s: hld up: effrt over 2f out: sn wknd* **100/1**

13 *9* **Berti** 2-9-3 0.................. JerryO'Dwyer 5 38
(J Pearce) *s.s: a bhd: lost tch fnl 3f* **125/1**

1m 46.96s (1.86) **Going Correction** +0.025s/f (Good) **13** Ran SP% **117.5**
Speed ratings (Par 97): **91,90,88,87,87 86,85,84,82,82 80,78,69**
toteswinger: 1&2 £7.40, 1&3 £31.90, 2&3 £8.40. CSF £40.50 TOTE £22.90: £3.60, £1.40, £4.80; EX 53.00.
Owner Sheikh Ahmed Al Maktoum **Bred** Darley **Trained** Newmarket, Suffolk

FOCUS
This juvenile maiden looked a fair heat, but it was run at an average pace and no doubt suited those racing handily.

NOTEBOOK
Opinion Poll(IRE) ◆ had looked clueless on his debut at Newmarket 25 days earlier, but had evidently learnt a bundle for the experience and showed vastly improved form to open his account. He was perfectly positioned when the race became serious and there was plenty to like about his attitude when asked to win the race. He has a choice middle-distance pedigree and should make up into a nice 3yo. (op 14-1)
Three Moons(IRE) again managed to find one too good, but did little wrong in defeat. With an official mark of 85, she rates the benchmark. While she is becoming expensive to follow, she is well up to going one better this year. (op 2-1 tchd 6-4 and 9-4 in a place)
Lord Chancellor(IRE), the first foal of a dam closely related to Act One, knew his job and was soon on the lead. He had the run of the race but kept to his task throughout and should not remain a maiden for long. (op 16-1)
La Tizona(IRE) did best of those who were given waiting rides and, as was the case at Goodwood 12 days earlier, shaped better than the bare form suggests. He now qualifies for a mark and is one to keep an eye on. (op 13-2)
Decision was another who raced handily and he performed close to his previous level. He now has the option of nurseries. (op 16-1 tchd 20-1)
Moresco proved one-paced and never looked like justifying support. He probably would have enjoyed a stronger early pace and is far from one to give up on. (op 9-4 tchd 5-2 in places)

6721 IVECO ALL BLACKS H'CAP — 1m 1f 218y
5:10 (5:10) (Class 5) (0-75,75) 3-Y-O+ — £3,238 (£963; £481; £240) Stalls High

Form RPR
6/30 **1** **Wiggy Smith**[15] 6346 9-9-8 73.................. FrankieMcDonald 3 81+
(H Candy) *hld up: rdn over 2f out: hdwy over 1f out: r.o to ld wl ins fnl f* **14/1**

2000 **2** *1* **Night Orbit**[5] 6607 4-8-12 66..................(v) RussellKennemore[(3)] 15 72
(Miss J Feilden) *chsd ldr: rdn and ev ch 2f out: edgd rt ins fnl f: styd on* **50/1**

4024 **3** *3/4* **Danetime Panther (IRE)**[15] 6346 4-9-9 74.................. NCallan 14 78
(P F I Cole) *a.p: rdn over 2f out: edgd rt fr over 1f out: styd on* **11/1**

234 **4** *nse* **Silent Applause**[28] 6007 5-9-0 65.................. JoeFanning 12 69
(Dr J D Scargill) *sn led: hdd 5f out: led again over 2f out: rdn and hdd wl ins fnl f* **14/1**

2034 **5** *1 1/4* **Drawn Gold**[26] 6056 4-9-0 65.................. TedDurcan 2 66
(R Hollinshead) *chsd ldrs: rdn over 1f out: no ex ins fnl f* **13/2**[2]

0461 **6** *3/4* **Jawaab (IRE)**[14] 6363 4-9-9 74.................. MartinDwyer 7 74+
(W R Muir) *hld up: hdwy over 3f out: rdn over 1f out: styd on same pce* **10/3**[1]

424 **7** *1 3/4* **Roodolph**[20] 6203 4-9-8 73.................. StephenCarson 13 69
(Eve Johnson Houghton) *prom: rdn over 2f out: edgd rt and no ex fnl f* **12/1**

006 **8** *3/4* **Folio (IRE)**[12] 6424 8-9-8 73.................. TPQueally 4 68
(W J Musson) *hld up: hdwy over 3f out: sn rdn: styd on same pce appr fnl f* **25/1**

0602 **9** *1/2* **Lunar Promise (IRE)**[50] 5370 6-9-7 72.................. JerryO'Dwyer 1 66
(Ian Williams) *s.i.s: hld up: rdn over 2f out: styd on fnl f: nvr nrr* **12/1**

0-44 **10** *2 1/2* **Magdalene**[182] 1383 4-9-2 67.................. ChrisCatlin 6 56
(Rae Guest) *hld up: rdn over 2f out: sme hdwy over 1f out: n.d* **14/1**

6033 **11** *3* **Red Wine**[24] 6107 9-9-4 **74**.......... DavidProbert(5) 10 57
(A J McCabe) *s.i.s: hld up: hmpd 5f out: rdn over 2f out: n.d* **14/1**
0500 **12** *½* **Pugilist**[11] 6450 6-9-0 **65**.......... JohnEgan 17 47
(B J Meehan) *prom: hmpd over 8f out: rdn over 3f out: wknd 2f out* **28/1**
-230 **13** *4½* **Two Left Feet**[15] 6346 3-9-5 **75**.......... AdamKirby 5 48
(W R Swinburn) *hld up: rdn over 3f out: sn hung rt and wknd* **25/1**
4140 **14** *1½* **Fossgate**[29] 5967 7-9-0 **65**.......... DarryllHolland 16 35
(J D Bethell) *mid-div: hdwy over 3f out: rdn and wknd over 1f out* **10/1**[3]
0032 **15** *4½* **Blindspin**[21] 6188 3-9-5 **75**.......... ShaneKelly 9 36
(M Dods) *trckd ldrs: plld hrd: led 5f out: rdn and hdd over 2f out: wknd and eased over 1f out* **10/1**[3]
2100 **16** *34* **Blakfrankisch (IRE)**[10] 6472 5-9-7 **72**.......... RichardKingscote 11 —
(Tom Dascombe) *stmbld s: a in rr: eased wl over 1f out* **16/1**

2m 7.33s (-0.57) **Going Correction** +0.025s/f (Good)
WFA 3 from 4yo+ 5lb **16** Ran SP% **124.0**
Speed ratings (Par 103): **103,102,101,101,100 99,98,97,97,95 93,92,89,87,84 57**
toteswinger: 1&2 £71.50, 1&3 £46.40, 2&3 £192.90. CSF £612.49 CT £7746.79 TOTE £18.20: £3.00, £12.30, £2.90, £4.10; EX 1098.10 Place 6 £77.83, Place 5 £54.74 .
Owner Mrs George Tricks **Bred** Mrs V M Tricks **Trained** Kingston Warren, Oxon

FOCUS
A modest handicap, run at a fair pace although it looked to favour prominent runners. Sound form.
Red Wine Official explanation: jockey said gelding suffered interference in running
Blakfrankisch(IRE) Official explanation: jockey said gelding stumbled leaving stalls
T/Plt: £124.70 to a £1 stake. Pool: £58,603.61. 342.83 winning tickets. T/Qpdt: £84.40 to a £1 stake. Pool: £2,717.20. 23.80 winning tickets. CR

6381 NEWCASTLE (L-H)
Tuesday, October 14

OFFICIAL GOING: Heavy (soft in places last 3f)
Wind: Almost nil Weather: Overcast

6722 LUMSDEN AND CARROLL/E.B.F. MAIDEN FILLIES' STKS 7f
2:20 (2:21) (Class 5) 2-Y-O **£3,561** (£1,059; £529; £264) **Stalls** High

Form RPR
2 **1** **Allformary**[13] 6381 2-9-0 0.......... TomEaves 2 73
(B Smart) *racd far side: mde all: clr over 2f out: drvn out: 1st of 5 in gp* **5/4**[1]
2 *2½* **Drop The Hammer** 2-9-0 0.......... RobertWinston 4 67+
(T P Tate) *rn green in rr far side: hdwy over 2f out: wnt 2nd ins fnl f: nt rch wnr: 2nd of 5 in gp* **16/1**
34 **3** *1½* **Miss Cracklinrosie**[23] 6151 2-9-0 0.......... TonyHamilton 10 63
(J R Weymes) *chsd stands' side ldrs: led that gp over 2f out: kpt on fnl f: nt rch far side ldrs: 1st of 8 in gp* **6/1**[2]
0250 **4** *2½* **Haulage Lady (IRE)**[32] 5859 2-9-0 60.......... DavidAllan 8 57
(Karen McLintock) *cl up stands' side: ev ch that gp over 2f out: one pce fnl f: 2nd of 8 in gp* **10/1**
4 **5** *2¼* **Caress The Soul (IRE)**[10] 6481 2-9-0 0.......... MickyFenton 1 51
(P T Midgley) *chsd wnr far side to ins fnl f: no ex: 3rd of 5 in gp* **13/2**[3]
0 **6** *6* **Canucatcher (IRE)**[7] 6559 2-9-0 0.......... GrahamGibbons 13 36
(T D Walford) *led stands' side to over 2f out: sn wknd: 3rd of 8 in gp* **66/1**
7 *shd* **Diamond Jo (IRE)** 2-9-0 0.......... PaulHanagan 9 36
(Mrs L Williamson) *midfield on stands' side: drvn over 3f out: sn outpcd: no imp fr 2f out: 4th of 8 in gp* **11/1**
0 **8** *¾* **Suitably Accoutred (IRE)**[17] 6291 2-8-11 0.......... AndrewMullen(3) 12 34
(Mrs A Duffield) *trckd stands' side ldrs tl wknd over 2f out: 5th of 8 in gp* **25/1**
0 **9** *2* **Elevate Bambina**[27] 6013 2-8-11 0.......... MichaelJStainton(3) 11 29
(R M Whitaker) *bhd and drvn along stands' side: nvr on terms: 6th of 8 in gp* **33/1**
10 *5* **Betsy The Best** 2-9-0 0.......... PaulMulrennan 5 16
(R Bastiman) *s.i.s: bhd stands' side: drvn 1/2-way: nvr on terms: 7th of 8 in gp* **50/1**
0 **11** *4½* **Alacity (IRE)**[10] 6481 2-9-0 0.......... JimmyQuinn 6 5
(N Bycroft) *in tch far side to 1/2-way: sn wknd: 4th of 5 in gp* **20/1**
U **12** *17* **Liberty Estelle (IRE)**[13] 6381 2-9-0 0.......... PJMcDonald 7 —
(G A Swinbank) *prom stands' side tl hung lft and wknd fr 3f out: last of 8 in gp* **14/1**
00 **13** *7* **Kannie Annie**[19] 6229 2-8-7 0.......... LanceBetts(7) 3 —
(T J Pitt) *cl up far side to 1/2-way: sn struggling: last of 5 in gp* **100/1**

1m 35.65s (8.25) **Going Correction** +0.675s/f (Yiel) **13** Ran SP% **118.0**
Speed ratings (Par 92): **79,76,74,71,69 62,62,61,58,53 48,28,20**
toteswinger: 1&2 £9.10, 1&3 £2.70, 2&3 £20.00. CSF £22.44 TOTE £2.20: £1.10, £6.00, £2.20; EX 28.60 Trifecta £69.70 Pool: £221.38 - 2.35 winning tickets..
Owner Alan D Crombie **Bred** Ms R A Myatt **Trained** Hambleton, N Yorks

FOCUS
Conditions were very testing and the ground was described as 'gluey, tacky, very tiring'. A modest maiden in which the field split into two with five towards the far side and the time was very slow.

NOTEBOOK
Allformary had finished runner-up behind an 86-rated rival on her debut over this course and distance two weeks earlier. She stood out in the paddock and started a heavily backed favourite. Setting the pace on the far side, she went clear coming to the final furlong but in the conditions had to be kept right up to her work. She should make a useful handicapper at three. (op 15-8)
Drop The Hammer, who cost just 1,500gns, recovered from a slow start to stay on and take second spot on the far side inside the final furlong. She looks a backward type who should do better at three. (op 20-1)
Miss Cracklinrosie, whose two previous outings were over 1m, took charge on the stands'-side group two furlongs out. She ran on all the way to the line but was never going to land a blow. A 1m nursery looks her best option. (tchd 11-2 and 7-1)
Haulage Lady(IRE), having her fifth start and rated 60, came out second best on the stands' side and helps set the level. (op 11-1 tchd 12-1)
Caress The Soul(IRE) had shown promise when fourth on her debut on much better ground at Redcar ten days earlier. She tracked the winner but tired badly and lost three places in the final furlong. The heavy ground was almost certainly against her. (op 4-1 tchd 7-2)
Canucatcher(IRE), last of 14 on her debut just a week ago, took them along on the stands' side for over four furlongs before dropping away. (op 50-1)

6723 EBF / UTS MAIDEN STKS (C&G) 7f
2:50 (2:51) (Class 5) 2-Y-O **£3,723** (£1,108; £553; £276) **Stalls** High

Form RPR
5 **1** **Trumpstoo (USA)**[21] 6187 2-9-0 0.......... PaulHanagan 6 72+
(R A Fahey) *mde all: shkn up over 2f out: kpt on wl fnl f* **9/2**
622 **2** *hd* **Custody (IRE)**[19] 6234 2-9-0 81.......... RobertWinston 3 72+
(Sir Michael Stoute) *t.k.h: trckd ldrs: smooth hdwy to chal appr fnl f: rdn along ins fnl f: edgd lft: nt go past* **2/1**[1]
3 **3** *3½* **Tiger Reigns**[20] 6213 2-9-0 0.......... TonyHamilton 1 64+
(M Dods) *hld up: rdn and hdwy over 1f out: kpt on fnl f: nt rch ldrs* **7/2**[3]
0 **4** *3½* **Stanstill (IRE)**[10] 6480 2-9-0 0.......... PJMcDonald 2 54
(G A Swinbank) *cl up tl rdn and wknd 1f out* **40/1**
0 **5** *1½* **Legal Legacy**[19] 6230 2-9-0 0.......... TomEaves 4 50
(M Dods) *t.k.h: trckd ldrs tl wknd over 1f out* **25/1**
6 *1* **Fuzzy Cat** 2-8-11 0.......... NeilBrown(3) 7 48
(T D Barron) *hld up: effrt and hdwy over 1f out: wknd ent fnl f* **11/1**
7 *12* **Bushveld (IRE)** 2-9-0 0.......... GregFairley 5 18+
(M Johnston) *dwlt: t.k.h: hdwy and prom after 3f: chsng ldrs and rdn whn swvd bdly lft over 1f out: sn wknd* **3/1**[2]

1m 35.32s (7.92) **Going Correction** +0.675s/f (Yiel) **7** Ran SP% **113.4**
Speed ratings (Par 95): **81,80,76,72,71 69,56**
toteswinger: 1&2 £2.70, 1&3 £2.60, 2&3 £2.30. CSF £13.70 TOTE £6.30: £2.70, £1.60; EX 18.00.
Owner Mrs Suzanne Hart **Bred** Matthews Stables **Trained** Musley Bank, N Yorks

FOCUS
A decent maiden on paper but run at a very steady gallop and as a result the time was very moderate. They raced in one group on the stands' side.

NOTEBOOK
Trumpstoo(USA) stepped up the pace coming to the final quarter mile but looked likely to finish second best when joined on his inner by Custody a furlong out. However, he showed much the more willing attitude and was a worthy winner in the end. This was just his second start and, a grand, big type, he looks sure to make a useful handicapper at three. (op 8-1)
Custody(IRE), a gelded son of Fusaichi Pegasus, was having his third start and is rated 81. Heavily opposed in the market, he sat on the heels of the two leaders stuck on the inner. He came through to move upsides a furlong out but when asked to go and win his race he carried his head high, hung left and was outbattled. Conditions may not have been in his favour but this looked a very good opportunity thrown away. (op 11-8 tchd 9-4 in a place)
Tiger Reigns, who looked very inexperienced on his debut three weeks earlier, kept on after being tapped for toe. He still looks very immature and should be capable of better at three. (op 9-2)
Stanstill(IRE) showed a lot more than on his debut ten days earlier but he is another who will not be seen to full advantage until next year.
Legal Legacy showed a bit more than well when beaten when coming in for market support on his debut 19 days earlier. (tchd 28-1)
Fuzzy Cat look a big weak type, another who can be expected to show more at three. (op 12-1 tchd 10-1)
Bushveld(IRE) looked very inexperienced beforehand and on the way to post. After a slow start he recovered to be on the heels of the leaders when swerving violently left and ending up towards the centre of the course just under two furlongs out. He has an awful lot to learn but clearly possesses ability. (op 7-2 tchd 4-1)

6724 NORTHUMBRIAN WATER H'CAP 6f
3:20 (3:20) (Class 5) (0-75,75) 3-Y-O+ **£2,914** (£867; £433; £216) **Stalls** High

Form RPR
0044 **1** **Lap Of Honour (IRE)**[13] 6385 4-8-13 **69**..........(p) JimmyQuinn 15 79
(Jennie Candlish) *plld hrd: trckd stands' side ldrs: led that gp over 1f out: r.o wl fnl f: 1st of 7 in gp* **9/1**
1106 **2** *1* **Shotley Mac**[10] 6482 4-8-10 **69**..........(b) DuranFentiman(3) 14 76
(N Bycroft) *cl up stands' side: effrt whn carried lft over 1f out: kpt on u.p fnl f: 2nd of 7 in gp* **16/1**
0442 **3** *nse* **Artsu**[7] 6556 3-8-12 **74**.......... GaryBartley(5) 11 81
(M L W Bell) *hld up stands' side: smooth hdwy 2f out: rdn and r.o fnl f: 3rd of 7 in gp* **7/1**[1]
6504 **4** *nse* **Glasshoughton**[8] 6532 5-9-5 **75**..........(p) PaulMulrennan 13 82
(M Dods) *hld up stands' side: hdwy over 1f out: r.o fnl f: 4th of 7 in gp* **12/1**
2555 **5** *¾* **Charles Parnell (IRE)**[13] 6388 5-9-3 **73**.......... DaleGibson 6 77+
(M Dods) *hld up far side: hdwy over 1f out: led that gp wl ins fnl f: nt rch stands' side ldrs: 1st of 10 in gp* **12/1**
5106 **6** *1* **Balakiref**[26] 6043 9-9-3 **73**.......... WilliamBuick 8 74
(M Dods) *hld up far side: hdwy over 1f out: kpt on fnl f: 2nd of 10 in gp* **8/1**[3]
6231 **7** *nk* **Avontuur (FR)**[12] 6411 6-8-5 **61**.......... PaulFessey 5 61
(Mrs R A Carr) *dwlt: sn in midfield far side: hdwy to ld that gp briefly ins fnl f: no ex towards fin: 3rd of 10 in gp* **14/1**
3600 **8** *2* **Cornus**[17] 6278 6-9-5 **75**..........(be) JamesDoyle 1 69
(A J McCabe) *trckd far side ldrs: led that gp appr fnl f to ins fnl f: no ex: 4th of 10 in gp* **10/1**
040 **9** *1½* **Steel Blue**[40] 5634 8-9-0 **70**..........(p) J-PGuillambert 2 59
(R M Whitaker) *w far side ldr tl no ex fnl f: 5th of 10 in gp* **20/1**
5010 **10** *hd* **First Swallow**[20] 6218 3-8-6 **63**.......... PaulHanagan 9 51
(R A Fahey) *t.k.h: led far side to appr fnl f: btn ins fnl f: 6th of 10 in gp* **16/1**
00-0 **11** *½* **Bravely (IRE)**[20] 6215 4-9-5 **75**.......... DavidAllan 16 62
(T D Easterby) *trckd stands' side ldrs: led that gp briefly over 1f out: sn no ex: 5th of 7 in gp* **33/1**
3310 **12** *¾* **Bid For Gold**[22] 6164 4-8-10 **66**.......... AndrewElliott 7 50
(Jedd O'Keeffe) *prom far side: sn rdn along: btn fnl f: 7th of 10 in gp* **20/1**
1116 **13** *hd* **Woodsley House (IRE)**[28] 5991 6-8-13 **72**.......... NeilBrown(3) 10 56
(A G Foster) *hld up far side: rdn and sme hdwy appr fnl f: nvr able to chal: 8th of 10 in gp* **15/2**[2]
100- **14** *½* **Captain Macarry (IRE)**[374] 6017 3-8-10 **67**.......... TomEaves 3 49
(B Smart) *towards rr stands' side: rdn over 1f out: btn fnl f: 9th of 10 in gp* **40/1**
1120 **15** *2¼* **Sea Salt**[22] 6178 5-8-12 **68**.......... GregFairley 17 43
(A J McCabe) *led stands' side tl hung lft and hdd over 1f out: sn wknd: 6th of 7 in gp* **16/1**
0015 **16** *5* **The Twelve Steps**[29] 5962 3-9-4 **75**..........(t) PJMcDonald 4 34
(G A Swinbank) *bhd far side: drvn over 2f out: nvr on terms: last of 10 in gp* **14/1**
4143 **17** *½* **Zabeel Tower**[16] 6314 5-9-4 **74**..........(p) TonyHamilton 12 31
(R Allan) *trckd ldrs stands' side tl wknd fr 2f out: last of 7 in gp* **8/1**[3]

1m 18.7s (3.50) **Going Correction** +0.675s/f (Yiel)
WFA 3 from 4yo+ 1lb **17** Ran SP% **126.8**
Speed ratings (Par 103): **103,101,101,101,100 99,98,96,94,93 93,92,91,88,81 80**
toteswinger: 1&2 £51.70, 1&3 £13.90, 2&3 £41.40. CSF £143.73 CT £1090.04 TOTE £9.80: £2.50, £4.70, £1.70, £4.20; EX 243.90 Trifecta £323.60 Part won. Pool: £437.37 - 0.57 winning tickets..
Owner P and Mrs G A Clarke **Bred** Ben Sangster **Trained** Basford Green, Staffs
■ Stewards' Enquiry : Paul Fessey one-day ban: used whip with excessive frequency (Oct 28)
Jimmy Quinn caution: used whip with excessiv e frequency

FOCUS
An ordinary handicap in which they split into two groups, those drawn one to ten electing to race on the far side leaving seven to race on the stands' side. There was precious little between the two sides at the line but the first four home were all drawn high. The form looks reasonable rated around the placed horses.

Sea Salt Official explanation: jockey said gelding hung left-handed throughout
Zabeel Tower Official explanation: jockey said, regarding running and riding, his orders were to be handy behind the leaders and produce the gelding late, but he was unable to make any progress from 2f out; trainer said that although it was dropping back in distance slightly, he believed the heavy ground would prove a test of stamina, and it was possible gelding was unsuited by the ground; vet said gelding returned lame

6725 PHIL BENTLEY IS 40 NOW MEDIAN AUCTION MAIDEN STKS 1m 4f 93y
3:50 (3:50) (Class 6) 3-4-Y-O £2,266 (£674; £337; £168) Stalls Low

Form RPR
-000 1 **Ice Bellini**[13] 6374 3-8-12 45 (v[1]) MickyFenton 2 58
(Miss Gay Kelleway) *hld up: hdwy and cl up 1/2-way: led over 2f out: kpt on wl fnl f* **25/1**
62 2 2 1/2 **Princess Rainbow (FR)**[29] 5963 3-8-12 0 JimmyQuinn 3 54
(Jennie Candlish) *plld hrd: hld up in last: swtchd to outside 4f out: hdwy over 2f out: chsd wnr appr fnl f: one pce ins fnl f* **2/9**[1]
0000 3 4 **Carlton Mac**[8] 6530 3-8-10 41 JamieKyne(7) 6 53
(N Bycroft) *prom: drvn and outpcd 5f out: rallied 2f out: styd on to take 3rd cl home* **66/1**
50 4 1 **The Little Master (IRE)**[13] 6400 4-9-7 0 MarcHalford(3) 9 51
(D R C Elsworth) *led to over 2f out: wknd over 1f out: lost 3rd nr fin* **10/1**[2]
00-0 5 12 **Starbougg**[40] 5637 4-9-5 48 PaulHanagan 1 27
(K G Reveley) *hld up: drvn and outpcd over 4f out: nvr on terms* **16/1**[3]
00 6 2 1/2 **Golondrina**[13] 6393 3-8-12 0 PaulMulrennan 7 23
(T J Fitzgerald) *chsd ldrs tl rdn and wknd over 3f out* **33/1**
00- 7 41 **Glamoroso (IRE)**[377] 5903 3-9-0 0 NeilBrown(3) 8 —
(A Kirtley) *in tch tl rdn and lost tch fr 4f out* **80/1**
00 8 27 **Kiss Me Hardy**[13] 6393 3-8-12 0 GrahamGibbons 5 —
(J D Bethell) *trckd ldrs tl wknd over 4f out* **50/1**

3m 1.27s (15.67) **Going Correction** +1.35s/f (Soft)
WFA 3 from 4yo 7lb **8** Ran SP% **108.3**
Speed ratings (Par 101): **101,99,96,96,88 86,59,41**
toteswinger: 1&2 £2.80, 1&3 £27.40, 2&3 £6.80. CSF £28.98 TOTE £15.50: £2.60, £1.10, £6.00; EX 49.70 TRIFECTA Not won..
Owner JCS Partnership **Bred** Boyce Bloodstock **Trained** Exning, Suffolk

FOCUS
This poor median auction maiden race looked a penalty kick beforehand for Princess Rainbow but it did not work out that way and the form looks very weak.

6726 FASTFLOW PIPELINE SERVICES H'CAP 1m 2f 32y
4:20 (4:20) (Class 5) (0-70,76) 3-Y-0+ £2,914 (£867; £433; £216)

Form RPR
6461 1 **Bavarian Nordic (USA)**[20] 6216 3-9-1 70 AndrewMullen(3) 11 81
(Mrs A Duffield) *trckd ldrs: led and qcknd over 2f out: kpt on strly fnl f* **6/1**[2]
1330 2 3 **Harry The Hawk**[111] 3368 4-9-9 70 GrahamGibbons 8 75
(T D Walford) *t.k.h: hld up: hdwy and squeezed through over 2f out: wnt 2nd over 1f out: r.o: no imp* **13/2**[3]
334- 3 nk **Rawdon (IRE)**[152] 6727 7-9-4 70 (v) GaryBartley(5) 10 74
(M L W Bell) *hld up on outside: hdwy to chse wnr over 2f out to over 1f out: kpt on fnl f* **10/1**
10 4 3 1/4 **Follow The Sun (IRE)**[20] 6221 4-8-11 58 TonyHamilton 2 56+
(Ronald O'Leary, Ire) *hld up: drvn over 3f out: styd on strly fnl f: nrst fin* **15/2**
5052 5 1/2 **Transmission (IRE)**[12] 6408 3-8-13 65 TomEaves 3 62+
(B Smart) *t.k.h in midfield: n.m.r over 3f out to over 2f out: sn rdn: kpt on fnl f: no imp* **5/1**[1]
660- 6 2 1/2 **Beresford Lady**[333] 6832 4-8-9 56 oh11 SilvestreDeSousa 4 48
(A D Brown) *t.k.h: trckd ldrs tl rdn and no ex fr 2f out* **80/1**
2066 7 3/4 **Dechiper (IRE)**[13] 6385 6-8-11 63 PatrickDonaghy(5) 1 53
(R Johnson) *hld up: n.m.r briefly over 2f out: sn rdn: nvr able to chal* **12/1**
4163 8 1 1/4 **Karmest**[10] 6487 4-9-1 69 (b) JamesRogers(7) 12 57
(A D Brown) *hld up: hdwy over 3f out: rdn and wknd fnl f* **10/1**
4520 9 6 **Doon Haymer (IRE)**[22] 6162 3-9-4 70 PaulMulrennan 9 46
(Miss L A Perratt) *led to over 2f out: sn rdn and wknd* **16/1**
0003 10 4 1/2 **Trouble Mountain (USA)**[26] 6050 11-9-4 65 (t) DaleGibson 13 32
(M W Easterby) *in tch: drvn over 3f out: wknd fr 2f out* **16/1**
2202 11 2 **Thornaby Green**[22] 6162 7-8-2 56 oh1 DeanHeslop(7) 5 19
(T D Barron) *plld hrd early: cl up tl wknd over 2f out* **9/1**
5501 12 1 1/2 **Giant Love (USA)**[7] 6551 3-9-10 76 6ex GregFairley 6 36
(M Johnston) *in tch: struggling over 5f out: sn lost pl: n.d after* **5/1**[1]

2m 26.8s (14.90) **Going Correction** +1.35s/f (Soft)
WFA 3 from 4yo+ 5lb **12** Ran SP% **121.6**
Speed ratings (Par 103): **94,91,91,88,88 86,85,84,79,76 74,73**
toteswinger: 1&2 £6.60, 1&3 £18.70, 2&3 £13.20. CSF £46.07 CT £393.23 TOTE £9.20: £2.70, £2.20, £4.30; EX 63.70 Trifecta £192.90 Part won. Pool: £260.81 - 0.20 winning tickets..
Owner Six Iron Partnership **Bred** Gainsborough Farm Llc **Trained** Constable Burton, N Yorks

FOCUS
The stalls could not be used because of the state of the ground on the adjacent jumps course and it was a flip start and a hand time. A modest handicap, the pace was not strong and the time was nearly 20secs slower than standard. Nevertheless, the form looks sound rated around the placed horses.

6727 GOWLAND AND DAWSON H'CAP (FOR AMATEUR RIDERS) 1m 4f 93y
4:50 (4:50) (Class 6) (0-65,65) 3-Y-0+ £1,977 (£608; £304) Stalls Low

Form RPR
0153 1 **Prince Rhyddarch**[23] 6155 3-10-3 61 MrRossSmith(7) 14 73
(Miss L A Perratt) *midfield: hdwy to ld over 2f out: styd on strly fnl f* **10/1**
6223 2 4 **Signalman**[28] 5993 4-10-12 56 MrSWalker 15 61
(P Monteith) *hld up in tch: n.m.r and swtchd rt bnd over 3f out: hdwy: edgd lft and chsd wnr appr fnl f: r.o* **13/8**[1]
4013 3 4 **Mister Pete (IRE)**[24] 6115 5-11-1 59 MissPRobson 6 58+
(W Storey) *midfield: n.m.r briefly and swtchd rt 3f out: kpt on fr 2f out: nt rch first two* **13/2**[2]
0040 4 1 3/4 **Bed Fellow (IRE)**[13] 6396 4-10-1 52 MissJKWilson(7) 11 48
(Paul Murphy) *t.k.h: led after 4f to over 2f out: sn no ex* **33/1**
4360 5 9 **Trance (IRE)**[40] 5637 8-10-10 54 (b) MissARyan 13 36
(T D Barron) *s.i.s: bhd and struggling: hung rt and kpt on fr 2f out: n.d* **12/1**
0005 5 dht **Hurricane Thomas (IRE)**[21] 6189 4-10-6 57 MissPhillipaTutty(7) 9 39
(R E Barr) *prom tl rdn and wknd over 2f out* **33/1**
0-15 7 3 1/4 **Front Rank (IRE)**[9] 5559 8-10-3 54 MissNSayer(7) 5 30
(Mrs Dianne Sayer) *prom tl lost pl 4f out: n.d after* **25/1**
0-04 8 nk **Shekan Star**[16] 6309 6-10-7 51 oh6 MrsCBartley 10 27
(K G Reveley) *hld up: rdn 4f out: sn no imp* **25/1**
0050 9 1 1/2 **Poppy Day**[28] 5993 5-10-4 51 oh3 MrOGreenall(3) 16 25
(M W Easterby) *led 4f: cl up tl wknd fr over 2f out* **20/1**
5620 10 12 **Bienheureux**[27] 6019 7-10-10 54 (t) MissEJJones 8 8
(Miss Gay Kelleway) *hld up: drvn over 3f out: sn wknd* **14/1**
0000 11 22 **Woody Valentine (USA)**[11] 5776 7-10-3 52 (p) MissECSayer(5) 3 —
(Mrs Dianne Sayer) *s.v.s: hdwy after 4f: wknd fr 5f out* **28/1**
0316 12 shd **Always Best**[40] 5637 4-10-4 51 oh2 MissJCoward(3) 4 —
(R Allan) *trckd ldrs tl wknd over 3f out* **7/1**[3]
0600 13 11 **Dushstorm (IRE)**[14] 6364 7-10-3 52 MrMPrice(5) 7 —
(R J Price) *hld up: rdn over 3f out: sn wknd* **16/1**
5-50 14 10 **Cripsey Brook**[13] 6395 10-11-0 65 MrCMcCormack(7) 2 —
(K G Reveley) *s.i.s: bhd: lost tch fr 1/2-way* **25/1**
-500 15 2 **Ergo (FR)**[7] 6551 4-10-6 57 (b) MissRebeccaSparkes(7) 17 —
(James Moffatt) *sn w ldrs: wknd over 4f out* **66/1**
-640 16 12 **Riverhill (IRE)**[79] 4451 5-10-7 51 oh1 MissTJackson 1 —
(Miss T Jackson) *towards rr: struggling 1/2-way: nvr on terms* **50/1**

3m 4.42s (18.82) **Going Correction** +1.35s/f (Soft)
WFA 3 from 4yo+ 7lb **16** Ran SP% **122.3**
Speed ratings (Par 101): **91,88,85,84,78 78,76,76,75,67 52,52,45,38,37 29**
toteswinger: 1&2 £7.60, 1&3 £12.10, 2&3 £2.80. CSF £23.62 CT £123.11 TOTE £12.70: £2.50, £1.40, £2.20, £8.10; EX 39.80 Trifecta £304.30 Part won. Pool: £411.27 - 0.49 winning tickets. Place 6 £26.92, Place 5 £18.69.
Owner Mr & Mrs Charles Villiers **Bred** Ian Murray Tough **Trained**
■ A first winner on his second ride for Ross Smith.

FOCUS
A low-grade amateur riders' handicap. The pace was strong in the driving rain and deteriorating underfoot conditions. The runner-up is the best guide to the form.
T/Jkpt: Not won. T/Plt: £17.80 to a £1 stake. Pool: £79,021.11. 3,222.71 winning tickets. T/Qpdt: £13.30 to a £1 stake. Pool: £4,099.20. 227.30 winning tickets. RY

6693 KEMPTON (A.W) (R-H)
Wednesday, October 15

OFFICIAL GOING: Standard
Wind: Moderate, across Weather: Overcast

6728 TURFTV H'CAP (DIV I) 1m 4f (P)
5:50 (5:51) (Class 6) (0-55,55) 3-Y-0+ £1,706 (£503; £252) Stalls Centre

Form RPR
-035 1 **Mayadeen (IRE)**[23] 6161 6-8-13 48 JamieMoriarty 9 57
(R A Fahey) *prom: rdn 4f out: struggling 3f out: prog on inner 2f out: drvn ahd ins fnl f: styd on* **6/1**[2]
0036 2 1 3/4 **Shouldntbethere (IRE)**[42] 5611 4-9-0 52 JackMitchell(3) 7 58
(Mrs P N Dutfield) *hld up in rr: gd prog over 3f out to trck ldr over 2f out: rdn to ld over 1f out: hdd and no ex ins fnl f* **11/2**[1]
0400 3 2 1/4 **Eddie Dowling**[14] 6386 3-8-10 52 SamHitchcott 12 54
(M R Channon) *settled in midfield: drvn over 3f out: lost pl and bk of main gp over 2f out: styd on u.p after: tk 3rd wl ins fnl f* **7/1**
6002 4 1 1/4 **Silver Surprise**[14] 6378 4-9-3 55 MarcHalford(3) 13 55
(J J Bridger) *hld up in last pair: rdn and struggling over 4f out: gd prog over 2f out: tried to cl on ldrs over 1f out: one pce after* **12/1**
0150 5 1 1/2 **Itsy Bitsy**[20] 6228 6-8-7 49 (p) DebraEngland(7) 6 47
(W J Musson) *dwlt: sn in midfield: outpcd and wd bnd 3f out: plugged on fr over 1f out* **25/1**
216 6 1 1/2 **Split The Wind (USA)**[28] 6019 4-9-4 53 EdwardCreighton 4 49
(Miss Sheena West) *led: clr after 3f: hdd & wknd over 1f out* **15/2**
0436 7 2 1/4 **Play Up Pompey**[32] 5912 6-8-12 47 HayleyTurner 11 39
(J J Bridger) *t.k.h early: hld up in rr: pushed along 1/2-way: gng bttr whn nt clr run on inner over 2f out: no prog after* **13/2**[3]
0624 8 2 **Flash Of Fire (USA)**[52] 5320 3-8-9 51 (v[1]) LPKeniry 3 40
(P R Chamings) *hld up bhd ldrs: rdn to dispute 2nd over 2f out: wknd rapidly wl over 1f out* **15/2**
1660 9 3 1/2 **Shandelight (IRE)**[25] 6136 4-9-1 50 (p) DO'Donohoe 1 33
(Mrs A Duffield) *t.k.h early: chsd clr ldr to over 2f out: wknd rapidly* **14/1**
0005 10 5 **Leitmotif (USA)**[67] 4879 3-8-6 48 (b) JimmyQuinn 2 23
(J L Dunlop) *t.k.h early: mostly trckd ldng pair: disp 2nd over 2f out: wknd rapidly wl over 1f out* **13/2**[3]
0-00 11 8 **Amicus**[160] 1938 3-8-11 53 WilliamBuick 10 15
(D K Ivory) *a in rr: lost tch over 3f out: t.o* **40/1**
6 12 6 **Captain Sirus (FR)**[21] 6206 5-9-1 50 (t) AdamKirby 8 3
(P Butler) *a in last pair: rdn 1/2-way: btn after: t.o* **66/1**

2m 35.38s (0.88) **Going Correction** +0.05s/f (Slow)
WFA 3 from 4yo+ 7lb **12** Ran SP% **114.5**
Speed ratings (Par 101): **99,97,96,95,94 93,92,90,88,85 79,75**
toteswinger: 1&2 £8.00, 1&3 £6.80, 2&3 £11.20. CSF £37.03 CT £235.83 TOTE £7.70: £2.40, £2.90, £2.90; EX 50.30.
Owner James Gaffney **Bred** Shadwell Estate Company Limited **Trained** Musley Bank, N Yorks

FOCUS
Most of the runners were struggling for form and only one contender had finished closer than four lengths to a winner on their previous start. Split The Wind ensured that the pace was strong. The form seems sound enough but this is not a race to be too positive about.

6729 TURFTV H'CAP (DIV II) 1m 4f (P)
6:20 (6:21) (Class 6) (0-55,55) 3-Y-0+ £1,706 (£503; £252) Stalls Centre

Form RPR
252 1 **Well Informed**[19] 6248 3-8-9 50 DeanMcKeown 6 59+
(E J O'Neill) *stdd s: hld up in last: gd prog fr 3f out to go 2nd over 1f out: shuffled along and led ins fnl f: in command after* **11/2**
0030 2 1 **Rosy Dawn**[9] 6541 3-8-4 48 MarcHalford(3) 3 55
(J J Bridger) *led: drew clr over 3f out: rdn 2f out: collared ins fnl f: kpt on* **40/1**
6000 3 2 1/2 **Prince Of Medina**[13] 6421 5-8-12 46 (t) SteveDrowne 11 49
(J R Best) *hld up in last trio: rdn and effrt over 3f out: prog fr 2f out: styd on to take 3rd fnl 75yds* **11/1**
5300 4 nse **Ocean Avenue (IRE)**[47] 5465 9-9-6 54 TedDurcan 10 57
(C A Horgan) *hld up in last trio: taken to wd outside and effrt over 2f out: prog over 1f out: styd on fnl f: no ch of rching ldrs* **5/1**[3]
500- 5 1 3/4 **Beau Torero (FR)**[203] 1907 10-8-12 49 RussellKennemore(3) 9 49
(B N Pollock) *sn chsd ldr: outpcd fr 3f out: lost 2nd over 1f out: wknd and lost 2 pls ins fnl f* **50/1**
5050 6 1 1/4 **Ever Dreaming (USA)**[53] 5291 3-9-0 55 LPKeniry 14 53
(A M Balding) *hld up in midfield on inner: effrt 3f out: chsd ldrs but outpcd 2f out: fdd* **7/2**[1]

4056 **7** 2 **Floodlight Fantasy**[7] 6570 5-9-2 **50**............................(v) HayleyTurner 7 45
(Dr R D P Newland) *towards rr: drvn 1/2-way: struggling after: brief effrt u.p over 2f out: sn btn* **10/1**

4363 **8** 1 3/4 **Amwell Brave**[85] 4275 7-8-8 **47**.............................. DavidProbert(5) 2 39
(J R Jenkins) *hld up in midfield: prog on outer over 3f out: nt qckn over 2f out: sn wknd: dismntd after fin* **9/2**[2]

0656 **9** 1/2 **Safebreaker**[33] 5868 3-8-9 **50**.............................. TonyCulhane 13 41
(N Tinkler) *t.k.h early: mostly in rr: brief effrt wl over 2f out: sn wknd* **10/1**

0600 **10** 4 **Medieval Maiden**[35] 5802 5-9-3 **51**.............................. IanMongan 4 36
(Mrs L J Mongan) *in tch in midfield: prog to dispute 3rd over 2f out: sn wknd u.p* **11/1**

231- **11** 17 **Kassuta**[227] 6573 4-8-12 **53**.............................. AndreaAtzeni(7) 12 11
(M J Gingell) *t.k.h early: chsd ldng trio: wknd rapidly u.p over 2f out: t.o* **20/1**

6300 **12** dist **Autograph Hunter**[21] 6208 4-9-0 **48**.............................. AdamKirby 5 —
(Peter Grayson) *chsd ldng pair: urged along after 4f: wknd rapidly 4f out: sn t.o: virtually p.u* **20/1**

2m 36.61s (2.11) **Going Correction** +0.05s/f (Slow)
WFA 3 from 4yo+ 7lb **59** Ran SP% **121.2**
Speed ratings (Par 101): **94,93,91,91,90 89,88,87,86,84 72,52**
toteswinger: 1&2 £65.20, 1&3 £12.00, 2&3 £56.10. CSF £220.83 CT £2354.97 TOTE £7.90: £2.20, £10.30, £3.30; EX 267.90.
Owner David Barlow **Bred** J A E Hobby **Trained** Averham Park, Notts
■ Stewards' Enquiry : Marc Halford five-day ban: careless riding (Oct 29-31, Nov 1-2)

FOCUS
The pace was only modest and the time was more than a second slower than the first division. That said, three of the first four came from the rear. The second got an easy lead and has been rated back to her 2yo best at face value.
Amwell Brave Official explanation: jockey said gelding hung right-handed

6730 TANYA RANDALL CLAIMING STKS 6f (P)
6:50 (6:50) (Class 6) 2-Y-O **£2,047** (£604; £302) **Stalls** High

Form RPR

030 **1** **Riflessione**[54] 5213 2-8-13 74.............................(p) LPKeniry 8 71+
(J S Moore) *hld up bhd ldrs: swtchd rt 2f out: led over 1f out: shkn up fnl f: decisively* **6/1**[2]

0055 **2** 1 1/2 **Hosanna**[31] 5937 2-9-0 57.............................(b[1]) EddieAhern 9 67
(B J Meehan) *t.k.h early and hld up at bk of main gp: prog on inner jst over 2f out: drvn and nt qckn over 1f out: chsd wnr ins fnl f: no imp* **10/1**[3]

2020 **3** nk **Night Seed (IRE)**[23] 6172 2-8-6 76.............................. RichardMullen 4 58
(R Hannon) *pushed along in rr bef 1/2-way: prog u.p 2f out: kpt on to take 3rd ins fnl f: no hdwy after* **9/4**[1]

2351 **4** 1 1/2 **Key To Love (IRE)**[22] 6191 2-8-3 72.............................. JimmyQuinn 7 51
(H J L Dunlop) *w ldr to 2f out: nt qckn after: fdd ins fnl f* **9/4**[1]

1620 **5** 2 1/4 **Sweet Smile (IRE)**[41] 5632 2-9-2 73.............................(p) NCallan 6 57
(K A Ryan) *in tch towards rr but sn pushed along: nvr gng pce to trble ldrs: kpt on fr over 1f out* **14/1**

600 **6** nk **River Style (IRE)**[9] 6534 2-8-10 0.............................. DaneO'Neill 10 50
(A P Jarvis) *mde most to over 1f out: steadily wknd* **33/1**

0005 **7** 1/2 **Missou Maiden**[8] 6555 2-8-8 56.............................(b) PaulMulrennan 5 46
(M H Tompkins) *outpcd and drvn in detached last: kpt on fnl 2f: nrst fin* **25/1**

0603 **8** 1 3/4 **Identity**[13] 6406 2-7-10 62.............................. DavidProbert(5) 1 34
(E J O'Neill) *racd wd: w ldrs: nt qckn over 2f out: sn wknd tamely* **10/1**[3]

2104 **9** 3 3/4 **Sienna Lake (IRE)**[21] 6207 2-8-6 60.............................. RichardSmith 2 28
(R Hannon) *pressed ldrs: nt qckn over 2f out: sn lost pl and btn* **16/1**

00 **10** 6 **Elusive Intentions (IRE)**[68] 4823 2-8-1 0.............................. LukeMorris(3) 12 —
(P D Evans) *chsd ldrs but sn drvn: wknd over 2f out* **66/1**

0 **11** 6 **Stevies Song**[77] 4536 2-8-5 0.............................. MarcHalford(3) 3 —
(D Flood) *nvr gng wl: a struggling in rr: t.o* **66/1**

1m 13.64s (0.54) **Going Correction** +0.05s/f (Slow) **11** Ran SP% **116.3**
Speed ratings (Par 93): **98,96,95,93,90 90,89,87,82,74 66**
toteswinger: 1&2 £7.40, 1&3 £2.20, 2&3 £8.10. CSF £61.86 TOTE £7.10: £1.90, £1.80, £1.40; EX 62.30.Riflessione was claimed by P Moulton for £12000.
Owner Tom & Evelyn Yates **Bred** Tom & Evelyn Yates **Trained** Upper Lambourn, Berks

FOCUS
A fair event of its type, four of the runners having an official rating in the 70s.

NOTEBOOK
Riflessione ◆ lost his chance when clipping heels with a rival at Bath last time but had an interesting chance on his third off a mark of 75 in a Polytrack nursery in August. He was always travelling well, got a nice split against the far rail and quickened up to win with some authority and justify a gamble that shortened his price from 8-1 to 6-1. (op 8-1 tchd 5-1)
Hosanna is only rated 57, so makes the form look a bit suspect but she was also nibbled at in the market, stuck on really well in the closing stages and probably found a fair bit of improvement in first-time blinkers. (op 14-1)
Night Seed(IRE) was well below her best at Leicester last time but set the standard on her pick of form, including a second to an 84-rated rival in a 6f Wolverhampton claimer last month. She never quite got into a threatening position but showed plenty of determination to finish as close as she did after being forced to race wide from a difficult draw. (tchd 11-4)
Key To Love(IRE) travelled enthusiastically up with the pace but her response to pressure was a bit limited. She had won in really good style over 5f at Folkestone last time, was probably a little too keen for her own good over this extra furlong and may be better suited by being ridden with a bit more restraint at this trip. (op 2-1 tchd 5-2)
Sweet Smile(IRE) received an early bump but made late headway from an unpromising position. His profile does have a couple of blips in it, but this was a fair effort in first-time cheekpieces on his all-weather debut. (op 12-1)

6731 DIGIBET SPORTS BETTING MAIDEN STKS 1m (P)
7:20 (7:21) (Class 4) 2-Y-O **£3,885** (£1,156; £577; £288) **Stalls** High

Form RPR

434 **1** **Markyg (USA)**[95] 3939 2-9-3 88.............................. NCallan 6 84+
(K R Burke) *hld up bhd ldrs: given a nudge by rival jst over 2f out: rdn and prog sn after: chal 1f out: led ins fnl f: styd on readily* **4/1**[2]

62 **2** 1/2 **History Lesson**[25] 6122 2-9-3 0.............................. RichardHughes 14 84+
(R Hannon) *disp ld over 1f: trckd ldrs after: squeezed through on inner over 1f out: led jst ins fnl f: sn hdd and nt qckn* **6/5**[1]

00 **3** 2 **Duar Mapel (USA)**[43] 5590 2-9-3 0.............................(b) PaulEddery 2 75
(G D Blake) *dwlt: rapid prog to ld over 6f out: drvn over 2f out: hdd and outpcd jst ins fnl f* **100/1**

35 **4** 3/4 **Fin Vin De Leu (GER)**[18] 6282 2-9-3 0.............................. RoystonFfrench 3 73
(M Johnston) *hld up in cl tch: swtchd lft jst over 2f out: sn nt qckn: kpt on again fr over 1f out: nt pce to chal* **12/1**

0 **5** 1 3/4 **Lady Drac (IRE)**[26] 6076 2-8-12 0.............................. MichaelHills 9 64
(B W Hills) *stdd s: prog on outer bef 1/2-way to trck ldrs: rdn to chal and upsides over 1f out: wknd ins fnl f* **13/2**[3]

04 **6** nk **King's La Mont (IRE)**[56] 5184 2-9-3 0.............................. JimCrowley 5 68
(Mrs A J Perrett) *disp ld over 1f: styd cl up: nt qckn 2f out: fdd fnl f* **10/1**

04 **7** nk **Dr Valentine (FR)**[15] 6359 2-9-3 0.............................. AdamKirby 11 68+
(S Kirk) *stdd s: hld up in last trio: two reminders fr 2f out: styd on steadily: nvr nr ldrs* **14/1**

6 **8** 3/4 **Augusta Gold (USA)**[28] 6025 2-9-3 0.............................. JamieSpencer 8 66
(B J Meehan) *trckd ldrs: cl up and rdn over 2f out: no room on inner over 1f out: reined bk and swtchd lft: one pce after* **20/1**

30 **9** 3/4 **Omokoroa (IRE)**[27] 6057 2-9-3 0.............................. PaulMulrennan 4 64
(M H Tompkins) *nvr on terms w ldrs: outpcd in rr over 2f out: kpt on fnl f* **50/1**

10 nk **Spiritual Treasure (USA)** 2-9-3 0.............................. PaulHanagan 1 64
(M A Magnusson) *dwlt: hld up wl in rr: outpcd over 2f out: pushed along and kpt on fnl f* **33/1**

11 2 3/4 **Jeunesse (IRE)** 2-8-12 0.............................. RichardKingscote 12 53
(R M Beckett) *a wl in rr: struggling wl over 2f out* **33/1**

0 **12** nk **Wahan (USA)**[12] 6438 2-9-3 0.............................. TedDurcan 13 57
(C E Brittain) *a wl in rr: last and shkn up 3f out: nvr on terms after* **66/1**

13 7 **Escapist** 2-9-3 0.............................. SteveDrowne 10 42
(H Morrison) *a towards rr: wknd over 2f out: wl bhd fnl f* **50/1**

1m 41.03s (1.23) **Going Correction** +0.05s/f (Slow) **13** Ran SP% **119.3**
Speed ratings (Par 97): **95,94,92,91,90 89,89,88,87,87 84,84,77**
toteswinger: 1&2 £1.40, 1&3 £15.70, 2&3 £17.60. CSF £8.64 TOTE £4.60: £1.50, £1.30, £20.20; EX 11.60.
Owner Mrs Maura Gittins **Bred** Robert S Evans **Trained** Middleham Moor, N Yorks

FOCUS
A decent event. The pace was a bit muddling but the two main form contenders filled the first two positions and pulled a little way clear of the rest, so the form looks solid.

NOTEBOOK
Markyg(USA) has a BHA rating of 88 and had strong form claims on his third in the Chesham Stakes at Royal Ascot, but he still did really well to overcome some traffic problems and find a good turn of foot to pounce late on his first run for three months. He is a big, scopey type who stayed the trip really well, should be capable of further progress and looks a decent prospect. (op 7-2 tchd 10-3)
History Lesson's latest second in a 7f Newbury maiden had been boosted by the winner finishing runner-up in a Group 3 at Newmarket next time. He was heavily backed and was hampered and harassed on the far rail in the straight before quickening through a gap. He was unlucky to meet interference, but may not have beaten the winner with a clear run. He is, however, a very likeable type, who has an athletic physique and should have a bright future over middle-distances next season. (op 13-8 tchd 7-4 in a place)
Duar Mapel(USA)'s proximity in third puts a slight blemish on the form. He had been well held at big prices on two previous starts, but has responded well to a positive ride and his dam was a quite useful winner on dirt in the US, so he possibly improved for the switch to Polytrack.
Fin Vin De Leu(GER) got involved in a damaging battle for the lead last time and had quite a bit to find with the principals here, but rallied well after being trapped for room in the straight and seems to be progressing. (op 16-1)
Lady Drac(IRE) also seems to have taken a step in the right direction. She raced keenly, hit the front at the two-furlong pole before fading and did hang a bit, but that is probably due to inexperience and she should be capable of further improvement. (op 15-2)
Dr Valentine(FR) Official explanation: jockey said gelding ran too free

6732 DIGIBET NURSERY 6f (P)
7:50 (7:54) (Class 5) (0-75,75) 2-Y-O **£2,590** (£770; £385; £192) **Stalls** High

Form RPR

253 **1** **Victoria Sponge (IRE)**[63] 4980 2-9-0 **68**.............................. DaneO'Neill 5 72+
(R Hannon) *hld up in last trio and wl off the pce: prog fr 2f out: clsd rapidly 1f out: drvn ahd fnl 100yds: a holding on* **9/2**[2]

304 **2** hd **Five Star Junior (USA)**[12] 6434 2-9-0 **68**.............................. JamieSpencer 4 71
(S A Callaghan) *hld up in last trio and wl off the pce: prog fr 2f out: clsd rapidly 1f out: pressed wnr fnl 100yds: a jst hld* **16/1**

5313 **3** 1 3/4 **Ray Of Joy**[20] 6223 2-9-7 **75**.............................. JimmyQuinn 6 73
(J R Jenkins) *hld up in 6th and wl off the pce: prog over 2f out: drvn ahd jst ins fnl f: hdd & wknd fnl 100yds* **5/1**[3]

61 **4** 1 **Cumana Bay**[33] 5860 2-9-6 **74**.............................. RichardHughes 8 69
(R Hannon) *pushed along in 7th and wl off the pce: prog u.p over 2f out: clsd to chal ins fnl f: fdd fnl 100yds* **4/1**[1]

3550 **5** 2 **Spit And Polish**[13] 6414 2-9-4 **72**.............................(b) EddieAhern 3 61
(J L Dunlop) *dwlt: last and wl off the pce: sme prog on inner fr 2f out: plugged on but nvr rchd ldrs* **25/1**

0042 **6** 3/4 **All Spin (IRE)**[19] 6246 2-9-7 **75**.............................. GregFairley 11 62+
(A P Jarvis) *chsd ldr's frntic pce: led over 2f out and edgd lft: sitting duck for deep clsrs over 1f out: hdd & wknd jst ins fnl f* **12/1**

5300 **7** 2 1/4 **Dotty's Brother**[27] 6051 2-8-11 **65**.............................(p) TPO'Shea 7 45
(Mrs A Duffield) *chsd clr ldng pair: lft in 2nd over 2f out: wknd rapidly fnl f* **50/1**

0554 **8** 5 **Multi Tasker**[156] 2049 2-8-11 **65**.............................. PaulFitzsimons 9 30
(Miss J R Tooth) *chsd ldng trio: u.p fr 1/2-way: no imp over 2f out: sn lost pl: wknd fnl f* **66/1**

2320 **9** 19 **Count Almaviva (USA)**[30] 5960 2-9-5 **73**.............................(b[1]) NCallan 2 —
(K A Ryan) *chsd clr ldng trio and sn pushed along: wknd over 2f out: t.o* **12/1**

0126 **10** 1 1/2 **Simple Rhythm**[33] 5866 2-8-10 **69**.............................. DavidProbert(5) 12 —
(N Tinkler) *led at furious pce: sddle slipped bdly and hdd over 2f out: no ch after* **14/1**

1m 13.42s (0.32) **Going Correction** +0.05s/f (Slow) **10** Ran SP% **90.1**
Speed ratings (Par 95): **99,98,96,95,92 91,88,81,56,54**
toteswinger: 1&2 £12.70, 1&3 £2.40, 2&3 £7.20. CSF £41.66 CT £158.83 TOTE £4.80: £2.30, £2.60, £1.30; EX 49.50.
Owner Simon Leech **Bred** Corrin Stud & Peter McCutcheon **Trained** East Everleigh, Wilts
■ Stewards' Enquiry : Jimmy Quinn one-day ban: careless riding (Oct 29)

FOCUS
A reasonable nursery run at a furious pace. It was weakened by the withdrawal of the favourite Whatyouwoodwishfor, who refused to enter the stalls (5/2, deduct 25p in the £ under R4).

NOTEBOOK
Victoria Sponge(IRE) had been unable to mount a challenge when favourite the last two times, but she was suited by the suicidal pace set by Simple Rhythm and just outgunned her rivals on her nursery debut to give Richard Hannon his 85th juvenile winner in Britain this year. She should not go up much for this narrow win and should be capable of further success, and should stay quite a bit further than this in time. (op 7-1)
Five Star Junior(USA) cost $140,000 in February and posted his best effort when returning from a break at Lingfield on his all-weather debut last time. He improved again stepped up to 6f and is a brother to a smart multiple dirt winner in the US, so could continue to thrive on the Polytrack. (op 12-1 tchd 20-1)
Ray Of Joy powered clear over course and distance last month and was unlucky when stopped in her tracks last time. She ran another creditable race and probably just ran into two better, less exposed and better handicapped rivals. (op 6-1)

Cumana Bay seemed to have every chance but was not quite good enough on her nursery debut. (op 7-2 tchd 9-2 in a place)
All Spin(IRE) lasted quite well after racing up with the brutal pace. He obviously has plenty of natural speed, seemed to handle the surface well and looks worth a try at 5f. (op 16-1)
Count Almaviva(USA) was reported to have hung badly right. Official explanation: jockey said colt hung right-handed (op 14-1)
Simple Rhythm Official explanation: jockey said saddle slipped

6733 DIGIBET.COM H'CAP — 6f (P)
8:20 (8:21) (Class 6) (0-52,52) 3-Y-O+ — **£2,047** (£604; £302) **Stalls** High

Form — RPR
0645 **1** **Hurricane Coast**[2] 6693 9-8-12 **50**........(b) TonyCulhane 4 64
(D Flood) *hld up in rr and confidently rdn: smooth prog fr 2f out: shkn up to ld ins fnl f: comf* **9/2**[2]
6364 **2** 1 3/4 **Musical Script (USA)**[19] 6251 5-9-0 **52**........(b) NCallan 10 61
(Mouse Hamilton-Fairley) *trckd ldrs: effrt 2f out: rdn to ld jst over 1f out: hdd and outpcd ins fnl f* **4/1**[1]
3050 **3** 1 3/4 **Nawaaff**[3] 6679 3-8-13 **52**........(v) TPO'Shea 5 55
(M R Channon) *in tch in rr: urged along over 2f out: prog over 1f out: styd on to take 3rd ins fnl f* **8/1**
4002 **4** nk **Reigning Monarch (USA)**[6] 6595 5-8-12 **50**........(p) SamHitchcott 8 52
(Miss Z C Davison) *rrd s: in rr: effrt whn nt clr run 2f out: prog over 1f out: kpt on but nt pce of ldng pair* **5/1**[3]
5056 **5** 1 **Majestical (IRE)**[16] 6335 6-8-13 **51**........(p) WilliamBuick 12 50
(R A Harris) *t.k.h early: trckd ldrs: cruised into ld 2f out: hdd jst over 1f out: immediately capitulated* **12/1**
0-00 **6** 3/4 **Up The Chimney**[7] 6571 4-9-0 **52**........ DaneO'Neill 2 48
(A P Jarvis) *s.i.s: rdn in last after 2f: kpt on fr over 1f out: n.d* **14/1**
1436 **7** 2 **Davids Mark**[170] 1687 8-8-9 **52**........ DavidProbert(5) 3 42
(J R Jenkins) *sn w ldrs on outer: nrly upsides 2f out: wknd rapidly over 1f out* **5/1**[3]
150 **8** 3 **Currency**[107] 3559 11-8-11 **52**........ TolleyDean(3) 6 32
(J M Bradley) *reluctant to enter stalls: w ldr: urged along furiously fr 1/2-way: losing pl qckly whn n.m.r 1f out* **33/1**
0040 **9** 1 **Planet Queen**[13] 6409 3-8-13 **52**........(v) DarrenWilliams 7 29
(K R Burke) *racd freely: led to 2f out: wknd* **20/1**
426 **10** 1 1/4 **Charlotte Grey**[32] 5916 4-8-5 **50**........ AndreaAtzeni(7) 9 23
(P J McBride) *chsd ldrs tl wknd jst over 2f out* **13/2**

1m 12.84s (-0.26) **Going Correction** +0.05s/f (Slow)
WFA 3 from 4yo+ 1lb — **10** Ran SP% **118.0**
Speed ratings (Par 101): **103,100,98,97,96 95,92,88,87,85**
toteswinger: 1&2 £5.80, 1&3 £8.00, 2&3 £11.10. CSF £23.20 CT £143.94 TOTE £6.10: £2.80, £1.80, £3.60; EX 25.90.
Owner Nadeem Ahmad **Bred** Ian H Wills **Trained** Wollerton, Shropshire

FOCUS
A modest event featuring some inconsistent types with modest strike-rates and a few contenders in the twilight of their career. That said, it was well run and the form looks sound.

6734 RACING UK H'CAP — 7f (P)
8:50 (8:51) (Class 4) (0-80,80) 3-Y-O+ — **£5,180** (£1,541; £770; £384) **Stalls** High

Form — RPR
5205 **1** **Countdown**[11] 6478 6-9-6 **80**........ AlanMunro 13 89
(M D Squance) *hld up wl in rr: swtchd to inner and dream run through fr 2f out: r.o to ld fnl 100yds: readily* **12/1**
1035 **2** 1 **Credit Swap**[22] 6194 3-9-2 **78**........ DaneO'Neill 4 84
(L M Cumani) *awkward s: keen early: hld up wl in rr: rdn and hanging 2f out: gd prog on outer over 1f out: r.o to take 2nd last strides* **5/1**[2]
2152 **3** shd **Gap Princess (IRE)**[17] 6314 4-8-10 **70**........ PaulHanagan 10 76
(R A Fahey) *cl up on inner: hmpd 1/2-way: rdn over 2f out: prog jst over 1f out: r.o to take 3rd last strides* **11/2**[3]
6060 **4** nk **Southandwest (IRE)**[16] 6346 4-9-2 **76**........ TPO'Shea 9 81
(J S Moore) *racd freely: mde most: hdd and outpcd fnl 100yds: lost 2 pls nr fin* **14/1**
4646 **5** hd **Harry Gee**[63] 4983 3-9-2 **78**........(b) SteveDrowne 6 82
(C Wragg) *chsd ldrs: rdn over 2f out: nt qckn over 1f out: kpt on fnl f but nvr able to chal* **10/1**
4054 **6** 1 **Purus (IRE)**[22] 6194 6-8-12 **75**........ LukeMorris(3) 11 81+
(R A Teal) *t.k.h early: trckd ldrs: cl up bhd ldng pair but nowhere to go jst over 1f out: trapped after and lost pls* **8/1**
0064 **7** 1/2 **Forest Dane**[14] 6402 8-8-12 **72**........ RoystonFfrench 2 72
(Mrs N Smith) *hld up in midfield on outer: rdn and effrt over 2f out: one pce and no real imp on ldrs* **15/2**
4510 **8** 1 **Rambling Light**[81] 4407 4-9-4 **78**........(p) LPKeniry 8 76
(A M Balding) *t.k.h early: w ldr: stl upsides jst over 1f out: wknd ins fnl f* **4/1**[1]
1500 **9** hd **Onceaponatime (IRE)**[22] 6194 3-9-4 **80**........ RichardHughes 14 77
(E A L Dunlop) *chsd ldrs: rdn over 2f out: no imp over 1f out: one pce* **16/1**
1503 **10** 1/2 **Charlie Delta**[14] 6402 5-8-3 **68**........(b) WilliamCarson(5) 1 64
(J G M O'Shea) *hld up in last pair: struggling 3f out: swtchd to inner and modest prog over 1f out: nvr rchd ldrs* **14/1**
0000 **11** 1 **Sweet Gale (IRE)**[23] 6178 4-8-8 **68**........ GregFairley 7 61
(Mike Murphy) *t.k.h early: hld up towards rr: brief effrt 2f out: sn no prog and btn* **12/1**
0000 **12** 10 **Centenerola (USA)**[25] 6124 3-8-10 **72**........(b[1]) MichaelHills 12 38
(B W Hills) *stdd s: t.k.h early: hld up in last pair: struggling fr 3f out: t.o* **28/1**
5630 **13** 3 1/4 **Always Ready**[13] 6420 3-9-1 **77**........(vt) NCallan 5 34
(C E Brittain) *trckd ldrs: shkn up over 2f out: sn wknd rapidly: t.o* **10/1**

1m 26.0s **Going Correction** +0.05s/f (Slow)
WFA 3 from 4yo+ 2lb — **13** Ran SP% **131.2**
Speed ratings (Par 105): **102,100,100,100,100 99,98,97,97,96 95,83,80**
toteswinger: 1&2 £13.40, 1&3 £20.30, 2&3 £5.40. CSF £78.01 CT £399.70 TOTE £13.50: £3.40, £2.60, £2.50; EX 156.50.
Owner David W Armstrong **Bred** Lady Fairhaven **Trained** Newmarket, Suffolk

FOCUS
A decent handicap. The pace was reasonable and they finished in a bunch. The form looks sound at face value.
Gap Princess(IRE) Official explanation: jockey said filly suffered interference in running
Purus(IRE) Official explanation: jockey said gelding was denied a clear run
Centenerola(USA) Official explanation: jockey said filly suffered interference at the start

6735 PANORAMIC BAR & RESTAURANT CLASSIFIED STKS — 1m (P)
9:20 (9:20) (Class 6) 3-Y-O+ — **£2,047** (£604; £302) **Stalls** High

Form — RPR
5/50 **1** **Charming Escort**[36] 5790 4-9-3 55........ AlanMunro 3 55
(T T Clement) *hld up in rr and racd on outer: rdn and plenty to do stl 2f out: gd prog jst over 1f out: drvn and r.o to ld post* **20/1**
3000 **2** nse **Royal Encore**[16] 6338 4-9-3 53........ EddieAhern 4 55
(J R Fanshawe) *hld up bhd ldrs: effrt 2f out: clsd jst over 1f out: drvn ahd fnl strides: hdd post* **8/1**
0030 **3** shd **Harting Hill**[48] 5428 3-9-0 55........ PatDobbs 9 55
(M P Tregoning) *hld up towards rr: rdn and effrt over 2f out: one of many clsng ins fnl f: upsides nr fin: jst hld* **11/2**[3]
-600 **4** 1/2 **Karate Queen**[108] 3524 3-9-0 52........ WilliamBuick 6 54
(A M Balding) *mde most: drew 2 l clr 2f out: hrd rdn fnl f: swamped nr fin* **16/1**
0002 **5** 1/2 **Headache**[40] 5684 3-9-0 53........(t) DaneO'Neill 1 52
(B W Duke) *prom: chsd ldr over 2f out: grad clsd fr 1f out but lost pls nr fin* **6/1**
00-1 **6** nk **Pembo**[37] 5748 3-8-7 50........ AndreaAtzeni(7) 2 52
(R A Harris) *mostly in midfield: hrd rdn over 2f out: edgd rt after: one of many clsng ins fnl f: no ex fnl 50yds* **10/1**
7 nse **Coughlans Locke (IRE)**[41] 5657 5-9-3 53........ JerryO'Dwyer 14 52
(Kieran P Cotter, Ire) *t.k.h early: hld up bhd ldrs: rdn over 2f out on inner: clsd fr jst over 1f out: jst outspded in bunch fin* **5/1**[2]
060 **8** 1 1/4 **Safaseef (IRE)**[53] 5261 3-9-0 54........ JamesDoyle 13 51+
(K A Morgan) *hld up towards rr: rdn and swtchd lft jst over 2f out: trying to cl whn nt clr run fr 1f out: kpt on* **16/1**
-000 **9** hd **Double Duty (IRE)**[34] 5836 3-9-0 55........(b) RichardHughes 8 48
(B J Meehan) *hld up in rr: last and stl hld up jst over 2f out: nt clr run wl over 1f out: styd on fnl f: too much to do* **12/1**
4000 **10** 2 **Tamdiid (USA)**[20] 6227 3-9-0 54........ LiamJones 12 44+
(C E Brittain) *trckd ldrs: rdn but stl in tch whn bdly squeezed out 2f out: no ch after* **8/1**
640 **11** nse **Zantic**[99] 3823 3-9-0 54........ LPKeniry 5 44
(P R Chamings) *a in last trio: rdn and brief effrt over 2f out: sn btn* **33/1**
0000 **12** 1/2 **Siena**[28] 6036 3-9-0 50........(v[1]) TGMcLaughlin 11 42
(Mrs C A Dunnett) *hld up in last pair: rdn and effrt on inner over 2f out: sn no prog* **33/1**
6203 **13** 7 **Ceili Mor (IRE)**[11] 6492 3-9-0 53........ J-PGuillambert 7 26
(M Johnston) *w ldr tl wknd rapidly over 2f out: t.o* **10/3**[1]

1m 40.5s (0.70) **Going Correction** +0.05s/f (Slow)
WFA 3 from 4yo+ 3lb — **13** Ran SP% **130.8**
Speed ratings (Par 101): **98,97,97,97,96 96,96,95,95,93 93,92,85**
toteswinger: 1&2 £14.80, 1&3 £15.10, 2&3 £7.70. CSF £184.98 TOTE £32.70: £6.00, £3.50, £2.70; EX 215.20 Place 6: £100.35 Place 5: £46.74.
Owner P Charalambous **Bred** Hyperion Bloodstock **Trained** Newmarket, Suffolk
■ Stewards' Enquiry : Andrea Atzeni four-day ban: careless riding (Oct 30-31, Nov 1-2)

FOCUS
An ordinary event, but some powerful yards were represented by lightly raced types. They finished in a bit of a heap and the form looks a bit muddling.
Charming Escort Official explanation: trainer's rep said, regarding running, that this was a drop in class.
Zantic Official explanation: vet said gelding bled from the nose
Ceili Mor(IRE) Official explanation: jockey had no explanation for the poor form shown
T/Jkpt: Not won. T/Plt: £192.00 to a £1 stake. Pool: £81,782.55. 310.86 winning tickets. T/Qpdt: £19.30 to a £1 stake. Pool: £7,496.38. 286.67 winning tickets. JN

6620 LINGFIELD (L-H)
Wednesday, October 15

OFFICIAL GOING: Standard
Wind: medium, half behind Weather: overcast

6736 FIGHTSPORT CLAIMING STKS — 7f (P)
2:20 (2:21) (Class 6) 3-Y-O+ — **£1,978** (£584; £292) **Stalls** Low

Form — RPR
3052 **1** **Trimlestown (IRE)**[49] 5389 5-9-2 64........(p) NCallan 3 74
(K A Ryan) *racd in midfield: rdn 3f out: hdwy over 2f out: burst between horse ent fnl f: led ins fnl f: r.o strly* **7/1**[2]
0041 **2** 1 **I Confess**[12] 6433 3-8-9 70........(b) RichardEvans(5) 10 71
(P D Evans) *led for 1f: styd chsng ldrs: ev ch and rdn 2f out: led 1f out: sn hdd: one pce after* **7/1**[2]
1130 **3** hd **One More Round (USA)**[29] 5994 10-8-8 65........(b) TPQueally 4 63
(Ollie Pears) *hld up in tch: trckd ldrs and nt clr run over 1f out: squeezed between horses ent fnl f: kpt on same pce u.p fnl f* **4/1**[1]
0043 **4** 2 **Deal Flipper**[12] 6433 3-7-13 62........ FrankieMcDonald 8 50
(P Winkworth) *dwlt: bhd: hdwy and rdn over 2f out: styd on fr over 1f out: edgd lft ins fnl f: nt rch ldrs* **8/1**
5303 **5** shd **Buy On The Red**[12] 6435 7-9-6 73........(p) MartinDwyer 7 69
(W R Muir) *chsd ldr after 1f: ev ch and rdn 2f out: led jst over 1f out: sn hdd: no ex fnl f* **7/1**[2]
4256 **6** 1 3/4 **Little Knickers**[14] 6387 3-8-9 67........(b) EdwardCreighton 2 55
(E J Creighton) *dwlt: sn pushed up into midfield: rdn and unable qck over 2f out: kpt on same pce fr over 1f out* **16/1**
0400 **7** 1/2 **Flying Bantam (IRE)**[27] 6043 7-8-8 69........ PaulHanagan 14 51
(R A Fahey) *stdd after s: hld up in rr: styd on fnl f: nvr trbld ldrs* **10/1**
55/ **8** nk **Brigydon (IRE)**[779] 4899 5-9-10 0........ AdamKirby 5 66
(J R Fanshawe) *in tch in midfield: rdn and edgd lft over 2f out: no imp after* **33/1**
0530 **9** nk **Rockfield Tiger (IRE)**[19] 6256 3-9-4 73........ ShaneKelly 13 61
(J A Osborne) *stdd s: hld up in rr: styd on fr over 1f out: nvr trbld ldrs* **12/1**
0240 **10** 1 1/4 **Crocodile Bay (IRE)**[11] 6482 5-9-1 74........ JamesO'Reilly(5) 1 58
(John A Harris) *s.i.s: sn pushed along: led after 1f: rdn wl over 1f out: hdd jst over 1f out: wknd qckly fnl f* **15/2**[3]
0300 **11** 9 **Hopeful Purchase (IRE)**[11] 6490 5-9-5 75........(b) DavidProbert(5) 11 38
(J R Gask) *racd on outer: nvr bttr than midfield: rdn 4f out: no ch last 2f* **11/1**
3200 **12** 3/4 **El Fuser**[19] 6254 3-9-4 65........(p) EddieAhern 6 32
(P J Makin) *chsd ldr for 1f: chsd ldrs after: shkn up over 3f out: lost pl over 2f out: no ch after* **20/1**
6400 **13** 1 3/4 **Rankayo Hitam (USA)**[13] 6417 3-9-0 70........(b) JohnEgan 12 23
(P F I Cole) *a bhd: rdn 4f out: nvr a factor* **14/1**

The Form Book, Raceform Ltd, Compton, RG20 6NL

0-00 **14** *11* **Obstructive**[15] 6354 4-8-13 75........................ AlanCreighton(3) 9 —
(E J Creighton) *dwlt: sn rdn along and in tch: rdn and wknd 3f out: wl bhd last 2f* **50/1**

1m 23.04s (-1.76) **Going Correction** -0.175s/f (Stan)
WFA 3 from 4yo+ 2lb **14** Ran SP% **127.7**
Speed ratings (Par 101): **103,101,101,99,99 97,96,96,95,94 84,83,81,68**
toteswinger: 1&2 £8.60, 1&3 £7.50, 2&3 £9.40. CSF £58.00 TOTE £6.00: £2.80, £3.20, £1.80; EX 53.90 Trifecta £57.80 Pool: £406.53 - 5.20 winning units..Trimlestown was claimed by P. D. Evans for £10,000.
Owner Mrs R G Hillen & B Walsh **Bred** Liam Brennan **Trained** Hambleton, N Yorks

FOCUS
An ordinary claimer, but they appeared to go a decent pace. The runner-up is the best guide, with the winner up 5lb on this years form.
El Fuser Official explanation: jockey said gelding hung left
Rankayo Hitam(USA) Official explanation: jockey said colt felt wrong behind

6737 DAWSON NEWS EBF MAIDEN STKS 7f (P)
2:50 (2:53) (Class 5) 2-Y-O **£3,885** (£1,156; £577; £288) **Stalls** Low

Form RPR

3 **1** **Axel Foley (USA)**[29] 5996 2-9-3 0........................ SteveDrowne 10 81+
(J R Best) *racd in midfield: hdwy on outer over 2f out: rdn over 1f out: drvn to ld ins fnl f: pushed out fnl 75yds: readily* **3/1**[2]

2 *1 1/4* **Cross Section (USA)** 2-8-12 0........................ JamieSpencer 7 71+
(E F Vaughan) *hld up wl in tch: rdn and chsd ldng pair jst over 2f out: hdwy jst over 1f out: ev ch ins fnl f: nt pce of wnr wl ins fnl f* **14/1**

64 **3** *nk* **Mirrored**[75] 4600 2-9-3 0........................ RyanMoore 1 75
(Sir Michael Stoute) *trckd ldrs: plld out off of rail 2f out: rdn jst over 1f out: pushed along over 1f out: kpt on wl fnl f to go 3rd towards fin* **9/2**[3]

4 *1 1/2* **Leelu** 2-8-12 0........................ NCallan 12 66
(D W P Arbuthnot) *chsd ldrs: wnt 2nd over 2f out: led 2f out: sn rdn: hdd ins fnl f: fdd fnl 50yds* **66/1**

2630 **5** *1* **Noble Jack (IRE)**[54] 5244 2-9-3 86........................ RichardHughes 13 69
(R Hannon) *hld up towards rr: hdwy over 2f out: drvn 2f out: styd on fnl f: nvr pce to rch ldrs* **9/1**

66 **6** *1* **Curacao**[13] 6412 2-9-3 0........................ JimCrowley 6 66+
(Mrs A J Perrett) *in tch in midfield: rdn and no real hdwy over 2f out: kpt on fnl f: nvr pce to threaten ldrs* **13/2**

0 **7** *1 3/4* **Duke Of Normandy (IRE)**[11] 6480 2-9-3 0........................ JoeFanning 5 62
(M Johnston) *chsd ldrs tl led over 2f out: rdn and hdd 2f out: wknd qckly fnl f* **12/1**

0 **8** *1* **Salybia Bay**[21] 6205 2-8-12 0........................ PatDobbs 2 55
(R Hannon) *s.i.s: sn in tch in midfield: rdn and unable qck over 2f out: plugged on same pce after* **20/1**

05 **9** *1* **Darwin's Dragon**[19] 6253 2-9-3 0........................ NelsonDeSouza 14 57
(P F I Cole) *stdd and dropped in rr after s: t.k.h: hld up in rr: sme hdwy 2f out: nvr trbld ldrs* **25/1**

0 **10** *3* **Derringbay (IRE)**[8] 6552 2-9-3 0........................ SaleemGolam 8 50
(M H Tompkins) *s.i.s: a towards rr: rdn and struggling 3f out: no ch fnl 2f* **66/1**

11 *1 3/4* **Great Bounder (CAN)** 2-9-3 0........................ HayleyTurner 4 45
(J R Best) *taken down early: s.i.s: t.k.h: hld up in rr: n.d* **14/1**

05 **12** *1 1/2* **Echo Forest**[16] 6333 2-9-3 0........................ LPKeniry 3 41
(J R Best) *led tl over 2f out: wknd qckly 2f out* **66/1**

13 *nk* **Lead Home (IRE)** 2-8-12 0........................ MartinDwyer 9 36
(B J Meehan) *t.k.h: hld up towards rr: rdn and struggling over 2f out: no ch last 2f* **33/1**

1m 25.01s (0.21) **Going Correction** -0.175s/f (Stan) **13** Ran SP% **124.3**
Speed ratings (Par 95): **91,89,89,87,86 85,83,82,80,77 75,73,73**
toteswinger: 1&2 £8.10, 1&3 £4.00, 2&3 £9.30. CSF £43.69 TOTE £4.90: £1.60, £3.90, £1.80; EX 46.80 Trifecta £98.10 Pool: £395.21 - 2.98 winning units..
Owner Kent Bloodstock **Bred** George Waggoner Stables Inc **Trained** Hucking, Kent

FOCUS
A fair-looking maiden though the pace seemed ordinary.

NOTEBOOK
Axel Foley(USA) ◆, a very promising third on his debut over course and distance last month, was rather weak in the betting here but the market got it wrong. He was having to be ridden along before starting the final turn, but once in line for home he produced a nice turn of foot down the wide outside to hit the front and did it well in the end. He can continue to improve, but won't be seen again this season. (op 5-2 tchd 9-4 and 7-2)
Cross Section(USA) ◆, a half-sister to three winners including the smart Il Warrd, was weak in the market for this debut but she ran a fine race, keeping on well having been up there from the start. She can improve and ought to win races. (op 15-2)
Mirrored, disappointing in two outings on turf during the summer, plugged on into third on this switch to sand but it's debatable whether he improved much on previous efforts. He can now be handicapped and that may be his best option as he is obviously nothing special. (op 5-1 tchd 11-2)
Leelu ◆, who cost just £600 as a yearling, belied her value with a cracking debut effort and she led the field into the straight before getting swamped by the front trio. Related to several winners at up to 1m4f on the dam's side, she is entitled to improve with racing and looks to have a future.
Noble Jack(IRE), placed three times from five starts and not disgraced in a very valuable sales race at Newmarket in August, set the standard with an official rating of 86. He did have an awkward wide draw to overcome, but really ought to have done better and perhaps the switch to sand didn't suit him. Either way he is not looking an easy horse to place. (op 11-4 tchd 3-1)
Curacao ◆ was very well backed beforehand, but as in his his two previous starts he seemed to find this trip inadequate and was doing all his best work late. He now qualifies for a mark and is bred to come into his own over middle-distances next season. (op 12-1)
Darwin's Dragon ◆, who had hinted at ability though unplaced in his two previous starts, pulled very hard out the back early from the outside stall before making a little late progress. He now qualifies for nurseries and could improve in that sphere. (tchd 33-1 in places)
Great Bounder(CAN), a half-brother to a couple of useful sprinters on dirt in the US and a stable-companion of the winner, missed the break and was then inclined to race in snatches at the back. He is almost certainly capable of improving with racing. (op 25-1)

6738 MENZIES DISTRIBUTION H'CAP 1m (P)
3:25 (3:26) (Class 5) (0-75,75) 3-Y-0+ **£2,590** (£770; £385; £192) **Stalls** High

Form RPR

4006 **1** **Prince Of Thebes (IRE)**[6] 6598 7-9-4 72........................ PaulDoe 4 78
(M J Attwater) *chsd ldr tl led 5f out: mde rest: rdn 2f out: hld on gamely fnl f: all out* **10/1**

0064 **2** *hd* **Daniel Thomas (IRE)**[15] 6363 6-9-5 73........................ EddieAhern 9 79
(Mrs A L M King) *s.i.s: towards rr: hdwy into midfield 3f out: rdn wl over 1f out: plld out ent fnl f: r.o strly fnl 100yds: snatched 2nd last stride* **14/1**

0360 **3** *shd* **Zero Cool (USA)**[74] 4627 4-9-7 75........................ RyanMoore 12 81
(G L Moore) *led for 3f out: pressed wnr after: rdn 2f out: hrd rdn and nt qckn fnl f: lost 2nd last stride* **9/2**[1]

4000 **4** *1 1/2* **Sam's Cross (IRE)**[44] 5580 3-9-3 74........................ DarrenWilliams 3 76
(K R Burke) *stdd after s: hld up in rr: rdn and hdwy over 1f out: r.o ins fnl f: nt rch ldrs* **14/1**

6000 **5** *shd* **Lend A Grand (IRE)**[36] 5789 4-9-1 69........................ LPKeniry 2 71
(Miss Jo Crowley) *hld up in rr: rdn and gd hdwy on inner wl over 1f out: kpt on but nvr able to rch ldrs* **20/1**

0142 **6** *nse* **Glencal**[23] 6178 4-9-1 69........................ TravisBlock 8 71
(H Morrison) *racd in mdfield on outer: rdn and hdwy over 2f out: chsd ldrs over 1f out: one pce fnl f* **8/1**[3]

000 **7** *nk* **Shake On It**[16] 6346 4-9-3 71........................ NCallan 6 72
(Eve Johnson Houghton) *chsd ldrs: rdn and effrt wl over 1f out: kpt om same pce fnl f* **9/1**

-453 **8** *3/4* **Spring Goddess (IRE)**[9] 6537 7-9-6 74........................ JamieSpencer 1 74
(A P Jarvis) *hld up in midfield on inner: n.m.r briefly 2f out: sn rdn and unable qck: kpt on same pce fnl f* **15/2**[2]

0035 **9** *nk* **Millfield (IRE)**[11] 6491 5-9-5 73........................ HayleyTurner 10 72
(P R Chamings) *stdd and dropped in bhd after s: t.k.h: rdn over 1f out: kpt on fnl f: nvr trbld ldrs* **15/2**[2]

5006 **10** *1/2* **Tinnarinka**[14] 6396 4-9-1 69........................ RichardHughes 7 67
(R Hannon) *racd on outer in midfield: rdn and unable qck over 2f out: plugged on same pce u.p fr over 1f out* **14/1**

4311 **11** *1 1/2* **Gazboolou**[14] 6380 4-9-4 72........................ DaneO'Neill 5 66
(David Pinder) *chsd ldrs: rdn over 2f out: no prog: wknd ent fnl f* **9/2**[1]

0510 **12** *4 1/2* **Colour Trooper (IRE)**[19] 6256 3-9-4 75........................ JimCrowley 11 59
(P Winkworth) *chsd ldrs: rdn over 2f out: wknd wl over 1f out: no ch and eased ins fnl f* **10/1**

1m 36.23s (-1.97) **Going Correction** -0.175s/f (Stan) course record
WFA 3 from 4yo+ 3lb **12** Ran SP% **123.9**
Speed ratings (Par 103): **102,101,101,100,100 100,99,99,98,98 96,92**
toteswinger: 1&2 £21.70, 1&3 £10.60, 2&3 £3.20. CSF £148.47 CT £741.69 TOTE £11.70: £4.10, £2.60, £2.10; EX 126.80 TRIFECTA Not won..
Owner Canisbay Bloodstock **Bred** Mrs A Rothschild & London Thoroughbred Services L **Trained** Epsom, Surrey

FOCUS
An ordinary handicap, but quite a competitive one. The early pace didn't appear that strong though, and that was probably a help to those that raced handily as the winner and third were at the sharp end throughout. The winner is rated close to his summer form.
Gazboolou Official explanation: trainer had no explanation for the poor form shown

6739 NEWS INTERNATIONAL EBF CONDITIONS STKS 6f (P)
4:00 (4:02) (Class 4) 2-Y-O **£4,415** (£1,321; £660; £330; £164) **Stalls** Low

Form RPR

2106 **1** **Global City (IRE)**[18] 6274 2-9-4 85........................(t) LDettori 5 93+
(Saeed Bin Suroor) *chsd ldr after 1f: chal and carried wd bnd 2f out: led ent fnl f: rdn clr fnl f: r.o strly* **15/8**[2]

521 **2** *3 1/4* **Spanish Baron (USA)**[60] 5089 2-9-4 78........................(t) EddieAhern 2 83
(R M H Cowell) *s.i.s: hdwy to ld after 1f: rdn and hung rt bnd 2f out: hdd ent fnl f: no ch w wnr after* **15/2**[3]

2010 **3** *1* **Blown It (USA)**[75] 4588 2-9-2 82........................ ShaneKelly 1 78
(J A Osborne) *hld up in last pl: hdwy on inner 2f out: sn ev ch and rdn: wknd fnl f* **12/1**

51 **4** *4 1/2* **Calligrapher (USA)**[20] 6230 2-9-4 91........................ PhilipRobinson 3 67+
(M A Jarvis) *led for 1f: chsd ldng pair but nvr looked happy after: rdn 3f out: wknd ent fnl f* **4/5**[1]

1230 **5** *nk* **Countrywide City (IRE)**[9] 6525 2-9-2 82........................ AlanMunro 4 64
(P W Chapple-Hyam) *racd in last pair: rdn and effrt 2f out: sn swtchd lft: wknd ent fnl f* **20/1**

1m 10.75s (-1.15) **Going Correction** -0.175s/f (Stan) 2y crse rec **5** Ran SP% **114.6**
Speed ratings (Par 97): **100,95,94,88,87**
toteswinger: 1&2 £10.10. CSF £15.90 TOTE £3.30: £1.60, £2.80; EX 15.10.
Owner Godolphin **Bred** Mrs Monica Hackett **Trained** Newmarket, Suffolk

FOCUS
This was a fair conditions event run in a course record for juveniles, helped by a slight tailwind in the straight.

NOTEBOOK
Global City(IRE), a Yarmouth maiden winner earlier in the season, looked to be crying out for a step up to 6f when finishing sixth off a mark of 89 on his nursery debut at Chester (poor draw didn't help) and he really came strong inside the final furlong, getting well on top in the final 100 yards. With the favourite failing to run a race it is hard to tell how much he achieved, but he was tried in a Group 3 on his third start and may well be capable of better at this distance. (op 11-4)
Spanish Baron(USA) has progressed with each run and scored narrowly at the third attempt on the turf here in August. He had work to do at the weights though, officially being rated 7lb inferior to the winner, and this was as good a run as connections could have hoped for. He ran wide into the straight but kept on well and continues to go the right way. (op 9-1 tchd 11-1 and 7-1)
Blown It(USA), whose Wolverhampton maiden win was sandwiched between two down-the-field runs in Group 2 events (latterly in first-time blinkers) was going without the headgear on this occasion and ran an improved race. He was produced to have every chance off the final bend, but could find no more inside the final furlong. (op 10-1)
Calligrapher(USA) was a huge disappointment. The form of his narrow Pontefract win had received a nice boost when the runner-up Film Set won tidily at Newbury next time and he set a high standard, being officially rated at least 6lb higher than all his rivals. This was his first try on the surface though, and he never looked happy, being ridden down the side of the track and never threatening to take part in the finish. He has already shown himself to be better than this and probably deserves another chance back on turf. Official explanation: trainer said, regarding running, that the gelding never travelled (op 4-6 tchd 8-13)
Countrywide City(IRE) is exposed and ran as though something was amiss at Pontefract last time on his nursery debut. He briefly looked a danger as they started to round the final bend, but he could not pick up in the straight and ended up well held.

6740 HIGGS INTERNATIONAL H'CAP 2m (P)
4:30 (4:30) (Class 6) (0-65,65) 3-Y-0+ **£2,047** (£604; £302) **Stalls** Low

Form RPR

1516 **1** **Coda Agency**[138] 2567 5-9-8 57........................ NCallan 1 71
(D W P Arbuthnot) *chsd ldrs: wnt 2nd over 2f out: led wl over 1f out: clr ent fnl f: styd on strly* **4/1**[1]

0505 **2** *4 1/2* **Forget It**[14] 6403 3-9-2 62........................ RichardHughes 10 71
(R Hannon) *led tl over 7f out: chsd ldrs after: rdn over 2f out: chsd wnr over 1f out: no imp* **9/2**[2]

5115 **3** *4 1/2* **Astrodome**[26] 6092 3-9-5 65........................ J-PGuillambert 3 69
(Sir Mark Prescott) *stdd s: hld up in rr: hdwy 3f out: rdn 2f out: styd on to 3rd ins fnl f: nvr nr ldng pair* **7/1**

0424 **4** *1* **The Composer**[16] 6329 6-9-6 55........................ SteveDrowne 2 57
(M Blanshard) *in tch in midfield: drvn jst over 2f out: sn unable qck: plugged on same pce* **8/1**

0032 **5** 1 1/4 **Irish Ballad**[32] 5917 6-9-1 **50**........................ NickyMackay 6 51
(S Dow) *chsd ldr: rdn to ld over 2f out: hdd wl over 1f out: wknd qckly jst over 1f out* **6/1**[3]

3306 **6** hd **Adage**[13] 6421 5-8-10 **45**........................(t) DaneO'Neill 11 46
(David Pinder) *stdd s: hld up towards rr: rdn and unable qck over 3f out: plugged on u.p fr over 1f out: nvr threatened ldrs* **10/1**

0-66 **7** 2 1/2 **Garrulous (UAE)**[63] 4978 5-9-9 **63**........................ DavidProbert(5) 4 61
(G L Moore) *t.k.h: hld up towards rr: hdwy over 3f out: chsd ldrs and rdn 2f out: sn btn* **7/1**

1305 **8** 7 **Champagne Shadow (IRE)**[182] 1408 7-9-11 **60**........(p) JerryO'Dwyer 5 49
(J Pearce) *hld up in midfield: rdn 5f out: drvn and wknd 3f out: wl bhd last 2f* **14/1**

063 **9** 1 **Beckenham's Secret**[46] 5489 4-8-10 **45**........................ ShaneKelly 9 33
(A W Carroll) *stdd s: hld up in rr: rdn 4f out: wknd wl over 2f out: no ch last 2f* **20/1**

5000 **10** 4 1/2 **Flame Creek (IRE)**[31] 5934 12-9-9 **58**........................ EdwardCreighton 12 41
(E J Creighton) *stdd s: hld up in rr: short lived effrt 3f out: wl bhd last 2f: eased ins fnl f* **20/1**

5620 **11** 1 **Daring Racer (GER)**[40] 5676 5-9-8 **57**........................ IanMongan 7 38
(Mrs L J Mongan) *chsd ldrs tl hdwy to ld over 7f out: rdn and hdd over 2f out: wknd qckly wl over 1f out: wl btn and eased ins fnl f* **14/1**

0/60 **12** 9 **Jomelamin**[51] 4811 6-8-10 **45**........................(t) EddieAhern 8 16
(M Sheppard) *hld up in midfield: lost pl 5f out: bhd and toiling over 3f out: t.o and eased fnl f* **33/1**

3m 22.53s (-3.17) **Going Correction** -0.175s/f (Stan)
WFA 3 from 4yo+ 11lb 12 Ran SP% **123.5**
Speed ratings (Par 101): **100,97,95,95,94 94,93,89,89,86 86,81**
toteswinger: 1&2 £6.50, 1&3 £8.50, 2&3 £8.00. CSF £22.03 CT £127.29 TOTE £5.60: £1.90, £2.60, £2.30; EX 22.60 Trifecta £182.60 Part won. Pool: £246.84 - 0.69 winning units..
Owner Banfield, Thompson **Bred** Baydon House Stud **Trained** Compton, Berks

FOCUS
A moderate staying handicap and the pace was very slow on the first circuit, but they still finished well spread out. Reasonable for for the grade.
Flame Creek(IRE) Official explanation: jockey said gelding hung left

6741 SMITHS NEWS H'CAP — 1m 2f (P)
5:00 (5:03) (Class 5) (0-70,70) 3-Y-O — **£2,590** (£770; £385; £192) **Stalls** Low

Form RPR

0024 **1** **Princess India (IRE)**[12] 6437 3-8-10 **62**........................ JimCrowley 7 71+
(P Winkworth) *s.i.s: t.k.h: hld up in rr: swtchd wl over 1f out: stl plenty to do ent fnl f: str run ins fnl f to ld nr fin* **4/1**[2]

1200 **2** 3/4 **Smarterthanuthink (USA)**[20] 6235 3-9-0 **66**........................ PaulHanagan 3 73
(R A Fahey) *led: rdn and hung rt fr 2f out: battled on gamely tl hdd and no ex nr fin* **16/1**

0000 **3** 1 3/4 **James Pollard (IRE)**[12] 6437 3-8-8 **60**........................ JamieSpencer 2 64
(D R C Elsworth) *t.k.h: hld up wl in tch: hdwy to chse ldr over 2f out: drvn over 1f out: hung rt and one pce fnl f* **9/4**[1]

2244 **4** nk **Valento**[9] 6544 3-9-0 **66**........................(p) StephenCarson 14 69
(Eve Johnson Houghton) *t.k.h: racd on outer in midfield: rdn and effrt wd bnd 2f out: chsd ldrs ins fnl f: kpt on same pce fnl 100yds* **9/1**

0301 **5** nk **Royal Straight**[29] 5994 3-9-4 **70**........................ NCallan 4 72
(B N Pollock) *hld up in midfield: hdwy on inner over 3f out: chsd ldng pair and drvn over 1f out: hung rt and one pce fnl f* **11/2**[3]

5-06 **6** 1 **Danse The Blues**[14] 6393 3-8-13 **65**........................ RichardHughes 12 65
(E A L Dunlop) *hld up in rr: rdn and effrt 3f out: hdwy 2f out: chsd ldrs ent fnl f: no imp fnl f* **15/2**

0063 **7** 1 1/2 **American Madness (USA)**[20] 6227 3-8-8 **60**........................ ShaneKelly 1 57
(M G Quinlan) *s.i.s: hld up towards rr: hdwy on inner over 1f out: kpt on but nvr rchd ldrs* **12/1**

5160 **8** 1/2 **Redsensor**[23] 6173 3-8-5 **57**........................ LiamJones 10 53
(M Quinn) *hld up in midfield: rdn and unable qck over 3f out: kpt on same pce u.p last 2f* **50/1**

630 **9** 1 1/2 **Soggy Dollar**[51] 5362 3-9-4 **70**........................ SaleemGolam 11 63
(M H Tompkins) *chsd ldr tl over 2f out: sn drvn: wknd ent fnl f* **33/1**

0200 **10** nk **Brave Mave**[30] 5964 3-9-1 **67**........................ AlanMunro 9 60
(W Jarvis) *stdd s: hld up in last pl: rdn 3f out: nvr nr ldrs* **16/1**

2300 **11** 1 **Speyside (IRE)**[13] 6422 3-9-1 **67**........................(p) EddieAhern 5 58
(J W Hills) *hld up towards rr: rdn and effrt 2f out: keeping on same pce and wl hld whn nt clr run and edging out rt ins fnl f* **14/1**

2302 **12** 2 1/4 **Just Mossie**[11] 6492 3-8-2 **57**........................(p) LukeMorris(3) 13 43
(W G M Turner) *chsd ldrs tl wknd u.p over 2f out: wl btn fnl f* **16/1**

20 **13** 1/2 **Nawaahi (IRE)**[30] 5962 3-8-13 **65**........................ JamesDoyle 8 50
(K A Morgan) *hld up in midfield: drvn 4f out: struggling fr over 2f out* **50/1**

44-0 **14** shd **Freedom Song**[86] 4253 3-9-4 **70**........................ SteveDrowne 6 55
(R Charlton) *in tch: drvn 4f out: wknd over 2f out* **12/1**

2m 5.31s (-1.29) **Going Correction** -0.175s/f (Stan) 14 Ran SP% **134.5**
Speed ratings (Par 101): **98,97,96,95,95 94,93,93,91,91 90,89,88,88**
toteswinger: 1&2 £19.10, 1&3 £3.40, 2&3 £15.10. CSF £75.17 CT £188.61 TOTE £6.00: £2.20, £7.30, £1.40; EX 101.90 TRIFECTA Not won. Place 6: £86.49 Place 5: £44.99 .
Owner The Hon Mrs C Cameron **Bred** C H Wacker Iii **Trained** Chiddingfold, Surrey

FOCUS
An ordinary if competitive handicap to end the card and as dramatic a finish as you are likely to see, even at Lingfield. Sound form, rated through the second and fourth.
James Pollard(IRE) Official explanation: jockey said colt ran too free and hung right in straight
Speyside(IRE) Official explanation: jockey said gelding was denied a clear run
T/Plt: £148.30 to a £1 stake. Pool: £63,629.32. 313.12 winning tickets. T/Qpdt: £112.20 to a £1 stake. Pool: £4,004.64. 26.40 winning tickets. SP

6333 BRIGHTON (L-H)
Thursday, October 16

OFFICIAL GOING: Good (good to soft in places; 7.4)
Wind: Moderate, half behind Weather: Fine

6745 EUROPEAN BREEDERS FUND MEDIAN AUCTION MAIDEN STKS — 7f 214y
2:30 (2:30) (Class 5) 2-Y-O — **£3,469** (£1,038; £519; £259; £129) **Stalls** Low

Form RPR

04 **1** **Tottie**[15] 6391 2-8-12 0........................ JimCrowley 12 80+
(Mrs A J Perrett) *sn trcking ldrs: effrt and hung lft fnl 2f: led ins fnl f: rdn clr* **5/1**[2]

023 **2** 2 1/4 **Roman Glory (IRE)**[14] 6425 2-9-3 82........................ RichardHughes 8 79
(B J Meehan) *prom: led over 2f out: hrd rdn over 1f out: hdd and no ex ins fnl f* **8/11**[1]

5 **3** 3 1/2 **Midnight In May (IRE)**[22] 6198 2-9-3 0........................ MartinDwyer 3 71
(W R Muir) *t.k.h: hdwy to ld after 2f: hdd over 2f out: wknd fnl f* **7/1**[3]

002 **4** 4 1/2 **Celtic Commitment**[24] 6165 2-9-3 70........................ PatDobbs 5 61
(R Hannon) *in tch: rdn 3f out: styd on same pce: no imp* **25/1**

5 1 **Repealed** 2-9-3 0........................ TravisBlock 4 59+
(H Morrison) *s.i.s: hld up in rr: rdn over 3f out: styd on fnl 2f* **28/1**

60 **6** 2 **Spring Secret**[90] 4151 2-9-3 0........................ CatherineGannon 10 55
(B Palling) *towards rr and wd: rdn over 3f out: mod late hdwy* **125/1**

503 **7** 3 **Phoenix Enforcer**[15] 6391 2-8-12 74........................ DO'Donohoe 11 43
(George Baker) *w ldrs tl wknd 2f out* **20/1**

0 **8** 1/2 **Astrobrava**[15] 6392 2-8-12 0........................ SaleemGolam 2 42
(M H Tompkins) *in rr of midfield: rdn and no hdwy fnl 3f* **100/1**

02 **9** 1 1/4 **Parc Des Princes (USA)**[17] 6333 2-9-3 0........................ WilliamBuick 9 44+
(A M Balding) *led 2f: rdn 4f out: wknd over 2f out* **9/1**

00 **10** 3 3/4 **New Adventure**[27] 6085 2-9-3 0........................ LPKeniry 1 36
(P F I Cole) *sn in tch on rail: rdn over 3f out: sn wknd* **66/1**

5503 **11** 3 3/4 **Buddy Marvellous (IRE)**[47] 5488 2-9-3 55........................ TGMcLaughlin 7 28
(R A Harris) *mid-div tl wknd 3f out* **100/1**

0000 **12** 11 **Ain't Talkin'**[8] 6572 2-9-3 58........................ PaulDoe 6 4
(M J Attwater) *s.s: towards rr: rdn 4f out: sn bhd* **100/1**

1m 37.4s (1.40) **Going Correction** +0.25s/f (Good) **12** Ran SP% **114.4**
Speed ratings (Par 95): **103,100,97,92,91 89,86,86,85,81 77,66**
toteswinger: 1&2 £2.50, 1&3 £4.40, 2&3 £2.90. CSF £8.26 TOTE £6.80: £1.80, £1.10, £2.10; EX 9.80 Trifecta £49.70 Pool: £247.44 - 3.68 winning units..
Owner J H Richmond-Watson **Bred** Lawn Stud **Trained** Pulborough, W Sussex

FOCUS
A modest-looking maiden and though the pace looked ordinary, they still finished well spread out and the form looks solid rated around the placed horses. The runners tended to come up the centre of the track.

NOTEBOOK
Tottie ◆, who had finished just behind Phoenix Enforcer at Nottingham last time, reversed that form in no uncertain terms. Tracking the leaders throughout, she took a little time to respond to her rider's urgings but she relished the final climb and was going away from her rivals at the line. She will be put away now, but she is bred to be suited by middle-distances and should make a fair handicapper next year. (op 9-2 tchd 11-2)
Roman Glory(IRE), who had run very well in maidens at the top tracks in his last two starts, was up with the pace the whole way and he had every chance, but was unable to cope with the filly late on. He set the standard with an official rating of 82 and it remains to be seen whether he has run close to that with nurseries in mind. (op 10-11 tchd 4-6)
Midnight In May(IRE), who ran green before showing some ability on his Goodwood debut, pulled his way to the front at halfway and battled on quite well when challenged. He may well come on again for this and will be especially interesting when handicapped after one more run. Official explanation: vet said colt was struck into (op 13-2 tchd 6-1)
Celtic Commitment was close enough if good enough, but couldn't stop the front three from getting away from him and looked short of pace. Already rated 70, he may be better off in nurseries, while he improved no end when stepped up to this trip on Polytrack last time, so it may be that he prefers that surface.
Repealed, a half-brother to the 1m2f-winner Masterofthecourt and the top-class Greys Inn, was the only newcomer in the field. He was inclined to run green out the back in the early stages, but showed a bit of ability as the contest progressed and is likely to improve with racing. (op 25-1 tchd 33-1)

6746 BOB DALEY MEMORIAL H'CAP — 7f 214y
3:00 (3:02) (Class 6) (0-60,60) 3-Y-O — **£2,331** (£693; £346; £173) **Stalls** Low

Form RPR

0123 **1** **Kannon**[69] 4825 3-9-3 **59**........................ JimCrowley 6 68
(W J Knight) *prom: led ins fnl 2f: jnd by runner-up ins fnl f: drvn to hold on: gamely* **13/2**[2]

6431 **2** nk **Croeso Cusan**[35] 5816 3-8-12 **59**........................ SophieDoyle(5) 2 67
(J L Spearing) *hld up towards rr: hdwy 2f out: drvn to join wnr ins fnl f: jst outpcd nr fin* **13/2**[2]

0000 **3** 4 1/2 **Mganga**[3] 6712 3-9-0 **56**........................(v[1]) TonyCulhane 8 54
(M R Channon) *dwlt: sn in midfield: effrt over 2f out: kpt on u.p to take 3rd wl ins fnl f: nt trble first 2* **16/1**

0034 **4** 1/2 **Hobson**[42] 5639 3-9-4 **60**........................ StephenCarson 3 57
(Eve Johnson Houghton) *led tl ins fnl 2f: wknd fnl f* **8/1**[3]

306 **5** 1 1/4 **Jemiliah**[21] 6227 3-8-7 **56**........................ RossAtkinson(7) 7 50
(B G Powell) *towards rr: rdn 3f out: styd on fnl 2f: nt rch ldrs* **25/1**

4303 **6** 1 3/4 **Island Treasure**[15] 6396 3-9-3 **59**........................ TravisBlock 16 49
(H Morrison) *mid-div and wd: rdn 3f out: no imp* **8/1**[3]

3220 **7** 1 1/2 **Plumage**[16] 6353 3-9-4 **60**........................ LPKeniry 15 46
(M Blanshard) *mid-div: hdwy and prom 4f out: hrd rdn and outpcd 2f out: btn whn hung lft ins fnl f* **11/1**

0026 **8** 2 1/4 **Rockjumper**[35] 5837 3-8-10 **55**........................ JackMitchell(3) 5 36
(Mrs T J Hill) *prom tl hung lft and btn jst over 2f out* **11/1**

1066 **9** nk **Lancaster Lad (IRE)**[17] 6332 3-9-3 **59**........................(p) GeorgeBaker 13 40
(A B Haynes) *towards rr: hdwy and in tch 2f out: hung lft and wknd over 1f out* **20/1**

1204 **10** 7 **Circadian Rhythm**[21] 6227 3-9-3 **59**........................ J-PGuillambert 4 23
(S C Williams) *plld hrd: prom: hmpd on rail 5f out: hrd rdn and wknd 2f out: eased whn wl btn over 1f out* **10/1**

5244 **11** 1 **Nikolaievich (IRE)**[17] 6332 3-9-1 **57**........................(p) MartinDwyer 1 19
(P F I Cole) *missed break and lost 10l: wl bhd most of way: rdn 3f out: eased whn unable to get into contention fnl 2f* **9/1**

5000 **12** 1 1/2 **Miss Clarice (USA)**[58] 5167 3-9-0 **56**........................(p) WilliamBuick 12 15
(B J Meehan) *mid-div: rdn 4f out: sn bhd* **25/1**

5060 **13** 8 **Follow The Band**[8] 6571 3-8-13 **55**........................ PatDobbs 14 —
(R Hannon) *prom 1f: sn rdn and lost pl: bhd and drvn along fnl 4f* **50/1**

10 **14** 26 **Casela Park (IRE)**[6] 6631 3-9-4 **60**........................ RichardHughes 10 —
(S Kirk) *bolted to post and awkward at s: trckd ldrs tl eased and taken v wd 3f out: virtually p.u* **5/1**[1]

1m 37.25s (1.25) **Going Correction** +0.25s/f (Good) 14 Ran SP% **121.6**
Speed ratings (Par 99): **103,102,98,97,96 94,93,90,90,83 82,81,73,47**
toteswinger: 1&2 £5.30, 1&3 £33.40, 2&3 £34.10. CSF £46.79 CT £680.18 TOTE £7.40: £2.80, £2.10, £5.20; EX 28.20 Trifecta £180.50 Part won. Pool: £244.04 - 0.58 winning units..
Owner Mrs W W Fleming **Bred** Stourbank Stud **Trained** Patching, W Sussex
■ A first century of winners for Jim Crowley, in only his second full season on the Flat.

FOCUS
A moderate three-year-old handicap, the front pair came well clear, and again the runners came up the middle of the track. The winning time was just 0.15 seconds faster than the opening two-year-old maiden. The winner is rated up 6lb.
Nikolaievich(IRE) Official explanation: jockey said gelding was reluctant to jump when gates opened

Casela Park(IRE) Official explanation: jockey said gelding bolted to post and then lost its action

6747 BRIGHTON RACECOURSE (S) STKS 1m 3f 196y

3:30 (3:33) (Class 6) 3-Y-O **£1,942** (£578; £288; £144) **Stalls** High

Form RPR

0300 **1** **Sparkling Montjeu (IRE)**[2] 6719 3-8-7 50 DO'Donohoe 5 53
(George Baker) *prom: rdn to ld over 3f out: hdd over 1f out: drvn to regain ld ins fnl f: styd on wl* **13/2**[3]

5020 **2** *1* **Threestoneburn (USA)**[10] 6541 3-8-0 52 AndreaAtzeni(7) 9 51
(J R Boyle) *towards rr: hdwy 3f out: led over 1f out: edgd lft and hdd ins fnl f: one pce* **7/1**

6034 **3** *1 1/4* **Fleurs De Censier**[13] 6447 3-8-7 48 WilliamBuick 8 49
(D M Simcock) *hld up in midfield: hdwy 5f out: edgd lft and pressed ldrs over 1f out: one pce fnl f* **9/1**

0023 **4** *1* **Oronsay**[9] 6562 3-8-7 47 TGMcLaughlin 2 47
(B R Millman) *hld up in rr: hdwy 3f out: drvn to press ldrs over 1f out: no ex fnl f* **13/2**[3]

0365 **5** *6* **Balais Folly (FR)**[9] 6562 3-8-7 42 (p) MCGeran(5) 1 43
(B Palling) *chsd ldrs tl hrd rdn and wknd qckly over 1f out* **12/1**

4043 **6** *2 1/4* **Ask Nicely**[26] 6111 3-8-7 45 MartinDwyer 11 34
(W R Muir) *sn chsng ldr: led 6f out tl over 3f out: n.m.r and wknd over 1f out* **9/2**[1]

4104 **7** *8* **Havanavich**[15] 6374 3-9-4 54 RichardHughes 10 32
(S Kirk) *hld up in midfield: rdn 3f out: no rspnse: hung lft whn btn* **9/2**[1]

0600 **8** *10* **Dickie Valentine**[37] 5787 3-8-12 43 (p) VinceSlattery 4 10
(M R Bosley) *sn led: hdd 6f out: wknd and hung rt 3f out* **20/1**

3045 **9** *6* **Hoar Frost**[10] 6541 3-8-13 47 TonyCulhane 6 2
(M R Channon) *chsd ldrs: rdn along fr 7f out: wknd over 3f out* **6/1**[2]

0 **10** *9* **Marikova**[10] 6541 3-8-2 ow2 PNolan(7) 3 —
(A B Haynes) *s.s: plld hrd in rr: rdn 1/2-way: no ch fnl 4f* **100/1**

0100 **11** *49* **Ericarrow (IRE)**[89] 3614 3-8-13 59 LPKeniry 7 —
(M F Harris) *in tch: rdn and wknd 5f out: bhd fnl 4f* **33/1**

2m 36.83s (4.13) **Going Correction** +0.25s/f (Good) 11 Ran SP% **116.2**
Speed ratings (Par 99): **96,95,94,93,89 88,83,76,72,66 33**
toteswinger: 1&2 £9.20, 1&3 £14.70, 2&3 £16.00. CSF £50.01 TOTE £8.60: £2.30, £3.00, £2.90; EX 57.30 TRIFECTA Not won..The winner was bought in 3600gns.
Owner Jerry Jamgotchian **Bred** Quay Bloodstock **Trained** Moreton Morrell, Warwicks

FOCUS
A weak seller and the form, rated around winner and third, is very unlikely to amount to much. The early pace looked steady and the field were spread out right across the track starting the final climb.

6748 ENTREMETTIER MAIDEN STKS 1m 3f 196y

4:00 (4:04) (Class 5) 3-Y-O+ **£3,027** (£906; £453; £226; £112) **Stalls** High

Form RPR

2532 **1** **Crusoe's Return**[12] 6470 3-9-3 75 PatCosgrave 2 76
(L M Cumani) *broke wl: stdd to trck ldrs: hrd rdn and hung lft over 1f out: styd on u.p to ld fnl 30yds* **7/2**[2]

-304 **2** *nk* **Crazy About You (IRE)**[34] 5864 3-8-12 68 MichaelHills 4 70
(B W Hills) *prom: led 2f out tl over 1f out: hrd rdn and kpt on fnl f: nt qckn nr fin* **7/1**

022 **3** *3/4* **Inquest**[34] 5864 3-9-3 74 JimCrowley 1 74
(Mrs A J Perrett) *t.k.h: hld up towards rr: hdwy over 2f out: led over 1f out: hrd rdn fnl f: hdd and one pce fnl 30yds* **3/1**[1]

0422 **4** *1 1/2* **Hawk Flight (IRE)**[14] 6416 3-9-3 70 GeorgeBaker 9 72
(W R Muir) *stdd s: patiently rdn in rr: hdwy and hung lft 2f out: rdn to chse ldrs whn veered lft 1f out: nt run on* **3/1**[1]

4432 **5** *8* **Mushtaaq (USA)**[21] 6226 3-9-3 73 (p) MartinDwyer 5 59
(M A Jarvis) *sn led: hdd & wknd 2f out: eased whn wl btn fnl f* **4/1**[3]

3600 **6** *10* **Snake Hips**[115] 3310 4-9-10 45 CatherineGannon 8 43
(B Palling) *chsd ldr tl wknd qckly 3f out* **200/1**

060 **7** *29* **Force Tradition (IRE)**[149] 2291 3-9-3 65 SaleemGolam 3 —
(M H Tompkins) *dwlt: hld up in 6th: dropped to rr and rdn 4f out: sn bhd* **40/1**

0 **8** *2 3/4* **Cadeaux Fax**[35] 5813 3-8-10 PNolan(7) 6 —
(A B Haynes) *prom to 1/2-way: lost pl and drvn along towards rr after: bhd fnl 3f* **250/1**

0 **9** *15* **Indiana Fox**[8] 6583 5-9-5 RichardHughes 7 —
(B G Powell) *hld up in rr: hdwy and in tch 3f out: shkn up and wknd over 2f out: eased* **33/1**

2m 35.8s (3.10) **Going Correction** +0.25s/f (Good)
WFA 3 from 4yo+ 7lb 9 Ran SP% **111.0**
Speed ratings (Par 103): **99,98,98,97,91 85,65,64,54**
toteswinger: 1&2 £5.10, 1&3 £3.30, 2&3 £4.30. CSF £25.91 TOTE £4.50: £1.60, £1.80, £1.40; EX 26.50 Trifecta £91.50 Pool: £593.74 - 4.80 winning units..
Owner Castle Down Racing **Bred** Meon Valley Stud **Trained** Newmarket, Suffolk

FOCUS
An ordinary maiden featuring some frustrating sorts. The early pace was pretty modest and there were four in a line across the track half a furlong from home, but the winning time was still over a second quicker than the seller and the form looks sound enough.
Indiana Fox Official explanation: jockey said mare lost its action

6749 TRANSPLANTS IN MIND H'CAP 6f 209y

4:30 (4:31) (Class 5) (0-70,70) 3-Y-O+ **£3,108** (£924; £462; £230) **Stalls** Low

Form RPR

012 **1** **Sendreni (FR)**[6] 6631 4-9-0 64 RichardHughes 7 72
(M Wigham) *in tch: bmpd 3f out: wnt rt and bmpd sn after: led wl over 1f out: c to stands' rail and hld on wl u.p fnl f* **11/4**[1]

0660 **2** *hd* **Benedetto**[9] 6554 3-9-4 70 (p) JimCrowley 3 77
(Mrs A J Perrett) *hld up towards rr: hdwy 2f out: rdn to chal over 1f out: r.o* **8/1**

4600 **3** *1 1/4* **Ten Pole Tudor**[15] 6380 3-8-13 65 LPKeniry 2 69
(R A Harris) *hld up in rr: hdwy to chal ins fnl 2f: nt qckn fnl 50yds* **40/1**

0600 **4** *3/4* **Flying Goose (IRE)**[4] 6671 4-9-6 70 TGMcLaughlin 13 72+
(R A Harris) *lost 12l s and wl bhd: styd alone on ins rail st: v gd hdwy to press stands' side ldrs over 1f out: one pce* **12/1**

0102 **5** *3/4* **Kinnego Bay (IRE)**[9] 6554 3-9-4 70 MichaelHills 11 70
(B W Hills) *prom tl hrd rdn and no ex over 1f out* **13/2**[3]

2202 **6** *hd* **Ten To The Dozen**[17] 6335 5-8-10 60 (b[1]) TonyCulhane 4 59
(P W Hiatt) *hld up in rr: rdn 3f out: styd on wl fnl f* **6/1**[2]

3006 **7** *1 3/4* **Palmetto Point**[17] 6338 4-9-0 64 (tp) TravisBlock 12 59
(H Morrison) *in tch and wd: effrt 3f out: hung lft and outpcd fnl 2f* **13/2**[3]

0003 **8** *3 1/4* **Cinnamon Hill**[17] 6338 4-9-0 64 StephenCarson 8 50
(Eve Johnson Houghton) *slt ld tl wknd wl over 1f out* **20/1**

3261 **9** *3 1/2* **Romantic Verse**[27] 6088 3-9-2 68 (b) LiamJones 9 45
(W J Haggas) *plld hrd: chsd ldrs: swtchd lft to avoid trble and bmpd 3f out: bmpd and wknd over 2f out* **6/1**[2]

-006 **10** *2 1/4* **Inka Dancer (IRE)**[16] 6357 6-8-9 59 CatherineGannon 10 29
(B Palling) *w ldr tl wknd ins fnl 2f: eased whn btn jst over 1f out* **33/1**

P30 **11** *nk* **Torquemada (IRE)**[24] 6178 7-8-8 58 (t) PaulDoe 6 28
(M J Attwater) *towards rr: rdn 3f out: sn bhd* **28/1**

1m 24.38s (1.28) **Going Correction** +0.25s/f (Good)
WFA 3 from 4yo+ 2lb 11 Ran SP% **114.3**
Speed ratings (Par 103): **102,101,100,99,98 98,96,92,88,86 85**
toteswinger: 1&2 £6.40, 1&3 £29.60, 2&3 £42.00. CSF £23.24 CT £708.40 TOTE £3.00: £1.40, £3.80, £8.70; EX 29.60 Trifecta £185.80 Part won. Pool: £251.16 - 0.40 winning units..
Owner Allan Darke **Bred** H H The Aga Khan's Studs Sc **Trained** Newmarket, Suffolk
■ Stewards' Enquiry : Richard Hughes four-day ban: improper riding (Oct 30-31,Nov 1-2)
Liam Jones three-day ban: careless riding (Oct 30-31, Nov 1)

FOCUS
An ordinary handicap, but an extraordinary race in some ways and quite a rough one too. The winner only needed to match previous sand form to score, with doubts over most of this field.

6750 SUSSEX NEWSPAPERS H'CAP 5f 59y

5:00 (5:00) (Class 5) (0-75,73) 3-Y-O+ **£3,027** (£906; £453; £226; £112) **Stalls** Low

Form RPR

0621 **1** **Rocker**[15] 6388 4-9-3 72 GeorgeBaker 13 82
(G L Moore) *confidently rdn fr last pl: c alone to stands' rail ent st: hdwy over 1f out: r.o to ld ins fnl f: readily* **5/1**[3]

4523 **2** *1 1/4* **Make My Dream**[17] 6340 5-9-2 71 JimCrowley 3 77
(J Gallagher) *prom: led over 1f out tl ins fnl f: nt pce of wnr* **5/2**[1]

6012 **3** *1/2* **Desperate Dan**[17] 6328 7-8-8 70 (b) PNolan(7) 5 74
(A B Haynes) *towards rr: hmpd 3f out: rdn and hdwy over 1f out: c towards stands' rail: kpt on* **17/2**

4023 **4** *1 1/4* **Hart Of Gold**[53] 5315 4-8-12 67 LPKeniry 2 67
(R A Harris) *in tch: drvn to press ldrs over 1f out: hung lft: no ex* **11/2**

1226 **5** *shd* **Matterofact (IRE)**[5] 6658 5-9-1 70 TGMcLaughlin 8 69
(M S Saunders) *in tch: drvn to press ldrs over 1f out: no ex ins fnl f* **3/1**[2]

4610 **6** *1 1/4* **Azygous**[17] 6339 5-8-8 63 (v[1]) StephenCarson 14 58
(J Akehurst) *sn rdn up to press ldr: led over 3f out tl over 1f out: wknd fnl f* **16/1**

0403 **7** *shd* **Cape Royal**[17] 6328 8-8-12 72 MCGeran(5) 7 66
(J M Bradley) *bhd: rdn and hdwy 2f out: pressed ldrs over 1f out: sn wknd* **12/1**

3030 **8** *6* **Kalligal**[15] 6388 3-8-7 62 RobertHavlin 6 35
(R Ingram) *led over 1f: prom tl hrd rdn and wknd over 1f out* **20/1**

63.24 secs (0.94) **Going Correction** +0.25s/f (Good) 8 Ran SP% **114.5**
Speed ratings (Par 103): **102,100,99,97,97 95,94,85**
toteswinger: 1&2 £3.50, 1&3 £3.60, 2&3 £6.30. CSF £17.96 CT £103.47 TOTE £5.00: £1.80, £1.10, £2.20; EX 16.40 Trifecta £35.90 Pool: £297.63 - 6.13 winning units. Place 6: £84.86 Place 5: £76.68.
Owner Sir Eric Parker **Bred** Sir Eric Parker **Trained** Woodingdean, E Sussex
■ Stewards' Enquiry : L P Keniry three-day ban: careless riding (Oct 30-31, Nov 1)

FOCUS
A modest sprint handicap, weakened further by six non-runners. The entire field came over to the stands' side this time and, despite what looked a decent pace, there were seven in a line across the track inside the last furlong. The form is best rated around the placed horses.
T/Jkpt: Not won. T/Plt: £23.80 to a £1 stake. Pool: £71,217.48. 2,177.19 winning tickets. T/Qpdt: £11.50 to a £1 stake. Pool: £3,837.34. 246.90 winning tickets. LM

6679 GREAT LEIGHS (A.W) (L-H)

Thursday, October 16

OFFICIAL GOING: Standard
Wind: Moderate, across Weather: dry, chilly

6751 ORWELL APPRENTICE H'CAP (DIV I) 1m (P)

5:50 (5:51) (Class 6) (0-55,55) 3-Y-O+ **£1,942** (£578; £288; £144) **Stalls** Centre

Form RPR

-565 **1** **Accolation**[35] 5832 4-8-5 46 oh1 CharlesEddery(3) 8 55
(Pat Eddery) *mde all: sn crossed to rail: jnd over 1f out: forged ahd ins fnl f: styd on wl* **6/1**

6003 **2** *3 3/4* **Fantasy Fighter (IRE)**[21] 6224 3-8-5 46 JamieKyne 9 46
(J J Quinn) *chsd wnr: clr w wnr over 2f out: upsides over 1f out: rdn and flashed tail 1f out: fnd little and btn fnl f* **15/2**

/0-5 **3** *1 1/2* **Keep Your Distance**[14] 6422 4-9-0 55 DebraEngland(3) 2 52
(P J McBride) *hld up towards rr: hdwy over 3f out: chsd clr ldng pair over 2f out: kpt on fnl f but nvr able to chal* **7/2**[2]

0003 **4** *2* **Wadnagin (IRE)**[36] 5797 4-8-6 47 JamesRogers(3) 3 39
(I A Wood) *hld up towards rr: v wd bnd 3f out: styd on u.p fnl f: nvr nr ldrs* **11/2**[3]

-000 **5** *3/4* **Miss Okaloosa**[129] 2898 3-8-8 49 (p) NSLawes 5 40
(D M Simcock) *hld up in rr: hdwy and rdn jst over 3f out: swtchd lft wl over 1f out: hld hd high and no imp after* **50/1**

0440 **6** *3/4* **Border Artist**[17] 6335 9-8-3 46 oh1 (p) TobyAtkinson(5) 6 35
(J Pearce) *hld up towards rr: hdwy over 3f out: rdn over 2f out: no imp last 2f* **20/1**

5000 **7** *3* **The Young Fella**[35] 5832 3-8-5 53 ow5 HollyHall(7) 11 35
(S A Callaghan) *in tch: rdn and outpcd over 2f out: n.d after* **16/1**

0000 **8** *5* **Talamahana**[35] 5832 3-8-2 46 oh1 (p) RichardRowe(3) 7 16
(A B Haynes) *hld up towards rr on outer: lost pl bnd over 3f out: no ch after* **40/1**

000- **9** *1* **Divine White**[13] 6311 5-8-6 49 oh1 ow3 BradleyRoper(5) 10 17
(P Bowen) *chsd ldrs: rdn over 3f out: sn struggling: no ch last 2f* **50/1**

3534 **10** *13* **Peas In A Pod**[12] 6492 3-8-11 52 (v[1]) RosieJessop 1 —
(J R Best) *chsd ldr tl over 2f out: sn rdn and struggling: wl bhd fnl f: t.o* **3/1**[1]

0006 **11** *57* **Ramblin Bob**[35] 5832 3-8-0 46 oh1 (t) MatthewLawson(5) 4 —
(W J Musson) *rrd and v awkward leaving stalls: sn veered bdly rt: continued t.o thrght* **12/1**

1m 42.04s (2.14) **Going Correction** +0.175s/f (Slow)
WFA 3 from 4yo+ 3lb 11 Ran SP% **113.4**
Speed ratings (Par 101): **96,92,90,88,88 87,84,79,78,65 8**
toteswinger: 1&2 £10.70, 1&3 £10.70, 2&3 Not won. CSF £46.83 CT £181.52 TOTE £6.80: £2.70, £2.30, £2.40; EX 58.60.
Owner Pat Eddery Racing (Law Society) **Bred** Brick Kiln Stud, Mrs L Hicks & Partners **Trained** Nether Winchendon, Bucks

FOCUS
A typically weak race of its type in which six of the runners competed from out of the handicap. It was run at a fair pace and nothing managed to land a blow from off the pace. The runner-up is the best guide but the form is not that solid.
Peas In A Pod Official explanation: vet said gelding scoped dirty

6752 ORWELL APPRENTICE H'CAP (DIV II) 1m (P)
6:20 (6:20) (Class 6) (0-55,55) 3-Y-O+ **£1,942** (£578; £288; £144) **Stalls** Centre

Form RPR
040 **1** **Margot Mine (IRE)**21 6228 3-8-2 47....(bt) MatthewLawson(5) 7 52
(J S Moore) *s.i.s: hld up bhd: hmpd bnd over 3f out: 9th whn swtchd rt and bmpd rival wl over 1f out: str run over 1f out to ld fnl 100yds: sn clr* **3/1**1

2630 **2** 2 1/4 **Reve Vert (FR)**28 6047 3-8-12 55.... DebraEngland(3) 9 55
(A W Carroll) *led: rdn wl over 1f out: kpt on tl hdd and nt pce of wnr fnl 100yds* **3/1**1

000- **3** 1 **Mocha Java**337 6809 5-8-8 45.... NSLawes 1 43
(M Salaman) *chsd ldrs: rdn to press ldr wl over 1f out: unable qckn u.p ins fnl f* **20/1**

5000 **4** 1/2 **General Tufto**9 6562 3-8-6 49.... RichardRowe(3) 3 46
(C Smith) *bhd: detached last 4f out: rdn and hdwy 3f out: bmpd wl over 1f out: kpt on fnl f: nvr quite getting to ldrs* **22/1**

0000 **5** hd **Tapas Lad (IRE)**24 6173 3-8-6 51 ow1....(v) BradleyRoper(5) 11 47
(G J Smith) *stdd and dropped in bhd after s: stdy hdwy over 3f out: rdn wl over 1f out: kpt on steadily fnl f: nvr quite getting to ldrs* **8/1**3

0000 **6** 2 **Marvin Gardens**30 6003 5-8-6 48.... TobyAtkinson(5) 2 39
(P S McEntee) *chsd ldr tl wl over 1f out: wknd u.p jst ins fnl f* **22/1**

0040 **7** 1/2 **Jimmy Dean**24 6173 3-8-5 45....(tp) SoniaEaton 5 35
(M Wellings) *t.k.h: hld up in midfield: hdwy over 2f out: rdn and no imp fr wl over 1f out* **25/1**

0005 **8** 5 **Tarraburn (USA)**29 6036 4-8-12 54.... AntiocoMurgia(5) 10 33
(G C H Chung) *chsd ldrs: rdn and struggling over 2f out: no ch fr over 1f out* **7/2**2

3400 **9** 23 **Our Dolly**51 5379 3-8-6 46.... JamieKyne 6 —
(Garry Moss) *chsd ldrs: rdn 5f out: struggling over 3f out: wl bhd and virtually p.u fnl f: t.o* **16/1**

00/0 **10** 32 **Jiggy Spriggy (IRE)**22 6208 5-8-5 45....(p) CharlesEddery(3) 8 —
(H J Collingridge) *racd wd in midfield: rdn 4f out: lost tch 3f out: t.o and virtually p.u fnl f* **11/1**

1m 43.35s (3.45) **Going Correction** +0.175s/f (Slow)
WFA 3 from 4yo+ 3lb 10 Ran SP% **114.9**
Speed ratings (Par 101): **89,86,85,85,85 83,82,77,54,22**
toteswinger: 1&2 £5.60, 1&3 £3.00, 2&3 £5.60. CSF £10.99 CT £152.17 TOTE £4.60: £2.00, £1.70, £6.70; EX 12.00.
Owner Far And Wide Brigade **Bred** T C Butler **Trained** Upper Lambourn, Berks

FOCUS
This second division of the apprentice riders' handicap was run at a sound enough pace, but the form looks very ordinary.
Tarraburn(USA) Official explanation: trainer said gelding had a breathing problem
Jiggy Spriggy(IRE) Official explanation: jockey said mare lost its action

6753 BANQUETING AT GREAT LEIGHS H'CAP 1m 2f (P)
6:50 (6:55) (Class 6) (0-50,50) 3-Y-O+ **£1,942** (£578; £288; £144) **Stalls** Low

Form RPR
0436 **1** **Ba Dreamflight**8 6584 3-7-13 46.... JamieKyne(7) 4 56
(H Morrison) *chsd ldrs: rdn 4f out: led narrowly over 2f out: kpt on gamely u.p: all out* **9/1**

0000 **2** nk **Darley Star**58 5167 3-8-8 48.... TedDurcan 2 57
(C E Brittain) *led tl over 8f out: chsd ldr after: chsd wnr over 2f out: ev ch after: unable qckn u.p fnl f* **20/1**

0345 **3** 3/4 **Marie Tempest**42 5631 3-8-7 47.... MichaelHills 10 55
(B W Hills) *racd in midfield: niggled along 8f out: swtchd rt and rdn over 4f out: rdn and hdwy over 3f out: ev ch 1f out: unable qckn fnl f* **7/2**1

0365 **4** 1 **Golden Brown (IRE)**33 5912 4-8-12 47.... DarrenWilliams 15 53
(David Pinder) *hld up in last pair: hdwy over 3f out: pressed ldrs ent fnl f: kpt on same pce u.p fnl f* **8/1**3

3500 **5** 3/4 **Summer Bounty**7 6594 12-8-12 47.... JerryO'Dwyer 11 51
(F Jordan) *stdd s: hld up in rr: hdwy over 3f out: chsd ldrs u.p ent fnl f: kpt on same pce fnl f* **33/1**

5050 **6** 2 1/2 **Hatch A Plan (IRE)**8 6570 7-9-0 49.... J-PGuillambert 7 48
(Mouse Hamilton-Fairley) *hld up in rr: rdn and hdwy on outer over 3f out: chsd ldrs u.p over 1f out: wknd ins fnl f* **5/1**2

0000 **7** nk **Samahir (USA)**14 6422 4-8-12 47.... AlanMunro 6 45
(T T Clement) *hld up in tch: pushed along and lost pl over 3f out: swtchd rt and hdwy wl over 1f out: edgd lft u.p fnl f: kpt on but nvr gng pce to chal ldrs* **9/1**

4006 **8** 2 3/4 **Dawn Wind**17 6331 3-8-10 50....(b1) PatCosgrave 9 43
(I A Wood) *s.i.s: towards rr: hdwy 4f out: drvn and chsd ldrs over 1f out: wknd ent fnl f* **50/1**

0000 **9** 7 **Aura**29 6032 3-8-8 48.... RichardMullen 8 27
(H J L Dunlop) *hld up in midfield: rdn and struggling over 3f out: no ch last 2f* **40/1**

3455 **10** 1 3/4 **Limelight (USA)**13 6447 3-8-7 47.... DO'Donohoe 1 22
(Sir Mark Prescott) *s.i.s: sn pushed along: led over 8f out: clr 6f out: drvn and hdd over 2f out: wknd over 1f out* **9/1**

0000 **11** 5 **Feeling (IRE)**11 4664 4-8-9 49 ow1.... GabrielHannon(5) 13 14
(T T Clement) *hld up towards rr: hdwy on outer over 4f out: hung bdly lft over 2f out: wknd wl over 1f out* **100/1**

0006 **12** shd **Hawkstar Express (IRE)**21 6228 3-7-12 45....(t) RosieJessop(7) 5 10
(J R Boyle) *racd in midfield: pushed along 7f out: rdn and wknd 4f out: no ch last 2f* **14/1**

2606 **13** 13 **Kijivu**32 5931 3-8-8 48.... WilliamBuick 14 —
(A J Lidderdale) *hld up in tch: rdn and struggling over 3f out: wl bhd 2f out: eased fnl f: t.o* **16/1**

2300 **14** 18 **Fantasy Crusader**33 5912 9-8-10 45.... JimmyQuinn 12 —
(R M H Cowell) *in tch in midfield: rdn 4f out: sn hmpd and dropped to last wl over 3f out: t.o last 2f* **20/1**

0060 **P** **King Of Sparta (USA)**51 5378 3-8-9 49 ow1.... MickyFenton 3 —
(T J Fitzgerald) *s.i.s: t.k.h: sn wl in tch: rdn 4f out: wkng whn bdly hmpd over 2f out: sn eased: p.u over 1f out* **8/1**3

2m 11.14s (2.54) **Going Correction** +0.175s/f (Slow)
WFA 3 from 4yo+ 5lb 15 Ran SP% **121.5**
Speed ratings (Par 101): **96,95,95,94,93 91,91,89,83,82 78,78,67,53,—**
toteswinger: 1&2 £23.00, 1&3 £20.90, 2&3 £23.00. CSF £186.64 CT £759.43 TOTE £10.80: £2.40, £5.00, £2.40; EX 269.80.
Owner BA Racing **Bred** Chippenham Lodge Stud Ltd **Trained** East Ilsley, Berks

FOCUS
This handicap was a seller in disguise. It was run at a decent early pace and provided a slow-motion finish. The form is rated around the runner-up and fourth.
Kijivu Official explanation: trainer said filly was unsuited by the track

6754 CASTLE HEDINGHAM H'CAP 1m 5f 66y(P)
7:20 (7:23) (Class 6) (0-65,64) 3-Y-O **£2,266** (£674; £337; £168) **Stalls** Low

Form RPR
0501 **1** **Highland Homestead**10 6541 3-8-8 61 6ex.... AndreaAtzeni(7) 4 69
(M R Hoad) *hld up in last pair: hdwy over 4f out: chsd clr ldr wl over 2f out: clsd steadily u.p: swtchd rt over 1f out: led fnl 100yds: styd on* **13/2**

0336 **2** nk **Bruki (IRE)**53 5322 3-9-0 60....(bt) JimmyQuinn 3 67
(M Botti) *prom in main gp: clsd over 4f out: led over 3f out: sn clr: rdn ent fnl f: hdd fnl 100yds: one pce* **7/2**3

4664 **3** 20 **Opera De Luna**15 6390 3-9-1 61.... DarrenWilliams 2 45
(D Shaw) *hld up in main gp: clsd on ldr over 4f out: wnt 2nd and rdn 3f out: sn btn: poor 3rd and eased fnl f* **2/1**1

0354 **4** 6 **Trinkila (USA)**13 6436 3-8-13 59.... AlanMunro 5 27
(P F I Cole) *chsd clr ldr: niggled along 10f out: rdn 5f out: wknd over 3f out: wl btn after: t.o* **11/4**2

5-50 **5** 13 **Greek Theatre (USA)**71 4732 3-9-2 62.... JerryO'Dwyer 6 11
(P S McEntee) *led and sn wl clr: c bk to field 4f out: hdd over 3f out: immediately btn: t.o last 2f* **22/1**

1060 **6** 1 **Emshabb**28 6049 3-9-4 64....(b1) LiamJones 1 11
(W J Haggas) *s.i.s: hld up in last pair: rdn over 4f out: lost tch over 3f out: t.o last 2f* **6/1**

2m 54.38s (0.78) **Going Correction** +0.175s/f (Slow) 6 Ran SP% **114.2**
Speed ratings (Par 99): **104,103,91,87,79 79**
toteswinger: 1&2 £3.10, 1&3 £1.10, 2&3 £3.10. CSF £29.82 TOTE £4.20: £4.00, £1.40; EX 34.20.
Owner Brick Farm Racing **Bred** Rowcliffe Stud **Trained** Lewes, E Sussex

FOCUS
A moderate staying handicap for three-year-olds. The first pair came nearly a distance clear with the runner-up the best guide to the level.

6755 COLNE MAIDEN STKS 6f (P)
7:50 (7:51) (Class 5) 2-Y-O **£3,885** (£1,156; £577; £288) **Stalls** Low

Form RPR
2 **1** **Audemar (IRE)**45 5572 2-9-3 0.... JamieSpencer 5 69+
(E F Vaughan) *trckd ldng pair: shkn up over 2f out: rdn and effrt wl over 1f out: edgd lft u.p: led ins fnl f: in command last 50yds* **1/5**1

0 **2** 1 1/4 **Dynamo Dane (IRE)**15 6389 2-9-3 0.... PatCosgrave 4 61+
(J G Given) *led tl 3f out: rdn to ld again over 1f out: edgd lft u.p and hdd ins fnl f: btn fnl 50yds* **20/1**3

0030 **3** 2 1/2 **Clerical (USA)**14 6414 2-8-10 50....(p) AndreaAtzeni(7) 1 53
(M J Gingell) *chsd ldr tl led 3f out: rdn 2f out: hdd over 1f out: wknd ins fnl f* **20/1**3

4 3/4 **Captain Carnival (IRE)** 2-9-3 0.... WilliamBuick 2 51+
(D W P Arbuthnot) *dwlt: in tch: rdn over 2f out: pressed ldrs over 1f out: kpt on same pce fnl f* **10/1**2

00 **5** 3 1/2 **Wunder Strike (USA)**9 6545 2-9-3 0.... DO'Donohoe 7 40
(M J Wallace, Australia) *a in last pair: rdn and outpcd 4f out: no ch after* **25/1**

6 11 **Always The Sun** 2-8-12 0.... MickyFenton 6 —
(P Leech) *a last: sn rdn along: lost tch 4f out: t.o and eased fnl f* **25/1**

1m 14.92s (1.22) **Going Correction** +0.175s/f (Slow) 6 Ran SP% **109.6**
Speed ratings (Par 95): **98,96,93,92,87 72**
toteswinger: 1&2 £5.50, 1&3 £4.70, 2&3 £9.80. CSF £6.91 TOTE £1.10: £1.02, £6.00; EX 6.10.
Owner Gute Freunde Partnership **Bred** Mrs Amanda Brudenell And Mr & Mrs R A **Trained** Newmarket, Suffolk

FOCUS
A very weak maiden which Audemar was entitled to win well. The form is rated around the third and fifth.

NOTEBOOK
Audemar(IRE) took full advantage of a golden opportunity to get off the mark and did not have to improve on the level of his Kempton debut second in September. He made very hard work of landing the odds, however, and still looked distinctly green as his rider had to get very serious at the furlong pole. It is probably more likely that he now needs a stiffer test though, as there is a lot of stamina on his dam's side and this will hardly damage his prospective handicap mark.
Dynamo Dane(IRE) got an aggressive ride and made the favourite pull out all the stops inside the final furlong. The step up a furlong was clearly to his liking and he is now getting the hang of things so could be placed to find an opening. (op 16-1)
Clerical(USA) has now run both of his most encouraging races at this venue, but he was still well held. With an official mark of 50 he helps to set the level of the form. (op 25-1)
Captain Carnival(IRE), whose dam was a winner over this trip, did not shape without ability on this racecourse bow and should come on nicely for the experience. (op 7-1)

6756 DOON NURSERY 1m (P)
8:20 (8:21) (Class 4) (0-85,84) 2-Y-O **£5,504** (£1,637; £818; £408) **Stalls** Centre

Form RPR
5201 **1** **Atabaas Allure (FR)**27 6087 2-9-0 77.... RoystonFfrench 4 81
(M Johnston) *chsd ldr: rdn and chal wl over 1f out: led jst ins fnl f: hld on gamely: all out* **4/1**1

2120 **2** 1/2 **Rapid Release (CAN)**76 4589 2-9-7 84.... J-PGuillambert 6 87
(Sir Mark Prescott) *chsd ldrs: squeezed between horses to chal ent fnl f: ev ch after: unable qckn fnl 100yds* **8/1**

01 **3** nk **Tobond (IRE)**15 6375 2-8-10 80.... AndreaAtzeni(7) 9 82
(M Botti) *hld up in tch: effrt and hung lft over 1f out: rdn and hung rt 1f out: pressed wnr and intimidated by rivals whip ins fnl f: nt qckn fnl 100yds* **9/2**2

1030 **4** 2 **Richo**9 6549 2-8-11 79.... FrederikTylicki(5) 1 77
(D H Brown) *led: rdn wl over 1f out: hdd jst ins fnl f: wknd fnl 100yds* **13/2**

532 **5** 3/4 **Kaloni (IRE)**29 6016 2-9-0 77.... MickyFenton 8 73
(Mrs P Sly) *hld up in midfield: rdn and effrt 2f out: pressed ldrs and drvn over 1f out: wknd ins fnl f* **9/1**

603 **6** 3/4 **Give Us A Song (USA)**19 6282 2-8-8 71.... TedDurcan 5 66+
(J S Moore) *t.k.h: hld up in midfield: effrt on inner and rdn wl over 1f out: kpt on same pce fnl f* **20/1**

0160 **7** 7 **Grand Honour (IRE)**14 6426 2-9-6 83.... JimmyQuinn 10 62
(P Howling) *hld up in last pair: rdn 3f out: wknd wl over 1f out: wl btn fnl f* **16/1**

501 **8** 3 1/2 **Master Fong (IRE)**22 6198 2-9-4 81.... MichaelHills 3 53
(B W Hills) *chsd ldrs: rdn 4f out: steadily lost pl: wl bhd fr over 1f out* **6/1**3

0150 **9** 6 **Swingfire (USA)**16 6362 2-8-9 72....(p) JamieSpencer 2 30
(R M H Cowell) *pushed along early: hld up in last pair: rdn and no rspnse over 2f out: wl bhd and eased ins fnl f* **14/1**

The Form Book, Raceform Ltd, Compton, RG20 6NL

030 **U** **Worth A King's**[28] 6057 2-8-7 **70**.. RyanMoore 7 —
(Sir Michael Stoute) *uns rdr leaving stalls* **6/1**[3]

1m 40.91s (1.01) **Going Correction** +0.175s/f (Slow) **10** Ran SP% **118.5**
Speed ratings (Par 97): **101,100,100,98,97 96,89,86,80,—**
toteswinger: 1&2 £4.70, 1&3 £3.90, 2&3 £13.10. CSF £36.94 CT £154.58 TOTE £4.80: £1.20, £2.50, £2.90; EX 22.40.
Owner Mrs R J Jacobs **Bred** Newsells Park Stud **Trained** Middleham Moor, N Yorks
■ Stewards' Enquiry : J-P Guillambert caution: careless riding.

FOCUS
This was a fair nursery, run at a sound pace. The race lost a fair amount of its interest when Worth A King's unseated Ryan Moore on coming out of the stalls but the form still looks solid rated around the second and fourth.

NOTEBOOK
Atabaas Allure(FR) followed up her Wolverhampton win 27 days earlier with a very gutsy effort from a 3lb higher mark. The extra furlong proved within range and she has now won both her outings in handicaps on this surface. Another rise in the weights is forthcoming, but further improvement cannot be ruled out. (op 11-4)
Rapid Release(CAN) had been left off since disappointing at Goodwood in July and was racing from a 6lb higher mark. He just missed out under top weight, getting the longer trip well, and showed his previous effort to be all wrong. This surface suits and there will no doubt be other days for him. (op 7-1 tchd 10-1)
Tobond(IRE), comfortably off the mark at Kempton 15 days previously, turned in an improved effort on this handicap bow yet failed to see out the extra furlong as well as the first pair. He remains on the up and a return to a sharper test could see him back to winning ways. (op 13-2)
Richo posted a better effort in defeat on this All-Weather debut, yet the aggressive tactics on this step up in trip found out his stamina and he effectively set the race up for the principals. (op 12-1)

6757 GREATLEIGHS.COM CLAIMING STKS 1m 2f (P)
8:50 (8:52) (Class 6) 3-Y-O **£2,266** (£674; £337; £168) **Stalls** Low

Form RPR
0420 **1** **Sabre Light**[14] 6424 3-8-9 72.......................(p) DavidProbert(5) 9 66+
(A Bailey) *hld up wl in tch: rdn and effrt wl over 2f out: led over 1f out: clr 1f out: pushed out fnl f: comf* **7/4**[1]
0F03 **2** *1 1/4* **Wabbraan (USA)**[71] 4750 3-8-10 56........................ RichardMullen 2 59
(D M Simcock) *chsd ldrs: drvn 5f out: lost pl and dropped to rr 4f out: rallied u.p 2f out: disp 2nd ins fnl f: kpt on but nvr trbld wnr* **20/1**
3 *nk* **Whentodream**[82] 3-9-3 75.. JohnEgan 5 65+
(M Botti) *plld hrd: hld up towards rr: plld to outer over 4f out: rdn and wd bnd 3f out: hdwy 2f out: hung lft but r.o to dispute 2nd ins fnl f: nvr gng pce to trble wnr* **16/1**[3]
-41 **4** *2 1/2* **Dazzling Begum**[9] 6562 3-8-8 0........................ JimmyQuinn 3 51
(J Pearce) *chsd ldr tl over 4f out and again over 3f out: rdn and ev ch briefly over 1f out: sn outpcd by wnr: wknd ins fnl f* **12/1**[2]
6660 **5** *1 3/4* **Pharaohs Queen (IRE)**[13] 6437 3-8-2 59.................. WilliamBuick 7 42
(E A L Dunlop) *hld up towards rr: hdwy 6f out: drvn 3f out: kpt on same pce last 2f* **12/1**[2]
06 **6** *hd* **Tropical Tradition (IRE)**[13] 6433 3-8-10 0.................. JimCrowley 8 50
(D W P Arbuthnot) *hld up in midfield: lost pl and dropped to rr over 3f out: sme hdwy u.p on inner over 1f out: nvr gng pce to trble ldrs* **20/1**
6000 **7** *4 1/2* **Little Firecracker**[21] 6227 3-8-4 53.................(p) SaleemGolam 10 35
(Miss M E Rowland) *hld up in midfield: lost pl 4f out: sn rdn: no imp u.p fr wl over 1f out* **66/1**
1-00 **8** *3 3/4* **Hold The Gold (IRE)**[12] 6467 3-9-8 78.................. JamieSpencer 1 53+
(E J O'Neill) *s.i.s: t.k.h: hld up in rr: rapid hdwy on outer to ld over 4f out: clr over 2f out: rdn and hdd over 1f out: immediately btn: eased ins fnl f* **7/4**[1]
2543 **9** *4* **Tank Commander**[10] 6541 3-8-10 55.......................... LiamJones 6 25
(W R Muir) *hld up in last pair: rapid hdwy on outer 5f out: chsd ldr over 4f out tl over 3f out: sn wknd* **12/1**[2]
5000 **10** *13* **Titfer (IRE)**[72] 4710 3-8-12 50.............................. TedDurcan 4 1
(A W Carroll) *led tl over 4f out: rdn and struggling over 3f out: wl bhd last 2f: eased fnl f: t.o* **66/1**

2m 10.51s (1.91) **Going Correction** +0.175s/f (Slow) **10** Ran SP% **114.2**
Speed ratings (Par 99): **99,98,97,95,94 94,90,87,84,74**
toteswinger: 1&2 £5.50, 1&3 £3.90, 2&3 £15.00. CSF £45.61 TOTE £3.50: £1.10, £4.80, £4.50; EX 63.80.Sabre Light was claimed by Mr Jeff Pearce for £12,000.
Owner A Bailey **Bred** D J And Mrs Deer **Trained** Newmarket, Suffolk

FOCUS
This claimer for three-year-olds was run at an average pace until halfway. The form is limited by the second with the winner a stone off his best.
Hold The Gold(IRE) Official explanation: vet said colt returned lame in right-hind

6758 TAY H'CAP 1m 2f (P)
9:20 (9:22) (Class 5) (0-75,75) 3-Y-O+ **£3,238** (£963; £481; £240) **Stalls** Low

Form RPR
1203 **1** **Suzi Spends (IRE)**[14] 6424 3-8-13 **72**.......................... JimmyQuinn 9 82+
(H J Collingridge) *hld up towards rr: hdwy over 3f out: chsd ldrs jst over 2f out: rdn to ld over 1f out: edgd lft but r.o wl fnl f* **11/4**[1]
15 **2** *1* **Vineyard**[64] 4984 3-9-2 **75**.. LiamJones 4 83
(W J Haggas) *t.k.h: hld up in midfield: rdn and effrt on inner wl over 1f out: chsd wnr ins fnl f: kpt on same pce fnl 100yds* **4/1**[2]
0004 **3** *3 1/2* **Master Pegasus**[7] 6599 5-8-12 **66**.......................... PatCosgrave 7 67
(J R Boyle) *hld up in midfield: hdwy over 3f out: chsd ldr over 2f out: rdn to ld wl over 1f out: sn hdd: wknd fnl f* **7/1**
31-0 **4** *1/2* **Phoenix Flight (IRE)**[13] 6450 3-9-2 **75**.................. J-PGuillambert 5 75+
(Sir Mark Prescott) *t.k.h: hld up in midfield: shuffled bk and dropped to rr over 4f out: swtchd rt and hdwy u.p over 1f out: kpt on but nvr gng pce to trble ldrs* **5/1**[3]
1440 **5** *1 3/4* **Monashee Rock (IRE)**[20] 6242 3-9-0 **73**.................. TGMcLaughlin 10 70
(M Salaman) *hld up in last pair: hdwy on outer 3f out: rdn wl over 1f out: no imp over 1f out* **25/1**
1033 **6** *3* **Supercast (IRE)**[17] 6346 5-9-5 **73**.......................... SamHitchcott 6 64
(N J Vaughan) *t.k.h: chsd ldrs: hdwy and w ldr over 4f out: led wl over 3f out: rdn over 2f out: hdd over 1f out: wknd fnl f* **12/1**
305 **7** *1* **Jo'Burg (USA)**[29] 6028 4-9-2 **70**.......................... JimCrowley 8 59
(Mrs A J Perrett) *s.i.s: t.k.h: hld up in rr: hdwy 4f out: rdn over 2f out: wknd wl over 1f out* **7/1**
6411 **8** *11* **Hamalka (IRE)**[19] 6275 3-8-7 **66** ow1.......................... MichaelHills 3 33
(B W Hills) *chsd ldr untl led over 4f out: rdn and hdd wl over 3f out: wknd qckly jst over 2f out* **10/1**
6124 **9** *1/2* **Shesha Bear**[32] 5935 3-8-8 **72**.......................... DavidProbert(5) 2 38
(W R Muir) *chsd ldrs tl lost pl 4f out: bhd and rdn 3f out: no ch after* **12/1**
1-0 **10** *28* **Hucking Heist**[109] 3529 4-9-7 **75**.......................... JohnEgan 1 —
(J R Best) *led tl over 4f out: sn rdn and lost pl: wl bhd and eased last 2f: t.o* **25/1**

2m 8.52s (-0.08) **Going Correction** +0.175s/f (Slow)
WFA 3 from 4yo+ 5lb **10** Ran SP% **120.5**
Speed ratings (Par 103): **107,106,103,103,101 99,98,89,89,66**
toteswinger: 1&2 £2.20, 1&3 £1.40, 2&3 £28.00. CSF £14.04 CT £69.41 TOTE £3.50: £2.00, £1.60, £2.70; EX 23.80 Place 6 £82.62, Place 5 £27.92..
Owner Greenstead Hall Racing **Bred** G Callanan **Trained** Exning, Suffolk

FOCUS
This was not just an ordinary handicap for the class which was run at an uneven pace. Nevertheless the form looks sound rated around the third and fourth.
T/Plt: £59.50 to a £1 stake. Pool: £68,631.11. 841.29 winning tickets. T/Qpdt: £11.20 to a £1 stake. Pool: £8,016.59. 528.92 winning tickets. SP

6578 NOTTINGHAM (L-H)
Thursday, October 16

OFFICIAL GOING: Good to soft (6.6)
Wind: light 1/2 behind Weather: changeable but mainly fine

6759 EUROPEAN BREEDERS' FUND MAIDEN STKS (DIV I) 1m 75y
1:40 (1:43) (Class 5) 2-Y-O **£3,412** (£1,007; £504) **Stalls** Low

Form RPR
4 **1** **Neuchatel (GER)**[7] 6597 2-9-3 0.......................... GregFairley 11 79+
(M Johnston) *trckd ldr: effrt to chal 2f out: rdn to ld wl over 1f out: kpt on wl u.p ins fnl f* **13/2**[3]
0 **2** *1/2* **Orbitor**[27] 6084 2-9-3 0.......................... HayleyTurner 10 78+
(M L W Bell) *t.k.h: trckd ldrs: swtchd rt and effrt over 2f out: sn rdn and edgd lft over 1f out: kpt on wl fnl f* **14/1**
3 *2 1/4* **Ebiayn (FR)** 2-9-3 0.......................... RHills 12 73+
(M A Jarvis) *trckd ldrs: hdwy 3f out: rdn and ev ch wl over 1f out: drvn and kpt on same pce fnl f* **6/1**[2]
2 **4** *hd* **Big Bound (USA)**[19] 6292 2-9-3 0.......................... LDettori 9 73
(J H M Gosden) *unruly at s: led: rdn along over 2f out: hdd wl over 1f out: sn drvn and wknd ins fnl f* **4/5**[1]
5 *1/2* **Blue Nymph** 2-8-12 0.......................... RichardKingscote 4 69+
(R M Beckett) *in rr: stdy hdwy fr wl over 2f out: rdn and kpt on ins fnl f: nrst fin* **20/1**
6 *5* **Whatami** 2-8-12 0.......................... TedDurcan 5 56
(E A L Dunlop) *hld up in tch: hdwy to chse ldrs wl over 2f out: sn rdn and no imp* **50/1**
7 *hd* **Wee Giant (USA)** 2-9-3 0.......................... JamieSpencer 6 60
(K A Ryan) *trckd ldrs: pushed along wl over 2f out: sn rdn and wknd wl over 1f out* **16/1**
8 *15* **Pezula** 2-8-12 0.......................... SteveDrowne 3 22
(R T Phillips) *a in rr* **100/1**
9 *14* **Battle Hero** 2-9-3 0..........................(v[1]) RyanMoore 2 —
(Sir Michael Stoute) *chsd ldrs lost pl and reminders 1/2-way: sn bhd* **14/1**
10 *1 1/2* **Rogalt (IRE)** 2-9-3 0.......................... TomEaves 7 —
(B Smart) *s.i.s: a bhd* **100/1**
0 **11** *4* **Mythical Thrill**[15] 6381 2-9-3 0.......................... TPQueally 13 —
(J G Given) *in tch: rdn along over 3f out: sn wknd and bhd* **100/1**

1m 48.73s (3.33) **Going Correction** +0.225s/f (Good) **11** Ran SP% **112.1**
Speed ratings (Par 95): **92,91,89,89,88 83,83,68,54,52 48**
toteswinger: 1&2 £6.90, 1&3 £4.70, 2&3 £8.60. CSF £84.13 TOTE £6.90: £1.80, £2.70, £2.10; EX 69.50.
Owner Sheikh Hamdan Bin Mohammed Al Maktoum **Bred** Darley Stud Management Snc/Gb **Trained** Middleham Moor, N Yorks

FOCUS
This looked the more interesting of the two divisions of this 1m maiden, despite the favourite going off a very short price. The winning time was slightly quicker than the second division and most of the principals can go forwards from here.

NOTEBOOK
Neuchatel(GER) shaped well on his debut at Great Leighs and is a nice-looking sort. He duly improved on that effort and provided his trainer with yet another course maiden win this season. The further he went the better he looked, despite showing signs of greenness, but he holds no fancy entries at the moment and it remains to be seen what route connections take with him. (op 7-1 tchd 15-2)
Orbitor was green on his debut but seemed to get the hang of things late on at Newmarket. It was much the same thing here, as he only really got going inside the final furlong and is sure to make up into a nice middle-distance sort next season. (op 16-1 tchd 20-1)
Ebiayn(FR), who cost 210,000gns, was a bit keen to post and held a prominent position during the race. He was produced to have every chance when the tempo increased but he did not appear to be subjected to a hard race once it was clear he would not win. (op 10-1)
Big Bound(USA) had looked a bit unlucky on his debut at Haydock but there was no questioning the promise he showed. A horse with plenty of size and scope, he reared up badly at the start while walking around and fell on his side before being loaded. One does have to question why he was allowed to run, considering the amount of punters' money he was carrying, but he did not show any obvious side effects during the race and only weakened late on. He will probably be a better three-year-old. (op 8-13 tchd 8-15)
Blue Nymph was a big eyecatcher in behind, as she got outpaced in the home straight before really getting the grasp of things late on. Had she been ridden with a bit more vigour inside the final 50yards, she may well have grabbed third.
Battle Hero will probably not be running for Sir Michael Stoute for much longer after this effort. (op 10-1)

6760 EUROPEAN BREEDERS' FUND MAIDEN STKS (DIV II) 1m 75y
2:10 (2:12) (Class 5) 2-Y-O **£3,412** (£1,007; £504) **Stalls** Low

Form RPR
0 **1** **Cygnet**[48] 5469 2-9-3 0.......................... DaneO'Neill 6 80
(L M Cumani) *mid-div: hdwy on inner 3f out: chal over 1f out: styd on to ld nr fin* **7/1**
223 **2** *shd* **Union Island (IRE)**[19] 6292 2-9-3 84.......................... JamieSpencer 7 80
(K A Ryan) *w ldrs: led 3f out: rdn over 1f out: hdd towards fin* **9/4**[1]
0 **3** *5* **Jedi**[14] 6425 2-9-3 0.......................... RyanMoore 5 69+
(Sir Michael Stoute) *chsd ldrs: outpcd and swtchd outside over 2f out: styd on same pce* **9/2**[3]
4 *1 1/4* **Cubism** 2-9-3 0.......................... GregFairley 1 67+
(M Johnston) *s.i.s: hdwy on ins 4f out: wknd appr fnl f* **7/2**[2]
0 **5** *3 1/4* **Halfway House**[13] 6438 2-9-3 0.......................... HayleyTurner 4 60+
(M L W Bell) *in rr: styd on fnl 3f: nvr nr ldrs* **16/1**
03 **6** *3/4* **Radegund Abbey**[15] 6384 2-9-3 0.......................... TedDurcan 9 58
(B Smart) *led after 1f: hdd over 3f out: wknd over 1f out* **25/1**

00 **7** *3* **Shakin John**[8] 6581 2-9-3 0 RobertWinston 8 52
(E J O'Neill) *in rr div: sme hdwy on outside over 2f out: nvr nr ldrs* **66/1**

0 **8** *1* **Zelos Diktator**[71] 4740 2-9-3 0 TPQueally 10 49
(J G Given) *reluctant to post: mid-div: reminders over 5f out: hung bdly lft over 2f out: nvr nr ldrs* **100/1**

0 **9** *1* **Sydney Cove (IRE)**[12] 6481 2-9-3 0 JoeFanning 12 47
(M Johnston) *trckd ldrs: chal 3f out: wknd over 1f out* **33/1**

50 **10** *1 3/4* **Best Bidder (USA)**[18] 6319 2-8-12 0 PaulHanagan 11 38
(R A Fahey) *t.k.h: led 1f: led over 3f out: sn hdd: lost pl 2f out* **10/1**

00 **11** *1* **Aziz (IRE)**[8] 6581 2-9-3 0 PaulEddery 13 41
(Miss D Mountain) *sn pushed along: sn chsng ldrs on outer: wknd 2f out* **100/1**

12 *11* **Red Margarita (IRE)** 2-8-12 0 TQuinn 3 13
(D R C Elsworth) *s.i.s: in rr: bhd fnl 2f* **33/1**

13 *7* **Tres Chic (FR)** 2-8-12 0 SteveDrowne 2 —
(S Curran) *in rr: sme hdwy over 3f out: sn wknd: bhd fnl 2f* **100/1**

1m 48.83s (3.43) **Going Correction** +0.225s/f (Good) **13** Ran SP% **112.8**
Speed ratings (Par 95): **91,90,85,84,81 80,77,76,75,73 72,61,54**
toteswinger: 1&2 £4.00, 1&3 £5.90, 2&3 £3.00. CSF £20.98 TOTE £8.10: £2.80, £1.20, £1.70; EX 22.30.
Owner Lady Milford Haven & The Hon Mrs Steel **Bred** Charlie Wyatt **Trained** Newmarket, Suffolk

FOCUS
The pace seemed generous early but very few got into the race when it mattered. The first two pulled nicely clear of the remainder and the form looks pretty sound.

NOTEBOOK
Cygnet, who was wearing a cross noseband, had been off the track for a while since a fair debut at Sandown but he showed plenty of heart for a battle to just get the better of the runner-up. He has an entry in the Derby next season, so one would imagine connections will try him in something decent at some stage to test him out. (op 15-2 tchd 8-1)
Union Island(IRE) had the best form on offer but once again got beat, although you could hardly fault his attitude too much.
Jedi appeared to get outpaced when the tempo increased before staying on. A half-brother to Hi Calypso and Warringah, the force is sure to be strong with him next season over much further and it would be some training feat by Sir Michael Stoute if he got him to run in the Bibury Cup at Salisbury next year, a race both the aforementioned horses ran in.
Cubism, whose dam was a half-sister to top-class two-year-old Medaaly and high-class Charnwood Forest, was settled towards the rear early before making up ground in the latter stages. He will be better for the run and shaped like a winner waiting to happen. (op 11-4)
Halfway House shaped with some promise just under a fortnight ago and did so again in this. Much like the stable's runner-up in the first division, he should make up into a nice middle-distance handicapper next season (tchd 14-1)
Shakin John stayed on well past some tired horses and will now have the options of handicaps. (op 50-1)

6761 T DENMAN & SONS NURSERY 1m 75y
2:40 (2:40) (Class 5) (0-70,70) 2-Y-O **£3,238** (£963; £481; £240) **Stalls** Low

Form RPR

2041 **1** **Digger Derek (IRE)**[9] 6549 2-9-8 **69** 6ex PaulHanagan 5 74
(R A Fahey) *led: rdn along 3f out: drvn and hdd briefly wl over 1f out: led again appr fnl f: kpt on gamely u.str.p towards fin* **6/1**[2]

640 **2** *hd* **Mykingdomforahorse**[53] 5314 2-9-4 **65** (v[1]) DarryllHolland 6 70
(M R Channon) *cl up: effrt 3f out: sn rdn and led briefly wl over 1f out: sn hung rt and hdd appr fnl f: drvn and ev ch tl no ex nr fin* **18/1**

0051 **3** *nse* **Recession Proof (FR)**[6] 6632 2-9-9 **70** 6ex JamieSpencer 3 74+
(S A Callaghan) *in rr: hdwy over 2f out: rdn over 1f out: chsng ldrs whn clr run ins fnl f: swtchd lft: drvn and squeezed through to have ev ch fnl 75yds tl no ex nr line* **7/4**[1]

152 **4** *1 1/2* **Hip Hip Hooray**[22] 6207 2-9-4 **65** HayleyTurner 16 66
(L A Dace) *hld up towards rr: hdwy over 2f out: sn swtchd ins and rdn to chal over 1f out: ev ch tl drvn and one pce wl ins fnl f* **20/1**

2050 **5** *shd* **Very Distinguished**[21] 6231 2-9-1 **62** EdwardCreighton 11 64+
(M G Quinlan) *in rr: hdwy over 2f out: rdn to chse ldrs over 1f out: n.m.r ins fnl f: kpt on u.p* **14/1**

2054 **6** *1* **Deal Clincher**[16] 6362 2-9-2 **66** LukeMorris(3) 14 65
(P Winkworth) *in tch: hdwy to chse ldrs over 3f out: sn rdn and edgd lft over 1f out: drvn and one pce ent fnl f* **10/1**

2000 **7** *1 1/4* **Tepmokea (IRE)**[33] 5895 2-9-7 **68** DarrenWilliams 7 64
(K R Burke) *trckd ldrs gng wl: effrt over 2f out: sn rdn and wknd over 1f out* **14/1**

5403 **8** *2 1/2* **Security Joan (IRE)**[17] 6330 2-9-6 **67** RyanMoore 1 58+
(R Hannon) *hld up towards rr: hdwy on inner 2f out: sn rdn and kpt on same pce* **20/1**

4124 **9** *1/2* **Musical Maze**[21] 6231 2-9-3 **67** DuranFentiman(3) 2 57
(W M Brisbourne) *s.i.s and bhd tl styd on fnl 2f* **14/1**

3065 **10** *4* **Mawjaat (IRE)**[44] 5585 2-9-5 **66** RHills 15 48
(J L Dunlop) *nvr bttr than midfield* **9/1**[3]

0050 **11** *6* **Kilsyth (IRE)**[19] 6291 2-9-0 **61** MickyFenton 12 30
(S Parr) *chsd ldrs: rdn along over 3f out and sn wknd* **66/1**

044 **12** *1* **Yeoman Of England (IRE)**[23] 6187 2-9-7 **68** TomEaves 17 35
(B Smart) *nvr nr ldrs* **16/1**

6000 **13** *hd* **Order Order**[20] 6240 2-9-4 **65** JamesDoyle 8 32
(H J L Dunlop) *chsd ldrs: rdn along 3f out: sn wknd* **66/1**

2026 **14** *1* **Johnny Rook (GER)**[85] 4305 2-9-7 **68** SteveDrowne 9 32
(E A L Dunlop) *a towards rr* **40/1**

030 **15** *6* **Mekong Miss**[12] 6473 2-9-4 **65** JoeFanning 10 17
(J Jay) *midfield: rdn along 1/2-way: sn wknd* **33/1**

1362 **16** *1 1/4* **Meydan Groove**[26] 6133 2-9-6 **67** RobertWinston 4 16
(R Johnson) *in rr fr 1/2-way* **28/1**

1m 48.77s (3.37) **Going Correction** +0.225s/f (Good) **16** Ran SP% **122.2**
Speed ratings (Par 95): **92,91,91,90,90 89,87,85,84,80 74,73,73,72,66 65**
toteswinger: 1&2 £22.30, 1&3 £3.00, 2&3 £12.20. CSF £101.42 CT £258.76 TOTE £7.60: £1.40, £4.00, £1.50, £2.90; EX 115.00.
Owner Dr W D Ashworth **Bred** Airlie Stud **Trained** Musley Bank, N Yorks
■ Stewards' Enquiry : Jamie Spencer two-day ban: used whip with excessive force and without giving colt time to respond (Oct 30-31)

FOCUS
This had the look of a very open nursery, despite the favourite being a short price and the form looks solid. The early pace was good and the first two home were up with the gallop throughout.

NOTEBOOK
Digger Derek(IRE) took a little while to get off the mark but was a comfortable winner of a nursery last time at Catterick. Stepped up a furlong in trip, he showed a really admirable attitude to hold off every challenge thrown at him and looks a tough handicapper in the making. (op 11-2)
Mykingdomforahorse, wearing a visor for the first time, shared the work with the winner in the early stages and also kept on well despite wandering under pressure. If the headgear works again, he should win before too long. (op 25-1)
Recession Proof(FR), returning to turf after a couple of spins on Polytrack, won by six lengths last time but faced very different conditions here. Going nowhere quickly for much of the race, the jockey did well to get him in with half a chance of victory but he was unable to force his mount's head past a couple of determined sorts. (op 15-8 tchd 2-1)
Hip Hip Hooray, trying 1m for the first time, made a big move at the midway point but did not quite get home. (op 25-1)
Very Distinguished looked a bit unlucky not to play a part in the finish as she got short of room when the front four came together late on. Official explanation: jockey said filly hung right-handed throughout (tchd 12-1)
Security Joan(IRE) stayed on from a long way back in the straight and caught the eye. (tchd 16-1)
Mawjaat(IRE) Official explanation: jockey said filly hung right-handed in home straight
Meydan Groove Official explanation: jockey said filly was never travelling

6762 WILDGOOSECONSTRUCTION.CO.UK MAIDEN STKS 1m 2f 50y
3:10 (3:11) (Class 5) 3-Y-O **£3,238** (£963; £481; £240) **Stalls** Low

Form RPR

1 **Covert Ambition** 3-9-3 0 LDettori 10 101+
(Saeed Bin Suroor) *hld up towards rr: effrt and rn v green over 3f out: edgd lft and qcknd to ld over 1f out: sn wnt wl clr: heavily eased last 75yds* **15/8**[1]

3420 **2** *7* **Arts Guild (USA)**[3] 6704 3-9-3 **76** RyanMoore 8 80
(W J Musson) *in tch: hdwy 4f out: led briefly 2f out: n.m.r appr fnl f: no ch w wnr* **9/2**[2]

62 **3** *2 1/4* **Streets Apart (USA)**[19] 6280 3-8-12 0 AdamKirby 3 70
(W R Swinburn) *led tl 2f out: one pce* **8/1**

6242 **4** *2 1/2* **Applaude**[12] 6487 3-9-3 **75** RobertWinston 15 70
(G A Swinbank) *trckd ldrs: chal over 2f out: hung rt and wknd over 1f out* **9/2**[2]

6 **5** *1* **Icy Cool (IRE)**[12] 6470 3-9-3 0 TPQueally 4 68+
(J Noseda) *hld up in rr: hdwy and swtchd outside over 2f out: kpt on: nvr nr ldrs* **33/1**

44 **6** *nse* **Time To Play**[19] 6280 3-9-0 0 MarcHalford(3) 16 68
(T T Clement) *mid-div: hdwy over 3f out: kpt on fnl 2f: nvr a threat* **100/1**

3- **7** *1/2* **Nasaq (USA)**[358] 6436 3-9-3 0 RHills 2 67
(M P Tregoning) *in tch: effrt to chse ldrs over 3f out: wknd over 1f out* **11/2**[3]

60 **8** *hd* **Qeyaada (USA)**[15] 6393 3-8-12 0 SteveDrowne 12 62
(E A L Dunlop) *prom: effrt over 3f out: wknd over 1f out* **20/1**

2553 **9** *6* **Eqbaal**[8] 6583 3-9-3 **81** (b) TedDurcan 6 55
(J L Dunlop) *chsd ldrs: chal over 3f out: wknd over 1f out: eased* **10/1**

0 **10** *11* **Purlando (GER)**[152] 2191 3-9-3 0 DaneO'Neill 5 33
(H Morrison) *s.i.s: a in rr* **100/1**

11 *1* **The Honorable (IRE)** 3-9-3 0 PaulHanagan 7 31
(R A Fahey) *mid-div: sn pushed along: lost pl 3f out* **50/1**

0450 **12** *2* **Toballa**[30] 6007 3-8-12 **49** DarryllHolland 9 22
(H J Collingridge) *w ldr: wknd over 3f out: sn bhd* **100/1**

000 **13** *8* **Little Rococoa**[157] 2046 3-9-3 0 JamesDoyle 14 11
(R J Price) *s.i.s: a in rr: bhd fnl 2f* **300/1**

6 **14** *1 1/4* **Sunset Resort (IRE)**[24] 6163 3-8-12 0 SladeO'Hara(5) 11 8
(A Berry) *chsd ldrs: drvn over 5f out: hung lft and wknd 4f out: sn bhd* **300/1**

0330 **15** *2 1/4* **Robert Burns (IRE)**[83] 4377 3-9-3 **68** (t) PaulEddery 1 4
(Miss D Mountain) *dwlt: in rr: eased over 2f out: sn bhd* **100/1**

2m 14.03s (1.53) **Going Correction** +0.225s/f (Good) **15** Ran SP% **121.0**
Speed ratings (Par 101): **102,96,94,92,91 91,91,91,86,77 76,75,68,67,66**
toteswinger: 1&2 £3.60, 1&3 £6.60, 2&3 £10.70. CSF £9.85 TOTE £2.80: £1.80, £1.60, £3.50; EX 13.50.
Owner Godolphin **Bred** Cyril Humphris **Trained** Newmarket, Suffolk

FOCUS
Races of this nature towards the end of a season generally do not take a great deal of winning, but one could not fail to be impressed by the winner. The early pace looked generous and the form appears relatively sound.
Applaude Official explanation: jockey said gelding hung right
Time To Play Official explanation: jockey said gelding hung left

6763 FLINT BISHOP H'CAP 1m 2f 50y
3:40 (3:41) (Class 3) (0-95,92) 3-Y-O+ **£7,771** (£2,312; £1,155; £577) **Stalls** Low

Form RPR

4211 **1** **Expresso Star (USA)**[8] 6582 3-9-2 **88** 6ex LDettori 1 104+
(J H M Gosden) *hld up: smooth hdwy 3f out: chal 2f out: rdn to ld 1 1/2 f out: styd on strly ins fnl f* **4/9**[1]

0302 **2** *3* **Suits Me**[20] 6249 5-9-7 **88** MickyFenton 5 98
(T P Tate) *led: rdn along wl over 2f out: hdd 1 1/2f out: kpt on same pce fnl f* **25/1**

1300 **3** *3* **Jaser**[52] 5360 3-9-6 **92** AlanMunro 11 96
(P W Chapple-Hyam) *hld up towards rr: hdwy 3f out: rdn 2f out: kpt on u.p to take 3rd ins fnl f* **14/1**

0260 **4** *3/4* **Conquisto**[35] 5843 3-9-2 **88** PhilipRobinson 4 91
(C G Cox) *hld up in rr: stdy hdwy on inner 3f out: rdn 2f out: kpt on same pce u.p ins fnl f* **16/1**

1114 **5** *1/2* **Mr Hichens**[34] 5865 3-9-3 **89** TPO'Shea 2 91
(B J Meehan) *prom: hdwy and cl up 3f out: rdn over 2f out: sn drvn and grad wknd appr fnl f* **11/1**[3]

5013 **6** *hd* **Rainbow Mirage (IRE)**[20] 6249 4-9-6 **87** DarryllHolland 6 88
(E S McMahon) *hld up towards rr: hdwy wl over 2f out: sn rdn and no imp appr fnl f* **10/1**[2]

25 **7** *1 1/2* **Indicible (FR)**[153] 2152 4-9-3 **84** DaneO'Neill 7 82
(A King) *trckd ldrs: effrt 3f out: rdn along 2f out and sn one pce* **25/1**

0300 **8** *shd* **Maramba (USA)**[29] 6034 3-9-3 **89** (t) RyanMoore 8 87
(Sir Michael Stoute) *prom: rdn along 3f out: drvn 2f out and grad wknd* **25/1**

024 **9** *hd* **Granston (IRE)**[21] 6233 7-9-1 **82** RobertWinston 13 80
(J D Bethell) *chsd ldrs: rdn along wl over 2f out: sn drvn and wknd wl over 1f out* **33/1**

2420 **10** *nk* **Ella Woodcock (IRE)**[28] 6041 4-9-1 **82** (p) ShaneKelly 10 79
(E J Alston) *hld up: a towards rr* **50/1**

4022 **11** *10* **Blue Spinnaker (IRE)**[27] 6070 9-9-4 **85** DaleGibson 9 62
(M W Easterby) *a in rr: bhd fnl 3f* **16/1**

2m 13.24s (0.74) **Going Correction** +0.225s/f (Good)
WFA 3 from 4yo+ 5lb **11** Ran SP% **121.5**
Speed ratings (Par 107): **106,103,101,100,100 100,98,98,98,98 90**
toteswinger: 1&2 £5.40, 1&3 £4.10, 2&3 £23.80. CSF £22.97 CT £96.63 TOTE £1.40: £1.10, £4.00, £3.70; EX 14.10.
Owner H R H Princess Haya Of Jordan **Bred** Stoneside Stable **Trained** Newmarket, Suffolk

FOCUS
Quite a good handicap, but the winner was well ahead of the Handicapper. The runner-up looks the best guide to the form, backed up by the third.

NOTEBOOK

Expresso Star(USA) was 5lb well-in under the penalty he picked up for an impressive five-length success over this course and distance the previous week and proved too good for this lot, readily completing the hat-trick. Having travelled well in about mid-division, he was made to work slightly harder this time, needing a few taps of the whip to pick up early-leader Suits Me, but he was well on top at the finish. Despite his US pedigree, he again showed a liking for easy ground, and all three of his wins have been gained on a soft surface. This was just his sixth start and he could be better than a handicapper next year. (op 8-15 tchd 8-13 and 4-6 in a place)

Suits Me took them along at a sensible pace considering the conditions and was allowed the run of the race. Although ultimately no match for the well-handicapped winner, he stuck on well in the straight and this was a decent effort off top weight. (op 12-1)

Jaser, trying 1m2f for the first time on his first start in almost two months, fared best of those held up, but basically got going too late having been outpaced at the top of the straight. He would have preferred a stronger pace, but still gives the impression some headgear might just sharpen him up (op 16-1 tchd 20-1)

Conquisto can be keen, so the steady pace cannot have been ideal, and like the third he got going too late having been held up (op 10-1 tchd 20-1)

Mr Hichens was produced with every chance if good enough, but not for the first time he carried his head a little proud. (op 10-1 tchd 8-1)

Rainbow Mirage(IRE) is another who was unsuited by a slow early gallop. (op 14-1)

6764 RACING UK ON CHANNEL 432 MAIDEN AUCTION STKS — 5f 13y

4:10 (4:11) (Class 5) 2-Y-O — £3,070 (£906; £453) Stalls High

Form				RPR
	1		**Harry Patch** 2-8-10 0 .... PhilipRobinson 2	77+
			(M A Jarvis) *w ldrs on outer: led over 1f out: edgd rt and hld on wl* **10/3**[2]	
225	2	¾	**Silent Wonder**[16] 6351 2-8-9 72 .... TomEaves 8	73
			(R M H Cowell) *chsd ldrs stands' side: swtchd lft and kpt on ins fnl f: no ex towards fin* **7/2**[3]	
2	3	*hd*	**Gilt Edge Girl**[28] 6051 2-8-8 0 .... DaneO'Neill 7	72
			(C G Cox) *w ldrs: led over 2f out tl over 1f out: no ex ins fnl f* **15/8**[1]	
U0	4	3 ¼	**Lucky Dan (IRE)**[74] 4658 2-8-10 0 .... PaulQuinn 13	62
			(Paul Green) *mid-div: kpt on fnl 2f: nvr rchd ldrs* **40/1**	
	5	3 ¼	**Tikka Masala (IRE)** 2-8-11 0 .... RichardKingscote 1	51
			(Tom Dascombe) *dwlt: mid-div on outer: hdwy over 2f out: fdd appr fnl f* **14/1**	
0	6	*nk*	**La Capriosa**[16] 6351 2-8-2 0 .... DavidProbert(5) 3	46
			(A J McCabe) *chsd ldrs on outer: wknd over 1f out* **66/1**	
600	7	3 ¼	**Pollish**[30] 5989 2-8-4 43 .... FrancisNorton 9	31
			(A Berry) *mid-div: nvr nr ldrs* **66/1**	
643	8	½	**Fasliyanne (IRE)**[157] 2054 2-8-7 71 .... JamieSpencer 4	33
			(K A Ryan) *led tl over 2f out: wknd over 1f out* **15/2**	
	9	2 ¾	**Old Sarum (IRE)** 2-8-10 0 .... TQuinn 12	26
			(D R C Elsworth) *s.s: sn detached: sme hdwy 2f out: nvr on terms* **33/1**	
	10	2	**Belle Choisir** 2-8-4 0 .... RoystonFfrench 11	13
			(B Smart) *s.s: detached in rr: nvr on terms* **11/1**	
00	11	2 ¼	**Its Alice**[12] 6489 2-8-5 0 .... PatrickMathers 6	5
			(Peter Grayson) *mid-div: wknd over 2f out* **200/1**	
000	12	6	**Flaming Ruby**[29] 6010 2-8-5 50 .... KimTinkler 5	—
			(N Tinkler) *chsd ldrs: lost pl over 2f out* **200/1**	
	13	5	**Heaveni Gift** 2-8-1 0 .... DominicFox(3) 10	—
			(S W Hall) *s.i.s: in rr: bhd fnl 2f* **200/1**	

61.12 secs (0.42) **Going Correction** +0.225s/f (Good) 13 Ran SP% **116.7**

Speed ratings (Par 95): **105,103,103,98,93 92,87,86,82,79 75,65,57**

toteswinger: 1&2 £3.50 1&3 £2.40, 2&3 £2.40. CSF £14.88 TOTE £4.80: £2.00, £1.70, £1.10; EX 14.90.

Owner Mrs Gay Jarvis **Bred** Red House Stud **Trained** Newmarket, Suffolk

FOCUS

Only a couple of these had shown form on the track, but the form looks fairly strong for the time of year with the placed horses setting the level. The race was the first of the final three to be run on the inner track.

NOTEBOOK

Harry Patch, an already gelded half-brother to Dichoh, a multiple 7f-1m winner, certainly knew his job and was probably value for a bit more than the winning margin, as he came from a much lower draw than the next two home. He is sure to make up in to a fair handicapper. (op 15-8)

Silent Wonder looked far from straightforward at Southwell last time and once again did not really convince that he wants to go past horses in a battle. (op 9-2 tchd 5-1)

Gilt Edge Girl, off for about a month since a decent racecourse debut, chased the leader throughout and ran another solid race. She ought to win a similar event if asked to before the end of the season. (op 2-1 tchd 7-4)

Lucky Dan(IRE) was behind early but kept on quite well inside the final furlong. The drop in trip did not suit him and he will be more effective over further. (op 50-1)

Tikka Masala(IRE), wearing a sheepskin noseband, changed hands for 32,000gns earlier this year and showed a bit of ability. (op 40-1)

Fasliyanne(IRE) had been absent since some reasonable efforts over this trip back in May. She showed a lot of early toe but weakened quickly in the latter stages. (op 9-1)

Old Sarum(IRE) Official explanation: jockey said gelding was slow into its stride

6765 OVAL GROUP H'CAP — 5f 13y

4:40 (4:41) (Class 5) (0-75,75) 3-Y-O — £3,238 (£963; £481; £240) Stalls High

Form				RPR
4004	1		**Harlech Castle**[17] 6340 3-9-0 71 .... (b) ShaneKelly 9	78
			(P F I Cole) *hld up in tch: hdwy 2f out: swtchd rt and rdn ent fnl f: kpt on to ld nr fin* **11/2**[3]	
6054	2	½	**Nickel Silver**[15] 6388 3-8-9 66 .... TomEaves 11	71
			(B Smart) *prom: effrt 2f out: rdn to ld over 1f out: drvn ins fnl f: hdd and nt qckn nr fin* **9/2**[2]	
0000	3	¾	**Calmdownmate (IRE)**[76] 4595 3-9-2 73 .... AndrewElliott 8	75
			(K R Burke) *cl up: rdn along 2f out: drvn and ev ch over 1f out: kpt on wl u.p fnl f* **40/1**	
5641	4	½	**Our Piccadilly (IRE)**[33] 5902 3-8-12 74 .... DavidProbert(5) 10	75
			(W S Kittow) *cl up: effrt 2f out: sn rdn and ev ch tl drvn and no ex wl ins fnl f* **4/1**[1]	
1400	5	*nk*	**Barraland**[12] 6486 3-9-1 72 .... TPO'Shea 3	71+
			(M R Channon) *chsd ldrs: effrt on outer 2f out: sn rdn and ev ch tl drvn and one pce ent fnl f* **16/1**	
1620	6	1	**Cheshire Rose**[22] 6218 3-8-4 68 .... DeanHeslop(7) 5	64
			(T D Barron) *midfield: hdwy 2f out: rdn to chse ldrs ent fnl f: sn drvn and kpt on same pce* **14/1**	
1404	7	¾	**Feeling Fresh (IRE)**[22] 6219 3-8-7 64 .... PaulQuinn 6	57+
			(Paul Green) *dwlt and squeezed out s: rr and reminders after 1f: hdwy 2f out: swtchd lft and rdn ent fnl f: kpt on: nrst fin* **10/1**	
2000	8	1 ½	**Helping Hand (IRE)**[93] 4047 3-8-6 63 .... HayleyTurner 2	51
			(R Hollinshead) *in tch on outer: hdwy 2f out: sn rdn and ch tl drvn and wknd ent fnl f* **20/1**	
2005	9	*nse*	**Andrasta**[18] 6308 3-8-4 61 oh4 .... FrancisNorton 7	49
			(A Berry) *in tch: rdn along 2f out: sn no imp* **33/1**	
6240	10	2 ½	**Bishopbriggs (USA)**[5] 6658 3-8-13 70 .... RobertWinston 4	49
			(S Parr) *chsd ldrs: rdn 2f out: sn drvn and wknd* **7/1**	
2620	11	½	**Rockfield Lodge (IRE)**[26] 6125 3-9-4 75 .... (b) AdamKirby 12	52
			(M E Rimmer) *chsd ldrs: swtchd lft and rdn wl over 1f out: sn btn* **9/1**	
0050	12	1	**Wavertree Princess (IRE)**[22] 6204 3-8-8 65 .... JamesDoyle 1	38
			(N P Littmoden) *a towards rr* **50/1**	
3000	13	6	**Coachhouse Lady (USA)**[28] 6053 3-9-2 73 .... (b[1]) DarryllHolland 13	25
			(K A Ryan) *sn led on stands' rail: rdn along 2f out: drvn and hdd over 1f out: wknd qckly and eased* **16/1**	

61.28 secs (0.58) **Going Correction** +0.225s/f (Good) 13 Ran SP% **115.7**

Speed ratings (Par 101): **104,103,102,101,100 99,97,95,95,91 90,89,79**

toteswinger: 1&2 £5.10, 1&3 £47.80, 2&3 £43.00. CSF £28.29 CT £898.89 TOTE £6.00: £2.00, £1.60, £13.60; EX 24.20.

Owner Elite Racing Club **Bred** Elite Racing Club **Trained** Whatcombe, Oxon

FOCUS

An ordinary handicap for the grade and at least five horses had a winning chance inside the final 100 yards. The form is sound enough rated through the runner-up.

Bishopbriggs(USA) Official explanation: jockey said gelding was unsuited by the ground

Coachhouse Lady(USA) Official explanation: jockey said filly hung right-handed

6766 BEST RACECOURSES ON TURFTV H'CAP — 5f 13y

5:10 (5:11) (Class 6) (0-65,65) 3-Y-O+ — £2,047 (£604; £302) Stalls High

Form				RPR
-130	1		**Dragon Flame (IRE)**[141] 2511 5-9-3 64 .... ShaneKelly 1	72
			(M Quinn) *racd alone far side: overall ldr: rdn over 1f out: jst lasted* **22/1**	
5034	2	½	**Sands Crooner (IRE)**[28] 6045 5-8-13 60 .... (v) TPQueally 14	67+
			(J G Given) *dwlt: hld up in rr: effrt and nt clr run 2f out: swtchd ins: styd on wl ins fnl f: jst hld* **7/1**[3]	
6000	3	*nk*	**Joyeaux**[9] 6564 6-8-10 60 .... (v) DuranFentiman(3) 13	65
			(L R James) *mid-div: hdwy 2f out: led stands' side gp jst ins fnl f: hung bdly lft: no ex towards fin* **11/1**	
5030	4	*hd*	**Colorus (IRE)**[54] 5260 5-9-2 63 .... JamieMoriarty 12	68
			(W J H Ratcliffe) *chsd ldrs: led stands' side gp over 1f out: no ex wl ins fnl f* **12/1**	
3223	5	¾	**Select Committee**[15] 6382 3-9-0 61 .... (p) TonyHamilton 10	63
			(J J Quinn) *sn chsng ldrs: kpt on same pce fnl f* **5/1**[2]	
2050	6	*nk*	**Filemot**[86] 4272 3-8-11 58 .... JohnEgan 4	59+
			(John Berry) *mid-div: effrt 2f out: kpt on same pce fnl f* **25/1**	
3421	7	1 ¼	**Tanley**[7] 6595 3-8-6 58 6ex .... (p) WilliamCarson(5) 8	54
			(J F Coupland) *chsd ldrs: fdd fnl f* **11/1**	
4000	8	2 ½	**The History Man (IRE)**[39] 5719 5-8-11 65 .... (e[1]) GarryWhillans(7) 15	52
			(M Mullineaux) *prom: wknd over 1f out* **22/1**	
2050	9	*nse*	**Twosheetstothewind**[50] 5401 4-8-12 59 .... RobertWinston 6	46
			(C R Dore) *led stands' side tl hdd & wknd over 1f out* **14/1**	
036	10	*nk*	**Tender Process (IRE)**[54] 5260 5-8-12 59 .... (v) PaulHanagan 2	45+
			(R A Fahey) *dwlt: sn chsng ldrs on outer: wknd appr fnl f* **7/2**[1]	
1136	11	1 ½	**Lake Chini (IRE)**[12] 6486 6-9-4 65 .... (b) DaleGibson 5	46
			(M W Easterby) *chsd ldrs: wknd over 1f out* **15/2**	
0210	12	1 ¾	**Littledodayno (IRE)**[40] 5709 5-9-2 63 .... FrancisNorton 7	37
			(M Wigham) *chsd ldrs: lost pl over 1f out* **17/2**	
000-	13	2	**Majestic Cheer**[48] 5485 4-8-12 59 ow1 .... AdamKirby 3	26+
			(John A Harris) *mid-div on outer: wknd 2f out* **50/1**	

61.62 secs (0.92) **Going Correction** +0.225s/f (Good) 13 Ran SP% **119.2**

Speed ratings (Par 101): **101,100,99,99,98 97,95,91,91,91 88,85,82**

toteswinger: 1&2 £29.00, 1&3 £37.60, 2&3 £17.30. CSF £163.28 CT £1867.83 TOTE £26.30: £7.10, £2.70, £3.50; EX 252.80 Place 6: £11.36 Place 5: £2.93.

Owner A Newby **Bred** Denis Hackett **Trained** Newmarket, Suffolk

FOCUS

Quite a few familiar names lined up for this sprint. The pace was sound as one would expect for a bunch of mainly seasoned handicappers. The fifth sets the standard.

Joyeaux Official explanation: jockey said gelding hung left in closing stages

T/Plt: £17.20 to a £1 stake. Pool: £53,819.15. 2,283.99 winning tickets. T/Qpdt: £3.10 to a £1 stake. Pool: £3,509.36. 832.70 winning tickets. JR

6767 - (Foreign Racing) - See Raceform Interactive

6728 KEMPTON (A.W) (R-H)

Friday, October 17

OFFICIAL GOING: Standard

Wind: Almost nil

6768 TRY BETDAQ FOR AN EXCHANGE CLASSIFIED STKS — 1m 2f (P)

5:45 (5:49) (Class 6) 3-Y-O+ — £2,047 (£604; £302) Stalls High

Form				RPR
5043	1		**Stand Guard**[16] 6374 4-9-3 53 .... IanMongan 10	66+
			(P Howling) *s.i.s: hld up in rr: gd hdwy over 4f out: led over 2f out: rdn clr: easily* **5/2**[1]	
0402	2	4 ½	**Turkish Sultan (IRE)**[9] 6570 5-8-12 47 .... (p) MCGeran(5) 9	57
			(J M Bradley) *hld up in rr: hdwy over 2f out: rdn to go 2nd ins fnl f* **20/1**	
0004	3	2	**Apache Dawn**[26] 5748 4-9-3 55 .... GeorgeBaker 6	53
			(G L Moore) *hld up in rr: hdwy over 3f out: chsd wnr 2f out: rdn and lost 2nd ins fnl f* **3/1**[2]	
5024	4	2 ¾	**Lady Valentino**[13] 6485 4-9-3 54 .... ShaneKelly 12	48
			(M Dods) *towards rr: styd on one pce fr over 2f out* **5/1**[3]	
0544	5	1 ¾	**West Lorne (USA)**[29] 6044 3-8-12 50 .... ChrisCatlin 13	44
			(E J O'Neill) *chsd ldrs: rdn over 2f out: sn btn* **17/2**	
2166	6	13	**Split The Wind (USA)**[2] 6728 4-8-12 53 .... DavidProbert(5) 14	18
			(Miss Sheena West) *led for 1f: led again 4f out: rdn and hdd over 2f out: sn wknd* **5/1**[3]	
-000	7	2	**El Dottore**[5] 6668 4-9-0 53 .... LukeMorris(3) 4	14
			(A W Carroll) *mid-div: rdn and wknd 2f out* **50/1**	
0100	8	1	**Muffett's Dream**[50] 5427 4-9-3 49 .... J-PGuillambert 2	12
			(J J Bridger) *trckd ldrs: rdn 3f out: sn wknd* **20/1**	
0-56	9	8	**Kinlochard**[10] 6566 3-8-12 53 .... StephenCarson 7	—
			(Eve Johnson Houghton) *a wl in rr* **33/1**	
2020	10	6	**Ardent Prince**[68] 4898 5-9-0 53 .... TolleyDean(3) 8	—
			(A J McCabe) *led after 1f: hdd 4f out: wkng whn hmpd 2f out* **14/1**	

2m 5.16s (-2.84) **Going Correction** -0.125s/f (Stan)

WFA 3 from 4yo+ 5lb 10 Ran SP% **118.5**

Speed ratings (Par 101): **106,102,100,98,97 86,85,84,78,73**

toteswinger: 1&2 £8.00, 1&3 £2.90, 2&3 £6.10. CSF £55.42 TOTE £3.70: £1.60, £2.60, £1.80; EX 66.30.

Owner The Circle Bloodstock I Limited **Bred** Juddmonte Farms Ltd **Trained** Newmarket, Suffolk

FOCUS
A very moderate classified contest in which Split The Wind and Ardent Prince took each other on for the lead and went off too fast, setting this up for those who were waited with. The time was fast and the form is worth taking at face value.
El Dottore Official explanation: jockey said gelding hung left throughout
Ardent Prince Official explanation: jockey said gelding had no more to give

6769 BET CHAMPIONS DAY - BETDAQ NURSERY 5f (P)
6:20 (6:20) (Class 4) (0-85,85) 2-Y-O **£3,885** (£1,156; £577; £288) **Stalls** High

Form RPR
4315 **1** **Sir Geoffrey (IRE)**[32] 5969 2-8-9 **76**........ TolleyDean(3) 12 82
(A J McCabe) *mde all: rdn over 1f out: r.o wl* **6/1**[3]
624 **2** *1* **Master Lightfoot**[16] 6389 2-8-13 **77**........(t) AdamKirby 10 79
(W R Swinburn) *trckd ldrs: rdn to go 2nd over 1f out: kpt on wl fnl f* **11/4**[1]
10 **3** *nk* **Rowayton**[43] 5642 2-9-2 **80**........ IanMongan 11 81
(J D Bethell) *s.i.s: towards rr: rdn and hdwy to go 3rd 1f out: r.o* **10/1**
0404 **4** *1 1/2* **Sweet Applause (IRE)**[4] 6696 2-8-11 **75**........ PaulHanagan 2 71
(A P Jarvis) *in tch: rdn over 1f out: kpt on one pce* **33/1**
421 **5** *nse* **Brenin Taran**[158] 2054 2-9-6 **84**........ RichardMullen 9 79+
(D M Simcock) *s.i.s: in rr: rdn and r.o fr over 1f out: nvr nrr* **11/2**[2]
6631 **6** *1/2* **Misty Glade**[10] 6547 2-8-5 **69** 6ex........(b) NickyMackay 1 63+
(B J Meehan) *mid-div on outside: kpt on one pce fr over 1f out* **14/1**
036 **7** *1* **Mazzola**[13] 6469 2-9-5 **83**........ SamHitchcott 5 73
(M R Channon) *prom early but sn mid-div: rdn and no hdwy fnl 2f* **16/1**
2014 **8** *2 3/4* **Azwa**[30] 6023 2-8-9 **73**........ SteveDrowne 4 53
(E A L Dunlop) *sn chsd wnr: wknd qckly over 1f out* **16/1**
2612 **9** *nk* **Cat Patrol**[33] 5937 2-9-0 **78**........ EddieAhern 6 57
(H J L Dunlop) *hld up: a in rr* **11/2**[2]
4420 **10** *nk* **Eldorado Days (IRE)**[11] 6525 2-9-0 **78**........ DarrenWilliams 8 56
(K R Burke) *chsd ldrs tl wknd over 1f out* **25/1**
2060 **11** *16* **Finnegan McCool**[27] 6118 2-9-7 **85**........ GeorgeBaker 7 5
(R M Beckett) *s.i.s: a bhd* **13/2**
4413 **12** *12* **Just The Lady**[20] 6274 2-8-11 **75**........ AdrianTNicholls 3 —
(D Nicholls) *rrd leaving stalls: a bhd* **16/1**

59.51 secs (-0.99) **Going Correction** -0.125s/f (Stan) **12** Ran SP% **125.2**
Speed ratings (Par 97): **102,100,99,97,97 96,95,90,90,89 64,44**
toteswinger: 1&2 £6.30, 1&3 £20.40, 2&3 £5.50. CSF £24.16 CT £155.96 TOTE £8.40: £2.40, £1.20, £5.00; EX 34.00.
Owner Dixon, Howlett & The Chrystal Maze Ptn **Bred** P Rabbitte **Trained** Babworth, Notts

FOCUS
A fair nursery on paper, but very much a draw race as the first three home emerged from the top three boxes. The form is rated through the second and fourth.

NOTEBOOK
Sir Geoffrey(IRE), drawn in stall 12, set an ordinary pace for the trip and the bare form needs treating with caution. He made all in a Redcar maiden two starts back and is clearly all right when able to dominate, but things will not always fall so kindly. He will apparently be kept on the go this winter. (op 8-1)
Master Lightfoot gave the impression he would be suited by the return to Polytrack when below form at Nottingham on his previous start, and he also had a tongue-tie fitted for the first time on this nursery debut. He tracked the winner throughout, but that one had clearly saved something in front and he was unable to go by when produced. (op 3-1)
Rowayton failed to beat a rival in a Salisbury Listed race last time, but she looked quite good when winning on her debut at Redcar. Although theoretically well drawn in stall 11, she raced further back than the front two and was doing all her best work at the finish. She fared best of those to race off the pace and this was a creditable effort. (op 6-1)
Sweet Applause(IRE) ◆ was able to race quite handy from stall two thanks to the lack of early pace in the race, but she ended up running keenly. Her early exertions ultimately told, but this was still a respectable effort from her low draw.
Brenin Taran was arguably the biggest eyecatcher, finishing well having been a long way off the modest pace. His promising trainer felt he was a Royal Ascot two-year-old after he won his maiden at Yarmouth in May, but he had not been seen since that success. This rates as a very pleasing return and he could be better than his mark of 84. (op 8-1)
Misty Glade was 7lb well in under the penalty she picked up for a 5l success at Catterick, but stall one gave her little chance. (op 10-1)
Finnegan McCool Official explanation: jockey said colt never travelled
Just The Lady Official explanation: jockey said filly had no more to give

6770 BET CHAMPIONS LEAGUE FOOTBALL - BETDAQ MEDIAN AUCTION MAIDEN STKS 6f (P)
6:50 (6:52) (Class 4) 2-Y-O **£3,885** (£1,156; £577; £144; £144) **Stalls** High

Form RPR
2 **1** **Aroundthebay**[17] 6358 2-8-12 0........ EddieAhern 4 74
(H J L Dunlop) *trckd ldr: rdn over 1f out: chal strly to ld fnl strides* **10/3**[2]
53 **2** *shd* **Comadoir (IRE)**[34] 5905 2-9-3 0........ TravisBlock 9 79
(Miss Jo Crowley) *led: rdn over 1f out: kpt on: hdd fnl strides* **11/4**[1]
3 **3** *3 3/4* **Jordaura**[18] 6342 2-9-3 0........ AdamKirby 3 68
(W R Swinburn) *in rr: rdn and hdwy fr over 1f out: wnt 3rd ins fnl f* **11/4**[1]
4 *1/2* **Goodison Glory (IRE)** 2-9-3 0........ PaulHanagan 10 66
(R A Fahey) *prom: rdn 1/2-way: wknd ins fnl f* **15/2**[3]
50 **4** *dht* **Seek The Fair Land**[30] 6031 2-9-3 0........ J-PGuillambert 6 66+
(J R Boyle) *in rr: rdn and hdwy over 1f out: r.o: nvr nrr* **12/1**
6 *3/4* **Flying Silks (IRE)** 2-9-3 0........ AdrianTNicholls 1 64+
(J R Gask) *wnt lft s: in rr: effrt on outside over 1f out: nvr nr to chal* **33/1**
7 *1 3/4* **Django Reinhardt** 2-8-12 0........ DavidProbert(5) 5 59
(J R Gask) *s.i.s: nvr on terms* **33/1**
23 **8** *1* **Corton Charlemagne (IRE)**[14] 6434 2-8-12 0........ ChrisCatlin 2 51
(Rae Guest) *trckd ldrs tl rdn and wknd over 1f out* **15/2**[3]
00 **9** *2* **Border Maid**[10] 6555 2-8-12 0........ SteveDrowne 8 45
(E A L Dunlop) *in rr: rdn 1/2-way: nvr on terms* **16/1**
0003 **10** *12* **Tobizzy**[18] 6333 2-8-12 50........ ShaneKelly 7 9
(J R Jenkins) *in tch tl wknd over 2f out* **33/1**

1m 12.55s (-0.55) **Going Correction** -0.125s/f (Stan) **10** Ran SP% **122.3**
Speed ratings (Par 97): **98,97,92,92,92 91,88,87,84,68**
toteswinger: 1&2 £3.80, 1&3 £2.70, 2&3 £3.50. CSF £13.50 TOTE £4.60: £1.50, £1.30, £1.70; EX 14.70.
Owner John F Jarvis **Bred** R G Levin **Trained** Lambourn, Berks
■ Stewards' Enquiry : Eddie Ahern three-day ban: used whip in incorrect place (Oct 31, Nov 1-2)

FOCUS
A modest juvenile maiden in which the first two home raced in the first two pretty much throughout. They finished clear and the form is easy to assess and pretty solid.

NOTEBOOK
Aroundthebay had been runner-up in a 7f maiden at Warwick when a 100-1 shot first-time up. She was well placed throughout, but made hard work of this and gave the impression she might be happier back up in trip next time. Whatever the case, things are likely to be tougher from now on. (tchd 3-1 and 7-2)
Comadoir(IRE) had his chance from the front, but he does not look quite as good as his official mark of 79 suggests and was just denied. (op 9-2)
Jordaura fared best of those to race off the pace but never threatened the front two. He didn't really improve on the form he showed when third on his debut at Windsor, but can be given a chance. (op 10-3)
Goodison Glory(IRE), a 40,000-euros son of first-season sire Tout Seul, had to be niggled early to hold his position and was unable to sustain an effort in the straight. This run should sharpen him plenty. (tchd 8-1)
Seek The Fair Land, dropped back from 7f, was last entering the straight, but he kept on nicely under hands-and-heels riding and very much caught the eye. Admittedly he was passing mainly beaten horses, but it will still be a surprise if he does not make his mark in handicaps at some point. (tchd 8-1)
Flying Silks(IRE) had the worst draw and ended up racing widest in the straight, but he was keeping on at the finish. (op 25-1)
Django Reinhardt started slowly but was making a bit of ground at the finish. Official explanation: jockey said gelding ran green (op 25-1)
Corton Charlemagne(IRE) was stuck out wide from stall two and was well below the form she showed on her first two starts. (op 11-2)

6771 BET BREEDERS CUP - BETDAQ CLAIMING STKS 1m (P)
7:20 (7:22) (Class 6) 3-Y-O+ **£2,047** (£604; £302) **Stalls** High

Form RPR
0543 **1** **Smokey Rye**[44] 5607 3-8-9 70........ SteveDrowne 11 66
(G L Moore) *hld up in tch: rdn to ld ins fnl f: hld on wl* **14/1**
0243 **2** *nk* **Fremen (USA)**[19] 6312 8-9-6 84........ AdrianTNicholls 10 73+
(D Nicholls) *slowly away: in rr: swtchd lft over 2f out: sustained run on outside to go 2nd cl home* **5/1**[3]
0004 **3** *hd* **Electric Warrior (IRE)**[12] 6510 5-9-6 88........ DarrenWilliams 6 73
(K R Burke) *a in tch: led ent fnl f: hdd ins fnl f and lost 2nd cl home* **5/2**[1]
4055 **4** *hd* **Teasing**[13] 6490 4-8-12 65........(v[1]) AdamKirby 14 64
(J Pearce) *s.i.s: hdwy on ins 2f out: r.o wl fnl f* **20/1**
0256 **5** *1 3/4* **Ballora (FR)**[8] 6605 3-8-9 75........ PatDobbs 7 60
(S Kirk) *s.i.s: towards rr: rdn and hdwy ins fnl 2f: nvr nrr* **6/1**
055P **6** *shd* **Wooden King (IRE)**[10] 6562 3-8-4 50........ JohnEgan 2 55
(P D Evans) *led after 1f: rdn and hdd ent fnl f: kpt on one pce* **66/1**
0500 **7** *nk* **Pha Mai Blue**[13] 6467 3-8-9 75........ DavidProbert(5) 9 64
(W J Knight) *in rr: hdwy over 2f out: one pce fnl f* **16/1**
3-30 **8** *nk* **Deo Valente (IRE)**[126] 3002 3-9-3 78........ EddieAhern 1 67
(B J Meehan) *led for 1f: trckd ldrs: rdn over 2f out: kpt on but n.d after* **20/1**
0141 **9** *nk* **Blacktoft (USA)**[6] 6659 5-9-4 71........(e) J-PGuillambert 12 64+
(S C Williams) *hld up in rr: kpt on one pce fnl 2f* **9/2**[2]
4000 **10** *1 1/4* **Count Ceprano (IRE)**[27] 6120 4-9-1 81........ GabrielHannon(5) 3 63
(M D I Usher) *in tch on outside: pushed along 3f out: no hdwy fnl 2f* **6/1**
0060 **11** *2 3/4* **Daring Dream (GER)**[27] 6108 3-9-0 60........(v) RichardMullen 8 54
(A P Jarvis) *mid-div: rdn 3f out: wknd over 1f out* **66/1**
0000 **12** *8* **Sky Quest (IRE)**[78] 4568 10-8-10 57........ TGMcLaughlin 5 28
(J R Boyle) *chsd ldrs tl wknd over 2f out* **80/1**
206 **13** *7* **Nok Twice (IRE)**[19] 6312 7-8-10 64........ RobertWinston 4 12
(K A Ryan) *t.k.h: lost tch wl over 2f out* **20/1**

1m 38.6s (-1.20) **Going Correction** -0.125s/f (Stan)
WFA 3 from 4yo+ 3lb **13** Ran SP% **123.0**
Speed ratings (Par 101): **101,100,100,100,98 98,98,97,97,96 93,85,78**
toteswinger: 1&2 £7.90, 1&3 £13.10, 2&3 £3.60. CSF £79.87 TOTE £16.40: £3.60, £1.90, £1.50; EX 52.10.
Owner Darrell Hinds Susan Bell Pat Butcher **Bred** Jeremy Hinds **Trained** Woodingdean, E Sussex
■ Stewards' Enquiry : John Egan caution: eased gelding closing stages and lost fifth place

FOCUS
A competitive claimer, but they went an ordinary pace and finished in a bit of a bunch. Messy form with the principals a stone+ off their best.
Wooden King(IRE) Official explanation: jockey said gelding ran too free
Nok Twice(IRE) Official explanation: jockey said gelding hung left in straight

6772 BETDAQ.CO.UK SPORTS BETTING H'CAP 1m (P)
7:50 (7:52) (Class 2) (0-100,98) 3-Y-O+
£11,215 (£3,358; £1,679; £840; £419; £210) **Stalls** High

Form RPR
0000 **1** **Samarinda (USA)**[41] 5695 5-8-13 **90**........ AdamKirby 4 98
(Mrs P Sly) *hld up in rr: hdwy on ins over 1f out: r.o wl to ld ins fnl f* **25/1**
4304 **2** *3/4* **Extraterrestrial**[19] 6307 4-8-13 **90**........ PaulHanagan 12 96
(R A Fahey) *trckd ldrs: rdn to go 2nd wl ins fnl f* **8/1**
4020 **3** *3/4* **Cape Hawk (IRE)**[20] 6269 4-9-7 **98**........ PatDobbs 9 103
(R Hannon) *led for 1f: led again 2f out: rdn and hdd ins fnl f: lost 2nd towards fin* **5/2**[1]
2166 **4** *3/4* **Maghya (IRE)**[20] 6266 3-8-10 **90**........ ShaneKelly 7 93
(W J Haggas) *trckd ldrs: chal 2f out: nt qckn ins fnl f* **9/2**[2]
0001 **5** *1/2* **Final Verse**[13] 6490 5-8-11 **88**........ AlanMunro 1 90
(M Salaman) *in rr: rdn and r.o fnl f: nvr nrr* **16/1**
0006 **6** *1 1/4* **Pride Of Nation (IRE)**[9] 6576 6-9-1 **92**........(p) EddieAhern 5 91
(J W Hills) *mid-div: hung rt fr over 1f out and nvr threatened to chal* **12/1**
5064 **7** *3/4* **Scartozz**[21] 6249 6-9-0 **91**........(b) JohnEgan 3 88
(M Botti) *t.k.h: mid-div: nvr on terms* **8/1**
4030 **8** *1 1/4* **Mastership (IRE)**[20] 6269 4-9-4 **95**........ RobertWinston 6 89+
(J J Quinn) *in rr: short of room over 2f out: nvr threatened to chal* **11/2**[3]
3210 **9** *1 1/4* **The Jostler**[37] 5795 3-8-7 **87**........ ChrisCatlin 10 78
(B W Hills) *mid-div: effrt 2f out: wknd over 1f out* **9/1**
5100 **10** *1/2* **Mut'Ab (USA)**[19] 6307 3-8-9 **89**........(b) RichardMullen 11 79
(C E Brittain) *led after 1f: hdd 2f out: wknd qckly fnl f* **40/1**

1m 38.62s (-1.18) **Going Correction** -0.125s/f (Stan)
WFA 3 from 4yo+ 3lb **10** Ran SP% **114.2**
Speed ratings (Par 109): **100,99,98,97,97 96,95,94,92,92**
toteswinger: 1&2 £, 1&3 £, 2&3 £. CSF £197.85 CT £616.86 TOTE £35.40: £9.30, £1.80, £1.10; EX 223.10.
Owner D Bayliss, T Davies, G Libson & P Sly **Bred** Gainsborough Farm Llc **Trained** Thorney, Cambs

FOCUS
A good handicap, but they went an ordinary pace until the straight and the winning time was slower than the previous claimer. The form is a bit messy with the winner back to something like last winter's best.

NOTEBOOK
Samarinda(USA) had mainly struggled since winning at Lingfield in February, but he was 3lb lower than when gaining that latest success and returned to form. He was held up off the modest pace, but got a good run up the inside in the straight and picked up well to take this in decisive fashion. His trainer reported he has been schooled over fences lately, including as recently as the day before this success, and that has apparently rekindled his enthusiasm. He showed little in two runs over hurdles in 2006, but could be given another chance at some point.
Extraterrestrial was well placed for much of the way, but he had to wait for a gap in the straight and was forced to switch back inside with his challenge. He kept on, but was basically beaten by a better one on the day. (tchd 15-2)

Cape Hawk(IRE) was another nicely placed considering the way the race was run and seemed to have his chance. (op 11-4 tchd 2-1)
Maghya(IRE) was never too far away and did not seem to have any excuses. (op 6-1)
Final Verse, claimed after winning at Wolverhampton last time, ran well for his new connections considering he raced keenly off the modest pace. He was keeping on at the finish and can do better in a stronger-run race. (op 20-1 tchd 25-1)
Pride Of Nation(IRE) is due to be dropped 2lb and was well held. (op 14-1)
Scartozz was too keen after being stuck out wide early on. Official explanation: jockey said horse hung right (tchd 9-1)
Mastership(IRE), back over 1m with the blinkers left off this time, was denied a clear run for much of the straight, but he did not run on when finally in the clear, even if it was too late, and he displayed a most awkward head carriage. He looks best avoided. Official explanation: jockey said, regarding running and riding, his orders were to settle gelding in 5th or 6th, and produce it late, adding that the slow pace shuffled it back in the field then, in the home straight, he found himself boxed in with nowhere to go, and when able to switch to get a run, it was too late to reach a challenging position. (op 5-1 tchd 4-1)

6773 TFM NETWORKS H'CAP (DIV I) 6f (P)
8:20 (8:22) (Class 6) (0-65,65) 3-Y-O+ **£1,706** (£503; £252) **Stalls High**

Form RPR
1004 **1** **Cool Sands (IRE)**[17] 6356 6-9-1 **61**....(v) J-PGuillambert 1 73+
(J G Given) *racd wd thrght: plenty to do whn rdn over 2f out: kpt on u.p to ld ins fnl f* **12/1**
5442 **2** *1 ¾* **Morse (IRE)**[16] 6377 7-8-12 **58**....(p) ShaneKelly 7 64
(J A Osborne) *chsd ldr to over 3f out: rdn to ld 1f out: nt qckn and hdd ins fnl f* **13/2**
1010 **3** *½* **Tous Les Deux**[7] 6631 5-9-5 **65**.... GeorgeBaker 11 69
(G L Moore) *hld up: swtchd lft 2f out: r.o wl to go 3rd ins fnl f* **11/4**[2]
0041 **4** *1* **Milne Bay (IRE)**[5] 6679 3-8-12 **59** 6ex....(t) RichardMullen 6 60
(D M Simcock) *mid-div: hdwy and gng wl over 2f out: rdn over 1f out: nt qckn fnl f* **5/2**[1]
000- **5** *1* **Polish World (USA)**[401] 5339 4-9-0 **63**.... LeeVickers(3) 12 61
(T J Etherington) *t.k.h: hdwy on ins 2f out: rdn and no hdwy ins fnl f* **25/1**
0035 **6** *2* **Hammer Of The Gods (IRE)**[35] 5867 8-9-5 **65**....(bt) RobertWinston 4 57
(G C Bravery) *sn led: rdn and hdd 1f out: fdd ins fnl f* **10/1**
1336 **7** *nse* **River Bounty**[53] 5346 3-9-4 **65**.... DarrenWilliams 2 56
(A P Jarvis) *in tch: wnt 2nd over 3f out: wknd fnl f* **33/1**
2225 **8** *shd* **Towy Boy (IRE)**[4] 6707 3-9-4 **65**....(t) AlanMunro 5 56
(I A Wood) *chsd ldrs: rdn over 2f out: sn btn* **10/1**
6450 **9** *1 ¼* **The Jailer**[71] 4767 5-8-11 **57**.... VinceSlattery 8 44
(J G M O'Shea) *a in rr* **16/1**
0534 **10** *nk* **Truly Divine**[29] 6063 3-8-12 **59**.... SteveDrowne 9 45
(E A L Dunlop) *s.i.s: rdn over 2f out: nvr on terms* **5/1**[3]

1m 12.7s (-0.40) **Going Correction** -0.125s/f (Stan)
WFA 3 from 4yo+ 1lb **10** Ran SP% **123.8**
Speed ratings (Par 101): **97,94,94,92,91 88,88,88,86,86**
toteswinger: 1&2 £15.00, 1&3 £9.10, 2&3 £4.60. CSF £93.27 CT £291.85 TOTE £15.40: £3.30, £1.70, £1.90; EX 80.00.
Owner Peter Swann **Bred** Rathasker Stud **Trained** Willoughton, Lincs

FOCUS
A modest sprint handicap run in a time 0.65sec slower than the second division. Ordinary form, but sound enough.

6774 TFM NETWORKS H'CAP (DIV II) 6f (P)
8:50 (8:50) (Class 6) (0-65,65) 3-Y-O+ **£1,706** (£503; £252) **Stalls High**

Form RPR
3202 **1** **Our Blessing (IRE)**[5] 6680 4-9-0 **60**.... RichardMullen 4 73
(A P Jarvis) *mde all: pushed out fnl f: a in command* **3/1**[1]
00 **2** *1 ¾* **Compton Classic**[81] 4478 6-8-4 **57**.... AndreaAtzeni(7) 10 64
(J R Boyle) *mid-div: rdn and hdwy to chse wnr over 1f out: hld on for 2nd* **5/1**[3]
4223 **3** *shd* **Rhapsilian**[18] 6334 4-8-12 **58**.... AdamKirby 6 65
(J A Geake) *hld up: t.k.h: hdwy over 1f out: sn wnt 3rd but hung rt and nt go by runner-up* **7/2**[2]
1514 **4** *2 ½* **Game Lady**[16] 6377 4-8-12 **58**.... AlanMunro 9 57
(I A Wood) *prom: chsd wnr over 2f out tl one pce fnl f* **11/2**
3000 **5** *¾* **Shot To Fame (USA)**[16] 6380 9-9-5 **65**.... GeorgeBaker 2 62
(S Kirk) *in rr tl hdwy over 1f out: r.o: nvr nrr* **14/1**
0000 **6** *nk* **Imperial Echo (USA)**[13] 6490 7-9-2 **62**....(v) TGMcLaughlin 11 58
(P Howling) *s.i.s: in rr: effrt 2f out: nvr nr to chal* **14/1**
0000 **7** *1 ¼* **Hollow Jo**[51] 5401 8-8-9 **55**.... ChrisCatlin 7 47
(J R Jenkins) *racd wd: in tch: rdn over 2f out: sn btn* **14/1**
3030 **8** *½* **Rainbow Fox**[32] 5965 4-9-3 **63**.... PaulHanagan 8 53
(R A Fahey) *mid-div: rdn over 2f out: no hdwy after* **11/2**
6340 **9** *½* **Valhillen**[45] 5592 3-9-1 **65**....(p) PatrickHills(3) 1 54
(M D I Usher) *trckd ldrs: rdn and wknd over 1f out* **18/1**
5060 **10** *6* **Ever Cheerful**[16] 6380 7-9-4 **64**....(p) SteveDrowne 5 33
(A B Haynes) *trckd wnr to over 2f out: sn wknd* **16/1**

1m 12.05s (-1.05) **Going Correction** -0.125s/f (Stan)
WFA 3 from 4yo+ 1lb **51** Ran SP% **125.8**
Speed ratings (Par 101): **102,99,99,96,95 94,93,92,91,83**
toteswinger: 1&2 £9.80, 1&3 £4.10, 2&3 £11.10. CSF £19.98 CT £59.10 TOTE £4.90: £1.60, £2.30, £1.90; EX 38.00.
Owner Eurostrait Ltd **Bred** Mrs N Quinn **Trained** Twyford, Bucks

FOCUS
Another modest sprint handicap and the winning time was 0.65sec quicker than the first division. The third gives the form a sound feel.
Rhapsilian Official explanation: jockey said filly hung right

6775 BARRETTSTOWN STUD H'CAP 1m 4f (P)
9:20 (9:23) (Class 5) (0-70,70) 3-Y-O+ **£2,590** (£770; £385; £192) **Stalls Centre**

Form RPR
5041 **1** **Graylyn Ruby (FR)**[14] 6436 3-9-1 **68**.... LukeMorris(3) 13 76
(J Jay) *trckd ldrs: led 2f out: hung bdly lft but had enough in hand to be in command fnl f* **11/2**[2]
2100 **2** *1 ¼* **Papradon**[9] 6577 4-9-7 **64**.... GeorgeBaker 7 70
(J R Best) *hld up: hdwy whn swtchd rt wl over 1f out: r.o u.p but nt rch wnr* **12/1**
4564 **3** *1 ¾* **Flam**[22] 6226 3-9-1 **65**....(p) EddieAhern 12 68
(J R Fanshawe) *mid-div: hdwy over 1f out: styd on to go 3rd ins fnl f* **7/1**[3]
0226 **4** *½* **Mista Rossa**[16] 6379 3-9-6 **70**.... TravisBlock 10 72
(H Morrison) *mid-div: rdn over 3f out: styd on fr over 1f out: nvr nrr* **7/1**[3]
3623 **5** *nk* **Dusk**[16] 6378 3-9-5 **69**....(b) RichardMullen 3 71
(J L Dunlop) *hld up: hdwy over 2f out: sn rdn: no ex ins fnl f* **11/2**[2]
210 **6** *½* **Granary Girl**[49] 5476 6-9-1 **58**.... AdamKirby 11 59
(J Pearce) *hld up in rr: gd hdwy over 2f out: ev ch over 1f out: fdd ins fnl f* **20/1**
5650 **7** *nk* **Fateful Attraction**[30] 6019 5-9-0 **57**....(b) AlanMunro 4 57
(I A Wood) *in rr: effrt on ins over 1f out: nvr a factor* **25/1**
0252 **8** *1 ¼* **Calzaghe (IRE)**[13] 6493 4-9-11 **68**....(v) DarrenWilliams 6 66
(K R Burke) *hld up in rr: effrt 2f out: nt qckn* **7/1**[3]
3300 **9** *1 ¾* **Rock Peak (IRE)**[49] 5465 3-9-4 **68**.... SteveDrowne 14 64
(H Morrison) *led for 4f: led again 4f out: hdd 2f out: wknd* **7/2**[1]
4415 **10** *3 ¾* **Lough Beg (IRE)**[142] 2512 5-9-5 **62**....(t) ChrisCatlin 9 52
(Miss Tor Sturgis) *mid-div: rdn over 2f out: sn btn* **16/1**
041 **11** *½* **Oasis Sun (IRE)**[30] 6019 5-8-8 **58**....(b) AndreaAtzeni(7) 1 47
(J R Best) *towards rr: rdn over 3f out: nvr on terms* **10/1**
3010 **12** *9* **Megalala (IRE)**[48] 5512 7-8-7 **55**.... DavidProbert(5) 8 29
(J J Bridger) *trckd ldr: led after 4f: hdd 4f out: wknd 2f out* **14/1**
0400 **13** *38* **Royal Premier (IRE)**[31] 6007 5-9-8 **65**....(v) VinceSlattery 2 —
(H J Collingridge) *trckd ldrs: rdn 4f out: wknd qckly: t.o* **25/1**

2m 33.39s (-1.11) **Going Correction** -0.125s/f (Stan)
WFA 3 from 4yo+ 7lb **13** Ran SP% **132.3**
Speed ratings (Par 103): **98,97,96,95,95 95,94,94,92,90 90,84,58**
toteswinger: 1&2 £18.60, 1&3 £8.30, 2&3 £20.00. CSF £76.24 CT £487.00 TOTE £7.00: £2.10, £5.90, £2.20; EX 125.10 Place 6 £29.43, Place 5 £17.02.
Owner Graham & Lynn Knight **Bred** Jonathan Jay **Trained** Newmarket, Suffolk

FOCUS
A modest middle-distance handicap. They went a good pace early, with Rock Peak and Megalala taking each other on up front, but they slowed up before the straight and the field bunched up as a result. The form looks sound though.
T/Plt: £25.10 to a £1 stake. Pool: £66,788.53. 1,935.32 winning tickets. T/Qpdt: £3.90 to a £1 stake. Pool: £6,809.68. 1,266.10 winning tickets. JS

6473
NEWMARKET (ROWLEY) (R-H)
Friday, October 17

OFFICIAL GOING: Good
Wind: Light, half behind Weather: Cloudy with sunny spells

6776 EBF FEDERATION OF BLOODSTOCK AGENTS MAIDEN STKS 6f
1:00 (1:02) (Class 4) 2-Y-O **£6,476** (£1,927; £963; £481) **Stalls High**

Form RPR
32 **1** **Run For The Hills**[80] 4510 2-9-3 0.... LDettori 2 92+
(J H M Gosden) *lw: mde all: edgd lft over 1f out: rdn out* **13/8**[1]
4532 **2** *1 ½* **Invincible Heart (GR)**[28] 6077 2-9-3 93.... JohnEgan 7 88
(Jane Chapple-Hyam) *a.p: rdn to chse wnr over 1f out: edgd lft ins fnl f: styd on* **9/2**[2]
0 **3** *nk* **Swiss Diva**[119] 3219 2-8-12 0.... JamieSpencer 6 82
(D R C Elsworth) *lw: a.p: rdn over 1f out: styd on u.p* **14/1**
43 **4** *3 ¾* **Izzi Mill (USA)**[112] 3456 2-8-12 0.... TQuinn 4 70
(D R C Elsworth) *bit bkwd: chsd wnr tl rdn and edgd rt over 1f out: wknd ins fnl f* **11/1**
5 *shd* **Balaagha (USA)** 2-8-12 0.... RHills 10 70
(M A Jarvis) *w'like: attractive: dwlt: hdwy 1/2-way: styd on same pce appr fnl f* **7/1**[3]
3 **6** *4* **Getcarter**[14] 6443 2-9-3 0.... PatDobbs 9 63
(R Hannon) *chsd ldrs: rdn over 2f out: wknd over 1f out* **8/1**
7 *hd* **Catigo (USA)** 2-8-12 0.... RyanMoore 12 57
(Sir Michael Stoute) *unf: scope: bit bkwd: chsd ldrs: lost pl over 2f out: styd on fr over 1f out* **10/1**
8 *¾* **Rapid Water** 2-9-3 0.... WilliamBuick 15 60+
(A M Balding) *w'like: bit bkwd: sn outpcd: styd on appr fnl f: nvr nrr* **50/1**
3 **9** *1 ¾* **Petsas Pleasure**[13] 6480 2-9-3 0.... AlanMunro 11 55
(L R James) *w'like: lw: prom: lost pl 4f out: n.d after* **25/1**
10 *1* **Fondant Fancy** 2-8-12 0.... EddieAhern 5 47
(H J L Dunlop) *w'like: bit bkwd: b.nr hind: s.i.s: outpcd* **100/1**
11 *1 ¼* **Desert Streak (FR)** 2-9-3 0.... DaneO'Neill 16 48
(H J L Dunlop) *w'like: bit bkwd: dwlt: outpcd* **66/1**
000 **12** *4 ½* **Hayley's Girl**[10] 6559 2-8-12 0....(b[1]) TravisBlock 1 30
(S W James) *prom: rdn over 3f out: wknd over 2f out* **150/1**
00 **13** *hd* **Red Horse (IRE)**[28] 6080 2-8-10 0.... MalinHolmberg(7) 14 34
(M L W Bell) *swtg: sn outpcd* **200/1**
14 *¾* **Al Qeddaaf (IRE)** 2-9-3 0.... MartinDwyer 3 32
(W J Haggas) *tall: unf: bit bkwd: dwlt: outpcd* **33/1**
15 *4* **Golden Pool (IRE)** 2-8-12 0.... HayleyTurner 13 15
(S A Callaghan) *w'like: sn outpcd* **66/1**

1m 10.93s (-1.27) **Going Correction** -0.10s/f (Good) **15** Ran SP% **117.9**
Speed ratings (Par 97): **104,102,101,96,96 91,90,89,87,86 84,78,78,77,71**
toteswinger: 1&2 £2.40, 1&3 £8.30, 2&3 £15.60. CSF £7.70 TOTE £2.60: £1.30, £1.90, £3.30; EX 7.70.
Owner Normandie Stud Ltd **Bred** Normandie Stud Ltd **Trained** Newmarket, Suffolk

FOCUS
An interesting maiden featuring a couple of expensive newcomers but the race was dominated by those with previous racecourse experience. The principals ended up racing towards the stands' side.

NOTEBOOK
Run For The Hills ◆, on whom Dettori made good use of the tail wind, broke quickly and made all the running. The form of his second outing at Goodwood had been working out working out (3rd, 4th 6th and 10th have won since) and, although he was returning from a break, he looked pretty straight and travelled well before finding plenty up the hill when asked. He should go in from this and will be aimed at the Pavilion Stakes (a 6f Listed race for three-year-olds) next spring. (op 2-1)
Invincible Heart(GR) came into this with fair and consistent form on varying ground and again ran his race. However, he was no match for the winner in the final furlong and he may prove most effective on soft, as his best performance ratings-wise prior to this was on that ground. (op 10-3)
Swiss Diva ran with plenty of credit against the colts on her first appearance since her debut 6f on fast ground in June. That race has thrown up a few winners and she overcame a sluggish start to chase the leaders before keeping on well up the hill and finishing clear of the remainder. (tchd 16-1)
Izzi Mill(USA), yet another returning from an absence, showed plenty of pace until fading in the closing stages and now qualifies for a handicap mark. She could be interesting if reappearing in that grade. (op 14-1)
Balaagha(USA), who is not over-big and got a bit warm beforehand, is a $750,000 half-sister to a multiple winner in the USA. She missed the break on this debut but soon recovered to chase the leading group and stayed on steadily in the closing stages. She should come on a fair amount for the experience. (tchd 8-1)
Getcarter, who put up an encouraging debut over 7f of this course two weeks previously, seemed to struggle to live up with the pace on this drop in trip and looks the sort who will find his level once handicapped. (op 17-2)

Catigo(USA), a $1.5m sister to high-class Aragorn, showed signs of ability despite looking as if the experience would do her good. (op 8-1)
Rapid Water, a son of Lochsong and half-brother to Lochridge and Loch Verdi, could not go the early pace but was getting the idea in the closing stages and should benefit from the experience.

6777 ANGLO HIBERNIAN BLOODSTOCK INSURANCE EBF MAIDEN STKS (DIV I) 1m

1:30 (1:35) (Class 4) 2-Y-O **£6,152** (£1,830; £914; £456) **Stalls** High

Form				RPR
25	1		**Mustaqer (IRE)**[35] 5859 2-9-3 0 RHills 12	84
			(B W Hills) *lw: led over 6f out: rdn jst over 1f out: edgd lft cl home: r.o* **3/1**[2]	
	2	*nk*	**Hyades (USA)** 2-9-3 0 TPQueally 11	84+
			(H R A Cecil) *str: hld up in mid-div: swtchd rt and hdwy over 2f out: rdn over 1f out: ev ch ins fnl f: r.o* **16/1**	
0	3	*½*	**Monetary Fund (USA)**[76] 4625 2-9-3 0 HayleyTurner 6	82
			(G A Butler) *hld up and bhd: pushed along over 2f out: hdwy over 1f out: rdn fnl f: styd on to take 3rd nr fin* **66/1**	
36	4	*hd*	**Coiled Spring**[11] 6539 2-9-3 0 JimCrowley 8	82
			(Mrs A J Perrett) *lw: hld up in tch: rdn over 2f out: swtchd lft over 1f out: styng on whn nt clr run nr fin* **15/2**[3]	
22	5	*1 ¼*	**Alhaque (USA)**[15] 6425 2-9-3 0 JamieSpencer 2	79
			(P W Chapple-Hyam) *lw: w ldrs: rdn and ev ch over 1f out: no ex ins fnl f* **15/8**[1]	
	6	*¾*	**Thin Red Line (IRE)** 2-9-3 0 RyanMoore 5	78+
			(E A L Dunlop) *w'like: str: bit bkwd: s.i.s: hld up in rr: pushed along over 2f out: rdn and r.o ins fnl f: nt rch ldrs* **33/1**	
06	7	*nk*	**Akmal**[16] 6384 2-9-3 0 (b[1]) MartinDwyer 14	77
			(J L Dunlop) *prom: rdn whn edgd lft wl over 1f out: fdd towards fin* **66/1**	
05	8	*8*	**Highway Magic (IRE)**[94] 4062 2-9-3 0 KShea 13	59
			(A P Jarvis) *led over 1f: w ldrs: rdn and wknd 2f out* **66/1**	
	9	*shd*	**Putra One (IRE)** 2-9-3 0 PhilipRobinson 3	59
			(M A Jarvis) *w'like: str: tall: scope: bit bkwd: dwlt: sn hld up in tch: shkn up over 2f out: wknd wl over 1f out* **14/1**	
	10	*5*	**Lombok** 2-9-3 0 TPO'Shea 9	48
			(G Wragg) *w'like: scope: str: bit bkwd: dwlt: a in rr* **25/1**	
	11	*1 ¾*	**Nbhan (USA)** 2-9-3 0 DaneO'Neill 4	44
			(L M Cumani) *w'like: athletic: hld up in mid-div: pushed along over 3f out: sn bhd* **12/1**	

1m 38.54s (-0.06) **Going Correction** -0.10s/f (Good) **11** Ran SP% **103.1**
Speed ratings (Par 97): **96,95,95,95,93 93,92,84,84,79 77**
toteswinger: 1&2 £9.50, 1&3 £41.50, 2&3 £93.90. CSF £34.59 TOTE £3.90: £1.20, £3.30, £12.60; EX 57.60.
Owner Hamdan Al Maktoum **Bred** Shadwell Estate Company Limited **Trained** Lambourn, Berks
■ Stewards' Enquiry : R Hills two-day ban: careless riding (Oct 31, Nov 1)

FOCUS
An interesting maiden containing a few with established form and a couple of well-bred newcomers. The form is rated at face value, although the proximity of the seventh is a potential concern. Unlike in the first race, they stayed centre to far side.

NOTEBOOK
Mustaqer(IRE), who was well supported in the market, made the vast majority of the running and showed a decent attitude when challenged late on. Runner-up in Listed company on his debut before pulling too hard when an odds-on failure on softer ground at Doncaster, he was tried in a different bridle here and has now apparently grown up. Considered a nice sort by connections, he should be able to hold his own in better company next season. (op 4-1 tchd 9-2)
Hyades(USA) ◆, a good-bodied sort, is probably the one to take from the race. A half-brother to Light Shift and Shiva amongst others, he travelled well off the pace before being delivered with his effort towards the far side of the field, and despite showing signs of inexperience he stayed on very gamely up the hill. Improvement looks certain and it would be no surprise to see him eventually turn out the best of these. (op 14-1)
Monetary Fund(USA), edgy beforehand and trapped out wide throughout, came off the bridle a long way from home but he responded and was finishing to good effect. His proximity could be seen as a problem as he was beaten a very long way on his Goodwood debut, but he has probably improved a lot since then and should be given the benefit of the doubt.
Coiled Spring, a disappointing favourite on soft ground at Windsor the previous week after showing promise on his debut here, returned to form and was staying on again after becoming outpaced. He now qualifies for a mark and is worth keeping an eye on. (op 8-1 tchd 7-1)
Alhaque(USA), already runner-up in a couple of maidens here that have only worked out reasonably, was a bit disappointing as he was always up with the pace and had every chance, but didn't seem to get home. This was a step backwards and he has a few questions to answer now. (op 2-1 tchd 9-4 and 5-2 in places)
Thin Red Line(IRE) ◆, on his toes beforehand on his racecourse debut, was noted staying on very nicely at the end. A 25,000gns half-brother to a three-time winner at up to 1m4f, he is one to watch out for, especially when stepped up in trip.
Akmal, who had been well beaten in his first two starts and was sporting first-time blinkers, appeared to show much improved form back on this better ground. He is qualified for a mark now.
Highway Magic(IRE) who was up there early but was keen on this return from three months off. He was beaten a fair way but is another that may do better now that he can be handicapped.
Putra One(IRE) travelled well behind the leaders before coming under pressure and dropping right out. The way he drifted in the market suggested this was probably needed and he is surely capable of better. (op 8-1)
Lombok, a full-brother to Asian Heights and half-brother to St Expedit, never figured after standing still as the stalls opened. (op 28-1)
Nbhan(USA), who was the subject of a gamble, was under pressure a long way out and was one of the first beaten. (op 33-1)

6778 ANGLO HIBERNIAN BLOODSTOCK INSURANCE EBF MAIDEN STKS (DIV II) 1m

2:00 (2:08) (Class 4) 2-Y-O **£6,152** (£1,830; £914; £456) **Stalls** High

Form				RPR
	1		**Mooakada (IRE)** 2-8-12 0 RHills 13	84+
			(J H M Gosden) *w'like: rangy: scope: s.i.s: hld up: hdwy over 3f out: led wl over 1f out: shkn up and styd on: eased nr fin* **11/2**[2]	
	2	*½*	**Times Up** 2-9-3 0 EddieAhern 14	84
			(J L Dunlop) *tall: angular: unf: scope: a.p: rdn and ev ch fr over 1f out: styd on* **33/1**	
0	3	*¾*	**Legislate**[27] 6117 2-9-3 0 MichaelHills 9	82+
			(B W Hills) *lw: hld up: hdwy over 2f out: rdn over 1f out: styd on* **7/2**[1]	
0	4	*1*	**Akbabend**[11] 6535 2-9-3 0 JoeFanning 12	80
			(M Johnston) *tall: unf: chsd ldr: rdn and ev ch over 1f out: styd on same pce ins fnl f* **14/1**	
	5	*3 ¾*	**Pachakutek (USA)** 2-9-3 0 JamieSpencer 3	72+
			(E F Vaughan) *w'like: s.i.s and hmpd s: hld up: hdwy and hung rt fr over 1f out: nrst fin* **12/1**	
0	6	*2 ½*	**Hi Fling**[30] 6029 2-9-3 0 MartinDwyer 6	66
			(B J Meehan) *w'like: lw: led: hdd wl over 1f out: wknd fnl f* **15/2**	
	7	*shd*	**Highland Glen** 2-9-3 0 RyanMoore 11	66
			(Sir Michael Stoute) *w'like: mid-div: rdn over 3f out: outpcd fnl 2f* **11/2**[2]	
00	8	*1 ¾*	**Play To Win (IRE)**[15] 6425 2-9-3 0 TQuinn 5	62
			(D R C Elsworth) *lw: chsd ldrs: rdn over 2f out: wknd over 1f out* **20/1**	
	9	*5*	**Dreamcoat** 2-9-3 0 RobertHavlin 2	51
			(J H M Gosden) *w'like: scope: str: bit bkwd: s.i.s: hld up: wknd over 2f out* **7/1**[3]	
	10	*4 ½*	**Carte D'Oro (IRE)** 2-8-12 0 AlanMunro 1	36
			(P W Chapple-Hyam) *unf: bit bkwd: s.i.s: hld up: hdwy over 3f out: hung rt and wknd wl over 1f out* **12/1**	
0	11	*nk*	**Bansha (IRE)**[9] 6581 2-9-3 0 RobertWinston 4	40
			(A Bailey) *wnt lft s: chsd ldrs: rdn: hung lft and wknd 2f out* **100/1**	
0	12	*4 ½*	**Captain Flack**[15] 6425 2-9-3 0 OscarUrbina 8	31
			(J A R Toller) *hld up: rdn 1/2-way: wknd 3f out* **100/1**	
	13	*3 ¼*	**Myshkin** 2-9-3 0 PhilipRobinson 10	23
			(M A Jarvis) *w'like: bit bkwd: chsd ldrs tl wknd over 3f out* **9/1**	

1m 38.65s (0.05) **Going Correction** -0.10s/f (Good) **13** Ran SP% **119.0**
Speed ratings (Par 97): **95,94,93,92,89 86,86,84,79,75 74,70,67**
toteswinger: 1&2 £33.40, 1&3 £5.50, 2&3 £23.00. CSF £183.17 TOTE £6.60: £2.90, £7.10, £1.60; EX 236.50.
Owner Hamdan Al Maktoum **Bred** Shadwell Estate Company Limited **Trained** Newmarket, Suffolk

FOCUS
The second division of this maiden did not look quite as strong as the first leg on paper and was run 0.11secs slower, but the form is rated positively. The runners raced middle to far side of the track.

NOTEBOOK
Mooakada(IRE) ◆, representing a yard with a good record in this race, caught the eye in the paddock but was easy to back beforehand. This Montjeu filly out of a mare from the family of Bint Shadayid was one of only two fillies in the race but travelled well before cruising into contention on the run into the Dip. She found what was required when asked and looks to have a future over middle distances. Her trainer clearly thinks so, as he was talking in terms of the Pretty Polly and the Oaks next year. (op 5-1 tchd 6-1)
Times Up ◆, a gelded half-brother to several winners such as Give Notice and Fearless Warrior, is bred to stay on the dam's side but he has clearly inherited some speed from his sire, who was basically a miler. He ran his race and, like the winner, is likely to make his mark over middle distances next year and should have little trouble winning a maiden on this evidence.
Legislate, a Dansili half-brother to 12 winners, including Tenby and Bristol Channel, had previous experience and was held up before making progress from the three-furlong marker. He appeared to have his chance but could never land a blow at the first two. (op 4-1)
Akbabend, who was always struggling on his debut on soft ground earlier in the month, seemed happier on this surface although, after briefly showing in front, was unable to go with the principals up the hill. (op 12-1 tchd 10-1)
Pachakutek(USA), who is a bit on the leg, is a 90,000gns son of a winning mare from the family of Dancing Rocks. He was backed at long prices but rather fell out of the stalls and was still last at halfway before staying on nicely in the last couple of furlongs. He looks sure to come on with this run under his belt. (op 16-1)
Hi Fling who was well backed beforehand, made the running and stepped up on his debut effort at Yarmouth. He was not given too hard a time when headed and looks the sort to do better next year. (op 14-1 tchd 7-1)
Highland Glen, edgy beforehand, and a Derby entry from the family of Phantom Gold, was a market drifter and ran as if the outing was needed. (op 4-1 tchd 7-1)
Play To Win(IRE) Official explanation: jockey said colt stumbled into the Dip.
Dreamcoat, a stable companion of the winner and a half-brother to Pipedreamer, was another to miss the break and looked as if the experience was needed. (op 11-2 tchd 15-2)
Carte D'Oro(IRE) missed the break then pulled too hard and not surprisingly dropped away in the latter stages. (op 16-1)

6779 PETER STONE MEMORIAL HOUGHTON CONDITIONS STKS 1m

2:35 (2:37) (Class 2) 2-Y-O

£12,462 (£3,732; £1,866; £934; £466; £234) **Stalls** High

Form				RPR
3123	1		**On Our Way**[20] 6267 2-9-3 103 TPQueally 6	107+
			(H R A Cecil) *lw: broke wl: hld up in tch: led over 1f out: sn hung lft: pushed out* **11/8**[1]	
421	2	*2 ¼*	**Ra Junior (USA)**[14] 6443 2-9-3 94 JamieSpencer 2	99
			(B J Meehan) *sn chsng ldr: led 4f out: rdn and hdd over 1f out: carried sltly lft ent fnl f: nt qckn* **3/1**[2]	
1	3	*nk*	**Mastery**[9] 6581 2-9-3 0 JoeFanning 1	98
			(M Johnston) *lw: a.p: rdn wl over 1f out: carried sltly lft ent fnl f: one pce* **5/1**[3]	
314	4	*1*	**Midnight Cruiser (IRE)**[36] 5825 2-9-1 86 RyanMoore 7	94
			(R Hannon) *hld up in rr: rdn over 2f out: hdwy over 1f out: swtchd rt ent fnl f: kpt on* **13/2**	
10	5	*3 ½*	**Cruikadyke**[19] 6317 2-9-3 100 JohnEgan 3	88
			(P F I Cole) *hld up: hdwy over 3f out: rdn 2f out: wknd ins fnl f* **10/1**	
0142	6	*1 ¼*	**Aurorian (IRE)**[13] 6466 2-9-3 88 DaneO'Neill 4	86
			(R Hannon) *prom: rdn 2f out: wknd fnl f* **20/1**	
060	7	*33*	**Moon Warrior**[38] 5778 2-8-12 30 LPKeniry 5	8
			(C Smith) *led 4f: wknd qckly: t.o* **200/1**	

1m 36.4s (-2.20) **Going Correction** -0.10s/f (Good) 2y crse rec **7** Ran SP% **111.5**
Speed ratings (Par 101): **107,104,104,103,99 98,65**
toteswinger: 1&2 £1.50, 1&3 £2.70, 2&3 £2.50. CSF £5.31 TOTE £2.10: £1.40, £2.00; EX 5.40.
Owner J R May **Bred** Whatton Manor Stud **Trained** Newmarket, Suffolk

FOCUS
This race has not gone to a true star in recent years, but winners tend to be useful enough and there is no reason to think this latest renewal was not right up to scratch, with the form looking solid. It was run in a fast time too, nearly two seconds quicker than either division of the maiden, even allowing for it being hand-timed, whereas the others were electronic. The winner ran to his pre-race mark but gave the impression there was more there if needed. He is a nice type and can go on from here.

NOTEBOOK
On Our Way, the Royal Lodge third, who looked outstanding beforehand, set a decent standard, and proved more than good enough despite hanging badly left when he hit the front. Held up while rank outsider Moon Warrior made the early running, he moved up readily on the far side of the group and gradually took the measure of Ra Junior, who had taken over up front, without Queally needing to resport to the whip. A big colt with a good stride, he is not the sort to do anything quickly, and his breeding suggests he is not sure to get that much more than 1m. However, he looked a class above his rivals here and may yet prove really smart next year. (tchd 15-8)
Ra Junior(USA) has progressed with every race. Back at 1m, the distance of his good Sandown second to Four Winds, he was up there all of the way and did not give in without a fight, but the winner was much too good for him. Brian Meehan felt he may have just been a bit flat today. (op 5-1)
Mastery, quite a good-bodied type, his debut win at Nottingham last week came in a maiden on soft ground, and this much better race on quicker ground represented a very different test. He went with the runner-up most of the way and ran as well as he was entitled to. (op 11-4)

Midnight Cruiser(IRE) had been too keen over 7f on his latest start so was ridden much more patiently this time. He was keeping on when switched right, and he got the longer trip fine. (op 10-1)
Cruikadyke, a York winner, has had stiff tasks on both starts since. He ran all right in Ireland, but this was nowhere near so good. (op 8-1 tchd 15-2)
Aurorian(IRE) was ridden handier than his stablemate Midnight Cruiser but seemed outclassed. He is bred to do better over further next year.

6780 GEORGIA HOUSE STUD DARLEY STKS (GROUP 3) 1m 1f

3:10 (3:12) (Class 1) 3-Y-O+

£36,900 (£13,988; £7,000; £3,490; £1,748; £877) **Stalls** High

Form RPR
502 **1** **Charlie Farnsbarns (IRE)**[5] 6670 4-9-3 105 RyanMoore 12 117
(B J Meehan) *a.p: pushed along over 2f out: rdn and swtchd lft over 1f out: hung lft and r.o to ld wl ins fnl f* **50/1**
2222 **2** *1 1/2* **Bankable (IRE)**[14] 6440 4-9-3 117 DaneO'Neill 17 114
(L M Cumani) *s.i.s: hdwy 1/2-way: chsd ldr over 1f out: rdn to ld ins fnl f: sn hdd and unable qckn* **5/2**[1]
/11- **3** *nk* **Kirklees (IRE)**[387] 5723 4-9-3 110 LDettori 7 113
(Saeed Bin Suroor) *lw: hld up in tch: plld hrd: rdn over 1f out: r.o* **11/2**[3]
4 *nse* **Sahpresa (USA)**[21] 6265 3-8-10 0 KJManning 5 110
(Rod Collet, France) *w'like: lw: s.i.s: hld up: hdwy over 1f out: sn edgd rt: r.o* **12/1**
1251 **5** *1* **Tranquil Tiger**[23] 6201 4-9-3 116 (b) TPQueally 18 111
(H R A Cecil) *sn led: rdn over 1f out: hdd and no ex ins fnl f* **15/2**
211 **6** *3 1/4* **Mawatheeq (USA)**[21] 6242 3-8-13 100 RHills 13 104
(M P Tregoning) *lw: chsd ldrs: rdn over 1f out: wknd ins fnl f* **4/1**[2]
-104 **7** *1 1/2* **General Eliott (IRE)**[14] 6440 3-8-13 108 ShaneKelly 9 101
(P F I Cole) *trckd ldrs: racd keenly: rdn over 2f out: wknd fnl f* **14/1**
1636 **8** *1 1/2* **Drumfire (IRE)**[13] 6499 4-9-3 107 RoystonFfrench 3 98
(M Johnston) *mid-div: hmpd and lost pl over 6f out: n.d after* **33/1**
665 **9** *1 1/2* **Stubbs Art (IRE)**[14] 6440 3-8-13 108 (b[1]) AlanMunro 16 95
(D R C Elsworth) *s.i.s: hld up: racd keenly: rdn and hung rt over 2f out: n.d* **16/1**
3215 **10** *1* **Yaddree**[13] 6476 3-8-13 107 PhilipRobinson 11 93
(M A Jarvis) *chsd ldrs: rdn over 2f out: wknd over 1f out* **11/1**
150 **11** *3/4* **Fanjura (IRE)**[14] 6440 3-8-13 99 JamieSpencer 15 91
(J Noseda) *hld up: rdn over 3f out: sme hdwy 2f out: wknd fnl f* **100/1**
1153 **12** *2 3/4* **Third Set (IRE)**[55] 5265 5-9-3 110 TedDurcan 4 85
(Saeed Bin Suroor) *s.i.s: hld up: a in rr* **20/1**
0264 **13** *13* **Regime (IRE)**[28] 6074 4-9-7 112 HayleyTurner 10 62
(M L W Bell) *prom: rdn over 2f out: sn wknd* **22/1**
4500 **14** *6* **Halicarnassus (IRE)**[28] 6074 4-9-3 110 DarryllHolland 2 45
(M R Channon) *hld up: plld hrd: hdwy over 6f out: rdn over 3f out: wknd over 2f out* **33/1**

1m 47.78s (-2.82) **Going Correction** -0.10s/f (Good)
WFA 3 from 4yo+ 4lb **14** Ran SP% **122.2**
Speed ratings (Par 113): **108,106,106,106,105 102,101,99,98,97 97,94,83,77**
toteswinger: 1&2 £27.30, 1&3 £32.20, 2&3 £3.00. CSF £168.65 TOTE £47.30: £9.00, £1.40, £2.00; EX 245.70.
Owner The English Girls **Bred** Tinnakill Partnership I **Trained** Manton, Wilts

FOCUS
A competitive-looking Group 3 with some established Pattern-class performers up against some unexposed three-year-olds, but in a race run at a fair pace the older horses dominated. The form looks reasonable, rated through the second and fourth.

NOTEBOOK
Charlie Farnsbarns(IRE) caused quite a shock under Moore, a late replacement for Eddie Ahern. He was always travelling strongly behind the leaders and really found his stride up the hill to hit the front well inside the final furlong. Comparatively lightly raced since finishing second to Authorized in the 2006 Racing Post Trophy, he has had his problems but this showed that when he is on song he is highly talented. He apparently needed his two recent runs to put him right and he may be capable of even better next year.
Bankable(IRE), who has not enjoyed much luck in finishing runner-up in his last four starts, was still the one to beat on official ratings but he managed to find one to beat him again. He seemed to be given every chance, as was always travelling well towards the far side of the group and he was produced in plenty of time, but the final climb seemed to just find him out. It may be that 1m is his ideal trip, but it has become an expensive business making excuses for him. He stays in training. (tchd 9-4, 11-4 and 3-1 in places)
Kirklees(IRE), having his first run in a year but successful after a similar layoff last season, raced quite keenly early and after coming off the bridle a fair way out, he was staying on at the line. It may be that he is at his best over the extra furlong now and there will be other opportunities. (op 9-2 tchd 6-1)
Sahpresa(USA), easy winner of a fillies' Listed event at Saint-Cloud last time, was carried back to last after three furlongs when Drumfire met serious interference just in front of her, so she did very well to stay on and finish so close. Still lightly raced, the very best of her is probably yet to be seen. (op 9-1)
Tranquil Tiger, in good form in Listed company this year, was trying his shortest trip since his racecourse debut. Positively ridden from the start, he tried his best to see it out but his rivals had the legs of him from the furlong pole. (op 10-1)
Mawatheeq(USA) was always handy and ran well on this step up in class. A progressive sort who was raised 15lb for destroying his rivals in an Ascot handicap last month, he remains unexposed and is likely to come into his own in Pattern company next season. (op 6-1)
General Eliott(IRE), just behind Bankable on his return from five months off here a couple of weeks ago, was trying this extra furlong for the first time and he had every chance, but didn't seem to get home. (op 12-1)
Stubbs Art(IRE) attracted some market support in the first-time blinkers, but he never looked happy in them and never figured. Considering that he finished third in both the English and Irish 2000 Guineas back in the spring, he has become very disappointing. (op 20-1)
Yaddree Official explanation: jockey said colt was struck into

6781 LANWADES STUD SEVERALS STKS (LISTED RACE) (F&M) 1m 2f

3:45 (3:47) (Class 1) 3-Y-O+

£24,978 (£9,468; £4,738; £2,362; £1,183; £594) **Stalls** High

Form RPR
2646 **1** **Barshiba (IRE)**[13] 6475 4-9-2 108 TQuinn 7 106
(D R C Elsworth) *lw: plld hrd early: hld up in tch: rdn to ld jst over 1f out: edgd rt ins fnl f: drvn out* **11/1**
0241 **2** *1/2* **Fragrancy (IRE)**[22] 6233 4-9-2 98 PhilipRobinson 11 105
(M A Jarvis) *hld up in rr: hdwy 2f out: rdn and r.o ins fnl f* **4/1**[2]
3-50 **3** *3* **In The Light**[48] 5506 4-9-2 100 RyanMoore 5 99
(Sir Michael Stoute) *led: rdn and hdd jst over 1f out: edgd lft ins fnl f: no ex* **14/1**
2414 **4** *1/2* **Spacious**[13] 6475 3-8-11 112 RobertWinston 8 98
(J R Fanshawe) *swtg: hld up towards rr: swtchd lft over 2f out: hdwy over 1f out: sn rdn: kpt on same pce ins fnl f* **11/4**[1]
0223 **5** *4 1/2* **Ronaldsay**[21] 6241 4-9-5 105 DaneO'Neill 3 92
(R Hannon) *hld up towards rr: rdn over 2f out: hdwy over 1f out: one pce fnl f* **7/1**[3]
0631 **6** *3/4* **Princess Taylor**[20] 6293 4-9-2 86 (t) DarryllHolland 6 88
(M Botti) *hld up in tch: pushed along over 2f out: rdn wl over 1f out: wknd fnl f* **25/1**
1-36 **7** *1 3/4* **Classic Legend**[21] 6241 3-8-11 90 JamieSpencer 10 84
(B J Meehan) *lw: hld up in mid-div: rdn over 2f out: wknd fnl f* **8/1**
5205 **8** *4 1/2* **Sweet Lilly**[27] 6106 4-9-5 108 EdwardCreighton 2 78
(M R Channon) *t.k.h early in rr: pushed along over 2f out: n.d* **14/1**
2160 **9** *1 1/4* **Classic Remark (IRE)**[54] 5331 3-9-0 108 LDettori 1 76
(H J L Dunlop) *hld up in mid-div: bhd fnl 2f* **16/1**
1312 **10** *5* **Moon Sister (IRE)**[30] 6034 3-8-11 100 AlanMunro 9 63
(W Jarvis) *w ldr tl rdn and wknd 2f out* **7/1**[3]
0000 **11** *5* **Raymi Coya (CAN)**[20] 6266 3-9-0 98 TedDurcan 4 56
(M Botti) *prom tl rdn and wknd wl over 1f out* **33/1**

2m 1.65s (-4.15) **Going Correction** -0.10s/f (Good)
WFA 3 from 4yo 5lb **11** Ran SP% **117.1**
Speed ratings (Par 111): **112,111,109,108,105 104,103,99,98,94 90**
toteswinger: 1&2 £12.70, 1&3 £32.00, 2&3 £15.50. CSF £54.45 TOTE £11.40: £3.00, £2.00, £5.00; EX 64.70.
Owner J C Smith **Bred** Littleton Stud **Trained** Newmarket, Suffolk

FOCUS
This looked a strongish field for a Listed race with the winner basically to form. The two principals came from either side of the pack.

NOTEBOOK
Barshiba(IRE), whose career may have been hindered by poor vision in her right eye, has run some cracking races in top company but has not always delivered when her sights were lowered, so this first win since Royal Ascot last year was not coming out of turn. She was immediately retired to the paddocks. (op 10-1 tchd 9-1)
Fragrancy(IRE), who got a bit warm beforehand, came from the back of the field on the near-side to make the winner fight and pulled clear of the rest. She was held up at the back of the field and given a lot to do, but in fairness she got to the winner's quarters in plenty of time and would not have gone by if they had raced for another 100 yards. She remains most progressive. (op 6-1)
In The Light, an ex-French filly, was given a really positive ride, and although the first two left her behind up the hill this was easily her best race over here on her third attempt. (tchd 16-1)
Spacious, who ought to have had this race at her mercy based on her 1000 Guineas form if she stayed the longer trip, was given a confident ride but she failed to pick up in the style one would have expected and, although she was plugging on up the hill, she could not even master In The Light, who herself was adrift of the two principals. One could not say definitively that she did not stay, for she may have been over the top after all, but this was nowhere near her best 1m form. (op 5-2 tchd 10-3)
Ronaldsay, last year's second, had a stiffer task with her 3lb penalty and was without the headgear connections felt had been a success last time, when she was unlucky in running. She made heavy weather of it here, labouring from some way out, and was beaten a long way in fifth. (op 5-1 tchd 9-2)
Princess Taylor had a lot to find on form and wasn't entitled to finish any closer. (tchd 22-1)
Classic Legend was popular in the betting but she has been below last year's form since her belated return to action. (op 14-1)
Classic Remark(IRE) Official explanation: jockey said filly lost its action

6782 EBF NATIONAL STUD BOADICEA FILLIES' STKS (LISTED RACE) 6f

4:20 (4:20) (Class 1) 3-Y-O+

£24,978 (£9,468; £4,738; £2,362; £1,183; £594) **Stalls** High

Form RPR
5110 **1** **Ethaara**[20] 6271 3-8-12 88 RHills 4 104
(W J Haggas) *lw: racd centre: chsd ldrs: led ins fnl f: r.o wl* **20/1**
612 **2** *1 1/2* **Medicea Sidera**[20] 6271 4-8-13 94 JamieSpencer 9 99
(E F Vaughan) *racd towards far side: a.p: rdn and ev ch ins fnl f: edgd lft: styd on same pce* **10/1**
0-32 **3** *1* **Bastakiya (IRE)**[15] 6430 3-8-12 93 LDettori 7 96
(J H M Gosden) *racd centre: chsd ldrs: rdn and ev ch ins fnl f: styd on same pce* **8/1**[3]
1144 **4** *1* **Red Dune (IRE)**[36] 5829 3-8-12 98 PhilipRobinson 5 93
(M A Jarvis) *racd centre: led that gp: tl rdn and hdd over 1f out: styd on same pce fnl f* **5/1**[2]
5325 **5** *nse* **Vital Statistics**[20] 6271 4-8-13 90 DaneO'Neill 3 92
(D R C Elsworth) *racd centre: dwlt: hld up: r.o ins fnl f: nrst fin* **33/1**
131 **6** *3/4* **Laddies Poker Two (IRE)**[21] 6239 3-8-12 98 TPQueally 6 90
(J Noseda) *lw: racd centre: hld up: hdwy over 2f out: overall ldr over 1f out: rdn and hdd ins fnl f: hld whn n.m.r towards fin* **11/8**[1]
4305 **7** *1/2* **How's She Cuttin' (IRE)**[6] 6651 5-8-13 83 (v) WilliamBuick 1 92+
(T D Barron) *racd centre: chsd ldr: nt clr run and lost pl over 1f out: running on whn n.m.r wl ins fnl f* **33/1**
1241 **8** *hd* **Masada (IRE)**[15] 6430 3-8-12 90 MartinDwyer 8 88
(B J Meehan) *racd towards far side: chsd ldrs: led overall wl over 1f out: sn hdd: edgd lft and no ex ins fnl f* **16/1**
0111 **9** *1* **Perfect Flight**[33] 5930 3-8-12 91 HayleyTurner 14 85
(M Blanshard) *racd far side: chsd ldrs: outpcd over 1f out: styd on ins fnl f* **14/1**
0050 **10** *2* **Spinning Lucy (IRE)**[20] 6271 3-8-12 92 MichaelHills 11 78
(B W Hills) *racd towards far side: chsd ldr tl overall ldr over 4f out: hdd wl over 1f out: wknd fnl f* **25/1**
5113 **11** *1/2* **Angus Newz**[15] 6430 5-9-2 90 (v) FrancisNorton 13 80
(M Quinn) *racd far side: led overall tl hdd over 4f out: rdn over 1f out: sn wknd* **25/1**
-045 **12** *4 1/2* **Silver Touch (IRE)**[124] 3063 5-8-13 106 DarryllHolland 10 62
(M R Channon) *racd towards far side: hld up: hdwy over 2f out: rdn over 1f out: sn wknd* **11/1**
0040 **13** *2* **Monaazalah (IRE)**[20] 6271 3-8-12 90 RobertHavlin 2 56
(Rae Guest) *racd centre: s.i.s: hld up: a in rr* **100/1**
4402 **14** *1 1/2* **Topflightcoolracer**[11] 6532 4-8-13 80 TedDurcan 15 51
(Mrs G S Rees) *racd far side: hld up: rdn and wknd over 2f out* **80/1**

1m 10.71s (-1.49) **Going Correction** -0.10s/f (Good)
WFA 3 from 4yo+ 1lb **14** Ran SP% **120.4**
Speed ratings (Par 108): **105,103,101,100,100 99,98,98,97,94 93,87,85,83**
toteswinger: 1&2 £36.10, 1&3 £35.00, 2&3 £12.10. CSF £198.15 TOTE £24.20: £5.90, £3.20, £2.40; EX 393.20.
Owner Hamdan Al Maktoum **Bred** Shadwell Estate Company Limited **Trained** Newmarket, Suffolk

FOCUS
A competitive Listed fillies' sprint with several of these having met each other recently. The field split into three early with a trio racing up the far rail, a group of four racing slightly wider, whilst the other seven came up the centre and it was from that group that most of the principals emerged. The form looks pretty straightforward with the runner-up and fifth close to previous Ascot form.

NOTEBOOK

Ethaara had finished behind a couple of these when stepped up to this level at Ascot last month, but she was a different proposition on this drop back in trip and, having been produced with her effort down the outside, she eventually stormed clear. She is likely to be retired to the paddocks now.

Medicea Sidera, having only her second try over a trip this short, stayed on strongly up the hill and fared much the best of those that raced more towards the far side of the track. She has gained all three of her wins on the July course so she obviously likes the Newmarket air. (op 14-1)

Bastakiya(IRE), lightly raced this year following a knee injury as a juvenile, had split Masada and Angus Newz in a Listed handicap here two weeks ago and was weighted to beat them both on these terms. She managed to do that and had every chance, but was done for finishing speed. (op 7-1)

Red Dune(IRE) was ridden positively on this drop to 6f for the first time, but was forced to give best to speedier types over the last couple of furlongs. (op 13-2 tchd 7-1)

Vital Statistics stayed on strongly in the closing stages, but she is without a win in well over two years so is hardly a betting proposition.

Laddies Poker Two(IRE), upped in class after winning a red-hot handicap at Ascot last time, was travelling better than anything entering the last two furlongs, but found nothing like as much as had seemed likely once off the bridle and was already beaten when getting short of room late on. She remains lightly raced and is probably worth another chance. (op 6-4 tchd 13-8 in places)

How's She Cuttin'(IRE), placed at this level in the summer but without a win since July of last year, was racing beyond the minimum trip for the first time in well over two years and she faced a huge task at the weights. However, she ran with a great deal of credit and would have finished even closer had she not been squeezed out between the eventual winner and Red Dune a furlong and a half out, and she was again short of room well inside the last furlong.

Silver Touch(IRE) had upwards of 8lb in hand of these rivals at the weights, but she was weak in the market and failed to get home after moving into a challenging position a furlong out. (op 8-1)

6783 SAKHEE'S SECRET AT WHITSBURY MANOR STUD H'CAP — 7f

4:55 (4:56) (Class 2) (0-100,100) 3-Y-0+

£12,462 (£3,732; £1,866; £934; £466; £234) **Stalls** High

Form — RPR

0001 **1** **Plum Pudding (IRE)**[13] 6478 5-9-6 **100** .... RyanMoore 13 — 112
(R Hannon) *mde all: drvn out and r.o wl fnl f* — **10/1**

2130 **2** 1 **Signor Peltro**[20] 6269 5-8-9 **89** .... DaneO'Neill 8 — 98
(H Candy) *hld up in mid-div: hdwy 2f out: rdn and chsd wnr fnl f: kpt on* — **9/1**

0010 **3** 1 1/4 **Slugger O'Toole**[13] 6478 3-8-12 **94** .... WilliamBuick 15 — 100
(B W Hills) *lw: a.p: rdn over 1f out: kpt on same pce fnl f* — **14/1**

3425 **4** 1 1/4 **Swift Gift**[125] 3039 3-8-6 **88** .... MartinDwyer 16 — 91
(B J Meehan) *lw: hld up in mid-div: hdwy 4f out: chsd wnr 2f out tl jst over 1f out: rdn and one pce fnl f* — **16/1**

4050 **5** hd **Aye Aye Digby (IRE)**[21] 6239 3-8-4 **86** .... FrankieMcDonald 3 — 88
(H Candy) *a.p: rdn and one pce fnl 2f* — **25/1**

3611 **6** 1/2 **Furnace (IRE)**[20] 6269 4-9-0 **94** .... HayleyTurner 1 — 95
(M L W Bell) *hld up: sn mid-div: rdn over 1f out: kpt on ins fnl f* — **9/2**[1]

5036 **7** nk **Carcinetto (IRE)**[43] 5644 6-8-6 **86** .... JohnEgan 7 — 86
(P D Evans) *a.p: rdn 2f out: fdd ins fnl f* — **50/1**

0422 **8** nk **Masai Moon**[13] 6478 4-8-12 **95** .... JamesMillman(3) 14 — 94
(B R Millman) *prom: rdn and wknd over 1f out* — **14/1**

0403 **9** 1 **Flipando (IRE)**[13] 6478 7-8-9 **89** .... FrancisNorton 10 — 85
(T D Barron) *lw: hld up towards rr: pushed along over 1f out: nvr trbld ldrs* — **9/1**

530 **10** nk **Giganticus (USA)**[20] 6269 5-9-4 **98** .... MichaelHills 11 — 94
(B W Hills) *swtg: prom tl wknd wl over 1f out* — **6/1**[2]

5464 **11** 1/2 **Damika (IRE)**[13] 6484 5-9-6 **100** .... JimCrowley 17 — 94
(R M Whitaker) *hld up in mid-div: rdn and hdwy on far rail over 1f out: wknd ins fnl f* — **9/1**

0360 **12** shd **King's Bastion (IRE)**[34] 5897 4-8-1 **86** oh1 Louis-PhilippeBeuzelin(5) 18 — 80
(M L W Bell) *hld up and bhd: rdn and short-lived effrt 2f out* — **22/1**

2363 **13** nse **We'll Come**[20] 6269 4-9-0 **94** .... (p) DarryllHolland 5 — 88
(M A Jarvis) *a in rr* — **7/1**[3]

4001 **14** 1 1/4 **Game Lad**[27] 6105 6-8-7 **87** oh2 ow1 .... (t) TedDurcan 9 — 77
(T D Easterby) *a towards rr* — **33/1**

640 **15** 9 **City Of The Kings (IRE)**[11] 6526 3-8-8 **90** .... JoeFanning 4 — 56
(G A Harker) *a in rr* — **50/1**

0600 **16** 1/2 **Fajr (IRE)**[121] 3122 6-9-1 **95** .... TPQueally 12 — 60
(Miss Gay Kelleway) *s.i.s: a bhd* — **33/1**

-40 **17** 62 **Somnus**[34] 5893 8-9-1 **95** .... (t) JamieSpencer 6 — —
(J J Quinn) *a in rr: virtually p.u fnl f* — **18/1**

1m 23.8s (-1.60) **Going Correction** -0.10s/f (Good)
WFA 3 from 4yo+ 2lb — **17** Ran SP% **126.5**
Speed ratings (Par 109): **105,103,102,101,100 100,99,99,98,98 97,97,97,95,85 85,14**
toteswinger: 1&2 £27.40, 1&3 £36.30, 2&3 £29.40. CSF £93.90 CT £1328.49 TOTE £6.40: £2.50, £2.70, £4.00, £3.60; EX 135.20.
Owner Hyde Sporting Promotions Limited **Bred** Tom Deane **Trained** East Everleigh, Wilts

FOCUS
A routine handicap in which they began in two distinct groups but merged just after halfway. The winner loves this track and put up another personal best. The placed horses ran to their marks. Sound form.

NOTEBOOK

Plum Pudding(IRE) loves a straight track and has never won anywhere but here. He looked terrific beforehand and dominated proceedings throughout, his success taking his record on the Rowley Mile to a remarkable six wins from 11 tries, every one of them in a handicap, and all but one in a double-figure field. This was the highest mark he has won from and looks a career best. (op 8-1)

Signor Peltro, who raced in the other group up the middle through the first half of the race, emerged from the pack as the only danger, but he was never quite getting to grips with the winner. He is a very capable handicapper but has not enjoyed the best of luck. (op 10-1 tchd 11-1)

Slugger O'Toole, a good winner here in the spring but well beaten last time, returned to form with a sound effort, despite getting very warm in the preliminaries. (tchd 16-1)

Swift Gift, taking on his elders for the first time and returning from four months off the track, did well in fourth, especially as he had pulled hard early on and was edging left in the closing stages.

Aye Aye Digby(IRE), who is gradually easing down the handicap, could not pick up from the run into the dip. (tchd 20-1)

Furnace(IRE), who was on a hat-trick, had been inclined to hang right, particularly when they were running down into the Dip. (op 6-1 tchd 13-2 in places)

Carcinetto(IRE), who had led the group that raced up the middle of the track, ran respectably before tiring up the hill.

Masai Moon could not reproduce his recent effort against the winner. (op 16-1)

Somnus Official explanation: vet said gelding bled from the nose

6784 THOROUGHBRED BREEDERS ASSOCIATION H'CAP — 1m 4f

5:30 (5:34) (Class 2) (0-100,97) 3-Y-0+

£12,462 (£3,732; £1,866; £934; £466; £234) **Stalls** Centre

Form — RPR

2400 **1** **Bandama (IRE)**[13] 6479 5-8-12 **84** .... TPQueally 7 — 94
(Mrs A J Perrett) *hld up in tch: rdn over 1f out: styd on to ld nr fin* — **14/1**

3005 **2** nk **Luberon**[22] 6233 5-9-5 **91** .... JoeFanning 6 — 101
(M Johnston) *led: clr 1/2-way: rdn and hdd nr fin* — **12/1**

0300 **3** 1 1/4 **John Terry (IRE)**[79] 4516 5-9-3 **89** .... JimCrowley 8 — 97
(Mrs A J Perrett) *a.p: chsd ldr 2f out: sn rdn: styd on same pce ins fnl f* — **20/1**

221 **4** 2 **Redesignation (IRE)**[36] 5843 3-9-1 **94** .... RyanMoore 3 — 99
(R Hannon) *hld up: hdwy over 1f out: styd on: nt rch ldrs* — **9/2**[1]

3331 **5** 3/4 **Greylami (IRE)**[23] 6202 3-8-8 **87** .... MichaelHills 2 — 91+
(T G Mills) *hld up: hdwy over 1f out: styd on: nt rch ldrs* — **5/1**[2]

5420 **6** 4 1/2 **Crete (IRE)**[6] 6646 6-9-6 **92** .... HayleyTurner 12 — 88
(W J Haggas) *hld up: racd keenly: hdwy u.p over 1f out: wknd ins fnl f* — **15/2**[3]

0005 **7** 1/2 **Whitcombe Minister (USA)**[6] 6649 3-9-2 **95** .... RobertHavlin 9 — 91
(Jamie Poulton) *hld up: styd on ins fnl f: nrst fin* — **18/1**

5540 **8** 3 3/4 **Samsons Son**[6] 6646 4-9-2 **88** .... LPKeniry 10 — 78
(J R Best) *prom: rdn over 2f out: sn wknd* — **9/1**

6050 **9** nk **Monte Alto (IRE)**[27] 6120 4-9-11 **97** .... DaneO'Neill 5 — 86
(L M Cumani) *lw: hld up: racd keenly: rdn and wknd over 1f out* — **9/2**[1]

5213 **10** nk **Crystal Rock (IRE)**[35] 5865 3-8-4 **83** oh3 .... WilliamBuick 11 — 72
(B W Hills) *chsd ldr tl rdn 2f out: wknd fnl f* — **17/2**

4000 **P** **Smart Instinct (USA)**[13] 6479 4-9-2 **88** .... RoystonFfrench 4 — —
(R A Fahey) *prom: 6th whn p.u and dismntd 3f out* — **25/1**

2m 30.03s (-3.47) **Going Correction** -0.10s/f (Good)
WFA 3 from 4yo+ 7lb — **11** Ran SP% **113.6**
Speed ratings (Par 109): **107,106,105,104,104 101,100,98,98,97** —
toteswinger: 1&2 £28.30, 1&3 £27.00, 2&3 £34.20. CSF £157.36 CT £2872.93 TOTE £17.70: £3.80, £3.10, £5.40; EX 106.00 Place 6 £72.36, Place 5 £48.95.
Owner Mrs S L Whitehead **Bred** Newberry Stud Farm Ltd **Trained** Pulborough, W Sussex
■ Ordination (11/1) was withdrawn after spreading a plate. R4 applies, deduct 5p in the £.

FOCUS
A decent handicap in which several were trying this trip for the first time and a few were backed, which suggests the form is solid. The pace was generous which meant that stamina was all-important and older horses filled the first three places.

NOTEBOOK

Bandama(IRE) looked the stable's second string on jockey bookings, but he had dropped to a mark 1lb lower than for his last win in June 2006. Although he hadn't won over the trip before, he had run enough good races over it to suggest that stamina wasn't an issue and he was produced with perfect timing to creep up the inside of the leader close to the line and win with a little bit in hand. He may go for the November Handicap and then on to Dubai early next year. (op 12-1)

Luberon, who likes to do it from the front, had been well below form in recent starts, but he can be a dangerous opponent when let loose in front and after setting a decent pace it did appear that he might see it through. However, he started to get tired up the final climb and was agonisingly nailed near the line. (tchd 14-1)

John Terry(IRE), not seen since flopping over more than a mile further at Goodwood in July, sat in third place for most of the way, clear of the main group, but although trying his best he could never quite reel in Luberon let alone contain his stable-companion. He may join his stablemate in the November Handicap prior to a possible hurdling campaign. (op 14-1)

Redesignation(IRE), raised 6lb for his victory over a subsequent winner at Sandown last month and well backed here, was trying this trip for the first time and, although he stayed on from last place, he was never getting there in time. (op 6-1)

Greylami(IRE), another trying this trip for the first time and also raised 6lb for beating a couple of subsequent winners at Goodwood last month, was weak in the market and, although it looked as though he might get involved when moving into contention inside the last two furlongs, he was making no further impression up the hill and may not have stayed. (op 7-2)

Monte Alto(IRE), still 5lb above his last winning mark and trying this trip for the first time, went off a well-backed favourite but he raced rather keenly in the pack and when eventually asked for his effort there was little there. (op 13-2)

Crystal Rock(IRE), yet another trying this trip for the first time and 3lb out of the weights, slipstreamed Luberon for a long way but found little off the bridle and appeared not to stay. (op 14-1)

T/Jkpt: Not won. T/Plt: £55.70 to a £1 stake. Pool: £65,101.25. 852.70 winning tickets. T/Qpdt: £12.20 to a £1 stake. Pool: £5,373.38. 323.95 winning tickets. CR

6480 REDCAR (L-H)

Friday, October 17

OFFICIAL GOING: Good (8.5)

Wind: Light, half behind Weather: Fine

6785 EUROPEAN BREEDERS' FUND MAIDEN FILLIES' STKS (DIV I) — 6f

1:40 (1:41) (Class 5) 2-Y-0 — £3,561 (£1,059; £529; £264) **Stalls** Centre

Form — RPR

6 **1** **Mythicism**[30] 6010 2-9-0 0 .... (t) PaulMulrennan 4 — 70
(B Smart) *a cl up: rdn to ld and hung rt over 1f out: drvn ins fnl f and kpt on u.p towards fin* — **9/2**[2]

0 **2** nk **Timeless Dream**[56] 5240 2-9-0 0 .... GregFairley 5 — 69
(P W Chapple-Hyam) *sn led: rdn along 2f out: hdd and carried rt over 1f out: drvn and kpt on wl fnl f: jst hld* — **9/2**[2]

5 **3** 4 **Makaykla**[9] 6578 2-9-0 0 .... DavidAllan 14 — 57
(E J Alston) *in tch: hdwy 2f out: rdn to chse ldng pair over 1f out: swtchd lft and drvn ent fnl f: sn one pce* — **8/1**[3]

4 2 **Sams Lass** 2-9-0 0 .... CatherineGannon 8 — 51
(M Mullineaux) *dwlt and towards rr: hdwy 2f out: styd on wl fnl f: nrst fin* — **66/1**

04 **5** 3 1/4 **Monaco Mistress (IRE)**[64] 5004 2-9-0 0 .... LeeEnstone 13 — 41
(P C Haslam) *in tch on outer: hdwy to chse ldrs over 2f out: sn rdn and kpt on same pce* — **9/1**

05 **6** 1 1/2 **Petella**[21] 6245 2-9-0 0 .... PJMcDonald 6 — 37
(C W Thornton) *in tch: pushed along and outpcd 1/2-way: styd on appr fnl f: nrst fin* — **8/1**[3]

36 **7** 3/4 **Diamond Daisy (IRE)**[10] 6548 2-8-11 0 .... AndrewMullen(3) 10 — 35
(Mrs A Duffield) *dwlt: sn in tch: effrt to chse ldrs over 2f out: sn rdn and wknd wl over 1f out* — **9/1**

500 **8** 2 **Lady Dunhill (IRE)**[6] 6655 2-8-11 0 ow2 .... GaryBartley(5) 3 — 31
(J S Goldie) *in rr: pushed along 1/2-way: swtchd rt 2f out: styd on ins fnl f: nrst fin* — **33/1**

The Form Book, Raceform Ltd, Compton, RG20 6NL

	9 *1*	**Oceanic Dancer (IRE)** 2-8-11 0 ... RussellKennemore(3) 12 (Mrs L Williamson) *prom: cl up 1/2-way and sn rdn: drvn and wknd 2f out* **50/1**	26
	10 *7*	**Desdamona (IRE)** 2-8-9 0 ... SladeO'Hara(5) 11 (A Berry) *s.i.s: a in rr* **100/1**	5
0	**11** *3/4*	**Miss Cameo (USA)**[13] 6481 2-9-0 0 ... DeanMcKeown 1 (R M Whitaker) *dwlt and a towards rr* **12/1**	2
05	**12** *2*	**Dahama**[17] 6360 2-9-0 0 ... NCallan 2 (C E Brittain) *cl up: pushed along 1/2-way: sn rdn and wknd over 2f out* **10/3**[1]	—
0	**13** *nk*	**Broomfield Buddy**[27] 6109 2-9-0 0 ... TonyHamilton 7 (D W Barker) *prom: rdn along 1/2-way and sn wknd* **150/1**	—
0	**14** *3/4*	**Rafta (IRE)**[10] 6548 2-8-11 0 ... DuranFentiman(3) 9 (W G Harrison) *a towards rr* **100/1**	—

1m 12.36s (0.56) **Going Correction** +0.15s/f (Good) **14** Ran SP% **118.4**
Speed ratings (Par 92): **102,101,96,93,89 87,86,83,82,72 71,69,68,67**
toteswinger: 1&2 £5.40, 1&3 £6.90, 2&3 £12.40. CSF £24.30 TOTE £5.40: £1.70, £1.70, £2.50; EX 30.50.
Owner Crossfields Racing **Bred** Bearstone Stud **Trained** Hambleton, N Yorks

FOCUS
Last year's winner Spinning Lucy went on to score in Listed company but this renewal had little strength in depth and is unlikely to be throwing up too many winners outside of modest handicap or selling company. The pace was sound and the first two pulled clear.

NOTEBOOK
Mythicism hinted at ability in a race that has worked out fairly well on soft on her debut and bettered that form over this longer trip fitted with a tongue-tie. She may progress further in ordinary nursery company. (tchd 7-2 and 5-1)
Timeless Dream was well beaten over 7f in a better race than this on her debut but she showed enough to suggest a similarly uncompetitive event can be found. (op 4-1 tchd 5-1)
Makaykla showed a glimmer of ability on her debut and fared a bit better over this longer trip on better ground. Modest handicaps will be the way forward with her. (op 11-1)
Sams Lass, a half-sister to three winners, was green but showed ability on this racecourse debut. She should improve but is likely to remain vulnerable in this grade. (op 50-1)
Monaco Mistress(IRE), upped in trip and back on a sound surface, failed to better her latest soft ground run but may do better in handicaps in due course. (op 12-1)
Petella is now qualified for a mark but will be suited by a much stiffer test of stamina. She is not one to write off yet. (op 7-1)
Dahama, back in trip, jumped off on terms this time but proved the big disappointment of the race. She looks best watched at present. Official explanation: jockey said filly never travelled and had no more to give final furlong (op 7-2 tchd 3-1)

6786 SAWFISH SOFTWARE LADIES' H'CAP (FOR LADY AMATEUR RIDERS) 1m 2f
2:10 (2:12) (Class 6) (0-60,60) 3-Y-O+ £2,307 (£709; £354) Stalls Low

Form			RPR
0040	**1**	**Neon Blue**[23] 6216 7-10-4 56 ... MissARyan 3 (R M Whitaker) *s.s: hdwy and swtchd outside over 3f out: styd on to ld wl ins fnl f* **10/1**	63
2020	**2** *nk*	**Thornaby Green**[3] 6726 7-10-3 55 ... MissGDGracey-Davison 2 (T D Barron) *chsd ldrs: chal 2f out: no ex towards fin* **9/1**[3]	61
3203	**3** *hd*	**Emperor's Well**[24] 6189 9-10-2 57 ... (b) MissJCoward(3) 8 (M W Easterby) *chsd ldrs: led over 2f out: hdd and no ex wl ins fnl f* **14/1**	63
6-01	**4** *4 1/2*	**Surprise Pension (IRE)**[25] 6161 4-10-6 58 ... MissADeniel 7 (J J Quinn) *in tch: effrt 3f out: one pce* **4/1**[2]	55
6205	**5** *1/2*	**Polish Corridor**[47] 5538 9-10-7 59 ... MissSBrotherton 5 (M Dods) *hld up in rr: hdwy over 3f out: kpt on fnl 2: nvr rchd ldrs* **7/2**[1]	55
5240	**6** *9*	**Desert Hawk**[11] 6538 7-10-7 59 ... MissEJJones 9 (W M Brisbourne) *in rr: kpt on fnl 3f: nvr nr ldrs* **16/1**	37
3060	**7** *1/2*	**Grethel (IRE)**[23] 6215 4-10-2 59 ... MissMMullineaux(5) 6 (A Berry) *mid-div: effrt over 3f out: nvr a factor* **25/1**	36
2500	**8** *7*	**Chin Wag (IRE)**[46] 5564 4-10-7 59 ... (p) MrsCBartley 10 (J S Goldie) *hld up in rr: nvr on terms* **16/1**	22
6420	**9** *shd*	**Hi Dancer**[118] 3279 5-9-11 56 ... MissEStead(7) 11 (P C Haslam) *hld up in rr: effrt on outside over 3f out: nvr on terms* **11/1**	18
0235	**10** *6*	**Natural Rhythm (IRE)**[29] 6042 3-9-12 60 ... (b) MissWGibson(5) 1 (Mrs R A Carr) *led tl hdd & wknd over 2f out* **16/1**	10
0055	**11** *4 1/2*	**Hurricane Thomas (IRE)**[3] 6727 4-9-12 57 ... (p) MissPhillipaTutty(7) 14 (R E Barr) *racd wd: chsd ldrs: sn pushed along: lost pl 4f out: sn bhd* **12/1**	—
0-0	**12** *3*	**Skylarker (USA)**[16] 6385 10-10-0 57 ... MissHCuthbert(5) 12 (T A K Cuthbert) *chsd ldrs: lost pl 3f out* **80/1**	—
-364	**13** *hd*	**Waterloo Corner**[17] 4537 6-9-13 58 ... MissLSutcliffe(7) 15 (R Craggs) *racd wd: prom tl lost pl after 3f: sn bhd* **16/1**	—
600-	**14** *1 3/4*	**Kiss Chase (IRE)**[393] 5555 4-9-13 56 ... (b) MissRKneller(5) 4 (J S Goldie) *prom: edgd rt and lost pl over 2f out* **12/1**	—
006	**15** *56*	**Miss Ferney**[20] 6275 4-9-13 56 ow1 ... MissRBastiman(5) 13 (A Kirtley) *t.k.h: prom: lost pl over 5f out: sn bhd: t.o: virtually p.u* **40/1**	—

2m 10.13s (3.03) **Going Correction** +0.15s/f (Good)
WFA 3 from 4yo+ 5lb **15** Ran SP% **122.7**
Speed ratings (Par 101): **93,92,92,89,88 81,81,75,75,70 66,64,64,62,18**
toteswinger: 1&2 £21.80, 1&3 £16.00, 2&3 £20.80. CSF £97.28 CT £1282.15 TOTE £14.30: £3.90, £3.60, £3.20; EX 149.70.
Owner Country Lane Partnership **Bred** R And Mrs Watson And Mrs A J Ralli **Trained** Scarcroft, W Yorks

FOCUS
A modest handicap featuring mainly exposed sorts. The pace was soon sound and the form is best rated through the third.
Miss Ferney Official explanation: trainer said filly was heavily in seaason

6787 REDCAR CONFERENCE CENTRE CLAIMING STKS 7f
2:45 (2:45) (Class 6) 2-Y-O £2,388 (£705; £352) Stalls Centre

Form			RPR
5322	**1**	**Digit**[32] 5966 2-8-4 57 ... SilvestreDeSousa 14 (B Smart) *in tch: hdwy 1/2-way: rdn to ld wl over 1f out: drvn out* **7/2**[1]	62
5055	**2** *1 1/4*	**Flyit (IRE)**[15] 6414 2-9-1 68 ... TonyCulhane 10 (M R Channon) *trckd ldrs gng wl: smooth hdwy to ld over 2f out: rdn: edgd lft and hdd wl over 1f out: sn drvn and kpt on u.p ins fnl f* **7/1**[3]	70
6506	**3** *1 3/4*	**Skruton (IRE)**[15] 6414 2-8-12 67 ... NCallan 17 (M G Quinlan) *hld up in midfield: hdwy wl over 2f out: rdn to chse ldrs over 1f out: kpt on u.p ins fnl f* **7/1**[3]	63
4065	**4** *nk*	**Premier Krug (IRE)**[35] 5866 2-8-4 58 ... CatherineGannon 15 (P D Evans) *outpcd and rdn along in rr 1/2-way: hdwy wl over 1f out: styd on strly ins fnl f: nrst fin* **22/1**	54
00	**5** *1 1/4*	**Paddyntrev Bakfavs (IRE)**[83] 4415 2-8-13 0 ... DavidAllan 4 (T D Easterby) *in tch: rdn along to chse ldrs over 2f out: drvn and kpt on same pce appr fnl f* **66/1**	60
526	**6** *1/2*	**Glan Lady (IRE)**[27] 6133 2-8-0 55 ... LiamJones 9 (J L Spearing) *led: rdn along 1/2-way: hdd over 2f out and sn drvn: kpt on same pce fr over 1f out* **9/1**	45
0540	**7** *3/4*	**Hatchet Man**[23] 6207 2-8-3 60 ... SaleemGolam 12 (P Winkworth) *midfield: effrt over 2f out and sn pushed along: rdn wl over 1f out: kpt on u.p ins fnl f: nrst fin* **20/1**	47
0253	**8** *nk*	**Iorek Byrnison**[45] 5591 2-8-7 58 ... PaulQuinn 1 (D Nicholls) *in tch: rdn along 2f out: sn drvn and no imp* **10/1**	50
3020	**9** *3/4*	**Raise All In (IRE)**[10] 6547 2-8-5 65 ... BMcHugh(7) 2 (N Wilson) *chsd ldrs: rdn along and ch 2f out: sn drvn and wknd appr fnl f* **14/1**	53
00	**10** *1/2*	**Curtain Up**[45] 5590 2-8-5 0 ... (b[1]) DaleGibson 7 (M W Easterby) *cl up: rdn along over 2f out and grad wknd* **100/1**	45
3	**11** *1 1/2*	**Risky Capital**[17] 6351 2-8-3 0 ... JimmyQuinn 13 (S A Callaghan) *chsd ldrs: rdn along 2f out: grad wknd* **4/1**[2]	39
5000	**12** *1/2*	**Buckers Beauty (IRE)**[44] 5606 2-8-1 57 ... AndrewMullen(3) 20 (P D Evans) *in tch on wd outside: pushed along 3f out: rdn over 2f out and sn no imp* **40/1**	39
0250	**13** *2*	**Sale Or Return (IRE)**[9] 6579 2-8-1 53 ... DuranFentiman(3) 16 (T D Easterby) *nvr nr ldrs* **33/1**	34
560	**14** *1 1/4*	**Betws Y Coed (IRE)**[69] 4870 2-8-12 57 ... (p) MickyFenton 11 (A Bailey) *sn pushed along in rr: effrt and hung lft 3f out: nvr a factor* **16/1**	39
0	**15** *9*	**Suprise Gift**[23] 6213 2-8-1 0 ... JamieKyne(7) 6 (J J Quinn) *midfield: rdn along 1/2-way and sn wknd* **40/1**	12
40	**16** *3 3/4*	**Blue Dagger (IRE)**[105] 3670 2-8-10 0 ... PatrickDonaghy(5) 18 (P C Haslam) *a bhd* **50/1**	10
4605	**17** *1 3/4*	**Winsome Hearts**[38] 5774 2-8-9 55 ... (b[1]) PaulMulrennan 3 (M W Easterby) *cl up on outer: rdn along 1/2-way and sn wknd* **25/1**	—
	18 *1*	**Petite Rocket (IRE)** 2-8-4 0 ... GregFairley 8 (A G Foster) *chsd ldrs: rdn along over 2f out and sn wknd* **66/1**	—
0	**19** *3 1/4*	**Secret Star (IRE)**[21] 6246 2-8-7 0 ... TonyHamilton 19 (R Bastiman) *a towards rr* **100/1**	—
0250	**R**	**El Portet**[38] 5778 2-8-9 58 ... (b[1]) PJMcDonald 5 (G M Moore) *ref to r: tk no part* **50/1**	—

1m 25.69s (1.19) **Going Correction** +0.15s/f (Good) **20** Ran SP% **128.5**
Speed ratings (Par 93): **99,97,95,95,93 93,92,92,91,90 88,88,86,84,74 70,68,66,63,—**
toteswinger: 1&2 £6.70, 1&3 £6.80, 2&3 £9.20. CSF £25.64 TOTE £4.00: £1.90, £3.00, £3.20; EX 18.50.
Owner B Smart **Bred** Bearstone Stud **Trained** Hambleton, N Yorks

FOCUS
Not a strong race. The pace was reasonable and the market leaders came to the fore in the closing stages.

NOTEBOOK
Digit, who had a good chance at the weights and who hails from an in-form yard, threw away a winning chance when hanging badly on soft last time but kept much straighter back on a sound surface to justify the market support. She is a fairly reliable sort who should continue to run well in this grade. (op 11-2)
Flyit(IRE) had been shaping as though worth another try over this trip and showed enough to suggest a similar event over this trip can be found. (op 6-1 tchd 11-2)
Skruton(IRE), the only previous winner in the field, had a decent chance at the weights and fared the best of the hold up horses on his first run over 7f. She'll find life tougher back in nurseries from her current mark, though. (op 11-2)
Premier Krug(IRE) is an exposed maiden who wasn't disgraced upped to this trip for the first time on this return to turf but she does not look the most consistent around. (op 20-1)
Paddyntrev Bakfavs(IRE) , who again lost ground at the start, showed his first worthwhile form down in grade after a break of nearly three months. He should stay 1m and may do better in modest nursery company.
Glan Lady(IRE), having her first run on a sound surface, was well beaten on Polytrack on her previous start and failed to reproduce her soft ground form back on turf. (op 8-1)

6788 EUROPEAN BREEDERS' FUND MAIDEN FILLIES' STKS (DIV II) 6f
3:20 (3:21) (Class 5) 2-Y-O £3,561 (£1,059; £529; £264) Stalls Centre

Form			RPR
0550	**1**	**Impressible**[36] 5834 2-9-0 64 ... DavidAllan 8 (E J Alston) *led 3f: led over 1f out: hld on towards fin* **7/2**[2]	63
	2 *1/2*	**Lily Jicaro (IRE)** 2-8-11 0 ... RussellKennemore(3) 7 (Mrs L Williamson) *mid-div: hung lft over 2f out: edgd lft and styd on wl ins fnl f* **12/1**	62
0002	**3** *2 1/4*	**Real Diamond**[63] 5043 2-9-0 53 ... SilvestreDeSousa 6 (A Dickman) *t.k.h: w ldr: led 3f out tl over 1f out: kpt on same pce* **10/1**	55
	4 *1 1/4*	**Jeunopse (IRE)** 2-9-0 0 ... PaulMulrennan 3 (B Smart) *s.s: detached in rr: hdwy over 1f out: styd on wl ins fnl f* **7/1**[3]	55+
0	**5** *nk*	**Dawn Wee**[9] 6578 2-9-0 0 ... PJMcDonald 14 (G R Oldroyd) *mid-div: outpcd over 2f out: kpt on fnl f* **40/1**	50
00	**6** *hd*	**Shining Times (IRE)**[10] 6548 2-9-0 0 ... PaulFessey 2 (D W Barker) *chsd ldrs: kpt on same pce appr fnl f* **40/1**	50
0	**7** *1*	**Forgotten Dreams (IRE)**[13] 6473 2-9-0 0 ... NCallan 5 (H J L Dunlop) *chsd ldrs: one pce fnl 2f* **2/1**[1]	47+
060	**8** *3/4*	**Valentine Bay**[31] 5989 2-8-7 48 ... DeanHeslop(7) 9 (M Mullineaux) *s.i.s: kpt on fnl 2f: nvr nr ldrs* **16/1**	44
0	**9** *3/4*	**Melkatant**[22] 6229 2-9-0 0 ... JimmyQuinn 11 (N Bycroft) *mid-div: outpcd and lost pl over 2f out* **50/1**	42
	10 *2 1/4*	**Fifer (IRE)** 2-9-0 0 ... TonyHamilton 1 (R A Fahey) *mid-div: drvn over 2f out: sn lost pl* **7/1**[3]	35
	11 *4*	**All The Nines (IRE)** 2-8-11 0 ... DuranFentiman(3) 4 (Miss V Haigh) *sn chsng ldrs: hung lft and lost pl over 1f out* **16/1**	23
60	**12** *2*	**Bun Penny**[27] 6110 2-9-0 0 ... GregFairley 10 (G M Moore) *mid-div: outpcd over 2f out: sn lost pl* **40/1**	17
000	**13** *14*	**Fizzy Friend**[72] 4734 2-8-11 34 ... NeilBrown(3) 13 (J R Weymes) *in rr: bhd fnl 2f* **100/1**	—

1m 13.73s (1.93) **Going Correction** +0.15s/f (Good) **13** Ran SP% **119.4**
Speed ratings (Par 92): **93,92,89,87,87 87,85,84,83,80 75,72,54**
toteswinger: 1&2 £11.70, 1&3 £4.70, 2&3 £17.80. CSF £43.90 TOTE £4.90: £1.90, £5.90, £2.10; EX 45.60.
Owner Mr & Mrs G Middlebrook **Bred** Mr & Mrs G Middlebrook **Trained** Longton, Lancs

FOCUS
A poor second division of this maiden fillies' race and a much slower time than part one. The form is weak, little better than a seller.

NOTEBOOK
Impressible, having her seventh start and rated just 64, regained the advantage and in the end did just enough. Low-grade nurseries now beckon. (op 4-1 tchd 10-3)
Lily Jicaro(IRE) went right then wandered left before picking up in good style on this racecourse debut. She should improve and find a modest event. (op 16-1)
Real Diamond, rated just 51, looks all speed. Keen to get on with it after taking charge in the end she did not get home anyway near as well as the first two. A drop back to five will suit. (op 13-2)
Jeunopse(IRE) ◆ is the one to take out of the race. Slowly away and detached in the rear, she put in some sterling work in the final furlong. (op 4-1)

Dawn Wee showed a fair bit more than on her soft ground debut nine days earlier.
Shining Times(IRE), having her third start, was another who seemingly turned in an improved effort. (op 50-1)
Forgotten Dreams(IRE), who made her debut in a valuable sales race at Newmarket two weeks earlier, was struggling to keep up soon after halfway and had no obvious excuse. (op 4-1)

6789 MARKET CROSS JEWELLERS MEDIAN AUCTION MAIDEN STKS 1m
3:55 (3:58) (Class 6) 2-Y-O **£2,388** (£705; £352) **Stalls** Centre

Form RPR

0 **1** **Shady Lady (IRE)**[71] 4780 2-8-12 0 .... GregFairley 10 69+
(M Johnston) *mde virtually all: rdn along 2f out: drvn over 1f out: kpt on wl u.p ins fnl f* **12/1**

2 *2* **Storming Sioux** 2-8-12 0 .... LiamJones 18 65+
(W J Haggas) *hld up: gd hdwy on outer over 2f out: rdn to chse ldrs over 1f out: edgd lft and kpt on fnl f* **11/1**

323 **3** *1 ½* **Popiel**[11] 6539 2-9-3 0 .... NCallan 12 67
(Saeed Bin Suroor) *a cl up: effrt over 2f out: sn rdn to chal and ev ch tl drvn: edgd lft and one pce ent fnl f* **5/6**[1]

56 **4** *nk* **Bigalo's Star (IRE)**[13] 6466 2-9-0 0 .... DuranFentiman(3) 7 66
(L A Mullaney) *cl up: effrt over 2f out: sn rdn and ev ch tl drvn and one pce ent fnl f* **10/1**

420 **5** *3 ½* **Forty Thirty (IRE)**[11] 6524 2-9-3 0 .... TonyCulhane 2 58
(M R Channon) *prom: hdwy and cl up 1/2-way: rdn along wl over 2f out and ev ch tl drvn: edgd rt and wknd over 1f out* **9/1**[3]

6 *1* **Distant Memories (IRE)** 2-9-3 0 .... MickyFenton 16 56+
(T P Tate) *in tch: hdwy to chse ldrs 3f out: rdn along over 2f out and kpt on same pce* **13/2**[2]

7 *½* **Sinchiroka (FR)** 2-9-3 0 .... JimmyQuinn 14 55+
(E F Vaughan) *towards rr: hdwy wl over 2f out: rdn and styd on appr fnl f: nrst fin* **20/1**

0 **8** *4* **Murrays Magic (IRE)**[29] 6037 2-8-12 0 .... SilvestreDeSousa 13 41
(D Nicholls) *midfield: hdwy to chse ldrs over 2f out: sn rdn and kpt on same pce* **66/1**

0 **9** *1 ¼* **Pattern Mark**[23] 6213 2-9-3 0 .... TonyHamilton 5 43
(Ollie Pears) *wnt rt s: sn in midfield: rdn along wl over 2f out and sn no imp* **100/1**

0 **10** *2* **Berriedale**[89] 4213 2-8-12 0 .... PaulQuinn 11 34
(Mrs A Duffield) *chsd ldrs: rdn along over 2f out and grad wknd* **100/1**

0 **11** *1 ¾* **Avitus**[22] 6230 2-9-3 0 .... DeanMcKeown 1 35
(Micky Hammond) *midfield: hdwy and in tch on outer over 2f out: sn rdn and wknd* **100/1**

0 **12** *4 ½* **Indigo Belle (IRE)**[24] 6187 2-8-9 0 .... AndrewMullen(3) 8 20
(Mrs A Duffield) *in tch: rdn along 1/2-way: sn wknd* **100/1**

05 **13** *¾* **Magical Night**[25] 6176 2-8-12 0 .... PJMcDonald 15 19+
(T D Walford) *nvr nr ldrs* **66/1**

00 **14** *1* **Transporter (IRE)**[16] 6381 2-9-3 0 .... DavidAllan 9 21
(T D Easterby) *in tch: rdn along 3f out: sn drvn and wknd* **100/1**

06 **15** *nse* **Swing It Ruby (IRE)**[28] 6089 2-8-12 0 .... CatherineGannon 19 16
(Miss V Haigh) *wnt rt s: in tch on outer tl rdn along over 3f out and sn wknd* **66/1**

16 *nk* **Top Tinker** 2-9-3 0 .... SaleemGolam 3 21
(M H Tompkins) *a towards rr* **50/1**

0 **17** *hd* **Prince Andjo (USA)**[21] 6253 2-9-3 0 .... PatrickMathers 17 20
(I W McInnes) *a towards rr* **66/1**

18 *7* **Net Value (USA)** 2-9-3 0 .... PaulMulrennan 4 5+
(B Smart) *chsd ldrs: rdn along 3f out: sn wknd* **25/1**

19 *¾* **Neva A Mull Moment (IRE)** 2-8-10 0 .... NSLawes(7) 20 —
(D Nicholls) *s.i.s: a in rr* **40/1**

0 **20** *1* **High Tensile**[16] 6381 2-8-12 0 .... PaulFessey 6 —
(J G Given) *in rr fr 1/2-way* **66/1**

1m 39.83s (1.83) **Going Correction** +0.15s/f (Good) **20 Ran SP% 128.4**
Speed ratings (Par 93): **96,94,92,92,88 87,87,83,81,79 78,73,72,71,71 71,71,64,63,62**
toteswinger: 1&2 £12.20, 1&3 £5.60, 2&3 £4.90. CSF £134.31 TOTE £15.90: £3.90, £3.00, £1.30; EX 205.60.
Owner Ascot In Mind **Bred** P D Savill **Trained** Middleham Moor, N Yorks

FOCUS
A maximum field but a race lacking much in the way of strength in depth and one in which the short-priced favourite proved disappointing. The pace was fair and the first two can be expected to improve.

NOTEBOOK
Shady Lady(IRE), well beaten on soft ground on her debut, turned in a much improved display on this quicker ground. She will have no problems with 1m2f, has a good attitude and is the type to progress further. (op 8-1)
Storming Sioux ◆, who was easy to back, took the eye on pedigree as a daughter of Fred Darling winner and Oaks-placed Sueboog and shaped with plenty of encouragement on her debut. She is open to plenty of improvement and is sure to win a similar event at the very least. (op 10-1 tchd 16-1)
Popiel looked to have solid claims but, although not beaten far, proved a disappointment. While he has shown enough to suggest he can win a modest maiden, he lacks much in the way of physical scope and this looks as good as he is. (op 10-11 tchd Evens)
Bigalo's Star(IRE) was the subject of a gamble and duly turned in an improved effort back on turf and on this first run on a sound surface. He pulled clear of the remainder and is more than capable of winning an ordinary handicap up to this trip. (op 66-1)
Forty Thirty(IRE), who didn't get home over 1m2f on his previous start, looked to have claims back over this trip but again proved disappointing. He looks one to have reservations about at present. (op 8-1)
Distant Memories(IRE), who is out of a 1m1f French Listed winner, was green and not totally disgraced on this racecourse debut. He is entitled to improve for the experience. (op 8-1)
Net Value(USA) Official explanation: jockey said colt hung right final 2f

6790 SAM HALL MEMORIAL H'CAP 1m 6f 19y
4:30 (4:31) (Class 5) (0-75,75) 3-Y-O+ **£3,238** (£963; £481; £240) **Stalls** Low

Form RPR

5341 **1** **Bollin Greta**[11] 6529 3-8-9 **65** 6ex .... DavidAllan 4 75+
(T D Easterby) *trckd ldrs: smooth hdwy over 3f out: chal 2f out: shkn up to ld 1f out: styd on strly towards fin* **5/1**[2]

2204 **2** *nk* **Motarid (USA)**[32] 5963 3-9-5 **75** .... (b[1]) PJMcDonald 1 84
(T D Walford) *trckd ldrs: led over 1f out: sn hdd: no ex ins fnl f* **10/1**

4563 **3** *3 ¼* **Garra Molly (IRE)**[11] 6529 3-8-9 **65** .... NCallan 7 70
(G A Swinbank) *hld up in rr: effrt over 3f out: styd on fnl f to snatch modest 3rd nr line* **11/2**[3]

1550 **4** *½* **Monterrico**[31] 5999 3-9-2 **72** .... GregFairley 8 76
(G Wragg) *trckd ldrs: led over 3f out: hdd over 1f out: kpt on same pce* **9/2**[1]

05-0 **5** *shd* **Top Tiger**[29] 6050 4-9-1 **62** .... LiamJones 14 66
(M H Tompkins) *t.k.h in rr: hdwy 3f out: kpt on wl fnl f* **16/1**

46-3 **6** *3 ¾* **Categorical**[177] 1304 5-9-4 **65** .... TonyHamilton 11 64
(K G Reveley) *trckd ldrs on outer: effrt over 3f out: wknd over 1f out* **18/1**

2340 **7** *½* **Lemonesse (USA)**[70] 4821 3-9-2 **72** .... JimmyQuinn 5 70
(H R A Cecil) *trckd ldrs: nt clr run 3f out: wknd over 1f out* **10/1**

1140 **8** *½* **Let It Be**[11] 6527 7-10-0 **75** .... TonyCulhane 13 72
(K G Reveley) *hld up in rr: hdwy over 3f out: nvr nr ldrs* **20/1**

034 **9** *1 ½* **River Danube**[34] 5887 5-9-5 **66** .... PaulMulrennan 6 61
(T J Fitzgerald) *set modest pce: qcknd 4f out: hdd over 3f out: lost pl over 1f out* **18/1**

1346 **10** *1 ½* **Kyber**[19] 6313 7-8-11 **63** ow2 .... GaryBartley(5) 9 56
(J S Goldie) *t.k.h towards rr on outer: effrt 3f out: nvr a threat* **14/1**

2105 **11** *hd* **Benhego**[18] 6329 3-8-12 **68** .... SaleemGolam 2 61
(S C Williams) *prom: hmpd bnd after 2f: effrt over 3f out: wknd 2f out* **9/2**[1]

1-4P **12** *25* **Hernando's Boy**[177] 1559 7-9-9 **70** .... PaulFessey 10 28
(K G Reveley) *hld up in rr: hdwy on inner over 3f out: wknd over 1f out: heavily eased* **25/1**

3m 12.37s (7.67) **Going Correction** +0.15s/f (Good)
WFA 3 from 4yo+ 9lb **12 Ran SP% 118.3**
Speed ratings (Par 103): **84,83,81,81,81 79,79,78,78,77 77,62**
toteswinger: 1&2 £9.20, 1&3 £4.40, 2&3 £16.50. CSF £54.32 CT £287.97 TOTE £4.40: £1.70, £3.00, £2.00; EX 61.90.
Owner Sir Neil Westbrook **Bred** Sir Neil & Exors Of Late Lady Westbrook **Trained** Great Habton, N Yorks
■ Stewards' Enquiry : Jimmy Quinn two-day ban: careless riding (Oct 31, Nov 1)

FOCUS
An ordinary handicap in which the gallop was only steady to the straight, but the first four all came here unexposed at the trip or progressive and this looks form to be fairly positive about. The fifth sets the level.
Top Tiger Official explanation: jockey said gelding ran too free
Hernando's Boy Official explanation: jockey said gelding had no more to give

6791 REDCARRACING.CO.UK MAIDEN STKS 6f
5:05 (5:07) (Class 5) 3-Y-O+ **£2,590** (£770; £385; £192) **Stalls** Centre

Form RPR

0300 **1** **Medici Time**[29] 6042 3-9-3 54 .... (v[1]) DavidAllan 13 70
(T D Easterby) *dwlt and towards rr: hdwy 1/2-way: rdn to chse ldrs over 1f out: styd on u.p to ld ins fnl f* **40/1**

5 **2** *1 ½* **Taqdeyr**[16] 6393 3-9-3 0 .... NCallan 1 65
(M A Jarvis) *s.i.s: rapid hdwy and cl up after 1f: led 1/2-way: rdn along 2f out: hdd and edgd lft over 1f out: drvn ins fnl f and kpt on towards fin* **8/13**[1]

25-5 **3** *½* **Liberty Ship**[214] 918 3-9-3 69 .... (t) JimmyQuinn 10 64
(J D Bethell) *cl up: rdn to ld over 1f out: drvn and hdd ins fnl f: no ex towards fin* **16/1**

2006 **4** *½* **Hansomis (IRE)**[15] 6409 4-8-13 52 .... PAspell 7 57
(B Mactaggart) *chsd ldrs: rdn along 2f out: drvn over 1f out: kpt on same pce ins fnl f* **50/1**

\- **5** *1 ¼* **Edmondstown Lass (IRE)**[14] 6454 3-8-12 74 .... TonyHamilton 16 53
(R A Fahey) *chsd ldrs: rdn along 2f out: drvn over 1f out and kpt on ins fnl f* **12/1**

0320 **6** *nk* **Pintano**[32] 5965 3-8-12 62 .... (b) FrederikTylicki(5) 2 57
(J Howard Johnson) *chsd ldrs: rdn along 2f out: drvn over 1f out and kpt on same pce* **7/1**[2]

0002 **7** *3* **Morocchius (USA)**[30] 6036 3-9-3 60 .... (p) PaulMulrennan 19 47
(Miss J A Camacho) *towards rr tl styd on fnl 2f: nrst fin* **16/1**

8 *2 ½* **This Ones For Pat (USA)** 3-9-3 0 .... TonyCulhane 5 39+
(S Parr) *s.i.s and in rr tl styd on fnl 2f: nrst fin* **50/1**

9 *¾* **Hitches Dubai (BRZ)** 3-8-7 0 .... SilvestreDeSousa 20 27+
(D Nicholls) *s.i.s and bhd tl styd on fnl 2f* **25/1**

0- **10** *2 ½* **Silk Gallery (USA)**[406] 5194 3-8-9 0 .... AndrewMullen(3) 15 24
(E J Alston) *chsd ldrs: rdn along 2f out: sn drvn and grad wknd* **28/1**

5600 **11** *1* **Tump Mac**[91] 4172 4-9-1 60 .... NeilBrown(3) 11 26
(N Bycroft) *a towards rr* **66/1**

06 **12** *¾* **Rosies Dawn**[7] 6633 3-8-12 0 .... DNolan 18 18
(D Carroll) *nvr nr ldrs* **150/1**

13 *½* **Dance Card** 3-8-12 0 .... GregFairley 6 17
(A G Foster) *s.i.s: pushed along and hdwy on outer 1/2-way: rdn 2f out and sn no imp* **11/1**[3]

0060 **14** *1* **Yorke's Folly (USA)**[22] 6232 7-8-13 44 .... (v) PaulFessey 17 14
(C W Fairhurst) *nvr nr ldrs* **100/1**

5500 **15** *nk* **Firewalker**[7] 6633 3-8-12 60 .... PJMcDonald 4 13
(P T Dalton) *sn led: rdn along and hdd 1/2-way: sn drvn and wknd* **100/1**

0-00 **16** *2 ½* **Northgate Lodge (USA)**[79] 4538 3-9-3 47 .... (b) MickyFenton 12 10
(M Brittain) *cl up: rdn along 1/2-way: sn wknd* **150/1**

00 **17** *3 ½* **Little Pandora**[21] 6254 4-8-13 0 .... CatherineGannon 14 —
(G P Kelly) *chsd ldrs: rdn along 1/2-way: wknd over 2f out* **150/1**

0 **18** *18* **Avatea (IRE)**[27] 6114 3-8-9 0 ow2 .... SladeO'Hara(3) 9 —
(A Berry) *sn outpcd and rdn along in rr: wl bhd fr 1/2-way* **200/1**

1m 12.29s (0.49) **Going Correction** +0.15s/f (Good)
WFA 3 from 4yo+ 1lb **18 Ran SP% 121.8**
Speed ratings (Par 103): **102,100,99,98,97 96,92,89,88,84 83,82,81,80,80 76,72,48**
toteswinger: 1&2 £14.30, 1&3 £52.90, 2&3 £4.70. CSF £64.23 TOTE £39.40: £9.30, £1.10, £2.90; EX 119.20.
Owner Mrs C A Hodgetts **Bred** Mrs Fiona Denniff **Trained** Great Habton, N Yorks
■ Stewards' Enquiry : Slade O'Hara one-day ban: used whip when out of contention with filly showing no response (Oct 31)

FOCUS
A truly run race but, with winner and fourth rated 54 and 52 respectively and the market leader disappointing, this form, rated around the exposed fourth, does not amount to much.
Hitches Dubai(BRZ) Official explanation: jockey said colt missed the break and ran green

6792 THANKS & SEE YOU NEXT SEASON H'CAP 7f
5:40 (5:41) (Class 5) (0-70,69) 3-Y-O **£2,914** (£867; £433; £216) **Stalls** Centre

Form RPR

3313 **1** **Strawberry Moon (IRE)**[15] 6411 3-9-2 **67** .... PaulMulrennan 14 74
(B Smart) *s.s: hdwy stands' side over 2f out: hrd rdn: edgd lft and r.o wl to ld nr fin* **6/1**[2]

200 **2** *hd* **Top Tribute**[16] 6393 3-8-9 **60** .... MickyFenton 20 66
(T P Tate) *sn in rr stands' side: gd hdwy over 1f out: edgd lft and styd on wl fnl 75yds* **40/1**

0532 **3** *1 ¼* **Bertie Vista**[27] 6116 3-8-8 **62** .... DuranFentiman(3) 1 65
(T D Easterby) *w ldrs far side: led jst ins fnl f: hdd and no ex fnl 50yds* **16/1**

1552 **4** *shd* **Red Skipper (IRE)**[29] 6042 3-8-11 **62** .... JimmyQuinn 12 65
(N Wilson) *mid-div centre: hdwy over 2f out: chsng ldrs whn hmpd ins fnl f: 3rd whn eased nr fin* **12/1**

The Form Book, Raceform Ltd, Compton, RG20 6NL

452 **5** *nk* **Ishiadancer**[21] 6254 3-8-11 **62**.................................. DavidAllan 5 64
(E J Alston) *w ldrs far side: led wl over 1f out: hdd jst ins fnl f: no ex* **10/1**

102 **6** *shd* **Chosen Forever**[7] 6628 3-8-13 **64**.......................... SilvestreDeSousa 3 66
(G R Oldroyd) *mid-div: hdwy far side over 2f out: upsides ins fnl f: no ex* **8/1**

0501 **7** *1* **Apollo Shark (IRE)**[23] 6219 3-8-13 **69**.................... FrederikTylicki(5) 17 68
(J Howard Johnson) *chsd ldrs: kpt on same pce fnl f* **7/2**[1]

3221 **8** *1½* **Maybe I Wont**[259] 393 3-9-2 **67**.. DNolan 8 62
(Lucinda Featherstone) *w ldrs: wknd fnl 75yds* **20/1**

-264 **9** *hd* **Tito (IRE)**[11] 6543 3-8-13 **67**....................................... NeilBrown(3) 6 61
(T D Barron) *in tch towards far side: kpt on wl fnl f* **7/1**[3]

0000 **10** *nk* **Rowaad**[10] 6566 3-8-9 **60**.. SaleemGolam 16 54
(A E Price) *in rr stands' side: hmpd 2f out: kpt on fnl f* **33/1**

0000 **11** *4* **Brother Barry (USA)**[16] 6385 3-8-9 **60**.................... PJMcDonald 11 43
(G A Swinbank) *chsd ldrs: kpt on same pce appr fnl f* **25/1**

204 **12** *½* **This Ones For Eddy**[18] 6339 3-8-13 **64**.......................... TonyCulhane 4 45
(S Parr) *chsd ldrs far side: lost pl over 1f out* **8/1**

4255 **13** *shd* **Orchestrion**[16] 6387 3-8-6 **60**........................... AndrewMullen(3) 10 41
(Miss T Jackson) *chsd ldrs: rdn 4f out: sn outpcd* **33/1**

0000 **14** *1* **Dhhamaan (IRE)**[32] 5965 3-8-9 **60**............................(b) LiamJones 13 38
(Mrs R A Carr) *led centre: edgd lft and hdd wl over 1f out: sn wknd* **50/1**

3203 **15** *1¾* **Orpenella**[17] 6356 3-8-7 **58**................................ CatherineGannon 18 32
(K A Ryan) *w ldrs stands' side: wkng whn edgd rt 2f out* **22/1**

-360 **16** *¾* **Rub Of The Relic (IRE)**[17] 6356 3-8-3 **61** ow3............ PaulPickard(7) 7 33
(P T Midgley) *sn towards rr* **33/1**

0340 **17** *2* **Irving Place**[17] 6357 3-8-11 **62**.............................. TonyHamilton 15 28
(R A Fahey) *sn in rr and drvn along: nvr a factor* **18/1**

0032 **18** *1½* **Blues Minor (IRE)**[14] 6433 3-8-9 **67**.............................. DeanHeslop(7) 2 29
(M Mullineaux) *chsd ldrs far side: lost pl over 1f out* **22/1**

034 **19** *3* **Half A Crown (IRE)**[43] 5636 3-8-6 **57**.......................... PaulFessey 9 11
(D W Barker) *t.k.h: trckd ldrs: wknd 2f out* **16/1**

5400 **20** *½* **Bohobe (IRE)**[65] 4988 3-8-1 **59**............................... RosieJessop(7) 19 12
(J G Given) *in rr stands' side: hmpd 2f out: sn wknd* **40/1**

1m 25.77s (1.27) **Going Correction** +0.15s/f (Good) **20 Ran SP% 138.0**
Speed ratings (Par 101): **98,97,96,96,95 95,94,92,92,92 87,87,87,85,83 83,80,79,75,75**
toteswinger: 1&2 £74.90, 1&3 £15.30, 2&3 £99.60. CSF £252.00 CT £3824.57 TOTE £9.00: £2.20, £7.70, £4.50, £3.50; EX 296.00 Place 6 £195.90, Place 5 £98.58.
Owner Mrs Julie Martin **Bred** Gerrardstown House Stud **Trained** Hambleton, N Yorks
■ Stewards' Enquiry : Paul Mulrennan two-day ban: careless riding (Oct 31, Nov 1); one-day ban: used whip with excessive frequency without giving filly time to respond (Nov 2)

FOCUS
A run-of-the-mill handicap but one run at a strong early gallop that collapsed and those coming from off the pace filled three of the first four places. The form looks sound with the four behind the winner close to their marks.

Rowaad Official explanation: jockey said colt was denied a clear run
Orpenella Official explanation: jockey said filly became unbalanced and had no more to give
Half A Crown(IRE) Official explanation: jockey said colt had no more to give
T/Plt: £87.30 to a £1 stake. Pool: £43,284.19. 361.75 winning tickets. T/Qpdt: £12.30 to a £1 stake. Pool: £3,863.60. 231.76 winning tickets. JR

6793 - 6805a (Foreign Racing) - See Raceform Interactive

6545 CATTERICK (L-H)
Saturday, October 18

OFFICIAL GOING: Good to soft (7.8)
Wind: Light, across Weather: Showers & sunny periods

6806 TOTEPLACEPOT APPRENTICE CLAIMING STKS 1m 3f 214y
1:25 (1:25) (Class 6) 3-Y-O+ **£2,388** (£705; £352) **Stalls** High

Form RPR

0165 **1** **Jafra (IRE)**[14] 6485 3-9-3 65............................(p) MichaelJStainton 11 62
(R M Whitaker) *hld up towards rr: hdwy over 4f out: effrt on outer wl over 1f out: rdn ent fnl f: drvn and styd on wl to ld nr fin* **10/3**[1]

5440 **2** *nk* **Dan Tucker**[24] 6216 4-9-7 63.......................... Louis-PhilippeBeuzelin(3) 1 61
(N Tinkler) *hld up in midfield: hdwy over 2f out: rdn to ld 1f out: hdd and no ex nr fin* **8/1**

5603 **3** *½* **Coco L'Escargot**[78] 4599 4-9-5 45.................................(v) DuranFentiman 2 56
(J R Jenkins) *prom: rdn along to chse ldng pair over 2f out: drvn wl over 1f out: kpt on wl undert press ins fnl f* **40/1**

3403 **4** *1¼* **Mister Fizzbomb (IRE)**[14] 6485 5-9-11 60..........................(v) NeilBrown 3 60
(J S Wainwright) *led: rdn along over 2f out: drvn and hdd 1f out: kpt on same pce* **11/2**[3]

5330 **5** *2¼* **Muncaster Castle (IRE)**[70] 4848 4-9-3 47.............. MatthewDavies(5) 4 53
(R F Fisher) *cl up: rdn along 3f out: drvn wl over 1f out and grad wknd* **25/1**

2160 **6** *3* **Shaylee**[12] 6529 3-8-12 55.. JamieMoriarty 15 45
(T D Walford) *hld up towards rr: hdwy and in tch 4f out: rdn along 3f out: drvn 2f out and sn no imp* **14/1**

2542 **7** *3½* **Court Of Appeal**[20] 6309 11-8-13 56...........................(tp) LanceBetts(5) 14 39
(B Ellison) *in tch: effrt to chse ldrs 4f out: rdn along 3f out and sn btn* **4/1**[2]

0461 **8** *10* **Jane Of Arc (FR)**[20] 6309 4-8-10 53..............................(p) GaryBartley(3) 9 18
(J S Goldie) *in midfield: rdn along 4f out: nvr a factor* **6/1**

1000 **9** *3* **Shenandoah Girl**[39] 5783 5-8-9 56..............................(p) KylieManser(5) 8 14
(Miss Gay Kelleway) *s.i.s: a in rr* **15/2**

5006 **10** *43* **Predictable (IRE)**[24] 6217 3-8-6 45.............................. AndrewMullen 13 —
(M W Easterby) *a in rr: rdn along over 4f out and sn bhd* **22/1**

00 **P** **Trusted Friend (USA)**[52] 5395 3-8-12 0.............................. WilliamBuick 6 —
(M Johnston) *prom: rdn along 5f out: sn wknd and bhd: t.o whn p.u wl over 1f out* **14/1**

2m 44.42s (5.52) **Going Correction** +0.375s/f (Good)
WFA 3 from 4yo+ 7lb **11 Ran SP% 119.6**
Speed ratings (Par 101): **96,95,95,94,93 91,88,82,80,51** —
toteswinger: 1&2 £5.10, 1&3 £15.20, 2&3 £43.30. CSF £30.42 TOTE £5.00: £1.90, £3.20, £5.60; EX 29.50.Dan Tucker was claimed by J. J. Best for £12,000.
Owner G B Bedford **Bred** J Webb **Trained** Scarcroft, W Yorks

FOCUS
A modest claimer for apprentice riders. The pace was only ordinary. The winner did not need to match his recent best with the third the chief doubt over the form.

Shenandoah Girl Official explanation: jockey said mare never travelled

6807 BET TOTEPOOL ON ALL UK RACING EBF NOVICE STKS 5f
1:55 (1:55) (Class 5) 2-Y-O **£4,209** (£1,252; £625; £312) **Stalls** Low

Form RPR

4006 **1** **Oasis Breeze**[26] 6172 2-8-11 78.............................. DuranFentiman(3) 1 82
(T D Easterby) *chsd wnr: styd on wl fnl f: led last stride* **9/1**

1036 **2** *shd* **To The Point**[12] 6540 2-9-0 87.. RichardMullen 5 82
(E S McMahon) *led: clr over 1f out: jst ct* **11/4**[2]

32 **3** *3* **York Key Bar**[17] 6383 2-8-5 0.. LanceBetts(7) 6 69
(B Ellison) *sn outpcd and in rr: hdwy over 2f out: kpt on wl fnl f* **13/2**[3]

1302 **4** *4* **Glamorous Spirit (IRE)**[25] 6183 2-9-0 87.......................... WilliamBuick 2 56
(J Noseda) *chsd ldrs: edgd rt over 1f out: sn fdd* **11/4**[2]

6103 **5** *3½* **Love You Louis**[25] 6183 2-9-2 85.. TomEaves 3 46
(J R Jenkins) *chsd ldrs: outpcd over 2f out: lost pl over 1f out* **14/1**

5410 **6** *hd* **Lucky Art (USA)**[21] 6274 2-9-0 87.......................... FrederikTylicki(5) 7 48
(J Howard Johnson) *sn chsng ldrs: drvn over 2f out: wknd over 1f out* **9/4**[1]

3460 **7** *13* **What A Fella**[18] 6350 2-8-12 58..............................(p) PaulMulrennan 8 —
(Mrs A Duffield) *chsd ldrs: lost pl over 2f out: sn bhd* **80/1**

61.40 secs (1.60) **Going Correction** +0.375s/f (Good) **7 Ran SP% 115.3**
Speed ratings (Par 95): **102,101,97,90,85 84,63**
toteswinger: 1&2 £8.70, 1&3 £37.80, 2&3 £10.30. CSF £34.58 TOTE £11.20: £2.70, £2.50; EX 56.50.
Owner Dale And Ann Wilsdon **Bred** P And Mrs A G Venner **Trained** Great Habton, N Yorks

FOCUS
This looked fairly competitive on paper, but very little got into it as To The Point set a strong pace, stretching his field out from an early stage. Straightforward form, the winner back to his best.

NOTEBOOK
Oasis Breeze, who has changed stables, had a fair bit to find with the best of these at the weights, and the return to 5f looked a negative, but the strong pace helped on that front and her stamina came to the fore in the closing stages as she stayed on best. She will be better suited by the return to 6f. (op 8-1)
To The Point showed blistering speed to lead these a merry dance and this sharp 5f looks ideal for her. She can win more races under these conditions. (op 10-3 tchd 5-2 in places)
York Key Bar stayed on from off the pace without landing a blow, but this sharp 5f was not a stiff enough test for him and he can do much better back up at 6f. (op 7-1)
Glamorous Spirit(IRE) could never get into it from off the pace. (op 2-1)
Lucky Art(USA) was struggling far too soon for this to be his true running. He looks to need faster conditions. (op 7-2 tchd 2-1)

6808 TOTESPORT 0800 221221 MEDIAN AUCTION MAIDEN STKS (DIV I) 7f
2:30 (2:30) (Class 6) 2-Y-O **£2,047** (£604; £302) **Stalls** Low

Form RPR

563 **1** **Senor Berti**[14] 6481 2-9-3 73.. TomEaves 2 72
(B Smart) *trckd ldrs: hdwy 2f out: effrt whn nt clr run over 1f out: swtchd rt and rdn ent fnl f: drvn and kpt on to ld last 50yds* **10/3**[2]

6326 **2** *1¼* **Tropical Blue**[90] 4214 2-8-12 72.. JackDean(5) 10 69
(Jennie Candlish) *cl up: effrt 2f out: rdn to ld over 1f out: drvn ins fnl f: hdd and no ex last 50yds* **8/1**

3 **3** *1* **Do The Deal (IRE)**[21] 6273 2-8-12 0.............................. GrahamGibbons 5 61
(J J Quinn) *prom: effrt 2f out: cl up and rdn over 1f out: ev ch tl drvn and nt qckn wl ins fnl f* **5/2**[1]

43 **4** *2* **Hector's House**[17] 6381 2-9-3 0.. TonyHamilton 3 61
(M Dods) *cl up: led 4f out: rdn over 2f out: drvn and hdd over 1f out: wknd ins fnl f* **7/2**[3]

0 **5** *1¾* **Stellarina (IRE)**[113] 3456 2-8-12 0.............................. RobertWinston 4 52
(G A Swinbank) *led 3f: cl up on outer tl rdn along and wknd appr fnl f* **8/1**

0 **6** *2½* **Challenging (UAE)**[23] 6234 2-8-12 0.............................. JamieMoriarty 7 46
(R D E Woodhouse) *dwlt: hdwy and in midfield 1/2-way: rdn along to chse ldrs 2f out: sn no imp* **100/1**

7 *1½* **Rupestrian** 2-9-3 0.. JoeFanning 1 47
(M Johnston) *dwlt: sn rdn along and outpcd: a towards rr* **13/2**

0400 **8** *nk* **Ernies Keep**[70] 4873 2-9-0 35.. DominicFox(3) 6 46
(W Storey) *sn rdn along and a towards rr* **150/1**

0 **9** *7* **Irish Saint (IRE)**[25] 6187 2-9-3 0.. WilliamBuick 9 29
(T J Pitt) *a towards rr* **33/1**

00 **10** *3¾* **Katie Girl**[32] 5989 2-8-12 0.. LiamJones 11 14
(Mrs G S Rees) *a bhd* **100/1**

1m 31.42s (4.42) **Going Correction** +0.375s/f (Good) **10 Ran SP% 115.0**
Speed ratings (Par 93): **89,87,86,84,82 79,77,77,69,64**
toteswinger: 1&2 £8.80, 1&3 £2.70, 2&3 £6.30. CSF £29.41 TOTE £5.60: £1.40, £2.80, £1.20; EX 18.50.
Owner A Turton & S Brown **Bred** T W R Chugg & Overbury Stallions Ltd **Trained** Hambleton, N Yorks

FOCUS
Just a fair maiden and the finish was dominated by those who had shown the best form so far. The poor eighth and the time limit the form.

NOTEBOOK
Senor Berti had the highest official rating of these, but he looked vulnerable here given he seemed fairly exposed. However, he relished the ease in the ground and, although he had to be switched out to get a clear run, he finished his race strongly, suggesting he would appreciate a stiffer test of stamina. (op 7-2 tchd 4-1)
Tropical Blue had yet to race on ground this soft but ran right up to form on his return from a 90-day break. Always close up, he stayed on well to go down fighting
Do The Deal(IRE) shaped with distinct promise on her debut, but it is hard to know whether showed improved form here. She responded to pressure to move through and challenge entering the final furlong, but she looked a touch one-paced in the closing stages. Perhaps she wants slightly better ground. (op 11-4 tchd 3-1)
Hector's House weakened in the closing stages, having raced on the sharp end throughout, and was a touch disappointing. (op 4-1 tchd 10-3)

6809 TOTESPORT BETXTRA FILLIES' NURSERY 7f
3:00 (3:01) (Class 4) (0-85,75) 2-Y-O **£3,885** (£1,156; £577; £288) **Stalls** Low

Form RPR

2401 **1** **Amber Sunset**[12] 6535 2-9-4 **75**.. LukeMorris(3) 7 78
(J Jay) *mde all: qcknd clr over 4f out: jst lasted* **3/1**[1]

55B5 **2** *½* **Antigua Sunrise (IRE)**[28] 6110 2-8-11 **65**.............................. TonyHamilton 1 67+
(R A Fahey) *chsd ldrs: outpcd 4f out: hdwy 2f out: styd on wl ins fnl f: nt quite rch wnr* **11/2**[3]

525 **3** *1* **Tiger Goddess (IRE)**[66] 4968 2-9-4 **72**.. LiamJones 3 71
(W J Haggas) *chsd ldrs: wnt 2nd over 3f out: kpt on same pce fnl f* **8/1**

040 **4** *13* **Orphaned Annie**[130] 2909 2-8-2 **63** ow4.............................. LanceBetts(7) 4 30
(B Ellison) *dwlt: kpt on fnl 2f: nvr on terms* **20/1**

3516 **5** *2* **Lady Salama**[50] 5451 2-8-11 **65**..............................(v[1]) AndrewElliott 6 27
(K R Burke) *in rr: bhd fnl 3f* **20/1**

0634 **6** *1* **Inthawain**[37] 5838 2-8-12 **66**.. TonyCulhane 9 25
(M R Channon) *hld up on outer: effrt over 2f out: sn btn* **9/1**

150 **7** *2* **It's Toast (IRE)**[14] 6477 2-8-11 **65**..............................(v[1]) WilliamBuick 5 19
(R M Beckett) *chsd ldrs: lost pl over 3f out* **3/1**[1]

31 **8** *2¾* **Via Mia**[29] 6089 2-9-7 **75**.. TomEaves 8 22
(P F I Cole) *w ldrs: lost pl over 3f out* **9/2**[2]

206 **9** *10* **Our Apolonia (IRE)**[35] 5883 2-7-10 **53** oh1 ow1...... DuranFentiman(3) 2 —
(A Berry) *chsd ldrs: hung and lost pl over 2f out* **25/1**

1m 29.96s (2.96) **Going Correction** +0.375s/f (Good) **9** Ran SP% **118.0**
Speed ratings (Par 94): **98,97,96,81,79 78,75,72,61**
toteswinger: 1&2 £3.80, 1&3 £6.50, 2&3 £7.30. CSF £19.72 CT £121.89 TOTE £4.60: £1.80, £1.50, £2.80; EX 22.90.
Owner David J Orchard **Bred** Southill Stud **Trained** Newmarket, Suffolk

FOCUS
An ordinary fillies' nursery and once again little got into this from off the pace. The winner continues to progress with forcing tactics and the runner-up shaped well.

NOTEBOOK
Amber Sunset was very strongly backed throughout the morning to follow up her recent Warwick win. That last start was her first try at 7f, after running so well over shorter in a valuable sales race at Ascot, and she looks well suited to this trip on a sharp track, although she doesn't look like she'll get any further given the speed he shows and how tired she got close home. (op 10-3)
Antigua Sunrise(IRE) looks to be crying out for another furlong, over which she has to be of interest off this sort of mark. (op 10-1)
Tiger Goddess(IRE), refreshed by a 66-day break, ran arguably her best race so far, making good headway to throw down a challenge before just lacking the finishing punch to tackle the winner. (op 7-1 tchd 9-1)
It's Toast(IRE) ran no race in a first-time visor. (op 4-1)

6810 TOTESCOOP6 CATTERICK DASH (HANDICAP STKS) 5f
3:35 (3:35) (Class 3) (0-95,98) 3-Y-0+ **£7,771** (£2,312; £1,155; £577) **Stalls** Low

Form RPR
2151 **1** **Judge 'n Jury**[7] 6650 4-9-4 **98**..................................(t) KevinGhunowa(3) 1 110
(R A Harris) *cl up far side: chal over 1f out: rdn to ld ins fnl f: kpt on wl* **11/2**[2]
6123 **2** *1* **Supermassive Muse (IRE)**[15] 6449 3-8-8 **85**........(p) GrahamGibbons 8 93
(E S McMahon) *in tch far side: hdwy 2f out: rdn and styd on to chse wnr ins fnl f: nt qckn towards fin: 2nd of 8 in gp* **9/1**
0013 **3** *1 1/4* **Captain Dunne (IRE)**[7] 6653 3-9-4 **98**..................... DuranFentiman(3) 4 102
(T D Easterby) *overall ldr far side: rdn along wl over 1f out: drvn and hdd ins fnl f: no ex: 3rd of 8 in gp* **5/1**[1]
2110 **4** *shd* **Haajes**[7] 6650 4-9-1 **95**...(t) TolleyDean(3) 14 98
(S Parr) *chsd ldrs stands' side: hdwy 2f out: sn rdn and kpt on ins fnl f: 1st of 7 in gp* **10/1**
5603 **5** *1/2* **Fol Hollow (IRE)**[7] 6651 3-8-9 **86**............................ AdrianTNicholls 13 87
(D Nicholls) *cl up stands' side: rdn along 2f out: drvn and one pce ent fnl f: 2nd of 7 in gp* **10/1**
0000 **6** *shd* **Luscivious**[18] 6354 4-7-11 **81** oh2.........................(b) StacyRenwick(7) 7 82
(A J McCabe) *dwlt: sn in tch far side: rdn along 2f out and kpt on same pce: 4th of 8 in gp* **16/1**
0650 **7** *1/2* **El Dececy (USA)**[18] 6352 4-8-5 **82**................................. PaulEddery 9 81
(S Parr) *led stands' side gp: rdn along 2f out: drvn and one pce appr fnl f: 3rd of 7 in gp* **20/1**
6043 **8** *1/2* **Misaro (GER)**[6] 6669 7-9-0 **91**.......................................(b) WilliamBuick 6 88
(R A Harris) *towards rr far side: hdwy wl over 1f out: sn rdn and kpt on ins fnl f: 5th of 8 in gp* **16/1**
1321 **9** *nk* **Hotham**[7] 6651 5-8-8 **85**.. JamieMoriarty 15 81
(N Wilson) *dwlt: in tch stands' side: rdn along 2f out and sn one pce: 4th of 7 in gp* **9/1**
00-0 **10** *1 3/4* **Roker Park (IRE)**[37] 5831 3-8-8 **85**........................... AndrewElliott 11 75
(K R Burke) *a towards rr stands' side: 5th of 7 in gp* **40/1**
242 **11** *shd* **Secret Asset (IRE)**[6] 6669 3-9-1 **92**............................ LiamJones 5 82
(W M Brisbourne) *in tch far side: rdn along 1/2-way: sn wknd 6th of 8 in gp* **6/1**[3]
0000 **12** *nk* **Indian Trail**[7] 6653 8-8-6 **90**...................................... NSLawes(7) 10 79
(D Nicholls) *prom stands' side: rdn along 2f out and grad wknd: 6th of 7 in gp* **16/1**
0260 **13** *1 1/4* **Mesbaah (IRE)**[20] 6307 4-8-2 **82**............................ AndrewMullen(3) 12 66
(R A Fahey) *a towards rr stands' side: 7th of 7 in gp* **20/1**
00- **14** *1/2* **Final Dynasty**[357] 6487 4-8-11 **88**.................................... JoeFanning 2 70
(Mrs G S Rees) *chsd ldrs far side: rdn along over 2f out and sn wknd: 7th of 8 in gp* **16/1**
1000 **15** *hd* **Total Impact**[21] 6289 5-8-7 **84**.................................... TonyHamilton 3 66
(R A Fahey) *a towards rr far side: 8th of 8 in gp* **16/1**

60.98 secs (1.18) **Going Correction** +0.375s/f (Good) **15** Ran SP% **125.9**
Speed ratings (Par 107): **105,103,101,101,100 100,99,98,98,95 95,94,92,91,91**
toteswinger: 1&2 £11.90, 1&3 £1.30, 2&3 £16.40. CSF £55.33 CT £278.06 TOTE £5.20: £1.90, £2.60, £3.10; EX 64.60 TRIFECTA Not won..
Owner Mrs Ruth M Serrell **Bred** C A Cyzer **Trained** Earlswood, Monmouths

FOCUS
A competitive sprint handicap in which the field split into two groups. The first three home came up the inside, close to the rail, but the stands' side group were not at all far behind them. Another improved effort from Judge 'N Jury with the next two close to their marks.

NOTEBOOK
Judge 'n Jury is a real credit to Ron Harris and he has done nothing but improve all season, winning here off a 28lb higher mark than when scoring at Warwick in April. Always tracking Captain Dunne up the inside, he proved too strong for that rival in the closing stages and this caps off a terrific season, although connections are considering going for another tilt at Doncaster next week. \n\x\x Harris thinks he will turn out to be a Group-class sprinter next season, and given the way he has improved this term, that could well be the case. (op 6-1)
Supermassive Muse(IRE) is more than capable of a big run off this sort of mark and he continued his excellent form, finishing strongly in the closing stages. (op 11-1)
Captain Dunne(IRE) was always front rank and he had every chance, but he couldn't sustain his effort in the final half-furlong. (tchd 9-2)
Haajes fared best of those to come up the stands' side, although he edged towards the centre in the closing stages. He bounced right back to form having run flat last time and he could well be capable of scoring off this mark. (tchd 11-1)
Fol Hollow(IRE) stayed on well up the stands' side to confirm the promise of his latest Musselburgh effort. (op 11-1 tchd 9-1)
Luscivious fluffed the start but came home strongly. Although not one to trust implicitly, he is well treated and looks one to keep an eye on. (op 18-1)

6811 TOTESPORT 0800 221221 MEDIAN AUCTION MAIDEN STKS (DIV II) 7f
4:10 (4:11) (Class 6) 2-Y-0 **£2,047** (£604; £302) **Stalls** Low

Form RPR
23 **1** **Goliaths Boy (IRE)**[7] 6655 2-9-3 0.................................. TonyHamilton 6 85+
(R A Fahey) *mde all: qcknd clr 2f out: unchal* **8/15**[1]
06 **2** *13* **Dillenda**[22] 6245 2-8-12 0... GrahamGibbons 2 46
(T D Easterby) *hld up towards rr: hdwy 3f out: chsd ldng pair wl over 1f out: styd on to take 2nd ins fnl f: no ch w wnr* **12/1**[3]
00 **3** *1 1/2* **Great Charter (USA)**[125] 3055 2-9-3 0................................ JoeFanning 9 47
(M Johnston) *chsd ldrs: rdn to chse wnr over 2f out: sn drvn and plugged on same pce* **6/1**[2]
00 **4** *3 1/2* **Le Petit Vigier**[31] 6008 2-8-12 0.......................................(t) AndrewElliott 4 34
(P Beaumont) *in tch: pushed along 1/2-way: rdn over 2f out: sn outpcd* **100/1**
5 *4 1/2* **Molesden Glen (IRE)** 2-9-3 0.. TomEaves 5 27
(B Smart) *sn outpcd and a in rr* **14/1**
00 **6** *1/2* **Strevelyn**[14] 6481 2-9-0 0.. AndrewMullen(3) 8 26
(Mrs A Duffield) *in tch: rdn along 1/2-way: sn outpcd* **40/1**
7 *2 1/2* **Madam'X** 2-8-12 0.. RobertWinston 3 15
(P F I Cole) *chsd ldrs: rdn along 3f out: sn wknd* **6/1**[2]
46 **8** *3/4* **Blue Noodles**[14] 6480 2-9-3 0... PaulMulrennan 10 18
(D W Barker) *stdd s: t.k.h and rapid hdwy to chse wnr after 1f: rdn along over 2f out and sn wknd* **14/1**
9 *8* **Mull Of Fire (IRE)** 2-8-12 0.. SladeO'Hara(5) 7 —
(A Berry) *dwlt: a bhd* **66/1**

1m 29.45s (2.45) **Going Correction** +0.375s/f (Good) **9** Ran SP% **119.8**
Speed ratings (Par 93): **101,86,84,80,75 74,71,71,61**
toteswinger: 1&2 £3.10, 1&3 £2.40, 2&3 £7.60. CSF £9.37 TOTE £1.40: £1.10, £2.50, £1.80; EX 7.40.
Owner Rob Lloyd Racing Limited **Bred** Mrs O M E McKeever **Trained** Musley Bank, N Yorks

FOCUS
A terribly weak maiden, even by Catterick standards with the impressive Goliaths Boy slamming his field by 13 lengths. His rating could underestimate him.

NOTEBOOK
Goliaths Boy(IRE) turned this into a procession, soon bagging the rail, and he never saw another rival, drawing right away in the straight and coming home in a canter. The standard-setter on form coming into this, he is clearly going the right way and although he did not beat much here, he couldn't have done it any more emphatically and he looks a nice type for nurseries, providing the handicapper doesn't get carried away with this. (op 4-5 tchd 5-6)
Dillenda plugged on for a remote second and she shapes as though a stiffer test of stamina might suit, but modest nurseries look the best she can hope for. (tchd 14-1)
Great Charter(USA) looks very modest and he didn't travel with any real fluency. It will be bitterly disappointing if he's not better than he's shown so far. (op 7-1)
Blue Noodles Official explanation: jockey said colt ran too free early stages

6812 TOTESWINGER H'CAP 1m 5f 175y
4:45 (4:45) (Class 6) (0-60,66) 3-Y-0+ **£2,266** (£674; £337; £168) **Stalls** Low

Form RPR
3203 **1** **Sir Sandicliffe (IRE)**[11] 6550 4-9-2 **58**........................ DeanHeslop(7) 5 71
(W M Brisbourne) *hld up in rr: hdwy into midfield 1/2-way: effrt over 2f out: rdn to ld over 1f out: clr ins fnl f* **8/1**
0351 **2** *3* **Mayadeen (IRE)**[3] 6728 6-9-5 **54** 6ex.......................... JamieMoriarty 7 63
(R A Fahey) *led 4f: cl up on inner: effrt 3f out: rdn over 2f out and ev ch: drvn and kpt on same pce ent fnl f* **14/1**
4002 **3** *3/4* **Eijaaz (IRE)**[11] 6551 7-9-10 **59**...................................... TonyHamilton 11 67
(G A Harker) *hld up in rr: hdwy over 3f out: effrt on outer over 2f out: rdn wl over 1f out: kpt on ins fnl f* **12/1**
6512 **4** *3* **Blue Jet (USA)**[16] 6421 4-9-5 **54**.................................... DeanMcKeown 1 58
(R M Whitaker) *s.i.s: sn in tch: chsd ldrs over 4f out: rdn and ev ch over 2f out: sn drvn and wknd ent fnl f* **13/2**[3]
0314 **5** *2* **Three Strings (USA)**[33] 5971 5-9-5 **59**................(p) FrederikTylicki(5) 12 60
(P D Niven) *prom: led after 4f: rdn along 3f out: drvn 2f out: hdd over 1f out and sn wknd* **7/2**[1]
0451 **6** *3 1/4* **Capal Dubh Alainn (IRE)**[11] 6550 3-9-8 **66**...............(vt) WilliamBuick 9 62
(T J Pitt) *chsd ldrs: rdn along 3f out: drvn 2f out and sn wknd* **9/2**[2]
0602 **7** *1 3/4* **Coronado's Gold (USA)**[11] 6550 7-8-13 **55**..................... LanceBetts(7) 15 49
(B Ellison) *t.k.h: trckd ldrs: hdwy and cl up 1/2-way: rdn along 3f out: drvn 2f out and grad wknd* **11/1**
8 *1* **Mega Steps (IRE)**[143] 5926 4-8-12 **52**........................... JackDean(5) 14 45
(Jennie Candlish) *bhd tl sme late hdwy* **40/1**
3420 **9** *1/2* **Wulimaster (USA)**[11] 6550 5-9-2 **51**............................. PaulMulrennan 8 43
(D W Barker) *hld up: hdwy 4f out: rdn along over 2f out: nvr rchd ldrs* **12/1**
055 **10** *2 1/4* **Spume (IRE)**[31] 6019 4-9-5 **57**......................................(t) TolleyDean(3) 13 46
(S Parr) *hld up in midfield: hdwy over 3f out and sn rdn along: drvn and outpcd 2f out: keeping on whn n.m.r ent fnl f* **8/1**
6205 **11** *1 1/2* **Simple Jim (FR)**[11] 6550 4-9-7 **56**........................... SilvestreDeSousa 6 43
(A D Brown) *in midfield: rdn along 4f out: sn wknd* **12/1**
0400 **12** *1/2* **Saluscraggie**[25] 6189 6-9-4 **56**................................ MichaelJStainton(3) 10 42
(R E Barr) *dwlt: a in rr* **20/1**
050- **13** *4* **Greenbelt**[224] 1042 7-9-5 **54**... DanielTudhope 2 34
(G M Moore) *chsd ldrs: rdn along over 4f out and sn wknd* **33/1**
0130 **14** *2 3/4* **Tykie Two**[102] 3820 4-9-3 **52**.. LiamJones 4 29
(S Wynne) *a bhd* **28/1**

3m 11.36s (7.76) **Going Correction** +0.375s/f (Good)
WFA 3 from 4yo+ 9lb **14** Ran SP% **127.6**
Speed ratings (Par 101): **92,90,89,88,87 85,84,83,83,82 81,80,78,77**
toteswinger: 1&2 £24.70, 1&3 £18.40, 2&3 £31.20. CSF £117.49 CT £1369.38 TOTE £9.50: £3.00, £3.30, £4.20; EX 175.40.
Owner The Blacktoffee Partnership **Bred** James Lombard **Trained** Great Ness, Shropshire

FOCUS
Competitive enough for the grade and plenty in with chances entering the final furlong. The winner ran his best race on turf since he was a 2yo, with the placed form sound enough.

6813 TOTEEXACTA H'CAP 7f
5:20 (5:20) (Class 5) (0-75,75) 3-Y-0+ **£2,590** (£770; £385; £192) **Stalls** Low

Form RPR
006 **1** **Bold Marc (IRE)**[30] 6052 6-9-3 **72**............................. DarrenWilliams 6 86+
(K R Burke) *led after 1f: qcknd clr 2f out: rdn ent fnl f: jst hld on* **4/1**[1]
6116 **2** *hd* **Keys Of Cyprus**[12] 6537 6-9-6 **75**............................ AdrianTNicholls 8 86
(D Nicholls) *prom: chsd wnr over 4f out: rdn over 2f out: drvn ent fnl f: styd on wl towards fin* **11/2**[3]
2314 **3** *2 1/4* **Turn Me On (IRE)**[20] 6314 5-9-3 **72**............................ DanielTudhope 9 77
(T D Walford) *hld up towards rr: hdwy on inner over 2f out: rdn over 1f out: kpt on ins fnl f: nrst fin* **5/1**[2]
3216 **4** *1 3/4* **Ubenkor (IRE)**[56] 5258 3-9-1 **72**.. TomEaves 4 72
(B Smart) *led 1f: styd prom: rdn along 2f out: drvn and one pce appr fnl f* **14/1**
0304 **5** *1 1/4* **River Thames**[21] 6278 5-9-1 **75**.................................. FrederikTylicki(5) 1 72
(K A Ryan) *chsd ldrs: effrt 2f out: sn rdn and styd on same pce* **13/2**
0346 **6** *2 3/4* **Ingleby Princess**[11] 6564 4-8-10 **65**................................ PaulFessey 5 54
(T D Barron) *towards rr tl styd on fnl 2f* **16/1**

6500 **7** ½ **San Silvestro (IRE)**[14] 6491 3-8-6 **66**......................(p) AndrewMullen[3] 3 54
(Mrs A Duffield) *in tch: hdwy to chse ldrs 3f out: rdn over 2f out: drvn and wknd* **16/1**

1330 **8** 1 ½ **Dream Express (IRE)**[20] 6314 3-9-1 **75**.......................... NeilBrown[3] 2 59
(M Dods) *plld hrd: trckd ldrs: effrt 2f out: swtchd outside and rdn over 1f out: sn btn* **14/1**

2000 **9** nk **King Of Rhythm (IRE)**[9] 6598 5-9-1 **70**.................................. DNolan 15 53
(D Carroll) *a towards rr* **16/1**

4440 **10** 3 ½ **Violent Velocity (IRE)**[14] 6482 5-9-6 **75**.................. GrahamGibbons 13 49
(J J Quinn) *nvr bttr than midfield* **9/1**

0000 **11** nse **Passion Fruit**[14] 6484 7-9-4 **73**...............................(v[1]) DeanMcKeown 14 47
(C W Fairhurst) *s.i.s: a in rr* **22/1**

0000 **12** shd **Sunnyside Tom (IRE)**[18] 6363 4-9-3 **72**...................... JamieMoriarty 10 45
(R A Fahey) *a towards rr* **25/1**

1226 **13** 9 **No Grouse**[42] 5708 8-8-12 **67**.............................. RobertWinston 11 16
(E J Alston) *a towards rr* **14/1**

103 **14** 6 **Yungaburra (IRE)**[18] 6357 4-8-7 **65**............................(t) TolleyDean[3] 7 —
(S Parr) *in midfield: rdn along over 2f out and sn wknd* **14/1**

5160 **15** 7 **Billy One Punch**[115] 3376 6-9-1 **70**.................................. JoeFanning 12 —
(D Shaw) *a bhd* **33/1**

1m 29.39s (2.39) **Going Correction** +0.375s/f (Good)
WFA 3 from 4yo+ 2lb **15** Ran SP% **130.8**
Speed ratings (Par 103): **101,100,98,96,94 91,91,89,89,85 84,84,74,67,66**
toteswinger: 1&2 £5.70, 1&3 £5.90, 2&3 £6.80. CSF £26.59 CT £120.46 TOTE £5.70: £2.50, £2.50, £2.00; EX 27.40 Place 6 £51.29, Place 5 £17.53..
Owner Market Avenue Racing Club Ltd **Bred** Eamon D Delany **Trained** Middleham Moor, N Yorks

FOCUS
A fair handicap and again it paid to be prominent. The form makes sense with the first two potentially well treated.
No Grouse Official explanation: jockey said gelding was unsuited by the good to soft ground
Yungaburra(IRE) Official explanation: jockey said gelding was unsuited by the good to soft ground
T/Plt: £68.00 to a £1 stake. Pool: £44,904.41. 481.45 winning tickets. T/Qpdt: £7.30 to a £1 stake. Pool: £3,260.50. 329.20 winning tickets. JR

6776 NEWMARKET (ROWLEY) (R-H)

Saturday, October 18

OFFICIAL GOING: Good (good to firm in places; 8.2)
Wind: Fresh, behind Weather: Cloudy with sunny spells

6814 VICTOR CHANDLER CHALLENGE STKS (GROUP 2) 7f

2:05 (2:06) (Class 1) 3-Y-O+

£56,770 (£21,520; £10,770; £5,370; £2,690; £1,350) **Stalls** Low

Form RPR

2423 **1** **Stimulation (IRE)**[41] 5742 3-9-1 114.......................... DarryllHolland 12 118
(H Morrison) *lw: racd far side: chsd ldr: rdn to ld ins fnl f: r.o* **9/2**[1]

4402 **2** 1 ¼ **Cat Junior (USA)**[28] 6123 3-9-1 115.......................... JamieSpencer 14 115
(B J Meehan) *racd far side: overall ldr: rdn over 1f out: hdd and unable qck ins fnl f: 2nd of 6 in gp* **9/1**

2102 **3** ½ **Laa Rayb (USA)**[20] 6322 4-9-3 115...................... RoystonFfrench 5 113
(M Johnston) *racd stands' side: chsd ldr: rdn to ld that gp 1f out: edgd rt: r.o: 1st of 9 in gp* **15/2**

2000 **4** 1 ¾ **Balthazaar's Gift (IRE)**[7] 6645 5-9-3 110...................... DaneO'Neill 11 109
(L M Cumani) *on toes: racd stands' side: s.i.s: hld up: hdwy over 1f out: r.o: nt rch ldrs: 2nd of 9 in gp* **20/1**

301 **5** hd **Express Wish**[46] 5586 4-9-3 104.................................. ShaneKelly 2 108
(J Noseda) *lw: racd stands' side: hld up: hdwy over 2f out: sn rdn: styd on: 3rd of 9 in gp* **16/1**

20-0 **6** shd **Duff (IRE)**[14] 6496 5-9-3 0.................................. KJManning 1 108
(Edward Lynam, Ire) *on toes: led stands' side: rdn and hdd 1f out: styd on same pce: 4th of 9 in gp* **16/1**

4050 **7** shd **Captain Marvelous (IRE)**[29] 6073 4-9-3 100.......................(p) RHills 4 107
(B W Hills) *on toes: racd stands' side: hld up in tch: outpcd over 2f out: swtchd rt and hdwy over 1f out: r.o: nt rch ldrs: 5th of 9 in gp* **40/1**

-410 **8** shd **Summit Surge (IRE)**[111] 3536 4-9-3 0...........................(t) JMurtagh 10 107
(G M Lyons, Ire) *chsd ldr in centre tl hung to stands' side over 2f out: rdn over 1f out: styd on same pce: 6th of 9 in gp* **20/1**

1332 **9** 1 ¼ **Major Cadeaux**[35] 5893 4-9-7 115.......................... RichardHughes 17 108
(R Hannon) *racd far side: chsd ldrs: rdn over 1f out: no ex: 3rd of 6 in gp* **5/1**[2]

0051 **10** 2 ½ **Royal Confidence**[37] 5829 3-8-12 103.......................... MichaelHills 15 94
(B W Hills) *racd far side: s.i.s: hdwy over 2f out: rdn and wknd over 1f out: 4th of 6 in gp* **14/1**

010 **11** nk **Baharah (USA)**[41] 5730 4-9-0 111.......................... HayleyTurner 13 93
(G A Butler) *warm: racd far side: hld up: rdn over 2f out: a in rr: 5th of 6th in gp* **20/1**

133 **12** 1 ½ **Ordnance Row**[15] 6440 5-9-3 109.......................... RyanMoore 3 92
(R Hannon) *racd stands' side: chsd ldrs tl rdn over 2f out: sn wknd 7th of 9 in gp* **8/1**

4521 **13** 1 **Il Warrd (IRE)**[14] 6484 3-9-1 109.......................... LDettori 7 90
(Saeed Bin Suroor) *led centre pair tl rdn and wknd over 1f out: 8th of 9 in gp* **7/1**[3]

1005 **14** 4 **Racer Forever (USA)**[21] 6285 5-9-3 108...........................(b) OPeslier 8 79
(J H M Gosden) *racd stands' side: hld up: effrt 2f out: sn wknd: last of 9 in gp* **16/1**

100 **15** 6 **Sharp Nephew**[15] 6440 3-9-1 99.......................... MartinDwyer 16 63
(B J Meehan) *racd far side: hld up in tch: plld hrd: rdn and wknd over 2f out: last of 6 in gp* **66/1**

1m 22.48s (-2.92) **Going Correction** -0.10s/f (Good)
WFA 3 from 4yo+ 2lb **15** Ran SP% **122.8**
Speed ratings (Par 115): **112,110,110,108,107 107,107,107,106,103 102,101,99,95,88**
toteswinger: 1&2 £10.80, 1&3 £7.80, 2&3 £9.70. CSF £42.12 TOTE £6.50: £2.80, £4.40, £4.30; EX 48.20 Trifecta £755.00 Pool £2,550.80 - 2.50 winning units..
Owner Michael Kerr-Dineen **Bred** Illuminatus Investments **Trained** East Ilsley, Berks

FOCUS
The going had dried out overnight so that 'good to firm in places' appeared in the description, but to offset that they were racing on fresh ground, having not used the stands'-side part of the course since May. There was a breeze behind the runners in the straight. A competitive renewal of this Group 2 but a race that has often thrown up a surprise winner, with four at 20-1 and one at 16-1 this century. However, on this occasion it fell to the well-backed favourite. They split into two groups and although the first two raced in the smaller far-side group any bias seemed due to pace not ground.

NOTEBOOK
Stimulation(IRE) ◆ won the Free Handicap over course and distance in the spring and, although the 2,000 Guineas may have come a bit early in his career, he had been running creditably in Group company since. Always close to the pace on the far side, he found plenty when asked to assert and scored cosily. He looks the sort who will get a mile at four and, relatively lightly raced, could make the step up to the highest level next season. (op 5-1 tchd 11-2 in places)
Cat Junior(USA), who was dropping in trip, made the running on the far side and held off all apart from the winner. This was a cracking effort from the St James's Palace and Prix Jean Prat fourth, especially as Brian Meehan revealed he had missed work owing to a corn, and, like the winner, he may have more to offer with another winter behind him. (op 17-2 tchd 8-1)
Laa Rayb(USA), who got warm in the paddock, has been steadily progressive this season and did best of the stands'-side group, having been close up, although never able to get near the pair on the far side. (op 17-2 tchd 9-1)
Balthazaar's Gift(IRE), who had not run over 7f since finishing fourth in this race last year, repeated the feat with the headgear he has worn of late left off. He missed the break but is usually held up anyway. (op 25-1)
Express Wish, whose best recent effort was back at 7f on soft, was stepping up in grade and ran creditably but may be more effective on an easier surface.
Duff(IRE) led up the stands' rail but was in trouble coming out of the Dip, although he was only run out of the places near the finish. (op 20-1)
Captain Marvelous(IRE), with cheekpieces replacing the blinkers he wore on his previous start, ran a fine race on ground which may have been on the fast side for him, especially as he raced more towards the centre of the track and had to come from off the pace. (op 50-1)
Summit Surge(IRE) was another to race towards the centre of the track and had his chance before hanging left, then running out of steam up the hill.
Major Cadeaux, carrying a 4lb penalty, got a good lead into the race on the far side from the principals, but may have found the ground faster than he prefers. (op 6-1)
Royal Confidence, representing a yard that had won this three times in the last ten years, came into this off the back of a win but missed the break and never got involved. (op 12-1)
Baharah(USA) never managed to get into the race. (tchd 18-1)
Ordnance Row probably found the combination of a drop in trip and fastish ground not playing to his strengths. Official explanation: jockey said gelding was unsuited by the track (op 9-1)
Il Warrd(IRE) raced up with the pace towards the centre of the track but was in trouble going into the Dip. Official explanation: jockey said colt was struck into early on (op 8-1)

6815 DARLEY DEWHURST STKS (GROUP 1) (ENTIRE COLTS & FILLIES) 7f

2:35 (2:37) (Class 1) 2-Y-O

£163,355 (£61,923; £30,990; £15,452; £7,740; £3,884) **Stalls** Low

Form RPR

5633 **1** **Intense Focus (USA)**[13] 6520 2-9-1 0..........................(vt[1]) KJManning 1 118
(J S Bolger, Ire) *lw: chsd ldrs: rdn to ld 1f out: edgd lft ins fnl f: all out* **20/1**

2351 **2** nse **Lord Shanakill (USA)**[28] 6119 2-9-1 112.......................... JimCrowley 12 117
(K R Burke) *lw: hld up: hdwy over 2f out: rdn and ev ch ins fnl f: r.o* **12/1**

1210 **3** nse **Finjaan**[15] 6442 2-9-1 110.................................. RHills 4 117
(M P Tregoning) *chsd ldr tl led 1/2-way: rdn and hdd over 1f out: ev ch and n.m.r ins fnl f: r.o* **20/1**

3512 **4** ½ **Shaweel**[34] 5946 2-9-1 119.................................. GregFairley 9 116
(M Johnston) *lw: chsd ldrs: led over 1f out: sn rdn and edgd lft: hdd 1f out: unable qck towards fin* **10/1**

21 **5** 1 **Delegator**[57] 5246 2-9-1 0.................................. JamieSpencer 8 114
(B J Meehan) *hld up: hdwy and hung rt over 1f out: styd on* **15/2**[3]

121 **6** nk **Ashram (IRE)**[16] 6428 2-9-1 0.................................. RyanMoore 10 113
(J W Hills) *s.i.s: hld up: hdwy on outer over 1f out: styd on* **9/2**[2]

1 **7** hd **Rip Van Winkle (IRE)**[86] 4353 2-9-1 0.................................. JMurtagh 13 114+
(A P O'Brien, Ire) *w'like: athletic: lw: hld up: r.o ins fnl f: eased towards fin* **6/4**[1]

213 **8** 1 ¼ **Huntdown (USA)**[15] 6442 2-9-1 112.................................. LDettori 5 109
(J H M Gosden) *hld up in tch: rdn over 2f out: styd on same pce fnl f* **15/2**[3]

1041 **9** 4 ½ **Ouqba**[17] 6401 2-9-1 108.................................. MartinDwyer 6 98
(B W Hills) *hld up: rdn 1/2-way: n.d* **50/1**

4111 **10** 1 ¼ **Soul City (IRE)**[20] 6317 2-9-1 110.......................... RichardHughes 3 95
(R Hannon) *on toes: led to 1/2-way: rdn and wknd over 1f out* **11/1**

310 **11** ½ **Galpin Junior (USA)**[15] 6442 2-9-1 87.......................... TedDurcan 2 94
(B J Meehan) *hld up: pushed along 1/2-way: rdn and wknd over 1f out* **66/1**

6340 **12** 7 **Prime Delivery (USA)**[49] 5507 2-9-1 97..........................(t) ShaneKelly 11 76
(R M H Cowell) *s.i.s: outpcd* **200/1**

6 **13** ½ **Egypt**[97] 4008 2-9-1 0.................................. EddieAhern 7 75
(A P O'Brien, Ire) *chsd ldrs: rdn 1/2-way: wknd 2f out* **200/1**

1m 23.33s (-2.07) **Going Correction** -0.10s/f (Good) **13** Ran SP% **120.8**
Speed ratings (Par 109): **107,106,106,106,105 104,104,103,98,96 96,88,87**
toteswinger: 1&2 £33.60, 1&3 £46.80, 2&3 £36.40. CSF £235.49 TOTE £22.70: £4.10, £4.50, £6.90; EX 166.30 TRIFECTA Not won..
Owner Mrs J S Bolger **Bred** Robert N Clay And Airlie Stud **Trained** Coolcullen, Co Carlow
■ A third successive Dewhurst win for the Bolger/Manning team, following the wins of Teofilo and New Approach.
■ Stewards' Enquiry : K J Manning one-day ban: used whip without giving colt time to respond (Nov 1)

FOCUS
On paper not the strongest renewal of a race that is traditionally the most significant juvenile event of the season and one that this century has already produced the winner of an English, Irish and French Guineas, a Prix du Jockey-Club and, most recently, two Epsom Derby winners. With several of the principals closely matched or yet to prove themselves at this level, it looked an opportunity for a new star to establish himself, but that did not happen as the race climaxed in a desperate finish between three relatively exposed performers. Only 2 lengths or so covered the first seven too, but the form seems sound enough. This year's juvenile crop as a whole looks as weak as any in the past decade.

NOTEBOOK
Intense Focus(USA) has been running with credit in top company for most of the season, and his form tied in nicely with top Irish colts such as Mastercraftsman and Bushranger, but he looked held by Soul City and Shaweel on form. Equipped with the combination of a first-time visor and a tongue tie, he got a good tow early and squeezed through a gap to lead a furlong from home. When the placed horses came back at him he looked likely to get beaten, but he responded in the manner of his sire Giant's Causeway and just held on. The result probably means the European champion juvenile colt will come from another race, but this colt, who is best on this sort of surface, will be trained for the 2,000 Guineas (for which he is 25-1), and his trainer thinks he might get the Derby distance. (op 25-1)
Lord Shanakill(USA), like the winner, had raced in many of the big juvenile contests and been placed in the Coventry, Vintage Stakes and Prix Morny before winning the Mill Reef. Able to get a lead on this return to 7f, he was produced to have every chance inside the final furlong but just could not quite get past. He is by a Breeders' Cup Sprint winner, but his dam is by Theatrical, so possibly the Guineas trip will not be beyond him. (op 16-1)

Finjaan, who got no run in the Middle Park, was stepping up in trip and was given a positive ride. Always prominent, he was headed by the winner entering the furlong but rallied strongly and lost out only narrowly. Whether he is aimed at the Guineas or returned to sprinting remains to be seen, but he will reportedly start off next season over 7f. (op 16-1)
Shaweel, winner of the Gimcrack and touched off by Mastercraftsman in Group 1 National Stakes with Intense Focus behind, was given a positive ride and led briefly before the winner went on. He only weakened in the closing stages and possibly is better suited by easier ground.
Delegator, whose maiden win on the July course had been boosted by the next two home, ran with credit on this step up in grade, although he did not get up the hill as well as the battle-hardened principals, tending to drift right. He is a grand sort and open to further improvement. (op 10-1 tchd 11-1 in a place)
Ashram(IRE), the impressive winner of a Group 3 over course and distance last time, came from off the pace to have his chance, but was out towards the centre of the track and his effort petered out in the closing stages. (op 4-1 tchd 5-1)
Rip Van Winkle(IRE) ◆ is probably better than the bare form suggests, as he was held up at the back and had a good deal to do to get involved. He got to the heels of the leaders but was not given a hard time once his chance of making the frame had gone. He can be expected to do better next season. (op 15-8)
Huntdown(USA) tracked the leaders and appeared to have his chance but failed to pick up in the closing stages on this step up in trip. (op 9-1 tchd 10-1 in places)
Ouqba appeared to be found out in this grade and has yet to prove himself at this trip.
Soul City(IRE), who looked to have gone in his coat and was on his toes, was closely matched with Lord Shanakill and Shaweel on Goodwood form and was the disappointment of the race, making the early running but dropping out tamely late on. He may have had excuses, though, as he has had a long season and had looked better with some cut in the ground. Official explanation: jockey said colt stopped quickly (op 9-1)
Galpin Junior(USA) has now been well held in both tries at this level. (op 50-1)

6816 EMIRATES AIRLINE CHAMPION STKS (GROUP 1) 1m 2f

3:10 (3:16) (Class 1) 3-Y-O+

£242,691 (£91,998; £46,041; £22,956; £11,499; £5,771) **Stalls** Low

Form RPR
2131 **1** **New Approach (IRE)**[41] 5732 3-8-12 0 KJManning 10 131
(J S Bolger, Ire) *lw: a.p: chsd ldr over 8f out: led 3f out: clr over 1f out: r.o wl* **6/5**[1]
3310 **2** *6* **Twice Over**[56] 5302 3-8-12 116 TPQueally 3 121+
(H R A Cecil) *lw: trckd ldrs: nt clr run and swtchd rt over 2f out: rdn to chse wnr over 1f out: no imp* **8/1**[3]
0012 **3** *1 1/2* **Linngari (IRE)**[41] 5742 6-9-3 119 RyanMoore 1 116
(Sir Michael Stoute) *hld up: rdn 1/2-way: swtchd rt and hdwy over 1f out: sn rdn and no imp* **12/1**
12 **4** *1 1/4* **Russian Cross (IRE)**[28] 6148 3-8-12 0 OPeslier 9 114+
(A Fabre, France) *w'like: hld up: hdwy and hmpd over 2f out: rdn over 1f out: styd on same pce* **5/1**[2]
2022 **5** *4 1/2* **Traffic Guard (USA)**[41] 5732 4-9-3 120 JohnEgan 6 105
(Jane Chapple-Hyam) *lw: hld up: hdwy 6f out: rdn over 2f out: hung lft and wknd over 1f out* **16/1**
4002 **6** *nk* **Full Of Gold (FR)**[23] 6237 3-8-12 0 (p) DBoeuf 7 104
(Mme C Head-Maarek, France) *tall: w'like: chsd ldrs: rdn over 2f out: wknd over 1f out* **40/1**
3314 **7** *8* **Pipedreamer**[56] 5276 4-9-3 117 LDettori 8 88
(J H M Gosden) *hld up: hdwy over 3f out: rdn and wknd over 1f out* **5/1**[2]
0052 **8** *1/2* **Upton Grey (IRE)**[21] 6276 3-8-12 92 RobertHavlin 11 87
(J H M Gosden) *sn pushed along to ld: hdd 3f out: wkng whn n.m.r over 1f out* **200/1**
2103 **9** *1/2* **Hebridean (IRE)**[81] 4505 3-8-12 0 JMurtagh 4 86
(A P O'Brien, Ire) *hld up: nt clr run over 2f out: swtchd rt: rdn and edgd lft over 1f out: n.d* **25/1**
6234 **10** *5* **City Leader (IRE)**[34] 5953 3-8-12 114 JamieSpencer 2 76
(B J Meehan) *s.i.s: hld up: rdn over 2f out: wknd over 1f out* **25/1**
1260 **11** *22* **Staying On (IRE)**[15] 6440 3-8-12 108 AdamKirby 5 32
(W R Swinburn) *trckd ldrs: racd keenly: lost pl over 4f out: wknd and eased over 2f out* **66/1**

2m 0.13s (-5.67) **Going Correction** -0.10s/f (Good) course record
WFA 3 from 4yo+ 5lb **11** Ran SP% **115.6**
Speed ratings (Par 117): **118,113,112,111,107 107,100,100,99,95 78**
toteswinger: 1&2 £2.80, 1&3 £5.60, 2&3 £12.40. CSF £10.82 TOTE £2.20: £1.10, £2.50, £3.70; EX 11.90 Trifecta £70.80 Pool £11,200.20 - 117.05 winning units..
Owner H R H Princess Haya Of Jordan **Bred** Lodge Park Stud **Trained** Coolcullen, Co Carlow
■ Stewards' Enquiry : T P Queally two-day ban: careless riding (Nov 1-2)

FOCUS
This did not look by any means a strong Champion Stakes, but it was redeemed in full by a stunning performance from the favourite who won with overwhelming authority and became the first Derby winner to succeed here since Sir Ivor in 1968. His time, wind assisted admittedly, took nearly a second off a course record that Palace Music set in 1984. He is rated the season's best turf horse now, although everything went right for him here.

NOTEBOOK
New Approach(IRE), who looked in terrific condition, stood out on form and was entitled to win well, but the drying ground was a negative and few can have expected a six-length demolition job like this after his relatively workmanlike win in the Irish Champion Stakes. With the same owner's Upton Grey in the field to make the pace for him, he raced handily and was more settled than usual. Having taken it up 3f out, Manning made full use of his stamina and soon had him in an unassailable lead. He was in a different class, and it was a fitting end to a superb career in which he won eight of his 11 starts, five of them at Group 1 level. He has been retired to Dalham Hall Stud. (op 5-4 tchd 11-10, 6-4 in places and 11-8 in places)
Twice Over, unbeaten in three races at Newmarket, was a decisive enough 'winner' of the separate race for second, picking up pretty well when switched to the outer but never having the slightest chance of troubling New Approach. It was a good effort from the Maisons-Laffitte Group 2 winner, and Henry Cecil, who had started the week with a stronger candidate in Phoenix Tower, who had to be scratched following an injury, was pleased with him. He felt the colt would have done better with more give underfoot, but so would the winner. (op 7-1)
Linngari(IRE), the only Group 1 winner in the field apart from New Approach, was having only his second run in Britain in three years. He ran an honest race in third and Sir Michael Stoute, who felt easier ground would have helped him, has him entered in Hong Kong, although he will be in no hurry to commit him. (op 10-1 tchd 14-1)
Russian Cross(IRE), though unproven at this level, had been progressing nicely, following a similar route to last year's winner Literato. Although he would have been closer except for being slightly hampered when Twice Over was switched, he failed to make the impression many had expected. (op 9-2 tchd 6-1)
Traffic Guard(USA) had excelled himself when beaten only half a length by New Approach in the Irish Champion, but the winner was clearly below his best that day. This time Traffic Guard was a bit below his best, but it's worth remembering that while he has had many chances in Group races he has not yet won one. Official explanation: jockey said colt lost his action (op 12-1)
Full Of Gold(FR) looked much the weaker of the two French challengers, and he was racing on the fastest ground he has encountered. The cheekpieces he had benefited from last time did not seem to do much for him here and he dropped right away.
Pipedreamer, just behind New Approach when the pair were beaten in the Juddmonte, ran a rare moderate race and never looked like getting involved. (op 7-1)
Upton Grey(IRE), who was supplemented, did his pacemaking job well and beat three horses with much better credentials.
Hebridean(IRE) would have been closer with better luck in running. (tchd 33-1 in a place)

6817 TOTESPORT.COM CESAREWITCH (HERITAGE H'CAP) 2m 2f

3:50 (3:58) (Class 2) 3-Y-O+

£99,696 (£29,856; £14,928; £7,472; £3,728; £1,872) **Stalls** High

Form RPR
-654 **1** **Caracciola (GER)**[70] 4843 11-9-6 98 EddieAhern 11 109
(N J Henderson) *lw: hld up in mid-div: smooth hdwy on outer 4f out: led over 1f out: styd on strly to forge clr ins fnl f* **50/1**
-130 **2** *3* **Arc Bleu (GER)**[13] 6510 7-8-13 91 JMurtagh 32 99
(A J Martin, Ire) *racd quite freely: trckd ldng pair: led over 3f out: hdd over 1f out: styd on same pce* **15/2**[2]
0-2 **3** *nk* **Mamlook (IRE)**[123] 3104 4-8-7 85 ow1 RyanMoore 28 93
(D E Pipe) *in tch: hdwy 6f out: chal 3f out: styd on same pce fnl f* **10/1**[3]
1111 **4** *5* **Askar Tau (FR)**[34] 5940 3-8-7 96 4ex MartinDwyer 14 98
(M P Tregoning) *t.k.h in midfield: outpcd over 5f out: hdwy over 3f out: sn chsng ldrs: kpt on same pce fnl 2f* **7/2**[1]
011- **5** *2* **Leg Spinner (IRE)**[76] 6335 7-9-7 102 RCColgan(3) 15 102
(A J Martin, Ire) *hld up in rr: hdwy over 3f out: swtchd lft over 1f out: styd on wl: nt rch ldrs* **28/1**
3000 **6** *nk* **Tilt**[81] 4508 6-8-11 89 (p) DaneO'Neill 8 89+
(B Ellison) *bhd: hdwy over 3f out: kpt on wl fnl f* **66/1**
13/3 **7** *nk* **Liberate**[123] 3104 5-8-9 87 (p) JamieSpencer 24 86
(P J Hobbs) *prom: edgd lft over 2f out: one pce* **15/2**[2]
3230 **8** *3/4* **Hue**[115] 3368 7-7-5 76 JamieKyne(7) 6 74+
(B Ellison) *lw: t.k.h in rr: hdwy 4f out: styd on fnl 2f: nvr trbld ldrs* **66/1**
4200 **9** *shd* **Inchpast**[19] 6329 7-7-12 76 oh1 (b) NickyMackay 12 74
(M H Tompkins) *in tch: effrt over 3f out: kpt on one pce* **100/1**
1210 **10** *3/4* **Four Miracles**[21] 6272 4-8-0 85 AshleyMorgan(7) 4 83
(M H Tompkins) *lw: in rr: hdwy over 3f out: kpt on fnl 2f: nvr nr ldrs* **66/1**
00-0 **11** *1 1/4* **Hernando Royal**[21] 6288 5-8-1 86 AndreaAtzeni(7) 1 82
(Dr R D P Newland) *s.i.s: in rr div: kpt on fnl 4f: nvr a factor* **100/1**
4100 **12** *nk* **Missoula (IRE)**[21] 6272 5-8-10 88 SamHitchcott 9 84
(Miss Suzy Smith) *wl in tch: effrt over 4f out: one pce* **25/1**
3100 **13** *1/2* **Always Bold (IRE)**[7] 6646 3-8-1 90 4ex RoystonFfrench 3 85
(M Johnston) *in tch: one pce fnl 4f* **66/1**
2211 **14** *1* **Hits Only Vic (USA)**[16] 6410 4-8-11 89 7ex DavidAllan 7 83
(D Carroll) *in rr div: kpt on fnl 3f: nvr nr ldrs* **16/1**
5/3 **15** *1* **Talenti (IRE)**[178] 1568 5-9-2 94 AlanMunro 18 87
(Miss E C Lavelle) *lw: chsd ldr: wknd over 2f out* **50/1**
022/ **16** *2* **Top The Charts**[15] 6460 6-8-3 81 (t) JohnEgan 30 72
(A J Martin, Ire) *mid-div: effrt over 2f out: sn btn* **14/1**
1031 **17** *5* **Daraahem (IRE)**[72] 4784 3-8-10 99 RHills 20 84
(B W Hills) *lw: in rr div: hdwy 4f out: nt clr run over 2f out: sn wknd: eased 1f out* **10/1**[3]
/240 **18** *1* **Souffleur**[21] 6288 5-8-4 82 HayleyTurner 17 66
(P Bowen) *prom: lost pl over 3f out* **25/1**
1312 **19** *4* **Bollin Felix**[36] 5853 4-8-9 87 4ex (b) TedDurcan 5 67
(T D Easterby) *on toes: hld up towards rr: nvr a factor* **20/1**
2110 **20** *nk* **Wicked Daze (IRE)**[57] 5229 5-9-4 96 J-PGuillambert 26 76
(Sir Mark Prescott) *in rr: bhd fnl 5f* **25/1**
0000 **21** *3/4* **Swan Queen**[36] 5853 5-8-9 87 JimmyQuinn 34 66
(J L Dunlop) *prom: lost pl over 3f out* **80/1**
4040 **22** *1* **Kasthari (IRE)**[21] 6272 9-8-5 83 ChrisCatlin 13 61
(J D Bethell) *prom: lost pl over 3f out* **100/1**
2540 **23** *3/4* **Whenever**[21] 6272 4-8-4 82 (b1) DaleGibson 22 59
(R T Phillips) *mid-div: lost pl over 3f out: sn bhd* **33/1**
4-40 **24** *3/4* **Downing Street (IRE)**[9] 4516 7-7-13 77 ow1 (v) FrancisNorton 19 53
(Jennie Candlish) *a towards rr* **100/1**
0-60 **25** *6* **Land 'n Stars**[20] 6306 8-9-4 96 RobertHavlin 29 65
(Jamie Poulton) *hmpd after 1f: a towards rr: bhd fnl 3f* **66/1**
0100 **26** *9* **Pippa Greene**[36] 5853 4-9-4 96 NCallan 16 55
(P F I Cole) *mid-div: lost pl over 3f out* **40/1**
3202 **27** *3 1/4* **Bogside Theatre (IRE)**[12] 6527 4-9-1 93 PJMcDonald 31 49
(G M Moore) *led tl over 3f out: sn lost pl* **25/1**
2105 **28** *3 1/2* **Mighty Moon**[49] 5498 5-7-12 76 oh1 PaulHanagan 33 28
(R A Fahey) *in tch: pushed along 7f out: lost pl over 3f out* **16/1**
1405 **29** *2 1/4* **Bulwark (IRE)**[36] 5854 6-9-9 101 (v) JimCrowley 21 51
(Ian Williams) *in tch: drvn 6f out: lost pl over 3f out* **33/1**
0104 **30** *2 1/2* **Baddam**[12] 6527 6-9-1 93 RichardHughes 2 40
(Ian Williams) *in tch: drvn 6f out: sn lost pl: bhd fnl 3f* **50/1**
-000 **31** *17* **Mudawin (IRE)**[60] 4843 7-8-3 86 DavidProbert(5) 27 14
(M F Harris) *in rr: bhd fnl 3f: t.o* **66/1**
1501 **32** *67* **Gee Dee Nen**[70] 4843 5-9-1 93 LDettori 23 —
(Jim Best) *chsd ldrs: drvn 5f out: lost pl over 3f out: sn bhd and eased: virtually p.u: hopelessly t.o* **14/1**

3m 48.3s (-6.50) **Going Correction** -0.10s/f (Good)
WFA 3 from 4yo+ 11lb **32** Ran SP% **141.0**
Speed ratings (Par 109): **110,108,108,106,105 105,105,104,104,104 103,103,103,103,102 101,99,99,97,97 96,96,96,95,93 89**
toteswinger: 1&2 £46.10, 1&3 £85.20, 2&3 £7.30. CSF £376.17 CT £4132.49 TOTE £62.70: £10.40, £2.70, £2.30, £2.50; EX 431.00 Trifecta £8681.90 Pool £22,291.37 - 1.90 winning units..

Owner P J D Pottinger **Bred** Frau I U A Brunotte **Trained** Upper Lambourn, Berks
■ Caracciola is the oldest ever winner of the Cesarewitch.

FOCUS
This historic long-distance handicap has often attracted the attention of the jumping trainers and last year the first four were better known as hurdlers or chasers. It was a similar case this year, with jumping stalwart Nicky Henderson training his second winner of the race following Landing Light in 2003. The usual large field lined up and, although in recent history a middle-to-high draw has proven essential, that wasn't the case this time. The form has a solid look to it, with the winner up 3lb on last year's mark.

NOTEBOOK
Caracciola(GER), last year's runner-up, was 6lb higher and had a modest draw, which perhaps accounts for his long odds. However, he appreciated the sounder surface and travelled strongly before settling the issue up the hill. Apparently he may race over hurdles again but this will be his last run on the Flat.
Arc Bleu(GER), who had gained his wins on soft ground but handles fast going over hurdles, was 6lb higher than for his Northumberland Plate win and ran a fine race, having been in the leading group throughout. He has not had much racing so can be expected to contest this sort of race for a while. (op 8-1 tchd 9-1, 10-1 in places)
Mamlook(IRE), who was narrowly beaten in the Ascot Stakes, made a bold bid to score in his first outing since. He had every chance but had nothing in reserve for the climb to the line. (op 7-1)

Askar Tau(FR) held a decent pitch in the main bunch, but did not have much room when he wanted to make a move before staying on steadily in the final 2f. He has gone up 39lb since his winning run started and, being only a three-year-old, could continue to go the right way. Connections suggested he will be given a Cup campaign next season. (op 9-2)
Leg Spinner(IRE), last year's winner, had not been seen on the Flat since, but he had been in action over hurdles this summer. However, he was 10lb higher than last season and only ran on late to pass beaten horses. (op 33-1)
Tilt has not won since May 2006 but is regularly in the frame in decent handicaps and finished third in the Chester Cup in the spring. He ran another sound race but could only keep on at one pace in the last 2f.
Liberate stays well and was closely matched with Mamlook on Ascot Stakes form. Like that gelding, he had not run since, but performed creditably in first-time cheekpieces, only to be left behind when the principals struck for home. (op 8-1)
Hue had to overcome a low draw and was quite keen early, so his rider had to settle him well in arrears. He was doing his best work late and just got past the Mark Tompkins pair.
Inchpast is a sound stayer and had some sort of chance halfway up the straight before lacking the extra gears at the business end.
Four Miracles, like her stable companion, had a chance halfway up the straight but lacked the pace to land a blow.
Hernando Royal had only won on sand on the Flat and never got involved from his poor draw. (op 66-1)
Missoula(IRE), the Ascot Stakes winner, was close enough at the 4f pole but had no more to give. Official explanation: trainer said mare was scoped later and shown to have bled (tchd 33-1 in a place)
Talenti(IRE) showed to the fore for a long way, but had done enough before reaching the 2f pole.
Bogside Theatre(IRE) was the early pacemaker, but not surprisingly he was done with soon after the 3f pole. (op 33-1)
Bulwark(IRE) was reportedly struck into. Official explanation: jockey said gelding was struck into
Gee Dee Nen, having his first run for connections and reasonably drawn, raced close to the pace early but suddenly came under pressure around 6f from home and dropped right out as if something was amiss. He was reported to have lost his action. Official explanation: jockey said gelding lost its action

6818 COUNTRYWIDE STEEL & TUBES ROCKFEL STKS (GROUP 2) (FILLIES) 7f

4:25 (4:34) (Class 1) 2-Y-O

£45,416 (£17,216; £8,616; £4,296; £2,152; £1,080) **Stalls** Low

Form				RPR
432	**1**		**Lahaleeb (IRE)**[20] 6318 2-8-12 102 .... DarryllHolland 10 (M R Channon) *racd stands' side: hld up: hdwy to ld overall over 1f out: edgd lft: rdn out* **11/1**	112
5112	**2**	*2 1/4*	**Aspen Darlin (IRE)**[15] 6441 2-8-12 111 .... (p) JimmyQuinn 17 (A Bailey) *led far side: rdn over 1f out: styd on: 1st of 6 in gp* **13/2**[3]	106
1541	**3**	*shd*	**Souter's Sister (IRE)**[15] 6439 2-8-12 104 .... DaneO'Neill 14 (R Hannon) *racd far side: prom: rdn over 1f out: styd on: 2nd of 6 in gp* **12/1**	106
0162	**4**	*nk*	**Baileys Cacao (IRE)**[20] 6319 2-8-12 97 .... RichardHughes 4 (R Hannon) *b.hind: lw: racd stands' side: s.i.s: hld up: hdwy over 1f out: r.o: nt rch ldrs: 2nd of 9 in gp* **11/1**	105
612	**5**	*1 1/4*	**Moonlife (IRE)**[15] 6439 2-8-12 103 .... LDettori 3 (Saeed Bin Suroor) *overall ldr on stands' side: tl hdd over 2f out: rdn and ev ch over 1f out: styd on same pce: 3rd of 9 in gp* **6/1**[2]	102
2021	**6**	*nk*	**Penny's Gift**[22] 6240 2-8-12 105 .... JamieSpencer 12 (R Hannon) *lw: racd far side: hld up in tch: rdn over 1f out: styd on: 3rd of 6 in gp* **8/1**	101
1	**7**	*1 1/4*	**Lassarina (IRE)**[29] 6076 2-8-12 0 .... MichaelHills 16 (B W Hills) *free to post: racd far side: chsd ldrs: rdn over 2f out: no ex fnl f: 4th of 6 in gp* **15/2**	98
04	**8**	*nk*	**Blas Ceoil (USA)**[8] 6637 2-8-12 0 .... KJManning 7 (J S Bolger, Ire) *w'like: scope: racd stands' side: prom: rdn over 1f out: no ex: 4th of 9 in gp* **16/1**	97
5421	**9**	*1 1/2*	**Purple Sage (IRE)**[21] 6273 2-8-12 82 .... RHills 1 (B W Hills) *racd stands' side: hld up in tch: nt clr run over 2f out: rdn over 1f out: no imp: 5th of 9 in gp* **33/1**	94
1	**10**	*1 1/4*	**Purissima (USA)**[12] 6531 2-8-12 0 .... RyanMoore 11 (Sir Michael Stoute) *leggy: scope: racd stands' side: hld up in tch: led over 2f out: hdd over 1f out: wknd fnl f: 6th of 9 in gp* **4/1**[1]	90
03	**11**	*1 1/2*	**Haakima (USA)**[31] 6013 2-8-12 0 .... NCallan 5 (C E Brittain) *racd stands' side: prom: rdn over 2f out: wknd over 1f out: 7th of 9 in gp* **66/1**	87
1120	**12**	*3*	**Rosabee (IRE)**[15] 6441 2-8-12 103 .... EdwardCreighton 15 (Miss V Haigh) *racd far side: sn pushed along in rr: wknd over 2f out: 5th of 6 in gp* **25/1**	79
205	**13**	*1 3/4*	**Marquesa (USA)**[13] 6519 2-8-12 0 .... JMurtagh 2 (David Wachman, Ire) *lean: angular: racd stands' side: hld up in tch: rdn and wknd over 1f out: 8th of 9 in gp* **8/1**	75
002	**14**	*1 1/4*	**Tamarah**[31] 6029 2-8-12 74 .... HayleyTurner 8 (Miss D Mountain) *racd stands' side: chsd ldr tl rdn over 2f out: wknd over 1f out: last of 9 in gp* **100/1**	72
6020	**15**	*7*	**Amosite**[26] 6172 2-8-12 75 .... EddieAhern 13 (J R Jenkins) *racd far side: w ldr tl rdn over 2f out: sn wknd: last of 6 in gp* **150/1**	54

1m 23.95s (-1.45) **Going Correction** -0.10s/f (Good) **15** Ran SP% **121.8**
Speed ratings (Par 104): **104,101,101,100,99 99,97,97,95,94 92,89,87,85,77**
toteswinger: 1&2 £16.30, 1&3 £30.20, 2&3 £10.90. CSF £79.63 TOTE £15.20: £3.70, £2.60, £3.30; EX 111.40.
Owner M Al-Qatami & K M Al-Mudhaf **Bred** Tom Twomey **Trained** West Ilsley, Berks

FOCUS
While last year's renewal was weak, this has often been a strong pointer to the following year's Classics, with the 2005 winner Speciosa and the 2006 winner Finsceal Beo both going on to land the 1,000 Guineas, and the 2004 winner Maids Causeway finishing second in it. On paper this looked a decent enough renewal, but the first three had all had plenty of racing and with the field racing in two distinct groups on either side of the track it was somewhat unsatisfactory. Lahaleeb is admirably progressive, but Aspen Darlin was a length or so off her recent best.

NOTEBOOK
Lahaleeb(IRE) was more exposed than most but, in fairness, she appeared to be trained with nurseries in mind to begin with, and since winning two of them, off just 72 and 74, she has gone from strength to strength, gaining soft-ground Group-race placings on her last two starts. This time she was held up in the stands' group, getting the cover she had lacked last time, and she made her effort widest of all. She went left when she hit the front, but it did not stop her going forward and she ran up the hill strongly for a clear-cut win, arguably proving even more effective on the drying ground. She will presumably be trained for the Guineas, but the stable has had several better candidates over the years. (op 12-1 tchd 10-1)
Aspen Darlin(IRE), who was keen to post, had run nine times but her best performance had been her most recent one when second in the Cheveley Park Stakes, and she confirmed that was no fluke by narrowly 'winning' the separate race up the opposite side of the track. A tough filly, she got the extra furlong all right and may get further. (tchd 6-1)
Souter's Sister(IRE) also went up the far side, and like Aspen Darlin, she was up there all the way. Her best effort had come on her tenth start, when a shock winner of the Oh So Sharp Stakes, and this was probably another small step up. (op 17-2 tchd 8-1)
Baileys Cacao(IRE), a front-running Listed winner on fast ground on the July course, was closing in fourth and did particularly well considering she had missed the break. (op 12-1)
Moonlife(IRE), second to Souter's Sister here last time, was given another positive ride, making good use of her draw near the stands' rail, but she was beaten fair and square. (tchd 13-2)
Penny's Gift, second in a sub-standard Lowther, was just staying on up the far side. (op 10-1)
Lassarina(IRE) had looked good at Newbury on her debut, but was free to post here. (op 7-1 tchd 8-1)
Blas Ceoil(USA), representing the Finsceal Beo team, ran respectably in eighth up the stands' side.
Purissima(USA) needed to improve considerably on her debut win over 6f at Warwick, impressive though that was. She got to the front going to 2f out but did not get home. This may have come too soon for her, and it was on different ground too, so she is worth another chance. (tchd 9-2)

6819 PRIDE STKS (GROUP 2) (F&M) 1m 4f

5:00 (5:07) (Class 1) 3-Y-O+

£60,829 (£23,058; £11,540; £5,753; £2,882; £1,446) **Stalls** High

Form				RPR
1111	**1**		**Crystal Capella**[22] 6241 3-8-10 98 .... RyanMoore 2 (Sir Michael Stoute) *chsd ldrs: rdn to ld over 1f out: hung rt ins fnl f: styd on gamely* **4/1**[3]	103+
12	**2**	*hd*	**Unsung Heroine (IRE)**[35] 5892 3-8-10 0 .... WMLordan 9 (T Stack, Ire) *lw: chsd ldr tl led over 2f out: rdn and hdd over 1f out: rallied and hmpd ins fnl f: styd on gamely* **11/8**[1]	102+
110	**3**	*2 1/2*	**Saphira's Fire (IRE)**[134] 2792 3-8-10 98 .... MartinDwyer 3 (W R Muir) *chsd ldrs: rdn over 2f out: styd on same pce fnl f* **16/1**	98
0062	**4**	*2*	**Under The Rainbow**[22] 6241 5-9-3 95 .... (p) NCallan 5 (B W Hills) *hld up: hdwy 1/2-way: over 2f out: no ex fnl f* **16/1**	95
0002	**5**	*1*	**Perihelion (IRE)**[20] 6321 3-8-10 0 .... JMurtagh 1 (A P O'Brien, Ire) *led: pushed along over 4f out: hdd over 2f out: styd on same pce appr fnl f* **16/1**	93
1011	**6**	*1/2*	**Armure**[26] 6171 3-8-10 82 .... PhilipRobinson 7 (M A Jarvis) *lw: hld up: effrt over 2f out: sn hung lft and outpcd: styd on ins fnl f* **16/1**	93
1	**7**	*shd*	**Shreyas (IRE)**[21] 6298 3-8-10 0 .... KJManning 6 (J S Bolger, Ire) *hld up: plld hrd: rdn over 2f out: hung rt fr over 1f out: no ex* **11/4**[2]	92+
6000	**8**	*14*	**Sail (IRE)**[21] 6298 3-8-10 0 .... JamieSpencer 8 (A P O'Brien, Ire) *hld up: hdwy over 2f out: wknd over 1f out: eased* **25/1**	70

2m 31.48s (-2.02) **Going Correction** -0.10s/f (Good)
WFA 3 from 5yo 7lb **8** Ran SP% **116.1**
Speed ratings (Par 115): **102,101,100,98,98 97,97,88**
toteswinger: 1&2 £3.70, 1&3 £3.30, 2&3 £7.30. CSF £10.07 TOTE £4.80: £1.70, £1.30, £1.80; EX 10.40.
Owner Sir Evelyn De Rothschild **Bred** Southcourt Stud **Trained** Newmarket, Suffolk
■ Stewards' Enquiry : Ryan Moore one-day ban: careless riding (Nov 1)

FOCUS
The first running of this fillies' Group 2, which has taken the place of Ascot's Princess Royal Stakes, lost some of its interest with the withdrawal of Dar Re Mi, but produced a good race between two game and progressive fillies. It was steadily run and the bare form is a bit messy, with neither of the first two probably at their best.

NOTEBOOK
Crystal Capella ◆ has improved steadily since winning her maiden at Newcastle in the spring and completed a five-timer under a strong ride from Ryan Moore. She managed to make the step up from Listed company and travelled well before challenging the favourite running into the Dip. She tended to wander about and got involved in a bumping match with the runner-up, but kept sticking her head out and just held on. (op 3-1)
Unsung Heroine(IRE) ◆, a cheaply bought and lightly raced filly, had the best form in the race, having finished a clear second to Conduit in the St Leger. With stamina not in doubt, she had plenty of use made of her and went on at the 3f pole. She responded well when the winner took her on and only just lost out despite the barging match. Presumably she will remain in training next season, as this was only her fourth start, and in that case may get the chance for revenge. (op 6-4 tchd 6-5)
Saphira's Fire(IRE), another lightly raced filly, had won the Pretty Polly here in the spring and was having her first outing since finishing out the back in the Oaks, when she was found to have several insect bites and did not handle the track. She travelled well in the wake of the leaders and was upsides the winner three furlongs out, but did not quite have the pace of the front pair. She is another who looks to have more to offer. (tchd 12-1)
Under The Rainbow, the only older filly in the line-up, had been narrowly beaten by Crystal Capella at Ascot last month but was 2lb worse off. She seemed to run her race again and is a fair yardstick for the form. (op 20-1)
Perihelion(IRE), a distant runner-up to Allegretto in the Park Hill, set a fair pace after the early dawdle and kept going after being headed, being beaten less far than she was at Doncaster. (op 12-1)
Armure was stepping up considerably in grade, having done her winning on Kempton's Polytrack, and never got into contention. (op 14-1)
Shreyas(IRE), narrowly beaten by Unsung Heroine on their debuts, did not help her cause by pulling in the early stages on this step up in trip. (op 9-2)
Sail(IRE) has gone backwards and has not made much impression at this sort of level since winning the Cheshire Oaks. (op 14-1)

6820 JOCKEY CLUB CUP (GROUP 3) 2m

5:35 (5:43) (Class 1) 3-Y-O+

£36,900 (£13,988; £7,000; £3,490; £1,748; £877) **Stalls** Low

Form				RPR
5-51	**1**		**Veracity**[12] 6527 4-9-0 108 .... LDettori 5 (Saeed Bin Suroor) *chsd ldr tl led over 2f out: rdn over 1f out: styd on* **5/2**[1]	112
5363	**2**	*1/2*	**Sagara (USA)**[20] 6306 4-9-0 109 .... (v) TedDurcan 3 (Saeed Bin Suroor) *lw: hld up: rdn 2f out: hdwy and hung rt fr over 1f out: r.o: nt rch wnr* **13/2**	111
0012	**3**	*nk*	**Fiulin**[16] 6427 3-8-4 102 .... JohnEgan 8 (M Botti) *lw: prom: rdn over 3f out: hung rt and outpcd 2f out: r.o ins fnl f* **9/2**[3]	111
21-	**4**	*nk*	**Host Nation**[538] 1341 5-9-0 105 .... JMurtagh 4 (Miss Venetia Williams) *a.p: rdn and hung rt over 1f out: styng on whn hung lft wl ins fnl f* **14/1**	111
2145	**5**	*2*	**Distinction (IRE)**[20] 6306 9-9-0 112 .... RyanMoore 2 (Sir Michael Stoute) *hld up: hdwy over 4f out: rdn over 1f out: styng on same pce whn hmpd wl ins fnl f* **7/2**[2]	108
0322	**6**	*1/2*	**Balkan Knight**[20] 6306 8-9-0 110 .... GeorgeBaker 9 (D R C Elsworth) *b.hind: hld up: swtchd lft over 2f out: hdwy over 1f out: sn rdn: nt rch ldrs* **11/2**	108

0402 **7** 3 1/2 **Classic Punch (IRE)**[15] 6444 5-9-0 107 .... TQuinn 1 103
(D R C Elsworth) *plld hrd: led after 1f: rdn over 3f out: hdd over 2f out: wknd ins fnl f* **16/1**

0542 **8** 7 **Big Robert**[21] 6286 4-9-0 99 .... MartinDwyer 6 95
(W R Muir) *s.i.s: hld up: rdn over 2f out: wknd over 1f out* **25/1**

R002 **9** 16 **Carte Diamond (USA)**[35] 5885 7-9-0 102 .... J-PGuillambert 7 76
(B Ellison) *b: led 1f: chsd ldrs: rdn over 3f out: wknd over 2f out* **16/1**

3m 28.94s (-1.86) **Going Correction** -0.10s/f (Good)
WFA 3 from 4yo+ 10lb **9** Ran SP% **120.0**
Speed ratings (Par 113): **100,99,99,99,98 98,96,92,84**
toteswinger: 1&2 £5.10, 1&3 £15.20, 2&3 £43.30. CSF £20.30 TOTE £3.50: £1.70, £2.60, £1.90; EX 20.20 Place 6 £1,469.75, Place 5 £561.98. .
Owner Godolphin **Bred** Darley **Trained** Newmarket, Suffolk
■ Stewards' Enquiry : J Murtagh two-day ban: careless riding (Nov 1-2)

FOCUS
A competitive enough affair, but it perhaps lacked a bit of class and the pace was far from strong, which contributed to a bunched finish and a slow time. Saeed Bin Suroor sent out the first two and Veracity did not need to match last year's best form.

NOTEBOOK
Veracity is a thorough stayer and was well ridden the way the race was run, because having accepted a lead from the hard-pulling Classic Punch, he was committed a good way from home. He got the better of the leader with two furlongs to go and an advantage of a couple of lengths stood him in good stead as the pack closed up the hill. He came here fresher than most and still relatively unexposed following just two runs for Godolphin. He stays in training. (op 3-1)
Sagara(USA) has been very disappointing since his Arc third, but he ran better here, running on well having been held up in rear and offering further evidence of the excellent form in which Godolphin are ending the season. The visor seemed to work well, and connections were pleased to see him more focused. He too remains in training. (op 8-1)
Fiulin, the only three-year-old in the field, ran a blinder in third and might have gone even closer had the pace been stronger or more use been made more of him, as he had looked a progressive stayer under more forcing tactics on his two most recent starts, and he was running on here after getting outpaced when the winner was pressing on. He is going to be even better next year. (op 6-1)
Host Nation did tremendously well considering he had been off the track for 538 days since his Group 3 win at Longchamp. Remarkably, he had reportedly changed hands for just 5,000gns last December, so he has presumably had his problems, but this was an encouraging return.
Distinction(IRE)'s Listed win at Sandown in the summer made him the form choice on Racing Post Ratings, but he threatened only briefly and was held when hampered well inside the final furlong. Successful in the 2005 Goodwood Cup and placed in the Gold Cup behind Westerner at York in 2005 and behind Yeats at Royal Ascot in 2006, he was a flagbearer for his owners Highclere Thoroughbreds season after season but has now been retired. (tchd 10-3 and 4-1)
Balkan Knight, last year's second, needs holding up until the last possible moment and so is hard to win with, but he has an ideal new partner in George Baker. Unfortunately, the pace was not strong enough for him. (tchd 9-2 and 6-1)
Classic Punch(IRE) was allowed to go on when he pulled hard under restraint in the early stages, but eventually paid for it. (op 14-1)
Carte Diamond(USA) was too keen. (op 14-1)
T/Plt: £328.90 to a £1 stake. Pool: £189,193.95. 419.90 winning tickets. T/Qpdt: £8.30 to a £1 stake. Pool: £9,717.06. 859.45 winning tickets. CR

6707 WOLVERHAMPTON (A.W) (L-H)
Saturday, October 18

OFFICIAL GOING: Standard
Wind: medium, behind Weather: dry

6821 CLEANVU H'CAP (DIV I) — 1m 141y(P)
6:20 (6:20) (Class 6) (0-65,67) 3-Y-0+ **£2,047** (£604; £302) **Stalls** Low

Form RPR

106U **1** **Bramalea**[19] 6332 3-9-1 **62** .... AdamKirby 1 73
(B W Duke) *in tch: rdn to chse ldr 2f out: led 1f out: hld on wl u.p: all out* **11/1**

634 **2** nk **Beetuna (IRE)**[5] 6712 3-9-2 **63** .... (v[1]) RoystonFfrench 2 74
(B Smart) *hld up in midfield on inner: hdwy and nt clr run over 2f out: sn swtchd off rail and hmpd: rdn to chse ldng pair over 1f out: edgd out rt 1f out: chsd wnr ins fnl f: r.o but nt quite rch wnr* **7/2**[2]

361 **3** 3 3/4 **Shunkawakhan (IRE)**[48] 5538 5-9-3 **60** .... PJMcDonald 8 62
(Miss L A Perratt) *chsd ldng pair tl led over 2f out: rdn 2f out: hdd 1f out: wknd fnl 100yds* **15/2**

1200 **4** 2 1/2 **Time To Regret**[24] 6211 8-9-4 **61** .... (p) PatrickMathers 9 57
(I W McInnes) *hld up in midfield: effrt on outer over 3f out: chsd ldrs wl over 1f out: no prog fr over 1f out* **33/1**

3651 **5** 1/2 **Imperial Lucky (IRE)**[8] 6628 5-9-10 **67** .... PatCosgrave 6 62
(M J Wallace, Australia) *dwlt: towards rr: effrt and rdn over 3f out: no imp u.p fr over 1f out* **13/2**[3]

0030 **6** 2 3/4 **The Wily Woodcock**[10] 6585 4-9-6 **63** .... ChrisCatlin 11 52
(G Wragg) *hld up in rr: rdn 4f out: sme hdwy fnl f: nvr trbld ldrs* **7/1**

2206 **7** nk **Libre**[6] 6671 8-9-5 **62** .... LPKeniry 3 50
(F Jordan) *hld up towards rr: rdn and effrt 3f out: no real hdwy: wl hld whn hung rt over 1f out* **14/1**

4000 **8** 1/2 **Solicitude**[130] 2917 5-9-0 **57** .... (p) PaulHanagan 12 44
(D Haydn Jones) *chsd ldrs: rdn to chse ldng pair 2f out: wknd over 1f out* **40/1**

4062 **9** nk **Out Of Nothing**[37] 5816 5-8-8 **58** .... AmyKathleenParsons(7) 10 44
(K M Prendergast) *hld up in rr: rdn and no hdwy over 3f out: nvr trbld ldrs* **20/1**

0051 **10** 11 **Cinerama (IRE)**[19] 6332 3-9-1 **62** .... SteveDrowne 4 23
(M P Tregoning) *in tch: rdn over 3f out: wknd over 2f out: no ch whn hmpd over 1f out* **10/3**[1]

0000 **11** 2 1/4 **Bertbrand**[8] 6634 3-9-1 **62** .... TonyCulhane 13 18
(D Flood) *stdd and dropped in bhd after s: effrt on outer 3f out: n.d* **33/1**

6000 **12** 3 1/4 **Indian Edge**[74] 4710 7-8-10 **58** .... RichardEvans(5) 5 6
(B Palling) *w ldr tl over 4f out: sn rdn: wknd over 2f out* **16/1**

3550 **13** 3 3/4 **Mr Burton**[8] 6628 4-9-3 **60** .... GregFairley 7 —
(M Mullineaux) *sn led: rdn and hdd over 2f out: wknd qckly* **33/1**

1m 50.83s (0.33) **Going Correction** +0.10s/f (Slow)
WFA 3 from 4yo+ 4lb **13** Ran SP% **119.8**
Speed ratings (Par 101): **102,101,98,96,95 93,93,92,92,82 80,77,74**
toteswinger: 1&2 £7.90, 1&3 £7.90, 2&3 £7.90. CSF £46.95 CT £327.87 TOTE £10.40: £2.60, £2.20, £2.20; EX 76.00.
Owner P J Cave **Bred** P J Cave **Trained** Lambourn, Berks

FOCUS
A moderate handicap run in a time just over three seconds slower than standard. The form looks fairly reliable rated around the placed horses.

Cinerama(IRE) Official explanation: jockey said filly moved poorly

6822 CLEAN WASTE SOLUTIONS MAIDEN STKS — 5f 20y(P)
6:50 (6:50) (Class 5) 3-Y-0+ **£2,729** (£806; £403) **Stalls** Low

Form RPR

1 **Tayyab (USA)**[288] 3-9-3 0 .... KShea 1 80
(M F De Kock, South Africa) *s.i.s: sn pushed up into midfield: hdwy to chse ldng pair over 2f out: wnt 2nd over 1f out: led wl ins fnl f: r.o wl* **9/2**[3]

0-00 **2** 1 **Cayman Fox**[14] 6486 3-8-12 66 .... PJMcDonald 4 71
(James Moffatt) *taken down early: led: rdn over 1f out: hdd and no ex wl ins fnl f* **7/2**[2]

600 **3** 1/2 **Madame Hoi (IRE)**[6] 6671 3-8-12 83 .... TonyCulhane 7 69
(M R Channon) *taken down early: hld up in rr: hdwy 1/2-way: rdn wl over 1f out: wnt 3rd ins fnl f: r.o but nt rch ldng pair* **6/1**

6023 **4** 3 3/4 **Royal Degree**[20] 6308 3-9-3 63 .... (t) RoystonFfrench 13 61
(B Smart) *in tch in midfield: rdn and effrt on outer 1/2-way: chsd ldrs and edgd lft over 1f out: no hdwy fnl f* **3/1**[1]

0540 **5** 1 1/2 **Molly Two**[33] 5970 3-8-9 50 .... DuranFentiman(3) 3 50
(L A Mullaney) *wnt lft s: chsd ldr tl over 1f out: wknd fnl f* **11/2**

0000 **6** 5 **Cool Fashion (IRE)**[26] 6173 3-8-12 43 .... (b) FrancisNorton 9 32
(Ollie Pears) *chsd ldrs: rdn and struggling 1/2-way: wl btn last 2f* **40/1**

2 **7** 1 1/2 **Titus Gent**[5] 6633 3-9-3 0 .... MickyFenton 12 32
(J Ryan) *sn outpcd towards rr: nvr trbld ldrs* **14/1**

06 **8** hd **Bedloe's Island (IRE)**[61] 5160 3-9-3 0 .... PaulHanagan 2 31
(R C Guest) *rrd s and v.s.a: a bhd* **16/1**

4506 **9** 1 **Run From Nun**[73] 4725 3-8-7 43 .... DavidProbert(5) 8 23
(John Berry) *a outpcd in rr: nvr a factor* **22/1**

003- **10** hd **Comic Tales**[629] 282 7-9-3 45 .... (p) GregFairley 6 27
(M Mullineaux) *sn outpcd in rr: nvr a factor* **66/1**

00- **11** 6 **Human Touch**[55] 3-8-12 65 .... ChrisCatlin 10 —
(G A Butler) *racd in midfield tl 1/2-way: sn toiling* **25/1**

62.02 secs (-0.28) **Going Correction** +0.10s/f (Slow) **11** Ran SP% **119.7**
Speed ratings (Par 103): **106,104,103,97,95 87,84,84,82,82 72**
toteswinger: 1&2 £6.20, 1&3 £3.90, 2&3 £7.50. CSF £20.36 TOTE £4.40: £1.90, £1.90, £2.80; EX 25.10.
Owner Sheikh Mohammed Bin Khalifa Al Maktoum **Bred** Al Adiyaat **Trained** South Africa

FOCUS
A modest maiden which was run at a strong pace. The form looks sound enough rated around the runner-up, fourth and fifth.

Bedloe's Island(IRE) Official explanation: jockey said gelding started awkwardly

6823 WOLVERHAMPTON-RACECOURSE.CO.UK CLAIMING STKS — 5f 20y(P)
7:20 (7:20) (Class 6) 3-Y-0+ **£2,047** (£604; £302) **Stalls** Low

Form RPR

0503 **1** **Blue Tomato**[6] 6680 7-8-10 84 .... WilliamCarson(5) 3 88+
(D Nicholls) *racd off the pce in midfield: hdwy 1/2-way: chsd ldr 2f out: rdn to ld ins fnl f: sn clr: easily* **2/1**[1]

4006 **2** 6 **Thunder Bay**[35] 5886 3-8-11 74 .... PaulHanagan 2 62
(R A Fahey) *racd off the pce in midfield: rdn 1/2-way: kpt on u.p fnl f to go 2nd cl home: no ch w wnr* **4/1**[2]

2422 **3** 1 1/4 **Harry Up**[30] 6045 7-8-12 84 .... (b) BMcHugh(7) 9 66+
(K A Ryan) *w ldrs: led and edgd lft over 2f out: sn clr: rdn over 1f out: hdd ins fnl f: sn no ch w wnr: lost 2nd cl home* **4/1**[2]

0-00 **4** hd **Alugat (IRE)**[123] 3112 5-8-5 48 .... HayleyTurner 10 51
(Mrs A Duffield) *sn outpcd in rr on outer: rdn 1/2-way: styd on u.p fnl f: nvr nr ldrs* **33/1**

360 **5** 1/2 **Mr Rooney (IRE)**[33] 5970 5-8-5 57 .... FrancisNorton 4 49
(A Berry) *led for 1f: sn outpcd in 3rd: plugged on same pce fnl f* **14/1**

6355 **6** 1 **The Little Fizzer (IRE)**[7] 6658 3-8-2 55 .... ChrisCatlin 7 43
(P D Evans) *bhd: rdn wl over 1f out: kpt on u.p fnl f: no ch* **7/1**[3]

0060 **7** nk **Jun Fan (USA)**[11] 6546 6-8-7 47 .... RoystonFfrench 8 47
(B Ellison) *bhd: hdwy u.p and swtchd rt ent fnl f: kpt on but nvr nr ldrs* **28/1**

5060 **8** 5 **Polish Star**[16] 6405 4-8-2 45 .... (v) DuranFentiman(3) 1 27
(Miss L A Perratt) *v.s.a: a wl bhd* **28/1**

000 **9** nk **Classic Encounter (IRE)**[15] 6449 5-8-12 72 .... MarcHalford(3) 6 35+
(D M Simcock) *taken down early: dwlt: sn w ldrs: led after 1f: hdd and bdly hmpd over 2f out: wknd qckly 2f out: eased fnl f* **10/1**

000 **10** 8 **Coconut Moon**[16] 6418 6-9-0 65 .... (b) TonyCulhane 11 6
(D Flood) *racd wd: a bhd* **25/1**

61.82 secs (-0.48) **Going Correction** +0.10s/f (Slow) **10** Ran SP% **115.3**
Speed ratings (Par 101): **107,97,95,95,94 92,92,84,83,70**
toteswinger: 1&2 £7.10, 1&3 £1.02, 2&3 £14.30. CSF £9.22 TOTE £2.00: £1.50, £2.00, £1.10; EX 9.80.
Owner Dab Hand Racing **Bred** Bearstone Stud **Trained** Sessay, N Yorks
■ Stewards' Enquiry : B McHugh two-day ban: careless riding (Nov 1-2)

FOCUS
Fast and furious in this claimer, with Harry Up and Classic Encounter matching strides up front but not the most solid race overall.

Polish Star Official explanation: jockey said gelding missed the break

6824 CLEANEVENT H'CAP — 2m 119y(P)
7:50 (7:50) (Class 6) (0-65,64) 3-Y-0+ **£2,388** (£705; £352) **Stalls** Low

Form RPR

0/0- **1** **Compton Court**[24] 6220 6-9-13 **61** .... (t) PatCosgrave 6 69+
(John G Carr, Ire) *hld up in midfield: shuffled bk and dropped to rr 4f out: rdn and hdwy 3f out: chal 1f out: drvn ins fnl f: led nr fin* **15/2**

3066 **2** hd **Adage**[3] 6740 5-8-11 **45** .... (tp) ChrisCatlin 9 53
(David Pinder) *in tch: rdn 3f out: drvn to ld narrowly over 1f out: kpt on tl hdd nr fin* **5/1**[3]

4656 **3** 1/2 **Squirtle (IRE)**[9] 6606 5-9-11 **62** .... LukeMorris(3) 1 69
(W M Brisbourne) *s.i.s: hld up in rr: hdwy on outer 5f out: chsd ldrs and drvn 2f out: ev ch ins fnl f: unable qckn cl home* **12/1**

2230 **4** 3 **Borrowdale**[16] 6421 3-9-6 **64** .... ShaneKelly 7 68
(J A Osborne) *chsd ldrs: edgd lft 4f out: chsd ldr gng wl over 2f out: ev ch and rdn wl over 1f out: fnd little: edgd lft and wknd fnl f* **7/2**[1]

6006 **5** 3 3/4 **Synonymy**[22] 6252 5-8-11 **45** .... (b) SteveDrowne 12 44
(M Blanshard) *chsd ldr tl led over 4f out: rdn over 3f out: hdd over 1f out: wknd qckly ent fnl f* **12/1**

2003 **6** 1 **Pairumani Pat (IRE)**[15] 6447 3-7-10 **45** .... AmyBaker(5) 13 43
(J Pearce) *bhd: niggled along early: hdwy on outer 4f out: rdn and no imp last 2f* **7/1**

6500 **7** hd **Peas 'n Beans (IRE)**[9] 6596 5-8-9 **48** .... (t) NicolPolli(5) 11 46
(T Keddy) *stdd and dropped in bhd after s: effrt and rdn 3f out: sn no hdwy: wl hld last 2f* **66/1**

3500 **8** 1 1/4 **Restart (IRE)**[11] 6550 7-8-13 **54** ow8.................... MrJPFeatherstone(7) 2 50+
(Lucinda Featherstone) *hld up towards rr: sme hdwy on outer whn hmpd over 3f out: no prog after* **25/1**

2-13 **9** 8 **Cumbrian Knight (IRE)**[126] 779 10-9-13 **61**................ PaulHanagan 4 48+
(J M Jefferson) *hld up in midfield: shuffled bk to rr over 4f out: hmpd over 3f out: no ch after* **12/1**

60-0 **10** 9 **Leonardo's Friend**[9] 6594 5-8-11 **45**.........................(b) HayleyTurner 10 21
(B G Powell) *hld up in midfield: hdwy 8f out: chsd ldrs and drvn over 3f out: wknd qckly over 2f out* **50/1**

0000 **11** 68 **Mean Machine (IRE)**[33] 5968 6-8-11 **45**.....................(tp) TonyCulhane 8 —
(D Flood) *led tl over 4f out: wkng whn hmpd 4f out: virtually p.u last 2f* **66/1**

3502 **B** **Soldiers Quest**[61] 5148 4-8-6 **45**................................ RichardEvans(5) 5 —
(P D Evans) *in tch: n.m.r on inner whn bdly hmpd and b.d over 3f out: dead* **4/1**[2]

3m 45.37s (3.57) **Going Correction** +0.10s/f (Slow)
WFA 3 from 4yo+ 10lb **12** Ran SP% **115.0**
Speed ratings (Par 101): **95,94,94,93,91 91,90,90,86,82 50,—**
toteswinger: 1&2 £27.30, 1&3 £27.30, 2&3 £0. CSF £42.61 CT £444.70 TOTE £6.80: £2.10, £2.10, £3.60; EX 38.70.
Owner Coleman Country Syndicate **Bred** Summertree Stud **Trained** Maynooth, Co. Kildare

FOCUS
A low-grade staying handicap and not a true test of stamina with the pace pretty steady for the first 1m4f. The time was nearly nine seconds outside standard and there were five more or less in line across the track a furlong and a half out. The third is the best guide to the level.
Cumbrian Knight(IRE) Official explanation: jockey said gelding suffered interference in runing

6825 CHRISSY RODGERS CLASSIC H'CAP 1m 1f 103y(P)
8:20 (8:22) (Class 6) (0-65,65) 3-Y-0+ **£2,388** (£705; £352) **Stalls** Low

Form RPR

5561 **1** **Hucking Heat (IRE)**[17] 6395 4-9-8 **65**..........................(p) HayleyTurner 7 73
(R Hollinshead) *chsd ldrs: wnt 2nd 7f out: rdn to ld over 1f out: hld on wl u.p ins fnl f: all out* **7/1**[3]

4256 **2** 1/2 **Lunar River (FR)**[16] 6422 5-9-7 **64**...............................(t) ChrisCatlin 1 71
(David Pinder) *hld up in tch: nt clr run 2f out tl over 1f out: sn swtchd lft: chsd wnner ins fnl f: hrd drvn and unable qckn fnl 50yds* **9/2**[2]

5606 **3** nk **Pelham Crescent (IRE)**[29] 6090 5-8-11 **59**............... DavidProbert(5) 2 65
(B Palling) *chsd ldr tl 7f out: styd handy: rdn and ev ch over 1f out: hung rt jst ins fnl f: nt qckn fnl 50yds* **7/2**[1]

2540 **4** 1/2 **Alexander Guru**[86] 4343 4-9-3 **60**................................. SteveDrowne 5 65
(M Blanshard) *t.k.h: hld up towards rr: rdn and hdwy jst over 2f out: swtchd rt 1f out: kpt on u.p fnl f but nvr quite pce to rch ldrs* **9/1**

4234 **5** 1 **Always Brave**[26] 6161 3-9-3 **64**.............................. RoystonFfrench 6 67
(M Johnston) *stdd s: t.k.h: hld up in tch: rdn and effrt on outer over 3f out: keeping on same pce whn swtchd lft ins fnl f* **15/2**

1600 **6** 2 **Lujano**[14] 6485 3-9-2 **63**.. PaulMulrennan 4 62
(Ollie Pears) *in tch: pushed along 4f out: rdn 3f out: kpt on same pce u.p last 2f* **25/1**

5026 **7** 1/2 **Torrens (IRE)**[74] 4701 6-8-13 **61**...............................(t) RichardEvans(5) 3 59
(P D Evans) *stdd s: hld up in rr: hdwy and hmpd 2f out: nvr trbld ldrs* **9/1**

-000 **8** 1 1/4 **Ambrosiano**[17] 6380 4-9-8 **65**..................................... ShaneKelly 10 60
(Miss E C Lavelle) *sn led: rdn 3f out: hdd over 1f out: wknd ent fnl f* **9/1**

0000 **9** 1 3/4 **Moment Of Clarity**[29] 6090 6-9-2 **59**....................(p) PaulHanagan 12 51
(R C Guest) *t.k.h: chsd ldrs: rdn over 3f out: wknd 2f out* **18/1**

0040 **10** nk **King's Icon (IRE)**[8] 6629 3-8-8 **62**........................ TobyAtkinson(7) 13 53
(M Wigham) *stdd s: t.k.h: hld up in last trio: rdn 3f out: no prog* **33/1**

3000 **11** 3 1/2 **Prince Charlemagne (IRE)**[47] 5576 5-8-12 **58**....(b) DuranFentiman(3) 9 42
(R M Stronge) *hld up in last trio: rdn and struggling over 3f out: wl btn last 2f* **16/1**

2060 **12** 7 **Hits Only Cash**[12] 6544 6-9-3 **60**.................................... TPQueally 11 29
(J Pearce) *t.k.h: hld up in midfield on outer: rdn 4f out: drvn and btn 3f out: wl bhd last 2f* **14/1**

2m 2.98s (1.28) **Going Correction** +0.10s/f (Slow)
WFA 3 from 4yo+ 4lb **12** Ran SP% **119.3**
Speed ratings (Par 101): **98,97,97,96,95 94,93,92,91,90 87,81**
toteswinger: 1&2 £7.80, 1&3 £0, 2&3 £7.80. CSF £38.74 CT £131.59 TOTE £8.10: £2.70, £1.50, £1.70; EX 27.90.
Owner Ed Weetman (haulage & Storage) Ltd **Bred** Thomas J Reid **Trained** Upper Longdon, Staffs
■ Stewards' Enquiry : Hayley Turner caution: careless riding

FOCUS
A routine handicap run at just a steady pace but the form appears solid enough.

6826 CLEANCONCIERGE H'CAP 1m 141y(P)
8:50 (8:50) (Class 5) (0-70,70) 3-Y-0+ **£3,238** (£963; £481; £240) **Stalls** Low

Form RPR

0614 **1** **Alfie Tupper (IRE)**[15] 6452 5-9-8 **70**................................ PatCosgrave 3 78+
(J R Boyle) *hld up in midfield: hdwy wl over 1f out: pressed ldrs ins fnl f: drvn to ld last stride* **9/4**[1]

5204 **2** shd **Claret And Amber**[7] 6663 6-9-4 **66**................................ ChrisCatlin 6 74
(W K Goldsworthy) *in tch: rdn and hdwy 3f out: led over 1f out: kpt on wl u.p tl hdd last stride* **6/1**[3]

0636 **3** 1 **It's A Dream (FR)**[14] 6485 5-9-3 **65**..............................(t) TPQueally 1 71
(M W Easterby) *s.i.s: hld up towards rr: swtchd to outer over 3f out: gd hdwy 2f out: pressed ldr ent fnl f: one pce fnl 100yds* **15/2**

52-3 **4** 4 **Prize Fighter (IRE)**[32] 5994 6-9-8 **70**........................ FrancisNorton 7 67
(A Berry) *dwlt: hdwy to ld after 1f tl over 4f out: chsd ldrs and rdn 2f out: wknd jst ins fnl f* **10/1**

1/50 **5** 1 **Keel (IRE)**[7] 6663 5-9-2 **64**.. LiamJones 8 58
(C R Dore) *stdd s: hld up in last: hdwy over 1f out: kpt on fnl f: nvr pce to rch ldrs* **50/1**

4000 **6** 1 **Royal Island (IRE)**[7] 6663 6-9-4 **66**........................... VinceSlattery 11 58
(M G Quinlan) *hld up bhd: rdn over 1f out: kpt on fnl f: nvr trbld ldrs* **50/1**

2605 **7** 3/4 **Green Diamond**[17] 6380 3-9-1 **67**................................. GregFairley 4 57
(M Johnston) *chsd ldrs: briefly outpcd and rdn 4f out: chsd ldrs and drvn 2f out: wknd ent fnl f* **6/1**[3]

365 **8** 3/4 **Madam President**[19] 6331 3-9-4 **70**................................ AdamKirby 2 58
(W R Swinburn) *in tch: lost pl 3f out: drvn and tried to rally over 1f out: no imp* **16/1**

0365 **9** 1 1/4 **Kensington (IRE)**[11] 6554 7-9-5 **67**............................... JamesDoyle 13 53
(P D Evans) *stdd s: t.k.h: hld up in rr: rdn and no hdwy jst over 2f out* **28/1**

0-00 **10** 3/4 **Writ (IRE)**[14] 6491 6-9-5 **67**.. TomEaves 10 51
(Miss L A Perratt) *led for 1f: chsd ldr after: rdn 3f out: wknd qckly over 1f out* **28/1**

0000 **11** 4 **Roman Maze**[15] 6452 8-9-8 **70**..................................... ShaneKelly 5 45
(W M Brisbourne) *t.k.h: hld up in midfield: rapid hdwy to ld over 4f out: riddn 3f out: hdd over 1f out: sn wknd* **33/1**

124 **12** 7 **Myfrenchconnection (IRE)**[8] 6629 4-9-3 **65**................. MickyFenton 9 24
(P T Midgley) *racd in midfield: rdn and hung rt over 2f out: sn struggling: wl bhd fnl f* **9/2**[2]

1m 50.81s (0.31) **Going Correction** +0.10s/f (Slow)
WFA 3 from 4yo+ 4lb **12** Ran SP% **118.0**
Speed ratings (Par 103): **102,101,101,97,96 95,95,94,93,92 89,82**
toteswinger: 1&2 £1.02, 1&3 £3.10, 2&3 £11.50. CSF £14.88 CT £87.94 TOTE £2.30: £1.50, £2.70, £1.30; EX 16.00.
Owner Epsom Equine Spa Partnership **Bred** Stone Ridge Farm **Trained** Epsom, Surrey

FOCUS
This run-of-the-mill handicap was run in a time very similar to that for the opener over the same trip. The form looks sound rated around the first three.
Myfrenchconnection(IRE) Official explanation: jockey said gelding hung right

6827 CLEANVU H'CAP (DIV II) 1m 141y(P)
9:20 (9:20) (Class 6) (0-65,65) 3-Y-0+ **£2,047** (£604; £302) **Stalls** Low

Form RPR

3240 **1** **Faithful Ruler (USA)**[35] 5915 4-9-8 **65**........................... PaulHanagan 3 77+
(R A Fahey) *hld up trcking ldrs: rdn and hdwy over 2f out: rdn to ld ent fnl f: r.o strly* **9/4**[1]

1120 **2** 2 1/4 **Rowan Lodge (IRE)**[18] 6353 6-9-1 **58**...................(b) JamieMoriarty 5 65
(Ollie Pears) *t.k.h: hld up in midfield: rdn and hdwy 2f out: chsd wnr ins fnl f: no imp* **10/1**

3000 **3** 3/4 **Putra Laju (IRE)**[54] 3822 4-9-0 **60**.............................(p) PatrickHills(3) 7 65
(J W Hills) *hld up towards rr: hdwy 3f out: rdn over 2f out: kpt on to go 3rd wl ins fnl f: no ch w wnr* **28/1**

0040 **4** 3/4 **Sir Billy Nick**[16] 6422 3-9-2 **63**...................................... TPQueally 1 67
(J Noseda) *chsd ldrs: rdn over 2f out: ev ch over 1f out: kpt on same pce fnl f* **4/1**[2]

400 **5** 3 **Pop Music (IRE)**[12] 6544 5-9-1 **58**.............................(v) JamesDoyle 11 55
(Ms J S Doyle) *chsd ldr: hanging rt over 3f out: drvn and chal over 2f out: led wl over 1f out: hdd ent fnl f: sn wknd* **22/1**

4000 **6** 3/4 **Machinate (USA)**[14] 6491 6-9-6 **63**................................... LiamJones 8 58
(W M Brisbourne) *hld up in rr: rdn and hdwy wl over 1f out: kpt on but nvr pce to threaten ldrs* **33/1**

3005 **7** 2 **Sedge (USA)**[8] 6628 8-9-1 **58**..(b) MickyFenton 4 48
(P T Midgley) *stmbld sn after s: t.k.h: hld up in tch: rdn over 2f out: no imp whn hung lft ent fnl f* **16/1**

4003 **8** hd **Fort Amhurst (IRE)**[15] 6452 4-9-5 **62**...........................(b[1]) DaleGibson 13 52
(M W Easterby) *taken down early: plld hrd: hld up in rr: rdn and effrt on outer over 2f out: no real hdwy* **12/1**

4230 **9** nk **Bold Indian (IRE)**[33] 5965 4-9-1 **58**........................... RoystonFfrench 2 47
(Miss L A Perratt) *racd keenly: led: jnd and rdn over 2f out: hdd wl over 1f out: wknd qckly ent fnl f* **6/1**[3]

6136 **10** nse **Paddy Rielly (IRE)**[15] 6447 3-9-0 **61**........................... VinceSlattery 9 50
(P D Evans) *stdd s: hld up in rr: nvr trbld ldrs* **16/1**

5201 **11** 2 **Apache Nation (IRE)**[16] 6408 5-9-1 **58**..................(b) PaulMulrennan 12 42
(M Dods) *hld up towards rr: rdn and struggling over 3f out: wl bhd last 2f* **11/1**

2063 **12** 2 1/4 **Red Tarn**[22] 6254 3-9-4 **65**...(t) TomEaves 6 44
(B Smart) *wnt rt s: in tch: rdn over 3f out: struggling 3f out: wl bhd fr wl over 1f out* **12/1**

1m 50.96s (0.46) **Going Correction** +0.10s/f (Slow)
WFA 3 from 4yo+ 4lb **72** Ran SP% **120.4**
Speed ratings (Par 101): **101,99,98,97,95 94,92,92,92,92 90,88**
toteswinger: 1&2 £19.30, 1&3 £19.30, 2&3 £19.30. CSF £25.80 CT £515.14 TOTE £1.80: £1.30, £2.70, £5.40; EX 26.80.
Owner George Murray **Bred** WinStar Farm LLC **Trained** Musley Bank, N Yorks

FOCUS
This was the slowest of the three races run over the trip and is best assessed through the third to recent course and distance form.
Bold Indian(IRE) Official explanation: jockey said gelding ran too free
T/Plt: £49.80 to a £1 stake. Pool: £80,838.87. 1,183.47 winning tickets. T/Qpdt: £6.50 to a £1 stake. Pool: £7,151.92. 802.68 winning tickets. SP

6828 - 6834a (Foreign Racing) - See Raceform Interactive

CAULFIELD (R-H)
Saturday, October 18
OFFICIAL GOING: Good to soft changing to good after 3.20

6835a BMW CAULFIELD CUP (GROUP 1) (H'CAP) 1m 4f
6:05 (6:05) 3-Y-0+

£685,022 (£165,198; £88,106; £48,458; £36,948; £33,040)

RPR

1 **All The Good (IRE)**[57] 5229 5-8-8 .... KerrinMcEvoy 6 118+
(Saeed Bin Suroor) *midfield on outside: hdwy arnd outside to go 5th ent st: led 1f out: r.o wl* **40/1**

2 3/4 **Nom Du Jeu (NZ)**[14] 4-8-10 ....(b) JeffLloyd 15 118+
(Murray Baker, New Zealand) **30/1**

3 1/2 **Barbaricus (AUS)**[6] 4-8-2 .... SBaster 17 109
(Danny O'Brien, Australia) **100/1**

4 3/4 **Mad Rush (USA)**[55] 5333 4-8-9 .... DMOliver 13 116+
(L M Cumani) *hld up in rr: disputing last 1 1/2f out: 11th jst over 1f out: styd on strly between rivals ins fnl f: fin wl* **10/1**

5 nk **Littorio (AUS)**[14] 4-8-7 ....(b) StevenKing 8 113
(Nigel Blackiston, Australia) **7/2**[1]

6 hd **Red Ruler (NZ)**[14] 4-8-7 .... CoreyBrown 1 112
(John Sargent, New Zealand) **11/1**

7 shd **Master O'Reilly (NZ)**[14] 6-8-12 .... VDuric 11 117+
(Danny O'Brien, Australia) **13/2**[3]

8 1 3/4 **Ice Chariot (AUS)**[14] 6-8-8 .... GSchofield 2 110
(Ron Maund, Australia) **30/1**

9 1/2 **Maldivian (NZ)**[14] 6-8-12 .... MRodd 14 113
(Mark Kavanagh, Australia) **20/1**

10 1/2 **Viewed (AUS)**[28] 5-8-8 ....(b) BShinn 12 109
(Bart Cummings, Australia) **40/1**

11 1/2 **Boundless (NZ)**[14] 4-8-6 .... DwayneDunn 5 106
(Stephen McKee, New Zealand) **15/1**

12 shd **Weekend Hussler (AUS)**[14] 4-8-13 .... BRawiller 9 113
(Ross McDonald, Australia) **6/1**[2]

13 1/2 **Douro Valley (AUS)**[7] 7-8-8 ....(b) JWinks 3 107
(Danny O'Brien, Australia) **16/1**

14 3 1/4 **Guillotine (NZ)**[7] 4-8-1 .... CraigAWilliams 16 95
(David Hayes, Australia) **12/1**

15 *shd* **Dolphin Jo (AUS)**[7] 6-8-5 ClareLindop 10 99
(Terry & Karina O'Sullivan, Australia) **40/1**
16 *4 1/4* **Riva San (AUS)**[14] 4-8-5 LNolen 7 92
(Peter G Moody, Australia) **20/1**
17 *1 1/2* **Fiumicino (NZ)**[14] 5-8-11 (b) StevenArnold 4 95
(John Hawkes, Australia) **66/1**
2m 27.45s (147.45) **17** Ran SP% **112.9**

Owner Godolphin **Bred** Mount Coote Partnership **Trained** Newmarket, Suffolk

NOTEBOOK
All The Good(IRE), a smart handicapper who ran away with the race Newbury staged to replace the abandoned Ebor in August, took the big step up to Grade 1 company and, always travelling well in midfield before making his effort, he hit the front in the straight and never looked like being reeled in. Having given Godolphin its first Australian Grade 1, he will now take his chance in the Melbourne Cup under a penalty.
Mad Rush(USA), another upgraded handicapper who won the Old Newton Cup over this trip and had since been touched off in a Group 2 at Longchamp, ran a really eyecatching race, coming from the back of the field turning in, having not got a run, to finish on the heels of the placed horses. He will renew rivalry with the winner in the Melbourne Cup, and is quoted as short as 3/1 in places to improve on stable companion Purple Moon's gallant second last season.

6350 SOUTHWELL (L-H)
Sunday, October 19

OFFICIAL GOING: Standard
Wind: strong and gusty 1/2 behind Weather: fine

6836 JANET LORD LETS PLAY BINGO MEMORIAL MEDIAN AUCTION MAIDEN STKS (DIV I) 7f (F)
1:40 (1:40) (Class 6) 3-5-Y-O **£2,866** (£846; £423) **Stalls** Low

Form RPR
5505 **1** **Isabella's Fancy**[45] 5652 3-8-12 48 (v[1]) RobertWinston 10 57
(J R Fanshawe) *trckd ldrs: led 3f out: sn qcknd clr: hrd rdn and hung lft over 1f out: jst lasted* **11/1**
4030 **2** *3/4* **Vogarth**[25] 6208 4-9-2 50 JamesMillman(3) 8 60
(B R Millman) *chsd ldrs: outpcd 4f out: hdwy over 2f out: styd on wl to take 2nd nr fin* **8/1**
045 **3** *hd* **My Mate Mal**[8] 6660 4-8-12 63 LanceBetts(7) 11 59
(B Ellison) *trckd ldrs: wnt 2nd 2f out: kpt on fnl f* **7/2**[2]
422 **4** *6* **Manchestermaverick (USA)**[85] 4412 3-9-3 63 TravisBlock 1 43
(H Morrison) *stmbld s: sn trcking ldrs: effrt 3f out: wknd over 1f out* **1/1**[1]
3600 **5** *nk* **Rub Of The Relic (IRE)**[2] 6792 3-9-3 58 LeeEnstone 5 42
(P T Midgley) *chsd ldrs: sn pushed along: outpcd 3f out: no threat after* **6/1**[3]
6060 **6** *7* **Sheik'N'Knotsterd**[27] 6163 3-9-3 50 ChrisCatlin 4 24
(J F Coupland) *led tl 3f out: wknd 2f out* **28/1**
0400 **7** *6* **Lechero (IRE)**[11] 6584 3-9-3 40 (p) J-PGuillambert 3 7
(John A Harris) *s.i.s: lost pl 4f out: sn bhd* **33/1**
-060 **8** *1 1/4* **Ugly Betty**[17] 6411 3-8-12 44 PatrickMathers 2 —
(Bruce Hellier) *s.i.s: in rr: bhd fnl 2f* **66/1**
0000 **9** *1/2* **Savanna's Gold**[45] 5631 4-9-0 42 (p) SaleemGolam 9 —
(G Prodromou) *chsd ldrs: lost pl 3f out* **80/1**
0050 **10** *2 1/2* **Frill A Minute**[45] 5636 4-8-10 40 ow1 SladeO'Hara(5) 6 —
(Miss L C Siddall) *chsd ldrs: reminders and outpcd 4f out: sn lost pl* **150/1**
1m 30.37s (0.07) **Going Correction** -0.05s/f (Stan)
WFA 3 from 4yo 2lb **10** Ran SP% **115.7**
Speed ratings (Par 101): **97,96,95,89,88 80,73,72,71,69**
toteswinger: 1&2 £8.30, 1&3 £5.70, 2&3 £5.90. CSF £90.69 TOTE £10.80: £2.20, £2.20, £1.40; EX 89.60 Trifecta £165.80 Pool £263.75 - 1.18 winning units..
Owner Mrs Nicolas Kairis **Bred** Bellow Hill Stud **Trained** Newmarket, Suffolk
■ Stewards' Enquiry : Robert Winston two-day ban: used whip with excessive frequency (Nov 2-3)
FOCUS
The favourite ran below form to further devalue what was already a very moderate older-horse maiden, and this is not a race to dwell on. It was the slowest of the three races over course and distance.
Manchestermaverick(USA) Official explanation: trainer had no explanation for the poor form shown

6837 MERCEDES-BENZ OF DERBY MAIDEN STKS 7f (F)
2:10 (2:12) (Class 4) 2-Y-O **£4,403** (£1,310; £654; £327) **Stalls** Low

Form RPR
5245 **1** **Zelloof (IRE)**[13] 6525 2-8-12 67 TedDurcan 12 74
(Saeed Bin Suroor) *w ldrs on outer: led appr fnl f: styd on wl* **10/3**[2]
0 **2** *1 1/2* **Inflammable**[44] 5672 2-8-12 0 J-PGuillambert 5 70
(Sir Mark Prescott) *sn chsng ldrs: led over 1f out: sn hdd and no ex* **7/1**
2200 **3** *2 1/2* **Seminole (IRE)**[15] 6474 2-9-3 77 (b) RobertHavlin 9 69
(J H M Gosden) *w ldrs on outside: chal over 2f out: styd on same pce fnl f* **5/1**
4 *1 3/4* **Majestic Bull (USA)** 2-9-3 0 RobertWinston 10 65
(E J O'Neill) *chsd ldrs on outer: one pce fnl 2f* **16/1**
24 **5** *2* **Saif Al Fahad (IRE)**[101] 3882 2-9-3 0 ChrisCatlin 7 60+
(E J O'Neill) *led tl 2f out: wknd fnl f* **7/2**[3]
0233 **6** *1/2* **Ysing Yi**[9] 6621 2-9-3 74 PaulMulrennan 8 58+
(K A Ryan) *w ldr: led and hung lft 2f out: sn hdd: wknd 1f out* **5/2**[1]
7 *7* **Mile High Lad (USA)** 2-9-3 0 DO'Donohoe 4 41
(George Baker) *chsd ldrs: outpcd over 4f out: lost pl 3f out* **25/1**
000 **8** *9* **Monte Mayor Eagle**[55] 5344 2-8-12 50 PaulHanagan 11 13
(D Haydn Jones) *prom on outer: rn wd bnd and lost pl over 4f out: sn bhd* **66/1**
9 *1/2* **First Blade** 2-9-3 0 DeanMcKeown 3 17
(S R Bowring) *s.i.s: in rr: bhd fnl 3f* **50/1**
0 **10** *30* **Always Gunner**[126] 3055 2-8-12 0 JamesO'Reilly(5) 1 —
(J O'Reilly) *dwlt: sn outpcd in rr: bhd fnl 3f: t.o* **150/1**
00 **11** *18* **Stevies Song**[4] 6730 2-8-12 0 SaleemGolam 2 —
(D Flood) *sn bhd: t.o 3f out* **100/1**
1m 29.84s (-0.46) **Going Correction** -0.05s/f (Stan) **11** Ran SP% **117.9**
Speed ratings (Par 97): **100,98,95,93,91 90,82,72,71,37 16**
toteswinger: 1&2 £6.20, 1&3 £5.10, 2&3 £8.30. CSF £26.45 TOTE £5.30: £1.80, £1.80, £2.10; EX 27.10 Trifecta £105.60 Pool £291.26 - 2.04 winning units..
Owner Godolphin **Bred** Darley **Trained** Newmarket, Suffolk
FOCUS
Some powerful owners and trainers represented, but this was an ordinary juvenile maiden. The winner is rated back to form.

NOTEBOOK
Zelloof(IRE) was forced to race wide throughout from stall 12, but that's not always a bad thing at this course and she stayed on strongly in the straight to get off the mark at the fifth attempt in decisive fashion. She looked better than the bare form when fifth off a mark of 70 in a 6f nursery at Pontefract last time and probably has a little bit more ability than her current rating of 67 suggests, but whatever the case, this will have boosted her paddock value. (op 11-4 tchd 7-2 and 4-1 in places)
Inflammable ◆ was backed at big prices and ran a nice race in second, keeping on well in the straight having tracked the pace early. This was a big improvement on the form she showed on her debut over 1m at Kempton and she should do even better over middle-distances next year. (op 18-1)
Seminole(IRE) seemed to be going quite well early in the straight, but he only plugged on at the one pace. He might be worth a try over 6f. (op 4-1 tchd 7-2)
Majestic Bull(USA), a $57,000 purchase, fared best of the newcomers and this was a respectable effort. He is entitled to come on for this. (tchd 14-1)
Saif Al Fahad(IRE), a stablemate of the fourth, raced well away from the winner tight against the inside rail and could not sustain his challenge. He now has the option of handicaps. (op 5-1)
Ysing Yi seemed inclined to hang slightly left in the straight and is not progressing. Official explanation: jockey said colt hung left (op 11-4 tchd 3-1)

6838 JOHN CARTER AUTUMN H'CAP 1m 6f (F)
2:40 (2:40) (Class 4) (0-85,77) 3-Y-O+ **£6,476** (£1,927; £963; £481) **Stalls** Low

Form RPR
-530 **1** **Keenes Day (FR)**[18] 6390 3-9-5 77 JoeFanning 10 94+
(M Johnston) *set mod pce: qcknd over 3f out: styd on strly to forge clr 1f out: eased towards fin* **9/2**[3]
2500 **2** *3 1/4* **Victory Quest (IRE)**[13] 6527 8-9-2 65 (v) RobertWinston 8 76
(Mrs S Lamyman) *sn chsng ldrs: kpt on same pce fnl 2f* **8/1**
4045 **3** *1* **Pass The Port**[9] 6630 7-9-12 75 PaulHanagan 7 85
(D Haydn Jones) *hld up in rr: hdwy 4f out: styd on same pce over 1f out* **15/2**
3012 **4** *1 1/4* **Spanish Conquest**[86] 4391 4-9-4 67 J-PGuillambert 9 75
(Sir Mark Prescott) *chsd ldrs: drvn over 3f out: one pce fnl 2f* **11/4**[1]
053 **5** *7* **Cotton Eyed Joe (IRE)**[21] 6313 7-10-0 77 PJMcDonald 6 75
(G A Swinbank) *hld up towards rr: hdwy to chse ldrs over 4f out: fdd over 1f out* **4/1**[2]
3204 **6** *1/2* **Exit To Luck (GER)**[166] 1904 7-9-5 68 (b) ChrisCatlin 1 65
(S Gollings) *w ldrs: lost pl over 1f out* **33/1**
5362 **7** *10* **The King And I (IRE)**[64] 5092 4-9-8 76 (b) DavidProbert(5) 5 59
(Miss E C Lavelle) *hld up towards rr: hdwy 4f out: wknd over 1f out* **6/1**
0055 **8** *1 3/4* **Silver Blue (IRE)**[8] 6662 5-9-1 64 CatherineGannon 11 45
(W K Goldsworthy) *hld up in rr: hdwy over 5f out: lost pl over 3f out* **20/1**
-000 **9** *1 1/4* **Mceldowney**[13] 6527 6-8-13 65 LeeVickers(3) 3 44
(M C Chapman) *t.k.h: trckd ldrs: lost pl over 3f out* **66/1**
6100 **10** *6* **Three Boars**[8] 6662 6-9-6 69 (b) TPQueally 4 40
(S Gollings) *hld up in rr: lost pl over 3f out: sn bhd* **14/1**
0-50 **11** *45* **Foursquare Flyer (IRE)**[6] 6708 6-8-12 68 (vt[1]) LanceBetts(7) 2 —
(T J Pitt) *prom: reminders and lost pl over 5f out: t.o 3f out* **80/1**
3m 7.21s (-1.09) **Going Correction** -0.05s/f (Stan)
WFA 3 from 4yo+ 9lb **11** Ran SP% **119.1**
Speed ratings (Par 105): **101,99,98,97,93 93,87,86,86,82 57**
toteswinger: 1&2 £7.30, 1&3 £6.30, 2&3 £8.10. CSF £39.74 CT £268.56 TOTE £4.60: £1.80, £2.70, £2.00; EX 49.80 Trifecta £126.40 Pool £331.55 - 1.94 winning units..
Owner Mrs R J Jacobs **Bred** Newsells Park Stud Ltd **Trained** Middleham Moor, N Yorks
FOCUS
This looked a fair staying handicap with plenty of regular All-Weather winners lining up, but Keenes Day set a modest gallop, which probably wouldn't have suited a few of these. The form has been taken at face value though.
Silver Blue(IRE) Official explanation: jockey said gelding would not face the kick back

6839 TOTESPORT.COM H'CAP 1m 3f (F)
3:15 (3:15) (Class 4) (0-85,84) 3-Y-O+ **£5,828** (£1,734; £866; £432) **Stalls** Low

Form RPR
4055 **1** **Ellmau**[11] 6582 3-8-13 80 ChrisCatlin 4 89
(E J O'Neill) *trckd ldr: led 3f out: edgd rt fnl f: hld on wl towards fin* **5/1**[2]
1013 **2** *1/2* **Persian Peril**[29] 6108 4-9-0 75 RobertWinston 8 83
(G A Swinbank) *t.k.h: trckd ldrs: wnt 2nd over 2f out: sn chalng: hung lft: carried rt and no ex wl ins fnl f* **6/1**
4200 **3** *8* **Invasian (IRE)**[44] 5677 7-9-1 81 (t) Louis-PhilippeBeuzelin(5) 1 76
(P W D'Arcy) *led: qcknd over 4f out: hdd 3f out: fdd over 1f out* **8/1**
1056 **4** *7* **Robustian**[114] 3440 5-9-9 84 (v) DO'Donohoe 9 67
(George Baker) *hld up in rr: hdwy over 3f out: wknd over 1f out* **11/2**[3]
5005 **5** *5* **Points Of View**[32] 6033 3-9-0 81 J-PGuillambert 7 55
(Sir Mark Prescott) *restless in stalls: hld up in rr: outpcd and hung rt over 3f out: sn lost pl* **4/1**[1]
5010 **6** *hd* **Giant Love (USA)**[5] 6726 3-8-11 78 RoystonFfrench 3 52
(M Johnston) *stmbld s: hld up in rr: drvn over 5f out: reminders and lost pl over 4f out* **13/2**
6000 **7** *1 1/2* **William's Way**[9] 6626 6-8-9 70 TGMcLaughlin 2 41
(I A Wood) *sn chsng ldrs: hrd drvn over 4f out: wknd 2f out* **14/1**
0366 **8** *1/2* **Just Two Numbers**[64] 5100 4-9-0 75 TedDurcan 6 45
(W Jarvis) *sn chsng ldrs: hrd drvn 4f out: wknd over 2f out* **11/2**[3]
2m 24.37s (-3.63) **Going Correction** -0.05s/f (Stan)
WFA 3 from 4yo+ 6lb **8** Ran SP% **112.8**
Speed ratings (Par 105): **111,110,104,99,96 95,94,94**
toteswinger: 1&2 £3.30, 1&3 £5.90, 2&3 £8.10. CSF £33.86 CT £233.60 TOTE £5.00: £1.70, £1.80, £2.20; EX 31.50 Trifecta £228.70 Part won. Pool £309.12 - 0.96 winning units..
Owner Premspace Ltd **Bred** Lady Hardy **Trained** Averham Park, Notts
■ Stewards' Enquiry : Chris Catlin one-day ban: careless riding (Nov 2); caution: used whip down shoulder in forehand position.
FOCUS
A fair handicap run at a good pace. The first pair came clear and ere the only ones to show their form.
Giant Love(USA) Official explanation: jockey said colt stumbled at the start
Just Two Numbers Official explanation: jockey said gelding resented the kickback

6840 CARL SWIFT BIRTHDAY CELEBRATIONS H'CAP 5f (F)
3:50 (3:50) (Class 5) (0-70,70) 3-Y-O+ **£3,753** (£1,108; £554) **Stalls** High

Form RPR
1300 **1** **Invincible Lad (IRE)**[31] 6039 4-9-3 69 PatCosgrave 8 90
(E J Alston) *chsd ldrs: rdn to ld over 1f out: wnt clr: heavily eased fnl 50yds* **10/1**
003 **2** *5* **Punching**[17] 6418 4-8-10 69 (b) KylieManser(7) 2 72
(Miss Gay Kelleway) *racd wd: led tl over 1f out: kpt on: no ch w wnr* **13/2**[2]

0012 **3** *1 3/4* **Spirit Of Coniston**[12] 6546 5-8-5 **60**........................ DuranFentiman(3) 7 56
(P T Midgley) *chsd ldrs: styd on same pce fnl 2f* **15/2**[3]

3120 **4** *hd* **Blakeshall Quest**[109] 3608 8-8-8 **60**..........................(b) PaulMulrennan 4 56
(R Brotherton) *chsd ldrs on outer: one pce fnl 2f* **33/1**

1605 **5** *3 1/4* **King Of Swords (IRE)**[15] 6486 4-8-13 **70**................. FrederikTylicki(5) 1 54
(N Tinkler) *prom far side: wknd over 1f out* **11/2**[1]

1164 **6** *hd* **Miss Daawe**[15] 6486 4-8-9 **68**.. LanceBetts(7) 14 51
(B Ellison) *dwlt: racd stands' side: in rr: kpt on fnl 2f: nvr a factor* **14/1**

3500 **7** *nk* **Grand Palace (IRE)**[8] 6658 5-8-11 **63**.......................(v) DarrenWilliams 6 45
(D Shaw) *chsd ldrs: wknd over 1f out* **16/1**

1505 **8** *1 1/4* **Nabeeda**[18] 6382 3-8-5 **57**.. JimmyQuinn 3 35
(M Brittain) *mid-div: outpcd over 2f out: no threat after* **12/1**

6502 **9** *nk* **Diminuto**[12] 6564 4-8-3 **60**................................. DavidProbert(5) 13 37
(M D I Usher) *racd stands' side: sn in rr: nvr on terms* **9/1**

0040 **10** *hd* **Weet A Surprise**[24] 6232 3-9-0 **66**.................................... HayleyTurner 5 42
(R Hollinshead) *sn outpcd and in rr: nvr on terms* **15/2**[3]

0120 **11** *1 1/2* **Spoof Master (IRE)**[31] 6046 4-9-2 **68**.....................(p) RobertWinston 9 39
(C R Dore) *racd stands' side: mid-div: lost pl over 2f out* **12/1**

3002 **12** *1 1/2* **Kings College Boy**[18] 6382 8-8-8 **60**.........................(b) PaulHanagan 11 25
(R A Fahey) *racd stands' side: sn in rr* **9/1**

3512 **13** *16* **Russian Rocket (IRE)**[33] 6006 6-9-3 **69**.............. TGMcLaughlin 12 —
(Mrs C A Dunnett) *racd stands' side: t.k.h: sn in rr: hamperd after 1f: bhd whn eased fnl f: t.o* **12/1**

58.33 secs (-1.37) **Going Correction** -0.175s/f (Stan) 13 Ran SP% **119.9**
Speed ratings (Par 103): **103,95,92,91,86 86,85,83,83,83 80,78,52**
toteswinger: 1&2 £24.40, 1&3 £21.20, 2&3 £8.10. CSF £73.92 CT £542.20 TOTE £11.90: £5.00, £3.40, £2.90; EX 124.60 TRIFECTA Not won..
Owner Con Harrington **Bred** Mrs Chris Harrington **Trained** Longton, Lancs

FOCUS
A modest sprint handicap and a high draw seemed to be a big disadvantage, as those drawn towards the stands' rail were always trailing the others, who were middle to far side. Improved form from the winner at face value.
Kings College Boy Official explanation: jockey said gelding hung both ways
Russian Rocket(IRE) Official explanation: jockey said gelding finished distressed

6841 CARLSBERG UK H'CAP — 1m (F)
4:25 (4:25) (Class 4) (0-80,80) 3-Y-0+ **£5,828** (£1,734; £866; £432) **Stalls** Low

Form RPR

3241 **1** **Dan Chillingworth (IRE)**[19] 6356 3-9-0 **77**...................(v) RobertWinston 8 85
(J R Fanshawe) *hld up in mid-div: eased out 2f out: r.o to ld last strides* **7/2**[1]

5543 **2** *hd* **Nevada Desert (IRE)**[31] 6052 8-8-13 **76**.................. MichaelJStainton(3) 2 84
(R M Whitaker) *sn led: hdd over 1f out: no ex nr fin* **12/1**

2400 **3** *nk* **Crocodile Bay (IRE)**[4] 6736 5-8-9 **74**........................ JamesO'Reilly(5) 7 81
(John A Harris) *t.k.h: trckd ldrs: swtchd lft over 2f out: led over 1f out: hdd and no ex towards fin* **25/1**

2210 **4** *1 1/4* **Golden Penny**[55] 5350 3-8-13 **76**....................................... TravisBlock 13 80
(H Morrison) *w ldrs: kpt on same pce appr fnl f* **9/1**

1610 **5** *3/4* **Kimono My House**[31] 6050 4-8-6 **66**.................................. PaulHanagan 10 68+
(J G Given) *in rr: drvn 4f out: hdwy on wd outside over 2f out: kpt on: nt rch ldrs* **9/1**

5553 **6** *2* **White Deer (USA)**[15] 6490 4-9-3 **77**...........................(b) AdrianTNicholls 6 75
(D Nicholls) *t.k.h towards rr: effrt over 2f out: kpt on fnl f* **13/2**[3]

2250 **7** *nse* **Mumbleswerve (IRE)**[43] 5695 4-9-1 **75**........................ J-PGuillambert 5 73
(W Jarvis) *hld up in rr: hdwy on inner over 2f out: hung lft and kpt on fnl f* **6/1**[2]

2042 **8** *1 1/4* **Claret And Amber**[1] 6826 6-8-1 **66**.............................. DavidProbert(5) 1 61
(W K Goldsworthy) *wl away and led early: sn mid-div: effrt over 2f out: fdd fnl f* **8/1**

0050 **9** *3 1/2* **Spinning**[15] 6482 5-9-0 **77**...(b) NeilBrown(3) 3 64
(T D Barron) *s.i.s: sme hdwy over 2f out: wknd over 1f out* **12/1**

2306 **10** *1 1/4* **Elusive Warrior (USA)**[19] 6356 5-8-6 **66** oh1.............(p) JamesDoyle 12 50
(A J McCabe) *w ldrs: edgd rt and wknd over 1f out* **25/1**

500 **11** *1/2* **Mr Garston**[87] 4345 5-8-10 **70**... PatCosgrave 11 53
(J R Boyle) *w ldrs on outer: wknd over 1f out* **33/1**

13-0 **12** *2 1/2* **Direct Debit (IRE)**[17] 6431 5-9-6 **80**................................ HayleyTurner 4 57
(M L W Bell) *chsd ldrs on ins: hrd drvn 3f out: lost pl over 1f out* **9/1**

2060 **13** *2 1/2* **Dado Mush**[106] 3725 5-9-0 **77**..(p) MarcHalford(3) 9 48
(T T Clement) *s.i.s: drvn 4f out: lost pl over 2f out* **25/1**

1m 42.46s (-1.24) **Going Correction** -0.05s/f (Stan)
WFA 3 from 4yo+ 3lb 13 Ran SP% **120.8**
Speed ratings (Par 105): **104,103,103,102,101 99,99,98,94,93 92,90,87**
toteswinger: 1&2 £8.20, 1&3 £23.00, 2&3 £43.90. CSF £45.76 CT £962.54 TOTE £3.60: £1.70, £2.30, £10.90; EX 33.20 Trifecta £159.70 Part won. Pool £215.86 - 0.10 winning units..
Owner R C Thompson **Bred** Ballylinch Stud **Trained** Newmarket, Suffolk

FOCUS
A fair handicap although there was no great pace on. The form looks sound enough though.

6842 CARLSBERG PROBABLY THE BEST H'CAP — 6f (F)
4:55 (4:55) (Class 4) (0-85,85) 3-Y-0+ **£5,957** (£1,772; £885; £442) **Stalls** Low

Form RPR

004 **1** **My Gacho (IRE)**[11] 6576 6-9-0 **80**..............................(b) J-PGuillambert 3 91
(M Johnston) *t.k.h towards rr: hdwy and swtchd lft over 2f out: styd on wl to ld last 100yds* **7/1**

0200 **2** *1 1/4* **Rasaman (IRE)**[8] 6651 4-8-13 **79**.................................(tp) JoeFanning 12 86
(K A Ryan) *w ldrs: led over 1f out: hdd and no ex ins fnl f* **14/1**

4312 **3** *1* **Makshoof (IRE)**[22] 6278 4-8-12 **81**................................(p) NeilBrown(3) 5 85
(K A Ryan) *trckd ldrs: chal 1f out: styd on same pce* **7/2**[1]

0600 **4** *1 1/2* **Xpres Maite**[6] 6710 5-9-5 **85**.......................................(b) DeanMcKeown 6 84
(S R Bowring) *led tl over 1f out: kpt on same pce* **16/1**

0331 **5** *nk* **Memphis Man**[20] 6340 5-9-1 **81**.. TGMcLaughlin 2 79
(P D Evans) *prom on ins: drvn 3f out: one pce* **16/1**

0452 **6** *nk* **Pawan (IRE)**[19] 6354 8-9-0 **85**..................................(b) AnnStokell(5) 11 82
(Miss A Stokell) *chsd ldrs on outer: kpt on same pce fnl 2f* **7/1**

5002 **7** *1 3/4* **San Jose City (IRE)**[17] 6420 3-8-13 **80**................................ DNolan 4 71
(D Carroll) *sn chsng ldrs: fdd fnl f* **6/1**[3]

6005 **8** *2* **Ingleby Arch (USA)**[47] 5594 5-8-9 **75**................................ PaulFessey 9 60
(T D Barron) *s.i.s: sme hdwy on inner over 2f out: wknd over 1f out* **5/1**[2]

0005 **9** *shd* **Quest For Success (IRE)**[13] 6532 3-8-9 **76**.................. PaulHanagan 10 61
(R A Fahey) *chsd ldrs: wknd appr fnl f* **8/1**

13-0 **10** *3 3/4* **Imprimis Tagula (IRE)**[115] 3394 4-8-11 **77**.....................(v[1]) JimmyQuinn 7 50
(A Bailey) *hmpd s: in rr: nvr a factor* **14/1**

U403 **11** *4 1/2* **Gone'N'Dunnett (IRE)**[62] 5152 9-8-0 **71** oh25..........(v) DavidProbert(5) 8 29
(Mrs C A Dunnett) *rrd s: a bhd* **50/1**

1m 15.54s (-0.96) **Going Correction** -0.05s/f (Stan)
WFA 3 from 4yo+ 1lb 11 Ran SP% **116.3**
Speed ratings (Par 105): **104,102,101,99,98 98,95,93,93,88 82**
toteswinger: 1&2 £18.70, 1&3 £5.70, 2&3 £9.30. CSF £99.42 CT £407.40 TOTE £8.80: £2.70, £4.60, £2.00; EX 93.70 TRIFECTA Not won..
Owner Grant Mercer **Bred** Mount Coote Stud **Trained** Middleham Moor, N Yorks

FOCUS
A fair sprint handicap and very competitive, with several of these still in with a chance two furlongs out. The form looks sound.
Imprimis Tagula(IRE) Official explanation: jockey said gelding suffered interference at start

6843 JANET LORD LETS PLAY BINGO MEMORIAL MEDIAN AUCTION MAIDEN STKS (DIV II) — 7f (F)
5:25 (5:25) (Class 6) 3-5-Y-0 **£2,866** (£846; £423) **Stalls** Low

Form RPR

0432 **1** **Dancing Maite**[6] 6707 3-9-3 61.. DeanMcKeown 4 68
(S R Bowring) *trckd ldrs: led 2f out: edgd rt ins fnl f: hld on wl* **2/1**[2]

4022 **2** *1/2* **Unbiased (IRE)**[11] 6571 3-9-3 67.....................................(b) ShaneKelly 7 67
(J L Dunlop) *trckd ldrs: chal over 1f out: no ex ins fnl f* **15/8**[1]

0 **3** *6* **Oskari**[13] 6530 3-9-3 0.. LeeEnstone 8 50
(P T Midgley) *in rr: hdwy over 4f out: sn chsng ldrs: styd on to take modest 3rd ins fnl f* **50/1**

430 **4** *2* **Reine De Violette**[23] 6254 3-8-12 68.............................. TPQueally 10 40
(H R A Cecil) *w ldrs on outer: chal over 2f out: sn rdn and fnd nil* **4/1**[3]

0000 **5** *2 1/4* **Vanatina (IRE)**[99] 3951 4-8-7 42.................................... DeanHeslop(7) 1 34
(W M Brisbourne) *led tl 2f out: wknd fnl f* **33/1**

055 **6** *4 1/2* **Thanxforthat (USA)**[80] 4560 3-8-10 55........................(p) JamieKyne(7) 3 27
(J J Quinn) *trckd ldrs: t.k.h: wknd over 1f out: eased ins fnl f* **11/2**

050 **7** *3 1/2* **Anna Lane**[86] 4379 3-8-12 45... PJMcDonald 9 12
(G A Swinbank) *sn outpcd and bhd: nvr on terms* **33/1**

4-60 **8** *4* **Modern Practice (IRE)**[30] 6091 3-9-3 49..................... EdwardCreighton 5 7
(Miss V Haigh) *in rr: outpcd and lost pl over 4f out: sn bhd* **50/1**

-000 **9** *8* **Tiegan An Josh**[13] 6530 3-8-9 16......................... DuranFentiman(3) 6 —
(A Crook) *sn outpcd and bhd* **200/1**

0-U0 **10** *1 3/4* **Captain Jack Black**[27] 6175 3-9-3 30.......................(be[1]) VinceSlattery 2 —
(M R Bosley) *in rr: outpcd and drvn over 3f out: styd far side: sn bhd* **100/1**

1m 29.48s (-0.82) **Going Correction** -0.05s/f (Stan)
WFA 3 from 4yo 2lb 10 Ran SP% **114.8**
Speed ratings (Par 101): **102,101,94,92,89 84,80,76,66,64**
toteswinger: 1&2 £1.30, 1&3 £21.90, 2&3 £18.10 CSF £5.87 TOTE £2.80: £1.20, £1.30, £6.40; EX 5.60 Trifecta £112.20 Pool £294.22 - 1.94 winning units. Place 6 £407.44, Place 5 £153.82..
Owner Stuart Burgan **Bred** S R Bowring **Trained** Edwinstowe, Notts

FOCUS
A very moderate maiden and the form is worth little. The first pair basically ran to form.
T/Jkpt: Not won. T/Plt: £783.70 to a £1 stake. Pool: £65,381.43. 60.90 winning tickets. T/Qpdt: £80.50 to a £1 stake. Pool: £5,006.64. 46.00 winning tickets. WG

6844 - (Foreign Racing) - See Raceform Interactive

4221 FAIRYHOUSE (R-H)
Sunday, October 19

OFFICIAL GOING: Soft to heavy

6845a IRISH STALLION FARMS JOE MCGRATH EUROPEAN BREEDERS FUND H'CAP (PREMIER HANDICAP) — 6f
2:25 (2:27) 3-Y-0+ **£31,113** (£9,128; £4,349; £1,481)

RPR

1 **Emily Blake (IRE)**[19] 6370 4-9-3 99.................................. PTownend(5) 17 103
(J C Hayden, Ire) *sn chsd ldrs: 4th 1/2-way: rdn into 2nd 1 1/2f out: led under 1f out: strly pressed fnl f: kpt on wl* **12/1**

2 *shd* **Nanotech (IRE)**[29] 6141 4-8-12 89... WJLee 18 93
(Jarlath P Fahey, Ire) *chsd ldrs: impr to chal ent st: led under 2f out: hdd under 1f out: kpt on wl: jst hld* **6/1**[1]

3 *2 1/2* **Dedo (IRE)**[19] 6367 3-9-1 93.................................... DPMcDonogh 16 90
(Kevin Prendergast, Ire) *chsd ldrs: 5th 1/2-way: rdn in 6th 2f out: styd on into 3rd 1f out: kpt on same pce fnl f* **8/1**[3]

4 *1* **Majestic Times (IRE)**[42] 5731 8-8-11 88...........................(b) FMBerry 14 82
(Liam McAteer, Ire) *towards rr: hdwy in 8th 2f out: rdn into 7th 1 1/2f out: 6th and no ex 1f out: kpt on same pce fnl f* **16/1**

5 *2* **Zhukhov (IRE)**[19] 6367 5-7-12 82............ AmyKathleenParsons(7) 6 70
(T G McCourt, Ire) *towards rr: hdwy into 9th 1 1/2f out: 8th 1f out: kpt on same pce fnl f* **9/1**

6 *hd* **Maundy Money**[29] 6141 5-9-4 95.................................. CO'Donoghue 7 82
(David Marnane, Ire) *mid-div: rdn in 7th 2f out: styd on into 4th 1f out: no ex fnl f* **10/1**

7 *2 1/2* **Impossible Dream (IRE)**[21] 6315 4-9-3 94........................ PJSmullen 3 73+
(A Kinsella, Ire) *chsd ldrs: 8th 1/2-way: lost pl ent st: rdn: mod 9th 1f out: kpt on same pce* **10/1**

8 *2* **Belclare (IRE)**[19] 6367 3-8-5 83.. MCHussey 15 56
(Tracey Collins, Ire) *chsd ldrs: cl 3rd 1/2-way: rdn 2f out: no ex in 5th 1f out: kpt on one pce* **16/1**

9 *2* **Nastrelli (IRE)**[19] 6367 5-8-10 87.. RPCleary 12 54
(M Halford, Ire) *towards rr: sme hdwy into 10th 1 1/2f out: rdn and no imp* **14/1**

10 *1 1/2* **Shining Armour (IRE)**[14] 6514 3-7-11 85..................(b) LFRoche(10) 1 48
(D K Weld, Ire) *towards rr for most: nvr a factor* **20/1**

11 *1/2* **First In Command (IRE)**[19] 6367 3-8-12 90...............(t) NGMcCullagh 9 51
(Daniel Mark Loughnane, Ire) *chsd ldrs: 7th 1/2-way: rdn in 5th 2f out: no ex in 6th 1 1/2f out: sn wknd* **7/1**[2]

12 *3/4* **Monthly Medal**[14] 6511 5-8-6 83.......................................(t) WMLordan 8 42
(Anthony Mullins, Ire) *chsd ldrs early: lost pl bef 1/2-way: rdn and no imp ent st* **14/1**

13 *1* **Wyatt Earp (IRE)**[9] 6624 7-8-12 89...(b) KLatham 5 45
(R A Fahey) *led: rdn and hdd under 2f out: no ex in 4th 1 1/2f out: sn wknd* **9/1**

14 *1/2* **Senor Benny (USA)**[14] 6514 9-9-11 105................... CPGeoghegan(3) 10 60
(M McDonagh, Ire) *chsd ldrs: 6th 1/2-way: rdn and wknd 2f out* **10/1**

15 *1* **Bunsen Burner (IRE)**[100] 3932 3-8-7 90............................ MHarley(5) 13 42
(J S Bolger, Ire) *mid-div: rdn and wknd ent st* **25/1**

16 24 **Domingues**[14] 6514 3-9-9 106..............(p) SFoley(5) 4 —
(Edward Lynam, Ire) *s.i.s: a towards rr: eased fnl f: t.o* **33/1**

1m 20.3s (7.80)
WFA 3 from 4yo+ 1lb **18 Ran SP% 129.5**
CSF £83.32 CT £412.47 TOTE £15.30: £2.90, £2.20, £2.20, £2.80; DF 83.30.
Owner Stephen Hayden **Bred** Francis J O'Toole **Trained** Kilcullen, Co Kildare

NOTEBOOK
Emily Blake(IRE) had performed with credit in fourth behind subsequent Cork Listed winner Almass over a furlong longer at the Curragh last month. She was certainly helped here when getting a dream run up the inner to challenge the favourite, and although she tired in the closing stages on this testing surface, she just did enough to hang on.
Wyatt Earp(IRE), a winner on fast ground at Chester last month, led until giving way in the straight. The testing ground certainly didn't play to his strengths.

6322 COLOGNE (R-H)
Sunday, October 19

OFFICIAL GOING: Soft

6852a WEIDENPESCHER STUTENPREIS (LISTED RACE) (F&M) 1m
3:10 (3:25) 3-Y-0+ **£9,559** (£2,941; £1,471; £735)

			RPR
1		**Magic Eye (IRE)** 3-8-12 .... APietsch 11	90
		(Andreas Lowe, Germany) **251/10**	
2	3/4	**Masako (IRE)**[21] 6323 3-8-12 .... THellier 5	88
		(W Hickst, Germany) **51/10**	
3	1 3/4	**Montrachet**[38] 5829 4-9-2 .... MickyFenton 2	85
		(M L W Bell) *a cl up: 3rd st on ins: disp 2nd 2f out: rdn and hung lft appr fnl f: kpt on* **153/10**	
4	nk	**Big Monologue (IRE)**[35] 3-8-12 .... TFarina 1	83
		(H-A Pantall, France) **43/10[2]**	
5	2 1/2	**Alexa (GER)**[21] 6323 4-9-2 .... TMundry 10	79
		(H J Groschel, Germany) **91/10**	
6	shd	**Nolas Lolly (IRE)**[32] 6034 4-9-2 .... JohnEgan 9	79
		(M Botti) *racd in 6th to st: moved outside: hrd rdn wl over 1f out: nvr able to chal* **48/10[3]**	
7	1 1/2	**Antonym (USA)**[91] 4233 4-9-2 .... AHelfenbein 4	75
		(Mario Hofer, Germany) **33/10[1]**	
8	14	**Dragon Days (GER)**[148] 3-8-12 .... AStarke 3	44
		(P Schiergen, Germany) **94/10**	
9	6	**Ordinata (GER)**[35] 5-9-2 .... ADeVries 7	31
		(Frau Ira Ferentschak, Germany) **33/10[1]**	
10	3	**Eneyda (IRE)** 3-8-12 .... JiriPalik 8	24
		(P Schiergen, Germany) **40/1**	

1m 41.77s (3.38)
WFA 3 from 4yo+ 3lb **10 Ran SP% 130.9**
WIN (including 10 euro stake) 261; PL 52, 28, 44; SF 2,671.
Owner Gestut Winterhauch **Bred** Glending Bloodstock **Trained** Germany

NOTEBOOK
Montrachet, who had trip and ground to suit, gained black type at the third attempt. She was always close to the pace but hung under pressure in the closing stages and had nothing in reserve.
Nolas Lolly(IRE), who earned place money on both her previous trips to Germany, seems to have lost her edge in recent runs and this softer ground may not have been in her favour, so in the circumstances she did not perform too badly.

6853a PREIS DES WINTERFAVORITEN (GROUP 3) 1m
4:15 (4:33) 2-Y-0
£62,500 (£22,794; £15,074; £7,574; £4,044; £1,985)

			RPR
1		**Globus (GER)** 2-9-2 .... THellier 1	—
		(U Ostmann, Germany) *mde all: wnt clr appr fnl f: pushed out* **21/10[2]**	
2	10	**Next Vision (IRE)**[28] 2-9-2 .... ADeVries 6	—
		(J Hirschberger, Germany) *racd in 3rd: wnt 2nd wl over 3f out: rdn wl over 1f out: one pce* **14/10[1]**	
3	2	**Enzio (GER)** 2-9-2 .... EPedroza 4	—
		(A Wohler, Germany) *racd in 4th: disp 3rd on ins st: rdn over 2f out: disp 2nd fr over 1f out to 150yds out: one pce* **26/10[3]**	
4	13	**Running Home (GER)** 2-9-2 .... JohnEgan 3	—
		(A Wohler, Germany) *cl up: disp 3rd st: swtchd outside 2f out: sn rdn and btn* **104/10**	
5	3	**Martell (GER)** 2-9-2 .... AStarke 2	—
		(P Schiergen, Germany) *sn rushed up to go 2nd: wknd wl over 3f out: last and btn st* **58/10**	
6	8	**Falun (GER)** 2-9-2 .... TMundry 5	—
		(A Trybuhl, Germany) *in rr: pushed along after 3f: 5th and btn st* **15/1**	

1m 42.25s (3.86) **6 Ran SP% 131.4**
WIN 31; PL 15,13; SF 46.
Owner Stall Dipoli **Bred** Herbert Schniepp **Trained** Germany

6518 LONGCHAMP (R-H)
Sunday, October 19

OFFICIAL GOING: Good to soft

6854a PRIX DU CONSEIL DE PARIS (GROUP 2) 1m 4f
2:20 (2:22) 3-Y-0+ **£54,485** (£21,029; £10,037; £6,691; £3,346)

			RPR
1		**Crossharbour**[35] 5954 4-9-4 .... SPasquier 6	111
		(A Fabre, France) *mde all: pushed along st: rdn and r.o 1 1/2f out: styd on gamely ins fnl f* **8/1**	
2	nk	**Purple Moon (IRE)**[25] 6201 5-9-2 .... JamieSpencer 5	109
		(L M Cumani) *prom: 2nd 1/2-way: pushed along st: rdn to chse ldr over 1 1/2f out: nrest at fin* **11/1**	
3	1	**Poseidon Adventure (IRE)**[21] 6324 5-9-2 ....(b) ASuborics 2	107
		(W Figge, Germany) *mid-div on ins: disputing 6th st: drvn 1 1/2f out: rdn and r.o in centre fnl f: wnt 3rd 50yds out: nrest at fin* **9/2[2]**	
4	3/4	**Belle Et Celebre (FR)**[29] 6148 3-8-13 .... IMendizabal 1	110
		(A De Royer-Dupre, France) *mid-div: pushed along disputing 3rd st: hrd rdn 1 1/2f out: wnt 3rd 100yds out to 50yds out: styd on* **10/1**	
5	nk	**Buenos Dias (IRE)**[50] 5529 3-8-9 .... ACrastus 4	105
		(E Lellouche, France) *hld up in 7th: disputing 6th st: pushed along in centre 1 1/2f out: disputing 3rd 1f out: rdn and no ex fnl 100yds* **46/10[3]**	
6	hd	**Prospect Wells (FR)**[35] 5953 3-9-0 .... OPeslier 8	110
		(A Fabre, France) *hld up in last: rdn over 1 1/2f out in centre: sme hdwy but n.d* **14/10[1]**	
7	4	**Candy Gift (ARG)**[24] 6237 5-9-2 .... MGuyon 3	99
		(A Fabre, France) *in tch: drvn and 5th st: sn rdn and one pce* **14/1**	
8	2 1/2	**Magadino (FR)**[49] 5557 7-9-2 .... TJarnet 7	95
		(Mme Brigitte Renk, Switzerland) *in tch: pushed along disputing 3rd st: drvn 1 1/2f out: sn one pce* **29/1**	

2m 34.7s (3.50)
WFA 3 from 4yo+ 7lb **8 Ran SP% 116.2**
PARI-MUTUEL: WIN 9.00; PL 2.70, 3.00, 2.30; DF 36.30.
Owner K Abdulla **Bred** Juddmonte Farms Ltd **Trained** Chantilly, France

NOTEBOOK
Crossharbour appreciated the change in tactics. He was smartly out of stalls and soon at the head of affairs then quickened things up rapidly entering the straight and built up a lead of several lengths but had to pull out all the stops to hold off the runner-up. The colt may now be campaigned overseas but no decision has been made as to whether he will stay in training as a five-year-old.
Purple Moon(IRE) having only his second race in nearly a year, put up a fine performance and one which bodes well for the future. He was dropped in behind the leader on the rail and then outpaced when things quickened up early in the straight. He then knuckled down to the task and closed on the winner throughout the final furlong and a half. The softish ground was not in his favour and he will now be campaigned in Hong Kong (hopefully in the Vase) and next year in Dubai.
Poseidon Adventure(IRE) was given an awful lot to do in a race which did not have much early pace. He was one of the last coming into the straight when the pace was suddenly increased. He was bought with a run up the centre of the track and finished really well.
Belle Et Celebre(FR), running over a mile and a half for the first time and the only runner in the field to carry a Group 1 penalty, this filly ran with credit. She shared second place in the early stages and then could not accelerate as well as the winner in the straight. She stayed on gamely at one pace and will remain in training as a four-year-old.

6855a PRIX DE CONDE (GROUP 3) 1m 1f
2:50 (2:56) 2-Y-0 **£29,412** (£11,765; £8,824; £5,882; £2,941)

			RPR
1		**Naval Officer (USA)**[29] 6147 2-8-11 ....(b) IMendizabal 5	107
		(J-C Rouget, France) *led: jnd 5f out: hdd 4f out: 3rd st: rdn to chse ldrs 1 1/2f out: chal fnl f: styd on to ld 100yds out: drvn out* **2/1[2]**	
2	nk	**King Of Sydney (USA)**[50] 2-8-11 .... J-PCarvalho 4	107
		(Mario Hofer, Germany) *hld up: disputing 5th st: sn rdn: styd on on ins: wnt 2nd nr fin* **25/1**	
3	1 1/2	**Becomes You**[41] 5769 2-8-8 .... SPasquier 6	101
		(M Delzangles, France) *hld up: disputing 5th st: pushed along to chse ldrs 1 1/2f out: nvr able to chal: fin 4th: plcd 3rd* **71/10[3]**	
4	nk	**Zafisio (IRE)**[36] 5898 2-8-11 .... DarryllHolland 3	101
		(P A Blockley) *2nd: jnd ldr 5f out: led 4f out: drvn st: rdn and hdd 2f out: styd on u.p: bmpd by Handsme Maestro cl home: fin 5th: plcd 4th* **12/1**	
5	1	**Handsome Maestro (IRE)**[26] 2-8-11 .... OPeslier 1	101
		(D Smaga, France) *prom: 2nd st: r.o to ld 2f out: wandered u.p 1f out: hdd 100yds out: bmpd Zafisio cl home: no ex: fin 3rd, nk & 1l: plcd 5th* **6/5[1]**	
6	20	**Ivan Poddubny** 2-8-11 .... TThulliez 2	61
		(A Shavuyev, Czech Republic) *hld up: last and rdn st: n.d* **19/1**	
7	1/2	**Canwinn (IRE)**[29] 6147 2-8-11 .... DBonilla 7	60
		(M R Channon) *in tch: 4th and pushed along st: no imp* **10/1**	

1m 53.5s (-3.00) **7 Ran SP% 116.8**
PARI-MUTUEL: WIN 3.00; PL 2.00, 6.20; SF 47.80.
Owner Joseph Allen **Bred** J Allen **Trained** Pau, France

NOTEBOOK
Naval Officer(USA), a powerful and long-striding colt, he was wearing blinkers for the first time. He was at the head of affairs earlier on but was restrained as another runner drew along side on the descent before the straight. The colt made his final effort on the outside and took the advantage at the furlong marker, then edged right at the final stages, but finally won with a little in hand. Not an easy ride but a very talented individual, he could go for the Criterium de Saint-Cloud if the ground remains good.
King Of Sydney(USA), held up for a late run he did not really get into the race until halfway up the straight. He made rapid progress up the far rail and took the runner-up position inside the final furlong, and, it will be no surprise to see him back in France for the Criterium de Saint-Cloud.
Becomes You, taking on much better company on this occasion, was promoted to third place by the Stewards. She ran a little green early on and was putting in her best work at the finish and is certainly a filly with a future.
Zafisio(IRE) initially finished fifth but was promoted to fourth as the Stewards felt that the third past the post had stopped him from obtaining the best possible position. He ran free early on and eventually went into the lead halfway down the hill to the straight. He was then outpaced before running on again when a gap closed in front of him a hundred yards from the post. Connections would have preferred more cut in the ground and they might send him back for the Criterium de Saint-Cloud next month.
Handsome Maestro(IRE), made favourite on this step up in grade and on easier ground, had his chance but wandered under pressure and hampered Zafisio, for which infringement he was demoted to fifth.
Canwinn(IRE) never recovered from an outside draw and was on the outside throughout the race. He was slightly hampered before the straight and, beaten shortly after, this performance is best forgotten as things simply did not go right for him.

6856 - (Foreign Racing) - See Raceform Interactive

6524 PONTEFRACT (L-H)
Monday, October 20

OFFICIAL GOING: Good to soft (good in places; 7.7)
Wind: Strong, mainly behind Weather: Overcast and windy

6857 TOTEPLACEPOT NURSERY 1m 4y
2:10 (2:11) (Class 5) (0-75,75) 2-Y-0 **£3,885** (£1,156; £577; £288) **Stalls Low**

Form				RPR
1552	1		**Fastnet Storm (IRE)**[31] 6086 2-9-7 75.............. MickyFenton 17	79
			(T P Tate) *mde all: rdn over 1f out: drvn and jnd ins fnl f: hld on gamely* **11/1**	
6123	2	shd	**Dubai Crest**[7] 6700 2-9-6 74.............. JimCrowley 16	78
			(Mrs A J Perrett) *trckd ldrs: swtchd outside and hdwy wl over 1f out: rdn and hung lft entgering fnl f: sn drvn and ev ch tl nt qckn nr line* **6/1[1]**	

000 **3** 1½ **Sampower Quin (IRE)**[11] 6597 2-8-10 **64** ow2........................ DNolan 5 64
(D Carroll) *trckd ldng pair: effrt on inner 2f out: rdn wl over 1f out: drvn and kpt on ins fnl f* **33/1**

062 **4** shd **Oriental Cavalier**[14] 6535 2-8-12 **66**.............................. HayleyTurner 14 66
(R Hollinshead) *chsd ldrs: hdwy 3f out: rdn and ev ch wl over 1f out: drvn and n.m.r jst ins fnl f: kpt on u.p* **11/1**

0665 **5** hd **Flying Lady (IRE)**[19] 6394 2-9-0 **68**...................................... TPO'Shea 4 68
(M R Channon) *hld up towards rr: hdwy into midfield over 3f out: rdn to chse ldrs over 1f out: drvn and n.m.r ins fnl f: kpt on towards fin* **14/1**

6013 **6** 2 **Woteva**[30] 6101 2-9-2 **70**...(p) RoystonFfrench 3 65
(B Ellison) *hld up towards rr: hdwy on inner 2f out: rdn to chse ldrs over 1f out: drvn and n.m.r ins fnl f: kpt on* **11/1**

436 **7** 1 **Wabi Sabi (IRE)**[20] 6360 2-8-11 **65**................................ MichaelHills 15 58
(B W Hills) *midfield: hdwy on outer over 2f out: rdn and hung lft over 1f out: kpt on same pce ins fnl f* **14/1**

054 **8** 1 **Itlaaq**[37] 5901 2-9-5 **73**.. TedDurcan 12 64
(J L Dunlop) *towards rr: pushed along 3f out: rdn and kpt on fnl 2f: nt rch ldrs* **8/1**[3]

4323 **9** ¾ **Chilly Filly (IRE)**[25] 6231 2-9-6 **74**............................ JoeFanning 13 63
(M Johnston) *dwlt and hld up towards rr tl styd on fnl 2f: nvr rch ldrs* **7/1**[2]

555 **10** hd **Embsay Crag**[19] 6383 2-8-10 **64**.................................... PJMcDonald 1 53
(Mrs K Walton) *hld up and bhd: hdwy and nt clr run on inner wl over 1f out: sn swtchd rt and hdwy 1f out: styd on strly ins fnl f: nrst fin* **33/1**

1311 **11** 1¾ **Dougie Peel**[37] 5909 2-8-11 **65**......................................(p) RobertWinston 8 50
(K A Ryan) *prom: rdn along 3f out: wknd wl over 1f out* **12/1**

2350 **12** 1 **Jimwil (IRE)**[24] 6247 2-9-0 **68**..................................... TonyHamilton 2 51
(M Dods) *a in rr* **16/1**

5100 **13** ¾ **Sergeant Pink (IRE)**[19] 6394 2-9-2 **70**.............................. ChrisCatlin 7 51
(S Gollings) *chsd wnr: rdn along over 2f out: drvn and wknd wl over 1f out* **25/1**

5044 **14** ¾ **Lost In Paris (IRE)**[11] 6603 2-8-11 **65**............................ DavidAllan 10 45
(T D Easterby) *midfield: rdn along over 2f out and sn wknd* **11/1**

601 **15** nk **Sharp Sovereign (USA)**[33] 6014 2-9-3 **74**..................... NeilBrown(3) 6 53
(T D Barron) *in tch: rdn along over 2f out and sn wknd* **12/1**

000 **16** 2½ **Highland Burn**[10] 6622 2-9-4 **72**.. TQuinn 9 45
(D R C Elsworth) *s.i.s: a in rr* **25/1**

1m 50.12s (4.22) **Going Correction** +0.40s/f (Good) **16** Ran SP% **119.4**
Speed ratings (Par 95): **94,93,92,92,92 90,89,88,87,87 85,84,83,82,82 80**
toteswinger: 1&2 £7.70, 1&3 £70.90, 2&3 £53.80. CSF £70.90 CT £2195.97 TOTE £12.60: £3.50, £1.90, £8.10, £2.90; EX 70.70.

Owner The Kittywake Partnership **Bred** Norelands Bloodstock **Trained** Tadcaster, N Yorks
■ Stewards' Enquiry : Jim Crowley one-day ban: careless riding (Nov 3)

FOCUS
There had been no rain overnight and strong winds ensured the ground was drying out all the time. However, it still seemed to be riding on the easy side. There was a headwind from the mile start to the 6f start, and a following wind up the straight. This was an open-looking nursery.

NOTEBOOK
Fastnet Storm(IRE) pinged the gates and crossed over from his wide draw to take the field along next to the inside rail. More or less left alone in front, he was able to conserve enough energy to just about hold off the closers in the straight, and these tactics clearly suit him well. He should get 1m4f next year.
Dubai Crest came with a strong run down the centre of the track once in line for home, but he tended to hang left and the winner battled on just the better. Despite the perceived disadvantage, he made it a one-two for the outside stalls.
Sampower Quin(IRE) had beaten very few horses in three starts in maiden company on the all-weather, and a mark of 62 seemed harsh, to say the least. However, he showed much-improved form on his handicap debut, albeit having tracked the leader on the rail throughout and therefore taken the shortest route home.
Oriental Cavalier, another handicap debutant, was representing a stable very much in form. Prominent throughout, he gave away ground to the likes of the winner and third by racing wide most of the way and, in the circumstances, it was a sound effort.
Flying Lady(IRE), dropping back from 1m2f, shaped better than her finishing position as she was travelling well as they entered the straight but could not find a way through from off the pace. A stronger gallop would undoubtedly have suited her better. (op 12-1)
Woteva did not travel well but did respond to pressure and kept on, albeit with the inside rail to help.

6858 TOTESWINGER MAIDEN AUCTION STKS 6f
2:40 (2:41) (Class 5) 2-Y-O **£3,238** (£963; £481; £240) **Stalls** Low

Form RPR

03 **1** **Speedy Guru**[35] 5959 2-8-4 0.......................................(t) FrankieMcDonald 2 73
(H Candy) *chsd ldrs on inner: hdwy 2f out: swtchd rt and rdn over 1f out: styd on to chal ins fnl f: drvn and led last 30yds* **9/2**[1]

5 **2** hd **Zegna (IRE)**[18] 6407 2-8-12 0.. JimCrowley 16 80
(B Smart) *led: rdn clr wl over 1f out: drvn ins fnl f: hdd and no ex last 30yds* **8/1**

225 **3** 3¾ **Hameildaeme**[41] 5785 2-8-0 **65** ow1......................... PatrickDonaghy(5) 1 62
(S C Williams) *hld up: hdwy on inner 2f out: swtchd rt and rdn to chse ldrs over 1f out: drvn and kpt on ins fnl f: nrst fin* **9/2**[1]

65 **4** 1 **Quick Single (USA)**[10] 6620 2-8-13 0..................................... TQuinn 9 67
(D R C Elsworth) *chsd ldrs: rdn along 1f out: drvn and edgd lft over 1f out: sn one pce* **5/1**[2]

54 **5** 2¾ **Kinigi (IRE)**[16] 6488 2-8-9 0.. ChrisCatlin 14 55
(S A Callaghan) *hld up towards rr: hdwy 2f out: swtchd rt and rdn over 1f out: kpt on ins fnl f: nrst fin* **33/1**

500 **6** ¾ **Distinctive Spirit (IRE)**[25] 6229 2-8-12 **67**..........(b[1]) SilvestreDeSousa 5 56
(K A Ryan) *in tch and sn rdn along: drvn 2f out: kpt on same pce* **25/1**

0545 **7** ½ **Secret City (IRE)**[13] 6547 2-8-10 **64**.............................(b) PatCosgrave 11 52
(R Bastiman) *chsd ldr: rdn 2f out: drvn over 1f out: wknd ins fnl f* **18/1**

0 **8** ¾ **Northern Flyer (GER)**[19] 6383 2-8-13 0............................ MickyFenton 12 53
(J J Quinn) *hld up: hdwy 2f out: kpt on ins fnl f: nt rch ldrs* **40/1**

000 **9** 1½ **El Guevara (IRE)**[35] 5959 2-8-13 0..................................(b[1]) JoeFanning 3 48
(K A Ryan) *s.i.s: a towards rr* **50/1**

30 **10** 1¼ **Mohawk Ridge**[19] 6383 2-8-8 0..................................... NeilBrown(3) 13 43
(M Dods) *a towards rr* **8/1**

00 **11** nk **Lady Zena**[19] 6383 2-8-7 0.. DaleGibson 10 38
(M W Easterby) *a towards rr* **100/1**

12 3½ **Asakusa** 2-8-7 0.. RoystonFfrench 8 27
(M Johnston) *midfield: rdn along over 2f out: nvr a factor* **9/1**

3 **13** ½ **Starla Dancer (GER)**[19] 6383 2-8-9 0................................ TonyHamilton 7 28
(R A Fahey) *chsd ldrs: rdn along over 2f out: drvn and wknd over 1f out* **6/1**[3]

14 1¼ **Spruzzo** 2-8-11 0.. DeanMcKeown 15 26
(C W Thornton) *s.i.s: a in rr* **100/1**

00 **15** 6 **Miss Jabba (IRE)**[17] 6432 2-8-4 0..................................... DO'Donohoe 6 1
(Miss J Feilden) *a towards rr* **66/1**

1m 19.3s (2.40) **Going Correction** +0.40s/f (Good) **15** Ran SP% **119.5**
Speed ratings (Par 95): **100,99,94,93,89 88,88,87,85,83 83,78,77,76,68**
toteswinger: 1&2 £10.40, 1&3 £4.90, 2&3 £18.40. CSF £38.48 TOTE £5.40: £1.60, £3.70, £2.40; EX 38.60.

Owner Henry Candy **Bred** Miss M Cornell **Trained** Kingston Warren, Oxon
■ Stewards' Enquiry : Jim Crowley one-day ban: failed to ride to draw (Nov 4)

FOCUS
A fairly ordinary maiden.

NOTEBOOK
Speedy Guru improved for the fitting of a tongue tie last time and the aid was again in place here. Nicely drawn, she was able to cling to the rail throughout and, when the leader began to paddle inside the final furlong, she was able to stay on past him to get off the mark at the third attempt. She should get 7f in handicap company. (op 5-1)
Zegna(IRE) is the one to take out of the race as he improved markedly on his debut effort at Ayr when far too green to do himself justice. He was slowly away that day but had clearly learned plenty for that experience as he was swiftly out of the stalls this time and set about trying to make most of the running. He had most of them on the stretch turning into the straight, but got a bit tired inside the last and was caught by the filly close home. A similar maiden should come his way, especially if he improves again for this second outing. (op 7-1 tchd 13-2)
Hameildaeme was dropping back in distance and was outpaced turning into the straight but then kept on to grab third. A daughter of Storming Home out of a mare who is from the family of Mysilv, she seemed to find this an insufficient test. (op 5-1 tchd 11-2)
Quick Single(USA), a US-bred who improved for the switch to Polytrack last time, showed good speed towards the outer but was one-paced in the straight. Now eligible for a handicap mark, he may find a race back on the all-weather. (op 9-2 tchd 11-2)
Kinigi(IRE) was never a threat but did stay on to be nearest at the finish. Another for whom handicaps are now an option, she is likely to appreciate a longer trip in that sphere.
Distinctive Spirit(IRE), who had an excuse at this track last time as he lost his action on the fast ground, had blinkers on for the first time but still needed plenty of rousting along to go the early pace.
Mohawk Ridge Official explanation: jockey said colt was denied a clear run

6859 TOTESUPER7 H'CAP 5f
3:10 (3:10) (Class 4) (0-85,84) 3-Y-O+ **£6,476** (£1,927; £963; £481) **Stalls** Low

Form RPR

1064 **1** **Kay Two (IRE)**[9] 6651 6-9-4 **84**.......................................(p) JimCrowley 5 94
(R J Price) *prominet: hdwy to chse ldr 2f out: rdn to chal over 1f out: drvn to ld ins fnl f: kpt on* **7/1**[1]

0000 **2** ½ **Dig Deep (IRE)**[23] 6278 6-8-1 **74**.................................... JamieKyne(7) 3 82
(J J Quinn) *in tch: hdwy on inner 2f out: rdn to chse ldrs over 1f out: swtchd outside and drvn ent fnl f: styd on wl* **16/1**

3313 **3** hd **Mr Wolf**[10] 6634 7-8-7 **73**...(p) TonyHamilton 8 80
(D W Barker) *led: rdn along 2f out: drvn over 1f out: hdd ins fnl f: no ex* **9/1**[3]

4002 **4** ¾ **Foxy Music**[9] 6651 4-9-0 **80**.. DeanMcKeown 2 85
(E J Alston) *prom: rdn along wl over 1f out: drvn ent fnl f and kpt on same pce towards fin* **10/1**

0604 **5** ¾ **He's A Humbug (IRE)**[10] 6623 4-8-11 **80**.........................(p) NeilBrown(3) 4 82
(K A Ryan) *hld up: hdwy on inner 2f out: sn rdn and styd on ins fnl f: nrst fin* **10/1**

3504 **6** ½ **Johannes (IRE)**[30] 6125 5-8-11 **77**................................ ChrisCatlin 11 77+
(E J O'Neill) *dwlt and towards rr: hdwy 2f out: swtchd rt and rdn over 1f out: kpt on wl fnl f: nrst fin* **15/2**[2]

5555 **7** hd **Charles Parnell (IRE)**[6] 6724 5-8-7 **73**............................ DaleGibson 15 73
(M Dods) *towards rr: hdwy and rdn over 1f out: styd on ins fnl f: nrst fin* **11/1**

5100 **8** hd **Divine Spirit**[31] 6066 7-8-12 **78**.................................. PhilipRobinson 7 77
(M Dods) *in tch: effrt 2f out: sn rdn and no imp fnl f* **10/1**

0040 **9** nse **Efistorm**[9] 6650 7-9-2 **82**.. HayleyTurner 16 81+
(C R Dore) *towards rr: hdwy 2f out: sn rdn and kpt on ins fnl f* **16/1**

0211 **10** 2¼ **Ridge Wood Dani (IRE)**[51] 5510 3-9-1 **81**........................ PatCosgrave 13 72
(E J Alston) *dwlt: a towards rr* **12/1**

0015 **11** 1 **Namir (IRE)**[23] 6278 6-8-11 **77**.....................................(vt) TedDurcan 12 64
(D Shaw) *in tch: swtchd rt and hdwy wl over 1f out: sn rdn and wknd ent fnl f* **9/1**[3]

2040 **12** 1½ **Speedy Senorita (IRE)**[16] 6486 3-7-13 **72**............ DeclanCannon(7) 14 54
(K R Burke) *nvr bttr than midfield* **33/1**

-000 **13** ¾ **Jack Rackham**[40] 5796 4-8-10 **76**............................... RoystonFfrench 1 55
(B Smart) *a in rr* **10/1**

0000 **14** 1 **Northern Empire (IRE)**[9] 6651 5-9-0 **80**............................ TPO'Shea 17 55
(K A Ryan) *a in rr* **50/1**

3030 **15** ½ **Gallery Girl (IRE)**[9] 6650 5-8-8 **74**.................................. DavidAllan 10 47
(T D Easterby) *s.i.s: a bhd* **14/1**

3200 **16** 4 **Shes Minnie**[101] 3905 5-8-9 **75** ow1............................... RobertWinston 9 34
(J G M O'Shea) *mdifield: hdwy and in tch 2f out: sn rdn and wknd over 1f out* **40/1**

64.63 secs (1.33) **Going Correction** +0.40s/f (Good) **16** Ran SP% **122.4**
Speed ratings (Par 105): **105,104,103,102,101 100,100,100,99,96 94,92,91,89,88 82**
toteswinger: 1&2 £40.60, 1&3 £8.30, 2&3 £46.80. CSF £115.73 CT £1032.75 TOTE £6.80: £2.40, £4.70, £1.80, £2.30; EX 99.10.

Owner Hugh B McGahon **Bred** Roger A Ryan **Trained** Ullingswick, H'fords

FOCUS
There looked to be plenty of pace on here and sure enough Mr Wolf, Foxy Music and Kay Two did ensure a good gallop, but on a day when it appeared that the pace was holding up, all three were able to keep on to fill the frame, and it was the topweight who came out on top. The form looks sound.
Namir(IRE) Official explanation: jockey said gelding had no more to give
Gallery Girl(IRE) Official explanation: jockey said mare reared leaving stalls

6860 TOTEPOOL SILVER TANKARD STKS (LISTED RACE) 1m 4y
3:40 (3:41) (Class 1) 2-Y-O **£22,708** (£8,608; £4,308; £2,148) **Stalls** Low

Form RPR

113 **1** **Playfellow (IRE)**[37] 5889 2-9-2 **109**................................. PhilipRobinson 2 99+
(M A Jarvis) *stdd s and hld up: hdwy over 2f out: rdn to ld 1f out: edgd lft and kpt on fnl f* **4/9**[1]

51 **2** 2¼ **Mishrif (USA)**[42] 5754 2-9-2 **92**...................................... AlanMunro 3 94
(P W Chapple-Hyam) *led: rdn along 2f out: drvn and hdd 1f out: kpt on same pce* **5/2**[2]

1233 **3** 2¾ **Laahig**[28] 6176 2-9-2 **90**...(b[1]) HayleyTurner 1 88
(G A Butler) *t.k.h: trckd ldng pair: rdn along and outpcd over 2f out* **20/1**

3000 **4** *6* **Danidh Dubai (IRE)**[17] 6439 2-8-11 98 TPO'Shea 4 70
(M R Channon) *chsd ldr: rdn along over 2f out: drvn and edgd lft wl over 1f out: wknd qckly* **14/1**[3]

1m 51.25s (5.35) **Going Correction** +0.40s/f (Good) **4** Ran SP% **109.3**
Speed ratings (Par 103): **89,86,84,78**
CSF £1.85 TOTE £1.50; EX 1.80.
Owner Sheikh Ahmed Al Maktoum **Bred** Darley **Trained** Newmarket, Suffolk

FOCUS
An interesting little Listed race.

NOTEBOOK
Playfellow(IRE), third in the Champagne Stakes last time out, looked to face a pretty straightforward task. Held up off a modest early gallop, he was a little keen but quickened up well to tackle Mishrif approaching the furlong pole. Although he had to be kept up to his work and was only workmanlike in victory, he did it readily enough in the end. A nice type with scope to improve further next year, he should get 1m2f and could well make his mark at Group level, although it may be he will be racing in Godolphin blue next term. (op 8-15)
Mishrif(USA) had good maiden form and deserved to take his chance in this better company. Allowed the run of the race out in front, he set an ordinary gallop and was well placed to quicken off the front entering the straight. He ran well, simply bumping into a smart rival, and, given his pedigree, could be interesting on the Polytrack if a suitable race can be found for him. (tchd 3-1)
Laahig, keen in the first-time blinkers, was the lowest-rated horse in the field and looked to have a stiff task. He could prove difficult to place, as his handicap mark will not make things easy if his attention is switched to running in nurseries. (op 18-1)
Danidh Dubai(IRE), the only filly in the field, has struggled since finishing third in the Albany Stakes at Royal Ascot. Easily seen off by the first two early in the straight, her rider was soon looking down, as though the filly had lost her action. (op 12-1 tchd 16-1)

6861 TOTEEXACTA BLUFF COVE H'CAP 2m 1f 216y
4:10 (4:10) (Class 5) (0-75,75) 3-Y-O+ **£3,885** (£1,156; £577; £288) **Stalls** Low

Form RPR
25 **1** **Mr Crystal (FR)**[32] 6054 4-9-4 68 NeilBrown(3) 6 77
(Micky Hammond) *hld up in rr: rapid hdwy on outer 4f out: led over 2f out and sn rdn: drvn and narrow advantage ent fnl f: hld on gamely* **8/1**

5011 **2** *shd* **Miss Serena**[18] 6421 3-8-9 67 MickyFenton 4 76
(Mrs P Sly) *trckd ldng pair: effrt over 2f out: rdn to chal over 1f out and ev ch tl no ex nr fin* **6/1**[3]

0002 **3** *8* **Unawatuna**[19] 6386 3-7-5 56 oh3 JamieKyne(7) 10 55
(Mrs K Walton) *hld up: hdwy over 5f out: effrt on inner 3f out and sn rdn: drvn and styd on same pce u.p appr fnl f* **16/1**

1200 **4** *½* **Bugsy's Boy**[8] 6672 4-9-9 70 RobertWinston 2 69
(George Baker) *trckd ldrs: effrt 3f out: rdn along 2f out: sn drvn and kpt on same pce* **17/2**

3-52 **5** *2* **First Look (FR)**[10] 6410 8-9-11 72 PaulFessey 9 68
(P Monteith) *hld up in rr: stdy hdwy 7f out: chsd ldrs over 4f out: sn rdn along and no imp fnl 2f* **12/1**

-340 **6** *2 ¼* **Gallileo Figaro (USA)**[11] 6606 5-9-10 71 JerryO'Dwyer 3 65
(N B King) *midfield: hdwy 5f out: rdn along over 3f out: sn no imp* **16/1**

5363 **7** *4* **Thewhirlingdervish (IRE)**[32] 6054 10-9-2 63 DavidAllan 12 52
(T D Easterby) *trckd ldrs: reminders 6f out: rdn along 4f out: sn wknd* **4/1**[1]

006 **8** *1 ¾* **Rare Ruby (IRE)**[8] 6672 4-9-0 61 (p) TPO'Shea 1 48
(Jennie Candlish) *chsd ldr: led wl over 3f out: sn rdn and hdd over 2f out: grad wknd* **16/1**

0134 **9** *shd* **At The Money**[8] 6672 5-9-7 68 DaleGibson 8 55
(J M P Eustace) *led: rdn along over 4f out: sn hdd & wknd 3f out* **9/2**[2]

0635 **10** *nk* **Historic Place (USA)**[34] 5993 8-8-9 56 oh7 (p) RoystonFfrench 7 42
(J A Geake) *a bhd* **14/1**

3333 **11** *16* **Mith Hill**[20] 6361 7-9-11 72 (p) ChrisCatlin 11 39
(Ian Williams) *chasd ldrs: rdn along over 4f out: sn wknd* **7/1**

0-06 **12** *46* **Monolith**[18] 6410 10-9-7 75 (b) ClGillies(7) 5 —
(L Lungo) *hld up in rr: gd hdwy to chse ldrs 1/2-way: rdn along 5f out: sn wknd and bhd* **33/1**

4m 7.50s (3.60) **Going Correction** +0.40s/f (Good)
WFA 3 from 4yo+ 11lb **12** Ran SP% **121.6**
Speed ratings (Par 103): **108,107,104,104,103 102,100,99,99,99 92,79**
toteswinger: 1&2 £12.90, 1&3 £28.50, 2&3 £14.20. CSF £56.92 CT £767.12 TOTE £11.00: £3.20, £2.30, £4.00; EX 84.40.
Owner S Henderson **Bred** Gerard Schence **Trained** Middleham Moor, N Yorks

FOCUS
A standard stayers' handicap and quite a stamina test. The winner and runner-up are both rated up 4lb.
At The Money Official explanation: trainer said gelding was unsuited by the good to soft (good in places) ground

6862 TOTETRIFECTA H'CAP 1m 2f 6y
4:40 (4:41) (Class 5) (0-75,75) 3-Y-O+ **£3,885** (£1,156; £577; £288) **Stalls** Low

Form RPR
4160 **1** **King Fingal (IRE)**[16] 6482 3-9-2 75 MickyFenton 8 85
(J J Quinn) *midfield: hdwy and in tch over 3f out: rdn to chse ldr wl over 1f out: drvn ins fnl f and styd on to ld last 75yds* **20/1**

5305 **2** *1 ¼* **Dream Of Olwyn (IRE)**[14] 6530 3-8-3 62 HayleyTurner 1 69
(J G Given) *prom: hdwy to ld over 3f out: rdn wl over 1f out: drvn ins fnl f: hdd and no ex last 75yds* **25/1**

6332 **3** *¾* **Ahlawy (IRE)**[10] 6629 5-8-7 68 (b) BradleyRoper(7) 9 74+
(M W Easterby) *hld up towards rr: hdwy 3f out: rdn to chse ldrs over 1f out: drvn and edgd lft ins fnl f: kpt on* **16/1**

1104 **4** *2 ½* **Force Group (IRE)**[11] 6607 4-8-13 74 AshleyMorgan(7) 12 75
(M H Tompkins) *trckd ldrs: effrt over 2f out: swtchd ins and rdn over 1f out: kpt on same pce ins fnl f* **3/1**[1]

4113 **5** *1* **Five Wishes**[52] 5454 4-8-13 67 (be) PAspell 5 66+
(M Dods) *chsd ldrs: rdn along on inner over 2f out: swtchd rt and drvn over 1f out: kpt on ins fnl f* **25/1**

0002 **6** *hd* **Night Orbit**[6] 6721 4-8-7 64 ow1 (v) RussellKennemore(3) 11 62
(Miss J Feilden) *prom: cl up 3f out: rdn along over 2f out: drvn and wknd over 1f out* **8/1**[3]

062 **7** *1 ¼* **Black Coffee**[63] 5150 3-8-9 68 PhilipRobinson 10 64
(W J Musson) *midfield: hdwy to chse ldrs 4f out: rdn along 2f out: drvn and wknd appr fnl f* **11/1**

4362 **8** *1 ¼* **Pitbull**[14] 6537 5-8-9 63 (p) AlanMunro 16 56
(Mrs G S Rees) *dwlt and in rr: hdwy over 2f out: rdn wl over 1f out: styd on ent fnl f: nt rch ldrs* **9/1**

5014 **9** *1 ¾* **Packers Hill (IRE)**[9] 6657 4-8-11 65 PJMcDonald 7 55
(G A Swinbank) *trckd ldrs: hdwy 3f out: rdn along over 2f out: drvn and wknd wl over 1f out* **13/2**[2]

10/0 **10** *2 ¼* **Cote D'Argent**[182] 1520 5-8-13 70 NeilBrown(3) 17 55
(L Lungo) *a towards rr* **66/1**

05-0 **11** *3 ¾* **Along The Nile**[12] 6582 6-9-7 75 DeanMcKeown 15 53
(K G Reveley) *hld up and bhd: nvr a factor* **50/1**

5 **12** *4 ½* **Blushing Heart**[12] 6583 4-8-13 67 AndrewElliott 4 36
(G M Moore) *nvr bttr than midfield* **66/1**

6454 **13** *1 ½* **Graceful Descent (FR)**[33] 6012 3-8-11 70 TonyHamilton 3 36
(R A Fahey) *in tch: rdn along 3f out: wknd over 2f out* **10/1**

0310 **14** *2 ½* **Lilburn (IRE)**[35] 5964 3-8-9 68 RobertWinston 14 29
(J R Fanshawe) *midfield: rdn along and lost pl over 2f out* **14/1**

1040 **15** *8* **Zuwaar**[7] 6703 3-8-10 69 (tp) ChrisCatlin 13 14
(Ian Williams) *a towards rr* **20/1**

-200 **16** *14* **Rahere (IRE)**[32] 6049 3-8-6 65 RoystonFfrench 6 —
(M Johnston) *led: rdn along 4f out: sn hdd & wknd* **16/1**

0006 **17** *13* **My Paris**[16] 6487 7-9-0 73 FrederikTylicki(5) 2 —
(Ollie Pears) *sddle slipped sn after s: t.k.h and chsd ldrs on inner tl wknd qckly over 3f out* **11/1**

2m 17.27s (3.57) **Going Correction** +0.40s/f (Good)
WFA 3 from 4yo+ 5lb **17** Ran SP% **125.8**
Speed ratings (Par 103): **101,100,99,97,96 96,95,94,93,91 88,84,83,81,75 63,53**
toteswinger: 1&2 £105.80, 1&3 £76.80, 2&3 £72.50. CSF £439.39 CT £7945.79 TOTE £29.80: £4.50, £5.90, £2.30, £1.40; EX 887.00 TRIFECTA Not won. Place 6 £171.64, Place 5 £49.69.
Owner Geoffrey Van Cutsem **Bred** The Lavington Stud **Trained** Settrington, N Yorks

FOCUS
A pretty competitive handicap and a shock result. Ordinary form, rated through the second and third.
Lilburn(IRE) Official explanation: jockey said gelding lost its action
My Paris Official explanation: jockey said saddle slipped
T/Jkpt: Not won. T/Plt: £100.10 to a £1 stake. Pool: £72,044.89. 525.33 winning tickets. T/Qpdt: £36.30 to a £1 stake. Pool: £3,822.20. 77.80 winning tickets. JR

6700 WINDSOR (R-H)
Monday, October 20

OFFICIAL GOING: Good to firm (good in places) changing to good to soft (good in places) after race 4 (4.00)
Wind: Moderate, half behind Weather: Overcast, rain from race 3 onwards

6863 LADBROKES/RACING POST WINNER, D A KELLY MEDIAN AUCTION MAIDEN STKS 5f 10y
2:30 (2:31) (Class 5) 2-Y-O **£3,753** (£1,108; £554) **Stalls** High

Form RPR
622 **1** **Kheleyf's Silver (IRE)**[13] 6548 2-8-12 68 RichardMullen 11 73
(B Smart) *mde all: drvn over 1f out: kpt on wl fnl f* **5/2**[1]

302 **2** *½* **Albertine Rose**[31] 6089 2-8-12 72 MartinDwyer 7 71
(W R Muir) *hld up bhd ldrs: prog to go 2nd jst over 1f out: drvn to chal ins fnl f: nt qckn last 75yds* **8/1**

05 **3** *1 ¾* **Desert Strike**[17] 6434 2-9-3 0 ShaneKelly 5 70
(P F I Cole) *prom: chsd wnr 2f out to jst over 1f out: one pce* **25/1**

2300 **4** *1* **Sonhador**[33] 6023 2-9-3 68 StephenCarson 12 66
(P Winkworth) *chsd ldrs: hrd rdn over 1f out: kpt on one pce* **14/1**

44 **5** *1 ½* **Hand Painted**[97] 4050 2-9-3 0 TravisBlock 15 61
(P J Makin) *in tch in midfield: eased off rail and effrt over 2f out: shkn up and kpt on: nvr trbld ldrs* **9/1**

6 **6** *1* **Diamond Twister (USA)**[21] 6342 2-9-3 0 SteveDrowne 14 57
(J R Best) *in tch but sn pushed along: struggling 2f out: kpt on u.p fnl f* **7/1**[3]

04 **7** *1 ¼* **Lujeanie**[21] 6342 2-9-0 0 JackMitchell(3) 9 53
(D K Ivory) *dwlt: rcvrd and sn in tch in midfield: outpcd fr 2f out* **33/1**

4402 **8** *1 ¾* **Rossett Rose (IRE)**[13] 6547 2-8-12 64 AdrianTNicholls 3 42
(M Brittain) *in tch in midfield on outer: outpcd fr 2f out* **33/1**

3533 **9** *hd* **You've Been Mowed**[20] 6350 2-8-12 69 DaneO'Neill 10 41
(D K Ivory) *chsd wnr to 2f out: steadily wknd* **8/1**

454 **10** *1 ¼* **Bartica (IRE)**[31] 6072 2-9-3 68 FrancisNorton 4 44+
(R Hannon) *dwlt: outpcd and bhd: jst sing to stay on fnl f but no ch and eased* **12/1**

5 **11** *1 ½* **Compton Blue**[11] 6600 2-9-3 0 RyanMoore 6 36
(R Hannon) *outpcd and bhd: nvr a factor: kpt on modestly fnl f* **11/1**

05 **12** *1 ¾* **Esprit De Midas**[19] 6389 2-9-3 0 JamieSpencer 13 39+
(K A Ryan) *stmbld sn after s: rdn at rr of main field: a struggling* **4/1**[2]

54 **13** *nk* **Mary West (IRE)**[13] 6548 2-8-12 0 JamieMoriarty 16 24
(R A Fahey) *prom tl wknd rapidly 2f out* **22/1**

14 *8* **Kiss A Prince** 2-8-12 0 JamesO'Reilly(5) 2 —
(D K Ivory) *s.s: outpcd and a t.o* **100/1**

15 *1 ¾* **Rio Ramus (IRE)** 2-9-0 0 LukeMorris(3) 8 —
(R A Teal) *taken down early and walked to post: s.s: rcvrd and jst in tch 1/2-way: hanging and green on outer after: wknd: t.o* **40/1**

59.68 secs (-0.62) **Going Correction** -0.175s/f (Firm) **15** Ran SP% **133.5**
Speed ratings (Par 95): **97,96,93,91,89 87,85,83,82,80 78,75,75,62,59**
toteswinger: 1&2 £4.30, 1&3 £34.60, 2&3 £45.90. CSF £24.33 TOTE £3.60: £1.40, £3.00, £13.30; EX 18.20 TRIFECTA Not won..
Owner H E Sheikh Rashid Bin Mohammed **Bred** Shane Doyle **Trained** Hambleton, N Yorks

FOCUS
An ordinary juvenile maiden. They raced stands' side and a high draw was an advantage.

NOTEBOOK
Kheleyf's Silver(IRE) had been narrowly beaten into second in similar races at Catterick on her last couple of starts, but she just proved good enough this time. Quickly away, she showed bags of early speed and kept on well in the straight once bagging the stands' rail. This will have boosted her paddock value, but this looks as good as she is. (op 3-1 tchd 7-2 in a place and 10-3 in places)
Albertine Rose arguably looked the most likely winner when produced with her chance inside the final two furlongs, and her rider didn't go for the whip until about 100 yards out, but she was unable to get there.
Desert Strike was far from ideally drawn, but he ran a good race, improving on the form he showed in a couple of starts on sand, and he now has the option of handicaps.
Sonhador has had a few chances, but this was a respectable effort. (op 20-1)
Hand Painted was never a threat, but he is entitled to be sharper for this first run in over three months and he should do better in handicaps, probably back over another furlong. (op 17-2 tchd 8-1)
Diamond Twister(USA) still looked green, but he was keeping on at the finish and can do better, possibly over further. (op 12-1)
Lujeanie gave the impression he will have more to offer now he is qualified for a handicap mark.

Esprit De Midas had looked to be getting the idea when fifth at Nottingham on his previous start but was the disappointment of the race. After stumbling slightly on leaving the stalls, he was immediately driven along but made no progress before being heavily eased close home. This good-looking son of Namid should do better back on easier ground, and he is now qualified for a handicap mark. He was reported to be lame on his near fore. Official explanation: vet said colt returned lame near-fore (op 11-2 tchd 6-1)

6864 LADBROKES ODDS ON VICTORIA NEWBURY SHOP CLAIMING STKS 6f

3:00 (3:01) (Class 6) 3-Y-0+ **£2,388** (£705; £352) **Stalls** High

Form RPR

1060 **1** **Stand In Flames**[26] 6200 3-8-7 78 ShaneKelly 4 76
(Pat Eddery) *sn trckd ldr: led 2f out: edgd lft over 1f out: drvn and hld on wl last 100yds* **10/1**

0034 **2** *hd* **Mutamared (USA)**[10] 6624 8-9-3 87 EddieAhern 2 84
(K A Ryan) *dwlt: hld up in rr: stdy prog on outer over 2f out and gng wl: drvn to chal 1f out: edgd lft: jst hld* **4/1**[1]

0000 **3** *nse* **Dressed To Dance (IRE)**[36] 5936 4-9-2 83 (v) JohnEgan 12 83
(P D Evans) *dwlt: wl in rr: prog over 2f out: hrd rdn to chal 1f out: edgd lft and nt qckn* **7/1**[3]

1010 **4** *nse* **Obe Brave**[17] 6448 5-8-10 75 JamieMoriarty 6 77
(R A Fahey) *hld up wl in rr: nt clr run over 2f out: prog wl over 1f out: styd on wl u.p fnl f: fin best* **8/1**

0234 **5** *3/4* **Hart Of Gold**[4] 6750 4-8-6 67 KevinGhunowa(3) 13 74
(R A Harris) *trckd ldrs: disp 2nd wl over 1f out: hrd rdn and edgd lft: nt qckn fnl f* **13/2**[2]

4600 **6** *1 1/4* **Scarlet Oak**[8] 6671 4-8-2 63 (p) WilliamBuick 5 63
(D J S Ffrench Davis) *dwlt: wl in rr: swtchd to inner and effrt 2f out: hrd rdn over 1f out: kpt on but nt rch ldrs* **33/1**

2440 **7** *4 1/2* **Tina's Best (IRE)**[8] 6675 3-8-5 76 FrancisNorton 15 52
(R Hannon) *s.i.s: wl in rr: modest prog fr over 1f out: nvr on terms* **13/2**[2]

1200 **8** *hd* **Farthermost (IRE)**[7] 6699 3-9-1 79 RyanMoore 10 62
(R Hannon) *chsd ldrs: lost pl over 2f out: rdn and no prog after* **4/1**[1]

1455 **9** *1 1/2* **Our Acquaintance**[21] 6328 3-8-12 65 (b) MartinDwyer 16 54
(W R Muir) *trckd ldrs: tried to chal on inner 2f out: sn wknd* **25/1**

032 **10** *1 1/4* **Trinculo (IRE)**[47] 5601 11-8-0 63 (b) AndreaAtzeni(7) 9 44
(R A Harris) *racd on outer: trckd ldrs: rdn over 2f out: sn lost pl* **16/1**

3400 **11** *4* **A Wish For You**[56] 5346 3-7-12 64 (p) CharlotteKerton(7) 3 30
(D K Ivory) *a in rr: swtchd to outer bef 1/2-way: no prog* **66/1**

3200 **12** *1 1/4* **Double Bill (USA)**[30] 6137 4-9-2 67 NelsonDeSouza 14 36
(P F I Cole) *led to 2f out: wknd rapidly* **33/1**

1000 **13** *9* **Gleaming Spirit (IRE)**[32] 6039 4-8-13 64 (v) RichardMullen 11 4
(A P Jarvis) *trckd ldrs tl wknd rapidly over 2f out: t.o* **25/1**

1m 11.75s (-1.25) **Going Correction** -0.175s/f (Firm)
WFA 3 from 4yo+ 1lb 13 Ran SP% **120.3**
Speed ratings (Par 101): **101,100,100,100,99 97,91,91,89,88 82,81,69**
toteswinger: 1&2 £10.00, 1&3 £14.00, 2&3 £3.60. CSF £47.81 TOTE £15.40: £3.40, £1.60, £2.20; EX 59.50 Trifecta £80.40 Part won. Pool: £108.66 - 0.20 winning units..Obe Brave was claimed by B. W. Duke for £9,000. Scarlet Oak was claimed by Gary P. Martin for £6,000.
Owner Chris Hardy **Bred** Chris E Hardy **Trained** Nether Winchendon, Bucks

FOCUS
A good, competitive claimer and the first four were covered by just over a head at the line. The principals drifted towards the middle of the track late on. The first three were all 8lb+ off their best efforts this term with the fifth looking the best guide to the form.
Dressed To Dance(IRE) Official explanation: jockey said filly missed the break
Gleaming Spirit(IRE) Official explanation: jockey said gelding failed to handle the ground

6865 RACINGDIARY.COM NURSERY 6f

3:30 (3:31) (Class 5) (0-70,69) 2-Y-0 **£3,753** (£1,108; £554) **Stalls** High

Form RPR

653 **1** **Final Salute**[25] 6229 2-9-5 67 (v) RichardMullen 10 71
(B Smart) *w ldrs 2f: lost pl 1/2-way: n.m.r over 1f out: got out and r.o strly fnl f to ld last strides* **16/1**

042 **2** *1/2* **Ben's Dream (IRE)**[19] 6389 2-9-7 69 WilliamBuick 2 72
(A M Balding) *trckd ldrs on outer: wnt 2nd over 2f out: rdn to ld ent fnl f: styd on: mown down last strides* **7/2**[1]

0450 **3** *1 1/4* **Mr Flannegan**[46] 5647 2-9-3 65 (v[1]) DaneO'Neill 11 64
(H Candy) *w ldr: led 1/2-way: hdd ent fnl f: one pce* **20/1**

3000 **4** *3* **Night Lily (IRE)**[20] 6362 2-9-3 68 LukeMorris(3) 8 58
(J Jay) *sn pushed along in midfield: lost pl and struggling 1/2-way: kpt on again u.p fr over 1f out* **14/1**

405 **5** *nk* **Graycliffe (IRE)**[19] 6384 2-9-3 65 JamieMoriarty 7 54
(R A Fahey) *dwlt: sn rcvrd to chse ldrs: hrd rdn over 2f out: outpcd fr over 1f out* **25/1**

0521 **6** *3/4* **Cocktail Party (IRE)**[12] 6579 2-9-1 63 EddieAhern 15 54+
(J W Hills) *hld up bhd ldrs: nt clr run 2f out: no ch after: modest late prog* **8/1**

0454 **7** *nk* **Assent (IRE)**[12] 6579 2-9-1 66 JamesMillman(3) 14 55+
(B R Millman) *stdd s: hld up in rr: swtchd to inner and nt clr run 2f out: bmpd over 1f out: kpt on fnl f* **15/2**

053 **8** *1/2* **Arachnophobia (IRE)**[19] 6389 2-9-1 63 PaulEddery 3 47
(Pat Eddery) *dwlt: wl in rr: prog on wd outside over 2f out: hld whn rdr dropped whip over 1f out* **6/1**[3]

4200 **9** *1/2* **Granski (IRE)**[22] 6305 2-9-7 69 RyanMoore 6 52+
(R Hannon) *led to 1/2-way: wknd wl over 1f out* **11/2**[2]

4520 **10** *hd* **Sea Crest**[46] 5633 2-9-4 66 AdrianTNicholls 9 48+
(M Brittain) *stdd s: hld up in last pair: shuffled along 1/2-way: nvr nr ldrs but styd on steadily* **33/1**

41 **11** *1 1/2* **Piccolinda**[36] 5939 2-9-6 68 MartinDwyer 1 46
(W R Muir) *w ldrs to over 2f out: steadily wknd* **12/1**

3040 **12** *1 1/4* **My Best Man**[18] 6414 2-9-7 69 TGMcLaughlin 4 43+
(B R Millman) *chsd ldrs on outer: rdn 2f out: fading whn n.m.r over 1f out* **25/1**

000 **13** *3/4* **Bob Stock (IRE)**[14] 6531 2-9-4 66 JohnEgan 13 38
(W J Musson) *stdd s: sn wl in rr and styd there: do bttr* **14/1**

0260 **14** *6* **Song Of Praise**[33] 6023 2-9-1 63 SteveDrowne 16 17
(M Blanshard) *hld up bhd ldrs on inner: losing grnd whn bmpd over 1f out: eased* **50/1**

030 **15** *49* **D'Nurse (IRE)**[52] 5461 2-9-2 67 PatrickHills(3) 12 —
(R Hannon) *a wl in rr: taken to outer 1/2-way: sn wknd: virtually p.u fnl f: dead* **25/1**

1m 12.56s (-0.44) **Going Correction** -0.175s/f (Firm) 15 Ran SP% **122.9**
Speed ratings (Par 95): **95,94,92,88,88 87,86,86,85,85 83,81,80,72,7**
toteswinger: 1&2 £16.60, 1&3 £109.60, 2&3 £26.80. CSF £66.69 CT £1194.18 TOTE £20.90: £4.50, £1.90, £8.00; EX 101.50 Trifecta £128.70 Part won. Pool: £174.00 - 0.39 winning units..
Owner H E Sheikh Rashid Bin Mohammed **Bred** Bricklow Ltd **Trained** Hambleton, N Yorks

FOCUS
A modest but competitive nursery.

NOTEBOOK
Final Salute showed himself on a good mark on his nursery debut. He did not enjoy the best of runs in the straight, having to be switched a couple of times, but his rider felt he might just be the type who is kept interested by finding a bit of trouble, and he picked up really well once in the clear. While he probably would have been an unlucky loser had he not got a run, it's still fair to say that the runner-up was a little unfortunate. (op 14-1 tchd 12-1)
Ben's Dream(IRE) was a little unfortunate as he was forced to race wide for much of the way from stall two, and was just caught. He showed loads of pace and should do even better back over 5f. (op 5-1)
Mr Flannegan seemed to have his chance in a first-time visor, and ran with credit.
Night Lily(IRE), representing an in-form yard, was keeping on at the finish having been outpaced.
Graycliffe(IRE) ran as though he will be happier back over further. Official explanation: jockey said colt hung left
Cocktail Party(IRE) had nowhere to go when looking to make her move inside the final two furlongs and is much better than she was able to show. Official explanation: jockey said filly hung right (tchd 10-1)
Assent(IRE) was blocked off when trying to pick up, but for which he would have finished closer. (op 8-1)
Arachnophobia(IRE) is a little better than he showed as he was stuck out wide throughout from his low draw and soon had to be driven along having started slowly. He had little chance of getting involved when stuck out towards the middle of the track in the straight and his rider had his whip knocked out of his hand over a furlong out, before easing off when held in the final 50 yards. Easier ground should suit better. (op 5-1)
Granski(IRE) showed early speed, but finished up well held and could not justify a market move. (op 8-1)
Bob Stock(IRE) caught the eye down the field but was reported to have a breathing problem. Official explanation: trainer's rep said colt had a breathing problem (op 12-1)

6866 LADBROKES ODDS ON JOHN BUTLER H'CAP 1m 3f 135y

4:00 (4:01) (Class 3) (0-90,92) 3-Y-0 **£9,714** (£2,890; £1,444; £721) **Stalls** Low

Form RPR

2123 **1** **Inchwood (IRE)**[30] 6127 3-9-4 89 DarryllHolland 8 100
(M A Jarvis) *led to over 5f out: pushed up to ld again over 2f out: pressed over 1f out: forged clr fnl f* **3/1**[1]

6-1 **2** *4 1/2* **Jaadull**[14] 6530 3-9-0 85 JamieSpencer 5 88
(M Johnston) *awkward s: hld up in last: prog and cl up 2f out: wnt 2nd fnl f but easily outpcd by wnr* **7/2**[2]

1513 **3** *1/2* **Fair Gale**[24] 6238 3-9-2 87 GeorgeBaker 7 89
(S Kirk) *cl up: wnt 2nd 2f out and sn chalng: brushed aside fnl f* **9/2**

1526 **4** *1* **King Supreme (IRE)**[16] 6479 3-8-8 79 (b) RyanMoore 3 79
(R Hannon) *hld up in 5th: effrt 3f out: tried to cl 2f out: sn nt qckn and btn* **4/1**[3]

116 **5** *nse* **Rowan Rio**[33] 6012 3-9-0 85 LiamJones 4 85
(W J Haggas) *mostly trckd wnr: quick move to ld over 5f out: hdd over 2f out: no ex* **15/2**

1232 **6** *27* **Summer Winds**[151] 2327 3-8-7 78 SteveDrowne 1 32
(T G Mills) *trckd ldrs: pushed along 4f out: wknd and eased wl over 2f out: t.o* **7/1**

2m 31.79s (2.29) **Going Correction** +0.325s/f (Good) 6 Ran SP% **109.7**
Speed ratings (Par 105): **105,102,101,101,100 82**
toteswinger: 1&2 £2.10, 1&3 £1.90, 2&3 £3.10. CSF £13.00 CT £40.86 TOTE £3.10: £1.70, £2.00; EX 7.40 Trifecta £26.70 Pool: £258.35 - 7.14 winning units..
Owner Sheikh Ahmed Al Maktoum **Bred** Woodcote Stud Ltd **Trained** Newmarket, Suffolk

FOCUS
This race was run in driving rain and the ground was duly changed afterwards to good to soft, good in places. A good three-year-old handicap, but the early pace was just steady. The winner showed herself on a fair mark, with the second up 4lb and the third to form.

NOTEBOOK
Inchwood(IRE) was allowed to dictate on her own terms early on and, although taken on and passed by Rowan Rio over half a mile out, her rider never looked worried. She picked up really nicely when asked in the straight and had clearly saved plenty for the relative dash to the line. This was a decent performance, regardless of the way the race was run, and she is progressing into a very useful filly. (op 5-2 tchd 9-4 and 10-3 in a place)
Jaadull, off the mark in a 1m Pontefract maiden last time, was held up in last after starting slowly and the steady pace cannot have been ideal. He stayed on in the straight, but was never getting to the winner, who enjoyed the run of the race. (op 11-4)
Fair Gale was never too far away, with his rider clearly alive to the lack of pace in the race, and he had his chance. (op 5-1)
King Supreme(IRE) might have preferred a stronger pace, but he basically looks high enough in the weights. (op 6-1)
Rowan Rio, whose rider tried to ensure Inchwood did not get things all her own way, was below form despite the rain arriving in time for him. (op 8-1 tchd 9-1)

6867 SUPERIOR SAUSAGE COMPANY H'CAP 1m 67y

4:30 (4:31) (Class 5) (0-70,70) 3-Y-0+ **£3,753** (£1,108; £554) **Stalls** High

Form RPR

034 **1** **Mister Ross**[48] 5587 3-8-12 65 RyanMoore 4 89
(G L Moore) *mde all: led field to centre over 3f out: drew rt away fr over 2f out: edgd rt to nr side rail 1f out: styd on strly* **5/1**[1]

4405 **2** *8* **Hawaana (IRE)**[18] 6416 3-9-3 70 PaulDoe 9 76
(Eve Johnson Houghton) *a chsng wnr: lft bhd fr over 2f out but clr of rest and in n.d of losing 2nd over 1f out* **8/1**[3]

4034 **3** *3 3/4* **Vigano (IRE)**[18] 6420 3-9-2 69 GeorgeBaker 13 66
(S Kirk) *trckd ldrs: prog to go 3rd over 3f out: lft bhd by ldng pair fr over 2f out: kpt on* **16/1**

5263 **4** *2 1/4* **Tanforan**[12] 6585 6-8-3 60 BillyCray(7) 7 52
(B P J Baugh) *hld up in midfield: effrt over 3f out: modest 4th over 1f out: no ch* **14/1**

3401 **5** *1 3/4* **Sofia's Star**[14] 6544 3-9-3 70 StephenCarson 6 58
(P Winkworth) *hld up: last 1/2-way: hrd rdn over 2f out: plugged on fnl 2f: no ch* **5/1**[1]

2103 **6** *1/2* **Run For Ede'S**[58] 5291 4-8-12 67 (p) JackDean(5) 14 54
(P M Phelan) *hld up in midfield: effrt over 3f out: sn rdn and no prog* **12/1**

3002 **7** *1 1/4* **Marvo**[8] 6675 4-9-6 70 SaleemGolam 2 54
(M H Tompkins) *hld up in last trio: rdn over 3f out: nvr on terms after* **7/1**[2]

650 **8** *1/2* **Cross The Line (IRE)**[56] 5350 6-9-0 64 RichardMullen 5 47
(A P Jarvis) *trckd ldrs: rdn over 3f out: sn lft bhd* **9/1**

0350 **9** *2* **Aegean Pride**[20] 6356 3-8-9 62 DaneO'Neill 11 40
(R Hannon) *dwlt: hld up towards rr: effrt on outer and sme prog 3f out: sn struggling* **12/1**

6005 **10** *4 1/2* **Summer Dancer (IRE)**[28] 6177 4-9-5 69 MartinDwyer 12 37
(D R C Elsworth) *t.k.h early: prom tl wknd 3f out: sn bhd* **8/1**[3]

4300 **11** *1 1/2* **Young Bertie**[21] 6336 5-9-4 68 (v) TravisBlock 10 33
(H Morrison) *trckd ldrs: rdn 3f out: wknd over 2f out* **12/1**

0404 **12** ½ **Wavertree Warrior (IRE)**[63] 5144 6-9-5 69 (v[1]) JamesDoyle 1 32
(N P Littmoden) *hld up in rr: c wd 4f out: sn rdn and struggling* **20/1**
0600 **13** 5 **Rock Anthem (IRE)**[28] 6177 4-8-13 63 ShaneKelly 8 15
(Mike Murphy) *s.s and lost at least 6 l: ct up at rr after 3f: wknd 3f out: sn bhd* **33/1**
1000 **14** 9 **The Gaikwar (IRE)**[12] 6570 9-8-0 57 (b) AndreaAtzeni(7) 3 —
(R A Harris) *nvr beyond midfield: rdn over 3f out: wknd: t.o* **25/1**
1m 46.24s (1.54) **Going Correction** +0.325s/f (Good)
WFA 3 from 4yo+ 3lb **14** Ran SP% **125.2**
Speed ratings (Par 103): **105,97,93,91,89 88,87,87,85,80 79,78,73,64**
toteswinger: 1&2 £7.80, 1&3 £15.80, 2&3 £38.70. CSF £44.82 CT £632.98 TOTE £4.10: £2.10, £2.90, £5.30; EX 58.50 TRIFECTA Not won..
Owner Mrs Patricia Pink **Bred** C D S Bryce And Mrs M Bryce **Trained** Woodingdean, E Sussex

FOCUS
A modest handicap in which the winner and second were 1-2 nearly throughout. The form has been rated at face value, with massive improvement from Mister Ross.

6868 SEASON FINALE AT ROYAL WINDSOR RACECOURSE H'CAP 1m 2f 7y
5:00 (5:00) (Class 6) (0-65,65) 3-Y-O £2,729 (£806; £403) **Stalls** Low

Form RPR
0000 **1** **Sainglend**[102] 3886 3-9-4 65 PaulDoe 8 76+
(S Curran) *trckd ldrs: effrt in centre to ld 2f out: sn hrd pressed: forged clr fnl f* **7/1**[3]
642 **2** 2 **Orange River (IRE)**[21] 6331 3-9-4 65 RyanMoore 3 71
(J H M Gosden) *dwlt: towards rr: rdn and prog over 3f out: jnd wnr wl over 1f out: one pce fnl f* **9/2**[2]
0640 **3** 1½ **Danamight (IRE)**[33] 6028 3-9-2 63 RichardMullen 7 66
(J L Dunlop) *hld up towards rr: prog and carried to far side fr 3f out: tried to chal over 1f out: one pce* **8/1**
1360 **4** 2¼ **Paddy Rielly (IRE)**[2] 6827 3-9-0 61 (p) JohnEgan 15 60
(P D Evans) *trckd ldng pair: nt qckn u.p 3f out and lost pl: kpt on again fr over 1f out* **9/1**
5353 **5** ½ **Coral Shores**[25] 6235 3-9-2 63 (v) DarrenWilliams 5 61
(P W Hiatt) *pressed ldr: led over 3f out to 2f out: nt qckn: kpt on fnl f* **14/1**
0351 **6** 1¼ **Catholic Hill (USA)**[19] 6374 3-8-13 60 JamieSpencer 2 55
(B J Meehan) *t.k.h early and hld up in midfield: hanging lft bnd 6f out: hung lft towards far side 3f out: on terms w ldrs 2f out: fdd* **7/2**[1]
0-45 **7** nk **Royal Manor**[23] 6275 3-9-1 62 DaneO'Neill 12 56
(N J Vaughan) *hld up in tch: gng wl enough over 3f out: nt qckn over 2f out: plugged on* **9/2**[2]
4000 **8** nk **Where's Susie**[82] 4524 3-9-0 61 (p) RobertHavlin 9 55
(D K Ivory) *hld up wl in rr: sme prog 2f out: kpt on fr over 1f out: nrst fin but n.d* **20/1**
0050 **9** 10 **Road To Hucking (GER)**[102] 3873 3-9-1 62 SteveDrowne 4 36
(J R Best) *sn hld up in midfield: no prog 3f out: wknd sn after* **50/1**
560 **10** 3¼ **Danesman**[47] 5608 3-9-4 65 GeorgeBaker 16 32
(G L Moore) *hld up in rr: no prog 3f out: sn bhd* **12/1**
-066 **11** 7 **Danse The Blues**[5] 6741 3-9-4 65 WilliamBuick 10 18
(E A L Dunlop) *chsd ldrs: rdn 4f out: wknd 3f out* **10/1**
1000 **12** 4½ **Mont Cervin**[9] 6663 3-9-4 65 PaulEddery 13 9
(Ian Williams) *dwlt: a wl in rr: bhd fnl 2f* **33/1**
3340 **13** 8 **Gang Show (IRE)**[18] 6417 3-9-3 64 (t) EddieAhern 11 —
(W J Musson) *led to over 3f out: wknd rapidly* **33/1**
5020 **14** 13 **Plenilune (IRE)**[26] 6216 3-9-4 65 (b[1]) AdrianTNicholls 6 —
(M Brittain) *a last: t.o* **25/1**
2m 14.29s (5.59) **Going Correction** +0.55s/f (Yiel) **14** Ran SP% **132.1**
Speed ratings (Par 99): **99,97,96,94,94 93,92,92,84,81 76,72,66,55**
toteswinger: 1&2 £8.60, 1&3 £9.70, 2&3 £10.30. CSF £40.41 CT £274.91 TOTE £8.30: £2.70, £2.30, £4.10; EX 68.60 TRIFECTA Not won. Place 6 £142.68, Place 5 £56.60.
Owner W J M Byrne **Bred** Penfold Bloodstock Ltd **Trained** Hatford, Oxon

FOCUS
A moderate handicap. They were spread across the track in the straight, but the main action took place towards the far rail. The winner returned to something like his 2yo form.
Where's Susie Official explanation: jockey said filly was denied a clear run
T/Plt: £65.10 to a £1 stake. Pool: £67,574.89. 756.96 winning tickets. T/Qpdt: £29.40 to a £1 stake. Pool: £3,684.80. 92.70 winning tickets. JN

6736 LINGFIELD (L-H)
Tuesday, October 21

OFFICIAL GOING: Standard
Wind: Moderate, across Weather: Fine

6876 FOREST ROW MAIDEN AUCTION STKS (DIV I) 7f (P)
2:00 (2:01) (Class 6) 2-Y-O £1,942 (£578; £288; £144) **Stalls** Low

Form RPR
00 **1** **Take The Micky**[34] 6031 2-8-11 0 ShaneKelly 7 74
(W J Knight) *prom: led jst ins fnl f: drvn out* **3/1**[2]
0 **2** 1¼ **Freepressionist**[14] 6555 2-8-4 0 WilliamBuick 10 64
(R A Teal) *led: rdn and sltly wd ent st: hdd jst ins fnl f: kpt on* **20/1**
4236 **3** hd **Our Day Will Come**[36] 5959 2-8-10 73 EddieAhern 8 69
(R Hannon) *in tch: effrt over 2f out: pressed runner-up fnl f: r.o* **2/1**[1]
4 2¼ **Zim Ho** 2-8-9 0 JimCrowley 1 62
(J Akehurst) *dwlt: sn in tch: n.m.r and lost pl 5f out: hmpd 4f out: rdn and hdwy over 1f out: nt rch first 3* **14/1**
66 **5** nk **Strathcal**[20] 6375 2-8-13 0 TravisBlock 4 66
(H Morrison) *towards rr: rdn 1/2-way: styd on fnl 2f: nrst fin* **5/1**[3]
0 **6** 1½ **Thaumatology (USA)**[20] 6375 2-8-8 0 RobertWinston 11 57
(M Botti) *mid-div: hdwy to press ldrs 4f out: outpcd fnl 2f* **14/1**
46 **7** nk **Noble Dictator**[76] 4747 2-8-11 0 SteveDrowne 3 59
(E F Vaughan) *towards rr: pushed along 3f out: styd on u.p appr fnl f: nt rch ldrs* **7/1**
0 **8** ½ **Duke's Emerald**[41] 5798 2-8-9 0 JoeFanning 12 56
(J A R Toller) *s.i.s: wd: bhd tl hdwy on outside 4f out: sn chsng ldrs: outpcd and btn 2f out* **33/1**
0 **9** 1¼ **Lambourn Genie (UAE)**[60] 5227 2-9-1 0 RichardKingscote 2 59
(Tom Dascombe) *t.k.h: prom: stdd towards rr after 2f: shkn up and sme hdwy ent st: sn wknd* **20/1**
10 1½ **Rubbinghousedotcom (IRE)** 2-8-11 0 IanMongan 9 51
(P M Phelan) *bhd: rdn 3f out: n.d* **40/1**
4004 **11** 1 **Captain Kallis (IRE)**[22] 6333 2-8-11 52 ChrisCatlin 5 49
(D J S Ffrench Davis) *plld hrd in rr: n.m.r on rail first bnd: rdn 1/2-way: nvr a factor* **33/1**
0000 **12** shd **Tightrope (IRE)**[24] 6282 2-8-4 54 AndreaAtzeni(7) 6 48
(T D McCarthy) *t.k.h: prom: rdn 1/2-way: wknd qckly over 1f out* **100/1**
1m 24.87s (0.07) **Going Correction** -0.15s/f (Stan) **12** Ran SP% **119.7**
Speed ratings (Par 93): **93,91,91,88,88 86,86,85,84,82 81,81**
toteswinger: 1&2 £21.80, 1&3 £2.90, 2&3 £11.40. CSF £69.30 TOTE £3.50: £1.80, £6.90, £1.10; EX 82.40.
Owner Botham, Dale, Nunns & Shopland **Bred** Peter Botham **Trained** Patching, W Sussex

FOCUS
A modest maiden auction event and a couple were tight for room rounding the first bend. Not many ever really got involved and the front three had quickened clear by the time the field reached the furlong pole.

NOTEBOOK
Take The Micky had disappointed at Yarmouth last time after showing ability on his Newmarket debut, but he confirmed the promise of that initial effort with a clear-cut victory here. Never far away, he produced a nice turn of foot to cut down the pacemaker and won going away. He will be put away now. (op 7-2)
Freepressionist, green on her Folkestone debut and up a furlong here, proved a totally different proposition this time under a positive ride. It seemed as though she might see it out and cause a surprise rounding the home turn, but she hung away to her right and the winner made full use of the gap she left up her inside. She obviously has a future. (op 25-1)
Our Day Will Come, already placed a couple of times and back up to a more suitable trip, set the standard with an official rating of 73. She did run into some traffic problems on the first bend, but she still had every chance and can't have too many excuses. She has already been beaten off a 1lb higher mark in a nursery, so it's difficult to know quite where she goes from here. (op 6-4)
Zim Ho, a half-brother to two winners over this trip, cost just £800 and although he was very well supported earlier in the day, he was relatively weak on track. He showed why there was money for him though with a very solid debut effort, especially as he pulled hard early and was another to meet trouble on the first bend. (op 10-1)
Strathcal never really threatened, but now qualifies for a mark so improvement is a possibility. (op 6-1)
Thaumatology(USA), around four lengths behind Strathcal on her Kempton debut, finished a bit closer this time after racing handily throughout and is another likely to come into her own in handicaps after one more run. (op 10-1)
Captain Kallis(IRE) Official explanation: jockey said colt ran too free
Tightrope(IRE) Official explanation: vet said colt had been struck into

6877 FOREST ROW MAIDEN AUCTION STKS (DIV II) 7f (P)
2:30 (2:36) (Class 6) 2-Y-O £1,942 (£578; £288; £144) **Stalls** Low

Form RPR
4202 **1** **Young Dottie**[18] 6432 2-8-4 71 CatherineGannon 9 75
(P M Phelan) *t.k.h: hld up in 6th: rdn and hdwy over 2f out: r.o to ld ins fnl f: sn clr* **7/1**[3]
602 **2** 4 **Piccolo Mondo**[22] 6342 2-8-9 77 JimCrowley 6 70
(P Winkworth) *chsd ldrs: rdn over 3f out: kpt on to take 2nd nr fin: nt pce of wnr* **7/2**[2]
5 **3** ½ **Test Match (IRE)**[11] 6621 2-8-13 0 MartinDwyer 5 73
(M P Tregoning) *sn rushed up to ld and set gd pce: rdn ent st: hdd & wknd ins fnl f* **6/5**[1]
23 **4** 3½ **Bea Menace (USA)**[15] 6534 2-8-10 0 JoeFanning 8 61
(P F I Cole) *prom: chsd ldr after 2f tl wknd over 1f out* **7/1**[3]
3004 **5** 2¾ **Lois Darlin (IRE)**[22] 6343 2-8-4 49 (b) TPO'Shea 7 48
(J S Moore) *sn outpcd and bhd: modest hdwy over 1f out: nvr trbld ldrs* **33/1**
6232 **6** 1¾ **Pokfulham (IRE)**[32] 6065 2-8-11 67 (v) DarrenWilliams 13 51
(A P Jarvis) *in tch: rdn over 3f out: sn btn* **9/1**
7 ¾ **Bari Bay** 2-8-4 0 WilliamBuick 1 42
(R M Beckett) *sn rdn along and detached in last pl: nvr nr ldrs* **10/1**
00 **8** 5 **Red Dagger (IRE)**[15] 6539 2-8-2 0 AndreaAtzeni(7) 10 34
(T D McCarthy) *towards rr: rdn over 4f out: bhd fnl 3f* **66/1**
9 22 **Romancingthestone** 2-8-4 0 PaulDoe 2 —
(I A Wood) *chsd ldr 2f: drvn along 1/2-way: sn wknd* **40/1**
1m 23.68s (-1.12) **Going Correction** -0.15s/f (Stan) 2y crse rec **9** Ran SP% **118.6**
Speed ratings (Par 93): **100,95,94,90,87 85,84,79,54**
toteswinger: 1&2 £4.30, 1&3 £2.90, 2&3 £1.80. CSF £32.39 TOTE £6.30: £1.80, £1.50, £1.40; EX 20.90.
Owner Tony Smith **Bred** Tony J Smith **Trained** Epsom, Surrey

FOCUS
Another modest maiden, but despite the smaller field they went a serious pace with several battling for the early lead. The winning time was 1.19 seconds faster than division one and they took 0.28 seconds off the two-year-old course record.

NOTEBOOK
Young Dottie had already made the frame a few times including when runner-up to a red-hot favourite over 1m here last time, so the strong gallop over this shorter trip was probably in her favour and she came from off the pace to cut down the leader well inside the last furlong and win going away. Currently rated 71, she was 1lb badly in with the runner-up at the weights so her future depends on how the handicapper views this. (op 8-1 tchd 5-1)
Piccolo Mondo, runner-up to a Stoute newcomer at Windsor last month in a maiden that has already produced a winner, raced prominently throughout but although he plugged on to take second he couldn't match the impetus of the winner. Rated 77, as with the filly his future may depend on how the handicapper interprets this. (tchd 3-1)
Test Match(IRE) ◆, fifth on his debut in a stronger-looking maiden on his debut over course and distance this month, soon won the battle for the early lead but he almost certainly did too much early and was running on empty inside the last furlong. A more conservative ride should see him break his duck before too long. (op 7-4 tchd 9-4)
Bea Menace(USA), placed on varying ground in her first two starts on turf, was another to have every chance having been up there from the off, but she didn't get home though it was later reported that she was in season. She now qualifies for a mark which will give her a few more options. Official explanation: vet said filly was in season (op 4-1)
Lois Darlin(IRE), previously placed at this track but beaten in a seller last time, plugged on for a remote fifth after fluffing the start but she is only rated 49 and probably didn't achieve much.

6878 MARSH GREEN (S) STKS 6f (P)
3:00 (3:05) (Class 6) 3-Y-O £1,978 (£584; £292) **Stalls** Low

Form RPR
0000 **1** **Connor's Choice**[9] 6681 3-9-0 55 ChrisCatlin 4 67
(Andrew Turnell) *trckd ldr: led over 1f out: hrd drvn fnl f: hld on narrowly nr fin* **7/1**[2]
0546 **2** shd **Celtic Spring (IRE)**[62] 5186 3-8-2 57 AndreaAtzeni(7) 3 61
(J R Boyle) *prom: drvn to chal over 1f out: kpt on u.p nr fin: narrowly hld* **5/1**[1]
020 **3** 3½ **Green Velvet**[26] 6224 3-8-9 54 RichardSmith 1 50
(P J Makin) *chsd ldrs: rdn over 2f out: one pce appr fnl f* **16/1**
6310 **4** ½ **Meridian Line (IRE)**[14] 6564 3-9-0 58 (b) RichardKingscote 10 53
(J G Portman) *hdwy to chse ldrs 3f out: rdn and outpcd 2f out: styd on fnl f* **5/1**[1]

0503 **5** ¾ **What Katie Did (IRE)**[18] 6448 3-9-0 65 ....(p) JackDean(5) 11 56
(J M Bradley) *trckd ldrs: hrd rdn wl over 1f out: one pce* **5/1**[1]
5050 **6** 1½ **Tea Cake (IRE)**[68] 5015 3-8-9 56 .... EddieAhern 9 41
(H J L Dunlop) *hld up in midfield: rdn over 2f out: no imp* **8/1**[3]
000 **7** ¾ **Usetheforce (IRE)**[7] 6716 3-9-0 60 .... ShaneKelly 7 44
(M J Wallace, Australia) *dwlt: towards rr: pushed along and briefly nt clr run 3f out: modest hdwy and hrd rdn over 1f out: n.d* **10/1**
0450 **8** 3½ **Blue Zenith (IRE)**[48] 5617 3-8-9 55 ....(b[1]) TPO'Shea 2 28
(J S Moore) *led tl wknd over 1f out* **10/1**
9 ¾ **Yxes (IRE)**[212] 3-8-9 55 .... EdwardCreighton 5 25
(E J Creighton) *dwlt: sn in mid-div: rdn over 3f out: sn wknd* **33/1**
4100 **10** ¾ **Hucking Harkness**[14] 6554 3-9-5 61 ....(b[1]) SteveDrowne 8 33
(J R Best) *in tch: rdn and wknd over 3f out: sn lost pl* **7/1**[2]
0-6 **11** *shd* **Hennalaine (IRE)**[10] 3446 3-8-9 0 .... JamesDoyle 12 22
(Miss J S Davis) *dwlt: rdn over 3f out: a bhd* **50/1**
0050 **12** 5 **Johnny McGurk**[8] 6707 3-9-0 54 ....(b) NeilPollard 6 11
(M E Rimmer) *a in rr gp: rdn 1/2-way: n.d after* **16/1**

1m 10.74s (-1.16) **Going Correction** -0.15s/f (Stan) 12 Ran SP% **121.0**
Speed ratings (Par 99): **101,100,96,95,94 92,91,86,85,84 84,78**
toteswinger: 1&2 £8.40, 1&3 £18.90, 2&3 £14.50. CSF £42.81 TOTE £9.80: £3.50, £2.70, £3.10; EX 59.90.There was no bid for the winner.
Owner Andrew Turnell **Bred** Mrs Claire Hollowood **Trained** Broad Hinton, Wilts

FOCUS
A moderate three-year-old seller and the race only concerned the front pair from the furlong pole. The time was fast and the form has been rated on the positive side.

6879 ASHURST WOOD MEDIAN AUCTION MAIDEN STKS 6f (P)
3:30 (3:32) (Class 6) 2-Y-0 **£2,266** (£674; £337; £168) **Stalls Low**

Form RPR
4304 **1** **Retro (IRE)**[9] 6677 2-9-3 77 .... EddieAhern 6 75
(R Hannon) *stdd s: sn trcking ldrs gng wl: led 1f out: rdn and r.o wl: in control fnl 50yds* **11/4**[1]
0033 **2** 1½ **Whisky Jack**[15] 6535 2-9-3 67 ....(b) MartinDwyer 2 71
(W R Muir) *hld up in midfield: rdn and hdwy 2f out: got through on rail to press wnr ins fnl f: hld fnl 50yds* **13/2**[3]
53 **3** 1 **My Best Bet**[29] 6158 2-8-12 0 .... EdwardCreighton 10 63
(M R Channon) *uns rdr bef loading: dwlt: bhd: rdn and styd on wl fnl 2f: nrst fin* **11/1**
3042 **4** *nk* **Five Star Junior (USA)**[6] 6732 2-9-3 68 .... ChrisCatlin 5 67
(S A Callaghan) *w ldr: led 3f out tl 1f out: no ex* **3/1**[2]
53 **5** 1¼ **Battle**[15] 6531 2-9-3 0 .... SteveDrowne 7 63
(H Morrison) *w ldrs: hrd rdn over 1f out: sn wknd* **11/4**[1]
00 **6** 1¼ **Hekaaya (IRE)**[12] 6600 2-8-12 0 .... WilliamBuick 9 54
(M P Tregoning) *trckd ldrs: rdn over 2f out: btn over 1f out* **18/1**
6 **7** 2½ **Molnaya (IRE)**[22] 6333 2-9-3 0 .... GeorgeBaker 11 52
(G L Moore) *dwlt: bhd: pushed along 3f out: n.d* **20/1**
8 ½ **Coeur Brule (FR)** 2-9-3 0 .... LiamJones 8 50
(J R Gask) *dwlt: sn rdn and detached in last pl: nvr trbld ldrs* **66/1**
06 **9** 1 **Aestival**[19] 6407 2-9-3 0 .... J-PGuillambert 1 47
(Sir Mark Prescott) *dwlt: sn rdn along towards rr: nvr a factor* **25/1**
00 **10** 1¾ **Merry May**[22] 6341 2-8-9 0 .... PatrickHills(3) 4 37
(R Hannon) *in tch on rail: rdn over 2f out: wknd ent st* **80/1**
0004 **11** 2 **Valdemar**[21] 6351 2-9-3 60 ....(p) SilvestreDeSousa 3 36
(A D Brown) *carried hd on one side: led 3f: hrd rdn and wknd qckly over 1f out* **33/1**

1m 11.41s (-0.49) **Going Correction** -0.15s/f (Stan) 2y crse rec 11 Ran SP% **119.5**
Speed ratings (Par 93): **97,95,93,91 89,86,85,84,82 79**
toteswinger: 1&2 £5.50, 1&3 £8.20, 2&3 £6.60. CSF £20.59 TOTE £4.10: £2.00, £1.30, £2.40; EX 18.90.
Owner Mrs J Wood **Bred** Seamus Phelan **Trained** East Everleigh, Wilts

FOCUS
A moderate maiden, but they went a decent pace early with four in a line battling for the lead entering the first bend.

NOTEBOOK
Retro(IRE) had been a bit disappointing since finishing a close third behind two 95-rated rivals at Kempton last month, but with an official rating of 77 he still set the standard in this. He held the perfect position throughout and after being produced to lead between horses inside the last furlong, he found plenty. He did no more than he was entitled to at the weights though, and his future lies in the hands of the handicapper. (op 7-2 tchd 4-1)
Whisky Jack, placed three times from six starts on turf, came from off the pace and put in a strong finish up the inside rail but could never get to the winner. He would have been 10lb better off with him in a handicap, so he has run right up to his mark. (op 7-1 tchd 6-1)
My Best Bet, third behind a subsequent winner in testing conditions at Hamilton last time, was held up off the pace but was finishing strongly at the line and may need a return to 7f on a quicker surface like this. (op 14-1 tchd 10-1)
Five Star Junior(USA), just beaten off a mark of 68 on his nursery debut at Kempton last time, should have done a bit better at the weights but he fared best of those that were battling for the early lead so deserves some credit for that. (op 2-1 tchd 7-2 and 4-1 in a place)
Battle, who has shown ability in both outings to date on turf, was another of those fighting for the early lead and he was still there when looking a little awkward rounding the home bend. He had little more to offer in the straight, but now gets a mark and he may improve for handicap company, especially on a more galloping track. (op 7-2)
Hekaaya(IRE), last in two Newbury maidens, ran a bit better here especially as she was trapped out wide throughout, and is another that may progress again now that she can be handicapped. (op 25-1)

6880 THREE BRIDGES H'CAP 6f (P)
4:00 (4:00) (Class 5) (0-70,69) 3-Y-0+ **£2,590** (£770; £385; £192) **Stalls Low**

Form RPR
4116 **1** **Lord Deevert**[87] 4413 3-8-6 62 .... JackDean(5) 12 68
(W G M Turner) *rdn to ld and crossed to ins rail fr wd draw after 1f: mde virtually all: hrd rdn and hld on wl fnl f* **25/1**
0343 **2** *nk* **Vigano (IRE)**[1] 6867 3-9-4 69 ....(v) GeorgeBaker 3 74
(S Kirk) *prom: drvn to press wnr fnl f: r.o: a narrowly hld* **7/2**[1]
1500 **3** *nse* **Kingsgate Castle**[8] 6706 3-9-1 66 ....(b) SteveDrowne 5 71
(J R Best) *chsd ldrs: hrd rdn over 1f out: r.o: a jst hld by wnr* **14/1**
-500 **4** 1¾ **Rydal (USA)**[34] 6020 7-8-12 62 ....(v) EddieAhern 1 61
(Miss Jo Crowley) *mid-div: hrd rdn and hdwy over 1f out: pressed wnr on rail ent fnl f: one pce fnl 75yds* **20/1**
0605 **5** *hd* **Sand Cat**[19] 6418 5-8-11 64 ....(b) MichaelJStainton(3) 10 63+
(G L Moore) *bhd: rdn and st: styd on wl on wl fnl f: nrst fin* **11/2**[3]
6431 **6** *nse* **Louphole**[18] 6435 6-9-5 69 .... TravisBlock 8 67
(P J Makin) *dwlt: hld up in rr: hdwy ent st: rdn to chse ldrs over 1f out: one pce* **5/1**[2]
0000 **7** ¾ **Hessian (IRE)**[31] 6125 4-9-4 68 .... ShaneKelly 11 64
(M D Squance) *in tch on outer: rdn ent st: styd on same pce* **25/1**
6000 **8** ½ **Liberty Belle (IRE)**[14] 6554 3-8-13 64 .... JimCrowley 4 58
(J R Best) *prom: hrd rdn and n.m.r over 1f out: sn wknd* **25/1**
5431 **9** *nk* **Chelsea Girl**[10] 6658 3-9-2 67 .... AdamKirby 6 60+
(C G Cox) *bmpd s: towards rr: rdn over 2f out: nvr able to chal* **7/2**[1]
2153 **10** *nk* **Bahamian Bliss**[35] 5998 3-8-13 64 .... CatherineGannon 2 57
(J A R Toller) *mid-div: rdn and outpcd 2f out: sn btn* **20/1**
0002 **11** ½ **Monsieur Reynard**[18] 6448 3-8-12 68 .... MCGeran(5) 7 59
(J M Bradley) *awkward s: plld hrd in midfield: rdn and no rspnse ent st* **16/1**
3113 **12** 2¾ **Commander Wish**[69] 4981 5-9-4 68 ....(p) LiamJones 9 50
(Lucinda Featherstone) *outpcd and bhd: no ch fnl 2f* **8/1**

1m 11.31s (-0.59) **Going Correction** -0.15s/f (Stan)
WFA 3 from 4yo+ 1lb 12 Ran SP% **121.2**
Speed ratings (Par 103): **97,96,96,94,93 93,92,92,91,91 90,87**
toteswinger: 1&2 £30.90, 1&3 £81.60, 2&3 £9.30. CSF £106.66 CT £1319.02 TOTE £34.00: £7.00, £1.90, £3.90; EX 220.40.
Owner Mrs M S Teversham **Bred** Mrs Monica Teversham **Trained** Sigwells, Somerset

FOCUS
An ordinary handicap, but quite competitive. The early pace looked solid, but the winner was able to dictate at the tempo he wanted and the winning time was 0.57 seconds slower than the seller. The form is a bit muddling.
Chelsea Girl Official explanation: jockey said filly jumped right on leaving stalls
Monsieur Reynard Official explanation: jockey said gelding ran too free

6881 WEATHERBYS BANK H'CAP 5f (P)
4:30 (4:32) (Class 5) (0-75,75) 3-Y-0+ **£2,590** (£770; £385; £192) **Stalls High**

Form RPR
0002 **1** **Wibbadune (IRE)**[10] 6658 4-9-2 73 .... AdamKirby 7 82+
(D Shaw) *patiently rdn in rr: shkn up and hdwy over 1f out: str run to ld nr fin* **5/1**[3]
5560 **2** ½ **Hereford Boy**[11] 6623 4-8-13 75 ....(b[1]) JamesO'Reilly(5) 2 82
(D K Ivory) *chsd ldrs: rdn to ld jst ins fnl f: hdd and outpcd nr fin* **9/2**[2]
4030 **3** 1¾ **Cape Royal**[5] 6750 8-8-12 72 .... KevinGhunowa(3) 4 73
(J M Bradley) *prom: effrt whn hung bdly rt and faltered over 1f out: rallied and r.o again fnl 50yds* **16/1**
2300 **4** *nk* **Asian Power (IRE)**[11] 6624 3-9-3 74 .... OscarUrbina 9 74
(P J O'Gorman) *hld up in 6th: rdn and r.o fr over 1f out: nrst fin* **7/1**
0335 **5** ½ **Angle Of Attack (IRE)**[26] 6232 3-9-2 73 .... SilvestreDeSousa 1 71
(A D Brown) *led: rdn 2f out: hdd & wknd jst ins fnl f* **4/1**[1]
0000 **6** *nse* **What Do You Know**[39] 5861 5-8-9 73 ....(v) AndreaAtzeni(7) 3 71
(A M Hales) *chsd ldrs tl wknd over 1f out* **15/2**
3010 **7** 1¾ **Enodoc**[20] 6388 3-9-0 71 .... MartinDwyer 5 63
(W R Muir) *prom: shkn up ent st: sn wknd* **8/1**
0123 **8** 2 **Desperate Dan**[5] 6750 7-8-9 73 ....(b) PNolan(7) 8 57
(A B Haynes) *missed break and lost 5 l: a detached last: drvn along after 2f: nvr rcvrd* **9/2**[2]

58.35 secs (-0.45) **Going Correction** -0.15s/f (Stan) 8 Ran SP% **114.3**
Speed ratings (Par 103): **97,96,93,92,92 92,89,86**
toteswinger: 1&2 £5.00, 1&3 £12.30, 2&3 £13.60. CSF £27.67 CT £334.29 TOTE £6.60: £2.20, £1.90, £4.80; EX 33.70.
Owner Simon Mapletoft Racing I **Bred** Ballyhane Stud **Trained** Danethorpe, Notts

FOCUS
A moderate sprint handicap, run at a strong pace and the leaders may have gone off too quick. The winner is back in top form and the race could have rated higher on paper.
Cape Royal Official explanation: jockey said gelding hung right
Enodoc Official explanation: jockey said gelding had no more to give

6882 SPELDHURST H'CAP 1m 4f (P)
5:00 (5:00) (Class 6) (0-60,63) 3-Y-0+ **£2,047** (£604; £302) **Stalls Low**

Form RPR
0201 **1** **Yes Eighteen (IRE)**[9] 6685 3-8-9 60 .... LanceBetts(7) 10 67
(J W Hills) *in tch: rdn to narrow ld 1f out: edgd lft and leant on runner-up: jnd fnl 75yds: jst prevailed* **7/1**[3]
5064 **2** *nse* **Generous Lad (IRE)**[13] 6577 5-9-6 57 ....(p) SteveDrowne 14 64
(A B Haynes) *chsd ldrs: rdn to ld briefly jst over 1f out: leant on by wnr fnl f: rallied wl to dispute ld fnl 75yds: jst pipped* **8/1**
5301 **3** ½ **Josr's Magic (IRE)**[21] 6353 4-9-9 60 .... RobertWinston 3 66
(H J Collingridge) *bhd: gd hdwy ent st: drvn to chse ldrs fnl f: r.o* **11/1**
0633 **4** *hd* **Corrib (IRE)**[15] 6538 5-9-3 54 .... CatherineGannon 9 60+
(B Palling) *mid-div: outpcd and towards rr over 2f out: rallied and r.o wl fnl f: clsng at fin* **20/1**
4344 **5** ½ **Best Selection**[34] 6019 4-9-6 57 ....(p) IanMongan 12 63+
(Mrs L J Mongan) *chsd ldrs: hrd rdn over 1f out: kpt on* **16/1**
5450 **6** ¾ **Go On Ahead (IRE)**[22] 6329 8-8-9 53 ....(p) RichardRowe(7) 2 57
(M J Coombe) *sn led: hdd jst over 1f out: 3rd and hld whn n.m.r on rail ins fnl f* **33/1**
0204 **7** *shd* **Good Effect (USA)**[15] 6538 4-9-6 57 ....(t) WilliamBuick 11 61
(C P Morlock) *prom tl wknd 1f out* **14/1**
5011 **8** *shd* **Highland Homestead**[5] 6754 3-8-12 63 6ex .... AndreaAtzeni(7) 16 67
(M R Hoad) *bhd: hdwy into midfield over 4f out: hrd rdn 2f out: styd on fnl f* **8/1**
2356 **9** 1 **Kangrina**[20] 6395 6-9-2 58 .... FrederikTylicki(5) 5 63+
(George Baker) *hld up towards rr: effrt whn nt clr run and snatched up early st: nvr able to chal* **17/2**
5013 **10** *shd* **Formidable Guest**[34] 6019 4-9-7 58 .... ChrisCatlin 8 60
(J Pearce) *mid-div: rdn and no imp fnl 2f* **13/2**[2]
0002 **11** ¾ **Pretty Demanding (IRE)**[75] 4799 4-9-9 60 .... TPO'Shea 6 61
(M G Quinlan) *trckd ldrs: rdn 2f out: sn outpcd* **12/1**
3160 **12** 1½ **Pab Special (IRE)**[41] 5799 5-9-6 57 .... PaulDoe 1 55
(B R Johnson) *bhd: rdn over 2f out: sme late hdwy* **33/1**
3150 **13** 2 **Looks The Business (IRE)**[64] 5154 7-9-2 58 ....(tp) JackDean(5) 13 53
(W G M Turner) *wd: in tch tl wknd 2f out* **25/1**
0052 **14** 6 **Silky Steps (IRE)**[18] 6436 3-9-2 60 .... EddieAhern 4 46+
(P J Makin) *mid-div: pushed along whn n.m.r on rail early st: n.d after* **9/2**[1]
15 3¼ **Able King (NZ)**[16] 8-9-3 54 .... JimCrowley 7 34
(M F Harris) *towards rr: rdn and n.d fnl 3f* **66/1**
5555 **16** ½ **Abounding**[9] 6668 4-9-8 59 .... GeorgeBaker 15 39
(M J Attwater) *pressed ldr: rdn over 2f out: wknd qckly ent st* **16/1**

2m 31.04s (-1.96) **Going Correction** -0.15s/f (Stan)
WFA 3 from 4yo+ 7lb 16 Ran SP% **127.2**
Speed ratings (Par 101): **100,99,99,99,99 98,98,98,97,97 97,96,94,90,88 88**
toteswinger: 1&2 £17.70, 1&3 £20.70, 2&3 £18.70. CSF £61.45 CT £632.57 TOTE £11.40: £3.00, £2.90, £3.90, £5.50; EX 69.20 Place 6: £65.91 Place 5: £48.31.
Owner Yes Eighteen **Bred** David F Byrne **Trained** Upper Lambourn, Berks

FOCUS
A moderate handicap, but the size of the field made it competitive. The early pace was modest though and they finished in a bit of a heap, but as often happens in such situations a couple got into real difficulties in the home straight. Ordinary form and rather messy, and it is doubtful if the winner had to improve on his Great Leighs win.
Best Selection Official explanation: jockey said filly was denied a clear run
T/Jkpt: Not won. T/Plt: £261.70 to a £1 stake. Pool: £59,400.84. 165.65 winning tickets. T/Qpdt: £152.90 to a £1 stake. Pool: £3,037.98. 14.70 winning tickets. LM

6057 YARMOUTH (L-H)
Tuesday, October 21

OFFICIAL GOING: Good (good to soft in places) changing to good to soft after race 3 (2.50)
There was a big bias towards front-runners at this meeting.
Wind: fresh across Weather: bright and breezy

6883 CRYSTAL CLEANING (S) STKS 1m 3f 101y
1:50 (1:50) (Class 6) 3-Y-O **£1,942** (£578; £288; £144) **Stalls** Low

Form RPR
0450 **1** **Hoar Frost**[5] 6747 3-9-0 52 DarryllHolland 1 57
(M R Channon) *mde virtually all: hrd pressed and drvn over 3f out: forged ahd ent fnl f: styd on dourly* **11/2**[3]
0002 **2** 4 1/2 **Ricci De Mare**[14] 6562 3-8-9 55 DavidProbert(5) 4 50
(A B Haynes) *chsd wnr: effrt and ev ch wl over 3f out: wknd fnl f* **9/2**[2]
00 **3** 1 3/4 **Colonel Sherman (USA)**[22] 6345 3-8-12 0 PatCosgrave 9 45
(Jane Chapple-Hyam) *s.i.s: t.k.h: hld up in rr: hdwy on inner over 3f out: swtchd rt ins fnl f: plugged on to snatch 3rd nr fin: nvr nr ldrs* **22/1**
0020 **4** nk **Near The Front**[14] 6562 3-8-5 55 (v) KylieManser(7) 10 45
(Miss Gay Kelleway) *chsd ldrs: hdwy 4f out: sn ev ch: wknd jst over 1f out: rdr dropped whip ins fnl f: lost 3rd nr fin* **16/1**
0005 **5** 2 1/2 **Bobal Girl**[9] 6685 3-8-8 52 ow1 (t) TPQueally 5 37
(E F Vaughan) *hld up in tch: rdn and edgd lft 3f out: no hdwy fnl 2f* **10/1**
020R **6** 1 **Bella Medici**[20] 6403 3-9-0 63 PaulMulrennan 3 41
(M H Tompkins) *dwlt: sn in tch in midfield: rdn and unable qck 3f out: no ch fr wl over 1f out* **3/1**[1]
050 **7** 3/4 **Watercolours (IRE)**[8] 6705 3-8-7 0 (p) RobertHavlin 2 33
(G L Moore) *dwlt: sn wl in tch: rdn over 3f out: struggling 3f out: no ch fnl 2f* **9/2**[2]
006- **8** 24 **Me Me Me**[419] 4946 3-8-12 45 TedDurcan 6 —
(E F Vaughan) *stdd s: hld up towards rr: rdn over 3f out: sn btn: virtually p.u fnl f: t.o* **10/1**
410 **9** 19 **Linby (IRE)**[20] 6374 3-9-5 54 TonyCulhane 7 —
(Miss Tor Sturgis) *s.i.s: hld up in last pair: rdn 3f out: sn wl btn: virtually p.u fnl f: t.o* **10/1**

2m 33.65s (4.95) **Going Correction** +0.125s/f (Good) **9** Ran SP% **114.3**
Speed ratings (Par 99): **87,83,82,82,80 79,79,61,47**
toteswinger: 1&2 £4.90, 1&3 £22.30, 2&3 £23.80. CSF £30.10 TOTE £7.10: £1.90, £1.50, £7.60; EX 31.40 TRIFECTA Not won..The winner was bought in for 3,400gns. Watercolours was claimed by J. S. Goldie for £5000.
Owner Chris & Karen Hoar **Bred** Mike Channon Bloodstock Ltd **Trained** West Ilsley, Berks
■ Stewards' Enquiry : Kylie Manser ten-day ban: failed to ride out for third place (Nov 4-13)

FOCUS
A very moderate seller and not a race to spend long on. The winner could be underrated but she had been beaten in sellers on her last three starts.
Bella Medici Official explanation: trainer said filly was unsuited by the good (good to soft in places) ground

6884 EBF/HARMAN BROS PLASTERING CONTRACTORS MAIDEN FILLIES' STKS (DIV I) 1m 3y
2:20 (2:33) (Class 5) 2-Y-O **£3,532** (£1,057; £528; £264; £131) **Stalls** High

Form RPR
1 **Bombina** 2-9-0 0 AlanMunro 5 77
(P W Chapple-Hyam) *loose bef s: led 1f: styd pressing ldrs tl led again ins fnl 3f: drvn and styd on strly thrght fnl f* **10/1**[3]
5 **2** 1 1/2 **Hometown**[27] 6205 2-9-0 0 RobertHavlin 6 74
(J H M Gosden) *trckd ldrs: wnt 2nd appr fnl 2f: effrt to get upsides appr fnl f: sn rdn and nt qckn* **12/1**
2 **3** 2 3/4 **Mezenah**[14] 6565 2-9-0 0 TedDurcan 3 68
(Saeed Bin Suroor) *chsd ldrs: rdn 2f out: no imp over 1f out: wknd ins fnl f* **4/7**[1]
4 1/2 **My Girl Jode** 2-9-0 0 PaulMulrennan 2 67
(M H Tompkins) *trckd ldrs: outpcd 1/2-way: hdwy 3f out: drvn and styd on fnl f but no imp on ldng trio whn stmbld cl home* **80/1**
0 **5** 3/4 **Tomintoul Star**[21] 6358 2-9-0 0 TPQueally 7 65
(H R A Cecil) *in tch: hdwy and drvn along to chse ldrs 3f out: hung lft over 1f out and sn one pce* **14/1**
0 **6** 2 1/4 **Alimarr (IRE)**[14] 6559 2-9-0 0 JamieSpencer 13 60
(B J Meehan) *s.i.s: and swtchd lft: hdwy 3f out: rdn and mod prog over 2f out: no ch fr over 1f out* **40/1**
0 **7** 1/2 **Spirit Of Dubai (IRE)**[20] 6392 2-9-0 0 RichardMullen 4 59
(D M Simcock) *sn chsng ldrs: rdn over 3f out: wknd fr 2f out* **9/1**[2]
0 **8** 2 **Admiring Glances**[14] 6559 2-9-0 0 JerryO'Dwyer 8 55
(J Pearce) *led after 1f: hdd 6f out: styd chsng ldrs tl rdn and wknd 3f out* **100/1**
9 7 **Bourn Fair** 2-9-0 0 TonyCulhane 9 39
(P J McBride) *rr: mod prog over 3f out: sn bhd* **100/1**
10 1 1/4 **Shaaridh (USA)** 2-9-0 0 RHills 1 36
(M Johnston) *led after 2f: hdd & wknd ins fnl 3f* **9/1**[2]
00 **11** shd **Blessing Belle (IRE)**[20] 6391 2-9-0 0 SaleemGolam 10 36
(M H Tompkins) *a towards rr: no ch fr 1/2-way* **150/1**
0 **12** 1 1/4 **Pinkalicious (IRE)**[14] 6559 2-9-0 0 MichaelHills 12 33
(M L W Bell) *a struggling in rr* **66/1**

1m 43.76s (3.16) **Going Correction** +0.125s/f (Good) **12** Ran SP% **114.9**
Speed ratings (Par 92): **89,87,84,84,83 81,80,78,71,70 70,69**
toteswinger: 1&2 £9.60, 1&3 £3.50, 2&3 £2.60. CSF £116.21 TOTE £14.50: £3.40, £2.00, £1.10; EX 168.00 Trifecta £236.50 Part won. Pool: £319.60 - 0.20 winning units..
Owner C G P Wyatt **Bred** Dukes Stud & Overbury Stallions Ltd **Trained** Newmarket, Suffolk

FOCUS
Quite a good juvenile fillies' maiden, but they went steady early on. They raced up the middle of the track.

NOTEBOOK
Bombina, who is out of a smart triple 6f-7f winner, produced a likeable effort on her racecourse debut, despite running loose beforehand and having to be walked to the start. She was withdrawn at Newmarket last month as a result of reported traffic problems, and then refused to enter the stalls at Warwick, so she clearly has her own ideas, but her attitude in the race itself could not be faulted. Always well placed, she was strongly pressed by Hometown inside the final quarter mile, but found plenty and was ultimately quite a decisive winner. She rates as a potential pattern-class filly and may be aimed at the Listed Montrose Stakes at Newmarket provided this has not taken too much out of her. (op 6-1)
Hometown improved on the form showed on her debut over this trip at Kempton, but probably ran into quite a decent type. (op 14-1 tchd 10-1)
Mezenah was easy to back ahead of her debut second at Leicester and she didn't seem to have any excuses this time. (op 4-6 tchd 8-11)
My Girl Jode, a daughter of Haafhd, half-sister to among others 1m2f winner Craft Fair, made a pleasing debut. She showed signs of inexperience, but was keeping on nicely at the finish. (op 50-1)
Tomintoul Star raced a little keenly in a cross noseband, but this was still an improvement on her first effort and she clearly has ability. (op 12-1)
Spirit Of Dubai(IRE), just as on her debut at Nottingham, showed real signs of ability, despite finishing up well held. She is probably still quite weak and we are unlikely to see the best of her this year. Official explanation: jockey said filly ran green (op 14-1)

6885 EBF/FIRSTBET TELEPHONE DEBIT BETTING 0800 230 0800 MAIDEN STKS 6f 3y
2:50 (3:00) (Class 5) 2-Y-O **£4,415** (£1,321; £660; £330; £164) **Stalls** High

Form RPR
6 **1** **Merry Diva**[22] 6341 2-8-12 0 AlanMunro 8 73
(C F Wall) *mde all: rdn 2f out: hld on wl u.p fnl f* **6/1**
3234 **2** 1/2 **Taazur**[17] 6480 2-9-3 77 RHills 7 76
(M Johnston) *chsd wnr thrght: ev ch u.p over 1f out: unable qck fnl f* **10/3**[2]
002 **3** 1 **Midnight Fantasy**[14] 6555 2-8-12 72 SaleemGolam 12 68
(Rae Guest) *chsd ldrs: rdn and unable qck 2f out: kpt on again u.p fnl f* **11/2**[3]
0 **4** nk **Drum Dragon**[15] 6531 2-8-5 0 AshleyMorgan(7) 6 67
(M H Tompkins) *s.i.s: t.k.h: sn hld up in midfield: hdwy over 2f out: chsd ldrs over 1f out: kpt on same pce fnl f* **66/1**
5 5 **Fat Chance** 2-8-7 0 WilliamCarson(5) 4 52
(Rae Guest) *s.i.s: bhd: rdn 2f out: kpt on fr over 1f out: nvr pce to trble ldrs* **33/1**
0 **6** hd **Moggy (IRE)**[14] 6565 2-8-5 0 MalinHolmberg(7) 11 52
(M L W Bell) *hld up in midfield: outpcd jst over 2f out: kpt on same pce fnl f* **33/1**
6 **7** 1/2 **The Happy Hammer (IRE)**[32] 6077 2-9-3 0 TPQueally 15 55
(T Keddy) *dwlt: sn in tch in midfield: rdn 2f out: sn struggling and outpcd: n.d fnl f* **8/1**
8 1 1/4 **Yughanni** 2-8-12 0 NCallan 3 46
(C E Brittain) *dwlt: t.k.h: hld up wl in tch: rdn 2f out: wknd wl over 1f out* **14/1**
9 1 1/4 **Valid Point (IRE)** 2-9-3 0 DO'Donohoe 1 48
(Sir Mark Prescott) *wnt lft and lost many l s: bhd: sme late hdwy: n.d* **20/1**
10 nse **Wedding List** 2-8-12 0 MichaelHills 10 42
(W J Haggas) *dwlt: sn wl in tch: rdn jst over 2f out: sn btn* **11/4**[1]
0 **11** nk **Supera (IRE)**[40] 5835 2-8-12 0 PaulMulrennan 5 41
(M H Tompkins) *in tch in midfield: rdn and struggling 1/2-way: no ch last 2f* **66/1**
12 1/2 **Thumberlina** 2-8-12 0 TGMcLaughlin 9 40
(Mrs C A Dunnett) *s.i.s: a bhd: struggling fr 1/2-way* **50/1**
13 shd **The Scorching Wind (IRE)** 2-9-3 0 JerryO'Dwyer 2 45
(S C Williams) *s.i.s: a bhd: rdn and toiling fr 1/2-way* **40/1**
0 **14** 3 3/4 **Sparks Alive**[18] 6434 2-8-12 0 DaneO'Neill 13 28
(D R C Elsworth) *s.i.s: a bhd: toiling fr 1/2-way* **33/1**

1m 16.54s (2.14) **Going Correction** +0.125s/f (Good) **14** Ran SP% **118.2**
Speed ratings (Par 95): **90,89,88,87,80 80,80,78,76,76 76,75,75,70**
toteswinger: 1&2 £4.80, 1&3 £7.90, 2&3 £3.30. CSF £23.96 TOTE £7.50: £2.50, £1.10, £2.30; EX 28.90 Trifecta £59.10 Part won. Pool: £79.95 - 0.98 winning units..
Owner Mrs Barry Green **Bred** Jeremy Green And Sons **Trained** Newmarket, Suffolk

FOCUS
The ground was changed to good to soft after this race, an ordinary juvenile maiden. They raced up the middle of the track.

NOTEBOOK
Merry Diva, a sister to the stable's Listed winner Paradise Isle, improved significantly on the form she showed on her debut at Windsor with a game effort. She showed good speed to lead up and kept responding to pressure to hold the Johnston horse at bay. There may well be more to come. (tchd 13-2)
Taazur had every chance if good enough, but he found one too strong and is now 0-8. (op 3-1)
Midnight Fantasy, runner-up at Folkestone on her previous start, was never too far away and seemed to have her chance. (op 9-2)
Drum Dragon improved on her debut effort, despite racing keenly. (op 50-1)
Fat Chance showed some ability on her debut.
Moggy(IRE) was well held, but showed definite signs of ability under an inexperienced apprentice and she should do better when handicapped. (op 25-1)
The Happy Hammer(IRE) was backed, but he could not build on the form of his debut effort. (op 10-1)
Yughanni was too keen.
Valid Point(IRE) completely blew the start and ran green, but this run was not without promise and he will know a lot more next time. (op 25-1)
Wedding List was popular on her debut, but she ran rather disappointingly. (op 7-2)
Supera(IRE) Official explanation: trainer said filly was unsuited by the good (good to soft in places) ground

6886 EVENTGUARD NURSERY 1m 3y
3:20 (3:27) (Class 5) (0-75,75) 2-Y-O **£3,367** (£1,002; £500; £250) **Stalls** High

Form RPR
6402 **1** **Mykingdomforahorse**[5] 6761 2-8-11 65 (v) DarryllHolland 8 70
(M R Channon) *led tl hdd 3f out: styd chsng ldr: rdn: hd high and styd on fr 1f out to ld fnl 75yds: hld on wl* **11/4**[1]
4341 **2** nk **Nizhoni Dancer**[36] 5960 2-9-7 75 AlanMunro 12 79
(C F Wall) *chsd ldrs: rdn over 2f out: kpt on ins fnl f and tk 2nd nr fin but a jst hld by wnr* **4/1**[3]
6010 **3** 1/2 **Balladiene (IRE)**[20] 6394 2-8-13 67 PaulMulrennan 6 70+
(M H Tompkins) *in tch tl drvn and outpcd 1/2-way: hdwy over 1f out: styd on wl thrght fnl f: tk 3rd and gng on cl home* **12/1**
000 **4** hd **Foxtrot Charlie**[34] 6026 2-8-13 67 (b[1]) StephenCarson 10 70
(P Winkworth) *s.i.s: sn prom: led 3f out: shkn up and edgd lft fr 1f out: fnd no ex and hdd fnl 75yds: wknd bk into 4th cl home* **16/1**

556 **5** *2* **Land Hawk (IRE)**[18] 6438 2-9-5 **73** ... PatCosgrave 9 71
(J Pearce) *s.i.s: hld up in rr: hdwy fr 2f out: styd on fnl f but nvr gng pce to rch ldrs* **7/2**[2]
002 **6** *11* **Chadwell Spring (IRE)**[24] 6282 2-9-0 **71** ... RussellKennemore(3) 11 45
(Miss J Feilden) *in tch: rdn 3f out: wknd ins fnl 2f* **33/1**
066 **7** *3* **Winning Band (IRE)**[12] 6600 2-8-7 **61** ow1 ... JamieSpencer 2 29
(B J Meehan) *sn rdn in rr and little rspnse* **11/1**
1363 **8** *3* **Asian Tale (IRE)**[9] 6666 2-9-7 **75** ... TGMcLaughlin 7 36
(A B Haynes) *s.i.s: rdn 5f out: a bhd* **14/1**
0500 **9** *3¼* **Yokozuna**[14] 6549 2-8-6 **60** ... (b) AndrewElliott 1 14
(Mrs R A Carr) *chsd ldrs: rdn 3f out: wknd over 2f out* **28/1**
604 **10** *1¼* **Miss Fritton (IRE)**[25] 6245 2-9-3 **71** ... DaneO'Neill 4 22
(R Hannon) *chsd ldrs over 5f* **15/2**

1m 42.5s (1.90) **Going Correction** +0.125s/f (Good) **10** Ran SP% **115.6**
Speed ratings (Par 95): **95,94,94,94,92 81,78,75,71,70**
toteswinger: 1&2 £2.10, 1&3 £7.40, 2&3 £9.60. CSF £13.53 CT £114.73 TOTE £3.00: £1.30, £1.70, £3.60; EX 11.10 Trifecta £7.70 Pool: £215.46 - 20.69 winning units..
Owner C C Buckley **Bred** Hunscote House Farm Stud **Trained** West Ilsley, Berks

FOCUS
A modest but competitive nursery run at an ordinary pace. They raced middle to stands' side.

NOTEBOOK
Mykingdomforahorse confirmed the promise he showed in a first-time visor at Nottingham on his previous start. Having enjoyed a soft lead early on, he looked in trouble when coming under strong pressure and passed inside the final two furlongs, but Darryll Holland conjured one last effort from him close home. He might not be totally straightforward, but he ought to improve again for a step up to 1m2f. (op 5-2 tchd 9-4 and 3-1)
Nizhoni Dancer was a winner over 7f on her nursery debut at Leicester, but she looked to need every yard of this 1m and just failed off a 5lb higher mark. Although her sire Bahamian Bounty is an influence for speed, there is loads of stamina on the dam's side of her pedigree, so she probably would have preferred a stronger pace, and she gives the impression she will benefit from a further step up in trip. (tchd 7-2)
Balladiene(IRE), a selling winner over this course and distance two starts back, was doing all her best work at the finish and is another who probably would have preferred a stronger pace.
Foxtrot Charlie travelled as well as anything, in the first-time blinkers on this nursery debut, but he failed to see his race out once in front. He looks worth another try in the headgear over 7f. (op 20-1)
Land Hawk(IRE) was well backed first-time up in nursery company, but he was never a threat and is another who might have preferred a better pace. (op 9-2 tchd 11-2, 6-1 in places)
Chadwell Spring(IRE) Official explanation: jockey said filly ran too freely early on
Winning Band(IRE) Official explanation: jockey said gelding never travelled
Miss Fritton(IRE) Official explanation: trainer's rep said filly was unsuited by the good to soft ground

6887 EBF/HARMAN BROS PLASTERING CONTRACTORS MAIDEN FILLIES' STKS (DIV II) 1m 3y
3:50 (3:56) (Class 5) 2-Y-0 **£3,532** (£1,057; £528; £264; £131) **Stalls** High

Form RPR
0 **1** **Take The Hint**[32] 6081 2-9-0 0 ... RobertHavlin 3 81+
(J H M Gosden) *s.i.s: sn in midfield: shkn up and hanging lft 3f out: outpcd over 2f out: modest 5th over 1f out: rdn and str burst ent fnl f: led fnl 100yds: readily* **7/2**[2]
0 **2** *1½* **Natural Flair (USA)**[20] 6391 2-9-0 0 ... AlanMunro 1 78
(P W Chapple-Hyam) *pressed ldr: ev ch and rdn jst over 2f out: led over 1f out: hdd and nt pce of wnr fnl 100yds* **4/1**[3]
63 **3** *3* **Holamo (IRE)**[24] 6291 2-9-0 0 ... JohnEgan 11 71
(M Botti) *trckd ldrs: hdwy and rdn over 2f out: ev ch over 1f out: wknd jst ins fnl f* **5/1**
53 **4** *2¼* **Mayaalah**[29] 6167 2-9-0 0 ... RHills 2 66
(J H M Gosden) *led: rdn and hdd over 1f out: sn btn* **9/4**[1]
5 *1* **Astrodiva** 2-9-0 0 ... PaulMulrennan 7 64
(M H Tompkins) *bhd: rdn over 3f out: hdwy past btn horses over 1f out: kpt on fnl f: nvr trbld ldrs* **100/1**
5 **6** *2¾* **Quiquillo (USA)**[29] 6166 2-9-0 0 ... TPQueally 6 58
(H R A Cecil) *pressed ldrs: rdn 2f out: wknd qckly over 1f out* **12/1**
7 *2* **In Step** 2-9-0 0 ... MichaelHills 8 54
(W J Haggas) *s.i.s: towards rr: rdn 1/2-way: sme hdwy 3f out: sn no imp* **12/1**
00 **8** *3¾* **In Her Shoes**[14] 6565 2-9-0 0 ... DarryllHolland 13 45
(B J Meehan) *a in rr: rdn 1/2-way: nvr trbld ldrs* **33/1**
9 *shd* **Nice Time (IRE)** 2-9-0 0 ... SaleemGolam 10 45
(M H Tompkins) *s.i.s: hld up in rr: struggling fr 1/2-way* **66/1**
10 *2* **Dubai Diva** 2-9-0 0 ... TedDurcan 9 41
(C F Wall) *stdd s: sn in tch in midfield: rdn 3f out: sn struggling: wl hld last 2f* **20/1**
0 **11** *3¼* **Red Stiletto**[97] 4080 2-8-9 0 ... WilliamCarson(5) 5 33
(Rae Guest) *a bhd: lost tch 1/2-way* **100/1**
12 *7* **Tagula Minx (IRE)** 2-9-0 0 ... PatCosgrave 4 18
(J Pearce) *chsd ldrs tl 1/2-way: wknd qckly 3f out: t.o fnl f* **100/1**

1m 42.07s (1.47) **Going Correction** +0.125s/f (Good) **12** Ran SP% **117.2**
Speed ratings (Par 92): **97,95,92,90,89 86,84,80,80,78 75,68**
toteswinger: 1&2 £3.50, 1&3 £4.80, 2&3 £4.90. CSF £17.09 TOTE £4.80: £1.70, £1.90, £2.30; EX 23.40 Trifecta £70.10 Pool: £197.10 - 2.08 winning units..
Owner K Abdulla **Bred** Juddmonte Farms Ltd **Trained** Newmarket, Suffolk

FOCUS
A fair fillies' maiden run in a time 1.69sec quicker than the first division, and 0.43sec faster than the earlier 0-75 nursery. They raced up the centre of the track.

NOTEBOOK
Take The Hint shaped well from a poor draw on her debut over 7f at Newmarket and confirmed that promise with a performance even better than the bare result suggests, as the track was favouring front runners. She was under pressure a fair way out, but gradually responded and was ultimately well on top at the line. She gave the impression this run will bring her on significantly again and she rates as a decent middle-distance prospect. (op 9-2 tchd 3-1)
Natural Flair(USA), whose trainer won the first division with a newcomer, stepped up on the form she showed on her debut at Nottingham and ran a good race behind the promising winner. (op 9-2 tchd 5-1)
Holamo(IRE) again showed ability and is now qualified for a handicap mark. (op 13-2)
Mayaalah, a stablemate of the winner, did not build on the form of her first two efforts and may have been unsuited by the ground. (op 15-8 tchd 13-8 and 5-2)
Astrodiva, out of a 1m6f winner, was keeping on nicely at the finish and this was a pleasing debut. She should do even better over further next year.

6888 NWES BEACON INNOVATION CENTRE CLAIMING STKS 1m 3y
4:20 (4:24) (Class 6) 3-Y-0+ **£2,331** (£693; £346; £173) **Stalls** High

Form RPR
2432 **1** **Desiderio**[75] 4766 3-9-3 77 ... (b) CharlesEddery(7) 5 78
(R Hannon) *mde all: shkn up over 1f out: hld on wl cl home* **7/1**
-300 **2** *¾* **Deo Valente (IRE)**[4] 6771 3-9-10 78 ... JamieSpencer 9 76
(B J Meehan) *hld up in tch: rdn and hdwy over 2f out: styd on u.p ins fnl f and tk 2nd cl home but a hld by wnr* **5/1**[2]
4000 **3** *nk* **Gee Ceffyl Bach**[29] 6178 4-7-11 49 ... (p) DavidProbert(5) 2 51
(John A Harris) *a chsng wnr: rdn over 1f out: kpt on same pce ins fnl f and lost 2nd cl home* **16/1**
0125 **4** *½* **Mick Is Back**[27] 6217 4-8-13 58 ... (p) DaneO'Neill 4 60
(G G Margarson) *s.i.s: sn in tch: chsd ldrs 1/2-way: styd on u.p ins fnl f but nvr gng pce to rch ldrs* **12/1**
4201 **5** *1¾* **Sabre Light**[5] 6757 3-9-4 72 ... JerryO'Dwyer 10 64+
(J Pearce) *sn rdn along towards rr: kpt on u.p fr 2f out: styd on ins fnl f but nvr in contention* **4/1**[1]
0033 **6** *shd* **Yakama (IRE)**[7] 6716 3-8-10 55 ... (bt) DO'Donohoe 14 56
(Mrs C A Dunnett) *s.i.s: in rr: rdn over 2f out and kpt on fnl f: nvr in contention* **12/1**
1410 **7** *1½* **Blacktoft (USA)**[4] 6771 5-9-8 77 ... (e) WilliamCarson(5) 3 67
(S C Williams) *sn wl there: rdn over 2f out: styd on same pce fr over 1f out* **6/1**[3]
0000 **8** *3* **Sun Catcher (IRE)**[21] 6356 5-8-9 62 ... (p) RobertHavlin 1 42
(P G Murphy) *chsd ldrs: rdn over 2f out: wknd fnl f* **25/1**
4000 **9** *¾* **High Five Society**[7] 6716 4-8-11 54 ... (bt) RoystonFfrench 7 42
(S R Bowring) *chsd ldrs: rdn 3f out: wknd fr 2f out* **25/1**
5340 **10** *2¾* **Peas In A Pod**[5] 6751 3-8-7 52 ... JackMitchell(3) 16 38
(J R Best) *chsd ldrs: rdn 3f out: wknd over 2f out* **14/1**
3462 **11** *2* **Al Rayanah**[25] 6255 5-8-6 54 ... (p) SaleemGolam 8 26
(G Prodromou) *s.i.s: sn chsng ldrs: wknd over 3f out* **6/1**[3]
5060 **12** *11* **Sleeping**[14] 6562 3-8-1 54 ow5 ... (b) AshleyMorgan(7) 11 —
(M H Tompkins) *s.i.s: a bhd* **66/1**
0 **13** *27* **Brakey Hill (USA)**[136] 2834 3-9-10 0 ... (b1) TedDurcan 12 —
(B J Meehan) *slowly away: a bhd* **40/1**

1m 41.9s (1.30) **Going Correction** +0.125s/f (Good)
WFA 3 from 4yo+ 3lb **13** Ran SP% **117.3**
Speed ratings (Par 101): **98,97,96,96,94 94,93,90,89,86 84,73,46**
toteswinger: 1&2 £7.00, 1&3 £38.90, 2&3 £27.60. CSF £39.76 TOTE £9.10: £3.10, £2.00, £7.60; EX 23.20 TRIFECTA Not won. Pool.
Owner Exors of the late Cathal M Ryan **Bred** Keith Freeman **Trained** East Everleigh, Wilts

FOCUS
A moderate claimer in which the field came up the centre of the track, and the time was fractionally faster than the best of the three earlier juvenile contests. The form is rated through the winner and second.
Deo Valente(IRE) Official explanation: jockey said gelding hung left final few furlongs

6889 GAMBAS SEAFOOD AND GRILL RESTAURANT H'CAP 7f 3y
4:50 (4:50) (Class 6) (0-65,64) 3-Y-0+ **£2,719** (£809; £303; £303) **Stalls** High

Form RPR
2155 **1** **Sarah Park (IRE)**[75] 4766 3-9-3 **63** ... JamieSpencer 6 76
(B J Meehan) *mde all: rdn over 2f out: drvn and styd on wl fnl f* **5/1**[1]
5200 **2** *2½* **Melt (IRE)**[14] 6564 3-8-9 **55** ... DaneO'Neill 1 61
(R Hannon) *hld up in tch in midfield: hdwy over 2f out: rdn to chse wnr 2f out: no ex jst ins fnl f* **14/1**
2310 **3** *3¼* **Avontuur (FR)**[7] 6724 6-9-3 **61** ... AndrewElliott 2 58
(Mrs R A Carr) *taken down early: cl up: chsd wnr 5f out tl 2f out: sn drvn and unable qck: kpt on same pce fnl f* **7/1**[2]
0135 **3** *dht* **West End Lad**[28] 6186 5-9-5 **63** ... (b) RoystonFfrench 7 60
(S R Bowring) *chsd ldrs: rdn over 2f out: unable qck u.p 2f out: plugged on same pce fnl f* **5/1**[1]
0310 **5** *½* **Poppets Sweetlove**[15] 6544 4-9-6 **64** ... RichardMullen 13 60+
(A B Haynes) *stdd s: hld up in midfield: rdn over 2f out: kpt on u.p fnl f: nvr pce to threaten ldrs* **9/1**
1000 **6** *1¾* **Avoncreek**[21] 6357 4-8-10 **54** ... TPQueally 8 45
(B P J Baugh) *stdd s: hld up in midfield: rdn and effrt over 2f out: kpt on u.p fnl f: nt pce to trble ldrs* **14/1**
0160 **7** *1¼* **Registrar**[31] 6125 6-9-4 **62** ... (p) SaleemGolam 9 50
(Mrs C A Dunnett) *in tch: rdn jst over 2f out: wknd over 1f out: no ch fnl f* **8/1**[3]
4053 **8** *1¾* **Paradise Island (IRE)**[40] 5816 3-9-0 **60** ... TGMcLaughlin 4 43
(E A L Dunlop) *stdd and bmpd s: t.k.h: hld up in rr: rdn and no rspnse jst over 2f out: wl hld fnl 2f* **12/1**
605 **9** *nk* **Second Opinion (IRE)**[14] 6566 3-8-8 **57** ... LukeMorris(3) 5 39
(J M P Eustace) *plld hrd: chsd wnr for 3f: rdn and btn wl over 2f out* **40/1**
6000 **10** *3¾* **Cavalry Guard (USA)**[144] 2561 4-9-2 **60** ... (p) RobertHavlin 10 32
(T D McCarthy) *chsd ldrs: rdn 3f out: wknd over 2f out: wl btn after* **66/1**
0036 **11** *1½* **Valentino Swing (IRE)**[11] 6628 5-9-3 **64** ... TolleyDean(3) 12 32
(Miss T Spearing) *hld up in midfield: lost pl and rdn 1/2-way: wl btn last 2f* **12/1**
3013 **12** *1½* **Avoca Dancer (IRE)**[41] 5801 5-9-4 **62** ... (p) NCallan 11 26
(Miss Gay Kelleway) *hld up in tch: rdn and btn over 2f out* **9/1**
0050 **13** *8* **Mansii**[20] 6395 3-9-4 **64** ... TonyCulhane 15 6
(P J McBride) *stdd and dropped in bhd after s: a in rr: toiling fr 1/2-way* **25/1**
-205 **14** *1¼* **Royal Sovereign (IRE)**[18] 6433 3-8-8 **59** ... WilliamCarson(5) 14 —
(G C H Chung) *chsd ldrs tl lost pl 1/2-way: sn rdn and hung lft: wl bhd last 2f* **25/1**

1m 28.31s (1.71) **Going Correction** +0.125s/f (Good)
WFA 3 from 4yo+ 2lb **14** Ran SP% **117.3**
Speed ratings (Par 101): **95,92,88,88,87 85,84,82,82,77 76,74,65,63**
toteswinger: SP & M £19.00; SP & WEL £2.70; M & WEL £10.80; SP & A £3.10; M & A £ 9.00. TOTE £7.20: £2.60, £5.10 Trifecta £113.80 Part won. Pool: £307.77 - 0.20 w/u. PL: WEL £1.20; A£1.40; TRI: SP/M/WEL £185.28, SP/M/A £188.43..
Owner Mrs J & D E Cash **Bred** George S O'Malley **Trained** Manton, Wilts

FOCUS
A modest handicap in which a low draw was an advantage, as they were spread across the track and those towards the far side had the call. Once again it paid to be bang on the pace. The form is rated through the second and the winner may do a little bit better.

6890 ONE ESTATES H'CAP 6f 3y
5:20 (5:22) (Class 6) (0-60,59) 3-Y-0+ **£2,719** (£809; £404; £202) **Stalls** High

Form RPR
0040 **1** **La Famiglia**[22] 6334 3-9-0 **55** ... DaneO'Neill 16 72
(H Candy) *mde all: drvn out fnl f* **13/2**[2]
0003 **2** *2½* **Joyeaux**[5] 6766 6-8-12 **55** ... DuranFentiman(3) 12 64
(L R James) *in tch: rdn to chse wnr 2f out: no imp thrght fnl f but hld on wl for 2nd* **17/2**
3436 **3** *1½* **City For Conquest (IRE)**[19] 6419 5-8-10 **50** ... PatCosgrave 13 54
(John A Harris) *slowly away: rr: rdn and hdwy fr 2f out: fin wl fnl f: nt rch ldrs* **16/1**

2565 **4** *shd* **Oi Vay Joe (IRE)**[48] 5601 4-9-5 **59**....................(b) AlanMunro 14 62
(W Jarvis) *chsd ldrs: rdn over 2f out: outpcd ins fnl f* **7/1**[3]
0043 **5** *nse* **Comrade Cotton**[8] 6693 4-8-12 **52**....................(vp[1]) JerryO'Dwyer 3 55
(J Ryan) *racd far side in gp of 3 and a jst in command that side but nt go pce of stands' side fr ins fnl 2f* **12/1**
-053 **6** *shd* **Whiskey Creek**[9] 6679 3-8-12 **53**.................... PaulEddery 11 56
(C A Dwyer) *chsd ldrs: rdn 3f out: styd on same pce fr over 1f out* **14/1**
6002 **7** *nk* **Interactive (IRE)**[8] 6706 5-9-4 **58**.................... AlanDaly 9 60
(Andrew Turnell) *hld up in rr: hdwy over 2f out: rdn and styd on to chse ldrs 1f out but nvr gng pce to chal and sn one pce* **7/2**[1]
66P0 **8** *nk* **Rough Rock (IRE)**[20] 6388 3-9-4 **59**.................... SaleemGolam 2 60
(G Prodromou) *racd far side and and disp ld that gp of 3 fr 2f out but nt gng pce of stands' side: one pce ins fnl f* **10/1**
3504 **9** *2* **Namu**[21] 6357 5-8-11 **54**.................... TolleyDean[(3)] 10 49
(Miss T Spearing) *in rr: rdn 1/2-way: nvr gng pce to be competitive* **8/1**
6020 **10** *4* **Swallow Forest**[29] 6159 3-8-6 **54**....................(b) DeanHeslop[(7)] 8 36
(T D Barron) *chsd ldrs: rdn 1/2-way: wknd fr 2f out* **25/1**
5013 **11** *2 ¾* **Just Spike**[76] 4749 5-9-1 **55**.................... TPQueally 5 28
(B P J Baugh) *racd far side in gp of 3 and dropped away fr 3f out* **15/2**
3364 **12** *2* **Night Premiere (IRE)**[14] 6564 3-9-1 **56**.................... RobertHavlin 7 23
(R Hannon) *chsd ldrs tl wknd qckly over 2f out* **14/1**

1m 14.91s (0.51) **Going Correction** +0.125s/f (Good)
WFA 3 from 4yo+ 1lb **12 Ran SP% 121.3**
Speed ratings (Par 101): **101,97,95,95,95 95,94,94,91,86 82,80**
toteswinger: 1&2 £9.80, 1&3 £26.90, 2&3 £23.80. CSF £62.39 CT £617.28 TOTE £7.50: £2.20, £2.90, £4.20; EX 52.50 Trifecta £181.30 Pool: £245.11 - 0.10 winning units. Place 6: £60.17 Place 5: £20.02.
Owner Acloque, Jones & Frost **Bred** Miss A M Rees **Trained** Kingston Warren, Oxon

FOCUS
A moderate sprint handicap. Three horses raced far side, but those towards the stands' rail very much held sway and a high draw was a big advantage. So too was a prominent ride once again. The form has been rated at face value with the unexposed winner up a stone on her maiden form.
T/Plt: £44.70 to a £1 stake. Pool: £50,918.42. 829.89 winning tickets. T/Qpdt: £21.80 to a £1 stake. Pool: £3,560.08. 120.30 winning tickets. SP

5555 DEAUVILLE (R-H)
Tuesday, October 21
OFFICIAL GOING: Turf course - very soft; all-weather - standard

6891a PRIX DES RESERVOIRS (GROUP 3) (FILLIES) (ROUND) 1m (R)
1:50 (1:56) 2-Y-O £29,412 (£11,765; £8,824; £5,882; £2,941)

RPR
1 **Article Rare (USA)**[36] 5987 2-8-9 .... ACrastus 105
(E Lellouche, France) *mde all: rdn over 2 l clr ins fnl f: r.o wl* **5/2**[2]
2 *1* **Ciel Rouge (FR)**[55] 2-8-9 .... IMendizabal 103
(J-C Rouget, France) *flipped over bkwards and uns in stalls bef r: racd in 4th: 3rd st: wnt 2nd ins fnl f: r.o* **11/2**
3 *shd* **Bufera (IRE)**[32] 6157 2-8-9 .... OPeslier 103
(Robert Collet, France) *hld up in rr: 5th st: wnt 4th under 2f out: stl 4th tl styd on wl down outside clsng stages* **12/1**
4 *1 ½* **Homebound (USA)**[53] 5486 2-8-9 .... C-PLemaire 99
(J-C Rouget, France) *racd in 3rd: 2nd st: rdn over 1 1/2f out: one pce* **8/5**[1]
5 *6* **Yakhy (FR)**[16] 2-8-9 .... JMartin 86
(B De Montzey, France) *a bhd* **30/1**
6 *nk* **Gainful (USA)**[18] 2-8-9 .... SPasquier 85
(D Smaga, France) *immediately pushed along in rr: 5th whn rdn 3f out: 6th and btn ent st* **5/1**[3]
7 *20* **Alta Fedelta** 2-8-9 .... MDemuro 41
(V Caruso, Italy) *plld hrd in 2nd: 4th st: sn wknd and eased* **15/1**

1m 48.7s (7.70) **7 Ran SP% 116.3**
PARI-MUTUEL: WIN 3.50; PL 2.30, 2.80; SF 23.30.
Owner Ecurie Wildenstein **Bred** Dayton Investments Ltd **Trained** Lamorlaye, France

NOTEBOOK
Article Rare(USA) is certainly a nice filly in the making and she won her first Group event in style. Her young jockey decided to make all the running at a sensible pace early on before then quickening things up early in the straight and the filly hung on well to win with something in hand. Her connections were worried about the very soft ground, but she coped with it well and she will now be put away. Her target is likely to be the Poule d'Essai des Pouliches.
Ciel Rouge(FR) reared up in the stalls, throwing her jockey to the ground, and her trainer only decided to let her take her chance after some deliberation. Quickly into stride and tracking the winner throughout, she looked outpaced early in the straight but ran on gamely to the line. She was found to have taken a knock on her near-fore hock, which probably happened when she played up at the start.
Bufera(IRE), on whom waiting tactics were employed, was brought with a run up the centre of the track and was putting in her best work at the end. A longer trip might suit her in the future.
Homebound(USA) was a rather disappointing favourite having been given every chance. She was always well up there, but couldn't really quicken in the straight and just stayed on one pace inside the final furlong. She was probably unsuited by the testing ground.

6665 BATH (L-H)
Wednesday, October 22
OFFICIAL GOING: Good to soft (6.9)
Wind: virtually nil Weather: Bright

6892 FMW CONSULTANCY MAIDEN STKS (DIV I) 1m 5y
2:00 (2:02) (Class 5) 2-Y-O £2,396 (£712; £356; £177) Stalls Low

Form RPR
43 **1** **Calaloo (IRE)**[15] 6553 2-9-3 0.................... SteveDrowne 11 77
(C R Egerton) *s.i.s: sn chsng ldr: led ins fnl 3f: styd on wl whn strly chal thrght fnl f* **16/1**
42 **2** *nk* **Antinori (IRE)**[16] 6539 2-9-3 0.................... AdamKirby 9 76
(W R Swinburn) *in tch: hdwy over 2f out: drvn to chal ins fnl f: no ex cl home* **10/3**[2]
0 **3** *1* **Longboat Key**[19] 6451 2-9-3 0.................... J-PGuillambert 4 74
(M Johnston) *chsd ldrs: rdn 3f out: chsd wnr over 2f out: nt qckn ins fnl f* **33/1**
2 **4** *nk* **Lasso The Moon**[13] 6602 2-9-3 0.................... TPO'Shea 3 73
(M R Channon) *s.i.s: bhd: pushed along 3f out: hdwy over 1f out: kpt on ins fnl f but nt rch ldrs* **10/11**[1]
5333 **5** *1 ½* **Admiral Sandhoe (USA)**[28] 6198 2-9-3 74.................... JimCrowley 8 70
(Mrs A J Perrett) *in tch: rdn to chse ldrs over 2f out: one pce fnl f* **6/1**[3]
0 **6** *6* **North Cape (USA)**[44] 5753 2-9-3 0.................... FrankieMcDonald 10 57
(H Candy) *towards rr and pushed along 3f out: sme prog fnl f* **20/1**
000 **7** *4* **Braishfield Lass**[23] 6330 2-8-12 44.................... TQuinn 14 43
(B G Powell) *in rr: mod prog fnl 2f* **200/1**
0 **8** *3* **Thief**[68] 5068 2-9-3 0.................... PatCosgrave 5 41
(L M Cumani) *s.i.s: sn in tch: pushed along 3f out: n.d after* **12/1**
0640 **9** *1 ¾* **Primo Dilettante**[28] 6207 2-9-3 58.................... PaulDoe 2 38
(W J Knight) *led tl hdd ins fnl 3f: sn wknd* **80/1**
0 **10** *5* **Lady Meg (IRE)**[89] 4367 2-8-12 0.................... CatherineGannon 6 22
(B Palling) *chsd ldrs 5f* **150/1**
00 **11** *nse* **Hart House**[10] 6665 2-8-12 0.................... VinceSlattery 13 21
(C J Gray) *a in rr* **200/1**
12 *4* **Ringo Zaar** 2-9-3 0.................... TPQueally 12 18
(A B Haynes) *prom to 1/2-way: sn wknd* **100/1**

1m 47.06s (6.26) **Going Correction** +0.80s/f (Soft) **12 Ran SP% 114.9**
Speed ratings (Par 95): **100,99,98,98,96 90,86,83,82,77 77,73**
toteswinger: 1&2 £7.20, 1&3 £23.30, 2&3 £15.20. CSF £66.12 TOTE £17.70: £3.30, £1.70, £6.80; EX 56.00 Trifecta £347.70 Part won. Pool: £469.97 - 0.10 winning units..
Owner Brimacombe, McNally, Rickman & Sangster **Bred** John Osborne **Trained** Chaddleworth, Berks

FOCUS
This looked just a fair maiden.

NOTEBOOK
Calaloo(IRE) stepped up markedly on his two previous efforts to score in a tight finish. His previous runs had been over shorter and there was always a good chance this step up to 1m was going to suit, his dam having been effective at up to 1m6f. Sent on three out, he repelled all challengers and pulled out extra close home to deny Antinori. He should stay 1m2f before long and it will be interesting to see what mark he is given for handicaps. (op 14-1 tchd 18-1)
Antinori(IRE) had finished a running-on second over this trip at Windsor last time, and he at least matched that form here, coming through to have every chance but not staying on as well as the winner close home. He is going the right way and will now be eligible for handicaps. (op 3-1 tchd 7-2)
Longboat Key comes from a yard whose juveniles often improve markedly for a run and this one was no exception. He was produced to have every chance and, on this evidence, will stay further next season. (op 50-1)
Lasso The Moon was a big disappointment. A most promising second on his debut at Newbury, he was understandably made a short-priced favourite to take this lesser contest but blew the start and lacked the pace to recover. Under pressure at halfway, he took an age to pick up and, having finally got going, ran on inside the final furlong for fourth. He was hardly flying at the finish, but this course may not have suited and he is worth another chance. (op 5-6 tchd 8-11)
Admiral Sandhoe(USA) challenged widest of all and looked the likely winner 1f out but could find no extra in the final 100 yards. (op 7-1)
Thief was another slowly away and unable to get into it. He will be one for handicaps next year. (op 18-1)

6893 FMW CONSULTANCY MAIDEN STKS (DIV II) 1m 5y
2:30 (2:33) (Class 5) 2-Y-O £2,396 (£712; £356; £177) Stalls Low

Form RPR
04 **1** **Blue Tango (IRE)**[15] 6552 2-9-3 0.................... JimCrowley 12 75
(Mrs A J Perrett) *chsd ldrs: pushed along 3f out: styd on u.p fnl f to ld fnl 50yds* **7/2**[2]
4 **2** *nk* **Mehendi (IRE)**[13] 6604 2-9-3 0.................... MartinDwyer 5 74
(B J Meehan) *chsd ldrs: slt ld ins fnl 2f: hrd drvn whn chal fr 1f out: hdd and no ex fnl 50yds* **11/4**[1]
66 **3** *1* **Whisky Galore**[13] 6604 2-9-3 0.................... AdamKirby 2 72
(C G Cox) *chsd ldrs: drvn to chal fr 1f out: wknd fnl 50yds* **6/1**
0 **4** *3 ¾* **Miss Kadee**[121] 3323 2-8-12 0.................... TGMcLaughlin 8 59
(P D Evans) *chsd ldrs: rdn 3f out: one pce fnl 2f* **100/1**
5 *nk* **Kris Kin Line (IRE)** 2-9-3 0.................... JamieSpencer 6 63
(Sir Michael Stoute) *sn slt ld: hdd 4f out: styd pressing ldrs tl wknd ins fnl 2f* **13/2**
6 *1 ¼* **Am I Blue** 2-8-12 0.................... FrancisNorton 11 55
(H J L Dunlop) *in rr: rdn along over 2f out: sme prog fnl f* **25/1**
7 *½* **Cool Libby (IRE)** 2-8-12 0.................... TPQueally 4 54
(A B Haynes) *in rr: pushed along and sme hdwy 3f out: nvr in contention* **50/1**
8 *¾* **Cool Hand Jake** 2-9-3 0.................... TravisBlock 9 57
(P J Makin) *s.i.s: rr unto: sme prog fnl 2f* **28/1**
42 **9** *¾* **Noordhoek Kid**[20] 6423 2-9-3 0.................... SteveDrowne 3 56
(C R Egerton) *pressed ldr: led 4f out: hdd & wknd qckly ins fnl 2f* **4/1**[3]
10 *11* **Stafford Charlie** 2-9-3 0.................... VinceSlattery 7 32
(J G M O'Shea) *slowly away: a in rr* **100/1**
50 **11** *3 ½* **Googoobarabajagal (IRE)**[44] 5753 2-9-3 0.................... TPO'Shea 1 24
(W S Kittow) *a in rr* **33/1**
0 **12** *4 ½* **Castlemaine**[15] 6552 2-8-12 0.................... RichardHughes 10 9
(R Hannon) *pressed ldrs: rdn and wknd qckly over 2f out* **20/1**

1m 49.93s (9.13) **Going Correction** +0.80s/f (Soft) **12 Ran SP% 115.4**
Speed ratings (Par 95): **86,85,84,80,80 79,78,78,77,66 62,58**
toteswinger: 1&2 £2.90, 1&3 £3.80, 2&3 £3.90. CSF £12.28 TOTE £4.70: £1.50, £1.40, £2.00; EX 14.70 Trifecta £71.60 Pool: £288.67 - 2.98 winning units..
Owner The Green Dot Partnership **Bred** Paul Ennis **Trained** Pulborough, W Sussex

FOCUS
This looked the weaker of the two divisions and the times seemed to confirm that, for all that they did not go much of a pace and came towards the stands' side.

NOTEBOOK
Blue Tango(IRE), who looked in need of this trip when fourth at Folkestone last time, had already shown himself to be effective with give in the ground and he toughed it out best in the final furlong. There is speed in his pedigree, but this trip clearly suits him best and there is a chance he may get a little further next season. (op 5-1 tchd 11-2)
Mehendi(IRE) looked the one to beat if improving on his debut fourth at Newbury, but he was slowly away, and, having caught up, had to be ridden to keep his place. He moved through to take it up over two out but in the end was outstayed by the winner. This probably represented a step forward and he will be capable of better next season. (tchd 5-2 and 3-1)
Whisky Galore, two places behind Mehendi at Newbury, was produced to have every chance over 1f out, but his stamina gave out in the final furlong. He should do better in handicaps and looks well worth a try at 7f. (op 8-1)
Miss Kadee, off since beating just one rival home on her debut at Windsor in June, was up 2f in trip and ran a much-improved race. She has a future at the right level (op 80-1 tchd 66-1)
Kris Kin Line(IRE), representing the connections of his Derby-winning sire, seemed to know his job well enough on this racecourse debut and found himself bang there on the speed. He was under pressure well over 2f out though and could find no extra inside the final furlong. This run should bring him on, but he is clearly no star. (op 9-2)
Am I Blue, a half-sister to the useful Prism, made some late headway and should come on. (op 33-1)

Cool Libby(IRE), a half-sister to a juvenile 1m winner, ran better than her finishing position implies and should find easier opportunities. Official explanation: jockey said filly suffered interference in running (op 40-1)

Noordhoek Kid could not build on his recent Great Leighs second, stopping quickly, and may be more of a handicap type. Official explanation: jockey said gelding suffered interference in running

Castlemaine Official explanation: jockey said filly had no more to give

6894 EBF TERRY LEIGH MEMORIAL MAIDEN STKS 5f 11y
3:00 (3:01) (Class 5) 2-Y-O **£3,561** (£1,059; £529; £264) **Stalls** Centre

Form RPR

20 **1** **Master Of Disguise**[20] 6426 2-9-3 0 AdamKirby 3 81
(C G Cox) *a gng wl: led on bit appr fnl f: comf* **13/2**[3]

3054 **2** 2 ¾ **Sharpener (IRE)**[15] 6555 2-8-12 66 RichardHughes 2 66
(R Hannon) *led: rdn 2f out: hdd appr fnl f and no ch w wnr ins fnl f but kpt on wl for 2nd* **8/1**

254 **3** 1 **Fitz Flyer (IRE)**[42] 5794 2-9-3 93 PaulMulrennan 9 67
(D H Brown) *s.i.s: sn puhed along and in tch 1/2-way: styd on u.p to take 3rd ins fnl f but no imp on ldng duo* **8/13**[1]

4 2 **Celestial Dream (IRE)** 2-8-7 0 DavidProbert(5) 8 55
(A M Balding) *trckd ldrs: pushed along over 1f out: sn one pce* **9/2**[2]

06 **5** 3 ½ **Art Fund (USA)**[14] 6575 2-9-3 0 RichardMullen 6 48
(G L Moore) *chsd ldrs: rdn 2f out and sn btn* **20/1**

0 **6** ¾ **Lana's Charm**[82] 4579 2-8-12 0 CatherineGannon 1 40
(P J Makin) *chsd ldr: rdn 1/2-way: wknd fr 2f out* **50/1**

7 1 ¼ **Genipabu (IRE)** 2-8-12 0 TPO'Shea 10 35
(M G Quinlan) *in tch: rdn and hung lft fr 3f out: sn bhd* **25/1**

00 **8** ¾ **Billy Smart (IRE)**[8] 6714 2-9-3 0 TQuinn 11 38
(D J S Ffrench Davis) *s.i.s: sn rdn and in tch: wknd 1/2-way* **66/1**

65.77 secs (3.27) **Going Correction** +0.55s/f (Yiel) **8 Ran SP% 116.6**

Speed ratings (Par 95): **95,90,89,85,80 79,77,75**

toteswinger: 1&2 £3.80, 1&3 £2.10, 2&3 £1.90. CSF £53.41 TOTE £6.70: £1.60, £2.10, £1.10; EX 35.60 Trifecta £131.90 Pool: £672.31 - 3.77 winning units..

Owner Courtenay Club **Bred** T R Lock **Trained** Lambourn, Berks

FOCUS

A modest sprint maiden won in good style.

NOTEBOOK

Master Of Disguise, runner-up over course and distance on his debut back in May, was not seen again until finishing down the field in the valuable sales race at Newmarket earlier this month, and this obviously represented a marked drop in grade. Always going strongly just in behind the speed, he cruised to the front over 1f out and just had to be nudged out to score comfortably. This softer ground is the key to him, and he will be put away now with next season in mind. (op 6-1 tchd 11-2)

Sharpener(IRE) appeared not to see out the 6f in soft ground at Folkestone last time and was happier back at this trip. She was no match for the winner though and will remain vulnerable to improvers. (tchd 10-1)

Fitz Flyer(IRE) set a high standard, having shown useful form in defeat in a sales race at Newmarket and then a conditions race at Doncaster, but he was slowly away and never travelled as his jockey would have liked. He stayed on without threatening the winner and looks well worth a try at 7f now. Official explanation: vet said colt finished sore behind (op 4-6 tchd 8-11)

Celestial Dream(IRE), the second known foal of smart sprinter Lochangel, travelled really strongly on this racecourse debut but could not quicken under pressure and found no extra in the final furlong. She should learn from the experience and may prefer faster ground. (op 13-2)

Art Fund(USA) is now qualified for a handicap mark and looks sure to fare better in that sphere.

6895 NASH PARTNERSHIP H'CAP 5f 161y
3:30 (3:31) (Class 6) (0-58,58) 3-Y-O+ **£1,942** (£578; £288; £144) **Stalls** Centre

Form RPR

0412 **1** **Kyllachy Storm**[23] 6334 4-8-10 55 WilliamCarson(5) 7 69
(R J Hodges) *trckd ldrs: led jst ins fnl f: styd on wl fnl f* **7/2**[1]

0400 **2** 2 ¼ **Harrison's Flyer (IRE)**[44] 5751 7-8-9 54 (p) JackDean(5) 11 60
(J M Bradley) *chsd ldrs: rdn and chsd wnr finmal f but a hld* **25/1**

5040 **3** ½ **Namu**[1] 6890 5-9-0 54 JimCrowley 17 58
(Miss T Spearing) *towards rr: rdn 1/2-way: hdwy over 1f out: kpt on but nt rch ldng duo* **9/1**

0120 **4** 1 ½ **Exit Strategy (IRE)**[49] 5601 4-8-13 56 (b) KevinGhunowa(3) 4 55
(R A Harris) *mid-div: rdn and hdwy fr 2f out: kpt on same pce ins fnl f* **8/1**[3]

2054 **5** 2 ½ **Eleanor Eloise (USA)**[10] 6681 4-9-1 55 (b[1]) J-PGuillambert 10 46
(J R Gask) *in rr: rdn 1/2-way: hdwy appr fnl f: gng on cl home* **9/1**

0200 **6** 1 ¾ **Our Fugitive (IRE)**[42] 5801 6-9-4 58 (v[1]) AdamKirby 5 43
(C Gordon) *chsd ldr: led appr fnl 2f: hdd sn after: wknd ins fnl f* **16/1**

044 **7** ¾ **Nordic Light (USA)**[23] 6334 4-8-10 50 (b) TravisBlock 3 32
(J M Bradley) *slt ld tl hdd appr fnl 2f: wknd fnl f* **16/1**

0020 **8** 3 ¼ **Mr Forthright**[51] 5582 4-8-8 48 (b) SteveDrowne 2 19
(J M Bradley) *mid-div: rdn and styd on same pce fnl 2f* **18/1**

2240 **9** 1 ¼ **Fast Freddie**[23] 6339 4-8-11 56 DavidProbert(5) 12 23
(S Parr) *pressed ldrs: rdn over 2f out: wknd over 1f out* **4/1**[2]

5460 **10** 2 **Caustic Wit (IRE)**[41] 5817 10-9-3 57 (p) TGMcLaughlin 9 17
(M S Saunders) *in rr: sme prog u.p fnl 2f: nvr in contention* **12/1**

0210 **11** hd **Willhewiz**[10] 6679 8-8-9 56 (v) DeanHeslop(7) 16 15
(W M Brisbourne) *chsd ldrs to 1/2-way* **12/1**

500 **12** 1 ¼ **Currency**[7] 6733 11-8-9 52 TolleyDean(3) 14 7
(J M Bradley) *sn outpcd* **33/1**

0400 **13** 1 **Last Of The Line**[23] 6338 3-8-9 57 (v) VictorSantos(7) 15 9
(H J L Dunlop) *a in rr* **33/1**

6060 **14** 8 **Night Prospector**[9] 6711 8-9-4 58 (b) JamieSpencer 6 —
(R A Harris) *chsd ldrs tl wknd qckly fr 2f out: eased ins fnl f* **12/1**

6000 **15** 2 ¾ **Jonny Ebeneezer**[7] 6232 9-9-1 55 TonyCulhane 1 —
(D Flood) *sn outpcd* **33/1**

0440 **16** 9 **Mr Funshine**[28] 6204 3-8-11 55 JackMitchell(3) 8 —
(Mrs P N Dutfield) *in tch: wknd and eased fr 2f out* **40/1**

1m 16.17s (4.97) **Going Correction** +0.55s/f (Yiel)

WFA 3 from 4yo+ 1lb **16 Ran SP% 128.5**

Speed ratings (Par 101): **88,85,84,82,79 76,75,71,69,67 66,65,63,53,49 37**

toteswinger: 1&2 £23.50, 1&3 £9.20, 2&3 £47.80. CSF £105.10 CT £799.67 TOTE £4.10: £1.10, £4.70, £3.70, £2.60; EX 95.00 Trifecta £186.10 Part won. Pool: £251.57 - 0.10 winning units..

Owner Mrs Angela Hart **Bred** Sir Eric Parker **Trained** Charlton Mackrell, Somerset

FOCUS

A moderate sprint handicap in which they came middle to stands' side. The winner produced a slight personal best and is perhaps the best guide to the form.

Fast Freddie Official explanation: jockey said gelding was unsuited by the good to soft ground

Night Prospector Official explanation: jockey said gelding hung right

6896 PROFAB WINDOWS MAIDEN FILLIES' STKS 1m 2f 46y
4:00 (4:05) (Class 5) 3-Y-O+ **£2,719** (£809; £404; £202) **Stalls** Low

Form RPR

53 **1** **Surrealism**[25] 6275 3-8-12 0 SteveDrowne 8 86+
(J H M Gosden) *trckd ldr: led over 2f out: forged clr fnl f: readily* **6/4**[1]

2245 **2** 2 ¾ **Ainia**[13] 6605 3-8-12 74 RichardMullen 14 80
(D M Simcock) *chsd ldrs: drvn to chal appr fnl 2f: styd chsng wnr but no ch fr over 1f out* **11/4**[2]

306 **3** 6 **Miss Brown To You (IRE)**[151] 2413 3-8-12 77 JamieSpencer 13 68
(M L W Bell) *chsd ldr: rdn over 3f out: wknd 2f out* **33/1**

4405 **4** 10 **Poyle Dee Dee**[22] 6363 3-8-12 68 RichardHughes 4 48
(R M Beckett) *in rr: rdn and sme hdwy fr 4f out: no ch w ldrs fnl 3f* **14/1**

3042 **5** 4 ½ **Crazy About You (IRE)**[6] 6748 3-8-12 67 MichaelHills 1 39
(B W Hills) *sn led: rdn over 3f out: hdd & wknd qckly over 2f out* **7/1**[3]

46-0 **6** 5 **Tomorrow's World (IRE)**[161] 2109 3-8-12 71 TGMcLaughlin 9 29
(M S Saunders) *in rr: mod prog fnl 3f* **25/1**

0/ **7** 7 **Rosemarkie**[707] 6486 4-9-3 0 FrankieMcDonald 15 15
(B J Llewellyn) *slowly away: a in rr* **100/1**

00 **8** 4 ½ **Indiana Fox**[6] 6748 5-9-3 0 TQuinn 7 6
(B G Powell) *a in rr* **100/1**

0 **9** 10 **Lady Hestia (USA)**[14] 6571 3-8-12 0 MartinDwyer 2 —
(M P Tregoning) *chsd ldrs: rdn 5f out: wknd qckly 4f out* **20/1**

0000 **10** 2 ¼ **Ubiquitous**[23] 6337 3-8-7 42 DavidProbert(5) 12 —
(S Dow) *chsd ldrs: wknd qckly over 3f out* **100/1**

06 **11** 5 **Sharki**[9] 6705 3-8-12 0 JimCrowley 5 —
(J H M Gosden) *chsd ldrs 5f* **20/1**

0300 **12** 1 **Poppy Red**[78] 4707 3-8-12 47 VinceSlattery 6 —
(C J Gray) *a in rr* **150/1**

2m 16.87s (5.87) **Going Correction** +0.80s/f (Soft)

WFA 3 from 4yo+ 5lb **12 Ran SP% 105.8**

Speed ratings (Par 100): **108,105,101,93,89 85,79,76,68,66 62,61**

toteswinger: 1&2 £1.40, 1&3 £6.30, 2&3 £12.40. CSF £3.90 TOTE £2.20: £1.20, £1.20, £3.60; EX 5.20 Trifecta £60.60 Pool: £201.57 - 2.46 winning units..

Owner H R H Princess Haya Of Jordan **Bred** Aston House Stud **Trained** Newmarket, Suffolk

■ Filigree Lace was withdrawn (13/2, deduct 10p in the £ under R4).

FOCUS

Two drew clear in what was an ordinary fillies' maiden in which they came across to the stands' side. The winner produced a step up with the second to form. There were some big gaps down the field and the form looks sound.

6897 M.J. CHURCH H'CAP 2m 1f 34y
4:30 (4:32) (Class 5) (0-75,71) 3-Y-O **£2,914** (£867; £433; £216) **Stalls** Low

Form RPR

011 **1** **Rutba**[49] 5613 3-8-8 58 (v) MartinDwyer 8 63
(M P Tregoning) *chsd ldrs 1/2-way: drvn to ld over 1f out: sn edgd lft: r.o strly fnl f* **3/1**[2]

5052 **2** 2 **Forget It**[7] 6740 3-8-12 62 RichardHughes 3 65
(R Hannon) *led: shkn up 1/2-way: rdn over 3f out: hdd over 2f out: edgd lft fr 2f out: styd on fnl f to hold 2nd but a wl hld by wnr* **7/2**[3]

0202 **3** shd **Corking (IRE)**[8] 6719 3-7-10 53 ow1 BillyCray(7) 7 56
(J L Flint) *chsd ldrs untl outpcd over 3f out: rallied u.p fr 2f out to press for 2nd ins fnl f but no ch w wnr* **12/1**

3250 **4** 2 ½ **Shaftesbury (IRE)**[170] 1871 3-9-1 65 SteveDrowne 4 65
(Jane Southcombe) *in rr and plenty to do whn rdn over 3f out: styd on u.p to cl on ldrs fr 2f out: no prog fnl f* **25/1**

6030 **5** 2 **Mary Athena (FR)**[27] 6226 3-8-1 56 DavidProbert(5) 1 53
(M G Quinlan) *hld up in rr: rdn and sme hdwy 4f out: wknd over 2f out* **20/1**

6643 **6** 1 ¼ **Opera De Luna**[6] 6754 3-8-11 61 DarrenWilliams 6 57
(D Shaw) *in rr tl hdwy to chse ldrs 4f out: styd stands' side and wknd over 2f out* **17/2**

2542 **7** 5 **Spiritonthemount (USA)**[110] 3671 3-9-7 71 TonyCulhane 2 61
(P W Hiatt) *chsd ldrs to 5f out: styd stands' side and wknd fr 3f out* **13/2**

0041 **8** 2 **Goldrenched (IRE)**[21] 6386 3-9-3 67 JamieSpencer 5 55
(M L W Bell) *chsd ldr: rdn 5f out: wknd ins fnl 3f* **11/4**[1]

4m 6.24s (14.34) **Going Correction** +0.80s/f (Soft) **8 Ran SP% 114.0**

Speed ratings (Par 101): **98,97,97,95,94 94,91,91**

toteswinger: 1&2 £1.80, 1&3 £3.90, 2&3 £3.00. CSF £13.89 CT £107.02 TOTE £3.80: £1.30, £1.70, £3.50; EX 12.90 Trifecta £85.20 Pool: £549.54 - 4.77 winning units..

Owner William Lea Screed Mac's Plaster & Home **Bred** Shadwell Estate Company Limited **Trained** Lambourn, Berks

FOCUS

The pace lifted a long way from home in this stayers' contest and they were all over the course in the final quarter-mile. The bare form is only modest but the winner may do better yet.

Shaftesbury(IRE) Official explanation: jockey said gelding hung both ways

Goldrenched(IRE) Official explanation: jockey said filly had no more to give

6898 PREMPRO RACING H'CAP 1m 3f 144y
5:00 (5:02) (Class 4) (0-80,80) 3-Y-O+ **£4,857** (£1,445; £722; £360) **Stalls** Low

Form RPR

3430 **1** **Spirit Of Adjisa (IRE)**[15] 6551 4-8-11 73 (b) DavidProbert(5) 12 83
(Pat Eddery) *chsd ldrs: led over 4f out: rdn over 2f out: hld on wl whn strly chal thrght fnl f* **7/1**[2]

1044 **2** nk **Force Group (IRE)**[2] 6862 4-8-10 74 AshleyMorgan(7) 8 84
(M H Tompkins) *mid-div: hdwy 6f out: chsd ldrs 3f out: chsd wnr 2f out: str chal fnl f: no ex cl home* **13/2**[1]

2000 **3** 3 ½ **Brave Mave**[7] 6741 3-8-3 67 FrancisNorton 2 71
(W Jarvis) *in rr: rdn over 3f out: hdwy fr 2f out: kpt on to take 3rd ins fnl f: nt rch ldrs* **8/1**

0330 **4** nk **Jadaara**[43] 5773 3-9-0 78 J-PGuillambert 16 82
(M Johnston) *chsd ldrs: rdn 4f out: one pce fnl 2f* **10/1**

6454 **5** 1 ¼ **Mae Cigan (FR)**[13] 6606 5-8-9 66 oh3 SteveDrowne 7 68
(M Blanshard) *in rr: rdn over 3f out: hdwy over 2f out: styd on fr over 1f out: nt rch ldrs* **7/1**[2]

4351 **6** 1 ¾ **Mistress Eva**[13] 6607 3-8-3 72 ow1 WilliamCarson(5) 11 71
(P Winkworth) *in rr: rdn over 3f out: styd on fr over 1f out: gng on cl home* **7/1**[2]

0-50 **7** nk **Cantabilly (IRE)**[10] 6671 5-8-8 70 MCGeran(5) 10 69
(R J Hodges) *chsd ldrs tl lost pl over 4f out: styd on again fnl 2f* **25/1**

6020 **8** 2 ¼ **Top Ticket (IRE)**[16] 6542 3-8-11 75 RichardMullen 15 70
(D M Simcock) *led tl hdd 9f out: lost pl over 3f out: sn rdn: n.d after* **12/1**

0000 **9** ¾ **William's Way**[3] 6839 6-8-13 76 PaulMulrennan 13 64
(I A Wood) *in rr: hdwy 6f out: no prog fnl 3f* **25/1**

110 **10** 3 1/2 **Fearless Warrior**[35] 6012 3-8-9 **73** ow1....................(b) RichardHughes 4 61
(J L Dunlop) *led 9f out: hdd over 4f out: wknd qckly over 2f out* **15/2**[3]
1335 **11** 2 **Hawridge King**[22] 6361 6-9-6 **80**.................................. JamesMillman(3) 5 65
(W S Kittow) *bhd tl sme prog fnl 2f* **16/1**
0350 **12** 3/4 **Venir Rouge**[67] 5092 4-9-1 **72**.................................. TGMcLaughlin 14 56
(M Salaman) *chsd ldrs: rdn over 3f out: sn btn* **12/1**
0005 **13** 1 1/2 **Prince Desire (IRE)**[9] 6703 3-8-3 **67**......................(p) CatherineGannon 3 48
(Tom Dascombe) *bhd fnl 4f* **20/1**
5136 **14** 6 **Apache Fort**[12] 6626 5-8-13 **70**.. TonyCulhane 6 42
(T Keddy) *chsd ldrs 1m* **20/1**
405- **15** 27 **Dundry**[359] 6545 7-9-2 **73**..(p) TravisBlock 9 —
(G L Moore) *chsd ldrs 1m: virtually p.u fnl 2f* **16/1**
0240 **16** 21 **Optimus (USA)**[13] 6607 6-8-10 **67**... TQuinn 1 —
(B G Powell) *a in rr: virtually p.u fnl 3f* **25/1**

2m 39.72s (9.12) **Going Correction** +0.80s/f (Soft)
WFA 3 from 4yo+ 7lb **16** Ran SP% **131.0**
Speed ratings (Par 105): **101,100,98,98,97 96,96,94,94,91 90,89,88,84,66 52**
toteswinger: 1&2 £11.40, 1&3 £27.20, 2&3 £27.20. CSF £51.78 CT £382.97 TOTE £6.30: £1.70, £2.50, £3.70, £1.90; EX 51.70 TRIFECTA Not won..
Owner Darr, Johnson, Weston & Whitaker **Bred** C J Haughey J Flynn And E Mulhern **Trained** Nether Winchendon, Bucks

FOCUS
A competitive handicap in which the winner and second produced improved form under claimers, with the runner-up to form.
Optimus(USA) Official explanation: jockey said gelding lost its action

6899 BETFAIR APPRENTICE TRAINING SERIES H'CAP 1m 5y
5:30 (5:30) (Class 5) (0-75,75) 3-Y-0+ **£2,719** (£809; £404; £202) **Stalls** Low

Form RPR
6411 **1** **Moves Goodenough**[14] 6585 5-9-2 **69**........................(b) DeanHeslop 2 84
(Andrew Turnell) *in tch: hdwy 3f out: drvn to ld wl over 1f out: sn clr: easily* **9/1**[3]
-653 **2** 6 **Prairie Storm**[145] 2564 3-9-4 **74**.. DavidProbert 5 75
(A M Balding) *chsd ldrs: led over 2f out: hdd wl over 1f out: kpt on but nvr any ch w easy wnr* **7/2**[2]
0601 **3** shd **Support Fund (IRE)**[10] 6671 4-9-0 **74** 6ex............... DanielBlackett(7) 12 75
(Eve Johnson Houghton) *mid-div: rdn and hdwy fr 3f out: disp 2nd fnl f but no ch w easy wnr* **16/1**
2113 **4** 1 1/4 **Effigy**[13] 6598 4-9-5 **75**... AmyScott(3) 9 73+
(H Candy) *in rr: stl plenty to do whn hdwy fr 2f out: fin wl but nt rch ldrs* **3/1**[1]
6613 **5** 3/4 **Grey Boy (GER)**[10] 6671 7-9-3 **70**...................................... AshleyMorgan 1 66
(A W Carroll) *in rr tl hdwy fr 3f out: styd on fnl f but nvr gng pce to chal* **16/1**
-041 **6** 1 3/4 **Barkass (UAE)**[21] 6385 4-9-1 **68**............................... FrederikTylicki 11 60
(B Ellison) *in tch: hdwy and rdn fr 3f out: nt rch ldrs and wknd ins fnl f* **3/1**[1]
6330 **7** 2 **Cool Ebony**[22] 6363 5-9-7 **74**............................... Louis-PhilippeBeuzelin 7 62
(P J Makin) *mid-div: rdn and hdwy fr 3f out: nvr rchd ldrs and wknd over 1f out* **11/1**
0005 **8** 2 1/2 **Very Well Red**[10] 6671 5-8-12 **65**... JackDean 8 47
(P W Hiatt) *slt ld 3f: led again 4f out: hdd & wknd over 2f out* **16/1**
0000 **9** 3 **Sky Quest (IRE)**[5] 6771 10-8-1 **61** oh4.................. NathanAlison(7) 6 36
(J R Boyle) *in tch: chsd ldrs and rdn 3f out: wknd 2f out* **66/1**
0/0- **10** 4 **Barodine**[167] 444 5-9-3 **70**.. MCGeran 14 36
(R J Hodges) *chsd ldrs 5f* **66/1**
0050 **11** 19 **Valart**[27] 6226 5-8-1 **61** oh16.......................................(t) GemmaElford(7) 15 —
(M R Bosley) *slowly away: sn chsd ldrs: wknd 4f out* **100/1**
031 **12** 4 1/2 **Willridge**[69] 5023 3-9-2 **72**... RossAtkinson 4 —
(Tom Dascombe) *led after 3f: hdd 4f out: wknd qckly 3f out* **25/1**
6652 **13** 2 1/2 **Candy Rose**[20] 6417 3-8-0 **61**.. KatiaScallan(5) 13 —
(M P Tregoning) *a in rr* **14/1**

1m 46.72s (5.92) **Going Correction** +0.80s/f (Soft)
WFA 3 from 4yo+ 3lb **13** Ran SP% **122.7**
Speed ratings (Par 103): **102,96,95,94,93 92,90,87,84,80 61,57,54**
toteswinger: 1&2 £8.20, 1&3 £28.60, 2&3 £14.80. CSF £41.17 CT £534.68 TOTE £7.90: £2.40, £1.70, £5.20; EX 61.10 TRIFECTA Not won. Place 6: £38.57 Place 5: £7.01..
Owner D Goodenough Removals & Transport **Bred** G Foster **Trained** Broad Hinton, Wilts

FOCUS
A low-grade handicap run in a modest time. Moves Goodenough showed improved form.
T/Plt: £27.30 to a £1 stake. Pool: £52,507.91. 1,401.06 winning tickets. T/Qpdt: £3.10 to a £1 stake. Pool: £4,326.40. 1,002.40 winning tickets. ST

6751 GREAT LEIGHS (A.W) (L-H)
Wednesday, October 22

OFFICIAL GOING: Standard
Wind: fresh, behind Weather: bright, chilly

6900 ALPHA MEDICAL H'CAP 1m (P)
2:10 (2:11) (Class 4) (0-85,85) 3-Y-0+ **£5,180** (£1,541; £770; £384) **Stalls** Centre

Form RPR
3612 **1** **Hall Hee (IRE)**[24] 6311 3-8-11 **78**.. PatDobbs 9 89
(M P Tregoning) *stdd and dropped in bhd after s: pushed along and hdwy over 2f out: rdn and pressed ldrs over 1f out: led jst ins fnl f: r.o wl* **3/1**[1]
-210 **2** 1 3/4 **Resurge (IRE)**[95] 4197 3-9-4 **85**.. ShaneKelly 1 92
(J Noseda) *s.i.s: sn bustled along to chsd ldrs: plld out off rail over 2f out: led wl 1f: sn rdn and hung rt: hdd jst ins fnl f: one pce* **6/1**
-004 **3** 2 3/4 **Amazing Star (IRE)**[12] 6625 3-9-4 **85**................................... NCallan 12 86
(M Halford, Ire) *hld up in midfield: hdwy over 2f out: pressed ldrs and rdn over 1f out: outpcd by ldng pair fnl f* **4/1**[2]
6305 **4** 3/4 **Obezyana (USA)**[35] 6035 6-8-8 **72**..................................... MickyFenton 6 71
(A Bailey) *wnt rt s: chsd ldr tl over 5f out: styd handy: rdn and ev ch whn carried rt wl over 1f out: wknd ins fnl f* **11/1**
0040 **5** 2 1/2 **Man Of Gwent (UAE)**[14] 6582 4-8-7 **71**................................... JohnEgan 14 64
(P D Evans) *bhd: detached last and rdn 4f out: styd on past btn horses fr jst over 1f out: nvr trbld ldrs* **14/1**
6000 **6** nk **Mount Hadley (USA)**[13] 6598 4-8-11 **75**........................(b) HayleyTurner 8 68
(G A Butler) *hmpd s: pushed along early: bhd: hdwy over 2f out: n.m.r briefly wl over 1f out: no imp fr jst over 1f out* **12/1**
5010 **7** 1/2 **Buxton**[18] 6471 4-9-5 **83**...(t) RobertHavlin 5 74
(R Ingram) *hld up wl in tch: rdn and effrt wl over 1f out: wknd ent fnl f* **18/1**
0004 **8** 1 3/4 **Mey Blossom**[18] 6471 3-8-7 **77** ow2.............................. RussellKennemore(3) 13 64
(R M Whitaker) *dropped in towards rr after s: rdn and little rspnse 3f out: nvr trbld ldrs* **25/1**
0500 **9** 3 1/2 **Silver Hotspur**[14] 6576 4-9-4 **82**.. DaneO'Neill 2 61
(C R Dore) *hld up in midfield: hdwy over 2f out: drvn and shortlived effrt on inner wl over 1f out: wknd qckly over 1f out* **33/1**
3320 **10** 1 3/4 **Moonlight Man**[13] 6598 7-9-1 **79**..................................(t) RobertWinston 4 54
(C R Dore) *led: rdn over 2f out: hdd wl over 1f out: wknd qckly over 1f out* **16/1**
6202 **11** 2 1/4 **Almoutaz (USA)**[29] 6194 3-9-2 **83**.. RHills 7 53
(B W Hills) *w ldrs: wnt 2nd over 5f out: pressed ldr and hung rt over 2f out: rdn 2f out: sn btn: eased fnl f* **9/2**[3]
0060 **12** 10 **Solent Ridge (IRE)**[51] 5580 3-9-2 **83**............................(b[1]) TedDurcan 10 30
(J S Moore) *hld up towards rr: rdn over 2f out: struggling wl over 1f out: no ch and eased fnl f* **25/1**

1m 39.73s (-0.17) **Going Correction** +0.025s/f (Slow)
WFA 3 from 4yo+ 3lb **12** Ran SP% **119.0**
Speed ratings (Par 105): **101,99,96,95,93 92,92,90,87,85 83,73**
toteswinger: 1&2 £3.50, 1&3 £3.40, 2&3 £5.70. CSF £19.95 CT £75.28 TOTE £4.30: £1.60, £1.80, £1.70; EX 24.60.
Owner Sheikh Ahmed Al Maktoum **Bred** Hawthorn Villa Stud **Trained** Lambourn, Berks

FOCUS
Quite a competitive handicap and the pace seemed a fair one with a trio of horses disputing the early lead. The winner is up 9lb and the second 6lb, with the third to form.
Man Of Gwent(UAE) Official explanation: jockey said gelding would not face the kick-back
Almoutaz(USA) Official explanation: jockey said colt hung badly right
Solent Ridge(IRE) Official explanation: jockey said gelding had no more to give

6901 MARKS TEY MAIDEN FILLIES' STKS 1m (P)
2:40 (2:42) (Class 4) 2-Y-0 **£5,828** (£1,734; £866; £432) **Stalls** Centre

Form RPR
4 **1** **Wajaha (IRE)**[19] 6443 2-9-0 0.. RHills 8 80+
(J H M Gosden) *hld up in last trio: hdwy on outer over 3f out: chsd ldr over 2f out: rdn to ld over 1f out: in command ins fnl f: eased nr fin* **8/11**[1]
63 **2** 2 3/4 **Charlotte Point (USA)**[12] 6620 2-9-0 0.. NCallan 3 72
(P F I Cole) *hld up wl in tch: effrt and bmpd rival wl over 2f out: chsd wnr jst ins fnl f: no imp on wnr* **11/2**[3]
20 **3** 3/4 **Furious Belle (IRE)**[22] 6360 2-9-0 0..................................... AlanMunro 5 70
(P W Chapple-Hyam) *chsd ldr unti led over 5f out: rdn 2f out: hdd over 1f out: wknd ent fnl f* **9/2**[2]
034 **4** 2 1/4 **Persian Memories (IRE)**[25] 6273 2-9-0 78........................ EddieAhern 7 65
(J L Dunlop) *dwlt: hld up in midfield: lost pl over 3f out: rdn and no hdwy over 2f out: plugged on steadily fnl f: no ch w ldrs* **11/2**[3]
0 **5** 1 **Cobos**[61] 5240 2-9-0 0.. RobertWinston 2 63
(M G Quinlan) *led tl over 5f out: chsd ldr tl over 2f out: wknd over 1f out* **100/1**
00 **6** 2 1/2 **Kiyari**[12] 6622 2-9-0 0.. TedDurcan 9 58
(M Botti) *stdd and dropped in bhd after s: rdn over 4f out: no ch fr wl over 1f out* **40/1**
000 **7** nk **Veiled**[12] 6622 2-9-0 0.. DO'Donohoe 4 57
(Sir Mark Prescott) *sn pushed along in rr: rdn 3f out: wl btn last 2f* **33/1**
00 **8** 7 **Mill Pond**[43] 5788 2-9-0 0... RoystonFfrench 6 42
(M Johnston) *chsd ldrs: rdn and wkng whn bmpd rival wl over 2f out: wl bhd last 2f* **33/1**

1m 41.49s (1.59) **Going Correction** +0.025s/f (Slow) **8** Ran SP% **116.2**
Speed ratings (Par 94): **93,90,89,87,86 83,83,76**
toteswinger: 1&2 £2.10, 1&3 £2.20, 2&3 £3.10. CSF £5.30 TOTE £2.00: £1.10, £1.30, £1.70; EX 5.20.
Owner Hamdan Al Maktoum **Bred** Shadwell Estate Company Limited **Trained** Newmarket, Suffolk

FOCUS
Not the strongest of maidens even though all eight fillies had previous racecourse experience.

NOTEBOOK
Wajaha(IRE) was all the rage following her promising fourth on her Newmarket debut and she duly justified the support. Wide throughout, she had to be kept up to work after taking over in front, but she still scored in taking style and we should be hearing a lot more of her next season. (op 10-11 tchd evens in places)
Charlotte Point(USA), who improved when switched to Polytrack for her second start, raced handily early but she lost a little momentum when slightly awkward on the home turn and needed to be vigorously ridden to get back into contention. She stayed on again late and, although she was not in the same league as the favourite, this was a fair effort. She has a few more options now that she can be handicapped. (op 4-1)
Furious Belle(IRE), a disappointing favourite at Warwick last time after showing plenty of promise on her Yarmouth debut (though admittedly the form of that race has not worked out), was upped in trip again. Given a positive ride, she was comfortably brushed aside when the favourite arrived and didn't appear to get home. She can now be handicapped. (tchd 6-1)
Persian Memories(IRE), the most experienced in the field and an Irish Oaks entry, plugged on late but could never get anywhere near the leading trio and seemed to find even this 1m trip inadequate. Her official mark of 78 provides a benchmark to the form and she may be better off in nurseries. (op 7-1 tchd 5-1)
Cobos, tailed off on her Newmarket debut, has changed stables in the meantime and at least she showed a little ability here, having been ridden close to the pace from the off. (op 66-1)
Veiled Official explanation: jockey said, regarding the running and riding, his orders were to be handy early on, but filly did not have the speed to establish a position, and thereafter struggled, adding that filly is still immature and needs time to strengthen

6902 STOUR H'CAP 6f (P)
3:10 (3:10) (Class 3) (0-95,94) 3-Y-0+
£7,477 (£2,239; £1,119; £560; £279; £140) **Stalls** Low

Form RPR
0211 **1** **Beat The Bell**[12] 6634 3-8-5 **86**.. NicolPolli(5) 6 96
(A Bailey) *chsd ldrs: rdn and effrt wl over 1f out: ev ch ent fnl f: led ins fnl f: rdn out: hld on* **11/4**[1]
0100 **2** hd **Mister Hardy**[33] 6069 3-8-7 **83**.. TonyHamilton 11 93
(R A Fahey) *stdd after s: hld up towards rr: hdwy over 2f out: swtchd to inner and rdn over 1f out: chsd wnr wl ins fnl f: clsng towards fin* **16/1**
0023 **3** 1 1/4 **Lone Wolfe**[12] 6624 4-8-12 **87**.. IanMongan 7 92
(Jane Chapple-Hyam) *led and crossed to rail: rdn 2f out: hdd ins fnl f: wknd towards fin* **11/2**[3]
2000 **4** 1/2 **Silver Wind**[12] 6624 3-8-4 **80**...(v) JimmyQuinn 1 83
(P D Evans) *racd in midfield on inner: rdn over 3f out: hdwy on inner over 1f out: chsd ldrs 1f out: kpt on same pce fnl 100yds* **4/1**[2]
0360 **5** 1/2 **Carcinetto (IRE)**[5] 6783 6-8-11 **86**.. DaneO'Neill 9 87
(P D Evans) *sn pushed along: rdn and struggling 1/2-way: hdwy 1f out: r.o wl ins fnl f: nvr rchd ldrs* **16/1**

3626 **6** *nk* **Orpenindeed (IRE)**[12] 6624 5-9-0 **89**................................(t) JohnEgan 4 89
(M Botti) *chsd ldrs: sltly hmpd after 1f: rdn and n.m.r fr wl over 1f out: swtchd rt ins fnl f: kpt on same pce* **9/2**[2]

3345 **7** *nk* **Matsunosuke**[10] 6669 6-9-5 **94**.............................. AlanMunro 2 93
(A B Coogan) *trckd ldrs: gng wl over 2f out: rdn and effrt over 1f out: pressed ldr ent fnl f: nt qckn: wknd fnl 100yds* **10/1**

0520 **8** *1* **Lodi (IRE)**[18] 6478 3-8-7 **83**..(t) RobertWinston 3 79
(J Akehurst) *s.i.s: bhd: hdwy over 3f out: rdn wl over 2f out: hung lft and no imp over 1f out* **16/1**

0015 **9** *nk* **Vhujon (IRE)**[18] 6471 3-8-12 **88**.................................. SimonWhitworth 5 83
(P D Evans) *s.i.s: hld up bhd: rdn over 1f out: swtchd rt 1f out: kpt on but nvr trbld ldrs* **20/1**

3000 **10** *nk* **Evens And Odds (IRE)**[11] 6653 4-9-3 **92**..........................(b) NCallan 12 85
(K A Ryan) *chsd ldrs on outer: rdn over 2f out: drvn over 1f out: wknd jst ins fnl f* **6/1**

0064 **11** *6* **Tabaret**[25] 6285 5-9-4 **93**..(p) DeanMcKeown 8 65
(R M Whitaker) *chsd ldr tl wl over 1f out: sn hung lft: wknd jst over 1f out: eased whn wl btn ins fnl f* **20/1**

3501 **12** *1 ¾* **Guilded Warrior**[25] 6277 5-8-13 **88**.................................. ChrisCatlin 10 54
(W S Kittow) *racd wd: bhd fr 1/2-way* **10/1**

1m 12.37s (-1.33) **Going Correction** +0.025s/f (Slow)
WFA 3 from 4yo+ 1lb **12** Ran SP% **122.8**
Speed ratings (Par 107): **109,108,107,106,105 105,104,103,103,102 94,92**
toteswinger: 1&2 £17.00, 1&3 £3.30, 2&3 £44.90. CSF £51.71 CT £241.76 TOTE £3.10: £1.60, £6.00, £1.90; EX 95.00.
Owner D J P Turner **Bred** D J P Turner **Trained** Newmarket, Suffolk

FOCUS
A competitive sprint handicap and there were five horses in a line across the track well inside the last furlong. Pretty sound form, with the winner maintaining his improvement.

NOTEBOOK
Beat The Bell had been hoisted 10lb for his recent easy Wolverhampton win, but it was not enough to stop him completing the hat-trick. Once again well handled by his young rider, he was always close to the pace and when the gap presented itself he made full use of it. It would be brave to say he cannot extend his winning sequence in his current mood and connections have their eyes on a possible trip to Dubai. (op 10-3 tchd 7-2)
Mister Hardy, well beaten in his only previous attempt on sand, was dropped right out from his wide draw and trailed the field for much of the way. He put in a powerful finish when switched to the inside rail in the home straight and this should give connections the courage to give him another try on Polytrack. (op 14-1)
Lone Wolfe, without a win since his racecourse debut but in front of both Orpenindeed and Silver Wind when third at Lingfield last time, ran a fine race from the front and never stopped trying. He continues to run well in defeat on this surface and deserves to win another race. (op 8-1)
Silver Wind, not at his best recently and well beaten on his sand debut last time, was having to be niggled along to go the pace at various stages, but stayed on strongly tight against the inside rail up the home straight and this was much better. (op 25-1)
Carcinetto(IRE) was forced to make her effort widest of all and although finishing well she was never going to get there. Still 4lb above her last winning mark, this effort suggests she needs a return to 7f but her recent efforts over that trip have been modest. (op 14-1)
Orpenindeed(IRE) tracked the leaders early and had every chance, but he has consistently found one or two to beat him in his previous 11 outings in this country and his handicap mark remains pretty static as a result. (op 13-2)
Matsunosuke, not disgraced in decent company this term, was always up there and was travelling as well as anything starting up the home straight, but he was never doing quite enough once off the bridle. He is without a win in over a year, but is still 3lb higher. (op 8-1)
Evens And Odds(IRE), well beaten lately but now 2lb lower than for his last win at Southwell in February, showed up for a long way despite being trapped out wide and he would be of special interest if finding another opportunity back on Fibresand.

6903 NEW HOLLAND CONDITIONS STKS 6f (P)
3:40 (3:41) (Class 3) 3-Y-0+ **£7,771** (£2,312; £1,155; £288; £288) **Stalls** Low

Form RPR

3350 **1** **Prohibit**[130] 3047 3-9-0 97.. RobertHavlin 8 108
(J H M Gosden) *hld up towards rr: hdwy over 1f out: led 1f out: edgd rt but a holding runner up fnl f: rdn out* **12/1**

313 **2** *¾* **Diriculous**[47] 5681 4-9-1 97.. JohnEgan 6 106
(T G Mills) *hld up in tch: hdwy to trck ldrs over 2f out: swtchd rt and effrt wl over 1f out: pressed wnr fnl f: kpt on same pce* **7/2**[1]

0 **3** *¾* **Hitchens (IRE)**[25] 6269 3-9-0 103.................................... GeorgeBaker 2 104
(G L Moore) *led narrowly tl hdd over 2f out: rdn 2f out: led again over 1f out: hdd 1f out: no ex fnl 100yds* **6/1**[3]

3400 **4** *nk* **Bonus (IRE)**[25] 6285 8-9-6 105................................(e[1]) HayleyTurner 10 108
(G A Butler) *s.i.s: sn detached in last pl and pushed along: stl last but in tch 2f out: hdwy over 1f out: kpt on fnl f: nvr rchd ldrs* **20/1**

0023 **4** *dht* **Ebraam (USA)**[18] 6468 5-9-1 99.. IanMongan 9 103
(P Howling) *hld up towards rr: hdwy on inner 2f out: chsd ldrs jst over 1f out: kpt on same pce u.p fnl f* **15/2**

0543 **6** *4* **Oldjoesaid**[29] 6184 4-9-1 103.. DaneO'Neill 1 90
(H Candy) *w ldr tl led narrowly over 2f out: sn rdn: hdd over 1f out: wknd fnl f* **7/2**[1]

2200 **7** *1 ½* **Advanced**[24] 6304 5-9-1 100.. NCallan 7 85
(K A Ryan) *towards rr: hdwy on outer and rdn over 2f out: drvn wl over 1f out: wknd jst over 1f out* **7/1**

5600 **8** *3 ½* **Mac Gille Eoin**[25] 6289 4-9-1 95.. ChrisCatlin 5 74
(J Gallagher) *prom on outer: rdn over 2f out: wknd over 1f out: no ch fnl f* **25/1**

04 **9** *9* **Biniou (IRE)**[43] 5781 5-9-1 100.. ShaneKelly 3 45
(R M H Cowell) *awkward leaving stalls and s.i.s: sn in tch in midfield: effrt on inner wl over 1f out: wknd qckly over 1f out: eased fnl f* **66/1**

10-5 **10** *3* **Major Eazy (IRE)**[11] 6645 3-9-0 100................................... EddieAhern 4 35
(B J Meehan) *w ldrs tl 1/2-way: sn rdn and struggling: wl bhd and eased fnl f* **11/2**[2]

1m 12.2s (-1.50) **Going Correction** +0.025s/f (Slow)
WFA 3 from 4yo+ 1lb **10** Ran SP% **116.2**
Speed ratings (Par 107): **111,110,109,108,108 103,101,96,84,80**
toteswinger: 1&2 £8.20, 1&3 £16.30, 2&3 £5.80. CSF £52.70 TOTE £11.70: £3.10, £1.70, £2.50; EX 67.70.
Owner K Abdulla **Bred** Juddmonte Farms Ltd **Trained** Newmarket, Suffolk

FOCUS
A decent conditions sprint and the winning time was 0.17 seconds faster than the preceding handicap. Sound conditions race form in the main, with the winner rated up 8lb on previous efforts.

NOTEBOOK
Prohibit, gelded since his last start, was returning from four months off and on this evidence the break has done him good. Given a patient ride, he found plenty when asked for his effort in the home straight and came between horses to win tidily. He seems to go well fresh, but he had a few pounds to find with most of his rivals on these terms, so this was a good effort. He looks capable of winning something even better on this surface if such a race can be found. (op 11-1 tchd 10-1)
Diriculous, a winner seven times on sand in the past year and unbeaten in two previous attempts here, raced close to the pace throughout and put in a strong late run down the wide outside, but the winner was always holding him (tchd 4-1)
Hitchens(IRE), joint best in at the weights for this sand debut, helped force the pace from the off and kept on very gamely when the challengers arrived. He seemed to handle the surface well enough and there will be another day. (op 7-1)
Ebraam(USA), a much-improved Polytrack sprinter in the past year, tried to get involved tight against the inside rail up the home straight, but whether racing on that strip helped him is debatable and he could never land a blow. (op 14-1)
Bonus(IRE), a multiple winner on Polytrack but well beaten on his return from nearly five months off here last time, was tried in a first-time eyeshield. Dropped right out early, he stayed on down the home straight but was never getting there in time. (op 14-1)
Oldjoesaid, yet to win beyond the minimum trip but one of those best in at these weights, helped set the pace but folded rather disappointingly. Just over a length behind Ebraam over this trip at Kempton in August, he enjoyed a 7lb pull, so the fact that he finished further behind that rival here suggests he was well below his best. (tchd 10-3)
Biniou(IRE) Official explanation: vet said that mare had lost both front shoes
Major Eazy(IRE), making his sand debut following a creditable return from a year off in a Group 3 at Ascot 11 days earlier, was well backed but after showing up for a while he dropped away tamely and there must be the strong possibility that he bounced. (op 9-1)

6904 GROUSE FILLIES' H'CAP 1m 2f (P)
4:10 (4:11) (Class 3) (0-90,90) 3-Y-0+
£7,477 (£2,239; £1,119; £560; £279; £140) **Stalls** Low

Form RPR

0000 **1** **Try Me (UAE)**[13] 6605 3-8-10 **82** ow2....................................... NCallan 1 89
(C E Brittain) *wnt rt s: mde all: set stdy gallop: rdn 2f out: hld on gamely u.p fnl f* **20/1**

2031 **2** *½* **Suzi Spends (IRE)**[6] 6758 3-8-6 **78** 6ex.......................... JimmyQuinn 4 84+
(H J Collingridge) *hld up in tch: n.m.r and bmpd over 2f out: nt clr run after tl gap opened 1f out: sn rdn: chsd wnr fnl 100yds: hld towards fin* **5/2**[1]

1115 **3** *1* **Oat Cuisine**[25] 6266 4-9-3 **84**.. HayleyTurner 7 88
(M L W Bell) *trckd ldr: rdn to chal wl over 1f out: edgd lft u.p over 1f out: unable qck fnl f* **4/1**[3]

0240 **4** *¾* **Rio Guru (IRE)**[20] 6415 3-8-6 **78**................................ EdwardCreighton 3 81
(M R Channon) *t.k.h: hld up in tch in rr: rdn and effrt over 1f out: edgd lft ent fnl f: kpt on same pce fnl 100yds* **16/1**

-552 **5** *1 ¾* **Red And White (IRE)**[9] 6704 3-8-5 **77**........................ RoystonFfrench 6 76
(M Johnston) *hld up in midfield on outer: rdn and edgd lft over 2f out: unable qck u.p 2f out: one pce after* **3/1**[2]

1-04 **6** *nk* **Mystery Sail (USA)**[83] 4571 3-8-5 **77**...........................(p) DO'Donohoe 2 75
(Mrs A J Perrett) *hld up in tch: effrt on inner and hung lft over 1f out: nt clr run after tl swtchd rt ins fnl f: nvr able to chal* **8/1**

0360 **7** *½* **Olympic City (BRZ)**[16] 6536 5-9-6 **90**............................ PatrickHills[(3)] 5 87
(M F De Kock, South Africa) *trckd ldng pair: rdn 2f out: pressed wnr over 1f out: wknd jst ins fnl f* **5/1**

05R0 **8** *5* **Lisathedaddy**[21] 6403 6-8-9 **83**..................................(p) KylieManser[(7)] 8 70
(B G Powell) *stdd s: hld up in last: rdn and btn wl over 1f out* **33/1**

2m 9.49s (0.89) **Going Correction** +0.025s/f (Slow)
WFA 3 from 4yo+ 5lb **8** Ran SP% **114.9**
Speed ratings (Par 104): **97,96,95,95,93 93,93,89**
toteswinger: 1&2 £7.80, 1&3 £10.80, 2&3 £3.60. CSF £70.44 CT £249.91 TOTE £34.30: £5.70, £1.50, £2.10; EX 100.60.
Owner Saeed Manana **Bred** Darley **Trained** Newmarket, Suffolk

FOCUS
A fair fillies' handicap, but it was something of a tactical affair with the winner making all at a steady pace. The form is ordinary at best and potentially midsleading given the slow gallop.

NOTEBOOK
Try Me(UAE), whose jockey put up 2lb overweight, was ideally placed to quicken from the front. She had struggled as a result of finishing five lengths behind the winner in the Cheshire Oaks, but the handicapper had given her a chance by dropping her back to a reasonable mark. It was, however, the way the race was run that was the determining factor in this result. Official explanation: trainer's rep said, regarding the apparent improvement in form, filly can be inconsistent and prefers to dominate its races, which it was able to do today (tchd 25-1)
Suzi Spends(IRE), who has a great record at this track, kept on well for pressure but just could not claw back the winner's advantage in the closing stages. She would have preferred a stronger gallop, but it was still a solid effort. (op 11-4)
Oat Cuisine, who has had a terrific season, was never too far off the pace but she was being rowed along leaving the back straight and, although she kept on for pressure, never looked like getting there. It could be that her long season is just catching up with her now. Official explanation: jockey said filly hung left in home straight (op 7-2)
Rio Guru(IRE) did best of those that were held up in rear, but she faced a tough task given the way the race was run.
Red And White(IRE) raced two or three horse-widths wide throughout and was one-paced and edged left under pressure in the straight. She was another who could have done with a stronger all-round gallop. (op 5-2 tchd 7-2)
Mystery Sail(USA), who was keen off the ordinary early pace and did not get the best of runs in the straight, was another who basically struggled to get involved having been held up. Official explanation: jockey said filly was denied a clear run (op 10-1 tchd 12-1)
Olympic City(BRZ) was another who raced keenly, and she dropped away after turning into the straight with every chance. (op 6-1)

6905 GREAT LEIGHS H'CAP 1m 2f (P)
4:40 (4:40) (Class 5) (0-70,76) 3-Y-0 **£3,238** (£963; £481; £240) **Stalls** Low

Form RPR

6331 **1** **Intabih (USA)**[9] 6712 3-9-10 **76** 6ex.................................... NCallan 6 89+
(C E Brittain) *hld up in midfield: hdwy over 2f out: rdn to ld over 1f out: clr 1f out: r.o wl: comf* **5/4**[1]

0621 **2** *1 ½* **Mick's Dancer**[12] 6629 3-9-3 **69**...................................... DO'Donohoe 3 79
(W R Muir) *t.k.h: hld up: stdd to last pl 8f out: swtchd rt and hdwy over 1f out: wnt 2nd 1f out: edgd lft and kpt on fnl f: nvr pce to rch wnr* **10/1**

4364 **3** *2 ¾* **Red Lily (IRE)**[16] 6529 3-9-0 **66**.................................(v[1]) RobertWinston 2 71
(J R Fanshawe) *hld up in midfield: rdn and hdwy 2f out: wnt 3rd jst ins fnl f: no ch w wnr* **13/2**[3]

1340 **4** *nk* **Moon Crystal**[20] 6422 3-9-1 **67**..(t) EddieAhern 10 71
(E A L Dunlop) *t.k.h: hld up in rr: hdwy and hmpd over 1f out: sn swtchd rt: disp 3rd ins fnl f: nvr trbld ldrs* **11/1**

2060 **5** *3 ½* **Taken (IRE)**[16] 6528 3-9-4 **70**.. JerryO'Dwyer 5 67
(Miss Gay Kelleway) *hld up wl in tch: rdn over 2f out: hrd drvn and chsd wnr briefly over 1f out: wknd fnl f* **25/1**

4042 **6** *3* **Colleoni (IRE)**[21] 6374 3-8-5 **57**...................................(v[1]) HayleyTurner 7 48
(G A Butler) *t.k.h: chsd ldr tl 8f out: chsd ldrs after: rdn wl over 2f out: hung lft over 1f out: sn wknd* **9/2**[2]

6635 **7** ¾ **Desert Thistle (IRE)**[15] 6558 3-9-0 66.....................(v) JimmyQuinn 8 55
(H J L Dunlop) *s.i.s: reminders early: hdwy to chse ldr 8f out: led over 2f out: rdn and hdd over 1f out: sn btn* **16/1**
450 **8** 1 ¾ **Joinedupwriting**[16] 6528 3-8-8 60.......................... DeanMcKeown 11 46
(R M Whitaker) *hld up in last trio: rdn wl over 1f out: no rspnse and wl btn after* **20/1**
0040 **9** ½ **Triple Dream**[20] 6422 3-9-1 67.......................... TedDurcan 1 52
(J L Dunlop) *t.k.h: chsd ldrs: rdn over 2f out: wknd qckly over 1f out* **9/1**
4006 **10** 3 ¾ **Classical Rhythm (IRE)**[19] 6437 3-8-6 61 ow1............ PatrickHills(3) 4 38
(J R Boyle) *led: rdn and hdd over 2f out: wknd qckly over 1f out: eased wl ins fnl f* **20/1**
2m 7.54s (-1.06) **Going Correction** +0.025s/f (Slow) 10 Ran SP% **122.6**
Speed ratings (Par 101): **105,103,101,101,98 96,95,94,93,90**
toteswinger: 1&2 £4.30, 1&3 £4.40, 2&3 £4.80. CSF £15.79 CT £66.67 TOTE £2.20: £1.40, £2.50, £1.50; EX 20.20 Place 6: £11.29 Place 5: £7.09.
Owner Saeed Manana **Bred** Dr George S Stefanis **Trained** Newmarket, Suffolk
FOCUS
An ordinary contest, but they went a more reasonable pace than in the preceding race and the winning time was almost two seconds quicker. The form is rated through the third, with another step forward from Intabih.
T/Jkpt: £76,745.30 to a £1 stake. Pool: £216,184.20. 2.00 winning tickets. T/Plt: £8.20 to a £1 stake. Pool: £61,998.51. 5,472.05 winning tickets. T/Qpdt: £5.10 to a £1 stake. Pool: £3,069.28. 439.46 winning tickets. SP

6768 KEMPTON (A.W) (R-H)
Wednesday, October 22

OFFICIAL GOING: Standard
Wind: Almost nil

6906 FIREWORK PARTY NIGHT HERE NOVEMBER 5TH NURSERY 5f (P)
5:50 (5:51) (Class 6) (0-60,60) 2-Y-O **£2,047** (£604; £302) **Stalls** High

Form RPR
000 **1** **Rainbow Seeker**[12] 6620 2-9-6 59..........................(b1) LiamJones 12 69+
(W J Haggas) *slowly away: sn chsng ldrs: led appr fnl f: pushed out: comf* **6/1**[3]
600 **2** 2 ¼ **Celtic Rebel (IRE)**[21] 6389 2-9-2 55.......................... PatCosgrave 10 57
(S A Callaghan) *t.k.h: chsd ldrs: r.o u.p to go 2nd ins fnl f* **9/4**[1]
6625 **3** 1 ½ **Imaginary Diva**[14] 6579 2-9-3 56..........................(v1) DaneO'Neill 6 53
(G G Margarson) *towards rr: hdwy on ins 2f out: rdn and r.o to go 3rd ins fnl f* **8/1**
030 **4** 1 **Imperial Skylight**[13] 6603 2-9-7 60.......................... SamHitchcott 2 53
(M R Channon) *racd wd: rdn and styd on to go 4th ins fnl f* **25/1**
6054 **5** 1 ½ **Miss Thippawan (USA)**[15] 6545 2-8-13 52............ SilvestreDeSousa 11 40
(P T Midgley) *led tl rdn and hdd appr fnl f: wknd ins fnl f* **6/1**[3]
00 **6** 1 ¾ **Kayceebee**[14] 6572 2-9-1 54.......................... RichardKingscote 7 35
(R M Beckett) *in rr: mde sme late hdwy* **13/2**
0503 **7** ½ **Claphands**[51] 5567 2-9-2 55..........................(p) GeorgeBaker 4 35
(G L Moore) *prom tl rdn and wknd over 1f out* **9/2**[2]
0045 **8** hd **Silver Salsa**[29] 6191 2-9-4 57.......................... TPQueally 3 36
(J R Jenkins) *rdn 1/2-way: a towards rr* **33/1**
3000 **9** 1 ¼ **True Britannia**[9] 6697 2-8-12 51.......................... AlanMunro 9 25
(S Kirk) *a in rr* **16/1**
2000 **10** 3 ¼ **Anacaona (IRE)**[14] 6572 2-9-5 58.......................... PatDobbs 8 21
(R Hannon) *chsd ldr to 2f out: wknd qckly* **25/1**
5000 **11** 1 ¼ **Drachenfels**[74] 4874 2-9-1 54.......................... ChrisCatlin 5 12
(K A Ryan) *outpcd thrght* **50/1**
60.65 secs (0.15) **Going Correction** +0.125s/f (Slow) 11 Ran SP% **120.4**
Speed ratings (Par 93): **103,99,97,95,93 90,89,89,87,81 79**
toteswinger: 1&2 £6.10, 1&3 £9.80, 2&3 £4.30. CSF £19.71 CT £114.69 TOTE £7.50: £2.50, £2.00, £3.10; EX 21.80.
Owner Dwayne Woods **Bred** Brook Stud Bloodstock Ltd **Trained** Newmarket, Suffolk
FOCUS
This was a moderate nursery in which a high draw proved a must. The form looks straightforward enough.
NOTEBOOK
Rainbow Seeker, dropping back from 7f, was blinkered for this switch to handicap company and broke his duck at the fourth time of asking. He was again slow to break, but soon recovered and was perfectly placed to strike when coming into the home straight. Showing a turn of foot when asked to seal the race, it was clear at the furlong pole he was the one to be on and obviously he has begun life in this sphere on a decent mark. He is entitled to show more as a sprinter, despite a likely rise up the handicap. Official explanation: trainer's rep said, regarding the apparent improvement in form, gelding was wearing blinkers for the first time and was down in trip from 7f to 5f
Celtic Rebel(IRE) had his chance on this nursery bow, but just lacked the turn of foot displayed by the winner. This was a definite step in the right direction, he has evidently now found his level, and a step back up to 6f should see him winning. (op 7-4 tchd 5-2)
Imaginary Diva, equipped with a first-time visor, remains winless and does not seem the most straightforward, but she did well from her modest draw. She is the best guide to this form.
Imperial Skylight, back down in trip, was tapped for toe, having been forced wide from his low draw. He was not disgraced. (tchd 20-1)
Miss Thippawan(USA) has now run her two most encouraging races on the all-weather, but she did get very much the run of the race out in front from her decent draw. Official explanation: jockey said filly hung left (tchd 13-2)

6907 BOOK KEMPTON TICKETS ON 0844 5793008 H'CAP 5f (P)
6:20 (6:23) (Class 6) (0-55,55) 3-Y-O+ **£2,047** (£604; £302) **Stalls** High

Form RPR
3642 **1** **Musical Script (USA)**[7] 6733 5-8-13 52..........................(b) DaneO'Neill 5 66
(Mouse Hamilton-Fairley) *a.p: led appr fnl f: r.o wl* **3/1**[1]
10-0 **2** 2 ½ **Sarah's Art (IRE)**[67] 5101 5-9-1 54.......................... MickyFenton 6 59+
(Stef Liddiard) *s.i.s: in rr tl hdwy and n.m.r over 1f out: swtchd lft: r.o to go 2nd cl home* **12/1**
0503 **3** shd **Nawaaff**[7] 6733 3-8-13 52..........................(v) TPO'Shea 12 57
(M R Channon) *a in tch: led briefly over 1f out: chsd wnr u.p tl lost 2nd cl home* **5/1**[3]
0320 **4** 1 ¾ **Billy Red**[23] 6334 4-9-2 55..........................(b) TPQueally 10 54
(J R Jenkins) *chsd ldrs: rdn and hung rt over 1f out: no ex fnl f* **5/1**[3]
5156 **5** nk **Welcome Approach**[10] 6679 5-9-2 55.......................... ChrisCatlin 2 53
(J R Weymes) *outpcd: gd hdwy on ins over 1f out: r.o: nvr nrr* **12/1**
3263 **6** 2 **Spic 'n Span**[9] 6707 3-8-13 55..........................(p) KevinGhunowa(3) 9 45
(R A Harris) *chsd ldrs: rdn 1/2-way: no hdwy fr over 1f out* **9/2**[2]
3660 **7** 2 ¼ **Wynberg (IRE)**[29] 6190 3-8-9 55.......................... HollyHall(7) 4 37
(S A Callaghan) *hld up: nvr on terms* **20/1**
0500 **8** 1 **Twosheetstothewind**[6] 6766 4-9-2 55..........................(p) LiamJones 11 34
(C R Dore) *led tl rdn and hdd over 1f out: wknd qckly* **9/1**
0004 **9** 2 ¾ **Diademas (USA)**[20] 6418 3-8-5 51.......................... AndreaAtzeni(7) 7 20
(M J Gingell) *prom on outside tl wknd 1/2-way* **12/1**
5000 **10** ¾ **Honest Value (IRE)**[20] 6419 3-8-13 52..........................(p) RichardThomas 8 18
(Mrs L C Jewell) *chsd ldr to 2f out: wknd qckly* **50/1**
5600 **11** ¾ **Dancing Mystery**[28] 6204 14-9-2 55..........................(b) StephenCarson 1 18
(E A Wheeler) *prom on outside tl wknd 1/2-way* **33/1**
60.50 secs **Going Correction** +0.125s/f (Slow) 11 Ran SP% **119.3**
Speed ratings (Par 101): **105,101,100,98,97 94,90,89,84,83 82**
toteswinger: 1&2 £8.90, 1&3 £4.30, 2&3 £15.60. CSF £41.10 CT £181.29 TOTE £4.00: £1.20, £3.20, £2.50; EX 51.60.
Owner The Composers **Bred** Juddmonte Farms Inc **Trained** Bramshill, Hants
■ Stewards' Enquiry : Holly Hall 12-day ban: in breach of Rule 158 (Nov 5-16)
FOCUS
A weak sprint and once again it was a real advantage to be drawn high. The form is rated through the winner and third.
Wynberg(IRE) Official explanation: jockey said, regarding the running and riding, her orders were to drop in and get the gelding covered up and go to the inside rail, then bring the gelding through the field and not get to the front too soon; trainer confirmed orders but said perhaps they had been overdone and jockey should have done more when becoming detached

6908 BOOK YOUR CHRISTMAS PARTY AT KEMPTON CLAIMING STKS 1m 2f (P)
6:50 (6:52) (Class 6) 3-4-Y-O **£2,047** (£604; £302) **Stalls** High

Form RPR
1302 **1** **Gross Prophet**[16] 6528 3-9-8 75.......................... RichardKingscote 9 72
(Tom Dascombe) *trckd ldrs: pushed wd 3f out: rdn and r.o to ld wl ins fnl f* **3/1**[1]
0340 **2** 1 **Blur**[41] 5833 3-8-7 47.......................... RichardThomas 12 55
(R Hannon) *trckd ldr: rdn to ld appr fnl f: hdd wl ins fnl f: no ex* **25/1**
0256 **3** ¾ **Mystic Art (IRE)**[73] 4902 3-9-0 68.......................... JohnEgan 8 61
(C R Egerton) *mid-div: pushed along 1/2-way: rdn and short of room over 1f out: r.o to go 3rd ins fnl f* **12/1**
050 **4** 1 **Jo'Burg (USA)**[6] 6758 4-9-10 70.......................... JimCrowley 14 64
(Mrs A J Perrett) *s.i.s: in rr: hdwy whn swtchd lft wl over 1f out: r.o ins fnl f: nvr nrr* **3/1**[1]
5453 **5** ½ **Themwerethedays**[9] 6712 3-8-12 64.......................... AdamKirby 2 56
(S Kirk) *hld up: hdwy over 1f out: kpt on fnl f: nvr nrr* **9/2**[2]
6300 **6** 1 ¼ **Soggy Dollar**[7] 6741 3-9-3 70.......................... SaleemGolam 6 58
(M H Tompkins) *mid-div: pushed along over 4f out: trckd ldrs over 1f out: wknd ins fnl f* **33/1**
0106 **7** nk **Red Current**[8] 6719 4-8-9 56.......................... KevinGhunowa(3) 11 47
(R A Harris) *trckd ldrs: rdn and ev ch over 1f out: wknd qckly ins fnl f* **10/1**
4000 **8** 7 **The Willowy Wigeon**[16] 6541 3-8-1 55.......................... FrankieMcDonald 4 27
(P Winkworth) *in rr: reminders after 4f: wl bhd fnl 3f* **25/1**
6/0- **9** shd **Andorn (GER)**[101] 4012 4-9-13 90.......................... TPQueally 10 48
(A P Stringer) *sn led: rdn and hdd appr fnl f: wknd rapidly* **8/1**
000 **10** 2 ¼ **Shake On It**[7] 6738 4-9-11 71.......................... DaneO'Neill 5 42
(Eve Johnson Houghton) *in tch on outside tl rdn and wknd 2f out* **6/1**[3]
2m 8.79s (0.79) **Going Correction** +0.125s/f (Slow)
WFA 3 from 4yo 5lb 10 Ran SP% **121.0**
Speed ratings (Par 101): **101,100,99,98,98 97,97,91,91,89**
toteswinger: 1&2 £27.00, 1&3 £12.40, 2&3 £37.60. CSF £89.18 TOTE £4.90: £1.50, £7.20, £4.20; EX 80.70.
Owner Alan Solomon **Bred** A David Solomon **Trained** Lambourn, Berks
FOCUS
Rather messy form and the proximity of the runner-up casts a doubt over the level.
Red Current Official explanation: jockey said filly ran too keenly

6909 DIGIBET MEDIAN AUCTION MAIDEN STKS 1m 4f (P)
7:20 (7:20) (Class 5) 3-5-Y-O **£3,238** (£963; £481; £240) **Stalls** Centre

Form RPR
3-06 **1** nk **War Anthem**[49] 5603 4-9-10 64..........................(b) PatCosgrave 5 71
(J R Boyle) *in rr: hdwy on ins 4f out: wnt 2nd 1f out: bmpd twice u.p nr fin: jst failed: fin 2nd, nk: awrdd r* **8/1**
45 **2** **Mvuto**[65] 5155 3-8-12 0.......................... AdamKirby 6 66
(C G Cox) *trckd ldr for 2f: rdn over 3f out: wnt 2nd over 2f out: wandered u.p and bmpd runner-up twice nr fin: jst hld on: fin 1st: disq & plcd 2nd* **3/1**[2]
2 **3** shd **Isabelonabicycle**[35] 6018 3-8-12 0.......................... MartinDwyer 10 66
(A M Balding) *rrd leaving stalls: hdwy after 4f: rdn 3f out: c wd fr over 1f out: kpt on fnl f: jst failed to go 2nd* **4/5**[1]
00 **4** 8 **Generous Star**[13] 6596 5-9-10 0..........................(p) JimmyQuinn 3 58
(J Pearce) *wnt 2nd after 2f: lost 2nd over 2f out: one pce after* **33/1**
505 **5** 2 ¼ **Lazeyma**[21] 6378 3-8-12 58..........................(p) PhilipRobinson 7 49
(M A Jarvis) *led tl rdn and hdd over 1f out: wknd* **15/2**[3]
0024 **6** 8 **Silver Surprise**[7] 6728 4-9-2 55.......................... MarcHalford(3) 9 37
(J J Bridger) *a in rr: no ch fnl 3f* **14/1**
00 **7** 25 **Enjoy The Mood**[25] 6275 5-9-5 0.......................... ChrisCatlin 2 —
(Ms N M Hugo) *a in rr* **80/1**
00 **8** 9 **Upstart (IRE)**[115] 3530 3-9-3 0.......................... TPQueally 4 —
(H R A Cecil) *in tch tl wknd over 3f out* **14/1**
00 **9** dist **Wrecker's Moon (IRE)**[55] 5426 3-8-11 0 ow2.......................... LeeVickers(3) 11 —
(T J Etherington) *in rr: lost tch 1/2-way: t.o* **66/1**
2m 36.37s (1.87) **Going Correction** +0.125s/f (Slow)
WFA 3 from 4yo+ 7lb 9 Ran SP% **122.4**
Speed ratings (Par 103): **97,98,97,92,90 85,68,62,—**
toteswinger: 1&2 £6.10, 1&3 £1.20, 2&3 £2.70. CSF £34.22 TOTE £12.30: £2.50, £1.10, £1.60; EX 46.60.
Owner David Grieve **Bred** Ms Linda Redmond And Mrs Mary Mayall **Trained** Epsom, Surrey
■ Stewards' Enquiry : Adam Kirby three-day ban: careless riding (Nov 5-7)
FOCUS
This moderate maiden was run at a fair pace and the first three came clear. The fourth casts doubt on the form and War Anthem, who got the race in the stewards' room, is probably the best guide.
Wrecker's Moon(IRE) Official explanation: jockey said filly finished distressed

6910 DIGIBET CASINO MAIDEN STKS 7f (P)
7:50 (7:53) (Class 4) 2-Y-O **£3,885** (£1,156; £577; £288) **Stalls** High

Form RPR
02 **1** **Redding Colliery (USA)**[13] 6597 2-9-3 0..........................(b) JohnEgan 6 83+
(Jane Chapple-Hyam) *mde all: clr 1/2-way: pushed out: unchal* **11/4**[1]
0 **2** 5 **New Beginning (FR)**[21] 6392 2-8-12 0.......................... JimmyQuinn 14 66
(H J L Dunlop) *a.p: wnt 2nd over 1f out: no ch w wnr* **50/1**
45 **3** ½ **Al Mugtareb (IRE)**[34] 6062 2-9-3 0.......................... RoystonFfrench 7 69
(M Johnston) *in rr: hdwy on ins over 1f out to go 3rd ins fnl f* **7/1**

4 hd **Mrs Beeton (IRE)** 2-8-12 0 AdamKirby 1 64
(W R Swinburn) *s.i.s and c over to ins fr wd draw: in rr tl gd hdwy appr fnl f: r.o strly: nvr nrr* **40/1**

4 5 1/2 **Mootriba**[30] 6166 2-8-12 0 (b) MartinDwyer 10 63
(W J Haggas) *mid-div: hdwy over 1f out: r.o: nvr nrr* **11/2**[3]

06 6 3/4 **Rosco Flyer (IRE)**[15] 6553 2-9-3 0 PatCosgrave 13 66
(J R Boyle) *s.i.s: hdwy over 1f out: kpt on: nvr nrr* **50/1**

7 1 **Lastroarofdtiger (USA)** 2-9-3 0 DarrenWilliams 8 63
(K R Burke) *mid-div: rdn over 2f out: kpt on one pce* **8/1**

2 8 1 1/4 **Swiss Art (IRE)**[14] 6574 2-9-0 0 KevinGhunowa(3) 12 60
(R A Harris) *in tch tl rdn and hung rt over 2f out* **12/1**

9 6 **Dialect** 2-8-12 0 JimCrowley 5 40
(Mrs A J Perrett) *slowly away: a towards rr* **8/1**

00 10 3 3/4 **Castleburg**[14] 6575 2-8-12 0 SteveDrowne 11 31
(G L Moore) *chsd wnr tl rdn and wknd over 1f out* **20/1**

11 9 **Arty Crafty (USA)** 2-8-12 0 ChrisCatlin 2 8
(Sir Mark Prescott) *slowly away and c over to stands' side: in rr and nvr on terms* **50/1**

33 12 3 1/2 **Caerus (USA)**[26] 6253 2-9-3 0 JamieSpencer 9 4
(W J Knight) *chsd ldrs tl wknd over 2f out* **3/1**[2]

00 13 6 **Manhattan Sunrise (USA)**[90] 4339 2-8-12 0 PaulEddery 3 —
(G D Blake) *racd wd: in tch tl wknd 1/2-way* **66/1**

54 14 3 3/4 **George Rex (USA)**[19] 6438 2-9-3 0 EddieAhern 4 —
(B J Meehan) *prom tl lost pl after 2f: sn bhd* **12/1**

1m 27.08s (1.08) **Going Correction** +0.125s/f (Slow) 14 Ran SP% **131.7**
Speed ratings (Par 97): **98,92,91,91,90 90,88,87,80,76 66,62,55,50**
toteswinger: 1&2 £63.40, 1&3 £10.40, 2&3 £63.40. CSF £172.92 TOTE £4.10: £1.10, £23.30, £3.10; EX 346.30.
Owner Mrs Fitri Hay **Bred** Gaineway T'Breds Ltd & 707 Stables **Trained** Lambourn, Berks

FOCUS
This juvenile maiden looked an interesting heat and it produced a clear-cut winner.

NOTEBOOK
Redding Colliery(USA) settled better after taking the race by the scruff of the neck early on and lengthened into a clear lead from the top of the home straight. There was no danger of him folding over this shorter trip and, while he got an uncontested lead, he still looked value for the winning margin. Very much suited to an artificial surface, it will be interesting to see how the handicapper reacts to this. (op 5-2)
New Beginning(FR), down in trip, showed the benefit of her debut experience at Nottingham and won the race for second. She looked suited by the sounder surface and will become eligible for a mark after her next outing. (op 66-1)
Al Mugtareb(IRE), who attracted good support, had shown modest form in two previous runs and was up in trip for this all-weather bow. He stayed on too late and appeared in need of the experience again, so should look more interesting now he is qualified for handicaps. His rider later reported that the colt had failed to handle the bend. Official explanation: jockey said colt failed to handle the bend (op 14-1)
Mrs Beeton(IRE), who lost ground with a tardy start and had it to do two furlongs out, put up an eyecatching debut effort. She stayed on nicely as the penny dropped and this half-sister to her yard's smart Stotsfold looks sure to improve for this. (op 33-1)
Mootriba took time to settle and probably ran near to the level of her debut form over course and distance in September. (op 6-1)
Rosco Flyer(IRE) did not shape without some ability and now has the option of handicaps.
Caerus(USA) now qualifies for a mark, but this was a disappointing effort and he has a little to prove. (op 10-3 tchd 11-4)
George Rex(USA) Official explanation: jockey said gelding suffered interference on bend out of back straight

6911 DIGIBET.COM H'CAP 7f (P)
8:20 (8:23) (Class 3) (0-95,95) 3-Y-O+

£7,477 (£2,239; £1,119; £560; £279; £140) Stalls High

Form RPR

1 **Il Grande Maurizio (IRE)**[40] 4-8-13 95 (t) AndreaAtzeni(7) 14 106
(S Santella, Italy) *a.p: led wl over 1f out: pushed out: comf* **16/1**

6-21 2 1/2 **Otaared**[21] 6393 3-9-3 94 PhilipRobinson 9 103
(M A Jarvis) *trckd ldr: led over 2f out: hdd wl over 1f out: kpt on: jst hld on for 2nd* **6/4**[1]

0000 3 hd **Bazroy (IRE)**[21] 6402 4-8-10 85 (b) JohnEgan 6 94
(P D Evans) *in rr tl hdwy on ins over 2f out: r.o to press runner-up ins fnl f* **16/1**

0663 4 1 3/4 **Lindoro**[14] 6576 3-8-12 89 (t) AdamKirby 12 93
(W R Swinburn) *hld up: rdn and hdwy over 1f out: r.o: nvr nrr* **7/1**[3]

4002 5 1 **Barney McGrew (IRE)**[25] 6289 5-9-3 92 TomEaves 8 93
(M Dods) *t.k.h in mid-div: hdwy over 1f out: nvr nrr* **10/1**

0000 6 1 **Hinton Admiral**[25] 6277 4-8-11 86 JamieMoriarty 2 85
(R A Fahey) *slowly away and swtchd to ins fr wd draw: hdwy appr fnl f: enver nrr* **16/1**

226 7 3 1/4 **Jeninsky (USA)**[16] 6532 3-8-7 84 JimmyQuinn 7 74
(Rae Guest) *in rr: mde sme late hdwy* **12/1**

/51- 8 1 3/4 **Kirk Michael**[312] 7159 4-8-8 83 ow1 DaneO'Neill 4 68
(H Candy) *racd wd in rr: mde sme late hdwy* **12/1**

1500 9 1 **Transfer**[79] 4682 3-8-6 83 MartinDwyer 13 65
(A M Balding) *led tl hdd over 2f out: wknd over 1f out* **14/1**

0200 10 9 **Royal Intruder**[10] 6676 3-9-1 95 PatrickHills(3) 11 53
(R Hannon) *chsd ldrs tl rdn and wknd over 2f out* **33/1**

0320 11 1 1/4 **Salient**[12] 6625 4-8-9 84 PaulDoe 5 39
(M J Attwater) *chsd ldrs tl rdn and wknd over 2f out* **33/1**

1540 12 3 1/4 **Markab**[25] 6269 5-9-3 92 PatCosgrave 3 38
(K A Morgan) *racd wd in mid-div: wknd over 2f out* **14/1**

12 13 12 **Baby Houseman**[116] 3500 3-9-0 91 EddieAhern 10 5
(J H M Gosden) *s.i.s: sn in tch: t.k.h: wknd 3f out* **5/1**[2]

1m 25.8s (-0.20) **Going Correction** +0.125s/f (Slow)
WFA 3 from 4yo+ 2lb 13 Ran SP% **130.5**
Speed ratings (Par 107): **106,105,105,103,102 100,97,95,94,83 82,78,64**
toteswinger: 1&2 £10.20, 1&3 £152.80, 2&3 £17.00. CSF £43.84 CT £456.91 TOTE £17.30: £3.00, £1.20, £4.70; EX 76.30.
Owner Federico Pierluigi **Bred** Michael O'Mahony **Trained** Italy

FOCUS
A good-quality handicap, run at a fair pace. The form looks sound, rated through the fourth.

NOTEBOOK
Il Grande Maurizio(IRE) has been prolific this year in Italy, did win on an artificial surface last time out, and had been allotted a mark of 95 for this British debut, which meant he would carry topweight in this. He had the rail draw and sat handy, before starting his challenge from the home turn. He dug deep when pressed from the furlong marker and was always doing enough to hold the placed horses.
Otaared, whose maiden win three weeks earlier has worked out well, held every chance on this handicap bow and did not look to do anything wrong in defeat. There will be other days for him and a return to 1m may help. (tchd 7-4 and 2-1 in a place and 15-8 in places)
Bazroy(IRE) was patiently ridden and found plenty when switched to the far rail with his challenge. He kept on for pressure and this was much more like it from him back over 7f. (op 14-1)
Lindoro had his chance, but could find only the same pace when put under pressure. He gives the form a good look. (op 11-1)
Barney McGrew(IRE) refused to settle through the first half of the race and that cannot have helped his cause. (op 12-1)
Baby Houseman Official explanation: jockey said filly lost her action

6912 PANORAMIC BAR & RESTAURANT H'CAP (DIV I) 1m (P)
8:50 (8:54) (Class 6) (0-50,50) 3-Y-O+ £1,706 (£503; £252) Stalls High

Form RPR

0600 1 **Zazous**[39] 5916 7-8-7 47 MarcHalford(3) 11 55
(J J Bridger) *prom tl hmpd and lost pl over 6f out: rdn and hdwy over 2f out: led jst ins fnl f: rdn out* **16/1**

0401 2 1 1/4 **Margot Mine (IRE)**[6] 6752 3-8-7 47 (bt) TPO'Shea 14 52+
(J S Moore) *s.i.s: hld up: hdwy on ins over 2f out: r.o to go 2nd wl ins fnl f* **2/1**[1]

502 3 3/4 **Moorside Diamond**[102] 3963 4-8-13 50 (b) SilvestreDeSousa 12 53
(A D Brown) *trckd ldr: led over 1f out: rdn and hdd jst ins fnl f: lost 2nd wl ins fnl f* **12/1**

0300 4 3/4 **Telephonist**[23] 6338 3-8-9 49 SteveDrowne 13 51
(J R Best) *mid-div: chal ldrs on ins 2f out: kpt on one pce fnl f* **33/1**

0400 5 1 1/4 **First Tracks (IRE)**[18] 6470 3-8-10 50 SimonWhitworth 4 49
(J W Hills) *hld up: hdwy 2f out: kpt on fnl f* **25/1**

4022 6 hd **Turkish Sultan (IRE)**[5] 6768 5-8-7 49 (p) MCGeran(5) 1 47
(J M Bradley) *in tch: kpt on one pce ins fnl 2f* **5/1**[2]

6506 7 1 3/4 **Ma Ridge**[88] 4412 4-8-10 47 RobertHavlin 10 41
(T D McCarthy) *led tl rdn and hdd over 1f out: fdd ins fnl f* **33/1**

0006 8 nse **Anduril**[9] 6693 7-8-13 50 (b) PatrickMathers 8 44
(I W McInnes) *s.i.s: sme late hdwy* **12/1**

0400 9 1 1/4 **Goose Green (IRE)**[9] 6693 4-8-13 50 JimmyQuinn 5 41
(R J Hodges) *towards rr: rdn over 2f out: nvr on terms* **12/1**

0455 10 2 1/4 **Lights Of Vegas**[14] 6570 4-8-11 48 ChrisCatlin 3 34
(S Kirk) *chsd ldrs: rdn 3f out: sn btn* **8/1**

0-16 11 3/4 **Pembo**[7] 6735 3-8-7 50 KevinGhunowa(3) 2 34
(R A Harris) *trckd ldr tl wknd wl over 1f out* **14/1**

2000 12 3 **Hollywood George**[20] 6419 4-8-12 49 (p) AdamKirby 7 26
(Miss M E Rowland) *chsd ldrs tl rdn and wknd 2f out* **10/1**

4605 13 1 **Artistic Light**[43] 5787 3-8-8 48 MartinDwyer 9 23
(W R Muir) *racd wd: chsd ldrs tl wknd over 2f out* **7/1**[3]

6 14 2 **Follow The Buzz**[88] 4429 4-8-10 47 oh1 ow1 MickyFenton 6 18
(M Wellings) *slowly away: a bhd* **50/1**

1m 41.82s (2.02) **Going Correction** +0.125s/f (Slow)
WFA 3 from 4yo+ 3lb 14 Ran SP% **130.0**
Speed ratings (Par 101): **94,92,92,91,90 89,88,88,86,84 83,80,79,77**
toteswinger: 1&2 £54.20, 1&3 £15.90, 2&3 £3.20. CSF £50.64 CT £384.65 TOTE £27.20: £3.80, £1.70, £3.30; EX 101.30.
Owner J J Bridger **Bred** Lordship Stud **Trained** Liphook, Hants

FOCUS
A poor handicap, run at a moderate pace. The first four came out of the four highest stalls. The form should be treated with caution although it makes sense at face value.
Hollywood George Official explanation: jockey said colt ran too free

6913 PANORAMIC BAR & RESTAURANT H'CAP (DIV II) 1m (P)
9:20 (9:22) (Class 6) (0-50,53) 3-Y-O+ £1,706 (£503; £252) Stalls High

Form RPR

0300 1 **The Grey One (IRE)**[27] 6228 5-8-5 47 (p) MCGeran(5) 9 62
(J M Bradley) *hld up in mid-div: rdn and str hdwy over 1f out: led jst ins fnl f: sn clr* **8/1**

6300 2 3 **Ugenius**[28] 6208 4-8-12 49 JohnEgan 3 57
(Mrs C A Dunnett) *a.p: led 2f out: rdn and hdd jst ins fnl f: nt pce of wnr* **20/1**

300- 3 nk **Saucy**[75] 4834 7-8-13 50 RichardKingscote 11 57
(Tom Dascombe) *mid-div: hdwy over 1f out: r.o wl fnl f* **6/1**[3]

3654 4 1 1/2 **Golden Brown (IRE)**[6] 6753 4-8-10 47 (p) ChrisCatlin 6 51
(David Pinder) *in rr: styd on fr over 1f out: nvr nrr* **4/1**[1]

40 5 1/2 **Bon Ton Roulet**[41] 5815 3-8-6 49 oh3 JimmyQuinn 12 49
(R Hannon) *in rr: rdn and hdwy on ins over 1f out: nvr nrr* **13/2**

4040 6 1/2 **Gracie's Gift (IRE)**[54] 5458 6-8-13 50 DaneO'Neill 5 52
(A G Newcombe) *mid-div: effrt over 1f out: kpt on one pce* **9/2**[2]

0002 7 1 3/4 **Lady Florence**[64] 5167 3-8-8 49 oh1 AlanMunro 7 46
(A B Coogan) *led tl hdd 2f out: wknd 1f out* **9/1**

3004 8 1 1/4 **Rowan Dancer**[16] 6541 3-8-10 50 PatCosgrave 4 45
(J R Boyle) *chsd ldrs tl rdn and wknd appr fnl f* **8/1**

4555 9 3 **My Flame**[47] 5684 3-8-10 50 EddieAhern 10 38
(J R Jenkins) *trckd ldrs: rdn 2f out: no further hdwy* **14/1**

0060 10 nk **Poppy Dean (IRE)**[90] 4326 3-8-2 49 oh2 DavidProbert(5) 1 34
(J G Portman) *trckd ldr: rdn over 2f out: sn btn* **20/1**

3005 11 1/2 **Stargazy**[23] 6335 4-8-11 48 LiamJones 8 34
(W G M Turner) *a towards rr* **16/1**

0003 12 3 **Frosty's Gift**[28] 6206 4-8-13 50 PatDobbs 13 29
(J C Fox) *in tch tl wknd 2f out* **16/1**

0000 13 3/4 **Lekezia (IRE)**[48] 5631 3-8-8 49 oh1 SimonWhitworth 2 25
(J W Hills) *a bhd* **33/1**

0040 14 8 **Monte Cassino (IRE)**[78] 4702 3-8-8 53 ow3 JamesO'Reilly(5) 14 12
(J O'Reilly) *t.k.h: chsd ldrs tl wknd over 2f out* **25/1**

1m 40.42s (0.62) **Going Correction** +0.125s/f (Slow)
WFA 3 from 4yo+ 3lb 14 Ran SP% **132.8**
Speed ratings (Par 101): **101,98,97,96,95 95,93,92,89,88 88,85,84,76**
toteswinger: 1&2 £16.50, 1&3 £6.50, 2&3 £43.20. CSF £173.47 CT £1088.54 TOTE £12.20: £3.30, £7.70, £2.60; EX 413.30 Place 6 £36.96, Place 5 £19.93.
Owner R Miles **Bred** Blackdown Stud **Trained** Sedbury, Gloucs

FOCUS
This second division of the 1m handicap was an open affair and run at a much more generous pace than the first. The form is sound.
Poppy Dean(IRE) Official explanation: jockey said filly ran too freely
Stargazy Official explanation: jockey said gelding ran too free
Monte Cassino(IRE) Official explanation: jockey said saddle slipped forward
T/Plt: £35.80 to a £1 stake. Pool: £72,440.78. 1,473.78 winning tickets. T/Qpdt: £9.90 to a £1 stake. Pool: £7,219.96. 537.10 winning tickets. JS

6914 - 6920a (Foreign Racing) - See Raceform Interactive

6891 DEAUVILLE (R-H)

Wednesday, October 22

OFFICIAL GOING: Turf course - very soft; all-weather - standard

6921a PRIX VULCAIN (LISTED RACE) — 1m 4f 110y

2:35 (2:34) 3-Y-O **£20,221** (£8,088; £6,066; £4,044; £2,022)

RPR

1 **Winkle (IRE)**[49] 5623 3-8-8 .... CSoumillon 7 94
(M Delzangles, France)

2 *2* **Angelo Minny (FR)**[39] 5927 3-9-2 .... OPeslier 6 99
(A Fabre, France)

3 *1 1/2* **Drill Sergeant**[11] 6646 3-8-11 .... JoeFanning 1 92
(M Johnston) *racd in 2nd bhd slow pce: pushed along and outpcd by wnr under 2f out: disputing 2nd over 1f out to 100yds out: styd on to hold 3rd* **71/10**[1]

4 *shd* **Pouvoir Absolu**[34] 3-8-11 ....(b) ACrastus 3 91
(E Lellouche, France)

5 *nse* **Court Canibal**[17] 6517 3-9-2 .... TThulliez 5 96
(M Delzangles, France)

6 *1/2* **Chirango (FR)**[19] 6464 3-8-11 .... SPasquier 2 91
(P Demercastel, France)

6 *dht* **Syvilla**[44] 5750 3-8-8 .... DBonilla 8 88
(Rae Guest) *wnt 3rd after 2f: disp 2nd over 1f out tl no ex last 100yds* **31/1**[2]

8 *hd* **Shawnee Saga (FR)**[19] 6464 3-8-11 .... DBoeuf 4 90
(W Baltromei, Germany)

2m 53.9s (7.50) **8** Ran SP% **15.5**
PARI-MUTUEL: WIN 2.40; PL 1.40, 3.00, 2.30; DF 15.00.
Owner H H Aga Khan **Bred** Haras De S A Aga Khan S C E A **Trained** France

NOTEBOOK
Drill Sergeant was totally unsuited by a lack of early pace. Tracking the winner for much of the way, he tried to get on terms early in the straight but was outpaced. He did stay on gamely in the final stages and battled in well to hold on to third. He is now likely to be gelded before being sent to Dubai for the Carnival Meeting.
Syvilla was tucked in behind the leader early on and was given every chance. She looked quite dangerous as the field turned for home, but she didn't go through with her challenge. Her jockey felt she didn't quite have the stamina for this class of opposition.

GEELONG (L-H)

Wednesday, October 22

OFFICIAL GOING: Good

6922a PETSTOCK GEELONG CUP (H'CAP) (GROUP 3) — 1m 4f 7y

6:25 (6:25) 4-Y-O+

£59,471 (£15,859; £7,930; £3,965; £2,203; £1,762)

RPR

1 **Bauer (IRE)**[61] 5229 5-8-10 .... DMOliver 15 113+
(L M Cumani) *midfield towards outside: hdwy over 2 1/2f out: cl 5th st on outside: led over 1f out: r.o strly* **5/1**[2]

2 *1* **Moatize (AUS)**[18] 4-8-5 ....(b) BShinn 2 105
(Bart Cummings, Australia) **9/1**

3 *hd* **Magic Instinct**[18] 6-8-5 .... LNolen 12 105
(Peter G Moody, Australia) **20/1**

4 *3/4* **Light Vision (NZ)**[18] 5-9-0 .... BMelham 9 112
(Robert Smerdon, Australia) **15/4**[1]

5 *1* **Guyno (NZ)**[18] 5-8-10 ....(b) BRawiller 1 107
(Lou Luciani, Australia) **8/1**

6 *1 1/2* **The Wolverine (NZ)**[11] 5-8-6 .... VDuric 10 100
(Leon Corstens, Australia) **6/1**[3]

7 *shd* **Zavite (NZ)**[11] 6-8-10 .... NashRawiller 4 104
(Anthony Cummings, Australia) **13/2**

8 *1 1/4* **Banana Man (AUS)** 5-8-5 ....(b) MichellePayne 14 97
(Michael Kent, Australia) **20/1**

9 *shd* **Chantal Sally (AUS)**[10] 6-8-5 .... NicholasHall 11 97
(J Symons & Sheila Laxon, Australia) **20/1**

10 *1 1/2* **Inkster (AUS)**[18] 4-8-5 .... CNewitt 13 95
(Mick Price, Australia) **25/1**

11 *shd* **Get Up Jude (AUS)**[18] 4-8-9 .... JasonTaylor 16 99
(Diane Poidevin-Laine, Australia) **12/1**

12 *2 1/4* **Glistening**[715] 6392 6-8-5 .... GChilds 3 91
(Michael Moroney, Australia) **30/1**

13 *1/2* **Fast Ruler (NZ)** 4-8-5 ....(b) DYendall 7 90
(Tony Vasil, Australia) **50/1**

14 *2* **Britomart (AUS)**[46] 5-8-5 .... PMertens 5 87
(Rick Hore-Lacy, Australia) **80/1**

15 *nk* **Dandaad (NZ)** 5-8-5 ....(b) StevenKing 8 87
(Bart Cummings, Australia) **25/1**

16 *2* **Foolish Lad (AUS)**[226] 8-8-5 ....(b) MPumpa 6 83
(Shane Oxlade, Australia) **100/1**

2m 30.16s (150.16) **16** Ran SP% **123.5**
.
Owner Aston House Stud & O T I Racing **Bred** Aston House Stud **Trained** Newmarket, Suffolk

NOTEBOOK
Bauer(IRE) was ideally placed throughout the race before quickening to the front down the home straight. He never looked like being caught once Oliver had made his move and this win should confirm his pace in the Melbourne Cup field early next month.

6745 BRIGHTON (L-H)

Thursday, October 23

OFFICIAL GOING: Good to soft
There was a strong headwind in the straight.
Wind: Strong, against Weather: Cloudy

6923 MARGARET JONES MEDIAN AUCTION MAIDEN STKS — 6f 209y

2:00 (2:02) (Class 5) 2-Y-O **£3,108** (£924; £462; £230) **Stalls** Low

Form RPR

53 **1** **Midnight In May (IRE)**[7] 6745 2-9-3 0.......... MartinDwyer 1 71
(W R Muir) *mde all: shkn up 2f out: pushed clr fnl f: comf* **7/4**[1]

00 **2** *2 3/4* **Rock Relief (IRE)**[19] 6488 2-9-3 0.......... J-PGuillambert 7 64
(Sir Mark Prescott) *hld up in rr of main gp: rdn and hdwy 2f out: chsd wnr fnl f: styd on: no imp* **25/1**

3 *1* **Men Bhavin Bradley (USA)** 2-9-3 0.......... ShaneKelly 2 61
(J Noseda) *cl up: drvn to chse wnr over 1f out tl ins fnl f: one pce* **8/1**

4 *1 1/4* **Where You Will** 2-8-12 0.......... MichaelHills 9 53
(W J Haggas) *prom: chsd wnr after 2f tl over 1f out: wknd fnl f* **9/1**

5 *1* **Feudal (IRE)** 2-9-3 0.......... RoystonFfrench 4 55
(M Johnston) *s.s: in rr of main gp: rdn 4f out: nt pce to chal* **4/1**[2]

005 **6** *3 1/4* **Lady Norlela**[79] 4705 2-8-12 48.......... RichardHughes 5 42
(R Hannon) *chsd wnr 2f: prom tl wknd over 1f out* **8/1**

6040 **7** *2 3/4* **Sharav**[29] 6207 2-9-3 60..........(b) StephenCarson 8 40
(Eve Johnson Houghton) *in tch tl wknd 2f out: hung lft whn btn* **14/1**

8 *3/4* **Telling Stories (IRE)** 2-8-12 0.......... JimCrowley 3 33
(M Johnston) *s.i.s: rn green: sn pushed along and wl bhd* **7/1**[3]

9 *22* **Eye For The Girls** 2-9-3 0.......... TPO'Shea 6 —
(M R Channon) *blind rt eye: v.s.a: sn t.o* **18/1**

1m 26.71s (3.61) **Going Correction** +0.45s/f (Yiel) **9** Ran SP% **116.9**
Speed ratings (Par 95): **97,93,92,91,90 86,83,82,57**
toteswinger: 1&2 £11.60, 1&3 £4.10, 2&3 £27.40. CSF £53.40 TOTE £2.30: £1.20, £4.90, £2.70; EX 49.80 Trifecta £280.30 Part won. Pool: £378.85, 0.20 winning units..
Owner C L A Edginton **Bred** Pat Grogan **Trained** Lambourn, Berks

FOCUS
Some big stables represented, but very few of these seemed seriously fancied and most of the newcomers ran green. It was all rather straightforward for the favourite, Midnight In May, who recorded a time 0.26 seconds slower than the following 0-75 nursery. They raced stands' side in the straight.

NOTEBOOK
Midnight In May(IRE) was too keen for his own good over 1m here last time, so this drop in trip suited, and rather than fight him Martin Dwyer let him stride on. He made just about every yard and this effort is even more creditable than the bare result suggests, as he was racing into a headwind. There is a chance he will be kept on the go and given a chance on the All-Weather. (op 5-2)
Rock Relief(IRE) ◆ had achieved an RPR in the 30s on his first two starts, including over 6f at Wolverhampton last time, but he proved suited by this step back up in trip and ran surprisingly well. This will not have helped his prospective handicap mark, but he is bred to come into his own over middle-distances and could be quite useful next year. (tchd 33-1)
Men Bhavin Bradley(USA), a $100,000 son of Officer, found a couple too good. This ground was probably softer than ideal, and he looked green, so better can be expected. (op 6-1 tchd 17-2)
Where You Will chased the eventual winner early on, but was rather one-paced when asked for her effort and does not look anything special. Official explanation: jockey said filly hung left (op 6-1 tchd 10-1)
Feudal(IRE) ran green throughout and will have learned plenty. (tchd 7-2 and 5-1)
Eye For The Girls Official explanation: jockey said colt was slowly away

6924 HARDINGS BAR & CATERING SERVICES NURSERY — 6f 209y

2:30 (2:33) (Class 5) (0-75,81) 2-Y-O **£3,367** (£1,002; £500; £250) **Stalls** Low

Form RPR

0440 **1** **Arushore (IRE)**[21] 6412 2-8-10 **64**.......... RichardHughes 15 68
(R Hannon) *hld up towards rr: hdwy and hrd rdn 2f out: str run to ld nr fin* **10/1**

0010 **2** *1/2* **My Kingdom (IRE)**[25] 6305 2-9-7 **75**..........(t) TravisBlock 10 78
(H Morrison) *chsd ldrs: led over 1f out: hrd rdn and kpt on fnl f: hdd nr fin* **6/1**[2]

4630 **3** *3 1/4* **Importer (IRE)**[21] 6412 2-9-4 **72**.......... MartinDwyer 1 66
(W R Muir) *prom: rdn and edgd bdly lft over 1f out: one pce* **12/1**

4011 **4** *1/2* **Amber Sunset**[5] 6809 2-9-10 **81** 6ex.......... LukeMorris(3) 3 74
(J Jay) *racd freely: led: claimed stands' rail over 2f out: hrd rdn and hdd over 1f out: no ex* **4/1**[1]

000 **5** *1 3/4* **Kyle Of Bute**[28] 6223 2-8-5 **59**..........(b) ChrisCatlin 14 47
(J L Dunlop) *in tch: lost pl and towards rr 3f out: swtchd lft over 2f out: rallied and styd on wl fnl f* **33/1**

5422 **6** *1* **Itainteasybeingme**[15] 6572 2-8-1 **62**.......... AndreaAtzeni(7) 8 48
(J R Boyle) *trckd ldrs: rdn 3f out: edgd bdly lft over 1f out: sn wknd* **9/1**[3]

620 **7** *1* **Fongoli**[23] 6358 2-8-5 **59**..........(v1) HayleyTurner 12 42
(B G Powell) *chsd ldrs 3f: losing pl whn squeezed for room over 2f out: styd on fnl f* **16/1**

5401 **8** *1 1/4* **Hum Cat (IRE)**[10] 6694 2-9-1 **69** 6ex.......... LPKeniry 13 49
(J S Moore) *in tch tl wknd and hung lft 2f out* **20/1**

5400 **9** *3/4* **Daily Double**[29] 6207 2-8-6 **60**..........(b1) RichardSmith 5 38
(R Hannon) *dwlt: mid-div after 2f: rdn 3f out: outpcd fnl 2f* **16/1**

5000 **10** *1* **Ayrus (USA)**[14] 6597 2-9-5 **73**.......... JimCrowley 6 48
(B J Meehan) *dwlt: bhd: pushed along 1/2-way: sme hdwy 2f out: n.d* **10/1**

1103 **11** *3 1/4* **Shadow Bay (IRE)**[15] 6574 2-9-7 **75**.......... RichardKingscote 2 42
(Tom Dascombe) *in tch: rdn and lost pl after 2f: sn bhd* **6/1**[2]

0003 **12** *3 1/2* **Baby Josr**[15] 6572 2-8-5 **59**..........(vt) PaulDoe 9 17
(I A Wood) *prom tl wknd and wandered over 2f out* **25/1**

435 **13** *1* **Surprise Party**[16] 6552 2-9-0 **71**.......... JackMitchell(3) 16 26
(C F Wall) *chsd ldrs on outside tl wknd over 2f out* **6/1**[2]

0050 **14** *102* **Missou Maiden**[8] 6730 2-8-8 **62**..........(b) PaulMulrennan 11 —
(M H Tompkins) *dwlt: sn wl bhd* **50/1**

1m 26.45s (3.35) **Going Correction** +0.45s/f (Yiel) **14** Ran SP% **124.0**
Speed ratings (Par 95): **98,97,93,93,91 90,88,87,86,85 81,77,76,—**
toteswinger: 1&2 £16.30, 1&3 £23.90, 2&3 £20.40. CSF £68.46 CT £767.85 TOTE £14.00: £5.20, £3.40, £4.30; EX 109.60 TRIFECTA Not won..
Owner A J Ilsley **Bred** Michael Woodlock & Seamus Kennedy **Trained** East Everleigh, Wilts

FOCUS
A modest but competitive nursery. The winning time was 0.26 seconds quicker than the previous juvenile maiden. Again, the main action took place stands' side.

The Form Book, Raceform Ltd, Compton, RG20 6NL

NOTEBOOK

Arushore(IRE) was well back early and had to wait for a gap when taken towards the near side in the straight, but that was probably no bad thing considering they were racing into a strong headwind. He stayed on strongly once in the clear, making his move as close to the rail as possible, rather than switching round the eventual runner-up. There is loads of stamina on the dam's side of his pedigree and he should be suited by a step back up in trip. (tchd 9-1 and 11-1)

My Kingdom(IRE), a surprise winner of a course-and-distance maiden two starts back, travelled well and looked the winner once taking over in the straight, but he was eventually worn down by a rival who had raced further back. (op 7-1)

Importer(IRE) was carried all the way across to the far rail by Itainteasybeingme and was not given a hard time once held by the front pair.

Amber Sunset was chasing a hat-trick, but she was too free in front and did not see her race out once bagging the stands' rail in the straight, with the headwind not helping matters. (op 7-2 tchd 9-2)

Kyle Of Bute is better than he showed, as he had nowhere to go almost as soon as he grabbed the stands' rail in the straight, and had to be switched. He finished well when in the clear.

Itainteasybeingme ruined his chance by hanging left down the camber in the straight. (tchd 8-1 and 10-1)

Hum Cat(IRE) seemed inclined to hang left in the straight and could not follow up his recent success in a Kempton claimer (op 16-1)

Shadow Bay(IRE) attracted support in the market, but ran disappointingly. Official explanation: jockey said gelding was unsuited by the track (op 15-2 tchd 11-2)

Baby Josr Official explanation: jockey said colt hung badly left throughout

Missou Maiden Official explanation: jockey said filly pulled itself up final 2f

6925 CONNOLLY'S RED MILLS HORSEFEEDS H'CAP — 5f 213y

3:05 (3:06) (Class 4) (0-80,80) 3-Y-O+ **£5,929** (£1,774; £887; £443; £220) **Stalls** Low

Form				RPR
0603	**1**		**The Tatling (IRE)**[12] 6650 11-8-10 **76** ... JackDean(5) 9 *(J M Bradley) hld up in rr travelling strly: hdwy and nt clr run ins fnl 2f: swtchd several times: plld wd and str run to ld ins fnl f* **10/1**	88+
6211	**2**	*1 ½*	**Rocker**[7] 6750 4-9-3 **78** 6ex ... JimCrowley 5 *(G L Moore) chsd ldrs: drvn to ld briefly jst ins fnl f: sn outpcd by wnr* **11/4**[1]	85
2502	**3**	*1*	**Feisty Royale**[31] 6160 3-8-10 **72** ... (b) RoystonFfrench 7 *(M Johnston) sn outpcd and detached in last tl r.o strly fnl f: gng on wl at fin* **7/1**	76
2000	**4**	*½*	**Malapropism**[22] 6388 8-8-5 **66** ... EdwardCreighton 6 *(M R Channon) prom: rdn and sltly outpcd 2f out: kpt on again ins fnl f* **14/1**	68
0102	**5**	*2 ¼*	**Peter Island (FR)**[10] 6699 5-9-5 **80** ... (v) ChrisCatlin 11 *(J Gallagher) led: claimed stands' rail st: hdd jst ins fnl f: hung lft and wknd* **6/1**	75
243	**6**	*¾*	**Mango Music**[16] 6557 5-9-5 **80** ... ShaneKelly 3 *(M Quinn) w ldr over 4f: 4th and hld whn squeezed for room ins fnl f* **5/1**[3]	73
0600	**7**	*nse*	**Bonnie Prince Blue**[17] 6532 5-9-1 **76** ... (b) MichaelHills 1 *(B W Hills) towards rr: rdn and n.d fnl 2f: styng on at fin* **9/2**[2]	69
3300	**8**	*¾*	**Cosmic Destiny (IRE)**[33] 6131 6-8-6 **67** ... LPKeniry 2 *(E F Vaughan) hld up towards rr gng wl: hdwy and nt clr run over 1f out: fnd little whn clr* **10/1**	57
0634	**9**	*9*	**Peopleton Brook**[12] 6650 6-8-0 **68** ow1 ... (t) RossAtkinson(7) 4 *(B G Powell) in tch: rdn to press ldrs 2f out: wknd 1f out: eased whn wl btn* **16/1**	29

1m 12.86s (2.66) **Going Correction** +0.45s/f (Yiel)
WFA 3 from 4yo+ 1lb **9** Ran SP% **119.0**
Speed ratings (Par 105): **100,98,96,96,93 92,91,90,78**
toteswinger: 1&2 £6.90, 1&3 £10.10, 2&3 £5.10. CSF £38.95 CT £213.07 TOTE £13.00: £2.90, £1.60, £2.30; EX 40.40 Trifecta £352.40 Part won. Pool: £476.23, 0.49 winning units..
Owner J M Bradley **Bred** Patrick J Power **Trained** Sedbury, Gloucs
■ Stewards' Enquiry : Jim Crowley two-day ban: careless riding (Nov 6-7)

FOCUS
A fair sprint handicap, but a strong headwind meant those held up were favoured as the pace collapsed. The Tatling basically ran to this year's form.
Mango Music Official explanation: jockey said mare suffered interference in running

6926 EUROPEAN BREEDERS' FUND MAIDEN STKS — 7f 214y

3:35 (3:35) (Class 4) 2-Y-O **£5,551** (£1,661; £830; £415; £206) **Stalls** Low

Form				RPR
32	**1**		**Headline Act**[29] 6199 2-9-3 0 ... RobertHavlin 3 *(J H M Gosden) hld up in rr: hdwy over 2f out: led jst ins fnl f: rdn out: readily* **10/11**[1]	78
6	**2**	*2 ½*	**Gitano Hernando**[15] 6581 2-9-3 0 ... TPQueally 9 *(M Botti) prom: led 2f out tl jst ins fnl f: kpt on same pce* **25/1**	73
05	**3**	*nk*	**Block Party**[33] 6117 2-9-3 0 ... SteveDrowne 6 *(R Charlton) hld up in tch: rdn to chse ldrs 2f out: hung lft fr over 1f out: kpt on* **11/2**[3]	72
00	**4**	*nk*	**Double Rubble (USA)**[21] 6425 2-9-3 0 ... ShaneKelly 7 *(J Noseda) hld up towards rr: rdn and hdwy 2f out: kpt on fnl f* **12/1**	71
4030	**5**	*3 ½*	**Rockfella**[22] 6376 2-9-3 70 ... TPO'Shea 5 *(D J Coakley) plld hrd: chsd ldrs: effrt 2f out: no ex appr fnl f* **33/1**	63
3	**6**	*10*	**Takeover Bid (USA)**[9] 6714 2-9-3 0 ... RoystonFfrench 2 *(M Johnston) chsd ldrs: lost pl 5f out: bhd and rdn 3f out* **3/1**[2]	41
0	**7**	*1 ¼*	**Carita Mia**[13] 6622 2-8-12 0 ... JimCrowley 8 *(G L Moore) mid-div on outside: wknd 1/2-way: sn bhd* **50/1**	34
05	**8**	*½*	**Sairaam (IRE)**[29] 6197 2-8-12 0 ... MartinDwyer 4 *(J L Dunlop) led tl 2f out: wknd over 1f out: eased whn wl btn fnl f* **14/1**	33
5004	**9**	*4 ½*	**Killmarnock**[42] 5811 2-9-3 58 ... WilliamBuick 1 *(R A Teal) w ldrs 3f: sn hanging and lost pl: bhd fnl 3f* **66/1**	28

1m 39.18s (3.18) **Going Correction** +0.45s/f (Yiel) **9** Ran SP% **117.4**
Speed ratings (Par 97): **102,99,99,98,95 85,84,83,79**
toteswinger: 1&2 £6.90, 1&3 £2.00, 2&3 £12.20. CSF £33.93 TOTE £1.90: £1.10, £5.90, £1.60; EX 28.50 Trifecta £153.90 Pool: £409.94, 1.97 winning units.
Owner K Abdulla **Bred** Juddmonte Farms Ltd **Trained** Newmarket, Suffolk

FOCUS
A reasonable maiden for the track. They all raced stands' side.

NOTEBOOK

Headline Act, beaten at odds-on over 1m1f at Goodwood on his previous start, got the job done this time, but he made quite hard work of it. He did not help his chance by continually edging right in the straight, doing Gitano Hernando few favours in the process, although Robert Havlin never went for the whip (he was possibly unable to when things got tight), and he was ultimately well on top at the line. The bare result slightly flatters him, as the runner-up lost momentum near the finish, but he can probably do better back on a more conventional track. (op Evens tchd 6-5 and 5-4 in a place)

Gitano Hernando ran a big race in defeat considering he was taken on for the lead and continually leaned on by the eventual winner in the closing stages. He ultimately had to snatch up slightly and, although held at the time, it looked to cost him around a length. (op 33-1)

Block Party, upped in trip, did not enjoy the clearest of runs when trying to make his move tight against the stands' rail, but he was not unlucky. (op 5-1)

Double Rubble(USA) never really looked like doing enough, but he now has the option of handicaps and should do better on a quicker surface. (op 16-1)

Rockfella was too keen for his own good.

Takeover Bid(USA) was in trouble a fair way out and could not confirm the promise he showed when third on his debut over 7f at Leicester. Official explanation: trainer had no explanation for the poor form shown (op 10-3 tchd 11-4)

Killmarnock Official explanation: jockey said gelding hung right

6927 SUSSEX NEWSPAPERS (S) H'CAP — 1m 1f 209y

4:05 (4:08) (Class 6) (0-60,59) 3-Y-O+ **£2,320** (£685; £342) **Stalls** High

Form				RPR
0005	**1**		**Siena Star (IRE)**[116] 3518 10-9-3 **53** ... MickyFenton 6 *(Stef Liddiard) chsd ldrs: led 6f out: jnd and carried lft by runner-up fnl 2f: hld on wl* **12/1**	62
3620	**2**	*hd*	**Black Falcon (IRE)**[44] 5776 8-8-8 **49** ... JamesO'Reilly(5) 8 *(John A Harris) t.k.h: trckd ldrs: disp ld and persistently edgd lft fnl 2f: outbattled* **4/1**[1]	58
0202	**3**	*2 ½*	**Threestoneburn (USA)**[7] 6747 3-8-2 **50** ... AndreaAtzeni(7) 10 *(J R Boyle) hld up towards rr: drvn to chse ldng pair ins fnl 2f: edgd lft: styd on same pce* **9/2**[2]	54
5103	**4**	*4*	**Josephine Malines**[36] 6015 4-9-5 **55** ... (p) PaulMulrennan 3 *(Mrs A Duffield) prom: rdn and outpcd 2f out: kpt on past btn rivals fnl f* **10/1**	51
506	**5**	*2 ¼*	**Ryan's Future (IRE)**[19] 6493 8-9-9 **59** ... LPKeniry 7 *(J S Moore) hld up towards rr: mod effrt 2f out: no imp* **7/1**	51
6200	**6**	*nk*	**Daring Racer (GER)**[8] 6740 5-9-7 **57** ... (p) IanMongan 1 *(Mrs L J Mongan) led 4f: hrd rdn and wknd 2f out: hung lft whn btn* **15/2**	48
3041	**7**	*½*	**Personify**[28] 6228 6-8-13 **52** ... (p) TolleyDean(3) 9 *(J L Flint) bhd: rdn 4f out: sme hdwy over 1f out: edgd lft: sn wknd* **9/2**[2]	42
3655	**8**	*2*	**Balais Folly (FR)**[7] 6747 3-8-3 **49** ... (p) MCGeran(5) 2 *(B Palling) uns rdr and loose gng to post: s.s: sn in midfield: effrt over 2f out: edgd lft and wknd over 1f out* **14/1**	35
5430	**9**	*11*	**Tank Commander**[7] 6757 3-8-11 **52** ... MartinDwyer 5 *(W R Muir) hld up towards rr: rdn 4f out: effrt 2f out: carried lft and wknd over 1f out: eased whn no ch fnl f* **13/2**[3]	16
5330	**10**	*13*	**Fairly Honest**[9] 6719 4-9-3 **53** ... ChrisCatlin 4 *(P W Hiatt) chsd ldrs: pushed along and lost pl over 4f out: n.d fnl 3f* **16/1**	—

2m 8.30s (4.70) **Going Correction** +0.45s/f (Yiel)
WFA 3 from 4yo+ 5lb **10** Ran SP% **123.3**
Speed ratings (Par 101): **99,98,96,93,91 91,91,89,80,70**
toteswinger: 1&2 £23.70, 1&3 £15.30, 2&3 £5.30. CSF £63.11 CT £259.65 TOTE £17.30: £4.40, £2.30, £1.90; EX 81.20 TRIFECTA Not won..There was no bid for the winner
Owner ownaracehorse.co.uk (Shefford) **Bred** Mrs T Brudenell **Trained** Great Shefford, Berks

FOCUS
Very moderate form, as you would expect, and they were all over the place in the straight. They went an ordinary pace. The first two had both fropped to fair marks.
Black Falcon(IRE) Official explanation: jockey said gelding hung left in straight
Balais Folly(FR) Official explanation: jockey said gelding hung left
Tank Commander Official explanation: jockey said gelding ran flat

6928 ROBIN MARTIN-JENKINS H'CAP — 7f 214y

4:40 (4:40) (Class 6) (0-63,68) 3-Y-O+ **£2,719** (£809; £404; £202) **Stalls** Low

Form				RPR
451	**1**		**Duty Doctor**[12] 6660 3-9-1 **61** ... WilliamBuick 7 *(S Kirk) hld up in midfield: rdn and hdwy 2f out: led jst over 1f out: hld on wl fnl f* **12/1**	69
3332	**2**	*½*	**Under Fire (IRE)**[23] 6364 5-8-9 **59** ... JemmaMarshall(7) 1 *(A W Carroll) led: rdn and hdd jst over 1f out: rallied wl* **16/1**	66
1231	**3**	*1 ¼*	**Kannon**[7] 6746 3-9-0 **65** 6ex ... Louis-PhilippeBeuzelin(5) 12 *(W J Knight) t.k.h in midfield: rdn to chse ldrs over 1f out: kpt on* **11/2**[2]	69
0600	**4**	*nk*	**Lordship (IRE)**[15] 6585 4-8-11 **57** ... LukeMorris(3) 11 *(A W Carroll) bhd: nt clr run over 2f out: gd hdwy fr over 1f out: swtchd rt wl ins fnl f: nrst fin* **20/1**	60+
0-00	**5**	*shd*	**Braddock (IRE)**[6] 6802 5-9-9 **66** 6ex ... (tp) RichardHughes 3 *(S Donohoe, Ire) t.k.h: prom: trckd ldr gng wl 3f out: hrd rdn and no ex over 1f out* **7/4**[1]	69
0-55	**6**	*¾*	**Moscow Oznick**[27] 6254 3-8-11 **62** ... DavidProbert(5) 5 *(N J Vaughan) prom tl rdn and outpcd fnl 2f* **11/1**[3]	63
2026	**7**	*¾*	**Ten To The Dozen**[7] 6749 5-9-3 **60** ... (b) ChrisCatlin 13 *(P W Hiatt) t.k.h: chsd ldrs: lost pl 3f out: stmbld over 2f out: styng on whn n.m.r fnl 50yds* **11/1**[3]	62+
2164	**8**	*2*	**Prince Valentine**[50] 5604 7-8-9 **52** ... (p) LPKeniry 10 *(G L Moore) stdd s: hld up in rr: shkn up and sme hdwy 2f out: hung lft and wknd 1f out* **16/1**	47
0052	**9**	*¾*	**Bidable**[16] 6560 4-8-6 **54** ... MCGeran(5) 4 *(B Palling) hld up towards rr: rdn and hdwy 2f out: wknd 1f out* **16/1**	47
000	**10**	*5*	**Bolton Hall (IRE)**[64] 2391 6-8-12 **60** ... WilliamCarson(5) 16 *(W K Goldsworthy) sn pressing ldr: wknd 3f out* **33/1**	42
1141	**11**	*3*	**Singleb (IRE)**[9] 6716 4-9-11 **68** 6ex ... SteveDrowne 8 *(G L Moore) hld up in rr: shkn up over 2f out: nvr nr ldrs* **11/2**[2]	43
3065	**12**	*3*	**Jemiliah**[7] 6746 3-8-7 **56** ... TolleyDean(3) 15 *(B G Powell) t.k.h in midfield on outer: wknd over 3f out: sn bhd: eased whn no ch ins fnl 2f* **50/1**	24
064	**13**	*½*	**Charlie Bear**[16] 6560 7-8-5 **50** oh2 ow1 ... KevinGhunowa(3) 6 *(Miss Z C Davison) t.k.h: prom tl wknd 2f out* **50/1**	18
1P00	**14**	*½*	**Ten Spot (IRE)**[67] 5119 3-8-9 **55** ... (bt) MickyFenton 2 *(Stef Liddiard) wnt rt s: chsd ldrs tl wknd and n.m.r 2f out* **66/1**	21

1m 39.38s (3.38) **Going Correction** +0.45s/f (Yiel)
WFA 3 from 4yo+ 3lb **14** Ran SP% **122.3**
Speed ratings (Par 101): **101,100,99,98,98 97,97,95,94,89 86,83,83,82**
toteswinger: 1&2 £14.00, 1&3 £16.80, 2&3 £21.90. CSF £185.03 CT £1218.81 TOTE £14.40: £3.80, £3.60, £2.50; EX 121.40 TRIFECTA Not won..
Owner J C Smith **Bred** Littleton Stud **Trained** Upper Lambourn, Berks
■ Stewards' Enquiry : Luke Morris caution: careless riding.
M C Geran caution: careless riding.

FOCUS
A moderate but competitive handicap, and straightforward form. They raced stands' side in the straight.

Jemiliah Official explanation: jockey said filly was denied a clear run

6929 BETTERBETCASINO.COM APPRENTICE H'CAP — 1m 3f 196y
5:10 (5:13) (Class 6) (0-55,55) 3-Y-0+ — **£2,590** (£770; £385; £192) **Stalls** High

Form — RPR

2260 **1** **She's So Pretty (IRE)**[51] 5583 4-9-4 **55**............(b) JemmaMarshall(3) 10 — 68
(G L Moore) *hld up in tch: smooth hdwy 2f out: led over 1f out: hung lft: drvn clr* **7/1**

0003 **2** 3 1/4 **Sagunt (GER)**[28] 6228 5-9-3 **54**.................. RossAtkinson(3) 4 — 62
(S Curran) *towards rr: rdn and hdwy 2f out: hung lft: styd on to take 2nd nr fin* **11/1**

P532 **3** 3/4 **Saloon (USA)**[11] 6668 4-9-4 **52**..........(t) Louis-PhilippeBeuzelin 6 — 59
(S Curran) *trckd ldrs: led 3f out tl over 1f out: one pce* **9/4**[1]

4003 **4** 7 **Eddie Dowling**[8] 6728 3-8-11 **52**.................. MCGeran 5 — 47
(M R Channon) *led 4f: prom tl wknd 2f out: hung lft whn btn* **5/1**[3]

2000 **5** 1 3/4 **Mighty Mover (IRE)**[73] 4936 6-9-3 **54**.......... AshleyMorgan(3) 9 — 47
(B Palling) *s.s: towards rr: rdn 3f out: sme late hdwy* **50/1**

1210 **6** 4 **Mixing**[15] 6577 6-9-6 **54**.................. DavidProbert 1 — 40
(M J Attwater) *chsd ldrs: hrd rdn over 2f out: sn wknd* **7/2**[2]

05-0 **7** 2 1/2 **Palanoverre (IRE)**[15] 6570 4-8-11 **48**.................. BillyCray(3) 3 — 30
(D J S Ffrench Davis) *hld up in rr: styd far side st: sme hdwy 2f out: sn wknd* **33/1**

0043 **8** 1 1/2 **Valentine Blue**[30] 6185 3-8-4 **50**..........(tp) PNolan(5) 8 — 30
(A B Haynes) *mid-div: reminders 1/2-way: hrd rdn and wknd 3f out* **20/1**

0600 **9** 1 3/4 **Bold Phoenix (IRE)**[10] 6693 7-8-9 **46** oh1..........(t) AndreaAtzeni(3) 2 — 23
(Miss Amy Weaver) *mid-div: outpcd 4f out: styd far side st: rallied to chse stands' side ldrs 2f out: wknd over 1f out* **16/1**

60-6 **10** 5 **Rajam**[102] 2643 10-8-12 **46** oh1..........(p) NicolPolli 7 — 15
(W K Goldsworthy) *chsd ldr: led after 4f tl 4f out: hrd rdn and wknd 3f out* **11/1**

4150 **11** 7 **Maddy**[47] 5710 3-8-10 **54**..........(p) MatthewDavies(3) 12 — 12
(George Baker) *prom: led 4f out tl 3f out: sn wknd* **12/1**

2m 38.68s (5.98) **Going Correction** +0.45s/f (Yiel)
WFA 3 from 4yo+ 7lb — **11** Ran SP% **122.1**
Speed ratings (Par 101): **98,95,95,90,89 86,85,84,83,79 75**
toteswinger: 1&2 £13.90, 1&3 £20.50, 2&3 £7.50. CSF £82.91 CT £232.06 TOTE £7.40: £2.40, £4.10, £1.50; EX 93.40 Trifecta £177.30 Pool: £342.72, 1.43 winning units. Place 6 £ 188.67, Place 5 £ 91.57.
Owner Miss S Bowles **Bred** Airlie Stud **Trained** Woodingdean, E Sussex
■ Stewards' Enquiry : M C Geran five-day ban: careless riding (Nov 6-10)

FOCUS
A very moderate handicap restricted to apprentices who had not ridden more than 25 winners. They raced middle to far side in the straight. The winner is rated to her best.
Maddy Official explanation: jockey said filly suffered interference in running
T/Jkpt: Not won. T/Plt: £156.80 to a £1 stake. Pool: £61,052.37. 284.06 winning tickets. T/Qpdt: £17.40 to a £1 stake. Pool: £3,777.19. 160.40 winning tickets. LM

6900 GREAT LEIGHS (A.W) (L-H)
Thursday, October 23

OFFICIAL GOING: Standard
Wind: strong behind Weather: cloudy, windy

6930 BANQUETING AT GREAT LEIGHS H'CAP — 1m 2f (P)
6:20 (6:20) (Class 6) (0-55,56) 3-Y-0+ — **£1,942** (£578; £288; £144) **Stalls** Low

Form — RPR

0002 **1** **Darley Star**[7] 6753 3-8-6 48.................. TedDurcan 6 — 59
(C E Brittain) *chsd ldr: rdn to ld 2f out: styd on wl u.p fnl f* **5/1**

3304 **2** 1 3/4 **King Of Connacht**[23] 6364 5-8-9 46 oh1..........(p) JamieSpencer 5 — 55+
(M Wellings) *hld up in midfield: hdwy and swtchd rt wl over 1f out: chsd wnr ent fnl f: drvn and nt qckn after: btn whn eased towards fin* **3/1**[1]

0-53 **3** 3 1/4 **Keep Your Distance**[7] 6751 4-9-4 55.................. JimmyQuinn 4 — 56
(P J McBride) *hld up wl in tch: hdwy to chse wnr wl over 1f out: sn rdn: outpcd by ldng pair fnl f* **4/1**[3]

2521 **4** 1/2 **Well Informed**[8] 6729 3-9-0 56 6ex.................. DeanMcKeown 2 — 56
(E J O'Neill) *stdd s and slowly away: hld up towards rr: hdwy jst over 2f out: rdn and brief effrt over 1f out: wl hld fnl f* **7/2**[2]

0000 **5** 3 1/2 **Samahir (USA)**[7] 6753 4-8-10 47..........(v[1]) RichardMullen 3 — 40
(T T Clement) *chsd ldng pair: rdn 2f out: wknd over 1f out* **10/1**

0100 **6** nk **Hallings Overture (USA)**[36] 6019 9-9-4 55..........(p) RichardKingscote 11 — 47
(C A Horgan) *stdd s: t.k.h: hld up in rr: hdwy on outer 3f out: rdn wl over 1f out: wknd jst over 1f out* **8/1**

0000 **7** 2 1/4 **Balerno**[10] 6693 9-8-13 50.................. PaulDoe 9 — 38
(Mrs L J Mongan) *hld up towards rr: rdn and struggling over 2f out: no ch fr over 1f out* **28/1**

030 **8** 5 **Credential**[38] 5961 6-9-2 53.................. J-PGuillambert 1 — 31
(John A Harris) *led tl rdn and hdd 2f out: wknd qckly over 1f out: eased whn wl btn ins fnl f* **14/1**

5000 **9** 5 **Elusive Deal (USA)**[17] 6529 3-8-7 52 ow1.......... RussellKennemore(3) 8 — 20
(Mrs L Williamson) *v.s.a: hld up bhd: rdn over 4f out: lost tch over 2f out* **66/1**

2m 8.27s (-0.33) **Going Correction** -0.05s/f (Stan)
WFA 3 from 4yo+ 5lb — **9** Ran SP% **115.7**
Speed ratings (Par 101): **99,97,95,94,91 91,89,85,81**
toteswinger: 1&2 £14.00, 1&3 £7.40, 2&3 £3.60. CSF £20.43 CT £65.71 TOTE £5.60: £2.40, £1.10, £1.80; EX 20.00.
Owner Mohammed Rashid **Bred** Darley **Trained** Newmarket, Suffolk

FOCUS
This had the look of a low-grade handicap. The form is straightforward.

6931 EPPING FOREST CLAIMING STKS — 6f (P)
6:50 (6:50) (Class 5) 2-Y-0 — **£3,238** (£963; £481; £240) **Stalls** Low

Form — RPR

4562 **1** **Timeteam (IRE)**[14] 6603 2-9-5 81.................. JamieSpencer 1 — 81
(S Kirk) *s.i.s: hld up in rr of main gp on inner: edgd out rt 2f out: rdn and swtchd rt jst over 1f out: ev ch ent fnl f: hrd rdn fnl f: led last strides* **11/8**[1]

5212 **2** hd **Gone Hunting**[26] 6281 2-9-2 84.................. JackDean(5) 5 — 82
(W G M Turner) *s.i.s: hld up in rr of main gp: rdn and hdwy on outer over 2f out: led ins fnl f: hdd last strides* **3/1**[2]

4210 **3** 2 1/4 **Rio Royale (IRE)**[103] 3941 2-9-7 79.................. JimCrowley 6 — 75
(Mrs A J Perrett) *hld up wl in tch: rdn and effrt 2f out: ev ch over 1f out: led jst ins fnl f: sn hdd: one pce fnl 100yds* **6/1**[3]

3514 **4** 1/2 **Key To Love (IRE)**[8] 6730 2-8-1 72.................. JimmyQuinn 2 — 54
(H J L Dunlop) *hld up in tch: hdwy and swtchd rt over 1f out: kpt on ins fnl f: nt pce to trble ldng pair* **13/2**

4200 **5** 2 1/4 **Eldorado Days (IRE)**[6] 6769 2-9-7 73..........(v[1]) TPQueally 11 — 67
(K R Burke) *chsd ldrs: rdn to chal wl over 1f out: wandered over 1f out: wknd ins fnl f* **16/1**

0000 **6** nk **Isabella Romee (IRE)**[29] 6214 2-8-4 60.................. FrankieMcDonald 14 — 49
(Jane Chapple-Hyam) *in tch: rdn over 2f out: keeping on same pce and looked hld whn short of room jst over 1f out: one pce fnl f* **40/1**

30 **7** 1/2 **Risky Capital**[6] 6787 2-8-6 0.................. HayleyTurner 8 — 50
(S A Callaghan) *w ldr: rdn to ld 2f out: hdd jst ins fnl f: sn wknd* **20/1**

6006 **8** 1 3/4 **River Style (IRE)**[8] 6730 2-8-6 47.................. RichardMullen 3 — 44
(A P Jarvis) *led narrowly tl rdn and hdd 2f out: wknd ent fnl f* **66/1**

2506 **9** 2 1/2 **Handful Of Magic**[15] 6573 2-8-1 57.................. CatherineGannon 13 — 32
(Tom Dascombe) *chsd ldrs: drvn over 2f out: wknd over 1f out* **33/1**

3 **10** hd **Bid To Dance**[71] 4986 2-8-1 0.................. NickyMackay 4 — 31
(K A Morgan) *s.i.s: in rr of main gp: drvn over 2f out: sn struggling: wl btn fnl f* **33/1**

6600 **11** 1 1/4 **Sericus (IRE)**[44] 5785 2-8-11 62..........(p) TedDurcan 7 — 38
(W Jarvis) *bhd: swtchd rt after 1f: lost tch over 3f out: nvr a factor* **16/1**

0400 **12** 1 **Kaada**[62] 5242 2-8-11 53.................. PaulDoe 12 — 35
(C E Brittain) *racd wd: a bhd: lost tch over 3f out: nvr a factor* **33/1**

0 **13** 11 **Che Castagna**[10] 6697 2-7-12 0.................. DominicFox(3) 9 — —
(Tom Dascombe) *sn rdn along in rr: lost tch 4f out: t.o last 2f* **66/1**

1m 13.28s (-0.42) **Going Correction** -0.05s/f (Stan) — **13** Ran SP% **125.5**
Speed ratings (Par 95): **100,99,96,96,93 92,92,89,86,86 84,83,68**
toteswinger: 1&2 £1.10, 1&3 £4.60, 2&3 £8.60. CSF £5.25 TOTE £2.50: £1.10, £1.70, £2.50; EX 7.60.Key To Love (IRE) was claimed by A. J. Chamberlain for £5,000
Owner R Gander **Bred** R N Auld **Trained** Upper Lambourn, Berks

FOCUS
A decent little claimer.

NOTEBOOK
Timeteam(IRE) has some useful form to his name and was beaten just a head off a mark of 75 in a nursery at Newbury last time. Dropping to this level for the first time, he was dropped in by Spencer and gradually weaved his way through the field. He had to fight hard in the end, Gone Hunting proving a real tough one to shake off, and he just edged it in a head-bobber. (op 15-8 tchd 2-1 in places)
Gone Hunting won in this grade at Wolverhampton two starts back and was not beaten far over course and distance last time. Held up early, he came widest of all in the straight and stayed on strongly for pressure, just losing out in a tight finish. He is a fair sort at this level. (op 11-4 tchd 10-3)
Rio Royale(IRE) had not been seen since running poorly at Ascot on his nursery debut back in July and it looked significant he was dropping in grade for this return. He was produced to have every chance and could not quicken from a furlong out. (op 9-1 tchd 10-1)
Key To Love(IRE) kept on at the one pace back in fourth and probably found this too good a race for the level. (tchd 6-1)
Eldorado Days(IRE) appeared to face a stiff task at the weights and he ran quite well considering in the first-time visor. (op 12-1)

6932 MOULSHAM HALL MAIDEN STKS — 5f (P)
7:20 (7:21) (Class 4) 2-Y-0 — **£3,885** (£1,156; £577; £288) **Stalls** Low

Form — RPR

6 **1** **Rublevka Star (USA)**[36] 6030 2-8-12 0.................. ShaneKelly 3 — 68
(J Noseda) *chsd ldng pair: swtchd lft wl over 1f out: hrd rdn ent fnl f: kpt on wl u.p to ld nr fin* **7/4**[1]

3U52 **2** 1/2 **Bees River (IRE)**[15] 6578 2-8-12 65.................. JamieSpencer 2 — 66
(A P Jarvis) *led: c to centre 2f out: drvn over 1f out: battled on wl tl hdd and no ex nr fin* **9/2**[3]

60 **3** shd **Chosen Son (IRE)**[39] 5939 2-9-3 0.................. TedDurcan 9 — 71
(P J O'Gorman) *s.i.s: sn swtchd to inner: hdwy 2f out: chsd ldrs 1f out: edgd rt fnl f but r.o wl to go 3rd nr fin* **25/1**

06 **4** 1/2 **La Capriosa**[7] 6764 2-8-7 0.................. DavidProbert(5) 4 — 64
(A J McCabe) *chsd ldr: rdn and ev ch over 1f out tl unable qck fnl 100yds* **33/1**

404 **5** 1 1/4 **Piste**[19] 6469 2-8-12 70.................. MartinDwyer 11 — 60
(B J Meehan) *chsd ldrs: rdn over 2f out: hrd rdn over 1f out: kpt on but nvr pce to rch ldrs* **8/1**

0 **6** shd **Liteup My World (USA)**[27] 6253 2-9-3 0.................. DaneO'Neill 1 — 64
(B Ellison) *in tch: pushed along wl over 3f out: rdn over 2f out: kpt on same pce fr over 1f out* **20/1**

43 **7** 3 1/4 **Rare Art**[15] 6578 2-9-3 0.................. HayleyTurner 12 — 51
(S A Callaghan) *s.i.s: sn swtchd rt: wl bhd: sme hdwy on inner over 1f out: n.d* **12/1**

2232 **8** 1 **Majuba (USA)**[16] 6545 2-9-3 82.................. PaulMulrennan 7 — 47
(K A Ryan) *in tch: rdn jst over 2f out: wknd qckly over 1f out: wl btn fnl f* **2/1**[2]

6360 **9** 1 1/4 **Fortune In Faith (USA)**[21] 6414 2-8-12 67.................. AdamKirby 6 — 38
(C G Cox) *bhd and rdn 1/2-way: n.d after* **33/1**

000 **10** 1/2 **Brown Lentic (IRE)**[11] 6677 2-9-3 0.................. SteveDrowne 8 — 41
(G L Moore) *towards rr: rdn 1/2-way: drvn and wknd 2f out: wl btn fnl f* **66/1**

11 1 1/2 **Fitz** 2-9-3 0.................. TGMcLaughlin 5 — 35
(M Salaman) *rrd s and v.s.a: a wl bhd* **100/1**

60.36 secs (0.16) **Going Correction** -0.05s/f (Stan) — **11** Ran SP% **123.7**
Speed ratings (Par 97): **96,95,95,94,92 92,86,84,82,81 79**
toteswinger: 1&2 £9.30, 1&3 £26.10, 2&3 £0. CSF £10.14 TOTE £2.90: £1.40, £1.80, £7.70; EX 13.30.
Owner Red Man Bloodstock **Bred** Grapestock Llc **Trained** Newmarket, Suffolk

FOCUS
This was just a modest maiden, although the time was decent, it being run in a 5f juvenile course record.

NOTEBOOK
Rublevka Star(USA) showed plenty of speed before fading into sixth on her debut at Yarmouth, and the drop in trip looked a good move. Driven to obtain a handy position, she took a while to engage top gear but got there in plenty of time. Although no star, she has a future at the right level. (op 6-4 tchd 5-4, 11-10 in places)
Bees River(IRE) was ridden positively and came down the middle of the track in the straight. Strongly pressed on both sides a furlong out, she kept finding and got run out of it only late on. (op 13-2)
Chosen Son(IRE) stuck towards the rail in the straight and it seemed to do him no harm, as he was staying on and only just lost out for second. He has improved with each run and is now qualified for handicaps. (op 40-1)
La Capriosa is another improving with experience and she stayed on right the way to the line. She can make an impact in handicaps. (op 50-1)
Piste kept on again close home and did not run too badly. (op 12-1)
Liteup My World(USA) improved on his first effort and seemed more effective at a sprint trip. (op 16-1)

Majuba(USA) had finished either second or third in each of his last six starts (all turf) and the switch to Polytrack clearly didn't suit. He found nothing for pressure and ran well below form. (op 9-4 tchd 5-2)

6933 NEW HOLLAND MAIDEN FILLIES' STKS 6f (P)
7:50 (7:51) (Class 4) 2-Y-O £3,885 (£1,156; £577; £288) **Stalls** Low

Form RPR

52 **1** **Minute Limit (IRE)**[10] [6697] 2-9-0 0........................ ShaneKelly 7 72
(J A Osborne) *in tch: hdwy 2f out: rdn to ld over 1f out: r.o wl* **9/2**[3]

2 *1* **Kind Heart** 2-9-0 0........................ J-PGuillambert 3 69
(Sir Mark Prescott) *s.i.s: bhd: hdwy 2f out: swtchd rt jst over 1f out: r.o wl fnl f: wnt 2nd towards fin: nt rch wnr* **20/1**

3 **3** *1* **Dareh (IRE)**[16] [6555] 2-9-0 0........................ TedDurcan 9 66
(Saeed Bin Suroor) *in tch: hdwy 2f out: rdn and unable qck over 1f out: kpt on to chse wnr briefly ins fnl f: nvr pce to chal wnr* **2/1**[1]

360 **4** *¾* **Peter's Gift (IRE)**[96] [4202] 2-9-0 72........................ PaulMulrennan 5 64
(K A Ryan) *racd in midfield: rdn 1/2-way: hdwy u.p and swtchd lft jst ins fnl f: styd on but nvr threatened ldrs* **16/1**

06 **5** *1 ½* **Romantic Queen**[42] [5835] 2-9-0 0........................ TGMcLaughlin 12 59
(E A L Dunlop) *s.i.s: wl bhd: hdwy on inner 2f out: kpt on fnl f: nt rch ldrs* **15/2**

040 **6** *nse* **Iliketoboogie**[10] [6697] 2-8-9 0........................ DavidProbert(5) 11 59
(A J McCabe) *led: rdn 2f out: hdd over 1f out: sn edgd rt: chsd wnr again briefly 1f out: sn wknd* **33/1**

4540 **7** *2 ¾* **Chatterszaha**[28] [6223] 2-9-0 65........................ SteveDrowne 2 51
(C Drew) *chsd ldrs: wnt 2nd 2f out tl 1f out: wknd qckly ins fnl f* **33/1**

2002 **8** *1 ¾* **Val De Flores**[11] [6666] 2-9-0 62........................ LPKeniry 8 46
(E F Vaughan) *chsd ldr tl 2f out: wknd u.p over 1f out* **12/1**

0 **9** *hd* **Miss Perfectionist**[34] [6083] 2-9-0 0........................ TPQueally 10 45
(S A Callaghan) *hld up off the pce in midfield: rdn 3f out: keeping on same pce whn sltly hmpd jst over 1f out* **33/1**

0000 **10** *½* **Fleur De'Lion (IRE)**[20] [6432] 2-9-0 52........................ MartinDwyer 6 44
(S Kirk) *in tch: rdn over 3f out: struggling 1/2-way: no ch fr wl over 1f out* **66/1**

0 **11** *2* **Taste Of Honey (IRE)**[24] [6327] 2-9-0 0........................ WilliamBuick 4 38
(D W P Arbuthnot) *a towards rr: rdn and struggling 1/2-way: n.d after* **10/1**

12 *nk* **Mandhooma** 2-9-0 0........................ RHills 1 37
(J H M Gosden) *s.i.s: a bhd: n.d* **7/2**[2]

1m 13.43s (-0.27) **Going Correction** -0.05s/f (Stan) 12 Ran SP% **123.2**
Speed ratings (Par 94): **99,97,96,95,93 93,89,87,87,86 83,83**
toteswinger: 1&2 £21.90, 1&3 £1.30, 2&3 £15.50. CSF £98.96 TOTE £5.90: £1.70, £5.80, £1.20; EX 76.10.
Owner Danny Durkan **Bred** Airlie Stud **Trained** Upper Lambourn, Berks

FOCUS
A fair fillies' maiden.

NOTEBOOK
Minute Limit(IRE) shaped with promise here on her debut before finishing second at Kempton last time, and she was able to put an end to a miserable run of form for her trainer. She came through to lead over a furlong out and stayed on well for pressure, suggesting there may be more to come in handicaps.
Kind Heart, half-sister to a 1m winner, comes from a yard whose juveniles often need a run to set them straight, and she shaped with a good deal of promise in second, staying on well under an educational ride. She is going to improve for a step up to 7f and looks a ready-made maiden winner. (op 18-1 tchd 16-1)
Dareh(IRE) shaped well when third on soft ground on her debut at Folkestone and was expected to improve with the experience under her belt. She was under pressure as they straightened for home, though, and never looked like winning, just finding the one pace for pressure. A step up to 7f is evidently required. (op 9-4 tchd 5-2 in places)
Peter's Gift(IRE) stayed on for strong pressure and appreciated the return to 6f. She would make more appeal in handicaps. (op 12-1)
Romantic Queen is now qualified for a mark and should fare better in handicaps. (op 10-1)
Mandhooma, whose trainer has been doing well with his juveniles here of late, was slowly into stride and never threatened to get involved. She showed signs of greenness but needs to leave this well behind if she is to be winning any time soon. (op 4-1 tchd 9-2 in a place)

6934 SHALFORD H'CAP 1m 6f (P)
8:20 (8:20) (Class 5) (0-75,75) 3-Y-O £2,914 (£867; £433; £216) **Stalls** Low

Form RPR

2341 **1** **Silk Hall (UAE)**[10] [6708] 3-9-6 74 6ex........................ DaneO'Neill 4 87
(D W P Arbuthnot) *hld up towards rr: hdwy gng wl over 3f out: chsd ldr 2f out: rdn to ld over 1f out: styd on wl and in command fnl f* **11/8**[1]

6245 **2** *1 ¾* **Trenchant**[71] [4992] 3-8-13 67........................(v[1]) AdamKirby 3 78
(J R Fanshawe) *hld up towards rr: rdn 6f out: hdwy u.p over 2f out: chsd wnr 1f out: no imp* **20/1**

-404 **3** *3 ¾* **Ragamuffin Man (IRE)**[11] [6678] 3-9-7 75........................(v[1]) PaulDoe 13 80
(W J Knight) *sn led: ridded wl over 2f out: hdd over 1f out: plugged on same pce fnl f* **8/1**[3]

0401 **4** *3 ¾* **Eventide**[20] [6447] 3-8-11 70........................ DavidProbert(5) 11 70
(W J Knight) *hld up in tch: travelling wl over 2f out: n.m.r briefly wl over 1f out: sn rdn and fnd little: wl hld fnl f: wnt 4th towards fin* **16/1**

4024 **5** *nk* **My Mate Max**[13] [6630] 3-9-6 74........................(p) GrahamGibbons 2 74
(R Hollinshead) *hld up in midfield: rdn and effrt on inner wl over 2f out: chsd ldng trio 1f out: no imp: lost 4th towards fin* **14/1**

6151 **6** *6* **Bushy Dell (IRE)**[34] [6092] 3-9-2 75........................ AmyBaker(5) 5 66
(Miss J Feilden) *chsd ldr for 2f: styd handy: rdn 2f out: wknd qckly over 1f out* **20/1**

6442 **7** *1 ¼* **Blue Citadel (USA)**[11] [6678] 3-8-12 66........................ JimCrowley 9 55
(Mrs A J Perrett) *hld up in midfield: hdwy on outer 8f out: sn chsng ldng pair: wnt 2nd 4f out: sn rdn: wknd 3f out: wl btn last 2f* **11/1**

1022 **8** *5* **China Pink**[32] [6155] 3-8-6 60........................ JimmyQuinn 7 42
(Sir Mark Prescott) *prom: chsd ldr after 2f tl rdn 4f out: chsd ldr again jst over 3f out tl 2f out: sn btn: hung rt over 1f out* **14/1**

3316 **9** *1* **Lady Sorcerer**[33] [6107] 3-9-1 69........................ DarrenWilliams 10 50
(A P Jarvis) *hld up bhd: hdwy over 4f out: rdn and no rspnse 2f out: wl btn after* **20/1**

021 **10** *2 ¼* **Drum Major (IRE)**[14] [6596] 3-9-3 71........................ RichardMullen 8 49
(G L Moore) *hld up in tch in midfield: rdn 4f out: drvn and wknd 2f out: eased whn no ch fnl f* **16/1**

0410 **11** *52* **Kritzia**[35] [6060] 3-8-11 65........................ TPQueally 14 —
(H R A Cecil) *chsd ldrs: rdn and lost pl qckly 5f out: t.o and virtually p.u last 2f* **5/1**[2]

0600 **12** *4* **Force Tradition (IRE)**[7] [6748] 3-8-11 65........................ PaulMulrennan 6 —
(M H Tompkins) *hld up bhd: rdn and toiling over 7f out: t.o and virtually p.u fr over 2f out* **100/1**

3m 0.89s (-2.31) **Going Correction** -0.05s/f (Stan) 12 Ran SP% **118.6**
Speed ratings (Par 101): **104,103,100,98,98 95,94,91,90,89 59,57**
toteswinger: 1&2 £5.60, 1&3 £6.30, 2&3 £17.00. CSF £38.50 CT £175.00 TOTE £2.50: £1.30, £5.50, £3.10; EX 41.50.
Owner Bonusprint **Bred** Darley **Trained** Compton, Berks

FOCUS
A moderate staying handicap but the time was good and this is solid form for the grade. The well-in Silk Hall probably improved on the bare form of his latest win.
Kritzia Official explanation: trainer's rep had no explanation for the poor form shown; vet said filly was lame left hind
Force Tradition(IRE) Official explanation: jockey said gelding had no more to give

6935 GREATLEIGHS.COM MEDIAN AUCTION MAIDEN STKS 1m (P)
8:50 (8:54) (Class 5) 3-4-Y-O £2,914 (£867; £433; £216) **Stalls** High

Form RPR

1 **Pink Ivory** 3-8-12 0........................ TedDurcan 1 77+
(Saeed Bin Suroor) *dwlt: hld up towards rr on inner: hdwy on inner 2f out: rn green over 1f out: edgd rt but led ins fnl f: stormed clr fnl 100yds* **4/1**[3]

2326 **2** *3 ¼* **Azure Mist**[10] [6712] 3-8-12 65........................ PaulMulrennan 8 68
(M H Tompkins) *led: rdn 2f out: hdd ins fnl f: no ch w wnr fnl 100yds* **9/4**[2]

2322 **3** *1* **Mazaris (IRE)**[12] [6660] 3-9-3 71........................ DaneO'Neill 6 71
(L M Cumani) *hld up towards rr: hdwy over 2f out: drvn to press ldr jst over 1f out: nt qckn and one pce fnl f* **6/4**[1]

624 **4** *1 ¾* **Quail Landing**[84] [4566] 3-8-12 66........................ MartinDwyer 2 62
(M P Tregoning) *trckd ldrs: rdn and effrt over 1f out: unable qck ent fnl f: one pce after* **7/1**

5 *1 ½* **Another Try (IRE)** 3-9-3 0........................ DarrenWilliams 3 63
(A P Jarvis) *s.i.s: hld up towards rr: hdwy jst over 2f out: rdn over 1f out: no imp fnl f* **25/1**

6- **6** *1* **To Be Or Not To Be**[309] [7190] 3-8-9 0........................ LukeMorris(3) 5 56
(John Berry) *t.k.h: chsd ldrs: rdn to chse ldr over 2f out: edgd lft and wknd over 1f out* **25/1**

0360 **7** *1 ¼* **Xandra (IRE)**[37] [6003] 3-8-9 46........................ JackMitchell(3) 7 53
(C F Wall) *s.i.s: hld up in rr: rdn 4f out: struggling over 2f out: no imp last 2f* **33/1**

0560 **8** *2 ½* **Misplaced Fortune**[85] [4540] 3-8-7 58........................ Louis-PhilippeBeuzelin(5) 9 47
(N Tinkler) *chsd ldr tl over 2f out: sn drvn: c wd 2f out: sn wknd* **16/1**

0 **9** *29* **Mr Skipiton (IRE)**[12] [6660] 3-9-3 0........................ JerryO'Dwyer 10 —
(B J McMath) *s.i.s: hld up in midfield on outer: rdn and lost pl wl over 3f out: virtually p.u fnl f: t.o* **40/1**

1m 40.26s (0.36) **Going Correction** -0.05s/f (Stan) 9 Ran SP% **122.2**
Speed ratings (Par 103): **96,92,91,90,88 87,86,83,54**
toteswinger: 1&2 £5.60, 1&3 £1.70, 2&3 £3.70. CSF £13.87 TOTE £4.90: £1.80, £1.10, £1.10; EX 19.20.
Owner Godolphin **Bred** Darley **Trained** Newmarket, Suffolk

FOCUS
An uncompetitive maiden in which the form horses did not set much of a standard. The winner can do better though, and the placed horses are rated to form.

6936 HOSPITALITY AT GREAT LEIGHS H'CAP 1m (P)
9:20 (9:23) (Class 5) (0-75,75) 3-Y-O £2,914 (£867; £433; £216) **Stalls** High

Form RPR

4000 **1** **Wing Play (IRE)**[24] [6337] 3-8-4 61 oh1........................(p) WilliamBuick 2 72+
(H Morrison) *hld up bhd: gd hdwy on inner 2f out: led over 1f out: hung rt but drvn clr fnl f: r.o wl* **14/1**

6602 **2** *3* **Benedetto**[7] [6749] 3-8-12 69........................(p) JimCrowley 4 73+
(Mrs A J Perrett) *s.i.s: hld up in rr: hdwy and nt clr run over 2f out: tl swtchd lft ent fnl f: chsd wnr fnl 100yds: nvr able to chal* **10/1**

3036 **3** *1* **Island Treasure**[7] [6746] 3-8-4 61 oh2........................ JimmyQuinn 6 63
(H Morrison) *t.k.h: hld up in tch: hdwy 2f out: ev ch over 1f out: sn rdn and outpcd by wnr: wl hld ins fnl f: lost 2nd fnl 100yds* **16/1**

4030 **4** *1 ¼* **Atabaas Pride**[12] [6663] 3-9-3 74........................ JoeFanning 7 73
(M Johnston) *towards rr: rdn and hdwy 3f out: chsd ldrs and rdn wl over 1f out: outpcd fnl f* **14/1**

1530 **5** *5* **Jollyhockeysticks**[11] [6683] 3-8-10 67........................ SamHitchcott 1 55+
(M R Channon) *hld up in midfield on inner: effrt and nt clr run 2f out: gap opened but bdly hmpd over 1f out: no ch after* **16/1**

0005 **6** *nse* **Zaarmit (IRE)**[13] [6631] 3-8-4 61 oh1........................(b) RichardMullen 8 49
(D M Simcock) *s.i.s: bhd: rdn wl over 1f out: swtchd lft over 1f out: no imp fnl f* **40/1**

4431 **7** *½* **Pension Policy (USA)**[11] [6683] 3-9-2 73 6ex........................ SteveDrowne 5 59
(R Charlton) *in tch: rdn and effrt 3f out: pressed ldrs 2f out: drvn and wknd over 1f out: wl btn fnl f* **2/1**[1]

30-3 **8** *1* **Red Expresso (IRE)**[12] [6660] 3-8-11 68........................ JamieSpencer 9 52+
(M L W Bell) *hld up in last trio: rdn 3f out: no hdwy u.p over 1f out: eased whn wl hld ins fnl f* **6/1**[3]

6605 **9** *¾* **Miss Emma May (IRE)**[20] [6446] 3-9-1 72........................(v) MartinDwyer 12 54
(D R C Elsworth) *t.k.h: chsd ldr after 1f: rdn wl over 2f out: wknd and edgd rt over 1f out* **25/1**

3053 **10** *½* **Ocean Legend (IRE)**[51] [5595] 3-9-3 74........................(t) SaleemGolam 10 55
(Miss J Feilden) *led for 1f out: chsd ldrs after: rdn over 3f out: wknd wl over 1f out* **8/1**

6402 **11** *1* **Wikaala (USA)**[11] [6683] 3-9-4 75........................(v[1]) RHills 11 54
(M P Tregoning) *led after 1f: rdn 2f out: hdd over 1f out: sn wl btn* **4/1**[2]

1m 39.53s (-0.37) **Going Correction** -0.05s/f (Stan) 11 Ran SP% **119.2**
Speed ratings (Par 101): **99,96,95,93,88 88,88,87,86,85 84**
toteswinger: 1&2 £33.80, 1&3 £9.60, 2&3 £40.50. CSF £148.56 CT £2272.59 TOTE £20.60: £5.60, £2.00, £6.10; EX 197.90 Place 6 £ 5.01, Place 5 £ 3.22.
Owner Watching Brief **Bred** Churchtown House Stud **Trained** East Ilsley, Berks

FOCUS
Any number looked in with a chance as they turned for home but Wing Play ultimately ran out an easy winner. He is rated to this year's form with the second close to his sand mark.
Wikaala(USA) Official explanation: jockey said gelding ran too free
T/Plt: £10.00 to a £1 stake. Pool: £75,259.26. 5,473.10 winning tickets. T/Qpdt: £6.50 to a £1 stake. Pool: £6,076.24. 690.70 winning tickets. SP

6405 AYR (L-H)
Friday, October 24
6937 Meeting Abandoned - waterlogged

[5889]DONCASTER (L-H)

Friday, October 24

OFFICIAL GOING: Good (good to soft in places; 7.9)

Thr ground was described as 'just on the dead side of good'.

Wind: breezy 1/2 against Weather: fine and sunny

6944 SOCIETY LIFESTYLE AND LEISURE MAGAZINE E B F MAIDEN STKS (C&G) 7f

1:50 (1:53) (Class 4) 2-Y-O £4,857 (£1,445; £722; £360) **Stalls** High

Form RPR

0 **1** **Roman Republic (FR)**[15] 6604 2-9-0 0 RoystonFfrench 10 80+
(M Johnston) *chsd ldrs: pushed along wl over 2f out: rdn wl over 1f out: styd on u.p ins fnl f to ld fnl 50yds* **11/4[1]**

432 **2** ¾ **Striker Torres (IRE)**[20] 6481 2-9-0 76 TomEaves 6 78
(B Smart) *led: qcknd over 2f out: pushed along wl over 1f out: drvn ent ins fnl f: hdd and no ex fnl 50yds* **9/2[3]**

3 ¾ **Meyyal (USA)** 2-9-0 0 RHills 14 76
(B W Hills) *trckd ldrs towards stands' rail: hdwy 2f out: sn swtchd lft and nt clr run over 1f out: rdn to chse ldng pair whn rn green and n.m.r ent fnl f: kpt on towards fin* **9/1**

4 ½ **Maverin (IRE)** 2-9-0 0 TPQueally 3 75
(J Noseda) *trckd ldrs: effrt 2f out: rdn and ch over 1f out: drvn and kpt on same pce ins fnl f* **25/1**

5 ¾ **Dream Win** 2-9-0 0 RichardMullen 13 73
(Sir Michael Stoute) *in tch pushed along and outpcd over 2f out: swtchd lft and hdwy over 1f out: styd on strly ins fnl f: nrst fin* **7/2[2]**

02 **6** ½ **Chapter And Verse (IRE)**[22] 6412 2-9-0 0 MichaelHills 16 72
(B W Hills) *cl up on stands' rail: effrt 2f out: sn rdn and ev ch tl drvn and wknd appr fnl f* **11/2**

7 2 ¾ **Jesse James (IRE)** 2-9-0 0 RobertHavlin 4 65
(J H M Gosden) *dwlt: hdwy on outer 1/2-way: rdn along 2f out and kpt on same pce appr fnl f* **6/1**

8 1 ½ **Francis Walsingham (IRE)** 2-9-0 0 AdamKirby 8 61
(J R Fanshawe) *dwlt and towards rr tl styd on fnl 2f* **22/1**

9 ½ **First Service (IRE)** 2-9-0 0 SteveDrowne 2 60
(R Charlton) *racd wd in midfield: hdwy iover 2f out: sn rdn and wknd wl over 1f out* **50/1**

10 3 ½ **Khayar (IRE)** 2-9-0 0 NCallan 5 51
(M H Tompkins) *a towards rr* **66/1**

0 **11** ¾ **Safari Song (IRE)**[13] 6655 2-9-0 0 PaulMulrennan 7 49
(B Smart) *chsd ldrs: rdn along 2f out: sn wknd* **66/1**

00 **12** 1 ¾ **Green Agenda**[20] 6474 2-9-0 0 J-PGuillambert 15 45
(M Johnston) *cl up: rdn along 3f out: sn wknd* **66/1**

13 3 **Nocturnal Lad (IRE)** 2-9-0 0 JerryO'Dwyer 9 37
(M G Quinlan) *cl up: rdn along 3f out: wknd over 2f out* **100/1**

0 **14** 1 ¾ **Top Tinker**[7] 6789 2-9-0 0 SaleemGolam 1 33
(M H Tompkins) *a in rr* **150/1**

15 4 **Carrimion** 2-9-0 0 DavidAllan 11 23
(T H Caldwell) *slowly into strride: a in rr* **200/1**

1m 29.5s (3.20) **Going Correction** +0.125s/f (Good) **15** Ran SP% **123.5**

Speed ratings (Par 97): **86,85,84,83,82 82,79,77,76,72 72,70,66,64,60**

toteswinger: 1&2 £4.60, 1&3 £14.40, 2&3 £9.70. CSF £14.97 TOTE £4.60: £2.00, £1.50, £3.10; EX 18.30 Trifecta £171.80 Part won. Pool: £232.22 -0.50 winning units..

Owner Sheikh Hamdan Bin Mohammed Al Maktoum **Bred** Famille Niarchos **Trained** Middleham Moor, N Yorks

FOCUS

A maiden featuring mostly unexposed juveniles and several promising performances.

NOTEBOOK

Roman Republic(FR), a 200,000gns son of Cape Cross and half-brother to a 1m winner out of a high-class dual 1m1f scorer, went off a short-priced favourite over 1m on his debut but was well beaten. He had been given Dewhurst and Racing Post Trophy entries, which indicated he was well regarded, and he was backed in to clear favourite again. Settling behind the leader, he was produced inside the final furlong and, after being ridden to get there, scored nicely in the end. He should go on from this and justify connections' faith. (op 3-1 tchd 7-2)

Striker Torres(IRE) looked slightly unfortunate not to score at Redcar last time and hit the bar again. However, he did little wrong, although perhaps he was slightly keen early, and has races in him. He would be no good thing to confirm the form with the trio behind him, though, all of whom showed plenty of ability on their debuts. (op 7-2)

Meyyal(USA) ◆, a half-brother to multiple middle-distance winner Mutamaasek, might have finished a little closer had his run not been slightly impeded when the first two came close together inside the last furlong. He looks sure to come on a good deal for the run. (op 16-1)

Maverin(IRE), a neat newcomer who was edgy and had two handlers in the paddock, is a half-brother to a 1m2f/1m4f winner. He saw a fair amount of daylight from his low draw but was in the firing line until fading in the final furlong. (op 33-1)

Dream Win ◆, a quality-looking colt with plenty of size and scope, is a half-brother to Quiff out of 1,000 Guineas winner Wince. He ran green when asked to go about his work before getting the idea and finishing on the heels of the placed horses. The experience will not be lost on him. (op 5-1)

Chapter And Verse(IRE) had the rail draw and raced up with the pace but failed to find an extra gear in the final furlong. He now qualifies for a handicap mark. (op 13-2)

Jesse James(IRE), a 130,000 euros half-brother to a 1m3f winner out of 1m2f winner, refused to go into the stalls on his intended debut and was relatively unfancied this time. He looked like taking a hand at around the quarter-mile pole, but was outpaced in the closing stages. He looks the type who will make a much better three-year-old. (op 5-1)

Francis Walsingham(IRE), a 140,000gns foal and half-brother to three winners from the family of Antonius Pius, was doing his best work in the closing stages and should benefit considerably for the outing. Both tall and narrow, he looks as though he will be much more the finished article next year (op 25-1)

6945 E B F QUINTIN GILBEY MAIDEN FILLIES' STKS 1m (R)

2:20 (2:27) (Class 4) 2-Y-O £5,180 (£1,541; £770; £384) **Stalls** Low

Form RPR

1 **Leocorno (IRE)** 2-9-0 0 RichardMullen 8 76
(Sir Michael Stoute) *hld up in rr: hdwy on inner over 2f out: nt clr run and swtchd outside over 1f out: r.o strly to ld fnl 50yds* **6/1[2]**

6 **2** ¾ **Queen Eleanor**[14] 6622 2-9-0 0 RobertHavlin 4 74
(J H M Gosden) *stdd s: hld up in rr: hdwy over 2f out: qcknd to ld 1f out: hdd and no ex towards fin* **7/1[3]**

3 2 ¼ **Ballet Dancer (IRE)** 2-9-0 0 PhilipRobinson 7 69
(M A Jarvis) *in rr: hdwy and plld wd over 2f out: styd on same pce fnl f* **8/1**

4 hd **Sweet Hollow** 2-9-0 0 IanMongan 14 69
(C G Cox) *chsd ldrs: kpt on same pce appr fnl f* **33/1**

5 **5** 1 ½ **Teeky**[95] 4256 2-9-0 0 TedDurcan 11 65
(J H M Gosden) *trckd ldr: led over 1f out: sn hdd and fdd* **6/1[2]**

00 **6** ¾ **Waheeba**[17] 6559 2-9-0 0 RHills 9 64
(J L Dunlop) *chsd ldrs: styd on same pce fnl 2f* **33/1**

7 ¾ **Silken Promise (USA)** 2-9-0 0 AdamKirby 1 62
(W R Swinburn) *mid-div: kpt on fnl 2f: nvr nr ldrs* **12/1**

8 ½ **Marillos Proterras** 2-9-0 0 TPO'Shea 2 61
(Mrs A Duffield) *s.i.s: in rr: c wd over 2f out: kpt on: nvr nr ldrs* **100/1**

4 **9** 2 **Special Bond**[14] 6622 2-9-0 0 SamHitchcott 3 57
(J A Osborne) *in rr: kpt on fnl 2f: nvr a factor* **12/1**

5 **10** nk **Martha's Girl (USA)**[16] 6580 2-9-0 0 DNolan 12 56
(D Carroll) *chsd ldrs: wknd over 1f out* **22/1**

0 **11** ½ **Morning Calm**[63] 5240 2-9-0 0 SteveDrowne 15 55
(R Charlton) *prom: wkng whn n.m.r over 1f out* **10/1**

0 **12** 1 **Labisa (IRE)**[63] 5241 2-9-0 0 DarryllHolland 6 53
(H Morrison) *mid-div on inner: nt clr run over 1f out: sn wknd* **14/1**

13 nk **Peintre D'Argent (IRE)** 2-9-0 0 TravisBlock 16 52
(H Morrison) *chsd ldrs: lost pl over 1f out* **18/1**

0 **14** 1 ½ **Marjury Daw (IRE)**[23] 6391 2-9-0 0 HayleyTurner 13 49
(J G Given) *led: hdd & wknd over 1f out* **33/1**

15 1 ½ **Aim To Achieve (IRE)** 2-9-0 0 MichaelHills 10 45
(B W Hills) *s.i.s: nvr on terms: hung rt and eased 1f out: lame* **9/2[1]**

1m 43.39s (2.39) **Going Correction** +0.125s/f (Good) **15** Ran SP% **120.9**

Speed ratings (Par 94): **93,92,90,89,88 87,86,86,84,84 83,82,82,80,79**

toteswinger: 1&2 £10.80, 1&3 £10.40, 2&3 £18.10. CSF £45.33 TOTE £7.00: £2.50, £2.70, £2.60; EX 42.80 Trifecta £194.20 Part won. Pool: £262.54 - 0.60 winning units.units..

Owner Ballymacoll Stud **Bred** Ballymacoll Stud Farm Ltd **Trained** Newmarket, Suffolk

FOCUS

Plenty of well-bred fillies from powerful connections and this looked a potentially decent maiden, although a winning time 2.67sec slower than the following nursery tempers enthusiasm somewhat.

NOTEBOOK

Leocorno(IRE) ◆, a half-sister to the top-class Golan as well as this year's Derby runner-up Tartan Bearer, was easy to back on-course but still proved good enough to make a winning debut. The effort is even more creditable than the bare result suggests, as she was behind a wall of horses early in the straight and had to be continually switched while trying to make ground. She was finally in the clear just over a furlong out and stayed on impressively to reel in Queen Eleanor, who had travelled as well as anything. A rangy filly with plenty of scope, the winner rates a very exciting three-year-old prospect and was given a quote of 16-1 for the Oaks by Blue Square. Her sire Pivotal has a ten per cent strike-rate with his runners over 1m4f-plus in Britain and Ireland, compared with 14 per cent over shorter, but there is enough stamina on the dam's side of her pedigree to think she will have no problems with middle-distances. (op 7-1)

Queen Eleanor ◆, who looked very fit, had caught the eye first time out when running on late in a Polytrack maiden at Lingfield and confirmed the promise with a good run behind the potentially smart winner. She travelled well for much of the way and did nothing wrong, but was simply beaten by a better one on the day. (op 5-1)

Ballet Dancer(IRE) ◆, a well-made newcomer who looked short of peak fitness, was niggled along early in the straight, but she stayed on well when switched out wide and this was a pleasing debut. (op 15-2 tchd 7-1 and 9-1)

Sweet Hollow, who stands over plenty of ground, looked very inexperienced beforehand. A 46,000gns half-sister to French 2,000 Guineas winner Victory Note, she ran green and gave the impression she will be a lot better for the experience. (op 28-1)

Teeky ◆, a half-sister to Sleeping Indian, had been off the track since running below expectations when 3-1 joint favourite at Yarmouth in July. She looked as though the run would do her good, but this was still an improvement and there should be much better to come again. (op 11-2 tchd 13-2)

Waheeba, easily the biggest filly in the line-up, improved on the form of her first two efforts and has the scope to make a fair handicapper. (op 20-1)

Silken Promise(USA), a lightly-made newcomer, showed ability on this debut for a stable not in the best of form. (op 14-1 tchd 16-1)

Marillos Proterras, who is very narrow, ended up out wide and ran a reasonable first race. (tchd 80-1)

Morning Calm Official explanation: jockey said filly was denied a clear run

Labisa(IRE) Official explanation: jockey said filly was denied a clear run

Aim To Achieve(IRE), a 190,000 euros daughter of Galileo, did not impress on the way to post and she was very slow to find her stride when the stalls opened, being last away and driven along. She eventually tagged on to the main group, but was in trouble over three furlongs out. Official explanation: vet said filly was found to be lame off-hind. (op 8-1)

6946 RACING POST NURSERY 1m (R)

2:55 (2:56) (Class 3) 2-Y-O £9,714 (£2,890; £1,444; £721) **Stalls** Low

Form RPR

322 **1** **Henderson Park**[13] 6655 2-9-3 **84** NCallan 18 91
(A G Foster) *trckd ldrs: gd hdwy 3f out: led 2f out: rdn clr appr last: styd on wl* **11/1**

1230 **2** 1 ¾ **Quatermain**[41] 5895 2-8-13 **80** TomEaves 7 83
(B Smart) *towards rr: hdwy over 2f out: rdn over 1f out: styd on strly ins fnl f: nt rch wnr* **16/1**

14 **3** nk **Parthenon**[37] 6025 2-9-7 **88** J-PGuillambert 16 90
(M Johnston) *s.i.s and bhd: hdwy on wd outside 3f out: rdn along 2f out: styd on strly u.p ins fnl f* **10/1[3]**

2332 **4** nk **Dr Jameson (IRE)**[18] 6534 2-8-8 **75** PaulHanagan 4 77
(R A Fahey) *trckd ldrs: effrt wl over 2f out: swtchd rt and rdn wl over 1f out: styd on u.p ins fnl f* **18/1**

6161 **5** hd **Zaaqya**[29] 6231 2-8-11 **78** RHills 13 79
(J L Dunlop) *midfield: hdwy on outer 3f out: chsd ldrs wl over 1f out: sn rdn and kpt on ins fnl f: nrst fin* **11/1**

010 **6** 1 ½ **Felday**[20] 6474 2-9-4 **85** SteveDrowne 10 83
(H Morrison) *trckd ldrs: effrt and hdwy over 2f out: rdn to chse wnr over 1f out: drvn and wknd ins fnl f* **14/1**

5053 **7** 1 ¼ **In Transit (IRE)**[11] 6694 2-8-3 **70** TPO'Shea 17 65
(M R Channon) *cl up: rdn along 3f out: led briefly over 2f out: hdd 2f out: sn drvn and grad wknd appr fnl f* **50/1**

541 **8** nk **Dialogue**[38] 5996 2-9-4 **85** RoystonFfrench 14 80
(M Johnston) *hld up towards rr: hdwy over 3f out: swtchd lft and rdn wl over 1f out: kpt on same pce appr fnl f* **12/1**

4550 **9** ¾ **Party Cat (IRE)**[12] 6673 2-8-7 **74** FrancisNorton 5 67
(R Hannon) *s.i.s and bhd: hdwy 2f out: rdn over 1f out: styd on ins fnl f: nrst fin* **33/1**

13 **10** 1 ¼ **Something Perfect (USA)**[20] 6466 2-9-1 **82** IanMongan 12 72
(H R A Cecil) *prom: rdn along 3f out: drvn over 2f out and sn wknd* **18/1**

31 **11** nk **Hunterview**[31] 6187 2-8-13 **80** PhilipRobinson 11 70
(M A Jarvis) *led: rdn along 3f out: drvn and hdd over 2f out: sn wknd* **6/1[1]**

341 **12** 1 **Kudu Country (IRE)**[31] 6187 2-8-13 **80** MickyFenton 15 67
(T P Tate) *midfield: hdwy on outer and in tch over 3f out: sn rdn and btn over 2f out* **14/1**

0315 **13** ¾ **Amethyst Dawn (IRE)**[44] 5791 2-8-10 **77** .... DavidAllan 2 63
(T D Easterby) *hld up towards rr: stdy hdwy on inner 3f out: rdn to chse ldrs 2f out: sn wknd* **12/1**

3125 **14** 2 ¼ **Thunderball**[27] 6284 2-9-2 **86** .... TolleyDean(3) 6 67
(A J McCabe) *a in rr* **16/1**

2104 **15** ¾ **Blazing Buck**[12] 6665 2-8-9 **76** .... JimmyQuinn 1 55
(H J L Dunlop) *hld up towards rr: sme hdwy on inner 3f out: sn rdn and wknd* **33/1**

20 **16** ½ **Kings Troop**[35] 6082 2-9-5 **86** .... TPQueally 8 64
(H R A Cecil) *chsd ldrs on inner: rdn along over 3f out: sn wknd* **25/1**

4322 **17** *nk* **Silver Print (USA)**[23] 6376 2-8-11 **78** .... DarryllHolland 3 55
(W R Swinburn) *a towards rr* **9/1**[2]

0041 **18** 5 **Sequillo**[25] 6344 2-8-8 **75** ow1 .... RichardHughes 9 41
(R Hannon) *midfield: effrt and sme hdwy 3f out: rdn along over 2f out: wkng whn hmpd wl over 1f out: sn lost action and eased* **6/1**[1]

1m 40.72s (-0.28) **Going Correction** +0.125s/f (Good) **18** Ran SP% **127.0**
Speed ratings (Par 99): **106,104,103,103,103 101,100,100,99,98 98,97,96,94,93 92,92,87**
toteswinger: 1&2 £34.90, 1&3 £37.30, 2&3 £51.60. CSF £175.81 CT £1896.12 TOTE £14.10: £2.90, £4.40, £3.10, £4.10; EX 299.20 TRIFECTA Not won. units..
Owner Lothian Recycling Limited **Bred** A M Tombs **Trained** Cousland, Midlothian

FOCUS
A big field for this decent nursery and an open betting market, but a clear-cut winner and the time was 2.67sec faster than the preceding fillies' maiden.

NOTEBOOK
Henderson Park, making his handicap debut having been placed in all three starts over 7f on good and easy ground, travelled well before kicking on just inside the two-furlong pole. He deserved this success, having been beaten no more than half a length in his previous outings, and readily reversed form with Quatermain, despite being on 4lb worse terms, and the effort was all the more meritorious considering he was drawn on the wide outside. He will not run again this year but should make a decent handicapper in 2009.
Quatermain had been unable to build on his defeat of Henderson Park at Redcar, but had come up against the subsequent Rockfel winner on his next start and the return to waiting tactics and good ground seemed to help. He came out of the pack but the winner had flown. (op 20-1 tchd 14-1)
Parthenon ◆ put up a fine effort under top weight, having been drawn wide, and lost a fair amount of ground at the start. He still had a fair bit to do at the two-furlong pole, but picked up down the outside and, with some useful form already in the book, looks sure to make up into a decent handicapper next season. (op 12-1 tchd 14-1)
Dr Jameson(IRE) had been placed on all four starts and the step up in trip held no fears. He raced just behind the pace but had to be switched before staying on in the final furlong, and this consistent type, who handles most ground, should be found a winning opportunity.
Zaaqya, a winner over the trip, was held up and did not pick up immediately before staying on late. She may be more effective on a faster surface. (op 12-1)
Felday, a 7f winner on easy ground, came to have his chance inside the last two furlongs before his effort petered out. (tchd 12-1)
In Transit(IRE), who has been busy, has dropped almost a stone since his nursery debut in July and was another who showed up until fading late on.
Dialogue, a winner over 7f on Polytrack and effective on a sound surface on turf, was held up on this handicap debut before staying on. (tchd 11-1)
Hunterview made the running but capitulated tamely once taken on. (op 11-2 tchd 7-1)
Sequillo appeared well enough placed for most of the way but failed to pick up when asked and was ultimately eased inside the last furlong after losing his action. Official explanation: jockey said colt ran flat. (op 13-2)

6947 RECTANGLE GROUP H'CAP 6f
3:30 (3:31) (Class 2) (0-100,100) 3-Y-O+ **£16,190** (£4,817; £2,407; £1,202) **Stalls** High

Form RPR

050 **1** **Skhilling Spirit**[27] 6269 5-8-7 **91** .... NeilBrown(3) 16 103
(T D Barron) *s.s: in rr: hdwy over 2f out: styd on wl to ld towards fin* **14/1**

230 **2** *nk* **Kaldoun Kingdom (IRE)**[35] 6069 3-8-8 **90** .... PaulHanagan 2 101
(R A Fahey) *hld up in mid-div: hdwy to ld over 1f out: hdd towards fin* **14/1**

1140 **3** 2 **Shifting Star (IRE)**[34] 6104 3-9-2 **98** .... AdamKirby 18 103
(W R Swinburn) *hld up in rr-div stands' side: hdwy 2f out: styd on wl fnl f* **8/1**[2]

0040 **4** ½ **Dhaular Dhar (IRE)**[26] 6304 6-9-5 **100** .... DanielTudhope 13 103
(J S Goldie) *hld up towards rr: hdwy over 1f out: styd on ins fnl f* **14/1**

5006 **5** 2 ¼ **Orpsie Boy (IRE)**[22] 6429 5-8-10 **94** .... LukeMorris(3) 21 90
(N P Littmoden) *in rr stands' side: styd on fnl 2f: nvr trbld ldrs* **12/1**

006 **6** ½ **Cape**[22] 6430 5-8-9 **90** ow1 .... DarryllHolland 10 84
(P Howling) *hld up in mid-div: effrt and n.m.r over 1f out: kpt on: nt rch ldrs* **16/1**

3605 **7** *nk* **Carcinetto (IRE)**[2] 6902 6-8-5 **86** .... JohnEgan 12 79
(P D Evans) *hld up in rr: hdwy over 1f out: kpt on wl: nt rch ldrs* **25/1**

0550 **8** ½ **Zomerlust**[27] 6277 6-7-12 **86** oh1 .... JamieKyne(7) 11 78
(J J Quinn) *mid-div: edgd rt over 1f out: kpt on: nvr nr ldrs* **20/1**

0403 **9** *nse* **Great Charm (IRE)**[28] 6239 3-8-5 **87** .... HayleyTurner 20 79
(M L W Bell) *chsd ldrs stands' side: kpt on same pce fnl 2f* **8/1**[2]

4100 **10** 1 **Ishetoo**[13] 6653 4-9-2 **97** .... IanMongan 22 85
(A Dickman) *trckd ldrs stands' side: t.k.h: fdd fnl f* **14/1**

01-5 **11** *hd* **Ponty Rossa (IRE)**[33] 6153 4-8-9 **90** .... DavidAllan 9 78
(T D Easterby) *chsd ldrs: one pce fnl 2f* **16/1**

002 **12** ¾ **Artimino**[20] 6468 4-9-0 **100** .... Louis-PhilippeBeuzelin(5) 8 85
(J R Fanshawe) *trckd ldrs on outer: effrt over 2f out: wknd 1f out* **7/1**[1]

0015 **13** 1 ¼ **Bond City (IRE)**[20] 6484 6-9-3 **98** .... PJMcDonald 3 79
(G R Oldroyd) *chsd ldrs on outer: wknd over 1f out* **25/1**

2140 **14** *nk* **Bel Cantor**[27] 6289 5-8-2 **90** ....(p) AndreaAtzeni(7) 5 70
(W J H Ratcliffe) *led tl hdd & wknd over 1f out* **16/1**

2460 **15** ½ **Fathom Five (IRE)**[13] 6653 4-9-1 **96** .... TomEaves 6 75
(B Smart) *w ldrs: wknd appr fnl f* **12/1**

5006 **16** *shd* **Prior Warning**[12] 6669 4-8-10 **91** ....(t) PaulEddery 15 69
(Miss D Mountain) *a in rr* **40/1**

3042 **17** 1 ¼ **Brassini**[12] 6676 3-8-8 **90** .... AlanMunro 19 64
(B R Millman) *chsd ldrs stands' side: wknd over 1f out* **10/1**[3]

0000 **18** 1 ¼ **Celtic Sultan (IRE)**[27] 6269 4-9-1 **96** .... MickyFenton 1 66
(T P Tate) *chsd ldrs on outer: hung rt and lost pl over 1f out* **20/1**

0060 **19** 8 **Capricorn Run (USA)**[27] 6285 5-9-3 **98** ....(p) SteveDrowne 4 43
(A J McCabe) *s.v.s: a detached in last* **33/1**

1m 12.88s (-0.72) **Going Correction** +0.125s/f (Good)
WFA 3 from 4yo+ 1lb **19** Ran SP% **126.1**
Speed ratings (Par 109): **109,108,105,105,102 101,101,100,100,99 98,97,96,95,95 95,93,91,81**
toteswinger: 1&2 £65.90, 1&3 £15.60, 2&3 £32.90. CSF £182.74 CT £1737.60 TOTE £18.00: £4.20, £3.90, £2.60, £2.70; EX 397.00 Trifecta £424.40 Part won. Pool: £573.58 - 0.10 winning units. units..
Owner I Hill **Bred** Pillar To Post Racing **Trained** Maunby, N Yorks

FOCUS
An ordinary sprint handicap for the grade and nine of the first ten were drawn in a double-figure stall. They tended to race up the middle of the track. Solid form.

NOTEBOOK
Skhilling Spirit completely blew the start, but he recovered to tag on to the main group and picked up strongly in the closing stages. He was well beaten over 7f at Ascot last time, but a reproduction of the sort of form he showed when fifth in the Ayr Gold Cup proved good enough. (op 16-1)
Kaldoun Kingdom(IRE) might just have hit the front a little too soon, but this was still a huge effort, as he was the only one in the first ten drawn in a single-figure stall. (op 20-1)
Shifting Star(IRE) seemed to have every chance if good enough and this was much better than his latest Ayr effort. (op 6-1)
Dhaular Dhar(IRE) looked unlucky not to finish a length or so closer, as he twice had to be switched when trying to stay on. This was his best cever run over a sprint trip.
Orpsie Boy(IRE), who made his move against the stands' rail, did not look to have any excuses. (op 16-1)
Cape, carrying 1lb overweight, travelled strongly but could find only the one pace when in the clear. (op 14-1)
Carcinetto(IRE), due to be dropped 2lb, stayed on again after getting outpaced mid-race. (op 22-1)
Great Charm(IRE) probably would have preferred softer ground. (tchd 15-2)
Artimino was poorly drawn as it turned out, but that was no excuse. (op 8-1)
Celtic Sultan(IRE) Official explanation: jockey said colt hung right-handed

6948 BETTING SHOP MANAGER OF THE YEAR H'CAP 1m 6f 132y
4:05 (4:06) (Class 4) (0-85,88) 3-Y-O+ **£6,476** (£1,927; £963; £481) **Stalls** Low

Form RPR

3311 **1** **Wells Lyrical (IRE)**[26] 6313 3-9-3 **83** .... TomEaves 8 94
(B Smart) *in tch: hdwy to trck ldrs over 4f out: rdn over 2f out: drvn to chal over 1f out: led ins fnl f and styd on wl* **8/1**[3]

0112 **2** ¾ **Soundbyte**[23] 6379 3-8-3 **69** .... TPO'Shea 3 79
(J Gallagher) *hld up and bhd: stdy hdwy 3f out: swtchd lft over 2f out: swtchd rt and rdn to chse ldrs over 1f out: drvn and styd on wl fnl f* **16/1**

4101 **3** *nse* **Neve Lieve (IRE)**[23] 6390 3-8-9 **75** .... DarryllHolland 1 85
(M Botti) *tracked ldr: led over 3f out: rdn 2f out: jnd and drvn over 1f out: hdd ins fnl f: kpt on* **12/1**

2202 **4** ¾ **Sleepy Hollow**[18] 6542 3-8-13 **79** .... SteveDrowne 4 88
(H Morrison) *in tch on inner: hdwy over 3f out: rdn to chse ldrs 2f out: drvn and ev ch over 1f out: kpt on same pce ins fnl f* **17/2**

01 **5** *nk* **Cape Tribulation**[16] 6584 4-9-12 **83** .... PaulHanagan 6 91
(J M Jefferson) *trckd ldrs: hdwy 3f out: rdn to chse ldrs 2f out: drvn over 1f out: kpt on same pce ins fnl f* **13/2**[2]

1000 **6** 6 **Puy D'Arnac (FR)**[27] 6279 5-9-5 **76** .... PJMcDonald 14 76
(G A Swinbank) *hld up towards rr: stdy jhdwy over 3f out: rdn along 2f out: kpt on: nt rch ldrs* **20/1**

4632 **7** ¾ **Haarth Sovereign (IRE)**[24] 6361 4-9-6 **77** .... AdamKirby 5 76
(W R Swinburn) *midfield: hdwy 4f out: rdn to chse ldrs over 2f out: sn drvn and grad wknd* **16/1**

0330 **8** *nk* **Red Wine**[10] 6721 9-8-10 **74** .... StacyRenwick(7) 13 73
(A J McCabe) *stdd s: hld up and bhd: swtchd outside and hdwy 3f out: rdn along wl over 1f out: kpt on: nt rch ldrs* **20/1**

-505 **9** ¾ **Tritonville Lodge (IRE)**[15] 6606 6-9-3 **74** .... AlanMunro 17 72
(Miss E C Lavelle) *prom: rdn along over 3f out: drvn over 2f out and grad wknd* **40/1**

2510 **10** 4 ½ **Nemo Spirit (IRE)**[111] 3719 3-9-6 **86** .... RichardMullen 7 77
(W R Muir) *midfield: hdwy on outer 4f out: chsd ldrs 3f out: sn rdn and wknd over 2f out* **50/1**

0002 **11** 3 **Lets Roll**[13] 6657 7-9-7 **78** .... DanielTudhope 9 65
(C W Thornton) *hld up towards rr: hdwy 3f out: rdn along over 2f out: sn no imp* **14/1**

004 **12** 3 **Minkowski**[27] 6272 5-10-3 **88** .... TPQueally 12 71
(J Noseda) *hld up in midfield: hdwy on outer over 3f out: rdn along wl over 2f out and sn wknd* **6/1**[1]

15-6 **13** 1 ¾ **Mirjan (IRE)**[33] 6154 12-10-0 **85** ....(b) JimCrowley 2 65
(L Lungo) *in tch on inner: rdn along over 3f out: sn drvn and wknd* **25/1**

1302 **14** ½ **Cleaver**[41] 5900 7-9-9 **80** .... RichardHughes 19 60
(Lady Herries) *a towards rr* **12/1**

3003 **15** 1 ¼ **Burnt Oak (UAE)**[15] 6606 6-8-9 **66** oh1 .... TedDurcan 15 44
(C W Fairhurst) *hld up: effrt and sme hdwy 3f out: sn rdn and wknd* **20/1**

63 **16** 1 ¾ **West With The Wind**[34] 6126 3-9-0 **80** .... MickyFenton 11 55
(T P Tate) *led: rdn along 4f out: hdd over 3f out and sn wknd* **20/1**

4216 **17** ¾ **Lough Diver (IRE)**[22] 6427 3-9-2 **82** .... NCallan 18 56
(M H Tompkins) *towards rr: sme hdwy over 3f out: sn rdn and btn* **50/1**

3011 **18** ½ **Opera Writer (IRE)**[18] 6538 5-8-7 **69** ....(p) DavidProbert(5) 10 43
(R Hollinshead) *prom: effrt over 3f out and: rdn over 2f out and sn wknd* **25/1**

2042 **19** 6 **Motarid (USA)**[7] 6790 3-8-9 **75** ....(b) GrahamGibbons 16 40
(T D Walford) *trckd ldrs: pushed along 4f out: rdn 3f out and sn wknd* **11/1**

1/00 **20** 2 ½ **Mikado**[27] 6288 7-9-9 **80** ....(p) GeorgeBaker 20 42
(Jonjo O'Neill) *hld up: a bhd* **50/1**

3m 8.72s (2.02) **Going Correction** +0.125s/f (Good)
WFA 3 from 4yo+ 9lb **20** Ran SP% **126.5**
Speed ratings (Par 105): **99,98,98,98,98 94,94,94,93,91 89,88,87,87,86 85,85,84,81,80**
toteswinger: 1&2 £33.20, 1&3 £20.60, 2&3 £39.60. CSF £114.56 CT £1546.07 TOTE £9.20: £2.30, £5.40, £3.70, £2.60; EX 240.60 TRIFECTA Not won..
Owner M Barber **Bred** Brittas House Stud **Trained** Hambleton, N Yorks

FOCUS
A fair handicap featuring a combination of well-established and unexposed performers and in the end the latter group dominated. The field raced up the centre of the track in the straight. The gallop appeared to be sound. The first five finished clear and this is solid form, with the winner up 9lb.
Red Wine ◆ Official explanation: jockey said, regarding running and riding, her orders were to drop to the rear and in the straight come wide and late as the gelding stops when hitting the front; trainer confirmed, adding that it needs to be brought with a late run.
Lough Diver(IRE) Official explanation: jockey said gelding was unsuited by the good (good to soft places) ground

6949 WEATHERBYS BANK H'CAP 1m 2f 60y
4:40 (4:42) (Class 4) (0-85,85) 3-Y-O **£6,476** (£1,927; £963; £481) **Stalls** Low

Form RPR

0024 **1** **Timetable**[20] 6467 3-8-13 **80** .... TPQueally 18 91+
(H R A Cecil) *hld up in rr: stdy hdwy on outside 3f out: led and carried hd high over 1f out: pushed out* **12/1**

4541 **2** 1 **Shaloo Diamond**[31] 6188 3-8-9 **79** .... MichaelJStainton(3) 5 85
(R M Whitaker) *trckd ldrs: led over 2f out: hdd over 1f out: kpt on wl* **16/1**

0225 **3** *hd* **St Jean Cap Ferrat**[11] 6704 3-9-4 **85** ....(v) TedDurcan 7 91
(G Wragg) *in tch: effrt over 2f out: kpt on wl fnl f* **13/2**[2]

3242 **4** *nk* **Special Reserve (IRE)**[25] 6345 3-8-10 **77**.............(p) RichardHughes 13 83+
(R Hannon) *hld up towards rr: stdy hdwy over 2f out: nt clr run and swtchd rt ins fnl f: kpt on* **15/2**[3]

4465 **5** *hd* **Mega Watt (IRE)**[42] 5865 3-8-8 **75**..............................(b[1]) AlanMunro 8 80
(W Jarvis) *mid-div: hdwy 3f out: keeping on same pce whn hmpd ins fnl f* **11/1**

0464 **6** *3 ¼* **Indian Skipper (IRE)**[18] 6528 3-8-8 **75**..................... PaulMulrennan 14 73
(M H Tompkins) *in rr: hdwy over 2f out: kpt on one pce fnl f* **18/1**

2311 **7** *nse* **Offshore Anna (IRE)**[33] 6155 3-8-11 **78**................. GrahamGibbons 19 76
(J J Quinn) *mid-div: drvn over 3f out: kpt on fnl f* **17/2**

0306 **8** *1 ¼* **Dauberval (IRE)**[18] 6542 3-9-0 **81**..................................(v[1]) AdamKirby 2 77
(S Kirk) *chsd ldrs: one pce fnl 2f* **16/1**

3240 **9** *nk* **Eton Fable (IRE)**[41] 5888 3-8-0 **74**.................... AndreaAtzeni(7) 15 69
(W J H Ratcliffe) *led tl over 2f out: wknd over 1f out* **50/1**

0-02 **10** *½* **Theonebox (USA)**[84] 4606 3-8-5 **77**........................ DavidProbert(5) 10 71
(N J Vaughan) *chsd ldrs: rdn 3f out: fdd over 1f out* **16/1**

1021 **11** *1 ½* **Ogre (USA)**[18] 6528 3-8-10 **77**.. JimmyQuinn 9 68
(P D Evans) *prom: drvn whn hmpd over 2f out: wknd over 1f out* **11/1**

16-0 **12** *shd* **Silver Regent (USA)**[11] 6704 3-9-1 **82**......................... JimCrowley 1 73
(Mrs A J Perrett) *mid-div: effrt over 3f out: sn btn* **6/1**[1]

-551 **13** *2* **Majeen**[25] 6345 3-8-11 **78**... MichaelHills 16 65
(W J Haggas) *trckd ldrs: effrt over 2f out: lost pl over 1f out* **11/1**

330 **14** *nse* **Wellington Square**[27] 6280 3-8-13 **80**.................... DarryllHolland 17 67
(H Morrison) *hld up in rr: hdwy on outside over 2f out: wknd over 1f out* **16/1**

3550 **15** *2 ¾* **Elk Trail (IRE)**[20] 6487 3-8-5 **72**............................ RoystonFfrench 6 53
(T P Tate) *chsd ldrs: lost pl and hmpd over 2f out* **33/1**

0320 **16** *4 ½* **Blindspin**[10] 6721 3-8-8 **75**... TomEaves 12 47
(M Dods) *t.k.h in rr: bhd fnl 2f* **50/1**

443 **17** *2 ½* **Hucking Hero (IRE)**[233] 799 3-8-11 **78**..................... SteveDrowne 11 45
(J R Best) *s.i.s: a in rr* **40/1**

5600 **18** *43* **Pegasus Again (USA)**[78] 4790 3-9-1 **82**.......................... JohnEgan 4 —
(T G Mills) *chsd ldrs: hmpd and lost pl over 2f out: sn bhd and eased: t.o* **40/1**

2m 11.31s (0.11) **Going Correction** +0.125s/f (Good) **18 Ran SP% 123.1**
Speed ratings (Par 103): **104,103,103,102,102 100,100,99,98,98 97,97,95,95,93 89,87,53**
toteswinger: 1&2 £44.50, 1&3 £18.70, 2&3 £29.30. CSF £184.92 CT £1369.49 TOTE £12.50: £2.80, £4.50, £2.20, £2.10; EX 188.90 Trifecta £169.70 Pool: £688.14 - 3.00 winning units..
Owner K Abdulla **Bred** Juddmonte Farms Ltd **Trained** Newmarket, Suffolk

FOCUS
A good three-year-old handicap and they raced up the middle of the track. The form looks sound and the winner should be capable of better.
Elk Trail(IRE) Official explanation: jockey said gelding suffered interference in running
Pegasus Again(USA) Official explanation: jockey said colt suffered interference in running

6950 AMATEUR JOCKEYS ASSOCIATION LADY RIDERS' H'CAP 1m 2f 60y
5:10 (5:12) (Class 4) (0-80,79) 3-Y-0+ **£4,996** (£1,549; £774; £387) **Stalls** Low

Form RPR

4530 **1** **Spring Goddess (IRE)**[9] 6738 7-9-11 **74**................. MissLEBurke(5) 12 83
(A P Jarvis) *hld up in rr: hdwy 3f out: led over 1f out: kpt on wl* **33/1**

634 **2** *¾* **Yetholm (USA)**[16] 6584 3-9-9 **72**................................ MrsRDobbin 8 80
(J R Fanshawe) *in rr: effrt on outer 4f out: edgd lft and styd on: chal ins fnl f: no ex* **13/2**[2]

6420 **3** *hd* **Holden Eagle**[55] 5491 3-9-9 **72**............................ MissCHannaford 16 79
(A G Newcombe) *mid-div: hdwy on outside 3f out: chal 1f out: kpt on same pce* **28/1**

5216 **4** *2 ½* **Dar Es Salaam**[13] 6657 4-10-7 **79**................................ MrsCBartley 5 81
(J S Goldie) *in tch: lost pl over 7f out: hdwy 3f out: styd on fnl f* **11/2**[1]

1030 **5** *½* **Red Birr (IRE)**[25] 6346 7-10-5 **77**.......................(t) MissSBrotherton 6 78
(P R Webber) *mid-div: effrt 3f out: kpt on same pce fnl f* **16/1**

002 **6** *1 ½* **Celtic Strand (IRE)**[29] 6235 3-9-4 **74**................... MissKECooper(7) 1 72
(T P Tate) *led tl over 1f out: grad wknd* **20/1**

2041 **7** *1 ¾* **New Star (UAE)**[21] 6450 4-10-6 **78**............................ MissEJJones 14 73
(W M Brisbourne) *in rr: hdwy over 3f out: w ldrs over 1f out: one pce* **16/1**

-055 **8** *2 ¾* **Harvest Warrior**[28] 6250 6-9-12 **73** ow1................... MissJCoward(3) 7 62
(T D Easterby) *s.i.s: styd on fnl 3f: nvr nr ldrs* **9/1**

5643 **9** *2 ½* **Thunderstruck**[14] 6629 3-9-7 **70**................................(b) MissARyan 9 54
(K A Ryan) *chsd ldrs: wknd 2f out* **15/2**

0620 **10** *½* **Nisaal (IRE)**[108] 3813 3-9-12 **75**................................ MissADeniel 18 58
(J J Quinn) *in rr div: hdwy 3f out: chsng ldrs 2f out: sn wknd* **25/1**

5402 **11** *1* **Inchloch**[146] 2623 6-10-1 **76**.................................... MissCDyson(3) 3 57
(Miss C Dyson) *mid-div: hdwy over 3f out: sn chsng ldrs: wknd over 1f out* **16/1**

0004 **12** *nk* **Fongs Gazelle**[14] 6626 4-10-3 **75**................................(v[1]) MissJAKidd 2 56
(M Johnston) *chsd ldrs: wknd over 1f out* **7/1**[3]

0103 **13** *shd* **Emirate Isle**[30] 6216 4-9-13 **71**..............................(p) MissLHorner 19 51
(C Grant) *chsd ldr: chal over 3f out: wknd over 1f out* **20/1**

1213 **14** *3 ½* **Nawamees (IRE)**[15] 6607 10-10-4 **76**........................ MissEFolkes 17 49
(P D Evans) *chsd ldrs: lost pl over 2f out* **12/1**

2040 **15** *3 ½* **Black Dahlia**[24] 6355 3-9-10 **78**............................ MissABevan(5) 11 44
(A J McCabe) *chsd ldrs: lost pl over 1f out* **16/1**

3022 **16** *4* **Prince Noel**[21] 6452 4-9-2 **65** oh1.................. MissBeverleyKendall(5) 4 23
(N Wilson) *a towards rr* **11/1**

0-00 **17** *2 ¼* **Skylarker (USA)**[7] 6786 10-9-2 **65** oh8.................. MissHCuthbert(5) 15 19
(T A K Cuthbert) *prom: lost pl over 2f out* **100/1**

0404 **18** *1 ¼* **Bed Fellow (IRE)**[10] 6727 4-9-0 **65** oh13.................. MissJKWilson(7) 13 16
(Paul Murphy) *rdr briefly lost iron sn after s: in rr: hung lft and bhd fnl 2f* **66/1**

2m 12.97s (1.77) **Going Correction** +0.125s/f (Good)
WFA 3 from 4yo+ 5lb **18 Ran SP% 124.8**
Speed ratings (Par 105): **97,96,96,94,93 92,91,89,87,86 85,85,85,82,79 76,74,73**
toteswinger: 1&2 £42.90, 1&3 £75.70, 2&3 £39.10. CSF £227.27 CT £6078.45 TOTE £42.00: £6.90, £2.10, £5.20, £2.10; EX 345.60 TRIFECTA Not won. Place 6: £499.35 Place 5: £271.45.
Owner Grant & Bowman Limited **Bred** Ballyhane Stud **Trained** Twyford, Bucks
■ Stewards' Enquiry : Miss A Ryan caution: used whip above from shoulder height

FOCUS
An ordinary lady riders' handicap in which the leaders appeared to go a decent gallop and it was not surprising that the principals came from well back. The winner is rated to his best AW form of the past year with the second up 7lb.
T/Jkpt: Not won. T/Plt: £729.20 to a £1 stake. Pool: £113,023.75. 113.14 winning tickets. T/Qpdt: £218.50 to a £1 stake. Pool: £7,827.60. 26.50 winning tickets. JR

6821 WOLVERHAMPTON (A.W) (L-H)
Friday, October 24

OFFICIAL GOING: Standard
Wind: Light, behind Weather: Fine and sunny

6951 LADBROKESPOKER.COM H'CAP (DIV I) 1m 141y(P)
6:20 (6:20) (Class 6) (0-55,55) 3-Y-0+ **£2,866** (£846; £423) **Stalls** Low

Form RPR

420 **1** **Malinsa Blue (IRE)**[23] 6395 6-9-3 **55**...................(p) J-PGuillambert 3 63
(B Ellison) *a.p: chsd ldr over 1f out: sn rdn and edgd lft: styd on to ld towards fin* **15/2**

5600 **2** *hd* **Kargan (IRE)**[36] 6042 3-8-9 **54**................................ NeilBrown(3) 8 62
(A G Foster) *s.i.s: hld up: hdwy over 2f out: rdn to ld wl ins fnl f: hdd towards fin* **14/1**

0000 **3** *1* **Tri Chara (IRE)**[34] 6116 4-9-1 **53**......................(p) WilliamBuick 6 58
(R Hollinshead) *chsd ldr tl led 2f out: rdn and hdd wl ins fnl f: styd on same pce* **8/1**

0226 **4** *1 ½* **Turkish Sultan (IRE)**[2] 6912 5-8-6 **49**................(p) MCGeran(5) 11 51+
(J M Bradley) *hld up: rdn over 1f out: r.o ins fnl f: nrst fin* **13/2**[3]

300 **5** *shd* **Champain Sands (IRE)**[28] 6250 9-8-8 **53**.................. BMcHugh(7) 10 55
(E J Alston) *hld up in tch: rdn over 1f out: no ex wl ins fnl f* **5/1**[2]

4656 **6** *1 ¾* **Semi Detached (IRE)**[28] 6255 5-9-1 **53**............. RichardKingscote 4 51
(J W Unett) *hld up in tch: rdn and hung lft fr over 1f out: no ex ins fnl f* **7/1**

0435 **7** *nse* **Comrade Cotton**[3] 6890 4-9-0 **52**..............................(v) JerryO'Dwyer 2 49
(J Ryan) *chsd ldrs: rdn over 1f out: no ex fnl f* **4/1**[1]

2250 **8** *nse* **Sceilin (IRE)**[58] 5407 4-9-3 **55**..(t) LPKeniry 5 52
(J Mackie) *hld up: rdn over 1f out: nvr trbld ldrs* **14/1**

006 **9** *1 ¾* **Social Rhythm**[54] 5538 4-8-13 **51**................................ ChrisCatlin 12 44
(A C Whillans) *s.s: effrt and nt clr run over 1f out: wknd ins fnl f* **10/1**

6030 **10** *7* **Roman History (IRE)**[20] 6485 5-9-0 **52**...............(p) SilvestreDeSousa 1 29
(Miss Tracy Waggott) *led: rdn and hdd 2f out: wknd over 1f out* **10/1**

1m 53.64s (3.14) **Going Correction** +0.125s/f (Slow)
WFA 3 from 4yo+ 4lb **10 Ran SP% 116.9**
Speed ratings (Par 101): **91,90,89,88,88 86,86,86,85,79**
CSF £106.82 CT £865.99 TOTE £5.90: £2.50, £5.50, £3.00; EX 142.80.
Owner Mrs Andrea M Mallinson **Bred** Martin Donovan **Trained** Norton, N Yorks

FOCUS
A moderate handicap and messy form, with the winner probably the best guide.

6952 BETTER PRICES, BIGGER WINS AT LADBROKES.COM H'CAP 7f 32y(P)
6:50 (6:51) (Class 4) (0-80,80) 3-Y-0+ **£5,459** (£1,612; £806) **Stalls** High

Form RPR

1061 **1** **Alexander Huricane (IRE)**[13] 6663 4-9-6 **78**.................. ChrisCatlin 1 93+
(K A Ryan) *hld up: hdwy over 2f out: led over 1f out: sn rdn: styd on* **3/1**[2]

5060 **2** *1 ¼* **Autumn Blades (IRE)**[11] 6695 3-9-0 **74**.................. JamieSpencer 6 82
(J W Hills) *s.i.s: hld up: hdwy over 1f out: sn rdn to chse wnr: styd on* **9/1**

0000 **3** *1* **Royal Envoy (IRE)**[14] 6634 5-8-12 **73**.................. TolleyDean(3) 10 79
(P Howling) *hld up: hdwy over 1f out: sn rdn: styd on* **25/1**

1523 **4** *1 ½* **Gap Princess (IRE)**[9] 6734 4-8-12 **70**..................... PaulHanagan 11 72
(R A Fahey) *hld up: hdwy over 1f out: rdn and hung lft ins fnl f: nt trble ldrs* **16/1**

0043 **5** *1 ½* **Mandarin Spirit (IRE)**[17] 6556 8-8-6 **69**............(p) WilliamCarson(5) 5 67
(G C H Chung) *hld up: hdwy over 1f out: no imp fnl f* **16/1**

1-62 **6** *1 ½* **Parisian Gift (IRE)**[94] 4284 3-9-5 **79**................ RichardKingscote 7 72
(Tom Dascombe) *trckd ldrs: racd keenly: rdn over 1f out: wknd fnl f* **8/1**[3]

0060 **7** *2 ¼* **Chjimes (IRE)**[24] 6356 4-9-0 **72**....................................... LPKeniry 4 60
(C R Dore) *trckd ldrs: plld hrd: nt clr run 2f out, sn rdn: wknd fnl f* **40/1**

0214 **8** *4* **Bahamian Kid**[14] 6634 3-8-10 **73**...................... RussellKennemore(3) 9 49
(R Hollinshead) *hld up: last over 2f out: n.d* **8/1**[3]

0000 **9** *1* **Fitzwarren**[24] 6356 7-8-6 **64** oh19.........................(v) SilvestreDeSousa 12 39
(A D Brown) *trckd ldr: racd keenly: rdn and ev ch 2f out: wknd 1f out* **200/1**

2101 **10** *1 ¼* **Without Prejudice (USA)**[11] 6695 3-9-6 **80** 6ex.............. ShaneKelly 8 51
(J Noseda) *hld up in tch: rdn 3f out: wknd wl over 1f out* **5/4**[1]

0003 **11** *1 ¼* **Westwood**[17] 6554 3-8-10 **70**....................................... RobertHavlin 3 38
(D Haydn Jones) *led: rdn and hdd over 1f out: sn wknd* **33/1**

1m 30.18s (0.58) **Going Correction** +0.125s/f (Slow)
WFA 3 from 4yo+ 2lb **11 Ran SP% 123.2**
Speed ratings (Par 105): **101,99,98,96,95 93,90,86,85,83 82**
CSF £31.21 CT £605.90 TOTE £4.80: £1.40, £3.00, £7.70; EX 45.00.
Owner N O'Callaghan, R Fagan & R O'Callaghan **Bred** Mrs M Fox **Trained** Hambleton, N Yorks

FOCUS
A fair handicap, run at a decent pace and the form looks sound. The winner is unbeaten here and is better than the bare form, with the second running to his mark.
Chjimes(IRE) Official explanation: jockey said gelding was denied a clear run
Without Prejudice(USA) Official explanation: trainer had no explanation for the poor form shown

6953 LADBROKESCASINO.COM MAIDEN STKS 5f 216y(P)
7:20 (7:20) (Class 5) 2-Y-0 **£3,885** (£1,156; £577; £288) **Stalls** Low

Form RPR

3 **1** **Fulham Broadway (IRE)**[25] 6327 2-9-3 0.................... JamieSpencer 10 71+
(E F Vaughan) *hld up: hdwy over 2f out: led on bit 1f out: edgd lft: shkn up and sn clr* **11/10**[1]

2 **2** *2 ½* **Nemorosa**[18] 6531 2-8-12 0.. LiamJones 3 55
(W J Haggas) *s.i.s: hld up: hdwy over 1f out: r.o to go 2nd wl ins fnl f: no ch w wnr* **5/2**[2]

3440 **3** *1 ¼* **Forever's Girl**[47] 5715 2-8-12 50.................................. DavidAllan 12 51
(G R Oldroyd) *led 1f: chsd ldr: rdn and ev ch over 1f out: styd on same pce* **66/1**

4 **4** *1* **Rainy Night**[125] 3259 2-9-3 0.................................. GrahamGibbons 9 53
(R Hollinshead) *led 5f out: rdn and hdd 1f out: wknd towards fin* **16/1**

5 **5** *½* **Ponting (IRE)**[25] 6341 2-9-3 0.................................... GeorgeBaker 4 51
(R M Beckett) *chsd ldrs: rdn over 2f out: hung lft fr over 1f out: no ex fnl f* **7/1**[3]

525 **6** *1* **Chambers (IRE)**[11] 6701 2-9-3 0.............................. J-PGuillambert 6 48
(M Johnston) *chsd ldrs: rdn over 1f out: wknd ins fnl f* **8/1**

4 **7** *4* **Captain Carnival (IRE)**[8] 6755 2-9-3 0......................... WilliamBuick 11 36
(D W P Arbuthnot) *prom: rdn 1/2-way: wkng whn hung lft over 1f out* **25/1**

05 **8** *4* **Dawn Wee**[7] 6788 2-8-12 0.. PJMcDonald 2 19
(G R Oldroyd) *s.i.s: a in rr* **66/1**

0500 **9** *1 ½* **Kilsyth (IRE)**[8] 6761 2-8-9 61.................................. TolleyDean(3) 8 15
(S Parr) *broke wl: stdd and sn lost pl: last and rdn 1/2-way: n.d after* **80/1**

The Form Book, Raceform Ltd, Compton, RG20 6NL

0 **10** *1* **Gore Hill (IRE)**[17] 6548 2-9-3 0 AndrewElliott 1 17
(K R Burke) *s.i.s: sn prom: rdn 1/2-way: wknd over 1f out* **50/1**

0 **11** *8* **Oasis On Island**[28] 6246 2-9-3 0 TomEaves 13 —
(B Smart) *s.i.s: sn pushed along in rr: rdn 1/2-way: wkng whn hung lft fr over 2f out* **25/1**

1m 15.94s (0.94) **Going Correction** +0.125s/f (Slow) **11** Ran SP% **119.6**
Speed ratings (Par 95): **98,94,93,91,91 89,84,79,77,75 65**
CSF £3.73 TOTE £1.80: £1.20, £1.40, £13.90; EX 5.60.
Owner Trevor C Stewart **Bred** Brian Killeen **Trained** Newmarket, Suffolk

FOCUS
A modest juvenile maiden. The easy winner rates value for further.

NOTEBOOK
Fulham Broadway(IRE) had been well backed when third on his debut at Bath 25 days previously and again received strong support. This time he rewarded his supporters and did the job in taking fashion, under a very confident ride. He had travelled sweetly before coming under pressure last time and again moved into contention with ease. His rider looked for dangers before giving him the office inside the final furlong and, coming clear under hands-and-heels riding, he rates value for a good bit further than the bare margin. He obviously has a future and should stay further as he matures. (op 11-8)
Nemorosa, runner-up on her debut at Warwick earlier this month, stayed on from off the pace without rating any sort of threat to the winner. Her dam scored over this trip, but she may need a stiffer test on this display and her turn should not be too far off. (op 11-4 tchd 10-3)
Forever's Girl posted her best effort yet on this return from a 47-day break, but was suited by racing handily and the fact she had been beaten twice previously in plating company puts the form into perspective.
Rainy Night was last seen finishing fourth on his debut at Haydock back in June and was faced with another furlong here. He ran a fair race from the front and is entitled to come on for the run, but will be of greater interest when eligible for a mark after his next outing. (tchd 14-1)

6954 BET NOW WITH LADBROKES ON 0800 777 888 NURSERY 1m 141y(P)
7:50 (7:50) (Class 4) (0-80,77) 2-Y-O **£5,459** (£1,612; £806) **Stalls** Low

Form RPR

0000 **1** **Tepmokea (IRE)**[8] 6761 2-8-12 **68** DarrenWilliams 5 70
(K R Burke) *mde virtually all: rdn clr and hung rt fr over 1f out: styd on* **12/1**

3452 **2** *3/4* **Rumble Of Thunder (IRE)**[36] 6058 2-9-5 **75** WilliamBuick 11 76
(D W P Arbuthnot) *hld up: hdwy over 2f out: rdn to chse wnr: hung rt and lft fr over 1f out: styd on* **8/1**

0513 **3** *nk* **Recession Proof (FR)**[8] 6761 2-9-0 **77** HollyHall(7) 8 79+
(S A Callaghan) *s.i.s: hld up: nt clr run over 2f out: hdwy over 1f out: r.o wl* **9/2**[1]

0053 **4** *1 1/2* **First Queen**[23] 6376 2-9-0 **70** DaneO'Neill 4 67
(L M Cumani) *hld up: nt clr run over 2f out: hdwy over 1f out: styd on same pce fnl f* **6/1**[3]

0136 **5** *hd* **Woteva**[4] 6857 2-9-0 **70** (p) DavidAllan 2 66
(B Ellison) *prom: rdn 1/2-way: styd on same pce fnl f* **9/1**

120 **6** *1* **Perfect Friend**[12] 6673 2-8-11 **67** RichardKingscote 10 61
(S Kirk) *s.i.s: sn outpcd: hdwy over 1f out: sn rdn and edgd lft: no imp ins fnl f* **10/1**

6040 **7** *3/4* **Shaker Style (USA)**[34] 6112 2-8-12 **68** (b) GrahamGibbons 3 61
(J D Bethell) *hld up: rdn over 2f out: r.o u.p ins fnl f: nrst fin* **50/1**

034 **8** *6* **La Diosa (IRE)**[18] 6539 2-9-4 **74** LiamJones 12 54
(W J Haggas) *s.i.s: outpcd* **12/1**

065 **9** *3/4* **Adios Juan**[43] 5811 2-9-1 **71** SaleemGolam 1 50
(S C Williams) *chsd ldrs tl rdn and wknd over 1f out* **7/1**

5210 **10** *1 1/2* **Aladdin's Lamp (IRE)**[18] 6525 2-9-2 **72** JamieSpencer 6 47
(M Johnston) *trckd ldrs: racd keenly: rdn: hung lft and wknd over 1f out* **5/1**[2]

002 **11** *3 1/4* **Champion Girl (IRE)**[17] 6552 2-8-10 **66** RobertHavlin 9 35
(D Haydn Jones) *hld up in tch: hmpd over 2f out: sn rdn and wknd* **14/1**

0100 **12** *6* **Cavendish Road (IRE)**[24] 6362 2-9-2 **72** (b[1]) SteveDrowne 7 28
(W R Muir) *sn chsng wnr: rdn and wknd over 1f out* **40/1**

1m 51.72s (1.22) **Going Correction** +0.125s/f (Slow) **12** Ran SP% **118.3**
Speed ratings (Par 97): **99,98,98,96,96 95,95,89,89,87 84,79**
CSF £104.54 CT £512.32 TOTE £17.30: £6.00, £2.70, £1.50; EX 160.10.
Owner Keep Racing **Bred** J H A Baggen **Trained** Middleham Moor, N Yorks
■ Stewards' Enquiry : Darren Williams caution: careless riding.
William Buick two-day ban: careless riding (Nov 7-8)

FOCUS
This was a modest nursery, but it had a very open look about it and the race was run at a solid pace.

NOTEBOOK
Tepmokea(IRE) won the battle for the early lead and eventually made just about all to get off the mark at the seventh attempt. He looked a sitting duck at the furlong marker, but dug deep and deserves credit. He did drift markedly right late on, not helping the runner-up, but is going the right way and evidently enjoyed the switch to this surface. (op 16-1)
Rumble Of Thunder(IRE), second on his nursery bow 36 days previously, was forced to race a lot more patiently on this all-weather debut as he was drawn wide. He also had to come wide into the home straight and was coming at the winner before being carried wide by that rival inside the final furlong. All considered, he has to be rated unlucky, but he has clearly begun life in nurseries on a fair mark and can be placed to go one better. (tchd 10-1)
Recession Proof(FR), a winner over course and distance on his penultimate start, was racing from another 7lb higher mark and performed with credit. He was unable to confirm Nottingham form with the winner, but did not get the best of passages from off the pace and there is little doubt he has another race within his compass. (tchd 4-1)
First Queen found just the same pace when asked for maximum effort, but did little wrong. She ought to get a bit further in time. (op 9-2 tchd 13-2)
Aladdin's Lamp(IRE) Official explanation: jockey said colt had no more to give

6955 LADBROKESPOKER.COM H'CAP (DIV II) 1m 141y(P)
8:20 (8:20) (Class 6) (0-55,55) 3-Y-O+ **£2,866** (£846; £423) **Stalls** Low

Form RPR

0650 **1** **Kirstys Lad**[31] 6189 6-9-1 **53** GeorgeBaker 12 60
(M Mullineaux) *a.p: chsd ldr 3f out: rdn to ld over 1f out: styd on* **7/2**[1]

0200 **2** *1 1/4* **Ardent Prince**[7] 6768 5-8-12 **53** TolleyDean(3) 10 57
(A J McCabe) *hld up: racd keenly: hdwy u.p over 1f out: edgd lft: styd on: nt rch wnr* **16/1**

0000 **3** *3/4* **Alberts Story (USA)**[89] 4458 4-8-11 **49** PaulHanagan 8 51
(R A Fahey) *a.p: rdn over 1f out: styd on* **6/1**

0-00 **4** *hd* **Plush**[104] 3951 5-9-3 **55** RichardKingscote 4 57
(Tom Dascombe) *s.i.s: hld up: racd keenly: r.o ins fnl f: nrst fin* **7/1**

6000 **5** *1/2* **Dushstorm (IRE)**[10] 6727 7-9-0 **52** LiamJones 11 53
(R J Price) *sn pushed along in rr: hdwy over 1f out: r.o* **16/1**

2500 **6** *1/2* **The Geester**[24] 6353 4-9-3 **55** (b) WilliamBuick 13 55
(S R Bowring) *s.i.s: hdwy to ld over 6f out: rdn and hdd over 1f out: no ex ins fnl f* **22/1**

2630 **7** *1/2* **Grand Value (USA)**[21] 6437 3-8-12 **54** PJMcDonald 1 52
(R Ford) *chsd ldrs: rdn over 1f out: styd on same pce fnl f* **20/1**

5620 **8** *7* **Welsh Opera**[59] 5378 3-8-13 **55** JimCrowley 7 37
(Mrs A J Perrett) *hld up: hdwy u.p over 2f out: wknd fnl f* **9/2**[2]

0403 **9** *6* **Sazerac (USA)**[49] 5684 3-8-10 **52** IanMongan 3 20
(P Howling) *hld up: hdwy over 2f out: rdn and wknd over 1f out* **11/2**[3]

10 **10** *3 1/2* **Flashy Max**[20] 6492 3-8-6 **53** PatrickDonaghy(5) 6 13
(Jedd O'Keeffe) *led: hdd over 6f out: chsd ldr tl rdn over 3f out: wknd 2f out* **15/2**

000- **11** *35* **Silent Storm**[318] 7111 8-9-3 **55** LPKeniry 2 —
(Peter Grayson) *a in rr: wknd over 2f out: eased* **28/1**

1m 52.12s (1.62) **Going Correction** +0.125s/f (Slow)
WFA 3 from 4yo+ 4lb **11** Ran SP% **118.7**
Speed ratings (Par 101): **97,95,95,95,94 94,93,87,82,79 47**
CSF £60.79 CT £331.72 TOTE £4.40: £1.70, £5.70, £2.30; EX 49.90.
Owner S A Pritchard **Bred** T S And Mrs Wallace **Trained** Alpraham, Cheshire

FOCUS
This second divison of the handicap was another weak affair and it was run at a steady pace. There was not much solid recent form to go on and the winner is rated back to something like his old winning form over course-and-distance.
Dushstorm(IRE) Official explanation: jockey said gelding was denied a clear run

6956 BET NOW WITH LADBROKES ON 0800 777 888 MEDIAN AUCTION MAIDEN STKS 1m 1f 103y(P)
8:50 (8:50) (Class 6) 3-5-Y-O **£2,729** (£806; £403) **Stalls** Low

Form RPR

4023 **1** **Barliffey (IRE)**[28] 6256 3-9-3 73 (v) TPO'Shea 5 71
(D J Coakley) *s.s: hld up: hmpd over 6f out: hdwy over 2f out: rdn and hung lft over 1f out: hung rt and styd on u.p to ld wl ins fnl f* **2/1**[2]

5265 **2** *3/4* **Indy Driver**[16] 6571 3-9-3 72 JamieSpencer 4 69
(J R Fanshawe) *hld up: hdwy over 2f out: hung lft over 1f out: rdn to ld 1f out: hung rt and hdd wl ins fnl f* **15/8**[1]

3000 **3** *1 1/2* **Speyside (IRE)**[9] 6741 3-9-0 67 (p) PatrickHills(3) 7 66
(J W Hills) *prom: hmpd and lost pl over 6f out: hdwy 4f out: led over 2f out: rdn and hdd 1f out: styd on same pce* **14/1**

3032 **4** *2* **Templetuohy Max (IRE)**[42] 5868 3-9-3 52 (v) JimmyQuinn 1 62
(J D Bethell) *chsd ldrs: rdn over 2f out: no ex fnl f* **10/1**

5 *2 1/2* **That'll Do Nicely (IRE)**[133] 5-9-7 0 PJMcDonald 3 57
(N G Richards) *s.s: hld up: hdwy over 2f out: styd on same pce appr fnl f* **7/1**[3]

005- **6** *6* **Whodunit (UAE)**[425] 4845 4-9-7 51 ChrisCatlin 9 44?
(P W Hiatt) *chsd ldrs: rdn and ev ch 2f out: wknd fnl f* **50/1**

0 **7** *10* **Gulnaz**[125] 3262 3-8-12 0 DaleGibson 8 18
(Mrs G S Rees) *s.i.s: a in rr* **66/1**

0406 **8** *2* **Tara's Garden**[80] 4708 3-8-12 58 SteveDrowne 2 14
(M Blanshard) *chsd ldrs: rdn 1/2-way: wknd 2f out* **25/1**

2606 **9** *10* **Great Knight (IRE)**[13] 6660 3-9-3 58 (v[1]) LiamJones 6 —
(W J Haggas) *hld: racd keenly: hdd over 2f out: sn rdn and wknd* **9/1**

60-6 **10** *4* **Beresford Lady**[10] 6726 4-9-2 45 SilvestreDeSousa 10 —
(A D Brown) *hdwy and edgd lft over 6f out: rdn over 3f out: sn wknd* **33/1**

2m 2.35s (0.65) **Going Correction** +0.125s/f (Slow)
WFA 3 from 4yo+ 4lb **10** Ran SP% **116.6**
Speed ratings (Par 101): **102,101,100,98,96 90,81,80,71,67**
CSF £5.95 TOTE £2.70: £1.60, £1.10, £4.60; EX 5.90.
Owner Fairfax Racing **Bred** Forenaghts Stud **Trained** West Ilsley, Berks

FOCUS
This weak maiden was run at a solid pace and the form makes sense, although it is doubtful if the principals had to match their best efforts.

6957 LADBROKESCASINO.COM H'CAP 2m 119y(P)
9:20 (9:20) (Class 4) (0-80,83) 3-Y-O+ **£5,180** (£1,541; £770; £384) **Stalls** Low

Form RPR

5301 **1** **Keenes Day (FR)**[5] 6838 3-9-7 **83** 6ex J-PGuillambert 7 96+
(M Johnston) *hld up in tch: led 2f out: sn rdn and edgd lft: styd on: eased nr fin* **5/4**[1]

0120 **2** *1 1/2* **Master At Arms**[21] 6220 5-9-4 **70** JerryO'Dwyer 9 81
(Daniel Mark Loughnane, Ire) *s.i.s: hld up: hdwy over 2f out: rdn to chse wnr over 1f out: edgd lft: styd on same pce ins fnl f* **5/1**[2]

1160 **3** *1 1/2* **Mohawk Star (IRE)**[12] 6672 7-9-0 **66** (v) JimCrowley 8 75
(I A Wood) *hld up: hdwy over 2f out: nt clr run and swtchd rt over 1f out: styd on* **14/1**

1040 **4** *hd* **Salute (IRE)**[12] 6672 9-9-6 **72** RobertHavlin 4 81
(P G Murphy) *a.p: chsd ldr over 3f out: hmpd over 2f out: sn rdn: styd on same pce fnl f* **10/1**

0/56 **5** *3 1/4* **Absolut Power (GER)**[24] 6361 7-10-0 **80** (v) SteveDrowne 3 85
(J A Geake) *led 2f: chsd ldr tl led over 4f out: rdn and hdd 2f out: wknd fnl f* **33/1**

0000 **6** *4* **Calculating (IRE)**[15] 6606 4-9-7 **73** DaneO'Neill 5 73
(M D I Usher) *hld up: nt clr run over 2f out: nvr trbld ldrs* **13/2**[3]

0036 **7** *5* **Abstract Folly (IRE)**[27] 6279 6-8-13 **65** GrahamGibbons 1 59
(J D Bethell) *chsd ldrs: rdn over 2f out: wknd over 1f out* **16/1**

2124 **8** *10* **River Kent**[20] 6493 3-7-13 **61** oh2 JimmyQuinn 6 43
(Mrs A Duffield) *sn prom: rdn and wknd over 2f out* **7/1**

-440 **9** *45* **Trew Style**[24] 6361 6-8-9 **61** oh2 SaleemGolam 2 —
(M H Tompkins) *s.i.s: hdwy to ld after 2f: rdn and hdd over 4f out: wknd over 3f out* **16/1**

3m 39.53s (-2.27) **Going Correction** +0.125s/f (Slow)
WFA 3 from 4yo+ 10lb **9** Ran SP% **117.4**
Speed ratings (Par 105): **110,109,108,108,106 105,102,98,76**
CSF £7.74 CT £60.33 TOTE £2.00: £1.30, £2.10, £2.40; EX 7.80 Place 6 £181.33, Place 5 £22.97 .
Owner Mrs R J Jacobs **Bred** Newsells Park Stud Ltd **Trained** Middleham Moor, N Yorks

FOCUS
A modest staying handicap, run at a sound pace. Solid form for the grade, the winner carrying his Southwell improvement over to Polytrack.
T/Plt: £123.20 to a £1 stake. Pool: £82,154.22. 486.45 winning tickets. T/Qpdt: £6.20 to a £1 stake. Pool: £8,730.59. 1,033.70 winning tickets. CR

6958 - 6962a (Foreign Racing) - See Raceform Interactive

[6793]DUNDALK (A.W) (L-H)

Friday, October 24

OFFICIAL GOING: Standard

6963a MERCURY STKS (LISTED RACE) 5f

8:40 (8:41) 2-Y-0+ **£23,933** (£7,022; £3,345; £1,139)

RPR

1 **Borderlescott**[19] 6518 6-10-3 .... PatCosgrave 7 105+
(R Bastiman) *chsd ldrs: 4th 1/2-way: hdwy to chal 1 1/2f out: narrow ld 1f out: strly pressed and kpt on wl fnl f* **4/5**[1]

2 *nk* **Invincible Ash (IRE)**[47] 5720 3-9-8 83 .... RPCleary 2 95+
(M Halford, Ire) *towards rr: hdwy in 6th 2f out: rdn into cl 3rd and chal 1f out: kpt on wl to press ldr ins fnl f: no ex cl home* **14/1**

3 *1/2* **Masta Plasta (IRE)**[17] 6568 5-10-0 .... CDHayes 8 99
(D Nicholls) *chsd ldrs: 3rd 1/2-way: impr to chal 1f out: kpt on fnl f: no ex cl home* **10/3**[2]

4 *1/2* **Peace Offering (IRE)**[22] 6429 8-10-0 .... AdrianTNicholls 1 98
(D Nicholls) *led: rdn and chal 1 1/2f out: hdd 1f out: kpt on same pce fnl f* **9/2**[3]

5 *1* **Brave Falcon (IRE)**[34] 6138 4-9-11 90 .... (p) KLatham 6 91
(Leo J Temple, Ire) *chsd ldrs: 5th 1/2-way: rdn in 6th 1 1/2f out: kpt on same pce fr over 1f out* **16/1**

6 *1 1/4* **Baggio (IRE)**[14] 6635 7-9-11 94 .... FMBerry 4 87
(Charles O'Brien, Ire) *dwlt: hld up: rdn into 6th 1f out: kpt on one pce* **12/1**

7 *1 1/4* **Senor Benny (USA)**[5] 6845 9-10-0 100 .... DPMcDonogh 9 85
(M McDonagh, Ire) *sn towards rr: rdn and no imp 2f out: kpt on one pce* **16/1**

8 *1 3/4* **Copper Dock (IRE)**[7] 6794 4-9-11 82 .... WJLee 3 76
(T G McCourt, Ire) *disp ld early: chsd ldr in 2nd: rdn in 4th and no ex 1 1/2f out: sn wknd* **20/1**

9 *3/4* **Tornadodancer (IRE)**[19] 6514 5-9-11 90 .... MHarley 5 73
(T G McCourt, Ire) *chsd ldrs: 6th 1/2-way: rdn and no ex 2f out* **25/1**

59.10 secs (59.10) **9 Ran SP% 131.5**
CSF £18.90 TOTE £1.70: £1.50, £3.30, £2.00; DF 36.10.
Owner James Edgar & William Donaldson **Bred** James Clark **Trained** Cowthorpe, N Yorks

FOCUS
Borderlescott, plus the Nicholls pair, were below their recent turf form. Step ups from the second and fifth.

NOTEBOOK
Borderlescott, for whom this wasn't the most suitable race as he had to carry a Group 1 penalty, nevertheless prevailed through a combination of class and toughness. Ridden early to get a position, he was being more or less pushed along throughout, but switching to the inside under two furlongs out, he got his head in front inside the last and won with more in hand than the margin suggests. He is likely to forego an invitation to race in Hong Kong in December and will be put away for next year, with the Temple Stakes and King's Stand the early-season targets. (op 11/8)
Invincible Ash(IRE) was the real surprise package of the race and if staying in training she is progressive enough to make up into a genuine performer at Listed or maybe even Group 3 level. Racing just off the pace on the inside rail, she quickened inside the last and kept going all the way to the line, but just wasn't able to get close enough to Borderlescott.
Masta Plasta(IRE) travelled best of the Nicholls duo most of the way and threw down his challenge on the outside a furlong out. He kept on well, but just wasn't good enough. (op 3/1)
Peace Offering(IRE) looked to have everything in his favour with the plum draw, and even though he got to the front early he drifted off the rail, especially off the home bend, and negated any advantage that would have given him. He could find no extra when headed a furlong out. (op 7/2)

6964 - (Foreign Racing) - See Raceform Interactive

SANTA ANITA (L-H)

Friday, October 24

OFFICIAL GOING: Pro-ride (aw) - fast; turf course - firm

6965a SENTIENT FLIGHT BREEDERS' CUP FILLY & MARES SPRINT (F&M) (PRO-RIDE) 7f

8:35 (8:38) 3-Y-0+ **£271,357** (£100,503; £50,251; £25,628; £12,563)

RPR

1 **Ventura (USA)**[47] 4-8-11 .... GKGomez 11 121
(Robert Frankel, U.S.A) *trckd over towards rail: three bhd her after 1f: str run on outside fr 2f out: 6th st: drvn to ld 150yds out: r.o strly* **3/1**[2]

2 *4* **Indian Blessing (USA)**[34] 3-8-8 .... JRVelazquez 4 109
(Bob Baffert, U.S.A) *sn pressing ldr: 2nd st: led 1 1/2f out to 150yds out: one pce* **9/4**[1]

3 *2* **Zaftig (USA)**[139] 3-8-8 .... RBejarano 5 104
(James Jerkens, U.S.A) *a cl up: 3rd st: one pce* **13/2**

4 *1 1/4* **Miraculous Miss (USA)**[48] 5-8-11 .... RADominguez 9 101
(Steven B Klesaris, U.S.A) *outpcd: 12th st: gd hdwy fnl f: nrest at fin* **25/1**

5 *nk* **Tizzy's Tune (USA)**[26] 5-8-11 .... ASolis 12 100
(Ronald McAnally, U.S.A) *disp early ld fr wd draw: 5th st: kpt on one pce* **33/1**

6 *nse* **Intangaroo (USA)**[61] 4-8-11 .... AQuinonez 2 100
(Gary Sherlock, U.S.A) *outpcd: 11th st: c down outside: styd on fnl f* **6/1**[3]

7 *1 1/4* **Magnificience (USA)**[26] 4-8-11 .... DFlores 1 97
(Bruce Headley, U.S.A) *s.i.s: last st: nvr a factor* **22/1**

8 *1 1/4* **Jazzy (ARG)**[41] 6-8-11 .... AGarcia 10 94
(Mark Hennig, U.S.A) *8th st: nvr a factor* **66/1**

9 *2* **Lady Sprinter (USA)**[174] 4-8-11 .... RRDouglas 3 88
(Juan J Reviriego, Argentina) *7th st on ins: wknd 1f out* **20/1**

10 *1 3/4* **La Tee (USA)**[20] 4-8-11 .... JKCourt 13 83
(Mark Glatt, U.S.A) *fast away on outside: led over 1f: wkng 9th st* **66/1**

11 *1 1/2* **Dearest Trickski (USA)**[61] 4-8-11 .... (b) MESmith 8 79
(John W Sadler, U.S.A) *led wl over 5f out to 1 1/2f out* **12/1**

12 *1 3/4* **Dream Rush (USA)**[41] 4-8-11 .... KDesormeaux 6 75
(William Phipps, U.S.A) *chsd ldrs: 5th st: sn wknd* **33/1**

13 *nk* **Tiz Elemental (USA)**[26] 4-8-11 .... JRosario 7 74
(Carla Gaines, U.S.A) *cl up to 1/2-way: 10th and btn st* **22/1**

1m 19.9s (79.90)
WFA 3 from 4yo+ 2lb **13 Ran SP% 117.3**
PARI-MUTUEL (including $2 stakes): WIN 7.60; PL (1-2) 3.40, 3.40; SHOW (1-2-3) 3.00, 2.40, 4.00; SF 25.40.
Owner Juddmonte Farms Inc **Bred** Juddmonte Farms Inc **Trained** USA
■ The first-ever running of a Breeders' Cup race on a synthetic track, and also the first steroid-free BC meeting.

FOCUS
This was the inaugural running of the Filly & Mares' Sprint. Some will argue that this type of race simply dilutes the overall quality of the two-day meeting, and it lacked current European interest, but this was still a high-class contest, arguably made all the more interesting and competitive by the introduction of Pro-Ride.

NOTEBOOK
Ventura(USA), chosen by the excellent Garrett Gomez ahead of Indian Blessing, landed a Polytrack Listed race at Kempton on her final start for Amanda Perrett last year, and has since won a Grade 2 on the same surface in the States, as well as a Grade 1 on turf, so she was well suited to this track. She was a long way behind early, but the strong pace was exactly what she needed and she produced a sustained burst when taken wide into the straight, ultimately drawing clear of the tiring favourite. She is obviously high class, and is now three from four on synthetics, but it has to be said absolutely everything went her way.
Indian Blessing(USA) is best known for her exploits on dirt, including victory in last year's Juvenile Fillies, but she holds the track record over this course and distance (on cushion track, the original replacement to dirt), and handled the surface beautifully. However, there was loads of pace on, as anticipated, and she looked to go off too quickly up front.
Zaftig(USA) had today's runner-up four lengths behind when winning a Grade 1 on the dirt at Belmont last time, but that was back in June and she could not confirm form under these different conditions.
Miraculous Miss(USA) was detached from the main bunch early, but she stayed on strongly in the straight once switched to the inside, confirming the leaders overdid things.
Intangaroo(USA) was disappointing, considering she had the race run to suit.

6966a GREY GOOSE BREEDERS' CUP JUVENILE FILLIES TURF 1m (T)

9:15 (9:16) 2-Y-0 **£312,060** (£115,578; £57,789; £29,472; £14,447)

RPR

1 **Maram (USA)**[23] 2-8-10 .... JLezcano 3 110
(Chad C Brown, U.S.A) *a in tch: 5th st on outside: hdwy to go 2nd 1f out: led 50yds out: all out* **9/1**[3]

2 *nse* **Heart Shaped (USA)**[21] 6441 2-8-10 .... JMurtagh 12 110
(A P O'Brien, Ire) *hld up towards rr: clsng up and 8th st: gd hdwy on outside fr over 1f out: hrd rdn ins fnl f: jst failed* **14/1**

3 *1* **Laragh (USA)**[15] 2-8-10 .... EPrado 2 108
(John Terranova II, U.S.A) *led to 50yds out: no ex* **11/4**[1]

4 *1* **Saucey Evening (USA)**[19] 2-8-10 .... GKGomez 11 105
(H Graham Motion, U.S.A) *pushed along over 2f out: 6th st: styd on: nrest at fin* **9/1**[3]

5 *1 1/2* **Emmy Darling (USA)**[53] 2-8-10 .... RBejarano 5 102
(John W Sadler, U.S.A) *prom: 4th st: disp 2nd 1f out: one pce* **25/1**

6 *1/2* **Consequence (USA)**[23] 2-8-10 .... JRVelazquez 7 101
(Claude McGaughey III, U.S.A) *towards rr: 9th st: kpt on one pce* **4/1**[2]

7 *1/2* **Sugar Mom (USA)**[27] 2-8-10 .... ECoa 8 100
(Wayne Catalano, U.S.A) *disp 5th: lost pl and 10th on outside st: sme late prog* **12/1**

8 *1 1/4* **C Karma (USA)**[40] 2-8-10 .... CVelasquez 4 97
(Gregory De Gannes, Canada) *prom: 4th st on ins: wknd fnl f* **9/1**[3]

9 *1 1/4* **Freedom Rings (USA)**[23] 2-8-10 .... AGarcia 6 94
(David Donk, U.S.A) *11th st: a bhd* **16/1**

10 *2* **Renda (USA)**[27] 2-8-10 .... SMadrid 9 90
(Juan D Arias, U.S.A) *chsd ldr: 2nd st: sn wknd* **12/1**

11 *hd* **April Pride**[62] 5266 2-8-10 .... DFlores 1 90
(James Cassidy, U.S.A) *disp 5th on ins: 7th and btn st* **20/1**

12 *2 3/4* **Beyond Our Reach (IRE)**[21] 6441 2-8-10 .... LDettori 10 84
(T Stack, Ire) *last most of way* **16/1**

1m 35.15s (1.28) **12 Ran SP% 119.1**
PARI-MUTUEL: WIN 24.20; PL (1-2) 13.20, 11.60; SHOW (1-2-3) 6.40, 6.60, 3.40; SF 350.20.
Owner Karen Woods & Saud Bin Khaled **Bred** Palides Investments N V Inc **Trained** USA

FOCUS
The first running of the Juvenile Fillies' Turf. A weak contest by Breeders' Cup standards, with the Pro-Ride version of this race far more prestigious, but it was at least competitive and should gain in popularity, particularly with the Europeans. They went a good pace. The runner-up is the bset guide to the form.

NOTEBOOK
Maram(USA) is now 3-3, with this success supplementing victories in a maiden and a Grade 3, but she did get first run on the runner-up.
Heart Shaped(USA) would have got there in another stride. This was her first try beyond 6f, but she got the trip well, having been dropped in from the widest stall of all, and she will have more options now.
Laragh(USA) went a good pace, but crucially she was unchallenged in front and still looked full of running entering the straight; indeed her rider took a look round. However, she was eventually worn down by a pair of strong finishers.
Saucey Evening(USA) looked to have something to find in this company but she finished strongly to take fourth and this was a big effort in defeat.
Emmy Darling(USA) might have found 1m, the longest trip she has tried to date, just stretching her a little on this first try on turf.
Beyond Our Reach(IRE) was never involved.

6967a BESSEMER TRUST BREEDERS' CUP JUVENILE FILLIES (GRADE 1) (PRO-RIDE) 1m 110y(D)

9:55 (9:56) 2-Y-0 **£542,714** (£201,005; £100,503; £51,256; £25,126)

RPR

1 **Stardom Bound (USA)**[27] 2-8-10 .... MESmith 10 118
(Christopher S Paasch, U.S.A) *last but one 3f out: str run on outside: 2nd st: led 1 1/2f out: sn clr: drvn out* **13/8**[1]

2 *1 1/2* **Dream Empress (USA)**[21] 6463 2-8-10 .... KDesormeaux 12 115
(Kenneth McPeek, U.S.A) *mid-div: hdwy and 6th on outside st: styd on to take 2nd 100yds out: r.o* **9/1**

3 *1 1/2* **Sky Diva (USA)**[20] 6500 2-8-10 .... RADominguez 4 112
(Steven B Klesaris, U.S.A) *prom: 3rd on ins st: edgd rt: kpt on same pce* **4/1**[2]

4 *nse* **Dave's Revenge (USA)**[54] 2-8-10 .... JRosario 7 111
(R Hess Jr, U.S.A) *mid-div: hdwy on ins and 4th st: one pce fnl f* **50/1**

5 *2 1/2* **Persistently (USA)**[20] 6500 2-8-10 .... AGarcia 2 106
(Claude McGaughey III, U.S.A) *last and hrd rdn 3f out: c wd st: r.o fr over 1f out: nvr nrr* **20/1**

6 *nk* **Van Lear Rose (CAN)**[19] 2-8-10 .... ChantalSutherland 6 105
(Catherine Day-Phillips, Canada) *6th and hrd rdn st: edgd out: styd on fnl f: nvr a danger* **33/1**

7 *3/4* **C. S. Silk (USA)**[48] 2-8-10 .... RAlbarado 8 104
(Dale Romans, U.S.A) *led to 1 1/2f out: one pce* **9/1**

8 *1* **Black Magic Mama (USA)**[27] 2-8-10 .... RBejarano 3 102
(Doug O'Neill, U.S.A) *a mid-div* **50/1**

9 *2* **Evita Argentina (USA)**[53] 2-8-10 .... ASolis 1 97
(John W Sadler, U.S.A) *bhd fnl 3f* **25/1**

10 3 1/2 **Doremifasollatido (USA)**[41] 2-8-10 .... ECoa 13 90
(James Jerkens, U.S.A) *a in rr* **20/1**

11 1 1/4 **Pursuit Of Glory (IRE)**[21] 6441 2-8-10 .... JMurtagh 11 87
(David Wachman, Ire) *a in rr: remained on ins ent st: sn rdn and btn* **8/1**[3]

12 3 3/4 **Be Smart (USA)**[21] 6463 2-8-10 .... GKGomez 5 79
(D Wayne Lukas, U.S.A) *chsd ldr to appr st: sn wknd* **16/1**

13 2 1/2 **Palacio De Amor (USA)**[27] 2-8-10 .... VEspinoza 9 74
(Myung Kwon Cho, U.S.A) *mid-div to st: sn wknd* **25/1**

1m 40.99s (-1.43) **13** Ran SP% **119.2**
PARI-MUTUEL: WIN 5.20; PL (1-2) 3.20, 8.80; SHOW (1-2-3) 2.20, 5.20, 3.60; SF 49.00.
Owner C R Cono LLC **Bred** F Gray, C Gray, J Youngblood **Trained** USA

FOCUS
A high-class juvenile contest and they went a good pace. Strong form.

NOTEBOOK
Stardom Bound(USA) was held up as usual, having been last to break, so the strong pace suited, and she produced a performance that was almost a carbon copy of her success in the course-and-distance Oak Leaf Stakes last time. Just as on her previous start, she was taken widest of all rounding the final bend to ensure a clear run, and once again, she produced a sustained burst that took her to the front in a remarkably short space of time. She understandably got tired in the final 100 yards or so, but was never in any danger and is clearly a top-class juvenile on the synthetics. She is due to be sold at the Fasig-Tipton November Sale on November 2 and it will be fascinating to see what she fetches.
Dream Empress(USA), well out the back early, looked to make her move towards the inner. However, her rider soon realised she had little chance of getting a run and manoeuvred her out wide, but by that time she found herself behind the winner, who had already begun to make her big move. She took a while to gain momentum once in the straight but finished strongly. On this evidence, there is not a lot between the front two.
Sky Diva(USA) looked to be going really well just in behind the leaders rounding the final bend but she had little room to make her move and was messed around when trying to negotiate a passage. She stayed on well when in the clear and this was a big run from a filly whose two previous wins had been gained on dirt. She should be capable of better again.
Dave's Revenge(USA) looked flattered by her debut success on the Polytrack, but that is seemingly not the case.
Persistently(USA) again gave the impression she already needs longer trips.
Pursuit Of Glory(IRE) did not get a chance to show what she might have been capable of, as she lost all momentum when blocked in her run just as she was trying to pick up rounding the final bend.

6968a FLY EMIRATES BREEDERS' CUP FILLY & MARE TURF (GRADE 1) (F&M) 1m 2f (T)

10:35 (10:37) 3-Y-O+ **£577,990** (£214,070; £107,035; £54,588; £26,759)

RPR

1 **Forever Together (USA)**[21] 6462 4-8-11 .... JRLeparoux 3 118
(Jonathan Sheppard, U.S.A) *hld up: 8th on outside st: str run fnl f to ld cl home* **5/1**[3]

2 3/4 **Sealy Hill (CAN)**[20] 6505 4-8-11 ....(b) PHusbands 1 116
(Mark Casse, Canada) *hld up in rr: 9th st: hdwy over 1f out: drvn to take 2nd last strides* **33/1**

3 hd **Wait A While (USA)**[27] 5-8-11 .... JRVelazquez 5 116
(Todd Pletcher, U.S.A) *a.p: 3rd st: led 100yds out tl ct cl home* **4/1**[2]

4 3/4 **Visit**[20] 6475 3-8-6 .... RyanMoore 4 114
(Sir Michael Stoute) *hld up in 8th: hdwy fr over 2f out and got through on ins: 4th st: led over 1 1/2f out: hrd rdn and hdd 100yds out* **10/1**

5 1/2 **Vacare (USA)**[27] 5-8-11 .... JValdiviaJr 2 113
(Christophe Clement, U.S.A) *trckd ldrs: 5th st: kpt on same pce* **16/1**

6 3/4 **Mauralakana (FR)**[27] 5-8-11 .... KDesormeaux 7 112
(Christophe Clement, U.S.A) *a in tch: 6th st: nvr able to chal* **7/1**

7 1/2 **Halfway To Heaven (IRE)**[20] 6475 3-8-8 ow2.................. JMurtagh 8 111
(A P O'Brien, Ire) *pressed ldr: 2nd st: 3rd 1f out: sn wknd* **5/2**[1]

8 3/4 **Dynaforce (USA)**[27] 5-8-11 .... AGarcia 6 109
(William Mott, U.S.A) *mid-div: nvr a factor* **12/1**

9 3/4 **Folk Opera (IRE)**[20] 6505 4-8-11 .... LDettori 9 108
(Saeed Bin Suroor) *led to over 1 1/2f out* **10/1**

10 3 3/4 **Pure Clan (USA)**[48] 5745 3-8-6 ....(b) EPrado 10 100
(Robert E Holthus, U.S.A) *last thrght* **14/1**

2m 1.58s (2.30)
WFA 3 from 4yo+ 5lb **10** Ran SP% **119.1**
PARI-MUTUEL: WIN 11.80; PL (1-2) 6.40, 36.20; SHOW (1-2-3) 4.80, 15.80, 3.60; SF 449.20.
Owner Augustin Stable **Bred** White Fox Farm **Trained** USA

FOCUS
The European challenge was not as strong as it has been for this race in years gone by and this looked a sub-standard Filly & Mare Turf. The pace was just ordinary for much of the way, but crucially, Folk Opera was continually pressed by Halfway To Heaven, who in turn was followed by Wait A While, and that trio would appear to have started 'racing' a little too soon.

NOTEBOOK
Forever Together(USA) benefited from three of her main rivals taking each other on early, and she stayed on from well back when produced with her effort up the centre of the track, seeing the trip out in style on her first run beyond 1m1f.
Sealy Hill(CAN), last year's Canadian Horse of the Year, was another to benefit the pacesetters doing a bit too much and she stayed on strongly to grab second just yards from the line.
Wait A While(USA) was 3-3 over this rather unusual course-and-distance, but she arguably did a bit too much in keeping tabs on Folk Opera and Halfway To Heaven, and this was a creditable effort considering that pair dropped right away.
Visit was given a superb ride in defeat by Breeders' Cup novice Ryan Moore, who found a lovely gap against the inside rail early in the straight, and the filly had every chance if good enough, but she simply did not stay.
Vacare(USA) seemed to have her chance.
Halfway To Heaven(IRE), carrying 2lb overweight, was not at her best. She's had a lot go her way this season, but her only previous win over this trip was gained in a very muddling renewal of the Nassau and she probably didn't stay under a handy ride. This was also her seventh outing of the campaign.
Folk Opera(IRE), who had been gifted the lead when winning the E P Taylor Stakes at Woodbine on her previous start, was forced to go quicker this time and finished up well beaten.

6969a BREEDERS' CUP LADIES CLASSIC (GRADE 1) (F&M) (PRO-RIDE) 1m 1f (D)

11:15 (11:17) 3-Y-O+ **£542,714** (£201,005; £100,503; £51,256; £25,126)

RPR

1 **Zenyatta (USA)**[27] 4-8-11 .... MESmith 1 124
(John Shirreffs, U.S.A) *hld up: last tl hdwy over 2f out: 6th on outside st: rdn to ld jst ins fnl f: pushed out and r.o wl* **1/2**[1]

2 1 1/2 **Cocoa Beach (CHI)**[27] 4-8-11 .... RADominguez 3 121
(Saeed Bin Suroor) *hld up in rr: 7th on ins st: qcknd through gap to ld narrowly at dist: hdd jst ins fnl f: r.o same pce* **7/1**[2]

3 1 1/2 **Music Note (USA)**[41] 3-8-7 .... JJCastellano 4 118
(Saeed Bin Suroor) *racd in 6th: clsd up on outside over 2f out: 5th st: kpt on to take 3rd 150yds out: one pce* **9/1**

4 2 1/4 **Carriage Trail (USA)**[19] 6523 5-8-11 .... KDesormeaux 5 114
(Claude McGaughey III, U.S.A) *disp 4th: 4th st: rdn 1f out: kpt on one pce* **8/1**[3]

5 2 **Hystericalady (USA)**[27] 5-8-11 .... GKGomez 2 110
(Jerry Hollendorfer, U.S.A) *led 1f: racd in cl 3rd: chal on outside 2f out: 3rd st: wknd fnl 150yds* **20/1**

6 nk **Ginger Punch (USA)**[27] 5-8-11 .... RBejarano 6 109
(Robert Frankel, U.S.A) *disp 4th on outside tl lost pl over 2f out: last st* **10/1**

7 nk **Santa Teresita (USA)**[27] 4-8-11 .... MCBaze 7 109
(Eric J Guillot, U.S.A) *pressed ldr: 2nd st: drvn to ld 1 1/2f out to dist: sn wknd* **50/1**

8 5 1/2 **Bear Now (USA)**[27] 4-8-11 .... ERosaDaSilva 8 98
(Reade Baker, Canada) *led after 1f to 1 1/2f out* **40/1**

1m 46.85s (-2.05)
WFA 3 from 4yo+ 4lb **8** Ran SP% **118.5**
PARI-MUTUEL: WIN 3.00; PL (1-2) 2.60, 4.60; SHOW (1-2-3) 2.10, 3.80, 3.80; SF 13.40.
Owner Mr & Mrs Jerome S Moss **Bred** Maverick Production Limited **Trained** USA

FOCUS
A decent renewal of the race formerly known as the Distaff.

NOTEBOOK
Zenyatta(USA) is now unbeaten in nine starts, eight of which have been on synthetic surfaces. Held up well out the back as usual, she made a big move about five-horse widths wide rounding the final bend and sustained her challenge into the straight. It's fair to say she had to work for this, but she looked a class act once in front and won with more authority than the official margin might suggest. Although taking nothing away from this mighty performance, it should be at least mentioned that the track very much played to her strengths, as the two other BC winners on the Pro-Ride course on the day were also held up, before swinging wide into the straight. Her connections plan to campaign her as a five-year-old.
Cocoa Beach(CHI), who was supplemented at huge expense, had to switch towards the inside with her challenge in the straight, but was basically just beaten by an exceptional filly.
Music Note(USA) is probably best suited to dirt, but she ran an honest race in defeat.
Carriage Trail(USA) seemed to have her chance and looks a good guide to the strength of the form.
Ginger Punch(USA), last year's winner, looks better suited to dirt.

6944 DONCASTER (L-H)

Saturday, October 25

OFFICIAL GOING: Good (good to soft in places; 7.8)
The ground had not changed overnight and was on the easy side of good but there was a brisk headwind to contend with.
Wind: fresh and blustery 1/2 against Weather: overcast, cool and breezy, light rain

6970 CROWNHOTEL-BAWTRY.COM NURSERY 7f

1:55 (1:56) (Class 3) 2-Y-O **£9,714** (£2,890; £1,444; £721) **Stalls** High

Form RPR

5212 **1** **Definitly**[35] 6118 2-9-7 **88**..................................... JamieSpencer 8 95
(R Charlton) *hld up in rr: gd hdwy on ins over 1f out: r.o to ld fnl strides* **5/2**[1]

3140 **2** hd **Satwa Laird**[21] 6474 2-9-3 **84**.. JimmyFortune 12 91
(E A L Dunlop) *hld up in rr: stdy hdwy over 1f out: chal wl ins fnl f: no ex* **10/1**

51 **3** shd **Greensward**[70] 5099 2-8-11 **78**.. JAHeffernan 9 84
(B J Meehan) *trckd ldrs: led over 1f out: hdd towards fin* **10/1**

3113 **4** 2 3/4 **Count Paris (USA)**[19] 6533 2-8-10 **77**............................ JoeFanning 11 76
(M Johnston) *mde most: hdd over 1f out: one pce* **13/2**[3]

0121 **5** 1/2 **Silent Hero**[25] 6362 2-8-10 **77**.................................... PhilipRobinson 14 75
(M A Jarvis) *t.k.h in rr: hdwy on ins 2f out: kpt on same pce ins fnl f* **5/1**[2]

5253 **6** 3 3/4 **Tiger Goddess (IRE)**[7] 6809 2-8-6 **73**.......................(v[1]) LiamJones 13 62
(W J Haggas) *chsd ldrs on ins: wknd appr fnl f* **16/1**

0360 **7** 1 1/2 **Admirable Duque (IRE)**[12] 6700 2-8-4 **71**........................ WMLordan 5 56
(D J S Ffrench Davis) *chsd ldrs on outer: wknd over 1f out* **100/1**

6313 **8** 2 1/2 **Daddy's Gift (IRE)**[23] 6414 2-9-4 **85**............................... DaneO'Neill 6 64
(R Hannon) *mid-div: wkng whn hmpd over 1f out and ins fnl f* **18/1**

021 **9** hd **Dubai Hills**[39] 5989 2-8-13 **80**... TedDurcan 10 58
(B Smart) *mid-div: effrt 2f out: no ch whn sltly hmpd appr fnl f* **9/1**

0140 **10** 1 **Red Humour (IRE)**[57] 5447 2-8-13 **80**............................. PaulHanagan 7 56
(B W Hills) *w ldrs: wknd over 1f out* **40/1**

5300 **11** 1/2 **Becausewecan (USA)**[35] 6101 2-8-4 **71**..................... RoystonFfrench 4 46
(M Johnston) *chsd ldrs: wkng whn n.m.r over 1f out* **20/1**

2213 **12** 1 **Brazilian Art**[26] 6344 2-9-0 **81**... RobertWinston 3 53
(P W Chapple-Hyam) *chsd ldrs: rdn over 2f out: wknd over 1f out* **20/1**

5423 **13** 3/4 **Roly Boy**[42] 5895 2-9-4 **85**... PatDobbs 1 55
(R Hannon) *trckd ldrs on outer: quite keen: lost pl over 1f out* **9/1**

025 **14** 3 1/4 **Damini (USA)**[24] 6392 2-8-8 **75**.. MJKinane 2 37
(Sir Michael Stoute) *chsd ldrs on wd outside: lost pl over 1f out* **20/1**

1m 27.29s (0.99) **Going Correction** +0.125s/f (Good) **14** Ran SP% **125.6**
Speed ratings (Par 99): **99,98,98,95,94 90,88,86,85,84 84,83,82,78**
toteswinger: 1&2 £7.00, 1&3 £8.40, 2&3 £19.90. CSF £28.01 CT £228.87 TOTE £3.10: £1.70, £3.60, £5.00; EX 38.70 TRIFECTA Not won..
Owner S Emmet And Miss R Emmet **Bred** S Emmet And Miss R Emmet **Trained** Beckhampton, Wilts

FOCUS
An interesting nursery and a race that usually falls to an improving type produced a good finish, with the first five, including most of the fancied horses, drawing clear.

NOTEBOOK
Definitly was held up at the back on this step up in trip before being brought with a run up the stands' rail. He looked like running out the clear winner as he came through, but it needed all Spencer's strength to get him home in a desperate finish. (tchd 11-4)
Satwa Laird was another who was settled in rear in the early stages and moved easily into contention at the same time as the winner before that rival picked up more readily when asked to challenge. He responded to pressure, though, was closing all the way to the line and deserves compensation. (op 12-1)
Greensward ◆, who was less experienced than his rivals, having just his third start, travelled well in the slipstream of the leaders before striking the front over a furlong out and then responded to pressure, only to be run down by the challengers on eaither side in the last 50 yards. He is possibly the one with the most scope and the horse to take out of the race. (tchd 11-1)
Count Paris(USA), whose wins have both been gained on soft ground, was given a positive ride on this sounder surface but failed to pick up when the principals committed. He may be most effective in more testing conditions. (op 8-1)
Silent Hero came into the race with a progressive profile and looked sure to be involved when produced at around the two-furlong pole, but he could not find another gear when it was needed. Still, he finished clear of the remainder. (op 7-1)

Tiger Goddess(IRE), who is still a maiden, ran quite well in a first-time visor although she was left behind by the first five in the closing stages. (op 14-1)
Admirable Duque(IRE), who had not gone on from a decent effort on his second start, ran better under a hold-up ride from his replacement jockey but was never in a challenging position.
Daddy's Gift(IRE) Official explanation: jockey said filly was denied a clear run
Red Humour(IRE) Official explanation: jockey said gelding hung both ways
Roly Boy, a winner over 7f on Polytrack, had to race on the outside of the field in the centre of the track and was in trouble before the two-furlong pole. (op 8-1)

6971 CORAL.CO.UK H'CAP 5f

2:25 (2:27) (Class 2) (0-100,105) 3-Y-0+

£31,155 (£9,330; £4,665; £2,335; £1,165; £585) **Stalls** High

Form — RPR

1511 **1** **Judge 'n Jury**[7] 6810 4-9-6 **105**..............(t) KevinGhunowa(3) 16 — 114
(R A Harris) *cl up: led over 2f out: qcknd appr last: sn rdn and kpt on strly* **13/2**[2]

2012 **2** ¾ **Fantasy Explorer**[28] 6290 5-7-12 **87**.............. JamieKyne(7) 22 — 94
(J J Quinn) *hld up towards rr: hdwy 2f out: swtchd rt and rdn over 1f out: drvn and chsd wnr ins fnl f: kpt on* **12/1**

6035 **3** shd **Fol Hollow (IRE)**[7] 6810 3-8-4 **86**.............. AdrianTNicholls 8 — 92
(D Nicholls) *led: rdn along and hdd over 2f out: cl up and drvn over 1f out: kpt on wl u.p ins fnl f* **14/1**

6205 **4** nk **River Falcon**[14] 6653 8-9-0 **96** ow1.............. DanielTudhope 3 — 101+
(J S Goldie) *towards rr: hdwy whn pushed lft wl over 1f out: sn rdn and styd on strly ins fnl f* **12/1**

0641 **5** nk **Kay Two (IRE)**[5] 6859 6-8-3 **90** 6ex..............(p) DavidProbert(5) 10 — 94
(R J Price) *prom: rdn along 2f out: drvn over 1f out and kpt on ins fnl f* **9/1**[3]

0666 **6** ½ **Patavellian (IRE)**[13] 6676 10-8-10 **92**..............(v) DaneO'Neill 17 — 94+
(R Charlton) *rr: hdwy over 1f out: rdn and styd on strly ins fnl f: nrst fin* **16/1**

3210 **7** ½ **Hotham**[7] 6810 5-8-4 **86** oh1.............. JimmyQuinn 21 — 86
(N Wilson) *hld up: hdwy wl over 1f out: sn drvn and styd on ins fnl f: nrst fin* **20/1**

0000 **8** ½ **Indian Trail**[7] 6810 8-8-4 **86**.............. PaulQuinn 14 — 85
(D Nicholls) *towards rr: hdwy 2f out: rdn over 1f out: kpt on ins fnl f: nrst fin* **33/1**

0001 **9** ½ **Piscean (USA)**[15] 6623 3-8-4 **86** oh3.............. LiamJones 1 — 83
(T Keddy) *hld up: hdwy on wd outside 1/2-way: rdn wl over 1f out: kpt on same pce ent fnl f* **33/1**

0133 **10** shd **Captain Dunne (IRE)**[7] 6810 3-8-13 **98**.............. DuranFentiman(3) 19 — 94
(T D Easterby) *cl up towards stands' rail: rdn 2f out and ev ch tl drvn and wknd appr fnl f* **14/1**

1104 **10** dht **Haajes**[7] 6810 4-8-10 **95**..............(t) TolleyDean(3) 18 — 91
(S Parr) *chsd ldrs: rdn along 2f out: sn drvn and kpt on same pce appr fnl f* **12/1**

0152 **12** hd **The Jobber (IRE)**[18] 6557 7-8-6 **88**.............. FrancisNorton 20 — 84
(M Blanshard) *in tch: effrt 2f out: sn rdn and no imp* **25/1**

1152 **13** hd **Cheveton**[14] 6653 4-8-9 **96**.............. Louis-PhilippeBeuzelin(5) 5 — 91
(R J Price) *s.i.s: hdwy 1/2-way: sn rdn and styd on appr fnl f: nvr a factor* **6/1**[1]

1001 **14** 1¼ **Hamish McGonagall**[14] 6653 3-9-4 **100**.............. DavidAllan 6 — 91
(T D Easterby) *cl up on outer: rdn along 2f out: sn drvn and grad wknd* **14/1**

0006 **15** shd **Luscivious**[7] 6810 4-7-11 **86** oh6.............. StacyRenwick(7) 9 — 76
(A J McCabe) *nvr bttr than midfield* **40/1**

6000 **16** ¾ **Aegean Dancer**[14] 6653 6-8-7 **89**.............. RoystonFfrench 15 — 76
(B Smart) *dwlt: sn chsng ldrs: rdn along 2f out and sn wknd* **25/1**

000 **17** ½ **Spirit Of Sharjah (IRE)**[29] 6239 3-8-13 **95**.............. MJKinane 7 — 81
(Miss J Feilden) *swtchd rt s and hld up in rr: hdwy 1/2-way: swtchd lft and rdn over 1f out: no hdwy* **33/1**

4011 **18** ½ **Tony The Tap**[22] 6449 7-8-10 **92**.............. RichardKingscote 2 — 76
(W R Muir) *a towards rr* **25/1**

1036 **19** nk **Green Park (IRE)**[14] 6651 5-8-5 **87**..............(b) PaulHanagan 13 — 70
(R A Fahey) *a in rr* **20/1**

1405 **20** ¾ **Turn On The Style**[45] 5793 6-9-4 **100**..............(b) PaulMulrennan 4 — 80
(J Balding) *towards rr: hdwy and in tch 1/2-way: sn rdn and wknd* **18/1**

59.82 secs (-0.68) **Going Correction** +0.125s/f (Good) **20 Ran SP% 124.2**
Speed ratings (Par 109): **110,108,108,108,107 106,106,105,104,104 104,104,103,101,101 100,99,98,98,97**
toteswinger: 1&2 £16.50, 1&3 £33.40, 2&3 £46.10. CSF £70.20 CT £1099.20 TOTE £6.20: £1.90, £3.40, £3.60, £3.00; EX 117.30 Trifecta £656.00 Pool: £1861.63 - 2.10 winning units..
Owner Mrs Ruth M Serrell **Bred** C A Cyzer **Trained** Earlswood, Monmouths

FOCUS
A good prize produced plenty of runners and a competitive sprint handicap in which the key form races appeared to be Musselburgh's York Sprint Cup and the Catterick Dash, and the latter proved more relevant. As in the opening race, the field raced towards the stands' rail. Judge 'n Jury maintained his remarkable recent progress, up another 5lb, and the form looks sound enough.

NOTEBOOK
Judge 'n Jury ◆ has been in blinding form, having won four of his six races since August, as a result of which he has gone up from a mark of 74 to 105. Carrying top weight, he was well backed and always in the firing line before showing in front travelling well over two furlongs out. Despite several challenges in the final furlong, he never looked like being reeled in and, sure to go up again, he is unlikely to run again this season. This bargain buy will have to contest Listed or Group races from now on, although he could well prove up to that class next year. (op 8-1)
Fantasy Explorer, whose trainer had been responsible for two winners of this race since 2001, was held up off the pace but came out of the pack to challenge entering the final furlong. However, he could never get to grips with the winner and would have been suited by faster ground and probably an extra furlong. (op 14-1)
Fol Hollow(IRE), 7lb better off with the winner for the three lengths he was beaten at Catterick, ran a fine race from a single-figure draw, although he ended up racing more towards the stands' side and suggests the form is sound.
River Falcon ran a typical race, being held up off the pace before finishing strongly, having not had the clearest of passages. He has been in good heart and, considering he would have preferred a softer surface, this offers encouragement if he reappears before the end of the turf campaign. (tchd 11-1)
Kay Two(IRE), another who has been running well and who was carrying a 6lb penalty for his win at Pontefract, also raced prominently but had to be switched at around the two-furlong pole before staying on. A stiffer track probably suits him better. Official explanation: jockey said gelding was denied a clear run
Patavellian(IRE) has not won since 2005 and has been racing mainly over 6f of late, but he produced a decent staying-on effort that suggests he may yet be able to end that long losing sequence.
Hotham, 9lb better off with the winner for four and a half lengths at Catterick, ran another decent race from a high draw, having tracked the early leader under the stands' rail.
Indian Trail, who has not won since September last year, has dropped 21lb this season and was staying on at the finish.
Piscean(USA), racing from 3lb out of the handicap, did well from a low draw on ground softer than he may prefer.
Cheveton lost his chance with a slow start and there was no way back in this dash. (op 13-2)
Hamish McGonagall, who won the big sprint at Musselburgh, showed his usual pace out in the centre but was away from the main action and faded.
Spirit Of Sharjah(IRE) was a useful juvenile but had appeared to lose his way this term. However, he is back with his original trainer and gave encouragement that he may be able to rediscover some of that old ability, as he ran better than the placings suggest, having been denied a run on more than one occasion.
Turn On The Style Official explanation: jockey said gelding reared as the gates opened

6972 RACINGPOST.COM STKS (REGISTERED AS THE DONCASTER STAKES) (LISTED RACE) 6f

3:00 (3:03) (Class 1) 2-Y-O

£23,704 (£8,964; £4,480; £2,240) **Stalls** High

Form — RPR

1403 **1** **Imperial Guest**[23] 6426 2-9-1 89.............. TonyCulhane 12 — 98
(G G Margarson) *in rr: hdwy 2f out: led jst ins fnl f: hld on towards fin* **50/1**

221 **2** ½ **Enderby Spirit (GR)**[24] 6389 2-9-1 83.............. PaulMulrennan 5 — 97
(B Smart) *trckd ldrs: chal jst ins fnl f: nt qckn towards fin* **14/1**

5136 **3** ½ **Absent Pleasure (USA)**[11] 6717 2-9-1 95.............. MJKinane 2 — 95
(B J Meehan) *hld up in rr: hdwy on outer 2f out: upsides ins fnl f: no ex nr fin* **14/1**

3611 **4** 2¼ **Noble Storm (USA)**[19] 6533 2-9-1 88.............. GrahamGibbons 9 — 88
(E S McMahon) *w ldrs: led over 2f out: hdd jst ins fnl f: wknd towards fin* **16/1**

1 **5** 1 **Dark Mischief**[138] 2893 2-9-1 85.............. DaneO'Neill 6 — 85
(H Candy) *s.i.s: in rr: styd on fnl 2f: nt rch ldrs* **10/1**[3]

1202 **6** 1½ **Favourite Girl (IRE)**[21] 6483 2-8-10 104.............. DavidAllan 1 — 76
(T D Easterby) *chsd ldrs on outer: wknd appr fnl f* **7/1**[2]

010 **7** 2 **Spiritofthewest (IRE)**[14] 6644 2-9-1 89.............. JohnEgan 4 — 75
(S Parr) *mid-div: effrt over 2f out: fdd over 1f out* **50/1**

01 **8** ½ **Hartley**[35] 6110 2-9-1 0.............. PhilipRobinson 13 — 73
(J D Bethell) *sn outpcd and in rr: kpt on fnl 2f: nvr on terms* **14/1**

2141 **9** 4 **Kingswinford (IRE)**[16] 6603 2-9-1 80.............. RobertWinston 10 — 61
(P D Evans) *mid-div: effrt over 2f out: lost pl over 1f out* **66/1**

1303 **10** 1¼ **Carnaby Haggerston (IRE)**[11] 6717 2-9-1 82..............(b[1]) JoeFanning 7 — 58
(K A Ryan) *led early: chsd ldrs: wknd appr fnl f* **66/1**

2332 **11** 14 **Sayif (IRE)**[22] 6442 2-9-1 118.............. JamieSpencer 8 — 16
(P W Chapple-Hyam) *sn led: hdd over 2f out: sn lost pl and eased* **4/6**[1]

1m 13.6s **Going Correction** +0.125s/f (Good) **11 Ran SP% 114.4**
Speed ratings (Par 103): **105,104,103,100,99 97,94,94,88,87 68**
toteswinger: 1&2 £35.10, 1&3 £52.00, 2&3 £16.20. CSF £614.88 TOTE £62.50: £9.70, £3.30, £3.80; EX 717.10 TRIFECTA Not won..
Owner John Guest **Bred** John Guest Racing Ltd **Trained** Newmarket, Suffolk
■ Able Master and La Brigitte were both withdrawn after giving trouble at the start. Rule 4 does not apply.

FOCUS
This Listed race often goes to an improver from one of the major yards.

NOTEBOOK
Imperial Guest took full advantage of the below-par effort of the favourite. Held up off the pace, he came through to lead inside the final furlong but had to be driven out to score. He has done well for the yard, having finished third in a sales race on his previous start, but the form of this race looks ordinary for the grade.
Enderby Spirit(GR), a winner over 5f on easy ground but a well-beaten second on his previous try at 6f, put up a decent effort and did not go down without a fight. He looks the sort to make up into a decent sprinter next season. (op 16-1)
Absent Pleasure(USA), who had not gone on since he beat the high-class Huntdown when winning his maiden, bounced back with a decent effort from off the pace. (op 12-1 tchd 16-1)
Noble Storm(USA), a dual Warwick nursery winner on soft ground, continued his progression but, after having every chance, was outpaced in the last furlong.
Dark Mischief was the least experienced runner but his win on his debut over 6f on fast ground in June had worked out well, with the next four home scoring since. He ran quite well after this long break. (op 13-2 tchd 6-1)
Favourite Girl(IRE), who had the second-highest official rating after being narrowly beaten in Ripon and Redcar Listed races, had her chance but had nothing more to give in the last two furlongs. (op 10-1)
Spiritofthewest(IRE) Official explanation: jockey said colt hung both ways
Carnaby Haggerston(IRE) probably ran too free in the first-time blinkers. (op 50-1)
Sayif(IRE) had what looked on paper something of a penalty kick, as he had been placed in the July Stakes, Vintage Stakes, Mill Reef Stakes and Middle Park and had plenty in hand judged on official ratings. He started odds-on and set off in front but was headed and dropped out quickly before the two-furlong pole, suggesting something was amiss. Official explanation: trainer had no explanation for the poor form shown (op 5-6)

6973 RACING POST TROPHY (GROUP 1) (ENTIRE COLTS & FILLIES) 1m (S)

3:35 (3:37) (Class 1) 2-Y-O

£122,623 (£46,483; £23,263; £11,599; £5,810; £2,916) **Stalls** High

Form — RPR

012 **1** **Crowded House**[21] 6474 2-9-0 98.............. JamieSpencer 10 — 121+
(B J Meehan) *lw: hld up in rr: hdwy and swtchd rt over 1f out: rdn and str run ent fnl f: sn hung bdly lft: led ins fnl f and sprinted clr* **7/1**[3]

1431 **2** 3½ **Jukebox Jury (IRE)**[28] 6267 2-9-0 112.............. RoystonFfrench 3 — 112+
(M Johnston) *hld up: n.m.r and outpcd wl over 2f out: sn rdn and gd hdwy to chal over 1f out: drvn and edgd rt appr fnl f: ev ch whn bmpd ins fnl f: kpt on: no ch w wnr* **2/1**[1]

1 **3** nk **Skanky Biscuit**[16] 6604 2-9-0 0.............. DBonilla 6 — 111
(B J Meehan) *hld up in rr: gd hdwy over 2f out: chsd ldrs over 1f out: rdn to ld ent fnl f: drvn: bmpd and hdd ins fnl f: kpt on same pce* **16/1**

0 **4** 3½ **Set Sail (IRE)**[87] 4517 2-9-0 0.............. SMLevey 14 — 103
(A P O'Brien, Ire) *rangy: led: rdn along over 2f out: drvn over 1f out: hdd ent fnl f: sn wknd* **66/1**

152 **5** 1 **Courageous (IRE)**[44] 5825 2-9-0 96.............. TedDurcan 7 — 101
(B Smart) *hld up towards rr: stdy hdwy over 2f out: rdn to chse ldrs whn hmpd appr fnl f: kpt on* **28/1**

0232 **6** 2 **Roman Glory (IRE)**[9] 6745 2-9-0 82.............. RobertWinston 12 — 96?
(B J Meehan) *chsd ldr: effrt 3f out: sn rdn along: drvn wl over 1f out and grad wknd appr fnl f* **100/1**

1202 **7** nk **Weald Park (USA)**[14] 6647 2-9-0 105.............. PatDobbs 1 — 96
(R Hannon) *hld up and bhd tl styd on fnl 2f: nvr a factor* **33/1**

110 **8** 1 **Sri Putra**[21] 6474 2-9-0 106.............. PhilipRobinson 2 — 93
(M A Jarvis) *lw: in tch: hdwy to chse ldrs on outer 3f out: rdn along over 2f out and sn wknd* **9/1**

1 **9** ¾ **Red Spider**[33] 6165 2-9-0 0.............. JimmyFortune 9 — 92
(J H M Gosden) *in tch: hdwy on outer over 3f out: chsd ldrs over 2f out: sn rdn: hung lft and wknd appr last* **8/1**

4 **10** *shd* **Indian Ocean (IRE)**[41] 5946 2-9-0 0 .... WMLordan 11 92
(A P O'Brien, Ire) *cmpt: trckd ldrs: effrt 2f out: sn rdn and edgd lft: btn whn n.m.r over 1f out* **14/1**

3 **11** *1 1/4* **Masterofthehorse (IRE)**[27] 6316 2-9-0 0 .... JAHeffernan 8 89
(A P O'Brien, Ire) *chsd ldrs: rdn along 2f out: sn drvn and wknd* **11/4**[2]

3144 **12** *3/4* **Midnight Cruiser (IRE)**[8] 6779 2-9-0 86 .... DaneO'Neill 15 87
(R Hannon) *t.k.h: hld up effrt and sme hdwy on outer 1/2-way: rdn along 3f out and sn btn* **100/1**

0 **13** *3* **Gibb River (IRE)**[35] 6122 2-9-0 0 .... JoeFanning 13 81
(P W Chapple-Hyam) *a towards rr* **66/1**

61 **14** *1 3/4* **Marching Time**[38] 6029 2-9-0 81 .... MJKinane 4 77
(Sir Michael Stoute) *chsd ldrs: rdn along over 2f out and sn wknd* **20/1**

1301 **15** *23* **Rising Prospect**[35] 6101 2-9-0 85 .... PJMcDonald 5 26
(G M Moore) *chsd ldrs: rdn along wl over 2f out: sn hung lft and wknd* **100/1**

1m 39.17s (-0.13) **Going Correction** +0.125s/f (Good) **15** Ran SP% **123.3**
Speed ratings (Par 109): **105,101,101,97,96 94,94,93,92,92 91,90,87,85,62**
toteswinger: 1&2 £4.80, 1&3 £24.70, 2&3 £11.80. CSF £20.78 TOTE £8.40: £2.50, £1.50, £3.50; EX 23.60 Trifecta £583.30 Pool: £24,832.90 - 31.50 winning units..

Owner J P Reddam, Mrs C Burrell & J Harvey **Bred** Car Colston Hall Stud **Trained** Manton, Wilts

FOCUS

A major juvenile contest that has produced five Classic winners, including three Derby winners, this century and another one is not out of the question after the success of Crowded House. He is rated the joint top juvenile of the year with Bushranger on RPRs, and the best winner of this race in the last 15 years.

NOTEBOOK

Crowded House ◆, outstanding in the paddock and a winner over 1m on Polytrack, had been runner-up in a valuable sales race when dropped to 7f last time (form that was later given even more kudos by the winner of that contest Donativum taking the Breeders' Cup Turf Juvenile). He travelled well under restraint, but just when the race was beginning in earnest Spencer had to switch him around two rivals to get a run. However, once in the clear, he picked up in impressive fashion but swerved left, giving his stablemate Skanky Biscuit a broadside in the process, which somewhat surprisingly did not even earn his rider a ban. Still, he strode clear in impressive fashion and was quoted at between 12-1 and 20-1 for the Derby and was offered at less for the 2000 Guineas, although his first outing next year is likely to be in the Dante Stakes. His sire is an influence for stamina, but he is out of a Woodman mare, so staying the Derby trip is not totally guaranteed. He looks one of the major contenders at this stage, though. (op 15-2 tchd 13-2)

Jukebox Jury(IRE), the winner of the Royal Lodge, offers a link to the form of Naaqoos through Longchamp runner-up Milanais. He set a reasonable standard but looked in trouble when caught on heels and having to be ridden along three furlongs out. However, he picked up well and had every chance going into the last furlong but, although he suffered slightly due to the antics of the winner, he would not have beaten him. (op 3-1)

Skanky Biscuit was one of the least experienced in the line-up. The half-brother to a couple of multiple winners was coming into the race having won a maiden on his debut but handled the step up in class well. Keen to post, he travelled well off the pace, came to have every chance inside the last furlong and arguably may have been second had he not been side-swiped by his stablemate Crowded House. He may not be quite in the winner's class but was clear of the remainder and on this evidence looks well up to winning Group races next season. (op 14-1)

Set Sail(IRE), a moderate walker, did best of the Aidan O'Brien trio, having made the running, and, although brushed aside by the first three, kept on quite well to hold off the rest.

Courageous(IRE) had finished ahead of Midnight Cruiser over 7f at the St Leger meeting here and confirmed the form over this longer trip, but never troubled the principals. (op 25-1)

Roman Glory(IRE), the Meehan third string, also earned prize-money and put up a fair effort for a maiden. The effort could blow his handicap mark, though.

Weald Park(USA) had been runner-up in a Group 2 but had a lot to find with the winner on Newmarket sales race form. However, he was beaten more than twice as far and is not up to this level.

Sri Putra, the Solario winner, was another who was probably out of his depth, having been well behind today's winner in the Newmarket sales race. He was too free and did not get much cover, and failed to confirm previous running with Weald Park. (op 12-1)

Red Spider was taking a big step up from his winning debut in a Polytrack maiden but showed up until edging left and weakening in the last furlong. (op 9-1)

Masterofthehorse(IRE), who looked very hard trained, travelled well enough in the wake of his stablemate Set Sail but then failed to find anything under pressure. (op 3-1)

Marching Time was another taking a big step up in class, having just got home in a Yarmouth maiden, and did not help his chances by running free early. (op 16-1)

6974 RICHARD (BONEY) JAMES HONE MEMORIAL H'CAP 1m 4f

4:10 (4:10) (Class 3) (0-95,93) 3-Y-O+ £9,714 (£2,890; £1,444; £721) Stalls Low

Form RPR

210 **1** **Times Vital (IRE)**[18] 6563 3-8-5 **82** .... DeanMcKeown 6 93+
(E J O'Neill) *hld up towards rr: hdwy on outside 3f out: edgd lft and led over 1f out: styd on strly* **9/2**[3]

6102 **2** *2 3/4* **Voice Coach (IRE)**[19] 6536 3-9-2 **93** .... MJKinane 10 99+
(Sir Michael Stoute) *prom: effrt: hung lft and outpcd over 3f out: styd on fnl 2f: tk 2nd nr fin* **5/2**[1]

1300 **3** *nk* **Hunting Country**[63] 5279 3-8-11 **88** .... RoystonFfrench 5 94
(M Johnston) *led: qcknd over 3f out: hdd over 1f out: styd on same pce* **15/2**

2150 **4** *1 3/4* **Full Speed (GER)**[86] 4565 3-8-6 **83** .... PJMcDonald 1 86
(G A Swinbank) *trckd ldrs: chal over 1f out: kpt on one pce* **20/1**

0015 **5** *3/4* **Taikoo**[25] 6355 3-8-2 **79** oh3 .... JimmyQuinn 9 81
(H Morrison) *chsd ldrs: drvn over 3f out: one pce* **16/1**

0441 **6** *3 1/4* **Night Hour (IRE)**[80] 4742 6-9-9 **93** .... TedDurcan 13 90
(Saeed Bin Suroor) *trckd ldrs: chal 3f out: wknd over 1f out: eased* **10/3**[2]

4200 **7** *1 1/4* **Ella Woodcock (IRE)**[9] 6763 4-8-10 **80** ....(p) DavidAllan 8 75
(E J Alston) *in rr: effrt over 3f out: edgd rt: nvr nr ldrs* **33/1**

2005 **8** *shd* **Birkside**[12] 6698 5-9-2 **86** ....(p) JoeFanning 12 81
(K A Ryan) *sn trcking ldrs: effrt over 2f out: wkng whn hmpd over 1f out* **14/1**

1615 **9** *3/4* **Amanda Carter**[29] 6238 4-9-1 **85** .... PaulHanagan 2 78
(R A Fahey) *t.k.h in midfield: effrt 3f out: sn lost pl* **12/1**

5404 **10** *1 1/2* **Prince Sabaah (IRE)**[21] 6479 4-8-11 **81** .... PatDobbs 3 72
(R Hannon) *mid-div: lost pl over 2f out* **10/1**

200- **11** *5* **Realism (FR)**[176] 6759 8-8-13 **83** ....(t) PaulMulrennan 4 66
(M W Easterby) *in rr: effrt over 3f out: lost pl 2f out* **40/1**

0500 **12** *2 1/4* **New Beginning (IRE)**[22] 6444 4-8-10 **80** oh5 ow1 .... RobertWinston 7 59
(Mrs S Lamyman) *s.s: effrt over 3f out: sn lost pl* **40/1**

2m 35.61s (0.51) **Going Correction** +0.125s/f (Good)
WFA 3 from 4yo+ 7lb **12** Ran SP% **123.5**
Speed ratings (Par 107): **103,101,100,99,99 97,96,96,95,94 91,89**
toteswinger: 1&2 £3.60, 1&3 £9.10, 2&3 £6.50. CSF £16.29 CT £85.33 TOTE £7.00: £1.90, £1.70, £3.40; EX 24.60 Trifecta £433.30 Part won. £585.59 - 0.80 winning units..

Owner G A Lucas **Bred** Miss Louise Fitzgerald **Trained** Averham Park, Notts

■ A winner for Dean McKeown shortly after being warned off for four years by the BHA.

FOCUS

A good handicap that has been dominated by raiders from southern yards this century but the sequence was ended by his relatively local trainer. There were several who look held by the handicapper now but the winner remains progressive.

NOTEBOOK

Times Vital(IRE) scored for relatively local trainer Eoghan O'Neill, understandably much to the delight of his rider, who had been given a four-year-ban earlier in the week which is due to come into force in the near future. The colt had looked progressive until disappointing at Leicester last time, which suggested he may have been over the top. However, that was clearly not the case as he came through travelling well and, after hitting the front inside the last, had enough in hand to prick his ears and idle before the line. He will go up a little for this but, providing he continues to progress, could give connections a lot of fun in good handicaps next season, and the Ebor does not look an unrealistic long-term target. (op 7-1 tchd 15-2)

Voice Coach(IRE), a lightly raced half-brother to the high-class Scottish Stage, was stepping up in trip, having been raised 6lb from his previous outing. He had every chance and seemed to get the trip but had no answer to the winner's challenge. He is another who will do better next year. (op 2-1 tchd 11-4)

Hunting Country, a dual 1m2f winner on a sound surface, made the running on this step up in trip and did not do much wrong. He was racing from 7lb above his latest winning mark and looks in the Handicapper's grip. (op 10-1)

Full Speed(GER) travelled nicely into the race but did not pick up as well as may have been expected and is another who looks held by the assessor. (op 16-1)

Taikoo, a 1m4f winner on soft, had the cheekpieces left off this time and seemed to run his race despite being 3lb out of the handicap.

Night Hour(IRE), who took the race last year for John Gosden, was 7lb higher and that was enough to stop him. (op 4-1 tchd 3-1)

Birkside was 2lb better off with Night Hour on recent Pontefract form and was back to his latest winning mark. He looked a big threat two furlongs from home before fading and is happier on a faster surface. (op 10-1)

Realism(FR), a winner over hurdles since he last ran on the Flat, was wearing a first-time tongue tie on this first start since May and this should have blown away the cobwebs before he returns to jumping. (op 50-1)

6975 1STSECURITYSOLUTIONS.CO.UK CONDITIONS STKS 7f

4:45 (4:45) (Class 2) 3-Y-O+

£12,462 (£3,732; £1,866; £934; £466; £234) Stalls High

Form RPR

0100 **1** **Mr Aviator (USA)**[31] 6201 4-8-11 106 .... DaneO'Neill 5 106
(R Hannon) *hld up: swtchd rt and hdwy over 2f out: rdn to chse ldrs over 1f out: styd on strly u.p ent fnl f: led fnl 100yds and sn clr* **13/2**

6245 **2** *1 3/4* **Welsh Emperor (IRE)**[21] 6496 9-9-4 112 ....(b) MickyFenton 7 108
(T P Tate) *led: rdn along 2f out: drvn over 1f out: hdd and no ex fnl 100yds* **6/1**[3]

3036 **3** *3/4* **Red Alert Day**[107] 3880 3-8-9 105 .... JohnEgan 2 99
(S A Callaghan) *in tch: hdwy over 2f out: rdn to chse ldr over 1f out: drvn ent fnl f and kpt on same pce* **8/1**

0060 **4** *nk* **Protector (SAF)**[21] 6484 7-8-11 95 ....(t) RobertWinston 9 98
(A G Foster) *in tch: hdwy over 2f out: rdn to chse ldr over 1f out: sn drvn and one pce ent fnl f* **11/1**

400- **5** *1* **Quito (IRE)**[470] 3506 11-8-11 100 ....(b) PaulMulrennan 11 95
(Mrs R A Carr) *dwlt: hld up in rr: hdwy over 2f out: rdn over 1f out: styd on ins fnl f: nrst fin* **28/1**

630 **6** *3/4* **Kay Gee Be (IRE)**[29] 6249 4-8-11 93 .... JoeFanning 4 97+
(W Jarvis) *hld up in tch: hdwy over 2f out: effrt whn hmpd and lost pl wl over 1f out: swtchd rt and rdn appr fnl f: styd on wl towards fin* **12/1**

1 **7** *1/2* **Sirocco Breeze**[18] 6566 3-8-9 86 .... TedDurcan 6 92
(Saeed Bin Suroor) *plld hrd: chsd ldrs: rdn along over 2f out: edgd lft wl over 1f out: sn drvn and one pce* **3/1**[1]

0600 **8** *3 3/4* **Aeroplane**[21] 6484 5-8-11 92 .... JamieSpencer 8 82
(S A Callaghan) *hld up: hdwy on outer over 2f out: rdn and edgd rt wl over 1f out: sn drvn and btn appr last* **10/1**

0050 **9** *7* **Sion Hill (IRE)**[33] 6178 7-9-0 55 ....(p) RoystonFfrench 1 66?
(John A Harris) *cl up: rdn along 1/2-way: sn wknd* **150/1**

0000 **10** *3/4* **Dabbers Ridge (IRE)**[35] 6104 6-9-4 92 .... PhilipRobinson 3 68
(B W Hills) *chsd ldrs: rdn along over 2f out: sn wknd* **12/1**

0011 **11** *2 1/4* **Plum Pudding (IRE)**[8] 6783 5-8-11 100 .... PatDobbs 10 55
(R Hannon) *dwlt: sn cl up: rdn along over 2f out: sn wknd* **7/2**[2]

1m 27.05s (0.75) **Going Correction** +0.125s/f (Good)
WFA 3 from 4yo+ 2lb **11** Ran SP% **122.9**
Speed ratings (Par 109): **100,98,97,96,95 94,94,89,81,81 78**
toteswinger: 1&2 £9.00, 1&3 £12.00, 2&3 £7.20. CSF £47.50 TOTE £8.10: £2.50, £2.50, £2.30; EX 54.70 Trifecta £384.30 Part won. Pool: £519.42 - 0.30 winning units..

Owner Mrs Sue Brendish **Bred** Dr Tom Keenan & Dr H G White Jr **Trained** East Everleigh, Wilts

■ Stewards' Enquiry : Ted Durcan one-day ban: failed to ride out to finish on colt who could have been placed (Nov 8)

FOCUS

A good conditions event not far off Listed level and dominated by the pair with the highest official marks. The form is messy though with the principals not at their best. The field raced down the centre of the track early but migrated towards the stands' rail in the closing stages.

NOTEBOOK

Mr Aviator(USA), the Royal Hunt Cup winner and a 1m2f winner on Polytrack, had not run over a trip this short since his debut. However, he appeared to have no problem with the pace and moved up smoothly to challenge the long-time leader before settling the issue with little fuss. He is a quality performer at his best and connections may be tempted to take him to Dubai for the carnival, as he is very adaptable regarding ground conditions. Official explanation: trainer had no explanation regarding the apparent improvement in form. (tchd 15-2)

Welsh Emperor(IRE), a 7f specialist who is best on soft ground, has been contesting Group races recently. He made the running as usual on this drop in grade and had most of his rivals in trouble at the two-furlong pole, but he had no answer when the winner ranged alongside. (op 11-2)

Red Alert Day, who has been placed in Listed and Group 3 races this season, put up a decent effort against his elders on his first run since July. He is another who handles most surfaces and is well up to winning a similar event. Official explanation: jockey said colt hung right (op 7-1)

Protector(SAF)'s form was mostly at shorter but he seemed to get the trip well enough and, having run at the Dubai carnival in 2007, could be in line for a return this winter. (op 14-1)

Quito(IRE), a multiple Listed winner who retired from racing in July 2007, was not suited by the quiet life and seemed to relish the return to the track, staying on from the rear in a manner which suggests the ability remains. (op 25-1)

Kay Gee Be(IRE) has not won for over a year but is still 5lb above his latest winning mark and had a difficult task judged on official ratings. (tchd 10-1)

Sirocco Breeze, who only made his debut at the beginning of the month, found this too much for him against seasoned campaigners at this stage of his career. Official explanation: jockey said colt ran too freely (op 7-2 tchd 4-1)

Aeroplane, struggling for form since the spring, moved up to have his chance before his effort petered out. Official explanation: jockey said horse hung right (op 12-1)

Plum Pudding(IRE) only wins over 7f and 1m at Newmarket and, although he came into the race in good form, he could not get an uncontested lead with Welsh Emperor in the race and it was no surprise to see him fade late on. (op 9-2)

6976 PERTEMPS PEOPLE DEVELOPMENT "HANDS AND HEELS" APPRENTICE SERIES FINAL H'CAP 7f

5:15 (5:15) (Class 4) (0-85,85) 3-Y-O **£6,476** (£1,927; £963; £481) **Stalls** High

Form RPR

0050 **1** **Quest For Success (IRE)**[6] 6842 3-8-9 **76** .... LanceBetts 10 83+
(R A Fahey) *hld up in mid-div: hdwy stands' side over 2f out: r.o to ld fnl 75yds* **13/2**

3116 **2** *1* **Internationaldebut (IRE)**[14] 6663 3-9-1 **82** .... KylieManser 1 86
(S Parr) *led after 1f: shkn up over 1f out: hdd towards fin* **6/1**[3]

1350 **3** *2 1/4* **Pavershooz**[29] 6239 3-9-1 **82** .... (t) NSLawes 6 80
(N Wilson) *trckd ldrs: t.k.h: wnt 2nd over 1f out: styd on same pce* **14/1**

0040 **4** *hd* **Mey Blossom**[3] 6900 3-8-8 **75** .... (p) DeclanCannon 5 72
(R M Whitaker) *chsd ldrs: one pce appr fnl f* **11/1**

4403 **5** *1* **Kiwi Bay**[12] 6710 3-8-13 **83** .... JohnCavanagh(3) 9 78+
(M Dods) *in rr and sn pushed along: hmpd after 2f: styd on fnl 2f: nt rch ldrs* **5/1**[2]

5464 **6** *1 1/4* **Astrodonna**[23] 6417 3-8-5 **72** .... AshleyMorgan 11 63+
(M H Tompkins) *hld up towards rr: hdwy stands' side over 2f out: kpt on: nvr trbld ldrs* **4/1**[1]

00-0 **7** *1 1/2* **Captain Macarry (IRE)**[11] 6724 3-8-4 **71** oh7 .... JamieKyne 7 58
(B Smart) *mid-div: hmpd after 2f: sn drvn along and outpcd* **20/1**

0000 **8** *1 3/4* **Carleton**[77] 4842 3-9-1 **85** .... DebraEngland(3) 8 68
(W J Musson) *s.s: swtchd stands' side and sme hdwy 4f out: wknd over 1f out* **12/1**

0005 **9** *1 1/4* **Always A Rock (IRE)**[25] 6352 3-8-11 **81** .... (b) MatthewLawson(3) 3 60
(M Johnston) *chsd ldrs on outer: wknd over 1f out* **6/1**[3]

1240 **10** *4* **Rubirosa (IRE)**[70] 5102 3-9-3 **84** .... DeanHeslop 2 52
(M Dods) *hmpd and stmbld s: effrt on outer over 2f out: lost pl over 1f out* **16/1**

0412 **11** *9* **I Confess**[10] 6736 3-8-4 **71** oh3 .... (b) CharlesEddery 4 15
(P D Evans) *led 1f: lost pl 2f out: sn bhd* **7/1**

1m 28.37s (2.07) **Going Correction** +0.125s/f (Good) **11 Ran SP% 124.4**

Speed ratings (Par 103): **93,91,89,89,87 86,84,82,81,76 66**

toteswinger: 1&2 £11.90, 1&3 £25.30, 2&3 £18.70. CSF £48.14 CT £552.67 TOTE £8.20: £3.00, £2.50, £5.70; EX 70.70 TRIFECTA Not won. Place 6 £534.41, Place 5 £226.05..

Owner Rob Lloyd Racing Limited **Bred** Desmond Monaghan **Trained** Musley Bank, N Yorks

FOCUS

A hands-and-heels handicap for relatively inexperienced apprentices. It was run at a steady pace. The winner was slightly better than the bare form with the second showing his best form race since last year's Racing Post Trophy.

T/Jkpt: Not won. T/Plt: £1,055.40 to a £1 stake. Pool: £106,193.21. 73.45 winning tickets. T/Qpdt: £154.30 to a £1 stake. Pool: £4,777.90. 22.90 winning tickets. JR

6600 NEWBURY (L-H)

Saturday, October 25

OFFICIAL GOING: Good to soft (soft in places and in back straight) changing to soft after race 1 (1.10)

Wind: Moderate, across Weather: Mainly cloudy

6977 HILDON E B F MAIDEN STKS (DIV I) 1m (S)

1:10 (1:14) (Class 4) 2-Y-O **£5,504** (£1,637; £818; £408) **Stalls** High

Form RPR

36 **1** **Monitor Closely (IRE)**[21] 6474 2-9-3 .... AlanMunro 12 83+
(P W Chapple-Hyam) *prom: led over 3f out: edgd rt wl over 1f out: drvn out* **8/11**[1]

2 *1* **London Bridge** 2-9-3 .... RobertHavlin 11 83+
(J H M Gosden) *hld up in midfield: briefly hmpd over 2f out: smooth hdwy whn carried rt and nt clr run fr wl over 1f out: swtchd lft: r.o wl: promising* **7/1**[2]

0 **3** *1 1/2* **All Guns Firing (IRE)**[11] 6720 2-9-3 .... NCallan 13 77
(M A Jarvis) *chsd ldrs: rdn over 2f out: carried rt by wnr wl over 1f out: kpt on same pce* **18/1**

0 **4** *hd* **Rupestrian**[7] 6808 2-9-3 .... GregFairley 4 77
(M Johnston) *in tch: drvn along over 3f out: chsd ldrs 2f out: one pce fnl f* **40/1**

5 *2 1/4* **Sonning Gate** 2-9-3 .... GeorgeBaker 14 74+
(D R C Elsworth) *hld up last wl off the pce: swtchd lft to far side over 1f out: shkn up and r.o promisingly: gng on wl at fin* **66/1**

6 *nk* **Cherish The Moment (IRE)** 2-9-3 .... MichaelHills 5 71
(B W Hills) *bhd: gd hdwy fnl 2f: nrst fin: should improve* **20/1**

5 **7** *1/2* **Midnight Bay**[12] 6665 2-9-3 .... EdwardCreighton 16 70+
(M R Channon) *chsd ldrs: rdn whn hmpd on rail wl over 1f out: swtchd lft: one pce* **66/1**

5 **8** *1/2* **King's Song (IRE)**[11] 6715 2-9-3 .... CSoumillon 6 69
(Sir Michael Stoute) *in tch: effrt over 2f out: hrd rdn and one pce wl over 1f out, btn wn carried left ins fnl f* **8/1**[3]

0 **9** *1/2* **Brunston**[16] 6604 2-9-3 .... RichardHughes 3 68
(R Charlton) *mid-div: rdn over 3f out: sme hdwy over 1f out: wknd fnl f* **20/1**

35 **10** *1 1/2* **Red Junior**[16] 6597 2-9-3 .... DarryllHolland 8 64
(B J Meehan) *hld up in midfield: effrt and edged rt over 2f out: sn rdn and hld by ldrs* **12/1**

11 *1/2* **Rebel Swing** 2-9-3 .... MartinDwyer 10 63
(W R Muir) *dwlt: sn in mid-div: rdn and no imp whn hmpd over 1f out* **66/1**

0 **12** *nk* **Going For Gold**[16] 6604 2-8-12 .... SteveDrowne 17 58
(R Charlton) *hld up in midfield: outpcd wn hmpd and swtchd lft over 2f out: n.d after* **33/1**

13 *3/4* **Ultimate** 2-9-3 .... TravisBlock 9 61
(H Morrison) *pressed ldr: hrd rdn 2f out: wknd over 1f out* **66/1**

0 **14** *6* **Litenup (IRE)**[33] 6166 2-8-12 .... JamesDoyle 15 43
(A J Lidderdale) *led over 4f: wknd over 2f out* **100/1**

15 *6* **Save My Blushes** 2-9-3 .... RichardMullen 2 35
(C G Cox) *sn bhd and rdn along: n.d fr 1/2-way* **66/1**

16 *5* **Green Endeavour (CAN)** 2-9-3 .... JimCrowley 18 24
(Mrs A J Perrett) *s.s: a bhd: no ch fnl 3f* **50/1**

17 *11* **Almutawaazin** 2-9-3 .... RHills 1 —
(M P Tregoning) *a towards rr: drvn along and no ch fnl 3f* **20/1**

18 *33* **Mellow Mixture** 2-9-3 .... PatCosgrave 7 —
(R Hannon) *v.s.a: a towards rr: no ch fnl 3f* **66/1**

1m 47.37s (7.67) **Going Correction** +1.00s/f (Soft) **18 Ran SP% 126.0**

Speed ratings (Par 97): **101,100,98,98,96 95,95,94,94,92 92,91,91,85,79 74,63,30**

toteswinger: 1&2 £3.50, 1&3 £6.80, 2&3 £3.50. CSF £5.08 TOTE £1.80: £1.70, £2.60, £3.90; EX 10.40.

Owner Lawrie Inman **Bred** Cliveden Stud Ltd **Trained** Newmarket, Suffolk

■ Stewards' Enquiry : Alan MunroM three-day ban: careless riding (Nov 8-10)

Robert HavlinM one-day ban: careless riding (Nov 8)

FOCUS

The official ground was amended to soft all round following this contest. An interesting maiden, though something of a rough race, and a longer-term view should be taken over many of these. The field raced centre-to-stands' side.

NOTEBOOK

Monitor Closely(IRE), who boasted the best form, having finished a decent sixth in the Tattersalls Timeform Million last time, was always up with the pace, and although he tended to edge over to the stands' rail towards the latter stages, he kept on finding what was required. Whether he would have scored had the runner-up not got into all sorts of trouble is doubtful. Connections believe he prefers better ground and he may now go for the Group 1 Criterium de Saint-Cloud over an extra 2f next month. (op 4-5 tchd 5-6 in places)

London Bridge ◆, a half-brother to three winners on the Flat at up to 1m4f plus the high-class hurdler Upgrade, travelled well in midfield before trying to get involved coming to the last 2f, but he then ran into trouble and was even more inconvenienced when hampered against the stands' rail when the eventual winner carried All Guns Firing across him passing the furlong pole. Considering how close he managed to get, despite all that, suggests he was probably the best horse in the race and we should be hearing plenty more of him. (tchd 8-1)

All Guns Firing(IRE), who looked the stable's second string when in mid-division in a Leicester maiden won by a stable companion on debut, was always up with the pace, and although the winner did him few favours 1f out, he did look third-best on merit. (op 20-1 tchd 16-1)

Rupestrian, well beaten on his Catterick debut seven days earlier, improved a good deal on that and was always close to the pace. Despite coming off the bridle a fair way out, he kept on well until tending to hang away to his left in the latter stages. He is going the right way and there are races to be won with him. (op 50-1)

Sonning Gate ◆, a half-brother to Resplendent Alpha, was switched off out the back before trying to get closer against the stands' rail, but when that route became blocked he was forced to switch out very wide and was noted finishing very strongly at the line. He should come on for this and will make his mark in due course. (op 50-1)

Cherish The Moment(IRE) ◆ was well behind early before finishing in eye-catching style on the wide outside and is another to keep in mind. (op 25-1)

Midnight Bay, well held behind previous winners in a Bath novice event on debut, was another to meet a bit of trouble in running but looked to have run his race by then. (tchd 80-1)

King's Song(IRE) seemed to have every chance and didn't appear to step up from his Leicester debut as might have been expected. (op 9-1)

Rebel Swing ◆ shaped with a bit of promise on this debut and this half-brother to two winners, including one over hurdles, should improve with racing. (op 100-1)

6978 HILDON E B F MAIDEN STKS (DIV II) 1m (S)

1:40 (1:48) (Class 4) 2-Y-O **£5,504** (£1,637; £818; £408) **Stalls** High

Form RPR

1 **Your Old Pal** 2-9-3 .... ShaneKelly 9 98+
(J Noseda) *hld up in midfield: hdwy to trck ldr 2f out: led 1f out: rdn clr* **33/1**

2 *6* **Classically (IRE)** 2-9-3 .... SteveDrowne 7 85
(R Charlton) *dwlt: bhd: gd hdwy over 1f out: r.o to take 2nd nr fin: nt rch wnr: should improve* **16/1**

4 **3** *nk* **Clowance House**[24] 6397 2-9-3 .... RichardMullen 16 84
(R Charlton) *chsd ldrs: rdn over 2f out: one pce appr fnl f* **3/1**[2]

2 **4** *3/4* **Kings Destiny**[17] 6581 2-9-3 .... NCallan 6 82
(M A Jarvis) *led: rdn and hdd 1f out: wknd fnl f* **5/4**[1]

5 *3* **Non Dom (IRE)** 2-9-3 .... DarryllHolland 4 76
(H Morrison) *prom: hrd rdn 2f out: wknd over 1f out* **25/1**

5 **6** *1* **Simon Gray**[24] 6397 2-9-3 .... RichardHughes 13 74
(R Hannon) *hld up in rr: c to stands' rail and gd hdwy fr 2f out: no further prog fnl f* **11/2**[3]

0 **7** *1* **Lennie Briscoe (IRE)**[19] 6539 2-9-3 .... GeorgeBaker 10 71
(S Kirk) *t.k.h: sn stdd towards rr: promising hdwy 2f out: wandered and btn fr over 1f out* **12/1**

0 **8** *1 1/4* **Mystic Prince**[16] 6602 2-9-3 .... DPMcDonogh 5 69
(B J Meehan) *in tch: hrd rdn and edged rt 2f out: wknd over 1f out* **66/1**

0 **9** *2 1/4* **Rowan Tiger**[16] 6604 2-9-3 .... PatCosgrave 2 64
(J R Boyle) *restless in stalls: dwlt: bhd and pushed along: sme late hdwy* **100/1**

0 **10** *1/2* **Newlyn Art**[12] 6702 2-9-3 .... RobertHavlin 11 63
(D R C Elsworth) *in tch: hrd rdn over 2f out: sn outpcd* **100/1**

11 *1* **Saint Chapelle (IRE)** 2-8-12 .... JimCrowley 17 55
(Mrs A J Perrett) *dwlt: sn in midfield: rdn over 3f out: sn outpcd* **33/1**

12 *1 1/4* **Woodlark Island (IRE)** 2-9-3 .... MartinDwyer 12 58
(M P Tregoning) *pressed ldr tl wknd over 2f out* **28/1**

13 *1 3/4* **Flapper (IRE)** 2-8-12 .... RHills 3 49
(J W Hills) *restless in stalls: mid-div: effrt over 2f out: wknd wl over 1f out* **40/1**

6 **14** *1 1/4* **Troubletimestwo (FR)**[11] 6715 2-9-3 .... TPQueally 15 51
(H J L Dunlop) *mid-div tl wknd 3f out: sn bhd* **50/1**

6 **15** *3* **Altimatum (USA)**[22] 6443 2-9-3 .... (t) AlanMunro 8 45
(P F I Cole) *prom 5f: sn lost pl* **20/1**

16 *dist* **Brooklyn Spirit** 2-9-3 .... AdamKirby 14 —
(C G Cox) *s.s and rdn early: a bhd: t.o 3f out: eased over 1f out* **33/1**

1m 46.07s (6.37) **Going Correction** +1.00s/f (Soft) **16 Ran SP% 127.2**

Speed ratings (Par 97): **108,102,101,100,97 96,95,94,92,91 90,89,87,86,83 —**

toteswinger: 1&2 £23.10, 1&3 £23.10, 2&3 £4.80. CSF £472.41 TOTE £32.90: £5.40, £3.40, £1.60; EX 499.90.

Owner Raffles Racing **Bred** Meon Valley Stud **Trained** Newmarket, Suffolk

FOCUS

Another interesting maiden, and again many of these will come into their own next season. However, the winning time was 1.3 seconds quicker than the first division, and it was won in devastating style.

NOTEBOOK

Your Old Pal ◆ ran right away from his rivals on this racecourse debut, having travelled like a dream throughout. Out of a half-sister to Mullins Bay and Stagecraft, he should get further and looks a very nice prospect for next season. (tchd 28-1)

Classically(IRE) ◆, who was weak in the market for this debut, did extremely well to come through and take second, as he was well behind early but stayed on very nicely towards the far side of the track in the latter stages. A 200,000gns half-brother to three winners, including the 1000 Guineas heroine Speciosa, he looks to have a bright future. (op 10-1)

Clowance House, who didn't get the best of runs when fourth on his Salisbury debut, raced close to the pace early but came off the bridle at halfway. To his credit, he kept plugging on and he should come into his own over middle distances next season. (op 4-1 tchd 9-2)

Kings Destiny, second to a runaway winner on his Nottingham debut, tried to make every yard but was keen enough in this ground and didn't get home. (op 11-8 tchd 11-10 & 6-4 in places)

Non Dom(IRE) ◆ showed up for a long way, but looked a little green on this debut, so he did well to hang in there for as long as did. A half-brother to five winners at up to 1m5f, he should do better with this experience under his belt and looks another for middle distances next season. (op 16-1)

Simon Gray, just behind Clowance House on his Salisbury debut, looked a possible danger when switched to make his effort up the stands' rail passing the 2f pole, but his effort soon flattened out. (op 8-1)

Lennie Briscoe(IRE) ran better than on his Windsor debut but looked very awkward inside the last 2f and may not have liked the ground. He may be one to watch out for when qualifying for a mark after one more run. Official explanation: jockey said colt hung right (op 16-1)

6979 MOUNTGRANGE STUD STKS (REGISTERED AS THE HORRIS HILL STAKES) (GROUP 3) (C&G) 7f (S)

2:10 (2:19) (Class 1) 2-Y-O

£28,385 (£10,760; £5,385; £2,685; £1,345; £675) Stalls High

Form				RPR
31	1		**Evasive**[22] 6438 2-8-12 90 ..... CSoumillon 2 (Sir Michael Stoute) *w ldr: led 4f out: drvn 3 l ahd over 1f out: tired fnl f: rdn out and jst lasted* **15/2**	109
2213	2	½	**Bonnie Charlie**[12] 6713 2-8-12 108 ..... RichardHughes 10 (R Hannon) *hld up in rr: hmpd over 2f out: gd hdwy to take 2nd ins fnl f: catching wnr at fin* **6/1**[3]	108
133	3	2 ¼	**Aahaykid (IRE)**[14] 6647 2-8-12 95 ..... FergusSweeney 6 (K R Burke) *hld up in midfield: effrt and swtchd rt over 2f out: styd on to take 3rd nr fin* **25/1**	102
0211	4	shd	**Rileyskeepingfaith**[14] 6647 2-8-12 101 ..... DarryllHolland 1 (M R Channon) *hld up towards rr: gd hdwy to dispute 2nd 2f out: one pce appr fnl f* **8/1**	102
0	5	4	**Splendorinthegrass (IRE)**[35] 6122 2-8-12 ..... SteveDrowne 11 (R Charlton) *s.s: hld up in rr of midfield: hdwy and prom 3f out: wknd over 1f out* **33/1**	92
3130	6	nk	**Jobe (USA)**[22] 6442 2-8-12 108 ..... NCallan 9 (K A Ryan) *chsd ldrs wd on stands' rail: disp 2nd 2f out: no ex 1f out* **10/1**	91
0101	7	hd	**Shampagne**[28] 6284 2-8-12 104 ..... MartinDwyer 13 (P F I Cole) *t.k.h early: held up in rr: rdn and sme hdwy 2f out: nvr rchd ldrs* **14/1**	91
2321	8	8	**Kingship Spirit (IRE)**[23] 6426 2-8-12 94 ..... ShaneKelly 4 (J Noseda) *t.k.h in midfield: effrt over 2f out: wknd wl over 1f out* **10/1**	71
2113	9	½	**Nasri**[21] 6474 2-8-12 96 ..... DPMcDonogh 3 (B J Meehan) *t.k.h: prom tl hrd rdn and wknd over 2f out* **10/3**[1]	69
1100	10	3 ¼	**Cry Of Freedom (USA)**[21] 6474 2-8-12 98 ..... (b[1]) GregFairley 12 (M Johnston) *prom: rdn 3f out: sn lost pl* **14/1**	61
01	11	1	**Bravo Echo**[11] 6714 2-8-12 ..... RichardMullen 8 (J H M Gosden) *sn led: hdd 4f out: wknd 2f out* **9/2**[2]	59
1120	12	10	**Lucky Redback (IRE)**[45] 5791 2-8-12 87 ..... JimCrowley 14 (R Hannon) *racd wd on stands' rail: bhd fnl 3f* **33/1**	34
1	13	2 ¾	**Folsomprisonblues (IRE)**[155] 2362 2-8-12 ..... ChrisCatlin 7 (E J O'Neill) *prom over 4f* **40/1**	27

1m 31.69s (5.99) **Going Correction** +1.00s/f (Soft) 13 Ran SP% **122.1**

Speed ratings (Par 105): **105,104,101,101,97 96,96,87,86,83 82,70,67**

toteswinger: 1&2 £5.90, 1&3 £43.90, 2&3 £51.00. CSF £51.55 TOTE £7.90: £2.90, £2.40, £7.30; EX 58.70 TRIFECTA Not won..

Owner Cheveley Park Stud **Bred** Cheveley Park Stud Ltd **Trained** Newmarket, Suffolk

■ Stewards' Enquiry : Fergus Sweeney three-day ban: careless riding (Nov 8-10)

FOCUS

A strong field by Group 3 standards, but it's a very long time since the Horris Hill went to a genuine Classic colt. In a race in which the majority raced up the middle of the track to begin with, they gradually edged over to the stands' side

NOTEBOOK

Evasive has more improving to do before he can be considered a serious 2000 Guineas candidate, but this was a big step up on his fast-ground maiden win at Newmarket and he could not be in better hands, so it was no surprise to see him quoted at a general 16-1 after following up on this very different ground. He was up there helping force it throughout and was clear going into the final furlong. (op 6-1 tchd 8-1 in a place)

Bonnie Charlie ◆'s Chantilly Group 3 third set the standard, but he had his stamina to prove. In the event, it was not an issue, as he finished really powerfully after losing ground and momentum when getting badly buffeted about between Shampagne and Aahaykid when still towards the rear over 2f out. It would have been interesting if he had avoided the interference, and he is clearly a very useful juvenile. (op 5-1 tchd 13-2 in a place)

Aahaykid(IRE) ran really well in third, reversing recent Ascot placings with Rileyskeepingfaith. (tchd 33-1)

Rileyskeepingfaith, who had his chance, has now come up short in several Group races. (op 12-1 tchd 15-2)

Splendorinthegrass(IRE) ◆ had made a pleasing debut in a maiden here, but one suspects he may have been stepped up to this grade principally because his owner sponsored the race. He did really well in fifth, particularly as he missed the break, and ought to have a maiden at his mercy.

Jobe(USA), not beaten far when only eighth in the Middle Park, came up the stands' rail, where he had every chance. (op 8-1)

Shampagne, keen early on, was a long way clear of the rest. (op 16-1)

Nasri, whose recent Newmarket third was given a massive boost at Santa Anita later in the day when Donativum and Crowded House were both Breeders' Cup winners, was too keen for his own good in the early stages. Official explanation: trainer said colt was unsuited by the soft ground (op 7-2 tchd 4-1)

Bravo Echo, who was one of the stand-outs in the paddock, was in trouble with more than 2f to go and hung across towards the stands' rail. Official explanation: trainer's rep said colt was unsuited by the soft ground (op 6-1)

6980 INTERCASINO.CO.UK ST SIMON STKS (GROUP 3) 1m 4f 5y

2:45 (2:50) (Class 1) 3-Y-O+

£36,900 (£13,988; £7,000; £3,490; £1,748; £877) Stalls Low

Form				RPR
5141	1		**Buccellati**[22] 6444 4-9-3 109 ..... (v) WilliamBuick 8 (A M Balding) *hld up in 4th: led wl over 1f out: edgd lft u.p fnl f: hrd drvn and hld on wl* **15/2**[3]	117
-201	2	1	**Blue Monday**[36] 6074 7-9-6 114 ..... SteveDrowne 3 (R Charlton) *led tl 5f out: led 3f out tl over 2f out: sltly outpcd: rallied wl to press wnr fnl 100yds: jst hld* **7/1**[2]	118
241	3	4	**Sell Out**[52] 5623 4-9-0 109 ..... AlanMunro 2 (G Wragg) *trckd ldng pair: outpcd over 2f out: styd on same pce to regain 3rd ins fnl f* **12/1**	106
0253	4	1	**Scintillo**[63] 5263 3-8-10 107 ..... (b[1]) RichardHughes 5 (R Hannon) *hld up in 5th: hdwy to ld briefly 2f out: wknd over 1f out* **25/1**	107
0-50	5	2	**Numide (FR)**[36] 6074 5-9-3 102 ..... GeorgeBaker 4 (G L Moore) *hld up last off the pce: effrt on outer 3f out: hrd rdn and no imp 2f out* **40/1**	104
0566	6	1 ¼	**Championship Point (IRE)**[41] 5932 5-9-6 107 ..... DarryllHolland 1 (M R Channon) *hld up in 6th: effrt 3f out: hrd rdn and btn 2f out* **33/1**	105
1556	7	nk	**Ask**[20] 6522 5-9-6 121 ..... CSoumillon 7 (Sir Michael Stoute) *t.k.h: trckd ldr: led 5f out tl 3f out: wkd qckly over 2f out* **8/13**[1]	104

2m 45.51s (10.01) **Going Correction** +1.00s/f (Soft)

WFA 3 from 4yo+ 7lb 7 Ran SP% **103.1**

Speed ratings (Par 113): **106,105,102,102,100 99,99**

toteswinger: 1&2 £3.10, 1&3 £4.70, 2&3 £5.00. CSF £42.72 TOTE £5.90: £2.60, £2.40; EX 29.00 Trifecta £236.40 Part won. Pool of £319.56 - 0.70 winning units..

Owner Mr & Mrs P McMahon & Mr & Mrs R Gorell **Bred** Burton Agnes Stud Co Ltd **Trained** Kingsclere, Hants

■ The first Group winner for apprentice title-chasing William Buick.

FOCUS

A small but select field for this Group 3, but it was weakened both by the withdrawal of Spanish Moon (7/1, deduct 10p in the £ under R4), who refused to enter the stalls, and by the favourite running a stinker. The early pace was very modest and didn't pick up until Ask took over in front at around halfway. Another personal best from Buccellati and the form seems sound enough on the face of things, although the favourite did not run his race.

NOTEBOOK

Buccellati seems to like the autumn, having completed a hat-trick at around this time last year, while he came into this off the back of a tidy win in a Newmarket Listed event. Patiently ridden, he was produced with his effort between horses coming to the last 2f and, despite wandering around a bit once in front, was always doing enough to keep his rivals at bay. Connections are hopeful that he may now get an invitation for Hong Kong. (tchd 8-1)

Blue Monday, a winner on his last two visits here, including when edging out Spanish Moon in the Arc Trial last month, set the modest early pace until headed by Ask turning in, but he was in front again passing the 2f pole and fought back in tenacious style after the winner had gone past him. He is very tough and there seems no reason why he shouldn't find further success at this level. (op 9-1)

Sell Out, winner of a fillies' Listed event at Chantilly last time, ran well considering she took quite a hold early and kept plugging away right to the end. (op 14-1)

Scintillo, without a win in a year and blinkered for the first time, was the only three-year-old in the field. Travelling well in mid-division, he looked a possible winner when delivered with his effort down the outside 2f from home, but he then starting to hang and folded as though his stamina gave out in the ground. (op 18-1 tchd 16-1)

Numide(FR), a long way behind Blue Monday here last month, was switched right off out the back and, though plugging on down the outside in the home straight, never looked like figuring. (tchd 33-1)

Championship Point(IRE), yet to convince over this far, was another held up in order to help him see out the trip in the ground, but he never managed to get involved.

Ask, who has been plying his trade at the very highest level since winning in Group 3 company at Sandown in April, pulled his way to the front at halfway but it wasn't long before he was being pressed again and he didn't put up much of a fight. Admittedly, he did race keenly early, but this was still hugely disappointing and perhaps his Arc effort took more out of him than first thought. Official explanation: trainer had no explanation for the poor form shown (op 8-11 tchd 4-5 in places)

6981 EBF INKERMAN LONDON FILLIES' H'CAP 7f (S)

3:20 (3:24) (Class 3) (0-95,95) 3-Y-O+ £9,066 (£2,697; £1,348; £673) Stalls High

Form				RPR
2-31	1		**Izzibizzi**[17] 6571 3-8-4 79 oh4 ..... ChrisCatlin 18 (E A L Dunlop) *dwlt: t.k.h in rr: swtchd lft to far side and gd hdwy fr 2f out: str run to ld fnl 100yds* **20/1**	86
2461	2	¾	**Just Like A Woman**[51] 5644 3-8-7 82 ..... HayleyTurner 1 (M L W Bell) *in tch: effrt over 2f out: styd on to take 2nd ins fnl f: just outpcd by winner fnl 50yds* **12/1**	87
1	3	nk	**Cosmopolitan**[148] 2566 3-8-5 80 ..... RichardMullen 12 (J H M Gosden) *restless in stalls: hld up in midfield: promising hdwy whn nt clr run and swtchd lft 1f out: r.o fnl f* **4/1**[1]	89+
0003	4	½	**Dressed To Dance (IRE)**[5] 6864 4-8-10 83 ..... (v) PatCosgrave 5 (P D Evans) *dwlt: bhd: rdn and gd hdwy over 1f out: nrst fin* **33/1**	86
0153	5	hd	**Amber Queen (IRE)**[44] 5841 3-8-6 81 ow1 ..... AlanMunro 7 (B W Hills) *prom: drvn to ld jst ins fnl f: hdd and one pce fnl 100yds* **8/1**[3]	83
3542	6	1 ¼	**Oceana Blue**[13] 6684 3-8-4 79 oh4 ..... (t) WilliamBuick 6 (A M Balding) *led over 1f: led over 2f out tl jst ins fnl f: no ex* **14/1**	78+
0060	7	½	**Steam Cuisine**[28] 6271 4-9-0 87 ..... TPO'Shea 3 (M G Quinlan) *hld up in midfield: hrd rdn over 2f out: hmpd and swtchd left over 1f out: styd on fnl f* **12/1**	85
500	8	¾	**Folly Lodge**[16] 6605 4-8-8 81 ow1 ..... SteveDrowne 16 (G Wragg) *dwlt: held up twrds rr: effort and n.m.r 2f out: r.o appr fnl f: nvr nrr* **16/1**	77+
3255	9	nse	**Vital Statistics**[8] 6782 4-9-3 90 ..... GeorgeBaker 10 (D R C Elsworth) *towards rr: rdn over 2f out: nt clr rn over 1f out: 7th and staying on whn hmpd on stands' rail nr fin* **12/1**	88+
5012	10	3	**Elysee Palace (IRE)**[15] 6625 3-9-0 89 ..... NCallan 8 (M A Jarvis) *prom: outpcd ins fnl 2f: btn whn hmpd ins fnl f: eased* **8/1**[3]	85+
0-34	11	2 ½	**Romany Princess (IRE)**[151] 2481 3-8-5 80 ..... GregFairley 9 (R Hannon) *hld up in tch: effrt over 2f out: wknd over 1f out* **25/1**	61
5-12	12	7	**Danae**[145] 2666 3-9-3 92 ..... FrankieMcDonald 11 (H Candy) *in tch on stands' rail tl 2f out: rdn and wknd 2f out* **10/1**	54
2301	13	1 ¾	**Badweia (USA)**[24] 6387 3-8-4 79 oh3 ..... (b) MartinDwyer 19 (J L Dunlop) *dwlt: bhd: drvn along over 3f out: nvr trbld ldrs* **16/1**	36
6623	14	¾	**Kay Es Jay (FR)**[28] 6277 3-9-1 90 ..... MichaelHills 2 (B W Hills) *held up towards rr: rdn 3f out: sn bhd* **16/1**	45
54-0	15	½	**Perfect Act**[190] 1441 3-8-10 85 ..... AdamKirby 14 (C G Cox) *hld up in midfield: effrt wn n.m.r on stands' rail over 2f out: sn wknd* **20/1**	39
4411	16	½	**Granary**[18] 6554 4-8-9 82 ..... FergusSweeney 13 (H Candy) *prom: led over 5f out tl wknd qckly 2f out: eased whn no ch fnl f* **6/1**[2]	34
1050	17	24	**Divine Power**[35] 6124 3-8-5 87 oh2 ow8 ..... RossAtkinson(7) 17 (R M Beckett) *towards rr: swtchd wd to far side and rdn 3f out: sn bhd* **50/1**	—

1m 32.13s (6.43) **Going Correction** +1.00s/f (Soft)

WFA 3 from 4yo 2lb 17 Ran SP% **131.3**

Speed ratings (Par 104): **103,102,101,101,101 99,99,98,98,94 91,83,81,80,80 79,52**

toteswinger: 1&2 £104.00, 1&3 £31.90, 2&3 £16.30. CSF £246.48 CT £1223.61 TOTE £32.10: £4.10, £1.80, £1.70, £5.30; EX 365.00.

Owner J Weatherby, Champneys **Bred** Broughton Bloodstock **Trained** Newmarket, Suffolk

■ Stewards' Enquiry : Richard Mullen four-day ban: careless riding (Nov 8-10, 12)

FOCUS
A very competitive fillies' handicap, and they seemed to go a decent gallop. It became a bit messy and a number met trouble. Improved form from the winner, with the runner-up the best guide and the third unlucky.

NOTEBOOK
Izzibizzi, who was 4lb out of the weights on this handicap debut, had decent form as a two-year-old but had struggled to beat a 66-rated rival when winning a Polytrack maiden last time, which didn't suggest she was well handicapped here off a mark of 79. Held up off the pace early, she had to circle the field in order to get a run but quickened up well down the outside and was well on top at the line. She has apparently grown up now, having been given a bit of time, and this improving filly may be capable of more. (op 25-1)
Just Like A Woman, successful from Kay Es Jay and Vital Statistics at Salisbury last month and weighted to confirm the form, was never too far off the pace from the outside stall and had every chance. She remains in decent form and there will be other days. (op 11-1)
Cosmopolitan ◆, not seen since making a successful debut from a couple of subsequent winners in a Goodwood maiden in May, gave some trouble in the stalls but ran her race once under way and may have finished even closer had she not run into the back of Amber Queen half a furlong from home. She remains unexposed. (op 9-2)
Dressed To Dance(IRE), still 4lb higher than when completing a hat-trick in June, put in some decent late work out towards the centre of the track and stamina didn't seem to be a problem here.
Amber Queen(IRE), relatively unexposed and proven in testing ground, was always up with the pace and kept on well. (op 11-1)
Oceana Blue ran her race, having been at the sharp end throughout, and wasn't swallowed up until well inside the last furlong. This was a decent effort, considering she was running off a 12lb higher mark than when last successful. (op 20-1)
Steam Cuisine, 1lb lower than when winning this race last year in similar conditions but without a victory since, plugged on late but was never a threat. (op 11-1)
Folly Lodge ◆ can be forgiven this effort as she endured a nightmare passage and can be rated quite a bit better than this. (op 25-1)
Vital Statistics, without a win in over two years and 7lb higher than when last in a handicap following a couple of fair efforts in Listed company, may well have been fighting for a place had she not been squeezed right out when trying to sneak between Oceana Blue and the stands' rail well inside the last furlong. Official explanation: jockey said filly suffered interference in running (op 14-1 tchd 11-1)
Elysee Palace(IRE), in good form lately but now 10lb higher than when successful over course and distance last month, showed up for a long way but seemed to have run her race when getting hampered well inside the last furlong. Official explanation: jockey said filly suffered interference in running (op 15-2 tchd 9-1)

6982 PLAY BLACKJACK AT INTERCASINO.CO.UK STKS (REGISTERED AS THE RADLEY STAKES) (LISTED RACE) (FILLIES) 7f (S)
3:55 (3:57) (Class 1) 2-Y-O

£17,031 (£6,456; £3,231; £1,611; £807; £405) Stalls High

Form RPR
14 **1** **Summer Fete (IRE)**[35] 6102 2-8-12 100 TomEaves 6 100
(B Smart) *in tch in centre: effrt over 2f out: edgd lft fnl f: styd on to ld fnl 75yds* **11/4**[1]
12 **2** *1 3/4* **Rosy Mantle**[29] 6240 2-8-12 85 SteveDrowne 5 96
(W R Muir) *hld up in rr in centre: hrd rdn and hdwy 2f out: styd on wl fnl f: took 2nd on line* **10/1**
2031 **3** *nse* **Yorksters Girl (IRE)**[24] 6381 2-8-12 88 RichardMullen 2 96
(M G Quinlan) *w ldrs in centre: led over 2f out: hrd rdn fnl f: hdd and no ex fnl 75yds* **25/1**
4103 **4** *nse* **Seradim**[51] 5642 2-8-12 100 AlanMunro 1 95
(P F I Cole) *w ldrs in centre: drv to press ldr ent fnl f: one pce* **14/1**
41 **5** *1 3/4* **Nora Mae (IRE)**[25] 6358 2-8-12 83 JamesDoyle 11 91
(S Kirk) *racd in centre gp: led 3f: hrd rdn and chalng over 1f out: no ex* **16/1**
311 **6** *5* **Honest Quality (USA)**[93] 4348 2-9-1 98 TPQueally 7 82
(H R A Cecil) *w ldrs in centre: led after 3f tl over 2f out: wknd wl over 1f out* **6/1**[2]
4210 **7** *1 1/4* **Purple Sage (IRE)**[7] 6818 2-8-12 82 MichaelHills 14 75
(B W Hills) *sn led stands' side quintet: outpcd by centre gp fnl 2f* **16/1**
1 **8** *3* **Enact**[26] 6342 2-8-12 CSoumillon 15 68
(Sir Michael Stoute) *dwlt: hld up in tch in stands' side quintet: effrt 3f out: sn wknd* **7/1**[3]
1 **9** *hd* **Cashleen (USA)**[29] 6245 2-8-12 NCallan 3 67
(K A Ryan) *t.k.h in rr in centre: rdn 3f out: n.d* **25/1**
12 **10** *12* **Such Optimism**[51] 5641 2-8-12 90 WilliamBuick 13 37
(R M Beckett) *chsd ldr in stands' side quintet: wknd over 2f out* **20/1**
1 **11** *8* **Club Tahiti**[16] 6600 2-8-12 RichardHughes 9 17
(R Charlton) *restless in stalls: dwlt: racd towards rr in stands' side quintet: rdn and n.d fnl 3f* **11/4**[1]
3 **12** *2 1/2* **Sussex Dancer (IRE)**[54] 5570 2-8-12 ShaneKelly 4 11
(J A Osborne) *dwlt: swtchd rt over 5f out to r in stands' side quintet: a bhd* **33/1**

1m 32.41s (6.71) **Going Correction** +1.00s/f (Soft) 12 Ran SP% 123.0
Speed ratings (Par 100): **101,99,98,98,96 91,89,86,86,72 63,60**
toteswinger: 1&2 £5.70, 1&3 £33.30, 2&3 £13.60. CSF £32.50 TOTE £4.00: £1.50, £2.70, £4.60; EX 35.40 Trifecta £341.10 Part won. Pool: £461.00 - 0.10 winning units..
Owner H E Sheikh Rashid Bin Mohammed **Bred** Darley **Trained** Hambleton, N Yorks

FOCUS
This looked a good renewal of what is traditionally one of the juvenile programme's stronger Listed events, and it was run in a time just 0.72 seconds slower than the Group 3 Horris Hill won by Evasive earlier in the afternoon. They raced in two groups and the finish was dominated by fillies who raced in the main pack up the centre.

NOTEBOOK
Summer Fete(IRE)'s heavy-ground Ayr fourth to the subsequent Cheveley Park and Rockfel second Aspen Darlin was form as good as any could boast going into the race and, considering that had been only her second race, she was entitled to improve again. Her ability to handle this ground was an obvious plus and, although she did not get to the front until well inside the final furlong, she was well on top at the finish, the extra furlong proving right up her street.\n\x\x Her jockey reckons she has the size and scope to train on, and she is a 33-1 chance with Stan James and VCbet for the 1000 Guineas. A mile will be no problem, but she is by Pivotal and give in the ground may well be important to her. (op 4-1 tchd 5-1)
Rosy Mantle, narrowly beaten by Penny's Gift in the sales race at Ascot, was a moderate fifth going into the final furlong but finished strongly and confirmed trainer William Muir's high opinion of her with an excellent effort in second. She has improved with every race and can do better again over further next year. (tchd 9-1 and 11-1)
Yorksters Girl(IRE) showed improved form, especially considering she raced widest of all on the far side, and was in front going into the final furlong. (op 20-1 tchd 16-1)
Seradim came here with sound credentials and was only just run out of the places. (op 12-1)
Nora Mae(IRE), who had helped force the pace, faded in the last furlong but was a long way clear of the rest. (tchd 20-1)
Honest Quality(USA), who looked to have a decent chance despite her penalty, was in trouble inside the final 2f and faded away after being bang up there. She had been off the track three months and might not have enjoyed the ground. (tchd 13-2)
Purple Sage(IRE) was beaten the best part of ten lengths but still did best of those who were at an apparent disadvantage coming up the stands' rail. The ground may have been a factor too, and while she did not advertise the Rockfel form, it would be wrong to read too much into it. (op 20-1)
Enact, last month's Windsor fast-ground winner, was another in the stands'-side group whose run can probably be excused. (op 11-2 tchd 5-1)
Such Optimism Official explanation: trainer said filly was unsuited by the soft ground
Club Tahiti, an impressive recent winner here on her debut, was another to come up the stands' side and her running is best forgiven, although for different reasons. She was all the rage in the morning, but ran no sort of race and was eventually allowed to come home in her own time. There was a suggestion when she was restless in the stalls that something might not be quite right, and when Hughes came back he said he did not think it was anything to do with the ground, and that he had not been entirely happy at the start, where she was sucking in air. He told the stewards that she was never travelling. Official explanation: jockey said filly never travelled (op 7-2 tchd 5-2)

6983 BATHWICK TYRES LADY JOCKEYS' CHAMPIONSHIP H'CAP 1m 4f 5y
4:30 (4:30) (Class 5) (0-75,75) 4-Y-O+ £3,123 (£968; £484; £242) Stalls Low

Form RPR
550/ **1** **Blazing Bailey**[184] 5615 6-9-8 62 MissSBrotherton 2 73+
(A King) *w ldrs: rdn 4f out: sltly outpcd over 2f out: rallied to ld ins fnl f: styd on wl* **6/4**[1]
3000 **2** *2 3/4* **Benfleet Boy**[13] 6675 4-9-11 70 MissCLWills(5) 11 76
(B G Powell) *w ldrs: led 3f out tl ins fnl f: one pce* **40/1**
2161 **3** *1 1/2* **Pocketwood**[18] 6558 6-10-7 75 MissEJJones 5 79
(Jean-Rene Auvray) *led tl 3f out: one pce appr fnl f* **12/1**
3323 **4** *hd* **Penang Cinta**[21] 6493 5-9-10 64 (p) MissEFolkes 14 67
(P D Evans) *hld up in rr of midfield: effrt and hrd rdn 2f out: styd on fnl f* **14/1**
46-1 **5** *1 1/2* **Kerayasi (FR)**[17] 6577 6-9-8 67 ow1 MissHayleyMoore(5) 7 68
(G L Moore) *hld up towards rr: rdn and styd on fnl 2f: nvr nrr* **11/2**[2]
3560 **6** *2 3/4* **Lady Friend**[23] 6415 6-10-0 71 MissMSowerby(3) 13 68
(J W Hills) *stdd s: plld hrd in rr: hrd rdn and sme hdwy 2f out: nt pce to chal* **25/1**
4350 **7** *3/4* **Great View (IRE)**[39] 5993 9-9-4 63 (p) MissHannahWatson(5) 9 58
(Mrs A L M King) *mid-div: rdn 4f out: sme hdwy 2f out: edgd lft and rt: sn fdd* **16/1**
4005 **8** *1 1/4* **Scania Classic**[12] 6708 7-9-8 67 oh1 ow6 MissHGrissell(5) 8 60
(M J Scudamore) *chsd ldrs early: settled in midfield after 4f: no hdwy fnl 3f* **66/1**
5550 **9** *nk* **Alfie Noakes**[24] 6403 6-9-13 67 MissGDGracey-Davison 4 60
(Mrs A J Perrett) *bhd: hrd rdn 2f out: nvr rchd ldrs* **10/1**
4451 **10** *1/2* **Right Option (IRE)**[29] 6252 4-9-9 70 (p) MissRachelKing(7) 1 62
(J L Flint) *trckd ldrs tl wknd over 2f out* **16/1**
1022 **11** *3* **Jenny Soba**[19] 6538 5-9-11 65 MissARyan 3 52
(Lucinda Featherstone) *mid-div tl hrd rdn and wknd over 2f out* **12/1**
053- **12** *shd* **Cape Greko**[151] 5769 6-10-3 71 MissADeniel 6 58
(B G Powell) *sn trcking ldrs: rdn and wknd over 2f out* **25/1**
3302 **13** *1* **Harry The Hawk**[11] 6726 4-9-9 70 MissERamstrom(7) 12 56
(T D Walford) *stdd s: hld up towards rr: rdn and n.d fnl 3f* **7/1**[3]

2m 49.21s (13.71) **Going Correction** +1.00s/f (Soft) 21 Ran SP% 122.4
Speed ratings (Par 103): **94,92,91,91,90 88,87,86,86,86 84,84,83**
toteswinger: 1&2 £25.40, 1&3 £3.80, 2&3 £80.00. CSF £93.39 CT £584.85 TOTE £2.50: £1.40, £11.70, £2.50; EX 78.50.
Owner Three Line Whip **Bred** A M Tombs **Trained** Barbury Castle, Wilts
■ Stewards' Enquiry : Miss E J Jones three-day ban: used whip with excessive frequency and when gelding showed no sign of response (Nov 10-11, 25)

FOCUS
A modest lady jockeys' handicap run at an ordinary pace, with the winning time 3.7 seconds slower than the moderately run St Simon Stakes. Very few got into it, and the first three home virtually held those positions throughout. Blazing Bailey can rate higher on the Flat over further and the form is sound enough.

6984 FRANK OSGOOD MEMORIAL H'CAP 1m 2f 6y
5:05 (5:07) (Class 2) (0-100,99) 3-Y-O+

£11,215 (£3,358; £1,679; £840; £419; £210) Stalls Low

Form RPR
1310 **1** **La Sarrazine (FR)**[38] 6034 3-8-5 88 MartinDwyer 8 96
(J R Fanshawe) *prom: carried lft and led 3f out: hdd 2f out: led over 1f out: rdn out and styd on wl* **20/1**
214 **2** *1 1/4* **Redesignation (IRE)**[8] 6784 3-8-10 93 JimCrowley 9 99
(R Hannon) *prom: rdn to chal 2f out: sltly outpcd 1f out: kpt on wl to regain 2nd nr fin* **7/1**[2]
423 **3** *shd* **Gold Sovereign (IRE)**[27] 6307 4-9-7 99 RHills 5 105+
(Saeed Bin Suroor) *chsd ldrs: hmpd, swrvd lft and bmpd over 3f out: slt ld 2f out tl over 1f out: edgd lft: one pce fnl f* **7/2**[1]
0006 **4** *shd* **Throne Of Power (USA)**[13] 6667 3-8-4 87 TPO'Shea 6 93
(M A Magnusson) *hld up in rr: rdn and styd on fnl 3f: nrst fin* **20/1**
4012 **5** *1 3/4* **Curzon Prince (IRE)**[27] 6307 4-9-0 95 JackMitchell(3) 13 97
(C F Wall) *hld up in 5th: effrt 3f out: styd on sme pce fnl 2f* **9/1**[3]
0334 **6** *2* **Kinsya**[13] 6667 5-8-10 88 NCallan 11 86
(M H Tompkins) *hld up towards rr on outer: promising hdwy over 2f out: rdn and one pce appr fnl f* **10/1**
0352 **7** *2 1/2* **Ramona Chase**[14] 6649 3-8-11 94 AdamKirby 3 87
(S Kirk) *hld up in rr: smooth hdwy into midfield 3f out: no imp whn squeezed for room jst over 1f out* **10/1**
130- **8** *3* **Wandle**[492] 2790 4-8-12 90 MichaelHills 2 77
(T G Mills) *midfield on ins: hmpd and carried lft 3f out: sn btn* **10/1**
5604 **9** *1/2* **William Blake**[12] 6698 3-8-5 88 GregFairley 14 74
(M Johnston) *bhd: rdn 3f out: nvr trbld ldrs* **14/1**
3113 **10** *4 1/2* **Closertobelieving**[22] 6445 3-8-9 92 TQuinn 1 69+
(D R C Elsworth) *mid-div: effrt whn bdly bmpd 3f out: drvn to chse ldrs whn hmpd over 1f out: heavily eased* **7/2**[1]
0263 **11** *1/2* **Capable Guest (IRE)**[19] 6536 6-8-12 90 (v) ChrisCatlin 4 66
(M R Channon) *hld up in midfield: outpcd over 2f out: sn lost pl* **20/1**
0203 **12** *24* **Cape Hawk (IRE)**[8] 6772 4-8-12 90 RichardHughes 7 18
(R Hannon) *hld up in rr: shkn up and n.d fnl 3f: eased whn no ch* **10/1**
-500 **13** *35* **Allanit (GER)**[14] 6649 4-9-4 96 ShaneKelly 12 —
(A P Stringer) *led and plld hrd: restrained 6 l ahd: edgd lft, hdd & wknd rapidly 3f out: virtually p.u fnl 2f* **66/1**

2m 17.55s (8.75) **Going Correction** +1.00s/f (Soft)
WFA 3 from 4yo+ 5lb 13 Ran SP% 125.8
Speed ratings (Par 109): **105,104,103,103,102 100,98,96,96,92 92,72,44**
toteswinger: 1&2 £35.30, 1&3 £22.60, 2&3 £6.60. CSF £155.92 CT £625.83 TOTE £28.60: £7.40, £3.10, £1.70; EX 229.10 Place 6 £573.44, Place 5 £447.18..
Owner Mr & Mrs Duncan Davidson **Bred** Benedikt Fassbender **Trained** Newmarket, Suffolk

FOCUS
A routine handicap, in which the ability to cope with testing ground was a paramount. Only a few were at their best but the form is sound enough.

NOTEBOOK
La Sarrazine(FR), a dual Ripon winner, is in her element with give in the ground and ran out a game winner, having raced to the fore in the main pack throughout. The only filly in the field, and taking on hardened older horses, she was 8lb higher here than for her last win and has progressed well. (tchd 22-1)
Redesignation(IRE), another soft-ground scorer this year, was up there disputing it with the winner in the chasing group and was coming back at the finish, where he just got the best of a three-way photo for second. (op 8-1 tchd 13-2)
Gold Sovereign(IRE) was well backed and looked the likely winner when he went narrowly to the front, but he had given Closertobelieving a hefty bump when switched left 3f out and was inclined to continue edging left all the way to the finish. (op 11-2 tchd 3-1)
Throne Of Power(USA) had become a bit disappointing but switched off better this time and saw his race out well, staying on to fight it out for second. (tchd 33-1)
Curzon Prince(IRE) continues to climb the handicap and was far from disgraced. (op 8-1 tchd 11-1)
Kinsya, whose mark has been gradually reducing, could not take advantage of what looked a decent chance under his preferred conditions. (op 8-1 tchd 11-1)
Ramona Chase would have been closer but for being squeezed out over a furlong from home. Official explanation: jockey said gelding was unsuited by the soft ground (op 15-2)
Wandle ran better than the bare facts suggest, as he had been off the track since June 2007 and was hampered when Gold Sovereign bumped Closertobelieving for the first time. (op 16-1)
Closertobelieving was hampered twice by Gold Sovereign, who bumped him particularly hard the first time. He was almost pulled up in the end and this can be ignored. (op 9-2 tchd 10-3)
Cape Hawk(IRE) Official explanation: jockey said gelding stopped quickly
Allanit(GER) Official explanation: jockey said colt ran too free
T/Plt: £1,181.30 to a £1 stake. Pool: £70,883.89. 43.80 winning tickets. T/Qpdt: £338.20 to a £1 stake. Pool: £5,028.60. 11.00 winning tickets. LM

6951 WOLVERHAMPTON (A.W) (L-H)
Saturday, October 25

OFFICIAL GOING: Standard
Wind: Fresh, behind Weather: Light rain

6985 BETTER PRICES, BIGGER WINS AT LADBROKES.COM APPRENTICE CLAIMING STKS — 1m 4f 50y(P)
6:15 (6:15) (Class 6) 3-Y-O+ — £3,070 (£906; £453) Stalls Low

Form — RPR
1360 **1** **Apache Fort**^{3} 6898 5-9-9 70 ....(b) RossAtkinson(3) 10 — 78
(T Keddy) *hld up in rr: stdy hdwy fr over 3f out: led 2f out styd on wl* **14/1**
1-01 **2** ¾ **Veloso (FR)**^{16} 6594 6-9-8 70 .... DavidProbert 9 — 72
(A J McCabe) *a.p: led wl over 2f out: hdd 2f out: kpt on but no imp fnl f* **2/1**^{1}
0540 **3** 1 **Peruvian Prince (USA)**^{14} 6659 6-9-5 70 .... BMcHugh(3) 6 — 71
(R A Fahey) *a in tch: rdn to go 3rd 2f out: styd on one pce* **10/1**^{2}
6020 **4** 1¼ **Lunar Promise (IRE)**^{11} 6721 6-9-10 72 .... JackDean 12 — 71
(Ian Williams) *hld up in rr: rdn 3f out: styd on ins fnl 2f: nvr nrr* **14/1**
6116 **5** 1¼ **Kingsholm**^{25} 6364 6-9-10 64 .... KellyHarrison 4 — 69
(K A Ryan) *mid-div: rdn and hdwy over 2f out: one pce and lost 4th wl ins fnl f* **14/1**
1004 **6** 4 **Inch Lodge**^{14} 6662 6-10-0 70 ....(t) MCGeran 3 — 66
(Miss D Mountain) *t.k.h: prom: rdn 3f out: wknd wl over 1f out* **14/1**
4535 **7** 13 **Themwerethedays**^{3} 6908 3-8-10 64 ....(v^{1}) MatthewBirch(5) 1 — 39
(S Kirk) *trckd ldrs tl rdn and wknd 4f out* **16/1**
5/05 **8** hd **Zeitgeist (IRE)**^{23} 6410 7-9-10 84 ....(v) PatrickDonaghy 5 — 41
(Miss L A Perratt) *a bhd: fin lame* **10/1**^{2}
0140 **9** 1¼ **Wind Flow**^{21} 6472 4-9-7 72 ....(b) MatthewDavies(3) 11 — 39
(C A Dwyer) *prom: led over 3f out: hdd wl over 2f out: wknd qckly* **12/1**^{3}
10 26 **Gasat (IRE)**^{19} 7-9-3 0 .... AndreaAtzeni(3) 2 — —
(Sabastiano Deledda, Italy) *led until rdn and hdd over 3f out: sn wknd: t.o* **2/1**^{1}
-630 **11** 43 **Cash On (IRE)**^{16} 6606 6-9-5 65 ....(p) JPHamblett(3) 8 — —
(Karen George) *a bhd: virtually p.u 1f out: t.o* **33/1**

2m 40.61s (-0.49) **Going Correction** +0.025s/f (Slow)
WFA 3 from 4yo+ 7lb — 11 Ran SP% 128.0
Speed ratings (Par 101): **102,101,100,100,99 96,87,87,86,69 40**
toteswinger: 1&2 £13.00, 1&3 £14.20, 2&3 £7.40. CSF £46.01 TOTE £19.00: £5.00, £1.10, £3.50; EX 88.90.
Owner Andrew Duffield **Bred** Juddmonte Farms Ltd **Trained** Newmarket, Suffolk

FOCUS
Not the worst race of its type but a muddling pace means the bare form may not be entirely reliable.
Apache Fort Official explanation: trainer's rep said, regarding the apparent improvement in form, that gelding may have been unsuited by the good to soft ground last time and appeared to benefit from a return to the all-weather.
Zeitgeist(IRE) Official explanation: jockey said gelding finished lame
Gasat(IRE) Official explanation: jockey had no explanation for the poor form shown

6986 LADBROKESPOKER.COM MAIDEN AUCTION STKS (DIV I) — 7f 32y(P)
6:45 (6:46) (Class 6) 2-Y-O — £2,719 (£809; £404; £202) Stalls High

Form — RPR
1 **Island Sunset (IRE)** 2-8-8 0 .... SteveDrowne 4 — 70+
(W R Muir) *mid-div: rdn and hdwy on outside over 2f out: led over 1f out: clr whn idled and hung lft ins fnl f* **16/1**
220 **2** ½ **Campbeltown Trader (IRE)**^{13} 6673 2-8-11 76 ..(v) RichardKingscote 9 — 72
(Tom Dascombe) *trckd ldrs: rdn over 2f out: wnt 2nd ent fnl f: styd on wl* **13/8**^{1}
05 **3** 2½ **Candilejas**^{22} 6451 2-8-8 0 .... JimmyQuinn 7 — 63
(D J Coakley) *towards rr: rdn over 2f out: hdwy over 1f out: r.o wl ins fnl f: nvr nrr* **13/2**
405 **4** 1½ **Spinight (IRE)**^{41} 5939 2-8-3 65 .... AndreaAtzeni(3) 5 — 61
(M Botti) *led for 1f: styd prom: one pce and lost 3rd ins fnl f* **9/2**^{2}
5 1½ **Inconspicuous Miss (USA)** 2-7-13 0 ow1 .... MatthewDavies(3) 11 — 53
(George Baker) *trckd ldr to 2f out: wknd fnl f* **16/1**
343 **6** 1½ **Miss Cracklinrosie**^{11} 6722 2-8-7 68 .... TomEaves 2 — 51
(J R Weymes) *in rr: rdn 3f out: nvr rchd ldrs* **6/1**
0053 **7** ¾ **Jobekani (IRE)**^{15} 6632 2-8-10 61 .... RussellKennemore(3) 6 — 55
(Mrs L Williamson) *t.k.h: led after 1f: rdn and hdd over 1f out: weqakened qckly* **5/1**^{3}
46 **8** 3 **Kristopher James (IRE)**^{22} 6451 2-8-9 0 .... TGMcLaughlin 1 — 43
(W M Brisbourne) *t.k.h: trckd ldrs early: sn lost pl and bhd after* **16/1**
6004 **9** 3 **Noworneva**^{24} 6394 2-8-10 48 .... WilliamBuick 3 — 37
(S Kirk) *a in rr* **25/1**
0045 **10** nse **Lois Darlin (IRE)**^{4} 6877 2-8-2 49 ....(v^{1}) LukeMorris(3) 10 — 32
(J S Moore) *t.k.h: chsd ldrs tl rdn over 3f out: sn wknd* **20/1**
05 **11** 24 **Tillagirl**^{114} 3652 2-8-5 0 .... SaleemGolam 8 — —
(G G Margarson) *slowly away: a bhd: t.o* **66/1**

1m 31.0s (1.40) **Going Correction** +0.025s/f (Slow) — 11 Ran SP% 128.3
Speed ratings (Par 93): **93,92,89,87,86 84,83,80,76,76 49**
toteswinger: 1&2 £13.60, 1&3 £10.70, 2&3 £3.50. CSF £45.58 TOTE £16.50: £3.30, £1.50, £2.50; EX 70.50.
Owner Mrs J M Muir **Bred** Rathasker Stud **Trained** Lambourn, Berks

FOCUS
A race lacking any strength and one in which the gallop was only fair. The winner ended up against the inside rail.

NOTEBOOK
Island Sunset(IRE), related to several winners, was relatively easy to back but showed plenty of ability on her debut and looks a bit better than the bare result suggests after running green. She is entitled to come on for this experience and should win more races. (op 14-1)
Campbeltown Trader(IRE), from a yard back among the winners, looks a reasonable yardstick and seemed to run his race, despite racing keenly and edging off a true line, on this all-weather debut. He is capable of winning a similar race but is likely to remain vulnerable to the more progressive types in this grade. (op 9-4 tchd 11-4)
Candilejas ◆, dropping in trip, caught the eye and is now qualified for a handicap mark. She will be one to keep an eye on returned to 1m and beyond in ordinary nursery company. (tchd 11-2)
Spinight(IRE) had the run of the race against the inside rail and did not fail through lack of stamina over this longer trip. Modest handicaps will be the way forward with him. (op 4-1)
Inconspicuous Miss(USA), a cheap purchase, hinted at ability after racing three deep from her double-figure draw on this debut run. She is entitled to improve for the run. (op 10-1)
Miss Cracklinrosie had shown ability at up to 1m on a testing surface on turf but found this far too much of a test of speed on this all-weather bow. She'll be suited by further if kept to Polytrack. (op 4-1)
Jobekani(IRE) was the subject of market support but this exposed sort had his limitations exposed back in this grade after being allowed his own way in front. (op 12-1)

6987 LADBROKESPOKER.COM NURSERY — 5f 216y(P)
7:20 (7:20) (Class 4) (0-80,78) 2-Y-O — £5,180 (£1,541; £770; £384) Stalls Low

Form — RPR
231 **1** **Joe Caster**^{17} 6578 2-9-3 77 .... LukeMorris(3) 9 — 80
(J M P Eustace) *hld up in rr: hdwy over 1f out: led ins fnl f: drvn out* **10/1**
2140 **2** 1¼ **Diddums**^{23} 6426 2-9-6 77 ....(b^{1}) LiamJones 2 — 77
(W J Haggas) *s.i.s: in rr tl hdwy over 3f out: chsd ldr over 2f out: kpt on fnl f* **5/6**^{1}
4401 **3** ½ **Mabait**^{29} 6247 2-9-5 76 .... DaneO'Neill 13 — 74
(L M Cumani) *in rr: rdn and styd on fr over 1f out: nvr nrr* **7/1**^{3}
4106 **4** ¾ **Bobbie Soxer (IRE)**^{21} 6477 2-9-2 73 .... JimmyQuinn 1 — 69
(J L Dunlop) *a.p: led over 2f out: rdn and hdd ins fnl f: lost 2 pls towards fin* **7/1**^{3}
0046 **5** ½ **Madison Belle**^{30} 6223 2-8-1 58 ow1 .... AndrewElliott 3 — 52
(K R Burke) *t.k.h: in tch whn sltly hmpd over 2f out: rdn and hung lft fr over 1f out: no ex fnl f* **40/1**
0000 **6** 1¼ **Calypso Girl (IRE)**^{21} 6469 2-8-11 68 .... TGMcLaughlin 6 — 59
(P D Evans) *in rr: mde sme late hdwy: nvr nr to chal* **50/1**
0004 **7** 4 **Venetian Lady**^{14} 6661 2-8-0 60 .... AndrewMullen(3) 4 — 39
(Mrs A Duffield) *slowly away: a bhd* **33/1**
2362 **8** 3½ **Musical Bridge**^{14} 6656 2-9-4 78 .... RussellKennemore(3) 7 — 46
(Mrs L Williamson) *in rr: rdn 1/2-way: nvr on terms* **16/1**
3154 **9** 7 **Common Diva**^{94} 4297 2-9-5 76 .... WilliamBuick 8 — 23
(A J McCabe) *chsd ldrs tl wknd over 2f out* **25/1**
2410 **10** 1½ **Flintlock (IRE)**^{13} 6666 2-9-2 73 ....(b) RobertHavlin 11 — 16
(J H M Gosden) *sn led: hdd over 2f out: wknd qckly* **6/1**^{2}
0106 **11** 1½ **Bermondsey Bob (IRE)**^{16} 6603 2-8-13 73 .... TolleyDean(3) 5 — 11
(J L Spearing) *trckd ldr: rdn and wkng whn hit rail 2f out* **20/1**

1m 16.15s (1.15) **Going Correction** +0.025s/f (Slow) — 11 Ran SP% 124.8
Speed ratings (Par 97): **93,91,90,89,89 87,82,77,68,66 64**
toteswinger: 1&2 £3.30, 1&3 £13.00, 2&3 £2.30. CSF £19.12 CT £74.19 TOTE £13.30: £3.30, £1.10, £1.50; EX 26.10.
Owner The Greek Myths **Bred** Ms G P Walker **Trained** Newmarket, Suffolk

FOCUS
A fairly competitive event run at a decent gallop and this form should prove reliable.

NOTEBOOK
Joe Caster ◆ is a progressive individual who was ridden much more patiently than at Nottingham and he turned in his best effort upped in trip for this all-weather and nursery debut. There was plenty to like about the way he went about his business and it will be a surprise if he doesn't win again on this surface (op 8-1)
Diddums, better than the bare form of his previous turf run, was heavily backed returned to Polytrack and showed more than enough after racing keenly in the first-time blinkers and after being slow into his stride to suggest a similar event can be found. (op 4-5 tchd 10-11)
Mabait had turned in an improved performance dropped to 6f on turf last month but shaped from his wide draw back on Polytrack as though the step up to 7f would be in his favour. He is still fairly unexposed and is the type to win again. (tchd 13-2)
Bobbie Soxer(IRE), who travelled strongly on her all-weather debut down in trip, may be a bit better than the bare form as she was up with the decent gallop throughout and kicked for home some way out. She has the ability to win a similar event on Polytrack. (tchd 8-1)
Madison Belle was not disgraced but she looks exposed and is likely to remain vulnerable to the more progressive types in this grade. (op 33-1)
Calypso Girl(IRE) turned in her best all-weather effort but is not the most reliable and did not really do enough to suggest she'd be winning a similar event from her current mark in the near future.
Musical Bridge Official explanation: jockey said colt hung right throughout
Bermondsey Bob(IRE) Official explanation: jockey said gelding loost its action

6988 LADBROKESPOKER.COM MAIDEN AUCTION STKS (DIV II) — 7f 32y(P)
7:50 (7:50) (Class 6) 2-Y-O — £2,719 (£809; £404; £202) Stalls High

Form — RPR
6036 **1** **Give Us A Song (USA)**^{9} 6756 2-8-9 68 .... LPKeniry 3 — 67
(J S Moore) *t.k.h: hld up in tch: rdn over 1f out: drvn to ld post: all out* **2/1**^{2}
6303 **2** shd **Importer (IRE)**^{2} 6924 2-8-13 72 .... SteveDrowne 4 — 71
(W R Muir) *prom: led wl over 1f out: r.o u.p: hdd post* **15/8**^{1}
0440 **3** 2½ **Yeoman Of England (IRE)**^{9} 6761 2-8-13 66 .... TomEaves 9 — 65
(B Smart) *in tch on outside: rdn and hung lft over 1f out but r.o to go 3rd ins fnl f* **6/1**
6 **4** hd **Feet Of Fury**^{16} 6601 2-8-6 0 .... WilliamBuick 11 — 57
(W M Brisbourne) *racd wd: towards rr: styd on fnl f: nvr nrr* **16/1**
64 **5** 3¾ **Carter**^{22} 6451 2-8-9 0 .... PatCosgrave 7 — 51
(W M Brisbourne) *s.i.s: towards rr: pushed along 3f out: nvr nr to chal* **12/1**
3040 **6** 1¼ **Mistress Mary**^{31} 6214 2-8-5 51 ....(v^{1}) SaleemGolam 6 — 44
(G G Margarson) *towards rr: rdn over 2f out: effrt over 1f out: sn btn* **50/1**
7 nk **Ballade De La Mer** 2-8-0 0 .... DavidProbert(5) 1 — 43
(A J McCabe) *s.i.s: nvr on terms* **33/1**

334 **8** *nk* **Denton Diva**[24] 6381 2-8-5 66.. DaleGibson 8 42
(M Dods) *chsd ldrs on outside: rdn 2f out: wknd appr fnl f* **11/1**
554 **9** *1 1/4* **Viking Awake (IRE)**[42] 5882 2-8-13 72........................ RichardKingscote 5 47
(J W Unett) *t.k.h: led after 2f: hdd wl over 1f out: sn wknd* **7/2[3]**
540 **10** *3 3/4* **Lady Gem**[35] 6110 2-8-8 53.. PaulMulrennan 2 33
(D H Brown) *led for 2f: rdn over 2f out: sn wknd* **33/1**
0 **11** *22* **Kathanikki Girl (IRE)**[14] 6661 2-8-5 0............................ LiamJones 10 —
(Mrs L Williamson) *racd wd: a bhd: t.o* **66/1**

1m 31.41s (1.81) **Going Correction** +0.025s/f (Slow) 11 Ran SP% **127.5**
Speed ratings (Par 93): **90,89,87,86,82 81,80,80,78,74 49**
toteswinger: 1&2 £2.70, 1&3 £19.70, 2&3 £19.20. CSF £6.69 TOTE £3.90: £1.30, £1.10, £5.20; EX 7.80.
Owner John Wells & Ernie Moore **Bred** Michelle Redding **Trained** Upper Lambourn, Berks

FOCUS
Another division lacking any strength and just a steady gallop to the straight.

NOTEBOOK
Give Us A Song(USA) had shown ability at a modest level on Polytrack and did enough to get off the mark at the fifth attempt. He is a consistent sort who will appreciate the return to 1m but will find life tougher against the unexposed sorts in handicaps from his current mark. (op 11-4)
Importer(IRE) has had a few chances but he is a reliable sort who ran creditably after enjoying the run of the race on only this second all-weather outing. While vulnerable to the better sorts in this grade, he has the ability to win a similarly uncompetitive event. (op 11-4 tchd 3-1 and 13-8)
Yeoman Of England(IRE), from a yard whose juveniles have been in good form, was not disgraced on this first try on the all-weather, despite carrying his head awkwardly and hanging into the whip. His future lies in ordinary handicaps over further but he may not be one for maximum faith. (op 12-1)
Feet Of Fury shaped as though better than the bare form as she attempted to come from off the pace on the wide outside on this all-weather debut. She will be of more interest once handicapped. (op 10-1)
Carter shaped as though this trip was on the short side and will be suited by the return to 1m and the step into ordinary nursery company. (op 8-1)
Viking Awake(IRE) Official explanation: jockey said colt ran too free

6989 LADBROKESCASINO.COM H'CAP 1m 141y(P)
8:20 (8:21) (Class 5) (0-75,75) 3-Y-O+ **£3,885** (£1,156; £577; £288) **Stalls** Low

Form RPR
6363 **1** **It's A Dream (FR)**[7] 6826 5-8-10 65............................(t) GrahamGibbons 5 79
(M W Easterby) *a.p: wnt 2nd over 2f out: led on bit ins fnl f: sn clr* **9/2[2]**
6355 **2** *3 1/2* **Hepburn Bell (IRE)**[62] 5305 3-9-0 73........................(v[1]) RobertWinston 3 79
(J R Fanshawe) *s.i.s: in rr tl hdwy 2f out: n.m.r sn after: r.o to go 2nd wl ins fnl f* **11/2[3]**
6141 **3** *3/4* **Alfie Tupper (IRE)**[7] 6826 5-9-4 73.................................. PatCosgrave 2 77
(J R Boyle) *mid-div: wnt 2nd over 1f out tl wl ins fnl f* **5/2[1]**
2465 **4** *1 1/4* **Glenridding**[22] 6452 4-9-3 72... PaulMulrennan 8 73
(J G Given) *led tl rdn and hdd ins fnl f: outpcd* **12/1**
2326 **5** *2 3/4* **Del Mar Sunset**[16] 6599 9-9-5 74..................................... LiamJones 11 69
(W J Haggas) *in rr: hdwy whn n.m.r 2f out: kpt on one pce: n.d* **6/1**
-010 **6** *3/4* **Ghost Dancer**[16] 6598 4-9-5 74....................................... DaneO'Neill 10 67
(L M Cumani) *nvr bttr than mid-div* **7/1**
0610 **7** *1 3/4* **Middlemarch (IRE)**[21] 6482 8-9-1 75..........................(p) GaryBartley(5) 12 64
(J S Goldie) *mid-div: rdn and no ch whn hung lft over 1f out* **20/1**
0000 **8** *1/2* **King Of Rhythm (IRE)**[7] 6813 5-8-13 68.............................. DNolan 1 56
(D Carroll) *trckd ldrs tl rdn and wknd over 1f out* **25/1**
0006 **9** *hd* **Royal Island (IRE)**[7] 6826 6-8-9 64.............................. VinceSlattery 4 51
(M G Quinlan) *a towards rr* **25/1**
4502 **10** *1 1/2* **Hilbre Court (USA)**[14] 6659 3-8-9 75............................ BillyCray(7) 13 59
(B P J Baugh) *racd wd: a bhd* **12/1**
5 **11** *1/2* **Dubburg (USA)**[126] 3286 3-9-1 74................................. ChrisCatlin 7 57
(W J Musson) *t.k.h: hld up: a bhd* **33/1**
1535 **12** *6* **Morbick**[211] 1065 4-9-2 71... TGMcLaughlin 6 40
(W M Brisbourne) *trckd ldr to over 2f out: wknd qckly* **11/1**
0000 **13** *3 1/4* **August Gale (USA)**[14] 6659 3-8-13 72............................ DaleGibson 9 33
(G P Kelly) *in tch: rdn over 3f out: sn bhd* **66/1**

1m 49.7s (-0.80) **Going Correction** +0.025s/f (Slow)
WFA 3 from 4yo+ 4lb 13 Ran SP% **129.5**
Speed ratings (Par 103): **104,100,100,99,96 96,94,94,93,92 92,86,83**
toteswinger: 1&2 £3.90, 1&3 £2.00, 2&3 £6.80. CSF £30.50 CT £79.67 TOTE £4.70: £2.00, £2.00, £1.80; EX 36.20.
Owner Matthew Green **Bred** Serge Bernereau Sarl **Trained** Sheriff Hutton, N Yorks

FOCUS
An ordinary handicap and one run at a fair gallop. The form looks pretty sound.

6990 BET NOW WITH LADBROKES ON 0800 777 888 H'CAP 5f 20y(P)
8:50 (8:50) (Class 4) (0-80,80) 3-Y-O+ **£5,180** (£1,541; £770; £384) **Stalls** Low

Form RPR
3001 **1** **Invincible Lad (IRE)**[6] 6840 4-8-13 75 6ex........................ PatCosgrave 5 86
(E J Alston) *s.i.s: sn in tch: hdwy to go 3rd 2f out: led jst ins fnl f: hung lft but in command after* **11/8[1]**
-221 **2** *1 1/4* **Anne Of Kiev (IRE)**[15] 6633 3-9-3 79.............................. RobertHavlin 11 86
(J H M Gosden) *towards rr: hdwy over 1f out: kpt on to go 2nd post* **5/1[2]**
4310 **3** *nse* **Chelsea Girl**[4] 6880 3-8-5 67.. JimmyQuinn 4 76+
(C G Cox) *in rr: hdwy on ins over 1f out: chsd wnr fnl f tl hmpd and lost 2nd post* **5/1[2]**
5100 **4** *3/4* **Rothesay Dancer**[33] 6164 5-8-5 72............................... KellyHarrison(5) 3 76
(J S Goldie) *mid-div: effrt and hung lft whn sltly hmpd over 1f out: r.o ins fnl f* **20/1**
0303 **5** *1* **Cape Royal**[4] 6881 8-8-5 70...................................... KevinGhunowa(3) 1 70
(J M Bradley) *led tl hdd over 3f out: led again wl over 1f out: rdn and hdd jst ins fnl f* **8/1[3]**
0150 **6** *nk* **Namir (IRE)**[5] 6859 6-8-5 70.................................(vt) DuranFentiman(3) 6 69
(D Shaw) *plld hrd: hld up in rr: hdwy over 1f out: kpt on but nvr nr to chal* **16/1**
5060 **7** *3/4* **Incomparable**[15] 6627 3-8-8 70.................................... AndrewElliott 9 67
(A J McCabe) *chsd ldrs on outside: rdn 2f out: wknd appr fnl f* **66/1**
0062 **8** *4 1/2* **Thunder Bay**[7] 6823 3-8-9 71...................................... JamieMoriarty 7 51
(R A Fahey) *a towards rr* **16/1**
032 **9** *2* **Bookiesindex Boy**[32] 6190 4-8-8 75.........................(v) DavidProbert(5) 2 48
(J R Jenkins) *s.i.s: sn trckd ldr: led over 3f out: hdd wl over 1f out: wknd qckly* **8/1[3]**
0500 **10** *4* **Magic Glade**[56] 5493 9-8-8 70...................................... PatrickMathers 8 29
(Peter Grayson) *chsd ldrs on outside: wknd 1/2-way* **20/1**

62.00 secs (-0.30) **Going Correction** +0.025s/f (Slow) 10 Ran SP% **120.4**
Speed ratings (Par 105): **103,101,100,99,98 97,96,89,86,79**
toteswinger: 1&2 £1.50, 1&3 £1.50, 2&3 £5.90. CSF £8.43 CT £29.31 TOTE £2.20: £1.40, £1.10, £2.30; EX 8.20.
Owner Con Harrington **Bred** Mrs Chris Harrington **Trained** Longton, Lancs
■ Stewards' Enquiry : Pat Cosgrave two-day ban: careless riding (Nov 8-9)

FOCUS
A fair handicap in which the pace was sound throughout. Solid form with the winner continuing to progress and the fourth a good guide.

6991 GRAND SLAM DARTS AT WOLVERHAMPTON CIVIC H'CAP 1m 4f 50y(P)
9:20 (9:20) (Class 5) (0-75,75) 3-Y-O **£3,885** (£1,156; £577; £288) **Stalls** Low

Form RPR
4360 **1** **Bois Joli (IRE)**[16] 6599 3-8-9 73.................................. AndreaAtzeni(7) 4 81
(M Botti) *hld up towards rr: hdwy u.p over 2f out: wnt 2nd over 1f out: styd on to ld ins fnl f: hld on* **7/1**
0031 **2** *nk* **Black Rain**[12] 6703 3-9-1 75...................................... JackMitchell(3) 5 82
(P J McBride) *in tch: hdwy over 1f out: r.o to go 2nd ins fnl f: jst failed* **7/2[1]**
4224 **3** *1 1/4* **Hawk Flight (IRE)**[9] 6748 3-8-8 70.............................. DavidProbert(5) 10 75
(W R Muir) *trckd ldrs: led wl over 2f out: rdn and hdd ins fnl f: sn lost 2nd* **5/1[2]**
3604 **4** *3 3/4* **Paddy Rielly (IRE)**[5] 6868 3-8-1 61 oh1......................(p) LukeMorris(3) 3 60
(P D Evans) *towards rr: hdwy over 1f out: kpt on one pce* **15/2**
2310 **5** *5* **Dramatic Solo**[35] 6127 3-9-0 71.................................(b) AndrewElliott 7 62
(K R Burke) *led tl hdd wl over 1f out: wknd over 1f out* **11/1**
2400 **6** *2 1/4* **Houri (IRE)**[24] 6379 3-9-1 72...................................... RichardKingscote 8 59
(R M Beckett) *nvr bttr than mid-div* **14/1**
04-3 **7** *10* **Orkney (IRE)**[186] 1549 3-8-6 63.................................... RoystonFfrench 9 34
(Miss J A Camacho) *a bhd* **16/1**
-206 **8** *3 1/2* **Elliwan**[14] 6659 3-9-4 75.. DaleGibson 11 41
(M W Easterby) *sn wl bhd and nvr on terms* **40/1**
3022 **9** *3 3/4* **Eureka Moment**[16] 6596 3-8-8 65.................................... SteveDrowne 6 25
(E A L Dunlop) *a towards rr and no hdwy whn rdn over 3f out* **11/2[3]**
1240 **10** *2 1/4* **River Kent**[1] 6957 3-8-4 61 oh2...................................... JimmyQuinn 12 17
(Mrs A Duffield) *trckd ldrs tl wknd 2f out* **7/1**
400 **11** *6* **Turjuman (USA)**[12] 6703 3-8-6 63.................................... ChrisCatlin 2 10
(W J Musson) *w ldr tl rdn over 3f out: sn wknd* **25/1**
5334 **12** *26* **Cheeky Download (IRE)**[33] 6168 3-9-0 71...................... TGMcLaughlin 1 —
(E A L Dunlop) *trckd ldrs tl rdn and wknd 1/2-way: t.o* **16/1**

2m 39.91s (-1.19) **Going Correction** +0.025s/f (Slow) 12 Ran SP% **124.1**
Speed ratings (Par 101): **104,103,102,100,97 95,88,86,84,82 78,61**
toteswinger: 1&2 £6.50, 1&3 £9.80, 2&3 £6.10. CSF £33.22 CT £139.82 TOTE £8.90: £1.80, £2.00, £1.90; EX 39.00 Place 6: £7.27 Place 5: £3.48.
Owner Effevi Snc Di Villa Felice & C **Bred** Effevi Snc **Trained** Newmarket, Suffolk
■ Stewards' Enquiry : Jack Mitchell caution: careless riding.

FOCUS
A run-of-the-mill handicap in which the gallop was an ordinary one. The form is sound, rated through the third.
Black Rain Official explanation: trainer said gelding lost a hind shoe
T/Plt: £10.00 to a £1 stake. Pool: £74,750.84. 5,438.11 winning tickets. T/Qpdt: £2.50 to a £1 stake. Pool: £6,761.40. 1,985.30 winning tickets. JS

5736 BADEN-BADEN (L-H)
Saturday, October 25

OFFICIAL GOING: Soft

6992a HEEL BADEN-WURTTEMBERG-TROPHY (GROUP 3) 1m 3f
3:15 (3:40) 3-Y-O+ **£22,059** (£9,191; £3,676; £1,838)

RPR
1 **Sommertag (GER)**[55] 5557 5-9-0.. THellier 2 101
(J Hirschberger, Germany) *chsd ldr tl led 1f out: styd on wl* **59/10**
2 *3/4* **White Lightning (GER)**[22] 6461 6-9-0................................. APietsch 6 100
(U Stech, Norway) *prom: 5th st: r.o wl fnl f: nrest at fin* **119/10**
3 *1 1/4* **Schutzenjunker (GER)**[22] 6461 3-8-9................................ FilipMinarik 3 99
(U Ostmann, Germany) *set str pce tl hdd 1f out: no ex* **53/10[3]**
4 *shd* **Prince Flori (GER)**[22] 6461 5-9-4....................................... TMundry 10 102
(S Smrczek, Germany) *hld up: short of room ent st: swtchd to wd outside: kpt on: nt trble ldrs* **13/10[1]**
5 *1 1/2* **Pont Des Arts (FR)**[56] 5528 4-9-2...................................... OPlacais 9 97
(K Schafflutzel, Switzerland) *last to st: styd on fnl stages* **33/1**
6 *2* **Zaungast (IRE)**[22] 6461 4-9-0.. ASuborics 7 92
(W Hickst, Germany) *prom: 4th st: no ex fr over 1f out* **24/10[2]**
7 *3* **Simonas (IRE)**[27] 9-9-0... EPedroza 4 87
(A Wohler, Germany) *hld up in rr: n.d* **11/1**
8 *8* **Duellant (IRE)**[22] 6461 3-8-9.. AStarke 5 74
(P Schiergen, Germany) *racd in 3rd: no ex fr 2f out* **166/10**
9 *dist* **Proud Boris (GER)**[22] 6461 4-9-2...................................... RJuracek 8 —
(J Hanacek, Czech Republic) *mid-div: wknd st: t.o* **45/1**

2m 23.25s (3.98)
WFA 3 from 4yo+ 6lb 9 Ran SP% **130.1**
(Including 10 Euros stake): WIN 69; PL 24, 30, 24; SF 1,190.
Owner Gestut Schlenderhan **Bred** Gestut Schlenderhan **Trained** Germany

6965 SANTA ANITA (L-H)
Saturday, October 25

OFFICIAL GOING: Pro-ride (aw) - fast; turf course - firm

6993a BREEDERS' CUP MARATHON (PRO-RIDE) 1m 4f
6:10 (6:11) 3-Y-O+ **£153,317** (£56,784; £28,392; £14,480; £7,098)

RPR
1 **Muhannak (IRE)**[29] 6261 4-9-0.. PJSmullen 4 112
(R M Beckett) *racd in 4th: hdwy arnd outside to ld narrowly 2f out: hrd drvn and 1 1/2 l clr 1f out: drvn out: hld on wl* **10/1**
2 *hd* **Church Service (USA)**[63] 5-9-0... EPrado 1 112
(Mike Mitchell, U.S.A) *hld up in last: clsd up arnd outside fr 2f out: stl last appr fnl f: r.o wl: nrst fin* **14/1**
3 *3/4* **Big Booster (USA)**[87] 7-9-0..(b) RBejarano 6 111
(Mike Mitchell, U.S.A) *racd in 7th: hdwy arnd outside to dispute 2nd briefly 100yds out: kpt on* **9/1[3]**
4 *1 1/4* **Delightful Kiss (USA)**[28] 4-9-0.. CHBorel 2 109
(Pete D Anderson, U.S.A) *racd in 6th: edgd rt and hdwy between rivals to go 4th ent st: wnt 2nd 1f out: lost 2nd and one pce fnl 100yds* **13/2[2]**

The Form Book, Raceform Ltd, Compton, RG20 6NL

5 ½ **Sixties Icon**[27] 6303 5-9-0 .... LDettori 3 108
(J Noseda) *racd in 5th: trcking ldrs in 4th gng wl whn n.m.r 2f out: bmpd and dropped to 6th ent st: kpt on fr over 1f out* **11/8**[1]
6 1 ½ **Cedar Mountain (IRE)**[104] 5-9-0 .... JJCastellano 7 106
(Neil Drysdale, U.S.A) *racd in 3rd: 3rd st: one pce fr over 1f out* **12/1**
7 2 ½ **Zappa (USA)**[28] 6-9-0 ....(b) GKGomez 5 102
(John W Sadler, U.S.A) *racd in 2nd: disp ld over 3 1/2f out to 2f out: 2nd st: wknd over 1f out* **12/1**
8 2 ¼ **Booyah (USA)**[34] 4-9-0 .... JTalamo 8 99
(Jerry Fanning, U.S.A) *set stdy pce: jnd 3 1/2f out: hdd 2f out: sn btn* **40/1**

2m 28.24s (148.24) **8** Ran SP% **99.0**
PARI-MUTUEL (including $2 stake): WIN 26.80; PL (1-2) 10.80, 9.60; SHOW (1-2-3) 6.20, 6.80, 6.80; SF 266.20.
Owner R A Pegum **Bred** Mount Coote Stud **Trained** Whitsbury, Hants

FOCUS
The first running of this event, but not the test of stamina it might have been thanks to a very modest early pace. It still proved too much for the pair that set the moderate tempo though, as they were the last two home.

NOTEBOOK
Muhannak(IRE) has done nothing but improve since joining his current yard, firstly winning a Kempton handicap in a fast time and then following up in a Dundalk Listed event, and his proven ability on Polytrack was a major asset on this surface. Given a fine ride by Pat Smullen, he tracked the leading trio going comfortably before making his effort four wide rounding the home turn, and that proved to be a race-winning move. Connections are already talking about returning here for the same race next year.
Church Service(USA), who has form on this track, was held up right out the back before being delivered down the wide outside in the stretch and, although he was closing down the winner at the line, he was never quite getting there.
Big Booster(USA), who has been successful over further than this, looked a possible winner when delivered down the outside in the stretch, but although staying on he lacked the necessary finishing pace. He would probably have preferred a much stronger early pace.
Delightful Kiss(USA), bidding for a hat-trick after winning a couple of Grade 3s, was patiently ridden before moving closer on the home bend. He gave Sixties Icon a bump as he angled out from the rail on the crown of the home bend and put himself in a challenging position, but there was little more to come from him after that.
Sixties Icon, who was held up off the pace for most of the way, was close enough turning in though admittedly he was rather locked away in a pocket. He did take quite a buffeting between Big Booster and Delightful Kiss straightening up for home, but whether that made the difference between victory and defeat is debatable and, as with some of his rivals, the lack of early pace was probably a greater handicap.

6994a BREEDERS' CUP TURF SPRINT 6f 110y
6:50 (6:52) 3-Y-0+ **£324,271** (£120,101; £60,050; £30,626; £15,013)

RPR

1 **Desert Code (USA)**[31] 4-9-0 ....(b) RMigliore 9 120
(David Hofmans, U.S.A) *12th early: 11th st: 9th appr fnl f: str run to ld cl home* **40/1**
2 ½ **Diabolical (USA)**[27] 6304 5-9-0 .... LDettori 8 119
(Saeed Bin Suroor) *midfield: 6th st: hdwy to ld jst over 1f out: hdd and no ex cl home* **11/2**[2]
3 1 **Storm Treasure (USA)**[21] 5-9-0 .... SXBridgmohan 6 116
(Steven Asmussen, U.S.A) *last to 1 1/2f out: styd on wl down outside fr over 1f out* **33/1**
4 ¾ **Fleeting Spirit (IRE)**[20] 6518 3-8-8 .... JMurtagh 2 110
(J Noseda) *hld up: 8th st: hdwy on ins to dispute 2nd 1f out to 100yds out: one pce* **5/1**[1]
5 nse **Heros Reward (USA)**[21] 6-9-0 .... JJCastellano 1 114
(Dale Capuano, U.S.A) *hld up: 7th st: hdwy towards ins to dispute 2nd 1f out to 100yds out: one pce* **20/1**
6 1 **Salute The Count (USA)**[54] 8-9-0 ....(b) ECoa 5 111
(Richard Dutrow Jr, U.S.A) *hld up in 13th: styd on down ins fr over 1f out: nrst fin* **25/1**
7 2 **True To Tradition (USA)**[21] 6-9-0 ....(b) KCarmouche 3 105
(Scott Lake, U.S.A) *in tch: 5th st: one pce fr over 1f out* **14/1**
8 ¾ **One Union (USA)**[31] 5-9-0 .... VEspinoza 12 103
(Richard E Mandella, U.S.A) *cl up: 4th st: sn rdn and one pce* **40/1**
9 1 **Get Funky (USA)**[31] 5-9-0 .... JValdivia 13 100
(John W Sadler, U.S.A) *midfield: 9th st: nvr a factor* **5/1**[1]
10 2 ½ **California Flag (USA)**[31] 4-9-0 ....(b) JTalamo 10 93
(Brian Koriner, U.S.A) *pressed ldr tl led 2f out: 2l clr 1 1/2f out: hdd jst over 1f out: wknd* **7/1**
11 ¾ **Mr. Nightlinger (USA)**[63] 4-9-0 .... HJTheriotII 14 91
(W Bret Calhoun, U.S.A) *led to 2f out: hung rt ent st: sn wknd* **13/2**[3]
12 nk **Rouse The Cat (USA)**[21] 4-9-0 ....(b) EPrado 7 90
(Ollie Figgins III, U.S.A) *nvr a factor* **16/1**
13 1 ¾ **Idiot Proof (USA)**[28] 4-9-0 .... GKGomez 11 85
(Clifford Sise Jr, U.S.A) *cl up: 3rd st: sn wknd* **14/1**
14 1 ½ **Only Answer**[41] 5955 4-8-11 .... OPeslier 4 77
(A Fabre, France) *towards rr: squeezed up over 1 1/2f out: sn rdn and btn* **16/1**

1m 11.6s (71.60)
WFA 3 from 4yo+ 1lb **14** Ran SP% **116.1**
PARI-MUTUEL: WIN 75.00; PL (1-2) 30.80, 7.60; SHOW (1-2-3) 21.00, 5.20, 9.20; SF 786.20.
Owner Tarabilla Farms Inc **Bred** Classic Star Llc **Trained** USA

FOCUS
Another new race for the Breeders' Cup and an unusual track by US standards, rather like watching a Breeders' Cup race being run around Brighton. The pace set by California Flag and Mr Nightlinger was breakneck and the pair paid for it by eventually dropping right out, whilst those held up were favoured and the eventual first and third came from a mile back.

NOTEBOOK
Desert Code(USA) had finished well behind California Flag and another couple of these rivals over course and distance last time when ridden prominently, but he was switched right off this time and the change of tactics worked a treat as he produced a smart turn of foot to nail the runner-up near the line.
Diabolical(USA), a multiple winner on turf and dirt in the US before moving to Godolphin, travelled powerfully in the middle of the field and looked sure to win when sweeping to the front passing the furlong pole, only to cruelly have the prize snatched from him near the line. He did everything right and was just plain unfortunate.
Storm Treasure(USA), held up last in the early stages as is his style, was brought with his effort widest off the final bend and, despite tending to wander about, he put in a storming late effort that was always falling a little short.
Fleeting Spirit(IRE) was racing over the longest trip she had ever attempted and also running around a bend for the first time. She was given a fine ride by Murtagh, who held her together and saved every ounce of energy he could by keeping the filly as close to the inside rail as possible. There was a point halfway up the stretch when it looked as though she might get involved, but the last half-furlong just seemed to find her out.
Heros Reward(USA), behind True To Tradition the last twice they had met, managed to reverse that form having been given a patient ride, but although he stayed on late he was never quite doing enough.
Only Answer never managed to get into the race at any stage.

6995a BREEDERS' CUP DIRT MILE (PRO-RIDE) 1m
7:30 (7:32) 3-Y-0+ **£271,357** (£100,503; £50,251; £25,628; £12,563)

RPR

1 **Albertus Maximus (USA)**[28] 4-9-0 .... GKGomez 7 121
(Vladimir Cerin, U.S.A) *towards rr: gd hdwy under 2f out to go 5th ent st: led 1f out: r.o strly* **11/2**[3]
2 1 ¼ **Rebellion**[31] 5-9-0 .... EPrado 10 118
(H Graham Motion, U.S.A) *s.i.s: last tl got dream split between rivals and hdwy jst under 1 1/2f out: styd on wl to take 2nd cl home* **20/1**
3 ½ **Two Step Salsa (USA)**[54] 3-8-10 .... MPedroza 5 116
(Julio C Canani, U.S.A) *set hot pce: hdd jst over 1f out: rallied to regain 2nd 100yds out: lost 2nd cl home* **25/1**
4 hd **My Pal Charlie (USA)**[35] 3-8-10 .... VEspinoza 11 116
(Albert Stall Jr, U.S.A) *towards rr tl gd hdwy under 2f out to go 2nd st: led briefly jst over 1f out: sn hdd: lost 2nd 100yds out* **12/1**
5 1 ¼ **Mast Track (USA)**[28] 4-9-0 ....(b) TBaze 4 115
(Robert Frankel, U.S.A) *midfield: hdwy on ins to go 3rd under 1 1/2f out: sn rdn and one pce* **12/1**
6 3 ¾ **Pyro (USA)**[21] 3-8-10 .... SXBridgmohan 6 106
(Steven Asmussen, U.S.A) *towards rr: sme late hdwy but nvr nr ldrs* **14/1**
7 1 ½ **Lewis Michael (USA)**[62] 5-9-0 ....(b) ECoa 1 104
(Wayne Catalano, U.S.A) *bmpd 1st turn: prom: 4th st: sn wknd* **5/1**[2]
8 ½ **Lord Admiral (USA)**[21] 6504 7-9-0 ....(b) JMurtagh 12 103
(Charles O'Brien, Ire) *in rr: effrt arnd outside 2f out: nt clr run ent st but sn btn* **33/1**
9 1 **Well Armed (USA)**[28] 5-9-0 .... AGryder 8 101
(Eoin Harty, U.S.A) *nvr travelling wl on outside: racd in 6th: rdn wl over 3f out: nvr a factor* **15/8**[1]
10 2 ½ **Slew's Tiznow (USA)**[57] 3-8-10 .... RBejarano 9 95
(Doug O'Neill, U.S.A) *nvr bttr than midfield* **20/1**
11 ½ **Slew's Tizzy (USA)**[29] 4-9-0 .... JRosario 3 95
(Doug O'Neill, U.S.A) *cl up on outside tl wknd 2f out* **33/1**
12 9 ¼ **Surf Cat (USA)**[28] 6-9-0 ....(b) DFlores 2 77
(Bruce Headley, U.S.A) *prom tl wknd 2f out* **12/1**

1m 33.41s (93.41)
WFA 3 from 4yo+ 3lb **12** Ran SP% **115.8**
PARI-MUTUEL: WIN 14.60; PL (1-2) 7.40, 16.00; SHOW (1-2-3) 5.40, 11.20, 12.80; SF 218.60.
Owner Brandon L & Marianne Chase **Bred** Marianne Chase & Brandon L Chase **Trained** USA

FOCUS
The second running of this race, which incidentally now looks terribly named, and the form is ordinary. However, it was at least competitive, and they went quick, favouring those held up.

NOTEBOOK
Albertus Maximus(USA) had finished just under two lengths behind Well Armed over 1m1f here last time, but that one failed to give his running and he reversed form in no uncertain terms. Given a nice waiting ride, he made some good headway towards the inside before being switched right at the top of the straight and ran on strongly. He looks to be improving and his jockey said he felt the horse still feels green under this sort of hold-up ride.
Rebellion, formerly trained by Mark Johnston, looked to have something to find at this level, but he ran a huge race under an exaggerated hold-up ride. He was last to break and stayed well out the back until making some headway round the final bend, and then finished really strongly in the straight, clearly having saved plenty. He was mainly passing beaten horses, but this was still a big run, especially as he had previously looked best at shorter distances.
Two Step Salsa(USA) ran a huge race considering he was going hard up front from the off. He looked set to drop away in the straight, just as all of those around him early had, but he stuck on most gamely.
My Pal Charlie(USA) was given a good ride in defeat and had his chance.
Mast Track(USA) did not seem to have an excuse.
Lord Admiral(USA) is better than he showed as he was checked in his run at a crucial stage and lost all momentum.
Well Armed(USA) was a big disappointment considering he beat today's winner last time. It was a surprise to see him ridden so aggressively considering the pace was so hot, and he was stuck wide when trying to lay up down the back straight, but he basically looked to have an off-day as he was one of the first beaten. His jockey said he was leaned on at the first turn and the horse didn't get the clear trip he needs, as he has a particularly long stride.

6996a BREEDERS' CUP MILE (GRADE 1) (TURF) 1m (T)
8:15 (8:19) 3-Y-0+ **£577,990** (£214,070; £107,035; £54,588; £26,759)

RPR

1 **Goldikova (IRE)**[48] 5740 3-8-9 ow2.. OPeslier 4 125+
(F Head, France) *trckd ldr in 2nd: 3rd under 6f out: 4th st: qcknd between rivals to ld 1f out: sn clr: r.o strly* **9/4**[1]
2 1 ¼ **Kip Deville (USA)**[48] 5-9-0 ....(b) CVelasquez 2 122
(Richard Dutrow Jr, U.S.A) *disp 4th: 5th st: ev ch briefly jst over 1f out: r.o but nt pce of wnr* **7/2**[2]
3 2 ½ **Whatsthescript (IRE)**[62] 4-9-0 .... GKGomez 11 116
(John W Sadler, U.S.A) *last to 1 1/2f out: styd on down outside to take 3rd last strides* **9/2**[3]
4 hd **Precious Kitten (USA)**[22] 6462 5-8-11 .... RBejarano 3 113
(Robert Frankel, U.S.A) *disp 4th: 3rd st: led jst under 1 1/2f out to 1f out: one pce* **12/1**
5 nk **US Ranger (USA)**[21] 6496 4-9-0 ....(b) JMurtagh 7 115
(A P O'Brien, Ire) *in rr: styd on towards ins fr over 1f out but nvr nr ldrs* **12/1**
6 nk **Awesome Gem (USA)**[28] 5-9-0 ....(b) TBaze 6 114
(Craig Dollase, U.S.A) *a midfield* **25/1**
7 1 **War Monger (USA)**[21] 6504 4-9-0 .... KDesormeaux 9 112
(William Mott, U.S.A) *towards rr: kpt on down outside fr over 1f out* **25/1**
8 hd **Bold Chieftain (USA)**[20] 5-9-0 ....(b) RBaze 8 112
(William Morey Jr, U.S.A) *midfield: one pce fnl 1 1/2f* **33/1**
9 1 ¾ **Thorn Song (USA)**[21] 6504 5-9-0 ....(b) RAlbarado 10 108
(Dale Romans, U.S.A) *led to 2f out: 2nd st: sn wknd* **20/1**
10 1 ½ **Daytona (IRE)**[62] 4-9-0 .... ASolis 5 104
(Dan L Hendricks, U.S.A) *wnt 2nd under 6f out: led 2f out to 1 1/2f out: wknd* **14/1**
11 ¾ **Shakis (IRE)**[21] 6504 8-9-0 .... AGarcia 1 102
(Kiaran McLaughlin, U.S.A) *towards rr: hdwy on ins to go 6th st: hmpd over 1f out and ins fnl f: eased* **16/1**

1m 33.4s (-0.47)
WFA 3 from 4yo+ 3lb **11** Ran SP% **114.5**
PARI-MUTUEL: WIN 5.60; PL (1-2) 4.00, 4.80; SHOW (1-2-3) 2.80, 3.40, 3.40; SF 27.20.
Owner Wertheimer Et Frere **Bred** Wertheimer Et Frere **Trained** France

FOCUS
A race that has traditionally been targeted by European stables, and France especially has a good record in the event having taken it with the Pascal Bary-trained pair Domedriver and Six Perfections in 2002 and 2003 respectively.
NOTEBOOK
Goldikova(IRE) was bidding for a four-timer following her wins over the girls in the Prix Chloe and Prix d'Astarte and from both sexes in the Prix du Moulin. There was a slight question mark against her on this quicker ground and with the possibility of a tactical race, but Peslier always had her in a handy position to reduce the risk of her getting caught on heels. She travelled kindly throughout and the only slight moment of concern came when it looked as though she might not get a run between Precious Kitten and Daytona over a furlong from home, but her rider didn't panic and waited for the gap to appear. When it did, she produced one of the most dazzling turns of foot seen by any horse at the top level in recent years.
Kip Deville(USA), last year's winner, was produced with every chance to follow up in these very different conditions and he certainly ran his race, but he was up against a true international superstar here.
Whatsthescript(IRE) has a decent record fresh, so his two-month absence since winning the Del Mar Mile was a positive. Switched right off in a detached last early, he was forced to come extremely wide in order to make his final effort and, though he stayed on strongly, he was being asked a huge question to make up so much ground in this company.
Precious Kitten(USA) was produced to hit the front coming to the last furlong, but she was soon swamped on either side by the front pair and then seemed to completely run out of petrol.
US Ranger(USA) only had the eventual third behind him for most of the way and he didn't seem to be helping his rider at all when asked to take closer order rounding the home bend. He did plug on, but it was a case of far too little too late.

6997a BESSEMER TRUST BREEDERS' CUP JUVENILE (GRADE 1) (C&G) (PRO-RIDE) 1m 110y(D)

8:55 (8:57) 2-Y-O **£577,990** (£214,070; £107,035; £54,588; £26,759)

RPR

1 **Midshipman (USA)**[27] 2-8-10 ....(b) GKGomez 10 118
(Bob Baffert, U.S.A) *pressed ldr tl led over 5f out: mde rest: drvn out* **5/1**[3]
2 1 1/4 **Square Eddie (CAN)**[21] 6503 2-8-10 .... RBejarano 4 115
(Doug O'Neill, U.S.A) *led narrowly tl hdd over 5f out: dropped to 3rd 3f out: rallied on ins to regain 2nd 1f out: sllightly short of room 100yds out: kpt on* **4/1**[1]
3 1/2 **Street Hero (USA)**[27] 2-8-10 ....(b) ASolis 7 114
(Myung Kwon Cho, U.S.A) *racd in 3rd tl wnt 2nd 3f out: hrd rdn and kpt on at one pce fr wl over 1f out* **9/2**[2]
4 1/2 **Terrain (USA)**[21] 6503 2-8-10 .... HJTheriotll 3 113+
(Albert Stall Jr, U.S.A) *towards rr: styd on fr over 1f out to take 4th cl home* **16/1**
5 1/2 **Pioneerof The Nile (USA)**[21] 6503 2-8-10 .... RAlbarado 9 112
(William Mott, U.S.A) *racd in 5th: one pce fnl 1 1/2f* **25/1**
6 nk **West Side Bernie (USA)**[28] 2-8-10 .... StewartElliott 12 111+
(Kelly Breen, U.S.A) *towards rr: styd on fnl 1 1/2f: nvr nr ldrs* **25/1**
7 1/2 **Gallant Son (USA)**[28] 2-8-10 .... LAMawing 2 110
(Frank Lucarelli, U.S.A) *a midfield* **16/1**
8 nk **Silent Valor (USA)**[27] 2-8-10 ....(b) EPrado 6 109
(Todd Pletcher, U.S.A) *in rr tl styd on fnl 1 1/2f* **20/1**
9 1 **Azul Leon (USA)**[27] 2-8-10 .... JRosario 5 107
(Doug O'Neill, U.S.A) *a in rr* **25/1**
10 nse **Munnings (USA)**[21] 6501 2-8-10 .... JRVelazquez 1 107
(Todd Pletcher, U.S.A) *cl up: 4th st: sn wknd* **15/2**
11 2 1/4 **Bushranger (IRE)**[22] 6442 2-8-10 .... JMurtagh 11 102+
(David Wachman, Ire) *forced to r wd in midfield: 7th st: sn btn* **11/2**
12 2 3/4 **Mine That Bird (USA)**[20] 2-8-10 .... ChantalSutherland 8 95
(Richard E Mandella, U.S.A) *midfield: wknd 1 1/2f out* **18/1**

1m 40.94s (-1.48) **12** Ran SP% **115.3**
PARI-MUTUEL: WIN 9.20; PL (1-2) 4.40, 5.00; SHOW (1-2-3) 3.20, 3.80, 4.40; SF 39.40.
Owner Darley Stable **Bred** Stonerside Stable **Trained** USA

FOCUS
The first Breeders' Cup race on the Pro-Ride track at this year's two-day meeting in which the early pace held up, as the first three were pretty much in the front three throughout. This looked a solid if fairly ordinary renewal and, with nothing getting into it from behind, the form needs treating with a little caution.
NOTEBOOK
Midshipman(USA) was just under a length behind Street Hero in the Norfolk Stakes over this course and distance last time, but he managed to reverse form with that rival, thanks in no small part to a great ride. Although he managed to get across from stall 11 to help force the early pace, his jockey felt he was running a little keen, and every time he tried to restrain, the horse threw his head back a little, so he had to be finessed round the first bend. From that point on, though, Gomez was happy with this long-striding colt, and he was soon travelling well. He took over from Square Eddie when that one dropped back slightly before the turn for home and was always holding that rival, who was trying to rally in the straight.
Square Eddie(CAN), runner-up in a Kempton Group 3 before winning a Grade 1 on the Polytrack at Keeneland for John Best, ran well on his debut for a new trainer. He may have finished even closer had he not surrendered the lead to the eventual winner over half a mile from home, as all he did was gallop in the straight. Things got a little tight towards the inside rail late on, but he was held at the time.
Street Hero(USA) was always well placed and had every chance if good enough, but he could not confirm recent form with today's winner.
Terrain(USA), nearly five lengths behind Square Eddie last time, finished well and fared best of those held up, but he was never getting there.
Pioneerof The Nile(USA) had to work hard to take a tight gap in the straight and that cannot have helped his chance.
West Side Bernie(USA) got going too late from the widest stall of all.
Bushranger(IRE) ran no race on this step up in trip and switch to a synthetic surface. Johnny Murtagh said, "maybe he didn't stay, but I don't think he liked the track anyway".

6998a GREY GOOSE BREEDERS' CUP JUVENILE TURF (GRADE 1) (C&G) 1m (T)

9:35 (9:38) 2-Y-O **£306,633** (£113,568; £56,784; £28,960; £14,196)

RPR

1 **Donativum**[21] 6474 2-8-10 .... LDettori 4 113+
(J H M Gosden) *towards rr early: 6th whn edgd outside ent st: hdwy between rivals to go 3rd 1f out: led 50yds out: r.o wl* **11/2**[3]
2 1/2 **Westphalia (IRE)**[42] 5889 2-8-10 .... JMurtagh 3 112
(A P O'Brien, Ire) *towards rr: hdwy on ins over 3f out: bhd ldrs gng wl in 4th 1 1/2f out: swtchd rt: led ins fnl f: hdd 50yds out* **3/1**[1]
3 1 3/4 **Coronet Of A Baron (USA)**[52] 2-8-10 .... AGarcia 7 108
(Eoin Harty, U.S.A) *cl up: 2nd st: led over 1f out to ins fnl f: one pce* **8/1**
4 hd **City Style (USA)**[35] 2-8-10 .... TMcNeil 2 108
(Cheryl Asmussen, U.S.A) *in rr: 11th st: styd on wl fnl f: fin strly* **25/1**
5 2 1/2 **Relatively Ready (USA)**[24] 2-8-10 .... CVelasquez 5 102
(David Donk, U.S.A) *in rr: 10th and rdn over 1 1/2f out: kpt on* **25/1**
6 nse **Vaquero (USA)**[20] 2-8-10 .... KDesormeaux 6 102
(Michael P Leahy, U.S.A) *towards rr: 11th over 1f out: kpt on* **25/1**
7 3/4 **Orthodox (USA)**[28] 2-8-10 ....(b) JKCourt 9 100
(John Glenney, U.S.A) *led to over 1f out: wknd* **50/1**
8 1 **Bittel Road (USA)**[20] 2-8-10 .... JRVelazquez 11 98
(Todd Pletcher, U.S.A) *racd in 2nd: 3rd st: wknd over 1f out* **5/1**[2]
9 1/2 **Ninth Client (USA)**[20] 2-8-10 .... JRLeparoux 1 96
(D Wayne Lukas, U.S.A) *nvr a factor* **25/1**
10 hd **Grand Adventure (USA)**[21] 2-8-10 .... RBejarano 12 96
(Mark Frostad, Canada) *cl up on outside: 5th st: wknd over 1f out* **11/2**[3]
11 3/4 **Skipadate (USA)**[21] 2-8-10 ....(b) SXBridgmohan 10 94
(Mark Casse, Canada) *cl up: rdn 3f out: 7th st: wknd fnl f* **12/1**
12 8 1/4 **Paddy The Pro (IRE)**[29] 6258 2-8-10 .... GKGomez 8 75
(Patrick Gallagher, U.S.A) *a bhd* **12/1**

1m 34.68s (0.81) **12** Ran SP% **116.3**
PARI-MUTUEL: WIN 13.60; PL (1-2) 7.00, 5.40; SHOW (1-2-3) 5.00, 3.80, 5.40; SF 47.20.
Owner H R H Princess Haya Of Jordan **Bred** Stratford Place Stud **Trained** Newmarket, Suffolk

FOCUS
The second running of this race and a decent pace was set by the outsider Orthodox. The winning time was just 1.28secs slower than Goldikova in the Mile and this was a triumph for Europe with Donativum just getting the better of Westphalia in a thrilling finish. The runner-up sets the level of a race lacking strength in depth.
NOTEBOOK
Donativum could hardly have received a more timely boost than when Crowded House, whom he beat in the Tattersalls Timeform Million last time out, was an impressive winner of the Racing Post earlier in the day, and even the sixth horse took the opening maiden at Newbury. Given a patient ride by Dettori, he didn't have a great deal of room to play with when both he and the runner-up went for the same gap between Coronet Of A Baron and Grand Adventure a furlong from home, but he held his ground and just found a superior turn of foot when both were out in the clear. The longer trip was certainly not a problem, at least not on a sharp track like this, and being a gelding it will be interesting to see what connections do with him now.
Westphalia(IRE), another trying 1m for the first time, was settled off the pace after taking an early bump but he travelled noticeably well. All dressed up with nowhere to go turning in, he had to switch right in order to get a run just as the winner was making his move, and it did look as though he had got first run on Donativum when the pair had got through the gap, but his rival cut him down close to the line. This was still a fine effort and he remains on course for the 2,000 Guineas.
Coronet Of A Baron(USA), whose narrow defeat by Midshipman at Del Mar the previous month was given a boost in the preceding contest, was produced to hit the front a furlong from home, but he had little left when the two Europeans were unleashed and he didn't appear to see out the extra furlong.
City Style(USA), proven over the trip albeit in lesser company, was given plenty to do and although staying on at the end, he faced a hopeless task.
Bittel Road(USA) was a bit disappointing as he was bang there on the home turn before fading tamely.

6999a SENTIENT FLIGHT GROUP BREEDERS' CUP SPRINT (GRADE 1) (PRO-RIDE) 6f (D)

10:15 (10:18) 3-Y-O+ **£542,714** (£201,005; £100,503; £51,256; £25,126)

RPR

1 **Midnight Lute (USA)**[62] 5-9-0 .... GKGomez 3 128
(Bob Baffert, U.S.A) *last tl hdwy arnd outside 2f out: 4th st: led ins fnl f: r.o strly* **10/3**[2]
2 1 3/4 **Fatal Bullet (USA)**[28] 3-8-11 ....(b) ERosaDaSilva 8 120
(Reade Baker, Canada) *pressed ldr tl led jst over 3f out: hdd ins fnl f: one pce* **4/1**[3]
3 1 3/4 **Street Boss (USA)**[28] 4-9-0 .... DFlores 1 117
(Bruce Headley, U.S.A) *hld up in 7th: hdwy towards outside 2f out: kpt on fnl f: nt pce of first two* **3/1**[1]
4 1 **In Summation (USA)**[28] 5-9-0 .... JRVelazquez 6 114
(Christophe Clement, U.S.A) *racd in 5th: kpt on at one pce fnl 2f* **8/1**
5 1 1/2 **Fabulous Strike (USA)**[28] 5-9-0 .... RADominguez 2 110
(Todd M Beattie, U.S.A) *pressed ldr early: racd in 3rd: one pce fnl 1 1/2f* **7/1**
6 1/2 **Sing Baby Sing (USA)**[21] 5-9-0 ....(b) JustinShepherd 7 108
(Jack Bruner, U.S.A) *racd in 7th: last st: nvr a factor* **28/1**
7 7 **Black Seventeen (USA)**[28] 4-9-0 ....(b) CLPotts 5 87
(Brian Koriner, U.S.A) *cl up: 2nd 2f out: sn wknd* **12/1**
8 3 3/4 **First Defence (USA)**[28] 4-9-0 .... JJCastellano 4 76
(Robert Frankel, U.S.A) *led narrowly tl hdd jst over 3f out: wknd 2f out* **12/1**

67.08 secs (-1.18)
WFA 3 from 4yo+ 1lb **8** Ran SP% **110.5**
PARI-MUTUEL: WIN 7.40; PL (1-2) 5.00, 6.60; SHOW (1-2-3) 3.20, 3.80, 2.40; SF 47.60.
Owner Watson & Weitman Performances & Pegram **Bred** Tom Evans, Macon Wilmil Equines & Marjac Farms **Trained** USA
■ Garrett Gomez became the first jockey to ride three Breeders' Cup winners on the same day.

FOCUS
They went quick up front, as you would expect.
NOTEBOOK
Midnight Lute(USA), just as when winning this race in the slop at Monmouth Park 12 months earlier, stayed on best of all from well back. This famous follow-up victory was gained in a time of 1m 7.08sec, which bettered the previous quickest Breeders' Cup time of 1m 7.77sec set by Kona Gold at Churchill Downs in 2000. This was a remarkable effort from the winner, and a brilliant training performance from Bob Baffert, as the five-year-old had managed just two runs since last year's victory, having suffered from a quarter crack, and was well beaten on his only starts this season over 7f in August. He was yet another winner on the Pro-Ride to make his move on the wide outside, and his momentum carried him past Fatal Bullet.
Fatal Bullet(USA) ran a huge race in defeat considering he took over the strong pace at halfway.
Street Boss(USA) made his move from a similar position to the winner, but he basically lacked that one's speed.
In Summation(USA) basically didn't seem quite good enough.
Fabulous Strike(USA) was below form having been unable to dominate.

7000a EMIRATES AIRLINE BREEDERS' CUP TURF (GRADE 1) 1m 4f (T)

11:00 (11:04) 3-Y-O+ **£866,985** (£301,508; £150,754; £76,884; £37,668)

RPR

1 **Conduit (IRE)**[42] 5892 3-8-9 .... RyanMoore 9 127
(Sir Michael Stoute) *dropped out in 8th: hdwy between rivals 2f out: wnt 5th ent st: styd on to ld 100yds out: r.o wl* **7/2**[2]
2 1 1/2 **Eagle Mountain**[22] 6440 4-9-0 .... KShea 11 123
(M F De Kock, South Africa) *racd in 4th: trcking ldrs gng wl ent st: rdn to ld 1f out: hdd and no ex last 100yds* **7/1**[3]
3 2 1/4 **Dancing Forever (USA)**[28] 5-9-0 ....(b) RRDouglas 6 119
(Claude McGaughey III, U.S.A) *racd in 6th: rdn to go cl 4th ent st: styd on to take 3rd cl home* **25/1**

4 *hd* **Soldier Of Fortune (IRE)**[20] 6522 4-9-0 JMurtagh 4 119
(A P O'Brien, Ire) *trckd pcemaker in 3rd tl led narrowly 4f out: pushed along 3f out: rdn and 1 l clr 1 1/2f out: hdd 1f out: lost 3rd cl home* **2/1**[1]

5 *5 1/4* **Out Of Control (BRZ)**[28] 5-9-0 GKGomez 10 111
(Robert Frankel, U.S.A) *racd in 2nd: pressed ldr 4f out to over 1 1/2f out: wknd* **16/1**

6 *3* **Red Rock Canyon (IRE)**[20] 6522 4-9-0 CO'Donoghue 7 106
(A P O'Brien, Ire) *set str pce to 4f out: one pce* **66/1**

7 *3/4* **Winchester (USA)**[77] 4887 3-8-9 (b) PJSmullen 5 107
(D K Weld, Ire) *racd in 9th: nvr a factor* **12/1**

8 *hd* **Better Talk Now (USA)**[48] 9-9-0 (b) RADominguez 1 105
(H Graham Motion, U.S.A) *detached in last tl sme late hdwy* **25/1**

9 *1 3/4* **Spring House (USA)**[28] 6-9-0 (b) JRVelazquez 8 102
(Julio C Canani, U.S.A) *racd in 7th: rdn and btn under 2f out* **25/1**

10 *3/4* **Red Rocks (IRE)**[105] 3995 5-9-0 (b) LDettori 2 101
(Mark Hennig, U.S.A) *racd in 5th: wknd over 2f out* **15/2**

11 *2* **Grand Couturier**[28] 5-9-0 AGarcia 3 98
(Robert Ribaudo, U.S.A) *t.o virtually thrght* **7/1**[3]

2m 23.42s (-3.23)
WFA 3 from 4yo+ 7lb **11** Ran SP% **118.9**
PARI-MUTUEL: WIN 13.60; PL (1-2) 8.40, 9.60; SHOW (1-2-3) 5.80, 6.40, 12.80; SF 107.20.
Owner Ballymacoll Stud **Bred** Ballymacoll Stud Farm Ltd **Trained** Newmarket, Suffolk

FOCUS
A race in which Europe has done especially well over the years and it also featured two previous winners in Better Talk Now and Red Rocks, though both were ultimately disappointing. They went very fast in this thanks to the Ballydoyle pacemaker Red Rock Canyon and the field were spread out over a wide area with a circuit left, but a test of stamina was just what connections of St Leger winner Conduit would have hoped for and he produced the goods to give Sir Michael Stoute a third win in the race following Pilsudski and Kalanisi.

NOTEBOOK
Conduit(IRE), given a patient ride by Ryan Moore, who was perfectly happy to let the pace-setters get on with it, got stronger as the race progressed and, once switched out wide to make his effort in the stretch, both his stamina and his undoubted finishing speed were there for all to see. He was going to be retired after the Leger, but connections were understandably delighted to have made the decision to come here and, in view of his trainer's superb record with older horses, it would be wonderful to see him return to the track next year.
Eagle Mountain, placed in last year's English and Irish Derby, was having his second start for the yard after winning on his return from a year off over 1m at Newmarket earlier in the month. Nothing was travelling better throughout the contest and he hit the front on the bridle soon after turning for home, but he couldn't get away and had no answer when the winner appeared. It's hard to be critical of a horse that has now run three such big races at the highest level over this trip, especially with the problems he has had, but it did look as though it was right on the limit of his stamina here.
Dancing Forever(USA) was produced to hold every chance turning for home, but lacked the speed of the front pair.
Soldier Of Fortune(IRE)'s performance is difficult to dissect. Soon racing right behind his pacemaker Red Rock Canyon, along with Out Of Control, he was presented with a gap on the inside when his stable companion moved off the rail racing down the back stretch, but he had to be ridden to go through it and when he needed to find more to fend off the challengers down the home straight, there was very little left. It's possible that he was still feeling the effects of his performance in the Arc and perhaps this ground was a bit quicker than he cares for.
Out Of Control(BRZ) had stamina doubts coming into this and after mixing it with the Ballydoyle pair for a long way, he had run his race by the time the field straightened up for home.
Grand Couturier looked to be the best of the home contingent coming into this, but he ran no sort of race.

7001a BREEDERS' CUP CLASSIC (GRADE 1) (PRO-RIDE) 1m 2f (D)
11:45 (11:52) 3-Y-O+ **£1,356,784** (£502,513; £251,256; £128,141; £62,814)

RPR

1 **Raven's Pass (USA)**[28] 6270 3-8-9 LDettori 8 128
(J H M Gosden) *held up in 10th, headway over 2f out, 4th straight on outside, led 1f out, driven out* **8/1**[3]

2 *1 3/4* **Henrythenavigator (USA)**[28] 6270 3-8-9 JRVelazquez 5 125
(A P O'Brien, Ire) *raced in 7th, pushed along over 2f out, 5th straight, stayed on well to take 2nd inside final f* **11/1**

3 *3/4* **Tiago (USA)**[28] 4-9-0 MESmith 3 123
(John Shirreffs, U.S.A) *held up in 11th, 8th straight, stayed on well to take 2nd close home* **25/1**

4 *nk* **Curlin (USA)**[28] 6373 4-9-0 RAlbarado 9 122
(Steven Asmussen, U.S.A) *raced in 8th, good headway around outside to lead just under 2f out, headed 1f out, one pace, lost 3rd close home* **6/4**[1]

5 *1 3/4* **Go Between (USA)**[62] 5-9-0 GKGomez 1 119+
(William Mott, U.S.A) *raced in 4th, lost place over 2f out, 9th straight, stayed on well from over 1f out* **15/2**[2]

6 *1/2* **Colonel John (USA)**[63] 3-8-9 EPrado 11 118
(Eoin Harty, U.S.A) *raced in 6th, headway towards outside to dispute lead briefly 2f out, 2nd straight, one pace* **10/1**

7 *nk* **Smooth Air (USA)**[28] 3-8-9 RBejarano 6 117
(Bennie F Stutts Jr, U.S.A) *raced in 5th, 6th straight, soon ridden and one pace* **66/1**

8 *nse* **Champs Elysees**[21] 6506 5-9-0 (b) AGarcia 12 117
(Robert Frankel, U.S.A) *held up in last, 10th straight, no real headway* **20/1**

9 *3/4* **Duke Of Marmalade (IRE)**[20] 6522 4-9-0 JMurtagh 4 116
(A P O'Brien, Ire) *raced in 3rd, led briefly over 2f out, soon headed and weakened* **9/1**

10 *7* **Fairbanks (USA)**[28] 5-9-0 RMigliore 10 102
(Todd Pletcher, U.S.A) *raced in 2nd, disputed lead briefly under 2 1/2f out, soon weakened* **33/1**

11 *1 3/4* **Student Council (USA)**[62] 6-9-0 SXBridgmohan 7 98
(Steven Asmussen, U.S.A) *held up in 9th, behind final 2f* **33/1**

12 *6 1/4* **Casino Drive (USA)**[13] 3-8-9 VEspinoza 2 86
(Kazuo Fujisawa, Japan) *set strong pace til headed under 2 1/2f out, weakened* **9/1**

1m 59.27s (-0.61)
WFA 3 from 4yo+ 5lb **12** Ran SP% **116.3**
PARI-MUTUEL: WIN 29.00; PL (1-2) 15.80, 22.00; SHOW (1-2-3) 8.00, 11.20, 7.00; SF 319.00.
Owner H R H Princess Haya Of Jordan **Bred** Stonerside Stable **Trained** Newmarket, Suffolk
■ Raven's Pass became the first Classic winner trained in Europe since Arcangues in 1993.

FOCUS
In theory, this year's Classic offered Flat racing fans the sort of contest they have always wanted to see. The very best dirt horses, competing against some of the top turf performers on a level playing field. However, while this was indeed both a great race, as well as a fascinating spectacle, it would be wrong to pretend that this new surface suits every horse equally.

NOTEBOOK
Raven's Pass(USA) had finally got the better of Henrythenavigator in the Queen Elizabeth II Stakes at Ascot last time, having finished behind that rival in the Guineas, St James's Palace, and the Sussex Stakes, and he just proved the stronger of the pair once again. He was the subject of a significant jockey change since his last run, with Dettori replacing Jimmy Fortune in the saddle, and the Italian got it absolutely spot on. Interestingly enough, earlier on the card Dettori had found a bit of trouble on Sixties Icon in the Marathon, having stuck towards the inside, and he clearly learnt plenty from that defeat. Having held his mount up well off the strong pace, he opted to circle the field rounding the final bend, like so many winners on the Pro-Ride over the two days, and not only did the horse enjoy a clear run throughout, he was able to keep the eventual runner-up slightly hemmed in early in the straight, forcing that one to switch inside. This was especially sweet for the winning rider, it being exactly ten years since his controversial defeat in this race aboard a wayward Swain. Raven's Pass had apparently worked brilliantly around Lingfield prior to this, and he handled the surface beautifully. The longer trip also posed him no problems at all, and this was a truly magnificent performance. While his defeat of Curlin cannot be taken literally, he still comprehensively beat some of the best dirt, synthetic and turf horses around on a fair surface, and did so in an astonishingly quick time of 1m 59.27sec, a new track record on the Pro-Ride. He can now be considered one of the very best racehorses in the world.
Henrythenavigator(USA) ran a fine race, for while Raven's Pass has been thriving of late, he has had a hard season and had looked to lose his edge on his last couple of starts. Firstly he had a winning sequence of four Group 1s ended on unsuitably soft ground in France, and was then beaten by today's winner for the first time at Ascot last month, although he was late in arriving at the course that day, and some observers felt he did not look hard fit. Whatever the case, his recent runs had suggested he was well worth a try at this longer distance, and the quick surface ought to have been in his favour as well. He ran a mighty race, and was a little unfortunate that he had to switch inside with his challenge, as he ideally would have made his move just where the winner was, but he was still beaten fair and square. He has now been retired.
Tiago(USA) was under pressure a long way out, but he gradually responded and grabbed third from Curlin near the line, confirming the leaders went off very quick.
Curlin(USA), who in the spring added the Dubai World Cup to his success in this race last year and is now the all-time leading money earner in US racing, had his chance when making a big move from the rear to take it up early in the straight. However, he could not get away from some of the other closers in the way he might have been able to on dirt, and he tired into fourth. His trainer was adamant that it was the surface that beat him, saying it rode more like a turf race, but his rider said he couldn't answer whether that had anything to do with it. Whatever the case, he's had a long, hard season, and this slightly below-par showing is easily excused.
Go Between(USA) was well placed early, but he lost his position at a crucial stage before keeping on again.
Duke Of Marmalade(IRE), the winner of five straight Group 1s on turf earlier in the year, came here off the back of a below-par effort in the Arc and ran as though he has had enough. He lasted longer than expected having come under pressure down the back straight, and even made it to the front over two furlongs out, but he simply didn't have the legs to get home. Like his stablemate in second, he has now been retired.

6992 BADEN-BADEN (L-H)
Sunday, October 26

OFFICIAL GOING: Soft

7005a BADENER SPRINT-CUP (GROUP 3) 7f
12:05 (12:12) 3-Y-O+ **£22,059** (£9,191; £3,676; £1,838)

RPR

1 **Chantilly Tiffany**[45] 5829 4-8-12 THellier 3 108
(E A L Dunlop) *hld up: last over 2f out: brought wd st: gd hdwy over 1f out: led ins fnl f: rdn out* **27/10**[1]

2 *2* **Rock Of Rochelle (USA)**[21] 6516 3-9-1 RMBurke 10 108
(A Kinsella, Ire) *chsd ldrs: 4th st: brought towards stands' side: ev ch ins fnl f: no ex clsng stages* **3/1**[2]

3 *1 1/4* **Key To Pleasure (GER)**[28] 8-9-0 AHelfenbein 6 102
(Mario Hofer, Germany) *mid-div: hdwy and styd towards far side st: narrow ldr 1f out to ins fnl f: kpt on same pce* **25/1**

4 *hd* **Aturo (FR)**[28] 4-9-0 LennartHammer-Hansen 12 101
(C Sprengel, Germany) *pressed ldr: 2nd st: ev ch ins fnl f: one pce* **24/1**

5 *3/4* **Prince Fasliyev**[49] 5738 4-9-2 FVeron 5 101
(H-A Pantall, France) *mid-div: hdwy wl over 1f out: ev ch 1f out: one pce* **98/10**

6 *3/4* **Lumiere Noire (FR)**[28] 4-8-12 TRicher 9 95
(R Gibson, France) *led: hrd rdn wl over 1f out: hdd 1f out: one pce* **12/1**

7 *1 1/2* **Idolino (GER)**[28] 6322 3-8-13 FilipMinarik 11 94
(J Hirschberger, Germany) *mid-div: nvr able to chal* **93/10**

8 *3/4* **Le Big (GER)**[102] 4-9-0 EPedroza 7 91
(U Stoltefuss, Germany) *a outpcd* **19/1**

9 *2 1/2* **Abbashiva (GER)**[56] 5553 3-9-1 TMundry 4 87
(P Rau, Germany) *trckd ldrs: 5th st: btn over 1f out* **56/10**[3]

10 *6* **Setareh (GER)**[42] 3-8-13 ASuborics 8 69
(P Olsanik, France) *mid-div: hdwy and 3rd st: btn over 1f out* **88/10**

11 *nk* **Alaska River (GER)**[77] 4912 4-9-2 AStarke 2 69
(P Schiergen, Germany) *a outpcd* **8/1**

12 *3* **Galaxie Des Sables (FR)**[120] 3517 4-8-12 J-PCarvalho 1 57
(Mme N Rossio, France) *s.i.s: a bhd* **42/1**

1m 27.12s (3.22)
WFA 3 from 4yo+ 2lb **12** Ran SP% **130.3**
(including ten euro stakes): WIN 37; PL 16, 18, 45; SF 109.
Owner Ballygallon Stud Limited **Bred** Ballygallon Stud Limited **Trained** Newmarket, Suffolk

NOTEBOOK
Chantilly Tiffany, who took a Listed race on her previous visit to Germany, had shown she could handle soft ground when runner-up in a similar race at Doncaster. She came from the back of the field to sweep into the lead entering the last furlong and success at this level further increases her paddock value.

7006a PREIS DER WINTERKONIGIN (GROUP 3) (FILLIES) 1m
2:15 (2:32) 2-Y-O

£44,118 (£16,912; £8,088; £4,412; £2,206; £1,471)

RPR

1 **Sworn Pro (GER)** 2-9-0 AHelfenbein 6 —
(Mario Hofer, Germany) *disp 2nd: 2nd st: led over 1f out: r.o wl* **306/10**

2 *1/2* **Prema (GER)** 2-9-0 ASuborics 7 —
(W Hickst, Germany) *a cl up: 3rd st: drvn and ev ch ins fnl f: no ex cl home* **103/10**

3 *1 1/2* **Wildfahrte (GER)** 2-9-0 TMundry 12 —
(P Rau, Germany) *mid-div: hdwy over 1f out: r.o u.p to get the best of a three-way fight for 3rd* **30/1**

4 *nse* **Anjella (GER)** 2-9-0 .... ShaneKelly 2 —
(J Hirschberger, Germany) *a in tch: 5th st: disp 3rd ins fnl f: kpt on* **52/10**[3]
5 *shd* **Dubai (IRE)** 2-9-0 .... FilipMinarik 13 —
(P Schiergen, Germany) *a in tch: 5th st: disp 3rd ins fnl f: kpt on* **101/10**
6 *1 1/2* **All Annalena (IRE)** 2-9-0 .... J-PCarvalho 9 —
(Andreas Lowe, Germany) *led: brought whole field to stands' side st: hdd over 1f out: kpt on u.p* **12/1**
7 *nk* **La Dawa**[28] 2-9-0 .... EPedroza 8 —
(A Wohler, Germany) *6th st: one pce fr over 1f out* **47/10**[2]
8 *1 1/4* **Auenwunder (GER)** 2-9-0 .... MCadeddu 5 —
(Frau K Haustein, Germany) *cl up to st: wknd over 1f out* **107/10**
9 *1 1/4* **Classic Summer (GER)** 2-9-0 .... FVeron 11 —
(M Trybuhl, Germany) *a towards rr* **77/1**
10 *2 1/2* **Lautenspielerin (GER)**[51] 5686 2-9-0 .... AGoritz 3 —
(Frau Marion Rotering, Germany) *hdwy and 7th st: sn btn* **29/1**
11 *1 1/2* **Serienhoehe (IRE)**[51] 5686 2-9-0 .... AStarke 1 —
(P Schiergen, Germany) *nvr nrr than mid-div* **8/5**[1]
12 *1* **Cordoba (GER)** 2-9-0 ....(b) LennartHammer-Hansen 4 —
(H Steinmetz, Germany) *s.i.s: a bhd* **34/1**
13 *5* **Oriental Time (GER)** 2-9-0 .... THellier 10 —
(U Ostmann, Germany) *s.i.s: a bhd* **19/2**

1m 43.42s (4.31) **13 Ran SP% 129.6**
WIN 316: PL 75, 44, 63. SF 4519.
Owner Gestut Wittekindshof **Bred** Gestut Wittekindshof **Trained** Germany

6854 LONGCHAMP (R-H)

Sunday, October 26

OFFICIAL GOING: Good to soft

7008a PRIX ROYAL-OAK (GROUP 1) 1m 7f 110y

2:50 (2:56) 3-Y-0+ **£105,037** (£42,022; £21,011; £10,496; £5,257)

RPR
1 **Yeats (IRE)**[22] 6497 7-9-4 .... JMurtagh 8 117
(A P O'Brien, Ire) *trckd pacemaker several ls clr of the rest: led 3f out: pushed along and 3l up st: rdn 2f out: pushed out and r.o wl* **9/2**[3]
2 *1 1/2* **Allegretto (IRE)**[45] 5826 5-9-1 .... RyanMoore 7 112
(Sir Michael Stoute) *disp 3rd: 3rd st: rdn and wnt 2nd over 2f out: kpt on u.p but only clsd up wl ins fnl f* **10/1**
3 *nk* **Veracity**[8] 6820 4-9-4 .... C-PLemaire 1 115
(Saeed Bin Suroor) *disp 3rd: 4th st: 3rd wl over 1f out: rallied to regain 3rd last strides* **15/1**
4 *snk* **Bannaby (FR)**[22] 6497 5-9-4 .... CSoumillon 11 115
(M Delcher Sanchez, Spain) *racd in 6th to st: hdwy over 1f out: disp 2nd 150yds out: one pce and lost 3rd last strides* **48/10**
5 *shd* **Watar (IRE)**[22] 6494 3-8-9 .... DBonilla 2 115
(F Head, France) *hld up: 9th st: hdwy wl over 1f out: nrest at fin* **5/2**[2]
6 *2 1/2* **Moonstone**[21] 6521 3-8-6 .... CO'Donoghue 5 110
(A P O'Brien, Ire) *racd in 5th: 5th st: rdn 2f out: one pce* **9/2**[3]
7 *4* **Le Miracle (GER)**[22] 6497 7-9-4 .... DBoeuf 3 107
(W Baltromei, Germany) *hld up: 7th st: hdwy on ins 2f out: 5th 1 1/2f out: sn btn* **28/1**
8 *2* **Getaway (GER)**[21] 6522 5-9-4 .... OPeslier 9 105
(A Fabre, France) *hld up: 8th st: no hdwy* **23/10**[1]
9 *2 1/2* **Ryan (IRE)**[35] 5-9-4 ....(b) RJuracek 6 102
(J Hanacek, Czech Republic) *10th st: a towards rr* **54/1**
10 *4* **Mikhail Fokine (IRE)**[43] 5921 3-8-9 .... SMLevey 12 99
(A P O'Brien, Ire) *led to 3f out: 2nd st: sn wknd* **9/2**[3]
11 *15* **Brisant (GER)**[21] 6517 6-9-4 .... TThulliez 4 81
(M Trybuhl, Germany) *a towards rr: last fr 4f out* **47/1**

3m 19.3s (-2.20) **Going Correction** +0.30s/f (Good)
WFA 3 from 4yo+ 9lb **11 Ran SP% 153.4**
Speed ratings: **117,116,116,116,115 114,112,111,110,108 100**
PARI-MUTUEL: WIN 5.50 (coupled with Moonstone & Mikhail Fokine); PL2.40, 3.20, 3.30; DF 26.30.
Owner Mrs John Magnier **Bred** Barronstown Stud & Orpendale **Trained** Ballydoyle, Co Tipperary

FOCUS
This race is often among the weaker Group 1s in the European Pattern, but this latest running, while still not out of the top drawer, looked stronger than in recent years with five of the 11 who went to post boasting winning form at the top level.

NOTEBOOK
Yeats(IRE) had achieved a fair deal more than any of his rivals previously. However, a disappointing effort when sent off odds-on for the Prix du Cadran here three weeks previously, plus below-par runs in his other two starts in France meant that he had a couple of questions hanging over him, and he was subsequently sent off at the type of price unimaginable when he was handing out convincing defeats to rivals a cut above these at Ascot and Goodwood in the summer. Those who kept the faith were richly rewarded as he banished the memories of his last outing with a commanding performance where once again the tactics of his connections paid off. He got a good lead from his pacemaker and, once Murtagh made his decisive move 3f out, he never looked like being reeled in. His connections have a seemingly perfect replacement for the seven-year-old in the shape of Septimus, but if Yeats still retains this enthusiasm for his racing next year, it could prove a tough decision to retire him and they are already talking in terms of him winning an unprecedented fourth Ascot Gold Cup.
Allegretto(IRE) had won this race 12 months previously, when she had faced nothing of the sort of quality of her conqueror today. Her only win in the period in between had come in a weak renewal of the Park Hill Stakes and, while she is undoubtedly a talented individual and this was a fine effort, she seems exposed when coming up against a rival of true Group 1 class.
Veracity has had a busy time of it recently – this was his third race in less than three weeks. Those exertions may have taken their toll although he did stick on again when beaten.
Bannaby(FR), whose run of consistent performances was rewarded with his win in the Prix du Cadran last time, posted another solid effort here and is a real credit to connections. While that sequence included wins over middle distances they were in lesser company, and if he is to continue to show his best at this level it is probably in out-and-out staying events.
Watar(IRE) has shown improvement since stepping up to this trip. The three-year-old was again doing his best work in the final stages, having come from a long way back, and could be an interesting prospect over further next year.
Moonstone, racing over this sort of a trip for the first time in what looked like an experiment after she disappointed when dropped back to 1m2f last time following her win in the Irish Oaks the time before. She was still going strongly when they turned for home, but struggled to go with them when the race heated up late on. If she is seen again, it would be no surprise if it was over shorter.
Le Miracle(GER), a regular visitor to France, has not won since taking the Cadran last season and was eased when beaten.
Getaway(GER), whose season has failed to deliver much after he looked destined for the very top when impressing at Newmarket back in May, was stepping back up in distance, which was expected to bring about improvement but did not, and this was disappointing.

6906 KEMPTON (A.W) (R-H)

Monday, October 27

OFFICIAL GOING: Standard
Wind: Modest, half against Weather: Sunny and bright

7009 BETDAQ THE BETTING EXCHANGE H'CAP 1m 2f (P)

2:10 (2:12) (Class 5) (0-75,74) 3-Y-0+ **£3,238** (£963; £481; £240) **Stalls** High

Form RPR
5200 1 **Ryedale Ovation (IRE)**[33] 6211 5-8-9 **60**.......... SimonWhitworth 9 69
(M Hill) *s.i.s: hld up wl bhd: hdwy 4f out: chsd ldng trio 2f out: str run to ld ent fnl f: r.o strly* **10/1**
0065 2 *1 3/4* **Risque Heights**[21] 6544 4-8-12 **63**.......... IanMongan 6 69
(J R Boyle) *towards rr: gd hdwy over 4f out: to chse ldng pair over 2f out: ev ch briefly over 1f out: hung rt and one pce fnl f* **7/1**[3]
1046 3 *3/4* **Krugerrand (USA)**[37] 6108 9-9-2 **67**.......... TonyCulhane 10 71
(W J Musson) *hld up wl bhd: hdwy and hung rt wl over 1f out: r.o wl to go 3rd wl ins fnl f: nt rch ldrs* **14/1**
4010 4 *1* **Afram Blue**[13] 6719 3-8-11 **67**..........(t) JimCrowley 2 69
(W J Knight) *s.i.s: wl bhd: hdwy u.p wl over 1f out: r.o fnl f: nt rch ldrs* **10/1**
/-05 5 *nk* **Remember Ramon (USA)**[18] 6599 5-9-7 **72**.......... RichardHughes 8 73
(J R Gask) *hld up in midfield: hdwy 5f out: chsd ldr clr of remainder over 2f out: led wl over 1f out: sn rdn: hdd ent fnl f: wknd* **11/8**[1]
50-0 6 *3/4* **Parnassian**[219] 963 8-8-9 **60**..........(v) RichardThomas 7 60
(J A Geake) *towards rr: hdwy on inner 5f out: kpt on steadily u.p last 2f: nvr pce to threaten ldrs* **20/1**
0243 7 *6* **Danetime Panther (IRE)**[13] 6721 4-9-9 **74**..........(b[1]) NCallan 4 62
(P F I Cole) *t.k.h: chsd ldrs: wnt 2nd 7f out: led over 2f out and sn clr w one rival: rdn and hdd wl over 1f out: sn wknd: wl btn fnl f* **4/1**[2]
-330 8 *5* **Dancing Sword**[143] 2785 3-8-9 **65**.......... JamesDoyle 13 43
(D Burchell) *in tch: rdn 3f out: sn struggling: wl btn fnl 2f* **25/1**
0060 9 *2* **Tinnarinka**[12] 6738 4-9-2 **67**.......... TPO'Shea 3 41
(R Hannon) *racd in midfield: rdn and lost pl over 3f out: wl btn fnl 2f* **25/1**
0000 10 *nk* **Uig**[15] 6667 7-8-13 **64**.......... HayleyTurner 5 37
(H S Howe) *racd in midfield: pushed along over 7f out: brief effrt over 3f out: wknd over 2f* **33/1**
4405 11 *12* **Monashee Rock (IRE)**[11] 6758 3-9-1 **71**.......... TGMcLaughlin 11 20
(M Salaman) *restless stalls: awkward and v.s.a: nvr on terms* **20/1**
3000 12 *1/2* **Hopeful Purchase (IRE)**[12] 6736 5-9-5 **70**..........(v[1]) J-PGuillambert 12 18
(J R Gask) *led at fast pce tl over 2f out: sn wknd: eased fr over 1f out: t.o* **14/1**
3040 13 *5* **Rowan River**[101] 4152 4-9-2 **67**.......... RichardKingscote 14 5
(Tom Dascombe) *chsd ldrs tl 4f out: sn struggling: t.o and eased fnl f* **33/1**
3000 14 *dist* **Turner's Touch**[31] 6243 6-8-4 **62**..........(b) JemmaMarshall(7) 1 —
(G L Moore) *dwlt: sn pushed up to chse ldr tl 7f out: wknd qckly over 3f out: t.o last 2f: virtually plld fnl f* **16/1**

2m 7.44s (-0.56) **Going Correction** +0.10s/f (Slow)
WFA 3 from 4yo+ 5lb **14 Ran SP% 135.1**
Speed ratings (Par 103): **106,104,104,103,102 102,97,93,91,91 82,81,77,—**
toteswinger: 1&2 £18.40, 1&3 £40.20, 2&3 £12.60. CSF £80.97 CT £1022.92 TOTE £13.00: £3.30, £2.50, £4.40; EX 151.20.
Owner Martin Hill **Bred** Hascombe And Valiant Studs **Trained** Littlehempston, Devon

FOCUS
An ordinary handicap for the grade and the pace was strong, suiting those held up. The form looks fairly solid.
Monashee Rock(IRE) Official explanation: jockey said filly sat down as stalls opened
Hopeful Purchase(IRE) Official explanation: jockey said gelding had no more to give

7010 RAY ANTELL BIG BIRTHDAY H'CAP 1m 4f (P)

2:40 (2:41) (Class 6) (0-60,60) 3-Y-0 **£2,047** (£604; £302) **Stalls** Centre

Form RPR
0052 1 **Epsom Salts**[23] 5379 3-8-10 **52**.......... JamesDoyle 13 63
(P M Phelan) *hld up in midfield: lost pl and bhd over 3f out: swtchd lft and hdwy over 2f out: r.o strly u.p to ld nr fin* **16/1**
0013 2 *shd* **Star Choice**[15] 6685 3-9-3 **59**.......... HayleyTurner 9 69
(M L W Bell) *hld up in tch: outpcd 4f out: hdwy and rdn over 2f out: chsd ldr over 1f out: led ins fnl f: r.o tl hdd and no ex nr fin* **10/3**[1]
3304 3 *4* **Piverina (IRE)**[13] 6719 3-8-8 **50**.......... RichardKingscote 7 54
(Miss J A Camacho) *s.i.s: towards rr: swtchd lft and hdwy jst over 2f out: r.o fnl f: wnt 3rd fnl 100yds: nt rch ldrs* **14/1**
3544 4 *1* **Trinkila (USA)**[11] 6754 3-9-1 **57**..........(b[1]) JimCrowley 8 59
(P F I Cole) *hld up in tch: rdn and outpcd 4f out: rallied u.p 2f out: kpt on u.p to go 4th fnl 100yds: nt pce to threaten ldrs* **14/1**
0302 5 *1/2* **Rosy Dawn**[12] 6729 3-8-5 **50**.......... MarcHalford(3) 10 52
(J J Bridger) *led: pushed clr w one rival over 3f out: drvn over 2f out: hdd ins fnl f: sn btn: wknd and lost 2 pls fnl 100yds* **20/1**
2066 6 *2 1/4* **Pinnacle Point**[28] 6337 3-8-12 **54**.......... RichardHughes 12 52
(G L Moore) *chsd ldr tl 6f out: styd handy: outpcd 4f out: hdwy on inner jst over 2f out: chsd ldr over 1f out tl ent fnl f: wl hld after* **7/1**
4501 7 *1 1/4* **Hoar Frost**[6] 6883 3-8-10 **52** 6ex.......... TPO'Shea 6 48
(M R Channon) *in tch in midfield: hdwy to chse ldrs over 5f out: drvn and unable qck 4f out: no ch w ldrs after* **16/1**
60 8 *1 3/4* **Historical Giant (USA)**[20] 6566 3-8-11 **53**.......... RHills 1 46+
(E F Vaughan) *bmpd s and s.i.s: dropped in bhd: effrt on outer over 3f out: n.d* **25/1**
4540 9 *1/2* **Purely By Chance**[26] 6390 3-9-1 **57**.......... JerryO'Dwyer 11 49
(J Pearce) *in tch in midfield: drvn wl over 4f out: outpcd 4f out: no ch fnl 2f* **20/1**
5214 10 *shd* **Well Informed**[4] 6930 3-9-0 **56**.......... J-PGuillambert 4 48
(E J O'Neill) *s.i.s: hld up bhd: nvr a factor* **4/1**[3]
0002 11 *4 1/2* **Testimonial**[64] 5320 3-9-2 **58**.......... NCallan 2 43
(B G Powell) *hld up in last trio: n.d* **25/1**
0006 12 *shd* **Aston Boy**[26] 6374 3-8-5 **47**.......... PaulDoe 3 32
(M Blanshard) *chsd ldrs: wnt 2nd 6f out: pushed clr w ldr over 3f out: drvn over 2f out: wknd 2f out* **50/1**
0300 13 *1 1/2* **Southern Mistral**[15] 6685 3-9-2 **58**.......... TGMcLaughlin 14 40
(M Wigham) *hld up in tch: lost pl over 4f out: no ch last 2f* **7/2**[2]

0660 **14** *5* **Enderby Light (FR)**[23] 6485 3-9-4 **60**............................ JamieMoriarty 5 34
(Ollie Pears) *wnt lft s: hld up in rr: nvr factor* **22/1**

2m 36.97s (2.47) **Going Correction** +0.10s/f (Slow) **14** Ran SP% **126.4**
Speed ratings (Par 99): **95,94,92,91,91 89,88,87,87,87 84,84,83,79**
toteswinger: 1&2 £12.00, 1&3 £28.50, 2&3 £9.70. CSF £66.10 CT £809.26 TOTE £18.30: £4.00, £2.50, £4.30; EX 79.90.
Owner The Epsom Racegoers **Bred** Heatherwold Stud **Trained** Epsom, Surrey
■ Stewards' Enquiry : James Doyle one-day ban: used whip with excessive frequency (Nov 10)
Hayley Turner one-day ban: used whip with excessive frequency (Nov 10)

FOCUS
A moderate 3yo handicap run at a fair pace, thanks to Rosy Dawn. The form has a sound look to it.
Historical Giant(USA) Official explanation: jockey said gelding suffered inference leaving stalls
Testimonial Official explanation: jockey said filly moved poorly throughout

7011 LOOK FOR BETTER ODDS AT BETDAQ MAIDEN STKS 7f (P)
3:10 (3:16) (Class 4) 2-Y-0 **£3,885** (£1,156; £577; £288) **Stalls** High

Form RPR
3 **1** **Ghanaati (USA)**[35] 6166 2-8-12 0.. RHills 11 84+
(B W Hills) *dwlt: sn in tch: hdwy over 2f out: led over 1f out: sn clr: v easily* **4/6**[1]
2 *6* **Laudatory** 2-9-3 0.. AdamKirby 5 72+
(W R Swinburn) *hld up in midfield: swtchd lft and hdwy wl over 1f out: chsd clr wnr ins fnl f: no imp* **14/1**
60 **3** *2 1/4* **Augusta Gold (USA)**[12] 6731 2-9-3 0..................(b[1]) RichardHughes 12 66
(B J Meehan) *led tl over 1f out: sn no ch w wnr: lost 2nd ins fnl f* **13/2**[2]
4 *5* **Ymir** 2-9-3 0.. PaulDoe 10 54
(M J Attwater) *t.k.h: hld up in midfield: lost pl 3f out: hdwy on inner 2f out: styd on to go 4th nr fin: no ch* **100/1**
064 **5** *nk* **Survivor's Song**[38] 6084 2-9-3 75.............................. JerryO'Dwyer 9 53
(D K Ivory) *chsd ldrs: wnt 2nd wl over 2f out tl wl over 1f out: sn wknd* **12/1**
03 **6** *1* **Eddie Boy**[34] 6187 2-9-3 0...................................... HayleyTurner 4 50
(M L W Bell) *s.i.s: hld up bhd: rdn over 2f out: modest late hdwy: nvr a factor* **7/1**[3]
0 **7** *nse* **Sermons Mount (USA)**[18] 6602 2-9-3 0......................... JimCrowley 14 50
(Mouse Hamilton-Fairley) *chsd ldr tl 4f out: wknd over 2f out* **66/1**
0 **8** *1/2* **Alternative Choice (USA)**[26] 6375 2-9-3 0................. JamesDoyle 13 49
(N P Littmoden) *chsd ldrs: wnt 2nd 4f out tl wl over 2f out: sn wknd* **16/1**
9 *2 1/2* **Blaise Tower** 2-9-3 0.. TGMcLaughlin 3 43
(G L Moore) *racd wd: a towards rr: no ch fr over 2f out* **50/1**
0 **10** *2 1/4* **Jonnie Skull (IRE)**[14] 6701 2-9-3 0.......................... RichardKingscote 8 37
(D R C Elsworth) *racd wd in midfield: rdn and struggling 1/2-way: wl btn fnl 3f* **80/1**
00 **11** *1/2* **Sydney Cove (IRE)**[11] 6760 2-9-3 0............................. J-PGuillambert 6 36
(M Johnston) *t.k.h: hld up bhd: toiling over 3f out: wl btn after* **20/1**
06 **12** *4 1/2* **Day In Dubai**[38] 6072 2-8-9 0................................... MarcHalford[(3)] 1 20
(J J Bridger) *racd wd: a in rr: hung lft bnd 3f out: wl btn whn edgd rt wl over 2f out* **80/1**
13 *20* **Dancelectic (IRE)** 2-9-3 0.......................................(t) NCallan 2 —
(D R Lanigan) *s.i.s: rn green in rr: t.o and eased fr over 1f out* **33/1**

1m 27.15s (1.15) **Going Correction** +0.10s/f (Slow) **13** Ran SP% **120.7**
Speed ratings (Par 97): **97,90,87,81,81 80,80,79,76,74 73,68,45**
toteswinger: 1&2 £4.60, 1&3 £2.30, 2&3 £8.80. CSF £11.78 TOTE £1.60: £1.10, £3.30, £1.60; EX 13.00.
Owner Hamdan Al Maktoum **Bred** Shadwell Farm LLC **Trained** Lambourn, Berks

FOCUS
A weak, uncompetitive maiden.

NOTEBOOK
Ghanaati(USA) was basically far superior to her rivals. Odds-on backers cannot have been too pleased with her antics before the start, as she proved very reluctant to load, but she was fine in the race itself and built on the promise she showed when poorly drawn on her debut over course and distance. She is beautifully bred and clearly has plenty of ability; it just has to be hoped her attitude does not get the better of her. (op 8-15 tchd 1-2)
Laudatory, a 55,000gns half-brother to a few winning sprinters, showed some ability on his debut, keeping on well in the separate race for second. He got this trip okay, but is bred to be suited by shorter. (tchd 16-1)
Augusta Gold(USA), dropped back a furlong with blinkers on for the first time, was well drawn and had his chance from the front. This looks as good as he is. (op 10-1)
Ymir showed some ability on his racecourse debut and should find his level once handicapped. (op 66-1)
Survivor's Song was flattered by his recent Newmarket fourth on this evidence. (op 10-1)
Eddie Boy was never involved. He had to be driven along for a few strides early after being slow to find his stride, and was then inclined to edge right when trying to make ground in the straight. The signs are he's not straightforward, but his connections have a few options, including headgear, and he is now qualified for a handicap mark. (tchd 8-1)

7012 BET VOLVO MASTERS GOLF - BETDAQ H'CAP 7f (P)
3:40 (3:41) (Class 6) (0-60,60) 3-Y-0+ **£2,047** (£604; £302) **Stalls** High

Form RPR
6421 **1** **Musical Script (USA)**[5] 6907 5-9-6 60 6ex.........................(b) NCallan 10 74
(Mouse Hamilton-Fairley) *dwlt: t.k.h: hld up in tch: hdwy to chse ldr over 1f out: led ins fnl f: r.o wl* **9/2**[1]
066 **2** *2* **Tignello (IRE)**[19] 6571 3-9-4 60.............................. RichardKingscote 11 68
(D R C Elsworth) *sn pushed up to ld: rdn over 2f out: drvn over 1f out: hdd ins fnl f: one pce* **9/2**[1]
0020 **3** *1* **Morocchius (USA)**[10] 6791 3-9-4 60...........................(p) HayleyTurner 3 65
(Miss J A Camacho) *fly-jmpd s and slowly away: hld up wl bhd: swtchd lft over 2f out: r.o fnl f: wnt 3rd wl ins fnl f: nt rch ldrs* **16/1**
3006 **4** *2* **Thabaat**[33] 6209 4-9-0 57...(b) KevinGhunowa[(3)] 7 57
(J M Bradley) *s.i.s: hld up in midfield: hdwy over 2f out: kpt on u.p but nvr pce to chal ldrs* **16/1**
0006 **5** *shd* **Imperial Echo (USA)**[10] 6774 7-9-6 60....................(v) TGMcLaughlin 14 60
(P Howling) *chsd ldr: rdn jst over 2f out: unable qck over 1f out: kpt on same pce fnl f* **17/2**
6034 **6** *2 1/4* **Convivial Spirit**[25] 6422 4-9-1 60..................................(vt[1]) JackDean[(5)] 4 54
(E F Vaughan) *hld up towards rr: rdn and effrt over 2f out: n.m.r 2f out: nvr able to chal* **13/2**[3]
4315 **7** *1/2* **Inquisitress**[28] 6338 4-9-1 58.................................... MarcHalford[(3)] 13 50
(J J Bridger) *hld up in tch: rdn and effrt jst over 2f out: n.m.r and swtchd lft over 1f out: no imp fnl f* **11/2**[2]
0340 **8** *1 1/4* **Motu (IRE)**[51] 5712 7-9-4 58....................................(v) PatrickMathers 9 47
(I W McInnes) *in tch: rdn over 2f out: hrd rdn and nt qckn 2f out: one pce after* **16/1**
6605 **9** *hd* **Boldinor**[26] 6377 5-9-2 56.. JimCrowley 12 44
(M R Bosley) *chsd ldrs: rdn 3f out: wknd 2f out* **12/1**
0200 **10** *1 3/4* **H Harrison (IRE)**[29] 6314 8-8-13 60.............................. BMcHugh[(7)] 2 44
(I W McInnes) *prom early: lost pl and bhd 4f out: rdn and effrt on outer 3f out: no hdwy fnl 2f* **10/1**
6403 **11** *nk* **Acquifer**[26] 6377 3-9-3 59..(b) RichardHughes 6 49+
(J L Dunlop) *hld up in midfield: effrt over 2f out: keeping on same pce whn n.m.r ins fnl f* **9/1**
0-00 **12** *4 1/2* **Avening**[26] 6377 8-9-2 56.. PaulDoe 8 27
(Eve Johnson Houghton) *racd on outer: rdn over 3f out: nvr trbld ldrs* **25/1**
0000 **13** *1/2* **Kayflaa (IRE)**[23] 6485 3-9-4 60...................................(bt[1]) JamieMoriarty 1 29
(T D Walford) *a in rr* **50/1**
30-0 **14** *21* **Lady Bower**[297] 38 3-9-2 58... AdamKirby 5 —
(Miss M E Rowland) *dropped in bhd sn after s: nvr a factor* **66/1**

1m 26.98s (0.98) **Going Correction** +0.10s/f (Slow)
WFA 3 from 4yo+ 2lb **14** Ran SP% **127.3**
Speed ratings (Par 101): **98,95,94,92,92 89,89,87,87,85 85,79,79,55**
toteswinger: 1&2 £5.20, 1&3 £14.70, 2&3 £21.30. CSF £24.90 CT £321.40 TOTE £4.20: £2.10, £1.10, £6.10; EX 29.70.
Owner The Composers **Bred** Juddmonte Farms Inc **Trained** Bramshill, Hants
■ Stewards' Enquiry : B McHugh four-day ban: careless riding (Nov 10, 12-14)
Kevin Ghunowa two-day ban: used whip above shoulder height (Nov 10,12)

FOCUS
A moderate handicap in which there was little solid recent form to go on. The winner did not have to improve much on his old form.

7013 TFM NETWORKS CLAIMING STKS 6f (P)
4:10 (4:10) (Class 6) 3-Y-0+ **£2,047** (£604; £302) **Stalls** High

Form RPR
0342 **1** **Mutamared (USA)**[7] 6864 8-9-6 87... NCallan 4 79+
(K A Ryan) *hld up in midfield: hdwy over 2f out: led ent fnl f: sn pushed clr: readily* **1/1**[1]
4632 **2** *1 3/4* **Brandywell Boy (IRE)**[27] 6357 5-8-9 68................................ BillyCray[(7)] 3 69+
(D J S Ffrench Davis) *racd on outer: towards rr: rdn over 2f out: hdwy over 1f out: r.o to chse wnr ins fnl f: no imp* **7/1**[3]
004 **3** *1/2* **C'Mon You Irons (IRE)**[61] 5403 3-9-7 75......................(b) JimCrowley 12 73
(M R Hoad) *hld up in tch: rdn and effrt wl over 1f out: n.m.r and swtchd lft jst over 1f out: kpt on to go 3rd ins fnl f* **9/1**
0002 **4** *3/4* **Who's Winning (IRE)**[15] 6681 7-8-10 55.............. RichardKingscote 6 59
(B G Powell) *towards rr: rdn and effrt over 2f out: hdwy u.p ent fnl f: kpt on but nvr trbld ldrs* **16/1**
2033 **5** *hd* **Monda**[33] 6208 6-8-2 50.. AmyBaker[(5)] 8 55
(M Hill) *hung rt thrght: w ldr tl led over 3f out: hdd ent fnl f: no ex and lost 3 pls ins fnl f* **14/1**
3130 **6** *hd* **Bazguy**[24] 6448 3-8-10 69..(b) TGMcLaughlin 11 59
(P D Evans) *led tl hdd over 3f out: w ldr after: rdn and ev ch over 2f out: kpt on same pce fnl f* **11/2**[2]
0663 **7** *3/4* **Lady Fas (IRE)**[72] 5090 5-7-12 45.............................. StacyRenwick[(7)] 5 50
(A W Carroll) *swtchd rt sn after s: hld up in rr: hdwy on inner over 2f out: n.m.r and swtchd lft jst ins fnl f: kpt on same pce* **66/1**
0060 **8** *nse* **Sovereignty (JPN)**[17] 6631 6-8-4 62.................. CharlotteKerton[(7)] 10 56
(D K Ivory) *t.k.h: hld up in tch: rdn and unable qck jst over 2f out: btn whn n.m.r over 1f out* **33/1**
6200 **9** *2 1/4* **Rockfield Lodge (IRE)**[11] 6765 3-9-7 73............................... AdamKirby 2 60
(M E Rimmer) *sn rdn and dropped in bhd after s: nvr trbld ldrs* **16/1**
5033 **10** *2 3/4* **Nawaaff**[5] 6907 3-8-13 50..(v) TPO'Shea 7 43
(M R Channon) *racd keenly: chsd ldrs: rdn jst over 2f out: wknd wl over 1f out* **14/1**
3360 **11** *6* **River Bounty**[10] 6773 3-8-3 62.................................. MatthewDavies[(7)] 1 21
(A P Jarvis) *in tch tl lost pl over 3f out: rdn and edgd rt wl over 2f out: no ch fr 2f out* **40/1**

1m 13.29s (0.19) **Going Correction** +0.10s/f (Slow)
WFA 3 from 5yo+ 1lb **11** Ran SP% **119.9**
Speed ratings (Par 101): **102,99,99,98,97 97,96,96,93,89 81**
toteswinger: 1&2 £2.90, 1&3 £3.90, 2&3 £9.60. CSF £8.51 TOTE £2.10: £1.10, £2.30, £2.80; EX 12.10.
Owner Errigal Racing **Bred** E J Hudson Jr, Irrevocable Trust & Kilroy T'Bred **Trained** Hambleton, N Yorks

FOCUS
A reasonable claimer, but Mutamared stood out at the weights and did not need to match his recent best. Sound form for the grade.
Monda Official explanation: jockey said mare hung right throughout

7014 TFM NETWORKS H'CAP 1m (P)
4:40 (4:40) (Class 4) (0-80,79) 3-Y-0+ **£5,180** (£1,541; £770; £384) **Stalls** High

Form RPR
0061 **1** **Prince Of Thebes (IRE)**[12] 6738 7-9-3 75................................ PaulDoe 6 83
(M J Attwater) *chsd ldrs: effrt to ld over 1f out: clr ins fnl f: rdn out* **13/2**
4460 **2** *1 1/4* **Palmerin**[40] 6028 3-9-1 76.. RichardHughes 4 81+
(R Hannon) *towards rr: outpcd over 2f out: hdwy u.p over 1f out: r.o to chse wnr ins fnl f: comf hld* **7/2**[2]
5230 **3** *2 3/4* **Will He Wish**[14] 6710 12-9-7 79.....................................(b) HayleyTurner 3 78
(S Gollings) *hld up in tch: rdn and effrt jst over 2f out: kpt on same pce u.p fnl f* **12/1**
2021 **4** *1* **Our Blessing (IRE)**[10] 6774 4-8-10 68.......................... DarrenWilliams 8 65
(A P Jarvis) *t.k.h: led: rdn jst over 2f out: hdd over 1f out: wknd ins fnl f* **8/1**
-210 **5** *1* **Pippbrook Gold**[15] 6675 3-9-0 75.................................... NCallan 2 69
(J R Boyle) *chsd ldrs: rdn and pressed ldrs wl over 1f out: wknd ins fnl f* **12/1**
134 **6** *nk* **Hallingdal (UAE)**[17] 6627 3-9-3 78.............................. JamesDoyle 5 72
(Ms J S Doyle) *stdd s: hld up in rr: effrt on outer over 2f out: no imp fr over 1f out* **2/1**[1]
0000 **7** *3 1/4* **Mister New York (USA)**[17] 6627 3-9-3 78................... KirstyMilczarek 7 64
(Noel T Chance) *racd in midfield: lost pl 4f out: hdwy on inner jst over 2f out: wknd ent fnl f* **20/1**
0642 **8** *53* **Daniel Thomas (IRE)**[12] 6738 6-9-3 75............................ JimCrowley 1 —
(Mrs A L M King) *s.i.s: hld up bhd: hdwy 4f out: drvn and no rspnse over 2f out: virtually p.u fr over 1f out: t.o* **11/2**[3]

1m 39.79s (-0.01) **Going Correction** +0.10s/f (Slow)
WFA 3 from 4yo+ 3lb **8** Ran SP% **115.5**
Speed ratings (Par 105): **104,102,100,99,98 97,94,42**
toteswinger: 1&2 £9.70, 1&3 £9.50, 2&3 £19.80. CSF £29.84 CT £268.41 TOTE £8.60: £2.50, £1.30, £4.40; EX 56.70 Place 6 £109.15, Place 5 £18.62..
Owner Canisbay Bloodstock **Bred** Mrs A Rothschild & London Thoroughbred Services L **Trained** Epsom, Surrey

FOCUS
A fair handicap run at just a steady pace. The winner is rated to his AW summer best and the favourite was disappointing.

Daniel Thomas(IRE) Official explanation: jockey said gelding stopped quickly
T/Jkpt: Not won. T/Plt: £224.20 to a £1 stake. Pool: £54,620.43. 177.82 winning tickets. T/Qpdt: £20.50 to a £1 stake. Pool: £4,130.29. 148.90 winning tickets. SP

6714 LEICESTER (R-H)

Monday, October 27

OFFICIAL GOING: Good to soft (soft patches; 7.0)
Wind: Light, behind Weather: Cloudy with sunny spells

7015 LADBROKES.COM MEDIAN AUCTION MAIDEN FILLIES' STKS — 5f 218y

1:30 (1:33) (Class 6) 2-Y-0 — **£2,590** (£770; £385; £192) **Stalls** Low

Form				RPR
34	**1**		**Bounty Box**[38] 6080 2-9-0 0 TedDurcan 18 (C F Wall) *trckd ldrs: led over 1f out: rdn out* **11/4**[1]	82
3645	**2**	*1 1/4*	**Slant (IRE)**[53] 5640 2-9-0 78 StephenCarson 7 (Eve Johnson Houghton) *hld up in tch: rdn to chse wnr fnl f: styd on* **11/2**	78
23	**3**	*2 3/4*	**Gilt Edge Girl**[11] 6764 2-9-0 0 SteveDrowne 6 (C G Cox) *chsd ldrs: rdn over 1f out: styd on same pce ins fnl f* **5/1**[3]	70
	4	*1*	**Three Ducks** 2-9-0 0 DaneO'Neill 12 (L M Cumani) *s.s: hld up: hdwy 2f out: rdn over 1f out: styd on* **15/2**	67
60	**5**	*nk*	**Chocolicious (IRE)**[31] 6245 2-9-0 0 TomEaves 9 (B Smart) *hld up: hdwy u.p and hung rt over 1f out: nt trble ldrs* **10/1**	66
230	**6**	*4 1/2*	**Positivity**[31] 6240 2-9-0 79 RoystonFfrench 10 (B Smart) *chsd ldr tl led 1/2-way: rdn and hdd over 1f out: wknd fnl f* **9/2**[2]	52
05	**7**	*1 1/4*	**On Cue (IRE)**[21] 6534 2-8-11 0 LukeMorris(3) 16 (J M P Eustace) *mid-div: hdwy over 2f out: hung rt over 1f out: wknd fnl f* **50/1**	49
	8	*3/4*	**Wightgold** 2-9-0 0 TQuinn 5 (H J L Dunlop) *s.s: in rr: nvr nrr* **50/1**	46
04	**9**	*nse*	**Equinity**[14] 6697 2-9-0 0 LiamJones 1 (J Pearce) *chsd ldrs: rdn over 2f out: wknd over 1f out* **33/1**	46
53	**10**	*nk*	**Makaykla**[10] 6785 2-9-0 0 DavidAllan 11 (E J Alston) *plld hrd and prom: rdn over 2f out: wknd over 1f out* **10/1**	45
	11	*7*	**Gracie's Games** 2-8-9 0 Louis-PhilippeBeuzelin(5) 8 (R J Price) *s.s: outpcd: hung rt fr 1/2-way* **100/1**	24
0	**12**	*1*	**Full Blue**[38] 6080 2-9-0 0 RichardMullen 4 (S C Williams) *mid-div: rdn 1/2-way: wknd 2f out* **40/1**	21
	13	*1/2*	**Gwerthybyd** 2-9-0 0 CatherineGannon 3 (B Palling) *s.s: outpcd* **100/1**	20
60	**14**	*3 1/2*	**Jarrah Bay**[40] 6016 2-9-0 0 AndrewElliott 2 (J G M O'Shea) *sn pushed along in rr: bhd whn hung rt over 2f out* **66/1**	9
60	**15**	*11*	**Flavour**[27] 6360 2-9-0 0 ShaneKelly 14 (A W Carroll) *led to 1/2-way: sn wknd* **150/1**	—

1m 14.88s (1.88) **Going Correction** +0.325s/f (Good) **15** Ran SP% **120.3**
Speed ratings (Par 90): **100,98,94,93,92 86,85,84,84,83 74,73,72,67,53**
toteswinger: 1&2 £6.00, 1&3 £3.30, 2&3 £7.50. CSF £17.13 TOTE £3.40: £1.70, £2.30, £1.50; EX 22.60 Trifecta £31.10 Pool: £142.98 - 3.40 winning units..
Owner John E Sims **Bred** Farmers Hill Stud **Trained** Newmarket, Suffolk

FOCUS
A fair maiden that was dominated by those with previous experience.

NOTEBOOK
Bounty Box, having shown promise in maidens over 6f on good and fast ground, handled this slower surface well and, picking up to lead over a furlong out, ran on too strongly for her rivals, who were close enough at the furlong pole. She is out of a decent mare who won here and stayed 1m1f, and should make up into a fair handicapper herself next season. (op 10-3 tchd 7-2 and 5-2)
Slant(IRE) was the most experienced runner in the line-up and, with an official mark of 78, set the standard. She settled in behind the leaders before moving up to challenge, but could never quite get to the winner and, as on breeding she should appreciate trips of around a mile, she may do better over further in time. (tchd 5-1 and 6-1)
Gilt Edge Girl was stepping up in trip after a couple of good efforts over the minimum. She was bang there entering the last furlong but did not seem to last home. She now qualifies for a handicap mark, though. (op 10-3)
Three Ducks, a half-sister to smart performers Three Wrens and Thames, did easily best of the newcomers and showed plenty of promise for the future. Held up off the pace, she made steady progress in the second half of the race and should know more next time. Being by Diktat she is likely to be best suited by soft ground. (op 10-1)
Chocolicious(IRE), whose most promising previous effort was on easy ground, ran her best race so far on a similar surface here and is another who will now be able to ply her trade in handicaps. (op 12-1 tchd 14-1)
Positivity had posted decent efforts on both her starts over 5f on a sound surface but had been well beaten in a sales race after a break and, despite showing up for a good way, she may be best back on a sound surface. Official explanation: jockey said filly ran too freely (op 5-1 tchd 6-1 and 4-1)
On Cue(IRE) did not run badly on this drop in trip and is another now qualified for handicaps.
Wightgold Official explanation: jockey said filly lost its action

7016 LADBROKES.COM HAYMARKET NURSERY — 7f 9y

2:00 (2:01) (Class 6) (0-65,65) 2-Y-0 — **£2,590** (£770; £385; £192) **Stalls** Low

Form				RPR
5550	**1**		**Embsay Crag**[7] 6857 2-9-3 64 NeilBrown(3) 17 (Mrs K Walton) *s.i.s: hld up: hdwy over 2f out: led ins fnl f: rdn out: edgd lft nr fin* **11/1**	66
050	**2**	*nk*	**Clerk's Choice (IRE)**[24] 6443 2-9-7 65 GeorgeBaker 14 (W Jarvis) *hld up: hdwy over 1f out: sn rdn: r.o* **12/1**	66
0644	**3**	*shd*	**Nimmy's Special**[14] 6709 2-9-2 60 TQuinn 4 (M Mullineaux) *s.i.s: swtchd rt and hdwy over 2f out: sn rdn: ev ch ins fnl f: styd on* **25/1**	61
000	**4**	*1/2*	**Polly's Choice (IRE)**[37] 6118 2-9-2 63 PatrickHills(3) 1 (R Hannon) *hld up: swtchd rt over 2f out: hdwy over 1f out: r.o u.p* **28/1**	63
5063	**5**	*1/2*	**Skruton (IRE)**[10] 6787 2-9-7 65 RichardMullen 12 (M G Quinlan) *chsd ldrs: rdn to ld 1f out: hdd and unable qck ins fnl f* **11/1**	63
6202	**6**	*1 1/4*	**West Leake (IRE)**[32] 6223 2-9-5 63 MichaelHills 18 (B W Hills) *chsd ldrs: led over 1f out: sn rdn and hdd: styd on same pce ins fnl f* **14/1**	58
253	**7**	*nse*	**Hameildaeme**[7] 6858 2-9-2 65 WilliamCarson(5) 7 (S C Williams) *prom: hmpd over 4f out: outpcd over 2f out: styd on ins fnl f* **5/1**[1]	60
1524	**8**	*3*	**Hip Hip Hooray**[11] 6761 2-9-7 65 CatherineGannon 11 (L A Dace) *chsd ldrs: hmpd over 4f out: lost pl over 2f out: n.d after* **5/1**[1]	53
0500	**9**	*1 1/4*	**Entrancer (IRE)**[54] 5606 2-9-2 60 ShaneKelly 13 (W R Muir) *trckd ldr: racd keenly: rdn over 2f out: wknd over 1f out* **50/1**	44
3620	**10**	*nk*	**Meydan Groove**[11] 6761 2-9-7 65 GrahamGibbons 5 (R Johnson) *s.i.s: hld up: rdn over 1f out: n.d* **25/1**	49
0205	**11**	*1/2*	**Always There (IRE)**[46] 5838 2-9-7 65 PatDobbs 10 (R Hannon) *led: rdn: edgd rt and hdd over 1f out: wknd fnl f* **16/1**	47
400	**12**	*1*	**Postman**[61] 5387 2-9-2 60 (v[1]) TedDurcan 9 (B Smart) *dwlt: hld up: rdn over 2f out: n.d* **7/1**[2]	40
0000	**13**	*1 3/4*	**Taste The Wine (IRE)**[14] 6700 2-9-6 64 SteveDrowne 8 (J R Best) *prom: hmpd and lost pl over 4f out: n.d after* **8/1**[3]	40
0002	**14**	*1 1/2*	**Protiva**[14] 6694 2-9-5 63 (v) DaneO'Neill 3 (A P Jarvis) *trckd ldrs: rdn over 2f out: wknd wl over 1f out* **18/1**	35
0300	**15**	*4 1/2*	**Game Roseanna**[17] 6632 2-9-2 60 LiamJones 6 (W M Brisbourne) *sn pushed along in rr: bhd fnl 3f* **50/1**	21
660	**16**	*5*	**Yeoman Blaze**[108] 3895 2-9-7 65 WilliamBuick 2 (A M Balding) *mid-div: rdn 1/2-way: sn lost pl* **20/1**	13
600	**17**	*3/4*	**Hill Cross (IRE)**[23] 6480 2-8-13 60 AndrewMullen(3) 15 (Mrs A Duffield) *chsd ldrs: rdn 1/2-way: wknd over 2f out* **50/1**	6

1m 29.27s (3.07) **Going Correction** +0.325s/f (Good) **17** Ran SP% **120.9**
Speed ratings (Par 93): **95,94,94,93,93 91,91,88,87,86 86,85,83,81,76 70,69**
toteswinger: 1&2 £25.00, 1&3 £38.30, 2&3 £42.80. CSF £125.15 CT £3322.80 TOTE £14.00: £3.20, £2.60, £5.50, £5.70; EX 152.30 TRIFECTA Not won..
Owner Keep The Faith Partnership **Bred** Mrs Glenda Swinglehurst **Trained** Middleham Moor, N Yorks

■ Stewards' Enquiry : Shane Kelly three-day ban: careless riding (Nov 10, 12-13)
Catherine Gannon three-day ban: careless riding (Nov 10, 12-13)

FOCUS
A modest but competitive nursery with only 5lb covering the whole field on official ratings. The field raced towards the stands' rail early but the principals came up the centre of the track and from off the pace.

NOTEBOOK
Embsay Crag had started at big prices on all his previous starts but had been unlucky in running when upped to a mile last time. The drop back to 7f seemed to suit ideally and, after travelling comfortably in the wake of the leaders, he picked up to show ahead inside the last and held off the late challengers on either side. Being from a predominantly jumping yard, connections hope he may jump hurdles in due course. Official explanation: trainer said, regarding the apparent improvement in form, that gelding had been fairly consistent but had suffered interference on its last run. (op 22-1)
Clerk's Choice(IRE), whose best effort was over 6f on Polytrack, had been well beaten in two runs on fast ground and put up an improved effort on this easier ground on his handicap debut, finishing best of all. (op 8-1)
Nimmy's Special, another whose best run was on Polytrack on her previous start, seems to be progressing and came to deliver a challenge on the wide outside before her effort flattened out close home. (tchd 22-1)
Polly's Choice(IRE) was another to catch the eye, being held up at the back before staying on well in the closing stages to end up on the heels of the winner. (op 25-1)
Skruton(IRE), a 6f winner on easy ground, came to have every chance over a furlong out but could not go on from that point. (op 12-1)
West Leake(IRE) looked the likely winner when coming through to lead over a furlong out but was then unable to resist those challenging on his outside, which is ironic as he had made his way over from the widest draw of all. (op 12-1)
Hameildaeme was well-backed and was prominent early but was being pushed along to hold her pitch before halfway, only to stay on again in the closing stages. (op 8-1)
Hip Hip Hooray got a slight bump when being ridden to improve her position soon after halfway and could only stay on at one pace from that point. Official explanation: jockey said filly suffered interference approaching 4f mark
Postman, fitted with a visor for the first time, was held up and never got involved, making only moderate headway late on. (op 13-2 tchd 8-1)
Taste The Wine(IRE) Official explanation: jockey said colt suffered interference approaching 4f mark

7017 LADBROKES.COM SIR GORDON RICHARDS CONDITIONS STKS — 1m 3f 183y

2:30 (2:31) (Class 3) 3-Y-0+ — **£7,569** (£2,265; £1,132; £566; £282) **Stalls** High

Form				RPR
5020	**1**		**Young Mick**[16] 6646 6-9-2 105 (v) DaneO'Neill 1 (G G Margarson) *s.i.s: sn chsng ldrs: rdn over 2f out: led ins fnl f: edgd rt: styd on* **6/5**[1]	102
-333	**2**	*1/2*	**Spanish Hidalgo (IRE)**[91] 4496 4-9-8 102 RichardMullen 3 (J L Dunlop) *chsd ldr tl led 2f out: rdn and hdd ins fnl f: edgd rt: styd on* **7/2**[2]	107
3326	**3**	*2*	**Acropolis (IRE)**[16] 6652 7-9-2 95 (v) TomEaves 4 (Miss L A Perratt) *chsd ldrs: rdn over 1f out: swtchd rt ins fnl f: styd on* **16/1**	98
4020	**4**	*nk*	**Classic Punch (IRE)**[9] 6820 5-9-8 105 TQuinn 5 (D R C Elsworth) *set stdy pce: qcknd over 3f out: rdn and hdd 2f out: styd on same pce ins fnl f* **7/2**[2]	104
200/	**5**	*3*	**Mon Michel (IRE)**[170] 5488 5-9-2 102 GeorgeBaker 2 (G L Moore) *hld up: rdn over 1f out: no imp* **6/1**[3]	93

2m 40.65s (6.75) **Going Correction** +0.325s/f (Good) **5** Ran SP% **110.1**
Speed ratings (Par 107): **90,89,88,88,86**
CSF £5.67 TOTE £2.10: £1.10, £1.70; EX 4.30.
Owner M F Kentish **Bred** M F Kentish **Trained** Newmarket, Suffolk

FOCUS
One of the feature races of the day attracted some decent performers and, despite the size of the field, produced a good finish. All five were still in with some sort of chance at the quarter-mile pole. The form looks messy and best rated around the placed horses.

NOTEBOOK
Young Mick came through to win his first race since September 2006. He had the highest adjusted official rating, was a well-backed favourite and was kept wide and close to the leaders throughout. He made hard work of getting past the runner-up until finding a length or so entering the final furlong and was in control from that point. His trainer suggested he might take his chance in the November Handicap now. (op 5-4 tchd 11-8 and 11-10)
Spanish Hidalgo(IRE), who is ideally suited by 1m6f, was sensibly ridden close to the pace on this drop in trip. He went to the front halfway up the straight and gave the winner a good fight, but seemed to falter for a stride or two going into the final furlong, which allowed the winner to go on, before battling back. He is up to winning more good races when there is cut in the ground. (op 10-3)
Acropolis(IRE) has not won for over four years but is fairly consistent and stays further. He looked a big threat at the quarter-mile pole, but did not get the clearest passage and could not find an extra gear to trouble the principals. (op 18-1 tchd 14-1)
Classic Punch(IRE), runner-up in a Listed race over this trip at Newmarket behind subsequent St Simon Stakes winner Buccellati, had been beaten over 2m either side of that race. He should have been suited by the return to this trip and was allowed to lead, but was being urged along soon after turning in and the response was limited. He has won on soft but on this evidence looks better on a sound surface. (op 10-3 tchd 4-1 in places)

Mon Michel(IRE), who has been running over hurdles since last seen on the Flat in September 2006 and who goes well on soft, ran pretty well on this first outing since May, despite never getting out of last place, and it should put him right for a return to jumping. (op 7-1 tchd 9-1)

7018 LADBROKESCASINO.COM CLAIMING STKS — 7f 9y
3:00 (3:03) (Class 5) 3-4-Y-O — **£2,590** (£770; £385; £192) **Stalls** Low

Form — RPR

4321 **1** — **Dancing Maite**[8] 6843 3-8-11 63 — DeanMcKeown 11 — 73
(S R Bowring) *s.i.s: hdwy over 4f out: led over 1f out: rdn out* **11/1**

0601 **2** 1 1/4 **Stand In Flames**[7] 6864 3-8-6 78 — ShaneKelly 15 — 65
(Pat Eddery) *w ldr tl led 4f out: rdn and hdd over 1f out: styd on* **6/4**[1]

1410 **3** 1/2 **Singleb (IRE)**[4] 6928 4-9-3 67 — GeorgeBaker 7 — 72
(G L Moore) *mid-div: hdwy over 2f out: sn rdn: r.o* **10/3**[2]

1000 **4** 3 3/4 **Restless Genius (IRE)**[21] 6532 3-8-11 73 — (t) WilliamBuick 13 — 58
(A M Balding) *chsd ldrs: rdn over 2f out: styd on same pce appr fnl f* **11/2**[3]

0500 **5** 3/4 **Opal Noir**[24] 6448 4-8-7 62 — RoystonFfrench 8 — 50
(Miss L A Perratt) *hld up: hdwy u.p over 1f out: nt trble ldrs* **40/1**

5034 **6** 1/2 **Royal Applord**[23] 6490 3-8-8 64 ow1 — (p) PaulMulrennan 10 — 52
(K A Ryan) *chsd ldrs: rdn over 2f out: styd on same pce* **14/1**

6004 **7** 3 3/4 **Semah Harold**[13] 6716 3-8-8 55 ow1 — (v[1]) GrahamGibbons 12 — 42
(E S McMahon) *chsd ldrs: rdn over 2f out: wknd over 1f out* **25/1**

062 **8** 2 1/4 **Blue Charm**[13] 6716 4-8-7 57 — (t) StephenCarson 3 — 33
(S Kirk) *hld up: rdn over 2f out: n.d* **14/1**

6655 **9** 1 1/2 **Tampopo (IRE)**[28] 6332 3-7-12 50 — NicolPolli(5) 2 — 27
(D J S Ffrench Davis) *sn outpcd: nvr nrr* **100/1**

-255 **10** 3 1/4 **Sylvias Grove**[147] 2670 3-8-10 68 — TomEaves 18 — 25
(B Smart) *s.i.s: sn prom: rdn and wknd over 2f out* **16/1**

440 **11** 3 **Foreign Rhythm (IRE)**[35] 6159 3-7-9 50 ow2(v) Louis-PhilippeBeuzelin(5) 5 — 7
(N Tinkler) *sn outpcd* **40/1**

5004 **12** 1/2 **Follow Your Spirit**[47] 5797 3-8-3 49 — CatherineGannon 14 — 8
(B Palling) *led 3f: sn rdn: wknd 2f out* **50/1**

0320 **13** 1/2 **Blues Minor (IRE)**[10] 6792 3-8-7 63 — RichardMullen 4 — 11
(M Mullineaux) *sn pushed along: a in rr:* **40/1**

5000 **14** shd **Copperbottomed (IRE)**[17] 6628 3-8-11 55 — (e) SteveDrowne 16 — 15
(P G Murphy) *prom: rdn and wknd 1/2-way* **50/1**

-006 **15** 3 3/4 **Up The Chimney**[12] 6733 4-8-13 49 — DaneO'Neill 1 — 5
(A P Jarvis) *sn outpcd* **100/1**

0-60 **16** 1/2 **Hennalaine (IRE)**[6] 6878 3-7-10 0 ow1 — (b[1]) DominicFox(3) 6 — —
(Miss J S Davis) *swvd lft s: a wl bhd* **66/1**

1m 28.54s (2.34) **Going Correction** +0.325s/f (Good)
WFA 3 from 4yo 2lb — **16** Ran SP% **124.6**
Speed ratings (Par 103): **99,97,97,92,91 91,87,84,82,79 75,75,74,74,70 69**
toteswinger: 1&2 £5.20, 1&3 £14.70, 2&3 £21.30. CSF £27.20 TOTE £12.30: £3.40, £1.10, £1.90; EX 39.20 Trifecta £148.70 Pool: £201.07 - 1.00 winning units..The winner was subject to a friendly claim.
Owner Stuart Burgan **Bred** S R Bowring **Trained** Edwinstowe, Notts
■ Stewards' Enquiry : Dean McKeown two-day ban: used whip with excessive frequency (Nov 10,12)

FOCUS
A typical claimer featuring the usual wide variation in ability judged on official ratings and dominated by the first four in the betting, although not in the order the market suggested. The form is rated around the third with the winner rated up a length but the second 10lb off her recent best.
Follow Your Spirit Official explanation: jockey said gelding was unsuited by the good to soft (soft in places) ground

7019 LADBROKES.COM H'CAP — 1m 60y
3:30 (3:31) (Class 3) (0-90,90) 3-Y-O+
£7,788 (£2,332; £1,166; £583; £291; £146) **Stalls** High

Form — RPR

1050 **1** — **Axiom**[37] 6130 4-9-2 85 — DaneO'Neill 13 — 98
(L M Cumani) *chsd ldrs: swtchd lft over 2f out: rdn to ld over 1f out: styd on* **11/4**[1]

3101 **2** 1/2 **Mangham (IRE)**[21] 6526 3-9-3 89 — PaulMulrennan 1 — 101
(D H Brown) *broke wl: stdd and lost pl over 6f out: hdwy 2f out: rdn to chse wnr fnl f: edgd rt: styd on* **8/1**[3]

120 **3** 1 **Charm School**[17] 6625 3-9-3 89 — (e[1]) RichardMullen 6 — 99
(J H M Gosden) *hld up: hdwy over 3f out: ev ch 2f out: sn rdn: nt clr run ins fnl f: styd on same pce* **9/2**[2]

1100 **4** 3 **Red Somerset (USA)**[15] 6667 5-8-13 87 — MCGeran(5) 12 — 90
(R J Hodges) *hld up in tch: outpcd over 2f out: rallied over 1f out: styd on* **16/1**

0010 **5** 1 **Red Rumour (IRE)**[30] 6283 3-9-1 87 — GeorgeBaker 7 — 88
(R M Beckett) *chsd ldr: rdn over 2f out: sn ev ch: wknd ins fnl f* **16/1**

1145 **6** 1/2 **Mr Hichens**[11] 6763 3-9-1 87 — TedDurcan 10 — 87
(B J Meehan) *led: rdn and hdd over 1f out: wknd ins fnl f* **9/1**

3005 **7** 2 1/2 **Prince Of Light (IRE)**[25] 6424 5-8-13 82 — RoystonFfrench 4 — 76
(M Johnston) *hld up: rdn over 2f out: nvr trbld ldrs* **16/1**

0450 **8** 3/4 **Danehillsundance (IRE)**[14] 6710 4-8-9 81 — TolleyDean(3) 3 — 73
(S Parr) *hld up: rdn over 4f out: hdwy over 3f out: wknd fnl f* **16/1**

0130 **9** nk **Nutkin**[40] 6035 4-8-11 80 — WilliamBuick 9 — 71
(J R Fanshawe) *hld up: rdn over 2f out: n.d* **10/1**

0242 **10** hd **The Snatcher (IRE)**[37] 6103 5-9-7 90 — PatDobbs 5 — 81
(R Hannon) *chsd ldrs: rdn over 2f out: wknd over 1f out* **12/1**

4005 **11** 1 1/4 **Barons Spy (IRE)**[15] 6670 7-8-12 86 — Louis-PhilippeBeuzelin(5) 14 — 74
(R J Price) *hld up: nt clr run and swtchd lft over 2f out: n.d* **33/1**

0/00 **12** 5 **Spectait**[9] 6536 6-9-1 84 — ShaneKelly 2 — 61
(Jonjo O'Neill) *hld up: rdn over 2f out: a in rr* **50/1**

0062 **13** 3 1/4 **Jewelled Dagger (IRE)**[16] 6654 4-9-5 88 — (b) TomEaves 11 — 57
(Miss L A Perratt) *trckd ldrs: racd keenly: n.m.r and wknd over 2f out* **9/1**

1m 46.13s (1.03) **Going Correction** +0.325s/f (Good)
WFA 3 from 4yo+ 3lb — **13** Ran SP% **121.2**
Speed ratings (Par 107): **107,106,105,102,101 101,98,97,97,97 96,91,87**
toteswinger: 1&2 £5.30, 1&3 £3.60, 2&3 £7.30. CSF £25.05 CT £102.88 TOTE £3.20: £1.60, £3.10, £2.00; EX 29.90 Trifecta £74.10 Pool: £310.75 - 3.10 winning units..
Owner DIC Racing Syndicate **Bred** Cheveley Park Stud Ltd **Trained** Newmarket, Suffolk

FOCUS
A decent, competitive handicap with only 10lb covering the entire field on official ratings and once again the race was dominated by those at the head of the market. The form has been rated positively and there could be more to come from the winner.

NOTEBOOK
Axiom ◆ was back on his favourite soft ground after three runs on sounder surfaces and justified favouritism with a little in hand. He got a good lead in the early stages and, once eased to the front over a furlong out, he always looked like holding on. He is due to go to the sales now, and as this was only his 11th run he has little mileage on the clock, and looks one to have on-side when there is cut in the ground. (op 4-1)
Mangham(IRE) handles any ground and this consistent type ran his race again, coming from off the pace to keep the winner up to his work, although never looking as if he would get past. He has risen 16lb in the handicap this year but like the winner was having just his 11th race and should continue to progress next term. (op 11-1)
Charm School, even less exposed than the first two, looked a decent sort on soft ground in the spring and had been given one run on Polytrack earlier in the month following a break. Fitted with an eyeshield for the first time, he moved up to lead at the quarter-mile pole, but could not respond when the first two challenged either side of him. (tchd 11-2)
Red Somerset(USA), a course-and-distance winner, settled nicely in the pack but could not find the extra gears under pressure needed to reach the first three.
Red Rumour(IRE) kept the leader company but rather took him on and had nothing in reserve when the challenges arrived.
Mr Hichens made the running but was taken on by Red Rumour and probably went a little too quickly as he had nothing left for the closing stages. (op 11-1)
Jewelled Dagger(IRE) raced close to the pace but took a strong hold and faded in the last quarter-mile. (op 8-1 tchd 10-1)

7020 EBF LADBROKES.COM FOSSE WAY MAIDEN STKS — 5f 218y
4:00 (4:05) (Class 4) 2-Y-O — **£5,180** (£1,541; £770; £384) **Stalls** Low

Form — RPR

224 **1** — **Master Rooney (IRE)**[33] 6213 2-9-3 87 — TedDurcan 11 — 87
(B Smart) *trckd ldrs: racd keenly: rdn to ld over 1f out: r.o* **11/4**[2]

03 **2** 3/4 **Swiss Diva**[10] 6776 2-8-12 0 — TQuinn 12 — 80
(D R C Elsworth) *hld up in tch: chsd wnr over 1f out: sn rdn and ev ch: unable qck nr fin* **15/8**[1]

3402 **3** 4 **Piazza San Pietro**[15] 6677 2-9-3 85 — SteveDrowne 7 — 73
(C G Cox) *trckd ldrs: rdn over 1f out: no ex ins fnl f* **11/4**[2]

02 **4** 1 1/4 **Megasecret**[28] 6341 2-9-3 0 — PatDobbs 6 — 69
(R Hannon) *chsd ldr tl led over 2f out: rdn and hdd over 1f out: styd on same pce* **10/1**[3]

U04 **5** 6 **Lucky Dan (IRE)**[11] 6764 2-9-3 0 — PaulMulrennan 5 — 51
(Paul Green) *led over 3f: sn rdn: wknd over 1f out* **40/1**

6 1 1/4 **Academy Of War (USA)** 2-9-3 0 — WilliamBuick 9 — 47+
(P W Chapple-Hyam) *s.s: hdwy over 2f out: hung lft and wknd over 1f out* **16/1**

0 **7** 1 **Sarasota Sunshine**[20] 6555 2-8-9 0 — LukeMorris(3) 4 — 39
(N P Littmoden) *hld up in tch: rdn over 2f out: sn wknd* **150/1**

8 1/2 **Bold Bomber** 2-9-3 0 — PaulQuinn 8 — 43
(Paul Green) *sn pushed along in rr: n.d* **100/1**

9 2 1/2 **Bravalto** 2-9-3 0 — TomEaves 3 — 35
(B Smart) *s.i.s: sn mid-div: rdn and wknd 1/2-way* **22/1**

0 **10** hd **Acclaim To Fame (IRE)**[45] 5859 2-9-0 0 — TolleyDean(3) 1 — 35
(S Parr) *hung rt thrght: prom: rdn over 3f out: sn wknd* **100/1**

11 6 **Jachol (IRE)** 2-9-3 0 — MichaelHills 10 — 17
(W J Haggas) *s.i.s: a in rr: bhd fr 1/2-way* **16/1**

12 33 **Thurston (IRE)** 2-8-12 0 — GabrielHannon(5) 2 — —
(D J S Ffrench Davis) *s.s: outpcd* **150/1**

1m 14.37s (1.37) **Going Correction** +0.325s/f (Good) — **12** Ran SP% **119.1**
Speed ratings (Par 97): **103,102,96,95,87 85,84,83,80,79 71,27**
toteswinger: 1&2 £1.70, 1&3 £2.50, 2&3 £1.70. CSF £8.19 TOTE £3.30: £1.40, £1.20, £1.50; EX 10.10 Trifecta £8.40 Pool: £624.40 - 54.92 winning units..
Owner H E Sheikh Rashid Bin Mohammed **Bred** Darley **Trained** Hambleton, N Yorks

FOCUS
An interesting little maiden and the winning time was just over half a second quicker than the earlier fillies' maiden over the same trip. Again the action all unfolded down the centre of the track and the front pair, who came clear, started from the two highest stalls, though admittedly they were amongst the market leaders and the first three were the trio that dominated the betting.

NOTEBOOK
Master Rooney(IRE), who pulled too hard when tried over an extra furlong last time, was deserted by Eaves in favour of stable-companion Bravalto, but he still proved good enough having been close to the pace throughout and he battled on well to keep the favourite at bay. Currently rated 87, the drop back to 6f suited him and he should prove competitive in sprint handicap company off this sort of mark. (op 3-1 tchd 5-2)
Swiss Diva, who ran very well off the back of a four-month break in a Newmarket maiden earlier this month, tracked the eventual winner throughout and was brought through to hold every chance but, despite doing her best, she found him too tough. She should be able to win a race and now qualifies for a mark, which gives her more options. (op 7-4 tchd 6-4 and 2-1)
Piazza San Pietro, the most experienced in the field and officially rated 2lb inferior to the winner, was nonetheless well backed. Racing more towards the stands' side than the other principals, he had every chance but was firmly put in his place by the front pair and is starting to look exposed. (op 9-2)
Megasecret raced prominently for a long way before finding it too much, but his second to a 73-rated rival on his second start left him with a bit to find with the eventual winner and third, so he probably ran his race. (tchd 9-1)
Lucky Dan(IRE) made much of the early running before fading, but now gets a mark. (op 33-1 tchd 28-1)
Academy Of War(USA) stood still as the stalls opened before showing a little ability mid-race, so he may well improve a bit for the experience. (op 12-1)

7021 LADBROKESCASINO.COM COPLOW H'CAP — 7f 9y
4:30 (4:32) (Class 5) (0-70,69) 3-Y-O+ — **£2,590** (£770; £385; £192) **Stalls** Low

Form — RPR

00 **1** — **Smarty Socks (IRE)**[39] 6056 4-8-9 60 — SilvestreDeSousa 6 — 74+
(P T Midgley) *trckd ldrs: led over 2f out: rdn over 1f out: r.o: eased nr fin* **33/1**

5565 **2** 1 1/2 **Rosie Says No**[20] 6564 3-8-5 58 — (p) RoystonFfrench 14 — 65
(R M H Cowell) *wnt lft s: a.p: rdn to chse wnr over 1f out: sn ev ch: edgd lft ins fnl f: styd on same pce* **16/1**

5244 **3** nk **Ours (IRE)**[15] 6671 5-9-0 65 — (p) PaulMulrennan 13 — 72
(John A Harris) *s.i.s and hmpd s: sn pushed along in rr: hdwy u.p over 1f out: r.o* **9/2**[2]

3420 **4** 5 **Castano**[35] 6177 4-9-4 69 — (p) DaneO'Neill 12 — 63
(B R Millman) *chsd ldrs: rdn over 1f out: wknd ins fnl f* **6/1**[3]

5041 **5** shd **Starlight Gazer**[21] 6537 5-9-4 69 — (vt) SteveDrowne 9 — 62
(J A Geake) *chsd ldrs: rdn over 2f out: wknd over 1f out* **7/1**

2260 **6** 1 1/4 **No Grouse**[9] 6813 8-8-9 65 — GaryBartley(5) 16 — 55
(E J Alston) *hld up: hdwy over 2f out: wknd over 1f out* **18/1**

0241 **7** 1 3/4 **Ken's Girl**[20] 6560 4-8-10 66 — Louis-PhilippeBeuzelin(5) 5 — 51
(W S Kittow) *led: rdn and hdd over 2f out: wknd over 1f out* **4/1**[1]

640 **8** 1/2 **Charlie Bear**[4] 6928 7-8-1 59 oh7 ow4 — RossAtkinson(7) 11 — 43
(Miss Z C Davison) *s.s: outpcd: nvr nrr* **33/1**

3001 **9** 4 **Medici Time**[10] 6791 3-8-11 64 — (v) DavidAllan 8 — 36
(T D Easterby) *hld up: hdwy 1/2-way: rdn and wknd over 2f out* **14/1**

0000 **10** 2 1/4 **Rowaad**[10] 6792 3-7-13 55 — LukeMorris(3) 1 — 22
(A E Price) *hld up: hdwy 1/2-way: wknd over 2f out* **40/1**

3405 **11** 3 1/4 **Out Of India**[25] 6419 6-8-4 55 oh5 .... PaulEddery 17 13
(P T Dalton) *trckd ldrs: racd keenly: rdn and wknd 2f out* **33/1**

0016 **12** 3/4 **Prince Golan (IRE)**[20] 6560 4-8-5 63 .... AlexEdwards(7) 2 19
(J W Unett) *chsd ldrs: rdn 1/2-way: wknd over 2f out* **16/1**

4045 **13** 1 **Angaric (IRE)**[82] 4736 5-9-2 67 .... TomEaves 4 20
(B Smart) *plld hrd and prom: wknd over 2f out* **10/1**

1m 27.8s (1.60) **Going Correction** +0.325s/f (Good)
WFA 3 from 4yo+ 2lb **13** Ran SP% **109.0**
Speed ratings (Par 103): **103,101,100,95,95 93,91,91,86,83 80,79,78**
toteswinger: 1&2 £108.00, 1&3 £33.60, 2&3 £14.20. CSF £420.61 CT £2523.49 TOTE £48.20: £11.10, £4.40, £1.20; EX 730.10 Trifecta £143.80 Part won. Pool: £194.35 - 0.10 winning units.Place 6 £17.79, Place 5 £11.44..
Owner R G Fell **Bred** Mick McGinn **Trained** Westow, N Yorks
■ Cheap Street was withdrawn after spreading a plate (11/1, deduct 5p in the £ under R4.)

FOCUS
A big field for this modest handicap and they spread across the track, and it produced a surprise winner. Nevertheless, the form looks sound enough rated around the placed horses, the first three finishing clear.
Smarty Socks(IRE) Official explanation: trainerr's rep said, regarding the apparent improvement in form, that gelding broke from the stalls better and got the run of the race on this occasion.
T/Plt: £26.70 to a £1 stake. Pool: £54,068.10. 1,474.92 winning tickets. T/Qpdt: £2.60 to a £1 stake. Pool: £3,188.17. 877.30 winning tickets. CR

6876 LINGFIELD (L-H)
Monday, October 27

OFFICIAL GOING: Standard
Wind: Light, across Weather: Sunny

7022 PLAY CLEOPATRA AT CORAL.CO.UK APPRENTICE H'CAP 6f (P)
1:50 (1:50) (Class 6) (0-53,52) 3-Y-0+ **£2,047** (£604; £302) **Stalls** Low

Form RPR

0630 **1** **The Hoofer (IRE)**[15] 6681 3-8-13 52 ....(t) FrederikTylicki 4 60
(I A Wood) *trckd ldr: rdn to ld wl over 1f out: kpt on wl fnl f* **15/2**[3]

0536 **2** 3/4 **Whiskey Creek**[6] 6890 3-8-13 52 ....(b[1]) MatthewDavies 12 58
(C A Dwyer) *t.k.h: racd wd: prog over 3f out: chsd wnr jst over 1f out: styd on but a hld* **6/1**[2]

4363 **3** 1 1/2 **City For Conquest (IRE)**[6] 6890 5-8-12 50 .... StacyRenwick 9 51
(John A Harris) *dwlt: mostly in last trio tl prog wl over 1f out: r.o wl to take 3rd nr fin* **15/2**[3]

1055 **4** 1/2 **Jayanjay**[34] 6190 9-8-12 50 .... DeanHeslop 10 50
(B R Johnson) *trckd ldrs: effrt to dispute 2nd over 1f out: one pce fnl f* **11/1**

0200 **5** hd **Franksalot (IRE)**[14] 6693 8-9-0 52 ....(b) BMcHugh 5 51
(I W McInnes) *wl in rr: rdn 2f out: styd on wl fnl f: nrst fin* **8/1**

3063 **6** 1 1/2 **Lithaam (IRE)**[20] 6546 4-8-12 50 ....(p) AdeleRothery 7 44
(J M Bradley) *mostly in midfield: effrt over 1f out: outpcd fnl f* **8/1**

5040 **7** 1 3/4 **Szaba**[174] 1897 3-8-11 50 .... ShaneCreighton 6 39
(J Akehurst) *chsd ldrs: rdn 2f out: steadily fdd fnl f* **25/1**

0560 **8** nk **Arfinnit (IRE)**[25] 6419 7-8-11 49 ....(p) KylieManser 8 37
(Mrs A L M King) *hld up in last trio: nvr on terms* **8/1**

4030 **9** 1 1/4 **Sazerac (USA)**[3] 6955 3-8-13 52 .... BillyCray 3 36
(P Howling) *awkward s: nvr beyond midfield and nt moving comf: n.d over 1f out* **17/2**

5354 **10** 1 1/2 **Shatter Resistant (IRE)**[14] 6707 3-8-5 51 .... MarieLequarre(7) 11 30
(M D Squance) *stdd s: hld up in rr and racd wd: nvr nr ldrs* **16/1**

3000 **11** nk **Piccostar**[135] 3021 5-8-8 49 ....(b) PNolan(3) 1 27
(A B Haynes) *led to wl over 1f out: wknd rapidly* **16/1**

440 **12** 4 **Nordic Light (USA)**[5] 6895 4-8-12 50 ....(b) AshleyMorgan 2 15
(J M Bradley) *a towards rr on inner: wknd 2f out* **5/1**[1]

1m 11.58s (-0.32) **Going Correction** -0.15s/f (Stan)
WFA 3 from 4yo+ 1lb **12** Ran SP% **122.3**
Speed ratings (Par 101): **96,95,93,92,92 90,87,87,85,83 83,77**
toteswinger: 1&2 £11.60, 1&3 £14.50, 2&3 £8.50. CSF £53.80 CT £363.69 TOTE £7.60: £2.30, £2.50, £2.70; EX 58.00.
Owner The Super Optimists **Bred** Hesmonds Stud Ltd **Trained** Upper Lambourn, Berks

FOCUS
A modest handicap for apprentice riders. It was run at a decent pace, but few got into it from behind. The form is sound, if limited.

7023 CORAL.CO.UK MEDIAN AUCTION MAIDEN STKS 1m (P)
2:20 (2:21) (Class 6) 2-Y-0 **£2,388** (£705; £352) **Stalls** High

Form RPR

0 **1** **Spiritual Treasure (USA)**[12] 6731 2-9-3 0 .... RyanMoore 4 74+
(M A Magnusson) *led after 1f to 1/2-way: drvn to ld again 2f out: asserted ent fnl f: styd on wl* **10/3**[2]

5 **2** 1 3/4 **Naheell**[30] 6292 2-9-3 0 .... PhilipRobinson 6 70
(M A Jarvis) *led 1f: chsd ldr to 1/2-way: drvn over 2f out: wnt 2nd 1f out: no imp on wnr* **4/1**[3]

0 **3** 1/2 **Colangnik (USA)**[142] 2821 2-8-12 0 .... KirstyMilczarek 7 64+
(J R Best) *hld up in last trio: nudged along and prog over 1f out: styd on encouragingly fnl f: nrst fin* **40/1**

6 **4** nk **Zulu Moon**[18] 6602 2-9-3 0 .... ChrisCatlin 8 68
(A M Balding) *hld up wl in rr: prog on outer over 3f out: chsd ldrs 2f out: hanging over 1f out: styd on ins fnl f* **10/1**

6 **5** 3/4 **It's A Mans World**[38] 6085 2-9-3 0 .... AlanMunro 2 67
(P W Chapple-Hyam) *trckd ldrs: outpcd 2f out: effrt to dispute 3rd 1f out: one pce after* **2/1**[1]

04 **6** 1/2 **Merton Lad**[35] 6165 2-9-3 0 .... RobertHavlin 3 66+
(T G Mills) *chsd ldrs: pushed along over 4f out: stl chsng 2f out: one pce fr over 1f out* **12/1**

06 **7** nk **Diktalina**[24] 6432 2-8-12 0 .... TPQueally 9 60
(W R Muir) *wl in rr: racd wdst of all over 3f out: drvn over 2f out: styd on fr over 1f out: n.d* **25/1**

56 **8** 2 1/2 **Sley (FR)**[20] 6555 2-8-12 0 .... JamieSpencer 12 54+
(B J Meehan) *hld up in rr: rapid prog to ld 1/2-way: hdd 2f out: wknd rapidly fnl f* **5/1**

00 **9** 1/2 **Viking Rock (IRE)**[15] 6665 2-9-3 0 .... EdwardCreighton 5 58
(M Salaman) *a in rr: last and struggling over 2f out: plugged on* **100/1**

10 shd **Flannel (IRE)** 2-9-3 0 .... RobertWinston 1 58
(J R Fanshawe) *s.i.s: sn rcvrd to midfield: lost pl and struggling in rr wl over 2f out: n.d after* **33/1**

60 **11** nse **Damselfly**[124] 3364 2-8-12 0 .... JoeFanning 11 53
(M Johnston) *chsd ldrs: rdn over 2f out: wknd rapidly jst over 1f out* **33/1**

00 **12** 2 **Midsummer Madness (IRE)**[15] 6682 2-8-12 0 .... FergusSweeney 10 49
(David Pinder) *a towards rr: struggling fr over 2f out* **100/1**

1m 38.28s (0.08) **Going Correction** -0.15s/f (Stan) **12** Ran SP% **124.0**
Speed ratings (Par 93): **93,91,90,90,89 89,88,86,85,85 85,83**
toteswinger: 1&2 £3.40, 1&3 £35.80, 2&3 £35.80. CSF £17.29 TOTE £4.00: £1.10, £1.90, £10.50; EX 19.90.
Owner Eastwind Racing Ltd and Martha Trussell **Bred** Robert B Trussell Jr **Trained** Upper Lambourn, Berks

FOCUS
A modest juvenile maiden.

NOTEBOOK
Spiritual Treasure(USA) was a massive springer in the market and did the job in good style under a shrewd front-running ride by Moore. He travelled enthusiastically up with the pace, did not get flustered when attacked by a rival on the outside some way out, and eventually quickened up to win with something in hand for his trainer who has a 71 per cent record at this track this year (5-7). (op 10-1)
Naheell raced prominently in the early stages, seemed to lose a bit of composure during the middle of the race but then stayed on strongly to take second. He may need a bit more time to strengthen up but seems to be getting the hang of things and looks a steadily progressive type who should be able to win races. (tchd 5-1)
Colangnik(USA) caught the eye staying on strongly from a long way back and stepped up significantly on her debut effort in a 6f Doncaster fillies' maiden. (op 33-1)
Zulu Moon also found improvement on his debut form and seemed to handle the surface well on his All-Weather debut. (op 11-1 tchd 12-1 and 9-1)
It's A Mans World set the standard on his promising sixth of 17 behind an 86-rated rival in a 1m Newmarket auction maiden on debut last month. He found a good early position against the far rail, but was tapped for speed when the pace quickened and may not have handled the Polytrack. (op 15-8)

7024 CORAL - BET BY PHONE 0800 242 232 NOVICE STKS 6f (P)
2:50 (2:51) (Class 4) 2-Y-0 **£3,885** (£1,156; £577; £288) **Stalls** Low

Form RPR

5621 **1** **Timeteam (IRE)**[4] 6931 2-9-2 81 .... JamieSpencer 2 87
(S Kirk) *hld up bhd ldng pair: effrt over 1f out: drvn and r.o to ld last 100yds* **2/1**[2]

41 **2** 1 **Son Of The Cat (USA)**[15] 6677 2-9-2 86 .... ChrisCatlin 4 84
(B Gubby) *sn pressed ldr: led narrowly over 1f out: hrd rdn and hdd last 100yds: kpt on* **15/8**[1]

0330 **3** 1/2 **Effort**[25] 6426 2-9-5 91 .... JoeFanning 3 86
(M Johnston) *mde most but pressed thrght: narrowly hdd and edgd rt over 1f out: kpt on u.p* **15/8**[1]

3306 **4** 10 **Handcuff**[15] 6666 2-8-12 61 .... FergusSweeney 5 49
(J Gallagher) *hld up bhd ldng pair: rdn and wknd 2f out* **25/1**[3]

1m 11.49s (-0.41) **Going Correction** -0.15s/f (Stan) 2y crse rec **4** Ran SP% **106.7**
Speed ratings (Par 97): **96,94,94,80**
CSF £5.95 TOTE £2.10; EX 4.60.
Owner R Gander **Bred** R N Auld **Trained** Upper Lambourn, Berks

FOCUS
A decent event. The three main contenders were closely matched in the market and at the finish.

NOTEBOOK
Timeteam(IRE) had a bit to find on form but probably benefited from sitting just behind his two main rivals, who had a sustained duel for the lead, and did find a fair turn of foot to gain the initiative in the closing stages and win with some authority. He has been running consistently during a busy campaign and seems to have a good attitude and constitution. This win over two rivals with higher official ratings will have a detrimental effect on his mark but he should continue to run well (op 13-8 tchd 6-4)
Son Of The Cat(USA) was a bit keen in the early stages but showed a willing attitude to keep going and eventually prevailed in his front-running battle with Effort, but could not repel the late thrust of the winner. This was a creditable effort on his third career start, he should be open to improvement and looks fairly treated for handicaps off a current mark of 86. (op 13-8 tchd 9-4)
Effort had a bit to prove after a lacklustre effort in a valuable sales race at Newmarket last time but seemed to spring back to life on his all-weather debut. He ran a brave race, particularly since he was conceding weight to his two main rivals. (op 11-4)
Handcuff, who had a daunting task at the weights, was in trouble some way out and finished well beaten. (op 33-1)

7025 WATCH RACING UK LIVE AT CORAL.CO.UK H'CAP 1m 4f (P)
3:20 (3:20) (Class 4) (0-85,85) 3-Y-0+ **£4,727** (£1,406; £702; £351) **Stalls** Low

Form RPR

0531 **1** **Falcativ**[26] 6379 3-8-10 79 .... JamieSpencer 6 94+
(L M Cumani) *stdd s: hld up in last trio: awkward and drvn over 2f out: prog after: clsd on ldr ins fnl f: led last 75yds: r.o wl* **11/8**[1]

0012 **2** 1/2 **War Of The Roses (IRE)**[17] 6626 5-9-0 79 .... JackMitchell(3) 4 94
(R Brotherton) *hld up in midfield: prog 3f out: rdn to ldover 1f out: r.o but collared last 75yds* **5/1**[2]

250 **3** 4 1/2 **Indicible (FR)**[11] 6763 4-9-6 82 .... FergusSweeney 11 89
(A King) *trckd ldrs: prog over 3f out: led wl over 2f out to over 1f out: outpcd* **12/1**

1113 **4** 1 1/2 **Mutamaasek (USA)**[254] 591 6-9-2 78 .... KirstyMilczarek 5 83
(Lady Herries) *trckd ldrs: effrt 2f out: outpcd over 1f out: kpt on fnl f* **15/2**[3]

0-25 **5** 1 1/4 **Limbo King**[17] 6626 4-8-11 73 .... RobertWinston 2 76
(J R Fanshawe) *hld up in midfield: lost pl on inner over 2f out: plld wd 2f out: sme prog over 1f out: no ch w ldrs* **9/1**

4554 **6** 1/2 **Press The Button (GER)**[21] 6536 5-9-7 83 .... AlanMunro 3 88+
(J R Boyle) *t.k.h: trckd ldng pair: trapped bhd wkng rival fr wl over 2f out and lost pl completely: nudged along and styd on fnl f: fin w plenty lft* **14/1**

5200 **7** 1 3/4 **Awatuki (IRE)**[18] 6607 5-9-5 81 .... RyanMoore 10 80
(J R Boyle) *awkward s: hld up in last pair: no prog u.p over 2f out: hanging over 1f out: kpt on fnl f* **20/1**

0000 **8** 3 **Polish Power (GER)**[40] 6033 8-9-9 85 .... EdwardCreighton 1 80
(J S Moore) *dwlt: hld up in last pair: u.p and no prog over 2f out: no ch* **16/1**

153- **9** hd **Nobelix (IRE)**[364] 6545 6-9-3 79 .... ChrisCatlin 8 73
(J R Gask) *pressed ldrs: effrt and upsides 3f out: wknd wl over 1f out* **33/1**

2106 **10** 3/4 **Demolition**[32] 6233 4-9-1 82 .... FrederikTylicki(5) 12 75
(N Wilson) *pressed ldr tl jst over 3f out: sn lost pl u.p* **11/1**

000 **11** hd **Agapanthus (GER)**[14] 6698 3-9-2 85 .... TPQueally 9 78
(A P Stringer) *in tch: rdn on outer over 3f out: wknd 2f out* **66/1**

4600 **12** nse **Prime Number (IRE)**[14] 6698 6-8-11 73 .... JoeFanning 7 66
(J Akehurst) *led to wl over 2f out: wknd* **33/1**

2m 28.1s (-4.90) **Going Correction** -0.15s/f (Stan) course record
WFA 3 from 4yo+ 7lb **12** Ran SP% **121.2**
Speed ratings (Par 105): **110,109,106,105,104 104,103,101,101,100 100,100**
toteswinger: 1&2 £3.00, 1&3 £6.00, 2&3 £13.20. CSF £7.78 CT £62.30 TOTE £2.00: £1.30, £2.00, £3.30; EX 11.60.

The Form Book, Raceform Ltd, Compton, RG20 6NL

Owner Scuderia Rencati Srl **Bred** Az Agr Francesca **Trained** Newmarket, Suffolk

FOCUS
A decent handicap run that seemed to be run at a bit of stop-start gallop, but the winner managed to record a new 1m4f track record, the first two finished clear of the rest and the form looks good for the grade. There is more to come from the winner and the runner-up also posted a personal best.

Press The Button(GER) Official explanation: jockey said gelding was denied a clear run on final bend

7026 PLAY CORAL SLOTS IN SHOP AND ONLINE MAIDEN STKS 7f (P)
3:50 (3:51) (Class 5) 3-Y-0+ **£2,729** (£806; £403) **Stalls** Low

Form				RPR
3423	1		**Pivka**[20] 6566 3-8-12 68 RyanMoore 1 (Sir Michael Stoute) *trckd ldrs: rdn to go 2nd 2f out: clsd on ldr 1f out: led last 100yds: sn clr* **7/2**[2]	84
03-0	2	2 1/2	**Lemon N Sugar (USA)**[14] 6705 3-8-12 68 TPQueally 7 (J Noseda) *w ldr: led 3f out: drew more than 2 l clr over 1f out: hdd last 100yds: wknd* **8/1**	77
2252	3	2	**Cape Rock**[21] 6543 3-9-3 70 JamieSpencer 2 (C A Horgan) *taken down early: dwlt: sn pulling and hld up towards rr: prog over 2f out: kpt on to take 3rd fnl f: no threat to ldng pair* **5/1**	76
22	4	2	**Party Frock**[41] 5995 3-8-12 0 RobertHavlin 12 (J H M Gosden) *hld up towards rr: prog fr 3f out: drvn over 2f out: sn outpcd: hanging over 1f out: kpt on fnl f* **9/4**[1]	66
0323	5	2 3/4	**Marraasi (USA)**[59] 5471 3-8-12 70 AlanMunro 10 (M P Tregoning) *trckd ldrs: effrt over 2f out: wl outpcd fr over 1f out* **4/1**[3]	59
	6	3/4	**Watson's Bay**[50] 5725 3-9-3 73 ChrisCatlin 3 (Miss Tor Sturgis) *mde most to 3f out: grad wknd fnl 2f* **33/1**	62
6-0	7	2	**Kara Tau**[70] 5160 3-9-0 0 JackMitchell(3) 11 (Stef Liddiard) *s.i.s: wl in rr: urged along and bhd 3f out: styd on fr over 1f out: no ch* **66/1**	56
0	8	3 1/2	**Planetary Motion (USA)**[26] 6393 3-9-3 0 JoeFanning 9 (M Johnston) *trckd ldrs: rdn over 2f out: steadily wknd fnl 2f* **14/1**	47
5060	9	hd	**Ma Ridge**[5] 6912 4-9-5 47 RichardThomas 13 (T D McCarthy) *w ldng pair: lost 2nd 2f out: wknd rapidly* **66/1**	46
	10	nk	**Orlando's Tale (USA)** 3-9-3 0 RobertWinston 5 (J R Fanshawe) *s.s: t.k.h and hld up in last pair: lft bhd by ldrs fr 3f out* **25/1**	45
00	11	11	**Miss Medusa**[26] 6393 3-8-12 0 ow5 (t) FrederikTylicki(5) 6 (Mrs C A Dunnett) *a in rr: wknd 1/2-way: t.o* **100/1**	16
00	12	15	**Alyseve**[26] 6393 3-8-12 0 FergusSweeney 14 (Mrs C A Dunnett) *nvr beyond midfield: wknd 1/2-way: wl t.o* **100/1**	—
0	13	hd	**Arch Event**[14] 6707 3-8-12 0 (p) EdwardCreighton 8 (J M Bradley) *hld up in midfield: wknd 1/2-way: wl t.o: rdn rt out* **100/1**	—

1m 22.78s (-2.02) **Going Correction** -0.15s/f (Stan) course record
WFA 3 from 4yo 2lb **13** Ran SP% **120.2**
Speed ratings (Par 103): **105,102,99,97,94 93,91,87,87,86 74,57,56**
toteswinger: 1&2 £7.50, 1&3 £5.10, 2&3 £9.80. CSF £31.06 TOTE £5.40: £2.00, £2.40, £1.70; EX 30.30.
Owner J Wigan & G Strawbridge **Bred** G Strawbridge & London Thoroughbred Services Ltd **Trained** Newmarket, Suffolk

FOCUS
An interesting maiden, with several powerful yards represented. The pace was decent and they finished fairly strung out, and the time was good. The form looks sound.

Planetary Motion(USA) Official explanation: jockey said colt jumped left on leaving stalls

7027 CORAL ON CHANNEL 4 TELETEXT PAGE 611 H'CAP 1m (P)
4:20 (4:20) (Class 5) (0-70,71) 3-Y-0+ **£2,729** (£806; £403) **Stalls** High

Form				RPR
0341	1		**Mister Ross**[7] 6867 3-9-7 71 6ex RyanMoore 8 (G L Moore) *w ldr: led after 3f: kicked on 2f out: hung bdly rt in st: ended against nr side rail but clr and in n.d fnl f* **1/2**[1]	84+
0000	2	3 1/2	**Hessian (IRE)**[6] 6880 4-9-7 68 JamieSpencer 10 (M D Squance) *hld up in last pair: smooth prog 2f out: led main gp ins fnl f but no ch w wnr* **10/1**[3]	73
02-0	3	1/2	**Certain Justice (USA)**[72] 5101 10-9-7 68 TPQueally 7 (Stef Liddiard) *hld up in last pair: rdn and struggling over 2f out: styd on u.p fnl f to take 3rd nr fin* **20/1**	72
4000	4	1/2	**Burnbrake**[31] 6242 3-9-5 69 RobertHavlin 6 (J A R Toller) *hld up in tch: effrt 2f out: rdn and styd on same pce fr over 1f out* **16/1**	71
4366	5	nk	**Sweet Kiss (USA)**[26] 6380 3-8-6 63 KylieManser(7) 2 (M J Attwater) *hld up in tch: nt clr run and swtchd lft to rail over 1f out: shuffled along and styd on steadily fnl f* **20/1**	65
4130	6	nk	**Dawson Creek (IRE)**[25] 6422 4-9-4 65 (t) ChrisCatlin 9 (B Gubby) *trckd ldrs: effrt to dispute 2nd wl over 1f out tl fdd ins fnl f* **15/2**[2]	66
0220	7	shd	**Onenightinlisbon (IRE)**[26] 6380 4-9-7 68 FergusSweeney 4 (J R Boyle) *trckd ldrs: effrt on outer to dispute 2nd 2f out: stl same pl 1f out: wknd* **10/1**[3]	69
000	8	2 1/2	**Silca Destination**[15] 6683 3-9-0 64 EdwardCreighton 1 (M R Channon) *led 3f: chsd wnr to 2f out: stl disputing 2nd 1f out: wknd rapidly* **33/1**	59
005	9	nk	**Pop Music (IRE)**[9] 6827 5-8-8 55 (v) AlanMunro 3 (Ms J S Doyle) *pressed ldrs tl wknd over 1f out* **25/1**	49
6000	10	hd	**Adantino**[14] 6706 9-9-0 64 (b) JamesMillman(3) 5 (B R Millman) *hld up in last pair: reminder 3f out: outpcd fr 2f out* **16/1**	58

1m 36.78s (-1.42) **Going Correction** -0.15s/f (Stan)
WFA 3 from 4yo+ 3lb **10** Ran SP% **124.7**
Speed ratings (Par 103): **101,97,97,96,96 95,95,93,93,92**
toteswinger: 1&2 £2.60, 1&3 £6.70, 2&3 £14.50. CSF £6.86 CT £63.27 TOTE £1.60: £1.10, £3.10, £5.80; EX 6.60 Place 6 £71.06, Place 5 £34.86..
Owner Mrs Patricia Pink **Bred** C D S Bryce And Mrs M Bryce **Trained** Woodingdean, E Sussex

FOCUS
A modest handicap. Mister Ross was very well in under his penalty and did not need to match his Windsor figure. The form seems sound.

T/Plt: £79.40 to a £1 stake. Pool: £46,847.83. 430.29 winning tickets. T/Qpdt: £8.90 to a £1 stake. Pool: £3,851.77. 316.80 winning tickets. JN

7028 - (Foreign Racing) - See Raceform Interactive

5728 LEOPARDSTOWN (L-H)
Monday, October 27

OFFICIAL GOING: Yielding to soft

7029a KILLAVULLAN STKS (GROUP 3) 7f
1:25 (1:25) 2-Y-0 **£33,507** (£9,830; £4,683; £1,595)

			RPR
1		**Rayeni (IRE)**[15] 6686 2-9-1 FMBerry 8 (John M Oxx, Ire) *mid-div: 6th 1/2-way: hdwy in 5th 1 1/2f out: impr to chal 1f out: led ins fnl 150yds: pushed out: comf* **7/2**[2]	110+
2	1 1/2	**Vitruvian Man**[27] 6368 2-9-1 MJKinane 1 (John M Oxx, Ire) *led: rdn and chal 1f out: hdd last 150yds: no ex: kpt on same pce* **11/10**[1]	104
3	1 1/2	**Gluteus Maximus (IRE)**[9] 6829 2-9-1 100 JAHeffernan 5 (A P O'Brien, Ire) *trckd ldrs: 5th 1/2-way: rdn in 5th 2f out: 6th 1 1/2f out: kpt on same pce fr 1f out* **20/1**	101
4	1/2	**Liebermann (GER)**[60] 5442 2-9-1 PJSmullen 3 (D K Weld, Ire) *chsd ldrs: 4th 1/2-way: rdn into 3rd 2f out: no ex fr 1f out: kpt on same pce* **12/1**	99
5	nk	**What's Up Pussycat (IRE)**[29] 6318 2-8-12 97 WMLordan 6 (David Wachman, Ire) *hld up in rr: rdn into 6th over 1f out: kpt on same pce fnl f* **16/1**	96
6	1 3/4	**Forest Storm**[44] 5924 2-8-12 102 KJManning 4 (J S Bolger, Ire) *chsd ldr: 2nd 1/2-way: rdn 2f out: no ex in 4th 1f out: kpt on one pce* **11/2**[3]	91
7	1	**Peter Tchaikovsky**[106] 4005 2-9-1 JMurtagh 2 (A P O'Brien, Ire) *hld up towards rr: rdn in 7th 2f out: no ex fr 1 1/2f out: kpt on one pce* **11/1**	92
8	5	**Vilasol (IRE)**[9] 6829 2-9-1 96 DPMcDonogh 7 (Kevin Prendergast, Ire) *chsd ldrs: 3rd 1/2-way: rdn in 4th 2f out: no ex fr 1 1/2f out and sn wknd* **20/1**	79

1m 33.85s (3.55) **Going Correction** +0.70s/f (Yiel) **8** Ran SP% **116.7**
Speed ratings: **107,105,103,103,102 100,99,93**
CSF £7.89 TOTE £4.00: £1.60, £1.10, £3.50; DF 9.00.
Owner H H Aga Khan **Bred** Hh The Aga Khan's Studs Sc **Trained** Currabeg, Co Kildare

NOTEBOOK
Rayeni(IRE), an impressive winner of a maiden on his debut at Naas, looked a smart type here, cutting down his rivals with a sustained run on the outside. A half-brother by Indian Ridge to a Sinndar filly who was a minor winner over 1m4f as a three-year-old this season, he is out of a Rainbow Quest mare who raced only twice and won over 1m2f. He looks likely to stay 1m2f in time but has enough pace to compete at a high level over 1m. (op 7/2 tchd 100/30)
Vitruvian Man proved more popular in the betting than his winning stable companion and set out to make all. He had the others in trouble a furlong down, but had no answer to Rayeni's superior acceleration. He remains a very useful middle-distance prospect. (op 5/4)
Gluteus Maximus(IRE) is a well-exposed sort who was having his ninth start. He produced one of his better efforts, more in keeping with a fair third behind Captain Ramius at Dundalk than with a more recent run at Cork. Though clearly useful enough, he is some way removed from the best of the stable's juveniles and might be hard enough to place next season. (op 16/1)

6642 SAINT-CLOUD (L-H)
Monday, October 27

OFFICIAL GOING: Heavy

7037a PRIX DE FLORE (GROUP 3) (F&M) 1m 2f 110y
1:20 (1:23) 3-Y-0+ **£29,412** (£11,765; £8,824; £5,882; £2,941)

			RPR
1		**Albisola (IRE)**[64] 5331 3-8-7 JVictoire 13 (Robert Collet, France) *in rr: last st: brought wdst of all and hdwy over 2f out: wnt 2nd on outside rail 1 1/2f out: styd on to ld cl home* **76/10**	116
2	nk	**Light Green (BRZ)**[22] 6521 4-8-10 CSoumillon 5 (A De Royer-Dupre, France) *hld up in rr: 12th st: hdwy racing alone on ins rail to ld over 2f out: wnt 2 l clr: hdd and no ex cl home* **43/10**[1]	112
3	2	**Tres Rapide (IRE)**[23] 6495 3-8-7 DBoeuf 9 (H-A Pantall, France) *hld up in rr: 11th st: hdwy down outside to go 3rd ins fnl f: kpt on* **11/2**[2]	111
4	1 1/2	**Tangaspeed (FR)**[43] 5952 3-8-7 TJarnet 14 (R Laplanche, France) *midfield: 5th st: hdwy on outside to go 2nd 2f out: one pce fnl 1 1/2f* **19/1**	108
5	3/4	**High Maintenance (FR)**[43] 5956 4-8-11 OPeslier 11 (A Fabre, France) *hld up: 9th st: kpt on down outside fnl 2f* **23/1**	105
6	snk	**La Boum (GER)**[23] 6495 5-8-11 J-BEyquem 4 (Robert Collet, France) *in rr: 13th st: hdwy towards ins to go 2nd briefly jst over 1 1/2f out: wknd* **24/1**	105
7	1	**Bahia Breeze**[64] 5332 6-8-11 SPasquier 7 (Rae Guest) *in tch: 7th st: rdn and one pce fr over 2f out* **24/1**	103
8	1 1/2	**Alix Road (FR)**[23] 6495 5-8-11 AlexisBadel 8 (Mme M Bollack-Badel, France) *cl up: 4th st: effrt over 2f out: sn btn* **25/1**	100
9	3	**Top Toss (IRE)**[86] 4657 3-8-10 C-PLemaire 2 (Y De Nicolay, France) *cl up: 3rd st: wknd under 2f out* **13/2**	99
10	nk	**Mahaatheer (IRE)**[31] 6264 3-8-7 DBonilla 10 (F Head, France) *led to over 2f out: wknd* **79/10**	96
11		**Antiquities**[99] 4234 3-8-7 MGuyon 3 (A Fabre, France) *hld up: 8th st: effrt over 2f out: sn wknd* **6/1**[3]	96
12		**Lady Deauville (FR)**[16] 6664 3-8-7 FrancisNorton 1 (P A Blockley) *racd keenly towards rr: 10th st: nvr a factor* **41/1**	96
13		**Loutka (FR)**[86] 4657 3-8-7 TThulliez 12 (A De Royer-Dupre, France) *prom: 2nd st: sn rdn and btn* **92/1**	96
14		**Goose Bay (GER)**[24] 3-8-13 AStarke 6 (P Schiergen, Germany) *midfield: 7th st: sn wknd* **13/1**	102

2m 18.6s (-1.00)
WFA 3 from 4yo+ 5lb **14** Ran SP% **116.3**
PARI-MUTUEL: WIN 8.60; PL 2.70, 1.80, 2.10; DF 26.90.
Owner G A Oldham **Bred** Citadel Stud **Trained** Chantilly, France

NOTEBOOK
Albisola(IRE), held up towards the rear of the field for much of the race, drifted towards the stands rail in the straight and finished well to get up on the line. She clearly appreciated the soft ground, but there are no plans for her and it is undecided if she stays in training next year.

Light Green(BRZ), another that was held up near the back of the field, stayed on the outside rail up the straight whilst most of the other runners drifted to the stands' rail. She finished well and was just caught on the line.
Tres Rapide(IRE), held up at the back of the field, made progress on the outside at the furlong marker and galloped on strongly to the line. Her trainer reported that she needs further and now goes for the Queen Elizabeth Commemorative Cup in Japan on November 16th.
Tangaspeed(FR), not far from the leaders on the outside for much of the race, battled well up the straight but was no threat to the first three.
Bahia Breeze was well placed just behind the leaders, but when the pace quickened in the straight she could not go with them and just stayed on at one pace.
Lady Deauville(FR) lost her place on the first turn and never really got back into the race. She had her ground, but her trainer reported that it just was not her day. She now goes for the Listed Prix Solitude at Fontainebleau on November 21st.

6806 CATTERICK (L-H)
Tuesday, October 28

OFFICIAL GOING: Good to soft (7.8)
Wind: light half against Weather: fine but very cool

7038 COWTHORPE MEDIAN AUCTION MAIDEN STKS — 5f 212y
1:30 (1:31) (Class 6) 2-Y-O — £2,047 (£604; £302) Stalls Low

Form — RPR
0023 **1** **Real Diamond**[11] 6788 2-8-12 57 .... SilvestreDeSousa 1 — 65
(A Dickman) *mde all: edgd rt fnl f: kpt on strly: cheekily* 6/1[2]
0 **2** ½ **Fifth Amendment**[21] 6545 2-8-12 0 .... SladeO'Hara(5) 2 — 69
(A Berry) *chsd ldrs: kpt on wl ins fnl f* 250/1
52 **3** 1 ¼ **Zegna (IRE)**[8] 6858 2-9-3 0 .... TomEaves 4 — 65
(B Smart) *trckd ldrs: t.k.h: hrd rdn 1f out: kpt on same pce* 2/5[1]
6044 **4** 2 ¼ **Grissom (IRE)**[17] 6656 2-9-3 62 .... FrancisNorton 3 — 58
(A Berry) *chsd ldrs: one pce fnl 2f* 8/1[3]
05 **5** nk **Legal Legacy**[14] 6723 2-9-3 0 .... TonyHamilton 9 — 57
(M Dods) *mid-div: outpcd and lost pl 4f out: styd on fnl 2f* 28/1
60 **6** 1 **Kiama Bay (IRE)**[21] 6545 2-9-3 0 .... GrahamGibbons 10 — 54
(J J Quinn) *sn in rr: kpt on fnl 2f: nvr nr ldrs* 33/1
05 **7** shd **Mr Freddy (IRE)**[42] 5988 2-9-3 0 .... JamieMoriarty 12 — 54
(R A Fahey) *mid-div: outpcd and lost pl 4f out: wandered fnl 2f: nvr a threat* 12/1
00 **8** 1 ¼ **Top Flight Splash**[24] 6488 2-8-12 0 .... AndrewElliott 11 — 45
(Mrs G S Rees) *prom: outpcd over 3f out: kpt on fnl f* 150/1
4005 **9** 2 ¾ **Miss Xu Xia**[41] 6009 2-8-7 38 ....(p) NataliaGemelova(5) 6 — 37
(G R Oldroyd) *prom: outpcd over 3f out: edgd rt 2f out: sn wknd* 200/1
0 **10** 1 ¼ **Valid Point (IRE)**[7] 6885 2-9-3 0 .... PaulMulrennan 5 — 38
(Sir Mark Prescott) *s.i.s: a in rr* 16/1
00 **11** hd **Avitus**[11] 6789 2-9-3 0 .... TonyCulhane 7 — 37
(Micky Hammond) *s.i.s: sn bhd* 150/1
00 **12** 14 **Addison De Witt**[51] 5716 2-9-0 0 .... NeilBrown(3) 8 — —
(Micky Hammond) *s.i.s: sn bhd: detached in last whn rn wd bnd 3f out* 125/1

1m 17.01s (3.41) **Going Correction** +0.50s/f (Yiel) — 12 Ran SP% 119.8
Speed ratings (Par 93): **97,96,94,91,91 89,89,88,84,82 82,63**
toteswinger: 1&2 £33.60, 1&3 £1.50, 2&3 £27.70. CSF £983.41 TOTE £6.10: £1.60, £19.20, £1.10; EX 618.30.
Owner John H Sissons **Bred** Capt J H Wilson **Trained** Sandhutton, N Yorks
■ Stewards' Enquiry : Silvestre De Sousa one-day ban: careless riding (Nov 12)

FOCUS
A decidedly ordinary juvenile maiden in which a low draw proved a real advantage. The time was reasonable but the likes of the ninth hold down the form.

NOTEBOOK
Real Diamond, placed on her last two outings, took full advantage of her inside berth and made all to open her account at the sixth time of asking. She handled the softer ground well, this sharp 6f was no doubt right up her street, and she rates value for a little further despite having had the run of the race. Her trainer does well with this type and she can now expect a mark of around 60 when moving back into a handicap. (op 13-2)
Fifth Amendment, drawn 2, had looked clueless on his debut at this venue earlier in the month, but he stepped up significantly on that effort and showed a lot more speed here. The extra furlong suited and he is evidently coming good, but will only look of real interest when eligible for a mark after his next outing. (op 200-1)
Zegna(IRE) had run a blinder from an awful draw at Pontefract eight days previously and looked to have an obvious chance on that form. He refused to settle through the first two furlongs and that did not help his cause, but there is no doubt he ran well below his previous level on this sharper track. Perhaps the race came too soon and he should find his feet next year in handicaps. (op 4-9 tchd 1-2)
Grissom(IRE) was never seriously in the hunt on this step back up in trip, but he still left the impression there could be better to come now he becomes eligible for a mark. (op 7-1 tchd 9-1 and 12-1 in a place)
Avitus Official explanation: jockey said gelding would not face the kickback caused by the loose ground

7039 RACINGUK.TV H'CAP — 1m 3f 214y
2:00 (2:01) (Class 6) (0-60,60) 3-Y-0+ — £2,047 (£604; £302) Stalls High

Form — RPR
00-0 **1** **Covert Mission**[19] 6596 5-8-13 50 .... GregFairley 1 — 61
(P D Evans) *chsd ldrs: drvn 6f out: led on inner wl over 1f out: edgd rt: styd on strly: readily* 16/1
-014 **2** 2 ¼ **Surprise Pension (IRE)**[11] 6786 4-9-8 59 .... GrahamGibbons 5 — 66
(J J Quinn) *chsd ldrs: wnt 2nd over 1f out: no imp* 9/2[2]
0201 **3** ½ **Stravita**[14] 6719 4-9-5 56 ....(p) TonyCulhane 4 — 63
(R Hollinshead) *mid-div: effrt over 3f out: swtchd rt appr fnl f: styd on* 15/2
3145 **4** 6 **Three Strings (USA)**[10] 6812 5-9-7 58 ....(p) TomEaves 2 — 55
(P D Niven) *led 2f: t.k.h: drvn 4f out: wknd appr fnl f* 13/2[3]
0631 **5** ¾ **Bollin Freddie**[49] 5776 4-8-11 48 .... TonyHamilton 3 — 44
(A J Lockwood) *dwlt: hdwy to ld after 2f: hdd & wknd wl over 1f out* 10/1
5/3- **6** ¾ **Onyergo (IRE)**[28] 1745 6-9-7 58 ....(t) DavidAllan 13 — 53
(M A Barnes) *mid-div: kpt on fnl 3f: nvr a factor* 22/1
0306 **7** hd **Right You Are (IRE)**[66] 5262 8-8-10 47 .... PaulQuinn 9 — 41
(Paul Green) *in rr: kpt on fnl 3f: nvr nr ldrs* 66/1
4034 **8** 6 **Mister Fizzbomb (IRE)**[10] 6806 5-9-6 60 ....(v) NeilBrown(3) 10 — 45
(J S Wainwright) *chsd ldrs: drvn 4f out: lost pl 3f out* 12/1
2406 **9** ¾ **Desert Hawk**[11] 6786 7-9-6 57 .... ShaneKelly 11 — 40
(W M Brisbourne) *in rr div: nvr on terms* 25/1
6020 **10** 3 ¾ **Its Moon (IRE)**[30] 6313 4-9-8 59 ....(v[1]) JamieMoriarty 15 — 36
(T D Walford) *reluctant in last and sn given reminders: nvr on terms* 15/2
2550 **11** 4 ½ **Orchestrion**[11] 6792 3-8-13 57 .... PJMcDonald 7 — 27
(Miss T Jackson) *mid-div: lost pl 4f out* 40/1
4053 **12** 1 ¼ **Top Man Dan (IRE)**[35] 5399 3-8-9 53 .... DNolan 6 — 21
(D Carroll) *prom: hmpd bnd after 3f: lost pl over 3f out* 16/1
3560 **13** ½ **Kangrina**[7] 6882 6-9-2 58 .... FrederikTylicki(5) 12 — 25
(George Baker) *chsd ldrs: effrt over 3f out: lost pl over 2f out* 4/1[1]
0004 **14** 14 **Royal Citadel (IRE)**[80] 4850 5-8-8 50 ....(v) KellyHarrison(5) 14 — —
(Mrs L B Normile) *in rr: t.o 3f out* 33/1

2m 43.75s (4.85) **Going Correction** +0.50s/f (Yiel)
WFA 3 from 4yo+ 7lb — 14 Ran SP% 118.7
Speed ratings (Par 101): **103,101,101,97,96 96,96,92,91,89 86,85,84,75**
toteswinger: 1&2 £23.80, 1&3 £16.90, 2&3 £6.50. CSF £81.47 CT £600.67 TOTE £27.70: £6.60, £1.80, £2.60; EX 135.70.
Owner Lost Souls Racing **Bred** Mrs Marian Harding **Trained** Pandy, Monmouths

FOCUS
This weak handicap was run at an even pace and again a low draw proved to be an advantage. The first three came clear and this is probably reasonable form for the grade.
Kangrina Official explanation: trainer said mare was unsuited by the good to soft ground

7040 GO RACING AT WETHERBY THIS FRIDAY H'CAP — 5f 212y
2:30 (2:30) (Class 5) (0-75,75) 3-Y-O — £2,590 (£770; £385; £192) Stalls Low

Form — RPR
0041 **1** **Harlech Castle**[12] 6765 3-9-4 75 ....(b) ShaneKelly 2 — 86
(P F I Cole) *chsd ldrs: led 2f out: styd on strly* 10/3[1]
3210 **2** 2 ½ **Splash The Cash**[95] 4397 3-8-7 67 .... NeilBrown(3) 10 — 70
(K A Ryan) *led on outside 2f: kpt on appr fnl f: no imp* 12/1
5323 **3** nk **Bertie Vista**[11] 6792 3-8-3 63 .... DuranFentiman(3) 5 — 65
(T D Easterby) *chsd ldrs: drvn over 3f out: styd on same pce fnl 2f* 6/1
4040 **4** 3 ¾ **Feeling Fresh (IRE)**[12] 6765 3-8-7 64 .... PaulQuinn 8 — 54
(Paul Green) *in rr: edgd rt and styd on appr fnl f: nvr nr to chal* 12/1
1122 **5** hd **Mandalay King (IRE)**[51] 5714 3-8-4 66 .... KellyHarrison(5) 9 — 55+
(Mrs Marjorie Fife) *hld up towards rr: hdwy to trck ldrs over 2f out: fdd appr fnl f* 11/2[3]
0000 **6** 3 ¼ **Bespoke Boy**[80] 4875 3-9-2 73 .... LeeEnstone 1 — 52
(P C Haslam) *w ldrs: led after 2f: hdd 2f out: wknd appr fnl f* 25/1
0005 **7** 1 **Royal Acclamation (IRE)**[28] 6357 3-8-5 62 .... SilvestreDeSousa 11 — 38
(G A Harker) *sn detached in rr: kpt on fnl 2f: nvr a factor* 10/1
511 **8** 3 ¼ **Chosen One (IRE)**[37] 6150 3-8-10 67 .... TomEaves 6 — 32
(B Smart) *chsd ldrs: hung rt and lost pl over 1f out* 4/1[2]
0545 **9** 1 ¼ **Style Award**[62] 5397 3-8-13 75 .... FrederikTylicki(5) 7 — 36
(W J H Ratcliffe) *sn chsng ldrs: wknd over 1f out* 8/1

1m 16.33s (2.73) **Going Correction** +0.50s/f (Yiel) — 9 Ran SP% 112.2
Speed ratings (Par 101): **101,97,97,92,92 87,86,82,80**
toteswinger: 1&2 £9.00, 1&3 £4.90, 2&3 £15.10. CSF £42.34 CT £228.56 TOTE £4.20: £1.30, £3.40, £2.00; EX 57.90.
Owner Elite Racing Club **Bred** Elite Racing Club **Trained** Whatcombe, Oxon

FOCUS
A modest sprint handicap for three-year-olds, run at a solid pace. The winer built on his Nottingham win and the next two were close to their marks.
Chosen One(IRE) Official explanation: jockey said colt was unsuited by the loose ground

7041 TURFTV.CO.UK H'CAP — 7f
3:00 (3:00) (Class 4) (0-85,84) 3-Y-O+ — £4,857 (£1,445; £722; £360) Stalls Low

Form — RPR
1062 **1** **Shotley Mac**[14] 6724 4-8-4 70 ....(b) FrancisNorton 7 — 78
(N Bycroft) *led early: chsd ldr: styd on to ld fnl 50yds* 8/1[2]
0061 **2** ¾ **Bold Marc (IRE)**[10] 6813 6-8-11 77 .... DarrenWilliams 13 — 83
(K R Burke) *sn led: qcknd over 2f out: hdd wl ins fnl f* 9/1
3244 **3** hd **Grazeon Gold Blend**[47] 5831 5-8-13 79 .... GrahamGibbons 10 — 85+
(J J Quinn) *mid-div: hdwy over 2f out: styd on wl fnl f* 12/1
0501 **4** ½ **Quest For Success (IRE)**[3] 6976 3-8-8 76 .... TonyHamilton 2 — 79
(R A Fahey) *chsd ldrs: kpt on same pce fnl f* 3/1[1]
3210 **5** 1 ¼ **Jonny Lesters Hair (IRE)**[24] 6471 3-8-8 76 .... DavidAllan 9 — 76
(T D Easterby) *chsd ldrs: kpt on same pce fnl f* 8/1[2]
1430 **6** 1 ½ **Zabeel Tower**[14] 6724 5-8-8 74 ....(v[1]) AndrewElliott 1 — 71
(R Allan) *s.i.s: hdwy on inner over 2f out: sn chsng ldrs: one pce appr fnl f* 16/1
3045 **7** 3 ¾ **River Thames**[10] 6813 5-8-8 74 .... PaulMulrennan 11 — 61
(K A Ryan) *sn chsng ldrs on outer: wknd over 1f out* 22/1
0442 **8** 1 ¼ **Hiccups**[51] 5717 8-8-12 78 .... TomEaves 4 — 61
(M Dods) *t.k.h: in tch: effrt 2f out: fdd fnl f* 17/2[3]
0043 **9** ½ **Daaweitza**[26] 6431 5-8-13 82 .... NeilBrown(3) 6 — 64
(B Ellison) *in rr: drvn over 2f out: nvr on terms* 8/1[2]
1420 **10** 2 ½ **Esoterica (IRE)**[39] 6070 5-8-6 77 ....(v) GaryBartley(5) 8 — 52
(J S Goldie) *in rr: effrt on outside over 2f out: nvr on terms* 20/1
0521 **11** ¾ **Trimlestown (IRE)**[13] 6736 5-8-4 70 .... GregFairley 12 — 43
(P D Evans) *charged gate and rdr temporarily lost irons: lost pl after 2f: sn bhd* 16/1
0010 **12** 9 **Game Lad**[11] 6783 6-9-1 84 ....(t) DuranFentiman(3) 5 — 33
(T D Easterby) *s.i.s: sn detached in rr: bhd fnl 3f* 11/1

1m 29.83s (2.83) **Going Correction** +0.50s/f (Yiel)
WFA 3 from 4yo+ 2lb — 12 Ran SP% 115.8
Speed ratings (Par 105): **103,102,101,101,99 98,93,92,91,89 88,77**
toteswinger: 1&2 £15.10, 1&3 £15.90, 2&3 £18.60. CSF £76.24 CT £873.47 TOTE £10.30: £3.50, £3.70, £3.70; EX 102.30.
Owner J A Swinburne **Bred** N Bycroft **Trained** Brandsby, N Yorks

FOCUS
A modest handicap, run at a sound pace, and few managed to get into it from the rear. The form is sound enough.
Daaweitza Official explanation: jockey said gelding was unsuited by the loose ground
Trimlestown(IRE) Official explanation: jockey said he lost his irons leaving stalls

7042 BOOK NOW FOR SUNDAY 28TH DECEMBER H'CAP — 1m 7f 177y
3:30 (3:30) (Class 5) (0-70,67) 3-Y-O+ — £2,590 (£770; £385; £192) Stalls Low

Form — RPR
1 **Quitit (IRE)**[27] 5656 3-8-13 60 ....(b) TonyCulhane 3 — 73
(Mrs S A Watt) *in tch: hdwy to chse ldrs over 5f out: led 2f out: drvn clr* 12/1
0133 **2** 5 **Mister Pete (IRE)**[14] 6727 5-9-5 59 .... DominicFox(3) 5 — 66
(W Storey) *hld up in rr: gd hdwy 7f out: sn chsng ldrs: led over 3f out tl 2f out: kpt on same pce* 5/1[2]
0340 **3** 2 ¾ **River Danube**[11] 6790 5-9-12 63 .... JamieMoriarty 12 — 67
(T J Fitzgerald) *hld up in rr: hdwy over 6f out: sn chsng ldrs: one pce fnl 2f* 16/1
3-44 **4** 4 **Aston Lad**[21] 6550 7-8-10 47 .... PaulMulrennan 11 — 46
(Micky Hammond) *hld up in rr: hdwy over 5f out: one pce fnl 3f* 7/1[3]

2031 **5** *hd* **Sir Sandicliffe (IRE)**[10] 6812 4-9-7 **65** .... DeanHeslop(7) 6 64
(W M Brisbourne) *hld up in mid-div: effrt on outside over 2f out: nvr trbld ldrs: eased nr fin* **5/1**[2]
0003 **6** *2* **Carlton Mac**[14] 6725 3-8-3 **50** .... FrancisNorton 13 47
(N Bycroft) *in rr: hdwy 6f out: nvr nr ldrs* **33/1**
4050 **7** *15* **Rocknest Island (IRE)**[28] 5385 5-8-9 **46** oh1 .... (p) TomEaves 8 25
(P D Niven) *in rr: pushed along over 7f out: nvr on terms* **28/1**
0 **8** *2 1/2* **Mega Steps (IRE)**[10] 6812 4-9-0 **51** .... AdrianTNicholls 10 27
(Jennie Candlish) *in rr: drvn 7f out: nvr on terms* **16/1**
9 *2 3/4* **Never Pink (FR)**[185] 1620 4-9-4 **55** .... JoeFanning 2 27
(Ian Williams) *chsd ldrs: led 5f out tl over 3f out: wknd fnl 2f* **10/1**
5633 **10** *3/4* **Garra Molly (IRE)**[11] 6790 3-9-6 **67** .... PJMcDonald 7 38
(G A Swinbank) *chsd ldrs: drvn over 3f out: sn wknd* **11/4**[1]
00-0 **11** *37* **Glamoroso (IRE)**[14] 6725 3-7-13 **51** oh1 ow5 .... NataliaGemelova(5) 14 —
(A Kirtley) *mid-div: chal over 5f out: wknd and eased over 2f out: t.o* **250/1**
3160 **12** *29* **Always Best**[14] 6727 4-8-11 **48** .... TonyHamilton 1 —
(R Allan) *mde most tl 5f out: sn lost pl and bhd: wl t.o* **12/1**
243- **13** *6* **Born West (USA)**[202] 7004 4-9-7 **61** .... JackMitchell(3) 15 —
(N B King) *w ldrs: rn in snatches: lost pl 7f out: sn bhd: wl t.o* **28/1**
0300 **14** *1 3/4* **Stolen Light (IRE)**[40] 6054 7-8-13 **50** .... (b) GregFairley 4 —
(A Crook) *w ldr: lost pl7f out: sn bhd: t.o 3f out* **100/1**

3m 41.88s (9.88) **Going Correction** +0.50s/f (Yiel)
WFA 3 from 4yo+ 10lb **14 Ran SP% 120.0**
Speed ratings (Par 103): **95,92,91,89,89 88,80,79,77,77 59,44,41,40**
toteswinger: 1&2 £19.50, 1&3 £47.20, 2&3 £21.90. CSF £68.93 CT £984.63 TOTE £14.20: £3.90, £2.10, £6.00; EX 110.80.
Owner Major E J Watt **Bred** Philip Brady **Trained** Brompton-on-Swale, N Yorks
■ The first Flat winner for Sharon Watt.
■ Stewards' Enquiry : Dean Heslop three-day ban: failed to ride out for best possible placing (Nov 12-14)

FOCUS
This staying handicap was run at a solid gallop and suited those coming from behind. Improvement from the winner, with the next two close to their recent handicap form.
Garra Molly(IRE) Official explanation: jockey said filly was unsuited by the loose ground

7043 COME RACING AGAIN NEXT TUESDAY H'CAP 5f
4:00 (4:00) (Class 6) (0-65,65) 3-Y-0+ **£2,047** (£604; £302) **Stalls Low**

Form RPR
0032 **1** **Joyeaux**[7] 6890 6-8-11 **61** .... DuranFentiman(3) 1 73
(L R James) *in rr: hdwy on ins over 3f out: led 1f out: styd on wl* **6/1**[2]
1023 **2** *2* **Wicked Wilma (IRE)**[26] 6405 4-8-9 **56** .... FrancisNorton 2 61
(A Berry) *led tl 1f out: kpt on same pce* **9/2**[1]
2235 **3** *1/2* **Select Committee**[12] 6766 3-8-13 **60** .... (v) GrahamGibbons 7 63
(J J Quinn) *in tch: hdwy 2f out: kpt on fnl f* **12/1**
360 **4** *shd* **Tender Process (IRE)**[12] 6766 5-8-11 **58** .... (b) TonyHamilton 11 61+
(R A Fahey) *sn outpcd and in rr: hdwy over 1f out: fin wl* **12/1**
5-53 **4** *dht* **Liberty Ship**[11] 6791 3-9-2 **63** .... (t) AndrewElliott 3 66
(J D Bethell) *in rr: hdwy to chse ldrs over 2f out: kpt on same pce appr fnl f* **14/1**
1520 **6** *1/2* **Ryedane (IRE)**[52] 5709 6-8-11 **58** .... (b) DavidAllan 9 59
(T D Easterby) *in rr: hdwy 2f out: styd on wl ins fnl f* **8/1**[3]
0252 **7** *1/2* **Metal Guru**[15] 6711 4-9-0 **64** .... (p) RussellKennemore(3) 5 63
(R Hollinshead) *in tch: effrt 2f out: kpt on same pce* **11/1**
0605 **8** *3/4* **Zamalik (USA)**[38] 6116 5-8-7 **57** .... JackMitchell(3) 10 54
(Mrs A Duffield) *in rr: edgd rt over 2f out: kpt on: nvr nr ldrs* **10/1**
0342 **9** *1 1/4* **Sands Crooner (IRE)**[12] 6766 5-9-1 **62** .... (v) PaulMulrennan 14 54
(J G Given) *mid-div on outer: effrt over 2f out: nvr nr ldrs* **14/1**
0515 **10** *nse* **Guto**[21] 6546 5-8-6 **58** .... KellyHarrison(5) 15 50
(W J H Ratcliffe) *sn swtchd to r alone stands' side: nvr nr ldrs* **14/1**
0304 **11** *2 1/4* **Colorus (IRE)**[12] 6766 5-9-3 **64** .... TomEaves 4 48
(W J H Ratcliffe) *chsd ldrs: lost pl over 1f out* **16/1**
0000 **12** *1* **The History Man (IRE)**[12] 6766 5-9-0 **61** .... (be) GregFairley 6 41
(M Mullineaux) *a towards rr* **25/1**
0020 **13** *6* **Kings College Boy**[9] 6840 8-8-13 **65** .... (b) FrederikTylicki(5) 8 24
(R A Fahey) *sn outpcd and bhd* **11/1**
3160 **14** *1* **Micky Mac (IRE)**[36] 6178 4-8-13 **60** .... JamieMoriarty 13 15
(T D Walford) *sn outpcd and in rr: bhd fnl 3f* **14/1**

62.12 secs (2.32) **Going Correction** +0.50s/f (Yiel) **14 Ran SP% 121.1**
Speed ratings (Par 101): **101,97,97,96,96 95,95,94,92,91 88,86,77,75**
toteswinger: 1&2 £9.60, 1&3 £9.60, 2&3 £8.40. CSF £33.25 CT £330.60 TOTE £7.80: £3.10, £1.70, £2.20; EX 22.80 Place 6: £241.31 Place 5: £196.55.
Owner PSB Holdings Ltd **Bred** Mrs Ann Jarvis **Trained** Norton, N Yorks

FOCUS
A wide-open sprint in which once more a low draw was a real advantage.
T/Jkpt: Not won. T/Plt: £212.00 to a £1 stake. Pool: £59,712.85. 205.60 winning tickets. T/Qpdt: £87.50 to a £1 stake. Pool: £3,529.70. 29.85 winning tickets. WG

6836 SOUTHWELL (L-H)
Tuesday, October 28

OFFICIAL GOING: Standard
Wind: Virtually nil Weather: Overcast and cold

7044 SOUTHWELL-RACECOURSE.CO.UK MAIDEN AUCTION STKS 6f (F)
1:50 (1:51) (Class 6) 2-Y-0 **£3,070** (£906; £453) **Stalls Low**

Form RPR
2405 **1** **Wotatomboy**[40] 6051 2-8-5 61 .... MichaelJStainton(3) 5 63
(R M Whitaker) *hmpd and squeezed out s: hdwy on inner 2f out: rdn over 1f out: edgd rt ins fnl f: styd on to ld fnl 100yds* **13/2**[3]
0040 **2** *nk* **Captain Kallis (IRE)**[7] 6876 2-8-10 52 .... FrankieMcDonald 2 64
(D J S Ffrench Davis) *t.k.h: mde most: rdn along 2f out: drvn ent fnl f: hdd and kpt on same pce fnl 100yds* **33/1**
052 **3** *4 1/2* **Trigger McCann**[17] 6661 2-8-9 72 .... LPKeniry 1 50
(J S Moore) *cl up: disp ld 1/2-way: rdn along 2f out and ev ch tl drvn ent fnl f and grad wknd* **2/1**[2]
323 **4** *1* **York Key Bar**[10] 6807 2-8-9 75 .... DaneO'Neill 4 47
(B Ellison) *cl up: rdn along 3f out: drvn and outpcd 2f out: styd on same pce u.p fnl f* **4/5**[1]
6000 **5** *nk* **Pollish**[12] 6764 2-8-4 38 .... SaleemGolam 3 41
(A Berry) *chsd ldrs: swtchd lft and hdwy wl over 1f out: sn rdn and wknd ent fnl f* **50/1**
5066 **6** *9* **Danderdandan**[26] 6406 2-8-11 36 .... (p) RobertWinston 7 21
(P T Midgley) *cl up: rdn along 3f out: drvn over 2f out and sn wknd* **25/1**
00 **7** *7* **Angelsbemine**[43] 5959 2-8-1 0 .... (v[1]) AndrewMullen(3) 6 —
(J R Norton) *sn outpcd and bhd fnl 3f* **100/1**

1m 16.79s (0.29) **Going Correction** -0.075s/f (Stan) **7 Ran SP% 112.0**
Speed ratings (Par 93): **95,94,88,87,86 74,65**
toteswinger: 1&2 £8.90, 1&3 £3.10, 2&3 £9.80. CSF £138.59 TOTE £7.20: £2.30, £13.50; EX 145.70.
Owner Giro Partnership **Bred** Hellwood Stud Farm **Trained** Scarcroft, W Yorks

FOCUS
A very poor maiden in which only a couple seemed to have any chance according to the market, but another reminder were it needed that this surface can turn the formbook upside down, especially with horses trying Fibresand for the first time. Selling-class form.

NOTEBOOK
Wotatomboy was racing beyond the minimum trip for the first time on this sand debut, but her prospects didn't look that good when she took quite a buffeting from the pair drawn either side of her after leaving the stalls and she soon found herself in last place. However, once switched over to the inside rail to make her effort, she picked up nicely and battled on well to score despite hanging away to her right throughout the last furlong. The longer trip seemed to suit her and connections may now look for a nursery before putting her away. (op 15-2 tchd 8-1)
Captain Kallis(IRE), back down in trip for this Fibresand debut, raced keenly up with the pace and battled on well under the circumstances, but he appeared to face a huge task on official ratings and his proximity doesn't do a lot for the form. (op 20-1)
Trigger McCann, another to race up with the pace from the start, put up little resistance once tackled. He had progressed in each of his three previous starts and was only just pipped in a Polytrack maiden last time, but it seemed that this surface didn't suit him so well. (op 7-4 tchd 9-4 in places)
York Key Bar was off the bridle and going nowhere from halfway. His form on turf gave him the winning of this, but he plainly failed to handle the surface and he should be given another chance back on turf, or even if trying Polytrack. (op 11-10)
Pollish ran well for a long way, but probably didn't achieve much. (op 33-1)

7045 LADBROKES BET NOW ON 0800 777 888 H'CAP 1m 6f (F)
2:20 (2:20) (Class 6) (0-65,65) 3-Y-0+ **£2,388** (£705; £352) **Stalls Low**

Form RPR
5002 **1** **Victory Quest (IRE)**[9] 6838 8-10-0 **65** .... (v) J-PGuillambert 9 73
(Mrs S Lamyman) *hld up towards rr: hdwy on outer over 4f out: rdn along 2f out: drvn to chse ldr ent fnl f: styd on u.p to ld nr fin* **4/1**[2]
0601 **2** *nk* **Bold Bobby Be (IRE)**[16] 6668 4-9-12 **63** .... (v) DaneO'Neill 6 71
(J L Dunlop) *hld up in rr: smooth hdwy over 3f out: led wl over 1f out: rdn ins fnl f: hdd and no ex nr fin* **11/4**[1]
0-06 **3** *1 3/4* **Jetta Joy (IRE)**[38] 6115 3-7-13 **48** oh1 ow2 .... AndrewMullen(3) 7 53
(Mrs A Duffield) *in tch: hdwy over 4f out: rdn along to chse ldrs 3f out: drvn wl over 1f out: kpt on u.p* **40/1**
321- **4** *2 1/4* **Dart**[321] 7125 4-9-12 **63** .... RobertWinston 4 65
(J R Fanshawe) *hld up towards rr: hdwy 3f out: rdn to chse ldrs wl over 1f out: sn one pce* **7/1**
3605 **5** *10* **Trance (IRE)**[14] 6727 8-8-11 **51** .... (b) MichaelJStainton(3) 8 39
(T D Barron) *sn outpcd and rdn along in rr: hdwy over 4f out: plugged on u.p fnl 2f: nvr nr ldrs* **12/1**
2350 **6** *nk* **Blue Hills**[16] 6668 7-9-6 **62** .... (b) WilliamCarson(5) 3 50
(P W Hiatt) *cl up: led after 4f: rdn along over 3f out: hdd wl over 2f out and sn wknd* **12/1**
0020 **7** *9* **Pretty Demanding (IRE)**[7] 6882 4-9-9 **60** .... JamesDoyle 11 35
(M G Quinlan) *chsd ldng pair: effrt and cl up over 4f out: rdn along over 3f out: sn drvn and wknd* **10/1**
5550 **8** *hd* **Abounding**[7] 6882 4-9-6 **57** .... FrankieMcDonald 10 32
(M J Attwater) *chsd ldrs on outer: rdn along over 3f out: drvn and wknd over 2f out* **16/1**
0020 **9** *8* **Satindra (IRE)**[213] 1086 4-9-7 **58** .... (tp) LPKeniry 5 21
(C R Dore) *chsd ldrs: rdn along over 4f out and sn wknd* **33/1**
2230 **10** *19* **Leyte Gulf (USA)**[22] 6538 5-9-7 **58** .... AdamKirby 1 —
(C C Bealby) *led: hdd after 4f: cl up tl rdn along 5f out and sn wknd* **9/2**[3]
006- **11** *73* **Winter Lane**[255] 7110 4-8-9 **46** oh1 .... (v) SaleemGolam 2 —
(J R Norton) *chsd ldrs: rdn along 1/2-way: sn lost pl and bhd* **125/1**

3m 7.02s (-1.28) **Going Correction** -0.075s/f (Stan)
WFA 3 from 4yo+ 9lb **11 Ran SP% 113.9**
Speed ratings (Par 101): **100,99,98,97,91 91,86,86,81,70 29**
toteswinger: 1&2 £2.70, 1&3 £38.20, 2&3 £14.70. CSF £14.69 CT £373.59 TOTE £4.20: £2.20, £1.10, £6.90; EX 18.20.
Owner P Lamyman **Bred** Miss Veronica Henley **Trained** Ruckland, Lincs

FOCUS
A moderate staying handicap, though the pace looked solid and the front four pulled a long way clear of the rest. It resulted in a thrilling finish between a horse with proven form on this surface against a progressive sort off the turf, a battle the course specialist eventually won. The 3rd was 3lb wrong but otherwise the form looks sound.

7046 LADBROKESPOKER.COM H'CAP 1m 4f (F)
2:50 (2:50) (Class 5) (0-75,75) 3-Y-0+ **£3,412** (£1,007; £504) **Stalls Low**

Form RPR
4611 **1** **Bavarian Nordic (USA)**[14] 6726 3-8-13 **75** .... AndrewMullen(3) 6 86+
(Mrs A Duffield) *a.p: effrt 3f out: effrt to ld and edgd lft wl over 1f out: rdn clr appr fnl f: styd on strly* **3/1**[2]
0132 **2** *2 1/2* **Persian Peril**[9] 6839 4-9-9 **75** .... RobertWinston 5 82
(G A Swinbank) *t.k.h: trckd ldng pair: cl up 1/2-way: led over 4f out: rdn along 3f out: hdd wl over 1f out: sn drvn and kpt on same pce* **6/4**[1]
-530 **3** *hd* **Turban Heights (IRE)**[19] 6607 4-9-6 **72** .... DaneO'Neill 2 79
(E J O'Neill) *hld up in tch: hdwy 3f out: rdn 2f out: drvn over 1f out: kpt on u.p fnl f* **6/1**[3]
0550 **4** *3 1/2* **Mikao (IRE)**[73] 5100 7-9-5 **71** .... SaleemGolam 7 72
(M H Tompkins) *led: rdn along and hdd over 4f out: drvn 3f out: wknd over 2f out* **10/1**
306 **5** *3/4* **Jackie Kiely**[17] 6662 7-9-3 **69** .... (t) J-PGuillambert 1 69
(R Brotherton) *hld up in rr: effrt over 3f out: sn rdn and no imp* **13/2**
-000 **6** *1 1/4* **Can Can Star**[19] 6607 5-8-12 **64** .... CatherineGannon 3 62
(A W Carroll) *t.k.h: trckd ldrs: hdwy and cl up over 4f out: rdn over 2f out and ev ch tl drvn and wknd wl over 1f out* **16/1**
1630 **7** *3* **Karmest**[14] 6726 4-8-8 **67** .... (b) JamesRogers(7) 4 60
(A D Brown) *s.i.s: a in rr* **14/1**

2m 42.08s (1.08) **Going Correction** -0.075s/f (Stan)
WFA 3 from 4yo+ 7lb **7 Ran SP% 114.3**
Speed ratings (Par 103): **93,91,91,88,88 87,85**
toteswinger: 1&2 £1.50, 1&3 £8.10, 2&3 £2.90. CSF £7.90 TOTE £4.90: £2.30, £1.30; EX 8.30.
Owner Six Iron Partnership **Bred** Gainsborough Farm Llc **Trained** Constable Burton, N Yorks

FOCUS
Not a bad little handicap on paper, but the early pace was very slow and that caused several to take a strong hold early, and it developed into something of a sprint over the last half-mile. The winner built on his previous winning form and there could be more to come from him.

Jackie Kiely Official explanation: jockey said gelding was unsuited by the slow early pace

7047 HOLD YOUR BIRTHDAY CELEBRATIONS AT SOUTHWELL RACECOURSE H'CAP 6f (F)
3:20 (3:21) (Class 4) (0-85,86) 3-Y-O+ £5,180 (£1,156; £1,156; £384) Stalls Low

Form RPR
6200 1 **Irish Pearl (IRE)**[17] 6651 3-9-1 82 FergusSweeney 3 91
(K R Burke) *cl up: rdn to ld 2f out: drvn ins fnl f and kpt on wl* **16/1**
3-00 2 1 1/4 **Imprimis Tagula (IRE)**[9] 6842 4-8-6 77 (v) NicolPolli(5) 5 82
(A Bailey) *midfield: hdwy 2f out: rdn over 1f out: styd on strly ins fnl f: nrst fin* **12/1**
0365 2 dht **Temple Of Thebes (IRE)**[26] 6430 3-9-4 85 DaneO'Neill 2 90
(E A L Dunlop) *trckd ldrs: hdwy over 2f out: rdn to chse wnr ent fnl f: sn drvn and kpt on same pce* **8/1**
4526 4 1 **Pawan (IRE)**[9] 6842 8-9-0 85 (b) AnnStokell(5) 10 87
(Miss A Stokell) *dwlt and rr: hdwy over 2f out: rdn to chse ldrs over 1f out: kpt on* **7/1[3]**
0000 5 3/4 **Total Impact**[10] 6810 5-9-0 83 AndrewMullen(3) 7 82+
(R A Fahey) *sn outpcd and bhd tl styd on fnl 2f: nrst fin* **25/1**
0400 6 1 3/4 **Efistorm**[8] 6859 7-9-2 82 RobertWinston 4 76
(C R Dore) *in tch on outer: hdwy to chse ldrs over 2f out: sn rdn and no imp* **10/1**
0002 7 1 **High Curragh**[39] 6066 5-8-13 79 LPKeniry 8 70
(K A Ryan) *prom: rdn along over 2f out: grad wknd* **4/1[2]**
055 8 3 1/2 **Loose Caboose (IRE)**[18] 6623 3-8-9 76 (b) JamesDoyle 1 55
(A J McCabe) *cl up on inner: rdn along and outpcd over 2f out: in tch and keeping on along inner u.p whn n.m.r over 1f out* **25/1**
1020 9 2 1/4 **Harbour Blues**[80] 4854 3-9-4 85 (t) CatherineGannon 9 57
(A W Carroll) *led: rdn along 3f out: hdd 2f out: grad wknd* **20/1**
0041 10 2 **My Gacho (IRE)**[9] 6842 6-9-6 86 6ex (b) J-PGuillambert 11 52
(M Johnston) *stmbld s: a outpcd and bhd* **9/4[1]**
2600 11 4 **Mesbaah (IRE)**[10] 6810 4-8-5 78 (b) BMcHugh(7) 6 31
(R A Fahey) *a outpcd in rr* **12/1**

1m 15.27s (-1.23) **Going Correction** -0.075s/f (Stan)
WFA 3 from 4yo+ 1lb 11 Ran SP% 117.2
Speed ratings (Par 105): **105,103,103,102,101 98,97,92,89,87 81**toteswinger: Irish Pearl & Temple of Thebes: £19.90, TOT & Imprimis Tagula £40.40, TOT & Imprimis Tagula £15.80. TOTE £24.10: £5.70 TRIFECTA PL: TOT £2.40; IT £2.70 EX: IP&TOT £84.80; IP & IT £111.10; CSF IP &TOT, £67.07; IP&IT £93.97; TRI: IP, TOT, IT27 Owner.

FOCUS
A decent sprint handicap though not many ever really got into it. The winner took well to the surface and is rated as running a personal best, but there is a slight doubt over the strength of the form with the fourth the best guide.
Total Impact ◆ Official explanation: jockey said gelding hung right
My Gacho(IRE) Official explanation: jockey said gelding stumbled leaving stalls, vet said gelding was coughing

7048 LADBROKES.COM H'CAP 7f (F)
3:50 (3:50) (Class 5) (0-75,75) 3-Y-O+ £3,412 (£1,007; £504) Stalls Low

Form RPR
3060 1 **Elusive Warrior (USA)**[9] 6841 5-8-12 65 (p) JamesDoyle 6 79
(A J McCabe) *mde all: rdn clr 2f out: drvn ins fnl f and styd on strly* **7/1**
003 2 4 **Crocodile Bay (IRE)**[9] 6841 5-8-12 70 JamesO'Reilly(5) 4 73
(John A Harris) *hld up: hdwy on inner wl over 2f out: rdn to chse wnr over 1f out: drvn and no imp ins fnl f* **2/1[1]**
55/0 3 2 3/4 **Brigydon (IRE)**[13] 6736 5-9-0 67 AdamKirby 5 63
(J R Fanshawe) *hld up: hdwy over 2f out: rdn over 1f out: kpt on ins fnl f: nrst fin* **8/1**
0041 4 hd **Cool Sands (IRE)**[11] 6773 6-8-13 66 (v) J-PGuillambert 9 61
(J G Given) *chsd ldrs on outer: rdn along wl over 2f out: drvn over 1f out: grad wknd* **4/1[2]**
312 5 2 1/4 **Ballycroy Boy (IRE)**[199] 1339 3-9-1 75 NicolPolli(5) 3 64
(A Bailey) *chsd ldrs: rdn along 3f out: drvn 2f out and kpt on same pce* **10/1**
6103 6 2 1/4 **Mister Jingles**[54] 5638 5-8-7 60 DeanMcKeown 2 43
(R M Whitaker) *cl up on inner: rdn along 3f out: drvn over 2f out and grad wknd* **12/1**
0035 7 1/2 **Jellytot (USA)**[76] 4961 5-7-13 59 oh14 MatthewLawson(7) 1 41
(J O'Reilly) *s.i.s: a in rr* **50/1**
0002 8 7 **Fools Gold**[28] 6356 3-9-6 75 PaulEddery 7 38
(G D Blake) *prom: rdn along 3f out: drvn over 2f out and sn wknd* **6/1[3]**
200 9 16 **Secret Gem (IRE)**[80] 4863 3-8-2 64 (t) RossAtkinson(7) 8 —
(Tom Dascombe) *chsd ldrs: lost pl 4f out and sn bhd* **16/1**

1m 28.36s (-1.94) **Going Correction** -0.075s/f (Stan)
WFA 3 from 5yo+ 2lb 9 Ran SP% 115.9
Speed ratings (Par 103): **108,103,100,100,97 94,94,86,68**
toteswinger: 1&2 £5.40, 1&3 £11.30, 2&3 £10.60. CSF £21.46 CT £116.42 TOTE £10.60: £2.70, £1.10, £3.00; EX 25.00.
Owner Brian Morton **Bred** Steve Peskoff **Trained** Babworth, Notts

FOCUS
A fair handicap run at a decent pace and again not many ever really got into it, with Elusive Warrior making all to record a personal best.
Cool Sands(IRE) Official explanation: jockey said gelding hung left

7049 LADBROKESCASINO.COM APPRENTICE H'CAP 6f (F)
4:20 (4:21) (Class 6) (0-50,50) 3-Y-O+ £2,388 (£705; £352) Stalls Low

Form RPR
5520 1 **Megalo Maniac**[48] 5797 5-8-12 48 (p) BMcHugh 10 63
(R A Fahey) *mde all: rdn wl over 1f out: kpt on* **5/2[1]**
6046 2 2 1/2 **Mrs Bun**[76] 4967 3-8-13 50 JPHamblett 9 57
(K A Ryan) *chsd wnr: rdn along 2f out: drvn over 1f out: no imp ins fnl f* **13/2**
0000 3 2 1/2 **Hollywood George**[6] 6912 4-8-13 49 (p) AdeleRothery 1 48
(Miss M E Rowland) *in tch on inner: hdwy over 2f out: rdn to chse ldng pair over 1f out: kpt on same pce* **9/1**
0634 4 3/4 **Bilboa**[21] 6546 3-8-12 49 (p) AshleyMorgan 12 46
(J M Bradley) *in tch: smooth hdwy to chse ldrs 2f out: sn rdn: edgd lft and no imp* **9/2[2]**
3633 5 2 1/4 **City For Conquest (IRE)**[1] 7022 5-9-0 50 StacyRenwick 13 39
(John A Harris) *racd wd: towards rr: hdwy 2f out: sn rdn and kpt on same pce* **6/1[3]**
0030 6 nk **Admiralcollingwood**[34] 6215 3-8-6 48 MatthewLawson(5) 6 36+
(C Grant) *hmpd and squeezed s: bhd tl styd on fnl 2f: nrst fin* **16/1**
060 7 shd **Rosies Dawn**[11] 6791 3-8-11 48 ShaneCreighton 7 36
(D Carroll) *bmpd s: midfield: hdwy and in tch 2f out: sn rdn and no imp* **16/1**
0606 8 2 1/2 **Sheik'N'Knotsterd**[9] 6836 3-8-13 50 JemmaMarshall 4 30
(J F Coupland) *chsd ldrs to 1/2-way: sn wknd* **50/1**
0000 9 shd **Solemn**[35] 6192 3-8-11 48 (p) MatthewDavies 3 28
(J M Bradley) *prom on inner: rdn along wl over 2f out: sn drvn and wknd* **33/1**
6250 10 3/4 **Our Kally**[61] 5421 3-8-6 50 SeanPalmer(7) 5 27
(M D I Usher) *a towards rr* **20/1**
0200 11 1/2 **Mr Forthright**[6] 6895 4-8-12 48 (b) BillyCray 11 24
(J M Bradley) *dwlt: a in rr* **14/1**
1600 12 3 1/4 **Stoneacre Donny (IRE)**[260] 522 4-8-11 47 RossAtkinson 2 12
(Peter Grayson) *a in rr* **20/1**
0000 U **Tenancy (IRE)**[45] 5916 4-8-8 47 (e) NSLawes(3) 8 —
(R C Guest) *uns rdr at s* **14/1**

1m 15.92s (-0.58) **Going Correction** -0.075s/f (Stan)
WFA 3 from 4yo+ 1lb 13 Ran SP% 123.9
Speed ratings (Par 101): **100,96,93,92,89 88,88,85,85,84 83,79,—**
toteswinger: 1&2 £4.40, 1&3 £8.60, 2&3 £13.90. CSF £18.43 CT £137.31 TOTE £3.70: £1.70, £3.10, £3.70; EX 22.90 Place 6: £660.63 Place 5: £37.52.
Owner A Long **Bred** E R W Stanley & New England Stud Farm Ltd **Trained** Musley Bank, N Yorks
■ Stewards' Enquiry : Matthew Lawson four-day ban: used whip with excessive frequency (Nov 12-15)

FOCUS
A weak race with over half the field maidens and very few came into it in any sort of form, but despite the moderate nature of the contest it was a keen betting heat with a few well backed. Again it paid to be up with the pace and not many ever got involved. The time was relatively good and the form may be above average for the lowly grade.
T/Plt: £2,336.40 to a £1 stake. Pool: £51,050.58. 15.95 winning tickets. T/Qpdt: £44.40 to a £1 stake. Pool: £4,736.60. 78.90 winning tickets. JR

6883 YARMOUTH (L-H)
Tuesday, October 28

OFFICIAL GOING: Soft (6.6)
Wind: modest, across Weather: bright, slightly overcast

7050 STRAIGHTFORWARDSOLUTIONS.CO.UK (S) STKS 1m 2f 21y
1:10 (1:11) (Class 6) 3-4-Y-O £1,942 (£578; £288; £144) Stalls Low

Form RPR
0022 1 **Ricci De Mare**[7] 6883 3-8-13 55 (p) JamieSpencer 3 58
(A B Haynes) *drvn along leaving stalls: chsd ldr: clsd 4f out: rdn over 2f out: outpcd and looked btn jst over 1f out: hrd rdn and rallied ins fnl f: led last strides* **9/2[3]**
1254 2 hd **Mick Is Back**[7] 6888 4-9-9 58 (p) RyanMoore 1 63
(G G Margarson) *t.k.h: hld up wl in tch: hdwy on inner over 3f out: drvn over 2f out: led over 1f out: looked wnr tl tired and hdd last strides* **9/2[3]**
0204 3 1/2 **Near The Front**[7] 6883 3-8-5 55 (v) KylieManser(7) 2 56
(Miss Gay Kelleway) *led: clr 6f out: jnd wl over 2f out: hdd over 1f out: rdn 1f out: kpt on fnl 100yds* **14/1**
-414 4 1 **Dazzling Begum**[12] 6757 3-8-13 54 ChrisCatlin 5 55
(J Pearce) *stdd s: hld up in rr: shkn up over 5f out: rdn 4f out: hdwy u.p 2f out: chsd ldrs ins fnl f: kpt on but nvr pce to quite rch ldrs* **3/1[1]**
0022 5 2 3/4 **Alfredtheordinary**[16] 6685 3-8-12 61 SamHitchcott 8 48
(M R Channon) *dwlt: hld up in rr: rdn and effrt wl over 2f out: keeping on same pce whn swtchd lft 1f out: no imp after* **4/1[2]**
2023 6 3 3/4 **Threestoneburn (USA)**[5] 6927 3-8-0 50 RosieJessop(7) 9 36
(J R Boyle) *t.k.h: racd on outer: hld up in midfield tl dropped to rr 6f out: toiling 3f out: n.d after* **13/2**
6000 7 1/2 **Una Auroraborealis**[20] 6583 3-8-7 44 HayleyTurner 6 35
(S W James) *hld up in midfield: hdwy to chse ldrs 4f out: rdn 3f out: wknd over 2f out* **25/1**
0005 8 12 **Samahir (USA)**[5] 6930 4-8-12 46 (v) AlanMunro 7 11
(T T Clement) *t.k.h: hld up towards rr: rdn over 3f out: sn wl btn* **12/1**

2m 15.57s (5.07) **Going Correction** +0.525s/f (Yiel)
WFA 3 from 4yo 5lb 8 Ran SP% 112.9
Speed ratings (Par 101): **100,99,99,98,96 93,93,83**
toteswinger: 1&2 £3.40, 1&3 £8.60, 2&3 £6.90. CSF £24.35 TOTE £4.20: £1.40, £1.60, £3.00; EX 15.80 Trifecta £127.70 Pool: £276.16 - 1.60winning units..The winner was bought by G. Smith for 5,000gns.
Owner L R Turland **Bred** Belgrave Bloodstock Ltd **Trained** Limpley Stoke, Bath

FOCUS
This was low-key contest and the early pace was a steady one. Ordinary selling form which seems to make sense despite the bunch finish.

7051 LOUNGE AT ANDOVER HOUSE BOUTIQUE HOTEL / EBF MAIDEN STKS 7f 3y
1:40 (1:41) (Class 5) 2-Y-O £3,974 (£1,189; £594; £297; £148) Stalls High

Form RPR
2 1 **Desert Creek (IRE)**[15] 6702 2-9-3 0 RyanMoore 9 81+
(Sir Michael Stoute) *mde all: shkn up over 1f out: drew clr ent fnl f: easily* **8/13[1]**
2 3 1/4 **Yirga** 2-9-3 0 LDettori 2 70
(Saeed Bin Suroor) *hld up in midfield: rdn and hdwy 3f out: chsd ldng pair over 1f out: kpt on to snatch 2nd on post: nvr able to chal wnr* **7/2[2]**
0 3 nse **Integria**[15] 6701 2-9-0 0 LukeMorris(3) 1 70
(J M P Eustace) *hld up in tch: hdwy 3f out: chsd wnr over 2f out: rdn 2f out: outpcd by wnr ent fnl f: lost 2nd on post* **50/1**
4 2 **Avoir Choisi (IRE)** 2-9-3 0 AlanMunro 12 65
(P W Chapple-Hyam) *taken down early: s.i.s: bhd: hdwy over 2f out: rdn over 1f out: styd on steadily to chse ldng trio ins fnl f: nvr nr ldrs* **25/1**
5 1/2 **Tiger Flash** 2-9-3 0 MichaelHills 6 64
(W J Haggas) *hld up towards rr: pushed along over 1f out: kpt on steadily ins fnl f: nvr nr ldrs* **10/1[3]**
0 6 1 1/4 **Sofonisba**[41] 6029 2-8-12 0 JamieSpencer 8 56
(M L W Bell) *t.k.h: hld up in rr: nt clr run and swtchd lft over 1f out: hdwy jst over 1f out: kpt on past btn horses ins fnl f: nvr nr ldrs* **40/1**
00 7 nk **Mister Standfast**[14] 6715 2-9-3 0 DaleGibson 5 60
(J M P Eustace) *chsd wnr for 3f: pushed along 3f out: rdn and unable qck 2f out: wl hld fnl f* **100/1**
05 8 1/2 **Halfway House**[12] 6760 2-9-3 0 HayleyTurner 3 59
(M L W Bell) *chsd ldrs: rdn and unable qck 2f out: one pce fr over 1f out* **25/1**
3500 9 1 3/4 **Confucius Captain (IRE)**[14] 6717 2-9-3 76 TPQueally 11 54
(J R Boyle) *hld up in midfield: effrt 3f out: rdn and no hdwy 2f out: wl btn fr over 1f out* **16/1**

0 **10** *1 1/2* **Ethics Girl (IRE)**[16] 6677 2-8-12 0 TPO'Shea 10 46
(John Berry) *in tch: rdn over 3f out: bhd last 2f* **100/1**

00 **11** *nk* **King Of Defence**[14] 6714 2-9-3 0 PhilipRobinson 7 50
(M A Jarvis) *chsd ldrs tl chsd wnr 4f out tl over 2f out: sn outpcd* **33/1**

12 *5* **Cosimo** 2-8-12 0 Louis-PhilippeBeuzelin(5) 4 37
(Sir Michael Stoute) *s.i.s: a bhd* **25/1**

1m 30.01s (3.41) **Going Correction** +0.30s/f (Good) **12** Ran SP% **120.0**
Speed ratings (Par 95): **92,88,88,85,85 83,83,83,81,79 78,73**
toteswinger: 1&2 £1.40, 1&3 £16.20, 2&3 £30.00. CSF £2.54 TOTE £1.60: £1.20, £1.50, £12.80; EX 3.70 Trifecta £84.30 Part won. Pool: £113.96 - 0.90 winning units..
Owner Saeed Suhail **Bred** Mount Coote Stud And M H Dixon **Trained** Newmarket, Suffolk

FOCUS
Just a fair maiden, but the winner looks to have a bright future.

NOTEBOOK
Desert Creek(IRE) ◆ ran out an easy winner. He really caught the eye when finishing second on his debut at Windsor, running on strongly close home having been outpaced over an inadequate 6f, and the extra furlong was always likely to suit. Soon in front, he was asked to lengthen approaching two out and readily responded, ultimately drawing right away under hands and heels riding. He coped just fine with this softer surface, really grabbing the ground as he raced away, and looks to have a very bright future. (op 8-11)
Yirga, whose dam is a half-sister to Breeders' Cup Juvenile winner Gilded Time, comes from a yard that are putting in a strong finish to the season and he stayed on to snatch second. No match for the winner, he should learn from the experience, and, although clearly no star, can win a maiden at some stage. (tchd 9-2)
Integria was just run out of second, but he still improved markedly on his debut effort and this speedily-bred individual can be expected to fare better again back at 6f.
Avoir Choisi(IRE), a half-brother to the useful Spinning Lucy, was a bit slow away and showed definite signs of greenness, but kept on inside the final furlong and should know a lot more next time. (op 12-1)
Tiger Flash, a 75,000gns two-year-old who is a half-brother to Royal Lodge winner Leo, stayed on having been outpaced and is another likely to learn from the experience. Official explanation: jockey said colt hung left (op 16-1)
Sofonisba Official explanation: jockey said filly was denied a clear run
King Of Defence (op 28-1)
Cosimo, who is a stablemate to the winner, never recovered from a slow start and is unlikely to be seen at his best until next season. Official explanation: jockey said colt missed the break (op 20-1)

7052 WEATHERBYS BLOODSTOCK INSURANCE NURSERY 7f 3y
2:10 (2:13) (Class 5) (0-70,70) 2-Y-O **£3,238** (£963; £481; £240) **Stalls** High

Form RPR

006 **1** **Lovely Thought**[78] 4926 2-8-8 **57** (b1) MichaelHills 6 61
(W J Haggas) *mde all: hrd pressed and rdn over 1f out: styd on wl to assert fnl 50yds* **16/1**

054 **2** *1 1/4* **Belated Silver (IRE)**[20] 6578 2-9-3 **66** RichardKingscote 4 67
(Tom Dascombe) *t.k.h: hld up in tch: chsd wnr over 1f out: sn ev ch: no ex and btn fnl 50yds* **4/1**[1]

0160 **3** *2 1/2* **Punch Drunk**[24] 6477 2-9-4 **67** ChrisCatlin 3 62
(J G Given) *chsd wnr tl over 1f out: rdn and stl ev ch tl wknd ins fnl f* **11/2**[3]

6300 **4** *3/4* **Innactualfact**[56] 5585 2-8-11 **60** KirstyMilczarek 9 53
(L A Dace) *hld up towads rr: shkn up and unable qck 2f out: kpt on u.p to go 4th ins fnl f: kpt on but nvr pce to rch ldrs* **20/1**

1021 **5** *1 1/2* **Rocket Rob (IRE)**[53] 5671 2-9-6 **69** JamieSpencer 2 58
(S A Callaghan) *stdd s: t.k.h: hld up bhd: rdn and effrt 2f out: drvn to chse ldng trio jst ins fnl f: no imp after* **9/2**[2]

606 **6** *1 1/2* **Dance Club (IRE)**[21] 6559 2-9-3 **66** AlanMunro 5 51
(W Jarvis) *hld up in tch: rdn wl over 2f out: wknd over 1f out* **8/1**

2325 **7** *1* **Lookafternumberone (IRE)**[43] 5960 2-9-7 **70** TPQueally 10 53
(J G Given) *chsd ldrs: rdn and hung lft over 2f out: wl btn over 1f out* **9/2**[2]

5266 **8** *nk* **Glan Lady (IRE)**[11] 6787 2-8-4 **53** WilliamBuick 1 35
(J L Spearing) *s.i.s: t.k.h: hld up in midfield: rdn over 2f out: wknd wl over 1f out* **10/1**

4500 **9** *26* **Al Mukaala (IRE)**[33] 6223 2-9-1 **64** RyanMoore 7 —
(C E Brittain) *hld up towards rr: rdn and lost tch 3f out: eased fnl f: t.o* **9/1**

5044 **10** *nk* **Helpmeronda**[71] 5153 2-9-2 **65** HayleyTurner 11 —
(S A Callaghan) *s.i.s: a bhd: struggling 3f out: eased fnl f* **20/1**

1m 29.1s (2.50) **Going Correction** +0.30s/f (Good) **10** Ran SP% **117.4**
Speed ratings (Par 95): **97,95,92,91,90 88,87,86,57,56**
toteswinger: 1&2 £12.80, 1&3 £20.10 2&3 £5.20. CSF £79.63 CT £402.69 TOTE £17.20: £4.60, £1.60, £2.30; EX 90.90 Trifecta £275.90 Part won. Pool: £327.97 - 0.90 winning units..
Owner Liam Sheridan **Bred** Whitsbury Manor Stud **Trained** Newmarket, Suffolk

FOCUS
This was just an ordinary nursery and not many got into it.

NOTEBOOK
Lovely Thought, sporting first-time blinkers on this handicap debut, was sent off in front by Michael Hills and outstayed the runner-up inside the final furlong. She hadn't shown much in maidens, but the headgear helped her to concentrate and it will be interesting to see whether she can build on this. Official explanation: trainer said, regarding the apparent improvement in form, that filly had been ungenuine in the past and may have benefitted from the blinkers today (op 14-1)
Belated Silver(IRE) was of obvious interest on this nursery debut and looked set to be suited by the return to7f, having found 5f far too sharp a test at Nottingham last time. He travelled best and Kingscote seemed confident racing towards the final furlong, but in the end he was outstayed. There are races to be won with him and it may be that 6f is his trip for the time being. (op 9-2 tchd 5-1 and 7-2)
Punch Drunk was prominent throughout and held on for third, recording her best run to date in nurseries. (op 13-2 tchd 5-1)
Innactualfact, subject of a morning gamble, kept on all too late and never looked like troubling the principals. She may do better on a faster surface. (op 16-1)
Rocket Rob(IRE), a narrow winner over 6f at Kempton last time, was 5lb higher for this return to turf and did not look as effective on this softer surface. He was under pressure before two out and never picked up. Official explanation: jockey said gelding was keen early on (op 7-2 tchd 5-1)
Dance Club(IRE) was another who seemed unsuited by the ground. (op 13-2)
Al Mukaala(IRE) Official explanation: jockey said colt was never travelling

7053 WEATHERBYS PRINTING CLAIMING STKS 1m 3y
2:40 (2:44) (Class 6) 3-4-Y-O **£2,137** (£635; £317; £158) **Stalls** High

Form RPR

0453 **1** **My Mate Mal**[9] 6836 4-8-9 63 LanceBetts(7) 6 68+
(B Ellison) *taken down early: t.k.h: chsd ldr tl led after 1f: mde rest: clr over 1f out: edgd lft fnl f: rdn out* **9/4**[1]

4350 **2** *2 1/4* **Comrade Cotton**[4] 6951 4-8-11 54 (v) MarcHalford(3) 4 58
(J Ryan) *dwlt: sn led: hdd after 1f: chsd wnr after: rdn over 2f out: drvn and one pce fr over 1f out* **6/1**

1600 **3** *5* **Redsensor**[13] 6741 3-8-5 55 LiamJones 5 40
(M Quinn) *in tch: chsd ldng pair and rdn over 3f out: sn outpcd: no imp fnl 2f* **7/2**[2]

5500 **4** *1 1/2* **Driven Snow**[111] 3845 3-8-2 62 HayleyTurner 3 34
(N P Littmoden) *s.i.s: hld up bhd: rdn and lost tch 3f out: kpt on u.p fnl f: nvr trbld ldrs* **9/2**[3]

003 **5** *1 3/4* **Gee Ceffyl Bach**[7] 6888 4-8-1 49 (p) DaleGibson 7 26
(John A Harris) *a bhd and nvr gng wl: drvn and lost tch 3f out: wl btn last 2f* **7/2**[2]

4000 **6** *29* **Lechero (IRE)**[9] 6836 3-8-3 40 (bt1) ChrisCatlin 2 —
(John A Harris) *chsd ldrs tl over 3f out: sn rdn and dropped out: t.o fr 2f out* **28/1**

1m 43.48s (2.88) **Going Correction** +0.30s/f (Good)
WFA 3 from 4yo 3lb **6** Ran SP% **111.1**
Speed ratings (Par 101): **97,94,89,88,86 57**
toteswinger: 1&2 £2.70, 1&3 £2.20, 2&3 £4.30. CSF £15.78 TOTE £3.10: £1.70, £3.60; EX 13.70.
Owner Black and White Diamond Partnership **Bred** Mrs A M Mallinson **Trained** Norton, N Yorks

FOCUS
A weak claimer rated through the runner-up, with little solid in behind.
Redsensor Official explanation: vet said gelding was lame

7054 E B F /MOULTON NURSERIES, SAM AND STEVE MAIDEN STKS 1m 3y
3:10 (3:12) (Class 5) 2-Y-O **£3,885** (£1,156; £577; £288) **Stalls** High

Form RPR

62 **1** **Al Marmoom (USA)**[14] 6715 2-9-3 0 LDettori 9 79
(Saeed Bin Suroor) *mde all: pushed clr over 1f out: in command fnl f: eased towards fin* **6/4**[1]

2 *1 1/4* **Taarab** 2-9-3 0 TedDurcan 6 76
(Saeed Bin Suroor) *s.i.s: hld up in midfield: hdwy 1/2-way: chsd ldng trio over 1f out: styd on to go 2nd fnl 100yds: nvr threatened wnr* **16/1**

3 *1 3/4* **Palacefield (IRE)** 2-9-3 0 JamieSpencer 12 72
(P W Chapple-Hyam) *chsd wnr: rdn and nt pce of wnr over 1f out: kpt on same pce: lost 2nd fnl 100yds* **16/1**

4 *3/4* **Hidden Brief** 2-8-12 0 PhilipRobinson 14 66
(M A Jarvis) *hld up bhd: shkn up and hdwy 3f out: pushed along and kpt on fnl f: snatched 4th nr fin* **16/1**

54 **5** *nk* **Ocean's Minstrel**[27] 6375 2-9-0 0 MarcHalford(3) 13 70
(J Ryan) *chsd ldrs: rdn 3f out: chsd ldng pair over 2f out: unable qck u.p 2f out: plugged on same pce* **66/1**

6 *1 1/4* **Grey Granite (IRE)** 2-9-3 0 AlanMunro 10 67
(W Jarvis) *dwlt: sn in tch in midfield: shkn up and outpcd jst over 2f out: kpt on fnl f* **66/1**

4625 **7** *1* **Doncosaque (IRE)**[22] 6524 2-9-3 75 TPQueally 3 65
(H R A Cecil) *hld up in midfield: rdn and unable qck jst over 2f out: edgd rt and kpt on fnl f* **8/1**[3]

03 **8** *1/2* **Incendo**[21] 6552 2-9-3 0 WilliamBuick 2 64
(J R Fanshawe) *s.i.s: hld up in midfield: rdn and outpcd over 2f out: edgd rt and kpt on same pce last 2f* **10/1**

4 **9** *2 3/4* **Kaolak (USA)**[67] 5246 2-9-3 0 JerryO'Dwyer 4 58
(J Ryan) *s.i.s: bhd: rdn 5f out: nvr trbld ldrs* **9/2**[2]

10 *nse* **Daniel Defoe (USA)** 2-9-3 0 RyanMoore 7 58
(Sir Michael Stoute) *in tch: rdn over 2f out: btn over 1f out* **9/1**

11 *2 1/4* **Sir Freddie** 2-9-3 0 RichardKingscote 15 53
(Lady Herries) *s.i.s: a towards rr: rdn 3f out: nvr a factor* **100/1**

12 *1/2* **Choral Service** 2-9-3 0 MichaelHills 11 52
(W J Haggas) *v.s.a: rn green and a bhd* **28/1**

13 *13* **Knock Three Times (IRE)** 2-8-12 0 HayleyTurner 1 18
(M L W Bell) *hld up in midfield: struggling over 3f out: wl bhd last 2f* **50/1**

14 *nk* **Golden Eagle** 2-8-12 0 Louis-PhilippeBeuzelin(5) 8 23
(Sir Michael Stoute) *in tch tl lost pl 1/2-way: wl bhd last 2f* **12/1**

15 *13* **Vin De Rose** 2-9-3 0 LiamJones 5 —
(S W Hall) *t.k.h early: hld up in rr: rdn and lost tch 1/2-way: t.o* **250/1**

1m 43.9s (3.30) **Going Correction** +0.30s/f (Good) **15** Ran SP% **123.5**
Speed ratings (Par 95): **95,93,92,91,90 89,88,88,85,85 83,82,69,69,56**
toteswinger: 1&2 £9.00, 1&3 £9.60, 2&3 £30.30. CSF £30.26 TOTE £2.20: £1.20, £5.30, £5.30; EX 31.90 Trifecta £260.50 Part won. Pool: £352.08 - 0.20 winning units..
Owner Godolphin **Bred** Dr Charles S Giles **Trained** Newmarket, Suffolk

FOCUS
An ordinary maiden won in good style by Al Marmoom. The race should produce winners.

NOTEBOOK
Al Marmoom(USA) set the standard having twice shown a fair level of ability in 7f maidens and the step up to 1m looked in his favour. Soon in front, he was asked to extend before two out and readily came clear, drifting on to the stands' rail in the process. He was eased close home and can be rated a good bit better than the bare form, so it will be interesting to see if connections decide to set him a stiffer test before the season is done with. (op 2-1 tchd 9-4 in a place)
Taarab got going inside the final furlong and stayed on to make it a one-two for Godolphin. He was given a nice introductory ride and is sure to benefit from further next season, his dam being a winner at up to 1m5f. (op 12-1)
Palacefield(IRE), whose dam was a half-sister to Bahri, had plenty to prove first time up in soft ground, given his breeding, and it found him out once asked to quicken. He travelled nicely though and can be expected to fare better on a sounder surface, possibly down in trip as well. (op 25-1 tchd 28-1)
Hidden Brief ◆, a sister to the high-class performer Hazarista, was representing a yard responsible for two of the last four winners of this contest, but they had both had a run and she looked in need of the experience. She ran on nicely close home, faring best of the fillies, and rates a bright prospect for next season, given her size and scope to improve. (op 14-1)
Ocean's Minstrel has shown a decent level of ability on all three starts in maidens and it will be interesting to see what mark he gets for handicaps.
Grey Granite(IRE), a half-brother to numerous winners who cost £52,000 at the breeze-ups, took a while to pick up once coming off the bridle, but was running on close home and will make a better 3yo.
Doncosaque(IRE) Official explanation: jockey said colt hung right
Incendo never got into it and was a shade disappointing. He is now qualified for a handicap mark. (tchd 12-1)
Kaolak(USA) ran way above market expectations when fourth at 100-1 on his Newmarket debut (good maiden) but the slower ground here led to a disappointing effort. (op 5-1 tchd 4-1)
Choral Service, a brother to the yard's high-class 1m-1m2f winner Chorist, was slowly away and ran as the market indicated he would on this racecourse debut. (op 33-1)

7055 GREAT YARMOUTH GLASS H'CAP 6f 3y
3:40 (3:44) (Class 5) (0-75,73) 3-Y-O+ **£2,849** (£847; £423; £211) **Stalls** High

Form RPR

5013 **1** **Doric Lady**[21] 6564 3-8-10 **65** KirstyMilczarek 13 82
(J A R Toller) *hld up off the pce in midfield: hdwy 2f out: led jst over 1f out: drew clr fnl f: readily* **10/1**

5550 **2** *3* **Charles Parnell (IRE)**[8] 6859 5-9-5 **73** DaleGibson 9 80
(M Dods) *t.k.h: hld up in tch: hdwy 2f out: sn rdn: chsd wnr ins fnl f: no imp* **6/1**[2]

-003 **3** 1 1/4 **Efisio Princess**73 [5091] 5-8-5 59 oh3 RichardThomas 5 62
(J E Long) *chsd ldr: rdn over 2f out: clsd over 1f out: ev ch briefly jst over 1f out: one pce fnl f* **9/1**

3103 **4** 1 **Avontuur (FR)**7 [6889] 6-8-7 61 LiamJones 14 61
(Mrs R A Carr) *chsd ldng pair: rdn over 2f out: clsd and pressed ldrs jst over 1f out: kpt on same pce fnl f* **13/2**3

1600 **5** 3/4 **Registrar**7 [6889] 6-8-8 62 (p) TGMcLaughlin 6 60
(Mrs C A Dunnett) *s.i.s: hld up bhd: rdn and hdwy 2f out: kpt on u.p fnl f: nt rch ldrs* **14/1**

6P00 **6** nk **Rough Rock (IRE)**7 [6890] 3-8-1 59 LukeMorris(3) 16 56
(G Prodromou) *s.i.s: bhd: hdwy and hung lft 3f out: kpt on but nvr pce to threaten ldrs* **14/1**

6055 **7** 2 3/4 **Dresden Doll (USA)**40 [6053] 3-8-13 68 JamieSpencer 8 56+
(M L W Bell) *racd off the pce in midfield: swtchd to r alone on far side after 1f: rdn and no hdwy 2f out* **16/1**

0500 **8** 1/2 **Linda Green**15 [6706] 7-8-10 64 EdwardCreighton 15 50
(M R Channon) *bhd: rdn over 3f out: styd on past btn horses fnl f: nvr nr ldrs* **20/1**

1660 **9** 3/4 **Luminous Gold**15 [6695] 3-9-2 71 AlanMunro 12 55
(C F Wall) *chsd ldrs: rdn over 2f out: wknd over 1f out* **4/1**1

4030 **10** 1 3/4 **Gone'N'Dunnett (IRE)**9 [6842] 9-8-5 59 oh13 (v) WilliamBuick 1 37
(Mrs C A Dunnett) *racd off the pce in midfield tl lost pl and bhd 1/2-way: sn drvn: n.d after* **33/1**

032 **11** 1 3/4 **Punching**9 [6840] 4-8-6 67 (b) KylieManser(7) 4 40
(Miss Gay Kelleway) *led at fast gallop: clr after 2f: wknd and hdd jst over 1f out: fdd qckly fnl f* **7/1**

600 **12** 6 **Fly Time**29 [6339] 4-8-4 61 oh14 ow2 MarcHalford(3) 10 15
(T T Clement) *stdd after s: a bhd* **100/1**

304 **13** 8 **Vienna Affair**42 [6003] 3-8-10 65 RyanMoore 7 —
(J R Fanshawe) *racd off the pce in midield: rdn and btn 2f out: eased fnl f* **15/2**

6100 **14** 3/4 **Applesnap (IRE)**18 [6634] 3-8-13 68 (b) HayleyTurner 11 —
(Miss Amy Weaver) *a bhd* **22/1**

1m 15.63s (1.23) **Going Correction** +0.30s/f (Good)
WFA 3 from 4yo+ 1lb 14 Ran SP% **123.2**
Speed ratings (Par 103): **103,99,97,96,95 94,90,90,89,86 84,76,65,64**
toteswinger: 1&2 £14.70, 1&3 £14.70, 2&3 £13.80. CSF £68.14 CT £589.54 TOTE £10.90: £2.80, £2.80, £3.80; EX 77.30 Trifecta £253.30 Part won. Pool: £342.306 - 0.20 winning units..
Owner Buckingham Thoroughbreds I **Bred** Minster Enterprises Ltd **Trained** Newmarket, Suffolk

FOCUS
This had the look of a competitive handicap and it was run at a really good gallop. The winner is rated up 12lb but the form makes sense.
Vienna Affair Official explanation: jockey said filly was never travelling
Applesnap(IRE) Official explanation: trainer said filly was unsuited by the soft ground

7056 NWES BEACON INNOVATION CENTRE H'CAP — 1m 2f 21y
4:10 (4:11) (Class 4) (0-85,85) 3-Y-O+ — £4,857 (£1,445; £722; £360) Stalls Low

Form — RPR

0040 **1** **Best Prospect (IRE)**22 [6536] 6-9-9 85 (t) JamieSpencer 4 94+
(M Dods) *stdd s: hld up in last pl: hdwy to chse ldr over 1f out: rdn to ld ent fnl f: kpt on wl* **4/1**

2122 **2** nk **Dark Prospect**26 [6424] 3-8-11 78 (p) PhilipRobinson 3 86
(M A Jarvis) *led: rdn 2f out: hdd ent fnl f: kpt on u.p but unable qck fnl 50yds* **11/4**2

1010 **3** 1/2 **Dr Livingstone (IRE)**16 [6667] 3-9-3 84 SteveDrowne 7 91+
(C R Egerton) *hld up in last pair: rdn and hdwy jst over 2f out: chal and hung lft ins fnl f: no ex fnl 50yds* **10/3**3

3140 **4** 3 **Dragon Slayer (IRE)**32 [6243] 6-8-11 73 ChrisCatlin 8 74
(John A Harris) *t.k.h: chsd ldr after 2f: rdn over 2f out: lost 2nd over 1f out: wknd 1f out* **16/1**

0344 **5** 2 1/2 **Buddy Holly**39 [6078] 3-9-0 81 RyanMoore 2 77
(Pat Eddery) *chsd ldr for 2f: chsd ldrs after: rdn 3f out: wknd u.p 1f out* **15/8**1

2m 14.45s (3.95) **Going Correction** +0.525s/f (Yiel)
WFA 3 from 4yo+ 5lb 5 Ran SP% **110.4**
Speed ratings (Par 105): **105,104,104,101,99**
toteswinger: 1&2 £6.90. CSF £15.22 TOTE £5.50: £2.00, £1.20; EX 8.80 Trifecta £23.50 Pool: £405.45 - 12.72 winning units. Place 6: £105.27 Place 5: £31.35 .
Owner D Neale **Bred** Farmers Hill Stud **Trained** Denton, Co Durham

FOCUS
A fair but trappy contest and rather muddling form which is rated around the runner-up and fourth.
Dr Livingstone(IRE) Official explanation: jockey said gelding hung badly left
T/Plt: £88.30 to a £1 stake. Pool: £56,100.51. 463.60 winning tickets. T/Qpdt: £30.20 to a £1 stake. Pool: £3,213.70. 78.70 winning tickets. SP

7057 - 7063a (Foreign Racing) - See Raceform Interactive

6930 **GREAT LEIGHS (A.W)** (L-H)
Wednesday, October 29

OFFICIAL GOING: Standard
Wind: modest across Weather: bright, chilly

7064 KEYSTONE H'CAP — 1m 5f 66y(P)
2:00 (2:00) (Class 5) (0-75,75) 3-Y-O+ — £2,914 (£867; £433; £216) Stalls Low

Form — RPR

-660 **1** **Garrulous (UAE)**14 [6740] 5-8-12 63 FergusSweeney 8 73
(G L Moore) *stdd and dropped in after s: hld up in tch: hdwy 4f out: chsd ldng trio over 2f out: drvn over 1f out: styd on wl fnl f to ld fnl stride* **12/1**

212 **2** shd **Alonso De Guzman (IRE)**82 [4817] 4-9-6 71 LDettori 6 81
(J R Boyle) *led: rdn jst over 2f out: clr 1f out: edgd rt u.p fnl f: hdd fnl stride* **5/4**1

00 **3** 2 1/2 **Augustus John (IRE)**61 [5454] 5-9-0 65 WilliamBuick 2 71
(S Parr) *hld up in tch: hdwy to chse ldr over 2f out: rdn 2f out: kpt on same pce fr over 1f out: lost 2nd ins fnl f* **12/1**

06-3 **4** 1 1/2 **Tender Falcon**20 [6594] 8-8-8 64 WilliamCarson(5) 5 68
(R J Hodges) *hld up in tch: chsd ldng trio and rdn 2f out: kpt on same pce fnl f* **7/1**3

0202 **5** 3 3/4 **Mustajed**18 [6662] 7-9-7 75 JamesMillman(3) 7 73
(B R Millman) *hld up towards rr: rdn 4f out: struggling 3f out: wl btn fr wl over 1f out* **8/1**

3300 **6** 2 3/4 **Red Wine**5 [6948] 9-9-2 74 StacyRenwick(7) 1 68
(A J McCabe) *t.k.h: hld up in last pl: lost tch 3f out: no ch after* **14/1**

00-6 **7** 19 **Dhehdaah**24 [1337] 7-9-5 70 AdamKirby 4 36
(Mrs P Sly) *chsd ldng pair: rdn over 5f out: wknd over 4f out: wl bhd last 2f* **11/1**

4605 **8** 3 **Inspirina (IRE)**43 [5992] 4-9-1 66 JimCrowley 3 27
(R Ford) *chsd ldr tl over 2f out: sn wknd u.p: wl bhd over 1f out* **11/2**2

2m 53.6s **Going Correction** -0.025s/f (Stan) 8 Ran SP% **113.8**
Speed ratings (Par 103): **99,98,97,96,94 92,80,78**
toteswinger: 1&2 £6.20, 1&3 £22.40, 2&3 £8.20. CSF £27.31 CT £192.05 TOTE £9.40: £2.10, £1.40, £4.90; EX 29.80 TRIFECTA Not won..
Owner Dr C A Barnett **Bred** Darley **Trained** Woodingdean, E Sussex

FOCUS
Despite the small field, this had the look of a difficult race on paper. The favourite set a fair tempo, so the form looks sound and should work out.

7065 GREAT MAPLESTEAD CLAIMING STKS — 6f (P)
2:30 (2:30) (Class 5) 2-Y-O — £3,238 (£963; £481; £240) Stalls Low

Form — RPR

1000 **1** **Smokey Ryder**17 [6666] 2-8-11 74 FergusSweeney 2 76
(G L Moore) *chsd ldr for 1f: trckd ldrs after: wnt 2nd wl over 3f out tl 3f out: chal on inner over 1f out: led jst ins fnl f: styd on wl* **9/2**3

1505 **2** 1/2 **Woolston Ferry (IRE)**22 [6549] 2-8-11 74 EdwardCreighton 1 74
(M R Channon) *dwlt: sn bustled along: towards rr: hdwy jst over 2f out: chsd ldrs and nt clr run ent fnl f: sn swtchd rt: r.o wl fnl 100yds: snatched 2nd last stride* **15/2**

2122 **3** hd **Gone Hunting**6 [6931] 2-8-11 84 JackDean(5) 8 78
(W G M Turner) *in tch in midfield: rdn over 3f out: hdwy on outer over 2f out: ev ch ent fnl f: one pce fnl 50yds* **85/40**2

1333 **4** 1 1/2 **Leftontheshelf (IRE)**32 [6281] 2-8-7 85 LiamJones 7 65
(J L Spearing) *chsd ldrs: wnt 2nd 3f out: drvn and ev ch over 1f out: no ex fnl 100yds* **7/4**1

2115 **5** 1 3/4 **Bold Account (IRE)**38 [6149] 2-9-0 69 AndrewElliott 5 67
(K R Burke) *led: drvn 2f out: hdd jst ins fnl f: wknd fnl 100yds* **14/1**

0566 **6** 11 **Flawless Diamond (IRE)**21 [6572] 2-7-13 55 (b) WilliamBuick 9 19
(J S Moore) *chsd ldr 5f out tl wl over 3f out: wknd over 2f out* **20/1**

5604 **7** nk **Turn To Dreams**21 [6572] 2-7-13 50 NickyMackay 6 18
(P D Evans) *s.i.s: in tch towards rr: rdn and wknd over 2f out: wl bhd over 1f out* **33/1**

8 3 1/4 **Outdroad** 2-8-4 0 CatherineGannon 4 13
(P M Phelan) *s.i.s: sn outpcd and detached in last pl: n.d* **66/1**

6050 **9** 2 **Ruasgreyasme (USA)**29 [6350] 2-8-2 52 ow2 ChrisCatlin 3 5
(W R Muir) *t.k.h: hld up towards rr: rdn over 2f out: wknd qckly 2f out: sn wl btn* **50/1**

1m 13.72s (0.02) **Going Correction** -0.025s/f (Stan) 9 Ran SP% **116.1**
Speed ratings (Par 95): **98,97,97,95,92 78,77,73,70**
toteswinger: 1&2 £8.00, 1&3 £3.50, 2&3 £5.60. CSF £36.43 TOTE £5.00: £1.50, £1.70, £1.10; EX 39.30 Trifecta £133.00 Pool: £309.29 - 1.72 winning units..
Owner Pleasure Palace Racing **Bred** Jeremy Hinds **Trained** Woodingdean, E Sussex

FOCUS
Not many runners but once again competitive stuff for the grade. The pace looked sound and all the right horses were involved in the finish, with the runner-up setting the standard.

NOTEBOOK
Smokey Ryder probably ran below expectations last time but the drop to this grade appeared to work the oracle. Always well placed, she kept running all the way to the line, down the inside rail, to just prevail. (op 8-1)
Woolston Ferry(IRE), who might have scored if he had made his effort down the middle of the course after rounding the home bend. It was tough luck on his rider, who was hoping for a gap between a wall of four horses in front of him. He did eventually pull wide for a clear run but ran out of time to catch the winner. (tchd 8-1)
Gone Hunting came through to have every chance but seemed to lack the pace of the first two home. It was another consistent performance though. (op 2-1 tchd 9-4)
Leftontheshelf(IRE) pulled very hard again despite the respectable pace set by the leader and failed to quicken when her jockey needed a response. (op 2-1 tchd 9-4 in a place)
Bold Account(IRE) fought on respectably when joined after making the early running and was miles clear of the remainder. (op 10-1)

7066 STAN JAMES H'CAP — 5f (P)
3:00 (3:00) (Class 4) (0-85,85) 3-Y-O+ — £5,180 (£1,541; £770; £384) Stalls Low

Form — RPR

4116 **1** **Arganil (USA)**34 [6232] 3-9-3 84 NCallan 1 95
(K A Ryan) *mde all: c to centre 2f out: rdn over 1f out: r.o wl fnl f* **10/3**2

0010 **2** nk **Piscean (USA)**4 [6971] 3-9-2 83 LiamJones 10 93
(T Keddy) *in tch: swtchd lft and hdwy wl over 1f out: chsd wnr ins fnl f: r.o but nvr quite getting to wnr* **3/1**1

0064 **3** 1 1/4 **Not My Choice (IRE)**16 [6743] 3-8-12 82 TolleyDean(3) 5 88
(S Parr) *s.i.s: hld up in last trio: rdn and hdwy on outer over 2f out: styd on wl u.p fnl f: wnt 3rd wl ins fnl f: nt rch ldng pair* **14/1**

6003 **4** 1/2 **Madame Hoi (IRE)**11 [6822] 3-8-10 77 TonyCulhane 4 81
(M R Channon) *hld up in last pair: hdwy on inner wl over 1f out: kpt on u.p fnl f: nt pce to rch ldrs* **25/1**

6322 **5** 1 **Brandywell Boy (IRE)**2 [7013] 5-7-11 71 oh3 BillyCray(7) 9 71
(D J S Ffrench Davis) *racd in midfield tl lost pl and dropped to rr 3f out: rdn over 2f out: kpt on fnl f but nvr pce to trble ldrs* **13/2**

0021 **6** hd **Wibbadune (IRE)**8 [6881] 4-8-12 79 6ex AdamKirby 2 81+
(D Shaw) *stdd s: hld up towards rr: hdwy into midfield 1/2-way: chsd wnr over 1f out: drvn ent fnl f: 4th and hld whn faltered wl ins fnl f* **4/1**3

0003 **7** 3/4 **Calmdownmate (IRE)**13 [6765] 3-8-6 73 AndrewElliott 3 70
(K R Burke) *chsd ldr tl 2f out: sn edgd lft u.p: plugged on same pce* **7/1**

1050 **8** 2 1/2 **First Order**18 [6651] 7-8-10 82 ow2 (v) AnnStokell(5) 6 70
(Miss A Stokell) *stdd and dropped in bhd after s: effrt u.p on iner over 1f out: nvr trbld ldrs* **33/1**

0516 **9** 2 1/4 **Almaty Express**128 [3320] 6-9-4 85 (b) ChrisCatlin 8 65
(J R Weymes) *chsd ldrs: rdn over 2f out: wknd ent fnl f* **16/1**

59.93 secs (-0.27) **Going Correction** -0.025s/f (Stan) 9 Ran SP% **113.2**
Speed ratings (Par 105): **101,100,98,97,96 95,94,90,87**
toteswinger: 1&2 £2.80, 1&3 £13.20, 2&3 £17.00. CSF £13.46 CT £119.42 TOTE £3.90: £1.70, £1.30, £5.70; EX 14.90 Trifecta £120.10 Pool: £332.71 - 2.05 winning units..
Owner The Big Moment **Bred** Colt Neck Stables, Llc **Trained** Hambleton, N Yorks

FOCUS
A lot of these came into this race in fair heart so that coupled with a decent pace set by the winner should mean the form is reliable.
First Order Official explanation: jockey said gelding missed the break

7067 MALTON NURSERY — 1m (P)
3:30 (3:30) (Class 4) (0-85,85) 2-Y-O — £3,885 (£1,156; £577; £288) Stalls Centre

Form — RPR

030U **1** **Worth A King'S**13 [6756] 2-8-1 70 Louis-PhilippeBeuzelin(5) 3 73
(Sir Michael Stoute) *hld up in tch in last pl: hdwy on inner 2f out: rdn and ev ch ent fnl f: pushed along to ld fnl 100yds: r.o wl* **15/2**

The Form Book, Raceform Ltd, Compton, RG20 6NL

013 **2** ½ **Tobond (IRE)**[13] 6756 2-9-4 **82**.. NCallan 1 84
(M Botti) *t.k.h: reluctant ldr tl over 4f out: trckd ldrs after: rdn to ld over 1f out: hung rt and cannoned into rival jst ins fnl f: hdd fnl 100yds: unable qck cl home* **7/2**[2]

060 **3** *hd* **Makhaaleb (IRE)**[39] 6122 2-8-9 **73**...(b[1]) RHills 7 74
(B W Hills) *t.k.h early: hld up in tch in rr: hdwy 4f out: ev ch 2f out: hung lft and cannoned into rival jst ins fnl f: nt qckn cl home* **9/1**

4214 **4** 1 ¼ **Starry Sky**[60] 5511 2-8-13 **77**.. J-PGuillambert 2 76
(Sir Mark Prescott) *t.k.h: hld up wl in tch: nt clr run briefly wl over 1f out: sn swtchd lft: chsd ldrs 1f out: kpt on same pce fnl f* **9/2**[3]

1062 **5** ½ **Wilbury Star (IRE)**[17] 6665 2-9-3 **81**.............................. RichardHughes 6 79
(R Hannon) *t.k.h: hld up in tch: rdn over 2f out: kpt on same pce fr over 1f out* **8/1**

643 **6** 4 ½ **Island Chief**[40] 6065 2-8-3 **67**.. ChrisCatlin 4 55
(K A Ryan) *rrd s and s.i.s: t.k.h: hld up in rr early: hdwy to chse ldr over 4f out: rdn and ev ch 2f out: wknd fnl f* **10/1**

512 **7** 3 ¼ **Guestofthenation (USA)**[41] 6038 2-9-7 **85**.......................... JoeFanning 5 66
(M Johnston) *w ldr tl led over 4f out: rdn over 2f out: hdd over 1f out: wknd qckly ent fnl f* **9/4**[1]

1m 41.15s (1.25) **Going Correction** -0.025s/f (Stan) **7** Ran SP% **113.1**
Speed ratings (Par 97): **92,91,91,90,89 85,81**
toteswinger: 1&2 £5.40, 1&3 £11.10, 2&3 £6.20. CSF £33.04 TOTE £8.80: £3.90, £2.60; EX 37.70.
Owner Mrs Denis Haynes **Bred** Wretham Stud **Trained** Newmarket, Suffolk
■ Stewards' Enquiry : R Hills caution: careless riding

FOCUS
The gallop set by the leader looked very ordinary, so it was not a massive surprise to see virtually the whole field have a chance of some description down the home straight. The runner-up helps set the level.

NOTEBOOK
Worth A King'S, held up early, could be spotted going well rounding the final bend and sneaked past his rivals up the inside rail. He kept on gamely for his young rider and shaped like a horse that will be better suited by a stiffer test. One would imagine that he will stay at least 1m2f next season. (op 13-2)
Tobond(IRE) looked to be going equally well over two furlongs out but could not quicken away from his rivals under a big weight (the bump he got late on had no real effect on the final result). He is still a horse to keep on the right side of though. (op 3-1 tchd 11-4)
Makhaaleb(IRE) had the blinkers fitted for his first start on the all-weather and in nursery company. Much like everything else in the race, he had every chance but was just not good enough on the day. (op 8-1 tchd 10-1)
Starry Sky seemed to be going the best of them about a furlong out but she could not produce a turn of foot. A stronger pace would have helped her. (op 11-2)
Wilbury Star(IRE) kept on well down the middle of the course without looking a serious threat. (tchd 9-1)
Guestofthenation(USA) dropped out quickly under pressure. There was no obvious reason why the favourite performed so badly. (op 3-1)

7068 TIPTREE H'CAP 1m (P)
4:00 (4:01) (Class 5) (0-75,74) 3-Y-0+ **£2,914** (£867; £433; £216) **Stalls** Centre

Form RPR
400 **1** **Titan Triumph**[17] 6675 4-9-3 **70**...(t) JimCrowley 9 80
(W J Knight) *stdd s: hld up in last: stl travelling wl over 2f out: c wd wl over 1f out: hdwy over 1f out: rdn to ld ins fnl f: comf* **15/2**

3054 **2** 1 **Obezyana (USA)**[7] 6900 6-9-0 **72**............................... NicolPolli[(5)] 4 80
(A Bailey) *dwlt: sn pushed up to chse ldrs: rdn over 2f out: chsd ldr over 1f out: ev ch jst ins fnl f: kpt on same pce fnl 100yds* **3/1**[2]

4616 **3** *hd* **Jawaab (IRE)**[15] 6721 4-9-7 **74**.. MartinDwyer 8 82
(W R Muir) *hld up in last pair: hdwy and nt clr run briefly wl over 1f out: sn swtchd lft: chsd ldrs ins fnl f: kpt on u.p* **9/4**[1]

0400 **4** 1 **Eastern Gift**[16] 6695 3-9-0 **70**... RichardHughes 2 75
(R Hannon) *led narrowly: rdn over 2f out: hdd ins fnl f: lost 2 pl towards fin* **9/2**[3]

0004 **5** 1 ¾ **Rapid City**[18] 6659 5-9-2 **72**..(p) TolleyDean[(3)] 3 73
(A J McCabe) *in tch: rdn jst over 2f out: wknd u.p ent fnl f* **9/2**[3]

0000 **6** 3 **Silca Destination**[2] 7027 3-8-8 **64**................................ EdwardCreighton 1 58
(M R Channon) *s.i.s: towards rr: rdn and effrt over 2f out: chsd ldrs and drvn over 1f out: wknd fnl f* **25/1**

6100 **7** 19 **Landucci**[25] 6490 7-9-2 **72**...(v) PatrickHills[(3)] 7 23
(J W Hills) *pressed ldr tl 2f out: wknd qckly over 1f out: eased fnl f* **18/1**

000 **8** 20 **Ticking**[112] 3834 5-8-7 **60** oh15.. LiamJones 5 —
(T Keddy) *in tch tl lost pl 1/2-way: t.o last 2f* **66/1**

1m 39.68s (-0.22) **Going Correction** -0.025s/f (Stan)
WFA 3 from 4yo+ 3lb **8** Ran SP% **114.5**
Speed ratings (Par 103): **100,99,98,97,96 93,74,54**
toteswinger: 1&2 £4.30, 1&3 £3.50, 2&3 £1.60. CSF £30.35 CT £67.76 TOTE £10.70: £2.00, £1.40, £1.40; EX 31.50 Trifecta £270.50 Part won. Pool: £365.55 - 0.40 winning units..
Owner Canisbay Bloodstock **Bred** Hesmonds Stud Ltd **Trained** Patching, W Sussex

FOCUS
The early gallop did not look anything special, which meant plenty had a chance as the race developed. The leader quickened the tempo just over two furlongs from home which, for a few strides, caught some of his rivals out. The winner did not have to improve on decent form to score with the runner-up and fourth setting the level.

7069 TALENTO MAIDEN STKS 1m 2f (P)
4:30 (4:31) (Class 4) 2-Y-0 **£3,885** (£1,156; £577; £288) **Stalls** Low

Form RPR
02 **1** **Orbitor**[13] 6759 2-9-3 0.. HayleyTurner 5 72
(M L W Bell) *dwlt: sn pushed along to get in tch: shkn up and hdwy over 2f out: rdn to ld wl over 1f out: in command ins fnl f: rdn out* **5/2**[2]

600 **2** ½ **State General (IRE)**[23] 6524 2-9-3 65.................................. LiamJones 4 71
(Miss J Feilden) *racd wl off the pce in midfield: pushed along 7f out: rdn 4f out: hdwy and swtchd lft over 1f out: edgd lft but styd on wl to go 2nd ins fnl f: nvr quite getting to wnr* **66/1**

04 **3** 1 ½ **Akbabend**[12] 6778 2-9-3 0... JoeFanning 11 68
(M Johnston) *chsd ldrs: rdn to chse wnr over 1f out: drvn ent fnl f: one pce fnl 100yds* **5/1**[3]

5540 **4** *hd* **Supernoverre (IRE)**[17] 6674 2-9-3 70.............................. JimCrowley 9 68
(Mrs A J Perrett) *squeezed out and short of room sn after s: hld up off the pce in midfield: rdn and effrt on outer over 2 fout: kpt on ins fnl f: styng on fin* **10/1**

4205 **5** 2 **Forty Thirty (IRE)**[12] 6789 2-9-3 72............................ EdwardCreighton 2 64
(M R Channon) *t.k.h: hld up in tch: hdwy to trck ldrs 3f out: rdn and unable qckn over 1f out: one pce fnl f* **28/1**

0 **6** ½ **Decorum (USA)**[20] 6604 2-9-3 0..(t) RobertHavlin 7 63
(J H M Gosden) *wnt rt s: bhd: rdn over 2f out: hdwy and edgd rt over 1f out: edgd lft fnl f: kpt on ins fnl f: nvr trbld ldrs* **10/1**

7 5 **Theola (IRE)** 2-8-12 0... SaleemGolam 12 49
(M H Tompkins) *s.i.s: bustled along early: bhd: rdn over 4f out: kpt on past btn horses fnl f: n.d* **100/1**

0 **8** 4 **Great Western (USA)**[20] 6602 2-9-3 0...................................... NCallan 6 47
(P F I Cole) *led tl 8f out: chsd ldr after tl 2f out: sn drvn: wknd over 1f out* **33/1**

0000 **9** 3 ¼ **Captain Walcot**[61] 5460 2-9-3 60.................................. RichardHughes 8 41
(R Hannon) *in tch in midfield: reminders 5f out: wknd over 2f out* **33/1**

04 **10** *nk* **Nicky Nutjob (GER)**[23] 6524 2-9-3 0.................................. AlanMunro 3 41
(P W Chapple-Hyam) *dwlt: sn pushed along to chse ldrs: rdn over 4f out: sn struggling: no ch last 2f* **10/1**

50 **11** 1 **Contretemps (USA)**[46] 5901 2-9-3 0...................................... LDettori 13 39
(Saeed Bin Suroor) *hdwy to ld after 2f: rdn and hdd wl over 1f out: btn over 1f out: virtually p.u ins fnl f* **2/1**[1]

0 **12** 7 **Ivory's Icon (IRE)**[98] 4305 2-9-3 0...................................... TravisBlock 1 26
(Miss Jo Crowley) *s.i.s: nvr gng wl in rr: reminders 8f out: lost tch 4f out* **66/1**

00 **13** 3 **Ermyn Lodge**[17] 6674 2-9-3 0.. ChrisCatlin 10 21
(P M Phelan) *s.i.s: a bhd* **66/1**

2m 8.50s (-0.10) **Going Correction** -0.025s/f (Stan) **13** Ran SP% **120.6**
Speed ratings (Par 97): **99,98,97,97,95 95,91,88,85,85 84,78,76**
toteswinger: 1&2 £29.10, 1&3 £3.80, 2&3 £34.00. CSF £177.96 TOTE £3.50: £1.20, £11.60, £2.10; EX 296.20 Trifecta £356.50 Part won. Pool: £481.88 - 0.40 winning units..
Owner C Headfort and P Robinson **Bred** Mr & Mrs G Middlebrook **Trained** Newmarket, Suffolk

FOCUS
Quite a few of the major stables were involved in this maiden, but two of the first four home had looked fairly exposed before this, which does give the form a dubious look. The two that set a good pace did not feature in the finish and the runner-up is likely to prove the key to the form.

NOTEBOOK
Orbitor had shown plenty of promise in a couple of previous maidens and duly got off the mark at the third time of asking. He is sure to make up into a useful 1m4f handicapper next season. (op 9-4 tchd 11-4)
State General(IRE), rated 65, stayed on really well after getting behind in the early stages of the race. His previous form was nothing special, which may hold the winner's performance down a bit.
Akbabend, who lost a shoe on the way to the start, chased the leaders and kept on at the one pace under pressure. A big, rangy-looking sort, he is almost certainly going to be a more potent force during next year. Official explanation: jockey said colt lost a shoe going to the start (op 10-3 tchd 11-2)
Supernoverre(IRE) had an official mark of 70, but it is open to debate as to whether he actually deserved it. He kept going for pressure and one could see him winning a staying handicap next season. (op 16-1)
Forty Thirty(IRE) travelled really strongly for a lot of the race but could not quicken. (op 25-1)
Decorum(USA), fitted with a tongue-tie, kept on quite well from off the gallop, despite running around under pressure. The latter will no doubt be better once he has grown into his huge frame. (op 11-1 tchd 8-1)
Contretemps(USA) set a very strong pace but stopped quickly inside the final furlong under pressure. Official explanation: vet said colt had a breathing problem (op 3-1)

7070 BANTERS H'CAP 1m 2f (P)
5:00 (5:00) (Class 5) (0-75,75) 3-Y-O **£2,914** (£867; £433; £216) **Stalls** Low

Form RPR
1-04 **1** **Phoenix Flight (IRE)**[13] 6758 3-9-3 **74**.......................... J-PGuillambert 1 87+
(Sir Mark Prescott) *in tch: effrt and rdn jst over 2f out: ev ch jst ins fnl f: drvn to ld fnl 50yds: styd on* **2/1**[1]

1655 **2** 1 **Bluejain**[27] 6417 3-9-1 **72**... NCallan 9 83
(Miss Gay Kelleway) *stdd s: hld up in rr: hdwy 3f out: swtchd lft wl over 1f out: rdn to ld over 1f out: sn hung rt: hdd fnl 50yds: no ex* **8/1**

643 **3** 2 ½ **Locum**[26] 6437 3-8-7 **64**.. SaleemGolam 6 70
(M H Tompkins) *chsd ldrs: rdn jst over 2f out: pressing ldrs jst ins fnl f: btn whn swtchd lft ins fnl f: outpcd fnl 100yds* **7/2**[2]

165 **4** 3 ½ **Wallonia (IRE)**[17] 6683 3-8-6 **63**..................................... HayleyTurner 10 62
(K A Ryan) *hld up in rr: hdwy over 3f out: chsd ldrs and drvn over 1f out: wknd ins fnl f* **16/1**

0225 **5** 1 ¼ **Alfredtheordinary**[1] 7050 3-8-4 **61**...................................... TPO'Shea 8 58
(M R Channon) *dwlt: sn in tch: hdwy to chse ldr over 5f out: led 2f out: sn drvn: hdd over 1f out: wknd fnl f* **11/1**

666 **6** 1 ¼ **Paint The Town Red**[33] 6256 3-9-3 **74**............................... ChrisCatlin 2 68
(H J Collingridge) *s.i.s: in rr: dropped to last pl and rdn over 3f out: sme hdwy u.p over 1f out: nvr trbld ldrs* **10/1**

100 **7** ¾ **Mooted (UAE)**[55] 5635 3-9-2 **73**.......................... RichardKingscote 4 66
(Miss J A Camacho) *t.k.h: hld up in midfield: rdn and unable qckn over 2f out: no imp fr wl over 1f out* **40/1**

2002 **8** 9 **Smarterthanuthink (USA)**[14] 6741 3-8-11 **68**..................... JimCrowley 7 43
(R A Fahey) *t.k.h: pressed ldr tl led over 6f out: rdn and hdd 2f out: sn wknd* **7/1**[3]

1240 **9** 10 **Shesha Bear**[13] 6758 3-8-13 **70**.. MartinDwyer 3 25
(W R Muir) *racd in midfield: rdn and lost pl wl over 3f out: no ch 2f out: eased fnl f: t.o* **20/1**

0541 **10** 24 **Basanti (USA)**[30] 6331 3-9-4 **75**...................................... MichaelHills 5 —
(B W Hills) *led tl over 6f out: rdn and dropped out qckly over 4f out: wl bhd and eased last 2f: t.o* **15/2**

2m 7.38s (-1.22) **Going Correction** -0.025s/f (Stan) **10** Ran SP% **121.4**
Speed ratings (Par 101): **103,102,100,97,96 95,94,87,79,60**
toteswinger: 1&2 £6.80, 1&3 £3.10, 2&3 £6.10. CSF £19.95 CT £55.88 TOTE £3.20: £1.30, £3.70, £1.90; EX 30.70 Trifecta £197.80 Pool: £540.04 - 2.02 winning units. Place 6: £48.64 Place 5: £26.67.
Owner W E Sturt - Osborne House Iv **Bred** Airlie Stud And Sir Thomas Pilkington **Trained** Newmarket, Suffolk

FOCUS
A tough-looking handicap to end the day on and a contest to be fairly positive about. The leader did not seem to go a really strong pace (at least three horses took a grip in behind) but it did turn into a real struggle late on.
Basanti(USA) Official explanation: jockey said filly was unsuited by the all-weather surface

T/Plt: £41.10 to a £1 stake. Pool: £48,484.96. 860.57 winning tickets. T/Qpdt: £8.30 to a £1 stake. Pool: £3,053.72. 270.70 winning tickets. SP

7009 KEMPTON (A.W) (R-H)

Wednesday, October 29

OFFICIAL GOING: Standard

Wind: Brisk, behind Weather: Cold

7071 EPSOM OWNERS & TRAINERS AWARDS DINNER NOV 22ND H'CAP (DIV I) 1m 4f (P)

5:50 (5:50) (Class 6) (0-65,65) 3-Y-0+ **£1,706** (£503; £252) **Stalls** Centre

Form RPR

0041 **1** **Bluebell Ridge (IRE)**[28] 6378 3-8-12 **58**.................. KirstyMilczarek 11 66
(D W P Arbuthnot) *trckd ldrs: drvn to ld on ins 2f out: rdn and hung lft fnl f: kpt on wl* **15/2**

2040 **2** ½ **Good Effect (USA)**[8] 6882 4-9-4 **57**..............................(t) GeorgeBaker 8 64
(C P Morlock) *hld up in rr: hdwy whn hung rt 2f out: sn plld lft and styd on fr over 1f out: qcknd to chse wnr wnr ins fnl f but a hld* **6/1**[3]

0130 **3** 1¾ **Formidable Guest**[8] 6882 4-9-5 **58**........................... JerryO'Dwyer 10 62
(J Pearce) *chsd ldrs: rdn and styd on to chse wnr over 1f out: a hld and outpcd for 2nd ins fnl f* **15/2**

4402 **4** 1½ **Dan Tucker**[11] 6806 4-9-10 **63**...(b) PaulDoe 13 65
(Jim Best) *chsd ldrs: rdn 2f out: styd on same pce fnl f* **5/1**[2]

1000 **5** 4 **Muffett's Dream**[12] 6768 4-8-11 **50** oh3.................. CatherineGannon 14 45
(J J Bridger) *led: rdn fr 3f out: hdd 2f out: wknd appr fnl f* **33/1**

6 ¾ **Last Emperor**[47] 5879 3-7-13 **50** oh2........................... BACurtis(5) 2 44
(John Joseph Murphy, Ire) *in rr: wd into st 3f out: sme prog fnl f* **33/1**

-000 **7** *hd* **Finished Article (IRE)**[163] 2245 11-8-11 **50** oh5.................. LPKeniry 7 44
(Mrs D Thomas) *in rr: mod prog fr over 1f out* **66/1**

-000 **8** ½ **Royal Tartan (USA)**[89] 4607 3-8-1 **50** oh5.................. LukeMorris(3) 4 43
(G L Moore) *a towards rr* **40/1**

5643 **9** *nk* **Flam**[12] 6775 3-9-5 **65**..(p) RobertWinston 5 57
(J R Fanshawe) *chsd ldrs: rdn 3f out: wknd 2f out* **11/4**[1]

0200 **10** 8 **One To Follow**[119] 3614 4-9-9 **62**.. IanMongan 3 42
(C G Cox) *chsd ldrs: rdn 3f out: wknd sn after* **5/1**[2]

0000 **11** 2½ **Abydos**[55] 5630 4-9-7 **60**... TPQueally 9 36
(A P Stringer) *a in rr* **16/1**

5320 **12** ½ **Vinces**[45] 5934 4-9-11 **64**.. FergusSweeney 6 39
(T D McCarthy) *chsd ldrs tl rdn and wknd 3f out* **13/2**

2m 35.47s (0.97) **Going Correction** +0.05s/f (Slow)
WFA 3 from 4yo+ 7lb **12** Ran SP% **126.8**
Speed ratings (Par 101): **98,97,96,95,92 92,92,91,91,86 84,84**
toteswinger: 1&2 £6.80, 1&3 £7.60, 2&3 £6.10. CSF £54.79 CT £364.02 TOTE £4.60: £2.90, £2.20, £3.10; EX 65.30.
Owner The Bluebell Ridge Partnership **Bred** Yeomanstown Stud **Trained** Compton, Berks
■ Stewards' Enquiry : Kirsty Milczarek caution: used whip in incorrect place.

FOCUS
An ordinary handicap run in a slower time than division one, and modest form. The winner is up 6lb but the likes of the seventh and eighth expose the form.

7072 DAY TIME, NIGHT TIME, GREAT TIME CLASSIFIED STKS 7f (P)

6:20 (6:21) (Class 6) 3-Y-0+ **£2,047** (£604; £302) **Stalls** High

Form RPR

/501 **1** **Charming Escort**[14] 6735 4-9-2 55............................ RobertWinston 13 61
(T T Clement) *chsd ldrs: rdn and carried rt and led over 1f out: hung rt ins fnl f: drvn out* **11/4**[2]

0000 **2** *shd* **Optical Illusion (USA)**[19] 6631 4-9-2 55....................... TonyHamilton 7 61
(R A Fahey) *mid-div: hdwy whn n.m.r and pushed rt appr fnl f: styd on u.p to press wnr cl home: jst failed* **9/2**[3]

-000 **3** 2 **Langham House**[41] 6049 3-9-0 55................................. NickyMackay 1 56
(J R Jenkins) *chsd ldrs: rdn and edgd rt 2f out: styd on to chse wnr ins fnl f: a hld and sn outpcd into 3rd* **25/1**

4 2½ **Sturgis (IRE)**[66] 5328 5-9-2 51.......................................(bt) RPCleary 2 49
(Paul W Flynn, Ire) *slowly away: in rr: rdn over 2f out: hdwy over 1f out: kpt on fnl f: nvr in contention* **14/1**

60 **5** ½ **Bold Diva**[28] 6377 3-9-0 55...(v) KirstyMilczarek 8 48
(A W Carroll) *mid-div: hdwy 3f out: chsd ldrs 2f out: n.m.r and carried rt appr fnl f: sn wknd* **12/1**

6302 **6** 1 **Reve Vert (FR)**[13] 6752 3-9-0 55.................................. ShaneKelly 11 45
(A W Carroll) *led: rdn over 2f out: hdd and hung rt over 1f out: sn wknd* **5/2**[1]

00-0 **7** 1 **Lady Charlemagne**[56] 5603 3-8-11 50...........................(v1) LukeMorris(3) 9 42
(N P Littmoden) *bmpd s: t.k.h in rr: nvr bttr than mid-div* **33/1**

000 **8** ½ **Bad Moon Rising**[99] 4278 3-9-0 51..................................... LPKeniry 5 41
(J Akehurst) *chsd ldrs: rdn over 3f out: wknd 2f out* **9/1**

6500 **9** 5 **Alabama Spirit (USA)**[135] 3086 3-9-0 55........................ IanMongan 6 27
(P Howling) *chsd ldrs: rdn 3f out: wknd qckly 2f out* **16/1**

-000 **10** ½ **Danse De Sioux (IRE)**[30] 6345 3-9-0 47....................... WilliamBuick 3 26
(M Madgwick) *slowly away: a in rr* **50/1**

540 **11** *nk* **Flight Of Fashion (IRE)**[67] 5278 3-9-0 55................... RichardThomas 4 25
(Dr J D Scargill) *bhd fr 1/2-way* **9/1**

1m 26.6s (0.60) **Going Correction** +0.05s/f (Slow)
WFA 3 from 4yo+ 2lb **11** Ran SP% **122.4**
Speed ratings (Par 101): **98,97,95,92,92 91,89,89,83,83 82**
toteswinger: 1&2 £3.70, 1&3 £30.10, 2&3 £35.00. CSF £16.19 TOTE £4.00: £1.10, £1.70, £10.00; EX 17.20.
Owner P Charalambous **Bred** Hyperion Bloodstock **Trained** Newmarket, Suffolk

FOCUS
A poor event in which two of the three previous winners in the race fought out the finish. The winner built on his previous win here and the form seems sound enough.

7073 KEMPTON.CO.UK MAIDEN AUCTION STKS 1m (P)

6:50 (6:50) (Class 4) 2-Y-0 **£3,885** (£1,156; £577; £288) **Stalls** High

Form RPR

323 **1** **Officer In Command (USA)**[20] 6597 2-8-8 78............. LukeMorris(3) 8 81
(J S Moore) *trckd ldrs: led over 1f out: styd on strly* **5/2**[2]

354 **2** 2¾ **Fin Vin De Leu (GER)**[14] 6731 2-8-11 77....................... NickyMackay 9 75
(M Johnston) *chsd ldr: rdn: hung rt and led appr 2f out: hdd over 1f out: sn no ch w wnr but hld on for 2nd* **7/1**[3]

3366 **3** *nk* **Brooksby**[16] 6700 2-8-6 67.......................................(b1) RichardThomas 10 69
(R Hannon) *sn led: rdn and hdd appr fnl 2f: kpt on same pce fnl f* **8/1**

4 1 **Gaily Noble (IRE)** 2-8-13 0.. FergusSweeney 7 74
(A B Haynes) *chsd ldrs: shkn up and one pce fnl f* **33/1**

32 **5** ½ **High Office**[35] 6213 2-8-11 0..................................... TonyHamilton 2 71
(R A Fahey) *hld up in rr and t.k.h: drvn and hdwy over 1f out: kpt on ins fnl f but nvr gng pce to be competitive* **7/4**[1]

00 **6** ¾ **Co Dependent (USA)**[28] 6375 2-8-11 0.............................. ShaneKelly 5 69
(J A Osborne) *in rr: shkn up and sme prog fr over 1f out: nvr in contention* **20/1**

00 **7** ¾ **Ritano (IRE)**[20] 6597 2-8-13 0.. JerryO'Dwyer 3 70
(B I Case) *t.k.h towards rr: hdwy on ins to chse ldrs and hung bdly rt fr over 2f out: wknd fnl f* **66/1**

52 **8** 3¾ **Cool Strike (UAE)**[26] 6451 2-8-9 0.. LPKeniry 1 57
(A M Balding) *s.i.s: sn chsng ldrs: rdn over 2f out: sn wknd* **12/1**

0 **9** 3¾ **Playful Asset (IRE)**[39] 6122 2-8-8 0............................... WilliamBuick 6 48
(R M Beckett) *chsd ldrs: rdn 3f out: sn wknd* **8/1**

1m 40.09s (0.29) **Going Correction** +0.05s/f (Slow) **9** Ran SP% **116.5**
Speed ratings (Par 97): **100,97,96,95,95 94,93,90,86**
toteswinger: 1&2 £2.70, 1&3 £5.10, 2&3 £13.50. CSF £20.27 TOTE £2.80: £1.20, £2.10, £2.80; EX 16.20.
Owner N Brunskill & J S Moore **Bred** Blooming Hills Inc **Trained** Upper Lambourn, Berks

FOCUS
A fair maiden and solid form, rated around the placed horses.

NOTEBOOK
Officer In Command(USA) came into the race with a rating of 78 and set a decent standard to aim at. Enjoying the run of the race in tracking the leader on the rail, once switched to challenge he picked up well to go clear from a furlong out. Whether he improved at all to win this is questionable, but he certainly seems to be going the right way, is clearly at home on Polytrack and can do better again in handicap company. (op 9-4)
Fin Vin De Leu(GER), whose mark of 77 looks to flatter him on what he has done to date, briefly hit the front two furlongs out, but he was easily brushed aside by the winner. He did rally to take second, though, and he looks sure to appreciate stepping up in distance next year, as his pedigree (dam won the Ribblesdale and the Prix de Royallieu) would suggest. (op 11-2 tchd 9-2)
Brooksby had the best of the draw and took them along in the first-time blinkers. She ran a perfectly sound race given that she had a bit to find with the likes of the first two strictly on the ratings. (tchd 13-2)
Gaily Noble(IRE), a half-brother to a 7f three-year-old winner out of an unraced sister to Mind Games, shaped well on his debut and is entitled to come on for the experience.
High Office, who had run with promise on his first two starts, was racing on Polytrack for the first time. He shaped better than his finishing position suggests as he did not get much luck in running, and handicaps over middle distances next year look sure to see him in a better light. (op 5-2 tchd 3-1)
Co Dependent(USA) was another who needed this for a mark. Held up out the back and taken wide round the turn into the straight, he kept on without being unduly punished, and he will be of far more interest once he appears in handicap company. He certainly cannot be given too high a rating on the bare form of his three runs to date. (op 25-1 tchd 18-1)

7074 DIGIBET MEDIAN AUCTION MAIDEN STKS 6f (P)

7:20 (7:21) (Class 5) 3-4-Y-0 **£2,590** (£770; £385; £192) **Stalls** High

Form RPR

0/4 **1** **Silaah**[21] 6571 4-9-4 0.. TGMcLaughlin 1 83+
(E A L Dunlop) *s.i.s: hld up in rr: shkn up and hdwy on ins over 2f out: trckd ldrs jst ins fnl f: qcknd to ld and hung lft fnl 50yds: readily* **4/1**[2]

0 **2** 1½ **Towy Valley**[23] 6543 3-8-12 0... AdamKirby 8 73
(C G Cox) *in tch: hdwy 3f out: rdn over 2f out: styd on to ld ins fnl f: hdd and outpcd fnl 50yds* **14/1**

3 ¾ **Spring Buck (IRE)** 3-9-3 0... NickyMackay 2 76+
(M Johnston) *in rr: pushed along and hdwy 3f out: rdn and styd on fr over 1f out: kpt on cl home but nvr gng pce to trble ldng duo* **15/2**

4543 **4** 2 **Kenton Street**[23] 6543 3-9-3 68................................ KirstyMilczarek 12 69
(J A R Toller) *broke wl: stdd towrds rr after 1f: hdwy over 2f out: styd on fnl f but nvr gng pce to press ldrs* **3/1**[1]

2033 **5** 3½ **Dark Camellia**[21] 6571 3-8-12 65.....................................(t) DaneO'Neill 4 53
(H J L Dunlop) *chsd ldrs: led over 2f out: sn u.p: hdd & wknd ins fnl f* **5/1**[3]

0 **6** 1½ **May Parkin (IRE)**[9] 6874 3-8-12 0.................................... RPCleary 9 48
(Eamon Tyrrell, Ire) *sn towards rr: rdn and hung rt over 2f out: sme prog over 1f out: nvr in contention* **25/1**

0 **7** *nk* **This Ones For Pat (USA)**[12] 6791 3-9-3 0..................... TonyCulhane 5 52
(S Parr) *in rr: drvn along over 3f out: modearte prog fnl f* **33/1**

20 **8** 1½ **Titus Gent**[11] 6822 3-8-10 0...................................... RyanPowell(7) 11 47
(J Ryan) *sn chsng ldrs: rdn over 2f out: wknd appr fnl f* **25/1**

-5 **9** *hd* **Edmondstown Lass (IRE)**[12] 6791 3-8-12 70................ TonyHamilton 6 42
(R A Fahey) *sn led: rdn and hdd over 2f out: wknd over 1f out* **11/2**

6- **10** 1½ **Mexilhoeira**[431] 4808 4-8-13 0....................................... JerryO'Dwyer 3 37
(J R Gask) *in rr: mod prog 2f out: nvr in contention* **40/1**

6-00 **11** 3¾ **My Pin Up**[136] 3064 3-8-12 67...[1] DarrenWilliams 10 25
(Christian Wroe) *chsd ldrs over 3f* **16/1**

1m 12.92s (-0.18) **Going Correction** +0.05s/f (Slow)
WFA 3 from 4yo 1lb **11** Ran SP% **114.4**
Speed ratings (Par 103): **103,101,100,97,92 90,90,88,88,86 81**
toteswinger: 1&2 £30.40, 1&3 £7.40, 2&3 £26.30. CSF £53.87 TOTE £5.20: £1.50, £5.00, £2.60; EX 67.80.
Owner Hamdan Al Maktoum **Bred** Bearstone Stud **Trained** Newmarket, Suffolk

FOCUS
The leaders went off too quick in this maiden. The first three were all unexposed and finished clear of the fourth whose recent form is pretty solid and the race is rated around him. There is more to come from the winner.

7075 DIGIBET.COM NURSERY 6f (P)

7:50 (7:51) (Class 3) (0-90,89) 2-Y-0 **£6,670** (£1,984; £991; £495) **Stalls** High

Form RPR

3216 **1** **Tropical Paradise (IRE)**[47] 5855 2-9-0 **85**..................... LukeMorris(3) 1 87
(P Winkworth) *cl up in 4th: rdn and hdwy over 1f out: styd on strly to ld fnl 50yds* **6/1**[3]

103 **2** ½ **Rowayton**[12] 6769 2-8-12 **80**... RobertWinston 4 81
(J D Bethell) *trckd ldrs in cl 3rd: drvn to ld ins fnl 2f: hdd and no ex fnl 50yds* **13/2**

21 **3** 2½ **Film Set (USA)**[20] 6601 2-9-7 **89**.. LDettori 3 82
(Saeed Bin Suroor) *trckd ldr: rdn over 2f out: sn no prog: hung lft and btn appr fnl f* **5/6**[1]

1011 **4** ¾ **Go Go Green (IRE)**[17] 6666 2-9-4 **86**................................. TonyCulhane 7 77
(S Parr) *led: rdn and hdd ins fnl 2f: sn btn* **3/1**[2]

1m 12.26s (-0.84) **Going Correction** +0.05s/f (Slow) **4** Ran SP% **107.2**
Speed ratings (Par 99): **107,106,103,102**
toteswinger: 1&2 £8.60. CSF £34.55 TOTE £7.60; EX 27.10.
Owner S Lovelace & R Muddle **Bred** George E McMahon **Trained** Chiddingfold, Surrey
■ Dakota Hills was withdrawn after proving unruly in the paddock (12/1, deduct 5p in the £ under R4).

FOCUS
A small-field nursery and a little bit of a turn up, with the two outsiders coming clear of the market leaders. The form is rated through the runner-up.

NOTEBOOK
Tropical Paradise(IRE) did not get home in a decent nursery over an extended 6f in soft ground last time, having had a lot of use made of her, but she was ridden far more patiently here, and it seemed to suit her as she came with a strong run once switched to challenge two furlongs out. She should get 7f on this surface. (old market tchd 11-2 and 13-2)
Rowayton shaped as though she would be suited by the return to 6f when running on late over the minimum trip here last time. This was a solid effort and this surface clearly suits her well, but perhaps her rider could have held on to her for a bit longer and delayed her challenge slightly. (old market op 6-1 tchd 7-1)
Film Set(USA) was dropping back a furlong after winning his maiden tidily at Newbury. Debuting on Polytrack, this son of Breeders' Cup Turf winner Johar was well enough placed entering the straight, but he was simply outpaced by the first two. It looked as though this trip was just too short for him. (old market op 4-5 tchd 11-10)
Go Go Green(IRE) was soon in front, where he likes to be, but found disappointingly little in the straight. He is a half-brother to Dhanyata, who won the Group 3 Sirenia Stakes over course and distance, so the switch to Polytrack from turf was not expected to cause him any problems, but perhaps he is simply not as effective on this surface as he is on softish ground on turf. (old market op 9-2)

7076 DIGIBET SPORTS BETTING H'CAP — 1m (P)
8:20 (8:22) (Class 6) (0-60,60) 3-Y-O+ — **£2,047** (£604; £302) **Stalls** High

Form — RPR
0430 **1** **Epidaurian King (IRE)**[61] 5474 5-9-5 **58**..................(v) DarrenWilliams 1 — 68+
(D Shaw) *s.i.s: hld up in rr: stl plenty to do whn hdwy on ins fr 2f out: qcknd to ld ins fnl f: readily* **25/1**
3322 **2** *1 1/2* **Under Fire (IRE)**[6] 6928 5-8-13 **59**........................ JemmaMarshall(7) 13 — 66
(A W Carroll) *led: pushed along over 2f out: hdd ins fnl f: kpt on wl but nt pce of wnr* **7/2**[1]
0010 **3** *shd* **Alucica**[103] 4168 5-9-3 **56**..(v) JimCrowley 11 — 62
(D Shaw) *towards rr: hdwy 3f out: pressed ldrs and hung rt over 1f out and ins fnl f: kpt on same pce* **14/1**
023 **4** *3/4* **Having A Ball**[22] 6560 4-9-4 **57**.................................. MartinDwyer 10 — 62
(P D Cundell) *in rr: rdn and hdwy over 2f out: styd on u.p fnl f: gng on cl home* **9/2**[2]
0002 **5** *1/2* **Royal Encore**[14] 6735 4-9-0 **53**................................ RobertWinston 9 — 59+
(J R Fanshawe) *s.i.s: hld up in rr: hdwy fr 3f out: styng on whn hmpd over 1f and ins fnl f: nt rcvr* **9/1**
0302 **6** *hd* **Mrs Jefferson (IRE)**[74] 5086 3-9-4 **60**............................ JamesDoyle 12 — 63
(J G Portman) *chsd ldrs: rdn over 2f out: wknd ins fnl f* **25/1**
5404 **7** *3/4* **Alexander Guru**[11] 6825 4-9-7 **60**.................................... SteveDrowne 5 — 61
(M Blanshard) *in tch: rdn 3f out: kpt on same pce fr over 1f out* **10/1**
0010 **8** *3/4* **Convallaria (FR)**[66] 5317 5-9-3 **56**...........................(b) RobertHavlin 3 — 56
(G Wragg) *in rr: rdn and hung bdly rt fr over 2f out: smeprog whn stl hanging fnl f* **16/1**
050 **9** *hd* **Valdan (IRE)**[20] 6599 4-9-7 **60**............................... RichardHughes 4 — 59
(P D Evans) *in rr: rdn over 2f out: hdwy over 1f out: kpt on cl home* **8/1**
060 **10** *1* **One Oi**[35] 6206 3-9-4 **60**... DaneO'Neill 6 — 57
(D W P Arbuthnot) *chsd ldrs: rdn 3f out: wknd over 1f out* **9/1**
3150 **11** *1* **Inquisitress**[2] 7012 4-8-12 **58**................................... RossAtkinson(7) 14 — 52
(J J Bridger) *sn chsng ldrs: rdn 3f out: wknd over 1f out* **7/1**[3]
-000 **12** *3* **Kaystar Ridge**[23] 6543 3-9-2 **58**.................................. JerryO'Dwyer 7 — 46
(D K Ivory) *chsd ldrs: rdn 3f out: wknd fr 2f out* **66/1**
3601 **13** *hd* **Dr Synn**[49] 5797 7-9-0 **53**.. KirstyMilczarek 2 — 40
(M J Attwater) *in tch on outside 4f out: rdn 3f out: wknd 2f out* **12/1**
0000 **14** *1 1/4* **Cavalry Guard (USA)**[8] 6889 4-9-7 **60**....................(p) FergusSweeney 8 — 44
(T D McCarthy) *chsd ldrs over 5f* **66/1**

1m 40.35s (0.55) **Going Correction** +0.05s/f (Slow)
WFA 3 from 4yo+ 3lb — **14** Ran SP% **124.0**
Speed ratings (Par 101): **99,97,97,96,96 95,95,94,94,93 92,89,89,87**
toteswinger: 1&2 £59.00, 1&3 £64.90, 2&3 £13.80. CSF £112.10 CT £1359.59 TOTE £31.00: £7.70, £1.60, £5.50; EX 248.20.
Owner Market Avenue Racing Club Ltd **Bred** Shadwell Estate Company Limited **Trained** Danethorpe, Notts

FOCUS
Moderate handicap form, but it looks sound rated through the placed horses with the winner back to last winter's best.
Royal Encore Official explanation: jockey said filly suffered interference in running
Convallaria(FR) Official explanation: jockey said mare hung badly right-handed

7077 BIG MAC'S BIRTHDAY CELEBRATION H'CAP — 7f (P)
8:50 (8:50) (Class 4) (0-80,80) 3-Y-O+ — **£5,180** (£1,541; £770; £384) **Stalls** High

Form — RPR
3032 **1** **April Fool**[23] 6544 4-8-6 **66** oh3...............................(v) MartinDwyer 2 — 76
(J A Geake) *led after 1f: drvn along 2f out: styd on strly thrght fnl f* **18/1**
0604 **2** *1 3/4* **Southandwest (IRE)**[14] 6734 4-9-2 **76**............................. TPO'Shea 10 — 81
(J S Moore) *in tch tl rdn and outpcd over 3f out: hrd drvn and hdwy over 1f out: styd on fnl f to take 2nd nr fin but no ch w wnr* **11/1**
5031 **3** *1/2* **Dvinsky (USA)**[16] 6699 7-9-6 **80**.......................................(b) IanMongan 13 — 84
(P Howling) *led 1f: styd chsng wnr: rdn over 2f out and no imp but kpt on: lost 2nd cl home* **9/1**
3504 **4** *1 1/2* **Mogok Ruby**[16] 6699 4-9-3 **77**...................................... RichardHughes 1 — 77
(L Montague Hall) *hld up in rr: hdwy fr 2f out: rdn and styd on wl fnl f but nt rch ldng trio* **14/1**
0054 **5** *1 1/4* **My Learned Friend (IRE)**[22] 6554 4-8-12 **72**............... SteveDrowne 5 — 68
(A M Balding) *chsd ldrs: rdn over 2f out: styd on same pce fnl f* **12/1**
6314 **6** *1/2* **Provence**[16] 6695 3-8-12 **74**.. MichaelHills 12 — 69
(B W Hills) *chsd ldrs: rdn over 2f out: wknd ins fnl f* **3/1**[1]
4603 **7** *1 1/2* **Cat Whistle**[28] 6380 3-8-7 **69**.. TonyHamilton 11 — 60
(R A Fahey) *in rr: hdwy fr 3f out: chsd ldrs 2f out: wknd fnl f* **10/1**
3600 **8** *1/2* **Jake The Snake (IRE)**[16] 6695 7-8-13 **73**..................... ShaneKelly 4 — 62
(A W Carroll) *in rr: rdn and hung lft 2f out: nvr in contention* **14/1**
0214 **9** *3/4* **Our Blessing (IRE)**[2] 7014 4-8-1 **68**.......................... MatthewDavies(7) 8 — 55
(A P Jarvis) *t.k.h in rr: nvr gng pce to be competitive* **10/1**
6640 **10** *shd* **Trafalgar Square**[16] 6695 6-8-9 **69**.............................. PaulDoe 7 — 56
(M J Attwater) *in rr: hung lft and no ch after 2f out* **7/1**[3]
3600 **11** *1* **Rabbit Fighter (IRE)**[19] 6634 4-8-9 **69** ow1..............(v) DarrenWilliams 3 — 53
(D Shaw) *a in rr* **20/1**
312 **12** *1/2* **Lake Windermere (IRE)**[16] 6695 3-8-12 **74**.................... RobertHavlin 6 — 57
(J H M Gosden) *in rr: hung bdly lft fr 3f out* **7/2**[2]

1m 24.88s (-1.12) **Going Correction** +0.05s/f (Slow)
WFA 3 from 4yo+ 2lb — **12** Ran SP% **127.3**
Speed ratings (Par 105): **108,106,105,103,102 101,100,99,98,98 97,96**
toteswinger: 1&2 £15.50, 1&3 £19.30, 2&3 £47.60. CSF £217.12 CT £1960.01 TOTE £18.40: £4.60, £3.60, £2.70; EX 258.80.
Owner Miss B Swire **Bred** Miss B Swire **Trained** Kimpton, Hants

FOCUS
A fair handicap, and fairly solid form for the grade with the winner producing a clear personal best.
Lake Windermere(IRE) Official explanation: jockey said filly hung badly left-handed

7078 EPSOM OWNERS & TRAINERS AWARDS DINNER NOV 22ND H'CAP (DIV II) — 1m 4f (P)
9:20 (9:23) (Class 6) (0-65,65) 3-Y-O+ — **£1,706** (£503; £252) **Stalls** Centre

Form — RPR
0532 **1** **Cossack Prince**[20] 6594 3-9-5 **65**....................................... IanMongan 7 — 73
(Mrs L J Mongan) *mde virtually all: hrd drvn fnl 2f: hld on all out* **3/1**[1]
2 *hd* **Grand Aurora (IRE)**[37] 6179 4-9-5 **58**......................(t) RichardHughes 2 — 66
(Paul W Flynn, Ire) *in rr: rdn over 3f out: styd on u.p fnl 2f: chsd wnr ins fnl f and clsng nr fin but a jst hld* **8/1**
4360 **3** *3 1/4* **Play Up Pompey**[10] 6728 6-8-11 **50** oh4........................... JimCrowley 4 — 52
(J J Bridger) *in rr: hdwy and n.m.r 2f out: styng on whn nt clr run over 1f out: srayed on ins fnl f but nt rch ldng duo* **20/1**
5232 **4** *1 1/4* **Auntie Mame**[28] 6400 4-9-11 **64**.. TPO'Shea 6 — 64
(D J Coakley) *in rr: rdn and hdwy over 3f out: styd on to chse ldrs over 1f out: kpt on same pce* **4/1**[2]
/006 **5** *1 1/2* **Cover Drive (USA)**[21] 6577 5-9-6 **59**.......................... EdwardCreighton 9 — 57
(Christian Wroe) *in rr: hdaay whn hmpd over 2f oiut: kpt on ins fnl f but nvr a threat* **11/1**
1400 **6** *1/2* **Fossgate**[15] 6721 7-9-10 **63**... MartinDwyer 11 — 60
(J D Bethell) *chsd ldrs: rdn 3f out: wknd over 1f out* **8/1**
0362 **7** *3 1/4* **Shouldntbethere (IRE)**[14] 6728 4-8-12 **54**.................. JackMitchell(3) 13 — 46
(Mrs P N Dutfield) *chsd ldrs: rdn over 3f out: wknd fr 2f out* **15/2**[3]
3630 **8** *nk* **Amwell Brave**[14] 6729 7-8-11 **50** oh3............................ NickyMackay 10 — 42
(J R Jenkins) *chsd ldrs: rdn 3f out: wknd 2f out* **8/1**
0410 **9** *24* **Oasis Sun (IRE)**[12] 6775 5-9-4 **57**.................................(b) SteveDrowne 1 — 10
(J R Best) *chsd ldrs: rdn 3f out: wknd fr 2f out* **8/1**
10 *1/2* **Grand Cru**[14] 5879 3-8-6 **57**... BACurtis(5) 8 — 9
(John Joseph Murphy, Ire) *chsd ldrs over a m* **20/1**
000 **11** *5* **Brathay (IRE)**[43] 5993 4-8-8 **50** oh5................................ LukeMorris(3) 5 — —
(Ian Williams) *mid-div: bhd fnl 5f* **25/1**

2m 34.87s (0.37) **Going Correction** +0.05s/f (Slow)
WFA 3 from 4yo+ 7lb — **11** Ran SP% **122.9**
Speed ratings (Par 101): **100,99,97,96,95 95,93,93,77,76 73**
toteswinger: 1&2 £5.70, 1&3 £22.70, 2&3 £35.90. CSF £28.12 CT £424.56 TOTE £4.60: £1.90, £4.00, £3.30; EX 51.30 Place 6: £1039.40 Place 5: £239.52.
Owner Mrs P J Sheen **Bred** Wyck Hall Stud Ltd **Trained** Epsom, Surrey

FOCUS
The quicker of the two divisions by 0.6 seconds, with the winner making all and rated to this year's best.
Oasis Sun(IRE) Official explanation: jockey said mare had no more to give
T/Jkpt: Not won. T/Plt: £2,195.40 to a £1 stake. Pool: £82,703.53. 27.50 winning tickets. T/Qpdt: £182.10 to a £1 stake. Pool: £7,579.36. 30.80 winning tickets. ST

6759 NOTTINGHAM (L-H)
Wednesday, October 29

OFFICIAL GOING: Heavy (soft in places on straight course)
Wind: Virtually nil Weather: Sunny and cold

7079 PADDOCKS CONFERENCE CENTRE AT NOTTINGHAM RACECOURSE (S) STKS — 1m 75y
1:10 (1:11) (Class 6) 2-Y-O — **£2,729** (£806; £403) **Stalls** Low

Form — RPR
0200 **1** **Shifting Gold (IRE)**[19] 6632 2-8-11 57...................(b1) PaulMulrennan 16 — 60
(K A Ryan) *sn led and clr: rdn along over 2f out: drvn ent fnl f: jst hld on* **16/1**
4100 **2** *nk* **Hollow Green (IRE)**[19] 6632 2-8-11 58.......................... RobertWinston 14 — 59
(P D Evans) *in tch: effrt and hdwy whn n.m.r over 3f out: rdn to chse wnr wl over 1f out: drvn ins fnl f and styd on wl towards fin* **9/2**[2]
0640 **3** *2 1/4* **Strikemaster (IRE)**[28] 6394 2-8-11 53.......................... SteveDrowne 11 — 54
(J W Hills) *towards rr: hdwy on wd outside 2f out: sn rdn and kpt on ins fnl f: nrst fin* **9/1**
60 **4** *3/4* **Fruitful Job (IRE)**[21] 6574 2-8-6 0..........................(p) KellyHarrison(5) 13 — 53
(A G Newcombe) *prom: rdn along 3f out: drvn 2f out and kpt on same pce* **100/1**
3526 **5** *3* **Cherry Belle (IRE)**[16] 6694 2-8-11 60......................(v) TGMcLaughlin 12 — 46
(P D Evans) *in tch: hdwy over 3f out: rdn along over 2f out: drvn to chse ldrs over 1f out: sn one pce* **7/1**[3]
000 **6** *nk* **Aziz (IRE)**[13] 6760 2-8-8 52.. DominicFox(3) 8 — 45
(Miss D Mountain) *bhd: hdwy over 2f out: sn rdn and kpt on ins fnl f: nt rch ldrs* **28/1**
00 **7** *3/4* **Bansha (IRE)**[12] 6778 2-8-11 0.. DaneO'Neill 9 — 44
(A Bailey) *dwlt and towards rr tl sme late hdwy* **12/1**
30 **8** *4 1/2* **Jaubertie**[39] 6133 2-8-3 0.. LukeMorris(3) 17 — 29
(W G M Turner) *in tch: rdn along 3f out: sn drvn and wknd 2f out* **40/1**
9 *1 1/4* **Invincible Brave (IRE)** 2-8-11 0...................................... JamieMoriarty 1 — 31
(R A Fahey) *chsd ldrs: rdn along on inner 3f out: drvn over 2f out and sn wknd* **12/1**
0 **10** *2 1/4* **Jack's House (IRE)**[47] 5866 2-8-11 0.....................(t) FrankieMcDonald 6 — 26
(Jane Chapple-Hyam) *dwlt: t.k.h and a towards rr* **8/1**
60 **11** *hd* **Barbeito**[21] 6574 2-8-5 0 ow2.. KevinGhunowa(3) 3 — 23
(D J S Ffrench Davis) *chsd wnr: rdn along 4f out: drvn 3f out and sn wknd* **22/1**
01 **12** *1 1/4* **Jonah's Cruising (IRE)**[21] 6574 2-8-11 68.................. JamieSpencer 15 — 23
(J R Boyle) *hld up towards rr: hdwy over 2f out: rdn and in tch wl over 1f out: sn drvn and wknd* **7/2**[1]
06 **13** *6* **Canucatcher (IRE)**[15] 6722 2-8-8 0 ow2.......................... GrahamGibbons 7 — 7
(T D Walford) *in tch: rdn along over 3f out and sn wknd* **50/1**
0050 **14** *6* **Real Dandy**[57] 5591 2-8-11 64.. TPQueally 5 — —
(J G Given) *t.k.h: hld up and a towards rr* **12/1**

1m 50.86s (5.46) **Going Correction** +0.65s/f (Yiel) — **14** Ran SP% **116.2**
Speed ratings (Par 93): **98,97,95,94,91 91,90,86,84,82 82,81,75,69**
toteswinger: 1&2 £19.80, 1&3 £32.30, 2&3 £9.70. CSF £80.49 TOTE £23.50: £5.90, £2.30, £2.90; EX 114.80.There was no bid for the winner.
Owner Hambleton Racing Ltd VIII **Bred** Watership Down Stud **Trained** Hambleton, N Yorks

FOCUS
An average affair for the grade in which the winner made all.

NOTEBOOK
Shifting Gold(IRE), tried in blinkers instead of cheekpieces, was drawn in stall 16 but was driven to get across and secure the early lead and seemed to enjoy bowling along in front. He was clear early in the home straight and, although he was reaching the end of his tether close home, the line was always going to come in time for him. He is obviously suited by turning tracks and testing ground.

Hollow Green(IRE), who already had a lot to do when she was hampered by Jaubertie with just under half a mile to run, went after the winner with 2f left and was closing him down in the last few strides. This was her first run at this level since her win over 7f in heavy ground at Leicester. (op 7-1 tchd 4-1)

Strikemaster(IRE), down in class, was last turning into the long straight, but he stayed on quite well down the outside to grab third. He could be worth another go over 1m2f. (op 16-1 tchd 17-2)

Fruitful Job(IRE), upped in trip and with the cheekpieces back on, ran a creditable race, chasing the winner and sticking on for fourth. He now gets a handicap mark.

Cherry Belle(IRE), another with form in this grade, was inconvenienced in a chain reaction involving her stablemate Hollow Green before plugging on late. (op 11-2 tchd 5-1)

Aziz(IRE) was well beaten at 100/1 in three maidens and this was slightly more encouraging. (op 40-1)

Jonah's Cruising(IRE) sold out of Mark Wallace's yard after winning a 7f Kempton claimer, was the pick on adjusted BHA figures, but after being dropped in from her high stall she was never able to get involved. Official explanation: jockey said filly was never travelling (op 5-2)

7080 OATH MAIDEN STKS (C&G) — 1m 75y

1:40 (1:41) (Class 4) 2-Y-O — £4,533 (£1,348; £674; £336) Stalls Low

Form — RPR

03 **1** **Jedi**[13] 6760 2-9-0 0 ... RyanMoore 8 — 78
(Sir Michael Stoute) *hld up in tch: hdwy on outer over 2f out: rdn to chse ldrs over 1f out: styd on to ld ins fnl f* **10/3**[2]

2 **2** *nk* **Dome Rocket**[17] 6674 2-9-0 0 ... ShaneKelly 5 — 77
(W J Knight) *trckd ldrs: hdwy over 3f out: cl up 2f out: rdn over 1f out: led ent fnl f: drvn and hdd ins fnl f: kpt on* **5/2**[1]

035 **3** *nk* **Decision**[15] 6720 2-9-0 79 ... SteveDrowne 4 — 77
(C G Cox) *a.p: cl up 1/2-way: rdn to ld briefly over 1f out: drvn and hdd ent fnl f: kpt on wl* **6/1**

30 **4** *1 1/4* **Sixties Swinger (USA)**[17] 6674 2-9-0 0 ... PhilipRobinson 9 — 74
(M A Jarvis) *led: rdn along 2f out: sn drvn and hdd: wknd ins fnl f* **8/1**

6 **5** *1* **Advisor (FR)**[21] 6580 2-9-0 0 ... JamieSpencer 13 — 72
(M L W Bell) *trckd ldrs: effrt over 2f out: rdn wl over 1f out: kpt on same pce ins fnl f* **4/1**[3]

03 **6** *3* **Tilos Gem (IRE)**[41] 6057 2-9-0 0 ... GregFairley 15 — 66
(M Johnston) *t.k.h: cl up: rdn along over 2f out: grad wknd* **12/1**

00 **7** *1 1/4* **Canmoss (USA)**[32] 6282 2-9-0 0 ... DaneO'Neill 10 — 63
(E J O'Neill) *in rr: hdwy wl over 2f out: rdn and kpt on ins fnl f: nrst fin* **66/1**

05 **8** *1/2* **Musigny (USA)**[21] 6581 2-9-0 0 ... RobertWinston 3 — 62
(W Jarvis) *in tch on inner: hdwy 3f out: effrt to chal 2f out and ev ch: sn rdn and wknd appr fnl f* **25/1**

0 **9** *3 1/4* **Teddy West (IRE)**[18] 6655 2-9-0 0 ... TonyHamilton 12 — 55
(Mrs L Williamson) *in rr tl sme late hdwy* **250/1**

10 *6* **Just Dan** 2-9-0 0 ... GrahamGibbons 16 — 43
(R Hollinshead) *dwlt: a towards rr* **100/1**

00 **11** *1 1/2* **Pattern Mark**[12] 6789 2-9-0 0 ... PaulMulrennan 1 — 39
(Ollie Pears) *hld up: a in rr* **150/1**

0 **12** *8* **Myshkin**[12] 6778 2-9-0 0 ...(b[1]) TedDurcan 2 — 23
(M A Jarvis) *a towards rr* **40/1**

00 **13** *1 3/4* **Fire King**[28] 6398 2-8-11 0 ...(v[1]) KevinGhunowa(3) 14 — 19
(J A Geake) *in tch: rdn along over 3f out and sn wknd* **200/1**

0 **14** *8* **Bluebaru**[103] 4169 2-9-0 0 ... JamieMoriarty 11 — —
(L R James) *a in rr* **150/1**

5 **15** *20* **Mister Wilberforce**[69] 5200 2-8-11 0 ...(p) RussellKennemore(3) 6 — —
(Mrs L Williamson) *midfield: rdn along over 3f out and sn wknd* **150/1**

1m 50.2s (4.80) **Going Correction** +0.65s/f (Yiel) — **15** Ran SP% **116.4**

Speed ratings (Par 97): **102,101,101,100,99 96,94,94,91,85 83,75,73,65,45**

toteswinger: 1&2 £3.50, 1&3 £5.40, 2&3 £5.00. CSF £11.38 TOTE £3.90: £1.80, £1.40, £1.90; EX 14.30.

Owner Philip Newton **Bred** Philip Newton **Trained** Newmarket, Suffolk

FOCUS

Solid maiden form with the front three setting the standard.

NOTEBOOK

Jedi ◆ enhanced his stable's already excellent record in this maiden and opened his account at the third time of asking. He had run distinctly green on his two previous outings, including over course and distance 13 days earlier, and again looked inexperienced. His rider sensibly wound him up for his effort earlier this time, and he mowed down rivals on the outside of the pack to win with a little up his sleeve. No doubt staying will be his game next season and this Derby entry is the type his trainer tends to excel with, so his three-year-old debut will be eagerly anticipated. (tchd 11-4 and 7-2)

Dome Rocket ◆, second at big odds on his debut at Goodwood 17 days earlier, showed a more professional attitude and did nothing wrong in defeat. He is another who will enjoy racing over middle distances next year and should make up into a nice handicapper, but can go one better in similar company before the season is out. (op 11-4 tchd 10-3)

Decision stuck gamely to his task and ran close to his recent level in defeat, helping to set the level of the form. He may prefer a switch to nurseries. (op 12-1)

Sixties Swinger(USA) had his chance and, despite lacking a gear change, finished closer to the runner-up than at Goodwood last time. He looks the type to do better with a winter on his back and now qualifies for a mark. (op 11-1)

Advisor(FR) improved on the level of his debut sixth over course and distance three weeks earlier, but paid late on for running freely through the early parts and may be better off dropping in trip for the short term. (op 2-1)

7081 CLEAN WASTE SOLUTIONS H'CAP — 5f 13y

2:10 (2:11) (Class 5) (0-75,75) 3-Y-O+ — £3,238 (£963; £481; £240) Stalls High

Form — RPR

3035 **1** **Cape Royal**[4] 6990 8-8-10 70 ...(t) KevinGhunowa(3) 8 — 81
(J M Bradley) *awlkward s: sn chsng ldrs: hdwy 2f out: rdn to ld over 1f out: kpt on u.p ins fnl f* **10/1**

5232 **2** *1/2* **Make My Dream**[13] 6750 5-9-0 71 ... TPO'Shea 3 — 80
(J Gallagher) *midfield: hdwy wl over 1f out: swtchd lft and rdn ent fnl f: kpt on wl towards fin* **5/1**

2265 **3** *3/4* **Matterofact (IRE)**[13] 6750 5-8-12 69 ... TGMcLaughlin 9 — 75
(M S Saunders) *trckd ldrs: hdwy 2f out: rdn ent fnl f and ev ch tl drvn and nt qckn fnl 100yds* **11/1**

6055 **4** *3/4* **King Of Swords (IRE)**[10] 6840 4-8-13 70 ... KimTinkler 6 — 73
(N Tinkler) *chsd ldrs: hdwy wl over 1f out: sn rdn and kpt on ins fnl f* **28/1**

1301 **5** *1/2* **Dragon Flame (IRE)**[13] 6766 5-8-11 68 ... ShaneKelly 13 — 70
(M Quinn) *prom: rdn along over 1f out: drvn and one pce ent fnl f* **11/1**

5602 **6** *1/2* **Hereford Boy**[8] 6881 4-8-13 75 ...(b) JamesO'Reilly(5) 7 — 75
(D K Ivory) *dwlt and rr: hdwy wl over 1f out: sn rdn and kpt on ins fnl f: nrst fin* **11/2**[2]

4100 **7** *1/2* **Blessed Place**[28] 6388 8-8-10 67 ...(t) DaneO'Neill 10 — 65
(D J S Ffrench Davis) *led: rdn along wl over 1f out: sn hdd and grad wknd* **28/1**

2040 **8** *nk* **Feelin Foxy**[28] 6388 4-8-13 70 ... TPQueally 11 — 67
(J G Given) *cl up: rdn along 2f out: drvn and edgd rt over 1f out and ent fnl f: sn wknd* **16/1**

0542 **9** *nse* **Nickel Silver**[13] 6765 3-8-11 68 ... TomEaves 2 — 65
(B Smart) *trckd ldrs: gd hdwy on outer 2f out: sn rdn and wknd appr fnl f* **5/1**[1]

1143 **10** *1/2* **Highland Warrior**[37] 6164 9-9-4 75 ... JamieMoriarty 15 — 70
(P T Midgley) *dwlt and towards rr: hdwy 2f out: rdn and keeping on whn n.m.r ent fnl f: sn no imp* **7/1**[3]

3355 **11** *1/2* **Angle Of Attack (IRE)**[8] 6881 3-8-9 73 ... JamesRogers(7) 14 — 66
(A D Brown) *in tch: hdwy to chse ldrs 2f out: sn rdn and edgd lft over 1f out: wknd* **16/1**

4156 **12** *1/2* **Killer Class**[40] 6066 3-8-6 68 ... KellyHarrison(5) 12 — 59+
(J S Goldie) *trckd ldrs: effrt whn n.m.r over 1f out: swtchd rt and rdn whn nt clr run ent fnl f and again ins fnl f: nt rcvr* **8/1**

2000 **13** *1 1/4* **Shes Minnie**[9] 6859 5-9-3 74 ... RobertWinston 4 — 61
(J G M O'Shea) *sn outpcd and a in rr* **50/1**

62.30 secs (1.60) **Going Correction** +0.40s/f (Good) — **13** Ran SP% **118.7**

Speed ratings (Par 103): **103,102,101,99,99 98,97,96,96,96 95,94,92**

toteswinger: 1&2 £6.30, 1&3 £17.40, 2&3 £11.60. CSF £58.06 CT £571.27 TOTE £10.00: £3.20, £1.50, £4.40; EX 54.20.

Owner E A Hayward **Bred** D R Brotherton **Trained** Sedbury, Gloucs

FOCUS

An ordinary sprint handicap in which Cape Royal did not even need to match this year's best. Solid form.

Killer Class Official explanation: jockey said filly was denied a clear run

7082 RACING UK ON CHANNEL 432 MAIDEN STKS — 5f 13y

2:40 (2:40) (Class 5) 2-Y-O — £2,914 (£867; £433; £216) Stalls High

Form — RPR

1 **Affluent** 2-8-12 0 ... SteveDrowne 4 — 70+
(R Charlton) *hld up: hdwy 2f out: cl up over 1f out: shkn up and qckned to ld ins fnl f: comf* **9/4**[2]

2252 **2** *1 1/2* **Silent Wonder**[13] 6764 2-9-3 73 ... TomEaves 2 — 69
(R M H Cowell) *cl up: led 2f out: jnd and rdn over 1f out: drvn and hdd ins fnl f: one pce* **11/8**[1]

4 **3** *1 1/4* **Mister Tinktastic (IRE)**[28] 6383 2-9-3 0 ... TonyHamilton 6 — 65
(M Dods) *t.k.h: cl up: rdn along wl over 1f out: kpt on same pce ins fnl f* **11/2**[3]

0 **4** *3 1/4* **Oceanic Dancer (IRE)**[12] 6785 2-8-9 0 ... RussellKennemore(3) 7 — 48
(Mrs L Williamson) *cl up: led briefly 1/2-way: sn rdn and hdd 2f out: hung lft and wknd wl over 1f out* **66/1**

0040 **5** *nk* **Louie's Lad**[23] 6540 2-9-3 49 ...(p) DaneO'Neill 3 — 52
(J A Geake) *led: rdn along and hdd 1/2-way: sn wknd* **50/1**

0 **6** *1 3/4* **Solis**[34] 6230 2-9-3 0 ... GrahamGibbons 8 — 46
(J J Quinn) *s.i.s: rr tl effrt and sme hdwy 1/2-way: sn rdn: hung lft and wknd* **12/1**

3 **7** *1/2* **Breakevie (IRE)**[22] 6545 2-8-12 0 ... JamieMoriarty 5 — 39
(R A Fahey) *chsd ldrs: rdn along 2f out: sn wknd* **9/1**

8 *18* **You'relikemefrank** 2-9-3 0 ... DavidAllan 1 — —
(J Balding) *wnt lft s: a in rr: wl outpcd fnl 2f* **40/1**

62.99 secs (2.29) **Going Correction** +0.40s/f (Good) — **8** Ran SP% **111.8**

Speed ratings (Par 95): **97,94,92,87,86 84,83,54**

toteswinger: 1&2 £1.50, 1&3 £2.50, 2&3 £2.30. CSF £5.40 TOTE £3.00: £1.10, £1.10, £1.70; EX 6.20.

Owner K Abdulla **Bred** Juddmonte Farms Ltd **Trained** Beckhampton, Wilts

FOCUS

A weak maiden in terms of overall strength, but the winner impressed and looks a nice handicap prospect for next year.

NOTEBOOK

Affluent is related to five winners, most notably Deportivo, who progressed to win a Group 2 as a three-year-old. She was relatively easy to back for this racecourse bow considering it looked an ordinary heat, but knew her job and won cosily in the end. She took time to find her full stride, but it was clear at the furlong marker she was the one to be on and she scored without her rider having to resort to the whip. This ground was little problem and, using the runner-up as a guide, she can now expect an official mark in the high 70s. (op 5-2 tchd 3-1)

Silent Wonder again managed to find one too good and has now finished second on four of his five career starts. Time may tell he bumped into a decent newcomer and with an official mark of 73 he may be better off in nurseries, though he does have a little to prove with his attitude. (op 5-4 tchd 11-10)

Mister Tinktastic(IRE) ◆, well backed, improved on the level of his Newcastle debut without being able to muster the speed of the first pair on this drop back to the minimum trip. He has some scope and ought to fare better when becoming eligible for a mark after his next run. (op 10-1)

Oceanic Dancer(IRE) raced more towards the stands' side and showed early speed, but failed to see out her race that well despite this being a drop in trip. She will be more interesting when qualified for a nursery mark. (tchd 80-1)

Louie's Lad displayed early dash, but was a spent force nearing the final furlong and with an official mark of 49 he helps to put the form into some perspective.

7083 CLEANEVENT H'CAP — 1m 75y

3:10 (3:10) (Class 4) (0-85,85) 3-Y-O+ — £7,447 (£2,216; £1,107; £553) Stalls Low

Form — RPR

0140 **1** **Angel Rock (IRE)**[27] 6424 3-8-13 80 ... TedDurcan 2 — 89
(M Botti) *led: rdn along and hdd wl over 1f out: drvn and rallied ent fnl f: styd on gamely to ld fnl 50yds* **16/1**

2112 **2** *nk* **Rhadegunda**[20] 6605 3-9-3 84 ... RyanMoore 1 — 92
(J H M Gosden) *trckd wnr: hdwy to ld wl over 1f out: rdn ent fnl f: sn drvn and edgd lft: hdd and no ex fnl 50yds* **13/8**[1]

0550 **3** *1 3/4* **Harvest Warrior**[5] 6950 6-8-8 72 ...(v[1]) DavidAllan 7 — 76
(T D Easterby) *dwlt: t.k.h and sn chsng ldng pair: hdwy on inner 2f out and sn ev ch tl rdn and one pce ent fnl f* **9/1**

4313 **4** *nk* **Jennie Jerome (IRE)**[44] 5964 3-8-10 77 ... DaneO'Neill 3 — 80+
(L M Cumani) *trckd ldrs: effrt over 2f out: sn rdn and sltly outpcd: drvn and styd on ins fnl f* **10/3**[2]

4306 **5** *nk* **Kingsdale Orion (IRE)**[50] 5772 4-9-7 85 ... JamieSpencer 9 — 88
(B Ellison) *hld up in tch: effrt over 2f out: rdn and edgd lft over 1f out: swtchd outside and kpt on ins fnl f: nrst fin* **4/1**[3]

34-6 **6** *4 1/2* **Ebert**[218] 1016 5-9-5 83 ... JamieMoriarty 8 — 75
(R A Fahey) *hld up: a in rr* **25/1**

0220 **7** *3 1/4* **Blue Spinnaker (IRE)**[13] 6763 9-9-0 85 ... BradleyRoper(7) 6 — 70
(M W Easterby) *hld up: a in rr* **8/1**

1m 51.57s (6.17) **Going Correction** +0.65s/f (Yiel)

WFA 3 from 4yo+ 3lb — **7** Ran SP% **112.0**

Speed ratings (Par 105): **95,94,92,92,92 87,84**

toteswinger: 1&2 £4.20 1&3 £8.90, 2&3 £4.00. CSF £40.90 CT £256.62 TOTE £17.70: £5.30, £1.40; EX 58.10.

Owner Tenuta Dorna Di Montaltuzzo SRL **Bred** Ascagnano S P A **Trained** Newmarket, Suffolk

FOCUS
A fair handicap in which the winner dictated a modest pace. Nothing got into the race from off the speed with the order changing very little. The form is rated through the third.

7084 PADDOCKS WEDDING VENUE WITH A DIFFERENCE MAIDEN STKS 1m 75y
3:40 (3:42) (Class 5) 3-Y-O £3,238 (£963; £481; £240) Stalls Low

Form RPR
52 **1** **Cara's Request (AUS)**[28] 6393 3-8-6 0 .... JamieSpencer 9 78+
(L M Cumani) *mde all: wd st to stands' rail: rdn and qckly clr 2f out: easily* **4/7**[1]
44 **2** 4 ½ **Manere Bay**[16] 6705 3-8-12 0 .... TedDurcan 11 61
(J L Dunlop) *hld up: hdwy 3f out: rdn to chse wnr 2f out: no imp appr last* **6/1**[2]
5 **3** ½ **Gargano (IRE)**[61] 5453 3-9-3 0 .... GregFairley 12 65
(M Johnston) *chsd wnr: rdn along over 2f out and sn one pce* **13/2**[3]
4 3 ¾ **Wing Diva (IRE)** 3-8-12 0 .... TomEaves 8 51
(B Smart) *hld up in rr: hdwy 3f out: rdn to chse ldrs fnl 2f: no imp* **16/1**
5 1 ¼ **Supaverdi (USA)** 3-8-12 0 .... SteveDrowne 6 48
(H Morrison) *chsd ldrs: rdn along 3f out: sn wknd* **8/1**
0- **6** 8 **Benitez Bond**[415] 5281 3-9-3 0 .... DavidAllan 10 35
(G R Oldroyd) *prom: rdn along over 3f out and sn wknd* **80/1**
0 **7** 6 **Peedee**[141] 2912 3-8-7 0 .... NataliaGemelova(5) 1 16
(G R Oldroyd) *chsd ldrs on inner: rdn along 1/2-way: sn wknd and bhd* **150/1**
8 5 **Highland Relish** 3-8-10 0 .... MatthewDavies(7) 5 10
(George Baker) *a in rr* **25/1**

1m 50.89s (5.49) **Going Correction** +0.65s/f (Yiel) **8 Ran SP% 114.0**
Speed ratings (Par 101): **98,93,93,89,88 80,74,69**
toteswinger: 1&2 £1.80, 1&3 £2.40, 2&3 £2.80. CSF £4.46 TOTE £1.50: £1.02, £1.60, £1.90; EX 4.50.
Owner Stewart Aitken **Bred** S Aitkin **Trained** Newmarket, Suffolk

FOCUS
This was a moderate maiden for three-year-olds and the time was slower than that for the seller. The easy winner was value for extra, with the runner-up the chief guide to the form.

7085 SAWFISH SOFTWARE H'CAP (FOR LADY AMATEUR RIDERS) 1m 2f 50y
4:10 (4:10) (Class 6) (0-65,65) 3-Y-O+ £2,307 (£709; £354) Stalls Low

Form RPR
3052 **1** **Dream Of Olwyn (IRE)**[9] 6862 3-9-13 **62** .... MissSBrotherton 9 69
(J G Given) *chsd ldrs on outer: hdwy to ld over 3f out: rdn clr over 1f out: kpt on* **7/2**[1]
4361 **2** 2 ¼ **Ba Dreamflight**[13] 6753 3-9-1 **55** ow3 .... MissVCartmel(5) 10 58
(H Morrison) *trckd ldrs: hdwy 3f out: rdn to chse wnr wl over 1f out: drvn and no imp ins fnl f* **7/1**
435 **3** ¾ **Proficiency**[37] 6163 3-9-9 **58** .... MrsCBartley 3 59
(T D Walford) *cl up: led over 4f out: rdn along and hdd over 3f out: drvn wl over 1f out and kpt on same pce* **33/1**
255- **4** hd **Jocheski (IRE)**[181] 6421 4-10-2 **60** .... MissCHannaford 14 61+
(A G Newcombe) *hld up towards rr: hdwy on wd outside over 2f out: sn rdn and styd on ins fnl f: nrst fin* **8/1**
0445 **5** ½ **Giddywell**[15] 6719 4-9-7 **51** .... MissADeniel 7 51
(R Hollinshead) *dwlt and hld up towards rr: hdwy over 3f out: rdn to chse ldrs over 2f out: kpt on same pce appr fnl f* **9/2**[2]
0030 **6** 7 **Trouble Mountain (USA)**[15] 6726 11-10-2 **63** .... (t) MissJCoward(3) 5 49
(M W Easterby) *chsd ldrs: rdn along and lost pl 1/2-way: n.d after* **14/1**
-100 **7** nk **Crispian (IRE)**[28] 6396 4-9-9 **60** .... MissALMurphy(7) 1 45
(Jamie Snowden) *dwlt: hdwy on inner over 3f out: sn rdn along and no imp fnl 2f* **50/1**
6005 **8** ½ **Rub Of The Relic (IRE)**[10] 6836 3-9-1 **55** .... MissWGibson(5) 13 39
(P T Midgley) *a towards rr* **33/1**
0220 **9** nk **Jenny Soba**[4] 6983 5-10-0 **65** .... MissStefaniaGandola(7) 11 48
(Lucinda Featherstone) *dwlt: a towards rr* **10/1**
0202 **10** 1 ¼ **Thornaby Green**[12] 6786 7-10-0 **58** .... MissGDGracey-Davison 8 39
(T D Barron) *in tch: rdn along over 4f out and sn wknd* **12/1**
2033 **11** ¾ **Emperor's Well**[12] 6786 9-9-11 **60** .... (b) MissJoannaMason(5) 4 39
(M W Easterby) *led: rdn along and hdd over 4f out: drvn 3f out and sn wknd* **16/1**
6202 **12** 6 **Black Falcon (IRE)**[6] 6927 8-9-7 **51** oh2 .... MissFayeBramley 12 18
(John A Harris) *chsd ldrs: rdn along over 3f out and sn wknd* **6/1**[3]

2m 18.66s (6.16) **Going Correction** +0.65s/f (Yiel)
WFA 3 from 4yo+ 5lb **12 Ran SP% 115.5**
Speed ratings (Par 101): **101,99,98,98,98 92,92,91,91,90 89,85**
toteswinger: 1&2 £7.50, 1&3 £10.10, 2&3 £26.00. CSF £26.65 CT £689.38 TOTE £4.20: £2.00, £2.50, £4.60; EX 32.80 Place 6: £20.56 Place 5: £4.88.
Owner Alex Owen **Bred** Crandon Park Stud **Trained** Willoughton, Lincs

FOCUS
A moderate handicap, confined to lady amateur riders. The pace was not bad, but again it paid to race prominently. The form is sound enough.
T/Plt: £52.40 to a £1 stake. Pool: £42,736.73. 594.31 winning tickets. T/Qpdt: £5.00 to a £1 stake. Pool: £3,308.50. 489.35 winning tickets. JR

7086 - 7087a (Foreign Racing) - See Raceform Interactive

7064
GREAT LEIGHS (A.W) (L-H)
Thursday, October 30

OFFICIAL GOING: Standard
Wind: Moderate, across

7088 GREATLEIGHS.COM H'CAP 1m (P)
6:20 (6:20) (Class 6) (0-60,59) 3-Y-O £1,942 (£578; £288; £144) Stalls Centre

Form RPR
505 **1** **Greek Theatre (USA)**[14] 6754 3-9-4 59 .... JerryO'Dwyer 4 64
(P S McEntee) *led to post: mde all: rdn wl over 1f out: clr over 1f out: kpt on: eased towards fin* **10/1**
0545 **2** 1 ¼ **Miss Understanding**[60] 5544 3-8-4 45 .... (v[1]) ChrisCatlin 8 47
(J R Weymes) *sn bhd and rdn along: c wd 2f out: hdwy over 1f out: r.o wl fnl f: snatched 2nd last strides: nvr able to chal wnr* **16/1**
4012 **3** ½ **Margot Mine (IRE)**[8] 6912 3-8-8 52 .... (bt) LukeMorris(3) 1 53
(J S Moore) *dwlt: sn bustled along in midfield: hdwy u.p on inner over 2f out: chsd wnr jst ins fnl f: no imp: lost 2nd last stride* **13/8**[1]
-404 **4** 4 **Felicia**[18] 6685 3-9-0 55 .... NCallan 5 47
(S C Williams) *dwlt: sn wl in tch: chsd wnr 2f out: sn no hdwy u.p: lost 2 pls fnl f* **9/4**[2]
3004 **5** 3 **Telephonist**[8] 6912 3-8-8 49 .... AlanMunro 11 34
(J R Best) *racd in midfield: rdn and effrt over 2f out: nvr trbld ldrs* **9/1**[3]
0400 **6** shd **Jimmy Dean**[14] 6752 3-8-4 45 .... (vt[1]) WilliamBuick 2 30
(M Wellings) *a towards rr: modest late hdwy: n.d* **22/1**
000 **7** 1 ½ **Tuxedo**[99] 4302 3-8-4 45 .... SaleemGolam 6 26
(P W Hiatt) *hung rt thrght: pressed wnr tl 2f out: sn hrd drvn and wknd* **12/1**
5000 **8** 5 **Fly In Johnny (IRE)**[24] 6541 3-7-13 45 .... (b[1]) NicolPolli(5) 10 15
(M R Hoad) *chsd ldrs: hrd rdn over 2f out: sn wknd* **28/1**
060 **9** 53 **Actress Annie**[22] 6571 3-8-4 45 .... HayleyTurner 9 —
(Mike Murphy) *hung bdly rt thrght: a bhd: t.o and virtually p.u fr over 3f out* **20/1**

1m 40.12s (0.22) **Going Correction** +0.025s/f (Slow) **9 Ran SP% 114.1**
Speed ratings (Par 99): **99,97,97,93,90 90,88,83,30**
CSF £145.54 CT £394.67 TOTE £11.50: £3.00, £2.40, £1.10; EX 122.50.
Owner Eventmaker Racehorses **Bred** Formal Gold Llc **Trained** Newmarket, Suffolk
■ Phil McEntee's first winner since serving a 12-month suspension.

FOCUS
A very moderate bunch lined up for this three-year-old handicap and most of them struggled to lay up with the strong early pace, but there were surprisingly few closers. The winner made all at a good pace and is rated to something like his 2yo form.
Greek Theatre(USA) Official explanation: trainer said, regarding the apparent improvement in form, that gelding appeared to benefit from a considerable drop in trip.
Tuxedo Official explanation: jockey said gelding hung right throughout
Actress Annie Official explanation: jockey said filly hung badly right

7089 ASPEN (S) STKS 1m 5f 66y(P)
6:50 (6:50) (Class 6) 3-Y-O+ £2,590 (£770; £385; £192) Stalls Low

Form RPR
-012 **1** **Veloso (FR)**[5] 6985 6-9-6 70 .... TolleyDean(3) 7 72+
(A J McCabe) *t.k.h: hdwy to chse ldr over 4f out: led 2f out: sn pushed clr: v easily* **1/2**[1]
0400 **2** 2 ¾ **Zuwaar**[10] 6862 3-9-1 67 .... ChrisCatlin 5 66
(Ian Williams) *stdd and dropped in bhd after s: pushed along over 6f out: outpcd 3f out: rallied u.p over 1f out: wnt 2nd ins fnl f: no ch w wnr* **7/1**[2]
0000 **3** 2 ½ **Shenandoah Girl**[12] 6806 5-9-4 55 .... (e[1]) NCallan 11 57
(Miss Gay Kelleway) *hld up in last trio: hdwy over 4f out: chsd ldr over 1f out: no imp: lost 2nd ins fnl f* **14/1**[3]
5000 **4** 1 ½ **Fantasy Ride**[24] 6538 6-9-9 56 .... JerryO'Dwyer 1 60
(J Pearce) *chsd ldr tl over 9f out: chsd ldrs after: nt clr run wl over 1f out: rdn and one pce fr over 1f out* **16/1**
6500 **5** 4 **Fateful Attraction**[13] 6775 5-8-12 56 .... (b) AlanMunro 10 43
(I A Wood) *chsd ldrs: wnt 2nd over 9f out: led 5f out tl 2f out: sn rdn: wknd over 1f out* **7/1**[2]
0056 **6** 3 ½ **Mighty Kitchener (USA)**[80] 4932 5-9-3 40 .... ShaneKelly 9 43
(P Howling) *hld up in rr: rdn and effrt over 2f out: no hdwy: nvr trbld ldrs* **25/1**
-000 **7** 1 **Amicus**[15] 6728 3-8-4 49 .... SaleemGolam 6 36
(D K Ivory) *stdd and dropped in bhd after s: rdn and no rspnse 3f out: nvr a factor* **50/1**
0-00 **8** 78 **Allahor**[23] 6560 3-8-9 55 .... JamesDoyle 4 —
(D J S Ffrench Davis) *t.k.h: led tl 5f out: sn dropped out and bhd: t.o and virtually p.u last 2f* **20/1**

2m 54.56s (0.96) **Going Correction** +0.025s/f (Slow)
WFA 3 from 5yo+ 8lb **8 Ran SP% 114.8**
Speed ratings (Par 101): **98,96,94,93,91 89,88,40**
CSF £4.42 TOTE £1.10: £1.02, £2.50, £3.70; EX 5.60.The winner was bought in for 8,000gns.
Owner Brian Morton **Bred** Jean Louis Pariente **Trained** Babworth, Notts

FOCUS
A standard seller run at a very steady early pace and in a slow time. The winner ran to his recent best but his main rivals have been below form recently. The third and fourth were close to their marks.

7090 PURPLE H'CAP 6f (P)
7:20 (7:22) (Class 6) (0-65,65) 3-Y-O+ £2,590 (£770; £385; £192) Stalls Low

Form RPR
3204 **1** **Billy Red**[8] 6907 4-8-10 **55** .... (b) TPQueally 2 67
(J R Jenkins) *mde all: rdn clr over 1f out: in n.d fnl f: rdn out* **14/1**
0130 **2** 3 ½ **Avoca Dancer (IRE)**[9] 6889 5-9-3 **62** .... (v[1]) ChrisCatlin 3 63
(Miss Gay Kelleway) *racd in midfield: hdwy u.p 2f out: kpt on u.p to go 2nd ins fnl f: no ch w wnr* **14/1**
2436 **3** ¾ **Norcroft**[18] 6680 6-9-0 **59** .... WilliamBuick 4 57
(Mrs C A Dunnett) *towards rr: rdn over 2f out: edgd out rt fr over 1f out: styd on u.p fnl f: wnt 3rd nr fin: nvr trbld wnr* **7/1**[3]
0000 **4** ½ **Top Bid**[26] 6486 4-8-10 **55** .... (b) DavidAllan 7 52
(T D Easterby) *chsd ldr: drvn and unable qck over 1f out: no ch w wnr fnl f: lost 2 pls ins fnl f* **20/1**
0000 **5** shd **Muktasb (USA)**[36] 6209 7-9-1 **60** .... (v) AdamKirby 5 56+
(D Shaw) *s.i.s: bhd: hdwy and rdn wl over 1f out: styd on fnl f: nvr trbld ldrs* **25/1**
0000 **6** ¾ **Follow The Flag (IRE)**[20] 6634 4-9-2 **64** .... (p) JackMitchell(3) 13 58
(A J McCabe) *towards rr: rdn 1/2-way: drvn over 1f out: kpt on ins fnl f: nvr nr wnr* **10/1**
0506 **7** ¾ **Elkhorn**[17] 6706 6-9-4 **63** .... (v) TomEaves 11 55
(Miss J A Camacho) *racd in midfield: drvn and effrt wl over 1f out: sn no imp* **9/1**
0600 **8** nk **Sovereignty (JPN)**[3] 7013 6-9-3 **62** .... SaleemGolam 14 53
(D K Ivory) *racd towards rr on outer: rdn and effrt over 2f out: nvr trbld ldrs* **25/1**
0224 **9** ¾ **Elusive Dreams (USA)**[20] 6631 4-8-11 **59** .... (v) TolleyDean(3) 9 47
(P Howling) *s.i.s: bhd: rdn 4f out: sme hdwy fnl f: n.d* **9/2**[1]
0020 **10** ½ **George The Second**[18] 6681 5-8-10 **55** .... RichardKingscote 10 44
(Miss Tor Sturgis) *chsd ldng pair: rdn and struggling jst over 2f out: wknd over 1f out: eased whn wl btn fnl f* **10/1**
0005 **11** nk **Shot To Fame (USA)**[13] 6774 9-9-4 **63** .... JimmyFortune 6 49
(S Kirk) *hld up in rr: shkn up ent fnl f: kpt on same pce: nvr nr ldrs* **10/1**
4402 **12** 6 **Grizedale (IRE)**[18] 6679 9-8-10 **55** .... (tp) IanMongan 8 22
(M J Attwater) *hld up in tch: drvn and effrt on inner wl over 2f out: sn nt qckn: wl btn fnl f* **5/1**[2]
6006 **13** ½ **Scarlet Oak**[10] 6864 4-8-11 **61** .... NicolPolli(5) 12 26
(A M Hales) *a towards rr: n.d* **16/1**
03 **14** 3 ¾ **Promise Of Love**[20] 6633 3-9-5 **65** .... HayleyTurner 1 18
(Miss Amy Weaver) *chsd ldrs: rdn 1/2-way: sn lost pl: wl bhd fnl f* **20/1**

1m 12.46s (-1.24) **Going Correction** +0.025s/f (Slow)
WFA 3 from 4yo+ 1lb **14 Ran SP% 121.1**
Speed ratings (Par 101): **109,104,103,102,102 101,100,100,99,98 98,90,89,84**
CSF £187.03 CT £993.91 TOTE £16.40: £5.40, £3.50, £2.60; EX 162.90.
Owner Mrs Irene Hampson **Bred** D R Tucker **Trained** Royston, Herts

FOCUS
A modest sprint handicap, and they didn't want to know the inside rail in the straight. The winner made all and is rated back to his best.
Elusive Dreams(USA) Official explanation: jockey said gelding missed the break
Grizedale(IRE) Official explanation: jockey had no explanation for the poor form shown

7091 BLUE TIT H'CAP — 1m 5f 66y(P)
7:50 (7:50) (Class 4) (0-85,79) 3-Y-O — £5,180 (£1,541; £770; £384) Stalls Low

Form — RPR
0513 1 **Precision Break (USA)**[30] 6355 3-9-4 79 NCallan 6 91+
(P F I Cole) *a travelling wl: trckd ldr tl led 3f out: sn clr: rdn over 1f out: styd on wl: eased nr fin* **2/1**[1]
1516 2 6 **Bushy Dell (IRE)**[7] 6934 3-8-9 75 AmyBaker(5) 2 76
(Miss J Feilden) *hld up in tch: rdn over 3f out: no ch w wnr last 2f: wnt modest 2nd fnl 100yds* **16/1**
0411 3 ½ **Graylyn Ruby (FR)**[13] 6775 3-8-11 75 LukeMorris(3) 1 75
(J Jay) *trckd ldrs: rdn wl over 3f out: chsd clr wnr over 2f out: no imp: lost 2nd fnl 100yds* **11/4**[2]
5140 4 12 **Spider Silk**[62] 5464 3-9-1 76 ShaneKelly 5 58
(W Jarvis) *stdd s: hld up in tch: rdn 4f out: sn lost tch: hung lft fnl f* **6/1**
0522 5 8 **Plaisterer**[17] 6703 3-8-11 72 AlanMunro 4 42
(C F Wall) *led: hdd 3f out: flashed tail whn hit w whip: sn wl btn* **11/2**
2264 6 26 **Mista Rossa**[13] 6775 3-8-8 69 TravisBlock 3 —
(H Morrison) *t.k.h: hld up in tch: shkn up over 5f out: lost tch qckly 4f out: virtually p.u last 2f* **9/2**[3]

2m 50.5s (-3.10) **Going Correction** +0.025s/f (Slow) **6** Ran SP% **113.7**
Speed ratings (Par 103): **110,106,106,98,93 77**
CSF £33.17 TOTE £1.70: £2.30, £5.20; EX 17.40.
Owner JMH Lifestyle Ltd **Bred** Gainesway Thoroughbreds Ltd **Trained** Whatcombe, Oxon

FOCUS
An ordinary three-year-old staying handicap. They went no pace early on, but the tempo increased significantly on the final circuit and they finished strung out. The winner enhanced his good Polytrack record but neither the second or third was well treated after recent wins.
Plaisterer Official explanation: trainer's rep said filly did not stay
Mista Rossa Official explanation: trainer's rep had no explanation for the poor form shown

7092 GREAT HORSLEY H'CAP — 5f (P)
8:20 (8:25) (Class 5) (0-70,70) 3-Y-O+ — £3,238 (£963; £481; £240) Stalls Low

Form — RPR
2621 1 **Wreningham**[35] 6224 3-8-7 59 ShaneKelly 3 70
(T Keddy) *mde all: rdn over 1f out: edgd rt u.p fnl f: hld on wl* **9/4**[2]
3151 2 nk **Pride Of Northcare (IRE)**[17] 6711 4-9-2 68 DarrenWilliams 2 78
(D Shaw) *stdd s: hld up towards rr: hdwy wl over 1f out: chsd wnr over 1f out: ev ch ins fnl f: unable qck fnl 100yds* **2/1**[1]
0/00 3 ¾ **Dazzling Bay**[135] 3111 8-9-4 70 DavidAllan 7 77
(T D Easterby) *dwlt: bhd: rdn and hdwy over 1f out: chsd ldng pair ins fnl f: kpt on: nt rch ldng pair* **18/1**
230 4 3 **Monte Major (IRE)**[51] 5770 7-8-5 57 (v) WilliamBuick 10 53
(D Shaw) *chsd ldr: rdn wl over 1f out: edgd lft and one pce ent fnl f* **11/1**
0501 5 ¾ **Multahab**[31] 6339 9-8-11 63 (t) NCallan 4 57
(M Wigham) *chsd ldrs: rdn and hanging rt fr 2f out: kpt on same pce ent fnl f* **6/1**[3]
0/0 6 nk **Great Fox (IRE)**[36] 6204 7-8-5 57 SaleemGolam 6 50
(S C Williams) *hld up in midfield: rdn and effrt over 1f out: hung lft and no prog fnl f* **22/1**
2600 7 1 ¼ **Blakeshall Diamond**[19] 6658 3-9-0 66 J-PGuillambert 12 54
(K G Wingrove) *towards rr on outer: rdn and effrt wd over 2f out: no imp over 1f out* **22/1**
4050 8 ¾ **Smokin Beau**[104] 4154 11-8-12 67 LukeMorris(3) 5 52
(N P Littmoden) *sn pushed along: chsd ldrs tl lost pl 1/2-way: bhd over 1f out* **12/1**
6106 9 12 **Azygous**[14] 6750 5-8-10 62 (v) AlanMunro 1 4
(J Akehurst) *s.i.s: sn wl detached in last pl* **8/1**

59.86 secs (-0.34) **Going Correction** +0.025s/f (Slow) **9** Ran SP% **119.5**
Speed ratings (Par 103): **103,102,101,96,95 94,92,91,72**
CSF £7.48 CT £60.50 TOTE £3.80: £1.70, £1.60, £5.30; EX 9.60.
Owner Mervyn Ayers **Bred** Executive Bloodlines Ltd **Trained** Newmarket, Suffolk
■ Stewards' Enquiry : Shane Kelly one-day ban: careless riding (Nov 14)

FOCUS
A good sprint handicap for the grade, but just as in the two earlier non-staying events, a handy ride proved advantageous, and the inside rail was again a no-go area. The winner is rated to his best nursery form.

7093 PEGASUS MAIDEN FILLIES' STKS — 1m (P)
8:50 (8:53) (Class 4) 2-Y-O — £3,885 (£1,156; £577; £288) Stalls Centre

Form — RPR
632 1 **Charlotte Point (USA)**[8] 6901 2-9-0 0 NCallan 4 76
(P F I Cole) *chsd ldrs tl wnt 2nd over 4f out: rdn to ld over 1f out: styd on wl: comf* **13/8**[1]
4 2 2 ½ **Catamarca (USA)**[18] 6682 2-9-0 0 JimmyFortune 3 71
(J H M Gosden) *chsd ldr tl over 4f out: rdn and unable qck over 2f out: chsd wnr ent fnl f: no imp fnl 100yds* **9/4**[2]
3 1 **Penperth** 2-8-11 0 LukeMorris(3) 5 68
(J M P Eustace) *s.i.s: bhd: pushed along over 4f out: rdn 3f out: hdwy on inner over 1f out: kpt on fnl f: wnt 3rd wl ins fnl f: nvr nr ldrs* **33/1**
4 hd **Luthien (IRE)** 2-9-0 0 AdamKirby 1 68
(W R Swinburn) *s.i.s: hld up in last pair: outpcd 3f out: hdwy over 1f out: kpt on fnl f: wnt 4th nr fin: nvr nr ldrs* **20/1**
03 5 ½ **Breadstick**[18] 6682 2-9-0 0 TravisBlock 9 67
(H Morrison) *sn led: rdn 2f out: hdd over 1f out: wknd ent fnl f* **6/1**[3]
0 6 4 **Arcola (IRE)**[29] 6391 2-9-0 0 RichardMullen 6 58
(D M Simcock) *s.i.s: t.k.h: hld up in midfield: chsd ldng trio and rdn over 2f out: sn outpcd: wl hld fnl f* **12/1**
7 6 **Salamon** 2-9-0 0 NelsonDeSouza 8 45
(P F I Cole) *s.i.s: t.k.h: hld up in midfield tl stdd to rr 5f out: rdn and struggling over 3f out: sn wl bhd* **20/1**
34 8 6 **Surrounded**[22] 6580 2-9-0 0 EdwardCreighton 7 32
(R W Price) *in tch: rdn and struggling over 2f out: wl bhd fr over 1f out* **7/1**
0 9 4 ½ **Blushing Dreamer (IRE)**[43] 6013 2-9-0 0 DarrenWilliams 2 22
(D Shaw) *stdd s: plld hrd: hld up in midfield: rdn and lost tch over 3f out: wl bhd last 2f* **66/1**

1m 40.58s (0.68) **Going Correction** +0.025s/f (Slow) **9** Ran SP% **117.3**
Speed ratings (Par 94): **97,94,93,93,92 88,82,76,72**
CSF £5.22 TOTE £2.60: £1.30, £1.30, £10.20; EX 6.20.
Owner C Wright & The Hon Mrs J M Corbett **Bred** Douglas S Arnold **Trained** Whatcombe, Oxon

FOCUS
An ordinary juvenile fillies' maiden and a straightforward success for Charlotte Point who stepped up on recent efforts. Pretty solid efforts.

NOTEBOOK
Charlotte Point(USA), who has been improving with racing, did what was required having enjoyed the run of the race, but she does not appeal as one to back in better company. (op 9-4)
Catamarca(USA) kept on after the winner got first run, but she was never getting there. A win will boost her paddock value, but she looks modest and it remains to be seen whether she is open to much more improvement. (op 7-4 tchd 5-2)
Penperth has a nice pedigree, being a half-sister to smart 1m2f winner Jedediah, out of a triple 6f-7f winner, and this was a pleasing debut. Having been slowest away, she was trying to make ground when stopped in her run rounding the final bend, but she kept on well against the arguably unfavoured inside rail without being given an unnecessarily hard time. She has the ability to win races. (op 40-1)
Luthien(IRE), who is out of a multiple 1m4f-1m6f winner, was out the back for much of the way, but stayed on nicely under hands-and-heels riding and will know more next time. (tchd 16-1)
Breadstick could not confirm recent course form with Catamarca, but now has the option of handicaps.
Arcola(IRE) is a longer-term prospect, but she still didn't really go on as one might have hoped from her debut effort. (op 14-1)
Surrounded was nowhere near the form she showed in a couple of runs on turf. Official explanation: jockey said filly did not handle the bend (op 12-1)
Blushing Dreamer(IRE) Official explanation: jockey said filly hung right

7094 HOUSE AND JACKSON H'CAP — 1m 2f (P)
9:20 (9:20) (Class 5) (0-70,66) 3-Y-O+ — £3,238 (£963; £481; £240) Stalls Low

Form — RPR
0000 1 **Lord Theo**[22] 6577 4-9-5 62 JamesDoyle 4 68
(N P Littmoden) *mde all: rdn 2f out: edgd rt ins fnl f: hld on wl* **9/2**[2]
5021 2 ½ **Classic Blue (IRE)**[22] 6570 4-8-12 55 WilliamBuick 2 60
(Ian Williams) *chsd ldr tl 4f out: rdn and effrt on inner wl over 1f out: chsd wnr over 1f out: kpt on but nvr quite getting to wnr* **15/8**[1]
/505 3 ¾ **Keel (IRE)**[12] 6826 5-9-2 62 LukeMorris(3) 3 66
(C R Dore) *hld up in tch: rdn over 2f out: disp 2nd ins fnl f: kpt on same pce fnl 100yds* **8/1**
2110 4 2 **Strike Force**[20] 6629 4-9-6 66 JackMitchell(3) 6 66
(K F Clutterbuck) *hld up in last trio: rdn and effrt wl over 1f out: kpt on but nt pce to quite rch ldrs* **5/1**[3]
3505 5 hd **Bavarica**[29] 6395 6-8-13 61 AmyBaker(5) 7 60
(Miss J Feilden) *t.k.h: hld up in last pl tl hdwy on outer to chse wnr 4f out: rdn over 1f out: one pce fnl f* **9/2**[2]
1030 6 2 ½ **Dinner Date**[28] 6422 6-9-7 64 J-PGuillambert 5 58
(T Keddy) *hld up in last trio: dropped to last and rdn over 3f out: swtchd rt wl over 1f out: no imp* **15/2**

2m 9.89s (1.29) **Going Correction** +0.025s/f (Slow) **6** Ran SP% **110.7**
Speed ratings (Par 103): **95,94,94,92,92 90**
CSF £13.01 TOTE £6.40: £2.80, £2.00; EX 8.40 Place 6 £33.35, Place 5 £17.41 .
Owner Mrs Karen Graham **Bred** Mike Perkins **Trained** Newmarket, Suffolk

FOCUS
A modest handicap and messy form with the winner making all - the fourth to do so on the card - at his own pace. The form does not look solid.
T/Plt: £25.40 to a £1 stake. Pool: £87,460.95. 2,509.67 winning tickets. T/Qpdt: £13.70 to a £1 stake. Pool: £6,989.70. 377.20 winning tickets. SP

7022 LINGFIELD (L-H)
Thursday, October 30

OFFICIAL GOING: Standard
Wind: Light, half against Weather: Cloudy becoming fine, cold

7095 EBF BET AT LADBROKES.COM MAIDEN FILLIES' STKS (DIV I) — 7f (P)
12:40 (12:42) (Class 5) 2-Y-O — £4,079 (£1,214; £606; £303) Stalls Low

Form — RPR
44 1 **King's Siren (IRE)**[21] 6601 2-9-0 0 WilliamBuick 9 73
(A M Balding) *hld up in midfield: prog on outer fr 3f out to press ldrs 2f out: shkn up to ld over 1f out: kpt on fnl f* **7/1**
2 ½ **Silk Trail** 2-9-0 0 LDettori 10 72
(Saeed Bin Suroor) *racd wd early: green and hanging in rr: gd prog on outer over 2f out: styd on wl to take 2nd last 50yds* **11/4**[2]
05 3 ¾ **Stellarina (IRE)**[12] 6808 2-9-0 0 TPO'Shea 8 70
(G A Swinbank) *prom: rdn to chse ldr over 2f out: upsides wl over 1f out: chsd wnr after: a hld and lost 2nd last 50yds* **33/1**
24 4 nk **Kouloura (IRE)**[43] 6016 2-9-0 0 NCallan 11 69
(M Botti) *hld up in midfield: gng strly over 2f out: prog over 1f out and swtchd to inner: kpt on same pce fnl f* **7/2**[3]
00 5 hd **Salybia Bay**[15] 6737 2-9-0 0 RyanMoore 6 69
(R Hannon) *trckd ldrs: rdn and effrt over 2f out: kpt on fnl f but nvr able to chal* **20/1**
6 2 ¼ **Novastasia (IRE)** 2-9-0 0 AdamKirby 7 63
(W R Swinburn) *mostly in last trio and rn green: gd prog over 1f out: styd on fnl f: nrst fin* **25/1**
00 7 1 ½ **Clodoline**[30] 6358 2-9-0 0 JoeFanning 13 59
(P F I Cole) *dropped in fr wd draw and hld up in last trio: effrt 2f out: promising hdwy over 1f out but hanging: no imp fnl f* **80/1**
0 8 1 ¾ **Arty Crafty (USA)**[8] 6910 2-9-0 0 J-PGuillambert 4 55+
(Sir Mark Prescott) *hld up towards rr on inner: gng strly over 2f out: nudged along and no prog over 1f out: do bttr* **50/1**
6 9 nk **Downstream**[18] 6677 2-9-0 0 RichardMullen 3 54
(D M Simcock) *prom: chsd ldr over 3f out to over 2f out: grad wknd* **50/1**
06 10 ¾ **Moggy (IRE)**[9] 6885 2-9-0 0 HayleyTurner 12 52
(M L W Bell) *hld up and sn last: modest prog on inner over 1f out: nvr on terms* **20/1**
03 11 ½ **West With The Wind (USA)**[23] 6559 2-9-0 0 AlanMunro 1 69+
(P W Chapple-Hyam) *hld up bhd ldrs on inner: shkn up and effrt over 2f out: trapped bhd wkng early ldr fr over 1f out and lost all ch* **5/2**[1]
02 12 ½ **Freepressionist**[9] 6876 2-9-0 0 JimCrowley 2 50
(R A Teal) *led to over 1f out: wknd rapidly on inner* **14/1**
0 13 12 **Diamond Til (IRE)**[17] 6697 2-9-0 0 SteveDrowne 5 20
(G L Moore) *chsd ldr to 1/2-way: sn wknd u.p: t.o* **33/1**

1m 24.79s (-0.01) **Going Correction** -0.125s/f (Stan) **13** Ran SP% **121.0**
Speed ratings (Par 92): **95,94,93,93,93 90,88,86,86,85 84,84,70**
CSF £24.73 TOTE £8.50: £2.80, £1.90, £9.20; EX 38.20 TRIFECTA Not won..
Owner J C Smith **Bred** Littleton Stud **Trained** Kingsclere, Hants
■ Stewards' Enquiry : L Dettori two-day ban: used whip with excessive frequency without giving filly time to respond (Nov 13-14)

FOCUS
A fair maiden on paper in which the balance of the time and the principals set the level.

NOTEBOOK
King's Siren(IRE) travelled well enough towards the outside of the bunch and kept on in gritty fashion up the centre of the track once into the straight. This track would not have been ideal for her but she looks to be progressing with racing, and it would not be a surprise to see her get a mile in handicap company next year, despite the fact that she is out of that speedy mare Blue Siren. (tchd 8-1)
Silk Trail, a half-sister to five winners, including Middle Park winner Lujain, showed signs of inexperience on her debut but was staying on well at the finish. She should be capable of winning a similar event. (op 3-1 tchd 5-2)
Stellarina(IRE) improved on her turf efforts on this Polytrack debut. Always well placed, she ran a solid race in third, and handicaps now become an option for her. (op 50-1)
Kouloura(IRE), a weak and disappointing favourite on her last start at Kempton, hung left that day so was expected to appreciate going this way round. Well backed in the morning, she kept on between horses, edging towards the rail inside the last, and did not seem to have too many excuses. (tchd 9-2)
Salybia Bay finished clear of the rest in fifth. She is another who is steadily progressing, and now has the option of going handicapping. (op 25-1)
Novastasia(IRE) was staying on steadily at the finish and should benefit considerably from this debut outing. She hails from a winning family – each of her four siblings has won at least one race – so there should be better to come from her. (op 33-1)
West With The Wind(USA), whose Leicester third set the standard here, shaped a lot better than her finishing position suggests. She went for a run up the inside approaching the furlong marker, but the gap closed completely on her and her rider was forced to sit up. She would have been involved in the battle for the places with a clear run. Official explanation: jockey said filly was denied a clear run (tchd 9-4 and 11-4)

7096 PLAY POKER AT LADBROKES.COM H'CAP 1m 2f (P)
1:10 (1:10) (Class 5) (0-75,72) 3-Y-O+ **£2,729** (£806; £403) **Stalls** Low

Form				RPR
316	**1**		**Bridgewater Boys**[101] 4254 7-9-2 **66**....(b) RyanMoore 4 (G L Moore) *mde all: stdy pce early: pressed fr 2f out and hrd rdn after: a jst holding on: all out* **11/4**[2]	74
P305	**2**	*hd*	**Trifti**[44] 5999 7-9-5 **69**.... TravisBlock 5 (Miss Jo Crowley) *trckd wnr: rdn to chal 2f out: almost upsides after but a jst hld* **13/2**	77
3013	**3**	*1 1/4*	**Josr's Magic (IRE)**[9] 6882 4-8-10 **60**.... AlanMunro 2 (H J Collingridge) *hld up in 5th: effrt over 2f out: tried to chal on inner over 1f out: nt qckn and hld fnl f* **7/2**[3]	65
0325	**4**	*2 1/4*	**Potentiale (IRE)**[34] 6243 4-9-8 **72**....(p) MichaelHills 7 (J W Hills) *hld up in 4th: wnt 3rd briefly over 2f out but nt qckn after and readily hld* **2/1**[1]	73
4050	**5**	*2 1/2*	**Monashee Rock (IRE)**[3] 7009 3-9-2 **71**.... TGMcLaughlin 1 (M Salaman) *hld up in detached last: rdn over 2f out: nt qckn and no imp on ldrs after* **16/1**	67
5040	**6**	*4*	**Spanish Diva**[20] 6629 4-8-12 **62**....(v[1]) NCallan 3 (S C Williams) *t.k.h early: trckd ldng pair to wl over 2f out: wkng tamely whn hmpd sn after* **10/1**	50

2m 5.19s (-1.41) **Going Correction** -0.125s/f (Stan)
WFA 3 from 4yo+ 5lb **6** Ran SP% **110.5**
Speed ratings (Par 103): **100,99,98,97,95 91**
CSF £19.63 TOTE £3.60: £2.00, £2.80; EX 16.10.
Owner Matthew Green & Richard Green **Bred** Southill Stud **Trained** Woodingdean, E Sussex

FOCUS
A tactical affair in which Ryan Moore was granted an easy lead. The first pair are rated to form at face value.

7097 EBF BET AT LADBROKES.COM MAIDEN FILLIES' STKS (DIV II) 7f (P)
1:40 (1:42) (Class 5) 2-Y-O **£4,079** (£1,214; £606; £303) **Stalls** Low

Form				RPR
04	**1**		**Awfeyaa**[30] 6360 2-9-0 0.... RHills 8 (W J Haggas) *hld up in midfield: prog on inner 2f out: trckd ldng trio 1f out: got through on ins fnl f to ld last 100yds: sn clr: comf* **9/1**	76+
30	**2**	*1 1/2*	**Suba (USA)**[41] 6076 2-9-0 0.... LDettori 12 (Saeed Bin Suroor) *sn led: rdn whn jnd 2f out: gained upper hand ent fnl f: swamped by wnr last 100yds* **4/1**[3]	72
	3	*1/2*	**My Verse** 2-9-0 0.... PhilipRobinson 10 (M A Jarvis) *chsd ldr: rdn to chal and upsides 2f out: kpt on same pce fr jst over 1f out* **15/2**	71
04	**4**	*hd*	**Badiat Alzaman (IRE)**[38] 6167 2-9-0 0.... MartinDwyer 13 (D M Simcock) *t.k.h early: hld up but wnt prom after 2f: chal and upsides 2f out: kpt on same pce fnl f* **13/2**	70+
266	**5**	*nk*	**Capitelli (IRE)**[18] 6674 2-9-0 82.... RyanMoore 2 (R Hannon) *trckd ldrs: rdn to chse ldng trio over 2f out: nt qckn and no imp over 1f out: one pce* **11/4**[1]	69
434	**6**	*1*	**Izzi Mill (USA)**[13] 6776 2-9-0 75.... DaneO'Neill 11 (D R C Elsworth) *tk v t.k.h early: hld up in midfield: effrt to chse ldrs over 2f out: sn rdn and no imp: kpt on* **3/1**[2]	67
00	**7**	*1*	**Dicey Affair**[21] 6600 2-9-0 0.... RichardMullen 3 (G L Moore) *dwlt: wl in rr: pushed along firmly fr over 2f out: styd on steadily fr wl over 1f out: nrst fin* **66/1**	64
	8	*2 1/2*	**Turning Top (IRE)** 2-9-0 0.... HayleyTurner 5 (S A Callaghan) *s.s: wl in rr: lost tch 3f out: shuffled along and kpt on steadily fnl 2f: nvr nr ldrs* **12/1**	58
0	**9**	*5*	**Madam'X**[12] 6811 2-9-0 0.... JoeFanning 9 (P F I Cole) *chsd ldrs: lost pl fr 3f out: wknd 2f out* **66/1**	46
0000	**10**	*3*	**Hayley's Girl**[13] 6776 2-9-0 48.... TravisBlock 4 (S W James) *racd awkwardly in rr: wl btn whn rn wd bnd 2f out* **80/1**	38
0	**11**	*1/2*	**Aigle De Mer (IRE)**[18] 6682 2-9-0 0.... JimmyFortune 1 (B J Meehan) *chsd ldrs tl wknd rapidly 3f out* **66/1**	37
	12	*1/2*	**Eurotanz (IRE)** 2-9-0 0.... SteveDrowne 6 (H Morrison) *dwlt: a in rr: lost tch wl over 2f out* **40/1**	36
	13	*2 1/4*	**Signella** 2-9-0 0.... AlanMunro 7 (P W Chapple-Hyam) *a in rr: struggling after 3f* **25/1**	30

1m 24.77s (-0.03) **Going Correction** -0.125s/f (Stan) **13** Ran SP% **126.5**
Speed ratings (Par 92): **95,93,92,92,92 91,89,87,81,77 77,76,74**
CSF £46.60 TOTE £12.70: £2.60, £2.00, £2.70; EX 49.20 Trifecta £120.50 Part won. Pool: £162.90 - 0.40 winning tickets..
Owner Hamdan Al Maktoum **Bred** Shadwell Estate Company Limited **Trained** Newmarket, Suffolk

FOCUS
Although run in almost an identical time to the first division, this looked the stronger of the two fillies' maidens. The second, fourth and sixth set the level.

NOTEBOOK
Awfeyaa, who improved on her debut effort to finish fourth at Warwick last time, took another step in the right direction by winning in taking style. Her rider went for a run up the inside turning into the straight and the filly quickened up well to challenge between horses inside the last and win under hands and heels. Well related, she looks a useful filly in the making, and should get a mile next year. (op 8-1 tchd 10-1)
Suba(USA) crossed over from her wide draw and took them along at a fair gallop. Not for the first time she flashed her tail under pressure, but she did not do a lot wrong, she simply came up against an improving and useful-looking rival. (op 3-1)
My Verse, who cost 115,000gns, is a half-sister to three winners, each of whom was at least useful. She ran well on her debut against more experienced fillies and should be capable of winning a similar race with this run under her belt. (tchd 13-2 and 8-1)
Badiat Alzaman(IRE), drawn widest of all, was again keen and could not get any cover. Her rider let her go towards the front, but she was always doing a bit too much and racing wide, so in the circumstances she ran a fair race to finish fourth. Handicaps are now open to her and she should do better when held up off a strong gallop. (op 6-1 tchd 11-2 and 7-1)
Capitelli(IRE), a beaten favourite over 1m1f at Goodwood last time, got a bit outpaced as they approached the turn into the straight, and this trip on this speed-favouring track looked an insufficient test for her. (op 4-1 tchd 9-2)
Izzi Mill(USA), who had shown fair form in three previous starts on turf over 6f, was well backed into 3-1 on this Polytrack debut, having been available at 15-2 in the morning, but she raced too keenly and as a result she had nothing left in reserve to deliver a challenge in the straight. (op 6-1)
Dicey Affair ran her best race to date on her third start, and she looks the type to be of far more interest in handicap company.

7098 EBF BET AT LADBROKES ON 0800 777 888 MAIDEN STKS 7f (P)
2:10 (2:12) (Class 5) 2-Y-O **£4,403** (£1,310; £654; £327) **Stalls** Low

Form				RPR
442	**1**		**Star Links (USA)**[29] 6398 2-9-3 78.... PatDobbs 3 (R Hannon) *pressed ldr: rdn to chal 2f out: narrow ld ins fnl f: edgd rt and hld on* **11/1**	83
6222	**2**	*nk*	**Custody (IRE)**[16] 6723 2-9-3 80....(v[1]) RyanMoore 4 (Sir Michael Stoute) *led: kicked on wl over 2f out: drvn over 1f out: narrowly hdd ins fnl f: edgd lft and jst hld* **5/2**[2]	82
0322	**3**	*1 1/2*	**Sandor**[29] 6397 2-9-3 82.... NCallan 10 (P J Makin) *trckd ldng pair: asked to chal whn hung bdly rt bnd 2f out and threw away ch: limited rspnse u.p after* **4/1**[3]	79
6	**4**	*3/4*	**Ajjaadd (USA)**[103] 4199 2-9-3 0.... LDettori 5 (Saeed Bin Suroor) *dwlt: sn chsd ldrs: outpcd and drvn over 2f out: tried to cl over 1f out: one pce fnl f* **5/4**[1]	77
	5	*shd*	**Cape Quarter (USA)** 2-9-3 0.... MichaelHills 6 (W J Haggas) *t.k.h early: hld up in rr: wl off the pce over 2f out: nudged along over 1f out: flashed home last 150yds: encouraging debut* **12/1**	76
	6	*1 1/2*	**Partner Shift (IRE)** 2-9-3 0.... JimmyFortune 1 (E A L Dunlop) *sltly impeded s: mostly in midfield: outpcd wl over 2f out: effrt over 1f out: no imp fnl f* **20/1**	73
0	**7**	*3 1/4*	**Sham Sheer**[28] 6423 2-9-3 0.... DaneO'Neill 7 (L M Cumani) *t.k.h early: hld up towards rr: outpcd over 2f out: shuffled along and n.d after* **33/1**	65
0	**8**	*1/2*	**Desert Streak (FR)**[13] 6776 2-9-3 0.... RichardMullen 11 (H J L Dunlop) *dwlt: rcvrd to chse ldrs on outer: outpcd over 2f out: fdd* **40/1**	63
6	**9**	*9*	**Kuanyao (IRE)**[17] 6702 2-9-3 0.... RichardSmith 8 (P J Makin) *dwlt: t.k.h early and hld up in rr: last 3f out: bhd rest of way* **33/1**	41
60	**10**	*1 1/4*	**Private Passion (IRE)**[17] 6701 2-9-3 0.... PaulEddery 9 (Pat Eddery) *nvr beyond midfield: wknd over 2f out* **40/1**	38
	11	*3*	**Sugarbaby Princess (IRE)** 2-8-12 0.... SamHitchcott 2 (S W James) *dwlt: nvr gng wl in rr: a bhd* **100/1**	25
00	**12**	*hd*	**Hilltop Artistry**[27] 6438 2-9-3 0.... TravisBlock 12 (S W James) *drvn in rr 4f out: sn bhd* **100/1**	30

1m 24.11s (-0.69) **Going Correction** -0.125s/f (Stan) **12** Ran SP% **126.5**
Speed ratings (Par 95): **98,97,95,95,94 93,89,88,78,77 73,73**
CSF £40.00 TOTE £12.40: £2.60, £1.10, £1.70; EX 41.60 Trifecta £46.10 Pool: £386.35 - 6.20 winning tickets..
Owner Coriolan Partnership V **Bred** Shell Bloodstock **Trained** East Everleigh, Wilts
■ Stewards' Enquiry : Ryan Moore one-day ban: careless riding (Nov 13)

FOCUS
Not many got into this as the first three were in those positions throughout. The time was fast and the principals have all been rated as having improved.

NOTEBOOK
Star Links(USA), who was unlucky to bump into a very useful colt of David Elsworth's at Salisbury last time, appreciated the drop in trip, was always prominent in a race dominated by the pace horses and, once he hit the front, was always comfortably holding the increasingly frustrating runner-up. He will apparently be put away now and brought back for a three-year-old campaign. (op 9-1 tchd 8-1)
Custody(IRE) had a visor on for the first time and Ryan Moore tried to make all on him, but once he was headed in the straight one got the impression that he was happy enough to play follow-the-leader in the closing stages. (op 3-1 tchd 10-3)
Sandor, placed in his last three starts, including twice around here, again made the frame, although he might have finished closer had he not swung very wide turning into the straight. (op 7-2 tchd 9-2)
Ajjaadd(USA), off the track since finishing a promising sixth over 6f at Newmarket on his debut, was a well-backed favourite, but he was a bit disappointing, getting outpaced running down the hill and then only finding the one pace in the straight, albeit after being switched to the inside rail. (op 2-1 tchd 9-4)
Cape Quarter(USA) ◆ was the eye-catcher. A son of Elusive Quality and half-brother to German 2,000 Guineas winners Dupont and Pacino, he was keen enough early on and by the time they turned into the straight he had been shuffled back towards the back of the field. Switched towards the inside on straightening up, he picked up really strongly inside the last and finished on the heels of the third-placed horse. Sure to come on a bundle for this debut effort, he looks one to keep onside. (tchd 10-1)
Partner Shift(IRE), who cost 100,000euros as a yearling, did not shape too badly on his debut and looks the type to do better next year. (op 14-1)

7099 EBF PLAY BINGO AT LADBROKES.COM FLEUR DE LYS FILLIES' STKS (LISTED RACE) 1m (P)
2:40 (2:41) (Class 1) 3-Y-O+
£22,708 (£8,608; £4,308; £2,148; £1,076; £540) **Stalls** High

Form				RPR
100	**1**		**Baharah (USA)**[12] 6814 4-9-3 109.... HayleyTurner 6 (G A Butler) *hld up towards rr: prog 3f out: chsng ldrs but nt on terms over 1f out: drvn and r.o strly fnl f to ld last stride* **11/4**[1]	105+
-200	**2**	*nse*	**Harvest Queen (IRE)**[26] 6475 5-9-0 106.... NCallan 12 (P J Makin) *dropped in fr wd draw: sn hld up in midfield: prog over 3f out: clsd on ldrs over 1f out: drvn ahd last 100yds: hdd post* **10/1**	102

0604 **3** *1* **Kylayne**[16] 6718 3-8-11 94.. RobertWinston 4 99
(P W D'Arcy) *pressed ldr after 1f: rdn to ld narrowly over 2f out: hdd and one pce last 100yds* **40/1**

1105 **4** *1* **Desert Chill (USA)**[32] 6323 3-8-11 93.. LDettori 5 97
(Saeed Bin Suroor) *led after 1f: narrowly hdd over 2f out but stl gng wl enough: rdn over 1f out: stl ch ins fnl f: wknd last 75yds* **14/1**

1301 **5** *1 ½* **Born Tobouggie (GER)**[16] 6718 3-8-11 102........................ TPQueally 11 93
(H R A Cecil) *dropped in fr wd draw and hld up in last: stl there over 2f out: prog on inner over 1f out: styd on but no hope of rching ldrs* **12/1**

-503 **6** *2* **In The Light**[13] 6781 4-9-0 101.. RyanMoore 9 90
(Sir Michael Stoute) *led 1f: stdd bhd ldrs: rdn 2f out: fdd sn after* **8/1**

1-41 **7** *nk* **Sourire**[81] 4917 3-9-0 90.. J-PGuillambert 3 91
(Sir Mark Prescott) *prom early: lost pl and towards rr 3f out: n.m.r 2f out: n.d after: plugged on fnl f* **20/1**

5310 **8** *1 ¼* **Shabiba (USA)**[27] 6440 3-9-0 103.. RHills 2 88
(M P Tregoning) *dwlt: hld up in midfield on inner: outpcd fr over 2f out: no ch w ldrs after* **9/2**[3]

2412 **9** *½* **Fragrancy (IRE)**[13] 6781 4-9-0 106.. PhilipRobinson 1 85
(M A Jarvis) *cl up on inner: rdn and grad wknd fr 2f out* **10/3**[2]

340 **10** *½* **Flure De Leise (IRE)**[118] 3705 3-8-11 0.. RPCleary 7 83
(Eamon Tyrrell, Ire) *a towards rr: pushed along 1/2-way: struggling 2f out* **66/1**

4004 **11** *nk* **Don't Forget Faith (USA)**[33] 6266 3-8-11 91.................. AdamKirby 10 82
(C G Cox) *racd wd towards rr: rdn and sme prog over 2f out: sn wknd* **25/1**

0402 **12** *2* **Dream Day**[16] 6718 3-8-11 98.. DaneO'Neill 8 77
(R Hannon) *a towards rr: rdn and no prog 2f out: wknd* **25/1**

1m 34.77s (-3.43) **Going Correction** -0.125s/f (Stan) course record
WFA 3 from 4yo+ 3lb **12** Ran SP% **118.9**
Speed ratings (Par 108): **112,111,110,109,108 106,106,104,104,103 103,101**
CSF £29.37 TOTE £4.40: £1.60, £3.80, £9.10; EX 43.30 TRIFECTA Not won..
Owner Erik Penser **Bred** Darley **Trained** Newmarket, Suffolk

FOCUS
A decent Listed contest for fillies and the two who eventually fought it out were both class-droppers. The winner broke the course record, knocking 0.43sec off the previous time. The exposed thrid is probably the best guide to the form.

NOTEBOOK
Baharah(USA), whose last two starts came in the Group 1 Matron Stakes and Group 2 Challenge Stakes, appreciated dropping back to a more realistic level, and racing on a surface that she is very comfortable on. Challenging between horses inside the last, she just got up in a photo, and this was a good effort conceding weight all round. Dubai could be on her agenda next year, although she will only race on turf there as she did not take to the dirt surface at Nad Al Sheba earlier this year. The short-term target is the Churchill Stakes, though, back here on November 22. (op 7-2)
Harvest Queen(IRE), whose trainer said she saw too much daylight in the Group 1 Sun Chariot at Newmarket last time, had no trouble getting cover here, and came with what looked like a winning challenge down the outside, only to be pipped on the post. A dual Listed winner last season, this is clearly her level. (op 14-1)
Kylayne did not get home over this trip at Leicester last time and, while she fared better on this sharper track, she again seemed to find her stamina ebbing away in the closing stages. (op 50-1 tchd 66-1)
Desert Chill(USA), held at this level on softish ground in France and Germany on her last two starts, ran a better race on her Polytrack debut. She made much of the running but did not quite see it out. (op 12-1 tchd 11-1)
Born Tobouggie(GER) did not settle out the back and, while she stayed on up the inside rail in the straight, she never really got involved. A more galloping track probably suits her better, as does a bit of give in the ground. (tchd 16-1)
In The Light reversed Newmarket form with Fragrancy over this shorter trip on this sharper track. It was a good effort as she was forced to race quite wide throughout. (op 15-2 tchd 7-1)
Sourire won a race at this level in Sweden last time, but she still came into the race the lowest-rated contender. She ran about as well as could be expected on her return from an 81-day break. (op 16-1)
Fragrancy(IRE) has improved for the step up to 1m2f recently and she just lacked the pace of the principals back over this trip. (op 5-2 tchd 9-4)

7100 EBF BETTER PRICES, BIGGER WINS AT LADBROKES.COM RIVER EDEN FILLIES' STKS (LISTED RACE) 1m 5f (P)
3:10 (3:11) (Class 1) 3-Y-O+
£22,708 (£8,608; £4,308; £2,148; £1,076; £540) **Stalls** Low

Form RPR

1160 **1** **Mischief Making (USA)**[151] 2650 3-8-8 94........................ TGMcLaughlin 10 99
(E A L Dunlop) *hld up towards rr: prog over 3f out: clsd on ldrs fr 2f out: edgd rt but led last 150yds: edgd lft but drvn clr sn after* **33/1**

-064 **2** *¾* **Samira Gold (FR)**[43] 6034 4-9-2 100.. DaneO'Neill 9 98
(L M Cumani) *stdd s: hld up towards rr: prog 3f out: rdn on outer over 2f out: tried to cl over 1f out: r.o ins fnl f to take 2nd nr fin* **4/1**[2]

2235 **3** *1* **Ronaldsay**[13] 6781 4-9-5 105..(b[1]) RyanMoore 5 99
(R Hannon) *trckd ldrs: rdn to go 2nd over 2f out: led narrowly jst over 1f out but fnd little in front: hdd last 150yds: outpcd and lost 2nd nr fin* **7/1**[3]

-000 **4** *1 ¼* **Silver Mitzva (IRE)**[34] 6241 4-9-2 92..(b) TedDurcan 4 95
(M Botti) *trckd ldr: led 3f out: kicked on over 2f out: hdd jst over 1f out: wknd ins fnl f* **33/1**

U43 **5** *shd* **Les Fazzani (IRE)**[67] 5311 4-9-2 100.. ShaneKelly 2 94+
(M J Wallace, Australia) *hld up in midfield: hmpd on inner wl over 3f out and lost pl: drvn over 2f out: styd on fr over 1f out: no ch to rch ldrs* **8/1**

3511 **6** *½* **Storyland (USA)**[26] 6415 3-8-8 92........................ KirstyMilczarek 7 94+
(W J Haggas) *hld up in last pair: hmpd 4f out: effrt over 2f out: kpt on fr over 1f out: no ch to rch ldrs* **7/2**[1]

4101 **7** *3* **Mount Lavinia (IRE)**[29] 6403 3-8-8 81........................ RichardKingscote 8 89
(R M Beckett) *hld up in last trio: rdn and no prog 3f out: plugged on* **12/1**

0116 **8** *2* **Armure**[12] 6819 3-8-8 90.. PhilipRobinson 11 86
(M A Jarvis) *prom: forced wd bnd 4f out: stl chsng ldrs but u.p over 2f out: sn wknd* **7/2**[1]

1565 **9** *4 ½* **Elmaleeha**[34] 6241 3-8-8 95.. RHills 1 79
(J L Dunlop) *led to 3f out: wknd rapidly wl over 1f out* **12/1**

2464 **10** *9* **Susie May**[34] 6241 4-9-2 95.. GeorgeBaker 3 66
(G L Moore) *trckd ldrs tl wknd 3f out: t.o* **10/1**

5605 **P** **Silk Affair (IRE)**[28] 6427 3-8-10 92 ow2.. NCallan 6 —
(M G Quinlan) *in tch: wkng whn hmpd 4f out: p.u sn after* **40/1**

2m 41.08s (-4.92) **Going Correction** -0.125s/f (Stan) course record
WFA 3 from 4yo 8lb **11** Ran SP% **120.9**
Speed ratings (Par 108): **110,109,108,108,108 107,105,104,101,96 —**
CSF £163.97 TOTE £42.80: £9.20, £2.00, £2.30; EX 275.60 Trifecta £369.00 Part won. Pool: £498.65 - 0.40 winning tickets..
Owner Cliveden Stud **Bred** Clivedon Stud Ltd **Trained** Newmarket, Suffolk

FOCUS
An open-looking fillies' Listed race with several progressive sorts stepping up in grade against older fillies already proven at this level. They seemed to go an even pace but the a number of the runners were affected by some scrimmaging on the top bend over 4f from home. The form looks solid with the fourth the best guide.

NOTEBOOK
Mischief Making(USA) was short of room for a few strides in the trouble half a mile from home, but recovered well to close down the leaders from the home turn and responded well when sent to the front. A previous winner on this surface, she had not run since finishing down the field in a Group 3 in France at the beginning of June but had run reasonably at this level on unsuitably fast going before that. This win has considerably increased her broodmare value and the fact that she broke the track record also speaks in her favour.
Samira Gold(FR), a progressive filly last season, had failed to build on that in three previous outings this season but travelled well on this all-weather debut and proved she stays the trip by running on in the wake of the winner through the final furlong. (op 13-2)
Ronaldsay is a consistent sort and had the highest official rating but had been held on both previous runs on Polytrack, although they were at Kempton and all her wins have been on left-handed tracks. She ran well in the first-time blinkers, despite being a little keen, and showed ahead going into the final furlong before the winner asserted. (op 13-2 tchd 11-2 and 15-2)
Silver Mitzva(IRE) went for home just inside the three-furlong marker and stayed there until being collared going into the final furlong. This was a decent effort considering she had a bit to find with the placed horses on official ratings.
Les Fazzani(IRE) was bidding to give her trainer a winner with his last runner before leaving for Australia. She came into this with a perfect record in two previous starts on Polytrack, albeit at shorter trips, but was a market drifter. She travelled well enough off the pace until squeezed out on the top bend after which she had an uphill struggle to get back into contention. She was staying on steadily and may be worth another try at around this distance. Official explanation: jockey said filly suffered interference in running (op 6-1 tchd 11-2)
Storyland(USA), a four-time winner at up to 1m4f on turf, was stepping up in grade for this all-weather debut but was in the rear when short of room on the top bend and could never get into a challenging position thereafter. Official explanation: jockey said filly suffered interference in running (op 4-1 tchd 9-2)
Mount Lavinia(IRE) had a lot to find on official ratings on this all-weather debut and failed to get involved. (op 16-1)
Armure, a three-time winner on Kempton's Polytrack, showed up from the start but had to be pulled out wide on the top bend. She was still close enough going into the final turn before fading and the impression is that this course did not suit her as well as the Sunbury track. Official explanation: jockey said filly suffered interference in running (op 3-1)
Elmaleeha Official explanation: jockey said filly hung right
Silk Affair(IRE) Official explanation: jockey said filly suffered interference in running

7101 PLAY CASINO AT LADBROKES.COM H'CAP 7f (P)
3:40 (3:41) (Class 3) (0-95,94) 3-Y-O+ **£7,641** (£2,273; £1,136; £567) **Stalls** Low

Form RPR

0062 **1** **Gallantry**[17] 6710 6-8-11 83.. TGMcLaughlin 2 92
(P Howling) *awkward s: hld up in strly run r: prog on inner and clr run through to ld 1f out: edgd rt and drvn out* **15/2**

2000 **2** *½* **Commander Cave (USA)**[33] 6283 3-9-6 94........................ RyanMoore 7 101
(R Hannon) *chsd ldrs: rdn on outer 3f out: rallied u.p over 1f out: wnt 2nd ins fnl f: styd on but a hld* **9/2**[2]

2000 **3** *nk* **Compton's Eleven**[18] 6676 7-8-9 81........................ EdwardCreighton 3 88
(M R Channon) *stdd s: hld up in last pair in strly run r: nt qckn and no prog 2f out: styd on fnl f to take 3rd nr fin* **14/1**

003 **4** *hd* **Secret Night**[18] 6684 5-8-8 80..(p) KirstyMilczarek 8 86+
(C G Cox) *hld up in tch: gng easily 2f out: trapped bhd rivals over 1f out: managed to squeeze through wl ins fnl f but too late to chal* **15/2**

0003 **5** *nk* **Bazroy (IRE)**[8] 6911 4-8-13 85..(b) RobertWinston 1 90
(P D Evans) *stdd s: hld up in tch: cl enough gng wl 2f out: effrt over 1f out: nt qckn* **9/2**[2]

5105 **6** *hd* **South Cape**[22] 6576 5-8-10 89.. MatthewDavies[(7)] 4 94
(M R Channon) *trckd ldng pair: rdn to go 2nd 2f out: drvn to ld over 1f out: hdd 1f out: no ex* **13/2**[3]

11 **7** *1 ¾* **Noble Citizen (USA)**[26] 6471 3-9-0 88........................ RichardMullen 6 88
(D M Simcock) *stmbld s but sn chsd ldr to 2f out: wknd fnl f* **9/4**[1]

5303 **8** *4 ½* **King's Caprice**[46] 5930 7-8-12 84..(t) TravisBlock 5 72
(J A Geake) *taken down early: led at brisk pce: edgd rt and hdd over 1f out: wknd rapidly* **14/1**

1m 22.61s (-2.19) **Going Correction** -0.125s/f (Stan) course record
WFA 3 from 4yo+ 2lb **8** Ran SP% **117.3**
Speed ratings (Par 107): **107,106,106,105,105 105,103,98**
CSF £42.22 CT £471.37 TOTE £10.70: £2.40, £1.80, £3.90; EX 58.20 Trifecta £418.70 Pool: £673.40 - 1.19 winning tickets..
Owner The Circle Bloodstock I Limited **Bred** Cheveley Park Stud Ltd **Trained** Newmarket, Suffolk
■ Stewards' Enquiry : T G McLaughlin two-day ban: careless riding (Nov 13-14)

FOCUS
A decent handicap which was run at a strong pace and in a time over a second below standard. The first six finished in a heap ahead of the pair who had raced in first and second. The form looks sound.

NOTEBOOK
Gallantry raced in rear after a sluggish start, but an inviting gap opened for him on the rail entering the straight and he took full advantage, showing ahead at the furlong pole and holding on to his lead despite edging right under pressure. He has never been out of the frame in seven visits to Lingfield and this is his trip. (op 13-2 tchd 6-1)
Commander Cave(USA) was in fine heart on both Polytrack and turf in the first half of the campaign and this was his best run for some time. He was always obliged to race on the outside of the field from his high draw and was one of the first to come under pressure, but ran on willingly down the straight. He will not mind a return to a mile. (op 8-1)
Compton's Eleven had not run on Polytrack since April 2006 but this was a good effort as he finished well down the outer after turning into the short straight in last place. He obviously acts on this surface but wins infrequently. (op 20-1 tchd 22-1)
Secret Night, who was third in this race two years ago, travelled well into the straight but her momentum was soon halted. She ran on in the final furlong but was always short of room and this was an encouraging effort. (op 8-1 tchd 9-1)
Bazroy(IRE) showed something of a return to form at Kempton and was 3lb well in, but despite getting the decent pace he requires he could never quite pick up in the straight, although he would have finished slightly closer had he not been hampered when the winner edged across him close home. (op 5-2)
South Cape was never far from the pace and had every chance with no evident excuses. He is up to winning on this surface. (op 15-2 tchd 6-1)
Noble Citizen(USA), who was 5lb higher on this hat-trick bid, had been allowed the run of the race when gaining both his recent wins. After stumbling leaving the stalls he had to be content with tracking the strong pace this time and he faded in the latter stages. (op 3-1 tchd 10-3)

King's Caprice made the running as he likes to but could not hold on in the straight and was soon on the retreat when headed. He is well handicapped these days, but has never won on sand and is possibly happiest over 6f. (op 12-1)

7102 BET AT LADBROKES.COM APPRENTICE H'CAP 7f (P)

4:10 (4:10) (Class 6) (0-60,60) 3-Y-O+ **£2,047** (£604; £302) **Stalls** Low

Form RPR

5500 **1** **Tilsworth Charlie**[23] 6564 5-8-12 **54**........................(b) FrederikTylicki(3) 9 62
(J R Jenkins) *trckd ldrs on outer: shkn up and prog to ld jst over 1f out: pushed out fnl f* **8/1**[3]

0122 **2** *¾* **Palais Polaire**[31] 6338 6-9-1 **54**..............................(p) JackDean 5 60
(J A Geake) *trckd ldng pair: effrt to chal on inner jst over 1f out: chsd wnr after: styd on but readily hld* **9/2**[2]

2061 **3** *1* **Scruffy Skip (IRE)**[18] 6681 3-8-10 **54**.................. MatthewDavies(3) 13 56
(Mrs C A Dunnett) *t.k.h early: hld up in rr on outer: prog 3f out: effrt over 1f out: chsd ldng pair fnl f but no imp* **8/1**[3]

300 **4** *nk* **Torquemada (IRE)**[14] 6749 7-8-10 **56**.........................(t) KierenFox(7) 11 58
(M J Attwater) *t.k.h: hld up and hld up in rr: prog over 1f out: styd on fnl f: nt rch ldrs* **20/1**

2050 **5** *½* **Royal Sovereign (IRE)**[9] 6889 3-9-1 **59**................. AshleyMorgan(3) 10 59
(G C H Chung) *restrained s: plld hrd and hld up in midfield: effrt 2f out: kpt on fnl f but nvr able to chal* **16/1**

0350 **6** *½* **Imperium**[38] 6178 7-9-1 **57**....................................(p) SophieDoyle(3) 14 57+
(Jean-Rene Auvray) *hld up in last pair: stl last 2f out: plld wd and fin wl fnl f: no ch* **11/1**

4-00 **7** *½* **Bronte's Hope**[36] 6209 4-9-2 **60**.................................... KatiaScallan(5) 4 58
(M P Tregoning) *disp ld to jst over 1f out: wknd ins fnl f* **12/1**

0045 **8** *nse* **Shaded Edge**[29] 6396 4-9-0 **53**..................................... WilliamCarson 7 51+
(D W P Arbuthnot) *trckd ldrs: cl up jst over 1f out: wknd ins fnl f* **9/4**[1]

0066 **9** *¾* **Mythical Charm**[67] 5312 9-8-5 **47**..........................(t) JemmaMarshall(3) 12 43
(J J Bridger) *s.s: hld up in last: effrt 2f out: kpt on fnl f: no ch* **20/1**

3406 **10** *2 ¼* **Greek Secret**[89] 4653 5-8-9 **48**.. JamesO'Reilly 3 38
(J O'Reilly) *stdd s: t.k.h in midfield early: lost pl 3f out: sn toiling in rr* **12/1**

-400 **11** *1* **Murrisk**[53] 5724 4-8-9 **55**... SJWilliams(7) 2 43
(Eamon Tyrrell, Ire) *disp ld to over 1f out: wknd rapidly* **20/1**

2200 **12** *¾* **Waterloo Dock**[126] 3397 3-9-1 **56**...................................... MCGeran 8 40
(M Quinn) *nvr beyond midfield: wknd wl over 1f out* **11/1**

1m 25.05s (0.25) **Going Correction** -0.125s/f (Stan)
WFA 3 from 4yo+ 2lb **12** Ran SP% **123.4**
Speed ratings (Par 101): **93,92,91,90,90 89,88,88,88,85 84,83**
CSF £44.38 CT £302.92 TOTE £8.50: £2.60, £2.10, £2.40; EX 47.10 Trifecta £136.20 Part won. Pool of £184.12 - 0.20 winning tickets. Place 6 £254.80, Place 5 £106.40.
Owner M Ng **Bred** Michael Ng **Trained** Royston, Herts

FOCUS
A moderate handicap and the slowest of the five races run over this distance on the card. The placed form set the level and the winner looked well treated even on last winter's sand form.
T/Jkpt: Not won. T/Plt: £303.30 to a £1 stake. Pool: £55,435.30. 133.40 winning tickets. T/Qpdt: £28.30 to a £1 stake. Pool: £4,238.95. 110.80 winning tickets. JN

7007 LONGCHAMP (R-H)

Thursday, October 30

OFFICIAL GOING: Soft

7103a CRITERIUM DE VITESSE (LISTED RACE) 5f (S)

1:50 (1:54) 2-Y-O **£20,221** (£8,088; £6,066; £4,044; £2,022)

RPR

1 **Doriana (FR)**[35] 6236 2-8-13 .... CSoumillon 5 101
(A De Royer-Dupre, France)

2 *snk* **Bluster (FR)**[75] 5112 2-9-2 .... DBoeuf 7 103
(Robert Collet, France)

3 *1 ½* **Eva Kant**[25] 2-8-13 .... CFiocchi 4 95
(R Menichetti, Italy)

4 *¾* **Good Bye My Friend (FR)**[11] 6856 2-9-2 .... TThulliez 3 95
(N Clement, France)

5 *nse* **Rose Hill Doloise (FR)**[19] 2-8-13 .... RMarchelli 1 92
(A Bonin, France)

6 *4* **Theoricienne (FR)**[19] 2-8-13 .... SPasquier 2 78
(Mme C Head-Maarek, France)

7 *2 ½* **Kokawango (FR)**[35] 6236 2-9-2 .... JVictoire 6 72
(M Roussel, France)

8 *shd* **Plotting**[30] 6351 2-8-13 .... DBonilla 8 68
(K A Ryan) *spd 2f: sn btn and hung lft (9/1)*

9 *8* **Alta Luna (FR)**[11] 6856 2-8-13 .... IMendizabal 9 40
(J-C Rouget, France)

59.30 secs (2.60) **9** Ran
PARI-MUTUEL: WIN 4.20; PL 1.80, 3.00, 5.10; DF 17.60.
Owner Ecurie La Perrigne **Bred** Sca De La Perrigne **Trained** Chantilly, France

NOTEBOOK
Plotting, caught a little flat footed leaving the stalls, quickly made up ground to sit on the outside just off the leaders and appeared to be cruising at half way. However she was soon struggling, dropped out of contention and was allowed to come home in her own time. She was found to have a nasty cut on her near-fore and it appeared that she had been struck into during the race.

6814 NEWMARKET (ROWLEY) (R-H)

Friday, October 31

OFFICIAL GOING: Good to soft (soft in places)
Wind: Light across Weather: Fine and sunny

7104 PRESTIGE VEHICLES EBF MAIDEN STKS 6f

12:05 (12:06) (Class 4) 2-Y-O **£5,180** (£1,541; £770; £384) **Stalls** High

Form RPR

1 **Catskill Mountain (IRE)** 2-9-3 0.................................... AlanMunro 5 93
(P W Chapple-Hyam) *chsd ldr: rdn over 1f out: hung rt and led ins fnl f: r.o wl* **11/1**

032 **2** *1 ½* **Swiss Diva**[4] 7020 2-8-12 0.. DaneO'Neill 11 84
(D R C Elsworth) *led: rdn over 1f out: hdd and unable qck ins fnl f* **5/4**[1]

00 **3** *8* **Royal Collection (IRE)**[17] 6720 2-9-3 0........................ HayleyTurner 6 65
(J Pearce) *hld up: racd keenly: r.o ins fnl f: nvr nrr* **22/1**

4 *nk* **Emirates Sports** 2-9-3 0.. LDettori 7 64
(Saeed Bin Suroor) *s.i.s: sn chsng ldrs: rdn and edgd rt over 1f out: sn wknd* **13/2**[3]

5 *½* **Formula (USA)** 2-9-3 0... RyanMoore 12 62
(R Hannon) *prom: rdn over 2f out: wknd over 1f out* **12/1**

6 *1* **Raaeidd (IRE)** 2-9-3 0... PhilipRobinson 3 59
(M A Jarvis) *chsd ldrs: rdn: hung rt and wknd over 1f out* **9/2**[2]

7 *¾* **Monsieur Kiss Kiss** 2-9-3 0... PatCosgrave 2 57
(G A Butler) *s.s: hdwy over 3f out: rdn over 2f out: wknd over 1f out* **40/1**

30 **8** *1* **Cheam Forever (USA)**[45] 5996 2-9-3 0......................... SteveDrowne 9 54
(R Charlton) *hld up: shkn up over 2f out: sn edgd rt and wknd* **14/1**

9 *½* **Aphrodite's Rock** 2-8-12 0.. TedDurcan 13 47
(Miss Gay Kelleway) *s.i.s: a in rr* **33/1**

0 **10** *1 ¼* **Jachol (IRE)**[4] 7020 2-9-3 0.. MichaelHills 10 49
(W J Haggas) *chsd ldrs tl rdn and wknd over 1f out* **33/1**

11 *1 ¾* **Papyrian** 2-9-3 0.. J-PGuillambert 4 43
(W Jarvis) *mid-div: sn pushed along: rdn 1/2-way: wknd wl over 1f out* **25/1**

12 *4* **Here Comes Danny** 2-9-3 0.. FrancisNorton 8 31
(M Wigham) *chsd ldrs tl rdn and wknd over 2f out* **50/1**

13 *16* **Kina Jazz** 2-8-13 0 ow1... AdamKirby 1 —
(M E Rimmer) *s.i.s: a in rr: wknd over 2f out* **100/1**

1m 13.52s (1.32) **Going Correction** +0.225s/f (Good) **13** Ran SP% **118.1**
Speed ratings (Par 97): **100,98,87,86,86 84,83,82,81,80 77,72,51**
toteswinger: 1&2 £6.10, 1&3 £48.00, 2&3 £14.50. CSF £23.48 TOTE £15.90: £2.90, £1.10, £7.00; EX 33.10.
Owner Mrs J Magnier, M Tabor & D Smith **Bred** Michael Collins **Trained** Newmarket, Suffolk

FOCUS
A typical backend Newmarket maiden featuring mainly unraced or inexperienced types, several of whom patently need further. Nevertheless, impressive efforts from the two principals in pulling so far clear.

NOTEBOOK
Catskill Mountain(IRE) ◆, a 95,000gns first foal of a 1m1f winner in France and already gelded, clearly knew his job and was in the front rank throughout. He picked up really well in the last quarter-mile and found extra to settle the issue in the last half-furlong. He should be decent next term, when the plan is to stick to sprinting. (op 16-1)
Swiss Diva, who had been placed behind useful sorts Run For The Hills and Master Rooney this month following break since debut in June, was clearly none the worse for her race at the beginning of the week and tried to make all. She drew clear of the rest, but the winner always looked to have her covered. Nevertheless she appears to have run her race and sets a fair standard. (op 7-4)
Royal Collection(IRE), who had been a little free on both his previous starts, was anchored this time before running on steadily for third. He now qualifies for a handicap mark and should not be overburdened, having been a fair way behind the principals. (op 25-1)
Emirates Sports, a 150,000gns half-brother to Plea Bargain and Dubai Time from the family of Time Charter, was a market drifter but showed up well until outpaced in the last two furlongs. This Derby entry will be much better over a mile and more next season. (op 10-3)
Formula(USA), a 90,000gns second foal of an unraced sister to Blush Rambler and Tendulkar, made an encouraging debut and looks to sure to benefit from the experience. (op 7-1)
Raaeidd(IRE), a half-brother to three winners including Baharah, out of a Ribblesdale winner, was yet another with stamina in his pedigree to show ability, having seen plenty of daylight and been quite keen in the early stages. (op 11-2, tchd 6-1 in places)
Monsieur Kiss Kiss was one of those slowly away on this debut. He ran on steadily in the latter stages, and this half-brother to three winners at up to 1m1f should be better for the run. (op 66-1)
Cheam Forever(USA), dropping in trip having been too keen to get home over 7f last time, was backed at long prices but never really figured. He now qualifies for a mark and may do better in handicaps. (op 20-1 tchd 11-1)
Papyrian, the 15th and last foal of his dam and a half-brother to eight winners including Grand Lodge, did not fare too badly considering he was completely unfancied in the betting. (op 40-1)

7105 EBF CHARLIE GUEST 80TH BIRTHDAY MAIDEN STKS (C&G) (DIV I) 7f

12:40 (12:40) (Class 4) 2-Y-O **£4,857** (£1,445; £722; £360) **Stalls** High

Form RPR

622 **1** **Emirates Roadshow (USA)**[17] 6714 2-9-0 82........................ LDettori 8 83
(Saeed Bin Suroor) *mde all: rdn over 1f out: edgd rt ins fnl f: r.o* **1/1**[1]

0 **2** *1 ¾* **Jesse James (IRE)**[7] 6944 2-9-0 0.............................. JimmyFortune 6 79
(J H M Gosden) *a.p: chsd wnr 2f out: rdn over 1f out: styd on same wl ins fnl f* **9/4**[2]

5 **3** *1 ¾* **Absinthe (IRE)**[30] 6375 2-9-0 0....................................... AdamKirby 14 74+
(W R Swinburn) *hld up: hdwy over 1f out: hung lft ins fnl f: styd on* **11/1**

4 *3 ¼* **Libel Law** 2-9-0 0.. PhilipRobinson 1 66+
(M A Jarvis) *s.i.s: hld up: hdwy 1/2-way: rdn over 1f out: nt trble ldrs* **18/1**

50 **5** *½* **Compton Blue**[11] 6863 2-9-0 0.. PatDobbs 4 65
(R Hannon) *chsd wnr 4f: wknd fnl f* **66/1**

6 *½* **Abulharith** 2-9-0 0.. AlanMunro 10 64
(P W Chapple-Hyam) *chsd ldrs: rdn over 1f out: wknd fnl f* **28/1**

7 *1 ¼* **Ithinkbest** 2-9-0 0.. RyanMoore 3 61+
(Sir Michael Stoute) *s.i.s: sn prom: rdn over 2f out: wknd over 1f out* **10/1**[3]

00 **8** *½* **Everaard (USA)**[32] 6342 2-9-0 0................................. RobertHavlin 11 59+
(D R C Elsworth) *prom: rdn over 2f out: wkng whn nt clr run over 1f out* **100/1**

30 **9** *¾* **Beat Up**[29] 6412 2-9-0 0... JimCrowley 12 57
(P R Chamings) *chsd ldrs tl rdn and wknd over 1f out* **25/1**

00 **10** *2* **Mr Prolific**[17] 6715 2-9-0 0... MichaelHills 13 52
(B W Hills) *chsd ldrs: rdn over 2f out: wknd over 1f out* **40/1**

0 **11** *hd* **Millharbour (IRE)**[114] 3853 2-9-0 0................................ ChrisCatlin 15 52
(B W Hills) *s.i.s: a in rr* **16/1**

12 *hd* **Rising Star** 2-8-11 0.. TolleyDean(3) 9 51
(J L Spearing) *s.i.s: outpcd* **100/1**

00 **13** *¾* **Timbaa (USA)**[17] 6714 2-8-7 0................................ CharlesEddery(7) 2 50
(Rae Guest) *s.s: hld up: a in rr* **100/1**

0 **14** *½* **Berti**[17] 6720 2-9-0 0... JerryO'Dwyer 7 48
(J Pearce) *hld up: rdn and wknd over 1f out* **200/1**

1m 27.26s (1.86) **Going Correction** +0.225s/f (Good) **14** Ran SP% **124.0**
Speed ratings (Par 97): **98,96,94,90,89 89,87,87,86,84 83,83,82,82**
toteswinger: 1&2 £2.00, 1&3 £3.50, 2&3 £6.00. CSF £3.16 TOTE £2.10: £1.10, £1.60, £2.10; EX 4.70.
Owner Godolphin **Bred** George Strawbridge Jr **Trained** Newmarket, Suffolk

FOCUS
A fair maiden run in a time 1.21 seconds quicker than the second division, but those with experience held sway. The winner was given a good ride and appeared to reproduce his recent form, while the third and fourth deserve credit for coming from the rear in a race in which it paid to be handy.

NOTEBOOK

Emirates Roadshow(USA) was able to get off the mark at the fourth time of asking. Given a prominent ride, he ran on strongly for pressure, but while he was the best horse on the day he does not look open to as much improvement as some of those in behind. (op 6-5 after early 11-8 in a place, 5-4 in places)

Jesse James(IRE) improved on his debut at Doncaster a week earlier. He should win an ordinary maiden if persevered with this year, and has the potential to progress into a very useful type over further next season (op 10-3)

Absinthe(IRE) stayed on well once switched towards the far rail, but he was never getting to the front pair. This was an improvement on his debut effort at Kempton and there should be better to come again, particularly in middle-distance handicaps next year. (tchd 9-1)

Libel Law ◆, a Kingmambo half-brother to useful multiple 1m-1m4f winner Criticism, out of very smart 1m2f-1m4f winner Innuendo, fared best of the newcomers. He looks well up to winning a similar race with the benefit of this experience and could be very useful over further next season. (op 16-1)

Compton Blue ran his best race yet despite this trip looking far enough on breeding. He is likely to prove best suited by sprint trips, though, and now has the option of handicaps. (op 50-1)

Abulharith, a 38,000gns purchase, is likely to come into his own over further in time. (op 25-1 tchd 33-1)

Ithinkbest was not given a hard time and is yet another likely to do better over further next year. (op 8-1, tchd 11-1 in a place)

Everaard(USA), up a furlong in trip, was staying on again having lost his place when short of room over a furlong out. He still looked green and it will be a surprise if he cannot do better in handicaps. (op 66-1)

7106 EBF CHARLIE GUEST 80TH BIRTHDAY MAIDEN STKS (C&G) (DIV II) 7f

1:15 (1:16) (Class 4) 2-Y-O **£4,857** (£1,445; £722; £360) **Stalls** High

Form				RPR
0	1		**Captain Dancer (IRE)**[28] 6443 2-9-0 0 ... MichaelHills 7 (B W Hills) *dwlt: sn chsng ldr: led over 1f out: rdn out* **11/4**[1]	76
00	2	1 3/4	**Royal Willy (IRE)**[28] 6438 2-9-0 0 ... J-PGuillambert 1 (W Jarvis) *hld up: hdwy 1/2-way: swtchd rt 2f out: chsd wnr over 1f out: no imp ins fnl f* **33/1**	72
	3	1	**Count Of Tuscany (USA)** 2-9-0 0 ... JimCrowley 10 (Mrs A J Perrett) *hld up in tch: rdn over 2f out: hung lft over 1f out: r.o* **3/1**[2]	69+
	4	1	**African Art (USA)** 2-9-0 0 ... MartinDwyer 3 (B J Meehan) *hld up: shkn up over 1f out: r.o ins fnl f: nt trble ldrs* **10/1**	67
0	5	3/4	**Nbhan (USA)**[14] 6777 2-9-0 0 ... DaneO'Neill 12 (L M Cumani) *chsd ldrs: rdn over 1f out: styd on* **16/1**	65
	6	nk	**Regeneration (IRE)** 2-9-0 0 ... HayleyTurner 2 (S A Callaghan) *s.i.s: hld up: shkn up over 2f out: hdwy over 1f out: styd on* **33/1**	64
00	7	1/2	**Cooper Island Kid (USA)**[29] 6423 2-9-0 0 ... MickyFenton 6 (P W D'Arcy) *led: rdn and hdd over 1f out: no ex ins fnl f* **100/1**	63
	8	1 1/2	**Anacreon (IRE)** 2-9-0 0 ... JimmyFortune 13 (J H M Gosden) *chsd ldrs: rdn over 1f out: wknd ins fnl f* **6/1**[3]	59
0	9	1	**Big Nige (IRE)**[17] 6715 2-9-0 0 ... JerryO'Dwyer 8 (J Pearce) *hld up in tch: racd keenly: rdn and nt clr run over 1f out: wknd ins fnl f* **66/1**	57
	10	3 1/2	**Hilbre Point (USA)** 2-9-0 0 ... TedDurcan 9 (B J Meehan) *s.s: hdwy over 2f out: wknd over 1f out* **7/1**	48
	11	1/2	**Royal Bet (IRE)** 2-9-0 0 ... RyanMoore 14 (Sir Michael Stoute) *prom: rdn over 2f out: sn wknd* **7/1**	47
	12	2	**Iron Man Of Mersey (FR)** 2-9-0 0 ... ShaneKelly 4 (A W Carroll) *s.i.s: a in rr* **50/1**	42
	13	21	**Soldier Soldier** 2-9-0 0 ... NickyMackay 5 (J R Jenkins) *s.i.s: a in rr: wknd over 2f out* **50/1**	—
	14	3	**Kirkson** 2-9-0 0 ... AlanMunro 11 (P W Chapple-Hyam) *prom: rdn over 4f out: wknd 1/2-way* **20/1**	—

1m 28.47s (3.07) **Going Correction** +0.225s/f (Good) **14** Ran SP% **123.0**

Speed ratings (Par 97): **91,89,87,86,85 85,84,83,82,78 77,75,51,47**

toteswinger: 1&2 £13.60, 1&3 £4.30, 2&3 £26.30. CSF £107.38 TOTE £3.90: £1.60, £6.40, £1.90; EX 127.50.

Owner R J Arculli **Bred** King Bloodstock And Swettenham Stud **Trained** Lambourn, Berks

■ Stewards' Enquiry : Jim Crowley one-day ban: careless riding (Nov 14)

FOCUS

The second division of this maiden was run 1.21secs slower than the first leg. Not a lot to go on, but a couple of longshots were uncomfortably close and the form is further undermined by Captain Dancer having finished five lengths behind the winner of the first division, Emirates Roadshow, over course and distance at the beginning of the month.

NOTEBOOK

Captain Dancer(IRE) was a well-backed favourite and built on the promise of his debut run with a straightforward success. He got a good lead before going on at the two-furlong pole and was always in control from that point. He should make a fair handicapper next season. (op 4-1)

Royal Willy(IRE) who had been well beaten in 7f maidens on fast and soft ground previously, ran better on this third outing although his proximity tends to raise doubts about the form. He seems to be going the right way though and now qualifies for a handicap mark.

Count Of Tuscany(USA), a half-brother to two winners out of a 7f winner from the family of Zafonic, was well supported for on this debut despite being from a yard that rarely have first-time juvenile out winners. He tracked the pace before staying on up the hill and this tall, scopey colt looks sure to come on a fair amount for the outing. (op 4-1)

African Art(USA), a 160,000euros first foal of an unraced half-sister to winners at 7f and a mile, was held up out the back before doing his best work up the hill, more or less following through the third. Although not having quite the size of that rival, he showed enough to suggest there are races in him given normal progress. (op 16-1)

Nbhan(USA), who was backed when well beaten on his debut over 1m here, ran another fair race and can make his mark in handicaps after one more outing. (op 14-1)

Regeneration(IRE) also showed promise, having been held up early, running on steadily in the wake of the placed horses. This half-brother to several winners at sprint trips looks as though he may need a little further. (op 25-1)

Cooper Island Kid(USA), who had been well beaten in both starts over 6f and 1m at Great Leighs, also limits the form but there is a fair chance that turf suits him better than Polytrack, as he made the running until headed at the two-furlong pole and only gradually faded. (op 66-1)

Anacreon(IRE), a 220,000gns half-brother to a sprint winner in France from the family of Satwa Queen, was easy in the market despite the current form of his yard but ran well up to a point before losing several places up the hill. (op 4-1)

Big Nige(IRE), 100-1 when last of 14 on his debut, finished a lot closer this time.

Royal Bet(IRE) showed signs of ability, doing well to get on the heels of the leading group at halfway having missed the break, before tiring in the latter stages. (op 5-1)

7107 EBF IGLOOS BOSRA SHAM FILLIES' STKS (LISTED RACE) 6f

1:50 (1:52) (Class 1) 2-Y-O

£17,031 (£6,456; £3,231; £1,611; £807; £405) **Stalls** High

Form				RPR
0216	1		**Penny's Gift**[13] 6818 2-8-12 103 ... RyanMoore 2 (R Hannon) *a.p: rdn to ld over 1f out: r.o* **6/4**[1]	96+
2102	2	3	**Qalahari (IRE)**[30] 6401 2-8-12 92 ... TPO'Shea 5 (D J Coakley) *hld up: hdwy over 1f out: r.o: nt rch wnr* **7/1**[2]	90+
3022	3	shd	**Albertine Rose**[11] 6863 2-8-12 70 ... MartinDwyer 1 (W R Muir) *chsd ldr tl led over 3f out: rdn and hdd over 1f out: styd on same pce* **50/1**	87
4102	4	shd	**Calahonda**[19] 6673 2-8-12 80 ... PhilipRobinson 9 (P W D'Arcy) *led: hdd over 3f out: rdn over 1f out: styd on same pce* **11/1**	86
0061	5	hd	**Oasis Breeze**[13] 6807 2-8-12 85 ... DavidAllan 11 (T D Easterby) *hld up: hdwy over 2f out: rdn over 1f out: styd on same pce* **16/1**	86
1	6	1 1/2	**Miss Eze**[24] 6555 2-8-12 0 ... AlanMunro 7 (G Wragg) *prom: rdn over 2f out: no ex fnl f* **8/1**[3]	81
411	7	3	**Happy Forever (FR)**[27] 6469 2-8-12 80 ... LDettori 6 (M Botti) *prom: rdn 2f out: wknd fnl f* **12/1**	72
5000	8	3/4	**Art Princess (USA)**[20] 6644 2-8-12 93 ... MichaelHills 4 (B W Hills) *hld up: rdn over 1f out: n.d* **7/1**[2]	70
1365	9	1	**Caranbola**[27] 6483 2-8-12 90 ... JimmyFortune 10 (M Brittain) *chsd ldrs: rdn over 2f out: wknd fnl f* **10/1**	67
	10	hd	**Flame Of Ireland (IRE)**[31] 6365 2-8-12 0 ... TedDurcan 8 (M J Grassick, Ire) *unruly bhd stalls: sn outpcd* **14/1**	66
1060	11	nk	**Coconut Shy**[20] 6644 2-8-12 90 ... (t) SaleemGolam 3 (G Prodromou) *chsd ldrs: rdn over 2f out: wknd fnl f* **33/1**	66

1m 13.23s (1.03) **Going Correction** +0.225s/f (Good) **11** Ran SP% **118.7**

Speed ratings (Par 100): **102,98,97,97,97 95,91,90,89,88 88**

toteswinger: 1&2 £4.10, 1&3 £9.70, 2&3 £11.90. CSF £12.18 TOTE £2.30: £1.30, £2.00, £6.90; EX 14.20.

Owner Malcolm Brown & Mrs Penny Brown **Bred** Capt A L Smith-Maxwell **Trained** East Everleigh, Wilts

FOCUS

An ordinary juvenile fillies' Listed contest in which they raced up the middle of the track and went a good pace. The winner did not need to be at her best as the form is very limited for the grade.

NOTEBOOK

Penny's Gift was a class apart. Dropping back in trip having run sixth in the Rockfel, she was always well placed and eventually pulled away after taking a few strides to really hit top gear. She has had plenty of racing, but still looks the type to make a three-year-old, when she should get 7f. Connections hope she could be a Guineas filly, but it is doubtful she will be good enough for a domestic classic. (tchd 11-8 and 13-8, tchd 7-4 and 15-8 in places)

Qalahari(IRE) ◆ put up an even better effort than it looked as she certainly did not get the run of things. Held up, she had nowhere to go when all of the other principals were making their moves, and she got going too late by the time she was switched far side. She finished her race in similar fashion at Salisbury last time, so she would surely have benefited from a more positive ride. (op 15-2 tchd 9-1)

Albertine Rose came into this a 70-rated maiden and showed improved form, albeit in a weak race by Listed standards. She is clearly capable when things fall right. (tchd 40-1)

Calahonda showed early speed but still gave the impression she is probably best suited by 7f for the time being. (op 14-1)

Oasis Breeze had something to find in this company. (op 14-1)

Miss Eze still looked inexperienced. (op 13-2 tchd 6-1)

7108 EBF IGLOOS FILLIES' H'CAP 1m 4f

2:25 (2:27) (Class 3) (0-90,89) 3-Y-O+

£8,723 (£2,612; £1,306; £653; £326; £163) **Stalls** Centre

Form				RPR
1220	1		**Spring Dream (IRE)**[20] 6646 5-9-2 **80** ... RyanMoore 6 (A King) *hld up: hdwy over 1f out: rdn to ld 1f out: swvd lft wl ins fnl f: styd on* **8/1**	90
414	2	1 1/4	**Interchange (IRE)**[29] 6415 3-8-10 **81** ... JimCrowley 8 (J R Fanshawe) *chsd ldrs: rdn over 1f out: styd on* **13/2**[2]	89
3020	3	3/4	**Encircled**[22] 6605 4-8-12 **76** ... RobertHavlin 3 (D Haydn Jones) *hld up: nt clr run over 2f out: swtchd rt and hdwy over 1f out: styd on* **20/1**	83
2600	4	1 1/4	**Candle**[20] 6646 5-9-11 **89** ... DaneO'Neill 9 (H Candy) *chsd ldr tl led over 2f out: rdn and hdd 1f out: no ex ins fnl f* **15/2**[3]	94
1	5	1	**Critical Acclaim**[39] 6168 3-8-11 **82** ... JimmyFortune 1 (J H M Gosden) *hld up: hdwy over 2f out: rdn and edgd rt over 1f out: no ex fnl f* **9/1**	85
1154	6	nk	**Quirina**[34] 6293 3-9-1 **86** ... SteveDrowne 7 (J H M Gosden) *hld up in tch: rdn over 2f out: no ex fnl f* **10/1**	89
1152	7	2	**Starfala**[29] 6415 3-9-2 **87** ... ShaneKelly 10 (P F I Cole) *led: rdn and hdd over 2f out: wknd fnl f* **4/1**[1]	87
10	8	5	**Mango Lady**[21] 6626 3-8-5 **76** ... MartinDwyer 2 (C F Wall) *hld up: rdn over 2f out: wknd over 1f out* **11/1**	68
2-10	9	2 3/4	**Island Vista**[35] 6241 3-8-11 **82** ... PhilipRobinson 5 (M A Jarvis) *hld up in tch: plld hrd: rdn over 2f out: wknd over 1f out* **4/1**[1]	69
1205	10	5	**Sea Chorus**[29] 6415 3-8-4 **75** ... (t) HayleyTurner 4 (M L W Bell) *chsd ldrs: rdn over 3f out: wknd over 2f out* **14/1**	54

2m 35.53s (2.03) **Going Correction** +0.225s/f (Good)

WFA 3 from 4yo+ 7lb **10** Ran SP% **115.1**

Speed ratings (Par 104): **102,101,100,99,99 98,97,94,92,89**

toteswinger: 1&2 £11.50, 1&3 £16.70, 2&3 £25.20. CSF £58.36 CT £1004.21 TOTE £10.20: £2.60, £2.70, £6.40; EX 70.80.

Owner W H Ponsonby **Bred** R N Auld **Trained** Barbury Castle, Wilts

FOCUS

A reasonable fillies' handicap. Spring Dream was one of several who looked as if they mght now be in the grip of the Handicapper, so this rates a personal best for her, and also for Interchange, who was far less exposed.

NOTEBOOK

Spring Dream(IRE), who had been the subject of steady support from double-figure prices, proved the strongest under a brave man's ride from Ryan Moore. He held the mare up off the pace and the gaps opened at the right time to allow her to get through nearest the rail over a furlong out and she scored well, despite jinking left inside the last furlong. She is consistent and won this off a mark 7lb higher than for her last success, so connections may opt to stick to the Flat with her, although she still qualifies for novices' hurdles. (op 17-2 tchd 7-1)

Interchange(IRE) adopted a similar route to the winner, sitting in the slipstream of the long-time leader before switching out and running on up the hill. She looks very much a galloper and, if kept in training, is likely to appreciate further. (op 8-1)

Encircled was perhaps the unlucky horse in the race, for after being held up at the back she was denied a run several times before finally getting through in the wake of the winner. Having only her second try over this trip, she stayed on well enough but could not close the gap. (op 16-1)
Candle appreciates even softer ground than this but was backed and looked likely to play a major part when going on at around the two-furlong pole. However, she was soon brushed aside when the winner committed and was run out of it up the hill. (op 12-1)
Critical Acclaim, the daughter of a Group 2 winner, had scored on her belated debut in a Polytrack maiden over this trip but the form had not worked out. Held up early, she made a significant forward move that brought her into contention on the run into the dip, but from that point she had nothing extra to offer. (op 11-2 tchd 5-1)
Quirina was in the right place most of the way but the response was limited in the latter stages and the longer trip may have found her out. (tchd 9-1)
Starfala had posted her best efforts on turf on faster ground and was 9lb above her last winning mark. She made the running but was quickly done with when headed at the quarter-mile mark. If kept in training she is likely to be seen to better effect on a sounder surface or back on Polytrack. (op 9-2 tchd 5-1)
Mango Lady, a winner over 1m4f on fast ground here last month, failed to figure on this easier surface. (op 12-1)
Island Vista, who was too keen over this trip in Listed company last time, settled better but found disappointingly little when pressure was applied. (op 7-2)
Sea Chorus also faded quickly and seems to have gone off the boil of late. (op 20-1)

7109 NGK SPARK PLUGS CONDITIONS STKS (RUN IN MEMORY OF REG DAY) 6f
3:00 (3:01) (Class 3) 2-3-Y-0
£7,477 (£2,239; £1,119; £560; £279; £140) **Stalls** High

Form RPR
0464 **1** **Khor Dubai (IRE)**[27] 6483 2-8-6 102 TedDurcan 5 86+
(Saeed Bin Suroor) *hld up: plenty to do over 1f out: rdn and edgd rt ins fnl f: r.o to ld nr fin* **11/4**[1]
104 **2** ¾ **Arabian Art (USA)**[39] 6174 3-8-13 78 CharlesEddery(7) 1 83
(H R A Cecil) *led and sn wl clr: rdn and edgd rt ins fnl f: hdd nr fin* **25/1**
21 **3** *hd* **Palace Moon**[97] 4431 3-9-11 88 SteveDrowne 4 87+
(H Morrison) *hld up: hdwy over 1f out: chsd ldr ins fnl f: r.o: edgd lft towards fin* **5/1**[2]
302 **4** *hd* **Kaldoun Kingdom (IRE)**[7] 6947 3-9-8 90 PaulHanagan 6 84+
(R A Fahey) *hld up: rdn and plenty to do over 1f out: swtchd rt and r.o wl ins fnl f* **11/4**[1]
0320 **5** *nk* **Polish Pride**[27] 6483 2-8-1 88 FrancisNorton 3 76
(M Brittain) *chsd clr ldr: rdn over 1f out: n.m.r towards fin: styd on* **8/1**[3]
3316 **6** *1* **Frognal (IRE)**[27] 6483 2-7-12 93 DavidProbert(5) 2 75
(B J Meehan) *hld up: plld hrd: hung rt fr 2f out: rdn and hdwy sn after: styng on whn hmpd towards fin* **11/4**[1]
0100 **7** *23* **Minwir (IRE)**[58] 5617 3-9-8 57 ShaneKelly 7 6
(M Quinn) *sn in rr: wknd over 2f out* **200/1**
1m 13.92s (1.72) **Going Correction** +0.225s/f (Good) 7 Ran SP% **112.1**
Speed ratings: **97,96,95,95,95 93,63**
toteswinger: 1&2 £6.60, 1&3 £3.10, 2&3 £5.60. CSF £68.51 TOTE £3.40: £1.90, £4.10; EX 51.90.
Owner Godolphin **Bred** K And Mrs Cullen **Trained** Newmarket, Suffolk

FOCUS
With the runner-up effectively getting loose up front the bare result is misleading, and this is not form to be positive about.

NOTEBOOK
Khor Dubai(IRE), the sixth two-year-old to win this in the last seven years, is better than the bare facts. He was dropped in from the start, so his rider was relying on his rivals to peg back the tearaway leader, and he took a while to get balanced when asked to close. He eventually found his stride and got up near the line to gain his third success of the season. This is his sort of level, but he might get 7f. (tchd 3-1 in places)
Arabian Art(USA), who had something to find at the weights with most of these, has bags of speed and was allowed far too much rope in front. Having built up a lead of around ten lengths by halfway she nearly held on, but she is obviously flattered by the bare result. (op 20-1)
Palace Moon ◆ had been off the track for three months since winning his maiden at Salisbury, and he had no easy task conceding weight all round. Although the form of the race as a whole is unreliable, he shaped with real credit and should make a nice four-year-old. (op 4-1 tchd 11-2)
Kaldoun Kingdom(IRE) was switched into the clear too late and could not get there. (op 5-2, tchd 3-1 in places)
Polish Pride seemed to have her chance. (op 9-1)

7110 BRIAN GROVES "LIFETIME IN RACING" H'CAP 2m
3:35 (3:35) (Class 3) (0-90,89) 3-Y-0+ **£9,066** (£2,697; £1,348; £673) **Stalls** Centre

Form RPR
1 **1** **Viper**[29] 6413 6-9-13 88 HayleyTurner 1 96
(R Hollinshead) *racd wd for the first 5 1/2f: chsd ldrs tl led over 10f out: rdn over 1f out: edgd rt ins fnl f: styd on wl* **4/1**
/565 **2** 1 ¾ **Absolut Power (GER)**[7] 6957 7-9-5 80 (v) SteveDrowne 4 86
(J A Geake) *led over 5f: chsd wnr: rdn over 1f out: styd on same pce ins fnl f* **8/1**
3600 **3** *1* **Ned Ludd (IRE)**[22] 6606 5-8-11 72 PatCosgrave 6 77
(J G Portman) *chsd ldr to over 10f out: remained handy: rdn over 1f out: no ex ins fnl f* **11/4**[1]
2202 **4** 3 ¼ **Callisto Moon**[15] 6329 4-8-9 70 JimCrowley 5 71
(Ian Williams) *racd wd tl over 10f out: prom: lost pl 1/2-way: rdn over 2f out: styd on ins fnl f: nt trble ldrs* **10/3**[2]
0303 **5** 3 ¾ **Grande Caiman (IRE)**[34] 6272 4-9-12 87 (b) RyanMoore 3 83
(R Hannon) *racd wd tl over 10f out: hld up: hdwy 1/2-way: rdn over 3f out: wknd over 1f out* **7/2**[3]
0-11 **6** *10* **Gala Evening**[192] 1547 6-10-0 89 AdamKirby 2 73
(J A B Old) *racd wd tl over 10f out: hld up: rdn and wknd over 2f out* **9/1**
3m 31.54s (0.74) **Going Correction** +0.225s/f (Good) 6 Ran SP% **113.1**
Speed ratings (Par 107): **107,106,105,104,102 97**
toteswinger: 1&2 £7.10, 1&3 £3.90, 2&3 £5.60. CSF £34.33 TOTE £3.80: £2.50, £4.50; EX 52.80.
Owner Geoff Lloyd **Bred** R Hollinshead **Trained** Upper Longdon, Staffs

FOCUS
Despite some decent prize-money, this was an ordinary staying handicap for the grade, featuring a smallish field made up of all-weather performers and hurdler/chasers. The winner was unexposed, however, and improved around 10lb on his debut win.

NOTEBOOK
Viper, a dual hurdles winner on sound surface, had run out a clear-cut scorer on his sole Flat start but looked to have been given a stiff enough mark for this handicap debut. He handled the easier ground, however, and Hayley Turner made good use of the his long stride, taking him to the front before the turn into the long straight and gradually winding things up. He is quite well handicapped should connections opt for a return to hurdles, but next year's Cesarewitch could well be in their thoughts following this improved performance. (op 7-2 tchd 9-2)
Absolut Power(GER) is lightly raced on the Flat and better known as a hurdler/chaser who is suited by a sound surface, but he ran well under a positive ride on this easier ground, leading early and then keeping tabs on the winner and staying on all the way to the line. (op 12-1)
Ned Ludd(IRE) had never won on the Flat but had dropped to his lowest-ever handicap mark and was sent off favourite. He got a good lead from the front two and had every chance passing the bushes, but failed to pick up and was run out of second place up the hill. (op 7-2, tchd 4-1 in places)
Callisto Moon, better known as a hurdler and last seen making his chasing debut, has had a consistent if luckless season on the Flat but was slightly disappointing. He was making little impression in the latter stages and probably found the easy ground against him. (op 9-2 tchd 3-1)
Grande Caiman(IRE), a four-time winner on Polytrack at up to 1m5f; had not won on turf but had slipped in weights and ran better in blinkers last time. However, they did not appear to have the same effect on this occasion and his rider was uneasy some way from home. Once under pressure he was soon beaten. (tchd 4-1)
Gala Evening, three times a winner over 2m on Kempton's Polytrack, had not run since April and was 5lb higher than for that last success. A drifter in the market, this outing was clearly needed and he never got out of last position. (op 9-2, tchd 10-1 in places)

7111 BETFAIR APPRENTICE TRAINING SERIES FINALE STKS (H'CAP) 1m
4:05 (4:05) (Class 5) (0-75,72) 3-Y-0 **£6,476** (£1,927; £963; £481) **Stalls** High

Form RPR
1545 **1** **Casino Night**[17] 6718 3-8-13 66 DeanHeslop 9 74
(R Johnson) *racd far side: chsd ldrs tl overall ldr 1/2-way: rdn and hung lft fr over 1f out: r.o* **10/1**
5600 **2** 1 ¾ **Misplaced Fortune**[8] 6935 3-8-2 58 StacyRenwick(3) 2 62
(N Tinkler) *racd centre: hld up: hdwy over 3f out: rdn to ld that gp over 1f out: ev ch ins fnl f: styd on same pce* **16/1**
0600 **3** 1 ½ **King Columbo (IRE)**[25] 6542 3-9-5 72 (v[1]) AmyBaker 1 72
(Miss J Feilden) *racd centre: prom: rdn over 2f out: edgd rt over 1f out: styd on* **9/1**
0331 **4** *hd* **Zeffirelli**[45] 6004 3-8-3 59 AshleyMorgan(3) 10 59
(M Quinn) *racd far side: overall ldr to 1/2-way: rdn and hung lft over 1f out: styd on same pce fnl f* **10/1**
1100 **5** 1 ¼ **Billberry**[23] 6585 3-8-11 64 (t) WilliamCarson 7 61
(S C Williams) *racd centre: led that gp: rdn over 3f out: hung lft and hdd over 1f out: styd on same pce* **9/1**
5524 **6** ¾ **Red Skipper (IRE)**[14] 6792 3-8-7 63 BMcHugh(3) 12 58
(N Wilson) *racd far side: chsd ldrs: rdn over 3f out: hung lft over 1f out: no ex* **11/2**[2]
0003 **7** ¾ **James Pollard (IRE)**[16] 6741 3-8-7 60 DavidProbert 11 54
(D R C Elsworth) *racd far side: plld hrd and prom: rdn over 3f out: hung lft and wknd over 1f out* **4/1**[1]
0605 **8** *shd* **Taken (IRE)**[9] 6905 3-9-3 70 FrederikTylicki 6 63
(Miss Gay Kelleway) *racd centre: prom: rdn over 3f out: wknd over 1f out* **13/2**[3]
4050 **9** 3 ½ **Cape Roberto (IRE)**[29] 6422 3-8-5 58 oh1 JemmaMarshall 5 43
(Jamie Poulton) *racd centre: chsd ldrs: racd keenly: rdn over 2f out: wknd over 1f out* **20/1**
1310 **10** 1 ½ **Oriental Girl**[29] 6417 3-9-0 67 (p) JackDean 8 49
(J A Geake) *racd far side: chsd ldrs: rdn and hung lft over 2f out: wknd over 1f out* **11/2**[2]
4500 **11** ¾ **Toballa**[15] 6762 3-8-2 58 oh12 CharlesEddery(3) 3 38
(H J Collingridge) *racd centre: hld up: rdn 1/2-way: a in rr* **40/1**
00-0 **12** 2 ½ **Chinese Profit**[38] 6192 3-8-6 62 BillyCray(3) 4 36
(G C Bravery) *racd centre: hld up: rdn and wknd over 2f out* **33/1**
1m 41.18s (2.58) **Going Correction** +0.225s/f (Good) 12 Ran SP% **118.3**
Speed ratings (Par 101): **96,94,92,92,91 90,89,89,86,84 83,81**
toteswinger: 1&2 £49.40, 1&3 £38.50, 2&3 £26.40. CSF £155.36 CT £1518.70 TOTE £8.50: £2.30, £6.10, £3.40; EX 172.40 Place 6 £ 37.18, Place 5 £ 21.36.
Owner Barry Robson **Bred** Kingsmead Breeders **Trained** Newburn, Tyne & Wear

FOCUS
A modest handicap restricted to apprentices who had not ridden more than 20 winners at the start of the Flat turf season. They went a good pace and raced across the track, with no apparent bias.
T/Plt: £115.70 to a £1 stake. Pool: £52,241.83. 329.60 winning tickets. T/Qpdt: £121.60 to a £1 stake. Pool: £3,617.80. 22.00 winning tickets. CR

6985 WOLVERHAMPTON (A.W) (L-H)
Friday, October 31

OFFICIAL GOING: Standard
Wind: Almost nil

7112 TOTESPORTGAMES.COM H'CAP (DIV I) 1m 141y(P)
6:20 (6:20) (Class 6) (0-52,53) 3-Y-0+ **£2,388** (£705; £352) **Stalls** Low

Form RPR
3001 **1** **The Grey One (IRE)**[9] 6913 5-8-10 53 6ex (p) MCGeran(5) 7 66
(J M Bradley) *towards rr: hdwy on outside over 2f out: wnt 2nd over 1f out: carried lft in fnl furlong tl led wl ins fnl f* **9/2**[2]
0005 **2** 1 ¼ **Dushstorm (IRE)**[7] 6955 7-8-11 49 JamesDoyle 3 59
(R J Price) *t.k.h: trckd ldrs: led 2f out: hung rt ent fnl f and hdd wl ins fnl f* **7/2**[1]
0200 **3** *4* **Dancing Duo**[37] 6208 4-8-10 48 (v) SaleemGolam 1 49
(D Shaw) *trckd ldrs: rdn over 2f out: styd on one pce to chse first 2 fnl f* **14/1**
060 **4** ½ **Social Rhythm**[7] 6951 4-8-10 51 (p) NeilBrown(3) 6 51+
(A C Whillans) *in rr: making hdwy but hung lft whn bmpd appr fnl f: one pce* **7/1**
4550 **5** 1 ½ **Lights Of Vegas**[9] 6912 4-8-10 48 TPQueally 2 44
(S Kirk) *prom: rdn 2f out: hung rt and no hdwy fr over 1f out* **10/1**
6004 **6** 2 ¾ **Karate Queen**[16] 6735 3-8-10 52 WilliamBuick 4 42
(A M Balding) *led tl narrowly hdd over 4f out: stl prom tl wknd wl over 1f out* **6/1**[3]
6000 **7** *nk* **Scutch Mill (IRE)**[34] 2957 6-8-7 52 (t) DeclanCannon(7) 11 41
(P C Haslam) *v.s.a: t.k.h and hld up in rr: hdwy on outside over 2f out: sn rdn and no further hdwy* **16/1**
410- **8** ½ **Lytham (IRE)**[371] 6479 7-8-12 50 VinceSlattery 13 38
(D J Wintle) *a towards rr though mde brief effrt over 3f out* **28/1**
5620 **9** *shd* **Highland Song (IRE)**[123] 3546 5-8-8 46 ChrisCatlin 9 34
(R F Fisher) *t.k.h: pressed ldr after 2f: led over 4f out: hdd 2f out: sn wknd* **28/1**
0410 **10** ½ **Personify**[8] 6927 6-8-11 52 (p) TolleyDean(3) 5 39
(J L Flint) *a struggling in rr* **6/1**[3]

0400 **11** *nk* **Oeuf A La Neige**[29] 6409 8-8-12 **50**........ TomEaves 8 36
(Miss L A Perratt) *a in rr* **12/1**

1m 54.15s (3.65) **Going Correction** +0.20s/f (Slow)
WFA 3 from 4yo+ 4lb **11** Ran SP% **117.7**
Speed ratings (Par 101): **91,89,86,85,84 82,81,81,80 80**
toteswinger: 1&2 £17.80, 1&3 £17.80, 2&3 £11.90. CSF £20.63 CT £205.72 TOTE £5.70: £1.90, £2.00, £5.70; EX 25.10.
Owner R Miles **Bred** Blackdown Stud **Trained** Sedbury, Gloucs
■ Stewards' Enquiry : T P Queally caution: careless riding

FOCUS
A low-grade handicap in which the pace slowed right up down the back straight before picking up on the approach to the home turn. The first pair pulled clear and this is probably fair form for the class despite the slow time.

7113 TOTESPORTCASINO.COM NURSERY 5f 20y(P)
6:50 (6:54) (Class 5) (0-75,75) 2-Y-O £3,885 (£1,156; £577; £288) **Stalls** Low

Form RPR

0001 **1** **Rainbow Seeker**[9] 6906 2-8-11 **65** 6ex........(b) KirstyMilczarek 5 79+
(W J Haggas) *s.i.s: sn in mid-div: hdwy to go 2nd 2f out: led ins fnl f: qcknd clr: comf* **11/8**[1]

4044 **2** *2 1/4* **Sweet Applause (IRE)**[14] 6769 2-9-5 **73**........ TPQueally 1 76
(A P Jarvis) *led: rdn over 1f out: hdd ins fnl f: nt pce of wnr* **4/1**[2]

1363 **3** *3 3/4* **Agnes Love**[27] 6469 2-8-10 **64**........ JamesDoyle 4 53
(J Akehurst) *mid-div: rdn 2f out: kpt on one pce to chse first 2 fnl f* **8/1**

1560 **4** *1* **Adozen Dreams**[31] 6350 2-8-5 **59**........(p) SilvestreDeSousa 11 45
(G R Oldroyd) *racd wd towards rr: styd on fr over 1f out: nvr nr to chal* **50/1**

1604 **5** *nk* **Transcentral**[19] 6666 2-9-0 **68**........ GrahamGibbons 8 53
(W M Brisbourne) *mid-div: rdn 3f out: no hdwy fr over 1f out* **16/1**

6002 **6** *3/4* **Celtic Rebel (IRE)**[9] 6906 2-8-1 **55**........ ChrisCatlin 7 37
(S A Callaghan) *s.i.s: rdn over 1f out: nvr on terms* **13/2**[3]

6430 **7** *1 1/4* **Fasliyanne (IRE)**[15] 6764 2-8-13 **67**........ JoeFanning 6 45
(K A Ryan) *in rr: mde sme late hdwy* **12/1**

1260 **8** *1/2* **Simple Rhythm**[16] 6732 2-9-1 **69**........ TomEaves 3 45
(N Tinkler) *t.k.h in mid-div: rdn 1/2-way: sn btn* **16/1**

650 **9** *nk* **Perfect Class**[30] 6389 2-8-8 **62**........ WilliamBuick 12 37
(C G Cox) *a towards rr* **16/1**

5440 **10** *nk* **Chimbonda**[67] 5363 2-9-4 **72**........(v[1]) TonyCulhane 10 46
(S Parr) *trckd ldr to 2f out: wknd over 1f out* **33/1**

3000 **11** *1/2* **Dotty's Brother**[16] 6732 2-8-1 **58**........(p) AndrewMullen(3) 2 30
(Mrs A Duffield) *chsd ldrs: rdn 2f out: sn wknd* **25/1**

002 **12** *nse* **Autumn Morning (IRE)**[27] 6489 2-8-4 **58** ow1........ GregFairley 13 30
(P D Evans) *a struggling in rr* **33/1**

62.51 secs (0.21) **Going Correction** +0.20s/f (Slow) **12** Ran SP% **123.6**
Speed ratings (Par 95): **106,102,96,94,94 93,91,90,89,89 88,88**
toteswinger: 1&2 £2.30, 1&3 £3.10, 2&3 £5.30. CSF £6.59 CT £35.05 TOTE £2.20: £1.30, £1.80, £2.30; EX 9.80.
Owner Dwayne Woods **Bred** Brook Stud Bloodstock Ltd **Trained** Newmarket, Suffolk

FOCUS
A reasonable nursery run at a strong pace, and the form ought to stand up with the winner capable of better still.

NOTEBOOK
Rainbow Seeker ◆ was 2lb well-in under the penalty he incurred for his Kempton win, and he followed up in the style of a progressive performer, quickly brushing aside the leader when asked to assert. The drop back in trip combined with the headgear has been the making of him and he should have more to offer. (op 7-4 tchd 15-8)
Sweet Applause(IRE), who was well-backed, showed bright pace to lead from the inside stall and had the majority of her rivals in trouble turning for home, but she was no match for the favourite. This was a creditable effort. (op 8-1)
Agnes Love ran well from a poor draw at Kempton and produced another good performance from this 2lb higher mark, chasing the pace and keeping on. (tchd 15-2)
Adozen Dreams, tried in cheekpieces for the first time, found herself having to race wide from her high draw but she was staying on well at the end and grabbed fourth on the line.
Transcentral ran better than on her two previous visits to Dunstall Park but is probably most effective at 6f. (tchd 14-1)
Celtic Rebel(IRE) was runner-up to Rainbow Seeker at Kempton but was beaten further here despite being 6lb better off. He gave himself work to do with a tardy start and looks ready for a return to 6f. (op 4-1)
Chimbonda Official explanation: jockey said colt moved poorly throughout

7114 TOTESPORTGAMES.COM H'CAP (DIV II) 1m 141y(P)
7:20 (7:20) (Class 6) (0-52,52) 3-Y-O+ £2,388 (£705; £352) **Stalls** Low

Form RPR

0/ **1** **Wakita (IRE)**[46] 5986 5-8-9 **47**........(t) TedDurcan 1 58+
(Aidan Anthony Howard, Ire) *racd in mid-div: smooth hdwy to ld over 1f out: r.o wl* **11/2**[3]

00-0 **2** *2* **Victory Spirit**[77] 5045 4-8-12 **50**........ TomEaves 12 57
(Miss L A Perratt) *in rr: hdwy and hung lft fr over 1f out: r.o ins fnl f to go 2nd toward fin* **20/1**

2500 **3** *3/4* **Winged Farasi**[188] 1626 4-8-9 **47**........ SamHitchcott 11 52
(Miss J E Foster) *in rr: rdn and hdwy to go 2nd 1f out: one pce and lost 2nd towards fin* **33/1**

3110 **4** *4* **Mr Chocolate Drop (IRE)**[241] 792 4-9-0 **52**........(b) SaleemGolam 6 48
(Miss M E Rowland) *mid-div: rdn to go 2nd 3f out: wknd appr fnl f* **12/1**

6544 **5** *2* **Golden Brown (IRE)**[9] 6913 4-8-9 **47**........(p) FergusSweeney 13 38
(David Pinder) *in rr: mde sme hdwy fr over 1f out* **9/2**[2]

2002 **6** *nk* **Ardent Prince**[7] 6955 5-8-10 **51**........ TolleyDean(3) 5 42
(A J McCabe) *in rr: rdn over 3f out: nvr nr to chal* **4/1**[1]

5600 **7** *3 1/4* **Beck**[18] 6693 4-8-7 **48**........ DuranFentiman(3) 4 31
(W M Brisbourne) *sn trckd ldr: led 3f out: hdd & wknd over 1f out* **18/1**

000 **8** *1 3/4* **Blockley (USA)**[152] 2640 4-8-12 **50**........ VinceSlattery 3 29
(Ian Williams) *slowly away: a bhd* **16/1**

4000 **9** *11* **Goose Green (IRE)**[9] 6912 4-8-10 **48**........ FrancisNorton 9 2
(R J Hodges) *chsd ldrs tl rdn and wknd 3f out* **8/1**

0200 **10** *3 1/2* **Faraday (IRE)**[9] 6189 5-8-13 **51**........(b) ShaneKelly 7 —
(N P Mulholland) *led tl hdd 3f out: rdn and sn wknd* **4/1**[1]

3305 **11** *10* **Muncaster Castle (IRE)**[13] 6806 4-9-0 **52**........ ChrisCatlin 2 —
(R F Fisher) *prom on ins tl wknd qckly over 4f out* **8/1**

1m 51.63s (1.13) **Going Correction** +0.20s/f (Slow) **59** Ran SP% **122.3**
Speed ratings (Par 101): **102,100,99,96,94 93,91,89,79,76 67**
toteswinger: 1&2 £14.10, 1&3 £60.70, 2&3 £148.60. CSF £113.66 CT £3399.06 TOTE £5.10: £1.80, £6.90, £9.30; EX 155.10.
Owner Mrs Ann D Coogan **Bred** M Coogan **Trained** Kildalkey, Co Meath

FOCUS
Another decidedly moderate contest, but it was run in a time over two seconds quicker than the first division. The form should prove sound and the winner could be worth more than the bare form.

Blockley(USA) Official explanation: jockey said gelding missed the break

7115 TOTESPORTBINGO.COM H'CAP 1m 141y(P)
7:50 (7:50) (Class 5) (0-70,70) 3-Y-O+ £3,885 (£1,156; £577; £288) **Stalls** Low

Form RPR

6342 **1** **Beetuna (IRE)**[13] 6821 3-9-1 **67**........(v) TomEaves 6 78
(B Smart) *a in tch: hdwy to ld 1f out: rdn out* **9/2**[3]

0001 **2** *1 3/4* **Wing Play (IRE)**[8] 6936 3-9-0 **66** 6ex........(p) WilliamBuick 1 73
(H Morrison) *trckd ldrs: ev ch 1f out: kpt on but no imp ins fnl f* **9/4**[1]

0032 **3** *1* **Crocodile Bay (IRE)**[3] 7048 5-9-3 **70**........ JamesO'Reilly(5) 4 75
(John A Harris) *t.k.h: trckd ldrs: led over 2f out: hdd 1f out and sn lost 2nd* **5/2**[2]

0420 **4** *1 1/2* **Claret And Amber**[12] 6841 6-9-6 **68**........ ChrisCatlin 5 69
(W K Goldsworthy) *mid-div: kpt on one pce fr over 1f out* **11/2**

0400 **5** *3 1/4* **King's Icon (IRE)**[13] 6825 3-8-0 **59** ow1........ TobyAtkinson(7) 9 53
(M Wigham) *in rr: mde sme late hdwy but nvr on terms* **25/1**

1200 **6** *2 1/2* **Tevez**[19] 6683 3-9-4 **70**........ TPQueally 2 58
(Miss Amy Weaver) *v.s.a: a in rr* **16/1**

1600 **7** *hd* **Billy One Punch**[13] 6813 6-9-3 **65**........ DarrenWilliams 10 53
(D Shaw) *hld up in rr: brief effrt over 1f out: nvr on terms* **16/1**

-200 **8** *1* **Raquel White**[213] 1127 4-8-11 **62**........ KevinGhunowa(3) 3 47
(J L Flint) *led tl hdd over 2f out: sn wknd* **28/1**

3015 **9** *1 1/2* **Royal Straight**[16] 6741 3-9-0 **69**........ RussellKennemore(3) 7 51
(B N Pollock) *slowly into st: sn in mid-div: rdn 3f out and sn wknd* **12/1**

0040 **10** *6* **John Potts**[37] 6216 3-8-4 **56**........ GregFairley 8 24
(B P J Baugh) *in tch on outside tl rdn and wknd 3f out* **66/1**

1m 52.42s (1.92) **Going Correction** +0.20s/f (Slow)
WFA 3 from 4yo+ 4lb **10** Ran SP% **121.2**
Speed ratings (Par 103): **99,97,96,95,92 90,89,89,87,82**
toteswinger: 1&2 £2.50, 1&3 £3.40, 2&3 £2.90. CSF £15.47 CT £32.49 TOTE £6.40: £2.00, £1.40, £1.10; EX 17.50.
Owner Prime Equestrian **Bred** David Kiersey And Denise Power **Trained** Hambleton, N Yorks
■ Stewards' Enquiry : Darren Williams one-day ban: careless riding (Nov 14)

FOCUS
This modest handicap looked to be steadily run and nothing got involved from the rear, but the form among the principals seems sound enough.
Tevez Official explanation: jockey said gelding hit its head on the stalls
Royal Straight Official explanation: jockey said gelding was upset in the stalls and missed the break

7116 OVER 100 GAMES AT TOTESPORTCASINO.COM H'CAP 1m 1f 103y(P)
8:20 (8:20) (Class 4) (0-85,85) 3-Y-O+ £5,180 (£1,541; £770; £384) **Stalls** Low

Form RPR

1632 **1** **Royal Amnesty**[28] 6450 5-8-13 **76**........(b) TomEaves 2 82+
(Miss L A Perratt) *slowly away: in rr: rdn whn n.m.r ent fnl f: swtchd rt ins fnl f: str burst to ld post* **5/2**[1]

-000 **2** *nk* **Hold The Gold (IRE)**[15] 6757 3-8-6 **73**........ ChrisCatlin 6 78
(E J O'Neill) *in rr: plenty to do whn swtchd rt over 1f out: r.o ins fnl f to go 2nd post* **9/1**

3265 **3** *nk* **Del Mar Sunset**[6] 6989 9-8-11 **74**........ KirstyMilczarek 3 78
(W J Haggas) *in tch on ins: hdwy to ld briefly wl ins fnl f: hdd and lost 2nd cl home* **9/2**[2]

0410 **4** *3/4* **New Star (UAE)**[7] 6950 4-9-1 **78**........ GrahamGibbons 7 80
(W M Brisbourne) *trckd ldr: rdn to ld over 1f out: hdd wl ins fnl f: no ex* **9/2**[2]

5-0 **5** *hd* **Saltagioo (ITY)**[21] 6625 4-9-8 **85**........ TedDurcan 1 87
(M Botti) *trckd ldrs: rdn over 2f out: nt qckn ins fnl f* **16/1**

0305 **6** *1 1/4* **Red Birr (IRE)**[7] 6950 7-9-0 **77**........(t) WilliamBuick 4 76
(P R Webber) *in tch: rdn over 2f out: hld whn hmpd appr fnl f: kpt on cl home* **8/1**

0050 **7** *3/4* **Prince Of Light (IRE)**[4] 7019 5-9-5 **82**........ GregFairley 8 80
(M Johnston) *sn led: rdn and hdd over 1f out: wknd ins fnl f* **5/1**[3]

0010 **8** *7* **Just Bond (IRE)**[27] 6482 6-9-8 **85**........ PJMcDonald 5 68
(G R Oldroyd) *a struggling in rr* **5/1**[3]

2m 3.35s (1.65) **Going Correction** +0.20s/f (Slow)
WFA 3 from 4yo+ 4lb **8** Ran SP% **125.3**
Speed ratings (Par 105): **100,99,99,98,98 97,96,90**
toteswinger: 1&2 £4.70, 1&3 £2.40, 2&3 £11.30. CSF £29.51 CT £102.80 TOTE £4.00: £1.30, £3.40, £1.60; EX 42.60.
Owner Mrs Francesca Mitchell **Bred** Brick Kiln Stud, Mrs L Hicks & Partners **Trained**

FOCUS
A fair handicap run at just an ordinary pace. It produced a blanket finish and this is probably not form to take too literally although it makes some sense.

7117 HOTEL & CONFERENCING AT WOLVERHAMPTON MAIDEN FILLIES' STKS 1m 141y(P)
8:50 (8:53) (Class 5) 2-Y-O £3,238 (£963; £481; £240) **Stalls** Low

Form RPR

32 **1** **Daylumney (IRE)**[49] 5870 2-9-0 0........ ChrisCatlin 4 73
(E J O'Neill) *trckd ldr: led wl over 2f out: rdn clr over 1f out but kpt up to work* **5/6**[1]

00 **2** *4 1/2* **Labisa (IRE)**[7] 6945 2-9-0 0........ TravisBlock 11 64
(H Morrison) *mid-div: rdn and hdwy to go 2nd 2f out: sn outpointed by wnr and jst hld on for 2nd* **11/2**[2]

0 **3** *shd* **Precocious Air (IRE)**[21] 6622 2-9-0 0........ TPQueally 2 63
(J A Osborne) *mid-div: hdwy over 1f out: r.o wl fnl f: jst failed to go 2nd* **13/2**[3]

4 *3/4* **Moonbeam Dancer (USA)** 2-9-0 0........ RichardMullen 8 62
(D M Simcock) *mid-div: styd on fr over 1f out: nvr nrr* **14/1**

6200 **5** *3 3/4* **Fongoli**[8] 6924 2-9-0 59........ WilliamBuick 7 54
(B G Powell) *prom: wnt 2nd briefly over 2f out: sn wknd* **11/1**

6 *1 1/2* **Passage To India (IRE)** 2-9-0 0........ ShaneKelly 6 51
(J A Osborne) *towards rr: c wd into st: styd on but nvr nr to chal* **14/1**

0 **7** *1 3/4* **Dubai Diva**[10] 6887 2-9-0 0........ TedDurcan 5 47
(C F Wall) *in tch whn nt clr run over 2f out: sn btn* **16/1**

0 **8** *5* **Vita Mia**[27] 6480 2-9-0 0........ TonyCulhane 12 37
(P C Haslam) *sltly bmpd on bnd 7f out: a in rr* **80/1**

00 **9** *4* **Step Fast (USA)**[34] 6291 2-9-0 0........ GregFairley 1 28
(M Johnston) *trckd ldrs tl rdn and wknd 3f out* **22/1**

10 *nk* **Silk Star (IRE)** 2-8-11 0........ RussellKennemore(3) 3 28
(Mrs L Williamson) *v.s.a: a bhd* **66/1**

000 **11** *7* **Bella Olympia**[106] 4109 2-8-9 37........(p) DavidProbert(5) 10 13
(A J McCabe) *led tl hdd wl over 2f out: wknd rapidly* **80/1**

The Form Book, Raceform Ltd, Compton, RG20 6NL

0 12 19 **Diamond Jo (IRE)**[17] 6722 2-9-0 0 TomEaves 13 —
(Mrs L Williamson) *a bhd: lost tch over 3f out* **33/1**
1m 53.21s (2.71) **Going Correction** +0.20s/f (Slow) 12 Ran SP% **122.1**
Speed ratings (Par 92): **95,91,90,90,86 85,84,79,76,75 69,52**
toteswinger: 1&2 £1.40, 1&3 £2.10 CSF £5.57 TOTE £2.10: £1.10, £1.90, £1.90; EX 6.80.
Owner Miss A H Marshall **Bred** Frank Dunne **Trained** Averham Park, Notts

FOCUS
Just a moderate fillies' maiden overall but a fair winner.

NOTEBOOK
Daylumney(IRE) was always well placed before being driven clear in the straight for a decisive victory. Runner-up here last time to Stevie Junior, who has gone on to frank the form, she is out of a Group 3-winning mare and may bid for some black type of her own in a Listed race at Marseilles next month. (tchd 8-11 and 10-11)
Labisa(IRE) made good progress around the field on the last turn and chased the winner home at a respectful distance. She is capable of gaining those all-important winning brackets and now has the option of handicaps. (op 5-1)
Precocious Air(IRE) ◆ ran a taking race on her second start. Caught on heels before the home turn, she ran on nicely once into the clear and would have been second with a bit further to run. Further improvement should be forthcoming next time. (op 9-1)
Moonbeam Dancer(USA), who is related to some useful performers in the US, ran a promising debut in fourthand should know more next time.
Fongoli, rated 59 and seemingly exposed, looked to run her race with no excuses. (op 14-1)
Passage To India(IRE), a stablemate of the third, made a satisfactory debut and the experience should not be lost. (op 11-1)
Dubai Diva, who is out of a half-sister to Arc winner Marienbard, showed more than on her turf debut and should improve in time. (op 25-1 tchd 14-1)

7118 STAY AT THE WOLVERHAMPTON HOLIDAY INN H'CAP 5f 216y(P)
9:20 (9:24) (Class 5) (0-70,69) 3-Y-O+ **£3,885** (£1,156; £577; £288) **Stalls** Low

Form				RPR
1565	1		**Welcome Approach**[9] 6907 5-8-5 55 oh1 ChrisCatlin 1 (J R Weymes) *in rr: rdn and hdwy appr fnl f: r.o to ld wl ins fnl f* **15/2**	64
5006	2	1	**Gwilym (GER)**[21] 6634 5-8-9 64 DavidProbert(5) 4 (D Haydn Jones) *t.k.h in tch: rdn to ld 1f out: hdd wl ins fnl f* **15/2**	69
3200	3	1	**Bentley**[41] 6132 4-8-12 62 (v) TPQueally 11 (J G Given) *in tch on outside: rdn 1/2-way: styd on wl fnl f* **16/1**	64
4330	4	½	**Coleorton Dancer**[37] 6218 6-9-1 65 (p) SilvestreDeSousa 10 (K A Ryan) *mid-div: hdwy on ins to go 2nd briefly 1f out: kpt on one pce* **7/1**[3]	65
0404	5	¾	**Another Genepi (USA)**[28] 6448 5-9-5 69 EdwardCreighton 7 (E J Creighton) *slowly away: sn pushed along in rr: hdwy over 1f out: kpt on* **18/1**	66
0234	6	¾	**Royal Degree**[13] 6822 3-8-12 63 (t) TomEaves 13 (B Smart) *mid-div: rdn and hdwy to go 3rd 2f out: wknd ins fnl f* **8/1**	58
4121	7	1	**Kyllachy Storm**[9] 6895 4-8-6 61 6ex WilliamCarson(5) 12 (R J Hodges) *trckd ldrs: wnt 2nd over 3f out: rdn and wknd appr fnl f* **9/4**[1]	52
0130	8	1 ½	**Just Spike**[10] 6890 5-8-0 57 ow2 BillyCray(7) 3 (B P J Baugh) *slowly away: drvn and hung bdly lft fr over 1f out: nvr on terms* **20/1**	43
1410	9	nk	**Music Box Express**[30] 6377 4-8-10 67 (t) MatthewDavies(7) 9 (George Baker) *led after 1f out: rdn and hdd 1f out: wknd qckly* **15/2**	52
1130	10	¾	**Commander Wish**[10] 6880 5-9-4 68 (p) WilliamBuick 5 (Lucinda Featherstone) *sn outpcd: a bhd* **11/2**[2]	50
0502	11	4	**Lambrini Lace (IRE)**[29] 6411 3-8-5 56 SaleemGolam 2 (Mrs L Williamson) *in tch tl wknd 1/2-way* **12/1**	23
400	12	8	**Bishopbriggs (USA)**[15] 6765 3-9-0 68 TolleyDean(3) 8 (S Parr) *led for 1f: rdn and wknd over 2f out: eased whn wl bhd fnl f* **16/1**	7

1m 15.07s (0.07) **Going Correction** +0.20s/f (Slow)
WFA 3 from 4yo+ 1lb 12 Ran SP% **134.5**
Speed ratings (Par 103): **107,105,104,103,102 101,100,98,97,96 91,80**
toteswinger: 1&2 £39.70, 1&3 £19.80, 2&3 £0. CSF £71.73 CT £930.20 TOTE £13.40: £3.80, £3.30, £7.00; EX 72.90 Place 6 £ 34.93, Place 5 £ 17.91.
Owner T A Scothern **Bred** P Wyatt And Ranby Hall **Trained** Middleham Moor, N Yorks

FOCUS
Fast and furious in this ordinary sprint, with the picture changing quickly in the final furlong. The form could be rated a bit higher but it will probably pat to take a slightly negative view.
Just Spike Official explanation: jockey said gelding missed the break
T/Plt: £44.30 to a £1 stake. Pool: £97,282.44. 1,600.53 winning tickets. T/Qpdt: £20.90 to a £1 stake. Pool: £7,872.88. 278.16 winning tickets. JS

7119 - 7125a (Foreign Racing) - See Raceform Interactive

6405 AYR (L-H)
Saturday, November 1

OFFICIAL GOING: Heavy (4.2)
Wind: Light, across Weather: Cloudy, bright

7126 GREENPARK GARAGE MAIDEN STKS 7f 50y
12:50 (12:50) (Class 5) 2-Y-O **£3,885** (£1,156; £577; £288) **Stalls** Low

Form				RPR
6	1		**Distant Memories (IRE)**[15] 6789 2-9-3 0 MickyFenton 2 (T P Tate) *mde all: pushed along 2f out: styd on strly* **5/1**[3]	80
02	2	2 ¼	**Inflammable**[13] 6837 2-8-12 0 J-PGuillambert 8 (Sir Mark Prescott) *trckd ldrs on outside: effrt and chsd wnr over 1f out: r.o fnl f* **11/8**[1]	70
632	3	7	**Hard Luck Story**[31] 6384 2-9-3 73 TomEaves 3 (Miss L A Perratt) *chsd wnr to over 1f out: wknd fnl f* **7/4**[2]	58
0	4	13	**Bushveld (IRE)**[18] 6723 2-9-3 0 RobertWinston 1 (M Johnston) *prom: effrt over 2f out: wknd over 1f out* **12/1**	27
0	5	1	**Desdamona (IRE)**[15] 6785 2-8-8 0 ow1 SladeO'Hara(5) 7 (A Berry) *hld up in tch: struggling over 2f out: sn btn* **150/1**	20
0	6	18	**Fifer (IRE)**[15] 6788 2-8-12 0 PaulHanagan 6 (R A Fahey) *t.k.h: in tch tl wknd over 2f out* **20/1**	—
0	7	5	**Mull Of Fire (IRE)**[14] 6811 2-8-10 0 KrishGundowry(7) 4 (A Berry) *bhd: struggling 3f out: sn wknd* **100/1**	—

1m 39.8s (6.40) **Going Correction** +0.95s/f (Soft) 7 Ran SP% **109.2**
Speed ratings (Par 96): **101,98,90,75,74 53,48**
toteswinger: 1&2 £1.70, 1&3 £2.20, 2&3 £1.10. CSF £11.23 TOTE £6.90: £2.70, £1.30; EX 13.30.
Owner JMH Lifestyle Ltd **Bred** Kildaragh Stud **Trained** Tadcaster, N Yorks

FOCUS
The ground was very testing and they came home well strung out. The winner stepped forward but the third was below his Newcastle figure in similar conditions.

NOTEBOOK
Distant Memories(IRE) had clearly learnt plenty from his first run over a mile on much less testing ground at Redcar two weeks earlier. A decent type, he made this a true test and, making the best of his way home, he never really looked like being overhauled. He should make a decent handicapper over a mile plus at three. (op 6-1 tchd 7-1)
Inflammable, runner-up on the all-weather at Southwell, was an uneasy favourite. Brought wide once in line for home, she never gave up trying but in truth was never going to get in a blow. By Montjeu out of a staying dam-line, she is sure to find an opportunity but she will not start her career in handicap company from anything like a lenient mark. (op 11-10 tchd Evens & 6-4 in places)
Hard Luck Story, the most experienced in the line-up, has an official rating of 73 after three previous starts. He kept close tabs on the winner, but dropped right away coming to the final furlong. It is doubtful if he ran anywhere near his official mark. (op 9-4)
Bushveld(IRE), dropped in at the start, tended to run too keenly and stopped to nothing in the end. (op 9-1 tchd 14-1)
Desdamona(IRE), beaten a long way on her debut at Redcar two weeks earlier, was out of contention and driven along turning in. (tchd 200-1)

7127 KELBURNE CONSTRUCTION LTD H'CAP 1m
1:25 (1:26) (Class 3) (0-90,88) 3-Y-O+ **£9,714** (£2,890; £1,444; £721) **Stalls** Low

Form				RPR
3022	1		**Suits Me**[16] 6763 5-9-6 88 MickyFenton 3 (T P Tate) *mde all: rdn stands' side 2f out: kpt on strly fnl f* **6/4**[1]	101+
3065	2	3	**Kingsdale Orion (IRE)**[3] 7083 4-9-3 85 TomEaves 4 (B Ellison) *trckd ldrs: drvn stands' side over 2f out: kpt on fnl f: wnt 2nd last 75yds* **11/4**[2]	91
0500	3	½	**Spinning**[13] 6841 5-8-0 75 (b) DeanHeslop(7) 5 (T D Barron) *rdr slow to remove blindfold: hld up: effrt and ev ch stands' side over 1f out: no ex and lost 2nd last 75yds* **7/1**	80
1314	4	8	**Wind Shuffle (GER)**[24] 6582 5-8-6 79 ow1 GaryBartley(5) 1 (J S Goldie) *prom: styd far side in st: effrt 2f out: sn rdn and wknd* **7/2**[3]	65
00-0	5	6	**Trafalgar Bay (IRE)**[43] 6069 5-9-5 87 AndrewElliott 2 (K R Burke) *hld up: rdn far side 3f out: sn wknd* **20/1**	60

1m 49.92s (6.12) **Going Correction** +0.95s/f (Soft) 5 Ran SP% **106.2**
Speed ratings (Par 107): **107,104,103,95,89**
toteswinger: 1&2 £3.60. CSF £5.36 TOTE £2.70: £1.30, £1.70; EX 6.20.
Owner D E Cook **Bred** R S A Urquhart **Trained** Tadcaster, N Yorks

FOCUS
A fair handicap. A slight personal best for the front-running winner, with the second rated to his latest mark.

NOTEBOOK
Suits Me, without a win this year but in fine form and 9lb higher than his last success at this track a year ago, won the battle of the front-runners. Brought wide in the home straight, he kept up the gallop all the way to the line. An admirable type, he had been led out unsold at Newmarket Sales on Thursday and is clearly very tough. He should continue to give connections plenty of fun at six. (op 2-1)
Kingsdale Orion(IRE), struggling since his win from a 3lb lower mark at Newcastle in June, stuck to his guns to claim second spot near the line. He should make his mark over hurdles this winter. (op 5-2 tchd 3-1)
Spinning, off the boil since his win at Newcastle in June, had the hood removed very late. Hard at work once in line for home, after going in pursuit of the winner he never really threatened and missed out on second spot near the line. He does not really appreciate conditions as testing as he encountered here. (op 9-2 tchd 4-1)
Wind Shuffle(GER), a winner five times this year, has risen 18lb in the ratings as a result. 3lb higher than when winning here in September, he is at his best with a rail on his left-hand side, so he stayed on the far side in the home straight. (tchd 3-1 and 4-1)

7128 KIDZPLAY H'CAP 1m 7f
2:00 (2:00) (Class 4) (0-85,80) 3-Y-O+
£7,477 (£2,239; £1,119; £560; £279; £140) **Stalls** Low

Form				RPR
0006	1		**Puy D'Arnac (FR)**[8] 6948 5-9-8 74 RobertWinston 9 (G A Swinbank) *t.k.h early: hld up: smooth hdwy over 2f out: led over 1f out: rdn and r.o wl* **3/1**[1]	83
1050	2	¾	**Mighty Moon**[14] 6817 5-9-9 75 PaulHanagan 5 (R A Fahey) *hld up: hdwy over 2f out: chsd wnr 1f out: kpt on fin* **9/2**[3]	83
-525	3	3 ¾	**First Look (FR)**[12] 6861 8-9-4 70 MickyFenton 4 (P Monteith) *prom: effrt over 3f out: edgd lft and outpcd 2f out: r.o fnl f* **5/1**	73
1320	4	nk	**Nero West (FR)**[47] 5967 7-9-4 70 (b) TomEaves 2 (Miss L A Perratt) *led: rdn over 4f out: hdd over 1f out: no ex* **9/1**	73
1421	5	8	**Grandad Bill (IRE)**[21] 6657 5-8-12 69 KellyHarrison(5) 7 (J S Goldie) *hld up: hdwy on outside over 2f out: rdn and wknd over 1f out* **4/1**[2]	61
50	6	6	**Blushing Heart**[12] 6862 4-8-11 63 PJMcDonald 1 (G M Moore) *prom tl rdn and wknd over 2f out* **28/1**	48
6-36	7	1 ¾	**Categorical**[15] 6790 5-8-13 65 TonyHamilton 3 (K G Reveley) *cl up: rdn over 3f out: sn lost pl* **8/1**	47
5-60	8	14	**Mirjan (IRE)**[8] 6948 12-9-9 80 (b) FrederikTylicki(5) 8 (L Lungo) *hld up ins: drvn fr 1/2-way: struggling fnl 5f* **12/1**	44
0	9	85	**Francesco (FR)**[21] 6652 4-9-3 72 AndrewMullen(3) 6 (Mrs L B Normile) *prom: rdn after 5f: lost tch fr 5f out* **20/1**	—

3m 36.07s (15.67) **Going Correction** +0.95s/f (Soft) 9 Ran SP% **116.9**
Speed ratings (Par 105): **96,95,93,93,89 85,85,77,32**
toteswinger: 1&2 £3.60, 1&3 £2.30, 2&3 £7.10. CSF £16.78 CT £65.41 TOTE £4.50: £1.90, £2.00, £1.40; EX 18.00.
Owner Barrow Brook Racing **Bred** Mrs Axelle Du Verdier **Trained** Melsonby, N Yorks

FOCUS
A fair handicap but few showed their form on this bad ground. The winner is rated back to something like his early-season form.
Francesco(FR) Official explanation: jockey said gelding was lame near-fore

7129 DAWN DEVELOPMENTS H'CAP 7f 50y
2:35 (2:36) (Class 4) (0-80,80) 3-Y-O+
£6,231 (£1,866; £933; £467; £233; £117) **Stalls** Low

Form				RPR
5014	1		**Quest For Success (IRE)**[4] 7041 3-9-2 78 PaulHanagan 3 (R A Fahey) *trckd ldr: led 2f out: styd on strly to go clr fnl f* **11/8**[1]	89
0100	2	4 ½	**Misphire**[46] 5991 5-9-2 77 (p) TonyHamilton 1 (M Dods) *prom: effrt over 2f out: chsd wnr ins fnl f: no imp* **4/1**[3]	76
5500	3	3	**Fire Up The Band**[39] 6184 9-7-13 66 oh4 KellyHarrison(5) 2 (A Berry) *led to 2f out: wknd fnl f* **20/1**	56
5044	4	¾	**Glasshoughton**[18] 6724 5-9-0 75 TomEaves 4 (M Dods) *t.k.h: hld up in tch: rdn over 2f out: nvr rchd ldrs* **3/1**[2]	64

0060 **5** *1 1/4* **Geojimali**[21] 6651 6-9-0 **80** .... GaryBartley(5) 5 66
(J S Goldie) *prom tl rdn and no ex over 1f out* **15/2**

0064 **6** *1 1/2* **Hansomis (IRE)**[15] 6791 4-8-8 **70** oh14 ow4........ PJMcDonald 6 50
(B Mactaggart) *hld up in tch: rdn over 2f out: sn wknd* **12/1**

1m 40.08s (6.68) **Going Correction** +0.95s/f (Soft)
WFA 3 from 4yo+ 1lb **6** Ran SP% **111.3**
Speed ratings (Par 105): **99,93,90,89,88 86**
toteswinger: 1&2 £1.60, 1&3 £3.30, 2&3 £15.20. CSF £7.07 TOTE £2.00: £1.80, £2.30; EX 8.00.
Owner Rob Lloyd Racing Limited **Bred** Desmond Monaghan **Trained** Musley Bank, N Yorks

FOCUS
A weak handicap run in a slower time than the later lesser handicap. The form has been rated through the winner, with doubts over the rest.

7130 CHRISTMAS PARTY NIGHTS AT AYR RACECOURSE NURSERY 7f 50y
3:10 (3:10) (Class 5) (0-75,75) 2-Y-O £3,885 (£1,156; £577; £288) **Stalls** Low

Form RPR

3000 **1** **Becausewecan (USA)**[7] 6970 2-8-13 **67**........ RobertWinston 4 69
(M Johnston) *trckd ldrs: rdn to ld over 1f out: styd on wl* **13/8**[1]

2636 **2** *2 1/4* **Verinco**[26] 6525 2-9-7 **75**........ TomEaves 5 72
(B Smart) *in tch: effrt over 2f out: chsd wnr ins fnl f: kpt on* **9/2**[3]

0444 **3** *3 1/4* **Grissom (IRE)**[4] 7038 2-8-8 **62**........ PaulHanagan 2 51
(A Berry) *cl up: chal over 1f out: wknd ins fnl f* **6/1**

1155 **4** *1* **Bold Account (IRE)**[3] 7065 2-9-1 **69**........ AndrewElliott 1 55
(K R Burke) *led to over 1f out: sn wknd* **15/8**[2]

0050 **5** *13* **Meg Jicaro**[24] 6579 2-7-5 **52** oh2........(p) MatthewLawson(7) 3 7
(Mrs L Williamson) *s.s: sn rcvrd and in tch: hung lft and wknd fr 3f out* **20/1**

1m 41.59s (8.19) **Going Correction** +0.95s/f (Soft) **5** Ran SP% **110.1**
Speed ratings (Par 96): **91,88,84,83,68**
CSF £9.23 TOTE £2.60: £1.50, £2.10; EX 10.20.
Owner Douglas Livingston **Bred** Tony Holmes & Walter Zent **Trained** Middleham Moor, N Yorks

FOCUS
Another race that was intended to be run over six furlongs. Mainly exposed types in this modest nursery run at just a steady pace in the bad ground to past the halfway mark, and they all came wide in the home straight. The form is rated through the first two.

NOTEBOOK
Becausewecan(USA), raised to 74 after finishing third at Redcar four outings earlier, has not covered himself in glory since but here, keeping tabs on the leader, he ran out a most convincing winner. A return to a mile will not be a problem. Official explanation: trainer had no explanation for the apparent improvement in form (op 2-1 tchd 9-4)
Verinco, who started life in nursery company from an 8lb higher mark, stuck on to claim second inside the last. This was his first try at this trip and on testing ground but he clearly has his limitations. (op 4-1)
Grissom(IRE), having his second outing in four days, did not see out the extra furlong. (op 4-1)
Bold Account(IRE), fifth in an all-weather claimer at Great Leighs three days earlier, took them along, but was readily put in his place and is not progressing. (op 9-4 tchd 7-4)
Meg Jicaro, 2lb out of the handicap, made an awkward start in first-time cheekpieces then ran too freely, before hanging left and dropping right away, her stamina for this trip unproven. Even so it was an unsatisfactory effort. (op 16-1)

7131 RACING UK H'CAP 7f 50y
3:45 (3:46) (Class 5) (0-75,72) 3-Y-O+ £3,885 (£1,156; £577; £288) **Stalls** Low

Form RPR

0620 **1** **Out Of Nothing**[14] 6821 5-7-12 **58**........ AmyKathleenParsons(7) 4 66
(K M Prendergast) *mde all: rdn and hld on gamely fnl 2f* **7/1**

0132 **2** *1 1/4* **Distant Pleasure**[30] 6409 4-8-5 **58**........ DaleGibson 6 63
(M Dods) *hld up: rdn and hdwy over 2f out: chsd wnr over 1f out: kpt on* **11/4**[1]

0600 **3** *1 1/4* **Grethel (IRE)**[15] 6786 4-8-2 **58** oh2........ AndrewMullen(3) 2 60
(A Berry) *prom: effrt over 2f out: one pce fnl f* **14/1**

1066 **4** *shd* **Balakiref**[18] 6724 9-9-5 **72**........ TonyHamilton 3 73
(M Dods) *in tch: drvn 2f out: one pce fnl f* **9/2**[2]

0304 **5** *8* **Yorkshire Blue**[30] 6411 9-8-3 **61**........(p) KellyHarrison(5) 1 41
(J S Goldie) *hld up in tch: effrt over 2f out: edgd rt and sn outpcd* **7/1**

2002 **6** *4* **Top Tribute**[15] 6792 3-8-9 **63**........ MickyFenton 9 32
(T P Tate) *plld hrd: cl up tl wknd over 1f out* **5/1**[3]

4200 **7** *1/2* **Jamieson Gold (IRE)**[28] 6487 5-9-5 **72**........(p) PaulHanagan 8 40
(Miss L A Perratt) *hld up: rdn 3f out: sn wknd* **8/1**

2164 **8** *5* **Ubenkor (IRE)**[14] 6813 3-9-4 **72**........ TomEaves 7 26
(B Smart) *t.k.h: in tch tl rdn and wknd fr 2f out* **11/2**

000 **9** *17* **Supremely Blessed**[38] 6217 4-8-5 **58** oh13........(v[1]) AndrewElliott 5 —
(D W Thompson) *bhd: struggling over 3f out: sn wknd* **100/1**

1m 39.3s (5.90) **Going Correction** +0.95s/f (Soft)
WFA 3 from 4yo+ 1lb **9** Ran SP% **120.7**
Speed ratings (Par 103): **104,102,101,101,91 87,86,81,61**
toteswinger: 1&2 £6.20, 1&3 £16.00, 2&3 £11.60. CSF £27.88 CT £273.63 TOTE £8.40: £2.50, £1.60, £3.50; EX 42.40.
Owner R J Parsons **Bred** E Young And Sons **Trained** Sellack, H'fords
■ Stewards' Enquiry : Amy Kathleen Parsons caution: used whip in incorrect place.

FOCUS
This looked a tight-knit 58-72 handicap. It was the quickest of the four races over course-and-distance and the form looks sound, with the winner rated to her best.

7132 CONFERENCES AT AYR RACECOURSE H'CAP 1m 1f 20y
4:20 (4:20) (Class 6) (0-60,58) 3-Y-O+ £2,590 (£770; £385; £96; £96) **Stalls** Low

Form RPR

0061 **1** **Brandane (IRE)**[19] 6693 3-9-1 **55**........ PaulHanagan 5 67
(R A Fahey) *trckd ldrs: led and edgd rt over 1f out: kpt on strly* **8/1**

05-2 **2** *2 3/4* **Dark Planet**[53] 5776 5-8-13 **50**........(v) AndrewElliott 10 56
(D W Thompson) *in tch: effrt over 2f out: chsd wnr over 1f out: r.o fnl f* **7/1**[3]

026U **3** *1/2* **Ulysees (IRE)**[44] 6040 9-8-11 **48**........(p) PJMcDonald 3 53
(Miss L A Perratt) *hld up: hdwy over 2f out: effrt over 1f out: kpt on same pce ins fnl f* **17/2**

1154 **4** *1 1/2* **Wednesdays Boy (IRE)**[30] 6408 5-9-6 **57**........(p) DavidAllan 7 59
(P D Niven) *towards rr: effrt over 2f out: no imp fnl f* **11/4**[1]

4040 **4** *dht* **Bed Fellow (IRE)**[8] 6950 4-8-9 **51**........ KellyHarrison(5) 12 53
(Paul Murphy) *prom: rdn over 2f out: one pce fnl f* **7/1**[3]

0535 **6** *1* **Boppys Pride**[24] 6585 5-8-6 **50**........ JamesRogers(7) 4 50
(P T Midgley) *hld up: hdwy over 2f out: no imp fnl f* **9/2**[2]

000 **7** *nk* **Defi (IRE)**[40] 6162 6-8-13 **50**........(bt) MickyFenton 1 49
(D A Nolan) *led to over 1f out: sn btn* **50/1**

2020 **8** *1* **Thornaby Green**[3] 7085 7-9-0 **58**........ DeanHeslop(7) 13 55
(T D Barron) *trckd ldr tl rdn and wknd over 1f out* **14/1**

3000 **9** *2* **Kirkby's Treasure**[30] 6408 10-8-10 **52**........ SladeO'Hara(5) 8 45
(A Berry) *in tch: rdn 3f out: btn fnl f* **28/1**

6043 **10** *nk* **Sarraaf (IRE)**[30] 6409 12-9-2 **53**........ TomEaves 6 45
(Miss L A Perratt) *midfield: effrt over 2f out: wknd fnl f* **10/1**

534U **11** *hd* **Scotty's Future (IRE)**[53] 5776 10-8-4 **48**........ DanielleMooney(7) 2 40
(A Berry) *bhd: rdn 3f out: nvr trbld ldrs* **20/1**

3/00 **12** *20* **Find Me (USA)**[179] 1521 4-8-13 **55**........ FrederikTylicki(5) 11 5
(L Lungo) *dwlt: bhd: struggling fnl 3f* **12/1**

2m 9.85s (11.45) **Going Correction** +0.95s/f (Soft)
WFA 3 from 4yo+ 3lb **12** Ran SP% **125.1**
Speed ratings (Par 101): **87,84,84,82,82 81,81,80,78,78 78,60**
toteswinger: 1&2 £9.70, 1&3 £15.80, 2&3 £11.10. CSF £65.50 CT £504.47 TOTE £8.10: £3.10, £3.10, £2.50; EX 61.30 Place 6 £10.79, Place 5 £6.19.
Owner R A Fahey **Bred** King Bloodstock **Trained** Musley Bank, N Yorks

FOCUS
A low-grade handicap run at a strong pace and in the end they were spread right across the track in the home straight. Considering the bad ground this is probably reasonable form for the low grade.
T/Plt: £22.90 to a £1 stake. Pool: £41,801.18. 1,329.58 winning tickets. T/Qpdt: £12.20 to a £1 stake. Pool: £2,770.18. 167.80 winning tickets. RY

7088 GREAT LEIGHS (A.W) (L-H)
Saturday, November 1
7133 Meeting Abandoned - Unsafe ground

7104 NEWMARKET (ROWLEY) (R-H)
Saturday, November 1
OFFICIAL GOING: Good to soft (soft in places)
Wind: Light, across Weather: Overcast

7140 CASINO AT BET365.COM EBF MAIDEN FILLIES' STKS (DIV I) 7f
11:50 (11:53) (Class 4) 2-Y-O £4,857 (£1,445; £722; £360) **Stalls** Low

Form RPR

1 **Apple Charlotte** 2-9-0 0........ IanMongan 11 83+
(H R A Cecil) *hld up in tch: racd keenly: led over 1f out: rdn and r.o wl* **9/1**

2 *1 3/4* **Miss Beat (IRE)** 2-9-0 0........(t) HayleyTurner 13 79+
(B J Meehan) *hld up: hdwy over 2f out: rdn 1f out: r.o* **20/1**

0 **3** *1/2* **Dialect**[10] 6910 2-9-0 0........ JimCrowley 10 77
(Mrs A J Perrett) *a.p: racd keenly: chsd ldr over 4f out: rdn and edgd rt over 1f out: styd on same pce ins fnl f* **17/2**

03 **4** *1* **Naizak**[32] 6358 2-9-0 0........ MartinDwyer 8 75
(J L Dunlop) *led: rdn and hdd over 1f out: styd on same pce* **12/1**

402 **5** *3 1/2* **Granny McPhee**[35] 6273 2-9-0 **81**........ TGMcLaughlin 4 66
(A Bailey) *prom: rdn over 1f out: wknd ins fnl f* **7/1**[2]

6 *3/4* **Entreat** 2-9-0 0........ LDettori 3 64
(Sir Michael Stoute) *prom: rdn over 2f out: wknd fnl f* **11/4**[1]

7 *nk* **Frosted** 2-9-0 0........ JimmyFortune 12 63
(J H M Gosden) *hld up: hdwy over 2f out: rdn over 1f out: wknd ins fnl f* **8/1**[3]

8 *nk* **You Say I Say (USA)** 2-9-0 0........ RichardMullen 14 63
(Sir Michael Stoute) *mid-div: hdwy over 2f out: nt clr run over 1f out: wknd ins fnl f* **14/1**

9 *1/2* **Idle Tears** 2-9-0 0........ RobertHavlin 9 61+
(J H M Gosden) *hld up: nt clr run over 1f out: nvr nr to chal* **25/1**

10 *hd* **Beauchamp Xiara** 2-9-0 0........ DaneO'Neill 17 61
(H Candy) *s.i.s: hld up: hdwy over 1f out: wknd ins fnl f* **50/1**

11 *1/2* **Full Of Love (IRE)** 2-9-0 0........ MichaelHills 1 60
(B W Hills) *s.i.s: hld up: n.d* **25/1**

12 *hd* **Flame Of Hestia (IRE)** 2-9-0 0........ JamieSpencer 16 59+
(J R Fanshawe) *wnt rt s: hld up: shkn up over 1f out: n.d* **12/1**

0 **13** *nse* **Nice Time (IRE)**[11] 6887 2-9-0 0........ SaleemGolam 15 59
(M H Tompkins) *s.i.s: hld up: rdn over 2f out: n.d* **100/1**

14 *1 1/4* **Cartoon** 2-9-0 0........ PhilipRobinson 18 56
(M A Jarvis) *hld up: rdn over 2f out: n.d* **10/1**

15 *4 1/2* **See That Girl** 2-9-0 0........ AlanMunro 5 45
(P W Chapple-Hyam) *s.i.s: plld hrd and sn prom: rdn and wkng whn n.m.r over 1f out* **20/1**

16 *1 3/4* **Dovedon Angel** 2-9-0 0........ WilliamBuick 2 40
(Miss Gay Kelleway) *chsd ldr over 2f: rdn and wknd 2f out* **66/1**

17 *1 3/4* **Rocky Heights (IRE)** 2-9-0 0........ TedDurcan 7 36
(J L Dunlop) *s.i.s: hld up: rdn and wknd over 2f out* **66/1**

1m 29.06s (3.66) **Going Correction** +0.40s/f (Good) **17** Ran SP% **125.1**
Speed ratings (Par 95): **95,93,92,91,87 86,86,85,85,84 84,84,84,82,77 75,73**
toteswinger: 1&2 £105.30, 1&3 £21.10, 2&3 £88.10. CSF £186.47 TOTE £12.40: £4.70, £8.60, £3.40; EX 237.40.
Owner De La Warr Racing **Bred** Hascombe And Valiant Studs **Trained** Newmarket, Suffolk

FOCUS
They raced up the stands' side in this maiden, which was full of interesting, well-bred newcomers, one of whom came out on top. Difficult to be confident about the level of the form, but the front two should be worth watching closely next year.

NOTEBOOK
Apple Charlotte ◆, a half-sister to this year's Ribblesdale second Arthur's Girl, was backed in from 20-1 in the morning. She saw plenty of daylight and was keen in the early stages, but she still had enough in reserve to run on strongly. By Royal Applause, she has more speed than Arthur's Girl, and one would imagine she will not be going much further than 1m next year. (op 14-1 tchd 16-1)
Miss Beat(IRE) ◆, by Beat Hollow out of Irish Oaks winner Bolas, is bred to come into her own over middle distances next season. She made a promising debut for a stable that had won a division of this contest twice in the previous three years. (op 25-1)
Dialect, who was slowly away and never competitive at Kempton on her debut, came in for support, having been available at 22-1 in the morning. The daughter of Diktat was likely to be suited by the ground and she showed the benefit of her debut by racing prominently. Although keener than ideal, she ran a sound race. (op 11-1)
Naizak tried to put her experience to good use and make all next to the stands' rail. Perhaps the ground was not ideal for the daughter of Medicean, but she looked simply to come up against some better fillies. (op 20-1)
Granny McPhee was another who had the benefit of experience, and she came here on the back of a decent effort over this trip at Chester. It is possible she would have preferred quicker ground, but with a mark of 81 she will not be easy to place. (op 13-2 tchd 5-1)
Entreat, a half-sister to Kabis Amigos, a modest performer but multiple winner over 7f-1m, was popular in the market. She was keeping on at the finish and is the type to do better next year. (op 3-1 tchd 7-2)
Frosted, the Cheveley Park second string based on jockey caps, cost 170,000gns and is a half-sister to Andronikos, who won three times over 6f in Listed company. She was not given a hard race on this debut and should repay the kindness. (op 5-1)

You Say I Say(USA), a half-sister to smart French performer Ershaad, did not get a clear run and also ran green. She shaped better than her finishing position suggests. (op 16-1)

7141 CASINO AT BET365.COM EBF MAIDEN FILLIES' STKS (DIV II) 7f

12:20 (12:30) (Class 4) 2-Y-O £4,857 (£1,445; £722; £360) Stalls Low

Form				RPR
	1		**Sariska** 2-9-0 0 JamieSpencer 14 *(M L W Bell) s.i.s: hdwy over 1f out: sn chsng ldr: shkn up to ld and edgd rt ins fnl f: r.o wl* 7/2[1]	86+
23	2	1 1/2	**Mezenah**[11] 6884 2-9-0 0 LDettori 8 *(Saeed Bin Suroor) led: rdn over 1f out: hdd and unable qck ins fnl f* 7/2[1]	80
0	3	1 1/2	**Fleurissimo**[25] 6559 2-9-0 0 SteveDrowne 17 *(J L Dunlop) hld up in tch: rdn over 1f out: styd on* 50/1	77
0	4	1 1/4	**Arabian Mirage**[45] 6030 2-9-0 0 TedDurcan 5 *(B J Meehan) chsd ldrs: rdn and hung lft over 1f out: styd on same pce* 40/1	73
	5	2	**Russian Spirit** 2-9-0 0 PhilipRobinson 16 *(M A Jarvis) chsd ldrs: rdn over 1f out: wknd ins fnl f* 16/1	68
	6	1 1/2	**Coming Back** 2-9-0 0 RobertHavlin 1 *(J H M Gosden) hld up: swtchd lft 2f out: styd on ins fnl f: nvr nr to chal* 25/1	65
	7	3/4	**Precious Secret (IRE)** 2-9-0 0 GeorgeBaker 11 *(C F Wall) chsd ldrs: rdn over 2f out: hung rt over 1f out: wknd fnl f* 40/1	63
	8	1/2	**At A Great Rate (USA)** 2-9-0 0 IanMongan 3 *(H R A Cecil) chsd ldrs: rdn over 2f out: wknd over 1f out* 9/1[3]	62
	9	1	**Halliwell House** 2-9-0 0 JimmyFortune 6 *(J H M Gosden) s.s: hld up: rdn and nt clr run over 1f out: sn hung rt: nvr nrr* 8/1[2]	59
	10	shd	**Beauchamp Xenia** 2-9-0 0 (t) DaneO'Neill 18 *(H Candy) hld up: nt clr run over 2f out: sn rdn: n.d* 50/1	59
	11	1	**Fisadara** 2-9-0 0 MartinDwyer 15 *(B W Hills) mid-div: hdwy 1/2-way: rdn over 2f out: wknd over 1f out* 12/1	56
	12	3/4	**Silent Act (USA)** 2-9-0 0 JimCrowley 13 *(Mrs A J Perrett) s.i.s: a in rr* 28/1	54
	13	3 1/4	**Flying Cloud (USA)** 2-9-0 0 AlanMunro 7 *(B J Meehan) s.i.s: sn outpcd* 25/1	46
04	14	1 3/4	**Myttons Maid**[43] 6065 2-9-0 0 TGMcLaughlin 12 *(A Bailey) hld up: rdn 1/2-way: nt clr run over 2f out: sn wknd* 200/1	42
4	15	6	**My Girl Jode**[11] 6884 2-9-0 0 SaleemGolam 4 *(M H Tompkins) prom: racd keenly: hmpd over 4f out: rdn and wknd over 1f out* 12/1	27
	16	4	**Alystar (IRE)** 2-9-0 0 ShaneKelly 2 *(P F I Cole) chsd ldrs: edgd rt over 4f out: rdn and wknd wl over 1f out* 14/1	17
	17	3	**Peace In Paradise (IRE)** 2-9-0 0 KirstyMilczarek 9 *(J A R Toller) s.s: sn outpcd* 66/1	9

1m 28.17s (2.77) **Going Correction** +0.40s/f (Good) **17 Ran SP% 115.4**
Speed ratings (Par 95): **100,98,96,95,92 91,90,89,88,88 87,86,82,80,73 69,65**
toteswinger: 1&2 £3.00, 1&3 £53.80, 2&3 £23.30. CSF £10.51 TOTE £4.40: £1.90, £1.60, £11.50; EX 18.70.

Owner Lady Bamford **Bred** Lady Bamford **Trained** Newmarket, Suffolk

FOCUS
This time the field tacked over to race on the far side and the winning time was 0.89sec quicker than the first division. The runner-up set a fair standard and the winner looks a particularly good prospect.

NOTEBOOK
Sariska ◆, a half-sister to the stable's very useful stayer Gull Wing, is by Pivotal and clearly has more speed about her as she put up a taking display on this debut. Well backed from 9-1 in the morning, she was brought with a well-timed challenge from off the pace to take Mezenah's measure inside the last furlong. Well regarded by her trainer, she will get further next year and looks a very useful prospect. She is likely to return in one of the Guineas trials. (op 7-1 tchd 15-2)
Mezenah, who did not got home when beaten at odds-on over 1m at Yarmouth last time, looked the one to beat dropped back to 7f. Soon sent to the front, she enjoyed the run of the race, and simply met one too good. Perhaps she can be found an opening on the Polytrack. (op 5-2 tchd 9-4)
Fleurissimo, who showed some ability at Leicester on her debut, stayed on well in the closing stages and shaped as though she will be seen to better effect next year over further.
Arabian Mirage was another to improve for her debut effort. That run came over 6f, and the extra furlong on softer ground suited the half-sister to high-class stayer Tungsten Strike.
Russian Spirit is from a family that improves with age, so it was encouraging that she was able to run so well on this debut. (op 14-1)
Coming Back, by Fantastic Light out of a mare from a top-class family, was green on this debut and the ground would probably have been soft enough for her. She should come into her own over middle distances next year.
Precious Secret(IRE), a half-sister to ten winners, is from a stable whose juveniles rarely win first time up. She should come on for this outing. (op 50-1)
At A Great Rate(USA), whose dam was a smart performer over 7f-1m and is from an excellent family, shaped with some promise.
Halliwell House, who cost 105,000gns, is a half-sister to Counterclaim, who only showed fair form at two but progressed to be placed at Group 2 level at three. Given plenty to do on this debut, she hung right once switched into the clear, but she can be expected to do better next year. (tchd 9-1)

7142 POKER AT BET365.COM ZETLAND CONDITIONS STKS 1m 2f

12:55 (1:01) (Class 2) 2-Y-O £9,346 (£2,799; £1,399; £700; £349; £175) Stalls Low

Form				RPR
4012	1		**Heliodor (USA)**[25] 6561 2-9-0 82 JimmyFortune 4 *(R Hannon) hld up: hdwy over 1f out: rdn to ld ins fnl f: r.o* 7/2[3]	82
01	2	1	**Ouster (GER)**[31] 6398 2-9-0 0 GeorgeBaker 2 *(D R C Elsworth) trckd ldrs: plld hrd: led over 1f out: edgd rt: hdd ins fnl f: styd on* 6/5[1]	80
024	3	1 3/4	**It's Dubai Dolly**[29] 6432 2-8-9 72 WandersonD'Avila 3 *(A J Lidderdale) led: rdn and hdd over 1f out: styd on same pce ins fnl f* 28/1	72
201	4	1 1/4	**Latin Tinge (USA)**[38] 6205 2-8-9 87 JamieSpencer 1 *(P F I Cole) s.i.s: hld up: swtchd rt over 3f out: hdwy over 2f out: sn rdn: no ex fnl f* 10/3[2]	70
052	5	shd	**Orthology (IRE)**[26] 6524 2-9-0 84 SaleemGolam 6 *(M H Tompkins) prom: rdn over 2f out: styd on same pce fnl f* 10/1	74
0505	6	1 1/2	**Very Distinguished**[16] 6761 2-8-9 61 EdwardCreighton 5 *(M G Quinlan) stdd s: racd keenly: hdwy over 3f out: rdn and ev ch over 1f out: no ex* 28/1	67
04	7	nk	**Darley Sun (IRE)**[33] 6330 2-9-0 0 RichardMullen 7 *(D M Simcock) chsd ldr: rdn over 2f out: wknd fnl f* 25/1	71

2m 12.4s (6.60) **Going Correction** +0.40s/f (Good) **7 Ran SP% 110.6**
Speed ratings (Par 102): **89,88,86,85,85 84,84**
toteswinger: 1&2 £105.30, 1&3 £21.10, 2&3 £88.10. CSF £7.53 TOTE £4.50: £1.90, £1.70; EX 8.70.

Owner Mrs J Wood **Bred** Kim Nardelli Et Al **Trained** East Everleigh, Wilts

FOCUS
This is normally quite a test for two-year-olds, but the field was nowhere near as strong as it used to be and the early pace was not strong either, so the form may is not the most reliable. They came up the stands' side, and Heliodor did not need to improve to win.

NOTEBOOK
Heliodor(USA), proven over the distance, settled much better than the favourite and was produced with a well-timed challenge inside the last furlong. The most experienced runner in the line-up, he has improved since being stepped up to 1m1f-plus, and thrives on racing. However, he would not be sure to stay much further than this next year. (op 11-2)
Ouster(GER) won his maiden impressively at Salisbury last time, and the form had been given a boost when the runner-up won at Lingfield on Thursday. A son of Lomitas, this longer trip promised to be right up his street, but he is a keen-going sort, and having sweated up beforehand, he proceeded to pull far too hard in the early stages. The pace just was not brisk enough for him and, while he came there travelling strongly a furlong and a half out, he was always going to be vulnerable to a rival who had preserved a bit more energy for the climb out of the Dip. He can prove this form all wrong when getting a stronger pace. (op 11-10 tchd 5-4 in places)
It's Dubai Dolly is another who has improved as she has stepped up in distance. Well placed in a steadily run race, she posted a personal best, and appears to be steadily progressive, although her performance underlines the questionable merit of the form. (op 25-1 tchd 33-1)
Latin Tinge(USA) was another who raced a bit too keenly through the early part of the race and could not sustain her effort in the closing stages. She is better than this effort suggests. (op 5-2 tchd 7-2)
Orthology(IRE), runner-up in a maiden over this distance last time, was perhaps not comfortable on the ground, the softest he has encountered. (op 11-1 tchd 12-1 in places)

7143 BET365 08000 322365 H'CAP 7f

1:30 (1:32) (Class 4) (0-85,82) 3-Y-O+ £5,180 (£1,541; £770; £384) Stalls Low

Form				RPR
1535	1		**Amber Queen (IRE)**[7] 6981 3-9-3 80 MichaelHills 6 *(B W Hills) chsd ldr: rdn to ld over 1f out: sn edgd rt: styd on gamely* 5/2[1]	89
6000	2	hd	**Bahiano (IRE)**[19] 6695 7-8-10 72 HayleyTurner 5 *(C E Brittain) hld up: hrd rdn over 1f out: edgd rt and r.o ins fnl f* 12/1	81
0000	3	1 1/2	**Carleton**[7] 6976 3-9-5 82 ChrisCatlin 4 *(W J Musson) hld up: hdwy over 1f out: sn rdn: styd on same pce towards fin* 16/1	86
1141	4	shd	**Hurricane Harriet**[25] 6564 3-8-10 73 OscarUrbina 11 *(R M H Cowell) chsd ldrs: rdn and ev ch over 1f out: styd on same pce wl ins fnl f* 5/1[2]	77
6000	5	nk	**Cornus**[18] 6724 6-8-11 73 (be) JamesDoyle 2 *(A J McCabe) hld up: hdwy whn hmpd over 1f out: swtchd lft: styd on* 17/2	80+
0546	6	2	**Purus (IRE)**[17] 6734 6-8-13 78 LukeMorris[(3)] 3 *(R A Teal) hld up: plld hrd: hdwy 1/2-way: rdn over 1f out: no ex ins fnl f* 6/1[3]	77
100	7	3 1/2	**Shindy (FR)**[28] 6491 3-8-9 72 JoeFanning 8 *(J A R Toller) chsd ldrs: rdn and ev ch over 1f out: hmpd sn after: wknd ins fnl f* 16/1	60
1060	8	1 1/4	**Twilight Star (IRE)**[28] 6471 4-9-2 78 TedDurcan 10 *(R A Teal) hld up: rdn and hung rt over 1f out: wknd fnl f* 10/1	64
5505	9	1 1/2	**Idle Power (IRE)**[20] 6676 10-9-5 81 PatCosgrave 9 *(J R Boyle) led: rdn and hdd over 1f out: wknd fnl f* 9/1	63
0602	10	shd	**Russian Reel**[29] 6435 3-9-0 77 (t) EdwardCreighton 7 *(E J Creighton) prom: rdn over 2f out: wknd 2f out* 25/1	57
4042	11	12	**Polmaily**[128] 3419 3-8-12 75 AlanMunro 1 *(J Akehurst) hld up: a in rr: rdn and wknd over 2f out* 14/1	23

1m 27.22s (1.82) **Going Correction** +0.40s/f (Good)
WFA 3 from 4yo+ 1lb **11 Ran SP% 119.1**
Speed ratings (Par 105): **105,104,103,102,102 100,96,94,93,93 79**
toteswinger: 1&2 £12.60, 1&3 £9.60, 2&3 £31.80. CSF £35.21 CT £408.31 TOTE £2.80: £1.50, £4.00, £4.40; EX 38.80.

Owner Lady Richard Wellesley **Bred** R A Bonnycastle And Marston Stud **Trained** Lambourn, Berks

■ Stewards' Enquiry : Hayley Turner one-day ban: used whip with excessive frequency (Nov 15)

FOCUS
In the continuing quest for the best ground, the field came up the centre of the track this time. Just an ordinary handicap, but sound enough form of its type.

7144 BET365.COM EBF MONTROSE FILLIES' STKS (LISTED RACE) 1m

2:10 (2:11) (Class 1) 2-Y-O £17,031 (£6,456; £3,231; £1,611; £807; £405) Stalls Low

Form				RPR
1	1		**Enticement**[31] 6391 2-8-12 0 JimmyFortune 5 *(Sir Michael Stoute) trckd ldrs: racd keenly: rdn over 1f out: styd on u.p to ld wl ins fnl f* 15/2[3]	99
025	2	shd	**Super Sleuth (IRE)**[29] 6439 2-8-12 99 MartinDwyer 3 *(B J Meehan) chsd ldrs: led over 1f out: sn rdn: hdd wl ins fnl f* 9/1	99
1	3	3/4	**Splashdown**[40] 6167 2-8-12 0 DaneO'Neill 11 *(L M Cumani) hld up in tch: rdn and ev ch fr over 1f out: no ex towards fin* 8/1	97
031	4	1/2	**Midday**[43] 6081 2-8-12 86 RichardMullen 4 *(H R A Cecil) hld up: hdwy over 2f out: sn rdn: r.o* 9/1	96
041	5	1/2	**Tottie**[16] 6745 2-8-12 80 JimCrowley 10 *(Mrs A J Perrett) hld up: hdwy over 2f out: nt clr run over 1f out: r.o* 16/1	95
122	6	nk	**Rosy Mantle**[7] 6982 2-8-12 85 SteveDrowne 8 *(W R Muir) chsd ldrs: rdn 1/2-way: outpcd over 2f out: r.o ins fnl f* 9/2[2]	94
512	7	1/2	**La Adelita (IRE)**[46] 6002 2-8-12 80 JamieSpencer 13 *(M L W Bell) hld up: hdwy over 2f out: rdn over 1f out: no ex ins fnl f* 10/1	93
2222	8	3 1/4	**Three Moons (IRE)**[18] 6720 2-8-12 81 PhilipRobinson 6 *(H J L Dunlop) led: rdn and hdd over 1f out: edgd rt: wknd ins fnl f* 16/1	86
4314	9	3/4	**Dream In Waiting**[28] 6477 2-8-12 83 ShaneKelly 7 *(P F I Cole) hld up: rdn over 2f out: n.d* 10/1	84
30	10	hd	**Lady Francesca**[28] 6473 2-8-12 0 HayleyTurner 1 *(W R Muir) hld up: rdn over 2f out: nt trble ldrs* 66/1	84
1306	11	1/2	**Ahla Wasahl**[28] 6473 2-8-12 88 TedDurcan 14 *(D M Simcock) hld up: rdn over 2f out: wknd over 1f out* 66/1	83
1	12	11	**Burgundy Ice (USA)**[25] 6559 2-8-12 0 LDettori 2 *(Saeed Bin Suroor) hld up: hdwy over 2f out: wknd over 1f out* 4/1[1]	59

1 13 *10* **Bombina**[11] 6884 2-8-12 0.. AlanMunro 9 37
(P W Chapple-Hyam) *chsd ldrs: rdn over 2f out: sn wknd* **9/1**

1m 40.49s (1.89) **Going Correction** +0.40s/f (Good) **13** Ran SP% **124.0**
Speed ratings (Par 101): **106,105,105,104,104 103,103,100,99,99 98,87,77**
toteswinger: 1&2 £22.60, 1&3 £6.50, 2&3 £22.30. CSF £76.41 TOTE £7.10: £2.40, £4.30, £3.50; EX 78.10 Trifecta £402.50 Part won. Pool: £544.00 - 0.20 winning units..
Owner The Queen **Bred** Ecoutila Partnership **Trained** Newmarket, Suffolk

FOCUS
An interesting and open-looking Listed race in which they came up the centre of the track. It featured five fillies who had won their only previous start and the form should stand up.

NOTEBOOK
Enticement ◆ is a daughter of Montjeu and bred to come into her own over middle distances next season. There was plenty to like about the way she dug deep under pressure to get the better of the more experienced Super Sleuth in the closing stages, and she was quoted at around 20-1 for the Oaks. One would imagine that she will be given her chance to prove her Epsom credentials in one of the trial races in the spring. (op 13-2 tchd 6-1 and 9-1 in places)
Super Sleuth(IRE), whose fifth in the Group 3 Oh So Sharp Stakes here last time represented just about the best form on offer, did very little wrong, simply finding one of the less-exposed fillies too strong. She deserves to win a race, and might be able to find a maiden on the Polytrack before the year is out. (op 11-1 tchd 12-1)
Splashdown, who defied negative market vibes and greenness to win at Kempton on her debut, again showed signs of inexperience. The type to do much better with a winter on her back, she should get at least 1m2f next year and looks a smart filly in the making. (op 7-1 tchd 9-1)
Midday, who got off the mark at the third attempt when stepped up to this distance here last time, saw out her race well on her first try on softish ground. Her dam won over 1m3f, but she is by Oasis Dream, so it remains to be seen what her best trip will be next season. (tchd 10-1)
Tottie only won a Brighton maiden last time but the form has been working out well, with the third winning a similar event next time and the runner-up finishing a highly creditable sixth in the Racing Post Trophy. She did not get the clearest of runs and, being by Fantastic Light, the ground was perhaps on the easy side for her, but she still shaped well and looks an interesting type for next year. (op 14-1)
Rosy Mantle, second over 7f at a similar level at Newbury a week earlier, got a bit unbalanced in the Dip and may have found this race coming a bit quick. (op 11-2)
La Adelita(IRE), who had ground conditions to suit, had been beaten in a nursery off 74 last time, so this was a sound effort in the circumstances. (op 14-1)
Burgundy Ice(USA), a well-bred daughter of Storm Cat who won at Leicester on her debut, found disappointingly little under pressure. Official explanation: jockey said gelding had a breathing problem (op 5-1 tchd 6-1)
Bombina, who stayed on strongly to win at Yarmouth on her debut, dropped out tamely after being up there early on, and presumably there was something amiss. Official explanation: trainer had no explanation for the poor form shown (op 8-1 tchd 13-2)

7145 BET365 JAMES SEYMOUR STKS (LISTED RACE) 1m 2f
2:45 (2:46) (Class 1) 3-Y-0+

£22,708 (£8,608; £4,308; £2,148; £1,076; £540) **Stalls** Low

Form RPR
4231 1 **With Interest**[21] 6654 5-9-2 103.. TedDurcan 10 113
(Saeed Bin Suroor) *s.i.s: hld up: hdwy over 2f out: rdn to ld ins fnl f: r.o* **14/1**
11-3 2 *1 1/4* **Kirklees (IRE)**[15] 6780 4-9-2 110.. LDettori 11 111
(Saeed Bin Suroor) *led over 8f out: rdn over 1f out: hdd and unable qck ins fnl f* **11/8**[1]
-110 3 *1* **Bronze Cannon (USA)**[134] 3193 3-8-12 103.................. JimmyFortune 8 109
(J H M Gosden) *chsd ldrs: rdn over 2f out: ev ch over 1f out: styd on same pce ins fnl f* **5/1**[2]
6360 4 *3/4* **Drumfire (IRE)**[15] 6780 4-9-2 107.. JoeFanning 7 107
(M Johnston) *chsd ldrs: rdn over 1f out: styd on same pce* **12/1**
0624 5 *1 3/4* **Under The Rainbow**[14] 6819 5-8-11 100..................(p) AlanMunro 5 99
(B W Hills) *led: hdd over 8f out: chsd ldr: rdn and ev ch wl over 1f out: no ex fnl f* **20/1**
0020 6 *4 1/2* **Lang Shining (IRE)**[28] 6476 4-9-2 102.................... RichardMullen 6 95
(Sir Michael Stoute) *hld up: rdn over 2f out: hung lft and wknd over 1f out* **12/1**
2216 7 *2 3/4* **Duncan**[29] 6444 3-8-12 99.. PhilipRobinson 2 89
(J L Dunlop) *plld hrd and prom: rdn: hung rt and wknd 2f out* **16/1**
102 8 *nse* **Mutajarred**[42] 6106 4-9-2 106.. MartinDwyer 4 89
(W J Haggas) *prom: rdn over 2f out: sn wknd* **10/1**
0560 9 *4 1/2* **Grand Passion (IRE)**[159] 2465 8-9-2 97.................. SteveDrowne 3 80
(G Wragg) *hld up: rdn and wknd over 2f out* **66/1**
11-2 10 *5* **Jack Dawkins (USA)**[26] 6526 3-8-12 93........................ JamieSpencer 1 70
(H R A Cecil) *hld up: rdn and wknd over 2f out* **15/2**[3]
166 11 *22* **Smokey Oakey (IRE)**[49] 5893 4-9-9 110........................ SaleemGolam 9 33
(M H Tompkins) *hld up in tch: rdn and wknd over 3f out* **25/1**

2m 7.00s (1.20) **Going Correction** +0.40s/f (Good)
WFA 3 from 4yo+ 4lb **11** Ran SP% **117.7**
Speed ratings (Par 111): **111,110,109,108,107 103,101,101,97,93 76**
toteswinger: 1&2 £6.20, 1&3 £13.60, 2&3 £3.40. CSF £33.03 TOTE £16.40: £4.10, £1.40, £2.10; EX 47.50 Trifecta £301.20 Pool: £569.90 - 1.40 winning units..
Owner Godolphin **Bred** George Strawbridge **Trained** Newmarket, Suffolk

FOCUS
Ordinary Listed form, but a slight personal best from the winner, who was the only hold-up horse in the frame.

NOTEBOOK
With Interest had scrambled home in a minor conditions race at Musselburgh last time, but that was a bit of a tactical affair, and the better pace on this more galloping track, coupled with a return to 1m2f suited him. He ran well in Dubai this year and looks a prime candidate to be given another Carnival campaign. (op 16-1)
Kirklees(IRE) promised to be suited by the return to 1m2f, but perhaps the ground was softer than ideal for him, and he could probably have done with an easier time on the front end. (tchd 5-4 and 6-4 in places)
Bronze Cannon(USA) had been off the track since disappointing in the King Edward VII Stakes at Royal Ascot. Twice a winner over course and distance in the spring, he ran a promising race, especially as he was a bit short of room inside the last furlong. His trainer might be able to find an opening for him on the continent before the year is out, but the son of Lemon Drop Kid has twice won on the Polytrack, so there could be something for him on that surface too, as long as connections choose to persevere for a while. (tchd 11-2)
Drumfire(IRE) was over seven lengths behind Kirklees in the Darley Stakes last time, but he finished a lot closer to him on this softer ground, and seemed to run up to his recent best. (op 16-1)
Under The Rainbow is a very useful mare and has been placed in Group company this season, but her last win came over course and distance in the Zetland Stakes three years ago. (tchd 16-1)
Lang Shining(IRE) had ground conditions to suit for the first time since he won the Spring Cup in April, but this was a step up in class and he could not pick up from off the pace. This looked one race too many at the end of a long season. (op 16-1)
Duncan pulled much too hard and gave himself little chance of getting home. Still lightly raced and open to improvement, he should get further next year if learning to settle better. Official explanation: jockey said colt ran too freely (tchd 20-1)
Mutajarred Official explanation: jockey said gelding had no more to give
Jack Dawkins(USA) Official explanation: trainer said colt was unsuited by the good to soft (soft in places) ground

7146 BET365 BEST ODDS GUARANTEED ON EVERY RACE H'CAP 1m
3:20 (3:21) (Class 2) (0-100,100) 3-Y-0+

£12,462 (£3,732; £1,866; £934; £466; £234) **Stalls** Low

Form RPR
6064 1 **Lucky Dance (BRZ)**[21] 6654 6-8-6 86 oh4........................ GregFairley 7 96
(A G Foster) *mde all: rdn over 1f out: styd on wl* **33/1**
0015 2 *1 3/4* **Final Verse**[15] 6772 5-8-7 87........................ KirstyMilczarek 6 93
(M Salaman) *hld up: hdwy over 2f out: rdn to chse wnr over 1f out: styd on* **40/1**
4030 3 *1/2* **Flipando (IRE)**[15] 6783 7-8-8 88........................ JamieSpencer 1 93
(T D Barron) *hld up: hdwy u.p over 1f out: hung rt: styd on* **10/1**
3265 4 *1 3/4* **Ellemujie**[28] 6467 3-8-8 90.. MartinDwyer 12 91
(D K Ivory) *hld up: hdwy over 3f out: rdn and hung lft over 1f out: styd on* **25/1**
3346 5 *1/2* **Kinsya**[7] 6984 5-8-6 86.. SaleemGolam 18 86
(M H Tompkins) *hld up: hdwy over 2f out: rdn over 1f out: styd on* **8/1**[3]
1153 6 *1/2* **Oat Cuisine**[10] 6904 4-8-1 86 oh2........................ DavidProbert(5) 4 85
(M L W Bell) *hld up: hdwy u.p over 1f out: nt trble ldrs* **9/1**
6003 7 *2 1/2* **Moynahan (USA)**[20] 6670 3-9-2 98........................ AlanMunro 16 91
(P F I Cole) *chsd ldrs: rdn over 2f out: wknd ins fnl f* **12/1**
2400 8 *nk* **Whistledownwind**[29] 6444 3-9-4 100........................ WilliamBuick 15 92
(J Noseda) *chsd ldrs: rdn over 1f out: hung rt and wknd fnl f* **16/1**
0066 9 *2* **Pride Of Nation (IRE)**[15] 6772 6-8-9 89........................ ShaneKelly 13 76
(J W Hills) *chsd ldrs: rdn over 2f out: wknd fnl f* **20/1**
0060 10 *nse* **Prior Warning**[8] 6947 4-8-3 86 oh1..................(t) DominicFox(3) 2 73
(Miss D Mountain) *hld up: rdn and hung rt fr over 3f out: nvr nrr* **50/1**
1136 11 *nse* **Aromatherapy**[35] 6283 3-8-7 89........................ SteveDrowne 5 76
(H R A Cecil) *prom: rdn over 2f out: hung rt and wknd over 1f out* **18/1**
2550 12 *2 1/4* **Vital Statistics**[7] 6981 4-8-10 90........................ DaneO'Neill 10 72
(D R C Elsworth) *hld up: rdn over 3f out: n.d* **16/1**
1350 13 *hd* **Zero Tolerance (IRE)**[21] 6649 8-8-10 93........................ NeilBrown(3) 8 75
(T D Barron) *chsd ldrs: rdn over 2f out: hung rt and wknd over 1f out* **12/1**
0100 14 *1/2* **Unshakable (IRE)**[28] 6476 9-9-0 94........................ PaulEddery 3 74
(Bob Jones) *hld up: rdn over 1f out: n.d* **22/1**
2100 15 *2 3/4* **The Jostler**[15] 6772 3-8-4 86 oh1........................ ChrisCatlin 9 60
(B W Hills) *hld up: rdn and wknd over 2f out* **50/1**
4233 16 *1* **Gold Sovereign (IRE)**[7] 6984 4-9-6 100........................ LDettori 17 72
(Saeed Bin Suroor) *chsd ldrs: rdn over 2f out: wknd over 1f out* **5/1**[2]
41 17 *1 1/4* **Lease Of Life (USA)**[19] 6705 3-8-8 90........................ MichaelHills 14 59
(B W Hills) *racd keenly: w ldrs tl wknd over 2f out* **4/1**[1]
61 18 *6* **Wasp (AUS)**[19] 6710 6-8-6 86.. JoeFanning 11 41
(W Jarvis) *chsd ldrs: rdn over 3f out: wknd 2f out* **16/1**

1m 39.8s (1.20) **Going Correction** +0.40s/f (Good)
WFA 3 from 4yo+ 2lb **18** Ran SP% **127.4**
Speed ratings (Par 109): **110,108,107,106,105 105,102,102,100,100 100,97,97,97,94 93,92,86**
toteswinger: 1&2 £166.10, 1&3 £75.30, 2&3 £46.20. CSF £996.82 CT £13276.39 TOTE £46.00: £6.00, £9.90, £2.30, £6.30; EX 1021.60 TRIFECTA Not won..
Owner Joshua Snellings **Bred** Haras San Francesco **Trained** Cousland, Midlothian

FOCUS
A typical end-of-season handicap and puzzling form to evaluate. The first two have both slipped in the handicap through the year.

NOTEBOOK
Lucky Dance(BRZ) had run well in a conditions event at Musselburgh behind With Interest, who won a Listed race earlier on this card, and despite being 4lb wrong at the weights he made just about all the running up the centre of the track. He seems to appreciate some cut in the ground and, having not got home over longer distances at various times this year, the bare mile, a trip over which he won on three occasions in Brazil, would appear to be his ideal distance. His connections are hoping to take him back to Dubai for the Carnival next year. (tchd 40-1 in places)
Final Verse ran quite well from a tough draw at Kempton last time and built on that with a good effort here, despite pulling for his head. Having shown he can handle the Polytrack, he should pay his way over the winter.
Flipando(IRE), held up for his usual late run, finished well and appreciated the return to 1m. A stronger pace would have probably helped. (op 7-1)
Ellemujie is handicapped to the hilt and was racing on ground which would probably not be ideal. A sound effort in the circumstances.
Kinsya, runner-up in this race last year off a 7lb higher mark, was expected to appreciate the drop back from 1m2f but, off an ordinary early gallop, he was staying on all too late. (op 10-1)
Oat Cuisine, who has held her form particularly well, apparently goes to the paddocks now. (op 11-1 tchd 12-1 in places)
Moynahan(USA) was taking a drop in class and running in a handicap for the first time. He did not get cover, though, raced keenly and was perhaps unsuited by the softish ground. (op 16-1)
Whistledownwind was another taking a drop in class and, in his case, a big step back in distance, too. He did not run too badly but perhaps 1m2f will turn out to be his best distance. (tchd 20-1)
Lease Of Life(USA) raced too keenly through the early parts and gave himself no chance of getting home. Official explanation: trainer had no explanation for the poor form shown (op 9-2 tchd 5-1 in places)

7147 BET365 BEN MARSHALL STKS (LISTED RACE) 1m
3:55 (3:55) (Class 1) 3-Y-0+

£22,708 (£8,608; £4,308; £2,148; £1,076; £540) **Stalls** Low

Form RPR
3011 1 **Virtual**[21] 6664 3-9-0 107.. JimmyFortune 7 117
(J H M Gosden) *hld up: hdwy over 2f out: rdn to ld wl ins fnl f* **4/1**[2]
1040 2 *1/2* **General Eliott (IRE)**[15] 6780 3-8-11 108........................ ShaneKelly 8 113
(P F I Cole) *prom: rdn and nt clr run over 2f out: ev ch ins fnl f: r.o* **12/1**
2031 3 *nk* **Alexandros**[20] 6670 3-8-11 108.. LDettori 5 112
(Saeed Bin Suroor) *chsd ldrs: rdn over 1f out: edgd lft ins fnl f: r.o* **7/1**[3]
2120 4 *1* **Dijeerr (USA)**[28] 6484 4-8-13 109..................(v) MartinDwyer 6 110
(Saeed Bin Suroor) *led: rdn over 1f out: hdd and unable qck wl ins fnl f* **20/1**
1361 5 *1* **Lucky Find (SAF)**[35] 6287 5-9-5 112........................ PatCosgrave 10 113
(M F De Kock, South Africa) *plld hrd and prom: rdn and ev ch fr over 1f out tl no ex wl ins fnl f* **17/2**
2222 6 *1* **Bankable (IRE)**[15] 6780 4-9-2 114.. DaneO'Neill 2 108
(L M Cumani) *s.i.s: hld up: hdwy over 2f out: rdn over 1f out: n.m.r and no ex ins fnl f* **11/8**[1]
-015 7 *3 1/4* **Without A Prayer (IRE)**[135] 3156 3-8-11 105.................. WilliamBuick 11 98
(R M Beckett) *hld up: rdn over 2f out: n.d* **28/1**
0500 8 *3 3/4* **Captain Marvelous (IRE)**[14] 6814 4-9-2 109.................. MichaelHills 12 92
(B W Hills) *hld up: rdn over 2f out: wknd over 1f out* **25/1**

The Form Book, Raceform Ltd, Compton, RG20 6NL

0106 **9** 1 1/4 **Calming Influence (IRE)**[29] 6440 3-9-0 107........................(t) TedDurcan 1 89
(Saeed Bin Suroor) *hld up: plld hrd: rdn over 2f out: wknd over 1f out* **20/1**
3630 **10** 18 **Babodana**[49] 5896 8-8-13 100........................ SaleemGolam 9 45
(M H Tompkins) *chsd ldr tl rdn over 3f out: wknd over 2f out* **40/1**
2240 **R** **Don't Panic (IRE)**[28] 6476 4-8-13 104........................ AlanMunro 3 —
(P W Chapple-Hyam) *ref to r* **12/1**
1m 40.2s (1.60) **Going Correction** +0.40s/f (Good)
WFA 3 from 4yo+ 2lb **11** Ran SP% **119.8**
Speed ratings (Par 111): **108,107,107,106,105 104,100,97,95,77** —
toteswinger: 1&2 £12.80, 1&3 £5.60, 2&3 £11.10. CSF £47.23 TOTE £5.50: £1.70, £3.80, £1.90; EX 60.00 Trifecta £646.30 Part won. Pool: £873.46 - 0.60 winning units. Place 6 £145.37, Place 5 £23.76.
Owner Cheveley Park Stud **Bred** Cheveley Park Stud Ltd **Trained** Newmarket, Suffolk

FOCUS
A fairly competitive Listed race. The progressive winner improved again and the placed horses ran to their recent best.

NOTEBOOK
Virtual has taken time to come to himself but he has progressed nicely this autumn, winning a handicap off 100 and picking up a French Listed race last time. Clearly very much at home in soft ground, he completed the hat-trick in good style, being delivered with a decisive late run from off the pace. Given the improvement he has shown this backend and considering he was a late foal, it is reasonable to expect he will do even better next season, when he should make his mark in Group company. (op 9-2 tchd 5-1)
General Eliott(IRE) settled better on this drop back to 1m and ran a sound race. This is his trip and level, and if he can stay clear of injury, in contrast to this year, he might be able to pick up a similar race next season. (tchd 14-1)
Alexandros was given a nice lead by his stablemate Dijeerr, but he did not convince with his attitude once asked to go on. It is questionable whether he was putting it all in at the finish and, while undoubtedly talented, he might not be entirely straightforward. (op 11-2)
Dijeerr(USA), who has proved largely consistent this season, wore the stable's third-string colours. He likes to make the running, got his own way out in front and kept on quite well after being headed, putting up another sound effort. (tchd 16-1)
Lucky Find(SAF), who made a successful British debut in a decent conditions event at Great Leighs last time, had to give weight all round as a result of winning a Group 3 race in Dubai earlier in the year. Given that he pulled far too hard and was carried right by Dijeerr in the closing stages, he did not run too badly, and if he returns to Dubai in the new year he will again be of interest, especially as the ground is likely to be more in his favour there. (op 8-1 tchd 9-1)
Bankable(IRE) was given the benefit of the doubt by punters and sent off favourite, but he again let them down, this time running as though a long season was finally catching up with him. He still has the potential to progress for another winter under his belt, but he will have a few questions to answer when he returns next year. (op 7-4 tchd 15-8)
Without A Prayer(IRE) was running for the first time since finishing fifth in the Hampton Court Stakes at Royal Ascot. This ground was plenty soft enough for him. (op 25-1)
Calming Influence(IRE) goes on soft ground, but he was another who simply failed to settle and had little hope of seeing his race out.
T/Plt: £134.40 to a £1 stake. Pool: £64,873.24. 352.31 winning tickets. T/Qpdt: £14.90 to a £1 stake. Pool: £5,772.44. 286.20 winning tickets. CR

7044 SOUTHWELL (L-H)
Sunday, November 2

OFFICIAL GOING: Standard
Wind: Moderate, half-behind. Weather: blustery and wet

7148 WATCH RACING UK LIVE AT CORAL.CO.UK MEDIAN AUCTION MAIDEN STKS 1m (F)
1:25 (1:25) (Class 5) 2-Y-O **£3,207** (£947; £473) **Stalls** Low

Form RPR
1 **Aboukir** 2-9-3 0........................ JamieSpencer 7 67
(P F I Cole) *chsd ldr: led over 5f out: rdn 2f out: hld on wl* **10/3**[3]
30 **2** 1/2 **Petsas Pleasure**[16] 6776 2-9-0 0........................ DuranFentiman(3) 3 65
(L R James) *trckd ldrs: chal 2f out: no ex ins fnl f* **3/1**[2]
0404 **3** 2 **Orphaned Annie**[15] 6809 2-8-5 57........................ LanceBetts(7) 5 56
(B Ellison) *chsd ldrs: kpt on same pce fnl 2f* **14/1**
0 **4** 1/2 **Telling Stories (IRE)**[10] 6923 2-8-12 0........................ JoeFanning 6 55
(M Johnston) *chsd ldrs: one pce fnl 2f* **12/1**
4 **5** 1/2 **Majestic Bull (USA)**[14] 6837 2-9-3 0........................ DeanMcKeown 9 59
(E J O'Neill) *led tl over 5f out: outpcd 2f out: kpt on fnl f* **7/4**[1]
6 4 1/2 **Royal Keva (IRE)** 2-9-3 0........................ SilvestreDeSousa 2 49
(A D Brown) *s.s: hdwy over 3f out: fdd over 1f out* **20/1**
0 **7** 18 **Flowerwood (IRE)**[39] 6205 2-8-7 0........................ NicolPolli(5) 8 4
(M G Quinlan) *chsd ldrs: lost pl over 2f out* **50/1**
00 **8** nk **Elevate Bambina**[19] 6722 2-8-9 0........................ MichaelJStainton(3) 4 4
(R M Whitaker) *sn outpcd and bhd* **50/1**
0 **9** 10 **Shy Prophet**[19] 6714 2-9-0 0........................ TolleyDean(3) 1 —
(A J McCabe) *drvn along to sn chse ldrs: lost pl over 4f out: sn bhd* **66/1**
4000 **10** 2 1/2 **Ernies Keep**[15] 6808 2-9-0 45........................ DominicFox(3) 12 —
(W Storey) *in rr: bhd fnl 4f* **250/1**
11 1 1/4 **Mrs Fox** 2-8-12 0........................ JamesDoyle 10 —
(N P Littmoden) *chsd ldrs: lost pl over 2f out: sn bhd* **33/1**
12 11 **Speak Freely** 2-8-12 0........................ DNolan 11 —
(C Smith) *s.i.s: sn in rr on outer: bhd fnl 4f* **66/1**
1m 45.57s (1.87) **Going Correction** -0.05s/f (Stan) **12** Ran SP% **113.8**
Speed ratings (Par 96): **88,87,85,85,84 80,62,61,51,49 47,36**
toteswinger: 1&2 £6.40, 1&3 £10.20, 2&3 £14.60. CSF £12.56 TOTE £3.60: £2.00, £1.50, £2.80; EX 15.50 Trifecta £25.60 Pool: £69.42 - 2.00 winning tickets..
Owner The Fairy Story Partnership **Bred** Deepwood Farm Stud **Trained** Whatcombe, Oxon

FOCUS
An ordinary maiden. The placed horses set the level, but the winner was green and can do better.

NOTEBOOK
Aboukir ◆, a son of Almutawakel and half-brother to Traphalgar, a three-time winner on the all-weather for the same connections, is bred to go on this surface and made a winning debut. Spencer had him in the van early and, although he had to get at him from a long way out, the colt overcame greenness and kept responding. A big, scopey sort, his dam won over 2m and he too should get a good deal further as he gets older. He could start his handicap career on a favourable mark. (op 7-2 tchd 3-1)
Petsas Pleasure struggled when dropped back to 6f on his second start in a better race than this at Newmarket last time, but he was popular in the market on this step up to a mile. He looked the likeliest winner at the top of the straight but in the end the newcomer just had that bit more ability. Handicaps are now open to him. (op 4-1)
Orphaned Annie had only shown moderate form in her previous four starts, but her dam won at up to 1m6f and the step up to a mile brought about an improved performance. (op 16-1)
Telling Stories(IRE), who raced wide round the turn out of the back straight, could only find the one pace in the last two and a half furlongs. Handicaps will provide her with better opportunities after one more run. (op 13-2 tchd 14-1)
Majestic Bull(USA) ran a decent race here on his debut when fourth to more experienced rivals. Stepping up a furlong in distance, the market did not want to know him, and he disappointed. Perhaps he will do better once handicapped after one more outing. (tchd 13-8 and 15-8)
Royal Keva(IRE) missed the break badly and struggled out the back for most of the race, but he did keep on. A half-brother to Karmest, who has won three times here, he can do better with this experience under his belt. Official explanation: jockey said gelding missed the break (op 16-1)

7149 CORAL - BET BY PHONE 0800 242 232 H'CAP 1m 4f (F)
2:00 (2:00) (Class 5) (0-70,65) 3-Y-O **£4,776** (£1,410; £705) **Stalls** Low

Form RPR
0001 **1** **Ice Bellini**[19] 6725 3-8-3 55........................(v) DavidProbert(5) 6 66
(Miss Gay Kelleway) *trckd ldrs: led 3f out: clr over 1f out* **6/1**
0050 **2** 8 **Oberlin (USA)**[94] 4564 3-9-2 63........................ TonyCulhane 7 61
(T Keddy) *chsd ldrs: led and qcknd over 4f out: hdd 3f out: kpt on to take modest 2nd jst ins fnl f* **6/1**
2140 **3** 2 3/4 **Well Informed**[6] 7010 3-8-9 56........................ DeanMcKeown 2 50
(E J O'Neill) *hld up in rr: hdwy 4f out: wnt 2nd over 2f out: one pce* **7/2**[2]
-325 **4** 1 **Gayanula (USA)**[244] 784 3-8-13 60........................ HayleyTurner 8 52
(Miss J A Camacho) *t.k.h towards rr: hdwy over 3f out: one pce fnl 2f* **5/1**[3]
1200 **5** 5 **Captain Mainwaring**[24] 6607 3-8-13 60........................ JamesDoyle 3 44
(N P Littmoden) *trckd ldrs: hrd rdn 3f out: wknd wl over 1f out* **3/1**[1]
-000 **6** nk **Amouretta**[71] 5269 3-7-13 51 oh6........................ AmyBaker(5) 1 35
(T T Clement) *led 1f: chsd ldrs: drvn over 5f out: lost pl over 3f out* **40/1**
0000 **7** 40 **Little Firecracker**[17] 6757 3-8-1 51 oh1................(p) DuranFentiman(3) 4 —
(Miss M E Rowland) *sn pushed along towards rr: lost pl 4f out: sn bhd: hopelessly t.o* **16/1**
1000 **8** 13 **Beautiful Lady (IRE)**[20] 6703 3-9-4 65................(b[1]) JamieSpencer 5 —
(P F I Cole) *led after 1f: hdd over 4f out: sn lost pl: bhd and eased 3f out: virtually p.u: hopelessly t.o* **15/2**
2m 40.82s (-0.18) **Going Correction** -0.05s/f (Stan) **8** Ran SP% **112.5**
Speed ratings (Par 102): **98,92,90,90,86 86,59,51**
toteswinger: 1&2 £7.70, 1&3 £1.80, 2&3 £4.50. CSF £40.19 CT £143.58 TOTE £6.90: £2.80, £2.10, £1.20; EX 25.10 TRIFECTA Not won..
Owner JCS Partnership **Bred** Boyce Bloodstock **Trained** Exning, Suffolk

FOCUS
A modest handicap, but it was taken apart by the lightly raced and improving Ice Bellini.

7150 CORAL ON CHANNEL 4 TELETEXT PAGE 611 H'CAP 1m 3f (F)
2:30 (2:30) (Class 3) (0-95,95) 3-Y-O+ **£9,390** (£2,794; £1,396; £697) **Stalls** Low

Form RPR
0313 **1** **Tarkheena Prince (USA)**[27] 6527 3-9-0 91........................ JamieSpencer 4 103+
(G A Swinbank) *hld up towards rr: stdy hdwy over 3f out: led over 1f out: rdn clr jst ins fnl f: heavily eased* **15/8**[1]
2056 **2** 2 1/2 **Dunaskin (IRE)**[22] 6106 8-9-9 95........................ DavidAllan 3 98
(B Ellison) *chsd ldrs: led 3f out tl over 1f out: no ch w wnr* **7/1**
3003 **3** 2 **Hunting Country**[8] 6974 3-8-12 89........................ JoeFanning 1 89
(M Johnston) *led 1f: trckd ldrs: n.m.r on ins over 2f out: styd on same pce fnl 2f* **11/4**[2]
0000 **4** 1/2 **Polish Power (GER)**[6] 7025 8-8-13 85........................ LPKeniry 2 84
(J S Moore) *trckd ldrs: wnt 2nd appr fnl f: kpt on same pce* **12/1**
040- **5** 1 1/2 **Drawback (IRE)**[13] 6475 5-8-4 81 oh11........................ DavidProbert(5) 6 77?
(Heather Dalton) *hld up in rr: hdwy over 4f out: one pce fnl 2f* **33/1**
1133 **6** 5 **Hurlingham**[31] 6410 4-9-3 89........................ GrahamGibbons 8 77
(M W Easterby) *hld up in rr: hdwy over 2f out: wknd and eased 1f out* **5/1**[3]
0-40 **7** 1/2 **Film Festival (USA)**[16] 2582 5-8-2 81........................ LanceBetts(7) 5 68
(B Ellison) *drvn to ld after 1f: hdd 3f out: lost pl 2f out* **9/1**
2m 25.13s (-2.87) **Going Correction** -0.05s/f (Stan)
WFA 3 from 4yo+ 5lb **7** Ran SP% **111.2**
Speed ratings (Par 107): **108,106,104,104,103 99,99**
toteswinger: 1&2 £3.00, 1&3 £1.70, 2&3 £2.70. CSF £14.75 CT £33.40 TOTE £2.20: £1.80, £3.60; EX 15.50 Trifecta £16.70 Pool: £176.34 - 7.80 winning tickets..
Owner G H Bell **Bred** Whitewood Stable Inc **Trained** Melsonby, N Yorks

FOCUS
A pretty decent handicap run at a good gallop, and there were plenty in with a chance at the top of the straight. Improved form again from the progressive winner, who was value for more like double the margin.

NOTEBOOK
Tarkheena Prince(USA) handles plenty of cut on turf and stamina is certainly his strong suit, so he had plenty going for him on his Fibresand debut. Once he hit the front a furlong and a half out he just steadily drew further and further clear for his fourth success of the campaign, and on this evidence there could be more to come from him, although apparently he will be put away until the spring now. He will certainly not be inconvenienced by stepping up in trip again. (op 9-4 tchd 5-2)
Dunaskin(IRE) had not run here before but his style of running is suited to this track and he kept plugging away after the eventual winner went on. He retains plenty of ability, but his current mark just leaves him vulnerable to more progressive rivals. (op 5-1)
Hunting Country looked keen to lead, but was denied that role by Film Festival. He ran a sound enough race, but might do better if turning up in a race where he is able to dominate. (op 3-1)
Polish Power(GER) has been out of form recently, but he has run well here in the past and this was more encouraging. (tchd 11-1)
Drawback(IRE), who ran well over hurdles last time out on his return from a year on the sidelines, faced a stiff task from 11lb out of the handicap.
Hurlingham got the decent pace he needs, but his career-high mark proved too much. (tchd 9-2)

7151 CORAL.CO.UK H'CAP 5f (F)
3:00 (3:01) (Class 3) (0-95,92) 3-Y-O+ **£8,742** (£2,601; £1,300; £649) **Stalls** High

Form RPR
3050 **1** **How's She Cuttin' (IRE)**[16] 6782 5-8-8 82................(v) JamieSpencer 1 99+
(T D Barron) *led: clr over 3f out: unchal: eased nr fin* **5/1**[2]
0060 **2** 3 **Luscivious**[8] 6971 4-8-6 85................(b) DavidProbert(5) 9 89
(A J McCabe) *hld up towards rr: effrt 2f out: styd on to take 2nd ins fnl f: no ch w wnr* **12/1**
3450 **3** 1 1/2 **Matsunosuke**[11] 6902 6-9-4 92........................ AlanMunro 4 91
(A B Coogan) *chsd ldrs: kpt on same pce fnl 2f* **7/1**
2111 **4** shd **Beat The Bell**[11] 6902 3-8-11 90........................ NicolPolli(5) 8 88+
(A Bailey) *sn outpcd and in rr: last 1f out: fin wl* **13/2**[3]
5264 **5** nk **Pawan (IRE)**[5] 7047 8-8-8 87 ow3................(b) AnnStokell(5) 2 84
(Miss A Stokell) *hmpd s: sn mid-div: sn pushed along: hdwy on wd outside 2f out: kpt on same pce* **12/1**
0604 **6** 3/4 **Bertoliver**[21] 6669 4-9-2 90........................ RichardKingscote 5 85
(Tom Dascombe) *chsd ldrs: one pce fnl 2f* **12/1**
0000 **7** 1/2 **Aegean Dancer**[8] 6971 6-8-12 86........................ TomEaves 11 79
(B Smart) *prom: kpt on same pce fnl 2f* **14/1**
156 **8** 1 1/4 **Rebel Duke (IRE)**[179] 1917 4-8-9 83........................ TonyHamilton 12 71
(D W Barker) *chsd ldrs: wknd fnl f* **20/1**

0353 9 1 **Fol Hollow (IRE)**[8] 6971 3-8-13 **87** AdrianTNicholls 7 72
(D Nicholls) *chsd ldrs: rdn 2f out: wknd fnl f* 4/1[1]

0000 10 ½ **Canadian Danehill (IRE)**[33] 6354 6-8-9 **83** (p) GrahamGibbons 10 66
(R M H Cowell) *mid-div: sn pushed along: nvr nr ldrs* 33/1

030 11 1 **Tartatartufata**[29] 6486 6-8-11 **85** (v) J-PGuillambert 3 64
(J G Given) *sn towards rr: nvr on terms* 16/1

4520 12 nk **Invincible Force (IRE)**[36] 6290 4-9-0 **88** (b) FrancisNorton 6 66
(Paul Green) *s.i.s: nvr wnt pce: a in rr* 11/1

57.79 secs (-1.91) **Going Correction** -0.20s/f (Stan) 12 Ran SP% **114.2**
Speed ratings (Par 107): **107,102,99,99,99 97,97,95,93,92 91,90**
toteswinger: 1&2 £16.10, 1&3 £7.70, 2&3 £24.00. CSF £61.31 CT £425.21 TOTE £6.10: £2.10, £4.80, £2.90; EX 70.60 Trifecta £225.50 Part won. Pool: £304.74 - 0.10 winning tickets..
Owner Chris McHale **Bred** A M Burke **Trained** Maunby, N Yorks

FOCUS
A good, competitive sprint handicap on paper, but in the event it was a one-horse race.

NOTEBOOK
How's She Cuttin'(IRE) pinged the gates and never saw another rival. She appreciates some dig on turf and clearly took to this surface very well, as she came home a most impressive winner. This win followed a very good seventh in a Listed race at Newmarket and she is clearly at the top of her game at present. She is in at Musselburgh on Friday, and could be interesting under a penalty, as she has such a good record at that particular track. (tchd 6-1)
Luscivious has struggled on turf this year, but the return to Fibresand brought about an improved display from him as he won the separate race for second quite well. He is back on his last winning mark now and should remain of interest for a similar race.
Matsunosuke is on an attractive mark at present, but he had never run on this surface before and his preference for fast ground on turf suggested he might not take to it. He ran a perfectly sound race in the circumstances. (op 9-1)
Beat The Bell came here chasing a four-timer following a hat-trick of wins over 6f on Polytrack. This was a different test, and he was not disgraced off a 4lb higher mark, but a return to 6f will definitely be in his favour. (op 11-2)
Pawan(IRE) had the decent gallop he needs and kept plugging away. Official explanation: jockey said gelding suffered interference at the start (op 10-1)
Bertoliver, who likes to make the running, simply could not match the winner's pace in the early stages. Official explanation: jockey said gelding had no more to give (op 10-1 tchd 9-1)
Rebel Duke(IRE) has gone well fresh in the past and came here having won both his previous starts over this course and distance. He ran as though needing it this time, though. (tchd 18-1 and 25-1)
Fol Hollow(IRE) has been in good heart on turf of late, but failed to translate that form to this artificial surface. (tchd 7-2)

7152 PLAY CLEOPATRA AT CORAL.CO.UK H'CAP — 6f (F)
3:35 (3:36) (Class 5) (0-75,73) 3-Y-0+ — £4,094 (£1,209; £604) Stalls Low

Form RPR

0414 1 **Cool Sands (IRE)**[5] 7048 6-8-11 **66** (v) J-PGuillambert 2 77
(J G Given) *chsd ldrs: sn drvn along: hrd rdn and styd on fnl 2f: led towards fin* 7/4[1]

4060 2 ½ **Steel City Boy (IRE)**[23] 6634 5-8-8 **68** ow1 AnnStokell(5) 1 77
(Miss A Stokell) *led: hung rt: hdd and no ex fnl 50yds* 7/1

0404 3 3½ **Feeling Fresh (IRE)**[5] 7040 3-8-9 **64** FrancisNorton 4 62
(Paul Green) *s.i.s: hdwy to chse ldrs over 3f out: kpt on same pce fnl 2f* 13/2

0400 4 ¾ **Steel Blue**[19] 6724 8-7-13 **59** DavidProbert(5) 7 54
(R M Whitaker) *chsd ldrs: effrt over 2f out: kpt on same pce* 3/1[2]

4045 5 ½ **Another Genepi (USA)**[2] 7118 5-9-0 **69** EdwardCreighton 6 63
(E J Creighton) *hld up in midfield: effrt over 2f out: kpt on one pce* 6/1[3]

0000 6 13 **Fitzwarren**[9] 6952 7-8-4 **59** oh14 (v) SilvestreDeSousa 8 11
(A D Brown) *chsd ldrs: brought wd over 2f out: sn lost pl and bhd* 80/1

3250 7 95 **Thunderousapplause**[149] 2787 4-9-0 **72** TolleyDean(3) 5 —
(A J McCabe) *stmbld s: in rr: detached in last whn eased 2f out: hopelessly t.o: virtually p.u* 11/1

1m 15.16s (-1.34) **Going Correction** -0.05s/f (Stan) 7 Ran SP% **111.1**
Speed ratings (Par 103): **106,105,100,99,99 81,—**
toteswinger: 1&2 £4.50, 1&3 £3.20, 2&3 £6.30. CSF £13.82 CT £60.57 TOTE £2.30: £1.70, £5.00; EX 15.90 Trifecta £33.60 Pool: £113.67 - 2.50 winning tickets..
Owner Peter Swann **Bred** Rathasker Stud **Trained** Willoughton, Lincs

FOCUS
Modest sprinting form, but the winner was back to his best and the second ran close to his spring level.

7153 PLAY CORAL SLOTS IN SHOP AND ONLINE H'CAP — 7f (F)
4:05 (4:20) (Class 5) (0-70,70) 3-Y-0+ — £3,753 (£1,108; £554) Stalls Low

Form RPR

001 1 **Smarty Socks (IRE)**[6] 7021 4-8-11 **62** 6ex SilvestreDeSousa 7 80+
(P T Midgley) *dwlt: sn chsng ldrs: effrt over 2f out: str run to ld 1f out: sn pushed clr: eased fnl 50yds* 5/2[2]

2555 2 3¾ **Whitbarrow (IRE)**[31] 6420 9-9-2 **70** (p) JamesMillman(3) 1 78
(B R Millman) *w ldr: led over 4f out: qcknd 3f out: hdd 1f out: no ch w wnr* 16/1

0601 3 2¼ **Elusive Warrior (USA)**[5] 7048 5-9-4 **69** 6ex JamesDoyle 2 71
(A J McCabe) *led tl over 4f out: rdn and edgd rt 2f out: no ex* 15/8[1]

2030 4 1½ **Orpenella**[16] 6792 3-8-11 **63** FrancisNorton 5 61
(K A Ryan) *trckd ldrs: rdn over 2f out: one pce* 12/1

0060 5 ½ **Royal Island (IRE)**[8] 6989 6-8-9 **60** VinceSlattery 3 57
(M G Quinlan) *in rr: drvn over 3f out: kpt on fnl 2f: nvr a threat* 14/1

0500 6 3 **Divertimenti (IRE)**[23] 6627 4-9-5 **70** (p) LPKeniry 9 58
(C R Dore) *trckd ldrs on outer: brought wd over 2f out: one pce* 14/1

3602 7 ¾ **Dancing Deano (IRE)**[43] 6132 6-8-10 **64** RussellKennemore(3) 8 50
(R Hollinshead) *swtchd lft s: w ldrs: rdn over 2f out: edgd rt and sn btn* 5/1[3]

000 8 20 **Paint Stripper**[62] 5565 3-8-1 **56** oh11 (p) DominicFox(3) 6 —
(W Storey) *chsd ldrs: drvn over 3f out: lost pl 3f out: eased and sn wl bhd: t.o* 66/1

1m 28.0s (-2.30) **Going Correction** -0.05s/f (Stan)
WFA 3 from 4yo+ 1lb 8 Ran SP% **108.4**
Speed ratings (Par 103): **111,106,104,102,101 98,97,74**
toteswinger: 1&2 £5.60, 1&3 £1.70, 2&3 £3.80. CSF £36.49 CT £78.31 TOTE £3.70: £1.50, £2.90, £1.20; EX 48.60 Trifecta £109.70 Pool: £379.58 - 2.56 winning tickets. Place 6 £58.11, Place 5 £32.63.
Owner R G Fell **Bred** Mick McGinn **Trained** Westow, N Yorks
■ Stewards' Enquiry : Russell Kennemore one-day ban: failed to ride to draw (Nov 17)

FOCUS
A decent handicap for the grade, with both the winner and the third still looking ahead of the Handicapper under their penalties and the second back down to a good mark.
T/Plt: £121.20 to a £1 stake. Pool: £62,320.99. 375.15 winning tickets. T/Qpdt: £23.20 to a £1 stake. Pool: £4,702.89. 149.60 winning tickets. WG

7154 - 7156a (Foreign Racing) - See Raceform Interactive

7028 LEOPARDSTOWN (L-H)
Sunday, November 2

OFFICIAL GOING: Soft (yielding to soft in straight)

7157a KNOCKAIRE STKS (LISTED RACE) — 7f
2:15 (2:15) 3-Y-0+ — £23,933 (£7,022; £3,345; £1,139)

RPR

1 **Almass (IRE)**[15] 6831 3-9-1 110 DPMcDonogh 4 112+
(Kevin Prendergast, Ire) *trckd ldrs: 6th 1/2-way: hdwy in 3rd 2f out: rdn to ld over 1f out: kpt on strly to go clr fnl f* 11/4[2]

2 4 **Girouette (IRE)**[48] 5983 3-8-12 89 MCHussey 7 95
(Tracey Collins, Ire) *hld up towards rr: hdwy in 6th 1 1/2f out: 3rd 1f out: kpt on fnl f: no ch w wnr* 16/1

3 ½ **Al Qasi (IRE)**[50] 5893 5-9-2 MJKinane 1 98+
(P W Chapple-Hyam) *chsd ldrs: 4th 1/2-way: 5th 2f out: nt clr run 1 1/2f out: prog fr 1f out: kpt on fnl f* 11/10[1]

4 1½ **Nanotech (IRE)**[14] 6845 4-9-2 93 WJLee 2 93
(Jarlath P Fahey, Ire) *chsd ldrs: 5th 1/2-way: rdn in 6th 2f out: kpt on same pce fr 1f out* 12/1

5 ½ **Tian Shan (IRE)**[28] 6516 4-9-5 107 (b) PJSmullen 6 94
(D K Weld, Ire) *chsd ldrs: led after 2f: rdn and hdd over 1f out: no ex and kpt on same pce* 7/1[3]

6 ½ **Russian Empress (IRE)**[29] 6484 4-8-13 94 PBBeggy 8 87
(David P Myerscough, Ire) *towards rr: 8th 2f out: short of room and swtchd 1 1/2f out: rdn in 8th 1f out: kpt on same pce fnl f* 16/1

7 ½ **Rain Rush (IRE)**[15] 6831 5-9-2 101 JAHeffernan 3 89+
(David Marnane, Ire) *towards rr: hdwy to 7th 2f out: rdn into 5th 1 1/2f out: no ex over 1f out* 14/1

8 1¼ **Teacht An Earraig (USA)**[36] 6298 3-8-12 102 KJManning 10 82
(J S Bolger, Ire) *chsd ldrs: 2nd 1/2-way: rdn 2f out: no ex in 4th 1f out: wknd fnl f* 14/1

9 3½ **Emily Blake (IRE)**[14] 6845 4-8-13 105 PTownend 5 73
(J C Hayden, Ire) *led: hdd after 2f: rdn in 4th 2f out: sn no ex and wknd 1 1/2f out* 9/1

10 12 **Cuilaphuca (IRE)**[126] 3532 4-8-13 95 PShanahan 9 40
(Tracey Collins, Ire) *mid-div: 7th 1/2-way: rdn and wknd ent st* 33/1

1m 31.12s (0.82) **Going Correction** +0.40s/f (Good)
WFA 3 from 4yo+ 1lb 10 Ran SP% **132.5**
Speed ratings: **111,106,105,104,103 103,102,101,97,83**
CSF £53.90 TOTE £4.00: £1.50, £7.70, £1.40; DF 130.30.
Owner Hamdan Al Maktoum **Bred** Shadwell Estate Co Ltd **Trained** Friarstown, Co Kildare

NOTEBOOK
Almass(IRE), a versatile filly who has now scored six times this season, was a cosy winner. (op 5/2)
Al Qasi(IRE), down in grade following two second-placed efforts in Group 2 contests at Newbury and Doncaster, turned into the straight in fourth position hugging the inside rail, but it soon became evident that he would struggle to find room to produce a challenge. Once the gap did appear, the race was out of his reach although he did show a late change of gear to challenge for the runner-up spot. He has to rate as unfortunate. (op 7/4)

7158a EYREFIELD STKS (LISTED RACE) — 1m 1f
2:45 (2:46) 2-Y-0 — £23,933 (£7,022; £3,345; £1,139)

RPR

1 **Mourayan (IRE)**[35] 6316 2-9-1 109 MJKinane 2 105+
(John M Oxx, Ire) *prom: chsd ldr in 2nd after 1f: chal ent st: led under 2f out: rdn and kpt on wl fnl f* 4/6[1]

2 2 **Oh Goodness Me**[14] 6847 2-8-12 99 KJManning 1 98
(J S Bolger, Ire) *led early: hdd after 1f: settled bhd ldrs: 3rd 1/2-way: rdn into 2nd 1 1/2f out: kpt on same pce fnl f: no imp wnr* 9/2[2]

3 ¾ **Aristocrat**[13] 6869 2-9-1 JAHeffernan 6 100
(A P O'Brien, Ire) *hld up in rr: hdwy on outer to 3rd 1f out: rdn and kpt on same pce fnl f* 6/1[3]

4 4 **The Bull Hayes (IRE)**[13] 6869 2-9-1 100 DPMcDonogh 3 92
(Mrs John Harrington, Ire) *settled bhd ldrs: 4th 1/2-way: rdn and dropped to rr 2f out: 5th and no imp over 1f out: kpt on same pce* 7/1

5 2 **Billys Dream**[13] 6873 2-8-12 CDHayes 5 85
(J T Gorman, Ire) *settled bhd ldrs: 5th 1/2-way: rdn in 4th 2f out: no ex over 1f out and kpt on one pce* 20/1

6 5½ **Shady Lady (IRE)**[16] 6789 2-8-12 GregFairley 4 74
(M Johnston) *led after 1f: rdn and hdd under 2f out: wknd 1 1/2f out* 11/1

2m 2.86s (8.76) **Going Correction** +0.40s/f (Good) 6 Ran SP% **118.1**
Speed ratings: **77,75,74,71,69 64**
CSF £4.53 TOTE £1.50: £1.10, £1.90; DF 4.60.
Owner H H Aga Khan **Bred** Hh The Aga Khan's Stud Sc **Trained** Currabeg, Co Kildare

NOTEBOOK
Mourayan(IRE) put up a satisfactory performance in winning for the second time in his career. He clearly has plenty of stamina as no sooner had the runner-up got to within a length of him he pulled out plenty more to win comfortably in the end, with a performance which certainly did his 2009 Classic prospects no harm. Connections stated afterwards their intention to start off next season in the Ballysax Stakes in a campaign geared towards the Epsom Derby. (op 4/5)

7159 - 7161a (Foreign Racing) - See Raceform Interactive

7037 SAINT-CLOUD (L-H)
Sunday, November 2

OFFICIAL GOING: Heavy

7162a PRIX PERTH (GROUP 3) — 1m
1:15 (1:27) 3-Y-0+ — £29,412 (£11,765; £8,824; £5,882; £2,941)

RPR

1 **Vertigineux (FR)**[84] 4915 4-9-3 PSogorb 3 113
(Mme C Dufreche, France) *sn disputing 2nd: 2nd st: drvn to ld appr fnl f: pushed out last 100yds* 487/10

2 hd **Gris De Gris (IRE)**[56] 5742 4-9-5 TThulliez 6 115
(A De Royer-Dupre, France) *led: brought field over to stands' side ent st: hdd appr fnl f: rallied and r.o same pce* 68/10[3]

3 ¾ **Racinger (FR)**[36] 6270 5-9-3 DBonilla 9 111
(F Head, France) *a cl up: 4th st: hrd rdn over 1f out: tk 3rd ins fnl f: r.o* 42/10[2]

4 1 1/2 **Bermuda Rye (IRE)**[23] 6643 3-8-11 .... TJarnet 4 104
(M Delzangles, France) *5th st: rdn and 3rd over 1f out: one pce fnl f* **10/1**

5 1 **Royal God (USA)**[56] 5738 3-8-11 .... WMongil 8 102
(F Head, France) *hld up: last st: gd hdwy wl over 1f out: rdn and one pce ins fnl f* **43/1**

6 shd **Passager (FR)**[23] 6643 5-8-13 .... SPasquier 11 102
(Mme C Head-Maarek, France) *s.i.s: towards rr to st: hdwy 2f out: nvr nr to chal* **28/10**[1]

7 5 **Chopastair (FR)**[24] 6612 7-9-3 .... J-BEyquem 15 95
(T Lemer, France) *disp 2nd: cl 3rd st: rdn and btn appr fnl f* **69/10**

8 snk **Quest For Honor**[50] 5926 4-8-13 .... ACrastus 14 90
(T Doumen, France) *in rr 2f out: nvr a factor* **10/1**

9 3/4 **Zenone (IRE)**[49] 4-8-13 .... SUrru 1 89
(Laura Grizzetti, Italy) *broke wl: hld up in mid-div: 8th st: n.d* **41/1**

10 3/4 **Silent Sunday (IRE)**[60] 5622 3-8-8 .... IMendizabal 5 84
(H-A Pantall, France) *in rr to st: nvr a factor* **47/1**

11 **Santiago (GER)**[57] 5743 6-8-13 .... CSoumillon 7 87
(H Blume, Germany) *mid-div: 7th and pushed along st: sn btn* **12/1**

12 **Boris De Deauville (IRE)**[29] 6499 5-9-3 .... DBoeuf 12 91
(S Wattel, France) *6th st: rdn and btn over 1f out* **50/1**

13 **Caesarine (FR)**[37] 6265 3-8-8 .... JVictoire 2 84
(A Fabre, France) *a in rr* **14/1**

14 **Turning For Home (FR)**[35] 6322 3-8-8 .... FVeron 13 84
(H-A Pantall, France) *mid-div and pushed along appr st: bhd fnl 2f* **78/1**

1m 45.7s (-1.80) **Going Correction** +0.10s/f (Good)
WFA 3 from 4yo+ 2lb **14** Ran SP% **126.1**
Speed ratings: **113,112,112,110,109 109,104,104,103,102 102,102,102,102**
PARI-MUTUEL: WIN 49.70; PL 9.70, 2.80, 2.30; DF 132.60.
Owner Mme C & P Dufreche **Bred** Patrick Dufreche **Trained** France

NOTEBOOK

Vertigineux(FR) was tucked in just behind the leader early on, and was always enjoying himself on the heavy ground. Asked to quicken one and a half out, he joined the battle for the lead and ran on bravely to score narrowly. This was his second Group 3 win of the season and the colt should certainly turn into a nice five-year-old and is certainly a soft-ground specialist. The Group 2 Prix du Muguet over the course and distance could be an early target next year.

Gris De Gris(IRE) made a very brave attempt to make all the running. He brought the field across to the stands' side, hugged the rail throughout the straight, battled on gamely to the line and was only beaten a head while trying to give a kilo to the winner. He may well now go back to a trainer in the South of France to be campaigned at Cagnes-Sur-Mer.

Racinger(FR), a Group 3 winner who has been used as a pacemaker for a stablemate, was running in his own right in this event. He pulled very hard in the early stages and then came across to the stands' rail, but battled on gamely to hold third place with a little in hand. He will not be seen out again this season.

Bermuda Rye(IRE), not far from the leaders rounding the final turn, he made good progress in the straight but could never make it in to third place.

7163a CRITERIUM INTERNATIONAL (GROUP 1) (C&F) 1m

2:20 (2:29) 2-Y-O £105,037 (£42,022; £21,011; £10,496; £5,257)

RPR

1 **Zafisio (IRE)**[14] 6855 2-9-0 .... DBoeuf 8 110
(P A Blockley) *a in tch: 7th st: rdn 2f out: led appr fnl f: drvn out* **28/1**

2 hd **Prince Siegfried (FR)**[29] 6474 2-9-0 .... WilliamBuick 11 109
(A M Balding) *a.p: 3rd st: swtchd lft over 1f out: c through narrow gap to chal 1f out: r.o u.p* **25/1**

3 1/2 **Silver Frost (IRE)**[23] 6642 2-9-0 .... SPasquier 6 108
(Y De Nicolay, France) *trckd ldr: 2nd st: led over 2f out: sn hrd rdn: hdd appr fnl f: r.o same pce* **56/10**

4 1 1/2 **Fuisse (FR)**[23] 6642 2-9-0 .... TGillet 5 105
(Mme C Head-Maarek, France) *a.p: 5th st: ev ch 1f out: one pce* **10/1**

5 1/2 **Calvados Blues (FR)**[43] 6147 2-9-0 .... TThulliez 9 104
(P Demercastel, France) *led: brought field to stands' side st: hdd over 2f out: sn rdn: one pce fr over 1f out* **15/1**

6 nse **Milanais (FR)**[28] 6520 2-9-0 .... TJarnet 1 103
(B De Watrigant, France) *6th st: rdn to chal wl over 1f out: ev ch 1f out: one pce* **36/10**[2]

7 shd **Le Havre (IRE)**[30] 2-9-0 .... IMendizabal 2 103
(J-C Rouget, France) *mid-div: hdwy on outside 1 1/2f out: one pce fnl f* **5/2**[1]

8 2 1/2 **Serva Jugum (USA)**[29] 6466 2-9-0 .... CSoumillon 4 98
(P F I Cole) *in rr: last and reminders st: nvr a factor* **47/10**[3]

9 2 **Salpado (FR)**[24] 6611 2-9-0 .... CNora 10 93
(R Martin Sanchez, Spain) *dwlt: hdwy and 4th st: btn over 1f out* **33/1**

10 nk **Apro Lunare (IRE)**[36] 2-9-0 .... CColombi 7 93
(Laura Grizzetti, Italy) *a in rr* **36/1**

11 8 **Surdoue (USA)**[42] 2-9-0 .... JVictoire 3 75
(Robert Collet, France) *10th st: rdn over 2f out: sn btn: eased fnl f* **22/1**

1m 46.1s (-1.40) **Going Correction** +0.10s/f (Good) **11** Ran SP% **115.6**
Speed ratings: **111,110,110,108,108 108,108,105,103,103 95**
PARI-MUTUEL: WIN 29.10; PL 6.80, 6.60, 2.50; DF 171.10.
Owner H Downs **Bred** Airlie Stud And Sir Thomas Pilkington **Trained** Lambourn, Berks
■ Stewards' Enquiry : William Buick 100eur fine: whip abuse

FOCUS

The last few winners of this have gone on to be disappointing, but the likes of Act One, Bago and Dalakhani have used this as a springboard to greater things in recent times, although this did not look a particularly strong renewal.

NOTEBOOK

Zafisio(IRE), who was providing his soon-to-be-warned-off trainer Paul Blockley with a first Group 1 winner, seemed to confirm the impression that this was not the strongest renewal. The winner of a Listed contest at Goodwood in September, he managed only fourth in a Group 3 at Longchamp last time and the marked improvement can presumably be put down to encountering a testing surface for the first time. He burst through a furlong out and found plenty for strong pressure to just edge out fellow British raider Prince Siegfried. This was his moment of glory and he is going to find life tough next season with the Group 1 winner's penalty, so connections may return for the 1m2f Criterium de Saint-Cloud later in the month.

Prince Siegfried(FR) has twice come up short in good races having won impressively on his debut, but the form of his latest seventh in a valuable sales race at Newmarket received two significant boosts with the high-profile victories of Donativum and Crowded House the previous weekend. Improving for the step up to 1m, he moved through about the same time as the winner and stayed on well, but was always just being held close home. He should make a decent three-year-old when he is likely to make the trip across the Channel again.

Silver Frost(IRE) did best of the home team. Seventh in the Prix Morny earlier in the season, he showed a marked improvement in form when stepping up to this distance for the first time in a Group 3 at the course last time. He was run out of it in the final 100 yards, having gone on a furlong out, but this still represented another step forward.

Fuisse(FR), runner-up to Silver Frost at the course last month, could only find the one pace under pressure but ran to form and is still lightly raced, so may improve again at three.

Calvados Blues(FR) has improved markedly since encountering a sound surface, winning a Group 3 at Longchamp last time, but there was a major doubt as to how he would cope back on testing ground. He led them into the straight, but could not pick up for pressure and was run out of the places.

Milanais(FR), who set the standard having finished runner-up to Naaqoos in the Lagardere on Arc day, had earlier shown smart form when finishing fourth in the Prix Morny and the step up to 1m for the first time looked to be in his favour. This was the heaviest ground he has encountered though and, having been produced to have every chance, he could find no extra.

Le Havre(IRE) was stepping up markedly in grade having won two minor races, including over course and distance last time and, though he lost his unbeaten record, this was still a fair effort.

Serva Jugum(USA) justified connections' high opinion of him when winning a conditions race on his debut at Kempton, but this was a totally different test, up markedly in grade on a testing surface, and he was never travelling. He plugged on late and will be a different horse back on a sounder surface.

[7112] WOLVERHAMPTON (A.W) (L-H)

Monday, November 3

OFFICIAL GOING: Standard
Wind: Light against Weather: Overcast

7164 WOLVERHAMPTON-RACECOURSE.CO.UK (S) STKS 7f 32y(P)

2:20 (2:22) (Class 6) 2-Y-O £2,047 (£604; £302) Stalls High

Form RPR

6210 1 **Smalljohn**[89] 4733 2-9-2 74..(v) TomEaves 2 73+
(B Smart) *chsd ldr tl led 4f out: clr over 2f out: comf* **10/11**[1]

04 2 5 **Statute Book (IRE)**[26] 6574 2-8-11 0.. AdamKirby 9 54
(S Kirk) *mid-div: hdwy 2f out: wnt 2nd over 1f out: no ch w wnr* **8/1**

00 3 3 1/4 **Admiring Glances**[13] 6884 2-8-6 0.. JimmyQuinn 10 41
(J Pearce) *hld up in tch: rdn over 2f out: hung lft over 1f out: styd on same pce* **16/1**

4 shd **Dead Cat Bounce (IRE)** 2-8-11 0.. ShaneKelly 4 46
(J A Osborne) *s.s: hld up: r.o ins fnl f: nvr nrr* **11/1**

0032 5 nk **Svindal (IRE)**[21] 6709 2-8-11 58..(b) SilvestreDeSousa 7 48+
(K A Ryan) *prom: hung lft over 2f out: nt clr run sn after: styd on same pce* **11/2**[2]

04 6 1/2 **Miss Kadee**[12] 6893 2-8-3 0.. LukeMorris(3) 12 39
(P D Evans) *sn pushed along in rr: rdn over 2f out: hung lft and styd on fnl f* **16/1**

30 7 7 **Bid To Dance**[11] 6931 2-8-6 0.. NickyMackay 6 21
(K A Morgan) *chsd ldrs: rdn over 3f out: wknd 2f out* **50/1**

2200 8 1 1/4 **Come On Buckers (IRE)**[24] 6632 2-9-0 65 ow1....(p) AlanCreighton(3) 1 29
(E J Creighton) *sn led: hdd 4f out: rdn and wknd over 1f out* **25/1**

3 9 18 **Wickedly Fast (USA)**[21] 6709 2-8-1 0 ow2..........(t) MatthewDavies(7) 3 —
(George Baker) *chsd ldrs: rdn whn hmpd over 2f out: sn wknd* **7/1**[3]

10 17 **Auctioniki** 2-8-6 0.. RichardKingscote 11 —
(B Palling) *s.s: outpcd* **66/1**

1m 30.27s (0.67) **Going Correction** +0.05s/f (Slow) **10** Ran SP% **118.8**
Speed ratings (Par 94): **98,92,88,88,88 87,79,78,57,38**
toteswinger: 1&2 £4.00, 1&3 £6.50, 2&3 £18.60. CSF £9.10 TOTE £2.10: £1.20, £2.30, £3.60; EX 10.40 Trifecta £135.80 Pool: £255.23 - 1.39 winning units..There was no bid for the winner. Dead Cat Bounce was claimed by Jeff Pearce £6,000.
Owner John Walsh & Reuben Glynn **Bred** W H R John And Partners **Trained** Hambleton, N Yorks

FOCUS

An ordinary seller, but Smalljohn looks better than this level and recorded a time quicker than both divisions of the juvenile maiden.

NOTEBOOK

Smalljohn had been off the track for the best part of three months and has left Declan Carroll's yard since his last run, but he was strongly supported. Having raced keenly in a share of the lead, he was allowed to stride on well before the straight and looked to have this in the bag from some way out, ultimately coming home well clear. (op 11-8)

Statute Book(IRE) was no match for the winner, but he was clear second best. (op 17-2 tchd 10-1)

Admiring Glances, dropped in trip and grade, ran a respectable race without ever looking like doing enough. If anything, she still looked a little green under pressure. (tchd 20-1)

Dead Cat Bounce(IRE) was niggled along a fair way out, but he kept on from a long way back and showed some ability at this lowly level first-time up. (op 8-1)

Svindal(IRE) lost ground when short of room leaving the back straight and is better than his finishing position suggests. (op 4-1 tchd 6-1)

Miss Kadee was never in contention after blowing the start. (tchd 25-1)

Auctioniki Official explanation: jockey said filly moved poorly throughout

7165 HOTEL & CONFERENCING AT WOLVERHAMPTON MAIDEN STKS (DIV I) 7f 32y(P)

2:50 (2:51) (Class 5) 2-Y-O £2,914 (£867; £433; £216) Stalls High

Form RPR

0 1 **Wee Giant (USA)**[18] 6759 2-9-3 0.. JamieSpencer 9 73+
(K A Ryan) *hld up in tch: rdn to ld ins fnl f: hung lft: r.o* **9/2**

5 2 nk **Yellow Printer**[22] 6677 2-9-3 0.. RichardKingscote 5 72
(Tom Dascombe) *chsd ldrs: ev ch fr over 2f out: r.o* **3/1**[2]

0 3 2 1/2 **Dancourt (IRE)**[20] 6714 2-9-3 0.. RyanMoore 2 66
(Sir Michael Stoute) *chsd ldrs: led 3f out: rdn and hung rt over 2f out: hdd and unable qck ins fnl f* **7/2**[3]

20 4 2 **Swiss Art (IRE)**[12] 6910 2-9-0 0.. KevinGhunowa(3) 3 61
(R A Harris) *prom: rdn over 2f out: styng on same pce whn hung lft fr over 1f out* **9/1**

5 1 1/4 **More Tea Vicar (IRE)** 2-8-12 0.. PaulHanagan 10 53
(R A Fahey) *sn pushed along in rr: hdwy 1/2-way: outpcd over 2f out: rdn and hung lft fr over 1f out: styd on* **40/1**

02 6 1 **New Beginning (FR)**[12] 6910 2-8-12 0.. JimmyQuinn 1 51
(H J L Dunlop) *chsd ldr: hmpd and lft in ld 1/2-way: sn hdd: rdn and wknd over 1f out* **2/1**[1]

0 7 24 **Pepin (IRE)**[28] 6531 2-8-12 0.. DavidProbert(5) 6 —
(D Haydn Jones) *s.s and swvd lft sn after s: outpcd* **66/1**

8 6 **Jerry's Agent (IRE)** 2-9-0 0.. RussellKennemore(3) 8 —
(J Balding) *dwlt: racd keenly in rr: hmpd and wknd 1/2-way* **100/1**

005 9 25 **Colin Staite**[115] 3902 2-9-3 44.. J-PGuillambert 7 —
(R Brotherton) *sn pushed along in rr: wknd 1/2-way* **150/1**

00 P **Manero**[24] 6620 2-9-3 0.. ShaneKelly 4 —
(J A Osborne) *led tl broke down and p.u 1/2-way* **14/1**

1m 30.35s (0.75) **Going Correction** +0.05s/f (Slow) **10** Ran SP% **121.0**
Speed ratings (Par 96): **97,96,93,91,90 88,61,54,26,—**
toteswinger: 1&2 £5.30, 1&3 £4.10, 2&3 £3.40. CSF £19.22 TOTE £8.30: £2.40, £2.70, £1.20; EX 24.30 Trifecta £102.20 Pool: £576.38 - 4.17 winning units..
Owner Errigal Racing **Bred** Barnett Enterprises **Trained** Hambleton, N Yorks

FOCUS
A modest juvenile maiden, and the winning time was fractionally slower than the two-year-old seller. Wee Giant built on his debut effort and can go on to better things.

NOTEBOOK
Wee Giant(USA) was well held on his debut over 1m on easy ground at Nottingham, but he improved for this switch to Polytrack, which is hardly surprising considering he is a half-brother to Harlan's Holiday, who was second in a Dubai World Cup. Having tracked the leaders towards the inside, it briefly looked as though he might struggle for a run at the top of the straight, but he ultimately had plenty of room and stayed on strongest of all. He had to work hard to see off Yellow Printer, and was inclined to edge left, but was always doing enough. This was an ordinary race, but there should be more to come as he gains further experience. (op 11-4)

Yellow Printer was always well placed and had his chance. This was an improvement on the form he showed when fifth on his debut over 6f at Goodwood. (op 7-2 tchd 4-1 and 11-4)

Dancourt(IRE), who did not show much on his debut at Leicester, had his chance but still looked inexperienced and probably needs more time. (op 4-1 tchd 9-2)

Swiss Art(IRE) was not quite up to this level, but he ran an honest race and is now qualified for a handicap mark. (op 12-1 tchd 14-1)

More Tea Vicar(IRE), making her debut, had to switch round Manero as that rival was being pulled up and is probably better than this. (tchd 50-1)

New Beginning(FR) was hampered by Manero when that one went wrong and she can be forgiven this. Official explanation: jockey said filly suffered interference and never travelled thereafter (tchd 15-8 after early 9-4 and 5-2)

Pepin(IRE) Official explanation: jockey said gelding ran very green

7166 PARADE RESTAURANT H'CAP — 1m 141y(P)
3:20 (3:21) (Class 6) (0-67,67) 3-Y-0 — £2,388 (£705; £352) Stalls Low

Form — RPR
3200 1 **Blues Minor (IRE)**[7] 7018 3-8-12 **63** ....(be[1]) EddieAhern 10 72
(M Mullineaux) *a.p: rdn to ld ins fnl f: r.o* **40/1**
3404 2 1 3/4 **Moon Crystal**[12] 6905 3-9-1 **66** ....(t) RyanMoore 7 71
(E A L Dunlop) *hld up: hmpd 7f out: hdwy over 2f out: rdn to ld 1f out: hung rt and lft: sn hdd: styd on* **7/2**[1]
0006 3 nk **Redarsene**[48] 6004 3-9-2 **67** .... GeorgeBaker 4 71+
(S Wynne) *hld up: hdwy over 1f out: rdn and nt clr run ins fnl f: r.o: nt rch ldrs* **6/1**[3]
0020 4 1/2 **Bookiebasher Babe (IRE)**[21] 6712 3-9-0 **65** ....(v[1]) FrancisNorton 12 68+
(M Quinn) *s.i.s: hld up: hdwy and edgd lft over 1f out: r.o* **20/1**
6006 5 1 **Lujano**[16] 6825 3-8-9 **60** .... PaulMulrennan 2 61
(Ollie Pears) *chsd ldrs: rdn and ev ch 1f out: styd on same pce* **22/1**
30-0 6 hd **Quick Off The Mark**[33] 6393 3-9-0 **65** .... TPQueally 5 65
(J G Given) *chsd ldr: rdn and ev ch over 1f out: edgd rt and no ex ins fnl f* **16/1**
2255 7 1/2 **Alfredtheordinary**[5] 7070 3-8-10 **61** .... EdwardCreighton 8 60
(M R Channon) *hld up: swtchd lft and r.o ins fnl f: nvr nrr* **14/1**
-556 8 1/2 **Moscow Oznick**[11] 6928 3-8-11 **62** .... ChrisCatlin 6 60
(N J Vaughan) *hld up: n.m.r 7f out: styd on u.p fr over 1f out: nvr nrr* **16/1**
06U1 9 3/4 **Bramalea**[16] 6821 3-8-11 **67** .... DavidProbert[(5)] 13 63
(B W Duke) *chsd ldrs: rdn over 2f out: wknd over 1f out* **15/2**
6510 10 1 3/4 **Talon (IRE)**[46] 6042 3-8-5 **56** ....(p) WilliamBuick 1 48+
(G A Swinbank) *led: rdn and hdd 1f out: edgd rt and no ex: eased* **10/1**
0000 11 2 3/4 **August Gale (USA)**[9] 6989 3-8-11 **62** ....(b[1]) DaleGibson 11 48
(G P Kelly) *s.i.s: a in rr* **33/1**
5451 12 shd **Casino Night**[3] 7111 3-8-8 **66** .... DeanHeslop[(7)] 9 52
(R Johnson) *chsd ldrs: rdn over 2f out: sn wknd* **17/2**
6433 13 9 **Sir Ike (IRE)**[32] 6417 3-8-11 **62** ....(t) FergusSweeney 3 27
(W S Kittow) *hld up in tch: rdn over 2f out: wknd over 1f out* **4/1**[2]

1m 51.44s (0.94) **Going Correction** +0.05s/f (Slow) — **13** Ran SP% **120.8**
Speed ratings (Par 98): **97,95,95,94,93 93,93,92,92,90 88,88,80**
toteswinger: 1&2 £15.10, 1&3 £55.60, 2&3 £7.20. CSF £172.80 CT £1036.57 TOTE £34.70: £9.30, £1.70, £2.40; EX 183.60 Trifecta £253.50 Part won. Pool: £342.66 - 0.10 winning units..
Owner Bluestone Partnership **Bred** Liam Queally **Trained** Alpraham, Cheshire

FOCUS
A very moderate handicap, although the winning time was 0.32 seconds quicker than following 61-75 handicap. The form makes sense at face value.
Talon(IRE) Official explanation: jockey said gelding lost its action in home straight
Sir Ike(IRE) Official explanation: jockey said colt lost its action in home straight

7167 BOOK TICKETS ONLINE AT WOLVERHAMPTON-RACECOURSE.CO.UK H'CAP — 1m 141y(P)
3:50 (3:50) (Class 5) (0-75,75) 3-Y-0+ — £3,238 (£963; £481; £240) Stalls Low

Form — RPR
2000 1 **Stark Contrast (USA)**[34] 6364 4-8-2 **61** oh4.... DavidProbert[(5)] 4 69
(M D I Usher) *led early: chsd ldrs: rdn to ld 1f out: edgd rt: r.o* **11/1**
4052 2 nk **Hawaana (IRE)**[14] 6867 3-8-13 **70** .... PaulDoe 8 77
(Eve Johnson Houghton) *s.i.s: sn rcvrd to ld: rdn and hung rt fr over 1f out: hdd 1f out: r.o* **11/4**[2]
000 3 1 1/2 **Avertis**[25] 6598 3-8-11 **75** ....(t) AndreaAtzeni[(7)] 9 79
(M Botti) *chsd ldr: rdn over 1f out: styd on same pce* **16/1**
3620 4 hd **Pitbull**[14] 6862 5-8-9 **63** ....(p) LiamJones 7 66
(Mrs G S Rees) *s.s: hdwy over 6f out: rdn over 1f out: edgd lft ins fnl f: r.o* **10/1**
0220 5 2 **Prince Noel**[10] 6950 4-9-0 **75** .... BMcHugh[(7)] 6 74
(N Wilson) *prom: rdn over 1f out: styd on same pce fnl f* **9/4**[1]
0003 6 1 3/4 **Aussie Blue (IRE)**[34] 6353 4-8-7 **61** oh2.... WilliamBuick 3 56
(R M Whitaker) *prom: outpcd over 3f out: rallied u.p over 1f out: edgd rt ins fnl f: eased towards fin* **9/2**[3]
106 7 1/2 **Climate (IRE)**[145] 2943 9-8-6 **63** .... LukeMorris[(3)] 1 57
(P D Evans) *hld up: rdn 1/2-way: n.d* **18/1**
2060 8 2 1/2 **Elliwan**[9] 6991 3-9-0 **71** .... DaleGibson 5 59
(M W Easterby) *s.i.s: last whn rdn 1/2-way: n.d* **40/1**
0000 9 1 1/2 **Ninth House (USA)**[31] 6452 6-9-4 **72** ....(t) AndrewElliott 2 56
(Mrs R A Carr) *s.i.s: rapid hdwy 5f out: chsd ldr over 3f out: sn rdn: wknd wl over 1f out* **11/1**

1m 51.76s (1.26) **Going Correction** +0.05s/f (Slow)
WFA 3 from 4yo+ 3lb — **9** Ran SP% **115.0**
Speed ratings (Par 103): **96,95,94,94,92 90,90,88,86**
toteswinger: 1&2 £8.10, 1&3 £18.80, 2&3 £7.80. CSF £41.26 CT £495.73 TOTE £12.60: £3.00, £1.50, £4.70; EX 66.10 Trifecta £207.10 Part won. Pool: £279.97 - 0.10 winning units..
Owner DMV Racing **Bred** Grousemont Farm **Trained** Upper Lambourn, Berks

FOCUS
The sort of race where sectional times would have come in handy. Visually they looked to go off quite quickly, but hand times suggest they were almost a second slower through the first half of the contest than in the previous class 6 handicap, and the overall time was 0.32 seconds slower. Very modest form.

7168 SPONSOR A RACE MEDIAN AUCTION MAIDEN STKS — 5f 20y(P)
4:20 (4:20) (Class 5) 2-Y-O — £4,094 (£1,209; £604) Stalls Low

Form — RPR
0 1 **Rulesn'Regulations**[92] 4665 2-9-3 0.... JimmyQuinn 1 82+
(M Salaman) *trckd ldrs: swtchd rt over 1f out: led ins fnl f: rdn and r.o strly* **5/1**
032 2 4 **Satwa Street (IRE)**[31] 6434 2-9-3 73.... RichardMullen 10 68
(D M Simcock) *trckd ldrs: racd keenly: led over 1f out: rdn and hdd ins fnl f: sn outpcd* **9/2**[3]
064 3 2 **La Capriosa**[11] 6932 2-8-7 64.... DavidProbert[(5)] 7 55
(A J McCabe) *chsd ldr: rdn and ev ch over 1f out: hung lft and no ex ins fnl f* **9/4**[2]
5 4 1/2 **Tikka Masala (IRE)**[18] 6764 2-8-12 0.... RichardKingscote 3 54
(Tom Dascombe) *led: rdn and hdd over 1f out: styng on same pce whn hmpd ins fnl f* **15/8**[1]
0 5 1 1/4 **Lupe Lamora**[45] 6089 2-8-12 0.... ShaneKelly 8 49
(J A Osborne) *s.i.s: hdwy over 1f out: no ex ins fnl f* **22/1**
650 6 2 1/2 **Wee Bizzom**[30] 6489 2-8-8 42 ow1.... SladeO'Hara[(5)] 9 41
(A Berry) *chsd ldrs: rdn over 3f out: hung lft and wknd over 1f out* **100/1**
7 2 1/4 **Waterstown (IRE)** 2-9-3 0.... PaulHanagan 2 37
(R A Fahey) *s.s: outpcd: nvr nrr* **16/1**
5560 8 2 **Wigan Pier**[26] 6573 2-8-12 50....(b[1]) WilliamBuick 6 25
(M D Squance) *prom: rdn 1/2-way: wknd over 1f out* **33/1**
00 9 7 **Rocket Ruby**[148] 2865 2-8-5 0.... LeeTopliss[(7)] 4 —
(D Shaw) *dwlt: outpcd* **40/1**
10 7 **Catman (IRE)** 2-8-12 0.... LPKeniry 5 —
(Peter Grayson) *s.i.s: a in rr: hung lft thrght: lost tch 1/2-way* **66/1**

62.23 secs (-0.07) **Going Correction** +0.05s/f (Slow) — **10** Ran SP% **118.5**
Speed ratings (Par 96): **102,95,92,91,89 85,82,78,67,56**
toteswinger: 1&2 £4.20, 1&3 £4.70, 2&3 £3.50. CSF £27.19 TOTE £5.00: £1.50, £1.10, £1.70; EX 30.80 Trifecta £96.00 Pool: £467.42 - 3.60 winning units..
Owner M Salaman **Bred** Marshalla Salaman **Trained** Baydon, Wilts

FOCUS
A weak sprint maiden, but quite an impressive performance from the well-backed Rulesn'Regulations, who showed improved form in a race rated through the runner-up.

NOTEBOOK
Rulesn'Regulations had been off the track for three months since showing speed on his debut over 6f at Newbury, and had refused to enter the stalls at Great Leighs last month. Always travelling noticeably strongly just in behind the leaders towards the inside, he was switched wide at the top of the straight and picked up really well, ultimately pulling right away to win by four lengths. The opposition was just modest, but he has plenty of scope and looks pretty useful. (op 15-2 tchd 8-1)

Satwa Street(IRE) offered a best RPR of 68 coming into this and he was basically no match for a potentially decent winner. (op 10-3 tchd 5-1)

La Capriosa will probably be better off in handicaps. (op 2-1)

Tikka Masala(IRE) was already held when hampered inside the final furlong. She should find her level when handicapped. (op 3-1)

7169 RACING ALL YEAR ROUND H'CAP — 1m 5f 194y(P)
4:50 (4:50) (Class 6) (0-60,60) 3-Y-0+ — £2,388 (£705; £352) Stalls Low

Form — RPR
2065 1 **Berry Baby (IRE)**[28] 6529 3-9-1 **59** .... HayleyTurner 7 69
(G A Butler) *hld up: hdwy and bmpd over 1f out: rdn to ld and hung lft ins fnl f: styd on* **4/1**[2]
0-01 2 nk **Covert Mission**[6] 7039 5-9-3 **56** 6ex.... LukeMorris[(3)] 6 66
(P D Evans) *a.p: rdn over 2f out: hung rt over 1f out: sn swtchd lft: ev ch ins fnl f: r.o* **6/1**[3]
2210 3 3 1/4 **Little Richard (IRE)**[26] 6577 9-9-10 **60** ....(p) AdamKirby 9 65
(M Wellings) *a.p: chsd ldr over 2f out: led over 1f out: hdd and nt clr run ins fnl f: no ex* **8/1**
0005 4 1/2 **Mighty Mover (IRE)**[11] 6929 6-8-11 **54** .... AshleyMorgan[(7)] 3 59
(B Palling) *hld up: hdwy u.p over 1f out: hung rt ins fnl f: styd on same pce* **25/1**
5124 5 1 **Blue Jet (USA)**[16] 6812 4-9-3 **53** ....(p) DeanMcKeown 11 56
(R M Whitaker) *hld up: hdwy 5f out: led over 2f out: rdn and hdd over 1f out: no ex* **4/1**[2]
3050 6 2 **Champagne Shadow (IRE)**[19] 6740 7-9-9 **59** ....(p) JerryO'Dwyer 2 60
(J Pearce) *prom: rdn over 3f out: hung lft 2f out: wknd ins fnl f* **11/1**
0460 7 1 1/4 **King Of The Beers (USA)**[8] 6022 4-9-5 **58** ....(p) KevinGhunowa[(3)] 10 57
(R A Harris) *chsd ldrs: rdn over 2f out: wknd ins fnl f* **66/1**
5040 8 6 **Qaasi (USA)**[66] 5456 6-9-0 **50** .... JimmyQuinn 5 40
(M Brittain) *chsd ldrs: rdn over 1f out: wknd fnl f* **16/1**
0005 9 3/4 **Taxman (IRE)**[51] 5917 6-9-0 **50** ....(p) DaneO'Neill 4 39
(A G Newcombe) *hld up: rdn over 3f out: n.d* **9/1**
0 10 4 1/2 **Able King (NZ)**[13] 6882 8-9-0 **50** .... LPKeniry 13 33
(M F Harris) *chsd ldr tl led over 3f out: rdn and hdd over 2f out: wknd over 1f out* **66/1**
0000 11 hd **Fenners (USA)**[30] 6493 5-9-1 **58** .... BradleyRoper[(7)] 12 41
(M W Easterby) *hld up: rdn over 4f out: n.d* **28/1**
6300 12 7 **Bold Adventure**[22] 6668 4-9-7 **57** .... TonyCulhane 1 30
(W J Musson) *s.i.s: hld up: a in rr: rdn over 4f out: sn wknd* **7/2**[1]
1300 13 8 **Tykie Two**[16] 6812 4-9-2 **52** .... LiamJones 8 14
(S Wynne) *led: rdn: hdd & wknd over 3f out* **33/1**

3m 7.40s (1.40) **Going Correction** +0.05s/f (Slow)
WFA 3 from 4yo+ 8lb — **13** Ran SP% **125.1**
Speed ratings (Par 101): **98,97,95,95,95 93,93,89,89,86 86,82,78**
toteswinger: 1&2 £7.50, 1&3 £7.90, 2&3 £11.70. CSF £28.65 CT £190.61 TOTE £5.00: £1.70, £2.50, £3.10; EX 38.40 Trifecta £173.10 Pool: £524.05 - 2.24 winning units..
Owner Woodcote Stud Ltd **Bred** Woodcote Stud Ltd **Trained** Newmarket, Suffolk

FOCUS
A moderate staying handicap run at an ordinary pace early on. Improvement from the first two, and the form could have been rated a bit higher.

7170 HOTEL & CONFERENCING AT WOLVERHAMPTON MAIDEN STKS (DIV II) — 7f 32y(P)
5:20 (5:21) (Class 5) 2-Y-0 — £2,914 (£867; £433; £216) Stalls High

Form — RPR
36 1 **Takeover Bid (USA)**[11] 6926 2-9-3 0.... JoeFanning 9 70
(M Johnston) *chsd ldr: led over 2f out: rdn out* **11/10**[1]

40 2 ¾ **Barbarian**[20] 6714 2-9-3 0........ MichaelHills 5 68
(B W Hills) *a.p: chsd wnr over 2f out: rdn and ev ch fr over 1f out: unable qck towards fin* **2/1**[2]
00 3 2 ¼ **Venture Capitalist**[40] 6197 2-9-3 0........ DaneO'Neill 6 63
(L M Cumani) *hld up: hdwy and edgd lft fr over 1f out: nt trble ldrs* **8/1**[3]
4 ¾ **Mullitovermaurice** 2-9-3 0........ TPQueally 4 61
(J G Given) *mid-div: hdwy over 2f out: rdn over 1f out: styd on same pce fnl f* **16/1**
5 1 **Hawkspring (IRE)** 2-9-3 0........(t) ChrisCatlin 7 58
(George Baker) *s.i.s: hld up: hdwy over 1f out: styd on same pce fnl f* **18/1**
00 6 1 **Duke's Emerald**[13] 6876 2-9-3 0........ JimmyQuinn 3 56
(J A R Toller) *s.s: rdn over 4f out: styd on ins fnl f: nvr nrr* **16/1**
00 7 1 **Miss Cameo (USA)**[17] 6785 2-8-12 0........ DeanMcKeown 10 48
(R M Whitaker) *s.i.s: hld up: styd on fnl f: n.d* **33/1**
0600 8 11 **Valentine Bay**[17] 6788 2-8-12 48........ EddieAhern 1 22
(M Mullineaux) *chsd ldrs tl wknd over 2f out* **25/1**
0 9 10 **Golden Pool (IRE)**[17] 6776 2-8-12 0........ WilliamBuick 8 —
(S A Callaghan) *chsd ldrs: sddle slipped over 4f out: led briefly over 3f out: wknd over 2f out* **33/1**
50 10 4 ½ **Mister Wilberforce**[5] 7080 2-9-0 0........(v[1]) RussellKennemore(3) 2 —
(Mrs L Williamson) *led: hdd briefly over 3f out: hdd & wknd over 2f out* **66/1**

1m 30.81s (1.21) **Going Correction** +0.05s/f (Slow) **10** Ran SP% **120.3**
Speed ratings (Par 96): **95,94,91,90,89 88,87,74,63,58**
toteswinger: 1&2 £1.90, 1&3 £4.40, 2&3 £3.50. CSF £3.37 TOTE £2.30: £1.30, £1.10, £1.80; EX 4.00 Trifecta £5.60 Pool: £471.56 - 61.31 winning units. Place 6 £60.06, Place 5 £43.80.
Owner Sheikh Hamdan Bin Mohammed Al Maktoum **Bred** Darley **Trained** Middleham Moor, N Yorks

FOCUS
A winning time 0.46 seconds slower than the first division, 0.54 seconds off the time recorded in the juvenile seller tempers enthusiasm somewhat. The winner can do better but this form is just modest.

NOTEBOOK
Takeover Bid(USA) failed to give his running at Brighton last time, but he had previously shown plenty of ability when third on his debut at Leicester and he was able to confirm that initial promise with a battling success. He is possibly even better than the bare result suggests, as he was checked slightly by Golden Pool when that one's saddle slipped leaving the back straight, and he looks a fair handicapper in the making (op Evens tchd 10-11)
Barbarian had his chance but was just held. He should be able to win an ordinary maiden, but now has the option of handicaps. (op 5-2)
Venture Capitalist ◆, bearing the same name as the 1994 Wokingham winner, kept on nicely for third having been poorly placed and very much caught the eye. He looks one to keep on side now he is qualified for a handicap mark. (op 10-1 tchd 12-1)
Mullitovermaurice, out of a multiple 1m-1m1f winner, made a pleasing debut and should find his level once handicapped. (op 12-1)
Hawkspring(IRE), who had a tongue-tie fitted for his debut, was green and looks a longer-term prospect. (op 12-1 tchd 20-1)
Duke's Emerald Official explanation: jockey said gelding missed the break
Golden Pool(IRE) Official explanation: jockey said filly's saddle slipped
Mister Wilberforce Official explanation: jockey said colt hung right throughout
T/Jkpt: Not won. T/Plt: £73.90 to a £1 stake. Pool: £70,385.67. 694.45 winning tickets. T/Qpdt: £33.30 to a £1 stake. Pool: £4,304.90. 95.60 winning tickets. CR

7171 - (Foreign Racing) - See Raceform Interactive

7038 CATTERICK (L-H)
Tuesday, November 4

OFFICIAL GOING: Heavy (soft in places; 7.0)
Wind: light 1/2 against Weather: overcast, becoming wet

7172 SPONSOR A RACE AT CATTERICK RACECOURSE MAIDEN AUCTION STKS 7f
1:20 (1:21) (Class 6) 2-Y-O £2,047 (£604; £302) Stalls Low

Form RPR
4 1 **Goodison Glory (IRE)**[18] 6770 2-9-1 0........ JamieMoriarty 7 78+
(R A Fahey) *chsd ldrs: stmbld bnd over 2f out: swtchd lft and styd on to ld jst ins fnl f: rdn clr* **9/4**[2]
3436 2 4 ½ **Miss Cracklinrosie**[10] 6986 2-8-7 67 ow1........ GrahamGibbons 3 59
(J R Weymes) *w ldr: led over 4f out: hdd jst ins fnl f: eased nr fin* **2/1**[1]
004 3 4 **Le Petit Vigier**[17] 6811 2-8-4 48........(t) AndrewElliott 4 46
(P Beaumont) *led tl over 4f out: fdd fnl f* **50/1**
00 4 6 **Murrays Magic (IRE)**[18] 6789 2-7-11 0........ AdeleRothery(7) 8 31
(D Nicholls) *chsd ldrs: wknd over 1f out* **14/1**
2 5 6 **Lily Jicaro (IRE)**[18] 6788 2-8-9 0 ow2........ RussellKennemore(3) 2 24
(Mrs L Williamson) *chsd ldrs: drvn over 3f out: lost pl over 2f out* **4/1**[3]
4 6 1 **Sleepy Valley (IRE)**[102] 4384 2-7-13 0........ JamieKyne(7) 1 15
(A Dickman) *trckd ldrs: stmbld bnd over 2f out: wknd over 1f out* **6/1**
00 7 7 **Melkatant**[18] 6788 2-8-4 0........ FrancisNorton 9 —
(N Bycroft) *sn outpcd and bhd* **20/1**
0 8 6 **Spruzzo**[15] 6858 2-8-11 0........ PJMcDonald 6 —
(C W Thornton) *s.i.s: a bhd* **80/1**

1m 33.79s (6.79) **Going Correction** +1.00s/f (Soft) **8** Ran SP% **113.0**
Speed ratings (Par 94): **101,95,91,84,77 76,68,61**
toteswinger: 1&2 £1.50, 1&3 £7.30, 2&3 £4.50. CSF £6.94 TOTE £2.40: £1.10, £1.10, £6.70; EX 6.70.
Owner Mrs Gill Gamon **Bred** Agricola Dell 'Olmo **Trained** Musley Bank, N Yorks

FOCUS
A weak juvenile maiden and, although the winner scored well, not a race to go overboard about.

NOTEBOOK
Goodison Glory(IRE) ◆ opened his account at the second attempt on this switch to turf. Given time to organise himself just off the leaders, he found extra when asked for an effort in between the final two furlong markers and eventually looked better the further he went over this longer trip. In good hands, he should make up into a fair handicapper next year. (op 2-1 tchd 7-4)
Miss Cracklinrosie set the standard with an official mark of 67 and was given a positive ride on this drop back a furlong and return to the turf. She had every chance and was a clear second-best, but was unable to cope with the winner. She has scope and ought to find her feet as a handicapper, but is probably a little flattered by her current rating. (op 11-4)
Le Petit Vigier was allotted a mark of 48 after being beaten a long way behind a stable companion of the winner over course and distance 17 days previously and she ran a little better here. She does put this form into some perspective (tchd 40-1 and 66-1)
Murrays Magic(IRE) was treading water from the two-furlong pole, but now becomes eligible for a mark and should fare better when faced with a sounder surface. (op 12-1 tchd 16-1)
Lily Jicaro(IRE) Official explanation: jockey said filly was unsuited by the heavy (soft in places) ground

7173 GO RACING AT DONCASTER THIS SATURDAY NURSERY 5f 212y
1:50 (1:50) (Class 4) (0-85,85) 2-Y-O £3,885 (£1,156; £577; £288) Stalls Low

Form RPR
4310 1 **Lucky Numbers (IRE)**[38] 6274 2-8-13 77........ PaulMulrennan 2 80
(Paul Green) *trckd ldr: led over 1f out: edgd lft ins fnl f: hld on wl* **17/2**[3]
2311 2 ¾ **Joe Caster**[10] 6987 2-9-2 83........ LukeMorris(3) 3 84
(J M P Eustace) *sn trcking ldrs: chal over 1f out: no ex wl ins fnl f* **7/4**[2]
3321 3 1 ¾ **The Kyllachy Kid**[33] 6407 2-9-7 85........ MickyFenton 5 81
(T P Tate) *hld up: effrt and swtchd lft over 2f out: edgd rt and kpt on same pce ins fnl f: nvr a threat* **1/1**[1]
1060 4 1 ¼ **Secret Venue**[24] 6656 2-8-4 68........ AndrewElliott 1 60
(Jedd O'Keeffe) *led: shkn up and qcknd 3f out: hdd over 1f out: one pce* **11/1**

1m 20.59s (6.99) **Going Correction** +1.00s/f (Soft) **4** Ran SP% **105.2**
Speed ratings (Par 98): **93,92,89,88**
CSF £22.23 TOTE £10.00; EX 30.80.
Owner Men Behaving Badly Two **Bred** Rory O'Brien **Trained** Lydiate, Merseyside

FOCUS
This was a fairly tight little nursery, and was run at a modest pace, and is best rated around the principals.

NOTEBOOK
Lucky Numbers(IRE) resumed winning ways with a game effort on this first run beyond the minimum trip. He was undone by the draw in a better race at Chester last time, but the return to this deeper surface helped and he found the extra distance much to his liking. It is possible he could now turn out under a penalty at Doncaster on Saturday. (op 13-2 tchd 6-1)
Joe Caster looked to be moving best of all nearing the furlong marker and he did little wrong once coming under pressure, but simply got outstayed by the winner. He has developed into a very consistent performer and still looks fairly handicapped, so perhaps a return to Polytrack over this trip can see him back in the winner's enclosure. (tchd 9-4)
The Kyllachy Kid, already proven on such ground, was found out by being held up on this return to a nursery and was not seen to best effect. He is a relentless galloper and can leave this behind when able to race more prominently. (op 11-10)
Secret Venue, 5lb lower, was a sitting duck from the top of the home straight, but kept to his task when headed. He probably found this extra furlong on such ground beyond him. Official explanation: jockey said gelding was unsuited by the heavy (soft in places) ground (op 9-1 tchd 15-2)

7174 HAMBLETON MAIDEN STKS 1m 3f 214y
2:20 (2:20) (Class 5) 3-Y-O+ £2,590 (£770; £385; £192) Stalls High

Form RPR
52 1 **Scarab (IRE)**[27] 6583 3-9-3 0........ GregFairley 1 83+
(M Johnston) *led early: trckd ldr: led 3f out: clr whn hung lft over 1f out: eased towards fin* **7/4**[1]
30 2 9 **West With The Wind**[11] 6948 3-9-3 78........ MickyFenton 8 65
(T P Tate) *led early: hdd 3f out: no ch w wnr* **9/2**[3]
0036 3 4 ½ **Carlton Mac**[7] 7042 3-9-3 50........(p) FrancisNorton 11 58
(N Bycroft) *chsd ldrs: outpcd 5f: kpt on to take modest 3rd 3f out* **22/1**
0000 4 16 **Sweet Seville (FR)**[39] 6248 4-9-4 42........ AndrewElliott 10 27
(Mrs G S Rees) *in rr: bhd 6f out: kpt on fnl 3f* **80/1**
0-00 5 10 **Glamoroso (IRE)**[7] 7042 3-9-3 32........ PAspell 13 16
(A Kirtley) *in rr: sme hdwy 6f out: wknd 2f out* **200/1**
0246 6 4 **Jiminor Mack**[56] 5776 5-8-13 45........(p) KellyHarrison(5) 4 5
(W J H Ratcliffe) *sn chsng ldrs: outpcd 5f out: wknd 3f out* **11/1**
6 7 7 **Tazbar (IRE)**[29] 6527 6-9-9 0........ TonyCulhane 9 —
(K G Reveley) *s.i.s: sn drvn along in rr: bhd fnl 5f: t.o 3f out* **9/4**[2]
00 8 1 ¾ **Gulnaz**[11] 6956 3-8-12 0........ DaleGibson 5 —
(Mrs G S Rees) *prom: lost pl 6f out: t.o 3f out* **100/1**
0-0 9 7 **Solid Silver**[27] 6583 7-9-9 0........ PaulMulrennan 12 —
(K G Reveley) *mid-div: drvn 6f out: sn lost pl: t.o 3f out* **8/1**
0 10 52 **Ring Bertie**[147] 2912 3-9-3 0........ TPQueally 6 —
(Micky Hammond) *prom: lost pl after 3f: sn bhd: t.o 3f out: virtually p.u* **100/1**

2m 50.1s (11.20) **Going Correction** +1.00s/f (Soft)
WFA 3 from 4yo+ 6lb **10** Ran SP% **112.8**
Speed ratings (Par 103): **102,96,93,82,75 73,68,67,62,27**
toteswinger: 1&2 £2.50, 1&3 £5.00, 2&3 £8.80. CSF £9.56 TOTE £2.50: £1.40, £1.40, £2.90; EX 9.20.
Owner Sheikh Hamdan Bin Mohammed Al Maktoum **Bred** Gainsborough Stud Management Ltd **Trained** Middleham Moor, N Yorks

FOCUS
An uncompetitive maiden in which the winner had little to beat in the end. The form is rated around the exposed third and might not prove too solid.
Tazbar(IRE) Official explanation: jockey said gelding never travelled

7175 BOOK ON-LINE AT CATTERICKBRIDGE.CO.UK H'CAP 7f
2:50 (2:50) (Class 4) (0-80,79) 3-Y-O+ £4,857 (£1,445; £722; £360) Stalls Low

Form RPR
0621 1 **Shotley Mac**[7] 7041 4-9-1 76 6ex........(b) FrancisNorton 4 85
(N Bycroft) *chsd ldrs: hrd drvn over 2f out: edgd rt over 2f out: styd on to ld fnl 75yds* **7/2**[2]
0612 2 1 ¼ **Bold Marc (IRE)**[7] 7041 6-8-9 77........ DeclanCannon(7) 9 83
(K R Burke) *led: hdd and no ex wl ins fnl f* **15/8**[1]
0-00 3 1 ¾ **Bravely (IRE)**[21] 6724 4-8-11 72........ DavidAllan 1 73+
(T D Easterby) *stmbld s: hld up in rr: n.m.r over 2f out: r.o to take 3rd ins fnl f* **9/1**
-000 4 4 **Captain Royale (IRE)**[35] 6352 3-8-6 68........ GregFairley 2 59
(Miss Tracy Waggott) *hld up in midfield: effrt 3f out: wknd appr fnl f* **40/1**
4306 5 2 ¾ **Zabeel Tower**[7] 7041 5-8-13 74........(p) TonyCulhane 6 58
(R Allan) *prom: effrt over 2f out: fdd over 1f out* **10/1**
1000 6 1 **Elusive Hawk (IRE)**[28] 6554 4-8-7 68........ TPQueally 7 49
(A P Stringer) *trckd ldrs: t.k.h: wknd over 1f out* **33/1**
2443 7 nse **Grazeon Gold Blend**[7] 7041 5-9-4 79........ GrahamGibbons 8 60
(J J Quinn) *chsd ldrs: hmpd over 2f out: wknd over 1f out* **4/1**[3]
4400 8 8 **Violent Velocity (IRE)**[17] 6813 5-8-5 73........ JamieKyne(7) 5 33
(J J Quinn) *s.i.s: in rr: bhd fnl 2f* **15/2**
000 9 nse **Paint Stripper**[2] 7153 3-8-0 65 oh20........(p) DominicFox(3) 3 25
(W Storey) *in rr: bhd fnl 2f* **80/1**

1m 33.11s (6.11) **Going Correction** +1.00s/f (Soft)
WFA 3 from 4yo+ 1lb **9** Ran SP% **114.5**
Speed ratings (Par 105): **105,103,101,97,93 92,92,83,83**
toteswinger: 1&2 £2.20, 1&3 £7.80, 2&3 £4.40. CSF £10.27 CT £52.68 TOTE £4.80: £1.50, £1.30, £3.10; EX 10.70.
Owner J A Swinburne **Bred** N Bycroft **Trained** Brandsby, N Yorks
■ Stewards' Enquiry : Francis Norton one-day ban: careless riding (Nov 18)

FOCUS
A modest handicap. The form has been taken at something like face value with the winner better than ever recently and up 7lb on the runner-up on their recent course meeting.

7176 GO RACING IN YORKSHIRE CLAIMING STKS 5f
3:20 (3:20) (Class 6) 3-Y-O+ £2,047 (£604; £302) Stalls Low

Form RPR
0006 1 **Godfrey Street**[28] 6557 5-9-0 74 (b) GregFairley 4 81
(A G Newcombe) *mde all: jst lasted* 16/1
0000 2 nk **Gleaming Spirit (IRE)**[15] 6864 4-8-1 62 (v) AndrewHeffernan(7) 6 74
(Peter Grayson) *t.k.h: sn in rr: hdwy over 1f out: wnt 2nd ins fnl f: styd on towards fin* 33/1
6050 3 2 **Zamalik (USA)**[7] 7043 5-8-3 57 AndrewMullen(3) 9 65
(Mrs A Duffield) *chsd ldrs: kpt on same pce appr fnl f* 6/1[3]
5031 4 ½ **Blue Tomato**[17] 6823 7-9-5 84 WilliamCarson(5) 7 81
(D Nicholls) *in rr: hdwy and swtchd centre over 1f out: kpt on* 6/1[3]
2201 5 1 ½ **Whozart (IRE)**[28] 6546 5-7-13 56 KellyHarrison(5) 5 56
(A Dickman) *chsd ldrs: edgd rt and fdd over 1f out* 11/4[1]
4006 6 hd **Efistorm**[7] 7047 7-9-5 81 LukeMorris(3) 8 73
(C R Dore) *in rr div: kpt on fnl 2f: nvr a threat* 3/1[2]
0200 7 2 ¼ **Kings College Boy**[7] 7043 8-7-11 65 (b) JamieKyne(7) 2 47
(R A Fahey) *chsd ldrs: outpcd over 2f out: sn pl* 7/1
4000 8 4 **Nacho Libre**[39] 6239 3-9-10 93 DaleGibson 3 52
(M W Easterby) *in rr: bhd fnl 2f* 14/1
5003 9 1 ½ **Fire Up The Band**[3] 7129 9-9-4 62 FrancisNorton 1 41
(A Berry) *chsd ldrs on outer: lost pl over 1f out* 14/1

63.29 secs (3.49) **Going Correction** +0.825s/f (Soft) 9 Ran SP% 114.9
Speed ratings (Par 101): **105,104,101,100,98 97,94,87,85**
toteswinger: 1&2 £40.50, 1&3 £13.20, 2&3 £31.90. CSF £418.27 TOTE £14.60: £4.20, £10.90, £2.40; EX 169.40.
Owner M K F Seymour **Bred** Miss S N Ralphs **Trained** Yarnscombe, Devon
■ Stewards' Enquiry : Andrew Mullen two-day ban: used whip with excessive frequency (Nov 18-19)

FOCUS
Few managed to land a blow from off the pace in this average claimer in which the winner made all. Sound enough form for the grade, rated around the runner-up.

7177 NATIONAL HUNT SEASON STARTS ON 3RD DECEMBER H'CAP 1m 5f 175y
3:50 (3:50) (Class 5) (0-75,74) 3-Y-O+ £2,590 (£770; £385; £192) Stalls Low

Form RPR
0023 1 **Eijaaz (IRE)**[17] 6812 7-9-1 61 PaulFessey 8 69
(G A Harker) *hld up in rr: hdwy over 4f out: led 2f out: hld on towards fin* 14/1
1332 2 ¾ **Mister Pete (IRE)**[7] 7042 5-8-10 59 DominicFox(3) 1 66
(W Storey) *hld up in rr: hdwy over 3f out: styd on to go 2nd 1f out: kpt on wl towards fin* 4/1[2]
3006 3 2 **Red Wine**[6] 7064 9-9-7 74 StacyRenwick(7) 10 78
(A J McCabe) *in rr: hdwy centre over 2f out: kpt on fnl f* 9/1
/3-6 4 hd **Onyergo (IRE)**[7] 7039 6-8-12 58 (t) DavidAllan 7 62
(M A Barnes) *trckd ldrs: t.k.h: led 4f out tl 2f out: kpt on same pce* 6/1[3]
-4P0 5 2 **Hernando's Boy**[18] 6790 7-9-8 68 TomEaves 6 69
(K G Reveley) *mid-div: hdwy to trck ldrs 6f out: one pce fnl 2f* 12/1
5-22 6 10 **Dark Planet**[3] 7132 5-8-9 55 oh5 (v) AndrewElliott 4 42
(D W Thompson) *trckd ldrs: drvn over 3f out: lost pl over 1f out* 17/2
602- 7 2 **Tiger King (GER)**[311] 5676 7-8-13 59 MickyFenton 5 43
(P Monteith) *led tl 4f out: lost pl over 1f out* 16/1
1 8 4 **Quitit (IRE)**[7] 7042 3-8-12 66 6ex (b) TonyCulhane 2 45
(Mrs S A Watt) *trckd ldrs: t.k.h: chal 3f out: wknd over 1f out* 11/8[1]
1100 9 44 **Me Fein**[28] 6558 4-9-2 62 TPQueally 11 —
(A P Stringer) *racd wd: trckd ldrs drvn and olost pl over 5f out: sn bhd: t.o 3f out* 40/1
0-06 10 1 ¾ **Mister Maq**[101] 4420 5-8-4 55 oh10 (b) KellyHarrison(5) 3 —
(A Crook) *t.k.h in mid-div: drvn over 5f out: sn lost pl and bhd: t.o 3f out* 100/1

3m 20.28s (16.68) **Going Correction** +1.00s/f (Soft)
WFA 3 from 4yo+ 8lb 10 Ran SP% 120.6
Speed ratings (Par 103): **92,91,90,90,89 83,82,80,54,53**
toteswinger: 1&2 £5.90, 1&3 £13.80, 2&3 £7.20. CSF £71.77 CT £550.58 TOTE £15.80: £4.20, £1.30, £2.40; EX 47.60 Place 6: £672.80 Place 5: £438.36.
Owner A S Ward **Bred** Shadwell Estate Company Limited **Trained** Thirkleby, N Yorks

FOCUS
This moderate staying handicap was run at a fair pace in the bad ground and the form is rated around the placed horses.
Red Wine Official explanation: jockey said, regarding running and riding, her orders were to hold the gelding up and produce it with a late run, adding that it was not going forward and does not respond to stronger handling; vet said gelding was found to be coughing.
T/Plt: £659.80 to a £1 stake. Pool: £44,429.71. 49.15 winning tickets. T/Qpdt: £97.60 to a £1 stake. Pool: £3,458.87. 26.20 winning tickets. WG

7148 SOUTHWELL (L-H)
Tuesday, November 4

OFFICIAL GOING: Standard
Wind: Nil Weather: Misty and rain

7178 HOSPITALITY AT SOUTHWELL RACECOURSE MEDIAN AUCTION MAIDEN STKS 1m (F)
1:00 (1:00) (Class 6) 3-5-Y-O £3,070 (£906; £453) Stalls Low

Form RPR
-450 1 **Salerosa (IRE)**[151] 2781 3-8-12 56 PatCosgrave 1 67
(Mrs A Duffield) *chsd ldrs: swtchd rt and hdwy over 2f out: sn rdn and led over 1f out: drvn and edgd lft ins fnl f: styd on wl* 11/1
0302 2 2 ¼ **Vogarth**[16] 6836 4-9-2 55 JamesMillman(3) 12 67
(B R Millman) *hld up in rr: stdy hdwy 3f out: swtchd lft and effrt 2f out: sn rdn and ev ch over 1f out: drvn and kpt on same pce ins fnl f* 6/1[3]
0630 3 1 ¼ **Red Tarn**[17] 6827 3-9-3 62 TomEaves 4 64
(B Smart) *chsd ldrs: pushed along 1/2-way: rdn 3f out and sn outpcd: styd on u.p appr fnl f: nrst fin* 8/1
0005 4 2 ¾ **Vanatina (IRE)**[16] 6843 4-8-9 42 DavidProbert(5) 2 53
(W M Brisbourne) *a.p: hdwy to chal over 2f out and ev ch tl rdn wl over 1f out and grad wknd* 33/1
2-20 5 nk **Girl Of Pangaea (GER)**[46] 6091 3-8-12 70 TGMcLaughlin 7 52
(E A L Dunlop) *hld up in rr: hdwy on inner 3f out: rdn to chse ldrs wl over 1f out: sn drvn and no imp* 4/1[2]
3262 6 8 **Azure Mist**[12] 6935 3-8-12 65 SaleemGolam 5 34
(M H Tompkins) *led: rdn along wl over 2f out: drvn wl over 1f out: sn hdd & wknd* 7/4[1]
6000 7 4 **Just Oscar (GER)**[27] 6570 4-9-5 47 DaneO'Neill 11 29
(W M Brisbourne) *in tch on outer: rdn along 1/2-way and sn btn* 20/1
5 8 ¾ **Another Try (IRE)**[12] 6935 3-9-3 0 DarrenWilliams 3 28
(A P Jarvis) *t.k.h: cl up: rdn along over 2f out: and sn wknd* 7/1
0020 9 6 **Myriola**[56] 5770 3-8-12 47 ChrisCatlin 10 —
(S Gollings) *in tch on outer: rdn along 1/2-way: sn wknd* 28/1
0500 10 10 **Frill A Minute**[16] 6836 4-8-9 37 SladeO'Hara(5) 9 —
(Miss L C Siddall) *midfield: rdn along 1/2-way: sn lost pl and bhd* 200/1
00 11 ½ **White Rose George**[168] 2269 3-8-12 0 JamesO'Reilly(5) 6 —
(J O'Reilly) *s.i.s: a in rr* 250/1
00 12 15 **Bandoran**[100] 4461 3-8-10 0 (b[1]) CharlotteKerton(7) 13 —
(J R Holt) *dwlt: a in rr* 150/1

1m 43.96s (0.26) **Going Correction** -0.075s/f (Stan)
WFA 3 from 4yo 2lb 12 Ran SP% 115.3
Speed ratings (Par 101): **95,92,91,88,88 80,76,75,69,59 59,44**
toteswinger: 1&2 £6.90, 1&3 £7.50, 2&3 £8.70. CSF £70.71 TOTE £21.80: £6.00, £1.60, £3.30; EX 97.90 Trifecta £240.80 Pool: £325.47 - 1.00 winning units..
Owner David K Barker **Bred** Pedro Rosas **Trained** Constable Burton, N Yorks

FOCUS
A very moderate maiden run at a strong pace and the form is limited by the proximity of the fourth, so not a race to rate positively.

7179 BOOK YOUR CHRISTMAS PARTY HERE MAIDEN AUCTION STKS 6f (F)
1:30 (1:30) (Class 6) 2-Y-O £3,070 (£906; £453) Stalls Low

Form RPR
3340 1 **Denton Diva**[10] 6988 2-8-5 62 WilliamBuick 4 66
(M Dods) *prom: hdwy to ld 2f out: rdn over 1f out: drvn and edgd lft ins fnl f: styd on* 9/2[2]
053 2 2 ¼ **Desert Strike**[15] 6863 2-8-6 71 DavidProbert(5) 3 65
(P F I Cole) *t.k.h: trckd ldrs: hdwy to chse wnr over 1f out: sn rdn and kpt on same pce ins fnl f* 5/6[1]
5 3 1 ¼ **Inconspicuous Miss (USA)**[10] 6986 2-8-1 0 ow3.. MatthewDavies(7) 8 59
(George Baker) *chsd ldrs: hdwy over 2f out: rdn wl over 1f out: sn edgd lft and kpt on same pce* 11/2[3]
0060 4 1 ½ **River Style (IRE)**[12] 6931 2-8-5 54 LiamJones 6 51
(A P Jarvis) *in tch: hdwy on inner over 2f out: rdn to chse ldrs wl over 1f out: drvn and wknd appr fnl f* 16/1
5 hd **Rascal In The Mix (USA)** 2-8-8 0 DeanMcKeown 1 56+
(R M Whitaker) *s.i.s: hld up in rr: stdy hdwy over 2f out: shkn up over 1f out: kpt on ins fnl f: nrst fin* 14/1
0040 6 3 ½ **Valdemar**[14] 6879 2-8-10 56 (v[1]) DaneO'Neill 2 45
(A D Brown) *led: rdn along and hdd 2f out: sn wknd* 20/1
06 7 2 ¾ **Meydan Style (USA)**[122] 3735 2-8-11 0 TolleyDean(3) 10 41
(J Balding) *stdd s: a in rr* 50/1
6 8 ¾ **Why Nee Amy**[145] 2979 2-8-4 0 ChrisCatlin 9 28
(Miss Gay Kelleway) *chsd ldrs on outer: rdn wl over 2f out and sn wknd* 16/1
5060 9 1 ½ **That Boy Ronaldo**[39] 6245 2-8-7 47 LPKeniry 5 27
(A Berry) *in tch on inner: rdn along 1/2-way: sn wknd* 50/1

1m 16.85s (0.35) **Going Correction** -0.075s/f (Stan) 9 Ran SP% 115.2
Speed ratings (Par 94): **94,91,89,87,87 82,78,77,75**
toteswinger: 1&2 £1.30, 1&3 £3.70, 2&3 £2.70. CSF £8.44 TOTE £5.90: £1.10, £1.10, £1.80; EX 6.40 Trifecta £27.80 Pool: £384.57 - 10.21winning units..
Owner Denton Hall Racing Ltd **Bred** Mrs Sally Roberts **Trained** Denton, Co Durham
■ Dean McKeown, already warned off for 4 yrs pending an appeal, had his licence removed after this ride and his career is over.
■ Stewards' Enquiry : Dean McKeown Matter referred to BHA, breach of Rule 157.

FOCUS
A very weak juvenile maiden and they did not go that quick early on. The form looks solid rated through the winner and fourth.

NOTEBOOK
Denton Diva, dropped back in trip and trying Fibresand for the first time, was always well placed and stayed on best in the straight to gain her first success at the fifth attempt. She is likely to be put away for the year and is expected to stay further next season. (op 13-2)
Desert Strike, upped to 6f for the first time, raced very keenly just in behind the lead early on and did not totally convince under pressure in the straight. (op 11-8)
Inconspicuous Miss(USA), dropped a furlong in trip and carrying 3lb overweight, plugged on for third and this was a respectable effort. She should ultimately find her level in low-grade handicaps. (op 4-1 tchd 6-1)
River Style(IRE) did not run badly considering she was keen early after getting stuck in behind the leading group. She would have preferred a stronger pace and has a little race in her. (op 14-1)
Rascal In The Mix(USA) drifted alarmingly in the betting beforehand and very much caught the eye on her racecourse debut. Having started slowly, she raced a little keenly under restraint through the first half of the contest, having been held up last of all, but she was going noticeably well entering the straight. She then closed to within around three or four lengths of the lead at the two-furlong pole, without her rider asking for an effort at that point, but the principals were well on their way by the time she came under some sort of pressure over a furlong out, and she was eventually just pushed out under hands-and-heels riding. In fairness, she did look inexperienced in the closing stages, but anyone who backed her, particularly for a place, would surely have preferred to see a much more energetic ride, as she was simply never in contention, despite looking to have something to offer. The Stewards found Dean McKeown in breach of the non-triers' rule (157) and referred the case to the BHA, who withdrew his licence to ride forthwith. Official explanation: jockey said, regarding running and riding, his orders were to jump out, get handy, and ride the race as he found it, adding that the filly, on her racecourse debut, has proved nervous in the stalls at home, was slowly away, a fact he reported at scales, further adding that having found himself behind the field filly somewhat resented the kickback and, as a result, had to be coaxed into a final effort in the home straight and would not have finished closer for a more vigorous ride; trainer said filly has a history of injury and has proved difficult to train (op 4-1)

7180 TOTESUPER7 H'CAP 7f (F)
2:00 (2:00) (Class 6) (0-50,50) 3-Y-O+ £3,070 (£906; £453) Stalls Low

Form RPR
5201 1 **Megalo Maniac**[7] 7049 5-8-12 48 (p) TonyHamilton 12 58+
(R A Fahey) *cl up: led after 1f: rdn clr wl over 1f out: drvn ins fnl f: kpt on wl towards fin* 5/4[1]
000 2 ½ **Betteras Bertie**[109] 4168 5-9-0 50 RobertWinston 4 59+
(M Brittain) *s.i.s and t.k.hin rr: hdwy on outer wl over 2f out: rdn wl over 1f out: drvn ins fnl f and styd on wl towards fin* 40/1
0260 3 ½ **Ten To The Dozen**[12] 6928 5-8-11 47 (b) ChrisCatlin 1 55
(P W Hiatt) *chsd ldrs: hdwy over 2f out: rdn wl over 1f out: kpt on u.p ins fnl f* 7/1[3]

5003 **4** 1 **Winged Farasi**[4] 7114 4-8-11 **47**.................................. FergusSweeney 8 52
(Miss J E Foster) *prom: rdn to chse wnr over 2f out: drvn over 1f out: kpt on same pce* **13/2**[2]

0200 **5** 1 3/4 **Stormin Heart (USA)**[65] 5544 3-8-13 **50**.......................(b) JoeFanning 14 50
(M Johnston) *midfield: hdwy towards outer wl over 2f out: rdn wl over 1f out: chsd ldrs and edgd lft ent fnl f: no imp after* **16/1**

4050 **6** nk **Out Of India**[8] 7021 6-9-0 **50**.. DaneO'Neill 7 49
(P T Dalton) *led 1f: cl up: rdn over 2f out: sn drvn and grad wknd* **16/1**

6000 **7** 1 1/4 **Bold Phoenix (IRE)**[12] 6929 7-8-12 **48**.................(bt) J-PGuillambert 3 44
(Miss Amy Weaver) *dwlt: sn outpcd in rr: stdy hdwy on inner over 2f out: rdn to chse ldrs over 1f out: sn one pce* **33/1**

0060 **8** 1/2 **Up The Chimney**[8] 7018 4-8-13 **49**............................... DarrenWilliams 2 44
(A P Jarvis) *hld up: hdwy over 2f out: rdn to chse ldrs wl over 1f out: drvn and wknd appr fnl f* **25/1**

023 **9** nk **Moorside Diamond**[13] 6912 4-8-9 **50**..........................(b) DavidProbert(5) 9 44
(A D Brown) *hld up in tch: hdwy over 2f out: sn rdn and no imp* **9/1**

0050 **10** 2 1/2 **Rocheport**[52] 5911 3-8-12 **49**...................................(p) SaleemGolam 13 36
(G C H Chung) *chsd ldrs: rdn along 3f out: sn drvn and wknd* **50/1**

0400 **11** 1 1/4 **Doctor Delta**[71] 5362 3-8-6 **50**.................................. AdamCarter(7) 10 34
(M Brittain) *a in rr* **40/1**

0400 **12** 2 3/4 **Monte Cassino (IRE)**[13] 6913 3-8-8 **50**.................... JamesO'Reilly(5) 11 26
(J O'Reilly) *a in rr* **66/1**

0600 **13** 1 **Autumn Charm**[28] 6560 3-8-12 **49**.............................(v[1]) TGMcLaughlin 5 23
(Lucinda Featherstone) *dwlt: a in rr* **16/1**

002- **14** 14 **Belinda Rose (IRE)**[327] 7134 4-8-13 **49**...................... PatCosgrave 6 —
(J G Given) *towards rr: rdn along 1/2-way: sn bhd* **25/1**

1m 30.58s (0.28) **Going Correction** -0.075s/f (Stan)
WFA 3 from 4yo+ 1lb **14** Ran SP% **116.9**
Speed ratings (Par 101): **95,94,93,92,90 90,88,88,88,85 83,80,79,63**
toteswinger: 1&2 £8.20, 1&3 £5.90, 2&3 £38.20. CSF £76.30 CT £280.80 TOTE £1.90: £1.40, £10.90, £2.50; EX 86.70 Trifecta £153.60 Part won. Pool: £207.65 - 0.50 winning units..
Owner A Long **Bred** E R W Stanley & New England Stud Farm Ltd **Trained** Musley Bank, N Yorks

FOCUS
A very moderate but competitive handicap with the winner not needing to match his previous win here but the form seems sound enough.

7181 TOTEEXACTA H'CAP 6f (F)
2:30 (2:30) (Class 3) (0-95,90) 3-Y-0 **£7,569** (£2,265; £1,132; £566; £282) **Stalls** Low

Form RPR

2001 **1** **Irish Pearl (IRE)**[7] 7047 3-9-2 **88** 6ex........................... FergusSweeney 3 104
(K R Burke) *mde all: rdn clr wl: over 1f out: styd on strly* **13/2**[3]

0411 **2** 2 3/4 **Harlech Castle**[7] 7040 3-8-10 **87** 6ex............................ DavidProbert(5) 5 94
(P F I Cole) *hld up: hdwy over 2f out: rdn over 1f out: drvn to chse wnr ins fnl f: no imp* **15/2**

1002 **3** nk **Mister Hardy**[13] 6902 3-9-0 **86**.. TonyHamilton 9 92
(R A Fahey) *chsd wnr: effrt 2f out and sn rdn: drvn over 1f out: kpt on same pce ins fnl f* **8/1**

-000 **4** 2 1/4 **Nastrelli (IRE)**[16] 6845 5-8-12 **87**.. NeilBrown(3) 4 86
(T D Barron) *hld up in rr: hdwy over 2f out: swtchd rt and rdn wl over 1f out: kpt on ins fnl f: nrst fin* **20/1**

2645 **5** nse **Pawan (IRE)**[2] 7151 8-8-8 **85** ow1................................(b) AnnStokell(5) 2 84
(Miss A Stokell) *chsd ldrs: rdn 2f out: sn one pce* **7/1**

3652 **6** 4 1/2 **Temple Of Thebes (IRE)**[7] 7047 3-8-13 **85**........................ DaneO'Neill 1 69
(E A L Dunlop) *chsd ldrs on inner: rdn along 2f out: sn drvn and wknd* **7/2**[2]

4300 **7** nk **Thebes**[31] 6478 3-9-4 **90**.. JoeFanning 6 73
(M Johnston) *in tch: hdwy to chse ldrs over 2f out: sn rdn and btn* **9/4**[1]

0000 **8** 3 3/4 **Northern Empire (IRE)**[15] 6859 5-8-4 **76** oh1........................ ChrisCatlin 7 47
(K A Ryan) *a towards rr* **16/1**

2056 **9** 21 **Sudden Impact (IRE)**[43] 6160 3-9-3 **89**.................................. PaulQuinn 8 —
(Paul Green) *racd wd: rdn along and bhd fr 1/2-way* **33/1**

1m 14.04s (-2.46) **Going Correction** -0.075s/f (Stan) **9** Ran SP% **115.3**
Speed ratings (Par 107): **113,109,108,105,105 99,99,94,66**
toteswinger: 1&2 £3.30, 1&3 £4.90, 2&3 £7.70. CSF £54.17 CT £399.10 TOTE £7.30: £2.40, £2.00, £2.20; EX 42.30 Trifecta £119.10 Pool: £499.24 - 3.10 winning units..
Owner M J Halligan **Bred** Jim Halligan **Trained** Middleham Moor, N Yorks

FOCUS
A good sprint handicap and a race to rate positively with the winner improved and the placed horses to previous marks.

NOTEBOOK
Irish Pearl(IRE) has mainly struggled on turf this year, but has looked a different filly since switching to Fibresand and is now 2-2 on the surface after defying a penalty for her recent course-and-distance success. She is clearly very useful on sand and will surely be kept on the go for the time being. (op 6-1 tchd 7-1)
Harlech Castle, chasing a hat-trick after a couple of wins on turf, was 12lb higher than when successful at Catterick last time, and 16lb above the mark he won off at Nottingham two starts back. He ran well behind a filly who is proving quite decent on this surface. (op 6-1 tchd 11-2)
Mister Hardy ran reasonably on this first try on Fibresand, but he was not helped by a 3lb rise for his recent Great Leighs second. (op 9-2)
Nastrelli(IRE) was sweating on his debut for a new trainer, but he kept on in the closing stages and could build on this if not getting as warm next time. (op 10-1)
Pawan(IRE) has been kept extremely busy and was not at his best turned out two days after running fifth over 5f at this track. (op 9-1)
Temple Of Thebes(IRE) was less than two lengths behind today's winner over course and distance last time, but she was not at her best and might not have been helped by sticking towards the inside rail. (op 11-2)
Thebes, back on Fibresand for the first time since winning his maiden, was very well backed but he ran most disappointingly. (op 3-1 tchd 7-2)

7182 TOTETRIFECTA H'CAP 5f (F)
3:00 (3:01) (Class 5) (0-70,70) 3-Y-0+ **£4,209** (£1,252; £625; £312) **Stalls** High

Form RPR

5150 **1** **Guto**[7] 7043 5-7-13 **58**... AndreaAtzeni(7) 8 67
(W J H Ratcliffe) *chsd ldrs: pushed along 1/2-way: rdn wl over 1f out: drvn ent fnl f: kpt on to ld nr fin* **12/1**

5000 **2** 1/2 **Grand Palace (IRE)**[16] 6840 5-8-9 **61**.....................(v) DarrenWilliams 4 68
(D Shaw) *chsd ldrs: hdwy over 1f out: rdn ent fnl f: led fnl 100yds: drvn: hdd and nt qckn nr fin* **12/1**

1225 **3** nk **Shakespeare's Son**[22] 6706 3-8-12 **69**........................ DavidProbert(5) 9 75
(H J Evans) *midfield: hdwy wl over 1f out swtchd lft and rdn ent fnl f: sn drvn and ev ch tl nt qckn fnl 50yds* **9/2**[2]

0602 **4** hd **Steel City Boy (IRE)**[2] 7152 5-8-10 **67**............................ AnnStokell(5) 1 72
(Miss A Stokell) *wnt bdly rt s: led: rdn along wl over 1f out: edgd rt 1f out: hdd and no ex wl ins fnl f* **4/1**[1]

0320 **5** nk **Bookiesindex Boy**[10] 6990 4-8-13 **70**...................(v) FrederikTylicki(5) 13 74
(J R Jenkins) *hld up: pushed along 1/2-way: gd hdwy over 1f out: rdn to chse ldrs ent fnl f: drvn and nt qckn fnl 100yds* **20/1**

0006 **6** nk **Jilly Why (IRE)**[41] 6218 7-8-4 **56**.......................................(b) WilliamBuick 7 59
(Paul Green) *hld up towards rr: hdwy over 1f out: n.m.r ent fnl f: swtchd rt and rdn: styd on wl towards fin* **7/1**[3]

0600 **7** hd **Incomparable**[10] 6990 3-9-1 **67**.. PatCosgrave 10 69
(A J McCabe) *chsd ldrs: rdn along 2f out: drvn over 1f out: kpt on same pce ins fnl f* **14/1**

0321 **8** 1/2 **Joyeaux**[7] 7043 6-8-12 **67** 6ex.................................... DuranFentiman(3) 11 67
(L R James) *hld up towards rr: hdwy 2f out: sn rdn and no imp ent fnl f* **11/1**

340 **9** shd **After The Show**[156] 2644 7-9-0 **66**....................................... SaleemGolam 2 66
(Rae Guest) *hmpd s: in tch: rdn along 2f out: sn one pce* **11/1**

0232 **10** 3 1/4 **Wicked Wilma (IRE)**[7] 7043 4-8-4 **56**.................................. ChrisCatlin 5 44
(A Berry) *cl up: rdn along 2f out: drvn over 1f out: sn edgd lft and wknd* **7/1**[3]

1200 **11** 1 1/4 **Spoof Master (IRE)**[16] 6840 4-9-0 **66**...................................(p) LPKeniry 6 50
(C R Dore) *a in rr* **16/1**

1623 **12** 3/4 **Nautical**[251] 719 10-7-12 **57**.. CharlotteKerton(7) 3 38
(J R Holt) *hmpd s: a in rr* **40/1**

0506 **13** 2 1/2 **Filemot**[19] 6766 3-8-5 **57**.. LiamJones 12 29
(John Berry) *chsd ldrs to 1/2-way: sn outpcd* **33/1**

3311 **14** 3/4 **Upstanding**[248] 767 3-9-2 **68**... RobertWinston 14 37
(M Brittain) *chsd ldrs: rdn along 1/2-way and sn wknd* **28/1**

60.22 secs (0.52) **Going Correction** +0.20s/f (Slow) **14** Ran SP% **121.4**
Speed ratings (Par 103): **103,102,101,101,100 100,100,99,99,93 91,90,86,85**
toteswinger: 1&2 £35.20, 1&3 £17.10, 2&3 £14.20. CSF £143.92 CT £757.71 TOTE £16.10: £5.50, £5.30, £2.50; EX 289.40 TRIFECTA Not won..
Owner W J H Ratcliffe **Bred** H B Hughes **Trained** Wensley, N Yorks
■ Stewards' Enquiry : Pat Cosgrave one-day ban: used whip with excessive force (Nov 18)

FOCUS
A modest but competitive sprint handicap and there seemed no significant draw bias. The form looks ordinary but sound enough for the grade with the third, fourth and fifth close to their marks.
Steel City Boy(IRE) Official explanation: jockey said gelding hung right
Upstanding Official explanation: jockey said filly had no more to give

7183 TOTESWINGER H'CAP 1m 4f (F)
3:30 (3:31) (Class 5) (0-75,73) 3-Y-0+ **£3,561** (£1,059; £529; £264) **Stalls** Low

Form RPR

5303 **1** **Turban Heights (IRE)**[7] 7046 4-9-7 **72**................................. ChrisCatlin 7 84
(E J O'Neill) *hld up towards rr: gd hdwy on outer to chse ldr 4f out: led 3f out: rdn wl over 2f out: drvn and edgd lft 1f out: styd on gamely* **11/4**[1]

0003 **2** 3/4 **Brave Mave**[13] 6898 3-8-9 **66**.. JoeFanning 9 77
(W Jarvis) *trckd ldrs gng wl: smooth hdwy to chse wnr over 2f out: rdn to chal over 1f out and ev ch tl drvn ins fnl f and no ex fnl 75yds* **7/1**[3]

0220 **3** 2 1/4 **Moonstreaker**[31] 6487 5-8-12 **66**............................ MichaelJStainton(3) 8 73
(R M Whitaker) *s.i.s: hld up in rr: hdwy on outer 3f out: rdn to chse ldng pair and hung lft over 1f out: drvn and kpt on same pce ins fnl f* **6/1**[2]

4540 **4** 4 1/2 **Graceful Descent (FR)**[15] 6862 3-8-11 **68**............................ TonyHamilton 5 68
(R A Fahey) *hld up: hdwy on outer 3f out: rdn to chse ldrs wl over 2f out: drvn and no imp fr wl over 1f out* **11/1**

2020 **5** 2 **Black Falcon (IRE)**[6] 7085 8-8-7 **63**............................ JamesO'Reilly(5) 2 60
(John A Harris) *chsd ldrs: rdn along 4f out: wknd 2f out* **9/1**

065 **6** shd **Jackie Kiely**[7] 7046 7-9-4 **69**..(t) J-PGuillambert 10 66
(R Brotherton) *hld up towards rr: effrt over 3f out: rdn and hdwy 2f out: sn no imp* **9/1**

2024 **7** 9 **Snake Skin**[165] 2354 5-8-9 **60**.. FergusSweeney 4 42
(J Gallagher) *cl up: led after 1f: rdn along and hdd 3f out: drvn and wknd fnl 2f* **28/1**

2046 **8** 1/2 **Exit To Luck (GER)**[16] 6838 7-9-2 **67**...........................(b) WilliamBuick 6 48
(S Gollings) *chsd ldrs on outer: rdn along 4f out: wknd over 2f out* **10/1**

5000 **9** 1/2 **Monfils Monfils (USA)**[11] 6626 6-9-3 **73**...................... DavidProbert(5) 1 54
(A J McCabe) *led 1f: cl up tl rdn along over 4f out: wknd 3f out* **20/1**

5053 **10** 3 3/4 **Keel (IRE)**[5] 7094 5-8-11 **62**... LiamJones 11 37
(C R Dore) *s.i.s and bhd: gd hdwy to chse ldrs 4f out: rdn along wl over 2f out and sn wknd* **12/1**

-062 **11** 9 **War Anthem**[13] 6909 4-9-8 **73**...(b) PatCosgrave 3 33
(J R Boyle) *in tch: rdn along 5f out: sn lost pl and bhd* **11/1**

2m 38.21s (-2.79) **Going Correction** -0.075s/f (Stan)
WFA 3 from 4yo+ 6lb **11** Ran SP% **115.1**
Speed ratings (Par 103): **106,105,104,101,99 99,93,93,92,90 84**
toteswinger: 1&2 £4.30, 1&3 £5.50, 2&3 £11.50. CSF £20.88 CT £106.42 TOTE £3.30: £1.50, £2.30, £2.00; EX 23.50 Trifecta £194.10 Part won. Pool: £262.34 - 0.40 winning units..
Owner Raymond N R Auld **Bred** R N Auld **Trained** Averham Park, Notts

FOCUS
A modest middle-distance handicap run at an ordinary pace and sound-looking form rated through the third.

7184 WEATHERBYS ALL WEATHER "HANDS AND HEELS" APPRENTICE SERIES H'CAP 1m (F)
4:00 (4:01) (Class 5) (0-70,69) 3-Y-0+ **£3,070** (£906; £453) **Stalls** Low

Form RPR

6105 **1** **Kimono My House**[16] 6841 4-9-3 **65**.................................. RosieJessop 9 78+
(J G Given) *trckd ldrs: hdwy to chse ldr over 2f out: rdn to ld over 1f out: kpt on* **9/4**[1]

0400 **2** 2 1/4 **Mozayada (USA)**[61] 5636 4-8-4 **55** oh10......................... AdamCarter(3) 10 60
(M Brittain) *led: rdn clr wl over 2f out: hdd over 1f out and kpt on same pce* **50/1**

0006 **3** 5 **Louisiade (IRE)**[93] 4603 7-8-11 **62** ow1....................(p) GarryWhillans(3) 7 56
(M C Chapman) *chsd ldrs on outer: rdn along and outpcd 3f out: styd on u.p fr 2f out: tk 3rd ins fnl f* **20/1**

1104 **4** 3 **Sularno**[97] 4529 4-9-2 **69**.. RyanClark(5) 2 56
(H Morrison) *dwlt and towards rr: hdwy 1/2-way: chsd ldrs 3f out: rdn over 2f out: sn one pce and lost 3rd ins fnl f* **3/1**[2]

4030 **5** 2 1/4 **Vicious Warrior**[27] 6582 9-9-2 **67**................................ BradleyRoper(3) 4 48
(R M Whitaker) *hld up towards rr: hdwy 3f out: rdn over 2f out and sn no imp* **13/2**

34U0 **6** 1 1/4 **Scotty's Future (IRE)**[3] 7132 10-8-6 **57** oh7 ow2.... KrishGundowry(3) 3 36
(A Berry) *sn outpcd and wl bhd tl styd on fnl 2f: nvr a factor* **33/1**

4531 **7** hd **My Mate Mal**[7] 7053 4-9-1 **66** 6ex............................... AnthonyBetts(3) 11 44
(B Ellison) *prom: rdn along wl over 2f out and sn wknd* **4/1**[3]

00- **8** 1 1/2 **Timewatch**[108] 5571 3-8-6 **59**.....................................(tp) DebraEngland(3) 5 34
(Miss J E Foster) *nvr nr ldrs* **40/1**

5064 **9** 5 **Dasheena**[35] 6353 5-8-5 **56**...(be) JamesRogers(3) 6 19
(A J McCabe) *a towards rr* **17/2**

0000 **10** *1 3/4* **Dance In Style**[109] 4142 7-8-5 **56** oh10 ow1..............(p) PaulPickard(3) 8 15
(A Crook) *prom: rdn along 1/2-way and sn wknd* **66/1**

0350 **11** *2 1/2* **Jellytot (USA)**[7] 7048 5-8-4 **55** oh10........................ MatthewLawson(3) 1 8
(J O'Reilly) *chsd ldrs on inner: rdn along 3f out and sn wknd* **33/1**

1m 42.0s (-1.70) **Going Correction** -0.075s/f (Stan)
WFA 3 from 4yo+ 2lb **11** Ran SP% **116.2**
Speed ratings (Par 103): **105,102,97,94,92 91,91,89,84,82 80**
toteswinger: 1&2 £29.00, 1&3 £14.40, 2&3 £26.00. CSF £138.10 CT £1824.65 TOTE £3.30: £1.30, £10.40, £4.60; EX 121.30 TRIFECTA Not won. Place 6: £93.72 Place 5: £24.74 .
Owner Tremousser Partnership **Bred** G And Mrs Middlebrook **Trained** Willoughton, Lincs

FOCUS
A modest handicap restricted to apprentices who had not ridden more than ten winners. The winner goes well here and, although the runner-up was 10lb out of the handicap, there seems no fluke about this.
T/Jkpt: Not won. T/Plt: £170.30 to a £1 stake. Pool: £55,525.87. 237.95 winning tickets. T/Qpdt: £36.40 to a £1 stake. Pool: £4,932.07. 100.10 winning tickets. JR

6664 MAISONS-LAFFITTE (R-H)
Tuesday, November 4

OFFICIAL GOING: Heavy

7185a PRIX MIESQUE (GROUP 3) (FILLIES) (STRAIGHT) 7f (S)
1:20 (1:22) 2-Y-O **£29,412** (£11,765; £8,824; £5,882; £2,941)

RPR

1 **Stefer (USA)**[24] 2-8-11 .... DBoeuf 4 103
(D Smaga, France) *dwlt: hld up last of trio on stands' rail: swtchd rt and hdwy wl over 1f out: drvn to ld 100yds out: drvn out* **41/10**[2]

2 *hd* **Entre Deux Eaux (FR)**[9] 2-8-11 .... IMendizabal 1 102
(Robert Collet, France) *led trio on stands' rail: drvn and ev ch 100yds out: unable qck cl home* **14/1**

3 *2* **Aiboa (IRE)** 2-8-11 .... CSoumillon 3 97
(L Urbano-Grajales, France) *led sextet on outside: overall ldr over 2f out: rdn and hdd 100yds out: one pce* **68/10**

4 *snk* **Bufera (IRE)**[16] 6891 2-8-11 .... JVictoire 6 97
(Robert Collet, France) *trckd ldr on stands' rail: rdn 2f out: styd on one pce fnl f* **47/10**[3]

5 *1/2* **Denomination (USA)**[30] 6519 2-8-11 .... TGillet 7 96
(Mme C Head-Maarek, France) *trckd ldr on outside: one pce fnl 2f* **34/10**[1]

6 *3* **Higha (FR)**[30] 6520 2-8-11 .... SPasquier 5 88
(P Demercastel, France) *hld up in rr: last 2f out: nvr a factor* **78/10**

7 *2 1/2* **Blue Fiji (IRE)**[40] 2-8-11 .... TThulliez 8 82
(P Bary, France) *trckd ldrs on outside tl wknd 2f out* **9/1**

8 *1 1/2* **My Sweet Baby (USA)**[44] 2-8-11 .... CFiocchi 9 78
(R Menichetti, Italy) *pressed ldr on outside tl wknd wl over 1f out* **17/1**

9 *2 1/2* **Novita (FR)**[44] 2-8-11 .... AStarke 2 72
(P Schiergen, Germany) *a towards rr: rdn and btn 2f out* **86/10**

1m 29.4s (1.10) **9** Ran SP% **116.7**
PARI-MUTUEL: WIN 5.10; PL 2.00, 3.20, 2.50; DF 32.90.
Owner Wafic Said **Bred** F Benillouche & Woodside Farms Llc **Trained** Lamorlaye, France

NOTEBOOK
Stefer(USA) was held up on the rail in third position for much of the race. At the furlong marker, her jockey switched her to the outside of the long-time leader and the pair battled all the way to the line. She ran on bravely and got her head in front where it mattered. She is still green but improving all the time and there are no definite plans at this time.
Entre Deux Eaux(FR) tried to make all in this 7f event and, when joined by the eventual winner, she put her head down and fought bravely all the way to the line. She lost nothing in defeat and a race of this calibre is should go her way in the future.
Aiboa(IRE), a Spanish-trained filly, raced prominently on the outside of the other eight runners and travelled sweetly throughout. She was caught a little for speed in the final furlong and her jockey reported that she would have been closer on better ground.
Bufera(IRE) raced just behind the leaders, but could not quicken in the latter stages of the race although she stayed on well to only just be denied third place on the line.

7186a CRITERIUM DE MAISONS-LAFFITTE (GROUP 2) 6f (S)
2:20 (2:20) 2-Y-O **£79,632** (£30,735; £14,669; £9,779; £4,890)

RPR

1 **Smooth Operator (GER)**[22] 6713 2-8-13 .... AHelfenbein 2 112
(Mario Hofer, Germany) *pressed ldr on rails: outpcd wl over 1f out: drvn 1 1/2f out: led 1f out: r.o wl* **31/10**[2]

2 *2* **Dalghar (FR)**[24] 2-8-13 .... CSoumillon 5 106
(A De Royer-Dupre, France) *led after 1f to 2f out: rallied to regain 2nd last strides* **1/1**[1]

3 *hd* **Lui Rei (ITY)**[72] 5330 2-8-13 .... DVargiu 4 105
(A Renzoni, Italy) *led 1f: pressed ldr on outside: led 2f out to 1f out: one pce* **7/2**[3]

4 *2* **Treasure (FR)**[22] 6713 2-8-10 .... DBoeuf 1 96
(Mme C Head-Maarek, France) *dwlt: last and outpcd 2f out: styd on fnl 150yds* **83/10**

5 *6* **All Speedy (FR)**[40] 6236 2-8-10 .... TJarnet 3 78
(Mlle S-V Tarrou, France) *racd in 4th: outpcd fr over 2f out* **10/1**

1m 15.3s (1.90) **5** Ran SP% **116.5**
PARI-MUTUEL: WIN 4.10; PL 1.60, 1.40; SF 9.30.
Owner Stall Jenny **Bred** Mario Hofer **Trained** Germany

NOTEBOOK
Smooth Operator(GER) raced in third early on the rail before moving into second one and a half furlongs out as the pace quickened. When the long-time leader tired he hit the front and galloped strongly to the line to win a shade cosily. Since being gelded, he has gone from strength to strength and this win was his third on the trot and his second Group race. He will not be seen out again this year and his trainer highlighted the Prix Djebel back over this course and distance next season, followed by a step up to a mile.
Dalghar(FR) tried to make all the running over this straight 7f. When the tempo increased he couldn't quicken on the holding ground and looked as if he would lose the runner-up spot, before finding a second wind to stay on and take second by the minimum distance. His jockey reported that he would have given the winner a harder time on better ground, but he is still inexperienced and should be a nice sprinter for next season.
Lui Rei(ITY), quickly out of the stalls, was pulling in the early stages so his jockey took him back to third in an attempt to settle him. He was the first to make his move on the outside, but could not go through with his run and stayed on at one pace to just get pipped for third.
Treasure(FR) was always struggling to with the first three and when the pace quickened two out, she couldn't go with the leaders and stayed on to come home in her own time.

7187a PRIX DE SEINE-ET-OISE (GROUP 3) 6f (S)
2:50 (2:51) 3-Y-O+ **£29,412** (£11,765; £8,824; £5,882; £2,941)

RPR

1 **Utmost Respect**[31] 6496 4-8-13 .... PaulHanagan 5 110
(R A Fahey) *a cl up: rdn to ld over 1f out: drvn out* **27/10**[1]

2 *1/2* **Tiza (SAF)**[30] 6518 6-8-13 .... CSoumillon 13 109
(A De Royer-Dupre, France) *racd in 11th tl hdwy through field fr 1 1/2f out: wnt 2nd 100yds out: kpt on* **4/1**[2]

3 *3/4* **Dunkerque (FR)**[22] 6743 3-8-11 .... WMongil 10 104
(Mme C Head-Maarek, France) *in tch in centre: hdwy to dispute 2nd momentarily 100yds out: one pce* **62/10**[3]

4 *hd* **Etoile Nocturne (FR)**[37] 4-8-8 .... DBoeuf 11 101
(W Baltromei, Germany) *towards rr tl styd on strly down ins fnl f: nrest at fin* **29/1**

5 *3/4* **Stern Opinion (USA)**[51] 5955 3-8-11 .... SPasquier 7 101
(P Bary, France) *led to over 1f out: one pce* **9/1**

6 *2 1/2* **Rock Harmonie (FR)**[30] 6518 3-8-8 .... JVictoire 4 91
(Mme C Head-Maarek, France) *prom tl one pce fnl 1 1/2f* **76/10**

7 *3/4* **Mood Music**[11] 4-8-11 ....(b) AHelfenbein 12 92
(Mario Hofer, Germany) *a towards rr* **13/1**

8 *1 1/2* **Salut L'Africain (FR)**[9] 3-8-11 .... GBenoist 9 87
(Robert Collet, France) *missed break: a towards rr* **9/1**

9 *1 1/2* **Rising Shadow (IRE)**[31] 6484 7-8-11 .... JimmyQuinn 6 83
(N Wilson) *missed break: rcvrd to r in midfield: reminder over 2f out: sn btn* **48/1**

10 *2* **Mariol (FR)**[30] 6518 5-8-13 .... SMaillot 2 79
(Robert Collet, France) *in tch on stands' side tl wknd 1 1/2f out* **9/1**

11 **Bellifiore (FR)**[58] 5738 4-8-8 .... TJarnet 14 —
(Mlle S-V Tarrou, France) *last to fnl 50yds* **77/10**

12 **Hunter Street**[123] 5732 5-8-11 .... CFiocchi 8 —
(R Menichetti, Italy) *2nd early: cl up tl wknd 2f out* **70/1**

1m 14.4s (1.00) **12** Ran SP% **128.0**
PARI-MUTUEL: WIN 3.70; PL 1.80, 1.90, 2.20; DF 8.50.
Owner The Rumpole Partnership **Bred** Heather Raw **Trained** Musley Bank, N Yorks

NOTEBOOK
Utmost Respect gained a deserved win. Racing not far from the leaders, he took the advantage at the furlong marker on the outside and held on well to resist the late challenge of the runner-up. He adored the soft ground and is unlikely to be raced on a fast surface in the future. He will now have a break and be aimed at all Group sprint races next year.
Tiza(SAF), another who loved the soft going, was held up near the back of the field before progressing to the middle of the pack at the furlong pole. His jockey conjured up a final late run from him and he was flying at the finish. He will next go for the Listed Prix Zeddaan at Fontainebleau on November 21st.
Dunkerque(FR) has produced some bold efforts of late since being brought back in distance. Racing on the outside and wearing cheekpieces, he ran on strongly to the line and just got pipped for second. He should be capable of taking a race in this category in the future.
Etoile Nocturne(FR), held up near the back of the field, produced a fine finishing effort and was not beaten far.
Rising Shadow(IRE) was never really seen with a chance and his trainer reported that this race came at the end of a long and hard season. Now being a seven-year-old, perhaps his best days are behind him.

FLEMINGTON (L-H)
Tuesday, November 4

OFFICIAL GOING: Good

7188a EMIRATES MELBOURNE CUP (GROUP 1) (H'CAP) 2m
4:00 (4:02) 3-Y-O+
£1,519,824 (£367,841; £185,022; £96,916; £66,079; £50,661)

RPR

1 **Viewed (AUS)**[3] 5-8-5 ....(b) BShinn 9 116
(Bart Cummings, Australia) *racd in 9th: hdwy to ld 2f out: 2 l clr appr fnl f: jst hld on* **40/1**

2 *nse* **Bauer (IRE)**[13] 6922 5-8-3 .... CoreyBrown 13 114
(L M Cumani) *towards rr: 16th 1/2-way: 9th on outside 2f out: wnt 2nd appr fnl f: r.o wl: jst failed* **20/1**

3 *2* **C'Est La Guerre (NZ)**[10] 4-8-7 .... BPrebble 5 117+
(John D Sadler, Australia) *towards rr: 17th 1/2-way: 14th whn angling out and nt clr run briefly 2f out: styd on wl down outside fnl 1 1/2f* **20/1**

4 *1/2* **Master O'Reilly (NZ)**[10] 6-8-9 .... VDuric 6 117
(Danny O'Brien, Australia) *in midfield: 11th 1/2-way: n.m.r over 2f out: styd on wl between horses fr over 1 1/2f out* **25/1**

5 *hd* **Profound Beauty (IRE)**[79] 5136 4-8-2 .... GBoss 2 110
(D K Weld, Ire) *racd in 10th: 4th towards outside 2f out: wnt 2nd 1 1/2f out: lost 2nd appr fnl f: one pce* **8/1**

6 *2* **Moatize (AUS)**[3] 4-7-12 ....(b) ClareLindop 19 104
(Bart Cummings, Australia) *cl up: 6th 1/2-way: wnt 2nd jst under 2f out: lost 2nd 1 1/2f out: one pce* **30/1**

7 *1* **Mad Rush (USA)**[17] 6835 4-8-6 .... DMOliver 4 111
(L M Cumani) *hld up: 15th 1/2-way: 11th 2f out: kpt on at same pce* **9/2**[1]

8 *1 3/4* **Nom Du Jeu (NZ)**[17] 6835 4-8-7 ....(b) JeffLloyd 1 110
(Murray Baker, New Zealand) *hld up: 13th 1/2-way: 13th 2f out: kpt on at same pce* **13/2**[3]

9 *nk* **Zipping (AUS)**[10] 7-8-7 .... DNikolic 16 109
(John D Sadler, Australia) *racd in 19th: hmpd by injured horse and dropped bk to last under 4f out: styd on wl down ins fnl 1 1/2f* **14/1**

10 *nk* **Newport (AUS)**[10] 6-8-2 .... ChrisSymons 15 104
(Paul Perry, Australia) *in rr: 18th 2f out: modest late hdwy* **60/1**

11 *nk* **Ice Chariot (AUS)**[3] 6-8-5 .... MRodd 22 107
(Ron Maund, Australia) *in rr: 21st 1/2-way: effrt on outside in 15th whn carried rt 2f out: one pce* **50/1**

12 *shd* **Guyno (NZ)**[13] 6922 5-8-3 ....(b) CNewitt 8 105
(Lou Luciani, Australia) *in rr: 20th 1/2-way: hdwy arnd outside to go 6th 2f out: sn wknd* **150/1**

13 *2 1/4* **Littorio (AUS)**[3] 4-8-4 .... StevenKing 17 103
(Nigel Blackiston, Australia) *last 1/2-way: a in rr* **30/1**

14 *1/2* **Varevees**[72] 5333 5-8-2 .... CraigAWilliams 23 101
(R Gibson, France) *in tch: 7th 1/2-way: 7th and rdn 2f out: sn btn* **100/1**

15 ½ **Boundless (NZ)**[17] 6835 4-8-3 .... GChilds 20 101
(Stephen McKee, New Zealand) *racd in 4th: led briefly over 2f out: sn hdd & wknd* **80/1**

16 *shd* **Red Lord (AUS)**[10] 5-8-2 .... NicholasHall 14 100
(Anthony Cummings, Australia) *in midfield: 12th 1/2-way: 10th 2f out: sn btn* **100/1**

17 *7* **Prize Lady (NZ)**[17] 7-8-0 ....(b) MSweeney 18 90
(Graeme Sanders, New Zealand) *in tch: 8th 1/2-way: wknd over 2f out* **60/1**

18 *1 ¾* **Septimus (IRE)**[52] 5921 5-9-3 .... JMurtagh 10 105
(A P O'Brien, Ire) *disp ld 3f then prom w 2 stablemates: 5l clr of rest 1/2-way: led narrowly under 3f out to over 2f out: wknd: fin lame* **6/1**[2]

19 *4* **Barbaricus (AUS)**[3] 4-7-13 ....(b) SBaster 3 83
(Danny O'Brien, Australia) *disp ld racing freely for 3f: 5th 1/2-way: 8th and wknd 2f out* **15/1**

20 *15* **Alessandro Volta**[52] 5892 3-7-13 ....(b) WMLordan 11 75
(A P O'Brien, Ire) *missed break: pushed along and swtchd outside after 1f: led after 3f: set str pce: hdd under 3f out: wknd* **40/1**

21 *dist* **Honolulu (IRE)**[53] 5854 4-8-8 .... CO'Donoghue 24 —
(A P O'Brien, Ire) *sn prom: 5l clr w 2 stablemates 1/2-way: wknd over 3f out: fin lame* **20/1**

P **Gallopin (NZ)**[10] 5-8-3 .... JWinks 21 —
(Danny O'Brien, Australia) *14th 1/2-way: broke down over 4f out: p.u* **30/1**

3m 20.4s (0.76)
WFA 3 from 4yo+ 9lb **24** Ran SP% **111.6**
WIN 46.50; PL 14.00, 6.50, 7.80; DF 553.20; SF 1156.00;Trifecta 22324.00.
Owner Dato Tan Chin Nam **Bred** I Johnson **Trained** Australia
■ Godolphin's Caulfield Cup winner All The Good missed the big race after picking up a training injury.

NOTEBOOK
Viewed(AUS) travelled well throughout and kicked clear halfway up the straight. Although he was being reeled in with every stride near the finish, he just held on to give his veteran trainer his 12th sucess in the race.
Bauer(IRE), winner of the Geelong Cup over half a mile shorter last month, was trying this trip for the first time. He came from out of the pack to close down the winner and finished to such good effect that it looked at first as if he had got there. This was the second successive time that his trainer has suffered a narrow defeat in this race and he deserves to pick up the prize, especially if he brings this one back again next season.
Profound Beauty(IRE), another stepping up in trip and handled by a trainer reponsible for two previous winners of this race, came to have her chance early in the straight but may have not lasted home on ground that was on the quick side for her.
Mad Rush(USA), who had made such an impression when a fast-finishing fourth in the Caulfield Cup that he was sent off favourite, came from well back to have a chance early in the straight but failed to pick up from that point and his rider reported he did not stay.
Septimus(IRE), who came into this unbeaten in staying races, was given a very positive ride along with his stable companions and, although he was still at the head of affairs turning in, he soon weakened and finished lame. With the time for the first mile 5secs faster than last year's running the consensus was that the trio went off too quickly and their trainer and all three riders came under fire from the local stewards, although ultimately no action was taken.

7071 KEMPTON (A.W) (R-H)

Wednesday, November 5

OFFICIAL GOING: Standard
Wind: Virtually nil Weather: Light rain

7189 CHAMPAGNE LANSON H'CAP 1m 2f (P)
5:50 (5:52) (Class 6) (0-60,60) 3-Y-O+ **£2,047** (£604; £302) **Stalls** High

Form RPR

0431 **1** **Stand Guard**[19] 6768 4-9-6 **58** .... IanMongan 1 78+
(P Howling) *sn trcking ldr: led over 3f out: drvn 4l clr over 2f out: styd on strly and in n.d fr over 1f out* **11/4**[1]

410 **2** *6* **Old Romney**[47] 6090 4-9-8 **60** ....(b) RichardHughes 6 65
(M Wigham) *hld up in rr: stdy hdwy fr 2f out: styd on strly fr over 1f out to take 2nd fnl 50yds but no ch w clr wnr* **11/1**

0642 **3** *¾* **Generous Lad (IRE)**[15] 6882 5-9-7 **59** ....(p) RobertHavlin 3 63
(A B Haynes) *s.i.s: hdwy 1/2-way: rdn and styd on to take 3rd wl ins fnl f but nvr in contention* **15/2**

0000 **4** *hd* **Sky Quest (IRE)**[14] 6899 10-8-10 **55** .... NathanAlison(7) 14 58
(J R Boyle) *in rr tl str run over 1f out: styd on wl to take 4th wl ins fnl f but nvr in contention* **66/1**

0212 **5** *½* **Classic Blue (IRE)**[6] 7094 4-9-3 **55** .... JimCrowley 2 57
(Ian Williams) *chsd ldrs: chsd wnr fr 2f out but nvr any ch: swamped for 2nd fnl 50yds* **13/2**

-450 **6** *½* **Royal Manor**[16] 6868 3-9-4 **60** .... NelsonDeSouza 13 61
(N J Vaughan) *chsd ldrs: rdn 3f out: wkng whn hung rt wl ins fnl f* **6/1**[3]

0-06 **7** *1 ½* **Parnassian**[9] 7009 8-9-8 **60** ....(v) RichardThomas 5 58
(J A Geake) *in rr: rdn over 2f out: styd on fnl f: nvr in contention* **25/1**

000 **8** *nk* **Tyrana (GER)**[236] 879 5-8-13 **54** .... TolleyDean(3) 9 55+
(J L Spearing) *chsd ldrs: rdn and keeping on same pce whn hmpd wl ins fnl f* **7/2**[2]

000 **9** *3 ¾* **Promise Maker (USA)**[30] 6530 3-9-2 **58** .... GrahamGibbons 12 48
(T D Walford) *chsd ldrs: rdn over 3f out: wknd over 1f out* **14/1**

1600 **10** *½* **Pab Special (IRE)**[15] 6882 5-9-5 **57** .... PaulDoe 11 46
(B R Johnson) *led tl hdd over 3f out: wknd fr 2f out* **16/1**

-660 **11** *3* **Sir Haydn**[49] 6019 8-9-5 **57** ....(v) MartinDwyer 7 40
(J R Jenkins) *s.i.s: in rr: rdn and sme prog 3f out: nvr in contention* **25/1**

550 **12** *1 ¼* **Spume (IRE)**[18] 6812 4-9-3 **55** ....(t[1]) TonyCulhane 4 36
(S Parr) *chsd ldrs: rdn over 3f out: wknd 2f out* **16/1**

0334 **13** *1 ½* **Karmei**[134] 3343 3-9-2 **58** .... JamesDoyle 10 36
(R Curtis) *sn rdn: a in rr* **100/1**

645/ **P** **New England**[738] 6240 6-9-6 **58** .... GeorgeBaker 8 —
(W M Brisbourne) *in tch to 1/2-way: sn wknd: p.u bef fin: dismntd: lame* **33/1**

2m 6.51s (-1.49) **Going Correction** +0.025s/f (Slow)
WFA 3 from 4yo+ 4lb **14** Ran SP% **128.2**
Speed ratings (Par 101): **106,101,100,100,100 99,98,98,95,94 92,91,90,—**
toteswinger: 1&2 £10.60, 1&3 £4.60, 2&3 £11.90. CSF £35.87 CT £219.98 TOTE £4.10: £1.90, £3.20, £2.00; EX 47.10.
Owner The Circle Bloodstock I Limited **Bred** Juddmonte Farms Ltd **Trained** Newmarket, Suffolk
■ Stewards' Enquiry : Nelson De Souza two-day ban: careless riding (Nov 19-20)

FOCUS
An ordinary event in which they went a steady early pace but the overall time was good for the grade and the form looks solid rated around the placed horses.

New England Official explanation: vet said gelding was lame left fore

7190 DIGIBET NURSERY 1m (P)
6:20 (6:24) (Class 5) (0-70,70) 2-Y-O **£2,590** (£770; £385; £192) **Stalls** High

Form RPR

3663 **1** **Brooksby**[7] 7073 2-9-4 **67** ....(b) RyanMoore 2 73
(R Hannon) *led after 1f: drvn and styd on strly fnl 2f* **9/2**[2]

1206 **2** *1 ¾* **Perfect Friend**[12] 6954 2-9-2 **65** .... PatDobbs 12 67
(S Kirk) *chsd ldrs: rdn and carried lft ins fnl f: tk 2nd sn after but no ch w wnr* **8/1**

3242 **3** *½* **Striding Edge (IRE)**[23] 6700 2-9-5 **68** .... MartinDwyer 5 69
(W R Muir) *chsd ldrs: wnt 2nd over 3f out: hrd drvn and no imp on wnr fr 2f out: lost 2nd wl ins fnl f* **6/1**[3]

0665 **4** *¾* **Herschel (IRE)**[24] 6673 2-9-4 **67** .... GeorgeBaker 14 66
(G L Moore) *hld up towards rr but in tch: rdn and hdwy fr 2f out: kpt on ins fnl f but nvr gng pce to be competitive* **7/4**[1]

460 **5** *1* **Noble Dictator**[15] 6876 2-9-1 **64** .... JamieSpencer 8 61
(E F Vaughan) *in rr: rdn and stl plenty to do 2f out: styd on ins fnl f: gng on cl home* **20/1**

0024 **6** *shd* **Celtic Commitment**[20] 6745 2-9-3 **66** .... RichardHughes 1 63
(R Hannon) *sn chsng ldrs: rdn and hld whn carried lft ins fnl f* **10/1**

665 **7** *nk* **Strathcal**[15] 6876 2-9-5 **68** .... RobertHavlin 6 64
(H Morrison) *s.i.s: bhd: hdwy over 2f out: styng on same pce whn n.m.r and eased wl ins fnl f* **14/1**

405 **8** *6* **Omnium Duke (IRE)**[29] 6553 2-9-7 **70** .... EddieAhern 4 53
(J W Hills) *mid-div and drvn along fr 3f out: no imp on ldrs: sn wknd* **12/1**

0260 **9** *1* **Johnny Rook (GER)**[20] 6761 2-9-2 **65** .... TGMcLaughlin 7 46
(E A L Dunlop) *led 1f: styd chsng wnr to 3f out: wknd over 2f out* **33/1**

0035 **10** *½* **Countess Zara (IRE)**[25] 6655 2-9-5 **68** .... WilliamBuick 9 48
(A M Balding) *broke wl: sn bhd: rdn and no ch fr over 2f out* **14/1**

0500 **11** *1 ¾* **Muhim**[35] 6394 2-9-2 **65** .... HayleyTurner 13 41
(C E Brittain) *chsd ldrs: rdn 3f out: wknd qckly 2f out* **11/1**

0500 **12** *shd* **Flashgun (USA)**[35] 6376 2-9-2 **65** .... ShaneKelly 11 41
(M G Quinlan) *s.i.s: a in rr* **50/1**

1m 40.2s (0.40) **Going Correction** +0.025s/f (Slow) **12** Ran SP% **128.1**
Speed ratings (Par 96): **99,97,96,96,95 94,94,88,87,87 85,85**
toteswinger: 1&2 £14.70, 1&3 £7.00, 2&3 £8.30. CSF £43.40 CT £231.11 TOTE £8.10: £2.20, £4.30, £2.30; EX 62.20.
Owner Pall Mall Partners **Bred** Stowell Hill Ltd **Trained** East Everleigh, Wilts

FOCUS
A modest event in which the field had managed just two wins in a total of 53 starts. It was run at a steady pace and few got into it from behind.

NOTEBOOK
Brooksby found a slight hint of improvement switched to forcing tactics with first-time blinkers on in a course-and-distance maiden auction last time. The headgear worked again and she did really well to dominate from a difficult draw under a shrewd tactical ride by Moore. She is unlikely to get such an easy time up front next time, but should not go up too much for this win and could progress again with headgear retained. (op 10-1)
Perfect Friend missed the break last time and had some traffic issues on her previous run, but showed a resilient attitude to keep battling on here, without ever really threatening the winner. (op 9-1 tchd 15-2)
Striding Edge(IRE) was always well placed and ran another creditable race but his consistency means that his mark is rising and he may continue to find it tough to fend off less-exposed rivals. (tchd 7-1)
Herschel(IRE), the heavily backed favourite, plugged on but it was a bit disappointing that he couldn't find a more potent finishing effort. His dam was a multiple 1m4f winner and he could do better faced with a stiffer test but has a bit to prove after this run. (op 11-4)
Noble Dictator stayed on fairly well down the outside but it is a concern that he was reluctant to enter the stalls, slow to exit them and displayed an awkward head carriage in the closing stages. (op 25-1)

7191 EUROPEAN BREEDERS' FUND MEDIAN AUCTION MAIDEN STKS 6f (P)
6:50 (6:52) (Class 5) 2-Y-O **£3,561** (£1,059; £529; £264) **Stalls** High

Form RPR

45 **1** **Sunniva Duke (IRE)**[40] 6246 2-9-3 0 .... RichardHughes 1 77
(R Hannon) *led over 4f out: rdn fr 2f out: styd on gamely whn strly chal fr over 1f out* **5/1**[3]

464 **2** *1* **Albaseet (IRE)**[30] 6531 2-9-3 74 .... RHills 3 74
(M P Tregoning) *chsd ldrs: veered lft over 3f out: drvn and qcknd to press wnr 1f out: fnd no ex u.p ins fnl f* **4/1**[2]

33 **3** *2* **Jordaura**[19] 6770 2-9-3 0 .... JamieSpencer 11 68
(W R Swinburn) *in tch: rdn and one pce over 2f out: styd on strly again ins fnl f and fin wl* **3/1**[1]

0332 **4** *¾* **Whisky Jack**[15] 6879 2-9-3 72 ....(b) MartinDwyer 4 66
(W R Muir) *in rr and hmpd over 3f out: drvn along over 2f out: styd on fnl f: nt rch ldrs* **11/2**

5 *nse* **Princess Cagliari** 2-8-12 0 .... RyanMoore 6 61
(R Hannon) *in rr: rdn and hdwy over 1f out: sn edging lft: styd on wl cl home* **14/1**

6 **6** *shd* **Flying Silks (IRE)**[19] 6770 2-9-3 0 .... ChrisCatlin 8 65
(J R Gask) *wnt rt s: t.k.h: chsng ldrs whn hmpd over 3f out: sn rcvrd: styd on same pce fnl f* **12/1**

3004 **7** *hd* **Sonhador**[16] 6863 2-9-3 68 .... JimCrowley 7 65
(P Winkworth) *led tl hdd over 4f out: rdn over 2f out: wknd fnl f* **10/1**

04 **8** *½* **Fly By Nelly**[23] 6701 2-8-12 0 .... SteveDrowne 2 58
(H Morrison) *prom: chsd wnr over 3f out: wknd over 1f out* **12/1**

9 *1 ½* **Hillside Lad** 2-9-3 0 .... GeorgeBaker 9 59
(R M Beckett) *bmpd s: in rr: rdn: v green and no ch fr over 2f out* **11/1**

00 **10** *6* **Lambourn Genie (UAE)**[15] 6876 2-9-3 0 .... RichardKingscote 5 41
(Tom Dascombe) *in rr whn hmpd over 3f out: hung lft and no ch fnl 2f* **66/1**

1m 13.96s (0.86) **Going Correction** +0.025s/f (Slow) **10** Ran SP% **118.0**
Speed ratings (Par 96): **95,93,91,90,89 89,89,88,86,78**
toteswinger: 1&2 £5.90, 1&3 £4.20, 2&3 £3.40. CSF £25.68 TOTE £6.90: £2.20, £2.10, £1.50; EX 28.90.
Owner Ballylinch Stud **Bred** Ballylinch Stud **Trained** East Everleigh, Wilts

FOCUS
Not a particularly strong event but several of the runners were closely matched on form and like the previous race it featured a runner dominating from a low draw.

NOTEBOOK
Sunniva Duke(IRE) swept into the lead from stall one and showed a really gritty attitude to repel a rival who appeared to be travelling better at one point in the final furlong. He probably did not cope with fast ground when well beaten at Haydock last time, but set the standard on his fourth at Goodwood in September and handled the surface well on this all-weather debut. (op 4-1)
Albaseet(IRE) was disappointing under a forcing ride last time and the switch to more patient tactics looked like they were going to pay off when he moved smoothly up to challenge in the closing stages, but he did not see out the trip as well as the winner. (tchd 11-2)

Jordaura got a bit restless in the stalls and was a little keen in the race. He managed to stay on without looking dangerous but was a bit disappointing and probably needs a stronger run race. He should, however, start life in handicaps on a fair mark, is closely related to the useful sprinter To The Roof, and could do better next year. Official explanation: jockey said colt missed the break (op 7-2 tchd 4-1 in a place)

Whisky Jack took a long while to get going but found a reasonable finishing burst. He is fairly exposed but has been running well since blinkers have been applied, has an official rating of 72 and gives the form a solid look. (op 5-1 tchd 9-2)

Princess Cagliari shaped with promise despite looking very green on her debut. She cost 45,000gns, is the third foal of a winner over an extended 7f and should benefit from this experience. (op 11-1)

Flying Silks(IRE) took a strong grip and was barged around the turn by the eventual second but did quite well to keep his composure and keep going. (op 16-1)

7192 DIGIBET.COM H'CAP — 6f (P)

7:20 (7:22) (Class 2) (0-100,104) 3-Y-O+

£11,215 (£3,358; £1,679; £840; £419; £210) **Stalls** High

Form — RPR

2151 **1** **Benllech**[61] [5681] 4-8-9 **91**.................... MartinDwyer 8 102
(D M Simcock) *hld up in rr: rapid hdwy insde fnl 2f: squeezed through ins fnl f to ld fnl 75yds: won gng away* **15/2**[3]

1114 **2** ¾ **Beat The Bell**[3] [7151] 3-8-3 **90**.................... NicolPolli(5) 5 99
(A Bailey) *chsd ldrs: rdn to ld over 1f out: hdd and styd on same pce fnl 75yds* **7/2**[1]

4004 **3** ¾ **Bonus (IRE)**[14] [6903] 8-9-8 **104**....................(e) HayleyTurner 10 111
(G A Butler) *hld up towards rr: stdy hdwy over 2f out: styd on to chse ldng duo wl ins fnl f but nvr quite gng pce to chal* **5/1**[2]

0234 **4** ¾ **Ebraam (USA)**[14] [6903] 5-9-3 **99**.................... IanMongan 11 103
(P Howling) *chsd ldrs: rdn and one pce over 2f out: rallied u.p to chal over 1f out: outpcd ins fnl f* **5/1**[2]

2000 **5** 1 ¼ **Al Muheer (IRE)**[39] [6269] 3-9-0 **96**.................... RyanMoore 4 96
(C E Brittain) *in rr: rdn and styd on fnl 2f: nvr gng pce to be competitive* **5/1**[2]

0065 **6** *shd* **Orpsie Boy (IRE)**[12] [6947] 5-9-3 **99**.................... KirstyMilczarek 6 99
(N P Littmoden) *in tch: rdn and styd on over 1f out: no ex under pessure ins fnl f* **8/1**

4050 **7** ¾ **Turn On The Style**[11] [6971] 6-9-1 **97**....................(b) PaulMulrennan 7 94
(J Balding) *chsd ldrs: rdn over 2f out: wknd ins fnl f* **16/1**

040 **8** 3 ¾ **Biniou (IRE)**[14] [6903] 5-8-13 **95**.................... ShaneKelly 1 80
(R M H Cowell) *s.i.s: t.k.h: rdn over 2f out: a bhd* **50/1**

0430 **9** 1 ½ **Misaro (GER)**[18] [6810] 7-8-9 **90**....................(b) LPKeniry 12 71
(R A Harris) *disp ld tl over 3f out: wknd over 1f out* **16/1**

-045 **10** 3 ¼ **Maltese Falcon**[235] [907] 8-9-4 **100**....................(t) NelsonDeSouza 9 70
(P F I Cole) *disp ld tl def advantage over 3f out: hdd & wknd qckly over 1f out* **14/1**

1m 11.47s (-1.63) **Going Correction** +0.025s/f (Slow) **10** Ran SP% **115.5**
Speed ratings (Par 109): **111,110,109,108,106 106,105,100,98,93**
toteswinger: 1&2 £3.30, 1&3 £3.80, 2&3 £4.40. CSF £33.59 CT £148.44 TOTE £7.50: £2.50, £1.80, £1.70; EX 32.00.

Owner Mohammed Al Shafar **Bred** Speedlith Group **Trained** Newmarket, Suffolk

FOCUS

A classy handicap run at a blistering pace and it produced an exciting finish. Solid form, with improved efforts from the first two.

NOTEBOOK

Benllech is highly progressive and found a really good turn of foot to pounce late from off the pace and record his sixth Polytrack win of the year. His mark has risen 23lb since January but he continues to defy the attentions of the handicapper and has a record of 112121511 since dropped back to 6f. (op 11-2)

Beat The Bell was well backed and ran a brave race in defeat on the toughest assignment of his career. He has improved considerably this autumn and landed a hat-trick on the Polytrack last month, before finding things happening a bit quickly over 5f on Fibresand last time. His mark keeps climbing but he should have some more room to successfully manoeuvre before the Handicapper takes control. (op 5-1 tchd 10-3)

Bonus(IRE), a 7f Listed winner here last December, ran near his best in a first-time eyeshield last time and put in another commendable effort with the headgear on again, conceding weight to two rivals who are firmly on the upgrade. (op 7-2)

Ebraam(USA) had every chance once he found a split in the closing stages but was not quite good enough in a useful contest. (op 9-2)

Al Muheer(IRE) knuckled down really from some way off the pace but could not land a blow, despite the race being run at a searing pace. He will probably be suited by returning to 7f. (op 11-1)

Maltese Falcon deserves a mention as he got involved in a gruelling battle for the lead but showed up quite well before fading on his first run for 235 days and would be of some interest when next competing on the all-weather at Lingfield, the scene of his last four wins. (op 12-1)

7193 DIGIBET FLOODLIT STKS (LISTED RACE) — 1m 4f (P)

7:50 (7:51) (Class 1) 3-Y-O+

£22,708 (£8,608; £4,308; £2,148; £1,076; £540) **Stalls** Centre

Form — RPR

6312 **1** **Spanish Moon (USA)**[47] [6074] 4-9-8 113.................... RyanMoore 6 117
(Sir Michael Stoute) *mde all: hrd rdn and hld on gamely fr over 1f out* **7/4**[1]

1052 **2** 2 ¼ **Re Barolo (IRE)**[39] [6287] 5-9-3 110....................(t) JimmyQuinn 8 108
(M Botti) *chsd ldrs: rdn to go 2nd wl over 1f out: kpt on to hold that position ins fnl f but no imp on wnr* **12/1**

2534 **3** *hd* **Scintillo**[11] [6980] 3-8-11 107....................(b) RichardHughes 1 108
(R Hannon) *hld up in rr: gd hdwy on ins fr 2f out: drvn to dispute 2nd ins fnl f: no imp on wnr and one pce into 3rd nr fin* **16/1**

-013 **4** ¾ **Ajhar (USA)**[38] [6303] 4-9-3 103.................... RHills 7 107
(M P Tregoning) *chsd ldrs: rdn over 2f out: styd on same pce over 1f out* **4/1**[2]

0020 **5** *nk* **Illustrious Blue**[47] [6074] 5-9-3 107.................... PaulDoe 5 106
(W J Knight) *in rr: rdn and hdwy on outside fr 2f out: kpt on cl home but nvr in contention* **8/1**

0044 **6** ½ **Dansant**[72] [5348] 4-9-8 110.................... EddieAhern 4 111
(G A Butler) *in tch: qcknd to chse wnr over 6f out: rdn to chal fr 3f out: outpcd fr 2f out and wknd qckly over 1f out* **11/2**[3]

0265 **7** 1 ¼ **Gravitas**[33] [6444] 5-9-3 105.................... JamieSpencer 2 104
(Saeed Bin Suroor) *s.i.s: hld up in rr: rdn and hdwy 2f out: nvr gng pce to be competitive and sn btn* **9/1**

-100 **8** 4 ½ **Emirates Skyline (USA)**[99] [4504] 5-9-3 108.................... TedDurcan 3 96
(Saeed Bin Suroor) *in tch: rdn and dropped to rr over 3f out* **14/1**

124 **9** 3 ¼ **Arthur's Girl**[109] [4196] 3-8-6 102.................... SteveDrowne 9 86
(G Wragg) *chsd ldrs: rdn to dispute 2nd over 2f out: wknd rapidly wl over 1f out* **14/1**

2m 32.61s (-1.89) **Going Correction** +0.025s/f (Slow)
WFA 3 from 4yo+ 6lb **9** Ran SP% **119.8**
Speed ratings (Par 111): **107,105,105,104,104 104,103,100,98**
toteswinger: 1&2 £5.70, 1&3 £12.00, 2&3 £30.60. CSF £26.36 TOTE £2.80: £1.10, £3.70, £5.00; EX 29.10.

Owner K Abdulla **Bred** Juddmonte Farms Inc **Trained** Newmarket, Suffolk

FOCUS

A competitive Listed event, with the majority of runners having a BHA rating between 107 and 113. The form is sound enough rated around the winner, third and fourth.

NOTEBOOK

Spanish Moon(USA), who just failed in a Group 3 at Newbury last month, was ridden more positively here, got an easy time up front and kept responding to pressure to eventually demoralise his rivals and surge clear in impressive style. He has given trouble at the stalls in the past but went in quietly then handled the surface really well on his all-weather debut and arguably ran right up to his best form. His trainer is an expert in coaxing improvement out of his older middle-distance performers and this one should be able to make his mark in Group company. (op 2-1 tchd 9-4)

Re Barolo(IRE) took a strong grip but gradually crept into contention and stayed on quite well. His 12 career wins have been at up to 1m2f and this was a commendable performance on his first try at this trip. (op 16-1)

Scintillo, the Group 1 Gran Criterium winner last October, responded well to second-time blinkers and showed determination to finish third on his first try on Polytrack. (op 18-1 tchd 20-1)

Ajhar(USA) ran respectably back at the scene of his course record-breaking handicap win in September, but his improvement seems to have levelled out. He could now find himself in the unforgiving territory of either having to concede lumps of weight in handicaps or not being quite good enough at this level. (op 5-1)

Illustrious Blue hindered his chance by racing keenly and then got outpaced before staying on again. He seems to retain all of his ability but is on a 16-race losing run and his hold-up tactics are proving difficult to execute successfully. (op 10-1)

Dansant, bidding for a repeat win in this race, probably paid the price for attacking the leader some way out and eventually faded on his return from a 72-day break. (op 5-1)

7194 AZURE H'CAP — 1m (P)

8:20 (8:20) (Class 6) (0-65,69) 3-Y-O+ **£2,047** (£604; £302) **Stalls** High

Form — RPR

0103 **1** **Tous Les Deux**[19] [6773] 5-9-6 **65**.................... GeorgeBaker 1 77
(G L Moore) *stdd s: hld up in rr tl stdy hdwy over 2f out: qcknd to ld over 1f out: styd on wl* **5/1**[2]

0000 **2** 2 **Salt Of The Earth (IRE)**[48] [6048] 3-9-1 **62**.................... HayleyTurner 11 69
(T G Mills) *chsd ldrs: disp 2nd over 2f out: rdn to chse wnr ins fnl f but no imp* **14/1**

0321 **3** 1 ¾ **April Fool**[7] [7077] 4-9-10 **69** 6ex....................(v) MartinDwyer 9 72+
(J A Geake) *pressed ldrs: led ins fnl 5f: rdn 2f out: hdd over 1f out: wknd ins fnl f* **7/4**[1]

6503 **4** *shd* **Fine Ruler (IRE)**[26] [6631] 4-9-4 **63**.................... VinceSlattery 14 66
(M R Bosley) *in tch: hdwy on ins to chse ldrs over 2f out: kpt on same pce ins fnl f* **16/1**

0003 **5** *hd* **Putra Laju (IRE)**[18] [6827] 4-8-12 **60**....................(p) PatrickHills(3) 5 62
(J W Hills) *in rr: rdn and hdwy on outside fr 2f out: kpt on ins fnl f but nvr gng pce to be competitive* **14/1**

2050 **6** 1 ¼ **Bauhaus Bourbon (USA)**[34] [6417] 3-9-4 **65**..........(b[1]) JamieSpencer 10 64
(P F I Cole) *sn chsng ldrs: rdn over 2f out: sn outpcd* **6/1**[3]

0103 **7** ½ **Alucica**[7] [7076] 5-8-11 **56**....................(v) JimCrowley 4 54
(D Shaw) *in rr: rdn 3f out: sme prog fr over 1f out: nvr gng pce to get nr ldrs* **10/1**

0000 **8** 1 ¼ **Sun Catcher (IRE)**[15] [6888] 5-9-4 **63**....................(e[1]) SteveDrowne 2 58
(P G Murphy) *in rr: rdn over 2f out: sme prog fnl f* **33/1**

3665 **9** *hd* **Sweet Kiss (USA)**[9] [7027] 3-8-11 **63**.................... DavidProbert(5) 13 58
(M J Attwater) *mid-div and rdn 3f out: nvr in contention* **14/1**

4500 **10** 5 **Silidan**[55] [5846] 5-9-5 **64**.................... RyanMoore 3 47
(G L Moore) *chsd ldrs: rdn over 3f out: wknd 2f out* **8/1**

0230 **11** 1 ¼ **Feasible**[42] [6211] 3-9-2 **63**....................(b) JamesDoyle 6 44
(J G Portman) *pressed ldrs 3f: wknd qckly over 2f out* **14/1**

-100 **12** 8 **High Class Problem (IRE)**[139] [3162] 5-8-9 **54**.................... ChrisCatlin 8 16
(D C O'Brien) *a in rr* **25/1**

55P6 **13** *nse* **Wooden King (IRE)**[19] [6771] 3-8-8 **55**.................... GregFairley 7 17
(P D Evans) *sn slt ld: hdd ins fnl 5f: wknd fr 3f out* **11/1**

1m 39.29s (-0.51) **Going Correction** +0.025s/f (Slow)
WFA 3 from 4yo+ 2lb **13** Ran SP% **134.4**
Speed ratings (Par 101): **103,101,99,99,98 97,97,95,95,90 89,81,81**
toteswinger: 1&2 £34.60, 1&3 £3.10, 2&3 £21.80. CSF £83.44 CT £183.45 TOTE £7.00: £2.60, £6.20, £1.50; EX 173.10.

Owner A Grinter **Bred** G And Mrs Middlebrook **Trained** Woodingdean, E Sussex

FOCUS

A modest handicap run at a decent early pace and the form looks reasonable rated around the fourth and fifth.

7195 CHAMPAGNE LANSON AT KEMPTON H'CAP (DIV I) — 6f (P)

8:50 (8:50) (Class 6) (0-52,52) 3-Y-O+ **£1,706** (£503; £252) **Stalls** High

Form — RPR

0003 **1** **Kindallachan**[24] [6681] 5-8-12 **50**....................(p) AlanMunro 1 59
(G C Bravery) *in rr: hdwy 3f out: styd on strly u.p fnl f to ld last strides* **5/1**[2]

0554 **2** *nk* **Jayanjay**[9] [7022] 9-8-12 **50**.................... DaneO'Neill 11 58
(B R Johnson) *chsd ldrs: rdn to chal 1f out: led ins fnl f: ct last strides* **11/2**[3]

5000 **3** 1 **Pentandra (IRE)**[103] [4381] 3-8-10 **48**.................... JimCrowley 7 53
(J G Given) *led 1f: styd chsng ldrs: led over 1f out: hdd and outpcd ins fnl f* **20/1**

4360 **4** *hd* **Davids Mark**[21] [6733] 8-8-13 **51**.................... HayleyTurner 3 55
(J R Jenkins) *in rr: rdn and stl plenty to do whn hdwy fr 2f out: str run ins fnl f and fin wl: nt rch ldrs* **13/2**

006 **5** ¾ **Faintly Hopeful**[43] [6192] 3-8-11 **49**.................... EddieAhern 2 51
(R A Teal) *in rr: hdwy fr 2f out: kpt on fnl f but nvr gng pce to be competitive* **20/1**

000 **6** *shd* **Affirmatively**[24] [6679] 3-9-0 **52**.................... ShaneKelly 10 53
(A W Carroll) *s.i.s: sn in tch: rdn over 2f out: kpt on fnl f but nvr a threat* **20/1**

0000 **7** 1 ¼ **Spanish Ace**[37] [6328] 7-8-7 **50**....................(p) JackDean(5) 5 47
(J M Bradley) *pressed ldrs: rdn 3f out: wknd fnl f* **20/1**

4400 **8** ¾ **Nordic Light (USA)**[9] [7022] 4-8-11 **49**....................(b) TravisBlock 6 44
(J M Bradley) *chsd ldrs: rdn over 2f out: wknd fnl f* **16/1**

4012 **9** *hd* **Piccolo Diamante (USA)**[53] [5916] 4-9-0 **52**....................(t) DNolan 4 46
(S Parr) *in rr: rdn over 2f out: sme prog ins fnl f* **11/4**[1]

The Form Book, Raceform Ltd, Compton, RG20 6NL

0565 **10** ¾ **Majestical (IRE)**[21] 6733 6-8-10 **48**..............................(p) WilliamBuick 12 40
(R A Harris) *led after 1f: hdd & wknd qckly over 1f out* **7/1**
1000 **11** *nse* **Desert Light (IRE)**[176] 2075 7-8-11 **49**....................(v) DarrenWilliams 8 41
(D Shaw) *outpcd most of way* **14/1**
0000 **12** 2 **Piccostar**[9] 7022 5-8-4 **49**.. PNolan(7) 9 34
(A B Haynes) *outpcd most of way* **33/1**
1m 13.86s (0.76) **Going Correction** +0.025s/f (Slow) **12** Ran SP% **119.1**
Speed ratings (Par 101): **95,94,93,93,92 91,90,89,88,87 87,85**
toteswinger: 1&2 £4.50, 1&3 £48.70, 2&3 £27.40. CSF £29.74 CT £519.15 TOTE £5.80: £2.10, £2.20, £6.10; EX 34.40.
Owner Herts And Hinds Racing Syndicate **Bred** F D Harvey **Trained** Cowlinge, Suffolk

FOCUS

A low-grade event that produced an exciting finish and another winner from a low draw. The early pace was modest and several of the hold-up performers pulled hard, so the form may not be reliable, although it looks reasonably sound on paper.

7196 CHAMPAGNE LANSON AT KEMPTON H'CAP (DIV II) 6f (P)

9:20 (9:23) (Class 6) (0-52,52) 3-Y-O+ **£1,706** (£503; £252) **Stalls** High

Form RPR
0604 **1** **River Kirov (IRE)**[24] 6679 5-8-12 **50**............................. RichardHughes 2 62
(M Wigham) *sn in tch: hdwy 2f out: chsd ldr ins fnl f: qcknd to ld fnl 75yds: readily* **3/1**[1]
0005 **2** ¾ **Bountiful Bay**[24] 6681 3-8-13 **51**.......................................(t) JamieSpencer 4 61
(B J Meehan) *sn led: rdn 2f out: hdd and no ex fnl 75yds* **8/1**
0024 **3** 1 ¾ **Reigning Monarch (USA)**[21] 6733 5-9-0 **52**....................(p) SaleemGolam 5 56
(Miss Z C Davison) *sn chsng ldr: rdn and effrt fr 2f out: no imp wknd into 3rd fnl f* **9/2**[2]
055 **4** *hd* **Duke Of Milan (IRE)**[109] 4186 5-9-0 **52**........................ HayleyTurner 9 55
(G C Bravery) *t.k.h in rr: rdn and hdwy over 1f out: styd on ins fnl f: nt rch ldrs* **8/1**
6344 **5** 2 ½ **Bilboa**[8] 7049 3-8-11 **49**..(p) DaneO'Neill 8 44
(J M Bradley) *in rr: hdwy fr 2f out: kpt on fnl f: nt trble ldrs* **17/2**
0002 **6** *nk* **Calabaza**[42] 6204 6-8-9 **50**... TolleyDean(3) 7 44
(M J Attwater) *chsd ldrs: rdn and outpcd 2f out: styd on again fnl f* **12/1**
000 **7** 1 ½ **Currency**[14] 6895 11-8-6 **49**.. JackDean(5) 10 39
(J M Bradley) *sn mid-div: rdn and one pce over 2f out* **25/1**
1204 **8** 1 **Exit Strategy (IRE)**[14] 6895 4-8-7 **48**.....................(b) KevinGhunowa(3) 6 34
(R A Harris) *outpcd: sme prog fnl f* **11/2**[3]
0410 **9** 2 ½ **Bye Baby Bunting**[55] 5832 3-8-12 **50**........................... RichardSmith 3 28
(B R Johnson) *chsd ldrs: rdn 3f out: wknd fr 2f out* **20/1**
6330 **10** *nse* **Bollin Franny**[37] 6339 4-8-6 **49**............................ NataliaGemelova(5) 12 27
(J E Long) *chsd ldrs over 3f* **7/1**
0006 **11** *nk* **Talcen Gwyn (IRE)**[37] 6328 6-8-11 **49**...............................(v) LPKeniry 1 26
(M F Harris) *s.i.s: t.k.h: a towards rr* **40/1**
6520 **12** 2 **Cranworth Blaze**[27] 6595 4-8-9 **47**................................. GregFairley 11 18
(T J Etherington) *outpcd* **20/1**
1m 13.51s (0.41) **Going Correction** +0.025s/f (Slow) **12** Ran SP% **127.3**
Speed ratings (Par 101): **98,97,94,94,91 90,88,87,84,83 83,80**
toteswinger: 1&2 £18.10, 1&3 £4.90, 2&3 £6.20. CSF £28.57 CT £113.94 TOTE £5.60: £2.00, £3.00, £2.00; EX 34.30 Place 6 £32.41, Place 5 £14.25..
Owner A Darke T Matthews M Wigham **Bred** Kildaragh Stud **Trained** Newmarket, Suffolk

FOCUS

A moderate handicap in which the early pace was steady and not many got into it from behind. The form is rated around the third with the winner building on a more encouraging effort latest and the second up 9lb.

Cranworth Blaze Official explanation: jockey said filly hung left in the straight

T/Plt: £27.90 to a £1 stake. Pool: £88,072.01. 2,297.77 winning tickets. T/Qpdt: £5.10 to a £1 stake. Pool: £7,889.96. 1,138.90 winning tickets. ST

7079 NOTTINGHAM (L-H)

Wednesday, November 5

OFFICIAL GOING: Heavy (5.1)

Wind: Virtually nil Weather: Overcast and damp

7197 PINNACLE RACING "FRIENDLY SUCCESSFUL RACEHORSE PARTNERSHIP" H'CAP 5f 13y

1:20 (1:21) (Class 6) (0-55,55) 3-Y-O+ **£2,047** (£604; £302) **Stalls** High

Form RPR
0004 **1** **Top Bid**[6] 7090 4-9-2 **55**...(b) DavidAllan 1 68
(T D Easterby) *mde virtually all far side: rdn clr over 2f out: kpt on wl u.p ins fnl f* **10/1**[3]
0002 **2** 1 ¾ **Jakeini (IRE)**[34] 6405 5-9-2 **55**..............................(v) GrahamGibbons 4 62
(E S McMahon) *prom far side: hdwy to chse wnr after 2f: rdn along wl over 1f out: drvn and kpt on ins fnl f: nt rch wnr: 2nd of 9 in gp* **9/2**[1]
4210 **3** ½ **Tanley**[20] 6766 3-9-1 **54**..(p) ChrisCatlin 12 59+
(J F Coupland) *cl up stands' side: hdwy to ld that gp over 1f out: sn rdn and kpt on ins fnl f: 1st of 7 in gp* **16/1**
00-0 **4** *hd* **Majestic Cheer**[20] 6766 4-8-9 **53**.................................. DavidProbert(5) 5 57
(John A Harris) *cl up far side: rdn along 1/2-way: drvn wl over 1f out: kpt on same pce: 3rd of 9 in gp* **10/1**[3]
-000 **5** *shd* **Fish Called Johnny**[32] 6486 4-8-11 **55**........................ SladeO'Hara(5) 2 59
(A Berry) *chsd ldrs far side: rdn along 1/2-way: kpt on u.p appr fnl f: 4th of 9 in gp* **33/1**
-003 **6** 1 ¼ **Mickleberry (IRE)**[67] 5501 4-8-10 **49**........................... AlanMunro 17 48
(M Brittain) *chsd ldrs stands' side: rdn along and outpcd 1/2-way: swtchd lft and hdwy over 1f out: kpt on ins fnl f: 2nd of 7 in gp* **14/1**
4002 **7** ½ **Harrison's Flyer (IRE)**[14] 6895 7-8-10 **54**....................(p) JackDean(5) 9 52
(J M Bradley) *in rr far side: rdn along over 2f out: kpt on ins fnl f: nrst fin: 5th of 9 in gp* **8/1**[2]
4000 **8** *shd* **El Potro**[24] 6679 6-8-12 **51**.. WilliamBuick 15 48
(J R Holt) *prom stands' side: rdn over 1f out: drvn and one pce ins fnl f: 3rd of 7 in gp* **12/1**
0404 **9** ¾ **Ursus**[35] 6382 3-9-1 **54**... PAspell 3 49
(C R Wilson) *chsd ldrs far side: rdn along 2f out: sn drvn and one pce: 6th of 9 in gp* **8/1**[2]
4400 **10** *nk* **Mr Funshine**[14] 6895 3-8-9 **51**.................................. JackMitchell(3) 13 44
(Mrs P N Dutfield) *chsd ldrs stands' side: hdwy wl over 1f out: rdn and wknd ent fnl f: 4th of 7 in gp* **20/1**
0403 **11** ½ **Namu**[14] 6895 5-9-0 **53**.. DaneO'Neill 10 45
(Miss T Spearing) *a towards rr far side: 7th of 9 in gp* **8/1**[2]
0001 **12** ¾ **Note Perfect**[34] 6405 3-9-0 **53**....................................(b) DaleGibson 8 42
(M W Easterby) *in tch far side: rdn along 2f out: sn drvn and wknd: 8th of 9 in gp* **12/1**
0160 **13** *hd* **Sunley Sovereign**[29] 6546 4-8-10 **49**........................(b) AndrewElliott 14 37
(Mrs R A Carr) *s.i.s and a in rr stands' side: 5th of 7 in gp* **16/1**
0460 **14** 1 ½ **Bold Minstrel (IRE)**[106] 4285 6-9-0 **53**........................ FrancisNorton 11 36
(M Quinn) *lad stands' side gp: rdn along and hdd over 1f out: sn wknd: 6th of 7 in gp* **22/1**
0462 **15** 3 ½ **Mrs Bun**[8] 7049 3-8-11 **50**... PaulMulrennan 16 20
(K A Ryan) *s.i.s and a in rr stands' side: last of 7 in gp* **8/1**[2]
0560 **16** 13 **Monashee Brave (IRE)**[192] 1642 5-9-0 **53**........................ PaulDoe 7 —
(M A Allen) *in tch far side: rdn along 1/2-way: sn wknd and bhd: last of 9 in gp* **20/1**
63.14 secs (2.44) **Going Correction** +0.525s/f (Yiel) **16** Ran SP% **131.4**
Speed ratings (Par 101): **101,98,97,97,96 94,94,93,92,92 91,90,89,87,81 61**
toteswinger: 1&2 £13.90, 1&3 £38.70, 2&3 £16.10. CSF £55.88 CT £784.13 TOTE £13.90: £2.50, £1.70, £4.50, £8.40; EX 87.90.
Owner John & Marilyn Williams **Bred** Southill Stud **Trained** Great Habton, N Yorks

FOCUS

A moderate sprint handicap. They split into two groups and four of the first five raced far side. The form makes sense at face value but this is not a race to be too positive about.

Mrs Bun Official explanation: jockey said filly jumped awkwardly, never travelling thereafter

7198 PINNACLE RACING "SMART WAY TO OWNERSHIP" MAIDEN STKS 5f 13y

1:55 (1:56) (Class 5) 2-Y-O **£3,238** (£963; £481; £240) **Stalls** High

Form RPR
430 **1** **Rare Art**[13] 6932 2-9-3 70... HayleyTurner 2 70
(S A Callaghan) *led far side: gp: cl up tl rdn to ld over 1f out: drvn ins fnl f and kpt on wl* **7/2**[3]
2522 **2** ½ **Silent Wonder**[7] 7082 2-9-3 73.. ShaneKelly 9 68
(R M H Cowell) *overall ldr stands' side: rdn along 2f out: hdd over 1f out: drvn ins fnl f and kpt on: 1st of 2 in gp* **5/4**[1]
00 **3** 4 **Sarasota Sunshine**[9] 7020 2-8-9 0.................................. LukeMorris(3) 1 49
(N P Littmoden) *hld up far side: hdwy 2f out: rdn to chse wnr ins fnl f: no imp: 2nd of 5 in gp* **66/1**
2306 **4** ¾ **Positivity**[9] 7015 2-8-12 79.. TomEaves 8 46
(B Smart) *chsd overall ldr stands' side: rdn along 2f out: sn drvn and one pce appr fnl f: 2nd of 2 in gp* **3/1**[2]
50 **5** 2 **Diamond Surprise**[39] 6273 2-8-12 0............................... J-PGuillambert 4 39
(P A Blockley) *chsd ldng pair far side: rdn along 2f out: sn one pce: 3rd of 5 in gp* **8/1**
0 **6** 2 **Genipabu (IRE)**[14] 6894 2-8-12 0.................................. DarryllHolland 3 32
(M G Quinlan) *chsd wnr far side to 1/2-way: sn wknd: 4th of 5 in gp* **28/1**
0 **7** 1 **Bold Bomber**[9] 7020 2-9-3 0... PaulQuinn 6 33
(Paul Green) *in tch far side: rdn along over 2f out: sn outpcd: last of 5 in gp* **12/1**
63.17 secs (2.47) **Going Correction** +0.525s/f (Yiel) **7** Ran SP% **115.4**
Speed ratings (Par 96): **101,100,93,92,89 86,84**
toteswinger: 1&2 £1.80, 1&3 £19.80, 2&3 £9.50. CSF £8.45 TOTE £5.40: £1.70, £1.60; EX 8.90.
Owner Matthew Green **Bred** Cheveley Park Stud Ltd **Trained** Newmarket, Suffolk
■ Stewards' Enquiry : Hayley Turner one-day ban: failed to ride to draw (Nov 19)

FOCUS

Not many runners and the morning favourite looked one to take on when considering his form figures. Despite the small field, they split into two groups. Just modest form.

NOTEBOOK

Rare Art, who had an official mark of 70, was quickly taken to the far rail and was always in full control of his bunch. He stayed on really strongly to hold his biggest rival towards the stands' side. One would imagine that he will find things tough in handicap company after being raised for this victory. (tchd 3-1)

Silent Wonder, who had a 3lb higher mark than the winner, brought a lot of placed form into the race and, once again, managed to accrue another second place. However, it is impossible to crab him on this occasion as he was on his own from an early stage. (op Evens tchd 6-4)

Sarasota Sunshine, beaten at 150/1 last time, kept on well behind Rare Art and claimed third place. She is now qualified for handicaps. (op 50-1 tchd 40-1)

Positivity could not stay on terms with Silent Wonder down the stands' side and was disappointing, considering she had the highest official mark of these. (op 7-2)

Diamond Surprise got outpaced at about halfway before staying on in the latter stages. She is now qualified for handicaps. (op 10-1 tchd 7-1)

7199 PINNACLE RACING "FOR QUALITY VISIT PINNACLERACING.CO.UK" NURSERY 5f 13y

2:30 (2:31) (Class 5) (0-70,70) 2-Y-O **£3,238** (£963; £481; £240) **Stalls** High

Form RPR
0463 **1** **Rio Cobolo (IRE)**[40] 6247 2-8-1 **50**...................................(v) ChrisCatlin 7 53
(Paul Green) *trckd ldrs: hdwy 2f out: rdn to ld ent fnl f: sn drvn and kpt on* **3/1**[2]
3040 **2** 1 **Bold Rose**[24] 6666 2-8-1 **55**.. DavidProbert(5) 2 54
(M D I Usher) *led: rdn along wl over 1f out: drvn and hdd ent fnl f: kpt on* **12/1**
3300 **3** 4 **Lisburn (IRE)**[40] 6247 2-9-7 **70**...................................... AlanMunro 3 55
(M Brittain) *cl up: ev ch 2f out: sn rdn and kpt on same pce appr fnl f* **7/2**[3]
5216 **4** *nk* **Cocktail Party (IRE)**[16] 6865 2-8-13 **62**........................... EddieAhern 8 46
(J W Hills) *hld up: hdwy 2f out: sn rdn and kpt on same pce fnl f* **15/8**[1]
0020 **5** 2 **Autumn Morning (IRE)**[5] 7113 2-8-1 **57**........................ AndreaAtzeni(7) 6 34
(P D Evans) *in tch: rdn along over 2f out: sn outpcd* **16/1**
0322 **6** 2 ½ **Blackwater Fort (USA)**[66] 5530 2-9-6 **69**........................ WilliamBuick 4 37
(J Gallagher) *cl up: rdn along over 2f out: sn drvn and wknd* **7/1**
0005 **7** 1 ¾ **Pollish**[8] 7044 2-8-0 **49** oh2 ow2...................................(b[1]) FrancisNorton 5 10
(A Berry) *chsd ldrs: rdn along over 2f out: sn wknd* **18/1**
63.20 secs (2.50) **Going Correction** +0.525s/f (Yiel) **7** Ran SP% **113.3**
Speed ratings (Par 96): **101,99,93,92,89 85,82**
toteswinger: 1&2 £8.70, 1&3 £3.20, 2&3 £8.00. CSF £36.40 CT £129.73 TOTE £4.00: £2.60, £4.00; EX 50.40.
Owner The Keely Gang **Bred** Yvonne & Gerard Kennedy **Trained** Lydiate, Merseyside

FOCUS

A weak nursery, in which the first two set the level. They were all taken to the far side of the track.

NOTEBOOK

Rio Cobolo(IRE) built on the promise he showed when third over 6f on quick ground in a first-time visor at Haydock on his previous start. He handled these very different conditions well, and is clearly versatile, but he had to work for it, and his connections think he is quite a lazy type. He should remain competitive in lowly company. (op 4-1)

Bold Rose had her chance under a positive ride against the far rail and stuck on gamely for pressure. This looks as good as she is. (op 20-1)

Lisburn(IRE) seemed to have every chance, but she does not look to be progressing. (op 5-2)

Cocktail Party(IRE) won a similar race over course and distance on soft ground last month, so she could have been expected to run better. She did not enjoy the best of trips when looking for a run, but basically just failed to pick up. (op 9-4 tchd 5-2)

Autumn Morning(IRE) was always struggling. (tchd 14-1)

7200 PINNACLE RACING "1ST FOR SERVICE 01845 597987" MAIDEN STKS 1m 75y

3:05 (3:09) (Class 5) 2-Y-O £3,238 (£963; £481; £240) **Stalls Low**

Form RPR

04 1 **Prohibition (IRE)**[22] 6714 2-9-3 0 DarryllHolland 6 77
(W J Haggas) *mde most: rdn clr 2f out: eased towards fin* **3/1**[1]

0 2 ¾ **Class Is Class (IRE)**[22] 6720 2-9-3 0 RyanMoore 8 75
(Sir Michael Stoute) *trckd ldrs: hdwy 3f out: rdn 2f out: chsd wnr whn edgd lft ins fnl f: kpt on wl towards fin* **10/3**[2]

3 1 ¾ **Petrovsky** 2-9-3 0 JoeFanning 4 71
(M Johnston) *prom: rdn along and sltly outpcd over 2f out: swtchd rt and hdwy over 1f out: kpt on ins fnl f* **7/1**

4 1 ½ **Everynight (IRE)** 2-8-10 0 AndreaAtzeni(7) 11 68
(M Botti) *trckd ldrs: hdwy 3f out: rdn 2f out: kpt on appr fnl f: nrst fin* **8/1**

0 5 3 ½ **Rebel Swing**[11] 6977 2-9-3 0 ShaneKelly 7 60
(W R Muir) *chsd ldrs: rdn along 3f out: kpt on same pce fnl 2f* **18/1**

5 6 3 ¾ **Non Dom (IRE)**[11] 6978 2-9-3 0 SteveDrowne 12 52
(H Morrison) *hld up: hdwy 3f out: kpt on fnl 2f: nvr nr ldrs* **6/1**[3]

0 7 ½ **Putra One (IRE)**[19] 6777 2-9-3 0 PhilipRobinson 17 51
(M A Jarvis) *cl up: rdn along 3f out: edgd lft over 2f out: grad wknd* **16/1**

8 3 **Crocus Rose** 2-8-12 0 JimmyQuinn 9 39
(H J L Dunlop) *dwlt and in rr tl styd on fnl 2f* **66/1**

9 1 ½ **Flodden Field** 2-9-3 0 AlanMunro 15 41
(P W Chapple-Hyam) *a in midfield* **25/1**

10 6 **Bernie The Bolt (IRE)** 2-9-3 0 LPKeniry 16 28
(A M Balding) *chsd ldrs: rdn along 3f out: wknd over 2f out* **66/1**

0 11 ¾ **Bollin Judith**[32] 6481 2-8-12 0 DavidAllan 3 21
(T D Easterby) *dwlt: a towards rr* **40/1**

12 ½ **Harvest Song (IRE)** 2-9-3 0 PatDobbs 14 25
(Sir Michael Stoute) *dwlt: a towards rr* **10/1**

00 13 hd **Marjury Daw (IRE)**[12] 6945 2-8-12 0 TPQueally 5 19
(J G Given) *chsd ldrs: rdn along over 3f out: wknd wl over 2f out* **66/1**

14 ½ **Endeavoured (IRE)** 2-9-3 0 TGMcLaughlin 2 23
(P D Evans) *a towards rr* **40/1**

2 15 8 **Drop The Hammer**[22] 6722 2-8-12 0 MickyFenton 10 1
(T P Tate) *a towards rr* **9/1**

0 16 3 ¾ **Kazbow (IRE)**[28] 6581 2-9-3 0 DaneO'Neill 13 —
(L M Cumani) *sn outpcd and bhd* **40/1**

17 16 **Aspirational (IRE)** 2-9-3 0 TomEaves 1 —
(B Palling) *s.i.s: a bhd* **66/1**

1m 52.09s (6.69) **Going Correction** +0.90s/f (Soft) **17 Ran SP% 133.3**
Speed ratings (Par 96): **102,101,99,98,94 90,90,87,85,79 79,78,78,77,69 66,50**
toteswinger: 1&2 £5.30, 1&3 £6.60, 2&3 £7.70. CSF £13.47 TOTE £4.50: £1.02, £3.10, £3.70; EX 16.60.

Owner Ms Nicola Mahoney **Bred** Kevin Buckley **Trained** Newmarket, Suffolk

FOCUS

A big field of maidens, and potentially a decent event, despite the ground, with some powerful yards represented. It paid to race handily and the first three home were in the leading half-dozen throughout, but a few of those behind should improve from this and will come into their own next season.

NOTEBOOK

Prohibition(IRE), whose fourth at Leicester last time has been boosted by the subsequent victories of the pair that finished immediately ahead of him, benefited from a well-judged front-running ride from Darryll Holland. Kicking for home approaching the final quarter-mile, he had the race won when passing the furlong pole and was able to take things very easy close home. He seemed to relish this ground, so could be especially interesting in the early part of the next turf season. (op 5-2 tchd 7-2)

Class Is Class(IRE), well beaten over a similar trip on his Leicester debut, was always close to the pace and kept plugging away, but could never quite get on terms with the favourite and is a little flattered by his proximity at the end. He is bred to stay further and should have little difficulty finding a race. (op 4-1 tchd 3-1)

Petrovsky ◆, whose half-brother was successful in testing conditions at Catterick the previous day, ran really well on this debut having been close to the pace from the off and he was still going forward at the line. He really should win races. (op 8-1 tchd 10-1)

Everynight(IRE) ◆ was backed right in from massive prices and justified the support with a very promising debut effort. Forced to make his effort wide, he stayed on well over the last couple of furlongs, but did show signs of greenness, so this half-brother to the winning-sprinter Rasaman is likely to do even better with this experience under his belt. (op 50-1)

Rebel Swing, who hinted at ability on his Newbury debut, was a little awkward beforehand, but he again showed distinct signs of ability and is one to keep in mind, especially once handicapped. (op 16-1 tchd 14-1)

Non Dom(IRE), who ran in the other division of that Newbury maiden when a very promising fifth, was again far from disgraced especially as he was off the bridle at halfway and was another forced to race wide. (op 9-2 tchd 4-1)

Putra One(IRE) didn't get home after racing up with the pace early and he may need better ground.

Crocus Rose was noted staying on late under hand-and-heels riding and being a half-sister to four winners at up to 2m including the high-class Ela Athena, she should really come into her own when presented with a decent test next term.

Harvest Song(IRE), a 290,000gns colt out of a dual winner over 1m2f and a stable companion of the runner-up, looked the yard's second string on jockey bookings but he did attract significant market support. He never got involved in the contest at any stage as it turned out, but obviously someone thinks that he possesses more ability than he was able to show. (op 16-1 tchd 22-1)

7201 PINNACLE RACING "ROYAL ASCOT WINNERS" CONDITIONS STKS 1m 75y

3:40 (3:40) (Class 2) 3-Y-O+ £12,462 (£3,732; £1,866; £934; £466) **Stalls Low**

Form RPR

1324 1 **Little White Lie (IRE)**[32] 6476 4-8-10 104 DarryllHolland 1 99+
(J R Jenkins) *mde all: rdn along over 2f out: drvn ent fnl f and kpt on* **8/11**[1]

1356 2 2 ½ **Easy Target (FR)**[32] 6484 3-9-2 100 TomEaves 5 100
(B Smart) *trckd wnr: hdwy to chal over 2f out: sn rdn and ev ch tl drvn ent fnl f and kpt on same pce* **11/2**[3]

3625 3 1 ¼ **Igor Protti**[46] 6123 6-8-10 105 (v) TedDurcan 4 89
(Saeed Bin Suroor) *trckd ldrs: effrt 3f out: rdn 2f out and kpt on same pce ent fnl f* **9/4**[2]

0500 4 14 **First Order**[7] 7066 7-8-10 80 AnnStokell 2 57
(Miss A Stokell) *t.k.h: cl up tl rdn along 3f out: wknd over 2f out* **100/1**

53-0 5 21 **Wannarock (IRE)**[198] 1527 3-8-8 70 PaulQuinn 3 9
(M C Chapman) *a in rr* **100/1**

1m 50.72s (5.32) **Going Correction** +0.90s/f (Soft)
WFA 3 from 4yo+ 2lb **5 Ran SP% 106.0**
Speed ratings (Par 109): **109,106,105,91,70**
toteswinger: 1&2 £2.80. CSF £4.87 TOTE £1.80: £1.10, £2.10; EX 4.00.

Owner The Three Honest Men **Bred** J L Hassett **Trained** Royston, Herts

FOCUS

A reasonable conditions race on paper, but Little White Lie was gifted the run of the race and set an ordinary pace under an expert front-running jockey. The winner did not need to be at his best with the main form danger disappointing in third.

NOTEBOOK

Little White Lie(IRE) took a while to hit top gear when first coming under pressure in the straight, but had saved plenty and gradually drew clear. Although we didn't learn a great deal from this success, he has enjoyed a terrific season and looks capable of further improvement. He may now be aimed at the Dubai Carnival in early 2009. (op 4-6 tchd 8-13)

Easy Target(FR), who is unproven over a trip this far, raced without cover off the modest pace for much of the way and had little chance with Little White Lie when that one kicked from the front in the straight. He would have been 12lb better off with the winner had this been a handicap. (op 7-1 tchd 5-1)

Igor Protti offered little under pressure and was well below form. Both the steady pace and testing ground were seemingly against him, and he probably wants a little further as well. (op 2-1 tchd 7-4)

First Order had loads to find with the front three at the weights and did not help his chance by racing keenly early on. (op 66-1)

7202 PINNACLE RACING "THRILL OF OWNERSHIP 01845 597987" H'CAP 1m 2f 50y

4:10 (4:11) (Class 5) (0-75,80) 3-Y-O+ £3,561 (£1,059; £529; £264) **Stalls Low**

Form RPR

6532 1 **Prairie Storm**[14] 6899 3-9-3 74 LPKeniry 14 85+
(A M Balding) *prom: hdwy 3f out: led 2f out: rdn ent fnl f and styd on wl* **7/2**[1]

0110 2 2 ½ **Opera Writer (IRE)**[12] 6948 5-8-10 68 (p) DavidProbert(5) 3 74
(R Hollinshead) *a.p: effrt to chse wnr over 1f out: drvn ins fnl f: kpt on same pce* **10/1**

2144 3 2 ½ **Highland Love**[32] 6487 3-8-13 70 MickyFenton 8 71
(J T Stimpson) *cl up: led wl over 2f out: rdn and hdd 2f out: sn drvn and kpt on same pce appr fnl f* **12/1**

0026 4 1 ¼ **Night Orbit**[16] 6862 4-8-12 68 (v) RussellKennemore(3) 7 67
(Miss J Feilden) *in midfield: hdwy on outer 3f out: rdn 2f out: styd on u.p ins fnl f: nrst fin* **16/1**

0306 5 1 ¼ **St Petersburg**[24] 6675 8-9-2 69 PatCosgrave 16 65
(J R Boyle) *bhd: hdwy 3f out: rdn over 2f out: styd on appr fnl f: nrst fin* **33/1**

0521 6 1 **Dream Of Olwyn (IRE)**[7] 7085 3-8-13 70 6ex TPQueally 11 64
(J G Given) *chsd ldrs: effrt 3f out: rdn 2f out: edgd lft and no imp appr fnl f* **4/1**[2]

505- 7 5 **Bobby Charles**[495] 3060 7-9-1 68 TomEaves 9 52
(Dr J D Scargill) *dwlt: in rr tl styd on fnl 2f: nvr nr ldrs* **14/1**

2-34 8 ¾ **Prize Fighter (IRE)**[18] 6826 6-9-2 69 (b) JoeFanning 1 52
(A Berry) *led: rdn along over 3f out: hdd wl over 2f out and grad wknd* **16/1**

-440 9 3 ¼ **Magdalene**[22] 6721 4-8-12 65 SaleemGolam 4 41
(Rae Guest) *in tch: rdn alon g 3f out: sn drvn and wknd* **12/1**

5606 10 1 **Lady Friend**[11] 6983 6-9-2 69 LiamJones 13 43
(J W Hills) *chsd ldrs: hdwy and cl up 3f out: sn rdn and grad wknd* **20/1**

1135 11 hd **Five Wishes**[16] 6862 4-8-13 66 (be) PJMcDonald 10 40
(M Dods) *nvr nr ldrs* **14/1**

2200 12 nk **Jenny Soba**[7] 7085 5-8-11 64 DNolan 2 37
(Lucinda Featherstone) *dwlt: a in rr* **33/1**

-020 13 1 ¾ **Theonebox (USA)**[12] 6949 3-9-1 75 LukeMorris(3) 12 45
(N J Vaughan) *in midfield: rdn along 4f out: sn wknd* **9/1**[3]

405 14 6 **Man Of Gwent (UAE)**[14] 6900 4-8-9 69 AndreaAtzeni(7) 15 27
(P D Evans) *sn outpcd and a in rr* **9/1**[3]

4600 15 29 **Piper's Song (IRE)**[48] 6052 5-9-6 73 FergusSweeney 5 —
(B G Powell) *s.i.s: a bhd* **33/1**

2m 20.3s (7.80) **Going Correction** +0.90s/f (Soft)
WFA 3 from 4yo+ 4lb **15 Ran SP% 125.4**
Speed ratings (Par 103): **104,102,100,99,98 97,93,92,90,89 89,88,87,82,59**
toteswinger: 1&2 £5.80, 1&3 £16.70, 2&3 £29.50. CSF £38.61 CT £385.97 TOTE £4.20: £2.00, £2.50, £3.30; EX 44.20 Place 6 £48.02, Place 5 £16.67..

Owner W V & Mrs E S Robins **Bred** Mrs Shirley Robins **Trained** Kingsclere, Hants

FOCUS

This looked a difficult race to work out. By now the ground looked very soft and half the field were beaten off by the three-furlong pole. Improved form from Prairie Storm, who could have more to offer.

T/Plt: £101.40 to a £1 stake. Pool: £52,719.62. 379.48 winning tickets. T/Qpdt: £43.50 to a £1 stake. Pool: £4,175.98. 70.92 winning tickets. JR

7088 GREAT LEIGHS (A.W) (L-H)

Thursday, November 6

OFFICIAL GOING: Standard

Wind: Virtually nil Weather: dry, mild

7204 DANIEL GALMICHE IN EDEN MAIDEN STKS (DIV I) 1m (P)

5:50 (5:52) (Class 5) 2-Y-O £3,238 (£963; £481; £240) **Stalls Centre**

Form RPR

0 1 **Laurie Grove (IRE)**[33] 6474 2-9-3 0 RobertHavlin 8 85
(T G Mills) *t.k.h early: chsd ldng pair: hdwy to chal over 1f out: rdn to ld ent fnl f: r.o strly* **4/1**[2]

04 2 2 **Kansai Spirit (IRE)**[35] 6425 2-9-3 0 JimmyFortune 12 81
(J H M Gosden) *led: rdn wl over 1f out: hdd ent fnl f: nt pce of wnr fnl 100yds* **4/5**[1]

3 3 **Manahej (USA)** 2-9-3 0 TedDurcan 10 74
(Saeed Bin Suroor) *chsd ldr tl wl over 1f out: sn rdn: outpcd by ldng pair over 1f out: kpt on same pce* **9/1**

0 4 2 **Woodlark Island (IRE)**[12] 6978 2-9-3 0 FergusSweeney 3 70
(M P Tregoning) *in tch: rdn and unable qck over 2f out: edging lft over 1f out: kpt on same pce* **40/1**

5 1 ½ **Elliptical (USA)** 2-9-3 0 HayleyTurner 6 66
(G A Butler) *in tch in midfield: rdn and unable qck over 2f out: plugged on same pce fr over 1f out* **20/1**

0 6 2 ¾ **Great Bounder (CAN)**[22] 6737 2-9-3 0 SteveDrowne 9 60
(J R Best) *hld up in midfield: rdn and struggling over 2f out: no ch fr over 1f out* **20/1**

7 hd **Lord Of The Dance (IRE)** 2-9-0 0 LukeMorris(3) 2 60
(J M P Eustace) *s.i.s: a towards rr: rdn and struggling 3f out* **15/2**[3]

00 **8** *4* **Great Western (USA)**[8] 7069 2-9-3 0................................ ShaneKelly 7 51
(P F I Cole) *hld up in rr: effrt and rdn on outer wl over 2f out: sn no imp: wl hld last 2f* **40/1**

0 **9** *13* **Oke Bay**[36] 6397 2-8-12 0.. WilliamBuick 1 17
(R M Beckett) *s.i.s: a bhd: pushed along 5f out: rdn and lost tch 3f out: wl bhd and eased fnl f* **66/1**

0 **10** *¾* **Dancelectic (IRE)**[10] 7011 2-9-3 0...................................(t) TPQueally 5 21
(D R Lanigan) *s.i.s: a bhd: rdn 4f out: wl bhd last 2f: eased fnl f* **100/1**

11 *1½* **Majd Aljazeera** 2-9-3 0... MartinDwyer 11 17
(D M Simcock) *rn green: chsd ldrs tl over 2f out: sn wknd: wl bhd and eased ins fnl f* **20/1**

1m 40.2s (0.30) **Going Correction** +0.025s/f (Slow) **11** Ran SP% **119.0**
Speed ratings (Par 96): **99,97,94,92,90 87,87,83,70,69 68**
toteswinger: 1&2 £2.40, 1&3 Not won, 2&3 £1.20. CSF £7.11 TOTE £6.20: £2.40, £1.02, £2.60; EX 10.70.
Owner Mrs L M Askew **Bred** Fragrant Partnership **Trained** Headley, Surrey

FOCUS
A fair maiden.

NOTEBOOK
Laurie Grove(IRE) had been set a stiff task on his debut in the Tattersalls Timeform Million, where he finished 17th, but this represented a much easier task. Always travelling well in behind the favourite, he was switched out to challenge early in the straight and, having taken his measure, was drawing clear at the line. By Danehill Dancer out of an unraced half-sister to Sun Chariot winner Kissogram, he looks a nice prospect for next season. (op 5-1 tchd 7-2)
Kansai Spirit(IRE) looked to have been found a good opportunity to get off the mark following a good fourth at Newmarket last time. He was sent off a short price, and things looked good for his backers when Fortune was able to get to the front without too much difficulty early on. He was able to dictate things throughout and was given every chance, but on the night he simply met one too good. (op 10-11 tchd Evens)
Manahej(USA), who cost $600,000 as a yearling, is out of a half-sister to two US stakes performers. The market suggested not too much was expected on his debut, and, having shown up well to the turn into the straight, the first two left him behind. He should do better in time. (op 13-2)
Woodlark Island(IRE) improved on his debut effort at Newbury and looks to be going the right way. Another run will make him eligible for a mark. (op 33-1)
Elliptical(USA), a half-brother to winners in the US and Japan, kept on to finish a creditable fifth on his debut. His dam was a multiple winning sprinter so he clearly gets his stamina from his sire. (op 25-1)
Great Bounder(CAN) raced wide throughout and shaped a bit better than his finishing position suggests. He needs one more run for a mark. (op 33-1)
Lord Of The Dance(IRE), a half-brother to high-class Major Cadeaux, was backed in from 20-1 in the morning but the money proved misplaced. (op 13-2 tchd 8-1)

7205 FORBURY HOTEL'S APARTMENTS AND PENTHOUSE NURSERY 6f (P)
6:20 (6:23) (Class 6) (0-65,65) 2-Y-O **£2,590** (£770; £385; £192) **Stalls** Low

Form RPR

0530 **1** **Arachnophobia (IRE)**[17] 6865 2-9-4 **62**........................... PaulEddery 13 66
(Pat Eddery) *sn pushed up to chse ldr: rdn wl over 3f out: drvn and ev ch over 1f out: led 1f out: styd on gamely fnl 100yds* **5/1**[2]

065 **2** *¾* **Romantic Queen**[14] 6933 2-9-4 **62**............................... TGMcLaughlin 2 64
(E A L Dunlop) *s.i.s: hld up in tch: hdwy on inner over 2f out: ev ch ent fnl f: unable qckn u.p fnl 100yds* **11/2**[3]

0026 **3** *¾* **Celtic Rebel (IRE)**[6] 7113 2-8-13 **57**............................ HayleyTurner 3 57
(S A Callaghan) *trckd ldrs travelling wl: effrt to chal over 1f out: drvn to ld jst over 1f out: hdd ent fnl f: one pce ins fnl f* **7/2**[1]

230 **4** *1¼* **Corton Charlemagne (IRE)**[20] 6770 2-9-6 **64**............. SaleemGolam 7 60
(Rae Guest) *stdd after s: hld up in rr: hdwy over 2f out: bmpd wl over 1f out: chsd ldrs and swtchd rt ins fnl f: styd on u.p: nt rch ldrs* **12/1**

060 **5** *hd* **Sister Clement (IRE)**[94] 4692 2-9-2 **60**......................... ShaneKelly 4 55
(C R Egerton) *s.i.s: sn in tch in midfield: hmpd and dropped to rr 4f out: rdn and hdwy over 2f out: styd on fnl f: nt rch ldrs* **10/1**

000 **6** *1* **Bulella**[36] 6389 2-9-0 **58**... MickyFenton 11 50
(Garry Moss) *dwlt: towards rr: rdn and c v wd 2f out: styd on fnl f: nt rch ldrs* **66/1**

6045 **7** *½* **Courageous Nature (IRE)**[29] 6574 2-8-11 **58**...........(b) TolleyDean[(3)] 5 49
(A J McCabe) *led: rdn jst over 2f out: hdd jst over 1f out: edgd rt and wknd fnl f* **14/1**

4054 **8** *2* **Spinight (IRE)**[12] 6986 2-9-0 **65**............................. AndreaAtzeni[(7)] 8 50
(M Botti) *in tch in midfield: rdn over 3f out: drvn and kpt on same pce fr wl over 1f out* **12/1**

0360 **9** *1¾* **Lady Mulligan**[35] 6414 2-9-4 **62**.............................. FergusSweeney 6 41
(M Blanshard) *t.k.h: hld up towards rr: rdn and effrt 2f out: sn edging lft and no imp* **33/1**

650 **10** *2¼* **Tricky Trev (USA)**[31] 6531 2-9-4 **62**.............................. PaulDoe 14 35
(S Curran) *chsd ldrs: rdn over 2f out: wkng whn hung lft and bmpd rival wl over 1f out: wl btn after* **9/1**

352 **11** *2* **Chasing Amy**[70] 5431 2-9-6 **64**..................................... TPQueally 12 31
(M G Quinlan) *dwlt: a towards rr: rdn and effrt on outer over 2f out: sn struggling: wl btn over 1f out* **14/1**

6641 **12** *1¼* **Tillers Satisfied (IRE)**[33] 6489 2-8-13 **60**.................. DavidProbert[(3)] 10 23
(R Hollinshead) *in tch: rdn and struggling over 2f out: wl bhd fnl f* **16/1**

6006 **13** *28* **Spinning Belle (IRE)**[24] 6697 2-9-4 **62**........................... MichaelHills 9 —
(J W Hills) *stdd and swtchd lft after s: a bhd: lost tch over 3f out: t.o and eased fr over 1f out* **25/1**

1m 14.03s (0.33) **Going Correction** +0.025s/f (Slow) **13** Ran SP% **116.2**
Speed ratings (Par 94): **98,97,96,94,94 92,92,89,87,84 81,79,42**
toteswinger: 1&2 £1.90, 1&3 £5.10, 2&3 £3.80. CSF £31.18 CT £112.14 TOTE £7.20: £2.60, £1.80, £2.30; EX 42.10.
Owner Pat Eddery Racing (Sharpo) **Bred** Michael Staunton **Trained** Nether Winchendon, Bucks
■ Stewards' Enquiry : Paul Eddery caution: careless riding

FOCUS
A modest, pretty open nursery on paper but the form looks fairly reliable with the third the best guide.

NOTEBOOK
Arachnophobia(IRE) has tended to be slow out of the gates and that threatened to be a problem here given his draw out in stall 13, but on this occasion he got out of the stalls quickly and was able to cross over and gain a prominent early pitch. He was being shoved along rounding the turn into the straight but, to his credit, kept responding, and he just saw it out that bit stronger than the eventual runner-up. He is likely to be kept on the go on the all-weather now. (op 8-1)
Romantic Queen was taking a drop in grade and looked to hold solid claims on her handicap debut. Well drawn, she saved ground on the inside the whole way round and had every chance. (op 4-1)
Celtic Rebel(IRE) has been appearing to be finding 5f on the short side of late, and so the return to 6f promised to suit. Another who was well drawn, he had been headed and was weakening when a little chopped for room inside the last. (op 11-2)
Corton Charlemagne(IRE), whose previous best effort came over this course and distance on her debut, followed the eventual runner-up through on the inside, but had to be switched off the rail to challenge. She ran a respectable race. (op 14-1)
Sister Clement(IRE) was returning from a three-month absence and running on the all-weather for the first time on her handicap debut. She was keeping on at the finish and might be capable of a bit better. (op 8-1)
Bulella ran quite well considering that she was drawn out wide, raced keenly off the early pace and also gave up plenty of ground running widest of all. This was her best effort to date and she is not without hope.
Tricky Trev(USA) Official explanation: jockey said colt hung left in straight
Tillers Satisfied(IRE) Official explanation: jockey said filly never travelled
Spinning Belle(IRE) Official explanation: jockey said filly stumbled on leaving stalls

7206 DALE CARNEGIE (S) STKS 6f (P)
6:50 (6:51) (Class 6) 3-Y-O+ **£2,590** (£770; £385; £192) **Stalls** Low

Form RPR

1306 **1** **Bazguy**[10] 7013 3-9-3 69..(b) RyanMoore 3 75
(P D Evans) *chsd ldrs: rdn over 2f out: drvn and ev ch over 1f out: led 1f out: hld on wl u.p* **9/2**[2]

2215 **2** *hd* **Doubtful Sound (USA)**[27] 6634 4-9-0 71...........(p) KevinGhunowa[(3)] 11 75
(R A Harris) *t.k.h: hld up in tch: hdwy to chal over 1f out: sn rdn: upsides wnr whn rdr dropped whip ins fnl f: a jst hld after* **6/1**[3]

6030 **3** *2½* **Mafaheem**[27] 6634 6-9-3 70...(p) JamieSpencer 4 67+
(A B Haynes) *hld up in rr: rdn and effrt on wd outside 2f out: r.o wl fnl f: snatched 3rd on line: nt rch ldng pair* **8/1**

0414 **4** *nse* **Pegasus Dancer (FR)**[24] 6711 4-9-3 60.........................(p) ChrisCatlin 14 67
(K A Ryan) *racd keenly: chsd ldr tl rdn to ld wl over 1f out: hdd 1f out: wknd fnl 100yds* **12/1**

030 **5** *hd* **Yungaburra (IRE)**[19] 6813 4-9-3 77...............................(t) WilliamBuick 6 66+
(S Parr) *s.i.s: bhd: rdn and effrt 2f out: r.o u.p fr over 1f out: nt rch ldrs* **10/3**[1]

1060 **6** *1½* **Azygous**[7] 7092 5-9-3 62... DaneO'Neill 1 61
(J Akehurst) *t.k.h: hld up in midfield: effrt on inner and n.m.r over 1f out: kpt on same pce u.p fnl f* **40/1**

4000 **7** *shd* **Flying Bantam (IRE)**[22] 6736 7-9-3 67......................... PaulHanagan 12 61
(R A Fahey) *hld up in tch: rdn 2f out: unable qck u.p over 1f out: one pce fnl f* **20/1**

20-0 **8** *nk* **Far Gone**[31] 6543 3-8-7 65... HayleyTurner 8 50
(M L W Bell) *towards rr: rdn 2f out: sme hdwy u.p over 1f out: nvr trbld ldrs* **11/1**

0300 **9** *1¼* **Sazerac (USA)**[10] 7022 3-8-5 50....................................... BillyCray[(7)] 13 51
(P Howling) *s.i.s: sn in midfield: rdn 2f out: hung lft and no imp fr over 1f out* **66/1**

0065 **10** *¾* **Imperial Echo (USA)**[10] 7012 7-9-3 60...................(v) TGMcLaughlin 5 54
(P Howling) *s.i.s: a bhd: rdn 3f out: nvr trbld ldrs* **33/1**

0300 **11** *½* **Jebel Tara**[50] 6020 3-8-12 70.. TedDurcan 9 47
(C E Brittain) *racd in midfield: rdn and struggling wl over 1f out: bhd fr wl over 1f out* **16/1**

12 *hd* **Signora Frasi (IRE)**[68] 5514 3-8-7 74......................... FergusSweeney 7 41
(A G Newcombe) *in tch: rdn jst over 2f out: wkng whn rdr dropped whip ent fnl f* **10/1**

2500 **13** *hd* **Forced Upon Us**[64] 5610 4-8-10 60........................... AndreaAtzeni[(7)] 2 51
(P J McBride) *s.i.s: sn bustled along: a in rr* **16/1**

0560 **14** *5* **Blackmalkin (USA)**[63] 5629 4-8-7 56................................. ShaneKelly 10 25
(M Quinn) *led: rdn and hdd wl over 1f out: sn wknd* **16/1**

1m 13.53s (-0.17) **Going Correction** +0.025s/f (Slow) **14** Ran SP% **121.1**
Speed ratings (Par 101): **102,101,98,98,98 96,95,95,93,92 92,91,91,85**
toteswinger: 1&2 £3.70, 1&3 £3.10, 2&3 Not won. CSF £30.85 TOTE £6.70: £2.90, £1.80, £3.20; EX 36.30.There was no bid for the winner. Doubtful Sound was claimed by Phil Pye for £10,000. Yungaburra was subject to a friendly claim.
Owner B McCabe & K J Mercer **Bred** Usk Valley Stud **Trained** Pandy, Monmouths

FOCUS
An ordinary seller and once again it paid to be near the pace. The runner-up and fourth set the level.
Yungaburra(IRE) Official explanation: jockey said gelding missed the break
Jebel Tara Official explanation: jockey said colt had no more to give
Blackmalkin(USA) Official explanation: vet said filly bled from the nose

7207 CERISE BAR AND RESTAURANT MAIDEN FILLIES' STKS 6f (P)
7:20 (7:21) (Class 5) 2-Y-O **£3,561** (£1,059; £529; £264) **Stalls** Low

Form RPR

4432 **1** **Fen Spirit (IRE)**[24] 6696 2-9-0 77................................ JimmyFortune 7 78
(J H M Gosden) *hld up bhd ldng pair: plld out and hdwy over 1f out: rdn to ld ent fnl f: rdn out* **7/4**[1]

2 **2** *3¼* **Kind Heart**[14] 6933 2-9-0 0... J-PGuillambert 3 68
(Sir Mark Prescott) *pressed ldr: shkn up to ld over 2f out: rdn and hdd ent fnl f: sn btn* **7/4**[1]

4 **3** *4* **Celestial Dream (IRE)**[15] 6894 2-9-0 0........................ WilliamBuick 5 56
(A M Balding) *racd keenly: set fast pce tl over 2f out: styd w ldr tl rdn over 1f out: sn wknd: eased whn btn ins fnl f* **3/1**[2]

4 *4½* **Broughtons Dream** 2-9-0 0.. ChrisCatlin 4 43
(W J Musson) *in rr of main gp: outpcd 4f out: no ch w ldrs after: kpt on past btn horses fnl f* **66/1**

220 **5** *1½* **My Sweet Georgia (IRE)**[45] 6172 2-9-0 78...................... PatCosgrave 6 38
(S A Callaghan) *s.i.s: sn pushed along in rr: sme late hdwy: nvr trbld ldrs* **12/1**[3]

0 **6** *¾* **Romancingthestone**[16] 6877 2-8-11 0........................ DavidProbert[(3)] 8 36
(I A Wood) *racd off the pce in midfield: effrt 1/2-way: wknd over 1f out: no ch fnl f* **66/1**

06 **7** *2½* **Sofonisba**[9] 7051 2-9-0 0... JamieSpencer 1 29
(M L W Bell) *racd off the pce in midfield: effrt 1/2-way: rdn and wknd over 1f out: wl btn fnl f* **14/1**

8 *9* **Fine Tolerance** 2-9-0 0.. FergusSweeney 2 —
(J R Boyle) *v.s.a: a detached in last: t.o fr 4f out* **50/1**

1m 14.08s (0.38) **Going Correction** +0.025s/f (Slow) **8** Ran SP% **117.0**
Speed ratings (Par 93): **98,93,88,82,80 79,76,64**
toteswinger: 1&2 £1.30, 1&3 £1.70, 2&3 £1.90. CSF £5.06 TOTE £2.40: £1.10, £1.30, £1.20; EX 6.90.
Owner C J Murfitt **Bred** Mrs M Kehoe **Trained** Newmarket, Suffolk

FOCUS
There was a good pace on here and the form looks sound enough rated around the first two.

NOTEBOOK
Fen Spirit(IRE) got a nice lead and, once switched out to challenge approaching the final furlong, drew clear for a comfortable success. Officially rated 77, it is unlikely that she had to improve to win this, but it is possible that there could be a bit more to come from her. (op 13-8 tchd 15-8)
Kind Heart shaped with plenty of promise on her debut over course and distance a fortnight earlier, but the way she raced that day, coupled with her pedigree, suggested that she would appreciate a step up in distance. It was understandable, therefore, that her rider was keen to make it a test, but the fact that the free-going Celestial Dream took her on for the lead merely resulted in the pair setting it up for the favourite. (op 2-1 tchd 5-2 and 9-4 in a place)

Celestial Dream(IRE) was free to post and in the race itself. She simply took too much out of herself to have anything in reserve for the closing stages, and a drop back to the minimum trip should help her. (op 7-2)
Broughtons Dream, a half-sister to Izzibizzi, a two-time winner running later on this card, stayed on past a few beaten horses in the straight and is the type who should do better once handicapped. (op 50-1)
My Sweet Georgia(IRE), debuting for her new stable, was very slowly away, soon got outpaced and struggled to get involved. She has plenty to prove now. (op 9-1)
Romancingthestone Official explanation: jockey said filly ran green
Fine Tolerance's gate did not open completely, meaning that the filly had to barge her way out of the stalls. It was hardly the ideal debut experience. Official explanation: jockey said filly was very slowly away (stall jammed) (op 33-1)

7208 FORBURY HOTEL ORIENT OPEN CONDITIONS STKS 1m 2f (P)
7:50 (7:53) (Class 3) 3-Y-0+ £7,771 (£2,312; £1,155; £577) **Stalls** Low

Form RPR
5501 **1** **Yahrab (IRE)**[53] 5942 3-9-0 102.................. RyanMoore 5 113
(C E Brittain) *mde all: rdn and qcknd over 2f out: styd on wl fnl f* **11/8**[2]
-310 **2** *1* **Eddie Jock (IRE)**[34] 6440 4-9-4 108.................. TedDurcan 3 111
(Saeed Bin Suroor) *t.k.h: trckd wnr tl over 7f out and again over 2f out: rdn and effrt over 1f out: swtchd rt 1f out: kpt on same pce fnl f* **5/6**[1]
0000 **3** *9* **Coeur De Lionne (IRE)**[89] 4844 4-9-4 97.................. JimmyFortune 4 93
(E A L Dunlop) *stdd s: hld up in last: wnt 3rd over 2f out: shkn up and no rspnse over 1f out* **12/1**[3]
3106 **4** *11* **Mafeking (UAE)**[188] 1766 4-9-4 88.................. AndrewElliott 1 71
(M R Hoad) *fly-jmpd s: t.k.h: in tch: chsd wnr over 7f out tl over 2f out: wknd u.p 2f out* **25/1**

2m 6.59s (-2.01) **Going Correction** +0.025s/f (Slow)
WFA 3 from 4yo+ 4lb 4 Ran SP% **108.2**
Speed ratings (Par 107): **109,108,101,92**
CSF £2.86 TOTE £2.40; EX 2.70.
Owner Saif Ali **Bred** Swettenham Stud **Trained** Newmarket, Suffolk

FOCUS
A small field for this conditions event and it was no surprise that it was something of a tactical affair. The winner had the run of the race and the runner-up was a little disappointing.

NOTEBOOK
Yahrab(IRE) had a bit to find with Eddie Jock at the weights, but he was proven over the distance and, allowed the run of the race out in front, was able to dictate a pace to suit himself. While the favourite failed to settle, he was always doing things easily in the lead, and, once kicked on entering the straight, he was never going to be dragged back. One would imagine that Dubai will be on his agenda again in the new year. (op 6-4)
Eddie Jock(IRE), who apparently lost his action when only seventh in the Group 3 Joel Stakes last time out, won on his previous visit here in September. Trying this longer trip for the first time, he did not help his chances of seeing it out by racing keenly in behind the eventual winner. A stronger-run race back over 1m will suit him better. (op Evens)
Coeur De Lionne(IRE) showed good form on the Polytrack last autumn but has been right out of form in two starts on turf this term. Returning from a three-month break, he showed a bit more here, and might be of more interest when he returns to Kempton, where he has recorded three wins. Official explanation: jockey said gelding lost its action (op 7-1)
Mafeking(UAE) faced a tough task in this company. He dropped out of things rounding the turn into the straight but should come on for this first outing since May. (op 20-1)

7209 DANIEL GALMICHE IN EDEN MAIDEN STKS (DIV II) 1m (P)
8:20 (8:22) (Class 5) 2-Y-0 £3,238 (£963; £481; £240) **Stalls** Centre

Form RPR
1 **Emirates Champion** 2-9-3 0.................. TedDurcan 1 77
(Saeed Bin Suroor) *s.i.s: sn chsng ldrs: wnt 2nd 2f out: led wl over 1f out: edgd rt ent fnl f: styd on wl: in command fnl 75yds* **9/2**[2]
0 **2** *2 1/2* **Cosimo**[9] 7051 2-9-3 0.................. RyanMoore 2 72
(Sir Michael Stoute) *chsd ldrs: pushed along 4f out: rdn and hdwy on inner wl over 1f out: chsd wnr 1f out: no imp and wl hld fnl 75yds* **14/1**[3]
3 *hd* **Invisible Man** 2-9-3 0.................. JimmyFortune 8 71
(J H M Gosden) *s.i.s: hld up in midfield: c wd and rdn wl over 1f out: no hdwy tl styd on ins fnl f: wnt 3rd wl ins fnl f: nvr trbld wnr* **1/3**[1]
4 *2* **Kimberley Downs (USA)** 2-9-3 0.................. GregFairley 6 67
(M Johnston) *pushed along and dropped to rr over 5f out: hdwy ins fnl f: r.o wl fnl 100yds: wnt 4th nr fin* **14/1**[3]
00 **5** *nk* **Lava Steps (USA)**[28] 6604 2-9-3 0.................. JamieSpencer 3 66
(P F I Cole) *led: rdn over 2f out: edgd rt and hdd wl over 1f out: wknd ins fnl f* **14/1**[3]
0 **6** *1/2* **Kattar**[76] 5246 2-9-3 0.................. MartinDwyer 7 65
(D M Simcock) *stdd after s: hld up in rr: hdwy and hung lft over 1f out: kpt on fnl f: nvr trbld ldrs* **14/1**[3]
0 **7** *1 3/4* **Bourn Fair**[16] 6884 2-8-12 0.................. DaneO'Neill 10 56
(P J McBride) *bhd: rdn and effrt on outer 2f out: sn no imp* **66/1**
0 **8** *6* **Green Endeavour (CAN)**[12] 6977 2-9-3 0.................. ShaneKelly 5 48
(Mrs A J Perrett) *s.i.s: hld up in midfield: rdn 3f out: wknd over 2f out: wl bhd fnl f* **33/1**
00 **9** *1 1/4* **Mountain Forest (GER)**[25] 6674 2-9-3 0.................. TravisBlock 4 45
(H Morrison) *prom: drvn over 2f out: sn struggling: wl bhd fnl f* **66/1**
050 **10** *3 1/2* **Highway Magic (IRE)**[20] 6777 2-9-3 70.................. DarrenWilliams 9 37
(A P Jarvis) *sn chsng ldr tl rdn 2f out: sn wknd: wl bhd fnl f* **33/1**

1m 41.52s (1.62) **Going Correction** +0.025s/f (Slow) 10 Ran SP% **128.7**
Speed ratings (Par 96): **92,89,89,87,87 86,84,78,77,74**
toteswinger: 1&2 £3.70, 1&3 £1.30, 2&3 Not won. CSF £69.42 TOTE £7.80: £1.50, £4.50, £1.02; EX 23.70.
Owner Godolphin **Bred** Gainsborough Stud Management Ltd **Trained** Newmarket, Suffolk

FOCUS
The slower of the two divisions by 1.32sec.

NOTEBOOK
Emirates Champion was always well placed on the inner and enjoyed the perfect trip. He ran around a bit inside the final furlong, simply as a result of greenness, but won very nicely, and this half-brother to 2000 Guineas runner-up Lend A Hand looks very much the type to progress from two to three. (op 7-2 tchd 11-2)
Cosimo, who missed the break and was always behind on his debut at Yarmouth, had clearly learnt a thing or two from that as he was smartly enough away this time. Niggled along from some way out, he kept on quite well, and the chances are he'll come into his own in handicaps next year.
Invisible Man was backed as though defeat was out of the question on his debut. A half-brother to five winners, he was drawn towards the outer and his rider appeared happy to tuck in off the pace, despite the current bias towards those racing more prominently. Switched entering the straight, he was a bit one-paced, although he was keeping on nicely at the finish. Had it not been for the market move this could have been described as a promising enough debut effort, but in the circumstances it was disappointing. (op 4-6)
Kimberley Downs(USA) was under the pump much of the way. Last turning into the straight, he was putting in his best work at the finish, and this half-brother to Free House, a top-class multiple Grade 1 dirt winner, looks sure to benefit considerably from the outing.
Lava Steps(USA), in front for much of the way, is now eligible for a mark, and he will have better chances in that sphere. (tchd 16-1)
Kattar looks another who will do better once eligible for handicaps, probably over further. (op 16-1)

7210 BROOKER BIRD MARKETING FILLIES' H'CAP 1m (P)
8:50 (8:52) (Class 4) (0-85,85) 3-Y-0+ £5,180 (£1,541; £770; £384) **Stalls** Centre

Form RPR
3063 **1** **Miss Brown To You (IRE)**[15] 6896 3-8-5 72.................. HayleyTurner 2 79
(M L W Bell) *mde all: set stdy gallop: rdn and qcknd wl over 1f out: styd on wl fnl f* **9/2**[2]
5301 **2** *1 1/4* **Spring Goddess (IRE)**[13] 6950 7-9-0 79.................. DaneO'Neill 5 83
(A P Jarvis) *trckd wnr: rdn and effrt over 1f out: kpt on same pce u.p fnl f* **13/2**[3]
200 **3** *1* **Naughty Frida (IRE)**[33] 6471 3-8-6 80.................. AndreaAtzeni(7) 3 82
(M Botti) *s.i.s: hld up in last pl: rdn and effrt wl over 1f out: drvn ent fnl f* **9/1**
-311 **4** *1 1/2* **Izzibizzi**[12] 6981 3-9-2 83.................. ChrisCatlin 4 81
(E A L Dunlop) *hld up in 3rd: shkn up and effrt over 1f out: rdn 1f out: unable qckn and one pce fnl f* **15/8**[1]
5R00 **R** **Lisathedaddy**[15] 6904 6-8-13 78.................. (p) RyanMoore 1 —
(B G Powell) *ref to r: tk no part* **16/1**

1m 42.49s (2.59) **Going Correction** +0.025s/f (Slow)
WFA 3 from 4yo+ 2lb 5 Ran SP% **82.2**
Speed ratings (Par 102): **88,86,85,84,—**
toteswinger: 1&2 £7.70. CSF £16.29 TOTE £4.60: £2.70, £3.10; EX 14.20.
Owner W J Gredley **Bred** P E Banahan **Trained** Newmarket, Suffolk

FOCUS
Likely front-runner Debonnaire ducked under the stalls and had to withdrawn (5/2, deduct 25p in the £ under R4), while Lisathedaddy refused to race, which left only four. The form makes sense at face value rated around the placed horses.

7211 MOLTON BROWN H'CAP 1m 2f (P)
9:20 (9:20) (Class 4) (0-80,78) 3-Y-0 £5,180 (£1,541; £770; £384) **Stalls** Low

Form RPR
2404 **1** **Rio Guru (IRE)**[15] 6904 3-9-3 77.................. EdwardCreighton 5 83
(M R Channon) *hld up in last pair: rdn and effrt on outer wl over 1f out: edgd lft but r.o wl fnl f to ld towards fin* **14/1**
6212 **2** *1/2* **Mick's Dancer**[15] 6905 3-8-11 71.................. MartinDwyer 6 76
(W R Muir) *chsd ldr: rdn to ld over 1f out: hdd and no ex towards fin* **4/1**[2]
3506 **3** *1 1/2* **Totally Focussed (IRE)**[33] 6467 3-9-4 78.................. JamieSpencer 3 80+
(S Dow) *stdd s: hld up in last pair: hdwy to chse ldrs 2f out: nt clr run and swtchd rt jst over 1f out: drvn ins fnl f: kpt on same pce fnl 100yds* **11/2**[3]
0-21 **4** *1/2* **Distinctive Image (USA)**[40] 6280 3-9-3 77.................. GrahamGibbons 7 78
(R Hollinshead) *chsd ldrs: rdn over 2f out: drvn over 1f out: kpt on same pce fnl f* **10/11**[1]
2326 **5** *shd* **Summer Winds**[17] 6866 3-9-2 76.................. ShaneKelly 1 77
(T G Mills) *led: rdn over 2f out: hdd over 1f out: no ex ins fnl f* **14/1**
0422 **6** *2 1/2* **Randama Bay (IRE)**[171] 2246 3-8-13 73.................. RyanMoore 2 69
(I A Wood) *trckd ldrs: rdn 3f out: drvn 2f out: wknd ent fnl f* **16/1**
3160 **7** *1 3/4* **Lady Sorcerer**[14] 6934 3-8-8 68.................. ChrisCatlin 4 60
(A P Jarvis) *t.k.h: hld up wl in tch: rdn and dropped to last 3f out: no imp last 2f* **22/1**

2m 8.98s (0.38) **Going Correction** +0.025s/f (Slow) 7 Ran SP% **111.3**
Speed ratings (Par 104): **99,98,97,97,96 94,93**
toteswinger: 1&2 £5.20, 1&3 £8.70, 2&3 £26.20. CSF £65.06 TOTE £11.60: £5.70, £2.20; EX 75.10 Place 6 £11.62, Place 5 £9.48 .
Owner Norman Court Stud **Bred** Des Vere Hunt Farm Co Ltd & Jack Moclair **Trained** West Ilsley, Berks

FOCUS
The early gallop was not that strong here, but they wound things up from some way out and the winner came from off the pace. The form is not rated that positively although the placed horses ran close to recent form.
T/Plt: £11.10 to a £1 stake. Pool: £82,126.84. 5,358.31 winning tickets. T/Qpdt: £4.70 to a £1 stake. Pool: £5,617.62. 870.31 winning tickets. SP

7095 LINGFIELD (L-H)
Thursday, November 6

OFFICIAL GOING: Standard
Wind: Almost nil Weather: Dank

7212 BET AT LADBROKES.COM CLAIMING STKS 6f (P)
1:20 (1:20) (Class 6) 2-Y-0 £2,729 (£806; £403) **Stalls** Low

Form RPR
2100 **1** **Rebecca De Winter**[110] 4190 2-8-8 88 ow2.................. RichardHughes 7 64+
(R Hannon) *trckd ldr: poised to chal gng easily 2f out: nudged into ld ins fnl f: cosily* **8/13**[1]
5525 **2** *1 1/4* **Readily**[108] 4243 2-8-4 61.................. WilliamBuick 6 57
(J G Portman) *led: rdn over 2f out: kpt on wl enough u.p but hdd and readily outpcd ins fnl f* **10/1**[3]
6040 **3** *1 1/2* **Turn To Dreams**[8] 7065 2-7-11 50.................. AndreaAtzeni(7) 9 52
(P D Evans) *racd wd in midfield: urged along fr 1/2-way: prog over 1f out: kpt on to take 3rd ins fnl f* **25/1**
0 **4** *hd* **Old Sarum (IRE)**[21] 6764 2-8-8 0.................. MarcHalford(3) 2 58
(D R C Elsworth) *stdd s: t.k.h and hld up in tch: effrt 2f out: disp 3rd fnl f: one pce* **25/1**
0100 **5** *1* **Tartan Turban (IRE)**[63] 5647 2-8-6 68.................. RichardSmith 5 50
(R Hannon) *dwlt: mostly in last pair: effrt on inner over 1f out: n.m.r fnl f: kpt on* **4/1**[2]
0445 **6** *hd* **Officer Mor (USA)**[68] 5488 2-9-2 65.................. DarrenWilliams 8 60
(K R Burke) *dwlt and hmpd s: sn in tch: nt qckn 2f out: hanging over 1f out: kpt on again last 100yds* **11/1**
0000 **7** *shd* **Fleur De'Lion (IRE)**[14] 6933 2-8-4 50.................. MartinDwyer 11 48
(S Kirk) *mostly in last pair: rdn over 2f out: detached in last over 1f out: styd on fnl f: nrst fin* **33/1**
5540 **8** *1/2* **Multi Tasker**[22] 6732 2-8-9 61.................. (b[1]) PaulFitzsimons 4 51
(Miss J R Tooth) *t.k.h: hld up bhd ldrs: rdn and fnd nthing 2f out: fdd fnl f* **22/1**
5030 **9** *1 1/4* **Claphands**[15] 6906 2-7-12 55.................. DavidProbert(3) 3 39
(M A Allen) *trckd ldr: stl cl up on inner 2f out: wknd fnl f* **16/1**

1m 12.02s (0.12) **Going Correction** -0.075s/f (Stan) 9 Ran SP% **120.2**
Speed ratings (Par 94): **96,94,92,92,90 90,90,89,88**
toteswinger: 1&2 £3.80, 1&3 £9.50, 2&3 £12.10. CSF £8.03 TOTE £2.00: £1.10, £2.40, £6.80; EX 11.50 Trifecta £82.40 Part won. Pool: £111.43 - 0.41 winning units..The winner was claimed by A. D. W. Pinder for £10,000.

Owner R Hannon **Bred** B W Hills & Cavendish Investing Ltd **Trained** East Everleigh, Wilts

FOCUS

An ordinary claimer weakened further by the three non-runners, two of whom would have been towards the head of the market. The winner did not have to run anywhere near previous form to score comfortably, and the third is the best guide to the level.

NOTEBOOK

Rebecca De Winter hadn't been seen since finishing out the back in the Weatherbys Super Sprint in July and she wasn't disgraced in the Queen Mary before that. She had upwards of 18lb in hand of these rivals (allowing for the 2lb overweight) on these terms and she had run well here on her debut, so the surface was never going to be a problem. Ridden with plenty of confidence on the shoulder of the leader, she never had to be put under any great pressure and was only asked to do just enough. She was subsequently claimed, but she may not be the easiest to place from now on. (op 4-7 tchd 4-6)

Readily, making her sand debut after four months off, tried to make all the running but although she kept on well enough, she found the winner much too classy. This appeared to be a decent effort at the weights, but it's probably best not to take the form at face value. (op 11-1 tchd 12-1)

Turn To Dreams, who had a mountain to climb on these terms, was off the bridle a fair way out but she plugged on under pressure and wasn't disgraced. (op 33-1)

Old Sarum(IRE), beaten a long way after a slow start on his Nottingham debut, was another being niggled a fair way out before staying on up the home straight. Despite the extra furlong, this still looked an inadequate test and he may have a bit more to offer over further once handicapped.

Tartan Turban(IRE), twice well beaten since winning a Windsor maiden in July, was on sand for the first time and did attract some market support, but he could only plug on at one pace in the straight and never really looked like getting involved. (op 5-1 tchd 11-2)

Officer Mor(USA), returning from a short break and another trying sand for the first time, can be given a little extra credit as he was given quite a hefty bump by the eventual winner exiting the stalls and didn't enjoy the clearest of runs in the home straight. (op 9-1 tchd 8-1 and 12-1)

7213 PLAY POKER AT LADBROKES.COM MAIDEN STKS 5f (P)

1:50 (1:50) (Class 5) 3-Y-O+ **£3,238** (£963; £481; £240) **Stalls High**

Form RPR

0000 **1** **Atheer Dubai (IRE)**[38] 6336 3-9-3 66 JamieSpencer 6 73
(E F Vaughan) mde all: charted wd crse thrght: hrd pressed fnl f: hld on **13/2**

0034 **2** *nk* **Madame Hoi (IRE)**[8] 7066 3-8-12 77 TonyCulhane 9 67
(M R Channon) mostly chsd wnr: urged along to chal fnl f: nt qckn and a hld **7/2**[2]

2006 **3** *¾* **North South Divide (IRE)**[30] 6556 4-9-3 70 LPKeniry 2 69
(Peter Grayson) t.k.h early: cl up: effrt over 1f out: pressed ldrs fnl f: kpt on **5/1**[3]

3 **4** *¾* **Maid Of Ailsa (USA)**[248] 777 3-8-12 0 LiamJones 8 61
(W J Haggas) hld up in tch: effrt over 1f out: nt qckn and hld fnl f **6/5**[1]

-420 **5** *2 ¾* **East Coast Girl (IRE)**[25] 6681 3-8-12 53 (b) TGMcLaughlin 3 51
(S W Hall) dwlt: t.k.h and hld up in tch: effrt and sme prog over 1f out: wknd tamely fnl f **33/1**

00 **6** *1 ¾* **This Ones For Pat (USA)**[8] 7074 3-9-0 0 TolleyDean[(3)] 4 50+
(S Parr) heavily restrained after 50yds: sn detached in last where t.k.h and green: nvr nr ldrs: styd on fnl f **12/1**

0 **7** *2 ¾* **Rindless**[27] 6633 3-8-9 0 DavidProbert[(3)] 1 35
(J F Panvert) prom on inner tl wknd 2f out **25/1**

30 **8** *2 ½* **Rightcar Dominic**[64] 5608 3-9-3 0 DaneO'Neill 5 31
(Peter Grayson) a in rr: last and struggling fr 1/2-way **33/1**

9 *6* **In With A Shout** 3-8-12 0 TPQueally 10 5
(J G Given) dwlt: racd wd and nvr on terms: wknd 2f out: t.o **16/1**

58.81 secs (0.01) **Going Correction** -0.075s/f (Stan) **9 Ran SP% 121.0**

Speed ratings (Par 103): **96,95,94,93,88 85,81,77,67**

toteswinger: 1&2 £6.00, 1&3 £6.10, 2&3 £4.20. CSF £30.52 TOTE £7.10: £1.60, £1.50, £1.90; EX 28.00 Trifecta £94.80 Pool: £270.49 - 2.11 winning units..

Owner Mohammed Rashid **Bred** Darley **Trained** Newmarket, Suffolk

FOCUS

A very moderate older-horse maiden, dominated by those that raced up with the pace from the start, and it was noticeable that the front pair raced wide throughout including in the home straight. The winner is rated to last year's all-weather form.

This Ones For Pat(USA) Official explanation: jockey said gelding suffered interference early on

7214 BET AT LADBROKES ON 0800 777 888 NOVICE STKS 7f (P)

2:20 (2:22) (Class 4) 2-Y-O **£3,885** (£1,156; £577; £288) **Stalls Low**

Form RPR

1 **1** **Saint Arch (CAN)**[30] 6553 2-9-5 90 JoeFanning 3 91
(M Johnston) trckd ldr: shkn up to ld over 1f out: idled and looked vulnerable whn pressed last 100yds: fnd ex and hld on gamely **4/7**[1]

0 **2** *hd* **Prayer Boat (IRE)**[25] 6688 2-8-12 0 JamieSpencer 4 84
(John Joseph Murphy, Ire) hld up in last: drvn and prog on outer over 1f out: r.o to press wnr last 100yds and looked likely wnr: jst foiled cl home **9/1**

64 **3** *1 ¾* **Ajjaadd (USA)**[7] 7098 2-8-12 0 TedDurcan 5 79
(Saeed Bin Suroor) hld up in 3rd: effrt 2f out: hanging and nt qckn over 1f out: wnt 2nd briefly ins fnl f: wl hld whn n.m.r nr fin **3/1**[2]

4416 **4** *1* **Watergate (IRE)**[95] 4666 2-9-2 90 J-PGuillambert 2 81
(Sir Mark Prescott) led: stdy pce to 4f out: rdn over 2f out: hdd and one pce over 1f out **6/1**[3]

5 *4* **On The Edge (IRE)**[53] 5947 2-8-12 0 TPQueally 1 67
(John Joseph Murphy, Ire) dwlt: in tch tl wknd 2f out **33/1**

1m 24.11s (-0.69) **Going Correction** -0.075s/f (Stan) **5 Ran SP% 115.9**

Speed ratings (Par 98): **100,99,97,96,92**

CSF £7.44 TOTE £1.50: £1.10, £2.60; EX 5.50.

Owner Sheikh Hamdan Bin Mohammed Al Maktoum **Bred** Ascot Thoroughbreds **Trained** Middleham Moor, N Yorks

■ Stewards' Enquiry : Jamie Spencer one-day ban: careless riding (Nov 20)

FOCUS

A fair little novice event, made more interesting by the two Irish challengers. The winner stepped up for his debut and the third and fourth help set the level.

NOTEBOOK

Saint Arch(CAN) probably put up a better performance than the winning margin would suggest. Firstly, he had to work to get the better of the early leader Watergate, then once in front had to find more in order to just hold off the strong late burst of the runner-up. He looks a typically tough Johnston inmate and it's likely that he can go on to even better things. (op 4-6, tchd 4-5 in a place)

Prayer Boat(IRE), who has faced some very stiff tasks in four previous outings in his homeland, was switched off out the back by Spencer before being brought wide with his effort off the final bend. He appeared likely to win entering the last furlong, but was up against a very game rival who would simply not be denied. (op 12-1 tchd 14-1)

Ajjaadd(USA), the only one of these to have raced on sand before when a beaten favourite in a course-and-distance maiden the previous week, had every chance but looked held when running out of room between the front pair near the line. He will probably need to drop back into maiden company if he is to win a race. (tchd 4-1)

Watergate(IRE), off for three months since a disappointing favourite on his nursery debut, tried to make all the running and, although this was better than at Newbury, he was still rather easily picked off. He may have just needed it. (op 11-2 tchd 13-2)

On The Edge(IRE), a stable-companion of the runner-up who has also been highly tried in Ireland, was rather locked away in a pocket on the inside turning for home, but the way he was left behind late on suggests it had little effect on his chance. (tchd 40-1)

7215 PLAY BINGO AT LADBROKES.COM H'CAP 7f (P)

2:50 (2:51) (Class 3) (0-90,90) 3-Y-O+ **£9,714** (£2,890; £1,444; £721) **Stalls Low**

Form RPR

5400 **1** **Markab**[15] 6911 5-9-4 90 PatCosgrave 7 101
(K A Morgan) led 1f: trckd ldr: led again wl over 1f out and drvn at least 2l clr: styd on wl **10/1**

2334 **2** *1 ¼* **Dingaan (IRE)**[70] 5424 5-8-10 85 DavidProbert[(3)] 4 93
(A M Balding) trckd ldrs: gng strly 2f out: asked for effrt over 1f out and ref to deliver: styd on to take 2nd ins fnl f: no ch of catching wnr **8/1**

0410 **3** *nk* **My Gacho (IRE)**[9] 7047 6-8-12 84 (b) J-PGuillambert 12 91+
(M Johnston) t.k.h early: hld up towards rr: rdn over 1f out: r.o wl fnl f to take 3rd: nrst fin **12/1**

5230 **4** *1 ¼* **Dichoh**[198] 1545 5-8-9 81 PhilipRobinson 3 84
(M A Jarvis) trckd ldrs on inner: effrt 2f out: kpt on same pce fnl f **10/1**

5200 **5** *hd* **Lodi (IRE)**[15] 6902 3-8-6 82 (t) TolleyDean[(3)] 9 85
(J Akehurst) hld up in last trio: rdn wl over 1f out: styd on wl fnl f: nrst fin **16/1**

0006 **6** *hd* **Hinton Admiral**[15] 6911 4-8-13 85 PaulHanagan 5 87
(R A Fahey) t.k.h early: hld up in midfield: urged along wl over 2f out: no prog tl styd on ins fnl f **4/1**[1]

5520 **7** *nk* **Basra (IRE)**[54] 5910 5-8-12 84 TravisBlock 6 86
(Miss Jo Crowley) trckd ldrs on outer: c wd bnd 2f out: drvn and kpt on same pce: nvr able to chal **22/1**

0621 **8** *¾* **Gallantry**[7] 7101 6-9-3 89 6ex TGMcLaughlin 8 92+
(P Howling) hld up in last trio: trapped behnd rivals fr over 1f out and no ch to make any prog **11/2**[3]

0200 **9** *hd* **Halsion Chancer**[29] 6576 4-8-12 84 SteveDrowne 11 83
(J R Best) t.k.h early: led after 1f to wl over 1f out: wknd fnl f **10/1**

0100 **10** *nk* **Buxton**[15] 6900 4-8-9 81 (t) RobertHavlin 1 79
(R Ingram) dwlt: hld up towards rr on inner: stl gng wl enough 2f out: pushed along and no real prog after: nvr nr ldrs **20/1**

0640 **11** *nk* **Little Edward**[25] 6669 10-9-3 89 GeorgeBaker 14 86
(R J Hodges) t.k.h early: hld up in rr and racd wdst of all: effrt over 2f out: plugged on fnl f but n.d **16/1**

102 **12** *1 ¼* **Victoria Reel**[29] 6576 3-8-12 85 RichardHughes 13 79
(R Hannon) stdd s: hld up in last trio: effrt on inner over 1f out: sn no prog **5/1**[2]

3200 **13** *1 ¾* **Salient**[15] 6911 4-8-10 82 PaulDoe 10 71
(M J Attwater) pressed ldng pair tl wknd rapidly over 1f out **14/1**

1m 22.59s (-2.21) **Going Correction** -0.075s/f (Stan) course record

WFA 3 from 4yo+ 1lb **13 Ran SP% 125.7**

Speed ratings (Par 107): **109,107,107,105,105 105,105,104,103,103 103,101,99**

toteswinger: 1&2 £19.70, 1&3 £39.20, 2&3 £19.90. CSF £92.44 CT £1027.76 TOTE £18.60: £6.50, £2.50, £5.70; EX 116.40 TRIFECTA Not won..

Owner Tight Lines Partnership **Bred** Shadwell Estate Company Limited **Trained** Little Marcle, H'fords

FOCUS

A decent and competitive handicap and another race where it paid to be handy. The pace set by Halsion Chancer was a decent one, but rather typically for a race like this at this venue, a few left it too late while a couple of others didn't get the clearest of runs. The winning time was just 0.4 seconds outside the course record and the form looks sound rated around the first three.

NOTEBOOK

Markab, well beaten on his return to sand last time, broke well enough but was happy to take a lead from the pacemaker before battling his way back to the front off the home bend. He saw his race out well from there and this was a decent effort off a 4lb higher mark than for his last win. Connections are eyeing a possible trip to Dubai. Official explanation: trainer said, regarding apparent improvement in form, gelding was able to adopt his usual front-running tactics which he had been unable to do from a wide draw last time (op 8-1 tchd 11-1)

Dingaan(IRE), usually there or thereabouts lately but without a win since June of last year, was always in touch but he looked very awkward when asked to go after the winner in the home straight and perhaps his lengthy losing run is easier to explain after this. (op 13-2)

My Gacho(IRE) ◆, who had excuses for his dire effort at Southwell last time, ran much better here and he was finishing in good style from off the pace. He seems equally happy on Polytrack and Fibresand, so could be in for a good winter. (op 16-1)

Dichoh, returning from seven months off, ran well until tiring in the latter stages and should come on for this. (op 8-1 tchd 15-2)

Lodi(IRE), not at his best in his last couple of starts, was another doing his best work late and this was better. Official explanation: jockey said gelding was denied a clear run (op 25-1)

Hinton Admiral, a dual winner in Listed company here in his younger days, was down to a mark 20lb lower than when returning from a lengthy layoff in the spring and he had been hinting at a return to form in his last couple of starts. Very well backed earlier in the day, he seemed to have every chance with few excuses, but he shouldn't be given up on just yet. Official explanation: jockey said gelding hung left (op 9-2 tchd 5-1)

Gallantry, carrying a 6lb penalty for his victory over course and distance seven days earlier when everything fell right for him, didn't find things panning out so well this time and he should be given another chance. (op 13-2 tchd 5-1)

Victoria Reel, off the same mark as when making a very encouraging sand debut at Kempton earlier this month, was disappointing but she was given a lot to do and may not have been helped by trying to make her effort tight against the inside rail. (op 11-2 tchd 6-1)

7216 BETTER PRICES, BIGGER WINS AT LADBROKES.COM H'CAP 2m (P)

3:20 (3:23) (Class 5) (0-70,69) 3-Y-O+ **£3,238** (£963; £481; £240) **Stalls Low**

Form RPR

0325 **1** **Irish Ballad**[22] 6740 6-8-11 49 NickyMackay 10 57
(S Dow) trckd ldrs: prog to ld jst over 2f out: sn hrd pressed: duelled w runner-up fr over 1f out: jst prevailed **12/1**

1603 **2** *nse* **Mohawk Star (IRE)**[13] 6957 7-9-9 66 (v) FrederikTylicki[(5)] 14 74
(I A Wood) hld up in midfield: prog on outer 3f out: rdn to chal 2f out: w wnr after: jst pipped **7/1**[2]

111 **3** *2 ½* **Rutba**[15] 6897 3-9-4 65 (v) MartinDwyer 8 70
(M P Tregoning) led after 2f and maintained stdy gallop: hdd and outpcd jst over 2f out: tried to rally over 1f out: kpt on same pce **3/1**[1]

003 **4** *½* **L'Homme De Nuit (GER)**[127] 3614 4-9-8 60 GeorgeBaker 3 64
(G L Moore) dwlt: hld up in last trio: stl there 3f out: prog on wd outside after: styd on wl fnl f: no ch of rching ldrs **10/1**

6-34 **5** *hd* **Tender Falcon**[8] 7064 8-9-12 64 HayleyTurner 4 68
(R J Hodges) hld up towards rr on inner: effrt but nt qckn over 2f out: styd on fr over 1f out: nt pce to chal **11/1**

0110 **6** ¾ **Highland Homestead**[16] 6882 3-8-11 **65**................. AndreaAtzeni(7) 12 68
(M R Hoad) *stdd s: hld up wl in rr: sme prog on outer over 3f out: chsng ldrs over 2f out: no real imp after* **14/1**
5420 **7** 1 ½ **Spiritonthemount (USA)**[15] 6897 3-9-8 **69**....................(b) ChrisCatlin 11 70
(P W Hiatt) *cl up: rdn 4f out: grad outpcd fr over 2f out* **12/1**
0000 **8** *nk* **Finished Article (IRE)**[8] 7071 11-8-6 **47** oh2.........(t) KevinGhunowa(3) 5 48
(Mrs D Thomas) *hld up in midfield: rdn 3f out: no real prog* **66/1**
5000 **9** *nk* **Restart (IRE)**[19] 6824 7-8-10 **48**................................(p) DNolan 13 48
(Lucinda Featherstone) *trckd ldr after 2f tl over 2f out: steadily fdd* **33/1**
0522 **10** *hd* **Forget It**[15] 6897 3-9-3 **64**.. RichardHughes 7 64
(R Hannon) *plld hrd: reluctant ldr 2f: styd cl up: nt qckn wl over 1f out: lost pl fnl f* **3/1**[1]
033 **11** 1 ¾ **Extreme Pleasure (IRE)**[59] 5750 3-9-4 **65**......................... PaulDoe 2 63
(W J Knight) *nvr beyond midfield: lost pl and struggling 4f out: n.d fnl 2f* **8/1**[3]
0006 **12** 3 ¾ **Vanishing Dancer (SWI)**[24] 6708 11-8-9 **47** oh2(bt) FrankieMcDonald 9 41
(Mrs D Thomas) *a wl in rr: struggling over 3f out* **66/1**
000- **13** ½ **Debord (FR)**[210] 5924 5-9-0 **52**....................................... AmirQuinn 6 45
(Jamie Poulton) *nvr beyond midfield: rdn 5f out: sn lost pl and struggling* **66/1**
0060 **14** *nk* **Our Glenard**[58] 5787 9-8-9 **47** oh2.............................. RichardThomas 1 40
(J E Long) *hld up in last trio: outpcd fr 3f out* **66/1**

3m 25.59s (-0.11) **Going Correction** -0.075s/f (Stan)
WFA 3 from 4yo+ 9lb **14** Ran SP% **122.0**
Speed ratings (Par 103): **97,96,95,95,95 95,94,94,93,93 92,91,90,90**
toteswinger: 1&2 £12.80, 1&3 £10.40, 2&3 £6.60. CSF £93.64 CT £321.60 TOTE £14.60: £3.20, £2.20, £2.00; EX 100.30 Trifecta £166.20 Part won. Pool: £224.71 - 0.10 winning tickets..
Owner Chua, White, Moore & Jurd **Bred** The Kingwood Partnership **Trained** Epsom, Surrey

FOCUS
A modest staying handicap and, with the early pace pedestrian, nothing like the test of stamina that it might have been. The tempo didn't increase until past halfway, but the race did at least provide a thrilling finish. The form makes sense although perhaps is not the soundest.

7217 PLAY CASINO AT LADBROKES.COM H'CAP 1m 2f (P)
3:50 (3:51) (Class 6) (0-60,60) 3-Y-0+ **£2,729** (£806; £403) **Stalls** Low

Form RPR
00-3 **1** **Saucy**[15] 6913 7-8-10 **50**.. RichardKingscote 11 60
(Tom Dascombe) *trckd ldrs: effrt 2f out: led and hung lft over 1f out: styd on wl* **8/1**
0260 **2** 1 **Torrens (IRE)**[19] 6825 6-9-4 **58**................................(t) TGMcLaughlin 4 66
(P D Evans) *trckd ldrs: effrt 2f out: drvn and r.o fnl f to take 2nd last 75yds* **6/1**[2]
345 **3** ¾ **Compton Falcon**[35] 6421 4-9-2 **56**...........................(v[1]) RichardHughes 7 63
(G A Butler) *hld up towards rr: prog to trck ldrs 2f out: effrt but hanging and nt qckn over 1f out: styd on to chse wnr ins fnl f: one pce and lost 2nd last 75yds* **10/3**[1]
1320 **4** ¾ **Tabulate**[50] 6019 5-9-4 **58**.. JimmyQuinn 5 64+
(P Howling) *hld up towards rr: effrt whn nt clr run wl over 1f out: renewed effrt and styd on wl fnl f* **7/1**[3]
1666 **5** *nse* **Split The Wind (USA)**[20] 6768 4-8-11 **51**................. EdwardCreighton 2 56
(Miss Sheena West) *led: rdn over 2f out: hdd over 1f out: outpcd* **20/1**
1500 **6** ¾ **Barathea Dreams (IRE)**[36] 6396 7-9-3 **57**........................ LPKeniry 13 61
(J S Moore) *hld up wl in rr and racd wd: rdn 2f out: styd on wl fnl f: nrst fin* **16/1**
-600 **7** *nk* **Yab Adee**[74] 5321 4-8-11 **58**.. KatiaScallan(7) 14 61+
(M P Tregoning) *s.s: hld up in last: shuffled along fr 2f out: reminder fnl f: fin wl* **16/1**
0040 **8** *nk* **Tenement (IRE)**[35] 6421 4-8-11 **51** ow1............................ AmirQuinn 6 53
(Jamie Poulton) *hld up wl in rr: effrt over 2f out: kpt on fnl f: no ch* **25/1**
413- **9** ½ **Majehar**[361] 6780 6-9-6 **60**.. DaneO'Neill 8 61
(A G Newcombe) *hld up wl in rr: stl gng strly 2f out: nudged along and styd on takingly fnl f: nvr nrr* **14/1**
4044 **10** 1 ½ **Felicia**[7] 7088 3-8-11 **55**... JamieSpencer 1 53
(S C Williams) *prom: cl enough over 1f out: sltly hmpd ent fnl f and wknd* **11/1**
0303 **11** 2 **Harting Hill**[22] 6735 3-8-11 **55**.. PatDobbs 10 49
(M P Tregoning) *hld up bhd ldrs: effrt over 2f out: no prog over 1f out: wknd* **11/1**
000/ **12** 1 ½ **Tecktal (FR)**[697] 6775 5-9-2 **56**....................................... PatCosgrave 3 47
(P M Phelan) *wl in tch tl wknd rapidly over 1f out* **25/1**
0-05 **13** ½ **Mystic Storm**[41] 4820 5-9-6 **60**...............................(t) GeorgeBaker 9 50
(B G Powell) *hld up wl in rr: stdy prog fr 8f out to go 3rd 4f out: wknd over 2f out* **20/1**
20/0 **14** 5 **Rahy's Crown (USA)**[47] 6136 5-8-13 **53**...................... J-PGuillambert 12 33
(G L Moore) *mostly chsd ldr to over 2f out: wknd rapidly* **10/1**

2m 5.73s (-0.87) **Going Correction** -0.075s/f (Stan)
WFA 3 from 4yo+ 4lb **14** Ran SP% **122.4**
Speed ratings (Par 101): **100,99,98,98,97 97,97,96,96,95 93,92,92,88**
toteswinger: 1&2 £14.30, 1&3 £10.70, 2&3 £7.50. CSF £53.27 CT £194.27 TOTE £11.40: £3.20, £2.70, £1.80; EX 48.60 Trifecta £114.40 Part won. Pool: £154.60 - 0.20 winning tickets. Place 6 £71.10, Place 5 £50.01.
Owner Mrs Bernadette Quinn **Bred** Wyck Hall Stud Ltd **Trained** Lambourn, Berks

FOCUS
A moderate handicap and not many came into this in much form, but the pace seemed generous enough. The runner-up sets the standard.
Saucy ◆ Official explanation: jockey said mare hung left in straight
Tabulate Official explanation: jockey said mare was denied a clear run
Majehar Official explanation: jockey said gelding was denied a clear run
Felicia Official explanation: jockey said filly had no more to give
Rahy's Crown(USA) Official explanation: jockey said gelding stopped quickly
T/Jkpt: Not won. T/Plt: £107.40 to a £1 stake. Pool: £55,362.72. 376.00 winning tickets. T/Qpdt: £28.30 to a £1 stake. Pool: £3,530.51. 92.10 winning tickets. JN

6651 MUSSELBURGH (R-H)
Friday, November 7

OFFICIAL GOING: Soft (6.1)
Wind: Virtually nil Weather: Bright and Dry

7218 INDEPENDENT DENTAL PRACTITIONERS AMATEUR RIDERS' H'CAP 5f
1:00 (1:00) (Class 6) (0-65,75) 3-Y-0+ **£2,186** (£677; £338; £169) **Stalls** Low

Form RPR
000U **1** **Tenancy (IRE)**[10] 7049 4-9-12 **46** ow1............................ MrCAHarris(7) 5 57
(R C Guest) *wnt rt s: mde most: rdn over 1f out: kpt on wl fnl f* **33/1**
0130 **2** 1 ¼ **Grimes Faith**[37] 6382 5-11-7 **62**......................................(p) MissARyan 4 69
(K A Ryan) *a.p: cl up 2f out: rdn and ev ch over 1f out tl one pce ins fnl f* **5/1**[1]
1560 **3** 2 ¾ **Obe One**[31] 6546 8-10-11 **52**.. MissSBrotherton 11 49
(A Berry) *towards rr: rdn along 2f out: hdwy over 1f out: styd on wl fnl f* **12/1**
0123 **4** *nk* **Spirit Of Coniston**[19] 6840 5-11-0 **60**......................... MissWGibson(5) 14 56
(P T Midgley) *cl up: rdn along wl over 1f out: sn edgd lft and one pce* **13/2**[2]
0636 **5** 1 ½ **Lithaam (IRE)**[11] 7022 4-10-2 **50**................................(p) MissHDavies(7) 13 40
(J M Bradley) *cl up: effrt and ev ch wl over 1f out: sn rdn and wknd ent fnl f* **11/1**
5024 **6** 2 **Lambency (IRE)**[40] 6310 5-11-0 **55**................................(p) MrsCBartley 8 38+
(J S Goldie) *hmpd s and in rr: swtchd rt and hdwy wl over 1f out: sn rdn and kpt on ins fnl f: nrst fin* **9/1**
1601 **7** *hd* **Conjecture**[39] 6334 6-11-1 **61**.. MissRBastiman(5) 9 43
(R Bastiman) *cl up: rdn along 2f out: grad wknd* **7/1**[3]
1506 **8** ¾ **Finsbury**[28] 6631 5-11-0 **60**.. MrPNorton(5) 12 40
(J S Goldie) *s.i.s and bhd tl styd on appr fnl f* **13/2**[2]
0030 **9** 2 **Fire Up The Band**[3] 7176 9-11-13 **75** ow13.............. MrMMcCarthy(7) 6 47
(A Berry) *hmpd s: chsd ldrs tl wknd wl over 1f out* **22/1**
3210 **10** 2 ¼ **Joyeaux**[3] 7182 6-11-12 **67** 6ex.. MissADeniel 1 31
(L R James) *sn in rr: swtchd rt and sme hdwy 2f out: sn rdn and nvr a factor* **5/1**[1]
1600 **11** 4 ½ **Sunley Sovereign**[2] 7197 4-10-8 **49**............................(b) MrSDobson 10 —
(Mrs R A Carr) *a towards rr* **16/1**
5035 **12** 5 **Quicks The Word**[107] 4293 8-10-9 **55**.......................... MissHCuthbert(5) 2 —
(T A K Cuthbert) *prom: rdn along wl over 1f out: sn wknd* **11/1**
400- **13** 3 **Optical Seclusion (IRE)**[424] 5282 5-10-4 **52** ow7. MrThomasHogg(7) 3 —
(A Berry) *a towards rr* **66/1**
5000 **14** 1 ¾ **Seafield Towers**[40] 6310 8-9-13 **45**................................ MrRossSmith(5) 7 —
(D A Nolan) *hmpd s: a in rr* **66/1**

64.32 secs (3.92) **Going Correction** +0.50s/f (Yiel) **14** Ran SP% **123.0**
Speed ratings (Par 101): **88,86,81,81,78 75,75,74,70,67 60,52,47,44**
toteswinger: 1&2 £37.30, 1&3 £92.20, 2&3 £14.50. CSF £192.70 CT £2198.70 TOTE £53.30: £12.50, £1.90, £4.70; EX 347.70.
Owner Pinewood Racing Limited **Bred** G A E And J Smith Bloodstock **Trained** Carburton, Notts
■ A first winner for Ciaran Harris.
■ Stewards' Enquiry : Mr Ross Smith three-day ban: careless riding (Nov 25, Dec 1,2)

FOCUS
The ground was described as soft and loose. A poor handicap and a shock result although the solid runner-up is a good guide to the form.
Joyeaux Official explanation: jockey said mare suffered interference in running

7219 ALEXANDER (STIRLING) & CO STEELMASTERS NURSERY 5f
1:30 (1:30) (Class 4) (0-85,85) 2-Y-0 **£5,180** (£1,541; £770; £384) **Stalls** Low

Form RPR
4443 **1** **Grissom (IRE)**[6] 7130 2-7-12 **62**.. PaulQuinn 4 69
(A Berry) *cl up: chal over 2f out: rdn to ld wl over 1f out: styd on strly u.p ins fnl f* **20/1**
0615 **2** 3 ¼ **Oasis Breeze**[7] 7107 2-9-7 **85**.. DavidAllan 1 80
(T D Easterby) *in tch: pushed along and sltly outpcd 1/2-way: rdn and hdwy 2f out: styd on u.p ins fnl f: no imp towards fin* **7/2**[3]
U522 **3** 1 ¾ **Bees River (IRE)**[15] 6932 2-8-1 **65**................................ PaulHanagan 2 54
(A P Jarvis) *led: rdn along 2f out: sn hdd and one pce ent fnl f* **9/4**[1]
1423 **4** 1 ¼ **Dispol Grand (IRE)**[30] 6579 2-8-2 **66**........................... JimmyQuinn 6 51
(P T Midgley) *trckd ldrs: hdwy 2f out: rdn and edgd lft over 1f out: sn wknd* **5/1**
1131 **5** 5 **Visterre (IRE)**[27] 6656 2-9-4 **82**..................................... TomEaves 3 49
(B Smart) *dwlt: sn rdn along and a in rr* **3/1**[2]
5256 **6** ¾ **Chambers (IRE)**[14] 6953 2-7-8 **65**........................... MatthewLawson(7) 5 29
(M Johnston) *chsd ldrs: rdn along 1/2-way: sn btn* **7/1**

63.11 secs (2.71) **Going Correction** +0.50s/f (Yiel) **6** Ran SP% **111.9**
Speed ratings (Par 98): **98,92,90,88,80 78**
toteswinger: 1&2 £8.60, 1&3 £6.60, 2&3 £2.40. CSF £86.75 CT £222.55 TOTE £16.50: £3.80, £2.70; EX 95.30.
Owner Jim & Helen Bowers **Bred** Michael McGlynn **Trained** Cockerham, Lancs

FOCUS
This looked a fair nursery but following a 33-1 shock in the first race on the card, there was another turn-up here. The form is rated slightly negatively with a number not running their race.

NOTEBOOK
Grissom(IRE) had run well behind Visterre here three starts back but had not appeared to have gone on from that, albeit he tackled a trip which proved too far for him at Ayr last time. He found the drop back to the minimum in testing ground bringing out the best in him, though, and, carrying bottom weight, he showed good speed throughout and saw the trip out really strongly. (tchd 22-1 and 25-1 in places)
Oasis Breeze finished fifth in a Listed race at Newmarket last time and was officially 2lb well in at the weights on this drop in grade. Racing on the rail, she was given every chance but just could not pick up well enough in the ground. The concession of 23lb to the winner proved just too much. (op 10-3 tchd 4-1)
Bees River(IRE) looked to hold strong claims, but having made the early running she did not see it out as well as the winner. Her best effort to date came on the Polytrack at Great Leighs and she might be suited by a return to the artificial surface. (op 5-2)
Dispol Grand(IRE) saw his race out well when winning on soft ground here in the summer off a 5lb lower mark, but on this occasion he was going up and down on the spot in the closing stages. (op 11-2 tchd 4-1)
Visterre(IRE), unbeaten in three previous starts here, was never going at any stage and patently failed to give her running. Her trainer was of the opinion that she was over the top. Official explanation: trainer had no explanation for the poor form shown (op 5-2)
Chambers(IRE) promised to be suited by the drop back to the minimum as he has plenty of pace, but he is by Green Desert and this soft ground was always going to be a concern. (op 10-1)

7220 E.B.F./ CORNHILL BUILDING SERVICES LTD MAIDEN FILLIES' STKS 7f 30y
2:00 (2:00) (Class 5) 2-Y-0 **£3,885** (£1,156; £577; £288) **Stalls** High

Form RPR
3604 **1** **Peter's Gift (IRE)**[15] 6933 2-9-0 68.............................. PaulMulrennan 2 59+
(K A Ryan) *mde all: rdn clr 2f out: comf* **4/6**[1]
06 **2** 2 ¾ **Challenging (UAE)**[20] 6808 2-9-0 0................................ PJMcDonald 3 53
(R D E Woodhouse) *chsd wnr: rdn along and outpcd over 2f out: styd on strly u.p ins fnl f: nt rch wnr* **20/1**
6454 **3** 2 ¾ **Jaslyn (IRE)**[70] 5473 2-9-0 48.. JimmyQuinn 4 46
(J R Weymes) *trckd ldng pair: hdwy 3f out: rdn to chse wnr over 2f out: sn drvn and one pce ent fnl f* **7/1**[3]

45 **4** *3* **Caress The Soul (IRE)**[24] 6722 2-9-0 0 .... JamieMoriarty 9 39
(P T Midgley) *trckd ldrs: pushed along wl over 2f out: sn rdn and no imp* **11/4**[2]

5 *12* **Golden Kiss** 2-8-9 0 .... KellyHarrison(5) 1 9
(Paul Murphy) *s.i.s: rn green and a in rr* **14/1**

1m 36.3s (6.00) **Going Correction** +0.60s/f (Yiel) **5** Ran SP% **110.6**
Speed ratings (Par 93): **89,85,82,79,65**
toteswinger: 1&2 £10.50 CSF £15.31 TOTE £1.40: £1.20, £3.20; EX 12.80.
Owner Mr & Mrs Julian And Rosie Richer **Bred** T C Chiang **Trained** Hambleton, N Yorks

FOCUS
A weak maiden devalued further by four non-runners and the winner beat mainly platers.

NOTEBOOK
Peter's Gift(IRE) posted a promising return from a three-month absence at Great Leighs last time and, having already earned a turf mark of 68, did not have to improve on that to take this. Sent to the front right from the start, she dominated throughout and did it easily enough in the end. The seventh furlong proved no problem and she has the potential to improve if kept on the go on the all-weather this winter. (op 4-5 tchd 8-15)
Challenging(UAE) stayed on best of the rest to take the runner-up spot. This was by far her best run to date, and handicaps should present her with easier opportunities in future. (op 16-1 tchd 28-1)
Jaslyn(IRE), returning from a 70-day break, was found out by a combination of soft ground and a step up in distance. A return to 6f should suit her. (op 9-1 tchd 10-1)
Caress The Soul(IRE), who was keen through the early parts, is another now eligible for a mark. Better ground might suit him. (tchd 3-1)
Golden Kiss, out of a dual-winner over 6f; was very slowly away, losing many lengths at the start, and trailed the field throughout on her debut. (op 12-1 tchd 11-1)

7221 E.B.F./REDMAN FISHER MAIDEN STKS 1m
2:30 (2:33) (Class 5) 2-Y-O **£3,885** (£1,156; £577; £288) **Stalls** High

Form RPR

05 **1** **Kiwi Moon**[24] 6714 2-9-3 0 .... TomEaves 8 66
(B Smart) *mde all: rdn clr over 2f out: kpt on u.p ins fnl f* **10/11**[1]

0 **2** *3 ¾* **Markadam**[37] 6381 2-9-0 0 .... MichaelJStainton(3) 3 58
(Miss S E Hall) *dwlt and towards rr: rn green and sn pushed along: hdwy 3f out: rdn over 2f out: styd on to chse wnr ins fnl f: kpt on* **18/1**

3 *4* **Mystical Spirit (IRE)** 2-8-12 0 .... JimmyQuinn 2 44
(J R Weymes) *in tch: pushed along 1/2-way: rdn 3f out: styd on same pce fnl 2f* **12/1**

6 **4** *1 ¾* **Quick Gourmet**[47] 6151 2-8-12 0 .... MickyFenton 7 40
(A G Foster) *chsd ldrs: hdwy 3f out: rdn to chse wnr 2f out: drvn and wknd ent fnl f* **20/1**

5 *3 ½* **The Bully Wee** 2-9-3 0 .... PaulHanagan 1 37
(J Jay) *chsd ldrs: rdn along 3f out: wknd over 2f out* **7/1**[3]

6 *¾* **Tillietudlem (FR)** 2-9-3 0 .... DanielTudhope 5 36
(J S Goldie) *a towards rr* **15/2**

7 *14* **Gomarhoom** 2-8-12 0 .... GregFairley 4 —
(M Johnston) *cl up: rdn along wl over 2f out: sn drvn and wknd qckly* **13/2**[2]

8 *31* **Greenbank Destiny** 2-8-7 0 .... KellyHarrison(5) 6 —
(W J H Ratcliffe) *s.i.s: a wl bhd* **12/1**

1m 47.67s (6.47) **Going Correction** +0.60s/f (Yiel) **8** Ran SP% **115.4**
Speed ratings (Par 96): **91,87,83,81,78 77,63,32**
toteswinger: 1&2 £6.90, 1&3 £3.90, 2&3 £16.10. CSF £20.81 TOTE £1.90: £1.10, £4.50, £2.40; EX 18.90.
Owner H E Sheikh Rashid Bin Mohammed **Bred** Tarworth Bloodstock Investments Ltd **Trained** Hambleton, N Yorks

FOCUS
A weak maiden with the winner roughly to form.

NOTEBOOK
Kiwi Moon made it third time lucky. The form of his fifth at Leicester last time had been boosted by the subsequent successes of the second, third and fourth, so he was always going to take plenty of beating in this company. Given a positive ride, he saw the trip out strongly on ground that made it hard work, and he very much looks the type to do better as he gets older. A scopey sort, he should make up into a middle-distance performer next year. (op Evens tchd 11-8)
Markadam, well held on his debut at Newcastle, kept plugging away and saw it out well. He needs one more outing for a mark and will be of more interest once eligible for handicaps. (op 28-1 tchd 16-1)
Mystical Spirit(IRE), a sister to Mystical Land who was a very smart sprinting juvenile in 2004, clearly has more stamina than her. This was a pleasing enough debut effort and she should improve for the outing. (tchd 9-1)
Quick Gourmet looked likely to finish second approaching the final furlong but in the end dropped right out. She simply did not get home. (tchd 16-1)
The Bully Wee, a half-brother to prolific winner Cristoforo, is bred to appreciate this sort of ground but he looked awkward to ride, perhaps through greenness. Official explanation: jockey said colt hung badly left in straight (op 12-1)
Gomarhoom, who is bred to make a middle-distance filly next term, was weak in the betting on her debut. Jig-jogging around the paddock beforehand, she was green going to the start and raced too keenly through the early part of the race. (op 3-1 tchd 7-1)

7222 EDINBURGH EVENING NEWS H'CAP 5f
3:00 (3:01) (Class 4) (0-85,85) 3-Y-O+ **£5,180** (£1,541; £770; £384) **Stalls** Low

Form RPR

0-00 **1** **Roker Park (IRE)**[20] 6810 3-9-1 **82** .... JamieMoriarty 5 91
(K R Burke) *chsd ldrs: hdwy over 1f out: rdn ent fnl f: styd on to ld last 75yds* **40/1**

1146 **2** *2* **Le Toreador**[35] 6449 3-8-11 **78** .... (t) PaulMulrennan 10 80
(K A Ryan) *led: rdn wl over 1f out: drvn ent fnl f: hdd and no ex last 75yds* **20/1**

4423 **3** *½* **Artsu**[24] 6724 3-8-8 **75** .... TomEaves 7 75
(M Dods) *chsd ldrs: rdn along and sltly outpcd over 1f out: kpt on u.p ins fnl f* **7/1**[3]

1430 **4** *shd* **Highland Warrior**[9] 7081 9-8-9 **76** ow1 .... MickyFenton 9 76
(P T Midgley) *in tch on outer: hdwy 2f out: rdn and ev ch ent fnl f: sn drvn: edgd lft and one pce towards fin* **12/1**

1004 **5** *1* **Rothesay Dancer**[13] 6990 5-8-0 **72** .... KellyHarrison(5) 1 68
(J S Goldie) *hld up: hdwy 2f out: sn rdn: chsd ldrs ent fnl f: sn drvn and one pce* **9/1**

6031 **6** *hd* **The Tatling (IRE)**[15] 6925 11-8-10 **80** .... NeilBrown(3) 11 75
(J M Bradley) *trckd ldrs: effrt 2f out: rdn appr last and sn one pce* **11/2**[1]

0200 **7** *nse* **Swift Princess (IRE)**[46] 6160 4-9-2 **83** .... (v) AndrewElliott 8 78
(K R Burke) *chsd ldrs: rdn over 1f out: drvn and kpt on same pce ins fnl f* **16/1**

2100 **8** *nse* **Hotham**[13] 6971 5-9-4 **85** .... DanielTudhope 4 80
(N Wilson) *hld up towards rr: hdwy 2f out and sn rdn: styd on ins fnl f: nrst fin* **6/1**[2]

0351 **9** *½* **Cape Royal**[9] 7081 8-8-7 **74** 6ex .... (t) DavidAllan 12 67
(J M Bradley) *cl up: rdn along wl over 1f out: drvn and wknd appr fnl f* **10/1**

5046 **10** *½* **Johannes (IRE)**[18] 6859 5-8-10 **77** .... PaulHanagan 3 68
(R A Fahey) *hld up: a towards rr* **11/2**[1]

4200 **11** *6* **John Keats**[49] 6066 5-8-8 **75** .... PJMcDonald 2 45
(J S Goldie) *a towards rr* **18/1**

1560 **12** *½* **Killer Class**[9] 7081 3-8-0 **72** oh3 ow1 .... PatrickDonaghy(5) 13 40
(J S Goldie) *chsd ldrs on outer: rdn along 2f out: sn wknd* **20/1**

5445 **13** *¾* **Blazing Heights**[53] 5970 5-8-4 **71** oh1 .... JimmyQuinn 6 36
(J S Goldie) *towards rr: hdwy 1/2-way: rdn and n.m.r wl over 1f out: sn wknd* **7/1**[3]

63.78 secs (3.38) **Going Correction** +0.50s/f (Yiel) **13** Ran SP% **119.9**
Speed ratings (Par 105): **92,88,88,87,86 85,85,85,84,84 74,73,72**
toteswinger: 1&2 £47.10, 1&3 £35.60, 2&3 £19.30. CSF £684.21 CT £6147.39 TOTE £39.40: £10.90, £4.60, £3.30; EX 855.00.
Owner T Alderson **Bred** Dr Dean Harron **Trained** Middleham Moor, N Yorks

FOCUS
A competitive sprint handicap and yet another shock result on the card. The runner-up is the best guide to the level.
Roker Park(IRE) Official explanation: trainer's rep had no explanation for the apparent improvement in form other than the gelding broke well and everything had gone well.

7223 WILLIE PARK TROPHY H'CAP 2m
3:30 (3:30) (Class 2) (0-100,95) 3-Y-O+
£12,462 (£3,732; £1,866; £934; £466; £234) **Stalls** High

Form RPR

5100 **1** **Nemo Spirit (IRE)**[14] 6948 3-8-13 **84** .... JimmyQuinn 8 96
(W R Muir) *mde all: qcknd over 3f out: rdn 2f out: sn clr and styd on strly* **6/1**[3]

2422 **2** *5* **Gordonsville**[27] 6652 5-9-4 **80** .... DanielTudhope 3 86
(J S Goldie) *hld up and bhd: hdwy wl over 2f out: rdn over 1f out styd on to chse wnr ins fnl f: sn no imp* **7/1**

3120 **3** *2 ¾* **Bollin Felix**[20] 6817 4-10-0 **90** .... (b) DavidAllan 7 93
(T D Easterby) *hld up in rr: pushed along over 3f out: sn rdn: drvn over 2f out: styd on ins fnl f: tk 3rd nr line* **6/4**[1]

4210 **4** *nk* **Sphinx (FR)**[32] 6527 10-9-5 **81** .... (b) PaulMulrennan 4 83
(E W Tuer) *t.k.h: chsd ldrs: rdn along over 3f out: drvn and one pce fnl 2f* **16/1**

1411 **5** *½* **Merchant Of Dubai**[27] 6652 3-9-10 **95** .... PJMcDonald 6 97
(G A Swinbank) *trckd wnr: hdwy and cl up 4f out: rdn 3f out and ev ch tl drvn 2f out and sn wknd* **11/4**[2]

0020 **6** *10* **Lets Roll**[14] 6948 7-9-2 **78** .... TomEaves 1 68
(C W Thornton) *hld up in rr: sme hdwy 6f out: rdn along over 3f out and nvr nr ldrs* **14/1**

-023 **7** *1 ½* **Los Nadis (GER)**[49] 6071 4-8-10 **72** .... PaulHanagan 5 60
(P Monteith) *chsd ldng pair: rdn along 4f out: drvn 3f out and sn wknd* **17/2**

3m 42.05s (5.95) **Going Correction** +0.60s/f (Yiel)
WFA 3 from 4yo+ 9lb **7** Ran SP% **116.5**
Speed ratings (Par 109): **109,106,105,104,104 99,98**
toteswinger: 1&2 £7.60, 1&3 £3.70, 2&3 £4.10. CSF £47.84 CT £94.58 TOTE £8.50: £4.70, £3.80; EX 62.90.
Owner Mrs Monique V Bruce Copp **Bred** Gainsborough Stud Management Ltd **Trained** Lambourn, Berks

FOCUS
A valuable handicap but the highest rated horse in the field was Merchant Of Dubai and he was rated 5lb below the ceiling for the race. It was always going to be a proper test in the ground but the winner had the run of the race. The runner-up and fourth help set the level.

NOTEBOOK
Nemo Spirit(IRE) showed that he has bucket-loads of stamina with a pillar-to-post success. Soft ground seems key to him as he was below his best on his last two starts, but granted his conditions he looks very useful, and next year he could well win a decent staying race. Longer term, he has size and scope to make a hurdler. (op 11-1 tchd 12-1 in places)
Gordonsville filled his usual position, staying on from off the pace to take second once again. He is a gift to Placepot punters. (op 6-1 tchd 8-1)
Bollin Felix, who likes to get his toe in, probably found the ground against him in the Cesarewitch last time, but he ran a better race here. He needs to find some more improvement to win off his current mark, though. (op 15-8)
Sphinx(FR) is a keen-going type and this time he pulled too hard for too long, meaning he had little left in the tank for the finish. (op 14-1)
Merchant Of Dubai, who made all over 1m6f here last time, simply failed to get home over this two-furlong longer trip. He remains capable of better back over a shorter distance. (op 9-4)
Lets Roll has not built on his good effort here two starts back. (op 12-1)

7224 BETTY JOYCE H'CAP 1m 1f
4:00 (4:00) (Class 4) (0-80,79) 3-Y-O+ **£5,180** (£1,541; £770; £384) **Stalls** High

Form RPR

3646 **1** **Bourse (IRE)**[77] 5221 3-8-4 **64** oh4 .... GregFairley 4 72
(A G Foster) *trckd ldrs: hdwy over 2f out: sn swtchd lft and rdn to ld 1f out: drvn out* **14/1**

3144 **2** *1 ¼* **Wind Shuffle (GER)**[6] 7127 5-9-2 **78** .... GaryBartley(5) 9 82
(J S Goldie) *led: rdn along and hdd 2f out: drvn over 1f out: kpt on u.p ins fnl f* **4/1**[1]

4404 **3** *1* **Island Music (IRE)**[44] 6216 3-8-0 **67** .... JamieKyne(7) 12 70
(J J Quinn) *trckd ldrs on inner: hdwy over 2f out: effrt and n.m.r over 1f out: swtchd lft and rdn ent fnl f: kpt on towards fin* **10/1**

1633 **4** *½* **Grand Diamond (IRE)**[28] 6628 4-8-2 **64** .... (p) KellyHarrison(5) 7 65
(J S Goldie) *trckd ldrs: smooth hdwy 3f out: led on bit 2f out: rdn and hdd 1f out: sn drvn and wkng whn n.m.r ins fnl f* **7/1**

1350 **5** *1* **Moheebb (IRE)**[30] 6582 4-9-3 **74** .... (b) AndrewElliott 10 73
(Mrs R A Carr) *hld up in rr: stdy hdwy on inner over 2f out: rdn to chse ldrs over 1f out: kpt on same pce* **6/1**[3]

5503 **6** *1 ¾* **Harvest Warrior**[9] 7083 6-9-0 **71** .... (v) DavidAllan 8 66+
(T D Easterby) *v s.i.s and bhd: hdwy over 2f out: kpt on appr last: nrst fin* **5/1**[2]

2000 **7** *¾* **Jamieson Gold (IRE)**[6] 7131 5-9-1 **72** .... TomEaves 5 66
(Miss L A Perratt) *chsd ldrs on outer: rdn along wl over 2f out: drvn and wknd over 1f out* **12/1**

2401 **8** *1 ¾* **Faithful Ruler (USA)**[20] 6827 4-9-0 **71** .... PaulHanagan 6 61
(R A Fahey) *trckd ldrs: effrt and hdwy over 3f out: sn rdn and wknd 2f out* **4/1**[1]

63 **9** *1 ½* **Solis (GER)**[46] 6162 5-8-11 **68** .... PaulMulrennan 11 55
(P Monteith) *a towards rr* **16/1**

140 **10** *21* **Addikt (IRE)**[25] 6704 3-9-5 **79** .... JamieMoriarty 2 23
(J R Turner) *a towards rr: bhd and eased fnl 2f* **16/1**

000 **11** *7* **Defi (IRE)**[6] 7132 6-8-9 **66** oh14 ow2..............................(bt) MickyFenton 1 —
(D A Nolan) *cl up: rdn along over 3f out and sn wknd* **50/1**

1m 59.98s (5.28) **Going Correction** +0.60s/f (Yiel)
WFA 3 from 4yo+ 3lb **11** Ran SP% **120.6**
Speed ratings (Par 105): **100,98,98,97,96 95,94,92,91,72 66**
toteswinger: 1&2 £12.30, 1&3 £14.00, 2&3 £12.90. CSF £71.14 CT £617.98 TOTE £14.20: £4.80, £1.90, £3.20; EX 99.40 Place 6 £1868.46, Place 5 £ 412.25.
Owner M Sawers **Bred** Darley **Trained** Cousland, Midlothian

FOCUS
An ordinary handicap but sound form rated around the placed horses.
Moheebb(IRE) Official explanation: jockey said saddle slipped
T/Plt: £1,164.60 to a £1 stake. Pool: £53,526.88. 33.55 winning tickets. T/Qpdt: £35.60 to a £1 stake. Pool: £3,863.72. 80.10 winning tickets. JR

7164 WOLVERHAMPTON (A.W) (L-H)

Friday, November 7

OFFICIAL GOING: Standard
Wind: Light behind Weather: Some drizzle after 7.50

7225 WOLVERHAMPTON HOLIDAY INN APPRENTICE H'CAP 5f 216y(P)

6:20 (6:20) (Class 5) (0-70,70) 3-Y-0+ **£3,885** (£1,156; £577; £288) **Stalls** Low

Form RPR

4000 **1** **Gainshare**[49] 6088 3-8-1 **57**.............................. DeanHeslop(5) 3 67
(Mrs R A Carr) *t.k.h in rr: c wd st: rdn and hdwy fnl f: r.o to ld last strides* **20/1**

/003 **2** *nk* **Dazzling Bay**[8] 7092 8-9-5 **70**..............................(b) DuranFentiman 7 79
(T D Easterby) *hld up and bhd: hdwy over 3f out: led ins fnl f: edgd rt and hdd last strides* **6/1**

1161 **3** *2* **Lord Deevert**[17] 6880 3-8-11 **65**.............................. JackDean(3) 12 68
(W G M Turner) *chsd ldr: rdn to ld over 1f out: edgd rt and hdd ins fnl f: no ex* **12/1**

0000 **4** *½* **Shes Minnie**[9] 7081 5-9-5 **70**.............................. KirstyMilczarek 4 71
(J G M O'Shea) *hld up towards rr: hdwy over 1f out: kpt on ins fnl f* **16/1**

0600 **5** *shd* **Chjimes (IRE)**[14] 6952 4-9-5 **70**.............................. LukeMorris 2 71+
(C R Dore) *hld up in mid-div: nt clr run on ins over 2f out: swtchd rt and hdwy whn nt clr run wl over 1f out: sn swtchd rt again: kpt on ins fnl f* **8/1**

5321 **6** *¾* **Siren Sound**[28] 6631 3-9-4 **69**.............................. TravisBlock 5 68
(H Morrison) *a.p: swtchd lft over 1f out: rdn and one pce fnl f* **3/1**[1]

0620 **7** *1 ¾* **Thunder Bay**[13] 6990 3-8-13 **67**..............................(p) FrederikTylicki(3) 1 60
(R A Fahey) *hld up and bhd: hrd rdn and hdwy on ins wl over 1f out: wknd wl ins fnl f* **11/2**[3]

0062 **8** *1 ½* **Gwilym (GER)**[7] 7118 5-8-13 **64**.............................. DavidProbert 10 52
(D Haydn Jones) *prom: rdn 2f out: wknd 1f out* **7/2**[2]

320 **9** *6* **Trinculo (IRE)**[18] 6864 11-8-7 **63**..............................(b) MatthewDavies(5) 9 32
(R A Harris) *led: rdn and hdd over 1f out: wknd fnl f* **16/1**

4600 **10** *¾* **Caustic Wit (IRE)**[16] 6895 10-7-13 **57** ow1.............................. JakePayne(7) 8 24
(M S Saunders) *hld up towards rr: hung rt fr over 3f out: rn wd st: n.d* **33/1**

4400 **11** *1 ½* **Mr Loire**[57] 5832 4-8-0 **56** oh8..............................(b) AndreaAtzeni(5) 11 18
(K G Wingrove) *s.s: outpcd* **33/1**

65-0 **12** *11* **Gifted Gamble**[34] 6490 6-8-12 **70**.............................. AndrewHeffernan(7) 6 —
(Peter Grayson) *prom: rdn over 2f out: sn wknd* **40/1**

1m 16.0s (1.00) **Going Correction** +0.225s/f (Slow) **12** Ran SP% **120.5**
Speed ratings (Par 103): **102,101,98,98,98 97,94,92,84,83 81,67**
toteswinger: 1&2 £25.00, 1&3 £0, 2&3 £22.70. CSF £134.18 CT £1556.02 TOTE £17.80: £7.90, £1.90, £3.70; EX 272.50.
Owner David W Chapman **Bred** Baroness Bloodstock & Redmyre Bloodstock **Trained** Stillington, N Yorks

■ Stewards' Enquiry : Frederik Tylicki caution: used whip without giving gelding time to respond.
Andrew Heffernan one-day ban: used whip when out of contention (Nov 21)

FOCUS
A modest handicap restricted to apprentices and straightforward form rated around the placed horses.

7226 HORIZONS RESTAURANT OVERLOOKS THE TRACK H'CAP (DIV I) 7f 32y(P)

6:50 (6:51) (Class 6) (0-62,64) 3-Y-0+ **£2,729** (£806; £403) **Stalls** High

Form RPR

613 **1** **Shunkawakhan (IRE)**[20] 6821 5-8-11 **60**..............................(p) AndrewMullen(3) 6 70
(Miss L A Perratt) *t.k.h in mid-div: hdwy wl over 1f out: led 1f out: rdn and hung lft ins fnl f: drvn out* **4/1**[2]

0000 **2** *nk* **Kirkie (USA)**[81] 5154 3-8-13 **60**.............................. DNolan 8 68
(S Parr) *s.i.s: hld up towards rr: led over 1f out: sn rdn and hdd: r.o* **50/1**

6501 **3** *1 ¼* **Kirstys Lad**[14] 6955 6-8-11 **57**.............................. TPQueally 10 63
(M Mullineaux) *hld up towards rr: hdwy on outside 2f out: c wd st: rdn over 1f out: edgd lft ins fnl f: kpt on* **6/1**[3]

00-5 **4** *¾* **Polish World (USA)**[21] 6773 4-9-1 **61**.............................. SaleemGolam 2 65
(T J Etherington) *plld hrd: a.p: rdn and nt qckn fnl f* **14/1**

4563 **5** *½* **Cap St Jean (IRE)**[89] 4891 4-8-7 **60**..............................(p) DavidKenny(7) 5 63+
(R Hollinshead) *s.s: hld up in rr: nt clr run over 1f out: r.o ins fnl f: nrst fin* **10/1**

4525 **6** *1 ¼* **Ishiadancer**[21] 6792 3-9-1 **62**.............................. PatCosgrave 11 60
(E J Alston) *t.k.h: w ldr: led 2f out: rdn and hdd over 1f out: wknd ins fnl f* **11/1**

0544 **7** *1* **Vanadium**[48] 6132 6-9-2 **62**.............................. GeorgeBaker 9 59
(G L Moore) *hld up in tch: rdn 2f out: wknd over 1f out* **9/4**[1]

2100 **8** *2* **Willhewiz**[16] 6895 8-8-9 **55**..............................(v) TGMcLaughlin 4 46
(W M Brisbourne) *t.k.h: prom tl wknd wl over 1f out: eased wl ins fnl f* **33/1**

0203 **9** *¾* **Morocchius (USA)**[11] 7012 3-8-13 **60**..............................(p) HayleyTurner 3 48+
(Miss J A Camacho) *hld up in mid-div: nt clr run on ins over 2f out: n.d after* **6/1**[3]

3400 **10** *½* **Motu (IRE)**[11] 7012 7-8-12 **58**..............................(v) PatrickMathers 12 46
(I W McInnes) *hld up in tch: rdn 3f out: wknd 2f out* **16/1**

0344 **11** *1* **Hobson**[22] 6746 3-8-12 **59**.............................. StephenCarson 1 43
(Eve Johnson Houghton) *t.k.h: led: hdd 2f out: sn rdn: wknd and eased ins fnl f* **7/1**

1m 32.07s (2.47) **Going Correction** +0.225s/f (Slow)
WFA 3 from 4yo+ 1lb **11** Ran SP% **126.7**
Speed ratings (Par 101): **94,93,92,91,90 89,88,85,85,84 83**
toteswinger: 1&2 £0, 1&3 £5.70, 2&3 £28.60. CSF £191.15 CT £1235.79 TOTE £5.40: £1.40, £20.50, £2.10; EX 190.80.
Owner Partick Thistle Racing Club **Bred** Matthew Duffy **Trained**

FOCUS
Not a bad race for the level, but the pace was steady through the first couple of furlongs or so and a few of these raced keenly early on. The time was modest but the form looks sound rated around the third, fourth and sixth.
Polish World(USA) Official explanation: jockey said gelding ran too freely
Hobson Official explanation: jockey said gelding hung right and ran too freely

7227 HOTEL & CONFERENCING AT WOLVERHAMPTON RACECOURSE MAIDEN STKS 7f 32y(P)

7:20 (7:22) (Class 5) 2-Y-O **£4,094** (£1,209; £604) **Stalls** High

Form RPR

1 **Elusive Fame (USA)** 2-9-3 0.............................. JoeFanning 5 81
(M Johnston) *a.p: wnt 2nd over 5f out: led over 2f out: rdn clr over 1f out: r.o wl* **9/1**

200 **2** *2 ¼* **Sign Of Approval**[34] 6474 2-9-3 78.............................. PatCosgrave 9 75
(K R Burke) *s.s: hld up in rr: hdwy 2f out: rdn over 1f out: swtchd lft and tk 2nd ins fnl f: nt trble wnr* **5/2**[1]

33 **3** *1 ¾* **Dareh (IRE)**[15] 6933 2-8-12 0.............................. TedDurcan 6 66
(Saeed Bin Suroor) *hld up in tch: rdn wl over 1f out: kpt on same pce fnl f* **5/1**[3]

2 **4** *nk* **Storming Sioux**[21] 6789 2-8-12 0.............................. LiamJones 3 65
(W J Haggas) *led 1f: prom: chsd wnr over 1f out: edgd lft and lost 2nd ins fnl f* **5/2**[1]

05 **5** *3 ½* **Cobos**[16] 6901 2-8-12 0.............................. RobertWinston 4 56
(M G Quinlan) *hld up in tch: rdn wl over 1f out: wknd ins fnl f* **28/1**

0 **6** *shd* **Captain Carey**[39] 6327 2-9-3 0.............................. VinceSlattery 2 61
(M S Saunders) *t.k.h in mid-div: no hdwy fnl 2f* **80/1**

6 **7** *¾* **Thin Red Line (IRE)**[21] 6777 2-9-3 0.............................. DaneO'Neill 12 59
(E A L Dunlop) *hld up in mid-div: effrt over 2f out: no further prog* **4/1**[2]

00 **8** *11* **Blushing Dreamer (IRE)**[8] 7093 2-8-12 0.............................. DarrenWilliams 7 27
(D Shaw) *hld up in rr: rdn over 3f out: sn struggling* **100/1**

43 **9** *1 ¼* **Rio Gael (IRE)**[65] 5599 2-9-3 0.............................. TGMcLaughlin 1 29
(M S Saunders) *hld up in mid-div: rdn and wknd over 2f out* **25/1**

10 *hd* **Sytygre** 2-9-3 0.............................. TonyHamilton 8 29
(Miss J A Camacho) *swtchd lft sn after s: rdn over 3f out: a in rr* **50/1**

0050 **11** *1 ¼* **Miss Xu Xia**[10] 7038 2-8-9 38..............................(p) DavidProbert(3) 11 21
(G R Oldroyd) *led after 1f tl over 2f out: wknd wl over 1f out* **200/1**

12 *1 ¼* **Matilda Poliport** 2-8-12 0.............................. SteveDrowne 10 18
(W R Swinburn) *t.k.h towards rr: n.m.r over 4f out: hmpd and lost pl over 3f out: sn struggling* **20/1**

1m 31.33s (1.73) **Going Correction** +0.225s/f (Slow) **12** Ran SP% **120.5**
Speed ratings (Par 96): **99,96,94,94,90 89,89,76,75,74 73,72**
toteswinger: 1&2 £16.90, 1&3 £5.10, 2&3 £3.70 CSF £31.19 TOTE £13.60: £3.30, £1.50, £1.60; EX 49.00.
Owner Mark Johnston Racing Ltd **Bred** Summer Wind Farm **Trained** Middleham Moor, N Yorks

FOCUS
An ordinary juvenile maiden.

NOTEBOOK
Elusive Fame(USA), a half-brother to quite useful dual 5f-1m winner Catstar out of a high-class 5f-1m winner in the US, knew his job and this was all rather straightforward. He picked up best having been well positioned and further enhanced his trainer's fine record at the track. (tchd 10-1)
Sign Of Approval might have been given the winner more of a race had he not completely missed the break. He was stuck behind a bunch of no-hopers for much of the way and got going too late to challenge the Johnston horse. Official explanation: jockey said colt was slowly away (op 11-4 tchd 3-1)
Dareh(IRE), beaten at 2-1 at Great Leighs last time, had her chance but looks just modest. (op 7-2)
Storming Sioux shaped well when second of 20 on her debut over 1m at Redcar, but she failed to build on that and was a little disappointing. (op 9-4 tchd 11-4)
Cobos was comfortably held, but she now has the option of handicaps. (op 33-1 tchd 25-1)
Captain Carey surprisingly finished so close as he was very keen for much of the way, but he obviously has ability. (op 100-1)
Thin Red Line(IRE) shaped nicely on his debut over 1m at Newmarket, but this drop in trip was totally against him. (op 15-2)
Sytygre Official explanation: jockey said gelding hung left
Matilda Poliport was bumped around all over the place down the back straight, so it's probably best to put a line through this debut effort. Official explanation: jockey said filly suffered interference in running (op 16-1)

7228 HORIZONS RESTAURANT OVERLOOKS THE TRACK H'CAP (DIV II) 7f 32y(P)

7:50 (7:51) (Class 6) (0-62,63) 3-Y-0+ **£2,729** (£806; £201; £201) **Stalls** High

Form RPR

3604 **1** **Tender Process (IRE)**[10] 7043 5-8-12 **58**..............................(b) TonyHamilton 5 71+
(R A Fahey) *hld up towards rr: hdwy wl over 1f out: led ins fnl f: comf* **13/2**[3]

4224 **2** *2 ¾* **Manchestermaverick (USA)**[19] 6836 3-8-13 **60**.............................. SteveDrowne 2 65
(H Morrison) *a.p: rdn wl over 1f out: kpt on one pce fnl f* **13/2**[3]

0500 **3** *hd* **Sion Hill (IRE)**[13] 6975 7-8-9 **55**..............................(p) ChrisCatlin 8 60
(John A Harris) *chsd ldr: ev ch wl over 1f out: kpt on same pce fnl f* **16/1**

4211 **3** *dht* **Musical Script (USA)**[11] 7012 5-9-3 **63** 6ex..............................(b) DaneO'Neill 3 68
(Mouse Hamilton-Fairley) *hld up in mid-div: hdwy over 2f out: ev ch ins fnl f: nt qckn* **5/2**[1]

1600 **5** *1* **Micky Mac (IRE)**[10] 7043 4-9-0 **60**.............................. GrahamGibbons 6 62
(T D Walford) *led: rdn wl over 1f out: hdd and no ex ins fnl f* **6/1**[2]

040 **6** *nk* **This Ones For Eddy**[21] 6792 3-8-12 **62**.............................. TolleyDean(3) 7 62
(S Parr) *hld up towards rr: rdn over 2f out: hdwy over 1f out: one pce fnl f* **10/1**

2366 **7** *2 ½* **The Salwick Flyer (IRE)**[48] 6116 5-8-7 **56**.............................. AndrewMullen(3) 9 51
(Miss L A Perratt) *prom: rdn 3f out: edgd lft over 1f out: wknd fnl f* **10/1**

0360 **8** *4 ½* **Valentino Swing (IRE)**[17] 6889 5-8-13 **62**..............................(p) JamesMillman(3) 1 45
(Miss T Spearing) *s.i.s: sn hld up in tch: rdn over 2f out: wknd wl over 1f out* **9/1**

0000 **9** *¾* **Cape Of Storms**[25] 6711 5-8-9 **58**..............................(v[1]) JackMitchell(3) 12 39
(R Brotherton) *s.s: a in rr* **20/1**

3000 **10** *3 ¼* **Danzig Fox**[62] 5709 3-8-11 **58**.............................. TPQueally 11 29
(M Mullineaux) *t.k.h towards rr: rdn over 2f out: sn struggling* **16/1**

1m 30.52s (0.92) **Going Correction** +0.225s/f (Slow)
WFA 3 from 4yo+ 1lb **10** Ran SP% **114.2**
Speed ratings (Par 101): **103,99,99,99,98 98,95,90,89,85**
toteswinger: 1&2 £8.70, 1&MS £3.90, 1&SH, £0, 2&MS £0.80, 2&SH £3.90. CSF £43.11 TOTE £9.30: £1.60, £1.80; EX 63.10 TRIFECTA 3rd pl MS 2.00; SH ; T/C 1-2-MS 52.00; 1-2-SH £248.90.
Owner J J Staunton **Bred** Timothy Coughlan **Trained** Musley Bank, N Yorks

FOCUS
A moderate handicap. The winning time was 1.55sec quicker than the first division, but they went steady in that contest and this looked the less competitive of the two races. The form looks solid rated around the placed horses and sixth.

7229 STAY AT THE WOLVERHAMPTON HOLIDAY INN NURSERY 1m 141y(P)
8:20 (8:20) (Class 4) (0-85,85) 2-Y-O £5,180 (£1,541; £770; £384) Stalls Low

Form RPR
5410 1 **Dialogue**[14] 6946 2-9-6 **84**.................... JoeFanning 2 89
(M Johnston) *chsd ldr: led 3f out: rdn over 1f out: r.o* **5/4**[1]
523 2 *1* **Free Thinker**[36] 6423 2-8-9 **76**.................... DavidProbert(3) 4 79
(P W D'Arcy) *a.p: chsd wnr over 2f out: rdn over 1f out: kpt on ins fnl f* **11/4**[2]
6113 3 *9* **Northern Tour**[131] 3522 2-9-7 **85**.................... JamieSpencer 5 69
(P F I Cole) *hld up in rr: rdn over 2f out: wnt 3rd 1f out: no ch w ldng pair* **11/2**
2144 4 *6* **Starry Sky**[9] 7067 2-8-13 **77**.................... J-PGuillambert 1 48
(Sir Mark Prescott) *led: hdd 3f out: wknd 2f out* **3/1**[3]
0006 5 *31* **Susurrayshaan**[32] 6534 2-7-9 **62** oh10.................... DuranFentiman(3) 6 —
(Mrs G S Rees) *prom tl wknd 3f out: t.o* **40/1**
1m 51.62s (1.12) **Going Correction** +0.225s/f (Slow) **5 Ran SP% 113.9**
Speed ratings (Par 98): **104,103,95,89,62**
toteswinger: 1&2 £4.00 CSF £5.26 TOTE £1.80: £1.20, £1.40; EX 7.80.
Owner Sheikh Hamdan Bin Mohammed Al Maktoum **Bred** Darley **Trained** Middleham Moor, N Yorks

FOCUS
An ordinary nursery for the grade that concerned only two of the five runners.

NOTEBOOK
Dialogue found this much less competitive than the big field he encountered at Doncaster last time and was always doing enough to hold off his only serious rival. He is now 2-2 on Polytrack, having won his maiden over 7f at Lingfield. (op 15-8 tchd 2-1)
Free Thinker, making his nursery debut after showing ability in all three of his starts in maidens, travelled well enough and kept on, but he simply found one too good. (op 2-1)
Northern Tour offered little on this significant step up in trip after over four months off. (op 7-2)
Starry Skymade the running but was easily beaten off and is not progressing. (op 9-2)

7230 WOLVERHAMPTON-RACECOURSE.CO.UK H'CAP 1m 5f 194y(P)
8:50 (8:51) (Class 4) (0-85,85) 3-Y-O+ £5,180 (£1,541; £770; £384) Stalls Low

Form RPR
5131 1 **Precision Break (USA)**[8] 7091 3-9-11 **85** 6ex.................... JamieSpencer 3 93+
(P F I Cole) *mde all: rdn and hung rt over 1f out: drvn out* **4/7**[1]
0165 2 *2 3/4* **Lochiel**[47] 6154 4-9-10 **76**.................... RobertWinston 5 80
(G A Swinbank) *chsd wnr: ev ch 2f out: rdn and sltly hmpd jst over 1f out: one pce* **15/2**[2]
0-01 3 *3/4* **Five Two**[14] 6964 5-9-2 **68**....................(t) EdwardCreighton 2 71
(Gavin Patrick Cromwell, Ire) *s.i.s: hld up and bhd: hdwy over 3f out: rdn wl over 1f out: one pce fnl f* **14/1**
10-4 4 *1 1/2* **Barawin (IRE)**[191] 1730 3-9-6 **80**.................... FrancisNorton 6 81
(K R Burke) *hld up: outpcd over 2f out: styd on towards fin* **20/1**
3500 5 *hd* **Venir Rouge**[13] 6898 4-9-5 **71**.................... KirstyMilczarek 7 72
(M Salaman) *hld up in tch: rdn over 2f out: wknd wl over 1f out* **14/1**
4213 6 *6* **Chookie Hamilton**[27] 6657 4-9-6 **72**.................... TonyHamilton 4 64
(Miss L A Perratt) *prom: pushed along over 3f out: sn wknd* **9/1**[3]
3601 7 *2 1/2* **Apache Fort**[13] 6985 5-8-13 **72**....................(b) RossAtkinson(7) 1 61
(T Keddy) *hld up: rdn 3f out: sn struggling: rdr dropped whip wl ins fnl f* **15/2**[2]
3m 11.58s (5.58) **Going Correction** +0.225s/f (Slow)
WFA 3 from 4yo+ 8lb **7 Ran SP% 115.3**
Speed ratings (Par 105): **93,91,91,90,90 86,85**
toteswinger: 1&2 £2.00, 1&3 £10.40, 2&3 £10.40 CSF £5.75 TOTE £1.30: £1.10, £3.00; EX 6.00.

Owner JMH Lifestyle Ltd **Bred** Gainesway Thoroughbreds Ltd **Trained** Whatcombe, Oxon
■ Stewards' Enquiry : Jamie Spencer one-day ban: careless riding (Nov 21)

FOCUS
An ordinary staying handicap and the form looks muddling.

7231 EVENING RACING - MISS THE TRAFFIC H'CAP 5f 20y(P)
9:20 (9:20) (Class 6) (0-60,60) 3-Y-O+ £3,070 (£906; £453) Stalls Low

Form RPR
5206 1 **Ryedane (IRE)**[10] 7043 6-8-13 **58**....................(b) DuranFentiman(3) 8 67
(T D Easterby) *hld up in tch: rdn to ld ins fnl f: drvn out* **7/2**[1]
0065 2 *1/2* **Admiral Bond (IRE)**[25] 6711 3-9-1 **60**....................(p) DavidProbert(3) 13 67
(G R Oldroyd) *hld up towards rr: hdwy on outside over 2f out: hung lft over 1f out: ev ch whn hung lft ins fnl f: kpt on* **10/1**
304 3 *2 1/4* **Monte Major (IRE)**[8] 7092 7-9-1 **57**....................(v) RobertWinston 9 56
(D Shaw) *a.p: rdn to ld 1f out: hdd and no ex ins fnl f* **14/1**
2300 4 *1/2* **Back In The Red (IRE)**[25] 6711 4-9-1 **60**....................(p) KevinGhunowa(3) 1 57
(R A Harris) *sn rdn and outpcd in rr: hdwy 1f out: kpt on ins fnl f: nvr nrr* **7/2**[1]
5 5 *hd* **Rightcar Lewis**[28] 6633 3-8-8 **57**.................... AndrewHeffernan(7) 3 53
(Peter Grayson) *s.i.s: hld up towards rr: hdwy on ins wl over 1f out: rdn and kpt on ins fnl f* **20/1**
5500 6 *3/4* **Walragnek**[83] 5101 4-9-1 **60**.................... LukeMorris(3) 11 54
(J G M O'Shea) *outpcd towards rr: rdn wl over 1f out: kpt on ins fnl f* **20/1**
605 7 *1* **Mr Rooney (IRE)**[20] 6823 5-8-9 **56**.................... SladeO'Hara(5) 5 46
(A Berry) *led: rdn wh edgd rt and hdd 1f out: wknd ins fnl f* **10/1**
0040 8 *1 1/4* **Fizzlephut (IRE)**[238] 875 6-9-0 **56**.................... PaulFitzsimons 2 42
(Miss J R Tooth) *prom tl wknd ins fnl f* **14/1**
0000 9 *1* **Helping Hand (IRE)**[22] 6765 3-9-4 **60**.................... HayleyTurner 10 42
(R Hollinshead) *swtchd lft sn after s: a bhd* **7/1**
5056 10 *3 1/2* **Just Joey**[25] 6711 4-9-3 **59**....................(b) ChrisCatlin 6 28
(J R Weymes) *chsd ldr to 2f out: wknd over 1f out* **13/2**[3]
-000 11 *15* **Daddy Cool**[84] 5050 4-8-10 **57**.................... JackDean(5) 4 —
(W G M Turner) *prom tl wknd over 2f out* **33/1**
63.33 secs (1.03) **Going Correction** +0.225s/f (Slow) **11 Ran SP% 127.6**
Speed ratings (Par 101): **100,99,95,94,94 93,91,89,88,82 58**
toteswinger: 1&2 £23.30, 1&3 £1.10, 2&3 £2.70 CSF £42.27 CT £154.14 TOTE £5.00: £2.00, £2.10, £2.30; EX 53.70 Place 6 £ 70.08, Place 5 £ 8.90.
Owner Ryedale Partners No 5 **Bred** Tally-Ho Stud **Trained** Great Habton, N Yorks

FOCUS
A moderate but very competitive sprint handicap rated around the first two.
T/Plt: £40.20 to a £1 stake. Pool: £98,100.59. 1,781.03 winning tickets. T/Qpdt: £4.60 to a £1 stake. Pool: £8,602.44. 1,375.02 winning tickets. KH

7232 - 7234a (Foreign Racing) - See Raceform Interactive

6958 DUNDALK (A.W) (L-H)
Friday, November 7

OFFICIAL GOING: Standard

7235a CARLINGFORD STKS (LISTED RACE) 1m 2f 150y
7:40 (7:40) 3-Y-O+ £23,933 (£7,022; £3,345; £1,139)

RPR
1 **Fiery Lad (IRE)**[42] 6261 3-9-1 106.................... EJMcNamara 8 104
(G M Lyons, Ire) *mid-div: hdwy in 7th 1/2-way: 4th 3f out: impr to ld under 2f out: rdn and chal 1f out: kpt on wl u.p fnl f* **5/2**[1]
2 *1 1/4* **Varsity**[11] 7034 5-9-2 99....................(tp) FMBerry 3 98+
(C F Swan, Ire) *s.i.s: hld up towards rr: hdwy in 5th 2f out: 2nd 1 1/2f out: chal 1f out: kpt on fnl f: nt match wnr* **8/1**
3 *4 1/2* **Northgate (IRE)**[42] 6261 3-9-1 97.................... CDHayes 14 93
(Joseph G Murphy, Ire) *in rr of mid-div: hdwy in 8th 2f out: 3rd 1 1/2f out: 4th and no ex 1f out: kpt on same pce fnl f* **25/1**
4 *shd* **Monteriggioni (IRE)**[21] 6798 6-9-5 101.................... PBBeggy 5 92
(John Geoghegan, Ire) *hld up towards rr: hdwy to 5th 1 1/2f out: rdn into 3rd 1f out: kpt on same pce fnl f* **14/1**
5 *3 1/2* **Cat By The Tale (USA)**[20] 6831 3-8-12 90....................(t) WMLordan 11 84
(David Wachman, Ire) *mid-div: rdn into 6th 1 1/2f out: no ex in 5th 1f out: kpt on same pce fnl f* **16/1**
6 *2* **Windsor Palace (IRE)**[11] 7034 3-9-1 101.................... JMurtagh 6 83
(A P O'Brien, Ire) *mid-div: 8th 1/2-way: rdn into 6th 2f out: no ex in 7th 1 1/2f out: kpt on one pce* **13/2**[3]
7 *5* **Quinmaster (USA)**[21] 6798 6-9-5 101....................(tp) RPCleary 9 72
(M Halford, Ire) *chsd ldr in 2nd: rdn in 4th and no ex 1 1/2f out: kpt on one pce* **14/1**
8 *1 3/4* **Don Julio A (ARG)**[36] 6431 4-9-5.................... WJLee 1 69
(N F Glynn, Ire) *mid-div early: towards rr bef 1/2-way: rdn into mod 9th 1f out: kpt on same pce fnl f* **33/1**
9 *2 1/2* **Mojito Royale (IRE)**[21] 6798 4-9-5 103....................(p) PTownend 7 64
(Eoin Doyle, Ire) *chsd ldrs: 6th 1/2-way: rdn and lost pl over 2f out: 9th 1 1/2f out: kpt on one pce* **12/1**
10 *4 1/2* **Kitty Hawk Miss (IRE)**[26] 6690 3-8-12 95....................(p) KJManning 12 54
(J S Bolger, Ire) *chsd ldrs: 5th 1/2-way: rdn and no ex 2f out* **10/1**
11 *13* **Soft Morning**[41] 6298 4-9-2.................... DPMcDonogh 13 28
(Sir Mark Prescott) *led: rdn and hdd under 2f out: no ex and sn wknd* **5/1**[2]
12 *1 3/4* **Bobs Pride (IRE)**[28] 6640 6-9-5 94.................... PJSmullen 10 28
(D K Weld, Ire) *chsd ldrs: 3rd 1/2-way: rdn in 4th 2f out: sn no ex and wknd* **9/1**
13 *1/2* **High Court Drama (IRE)**[204] 1435 3-9-1 93.................... MJKinane 4 28
(P D Deegan, Ire) *chsd ldrs: 4th 1/2-way: rdn and wknd ent st* **8/1**
14 *7* **Farinelli**[21] 6798 5-9-5 99.................... CO'Donoghue 2 13
(Mrs John Harrington, Ire) *chsd ldrs early: 9th 1/2-way: rdn and wknd bef st* **12/1**
2m 11.52s (131.52)
WFA 3 from 4yo+ 5lb **14 Ran SP% 141.3**
CSF £27.54 TOTE £3.60: £1.60, £2.80, £7.50; DF 23.70.
Owner W Bellew **Bred** Ken Carroll **Trained** Dunsany, Co. Meath
■ Stewards' Enquiry : D P McDonogh vet said filly was found to have two small cuts on the outside of its right hind leg

NOTEBOOK
Fiery Lad(IRE) came into the race boasting a record of four wins and three placed efforts from seven starts at Dundalk and tackling Listed company for the second successive time, he got it right in decisive fashion. Big plans now await and it wouldn't be a surprise to see him line up in a Group contest early next year, with his previous third-placed effort having been boosted by Muhannak at the Breeders' Cup. (op 3/1)
Soft Morning has not won since landing a Listed event on the sand at Deauville almost a year ago and she ran no sort of race this time, dropping out tamely having made the early running. (op 3/1)

7236 - 7238a (Foreign Racing) - See Raceform Interactive

6970 DONCASTER (L-H)
Saturday, November 8

OFFICIAL GOING: Soft (5.8)
Wind: Moderate half against Weather: Fine

7239 MOLLART COX APPRENTICE H'CAP 7f
12:25 (12:26) (Class 4) (0-85,84) 3-Y-O+ £5,180 (£1,541; £770; £384) Stalls High

Form RPR
1002 1 **Misphire**[7] 7129 5-8-12 **76**.................... KirstyMilczarek 13 85
(M Dods) *hmpd s: chsd ldrs: hmpd and pushed lft ins fnl f: led last 50yds* **20/1**
0005 2 *3/4* **Cornus**[7] 7143 6-8-9 **73**....................(be) DavidProbert 19 80
(A J McCabe) *hld up in mid-div stands' side: smooth hdwy over 2f out: led and edgd lft jst ins fnl f: hdd and no ex towards fin* **9/1**[2]
6200 3 *nk* **Nisaal (IRE)**[15] 6950 3-8-10 **75** ow2.................... TravisBlock 17 80
(J J Quinn) *mid-div: hdwy over 2f out: kpt on wl ins fnl f* **40/1**
4200 4 *shd* **Esoterica (IRE)**[11] 7041 5-8-9 **76**....................(b) GaryBartley(3) 5 82
(J S Goldie) *mid-div: gd hdwy over 1f out: styng on same pce whn carried lft wl ins fnl f* **40/1**
4035 5 *1/2* **Kiwi Bay**[14] 6976 3-9-3 **82**.................... JamieMoriarty 16 86
(M Dods) *mid-div: hdwy over 2f out: styd on fnl f* **33/1**
0011 6 *shd* **Smarty Socks (IRE)**[6] 7153 4-8-7 **71** 6ex.................... RussellKennemore 1 75+
(P T Midgley) *racd alone far side tl swtchd rt after 1f: w ldrs: led over 2f out: hdd and hung rt ins fnl f: no ex* **5/1**[1]
0605 7 *1/2* **Geojimali**[7] 7129 6-8-11 **78**.................... KellyHarrison(3) 20 81
(J S Goldie) *hld up in rr stands' side: hdwy over 1f out: styd on wl towards fin* **20/1**
0664 8 *1/2* **Balakiref**[7] 7131 9-8-1 **70**.................... AndreaAtzeni(5) 3 72
(M Dods) *in rr on outer: hdwy over 2f out: styd on fnl f* **14/1**
0652 9 *hd* **Kingsdale Orion (IRE)**[7] 7127 4-9-0 **83**.................... BMcHugh(5) 7 84
(B Ellison) *mid-div: rdn 3f out: kpt on: nt rch ldrs* **20/1**
1162 10 *nk* **Internationaldebut (IRE)**[14] 6976 3-9-3 **82**.................... TolleyDean 15 81
(S Parr) *led tl over 2f out: fdd fnl f* **20/1**
0450 11 *nk* **River Thames**[11] 7041 5-8-8 **72**.................... NeilBrown 2 71
(K A Ryan) *mid-div on outer: hdwy over 2f out: sn chsng ldrs: one pce* **12/1**

6211 **12** *nk* **Shotley Mac**[4] 7175 4-9-1 **79** 6ex....(b) DuranFentiman 10 78
(N Bycroft) *chsd ldrs: one pce fnl 2f* **10/1**[3]
0003 **13** *1* **Compton's Eleven**[9] 7101 7-8-10 **81**.... AliceHaynes(7) 6 77
(M R Channon) *in rr: swtchd lft 3f out: chsng ldrs on outer over 1f out: sn fdd* **33/1**
0505 **14** *1/2* **Aye Aye Digby (IRE)**[22] 6783 3-9-0 **84**.... AmyScott(5) 12 78
(H Candy) *hmpd s: mid-div: kpt on fnl 2f: nvr rchd ldrs* **12/1**
5500 **15** *3/4* **Zomerlust**[15] 6947 6-9-1 **84**.... JamieKyne(5) 11 77
(J J Quinn) *mid-div: rdn over 2f out: kpt on fnl f* **18/1**
0531 **16** *1 1/4* **Sadeek**[134] 3443 4-9-2 **80**.... JackMitchell 21 69
(B Smart) *chsd ldrs stands' side: wknd over 1f out* **9/1**[2]
3315 **17** *1 1/4* **Memphis Man**[20] 6842 5-9-3 **81**.... LukeMorris 4 67
(P D Evans) *hld up in rr: effrt 3f out: nvr a factor* **18/1**
0000 **18** *1/2* **Jack Rackham**[19] 6859 4-8-10 **74**.... MarcHalford 8 58
(B Smart) *a towards rr* **33/1**
0003 **19** *3* **Carleton**[7] 7143 3-8-10 **82**.... DebraEngland(7) 18 57
(W J Musson) *chsd ldrs stands' side: wknd 2f out* **16/1**
0020 **20** *2 3/4* **High Curragh**[11] 7047 5-8-11 **78** ow1.... FrederikTylicki(3) 14 47
(K A Ryan) *chsd ldrs: hrd rdn over 2f out: sn lost pl* **14/1**
3060 **21** *6* **Burning Incense (IRE)**[26] 6710 5-9-4 **82**....(p) AndrewMullen 22 35
(M Dods) *hld up in rr stands' side: lost pl 2f out: sn bhd and eased* **16/1**

1m 33.2s (6.90) **Going Correction** +0.85s/f (Soft)
WFA 3 from 4yo+ 1lb **21** Ran SP% **129.5**
Speed ratings (Par 105): **94,93,92,92,92 92,91,90,90,90 89,89,88,87,87 85,84,83,80,77 70**
toteswinger: 1&2 £36.60, 1&3 £48.40, 2&3 £58.50. CSF £177.29 CT £7041.31 TOTE £27.90: £4.80, £2.20, £13.50, £12.30; EX 118.10 Trifecta £216.00 Pool: £291.91 - 1.00 winning ticket..
Owner Transpennine Partnership **Bred** P T Tellwright **Trained** Denton, Co Durham
■ David Probert, runner-up here, shared the apprentice title with William Buick. Both rode 50 winners.
■ Stewards' Enquiry : David Probert 15-day ban: careless riding (1 for offence and 14 under totting-up procedure - three days deferred until March 28th, 2009) (Nov 28-Dec 9)
Kirsty Milczarek one-day ban: careless riding (Nov 22)

FOCUS
After 0.5mm of rain overnight the ground was described as soft, and a strong headwind made it quite a test up the straight. This looked a competitive handicap for apprentices, and the whole field came centre to stands' side. The form looks pretty sound rated around the first two.
Aye Aye Digby(IRE) Official explanation: jockey said colt was hampered at start

7240 TOTESPORT BETXTRA E B F MAIDEN STKS 6f
12:55 (12:57) (Class 4) 2-Y-O **£5,504** (£1,637; £818; £408) **Stalls** High

Form RPR
02 **1** **Dynamo Dane (IRE)**[23] 6755 2-9-3 0.... TPQueally 17 69
(J G Given) *racd wd: cl up: led over 2f out: rdn and hung bdly lft ent fnl f: kpt on* **10/1**
0 **2** *1 1/4* **Al Qeddaaf (IRE)**[22] 6776 2-9-3 0.... RHills 6 65
(W J Haggas) *prom: pushed along and sltly outpcd 2f out: sn rdn and styd on wl fnl f* **11/1**
4400 **3** *nk* **Chimbonda**[8] 7113 2-9-0 70.... TolleyDean(3) 7 64
(S Parr) *led: hdd over 2f out and sn rdn along: drvn ent fnl f: kpt on same pce* **10/1**
5 **4** *nk* **Kingshill Prince**[33] 6535 2-9-3 0.... ChrisCatlin 2 63
(W J Musson) *s.i.s and bhd: hdwy 1/2-way: styd on strly ent fnl f: nrst fin* **12/1**
36 **5** *hd* **Getcarter**[22] 6776 2-9-3 0.... RichardHughes 8 63
(R Hannon) *in tch: hdwy to chse ldrs 2f out: sn rdn and one pce ins fnl f* **5/2**[1]
0 **6** *1* **Bravalto**[12] 7020 2-9-3 0.... PaulMulrennan 3 60
(B Smart) *prom: rdn along 2f out: grad wknd* **9/1**
0 **7** *3/4* **Monsieur Kiss Kiss**[8] 7104 2-9-3 0.... HayleyTurner 12 57
(G A Butler) *chsd ldrs: rdn along over 2f out: drvn and no imp fr over 1f out* **11/2**[2]
0 **8** *hd* **The Scorching Wind (IRE)**[18] 6885 2-9-3 0.... SaleemGolam 13 57
(S C Williams) *s.i.s and in rr: hdwy over 2f out: kpt on appr fnl f: nrst fin* **50/1**
0 **9** *1 3/4* **Sircozy (IRE)**[32] 6552 2-8-12 0.... WilliamCarson(5) 5 51
(S C Williams) *nvr bttr than midfield* **33/1**
10 *1 1/4* **Zeyadah (IRE)** 2-8-12 0.... PhilipRobinson 4 43
(M A Jarvis) *prom: rdn along over 2f out and sn wknd* **7/1**[3]
0 **11** *4 1/2* **Gracie's Games**[12] 7015 2-8-7 0.... SophieDoyle(5) 1 29
(R J Price) *a towards rr* **100/1**
00 **12** *5* **Jachol (IRE)**[8] 7104 2-9-3 0.... MichaelHills 9 19
(W J Haggas) *a towards rr* **16/1**
000 **13** *1/2* **Red Horse (IRE)**[22] 6776 2-9-3 0.... JamieSpencer 11 18
(M L W Bell) *a in rr* **17/2**
0 **14** *1* **Raffys Rock (IRE)**[32] 6552 2-9-3 0.... J-PGuillambert 15 15
(S C Williams) *midfield: rdn along 1/2-way and sn wknd* **66/1**
0 **15** *6* **Net Value (USA)**[22] 6789 2-9-3 0....(b[1]) TomEaves 10 —
(B Smart) *a towards rr* **22/1**

1m 19.48s (5.88) **Going Correction** +0.85s/f (Soft) **15** Ran SP% **128.8**
Speed ratings (Par 98): **94,92,91,91,91 89,88,88,86,84 78,72,71,70,62**
toteswinger: 1&2 £16.10, 1&3 £36.60, 2&3 £21.80. CSF £119.37 TOTE £11.60: £3.00, £3.50, £4.60; EX 121.40 TRIFECTA Not won..
Owner Hintlesham Racing **Bred** Malm Partnership **Trained** Willoughton, Lincs

FOCUS
This looked a fairly modest maiden on paper, and the result seemed to bear that out. The level is fluid with the third setting the level and also limiting the form.

NOTEBOOK
Dynamo Dane(IRE) improved quite a bit on his debut outing when giving 1-5 shot Audemar a race at Great Leighs last time, and he continued his progress with success here. From the highest draw, he raced apart from the rest of the field in the early stages, but gradually drifted towards the centre of the track from two and a half furlongs out, and then drifted further left inside the last when well on top. He is clearly improving with racing and his trainer suggested that he did not think that the son of Danehill Dancer needed the ground this soft. (op 17-2 tchd 11-1)
Al Qeddaaf(IRE) got outpaced from two and a half furlongs out before running on strongly again in the closing stages. Both his pedigree and style of running suggest he will come into his own over middle distances next season, and to qualify for a handicap mark he needs one more outing. (op 10-1 tchd 9-1)
Chimbonda, who went without the headgear this time, came into the race with an official mark of 70. He got the trip well enough considering the testing conditions and is probably the best guide to the level of the form. (op 16-1)
Kingshill Prince, who caught the eye of the Stewards on his debut, was another who came home well and shaped as though he will do a lot better when stepped up in distance next year. There is a good deal of stamina on his dam's side and, as a half-brother to five winners, he will be interesting once eligible for handicaps. (op 14-1 tchd 11-1)
Getcarter was too keen through the early stages and as a result did not get home. He seemed to handle the ground well enough but needs to learn to settle. Handicaps are now open to him. (tchd 11-4)
Bravalto, beaten a long way on his debut, ran a better race this time, but he is another bred to improve for longer trips next year. (op 20-1)
Zeyadah(IRE) is a sister to Jadaara, who won on her only start at two over 7.5f, and is also a half-sister to two other winners, including a useful horse called Almaram, who has won five times in Dubai. She looked interesting on paper but was weak in the betting and, having shown up well to two furlongs out, she dropped out tamely. (op 5-1)

7241 TOTESPORT.COM NURSERY 6f
1:30 (1:32) (Class 4) (0-85,85) 2-Y-O **£6,476** (£1,927; £963; £481) **Stalls** High

Form RPR
1 **1** **Harry Patch**[23] 6764 2-9-0 **78**.... PhilipRobinson 12 86+
(M A Jarvis) *w ldrs: shkn up to ld over 1f out: r.o strly: eased towards fin* **4/1**[1]
1410 **2** *1 1/4* **Kingswinford (IRE)**[14] 6972 2-9-2 **80**.... JimmyFortune 15 85
(P D Evans) *in rr: hdwy over 2f out: styd on to take 2nd ins fnl f* **11/1**
3101 **3** *1 1/2* **Lucky Numbers (IRE)**[4] 7173 2-9-3 **81** 6ex.... RyanMoore 13 81
(Paul Green) *trckd ldrs: effrt 2f out: styd on same pce fnl f* **8/1**[3]
6531 **4** *2 1/4* **Final Salute**[19] 6865 2-8-9 **73**....(v) TomEaves 14 66
(B Smart) *hld up in rr towards stands' side: hdwy over 2f out: kpt on same pce fnl f* **14/1**
5331 **5** *nse* **Doric Echo**[37] 6406 2-9-3 **81**.... PaulHanagan 7 74
(B Smart) *w ldrs: kpt on same pce appr fnl f* **14/1**
530 **6** *1 3/4* **Veroon (IRE)**[50] 6080 2-8-8 **72**.... TPQueally 3 60
(J G Given) *chsd ldrs far side: kpt on same pce fnl 2f* **16/1**
3130 **7** *3/4* **Daddy's Gift (IRE)**[14] 6970 2-9-6 **84**.... RichardHughes 16 70
(R Hannon) *racd stands' side: edgd lft over 2f out: kpt on: nvr rchd ldrs* **14/1**
21 **8** *2* **Outofoil (IRE)**[87] 4974 2-9-3 **81**.... GeorgeBaker 2 61
(R M Beckett) *swvd lft s: mid-div on outer: hdwy over 2f out: nvr nr ldrs* **12/1**
1134 **9** *shd* **Count Paris (USA)**[14] 6970 2-8-13 **77**.... JoeFanning 5 56
(M Johnston) *w ldrs: fdd over 1f out* **5/1**[2]
61 **10** *1 1/2* **Mythicism**[22] 6785 2-9-0 **78**....(t) PaulMulrennan 6 53
(B Smart) *led tl hdd & wknd over 1f out* **16/1**
34 **11** *1* **Ruby Tallulah**[37] 6414 2-8-11 **75**.... LPKeniry 11 47
(C R Dore) *s.i.s: effrt and n.m.r over 1f out: nvr a factor* **25/1**
3622 **12** *3/4* **Lakeman (IRE)**[32] 6549 2-9-4 **82**.... TonyHamilton 8 52
(B Ellison) *mid-div: effrt over 2f out: lost pl over 1f out* **8/1**[3]
10 **13** *3 3/4* **Regal Lyric (IRE)**[30] 6603 2-8-11 **75**.... MickyFenton 10 33
(T P Tate) *in rr: hung rt 2f out: sn bhd* **33/1**
0114 **14** *1/2* **Amber Sunset**[16] 6924 2-8-12 **79**.... LukeMorris(3) 9 36
(J Jay) *w ldrs: wknd 2f out* **16/1**
0100 **15** *22* **Spiritofthewest (IRE)**[14] 6972 2-9-4 **85**.... TolleyDean(3) 4 —
(S Parr) *chsd ldrs towards far side: hung rt and lost pl over 2f out: sn bhd and eased* **16/1**

1m 18.05s (4.45) **Going Correction** +0.85s/f (Soft) **15** Ran SP% **125.2**
Speed ratings (Par 98): **104,102,100,97,97 94,93,91,91,89 87,86,81,81,51**
toteswinger: 1&2 £13.10, 1&3 £7.20, 2&3 £21.20. CSF £49.76 CT £278.51 TOTE £4.00: £2.10, £4.10, £3.00; EX 60.10 Trifecta £367.90 Part won. Pool: £497.19 - 0.70 winning tickets..
Owner Mrs Gay Jarvis **Bred** Red House Stud **Trained** Newmarket, Suffolk

FOCUS
A competitive nursery featuring one or two interesting types and the first two are progressive.

NOTEBOOK
Harry Patch ◆ made a successful debut at Nottingham over the minimum trip and looked fairly handicapped on a mark of 78. The step up to 6f promised to suit, and that was certainly the case, as he travelled strongly and sealed matters when quickening up with over a furlong to run. He was still showing signs of greenness in the closing stages and looks very much the type to go on from two to three, so there should be plenty more to come from him next season.
Kingswinford(IRE) was outclassed in a Listed race last time out but his previous efforts in handicap company had suggested he was progressing quite nicely. He tracked the winner through, and while he could not match that one's acceleration from a furlong and a half out, he kept plugging away and saw the trip out strongly. His performance is a good guide to the level of the form. (op 12-1)
Lucky Numbers(IRE), who is very much at home with plenty of give in the ground, ran a solid race under his penalty for winning a weak race at Catterick last time. (op 10-1)
Final Salute kept on quite well from off the pace but this ground might not have been ideal for this son of Royal Applause. (op 16-1)
Doric Echo, a stablemate of the fourth, had already proved his effectiveness in testing conditions, but a 9lb rise for his win at Ayr last month probably did for his chances. (op 16-1 tchd 12-1)
Veroon(IRE), who is a half-brother to a couple of horses won on soft ground, was isolated from the main action in the closing stages, as the principals all challenged more towards the stands' side, so it was a fair effort from him in the circumstances. (tchd 18-1)
Daddy's Gift(IRE) ran her race but looks a little high in the handicap now. (tchd 12-1)
Regal Lyric(IRE) Official explanation: jockey said colt hung right
Amber Sunset Official explanation: jockey said filly had no more to give
Spiritofthewest(IRE) Official explanation: jockey said colt hung badly right throughout

7242 TOTESPORTCASINO.COM E B F GILLIES FILLIES' STKS (LISTED RACE) 1m 2f 60y
2:05 (2:07) (Class 1) 3-Y-O+ **£26,667** (£10,084; £5,040; £2,520) **Stalls** Low

Form RPR
435 **1** **Les Fazzani (IRE)**[9] 7100 4-9-0 100.... DarryllHolland 6 109
(K A Ryan) *prom: trckd ldr 1/2-way: hdwy to ld wl over 2f out: rdn and edgd rt wl over 1f out: sn clr* **7/2**[1]
1600 **2** *7* **Classic Remark (IRE)**[22] 6781 3-8-13 106.... MickyFenton 9 98
(H J L Dunlop) *hld up in rr: hdwy 3f out: rdn wl over 1f out: chse wnr ent fnl f: sn drvn and no imp* **20/1**
12-6 **3** *1* **Kahara**[49] 6127 4-9-0 85.... DaneO'Neill 4 93
(L M Cumani) *hld up towards rr: hdwy 3f out: rdn along wl over 1f out: kpt on ins fnl f* **11/2**
0031 **4** *2 1/4* **Insaaf**[87] 4970 3-8-10 94....(v) RHills 8 89
(W J Haggas) *led: rdn along and hdd wl: over 2f out: drvn wl over 1f out and sn one pce* **4/1**[2]
4142 **5** *6* **Interchange (IRE)**[8] 7108 3-8-10 81.... JimCrowley 5 77
(J R Fanshawe) *hld up in tch: effrt 4f out: rdn along 3f out and sn btn* **7/1**
531 **6** *1/2* **Surrealism**[17] 6896 3-8-10 79.... JimmyFortune 1 76
(J H M Gosden) *trckd ldrs: effrt and hdwy on inner 3f out: rdn over 2f out: sn drvn and btn* **5/1**[3]
-410 **7** *7* **Sourire**[9] 7099 3-8-13 90.... J-PGuillambert 10 65
(Sir Mark Prescott) *hld up: effrt 4f out: rdn along 3f out and nvr a factor* **25/1**
13 **8** *3 3/4* **Summer's Lease**[30] 6605 3-8-10 81.... JamieSpencer 3 54
(M L W Bell) *chsd ldr: pushed along over 4f out: rdn and wknd over 3f out* **11/2**

0203 9 18 **Encircled**[8] 7108 4-9-0 76.. MichaelHills 2 18
(D Haydn Jones) *a in rr* **33/1**

2m 17.64s (6.44) **Going Correction** +0.85s/f (Soft)
WFA 3 from 4yo 4lb **9 Ran SP% 113.7**
Speed ratings (Par 108): **108,102,101,99,95 94,89,86,71**
toteswinger: 1&2 £9.80, 1&3 £4.60, 2&3 £13.40. CSF £73.28 TOTE £3.90: £1.50, £3.60, £2.20; EX 45.10 Trifecta £403.20 Pool: £1,057.15 - 1.94 winning tickets..
Owner Mike & Denise Dawes **Bred** J Erhardt And Mrs J Schonwalder **Trained** Hambleton, N Yorks

FOCUS

This looked a modest race for the class, featuring only two fillies who could boast a three-figure BHA rating. Those two filled the first two places but not form to take too literally with few showing their form on the ground.

NOTEBOOK

Les Fazzani(IRE), who was unlucky in running at Lingfield last time and had since switched stables to join Kevin Ryan, has always appreciated plenty of cut in the ground, and, back over her best distance, ran out an easy winner. She steadily drew further and further clear over the final two furlongs, her rider letting her edge over to the stands' rail in the closing stages. That is it for the year now, but she will apparently stay in training next season. (tchd 10-3)

Classic Remark(IRE) had been disappointing in her last two starts but her trainer was confident of a better showing on this soft ground, and she justified his opinion. However, she had no chance with the winner, and it has to be said that her current mark of 106, gained as a result of finishing close up in a tactical Nassau Stakes, greatly flatters her. (op 16-1 tchd 14-1)

Kahara was having only her second start of the campaign having suffered niggling problems throughout the season. This distance would have been on the short side for her but the ground made it much more of a test and, given that she only has a rating of 85, connections will no doubt be pleased that she has gained some black type. (op 7-1)

Insaaf, returning from a three-month break, had won her previous two starts on soft ground but she had not run over further than a mile before. Being by Averti, her stamina was clearly going to be in doubt, but she was ridden as though connections had no concerns. As it happens she did not see it out, but it was a bold effort. (op 9-2 tchd 7-2)

Interchange(IRE), a well-bred, lightly-raced daughter of Montjeu, had a lot to find at this level, and the drop back in trip was not in her favour. She has the potential to do better if kept in training as a four-year-old. (op 9-1)

Surrealism, who is a half-sister to this year's Melbourne Cup runner-up Bauer, was taking a big step in class after her win in a Bath maiden last time. She ran well for a long way and is another who is bred to get better as she gets older. (op 11-2 tchd 6-1)

7243 TOTESPORTGAMES.COM WENTWORTH STKS (LISTED RACE) 6f

2:35 (2:40) (Class 1) 3-Y-O+ **£26,667** (£10,084; £5,040; £2,520) **Stalls** High

Form RPR

-133 **1** **Icelandic**[35] 6484 6-9-3 104..(t) HayleyTurner 10 112+
(Frank Sheridan) *trckd ldrs: smooth hdwy and pushed towards ins 2f out: shkn up and led over 1f out: sn qcknd clr: rdn out* **11/1**

451 **2** 2 1/2 **Against The Grain**[50] 6069 5-9-3 91.. JoeFanning 5 104
(L Lungo) *chsd ldr on outer: kpt on wl fnl f: no ch w wnr* **11/1**

2601 **3** 2 **Chief Editor**[42] 6289 4-9-3 107.. PhilipRobinson 14 98
(M A Jarvis) *trckd ldrs: effrt and edgd rt 2f out: styd on ins fnl f* **5/1**[2]

5111 **4** hd **Judge 'n Jury**[14] 6971 4-9-3 109..(t) KevinGhunowa 9 97
(R A Harris) *chsd ldrs: kpt on same pce fnl f: lost 3rd nr line* **7/1**

2452 **5** 2 1/4 **Welsh Emperor (IRE)**[14] 6975 9-9-3 112..(b) MickyFenton 1 91
(T P Tate) *racd wd: overall ldr: hdd over 1f out: wknd wl ins fnl f* **16/1**

-110 **6** 1/2 **Perfect Polly**[28] 6645 3-9-1 103.. ShaneKelly 11 87
(J Noseda) *chsd ldrs: one pce fnl 2f* **20/1**

1110 **7** hd **Perfect Flight**[22] 6782 3-8-12 91.. KirstyMilczarek 16 84
(M Blanshard) *in rr div stands' side: hdwy and hmpd 2f out: kpt on nvr trbld ldrs* **28/1**

1310 **8** 2 3/4 **Main Aim**[37] 6429 3-9-3 100.. RyanMoore 13 80
(Sir Michael Stoute) *in rr: hdwy over 2f out: kpt on fnl f: nvr nr ldrs* **7/2**[1]

5000 **9** 1/2 **Aahayson**[35] 6468 4-9-6 105..(p) AndrewElliott 15 82
(K R Burke) *chsd ldrs stands' side: wknd over 1f out* **14/1**

00-5 **10** 1 1/4 **Quito (IRE)**[14] 6975 11-9-3 98..(b) PaulMulrennan 8 75
(Mrs R A Carr) *mid-div: kpt on fnl 2f: nvr on terms* **33/1**

0560 **11** 1 1/4 **Sudden Impact (IRE)**[4] 7181 3-8-12 89.. TPQueally 12 66
(Paul Green) *in rr: swtchd lft over 2f out: hdwy on wd outside over 1f out: nvr on terms* **100/1**

2002 **12** 1 1/2 **Zidane**[28] 6645 6-9-6 108.. JamieSpencer 4 70
(J R Fanshawe) *hld up towards rr: hdwy over 2f out: wknd fnl f* **11/2**[3]

066 **13** 3 **Cape**[15] 6947 5-8-12 89.. DarryllHolland 2 53
(P Howling) *mid-div: hdwy on outside over 2f out: wknd over 1f out* **50/1**

-030 **14** 6 **Philario (IRE)**[133] 3488 3-9-3 103.. JimCrowley 7 40
(K R Burke) *hld up in mid-div: effrt over 2f out: sn wknd* **50/1**

501 **15** 4 1/2 **Skhilling Spirit**[15] 6947 5-9-3 97.. NeilBrown 17 26
(T D Barron) *virtually ref to r: hopelessly detached in last tl past two eased rivals ins fnl f* **12/1**

1130 **16** 1/2 **Angus Newz**[22] 6782 5-9-1 89.. FrancisNorton 3 23
(M Quinn) *chsd ldrs on outer: lost pl over 2f out: eased ins fnl f* **50/1**

1000 **17** 11 **Galeota (IRE)**[28] 6645 6-9-6 100.. RichardHughes 6 —
(R Hannon) *chsd ldrs: lost pl over 1f out: eased ins fnl f* **22/1**

1m 16.47s (2.87) **Going Correction** +0.85s/f (Soft) **17 Ran SP% 126.1**
Speed ratings (Par 111): **114,110,108,107,104 104,103,100,99,97 96,94,90,82,76 75,60**
toteswinger: 1&2 £23.20, 1&3 £18.20, 2&3 £18.40. CSF £121.01 TOTE £16.10: £4.30, £4.00, £2.60; EX 185.00 Trifecta £1290.20 Part won. Pool: £1,743.57 - 0.64 winning tickets..
Owner Scuderia A4/5 **Bred** Cheveley Park Stud Ltd **Trained** Stoke Heath, Shropshire
■ Stewards' Enquiry : Philip Robinson caution: careless riding.

FOCUS

This looked a good race for the grade, with ten of the 17 runners with BHA marks of at least 100. The form is rated conservatively but the first two are both rated improvers.

NOTEBOOK

Icelandic scored in convincing fashion, having run well in defeat in similar company in his last two starts, but those runs came over 7f and the drop back to sprinting brought about dramatic improvement. Always travelling well off the pace, he cruised up alongside Judge 'N Jury a furlong and a half out and, when Turner pressed the button at the furlong pole, he quickened away in great style. He might be a six-year-old, but he is unexposed as a sprinter, and on this performance he looks capable of winning in Group company over 6f next year, granted soft ground. (op 10-1)

Against The Grain is a rapidly improving sprinter and followed up his clear-cut win in the Ayr Silver Cup with a cracking effort. Like the winner, plenty of give in the ground looks essential to him, and he could well make his mark at this level next year as he too remains fairly unexposed despite his age. (op 16-1)

Chief Editor was an impressive winner of a handicap at Haydock last time off 97, and this softer ground, if anything, promised to suit him even better. He ran a sound-enough race but the turn of foot he possesses was absent this time. (op 4-1)

Judge 'n Jury has been in cracking form this autumn, progressing through the handicapping ranks, but the sixth furlong on this step up to Listed company was the worry, and it eventually found him out. A tough sort who takes his racing well, he will be a valid candidate for honours at Listed/Group 3 level over the minimum trip next season when the ground is not too fast. (op 8-1)

Welsh Emperor(IRE) is at his best when dominating in a small field over 7f these days but put up a sound effort on this drop in trip. (tchd 11-1)

Perfect Polly, a winner at this level against her own sex back in May, has had an interrupted campaign and did not fare too badly. (tchd 22-1)

Perfect Flight did not get the best of runs and acquitted herself well on her return to a soft surface and her rider reported that she suffered interference. Official explanation: jockey said filly suffered interference (tchd 33-1)

Main Aim was disappointing. He was taken off his feet over 5f on fast ground at Newmarket last time and the return to 6f on easier ground promised to suit, but he never got competitive. (op 11-2)

Zidane should not have had any problems with the conditions, but this might have been one race too many at the end of a long season. (op 5-1 tchd 6-1)

7244 £2 MILLION TOTESCOOP6 NOVEMBER H'CAP (HERITAGE HANDICAP) 1m 4f

3:10 (3:13) (Class 2) 3-Y-O+
£52,963 (£15,861; £7,930; £3,969; £1,980; £994) **Stalls** Low

Form RPR

0120 **1** **Tropical Strait (IRE)**[57] 5853 5-8-13 95.. MartinDwyer 22 105
(D W P Arbuthnot) *in tch: hdwy over 3f out: swtchd lft 2f out: rdn to ld over 1f out: drvn and hung lft ins fnl f: kpt on wl* **20/1**

3113 **2** 1/2 **The Betchworth Kid**[37] 6427 3-8-9 97.. HayleyTurner 18 106
(M L W Bell) *hld up towards rr: hdwy 4f out: rdn 2f out: sltly hmpd over 1f out and ev ch tl drvn ins fnl f and no ex towards fin* **9/2**[1]

320 **3** 2 **Tastahil (IRE)**[28] 6646 4-8-13 95.. RHills 11 101
(B W Hills) *chsd ldrs: hdwy 3f out: rdn along whn sltly hmpd 2f out: sn drvn and kpt on wl fnl f* **10/1**

0562 **4** 2 **Dunaskin (IRE)**[6] 7150 8-8-13 95.. TonyHamilton 7 98
(B Ellison) *chsd ldr: led 3f out and sn rdn: drvn and hdd over 1f out: kpt on u.p ins fnl f* **40/1**

2110 **5** 3 1/4 **Hits Only Vic (USA)**[21] 6817 4-8-13 95.. DavidAllan 8 92
(D Carroll) *midfield: effrt to chse ldrs 3f out: rdn along and sltly outpcd 2f out: kpt on u.p ins fnl f* **10/1**

2231 **6** 3/4 **First Avenue**[33] 6536 3-8-7 95..(p) PhilipRobinson 3 91
(M A Jarvis) *a.p: effrt 3f out: rdn over 2f out: drvn and wknd appr fnl f* **17/2**[3]

1-10 **7** 1 **Magicalmysterytour (IRE)**[28] 6646 5-9-4 100.. EddieAhern 19 95
(W J Musson) *in tch: hdwy on stands' rails 3f out: rdn along and n.m.r 2f out: sn drvn and no imp* **14/1**

500 **8** 5 **Group Captain**[28] 6646 6-9-0 96.. RichardHughes 23 83
(H J Collingridge) *hld up in rr: hdwy 3f out: rdn along whn hmpd 2f out: sn drvn and no imp* **25/1**

0050 **9** nk **Ladies Best**[28] 6649 4-8-12 94..(tp) TGMcLaughlin 12 80
(B Ellison) *hld up: hdwy on outer 3f out: rdn whn sltly hmpd 2f out: sn drvn and no imp* **50/1**

0020 **10** 3 1/4 **Carte Diamond (USA)**[21] 6820 7-9-4 100.. PaulHanagan 2 81
(B Ellison) *led: rdn along 4f out: hdd 3f out and grad wknd* **33/1**

1500 **11** 3/4 **Ajaan**[78] 5229 4-9-2 98..(b) TPQueally 21 78
(H R A Cecil) *nvr nr ldrs* **16/1**

0500 **12** 3 1/4 **Greek Envoy**[56] 5894 4-8-8 90.. RobertWinston 16 65
(T P Tate) *towards rr: sme hdwy on outer whn sltly hmpd 2f out: nvr a factor* **28/1**

2440 **13** 1 1/2 **Mull Of Dubai**[28] 6646 5-8-10 92.. MickyFenton 5 64
(T P Tate) *hld up towards rr: hdwy on wd outside 3f out: rdn over 2f out: hmpd 2f out and sn btn* **16/1**

5420 **14** 1 1/4 **Big Robert**[21] 6820 4-9-3 99.. AndrewElliott 4 69
(K R Burke) *s.i.s: hdwy to chse ldrs after 4f: rdn along 4f out and sn wknd* **50/1**

-410 **15** 1 1/4 **Celtic Spirit (IRE)**[189] 1812 5-9-0 97 ow1..(p) GeorgeBaker 17 64
(G L Moore) *nvr nr ldrs* **25/1**

2121 **16** nk **Electrolyser (IRE)**[32] 6563 3-8-7 95.. SteveDrowne 15 63
(C G Cox) *in tch: effrt 3f out: rdn along over 2f out and sn wknd* **5/1**[2]

0/ **17** 5 **Menwaal (FR)**[27] 6690 6-9-0 96.. JamieSpencer 6 56
(Michael David Murphy, Ire) *in tch: hdwy over 4f out: rdn along over 3f out: wknd over 2f out* **10/1**

3263 **18** 7 **Acropolis (IRE)**[12] 7017 7-8-12 94..(b[1]) TomEaves 10 52
(Miss L A Perratt) *in tch: effrt over 3f out: sn rdn and wknd* **50/1**

4011 **19** 5 **Night Crescendo (USA)**[28] 6646 5-8-12 94..(p) JimCrowley 20 44
(Mrs A J Perrett) *prom: rdn along 3f out: sn wknd* **14/1**

1100 **20** 18 **Wicked Daze (IRE)**[21] 6817 5-8-12 94.. ChrisCatlin 13 15
(Ian Williams) *a bhd* **66/1**

30-2 **21** dist **Cold Quest (USA)**[27] 6667 4-8-12 94.. JimmyFortune 14 —
(Miss L A Perratt) *a towards rr: lost pl and wl bhd fnl 4f* **28/1**

2m 42.19s (7.09) **Going Correction** +0.85s/f (Soft)
WFA 3 from 4yo+ 6lb **21 Ran SP% 129.9**
Speed ratings (Par 109): **110,109,108,107,104 104,103,100,100,97 97,95,94,93,92 92,89,88,85,73 —**
toteswinger: 1&2 £66.60, 1&3 £83.80, 2&3 £22.30. CSF £102.59 CT £1002.71 TOTE £31.00: £6.50, £1.90, £2.70, £8.60; EX 388.10 Trifecta £4998.00 Pool: £56,734.17 - 8.40 winning tickets..
Owner Francis Ward and Anthony Ward **Bred** George Ward **Trained** Compton, Berks

FOCUS

A typically competitive November Handicap run at a good gallop, and they came across to the stands' side in the straight, causing some general bunching next to the rail. The form still looks sound rated around the runner-up and fourth. The two declared topweights, Presvis and Young Mick, were non-runners.

NOTEBOOK

Tropical Strait(IRE) ran poorly in the Mallard Handicap last time (race came too quick according to his trainer) but his previous second to subsequent Caulfield Cup winner All The Good at Newbury back in August suggested he was once again handicapped to run well in this race, having finished fourth to Malt Or Mash in the race last year. He was a little tight for room behind the leaders but the gaps appeared for him from two furlongs out and he quickened up well. Always holding the persistent challenge of The Betchworth Kid in the closing stages, he dispelled his trainer's fear that the ground would be too soft for him. He will not go hurdling but will be trained for the Ebor next year. Official explanation: trainer had no explanation for the apparent improvement in form (op 25-1 tchd 33-1)

The Betchworth Kid, a well-backed favourite representing an age group that had produced five of the last ten winners of this race, he had won the Mallard in great style (today's winner behind) before finding the fast ground all against him at Newmarket on his next start. Plenty of people expected to see him return to his best back on soft ground and they were not wrong. After failing in his attempt to get a run up the nearside rail, he weaved his way through from the back of the field, and had every chance but simply met one too good at the weights. There is every chance that he will do better next year, and connections hope he will be good enough to tackle the Cup races. (op 6-1)

Tastahil(IRE) ◆ is a half-brother to Hattan, who has won two Group 3 races this year as a six-year-old, so he is certainly bred to improve with age. He has looked steadily progressive this season and this was another career-best effort, so he could do even better next year as a five-year-old. (op 12-1)

Dunaskin(IRE), prominent throughout, grabbed the stands'-side rail in the straight and kept on stoutly. This was a good effort off a mark 6lb higher than he has ever won off. (op 50-1)

Hits Only Vic(USA), who finished in midfield in the Cesarewitch last time, appreciated the return to soft ground, but, after a successful campaign in which he has won five times, the Handicapper looks to have his measure now. (op 20-1)
First Avenue had been put up 9lb for winning at Warwick last time, and that looked on the harsh side. He had his chance two furlongs out but simply could not sustain his effort in the closing stages. (op 10-1 tchd 11-1 and 8-1)
Magicalmysterytour(IRE), 9lb higher than when getting the better of Tastahil over this course and distance in September, could not confirm that form on 5lb worse terms. (op 12-1)
Group Captain, who won this race when it was held at Windsor in 2006, had shown little in three previous starts on the level this term, but he had dropped to a more realistic mark as a result and put up a more encouraging effort.
Ladies Best, debuting for his new stable, was a bit too keen for his own good in the first-time cheekpieces and tongue tie.
Ajaan was expected to be happier back on soft ground having got jarred up in the middle of the year, but he was disappointing. (tchd 18-1)
Electrolyser(IRE), a progressive three-year-old, was disappointing as he was already beginning to struggle when tightened up for room early in the straight. (op 4-1 tchd 11-2)
Cold Quest(USA) Official explanation: jockey said gelding ran too free early and then lost its action in straight

7245 TOTESPORTBINGO.COM H'CAP 7f
3:45 (3:48) (Class 2) (0-100,100) 3-Y-O+ **£25,904** (£7,708; £3,852; £1,924) **Stalls** High

Form RPR

5200 **1** **Invincible Force (IRE)**[6] 7151 4-8-7 **88**....................(b) FrancisNorton 21 100
(Paul Green) *chsd ldrs stands' side: swtchd lft after 2f: led appr fnl f: hld on towards fin* **33/1**

0025 **2** *hd* **Barney McGrew (IRE)**[17] 6911 5-8-11 **92**.................. TonyHamilton 12 103
(M Dods) *t.k.h in mid-div: hdwy over 2f out: chal jst ins fnl f: no ex nr fin* **33/1**

1203 **3** *1/2* **Charm School**[12] 7019 3-8-10 **92**.................................. JimmyFortune 5 101+
(J H M Gosden) *in rr: hdwy and nt clr run over 2f out: swtchd rt: styd on strly fnl f: fin strly* **11/2**[2]

3630 **4** *1 3/4* **We'll Come**[22] 6783 4-8-13 **94**.....................................(b) DarryllHolland 9 99
(M A Jarvis) *in rr: hdwy and nt clr run over 2f out: r.o fnl f* **12/1**

0501 **5** *nk* **Axiom**[12] 7019 4-8-11 **92**.................................... DaneO'Neill 11 96
(L M Cumani) *hld up towards rr: hdwy over 2f out: chsng ldrs 1f out: kpt on same pce* **3/1**[1]

0303 **6** *3/4* **Flipando (IRE)**[7] 7146 7-8-8 **89**.................................... PaulFessey 19 91
(T D Barron) *trckd ldrs: effrt 2f out: kpt on wl fnl f* **16/1**

5001 **7** *1/2* **Phantom Whisper**[27] 6676 5-9-0 **95**............................ TGMcLaughlin 8 96
(B R Millman) *dwlt: hdwy and edgd lft over1 f out: styd on ins fnl f* **33/1**

0620 **8** *hd* **Jewelled Dagger (IRE)**[12] 7019 4-8-5 **86**......................(b) JoeFanning 10 87
(Miss L A Perratt) *led tl hdd appr fnl f: fdd* **25/1**

0404 **9** *1 1/4* **Dhaular Dhar (IRE)**[15] 6947 6-9-5 **100**...................... DanielTudhope 14 97
(J S Goldie) *t.k.h in midfield: hdwy and swtchd stands' side over 1f out: kpt on wl* **14/1**

0113 **10** *shd* **Medici Pearl**[35] 6482 4-8-9 **90**..................................... DavidAllan 3 87
(T D Easterby) *in rr: hdwy over 2f out: hung lft and kpt on same pce fnl f: nvr nr to chal* **9/1**[3]

0641 **11** *1 1/4* **Lucky Dance (BRZ)**[7] 7146 6-8-11 **92**.......................... GregFairley 13 86
(A G Foster) *chsd ldrs: one pce fnl 2f* **10/1**

0300 **12** *1* **Mastership (IRE)**[22] 6772 4-9-0 **95**............................ GrahamGibbons 1 86
(J J Quinn) *mid-div: effrt over 2f out: wkng whn hmpd over 1f out* **22/1**

1040 **13** *1* **Haajes**[14] 6971 4-8-11 **95**..(t) TolleyDean(3) 4 83
(S Parr) *in rr div: drvn 3f out: nvr a factor* **33/1**

2000 **14** *3/4* **Advanced**[17] 6903 5-9-2 **97**.. JamieSpencer 16 83
(K A Ryan) *hld up in rr: effrt stands' side 2f out: nvr nr ldrs* **14/1**

0150 **15** *nse* **Bond City (IRE)**[15] 6947 6-9-0 **95**.............................. PJMcDonald 15 81
(G R Oldroyd) *chsd ldrs: wknd over 1f out* **40/1**

4220 **16** *1 1/2* **Masai Moon**[22] 6783 4-8-10 **94**............................... JamesMillman(3) 7 76
(B R Millman) *chsd ldrs: lost pl 2f out* **20/1**

0000 **17** *6* **Celtic Sultan (IRE)**[15] 6947 4-8-12 **93**........................ MickyFenton 20 59
(T P Tate) *dwlt: sn chsng ldrs stands' side: wkng whn hmpd and eased over 1f out* **40/1**

0604 **18** *nk* **Protector (SAF)**[14] 6975 7-9-2 **97**............................(t) RobertWinston 18 62
(A G Foster) *mid-div: lost pl over 2f out* **12/1**

0100 **19** *1 1/4* **Sir Xaar (IRE)**[35] 6478 5-8-7 **88** ow2.............................(v) TomEaves 2 50
(B Smart) *chsd ldrs: wknd 2f out* **50/1**

1-50 **20** *4* **Ponty Rossa (IRE)**[15] 6947 4-8-3 **87**.......................... DuranFentiman(3) 17 38
(T D Easterby) *mid-div: lost pl over 2f out* **25/1**

3100 **21** *21* **Wyatt Earp (IRE)**[20] 6845 7-8-7 **88**.................................(b) PaulHanagan 6 —
(R A Fahey) *in tch: lost pl over 2f out: eased whn bhd ins fnl f* **40/1**

1m 31.86s (5.56) **Going Correction** +0.85s/f (Soft)
WFA 3 from 4yo+ 1lb 21 Ran SP% 131.9
Speed ratings (Par 109): **102,101,101,99,98 98,97,97,95,95 94,93,91,91,91 89,82,82,80,76 52**
toteswinger: 1&2 £146.20, 1&3 £26.50, 2&3 £73.10. CSF £877.43 CT £6871.01 TOTE £40.80: £5.60, £7.20, £2.30, £3.60; EX 2327.80 TRIFECTA Not won. Place 6: £2986.55 Place 5: £342.99.

Owner Terry Cummins **Bred** Robert Wilson **Trained** Lydiate, Merseyside
■ Stewards' Enquiry : T G McLaughlin two-day ban: careless riding (Nov 29-30)

FOCUS
The final turf race of the season, and a competitive affair on paper. It produced a puzzling result with two 33-1 shots fighting out the finish. The form looks sound rated around the first two.

NOTEBOOK
Invincible Force(IRE) has done the vast majority of his racing over sprint distances and on the rare occasions he has tried this trip in the past he has not seen it out. It was therefore something of a surprise to see him bounce back to winning form. He was racing off a fair mark, though, and while not always the brightest from the stalls, importantly, he got away on terms this time.
Barney McGrew(IRE) has done all his winning on turf on good ground or faster, so these conditions did not look likely to suit, but he settled better just off the pace this time and picked up when his rider went for him. Any rise in the weights will not make things easy for him when he reappears on turf in the spring, though, as he is already 2lb higher than when last successful. (op 28-1)
Charm School, the least exposed runner in the line-up, having only had four previous starts, won his maiden over this course and distance in March. He reversed recent Leicester form with Axiom on 4lb better terms and, in staying on strongly, gave every indication that a return to a mile will suit him. He has the potential to improve quite a bit as a four-year-old next season. (op 7-1)
We'll Come has a poor strike-rate but he has run plenty of good races in defeat and this was another one, arguably on ground softer than ideal.
Axiom looked to have plenty going for him despite being dropped in distance. When he challenged the leaders a furlong out he looked sure to pull clear but, strangely, he weakened, eventually dropping out of the places. (op 7-2)
Flipando(IRE), who is as tough as they come, again finished his race off well, but he needs a very strong pace over this trip nowadays.
Phantom Whisper, who came here on the back of a win at Goodwood over 6f, was stepping back up in trip and class. This distance stretches his stamina.
Jewelled Dagger(IRE), for whom this trip was probably on the short side, as he has won at up to 1m1f, did his best but this track would not be the ideal one for his style of running.
Medici Pearl had been in good form of late at up to a mile and is well suited by soft ground but he hung under pressure and never got into contention. (op 12-1)
T/Jkpt: Not won. T/Plt: £2,194.10 to a £1 stake. Pool: £127,443.09. 42.40 winning tickets. T/Qpdt: £45.30 to a £1 stake. Pool: £11,385.75. 185.60 winning tickets. JR

7225 WOLVERHAMPTON (A.W) (L-H)
Saturday, November 8

7246 Meeting Abandoned - Floodlight failure
Meeting abandoned an hour after the scheduled 6.20 first-race time.

6325 SAN SIRO (R-H)
Saturday, November 8

OFFICIAL GOING: Heavy

7253a PREMIO CHIUSURA (GROUP 3) 7f
2:15 (2:35) 2-Y-O+ **£26,801** (£11,793; £6,432; £3,216)

RPR

1 **White Snow (IRE)**[125] 3808 4-9-3 .... MEsposito 8 95
(G Miliani, Italy) *in midfield: hdwy whn hrd rdn 2f out: styd on u.str.p to ld 100yds out: drvn out*

2 *snk* **Gesture**[120] 3938 6-9-10 .... DGrilli 10 102
(E Russo, Italy) *a cl up: hrd rdn to press wnr clsng stages: jst hld*

3 *1 3/4* **Remarque (IRE)**[181] 2029 3-9-7 ....(b) GMarcelli 16 95
(L Riccardi, Italy) *led in centre: 3 l clr 1/2-way: hdd 100yds out: one pce*

4 *nk* **Adragon (ITY)**[34] 2-8-1 .... DPorcu 12 94
(L Mariani, Italy) *cl up in 4th or 5th: kpt on fnl 2f: jst missed 3rd*

5 *3 1/2* **Rockhorse (IRE)**[58] 3-9-7 .... NPinna 9 85
(B Grizzetti, Italy) *in midfield in centre: kpt on fnl 2f*

6 *snk* **Sottone**[83] 2-8-1 .... GSanna 13 85
(B Grizzetti, Italy) *racd in 6th or 7th: rdn and unable qck 1 1/2f out*

7 *nk* **Titus Shadow (IRE)**[48] 4-9-10 .... SLandi 11 86
(B Grizzetti, Italy) *cl up on stands' side: one pce fnl 2f*

8 *2 1/2* **Blue Damask (USA)**[104] 5-9-7 .... LSorrentino 17 76
(G Raveneau, Switzerland) *chsd clr ldr: btn over 1f out*

9 *4* **Zenone (IRE)**[6] 7162 4-9-7 .... SUrru 5 65
(Laura Grizzetti, Italy) *a in midfield*

10 *shd* **Tibroso (ITY)**[34] 4-9-7 .... URispoli 1 65
(U Rispoli, Italy) *prom on stands' rail tl wknd 2f out*

11 *1* **Yacht Woman (USA)**[160] 3-9-3 .... ASanna 14 59
(E Borromeo, Italy) *racd in 3rd in centre: wknd 1 1/2f out*

12 *1 3/4* **Polar Wind (ITY)**[48] 4-9-7 .... LManiezzi 7 58
(L Maniezzi, Italy) *nvr a factor*

13 *shd* **Salisburgo (ITY)**[146] 5-9-7 .... MMonteriso 2 57
(V di Napoli, Italy) *a in rr*

14 *3/4* **Eldest (IRE)**[55] 3-9-7 .... MDemuro 15 56
(V Caruso, Italy) *cl up in centre tl wknd over 2f out*

15 *1 3/4* **Vattene (IRE)**[41] 3-9-3 .... NMurru 3 48
(M Gasparini, Italy) *a in rr*

16 *18* **L'Indiscreta**[41] 3-9-3 .... DVargiu 6 —
(B Grizzetti, Italy) *a in rr: t.o fnl f*

17 *3* **Mubaashir (IRE)**[411] 5685 4-9-7 .... MTellini 4 —
(A Bianco, Italy) *a in rr: t.o fnl f*

1m 24.0s (-4.20) 17 Ran
(including 1 Euro stake): WIN 11.04 (coupled with Rockhorse); PL 4.02, 2.17, 10.83; DF 42.15.
Owner L P A Stud **Bred** Razza Del Velino **Trained** Italy

7189 KEMPTON (A.W) (R-H)
Sunday, November 9

OFFICIAL GOING: Standard
Wind: Moderate across changing to moderate half-behind Weather: Raining

7254 BET MULTIPLES - BETDAQ H'CAP (DIV I) 6f (P)
2:00 (2:00) (Class 6) (0-60,60) 3-Y-O+ **£1,706** (£503; £252) **Stalls** High

Form RPR

2345 **1** **Hart Of Gold**[20] 6864 4-9-1 **60**...................................(p) KevinGhunowa(3) 8 71
(R A Harris) *trckd ldng pair: rdn to chal over 1f out: led ent fnl f: r.o strly* **7/2**[1]

0005 **2** *1 1/4* **Muktasb (USA)**[10] 7090 7-9-2 **58**.................................(v) AdamKirby 4 65
(D Shaw) *s.i.s: hld up towards rr: gd hdwy on inner over 2f out: chsd ldrs 1f out: r.o to snatch 2nd last strides: nt rch wnr* **9/1**

6301 **3** *hd* **Simpsons Gamble (IRE)**[215] 1254 5-9-1 **57**..............(p) EddieAhern 10 63
(R A Teal) *trckd ldng trio: effrt jst over 2f out: ev ch over 1f out: chsd wnr fnl f: one pce: lost 2nd last strides* **12/1**

3640 **4** *1 1/2* **Night Premiere (IRE)**[19] 6890 3-8-13 **55**.......................... PatDobbs 5 57
(R Hannon) *chsd ldr: rdn and ev ch 2f out tl 1f out: one pce fnl f* **16/1**

4363 **5** *1/2* **Norcroft**[10] 7090 6-9-2 **58**..(p) TGMcLaughlin 1 58
(Mrs C A Dunnett) *stdd s and dropped in bhd: bustled along after 2f: rdn wl over 2f out: swtchd rt over 2f out: styd on fnl f: nvr able to chal* **7/1**[2]

5035 **6** *shd* **What Katie Did (IRE)**[19] 6878 3-8-13 **60**......................(p) JackDean(5) 11 60
(J M Bradley) *led: rdn over 2f out: hdd ent fnl f: wknd fnl 100yds* **16/1**

0545 **7** *nk* **Eleanor Eloise (USA)**[18] 6895 4-8-12 **54**....................(b) LiamJones 12 53
(J R Gask) *in tch in midfield: rdn and hung lft over 2f out: kpt on same pce fr over 1f out* **15/2**[3]

4020 **8** *1/2* **Grizedale (IRE)**[10] 7090 9-8-13 **55**............................(tp) PaulDoe 3 52
(M J Attwater) *hld up in rr: rdn and little rspnse 2f out: kpt on fnl f: nvr pce to threaten ldrs* **10/1**

3104 **9** *hd* **Meridian Line (IRE)**[19] 6878 3-8-11 **56**.......................(b) TolleyDean(3) 9 52
(J G Portman) *rrd s and v.s.a: bhd: rdn and effrt on inner over 2f out: nvr trbld ldrs* **22/1**

5001 **10** *1/2* **Tilsworth Charlie**[10] 7102 5-8-11 **58**.....................(b) FrederikTylicki(5) 2 53
(J R Jenkins) *racd in midfield on outer: rdn over 2f out: no imp* **15/2**[3]

0120 **11** *3 3/4* **Piccolo Diamante (USA)**[4] 7195 4-8-10 **52**...................(t) ChrisCatlin 6 35
(S Parr) *a bhd: rdn 3f out: no prog* **8/1**

6230 **12** *10* **Nautical**[5] 7182 10-9-1 **57**........ JerryO'Dwyer 7 8
(J R Holt) *in tch in midfield: rdn and struggling over 2f out: wl btn whn eased ins fnl f* **18/1**

1m 12.6s (-0.50) **Going Correction** +0.025s/f (Slow) **12** Ran SP% **117.5**
Speed ratings (Par 101): **104,102,102,100,99 99,98,98,97,97 92,78**
toteswinger: 1&2 £9.50, 1&3 £6.90, 2&3 £15.90. CSF £34.44 CT £348.88 TOTE £3.30: £1.50, £3.50, £3.30; EX 42.30.
Owner Ridge House Stables Ltd **Bred** Bearstone Stud **Trained** Earlswood, Monmouths

FOCUS
The first division of a moderate sprint handicap.

7255 BET MULTIPLES - BETDAQ H'CAP (DIV II) 6f (P)
2:30 (2:30) (Class 6) (0-60,60) 3-Y-O+ **£1,706** (£503; £252) **Stalls** High

Form RPR
4030 **1** **Namu**[4] 7197 5-8-11 **53**........(p) DaneO'Neill 12 63
(Miss T Spearing) *hld up in mid-div: hdwy fr 2f out: led ins fnl f: drvn out* **12/1**

2550 **2** *1* **Dualagi**[33] 6564 4-9-4 **60**........ GeorgeBaker 10 67
(M R Bosley) *hld up in rr: hdwy over 1f out: str run to chse wnr ins fnl f but a hld* **15/2**[3]

0024 **3** *1* **Who's Winning (IRE)**[13] 7013 7-8-13 **55**........ MichaelHills 8 59
(B G Powell) *hld up towards rr: hdwy fr 2f out: styd on to go 3rd ins fnl f but no imp on ldng duo nr fin* **13/2**[2]

0230 **4** *1* **Afton View (IRE)**[79] 5223 3-9-0 **56**........ ChrisCatlin 6 57
(S Parr) *pressed ldr and stl upsides ins fnl 2f: wknd fnl 100yds* **16/1**

2233 **5** *1 1/4* **Rhapsilian**[23] 6774 4-9-2 **58**........(p) SteveDrowne 11 55
(J A Geake) *narrow ldr and kpt slt advantage tl hdd ins fnl f: wknd fnl 100yds* **4/1**[1]

0000 **6** *nk* **Hollow Jo**[23] 6774 8-8-10 **52**........ MickyFenton 1 48
(J R Jenkins) *in tch: rdn and styd on over 1f out: nvr gng pce to be competitive* **16/1**

0020 **7** *3/4* **Harrison's Flyer (IRE)**[4] 7197 7-8-7 **54**........(p) JackDean(5) 9 47
(J M Bradley) *chsd ldrs: rdn over 2f out: wknd fnl f* **14/1**

4422 **8** *2 1/4* **Morse (IRE)**[23] 6773 7-9-2 **58**........(p) ShaneKelly 4 44
(J A Osborne) *in tch: rdn and nt clr run 2f out: sn btn* **4/1**[1]

306 **9** *1* **Hamaasy**[39] 6377 7-8-13 **58**........ KevinGhunowa(3) 7 41
(R A Harris) *chsd ldrs: rdn 3f out: wknd over 1f out* **14/1**

1210 **10** *hd* **Patavium Prince (IRE)**[46] 6200 5-9-3 **59**........ TravisBlock 2 41
(Miss Jo Crowley) *chsd ldrs: rdn 3f out: wknd fr 2f out* **13/2**[2]

1000 **11** *2 1/2* **Minwir (IRE)**[9] 7109 3-9-1 **57**........(v) RobertWinston 5 31
(M Quinn) *outpcd in rr thrght* **20/1**

6000 **12** *1 3/4* **Caustic Wit (IRE)**[2] 7225 10-8-7 **56**........ JakePayne(7) 3 25
(M S Saunders) *a outpcd in rr* **40/1**

1m 13.24s (0.14) **Going Correction** +0.025s/f (Slow) **12** Ran SP% **118.4**
Speed ratings (Par 101): **100,98,97,96,94 93,92,89,88,88 85,82**
toteswinger: 1&2 £13.00, 1&3 £12.30, 2&3 £7.90. CSF £99.11 CT £645.81 TOTE £14.20: £4.00, £2.90, £1.70; EX 110.00.
Owner Advantage Chemicals Holdings Ltd **Bred** Philip Graham Harvey **Trained** Alcester, Warwicks
■ Stewards' Enquiry : Robert Winston 15-day ban: excessive use of the whip (1 for offence and 14 under totting-up procedure - three days deffered until March 28th, 2009) (Nov 30, Dec 3-13)

FOCUS
This was run in a quicker time than the first division and looked the stronger of the two races.
Minwir(IRE) Official explanation: matter referred; used whip without giving gelding time to respond.

7256 REGISTER NOW @ BETDAQPOKER.CO.UK MEDIAN AUCTION MAIDEN STKS 1m (P)
3:00 (3:02) (Class 5) 3-5-Y-O **£2,729** (£806; £403) **Stalls** High

Form RPR
3300 **1** **Wellington Square**[16] 6949 3-9-3 77........ JimmyFortune 3 76
(H Morrison) *hld up in midfield: hdwy and rdn over 2f out: hrd rdn to ld jst over 1f out: drvn clr fnl f* **3/1**[1]

00 **2** *5* **Fancy Footsteps (IRE)**[163] 2560 3-8-12 0........ AdamKirby 7 59
(C G Cox) *led for 1f: chsd ldr after: rdn and ev ch 2f out: led briefly over 1f out: no ch w wnr fnl f: hld on for 2nd* **12/1**

044 **3** *nk* **Parson's Punch**[148] 3022 3-9-3 68........ SimonWhitworth 13 64
(P D Cundell) *dwlt: sn pushed up to ld after 1f: jnd and pushed along 2f out: hdd over 1f out: kpt on same pce fnl f* **3/1**[1]

0336 **4** *3/4* **Yakama (IRE)**[19] 6888 3-9-3 48........(b) TGMcLaughlin 2 62
(Mrs C A Dunnett) *s.i.s: bhd: swtchd lft and hdwy over 2f out: rdn 2f out: styd on fnl f: no threat to wnr* **25/1**

2002 **5** *3/4* **Melt (IRE)**[19] 6889 3-8-12 57........ DaneO'Neill 6 55
(R Hannon) *in tch in midfield: rdn 3f out: outpcd over 1f out: plugged on same pce fnl f* **7/2**[2]

4254 **6** *8* **Caro George (USA)**[61] 5790 3-8-12 66........ SteveDrowne 5 37
(R Charlton) *chsd ldrs: pushed along over 3f out: drvn and unable qck over 2f out: sn wl btn* **13/2**[3]

0000 **7** *3/4* **Classy Affair**[53] 6032 4-9-0 42........ SaleemGolam 11 35
(D Morris) *chsd ldrs: rdn wl over 2f out: wknd qckly 2f out* **80/1**

05 **8** *5* **Jayarbee (IRE)**[58] 5864 3-8-12 0........ JimCrowley 1 24
(P J McBride) *a bhd: rdn and lost tch wl over 2f out* **12/1**

00 **9** *3 1/4* **Lady Hestia (USA)**[18] 6896 3-8-5 0........ KatiaScallan(7) 4 16
(M P Tregoning) *in tch on outer: lost pl over 3f out: lost tch over 2f out* **20/1**

00 **10** *15* **Deep Waters (IRE)**[185] 1926 3-9-3 0........ GeorgeBaker 8 —
(S Dow) *a towards rr: lost tch qckly over 2f out: eased fnl f: t.o* **66/1**

1m 39.77s (-0.03) **Going Correction** +0.025s/f (Slow)
WFA 3 from 4yo 2lb **10** Ran SP% **112.3**
Speed ratings (Par 103): **101,96,95,94,94 86,85,80,77,62**
toteswinger: 1&2 £6.50, 1&3 £3.00, 2&3 £8.30. CSF £35.26 TOTE £3.50: £1.40, £2.70, £1.60; EX 46.50.
Owner Roger Barby & Sir T Cassel **Bred** J A Peat **Trained** East Ilsley, Berks
■ L'Hirondelle was withdrawn after refusing to enter the stalls. R4 applies, deduct 5p in the £.

FOCUS
A weak maiden that concerned no more than a handful of runners.

7257 BET PREMIER LEAGUE FOOTBALL - BETDAQ NURSERY (DIV I) 1m (P)
3:30 (3:31) (Class 6) (0-60,60) 2-Y-O **£1,706** (£503; £252) **Stalls** High

Form RPR
0000 **1** **True Britannia**[18] 6906 2-8-12 **51**........ JamesDoyle 6 55
(S Kirk) *led 1f: styd chsng ldr: led over 1f out: drvn and hld on wl fnl f* **20/1**

000 **2** *nk* **Winterbrook King**[33] 6553 2-9-4 **57**........ GeorgeBaker 14 60
(J R Best) *in rr but in tch: hdwy fr 2f out: styd on strly fnl f: clsng nr fin but a jst hld* **8/1**

2050 **3** *2* **Josiah Bartlett (IRE)**[26] 6720 2-9-4 **57**........ LiamJones 5 56
(J W Hills) *in rr: hdwy on outside fr 2f out: kpt on fnl f but nvr gng pce to trble ldng duo* **18/1**

550 **4** *1 3/4* **Itsher**[70] 5530 2-9-0 **58**........ WilliamCarson(5) 1 53
(S C Williams) *led after 1f: rdn over 2f out: hdd over 1f out: wknd ins fnl f* **20/1**

0014 **5** *nk* **Barcode**[32] 6573 2-9-2 **55**........ FrancisNorton 9 49
(R Hannon) *in rr: rdn over 2f out: hdwy over 1f out: kpt on fnl f but nvr gng pce to be competitive* **8/1**

0026 **6** *nk* **Hold The Bucks (USA)**[57] 5914 2-9-5 **58**........ LPKeniry 12 52
(J S Moore) *chsd ldrs but nvr gng pce to chal: rdn over 2f out: wknd ins fnl f* **9/2**[1]

2446 **7** *2 1/4* **Frame And Cover**[72] 5473 2-8-10 **52**........ KevinGhunowa(3) 11 41
(Miss J S Davis) *in rr: rdn 3f out: hdwy over 1f out: kpt on but nvr in contention* **50/1**

4050 **8** *1/2* **Redhead (IRE)**[57] 5914 2-9-7 **60**........ JimmyFortune 3 48
(R Hannon) *in tch: rdn and no imp fr 3f out: no ch fnl 2f* **9/1**

560 **9** *hd* **Loulou (USA)**[31] 6597 2-9-7 **60**........ HayleyTurner 4 47
(S A Callaghan) *in rr: drvn along over 2f out: mod prog ins fnl f* **7/1**[3]

6600 **10** *hd* **Welcome Applause (IRE)**[46] 6207 2-9-6 **59**........ JimmyQuinn 10 46
(M G Quinlan) *in rr: sme prog u.p 2f out but nvr gng pce to get competitive* **16/1**

0200 **11** *4* **Ba Globetrotter**[41] 6343 2-9-1 **54**........ EdwardCreighton 13 32
(M R Channon) *chsd ldrs: rdn 3f out: wknd qckly over 1f out* **16/1**

5040 **12** *1 1/2* **Royal Max (IRE)**[46] 6214 2-9-0 **53**........ AdamKirby 8 28
(C G Cox) *chsd ldrs tl wknd 2f out* **9/1**

214 **13** *1 1/2* **Bounty Reef**[33] 6561 2-9-5 **58**........ RobertWinston 7 29
(P D Evans) *chsd ldrs: rdn over 2f out: sn btn: eased whn no ch ins fnl f* **6/1**[2]

505 **14** *30* **Mr Redford**[77] 5316 2-9-3 **56**........ SteveDrowne 2 —
(N P Littmoden) *chsd ldrs: drvn along 1/2-way: wknd qckly 3f out: t.o* **10/1**

1m 41.79s (1.99) **Going Correction** +0.025s/f (Slow) **14** Ran SP% **124.8**
Speed ratings (Par 94): **91,90,88,86,86 86,84,83,83,83 79,77,76,46**
toteswinger: 1&2 £67.60, 1&3 £81.40, 2&3 £63.60. CSF £175.27 CT £3044.54 TOTE £31.40: £6.30, £3.70, £6.30; EX 320.30.
Owner T R Lock **Bred** Cleaboy Farms Co **Trained** Upper Lambourn, Berks

FOCUS
This looked the weaker of the two divisions.

NOTEBOOK
True Britannia struggled to make an impact in a handful of runs over sprint distances, including at this course last month, but she is related to plenty of 1m-plus winners and showed a marked improvement for the step up in trip. Always well positioned, she was ridden off the final bend and raced on with long-time leader Itsher. In front over 1f out, she stayed on well and, despite getting a little tired in the final half furlong, always looked to be holding the runner-up. She was winning off a mark of just 51 and remains capable of better at this distance.
Winterbrook King looked to have been given a tough opening mark considering he achieved very little in three maidens, but he is from a good yard and the step back up to 1m was always likely to suit. Held up on the inside, he began to stay on when switched left over 2f out and really came strong inside the final furlong, but was never quite getting there. This was only his fourth run and he remains open to further improvement. (op 12-1)
Josiah Bartlett(IRE), 3lb lower than when beaten a nose at Wolverhampton in August, was widest of all in the straight and stayed on with the runner-up, but lacked any acceleration at the business end. His half-brother was placed over hurdles and he looks worth a try at further. (op 20-1)
Itsher, up in trip for this handicap debut, raced a few lengths clear with the winner early in the straight and showed up well for a long way, but she could find no extra from 1f out. This was still an improved effort. (op 18-1 tchd 16-1)
Barcode, winner of a 5f claimer at Bath two starts back, had never tried this trip before, but she really began to motor inside the final 2f and came home strongly for fifth. Now she seems to have shown she stays, it would not surprise to see her ridden more prominently next time. (op 17-2 tchd 9-1)
Hold The Bucks(USA), who has yet to win a race, was asked for his effort soon after turning for home, but could only find the one pace and never looked like winning. (tchd 5-1)
Loulou(USA), a well-bred filly that cost $300,000, failed to progress in maidens and never got involved following a sluggish start. (tchd 13-2)
Royal Max(IRE) Official explanation: vet said that colt had struck into itself
Bounty Reef, outclassed in a conditions race at Leicester last time when she may not have stayed the 1m2f trip, emptied from over 1f out and may be feeling the effects of a long season. Official explanation: jockey said filly had no more to give (op 11-2)
Mr Redford Official explanation: jockey said gelding never travelled

7258 BET PREMIER LEAGUE FOOTBALL - BETDAQ NURSERY (DIV II) 1m (P)
4:00 (4:02) (Class 6) (0-60,60) 2-Y-O **£1,706** (£503; £252) **Stalls** High

Form RPR
006 **1** **Roar Of Applause**[52] 6062 2-9-7 **60**........ EddieAhern 8 63
(B J Meehan) *hld up wl in tch: rdn and effrt 2f out: drvn to ld ins fnl f: hld on wl fnl 100yds* **5/1**[2]

0002 **2** *1/2* **Highland River**[32] 6573 2-9-5 **58**........ GeorgeBaker 6 60
(D R C Elsworth) *t.k.h: hld up in midfield: hdwy jst over 2f out: rdn and ev ch ent fnl f: unable qck fnl 100yds* **9/2**[1]

000 **3** *1/2* **Brer Rabbit**[90] 4926 2-9-6 **59**........ MichaelHills 12 60
(B W Hills) *plld hrd early: hld up in rr: hdwy on outer over 2f out: pressed ldrs ent fnl f: kpt on but nt quite gng pce to rch ldng pair* **14/1**

0000 **4** *shd* **Captain Walcot**[11] 7069 2-9-4 **57**........(b[1]) PatDobbs 10 58
(R Hannon) *led tl hdd over 2f out: drvn to ld again over 1f out: hung lft and hdd ins fnl f: no ex fnl 100yds* **10/1**

0600 **5** *1 1/4* **Lucky Punt**[41] 6343 2-9-0 **53**........ JimmyFortune 5 51
(B G Powell) *t.k.h: hld up in rr: hdwy and rdn over 2f out: chsd ldrs over 1f out: keeping on same pce whn short of room briefly ins fnl f* **17/2**

4453 **6** *2 1/4* **Tarawa Atoll**[52] 6059 2-8-11 **50**........ EdwardCreighton 13 43
(M R Channon) *t.k.h: hld up towards rr: rdn and no real hdwy over 2f out: hdwy ent fnl f: kpt on but nvr gng pce to trble ldrs* **10/1**

3000 **7** *1* **Nun Today (USA)**[27] 6709 2-9-2 **55**........(b) LPKeniry 7 46
(J S Moore) *pressed ldr tl rdn to ld over 2f out: edgd rt u.p 2f out: hdd over 1f out: wknd qckly fnl f* **16/1**

000 **8** *1 1/4* **Pure Crystal**[31] 6597 2-9-4 **57**........ JerryO'Dwyer 11 45
(M G Quinlan) *hld up towards rr: rdn and effrt on inner over 2f out: no imp fr wl over 1f out* **9/1**

400 **9** *1/2* **Terracotta Warrior**[106] 4421 2-8-11 **53**........ LukeMorris(3) 14 40
(J Jay) *in tch on inner: rdn and unable qck over 2f out: wknd 2f out* **12/1**

000 **10** *3/4* **Viking Rock (IRE)**[13] 7023 2-9-7 **60**........ NeilChalmers 1 45
(M Salaman) *stdd s and dropped in bhd: nvr trbld ldrs* **25/1**

1002 **11** *1 1/4* **Hollow Green (IRE)**[11] 7079 2-9-5 **58**........ RobertWinston 3 40
(P D Evans) *chsd ldrs: rdn over 3f out: wknd u.p wl over 1f out: btn and eased ins fnl f* **8/1**[3]

0550 **12** 1¼ **Lady Angelica**[44] 6240 2-8-13 **52**............................(e[1]) RichardThomas 9 32
(Dr J D Scargill) *hld up in midfield: rdn and n.m.r over 2f out: drvn and no imp 2f out: sn wknd* **50/1**

000 **13** 1½ **Sparkaway**[53] 6031 2-9-1 **54**.. ChrisCatlin 4 30
(W J Musson) *stdd after s: bhd: rdn and toiling over 3f out: nvr a factor* **12/1**

3004 **14** 5 **Innactualfact**[12] 7052 2-9-5 **58**.. HayleyTurner 2 23
(L A Dace) *t.k.h: chsd ldrs on outer: rdn wl over 2f out: wknd 2f out: wl bhd and eased ins fnl f* **10/1**

1m 43.54s (3.74) **Going Correction** +0.025s/f (Slow) **14** Ran SP% **127.5**
Speed ratings (Par 94): **82,81,81,80,79 77,76,75,74,73 72,71,69,64**
toteswinger: 1&2 £6.30, 1&3 £19.00, 2&3 £18.10. CSF £29.52 CT £320.28 TOTE £5.90: £2.30, £2.50, £5.80; EX 32.60.
Owner Raymond Tooth **Bred** Southcourt Stud **Trained** Manton, Wilts

FOCUS
This second division looked the stronger of the two on paper, and little should be read into the fact the time was slower, as they went just a steady pace.

NOTEBOOK
Roar Of Applause, up in trip for this handicap debut following three runs in maidens, was subject to good support beforehand and always held an ideal sit just in behind the leaders. He took a while to engage top gear, but really ran on well inside the final furlong and was always doing too much for Highland River. He has a bit of scope and could improve again off a stronger pace. Official explanation: trainer's rep said, regarding the apparent improvement in form, that gelding was an improving sort, and was suited by the trip and the all-weather surface. (op 8-1)
Highland River left his form in maidens well behind when second off a 2lb lower mark over 6f at this course on his nursery debut, and the step back up to 1m looked in his favour, his half-brother being a three-time winner at the distance. He moved through to look a big threat 2f out and stayed on well for pressure, but the winner had the legs of him inside the final furlong. He is going the right way and a truer gallop should enable him to settle better. (op 4-1 tchd 5-1)
Brer Rabbit showed just moderate form in three sprint maidens earlier in the year, but she had been given a break and returned with a much-improved effort on this nursery debut. She saw the trip out well, for all that it was not a proper test at the distance, and could win something similar if settling better. (op 10-1)
Captain Walcot, who looked a non-stayer over 1m2f at Great Leighs last time, had earlier shown just moderate form and the first-time blinkers needed to make a big difference. He was always on the pace and still held a narrow lead over 1f out, but in the end was done for a change of gear, just losing out on the places. This was an improved effort. (op 17-2)
Lucky Punt kept on to record one of his better efforts. (op 10-1 tchd 8-1)
Tarawa Atoll found her stride all too late. (tchd 9-1)
Nun Today(USA) raced on with Captain Walcot, but was visibly tiring from over 1f out and emptied in the final half-furlong.
Viking Rock(IRE) Official explanation: jockey said gelding missed the break

7259 E B F BETDAQ.CO.UK MEDIAN AUCTION MAIDEN FILLIES' STKS 1m (P)
4:30 (4:31) (Class 4) 2-Y-0 £4,533 (£1,348; £674; £336) Stalls High

Form RPR

33 **1** **Greenisland (IRE)**[30] 6622 2-9-0 0.......................... RobertHavlin 13 77
(H Morrison) *mde all: hrd drvn whn chal thrght fnl f but a jst in command* **5/2**[1]

05 **2** nk **Efficiency**[59] 5812 2-9-0 0... LPKeniry 6 76
(M Blanshard) *in tch: shkn up and no immediate rspnse over 2f out: str run appr fnl f to chse wnr and styd on strly ins fnl f but a jst hld* **33/1**

03 **3** 1 **Colangnik (USA)**[13] 7023 2-9-0 0.............................. SteveDrowne 10 74
(J R Best) *chsd ldrs tl drvn and outpcd over 2f out: styd on again fnl f and fin wl: gng on cl home* **6/1**

2363 **4** ½ **Our Day Will Come**[19] 6876 2-9-0 71.......................... EddieAhern 12 73
(R Hannon) *chsd wnr: rdn and no imp over 2f out: lost 2nd over 1f out and styd on same pce ins fnl f* **7/2**[2]

4 **5** 8 **Leelu**[25] 6737 2-9-0 0.. DaneO'Neill 8 55
(D W P Arbuthnot) *in tch whn snatched up after 2f: styd in tch: rdn and one pce over 2f out: styd on again fnl f* **9/2**[3]

0 **6** 1 **Tagula Minx (IRE)**[19] 6887 2-9-0 0............................ JimmyQuinn 7 53
(J Pearce) *in rr: pushed along 3f out: sme hdwy fnl 2f* **100/1**

005 **7** 1¾ **Salybia Bay**[10] 7095 2-9-0 68.................................... JimmyFortune 2 49
(R Hannon) *in rr tl mod late prog fnl f* **8/1**

8 2 **Vella** 2-9-0 0.. JamesDoyle 11 45
(H J L Dunlop) *drvn to chse ldrs: rdn over 3f out: wknd over 2f out* **50/1**

00 **9** 3¼ **Pinkalicious (IRE)**[19] 6884 2-9-0 0.............................. JimCrowley 9 38
(M L W Bell) *a in rr* **50/1**

00 **10** hd **Carita Mia**[17] 6926 2-9-0 0.. AdamKirby 4 37
(G L Moore) *s.i.s: a towards rr* **50/1**

0 **11** 3¼ **Knock Three Times (IRE)**[12] 7054 2-9-0 0................ HayleyTurner 3 30
(M L W Bell) *s.i.s: a in rr* **33/1**

0 **12** 1¾ **Wightgold**[13] 7015 2-9-0 0.. FrancisNorton 1 26
(H J L Dunlop) *chsd ldrs tl rdn and wknd qckly 3f out* **50/1**

P **Anna Ivanovna** 2-9-0 0.. RobertWinston 5 —
(J R Fanshawe) *in rr tl p.u over 2f out: lame* **10/1**

1m 40.96s (1.16) **Going Correction** +0.025s/f (Slow) **13** Ran SP% **118.2**
Speed ratings (Par 95): **95,94,93,93,85 84,82,80,77,77 73,72,—**
toteswinger: 1&2 £21.20, 1&3 £4.30, 2&3 £35.50. CSF £97.73 TOTE £3.90: £1.20, £10.20, £2.70; EX 104.20.
Owner Stonethorn Stud Farms Limited **Bred** Stonethorn Stud Farms Ltd **Trained** East Ilsley, Berks

FOCUS
Just an ordinary maiden, though the time was quicker than that recorded in either division of the nursery.

NOTEBOOK
Greenisland(IRE), narrowly denied at Lingfield last time, had the best of the draw here and made full use of it. Setting just a steady pace early on, she was asked to kick on over 2f out, but couldn't get away and looked vulnerable when the runner-up came to challenge 1f out. She found extra, though, and was always holding on close home. Everything went her way here and how she gets on in future depends on what mark she is given by the Handicapper. (op 9-4 tchd 11-4)
Efficiency ran a much-improved race and looked the winner when coming with a strong challenge 1f out, but could not pull out any extra close home. She is now qualified for handicaps and should fare better in that sphere.
Colangnik(USA) stepped up on her debut effort when keeping on into third at Lingfield last month and there was every chance she had improved again. Unable to quicken when first asked for an effort, she kept working away and stayed on well close home to grab third. She will be an interesting one for handicaps. (op 7-1)
Our Day Will Come is largely consistent and has looked worth a try at this trip for a while now. She tracked the winner into the straight and was produced to have every chance, but was already beaten when briefly squeezed over 1f out. Run out of third late on, perhaps 7f is her trip after all. (tchd 10-3)
Leelu shaped really promisingly when fourth on her debut at Lingfield, but she wanted to go faster early on and had to be restrained in behind the leaders. She failed to pick up when asked for an effort anyway and could not build on that initial promise. (op 11-2)
Anna Ivanovna, a well-bred debutante whose yard has not had a 2yo winner in 2008, was still in rear when badly breaking down early in the straight. (op 14-1)

7260 TFM NETWORKS CLAIMING STKS 1m 3f (P)
5:00 (5:07) (Class 6) 3-Y-O £2,047 (£604; £302) Stalls High

Form RPR

2015 **1** **Sabre Light**[19] 6888 3-8-13 70..........................(p) JerryO'Dwyer 3 74
(J Pearce) *dwlt: hld up towards rr: hdwy over 4f out: rdn over 2f out: chsd ldr wl over 1f out: drvn to ld ins fnl f: r.o wl* **5/2**[1]

2563 **2** ¾ **Mystic Art (IRE)**[18] 6908 3-8-11 65.......................... SteveDrowne 1 71
(C R Egerton) *chsd ldr after 2f: led over 2f out: sn rdn: hdd ins fnl f: kpt on same pce fnl 100yds* **7/2**[2]

2253 **3** 3¾ **Ambrose Princess (IRE)**[26] 6719 3-8-3 55............ KevinGhunowa(3) 2 60
(R A Harris) *chsd ldrs: rdn 3f out: chsd ldr over 2f out tl over 1f out: sn outpcd by ldng pair: plugged on* **8/1**

3402 **4** 5 **Blur**[18] 6908 3-8-4 52.. FrancisNorton 6 49
(R Hannon) *chsd ldr for 2f: chsd ldrs after: rdn wl over 2f out: sn struggling: no ch fr wl over 1f out* **7/1**[3]

3025 **5** 4 **Rosy Dawn**[13] 7010 3-8-3 49 ow2.............................. MarcHalford(3) 4 44
(J J Bridger) *sn pushed up to ld: rdn and hdd over 2f out: wknd qckly 2f out* **20/1**

0236 **6** nk **Threestoneburn (USA)**[12] 7050 3-8-1 50...................... LiamJones 10 39
(J R Boyle) *hld up in last pair: nvr a factor* **25/1**

1050 **7** nk **Haydens Mark**[30] 6626 3-8-13 70.................................. TGMcLaughlin 7 50
(D G Bridgwater) *hld up in midfield: rdn and no rspnse over 2f out: sn wl btn* **16/1**

0-06 **8** 5 **Veras Joy**[138] 3342 3-8-6 30 ow2...............................(p) SaleemGolam 8 35
(Miss Z C Davison) *s.i.s: a bhd: wl btn whn n.m.r over 2f out* **100/1**

0223 **9** 3½ **Inquest**[24] 6748 3-9-7 73.. JimCrowley 9 44
(Mrs A J Perrett) *hld up in midfield: rdn over 2f out: no rspnse and sn btn* **5/2**[1]

2m 20.53s (-1.37) **Going Correction** +0.025s/f (Slow) **9** Ran SP% **118.5**
Speed ratings (Par 98): **105,104,101,98,95 94,94,91,88**
toteswinger: 1&2 £3.30, 1&3 £6.30, 2&3 £6.40. CSF £11.57 TOTE £3.30: £1.40, £1.80, £2.50; EX 14.30.Ambrose Princess was claimed by M. Scudamore Jnr for £10,000
Owner Fran O'Brien **Bred** D J And Mrs Deer **Trained** Newmarket, Suffolk

FOCUS
The rain really started to tip down before this uncompetitive claimer.
Inquest Official explanation: trainer had no explanation for the poor form shown

7261 TFM NETWORKS H'CAP 1m 3f (P)
5:30 (5:36) (Class 6) (0-65,65) 3-Y-0+ £2,047 (£604; £302) Stalls High

Form RPR

2601 **1** **She's So Pretty (IRE)**[17] 6929 4-9-6 **62**..............(b) GeorgeBaker 1 75
(G L Moore) *stdd in rr after 3f: stl plenty to do 3f out: gd hdwy fr 2f out to chse ldr over 1f out: r.o strly to ld fnl 30yds* **9/2**[2]

500 **2** ½ **Valdan (IRE)**[11] 7076 4-9-3 **59**.. DaneO'Neill 9 71
(P D Evans) *in rr: gd hdwy on outside over 3f out to ld wl over 2f out and sn clr: styd on wl tl hdd and no ex fnl 30yds* **11/1**

6600 **3** 6 **Sir Haydn**[4] 7189 8-8-11 **58** ow1................................(v) FrederikTylicki(5) 13 59
(J R Jenkins) *in rr: hdwy fr 3f out: styd fnl f but no ch w ldng duo* **10/1**

1303 **4** ¾ **Formidable Guest**[11] 7071 4-9-1 **57**.......................... RobertHavlin 5 57
(J Pearce) *in rr tl styd on fnl 2f but nvr in contention* **6/1**[3]

3643 **5** 2½ **Red Lily (IRE)**[18] 6905 3-9-4 **65**..............................(v) RobertWinston 2 61+
(J R Fanshawe) *towards rr: hdwy 3f out: styng on whn n.m.r ins fnl 2f: styd on again but no ch w ldrs whn bdly hmpd appr fnl f and nt rcvr* **3/1**[1]

05-6 **6** ½ **Whodunit (UAE)**[16] 6956 4-8-9 **51**.................................... ChrisCatlin 7 46
(P W Hiatt) *chsd ldr: drvn to chal wl over 2f out: wknd qckly over 1f out* **33/1**

344 **7** 3¾ **Silent Applause**[26] 6721 5-9-9 **65**.............................. SteveDrowne 6 53
(Dr J D Scargill) *chsd ldrs: rdn over 3f out: wknd fr 2f out* **13/2**

0660 **8** 1¼ **Danse The Blues**[20] 6868 3-9-1 **62**............................ TGMcLaughlin 8 48
(E A L Dunlop) *in tch: chsd ldrs 3f out: wknd over 2f out* **10/1**

006- **9** ½ **Miss Habershon**[19] 6060 4-8-13 **55**.............................. TravisBlock 11 40
(Nick Mitchell) *led tl hdd & wknd qckly wl over 2f out* **50/1**

4005 **10** 1 **King's Icon (IRE)**[9] 7115 3-8-2 **56**.......................... TobyAtkinson(7) 4 39
(M Wigham) *a in rr* **20/1**

0245 **11** 8 **Touch Of Style (IRE)**[89] 4953 4-9-8 **64**........................ JimCrowley 10 33
(J R Boyle) *chsd ldrs: rdn 4f out: wknd over 3f out* **6/1**[3]

3603 **12** 1¼ **Play Up Pompey**[11] 7078 6-8-6 **51** oh1.......................... MarcHalford(3) 14 18
(J J Bridger) *chsd ldrs tl wknd qckly over 3f out* **18/1**

4620 **13** 17 **Al Rayanah**[19] 6888 5-8-12 **54**....................................(p) SaleemGolam 3 —
(G Prodromou) *s.i.s: a in rr* **20/1**

2m 21.47s (-0.43) **Going Correction** +0.025s/f (Slow) **13** Ran SP% **131.3**
WFA 3 from 4yo+ 5lb
Speed ratings (Par 101): **102,101,97,96,94 94,91,90,90,89 84,83,70**
toteswinger: 1&2 £16.40, 1&3 £11.50, 2&3 £36.00. CSF £56.86 CT £497.95 TOTE £5.20: £2.00, £3.90, £3.30; EX 49.70 Place 6 £455.81, Place 5 £160.25..
Owner Miss S Bowles **Bred** Airlie Stud **Trained** Woodingdean, E Sussex

FOCUS
Two came clear in what was a low-grade handicap.
Red Lily(IRE) Official explanation: jockey said filly was denied a clear run
T/Plt: £810.70 to a £1 stake. Pool: £76,850.51. 69.20 winning tickets. T/Qpdt: £69.70 to a £1 stake. Pool: £6,342.20. 67.30 winning tickets. SP

5951 CAPANNELLE (R-H)
Sunday, November 9

OFFICIAL GOING: Heavy
Only the second day's racing in Italy after a blank month due to strike action.

7262a PREMIO RIBOT (GROUP 2) 1m
1:50 (1:55) 3-Y-0+ £42,188 (£18,563; £10,125; £5,063)

RPR

1 **Pressing (IRE)**[63] 5742 5-9-2.. MJKinane 7 114
(M A Jarvis) *4th early on outside: wnt 3rd after 3f: shkn up to ld 2f out: edgd rt: pushed out: r.o strly* **30/100**[1]

2 4½ **Project Dane (IRE)**[189] 4-9-2.................................... GBietolini 5 104
(L Polito, Italy) *set str pce: hdd 2f out: readily outpcd by wnr but kpt on to hold 2nd* **8/1**[3]

3 1½ **Farrel (IRE)**[119] 4010 3-9-1.. DVargiu 6 102
(B Grizzetti, Italy) *racd in 5th: pushed along and wnt 4th down outside 3f out: kpt on at same pce u.p fnl 2f* **7/2**[2]

The Form Book, Raceform Ltd, Compton, RG20 6NL

4 1/2 **Sopran Promo (IRE)**[42] 6325 4-9-2 .... MDemuro 1 99
(B Grizzetti, Italy) *dropped out in last: styd on down outside fr over 2f out* **13/1**

5 1/2 **Pedra Pompas**[95] 4-9-2 .... NMurru 2 98
(M Gasparini, Italy) *3rd early: 4th 1/2-way: rdn and one pce fr over 2f out* **27/1**

6 1 1/4 **Stettino (ITY)**[58] 3-9-2 .... MMonteriso 3 97
() *racd in 2nd: one pce fnl 3f* **28/1**

7 10 **Touch Of Mida**[175] 3-9-1 .... MPasquale 4 73
(G Pucciatti, Italy) *racd in 6th: a bhd* **22/1**

1m 39.8s
WFA 3 from 4yo+ 2lb 7 Ran SP% **128.8**
(including 1 Euro stake): WIN 1.28; PL 1.05, 1.33; DF 3.71.
Owner Gary A Tanaka **Bred** Azienda Agricola Del Parco **Trained** Newmarket, Suffolk

NOTEBOOK
Pressing(IRE), who was long odds-on to add to his success in Istanbul's Topkapi Trophy two months ago, handled this very different ground (although it was not as soft as the official description), and outclassed his rival as expected. He is now on course for the Hong Kong Mile in the middle of next month.

7263a PREMIO ROMA AT THE RACES (GROUP 1) 1m 2f

3:25 (3:39) 3-Y-0+ £79,412 (£34,941; £19,059; £9,529)

RPR

1 **Estejo (GER)**[42] 6325 4-9-2 .... DPorcu 6 108
(R Rohne, Germany) *mde all: hrd rdn under 2f out: hld on gamely whn strly pressed fnl 1 1/2f*

2 3/4 **Permesso**[35] 3-9-0 .... MMonteriso 10 108
(F & L Camici, Italy) *hld up in rr: 11th st: remained in rr tl styd on strly fnl 1 1/2f: fin wl to take 2nd on line*

3 nse **Once More Dubai (USA)**[35] 3-9-0 ....(bt) GBietolini 7 108
(Gianluca Bietolini, Italy) *in rr: 10th st: hdwy over 2f out: angled to outside fr under 2f out: str run to go 2nd 150yds out: lost 2nd on line*

4 1/2 **Papetti (ITY)**[70] 3-9-0 ....(t) TThulliez 8 107
(B Grizzetti, Italy) *racd in 4th: wnt 2nd 2f out: one pce and lost 2nd 150yds out: lost 3rd cl home*

5 1 1/2 **Basaltico (IRE)**[11] 7087 4-9-2 ....(t) URispoli 4 102
(A & G Botti, Italy) *midfield: 6th st: hdwy on ins to dispute 3rd briefly over 1f out: one pce*

6 2 **Ul Zincarlin (IRE)**[49] 5-9-2 .... PBorelli 9 98
(S Santella, Italy) *hld up: 8th st: nvr a factor*

7 1 1/4 **Freemusic (IRE)**[35] 4-9-2 ....(t) GMarcelli 12 95
(L Riccardi, Italy) *hld up in last: modest late hdwy*

8 nk **Nahoodh (IRE)**[36] 6475 3-8-10 .... LDettori 3 93
(M Johnston) *racd in 5th: rdn 2 1/2f out: sn btn*

9 nk **Selmis**[56] 4-9-2 .... MDemuro 11 94
(V Caruso, Italy) *hld up in 9th: nvr a factor*

10 3 1/2 **Gimmy (IRE)**[42] 6325 4-9-2 ....(t) SUrru 1 87
(B Grizzetti, Italy) *racd in 2nd tl wknd under 2f out*

11 3 1/2 **Cima De Triomphe (IRE)**[35] 6522 3-9-0 ....(t) MJKinane 5 82
(B Grizzetti, Italy) *racd in 3rd: wknd 2f out*

12 dist **Storm Mountain (IRE)**[42] 6325 5-9-2 ....(tp) DVargiu 2 —
(B Grizzetti, Italy) *midfield: 7th st: wknd 3f out: t.o*

2m 6.70s (3.40)
WFA 3 from 4yo+ 4lb 12 Ran
(including 1 Euro stake): WIN 46.21; PL 16.91, 4.17, 3.09; SF 421.40..
Owner G Martone **Bred** Gestut Schallern **Trained** Germany

NOTEBOOK
Nahoodh(IRE), stepping up in trip having raced alsmost exclusively at a mile this season, was in trouble before stamina became an issue and, although she handles cut in the ground, probably found this ground too soft at the end of a long season.

2879 KREFELD (R-H)

Sunday, November 9

OFFICIAL GOING: Heavy

7264a HERZOG VON RATIBOR-RENNEN (GROUP 3) 1m 110y

1:05 (1:18) 2-Y-0 £22,059 (£7,353; £4,044; £2,206; £1,103)

RPR

1 **Peligroso (FR)**[21] 2-9-2 .... J-PCarvalho 2 —
(Mario Hofer, Germany) *uns rdr bef s and rn loose: racd in 4th on ins: swtchd outside and 3rd st: led appr fnl f: r.o wl* **68/10**

2 4 1/2 **Mantoro (GER)** 2-9-2 .... AHelfenbein 5 —
(Mario Hofer, Germany) *led: rn v wd on first turn and lost pl after 1f: regained ld after 3f: hdd appr fnl f: no ex* **41/10**[3]

3 2 1/2 **Anjella (GER)**[14] 7006 2-9-1 .... FilipMinarik 4 —
(J Hirschberger, Germany) *hld up in 5th: 4th st: kpt on fnl 1 1/2f but nvr nr ldrs* **36/10**[2]

4 3 **Julius Caesar (GER)** 2-9-2 .... AStarke 6 —
(P Schiergen, Germany) *lft in ld after 1f: hdd after 3f: pushed along under 3f out: btn over 2f out* **6/10**[1]

5 3 **Turgenjew (IRE)** 2-9-2 .... VSchulepov 3 —
(H J Groschel, Germany) *a in rr* **17/2**

6 17 **Marangu (IRE)** 2-9-2 .... EPedroza 7 —
(W Hickst, Germany) *t.k.h early: cl up in 3rd tl wknd 3f out* **119/10**

1m 51.43s (4.83) 6 Ran SP% **134.9**
TOTE: WIN 78; PL 38, 29; SF 396.
Owner M Hofer & Stall Steigenberger **Bred** Stall Undosa **Trained** Germany

7178 SOUTHWELL (L-H)

Monday, November 10

OFFICIAL GOING: Standard
Wind: Virtually nil Weather: Overcasty and rain

7265 RACING POST AMATEUR RIDERS' H'CAP 1m 6f (F)

12:10 (12:11) (Class 6) (0-65,61) 3-Y-0+ £1,977 (£608; £304) Stalls Low

Form RPR

-130 1 **Cumbrian Knight (IRE)**[23] 6824 10-11-4 **61**.......... MissNJefferson(3) 5 69
(J M Jefferson) *dwlt: hld up in rr: stdy hdwy 5f out: chsd ldrs over 2f out: rdn over 1f out: styd on to ld ins fnl f* **8/1**[3]

0334 2 3/4 **York Cliff**[44] 6279 10-11-0 **57**....................(e[1]) MrBenBrisbourne(3) 9 64
(W M Brisbourne) *in tch: hdwy over 4f out: rdn to ld over 1f out: drvn and hdd ins fnl f: no ex towards fin* **17/2**

3506 3 nk **Blue Hills**[13] 7045 7-11-6 **60**....................(b) MrsMarieKing 10 67
(P W Hiatt) *chsd ldng pair: hdwy on inner over 3f out: led wl over 2f out: rdn and hdd over 1f out: sn drvn and kpt on ins fnl f* **4/1**[1]

0000 4 nk **Hunting Haze**[85] 3399 5-9-12 **45**.................... MrsDWilkinson(7) 8 51
(A Crook) *hld up in rr: stdy hdwy 5f out: cl up over 2f out: rdn and ev ch over 1f out: one pce* **80/1**

4506 5 5 **Go On Ahead (IRE)**[20] 6882 8-10-13 **53**....................(p) MrsMRoberts 6 52
(M J Coombe) *led 4f: cl up tl led again over 3f out: sn rdn and hdd wl over 2f out: grad wknd* **7/1**[2]

0000 6 2 **Flame Creek (IRE)**[26] 6740 12-11-1 **55**.................... MissARyan 7 51
(E J Creighton) *hld up towards rr: hdwy 4f out: rdn along over 2f out: drvn: hung lft and wknd over 1f out* **12/1**

4050 7 3 1/2 **Ronsard (IRE)**[5] 5993 6-9-12 **45**.................... MrTCooper(7) 11 36
(P D Evans) *dwlt and hld up towards rr: sme hdwy 3f out: nvr nr ldrs* **14/1**

0050 8 11 **Able Dara**[128] 3718 5-10-5 **45**.................... MrSDobson 13 21
(N Bycroft) *in tch: hdwy to chse ldrs over 4f out: rdn along over 3f out: wknd over 2f out* **11/1**

66-5 9 shd **Joshua**[12] 154 3-9-11 **45**.................... MrSWalker 1 21
(D E Cantillon) *t.k.h: trckd ldrs: pushed along 1/2-way: rdn along 5f out and sn wknd* **4/1**[1]

1600 10 6 **Cragganmore Creek**[69] 5593 5-10-4 **49**....................(v) MrBMMorris(5) 4 16
(D Morris) *chsd ldr tl led after 4f: rdn along over 4f out: hdd over 3f out and sn wknd* **9/1**

-400 11 7 **Katie Kingfisher**[225] 606 4-9-12 **45**....................(p) MrJPearce(7) 14 3
(M E Rimmer) *s.i.s and a bhd* **80/1**

0P0- 12 46 **I'm Agenius**[373] 6642 5-9-12 **45**.................... MissCBoxall(7) 2 —
(P A Blockley) *in tch: rdn along 1/2-way: wknd 5f out: t.o fnl 3f* **25/1**

050- 13 58 **Snowflight**[410] 5755 4-10-5 **50**.................... MissWGibson(5) 12 —
(P T Midgley) *chsd ldrs to 1/2-way: sn lost pl and t.o fnl 3f* **14/1**

3m 11.46s (3.16) **Going Correction** -0.075s/f (Stan)
WFA 3 from 4yo+ 8lb 13 Ran SP% **119.8**
Speed ratings (Par 101): **87,86,86,86,83 82,80,73,73,70 66,40,7**
toteswinger: 1&2 £3.90, 1&3 £6.90, 2&3 £6.70. CSF £74.05 CT £316.36 TOTE £7.30: £2.30, £1.90, £1.70; EX 29.90 Trifecta £31.40 Pool: £102.41 - 2.41 winning units..
Owner J M Jefferson **Bred** John P A Kenny **Trained** Norton, N Yorks

FOCUS
A moderate amateur riders' staying handicap. Both Cragganmore Creek and Go On Ahead went off far too quickly and those held up were at an advantage. The winner is rated back to something like his best form of two winters ago.

7266 RACINGPOST.COM MEMBERS CLUB NURSERY (DIV I) 7f (F)

12:40 (12:40) (Class 5) (0-60,60) 2-Y-0 £2,627 (£775; £388) Stalls Low

Form RPR

545 1 **Kinigi (IRE)**[21] 6858 2-9-3 **56**.................... JamieSpencer 9 60
(S A Callaghan) *hld up in tch: hdwy on outer over 2f out: rdn to chal over 1f out: sn edgd lft: drvn to ld ins fnl f: jst hld on* **15/8**[2]

0043 2 shd **Le Petit Vigier**[6] 7172 2-8-9 **48**....................(t) AndrewElliott 6 52
(P Beaumont) *cl up: led on inner 3f out: rdn 2f out: drvn over 1f out: hdd ins fnl f: rallied wl towards fin: jst failed* **14/1**

660 3 hd **Cut And Thrust (IRE)**[35] 6539 2-9-5 **58**.................... PhilipRobinson 10 61
(M A Jarvis) *cl up on outer: effrt over 2f out: sn rdn to chal and ev ch tl drvn ins fnl f and no ex towards fin* **6/4**[1]

600 4 4 **Barbeito**[12] 7079 2-8-6 **45**.................... SaleemGolam 7 38
(D J S Ffrench Davis) *chsd ldrs: rdn along over 2f out: drvn and one pce fr over 1f out* **25/1**

0500 5 1 **Miss Xu Xia**[3] 7227 2-8-3 **45**....................(p) DuranFentiman(3) 8 36
(G R Oldroyd) *dwlt and towards rr: hdwy over 2f out: sn rdn and kpt on same pce appr fnl f* **33/1**

2001 6 hd **Shifting Gold (IRE)**[12] 7079 2-9-7 **60**....................(b) PaulMulrennan 2 50
(K A Ryan) *rdn along early to ld: hdd and rdn 3f out: drvn and wknd wl over 1f out: n.m.r appr fnl f* **13/2**[3]

0000 7 1 1/2 **Four Green Fields (IRE)**[89] 4982 2-8-0 **46** ow1.............. AmyScott(7) 1 33
(B W Duke) *sooun outpcd and rr 1/2-way: hdwy 2f out: styd on appr last: nrst fin* **50/1**

5600 8 1 **Betws Y Coed (IRE)**[24] 6787 2-8-13 **52**....................(p) NeilChalmers 3 36
(A Bailey) *dwlt: a in rr* **20/1**

0425 9 18 **Royal Premium**[70] 5560 2-9-0 **53**....................(p) PaulFessey 4 —
(H A McWilliams) *cl up: rdn along 3f out: sn drvn and wknd over 2f out* **33/1**

1m 30.21s (-0.09) **Going Correction** -0.075s/f (Stan) 9 Ran SP% **111.2**
Speed ratings (Par 96): **97,96,96,92,90 90,89,87,67**
toteswinger: 1&2 £3.20, 1&3 £1.50, 2&3 £5.00. CSF £23.22 CT £45.78 TOTE £3.10: £1.20, £2.50, £1.10; EX 27.60 Trifecta £56.00 Pool: £299.04 - 3.95 winning units..
Owner James M Egan **Bred** Corduff Stud **Trained** Newmarket, Suffolk

FOCUS
A reasonable nursery for such a lowly level and there was very little between the front three, although the winning time was slightly slower than the second division. The first three came clear and the form seems sound.

NOTEBOOK
Kinigi(IRE) appreciated the return to 7f on her nursery debut and showed herself on a good mark. She made hard work of this, but the front three were clear of the remainder and she is entitled to come on again. (op 7-4)
Le Petit Vigier, having his first start in a nursery, handled the Fibresand well and kept on really gamely for strong pressure in the straight. She is at the right end of the handicap to pick up a small race and she looks likely to stay further. (op 12-1)
Cut And Thrust(IRE), dropped a furlong in trip on his first start in a nursery, had his chance but just found the two horses on either side of him too strong. (op 7-4)
Barbeito probably ran her best race yet in fourth but she was still beaten a fair way. (op 28-1)

Shifting Gold(IRE), the winner of a 1m seller on heavy ground at Nottingham on his previous start, was well below form on his first try on Fibresand. (op 5-1 tchd 7-1)

7267 RACINGPOST.COM LIVE REPORTER H'CAP (DIV I) — 1m (F)

1:10 (1:10) (Class 6) (0-60,59) 3-Y-0+ — **£1,706** (£503; £252) **Stalls** Low

Form — RPR

0234 **1** — **Having A Ball**[12] 7076 4-9-2 **57** ... JamieSpencer 10 — 68
(P D Cundell) *hld up towards rr: gd hdwy on wd outside over 2f out: rdn to ld ent fnl f: sn edgd lft and drvn out* **9/4**[1]

0000 **2** 1 1/2 **Boss Hog**[168] 2451 3-9-1 **58** ... J-PGuillambert 5 — 66
(P A Blockley) *trckd ldrs: hdwy to ld over 2f out: sn rdn: drvn and hdd ent fnl f: kpt on same pce* **8/1**[3]

2004 **3** nk **Time To Regret**[23] 6821 8-9-4 **59** ...(p) AndrewElliott 9 — 66
(I W McInnes) *in tch: hdwy 3f out: rdn to chal 2f out: ev ch tl drvn and one pce ins fnl f* **12/1**

002 **4** 1/2 **Betteras Bertie**[6] 7180 5-8-9 **50** ... RobertWinston 2 — 56
(M Brittain) *s.i.s and bhd: hdwy on inner wl over 2f out: rdn to chse ldrs over 1f out: drvn and kpt on ins fnl f* **7/1**[2]

6201 **5** 1 1/4 **Out Of Nothing**[9] 7131 5-8-9 **55** ... AmyKathleenParsons(5) 6 — 58
(K M Prendergast) *trckd ldrs: hdwy 3f out: rdn and ev ch 2f out: wknd appr fnl f* **10/1**

3000 **6** 1 1/4 **Blue Empire (IRE)**[106] 4451 7-9-0 **55** ...(p) TonyHamilton 12 — 55
(Ollie Pears) *dwlt and towards rr: hdwy over 2f out: rdn to chse ldrs over 1f out: swtchd outside and drvn ent fnl f: no imp* **16/1**

0000 **7** 9 **Government (IRE)**[17] 3691 7-7-13 **45** ...(b) AmyBaker(5) 1 — 25
(M C Chapman) *led: rdn along 3f out: hdd over 2f out and sn wknd* **66/1**

0552 **8** 1 **Tuscan Treaty**[95] 4772 8-8-4 **45** ... LiamJones 4 — 22
(R W Price) *chsd ldrs: rdn along 3f out: drvn over 2f out and sn wknd* **14/1**

5050 **9** 3 1/2 **Sydneyroughdiamond**[44] 5454 6-8-4 **45** ...(e1) FrancisNorton 13 — 14
(M Mullineaux) *a towards rr* **50/1**

0500 **10** hd **Dry Speedfit (IRE)**[35] 6541 3-8-12 **55** ... PaulMulrennan 7 — 24
(Micky Hammond) *s.i.s: a in rr* **8/1**[3]

6400 **11** 1/2 **Riverhill (IRE)**[27] 6727 5-8-6 **47** ...(tp) PaulFessey 3 — 15
(Miss T Jackson) *cl up: rdn along 1/2-way: sn wknd* **25/1**

1034 **12** 2 **Josephine Malines**[18] 6927 4-8-9 **53** ...(p) AndrewMullen(3) 14 — 16
(Mrs A Duffield) *a in rr* **14/1**

0066 **13** 20 **Veronicas Way**[34] 6562 3-8-2 **45** ... FrankieMcDonald 8 — —
(G J Smith) *chsd ldrs to 1/2-way: sn wknd* **16/1**

1m 42.45s (-1.25) **Going Correction** -0.075s/f (Stan)
WFA 3 from 4yo+ 2lb — **13** Ran SP% **114.7**
Speed ratings (Par 101): **103,101,101,100,99 98,89,88,84,84 84,82,62**
toteswinger: 1&2 £5.20, 1&3 £8.20, 2&3 £21.40. CSF £18.33 CT £176.51 TOTE £2.60: £1.20, £3.50, £3.90; EX 20.00 Trifecta £143.50 Part won. Pool: £193.94 - 0.41winning units..
Owner Miss M C Fraser **Bred** R G Percival **Trained** Compton, Berks

FOCUS
A moderate but competitive handicap, and the form seems sound. The winning time was 0.78 seconds slower than the second division.
Riverhill(IRE) Official explanation: jockey said gelding hung left throughout

7268 E B F RACINGPOST.COM MAIDEN STKS — 6f (F)

1:45 (1:46) (Class 5) 2-Y-0 — **£3,753** (£1,108; £554) **Stalls** Low

Form — RPR

0402 **1** — **Captain Kallis (IRE)**[13] 7044 2-9-3 64 ... FrankieMcDonald 5 — 64
(D J S Ffrench Davis) *trckd ldr: hdwy to chal over 2f out: rdn over 1f out: drvn to ld ins fnl f: kpt on* **5/1**[2]

2 3/4 **Good Humoured** 2-9-3 0 ... J-PGuillambert 7 — 62
(Sir Mark Prescott) *trckd ldrs: hdwy over 2f out: chal wl over 1f out: rdn and ev ch ins fnl f: nt qckn last 50yds* **7/4**[1]

006 **3** 1/2 **Oisin's Boy**[28] 6701 2-9-3 60 ... PatCosgrave 4 — 60
(J R Boyle) *led: rdn along over 2f out: drvn over 1f out: hdd ins fnl f and kpt on same pce* **15/2**[3]

04 **4** 6 **Hawk's Eye**[42] 6341 2-9-3 0 ... JamieSpencer 1 — 42
(E F Vaughan) *t.k.h: chsd ldrs: rdn along over 2f out and sn btn* **7/4**[1]

5 1/2 **Fantasy Gladiator** 2-9-3 0 ... MickyFenton 6 — 41
(R M H Cowell) *s.i.s: rapid hdwy on outer to join ldrs after 2f: cl up tl rdn over 2f out: edgd lft and wknd* **25/1**

6 2 1/4 **Aaman (IRE)** 2-9-3 0 ... LiamJones 2 — 34
(E F Vaughan) *s.i.s: a in rr* **20/1**

00 **7** 18 **Bluebaru**[12] 7080 2-9-3 0 ... JamieMoriarty 3 — —
(L R James) *chsd ldrs: rdn along 1/2-way: sn wknd* **100/1**

1m 16.0s (-0.50) **Going Correction** -0.075s/f (Stan) — **7** Ran SP% **110.8**
Speed ratings (Par 96): **100,99,98,90,89 86,62**
toteswinger: 1&2 £2.10, 1&3 £3.50, 2&3 £3.00. CSF £13.28 TOTE £5.80: £1.70, £2.00; EX 16.00.
Owner Hargood Limited **Bred** Pipe View Stud **Trained** Lambourn, Berks

FOCUS
A weak, uncompetitive juvenile maiden. The winner reproduced his recent improved course form.

NOTEBOOK
Captain Kallis(IRE) probably only had to run to the same sort of level as when second over course and distance on his previous start. He is clearly well suited to Fibresand. (op 11-2 tchd 6-1)
Good Humoured, a 62,000gns purchase, out of a useful multiple 1m-1m2f winner, was well backed on his racecourse debut but found one too good. Having tracked the pace early, his jockey appeared confident early in the straight, and he duly went very short in-running, but he looked green when coming under pressure. He ran to just a moderate level, but will know more next time and really ought to improve when stepped up in trip. (op 10-3)
Oisin's Boy showed plenty of early speed, but he was readily outpaced in the straight and might want 7f. (op 8-1 tchd 7-1)
Hawk's Eye probably would have won had he built on his latest fourth at Windsor, but he never really looked comfortable. He was a touch keen early and found little when taken very wide (out of the kickback) in the straight. This surface probably didn't suit, and he now has the option of handicaps, but his attitude looks questionable. Official explanation: jockey said colt ran too freely (op Evens)
Fantasy Gladiator recovered from a slow start to show plenty of speed mid-race, but he weakened in the straight. Official explanation: jockey said gelding hung left (op 14-1)

7269 RACINGPOST.COM MEMBERS CLUB NURSERY (DIV II) — 7f (F)

2:15 (2:15) (Class 5) (0-60,59) 2-Y-0 — **£2,627** (£775; £388) **Stalls** Low

Form — RPR

000 **1** — **Kladester (USA)**[54] 6008 2-9-3 **55** ...(t) PaulMulrennan 5 — 63+
(B Smart) *prom: rdn along and sltly outpcd 3f out: hdwy on outer over 2f out: rdn and hung lft over 1f out: styd on to ld ent fnl f: sn clr* **10/3**[1]

460 **2** 4 **Kristopher James (IRE)**[16] 6986 2-9-5 **57** ... TGMcLaughlin 1 — 55
(W M Brisbourne) *chsd ldrs on inner: swtchd rt and hdwy over 2f out: rdn and ch whn hmpd over 1f out: kpt on u.p ins fnl f* **11/2**[3]

6000 **3** 2 1/2 **Cool Sonata (IRE)**[67] 5632 2-8-7 **45** ... FrancisNorton 2 — 37
(M Brittain) *led: pushed along and hdd 3f out: rdn and keeping on whn sltly hmpd over 1f: sn one pce* **4/1**[2]

000 **4** 1 1/4 **Dontforgetshovel**[42] 6343 2-8-7 **45** ...(v1) LiamJones 9 — 34
(J Pearce) *plld hrd: chsd ldrs: led 3f out: rdn and hung lft wl over 1f out: drvn and hdd ent fnl f: wknd* **9/1**

0000 **5** 2 3/4 **Daily Planet (IRE)**[52] 6086 2-8-5 **50** ...(p) AmyScott(7) 8 — 32
(B W Duke) *in rr tl styd on fnl 2f: nrst fin* **14/1**

0600 **6** 3/4 **Moon Warrior**[24] 6779 2-8-0 **45** ... AndrewHeffernan(7) 4 — 25
(C Smith) *chsd ldrs on inner: rdn along over 2f out: sn drvn and no imp* **33/1**

004 **7** 3 1/2 **Star Of Sophia (IRE)**[51] 6133 2-8-4 **45** ...(v) AndrewMullen(3) 10 — 16
(Mrs A Duffield) *a in rr* **11/1**

050 **8** 6 **Dawn Wee**[17] 6953 2-8-12 **53** ... DuranFentiman(3) 7 — 9
(G R Oldroyd) *chsd ldrs: rdn along 3f out and sn wknd* **11/1**

01 **9** 1 **Captain Cavendish (IRE)**[28] 6709 2-9-7 **59** ...(v1) MickyFenton 6 — 13
(A Bailey) *chsd ldrs: rdn along 1/2-way: sn wknd* **4/1**[2]

1m 30.13s (-0.17) **Going Correction** -0.075s/f (Stan) — **9** Ran SP% **114.7**
Speed ratings (Par 96): **97,92,89,88,85 84,80,73,72**
toteswinger: 1&2 £6.00, 1&3 £3.70, 2&3 £5.40. CSF £21.70 CT £74.78 TOTE £3.80: £1.80, £1.20, £1.80; EX 18.20 Trifecta £193.40 Part won. Pool: £261.47 - 0.91winning units..
Owner Prime Equestrian **Bred** Malec Thoroughbreds, Inc **Trained** Hambleton, N Yorks
■ Stewards' Enquiry : Paul Mulrennan three-day ban: careless riding (Nov 24-26)

FOCUS
The winning time was fractionally quicker than the first division, but this still looked the weaker of the two races overall. The winner put in a decent performance for the grade and this form could have been rated higher.

NOTEBOOK
Kladester(USA) ◆ had shown very limited form in three runs in turf maidens, but he proved well suited by the Fibresand on his nursery debut and stayed on strongly having been under pressure a fair way out. This didn't take much winning, but he had been off for almost two months and looks the type to improve with racing. Official explanation: trainer said, regarding the apparent improvement in form, that gelding may have appreciated the fibresand and the reapplication of a tongue tie. (op 13-2)
Kristopher James(IRE) did well to regain his momentum after being short of room and bumped two furlongs out, but he did not look unlucky. (op 4-1)
Cool Sonata(IRE) showed early speed but she finished up well held. (op 9-2)
Dontforgetshovel raced far too freely in a first-time visor and it was a surprise to see him last so long. (op 14-1)
Captain Cavendish(IRE) Official explanation: jockey said gelding never travelled

7270 RACINGPOST.COM LIVE REPORTER H'CAP (DIV II) — 1m (F)

2:45 (2:47) (Class 6) (0-60,59) 3-Y-0+ — **£1,706** (£503; £252) **Stalls** Low

Form — RPR

4002 **1** — **Mozayada (USA)**[6] 7184 4-8-6 **45** ... FrancisNorton 9 — 66+
(M Brittain) *prom: smooth hdwy to ld over 2f out: rdn clr over 1f out: comf* **9/4**[1]

30 **2** 3 3/4 **Barataria**[71] 5538 6-8-12 **54** ... JackMitchell(3) 11 — 63
(R Bastiman) *dwlt and bhd: hdwy wl over 2f out: rdn wl over 1f out: styd on to chse wnr ins fnl f sn no imp* **11/1**

1026 **3** 1 **Bert's Memory**[150] 2988 4-8-3 **45** ...(b) DuranFentiman(3) 8 — 52
(J Mackie) *trckd ldrs: hdwy over 2f out: rdn and ev ch wl over 1f out: sn drvn and kpt on same pce* **16/1**

054- **4** 2 3/4 **Mambo Sun**[599] 732 5-9-4 **57** ... RobertWinston 12 — 57
(P A Blockley) *in tch: hdwy 3f out: rdn to chse ldrs 2f out: sn drvn and kpt on same pce* **5/1**[2]

0000 **5** 2 1/4 **Dark Champion**[34] 6546 8-8-6 **45** ...(v) PaulQuinn 6 — 40
(R E Barr) *cl up: rdn over 2f out and ev ch tl drvn and wknd appr fnl f* **50/1**

500 **6** 1 3/4 **Spume (IRE)**[5] 7189 4-9-2 **55** ...(bt) TonyCulhane 13 — 46
(S Parr) *midfield: hdwy 3f out: rdn along over 2f out and sn no imp* **12/1**

3502 **7** 1 1/4 **Comrade Cotton**[13] 7053 4-8-13 **52** ...(p) MickyFenton 1 — 40
(J Ryan) *towards rr: sme hdwy over 2f out: sn rdn and nvr nr ldrs* **10/1**

0000 **8** 2 **So Sublime**[92] 4901 3-8-11 **55** ...(t) RussellKennemore(3) 3 — 39
(M C Chapman) *trckd ldrs: effrt over 2f out and sn rdn: drvn wl over 1f out and grad wknd* **66/1**

604 **9** 1 **Carefree**[103] 4540 4-8-6 **45** ... AndrewElliott 10 — 26
(Mrs R A Carr) *a towards rr* **12/1**

3314 **10** 2 **Zeffirelli**[10] 7111 3-9-4 **59** ... RobertHavlin 5 — 36
(M Quinn) *led: rdn along 3f out: drvn and hdd over 2f out: sn wknd* **13/2**[3]

0600 **11** 13 **Rosies Dawn**[13] 7049 3-8-4 **45** ... FrankieMcDonald 4 — —
(D Carroll) *chsd ldrs on inner: rdn along 1/2-way: sn lost pl and bhd* **25/1**

5356 **12** 2 3/4 **Boppys Pride**[9] 7132 5-8-9 **48** ... JamieMoriarty 2 — —
(P T Midgley) *s.i.s: a in rr* **14/1**

5246 **13** 5 **Abbeygate**[238] 916 7-8-8 **47** ... LiamJones 14 — —
(T Keddy) *chsd ldrs on outer: rdn along 1/2-way: sn lost pl and bhd* **14/1**

1m 41.67s (-2.03) **Going Correction** -0.075s/f (Stan)
WFA 3 from 4yo+ 2lb — **13** Ran SP% **120.1**
Speed ratings (Par 101): **107,103,102,99,97 95,94,92,91,89 76,73,68**
toteswinger: 1&2 £8.10, 1&3 £11.20, 2&3 £35.80. CSF £28.27 CT £332.15 TOTE £2.70: £1.50, £3.60, £4.00; EX 40.80 TRIFECTA Not won..
Owner Mel Brittain **Bred** Shadwell Farm LLC **Trained** Warthill, N Yorks
■ Stewards' Enquiry : Frankie McDonaldJ caution: used whip down shoulder in forehand position

FOCUS
A moderate handicap, but Mozayada recorded a time 0.78 seconds quicker than the first division and looks better than this grade. The winner took advantage of being well in and the form seems sound.

7271 RACING POST WEEKENDER H'CAP — 2m (F)

3:20 (3:20) (Class 5) (0-75,72) 3-Y-0+ — **£2,729** (£806; £403) **Stalls** Low

Form — RPR

21-4 **1** — **Dart**[13] 7045 4-9-5 **63** ... JamieSpencer 1 — 73+
(J R Fanshawe) *prom: effrt to ld over 2f out: rdn clr over 1f out: styd on strly* **5/2**[1]

2000 **2** 3 **Inchpast**[23] 6817 7-10-0 **72** ...(b) PaulMulrennan 2 — 76
(M H Tompkins) *stmbld s: hld up: gd hdwy on outer over 3f out: rdn to chal over 2f out: ever ch tl drvn and kpt on same pce appr last* **4/1**[2]

3403 **3** nk **River Danube**[13] 7042 5-9-3 **61** ... JamieMoriarty 4 — 65
(T J Fitzgerald) *trckd ldrs: effrt 4f out: rdn along 3f out: drvn and kpt on same pce fr over 1f out* **8/1**[3]

0021 **4** 3/4 **Victory Quest (IRE)**[13] 7045 8-9-11 **69** ...(v) J-PGuillambert 7 — 72
(Mrs S Lamyman) *prom: hdwy to ld over 4f out: rdn along and hdd over 2f out: sn drvn and kpt on same pce* **5/2**[1]

1000 **5** 1 3/4 **Three Boars**[22] 6838 6-9-8 **66** ...(b) RobertWinston 3 — 67
(S Gollings) *hld up: effrt 4f out: pushed along 3f out: rdn and one pce fnl 2f* **8/1**[3]

The Form Book, Raceform Ltd, Compton, RG20 6NL

0502 **6** 3/4 **Oberlin (USA)**[8] 7149 3-8-10 **63** .... TonyCulhane 5 63
(T Keddy) *led: rdn along and hdd over 4f out: drvn wl over 2f out and grad wknd* **9/1**

/054 **7** 2 **Nounou**[145] 2393 7-8-9 **56** .... (t) MarcHalford[(3)] 6 54
(Miss J E Foster) *hld up in tch: hdwy 4f out: rdn along over 2f out: sn drvn and wknd* **33/1**

3m 52.63s (7.13) **Going Correction** -0.075s/f (Stan)
WFA 3 from 4yo+ 9lb 7 Ran SP% **112.3**
Speed ratings (Par 103): **79,77,77,76,76 75,74**
toteswinger: 1&2 £2.60, 1&3 £4.10, 2&3 £5.60. CSF £12.25 TOTE £2.20: £1.30, £2.20; EX 14.50.
Owner Dr Catherine Wills **Bred** St Clare Hall Stud **Trained** Newmarket, Suffolk

FOCUS
An ordinary staying handicap and they went very steady early. The form makes sense at face value but may not be the most solid.

7272 RACEFORM UPDATE H'CAP 1m 4f (F)
3:50 (3:51) (Class 6) (0-65,64) 3-Y-O+ **£2,047** (£604; £302) **Stalls** Low

Form RPR

0060 **1** **Kylkenny**[33] 6577 13-8-6 **55** .... (t) RyanClark[(7)] 5 69
(H Morrison) *hld up towards rr: smooth hdwy on inner over 3f out: led wl over 2f out: rdn clr wl over 1f out: hung rt ins fnl f: kpt on strly* **14/1**

3612 **2** 7 **Ba Dreamflight**[12] 7085 3-8-8 **56** .... RobertHavlin 3 59
(H Morrison) *hld up: hdwy to trck ldrs 1/2-way: effrt 3f out: rdn along and ev ch over 2f out: drvn wl over 1f out: kpt on: no ch w wnr* **7/1**[3]

1263 **3** 3/4 **Elite Land**[34] 6551 5-9-8 **64** .... JamieSpencer 4 66
(K A Ryan) *stdd s: hld up and bhd: hdwy on wd outside wl over 2f out: rdn wl over 1f out: drvn and kpt on ins fnl f* **3/1**[1]

5-05 **4** 1 **Top Tiger**[24] 6790 4-9-6 **62** .... PaulMulrennan 7 62
(M H Tompkins) *trckd ldr: led 4f out: rdn along and hdd wl over 2f out: sn drvn and one pce* **6/1**[2]

0 **5** nk **Never Pink (FR)**[13] 7042 4-8-10 **52** .... LiamJones 6 52
(Ian Williams) *in tch: hdwy 4f out: rdn along wl over 2f out: sn drvn and kpt on same pce* **9/1**

0205 **6** nse **Black Falcon (IRE)**[6] 7183 8-9-0 **63** .... StacyRenwick[(7)] 8 63
(John A Harris) *trckd ldrs whn n.m.r and stmbld bnd over 9f out: effrt 4f out: rdn along 3f out: sn drvn and wknd fnl 2f* **15/2**

0363 **7** 3 1/2 **Carlton Mac**[6] 7174 3-8-2 **50** oh2 .... (p) FrancisNorton 2 44
(N Bycroft) *chsd ldrs: rdn along 5f out: sn wknd* **12/1**

-012 **8** 2 1/4 **Covert Mission**[7] 7169 5-9-0 **56** .... RobertWinston 9 47
(P D Evans) *chsd ldrs on outer: hdwy and cl up 4f out: rdn along over 2f out: sn drvn and wknd wl over 1f out* **3/1**[1]

4-10 **9** 25 **Tiegs (IRE)**[204] 1206 6-8-5 **50** oh3 .... MarcHalford[(3)] 1 1
(P W Hiatt) *led: rdn along and hdd 4f out: wknd qckly* **40/1**

2m 37.8s (-3.20) **Going Correction** -0.075s/f (Stan)
WFA 3 from 4yo+ 6lb 9 Ran SP% **115.3**
Speed ratings (Par 101): **107,102,101,101,100 100,98,97,80**
toteswinger: 1&2 £11.60, 1&3 £9.30, 2&3 £4.90. CSF £107.83 CT £376.60 TOTE £20.80: £4.40, £2.60, £1.60; EX 56.30 Trifecta £232.20 Part won. Pool: £313.81 - 0.10 winning units. Place 6: £15.32 Place 5: £6.53 .
Owner Mrs M D W Morrison **Bred** R M , P J And S R Payne **Trained** East Ilsley, Berks
■ A first winner for Ryan Clark, and a final racecourse appearance for Kylkenny.

FOCUS
A moderate handicap.
Black Falcon(IRE) Official explanation: jockey said gelding hung left
T/Plt: £21.10 to a £1 stake. Pool: £35,667.77. 1,231.69 winning tickets. T/Qpdt: £12.60 to a £1 stake. Pool: £3,427.58. 199.90 winning tickets. JR

7225 WOLVERHAMPTON (A.W) (L-H)
Monday, November 10

OFFICIAL GOING: Standard
Wind: Light behind Weather: Cloudy

7273 RACING POST MEDIAN AUCTION MAIDEN STKS 5f 216y(P)
2:05 (2:07) (Class 5) 2-Y-O **£3,070** (£906; £453) **Stalls** Low

Form RPR

0223 **1** **Albertine Rose**[10] 7107 2-8-12 **87** .... MartinDwyer 5 73+
(W R Muir) *mde all: shkn up over 1f out: pushed out* **1/3**[1]

020 **2** 2 **Freepressionist**[11] 7095 2-8-12 65 .... EddieAhern 7 67
(R A Teal) *a.p: chsd wnr over 2f out: rdn wl over 1f out: no imp* **20/1**

06 **3** 2 1/4 **Captain Carey**[3] 7227 2-9-3 0 .... VinceSlattery 6 65
(M S Saunders) *t.k.h in mid-div: hdwy over 2f out: kpt on ins fnl f* **80/1**

4 3/4 **Choisharp (IRE)** 2-8-10 0 .... AndreaAtzeni[(7)] 8 63
(M Botti) *hld up and bhd: hdwy on outside wl over 1f out: kpt on ins fnl f* **14/1**[3]

4540 **5** 2 1/2 **Bartica (IRE)**[21] 6863 2-9-0 66 .... PatrickHills[(3)] 1 56
(R Hannon) *prom: rdn 2f out: wknd ins fnl f* **16/1**

6 8 **Jolly Ranch** 2-8-12 0 .... SimonWhitworth 4 27
(A G Newcombe) *a bhd* **100/1**

426 **7** 7 **All Spin (IRE)**[26] 6732 2-9-3 73 .... DaneO'Neill 9 11
(A P Jarvis) *prom: rdn over 2f out: sn wknd: eased over 1f out* **8/1**[2]

8 5 **Patronne** 2-8-12 0 .... TPQueally 2 —
(Sir Mark Prescott) *t.k.h: stdd into mid-div after 1f: bhd fnl 2f* **22/1**

9 12 **Trick Or Two** 2-9-3 0 .... LPKeniry 3 —
(S Kirk) *s.i.s: a in rr* **33/1**

1m 15.33s (0.33) **Going Correction** +0.05s/f (Slow) 9 Ran SP% **113.0**
Speed ratings (Par 96): **99,96,93,92,89 78,69,62,46**
toteswinger: 1&2 £3.90, 1&3 £14.20, 2&3 £3.90. CSF £12.87 TOTE £1.50: £1.02, £3.40, £15.10; EX 9.60.
Owner Mr & Mrs G Middlebrook **Bred** Mr & Mrs G Middlebrook **Trained** Lambourn, Berks

FOCUS
Straightforward for the winner, who had a good deal in hand on Newmarket form. The race has been rated around the placed horses.

NOTEBOOK
Albertine Rose set the standard on her seconds over course and distance and at Windsor, let alone her seemingly much-improved effort when third at 50-1 in a Newmarket fillies' Listed event last time. She was sent off a hot favourite, free-wheeled into an early lead and was a comfortable winner. A 17lb rise for her previous run could make life tough when switched back to handicaps but she has a good attitude, seems tactically adaptable and could improve again over a slightly stiffer test. (op 4-11 tchd 2-5)
Freepressionist has looked a bit headstrong on three previous runs, but appreciated this return to sprinting and ran a creditable race behind a rival with a much higher rating. She looks on a feasible mark of 65 and could make an impact when sent handicapping. (op 22-1)
Captain Carey stumbled on his debut and was too keen over 7f here three days earlier but showed some ability, staying on steadily behind the first two dropped in trip, and modest handicaps look the way forward after this. (op 66-1)
Choisharp(IRE), a £16,000 purchase, took a little while to get the hang of things but stayed on quite well from a long way back and showed some promise on his debut. (op 12-1 tchd 16-1)
All Spin(IRE) was a sitting duck for finishers after chasing a frantic pace over 6f at Kempton last time. He was a clear second favourite here and ridden with a bit more restraint, but was in trouble a long way out.
Patronne was very weak in the market on her debut. Her dam was placed over 1m6f and is a half-sister to high-class 1m4f+ performers Classic Cliche and My Emma, so she should do better in time, particularly over middle-distances next year. (op 16-1 tchd 25-1)

7274 RACINGPOST.COM MEDIAN AUCTION MAIDEN STKS 1m 4f 50y(P)
2:35 (2:35) (Class 6) 3-5-Y-O **£2,729** (£806; £403) **Stalls** Low

Form RPR

3042 **1** **Azabu Juban (IRE)**[224] 1119 3-8-8 70 .... LukeMorris[(3)] 8 52
(J Jay) *hld up and bhd: hdwy over 3f out: sn rdn: led over 1f out: edgd rt ins fnl f: r.o* **9/4**[2]

0324 **2** 1 **Templetuohy Max (IRE)**[17] 6956 3-9-2 54 .... (v) JimmyQuinn 5 55
(J D Bethell) *t.k.h in mid-div: hdwy 3f out: ev ch over 1f out: nt qckn ins fnl f* **15/8**[1]

4-30 **3** 1 1/4 **Orkney (IRE)**[16] 6991 3-9-2 61 .... TomEaves 1 53
(Miss J A Camacho) *led 1f: chsd ldr: led 8f out: rdn over 2f out: hdd over 1f out: no ex ins fnl f* **9/2**[3]

3506 **4** nse **Amwell House**[29] 6678 3-9-2 45 .... EddieAhern 2 53
(J R Jenkins) *a.p: wnt 2nd 7f out: ev ch wl over 1f out: sn rdn: one pce fnl f* **7/1**

0400 **5** 21 **John Potts**[10] 7115 3-9-2 54 .... JoeFanning 4 19
(B P J Baugh) *hld up: rdn 3f out: sn struggling* **33/1**

0000 **6** 2 3/4 **Little Rococoa**[25] 6762 3-8-11 30 .... SophieDoyle[(5)] 6 15
(R J Price) *dwlt: a in rr* **100/1**

0045 **7** 3 **Crimsonwing (IRE)**[7] 6436 3-8-4 53 .... (b[1]) AndreaAtzeni[(7)] 3 5
(A M Hales) *led after 1f: hdd 8f out: rdn and wknd over 3f out* **8/1**

2m 43.42s (2.32) **Going Correction** +0.05s/f (Slow) 7 Ran SP% **111.3**
Speed ratings (Par 101): **94,93,92,92,78 76,74**
toteswinger: 1&2 £1.10, 1&3 £5.60, 2&3 £1.10. CSF £6.47 TOTE £2.80: £1.80, £2.10; EX 8.30.
Owner David Fremel **Bred** P F Corbet **Trained** Newmarket, Suffolk

FOCUS
A weak auction maiden, weakened by the withdrawal of the morning favourite Isabelonabicycle. The early pace was modest and although the two in the market filled the first two positions, the form is held down by the proximity of the fourth who has a BHA rating of 45.
Little Rococoa Official explanation: jockey said gelding gurgled

7275 RACINGPOST.COM MEMBERS' CLUB CLAIMING STKS 7f 32y(P)
3:05 (3:06) (Class 6) 2-Y-O **£3,070** (£906; £453) **Stalls** High

Form RPR

5052 **1** **Woolston Ferry (IRE)**[12] 7065 2-9-0 74 .... EdwardCreighton 5 77
(M R Channon) *hld up in tch: led over 1f out: r.o wl* **11/4**[2]

2101 **2** 4 **Smalljohn**[7] 7164 2-8-13 74 .... (v) TomEaves 1 66
(B Smart) *led: rdn over 2f out: hdd over 1f out: one pce* **7/4**[1]

0635 **3** 3 1/2 **Skruton (IRE)**[14] 7016 2-8-1 65 .... NicolPolli[(5)] 8 51
(M G Quinlan) *sn chsng ldr: rdn and lost 2nd 2f out: wknd ins fnl f* **8/1**

004 **4** 1 **Polly's Choice (IRE)**[14] 7016 2-8-6 64 ow1 .... PatrickHills[(3)] 10 51
(R Hannon) *hld up in rr: rdn and hdwy on ins over 2f out: hung lft over 1f out: one pce* **9/1**

3110 **5** 4 **Dougie Peel**[21] 6857 2-8-9 62 .... (p) DarryllHolland 6 41
(K A Ryan) *hld up in mid-div: hdwy 5f out: wknd over 2f out* **11/2**[3]

6436 **6** 1 1/4 **Island Chief**[12] 7067 2-8-11 63 .... (p) JoeFanning 12 40
(K A Ryan) *prom: chsd ldr over 5f out to 3f out: wknd over 2f out* **20/1**

7 1 1/2 **Hint Of Honey** 2-8-8 0 .... SimonWhitworth 7 34
(A G Newcombe) *s.s: nvr nr ldrs* **100/1**

4050 **8** hd **She's A Shaw Thing**[37] 6483 2-8-11 75 .... (v[1]) DaneO'Neill 2 36
(P D Evans) *s.i.s: t.k.h: sn mid-div: wknd over 2f out* **8/1**

0640 **9** 1/2 **Accomplishment (IRE)**[41] 6351 2-8-8 58 .... JimmyQuinn 9 32
(A P Jarvis) *a towards rr* **66/1**

0 **10** 6 **Invincible Brave (IRE)**[12] 7079 2-8-9 0 .... PaulHanagan 4 18
(R A Fahey) *hld up in tch: lost pl 4f out: rdn and struggling 3f out* **33/1**

1m 29.89s (0.29) **Going Correction** +0.05s/f (Slow) 10 Ran SP% **120.8**
Speed ratings (Par 94): **100,95,91,90,85 84,82,82,81,74**
toteswinger: 1&2 £2.50, 1&3 £5.30, 2&3 £4.00. CSF £8.11 TOTE £4.20: £1.40, £1.50, £2.20; EX 9.30.Woolston Ferry was subject to a friendly claim.
Owner Capital **Bred** Tim Taylor **Trained** West Ilsley, Berks

FOCUS
This claimer was run at a decent pace. The field finished strung out and the first two home both had strong form claims and an official rating of 74, so the form should be reliable. The winner is rated back to his best.

NOTEBOOK
Woolston Ferry(IRE) encountered a number of traffic problems before snatching second in a 6f Great Leighs claimer last time but had no trouble finding a run here. He travelled smoothly, moved ominously up to press his main market rival in the closing stages and powered clear for an authoritative success. He clearly appreciated the return to 7f and is a very consistent and likeable type, who should continue to run well. (tchd 5-2)
Smalljohn thrashed his rivals in a course-and-distance seller last time and was well drawn to attack in this race, but he did not get an easy time up front and was harassed by Island Chief some way out. He had no answer to the winner's finishing kick, but deserves credit for battling on and finishing clear of the rest, after his potentially damaging mid-race tussle. (op 6-4 tchd 2-1)
Skruton(IRE) was not far behind the first two turning for home but could not sustain her effort. She is fairly consistent but has found life tough and has looked a bit of an awkward ride at times since winning a 6f Lingfield maiden on good to soft in May. (op 11-1)
Polly's Choice(IRE) was a close fourth in a 17-runner Leicester nursery last time but she never got competitive switched back to Polytrack, faced with a difficult task at the weights. (op 12-1 tchd 14-1)
Dougie Peel is a triple claimer/seller winner since July, but he met several rivals on unfavourable terms here, and was forced to race wide and never got into contention. (op 15-2 tchd 8-1 and 5-1)

7276 RACINGPOST.COM LIVE REPORTER H'CAP 5f 20y(P)
3:40 (3:40) (Class 5) (0-75,75) 3-Y-O+ **£3,885** (£1,156; £577; £288) **Stalls** Low

Form RPR

3420 **1** **Sands Crooner (IRE)**[13] 7043 5-9-4 **75** .... (v) TPQueally 5 83
(J G Given) *s.i.s: in rr: hdwy over 1f out: rdn and r.o wl to ld fnl stride* **10/1**

-002 **2** shd **Cayman Fox**[23] 6822 3-8-12 **69** .... PaulHanagan 10 77
(James Moffatt) *led: rdn ins fnl f: hdd last stride* **20/1**

310 **3** 3/4 **Silvanus (IRE)**[38] 6435 3-9-1 **72** .... (b[1]) EddieAhern 9 77
(W J Haggas) *hld up and bhd: hdwy whn n.m.r 2f out: swtchd lft over 1f out: rdn and kpt on ins fnl f* **9/1**

3205 **4** ½ **Bookiesindex Boy**[6] 7182 4-8-13 **70**........(v) DarryllHolland 3 74
(J R Jenkins) *hld up in tch: rdn over 1f out: kpt on ins fnl f* **9/2**[2]

0631 **5** 1 ½ **Tangerine Trees**[28] 6707 3-8-8 **65**........ TomEaves 6 63
(B Smart) *a.p: hung lft over 1f out: one pce fnl f* **8/1**

1512 **6** ½ **Pride Of Northcare (IRE)**[11] 7092 4-8-13 **70**........(v[1]) DarrenWilliams 7 66
(D Shaw) *hld up in mid-div: rdn and hdwy over 1f out: no further prog fnl f* **10/3**[1]

0202 **7** ½ **Russian Symphony (USA)**[87] 5046 7-9-2 **73**........(b) DaneO'Neill 11 68
(C R Egerton) *s.i.s: in rr: rdn wl over 1f out: nvr nrr* **12/1**

5122 **8** nk **Figaro Flyer (IRE)**[152] 2950 5-9-0 **71**........ JimmyQuinn 2 64
(P Howling) *plld hrd in mid-div: hdwy on ins wl over 1f out: fdd towards fin* **15/2**

015 **9** nk **Princess Rose Anne (IRE)**[38] 6435 3-9-4 **75**........(p) LPKeniry 12 67
(E F Vaughan) *bhd: rdn jst over 1f out: nvr nr ldrs* **28/1**

303 **10** 2 ¼ **Another Socket**[30] 6658 3-8-10 **67**........ GrahamGibbons 1 51
(E S McMahon) *s.i.s: chsd ldr after 1f: swtchd rt over 1f out: sn rdn: wknd ins fnl f* **5/1**[3]

2653 **11** 1 ¼ **Matterofact (IRE)**[12] 7081 5-8-2 **66**........ JakePayne(7) 8 46
(M S Saunders) *hld up in mid-div: c wd st: sn bhd* **20/1**

0006 **12** 7 **Bespoke Boy**[13] 7040 3-8-11 **68**........(p) LeeEnstone 13 23
(P C Haslam) *prom 3f* **66/1**

62.37 secs (0.07) **Going Correction** +0.05s/f (Slow) 12 Ran SP% **122.1**
Speed ratings (Par 103): **101,100,99,98,96 95,94,94,93,90 88,77**
toteswinger: 1&2 £46.80, 1&3 £15.60, 2&3 £52.20. CSF £200.87 CT £1905.20 TOTE £10.00: £3.80, £9.60, £4.10; EX 201.50.
Owner Danethorpe Racing Partnership **Bred** Peter Molony **Trained** Willoughton, Lincs

FOCUS
A competitive handicap run at a furious pace. Sound form, with a slight personal best from the winner.

7277 RACING POST WEEKENDER H'CAP — 7f 32y(P)
4:10 (4:11) (Class 5) (0-75,75) 3-Y-O+ **£3,885** (£1,156; £577; £288) **Stalls** High

Form RPR

0000 **1** **Mister New York (USA)**[14] 7014 3-9-2 **73**........ GeorgeBaker 10 83
(Noel T Chance) *hld up towards rr: hdwy over 2f out: rdn over 1f out: edgd lft and led ins fnl f: r.o wl* **14/1**

0012 **2** 1 ¾ **Wing Play (IRE)**[10] 7115 3-8-11 **68**........(p) TravisBlock 6 73
(H Morrison) *hld up in mid-div: hdwy over 3f out: rdn wl over 1f out: led jst ins fnl f: sn hdd: nt qckn* **9/2**[2]

3304 **3** 2 ¾ **Coleorton Dancer**[10] 7118 6-8-8 **64**........ MartinDwyer 3 63
(K A Ryan) *broke wl: stdd into mid-div after 1f: lost pl over 2f out: hdwy on ins wl over 1f out: edgd lft wl ins fnl f: kpt on* **10/1**

4120 **4** hd **I Confess**[16] 6976 3-8-11 **68**........(b) DaneO'Neill 11 65
(P D Evans) *chsd ldr: led over 5f out: rdn wl over 1f out: hdd jst ins fnl f: one pce* **16/1**

5466 **5** 3 ½ **Purus (IRE)**[9] 7143 6-9-5 **75**........ EddieAhern 9 64
(R A Teal) *sn prom: rdn over 1f out: wkng whn hmpd on inner ins fnl f* **13/2**[3]

4200 **6** hd **Chief Exec**[184] 2010 6-9-2 **72**........(p) TPQueally 12 60
(J R Gask) *s.i.s: hld up in rr: rdn and hung lft fr over 1f out: nvr trbld ldrs* **25/1**

4204 **7** shd **Castano**[14] 7021 4-8-11 **67**........(p) DarryllHolland 2 55
(B R Millman) *s.i.s: hld up in rr: swtchd rt to outside wl over 1f out: n.d* **7/1**

402 **8** 2 **Idesia (IRE)**[29] 6671 4-8-12 **68**........(t) AdamKirby 1 51
(W R Swinburn) *prom 5f* **11/4**[1]

0323 **9** ½ **Crocodile Bay (IRE)**[10] 7115 5-8-13 **74**........ JamesO'Reilly(5) 8 55
(John A Harris) *sn prom: lost pl over 3f out: bhd fnl 2f* **8/1**

50 **10** 4 ½ **Herbert Crescent**[36] 6511 3-9-1 **72**........ PaulHanagan 7 40
(Ollie Pears) *half-rrd and s.i.s: short-lived effrt on outside 3f out* **28/1**

0000 **11** 1 ½ **Dhhamaan (IRE)**[24] 6792 3-9-1 **75**........(b) MichaelJStainton(3) 4 39
(Mrs R A Carr) *plld hrd: prom: rdn and wknd over 1f out* **25/1**

0R00 **12** 40 **Chrystal Venture (IRE)**[160] 2705 3-8-10 **70**........(p) TolleyDean(3) 5 —
(A J McCabe) *led over 1f: prom tl rdn and wknd qckly 2f out* **40/1**

1m 29.26s (-0.34) **Going Correction** +0.05s/f (Slow)
WFA 3 from 4yo+ 1lb 12 Ran SP% **117.0**
Speed ratings (Par 103): **103,101,97,97,93 93,93,91,90,85 83,37**
toteswinger: 1&2 £15.40, 1&3 £24.60, 2&3 £9.40. CSF £72.20 CT £681.00 TOTE £13.80: £3.30, £1.70, £3.00; EX 100.20.
Owner Chance, Talbot & Taylor **Bred** J S McDonald **Trained** Upper Lambourn, Berks
■ Stewards' Enquiry : Martin Dwyer one-day ban: careless riding (Nov 24)

FOCUS
A fair handicap run at a reasonable pace and it produced another come-from-behind winner. Sound form.
Castano Official explanation: jockey said gelding missed the break

7278 WOLVERHAMPTON-RACECOURSE.CO.UK H'CAP — 1m 141y(P)
4:40 (4:41) (Class 4) (0-80,80) 3-Y-O+ **£5,180** (£1,541; £770; £384) **Stalls** Low

Form RPR

5003 **1** **Spinning**[9] 7127 5-8-10 **73**........(b) NeilBrown(3) 2 82
(T D Barron) *hld up in rr: c wd st: rdn and hdwy over 1f out: edgd lft fnl f: r.o to ld nr fin* **7/1**

5350 **2** ½ **Morbick**[16] 6989 4-8-10 **70**........ GrahamGibbons 6 78
(W M Brisbourne) *a.p: rdn to ld ins fnl f: hdd nr fin* **16/1**

6163 **3** nse **Jawaab (IRE)**[12] 7068 4-9-0 **74**........ MartinDwyer 4 82
(W R Muir) *hld up in mid-div: hdwy over 2f out: rdn over 1f out: ev ch wl ins fnl f: kpt on* **7/2**[1]

3-00 **4** ½ **Direct Debit (IRE)**[22] 6841 5-9-0 **77**........ LukeMorris(3) 7 84
(M L W Bell) *w ldr: led over 5f out: rdn wl over 1f out: hdd ins fnl f: nt qckn* **14/1**

5540 **5** 4 **Celtic Change (IRE)**[93] 4876 4-9-1 **75**........(p) TomEaves 10 73
(M Dods) *hld up in mid-div: rdn and carried hd high over 1f out: kpt on ins fnl f: nt trble ldrs* **8/1**

2303 **6** nse **Will He Wish**[14] 7014 12-9-3 **77**........(b) DarryllHolland 11 74
(S Gollings) *hld up in rr: rdn over 2f out: wknd over 1f out* **10/1**

1031 **7** nk **Justcallmehandsome**[175] 2262 6-8-13 **80**........(v) BillyCray(7) 8 77
(D J S Ffrench Davis) *hld up in mid-div: hdwy over 3f out: ev ch over 2f out: hung lft and wknd over 1f out* **11/1**

6336 **8** 1 **Resplendent Ace (IRE)**[47] 6210 4-9-0 **74**........ TGMcLaughlin 1 68
(P Howling) *hld up towards rr: nt clr run and swtchd rt ins fnl f: n.d* **20/1**

5000 **9** hd **Silver Hotspur**[19] 6900 4-9-5 **79**........ DaneO'Neill 5 73
(C R Dore) *s.i.s: hld up towards rr: hdwy on ins over 2f out: rdn over 1f out: wknd ins fnl f* **40/1**

1042 **10** 8 **Wisdom's Kiss**[30] 6663 4-9-2 **76**........(b) JimmyQuinn 12 52
(J D Bethell) *s.i.s: a towards rr* **4/1**[2]

2200 **11** 4 **Nightjar (USA)**[35] 6526 3-9-2 **79**........ JoeFanning 3 45
(M Johnston) *led: hdd over 5f out: w ldr tl wknd over 2f out* **11/2**[3]

3200 **12** 12 **Moonlight Man**[19] 6900 7-9-3 **77**........(t) LPKeniry 13 16
(C R Dore) *prom tl rdn and wknd over 2f out* **33/1**

1m 50.41s (-0.09) **Going Correction** +0.05s/f (Slow)
WFA 3 from 4yo+ 3lb 12 Ran SP% **121.3**
Speed ratings (Par 105): **102,101,101,101,97 97,97,96,96,89 85,74**
toteswinger: 1&2 £20.10, 1&3 £7.00, 2&3 £14.10. CSF £113.47 CT £464.91 TOTE £7.50: £2.70, £4.60, £2.20; EX 136.00 Place 6: £127.24 Place 5: £97.96.
Owner Mrs J Hazell **Bred** Cheveley Park Stud **Trained** Maunby, N Yorks

FOCUS
This was run at a fair pace and produced an exciting finish. The first four were clear of the rest and the form should work out.
Wisdom's Kiss Official explanation: jockey said gelding never travelled
T/Jkpt: £30,077.10 to a £1 stake. Pool: £84,724.36. 2.00 winning tickets. T/Plt: £61.00 to a £1 stake. Pool: £75,242.64. 900.23 winning tickets. T/Qpdt: £31.80 to a £1 stake. Pool: £4,268.80. 99.22 winning tickets. KH

7265 SOUTHWELL (L-H)
Wednesday, November 12

OFFICIAL GOING: Standard
Racing was delayed 25 minutes after serious hold-ups on the M1.
Wind: Light behind Weather: Fine and dry

7279 HOSPITALITY AT SOUTHWELL RACECOURSE MAIDEN AUCTION STKS — 5f (F)
12:10 (12:36) (Class 6) 2-Y-O **£2,047** (£604; £302) **Stalls** High

Form RPR

5222 **1** **Silent Wonder**[7] 7198 2-8-9 73........(p) EddieAhern 5 68
(R M H Cowell) *led 1f: cl up: effrt 2f out and sn led: rdn and edgd rt over 1f out: clr ins fnl f* **1/4**[1]

3240 **2** 3 **Dedante**[126] 3846 2-8-8 64 ow5........(b[1]) JamesO'Reilly(5) 7 61
(D K Ivory) *cl up: led after 1f: rdn along and hdd wl over 1f out: sltly hmpd over 1f out: sn drvn and kpt on same pce* **17/2**[2]

5400 **3** 2 ¾ **Lady Gem**[18] 6988 2-8-8 49........ PaulMulrennan 8 46
(D H Brown) *midfield: rdn along 1/2-way: hdwy u.p wl over 1f out: kpt on over 1f out: nrst fin* **12/1**[3]

0 **4** 2 ¼ **Fitz**[20] 6932 2-8-9 0........ TGMcLaughlin 1 39
(M Salaman) *wnt rt s and sn outpcd in rr: rdn along 1/2-way: styd on appr fnl f: nrst fin* **12/1**[3]

000 **5** 1 **Rocket Ruby**[9] 7168 2-8-3 0 ow6........ LeeTopliss(7) 4 36
(D Shaw) *chsd ldrs: rdn along over 2f out and grad wknd* **40/1**

506 **6** ¾ **Wee Bizzom**[9] 7168 2-8-4 42........ FrancisNorton 9 28
(A Berry) *s.i.s: sn rdn along and a in rr* **66/1**

0 **7** 6 **You'relikemefrank**[14] 7082 2-8-7 0 ow1........ RussellKennemore(3) 2 12
(J Balding) *chsd ldng pair: rdn along over 2f out: sn drvn and wknd* **40/1**

0400 **8** 1 **Lemon Dash**[56] 6009 2-8-1 45........ DuranFentiman(3) 3 3
(L A Mullaney) *sn rdn and a outpcd in rr* **40/1**

60.13 secs (0.43) **Going Correction** -0.05s/f (Stan) 8 Ran SP% **114.7**
Speed ratings (Par 94): **94,89,84,81,79 78,68,67**
toteswinger: 1&2 £1.50, 1&3 £1.80, 2&3 £2.60. CSF £3.02 TOTE £1.10: £1.02, £1.40, £2.40; EX 3.20 Trifecta £13.10 Pool: £303.27 - 17.04 winning units..
Owner Khalifa Dasmal **Bred** K A Dasmal **Trained** Six Mile Bottom, Cambs

FOCUS
A weak maiden won in facile style by the long odds-on favourite. The placed horses dictate the level.

NOTEBOOK
Silent Wonder, who had finished runner-up in five of his previous six starts and was beaten at odds of 13-8 or shorter in four of those, had run poorly when tried on this surface before, but that was over 6f around a bend and he looked much happier over this straight 5f. Breaking well but soon content to get a lead from Dedante, once sent back past that filly the race was well and truly in the bag. He had 13lb in hand of the second taking into account the runner-up's overweight, so his mark shouldn't be affected too much and that will be important with handicaps in mind. (op 2-7 after early 1-3)
Dedante, blinkered for the first time on this first outing since July, showed plenty of early speed but looked well held when appearing to get a crack across the face coming to the last furlong. The 5lb overweight wouldn't have helped, but it wasn't the difference. (op 8-1)
Lady Gem, back down to the minimum trip for the first time since her debut, stayed on without offering a threat and probably achieved as much as she was entitled to at the weights. (op 10-1)
Fitz attracted some market support, but as on his debut he gave away ground at the start and struggled to go the pace which is fatal over this straight 5f. He also still looked green, but he did show a little bit later on and doesn't look completely devoid of ability. (op 16-1)
Rocket Ruby, carrying 6lb overweight, hung right over to the far rail under pressure and isn't seeing her races out at present. (tchd 50-1)

7280 SOUTHWELL-RACECOURSE.CO.UK CLAIMING STKS — 1m 4f (F)
12:40 (1:00) (Class 6) 3-Y-O+ **£2,047** (£604; £302) **Stalls** Low

Form RPR

4-30 **1** **La Estrella (USA)**[13] 5423 5-9-13 80........ DaneO'Neill 3 86
(D E Cantillon) *trckd ldrs: hdwy over 3f out: rdn to ld wl over 1f out: drvn and edgd lft ent fnl f: kpt on wl* **5/2**[2]

0121 **2** 2 ½ **Veloso (FR)**[13] 7089 6-9-3 68........ PatCosgrave 4 72
(A J McCabe) *trckd ldrs: hdwy 4f out: led wl over 2f out: rdn and hdd wl over 1f out: drvn ent fnl f and kpt on same pce* **2/1**[1]

5600 **3** 2 **Kangrina**[15] 7039 6-8-8 56 ow2........ EddieAhern 8 60
(George Baker) *trckd ldrs: hdwy 4f out: effrt over 2f out: sn rdn and ev ch tldrvn and one pce appr fnl f* **6/1**

3610 **4** 1 ¾ **Sudden Impulse**[38] 6007 7-8-10 68........ AndrewElliott 9 59
(A D Brown) *trckd ldr: led 4f out: rdn along and hdd wl over 2f out: sn drvn and wknd over 1f out* **17/2**

1403 **5** 16 **Well Informed**[10] 7149 3-8-2 55........ FrancisNorton 10 31
(E J O'Neill) *trckd ldrs: hdwy on outer 4f out: rdn along over 2f out: sn drvn and wknd wl over 1f out* **7/2**[3]

-040 **6** 7 **Pure Scandal**[28] 1913 3-8-10 50........(p) BradleyRoper(7) 1 35
(M W Easterby) *sn rdn along and outpcd in rr: sme hdwy to cl up 1/2-way: rdn and wknd over 3f out: sn bhd* **50/1**

5000 **7** 9 **Brutus Maximus**[80] 5303 5-9-5 40........(p) PatrickMathers 7 17
(I W McInnes) *reminders s and sn led: pushed along over 5f out: rdn and hdd 4f out: sn wknd* **66/1**

The Form Book, Raceform Ltd, Compton, RG20 6NL

000/ **8** *54* **Our Serendipity**[825] 4297 5-8-4 30 PaulQuinn 5 —
(R M Whitaker) *prom on inner: rdn along over 5f out and sn wknd* **100/1**

2m 39.89s (-1.11) **Going Correction** -0.125s/f (Stan)
WFA 3 from 4yo+ 6lb **8** Ran SP% **113.4**
Speed ratings (Par 101): **98,96,95,93,83 78,72,36**
toteswinger: 1&2 £1.70, 1&3 £5.50, 2&3 £3.60. CSF £7.76 TOTE £3.70: £1.10, £1.10, £2.40; EX 5.90 Trifecta £28.50 Pool: £124.94 - 3.24 winning units..
Owner Mrs J Hart C Lynas & M Freedman **Bred** Five Horses Ltd And Theatrical Syndicate **Trained** Newmarket, Suffolk

FOCUS
A fair claimer and the pace was nothing to write home about, though the front four came right away. A good effort for the grade from the winner.

7281 MEMBERSHIP AT SOUTHWELL NURSERY 6f (F)
1:15 (1:30) (Class 6) (0-65,65) 2-Y-O **£2,047** (£604; £302) **Stalls** Low

Form RPR

000 **1** **Top Flight Splash**[15] 7038 2-8-5 **49** DaleGibson 9 51
(Mrs G S Rees) *cl up: led 1/2-way: rdn along wl over 1f out: drvn ent fnl f and kpt on gamely* **16/1**

0006 **2** *1 1/2* **Bulella**[6] 7205 2-9-0 **58** MickyFenton 2 56
(Garry Moss) *dwlt: hdwy and in tch 1/2-way: effrt to chse ldng pair wl over 1f out: sn rdn and kpt on ins fnl f* **8/1**

0450 **3** *1 1/4* **Courageous Nature (IRE)**[6] 7205 2-8-12 **56** (b) PatCosgrave 3 50
(A J McCabe) *trckd ldrs: hdwy wl over 2f out: rdn to challnge wl over 1f out and ev ch tl drvn and one pce ins fnl f* **7/2**[1]

040 **4** *nk* **Lujeanie**[23] 6863 2-9-1 **64** JamesO'Reilly(5) 7 57
(D K Ivory) *towards rr and rdn along 1/2-way: hdwy 2f out: styd on wl fnl f: nrst fin* **4/1**[2]

2500 **5** *4 1/2* **Sale Or Return (IRE)**[26] 6787 2-8-4 **51** (b) DuranFentiman(3) 1 31
(T D Easterby) *cl up on inner: rdn along 3f out: drvn over 2f out and sn wknd* **8/1**

00 **6** *2* **Katie Higgins**[34] 6600 2-8-11 **55** LiamJones 10 29
(J L Spearing) *nvr bttr than midfield* **14/1**

2264 **7** *1/2* **Red Cell (IRE)**[62] 5834 2-9-7 **65** (b) PatrickMathers 4 37
(I W McInnes) *led: rdn along and hdd 3f out: drvn over 2f out and sn wknd* **13/2**

6200 **8** *1/2* **Meydan Groove**[16] 7016 2-9-5 **63** GrahamGibbons 5 34
(R Johnson) *sn outpcd and a bhd* **5/1**[3]

0050 **9** *14* **Abitofaboost (IRE)**[56] 6009 2-7-11 **48** ow3 AndrewHeffernan(7) 8 —
(Peter Grayson) *a in rr* **28/1**

1m 16.39s (-0.11) **Going Correction** -0.125s/f (Stan) **9** Ran SP% **110.4**
Speed ratings (Par 94): **95,93,91,90,84 82,81,80,62**
toteswinger: 1&2 £24.30, 1&3 £11.60, 2&3 £7.30. CSF £128.33 CT £532.09 TOTE £22.20: £5.10, £3.50, £1.50; EX 276.70 TRIFECTA Not won..
Owner P Bamford **Bred** Dandy's Farm **Trained** Sollom, Lancs

FOCUS
A weak nursery with only three of the nine runners having hit the target before and four had never previously made the frame, but the latter group provided the first two home. The winner could be capable of a bit more.

NOTEBOOK
Top Flight Splash was one of three disputing the early lead and she kept on going to achieve a very game victory. The switch to Fibresand suited her and her initial handicap mark of 49 was obviously well within her compass, so her prospects depend on what the Handicapper does with her now. She would have to be seriously considered if returned to this surface. Official explanation: trainer's rep said, regarding the apparent improvement in form, that filly has improved with her racing and had run well last time. (tchd 18-1)
Bulella was another with modest form figures coming into this, but she had undoubtedly run much better than her finishing position would have suggested on her nursery debut at Great Leighs last time. Never far away here, she kept on well to secure the runner-up spot and she should be able to find a race like this at some stage. (op 7-1)
Courageous Nature(IRE), just behind Bulella at Great Leighs and 2lb better off, travelled smoothly just behind the leaders and looked a big danger when ranging alongside the winner passing the 2f pole, but he found him a very tough nut to crack and he had no more to give inside the last furlong.
Lujeanie ◆ wasn't at all disgraced on this sand and nursery debut. Firstly, he missed the break, then got badly outpaced rounding the bend, and finally tried to make his effort tight against the inside rail which isn't always ideal here. The fact that he finished so close does him credit and he is one to watch for a similar event. (tchd 7-2)
Sale Or Return(IRE) showed up for a while, but is exposed as modest. (op 11-1)
Red Cell(IRE) dropped out after showing early speed and he does look happier over the minimum trip. (op 11-2 tchd 7-1)

7282 PLAY GOLF AT SOUTHWELL GOLF CLUB MEDIAN AUCTION MAIDEN STKS 1m (F)
1:50 (1:55) (Class 6) 2-Y-O **£2,047** (£604; £302) **Stalls** Low

Form RPR

52 **1** **Hometown**[22] 6884 2-8-12 0 JimmyFortune 12 69
(J H M Gosden) *cl up on outer: hdwy over 2f out: rdn tpo ld over 1f out and sn hung lft: drvn and kpt on ins fnl f* **8/13**[1]

2 *1 1/4* **Assail** 2-9-3 0 TravisBlock 5 72
(H Morrison) *hld up: hdwy 3f out: effrt and ev ch whn hmpd over 1f out: kpt on ins fnl f* **10/1**[3]

5 **3** *1 1/2* **Molesden Glen (IRE)**[25] 6811 2-9-3 0 TomEaves 4 69+
(B Smart) *led: rdn along and hdd 3f out: drvn and ev ch whn bdly hmpd over 1f out: kpt on wl u.p fnl f* **33/1**

6 **4** *shd* **Royal Keva (IRE)**[10] 7148 2-9-3 0 GrahamGibbons 3 68
(A D Brown) *chsd ldrs on inner: rdn along wl over 2f out: drvn over 1f out: kpt on same pce* **16/1**

45 **5** *1/2* **Majestic Bull (USA)**[10] 7148 2-9-3 0 DaneO'Neill 2 67
(E J O'Neill) *cl up: led 3f out: rdn over 2f out: drvn and hdd over 1f out: grad wknd* **9/2**[2]

6 *9* **Broughton Beck (IRE)** 2-9-3 0 FrankieMcDonald 1 47
(R F Fisher) *s.i.s: bhd tl sme late hdwy* **100/1**

500 **7** *1 1/2* **Ready To Prime**[44] 6341 2-8-7 45 JamesO'Reilly(5) 6 39
(D K Ivory) *chsd ldrs: rdn along wl over 2f out: sn drvn and wknd fnl 2f* **100/1**

0 **8** *1* **First Blade**[24] 6837 2-9-3 0 LPKeniry 9 42
(S R Bowring) *cl up: rdn along wl over 2f out and grad wknd* **100/1**

0006 **9** *3/4* **Aziz (IRE)**[14] 7079 2-9-3 50 (b) FergusSweeney 11 40
(Miss D Mountain) *chsd ldrs: rdn along 3f out: sn wknd* **66/1**

0 **10** *1/2* **Ballade De La Mer**[18] 6988 2-8-12 0 AndrewElliott 7 34
(A J McCabe) *in tch: rdn along over 3f out and sn wknd* **50/1**

11 *10* **Art Discovery (IRE)** 2-9-3 0 PaulMulrennan 13 17
(M H Tompkins) *s.i.s: a bhd* **20/1**

0 **12** *shd* **Marillos Proterras**[19] 6945 2-8-12 0 PatCosgrave 8 12
(Mrs A Duffield) *racd wd: nvr a factor* **12/1**

1m 43.71s (0.01) **Going Correction** -0.125s/f (Stan) **12** Ran SP% **116.9**
Speed ratings (Par 94): **94,92,91,91,90 81,80,79,78,77 67,67**
toteswinger: 1&2 £4.60, 1&3 £7.00, 2&3 £17.40. CSF £7.32 TOTE £1.70: £1.02, £2.70, £7.80; EX 8.60 Trifecta £36.70 Pool: £270.83 - 5.45 winning units..
Owner H R H Princess Haya Of Jordan **Bred** Gainsborough Stud Management Ltd **Trained** Newmarket, Suffolk

FOCUS
A modest and fairly uncompetitive maiden, though a couple did hint at better to come. The winner did not have to reproduce her previous turf form.

NOTEBOOK
Hometown had finished runner-up in an ordinary Yarmouth maiden last time and probably only needed repeat that to take this. Travelling well enough behind the leaders, she did tend to drift away to her left under pressure when produced with her effort, but she was always doing enough. She doesn't look anything special, but she should be able to hold her own in handicaps. (op 8-11, tchd 4-5 in a place)
Assail ◆, a brother to a winning juvenile sprinter, is the one to take from the race though. Given a patient ride, he eventually stayed on really well between horses up the home straight despite showing distinct signs of greenness and he can be expected to have learnt a good deal from this, so the future looks bright. (op 12-1)
Molesden Glen(IRE) ◆ ran much better than on his Catterick debut under a positive ride and kept on well despite getting squeezed out between the front pair a furlong from home. He wouldn't need to improve much on this, if at all, in order to win a maiden on sand.
Royal Keva(IRE) was much more organised than on his debut here earlier in the month, and he stayed on well considering he was being pumped along a fair way out. He looks the sort for handicaps after one more run. (op 12-1 tchd 20-1)
Majestic Bull(USA) was never far away and had every chance, but he doesn't seem to be progressing. He now qualifies for a mark which will at least provide him with a few more options. (tchd 5-1 and 11-2 in places)
Broughton Beck(IRE), a half-brother to four winners at up to 1m4f, lost all chance at the start but he did make a little late progress to finish best of the rest. (op 66-1)

7283 HOSPITALITY AT SOUTHWELL RACECOURSE (S) STKS 1m (F)
2:25 (2:25) (Class 6) 2-Y-O **£2,047** (£604; £302) **Stalls** Low

Form RPR

5 **1** **Hawkspring (IRE)**[9] 7170 2-8-11 0 (t) DaneO'Neill 11 59
(George Baker) *trckd ldrs: hdwy over 3f out: rdn to chse ldrs 2f out: drvn to ld over 1f out: kpt on u.p ins fnl f* **7/4**[1]

0325 **2** *1* **Svindal (IRE)**[9] 7164 2-8-11 58 (b) PaulMulrennan 9 57
(K A Ryan) *cl up: led 1/2-way: rdn wl over 2f out: sn drvn and hdd over 1f out: kpt on u.p ins fnl f* **5/1**[3]

010 **3** *nse* **Jonah's Cruising (IRE)**[14] 7079 2-8-12 65 PatCosgrave 1 58
(J R Boyle) *hld up in tch: hdwy on inner wl over 2f out: rdn to chse ldrs over 1f out: sn drvn and ev ch tl no ex wl ins fnl f* **10/3**[2]

6000 **4** *1/2* **Betws Y Coed (IRE)**[2] 7266 2-8-1 52 (p) NicolPolli(5) 8 51
(A Bailey) *rr: hdwy over 2f out: sn rdn: kpt on u.p ins fnl f: nrst fin* **7/1**

0000 **5** *1/2* **Braishfield Lass**[21] 6892 2-8-6 50 DaleGibson 4 49
(B G Powell) *cl up on inner: effrt 3f out: rdn to chal over 2f out and ev ch tl drvn over 1f out and wknd ins fnl f* **18/1**

046 **6** *3* **Miss Kadee**[9] 7164 2-8-3 0 LukeMorris(3) 5 43
(P D Evans) *rrd s: sn in tch: effrt to chse ldrs 3f out: rdn over 2f out and sn one pce* **6/1**

7 *6* **Beamon (USA)** 2-8-11 0 (b1) FergusSweeney 2 35
(Miss D Mountain) *a towards rr* **28/1**

6000 **8** *10* **Captain Cromby (IRE)**[56] 6009 2-8-11 44 (v1) GrahamGibbons 6 13
(J R Weymes) *led: rdn along and hdd 1/2-way: drvn along 3f out and sn wknd* **28/1**

00 **9** *98* **Secret Star (IRE)**[26] 6787 2-8-11 0 TonyHamilton 7 —
(R Bastiman) *cl up: rdn along and wknd qckly over 4f out: sn bhd and virtually p.u over 2f out* **80/1**

1m 44.41s (0.71) **Going Correction** -0.125s/f (Stan) **9** Ran SP% **116.3**
Speed ratings (Par 94): **91,90,89,89,88 85,79,69,—**
toteswinger: 1&2 £2.70, 1&3 £1.80, 2&3 £2.70. CSF £10.80 TOTE £2.50: £1.10, £1.10, £1.80; EX 8.70 Trifecta £21.10 Pool: £262.04 - 9.19 winning units..The winner was bought by S. Parr for 8,000gns.
Owner Mrs Susan Roy **Bred** Mrs S M Roy **Trained** Moreton Morrell, Warwicks

FOCUS
A moderate seller and the winning time was 0.7 seconds slower than the preceding maiden. The pace was solid enough with a three-way battle for the early lead, but there wasn't much covering the first five at the line and the form looks modest at best, if fairly sound among the principals.

NOTEBOOK
Hawkspring(IRE), far from disgraced in a Wolverhampton maiden on his debut, made the most of this drop in class but it proved very hard work for him to put the race to bed once brought through to lead towards the nearside of the track. He was sold for 8,000gns at the subsequent auction, but he will need to improve again from this if he is to prove competitive outside this level. (op 15-8 tchd 13-8 and 2-1 in a place)
Svindal(IRE), who has been running pretty well in sellers on turf and Polytrack recently, was one of the trio vying for the early lead and he kept on to just retain second, but it's not hard to see why he wears blinkers as he didn't really convince that he was giving it absolutely everything, so he doesn't really appeal as a betting proposition. (op 7-2)
Jonah's Cruising(IRE), beaten a long way on heavy ground last time on her debut for the yard after winning a Polytrack claimer, seemed happier back on sand, albeit on this different surface, and she plugged on having been delivered with her effort more towards the inside of the track. (op 5-1)
Betws Y Coed(IRE), well beaten in a nursery here two days earlier, stayed on to finish fourth but probably didn't achieve much. (op 15-2 tchd 8-1)
Braishfield Lass, another of those fighting for the early lead, ran a bit better on this drop in grade but will need to find a very moderate affair if she is to win a race. (op 25-1 tchd 33-1)

7284 PLAY GOLF AT SOUTHWELL GOLF CLUB H'CAP 1m (F)
3:00 (3:01) (Class 5) (0-70,70) 3-Y-O+ **£2,729** (£806; £403) **Stalls** Low

Form RPR

0116 **1** **Smarty Socks (IRE)**[4] 7239 4-9-3 **67** 6ex JamieMoriarty 5 81+
(P T Midgley) *trckd ldrs: smooth hdwy 2f out: swtchd rt and effrt to ld ent fnl f: rdn clr* **15/8**[2]

1353 **2** *1 1/2* **West End Lad**[22] 6889 5-8-12 **62** (b) DaneO'Neill 3 73
(S R Bowring) *cl up: rdn along and sltly outpcd 2f out: drvn and rallied ent fnl f: kpt on* **13/2**[3]

1051 **3** *1* **Kimono My House**[8] 7184 4-8-8 **65** RosieJessop(7) 9 74
(J G Given) *trckd ldng pair: smooth hdwy 3f out: rdn to ld over 2f out: drvn and hdd ent fnl f: one pce* **6/4**[1]

0010 **4** *2* **Trans Sonic**[35] 6585 5-9-6 **70** (v) PaulMulrennan 6 74
(A J Lockwood) *led: rdn along and hdd over 2f out: drvn and one pce fr over 1f out* **14/1**

6300 **5** *1 ¼* **Karmest**[15] 7046 4-9-2 **66** .... GrahamGibbons 4 67
(A D Brown) *sn rdn along towards rr: hdwy on outer over 2f out: kpt on u.p appr fnl f: nrst fin* **12/1**

100 **6** *18* **Blue Savannah (FR)**[48] 6227 3-7-11 **56** oh1 .... AndreaAtzeni(7) 7 16
(G J Smith) *chsd ldrs: rdn along over 3f out: sn drvn and wknd* **20/1**

00-0 **7** *3 ¼* **Gem Bien (USA)**[58] 5961 10-7-13 **56** oh11 ....(p) CharlotteKerton(7) 1 8
(T T Clement) *dwlt: a in rr* **100/1**

1m 41.67s (-2.03) **Going Correction** -0.125s/f (Stan)
WFA 3 from 4yo+ 2lb 7 Ran SP% **108.2**
Speed ratings (Par 103): **105,103,102,100,99 81,78**
toteswinger: 1&2 £1.80, 1&3 £1.50, 2&3 £2.20. CSF £12.75 CT £18.27 TOTE £2.40: £1.60, £1.80; EX 9.70 Trifecta £16.30 Pool: £191.06 - 8.67 winning units..
Owner R G Fell **Bred** Mick McGinn **Trained** Westow, N Yorks
■ Greek Theatre (12/1) was withdrawn after refusing to enter the stalls. R4 applies, deduct 5p in the £.
■ Stewards' Enquiry : Dane O'Neill six-day ban: used whip with excessive frequency without giving gelding time to respond (Nov 26-Dec 1)

FOCUS
A fair little handicap featuring a couple that have been in good form at this track lately and the pair dominated the market. The winner did it nicely.

7285 BOOK YOUR TICKETS ONLINE AT SOUTHWELL-RACECOURSE.CO.UK H'CAP 1m 6f (F)
3:30 (3:30) (Class 6) (0-60,61) 3-Y-0+ **£2,047** (£604; £302) **Stalls** Low

Form RPR

4/0- **1** **Elaala (USA)**[12] 4380 6-9-1 **49** .... RobertWinston 10 57
(B D Leavy) *in tch: hdwy 3f out: rdn 2f out: drvn to chse ldr appr last: styd on u.p to ld nr line* **4/1[2]**

0006 **2** *hd* **Flame Creek (IRE)**[2] 7265 12-9-7 **55** .... EdwardCreighton 7 63
(E J Creighton) *hld up in rr: hdwy over 3f out: rdn to ld over 2f out: drvn ins fnl f: edgd lft and hdd nr line* **8/1**

0011 **3** *½* **Ice Bellini**[10] 7149 3-8-12 **61** 6ex ....(v) AndreaAtzeni(7) 3 68
(Miss Gay Kelleway) *trckd ldng pair: effrt 3f out: rdn over 2f out: drvn over 1f out: kpt on u.p ins fnl f* **3/1[1]**

2050 **4** *¾* **Simple Jim (FR)**[25] 6812 4-9-5 **53** .... AndrewElliott 2 59
(A D Brown) *hld up and bhd: hdwy on outer 3f out: rdn 2f out: kpt on u.p appr last: nrst fin* **10/1**

-063 **5** *2* **Jetta Joy (IRE)**[15] 7045 3-8-8 **57** ow8 .... SamuelDrury(7) 5 60
(Mrs A Duffield) *in tch: effrt and hdwy to chse ldrs 3f out: rdn along and outpcd 2f out: kpt on u.p ins fnl f* **13/2[3]**

0400 **6** *1 ½* **Rare Coincidence**[30] 6708 7-9-10 **58** ....(p) DaneO'Neill 1 59
(R F Fisher) *trckd ldrs: effrt over 2f out: swtchd rt and rdn wl over 1f out: sn no imp* **10/1**

-300 **7** *¾* **Florentino**[25] 5993 4-8-11 **45** .... FergusSweeney 6 45
(C W Thornton) *trckd ldng pair: hdwy over 4f out: rdn to ld briefly 3f out: drvn and hdd over 2f out: grad wknd* **16/1**

0035 **8** *2 ½* **Just Waz (USA)**[170] 2467 6-8-9 **46** .... MichaelJStainton(3) 8 43
(R M Whitaker) *led 3f: cl up tl rdn along over 3f out and grad wknd* **7/1**

0004 **9** *4 ½* **Tapaellya (IRE)**[41] 6421 4-8-13 **47** .... RichardThomas 11 37
(J E Long) *cl up: led after 3f: rdn along and hdd 3f out: sn wknd* **16/1**

0500 **10** *13* **Ronsard (IRE)**[2] 7265 6-8-11 **45** .... PatCosgrave 4 17
(P D Evans) *hld up: a towards rr* **12/1**

3m 8.09s (-0.21) **Going Correction** -0.125s/f (Stan)
WFA 3 from 4yo+ 8lb 10 Ran SP% **119.6**
Speed ratings (Par 101): **95,94,94,94,93 92,91,90,87,80**
CSF £37.16 CT £110.86 TOTE £5.50: £1.80, £2.60, £1.40; EX 38.50 Trifecta £73.00 Pool: £149.97 - 1.52 winning units..
Owner Moorland Racing **Bred** Shadwell Farm LLC **Trained** Forsbrook, Staffs
■ Stewards' Enquiry : Robert Winston two-day ban: used whip with excessive frequency (Nov 26-27)

FOCUS
A modest staying event and they didn't go much of a gallop, but even so none of those that helped set the pace figured in the finish. The form is sound enough although the fifth is a bit of a worry.

7286 CALL 01636 814481 TO SPONSOR A RACE H'CAP 6f (F)
4:00 (4:02) (Class 5) (0-70,72) 3-Y-0+ **£2,729** (£806; £403) **Stalls** Low

Form RPR

0033 **1** **Efisio Princess**[15] 7055 5-8-5 **57** ow1 .... RichardThomas 1 73
(J E Long) *chsd ldrs: hdwy over 2f out: led wl over 1f out: rdn and edgd rt ins fnl f: kpt on strly* **11/1**

4141 **2** *3 ¼* **Cool Sands (IRE)**[10] 7152 6-9-6 **72** 6ex ....(v) J-PGuillambert 6 78
(J G Given) *dwlt: hdwy 1/2-way: rdn to chse ldrs over 1f out: drvn to chse wnr ins fnl f: sn edgd lft and no imp* **11/4[2]**

5552 **3** *nk* **Whitbarrow (IRE)**[10] 7153 9-9-1 **70** ....(p) JamesMillman(3) 5 75
(B R Millman) *a.p: effrt 2f out: sn rdn and kpt on same pce ent fnl f* **7/4[1]**

3650 **4** *2* **Kensington (IRE)**[25] 6826 7-8-13 **65** ....(p) JamesDoyle 7 63
(P D Evans) *hld up: hdwy over 2f out: swtchd outside and rdn over 1f out: kpt on ins fnl f: nrst fin* **6/1[3]**

1240 **5** *2* **Kingsmaite**[135] 3567 7-8-8 **60** ....(b) LPKeniry 4 52
(S R Bowring) *cl up: rdn along 2f out: sn drvn and wknd over 1f out* **11/1**

1204 **6** *½* **Blakeshall Quest**[24] 6840 8-8-7 **59** ....(b) PaulMulrennan 2 49
(R Brotherton) *led: rdn along over 2f out: hdd wl over 1f out and grad wknd* **16/1**

4000 **7** *4 ½* **A Wish For You**[23] 6864 3-8-7 **64** ow1 ....(b[1]) JamesO'Reilly(5) 8 40
(D K Ivory) *towards rr and sn pushed along: hdwy on inner and in tch over 1f out: sn rdn and wknd* **66/1**

00U1 **8** *3 ½* **Tenancy (IRE)**[5] 7218 4-8-4 **56** 6ex oh3 .... JimmyQuinn 11 21
(R C Guest) *chsd ldrs: effrt over 2f out: sn rdn and btn* **14/1**

5140 **9** *1 ¾* **Witchry**[36] 6556 6-9-0 **66** .... FergusSweeney 10 25
(A G Newcombe) *a towards rr* **14/1**

5525 **10** *¾* **Thoughtsofstardom**[75] 5474 5-8-5 **62** .... KellyHarrison(5) 3 19
(P S McEntee) *cl up: rdn along over 2f out and sn wknd* **20/1**

0606 **11** *5* **Kissi Kissi**[279] 469 5-8-4 **56** oh11 ....(vt) NeilChalmers 9 —
(Garry Moss) *dwlt: a in rr* **66/1**

1m 14.6s (-1.90) **Going Correction** -0.125s/f (Stan) 11 Ran SP% **120.9**
Speed ratings (Par 103): **107,102,102,99,96 96,90,85,83,82 75**
CSF £42.16 CT £83.57 TOTE £15.50: £3.00, £1.50, £1.40; EX 49.80 Trifecta £246.20 Pool: £382.62 -1.15 winning units. Place 6: £8.70 Place 5: £8.06.
Owner Miss M B Fernandes **Bred** Mrs A Yearley **Trained** Caterham, Surrey

FOCUS
A routine Fibresand sprint handicap run at a strong pace with another three-way battle for the early lead. Fair form for the grade, and a race which sould work out.
T/Plt: £18.50 to a £1 stake. Pool: £34,438.19. 1,355.26 winning tickets. T/Qpdt: £8.70 to a £1 stake. Pool: £2,739.68. 231.94 winning tickets. JR

7273 WOLVERHAMPTON (A.W) (L-H)
Wednesday, November 12

OFFICIAL GOING: Standard
Wind: Nil Weather: Fine

7287 HOTEL & CONFERENCING AT WOLVERHAMPTON APPRENTICE H'CAP 1m 141y(P)
6:20 (6:21) (Class 6) (0-55,55) 3-Y-0+ **£2,729** (£806; £403) **Stalls** Low

Form RPR

-004 **1** **Plush**[19] 6955 5-9-4 **55** .... RossAtkinson 3 64+
(Tom Dascombe) *s.i.s: t.k.h in rr: hdwy 2f out: led over 1f out: hung rt ins fnl f: r.o wl* **11/2[2]**

-650 **2** *2 ½* **Eternal Optimist (IRE)**[53] 6116 3-8-10 **55** .... KrishGundowry(5) 2 58
(Paul Green) *hld up in mid-div: hdwy over 3f out: hung rt over 2f out: c wd st: rdn wl over 1f out: kpt on ins fnl f: nt trble wnr* **10/1**

0430 **3** *hd* **Sarraaf (IRE)**[11] 7132 12-9-2 **53** .... AshleyMorgan 6 56
(Miss L A Perratt) *hld up in rr: hdwy 2f out: kpt on same pce fnl f* **14/1**

0/1 **4** *nk* **Wakita (IRE)**[12] 7114 5-8-12 **54** ....(t) BradleyRoper(5) 10 56
(Aidan Anthony Howard, Ire) *hld up towards rr: hdwy over 2f out: rdn over 1f out: kpt on one pce fnl f* **3/1[1]**

5003 **5** *nse* **Sion Hill (IRE)**[5] 7228 7-9-4 **55** ....(p) BillyCray 9 57
(John A Harris) *w ldr: led 7f out: rdn over 2f out: hung rt and hdd over 1f out: one pce fnl f* **15/2**

000 **6** *8* **Welcome Releaf**[43] 6353 5-9-2 **53** ....(v) SophieDoyle 4 36
(P Leech) *led over 1f: chsd ldr: rdn and ev ch 2f out: wknd fnl f* **33/1**

0003 **7** *1 ¼* **Tri Chara (IRE)**[19] 6951 4-8-11 **53** ....(v) DavidKenny(5) 8 33
(R Hollinshead) *t.k.h towards rr: hdwy over 3f out: nt clr run briefly wl over 1f out: sn wknd* **6/1[3]**

0000 **8** *1 ¾* **Kabis Amigos**[53] 6116 6-9-0 **54** ....(p) NSLawes(3) 5 30
(S T Mason) *prom: rdn 3f out: wknd over 1f out* **40/1**

2500 **9** *2 ¼* **Sceilin (IRE)**[19] 6951 4-8-13 **53** ....(t) RosieJessop(3) 7 24
(J Mackie) *hld up in tch: pushed along and wknd over 3f out* **7/1**

1060 **10** *1 ¾* **Red Current**[21] 6908 4-9-3 **54** .... MatthewDavies 1 21
(R A Harris) *prom tl rdn and wknd over 2f out* **8/1**

00-0 **11** *½* **Kiss Chase (IRE)**[26] 6786 4-9-3 **54** .... ShaneCreighton 13 20
(J S Goldie) *a towards rr* **33/1**

-533 **12** *¾* **Keep Your Distance**[20] 6930 4-9-2 **53** .... AndreaAtzeni 12 17
(P J McBride) *hld up in tch: pushed along and wknd over 3f out* **7/1**

1m 51.81s (1.31) **Going Correction** +0.10s/f (Slow)
WFA 3 from 4yo+ 3lb 12 Ran SP% **126.6**
Speed ratings (Par 101): **98,95,95,95,95 88,87,85,83,81 81,80**
toteswinger: 1&2 £0.00, 1&3 £0.00, 2&3 £0.00. CSF £63.10 CT £757.33 TOTE £7.30: £1.40, £6.80, £7.30; EX 180.90.
Owner John Reed **Bred** Cheveley Park Stud Ltd **Trained** Lambourn, Berks
■ Stewards' Enquiry : Shane Creighton two-day ban: careless riding (Nov 26-27)

FOCUS
A low-grade, but tight, handicap comprising exposed sorts. The pace was sound and the winner ended up in the centre in the straight. The first five finished clear. Modest form overall but the winner did it nicely.

7288 SPONSOR A RACE BY CALLING 01902 390009 H'CAP (DIV I) 5f 216y(P)
6:50 (6:52) (Class 6) (0-65,65) 3-Y-0+ **£2,047** (£604; £302) **Stalls** Low

Form RPR

1303 **1** **One More Round (USA)**[28] 6736 10-9-4 **65** ....(b) JamesDoyle 4 80
(P D Evans) *in rr: nt clr run over 2f out: plld out ent st: gd hdwy over 1f out: led ins fnl f: readily* **7/2[1]**

0050 **2** *3 ½* **Tudor Prince (IRE)**[49] 6200 4-9-4 **65** .... JimCrowley 6 69
(A W Carroll) *a.p: wnt 2nd over 2f out: rdn to ld 1f out: hdd ins fnl f: one pce* **4/1[2]**

0030 **3** *1 ½* **Argentine (IRE)**[77] 5392 4-8-7 **54** .... PaulMulrennan 3 53
(L Lungo) *led after 1f: hdd 1f out: one pce* **6/1[3]**

5651 **4** *1* **Welcome Approach**[12] 7118 5-8-13 **60** .... DarryllHolland 9 56
(J R Weymes) *hld up towards rr: hdwy wl over 1f out: one pce fnl f* **7/2[1]**

0246 **5** *nk* **Lambency (IRE)**[5] 7218 5-8-3 **55** .... KellyHarrison(5) 11 50+
(J S Goldie) *hld up towards rr: c wd st: gd late prog: nrst fin* **12/1**

4043 **6** *1 ½* **Feeling Fresh (IRE)**[10] 7152 3-9-2 **63** ....(v) FrancisNorton 10 53
(Paul Green) *mid-div: hdwy 1f out: sn no imp* **15/2**

0200 **7** *1* **Myriola**[8] 7178 3-8-4 **51** oh4 .... HayleyTurner 8 38
(S Gollings) *prom tl wknd ins fnl f* **33/1**

2324 **8** *½* **Forrest Star**[45] 6308 3-8-10 **57** .... TomEaves 12 42
(Miss L A Perratt) *t.k.h in tch: rdn and hung lft over 1f out: wknd ins fnl f* **11/1**

1650 **9** *nk* **Dalarossie**[45] 6308 3-9-1 **62** .... JimmyQuinn 7 46
(E J Alston) *t.k.h: led 1f: chsd ldr tl rdn over 2f out: wknd ins fnl f* **12/1**

6000 **10** *13* **Stoneacre Donny (IRE)**[15] 7049 4-7-11 **51** oh6... AndrewHeffernan(7) 1 —
(Peter Grayson) *a in rr: no ch fnl 2f* **28/1**

0000 **11** *3 ¼* **Desert Light (IRE)**[7] 7195 7-8-1 **51** oh2 ....(v) DuranFentiman(3) 2 —
(D Shaw) *mid-div: rdn over 2f out: wknd over 1f out: eased ins fnl f* **16/1**

1m 15.1s (0.10) **Going Correction** +0.10s/f (Slow) 11 Ran SP% **126.5**
Speed ratings (Par 101): **103,98,96,95,94 92,91,90,90,72 68**
toteswinger: 1&2 £10.20, 1&3 £5.30, 2&3 £0.00. CSF £18.95 CT £86.46 TOTE £5.60: £1.90, £2.30, £3.10; EX 23.20.
Owner Mrs I M Folkes **Bred** Kenneth L Ramsey And Sarah K Ramsey **Trained** Pandy, Monmouths

FOCUS
An ordinary handicap in which the pace was sound throughout and the time was a bit quicker than division one. The winner again came down the middle of the course and is rated about a length off last winter's best. Sound, but moderate form.

7289 BOOK YOUR CHRISTMAS PARTY NOW MEDIAN AUCTION MAIDEN STKS 7f 32y(P)
7:20 (7:23) (Class 6) 2-Y-0 **£2,729** (£806; £403) **Stalls** High

Form RPR

00 **1** **Double Act**[30] 6701 2-9-3 0 ....(t) TPQueally 9 76
(J Noseda) *w ldr: rdn over 1f out: led wl ins fnl f: r.o* **14/1**

6 **2** *¾* **Partner Shift (IRE)**[13] 7098 2-9-3 0 .... JamieSpencer 2 74
(E A L Dunlop) *led: rdn and edgd rt over 1f out: hdd wl ins fnl f: nt qckn* **10/11[1]**

3 *1* **Rosika** 2-8-12 0 .... RyanMoore 3 67+
(Sir Michael Stoute) *a.p: r.o one pce fnl f* **9/2[3]**

4 *2 ¼* **Debussy (IRE)** 2-9-3 0 .... JimmyFortune 8 66+
(J H M Gosden) *hld up: hdwy over 2f out: one pce fnl f* **15/8[2]**

03 **5** *1 ½* **Integria**[15] 7051 2-9-0 0 .... LukeMorris(3) 7 63
(J M P Eustace) *prom: rdn and wkng whn edgd lft over 1f out* **13/2**

6 3/4 **Leceile (USA)** 2-8-12 0 .... LiamJones 12 56+
(W J Haggas) *hld up: pushed along and no hdwy fnl 2f* **28/1**
0 7 6 **Coeur Brule (FR)**[22] 6879 2-9-3 0 .... TravisBlock 10 46
(J R Gask) *s.i.s: a in rr* **66/1**
6 8 1 **Always The Sun**[27] 6755 2-8-12 0 .... (p) MickyFenton 4 39
(P Leech) *hld up: n.m.r on ins over 2f out: sn bhd* **100/1**
00 9 1 1/4 **Arty Crafty (USA)**[13] 7095 2-8-12 0 .... J-PGuillambert 11 35
(Sir Mark Prescott) *a in rr* **25/1**

1m 32.35s (2.75) **Going Correction** +0.10s/f (Slow) **9 Ran SP% 135.1**
Speed ratings (Par 94): **88,87,86,83,81 80,74,72,71**
toteswinger: 1&2 £13.30, 1&3 £13.30, 2&3 £1.50. CSF £31.90 TOTE £18.90: £2.90, £1.30, £1.60; EX 84.30.
Owner Highclere Thoroughbred Racing (VC2) **Bred** Cheveley Park Stud Ltd **Trained** Newmarket, Suffolk

FOCUS
A maiden lacking much in the way of strength in depth and a muddling gallop means this bare form may not be entirely reliable. The winner and second were in the front two positions throughout and continued the evening's trend of racing in the centre in the straight.

NOTEBOOK
Double Act, fitted with a tongue-tie, was always well placed considering the way this race unfolded and, after running green when initially asked for his effort, he knuckled down well to register his best effort. He should stay 1m and may progress in ordinary handicap company. (op 11-1)
Partner Shift(IRE), who showed promise on his debut, was well placed in a muddling event, got first run on the rest and turned an improved effort. Things went his way here but he's capable of winning a small event. (op 7-4 tchd 4-5)
Rosika, a half-sister to smart middle-distance filly Rambling Rose (dam of Notnowcato), had the run of the race and showed ability on this debut. She will have no problems with further and is likely to be placed to best advantage. (op 4-1)
Debussy(IRE), the first foal of a useful half-sister to top middle-distance performer Belmez, was not disgraced given the way this debut race unfolded and that he was too green to do himself justice. He is in very good hands and is entitled to improve. (op 5-2 tchd 3-1)
Integria had the run of the race but failed to build on his improved soft-ground turf run. He is likely to remain vulnerable to the better types in this grade. (tchd 7-1)
Leceile(USA), a $160,000 purchase, hails from a yard whose newcomers invariably improve for a run.
Arty Crafty(USA) again did not show much but she is the type to leave this form behind over further in handicaps in due course.

7290 HOTEL & CONFERENCING AT WOLVERHAMPTON H'CAP 5f 20y(P)
7:50 (7:52) (Class 4) (0-85,84) 3-Y-O+ **£5,828** (£1,734; £866; £432) **Stalls Low**

Form RPR
4223 1 **Harry Up**[25] 6823 7-9-2 82 .... (p) JamieSpencer 2 93
(K A Ryan) *mde all: clr whn rdn wl over 1f out: all out* **13/2**
3100 2 nk **Even Bolder**[49] 6200 5-8-12 78 .... StephenCarson 1 88+
(E A Wheeler) *hld up in tch: rdn and wnt 2nd ins fnl f: kpt on* **8/1**
305 3 1 1/2 **Yungaburra (IRE)**[6] 7206 4-8-11 77 .... (t) AdamKirby 9 82
(S Parr) *stdd s: hld up towards rr: hdwy whn n.m.r briefly over 1f out: r.o ins fnl f* **8/1**
6415 4 2 3/4 **Kay Two (IRE)**[18] 6971 6-9-4 84 .... (p) JimCrowley 6 79
(R J Price) *chsd wnr: rdn wl over 1f out: lost 2nd and wknd ins fnl f* **9/2**[2]
0643 5 1 1/2 **Not My Choice (IRE)**[14] 7066 3-9-2 82 .... TonyCulhane 8 71
(S Parr) *s.i.s: hld up towards rr: rdn over 2f out: hdwy on ins over 1f out: no further prog fnl f* **18/1**
062 6 hd **Mambo Spirit (IRE)**[33] 6623 4-9-0 80 .... TPQueally 3 69+
(J G Given) *s.i.s: hld up towards rr: hdwy on outside over 2f out: rdn wl over 1f out: one pce whn edgd lft ins fnl f* **3/1**[1]
223 7 1 1/4 **Best One**[33] 6623 4-8-10 76 .... (b) JoeFanning 7 60
(R A Harris) *chsd ldrs: wknd wl over 1f out* **11/2**[3]
4566 8 2 1/4 **Woodcote (IRE)**[33] 6623 6-8-12 78 .... (vt) LPKeniry 10 54
(P R Chamings) *prom: disp 2nd 2f out: rdn and edgd rt over 1f out: sn wknd* **25/1**
501 9 1 3/4 **Timber Treasure (USA)**[106] 4502 4-9-0 80 .... (b) FrancisNorton 4 50
(Paul Green) *a towards rr* **15/2**
5160 10 1 1/4 **Almaty Express**[14] 7066 6-9-4 84 .... (b) DarryllHolland 11 49
(J R Weymes) *chsd ldrs: lost pl over 3f out: sn bhd* **20/1**
4110 11 4 **Geoffdaw**[59] 5936 3-8-10 76 .... RobertWinston 12 27
(P D Evans) *a in rr* **14/1**

61.52 secs (-0.78) **Going Correction** +0.10s/f (Slow) **11 Ran SP% 126.4**
Speed ratings (Par 105): **110,109,107,102,100 100,98,94,91,89 83**
toteswinger: 1&2 £17.70, 1&3 £14.70, 2&3 £17.70. CSF £62.35 CT £444.83 TOTE £6.10: £1.50, £3.80, £2.70; EX 83.40.
Owner The Fishermen **Bred** J E Rose **Trained** Hambleton, N Yorks

FOCUS
Mainly exposed performers in this fair handicap. The pace was sound and the action again unfolded in the centre. Sound form, the winner back to his best and the runner-up rated to his turf form.

7291 WOLVERHAMPTON HOLIDAY INN H'CAP 1m 1f 103y(P)
8:20 (8:20) (Class 2) (0-100,92) 3-Y-O+ **£8,403** (£8,403; £1,926; £962) **Stalls Low**

Form RPR
0025 1 **Nanton (USA)**[32] 6654 6-8-7 83 .... KellyHarrison(5) 2 91
(J S Goldie) *led early: a.p: slt ld jst over 1f out: jnd post* **4/1**[2]
0221 1 dht **Suits Me**[11] 7127 5-9-7 92 .... MickyFenton 3 100
(T P Tate) *sn led: narrowly hdd jst over 1f out: edgd lft ins fnl f: jnd ldr post* **7/1**
0152 3 2 1/4 **Final Verse**[11] 7146 5-9-4 89 .... LPKeniry 6 92+
(M Salaman) *t.k.h in mid-div: swtchd lft and hdwy ins fnl f: r.o wl to take 3rd nr fin* **13/2**[3]
0100 4 3/4 **Just Bond (IRE)**[12] 7116 6-8-9 83 .... DuranFentiman(3) 7 85
(G R Oldroyd) *hld up in rr: rdn and hdwy over 1f out: kpt on ins fnl f* **28/1**
3311 5 nk **Intabih (USA)**[21] 6905 3-8-8 82 .... EddieAhern 5 83
(C E Brittain) *hld up in mid-div: hdwy over 2f out: rdn over 1f out: one pce fnl f* **7/4**[1]
1-40 6 1/2 **Robby Bobby**[193] 1806 3-8-11 85 .... JoeFanning 4 85
(M Johnston) *sn chsng ldr: ev ch wl over 1f out: sn rdn: edgd lft and wknd ins fnl f* **12/1**
5525 7 nk **Heroes**[34] 6598 4-8-8 79 .... HayleyTurner 9 78
(J R Boyle) *hld up towards rr: hdwy wl over 1f out: no imp fnl f* **14/1**
3465 8 3/4 **Kinsya**[11] 7146 5-9-0 85 .... PaulMulrennan 8 83
(M H Tompkins) *prom: rdn over 1f out: wknd ins fnl f* **8/1**
0002 9 3 1/2 **Hold The Gold (IRE)**[12] 7116 3-7-11 78 oh4 .... AndreaAtzeni(7) 10 68
(E J O'Neill) *s.i.s: hld up in rr: rdn and sme hdwy on ins wl over 1f out: wknd fnl f* **14/1**
0 10 3 1/2 **Boo**[18] 2904 6-9-6 91 .... RobertWinston 1 74
(J W Unett) *hld up in tch: wknd wl over 1f out* **40/1**
2630 11 4 **Capable Guest (IRE)**[18] 6984 6-9-5 90 .... (v) TonyCulhane 12 65
(M R Channon) *a towards rr: no ch whn eased fnl f* **16/1**
4104 12 17 **New Star (UAE)**[12] 7116 4-8-7 78 oh1 .... JamesDoyle 11 17
(W M Brisbourne) *hld up in mid-div: rdn 3f out: sn bhd* **20/1**

2m 0.24s (-1.46) **Going Correction** +0.10s/f (Slow)
WFA 3 from 4yo+ 3lb **12 Ran SP% 130.9**
Speed ratings (Par 109): **110,110,108,107,107 106,106,105,102,99 95,80**toteswinger: Suits Me and Final Verse £11.60; Suits Me and Nanton £6.10; Nanton and Final Verse £6.10. TRIFECTA WIN:SM£5.20; N£4.00; PL: SM&N£1.90; N&SM£2.80; EX: SM&N£20.60; N&SM£21.50; CSF:SM&N£19.16; N&SM£17.71; TRI:SM/N/FV £101.89; N/SM/FV.
Owner J S Morrison **Bred** Samuel H And Mrs Rogers, Jr **Trained** Uplawmoor, E Renfrews

FOCUS
Just a fair pace to this valuable handicap and those racing up with the pace held the edge. For the first time on the evening, the principals ended up against the inside rail in the straight. The form may not be as strong as it might have been. Nanton is rated in line with the balance of his turf form, with fellow dead-heater Suits Me running another personal best.

NOTEBOOK
Nanton(USA) was an interesting runner as he was able to race from a 7lb lower mark than when a fine second in the Cambridgeshire. He turned in his best effort on this surface, despite not finding as much off the bridle as seemed likely for a long way, and is the type to win again on this surface. (op 11-2)
Suits Me showed a good attitude on this first all-weather run for over a year. He's a reliable sort who goes on most ground and should continue to give it his best shot. He'll be of interest if returned to hurdles this winter. (op 11-2)
Final Verse may be a bit better than this bare form as he fared the best of those to come off just an ordinary gallop. A more truly run race around 1m may be more to his liking and he should be able to pick up a handicap away from progressive sorts this winter. (op 7-1)
Just Bond(IRE), a prolific winner at this course, was also not disgraced given the way this race unfolded. A more end-to-end gallop would have suited but he has little margin for error from his current mark and consistency has not been his strongest suit of late.
Intabih(USA), the one progressive performer in the race, proved a bit of a disappointment back against his elders. However as one who has only had five all-weather starts, he would not be one to write off yet. (op 9-4 tchd 5-2 in places)
Robby Bobby, making his all-weather debut and having his first run since May, had the run of the race and showed up well until tiring late on. He is entitled to improve for this experience. (op 10-1)

7292 SPONSOR A RACE BY CALLING 01902 390009 H'CAP (DIV II) 5f 216y(P)
8:50 (8:51) (Class 6) (0-65,65) 3-Y-O+ **£2,047** (£604; £302) **Stalls Low**

Form RPR
0002 1 **Grand Palace (IRE)**[8] 7182 5-9-0 61 .... (v) DarrenWilliams 1 71
(D Shaw) *hld up in tch: rdn to ld jst ins fnl f: drvn out* **2/1**[1]
4000 2 shd **Bishopbriggs (USA)**[12] 7118 3-9-4 65 .... AdamKirby 12 74
(S Parr) *led: rdn and hdd jst ins fnl f: r.o* **20/1**
1000 3 2 1/2 **Willhewiz**[5] 7226 8-8-8 55 .... (v) TGMcLaughlin 3 56
(W M Brisbourne) *plld hrd: a.p: wnt 2nd over 3f out: ev ch over 2f out: rdn and edgd rt wl over 1f out: kpt on one pce fnl f* **8/1**
-500 4 nk **Chookie Heiton (IRE)**[48] 6232 10-9-4 65 .... TomEaves 2 65
(Miss L A Perratt) *hld up towards rr: rdn and hdwy over 1f out: kpt on ins fnl f* **16/1**
5060 5 3/4 **Finsbury**[5] 7218 5-8-13 60 .... HayleyTurner 11 64+
(J S Goldie) *s.s: in rr: hmpd wl over 1f out: gd late hdwy: nrst fin* **10/3**[2]
2100 6 1 1/2 **Littledodayno (IRE)**[27] 6766 5-9-1 62 .... FrancisNorton 5 55
(M Wigham) *towards rr: rdn and r.o ins fnl f: n.d* **6/1**[3]
0-04 7 shd **Majestic Cheer**[7] 7197 4-8-6 53 .... FrankieMcDonald 8 46
(John A Harris) *hld up in tch: rdn wl over 1f out: wknd wl ins fnl f* **16/1**
020 8 1 1/4 **Diminuto**[24] 6840 4-8-6 60 .... JemmaMarshall(7) 9 49
(M D I Usher) *chsd ldr tl over 3f out: wknd over 2f out* **12/1**
50-0 9 1 1/2 **Bourbon Balistic**[49] 6219 3-8-9 56 .... TPQueally 10 40
(Mrs A Duffield) *plld hrd: prom: rdn and wkng whn edgd lft over 1f out* **16/1**
000 10 1 **The Cube**[105] 4542 4-8-4 51 oh6 .... (b) DaleGibson 4 32
(J Balding) *s.i.s: t.k.h: a in rr* **40/1**
0550 11 2 1/4 **Dresden Doll (USA)**[15] 7055 3-9-4 65 .... JamieSpencer 6 39
(M L W Bell) *hld up in mid-div: rdn over 2f out: wkng whn edgd lft wl over 1f out* **7/1**
0060 12 1 3/4 **Talcen Gwyn (IRE)**[7] 7196 6-8-4 51 oh2 .... JimmyQuinn 7 19
(M F Harris) *s.i.s: a towards rr* **40/1**

1m 15.52s (0.52) **Going Correction** +0.10s/f (Slow) **12 Ran SP% 129.3**
Speed ratings (Par 101): **100,99,96,96,95 93,93,91,89,88 85,82**
toteswinger: 1&2 £0.00, 1&3 £2.40, 2&3 £0.00. CSF £53.92 CT £295.36 TOTE £3.50: £1.80, £5.30, £2.70; EX 109.50.
Owner ownaracehorse.co.uk (Shakespeare) **Bred** D McDonnell And Tower Bloodstock **Trained** Danethorpe, Notts

FOCUS
A run-of-the-mill sprint which again saw the prominent racers hold sway and the first three raced in the centre in the straight. Sound form, with the first two back to their best.
Finsbury Official explanation: jockey said gelding was denied a clear run
Talcen Gwyn(IRE) Official explanation: jockey said gelding was slowly away and hung right

7293 STAY AT THE WOLVERHAMPTON HOLIDAY INN H'CAP 2m 119y(P)
9:20 (9:21) (Class 6) (0-65,65) 3-Y-O+ **£2,729** (£806; £403) **Stalls Low**

Form RPR
2 1 **Laurel Creek (IRE)**[33] 6630 3-9-5 65 .... EddieAhern 12 75+
(M J Grassick, Ire) *hld up in mid-div: hdwy over 6f out: led 2f out: clr over 1f out: comf* **7/4**[1]
4002 2 1 3/4 **Zuwaar**[13] 7089 3-8-13 59 .... (t) JimCrowley 7 67
(Ian Williams) *hld up in tch: rdn and chsd wnr over 1f out: no imp* **7/1**[3]
6563 3 2 1/4 **Squirtle (IRE)**[25] 6824 5-9-11 65 .... LukeMorris(3) 9 70
(W M Brisbourne) *hld up in mid-div: lost pl on ins over 3f out: sn rdn: hdwy 2f out: styd on one pce fnl f* **14/1**
00-0 4 1/2 **Market Watcher (USA)**[28] 5372 7-9-2 53 .... JamieMoriarty 10 58
(Seamus Fahey, Ire) *hld up towards rr: stdy hdwy over 5f out: rdn wl over 1f out: one pce fnl f* **12/1**
-352 5 3 1/4 **Blushing Hilary (IRE)**[130] 3718 5-9-2 53 .... JerryO'Dwyer 1 54
(Mrs S J Humphrey) *hld up in tch: wnt 2nd 8f out: led over 3f out: rdn and hdd 2f out: wknd fnl f* **16/1**
3431 6 3 1/4 **Kokkokila**[34] 6606 4-9-13 64 .... KirstyMilczarek 8 61
(Lady Herries) *hld up towards rr: hdwy over 2f out: wknd over 1f out: eased ins fnl f* **3/1**[2]
3414 7 1 **Merrymaker**[30] 6708 8-9-6 60 .... DuranFentiman(3) 6 56
(W M Brisbourne) *hld up in rr: hdwy over 3f out: wknd wl over 1f out* **8/1**
00- 8 1/2 **Golden Hare (IRE)**[16] 6593 7-9-1 52 .... RobertWinston 4 47
(Aidan Anthony Howard, Ire) *hld up in mid-div: short-lived effrt on outside over 2f out* **33/1**
0653 9 2 **Rehearsal**[45] 6309 7-9-7 58 .... PaulMulrennan 13 51
(L Lungo) *stdd s: a in rr* **12/1**

3460 **10** 12 **Kyber**[26] 6790 7-8-8 **50** GaryBartley(5) 11 28
(J S Goldie) *led after 2f tl over 3f out: wknd over 2f out* **12/1**
0546 **11** 1 **Sleepy Mountain**[37] 6538 4-9-0 **56** WilliamCarson(5) 3 33
(A Middleton) *led after 1f tl after 2f: prom tl rdn and wknd over 3f out* **20/1**
0230 **12** 9 **Depraux (IRE)**[40] 5396 5-9-8 **59** TomEaves 2 25
(G M Moore) *led 1f: prom tl rdn and wknd over 5f out* **20/1**

3m 43.2s (1.40) **Going Correction** +0.10s/f (Slow)
WFA 3 from 4yo+ 9lb 12 Ran SP% **133.1**
Speed ratings (Par 101): **100,98,97,97,96 94,94,93,92,87 86,82**
toteswinger: 1&2 £5.90, 1&3 £13.40, 2&3 £36.20. CSF £16.60 CT £151.66 TOTE £3.20: £1.10, £2.40, £3.70; EX 32.70 Place 6: £ 263.05 Place 5: £61.50.
Owner Dont Tell The Missus Syndicate **Bred** Tetsu Nakata **Trained** Pollardstown, Co Kildare

FOCUS
Another ordinary handicap and a reasonable pace. The winner hugged the inside rail all the way up the straight and it is doubtful if he had to improve on his latest second here.
Kokkokila Official explanation: jockey said filly hung right in home straight
T/Plt: £232.30 to a £1 stake. Pool: £99,720.15. 313.27 winning tickets. T/Qpdt: £20.00 to a £1 stake. Pool: £9,162.56. 338.30 winning tickets. KH

7203 SAINT-CLOUD (L-H)
Wednesday, November 12

OFFICIAL GOING: Heavy

7294a CRITERIUM DE SAINT-CLOUD (GROUP 1) (C&F) 1m 2f
2:05 (2:09) 2-Y-0 **£105,037** (£42,022; £21,011; £10,496; £5,257)

RPR
1 **Fame And Glory**[21] 6917 2-9-0 JMurtagh 4 113
(A P O'Brien, Ire) *a cl up: 3rd st: brought wd: rdn 1 1/2f out: led 100yds out: drvn out* **31/10**[2]
2 1/2 **Drumbeat (IRE)**[45] 6317 2-9-0 CO'Donoghue 11 112
(A P O'Brien, Ire) *in rr: 10th st: hdwy between horses and rdn under 2f out: styd on to take 2nd last 50yds* **31/10**[2]
3 3/4 **Feels All Right (IRE)**[21] 2-9-0 OPeslier 5 111
(A Fabre, France) *midfield: 6th st: hdwy to ld narrowly 1f out tl hdd 100yds out: one pce* **29/10**[1]
4 nk **Age Of Aquarius (IRE)**[54] 6096 2-9-0 JAHeffernan 9 110
(A P O'Brien, Ire) *in tch: 5th st: styd on u.p fnl 2f* **31/10**[2]
5 snk **Zafisio (IRE)**[10] 7163 2-9-0 DBoeuf 10 110
(P A Blockley) *in tch on outside tl led at slow pce after 4f: hdd 1f out: one pce* **4/1**[3]
6 1 1/2 **Hail Caesar (IRE)**[45] 6316 2-9-0 CSoumillon 8 107
(A P O'Brien, Ire) *in rr: 8th st: kpt on fnl 1 1/2f but nvr a factor* **31/10**[2]
7 nk **Topclas (FR)**[33] 6642 2-9-0 IMendizabal 1 107+
(P Demercastel, France) *hld up: 7th st: cut corner down centre to go prom over 2f out: stl ev ch 1f out: sn one pce and eased* **15/1**
8 nk **King Of Sydney (USA)**[24] 6855 2-9-0 J-PCarvalho 6 106+
(Mario Hofer, Germany) *ref to settle in midfield: stl pulling 4f out: 9th st: rdn down wd outside 2f out: one pce* **83/10**
9 8 **Blaze Of Fire**[26] 2-9-0 SPasquier 3 92
(Mme C Head-Maarek, France) *prom racing keenly early: 2nd st: btn 2f out* **54/10**
10 4 **Entre Deux Eaux (FR)**[8] 7185 2-8-11 JVictoire 2 82
(Robert Collet, France) *set slow pce for 4f: 4th st: wknd 1 1/2f out* **14/1**
11 20 **Turin Lady (IRE)**[24] 6847 2-8-11 PShanahan 7 46
(Tracey Collins, Ire) *towards rr early: hdwy down outside to dispute 4th 4f out: wknd 3f out* **12/1**

2m 19.9s (3.90) 11 Ran SP% **190.2**
PARI-MUTUEL: WIN 4.10 (coupled with Drumbeat & Age Of Aquarius & Hail Caesar); PL 3.00, 7.90, 1.70; DF 104.20.
Owner Derrick Smith **Bred** Ptarmigan Bloodstock & Miss K **Trained** Ballydoyle, Co Tipperary
■ Stewards' Enquiry : J A Heffernan 200eur fine: whip abuse
C O'Donoghue 200eur fine: whip abuse
J Murtagh 400eur fine: whip abuse
O Peslier 400eur fine: whip abuse

FOCUS
A typically weak renewal of this Group 1, in which Aidan O'Brien saddled the first two and the fourth.

NOTEBOOK
Fame And Glory made a winning debut over 1m at Navan last month in similar ground. Always well placed and towards the outside of the field, he tacked across to the stands' side entering the straight. He picked up from a furlong and a half out and ran on really well under strong pressure. He is bred to get at least 1m4f and further improvement looks certain, particularly when there is some cut in the ground. He will be trained for a Derby in 2009.
Drumbeat(IRE) appreciated the cut in the ground and ran the best race of his career to date. He was held up in the early stages and still had plenty to do in the straight, but he was brought with a run up the centre of the track and battled gamely to the line. He is another with considerable scope for improvement.
Feels All Right(IRE), on whom waiting tactics were employed, challenged for the lead at the furlong marker. He was just a little one-paced in the latter stages and connections felt that this was the limit of his stamina, but he is expected to come on as a three-year-old.
Age Of Aquarius(IRE), a beautifully bred son of Galileo running on turf for the first time, put up a very promising performance. He started his challenge from a furlong and a half out and was putting in his best work at the finish. He looks a smart colt who is sure to turn into a decent three-year-old.
Zafisio(IRE) was totally unsuited by the lack of early pace. Halfway down the back straight his jockey looked over a shoulder, but there were no takers to set the pace so he went on towards the outside of the field. He was asked for an effort early in the straight, held the advantage until the furlong marker and battled on gamely. It was a really game effort considering he had a nightmare trip over to France due to bad weather in the channel.

7204 GREAT LEIGHS (A.W) (L-H)
Thursday, November 13

OFFICIAL GOING: Standard
Wind: Fairly strong, behind Weather: light rain

7295 WILD CHERRY H'CAP 5f (P)
6:50 (6:50) (Class 6) (0-65,65) 3-Y-0+ **£2,590** (£770; £385; £192) **Stalls** Low

Form RPR
0400 **1** **Fizzlephut (IRE)**[6] 7231 6-8-9 **56** WandersonD'Avila 2 65
(Miss J R Tooth) *taken down early: wnt rt s: chsd ldrs: led over 1f out: styd on gamely fnl f: all out* **25/1**
043 **2** 3/4 **Monte Major (IRE)**[6] 7231 7-8-8 **55** (v) JimmyQuinn 9 61
(D Shaw) *in tch: hdwy over 1f out: drvn ent fnl f: wnt 2nd wl ins fnl f: r.o but nt rch wnr* **5/1**[3]
2103 **3** shd **Tanley**[8] 7197 3-8-7 **54** (p) LPKeniry 4 60
(J F Coupland) *awkward s: sn in midfield: hdwy on inner 2f out: chsd ldng pair ent fnl f: r.o but nt rch wnr* **4/1**[2]
2041 **4** 1 **Billy Red**[14] 7090 4-9-1 **62** (b) TPQueally 7 64
(J R Jenkins) *led: rdn and hung rt over 1f out: hdd over 1f out: one pce fnl f: lost 2 pls wl ins fnl f* **6/1**
6501 **5** 1 1/4 **Desert Opal**[70] 5626 8-8-13 **63** (b) LukeMorris(3) 12 61+
(C R Dore) *towards rr on outer: rdn 1/2-way: hdwy and c v wd bnd 2f out: kpt on but nvr trbld ldrs* **16/1**
6340 **6** hd **Peopleton Brook**[21] 6925 6-9-4 **65** (t) GeorgeBaker 3 62
(B G Powell) *dwlt: towards rr: rdn and effrt wl over 1f out: kpt on: nvr threatened ldrs* **12/1**
0/06 **7** 1 **Great Fox (IRE)**[14] 7092 7-8-7 **54** SaleemGolam 5 48
(S C Williams) *in tch: effrt to chse ldrs over 1f out: no ex u.p fnl f* **12/1**
0560 **8** 3 1/4 **Just Joey**[6] 7231 4-8-12 **59** (b) DarryllHolland 11 41
(J R Weymes) *in tch: sn bustled along: drvn and wknd over 1f out* **33/1**
6211 **9** 1 3/4 **Wreningham**[14] 7092 3-9-1 **62** JamieSpencer 8 38+
(T Keddy) *stmbld bdly s: nvr able to rcvr: a bhd* **7/2**[1]
262 **10** hd **Pic Up Sticks**[45] 6339 9-9-0 **61** MichaelHills 1 36
(B G Powell) *dwlt: a bhd* **7/1**
0000 **11** 2 **Daddy Cool**[6] 7231 4-8-10 **57** HayleyTurner 6 25
(W G M Turner) *a in rr: drvn and no hdwy fr 1/2-way* **66/1**
5340 **12** nk **Triskaidekaphobia**[31] 6711 5-8-12 **59** (t) PaulFitzsimons 10 26
(Miss J R Tooth) *chsd ldr tl over 2f out: wknd qckly 2f out: eased fnl f* **33/1**

60.18 secs (-0.02) **Going Correction** +0.10s/f (Slow) 12 Ran SP% **118.2**
Speed ratings (Par 101): **104,102,102,101,99 98,97,91,89,88 85,85**
toteswinger: 1&2 £22.80, 1&3 £22.80, 2&3 £11.10. CSF £142.61 CT £631.25 TOTE £27.80: £9.40, £2.50, £1.60; EX 212.70.
Owner Miss J R Tooth **Bred** Tally-Ho Stud **Trained** Upper Lambourn, Berks

FOCUS
A modest sprint handicap but solid form for the grade.
Wreningham Official explanation: trainer said, regarding the poor form shown, gelding stumbled at start and as a result was unable to dominate from the front as it prefers to do.

7296 JUNIPER H'CAP 1m 6f (P)
7:20 (7:20) (Class 5) (0-75,70) 3-Y-0+ **£3,238** (£963; £481; £240) **Stalls** Low

Form RPR
1 **Weybridge Light**[35] 6608 3-8-11 **57** (b) JamieSpencer 5 61
(Eoin Griffin, Ire) *t.k.h: chsd ldr tl led after 2f tl over 9f out: led again 2f out: sn hung rt: drvn over 1f out: styd on wl* **5/2**[2]
0220 **2** 1 **Eureka Moment**[19] 6991 3-9-4 **64** EddieAhern 3 67
(E A L Dunlop) *hld up in tch: trckd ldrs gng wl over 2f out: chsd wnr and rdn over 1f out: kpt on same pce fnl f* **10/1**
-345 **3** 1 1/4 **Tender Falcon**[7] 7216 8-9-10 **62** GeorgeBaker 8 63
(R J Hodges) *stdd after s: hld up in last pl: hdwy over 3f out: chsd ldng pair and hung lft u.p over 1f out: one pce fnl f* **7/1**[3]
004 **4** 2 1/4 **Generous Star**[22] 6909 5-9-8 **60** DaneO'Neill 1 58
(J Pearce) *s.i.s: hld up in last trio: shkn up 4f out: hdwy over 2f out: chsd ldrs and rdn jst over 1f out: no imp fnl f* **25/1**
3105 **5** 2 1/4 **Dramatic Solo**[19] 6991 3-9-10 **70** (b) AndrewElliott 2 65
(K R Burke) *t.k.h: led for 2f: chsd ldrs after tl wknd u.p over 1f out* **15/2**
5000 **6** 9 **Peas 'n Beans (IRE)**[26] 6824 5-8-9 **47** oh2 (t) LiamJones 4 29
(T Keddy) *t.k.h: chsd ldr after 2f tl led over 9f out: rdn and hdd 2f out: wknd qckly over 1f out* **33/1**
6012 **7** 8 **Bold Bobby Be (IRE)**[16] 7045 4-10-0 **66** (v) JimmyQuinn 6 37
(J L Dunlop) *dwlt: plld hrd: hld up in last trio: rdn over 2f out: sn btn* **11/8**[1]
6 **8** 32 **Last Emperor**[15] 7071 3-7-11 **48** NicolPolli(5) 7 —
(John Joseph Murphy, Ire) *t.k.h: chsd ldrs: lost pl and rdn over 3f out: t.o last 2f* **33/1**

3m 5.54s (2.34) **Going Correction** +0.10s/f (Slow)
WFA 3 from 4yo+ 8lb 8 Ran SP% **113.8**
Speed ratings (Par 103): **97,96,95,94,93 88,83,65**
toteswinger: 1&2 £9.50, 1&3 £3.70, 2&3 £3.30. CSF £26.31 CT £152.21 TOTE £3.50: £1.10, £3.00, £2.30; EX 28.70.
Owner Weybridge Group Limited **Bred** Hascombe And Valiant Studs **Trained** Slieverue, Co. Kilkenny

FOCUS
A very moderate staying handicap for the grade and they went a steady pace early on. The runner-up is rated to her recent best.

7297 HOSPITALITY AT GREAT LEIGHS CLAIMING STKS 6f (P)
7:50 (7:51) (Class 5) 3-Y-0+ **£3,238** (£963; £481; £240) **Stalls** Low

Form RPR
6266 **1** **Orpenindeed (IRE)**[22] 6902 5-8-8 87 (tp) AndreaAtzeni(7) 1 89
(M Botti) *mde all: pushed clr over 1f out: in command fnl f: easily* **6/4**[1]
6400 **2** 3 1/4 **Little Edward**[7] 7215 10-9-2 89 GeorgeBaker 4 79
(R J Hodges) *stdd after s: plld hrd: hld up in rr: hdwy over 2f out: chsd ldng pair and rdn over 1f out: no ch w wnr fnl f: wnt 2nd fnl 100yds* **9/2**[3]
3421 **3** 1 **Mutamared (USA)**[17] 7013 8-9-2 86 JamieSpencer 5 76
(K A Ryan) *t.k.h: hld up in midfield: hdwy over 2f out: chsd wnr and rdn wl over 1f out: btn 1f out: lost 2nd fnl 100yds* **13/8**[2]
4 2 1/4 **Fairyville (IRE)**[16] 7059 3-7-8 52 NicolPolli(5) 2 52
(John Joseph Murphy, Ire) *chsd ldrs on inner: effrt u.p 2f out: outpcd over 1f out: kpt on same pce after* **50/1**
0004 **5** 1/2 **Silver Wind**[22] 6902 3-9-2 79 (v) RobertWinston 9 67
(P D Evans) *racd on outer: a towards rr: rdn 1/2-way: nvr trbld ldrs* **10/1**
3035 **6** 1/2 **Buy On The Red**[29] 6736 7-8-7 72 (v[1]) HayleyTurner 7 57
(W R Muir) *dwlt: sn chsng ldrs: rdn over 2f out: wknd over 1f out* **16/1**
0063 **7** 1/2 **Scots W'Hae**[35] 6595 3-8-4 47 (p) NeilChalmers 8 52
(A Bailey) *a in rr: n.d* **50/1**
8 13 **Baileys Brazilian**[106] 3-7-13 61 JimmyQuinn 3 6
(C A Dwyer) *t.k.h: chsd ldr tl 2f out: sn wknd* **66/1**

1m 12.52s (-1.18) **Going Correction** +0.10s/f (Slow) 8 Ran SP% **118.5**
Speed ratings (Par 103): **111,106,105,102,101 101,100,83**
toteswinger: 1&2 £2.90, 1&3 £1.10, 2&3 £1.10. CSF £9.28 TOTE £3.50: £1.20, £1.30, £1.10; EX 10.20.
Owner Giuliano Manfredini **Bred** Alexander Pereira **Trained** Newmarket, Suffolk

FOCUS
A decent claimer and the winner is the best guide to the level.

7298 BEECH NURSERY 1m (P)
8:20 (8:20) (Class 5) (0-75,72) 2-Y-O £3,885 (£1,156; £577; £288) Stalls Centre

Form RPR

0001 1 **Becausewecan (USA)**[12] 7130 2-9-7 **72** RobertWinston 1 75
(M Johnston) *chsd ldr tl 6f out: styd handy: n.m.r on inner over 1f out: ev ch and hrd drvn ins fnl f: led fnl 100yds: r.o* **9/2**[3]

0246 2 ¾ **Celtic Commitment**[8] 7190 2-9-1 **66** PatDobbs 4 67
(R Hannon) *led: rdn wl over 1f out: battled on gamely u.p tl hdd and no ex fnl 100yds* **6/1**

023 3 1½ **Charlie Smirke (USA)**[43] 6375 2-9-5 **70** GeorgeBaker 2 68
(G L Moore) *in tch: hung rt fr 4f out: pushed along and hdwy over 3f out: rdn to chse ldr wl over 1f out: edgd lft u.p: one pce ins fnl f* **7/4**[1]

4543 4 1½ **Jaslyn (IRE)**[6] 7220 2-7-12 **49** oh1 JimmyQuinn 7 44
(J R Weymes) *stdd and dropped in bhd after s: hld up in rr: hdwy 2f out: chsd ldrs and rdn ent fnl f: sn no imp* **25/1**

5460 5 3½ **Voulez Vous**[131] 3734 2-9-6 **71** DaneO'Neill 9 58
(E J O'Neill) *stdd and dropped in bhd after s: plld hrd: hld up in rr: rdn and struggling 3f out: nvr trbld ldrs* **16/1**

034 6 ¾ **Naizak**[12] 7140 2-9-7 **72** RHills 6 57
(J L Dunlop) *chsd ldrs tl wnt 2nd 6f out: rdn wl over 1f out: fnd little and sn btn: wknd fnl f* **5/2**[2]

060 7 1½ **Sweet Virginia (USA)**[99] 4740 2-7-8 **52** oh4 ow3 AndreaAtzeni[(7)] 5 34
(K R Burke) *racd on outer: in midfield: rdn over 4f out: struggling 3f out: no ch after* **33/1**

1m 41.53s (1.63) **Going Correction** +0.10s/f (Slow) 7 Ran SP% **110.1**
Speed ratings (Par 96): **95,94,92,91,87 87,85**
toteswinger: 1&2 £22.40, 1&3 £5.00, 2&3 £6.40. CSF £28.72 CT £59.15 TOTE £5.90: £3.50, £2.90; EX 27.50.
Owner Douglas Livingston **Bred** Tony Holmes & Walter Zent **Trained** Middleham Moor, N Yorks
■ Stewards' Enquiry : Robert Winston two-day ban: used whip with excessive frequency without giving colt time to respond (Nov 28-29)

FOCUS
A pretty modest nursery.

NOTEBOOK
Becausewecan(USA) gamely defied a 5lb rise for his recent success over 7f on heavy ground at Ayr. He was taken on for the early lead and looked in trouble rounding the final bend, but he squeezed through a tight gap between Celtic Commitment and the inside rail under a forceful ride in the straight. He took nine goes to get off the mark, but is progressing now and proved well suited by this first taste of Polytrack.
Celtic Commitment edged left under pressure in the straight, but he basically had every chance if good enough. He remains a maiden. (op 4-1)
Charlie Smirke(USA) looked to have every chance judged on the form he had shown in three runs over 7f in maidens (the last two on Polytrack), and he was well backed, but he proved disappointing. He never really travelled and looked laboured under pressure in the straight, suggesting some headgear may be needed. Official explanation: jockey said colt hung right (tchd 2-1)
Jaslyn(IRE), 1lb out of the handicap, did not run badly on this first try beyond 7f, but it remains to be seen what he actually achieved. (op 20-1)
Naizak had shown ability in maiden company, but she offered little on her nursery debut and may have had enough for the year. (op 11-4)

7299 ASH H'CAP 1m (P)
8:50 (8:51) (Class 4) (0-85,85) 3-Y-O+ £5,180 (£1,541; £770; £384) Stalls Centre

Form RPR

1214 1 **Mahadee (IRE)**[31] 6704 3-8-13 **80** (b) JamieSpencer 8 95+
(C E Brittain) *hld up wl in tch: chsd ldr 2f out: sn ev ch: rdn to ld ent fnl f: sn clr: easily* **9/4**[1]

0360 2 3½ **Premier Danseur (IRE)**[57] 6033 3-8-13 **80** RobertWinston 4 85
(M Johnston) *hld up in rr: rdn over 2f out: swtchd rt and hdwy over 1f out: kpt on u.p fnl f: wnt 2nd towards fin: no ch w wnr* **16/1**

5202 3 nk **Abbondanza (IRE)**[46] 6312 5-9-6 **85** (p) DaneO'Neill 9 89
(Miss L A Perratt) *chsd ldr after 1f: led 2f out: sn rdn: hdd ent fnl f: no ch w wnr after: lost 2nd towards fin* **10/1**

4602 4 1½ **Palmerin**[17] 7014 3-8-11 **78** EddieAhern 2 79
(R Hannon) *hld up towards rr: effrt and rdn 2f out: kpt on same pce u.p after* **9/2**[3]

0542 5 1¼ **Obezyana (USA)**[15] 7068 6-8-7 **72** MickyFenton 3 70
(A Bailey) *short of room and swtchd lft sn after s: hld up in last: effrt on outer over 2f out: nvr trbld ldrs* **4/1**[2]

3400 6 nse **Resplendent Nova**[61] 5908 6-9-0 **79** JimmyQuinn 1 77
(P Howling) *hld up in rr: effrt on inner wl over 1f out: kpt on past btn horses but nvr trbld ldrs* **12/1**

6122 7 2¾ **Bold Marc (IRE)**[9] 7175 6-8-13 **78** DarrenWilliams 7 70
(K R Burke) *led for 1f: steadily lost pl and dropped to midfield: rdn over 2f out: no hdwy fr wl over 1f out* **11/1**

0611 8 2 **Prince Of Thebes (IRE)**[17] 7014 7-9-1 **80** PaulDoe 6 67
(M J Attwater) *t.k.h: hld up towards rr: hdwy to chse ldrs over 4f out: rdn and unable qck over 2f out: wknd over 1f out* **15/2**

0133 9 6 **King's Ransom**[178] 2262 5-8-12 **77** DarryllHolland 13 50
(S Gollings) *led after 1f: rdn and hdd 2f out: sn wknd: wl bhd and eased ins fnl f* **14/1**

0000 10 4 **Super Frank (IRE)**[34] 6627 5-8-7 **77** NicolPolli[(5)] 5 41
(J Akehurst) *racd on outer in midfield: rdn and struggling 3f out: wl bhd fnl f* **33/1**

1m 39.36s (-0.54) **Going Correction** +0.10s/f (Slow)
WFA 3 from 4yo+ 2lb 10 Ran SP% **121.3**
Speed ratings (Par 105): **106,102,102,100,99 99,96,94,88,84**
toteswinger: 1&2 £36.40, 1&3 £7.70, 2&3 Not won. CSF £44.52 CT £321.90 TOTE £3.90: £1.80, £2.70, £2.10; EX 80.10.
Owner Saeed Manana **Bred** Darley **Trained** Newmarket, Suffolk
■ Stewards' Enquiry : Dane O'Neill caution: careless riding

FOCUS
A fair handicap run at a good pace and the fourth looks the best guide in a sound contest.
Obezyana(USA) Official explanation: jockey said gelding was hampered leaving stalls; vet said after routine testing after race he found the gelding showing signs of set fast.

7300 WILLOW MEDIAN AUCTION MAIDEN STKS 1m 2f (P)
9:20 (9:20) (Class 5) 3-5-Y-O £3,238 (£963; £481; £240) Stalls Low

Form RPR

50-4 1 **Incarnation (IRE)**[87] 5155 3-8-12 69 DaneO'Neill 4 66+
(L M Cumani) *led after 1f: mde rest: rdn and qcknd clr over 1f out: in command fnl f: easily* **4/9**[1]

0000 2 3½ **Mayfair's Future**[41] 6437 3-9-3 55 TPQueally 2 61
(J R Jenkins) *plld hrd: led for 1f: chsd ldr after: rdn and unable qckn over 1f out: no ch w wnr fnl f* **12/1**[3]

446 3 1½ **Time To Play**[28] 6762 3-9-3 66 KirstyMilczarek 3 58
(T T Clement) *trckd ldrs: rdn and unable qck over 1f out: wl hld fnl f* **5/2**[2]

000/ 4 3 **Kentavr's Dream**[767] 5847 5-9-2 0 JimmyQuinn 5 47
(P Howling) *hld up in last pair: rdn 2f out: sn outpcd: wl hld fnl f* **33/1**

0- 5 10 **Apocalypto (IRE)**[554] 1587 4-9-4 0 AlanCreighton[(3)] 1 32
(E J Creighton) *t.k.h: hld up in last pair: rdn over 2f out: wknd wl over 1f out: wl btn fnl f* **33/1**

2m 13.38s (4.78) **Going Correction** +0.10s/f (Slow)
WFA 3 from 4yo+ 4lb 5 Ran SP% **111.4**
Speed ratings (Par 103): **84,81,80,77,69**
CSF £7.42 TOTE £1.40: £1.02, £4.80; EX 6.00 Place 6 £62.77, Place 5 £27.52 .
Owner Paul Moulton **Bred** Bruno Faust **Trained** Newmarket, Suffolk
■ Stewards' Enquiry : T P Queally one-day ban: careless riding (Nov 27)

FOCUS
A terrible maiden and certainly not a race to dwell on, with the second the best guide to the level.
T/Plt: £73.80 to a £1 stake. Pool: £106,994.21. 1,057.98 winning tickets. T/Qpdt: £11.30 to a £1 stake. Pool: £8,011.44. 521.44 winning tickets. SP

7212 LINGFIELD (L-H)
Thursday, November 13

OFFICIAL GOING: Standard
Wind: Moderate, behind Weather: Overcast, drizzly

7301 ASHURST WOOD APPRENTICE H'CAP 1m 5f (P)
12:50 (12:50) (Class 5) (0-75,74) 3-Y-O+ £2,729 (£806; £403) Stalls Low

Form RPR

0521 1 **Epsom Salts**[17] 7010 3-8-5 **60** oh2 RosieJessop 5 66
(P M Phelan) *chsd ldr: rdn over 2f out: lft in ld over 1f out: pushed out and kpt on wl* **3/1**[2]

122 2 ¾ **Alonso De Guzman (IRE)**[15] 7064 4-9-7 **74** MatthewBirch[(5)] 7 79+
(J R Boyle) *led: pushed along 3f out: rn wd bnd 2f out and hdd over 1f out: tried to cl again but nt qckn fnl f* **13/8**[1]

0006 3 hd **Can Can Star**[16] 7046 5-8-9 **60** DebraEngland[(3)] 1 65
(A W Carroll) *heavily restrained s and wl detached in last pair: trying to creep clsr whn nt clr run briefly 2f out: prog after: rdn and styd on fnl f: too much to do* **14/1**

2106 4 5 **Mixing**[21] 6929 6-8-9 **64** KierenFox[(7)] 4 62
(M J Attwater) *trckd ldng pair to over 5f out: outpcd 3f out: wnt 3rd again over 2f out: no imp* **12/1**

5410 5 1½ **Mr Napoleon (IRE)**[35] 6607 6-9-8 **70** PNolan 6 65
(G L Moore) *stdd s: hld up in 4th: pushed along and no prog 3f out: n.d fnl 2f* **7/2**[3]

0063 6 9 **Red Wine**[9] 7177 9-9-9 **71** AmyScott 2 53
(A J McCabe) *heavily restrained s and wl detached in last pair: plld way through to go 2nd over 5f out to over 3f out: wknd: t.o* **8/1**

2m 45.3s (-0.70) **Going Correction** -0.05s/f (Stan)
WFA 3 from 4yo+ 7lb 6 Ran SP% **110.8**
Speed ratings (Par 103): **100,99,99,96,95 89**
toteswinger: 1&2 £1.90, 1&3 £7.60, 2&3 £6.20. CSF £8.07 TOTE £3.30: £1.80, £1.40; EX 7.40.
Owner The Epsom Racegoers **Bred** Heatherwold Stud **Trained** Epsom, Surrey

FOCUS
A modest apprentice handicap, but they went a reasonable pace thanks to the favourite and the field finished well spread out, but the form looks messy.

7302 HARTFIELD H'CAP (DIV I) 1m (P)
1:20 (1:22) (Class 5) (0-75,75) 3-Y-O+ £2,388 (£705; £352) Stalls High

Form RPR

4001 1 **Titan Triumph**[15] 7068 4-9-3 **72** (t) JimCrowley 9 78+
(W J Knight) *hld up in rr: plenty to do over 2f out but gng strly: eased to outer over 1f out: str run to ld fnl 75yds* **4/1**[1]

0004 2 ½ **Sam's Cross (IRE)**[29] 6738 3-9-2 **73** DarrenWilliams 5 78
(K R Burke) *t.k.h early: hld up bhd ldrs: prog over 2f out: hrd rdn to ld last 150yds: hdd and hld fnl 75yds* **9/2**[2]

5100 3 ½ **Rambling Light**[29] 6734 4-9-6 **75** (p) LPKeniry 1 79
(A M Balding) *trckd ldrs: gng easily over 2f out: effrt on inner over 1f out: upsides ent fnl f: nt qckn fnl 150yds* **6/1**

0000 4 nse **Straight And Level (CAN)**[58] 5999 3-8-11 **68** ow1 TravisBlock 4 72
(Miss Jo Crowley) *led after 2f: kicked on over 3f out: hrd pressed over 1f out: hdd and one pce last 150yds* **25/1**

0423 5 1¼ **Carmenero (GER)**[31] 6695 5-9-3 **72** HayleyTurner 11 73
(W R Muir) *hld up in midfield: rdn and effrt on inner 2f out: prog to chse ldrs 1f out: kpt on but no real imp* **5/1**[3]

2200 6 3 **Onenightinlisbon (IRE)**[17] 7027 4-8-12 **67** PatCosgrave 2 61
(J R Boyle) *led at slow pce for 2f: chsd ldr to wl over 1f out: sn lost pl u.p* **20/1**

5431 7 ½ **Smokey Rye**[27] 6771 3-8-13 **70** SteveDrowne 12 63
(G L Moore) *stdd s: sn pushed up into midfield: drvn and outpcd over 2f out: no imp on ldrs after* **11/1**

6060 8 ½ **Bombardier Wells**[120] 4090 3-8-13 **70** StephenCarson 6 62
(Eve Johnson Houghton) *trckd ldng pair to 3f out: grad outpcd and losing pls after* **25/1**

1555 9 2 **Murrin (IRE)**[45] 6346 4-9-4 **73** RobertHavlin 3 60+
(T G Mills) *stdd s: hld up in last in slowly run r: outpcd fr 3f out: nvr on terms after* **11/2**

0000 10 1 **Brunelleschi**[45] 6340 5-8-9 **67** LukeMorris[(3)] 10 52
(P L Gilligan) *stdd s: hld up in last trio in slowly run r: outpcd over 2f out: no ch after* **33/1**

662 11 7 **Ivory Lace**[34] 6627 7-9-5 **74** JamieSpencer 8 43
(S Woodman) *stdd s: hld up in last trio: outpcd fr 3f out: no ch after: t.o* **9/1**

1m 38.63s (0.43) **Going Correction** -0.05s/f (Stan)
WFA 3 from 4yo+ 2lb 11 Ran SP% **118.2**
Speed ratings (Par 103): **95,94,94,93,92 89,89,88,86,85 78**
toteswinger: 1&2 £8.10, 1&3 £8.90, 2&3 £6.10. CSF £20.87 CT £110.11 TOTE £6.20: £2.10, £1.80, £2.30; EX 34.80 Trifecta £86.90 Pool: £196.14 - 1.67 winning units..
Owner Canisbay Bloodstock **Bred** Hesmonds Stud Ltd **Trained** Patching, W Sussex

FOCUS
The first division of this moderate handicap was run at a very steady gallop. The placed horses set the standard.

Ivory Lace Official explanation: jockey said mare never travelled; trainer later said mare was found to be in season after the race

7303 EUROPEAN BREEDERS' FUND MEDIAN AUCTION MAIDEN STKS 5f (P)
1:50 (1:50) (Class 5) 2-Y-O £3,561 (£1,059; £529; £264) Stalls High

Form RPR

0322 **1** **Satwa Street (IRE)**[10] 7168 2-9-3 73 .... HayleyTurner 2 84
(D M Simcock) *mde all: shkn up and drew rt away wl over 1f out: rdn out* **2/1**[2]

024 **2** *6* **Megasecret**[17] 7020 2-9-3 75 .... DaneO'Neill 5 62
(R Hannon) *t.k.h early: trckd wnr after 1f: rdn and nt qckn wl over 1f out and easily lft bhd: kpt on* **5/6**[1]

0643 **3** *3* **La Capriosa**[10] 7168 2-8-12 64 .... EddieAhern 7 47
(A J McCabe) *prom but forced to r wd: wl outpcd fr 2f out: plugged on* **6/1**[3]

5600 **4** *½* **Wigan Pier**[10] 7168 2-8-12 50 ....(e[1]) SaleemGolam 3 45
(M D Squance) *trckd ldrs: rdn and easily outpcd fr 2f out* **50/1**

5 **5** *nse* **Cindy Incidentally**[51] 6183 2-8-12 0 .... LPKeniry 1 45
(Miss Gay Kelleway) *chsd wnr 1f: wl in tch 2f out: sn wknd* **40/1**

6 **6** *¾* **Piccaso's Sky**[200] 1640 2-9-3 0 .... SteveDrowne 4 47
(A B Haynes) *pushed along in last after 2f: outpcd 2f out* **22/1**

0 **7** *19* **Rio Ramus (IRE)**[24] 6863 2-9-0 0 .... LukeMorris(3) 6 —
(R A Teal) *taken down early: prom 2f: wl btn whn virtually rn off the crse bnd 2f out: t.o* **33/1**

58.58 secs (-0.22) **Going Correction** -0.05s/f (Stan) 2y crse rec **7 Ran SP% 113.9**
Speed ratings (Par 96): **99,89,84,83,83 82,52**
toteswinger: 1&2 £1.60, 1&3 £1.30, 2&3 £1.80. CSF £3.94 TOTE £3.00: £1.10, £1.10; EX 4.70.
Owner Khalifa Dasmal **Bred** Ditta Nardi Raffaele **Trained** Newmarket, Suffolk

FOCUS
A very moderate sprint maiden and the market suggested it was a three-horse race. The pace was decent enough with four horses in a line across the track vying for the early lead.

NOTEBOOK
Satwa Street(IRE), in the frame in similar events on Polytrack in his last three starts, was sent straight into the lead by replacement-rider Hayley Turner and, railing like a greyhound, had shot clear by the time he reached the furlong pole. He may not have beaten much here, but there should be enough sprint handicaps on Polytrack this winter to keep him occupied and he should win one or two. (op 7-4, tchd 9-4 in a place)
Megasecret, down to the minimum trip for the first time on this sand debut, officially had 2lb in hand of the winner on official ratings. After missing the break slightly, he was soon up amongst the leaders but he was inclined to take a keen hold once there. Under pressure turning for home, he didn't look that keen and could do nothing to stop the winner from scooting away from him. It looks a case of back to the drawing board. (op 10-11, tchd evens in places)
La Capriosa, a couple of lengths behind Satwa Street at Wolverhampton last time, raced prominently from the outside stall but was well and truly put in her place from the home bend. (op 11-2)
Wigan Pier, already exposed as modest and a long way behind Satwa Street and La Capriosa at Wolverhampton last time, had a first-time eyeshield replacing the blinkers. She plugged on to finish much closer to La Capriosa this time, but probably still didn't achieve much.
Cindy Incidentally, who faced a huge task against previous winners in a Beverley novice event on her debut and duly finished tailed off, was restrained after breaking well but she ended up well beaten and looks very modest. (op 33-1)
Rio Ramus(IRE) Official explanation: jockey said gelding hung right

7304 THREE BRIDGES MAIDEN STKS 1m 4f (P)
2:20 (2:23) (Class 5) 3-Y-O+ £2,729 (£806; £403) Stalls Low

Form RPR

420 **1** **Sibi Saba (USA)**[87] 5155 3-8-12 70 ....(t) JamieSpencer 9 78
(Saeed Bin Suroor) *hld up in midfield: shkn up and prog over 2f out: drvn to ld ins fnl f: kpt on wl* **13/2**

4202 **2** *1 ¼* **Arts Guild (USA)**[28] 6762 3-9-3 75 .... JimmyFortune 3 81
(W J Musson) *trckd ldng pair to 1/2-way: styd cl up: effrt 2f out: upsides ent fnl f: carried hd high and fnd nil* **3/1**[2]

3022 **3** *hd* **Amhooj**[112] 4342 3-8-12 76 .... RHills 4 76
(M P Tregoning) *trckd ldr: led wl over 2f out: drvn and hdd ins fnl f: nt qckn* **6/4**[1]

43 **4** *¾* **Dayia (IRE)**[35] 6596 4-9-4 0 .... JimmyQuinn 6 74+
(J Pearce) *dwlt and rousted along early: last tl 1/2-way: outpcd and struggling 3f out: styd on fnl 2f: nrst fin* **9/2**[3]

04 **5** *1* **Euroceleb (IRE)**[71] 5612 3-8-12 0 .... EdwardCreighton 2 73
(H Morrison) *trckd ldng pair 1/2-way: cl enough 2f out: rdn and fnd nil over 1f out* **20/1**

6 *1 ½* **El Diego (IRE)**[391] 6322 4-9-9 80 .... JerryO'Dwyer 8 75
(J R Gask) *stdd s: hld up towards rr: rdn 3f out: one pce and no imp fnl 2f* **10/1**

0 **7** *25* **Middle Of Nowhere (USA)**[133] 3628 3-9-3 0 ....(t) EddieAhern 1 35
(M A Magnusson) *led to wl over 2f out: wknd rapidly: t.o* **20/1**

00 **8** *nk* **Delerios**[188] 1957 3-9-3 0 .... LPKeniry 5 35
(J R Best) *unruly bef gng into stalls: dropped to last 1/2-way: t.o 3f out* **66/1**

2m 29.68s (-3.32) **Going Correction** -0.05s/f (Stan)
WFA 3 from 4yo 6lb **8 Ran SP% 116.6**
Speed ratings (Par 103): **109,108,108,107,106 105,89,89**
toteswinger: 1&2 £4.10, 1&3 £3.30, 2&3 £2.30. CSF £26.33 TOTE £7.40: £1.60, £1.30, £1.10; EX 27.80 Trifecta £74.80 Pool: £527.89 - 5.22 winning units..
Owner Godolphin **Bred** Stonestreet Mares Llc **Trained** Newmarket, Suffolk

FOCUS
A fairly weak maiden that was run at a slow early gallop but the overall time was very good for the grade. The form looks sound rated around the placed horses.

7305 EUROPEAN BREEDERS' FUND FILLIES' H'CAP 1m 2f (P)
2:50 (2:50) (Class 3) (0-90,83) 3-Y-O £9,066 (£2,697; £1,348; £673) Stalls Low

Form RPR

0312 **1** **Suzi Spends (IRE)**[22] 6904 3-9-4 81 .... JimmyQuinn 5 86+
(H J Collingridge) *hld up in 4th: effrt 2f out: drvn and r.o to ld fnl 150yds: in command after* **11/4**[1]

4041 **2** *1* **Rio Guru (IRE)**[7] 7211 3-9-6 83 6ex .... EdwardCreighton 1 83
(M R Channon) *hld up in last: pushed along 3f out: no prog tl drvn and kpt on fnl f to snatch 2nd on line* **8/1**

2165 **3** *hd* **Red Linnet**[185] 2045 3-8-13 76 .... HayleyTurner 3 76
(M L W Bell) *trckd ldng pair: rn in snatches fr 4f out: drvn to chal on inner 1f out: nt qckn* **3/1**[2]

-046 **4** *½* **Mystery Sail (USA)**[22] 6904 3-8-11 74 ....(p) JimCrowley 4 73
(Mrs A J Perrett) *trckd ldr: chal gng wl 2f out: hanging and fnd nil over 1f out: stl ev ch ins fnl f: one pce* **9/2**[3]

3304 **5** *½* **Jadaara**[22] 6898 3-9-0 77 .... JoeFanning 6 75
(M Johnston) *led: hrd pressed 2f out: hdd & wknd fnl 150yds* **11/4**[1]

2m 4.01s (-2.59) **Going Correction** -0.05s/f (Stan) **5 Ran SP% 107.6**
Speed ratings (Par 103): **108,107,107,106,106**
toteswinger: 1&2 £6.60. CSF £21.76 TOTE £2.80: £1.90, £2.70; EX 12.80.
Owner Greenstead Hall Racing **Bred** G Callanan **Trained** Exning, Suffolk

FOCUS
By far the classiest race on the card featuring some in-form or unexposed fillies, but the whole field were still within a length or so of each other passing the furlong pole and the quintet finished in a heap. The first two and the fourth were close to previous form and the race is rated at a face value.

NOTEBOOK
Suzi Spends(IRE), who had finished a couple of lengths in front of Rio Guru at Great Leighs last time but was actually 2lb better off, was having her first try here and she was relatively weak in the market. After having been held up off the pace, she was brought widest in order to make her effort but she quickened up nicely and was well on top at the line. She will now be put away until the spring and connections are hopeful that she will develop into a Listed-class filly. (op 9-4 tchd 2-1)
Rio Guru(IRE), carrying a 6lb penalty for her recent Great Leighs victory and also weak in the market, she was held up last early but although she finished well, her old rival had gone beyond recall. She probably needs a stronger pace than she got here. (op 6-1)
Red Linnet, a winner over 1m4f here in February and having her first start since May, was well supported in the market. Settled in the middle of the field early, she became outpaced half a mile from home and, although she put herself in with a chance tight against the inside rail starting up the home straight, she could never find the required turn of foot. She wouldn't have been suited by the way the race was run over this trip, but she doesn't have that many miles on the clock so is worth another chance. (op 5-1)
Mystery Sail(USA), behind both Suzi Spends and Rio Guru at Great Leighs last time, was weighted to finish right alongside the pair on these revised terms. She was always in a good position, but she put her head to one side when asked to pick up soon after turning in and found little. She has questions to answer now. (tchd 5-1)
Jadaara, well beaten in her only previous try on Polytrack though that was after a ten-month absence, raced enthusiastically in the lead and was still just about in front passing the furlong pole before being done for finishing speed. (op 5-2 tchd 9-4)

7306 FOREST ROW NURSERY 7f (P)
3:20 (3:21) (Class 5) (0-75,74) 2-Y-O £3,885 (£1,156; £577; £288) Stalls Low

Form RPR

0542 **1** **Belated Silver (IRE)**[16] 7052 2-9-2 69 .... RichardKingscote 6 74+
(Tom Dascombe) *sn trckd ldng pair: wnt 2nd 2f out: rdn to ld over 1f out: asserted ins fnl f* **5/2**[1]

3133 **2** *1 ¼* **Ray Of Joy**[29] 6732 2-9-7 74 .... EddieAhern 10 76
(J R Jenkins) *led: set stdy pce to 3f out: drvn 2f out: hdd over 1f out: kpt on same pce* **11/1**

2423 **3** *¾* **Black N Brew (USA)**[33] 6661 2-9-3 70 .... SteveDrowne 4 70
(J R Best) *racd wd in midfield: hrd rdn and effrt 2f out: r.o to take 3rd ins fnl f: nrst fin* **8/1**

0021 **4** *1* **Ditto Ditto**[33] 6661 2-9-2 69 .... TPQueally 12 67
(D R Lanigan) *hld up in last trio: stl there whn nt clr run briefly jst over 1f out: shkn up and r.o strly fnl f: no ch of rching ldrs* **14/1**

614 **5** *shd* **Cumana Bay**[29] 6732 2-9-5 72 .... DaneO'Neill 7 69
(R Hannon) *hld up in midfield: nt qckn over 2f out: styd on fr over 1f out: nt pce to rch ldrs* **15/2**[3]

304 **6** *1* **Deyas Dream**[52] 6172 2-9-2 69 .... LPKeniry 5 64
(A M Balding) *hld up in midfield: no prog 2f out: nt clr run 1f out: r.o fnl 100yds: no ch* **8/1**

0430 **7** *¾* **Dream Date (IRE)**[40] 6477 2-8-10 66 ....(t) GilmarPereira(3) 9 59
(W J Haggas) *hld up in last trio: stl there over 1f out: swtchd rt ent fnl f: styd on: no ch* **14/1**

1540 **8** *hd* **Common Diva**[19] 6987 2-9-7 74 .... PatCosgrave 13 67
(A J McCabe) *racd wd: hld up: prog 3f out: outpcd 2f out: one pce after* **50/1**

4003 **9** *½* **Chimbonda**[5] 7240 2-9-3 70 .... JimCrowley 8 61
(S Parr) *chsd ldr to 2f out: wknd ins fnl f* **16/1**

001 **10** *½* **It's A Game (USA)**[31] 6697 2-9-6 73 .... JimmyFortune 14 63
(J H M Gosden) *hld up in last trio fr wd draw: stl there over 1f out: no ch whn nt clr run ent fnl f: kpt on* **11/1**

040 **11** *shd* **Equinity**[17] 7015 2-8-10 63 .... JimmyQuinn 3 53
(J Pearce) *chsd ldrs: nt qckn u.p over 2f out: wknd ins fnl f* **40/1**

654 **12** *nk* **Quick Single (USA)**[24] 6858 2-9-0 70 .... MarcHalford(3) 2 59
(D R C Elsworth) *dwlt: sn rchd midfield: rdn over 2f out: no prog: wknd fnl f* **13/2**[2]

600 **13** *1 ¼* **Damselfly**[17] 7023 2-8-5 58 .... JoeFanning 1 44
(M Johnston) *chsd ldrs on inner: outpcd over 2f out: wknd fnl f* **40/1**

1m 25.17s (0.37) **Going Correction** -0.05s/f (Stan) **13 Ran SP% 118.6**
Speed ratings (Par 96): **95,93,92,91,91 90,89,89,88,88 87,87,86**
toteswinger: 1&2 £6.60, 1&3 £4.70, 2&3 £10.90. CSF £30.68 CT £204.94 TOTE £2.70: £1.50, £3.10, £2.70; EX 34.00 Trifecta £80.50 Pool: £407.32 - 3.74 winning units..
Owner Mrs M Findlay **Bred** Peter Kelly **Trained** Lambourn, Berks

FOCUS
The lack of pace meant few got into this and the form is probably not worth much.

NOTEBOOK
Belated Silver(IRE), runner-up in a 7f soft-ground nursery at Yarmouth last month, was 3lb higher here, but is bred to be effective on this surface and he got on top close home. He did have an ideal sit throughout though and probably needs to improve to defy a rise. (op 3-1 tchd 2-1)
Ray Of Joy, down 1lb from last time, has been progressing well, winning at Kempton before looking a shade unlucky next time, and she ran another fine race on this rise in trip. She was able to kick off the front having gone just a steady gallop though, and the others were closing as they reached the line, so it is fair to say she was a little flattered. (op 10-1 tchd 9-1)
Black N Brew(USA) ran well off similar marks earlier in the season and was not beaten far behind Ditto Ditto in a maiden at Wolverhampton last month. He was able to reverse form with the latter, who got going too late, and gave the impression he will be better suited by a more truly run contest. (tchd 9-1)
Ditto Ditto ◆, off the mark at the fourth attempt in maidens, looked reasonably weighted for this handicap debut, but found himself held up in a slowly-run race and was still disputing last with a furlong to run. He was staying on when denied a clear run over a furlong out, but still saw his race out strongly and can be rated a good deal better than the bare form. He is one to watch out for in a similar contest. (op 8-1)
Cumana Bay was under the pump turning in and she was another that would not have been suited by the way the race was run. (op 8-1)
Deyas Dream was trying to stay on when denied a clear run over a furlong out and she should probably have been a length or so closer. (op 9-1 tchd 11-1)
Dream Date(IRE), unable to make an impact on her nursery debut, was expected to fare better here in a first-time tongue it, but she was held up in rear and never threatened to get involved. Official explanation: vet said filly had been struck into (op 12-1 tchd 16-1)
It's A Game(USA), who had a difficult draw to overcome, raced in the rear, but was beginning to make some headway when stopped dead in her run inside the final furlong. This form can be safely ignored. Official explanation: jockey said filly was denied a clear run (op 8-1 tchd 15-2 and 12-1)

Quick Single(USA) looked one of the more interesting ones on this nursery debut, but he was under pressure turning in and faded disappointingly. He had shaped with a good deal of promise in maidens and probably deserves another chance. (op 7-1 tchd 11-2)

7307 HARTFIELD H'CAP (DIV II) 1m (P)
3:50 (3:52) (Class 5) (0-75,75) 3-Y-O+ **£2,388** (£705; £352) **Stalls** High

Form RPR

4231 **1** **Pivka**[17] 7026 3-9-3 **74**........................ JimmyFortune 6 87
(Sir Michael Stoute) *trckd ldrs: prog to go 3rd 2f out: rdn to ld over 1f out: sn wl in command* **4/6**[1]

4004 **2** *1 ¼* **Eastern Gift**[15] 7068 3-8-12 **69**........................ DaneO'Neill 5 79
(R Hannon) *hld up in midfield: rdn and prog over 2f out: chsd wnr fnl f: r.o but readily hld* **8/1**[2]

2105 **3** *2 ¼* **Pippbrook Gold**[17] 7014 3-9-2 **73**........................ FergusSweeney 10 78
(J R Boyle) *mostly trckd ldr: rdn to ld narrowly over 2f out: hdd and one pce over 1f out* **16/1**

1036 **4** *nk* **Run For Ede'S**[24] 6867 4-8-11 **66**........................(p) TPQueally 2 70
(P M Phelan) *t.k.h: hld up bhd ldng trio: nt qckn over 2f out: hanging over 1f out: styd on ins fnl f* **16/1**

0000 **5** *1 ¾* **Networker**[118] 4162 5-9-0 **69**........................ JimmyQuinn 9 69+
(P J McBride) *stdd s: hld up in last trio: stl there and pulling over 2f out: sme prog over 1f out: reminders ins fnl f: nvr nr ldrs* **16/1**

0003 **6** *hd* **My Shadow**[32] 6683 3-8-13 **70**........................ NickyMackay 8 70
(S Dow) *t.k.h early: hld up tl wnt prom over 5f out: rdn to chal over 2f out: wknd over 1f out* **20/1**

4040 **7** *½* **Wavertree Warrior (IRE)**[24] 6867 6-9-6 **75**........................(b) JamesDoyle 4 74
(N P Littmoden) *a in midfield: rdn 3f out: no prog fnl 2f* **16/1**

0002 **8** *hd* **Hessian (IRE)**[17] 7027 4-8-13 **68**........................ JamieSpencer 11 66
(M D Squance) *hld up in last trio: stl there 2f out: hanging over 1f out: nvr nr ldrs* **9/1**[3]

003 **9** *½* **Haasem (USA)**[45] 6336 5-8-11 **66**........................ EddieAhern 7 63
(J R Jenkins) *hld up in last trio: shuffled along over 1f out: nvr nr ldrs* **12/1**

6013 **10** *2* **Support Fund (IRE)**[22] 6899 4-9-4 **73**........................ StephenCarson 3 65
(Eve Johnson Houghton) *taken down early: dwlt: sn in midfield: rdn 3f out: wknd 2f out* **20/1**

4000 **11** *10* **Zafonical Storm (USA)**[44] 6363 4-8-10 **72**........................ AmyScott(7) 1 41
(B W Duke) *led to over 2f out: wknd rapidly: t.o* **33/1**

1m 37.93s (-0.27) **Going Correction** -0.05s/f (Stan)
WFA 3 from 4yo+ 2lb **33** Ran SP% **124.8**
Speed ratings (Par 103): **99,97,95,95,93 93,92,92,92,90 80**
toteswinger: 1&2 £3.30, 1&3 £5.00, 2&3 £19.10. CSF £6.99 CT £58.46 TOTE £1.70: £1.10, £3.00, £4.30; EX 10.50 Trifecta £189.30 Pool: £757.40 - 2.97 winning units. Place 6: £7.66 Place 5: £6.14 .
Owner J Wigan & G Strawbridge **Bred** G Strawbridge & London Thoroughbred Services Ltd **Trained** Newmarket, Suffolk

FOCUS
The winning time was 0.7 seconds faster than the first division and the third is the best guide to the level.
Networker ◆ Official explanation: jockey said gelding was denied a clear run
Hessian(IRE) Official explanation: jockey said filly hung right
T/Plt: £9.00 to a £1 stake. Pool: £36,359.43. 2,940.61 winning tickets. T/Qpdt: £3.40 to a £1 stake. Pool: £2,780.36. 592.46 winning tickets. JN

7254 KEMPTON (A.W) (R-H)
Friday, November 14

OFFICIAL GOING: Standard
Wind: Almost nil

7308 BET CHELTENHAM - BETDAQ NURSERY 5f (P)
5:50 (5:51) (Class 5) (0-75,76) 2-Y-O **£2,590** (£770; £385; £192) **Stalls** High

Form RPR

6316 **1** **Misty Glade**[28] 6769 2-9-6 **74**........................(b) NickyMackay 12 81
(B J Meehan) *mid-div tl hdwy on outside 2f out: led ent fnl f: rdn out* **7/1**

006 **2** *1 ½* **Final Rhapsody**[32] 6696 2-8-10 **64**........................ LPKeniry 7 66
(J A Geake) *a.p: wnt 2nd ent fnl f: kpt on* **12/1**

603 **3** *hd* **Chosen Son (IRE)**[22] 6932 2-9-2 **70**........................ JerryO'Dwyer 10 71
(P J O'Gorman) *in rr: making gd hdwy whn carried rt appr fnl f: rallied ins fnl f* **6/1**[3]

1 **4** *¾* **Casual Style**[128] 3830 2-9-5 **73**........................ GeorgeBaker 6 71
(D E Pipe) *s.i.s: making hdwy whn swtchd rt over 1f out: fnd no room and swtchd lft: r.o* **9/2**[2]

1500 **5** *3 ¼* **Royal Raider**[77] 5473 2-9-0 **75**........................ AndreaAtzeni(7) 11 61
(P D Evans) *in rr tl mde sme late hdwy* **8/1**

2542 **6** *½* **Sally's Dilemma**[179] 2239 2-8-11 **70**........................(t) JackDean(5) 1 55
(W G M Turner) *wnt lft s: sn trckd ldr: wknd fnl f* **33/1**

0542 **7** *¾* **Sharpener (IRE)**[23] 6894 2-9-1 **69**........................ RyanMoore 3 51
(R Hannon) *hmpd s: sn trckd ldrs: wknd over 1f out* **4/1**[1]

1155 **8** *1* **Fangfoss Girls**[41] 6469 2-8-9 **70**........................ ChrisHough(7) 9 48
(D M Simcock) *fly-jmpd s: a towards rr* **10/1**

5144 **9** *2 ½* **Key To Love (IRE)**[22] 6931 2-8-9 **63**........................ JamesDoyle 2 32
(A J Chamberlain) *wnt rt s but in tch to 1/2-way* **25/1**

2113 **10** *hd* **Pressed For Time (IRE)**[58] 6017 2-8-10 **64**........................(t) EdwardCreighton 4 33
(E J Creighton) *led tl rdn and hdd ent fnl f: wknd qckly* **6/1**[3]

3226 **11** *6* **Blackwater Fort (USA)**[9] 7199 2-9-1 **69**........................ FergusSweeney 8 16
(J Gallagher) *a struggling in rr* **10/1**

61.03 secs (0.53) **Going Correction** +0.225s/f (Slow) **11** Ran SP% **123.0**
Speed ratings (Par 96): **104,101,101,100,94 94,92,91,87,86 77**
toteswinger: 1&2 £25.00, 1&3 £15.40, 2&3 £21.50. CSF £92.14 CT £554.46 TOTE £9.20: £2.20, £3.60, £2.70; EX 175.50.
Owner Exors of the Late F C T Wilson **Bred** Mrs C R Philipson & Mrs H G Lascelles **Trained** Manton, Wilts

FOCUS
An ordinary nursery in which the leaders went too fast.

NOTEBOOK
Misty Glade, in contrast to last time out when drawn in stall one, had bagged the best of the draw this time and she enjoyed the perfect trip, racing in midfield on the rail before being switched out to challenge turning into the straight. She saw her race out strongly, as befits a filly who has already won over 6f and placed over 7f, and clearly the strongly run race suited her well. (op 17-2 tchd 13-2)
Final Rhapsody, running in a handicap for the first time, was fast away and got the inside rail, tracking the pacesetting duo. She had every chance. (op 14-1)
Chosen Son(IRE) travelled well held up in midfield, but he went for a gap which closed on him a furlong and a half out, and the loss of momentum no doubt cost him second place. On this evidence he can win a similar event off his current mark. Official explanation: jockey said gelding was denied a clear run (op 5-1)
Casual Style, who bolted up in a seller at Catterick in her one and only previous start back in July, was making her debut for the Pipe stable. Chased along towards the back of the field early on, she found them coming back to her in the straight, but she was always staying on a bit too late. She will have possibilities in similar company if sharper from the gate. (op 11-2)
Royal Raider, off the track since getting beaten at odds-on in a Wolverhampton claimer in August, was another who struggled to go the early gallop, but picked off a few rivals late on. (tchd 7-1)
Sharpener(IRE) was a bit disappointing on her handicap debut, although she was drawn low and raced slightly wider than ideal. (op 10-3)

7309 BETDAQ THE BETTING EXCHANGE CLAIMING STKS 1m 2f (P)
6:20 (6:21) (Class 6) 3-Y-O+ **£2,047** (£604; £302) **Stalls** High

Form RPR

3000 **1** **Sign Of The Cross**[45] 6352 4-9-1 78........................ DaneO'Neill 1 77
(J R Fanshawe) *towards rr: hdwy on outside over 2f out: led 1f out: sn clr* **16/1**

2001 **2** *3 ¼* **Ryedale Ovation (IRE)**[18] 7009 5-9-7 64........................ SimonWhitworth 11 76
(M Hill) *led tl rdn and hdd 1f out: hld on for 2nd* **12/1**

1165 **3** *hd* **Kingsholm**[20] 6985 6-8-11 64........................ JamieSpencer 2 66
(K A Ryan) *mid-div: rdn and hdwy on outside over 1f out: nvr nrr* **4/1**[2]

0554 **4** *½* **Teasing**[28] 6771 4-9-6 69........................ RobertHavlin 8 74
(J Pearce) *in rr: hdwy over 1f out: r.o fnl f: nvr nrr* **16/1**

3161 **5** *nk* **Bridgewater Boys**[15] 7096 7-9-1 70........................(b) RyanMoore 6 68
(G L Moore) *trckd ldr: rdn over 2f out: one pce fnl f* **4/1**[2]

6420 **6** *1* **Wrighty Almighty (IRE)**[33] 6671 6-9-2 69........................(t) LPKeniry 13 69+
(P R Chamings) *t.k.h in mid-div: making hdwy on ins whn short of room ins fnl f* **11/1**

0204 **7** *shd* **Lunar Promise (IRE)**[20] 6985 6-9-3 68........................ GeorgeBaker 3 68
(Ian Williams) *in rr: rdn over 2f out: hdwy fr over 1f out but nvr nr to chal* **7/2**[1]

0045 **8** *¾* **Rapid City**[16] 7068 5-9-1 70........................(p) JamesDoyle 10 65
(A J McCabe) *prom: rdn over 2f out: wknd over 1f out* **7/1**[3]

4100 **9** *1* **Blacktoft (USA)**[24] 6888 5-9-11 75........................(e) J-PGuillambert 9 73+
(S C Williams) *in rr: hdwy whn n.m.r fr wl over 1f out: nvr on terms* **12/1**

0000 **10** *¾* **Prince Charlemagne (IRE)**[27] 6825 5-8-7 55........................(p) FrankieMcDonald 4 53
(R M Stronge) *stdd s: a in rr* **50/1**

4500 **11** *3 ½* **Danski**[11] 3090 5-9-7 72........................ IanMongan 12 60
(Mrs L J Mongan) *prom: rdn 3f out: wknd over 1f out* **33/1**

1223 **12** *6* **Yakimov (USA)**[159] 2867 9-9-3 85........................ PaulMulrennan 5 44
(Ollie Pears) *mid-div tl wknd over 2f out* **7/1**[3]

2m 8.02s (0.02) **Going Correction** +0.225s/f (Slow)
WFA 3 from 4yo+ 4lb **12** Ran SP% **127.6**
Speed ratings (Par 101): **108,105,105,104,104 103,103,103,102,101 98,94**
toteswinger: 1&2 £35.60, 1&3 £13.30, 2&3 £12.10. CSF £209.34 TOTE £20.40: £5.00, £3.30, £2.20; EX 485.80.The winner was claimed by G L Moore for £9,000
Owner T R G Vestey **Bred** T R G Vestey **Trained** Newmarket, Suffolk

FOCUS
A fair claimer with the runner-up perhaps the best guide to the form, which is a bit muddling.
Wrighty Almighty(IRE) Official explanation: jockey said gelding was denied a clear run
Lunar Promise(IRE) Official explanation: jockey said gelding hung left throughout
Yakimov(USA) Official explanation: jockey said gelding never travelled

7310 BET MULTIPLES - BETDAQ CLASSIFIED STKS 1m 3f (P)
6:50 (6:53) (Class 6) 3-Y-O+ **£2,047** (£604; £302) **Stalls** High

Form RPR

066 **1** **Tropical Tradition (IRE)**[29] 6757 3-8-12 55........................ DaneO'Neill 12 65
(D W P Arbuthnot) *mid-div: wnt 2nd 2f out: styd on to ld jst ins fnl f: rdn out* **9/2**[2]

5444 **2** *2* **Trinkila (USA)**[18] 7010 3-8-12 55........................(b) AlanMunro 13 61
(P F I Cole) *led tl rdn and hdd jst ins fnl f: kpt on one pce* **4/1**[1]

504 **3** *1* **The Little Master (IRE)**[31] 6725 4-9-0 50........................ MarcHalford(3) 8 59
(D R C Elsworth) *in rr tl hdwy 2f out: styd on to chse first 2 fnl f* **12/1**

003 **4** *2* **Colonel Sherman (USA)**[24] 6883 3-8-12 50........................ AdamKirby 6 56
(L A Dace) *in rr: styd on fnl 2f: nvr nr to chal* **25/1**

3000 **5** *3 ¾* **Southern Mistral**[18] 7010 3-8-12 55........................ FrancisNorton 11 49
(M Wigham) *mid-div: plugged on one pce fnl 2f* **15/2**

0-00 **6** *3 ¾* **Womaniser (IRE)**[92] 5020 4-9-3 44........................ TonyCulhane 4 42
(T Keddy) *slowly away: rdn 3f out: nvr on terms* **7/1**

4144 **7** *2* **Dazzling Begum**[17] 7050 3-8-12 54........................ RobertHavlin 9 39
(J Pearce) *prom tl wknd over 2f out* **6/1**

0552 **8** *nse* **Too Grand**[72] 5607 3-8-12 54........................ NeilChalmers 2 38
(J J Bridger) *in rr and nvr on terms* **14/1**

6130 **9** *5* **Intersky Melody (USA)**[51] 6217 3-8-12 55........................ EdwardCreighton 7 29
(E J Creighton) *a towards rr: fin lame* **12/1**

0-50 **10** *nk* **First In Show**[37] 6571 3-8-12 49........................ LPKeniry 14 29
(A M Balding) *trckd ldr: wnt 2nd over 3f out: wknd rapidly 2f out* **11/2**[3]

11 *30* **Kingly (IRE)**[152] 3071 3-8-12 42........................ JerryO'Dwyer 5 —
(John Joseph Murphy, Ire) *trckd ldr to over 3f out: wknd qckly: t.o* **25/1**

606 **12** *5* **Bathwick Minstrel**[114] 4302 3-8-12 45........................ FergusSweeney 1 —
(A B Haynes) *mid-div tl wknd over 3f out: t.o* **33/1**

0000 **13** *8* **Aura**[29] 6753 3-8-12 45........................ JamesDoyle 3 —
(H J L Dunlop) *prom: rdn 4f out: sn wknd: t.o whn virtually p.u 1f out* **33/1**

2m 23.28s (1.38) **Going Correction** +0.225s/f (Slow)
WFA 3 from 4yo 5lb **13** Ran SP% **127.7**
Speed ratings (Par 101): **103,101,100,99,96 93,92,92,88,88 66,63,57**
toteswinger: 1&2 £4.80, 1&3 £14.30, 2&3 £12.70. CSF £23.69 TOTE £5.80: £2.00, £1.70, £4.00; EX 26.90.
Owner George Ward **Bred** George Ward **Trained** Compton, Berks

FOCUS
A moderate event, the highlight of which was the gamble on the Tom Keddy-trained Womaniser. The form is limited but sound for the grade.
Tropical Tradition(IRE) Official explanation: trainer said, regarding the apparent improvement in form, that gelding had run green on its first run, and ran well on its last at Great Leighs, having been baulked in running.
Intersky Melody(USA) Official explanation: jockey said gelding hung right throughout; vet said gelding returned lame in front
Aura Official explanation: jockey said filly stopped quickly

7311 BETDAQ.CO.UK EBF MAIDEN STKS (DIV I) 7f (P)
7:20 (7:27) (Class 4) 2-Y-O **£4,209** (£1,252; £625; £312) **Stalls** High

Form RPR

2 **1** **Laudatory**[18] 7011 2-9-3 0........................ AdamKirby 8 74
(W R Swinburn) *towards rr: hdwy on ins 2f out: sustained run to ld ins fnl f* **4/1**[3]

2 *1* **Pezula Bay** 2-9-3 0........................ TPQueally 1 72
(J Noseda) *slowly away: in rr: n.m.r over 2f out hdwy over 1f out: n.m.r ins fnl f but r.o to take 2nd cl home* **16/1**

2 **3** *shd* **Yirga**[17] 7051 2-9-3 0 JamieSpencer 6 71
(Saeed Bin Suroor) *trckd ldr: led wl over 1f out: veered bdly rt then wnt lft bef hdd ins fnl f: lost 2nd cl home* **2/1**[1]
0 **4** *1/2* **Blaise Tower**[18] 7011 2-9-3 0 GeorgeBaker 4 70
(G L Moore) *a front rnk: rdn and kpt on ins fnl f* **33/1**
05 **5** *nk* **Nbhan (USA)**[14] 7106 2-9-3 0 DaneO'Neill 3 69
(L M Cumani) *in rr: styd on fr over 1f out: nvr nrr* **14/1**
4 **6** *2 1/2* **Zim Ho**[24] 6876 2-9-3 0 AlanMunro 14 63
(J Akehurst) *t.k.h: led tl hdd over 1f out: wknd ins fnl f* **11/1**
7 *3* **Tahfeez (IRE)** 2-8-12 0 RyanMoore 9 51
(Sir Michael Stoute) *prom tl wknd wl over 1f out* **12/1**
502 **8** *1 1/2* **Head Down**[147] 3219 2-9-3 83 PatDobbs 7 52
(R Hannon) *in tch: rdn over 2f out: sn btn* **9/4**[2]
9 *1* **Lady Trish** 2-8-12 0 RobertWinston 2 44
(J R Fanshawe) *slowly away: a bhd* **33/1**
0 **10** *3/4* **Fine Tolerance**[8] 7207 2-8-12 0 RobertHavlin 11 42
(J R Boyle) *mid-div: rdn and wknd 2f out* **50/1**
11 *11* **Tahkeem** 2-8-12 0 RHills 10 15
(M P Tregoning) *s.i.s: a in rr* **14/1**

1m 29.44s (3.44) **Going Correction** +0.225s/f (Slow) **11 Ran SP% 127.2**
Speed ratings (Par 98): **89,87,87,87,86 83,80,78,77,76 64**
toteswinger: 1&2 £14.50, 1&3 £2.50, 2&3 £8.90. CSF £70.93 TOTE £6.10: £1.70, £6.30, £1.30; EX 77.40.
Owner Exors Of The Late Mrs P W Harris **Bred** Whitsbury Manor Stud & Pigeon House Stud **Trained** Aldbury, Herts
■ Outsiders Pezula and Sparks Alive were withdrawn after giving trouble at the stalls. No R4.

FOCUS
A fair maiden on paper, featuring one or two interesting types from the bigger stables.

NOTEBOOK
Laudatory ran into a useful-looking rival here on his debut and for a moment it looked as though second was the best he would achieve again, but he took full advantage of the favourite's antics to land an unlikely success. A nice type, he looks to have a future, and despite his pedigree he seems to stay 7f well. (op 7-2 tchd 3-1)
Pezula Bay is a half-brother to Easy Lover, who won twice at two, including over this course and distance, but he was weak in the market on his debut. Drawn out in stall one, he was slowly away and ran green, but his rider got him over to the inside rail and that did him no harm. Keeping on well at the finish, he looks sure to come on a bundle for this, and should be capable of winning a similar race. (op 14-1)
Yirga looked to hold sound claims on his debut second at Yarmouth, and all looked to be going well when he was asked to go on a furlong and a half out, as he quickened up nicely. But he then veered violently right and lost all momentum, letting the winner up his inside. He clearly has a few questions to answer now. (op 5-2)
Blaise Tower was well held on his debut and his pedigree suggests he will come into his own over middle distances next year, so in the circumstances this was an encouraging effort. (op 16-1)
Nbhan(USA) has now had the three runs required for a mark and will be of more interest once he steps into handicap company. (op 12-1)
Zim Ho got a bit warm beforehand and dropped out after being headed inside the final 2f. (tchd 10-1 and 12-1)

7312 BETDAQ.CO.UK EBF MAIDEN STKS (DIV II) 7f (P)
7:50 (7:54) (Class 4) 2-Y-O £4,209 (£1,252; £625; £312) Stalls High

Form RPR
6 **1** **Raaeidd (IRE)**[14] 7104 2-9-3 0 DarryllHolland 9 75
(M A Jarvis) *t.k.h: in tch: hdwy over 1f out: shkn up to ld towards fin* **2/1**[1]
2 *3/4* **Aurora Sky (IRE)** 2-8-12 0 AlanMunro 12 68
(J Akehurst) *a.p: rdn to ld 1/2f out: hdd towards fin* **25/1**
3 *1* **Alsahil (USA)** 2-9-3 0 RHills 6 70
(M P Tregoning) *in tch: led wl over 1f out: hdd 1/2f out: no ex* **11/2**
4 *1/2* **Visite Royale (USA)** 2-8-12 0 RyanMoore 4 64
(Sir Michael Stoute) *trckd ldrs: rdn and sltly outpcd 2f out: styd on fnl f* **11/4**[2]
5 *3* **Fortuni (IRE)** 2-9-3 0 J-PGuillambert 3 62
(Sir Mark Prescott) *s.i.s: in rr: hdwy over 1f out: nvr nrr* **16/1**
6 *1/2* **Global** 2-9-3 0 PatDobbs 13 60
(R Hannon) *towards rr: hdwy over 2f out: one pce appr fnl f* **12/1**
5 **7** *4 1/2* **On The Edge (IRE)**[8] 7214 2-9-3 0 JerryO'Dwyer 14 49
(John Joseph Murphy, Ire) *led tl hdd wl over 1f out: sn btn* **16/1**
0 **8** *1 1/4* **Rubbinghousedotcom (IRE)**[24] 6876 2-9-3 0 IanMongan 2 46
(P M Phelan) *trckd ldr tl rdn and fdd ins fnl 2f* **66/1**
0 **9** *3/4* **Endeavoured (IRE)**[9] 7200 2-9-3 0 JimmyQuinn 10 44
(P D Evans) *mid-div: rdn over 2f out: sn outpcd* **40/1**
00 **10** *hd* **Jonnie Skull (IRE)**[18] 7011 2-9-0 0 MarcHalford(3) 7 44
(D R C Elsworth) *s.i.s: sn in mid-div: rdn and wknd over 2f out* **50/1**
11 *1 3/4* **Spin Sister** 2-8-12 0 FergusSweeney 8 34
(J Gallagher) *a bhd* **50/1**
12 *3/4* **Tropical Duke (IRE)** 2-9-3 0 DaneO'Neill 5 37
(D W P Arbuthnot) *mid-div on outside: rdn and wknd over 2f out* **16/1**
0 **13** *8* **Hope Junior (USA)**[36] 6604 2-9-3 0 JamieSpencer 11 17
(B J Meehan) *a towards rr* **9/2**[3]

1m 29.14s (3.14) **Going Correction** +0.225s/f (Slow) **13 Ran SP% 130.6**
Speed ratings (Par 98): **91,90,89,88,85 84,79,77,77,76 74,73,64**
toteswinger: 1&2 £22.40, 1&3 £4.40, 2&3 £42.30. CSF £67.62 TOTE £3.00: £1.40, £5.50, £2.00; EX 104.60.
Owner Sheikh Ahmed Al Maktoum **Bred** Darley **Trained** Newmarket, Suffolk

FOCUS
They did not seem to go much pace in the early stages, but the final time was 0.3sec quicker than that clocked in the first division.

NOTEBOOK
Raaeidd(IRE) had not run badly on his debut at Newmarket, but that previous experience, coupled with a switch to Polytrack – he is a half-brother to that smart filly Baharah, who has won in Listed company on this surface – promised to see him in a much better light. He looked to be making hard work of it early in the straight, but he really found his stride inside the last and in the end won a shade comfortably. He looks the type to make a better three-year-old, and on this evidence a step up to a mile will be in his favour. (op 9-4)
Aurora Sky(IRE) raced a bit keenly, but held a good position throughout next to the inside rail, and when the gap opened up at the intersection, she grabbed it. She was run out of it late on by a more experienced colt, but this was a promising debut effort, especially considering that her stable's two-year-olds rarely figure in this type of event.
Alsahil(USA), whose dam is a half-sister to Group 2 winners Makderah and Oriental Fashion, is bred to make up into a middle-distance colt next season. He raced fairly wide most of the way and that probably told in the closing stages, but it was a promising enough debut effort. (op 5-1 tchd 6-1)
Visite Royale(USA), closely related to Duchess Royale, who won twice at up to 1m2f, was another who did not shape too badly on her debut, finishing nicely in front of the rest. (op 9-4 tchd 10-3)
Fortuni(IRE), a son of Montjeu who cost 300,000euros, holds a Derby entry. Slowly away, he raced towards the back of the field for most of the race, but caught the eye staying on nicely at the finish. He will be of far more interest when stepped up to middle distances next year. (tchd 20-1)

7313 BETDAQ.CO.UK H'CAP 1m (P)
8:20 (8:22) (Class 2) (0-100,95) 3-Y-O+
£11,215 (£3,358; £1,679; £840; £419; £210) Stalls High

Form RPR
0002 **1** **Commander Cave (USA)**[15] 7101 3-9-5 95 RyanMoore 10 105
(R Hannon) *a.p on ins: led over 2f out: sn clr: comf* **5/2**[2]
0030 **2** *2* **Moynahan (USA)**[13] 7146 3-9-5 95 AlanMunro 5 100
(P F I Cole) *in tch: rdn over 2f out: kpt on to go 2nd ins fnl f: no ch w wnr* **15/2**
5005 **3** *2* **Kayak (SAF)**[35] 6625 6-9-0 88 (b) DarryllHolland 4 88
(D M Simcock) *led tl rdn and hdd over 2f out: kpt on but lost 2nd ins fnl f* **16/1**
1344 **4** *1* **Councellor (FR)**[32] 6710 6-8-11 85 (t) JimmyQuinn 7 83
(Stef Liddiard) *t.k.h: trckd ldr to over 2f out: kpt on one pce after* **11/1**
-011 **5** *1/2* **Multakka (IRE)**[36] 6598 5-8-11 85 RHills 6 82
(M P Tregoning) *s.i.s: hdwy over 2f out: one pce fnl f* **9/4**[1]
0001 **6** *shd* **Samarinda (USA)**[28] 6772 5-9-6 94 AdamKirby 2 91+
(Mrs P Sly) *slowly away: in rr: styd on one pce ins fnl 2f* **9/1**
2051 **7** *2* **Countdown**[30] 6734 6-8-9 83 EddieAhern 9 75
(M D Squance) *in tch tl lost pl 1/2-way: nvr on terms after* **16/1**
5023 **8** *2 1/4* **Murfreesboro**[79] 5405 5-8-12 86 FrancisNorton 3 73
(D Shaw) *a in rr* **16/1**
306 **9** *3/4* **Kay Gee Be (IRE)**[20] 6975 4-9-5 93 TPQueally 1 78
(W Jarvis) *trckd ldrs on outside tl lost pl 3f out* **14/1**
3342 **10** *nk* **Dingaan (IRE)**[8] 7215 5-8-11 85 LPKeniry 8 70
(A M Balding) *t.k.h: in rr whn swtchd lft 2f out: nvr on terms* **7/1**[3]

1m 39.88s (0.08) **Going Correction** +0.225s/f (Slow)
WFA 3 from 4yo+ 2lb **10 Ran SP% 126.3**
Speed ratings (Par 109): **108,106,104,103,102 102,100,98,97,97**
toteswinger: 1&2 £6.80, 1&3 £15.00, 2&3 £22.70. CSF £24.19 CT £272.85 TOTE £3.60: £1.90, £1.80, £3.60; EX 24.20.
Owner Sir David Seale **Bred** R D Hubbard **Trained** East Everleigh, Wilts
■ Stewards' Enquiry : T P Queally two-day ban: careless riding (Nov 28-29)

FOCUS
A decent handicap, although the top-weight's mark was 6lb below the ceiling for the race. Not much got into it from the rear. The winner is rated back to his best early 3yo form.

NOTEBOOK
Commander Cave(USA), who had the best of the draw, had the rail to help rounding the turn into the straight and picked off the leader soon afterwards. He went for home plenty soon enough, but kept galloping on strongly, and this looked a career-best effort from him. His connections have a couple of races on the Polytrack in mind for him before the year is out, but at this rate he could be a candidate for honours out in Dubai in the new year. The dirt surface out there should certainly suit him. (op 9-4)
Moynahan(USA) completed a one-two for the three-year-olds in the race. More at home on this surface than the soft ground he raced on at Newmarket last time, he has dropped back to a mark off which he can be competitive in handicap company, and having proven his ability to handle this surface he will be interesting in similar company. (op 17-2 tchd 10-1)
Kayak(SAF) set a decent gallop out in front, so it is to his credit that he was able to hang on to third place. He could do with dropping a few more pounds in the handicap, though. (op 20-1 tchd 14-1)
Councellor(FR) put up another sound effort in defeat. The handicapper knows where he stands with him, though, so he is likely to remain vulnerable to more progressive animals. (op 14-1 tchd 10-1)
Multakka(IRE) was 6lb higher and up in class chasing a hat-trick, and having raced quite keenly in the early stages, he was not quite up to the task. (op 5-2 tchd 11-4)
Samarinda(USA) has a good record here, having won three times over this distance in the past, but, running off a 4lb higher mark for his most recent success, he could never get close enough to throw down a challenge. (op 12-1 tchd 14-1)

7314 LOOK FOR BETTER ODDS AT BETDAQ H'CAP 1m 4f (P)
8:50 (8:52) (Class 4) (0-85,83) 3-Y-O+ £5,180 (£1,541; £770; £384) Stalls Centre

Form RPR
5546 **1** **Press The Button (GER)**[18] 7025 5-9-10 83 PatCosgrave 6 91
(J R Boyle) *trckd ldrs: led over 1f out: r.o wl* **4/1**[1]
6010 **2** *1 1/4* **Apache Fort**[7] 7230 5-8-13 72 (b) TonyCulhane 14 78
(T Keddy) *mid-div: hdwy over 2f out: wnt 2nd appr fnl f: no imp on wnr* **20/1**
2150 **3** *1 1/2* **Bassinet (USA)**[99] 4771 4-9-3 76 GeorgeBaker 13 80
(J A R Toller) *in rr: gd hdwy over 1f out: r.o: nvr nrr* **14/1**
0155 **4** *1 1/4* **Taikoo**[20] 6974 3-8-11 76 SteveDrowne 3 78
(H Morrison) *trckd ldr: led 7f out: hdd over 1f out: no ex ins fnl f* **8/1**
4-16 **5** *nse* **Sam Lord**[118] 4191 4-9-10 83 DaneO'Neill 11 85+
(A King) *in rr: hdwy whn swtchd rt ins fnl f: r.o: nvr nrr* **8/1**
4646 **6** *nk* **Indian Skipper (IRE)**[21] 6949 3-8-8 73 PaulMulrennan 8 74
(M H Tompkins) *towards rr: hdwy on ins 2f out: kpt on one pce* **15/2**
05-0 **7** *1/2* **Dundry**[23] 6898 7-8-13 72 (p) FergusSweeney 4 72+
(G L Moore) *in tch: kpt on one pce ins fnl 2f* **16/1**
3265 **8** *1 3/4* **Summer Winds**[8] 7211 3-8-11 76 HayleyTurner 12 73
(T G Mills) *trckd ldrs: rdn over 2f out: wknd over 1f out* **13/2**[3]
1650 **9** *1 1/4* **Aegean Prince**[69] 5699 4-9-5 78 PatDobbs 9 73
(R Hannon) *in rr: nvr on terms* **16/1**
5264 **10** *1* **King Supreme (IRE)**[25] 6866 3-8-12 77 (b) RyanMoore 5 71
(R Hannon) *a towards rr* **4/1**[1]
0-00 **11** *2 1/4* **Woolfall Blue (IRE)**[46] 6346 5-9-4 77 AdamKirby 1 67
(G G Margarson) *led for 5f: rdn over 2f out: wknd qckly over 1f out* **25/1**
4430 **12** *1/2* **Hucking Hero (IRE)**[21] 6949 3-8-12 77 LPKeniry 10 66
(J R Best) *a bhd* **25/1**
0000 **13** *1 3/4* **Agapanthus (GER)**[18] 7025 3-9-1 80 TPQueally 7 67
(A P Stringer) *hld up in rr: rdn over 2f out: sn btn* **50/1**
1134 **14** *hd* **Mutamaasek (USA)**[18] 7025 6-9-5 78 KirstyMilczarek 2 64
(Lady Herries) *in rr: hdwy 5f out: rdn and wknd over 2f out* **11/2**[2]

2m 36.21s (1.71) **Going Correction** +0.225s/f (Slow)
WFA 3 from 4yo+ 6lb **14 Ran SP% 135.6**
Speed ratings (Par 105): **103,102,101,100,100 100,99,98,97,97 95,95,94,93**
toteswinger: 1&2 £17.70, 1&3 £24.30, 2&3 £88.50. CSF £100.10 CT £1091.12 TOTE £6.00: £2.80, £6.10, £3.20; EX 179.00.
Owner Brian McAtavey **Bred** Gestut Sommerberg **Trained** Epsom, Surrey

The Form Book, Raceform Ltd, Compton, RG20 6NL

FOCUS
Quite an open handicap. It was not that strongly run and it seemed best to race prominently. The winner was back to his best with the runner-up to form.

7315 BACK OR LAY AT BETDAQ H'CAP 6f (P)
9:20 (9:21) (Class 5) (0-75,75) 3-Y-0+ **£2,590** (£770; £385; £192) **Stalls** High

Form RPR
6052 **1** **Resplendent Alpha**[55] 6125 4-9-2 **73** .... JimmyQuinn 11 85
(P Howling) *stdd s: hdwy on ins 2f out: r.o to ld ins fnl f: r.o wl* **8/1**
6115 **2** 1 1/2 **Tubby Isaacs**[46] 6340 4-9-1 **72** .... SteveDrowne 7 79+
(P J Makin) *slowly away: hdwy whn short of room 2f out: rallied and r.o to go 2nd nr fin but no ch w wnr* **5/4**[1]
3004 **3** 3/4 **Asian Power (IRE)**[24] 6881 3-9-1 **72** .... DarryllHolland 12 77
(P J O'Gorman) *led after 2f: rdn and hdd ins fnl f: lost 2nd nr fin* **11/2**[2]
0204 **4** shd **Magical Speedfit (IRE)**[50] 6232 3-9-1 **72** .... DaneO'Neill 9 77
(G G Margarson) *a in tch: rdn over 2f out: kpt on one pce* **22/1**
2322 **5** 1 1/4 **Make My Dream**[16] 7081 5-9-2 **73** .... FergusSweeney 8 74
(J Gallagher) *mid-div: kpt on one pce ins fnl 2f* **10/1**
043 **6** 2 3/4 **C'Mon You Irons (IRE)**[18] 7013 3-8-8 **72** ....(b) AndreaAtzeni(7) 3 64
(M R Hoad) *in tch: rdn over 2f out: no hdwy after* **14/1**
0003 **7** 1 3/4 **Royal Envoy (IRE)**[21] 6952 5-9-2 **73** .... IanMongan 2 59
(P Howling) *in tch on outside: wknd over 1f out* **13/2**[3]
0350 **8** shd **Millfield (IRE)**[30] 6738 5-9-1 **72** .... TravisBlock 5 58
(P R Chamings) *slowly away: a towards rr* **14/1**
2204 **9** 2 **Charles Darwin (IRE)**[38] 6556 5-9-3 **74** .... LPKeniry 10 54
(M Blanshard) *chsd ldrs tl wknd qckly appr fnl f* **16/1**
4040 **10** 11 **Doctor Hilary**[33] 6680 6-9-4 **75** ....(v) RobertHavlin 6 19
(A B Haynes) *outpcd: a bhd* **33/1**
0550 **11** 3/4 **Loose Caboose (IRE)**[17] 7047 3-9-3 **74** ....(p) PatCosgrave 4 16
(A J McCabe) *led for 2f: rdn over 2f out: wknd qckly* **25/1**

1m 13.9s (0.80) **Going Correction** +0.225s/f (Slow) 11 Ran SP% **123.7**
Speed ratings (Par 103): **103,101,100,99,98 94,92,92,89,74 73**
toteswinger: 1&2 £6.60, 1&3 £5.80, 2&3 £3.50. CSF £18.94 CT £67.41 TOTE £11.10: £2.90, £1.30, £2.20; EX 27.20 Place 6 £ 219.01, Place 5 £ 61.52.
Owner The Oh So Sharp Racing Partnership **Bred** Sunley Stud **Trained** Newmarket, Suffolk

FOCUS
A fair handicap run in an ordinary time for the grade. The form is probably pretty sound.
Tubby Isaacs Official explanation: jockey said gelding missed the break
Doctor Hilary Official explanation: trainer said gelding was found to have been struck into
T/Plt: £313.40 to a £1 stake. Pool: £88,423.44. 205.91 winning tickets. T/Qpdt: £19.10 to a £1 stake. Pool: £8,125.58. 313.60 winning tickets. JS

7279 SOUTHWELL (L-H)
Friday, November 14

OFFICIAL GOING: Standard
Wind: Light behind Weather: Dry and overcast

7316 SOUTHWELL-RACECOURSE.CO.UK H'CAP (DIV I) 7f (F)
12:10 (12:10) (Class 6) (0-60,63) 3-Y-0+ **£1,706** (£503; £252) **Stalls** Low

Form RPR
4620 **1** **Mrs Bun**[9] 7197 3-8-9 **50** ....(p) DarryllHolland 5 61
(K A Ryan) *in tch on outer: hdwy 2f out: rdn over 1f out: styd on ins fnl f to ld last 75yds* **14/1**
0024 **2** 3/4 **Betteras Bertie**[4] 7267 5-8-10 **50** .... FrancisNorton 12 59
(M Brittain) *dwlt: in tch: hdwy over 2f out: chsd ldrs whn swtchd lft and rdn over 1f out: styd on to ld jst ins fnl f: drvn and hdd last 75yds* **3/1**[2]
0000 **3** 1 1/4 **Solicitude**[27] 6821 5-9-1 **55** ....(p) PatCosgrave 9 61
(D Haydn Jones) *cl up: led 3f out: rdn 2f out: drvn wl over 1f out: hdd jst ins fnl f: kpt on same pce* **9/1**
0050 **4** 1 **Sedge (USA)**[27] 6827 8-9-1 **55** ....(p) JamieMoriarty 2 58
(P T Midgley) *towards rr and pushed along: rdn and hdwy over 2f out: kpt on wl fnl f: nrst fin* **16/1**
6041 **5** 1 3/4 **Tender Process (IRE)**[7] 7228 5-9-9 **63** 6ex........(b) PaulHanagan 10 61
(R A Fahey) *cl up: effrt and ev ch over 2f out: sn rdn and one pce* **5/2**[1]
0003 **6** 1 1/4 **Hollywood George**[17] 7049 4-8-0 **47** ....(p) AdeleRothery(7) 3 42
(Miss M E Rowland) *trckd ldrs: hdwy 3f out: effrt and ev ch 2f out: sn rdn and wknd appr fnl f* **25/1**
0006 **7** 3 1/4 **Marvin Gardens**[29] 6752 5-8-0 **45** .... KellyHarrison(5) 6 31
(P S McEntee) *trckd ldrs on inner: hdwy over 2f out: rdn wl over 1f out and grad wknd* **66/1**
0002 **8** 3 3/4 **Kirkie (USA)**[7] 7226 3-9-5 **60** .... DNolan 7 36
(S Parr) *led: rdn along and hdd 3f out: drvn over 2f out and grad wknd* **11/2**[3]
10-0 **9** 1 1/4 **Whistleupthewind**[169] 2550 5-8-10 **53** .... LukeMorris(3) 11 26
(J M P Eustace) *nvr nr ldrs* **50/1**
3500 **10** nk **Jellytot (USA)**[10] 7184 5-8-12 **57** ow12........ JamesO'Reilly(5) 1 29
(J O'Reilly) *a towards rr* **80/1**
5000 **11** nk **Alabama Spirit (USA)**[16] 7072 3-8-11 **52** .... EdwardCreighton 14 23
(P Howling) *a in rr* **33/1**
0613 **12** 31 **Scruffy Skip (IRE)**[15] 7102 3-8-13 **54** .... HayleyTurner 13 —
(Mrs C A Dunnett) *in tch on outer: rdn along after 2f: sn lost pl and bhd* **7/1**
0000 **U** **Sir Douglas**[154] 2988 5-9-3 **57** ....(t) DavidAllan 4 —
(M A Barnes) *stmbld and uns rdr leaving stalls* **33/1**

1m 28.38s (-1.92) **Going Correction** -0.35s/f (Stan)
WFA 3 from 4yo+ 1lb 13 Ran SP% **118.4**
Speed ratings (Par 101): **96,95,93,92,90 89,85,81,79,79 79,43,—**
toteswinger: 1&2 £10.20, 1&3 £26.90, 2&3 £8.40. CSF £53.29 CT £427.47 TOTE £14.90: £2.10, £1.40, £2.90; EX 76.30 TRIFECTA Not won..
Owner Guy Reed **Bred** Guy Reed **Trained** Hambleton, N Yorks

FOCUS
An open race for this moderate handicap but it seemed best to race close to the pace and the principals came centre to stands' side in the straight. Sound form.

7317 PLAY GOLF AT SOUTHWELL GOLF CLUB CLAIMING STKS 7f (F)
12:40 (12:40) (Class 6) 3-Y-0+ **£2,047** (£604; £302) **Stalls** Low

Form RPR
0455 **1** **Another Genepi (USA)**[12] 7152 5-8-9 67........(b) EdwardCreighton 4 74
(E J Creighton) *trckd ldrs: hdwy wl over 2f out: sn cl up: rdn to ld over 1f out: drvn ins fnl f and kpt on wl* **25/1**
0004 **2** 3/4 **Nastrelli (IRE)**[10] 7181 5-9-3 87........ NeilBrown(3) 1 83
(T D Barron) *hld up: hdwy over 2f out: rdn over 1f out: styd on wl u.p ins fnl f* **6/1**
6020 **3** 1 1/2 **Dancing Deano (IRE)**[12] 7153 6-8-11 64........ RussellKennemore(3) 5 73
(R Hollinshead) *trckd ldrs: hdwy 3f out: cl up 2f out: rdn and ev ch over 1f out: drvn and one pce ins fnl f* **16/1**
6045 **4** 1/2 **He's A Humbug (IRE)**[25] 6859 4-9-6 80........(p) DarryllHolland 11 78
(K A Ryan) *chsd ldrs towards outer: effrt over 2f out: rdn wl over 1f out: kpt on u.p ins fnl f* **5/1**[3]
6013 **5** 1 1/4 **Elusive Warrior (USA)**[12] 7153 5-8-12 73........(p) JamesDoyle 12 66
(A J McCabe) *cl up: led over 3f out: rdn over 2f out: drvn and hdd over 1f out: sn wknd* **9/2**[2]
0106 **6** 3 1/4 **Flying Applause**[43] 6416 3-9-1 74........ LPKeniry 10 61
(S R Bowring) *led: rdn along and hdd over 3f out: drvn over 2f out and grad wknd* **12/1**
0251 **7** hd **Varadouro (BRZ)**[109] 4476 6-9-6 78........ RichardKingscote 3 65
(Tom Dascombe) *in tch on inner: rdn along wl over 2f out: drvn and wknd wl over 1f out* **9/4**[1]
125 **8** 2 **Ballycroy Boy (IRE)**[17] 7048 3-9-11 75........ NeilChalmers 2 66
(A Bailey) *hld up: in rr tl sme late hdwy* **20/1**
0346 **9** 1/2 **Royal Applord**[18] 7018 3-8-11 68........(p) PaulMulrennan 14 50
(K A Ryan) *dwlt: sn prom: rdn along 3f out: drvn over 2f out and sn wknd* **16/1**
0000 **10** nk **Flying Bantam (IRE)**[8] 7206 7-8-6 67........ PaulHanagan 13 43
(R A Fahey) *nvr nr ldrs* **14/1**
0000 **11** 1 **Copperbottomed (IRE)**[18] 7018 3-8-8 52........(e) FrancisNorton 9 44
(P G Murphy) *a towards rr* **50/1**
5004 **12** 2 1/2 **Mystic Roll**[49] 6255 5-8-12 52........ FrankieMcDonald 7 40
(Jane Chapple-Hyam) *a in rr* **33/1**
03- **13** nk **World Of Choice (USA)**[387] 6417 3-9-5 0........ DaleGibson 6 47
(M W Easterby) *dwlt: a in rr* **28/1**
0 **14** 16 **Highland Relish**[16] 7084 3-8-1 0 ow3........ MatthewDavies(7) 8 —
(George Baker) *sn rdn along and a bhd* **100/1**

1m 27.68s (-2.62) **Going Correction** -0.35s/f (Stan)
WFA 3 from 4yo+ 1lb 14 Ran SP% **124.0**
Speed ratings (Par 101): **100,99,97,96,95 91,91,89,88,88 87,84,83,65**
toteswinger: 1&2 £22.70, 1&3 £25.70, 2&3 £24.50. CSF £166.06 TOTE £21.00: £6.90, £2.90, £5.80; EX 143.70 TRIFECTA Not won..
Owner A S Reid **Bred** Joseph Lacombe Stables Inc **Trained** Mill Hill, London NW7

FOCUS
A typical claimer with the runners possessing a range of abilities but the time was seven tenths of a second faster than the opener. Again it seemed best to race close to the leaders. The form is sound enough with the winner back to the level of her best.

7318 SOUTHWELL-RACECOURSE.CO.UK MAIDEN AUCTION STKS 7f (F)
1:10 (1:10) (Class 6) 2-Y-0 **£2,047** (£604; £302) **Stalls** Low

Form RPR
00 **1** **Moon Lightning (IRE)**[45] 6359 2-9-1 0........ PaulMulrennan 1 67
(M H Tompkins) *trckd ldrs on inner: smooth hdwy 3f out: led 1 1/2f out: rdn ins fnl f and styd on wl* **15/2**
2 1 3/4 **Navy (USA)** 2-8-4 0........ SRuis 3 52
(D W P Arbuthnot) *cl up: led after 2 1/2f: rdn 2f out: hdd 1 1/2f out: edgd rt and kpt on ins fnl f* **8/1**
050 **3** 1 3/4 **Darwin's Dragon**[30] 6737 2-8-13 72........ LPKeniry 10 56
(P F I Cole) *chsd ldrs: swtchd lft over 2f out and sn rdn: drvn and kpt on same pce appr fnl f* **10/3**[1]
40 **4** 1 **Special Bond**[21] 6945 2-8-10 0........ TPQueally 8 51
(J A Osborne) *trckd ldrs: hdwy over 2f out: rdn wl over 1f out: sn drvn and no imp appr fnl f* **10/3**[1]
5 1 1/4 **Magical Destiny (IRE)** 2-9-3 0........ TomEaves 5 60+
(B Smart) *s.i.s and sn rdn along: bhd tl styd on wl fnl 2f: nrst fin* **5/1**[2]
0 **6** 1 **Paint Splash**[34] 6655 2-8-4 0........ PaulFessey 11 39
(T D Barron) *in tch on outer: rdn along and outpcd 3f out: styd on u.p fnl 2f* **14/1**
0600 **7** 2 **That Boy Ronaldo**[10] 7179 2-8-8 47........ FrancisNorton 9 38
(A Berry) *in rr tl sme late hdwy* **100/1**
8 2 **Vodka Shot (USA)** 2-8-10 0........ HayleyTurner 4 35
(M L W Bell) *chsd ldrs: rdn along over 2f out: sn drvn and wknd* **6/1**[3]
00 **9** 1 3/4 **Jack's House (IRE)**[16] 7079 2-8-11 0........(t) FrankieMcDonald 7 32
(Jane Chapple-Hyam) *led 2 1/2f: cl up tl rdn along wl over 2f out and sn wknd* **16/1**
50 **10** 15 **Reigning In Rio (IRE)**[133] 3669 2-8-10 0........ DarryllHolland 6 —
(P C Haslam) *cl up: rdn along 3f out: sn wknd* **14/1**

1m 29.41s (-0.89) **Going Correction** -0.35s/f (Stan) 10 Ran SP% **120.2**
Speed ratings (Par 94): **91,89,87,85,84 83,81,78,76,59**
toteswinger: 1&2 £10.80, 1&3 £6.50, 2&3 £6.50. CSF £68.25 TOTE £9.50: £3.20, £2.90, £1.30; EX 109.00 TRIFECTA Not won..
Owner David P Noblett **Bred** Miss Carmel McGinn **Trained** Newmarket, Suffolk

FOCUS
An open-looking median auction and not surprisingly the time was slower than the preceding older-horse races over the trip.

NOTEBOOK
Moon Lightning(IRE), a market drifter on this all-weather debut, was always going well and got the better of the newcomer over a furlong out to win nicely. He should not be overburdened in handicaps after this success. (op 11-2)
Navy(USA), a $3,200 half-sister to a multiple US winner, put up a fine effort on this debut. She dwelt at the start but soon recovered to lead and went well until the more experienced winner took her measure. She has a bit of size about her and looks to have scope for improvement with this under her belt. (tchd 10-1)
Darwin's Dragon, whose best effort in three starts was over 7f on Polytrack, settled behind the leaders but had to work hard to deliver a challenge and had nothing in reserve for the last furlong. (op 7-2 tchd 4-1 and 3-1)
Special Bond made a rather tardy start but got through on the rail to be close enough early in the straight, only for the effort to flatten out. She now qualifies for a handicap mark. (op 7-2 tchd 3-1)
Magical Destiny(IRE) cost 55,000gns earlier this year but was resold recently for only £800. He missed the break badly and was virtually tailed off leaving the back straight, but got the hang of things once in line for home and passed a number of rivals to reach his final placing. (op 7-1 tchd 15-2)
Vodka Shot(USA) tracked the leaders but was quite keen and gradually faded under pressure. (tchd 5-1 and 13-2, tchd 7-1 in places)

7319 HOSPITALITY PACKAGES AVAILABLE (S) STKS 6f (F)
1:40 (1:40) (Class 6) 2-Y-0 **£2,047** (£604; £302) **Stalls** Low

Form RPR
0000 **1** **Monte Mayor Eagle**[26] 6837 2-8-6 47........(b[1]) FrancisNorton 3 55
(D Haydn Jones) *midfield: gd hdwy over 2f out: swtchd rt and rdn over 1f out: styd on to ld ins fnl f: sn edgd lft: kpt on* **25/1**

4403 **2** 2 1/2 **Forever's Girl**[21] 6953 2-8-3 65 .... DuranFentiman(3) 2 48
(G R Oldroyd) *trckd ldrs: hdwy wl over 2f out: rdn to ld over 1f out: drvn and hdd ins fnl f: kpt on same pce* **9/4**[1]

4503 **3** 2 1/2 **Courageous Nature (IRE)**[2] 7281 2-9-2 56 ....(b) PatCosgrave 7 50
(A J McCabe) *chsd ldrs: hdwy over 2f out: rdn wl over 1f out: kpt on same pce* **10/3**[2]

0004 **4** 3/4 **Dontforgetturshovel**[4] 7269 2-8-11 42 ....(v) TPQueally 10 43
(J Pearce) *prom: effrt to ld over 2f out: rdn and hdd over 1f out: sn drvn and wknd* **6/1**

0 **5** 5 **Waterstown (IRE)**[11] 7168 2-8-11 0 .... PaulHanagan 6 28
(R A Fahey) *prom: rdn along over 2f out: sn drvn and wknd over 1f out* **5/1**[3]

5000 **6** 1 3/4 **Kneesy Earsy Nosey**[57] 6059 2-8-11 44 .... HayleyTurner 4 23
(Miss A Stokell) *towards rr: rdn along and sme hdwy fnl 2f: nvr a factor* **10/1**

0030 **7** 1/2 **Sorrel Ridge (IRE)**[37] 6579 2-8-6 48 .... NicolPolli(5) 13 21
(M G Quinlan) *led: rdn along 3f out: drvn and hdd over 2f out: sn wknd* **16/1**

6006 **8** 1 1/2 **Moon Warrior**[4] 7269 2-8-4 30 .... AndrewHeffernan(7) 8 17
(C Smith) *a towards rr* **50/1**

00 **9** 1 1/4 **Eyesore**[57] 6051 2-7-13 0 .... StacyRenwick(7) 12 8
(R C Guest) *cl up: rdn along wl over 2f out and sn wknd* **66/1**

0 **10** 1 **Belle Choisir**[29] 6764 2-8-7 0 ow1 .... TomEaves 1 6
(B Smart) *a in rr* **18/1**

0 **11** 3 1/2 **Senorita Mirasol**[123] 4027 2-8-6 0 .... PaulFessey 5 —
(K A Ryan) *dwlt: a in rr* **14/1**

1m 15.65s (-0.85) **Going Correction** -0.35s/f (Stan) 11 Ran SP% **119.0**
Speed ratings (Par 94): **91,87,84,83,76 74,73,71,70,68 64**
toteswinger: 1&2 £14.50, 1&3 £23.10, 2&3 £2.20. CSF £81.48 TOTE £31.90: £7.20, £1.30, £1.80; EX 120.00 TRIFECTA Not won..The winner was bought in for 4,250gns
Owner Miss Gillian Byrne **Bred** Ink Pot Partnership **Trained** Efail Isaf, Rhondda C Taff

FOCUS
A typical juvenile seller.

NOTEBOOK
Monte Mayor Eagle swept down the outside to catch the favourite inside the last furlong. She had been well beaten on her previous runs on a good and fast ground and Polytrack, but this daughter of Captain Rio proved well suited by this more testing surface. (op 16-1)
Forever's Girl, whose best previous efforts were on Polytrack and here on Fibresand, was produced to have every chance and beat the rest well enough, but could do nothing about the winner's late challenge. She looks capable of winning a similar contest. (op 10-3)
Courageous Nature(IRE), another proven on this surface, was produced over a furlong out but could only keep on at the one pace. (op 9-4)
Dontforgetturshovel was again keen in the visor despite the drop in trip and might be worth running at 5f and being given his head. (op 7-1 tchd 8-1 and 11-2)
Waterstown(IRE) showed up early and kept going in the straight. (tchd 13-2)

7320 SOUTHWELL-RACECOURSE.CO.UK H'CAP (DIV II) 7f (F)
2:15 (2:15) (Class 6) (0-60,60) 3-Y-0+ **£1,706** (£503; £252) **Stalls** Low

Form RPR

0021 **1** **Mozayada (USA)**[4] 7270 4-8-11 51 6ex .... FrancisNorton 9 75+
(M Brittain) *mde all: shkn up and qckn clr over 2f out: comf* **4/5**[1]

3002 **2** 2 3/4 **Ugenius**[23] 6913 4-8-9 49 .... TPQueally 7 66
(Mrs C A Dunnett) *hld up in midfield: hdwy on inner over 2f out: rdn wl over 1f out: styd on to chse wnr ins fnl f: no imp* **14/1**

5652 **3** 1 3/4 **Rosie Says No**[18] 7021 3-9-4 59 ....(p) EddieAhern 3 70
(R M H Cowell) *in tch on inner: hdwy over 2f out: rdn wl over 1f out: kpt on u.p fnl f* **9/1**[3]

0656 **4** 1 3/4 **Jojesse**[60] 5970 4-8-5 45 .... PaulQuinn 10 52
(G A Swinbank) *towards rr: wd st: gd hdwy on outer 2f out: sn rdn and styd on appr fnl f: nrst fin* **33/1**

1222 **5** 1/2 **Palais Polaire**[15] 7102 6-9-1 55 ....(p) TravisBlock 1 61
(J A Geake) *trckd ldrs: hdwy to chse wnr wl over 2f out: sn rdn and wknd over 1f out* **16/1**

0050 **6** 3/4 **Very Well Red**[23] 6899 5-8-1 48 .... MatthewDavies(7) 12 52
(P W Hiatt) *cl up: rdn along over 2f out: sn drvn and grad wknd* **8/1**[2]

2504 **7** 1 **Outer Hebrides**[32] 6693 7-8-8 53 ....(v) MCGeran(5) 11 54
(J M Bradley) *chsd ldrs: rdn along over 2f out: grad wknd* **20/1**

0032 **8** 1/2 **Fantasy Fighter (IRE)**[29] 6751 3-8-5 46 .... HayleyTurner 6 45
(J J Quinn) *plld hrd: chsd ldrs: rdn along wl over 2f out and sn wknd* **16/1**

0002 **9** 1 3/4 **Optical Illusion (USA)**[16] 7072 4-9-1 55 .... PaulHanagan 13 50
(R A Fahey) *chsd ldrs: rdn along wl over 2f out: sn drvn and wknd* **14/1**

0503 **10** 1 1/2 **Zamalik (USA)**[10] 7176 5-9-2 56 .... PatCosgrave 14 47
(Mrs A Duffield) *towards rr: wd st: effrt and sme hdwy on outer 2f out: sn rdn and nvr a factor* **14/1**

6630 **11** hd **Lady Fas (IRE)**[18] 7013 5-7-12 45 .... StacyRenwick(7) 4 36
(A W Carroll) *a towards rr* **40/1**

0050 **12** 1 3/4 **Royal Acclamation (IRE)**[17] 7040 3-9-5 60 .... PaulFessey 8 45
(G A Harker) *sn rdn along and a in rr* **33/1**

1m 27.61s (-2.69) **Going Correction** -0.35s/f (Stan)
WFA 3 from 4yo+ 1lb 50 Ran SP% **121.5**
Speed ratings (Par 101): **101,97,95,93,93 92,91,90,88,87 86,84**
toteswinger: 1&2 £8.00, 1&3 £2.90, 2&3 £15.00. CSF £13.63 CT £72.78 TOTE £1.90: £1.30, £3.50, £2.30; EX 13.60 Trifecta £57.80 Pool: £409.93, 5.24 winning units.
Owner Mel Brittain **Bred** Shadwell Farm LLC **Trained** Warthill, N Yorks

FOCUS
Another modest handicap though the winning time was 0.77 seconds faster than the first division. Solid form for the grade awith further improvement from Mozayada.

7321 HOSPITALITY AT SOUTHWELL RACECOURSE MAIDEN STKS 7f (F)
2:50 (2:52) (Class 5) 3-Y-0 **£2,729** (£806; £403) **Stalls** Low

Form RPR

52 **1** **Taqdeyr**[28] 6791 3-9-3 0 .... DarryllHolland 5 88+
(M A Jarvis) *t.k.h: trckd ldrs: hdwy to ld on bit over 2f out: sn pushed clr: easily* **2/5**[1]

0045 **2** 7 **Balata**[36] 4090 3-9-3 65 .... TPQueally 8 63
(B R Millman) *chsd ldrs: hdwy on outer 2f out: sn rdn and kpt on ent fnl f: no ch w wnr* **8/1**[2]

00- **3** 2 3/4 **Daggerman**[426] 5428 3-9-3 0 .... GrahamGibbons 3 55
(P A Blockley) *led: rdn and hdd over 2f out: sn drvn and one pce* **66/1**

4 2 1/4 **Sixth Zak** 3-9-3 0 .... PaulEddery 6 49
(S R Bowring) *cl up: rdn along over 2f out: drvn wl over 1f out and kpt on same pce* **33/1**

53 **5** shd **Superior Duchess**[71] 5652 3-8-12 0 .... FrankieMcDonald 1 44
(Jane Chapple-Hyam) *chsd ldrs: rdn along on inner 2f out: drvn wl over 1f out and sn outpcd* **8/1**[2]

4540 **6** 1 **Imperial Djay (IRE)**[102] 4686 3-8-10 60 .... StacyRenwick(7) 10 46
(G J Smith) *in rr: hdwy 2f out: swtchd lft and rdn over 1f out: kpt on ins fnl f: nrst fin* **20/1**

000 **7** 1 1/4 **Curly Brown**[32] 6707 3-9-3 45 ....(p) NeilChalmers 4 43
(A Bailey) *dwlt: hdwy 1/2-way: rdn to chse ldrs over 2f out: sn wknd* **66/1**

-50 **8** 1 3/4 **Edmondstown Lass (IRE)**[16] 7074 3-8-12 63 ....(p) PaulHanagan 12 33
(R A Fahey) *t.k.h: chsd ldrs: rdn along 3f out and sn outpcd* **14/1**[3]

000 **9** 5 **Lavender And Lace**[82] 5318 3-8-7 40 ....(bt[1]) KellyHarrison(5) 7 20
(T Keddy) *a in rr* **66/1**

3-05 **10** 2 3/4 **Wannarock (IRE)**[9] 7201 3-9-0 70 .... RussellKennemore(3) 2 17
(M C Chapman) *a in rr* **18/1**

11 8 **Mickys Mate** 3-9-3 0 .... TomEaves 11 —
(A Crook) *in tch on wd outside: rdn along 1/2-way: sn lost pl and bhd* **25/1**

1m 27.24s (-3.06) **Going Correction** -0.35s/f (Stan) 11 Ran SP% **121.6**
Speed ratings (Par 102): **103,95,91,89,89 88,86,84,78,75 66**
toteswinger: 1&2 £2.50, 1&3 £13.70, 2&3 £25.60. CSF £4.08 TOTE £1.40: £1.10, £1.90, £15.40; EX 5.20 Trifecta £471.80 Part won. Pool: £637.64, 0.67 winning units..
Owner Richie Baines & Stephen Dartnell **Bred** Darley **Trained** Newmarket, Suffolk

FOCUS
A modest and uncompetitive three-year-old maiden and they bet 14-1 bar three, but in the event it was a one-horse race and a very easy first success for the hot favourite. The form is rated around the runner-up. The time was 0.37secs faster than the next quickest of the five races over the trip on the day.
Curly Brown Official explanation: jockey said gelding missed the break
Lavender And Lace Official explanation: trainer said filly finished distressed

7322 HOSPITALITY AT SOUTHWELL RACECOURSE H'CAP 1m 4f (F)
3:25 (3:25) (Class 6) (0-52,52) 3-Y-0+ **£2,047** (£604; £302) **Stalls** Low

Form RPR

-300 **1** **Fortunella**[137] 3555 3-8-8 49 .... KirstyMilczarek 12 56
(Miss Gay Kelleway) *trckd ldrs: hdwy 4f out: rdn to ld 1 1/2f out: drvn and edgd lft ent fnl f: hld on* **11/1**

3043 **2** 3/4 **Piverina (IRE)**[18] 7010 3-8-9 50 .... TomEaves 11 55
(Miss J A Camacho) *midfield: hdwy 4f out: rdn to chse ldrs 2f out: drvn and kpt on ins fnl f* **4/1**[1]

3001 **3** shd **Sparkling Montjeu (IRE)**[2] 6747 3-8-11 52 .... EddieAhern 8 57
(George Baker) *hld up in tch: hdwy 3f out: rdn wl over 1f out: sn drvn and styd on ins fnl f* **4/1**[1]

6315 **4** 1 **Bollin Freddie**[17] 7039 4-8-13 48 .... TonyHamilton 14 51
(A J Lockwood) *cl up: effrt to chal 3f out: sn rdn and ev ch tl drvn and one pce appr fnl f* **9/2**[2]

2-00 **5** 2 1/2 **Intensifier (IRE)**[33] 6668 4-9-2 51 ....(v[1]) GrahamGibbons 6 50
(D L Williams) *led: rdn along 3f out: drvn and hdd 1 1/2f out: grad wknd* **5/1**[3]

5005 **6** 5 **Summer Bounty**[29] 6753 12-8-11 46 .... PaulHanagan 5 37
(F Jordan) *hld up in rr: hdwy 3f out: rdn along 2f out and sn no imp* **14/1**

0400 **7** 1 1/2 **Qaasi (USA)**[11] 7169 6-9-1 50 .... DavidAllan 3 39
(M Brittain) *trckd ldng pair: rdn along over 3f out: wknd over 2f out* **7/1**

3000 **8** 1/2 **Tykie Two**[11] 7169 4-9-3 52 .... JamieMoriarty 10 40
(S Wynne) *in tch: rdn along and lost pl 1/2-way: sn bhd* **16/1**

2264 **9** 1 **Turkish Sultan (IRE)**[21] 6951 5-8-9 49 ....(p) MCGeran(5) 7 35
(J M Bradley) *t.k.h: hld up towards rr: effrt over 3f out: sn rdn and nvr a factor* **10/1**

0-60 **10** 1 1/4 **Beresford Lady**[21] 6956 4-8-11 46 .... AndrewElliott 13 30
(A D Brown) *a towards rr* **25/1**

040 **11** 1 1/2 **Martingrange Lass (IRE)**[32] 6742 3-7-12 46..(b[1]) AndrewHeffernan(7) 2 28
(S Parr) *plld hrd: chsd ldrs and sddle slipped after 2f: rdn along and lost pl over 3f out: sn bhd* **50/1**

2m 38.04s (-2.96) **Going Correction** -0.35s/f (Stan)
WFA 3 from 4yo+ 6lb 11 Ran SP% **123.1**
Speed ratings (Par 101): **95,94,94,93,92 88,87,87,86,85 84**
toteswinger: 1&2 £15.00, 1&3 £15.20, 2&3 £3.80. CSF £57.34 CT £215.16 TOTE £18.90: £4.80, £2.10, £1.50; EX 97.00 TRIFECTA Not won..
Owner Miss Gay Kelleway **Bred** Wyck Hall Stud Ltd **Trained** Exning, Suffolk

FOCUS
A very moderate handicap and very few got competitive. Ordinary form, but pretty sound.
Martingrange Lass(IRE) Official explanation: jockey said saddle had slipped

7323 BOOK ONLINE AT SOUTHWELL-RACECOURSE.CO.UK H'CAP 5f (F)
3:55 (3:55) (Class 5) (0-75,74) 3-Y-0+ **£2,590** (£770; £385; £192) **Stalls** High

Form RPR

6000 **1** **Incomparable**[10] 7182 3-8-11 67 ....(p) PatCosgrave 2 71
(A J McCabe) *mde most: rdn over 1f out: edgd rt and drvn ins fnl f: kpt on wl* **4/1**[1]

-534 **2** 1 **Liberty Ship**[17] 7043 3-8-8 64 ow2 ....(t) GrahamGibbons 11 64
(J D Bethell) *dwlt: sn in tch: hdwy to chse ldrs 2f out: rdn wl over 1f out: drvn to chal ins fnl f: nt qckn last 100yds* **5/1**[2]

4550 **3** 1 1/2 **Our Acquaintance**[25] 6864 3-8-8 64 ow1 ....(b) EddieAhern 6 59
(W R Muir) *chsd ldrs: pushed along and hdwy on wd outside over 2f out: drvn over 1f out: one pce ins fnl f* **14/1**

3040 **4** 1 1/4 **Colorus (IRE)**[17] 7043 5-8-2 63 ....(p) KellyHarrison(5) 9 63+
(W J H Ratcliffe) *trckd ldrs: effrt whn n.m.r and then hmpd over 1f out: swtchd rt and rdn ent fnl f: styd on strly towards fin* **10/1**

4000 **5** hd **Monte Cassino (IRE)**[10] 7180 3-8-11 72 oh10 ow12 JamesO'Reilly(5) 12 62
(J O'Reilly) *cl up: rdn along over 2f out: drvn over 1f out: wknd ent fnl f* **66/1**

5420 **6** nk **Nickel Silver**[16] 7081 3-8-12 68 .... TomEaves 3 57
(B Smart) *a.p: rdn wl over 1f out: drvn and wknd ins fnl f* **4/1**[1]

0200 **7** 1 **Head To Head (IRE)**[66] 5770 4-7-11 60 oh15 .... TerenceFury(7) 1 45
(A D Brown) *wnt lft s: a towards rr* **50/1**

0104 **8** nk **Tyrannosaurus Rex (IRE)**[79] 5401 4-8-6 62 .... PaulHanagan 7 46
(D Shaw) *midfield: rdn along 1/2-way: n.d* **5/1**[2]

4304 **9** 2 3/4 **Highland Warrior**[7] 7222 9-9-4 74 .... JamieMoriarty 5 48
(P T Midgley) *dwlt: a towards rr* **7/1**[3]

0002 **10** 1 1/4 **Gleaming Spirit (IRE)**[10] 7176 4-7-13 62 ....(v) AndrewHeffernan(7) 4 32
(Peter Grayson) *chsd ldrs: rdn along 1/2-way: sn wknd* **15/2**

-600 **11** shd **Count Cougar (USA)**[192] 1901 8-8-11 70 .... MichaelJStainton(3) 8 39
(S P Griffiths) *cl up: rdn along 1/2-way: sn wknd* **16/1**

59.07 secs (-0.63) **Going Correction** -0.05s/f (Stan) 11 Ran SP% **122.7**
Speed ratings (Par 103): **103,101,99,97,96 96,94,94,89,87 87**
toteswinger: 1&2 £6.20, 1&3 £11.00, 2&3 £11.80. CSF £24.97 CT £268.28 TOTE £5.10: £1.70, £2.40, £2.40; EX 31.30 TRIFECTA Not won. Place 6 £ 102.17, Place 5 £ 28.42.
Owner Paul J Dixon & Brian Morton **Bred** Mrs Yvette Dixon **Trained** Babworth, Notts

The Form Book, Raceform Ltd, Compton, RG20 6NL

FOCUS
A modest handicap and muddling form with the fifth finishing closer than he was entitled to from a long way out of the weights.
Colorus(IRE) Official explanation: jockey said gelding was denied a clear run
T/Plt: £76.60 to a £1 stake. Pool: £38,681.67. 368.38 winning tickets. T/Qpdt: £3.80 to a £1 stake. Pool: £3,793.04. 731.00 winning tickets. JR

7324 - (Foreign Racing) - See Raceform Interactive

7232 DUNDALK (A.W) (L-H)
Friday, November 14

OFFICIAL GOING: Standard

7325a BOYLESPORTS.COM H'CAP 6f
6:40 (6:44) 3-Y-0+ **£12,445** (£3,651; £1,739; £592)

RPR
1 **Romeo's On Fire (IRE)**[35] 6635 4-8-4 78 (p) MCHussey 3 82+
(G M Lyons, Ire) *s.i.s: towards rr: hdwy in 6th 1 1/2f out: 4th 1f out: styd on to ld last 100yds: kpt on wl* **12/1**
2 ½ **Soap Wars**[35] 6635 3-9-2 90 JMurtagh 10 92
(M Halford, Ire) *mid-div: 8th 1/2-way: hdwy to go 3rd 1 1/2f out: styd on to ld briefly last 150yds: 2nd and kpt on same pce ins fnl 100yds* **9/2[2]**
3 ¾ **Fourpenny Lane**[7] 7234 3-9-8 101 (p) PTownend(5) 5 101
(Ms Joanna Morgan, Ire) *hld up towards rr: hdwy in 7th 2f out: sn short of room: swtchd 1 1/2f out: 7th 1f out: kpt on wl fnl f* **5/1[3]**
4 ½ **Advanced**[6] 7245 5-9-9 97 WMLordan 12 96
(K A Ryan) *chsd ldrs: 6th 1/2-way: hdwy to 2nd 1 1/2f out: rdn and no ex ins fnl f: kpt on same pce* **8/1**
5 ¾ **Tornadodancer (IRE)**[21] 6963 5-8-11 90 MHarley(5) 6 86
(T G McCourt, Ire) *chsd ldrs: impr to ld under 2f out: rdn and strly pressed ins fnl f: hdd 150yds and no ex* **20/1**
6 1 ½ **Baggio (IRE)**[21] 6963 7-9-6 94 FMBerry 9 86
(Charles O'Brien, Ire) *mid-div: 7th 1/2-way: rdn in 7th 1 1/2f out: 5th and no ex 1f out: kpt on same pce* **6/1**
7 ½ **Nortburn**[23] 6915 4-8-4 83 EJMcNamara(5) 7 73
(G M Lyons, Ire) *towards rr: hdwy to 8th 2f out: rdn in 9th and no imp 1f out: kpt on same pce* **9/1**
8 4 ½ **Fly By Magic (IRE)**[45] 6367 4-8-9 83 DPMcDonogh 8 60
(Patrick Carey, Ire) *chsd ldrs: 5th 1/2-way: rdn 1 1/2f out: no ex in 6th 1f out: kpt on one pce* **20/1**
9 1 ¾ **Boule Masquee**[45] 6367 4-8-2 79 PBBeggy(3) 11 51
(David P Myerscough, Ire) *towards rr for most: nvr a factor* **20/1**
10 1 **He's Got Rhythm (IRE)**[21] 6961 3-8-6 80 CO'Donoghue 4 49
(David Marnane, Ire) *mid-div: rdn and wknd 1/2-way: kpt on one pce st* **7/1**
11 2 **Nanotech (IRE)**[12] 7157 4-9-8 96 PJSmullen 2 59
(Jarlath P Fahey, Ire) *chsd ldrs: 4th 1/2-way: short of room 2f out: no ex in 8th 1 1/2f out* **4/1[1]**
12 1 ¼ **Empirical Power (IRE)**[55] 6141 7-9-12 103 SMGorey(3) 13 62
(Edward Lynam, Ire) *chsd ldr in 2nd: impr to ld briefly 2f out: sn hdd: no ex in 4th 1 1/2f out: sn wknd* **8/1**
13 1 ½ **Luminaire (IRE)**[18] 7033 3-8-3 80 (b) DJMoran(3) 1 34
(J S Bolger, Ire) *led: rdn and hdd 2f out: sn wknd* **12/1**
14 14 **Fairy Flow (IRE)**[23] 6915 4-7-11 78 oh4 DEMullins(7) 14 —
(Ms Joanna Morgan, Ire) *mid-div: rdn and wknd ent st* **13/2**
1m 11.78s (71.78) **14 Ran SP% 156.9**
CSF £83.05 CT £340.34 TOTE £20.20: £4.30, £2.30, £3.20; DF 199.40.
Owner Glenview House Stud **Bred** Fighting Countess Syndicate **Trained** Dunsany, Co. Meath
■ Stewards' Enquiry : S M Gorey one-day ban: careless riding (Nov 28)

NOTEBOOK
Advanced, the former Ayr Gold Cup winner, ran a solid race. He was in an ideal position most of the way and produced his challenge a furlong out, but could only keep on at the one pace after having had every chance.

7328a IRISH STALLION FARMS EUROPEAN BREEDERS FUND COOLEY FILLIES STKS (LISTED RACE) 1m
8:10 (8:11) 3-Y-0+ **£23,933** (£7,022; £3,345; £1,139)

RPR
1 **Jalmira (IRE)**[21] 6960 7-9-0 106 WJLee 3 101+
(C F Swan, Ire) *chsd ldrs: 2nd 1/2-way: impr to ld under 2f out: rdn and kpt on wl fr over 1f out* **7/4[1]**
2 1 ¼ **Kylayne**[15] 7099 3-8-12 JMurtagh 10 97
(P W D'Arcy) *chsd ldrs: 7th 1/2-way: hdwy in 5th 1 1/2f out: rdn into 3rd 1f out: kpt on same pce fnl f to go 2nd cl home* **7/1**
3 hd **Crossing**[75] 5547 7-9-0 95 MCHussey 7 97
(William J Fitzpatrick, Ire) *chsd ldrs: 5th 1/2-way: hdwy to 3rd 1 1/2f out: rdn into 2nd 1f out: kpt on same pce fnl f: lost 2nd cl home* **20/1**
4 ¾ **Solas Na Greine (IRE)**[33] 6689 3-8-12 92 KJManning 5 95+
(J S Bolger, Ire) *mid-div: 8th 1/2-way: rdn in 9th 1 1/2f out: 8th 1f out: swtchd ins fnl f and kpt on wl* **16/1**
5 ½ **Kalidaha (IRE)**[33] 6689 3-8-12 99 MJKinane 14 94
(John M Oxx, Ire) *hld up towards rr: hdwy in 9th 1 1/2f out: rdn into 5th 1f out: kpt on same pce fnl f* **3/1[2]**
6 1 ½ **Dimenticata (IRE)**[33] 6689 4-9-3 103 (b) CDHayes 11 93
(Kevin Prendergast, Ire) *towards rr: sme late hdwy in 10th 1f out: kpt on same pce fnl f* **12/1**
7 hd **Patio**[21] 6960 3-8-12 99 DJMoran 9 90
(David Marnane, Ire) *mid-div: rdn in 7th 2f out: 6th 1 1/2f out: kpt on one pce* **12/1**
8 ½ **Gist (IRE)**[21] 6960 5-9-0 95 (b) NGMcCullagh 1 89
(W J Martin, Ire) *chsd ldrs: 6th 1/2-way: rdn in 7th 1 1/2f out: kpt on one pce* **25/1**
9 nk **Sharleez (IRE)**[33] 6689 3-8-12 103 FMBerry 6 88
(John M Oxx, Ire) *hld up in rr: sme hdwy in 9th 1f out: kpt on one pce* **11/2[3]**
10 ½ **Tis Mighty (IRE)**[33] 6689 5-9-0 97 PShanahan 4 87
(P J Prendergast, Ire) *nvr a factor* **14/1**
11 ½ **Lunduv (IRE)**[23] 6920 3-8-12 92 (b[1]) PJSmullen 12 86
(D K Weld, Ire) *prom early: sn chsd ldrs: 3rd 1/2-way: rdn in 4th 1 1/2f out: no ex in 5th 1f out: sn wknd* **7/1**
12 shd **Mid Mon Lady (IRE)**[28] 6799 3-8-12 89 WMLordan 8 85
(H Rogers, Ire) *led after 2f: rdn and hdd under 2f out: no ex in 2nd 1 1/2f out: wknd over 1f out* **16/1**
13 3 **Miss Gorica (IRE)**[21] 6960 4-9-0 101 DPMcDonogh 13 78
(Ms Joanna Morgan, Ire) *a towards rr* **9/1**
14 1 **Dani's Girl (IRE)**[14] 5733 5-9-0 93 CPGeoghegan 2 76
(P A Fahy, Ire) *led early: hdd after 2f: chsd ldrs: 4th 1/2-way: rdn in 5th 2f out: no ex in 8th 1 1/2f out: sn wknd* **25/1**
1m 37.47s (97.47)
WFA 3 from 4yo+ 2lb **14 Ran SP% 158.0**
CSF £20.58 TOTE £3.70: £2.30, £2.10, £8.20; DF 23.60.
Owner Green Dragon Syndicate **Bred** Ivan & Mrs Eileen Heanen **Trained** Cloughjordan, Co Tipperary

NOTEBOOK
Jalmira(IRE) thoroughly deserved this win and was value for a bit further. (op 11/4)
Kylayne is a decent performer at this level and certainly justified the decision to send her over. She raced very prominently, although she did come under pressure three furlongs out and looked as though she would back-pedal. She kept going though and deservedly picked up second place prizemoney while being no match for the winner. (op 7/1 tchd 8/1)

7329 - 7331a (Foreign Racing) - See Raceform Interactive

7295 GREAT LEIGHS (A.W) (L-H)
Saturday, November 15

OFFICIAL GOING: Standard
Wind: Light, half-behind Weather: Mostly sunny

7332 E B F HAVEN HOUSE BUDDIES MAIDEN FILLIES' STKS (DIV I) 1m (P)
1:20 (1:20) (Class 5) 2-Y-O
£3,925 (£1,175; £587; £294; £146; £73) **Stalls** Centre

Form RPR
1 **Cascata (IRE)** 2-9-0 0 DaneO'Neill 5 71
(L M Cumani) *hld up on ins: swtchd rt and hdwy over 1f out: r.o wl to ld ins fnl f* **4/1[3]**
0 2 1 ¼ **Rag And Bone (CAN)**[33] 6697 2-9-0 0 JamieSpencer 1 68
(B J Meehan) *led tl rdn and hdd ins fnl f: edgd lft towards fin* **14/1**
3 1 ¼ **Rum Raisin**[29] 6801 2-9-0 0 JerryO'Dwyer 8 65
(John Joseph Murphy, Ire) *towards rr: hdwy on ins over 1f out: rdn and wnt 3rd post* **20/1**
534 4 shd **Mayaalah**[25] 6887 2-9-0 76 RHills 3 65
(J H M Gosden) *trckd ldrs: rdn and no ex ins fnl f: sltly impeded and lost 3rd last strides* **9/4[1]**
5 ½ **Faldal**[124] 4035 2-9-0 0 RichardKingscote 10 64
(Tom Dascombe) *trckd ldrs on outside: rdn over 1f out: one pce after* **16/1**
06 6 2 ¼ **Thaumatology (USA)**[25] 6876 2-8-7 0 AndreaAtzeni(7) 9 59
(M Botti) *trckd ldr tl wknd fnl f* **12/1**
0 7 ½ **Flapper (IRE)**[21] 6978 2-9-0 0 EddieAhern 12 58
(J W Hills) *steaded s: sn swtchd lft: towards rr: sme: late hdwy* **16/1**
0 8 ½ **Precious Secret (IRE)**[14] 7141 2-9-0 0 JimCrowley 7 57
(C F Wall) *trckd ldrs: rdn over 2f out: wknd appr fnl f* **5/2[2]**
00 9 ¾ **Astrobrava**[30] 6745 2-9-0 0 PaulMulrennan 6 55
(M H Tompkins) *towards rr: rdn over 2f out: nvr on terms* **66/1**
6 10 6 **Clinging Vine (USA)**[54] 6166 2-9-0 0 RyanMoore 11 42
(R Hannon) *a in rr* **6/1**
0 P **My Baby Love**[60] 5996 2-9-0 0 J-PGuillambert 4 —
(J Akehurst) *sn rdn along in rr: t.o 1/2-way: p.u over 2f out* **66/1**
1m 42.83s (2.93) **Going Correction** 0.0s/f (Stan) **11 Ran SP% 127.5**
Speed ratings (Par 93): **85,83,82,82,81 79,79,78,77,71** —
toteswinger: 1&2 £28.90, 1&3 £28.90, 2&3 £28.90. CSF £63.36 TOTE £6.00: £1.80, £4.40, £5.80; EX 68.70 TRIFECTA Not won..
Owner S Stuckey **Bred** Barton Bloodstock & Villiers Synd **Trained** Newmarket, Suffolk

FOCUS
An ordinary fillies' maiden and the time was slow.

NOTEBOOK
Cascata(IRE), a 95,000gns half-sister to high-class multiple 1m4f winner Grammarian, produced a likable effort on this debut. She showed signs of greenness when first coming under pressure, but stayed on strongly in the straight. The proximity of Rum Raisin suggests the winner probably only ran to a fair level, but she can step up significantly on the bare form over middle-distances next year and rates as a useful prospect. (op 11-2)
Rag And Bone(CAN) was allowed her own way in front and stepped up significantly on the form she showed when beating just one home on her debut over 6f at Kempton. (op 12-1)
Rum Raisin's best RPR coming into this was just 50, so her proximity suggests the form is just modest. However, it's fair to say she could have improved for the step up in trip and switch to Polytrack and, if anything, she might even be a little better than the bare result, as she ended up making her move against the often unfavoured inside rail after having to wait for a run.
Mayaalah, back on Polytrack, seemed to have her chance. She is not progressing and might have had enough for the year. Official explanation: jockey said, regarding riding, that he eased the filly as a precaution to avoid potentially clipping the heels of Rag And Bone, placed 2nd, which showed sings of hanging across at the winning line. (op 2-1 tchd 7-4)
Faldal, making her debut for a new trainer, probably improved slightly on the form she showed at Killarney on her only previous start four months earlier, but she carried her head awkwardly under pressure.
Thaumatology(USA) now has the option of handicaps.
Flapper(IRE) hinted at ability and only needs one more run for a mark.
Precious Secret(IRE) was beaten turning form home and this was very disappointing considering she shaped nicely on her debut over 7f at Newmarket. (tchd 11-4)
My Baby Love Official explanation: jockey said filly lost its action; vet said filly was found to have been struck into

7333 SUE IRWIN MEMORIAL MAIDEN STKS 6f (P)
1:55 (1:55) (Class 5) 2-Y-O **£3,238** (£963; £481; £240) **Stalls** Low

Form RPR
4 1 **Emirates Sports**[15] 7104 2-9-3 0 JamieSpencer 8 80
(Saeed Bin Suroor) *led after 1f: edgd rt appr fnl f: rdn out* **9/4[1]**
0 2 1 ¼ **Wedding List**[25] 6885 2-8-12 0 MichaelHills 2 72
(W J Haggas) *led for 1f: clsng on wnr whn carried sltly rt appr fnl f: kpt on* **5/1[2]**
2 3 1 ½ **Arctic Freedom (USA)**[141] 3456 2-8-12 0 JimmyFortune 3 67
(E A L Dunlop) *chsd ldrs: hdwy over 1f out: no imp on first 2 ins fnl f* **9/4[1]**
03 4 1 ¼ **Dancourt (IRE)**[12] 7165 2-9-3 0 RyanMoore 1 68
(Sir Michael Stoute) *s.i.s: sn chsd ldrs: no hdwy whn edgd lft ins fnl f* **6/1[3]**
5 shd **Major Phil (IRE)** 2-9-3 0 DaneO'Neill 6 68
(L M Cumani) *mid-div: rdn 2f out: styd on: nvr nr to chal* **16/1**
0 6 1 **Rebel City**[100] 4778 2-9-3 0 ShaneKelly 11 65
(S A Callaghan) *towards rr: rdn 2f out: sme hdwy fnl f* **33/1**
60 7 1 ¾ **Thin Red Line (IRE)**[8] 7227 2-9-3 0 TGMcLaughlin 9 60
(E A L Dunlop) *a in rr* **16/1**

					RPR
	8	nk	**Die Haard** 2-9-3 0 ... PaulHanagan 5		59
			(J R Gask) *mid-div: rdn 1/2-way: no hdwy fnl 2f*	**40/1**	
06	9	5	**Liteup My World (USA)**[23] 6932 2-9-3 0 ... J-PGuillambert 4		44
			(B Ellison) *plld hrd: a in rr*	**16/1**	
0	10	1/2	**Tagula Night (IRE)**[124] 4024 2-9-3 0 ... (t) AdamKirby 10		42
			(W R Swinburn) *a bhd*	**20/1**	
	11	nk	**Lucky Fortune (IRE)** 2-9-3 0 ... MickyFenton 7		41
			(Miss Amy Weaver) *a towards rr*	**50/1**	

1m 13.97s (0.27) **Going Correction** 0.0s/f (Stan) **11** Ran SP% **122.2**
Speed ratings (Par 96): **98,96,94,92,92 91,88,88,81,81 80**
toteswinger: 1&2 £8.50, 1&3 £1.10, 2&3 £2.90. CSF £14.03 TOTE £2.80: £1.70, £2.40, £1.10; EX 25.40 Trifecta £108.60 Pool: £202.68 - 1.38 winning units..
Owner Godolphin **Bred** W And R Barnett Ltd **Trained** Newmarket, Suffolk

FOCUS
A reasonable sprint maiden.

NOTEBOOK
Emirates Sports is hardly bred for sprint trips but he showed plenty of early speed to lead and ran on strongly, despite edging badly right under pressure in the straight. This was an improvement on the form he showed on his debut over this trip at Newmarket and he looks quite useful. (op 15-8)
Wedding List flopped when fancied on her debut at Yarmouth, but this was a lot better. She was carried right by the winner in the straight but was basically beaten by a better one on the day. She should have no problem winning a race if persevered with this winter. (op 7-1)
Arctic Freedom(USA) had not been seen since finishing second in an ordinary maiden over this trip on the July course nearly five months ago. She ran with credit and should pick up a modest race. (op 3-1 tchd 2-1 in a place)
Dancourt(IRE) was unsuited by the drop back in trip, but he is now qualified for a handicap mark and should do better over further. (op 5-1)
Major Phil(IRE) ◆, a 32,000gns half-brother to a number of winners from 6f to 1m2f, caught the eye, running on late. This was a pleasing debut and he looks one to keep on-side. (op 14-1 tchd 25-1)
Rebel City should find his level once handicapped. (op 20-1)
Thin Red Line(IRE) should be capable of better over longer trips now he is qualified for a handicap mark. (op 14-1)
Liteup My World(USA) Official explanation: jockey said colt ran too free

7334 HAVEN HOUSE FAMILIES CONDITIONS STKS 6f (P)
2:30 (2:30) (Class 3) 2-Y-O

£6,854 (£2,052; £1,026; £513; £256; £128) **Stalls** Low

Form					RPR
1024	1		**Calahonda**[15] 7107 2-8-9 87 ... RobertWinston 2		87
			(P W D'Arcy) *trckd ldr: led over 1f out: r.o wl*	**7/2**[3]	
412	2	3/4	**Son Of The Cat (USA)**[19] 7024 2-9-0 85 ... (t) MichaelHills 1		90
			(B Gubby) *in tch in 3rd pl: wnt 2nd over 1f out: rdn and edgd lft: nt qckn cl home*	**4/1**	
5322	3	1 3/4	**Invincible Heart (GR)**[29] 6776 2-9-0 89 ... AlanMunro 5		85
			(Jane Chapple-Hyam) *chsd ldr: rdn over 1f out: kpt on one pce*	**13/8**[1]	
6211	4	nk	**Timeteam (IRE)**[19] 7024 2-9-3 88 ... JamieSpencer 3		87
			(S Kirk) *s.i.s: hld up: rdn over 1f out: kpt on: n.d*	**3/1**[2]	
02	5	4	**Prayer Boat (IRE)**[9] 7214 2-9-0 0 ... JerryO'Dwyer 6		72
			(John Joseph Murphy, Ire) *hld up in rr: nvr on terms*	**11/1**	
035	6	2 1/2	**Love You Louis**[28] 6807 2-9-0 82 ... (v[1]) JimCrowley 4		64
			(J R Jenkins) *led: rdn over 2f out: hdd over 1f out: wknd fnl f*	**25/1**	
5204	7	7	**River Rye (IRE)**[50] 6247 2-8-12 73 ... LPKeniry 7		41
			(J S Moore) *slowly away: a bhd*	**25/1**	

1m 13.13s (-0.57) **Going Correction** 0.0s/f (Stan) **7** Ran SP% **121.3**
Speed ratings (Par 100): **103,102,99,99,93 90,81**
toteswinger: 1&2 £4.70, 1&3 £2.50, 2&3 £1.60. CSF £19.39 TOTE £4.20: £2.10, £3.00; EX 21.60.
Owner Gongolphin & Racing **Bred** Eurostrait Ltd **Trained** Newmarket, Suffolk

FOCUS
A reasonable juvenile conditions contest run at a very strong pace.

NOTEBOOK
Calahonda was fourth in a 6f Listed race last time, but both her previous wins were gained over 7f, so a proper test at this trip was ideal. She is very tough but was entitled to win this as she was best off at the weights and had 7lb in hand of the runner-up on official figures. She is likely to be put away until next year. (tchd 4-1)
Son Of The Cat(USA) seemed to run his best race yet in a first-time tongue-tie. (op 9-2)
Invincible Heart(GR) remains a maiden and is crying out for a drop back to 5f. (op 2-1)
Timeteam(IRE) looked well placed considering the strong pace but didn't really pick up in the straight. He had won his last two starts but this was tougher. (op 10-3 tchd 7-2)
Prayer Boat(IRE) was below the form he showed when second in a 7f novice event at Lingfield on his previous outing. (op 8-1 tchd 12-1 and 14-1 in a place)
Love You Louis went off too fast in a first-time visor.

7335 HAVEN HOUSE VOLUNTEERS NURSERY 6f (P)
3:05 (3:05) (Class 3) 2-Y-O

£7,788 (£2,332; £1,166; £583; £291; £146) **Stalls** Low

Form					RPR
5002	1		**Whatyouwoodwishfor (USA)**[40] 6525 2-8-9 72 ... PaulHanagan 5		74
			(R A Fahey) *mde all: kpt on u.p fnl f: hld on*	**5/1**[2]	
245	2	nk	**Saif Al Fahad (IRE)**[27] 6837 2-8-5 68 ... FrancisNorton 4		69
			(E J O'Neill) *t.k.h: in tch: r.o u.p to go 2nd post*	**10/1**	
0011	3	hd	**Rainbow Seeker**[15] 7113 2-8-13 76 ... (b) LiamJones 3		77
			(W J Haggas) *nvr out of first 3: edgd rt but stl 2nd over 1f out: lost 2nd post*	**9/4**[1]	
1032	4	nk	**Rowayton**[17] 7075 2-9-6 83 ... RobertWinston 1		83
			(J D Bethell) *s.i.s: sn prom: t.k.h: rdn over 1f out: kpt on fnl f*	**7/1**	
3112	5	3 1/2	**Joe Caster**[11] 7173 2-9-4 84 ... LukeMorris(3) 7		77+
			(J M P Eustace) *in rr whn short of room on ins over 2f out: rallied over 1f out but nvr nr to chal*	**13/2**[3]	
10	6	nse	**Cool Art (IRE)**[44] 6426 2-8-13 76 ... JamieSpencer 6		65
			(S A Callaghan) *hld up: nvr nr to chal*	**5/1**[2]	
0405	7	1 3/4	**Red Rossini (IRE)**[34] 6666 2-8-11 74 ... RyanMoore 8		58
			(R Hannon) *sn trckd wnr: rdn and wknd fnl f*	**7/1**	
40	8	1 1/2	**Ruby Tallulah**[7] 7241 2-8-11 74 ... LPKeniry 10		53
			(C R Dore) *a bhd*	**16/1**	
2010	9	23	**Plotting**[16] 7103 2-8-9 72 ... DarryllHolland 2		—
			(K A Ryan) *racd wd in rr: lost tch 1/2-way: t.o*	**16/1**	

1m 13.49s (-0.21) **Going Correction** 0.0s/f (Stan) **9** Ran SP% **123.3**
Speed ratings (Par 100): **101,100,100,99,95 95,92,90,60**
toteswinger: 1&2 £9.70, 1&3 £2.20, 2&3 £9.20. CSF £57.62 CT £146.68 TOTE £6.40: £1.70, £4.80, £1.90; EX 81.30 TRIFECTA Not won..
Owner Mel Roberts & Ms Nicola Meese 1 **Bred** Manganaro Llc **Trained** Musley Bank, N Yorks

FOCUS
Just a fair sprint nursery and not quite as good as the class of race suggests.

NOTEBOOK
Whatyouwoodwishfor(USA) refused to enter the stalls when strongly supported for a lesser race at Kempton last month, but all went according to plan this time. He enjoyed the run of the race under a positive ride and, in the process, did the favourite few favours, but he seemed inclined to edge left in the straight, despite having the rail to run against. This was a fair effort off a mark 6lb higher than when second at Pontefract on his nursery debut, but he was given a hard ride and only just hung on. (tchd 11-2)
Saif Al Fahad(IRE), dropped back in trip on his first start in a nursery, would probably have won had he not been inclined to lug left under pressure. (op 14-1 tchd 16-1)
Rainbow Seeker, bidding for a hat-trick following two wins over 5f, could not defy an 11lb rise for his latest success, and a mark 17lb higher than when gaining his first victory. He got slightly squeezed up after a couple of furlongs and was stuck in behind the winner for much the way. (op 5-2)
Rowayton was a little keen and was not at her best. She seems better suited to Kempton. (op 11-2)
Joe Caster is better than this as he was badly hampered rounding the final bend. (op 5-1)
Cool Art(IRE) does not seem to be progressing. (op 6-1)
Plotting Official explanation: jockey said filly hung right and moved poorly

7336 HAVEN HOUSE NURSES MAIDEN STKS (C&G) 1m (P)
3:35 (3:38) (Class 4) 2-Y-O

£4,361 (£1,306; £653; £326; £163; £81) **Stalls** Centre

Form					RPR
	1		**Father Time** 2-9-0 0 ... TPQueally 2		86
			(H R A Cecil) *mid-div and a gng wl: gd hdwy to ld over 1f out: edgd rt ins fnl f: r.o*	**7/1**	
24	2	1	**Kings Destiny**[21] 6978 2-9-0 0 ... DarryllHolland 13		84
			(M A Jarvis) *a.p: wnt 2nd and ev ch over 1f out: kpt on*	**6/4**[1]	
	3	shd	**December Draw (IRE)** 2-9-0 0 ... ShaneKelly 16		84
			(W J Knight) *in rr: rdn over 3f out: gd hdwy on ins fr 2f out: jst failed to go 2nd*	**33/1**	
06	4	3	**Decorum (USA)**[17] 7069 2-9-0 0 ... (t) JimmyFortune 4		77
			(J H M Gosden) *trckd ldrs: led over 2f out: hdd over 1f out: fdd ins fnl f*	**16/1**	
3	5	3 1/2	**Petrovsky**[10] 7200 2-9-0 0 ... RobertWinston 1		69
			(M Johnston) *chsd ldrs wknd over 1f out*	**9/4**[2]	
	6	1	**Wee Sonny (IRE)** 2-9-0 0 ... RichardKingscote 6		67
			(Tom Dascombe) *mid-div: rdn 1/2-way: hdwy over 1f out: nvr nr to chal*	**25/1**	
0	7	5	**Cayman Sky**[104] 4665 2-9-0 0 ... (b[1]) PatDobbs 10		56
			(R Hannon) *trckd ldr: rdn over 2f out: sn btn*	**33/1**	
0	8	hd	**Sir Freddie**[18] 7054 2-9-0 0 ... KirstyMilczarek 9		56
			(Lady Herries) *prom on outside no hdwy fnl 2f*	**66/1**	
	9	1 3/4	**Philmack Dot Com** 2-9-0 0 ... MickyFenton 3		52
			(Miss Amy Weaver) *chsd ldrs: rdn over 3f out: wknd 2f out*	**66/1**	
0	10	1 1/4	**Flodden Field**[10] 7200 2-9-0 0 ... AlanMunro 5		49
			(P W Chapple-Hyam) *towards rr and outpcd 2f out*	**33/1**	
	11	1 3/4	**Transformer (IRE)** 2-9-0 0 ... PaulHanagan 11		45
			(W J Knight) *a in rr*	**33/1**	
	12	1	**Windpfeil (IRE)** 2-9-0 0 ... JimCrowley 15		43
			(J H M Gosden) *slowly away: a in rr*	**33/1**	
	13	1 1/4	**Peak (IRE)** 2-9-0 0 ... SteveDrowne 7		40
			(H Morrison) *slowly away: a in rr*	**50/1**	
	14	1 1/2	**Keypit** 2-9-0 0 ... AdamKirby 12		37
			(W R Swinburn) *a bhd*	**50/1**	
54	15	28	**Emirates World (IRE)**[39] 6553 2-9-0 0 ... (v[1]) JamieSpencer 8		—
			(Saeed Bin Suroor) *led tl hdd over 2f out: wnt wd into st and eased*	**13/2**[3]	

1m 39.75s (-0.15) **Going Correction** 0.0s/f (Stan) **15** Ran SP% **127.9**
Speed ratings (Par 98): **100,99,98,95,92 91,86,86,84,83 81,80,79,77,49**
toteswinger: 1&2 £3.80, 1&3 £31.50, 2&3 £21.30. CSF £17.64 TOTE £7.20: £2.50, £1.10, £5.80; EX 16.80 TRIFECTA Not won..
Owner K Abdulla **Bred** Juddmonte Farms Ltd **Trained** Newmarket, Suffolk
■ Stewards' Enquiry : T P Queally caution: careless riding.

FOCUS
A big field for this maiden and the form looks useful. The winning time was impressive, significantly faster than both divisions of the fillies' maiden, and also quicker than the two-year-old claimer won by a horse rated 77.

NOTEBOOK
Father Time ◆, a brother to the stable's high-class 1m2f filly Passage Of Time, made a pleasing introduction. Having travelled well a fair way back, he picked up nicely in the straight and sustained his effort all the way to the line. He could be quite decent over further next season. (op 11-2)
Kings Destiny who had shown plenty of ability in two soft-ground maidens, seemed to run his race and probably just came up against a decent type. He now has the option of handicaps but will probably be better off sticking to maidens if persevered with this year. (op 11-8)
December Draw(IRE), a 25,000gns purchase, was another to make a pleasing debut. He was well behind early but produced a big effort against the inside rail in the straight and clearly has plenty of ability.
Decorum(USA) ◆ showed up well for much of the way and will have more options now he is qualified for a handicap mark. (op 20-1)
Petrovsky did not confirm the promise of his encouraging debut third at Nottingham and has to be considered disappointing. He was struggling from some way out, although he was keeping on at the finish, and can be given another chance. (op 3-1)
Wee Sonny(IRE) was green but he showed ability and will have learnt plenty.
Sir Freddie hinted at ability and will be one to watch when upped in trip and sent handicapping.
Emirates World(IRE), sporting a first-time visor, was in trouble when hanging badly right off the final bend. Official explanation: jockey said, regarding running and riding, colt hung badly right around final bend and when entering home straight, and bearing in mind it had tired having raced prominently hitherto, he felt it prudent to allow it to come home in its own time (op 7-1)

7337 E B F HAVEN HOUSE BUDDIES MAIDEN FILLIES' STKS (DIV II) 1m (P)
4:05 (4:07) (Class 5) 2-Y-O

£3,925 (£1,175; £587; £294; £146; £73) **Stalls** Centre

Form					RPR
00	1		**Nice Time (IRE)**[14] 7140 2-9-0 0 ... PaulMulrennan 7		69
			(M H Tompkins) *in rr on ins: hdwy fr 2f out: styd on u.p to ld nr fin*	**33/1**	
3	2	hd	**Penperth**[16] 7093 2-8-11 0 ... LukeMorris(3) 2		69
			(J M P Eustace) *a.p: led over 1f out: hrd rdn and hdd nr fin*	**9/1**	
5	3	nk	**More Tea Vicar (IRE)**[12] 7165 2-9-0 0 ... PaulHanagan 10		68
			(R A Fahey) *hld up in rr: hdwy over 1f out: kpt on u.str.p*	**20/1**	
3	4	1	**Ballet Dancer (IRE)**[22] 6945 2-9-0 0 ... DarryllHolland 6		66
			(M A Jarvis) *towards rr: rdn fr 1/2-way: kpt on u.p ins fnl 2f: nvr nrr*	**1/1**[1]	
06	5	1/2	**Alimarr (IRE)**[25] 6884 2-9-0 0 ... EddieAhern 3		65
			(B J Meehan) *mid-div: styd on ins fnl 2f*	**20/1**	
2665	6	1	**Capitelli (IRE)**[16] 7097 2-9-0 76 ... PatDobbs 1		63
			(R Hannon) *led: rdn 2f out: hdd over 1f out: one pce after*	**4/1**[3]	

The Form Book, Raceform Ltd, Compton, RG20 6NL

00 **7** *1* **Dubai Diva**[15] 7117 2-9-0 0 AlanMunro 11 61
(C F Wall) *in tch on outside: no hdwy fr over 1f out* **33/1**
5 **8** *1/2* **Valletta**[49] 6291 2-9-0 0 JimmyFortune 5 60
(J H M Gosden) *trckd ldr: rdn over 1f out: wknd fnl f* **7/2**[2]
00 **9** *5* **Bourn Fair**[9] 7209 2-9-0 0 DaneO'Neill 8 49
(P J McBride) *hld up in rr: nvr on terms* **66/1**
0 **10** *2* **Peintre D'Argent (IRE)**[22] 6945 2-9-0 0 SteveDrowne 9 44
(H Morrison) *in tch: rdn over 2f out: wknd over 1f out* **25/1**
11 *2 3/4* **Sashay Queen (USA)** 2-9-0 0 RyanMoore 4 38
(Sir Michael Stoute) *s.i.s: sn in tch: rdn and wknd over 2f out* **8/1**

1m 41.8s (1.90) **Going Correction** 0.0s/f (Stan) **11** Ran SP% **134.1**
Speed ratings (Par 93): **90,89,89,88,88 87,86,85,80,78 75**
toteswinger: 1&2 £39.50, 1&3 £62.00, 2&3 £15.40. CSF £316.45 TOTE £95.00: £12.90, £2.30, £3.80; EX 638.50 TRIFECTA Not won..
Owner Mrs Claudia Wiggins **Bred** Peter Mooney **Trained** Newmarket, Suffolk

FOCUS
They finished in a bit of a bunch and this looked like a rather ordinary fillies' maiden. The winning time was almost a second quicker than the first division but still much slower than the colts' and geldings' juvenile maiden, and also slower than the following claimer.

NOTEBOOK
Nice Time(IRE) had been well held in two turf maidens, but she produced an improved effort on this switch to Polytrack, seemingly benefiting from the step back up to 1m. She had to squeeze through a tight gap against the inside rail and showed a good attitude. She will now be put away until next year and her trainer thinks she will get 1m2f. (op 50-1)
Penperth confirmed the promise she showed when third over course and distance on her debut and did nothing wrong. She's a likeable filly. (op 8-1)
More Tea Vicar(IRE) can arguably be considered a little unlucky, as she was travelling well turning for home but had to wait longer than ideal for a run and also had to switch with her challenge.
Ballet Dancer(IRE) didn't really travel and was off the bridle a fair way out. She plugged on but was never getting there and could not confirm the promise she showed on her debut at Doncaster. (op 11-8)
Alimarr(IRE) now has the option of handicaps.
Capitelli(IRE) seems to be regressing.
Dubai Diva is another who can now compete in handicaps.
Valletta could not confirm the promise of her debut effort. (tchd 3-1)

7338 HAVEN HOUSE CHILDRENS MEMORIAL CLAIMING STKS 1m (P)
4:35 (4:35) (Class 5) 2-Y-O £2,590 (£770; £385; £192) **Stalls Centre**

Form RPR
6250 **1** **Doncosaque (IRE)**[18] 7054 2-9-1 77 TPQueally 7 71
(H R A Cecil) *trckd ldr: led over 1f out: r.o wl: comf* **8/11**[1]
45 **2** *3 1/2* **Mootriba**[24] 6910 2-9-2 0 RyanMoore 6 64
(W J Haggas) *hld up in rr: hdwy on outside 2f out: r.o to chse wnr ins fnl f* **13/8**[2]
0266 **3** *1 1/4* **Hold The Bucks (USA)**[6] 7257 2-8-10 58 LukeMorris(3) 3 59
(J S Moore) *racd in 4th pl: kpt on one pce to go 3rd ins fnl f* **14/1**[3]
4536 **4** *3/4* **Tarawa Atoll**[6] 7258 2-8-6 50 EdwardCreighton 2 50
(M R Channon) *trckd ldrs: rdn over 2f out: wknd ins fnl f* **16/1**
1000 **5** *3 1/2* **Cavendish Road (IRE)**[22] 6954 2-8-11 68 (bt) SteveDrowne 4 47
(W R Muir) *led to over 1f out: wknd ins fnl f* **14/1**[3]
000 **6** *6* **Border Maid**[29] 6770 2-8-3 55 PaulHanagan 8 26
(E A L Dunlop) *rdn 1/2-way: a bhd* **25/1**
0 **7** *hd* **Ringo Zaar**[24] 6892 2-8-13 0 DaneO'Neill 5 36
(A B Haynes) *hld up: a bhd* **40/1**

1m 40.85s (0.95) **Going Correction** 0.0s/f (Stan) **7** Ran SP% **121.5**
Speed ratings (Par 96): **95,91,90,89,86 80,79**
toteswinger: 1&2 £1.20, 1&3 £3.50, 2&3 £3.50. CSF £2.38 TOTE £1.80: £1.20, £1.90; EX 2.80 Trifecta £16.70 Pool £795.58 - 35.21 winning units..Doncosaque was claimed by Horses First Racing Limited for £12,000.
Owner Gestut Ammerland **Bred** Ammerland Verwaltung Gmbh **Trained** Newmarket, Suffolk

FOCUS
An ordinary juvenile claimer.

NOTEBOOK
Doncosaque(IRE) was the best off at the weights on this drop into claiming company and he found this a suitable opportunity to get off the mark at the sixth attempt. He seemed to carry his head at a slight angle under pressure but he still found plenty when asked. (op 4-5 tchd 5-6 and 10-11 in a place)
Mootriba was dropped in grade, but she had no easy task conceding 1lb to a colt rated 77. She was without the blinkers she wore for her first two starts and was up to 1m for the first time but she seemed to run her race. (op 7-4 tchd 15-8)
Hold The Bucks(USA) would have been 17lb better off with the winner had this been a handicap. (tchd 12-1)
Tarawa Atoll probably ran close to her official mark of 50, but that wasn't good enough. (op 18-1)

7339 HAVEN HOUSE SUPPORTERS CONDITIONS STKS 1m 1f 46y(P)
5:05 (5:05) (Class 3) 3-Y-O+ £8,095 (£2,408; £1,203; £601) **Stalls Low**

Form RPR
0046 **1** **Orchard Supreme**[34] 6670 5-9-0 100 RyanMoore 2 107
(R Hannon) *hld up in last pl tl shkn up and hdwy 2f out: edgd rt and led 1f out: rdn out* **4/1**[3]
-434 **2** *1 3/4* **Banknote**[34] 6670 6-9-0 100 FrancisNorton 4 103
(A M Balding) *led: rdn: sltly impeded and hdd 1f out: kpt on one pce* **6/5**[1]
1-20 **3** *1* **Jack Dawkins (USA)**[14] 7145 3-8-11 93 TPQueally 3 101
(H R A Cecil) *trckd ldr: rdn over 2f out: nt qckn fr over 1f out* **13/8**[2]
2000 **4** *5* **Evident Pride (USA)**[108] 4528 5-9-0 93 DaneO'Neill 1 90
(B R Johnson) *racd in 3rd pl to 2f out: rdn 2f out: wknd and eased ins fnl f* **10/1**

1m 57.9s (117.90)
WFA 3 from 5yo+ 3lb **4** Ran SP% **112.6**
CSF £9.69 TOTE £5.30; EX 8.70 Place 6 £694.39, Place 5 £163.16..
Owner Brian C Oakley **Bred** Mrs M H Goodrich **Trained** East Everleigh, Wilts
■ The only race on the card not for two-year-olds.
■ Stewards' Enquiry : Ryan Moore caution: careless riding.

FOCUS
Not much between these four on official figures and it developed into something of a sprint in the straight, as there was no pace on for much of the way. Not the most solid piece of form.

NOTEBOOK
Orchard Supreme basically picked up best in the dash to the line, despite edging right under pressure. He has now won at all four Polytrack courses in Britain.
Banknote was allowed to lead at a steady pace but he was not at his best. He kept on when headed but was held when slightly impeded by the winner. (op 13-8)
Jack Dawkins(USA) seemed totally unsuited by the lack of pace and can be forgiven this effort. (op 11-8 tchd 7-4)
Evident Pride(USA) seems to have lost his way. (op 9-1 tchd 8-1)
T/Plt: £775.50 to a £1 stake. Pool: £42,548.50. 40.05 winning tickets. T/Qpdt: £81.90 to a £1 stake. Pool: £2,855.56. 25.80 winning tickets. JS

7287 WOLVERHAMPTON (A.W) (L-H)
Saturday, November 15

OFFICIAL GOING: Standard
Wind: Almost nil Weather: Overcast

7340 BOOK ONLINE AT WOLVERHAMPTON-RACECOURSE.CO.UK H'CAP (DIV I) 1m 141y(P)
6:20 (6:20) (Class 6) (0-60,60) 3-Y-O+ £2,047 (£604; £302) **Stalls Low**

Form RPR
0041 **1** **Plush**[3] 7287 5-8-7 55 RossAtkinson(7) 9 65+
(Tom Dascombe) *s.s: hld up: plenty to do turning for home: hdwy over 1f out: hung lft and r.o wl to ld nr fin* **5/4**[1]
4025 **2** *hd* **Moyoko (IRE)**[157] 2943 5-8-10 51 PatCosgrave 3 61
(M Salaman) *mid-div: hdwy over 2f out: rdn and hung lft ins fnl f: led briefly nr fin: r.o* **12/1**
4506 **3** *1 1/2* **Royal Manor**[10] 7189 3-9-0 58 FergusSweeney 5 64
(N J Vaughan) *sn led: clr 2f out: sn rdn: hung lft fnl f: hdd nr fin* **8/1**[3]
4030 **4** *2 1/4* **Merrion Tiger (IRE)**[89] 5162 3-9-0 58 TomEaves 7 59
(A G Foster) *hld up: rdn over 3f out: hdwy over 1f out: edgd lft: nt rch ldrs* **7/1**[2]
0006 **5** *1 3/4* **Machinate (USA)**[28] 6827 6-9-5 60 LiamJones 2 57
(W M Brisbourne) *prom: rdn to chse wnr over 1f out: no ex fnl f* **20/1**
0000 **6** *1/2* **Miss Clarice (USA)**[30] 6746 3-8-9 53 ow1 (p) RobertWinston 6 49
(B J Meehan) *mid-div: rdn over 3f out: hdwy over 2f out: hmpd and lost pl wl over 1f out: hung lft: n.d after* **33/1**
0400 **7** *3/4* **All You Need (IRE)**[47] 6334 4-8-12 56 RussellKennemore(3) 12 50
(R Hollinshead) *hld up: plld hrd: hmpd 3f out: styd on towards fin* **25/1**
1104 **8** *nk* **Mr Chocolate Drop (IRE)**[15] 7114 4-8-9 50 (b) LPKeniry 10 43
(Miss M E Rowland) *hld up: plld hrd: hdwy over 2f out: rdn and wknd over 1f out* **33/1**
1202 **9** *3/4* **Rowan Lodge (IRE)**[28] 6827 6-9-4 59 (b) JamieMoriarty 11 51
(Ollie Pears) *hld up: rdn and hung lft over 1f out: n.d* **16/1**
0043 **10** *hd* **Time To Regret**[5] 7267 8-9-4 59 (p) PatrickMathers 1 50
(I W McInnes) *chsd ldrs: rdn over 2f out: wknd over 1f out* **9/1**
0052 **11** *2* **Dushstorm (IRE)**[15] 7112 7-8-11 52 JamesDoyle 8 39
(R J Price) *hld up: rdn over 2f out: c wd ent st: n.d* **10/1**
-500 **12** *1/2* **Foursquare Flyer (IRE)**[27] 6838 6-9-3 58 (vt) RobertHavlin 13 43
(T J Pitt) *chsd ldr over 6f out: rdn over 2f out: wknd over 1f out* **80/1**
500- **13** *18* **Lunar Limelight**[416] 5729 3-8-11 55 TravisBlock 4 —
(P J Makin) *prom: rdn over 3f out: wknd over 2f out* **40/1**

1m 50.89s (0.39) **Going Correction** +0.05s/f (Slow)
WFA 3 from 4yo+ 3lb **13** Ran SP% **118.9**
Speed ratings (Par 101): **100,99,98,96,94 94,93,93,92,92 90,90,74**
toteswinger: 1&2 £8.80, 1&3 £18.90, 2&3 £20.80. CSF £15.95 CT £95.40 TOTE £2.30: £1.40, £5.00, £3.10; EX 23.20.
Owner John Reed **Bred** Cheveley Park Stud Ltd **Trained** Lambourn, Berks

FOCUS
A modest handicap in which the pace was only fair and the form is ordinary. The principals ended up near the inside rail.
All You Need(IRE) Official explanation: jockey said gelding suffered interference in running
Rowan Lodge(IRE) Official explanation: jockey said gelding hung left-handed throughout

7341 EUROPEAN BREEDERS' FUND MAIDEN FILLIES' STKS 7f 32y(P)
6:50 (6:51) (Class 5) 2-Y-O £3,885 (£1,156; £577; £288) **Stalls High**

Form RPR
04 **1** **Arabian Mirage**[14] 7141 2-9-0 0 JamieSpencer 8 81
(B J Meehan) *mde all: rdn clr over 1f out: hung lft ins fnl f: jst hld on* **10/11**[1]
2 *1/2* **Flora Trevelyan** 2-9-0 0 AdamKirby 1 80
(W R Swinburn) *s.s: sn prom: rdn to chse wnr over 1f out: fin wl* **8/1**[3]
22 **3** *5* **Nemorosa**[22] 6953 2-9-0 0 LiamJones 11 68
(W J Haggas) *chsd wnr tl rdn over 1f out: styd on same pce* **11/4**[2]
6 **4** *5* **Passage To India (IRE)**[15] 7117 2-9-0 0 ShaneKelly 6 55
(J A Osborne) *hld up: shkn up over 1f out: nvr nr to chal* **20/1**
5 *3/4* **Volochkova (USA)** 2-9-0 0 RobertWinston 9 53
(J R Fanshawe) *hld up: hdwy 1/2-way: rdn and wknd wl over 1f out* **33/1**
6 *6* **Chic Shanique (USA)** 2-9-0 0 RichardKingscote 10 39
(Tom Dascombe) *hld up: pushed along over 2f out: n.d* **20/1**
7 *nse* **Luckier (IRE)** 2-9-0 0 LPKeniry 3 39
(S Kirk) *chsd ldrs: rdn and wknd over 2f out: in rr whn hung rt over 1f out* **33/1**
8 *2 1/4* **Gurteen Diamond** 2-9-0 0[1] FergusSweeney 12 33
(N J Vaughan) *s.i.s: rdn over 2f out: a in rr* **66/1**
9 *hd* **Seminal Moment** 2-9-0 0 PatCosgrave 5 33
(J G Given) *s.i.s: hld up: rdn over 2f out: a in rr* **33/1**
04 **10** *2 3/4* **Telling Stories (IRE)**[13] 7148 2-9-0 0 JoeFanning 7 26
(M Johnston) *chsd ldrs: rdn 1/2-way: sn wknd* **14/1**
0 **11** *3/4* **Chic Retreat (USA)**[76] 5535 2-9-0 0 MickyFenton 4 24
(M L W Bell) *plld hrd and prom: rdn and wknd over 2f out* **16/1**
12 *38* **Risque Belle** 2-8-13 0 ow2 AlanCreighton(3) 2 —
(E J Creighton) *s.i.s: hld up: rdn 1/2-way: sn wknd* **100/1**

1m 29.42s (-0.18) **Going Correction** +0.05s/f (Slow) **12** Ran SP% **123.5**
Speed ratings (Par 93): **103,102,96,91,90 83,83,80,80,77 76,33**
toteswinger: 1&2 £5.30, 1&3 £1.20, 2&3 £10.60. CSF £9.12 TOTE £1.80: £1.40, £2.50, £1.10; EX 15.70.
Owner Plantation Stud **Bred** Minster Stud **Trained** Manton, Wilts

FOCUS
A fair race of its type. The pace was reasonable and the winner edged over to the inside rail in the closing stages.

NOTEBOOK
Arabian Mirage looked the one to beat on turf form and she turned in her best effort after being allowed to dominate. Her pedigree suggests she should have no problems with 1m. (op 11-8 tchd 6-4)
Flora Trevelyan ◆ is the one to take out of the race. A half-sister to several very useful sorts up to middle distances, turned in an eyecatching display after missing a beat at the start to bustle up the more experienced winner. She has plenty of scope, will be suited by the step up to 1m and is sure to win a similar event at the very least. (op 7-1 tchd 10-1)
Nemorosa had the run of the race and ran creditably upped to this trip for the first time. She looks a good guide to the worth of the form and is likely to be placed to best effect in run-of-the-mill handicaps. (op 9-4)
Passage To India(IRE), having her second start, again hinted at ability on Polytrack without being knocked about. She is open to improvement and will be of much more interest once handicapped. (op 22-1 tchd 18-1)

Volochkova(USA) took the eye on pedigree and hinted at ability on this debut. She is entitled to improve for the experience but looks more of a longer term handicap prospect.
Chic Shanique(USA) was nibbled at in the market but offered only minimal encouragement on this debut. She should do better in handicaps in due course. (op 18-1 tchd 22-1)
Luckier(IRE), a half-sister to a juvenile 5f winner, ran as though the race was needed on her debut. (op 25-1)

7342 WOLVERHAMPTON-RACECOURSE.CO.UK FILLIES' H'CAP 1m 1f 103y(P)
7:20 (7:20) (Class 5) (0-70,70) 3-Y-0+ £3,238 (£963; £481; £240) Stalls Low

Form RPR
6435 1 **Red Lily (IRE)**[6] 7261 3-9-2 **65**....................(v) RobertWinston 7 74
(J R Fanshawe) *a.p: rdn over 2f out: styd on u.p to ld wl ins fnl f* **6/1**[3]
223 2 *nk* **Vine Street (IRE)**[49] 6280 3-9-0 **63**.................... DarryllHolland 11 71
(M A Jarvis) *sn led: rdn clr over 1f out: hdd wl ins fnl f: styd on* **4/1**[1]
5055 3 *1 1/4* **Bavarica**[16] 7094 6-8-10 **59**.................... RussellKennemore(3) 6 64+
(Miss J Feilden) *hld up: racd keenly: hdwy and hmpd 1f out: swtchd lft: r.o: nt rch ldrs* **16/1**
1300 4 *1* **Aphrodisia**[108] 4520 4-9-7 **67**.................... GeorgeBaker 5 70
(S C Williams) *dwlt: hld up: rdn over 2f out: hdwy over 1f out: nt clr run and swtchd lft sn after: styd on* **13/2**
2565 5 *shd* **Ballora (FR)**[29] 6771 3-9-7 **70**.................... PatDobbs 3 73
(S Kirk) *hld up: nt clr run 2f out: hdwy over 1f out: edgd lft and r.o ins fnl f: nrst fin* **9/1**
3204 6 *2 1/2* **Tabulate**[9] 7217 5-8-12 **58**.................... JimmyQuinn 4 56
(P Howling) *hld up: hdwy over 2f out: rdn and edgd rt 1f out: no ex* **10/1**
2324 7 *2 3/4* **Auntie Mame**[17] 7078 4-9-3 **63**.................... JoeFanning 1 55
(D J Coakley) *chsd ldrs: rdn over 2f out: wknd ins fnl f* **13/2**
2562 8 *shd* **Lunar River (FR)**[28] 6825 5-9-5 **65**....................(t) FergusSweeney 9 57
(David Pinder) *hld up: rdn over 2f out: n.d* **8/1**
0-6 9 *hd* **Distant Piper (IRE)**[19] 7032 5-9-5 **65**.................... PatCosgrave 2 56
(Adrian McGuinness, Ire) *prom: rdn over 3f out: wknd over 1f out* **28/1**
0505 10 *3* **Monashee Rock (IRE)**[16] 7096 3-9-5 **68**.................... TGMcLaughlin 8 53
(M Salaman) *s.i.s: hld up: a in rr* **40/1**
0-31 11 *hd* **Saucy**[9] 7217 7-8-8 **54**.................... RichardKingscote 12 39
(Tom Dascombe) *trckd ldr: racd keenly: rdn over 2f out: wknd over 1f out* **5/1**[2]
6003 12 *2 3/4* **Grethel (IRE)**[14] 7131 4-8-10 **56**.................... TomEaves 10 35
(A Berry) *prom tl rdn and wknd over 2f out* **33/1**

2m 1.84s (0.14) **Going Correction** +0.05s/f (Slow)
WFA 3 from 4yo+ 3lb 12 Ran SP% **122.5**
Speed ratings (Par 100): **101,100,99,98,98 96,93,93,93,91 90,88**
toteswinger: 1&2 £5.00, 1&3 £15.90, 2&3 Not won. CSF £30.84 CT £377.96 TOTE £9.60: £2.70, £1.80, £3.60; EX 19.10.
Owner Lord Halifax **Bred** Lord Halifax **Trained** Newmarket, Suffolk
■ Stewards' Enquiry : Russell Kennemore two-day ban: careless riding (Nov 29-30)
George Baker caution: used whip down shoulder in forehand position.
Joe Fanning two-day ban: careless riding (Nov 29 & 30)

FOCUS
An ordinary handicap in which the pace was only fair. The principals raced in the centre in the straight and the form is rated around the third and fourth.
Aphrodisia Official explanation: jockey said filly missed the break
Saucy Official explanation: jockey said mare ran flat

7343 EUROPEAN BREEDERS' FUND AT WOLVERHAMPTON MAIDEN STKS 1m 1f 103y(P)
7:50 (7:50) (Class 5) 2-Y-0 £3,885 (£1,156; £577; £288) Stalls Low

Form RPR
62 1 **Gitano Hernando**[23] 6926 2-9-3 0.................... JimmyQuinn 3 87
(M Botti) *trckd ldrs: rdn to ld over 1f out: r.o wl* **9/2**[3]
22 2 *4 1/2* **Dome Rocket**[17] 7080 2-9-3 0.................... ShaneKelly 12 79
(W J Knight) *chsd ldrs: rdn and ev ch over 1f out: hung lft and no ex fnl f* **9/4**[1]
52 3 *5* **Naheell**[19] 7023 2-9-3 0.................... DarryllHolland 9 70
(M A Jarvis) *chsd ldr: led 1/2-way: rdn and hdd over 1f out: hung lft and wknd fnl f* **7/2**[2]
04 4 *3* **Rupestrian**[21] 6977 2-9-3 0.................... JoeFanning 1 65
(M Johnston) *led to 1/2-way: sn rdn: wknd 2f out: sn hung lft* **6/1**
00 5 *2 3/4* **Irish Saint (IRE)**[28] 6808 2-9-3 0.................... RobertHavlin 6 60
(T J Pitt) *prom: hmpd and lost pl after 1f: n.d after* **100/1**
0 6 *1/2* **Mellow Mixture**[21] 6977 2-9-3 0.................... PatDobbs 8 59
(R Hannon) *hld up in tch: rdn over 3f out: wknd over 2f out* **33/1**
0 7 *nk* **In Step**[25] 6887 2-8-12 0.................... LiamJones 11 53
(W J Haggas) *prom: rdn over 3f out: wknd over 2f out* **20/1**
8 *1/2* **Vaglefield** 2-9-3 0.................... JimmyFortune 4 57
(J H M Gosden) *prom: pushed along over 2f out: sn wknd* **8/1**
0 9 *3 1/2* **Just Dan**[17] 7080 2-9-3 0.................... GrahamGibbons 5 51
(R Hollinshead) *s.i.s: hld up: a in rr: wknd over 2f out* **66/1**
0 10 *shd* **Lend A Light**[38] 6580 2-9-3 0.................... PatrickMathers 10 51
(I W McInnes) *hld up: rdn and wknd over 2f out* **40/1**
00 11 *16* **Dancelectic (IRE)**[9] 7204 2-9-3 0....................(t) LPKeniry 13 22
(D R Lanigan) *s.i.s: hld up: a in rr: wknd 3f out* **150/1**
12 *4* **Cumbrian Gold (USA)** 2-9-3 0.................... TomEaves 2 15
(B Smart) *dwlt: outpcd* **10/1**

2m 1.57s (-0.13) **Going Correction** +0.05s/f (Slow) 12 Ran SP% **118.9**
Speed ratings (Par 96): **102,98,93,90,88 88,87,87,84,84 69,66**
toteswinger: 1&2 £2.50, 1&3 £4.50, 2&3 £1.10. CSF £14.54 TOTE £6.10: £2.00, £1.30, £1.20; EX 19.00.
Owner Mrs R J Jacobs **Bred** Newsells Park Stud Limited **Trained** Newmarket, Suffolk

FOCUS
An interesting event in which the market leaders dominated. The pace was fair and the first three ended up near the inside rail in the straight.

NOTEBOOK
Gitano Hernando ◆ has progressed with every outing and turned in easily his best effort on his all-weather debut. There was plenty to like about the way he got the job done, he will have no problems staying further and is one to keep on the right side in handicaps. (op 5-1)
Dome Rocket had shaped with promise on his two turf starts and, although hanging under pressure on this all-weather debut, seemed to translate the form to Polytrack. His yard does well with its all-weather runners and he looks sure to pick up a similar event at some point. (op 11-4)
Naheell is a steadily progressive sort who had the run of the race and looked to give it his best shot against a couple of fair types over this longer trip. He is likely to be placed to advantage. (op 3-1)
Rupestrian was easy to back and failed to reproduce his improved Newbury run on this first outing on an artificial surface. He is in good hands, though, may be suited by a stiffer test of stamina and would not be one to write off. (op 7-2 tchd 13-2)
Irish Saint(IRE) showed his first signs of ability on this all-weather debut and modest handicaps will be the way forward with him. (tchd 150-1)
Mellow Mixture, who is likely to remain vulnerable in this type of event is another for whom modest handicaps may prove a better option. (op 40-1)
Cumbrian Gold(USA) attracted plenty of support at big odds but offered little in the way of promise on this debut. (op 33-1)

7344 STAY AT THE WOLVERHAMPTON HOLIDAY INN MAIDEN STKS 1m 141y(P)
8:20 (8:22) (Class 5) 3-Y-0+ £2,729 (£806; £403) Stalls Low

Form RPR
63 1 **Shamali**[40] 6530 3-9-3 0.................... TonyCulhane 2 89+
(W J Haggas) *mde all: rdn over 1f out: styd on wl* **10/11**[1]
0 2 *3 3/4* **Spouk**[175] 2413 3-8-12 0.................... DaneO'Neill 9 76+
(L M Cumani) *a.p: chsd wnr 1/2-way: rdn overb 1f out: eased whn hld towards fin* **15/8**[2]
5 3 *2 3/4* **Supaverdi (USA)**[17] 7084 3-8-12 0.................... TravisBlock 11 69+
(H Morrison) *s.i.s: hld up: hdwy over 2f out: r.o ins fnl f: nt rch ldrs* **16/1**
6-6 4 *1* **To Be Or Not To Be**[23] 6935 3-8-12 0.................... TGMcLaughlin 8 67
(John Berry) *hld up: hdwy 1/2-way: rdn over 1f out: no ex fnl f* **66/1**
/ 5 *3* **Desert Vision**[224] 4-8-13 0....................(t) BradleyRoper(7) 1 65
(M W Easterby) *chsd ldrs: outpcd over 3f out: hung lft over 1f out: no imp* **50/1**
5 6 *3/4* **That'll Do Nicely (IRE)**[22] 6956 5-9-6 0.................... PaulMulrennan 4 63
(N G Richards) *hmpd s: hld up: hdwy on outside over 2f out: wknd fnl f* **25/1**
0 7 *1/2* **Yvonne Evelyn (USA)**[60] 5995 3-8-12 0.................... J-PGuillambert 7 57
(J R Gask) *hld up: racd keenly: styd on ins fnl f: nvr nrr* **100/1**
04- 8 *2 1/4* **Lady Asheena**[373] 6737 3-8-9 0.................... LukeMorris(3) 3 52
(J Jay) *wnt rt s: hld up: rdn over 2f out: n.d* **66/1**
9 *2 1/2* **Metternich (USA)** 3-9-3 0....................(t) JimmyFortune 6 51
(J H M Gosden) *chsd ldrs: rdn over 3f out: hung lft and wknd 2f out* **9/1**[3]
0 10 *11* **Amber Moon**[252] 837 3-8-12 0.................... ShaneKelly 10 21
(J A Osborne) *hld up: rdn and wknd 3f out* **33/1**
11 *nk* **Fashion Week** 3-9-3 0.................... JoeFanning 12 25
(M Johnston) *s.i.s: hdwy over 6f out: rdn and wknd 3f out* **18/1**
0 12 *1/2* **Foolish Optimist**[56] 6114 3-8-6 0 ow1.................... KrishGundowry(7) 5 20
(Paul Green) *hld up in tch: rdn and wknd over 2f out* **66/1**
00- 13 *5* **Sparkling Silver**[341] 7097 3-8-12 0....................[1] RobertHavlin 13 —
(T J Pitt) *hld up: rdn 1/2-way: wknd 3f out* **125/1**

1m 51.36s (0.86) **Going Correction** +0.05s/f (Slow)
WFA 3 from 4yo+ 3lb 13 Ran SP% **123.3**
Speed ratings (Par 103): **98,94,92,91,88 88,87,85,83,73 73,72,68**
toteswinger: 1&2 £1.40, 1&3 £2.00, 2&3 Not won. CSF £2.65 TOTE £2.10: £1.10, £1.20, £3.40; EX 3.80.
Owner Abdulla Al Khalifa **Bred** Sheikh Abdulla Bin Isa Al-Khalifa **Trained** Newmarket, Suffolk

FOCUS
A race lacking much strength in depth but the form makes sense at face value. The early gallop was on the steady side and the winner and second came down the centre in the straight.
Supaverdi(USA) Official explanation: jockey said filly missed the break
That'll Do Nicely(IRE) Official explanation: jockey said gelding suffered interference at start
Lady Asheena Official explanation: jockey said filly jumped right leaving stalls
Metternich(USA) Official explanation: jockey said colt hung left

7345 BOOK ONLINE AT WOLVERHAMPTON-RACECOURSE.CO.UK H'CAP (DIV II) 1m 141y(P)
8:50 (8:50) (Class 6) (0-60,59) 3-Y-0+ £2,047 (£604; £302) Stalls Low

Form RPR
6000 1 **Gramm**[145] 3329 5-9-1 **55**.................... GrahamGibbons 5 63
(M W Easterby) *hld up: hdwy over 1f out: rdn to ld ins fnl f: r.o* **16/1**
0025 2 *1/2* **Royal Encore**[17] 7076 4-8-13 **53**.................... RobertWinston 13 60+
(J R Fanshawe) *hld up: hdwy over 2f out: rdn over 1f out: r.o* **8/1**
0065 3 *nse* **Lujano**[12] 7166 3-9-1 **58**.................... PaulMulrennan 12 65
(Ollie Pears) *chsd ldr tl led over 2f out: rdn over 1f out: hung rt and hdd ins fnl f: r.o* **12/1**
2564 4 *1/2* **The City Kid (IRE)**[95] 4946 5-9-5 **59**.................... MickyFenton 4 65
(Miss Gay Kelleway) *trckd ldrs: plld hrd: rdn over 1f out: r.o* **9/2**[3]
5013 5 *1 1/4* **Kirstys Lad**[8] 7226 6-9-3 **57**.................... GeorgeBaker 6 60
(M Mullineaux) *a.p: chsd ldr 2f out: sn rdn: edgd lft ins fnl f: styd on same pce* **11/4**[1]
0440 6 *3 1/2* **Felicia**[9] 7217 3-8-9 **52**.................... SaleemGolam 1 47
(S C Williams) *mid-div: hmpd and lost pl over 7f out: styd on ins fnl f: nt trble ldrs* **16/1**
0035 7 *1 1/4* **Putra Laju (IRE)**[10] 7194 4-9-2 **59**....................(p) PatrickHills(3) 7 51
(J W Hills) *prom: racd keenly: rdn over 1f out: hung lft and wknd fnl f* **4/1**[2]
505 8 *1 3/4* **Charming Tale (USA)**[34] 6679 3-8-11 **54**....................(b) DaneO'Neill 10 42
(B J Meehan) *hld up: rdn over 3f out: a in rr* **12/1**
0000 9 *nk* **Moment Of Clarity**[28] 6825 6-8-8 **55**....................(p) StacyRenwick(7) 2 42
(R C Guest) *prom: rdn over 2f out: wknd over 1f out* **16/1**
4201 10 *5* **Malinsa Blue (IRE)**[22] 6951 6-9-4 **58**....................(p) J-PGuillambert 8 34
(B Ellison) *led: hdd over 2f out: rdn and wknd over 1f out* **8/1**

1m 53.3s (2.80) **Going Correction** +0.05s/f (Slow)
WFA 3 from 4yo+ 3lb 10 Ran SP% **120.1**
Speed ratings (Par 101): **89,88,88,88,86 83,82,81,80,76**
toteswinger: 1&2 Not won, 1&3 Not won, 2&3 Not won. CSF £141.89 CT £1658.53 TOTE £17.20: £7.70, £3.40, £2.80; EX 150.10.
Owner Kevin McConnell **Bred** R Croft, W Hogan & Tweenhills Farm & Stud **Trained** Sheriff Hutton, N Yorks

FOCUS
A modest handicap in which the gallop was steady and the bare form looks messy and may not be entirely reliable. The winner raced against the inside rail in the straight.
The City Kid(IRE) Official explanation: vet said mare was struck into

7346 SPONSOR A RACE BY CALLING 01902 390009 H'CAP 5f 20y(P)
9:20 (9:20) (Class 5) (0-70,70) 3-Y-0+ £3,238 (£963; £481; £240) Stalls Low

Form RPR
2400 1 **Fast Freddie**[24] 6895 4-9-0 **66**.................... AdamKirby 11 79
(S Parr) *chsd ldr: led 4f out: rdn clr and edgd rt over 1f out: r.o* **7/2**[2]
000 2 *3 3/4* **Mayoman (IRE)**[60] 5991 3-9-1 **67**.................... TomEaves 8 67
(M Mullineaux) *hld up: racd keenly: hdwy over 1f out: rdn and no imp fnl f* **16/1**
3400 3 *3/4* **Triskaidekaphobia**[2] 7295 5-8-7 **59**....................(t) PaulFitzsimons 2 56
(Miss J R Tooth) *led 1f chsd ldrs: rdn over 1f out: styd on same pce* **6/1**
320 4 *1/2* **Punching**[18] 7055 4-8-12 **69**....................(b) MarkFlynn(5) 4 64
(Miss Gay Kelleway) *edgd rt s: hdwy over 3f out: rdn over 1f out: styd on same pce* **10/3**[1]
0/ 5 *1 1/2* **Meancog (IRE)**[141] 3468 4-8-9 **64**.................... LukeMorris(3) 6 54
(J S Moore) *prom: nt clr run and lost pl over 3f out: n.d after* **18/1**

The Form Book, Raceform Ltd, Compton, RG20 6NL

2000 6 3/4 **Spoof Master (IRE)**[11] 7182 4-8-12 **64**...(p) LPKeniry 7 51
(C R Dore) *trckd ldrs: rdn over 1f out: no ex* **10/1**
5000 7 3 1/4 **Magic Glade**[21] 6990 9-8-6 **65**... AndrewHeffernan(7) 5 40
(Peter Grayson) *hmpd s: hdwy over 3f out: rdn and wknd wl over 1f out* **10/1**
0004 8 1 1/2 **Shes Minnie**[8] 7225 5-9-2 **68**... RobertWinston 10 38
(J G M O'Shea) *sn pushed along in rr: hdwy 1/2-way: rdn and wknd over 1f out* **4/1**[3]
0544 9 1/2 **Rathmolyon**[36] 6633 3-8-9 **61**... RobertHavlin 3 29
(D Haydn Jones) *chsd ldrs tl rdn and wknd over 1f out* **12/1**
61.94 secs (-0.36) **Going Correction** +0.05s/f (Slow) **9** Ran SP% **116.6**
Speed ratings (Par 103): **104,98,96,96,93 92,87,84,84**
toteswinger: 1&2 £4.80, 1&3 £2.90, 2&3 £7.60. CSF £57.89 CT £329.77 TOTE £4.70: £1.80, £3.80, £1.90; EX 116.80 Place 6 £24.38, Place 5 £16.96..
Owner Gordon Crawford **Bred** New Hall Stud **Trained** Bawtry, S Yorks
FOCUS
Four non-runners and a field of exposed handicappers. The pace was sound and the winner raced in the centre in the straight, so the form looks fair for the grade.
T/Plt: £49.70 to a £1 stake. Pool: £94,378.12. 1,385.70 winning tickets. T/Qpdt: £20.50 to a £1 stake. Pool: £6,441.58. 232.20 winning tickets. CR

7347 - (Foreign Racing) - See Raceform Interactive

TOULOUSE
Tuesday, November 11

OFFICIAL GOING: Very soft

7348a PRIX FILLE DE L'AIR (GROUP 3) (F&M) 1m 2f 110y
1:50 (1:58) 3-Y-0+ **£29,412** (£11,765; £8,824; £5,882; £2,941)

RPR
1 **La Boum (GER)**[15] 7037 5-8-11 ... TJarnet 7 103
(Robert Collet, France) *a in tch in tightly packed field: 10th st: hdwy wl over 1f out: drvn to ld in centre jst ins fnl f: drvn out* **107/10**
2 1 **Rainbow Dancing**[16] 7007 3-8-8 ... DBoeuf 1 103
(Mlle H Van Zuylen, France) *a.p: 4th st: brought wd: drvn over 1f out: kpt on same pce* **15/1**
3 nk **Folle Allure (FR)**[39] 6465 3-8-8 ... IMendizabal 12 102
(J-C Rouget, France) *hld up in rr: cut corner and styd nrest to far side ent st: sn prom: ev ch 1f out: one pce* **10/1**
4 nk **Tangaspeed (FR)**[15] 7037 3-8-8 ... J-BEyquem 13 102
(R Laplanche, France) *towards rr to st: brought to stands' side: r.o u.p but nvr able to chal* **7/1**
5 1 3/4 **Alpine Rose (FR)**[46] 6264 3-8-8 ... CSoumillon 11 99
(J-C Rouget, France) *a.p: 3rd st: c to stands' rail: one pce fr over 1f out* **9/2**[2]
6 1/2 **Cymbal (IRE)**[23] 3-8-8 ...(b) MGuyon 4 98
(H-A Pantall, France) *a.p: 2nd st: led wl over 1f out to jst ins fnl f: sn wknd* **69/10**[3]
7 nk **Alamanni (USA)**[37] 6521 4-8-11 ... ASanna 2 95
(E Borromeo, Italy) *led 1 1/2f: 6th st: one pce* **42/1**
8 1 3/4 **Epic Similie**[39] 6465 3-8-8 ... JVictoire 8 94
(H-A Pantall, France) *towards rr to st: nvr a factor* **69/10**[3]
9 hd **Kareemah (IRE)**[35] 6567 3-8-8 ... FBlondel 3 93
(J E Hammond, France) *midfield: 5th st on ins: rdn and btn over 1f out* **11/4**[1]
10 1 1/2 **Abril (FR)**[48] 6222 3-8-8 ... OscarUrbina 9 90
(G Arizkorreta Elosegui, Spain) *midfield: 8th st on outside: sn btn* **108/1**
11 **Blue Ridge View (FR)**[23] 4-8-11 ... EDelbarba 5 —
(C Delcher Sanchez, Spain) *led after 1 1/2f tl hdd wl over 1f out* **75/1**
12 **Stella Di Quattro**[30] 6691 4-8-11 ... WMongil 6 —
(U Ostmann, Germany) *prom tl 7th and rdn st* **10/1**
13 **Class Attraction (IRE)**[29] 4-8-11 ... TGillet 10 —
(J E Hammond, France) *last most of way* **12/1**
2m 17.52s (137.52)
WFA 3 from 4yo+ 4lb **13** Ran SP% **127.9**
PARI-MUTUEL (including 1 Euro stake): WIN 11.70; PL 4.10, 4.90, 3.60; DF 78.60.
Owner E Trussardi **Bred** Gestut Karlshof **Trained** Chantilly, France

NOTEBOOK
La Boum(GER) seemed to appreciate being given a waiting ride. Well behind in the early stages, she came with a late challenge up the centre of the track to take the lead running into the final furlong. She adored the testing ground, and will go to the Tattersalls Sales in December.
Rainbow Dancing ran a little free early on and was always in the leading group. She stayed on well in the straight and did not go down without a fight.
Folle Allure(FR), last turning into the straight, came with a late run and finished best of all.
Tangaspeed(FR) began her challenge rounding the final turn and made her challenge up the stands' rail. She stayed on bravely inside the final furlong and only lost third place in the final 50 yards.

7262 CAPANNELLE (R-H)
Sunday, November 16

OFFICIAL GOING: Heavy

7349a PREMIO CARLO E FRANCESCO ALOISI (GROUP 3) 6f
2:45 (3:00) 2-Y-0+ **£26,801** (£11,793; £6,432; £3,216)

RPR
1 **Overdose**[77] 5553 3-10-2 ... ASuborics 8 123
(S Ribarszki, Hungary) *mde all: sn racing on stands' rails: 3 l clr at 1/2-way: pushed along and wnt steadily clr fr 2f out: easily* **1/2**[1]
2 10 **Black Mambazo (IRE)**[42] 6518 3-9-8 ... GMarcelli 3 85
(L Riccardi, Italy) *chsd wnr: kpt on one pce fr 2f out* **97/10**
3 nse **Titus Shadow (IRE)**[8] 7253 4-9-12 ... DVargiu 10 89
(B Grizzetti, Italy) *a.p in main gp: 3rd 2f out: r.o fnl f to jst miss 2nd* **138/10**
4 3/4 **Gesture**[8] 7253 6-9-12 ... CColombi 12 87
(E Russo, Italy) *a.p towards outside: rdn 2f out: one pce* **66/10**[3]
5 2 1/2 **L'Indiscreta**[8] 7253 3-9-5 ... SUrru 2 72
(B Grizzetti, Italy) *towards rr tl hdwy wl over 1f out: nvr a factor* **138/10**
6 2 1/4 **Reykon (IRE)**[56] 4-9-8 ... GBietolini 15 68
(A Renzoni, Italy) *trckd ldr of gp on outside: hdwy to dispute 3rd wl over 1f out: one pce* **32/1**
7 1/2 **Polar Wind (ITY)**[8] 7253 4-9-8 ... LManiezzi 1 67
(R Menichetti, Italy) *outpcd early: kpt on u.p on stands' rails: nvr a factor* **59/10**[2]
8 4 **Docksil**[56] 4-9-5 ... MDemuro 11 52
(B Grizzetti, Italy) *prom in main gp 4f* **20/1**
9 nk **Salar Micol (ITY)**[168] 3-9-5 ... MMonteriso 9 51
(M Marcialis, Italy) *nvr nrr than mid-div* **23/1**
10 1 3/4 **Yacht Woman (USA)**[8] 7253 3-9-5 ... ASanna 5 46
(E Borromeo, Italy) *outpcd and in rr: rdn 2f out: no real prog* **91/1**
11 shd **Jordan Strada (ITY)**[210] 4-9-8 ... URispoli 13 48
(A Renzoni, Italy) *led gp on outside 4f* **51/1**
12 1 1/2 **Dream Impact (USA)**[189] 2029 7-9-8 ... PAragoni 7 44
(L Riccardi, Italy) *a outpcd* **17/1**
13 6 **Lady Marmelade (ITY)**[119] 5-9-5 ... MEsposito 14 23
(D Ducci, Italy) *bhd fnl 2f* **35/1**
14 1/2 **Rubro Meridio (IRE)**[415] 5-9-8 ...(b) SBasile 4 24
(I Bugattella, Italy) *a outpcd* **24/1**
15 1/2 **Thinking Robins (IRE)**[119] 5-9-8 ... CDiStasio 16 23
(I Bugattella, Italy) *in tch on wd outside tl wknd over 2f out* **24/1**
16 nse **Magritte (ITY)**[16] 3-9-5 ... CFiocchi 6 20
(R Menichetti, Italy) *prom: 4th over 2f out: sn wknd* **59/10**[2]
1m 10.0s (-0.30) **16** Ran SP% **163.0**
TOTE: WIN 1.51; PL 1.24, 2.19, 3.18; DF 7.82.
Owner S C H Racing Team **Bred** Mr & Mrs G Robinson **Trained** Hungary

4916 HANOVER (L-H)
Sunday, November 16

OFFICIAL GOING: Soft

7350a LANDO-TROPHY (EX HESSEN-POKAL) (GROUP 3) 1m 2f
2:00 (2:02) 3-Y-0+ **£23,529** (£7,353; £3,676; £2,206)

RPR
1 **Lady Deauville (FR)**[20] 7037 3-8-7 ... HayleyTurner 3 113
(P A Blockley) *trckd ldr tl led over 3f out: drvn over 1f out: pushed out fnl f and r.o wl* **32/10**[2]
2 3 **Prince Flori (GER)**[22] 6992 5-9-3 ... EPedroza 7 113
(S Smrczek, Germany) *racd in 4th to st: chsd wnr fr 2f out: rdn over 1f out: one pce* **11/10**[1]
3 2 1/2 **Lord Hill (GER)**[35] 6692 4-9-1 ... THellier 6 106
(C Zeitz) *led to over 3f out: 2nd st: one pce fnl 2f* **63/10**[3]
4 1 **Adolfina (GER)**[70] 5737 3-8-7 ... ASchikora 5 100
(W Figge, Germany) *s.i.s: 5th st: kpt on u.p to take 4th wl ins fnl f* **99/10**
5 nk **Angel Dragon (GER)**[14] 3-8-7 ... AStarke 4 99
(P Schiergen, Germany) *racd in 3rd to st: one pce fnl 2f* **32/10**[2]
6 11 **Davidoff (GER)**[19] 7063 4-8-13 ... FilipMinarik 1 79
(P Schiergen, Germany) *last st: a in rr* **8/1**
7 3 **Ordinata (GER)**[28] 6852 5-8-10 ... LennartHammer-Hansen 2 70
(Frau Ira Ferentschak, Germany) *racd in 5th: 6th st: sn btn* **24/1**
2m 12.3s (132.30)
WFA 3 from 4yo+ 4lb **7** Ran SP% **133.2**
TOTE: WIN 42; PL 14, 12, 18; SF 125.
Owner P J Hughes Developments Ltd **Bred** Aerial Bloodstock Et Al **Trained** Lambourn, Berks
■ Hayley Turner was riding her first Group-race winner, and became the first woman to win a Group race in Germany.

NOTEBOOK
Lady Deauville(FR) was below her best at Saint-Cloud last time but bounced back to form in great style here. A winner of five Listed races in her career to date, she was notching her first Group win here, confirming her liking for both this trip and soft ground. It has yet to be decided whether she will stay in training at four.

7308 KEMPTON (A.W) (R-H)
Monday, November 17

OFFICIAL GOING: Standard
Wind: Light, half against Weather: Dull, rain Race 4 onwards

7353 TRY BETDAQ FOR AN EXCHANGE CLAIMING STKS 1m 2f (P)
1:40 (1:41) (Class 6) 2-Y-O **£2,047** (£604; £302) **Stalls** High

Form RPR
5404 1 **Supernoverre (IRE)**[19] 7069 2-9-7 70... JimCrowley 13 67
(Mrs A J Perrett) *trckd ldrs on inner: hanging briefly over 1f out: led 1f out: sn in command: pushed out firmly* **2/1**[1]
6005 2 1 **Lucky Punt**[8] 7258 2-8-12 53... MichaelHills 12 56
(B G Powell) *hld up in midfield on inner: effrt over 1f out: styd on to go 2nd ins fnl f: nvr really able to threaten wnr* **20/1**
3 3 1/4 **Cafe Mystique (IRE)**[20] 2-9-7 0... AdamKirby 7 60+
(R Pritchard-Gordon, France) *dwlt: hld up in rr on inner: effrt whn nt clr run over 1f out: styd on wl fnl f to take 3rd last strides* **25/1**
6403 4 hd **Strikemaster (IRE)**[19] 7079 2-8-13 57... SteveDrowne 9 51
(J W Hills) *sn pushed along in midfield: u.p 3f out: styd on fr over 1f out to press for 3rd nr fin* **16/1**
2000 5 shd **Ba Globetrotter**[8] 7257 2-8-3 54... MatthewDavies(7) 4 48
(M R Channon) *prom on outer: prog to ld 2f out: hdd & wknd 1f out* **25/1**
1105 6 hd **Dougie Peel**[7] 7275 2-8-11 62...(p) EddieAhern 14 48
(K A Ryan) *led to 2f out: wknd fnl f* **10/3**[2]
0145 7 hd **Barcode**[8] 7257 2-8-9 55... PatrickHills(3) 8 49
(R Hannon) *trckd ldrs: rdn and nt qckn over 1f out: kpt on same pce after* **12/1**
05 8 1 1/2 **Paddythefish (USA)**[72] 5696 2-9-3 0... FergusSweeney 11 51
(K R Burke) *hld up towards rr: effrt over 2f out towards outer: one pce over 1f out* **7/1**[3]
0646 9 1/2 **Give (IRE)**[59] 6086 2-8-7 56...(p) KevinGhunowa(3) 2 43
(R A Harris) *hld up in midfield on outer: nt qckn over 1f out: fdd* **28/1**
0430 10 nk **Hassadin**[49] 6330 2-8-11 66...(tp) DaneO'Neill 5 46+
(A B Haynes) *mostly chsd ldr to jst over 2f out: wkng whn n.m.r fnl f* **7/1**[3]
00 11 1 1/2 **Knock Three Times (IRE)**[8] 7259 2-8-4 0... HayleyTurner 6 34
(M L W Bell) *hld up in last pair: urged along and no real prog on inner over 1f out* **50/1**

0500 **12** *hd* **Against The Rules**75 5606 2-8-12 57.......(p) MickyFenton 10 42
(Miss Gay Kelleway) *dwlt: hld up towards rr on outer: hanging u.p wl over 1f out: no prog* **10/1**

000 **13** *15* **Pinkalicious (IRE)**8 7259 2-8-5 0 ow1....... MartinDwyer 1 8
(M L W Bell) *sn last: wknd over 2f out: t.o* **50/1**

2m 11.11s (3.11) **Going Correction** +0.125s/f (Slow) **13 Ran SP% 123.9**
Speed ratings (Par 94): **92,91,88,88,88 88,88,86,86,86 85,84,72**
toteswinger: 1&2 £11.90, 1&3 £17.80, 2&3 £70.30. CSF £53.23 TOTE £3.20: £1.30, £3.50, £9.90; EX 53.10.
Owner Cotton, James, Slade, Tracey **Bred** Derek Veitch And Saleh Ali Hammadi **Trained** Pulborough, W Sussex

FOCUS
This juvenile claimer was run at a fair pace and the first pair – both drawn high – came clear. The form is modest but solid.

NOTEBOOK
Supernoverre(IRE) got the ideal trip round and opened his account readily on this drop in grade. He stays well and, while he did not have to improve on his last-time-out maiden form to take this, looks a cut above plating class. However, whether he is really up to his current official mark has to be in doubt. (op 9-4 tchd 5-2 in places)
Lucky Punt again took time to settle just off the pace, but he stayed on to finish a clear second-best on this first run beyond 1m and it was his most encouraging effort to date. (op 16-1)
Cafe Mystique(IRE) was hard to assess, having previously been unplaced in two moderate races over 9f in the provinces, but this grade and the switch to the all-weather saw him improve. He can be rated a bit better than the bare form as he made a sluggish start and then found a little trouble when trying to stay on from 2f out. (op 33-1)
Strikemaster(IRE) ran in snatches and, having to be switched inside the final furlong, was doing his best work too late in the day on this return to the longer trip. (tchd 14-1)
Ba Globetrotter had to come wide into the home straight and held every chance. This is his grade.
Paddythefish(USA) Official explanation: jockey said colt was denied a clear run

7354 REGISTER NOW @ BETDAQPOKER.CO.UK H'CAP 1m 2f (P)
2:10 (2:11) (Class 5) (0-70,70) 3-Y-0+ **£2,590** (£770; £385; £192) **Stalls** High

Form RPR

4311 **1** **Stand Guard**12 7189 4-9-8 70....... IanMongan 4 84+
(P Howling) *trckd ldr: led over 2f out: drvn 3l clr over 1f out: all out but unchal* **2/1**1

5110 **2** *1* **Action Impact (ARG)**65 5910 4-9-8 70....... GeorgeBaker 8 82
(G L Moore) *towards rr: pushed along and prog over 2f out: styd on to take 2nd ent fnl f: clsd on wnr but nvr able to chal* **5/1**2

0603 **3** *2* **Rehabilitation**101 4819 3-9-2 68.......(t) AdamKirby 10 76
(W R Swinburn) *prom: u.p 3f out: chsd wnr over 1f out: no imp: lost 2nd ent fnl f* **7/1**

5002 **4** *½* **Valdan (IRE)**8 7261 4-8-11 59....... DaneO'Neill 6 66
(P D Evans) *hld up in rr: prog on wd outside fr 3f out to chse ldrs over 1f out: one pce after* **6/1**3

5651 **5** *3½* **Ministerofinterior**67 5813 3-8-7 59....... FergusSweeney 3 59
(G L Moore) *wl in rr: rdn over 2f out: no prog tl styd on fnl f: nrst fin* **20/1**

5632 **6** *shd* **Mystic Art (IRE)**8 7260 3-8-13 65....... SteveDrowne 7 65
(C R Egerton) *t.k.h early: racd wd in tch: lost pl 3f out: drvn and fnd nil over 1f out: kpt on* **11/1**

3042 **7** *nse* **King Of Connacht**25 6930 5-8-8 56 oh8.......(p) MartinDwyer 9 56
(M Wellings) *t.k.h early in midfield: rdn 3f out: stl chsng ldrs over 1f out: wknd fnl f* **20/1**

0550 **8** *1¼* **Silver Blue (IRE)**29 6838 5-8-12 60....... SaleemGolam 2 57
(W K Goldsworthy) *dwlt: a in rr: rdn over 2f out: no real prog* **20/1**

5611 **9** *½* **Hucking Heat (IRE)**30 6825 4-9-5 67.......(p) HayleyTurner 1 63
(R Hollinshead) *sn trckd ldrs on outer fr wd draw: drvn 3f out: wknd over 1f out* **12/1**

0660 **10** *1* **Mythical Charm**18 7102 9-8-5 56 oh11.......(t) MarcHalford(3) 11 50
(J J Bridger) *hld up on inner and sn in midfield: no prog 2f out: wknd over 1f out* **50/1**

0150 **11** *hd* **Royal Straight**17 7115 3-9-2 68....... JimCrowley 13 62
(B N Pollock) *trckd ldrs on inner: gng wl enough over 2f out: drvn and no prog over 1f out: wknd* **20/1**

6000 **12** *2½* **Piper's Song (IRE)**12 7202 5-9-7 69....... PatCosgrave 5 58
(B G Powell) *v awkward s and drvn in rr early: nvr a factor: u.p and struggling 3f out* **33/1**

3222 **13** *2½* **Under Fire (IRE)**19 7076 5-9-0 62....... ShaneKelly 12 46
(A W Carroll) *led to over 2f out: wknd tamely and rapidly over 1f out* **12/1**

2m 7.46s (-0.54) **Going Correction** +0.125s/f (Slow)
WFA 3 from 4yo+ 4lb **13 Ran SP% 124.5**
Speed ratings (Par 103): **107,106,104,104,101 101,101,100,99,99 98,96,94**
toteswinger: 1&2 £2.80, 1&3 £5.00, 2&3 £8.80. CSF £10.50 CT £63.06 TOTE £2.90: £1.50, £2.00, £2.40; EX 13.80.
Owner The Circle Bloodstock I Limited **Bred** Juddmonte Farms Ltd **Trained** Newmarket, Suffolk

FOCUS
A moderate but competitive enough handicap and the form looks sound and worth being positive about.

7355 BET PREMIER LEAGUE FOOTBALL - BETDAQ H'CAP 1m 4f (P)
2:40 (2:42) (Class 6) (0-60,60) 3-Y-0+ **£2,047** (£604; £302) **Stalls** Centre

Form RPR

160- **1** **Little Carmela**399 6235 4-9-8 59....... SaleemGolam 14 69
(S C Williams) *hld up in rr on inner: prog over 2f out: dashed through to ld wl over 1f out: in command after: rdn out* **14/1**

2602 **2** *2* **Torrens (IRE)**11 7217 6-9-7 58.......(t) DaneO'Neill 12 64
(P D Evans) *hld up bhd ldrs on inner: nt qckn over 2f out: styd on to take 2nd over 1f out: no imp on wnr* **7/2**1

0402 **3** *shd* **Good Effect (USA)**19 7071 4-9-8 59....... GeorgeBaker 4 65+
(C P Morlock) *hld up wl in rr: nt clr run 2f out and swtchd out wd: styd on wl fnl f to take 3rd on post* **5/1**2

0004 **4** *shd* **Sky Quest (IRE)**12 7189 10-8-11 55....... NathanAlison(7) 11 61
(J R Boyle) *hld up in rr: prog on wd outside over 2f out: disp 2nd over 1f out: pushed along and one pce* **20/1**

3620 **5** *1* **Shouldntbethere (IRE)**19 7078 4-9-0 54....... JackMitchell(3) 2 58
(Mrs P N Dutfield) *hld up in last pair: urged along and sme prog on outer 2f out: one pce and readily hld fnl f* **14/1**

5156 **6** *1½* **Atlantic Gamble (IRE)**237 1020 8-9-5 56.......(p) AndrewElliott 13 58
(K R Burke) *cl up on inner: led over 2f out to wl over 1f out: fdd* **20/1**

6423 **7** *½* **Generous Lad (IRE)**12 7189 5-9-7 58.......(p) SteveDrowne 10 59
(A B Haynes) *trckd ldrs: pushed along over 3f out: nt qckn over 2f out: fdd* **7/2**1

0004 **8** *½* **Fantasy Ride**18 7089 6-9-2 53.......(b) PatCosgrave 3 53
(J Pearce) *dwlt: sn in midfield: hanging and fnd nil over 2f out: one pce after* **8/1**3

-050 **9** *1¼* **Mystic Storm**11 7217 5-9-4 55.......(t) MichaelHills 6 53
(B G Powell) *hld up and mostly in last pair: struggling over 2f out* **20/1**

0200 **10** *5* **Satindra (IRE)**11 7045 4-9-5 56.......(t) EddieAhern 8 46
(C R Dore) *led: rdn and hdd over 2f out: sn btn and eased* **20/1**

0240 **11** *2¾* **Snake Skin**13 7183 5-9-7 58....... JimCrowley 7 44
(J Gallagher) *mostly trckd ldr to wl over 2f out: sn wknd rapidly* **14/1**

0510 **U** **Shraayef**61 6019 3-8-10 60....... AndreaAtzeni(7) 1 —
(M Botti) *stmbld and uns rdr leaving stalls* **8/1**3

2m 37.48s (2.98) **Going Correction** +0.125s/f (Slow)
WFA 3 from 4yo+ 6lb **12 Ran SP% 122.4**
Speed ratings (Par 101): **95,93,93,93,92 91,91,91,90,87 85,—**
toteswinger: 1&2 £11.90, 1&3 £17.80, 2&3 £70.30. CSF £60.89 CT £282.38 TOTE £17.90: £4.00, £1.60, £2.00; EX 77.00.
Owner O Pointing **Bred** O Pointing **Trained** Newmarket, Suffolk
■ Stewards' Enquiry : Nathan Alison ten-day ban: failed to ride out for 3rd place (Dec 1-10)

FOCUS
An ordinary handicap, run at a moderate early pace but straightforward form for the grade.

7356 BETDAQ.CO.UK MAIDEN AUCTION STKS 6f (P)
3:10 (3:14) (Class 4) 2-Y-0 **£3,885** (£1,156; £577; £288) **Stalls** High

Form RPR

1 **Lexlenos (IRE)** 2-8-5 0....... MarcHalford(3) 12 66
(D R C Elsworth) *hld up towards rr: sme prog on inner 2f out: styd on to ld fnl 100yds: jst hld on* **20/1**

66 **2** *hd* **Diamond Twister (USA)**28 6863 2-8-13 0....... SteveDrowne 7 71
(J R Best) *hld up bhd ldrs: pushed along to cl fr 2f out: wnt 2nd wl ins fnl f: rdn to press wnr nr fin: jst hld* **4/1**2

0 **3** *1¼* **Hillside Lad**12 7191 2-8-11 0....... JimCrowley 9 65
(R M Beckett) *led: narrowly hdd over 2f out: carried hd high and hung lft after: narrow ld fnl f: hdd and btn fnl 100yds* **14/1**

5 **4** *1¼* **Princess Cagliari**12 7191 2-8-11 0....... DaneO'Neill 10 61
(R Hannon) *in tch in midfield on inner: rdn over 2f out: kpt on same pce: nvr able to chal* **3/1**1

3 **5** *shd* **Bobs Dreamflight**165 2759 2-8-9 0....... MartinDwyer 2 59
(D K Ivory) *fast away fr wd draw: w ldr: narrow ld over 2f out: carried lft after: hdd fnl f: wknd nr fin* **3/1**1

00 **6** *½* **Golden Pool (IRE)**14 7170 2-8-8 0....... EddieAhern 11 56
(S A Callaghan) *trckd ldng pair: gng wl enough over 2f out: rdn and nt qckn wl over 1f out: wknd ins fnl f* **8/1**3

7 *4½* **Sicilian Warrior (USA)** 2-8-13 0....... ShaneKelly 6 48
(P F I Cole) *hld up in midfield: hanging bdly and green over 2f out: wknd* **4/1**2

0 **8** *5* **Outdroad**19 7065 2-8-9 0....... JamesDoyle 1 29
(P M Phelan) *in tch on outer: rdn 1/2-way: sn struggling* **80/1**

9 *hd* **Contradiktive (IRE)** 2-8-10 0 ow1....... PatCosgrave 8 29
(J R Boyle) *s.i.s: rn green in rr: struggling fr 1/2-way* **25/1**

06 **10** *½* **Trusted Venture (USA)**37 6661 2-8-2 0....... AndreaAtzeni(7) 4 27
(J R Best) *a in rr: u.p in last pair bef 1/2-way* **20/1**

00 **11** *24* **Diamond Til (IRE)**18 7095 2-8-11 0....... FergusSweeney 5 —
(G L Moore) *chsd ldrs to 1/2-way: wknd rapidly: t.o* **40/1**

1m 14.33s (1.23) **Going Correction** +0.125s/f (Slow) **11 Ran SP% 124.8**
Speed ratings (Par 98): **96,95,94,92,92 91,85,78,78,78 46**
toteswinger: 1&2 £25.10, 1&3 £34.40, 2&3 £8.60. CSF £99.90 TOTE £22.60: £6.80, £2.10, £2.90; EX 209.90.
Owner Calypso Bloodstock & Partner **Bred** Airlie Stud **Trained** Newmarket, Suffolk
■ Stewards' Enquiry : Jim Crowley three-day ban: careless riding (Dec 1-3)

FOCUS
An ordinary juvenile maiden with the fifth rated 10lb below his debut form.

NOTEBOOK
Lexlenos(IRE), who had the best draw in stall 12, was held up on the rail, and picked up well from a furlong out to just edge out the more experienced Diamond Twister. A half-sister to six winners, she has the size to improve from two to three and, based on this bare form, she should start off in handicaps off a fair mark. (op 14-1)
Diamond Twister(USA) had run with promise in his first two starts on turf and he improved for the switch to Polytrack. Now eligible for a handicap mark, he should make his presence felt in that sphere, perhaps over a little further. (tchd 6-1)
Hillside Lad was quickly away and set out to make all next to the inside rail, but he did not help himself by hanging left from 2f out, carrying Bobs Dreamflight with him, and he is clearly still learning about the game. (op 13-2)
Princess Cagliari appeared to run to about the same level as on her debut and is a fair guide to the quality of the form. (tchd 11-4 and 10-3)
Bobs Dreamflight set the standard with his debut effort at Sandown, but that came way back in June and clearly all had not gone swimmingly since. He might come on for this outing, but lacks scope and may struggle next year. (tchd 5-2 and 10-3)

7357 BETDAQ THE BETTING EXCHANGE H'CAP 6f (P)
3:40 (3:42) (Class 6) (0-58,58) 3-Y-0+ **£2,047** (£604; £302) **Stalls** High

Form RPR

3004 **1** **Back In The Red (IRE)**10 7231 4-8-13 58.......(b1) KevinGhunowa(3) 10 75
(R A Harris) *mde all: rdn 2l clr over 2f out: kpt on wl and further ahd ins fnl f: unchal* **11/1**

6041 **2** *2* **River Kirov (IRE)**12 7196 5-9-0 56....... JimCrowley 9 66
(M Wigham) *chsd ldrs: rdn over 2f out: prog on inner over 1f out: styd on to take 2nd ins fnl f: no ch of catching wnr* **7/2**1

0052 **3** *1½* **Muktasb (USA)**8 7254 7-9-2 58.......(v) AdamKirby 1 64+
(D Shaw) *dwlt: dropped in fr wd draw and hld up in last pair: pushed along on inner 2f out: prog over 1f out: rdn and styd on wl to take 3rd fnl 50yds: nvr nr wnr* **8/1**

0000 **4** *½* **Kaystar Ridge**19 7076 3-8-8 55.......(bt1) JamesO'Reilly(5) 12 59
(D K Ivory) *t.k.h early: prom: drvn and outpcd 2f out: kpt on same pce after* **25/1**

6404 **5** *1½* **Night Premiere (IRE)**8 7254 3-8-10 55....... PatrickHills(3) 6 54
(R Hannon) *chsd wnr: drvn and no imp over 1f out: wknd rapidly ins fnl f* **20/1**

0414 **6** *shd* **Milne Bay (IRE)**31 6773 3-9-1 57.......(t) MartinDwyer 3 56
(D M Simcock) *chsd ldrs: rdn and outpcd over 2f out: nvr on terms after: plugged on* **9/2**3

6451 **7** *nk* **Hurricane Coast**33 6733 9-9-1 57.......(b) JamesDoyle 4 55
(D Flood) *hld up in rr: pushed along fr 2f out: kpt on fnl f: nvr nr ldrs* **12/1**

0301 **8** *1¼* **Namu**8 7255 5-9-2 58 6ex.......(p) DaneO'Neill 5 52
(Miss T Spearing) *hld up in last pair: shkn up over 2f out: modest late prog* **10/1**

006 **9** *nk* **This Ones For Pat (USA)**11 7213 3-8-13 55....... MichaelHills 11 48+
(S Parr) *s.i.s: t.k.h early: hld up in rr: shkn up over 2f out: nvr a factor* **4/1**2

3013 **10** *2¾* **Simpsons Gamble (IRE)**8 7254 5-9-1 57.......(p) EddieAhern 2 41
(R A Teal) *a in rr: struggling over 2f out* **7/1**

The Form Book, Raceform Ltd, Compton, RG20 6NL

1040 **11** *5* **Meridian Line (IRE)**^{8} 7254 3-9-0 **56**............................(b) PatCosgrave 8 24
(J G Portman) *chsd ldrs tl wknd rapidly 2f out* **33/1**

1m 13.34s (0.24) **Going Correction** +0.125s/f (Slow) 11 Ran SP% **120.7**
Speed ratings (Par 101): **103,100,98,97,95 95,95,93,93,89 82**
toteswinger: 1&2 £9.60, 1&3 £11.50, 2&3 £4.30. CSF £49.64 CT £341.83 TOTE £14.30: £4.00, £1.80, £3.40; EX 55.10.
Owner Mrs Ruth M Serrell **Bred** Mrs Rachanee Butler **Trained** Earlswood, Monmouths

FOCUS
This was a tight handicap for the grade with only 3lb covering the entire field, but it was run at an uneven pace and those racing handily were at a notable advantage. The form looks solid enough for the grade.

7358 BET MULTIPLES - BETDAQ H'CAP (DIV I) 7f (P)
4:10 (4:10) (Class 6) (0-65,71) 3-Y-O+ **£1,706** (£503; £252) **Stalls** High

Form RPR

0040 **1** **Tobar Suil Lady (IRE)**^{66} 5867 3-9-0 **61**............................ AdamKirby 5 69+
(J L Spearing) *hld up in last pair: threaded through fr 2f out: pushed along and r.o wl fnl f to ld fnl strides* **33/1**

1306 **2** *½* **Dawson Creek (IRE)**^{21} 7027 4-9-4 **64**........................(t) MichaelHills 13 70
(B Gubby) *led: fought on wl whn drvn fnl 2f: looked like holding on tl collared last strides* **15/2**

0335 **3** *¾* **Dark Camellia**^{19} 7074 3-9-1 **62**....................................(t) JamesDoyle 7 66
(H J L Dunlop) *hld up bhd ldrs: prog to go 2nd over 1f out: hrd rdn and hld by ldr ins fnl f: lost 2nd nr fin* **33/1**

060 **4** *½* **King's Colour**^{35} 6705 3-8-10 **60**.............................. JackMitchell$^{(3)}$ 1 63
(B R Johnson) *dropped in fr wdst draw and hld up in last pair: taken towards outer and shkn up over 1f out: gd prog to press ldrs ins fnl f: no ex nr fin* **33/1**

5034 **5** *1 ½* **Fine Ruler (IRE)**^{12} 7194 4-9-2 **62**........................... VinceSlattery 11 61
(M R Bosley) *dwlt: hld up in rr: rdn and effrt on inner 2f out: chsng ldrs u.p 1f out but nt on terms: one pce* **12/1**

043 **6** *1 ¾* **Cheap Street**^{35} 6706 4-9-5 **65**.................................... EddieAhern 14 59
(J G Portman) *chsd ldng pair: hrd rdn to chse ldr 2f out to over 1f out: wknd fnl f* **7/1**

2242 **7** *½* **Manchestermaverick (USA)**^{10} 7228 3-8-13 **60**.......... SteveDrowne 4 53
(H Morrison) *chsd ldr to 2f out: grad wknd* **8/1**

3031 **8** *hd* **One More Round (USA)**^{5} 7288 10-9-11 **71** 6ex.........(b) PatCosgrave 9 63
(P D Evans) *dwlt and n.m.r s: sn rcvrd to trck ldrs on inner: wl plcd 2f out: sn shkn up and fnd nil* **3/1**^{1}

5000 **9** *½* **Silidan**^{12} 7194 5-9-1 **61** ow1.. GeorgeBaker 3 52
(G L Moore) *stdd s: tk v t.k.h early and hld up on outer: shuffled along and minimal prog 2f out: nvr nr ldrs* **12/1**

0200 **10** *1 ¼* **Grizedale (IRE)**^{8} 7254 9-8-9 **55**................................(tp) PaulDoe 8 43
(M J Attwater) *n.m.r s: hld up towards rr and nvr wl plcd: no prog fnl 2f* **16/1**

2113 **11** *hd* **Musical Script (USA)**^{10} 7228 5-9-5 **65**......................(b) DaneO'Neill 6 52
(Mouse Hamilton-Fairley) *t.k.h in midfield: effrt on outer over 2f out: no imp over 1f out: fdd ins fnl f* **11/2**^{2}

0364 **12** *7* **Roundthetwist (IRE)**^{107} 4629 3-8-4 **58**...................... NoraLooby$^{(7)}$ 12 26
(K R Burke) *chsd ldrs: lost pl 2f out: sn wknd* **33/1**

0500 **13** *7* **Cape Roberto (IRE)**^{17} 7111 3-8-9 **56** ow1......................... ShaneKelly 2 5
(Jamie Poulton) *racd wd: nvr beyond midfield: wknd over 2f out: t.o* **28/1**

6003 **14** *nk* **Ten Pole Tudor**^{32} 6749 3-9-1 **65**............................ KevinGhunowa$^{(3)}$ 10 13
(R A Harris) *chsd ldrs tl wknd rapidly wl over 2f out: t.o* **13/2**^{3}

1m 26.95s (0.95) **Going Correction** +0.125s/f (Slow)
WFA 3 from 4yo+ 1lb 14 Ran SP% **125.6**
Speed ratings (Par 101): **99,98,97,97,95 93,92,92,91,90 90,82,74,73**
toteswinger: 1&2 £84.40, 1&3 £84.50, 2&3 £31.60. CSF £266.34 CT £8283.14 TOTE £56.80: £20.30, £2.90, £5.10; EX 708.80.
Owner Eye Opener Syndicate **Bred** Roland H Alder **Trained** Kinnersley, Worcs

FOCUS
A moderate handicap, run at a fair pace and the form is only ordinary.

7359 BET MULTIPLES - BETDAQ H'CAP (DIV II) 7f (P)
4:40 (4:43) (Class 6) (0-65,65) 3-Y-O+ **£1,706** (£503; £252) **Stalls** High

Form RPR

0002 **1** **Salt Of The Earth (IRE)**^{12} 7194 3-9-2 **63**..................... HayleyTurner 10 73
(T G Mills) *trckd ldng pair: wnt 2nd over 2f out: pushed along and clsd grad on ldr: led fnl 50yds* **11/2**^{3}

0600 **2** *½* **Daring Dream (GER)**^{31} 6771 3-8-11 **58**......................... DaneO'Neill 8 67
(A P Jarvis) *mde most: drvn 2f out: kpt on but worn down fnl 50yds* **16/1**

5000 **3** *¾* **Mr Garston**^{29} 6841 5-9-5 **65**..(t) PatCosgrave 12 72
(J R Boyle) *hld up towards rr on inner: prog over 2f out: disp 2nd over 1f out: nt qckn and hld ins fnl f* **9/2**^{1}

6230 **4** *1 ¾* **Overstayed (IRE)**^{47} 6382 5-8-9 **55**............................ NeilChalmers 13 57
(A Bailey) *trckd ldrs: pushed along and nt qckn over 2f out: wnt modest 4th wl over 1f out: kpt on but nvr rchd ldng trio* **9/1**

5502 **5** *1 ¾* **Dualagi**^{8} 7255 4-9-0 **60**.. VinceSlattery 14 58
(M R Bosley) *plld hrd: hld up in last pair: rdn and sme prog on inner 2f out: kpt on but nvr on terms w ldrs* **12/1**

6504 **6** *2 ¼* **Kensington (IRE)**^{5} 7286 7-9-5 **65**............................(p) SteveDrowne 1 56
(P D Evans) *racd on outer: chsd ldrs: rdn over 2f out: sn outpcd and btn* **8/1**

3600 **7** *¾* **Valentino Swing (IRE)**^{10} 7228 5-9-0 **60**........................ AdamKirby 9 49
(Miss T Spearing) *dwlt: hld up in last pair: modest prog u.p fr 2f out: nvr on terms* **16/1**

-420 **8** *¾* **Somerset Falls (UAE)**^{45} 6452 3-9-1 **62**..................... J-PGuillambert 11 49
(M Johnston) *towards rr: hrd rdn and no prog over 2f out: no ch after* **5/1**^{2}

2313 **9** *2* **Kannon**^{25} 6928 3-9-4 **65**.. DarrenWilliams 2 47
(Miss M E Rowland) *hld up in midfield towards outer: outpcd over 2f out: n.d after* **12/1**

0243 **10** *1 ½* **Who's Winning (IRE)**^{8} 7255 7-8-9 **55**....................... MichaelHills 4 33
(B G Powell) *hld up in rr and racd wd: rdn and no prog over 2f out* **12/1**

4650 **11** *2 ¼* **Kinout (IRE)**^{37} 6658 3-9-1 **62**................................... MartinDwyer 3 34
(K A Ryan) *t.k.h: trckd ldr to over 2f out: wknd: eased over 1f out* **10/1**

6010 **12** *1 ¾* **Dr Synn**^{19} 7076 7-8-7 **53**.. PaulDoe 6 20
(M J Attwater) *rousted along early on outer: struggling fr wl over 2f out* **16/1**

6000 **13** *8* **Free Tussy (ARG)**^{49} 6336 4-9-5 **65**..........................(t) GeorgeBaker 5 11
(G L Moore) *chsd ldrs: rdn 1/2-way: wknd over 2f out: t.o* **14/1**

1m 26.49s (0.49) **Going Correction** +0.125s/f (Slow)
WFA 3 from 4yo+ 1lb 13 Ran SP% **127.8**
Speed ratings (Par 101): **102,101,100,98,96 94,93,92,90,88 85,83,74**
toteswinger: 1&2 £22.80, 1&3 £7.40, 2&3 £18.90. CSF £97.35 CT £444.78 TOTE £7.30: £2.30, £5.40, £1.70; EX 179.70.
Owner Mrs Yvonne Russell **Bred** Bayview Properties Ltd **Trained** Headley, Surrey

FOCUS
This second division of the 7f handicap was a wide-open heat and few managed to get into it from off the pace. It was a notably quicker time than the first and the race could rate a bit higher.

7360 BETDAQ.CO.UK H'CAP 1m (P)
5:10 (5:28) (Class 5) (0-70,70) 3-Y-O+ **£2,590** (£770; £385; £192) **Stalls** High

Form RPR

0042 **1** **Eastern Gift**^{4} 7307 3-9-3 **69**.. DaneO'Neill 14 77
(R Hannon) *trckd ldrs on inner: effrt 2f out: drvn to chse ldr ins fnl f: styd on wl to ld last stride* **11/4**^{1}

6000 **2** *shd* **Jake The Snake (IRE)**^{19} 7077 7-9-6 **70**.................... HayleyTurner 11 78
(A W Carroll) *t.k.h early: trckd ldr 3f: styd prom: effrt over 2f out: led over 1f out: drvn fnl f: hdd last stride* **10/1**

0004 **3** *2* **Restless Genius (IRE)**^{21} 7018 3-9-4 **70**.....................(t) SteveDrowne 3 73+
(A M Balding) *hld up towards rr: prog on outer 2f out: drvn and r.o fnl f to snatch 3rd last stride* **12/1**

6 **4** *nk* **Watson's Bay**^{21} 7026 3-9-2 **68**................................... FergusSweeney 10 71
(Miss Tor Sturgis) *hld up towards rr on inner: effrt over 2f out: prog to chse ldrs over 1f out: styd on: nvr able to chal* **33/1**

3000 **5** *hd* **Young Bertie**^{28} 6867 5-9-1 **65**..(v) GeorgeBaker 1 67
(H Morrison) *mde most to over 1f out: fdd ins fnl f* **12/1**

6400 **6** *½* **Trafalgar Square**^{19} 7077 6-9-3 **67**................................... JimCrowley 6 68+
(M J Attwater) *t.k.h: hld up in last pair: prog 2f out: r.o fnl f: nvr nrr and no ch* **10/1**

0043 **7** *2* **Master Pegasus**^{32} 6758 5-9-1 **65**................................... PatCosgrave 5 62
(J R Boyle) *chsd ldrs: rdn and nt qckn over 2f out: one pce after* **5/1**^{2}

6004 **8** *1 ½* **Flying Goose (IRE)**^{32} 6749 4-9-2 **69**...................... KevinGhunowa$^{(3)}$ 12 62
(R A Harris) *s.s: hld up in last pair: prog 2f out: no imp on ldrs over 1f out: nvr on terms* **9/1**

4042 **9** *¾* **Moon Crystal**^{14} 7166 3-9-0 **66**..(bt^{1}) ShaneKelly 9 57
(E A L Dunlop) *s.i.s: sn rcvrd into midfield: no prog 2f out: fdd* **8/1**^{3}

2252 **10** *shd* **Diego Rivera**^{86} 5268 3-9-1 **67**... EddieAhern 2 58
(P J Makin) *hld up in rr: shkn up and no prog over 2f out: no ch after* **14/1**

6000 **11** *¾* **Billy One Punch**^{17} 7115 6-8-13 **63**........................... DarrenWilliams 13 52
(D Shaw) *hld up in midfield: rdn over 2f out: no rspnse: wknd over 1f out* **10/1**

6U10 **12** *2 ¼* **Bramalea**^{14} 7166 3-9-1 **67**.. AdamKirby 4 51
(B W Duke) *t.k.h early: chsd ldr after 3f to over 2f out: wknd* **16/1**

6001 **13** *4* **Zazous**^{26} 6912 7-8-3 **56** oh4.. MarcHalford$^{(3)}$ 8 31
(J J Bridger) *t.k.h early: chsd ldrs on outer: cl enough over 2f out: wknd rapidly* **25/1**

1m 40.31s (0.51) **Going Correction** +0.125s/f (Slow)
WFA 3 from 4yo+ 2lb 13 Ran SP% **126.4**
Speed ratings (Par 103): **102,101,99,99,99 98,96,95,94,94 93,91,87**
toteswinger: 1&2 £10.70, 1&3 £12.00, 2&3 £28.50. CSF £33.20 CT £311.79 TOTE £4.20: £1.80, £3.50, £5.00; EX 41.90 Place 6: £697.50, Place 5: £263.12..
Owner J A Lazzari **Bred** P And Mrs A G Venner **Trained** East Everleigh, Wilts
■ Stewards' Enquiry : Fergus Sweeney two-day ban: careless riding (Dec 1-2)

FOCUS
This modest handicap was run at an average pace and the first pair pulled clear in a bobbing finish. The form is a bit messy with the winner not needing to run to his previous mark.
T/Jkpt: Not won. T/Plt: £463.70 to a £1 stake. Pool: £65,561.63. 103.20 winning tickets. T/Qpdt: £202.00 to a £1 stake. Pool: £3,849.70. 14.10 winning tickets. JN

7340 WOLVERHAMPTON (A.W) (L-H)
Monday, November 17

OFFICIAL GOING: Standard
Wind: Almost nil Weather: Overcast and damp, heavy shower for 4.30

7361 BOOK TICKETS ONLINE CLAIMING STKS 5f 216y(P)
2:00 (2:01) (Class 5) 2-Y-O **£3,238** (£963; £481; £240) **Stalls** Low

Form RPR

006 **1** **Deckchair**^{35} 6709 2-8-2 56..(v) LiamJones 9 55
(H J Collingridge) *hld up in mid-div: hdwy wl over 1f out: rdn to ld ent fnl f: sn hung lft: r.o* **16/1**

4456 **2** *1 ¾* **Officer Mor (USA)**^{11} 7212 2-9-1 65... NCallan 5 63
(K R Burke) *a.p: rdn over 1f out: ev ch jst ins fnl f: nt qckn* **11/2**^{3}

0304 **3** *1 ¼* **Imperial Skylight**^{26} 6906 2-8-9 57........................... EdwardCreighton 10 53
(M R Channon) *hld up in tch: c wd st: rdn and edgd lft fr over 1f out: kpt on* **7/1**

5252 **4** *½* **Readily**^{11} 7212 2-8-4 61.. FrankieMcDonald 3 47
(J G Portman) *led: hdd over 2f out: rdn and ev ch 1f out: one pce* **5/1**^{2}

0205 **5** *½* **Autumn Morning (IRE)**^{12} 7199 2-8-0 53........................ LukeMorris$^{(3)}$ 4 44+
(P D Evans) *s.i.s: hld up and bhd: rdn 3f out: hdwy whn swtchd rt over 1f out: edgd lft ent fnl f: one pce* **20/1**

05 **6** *1 ¾* **Lupe Lamora**^{14} 7168 2-8-1 0... FrancisNorton 12 37
(J A Osborne) *hld up towards rr: nvr trbld ldrs* **15/2**

1234 **7** *¾* **Faraway Sound (IRE)**^{91} 5159 2-9-2 75............................ LeeEnstone 1 50
(P C Haslam) *w ldr: led over 2f out: rdn wl over 1f out: hdd ent fnl f: wknd* **5/1**^{2}

1005 **8** *2* **Tartan Turban (IRE)**^{11} 7212 2-8-4 64........................ CharlesEddery$^{(7)}$ 7 39
(R Hannon) *hld up and bhd: n.d* **7/1**

2130 **9** *1 ¼* **Jubilee Juggins (IRE)**^{39} 6603 2-8-9 70................(b^{1}) KirstyMilczarek 8 33
(N P Littmoden) *prom: rdn whn carried sltly lft over 1f out: sn wknd* **9/2**^{1}

5604 **10** *nk* **Adozen Dreams**^{17} 7113 2-8-0 55.........................(p) DuranFentiman$^{(3)}$ 2 26
(G R Oldroyd) *s.i.s: sn prom: rdn and wknd jst over 1f out* **16/1**

0403 **11** *2 ½* **Turn To Dreams**^{11} 7212 2-8-4 57.......................... CatherineGannon 11 20
(P D Evans) *in rr: rdn over 2f out: sn struggling* **25/1**

1m 15.52s (0.52) **Going Correction** +0.025s/f (Slow) 11 Ran SP% **124.0**
Speed ratings (Par 96): **97,94,93,92,91 89,88,85,84,83 80**
toteswinger: 1&2 £31.70, 1&3 £22.80, 2&3 £12.40. CSF £107.22 TOTE £20.80: £3.60, £2.40, £3.40; EX 316.00 TRIFECTA Not won..
Owner Dave Clayton **Bred** Whitsbury Manor Stud **Trained** Exning, Suffolk

FOCUS
A moderate claimer and, although the form is weak, it looks reliable enough.

NOTEBOOK
Deckchair was able to get off the mark at the fifth attempt on this drop back to sprinting. She had something in hand at the weights over the runner-up and the third, so probably didn't have to improve on her official mark of 56. It has to be said, though, that she didn't look straightforward, as she hung left once in front.
Officer Mor(USA) had to switch towards the inside rail with his challenge, but he had his chance. He would have been 4lb better off with the winner in a handicap. (op 13-2 tchd 7-1)
Imperial Skylight had something to find with the front two at the weights, but he ran well considering he was caught wide for much of the way. (op 14-1)
Readily was given a positive ride, but she ran well below her official mark of 61. (op 6-1)

Autumn Morning(IRE) was always struggling after starting slowly.
Jubilee Juggins(IRE), dropped in grade, found nothing under pressure in first-time blinkers. (op 4-1)

7362 HOTEL & CONFERENCING AT WOLVERHAMPTON MAIDEN STKS 5f 216y(P)
2:30 (2:30) (Class 5) 3-Y-O+ **£2,729** (£806; £403) **Stalls** Low

Form RPR
0342 **1** **Madame Hoi (IRE)**[11] 7213 3-8-12 74 TonyCulhane 11 65
(M R Channon) *a.p: wnt 2nd over 3f out: led jst over 1f out: drvn out* **9/2**[3]
6200 **2** *1 ¾* **Welsh Opera**[24] 6955 3-8-12 53 (t) RichardKingscote 9 59
(S C Williams) *a.p: rdn and ev ch over 1f out: nt qckn ins fnl f* **14/1**
5 **3** *2* **Absa Lutte (IRE)**[10] 7233 5-8-12 65 (t) LPKeniry 5 53+
(Jarlath P Fahey, Ire) *s.s: hld up and bhd: hdwy over 2f out: hrd rdn over 1f out: kpt on to take 3rd towards fin* **5/2**[2]
0 **4** *½* **Cabopino (IRE)**[192] 1971 3-8-12 0 JamieSpencer 10 51
(K R Burke) *hld up in tch: rdn over 2f out: one pce whn edgd lft ins fnl f* **9/1**
04/0 **5** *2 ½* **Prix Masque (IRE)**[149] 3268 4-9-3 47 RichardThomas 7 48
(Christian Wroe) *towards rr: rdn over 2f out: kpt on ins fnl f: n.d* **66/1**
3046 **6** *¾* **Laureldean Dream (USA)**[75] 5617 3-8-12 66 (t) RobertWinston 2 41
(P W Chapple-Hyam) *sn w ldr: lost 2nd over 3f out: rdn over 2f out: wknd wl over 1f out* **11/1**
3234 **7** *2 ½* **Shakedown**[41] 6566 3-9-3 67 NCallan 8 38
(E S McMahon) *t.k.h: led: rdn and hung lft whn hdd jst over 1f out: wknd qckly ins fnl f* **15/8**[1]
0003 **8** *1 ½* **Pentandra (IRE)**[12] 7195 3-8-12 48 TPQueally 12 28
(J G Given) *t.k.h: stdd into mid-div over 4f out: short-lived effrt on outside over 2f out* **16/1**
9 *1 ¼* **Japura (USA)**[533] 2285 4-9-3 0 RobertHavlin 4 29
(T J Pitt) *s.i.s: a bhd* **9/1**
00 **10** *12* **Foolish Optimist**[2] 7344 3-8-5 0 KrishGundowry(7) 1 —
(Paul Green) *hld up in tch: wknd wl over 2f out* **80/1**
0 **11** *5* **In With A Shout**[11] 7213 3-8-12 0 PaulMulrennan 6 —
(J G Given) *a in rr* **40/1**

1m 15.09s (0.09) **Going Correction** +0.025s/f (Slow) 11 Ran SP% **127.6**
Speed ratings (Par 103): **100,97,95,94,91 90,86,84,83,67 60**
toteswinger: 1&2 £4.20, 1&3 £1.40, 2&3 £36.20. CSF £71.32 TOTE £5.10: £1.10, £8.50, £1.70; EX 59.20 TRIFECTA Not won..
Owner Norman Court Stud **Bred** Brownstown Stud Partnership **Trained** West Ilsley, Berks

FOCUS
A weak maiden rated around the runner-up to this year's form, although the proximity of the fifth raises doubts.
Absa Lutte(IRE) Official explanation: jockey said mare missed the break

7363 WOLVERHAMPTON-RACECOURSE.CO.UK (S) STKS 7f 32y(P)
3:00 (3:01) (Class 6) 3-Y-O+ **£2,047** (£604; £302) **Stalls** High

Form RPR
0360 **1** **Samurai Warrior**[99] 4891 3-9-0 55 RobertWinston 3 68
(P D Evans) *chsd ldr: led 2f out: hrd rdn and hung rt 1f out: drvn out* **14/1**
620 **2** *nk* **Blue Charm**[21] 7018 4-9-1 60 LPKeniry 7 68
(S Kirk) *hld up in tch: rdn whn swtchd lft and wnt 2nd 1f out: r.o* **3/1**[1]
0000 **3** *¾* **Lytton**[35] 6710 3-9-0 75 LiamJones 5 65
(R Ford) *hld up and bhd: hdwy wl over 1f out: rdn and edgd lft ins fnl f: kpt on* **11/2**[2]
060 **4** *3 ½* **Climate (IRE)**[14] 7167 9-9-4 60 (p) LukeMorris(3) 4 63
(P D Evans) *hld up in mid-div: rdn and hdwy over 1f out: one pce fnl f* **12/1**
3026 **5** *3 ¼* **Mrs Jefferson (IRE)**[19] 7076 3-9-1 59 TPQueally 1 48
(J G Portman) *prom: rdn wl over 1f out: sn wknd* **8/1**
2000 **6** *3* **El Fuser**[33] 6736 3-9-0 60 TravisBlock 2 39
(P J Makin) *led: rdn and hdd 2f out: wknd fnl f* **10/1**
300 **7** *1* **Just Jimmy (IRE)**[34] 6716 3-9-6 55 (v[1]) TomEaves 9 42
(P D Evans) *plld hrd in rr: rdn over 2f out: nvr nr ldrs* **22/1**
0 **8** *½* **Lucky Forteen**[59] 6091 5-8-10 0 TonyCulhane 10 31
(P W Hiatt) *a bhd* **100/1**
5635 **9** *9* **Cap St Jean (IRE)**[10] 7226 4-9-0 60 (p) DavidKenny(7) 6 18
(R Hollinshead) *s.s: lft in rr: no ch fnl 3f* **11/2**[2]
5000 **10** *¾* **Forced Upon Us**[11] 7206 4-9-7 58 (v[1]) NCallan 11 16
(P J McBride) *prom tl rdn and wknd over 2f out* **7/1**
36-0 **11** *6* **Prince Tum Tum (USA)**[314] 85 8-9-1 82 TGMcLaughlin 8 —
(P Howling) *hld up in mid-div: rdn over 2f out: sn wknd* **13/2**[3]
6-0 **12** *10* **Mexilhoeira**[19] 7074 4-8-10 0 JerryO'Dwyer 12 —
(J R Gask) *plld hrd in rr: lost tch fnl 2f* **66/1**

1m 29.11s (-0.49) **Going Correction** +0.025s/f (Slow)
WFA 3 from 4yo+ 1lb 12 Ran SP% **123.0**
Speed ratings (Par 101): **103,102,101,97,94 90,89,88,78,77 70,59**
toteswinger: 1&2 £31.70, 1&3 £22.80, 2&3 £12.40. CSF £57.52 TOTE £19.90: £6.10, £1.80, £2.70; EX 86.30 TRIFECTA Not won..There was no bid for the winner.
Owner Mrs I M Folkes **Bred** Lady Lonsdale **Trained** Pandy, Monmouths
■ Stewards' Enquiry : Robert Winston caution: careless riding; one-day ban: used whip with excessive frequency (Dec 1)

FOCUS
A standard seller but not bad form rated through the runner-up.
Mexilhoeira Official explanation: jockey said filly hung right

7364 WOLVERHAMPTON HOLIDAY INN H'CAP 1m 4f 50y(P)
3:30 (3:30) (Class 5) (0-75,74) 3-Y-O+ **£3,238** (£963; £481; £240) **Stalls** Low

Form RPR
-055 **1** **Remember Ramon (USA)**[21] 7009 5-9-7 71 NCallan 4 80
(J R Gask) *set modest pce: qcknd clr 2f out: shkn up over 1f out: r.o wl* **2/1**[1]
433 **2** *2* **Locum**[19] 7070 3-8-7 63 PaulMulrennan 3 69+
(M H Tompkins) *hld up in tch: rdn and hung lft whn wnt 2nd 1f out: nt trble wnr* **15/2**
4113 **3** *2 ½* **Graylyn Ruby (FR)**[18] 7091 3-9-1 74 LukeMorris(3) 7 76
(J Jay) *t.k.h: sn chsng wnr: rdn over 2f out: lost 2nd 1f out: one pce* **9/2**[2]
5000 **4** *¾* **New Beginning (IRE)**[23] 6974 4-9-8 72 RobertWinston 1 73
(Mrs S Lamyman) *prom: rdn over 2f out: wknd wl over 1f out* **14/1**
-013 **5** *½* **Five Two**[10] 7230 5-9-4 68 (t) EdwardCreighton 9 68
(Gavin Patrick Cromwell, Ire) *hld up in rr: hdwy on outside over 3f out: rdn and wkng whn hung lft jst over 1f out* **5/1**[3]
0345 **6** *1 ¾* **Drawn Gold**[34] 6721 4-9-0 64 GrahamGibbons 6 61
(R Hollinshead) *hld up in mid-div: hdwy over 5f out: rdn and wknd 2f out* **15/2**
1404 **7** *nse* **Dragon Slayer (IRE)**[20] 7056 6-9-0 71 AshleyMorgan(7) 2 68
(John A Harris) *t.k.h in tch: rdn wl over 1f out: wknd ent fnl f* **16/1**
2110 **8** *nk* **Swords**[44] 6472 6-9-3 67 DarryllHolland 8 64
(R E Peacock) *t.k.h: a in rr* **13/2**
4-00 **9** *¾* **Freedom Song**[33] 6741 3-8-10 66 RichardKingscote 5 61
(R Charlton) *a bhd* **22/1**

2m 43.45s (2.35) **Going Correction** +0.025s/f (Slow)
WFA 3 from 4yo+ 6lb 9 Ran SP% **121.9**
Speed ratings (Par 103): **93,91,90,89,89 88,87,87,87**
toteswinger: 1&2 £3.50, 1&3 £3.20, 2&3 £6.70. CSF £19.18 CT £64.21 TOTE £2.20: £1.10, £3.10, £2.10; EX 21.40 Trifecta £117.70 Part won. Pool: £159.13, 0.43 - winning units..
Owner Horses First Racing Limited **Bred** Bruce T Hundley **Trained** Sutton Veny, Wilts

FOCUS
An ordinary handicap, but the pace was modest which caused a few to take a keen grip and those that raced handily were at a big advantage. The runner-up is a solid marker backed up here by the third.
Drawn Gold Official explanation: vet said gelding was struck into on off-fore leg
Swords Official explanation: jockey said gelding ran too free

7365 WOLVERHAMPTON-RACECOURSE.CO.UK H'CAP 5f 20y(P)
4:00 (4:00) (Class 3) (0-95,95) 3-Y-O+ **£7,771** (£2,312; £1,155; £577) **Stalls** Low

Form RPR
1161 **1** **Arganil (USA)**[19] 7066 3-8-10 87 NCallan 5 100+
(K A Ryan) *sn led: rdn fnl f: drvn out* **5/2**[2]
1520 **2** *2* **The Jobber (IRE)**[23] 6971 7-8-10 87 FrancisNorton 8 93
(M Blanshard) *t.k.h in tch: swtchd lft after 1f: chsd wnr over 1f out: rdn and no imp ins fnl f: jst hld on for 2nd* **10/1**
000 **3** *shd* **Fyodor (IRE)**[51] 6290 7-9-4 95 (v) LPKeniry 4 101
(C R Dore) *hld up in rr: hdwy wl over 1f out: swtchd rt jst ins fnl f: rdn and kpt on: jst failed to take 2nd* **14/1**
4503 **4** *¾* **Matsunosuke**[15] 7151 6-8-13 90 DarryllHolland 1 93
(A B Coogan) *led early: sn stdd into mid-div: hmpd over 2f out: c wd st: r.o ins fnl f* **9/4**[1]
0602 **5** *1 ¼* **Luscivious**[15] 7151 4-8-3 85 (b) EJMcNamara(5) 3 83
(A J McCabe) *carried rt s: hld up in rr: hdwy on ins over 2f out: rdn and one pce fnl f* **7/1**[3]
6046 **6** *1* **Bertoliver**[15] 7151 4-8-11 88 RichardKingscote 10 83
(Tom Dascombe) *w ldrs: wnt 2nd 3f out: rdn over 1f out: wknd wl ins fnl f* **8/1**
0150 **7** *shd* **Vhujon (IRE)**[26] 6902 3-8-10 87 TGMcLaughlin 6 81
(P D Evans) *a bhd* **16/1**
1204 **8** *4 ½* **Soopacal (IRE)**[191] 1999 3-9-0 91 TomEaves 9 69
(B Smart) *hld up in mid-div: bmpd on outside over 2f out: c wd st: sn bhd* **11/1**
1600 **9** *nse* **Almaty Express**[5] 7290 6-8-7 84 (b) JoeFanning 7 62
(J R Weymes) *sn w ldr: lost 2nd 3f out: wknd wl over 1f out* **28/1**

61.23 secs (-1.07) **Going Correction** +0.025s/f (Slow) 9 Ran SP% **116.4**
Speed ratings (Par 107): **109,105,105,104,102 100,100,93,93**
toteswinger: 1&2 £4.90, 1&3 £8.80, 2&3 £22.80. CSF £28.14 CT £296.05 TOTE £2.80: £1.30, £3.80, £5.50; EX 27.40 Trifecta £186.00 Part won. Pool: £251.46, 0.43 - winning units..
Owner The Big Moment **Bred** Colt Neck Stables, Llc **Trained** Hambleton, N Yorks

FOCUS
A decent sprint handicap with the winner progressive and the runner-up to his recent turf best.

NOTEBOOK
Arganil(USA) ◆ looked very useful in defying a 3lb rise for his recent Great Leighs success. He was not exactly left alone up front, but was still able to set a sensible pace and was possibly able to get a breather in rounding the final bend, before running on strongly in the straight. Although plenty went his way, he is improving nicely and is now 4-7 lifetime, as well as 2-2 on Polytrack. (op 10-3 tchd 9-4)
The Jobber(IRE) was a winner at Lingfield on his last start on Polytrack, so the surface was not a problem, and he ran well behind the rapidly improving winner. Official explanation: jockey said gelding finished distressed (op 15-2)
Fyodor(IRE), picked up out of William Haggas's yard for 10,000gns since his last run, was kidded into contention but was never getting there. He is the sort of horse who needs everything to fall right. (op 12-1 tchd 16-1)
Matsunosuke is better than he showed as he was badly hampered when Almaty Express, who was directly in front of him, began to struggle, and he had to switch wide of that rival. (op 5-2 tchd 11-4)
Luscivious was on a winning mark, but he was never involved having been held up. (op 6-1 tchd 15-2)
Bertoliver is probably better when able to dominate. (tchd 9-1)

7366 DINE IN THE HORIZONS RESTAURANT H'CAP 2m 119y(P)
4:30 (4:30) (Class 5) (0-75,72) 3-Y-O+ **£3,238** (£963; £481; £240) **Stalls** Low

Form RPR
216- **1** **Bank On Benny**[22] 7004 6-9-3 66 (bt[1]) EJMcNamara(5) 6 77
(E McNamara, Ire) *t.k.h: a.p: led over 3f out: clr over 2f out: rdn out* **16/1**
1/61 **2** *2 ¼* **Pseudonym (IRE)**[9] 6329 6-9-7 65 (t) LPKeniry 4 73
(M F Harris) *hld up towards rr: hdwy 2f out: wnt 2nd jst ins fnl f: styd on: nt trble wnr* **25/1**
0214 **3** *3 ¾* **Victory Quest (IRE)**[7] 7271 8-9-11 69 (v) RobertWinston 3 73
(Mrs S Lamyman) *prom: rdn and outpcd over 2f out: styd on to take 3rd nr fin* **22/1**
6032 **4** *hd* **Mohawk Star (IRE)**[11] 7216 7-9-11 69 (v) NCallan 11 73
(I A Wood) *hld up: hdwy over 4f out: rdn and chsd wnr wl over 2f out tl jst ins fnl f: wknd* **10/1**
5633 **5** *2 ½* **Squirtle (IRE)**[5] 7293 5-9-4 65 LukeMorris(3) 2 66
(W M Brisbourne) *hld up and bhd: rdn 3f out: styd on fnl f: nvr nrr* **16/1**
1-41 **6** *1* **Dart**[7] 7271 4-9-11 69 6ex JamieSpencer 10 68
(J R Fanshawe) *hld up and bhd: hdwy over 4f out: rdn over 2f out: wknd 1f out* **1/1**[1]
6436 **7** *hd* **Opera De Luna**[26] 6897 3-8-4 57 LiamJones 9 56
(D Shaw) *hld up in rr: hdwy on outside 4f out: btn whn hung lft fr over 1f out* **33/1**
0002 **8** *5* **Inchpast**[7] 7271 7-10-0 72 (b) PaulMulrennan 1 65
(M H Tompkins) *hld up: rdn over 4f out: a bhd* **7/2**[2]
2256 **9** *7* **Urban Warrior**[48] 5465 4-9-8 66 DarryllHolland 7 51
(Ian Williams) *chsd ldr tl over 3f out: rdn and wknd over 2f out* **8/1**
4200 **10** *18* **Spiritonthemount (USA)**[11] 7216 3-8-13 66 (b) TonyCulhane 8 29
(P W Hiatt) *a bhd: t.o* **16/1**
5522 **11** *14* **Into The Light**[35] 6708 3-9-1 68 GrahamGibbons 5 14
(E S McMahon) *led: hdd over 3f out: wknd qckly over 2f out: t.o* **9/2**[3]

3m 41.26s (-0.54) **Going Correction** +0.025s/f (Slow)
WFA 3 from 4yo+ 9lb 11 Ran SP% **139.4**
Speed ratings (Par 103): **102,100,99,99,97 97,97,94,91,83 76**
toteswinger: 1&2 £63.80, 1&3 £35.80, 2&3 £27.10. CSF £407.51 CT £8570.99 TOTE £20.10: £4.40, £7.00, £5.10; EX 445.50 TRIFECTA Not won..
Owner Aidan Ryan **Bred** Gilridge Bloodstock Ltd **Trained** Rathkeale, Co. Limerick

FOCUS
A reasonable staying handicap run at a fair pace and the form looks sound.
Opera De Luna Official explanation: jockey said filly hung left in straight
Inchpast Official explanation: jockey said gelding never travelled
Spiritonthemount(USA) Official explanation: jockey said gelding ran poorly throughout

7367 RINGSIDE SUITE H'CAP (DIV I) 1m 141y(P)
5:00 (5:00) (Class 6) (0-65,65) 3-Y-0+ **£1,706** (£503; £252) **Stalls** Low

Form RPR
0006 **1** **Follow The Flag (IRE)**[18] 7090 4-9-4 **62**....................(p) RobertWinston 1 71
(A J McCabe) *hld up in mid-div: hdwy on ins over 2f out: rdn wl over 1f out: led wl ins fnl f: drvn out* **4/1**[2]
0135 **2** *1/2* **Kirstys Lad**[2] 7345 6-8-13 **57**.................................... DarryllHolland 6 65
(M Mullineaux) *a.p: led over 2f out: rdn and hdd wl ins fnl f: nt qckn* **11/8**[1]
0-60 **3** *3* **Distant Piper (IRE)**[2] 7342 5-9-2 **65**.......................... EJMcNamara(5) 7 66
(Adrian McGuinness, Ire) *hld up in rr: rdn and hdwy over 1f out: kpt on to take 3rd towards fin* **14/1**
4406 **4** *1* **Felicia**[2] 7345 3-8-2 **52**.. LukeMorris(3) 2 51
(S C Williams) *a.p: wnt 2nd 2f out: rdr sn lost reins: rdn and one pce fnl f* **7/1**
4040 **5** *2* **Alexander Guru**[19] 7076 4-9-1 **59**.............................. FrancisNorton 10 54
(M Blanshard) *t.k.h in mid-div: hdwy over 4f out: hung lft fr over 1f out: eased whn btn ins fnl f* **9/2**[3]
6502 **6** *1/2* **Eternal Optimist (IRE)**[5] 7287 3-8-2 **56** ow1.......(p) KrishGundowry(7) 5 49
(Paul Green) *hld up in rr: nvr trbld ldrs* **7/1**
4034 **7** *5* **Liberty Valance (IRE)**[97] 4943 3-9-3 **64**................................ LPKeniry 9 46
(S Kirk) *a bhd* **16/1**
0 **8** *nse* **Dontpaytheferryman (USA)**[31] 5261 3-8-10 **57**......... TGMcLaughlin 3 39
(P D Evans) *hld up in tch: pushed along over 3f out: sn wknd* **10/1**
1000 **9** *7* **Hit The Roof**[247] 900 3-9-2 **63**.. TPQueally 4 29
(J G Given) *led: hdd over 2f out: rdn and wknd wl over 1f out* **16/1**
1m 50.42s (-0.08) **Going Correction** +0.025s/f (Slow)
WFA 3 from 4yo+ 3lb **9** Ran SP% **132.8**
Speed ratings (Par 101): **101,100,97,97,95 94,90,90,84**
toteswinger: 1&2 £2.20, 1&3 £14.10, 2&3 £7.50. CSF £11.60 CT £81.05 TOTE £5.80: £1.70, £1.50, £3.60; EX 14.60 Trifecta £179.70 Part won. Pool: £242.90, 0.27 - winning units..
Owner S Gillen **Bred** Martin Francis **Trained** Babworth, Notts
■ Stewards' Enquiry : Robert Winston one-day ban: used whip with excessive frequency without giving gelding time to respond (Dec 2)
FOCUS
A moderate handicap, although the time was 0.59 seconds quicker than the second division and modest form rated around those in the frame behind the winner.

7368 RINGSIDE SUITE H'CAP (DIV II) 1m 141y(P)
5:30 (5:30) (Class 6) (0-65,65) 3-Y-0+ **£1,706** (£503; £252) **Stalls** Low

Form RPR
2443 **1** **Ours (IRE)**[21] 7021 5-9-7 **65**..(p) DarryllHolland 7 74+
(John A Harris) *hld up towards rr: smooth prog on ins wl over 1f out: shkn up to ld jst ins fnl f: pushed out* **11/4**[1]
0011 **2** *3/4* **The Grey One (IRE)**[17] 7112 5-8-10 **59**..........................(p) MCGeran(5) 8 67
(J M Bradley) *hld up in tch: rdn and ev ch 1f out: nt qckn* **13/2**
0-06 **3** *2 1/4* **Quick Off The Mark**[14] 7166 3-9-2 **63**................................ TPQueally 3 65
(J G Given) *chsd ldr: rdn to ld over 1f out: hdd jst ins fnl f: no ex* **6/1**
0160 **4** *1 1/2* **Prince Golan (IRE)**[21] 7021 4-9-4 **62**.......................... RobertWinston 9 61
(J W Unett) *s.i.s: hld up in rr: hdwy over 3f out: rdn over 2f out: one pce fnl f* **14/1**
0604 **5** *shd* **Pearl Dealer (IRE)**[108] 4605 3-9-0 **64**..........................(t) LukeMorris(3) 10 63
(N J Vaughan) *s.i.s: t.k.h in rr: hrd rdn over 1f out: sme late prog: n.d* **9/2**[3]
2005 **6** *1/2* **Stormin Heart (USA)**[13] 7180 3-8-4 **51** oh3..................(b) JoeFanning 4 49
(M Johnston) *led: rdn and hdd over 1f out: wknd ins fnl f* **15/2**
0520 **7** *1/2* **Dushstorm (IRE)**[2] 7340 7-8-1 **52**.............................. RossAtkinson(7) 1 48
(R J Price) *hld up in mid-div: n.m.r briefly over 2f out: sn wknd* **7/2**[2]
0-30 **8** *2 1/2* **Flagstone (USA)**[43] 1482 4-8-11 **55**.............................. TGMcLaughlin 5 46
(Ian Williams) *a bhd* **18/1**
0000 **9** *3 1/4* **Daraiym (IRE)**[136] 3671 3-8-4 **51** oh1................................ FrancisNorton 6 34
(Paul Green) *prom: reminders sn after s: wknd wl over 1f out* **25/1**
1m 51.01s (0.51) **Going Correction** +0.025s/f (Slow)
WFA 3 from 4yo+ 3lb **9** Ran SP% **122.2**
Speed ratings (Par 101): **98,97,95,94,93 93,93,90,87**
toteswinger: 1&2 £6.50, 1&3 £5.30, 2&3 £8.20. CSF £22.73 CT £103.99 TOTE £4.30: £1.50, £1.20, £2.60; EX 14.10 Trifecta £98.90 Pool: £184.57, 1.38 - winning units. Place 6: £2,037.13, Place 5: £458.59..
Owner D A Spencer **Bred** David John Brown **Trained** Eastwell, Leics
■ Stewards' Enquiry : Luke Morris one-day ban: careless riding (Dec 1)
FOCUS
They went a good pace thanks to Stormin Heart, but the winning time was still 0.59 seconds slower than the first division. The form looks solid enough with the first four all close to previous form.
T/Plt: £2,240.40 to a £1 stake. Pool: £58,773.43. 19.15 winning tickets. T/Qpdt: £215.70 to a £1 stake. Pool: £5,509.15. 18.90 winning tickets. KH

7316 SOUTHWELL (L-H)
Tuesday, November 18

OFFICIAL GOING: Standard
Wind: Light half across Weather: Fine and dry

7369 CALL 01636 814418 TO SPONSOR A RACE H'CAP (DIV I) 6f (F)
12:20 (12:28) (Class 6) (0-50,50) 3-Y-0+ **£1,706** (£503; £252) **Stalls** Low

Form RPR
0U10 **1** **Tenancy (IRE)**[6] 7286 4-8-7 **50**.................................. JamesO'Reilly(5) 5 61
(R C Guest) *mde all: jnd and rdn over 2f out: drvn over 1f out: kpt on gamely ins fnl f* **7/1**[2]
0405 **2** *hd* **Tadlil**[66] 5916 6-8-3 **46**..(v) MCGeran(5) 6 56
(J M Bradley) *dwlt: sn trcking ldrs: hdwy to join wnr over 2f out: rdn and ev ch wl over 1f out: drvn ins fnl f: edgd lft and one pce* **8/1**
260 **3** *1 3/4* **Charlotte Grey**[34] 6733 4-8-9 **50** ow1............................ JackMitchell(3) 3 55
(P J McBride) *in tch on inner: effrt to chse ldrs wl over 1f out and sn rdn: drvn ent fnl f: kpt on same pce* **15/2**[3]
0054 **4** *1/2* **Vanatina (IRE)**[14] 7178 4-8-5 **46** oh1............................ DuranFentiman(3) 4 49
(W M Brisbourne) *cl up: rdn over 2f out: drvn over 1f out and kpt on same pce* **7/1**[2]
2000 **5** *2* **Head To Head (IRE)**[4] 7323 4-8-8 **46** oh1.................. GrahamGibbons 1 43+
(A D Brown) *awkward s and towards rr: hdwy on inner whn hmpd over 3f out: rdn 2f out: styd on ins fnl f: nrst fin* **8/1**
0506 **6** *3/4* **Out Of India**[14] 7180 6-8-7 **48**.................................. KevinGhunowa(3) 13 42
(P T Dalton) *in tch: effrt over 2f out: sn rdn and kpt on same pce appr fnl f* **6/1**[1]
300 **7** *1/2* **Rossini Byline (IRE)**[104] 4725 3-8-12 **50**........................(b[1]) LiamJones 2 43
(J L Spearing) *cl up on inner: rdn along over 2f out and sn one pce* **14/1**
0500 **8** *1 1/4* **Northern Chorus (IRE)**[42] 6546 5-8-9 **47**..........(v) ChrisCatlin 10 36
(J O'Reilly) *towards rr: rdn and sme hdwy on wd outside 2f out: no imp appr fnl f* **14/1**
4000 **9** *shd* **Riverhill (IRE)**[8] 7267 5-8-9 **47**...................................(bt[1]) TomEaves 7 35
(Miss T Jackson) *a towards rr* **18/1**
0300 **10** *hd* **Gone'N'Dunnett (IRE)**[21] 7055 9-8-9 **47** ow1..........(p) TGMcLaughlin 11 35
(Mrs C A Dunnett) *in tch on inner: rdn along 1/2-way: sn wknd* **14/1**
0000 **11** *1 1/2* **Nabra**[116] 4383 4-8-8 **46** oh1.. JimmyQuinn 8 29
(M Brittain) *in tch: rdn along wl over 2f out and sn wknd* **16/1**
0600 **12** *7* **Union Jack Jackson (IRE)**[129] 3952 6-8-8 **46** oh1.....(b) DaleGibson 12 7
(John A Harris) *midfield: rdn along on outer wl over 2f out: sn wknd* **20/1**
3064 **13** *2 1/2* **Stoneacre Chris (USA)**[47] 6405 3-8-3 **48**.......... AndrewHeffernan(7) 14 1
(Peter Grayson) *sn outpcd and a in rr* **20/1**
54 **14** *1 1/2* **Geordie Dancer (IRE)**[78] 5562 6-8-4 **49** oh1 ow3(b) KrishGundowry(7) 9 —
(A Berry) *bolted bef s: in tch tl rdn along: edgd lft and wknd 1/2-way* **25/1**
1m 14.4s (-2.10) **Going Correction** -0.325s/f (Stan) **14** Ran SP% **117.8**
Speed ratings (Par 101): **101,100,98,97,95 94,93,91,91,91 89,80,76,74**
toteswinger: 1&2 £15.10, 1&3 £10.80, 2&3 £10.70. CSF £58.78 CT £436.61 TOTE £8.80: £2.90, £3.30, £2.20; EX 79.50 TRIFECTA Not won..
Owner Pinewood Racing Limited **Bred** G A E And J Smith Bloodstock **Trained** Carburton, Notts
■ Stewards' Enquiry : Krish Gundowry two-day ban: careless riding (Dec 2-3), further one-day ban: careless riding (Dec 4)
James O'Reilly one-day ban: used whip down shoulder in forehand position (Dec 2)
FOCUS
A moderate sprint handicap in which few were ever involved and the third is the best guide to the form.
Riverhill(IRE) Official explanation: jockey said gelding hung left
Geordie Dancer(IRE) Official explanation: vet said gelding finished lame

7370 SOUTHWELL-RACECOURSE.CO.UK (S) STKS 7f (F)
12:50 (12:54) (Class 6) 2-Y-O **£2,047** (£604; £302) **Stalls** Low

Form RPR
5005 **1** **Miss Xu Xia**[8] 7266 2-8-4 38.......................................(p) DuranFentiman(3) 4 46
(G R Oldroyd) *in tch: hdwy to chse ldrs 2f out: rdn and styd on to ld over 1f out: drvn ins fnl f and hld on wl towards fin* **33/1**
1030 **2** *1/2* **Shadow Bay (IRE)**[26] 6924 2-9-3 73........................ RichardKingscote 3 59+
(Tom Dascombe) *chsd ldrs: rdn along and lost pl 1/2-way: towards rr and swtchd wd wl over 2f out: rdn and hdwy wl over 1f out: drvn and edgd lft ins fnl f: kpt on* **11/10**[1]
4366 **3** *3/4* **Island Chief**[8] 7275 2-8-12 63..(b[1]) NCallan 2 48
(K A Ryan) *sn led: rdn along over 2f out: sn hdd and drvn: rallied u.p and ev ch ent fnl f: no ex towards fin* **10/3**[2]
6004 **4** *3/4* **Barbeito**[8] 7266 2-8-7 42..(v[1]) SaleemGolam 5 41
(D J S Ffrench Davis) *trckd ldng pair: effrt over 2f out: rdn and ev ch over 1f out: drvn ent fnl f and one pce* **12/1**
2530 **5** *2 3/4* **Iorek Byrnison**[32] 6787 2-8-5 57..............................(v[1]) AdeleRothery(7) 1 39
(D Nicholls) *trckd ldrs: rdn along wl over 2f out: sn drvn and kpt on same pce* **11/2**[3]
6000 **6** *2 1/4* **That Boy Ronaldo**[4] 7318 2-8-7 42.. JoeFanning 9 29
(A Berry) *cl up: rdn to ld over 2f out: drvn and hdd over 1f out: sn wknd* **22/1**
0060 **7** *1 3/4* **Moon Warrior**[4] 7319 2-8-5 30.............................. AndrewHeffernan(7) 11 29
(C Smith) *nvr nr ldrs* **100/1**
000 **8** *9* **Angelsbemine**[21] 7044 2-8-3 35 ow3............................ DavidKenny(7) 10 5
(J R Norton) *chsd ldrs on outer: rdn along bef 1/2-way: sn wknd* **150/1**
0005 **9** *2 3/4* **Spiritual Bond**[36] 6709 2-8-4 52.................................. KevinGhunowa(3) 6 —
(R A Harris) *a towards rr* **14/1**
00 **10** *9* **Clodazone (IRE)**[78] 5571 2-8-2 0.................................... NicolPolli(5) 7 —
(M G Quinlan) *s.i.s: a in rr* **33/1**
1m 29.33s (-0.97) **Going Correction** -0.325s/f (Stan) **10** Ran SP% **112.3**
Speed ratings (Par 94): **92,91,90,89,86 84,82,71,68,58**
toteswinger: 1&2 £10.70, 1&3 £11.00, 2&3 £1.50. CSF £66.85 TOTE £38.10: £6.60, £1.10, £1.10; EX 108.40 TRIFECTA Not won..There was no bid for the winner.
Owner R C Bond **Bred** Yapham Mill Stud **Trained** Brawby, N Yorks
FOCUS
A very moderate event with several lowly rated horses involved in the finish.
NOTEBOOK
Miss Xu Xia had been well beaten in a course-and-distance nursery off 45 the previous week, so the more fancied runners surely ran below form, and she was able to take advantage to gain her first success at the ninth attempt. To be fair, she must have improved a little on her official mark of 38, but things are likely to be tougher under a penalty in this grade. (op 40-1)
Shadow Bay(IRE) did not travel at all early and looked beaten after a couple of furlongs, but he finally responded to pressure in the straight. He might not have appreciated the kickback and is better than he showed, but he's not one for maximum confidence. (tchd Evens)
Island Chief was driven to lead in first-time blinkers (replacing cheekpieces), but he was run out of it late on. He looks flattered by his official mark. (tchd 7-2)
Barbeito had her chance in a first-time visor but was unable to confirm recent course-and-distance placings with Miss Xu Xia. (op 16-1)
Iorek Byrnison looked a difficult ride in a first-time visor. (op 5-1)

7371 EUROPEAN BREEDERS' FUND MEDIAN AUCTION MAIDEN STKS 7f (F)
1:20 (1:21) (Class 5) 2-Y-O **£3,561** (£1,059; £529; £264) **Stalls** Low

Form RPR
645 **1** **Holberg (UAE)**[40] 6602 2-9-3 75.. JoeFanning 5 77
(M Johnston) *sn pushed along to trck ldng pair: hdwy over 2f out: rdn and edgd lft over 1f out: led ent fnl f: sn drvn and kpt on wl towards fin* **11/8**[1]
5000 **2** *1 1/2* **Confucius Captain (IRE)**[21] 7051 2-9-3 72.................. FergusSweeney 6 73
(J R Boyle) *cl up: rdn to ld wl over 2f out: drvn over 1f out: hdd ent fnl f: no ex fnl 100yds* **8/1**
2520 **3** *1 3/4* **Today's The Day**[53] 6240 2-8-12 75......................................(p) NCallan 3 64
(M A Jarvis) *led: rdn along 3f out and sn hdd: drvn wl over 1f out: kpt on same pce appr fnl f* **9/4**[2]
4 *4 1/2* **Dante Deo (USA)** 2-8-12 0.. JamieSpencer 4 53
(T D Barron) *dwlt: in tch on outer: hdwy over 2f out: chsd ldrs wl over 1f out: sn rdn and btn appr fnl f* **13/2**[3]
4 **5** *1 1/2* **Mullitovermaurice**[15] 7170 2-9-3 0.................................. PaulMulrennan 2 54
(J G Given) *trckd ldrs on inner: rdn along wl over 2f out: drvn and wknd wl over 1f out* **8/1**

00 **6** *12* **Net Value (USA)**[10] 7240 2-9-3 0 TomEaves 1 24
(B Smart) *dwlt: a in rr: rdn along and outpcd fr wl over 2f out* **50/1**

1m 27.61s (-2.69) **Going Correction** -0.325s/f (Stan) **6** Ran SP% **110.4**
Speed ratings (Par 96): **102,100,98,93,91 77**
toteswinger: 1&2 £3.70, 1&3 £2.70, 2&3 £3.50. CSF £12.64 TOTE £2.10: £1.20, £5.10; EX 13.40.
Owner Sheikh Hamdan Bin Mohammed Al Maktoum **Bred** Darley **Trained** Middleham Moor, N Yorks
■ Stewards' Enquiry : Tom Eaves one-day ban: used whip with excessive force (Dec 2)

FOCUS
A fair juvenile maiden rated around the first two.

NOTEBOOK
Holberg(UAE) found this easier than his previous three assignments. He was inclined to edge left slightly under pressure in the straight, but gradually worked his way to the front. An official mark of 75 probably has him about right for now, but he looks as though he will be suited by 1m in time. (op 5-4 tchd 6-4)
Confucius Captain(IRE) had his chance and ran a respectable race. He would have been 3lb better off with the winner in a handicap. (op 9-1)
Today's The Day, trying Fibresand for the first time after nearly two months off, was well below her official mark of 75 and seems to be regressing. (op 5-2)
Dante Deo(USA), a half-sister to Angel Smoke, a three-time winner on turf and dirt, showed ability on her debut and should improve. (op 11-2 tchd 15-2)
Mullitovermaurice seemed to run below the form he showed on his debut over this trip at Wolverhampton. (op 10-1)

7372 MEMBERSHIP AT SOUTHWELL GOLF CLUB NURSERY 6f (F)
1:50 (1:51) (Class 6) (0-60,60) 2-Y-O £2,047 (£604; £302) Stalls Low

Form RPR
0465 **1** **Madison Belle**[24] 6987 2-9-3 **56** DarrenWilliams 13 67
(K R Burke) *prom: hdwy over 2f out: rdn to ld 1 1/2f out: kpt on strly u.p fnl f* **16/1**
4631 **2** *3½* **Rio Cobolo (IRE)**[13] 7199 2-9-3 **56** (v) ChrisCatlin 11 57
(Paul Green) *a.p: effrt over 2f out: rdn to chse wnr over 1f out: drvn and edgd lft ent fnl f: kpt on same pce* **11/2**[3]
0062 **3** *2* **Bulella**[6] 7281 2-9-0 **53** MickyFenton 9 48
(Garry Moss) *dwlt and towards rr: rdn along and hdwy wl over 2f out: drvn over 1f out: styd on ins fnl f: nrst fin* **4/1**[2]
0063 **4** *hd* **Oisin's Boy**[8] 7268 2-9-7 **60** FergusSweeney 10 54
(J R Boyle) *chsd ldrs: rdn along over 2f out: drvn over 1f out: kpt on same pce* **7/1**
6603 **5** *1¾* **Cut And Thrust (IRE)**[8] 7266 2-9-5 **58** (p) NCallan 2 47
(M A Jarvis) *chsd ldrs: n.m.r 3f out: rdn over 2f out: kpt on same pce* **5/2**[1]
06 **6** *shd* **Katie Higgins**[6] 7281 2-9-2 **55** (b[1]) LiamJones 1 43
(J L Spearing) *towards rr tl styd on u.p on inner fnl 2f: nrst fin* **40/1**
0406 **7** *hd* **Iliketoboogie**[26] 6933 2-9-7 **60** (p) JamieSpencer 7 48
(A J McCabe) *led: rdn along wl over 2f out: drvn and hdd 1 1/2f out: wknd ent fnl f* **14/1**
000 **8** *½* **Dark Desert**[80] 5488 2-8-11 **50** LPKeniry 5 36
(A G Newcombe) *bmpd s and bhd tl styd on fnl 2f* **66/1**
0530 **9** *1* **Jessica Mary (IRE)**[64] 5966 2-9-2 **55** (v[1]) TomEaves 6 38
(B Smart) *dwlt and wnt lft s: a towards rr* **16/1**
0406 **10** *3¼* **Valdemar**[14] 7179 2-9-1 **54** (p) GrahamGibbons 3 28
(A D Brown) *in tch: rdn along wl over 2f out: drvn wl over 1f out and sn wknd* **25/1**
000 **11** *shd* **Alderbed**[100] 4890 2-8-11 **50** (v[1]) EdwardCreighton 14 23
(George Baker) *dwlt: a in rr* **16/1**
0050 **12** *4½* **Time Loup**[62] 6009 2-8-13 **52** PaulEddery 4 —
(S R Bowring) *prom: rdn along 1/2-way: sn wknd* **20/1**
0000 **13** *9* **Dark Ranger**[41] 6572 2-8-13 **52** RobertHavlin 8 —
(T J Pitt) *a in rr* **28/1**

1m 15.28s (-1.22) **Going Correction** -0.325s/f (Stan) **13** Ran SP% **116.8**
Speed ratings (Par 94): **95,90,87,87,85 84,84,84,82,78 78,72,60**
toteswinger: 1&2 £17.50, 1&3 £15.30, 2&3 £5.30. CSF £94.23 CT £351.36 TOTE £22.90: £4.40, £2.40, £2.00; EX 177.30 TRIFECTA Not won..
Owner Paul Sweeting & Mrs L Wright **Bred** Paul Sweeting **Trained** Middleham Moor, N Yorks

FOCUS
A moderate nursery but not that competitive as they went 14-1 bar four. In the race itself very few got competitive but the form makes sense and is worth rating at face value for now.

NOTEBOOK
Madison Belle ran out a surprise but ultimately comfortable winner. She had been beaten in eight previous starts but had not run badly on Polytrack and had dropped 9lb since her first try on the all-weather. She really took to this surface though and, despite not handling the turn, found plenty to lead halfway up the straight and was in command thereafter. She will go up a bit for this and may be worth turning out under a penalty. (op 14-1)
Rio Cobolo(IRE), raised 6lb for his recent heavy-ground win, has improved for the fitting of a visor and put up a decent effort on his first try here. He gets this distance but a return to the minimum trip may be in his favour on this surface. (op 5-1)
Bulella missed the break slightly and was always playing catch-up. She was closest at the finish and can be given another chance. (op 10-3)
Oisin's Boy chased the leaders throughout but was unable to close the gap once in line for home. (tchd 6-1)
Cut And Thrust(IRE), tried in cheekpieces, tracked the leaders but was carried back by the fading Time Loup on the home turn and was never able to get back into contention from that point. Official explanation: jockey said gelding was hampered on bend: vet said gelding lost a shoe (tchd 9-4)
Katie Higgins, equipped with blinkers for the first time, finished much closer to Bulella than on their previous meeting here despite being worse off at the weights. She was doing her best work late and may be worth another try over 7f.
Iliketoboogie was keen to post and ran too free early in the race. (op 12-1)
Time Loup Official explanation: jockey said colt lost its action on bend

7373 HOSPITALITY AT SOUTHWELL RACECOURSE (S) STKS 1m (F)
2:20 (2:20) (Class 6) 3-Y-O+ £2,047 (£604; £302) Stalls Low

Form RPR
0416 **1** **Barkass (UAE)**[27] 6899 4-9-6 68 GeorgeBaker 12 69
(B Ellison) *hld up in midfield: gd hdwy over 2f out: rdn over 1f out: styd on to ld jst ins fnl f: r.o wl* **11/4**[1]
0004 **2** *1¼* **Captain Royale (IRE)**[14] 7175 3-8-12 65 NCallan 8 60
(Miss Tracy Waggott) *trckd ldrs: hdwy over 2f out: chse ldr wl over 1f out: rdn to ld jst over 1f out: drvn and edgd lft ent fnl f: sn hdd and no ex* **10/1**
0-30 **3** *1¼* **Red Expresso (IRE)**[26] 6936 3-8-12 66 (v[1]) JamieSpencer 7 57
(M L W Bell) *hld up: hdwy 3f out: rdn along over 2f out: drvn over 1f out: kpt on u.p ins fnl f* **7/2**[3]
5505 **4** *1¾* **Lights Of Vegas**[18] 7112 4-9-0 46 (bt[1]) LPKeniry 6 53
(S Kirk) *cl up: led over 3f out: rdn 2f out: drvn and hdd jst over 1f out: wknd ins fnl f* **40/1**
0135 **5** *1* **Elusive Warrior (USA)**[4] 7317 5-9-6 73 (p) JamesDoyle 14 57
(A J McCabe) *prom on outer: effrt 3f out: rdn over 2f out: drvn and one pce fr over 1f out* **3/1**[2]
0005 **6** *nse* **Tapas Lad (IRE)**[33] 6752 3-9-1 48 (v) KevinGhunowa[(3)] 4 57
(G J Smith) *dwlt: sn trcking ldrs: effrt over 2f out: sn rdn and kpt on same pce appr fnl f* **66/1**
2603 **7** *7* **Ten To The Dozen**[14] 7180 5-9-6 49 ChrisCatlin 11 40
(P W Hiatt) *midfield and rdn along 1/2-way: drvn over 2f out: plugged on u.p fr wl over 1f out: nvr nr ldrs* **11/1**
6550 **8** *4½* **Tampopo (IRE)**[22] 7018 3-8-12 48 FrankieMcDonald 9 24
(D J S Ffrench Davis) *cl up: rdn along over 2f out: grad wknd* **40/1**
0000 **9** *½* **Little Firecracker**[16] 7149 3-8-13 46 AdamKirby 10 24
(Miss M E Rowland) *a in rr* **66/1**
3000 **10** *hd* **Autograph Hunter**[34] 6729 4-8-7 46 AndrewHeffernan[(7)] 5 23
(Peter Grayson) *a in rr* **50/1**
4U06 **11** *1* **Scotty's Future (IRE)**[14] 7184 10-8-9 47 SladeO'Hara[(5)] 3 20
(A Berry) *sn outpcd and bhd* **50/1**
0263 **12** *½* **Bert's Memory**[8] 7270 4-8-12 45 (b) DuranFentiman[(3)] 2 20
(J Mackie) *led: rdn along and hdd over 3f out: sn drvn and wknd* **12/1**
3060 **13** *nse* **Right You Are (IRE)**[21] 7039 8-9-0 45 (v[1]) TomEaves 13 19
(Paul Green) *chsd ldrs: rdn along wl over 2f out: sn wknd* **25/1**
5000 **R** **Dry Speedfit (IRE)**[8] 7267 3-8-12 55 (v[1]) PaulMulrennan 1 —
(Micky Hammond) *ref to r: tk no part* **33/1**

1m 41.63s (-2.07) **Going Correction** -0.325s/f (Stan)
WFA 3 from 4yo+ 2lb **14** Ran SP% **117.6**
Speed ratings (Par 101): **97,95,94,92,91 91,84,80,79,79 78,78,77,—**
toteswinger: 1&2 £6.80, 1&3 £4.50, 2&3 £5.80. CSF £28.42 TOTE £3.00: £1.70, £3.60, £2.40; EX 38.70 Trifecta £164.70 Part won. Pool: £222.69, 0.84 winning units..There was no bid for the winner.
Owner Jelly Fish **Bred** Darley **Trained** Norton, N Yorks

FOCUS
A typical seller and muddling form with the seventh the best guide.

7374 PLAY GOLF AT SOUTHWELL GOLF CLUB H'CAP 1m (F)
2:50 (2:55) (Class 5) (0-75,74) 3-Y-O+ £2,729 (£806; £403) Stalls Low

Form RPR
003 **1** **Avertis**[15] 7167 3-8-12 **74** (t) AndreaAtzeni[(7)] 2 82
(M Botti) *mde virtually all: rdn 2f out: drvn ent fnl f and kpt on gamely* **8/1**
0530 **2** *¾* **Ocean Legend (IRE)**[26] 6936 3-9-4 **73** SaleemGolam 1 79
(Miss J Feilden) *a.p: chsd wnr over 2f out: rdn to chal over 1f out and ev ch tl drvn and no ex wl ins fnl f* **5/1**[3]
3 *8* **Crystal Crown (IRE)**[41] 6590 4-9-5 **72** (t) JamieSpencer 4 60
(David Wachman, Ire) *in tch: rdn along 3f out: drvn 2f out: sn one pce* **3/1**[1]
0060 **4** *2* **Classical Rhythm (IRE)**[27] 6905 3-8-4 **59** oh2 (b[1]) ChrisCatlin 3 42
(J R Boyle) *towards rr: effrt and hdwy wl over 2f out: sn rdn and one pce* **16/1**
5/03 **5** *3* **Brigydon (IRE)**[21] 7048 5-8-12 **65** AdamKirby 6 41
(J R Fanshawe) *in tch: hdwy to chse ldrs 3f out and sn rdn: drvn 2f out and sn btn* **7/2**[2]
0600 **6** *¾* **Dado Mush**[30] 6841 5-9-6 **73** (p) KirstyMilczarek 8 47
(T T Clement) *in rr tl styd on fnl 2f: nvr a factor* **12/1**
000 **7** *3¼* **Mooted (UAE)**[20] 7070 3-9-0 **69** (e[1]) TomEaves 7 35
(Miss J A Camacho) *prom: rdn along 1/2-way and sn wknd* **16/1**
5110 **8** *8* **Top Jaro (FR)**[41] 6585 5-8-4 **60** DuranFentiman[(3)] 5 7
(Mrs R A Carr) *cl up: rdn along over 3f out and sn wknd* **13/2**

1m 40.34s (-3.36) **Going Correction** -0.325s/f (Stan)
WFA 3 from 4yo+ 2lb **8** Ran SP% **107.8**
Speed ratings (Par 103): **103,102,94,92,89 88,84,76**
toteswinger: 1&2 £15.10, 1&3 £10.80, 2&3 £10.70. CSF £40.66 CT £110.88 TOTE £9.10: £2.20, £2.20, £1.20; EX 40.50 Trifecta £264.00 Pool: £371.30, 1.04 winning units..
Owner Dr Ornella Carlini Cozzi **Bred** Mrs Sally Doyle **Trained** Newmarket, Suffolk

FOCUS
A weak handicap for the grade and the front two pulled well clear. The form is rated around the first two to previous marks.
Brigydon(IRE) Official explanation: trainer's rep had no explanation for the poor form shown

7375 CALL 01636 814418 TO SPONSOR A RACE H'CAP (DIV II) 6f (F)
3:20 (3:21) (Class 6) (0-50,51) 3-Y-O+ £1,706 (£503; £252) Stalls Low

Form RPR
6335 **1** **City For Conquest (IRE)**[21] 7049 5-8-11 **49** ChrisCatlin 14 57
(John A Harris) *stdd and swtchd lft s: in rr tl rdn along and hdwy wl over 1f out: swtchd lft and drvn ins fnl f: led nr fin* **8/1**[3]
0526 **2** *½* **Mister Incredible**[259] 790 5-8-3 **46** oh1 (v) MCGeran[(3)] 6 52
(J M Bradley) *trckd ldrs: smooth hdwy to ld over 1f out: rdn ent fnl f: hdd and no ex nr fin* **10/1**
00 **3** *1¾* **Double Carpet (IRE)**[57] 6178 5-8-8 **46** oh1 PaulFessey 1 46
(G Woodward) *led: rdn along 2f out: drvn and hdd over 1f out: kpt on same pce* **8/1**[3]
5650 **4** *nk* **Majestical (IRE)**[13] 7195 6-8-5 **46** (b) KevinGhunowa[(3)] 4 45
(R A Harris) *chsd ldrs: hdwy over 2f out: sn rdn and ev ch tl drvn and one pce ent fnl f* **10/1**
0036 **5** *¾* **Mickleberry (IRE)**[13] 7197 4-8-11 **49** JimmyQuinn 11 46
(M Brittain) *in tch: rdn along over 2f out: drvn over 1f out: kpt on ins fnl f* **6/1**[2]
0000 **6** *½* **Sherjawy (IRE)**[78] 5582 4-8-8 **46** (b) SaleemGolam 7 41
(Miss Z C Davison) *towards rr tl styd on fnl 2f* **12/1**
5550 **7** *2¼* **My Flame**[27] 6913 3-8-10 **48** (p) MickyFenton 9 36
(J R Jenkins) *cl up: rdn along over 2f out: drvn and hung lft over 1f out: wkng whn eased ins fnl f* **11/1**
0005 **8** *shd* **Fish Called Johnny**[13] 7197 4-8-8 **51** ow3 SladeO'Hara[(5)] 3 39
(A Berry) *in tch: rdn along wl over 2f out: drvn and wknd wl over 1f out* **8/1**[3]
0036 **9** *hd* **Hollywood George**[4] 7316 4-8-2 **47** (p) AdeleRothery[(7)] 10 34
(Miss M E Rowland) *trckd ldrs: hdwy wl over 2f out: rdn and ev ch wl over 1f out: sn wknd* **5/1**[1]
0000 **10** *3¼* **Arrabiata**[89] 5203 3-8-8 **46** oh1 (b) FrankieMcDonald 12 23
(C N Kellett) *a in rr* **50/1**
0000 **11** *7* **Desert Hunter (IRE)**[97] 4961 5-8-9 **47** oh1 ow1 PaulMulrennan 5 —
(Micky Hammond) *a towards rr* **9/1**
000 **12** *3¼* **Rue Soleil**[126] 4047 4-8-8 **46** oh1 GrahamGibbons 8 —
(J R Weymes) *a towards rr* **50/1**

The Form Book, Raceform Ltd, Compton, RG20 6NL

00-0 P **Silent Storm**[25] 6955 8-8-5 50 .... AndrewHeffernan(7) 13 —
(Peter Grayson) *v.s.a and bhd whn p.u and dismntd bef 1/2-way* **22/1**
1m 15.32s (-1.18) **Going Correction** -0.325s/f (Stan) **13** Ran SP% **116.8**
Speed ratings (Par 101): **94,93,91,90,89 88,85,85,85,81 71,67,—**
toteswinger: 1&2 £6.40, 1&3 £10.50, 2&3 £17.80. CSF £82.39 CT £680.99 TOTE £4.70: £1.90, £3.90, £3.40; EX 53.00 Trifecta £185.20 Part won. Pool: £250.37, 0.42 winning units..
Owner M F Schofield **Bred** Ballyhane Stud **Trained** Eastwell, Leics
■ Stewards' Enquiry : Adele Rothery caution: used whip down shoulder in forehand position.

FOCUS
A very moderate sprint handicap run in a time 0.72 seconds slower than the first division. The winner is rated basically to form with the runner-up posting his best mark of the year.

7376 SOUTHWELL-RACECOURSE.CO.UK H'CAP 1m 4f (F)
3:50 (3:51) (Class 6) (0-65,65) 3-Y-0+ £2,047 (£604; £302) Stalls Low

Form RPR
1454 1 **Three Strings (USA)**[21] 7039 5-9-1 56 ....(p) PaulMulrennan 2 65
(P D Niven) *prom: hdwy to join ldr over 3f out: led 2f out and sn rdn: drvn and kpt on wl fnl f* **14/1**
003- 2 1 1/4 **Bluecrop Boy**[437] 4535 4-8-10 51 oh6 ....(v[1]) FrankieMcDonald 10 58
(D J S Ffrench Davis) *a.p: effrt over 2f out: rdn wl over 1f out: drvn to chse wnr ins fnl f: no imp towards fin* **66/1**
-060 3 2 1/4 **Parnassian**[13] 7189 8-9-0 55 ....(v) RichardThomas 4 58
(J A Geake) *in tch: pushed along over 4f out: rdn along 3f out: drvn wl over 1f out: kpt on wl u.p ins fnl f* **16/1**
4434 4 shd **Sabancaya**[83] 5399 3-8-10 57 .... MickyFenton 7 60
(Mrs P Sly) *hld up in midfield: hdwy to trckd ldrs over 4f out: effrt over 2f out and sn rdn: drvn over 1f out and kpt on same pce* **7/1**[3]
6303 5 1/2 **Red Tarn**[14] 7178 3-8-13 60 .... TomEaves 1 62
(B Smart) *chsd ldrs: rdn along and outpcd over 3f out: drvn 2f out: styd on appr fnl f* **16/1**
0046 6 1 **Inch Lodge**[24] 6985 6-9-10 65 ....(t) PaulEddery 14 65
(Miss D Mountain) *cl up: led after 2f: rdn along and jnd over 3f out: hdd 2f out and grad wknd* **14/1**
2450 7 1/2 **Touch Of Style (IRE)**[9] 7261 4-9-9 64 ....(e[1]) FergusSweeney 12 64
(J R Boyle) *in tch: hdwy to chse ldrs wl over 2f out: sn rdn and kpt on same pce appr fnl f* **16/1**
4200 8 nk **Mid Valley**[44] 4261 5-8-11 52 .... J-PGuillambert 9 51
(J R Jenkins) *hld up in rr: stdy hdwy over 3f out: rdn 2f out: drvn and no imp appr fnl f* **9/1**
0113 9 3 1/2 **Ice Bellini**[6] 7285 3-9-4 65 ....(v) KirstyMilczarek 13 59
(Miss Gay Kelleway) *hld up in rr: hdwy 3f out: rdn wl over 1f out: nvr nr ldrs* **7/2**[2]
000- 10 1 1/4 **Que Beauty (IRE)**[393] 6384 3-7-12 52 oh6 ow1.... AndrewHeffernan(7) 5 44
(R C Guest) *a in rr* **50/1**
3513 11 6 **Summer Lodge**[26] 6662 5-9-9 64 .... JamieSpencer 6 46
(A J McCabe) *hld up: a in rr* **5/2**[1]
4/00 12 3 **Liberty Seeker (FR)**[12] 602 9-8-11 52 .... ChrisCatlin 11 29
(John A Harris) *hld up: rdn along 1/2-way: a in rr* **20/1**
3254 13 1/2 **Gayanula (USA)**[16] 7149 3-8-11 58 .... TonyHamilton 8 34
(Miss J A Camacho) *midfield: effrt on inner 3f out: rdn along over 2f out and sn wknd* **14/1**
0334 14 2 1/2 **Bonny Bright Eyes**[112] 4498 3-8-0 52 oh5 ow1....(t) KellyHarrison(5) 3 24
(Miss Kate Milligan) *led 2f: prom tl rdn along 4f out and sn wknd* **50/1**
2m 37.03s (-3.97) **Going Correction** -0.325s/f (Stan)
WFA 3 from 4yo+ 6lb **14** Ran SP% **121.1**
Speed ratings (Par 101): **100,99,97,97,97 96,96,96,93,92 88,86,86,84**
toteswinger: 1&2 £91.60, 1&3 £34.10, 2&3 £177.60. CSF £752.04 CT £13933.76 TOTE £18.30: £3.30, £16.20, £6.60; EX 942.90 TRIFECTA Not won. Place 6: £38.87, Place 5: £9.41..
Owner The Wednesday Club **Bred** Gaucho Ltd **Trained** Barton-le-Street, N Yorks

FOCUS
A moderate middle-distance handicap run at a good pace but ordinary form for the grade.
Gayanula(USA) Official explanation: trainer had no explanation for the poor form shown
T/Plt: £35.80 to a £1 stake. Pool: £49,441.28. 1,005.39 winning tickets. T/Qpdt: £14.60 to a £1 stake. Pool: £3,555.65. 180.10 winning tickets. JR

7353 KEMPTON (A.W) (R-H)
Wednesday, November 19

OFFICIAL GOING: Standard
Wind: Almost Nil Weather: Dark

7377 BOOK NOW FOR BOXING DAY H'CAP 5f (P)
5:50 (5:51) (Class 6) (0-65,65) 3-Y-0+ £2,047 (£604; £302) Stalls High

Form RPR
5015 1 **Desert Opal**[6] 7295 8-9-2 63 ....(b) LiamJones 11 76
(C R Dore) *trckd ldrs and racd on inner: eased off rail 2f out: effrt to ld ent fnl f: styd on wl* **4/1**[1]
0052 2 1 **Bountiful Bay**[14] 7196 3-8-7 54 ....(t) MartinDwyer 9 63
(B J Meehan) *s.s: rousted along to rch midfield after 2f: prog over 1f out: tried to chal on inner 1f out: nt pce of wnr* **4/1**[1]
6001 3 3/4 **Bluebok**[48] 6418 7-8-11 63 ....(bt) JackDean(5) 10 69
(J M Bradley) *w ldr: led 2f out: drvn and hdd ent fnl f: one pce* **14/1**
0606 4 2 **Azygous**[13] 7206 5-8-13 60 .... DaneO'Neill 6 59
(J Akehurst) *bmpd sn after s: hld up towards rr: nt clr run 2f out: prog over 1f out: no imp fnl f* **10/1**
3050 5 nse **Joss Stick**[62] 6045 3-8-13 60 .... LPKeniry 3 59
(R A Harris) *hld up and racd wd: nvr on terms w ldrs: hanging wl over 1f out: sme prog after: n.d* **20/1**
0600 6 1 1/4 **Night Prospector**[28] 6895 8-8-5 55 ....(b) KevinGhunowa(3) 4 49
(R A Harris) *racd wd: hld up in tch: gng wl enough 1/2-way: fnd nil 2f out: btn after* **16/1**
620 7 hd **Pic Up Sticks**[6] 7295 9-9-0 61 .... NCallan 1 55
(B G Powell) *stdd s: dropped in fr wd draw and hld up last: prog to chse ldrs over 1f out: fdd fnl f* **17/2**[3]
002 8 2 **Bishopbriggs (USA)**[7] 7292 3-9-4 65 .... AdamKirby 8 52
(S Parr) *chsd ldrs on outer: lost pl fr 1/2-way: wl in rr and btn over 1f out* **4/1**[1]
0120 9 2 3/4 **Edie Superstar (USA)**[39] 6658 3-9-4 65 ....(v) EddieAhern 12 42
(M A Magnusson) *led to 2f out: wknd rapidly fnl f* **7/1**[2]
6000 10 1 1/4 **Blakeshall Diamond**[20] 7092 3-9-1 62 .... J-PGuillambert 7 34
(K G Wingrove) *chsd ldrs to 1/2-way: sn lost pl and wl in rr* **20/1**
59.71 secs (-0.79) **Going Correction** +0.075s/f (Slow) **10** Ran SP% **114.2**
Speed ratings (Par 101): **109,107,106,103,102 100,100,97,93,91**
toteswinger: 1&2 £4.40, 1&3 £9.90, 2&3 £5.70. CSF £18.50 CT £174.15 TOTE £5.90: £2.00, £1.80, £4.80; EX 22.70.
Owner Mrs Louise Marsh **Bred** Juddmonte Farms **Trained** West Pinchbeck, Lincs

FOCUS
A modest handicap run at a decent pace. The first three pulled a little way clear of the rest.
Azygous Official explanation: jockey said gelding suffered interference shortly after start
Bishopbriggs(USA) Official explanation: jockey said gelding never travelled

7378 TFM NETWORKS CLAIMING STKS 6f (P)
6:20 (6:20) (Class 6) 3-Y-0+ £2,047 (£604; £302) Stalls High

Form RPR
3225 1 **Brandywell Boy (IRE)**[21] 7066 5-8-7 68 .... BillyCray(7) 11 77
(D J S Ffrench Davis) *towards rr: rdn over 2f out: prog after: got through to chal 1f out: urged along and sustained effrt to ld last 75yds* **8/1**
4002 2 shd **Little Edward**[6] 7297 10-9-4 87 .... GeorgeBaker 10 81
(R J Hodges) *t.k.h early: hld up bhd ldrs: smooth prog to trck ldr 2f out: sn rdn: upsides ins fnl f: jst pipped* **3/1**[1]
3061 3 1 **Bazguy**[13] 7206 3-8-9 72 ....(b) JamesDoyle 9 69
(P D Evans) *prom: rdn over 2f out: grad clsd u.p: upsides ins fnl f: nt qckn nr fin* **11/1**
0102 4 1 1/4 **Came Back (IRE)**[96] 5050 5-8-12 93 .... NCallan 2 70+
(K A Ryan) *t.k.h early: trckd ldr: led over 2f out: rdn over 1f out: hdd last 75yds: btn whn squeezed out sn after* **4/1**[3]
5210 5 nk **Trimlestown (IRE)**[22] 7041 5-9-2 70 .... DaneO'Neill 7 71
(P D Evans) *awkward s: mostly last: shkn up and hanging over 2f out: styd on fr over 1f out: nrst fin but n.d* **12/1**
3050 6 1 1/2 **Don Pele (IRE)**[49] 6402 6-8-12 70 ....(b) LPKeniry 1 62
(R A Harris) *hld up on outer: stdy prog to trck ldrs 1/2-way: rdn over 2f out: nt qckn and hld after* **22/1**
3123 7 1/2 **Makshoof (IRE)**[31] 6842 4-9-3 80 ....(p) ChrisCatlin 4 65
(K A Ryan) *a towards rr: wd and drvn wl over 2f out: plugged on but no ch* **7/2**[2]
3451 8 1 1/2 **Hart Of Gold**[10] 7254 4-8-7 60 ....(p) KevinGhunowa(3) 8 54
(R A Harris) *plld hrd: hld up bhd ldrs: lost pl and rdn 1/2-way: brief effrt again 2f out: no prog* **10/1**
4100 9 3/4 **Angel Voices (IRE)**[39] 6650 5-7-11 66 ....(p) DeclanCannon(7) 6 45
(K R Burke) *t.k.h early: led to over 2f out: sn btn* **12/1**
0005 10 1/2 **Professor Malone**[72] 5749 3-8-8 47 .... NeilChalmers 5 48
(J C Tuck) *dwlt: hld up in last pair: swtchd to r against far rail over 2f out: no prog* **100/1**
0630 11 3 **Briannsta (IRE)**[51] 6334 6-8-8 51 .... RichardThomas 3 38
(J E Long) *nvr on terms and rdn in rr bef 1/2-way: nvr a factor* **66/1**
1m 13.04s (-0.06) **Going Correction** +0.075s/f (Slow) **11** Ran SP% **118.0**
Speed ratings (Par 101): **103,102,101,99,99 97,96,94,93,93 89**
toteswinger: 1&2 £6.30, 1&3 £5.70, 2&3 £7.10. CSF £32.04 TOTE £7.20: £2.40, £1.50, £4.10; EX 33.50.Bazguy was claimed by Mr J. O'Reilly for £7,000.
Owner P B Gallagher **Bred** Mountarmstrong Stud **Trained** Lambourn, Berks

FOCUS
A decent claimer, three of the runners had an official rating of between 80 and 93. It was run at a steady pace and produced a tight finish, but the form looks a bit dubious.
Hart Of Gold Official explanation: jockey said gelding ran too free

7379 TFM NETWORKS MEDIAN AUCTION MAIDEN STKS 1m 4f (P)
6:50 (6:53) (Class 6) 3-5-Y-0 £2,047 (£604; £302) Stalls Centre

Form RPR
6000 1 **Yab Adee**[13] 7217 4-9-9 58 .... MartinDwyer 6 67
(M P Tregoning) *trckd ldr: led over 2f out: sn rdn and wl clr* **11/10**[1]
00 2 5 **Dontpaytheferryman (USA)**[2] 7367 3-9-3 57....(t) TGMcLaughlin 3 59
(P D Evans) *hld up in last: stl there 3f out: prog over 2f out: wnt 2nd over 1f out: kpt on but no ch w wnr* **10/1**[3]
006- 3 1 1/4 **Bring It On Home**[11] 5273 4-9-9 62 .... GeorgeBaker 8 57
(G L Moore) *awkward s and s.i.s: hld up in 7th: rdn and laboured prog fr 3f out: wnt modest 3rd jst over 1f out: kpt on* **5/2**[2]
400 4 7 **Martingrange Lass (IRE)**[5] 7322 3-8-12 46....(t) AdamKirby 10 41
(S Parr) *led to over 2f out: sn no ch w wnr: wknd over 1f out* **33/1**
6033 5 1 **Coco L'Escargot**[14] 6806 4-9-4 52 ....(v) DarryllHolland 1 39
(J R Jenkins) *hld up in last pair: rdn over 3f out on outer: no ch fr over 2f out: plugged on* **12/1**
-060 6 3/4 **Veras Joy**[10] 7260 3-8-9 30 ....(p) KevinGhunowa(3) 9 38
(Miss Z C Davison) *hld up in midfield: mostly u.p fr 1/2-way: sme prog to modest 3rd over 2f out: wknd over 1f out* **66/1**
0606 7 1 3/4 **Bonzo**[55] 6226 3-9-3 53 .... JimmyQuinn 4 40
(P Howling) *trckd ldrs: rdn 5f out: grad wknd fnl 3f* **10/1**[3]
0006 8 3/4 **Little Rococoa**[9] 7274 3-9-3 30 ....(t) JamesDoyle 7 39
(R J Price) *s.v.s: in tch in rr: outpcd whn brief effrt over 2f out: sn wknd* **100/1**
0045 9 5 **Telephonist**[20] 7088 3-8-12 47 .... LPKeniry 2 26
(J R Best) *in tch on outer: rdn over 3f out: sn wknd* **16/1**
00 10 10 **Cadeaux Fax**[34] 6748 3-8-10 0 .... PNolan(7) 11 15
(A B Haynes) *t.k.h early: chsd ldng pair tl wknd rapidly over 3f out: t.o* **100/1**
2m 37.98s (3.48) **Going Correction** +0.075s/f (Slow)
WFA 3 from 4yo 6lb **10** Ran SP% **114.4**
Speed ratings (Par 101): **91,87,86,82,81 81,79,79,76,69**
toteswinger: 1&2 £6.70, 1&3 £1.10, 2&3 £5.90. CSF £13.38 TOTE £2.10: £1.10, £2.70, £1.60; EX 14.00.
Owner M P N Tregoning **Bred** Darley **Trained** Lambourn, Berks

FOCUS
This had the look of a weak seller rather than a maiden, with the field holding official marks that ranged between 30 and 62. The form looks sound rated around the placed horses.

7380 DIGIBET E B F MEDIAN AUCTION MAIDEN STKS 7f (P)
7:20 (7:23) (Class 5) 2-Y-0 £3,561 (£1,059; £529; £264) Stalls High

Form RPR
03 1 **Dialect**[18] 7140 2-8-12 0 .... JimCrowley 14 74
(Mrs A J Perrett) *t.k.h: trckd ldrs: effrt to go 2nd over 2f out: r.o to ld jst over 1f out: drvn and fnd enough* **11/4**[1]
4 2 nk **Gaily Noble (IRE)**[21] 7073 2-9-3 0 .... FergusSweeney 4 78
(A B Haynes) *sn led: hrd pressed fr 2f out: hdd jst over 1f out: kpt on wl fnl f* **11/2**[2]
4 3 3 **Three Ducks**[23] 7015 2-8-12 0 .... DaneO'Neill 7 66
(L M Cumani) *dwlt: t.k.h and rcvrd into midfield: effrt over 2f out: styd on to take 3rd fnl f: no imp on ldng pair* **11/4**[1]
4 1/2 **Dhania (IRE)** 2-9-0 0 .... LukeMorris(3) 5 70
(R A Teal) *in tch in midfield: rdn and effrt whn trapped bhd wkng rival and lost grnd 2f out: styd on again fnl f: nrly snatched 3rd* **100/1**
5 1 **All For You (IRE)** 2-8-12 0 .... ChrisCatlin 11 62+
(D R Lanigan) *t.k.h early: wl plcd: effrt to dispute 2nd over 2f out: green and nt qckn sn after: fdd* **6/1**[3]

4 **6** *2* **Ymir**[23] 7011 2-9-3 0 .... PaulDoe 10 62
(M J Attwater) *chsd ldrs on outer: shkn up and nt qckn over 2f out: steadily fdd over 1f out* **20/1**

7 *2* **Lucerne** 2-8-12 0 .... ShaneKelly 9 52
(W J Knight) *dwlt: towards rr: rdn over 2f out: plugged on: nvr on terms* **20/1**

8 *1 1/2* **Sitwell** 2-9-3 0 .... RobertWinston 6 53
(J R Fanshawe) *s.s: rn green in last and early reminders: nvr on terms: modest late prog* **25/1**

9 *shd* **Tuppenny Piece** 2-8-12 0 .... AdamKirby 13 48
(W R Swinburn) *dwlt: mostly wl in rr: nvr a factor: modest late prog* **16/1**

10 *shd* **Okba (USA)** 2-8-12 0 .... MartinDwyer 12 48
(M P Tregoning) *hld up in midfield and rn green: no prog over 2f out: wknd over 1f out* **12/1**

04 **11** *2 3/4* **Old Sarum (IRE)**[13] 7212 2-9-0 0 .... MarcHalford(3) 1 46
(D R C Elsworth) *plld hrd: pressed ldr to over 2f out: wknd rapidly* **25/1**

0 **12** *nk* **Cousin Charlie**[41] 6604 2-9-3 0 .... GeorgeBaker 2 45
(S Kirk) *dwlt: a wl in rr: no prog fnl 2f* **25/1**

13 *1* **Tattercoats (FR)** 2-8-12 0 .... NCallan 8 38
(D M Simcock) *towards rr whn bmpd against rail after 2f: brief effrt over 2f out: sn wknd* **33/1**

0 **14** *3* **Cool Libby (IRE)**[28] 6893 2-8-12 0 .... TPQueally 3 30
(A B Haynes) *a towards rr: rdn over 2f out: wknd* **50/1**

1m 26.9s (0.90) **Going Correction** +0.075s/f (Slow) **14** Ran SP% **123.5**
Speed ratings (Par 96): **97,96,93,92,91 89,86,85,85,85 81,81,80,76**
toteswinger: 1&2 £3.10, 1&3 £1.40, 2&3 £5.70. CSF £16.44 TOTE £3.40: £1.50, £2.40, £1.50; EX 30.40.
Owner K Abdulla **Bred** Juddmonte Farms Ltd **Trained** Pulborough, W Sussex
■ Stewards' Enquiry : Luke Morris four-day ban: careless riding (Dec 3-6)

FOCUS
A fair median auction race. They finished fairly strung out and nothing really got into it from behind.

NOTEBOOK
Dialect was supported when finding significant improvement on her debut effort, when third of 17 in a Newmarket maiden this month. She was a bit weak in the market here and had a bit to prove back on this surface, but has handled the Polytrack well. She raced near the pace, quickened at the furlong pole and showed determination to hang on in the closing stages. She is not particularly imposing, but is open to further progress and should receive a realistic mark for handicaps. (op 5-2 tchd 4-1)
Gaily Noble(IRE) snatched the lead from stall four and had the run of the race, but he finished clear of the third and stepped up on his promising fourth over 1m here on his debut. He seems to have a willing attitude and quite a bit of natural speed, so should be able to pick up a similar event. (op 13-2 tchd 7-1)
Three Ducks stayed on quite well after a slow start when fourth on her debut in a 6f Leicester maiden last month, but looked a bit one paced when asked for her effort over this longer trip. It is a bit disappointing that she does not seem to have built on her debut promise, but she is related to some useful types and should do better in time. (op 3-1)
Dhania(IRE) looked very inexperienced, but seemed to be getting the hang of things in the closing stages and has run a promising race at 100-1 on his debut. (op 80-1)
All For You(IRE) also offered plenty of encouragement on her debut. She displayed a good cruising speed, showed up well for a long way and should improve for this run. (op 5-1)

7381 DIGIBET.COM CONDITIONS STKS 7f (P)
7:50 (7:52) (Class 3) 3-Y-O+
£7,477 (£2,239; £1,119; £560; £279; £140) **Stalls** High

Form RPR

0053 **1** **Confuchias (IRE)**[60] 6104 4-9-4 101 .... DarrenWilliams 6 110
(K R Burke) *chsd ldrs: rdn over 2f out: prog over 1f out: drvn and r.o to ld wl ins fnl f* **7/1**

50-0 **2** *1 1/4* **Mac Love**[61] 6073 7-8-11 101 .... MickyFenton 11 100
(Stef Liddiard) *plld hrd: hld up in midfield: chsng ldrs and pushed along over 1f out: no impact tl styd on wl last 100yds: tk 2nd fnl strides* **20/1**

110 **3** *1/2* **Noble Citizen (USA)**[20] 7101 3-8-10 88 .... MartinDwyer 9 99
(D M Simcock) *trckd ldr: tried to chal over 2f out: no imp over 1f out: kpt on again last 100yds* **6/1**[3]

0363 **4** *nk* **Red Alert Day**[25] 6975 3-8-10 103 .... ShaneKelly 7 102+
(S A Callaghan) *dwlt: t.k.h early and sn prom: effrt on inner over 2f out: trying to chal whn no room jst ins fnl f: kpt on nr fin* **5/2**[2]

0005 **5** *nk* **Al Muheer (IRE)**[14] 7192 3-8-10 94 .... NCallan 1 97
(C E Brittain) *trckd ldrs: effrt on outer to press ldng pair 2f out: nt qckn over 1f out: kpt on* **7/1**

1152 **6** *hd* **Mr Lambros**[270] 679 7-8-11 92 .... (vt) DarryllHolland 10 96
(Miss Gay Kelleway) *reluctant to enter stalls: dwlt: sn led: drvn and pressed 2f out: edgd rt but holding rivals tl wknd and hdd wl ins fnl f: swamped for pls nr fin* **10/1**

106- **7** *2 1/4* **Green Oasis (USA)**[479] 3988 3-8-5 93 .... (t) ChrisCatlin 8 85
(E J O'Neill) *plld hrd: hld up in last pair: eased fr ins to outer fr 2f out: nvr gng pce to threaten* **20/1**

0043 **8** *2 1/4* **Bonus (IRE)**[14] 7192 8-9-5 104 .... EddieAhern 3 92
(G A Butler) *hld up in last: plld out over 2f out: shkn up and no prog wl over 1f out* **2/1**[1]

0-50 **9** *1 3/4* **Quito (IRE)**[11] 7243 11-8-11 90 .... (b) PaulMulrennan 4 80
(Mrs R A Carr) *stdd s: t.k.h early and hld up in rr: urged along bef 1/2-way: struggling over 2f out* **20/1**

6455 **10** *nse* **Pawan (IRE)**[15] 7181 8-8-9 83 ow3 .... (b) AnnStokell(5) 2 82
(Miss A Stokell) *hld up in midfield on outer: shuffled along vigorously over 2f out: wknd* **40/1**

1m 25.95s (-0.05) **Going Correction** +0.075s/f (Slow)
WFA 3 from 4yo+ 1lb **10** Ran SP% **127.0**
Speed ratings (Par 107): **103,101,101,100,100 100,97,94,92,92**
toteswinger: 1&2 £24.90, 1&3 £11.50, 2&3 £27.60. CSF £145.16 TOTE £8.50: £1.80, £6.30, £2.90; EX 187.40.
Owner Pattern Racing UK Ltd **Bred** Mrs Vanessa Hutch **Trained** Middleham Moor, N Yorks
■ Stewards' Enquiry : Darryll Holland three-day ban: careless riding (Dec 3-5)

FOCUS
A decent conditions event but it was run at a muddling pace and involved one hard-luck story. The form may not be entirely reliable and is best rated around the winner and third.

NOTEBOOK
Confuchias(IRE) was third on heavy ground in the Ayr Gold Cup last time and had a few questions to answer stepped back up to 7f on his all-weather debut and was under pressure some way out, but kept grinding away and eventually utilised his sprinting speed to strike off the moderate gallop and win in fairly decisive fashion. (op 11-2)
Mac Love put in an incredible performance in this race. He pulled violently in the early stages and gave his rider a torrid time, but then did really well to find a finishing effort. He could have an interesting chance if settling better off a stronger pace next time. (op 25-1)
Noble Citizen(USA), a quietly progressive, dual 7f handicap winner since May, ran creditably, particularly as he was unable to adopt his favoured front-running role and faced a tough task at the weights. (op 10-1)
Red Alert Day had strong claims on his third in a Listed event at Newmarket in May. He travelled sweetly into contention on the far side but was badly baulked as the leader drifted right. He was unlucky not to have finished quite a bit closer but it is hard to say that he would have won with a clear run. (tchd 11-4)
Al Muheer(IRE) ran a fair race stepped back up to 7f after his decent 6f run off a mark of 96 here last time, but the steady pace did not play to his strengths. (op 10-1)
Bonus(IRE) ran a mighty race off a mark of 104 over 6f here last time. He was heavily backed to successfully concede weight to all his rivals as well as age to most of them, but he was undone by the modest tempo and faced a forlorn task trying to get into the argument under a patient ride. (op 11-4 tchd 7-2 and 4-1 in a place)

7382 DIGIBET CASINO H'CAP (DIV I) 7f (P)
8:20 (8:20) (Class 6) (0-55,55) 3-Y-O+ **£1,706** (£503; £252) **Stalls** High

Form RPR

1200 **1** **Piccolo Diamante (USA)**[10] 7254 4-8-13 52 .... (t) AdamKirby 12 61
(S Parr) *mounted on crse: hld up towards rr: prog to chse ldrs 2f out: swtchd to inner and hrd rdn fr over 1f out: forced ahd last 100yds* **9/1**

2011 **2** *hd* **Megalo Maniac**[15] 7180 5-9-2 55 .... (p) PaulHanagan 8 63
(R A Fahey) *mounted on crse: trckd ldng pair: effrt to ld wl over 1f out: sn pressed and drvn: hdd last 100yds: kpt on wl* **9/2**[2]

3620 **3** *1/2* **Takitwo**[43] 6560 5-9-0 53 .... (v[1]) DaneO'Neill 11 60
(P D Cundell) *trckd ldrs: rdn to chal wl over 1f out: nrly upsides ent fnl f: nt qckn* **4/1**[1]

3506 **4** *1/2* **Imperium**[20] 7102 7-9-2 55 .... (p) TGMcLaughlin 2 61
(Jean-Rene Auvray) *stdd s: hld up in last: stdy prog fr 2f out: rdn and nt qckn 1f out: styng on again nr fin* **12/1**

5040 **5** *1/2* **Outer Hebrides**[5] 7320 7-8-9 53 .... (v) MCGeran(5) 9 57
(J M Bradley) *racd wd and hld up in rr: sme prog 2f out: nt qckn over 1f out: styd on ins fnl f* **7/1**

4000 **6** *2* **Motu (IRE)**[12] 7226 7-8-11 55 .... (b) KellyHarrison(5) 3 54
(I W McInnes) *t.k.h early: pressed ldr to 2f out: grad wknd fnl f* **28/1**

2032 **7** *shd* **Fun In The Sun**[37] 6693 4-9-1 54 .... GeorgeBaker 4 53
(A B Haynes) *hld up in midfield and racd wd: shkn up and nt qckn 2f out: sme prog jst over 1f out: nt pce to chal* **6/1**[3]

3004 **8** *3/4* **Torquemada (IRE)**[20] 7102 7-9-2 55 .... (t) PaulDoe 7 52
(M J Attwater) *hld up in last pair: effrt on outer 2f out: kpt on same pce and nvr threatened* **20/1**

0003 **9** *3/4* **Langham House**[21] 7072 3-8-13 53 .... DarryllHolland 13 48
(J R Jenkins) *led: hung lft and hdd wl over 1f out: wknd* **13/2**

5P60 **10** *nk* **Wooden King (IRE)**[14] 7194 3-8-12 52 .... (v) JamesDoyle 5 46
(P D Evans) *t.k.h: hld up in midfield: rdn over 2f out: no prog* **33/1**

5100 **11** *1/2* **Talon (IRE)**[16] 7166 3-9-1 55 .... (p) RobertWinston 6 48
(G A Swinbank) *t.k.h early: trckd ldng pair: rdn 3f out: wknd fnl 2f* **16/1**

4500 **12** *1 3/4* **The Jailer**[33] 6773 5-9-2 55 .... VinceSlattery 14 43
(J G M O'Shea) *reluctant to enter stalls: hld up bhd ldrs: rdn over 2f out: lost pl wl over 1f out* **16/1**

6505 **13** *1 1/4* **Double Valentine**[151] 3266 5-8-13 52 .... KirstyMilczarek 1 36
(R Ingram) *racd on outer: chsd ldrs: rdn over 2f out: wknd over 1f out* **20/1**

1m 26.67s (0.67) **Going Correction** +0.075s/f (Slow)
WFA 3 from 4yo+ 1lb **13** Ran SP% **123.7**
Speed ratings (Par 101): **99,98,98,97,97 94,94,93,92,92 92,90,88**
toteswinger: 1&2 £18.70, 1&3 £11.20, 2&3 £2.10. CSF £48.63 CT £195.02 TOTE £11.20: £3.50, £1.70, £2.20; EX 63.80.
Owner W Mckay, D Cornan, M Morris, P Reid **Bred** Pamela Linahan **Trained** Bawtry, S Yorks
■ Stewards' Enquiry : Dane O'Neill one-day ban: used whip with excessive frequency (Dec 3)
Adam Kirby two-day ban: used whip with excessive frequency (Dec 3-4)

FOCUS
An ordinary race but solid enough for the grade rated around the first three.
Langham House Official explanation: jockey said gelding hung left

7383 DIGIBET CASINO H'CAP (DIV II) 7f (P)
8:50 (8:50) (Class 6) (0-55,55) 3-Y-O+ **£1,706** (£503; £252) **Stalls** High

Form RPR

0100 **1** **Convallaria (FR)**[21] 7076 5-9-2 55 .... (b) ChrisCatlin 10 64
(G Wragg) *t.k.h early: hld up in last pair: hmpd over 2f out: prog over 1f out: drvn and styd on wl to ld last stride* **9/1**

0003 **2** *shd* **Solicitude**[5] 7316 5-9-2 55 .... (p) TPQueally 8 64
(D Haydn Jones) *dwlt: hld up in midfield: prog against far rail over 2f out: drvn ahd ins fnl f: hdd post* **7/2**[1]

0040 **3** *1 1/2* **Charmel's Lad**[51] 6334 3-8-13 53 .... (t) AdamKirby 14 58
(W R Swinburn) *dwlt: hld up in rr: rdn over 2f out: prog over 1f out: styd on to take 3rd nr fin* **10/1**

2304 **4** *nk* **Overstayed (IRE)**[2] 7359 5-9-2 55 .... NeilChalmers 3 59
(A Bailey) *led at decent pce: 3l clr 3f out: hung lft fr over 2f out: tied up and hdd ins fnl f* **9/2**[2]

2040 **5** *hd* **Guildenstern (IRE)**[70] 5801 6-9-2 55 .... JimmyQuinn 6 58
(P Howling) *t.k.h early: trckd ldrs and racd wd: tried to cl fr 2f out: one pce and nvr quite got there* **7/1**[3]

0064 **6** *1 1/4* **Thabaat**[23] 7012 4-9-2 55 .... (b) DaneO'Neill 2 55
(J M Bradley) *dwlt: t.k.h early: hld up in rr: drvn and prog 2f out: no imp on ldrs fnl f* **11/1**

0006 **7** *2 1/4* **Hollow Jo**[10] 7255 8-8-13 52 .... DarryllHolland 7 46
(J R Jenkins) *hld up in last pair: rdn and no prog over 2f out: modest late hdwy* **10/1**

5060 **8** *nk* **Filemot**[15] 7182 3-8-12 52 .... LiamJones 11 45
(John Berry) *chsd ldng pair: rdn wl over 2f out: fdd over 1f out* **25/1**

0060 **9** *shd* **This Ones For Pat (USA)**[2] 7357 3-8-8 55 .... AndreaAtzeni(7) 4 48
(S Parr) *stdd s: t.k.h and sn chsd ldr: rdn to try to cl fr 2f out: wknd fnl f* **7/1**[3]

6130 **10** *1/2* **Scruffy Skip (IRE)**[5] 7316 3-9-0 54 .... TGMcLaughlin 5 45
(Mrs C A Dunnett) *chsd ldrs: u.p over 2f out: no real imp over 1f out: wknd* **20/1**

6-00 **11** *17* **Kara Tau**[23] 7026 3-9-1 55 .... MickyFenton 13 1
(Stef Liddiard) *wnt rt s: hld up towards rr: bdly hmpd over 2f out: nt rcvr: t.o* **14/1**

1m 27.07s (1.07) **Going Correction** +0.075s/f (Slow)
WFA 3 from 4yo+ 1lb **11** Ran SP% **117.2**
Speed ratings (Par 101): **96,95,94,93,93 92,89,89,89,88 69**
toteswinger: 1&2 £9.70, 1&3 £15.50, 2&3 £11.50. CSF £40.37 CT £327.87 TOTE £11.00: £3.50, £1.10, £3.90; EX 37.30.
Owner Mrs Claude Lilley **Bred** Jan Krzywicki **Trained** Newmarket, Suffolk
■ The final winner for Geoff Wragg.
■ Stewards' Enquiry : T P Queally one-day ban: careless riding (Dec 3)

FOCUS
They went a decent pace in this modest handicap and it produced a thrilling finish. The form seems sound enough with the runner-up looking the best guide to the form.

7384 RACING UK LIVE ON CHANNEL 432 H'CAP — 6f (P)
9:20 (9:21) (Class 4) (0-80,80) 3-Y-0+ **£5,180** (£1,541; £770; £384) **Stalls** High

Form — RPR

0032 **1** **Dazzling Bay**[12] 7225 8-8-9 **74**..........(b) DuranFentiman(3) 12 — 87
(T D Easterby) *t.k.h early: racd on inner: trckd ldrs: wnt 2nd over 1f out: led 1f out: pushed clr and r.o wl* **8/1**

0/41 **2** *1 1/4* **Silaah**[21] 7074 4-9-1 **77**.......... TGMcLaughlin 11 — 90+
(E A L Dunlop) *dwlt: hld up in last pair: gd prog on inner fr 2f out: clsng whn no room and swtchd lft jst ins fnl f: r.o to take 2nd last 50yds* **2/1**[1]

0313 **3** *1* **Dvinsky (USA)**[21] 7077 7-9-4 **80**..........(b) JimmyQuinn 8 — 86
(P Howling) *mde most and racd on inner: drvn and hdd 1f out: fdd and lost 2nd last 50yds* **3/1**[2]

6630 **4** *1 1/4* **Distinctly Game**[127] 4058 6-9-2 **78**.......... ChrisCatlin 9 — 80
(K A Ryan) *hld up towards rr: effrt over 2f out: prog to chse ldrs over 1f out: kpt on but no imp* **12/1**

053 **5** *3 1/4* **Yungaburra (IRE)**[7] 7290 4-9-1 **77**..........(t) AdamKirby 2 — 69
(S Parr) *s.i.s: hld up in last pair: sme prog fr 2f out: nvr remotely on terms w ldrs* **9/1**

6026 **6** *1 1/4* **Hereford Boy**[21] 7081 4-9-0 **76**.......... RobertHavlin 10 — 64
(D K Ivory) *hld up towards rr: effrt over 2f out: nvr gng pce to threaten* **14/1**

2002 **7** *1 1/4* **Rasaman (IRE)**[31] 6842 4-9-4 **80**..........(tp) NCallan 5 — 64
(K A Ryan) *t.k.h early: pressed ldr to over 1f out: wknd* **7/1**[3]

5004 **8** *3/4* **First Order**[14] 7201 7-8-11 **78**..........(v) AnnStokell(5) 7 — 59
(Miss A Stokell) *trckd ldrs: knitted along furiously and no prog 2f out: wknd* **33/1**

6020 **9** *1* **Russian Reel**[18] 7143 3-8-12 **77**..........(t) AlanCreighton(3) 6 — 55
(E J Creighton) *rousted along early: nvr gng that wl in rr: stmbld jst over 2f out: no prog* **50/1**

0066 **10** *9* **Efistorm**[15] 7176 7-9-2 **78**.......... DaneO'Neill 4 — 27
(C R Dore) *w ldrs but racd three off rail: rdn over 2f out: sn wknd rapidly* **20/1**

0000 **11** *6* **Canadian Danehill (IRE)**[17] 7151 6-9-3 **79**..........(p) EddieAhern 1 — 9
(R M H Cowell) *w ldrs but wdst of all: lost plenty of grnd bnd bef 3f out: sn btn and bhd* **25/1**

0253 **12** *1* **Lucayos**[66] 5936 5-9-4 **80**.......... DarrenWilliams 3 — 7
(K R Burke) *w ldrs but racd wd: lost grnd bnd 3f out: wknd rapidly over 2f out* **14/1**

1m 12.35s (-0.75) **Going Correction** +0.075s/f (Slow) **12** Ran SP% **126.5**
Speed ratings (Par 105): **108,106,105,103,99 97,95,94,93,81 73,72**
toteswinger: 1&2 £8.50, 1&3 £11.30, 2&3 £2.30. CSF £25.13 CT £63.88 TOTE £9.10: £2.40, £1.60, £1.90; EX 34.30 Place 6 £32.79, Place 5 £17.17..
Owner Ghmw Racing **Bred** T And M A Bibby **Trained** Great Habton, N Yorks

FOCUS
An intriguing handicap involving a number of reliable multiple all-weather winners. The form is solid for the grade with the third setting the standard.
Yungaburra(IRE) Official explanation: jockey said gelding hung badly left
First Order Official explanation: jockey said gelding hung left
T/Plt: £72.70 to a £1 stake. Pool: £91,962.36. 922.25 winning tickets. T/Qpdt: £17.90 to a £1 stake. Pool: £7,020.58. 289.62 winning tickets. JN

7301 LINGFIELD (L-H)
Wednesday, November 19

OFFICIAL GOING: Standard
Wind: Light, half-against Weather: Sunny

7385 THREE BRIDGES AMATEUR RIDERS' H'CAP — 1m 4f (P)
12:00 (12:00) (Class 5) (0-70,70) 3-Y-0+ **£2,637** (£811; £405) **Stalls** Low

Form — RPR

5211 **1** **Epsom Salts**[6] 7301 3-10-3 **58**.......... MrSWalker 9 — 70+
(P M Phelan) *a.p: led over 2f out: sn clr: rdn out* **9/4**[1]

3254 **2** *1 1/2* **Potentiale (IRE)**[20] 7096 4-11-2 **70**..........(p) MrJoshuaMoore(5) 11 — 77
(J W Hills) *s.i.s: hld up in rr: hdwy on outside 2f out: styd on to go 2nd ins fnl f* **7/2**[2]

0264 **3** *1/2* **Night Orbit**[14] 7202 4-10-12 **66**..........(v) MrRBirkett(5) 6 — 72
(Miss J Feilden) *mid-div: hdwy over 3f out: chsd wnr over 1f out tl ins fnl f* **12/1**

0000 **4** *3/4* **William's Way**[28] 6898 6-10-10 **66**.......... MrCMartin(7) 1 — 71
(I A Wood) *hld up: hdwy on ins over 2f out: styd on: nvr nrr* **25/1**

1104 **5** *3 3/4* **Strike Force**[20] 7094 4-10-11 **65**.......... MissALHutchinson(5) 4 — 64
(K F Clutterbuck) *plld hrd: in rr: hdwy on outside over 1f out: nvr nr to chal* **16/1**

1300 **6** *nk* **Schinken Otto (IRE)**[8] 4556 7-10-4 **56** oh2.......... MissNJefferson(3) 3 — 54
(J M Jefferson) *slowly away in rr tl hdwy 2f out: styd on: nvr nr to chal* **14/1**

6000 **7** *3 1/4* **Medieval Maiden**[35] 6729 5-10-2 **56** oh8.......... MissAWallace(5) 14 — 49
(Mrs L J Mongan) *mid-div: hdwy whn swtchd rt over 1f out: nvr nr to chal* **50/1**

1-45 **8** *1 1/2* **Highest Esteem**[291] 406 4-10-13 **67**..........(p) MissHayleyMoore(5) 2 — 58
(G L Moore) *hld up in mid-div: rdn over 2f out: no hdwy after* **9/1**

0040 **9** *2* **Corlough Mountain**[36] 6719 4-10-0 **56** oh1.......... MissMBryant(7) 7 — 44
(P Butler) *s.i.s: a towards rr* **66/1**

4130 **10** *shd* **Home**[96] 5040 3-10-4 **66**.......... MissLGray(7) 10 — 53
(C Gordon) *trckd ldrs: rdn 3f out: wknd 2f out* **25/1**

21-0 **11** *3/4* **Zelos (IRE)**[111] 4568 4-11-2 **68**.......... MrMJJSmith(3) 5 — 54
(D G Bridgwater) *hld up in tch: rdn and wknd over 2f out* **33/1**

5005 **12** *1 3/4* **Venir Rouge**[12] 7230 4-11-2 **70**.......... MrAshleePrice(5) 15 — 53
(M Salaman) *t.k.h: prom: rdn over 4f out: wknd over 2f out* **16/1**

1402 **13** *2 3/4* **Snowberry Hill (USA)**[217] 1408 5-10-2 **56**.......... MrJPFeatherstone(5) 12 — 35
(Lucinda Featherstone) *prom: led after 3f: rdn and hdd over 2f out: wknd qckly* **7/1**[3]

1600 **14** *1* **Lady Sorcerer**[13] 7211 3-10-4 **64**.......... MissLEBurke(5) 8 — 41
(A P Jarvis) *saddle slipped sn after s: a in rr* **25/1**

3340 **15** *1 1/4* **Karmei**[14] 7189 3-10-1 **56** oh4.......... MissFayeBramley 16 — 31
(R Curtis) *s.i.s: sn prom: rdn and wknd over 3f out* **50/1**

60 **16** *27* **Captain Sirus (FR)**[35] 6728 5-10-2 **56** oh8.......... MissZoeLilly(5) 13 — —
(P Butler) *led over 3f: wknd 4f out: t.o* **66/1**

2m 31.57s (-1.43) **Going Correction** -0.175s/f (Stan)
WFA 3 from 4yo+ 6lb **16** Ran SP% **123.0**
Speed ratings (Par 103): **97,96,95,95,92 92,90,89,87,87 87,86,84,83,82 64**
toteswinger: 1&2 £13.70, 1&3 £13.80, 2&3 £10.90. CSF £8.69 CT £80.04 TOTE £2.80: £1.50, £1.10, £2.70, £3.60; EX 11.10 Trifecta £94.30 Part won. Pool: £127.50 - 0.50 winning units..
Owner The Epsom Racegoers **Bred** Heatherwold Stud **Trained** Epsom, Surrey
■ Stewards' Enquiry : Mr Joshua Moore two-day ban: careless riding (Dec 8, Jan 2)

FOCUS
A modest amateur riders' handicap, but competitive nonetheless. The pace appeared ordinary. Sound form for the grade, with the winner value for a bit extra.
Lady Sorcerer Official explanation: jockey said saddle slipped

7386 FOREST ROW H'CAP (DIV I) — 7f (P)
12:30 (12:32) (Class 4) (0-85,85) 3-Y-0+ **£4,403** (£1,310; £654; £327) **Stalls** Low

Form — RPR

4103 **1** **My Gacho (IRE)**[13] 7215 6-9-5 **85**..........(b) J-PGuillambert 7 — 99
(M Johnston) *a.p: led appr 2f out: sn clr: pushed out fnl f* **11/2**[3]

0001 **2** *2 3/4* **Mister New York (USA)**[9] 7277 3-8-12 **79** 6ex.......... JimCrowley 8 — 86
(Noel T Chance) *hld up on outside: hdwy over 1f out to chse wnr ins fnl f* **5/1**[2]

4-00 **3** *1 1/4* **Perfect Act**[25] 6981 3-8-13 **80**.......... AdamKirby 10 — 84
(C G Cox) *hld up in rr: hdwy over 1f out: r.o to go 3rd ins fnl f* **10/1**

/000 **4** *1/2* **Spectait**[23] 7019 6-9-0 **80**.......... ShaneKelly 6 — 82
(Jonjo O'Neill) *slowly away: in rr tl mde late hdwy: nvr nrr* **40/1**

0020 **5** *3/4* **Hessian (IRE)**[6] 7307 4-8-5 **71** oh3.......... JimmyQuinn 4 — 71
(M D Squance) *t.k.h: in tch: kpt on one pce fnl f* **16/1**

0460 **6** *shd* **Johannes (IRE)**[12] 7222 5-8-9 **75**.......... PaulHanagan 3 — 75
(R A Fahey) *slowly away: in rr: kpt on fnl f but nvr on terms* **13/2**

0030 **7** *hd* **Compton's Eleven**[11] 7239 7-9-0 **80**.......... EdwardCreighton 1 — 79
(M R Channon) *sn rdn in rr: nvr on terms* **14/1**

0002 **8** *1/2* **Bahiano (IRE)**[18] 7143 7-8-10 **76** ow1.......... NCallan 5 — 74
(C E Brittain) *in tch: rdn 2f out: wknd fnl f* **6/1**

5632 **9** *3/4* **Caprio (IRE)**[141] 3571 3-8-6 **73**.......... RichardKingscote 11 — 69
(Tom Dascombe) *c fr wd draw to join ldr: led 3f out: hdd appr 2f out: wknd fnl f* **10/1**

4500 **10** *1 1/2* **Danehillsundance (IRE)**[23] 7019 4-8-13 **79**.......... JamieSpencer 2 — 77+
(S Parr) *trckd ldrs: rdn over 2f out: wknd fnl f* **9/2**[1]

6000 **11** *3/4* **Pegasus Again (USA)**[26] 6949 3-8-10 **77**.......... JoeFanning 9 — 67
(T G Mills) *led tl hdd 3f out: wknd appr fnl f* **12/1**

1m 22.63s (-2.17) **Going Correction** -0.175s/f (Stan) course record
WFA 3 from 4yo+ 1lb **11** Ran SP% **118.7**
Speed ratings (Par 105): **105,101,100,99,99 98,98,98,97,95 94**
toteswinger: 1&2 £5.30, 1&3 £15.10, 2&3 £29.00. CSF £33.52 CT £272.30 TOTE £4.20: £1.70, £2.40, £4.60; EX 25.90 Trifecta £283.60 Part won. Pool: £383.33 - 0.72 winning units..
Owner Grant Mercer **Bred** Mount Coote Stud **Trained** Middleham Moor, N Yorks

FOCUS
A fair handicap and the pick of the times over course and distance. A new personal best from My Gacho with the runner-up to form.
Danehillsundance(IRE) Official explanation: jockey said colt was denied a clear run

7387 COLEMANS HATCH MAIDEN STKS — 1m 2f (P)
1:00 (1:02) (Class 5) 3-Y-0+ **£2,729** (£806; £403) **Stalls** Low

Form — RPR

26-0 **1** **Shavansky**[39] 6079 4-9-7 77.......... StephenCarson 6 — 81+
(C J Mann) *sn trckd ldr: led appr fnl f: rdn out* **6/1**

4-0 **2** *2 3/4* **Wine 'n Dine**[199] 1840 3-9-3 0.......... GeorgeBaker 1 — 73
(G L Moore) *hld up in rr: rdn over 2f out: hdwy over 1f out: r.o to go 2nd nr fin* **9/2**[3]

3 *1/2* **Annabelle's Charm (IRE)** 3-8-12 0.......... JamieSpencer 10 — 67
(L M Cumani) *led after 2f: rdn hdd appr fnl f: one pce and lost 2nd nr fin* **9/4**[1]

05 **4** *nk* **Antillia**[37] 6705 3-8-12 0.......... EddieAhern 2 — 66
(C F Wall) *trckd ldrs: rdn over 3f out: one pce fnl f* **12/1**

5 *1/2* **Cape Express (IRE)** 3-9-3 0.......... NCallan 8 — 70+
(M A Jarvis) *slowly away: sn prom: rdn 3f out: no hdwy fnl 2f* **7/2**[2]

640- **6** *1 1/2* **Musashi (IRE)**[342] 3-9-3 68.......... FrankieMcDonald 5 — 67
(Jane Chapple-Hyam) *mid-div: pushed along 3f out: one pce fr over 1f out* **20/1**

30 **7** *1/2* **Winter Miss (USA)**[77] 5612 3-8-12 0.......... ShaneKelly 7 — 61
(J Noseda) *racd wd: nvr bttr than mid-div* **10/1**

8 *9* **Bantu** 3-8-12 0.......... JimmyFortune 4 — 43
(J H M Gosden) *a towards rr* **10/1**

6-06 **9** *10* **Tomorrow's World (IRE)**[28] 6896 3-8-12 66.......... TGMcLaughlin 3 — 23
(M S Saunders) *led for 2f: rdn over 3f out: wknd 2f out* **33/1**

0000 **10** *31* **Alright Chuck**[58] 6175 4-9-7 32.......... ChrisCatlin 11 — —
(P W Hiatt) *a in rr and sn outpcd: t.o* **100/1**

2m 4.93s (-1.67) **Going Correction** -0.175s/f (Stan)
WFA 3 from 4yo 4lb **10** Ran SP% **120.0**
Speed ratings (Par 103): **99,96,96,96,95 94,94,86,78,54**
toteswinger: 1&2 £8.60, 1&3 £6.10, 2&3 £4.40. CSF £33.73 TOTE £7.20: £1.60, £1.80, £1.50; EX 42.50 Trifecta £263.20 Part won. Pool: £355.81 - 0.42 winning units..
Owner John Southway & Andrew Hughes **Bred** George Strawbridge **Trained** Upper Lambourn, Berks

FOCUS
An interesting maiden with some expensive three-year-olds making their belated debuts, but in a race run at only a modest pace it was those with previous experience that came to the fore. The form has been rated around the runner-up.
Alright Chuck Official explanation: jockey said gelding had no more to give

7388 EUROPEAN BREEDERS' FUND MAIDEN STKS — 6f (P)
1:30 (1:33) (Class 5) 2-Y-0 **£3,561** (£1,059; £529; £264) **Stalls** Low

Form — RPR

0322 **1** **Swiss Diva**[19] 7104 2-8-12 83.......... JamieSpencer 11 — 82+
(D R C Elsworth) *a.p: wnt 2nd over 2f out: shkn up to ld ins fnl f: sn clr* **1/4**[1]

0040 **2** *4 1/2* **Sonhador**[14] 7191 2-9-3 68.......... JimCrowley 6 — 67
(P Winkworth) *hld up in mid-div: rdn and r.o to go 2nd wl ins fnl f* **12/1**[2]

260 **3** *3/4* **All Spin (IRE)**[9] 7273 2-9-3 73.......... NCallan 10 — 65
(A P Jarvis) *led tl rdn and hdd ins fnl f: lost 2nd towards fin* **22/1**

2545 **4** *1 1/4* **Barnezet (GR)**[44] 6540 2-8-12 67.......... PatDobbs 12 — 56
(R Hannon) *t.k.h: hld up in mid-div: rdn to chse ldrs 2f out: wknd ins fnl f* **14/1**[3]

00 **5** *1* **Newlyn Art**[25] 6978 2-9-0 0.......... MarcHalford(3) 9 — 58+
(D R C Elsworth) *s.i.s: in rr: hdwy on ins appr fnl f: nvr nrr* **16/1**

6 **6** 3 ¾ **Little Blacknumber**[88] 5286 2-8-9 0 PatrickHills(3) 4 42
(R Hannon) *slowly away: sn mid-div: rdn over 2f out: sn btn* **25/1**

00 **7** *hd* **Cavitie**[49] 6381 2-9-3 0 EdwardCreighton 7 46
(E J Creighton) *s.i.s: a in rr* **80/1**

60 **8** ¾ **Molnaya (IRE)**[29] 6879 2-9-3 0 (t) FrankieMcDonald 5 44
(Jane Chapple-Hyam) *trckd ldr tl rdn over 2f out: sn wknd* **40/1**

000 **9** 6 **Red Dagger (IRE)**[29] 6877 2-9-3 40 RobertHavlin 8 26
(T D McCarthy) *disp 2nd tl weakeend over 2f out* **80/1**

10 3 ½ **Avrilo** 2-8-12 0 TGMcLaughlin 3 10
(M S Saunders) *sn outpcd: a bhd* **50/1**

11 7 **Pethers Dancer (IRE)** 2-9-3 0 MartinDwyer 2 —
(W R Muir) *s.i.s: outpcd thrght* **25/1**

69.99 secs (-1.91) **Going Correction** -0.175s/f (Stan) 2y crse rec **11** Ran SP% **119.2**
Speed ratings (Par 96): **105,99,98,96,95 90,89,88,80,76 66**
toteswinger: 1&2 £2.30, 1&3 £3.30, 2&3 £10.50. CSF £3.76 TOTE £1.20: £1.02, £2.30, £4.50; EX 4.60 Trifecta £59.80 Pool: £387.56 - 4.79 winning units..

Owner Lordship Stud **Bred** Lordship Stud **Trained** Newmarket, Suffolk

FOCUS
A one-sided maiden on paper and that was how it turned out, Swiss Diva scoring with plenty in hand. The form looks pretty solid.

NOTEBOOK
Swiss Diva ultimately ran out an easy winner. She had in excess of 16lb in hand of her rivals on adjusted official figures following three placed efforts in turf maidens last month and faced a simple task if she took to this surface. She took a bit of time to find her full stride once in line for home, but once getting to the leader she won going away and shaped as if she will will stay another furlong. She is a half-sister to the same connections' smart colt Swiss Franc, and they were keen to get a win out of her as a two-year-old. The three that chased her home all looked thoroughly exposed as no better than fair, and she did not have to be at her best to take this. The form looks pretty solid. (op 2-7 and 1-2 in places)
Sonhador, who was caught on heels going into the first bend, ran on to go second inside the last, seeming to allay stamina fears under this change of tactics. He is none too consistent but capable of picking up a little race one day. (op 11-1)
All Spin(IRE) possessed the pace to lead despite his wide draw, but was no match in the end for the favourite and was run out of second late on. He is not progressing. (op 20-1 tchd 25-1)
Barnezet(GR) is an exposed performer, but she ran her race and showed that she acts on this surface. (tchd 20-1)
Newlyn Art ◆, a stablemate of the winner, ran a nice race, keeping on steadily from the back of the field for fifth on this all-weather bow. He is now eligible for handicaps and is one to keep an eye on, perhaps over further. (op 25-1 tchd 28-1)
Little Blacknumber, who is out of an unraced half-sister to smart sprinter Baltic King, was not discredited on her return from nearly three months off following her debut. (tchd 33-1)
Molnaya(IRE), who was formerly trained by Gary Moore, is now eligible for handicaps. (op 33-1)

7389 ASHURST WOOD CLAIMING STKS 7f (P)
2:00 (2:01) (Class 6) 2-Y-O **£2,047** (£604; £302) **Stalls** Low

Form RPR

106 **1** **Cool Art (IRE)**[4] 7335 2-9-2 76 (b¹) JamieSpencer 8 77
(S A Callaghan) *hld up: hdwy over 1f out: r.o to ld ins fnl f and sn in command* **3/1**[2]

2103 **2** 1 ¼ **Rio Royale (IRE)**[27] 6931 2-9-2 78 JimCrowley 4 74
(Mrs A J Perrett) *a in tch: wnt 2nd 2f out: led briefly 1f out: nt pce of wnr* **4/1**[3]

0521 **3** *nk* **Woolston Ferry (IRE)**[9] 7275 2-9-0 74 EdwardCreighton 3 71+
(M R Channon) *in rr and sn pushed along: styd on fnl f: nvr nrr* **1/1**[1]

0020 **4** 1 ½ **Protiva**[23] 7016 2-8-6 62 (v) PaulHanagan 6 59
(A P Jarvis) *led tl rdn and hdd 1f out: one pce after* **33/1**

5505 **5** 3 ¼ **Elusive Ronnie (IRE)**[42] 6572 2-8-0 51 LukeMorris(3) 5 48
(R A Teal) *hld up in tch: no hdwy ins fnl 2f* **40/1**

0044 **6** *shd* **Polly's Choice (IRE)**[9] 7275 2-7-13 64 JimmyQuinn 10 44
(R Hannon) *a in rr* **10/1**

2600 **7** 6 **Johnny Rook (GER)**[14] 7190 2-8-3 62 (b¹) ChrisCatlin 2 33
(E A L Dunlop) *trckd ldr to 2f out: wknd qckly* **20/1**

0 **8** 17 **Thurston (IRE)**[23] 7020 2-8-9 0 ow3 GabrielHannon(5) 9 1
(D J S Ffrench Davis) *chsd ldrs tl hung bdly rt ent st and wknd qckly: t.o* **66/1**

1m 24.13s (-0.67) **Going Correction** -0.175s/f (Stan) **8** Ran SP% **115.7**
Speed ratings (Par 94): **96,94,94,92,88 88,81,62**
toteswinger: 1&2 £2.70, 1&3 £1.40, 2&3 £1.50. CSF £15.02 TOTE £4.20: £1.40, £1.60, £1.10; EX 14.30 Trifecta £20.10 Pool: £397.53 - 14.59 winning units..

Owner Matthew Green **Bred** Azienda Agricola Robiati Angelo **Trained** Newmarket, Suffolk

FOCUS
A modest and uncompetitive claimer and although the trio that dominated the market also dominated the finish, it wasn't in the order that many would have expected. The form looks solid.

NOTEBOOK
Cool Art(IRE), whose two wins to date had been at 6f, had become disappointing but he had blinkers on for the first time here and they did the trick. Always travelling well on the inside behind the leaders, once switched out wide by Jamie Spencer on reaching the home straight he found more than enough. He has now won twice here so obviously likes this surface. (op 7-2)
Rio Royale(IRE), who ran well when dropped to this level on his return from three months off at Great Leighs last time, was never far from the leaders and he had his chance, but found the winner's turn of foot too much. He would have been 2lb worse off with him in a handicap so this looks about as good as he is. (op 9-2 tchd 5-1)
Woolston Ferry(IRE), unfortunate not to be unbeaten in three previous starts on Polytrack and much the best-in at these weights, went off a very well-backed favourite but his supporters were soon getting nervous as he wasn't travelling at all well from an early stage and dropped himself out last. He did eventually respond to pressure and despite making his effort closer to the inside rail than is probably ideal, was catching the front two at the line. However, he had at least 5lb in hand of these rivals at the weights which shows that he was well below form here. Perhaps he needs a rest now. (op 10-11)
Protiva, whose best effort so far was when visored for the first time two starts back, had the run of the race out in front and wasn't completely disgraced.
Elusive Ronnie(IRE) struggled on to finish best of the rest but he had plenty to find at these weights, so at least ran close to his mark.
Thurston(IRE) Official explanation: jockey said colt hung badly right throughout

7390 FOREST ROW H'CAP (DIV II) 7f (P)
2:30 (2:31) (Class 4) (0-85,82) 3-Y-O+ **£4,403** (£1,310; £654; £327) **Stalls** Low

Form RPR

1620 **1** **Internationaldebut (IRE)**[11] 7239 3-9-3 81 AdamKirby 9 92+
(S Parr) *hld up in rr: rdn and hdwy over 1f out: r.o to ld ins fnl f* **3/1**[1]

4235 **2** 1 ¼ **Carmenero (GER)**[6] 7302 5-8-9 72 MartinDwyer 3 79
(W R Muir) *a.p: r.o u.p fnl f to go 2nd towards fin* **15/2**

-340 **3** ¾ **Romany Princess (IRE)**[25] 6981 3-9-2 82 DaneO'Neill 8 85
(R Hannon) *trckd ldr: led 2f out: rdn and hdd ins fnl f: lost 2nd towards fin* **6/1**[3]

1/-0 **4** *nse* **Stanley Goodspeed**[37] 6699 5-9-3 80 GeorgeBaker 6 85
(J W Hills) *hld up: rdn and hdwy appr fnl f: r.o: nvr nrr* **16/1**

0600 **5** *hd* **Twilight Star (IRE)**[18] 7143 4-8-13 76 DarryllHolland 10 80
(R A Teal) *hld up: hdwy appr fnl f: rdn and one pce* **12/1**

6113 **6** ¾ **Fiefdom (IRE)**[40] 6627 6-8-12 75 PatrickMathers 4 77
(I W McInnes) *hld up: rdn 2f out: nvr on terms* **10/1**

1000 **7** ½ **Buxton**[13] 7215 4-9-2 79 (t) RobertHavlin 5 80
(R Ingram) *a.p on outside: rdn 2f out: fdd ins fnl f* **8/1**

0-05 **8** 2 **Shustraya**[265] 733 4-9-5 82 EddieAhern 2 78
(P J Makin) *trckd ldrs: rdn 2f out: wknd ins fnl f* **33/1**

3213 **9** ¾ **April Fool**[14] 7194 4-8-7 70 (v) LPKeniry 7 64
(J A Geake) *led tl hdd 2f out: sn wknd* **9/2**[2]

346 **10** 2 **Hallingdal (UAE)**[23] 7014 3-8-13 77 JamesDoyle 1 65
(Ms J S Doyle) *a in rr* **13/2**

1m 23.03s (-1.77) **Going Correction** -0.175s/f (Stan)
WFA 3 from 4yo+ 1lb **10** Ran SP% **119.3**
Speed ratings (Par 105): **103,101,100,100,100 99,99,96,95,93**
toteswinger: 1&2 £5.50, 1&3 £12.20, 2&3 £11.20. CSF £26.68 CT £132.61 TOTE £3.90: £2.10, £3.10, £2.70; EX 35.40 Trifecta £199.50 Part won. Pool: £269.61 - 0.42 winning units..

Owner W McKay, J Barton **Bred** Ennistown Stud **Trained** Bawtry, S Yorks

FOCUS
The time was 0.43 seconds slower than that for the first division, which looked the stronger event overall. The form looks sound enough rated around the placed horses and the winner could have more to offer.

7391 EVENT IMAGE FOR PHOTO FINISH NURSERY 1m (P)
3:00 (3:01) (Class 4) (0-85,83) 2-Y-O **£4,533** (£1,348; £674; £336) **Stalls** High

Form RPR

41 **1** **Goodison Glory (IRE)**[15] 7172 2-9-0 76 PaulHanagan 8 78
(R A Fahey) *hld up on outside: hdwy 2f out: rdn to ld jst ins fnl f: drvn out* **13/2**[3]

041 **2** ¾ **Blue Tango (IRE)**[28] 6893 2-9-1 77 JimCrowley 5 77
(Mrs A J Perrett) *hld up in tch: rdn and r.o fnl f to go 2nd cl home* **11/1**

4522 **3** *nk* **Rumble Of Thunder (IRE)**[26] 6954 2-9-0 76 DaneO'Neill 4 76
(D W P Arbuthnot) *trckd ldr: hung rt over 2f out: rallied and led briefly 1f out: kpt on* **9/4**[2]

41 **4** *hd* **Neuchatel (GER)**[34] 6759 2-9-4 80 JoeFanning 7 79
(M Johnston) *hld up in tch: effrt and ev ch 1f out: nt qckn ins fnl f* **11/10**[1]

000 **5** 2 ¾ **Vien (IRE)**[87] 5314 2-7-12 60 JimmyQuinn 2 53
(R Hannon) *in tch tl rdn and one pce fr over 1f out* **20/1**

1133 **6** 5 **Northern Tour**[12] 7229 2-9-7 83 JamieSpencer 1 65
(P F I Cole) *led tl rdn and hdd 1f out: sn btn and eased* **14/1**

1m 36.38s (-1.82) **Going Correction** -0.175s/f (Stan) 2y crse rec **6** Ran SP% **111.5**
Speed ratings (Par 98): **102,101,100,100,98 93**
toteswinger: 1&2 £6.90, 1&3 £3.90, 2&3 £4.30. CSF £67.05 CT £204.49 TOTE £6.70: £2.20, £3.40; EX 28.50 Trifecta £87.60 Pool: £510.75 - 4.31 winning units..

Owner Mrs Gill Gamon **Bred** Agricola Dell 'Olmo **Trained** Musley Bank, N Yorks

FOCUS
A fair nursery featuring a couple of unexposed and progressive types. The pace looked a fair one, but the pair who raced widest filled the first two places and that may have been significant. The third helps set the level and there could be more to come from the winner.

NOTEBOOK
Goodison Glory(IRE), winner of a heavy-ground Catterick maiden earlier this month, was kept out wide out of trouble throughout and he quickened up nicely when asked to go and win his race. This was only his third outing so he is entitled to carry on improving. (op 5-1)
Blue Tango(IRE), who had improved in each of his three previous starts, was making his sand and handicap debut but his price virtually doubled in the market beforehand which didn't bode well. Held up last early, he put in a powerful finish down the wide outside and although the winner had gone beyond recall, this effort was still encouraging enough to make him worth another try on Polytrack. (op 6-1 tchd 12-1)
Rumble Of Thunder(IRE), who ran really well on his sand debut at Wolverhampton last time despite not enjoying the smoothest of passages, was backed to break his duck at the sixth attempt and he travelled well on the shoulder of the leader, but looked awkward on the home turn and although he hit the front briefly at the furlong pole, he couldn't see it out. (op 11-4)
Neuchatel(GER), the form of whose Nottingham maiden victory last month has since been boosted, went off a well-backed favourite but although he had every chance starting up the home straight, he couldn't match the finishing pace of the front pair and may not have been on the most favoured part of the track. He remains unexposed and is almost certainly better than this. (op 6-4 tchd 13-8 in places)
Vien(IRE), making his sand and handicap debut after finishing well beaten in three turf maidens, wasn't disgraced though he never really looked like winning either. (op 25-1 tchd 33-1)
Northern Tour, well beaten when stepped up to an extended 1m at Wolverhampton last time, made much of the running and may not have been helped by sticking to the inside rail throughout, but he still dropped out very tamely when challenged and his stamina for the trip remains an issue. (op 10-1 tchd 9-1)

7392 MARSH GREEN H'CAP 1m (P)
3:30 (3:30) (Class 6) (0-55,61) 3-Y-O+ **£2,047** (£604; £302) **Stalls** High

Form RPR

4600 **1** **General Feeling (IRE)**[98] 4961 7-9-0 53 PaulHanagan 12 63
(S T Mason) *trckd ldr: led wl over 1f out: sn clr: comf* **33/1**

0600 **2** 3 **One Oi**[21] 7076 3-9-0 55 MartinDwyer 10 58
(D W P Arbuthnot) *chsd ldrs: rdn and r.o to go 2nd nr fin* **9/1**[3]

1605 **3** *nk* **Landikhaya (IRE)**[120] 4280 3-9-0 55 (p) DarryllHolland 9 57
(D K Ivory) *sn led: hdd wl over 1f out: rdn and lost 2nd nr fin* **20/1**

6000 **4** 1 **Pab Special (IRE)**[14] 7189 5-9-1 54 DaneO'Neill 3 54
(B R Johnson) *mid-div: rdn 2f out: kpt on fnl f* **9/1**[3]

050 **5** *nk* **Pop Music (IRE)**[23] 7027 5-8-13 52 (v) JamesDoyle 6 51
(Ms J S Doyle) *trckd ldrs: rdn 2f out: one pce fnl f* **12/1**

0411 **6** 1 ¾ **Plush**[4] 7340 5-9-1 61 6ex RossAtkinson(7) 5 56+
(Tom Dascombe) *v.s.a and plld hrd in rr: sme late hdwy: nvr on terms* **1/1**[1]

0506 **7** 1 ¼ **Quality Street**[103] 4824 6-9-2 55 (p) JimCrowley 4 47
(P Butler) *in rr: effrt over 1f out: nvr nr to chal* **16/1**

5520 **8** ½ **Too Grand**[5] 7310 3-8-13 54 NeilChalmers 11 45
(J J Bridger) *in rr: rdn 1/2-way: nvr on terms* **16/1**

0000 **9** 1 ¼ **Cavalry Guard (USA)**[21] 7076 4-9-2 55 (p) RobertHavlin 1 43
(T D McCarthy) *chsd ldrs tl rdn and wknd wl over 1f out* **50/1**

06-0 **10** ½ **Miss Habershon**[10] 7261 4-9-2 55 TravisBlock 8 42
(Nick Mitchell) *trckd ldrs: rdn over 2f out: wknd over 1f out* **33/1**

0102 **11** 2 ½ **Batchworth Blaise**[49] 6396 5-9-1 54 StephenCarson 7 35
(E A Wheeler) *slowly away: t.k.h: rdn and wknd 2f out* **8/1**[2]

1500 **12** *nk* **Inquisitress**[21] 7076 4-9-2 **55** .... EddieAhern 2 36
(J J Bridger) *a in rr* **14/1**

1m 37.12s (-1.08) **Going Correction** -0.175s/f (Stan)
WFA 3 from 4yo+ 2lb 12 Ran SP% **119.8**
Speed ratings (Par 101): **98,95,94,93,93 91,90,89,88,88 85,85**
toteswinger: 1&2 £28.60, 1&3 £61.60, 2&3 £18.90. CSF £301.53 CT £3627.47 TOTE £34.30: £7.50, £1.90, £4.40; EX 530.70 TRIFECTA Not won. Place 6: £6.39, Place 5: £4.51..
Owner Mrs Gillian Mason **Bred** John Graham And Leslie Laverty **Trained** Castle Bytham, Lincs

FOCUS
This low-grade handicap was run at only a steady pace, and nothing was able to get into the race from the rear. The time was 0.74 seconds slower than the preceding claimer and the form should be treated with some caution. The winner is rated up 4lb.
Plush Official explanation: jockey said gelding hung badly left in straight
Batchworth Blaise Official explanation: jockey said gelding ran too free
Inquisitress Official explanation: jockey said filly reared when stalls opened
T/Jkpt: Not won. T/Plt: £18.10 to a £1 stake. Pool: £37,048.41. 1,491.55 winning tickets. T/Qpdt: £4.30 to a £1 stake. Pool: £4,077.28. 696.60 winning tickets. JS

7332 GREAT LEIGHS (A.W) (L-H)
Thursday, November 20

OFFICIAL GOING: Standard
Wind: Fresh, across Weather: Dry, chilly wind

7393 AUDLEY END H'CAP — 5f (P)
6:50 (6:52) (Class 5) (0-75,81) 3-Y-O+ **£3,238** (£963; £481; £240) **Stalls** Low

Form RPR
154 **1** **Ivory Silk**[39] 6680 3-9-3 **74** .... (b[1]) ChrisCatlin 5 88
(J R Gask) *bhd: nt clr run and swtchd rt over 1f out: str run to ld ins fnl f: r.o wl* **6/1[3]**
2152 **2** *1* **Doubtful Sound (USA)**[14] 7206 4-8-7 **71** .... (p) AndreaAtzeni[(7)] 10 81
(R Hollinshead) *towards rr: hdwy over 1f out: rdn to ld ins fnl f: sn hdd and no ex* **10/1**
4001 **3** *2 ¼* **Fast Freddie**[5] 7346 4-9-1 **72** 6ex .... AdamKirby 1 74+
(S Parr) *chsd ldr tl led 2f out: rdn over 1f out: hdd ins fnl f: no ex fnl 100yds* **5/4[1]**
103 **4** *½* **Silvanus (IRE)**[10] 7276 3-9-1 **72** .... (b) EddieAhern 2 73
(W J Haggas) *trckd ldrs: effrt to chse ldr over 1f out: kpt on same pce u.p fnl f* **11/2[2]**
4201 **5** *hd* **Sands Crooner (IRE)**[10] 7276 5-9-10 **81** 6ex .... (v) TPQueally 6 81
(J G Given) *s.i.s: bhd: hdwy on inner over 1f out: kpt on fnl f: nt rch ldrs* **16/1**
4530 **6** *½* **Gold Express**[40] 6650 5-8-11 **68** .... JimCrowley 12 66+
(P J O'Gorman) *s.i.s: bhd: styd on fr over 1f out: nvr trbld ldrs* **11/1**
2044 **7** *½* **Magical Speedfit (IRE)**[6] 7315 3-9-1 **72** .... DaneO'Neill 8 68
(G G Margarson) *in tch in midfield: rdn wl over 1f out: no imp u.p over 1f out* **25/1**
0414 **8** *1 ½* **Billy Red**[7] 7295 4-8-5 **62** .... (b) HayleyTurner 9 53
(J R Jenkins) *pressed ldrs: rdn wl over 2f out: wknd ent fnl f* **14/1**
560 **9** *2 ¼* **Playful**[38] 6699 5-9-4 **75** .... GeorgeBaker 7 58
(R M Beckett) *in tch: rdn 2f out: struggling whn hmpd over 1f out: wknd fnl f* **15/2**
0000 **10** *4 ½* **Northern Empire (IRE)**[16] 7181 5-9-1 **72** .... NCallan 11 38
(K A Ryan) *rrd s and v.s.a: racd wd: nvr trbld ldrs* **10/1**
0300 **11** *6* **Ten Down**[81] 5531 3-9-1 **72** .... ShaneKelly 4 17
(M Quinn) *led tl rdn and hdd 2f out: sn wknd: wl bhd and eased ins fnl f* **20/1**

59.25 secs (-0.95) **Going Correction** -0.025s/f (Stan) 11 Ran SP% **133.6**
Speed ratings (Par 103): **106,104,100,100,99 98,98,95,92,84 75**
toteswinger: 1&2 £44.20, 1&3 £9.60, 2&3 £9.30. CSF £74.09 CT £129.22 TOTE £14.70: £3.10, £3.70, £1.10; EX 103.10.
Owner Horses First Racing Limited **Bred** K T Ivory **Trained** Sutton Veny, Wilts
■ Stewards' Enquiry : Andrea Atzeni one-day ban: careless riding; remedial training (Jan 15)

FOCUS
A run-of-the-mill handicap but a strong pace resulted in a new track record. The winner raced in the centre in the straight and recorded a clear personal best. This form looks reliable.

7394 CHRISTMAS PARTIES AT GREAT LEIGHS H'CAP — 6f (P)
7:20 (7:20) (Class 3) (0-95,95) 3-Y-O+
£7,477 (£2,239; £1,119; £560; £279; £140) **Stalls** Low

Form RPR
003 **1** **Fyodor (IRE)**[3] 7365 7-9-4 **95** .... LPKeniry 4 109+
(C R Dore) *t.k.h: hld up towards rr: stdy hdwy 1/2-way: chal on bit ent fnl f: shkn up to ld ins fnl f: pushed clr: easily* **8/1**
400 **2** *2* **Biniou (IRE)**[15] 7192 5-8-13 **90** .... EddieAhern 2 95
(R M H Cowell) *stdd after s: hld up in rr: nt clr run over 1f out: hdwy 1f out: kpt on wl to snatch 2nd on post: no ch w wnr* **10/1**
0233 **3** *shd* **Lone Wolfe**[29] 6902 4-8-10 **87** .... IanMongan 1 92
(Jane Chapple-Hyam) *chsd ldr tl led 2f out: sn rdn: hdd ins fnl f: nt pce of wnr: lost 2nd on post* **9/2[3]**
0011 **4** *1 ½* **Irish Pearl (IRE)**[16] 7181 3-9-4 **95** .... FergusSweeney 6 95
(K R Burke) *trckd ldng pair: swtchd ins and effrt wl over 1f out: pressed ldrs ent fnl f: wknd ins fnl f* **7/2[2]**
6435 **5** *¾* **Not My Choice (IRE)**[8] 7290 3-8-5 **82** .... (p) ChrisCatlin 5 80
(S Parr) *led tl hdd 2f out: sn drvn: wknd jst ins fnl f* **11/1**
4 **6** *½* **Epic Odyssey**[51] 6367 3-8-9 **86** .... MartinDwyer 7 82
(J R Boyle) *chsd ldrs: rdn 2f out: wknd ent fnl f* **12/1**
0300 **7** *¾* **Tartatartufata**[18] 7151 6-8-5 **82** .... (v) LiamJones 8 76
(J G Given) *chsd ldrs: rdn over 2f out: lost pl 2f out: kpt on same pce after* **33/1**
0660 **8** *2* **Cape**[12] 7243 5-8-11 **88** .... JimmyQuinn 9 75
(P Howling) *dropped in bhd after s: rdn 1/2-way: nvr trbld ldrs* **8/1**
4112 **9** *36* **Harlech Castle**[16] 7181 3-8-10 **87** .... (b) ShaneKelly 3 —
(P F I Cole) *nvr gng wl: midfield and pushed along tl dropped to rr over 3f out: wl bhd and eased over 1f out* **3/1[1]**

1m 12.35s (-1.35) **Going Correction** -0.025s/f (Stan) 9 Ran SP% **115.7**
Speed ratings (Par 107): **108,105,105,103,102 101,100,97,49**
toteswinger: 1&2 £29.40, 1&3 £2.90, 2&3 £21.60. CSF £84.48 CT £405.61 TOTE £10.90: £2.70, £2.30, £2.40; EX 81.40.
Owner Liam Breslin **Bred** E J Banks And D I Scott **Trained** West Pinchbeck, Lincs

FOCUS
A valuable handicap, but one that took less winning than seemed likely with the two market leaders disappointing to varying degrees. The pace was sound enough and the winner raced towards the centre. He has been rated back to his best form of a couple of years back.

NOTEBOOK
Fyodor(IRE), with the headgear left off, confirmed himself as good as ever on this second start for his new yard and showed he is equally effective over 6f as over 5f. This strong traveller won with more in hand than the official margin suggests and he should be able to pick up another decent sprint this winter when things drop right. (op 7-1)
Biniou(IRE) has been disappointing but turned in a much more encouraging display. However, consistency has not been his strongest suit, he is still high enough in the weights and it remains to be seen whether this can be built on next time. (op 25-1)
Lone Wolfe has been running well on Polytrack and again seemed to give it his best shot. He looks a good guide to this form and he should continue to go well either over this trip or over 7f. (op 7-2 tchd 5-1)
Irish Pearl(IRE) had shown improved form from the front on Fibresand but was found out on this quicker surface from this 7lb higher mark in a race where she was unable to dominate. The return to that slower surface should suit. (op 4-1)
Not My Choice(IRE) had missed the break on his two previous starts but jumped out much better in first-time cheekpieces and almost certainly did too much too soon. His stable has been in form but he has little margin for error from this mark. (op 9-1 tchd 8-1)
Epic Odyssey, back on Polytrack on this first run for new connections, shaped as though this run was just needed. He will have to show a bit more before he is worth a bet, though. (op 14-1)
Harlech Castle was closely matched with Irish Pearl on recent Fibresand form but ran as though something amiss. He had looked progressive up to this point. Official explanation: trainer's rep said colt never travelled (op 10-3 tchd 7-2 and 11-4)

7395 THORPE-LE-SOKEN MAIDEN STKS — 1m (P)
7:50 (7:51) (Class 5) 3-4-Y-O **£2,590** (£770; £385; £192) **Stalls** Centre

Form RPR
44 **1** **Lyceana**[43] 6583 3-8-9 0 .... NCallan 7 76+
(M A Jarvis) *chsd ldr tl led over 2f out: clr and rdn over 1f out: in n.d after: eased wl ins fnl f* **7/1[3]**
06 **2** *3* **Ibbetson (USA)**[43] 6583 3-9-0 0 .... AdamKirby 2 71
(W R Swinburn) *in tch: hdwy to chse clr wnr wl over 1f out: no imp: kpt on* **8/1**
0 **3** *2 ¼* **Roleplay (IRE)**[38] 6705 3-8-6 0 .... (b[1]) LukeMorris[(3)] 5 61
(J M P Eustace) *towards rr: hdwy over 2f out: rdn and effrt on inner over 1f out: wnt modest 3rd over 1f out: nvr nr ldng pair* **66/1**
23- **4** *nse* **Bullet Man (USA)**[419] 5780 3-9-0 0 .... DaneO'Neill 8 66+
(L M Cumani) *in tch tl rdn and outpcd over 3f out: sme hdwy over 1f out: plugged on fnl f: no ch w ldrs* **6/4[1]**
2 **5** *6* **Fosool (IRE)**[219] 1379 3-8-9 0 .... RHills 3 47
(E A L Dunlop) *fly-jmpd s and v.s.a: rapid hdwy to chse ldrs over 6f out: rdn and short of room briefly jst over 2f out: sn wknd* **13/8[2]**
6 *nk* **Celtic Gold (USA)**[19] 4-9-2 0 .... (t) ChrisCatlin 10 51
(Andrew Turnell) *s.i.s: bhd: lost tch 3f out: kpt on past btn horses fnl f: n.d* **28/1**
7 *1 ¾* **Kipchak (IRE)** 3-9-0 0 .... EddieAhern 4 47
(C E Brittain) *led to s: t.k.h: hld up in rr: nvr a factor* **12/1**
00 **8** *1 ¼* **Gun For Sale (USA)**[124] 4195 3-9-0 0 .... TravisBlock 11 44
(P J Makin) *hld up in last trio: rdn and struggling 3f out: nvr trbld ldrs* **66/1**
0000 **9** *shd* **Rumline**[70] 5837 3-8-9 49 .... FergusSweeney 6 39
(W S Kittow) *led tl over 2f out: wknd qckly wl over 1f out* **66/1**
00 **10** *16* **Ashton Heights**[65] 6003 3-8-9 0 .... MarkFlynn[(5)] 9 7
(Miss Gay Kelleway) *in tch on outer: rdn and wknd qckly 3f out: t.o fnl f* **100/1**

1m 39.78s (-0.12) **Going Correction** -0.025s/f (Stan)
WFA 3 from 4yo 2lb 10 Ran SP% **118.3**
Speed ratings (Par 103): **99,96,93,93,87 87,85,84,84,68**
toteswinger: 1&2 £11.70, 1&3 Not won, 2&3 £3.90. CSF £60.15 TOTE £7.50: £1.80, £1.90, £12.80; EX 40.20.
Owner Cromhall Stud **Bred** Derek R Price **Trained** Newmarket, Suffolk

FOCUS
Little strength in depth and, with the two market leaders running below expectations, this race did not take as much winning as seemed likely. The pace was only fair and the winner raced two or three widths off the inside rail in the straight. The form seems sound enough.

7396 WEATHERBYS ALL-WEATHER "HANDS AND HEELS" APPRENTICE CLAIMING STKS — 1m (P)
8:20 (8:20) (Class 5) 3-Y-O+ **£2,590** (£770; £385; £192) **Stalls** Centre

Form RPR
0043 **1** **Electric Warrior (IRE)**[34] 6771 5-9-0 **85** .... MatthewLawson[(3)] 2 73
(K R Burke) *pressed ldr tl led over 4f out: rdn 2f out: clr ent fnl f: comf* **8/15[1]**
5425 **2** *4* **Obezyana (USA)**[7] 7299 6-9-9 **72** .... NSLawes 6 70
(A Bailey) *chsd clr ldng par: clsd 4f out: chsd wnr over 3f out: rdn and chal 2f out: wknd ent fnl f* **7/2[2]**
0000 **3** *9* **Zeeran**[92] 5186 3-8-8 **40** .... (t) RichardRowe[(3)] 4 39?
(C E Brittain) *v.s.a and lost many l s: nvr a factor: wnt modest 3rd over 1f out* **25/1**
403- **4** *28* **Idealist (GER)**[361] 6-9-11 **95** .... CharlesEddery 3 —
(A P Stringer) *led tl over 4f out: chsd wnr tl over 3f out: sn wknd: t.o fnl f* **9/2[3]**

1m 41.18s (1.28) **Going Correction** -0.025s/f (Stan)
WFA 3 from 5yo+ 2lb 4 Ran SP% **109.5**
Speed ratings (Par 103): **92,88,79,51**
toteswinger: 1&2 £4.20. CSF £2.79 TOTE £1.70; EX 2.00.
Owner Market Avenue Racing Club Ltd **Bred** Limestone Stud **Trained** Middleham Moor, N Yorks

FOCUS
An uncompetitive race run in a slow time. Messy form and it is doubtful if either of the front pair were at their best.
Zeeran Official explanation: jockey said colt resented tongue strap

7397 GREATLEIGHS.COM MEDIAN AUCTION MAIDEN STKS — 1m (P)
8:50 (8:50) (Class 5) 2-Y-O **£3,561** (£1,059; £529; £264) **Stalls** Centre

Form RPR
5220 **1** **Mannlichen**[61] 6101 2-9-3 **79** .... JoeFanning 11 78+
(M Johnston) *sn led: hdd after 1f: chsd ldr after tl led jst over 2f out: edgd lft u.p over 1f out: styd on wl: a holding runner up fnl 50yds* **3/1[2]**
0 **2** *½* **Barwell Bridge**[182] 2324 2-9-3 0 .... GeorgeBaker 12 77+
(S Kirk) *chsd ldrs: chsd ldng pair and rdn over 2f out: chsd clr wnr over 1f out: edgd lft but kpt on wl fnl f: nvr quite getting to wnr* **9/4[1]**
40 **3** *3 ¾* **Kaolak (USA)**[23] 7054 2-9-3 0 .... ChrisCatlin 1 69
(J Ryan) *s.i.s: sn rdn and hdwy to ld after 1f: rdn and hdd jst over 2f out: swtchd rt over 1f out: wl hld by ldng pair after* **9/1**
0 **4** *1 ½* **Eastern Warrior**[42] 6604 2-9-3 0 .... EddieAhern 4 65+
(J W Hills) *t.k.h: hld up in rr: outpcd 3f out: rdn and styd on fr over 1f out: gng on fin: nvr trbld ldrs* **5/1[3]**

60 **5** *shd* **Caravan Of Dreams (IRE)**^{112} 4554 2-8-12 0........................ NCallan 10 60
(M A Jarvis) *in tch: chsd ldng trio and outpcd u.p over 2f out: kpt on same pce after* **25/1**

00 **6** *½* **Sky Gate (USA)**^{41} 6620 2-9-3 0........................ ShaneKelly 9 64
(B J Meehan) *in tch in midfield: rdn and outpcd 3f out: rallied ent fnl f: kpt on but nvr trbld ldrs* **20/1**

00 **7** *hd* **Free Falling**^{90} 5240 2-8-12 0........................ DaneO'Neill 3 59+
(L M Cumani) *s.i.s: hld up in rr: outpcd over 3f out: styd on fnl f: nvr trbld ldrs* **22/1**

8 *2 ½* **Bathwick Pursuit** 2-9-3 0........................ NeilChalmers 13 58
(A M Balding) *stdd after s: t.k.h: hld up bhd: outpcd and rdn 3f out: kpt on fnl f: nt pce to trble ldrs* **66/1**

64 **9** *shd* **When Doves Cry**^{119} 4328 2-8-12 0........................ MichaelHills 2 53
(B W Hills) *a towards rr: struggling over 3f out: no ch last 2f* **10/1**

0 **10** *1 ¾* **Bernie The Bolt (IRE)**^{15} 7200 2-9-3 0........................ LPKeniry 7 54
(A M Balding) *in tch in midfield: rdn and outpcd 3f out: no ch w ldrs after* **50/1**

05 **11** *6* **Rebel Swing**^{15} 7200 2-9-3 0........................ MartinDwyer 8 41
(W R Muir) *towards rr: rdn 4f out: struggling over 3f out: wl bhd fnl 2f* **7/1**

12 *23* **Mountain Ridge (IRE)**^{27} 6959 2-9-3 0........................ JerryO'Dwyer 5 —
(John Joseph Murphy, Ire) *chsd ldrs: rdn and struggling 3f out: wl bhd fnl 2f: t.o* **66/1**

1m 40.48s (0.58) **Going Correction** -0.025s/f (Stan) **12** Ran SP% **121.9**
Speed ratings (Par 96): **96,95,91,90,90 89,89,86,86,85 79,56**
toteswinger: 1&2 £5.20, 1&3 £4.20, 2&3 £5.70. CSF £9.77 TOTE £4.90: £1.40, £1.60, £3.40; EX 21.50.

Owner Graham Mezzone **Bred** Miss K Rausing **Trained** Middleham Moor, N Yorks

FOCUS
An ordinary maiden but one run at a decent gallop, and this race could throw up a couple of winners. The first two pulled clear and the winner raced against the inside rail in the straight.

NOTEBOOK
Mannlichen, the most experienced in the field, had been bogged down in heavy ground on his previous start but returned to his best to get off the mark at the fifth attempt on this All-Weather debut. He had the rail to help but showed a good attitude and he may be capable of further progress in handicaps as he strengthens up. (op 9-2 tchd 11-2)

Barwell Bridge ◆ had shown ability in a race that threw up numerous winners in May and, although not seen since, was well supported over this longer trip for this All-Weather debut. He showed improved form, despite running green, to pull clear of the rest and looks sure to win a similar event. (op 5-2 tchd 7-4)

Kaolak(USA) had not been at his best on soft ground on his previous start but shaped better on this all-weather debut, despite losing ground at the start. The step into ordinary handicaps will suit and he's open to improvement. (op 15-2)

Eastern Warrior ◆ looked to be travelling well for much of the way, but his jockey found all sorts of trouble. He did well to finish so close and is much better than his finishing position suggests. Official explanation: jockey said gelding suffered interference in running throughout (op 8-1 tchd 9-2)

Caravan Of Dreams(IRE) was not disgraced on this All-Weather debut. (op 20-1)

Sky Gate(USA) is also qualified for a mark and may do better. (op 16-1)

Free Falling was not knocked about on this All-Weather debut and first run for three months. (op 20-1 tchd 25-1)

When Doves Cry Official explanation: jockey said filly was hampered on bend

7398 WIVENHOE H'CAP 1m 2f (P)
9:20 (9:20) (Class 4) (0-80,80) 3-Y-O+ **£4,857** (£1,445; £722; £360) **Stalls Low**

Form RPR

2000 **1** **Awatuki (IRE)**^{24} 7025 5-9-6 **78**........................ PatCosgrave 4 87
(J R Boyle) *trckd ldrs: wnt 2nd gng wl over 2f out: led wl over 1f out: drvn clr ins fnl f: r.o wl* **10/1**

0060 **2** *2 ½* **Folio (IRE)**^{37} 6721 8-8-13 **71**........................ ChrisCatlin 6 75
(W J Musson) *in tch in midfield: hdwy to chse ldrs 3f out: chsd wnr wl over 1f out: sn drvn: nt pce of wnr fnl 100yds* **8/1**

6552 **3** *¾* **Bluejain**^{22} 7070 3-8-13 **75**........................ NCallan 11 78
(Miss Gay Kelleway) *t.k.h: hld up in last trio: hdwy over 3f out: drvn over 1f out: kpt on to chse ldng pair ins fnl f: no imp fnl 100yds* **11/4**^{1}

0500 **4** *½* **Prince Of Light (IRE)**^{20} 7116 5-9-8 **80**........................ JoeFanning 5 82
(M Johnston) *chsd ldr tl over 2f out: drvn wl over 1f out: hung rt and one pce fnl f* **5/1**

2350 **5** *¾* **Yankee Storm**^{117} 4440 3-8-13 **75**........................(p) RobertWinston 1 75
(P W D'Arcy) *t.k.h: hld up towards rr: hdwy over 2f out: n.m.r wl over 1f out: sn drvn: keeping on same pce whn n.m.r fnl f* **14/1**

6-00 **6** *hd* **Silver Regent (USA)**^{27} 6949 3-9-3 **79**........................ JimCrowley 10 79
(Mrs A J Perrett) *dwlt: dropped in bhd after s: swtchd rt and hdwy 3f out: c wd and rdn 2f out: kpt on same pce u.p* **7/2**^{2}

7 *13* **Summercove (IRE)**^{104} 4835 3-8-5 **67**........................ MartinDwyer 3 41
(John Joseph Murphy, Ire) *dwlt: sn chsng ldrs: rdn over 3f out: wknd over 2f out* **33/1**

/0-0 **8** *1 ¼* **Andorn (GER)**^{29} 6908 4-9-8 **80**........................ TPQueally 7 51
(A P Stringer) *led: clr 7f out tl 4f out: rdn and hdd wl over 1f out: sn wknd* **25/1**

3602 **9** *6* **Premier Danseur (IRE)**^{7} 7299 3-9-4 **80**........................ MichaelHills 9 39
(M Johnston) *a bhd: pushed along 6f out: nvr travelling after: rdn and lost tch 3f out* **4/1**^{3}

051- **10** *37* **Pharaohs Justice (USA)**^{335} 7208 3-8-13 **75**........................ JamesDoyle 8 —
(N P Littmoden) *in tch in midfield: rdn and struggling over 3f out: t.o fnl f* **20/1**

2m 7.04s (-1.56) **Going Correction** -0.025s/f (Stan)
WFA 3 from 4yo+ 4lb **10** Ran SP% **124.0**
Speed ratings (Par 105): **105,103,102,102,101 101,90,89,85,55**
toteswinger: 1&2 £10.60, 1&3 £12.70, 2&3 £3.10. CSF £90.56 CT £287.65 TOTE £12.80: £3.70, £1.80, £1.50; EX 96.10 Place 6 £103.42, Place 5 £68.59.

Owner Allen B Pope **Bred** Yeomanstown Stud **Trained** Epsom, Surrey

FOCUS
Few progressive sorts in a fair handicap. The pace was soon reasonable and the action unfolded in the centre in the straight. The winner is rated back to his best and the fifth is a slight doubt over the form.

Premier Danseur(IRE) Official explanation: trainer had no explanation for the poor form shown
T/Plt: £223.00 to a £1 stake. Pool: £113,219.51. 370.55 winning tickets. T/Qpdt: £32.70 to a £1 stake. Pool: £7,414.24. 167.60 winning tickets. SP

7361 WOLVERHAMPTON (A.W) (L-H)
Friday, November 21

OFFICIAL GOING: Standard
Wind: fresh, across Weather: showers

7399 COME EVENING RACING AT WOLVERHAMPTON APPRENTICE H'CAP 5f 216y(P)
6:20 (6:22) (Class 6) (0-65,71) 3-Y-O+ **£2,729** (£806; £403) **Stalls Low**

Form RPR

53 **1** **Absa Lutte (IRE)**^{4} 7362 5-9-0 **65**........................(t) CPHarrison$^{(5)}$ 9 74
(Jarlath P Fahey, Ire) *v.s.a: stdy hdwy fr over 3f out: rdn over 1f out: led jst ins fnl f: hld on* **8/1**^{3}

36-0 **2** *nk* **Richelieu**^{52} 6366 6-9-4 **64**........................ CO'Farrell 8 72
(J J Lambe, Ire) *in rr: hdwy over 2f out: ev ch ins fnl f: no ex cl home* **10/1**

5060 **3** *1 ¾* **Elkhorn**^{22} 7090 6-9-0 **60**........................(v) AmyScott 7 63+
(Miss J A Camacho) *in rr: outpcd 1/2-way: styd on fr over 1f out: nvr nrr* **8/1**^{3}

020 **4** *nk* **Bishopbriggs (USA)**^{2} 7377 3-9-0 **65**........................ AnthonyBetts$^{(5)}$ 13 67
(S Parr) *chsd ldrs: rdn and ev ch appr fnl f: one pce ins fnl f* **9/2**^{2}

0000 **5** *1 ½* **Helping Hand (IRE)**^{14} 7231 3-8-11 **57**........................ CharlesEddery 1 54
(R Hollinshead) *led tl rdn and hdd jst ins fnl f: fdd* **12/1**

0000 **6** *3 ¼* **Caustic Wit (IRE)**^{12} 7255 10-8-2 **55**........................(p) JakePayne$^{(7)}$ 10 42
(M S Saunders) *nvr bttr than mid-div* **66/1**

0310 **7** *nk* **One More Round (USA)**^{4} 7358 10-9-6 **71** 6ex.(b) MatthewLawson$^{(5)}$ 2 57
(P D Evans) *slowly away: in rr: rn wd fr over 2f out: nvr on terms* **9/4**^{1}

0000 **8** *½* **Danzig Fox**^{14} 7228 3-8-9 **55**........................(e^{1}) PNolan 6 39
(M Mullineaux) *mid-div: effrt 1/2-way: sn btn* **22/1**

2300 **9** *3 ½* **Nautical**^{12} 7254 10-8-6 **55**........................ RichardRowe$^{(3)}$ 12 28
(J R Holt) *a towards rr* **33/1**

0652 **10** *½* **Admiral Bond (IRE)**^{14} 7231 3-9-2 **62**........................(p) NSLawes 4 33
(G R Oldroyd) *chsd ldrs: rdn 2f out: sn wknd* **8/1**^{3}

1302 **11** *nk* **Avoca Dancer (IRE)**^{22} 7090 5-8-11 **62**........................(b^{1}) DavidKenny$^{(5)}$ 5 32
(Miss Gay Kelleway) *a in rr* **12/1**

0000 **12** *4 ½* **Orchestrator (IRE)**^{21} 2917 4-8-6 **57**........................ TobyAtkinson$^{(5)}$ 3 13
(W Clay) *in tch tl wknd 2f out* **66/1**

1m 15.76s (0.76) **Going Correction** +0.275s/f (Slow) **12** Ran SP% **117.0**
Speed ratings (Par 101): **105,104,102,101,99 95,95,94,89,89 88,82**
toteswinger: 1&2 £34.30, 1&3 £34.30, 2&3 £0.00. CSF £81.90 CT £662.65 TOTE £7.10: £2.50, £4.40, £3.70; EX 95.90.

Owner Beechwood Aris Syndicate **Bred** Ian Amond **Trained** Monasterevin, Co. Kildare
■ The first winner in Britain for both Jarlath Fahey and Connor Harrison.

FOCUS
A moderate sprint handicap restricted to apprentices who had not ridden more than ten winners, and they went very quick up front, favouring those held up. The first two home were Irish trained, thanks in no small part to a couple of decent young riders. Not easy form to pin down and it could be underrated.

7400 SPONSOR A RACE AT WOLVERHAMPTON H'CAP (DIV I) 1m 5f 194y(P)
6:50 (6:52) (Class 6) (0-65,65) 3-Y-O+ **£2,388** (£705; £352) **Stalls Low**

Form RPR

034 **1** **L'Homme De Nuit (GER)**^{15} 7216 4-9-9 **60**........................(p) GeorgeBaker 11 71
(G L Moore) *towards rr: hdwy over 4f out: rdn to ld 1f out: all out* **4/1**^{2}

-356 **2** *¾* **Baan (USA)**^{89} 5321 5-9-9 **60**........................ JimmyQuinn 10 70
(H J Collingridge) *mid-div: hdwy 2f out: ev ch 1f out: kpt on but edgd rt ins fnl f* **14/1**

03 **3** *1* **Augustus John (IRE)**^{23} 7064 5-10-0 **65**........................ NCallan 13 74
(S Parr) *a in tch: led over 3f out: hrd rdn and hdd 1f out: no ex towards fin* **7/1**

0411 **4** *1* **Bluebell Ridge (IRE)**^{23} 7071 3-9-3 **62**........................ ChrisCatlin 8 70+
(D W P Arbuthnot) *hld up: effrt to chse ldrs 4f out: one pce fnl f* **5/1**^{3}

4165 **5** *10* **Foreign King (USA)**^{128} 4087 4-9-12 **63**........................ LPKeniry 9 57
(J W Mullins) *trckd ldr: led over 4f out: hdd over 3f out: wknd over 2f out* **25/1**

0506 **6** *3 ½* **Champagne Shadow (IRE)**^{18} 7169 7-9-5 **56**........................(p) JerryO'Dwyer 6 45
(J Pearce) *mid-div tl lost pl 5f out: nvr on terms after* **14/1**

6063 **7** *4* **Pelham Crescent (IRE)**^{34} 6825 5-9-3 **59**........................ MCGeran$^{(5)}$ 4 42
(B Palling) *s.i.s: a towards rr* **14/1**

0022 **8** *13* **Zuwaar**^{9} 7293 3-9-0 **59**........................ JimCrowley 1 24
(Ian Williams) *s.i.s: sn mid-div: rdn and wknd over 2f out* **3/1**^{1}

0004 **9** *11* **Sweet Seville (FR)**^{17} 7174 4-8-9 **46** oh1........................ DaleGibson 7 —
(Mrs G S Rees) *a in rr* **50/1**

0003 **10** *hd* **Prince Of Medina**^{37} 6729 5-8-9 **46**........................(t) SteveDrowne 12 —
(J R Best) *in tch tl rdn 4f out: sn wknd* **16/1**

2065 **11** *3 ½* **Bond Casino**^{56} 6248 4-8-6 **46** oh1........................ DuranFentiman$^{(3)}$ 3 —
(G R Oldroyd) *led tl hdd over 4f out: wknd qckly* **14/1**

3300 **12** *¾* **Still Dreaming**^{29} 4105 4-8-2 **46** oh1........................ RossAtkinson$^{(7)}$ 5 —
(R J Price) *a bhd* **20/1**

000 **13** *86* **Bandoran**^{17} 7178 3-8-1 **46** oh1........................ FrankieMcDonald 2 —
(J R Holt) *in tch tl lost pl 1/2-way: t.o* **100/1**

3m 8.15s (2.15) **Going Correction** +0.275s/f (Slow)
WFA 3 from 4yo+ 8lb **13** Ran SP% **118.3**
Speed ratings (Par 101): **104,103,103,102,96 94,92,85,78,78 76,76,27**
toteswinger: 1&2 £3.30, 1&3 £3.20, 2&3 £0.00. CSF £56.33 CT £385.55 TOTE £5.60: £1.40, £4.60, £2.00; EX 63.90.

Owner David & Jane George **Bred** Gestut Karlshof **Trained** Woodingdean, E Sussex

FOCUS
The first four pulled well clear off a reasonable pace and the form among the principals looks very solid for the grade and should work out. The winner is rated up 3lb. The winning time was 2.34 seconds quicker than the second division, although that race was steadily run.

7401 SPONSOR A RACE AT WOLVERHAMPTON H'CAP (DIV II) 1m 5f 194y(P)
7:20 (7:21) (Class 6) (0-65,65) 3-Y-O+ **£2,388** (£705; £352) **Stalls Low**

Form RPR

3251 **1** **Irish Ballad**^{15} 7216 6-9-1 **52**........................ NickyMackay 8 57
(S Dow) *trckd ldrs: rdn 3f out: kpt on u.p to ld cl home* **4/1**^{1}

-054 **2** *hd* **Top Tiger**^{11} 7272 4-9-11 **62**........................ PaulMulrennan 10 67
(M H Tompkins) *hld up: hdwy on outside over 3f outkpt on u.str.p fnl f: jst failed* **15/2**

0315 **3** *nk* **Sir Sandicliffe (IRE)**^{24} 7042 4-10-0 **65**........................ TGMcLaughlin 4 70
(W M Brisbourne) *in rr: hdwy and plenty to do over 1f out: swtchd rt and str jun fnl f: clsng fast on first 2* **10/1**

5063 **4** ½ **Blue Hills**[11] 7265 7-9-9 **60**........................(b) DarrenWilliams 5 64
(P W Hiatt) *led at stdy pce: qcknd 3f out: strly rdn: hd and lost 2 more pls towards fin* **9/2**[2]
2013 **5** *nse* **Stravita**[24] 7039 4-9-5 **56**........................(p) GrahamGibbons 7 60
(R Hollinshead) *in rr: hdwy over 2f out: kpt on u.p fnl f* **13/2**[3]
0/00 **6** 2½ **Rahy's Crown (USA)**[15] 7217 5-8-12 **49**........................ FrancisNorton 9 49
(G L Moore) *stdd s: swtchd rt and hdwy 4f out: wknd fnl f* **4/1**[1]
0006 **7** *hd* **Peas 'n Beans (IRE)**[8] 7296 5-8-9 **46** oh1........................ LiamJones 3 46
(T Keddy) *in rr: sme late hdwy: nvr on terms* **28/1**
5400 **8** *shd* **Purely By Chance**[25] 7010 3-8-9 **54**........................(b[1]) JimmyQuinn 12 54
(J Pearce) *sn trckd ldr: rdn 3f out: wknd appr fnl f* **20/1**
6444 **9** *16* **Reminiscent (IRE)**[238] 1062 9-8-9 **46** oh1........................(v) JoeFanning 6 23
(B P J Baugh) *in tch tl lost pl over 6f out* **22/1**
4-00 **10** *9* **Astania**[137] 3799 3-9-6 **65**........................ RobertWinston 13 30
(P W D'Arcy) *mid-div tl wknd over 3f out* **12/1**
040/ **11** *hd* **King's Jester (IRE)**[140] 2902 6-9-2 **60**........................(b[1]) CO'Farrell(7) 1 25
(J J Lambe, Ire) *t.k.h: trckd ldrs tl lost pl over 4f out* **20/1**
006 **12** *23* **Golondrina**[38] 6725 3-8-2 **47** oh1 ow1........................(e[1]) ChrisCatlin 2 —
(T J Fitzgerald) *a bhd: t.o* **50/1**

3m 10.49s (4.49) **Going Correction** +0.275s/f (Slow)
WFA 3 from 4yo+ 8lb **42** Ran SP% **119.3**
Speed ratings (Par 101): **98,97,97,97,97 95,95,95,86,81 81,68**
toteswinger: 1&2 £16.00, 1&3 £8.50, 2&3 £0.00. CSF £31.75 CT £285.26 TOTE £5.40: £2.20, £2.70, £2.30; EX 59.20.
Owner Chua, White, Moore & Jurd **Bred** The Kingwood Partnership **Trained** Epsom, Surrey
■ Stewards' Enquiry : Darren Williams three-day ban: used whip with excessive frequency (Dec 5-7)
C O'Farrell caution: used whip with excessive frequency.

FOCUS
This looked a reasonable staying handicap for the grade but the form is modest and needs treating with caution. They went a modest pace for much of the way, resulting in a time 2.34 seconds slower than the first division, and there was a bunch finish with the seventh too close for comfort.
Purely By Chance Official explanation: jockey said filly hung right
Astania Official explanation: jockey said filly had no more to give

7402 RINGSIDE CONFERENCE SUITE MAIDEN AUCTION STKS 7f 32y(P)
7:50 (7:53) (Class 6) 2-Y-O **£2,729** (£806; £403) **Stalls** High

Form RPR
53 **1** **Inconspicuous Miss (USA)**[17] 7179 2-8-0 0 ow3.. MatthewDavies(7) 8 66
(George Baker) *trckd ldrs: led jst ins fnl f: rdn out* **15/2**[3]
60 **2** ½ **Why Nee Amy**[17] 7179 2-8-4 0........................ LiamJones 4 65+
(Miss Gay Kelleway) *trckd ldrs: chalng whn short of room on ins and swtchd rt ent fnl f: fin wl on outside: wnt 2nd nr fin: possibly unlucky* **25/1**
3 *nse* **Monsieur Fillioux (USA)** 2-8-13 0........................ AdamKirby 9 71
(J R Fanshawe) *mid-div: hdwy 2f out: chsd wnr ins fnl f tl lost 2nd cl home* **9/1**
4 1½ **Ajara (IRE)** 2-8-6 0........................ ChrisCatlin 5 60
(N J Vaughan) *hld up: swtchd rt 3f out: sn mde hdwy: styd on ins fnl f* **6/1**[2]
5 1¼ **Watch The Master** 2-8-9 0........................ JerryO'Dwyer 6 60+
(B I Case) *in rr: hdwy on outside over 2f out: kpt on: nvr nr to chal* **50/1**
00 **6** *nk* **Short Sharp Shock**[38] 6715 2-8-9 0........................ PaulMulrennan 11 59
(J Mackie) *trckd ldr: ev ch over 1f out tl one pce ins fnl f* **28/1**
7 ½ **Missed Mondays** 2-8-4 0........................ FrancisNorton 7 53
(A Berry) *t.k.h: trckd ldrs tl lost pl 1/2-way* **33/1**
02 **8** ½ **Ucantmissme**[42] 6620 2-8-13 0........................ DaneO'Neill 1 61
(D W P Arbuthnot) *led tl rdn and hdd jst ins fnl f: fdd qckly* **4/7**[1]
9 2¼ **Witch Of The Wave (IRE)** 2-8-4 0........................ FrankieMcDonald 3 46
(Miss J S Davis) *slowly away: nvr nr to chal* **66/1**
10 ½ **Special Adviser** 2-8-11 0........................ GregFairley 2 52
(T J Etherington) *mid-div: rdn 2f out: no hdwy after* **20/1**
11 *19* **Minibuzz** 2-8-9 0........................ DaleGibson 10 3
(Mrs G S Rees) *slowly away: a bhd: t.o* **66/1**
0 **12** 3¼ **Trick Or Two**[11] 7273 2-8-6 0........................ MatthewBirch(7) 12 —
(S Kirk) *trckd ldrs tl wknd qckly over 2f out: t.o* **80/1**

1m 33.23s (3.63) **Going Correction** +0.275s/f (Slow) **12** Ran SP% **120.9**
Speed ratings (Par 94): **90,89,89,87,86 85,85,84,82,81 59,56**
toteswinger: 1&2 £7.40, 1&3 £2.40, 2&3 £10.20. CSF £174.97 TOTE £10.50: £1.90, £9.90, £2.60; EX 134.40.
Owner Jerry Jamgotchian **Bred** Jerry Jamgotchian **Trained** Moreton Morrell, Warwicks

FOCUS
The odds-on favourite ran well below form, weakening what was already a modest maiden, and there was a bunch finish.

NOTEBOOK
Inconspicuous Miss(USA) had run to just a moderate level of form on her first two starts, first over this course and distance and then over 6f at Southwell, and this was such a weak race she probably didn't have to improve a great deal. She carried 3lb overweight. (tchd 7-1)
Why Nee Amy probably should have won and looked unlucky. She was cruising towards the inside turning for home, but had nowhere to go and had to be switched with her challenge. She finished well when finally in the clear, but the line came too soon. Having said all that, it would be unwise to get carried away as this was not much of a race, even though she is now qualified for handicaps. (op 20-1)
Monsieur Fillioux(USA), who proved reluctant to load, was not given an unnecessarily hard time once his chance had gone late on and he looks likely to improve on this modest introduction. (tchd 17-2)
Ajara(IRE), a half-sister to a few winners, including 7f-1m scorer Bolodenka (also successful over hurdles), was supported on her racecourse debut and finished nicely to take fourth. This is ordinary form, but she can improve plenty. (op 15-2)
Watch The Master, a 4,000gns purchase, out of a 7f winner, stayed on from well back but was never seriously involved. (op 40-1)
Missed Mondays cost just 600 euros, but she caught the eye, albeit in a weak race, and looks to have some ability. (op 25-1)
Ucantmissme is probably going to prove best suited by sprint trips in the long term, but should still have been able to take care of this lot and was disappointing. Official explanation: trainer had no explanation for the poor form shown (op 4-6)

7403 DINE IN THE PARADE RESTAURANT MAIDEN STKS 7f 32y(P)
8:20 (8:22) (Class 5) 3-4-Y-O **£2,590** (£770; £385; £192) **Stalls** High

Form RPR
33- **1** **Pivotal Queen (IRE)**[477] 4102 3-8-12 0........................ DaneO'Neill 4 73+
(L M Cumani) *trckd ldrs: rdn over 2f out: styd on on ins fnl f to ld u.p towards fin* **2/1**[2]
224 **2** *hd* **Party Frock**[25] 7026 3-8-12 70........................ JimmyFortune 8 72
(J H M Gosden) *trckd ldr: rdn to ld over 1f out: edgd lft u.p and hdd towards fin* **6/4**[1]
2626 **3** 2¼ **Azure Mist**[17] 7178 3-8-12 65........................ PaulMulrennan 9 66
(M H Tompkins) *led tl rdn and hdd over 1f out: nt qckn and lost 2nd ins fnl f* **8/1**[3]
5256 **4** *nk* **Ishiadancer**[14] 7226 3-8-12 60........................ PatCosgrave 11 65
(E J Alston) *mid-div: hdwy over 1f out: styd on fnl f but nvr a danger* **12/1**
00 **5** *6* **Mr Skipiton (IRE)**[29] 6935 3-9-3 0........................ StephenCarson 2 54
(B J McMath) *t.k.h in mid-div: rdn over 2f out: snb eaten* **100/1**
6 ½ **Jayyid (IRE)** 3-9-3 0........................ NCallan 7 53
(C E Brittain) *slowly away: a in rr* **12/1**
6 **7** 1¼ **Focail Eile**[224] 1311 3-9-3 0........................ GrahamGibbons 5 49
(E S McMahon) *a bhd* **20/1**
0 **8** 4½ **Japura (USA)**[4] 7362 4-9-4 0........................ GregFairley 10 37
(T J Pitt) *in rr: rdn over 2f out and nvr on terms* **33/1**
0020 **9** ½ **Kirkie (USA)**[7] 7316 3-9-3 63........................(tp) AdamKirby 3 36
(S Parr) *chsd ldrs tl rdn and wknd over 2f out* **11/1**

1m 32.07s (2.47) **Going Correction** +0.275s/f (Slow)
WFA 3 from 4yo 1lb **9** Ran SP% **116.9**
Speed ratings (Par 103): **96,95,93,92,86 85,84,78,78**
toteswinger: 1&2 £2.10, 1&3 £5.30, 2&3 £1.90. CSF £5.34 TOTE £3.00: £1.10, £1.50, £1.60; EX 5.40.
Owner Tsega Horses **Bred** Tsega Breeding Limited **Trained** Newmarket, Suffolk

FOCUS
A modest maiden that only concerned four of the nine runners. The form makes a fair bit of sense at face value.

7404 WOLVERHAMPTON-RACECOURSE.CO.UK H'CAP 1m 4f 50y(P)
8:50 (8:50) (Class 2) (0-100,107) 3-Y-O+ **£12,616** (£3,776; £1,888; £944; £470) **Stalls** Low

Form RPR
4136 **1** **Millville**[212] 1568 8-10-1 **107**........................ JimmyFortune 2 114
(M A Jarvis) *hld up in rr: rdn and hdwy 3f out: wnt 2nd over 1f out: edgd rt and led ins fnl f: drvn out* **6/1**[2]
0006 **2** ½ **Tilt**[34] 6817 6-8-10 **88** ow1........................(p) DaneO'Neill 1 94
(B Ellison) *slowly away: in rr: rdn and hdwy over 2f out: kpt on wl fnl f to go 2nd cl home* **12/1**
5461 **3** *hd* **Press The Button (GER)**[7] 7314 5-8-11 **89** 6ex........................ PatCosgrave 12 95
(J R Boyle) *trckd ldr: led 4f out: rdn and hdd ins fnl f: lost 2nd cl home* **8/1**
2535 **4** *7* **Slip**[40] 6667 3-7-10 **87**........................ AndreaAtzeni(7) 11 82
(J R Boyle) *in rr: rdn and hdwy 2f out: hng lft over 1f out: one pce fnl f* **12/1**
5 1¾ **Rock Soleil**[56] 4-8-12 **90**........................ TPQueally 7 82
(Jane Chapple-Hyam) *in tch on ins: rdn 3f out: wknd over 1f out* **16/1**
0000 **6** 2¼ **Profit's Reality (IRE)**[46] 6536 6-8-13 **91**........................(p) GrahamGibbons 8 79
(M J Attwater) *in tch: chsd ldr 4f out tl wknd over 1f out* **20/1**
1006 **7** *5* **Sgt Schultz (IRE)**[174] 2593 5-9-0 **92**........................ LPKeniry 3 72
(J S Moore) *hld up in mid-div: rdn over 2f out: sn btn* **20/1**
4001 **8** *12* **Bandama (IRE)**[35] 6784 5-9-3 **95**........................ JimCrowley 9 56
(Mrs A J Perrett) *hld up in mid-div: lost pl over 3f out* **15/2**[3]
3011 **9** *19* **Keenes Day (FR)**[28] 6957 3-8-6 **90**........................ JoeFanning 6 21
(M Johnston) *led tl hdd 4f out: sn wknd: eased: t.o* **10/3**[1]
0050 **10** ¾ **Birkside**[27] 6974 5-8-10 **88**........................(p) NCallan 10 17
(K A Ryan) *trckd ldrs: outpcd over 3f out: wknd wl over 1f out: eased: t.o* **6/1**[2]
-04 **P** **King's Head (IRE)**[55] 2830 5-9-1 **93**........................(p) GeorgeBaker 4 —
(G L Moore) *mid-div tl rdn and wknd 4f out: t.o whn p.u over 1f out* **10/1**

2m 40.72s (-0.38) **Going Correction** +0.275s/f (Slow)
WFA 3 from 4yo+ 6lb **11** Ran SP% **114.4**
Speed ratings (Par 109): **112,111,111,106,105 104,100,92,80,79** —
toteswinger: 1&2 £15.20, 1&3 £3.40, 2&3 £21.00. CSF £73.65 CT £573.02 TOTE £6.20: £2.30, £3.70, £3.30; EX 72.50.
Owner T G Warner **Bred** Red House Stud **Trained** Newmarket, Suffolk

FOCUS
Not the strongest race for the grade but the pace was fair and the form looks sound with the first three clear. Millville is rated basically to his best.

NOTEBOOK
Millville obviously posted a terrific effort under his big weight off a mark of 107, but it has to be said this looked an ordinary handicap for the grade. He was enhancing an already impressive All-Weather record (now 7-17 on sand), but things are likely to get tougher and he is 0-3 in Listed company. This was his first run in seven months, but he has a history of going well fresh.
Tilt, carrying 1lb overweight, looked to be going nowhere for much of the way, but he finally responded to pressure late on and looked as though he would have got up in another few yards. He could even be considered a little unlucky as he was slightly checked in his run around a furlong out.
Press The Button(GER), carrying a penalty for his recent Kempton success, tried to nick this when kicking clear leaving the back straight and posted a brave effort in defeat. (op 13-2)
Slip ran with credit on his first start since leaving Marcus Tregoning and can build on this. (tchd 11-1)
Rock Soleil, an ex-French colt who was picked up for 35,000gns by his new connections, made a creditable British debut. (tchd 18-1)
Sgt Schultz(IRE) was well held on his return from nearly six months off, but he can do better when returned to Lingfield, where he has achieved seven of his eight best RPRs. (tchd 22-1)
Keenes Day(FR) was chasing a hat-trick, but something was seemingly amiss. (op 7-2 tchd 4-1 and 3-1)
Birkside was another to run too bad to be true. (tchd 11-2)
King's Head(IRE) Official explanation: jockey said gelding lost its action

7405 STAY AT THE WOLVERHAMPTON HOLIDAY INN H'CAP 1m 141y(P)
9:20 (9:21) (Class 5) (0-70,70) 3-Y-O+ **£3,885** (£1,156; £577; £288) **Stalls** Low

Form RPR
0062 **1** **Hyde Lea Flyer**[39] 6712 3-9-1 **67**........................ GrahamGibbons 13 76
(E S McMahon) *s.i.s: hld up: hdwy on outside over 2f out: sustained run u.p to ld wl ins fnl f* **4/1**[2]
0200 **2** ¾ **Maximus Aurelius (IRE)**[126] 4156 3-8-13 **68**........................ LukeMorris(3) 10 76
(J Jay) *hld up: hdwy 2f out: led briefly ins fnl f: kpt on* **33/1**
3502 **3** ¾ **Morbick**[11] 7278 4-9-7 **70**........................ TGMcLaughlin 5 76
(W M Brisbourne) *mid-div: hdwy to ld wl over 1f out: hdd and lost 2nd ins fnl f* **10/3**[1]
0520 **4** 1½ **Davenport (IRE)**[121] 4309 6-9-4 **70**........................(p) JamesMillman(3) 1 73
(B R Millman) *in tch: rdn over 1f out: kpt on one pce fnl f* **17/2**
0012 **5** *5* **Ryedale Ovation (IRE)**[7] 7309 5-9-1 **64**........................ SimonWhitworth 6 55
(M Hill) *hld up: nvr on terms* **9/2**[3]
2001 **6** *2* **Blues Minor (IRE)**[18] 7166 3-9-1 **67**........................(be) GeorgeBaker 12 53
(M Mullineaux) *trckd ldrs: rdn 2f out: wknd over 1f out* **9/1**
0600 **7** *2* **Elliwan**[18] 7167 3-8-13 **65**........................ DaleGibson 4 47
(M W Easterby) *hld up: nvr on terms* **16/1**

0001 **8** *2* **Stark Contrast (USA)**[18] 7167 4-8-8 **64**.................... SeanPalmer(7) 8 41
(M D I Usher) *trckd ldr: led over 3f out: hdd & wknd wl over 1f out* **16/1**

02 **9** *3 ¾* **Evelith Regent (IRE)**[48] 6485 5-8-13 **62**.................... RobertWinston 3 31
(G A Swinbank) *trckd ldrs tl rdn and wknd over 1f out* **6/1**

1-30 **10** *11* **Shepherds Warning (IRE)**[172] 2670 3-9-1 **67**.................... JimCrowley 2 10
(N J Vaughan) *led tl hdd over 3f out: sn rdn and wknd wl over 1f out* **16/1**

0-05 **11** *14* **Effingham (IRE)**[51] 6385 3-9-0 **66**.................... ChrisCatlin 11 —
(N J Vaughan) *a bhd: t.o* **14/1**

1m 51.86s (1.36) **Going Correction** +0.275s/f (Slow)
WFA 3 from 4yo+ 3lb 11 Ran SP% **123.3**
Speed ratings (Par 103): **104,103,102,101,96 95,93,91,88,78 66**
toteswinger: 1&2 £6.70, 1&3 £19.80, 2&3 £2.60. CSF £131.59 CT £511.16 TOTE £5.70: £2.50, £11.00, £1.50; EX 287.60 Place 6: £415.86 place 5: £127.56.
Owner Kemmel Partnership **Bred** Hesmonds Stud Ltd **Trained** Lichfield, Staffs
■ Stewards' Enquiry : Graham Gibbons caution: careless riding.

FOCUS
A modest but competitive handicap. They went quick up front and those waited with were favoured. The form is sound.
T/Plt: £472.90 to a £1 stake. Pool: £102,744.36. 158.60 winning tickets. T/Qpdt: £39.20 to a £1 stake. Pool: £9,401.91. 177.30 winning tickets. JS

7413 - (Foreign Racing) - See Raceform Interactive

7385
LINGFIELD (L-H)
Saturday, November 22

OFFICIAL GOING: Standard
Wind: fairly strong against Weather: brigth spells, chilly wind

7414 PLAY POKER AT LADBROKES.COM H'CAP (DIV I) 6f (P)
12:00 (12:02) (Class 6) (0-60,60) 3-Y-0+ **£1,706** (£503; £252) **Stalls** Low

Form RPR

4500 **1** **River Thames**[14] 7239 5-9-4 **60**.................... NCallan 7 74
(K A Ryan) *lw: in tch: hdwy on inner over 2f out: led jst over 1f out: styd on wl* **2/1**[1]

0523 **2** *2 ½* **Muktasb (USA)**[5] 7357 7-9-3 **59**....................(v) AdamKirby 9 65
(D Shaw) *bhd: hdwy over 2f out: rdn wl over 1f out: styd on fnl f to go 2nd last stride: nvr trbld wnr* **4/1**[2]

2304 **3** *shd* **Afton View (IRE)**[13] 7255 3-8-13 **55**.................... DaneO'Neill 3 61
(S Parr) *chsd ldr after 1f: rdn to chal 2f out: chsd wnr fnl f: no imp: lost 2nd last stride* **14/1**

2006 **4** *nk* **Our Fugitive (IRE)**[31] 6895 6-9-1 **57**....................(v) JimCrowley 2 62
(C Gordon) *led: sn clr: rdn and hld hd high 2f out: hdd jst over 1f out: one pce* **10/1**

000 **5** *1 ¼* **Loyal Royal (IRE)**[53] 6357 5-8-7 **54**....................(b[1]) MCGeran(5) 5 55
(J M Bradley) *dwlt: t.k.h: chsd ldr for 1f: chsd ldrs after tl rdn and unable qck over 2f out: one pce after* **16/1**

5600 **6** *1 ½* **Gambling Jack**[53] 6357 3-8-13 **55**.................... ShaneKelly 1 51
(A W Carroll) *dwlt: sn in midfield: rdn and unable qck 3f out: plugged on same pce after* **12/1**

4500 **7** *nk* **Blue Zenith (IRE)**[32] 6878 3-8-8 **50**.................... LPKeniry 12 45
(J S Moore) *racd off the pce in midfield: rdn wl over 3f out: nvr pce to threaten ldrs* **50/1**

6514 **8** *1 ¼* **Welcome Approach**[10] 7288 5-9-4 **60**.................... ChrisCatlin 6 51
(J R Weymes) *sn pushed along in rr: nvr a factor* **8/1**

0050 **9** *nk* **Shot To Fame (USA)**[23] 7090 9-9-4 **60**.................... GeorgeBaker 11 50
(S Kirk) *lw: a towards rr: rdn over 2f out: n.d* **13/2**[3]

55 **10** *½* **Rightcar Lewis**[15] 7231 3-8-6 **55**.................... AndrewHeffernan(7) 10 44
(Peter Grayson) *a bhd: nvr a factor* **50/1**

-000 **11** *½* **Bronte's Hope**[23] 7102 4-9-1 **57**....................(p) PatDobbs 4 44
(M P Tregoning) *racd off the pce in midfield: rdn over 2f out: sn struggling* **8/1**

1m 11.58s (-0.32) **Going Correction** +0.025s/f (Slow) 11 Ran SP% **122.1**
Speed ratings (Par 101): **103,99,99,99,97 95,95,93,93,92 91**
toteswinger: 1&2 £2.40, 1&3 £8.70, 2&3 £6.50. CSF £10.02 CT £92.26 TOTE £2.70: £1.30, £1.40, £3.20; EX 14.40 Trifecta £81.10 Part won. Pool: £109.62 - 0.50 winning units..
Owner Whitestonecliffe Racing Partnership **Bred** G And Mrs Middlebrook **Trained** Hambleton, N Yorks

FOCUS
A moderate sprint handicap run at a strong pace and in a good time. Solid form and the winner can win again.

7415 BET AT LADBROKES.COM (S) STKS 1m (P)
12:25 (12:28) (Class 6) 2-Y-0 **£1,978** (£584; £292) **Stalls** High

Form RPR

2663 **1** **Hold The Bucks (USA)**[7] 7338 2-8-8 **63**.................... LukeMorris(3) 7 64+
(J S Moore) *towards rr: rdn 3f out: nt clr run jst over 2f out: hdwy u.p ent fnl f: led wl ins fnl f: r.o strly* **11/4**[1]

0103 **2** *¾* **Jonah's Cruising (IRE)**[10] 7283 2-8-11 **61**.................... PatCosgrave 2 60
(J R Boyle) *chsd ldr for 2f: effrt between horses 2f out: rdn to ld over 1f out: hdd and no ex wl ins fnl f* **11/4**[1]

0503 **3** *1 ¾* **Josiah Bartlett (IRE)**[13] 7257 2-8-11 **57**.................... LiamJones 3 57
(J W Hills) *hld up wl in tch: hdwy on inner over 2f out: ev ch 1f out: fdd fnl 50yds* **8/1**[3]

00 **4** *½* **Ringo Zaar**[7] 7338 2-8-11 **0**....................(b[1]) FergusSweeney 11 55
(A B Haynes) *in tch: chsd ldr after 2f: ev ch and rdn 2f out: kpt on same pce fnl f* **66/1**

5 *¾* **Liberty Beau (IRE)** 2-8-8 **0**.................... MarcHalford(3) 9 54+
(D R C Elsworth) *s.i.s: in tch in rr: rdn and unable qck over 2f out: styd on wl fnl f: gng on fin* **12/1**

0005 **6** *nk* **Braishfield Lass**[10] 7283 2-8-6 **51**.................... ChrisCatlin 12 48
(B G Powell) *in tch: rdn and unable to quicke over 2f out: plugged on same pce* **20/1**

5364 **7** *¾* **Tarawa Atoll**[7] 7338 2-8-6 **54**.................... EdwardCreighton 10 46
(M R Channon) *towards rr: rdn and effrt over 2f out: nvr pce to trble ldrs* **8/1**[3]

003 **8** *nk* **Admiring Glances**[19] 7164 2-8-6 **50**.................... JimmyQuinn 5 46
(J Pearce) *in tch: rdn 3f out: no imp u.p fr over 1f out* **11/2**[2]

0300 **9** *3 ¼* **Claphands**[16] 7212 2-8-6 **55**.................... PaulDoe 8 39
(M A Allen) *led: rdn jst over 2f out: hdd over 1f out: wknd qckly ins fnl f* **25/1**

000 **10** *6* **Calypso Prince**[85] 5460 2-8-11 **52**.................... HayleyTurner 4 30
(M D I Usher) *toward rr: sn drvn and no prog over 2f out: nvr trbld ldrs* **20/1**

5400 **11** *3 ¾* **Multi Tasker**[16] 7212 2-8-11 **60**....................(e[1]) PaulFitzsimons 6 22
(Miss J R Tooth) *dwlt: a towards rr: reminders over 4f out: hrd drvn and no prog 3f out* **20/1**

12 *17* **Bee Bounty** 2-8-6 **0**.................... FrankieMcDonald 1 —
(J G Portman) *w'like: bit bkwd: rn green: sn detached in last pl: t.o* **50/1**

1m 40.0s (1.80) **Going Correction** +0.025s/f (Slow) 12 Ran SP% **120.2**
Speed ratings (Par 94): **92,91,89,89,88 87,87,86,83,77 73,56**
toteswinger: 1&2 £2.50, 1&3 £1.60, 2&3 £6.00. CSF £8.73 TOTE £3.90: £1.70, £1.60, £1.80; EX 10.50 Trifecta £31.60 Pool: £165.70 - 3.88 winning units..There was no bid for the winner.
Owner E Moore & J S Moore **Bred** David E Hager Ii **Trained** Upper Lambourn, Berks

FOCUS
A standard juvenile seller.

NOTEBOOK
Hold The Bucks(USA) was the best off at the weights so he was entitled to win this. He was off the bridle a fair way out, and then got stopped in his run when trying to stay on rounding the final turn, but he found plenty when in the clear in the straight to gain his first success at the 11th attempt. (tchd 7-2)
Jonah's Cruising(IRE) had every chance but was just run out of it. She would have been 2lb better off with the winner had this been a handicap. (tchd 10-3)
Josiah Bartlett(IRE) was a little keen early and was short of room on the first bend, but he had his chance against the inside rail in the straight. He touched 1.3 in-running, but could not sustain his challenge. (op 9-2 tchd 4-1)
Ringo Zaar was given a positive ride in first-time blinkers and had his chance.
Liberty Beau(IRE) ◆, a £12,000 first foal of a prolific 7f-1m3f winner, who was also successful over hurdles, recovered from a slow start and travelled well to a point, but he was outpaced turning for home, before keeping on all too late. The way he finished his race suggests he can win a similar event with the benefit of this experience. (op 16-1)

7416 PLAY POKER AT LADBROKES.COM H'CAP (DIV II) 6f (P)
12:55 (12:57) (Class 6) (0-60,60) 3-Y-0+ **£1,706** (£503; £252) **Stalls** Low

Form RPR

0412 **1** **River Kirov (IRE)**[5] 7357 5-9-0 **56**.................... RichardHughes 9 68+
(M Wigham) *lw: hld up wl in tch in midfield: chsng ldrs and n.m.r over 1f out tl ins fnl f: qcknd to ld nr fin* **2/1**[1]

202 **2** *½* **Blue Charm**[5] 7363 4-9-4 **60**.................... GeorgeBaker 8 70
(S Kirk) *hld up towards rr: hdwy on outer 2f out: ev ch ins fnl f: unable qck nr fin* **5/2**[2]

0356 **3** *nse* **What Katie Did (IRE)**[13] 7254 3-8-11 **58**....................(p) JackDean(5) 5 68
(J M Bradley) *chsd ldrs: rdn and ev ch over 1f out: led ins fnl f: hdd and no ex nr fin* **16/1**

406 **4** *1 ¼* **This Ones For Eddy**[15] 7228 3-9-4 **60**....................(tp) AdamKirby 7 66
(S Parr) *lw: s.i.s: in rr: plld out and hdwy on outer over 1f out: r.o fnl f: nt rch ldrs* **11/1**

432 **5** *¾* **Monte Major (IRE)**[9] 7295 7-9-1 **57**....................(v) JimmyQuinn 12 60
(D Shaw) *t.k.h: hld up trcking ldrs: ev ch 1f out: nt qckn u.p fnl 100yds* **11/1**

0001 **6** *1* **Connor's Choice**[32] 6878 3-9-4 **60**.................... ChrisCatlin 4 60
(Andrew Turnell) *chsd ldr tl led over 2f out: rdn over 1f out: hdd ins fnl f: wknd towards fin* **15/2**[3]

2100 **7** *nk* **Patavium Prince (IRE)**[13] 7255 5-8-13 **55**.................... TravisBlock 3 54
(Miss Jo Crowley) *in tch in midfield: effrt and n.m.r over 1f out: kpt on same pce fnl f* **16/1**

5200 **8** *2* **Forever Changes**[94] 5186 3-9-1 **57**.................... RobertWinston 6 50
(L Montague Hall) *in tch in midfield: shuffled bk and dropped to rr over 2f out: swtchd rt over 1f out: kpt on fnl f but nvr threatened ldrs* **25/1**

060 **9** *nk* **Great Fox (IRE)**[9] 7295 7-8-8 **50**.................... PaulHanagan 11 42
(S C Williams) *lw: racd wd: t.k.h: hld up towards rr tl hdwy to press ldrs wl over 3f out: hung lft and wknd over 1f out* **14/1**

3500 **10** *nse* **Mind Alert**[187] 2263 7-8-13 **55**....................(v) DarrenWilliams 10 47
(D Shaw) *bit bkwd: stdd and dropped in bhd after s: sme hdwy on inner over 1f out: no imp fnl f* **33/1**

006 **11** *2* **Affirmatively**[17] 7195 3-8-10 **52**.................... ShaneKelly 1 37
(A W Carroll) *chsd ldrs early: lost pl and rdn 1/2-way: bhd fnl f* **25/1**

3650 **12** *3 ½* **Stoneacre Sarah**[122] 4308 3-8-6 **55**.................... AndrewHeffernan(7) 2 29
(Peter Grayson) *led tl over 2f out: wknd qckly over 1f out* **50/1**

1m 11.85s (-0.05) **Going Correction** +0.025s/f (Slow) 12 Ran SP% **121.4**
Speed ratings (Par 101): **101,100,100,98,97 96,95,93,92,92 90,85**
toteswinger: 1&2 £3.10, 1&3 £12.90, 2&3 £14.30. CSF £6.77 CT £63.42 TOTE £3.10: £1.40, £1.40, £3.00; EX 7.60 Trifecta £117.60 Pool: £174.82 - 1.10 winning units..
Owner A Darke T Matthews M Wigham **Bred** Kildaragh Stud **Trained** Newmarket, Suffolk

FOCUS
A moderate handicap and there wasn't much pace on early, resulting in a time 0.27 seconds slower than the first division. Solid form for the grade with the winner still 45lb off last winter's best.
Great Fox(IRE) Official explanation: jockey said horse ran too free and hung right

7417 E B F BET AT LADBROKES ON 0800 777 888 MAIDEN STKS 5f (P)
1:30 (1:31) (Class 5) 2-Y-0 **£3,885** (£1,156; £577; £288) **Stalls** High

Form RPR

5420 **1** **Sharpener (IRE)**[8] 7308 2-8-12 **69**.................... RichardHughes 5 70
(R Hannon) *in tch: lft wev ch bnd 2f out: sn rdn: led fnl 100yds: styd on wl* **3/1**[2]

4642 **2** *nk* **Albaseet (IRE)**[17] 7191 2-9-3 **75**.................... RHills 3 74
(M P Tregoning) *lw: led: hung rt and c centre bnd 2f out: hrd pressed and rdn after: hdd fnl 100yds: no ex* **10/11**[1]

5 **3** *3 ¾* **Fantasy Gladiator**[12] 7268 2-9-3 **0**.................... MickyFenton 1 61+
(R M H Cowell) *tall: scope: s.i.s: bhd: rn wd and outpcd bnd 2f out: styd on wl fnl f: wnt 3rd nr fin* **16/1**

640 **4** *hd* **Africa's Star (IRE)**[121] 4337 2-8-12 **70**.................... NCallan 8 55
(M A Jarvis) *chsd ldrs on outer: hung rt and wd bnd jst over 2f out: outpcd by ldng pair 1f out: lost 3rd nr fin* **5/1**[3]

0030 **5** *3 ¾* **Chimbonda**[9] 7306 2-9-3 **68**.................... AdamKirby 4 46
(S Parr) *chsd ldr: carried wd bnd 2f out: sn drvn and struggling: wl btn fnl f* **6/1**

0 **6** *3 ½* **Contradiktive (IRE)**[5] 7356 2-9-3 **0**.................... PatCosgrave 6 34
(J R Boyle) *pushed along early: in tch towards rr: rdn and wknd jst over 2f out* **40/1**

00 **7** *2 ½* **Music In The Glen**[43] 6621 2-8-12 **0**.................... LPKeniry 7 20
(P Leech) *dwlt: in tch tl rdn and struggling over 2f out: wl btn fnl f* **66/1**

0500 **8** *½* **Abitofaboost (IRE)**[10] 7281 2-8-5 **38**.................... AndrewHeffernan(7) 2 18
(Peter Grayson) *dwlt: in tch in midfield: rdn over 2f out: wknd wl over 1f out* **66/1**

59.93 secs (1.13) **Going Correction** +0.025s/f (Slow) 8 Ran SP% **119.6**
Speed ratings (Par 96): **91,90,84,84,78 72,68,67**
toteswinger: 1&2 £1.10, 1&3 £9.20, 2&3 £5.00. CSF £6.41 TOTE £4.40: £1.50, £1.10, £2.50; EX 7.60 Trifecta £60.40 Pool: £430.63 - 5.27 winning units..
Owner Mrs J Wood **Bred** Dr Myles Sweeney **Trained** East Everleigh, Wilts

FOCUS
A weak sprint maiden, but the front two look to have run close to their marks.

NOTEBOOK

Sharpener(IRE) tracked the early pace and nipped through the inner on the turn into the straight, taking full advantage of the favourite's waywardness. (op 11-4 tchd 7-2)

Albaseet(IRE) arguably would have won had he not swung wide off the final turn, clearly failing to handle the tight bend. He recovered his momentum and kept on, but was just held. (op 11-10 tchd 6-5)

Fantasy Gladiator ◆ showed ability on his debut over 6f at Southwell and he built on that effort with an eye-catching display. He raced in last for much of the way having missed the kick, and this track was not ideal for such a big horse, but he motored home once balanced in the straight. He is still learning, but could be a fair sprinter in time, particularly on a more galloping track.

Africa's Star(IRE), returning from four months off, went wide on the final bend having already been stuck out from the highest stall of all, and she offered little for pressure. She was below her official mark of 70 and has something to prove. Official explanation: jockey said filly hung right (op 9-2 tchd 4-1)

7418 BETTER PRICES, BIGGER WINS AT LADBROKES.COM H'CAP 7f (P)

2:10 (2:11) (Class 2) (0-100,105) 3-Y-O+ **£11,527** (£3,430; £1,714; £856) **Stalls** Low

Form RPR

1250 **1** **Atlantic Story (USA)**[56] 6269 6-9-8 **103**....................(t) RyanMoore 3 115
(M W Easterby) *t.k.h: hld up wl in tch: hdwy to chse ldr over 1f out: drvn to ld jst ins fnl f: styd on wl* **7/2**[1]

4001 **2** *1* **Markab**[16] 7215 5-9-0 **95**.................... PatCosgrave 1 104
(K A Morgan) *lw: led: rdn over 1f out: hdd jst ins fnl f: kpt on same pce* **13/2**

0001 **3** *½* **Majuro (IRE)**[53] 6352 4-8-7 **88**.................... ChrisCatlin 9 96
(K A Ryan) *chsd ldr tl over 1f out: kpt on same pce u.p fnl f* **7/1**

1142 **4** *1 ½* **Beat The Bell**[17] 7192 3-8-5 **92**.................... NicolPolli(5) 11 96
(A Bailey) *hld up wl in tch in rr: hdwy to chse ldng trio ent fnl f: no imp fnl f* **10/1**

1031 **5** *1 ½* **My Gacho (IRE)**[3] 7386 6-8-10 **91** 6ex....................(b) J-PGuillambert 8 91
(M Johnston) *chsd ldrs on outer: rdn and outpcd over 1f out: styd on again u.p ins fnl f* **5/1**[2]

4254 **6** *nse* **Swift Gift**[36] 6783 3-8-5 **87**.................... MartinDwyer 5 86
(B J Meehan) *lw: stdd s: hld up in tch in rr: hdwy on inner over 1f out: no imp fnl f* **6/1**[3]

2344 **7** *nk* **Ebraam (USA)**[17] 7192 5-9-3 **98**.................... IanMongan 2 97
(P Howling) *t.k.h: hld up in tch: dropped to rr over 2f out: drvn and effrt over 1f out: no hdwy fnl f* **12/1**

0141 **8** *hd* **Quest For Success (IRE)**[21] 7129 3-8-5 **87**.................... PaulHanagan 7 85
(R A Fahey) *chsd ldrs: rdn 2f out: wknd ent fnl f* **12/1**

0600 **9** *shd* **Capricorn Run (USA)**[29] 6947 5-9-0 **95**....................(v) AdamKirby 10 93
(A J McCabe) *v.s.a: bhd: brief effrt on outer over 2f out: no ch ins fnl f* **10/1**

6000 **10** *4* **Fajr (IRE)**[36] 6783 6-9-10 **105**....................(b) RichardHughes 4 97
(Miss Gay Kelleway) *stdd s: hld up wl in tch: rdn and btn over 1f out: eased whn no ch fnl f* **20/1**

1m 22.76s (-2.04) **Going Correction** +0.025s/f (Slow) course record
WFA 3 from 4yo+ 1lb **10** Ran SP% **117.3**
Speed ratings (Par 109): **112,110,110,108,106 106,106,106,106,101**
toteswinger: 1&2 £5.90, 1&3 £6.70, 2&3 £10.70. CSF £26.36 CT £155.79 TOTE £3.60: £1.80, £2.40, £3.10; EX 22.60 Trifecta £162.60 Pool: £ 712.18 - 3.24 winning units..
Owner Matthew Green **Bred** Arthur I Appleton **Trained** Sheriff Hutton, N Yorks

FOCUS

A high-class handicap and solid form that should work out. A clear personal best from Atlantic Story.

NOTEBOOK

Atlantic Story(USA) ◆ found this all rather straightforward and is now 11-16 on sand. He was without the blinkers he often wears, and was a little keen early, but he was still a most decisive winner. This is the highest mark he has ever won off, but he is at the very least a Listed horse over 7f-1m on Polytrack and must be worth taking to the States, as there will be few worthwhile opportunities in Britain this winter. (tchd 4-1)

Markab ran a big race off a mark 5lb higher than when winning over course and distance on his previous start and simply ran into a very decent rival for the grade. (op 9-2 tchd 7-1)

Majuro(IRE), an impressive winner over 1m on Fibresand when with Mick Easterby last time, was given a positive ride and kept on the line. He is clearly very useful on sand and should do well for his new yard this winter. (op 14-1)

Beat The Bell had to wait for a gap, but he kept on reasonably well when in the clear. This was his first run beyond 6f and he will probably do better back over sprint trips. (op 9-1 tchd 12-1)

My Gacho(IRE), carrying a penalty for his success over course and distance three days earlier, was a little keen early and made only limited progress in the straight, despite coming under strong pressure. (op 11-2)

Swift Gift tried to make a move from the rear towards the inside rail, but he could make no impression. (op 8-1)

Capricorn Run(USA) Official explanation: jockey said gelding was slowly away

Fajr(IRE) Official explanation: trainer said gelding moved poorly

7419 E B F PLAY BINGO AT LADBROKES.COM FILLIES' H'CAP 1m (P)

2:40 (2:41) (Class 4) (0-85,84) 3-Y-O+ **£4,857** (£1,445; £722; £360) **Stalls** High

Form RPR

3403 **1** **Romany Princess (IRE)**[3] 7390 3-9-2 **80**.................... RyanMoore 7 88
(R Hannon) *lw: t.k.h: hld up wl in tch: hdwy over 1f out: drvn to ld ins fnl f: hld on wl u.p* **5/1**[2]

0034 **2** *½* **Secret Night**[23] 7101 5-9-4 **80**....................(p) IanMongan 12 87+
(C G Cox) *hld up in rr: hdwy wl over 1f out: n.m.r ent fnl f: r.o wl u.p to go 2nd nr fin: nt quite rch wnr* **13/2**

020 **3** *nk* **Victoria Reel**[16] 7215 3-9-6 **84**.................... RichardHughes 6 90
(R Hannon) *chsd ldng pair: squeezed between horses to chal over 1f out: led and edgd rt ent fnl f: hdd ins fnl f: unable qck towards fin* **7/1**

6030 **4** *nk* **Cat Whistle**[24] 7077 3-8-4 **68**.................... PaulHanagan 10 74
(R A Fahey) *stdd after s: t.k.h: hld up in rr: hdwy 2f out: n.m.r briefly jst ins fnl f: r.o: nt rch ldrs* **16/1**

3134 **5** *1* **Jennie Jerome (IRE)**[24] 7083 3-8-12 **76**.................... DaneO'Neill 9 79
(L M Cumani) *lw: chsd ldrs: rdn and unable qck jst over 2f out: kpt on same pce u.p fnl f* **4/1**[1]

3012 **6** *¾* **Spring Goddess (IRE)**[16] 7210 7-9-3 **79**.................... JimmyFortune 3 81
(A P Jarvis) *hld up in tch on inner: effrt to chse ldrs and drvn ent fnl f: wknd fnl 100yds* **12/1**

6620 **7** *1* **Ivory Lace**[9] 7302 7-8-12 **74**.................... JimCrowley 4 73
(S Woodman) *in tch in midfield: nudged along and lost pl over 2f out: kpt on u.p fnl f: nvr trbld ldrs* **25/1**

0631 **8** *shd* **Miss Brown To You (IRE)**[16] 7210 3-8-11 **75**.................... NCallan 2 74
(M L W Bell) *chsd ldr: drvn and ev ch wl over 1f out: wkng whn short of room ins fnl f: eased after* **6/1**[3]

003 **9** *2* **Naughty Frida (IRE)**[16] 7210 3-9-2 **80**.................... JimmyQuinn 11 74
(M Botti) *stdd after s: in rr: hdwy into midfield 4f out: rdn and unable qck over 1f out: one pce fnl f* **14/1**

5340 **10** *2 ½* **Paradise Dancer (IRE)**[154] 3272 4-8-12 **74**.................... JamieSpencer 1 63
(J A R Toller) *led: rdn 2f out: hdd ent fnl f: wknd qckly* **16/1**

-305 **11** *2 ¼* **Bermacha**[191] 2118 3-8-6 **70**.................... MartinDwyer 8 54
(W R Muir) *lw: hld up in rr: rdn and struggling over 2f out: nvr trbld ldrs* **20/1**

3114 **12** *¾* **Izzibizzi**[16] 7210 3-9-5 **83**.................... ChrisCatlin 5 65
(E A L Dunlop) *taken down early: a in rr: rdn and struggling over 2f out: no ch last 2f* **8/1**

1m 36.8s (-1.40) **Going Correction** +0.025s/f (Slow)
WFA 3 from 4yo+ 2lb **12** Ran SP% **122.6**
Speed ratings (Par 102): **108,107,107,106,105 105,104,104,102,99 97,96**
toteswinger: 1&2 £10.70, 1&3 £8.70, 2&3 £10.70. CSF £39.03 CT £238.00 TOTE £7.60: £2.40, £2.40, £3.10; EX 44.30 Trifecta £587.10 Part won. Pool: £793.45 - 0.10 winning units..
Owner Con Harrington **Bred** St Simon Foundation **Trained** East Everleigh, Wilts
■ Stewards' Enquiry : Richard Hughes caution: careless riding.

FOCUS

A fair and very competitive fillies' handicap, and sound form.

Miss Brown To You(IRE) Official explanation: jockey said filly suffered interference inside final furlong

7420 BET AT LADBROKES ON 0800 777 888 CHURCHILL STKS (LISTED RACE) 1m 2f (P)

3:20 (3:23) (Class 1) 3-Y-O+

£22,708 (£8,608; £4,308; £2,148; £1,076; £540) **Stalls** Low

Form RPR

5011 **1** **Yahrab (IRE)**[16] 7208 3-8-12 109.................... JamieSpencer 3 116
(C E Brittain) *mde all: rdn jst over 2f out: edgd lft hld on gamely u.p fnl 100yds: all out* **15/2**

1001 **2** *¾* **Baharah (USA)**[23] 7099 4-8-13 109.................... HayleyTurner 1 111
(G A Butler) *lw: in tch: rdn and jostled jst over 2f out: chsd wnr jst over 1f out: hrd drvn and ev ch ins fnl f: n.m.r and edgd lft: unable qck fnl 50yds* **5/1**[2]

2002 **3** *1* **Harvest Queen (IRE)**[23] 7099 5-8-11 106.................... EddieAhern 7 107
(P J Makin) *hld up in midfield: nt clr run jst over 2f out: hdwy over 1f out: r.o wl u.p fnl f: wnt 3rd towards fin: n.m.r fnl strides* **16/1**

0522 **4** *nk* **Re Barolo (IRE)**[17] 7193 5-9-2 110....................(t) JimmyQuinn 6 114+
(M Botti) *lw: hld up in tch towards rr: short of room and lost pl jst over 2f out: rallied u.p jst over 1f out: r.o fnl f nt rch ldrs* **8/1**

1103 **5** *½* **Bronze Cannon (USA)**[21] 7145 3-8-12 104.................... JimmyFortune 4 110
(J H M Gosden) *lw: in tch: effrt and jostled jst over 1f out: chsd ldng pair ent fnl f: one pce and lost 2 pls wl ins fnl f: btn whn n.m.r nr fin* **5/2**[1]

0134 **6** *½* **Ajhar (USA)**[17] 7193 4-9-2 103.................... RHills 2 109
(M P Tregoning) *chsd ldr: rdn 2f out: lost 2nd pl jst over 1f out: wknd fnl f* **9/1**

0461 **7** *4* **Orchard Supreme**[7] 7339 5-9-2 100.................... RyanMoore 5 101+
(R Hannon) *hld up in midfield: nr side rein broke and wnt rt 6f out: hdwy to press ldrs over 4f out: rdn 2f out: wknd over 1f out* **16/1**

1013 **8** *shd* **Philatelist (USA)**[211] 1596 4-9-2 106.................... NCallan 8 101
(M A Jarvis) *chsd ldrs: rdn over 2f out: wknd ent fnl f* **11/2**[3]

5600 **9** *shd* **Grand Passion (IRE)**[21] 7145 8-9-2 105.................... SteveDrowne 9 101
(G Wragg) *pushed along early: hld up towards rr: rdn over 2f out: no imp* **12/1**

3360 **10** *½* **Scamperdale**[145] 3561 6-9-2 87.................... TPQueally 10 100?
(B P J Baugh) *stdd s: hld up in rr: rdn whn hmpd wl over 1f out: nvr trbld ldrs* **66/1**

1001 **P** **Mr Aviator (USA)**[28] 6975 4-9-2 106.................... RichardHughes 11 —
(R Hannon) *hld up in rr: rdn and effrt whn p.u lame wl over 1f out* **7/1**

2m 5.81s (-0.79) **Going Correction** +0.025s/f (Slow)
WFA 3 from 4yo+ 4lb **11** Ran SP% **126.9**
Speed ratings (Par 111): **104,103,102,102,101 101,98,98,98,97 —**
toteswinger: 1&2 £9.20, 1&3 £19.20, 2&3 £22.20. CSF £48.65 TOTE £10.00: £2.60, £2.60, £5.00; EX 63.50 Trifecta £684.10 Part won. Pool: £924.53 - 0.70 winning units..
Owner Saif Ali **Bred** Swettenham Stud **Trained** Newmarket, Suffolk
■ Stewards' Enquiry : Jamie Spencer caution: careless riding.
Hayley Turner one-day ban: careless riding (Dec 6)

FOCUS

A reasonable Listed contest. The form is a bit messy with the winner, who is rated up 3lb, dictating a steady pace. The next two were close to this year's form.

NOTEBOOK

Yahrab(IRE) has taken a while to fulfil his potential, but he has not looked back since switching to Polytrack and followed up a couple of victories in slightly lesser races over this trip at Great Leighs to complete the hat-trick. Having set off at a decent pace, he managed to get a good breather in down the back straight. He seemed to squeeze up Baharah ever so slightly approaching the final bend, but kept finding for pressure and looked the winner on merit. His connections think he will get 1m4f, but he might be given a break now. (op 9-1)

Baharah(USA), racing beyond 1m for the first time, could be considered a little unlucky as she lost her place when squeezed slightly just before the final bend. She recovered to have a chance in the straight, but was always just being held. (op 9-2 tchd 4-1)

Harvest Queen(IRE), trying her furthest trip to date, travelled kindly for a long way, but her rider took a while to get serious, possibly as a result of traffic problems. She kept on once switched, but was never getting there. (op 12-1)

Re Barolo(IRE) was shuffled back when hampered on the turn into the straight and got going all too late. He is better than he showed. (op 15-2 tchd 9-1)

Bronze Cannon(USA) was slightly squeezed up against the inside rail early on the final turn and could find only the one pace in the straight. (op 7-2 tchd 9-2)

Ajhar(USA) was well enough placed if good enough, but he probably wants a little further and has yet to prove he is quite up to this level. (op 11-1 tchd 12-1)

Orchard Supreme finished surprisingly close considering he charted a very wide course after his rein broke around six furlongs out. Official explanation: jockey said rein broke (op 20-1 tchd 22-1 and 12-1)

Philatelist(USA), who looked fit enough, has a good record on sand, but he was nowhere near his best this time. (op 13-2 tchd 5-1)

Grand Passion(IRE), unable to repeat last year's win, was his trainer's final runner. (tchd 10-1 and 14-1)

Mr Aviator(USA) unfortunately had to be pulled up as something appeared to go badly amiss. (op 8-1 tchd 6-1)

7421 BETTER PRICES, BIGGER WINS AT LADBROKES.COM GOLDEN ROSE STKS (LISTED RACE) 6f (P)

3:50 (3:53) (Class 1) 3-Y-O+

£22,708 (£8,608; £4,308; £2,148; £1,076; £540) **Stalls** Low

Form RPR

0-06 **1** **Duff (IRE)**[35] 6814 5-9-4 0.................... KJManning 10 116
(Edward Lynam, Ire) *chsd ldng pair: wnt 2nd wl over 1f out: rdn ld jst over 1f out: clr ins fnl f: rdn out* **5/1**[3]

0450 **2** 2 1/4 **Maltese Falcon**[17] 7192 8-9-2 98..............................(t) NelsonDeSouza 3 107
(P F I Cole) *led: rdn 2f out: hdd jst over 1f out: no ch w wnr after but hld on for 2nd* **14/1**

3-36 **3** 1/2 **Swiss Franc**[160] 3063 3-9-2 105.. RyanMoore 2 105
(D R C Elsworth) *t.k.h: hld up in tch: rdn and unable qck 2f out: kpt on fnl f: nt threaten wnr* **8/1**

0501 **4** 1 **How's She Cuttin' (IRE)**[20] 7151 5-8-11 91..............(v) RobertWinston 5 97
(T D Barron) *chsd ldr tl wl over 1f out: outpcd by ldng pair over 1f out: one pce after* **10/1**

00 **5** hd **Smarten Die (IRE)**[50] 5-9-2 0.. JimCrowley 6 101
(Frau E Mader, Germany) *hld up towards rr: rdn and no hdwy jst over 2f out: kpt on fnl f: nvr pce to trble wnr* **25/1**

1011 **6** 1/2 **Ceremonial Jade (UAE)**[56] 6285 5-9-2 107..................(t) JimmyQuinn 9 100+
(M Botti) *lw: dwlt: towards rr: rdn and effrt jst over 2f out: plugged on but nvr pce to threaten wnr* **2/1**[1]

3501 **7** nk **Prohibit**[31] 6903 3-9-2 103.. JimmyFortune 7 102+
(J H M Gosden) *lw: stdd after s: hld up in rr: hdwy and nt clr run fr over 1f out: tl swtchd rt ins fnl f: nvr able to chal* **4/1**[2]

0300 **8** shd **Philario (IRE)**[14] 7243 3-9-2 100.................................. FergusSweeney 1 98
(K R Burke) *chsd ldrs: drvn and struggling over 2f out: no ch w ldrs last 2f* **12/1**

4040 **9** nk **Salsa Steps (USA)**[56] 6271 4-8-11 95............................(t) SteveDrowne 8 92
(H Morrison) *dwlt: sn pushed along: bhd and rdn over 2f out: n.d* **7/1**

1m 10.38s (-1.52) **Going Correction** +0.025s/f (Slow) course record **9** Ran SP% **120.9**
Speed ratings (Par 111): **111,108,107,106,105 105,104,104,104**
toteswinger: 1&2 £9.40, 1&3 £6.30, 2&3 £14.00. CSF £75.04 TOTE £6.40: £2.00, £3.40, £2.00; EX 123.00 Trifecta £740.00 Part won. Pool: £1000.02 - 0.40 winning units. Place 6: £13.95 Place 5: £8.68.
Owner Kilboy Estate **Bred** Kilboy Estate **Trained** Dunshaughlin, Co Meath
■ The last leg of a Scoop6 that had rolled over for 11 weeks. Eight winning tickets shared a record win fund of £3,496,091

FOCUS
An ordinary Listed sprint but quite an impressive performance from Duff, who is rated back to something like his best. Sound form.

NOTEBOOK
Duff(IRE) ◆, dropped back to 6f for the first time since his juvenile days and having his first go on sand, was always well placed and could be called the winner from over a furlong out. He is likely to be kept on the go and may well step back up in trip for another Listed contest at either Deauville or Kempton. (op 9-2 tchd 11-2)
Maltese Falcon was able to dominate, as he likes to, but he was no match for the winner. (op 12-1)
Swiss Franc, trying Polytrack for the first time on this first run since June, was a touch keen early and took a while to pick up when first coming under pressure, but he kept on well enough to grab a place.
How's She Cuttin'(IRE) had something to find at this level having won off just 82 over 5f at Southwell on her previous start, but she ran a fine race in fourth, just missing out on some black type. (tchd 9-1)
Smarten Die(IRE), trained in Germany, was never seriously involved but he didn't run badly. (op 33-1)
Ceremonial Jade(UAE) was slow to get going and was then trapped out wide for much of the way. He offered little for pressure and basically had an off day. (op 11-4 tchd 3-1)
Prohibit is much better than he showed as he was given a lot to do and continually found trouble in running. Official explanation: jockey said gelding was denied a clear run (op 7-2)
T/Plt: £12.10 to a £1 stake. Pool: £60,564.14. 3,649.92 winning tickets. T/Qpdt: £16.80 to a £1 stake. Pool: £3,231.90. 141.80 winning tickets. SP

7399 WOLVERHAMPTON (A.W) (L-H)
Saturday, November 22

OFFICIAL GOING: Standard
Wind: Almost nil Weather: Fine

7422 SOUL NIGHT MAIDEN STKS (DIV I) 1m 141y(P)
6:20 (6:20) (Class 5) 2-Y-O £2,914 (£867; £433; £216) Stalls Low

Form RPR

4 **1** **Kimberley Downs (USA)**[16] 7209 2-9-3 0.......................... GregFairley 4 80+
(M Johnston) *led early: a.p: rdn to ld ins fnl f: r.o* **9/1**[3]

2 **2** 1/2 **Miss Beat (IRE)**[21] 7140 2-8-12 0..................................(t) JamieSpencer 1 74
(B J Meehan) *t.k.h in tch: swtchd rt jst over 2f out: rdn and kpt on ins fnl f* **8/13**[1]

30 **3** 1 1/4 **Sussex Dancer (IRE)**[28] 6982 2-8-12 0.......................... ShaneKelly 10 71
(J A Osborne) *sn chsng ldr: led 2f out: rdn and hung lft over 1f out: hdd and nt qckn ins fnl f* **28/1**

00 **4** 3 1/4 **Big Nige (IRE)**[22] 7106 2-9-3 0.................................... JerryO'Dwyer 5 69
(J Pearce) *hld up in mid-div: hdwy on ins over 2f out: swtchd lft over 1f out: rdn and one pce fnl f* **50/1**

56 **5** 4 **Non Dom (IRE)**[17] 7200 2-9-3 0.................................... GeorgeBaker 8 61
(H Morrison) *towards rr: pushed along over 3f out: rdn and hung lft over 1f out: nvr nr ldrs* **9/1**[3]

00 **6** 1 **Bollin Judith**[17] 7200 2-8-12 0...................................... PaulMulrennan 6 54
(T D Easterby) *in rr: sme late prog: n.d* **66/1**

0 **7** 1 **Mile High Lad (USA)**[34] 6837 2-9-3 0.............................. ChrisCatlin 7 57
(George Baker) *prom: pushed along over 3f out: rdn and wknd 2f out* **40/1**

6 **8** 1/2 **Broughton Beck (IRE)**[10] 7282 2-9-3 0................. FrankieMcDonald 11 56
(R F Fisher) *dwlt: impr into mid-div over 6f out: short-lived effrt on outside 3f out* **100/1**

5232 **9** 1/2 **Free Thinker**[15] 7229 2-9-3 79.. AdamKirby 12 54
(P W D'Arcy) *sn led: hdd 2f out: rdn over 1f out: wkng whn hung rt jst ins fnl f* **4/1**[2]

0 **10** 6 **Cumbrian Gold (USA)**[7] 7343 2-9-3 0.............................. TomEaves 9 42
(B Smart) *in tch tl wknd wl over 3f out* **100/1**

60 **11** 1 3/4 **Refuse To Decline**[151] 3349 2-8-12 0.......................... MartinDwyer 3 33
(D M Simcock) *a towards rr* **66/1**

1m 52.57s (2.07) **Going Correction** +0.05s/f (Slow) **11** Ran SP% **114.7**
Speed ratings (Par 96): **92,91,90,87,84 83,82,81,81,76 74**
toteswinger: 1&2 £1.10, 1&3 £11.50, 2&3 £11.50. CSF £14.44 TOTE £13.10: £2.40, £1.02, £5.60; EX 23.00.
Owner Favourites Racing XIX **Bred** Gaines-Gentry Thoroughbreds **Trained** Middleham Moor, N Yorks
■ Stewards' Enquiry : Shane Kelly one-day ban: careless riding (Dec 6)

FOCUS
A race lacking strength in depth and one in which the early pace was only fair at best. The first three, who pulled clear in the closing stages, raced just off the inside rail in the straight.

NOTEBOOK
Kimberley Downs(USA) had shown ability on his debut but turned in an improved effort, in the process showing a good attitude under pressure. He should have no problems with 1m2f, is in good hands and is the type to progress further. (op 6-1)
Miss Beat(IRE) was well supported following her promising turf debut but, while running creditably, failed to build on that performance on this all-weather debut after racing keenly. She is capable of winning a similar event but she lacks physical scope and this may be as good as she is. (op 5-6)
Sussex Dancer(IRE) was well beaten in soft last time but had the run of the race and reproduced the form shown when dividing subsequent winners on her debut at Kempton. She should be able to pick up a minor event on Polytrack. (op 20-1)
Big Nige(IRE) has improved with each of his starts and turned in his best effort yet on this all-weather debut. He is the type to fare best in run-of-the-mill handicaps on this surface.
Non Dom(IRE), making his all-weather debut, was easy to back and again showed ability. He will be one to look out for in ordinary handicaps granted a stiffer test. (tchd 12-1)
Bollin Judith, having her first run on artificial surfaces, shaped as though a stiffer test of stamina would be in her favour. She is now qualified for a mark.

7423 WOLVERHAMPTON-RACECOURSE.CO.UK CLAIMING STKS 1m 141y(P)
6:50 (6:50) (Class 6) 3-Y-O+ £1,978 (£584; £292) Stalls Low

Form RPR

-004 **1** **Direct Debit (IRE)**[12] 7278 5-9-0 78.......................... JamieSpencer 13 81
(M L W Bell) *hld up in tch: led wl over 1f out: sn rdn and edgd lft: drvn out* **11/4**[1]

0230 **2** 2 1/4 **Murfreesboro**[8] 7313 5-9-6 85....................................(v) AdamKirby 10 82
(D Shaw) *t.k.h in rr: hdwy over 2f out: rdn and hung lft ins fnl f: wnt 2nd towards fin* **5/1**

3315 **3** 1/2 **Willkandoo (USA)**[40] 6710 3-9-3 84..................(p) PaulMulrennan 11 81
(K A Ryan) *t.k.h: led over 1f: chsd ldr: ev ch over 2f out: rdn over 1f out: one pce fnl f* **4/1**[2]

0-10 **4** nk **Clear Sailing**[71] 5858 5-8-10 79..............................(p) ChrisCatlin 3 70
(George Baker) *dwlt: t.k.h in rr: swtchd rt 5f out: hdwy on outside to ld 3f out: hdd wl over 1f out: one pce fnl f* **9/2**[3]

1000 **5** 1 **Blacktoft (USA)**[8] 7309 5-9-4 73..........................(e) J-PGuillambert 9 76
(S C Williams) *hld up towards rr: rdn and hdwy over 2f out: no imp fnl f* **7/1**

/5 **6** 1/2 **Desert Vision**[7] 7344 4-9-9 0.......................................(t) DaleGibson 7 80
(M W Easterby) *plld hrd in mid-div: lost pl 6f out: hdwy over 1f out: sn edgd lft: n.d* **40/1**

0040 **7** 4 1/2 **Mystic Roll**[8] 7317 5-8-3 50.. AndreaAtzeni(7) 1 56
(Jane Chapple-Hyam) *bhd fnl 3f* **25/1**

0604 **8** 6 **Climate (IRE)**[5] 7363 9-8-11 60....................................(p) JamesDoyle 8 43
(P D Evans) *a towards rr* **20/1**

3230 **9** 3 **Crocodile Bay (IRE)**[12] 7277 5-8-12 70.................. JamesO'Reilly(5) 12 42
(John A Harris) *prom tl rdn and wknd over 2f out* **14/1**

-160 **10** 11 **Pembo**[31] 6912 3-8-10 50.. JoeFanning 5 13
(R A Harris) *prom tl wknd over 3f out* **40/1**

1006 **11** 3 3/4 **Blue Savannah (FR)**[10] 7284 3-8-5 52...............(b[1]) FrankieMcDonald 6 —
(G J Smith) *led 7f out to 3f out: sn rdn and wknd* **80/1**

1m 50.96s (0.46) **Going Correction** +0.05s/f (Slow)
WFA 3 from 4yo+ 3lb **11** Ran SP% **115.4**
Speed ratings (Par 101): **99,97,96,96,95 94,90,85,82,73 69**
toteswinger: 1&2 £4.20, 1&3 £8.80, 2&3 £10.00. CSF £15.32 TOTE £3.30: £1.30, £2.20, £1.10; EX 17.30.The winner was claimed by Mark Wellings for £9,000. Willkandoo was claimed by D. M. I. Simcock for £15,000.
Owner Billy Maguire **Bred** Hawthorn Villa Stud **Trained** Newmarket, Suffolk

FOCUS
A mixed bag of exposed performers, although the principals set a fair standard for the grade and the race could rate higher. The pace was just an ordinary one and the winner raced centre to far side in the straight.
Willkandoo(USA) Official explanation: jockey said gelding ran too freely
Blue Savannah(FR) Official explanation: jockey said filly had no more to give

7424 SOUL NIGHT MAIDEN STKS (DIV II) 1m 141y(P)
7:20 (7:21) (Class 5) 2-Y-O £2,914 (£867; £433; £216) Stalls Low

Form RPR

04 **1** **Bushveld (IRE)**[21] 7126 2-9-3 0...................................... JoeFanning 11 78+
(M Johnston) *hld up in tch: led over 4f out: pushed clr fr over 1f out: eased towards fin* **11/1**

2 **2** 2 **Captainrisk (IRE)**[124] 4256 2-8-10 0.......................... AndreaAtzeni(7) 2 70
(M Botti) *hld up in tch: nt clr run over 2f out: rdn fnl f: wnt 2nd towards fin: no ch w wnr* **11/4**[1]

5 **3** 1 **Elliptical (USA)**[16] 7204 2-9-3 0.................................... HayleyTurner 3 68
(G A Butler) *a.p: pushed along over 3f out: chsd wnr over 1f out: sn rdn: no imp* **9/2**[3]

4 **4** 1 **Moonbeam Dancer (USA)**[22] 7117 2-8-12 0................. MartinDwyer 6 61
(D M Simcock) *hld up in tch: outpcd 2f out: styd on ins fnl f* **3/1**[2]

5 shd **Appropriate (IRE)** 2-8-12 0... LiamJones 9 61+
(W J Haggas) *hld up and bhd: c wd st: pushed along and styd on ins fnl f: bttr for r* **10/1**

0 **6** hd **Ultimate**[28] 6977 2-9-3 0.. SteveDrowne 8 65
(H Morrison) *t.k.h: a.p: chsd wnr over 2f out tl over 1f out: no ex ins fnl f* **13/2**

00 **7** 6 **Just Dan**[7] 7343 2-9-3 0.. GrahamGibbons 1 53
(R Hollinshead) *s.i.s: in rr: shortlived effrt on ins 2f out* **17/2**

8 4 1/2 **Tinshu (IRE)** 2-8-12 0.. ChrisCatlin 12 38
(D Haydn Jones) *a in rr* **33/1**

00 **9** 3 1/2 **Lend A Light**[7] 7343 2-9-3 0.. PatrickMathers 5 36
(I W McInnes) *led: hdd over 4f out: rdn and wknd wl over 1f out* **50/1**

10 1 1/4 **Diktaram** 2-9-3 0.. PaulMulrennan 4 33
(J R Weymes) *prom early: stdd and lost pl after 1f: towards rr after* **50/1**

0 **11** 17 **Carrimion**[29] 6944 2-9-0 0...................................... DuranFentiman(3) 10 —
(T H Caldwell) *hld up in mid-div: pushed along over 3f out: wknd over 2f out* **200/1**

1m 53.34s (2.84) **Going Correction** +0.05s/f (Slow) **11** Ran SP% **118.5**
Speed ratings (Par 96): **89,87,86,85,85 85,79,75,72,71 56**
toteswinger: 1&2 £11.40, 1&3 £3.70, 2&3 £4.00. CSF £41.43 TOTE £11.10: £2.80, £2.10, £2.40; EX 22.20.
Owner Sheikh Hamdan Bin Mohammed Al Maktoum **Bred** Darley **Trained** Middleham Moor, N Yorks

FOCUS
Another ordinary maiden (winner raced in the centre) and another gallop that suited the prominent racers, but a much improved performance on his all-weather debut from the winner.

NOTEBOOK
Bushveld(IRE) ◆, who had been bogged down in heavy ground on his first two starts, turned in a much improved display. He was value for at least double the winning margin and is the type to win more races on this surface. (op 8-1 tchd 12-1)

Captainrisk(IRE) had been off the course for four months but ran to a similar level as on that turf debut. His stable does well on artificial surfaces and he should be able to pick up a minor event around this trip. (op 7-2)
Elliptical(USA) had the run of the race and again showed ability. The step up to 1m2f may well be more to his liking and he will be of more interest once handicapped. (op 5-1)
Moonbeam Dancer(USA), who had run creditably on her debut, attracted support but, while running to a similar level, left the impression that a much stiffer test of stamina would suit. (op 4-1 tchd 11-4)
Appropriate(IRE) ◆, easy to back, is the one to take out of the race, despite her rider reporting a breathing problem. The filly, who is related to a couple of fair middle-distance winners, made up plenty of ground from an unpromising position without being knocked about. She is open to improvement, especially as she goes up in distance, and looks one to keep an eye on in similar company. Official explanation: jockey said filly had a breathing problem (op 7-1 tchd 13-2)
Ultimate was easy to back on his all-weather debut and, although not totally disgraced, he is going to have to settle better than he did here if he is to progress. (op 4-1 tchd 7-2)

7425 DINE IN HORIZONS CLAIMING STKS — 1m 141y(P)
7:50 (7:51) (Class 6) 2-Y-O — £2,388 (£705; £352) Stalls Low

Form				RPR
2501	1		**Doncosaque (IRE)**[7] 7338 2-8-11 78 ... TPQueally 13 — (J R Gask) *mde all: drew clr fnl f: easily* — 8/13[1]	74+
0004	2	6	**Betws Y Coed (IRE)**[10] 7283 2-7-9 52 ...(p) NicolPolli(5) 4 — (A Bailey) *a.p: rdn over 2f out: kpt on to take 2nd last strides: no ch w wnr* — 18/1	50
1056	3	nk	**Dougie Peel**[5] 7353 2-8-7 60 ...(p) ChrisCatlin 3 — (K A Ryan) *a.p: rdn over 2f out: chsd wnr fnl f: no imp: lost 2nd last strides* — 11/2[2]	56
03	4	1	**Precocious Air (IRE)**[22] 7117 2-8-9 0 ... ShaneKelly 11 — (J A Osborne) *bmpd s: sn chsng wnr: rdn and ev ch over 2f out: lost 2nd 1f out: one pce* — 7/1[3]	56
0	5	1/2	**Vodka Shot (USA)**[8] 7318 2-8-3 0 ... HayleyTurner 12 — (M L W Bell) *hld up and bhd: rdn wl over 1f out: styd on ins fnl f: nrst fin* — 20/1	49+
00	6	shd	**In Step**[7] 7343 2-8-4 0 ... LiamJones 10 — (W J Haggas) *hmpd s: hld up and bhd: hdwy wl over 1f out: sn rdn: one pce fnl f* — 14/1	50
000	7	2 1/2	**Jack's House (IRE)**[8] 7318 2-8-0 54 ... AndreaAtzeni(7) 7 — (Jane Chapple-Hyam) *hld up in tch: rdn over 2f out: wknd over 1f out* 33/1	48
0050	8	9	**Indian Blade (IRE)**[47] 6535 2-8-5 50 ow1 ...(p) MartinDwyer 5 — (M D I Usher) *hld up in mid-div: wknd over 2f out* — 50/1	27
0000	9	6	**Coral Point (IRE)**[63] 6135 2-8-4 50 ... JimmyQuinn 2 — (S Kirk) *s.i.s: mid-div: reminders over 5f out: rdn over 3f out: sn bhd* 40/1	13
0	10	9	**Sytygre**[15] 7227 2-8-8 0 ow1 ... TomEaves 8 — (Miss J A Camacho) *bmpd s: plld hrd in mid-div: pushed wd bnd after 1f: sn bhd* — 100/1	—
000	11	4	**Franali (IRE)**[105] 4847 2-8-6 49 ... PaulHanagan 1 — (R F Fisher) *hld up in tch: wknd over 2f out* — 40/1	—
000	12	16	**Blushing Dreamer (IRE)**[15] 7227 2-7-11 37 ...(v[1]) DuranFentiman(3) 6 — (D Shaw) *stdd s: plld hrd in rr: lost tch 3f out: t.o* — 80/1	—
0466	P		**Miss Kadee**[10] 7283 2-8-0 53 ...(v[1]) CatherineGannon 9 — (P D Evans) *wnt rt s: t.k.h: pushed wd bnd after 1f: sn hung bdly rt: p.u over 6f out* — 33/1	—

1m 51.34s (0.84) **Going Correction** +0.05s/f (Slow) 13 Ran SP% **121.4**
Speed ratings (Par 94): **98,92,92,91,91 90,88,80,75,67 63,49,—**
toteswinger: 1&2 £9.80, 1&3 £1.50, 2&3 £12.80. CSF £14.01 TOTE £1.70: £1.20, £3.50, £2.10; EX 21.20.The winner was claimed by Paul Howling for £12,000.
Owner Horses First Racing Limited **Bred** Ammerland Verwaltung Gmbh **Trained** Sutton Veny, Wilts
■ Stewards' Enquiry : T P Queally four-day ban: careless riding Dec 6-9); one-day ban: failed to ride to draw (Dec 10)

FOCUS
An uncompetitive event and an ordinary gallop but the time was quicker than both divisions of the maiden.

NOTEBOOK
Doncosaque(IRE), the market leader and clear form pick, proved far too good for some inferior rivals on this first run for an in-form stable. He probably did not have to improve to notch his second successive claiming win but, although life will be tougher in handicaps from his current 78 mark, he may be capable of a little better. He was claimed by Paul Howling. (op 8-11)
Betws Y Coed(IRE) had a bit to find at the weights but ran creditably to confirm herself as good on Polytrack as on Fibresand. Modest handicaps around this trip are likely to provide her with her best chance of success. (op 20-1)
Dougie Peel was not disgraced dropping back in distance, but remains below the form that saw him win at Great Leighs in September. (op 15-2)
Precocious Air(IRE) was not disgraced dropped in grade and may do better in run-of-the-mill handicaps on this surface. (tchd 6-1 and 8-1)
Vodka Shot(USA) was ridden with more patience than on her debut at Southwell and was not disgraced considering the way this race panned out. (tchd 22-1)
In Step was not disgraced and is now qualified for a mark. She may be capable of a little better in modest handicaps. (op 10-1)
Blushing Dreamer(IRE) Official explanation: jockey said filly hung right
Miss Kadee Official explanation: jockey said filly hung badly right

7426 WOLVERHAMPTON-RACECOURSE.CO.UK NURSERY — 7f 32y(P)
8:20 (8:21) (Class 4) (0-85,84) 2-Y-O — £5,180 (£1,541; £770; £384) Stalls High

Form				RPR
0132	1		**Tobond (IRE)**[24] 7067 2-9-0 84 ... AndreaAtzeni(7) 5 — (M Botti) *hld up in tch: rdn to ld wl ins fnl f: readily* — 11/4[2]	90+
6041	2	1 1/2	**Peter's Gift (IRE)**[15] 7220 2-8-3 66 ... ChrisCatlin 2 — (K A Ryan) *led: hrd rdn and hdd wl ins fnl f: nt qckn* — 7/2[3]	68
1600	3	2 3/4	**Grand Honour (IRE)**[37] 6756 2-9-4 81 ... JimmyQuinn 4 — (P Howling) *hld up: hdwy 2f out: rdn over 1f out: one pce* — 14/1	77
2100	4	1 1/4	**Aladdin's Lamp (IRE)**[29] 6954 2-8-7 70 ... JoeFanning 6 — (M Johnston) *sn chsng ldr: ev ch over 2f out: rdn wl over 1f out: wknd ins fnl f* — 7/1	63
0021	5	1/2	**Whatyouwoodwishfor (USA)**[7] 7335 2-8-12 75 ... PaulHanagan 1 — (R A Fahey) *prom: rdn and wkng whn edgd rt over 1f out* — 7/4[1]	66
6362	6	1/2	**Verinco**[21] 7130 2-9-0 77 ... TomEaves 3 — (B Smart) *hld up in last: rdn 3f out: no rspnse* — 12/1	67

1m 30.29s (0.69) **Going Correction** +0.05s/f (Slow) 6 Ran SP% **112.1**
Speed ratings (Par 98): **98,96,93,91,91 90**
toteswinger: 1&2 Not won, 1&3 £9.90, 2&3 £17.70. CSF £12.70 TOTE £3.80: £1.70, £2.30; EX 12.80.
Owner Giuliano Manfredini **Bred** David John Brown **Trained** Newmarket, Suffolk

FOCUS
Five of the six were previous winners but, in keeping with previous races on this card, the gallop was an ordinary one. The market leader disappointed and the winner raced in the centre in the straight.

NOTEBOOK
Tobond(IRE) ◆ is a steadily progressive sort who posted his best effort back in trip to win with something in hand. A stronger gallop would have suited and he's the type to go in again. (op 9-4)
Peter's Gift(IRE) ◆ had much more to do than when winning an uncompetitive soft-ground maiden on her previous start, but she had the run of the race and ran to her best. She pulled clear of the remainder and should win a race on artificial surfaces. (op 11-2 tchd 6-1)
Grand Honour(IRE) proved suited by the return to this trip and bettered his latest efforts over 6f and 1m, but he seems to have little room for manoeuvre from his current mark. (op 12-1)
Aladdin's Lamp(IRE) had the run of the race and, although he bettered the form of his two previous starts, will have to show more before he is a solid betting proposition. (op 13-2 tchd 6-1)
Whatyouwoodwishfor(USA) showed improved form over 6f on his all-weather debut on his previous start but was beaten before stamina became an issue over this longer trip. However, he is in good hands and would not be one to write off yet. Official explanation: jockey said colt hung left (op 2-1 tchd 9-4 in places)
Verinco, an exposed maiden, failed to build on his latest turf run on this all-weather debut. He'll have to show a fair bit more before he's worth a bet on Polytrack. (op 10-1 tchd 17-2)

7427 HOTEL & CONFERENCING AT WOLVERHAMPTON H'CAP — 1m 4f 50y(P)
8:50 (8:50) (Class 6) (0-55,57) 3-Y-O+ — £2,388 (£705; £352) Stalls Low

Form				RPR
5-04	1		**Amazing King (IRE)**[22] 4503 4-9-1 53 ... JamieSpencer 6 — (P A Kirby) *hld up towards rr: hdwy to ld wl over 1f out: shkn up ins fnl f: r.o wl* — 3/1[1]	68+
3300	2	1 1/2	**Lapina (IRE)**[41] 6672 4-9-2 54 ...(b) ShaneKelly 3 — (A Middleton) *hld up in rr: c wd st: hdwy wl over 1f out: kpt on ins fnl f* — 25/1	67
453	3	4	**Compton Falcon**[16] 7217 4-9-3 55 ...(b[1]) HayleyTurner 5 — (G A Butler) *plld hrd early in rr: stmbld 5f out: rdn and edgd lft fr over 1f out: one pce* — 4/1[2]	61
0000	4	hd	**Fenners (USA)**[19] 7169 5-9-3 55 ...(p) PaulMulrennan 7 — (M W Easterby) *hld up in mid-div: hdwy over 2f out: rdn over 1f out: one pce whn carried lft towards fin* — 7/1[3]	61
0060	5	2	**Terminate (GER)**[53] 6364 6-9-1 53 ... TGMcLaughlin 1 — (Ian Williams) *hld up towards rr: nt clr run 2f out: styd on fnl f: n.d* 15/2	56
4060	6	4	**Desert Hawk**[25] 7039 7-9-0 55 ... LukeMorris(3) 2 — (W M Brisbourne) *hld up in mid-div: nt clr run whn rdn and swtchd lft over 1f out: no hdwy fnl f* — 16/1	51
6334	7	1 3/4	**Corrib (IRE)**[32] 6882 5-9-3 55 ... CatherineGannon 12 — (B Palling) *hld up in tch: rdn wl over 1f out: wknd ent fnl f* — 12/1	48
4442	8	2 1/2	**Trinkila (USA)**[8] 7310 3-8-13 57 ...(b) JoeFanning 9 — (P F I Cole) *led: rdn and hdd wl over 1f out: sn wknd and hmpd* — 8/1	46
550/	9	hd	**Amron Hill**[20] 6899 5-9-1 53 ... GrahamGibbons 10 — (R Hollinshead) *prom: chsd ldr over 3f out to 2f out: sn wknd* — 16/1	42
0006	10	1/2	**Check Up (IRE)**[41] 6668 7-9-0 52 ... ChrisCatlin 8 — (J L Flint) *chsd ldr tl over 3f out: wknd wl over 1f out* — 20/1	40
0054	11	9	**Mighty Mover (IRE)**[19] 7169 6-8-8 53 ... AshleyMorgan(7) 11 — (B Palling) *s.s whn rdr late to remove blindfold: plld hrd in rr: hdwy on outside over 2f out: wknd wl over 1f out* — 14/1	27
0000	12	7	**Abydos**[24] 7071 4-9-3 55 ... TPQueally 4 — (A P Stringer) *hld up in tch: wkng whn n.m.r over 2f out* — 9/1	18

2m 41.87s (0.77) **Going Correction** +0.05s/f (Slow)
WFA 3 from 4yo+ 6lb 12 Ran SP% **125.1**
Speed ratings (Par 101): **99,98,95,95,93 91,90,88,88,87 81,77**
toteswinger: 1&2 £15.50, 1&3 £2.00, 2&3 Not won. CSF £89.93 CT £319.76 TOTE £3.90: £2.50, £7.00, £1.80; EX 213.00.
Owner The New Venture Partnership **Bred** Kraemer Partnership **Trained** Castleton, N Yorks
■ Stewards' Enquiry : Paul Mulrennan caution: careless riding.

FOCUS
A low-grade handicap run at a reasonable gallop and the hold-up horses came to the fore in the straight. The first two, who raced in the centre, pulled clear in the closing stages and the form has been rated slightly positively.

7428 CHRISTMAS PARTY TIME AT WOLVERHAMPTON H'CAP — 5f 216y(P)
9:20 (9:21) (Class 5) (0-75,74) 3-Y-O+ — £3,238 (£963; £481; £240) Stalls Low

Form				RPR
1522	1		**Doubtful Sound (USA)**[2] 7393 4-8-8 71 ...(p) AndreaAtzeni(7) 13 — (R Hollinshead) *hld up in tch: led over 1f out: r.o strly* — 3/1[1]	88
0401	2	3 1/2	**Princess Valerina**[46] 6556 4-9-2 72 ... TPQueally 1 — (D Haydn Jones) *hld up towards rr: hdwy on ins over 1f out: rdn and wnt 2nd ins fnl f: no ch w wnr* — 10/1	77
6315	3	1 1/4	**Tangerine Trees**[12] 7276 3-8-8 64 ... TomEaves 10 — (B Smart) *led over 1f: w ldr: led wl over 1f out: sn rdn and hdd: one pce* — 11/1	65
6630	4	nk	**Lekita**[73] 5800 3-9-2 72 ... AdamKirby 7 — (W R Swinburn) *a.p: rdn and one pce fnl f* — 7/1[3]	72
531	5	nk	**Absa Lutte (IRE)**[1] 7399 5-8-9 65 ...(t) LPKeniry 12 — (Jarlath P Fahey, Ire) *s.i.s: hld up in rr: rdn on outside over 1f out: kpt on ins fnl f: nvr nrr* — 7/1[3]	64
2400	6	1	**Tyfos**[70] 5886 3-9-4 74 ... GeorgeBaker 4 — (W M Brisbourne) *w ldr: led over 4f out tl wl over 1f out: sn wknd* — 16/1	70
6000	7	1	**Rabbit Fighter (IRE)**[24] 7077 4-8-10 66 ...(v) DarrenWilliams 8 — (D Shaw) *t.k.h in rr: sme late prog: n.d* — 16/1	59
2140	8	1/2	**Bahamian Kid**[29] 6952 3-9-2 72 ...(p) GrahamGibbons 3 — (R Hollinshead) *prom: rdn wl over 1f out: wknd ins fnl f* — 6/1[2]	63
1122	9	shd	**Royal Challenge**[43] 6634 7-9-3 73 ... PatrickMathers 2 — (I W McInnes) *hld up in mid-div: rdn wl over 1f out: wknd ins fnl f* — 3/1[1]	64
0-00	10	2 3/4	**No Page (IRE)**[63] 6137 3-8-13 69 ... LiamJones 9 — (J L Spearing) *a towards rr* — 50/1	51
2102	11	7	**Splash The Cash**[25] 7040 3-8-11 67 ...(p) ChrisCatlin 11 — (K A Ryan) *prom tl wknd 2f out* — 12/1	27

1m 14.11s (-0.89) **Going Correction** +0.05s/f (Slow) 11 Ran SP% **128.1**
Speed ratings (Par 103): **107,102,100,100,99 98,97,96,96,92 83**
toteswinger: 1&2 £3.90, 1&3 £31.90, 2&3 £62.00. CSF £39.18 CT £315.26 TOTE £5.30: £1.90, £3.30, £3.50; EX 66.00 Place 6 £12.30, Place 5 £8.74.
Owner Phil Pye **Bred** Millsec, Ltd **Trained** Upper Longdon, Staffs

FOCUS
A run-of-the-mill sprint handicap featuring mainly exposed types. The winner raced centre to far side in the straight and posted a clear personal best in a good time for the grade. Solid form.
Absa Lutte(IRE) Official explanation: jockey said mare ran too freely early stages
Royal Challenge Official explanation: jockey said gelding had no more to give
T/Plt: £15.50 to a £1 stake. Pool: £107,922.80. 5,059.36 winning tickets. T/Qpdt: £7.60 to a £1 stake. Pool: £6,454.05. 626.36 winning tickets. KH

7294 SAINT-CLOUD (L-H)

Saturday, November 22

OFFICIAL GOING: Heavy

7429a PRIX DENISY (LISTED) 1m 7f 110y

2:20 (2:20) 3-Y-0+ £19,118 (£7,647; £5,735; £3,824; £1,912)

RPR

1 **Latin Mood (FR)**[17] 5-9-1 CSoumillon 8 105
(P Demercastel, France)

2 6 **Quartz Jem (IRE)**[46] 6569 4-9-1 IMendizabal 10 98
(Mme Pia Brandt, France)

3 1 1/2 **Fully Funded (USA)**[46] 6569 3-8-7 SPasquier 1 98
(Mme C Head-Maarek, France)

4 8 **Green Tango (FR)**[17] 5-9-1 JCrocquevieille 12 88
(P Van De Poele, France)

5 2 **High Maintenance (FR)**[26] 7037 4-9-1 MGuyon 3 86
(A Fabre, France)

6 hd **Nemo Spirit (IRE)**[15] 7223 3-8-7 FrancisNorton 11 87
(W R Muir) *led: hdd and 3rd 1/2-way: rdn appr st: kpt on at one pce* **25/1**[3]

7 2 1/2 **Shawnee Saga (FR)**[31] 6921 3-8-7 DBoeuf 6 84
(W Baltromei, Germany)

8 20 **Gassin (FR)**[26] 5-9-1 TGillet 2 61
(J Bertran De Balanda, France)

9 4 **Mission Secrete (IRE)**[110] 3-8-4 ACrastus 5 54
(E Lellouche, France)

10 6 **Mont Joux (FR)**[18] 6-9-1 GBenoist 7 50
(H Billot, France)

0 **Spanish Hidalgo (IRE)**[26] 7017 4-9-1 DBonilla 9 —
(J L Dunlop) *hld up towards rr: moved up to 5th 1/2-way: 6th and sn btn st* **17/1**[2]

0 **Alma Mater**[48] 6517 5-8-11 J-BEyquem 4 —
(Sir Mark Prescott) *prom: 4th 1/2-way: rdn 3 1/2f out: sn btn and eased* **12/1**[1]

3m 40.0s (1.30)
WFA 3 from 4yo+ 8lb **12 Ran SP% 17.1**
PARI-MUTUEL: WIN 3.30; PL 1.50, 2.20, 2.30; DF 11.00.
Owner Naji Pharaon **Bred** N Pharaon **Trained** France

NOTEBOOK
Nemo Spirit(IRE) broke well from the stalls and led in the early part of this staying event. Passed by the winner on the back straight when the pace picked up, he stayed on bravely but one-paced in the final stages.
Spanish Hidalgo(IRE) never looked like finishing in the first six.
Alma Mater was well up in the early stages but was a spent force early in the straight.

2743 FONTAINEBLEAU

Friday, November 21

OFFICIAL GOING: Heavy

7430a PRIX ZEDDAAN (LISTED RACE) 6f

12:50 (12:52) 2-Y-0 £20,221 (£8,088; £6,066; £4,044; £2,022)

RPR

1 **Doriana (FR)**[22] 7103 2-8-12 CSoumillon 2 —
(A De Royer-Dupre, France)

2 1 1/2 **Mantadive (FR)**[16] 2-8-8 SRuis 7 —
(Mme N Rossio, France)

3 1/2 **Lutece Eria (FR)** 2-8-8 ARoussel 3 —
(C Diard, France)

4 1/2 **Bluster (FR)**[22] 7103 2-8-11 DBoeuf 12 —
(Robert Collet, France)

5 1 **Rose Hill Doloise (FR)**[22] 7103 2-8-8 RMarchelli 9 —
(A Bonin, France)

6 3 **Chausson Dore (IRE)**[16] 2-8-8 MGuyon 10 —
(A Fabre, France)

7 nk **Signorinasilvani (IRE)**[16] 2-8-8 JVictoire 8 —
(Rod Collet, France)

8 shd **Good Bye My Friend (FR)**[22] 7103 2-8-11 TThulliez 6 —
(N Clement, France)

9 3/4 **Eva Kant**[22] 7103 2-8-8 CFiocchi 14 —
(R Menichetti, Italy)

10 2 1/2 **Zibeling (IRE)**[21] 2-8-8 THuet 1 —
(Robert Collet, France)

11 **Aseena (IRE)**[57] 6236 2-8-8 RCMontenegro 4 —
(Thomas Demeaulte, France)

12 **Skid Solo (IRE)**[7] 2-8-11 IMendizabal 5 —
(Mme G Rarick, France)

13 **Lan Force (ITY)**[68] 5951 2-8-8 DBonilla 13 —
(A Renzoni, Italy)

14 **Definightly**[27] 6970 2-8-11 SPasquier 11 —
(R Charlton) *missed break: in rr: brief effrt over 2f out: sn btn: eased ins fnl f* **13/2**[1]

1m 10.9s (70.90) **14 Ran SP% 13.3**
PARI-MUTUEL (including 1 Euro stake): WIN 6.10; PL 2.30, 12.60, 6.90;DF 154.00.
Owner Ecurie La Perrigne **Bred** Sca De La Perrigne **Trained** Chantilly, France

7431a PRIX SOLITUDE (LISTED RACE) (FILLIES) 1m 1f

1:20 (1:21) 3-Y-0 £20,221 (£8,088; £6,066; £4,044; £2,022)

RPR

1 **Rhadegunda**[23] 7083 3-8-12 SPasquier 9 97
(J H M Gosden) *in tch: 6th st: brought to outside rail and led 2f out: rdn out* **59/10**[1]

2 1 1/2 **Synergy (FR)** 3-9-2 RonanThomas 6 98
(Y Durepaire, Spain)

3 1 1/2 **Sweet And Sour (IRE)**[29] 3-8-12 THuet 3 91
(Robert Collet, France)

4 nse **Sakza (IRE)**[26] 7007 3-8-12 CSoumillon 12 91
(M Delzangles, France)

5 1 1/2 **Kirkinola**[23] 3-8-12 DBonilla 2 88
(C Laffon-Parias, France)

6 2 **The World**[125] 3-8-12 MGuyon 1 84
(A Fabre, France)

7 3/4 **Bergamask (USA)**[29] 3-8-12 FVeron 10 82
(H-A Pantall, France)

8 2 **Place De L'Etoile (IRE)**[18] 7171 3-8-12 TGillet 4 78
(J E Hammond, France)

9 2 1/2 **Romance Bere (FR)**[69] 5925 3-8-12 IMendizabal 14 73
(Thomas Demeaulte, France)

10 2 **Tubular Bells (USA)**[26] 7007 3-8-12 JVictoire 11 68
(H-A Pantall, France)

11 **Moonlight Danceuse (IRE)**[21] 3-8-12 TThulliez 5 68
(F Doumen, France)

12 **Estrela Helen (FR)**[21] 3-8-12 MickaelForest 13 68
(P Bary, France)

13 **Lady MB (FR)**[33] 3-8-12 MSautjeau 8 68
(J De Roualle, France)

14 **Time To Beat (GER)**[16] 7203 3-8-12 DBoeuf 7 68
(W Baltromei, Germany)

1m 56.1s (116.10) **14 Ran SP% 14.5**
PARI-MUTUEL: WIN 6.90; PL 2.80, 6.50, 3.40; DF 68.40.
Owner A E Oppenheimer **Bred** Hascombe And Valiant Studs **Trained** Newmarket, Suffolk

NOTEBOOK
Rhadegunda, runner-up in a heavy-ground Nottingham handicap last time, ran out a comfortable winner on this first venture into listed company. She was John Gosden's 100th winner in 2008.

7414 LINGFIELD (L-H)

Monday, November 24

OFFICIAL GOING: Standard

Wind: Strong, against Weather: Cloudy becoming fine

7433 ASHURST WOOD H'CAP (DIV I) 7f (P)

12:00 (12:01) (Class 6) (0-58,58) 3-Y-0+ £1,706 (£503; £252) Stalls Low

Form RPR

5020 1 **Comrade Cotton**[14] 7270 4-8-11 52 (p) AdamKirby 8 60
(J Ryan) *trckd ldng trio: effrt wl over 1f out: hrd rdn to ld fnl 100yds: hld on* **8/1**

5600 2 nk **Surwaki (USA)**[101] 5069 6-9-3 58 EddieAhern 10 65
(R M H Cowell) *led: dictated stdy pce tl kicked on over 2f out: drvn and hdd fnl 100yds: kpt on wl* **11/2**[2]

5011 3 nk **Charming Escort**[26] 7072 4-9-1 56 RobertWinston 5 62
(T T Clement) *t.k.h early: hld up in midfield: effrt towards inner and forced to weave way through: tried to chal fnl 100yds: jst hld* **8/1**

6003 4 nk **Nikki Bea (IRE)**[84] 5575 5-8-11 52 PaulDoe 7 57
(Jamie Poulton) *hld up in abt 8th: effrt 2f out: prog and rdn ent fnl f: styd on wl: nvr quite able to chal* **7/1**

3635 5 nk **Norcroft**[15] 7254 6-9-2 57 TGMcLaughlin 6 61
(Mrs C A Dunnett) *hld up in last trio in steadily run r: effrt on wd outside 2f out: drvn and r.o fnl f: no ex last strides* **15/2**

2240 6 1/2 **Elusive Dreams (USA)**[25] 7090 4-9-2 57 (v) JimmyQuinn 4 60
(P Howling) *t.k.h early: trckd ldng pair: wnt 2nd wl over 1f out: rdn to chal ent fnl f: nt qckn and sn hld: lost several pls nr fin* **5/1**[1]

2000 7 1 1/4 **Grizedale (IRE)**[7] 7358 9-8-13 54 (tp) IanMongan 9 54
(M J Attwater) *racd wd: hld up bhd ldrs: effrt 2f out: nt qckn whn rdn over 1f out: no prog after* **16/1**

0010 8 shd **Tilsworth Charlie**[15] 7254 5-9-3 58 (b) GeorgeBaker 12 57
(J R Jenkins) *hld up fr outside draw and racd wd in midfield: effrt over 1f out: hanging lft and nt qckn* **16/1**

1030 9 1 3/4 **Alucica**[19] 7194 5-9-1 56 (v) JimCrowley 1 51
(D Shaw) *settled in midfield on inner: rdn 2f out: stl cl enough jst over 1f out: wknd fnl 100yds* **12/1**

0 10 5 **L'Art Du Silence (IRE)**[143] 3690 3-9-2 58 (p) PatCosgrave 2 39
(J R Boyle) *scrubbed along in rr and nvr gng wl: no prog* **6/1**[3]

500 11 2 3/4 **Sea Swell (USA)**[51] 6470 3-9-0 56 (t) ShaneKelly 3 30
(G A Butler) *stdd s: hld up in last: nvr a factor: rdn and no prog over 2f out* **16/1**

-021 12 1 1/4 **Station Place**[121] 4412 3-9-0 56 JamieSpencer 11 26+
(A B Haynes) *trckd ldr to wl over 1f out: wkng whn squeezed out ent fnl f: eased* **20/1**

1m 25.66s (0.86) **Going Correction** -0.025s/f (Stan)
WFA 3 from 4yo+ 1lb **12 Ran SP% 122.9**
Speed ratings (Par 101): **94,93,93,92,92 92,90,90,88,82 79,78**
toteswinger: 1&2 £17.60, 1&3 £16.50, 2&3 £16.90. CSF £53.61 CT £380.34 TOTE £11.60: £3.70, £3.30, £2.00; EX 80.40 TRIFECTA Not won..
Owner John Ryan Racing Partnership **Bred** Jeremy Gompertz **Trained** Newmarket, Suffolk
■ Stewards' Enquiry : Pat Cosgrave one-day ban: careless riding (Dec 8)

FOCUS
A moderate handicap run at an ordinary pace and typical Lingfield form, with the first eight covered by just under three lengths. The form is modest.

7434 EUROPEAN BREEDERS' FUND MAIDEN STKS (DIV I) 1m (P)

12:30 (12:31) (Class 5) 2-Y-0 £3,238 (£963; £481; £240) Stalls High

Form RPR

5 1 **Sonning Gate**[30] 6977 2-9-3 0 GeorgeBaker 7 74+
(D R C Elsworth) *hld up in tch: smooth prog over 2f out to go 2nd wl over 1f out: shkn up to ld 1f out: rn green but sn wl in command* **9/4**[1]

5 2 1 1/2 **Fortuni (IRE)**[10] 7312 2-9-3 0 J-PGuillambert 2 71+
(Sir Mark Prescott) *stdd s: hld up in last trio: pushed along 1/2-way and green after: prog 2f out: styd on wl to take 2nd nr fin: do bttr* **7/2**[2]

6 3 3/4 **Leceile (USA)**[12] 7289 2-8-12 0 TonyCulhane 9 61
(W J Haggas) *prom: wnt 2nd 1/2-way: led over 2f out: drvn and hdd 1f out: one pce* **33/1**

3 4 1 **Lord Chancellor (IRE)**[41] 6720 2-9-3 0 JamieSpencer 3 64+
(M Johnston) *trckd ldrs on inner: lost pl 1/2-way: plld out and effrt over 2f out: rdn and kpt on fr over 1f out: nt pce to threaten* **9/4**[1]

56 5 hd **Simon Gray**[30] 6978 2-9-3 0 RichardHughes 4 63+
(R Hannon) *led 2f: trckd ldrs after: effrt on inner over 1f out: chal ent fnl f: fdd fnl 100yds* **4/1**[3]

06 6 1 **Great Bounder (CAN)**[18] 7204 2-9-3 0 SteveDrowne 8 61
(J R Best) *led after 2f to over 2f out: shkn up and stl cl up over 1f out: fdd fnl f* **33/1**

The Form Book, Raceform Ltd, Compton, RG20 6NL

0 **7** ½ **Eurotanz (IRE)**[25] 7097 2-8-12 0 .... TravisBlock 6 55
(H Morrison) *trckd ldrs: rdn 3f out: tried to cl over 1f out: nt qckn and hld after* **66/1**

8 *5* **Rockson (IRE)** 2-8-12 0 .... MichaelHills 5 44
(B W Hills) *dwlt and rousted along to rchy midfield: rdn and no prog over 2f out: fdd* **14/1**

9 *shd* **Dulce Domum** 2-8-12 0 .... DaneO'Neill 11 44
(A B Haynes) *hld up in last pair: rdn over 2f out: no prog* **66/1**

00 **10** *nse* **Top Tinker**[31] 6944 2-8-10 0 .... AshleyMorgan(7) 1 49
(M H Tompkins) *a towards rr: struggling in last pair wl over 2f out* **100/1**

00 **11** *shd* **Ma Patrice**[61] 6205 2-8-12 0 .... AdamKirby 10 44
(T D McCarthy) *prom tl wknd wl over 2f out* **100/1**

1m 39.08s (0.88) **Going Correction** -0.025s/f (Stan) **11** Ran SP% **121.3**
Speed ratings (Par 96): **94,92,91,90,90 89,89,84,83,83 83**
toteswinger: 1&2 £3.90, 1&3 £17.30, 2&3 £15.60. CSF £10.70 TOTE £3.80: £1.30, £1.20, £8.20; EX 13.70 Trifecta £172.80 Pool: £296.58, 1.27 winning units..
Owner A Heaney **Bred** Sunley Stud **Trained** Newmarket, Suffolk

FOCUS
An interesting maiden for the time of year and a likeable winner, although this bare form cannot be pitched much higher.

NOTEBOOK
Sonning Gate ◆ confirmed the promise he showed when a running-on fifth over this trip on his debut at Newbury. A half-brother to a triple Polytrack winner, the switch to this surface was in his favour, and he took this in tidy style. It's fair to say that some sort of excuse can be made for his three main market rivals, but he still looked very green when coming under pressure and can step forward significantly on the bare form. He has plenty of size and should make a lovely three-year-old, particularly on a more galloping track. (tchd 2-1 and 5-2)
Fortuni(IRE) ◆ was equally as promising as the winner and stepped up on the form he showed on his debut over 7f at Kempton, but still looked green. He didn't travel very well, but gradually responded to pressure and was going on at the finish as his stamina kicked in. He should have no trouble at all winning a similar event if persevered with this year, but we are unlikely to see the best of him until he steps up to middle distances next season. He has loads of scope and rates as a very useful prospect. (op 11-2)
Leceile(USA) moved well for much of the way and improved significantly on the form she showed on her debut over 7f at Wolverhampton. She should win a maiden and would have an obvious chance in fillies-only company.
Lord Chancellor(IRE) was the least imposing of the market principals in the paddock and also got warm. After losing his position towards the inside, he swung wide with his effort, but lacked the pace to get involved. He already looks in need of 1m2f. Official explanation: jockey said colt hung left in straight (op 2-1 tchd 15-8)
Simon Gray was a little keen early and could not sustain his effort. His rider was not hard on him once his winning chance had gone and he now has the option of handicaps. (op 3-1 tchd 9-2)
Great Bounder(CAN) ◆ showed ability and could do better over shorter now he is eligible for a handicap mark. (op 40-1)

7435 PHOTO FINISH FOR CHRISTMAS GIFTS @ EVENTIMAGE.TV H'CAP 6f (P)
1:00 (1:00) (Class 5) (0-70,74) 3-Y-0+ **£2,729** (£806; £403) **Stalls** Low

Form RPR

6005 **1** **Chjimes (IRE)**[17] 7225 4-9-4 **70** .... LPKeniry 2 79
(C R Dore) *racd keenly: trckd ldrs: effrt to ld jst over 1f out: kpt on wl enough fnl f* **8/1**

010 **2** *1* **The Cayterers**[42] 6706 6-8-12 **69** .... MCGeran(5) 10 75
(A W Carroll) *hld up in last trio: prog over 1f out: styd on wl to take 2nd fnl 75yds: edgd rt and unable to chal* **12/1**

0640 **3** *nk* **Forest Dane**[40] 6734 8-9-4 **70** .... GeorgeBaker 11 75
(Mrs N Smith) *hld up in last trio: prog towards inner over 1f out: n.m.r wl ins fnl f but styd on to take 3rd nr fin* **7/1**[2]

2251 **4** ½ **Brandywell Boy (IRE)**[5] 7378 5-9-1 **74** 6ex .... BillyCray(7) 4 77
(D J S Ffrench Davis) *t.k.h early: pressed ldrs and racd towards outer: rdn 2f out: chsd wnr jst ins fnl f: nt qckn and hld after* **5/1**[1]

0020 **5** *1* **Interactive (IRE)**[34] 6890 5-9-1 **67** .... AlanDaly 9 67
(Andrew Turnell) *racd wd: hld up in midfield: nt qckn and looked wl btn over 1f out: styd on again fnl 150yds* **10/1**

451 **6** *nse* **Motivated Choice**[49] 6543 3-9-1 **67** .... DaneO'Neill 7 67+
(L M Cumani) *hld up in midfield: lost pl 2f out: shkn up and nt qckn over 1f out: kpt on* **7/1**[2]

6600 **7** ½ **Lieutenant Pigeon**[42] 6695 3-9-3 **69** .... PaulEddery 8 67
(G D Blake) *hld up in rr: dropped to last pair 1/2-way: pushed along over 1f out: styd on steadily* **22/1**

2054 **8** ½ **Bookiesindex Boy**[14] 7276 4-9-4 **70** .... (v) RichardHughes 1 67
(J R Jenkins) *w ldr: led 2f out to jst over 1f out: wknd fnl 100yds* **14/1**

1613 **9** *shd* **Lord Deevert**[17] 7225 3-8-8 **65** .... JackDean(5) 5 61
(W G M Turner) *narrow ld to 2f out: wknd jst over 1f out* **15/2**[3]

3606 **10** *2* **Cativo Cavallino**[42] 6695 5-9-3 **69** .... RichardThomas 6 59+
(J E Long) *prom but racd wd: rdn 1/2-way: lost pl wl over 1f out: no ch whn squeezed out ins fnl f* **9/1**

0303 **11** 2¾ **Mafaheem**[18] 7206 6-9-4 **70** .... JamieSpencer 12 51
(A B Haynes) *a in rr and wd: shkn up and no prog 2f out* **12/1**

0021 **12** *3* **Grand Palace (IRE)**[12] 7292 5-8-13 **65** .... (v) DarrenWilliams 3 37
(D Shaw) *trckd ldrs on inner: rdn over 2f out: wknd over 1f out: eased whn no ch* **7/1**[2]

1m 11.71s (-0.19) **Going Correction** -0.025s/f (Stan) **12** Ran SP% **122.5**
Speed ratings (Par 103): **100,98,98,97,96 96,95,94,94,92 88,84**
toteswinger: 1&2 £63.30, 1&3 £11.10, 2&3 £68.80. CSF £103.77 CT £727.32 TOTE £12.50: £3.20, £4.10, £3.00; EX 167.40 TRIFECTA Not won..
Owner Sean J Murphy **Bred** Morgan O'Flaherty **Trained** West Pinchbeck, Lincs

FOCUS
A modest but very competitive sprint handicap and a few of these came into this on good marks. The form looks sound with the third the best guide.

7436 FOREST ROW CLAIMING STKS 7f (P)
1:30 (1:30) (Class 6) 3-Y-0+ **£1,978** (£584; £292) **Stalls** Low

Form RPR

3100 **1** **Monkey Glas (IRE)**[117] 4522 4-9-3 93 .... (v) AndrewElliott 1 77
(K R Burke) *sn trckd ldr: led after 2f: drvn at least 3l clr jst over 2f out: tired fnl f: hld on* **11/8**[1]

1204 **2** *nk* **I Confess**[14] 7277 3-9-0 67 .... (b) TGMcLaughlin 11 73
(P D Evans) *hld up bhd ldrs: rdn and prog to chse wnr wl over 1f out: clsd fnl f: nt find enough* **7/1**

3652 **3** ¾ **Desert Dreamer (IRE)**[167] 2917 7-9-3 80 .... RichardKingscote 7 76+
(Tom Dascombe) *hld up wl off the pce: clsd gng wl fr 3f out: wnr already kicked clr whn nt clr run wl over 1f out: wnt 3rd jst over 1f out: styd on but post c too sn* **10/3**[2]

3500 **4** 1¾ **Aegean Pride**[35] 6867 3-8-7 60 .... FrancisNorton 6 59
(R Hannon) *hld up wl off the pce: stdy prog on outer 3f out: outpcd 2f out: rdn and kpt on fr over 1f out* **10/1**

0600 **5** *6* **Bombardier Wells**[11] 7302 3-8-11 67 .... StephenCarson 4 47
(Eve Johnson Houghton) *hld up wl off the pce: struggling 3f out: no real ch after* **20/1**

6012 **6** 2½ **Stand In Flames**[28] 7018 3-8-9 78 .... ShaneKelly 3 38
(Pat Eddery) *led 2f: chsd wnr to 2f out: wknd* **5/1**[3]

0040 **7** *hd* **Follow Your Spirit**[28] 7018 3-8-9 49 .... CatherineGannon 2 38
(B Palling) *tk v t.k.h early: trckd ldng pair: rdn over 2f out: wnt 2nd briefly 2f out: sn wknd* **50/1**

8 *7* **Special Chapter (IRE)** 3-8-8 0 ow1 .... SteveDrowne 5 18
(A B Haynes) *dwlt: sn t.o* **50/1**

2000 **9** 2½ **Millfields Dreams**[65] 6125 9-8-10 68 .... (p) LPKeniry 9 13
(P Leech) *chsd ldrs: u.p 1/2-way: wknd over 2f out: t.o* **14/1**

1m 24.31s (-0.49) **Going Correction** -0.025s/f (Stan)
WFA 3 from 4yo+ 1lb **9** Ran SP% **118.8**
Speed ratings (Par 101): **101,100,99,97,90 88,87,79,77**
toteswinger: 1&2 £3.00, 1&3 £2.10, 2&3 £4.80. CSF £12.19 TOTE £2.10: £1.40, £1.60, £1.30; EX 11.40 Trifecta £36.00 Pool: £226.06, 4.64 winning units..Monkey Glas was claimed by Horses First Racing Limited for £12,000.
Owner Mrs Elaine M Burke **Bred** D Bourke And Yuriy Meduedyev **Trained** Middleham Moor, N Yorks

FOCUS
A typical claimer in which the winner was well below his best in beating a rival rated considerably lower. The runner-up is rated to this year's best.
Desert Dreamer(IRE) Official explanation: jockey said gelding was denied a clear run

7437 ASHURST WOOD H'CAP (DIV II) 7f (P)
2:00 (2:01) (Class 6) (0-58,62) 3-Y-0+ **£1,706** (£503; £252) **Stalls** Low

Form RPR

5063 **1** **Royal Manor**[9] 7340 3-9-2 **58** .... FergusSweeney 11 70+
(N J Vaughan) *fast away fr wd draw: mde all: set mod pce tl kicked on over 2f out: at least 2 l clr ent fnl f: all out* **7/2**[1]

0022 **2** ½ **Ugenius**[10] 7320 4-8-12 **53** .... TGMcLaughlin 4 62
(Mrs C A Dunnett) *trckd ldrs: rdn over 2f out: picked up over 1f out: wnt 2nd fnl 100yds: gaining fast on wnr fin* **7/1**[2]

0025 **3** 1½ **Melt (IRE)**[15] 7256 3-9-1 **57** .... RichardHughes 9 61
(R Hannon) *trckd wnr: rdn over 2f out: no imp over 1f out: one pce and lost 2nd fnl 100yds* **8/1**

0346 **4** ½ **Convivial Spirit**[28] 7012 4-9-3 **58** .... (t) LPKeniry 10 62
(E F Vaughan) *hld up in midfield: effrt 2f out: hrd rdn and no prog over 1f out: styd on wl fnl 150yds: gaining at fin* **15/2**[3]

4510 **5** *1* **Hurricane Coast**[7] 7357 9-9-2 **57** .... (b) TonyCulhane 12 58
(D Flood) *hld up bhd ldrs on outer: outpcd 2f out: nt qckn over 1f out: kpt on* **8/1**

5450 **6** *1* **Eleanor Eloise (USA)**[15] 7254 4-8-11 **52** .... SteveDrowne 1 50
(J R Gask) *chsd ldng pair to over 1f out: fdd fnl f* **8/1**

0545 **7** *hd* **Upstairs**[158] 3162 4-8-13 **57** .... MarcHalford(3) 2 55
(D R C Elsworth) *hld up in midfield on inner: effrt and sme prog over 1f out: shkn up and no hdwy fnl f* **8/1**

0520 **8** ¾ **Bidable**[32] 6928 4-8-11 **52** .... CatherineGannon 5 48+
(B Palling) *t.k.h early: hld up in last pair: sme prog but no ch whn short of room jst ins fnl f: nvr nr ldrs and eased fnl 50yds* **12/1**

0040 **9** 2¼ **Torquemada (IRE)**[5] 7382 7-8-7 **55** .... (t) KierenFox(7) 7 45
(M J Attwater) *s.i.s: t.k.h early and hld up in last pair: prog on outer 3f out: lost pl and struggling 2f out* **16/1**

U050 **10** 1¾ **Dynamo Dave (USA)**[43] 6683 3-8-9 **56** ow1 .... GabrielHannon(5) 8 40
(M D I Usher) *hld up in rr: urged along and no prog over 2f out* **33/1**

42 **11** ½ **Charlie Allnut**[63] 6173 3-9-1 **57** .... (p) ChrisCatlin 6 39
(S Wynne) *a towards rr: rdn and no prog over 2f out* **7/1**[2]

1m 25.19s (0.39) **Going Correction** -0.025s/f (Stan)
WFA 3 from 4yo+ 1lb **11** Ran SP% **119.9**
Speed ratings (Par 101): **96,95,93,93,92 90,90,89,87,85 84**
toteswinger: 1&2 £3.90, 1&3 £5.80, 2&3 £10.70. CSF £28.14 CT £190.10 TOTE £3.70: £1.50, £2.40, £3.20; EX 31.10 Trifecta £109.00 Pool: £241.64, 1.64 winning units..
Owner Owen Promotions Limited **Bred** Newsells Park Stud Limited **Trained** Hampton, Cheshire

FOCUS
The quicker of the two divisions by 0.47sec. Sound form for the grade, with the winner a bit better than the bare form.
Bidable Official explanation: jockey said filly was denied a clear run

7438 EUROPEAN BREEDERS' FUND MAIDEN STKS (DIV II) 1m (P)
2:35 (2:36) (Class 5) 2-Y-O **£3,238** (£963; £481; £240) **Stalls** High

Form RPR

1 **Haashed (USA)** 2-9-3 0 .... JamieSpencer 6 90+
(M Johnston) *sn trckd ldr: cruised into ld wl over 1f out and brought wd: shkn up briefly ent fnl f: in n.d after: promising* **7/4**[1]

5 **2** *2* **Formula (USA)**[24] 7104 2-9-3 0 .... RichardHughes 10 83+
(R Hannon) *cl up: trckd ldng pair over 2f out: brought wd in st: wnt 2nd 1f out: rdn and styd on wl enough but no imp* **9/4**[2]

335 **3** *6* **Featherweight (IRE)**[43] 6674 2-8-12 75 .... MichaelHills 3 65
(B W Hills) *sn led: rdn and hdd wl over 1f out: brushed aside* **3/1**[3]

06 **4** 3¾ **Kattar**[18] 7209 2-9-0 0 .... MarcHalford(3) 2 62
(D M Simcock) *trckd ldrs: rdn to chse ldng trio over 2f out: easily lft bhd* **9/1**

0 **5** 1¾ **Windpfeil (IRE)**[9] 7336 2-9-3 0 .... NickyMackay 4 58+
(J H M Gosden) *wl in rr: rdn over 3f out: modest prog to take remote 5th wl over 1f out: kpt on* **25/1**

6 1½ **Maison D'Or** 2-9-3 0 .... SteveDrowne 8 54+
(R Ingram) *wl in rr: rdn over 3f out: plugged on into remote 6th over 1f out* **50/1**

7 1½ **Joannadarc (USA)** 2-8-12 0 .... PatCosgrave 1 46+
(S A Callaghan) *s.s: hld up in last pair: sme prog 3f out: nudged along and nvr on terms* **33/1**

0000 **8** *8* **Prima Fonteyn**[113] 4666 2-8-12 46 .... NeilChalmers 9 29
(Miss Sheena West) *w ldrs 2f: steadily lost grnd: wl bhd over 1f out* **66/1**

00 **9** *13* **Green Endeavour (CAN)**[18] 7209 2-9-3 0 .... JimCrowley 5 5
(Mrs A J Perrett) *in tch tl wknd over 2f out: t.o* **25/1**

0P **10** *51* **My Baby Love**[9] 7332 2-8-12 0 .... J-PGuillambert 11 —
(J Akehurst) *in tch in rr to 3f out: wknd rapidly: t.o and virtually p.u over 1f out* **66/1**

1m 37.55s (-0.65) **Going Correction** -0.025s/f (Stan) **10** Ran SP% **117.7**
Speed ratings (Par 96): **102,100,94,90,88 87,85,77,64,13**
toteswinger: 1&2 £2.00, 1&3 £2.10, 2&3 £2.70. CSF £5.63 TOTE £2.70: £1.30, £1.50, £1.10; EX 6.70 Trifecta £19.20 Pool: £567.50, 21.79 winning units..

Owner Hamdan Al Maktoum **Bred** London Thoroughbred Services Ltd **Trained** Middleham Moor, N Yorks

FOCUS
A winning time 1.53secs quicker than the first division, which looked a good race, and the wide margin back to the third suggests that the front two are very decent. Haashed could go on to much better things.

NOTEBOOK
Haashed(USA) ◆ created a fine impression on his debut. A $450,000 half-brother to the stable's smart 1m2f winner Zaham, he was always travelling well on the speed and needed mainly just hands-and-heels riding to keep Formula at bay. According to connections he may well be given another spin on the sand this winter, but whatever they opt for he rates as a very smart prospect. (op 5-2 tchd 11-4 in a place)
Formula(USA) ◆ posted a big effort in defeat, pulling well clear of all bar the very useful winner, and this was a significant improvement on the form he showed on his debut over 6f at Newmarket. A similar race should be a formality next time. (op 2-1 tchd 15-8 and 5-2)
Featherweight(IRE) was no match whatsoever for the front pair, but she looks to have run into a couple of very smart colts. (op 9-4)
Kattar ◆ was nibbled at in the market and travelled well early, but he was left behind when it mattered in what was a hot race. He should find his level now he is eligible for a handicap mark. (op 10-1)
Windpfeil(IRE) is probably more of a long-term prospect.

7439 MARSH GREEN H'CAP — 1m (P)
3:05 (3:06) (Class 4) (0-85,85) 3-Y-O+ £4,727 (£1,406; £702; £351) Stalls High

Form RPR
0012 1 **Mister New York (USA)**[5] 7386 3-8-13 **80** ... JimCrowley 11 89
(Noel T Chance) *hld up in last trio: wound up on wd outside fr over 2f out: sustained run fr over 1f out: to ld nr fin* **8/1**
1003 2 ½ **Rambling Light**[11] 7302 4-8-11 **76** ... (v[1]) LPKeniry 5 84
(A M Balding) *hld up in midfield: eased towards outer wl over 1f out: prog to ld 1f out: r.o: hdd nr fin* **8/1**
6110 3 1¼ **Prince Of Thebes (IRE)**[11] 7299 7-9-1 **80** ... PaulDoe 4 84
(M J Attwater) *t.k.h early: hld up bhd ldrs: rdn and cl up 2f out: styd on same pce fr over 1f out* **20/1**
2304 4 hd **Dichoh**[18] 7215 5-9-2 **81** ... MichaelHills 7 85
(M A Jarvis) *hld up in rr: effrt over 1f out: threaded through after: styd on wl fnl f but nvr able to chal* **13/2**[2]
1400 5 1¾ **The Kiddykid (IRE)**[42] 6710 8-9-4 **83** ... TGMcLaughlin 3 82
(P D Evans) *t.k.h: hld up in rr: effrt over 1f out: kpt on fnl f: nvr rchd ldrs* **20/1**
2020 6 nse **Den's Gift (IRE)**[43] 6675 4-9-2 **81** ... (b) AdamKirby 10 80
(C G Cox) *led to over 5f out: pressed ldr: rdn over 2f out: upsides 1f out on inner: fdd* **13/2**[2]
6-01 7 nk **Shavansky**[5] 7387 4-9-4 **83** 6ex ... StephenCarson 8 81
(C J Mann) *t.k.h early: pressed ldr: led over 5f out: mde most after tl hdd & wknd 1f out* **11/1**
3444 8 1¼ **Councellor (FR)**[10] 7313 6-9-5 **84** ... (t) PatCosgrave 12 79
(Stef Liddiard) *pressed ldrs on outer: rdn over 2f out: fdd fnl f* **16/1**
6024 9 1 **Palmerin**[11] 7299 3-8-11 **78** ... RichardHughes 9 70
(R Hannon) *hld up bhd ldrs on outer: nt qckn over 1f out: sn lost pl* **15/2**
6210 10 ¾ **Gallantry**[18] 7215 6-9-6 **85** ... JimmyQuinn 6 75+
(P Howling) *missed s bdly and lost at least 5 l: in tch in last pair after 2f: effrt on inner over 1f out: no real prog* **6/1**[1]
-406 11 2½ **Robby Bobby**[12] 7291 3-9-2 **83** ... JamieSpencer 1 66
(M Johnston) *t.k.h early: hld up bhd ldrs: pushed along over 1f out: folded tamely* **7/1**[3]
1-20 12 11 **Alpes Maritimes**[208] 1719 4-9-6 **85** ... GeorgeBaker 2 39
(G L Moore) *hld up in last pair: shkn up and no prog over 2f out* **8/1**

1m 36.24s (-1.96) **Going Correction** -0.025s/f (Stan) course record
WFA 3 from 4yo+ 2lb 12 Ran SP% **122.3**
Speed ratings (Par 105): **108,107,106,106,104 104,103,102,101,100 98,87**
toteswinger: 1&2 £19.30, 1&3 £24.80, 2&3 £36.80. CSF £72.99 CT £1259.62 TOTE £11.20: £2.90, £3.40, £6.70; EX 98.10 TRIFECTA Not won..
Owner Chance, Talbot & Taylor **Bred** J S McDonald **Trained** Upper Lambourn, Berks

FOCUS
A good, competitive handicap, and solid form.
Gallantry Official explanation: jockey said gelding missed the break

7440 ANNA BUSBRIDGE MEMORIAL H'CAP — 1m 2f (P)
3:35 (3:35) (Class 6) (0-65,65) 3-Y-O+ £2,047 (£604; £302) Stalls Low

Form RPR
0063 1 **Can Can Star**[11] 7301 5-9-3 **60** ... ShaneKelly 2 68+
(A W Carroll) *hld up in midfield: prog on inner over 2f out: disp 3rd jst over 1f out: styd on wl fnl f: led post* **6/1**[2]
0001 2 shd **Lord Theo**[25] 7094 4-9-7 **64** ... JamesDoyle 12 72
(N P Littmoden) *led: drew clr fr 1/2-way: 8 l clr 3f out: tired and drvn over 1f out: eased briefly 50yds out: hdd post* **17/2**
0051 3 nse **Siena Star (IRE)**[32] 6927 10-9-1 **58** ... PatCosgrave 11 66
(Stef Liddiard) *chsd ldr: 8 l down 3f out: clsd grad fr 2f out: gaining at fin but lost 2nd last strides* **8/1**
0652 4 1¼ **Risque Heights**[28] 7009 4-9-6 **63** ... GeorgeBaker 9 68
(J R Boyle) *hld up wl in rr: prog on outer to go prom in chsng gp 3f out: disp 3rd jst over 1f out: kpt on same pce after* **2/1**[1]
5644 5 2 **The City Kid (IRE)**[9] 7345 5-9-2 **59** ... RichardHughes 8 60
(Miss Gay Kelleway) *mostly chsd clr ldng pair: drvn over 2f out: one pce and lost pl jst over 1f out* **12/1**
0000 6 3 **Our Kes (IRE)**[45] 6629 6-9-7 **64** ... IanMongan 4 59+
(P Howling) *hld up wl in rr: effrt on wd outside over 2f out: nvr any ch: plugged on* **25/1**
6045 7 ½ **Pearl Dealer (IRE)**[7] 7368 3-9-0 **64** ... (t) LukeMorris(3) 5 58
(N J Vaughan) *wl plcd in chsng gp: rdn wl over 2f out: no imp as others sed to cl: fdd* **7/1**[3]
2443 8 1½ **Cherri Fosfate**[28] 7032 4-9-3 **65** ... (b) MarkFlynn(5) 6 56
(Paul W Flynn, Ire) *hld up in midfield: no prog whn pack tried to cl on clr ldr over 2f out* **25/1**
0065 9 hd **Cover Drive (USA)**[26] 7078 5-9-0 **57** ... EdwardCreighton 3 48
(Christian Wroe) *stdd s: hld up in last pair: effrt on outer over 2f out: no real prog* **12/1**
640 10 1¾ **Cape Of Luck (IRE)**[12] 6577 5-9-3 **60** ... (p) CatherineGannon 10 48
(P M Phelan) *hld up in last pair: no real prog whn pack tried to cl on runaway ldr over 2f out* **10/1**
6003 11 3¾ **Sir Haydn**[15] 7261 8-8-12 **55** ... (v) RichardKingscote 7 35
(J R Jenkins) *t.k.h early: prom in chsng gp: rdn and lost pl 3f out: sn btn* **14/1**
0404 12 4 **Sir Billy Nick**[37] 6827 3-9-1 **62** ... ChrisCatlin 1 34
(S Wynne) *hld up in midfield: lost pl and btn 3f out: sn bhd* **12/1**

2m 5.52s (-1.08) **Going Correction** -0.025s/f (Stan)
WFA 3 from 4yo+ 4lb 12 Ran SP% **128.3**
Speed ratings (Par 101): **103,102,102,101,100 97,97,96,96,94 91,88**
toteswinger: 1&2 £9.00, 1&3 £11.60, 2&3 £11.90. CSF £61.34 CT £423.36 TOTE £9.80: £2.10, £2.80, £3.30; EX 84.80 Trifecta £409.80 Part won. Pool: £553.85, 0.30 winning units. Place 6: £60.76, Place 5: £13.17..
Owner K F Coleman **Bred** A W And I Robinson **Trained** Cropthorne, Worcs

FOCUS
A moderate handicap, but a race with a dramatic conclusion, as Lord Theo, who built up a big lead after setting a good pace, and was still around seven lengths clear at the top of the straight, was nabbed on the post after his jockey glanced at the big screen yards from the line. The form is sound enough rated around the placed horses.
Cover Drive(USA) Official explanation: jockey said gelding hung right
Cape Of Luck(IRE) Official explanation: jockey said gelding hung left
T/Plt: £138.30 to a £1 stake. Pool: £45,248.13. 238.76 winning tickets. T/Qpdt: £9.80 to a £1 stake. Pool: £4,725.40. 356.40 winning tickets. JN

7369 SOUTHWELL (L-H)
Tuesday, November 25

OFFICIAL GOING: Standard
A strong tailwind helped propel the runners up the home straight.
Wind: Fresh behind Weather: Fine and dry

7441 PLAY GOLF AT SOUTHWELL GOLF CLUB AMATEUR RIDERS' H'CAP (DIV I) — 1m (F)
12:10 (12:11) (Class 6) (0-60,60) 3-Y-O+ £1,648 (£507; £253) Stalls Low

Form RPR
4501 1 **Salerosa (IRE)**[21] 7178 3-11-2 **57** ... MrSWalker 8 65
(Mrs A Duffield) *trckd ldrs: pushed along and hdwy wl over 2f out: rdn to ld ent fnl f: drvn and kpt on wl towards fin* **4/1**[1]
0002 2 ¾ **Boss Hog**[15] 7267 3-11-5 **60** ... MissFayeBramley 5 66
(P A Blockley) *prom: hdwy to trck ldrs 3f out: rdn to ld 2f out: drvn over 1f out: hdd ent fnl f: kpt on u.p* **15/2**
54-4 3 nk **Mambo Sun**[15] 7270 5-10-11 **57** ... MissCBoxall(7) 11 63
(P A Blockley) *hld up in midfield: hdwy over 2f out: rdn to chal over 1f out: ev ch tl drvn and one pce wl ins fnl f* **13/2**[3]
0063 4 3½ **Louisiade (IRE)**[21] 7184 7-11-2 **60** ... (p) MrKJames(5) 6 58
(M C Chapman) *hld up: hdwy on inner over 2f out: rdn to chse ldrs over 1f out: kpt on same pce ent fnl f* **16/1**
0112 5 ¾ **The Grey One (IRE)**[8] 7368 5-10-13 **59** ... (p) MissHDavies(7) 14 56
(J M Bradley) *hld up in rr: wd st: hdwy on outer wl over 1f out: kpt on ins fnl f: nt rch ldrs* **11/2**[2]
0504 6 ½ **Sedge (USA)**[11] 7316 8-10-10 **54** ... (be) MissWGibson(5) 7 49
(P T Midgley) *dwlt and rr: hdwy wl over 2f out: sn rdn: styd on ins fnl f: nrst fin* **12/1**
6430 7 hd **Aggbag**[207] 1780 4-10-10 **54** ... MissAWallace(5) 4 49
(B P J Baugh) *chsd ldrs on inner: rdn along over 2f out and sn one pce* **20/1**
1036 8 6 **Mister Jingles**[28] 7048 5-11-3 **59** ... MissNJefferson(3) 9 40
(R M Whitaker) *cl up: rdn along over 2f out: drvn wl over 1f out and sn wknd* **10/1**
6030 9 2¾ **Ten To The Dozen**[7] 7373 5-10-10 **49** ... (b) MrsMarieKing 10 24
(P W Hiatt) *sn led: rdn along 3f out: hdd 2f out and sn wknd* **16/1**
0120 10 10 **Uhuru Peak**[55] 6396 7-11-2 **55** ... (bt) MissSBrotherton 3 7
(M W Easterby) *dwlt: sn chsng ldrs: rdn along 3f out and sn wknd* **10/1**
1654 11 ½ **Wallonia (IRE)**[27] 7070 3-11-5 **60** ... MrSDobson 13 10
(K A Ryan) *chsd ldrs on outer: rdn along wl over 2f out: sn wknd* **8/1**
000- 12 1¼ **The Tinker Man**[474] 4313 4-10-11 **50** ... MrLeeNewnes 12 —
(M D I Usher) *cl up: rdn along 3f out and sn wknd* **40/1**
0006 13 1½ **Blue Empire (IRE)**[15] 7267 7-10-6 **52** ... (p) MrBenHamilton(7) 2 —
(Ollie Pears) *s.i.s: a in rr* **20/1**

1m 46.26s (2.56) **Going Correction** +0.05s/f (Slow)
WFA 3 from 4yo+ 2lb 13 Ran SP% **121.2**
Speed ratings (Par 101): **89,88,87,84,83 83,83,77,74,64 63,62,61**
toteswinger: 1&2 £7.70, 1&3 £7.50, 2&3 £15.60. CSF £33.05 CT £202.91 TOTE £4.50: £1.60, £3.00, £3.70; EX 41.20 Trifecta £53.20 Part won. Pool: £71.90, 0.20 winning units..
Owner David K Barker **Bred** Pedro Rosas **Trained** Constable Burton, N Yorks

FOCUS
This was a moderate amateur riders' handicap in which the front three pulled clear. The time was a shade quicker than that for division two and this is sound form for a race of this nature.

7442 PLAY GOLF AT SOUTHWELL GOLF CLUB AMATEUR RIDERS' H'CAP (DIV II) — 1m (F)
12:40 (12:40) (Class 6) (0-60,60) 3-Y-O+ £1,648 (£507; £253) Stalls Low

Form RPR
3022 1 **Vogarth**[21] 7178 4-10-9 **55** ... MrPMillman(7) 14 64
(B R Millman) *cl up: led over 3f out: rdn clr 2f out: drvn ins fnl f: kpt on* **5/1**[1]
02 2 1¼ **Barataria**[15] 7270 6-10-11 **55** ... MissRBastiman(5) 6 61+
(R Bastiman) *v.s.a and bhd: hdwy over 3f out: rdn 2f out: styd on strly ent fnl f: nt rch wnr* **11/2**[2]
0405 3 1 **Outer Hebrides**[6] 7382 7-10-8 **52** ... (v) MissSBradley(5) 4 56
(J M Bradley) *prom: effrt over 2f out: rdn to chse wnr wl over 1f out: kpt on ins fnl f* **12/1**
2405 4 1½ **Kingsmaite**[13] 7286 7-10-12 **58** ... (b) MrKApark(7) 13 59
(S R Bowring) *sn led: rdn along and hdd over 3f out: drvn 2f out and kpt on same pce* **10/1**
0553 5 shd **Bavarica**[10] 7342 6-11-1 **59** ... (e) MrRBirkett(5) 8 59
(Miss J Feilden) *in tch: hdwy 3f out: rdn along 2f out: sn drvn and kpt on same pce* **5/1**[1]
2005 6 1¾ **Magical Song**[103] 2704 3-10-11 **52** ... (b) MissFayeBramley 2 47
(P A Blockley) *prom: rdn along wl over 2f out: sn one pce* **20/1**
6000 7 14 **Inontime (IRE)**[20] 2861 3-10-8 **56** ... (p) MrHGMiller(7) 12 19
(Jean-Rene Auvray) *chsd ldrs: rdn along 3f out and sn wknd* **40/1**
0034 8 2¾ **Winged Farasi**[21] 7180 4-10-6 **48** ... (p) MrAEKinirons(3) 7 6
(Miss J E Foster) *s.i.s: a towards rr* **6/1**[3]
0404 9 1¾ **Bed Fellow (IRE)**[24] 7132 4-10-4 **50** ... (p) MissJKWilson(7) 11 4
(Paul Murphy) *s.i.s: sn in tch: rdn along 3f out and sn wknd* **14/1**
1352 10 3 **Kirstys Lad**[8] 7367 6-10-13 **57** ... MissMMullineaux(5) 3 4
(M Mullineaux) *midfield: rdn along 1/2-way: sn wknd* **8/1**

150- **11** *hd* **Nota Liberata**[378] 5557 4-11-0 **60**................................ MissVCoates(7) 1 6
(Ollie Pears) *chsd ldrs on inner: rdn along over 3f out and sn wknd* **25/1**
6000 **12** *1/2* **Tump Mac**[39] 6791 4-10-9 **55**.................................... MrSebSpencer(7) 9 —
(N Bycroft) *a in rr* **66/1**
0065 **13** *3 3/4* **Machinate (USA)**[10] 7340 6-11-2 **58**................(e1) MrBenBrisbourne(3) 5 —
(W M Brisbourne) *s.i.s: a bhd* **10/1**
1m 46.54s (2.84) **Going Correction** +0.05s/f (Slow)
WFA 3 from 4yo+ 2lb **53** Ran SP% **119.2**
Speed ratings (Par 101): **87,85,84,83,83 81,67,64,62,59 59,59,55**
toteswinger: 1&2 £4.20, 1&3 £10.40, 2&3 £13.90. CSF £30.64 CT £330.33 TOTE £7.20: £1.90, £2.10, £5.80; EX 40.50 Trifecta £91.10 Part won. Pool: £123.19, 0.43 winning units..
Owner P Millman **Bred** Rosyground Stud **Trained** Kentisbeare, Devon
■ A first winner for 16-year-old jockey Patrick Milman, son of trainer Rod.

FOCUS
Another moderate contest in which the front six pulled miles clear of the others and the winning time was 0.28 seconds slower than the first division. The form looks sound enough.

7443 SOUTHWELL-RACECOURSE.CO.UK CLAIMING STKS 7f (F)
1:10 (1:10) (Class 6) 2-Y-O **£2,047** (£604; £302) **Stalls** Low

Form RPR
5451 **1** **Kinigi (IRE)**[15] 7266 2-7-9 59........................... AndreaAtzeni(7) 10 53
(S A Callaghan) *prom on outer: effrt to ld over 2f out and sn rdn: drvn ins fnl f and kpt on wl* **10/11**[1]
3252 **2** *shd* **Svindal (IRE)**[13] 7283 2-8-9 58.......................(b) FrancisNorton 6 60
(K A Ryan) *trckd ldrs: hdwy over 2f out: rdn to chal over 1f out: drvn ins fnl f and ev ch tl no ex nr fin* **6/1**[3]
1012 **3** *nse* **Smalljohn**[15] 7275 2-9-5 74..............................(v) TomEaves 5 70
(B Smart) *led: rdn along and hdd over 2f out: drvn over 1f out: rallied ins fnl f and ev ch tl no ex nr fin* **11/4**[2]
06 **4** *8* **Paint Splash**[11] 7318 2-8-8 0.............................. GrahamGibbons 3 39
(T D Barron) *chsd ldrs: rdn along over 2f out and sn one pce* **20/1**
5033 **5** *6* **Courageous Nature (IRE)**[11] 7319 2-8-11 55.............(p) PatCosgrave 2 27
(A J McCabe) *trckd ldrs: effrt over 2f out and sn rdn: swtchd rt and drvn over 1f out: sn wknd* **18/1**
430 **6** *6* **Rio Gael (IRE)**[18] 7227 2-9-5 60.............................(p) TGMcLaughlin 1 20
(M S Saunders) *chsd ldrs on inner: rdn along 3f out and sn wknd* **40/1**
7 *nse* **First Hand** 2-9-0 0.. DaleGibson 8 15
(M W Easterby) *s.i.s and a in rr* **80/1**
600 **8** *1/2* **Lonsdale Lad**[71] 5959 2-8-10 40.......................... JamesO'Reilly(5) 4 15
(R C Guest) *in tch: rdn along over 3f out and sn wknd* **100/1**
1326 **9** *1 1/4* **Rose Of Coma (IRE)**[77] 5774 2-8-10 59.......................... ChrisCatlin 7 6
(Miss Gay Kelleway) *a in rr* **12/1**
4460 **10** *1 3/4* **Frame And Cover**[16] 7257 2-8-10 50............................. SteveDrowne 9 —
(Miss J S Davis) *prom: rdn along 1/2-way and sn wknd* **50/1**
1m 31.36s (1.06) **Going Correction** +0.05s/f (Slow) **10** Ran SP% **117.7**
Speed ratings (Par 94): **95,94,94,85,78 71,71,71,69,67**
toteswinger: 1&2 £3.50, 1&3 £1.90, 2&3 £3.00. CSF £6.92 TOTE £1.70: £1.30, £1.40, £1.10; EX 7.80 Trifecta £21.70 Pool: £491.27, 16.70 winning units..The winner was claimed by C R Dore for £4,000.
Owner James M Egan **Bred** Corduff Stud **Trained** Newmarket, Suffolk

FOCUS
An ordinary claimer. Only three mattered in the market and the trio pulled a long way from the others to battle out the finish. The runner-up helps set the level, with the winner 8lb below form in success.

NOTEBOOK
Kinigi(IRE) was dropping in class after running out the narrow winner of a course-and-distance nursery 15 days previously, and he was sent off a well-backed favourite. Kept wide from her outside stall, she looked like winning comfortably when sent for home off the final bend, but she could never quite shake off her two nearest pursuers and, after hanging right over to the stands' rail, had to battle hard in order to prevail with nothing to spare. She was subsequently claimed by Conor Dore. (op 5-4 tchd 11-8)
Svindal(IRE), who had finished nearly nine lengths behind Smalljohn at Wolverhampton this month and was 5lb better off, attracted market support and managed to turn that form around. He hasn't always looked the easiest of rides, but didn't do much wrong here and kept battling away between his two main rivals all the way to the line. (op 15-2)
Smalljohn, who has been in decent form over this trip on turf and Polytrack lately, was given his usual positive ride. He didn't respond immediataly when his two market rivals swept around his outside off the final bend, but he eventually put his head down and never stopped trying. (op 9-4)
Paint Splash, dropping in class for this third outing, was left for dead by the big three over the last couple of furlongs, but in turn pulled clear of the rest. She has a few more options now that she qualifies for a mark. Official explanation: vet said filly bled from the nose (op 25-1)
Courageous Nature(IRE), well held in his only previous try over this trip, had cheekpieces replacing the blinkers, but it made little difference as he was completely left behind up the home straight. (op 14-1)

7444 BOOK YOUR TICKETS ONLINE AT SOUTHWELL-RACECOURSE.CO.UK H'CAP 5f (F)
1:40 (1:41) (Class 6) (0-55,55) 3-Y-O+ **£2,047** (£604; £302) **Stalls** High

Form RPR
5006 **1** **The Geester**[32] 6955 4-8-13 **54**..................................(b) PaulEddery 7 65
(S R Bowring) *cl up: led after 1f: rdn ent fnl f: kpt on wl* **15/2**[3]
2636 **2** *3/4* **Spic 'n Span**[34] 6907 3-8-7 **55**...................................(b) AndreaAtzeni(7) 3 63
(R A Harris) *hmpd s: sn cl up: rdn and ev ch over 1f out tl drvn and one pce ins fnl f* **15/2**[3]
0066 **3** *shd* **Jilly Why (IRE)**[21] 7182 7-9-0 **55**..............................(b) ChrisCatlin 4 63
(Paul Green) *wnt lft s: prom tl lost pl and pushed along after 1 1/2f: swtchd lft to far rail and rdn along 1/2-way: hdwy wl over 1f out: styd on u.p ins fnl f* **5/2**[1]
6006 **4** *nk* **Night Prospector**[6] 7377 8-9-0 **55**..............................(b) ShaneKelly 6 62
(R A Harris) *led 1f: cl up tl outpcd and rdn along 1/2-way: drvn over 1f out: styd on u.p ins fnl f* **11/1**
004 **5** *1/2* **Alugat (IRE)**[38] 6823 5-8-11 **52**..............................(p) PatCosgrave 8 57
(Mrs A Duffield) *cl up: rdn along 2f out: drvn over 1f out and kpt on same pce* **11/1**
0243 **6** *nk* **Reigning Monarch (USA)**[20] 7196 5-8-11 **52**........................ LPKeniry 1 56
(Miss Z C Davison) *cl up: rdn along and ev ch 2f out: drvn: edgd rt and wknd ent fnl f* **7/2**[2]
4205 **7** *2 3/4* **East Coast Girl (IRE)**[19] 7213 3-8-9 **53**......................(b) LukeMorris(3) 2 47
(S W Hall) *hmpd s: sn cl up: rdn along wl over 1f out and ch tl drvn: edgd lft and wknd ent fnl f* **20/1**
0003 **8** *1* **Willhewiz**[13] 7292 8-8-12 **53**......................................(v) TGMcLaughlin 13 43
(W M Brisbourne) *a towards rr* **16/1**
0200 **9** *shd* **Swallow Forest**[35] 6890 3-8-6 **52**..............................(v1) DeanHeslop(5) 5 42
(T D Barron) *sn outpcd and a towards rr* **15/2**[3]
0006 **10** *1* **Caustic Wit (IRE)**[4] 7399 10-8-8 **52**..............................(p) TolleyDean(3) 9 38
(M S Saunders) *a in rr* **16/1**
0010 **11** *1 3/4* **Note Perfect**[20] 7197 3-8-12 **53**......................................(b) DaleGibson 12 33
(M W Easterby) *a towards rr* **22/1**
30 **12** *2 3/4* **Lady Bahia (IRE)**[43] 6711 7-8-7 **55**........................ AndrewHeffernan(7) 14 25
(Peter Grayson) *s.i.s: a in rr* **40/1**
59.70 secs **Going Correction** +0.025s/f (Slow) **12** Ran SP% **126.1**
Speed ratings (Par 101): **101,99,99,99,98 97,93,91,91,90 87,82**
toteswinger: 1&2 £11.60, 1&3 £7.50, 2&3 £4.90. CSF £65.49 CT £186.36 TOTE £12.40: £3.50, £2.70, £1.80; EX 91.80 TRIFECTA Not won..
Owner Mrs Anne & Fred Cowley **Bred** P O'Boyle **Trained** Edwinstowe, Notts

FOCUS
A moderate sprint handicap in which recent winning form was thin on the ground and just 3lb covered the entire field. As is usually the case, the race was dominated by those drawn low to middle and the front six finished in a bunch. The principals were always prominent and the form seems sound.

7445 EUROPEAN BREEDERS' FUND NOVICE STKS 1m (F)
2:10 (2:10) (Class 5) 2-Y-O **£3,885** (£1,156; £577; £288) **Stalls** Low

Form RPR
22 **1** **Kind Heart**[19] 7207 2-8-7 0.. J-PGuillambert 3 77+
(Sir Mark Prescott) *cl up: led on bit 1/2-way: pushed clr 2f out: easily* **6/5**[1]
0310 **2** *4 1/2* **Captain Imperial (IRE)**[88] 5447 2-9-2 76........................ MickyFenton 4 68+
(T P Tate) *led: pushed along and hdd over 3f out: rdn over 2f out and sn one pce* **3/1**[3]
01 **3** *5* **Alexander Gulch (USA)**[111] 4740 2-9-5 88........................ ChrisCatlin 5 60+
(K A Ryan) *cl up: rdn along over 3f out and sn btn* **15/8**[2]
3 **4** *5* **Mystical Spirit (IRE)**[18] 7221 2-8-7 0.............................. JimmyQuinn 1 37
(J R Weymes) *s.i.s: outpcd and bhd tl styd on fnl 2f: tk 4th nr fin* **25/1**
0006 **5** *3/4* **Kneesy Earsy Nosey**[11] 7319 2-8-9 40 ow7................. AnnStokell(5) 2 42
(Miss A Stokell) *chsd ldrs: rdn along 3f out and sn wknd* **150/1**
1m 44.54s (0.84) **Going Correction** +0.05s/f (Slow) **5** Ran SP% **109.7**
Speed ratings (Par 96): **97,92,87,82,81**
CSF £5.18 TOTE £2.10: £1.20, £1.90; EX 6.50.
Owner B Haggas **Bred** J B Haggas **Trained** Newmarket, Suffolk

FOCUS
A modest novice event, but the pace looked decent enough and they finished very well spread out. The principals can all do better.

NOTEBOOK
Kind Heart, runner-up in both of her previous starts over 6f at Great Leighs, moved smoothly to the front on the inside at around halfway and had little trouble in forging clear from her only possible danger up the home straight. With her main market rival running a shocker it remains to be seen what the form is worth, but she could hardly have done any more. The extra two furlongs certainly wasn't a problem and neither was the surface. (op 5-4 after early 11-8)
Captain Imperial(IRE), off since finishing last on his nursery debut in August, set the early pace but couldn't respond when the winner crept up his inside rounding the home bend and could only plug on for a respectable second. (op 7-2 tchd 4-1)
Alexander Gulch(USA), who hadn't been seen since winning at Pontefract in August, came off the bridle at halfway and was quickly left behind. He was in trouble before the extra two furlongs would have become an issue and he would have been 9lb worse off with the runner-up in a handicap, which demonstrates how moderate this performance was. However, any horse can be forgiven a poor debut effort on this unique surface and he shouldn't be given up on just yet. (op 13-8 tchd 2-1)
Mystical Spirit(IRE), third of eight, though beaten a fair way in a soft-ground maiden over a furlong further on her Musselburgh debut this month, walked out of the stalls and was never really travelling. (op 16-1)

7446 CALL 01636 814481 TO SPONSOR A RACE MAIDEN STKS 1m 4f (F)
2:40 (2:41) (Class 5) 3-Y-O+ **£2,729** (£806; £403) **Stalls** Low

Form RPR
302 **1** **West With The Wind**[21] 7174 3-9-3 75........................ MickyFenton 12 84+
(T P Tate) *mde all: rdn clr wl over 2f out: styd on wl* **6/4**[1]
60 **2** *7* **Colourful Move**[83] 5612 3-9-3 0.................................... SteveDrowne 5 70
(P G Murphy) *chsd ldrs: rdn along and sltly outpcd 4f out: hdwy to chse wnr wl over 1f out: sn drvn and no imp* **40/1**
53-0 **3** *4 1/2* **Fly With The Stars (USA)**[182] 2488 3-9-3 77..................... ChrisCatlin 6 63
(E J O'Neill) *chsd wnr: rdn along 4f out: drvn wl over 2f out and kpt on same pce* **5/1**[3]
4 *2 1/4* **Miracle Steps (CAN)**[25] 7122 3-8-12 0............................ ShaneKelly 7 54
(Andrew Oliver, Ire) *chsd ldrs: rdn along over 3f out: drvn over 2f out and sn one pce* **11/1**
4 **5** *9* **Sixth Zak**[11] 7321 3-9-3 0.. PaulEddery 2 45
(S R Bowring) *trckd ldrs: hdwy over 4f out: rdn to chse wnr wl over 2f out: sn wknd and eased* **16/1**
0500 **6** *1 1/2* **Able Dara**[15] 7265 5-9-9 41.. JimmyQuinn 4 43
(N Bycroft) *in rr and pushed along 1/2-way: sme hdwy over 3f out: nvr a factor* **50/1**
-060 **7** *1 1/4* **Tomorrow's World (IRE)**[6] 7387 3-8-12 66..............(b1) TGMcLaughlin 1 36
(M S Saunders) *in rr and rdn along after 4f: nvr a factor* **33/1**
8 *6* **Goodnight Dick (IRE)**[14] 3936 8-9-4 0........................ KellyHarrison(5) 9 31
(Paul Murphy) *in tch: pushed along and lost pl 1/2-way: bhd fnl 4f* **100/1**
-000 **9** *38* **Charlie Green (IRE)**[167] 2954 3-8-10 41.............. KrishGundowry(7) 11 —
(Paul Green) *midfield: rdn along over 4f out and sn wknd* **100/1**
0/00 **10** *6* **Aggi Mac**[277] 657 7-9-4 30...................................(b) AndrewElliott 10 —
(L R James) *dwlt: reminders after s and sn in midfield: rdn alonmg over 4f out and sn wknd* **100/1**
11 *35* **Mugs Game (IRE)**[27] 5-9-9 0... LPKeniry 8 —
(A J Martin, Ire) *s.i.s: a bhd* **20/1**
P **Shiwawa**[17] 6-9-9 0... RobertWinston 3 —
(G A Swinbank) *s.i.s and reminders after s: rdn along in rr after 3f: p.u over 5f out* **2/1**[2]
2m 39.68s (-1.32) **Going Correction** +0.05s/f (Slow)
WFA 3 from 5yo+ 6lb **12** Ran SP% **119.3**
Speed ratings (Par 103): **106,101,98,96,90 89,89,85,59,55 32,—**
toteswinger: 1&2 £17.10, 1&3 £2.90, 2&3 £22.60. CSF £79.82 TOTE £2.90: £1.30, £10.00, £1.70; EX 126.40 Trifecta £434.00 Part won. Pool: £586.61, 0.85 winning units..
Owner The Ivy Syndicate **Bred** Newsells Park Stud **Trained** Tadcaster, N Yorks

FOCUS
A modest older-horse maiden, but made a bit more interesting by a decent bumper performer and a couple of challengers from Ireland. The contest also saw some interesting betting patterns, with Shiwawa very weak just before the off, whilst the winner was very well supported late and ended up going off favourite. The winner set a good standard for the time of year based on his early season forn and is rated back to something like that level.
Able Dara Official explanation: jockey said gelding hung right

Shiwawa Official explanation: vet said gelding returned in a distressed state

7447 MEMBERSHIP AT SOUTHWELL GOLF CLUB H'CAP 1m 4f (F)
3:10 (3:10) (Class 5) (0-70,70) 3-Y-0+ **£2,729** (£806; £403) **Stalls** Low

Form RPR

0032 **1** **Brave Mave**[21] 7183 3-9-1 **69** SteveDrowne 10 83
(W Jarvis) *trckd ldng pair: hdwy to chse ldr 4f out: rdn to chal 2f out: drvn to ld ins fnl f: edgd lft and styd on wl* **4/1**[1]

2-12 **2** 1 1/4 **Pertemps Networks**[215] 1589 4-9-8 **70** GrahamGibbons 5 82
(M W Easterby) *cl up: led over 4f out: rdn along over 2f out: drvn over 1f out: hdd ins fnl f: one pce* **11/2**[3]

0421 **3** 3/4 **Azabu Juban (IRE)**[15] 7274 3-8-10 **67** LukeMorris(3) 2 78
(J Jay) *trckd ldrs: hdwy to chse ldng pair over 2f out: rdn to chal over 1f out and ev ch tl drvn and one pce ins fnl f* **16/1**

6104 **4** 8 **Sudden Impulse**[13] 7280 7-9-6 **68** TomEaves 14 66
(A D Brown) *hld up towards rr: hdwy 4f out: rdn along 3f out: drvn 2f out: kpt on u.p ins fnl f: nt rch ldrs* **25/1**

2203 **5** 1 3/4 **Moonstreaker**[21] 7183 5-9-1 **66** MichaelJStainton(3) 11 61
(R M Whitaker) *dwlt and reminders after s: towards rr tl hdwy 4f out: rdn along wl over 2f out: sn drvn and no imp fr wl over 1f out* **11/2**[3]

0120 **6** 1/2 **Bold Bobby Be (IRE)**[12] 7296 4-9-4 **66** (v) JimmyQuinn 7 60
(J L Dunlop) *hld up: gd hdwy 5f out: n.m.r on inner 4f out: chsd ldrs over 2f out: sn rdn and one pce* **9/2**[2]

5406 **7** 3 3/4 **Vanquisher (IRE)**[110] 4785 4-8-9 **57** ChrisCatlin 12 45
(Ian Williams) *midfield: effrt on wd outside 4f out: rdn along and sme hdwy 3f out: nvr a factor* **10/1**

0466 **8** 1 1/4 **Inch Lodge**[7] 7376 6-9-3 **65** (t) PaulEddery 8 51
(Miss D Mountain) *led: rdn along and hdd 4f out: sn wknd* **16/1**

5026 **9** 8 **Oberlin (USA)**[15] 7271 3-7-13 **60** AndreaAtzeni(7) 4 34
(T Keddy) *a in rr* **12/1**

5050 **10** 9 **Eseej (USA)**[73] 5913 3-8-10 **64** ow1 DarrenWilliams 13 23
(P W Hiatt) *chsd ldrs on outer: rdn along over 4f out: drvn 3f out and sn wknd* **25/1**

2056 **11** 5 **Black Falcon (IRE)**[15] 7272 8-8-7 **60** JamesO'Reilly(5) 3 11
(John A Harris) *a in rr* **14/1**

4006 **12** 3/4 **Houri (IRE)**[31] 6991 3-8-9 **70** (vt[1]) AndrewHeffernan(7) 6 20
(J T Stimpson) *t.k.h: in tch: rdn along over 4f out and sn wknd* **25/1**

1000 **13** 35 **Me Fein**[21] 7177 4-9-5 **67** TPQueally 1 —
(A P Stringer) *chsd ldrs: rdn along over 5f out and sn wknd* **16/1**

2m 39.68s (-1.32) **Going Correction** +0.05s/f (Slow)
WFA 3 from 4yo+ 6lb **13 Ran SP% 121.6**
Speed ratings (Par 103): **106,105,104,99,98 97,95,94,89,83 79,79,56**
toteswinger: 1&2 £4.00, 1&3 £7.20, 2&3 £6.20. CSF £25.41 CT £313.61 TOTE £3.00: £2.00, £2.60, £3.80; EX 20.50 Trifecta £106.40 Part won. Pool: £143.87, 0.73 winning units..
Owner J W Munroe Construction Ltd **Bred** Genesis Green Stud Ltd **Trained** Newmarket, Suffolk

FOCUS
An ordinary middle-distance handicap, but quite a competitive one and the pace was honest enough. The front trio were handy throughout before finishing clear and the winning time was identical to the preceding maiden. Probably fair form for the grade.

Eseej(USA) Official explanation: jockey said gelding hung badly right

7448 HOSPITALITY AT SOUTHWELL RACECOURSE H'CAP 6f (F)
3:40 (3:42) (Class 5) (0-75,75) 3-Y-0+ **£2,729** (£806; £403) **Stalls** Low

Form RPR

0050 **1** **Ingleby Arch (USA)**[37] 6842 5-9-2 **73** TomEaves 8 90
(T D Barron) *chsd ldrs: hdwy on outer 2f out: rdn to ld ent fnl f: sn drvn and styd on wl* **3/1**[2]

5502 **2** 1 1/4 **Charles Parnell (IRE)**[28] 7055 5-9-2 **73** DaleGibson 11 86
(M Dods) *hld up: hdwy over 2f out: swtchd lft and rdn over 1f out: chsd wnr ins fnl f: drvn and no imp towards fin* **8/1**

0331 **3** 3 1/4 **Efisio Princess**[13] 7286 5-8-8 **65** RichardThomas 1 68
(J E Long) *chsd ldrs: hdwy wl over 2f out: rdn to ld briefly over 1f out: drvn and hdd ent fnl f: one pce* **6/4**[1]

0001 **4** 3/4 **Incomparable**[11] 7323 3-8-13 **70** (p) PatCosgrave 7 70
(A J McCabe) *cl up: rdn to ld 2f out: drvn and hdd over 1f out: wknd ins fnl f* **15/2**[3]

0006 **5** 1 **Elusive Hawk (IRE)**[21] 7175 4-9-2 **73** TPQueally 3 70
(A P Stringer) *dwlt: held up in midfield: hdwy over 2f out: effrt whn nt clr run and swtchd lft over 1f out: sn rdn and no imp* **10/1**

5002 **6** 3/4 **Peter's Storm (USA)**[64] 6169 3-9-4 **75** FrancisNorton 10 70+
(K A Ryan) *s.i.s and bhd: hdwy 2f out: rdn and styd on ins fnl f: nrst fin* **16/1**

0150 **7** 3/4 **Princess Rose Anne (IRE)**[15] 7276 3-9-2 **73** LPKeniry 5 65
(E F Vaughan) *chsd ldrs: hdwy over 2f out: sn rdn and ev ch tl drvn and wknd over 1f out* **20/1**

250 **8** nk **Ballycroy Boy (IRE)**[11] 7317 3-9-2 **73** MickyFenton 14 64
(A Bailey) *a towards rr* **14/1**

0043 **9** 3 **Asian Power (IRE)**[11] 7315 3-9-1 **72** TGMcLaughlin 12 54
(P J O'Gorman) *stdd and swtchd lft s: a towards rr* **12/1**

500 **10** 4 **Herbert Crescent**[15] 7277 3-8-12 **69** JamieMoriarty 9 38
(Ollie Pears) *a towards rr* **40/1**

6000 **11** 4 1/2 **Count Cougar (USA)**[11] 7323 8-8-8 **65** SimonWhitworth 4 19
(S P Griffiths) *led: rdn along and hdd 2f out: grad wknd* **28/1**

0030 **12** 1 1/2 **Westwood**[32] 6952 3-8-10 **67** ChrisCatlin 13 17
(D Haydn Jones) *chsd ldrs on outer: rdn along over 2f out and sn wknd* **20/1**

1m 15.5s (-1.00) **Going Correction** +0.05s/f (Slow) **12 Ran SP% 132.6**
Speed ratings (Par 103): **108,106,102,101,99 98,97,97,93,87 81,79**
toteswinger: 1&2 £7.80, 1&3 £3.80, 2&3 £7.00. CSF £29.94 CT £53.79 TOTE £5.30: £2.50, £2.90, £1.10; EX 37.60 Trifecta £61.70 Pool: £833.94, 10.00 winning units. Place 6: £10.90, Place 5: £5.62..
Owner Dave Scott **Bred** Alexander-Groves Thoroughbreds **Trained** Maunby, N Yorks

FOCUS
An ordinary sprint handicap, but at least a few came into it in fair form. Solid form and a decent race for the grade.

Ingleby Arch(USA) Official explanation: trainer had no explanation for the poor form shown

Peter's Storm(USA) Official explanation: jockey said gelding reared as stalls opened and was slowly away

T/Jkpt: Not won. T/Plt: £26.50 to a £1 stake. Pool: £48,796.20. 1,343.30 winning tickets. T/Qpdt: £5.10 to a £1 stake. Pool: £2,997.18. 432.52 winning tickets. JR

7429 SAINT-CLOUD (L-H)
Tuesday, November 25

OFFICIAL GOING: Heavy

7449a PRIX ISONOMY (LISTED RACE) 1m
1:20 (1:20) 2-Y-O **£20,221** (£8,088; £6,066; £4,044; £2,022)

RPR

1 **Entre Deux Eaux (FR)**[13] 7294 2-8-12 IMendizabal 5 —
(Robert Collet, France)

2 nk **Stormy Weather (FR)**[46] 6642 2-8-11 YLerner 8 —
(J-L Pelletan, France)

3 2 1/2 **Hermoun (FR)**[14] 7347 2-8-11 GBenoist 2 —
(X Nakkachdji, France)

4 3/4 **Goliaths Boy (IRE)**[38] 6811 2-8-11 TonyHamilton 6 —
(R A Fahey) *midfield on outside: hdwy on outside to go 2nd 1/2-way: ev ch over 2 1/2f out tl hrd rdn and one pce over 2f out* **46/10**[1]

5 1 **Playwithmyheart**[13] 2-8-8 DBonilla 7 —
(T Doumen, France)

6 5 **Wood White (USA)**[14] 7347 2-8-11 CFiocchi 1 —
(R Menichetti, Italy)

7 15 **Guerande (IRE)**[21] 2-8-8 SPasquier 3 —
(A De Royer-Dupre, France)

8 1 1/2 **Laguna Salada (IRE)**[59] 2-8-12 DPorcu 4 —
(R Feligioni, Italy)

1m 49.2s (1.70) **8 Ran SP% 17.9**
PARI-MUTUEL: WIN 3.60; PL 1.60, 2.70, 3.20; DF 15.60.
Owner R Jesus **Bred** R Jesus **Trained** Chantilly, France

NOTEBOOK
Goliaths Boy(IRE), on the outside just behind the leaders, moved up to second just before turning for home. He looked to be in with a chance in the straight, but could not quicken on the ground and was rather one paced.

7450a PRIX CERES (LISTED RACE) (FILLIES) 7f
1:50 (1:58) 3-Y-O **£20,221** (£8,088; £6,066; £4,044; £2,022)

RPR

1 **Japan (GER)**[63] 3-8-12 DBoeuf 9 96
(D Smaga, France)

2 1/2 **Verba (FR)**[40] 6767 3-9-1 SPasquier 10 98
(R Gibson, France)

3 3/4 **Maree Basse (IRE)**[40] 6767 3-8-12 IMendizabal 1 93
(J-C Rouget, France)

4 1 1/2 **Just Like A Woman**[31] 6981 3-8-12 HayleyTurner 8 89
(M L W Bell) *midfield: 8th st: rdn over 2f out: kpt on steadily u.str.p* **11/1**[1]

5 snk **Roscoff (IRE)**[20] 7203 3-8-12 (b) TGillet 15 88
(Robert Collet, France)

6 nk **Halong Bay (FR)**[40] 3-8-12 TThulliez 11 87
(N Clement, France)

7 1 **Tudor Court (IRE)**[51] 3-8-12 (b) MGuyon 12 85
(H-A Pantall, France)

8 2 1/2 **Atullia (GER)**[51] 3-8-12 TJarnet 4 78
(T Clout, France)

9 6 **Mona Lisa (GER)**[23] 3-8-12 ASuborics 7 62
(Mario Hofer, Germany)

10 snk **Red Tulip (FR)**[33] 3-8-12 SRuis 14 61
(Mme C Head-Maarek, France)

11 **Head On (FR)**[71] 3-8-12 WMongil 6 61
(Mme C Head-Maarek, France)

12 **Sweet And Sour (IRE)**[4] 7431 3-8-12 THuet 16 61
(Robert Collet, France)

13 **Carved Emerald**[97] 3-8-12 (b) MaximeFoulon 3 61
(R Gibson, France)

14 **Ecume Du Jour (FR)**[88] 3-8-12 JAuge 2 61
(F Rohaut, France)

15 **Trully Belle (IRE)**[33] 3-8-12 GBenoist 13 61
(D Smaga, France)

1m 34.9s (2.70) **15 Ran SP% 8.3**
PARI-MUTUEL: WIN 9.80; PL 2.00, 1.30, 3.10; DF 9.30.
Owner M Parrish **Bred** Gestut Trona **Trained** Lamorlaye, France

NOTEBOOK
Just Like A Woman came under pressure coming out of the turning for home and looked to be struggling on the heavy ground. She stayed on well up the straight all the way to the line and was not beaten far.

7422 WOLVERHAMPTON (A.W) (L-H)
Wednesday, November 26

OFFICIAL GOING: Standard
Wind: Light behind Weather: Overcast

7451 BOOK TICKETS ONLINE NURSERY (DIV I) 5f 216y(P)
6:20 (6:22) (Class 6) (0-65,64) 2-Y-0 **£2,388** (£705; £352) **Stalls** Low

Form RPR

3300 **1** **Ridgeway Silver**[45] 6666 2-8-13 **61** GabrielHannon(5) 3 65
(M D I Usher) *hld up: hdwy over 1f out: r.o to ld wl ins fnl f* **40/1**

2000 **2** 1 1/4 **Come On Buckers (IRE)**[23] 7164 2-9-0 **60** AlanCreighton(3) 6 60
(E J Creighton) *chsd ldrs: led and edgd lft over 1f out: rdn and hdd wl ins fnl f* **66/1**

2026 **3** 2 **West Leake (IRE)**[30] 7016 2-9-6 **63** MichaelHills 2 57
(B W Hills) *a.p: n.m.r over 1f out: sn rdn to chse ldr: no ex ins fnl f* **7/2**[2]

503P **4** hd **Danzadil (IRE)**[88] 5511 2-9-5 **62** EddieAhern 1 56
(R A Teal) *s.s: bhd: hdwy over 1f out: sn rdn: styd on* **25/1**

4300 **5** 6 **Fasliyanne (IRE)**[26] 7113 2-9-7 **64** ChrisCatlin 4 40
(K A Ryan) *sn led: hdd 5f out: remained w ldr tl rdn over 1f out: wknd fnl f* **25/1**

4651 **6** shd **Madison Belle**[8] 7372 2-9-5 **62** 6ex DarrenWilliams 7 37
(K R Burke) *hld up: plld hrd: rdn and edgd lft over 1f out: n.d* **10/1**

4025 **7** 1 **Kitty Allen**[127] 4270 2-8-9 **59** AndreaAtzeni(7) 5 31
(M Botti) *s.i.s and stmbld sn after s: hld up: rdn and hung lft over 1f out: n.d* **9/2**[3]

3221 **8** 4 ½ **Digit**[40] 6787 2-9-7 **64**........ TomEaves 12 23
(B Smart) *led 5f out: rdn: hung lft and hdd over 1f out: sn wknd* **11/1**
3600 **9** 4 ½ **Lady Mulligan**[20] 7205 2-9-1 **58**........ FergusSweeney 11 3
(M Blanshard) *chsd ldrs: rdn over 2f out: wknd over 1f out* **40/1**
0263 **10** *nse* **Celtic Rebel (IRE)**[20] 7205 2-9-1 **58**........ HayleyTurner 8 3
(S A Callaghan) *broke wl and led early: chsd ldrs: rdn over 2f out: wknd over 1f out* **5/2**[1]
005 **11** 1 ½ **Cafe Fiore (IRE)**[53] 6488 2-8-13 **56**........ GregFairley 9 —
(T J Pitt) *chsd ldrs: rdn 1/2-way: wknd over 2f out* **11/2**
0024 **12** 3 ¾ **Intrepid Lady (IRE)**[86] 5581 2-9-3 **60**........ EdwardCreighton 13 —
(J C Tuck) *sn pushed along in rr: wknd 1/2-way* **66/1**

1m 16.91s (1.91) **Going Correction** +0.175s/f (Slow) **12** Ran SP% **117.3**
Speed ratings (Par 94): **94,92,89,89,81 81,79,73,67,67 65,60**
toteswinger: 1&2 £34.40, 1&3 £26.20, 2&3 £28.80. CSF £1526.69 CT £11108.17 TOTE £52.50: £14.70, £12.50, £1.70; EX 656.60.
Owner I Sheward **Bred** B Mills **Trained** Upper Lambourn, Berks
■ Stewards' Enquiry : Alan Creighton four-day ban: used whip with excessive frequency (Dec 10-13)

FOCUS
A modest nursery run at a good gallop, and it produced a shock result.

NOTEBOOK
Ridgeway Silver, who had dropped back to the mark she won off on her handicap debut at Salisbury in July, put behind her a couple of modest efforts to get back on the scoresheet. The good pace and sound surface undoubtedly suited her and, not for the first time in her career, she gave the impression that she will get 7f. (op 33-1)
Come On Buckers(IRE) has not been getting home over further and he appreciated dropping back to 6f. The more patiently ridden winner had that bit more in reserve at the finish, but it was still a good effort, and it showed that he does not need headgear. (tchd 50-1)
West Leake(IRE) did not get home over 7f at Leicester last time but had no excuses here, as he enjoyed the run of things, getting a good tow into the straight and saving ground on the inside all the way. (op 4-1)
Danzadil(IRE), not seen since finishing lame at Sandown in August, had previously looked to find 6f on the short side. This run confirmed that view, as she was slowly away, struggled towards the rear through the early parts, but then finished strongly. She will be interesting next time with this run under her belt. (op 28-1 tchd 20-1)
Fasliyanne(IRE), who was stepping up to 6f for the first time, showed good early speed, but she was taken on at the head of affairs and the result was that she simply helped set the race up for a closer. (op 20-1)
Madison Belle was officially 6lb well in at the weights under her penalty, but she had to prove that she could be as effective back on Polytrack as she is on Fibresand. The evidence of this run suggests she is simply a Fibresand filly through and through. (op 6-1)
Kitty Allen, who was the subject of a market move, stumbled early on and was taken very wide rounding the turn into the straight. She could never get close enough to land a blow. (op 12-1)
Celtic Rebel(IRE) has now disappointed on both his visits here. (op 3-1 tchd 7-2)

7452 ENJOY EVENING RACING MEDIAN AUCTION MAIDEN FILLIES' STKS 5f 216y(P)
6:50 (6:51) (Class 6) 2-Y-O **£2,729** (£806; £403) **Stalls** Low

Form RPR
0202 **1** **Freepressionist**[16] 7273 2-9-0 68........ EddieAhern 5 72+
(R A Teal) *trckd ldr: racd keenly: rdn to ld and edgd lft over 1f out: r.o wl* **13/8**[2]
2034 **2** 3 ½ **Our Wee Girl (IRE)**[138] 3908 2-9-0 75........ GeorgeBaker 13 60
(S Kirk) *sn led: rdn: edgd lft and hdd over 1f out: styd on same pce fnl f* **6/5**[1]
00 **3** 1 ¾ **Gracie's Games**[18] 7240 2-8-7 0........ AndreaAtzeni(7) 4 54
(R J Price) *mid-div: hdwy 2f out: sn rdn and hung lft: styd on* **33/1**
66 **4** ½ **Little Blacknumber**[7] 7388 2-9-0 0........ PatDobbs 1 53
(R Hannon) *hld up: hdwy and hung lft fr over 1f out: styd on* **11/1**[3]
5 ¾ **Devon Diva** 2-9-0 0........ SimonWhitworth 2 51
(M Hill) *s.s: outpcd: r.o ins fnl f: nrst fin* **14/1**
0 **6** 1 **Gwerthybyd**[30] 7015 2-9-0 0........ CatherineGannon 3 48
(B Palling) *prom: rdn over 2f out: styd on same pce appr fnl f* **80/1**
7 4 **Nairana** 2-9-0 0........ J-PGuillambert 6 36+
(J G Given) *s.s: outpcd: swtchd lft over 1f out: styng on whn eased ins fnl f* **25/1**
5000 **8** 4 **Cash In The Attic**[49] 6572 2-9-0 53........ EdwardCreighton 12 24
(M R Channon) *chsd ldrs: rdn over 2f out: sn wknd* **25/1**
0 **9** *shd* **Thumberlina**[36] 6885 2-9-0 0........ TGMcLaughlin 8 23
(Mrs C A Dunnett) *hld up: rdn 1/2-way: sn wknd* **50/1**
065 **10** 3 ¼ **Shirley High**[46] 6661 2-9-0 54........ JimmyQuinn 7 13
(P Howling) *chsd ldrs: rdn over 2f out: hung lft and wknd over 1f out* **11/1**[3]

1m 16.94s (1.94) **Going Correction** +0.175s/f (Slow) **10** Ran SP% **120.7**
Speed ratings (Par 91): **94,89,87,86,85 84,78,73,73,68**
toteswinger: 1&2 £1.30, 1&3 £15.30, 2&3 £18.10. CSF £3.88 TOTE £2.60: £1.10, £1.10, £8.60; EX 5.00.
Owner Free Press Racing **Bred** C N And Mrs Hart **Trained** Ashtead, Surrey

FOCUS
A modest maiden in which only two counted in the market.

NOTEBOOK
Freepressionist, second to an 87-rated filly over this course and distance last time out, had nothing of that quality to beat this time. She tracked her only serious market rival to the entrance to the straight before taking her measure approaching the furlong marker. This told us nothing we did not already know, but no doubt her success will have come as a relief to her trainer as his last winner came all the way back in June. (op 7-4 tchd 6-4)
Our Wee Girl(IRE) came into the race with the highest official rating, but she had been off the track since July and had to prover her stamina over this distance. The fact that she was backed into favouritism suggested connections were confident, but in the end she did not see it out as well as the winner. A drop back to the minimum trip should be in her favour. (op 15-8 tchd 2-1)
Gracie's Games ran her best race to date on her third start and is now eligible for a handicap mark. She will have better chances in that sphere. (op 50-1)
Little Blacknumber was a bit smarter away from the gates this time and is another who looks to be getting her act together in time for the move into handicap company. (op 7-1)
Devon Diva, who is by Ormonde Stakes winner Systematic out of a half-sister to that prolific sprinter Venture Capitalist, missed the break and ran green before staying on a little towards the finish. She should come on for this debut. (op 16-1)

7453 BOOK NOW FOR BOXING DAY MEDIAN AUCTION MAIDEN STKS 5f 216y(P)
7:20 (7:21) (Class 6) 3-5-Y-O **£2,388** (£705; £352) **Stalls** Low

Form RPR
0060 **1** **Marvin Gardens**[12] 7316 5-9-3 45........(b[1]) JerryO'Dwyer 7 58
(P S McEntee) *mde all: rdn and edgd lft fnl f: styd on* **40/1**
0063 **2** 2 ½ **North South Divide (IRE)**[20] 7213 4-9-3 69........ LPKeniry 3 50
(Peter Grayson) *half-rrd s: chsd wnr: rdn over 1f out: styd on same pce fnl f* **10/11**[1]
0000 **3** ½ **Mr Rev**[133] 4084 5-8-12 50........(p) MCGeran(5) 8 48
(J M Bradley) *hld up: hdwy and hung lft over 1f out: styd on same pce fnl f* **9/1**
3445 **4** 4 **Bilboa**[21] 7196 3-8-12 47........(p) JackDean(5) 6 36
(J M Bradley) *hld up: plld hrd: nt clr run and swtchd rt wl over 2f out: hdwy and edgd lft over 1f out: wknd ins fnl f* **7/1**[3]
00/0 **5** 1 ½ **Alocin (IRE)**[61] 6260 5-9-3 58........ J-PGuillambert 2 31
(W A Murphy, Ire) *prom: rdn 1/2-way: wknd over 1f out: eased ins fnl f* **14/1**
0006 **6** 8 **Rose De Rita**[62] 6224 3-8-12 31........ VinceSlattery 4 —
(L P Grassick) *hld up: rdn over 2f out: a in rr* **100/1**
-06 **7** 4 **Enlightened**[51] 6543 3-8-12 0........ SteveDrowne 1 —
(J H M Gosden) *dwlt: hld up: hdwy over 2f out: sn rdn: wknd fnl f* **3/1**[2]
0-0 **8** 11 **Princess Namid (IRE)**[71] 6004 3-8-12 0........ ChrisCatlin 5 —
(R A Harris) *chsd ldrs: rdn and wknd over 2f out* **100/1**

1m 17.22s (2.22) **Going Correction** +0.175s/f (Slow) **8** Ran SP% **111.0**
Speed ratings (Par 101): **92,88,88,82,80 70,64,50**
toteswinger: 1&2 £7.50, 1&3 £21.00, 2&3 £3.80. CSF £73.42 TOTE £35.50: £7.10, £1.02, £3.00; EX 114.30.
Owner H R Moszkowicz **Bred** Henry And Mrs Rosemary Moszkowicz **Trained** Newmarket, Suffolk

FOCUS
A weak maiden.
Enlightened Official explanation: jockey said filly bled from the nose

7454 BOOK TICKETS ONLINE NURSERY (DIV II) 5f 216y(P)
7:50 (7:51) (Class 6) (0-65,64) 2-Y-O **£2,388** (£705; £352) **Stalls** Low

Form RPR
533 **1** **My Best Bet**[36] 6879 2-9-6 **63**........ EdwardCreighton 4 68+
(M R Channon) *hld up: hdwy: hmpd and swtchd rt over 1f out: edgd lft and r.o to ld wl ins fnl f* **11/4**[1]
006 **2** 1 ¾ **Hellbender (IRE)**[51] 6531 2-9-3 **60**........ GeorgeBaker 10 60+
(S Kirk) *hld up: hdwy over 1f out: rdn to ld ins fnl f: sn hdd and unable qck* **13/2**
006 **3** ½ **Miss Tikitiboo (IRE)**[70] 6016 2-9-1 **58**........ LPKeniry 6 56
(E F Vaughan) *hld up: r.o ins fnl f: nt rch ldrs* **40/1**
0303 **4** 1 **Clerical (USA)**[41] 6755 2-8-6 **56**........(p) AndreaAtzeni(7) 8 51
(M J Gingell) *chsd ldrs: led over 1f out: sn rdn: hdd ins fnl f: styd on same pce* **16/1**
6500 **5** ½ **Tricky Trev (USA)**[20] 7205 2-9-3 **60**........(b[1]) PaulDoe 3 54
(S Curran) *prom: rdn and bmpd over 1f out: styd on same pce* **7/2**[2]
U045 **6** 2 ½ **Lucky Dan (IRE)**[30] 7020 2-9-7 **64**........ ChrisCatlin 11 50
(Paul Green) *sn led: rdn and hung rt over 1f out: sn hdd: no ex ins fnl f* **16/1**
4032 **7** 1 ½ **Forever's Girl**[12] 7319 2-9-0 **60**........ DuranFentiman(3) 7 42
(G R Oldroyd) *s.i.s: hdwy u.p over 1f out: wknd ins fnl f* **16/1**
0005 **8** ¾ **Cavendish Road (IRE)**[11] 7338 2-9-4 **61**........(bt) SteveDrowne 2 40
(W R Muir) *prom: rdn and nt clr run over 2f out: wknd fnl f* **16/1**
6503 **9** 2 **Abhainn (IRE)**[53] 6489 2-8-13 **56**........ CatherineGannon 12 29
(B Palling) *chsd ldr: rdn whn hmpd over 1f out: sn wknd* **14/1**
2566 **10** ¾ **Chambers (IRE)**[19] 7219 2-9-5 **62**........ GregFairley 13 33
(M Johnston) *chsd ldrs: rdn over 2f out: wknd over 1f out* **11/2**[3]
6433 **11** 2 ½ **La Capriosa**[13] 7303 2-9-2 **62**........ TolleyDean(3) 5 26
(A J McCabe) *hld up: a in rr: rdn over 2f out: wkng whn hung lft over 1f out* **16/1**

1m 16.32s (1.32) **Going Correction** +0.175s/f (Slow) **11** Ran SP% **116.1**
Speed ratings (Par 94): **98,95,95,93,93 89,87,86,84,83 79**
toteswinger: 1&2 £6.30, 1&3 £23.70, 2&3 £44.40. CSF £20.51 CT £588.91 TOTE £3.00: £1.10, £3.60, £12.40; EX 22.00.
Owner Phil Jen Racing **Bred** Phil Jen Racing **Trained** West Ilsley, Berks

FOCUS
There was a good pace on here, it was the quicker of the two divisions by 0.59sec, and the principals came from off the speed.

NOTEBOOK
My Best Bet appreciated the decent gallop and finished her race off really strongly once switched out in the straight. Nicely on top at the finish, she can improve again, especially over 7f, as both her pedigree and style of running suggest that she will appreciate a step up in distance. (op 3-1 tchd 7-2)
Hellbender(IRE) is by Exceed And Excel, whose progeny have a good record on Polytrack, so an improved effort on his handicap debut was not a huge surprise. He simply ran into a better handicapped rival, but it was still a sound effort, and he should be able to find a similar race. (op 4-1)
Miss Tikitiboo(IRE), dropping back to sprinting on her handicap debut, was in last place entering the straight but finished well as the leaders hit the wall. There is plenty of speed in her pedigree, but her dam did win over 1m3f so it remains to be seen what her best distance will end up being. (op 25-1)
Clerical(USA) enjoyed a good run through, tracking the leader on the rail, but he had been put up 6lb for running well in a maiden at Great Leighs last time, and that rise seemed to find him out. (op 12-1 tchd 8-1)
Tricky Trev(USA) looked dangerous at the top of the straight but he did not get home. A drop back to the minimum trip might help him as he has tended to weaken at the end of each of his races over 6f. (op 6-1)
Lucky Dan(IRE) had a lot of use made of him to get to the front from his wide draw, and he was not left alone in front. He paid for setting too strong a gallop. (op 8-1 tchd 18-1)

7455 HOTEL & CONFERENCING AT WOLVERHAMPTON H'CAP 2m 119y(P)
8:20 (8:21) (Class 6) (0-65,65) 3-Y-O+ **£2,729** (£806; £403) **Stalls** Low

Form RPR
11-3 **1** **Lady Pilot**[11] 1551 6-10-0 **65**........ RichardThomas 13 74+
(Jim Best) *hld up: hdwy to ld over 3f out: rdn over 1f out: jst hld on* **9/1**
0540 **2** *nk* **Nounou**[16] 7271 7-9-0 **54**........(tp) MarcHalford(3) 8 63
(Miss J E Foster) *hld up: hdwy over 2f out: rdn and edgd lft over 1f out: styd on wl* **25/1**
0044 **3** 3 ¾ **Generous Star**[13] 7296 5-9-7 **58**........ JimmyQuinn 5 62
(J Pearce) *s.i.s: sn prom: rdn over 2f out: edgd lft fr over 1f out: styd on same pce fnl f* **10/1**
/612 **4** 2 ¼ **Pseudonym (IRE)**[9] 7366 6-10-0 **65**........(t) LPKeniry 6 66
(M F Harris) *hld up in tch: rdn over 2f out: hung lft over 1f out: wknd ins fnl f* **2/1**[1]
5130 **5** 1 ½ **Summer Lodge**[8] 7376 5-9-13 **64**........ AdamKirby 4 64
(A J McCabe) *chsd ldr: rdn over 2f out: wknd fnl f* **17/2**[3]
0062 **6** 1 **Flame Creek (IRE)**[14] 7285 12-9-7 **58**........ EdwardCreighton 9 56
(E J Creighton) *hld up: rdn over 1f out: styd on ins fnl f: nvr nrr* **16/1**
0005 **7** 3 **Three Boars**[16] 7271 6-9-5 **63**........(b) AndreaAtzeni(7) 1 58
(S Gollings) *hld up in tch: nt clr run and lost pl over 3f out: n.d after* **14/1**

6335 **8** *nk* **Squirtle (IRE)**[9] 7366 5-9-11 **65**.................................... LukeMorris(3) 11 59
(W M Brisbourne) *hld up: rdn over 3f out: sme hdwy over 2f out: wkng whn hung lft over 1f out* **9/1**

0065 **9** *1¼* **Synonymy**[39] 6824 5-8-9 **46** oh1..............................(b) FergusSweeney 2 39
(M Blanshard) *hld up: rdn over 2f out: a in rr* **9/2**[2]

3525 **10** *½* **Blushing Hilary (IRE)**[14] 7293 5-9-2 **53**......................(p) JerryO'Dwyer 3 45
(Mrs S J Humphrey) *chsd ldrs tl wknd over 3f out* **25/1**

/0-1 **11** *1½* **Elaala (USA)**[14] 7285 6-8-11 **53**.............. PatrickDonaghy(5) 10 44
(B D Leavy) *chsd ldrs tl rdn and wknd over 2f out* **12/1**

6600 **12** *5* **Enderby Light (FR)**[30] 7010 3-8-9 **55**...........................(b[1]) TomEaves 12 40
(Ollie Pears) *hld up: rdn and wknd over 2f out:* **40/1**

0330 **13** *14* **Extreme Pleasure (IRE)**[20] 7216 3-9-3 **63**........................ ShaneKelly 7 31
(W J Knight) *led: rdn and hdd over 3f out: wknd over 2f out* **14/1**

3m 48.6s (6.80) **Going Correction** +0.175s/f (Slow)
WFA 3 from 5yo+ 9lb **13** Ran SP% **128.2**
Speed ratings (Par 101): **91,90,89,88,87 86,85,85,84,84 83,81,74**
toteswinger: 1&2 £0.00, 1&3 £31.90, 2&3 £31.90. CSF £229.85 CT £2323.25 TOTE £12.70: £2.80, £20.20, £2.80; EX 662.00.
Owner Odds On Racing **Bred** Genesis Green Stud Ltd **Trained** Lewes, E Sussex

FOCUS
An ordinary staying handicap run at a steady pace.

7456 STAY AT THE WOLVERHAMPTON HOLIDAY INN H'CAP 5f 20y(P)
8:50 (8:51) (Class 4) (0-80,80) 3-Y-O+ **£5,677** (£1,699; £849; £424; £211) **Stalls Low**

Form RPR

0535 **1** **Yungaburra (IRE)**[7] 7384 4-9-1 **77**..................................(bt) AdamKirby 1 92
(S Parr) *hld up in tch: rdn to ld and hmpd ins fnl f: r.o wl* **3/1**[2]

2020 **2** *2* **Russian Symphony (USA)**[16] 7276 7-8-9 **71**................(b) ShaneKelly 4 79
(C R Egerton) *s.i.s: sn pushed along in rr: rdn over 1f out: r.o wl ins fnl f: nt rch wnr* **10/1**

1002 **3** *¾* **Even Bolder**[14] 7290 5-9-4 **80**.. StephenCarson 3 85
(E A Wheeler) *a.p: rdn over 1f out: hung lft and styd on same pce ins fnl f* **11/4**[1]

131 **4** *1* **Garlogs**[190] 2292 5-9-0 **76**.. HayleyTurner 5 78
(R Hollinshead) *sn led: rdn over 1f out: hung lft and hdd ins fnl f: no ex* **8/1**[3]

0316 **5** *hd* **The Tatling (IRE)**[19] 7222 11-8-13 **80**.......................... JackDean(5) 7 81
(J M Bradley) *hld up: hung lft over 1f out: r.o ins fnl f: nrst fin* **16/1**

1050 **6** *1* **Choisette**[70] 6011 3-8-4 **66**.. GregFairley 2 63
(B Smart) *chsd ldr: rdn and ev ch whn hmpd ins fnl f: nt rcvr* **12/1**

0454 **7** *nk* **He's A Humbug (IRE)**[12] 7317 4-8-11 **78**................ JamesO'Reilly(5) 8 74
(J O'Reilly) *chsd ldrs: rdn over 1f out: no ex fnl f* **14/1**

6206 **8** *2½* **Cheshire Rose**[41] 6765 3-8-0 **67**.................................... DeanHeslop(5) 9 54
(T D Barron) *mid-div: rdn over 3f out: sn lost pl* **33/1**

4355 **9** *shd* **Not My Choice (IRE)**[6] 7394 3-9-4 **80**............................ ChrisCatlin 6 67
(S Parr) *hood removed late: s.i.s: hld up: plld hrd: rdn over 1f out: n.d* **14/1**

660 **10** *4½* **Drifting Gold**[126] 4313 4-8-8 **70**..................................(b) SteveDrowne 10 41
(C G Cox) *chsd ldrs: rdn over 1f out: wknd fnl f* **20/1**

0321 **11** *2½* **Dazzling Bay**[7] 7384 8-9-1 **80** 6ex........................(b) DuranFentiman(3) 11 42
(T D Easterby) *mid-div: rdn 1/2-way: sn wknd* **17/2**

62.12 secs (-0.18) **Going Correction** +0.175s/f (Slow) **11** Ran SP% **117.0**
Speed ratings (Par 105): **108,104,103,102,101 100,99,95,95,88 84**
toteswinger: 1&2 £19.20, 1&3 £6.50, 2&3 £19.20. CSF £33.23 CT £91.92 TOTE £4.80: £1.40, £5.10, £1.20; EX 38.10.
Owner Willie McKay **Bred** Newlands House Stud **Trained** Bawtry, S Yorks

FOCUS
Not a bad little sprint handicap.

7457 WOLVERHAMPTON-RACECOURSE.CO.UK H'CAP 1m 141y(P)
9:20 (9:20) (Class 4) (0-80,80) 3-Y-O+ **£5,828** (£1,734; £866; £432) **Stalls Low**

Form RPR

2- **1** **Princely Hero (IRE)**[49] 6591 4-8-11 **79**...................... AndreaAtzeni(7) 10 88
(M Botti) *hld up: hdwy over 1f out: rdn to ld and hung lft ins fnl f: r.o* **12/1**

0061 **2** *½* **Follow The Flag (IRE)**[9] 7367 4-8-7 **68** 6ex..............(p) JimmyQuinn 3 76
(A J McCabe) *hld up: hdwy over 1f out: rdn to ld ins fnl f: sn hdd: styd on u.p* **10/1**

0020 **3** *¾* **Hold The Gold (IRE)**[14] 7291 3-8-10 **74**......................... ChrisCatlin 9 80
(E J O'Neill) *s.i.s: hld up: hdwy over 1f out: hung lft and r.o ins fnl f* **7/1**

5036 **4** *2* **Harvest Warrior**[19] 7224 6-8-6 **70**........................... DuranFentiman(3) 4 72
(T D Easterby) *s.i.s: hld up: r.o fnl f: nt trble ldrs* **16/1**

2000 **5** *hd* **Moonlight Man**[16] 7278 7-9-0 **75**..................................(t) LPKeniry 12 76
(C R Dore) *hld up: rdn over 2f out: r.o fnl f: nt trble ldrs* **40/1**

0310 **6** *nk* **Justcallmehandsome**[16] 7278 6-8-12 **80**....................(v) BillyCray(7) 8 81
(D J S Ffrench Davis) *hld up: rdn over 2f out: styd on towards fin: nt trble ldrs* **10/1**

5023 **7** *hd* **Morbick**[5] 7405 4-8-11 **72**.. TGMcLaughlin 2 72
(W M Brisbourne) *chsd ldrs: rdn over 1f out: hmpd ins fnl f: styd on same pce* **11/4**[1]

0042 **8** *1¼* **Sam's Cross (IRE)**[13] 7302 3-8-11 **75**.................... DarrenWilliams 5 73+
(K R Burke) *hld up in tch: rdn over 1f out: hmpd ins fnl f: no ex* **4/1**[2]

1330 **9** *2* **King's Ransom**[13] 7299 5-9-0 **75**.. ShaneKelly 6 68
(S Gollings) *led: rdn over 2f out: hung rt and hdd ins fnl f: wknd towards fin* **25/1**

0040 **10** *1½* **Flying Goose (IRE)**[9] 7360 4-8-8 **69**........................ FergusSweeney 7 58
(R A Harris) *s.i.s: hld up: n.d* **22/1**

5250 **11** *1¾* **Heroes**[14] 7291 4-9-2 **77**..(p) PatCosgrave 1 65
(J R Boyle) *chsd ldrs: rdn over 1f out: hmpd and wknd ins fnl f* **6/1**[3]

2000 **12** *½* **Nightjar (USA)**[16] 7278 3-8-10 **74**.................................... GregFairley 11 58
(M Johnston) *chsd ldr: rdn over 2f out: wknd fnl f* **20/1**

1m 50.39s (-0.11) **Going Correction** +0.175s/f (Slow)
WFA 3 from 4yo+ 3lb **12** Ran SP% **120.6**
Speed ratings (Par 105): **107,106,105,104,103 103,103,102,100,99 97,97**
toteswinger: 1&2 £45.40, 1&3 £45.40, 2&3 £16.20. CSF £122.38 CT £929.94 TOTE £14.90: £4.60, £3.80, £3.40; EX 218.80 Place 6: £ 167.69 Place 5: £31.75 .
Owner Giuseppe Piccinni **Bred** Morristown Lattin Stud **Trained** Newmarket, Suffolk
■ Stewards' Enquiry : Shane Kelly two-day ban: careless riding (Dec 10 - 11)
Andrea Atzeni one-day ban: careless riding (Dec 10)

FOCUS
A fairly open handicap on paper.
T/Plt: £179.50 to a £1 stake. Pool: £100,004.86. 406.55 winning tickets. T/Qpdt: £41.60 to a £1 stake. Pool: £8,044.57. 142.90 winning tickets. CR

7393 GREAT LEIGHS (A.W) (L-H)
Thursday, November 27

OFFICIAL GOING: Standard
Wind: fresh, behind Weather: dry

7458 FREE HORSE RACING BETS @ FREEBETS.CO.UK MAIDEN STKS 6f (P)
6:50 (6:51) (Class 4) 2-Y-O **£5,180** (£1,541; £770; £384) **Stalls Low**

Form RPR

02 **1** **Wedding List**[12] 7333 2-8-12 0.. MichaelHills 1 82+
(W J Haggas) *mde all: c to centre 2f out: styd on strly: comf* **11/8**[1]

3403 **2** *2¾* **Poyle Meg**[45] 6696 2-8-12 80...(p) JimCrowley 5 71
(R M Beckett) *sn rdn along and towards rr: hdwy u.p on inner 2f out: styd on fnl f: chsd wnr fnl 100yds: nvr threatened wnr* **5/2**[2]

6 **3** *1* **Cabernet Sauvignon**[90] 5469 2-9-3 0.............................. EddieAhern 11 73+
(J W Hills) *s.i.s: bhd: hdwy on inner over 3f out: chsd ldrs u.p over 1f out: kpt on to go 3rd wl ins fnl f: no ch w wnr* **9/1**[3]

00 **4** *nk* **Miss Perfectionist**[35] 6933 2-8-12 0.............................. JimmyQuinn 12 67
(S A Callaghan) *hld up in midfield: hdwy and nt clr run briefly 2f out: hdwy over 1f out: rdn and kpt on fnl f: wnt 4th towards fin* **66/1**

5 *1* **Keep Icy Calm (IRE)** 2-8-12 0............................... RichardKingscote 2 64
(M F De Kock, South Africa) *chsd ldrs: hdwy to chse wnr over 2f out: rdn and flashed tail 1f out: no imp on wnr after: fdd and lost 3 pls fnl 100yds* **16/1**

0 **6** *1½* **Tahfeez (IRE)**[13] 7311 2-8-12 0..................................... MartinDwyer 3 60
(Sir Michael Stoute) *sn pushed along: in tch in midfield: drvn over 1f out: no real hdwy: wknd ins fnl f* **20/1**

6 **7** *1* **Novastasia (IRE)**[28] 7095 2-8-12 0.................................... AdamKirby 14 57
(W R Swinburn) *towards rr: pushed along and hdwy over 2f out: kpt on same pce fnl f: nt threaten ldrs* **12/1**

6 **8** *1¾* **Aaman (IRE)**[17] 7268 2-9-3 0.. LPKeniry 9 56
(E F Vaughan) *s.i.s: sn rdn along and outpcd in rr: styd on past btn horses fnl f: nvr a factor* **66/1**

0 **9** *½* **Lucky Fortune (IRE)**[12] 7333 2-9-3 0.............................. HayleyTurner 6 55
(Miss Amy Weaver) *restless in stalls: s.i.s: sn outpcd in rr: styd on past btn horses fnl f: nvr a factor* **100/1**

205 **10** *1¼* **My Sweet Georgia (IRE)**[21] 7207 2-8-12 75................ PatCosgrave 10 46
(S A Callaghan) *a towards rr: n.d* **20/1**

60 **11** *¾* **Always The Sun**[15] 7289 2-8-12 0................................(p) MickyFenton 8 44
(P Leech) *chsd ldr tl over 2f out: wknd wl over 1f out* **100/1**

0242 **12** *½* **Megasecret**[14] 7303 2-9-3 73.. ChrisCatlin 4 47
(R Hannon) *t.k.h: hld up in tch: rdn and edgd rt wl over 1f out: sn wknd* **16/1**

6 **13** *½* **No Nightmare (USA)**[125] 4359 2-8-12 0............................(t) JohnEgan 7 41
(Jane Chapple-Hyam) *racd on outer: in tch in midfield: rdn over 2f out: wknd wl over 1f out* **18/1**

00 **14** *6* **Oasis On Island**[34] 6953 2-9-3 0.. TomEaves 13 28
(B Smart) *chsd ldrs tl wknd over 2f out: sltly hmpd wl over 1f out: wl bhd whn hung lft over 1f out* **66/1**

1m 12.9s (-0.80) **Going Correction** -0.075s/f (Stan) **14** Ran SP% **121.4**
Speed ratings (Par 98): **102,98,97,96,95 93,91,89,88,87 86,85,84,76**
toteswinger: 1&2 £2.20, 1&3 £9.50, 2&3 £32.90. CSF £4.33 TOTE £2.50: £1.40, £1.60, £1.90; EX 6.10.
Owner Cheveley Park Stud **Bred** Cheveley Park Stud Ltd **Trained** Newmarket, Suffolk

FOCUS
An ordinary maiden despite the size of the field and the market suggested it was basically a two-horse race, but nonetheless a nice performance from the favourite. The runner-up has been rated as running 8lb below her best.

NOTEBOOK
Wedding List, who had improved from her debut to finish runner-up to a Godolphin colt over course and distance last time, made full use of the inside stall and was soon bowling along in front. Switched out to the centre of the track on reaching the home straight, she never looked like getting caught and she should continue to improve with racing. (op 13-8 tchd 7-4)
Poyle Meg, already placed a few times and just behind a subsequent winner on her sand debut at Kempton last time, was given plenty to do and, although she finished with quite a rattle tight against the inside rail, she never had a hope of getting near the winner. She is starting to look a bit exposed, but on this evidence may be worth a try over 7f. (tchd 3-1 in places)
Cabernet Sauvignon ◆, not seen since showing promise in a Sandown maiden in August which produced a couple of winners, attracted a bit of market support beforehand and stayed on to finish a respectable third. The drop in trip probably didn't help him and there should be a race like this in him back over further. (op 12-1)
Miss Perfectionist, well beaten in her two previous starts, showed a lot more this time and becomes of more interest now that she qualifies for a mark. (op 50-1)
Keep Icy Calm(IRE), a 105,000euros half-sister to a modest winning sprinter, was the only newcomer in the field. She travelled well in the slipstream of the winner and stayed in touch until getting tired late on. She should come on for this. (op 12-1)
Tahfeez(IRE), in midfield on her Kempton debut earlier this month, didn't achieve that much more here and looks modest. (op 16-1)

7459 FREE FOOTBALL BETS @ FREEBETS.CO.UK H'CAP 1m 6f (P)
7:20 (7:20) (Class 4) (0-85,82) 3-Y-O+ **£4,857** (£1,445; £722; £360) **Stalls Low**

Form RPR

3031 **1** **Turban Heights (IRE)**[23] 7183 4-9-7 **77**........................ ChrisCatlin 6 86+
(E J O'Neill) *t.k.h: hld up in last trio: hdwy and rdn over 3f out: chsd ldrs and swtchd rt wl over 1f out: drvn 1f out: styd on gamely to ld fnl 100yds* **11/4**[1]

16-1 **2** *¾* **Bank On Benny**[10] 7366 6-9-2 **72** 6ex..........................(bt) JohnEgan 3 80
(P W D'Arcy) *hld up in tch: chsd ldr over 2f out: ev ch wl over 1f out: rdn to ld ins fnl f: hdd and one pce fnl 100yds* **4/1**[3]

0156 **3** *1* **Clear Reef**[93] 5376 4-9-5 **75**.. TGMcLaughlin 7 82+
(Jane Chapple-Hyam) *t.k.h: hld up in last pl: hdwy on inner jst over 2f out: pressed ldrs ins fnl f: no ex u.p fnl 100yds* **8/1**

0102 **4** *2* **Apache Fort**[13] 7314 5-9-4 **74**..(b) TonyCulhane 5 78
(T Keddy) *chsd ldrs tl wnt 2nd over 6f out: led wl over 2f out: c centre st: sn drvn: hdd ins fnl f: wknd fnl 100yds* **9/1**

2020 **5** *6* **Quince (IRE)**[54] 6479 5-9-12 **82**......................................(v) JimmyQuinn 1 78
(J Pearce) *chsd ldr tl over 6f out: chsd ldrs after: rdn over 2f out: wknd wl over 1f out: no ch fnl f* **12/1**

0061 **6** *2½* **Puy D'Arnac (FR)**[26] 7128 5-9-8 **78**................................ EddieAhern 2 70
(G A Swinbank) *hld up in midfield: rdn and unable qck 2f out: sn btn: no ch fnl f* **3/1**[2]

1503 **7** *10* **Bassinet (USA)**[13] 7314 4-9-6 **76**.................................. GeorgeBaker 4 54
(J A R Toller) *led tl wl over 2f out: sn struggling: wl btn over 1f out: eased ins fnl f* **11/2**

3m 3.14s (-0.06) **Going Correction** -0.075s/f (Stan) 7 Ran SP% **115.9**
Speed ratings (Par 105): **97,96,96,94,91 90,84**
toteswinger: 1&2 £4.50, 1&3 £10.40, 2&3 £4.80. CSF £14.50 TOTE £4.60: £2.60, £2.30; EX 15.20.
Owner Raymond N R Auld **Bred** R N Auld **Trained** Averham Park, Notts

FOCUS
A fair staying handicap in which the pace was only fair and all seven runners were within a couple of lengths of each other passing the two-furlong pole. The race has been rated around the fourth.
Bassinet(USA) Official explanation: Jockey said filly ran too free

7460 FREE BINGO @ FREEBETS.CO.UK NURSERY 6f (P)
7:50 (7:50) (Class 4) (0-85,84) 2-Y-O **£5,180** (£1,541; £770; £384) **Stalls** Low

Form RPR

1125 **1** **Joe Caster**[12] 7335 2-9-4 **84**.................................. LukeMorris(3) 3 88
(J M P Eustace) *dwlt: racd in last pair: hdwy 2f out: rdn to chse ldr over 1f out: chal and edgd rt ent fnl f: led ins fnl f: r.o wl and forged ahd fnl 50yds* **6/1**

0215 **2** *1 1/2* **Rocket Rob (IRE)**[30] 7052 2-7-12 **68**.................................. AndreaAtzeni(7) 1 68
(S A Callaghan) *pressed ldr: led 2f out: sn rdn: hrd pressed ent fnl f: hdd ins fnl f: one pce fnl 100yds* **3/1**[1]

3041 **3** *2 1/4* **Retro (IRE)**[37] 6879 2-8-13 **76**.................................. EddieAhern 2 69
(R Hannon) *hld up in tch: sltly hmpd ent fnl f: sn rdn and nt qckn: kpt on same pce fnl f* **5/1**[3]

2452 **4** *nk* **Saif Al Fahad (IRE)**[12] 7335 2-8-7 **70**.................................. ChrisCatlin 8 62
(E J O'Neill) *chsd ldrs: rdn over 2f out: kpt on same pce u.p fr over 1f out* **11/2**

301 **5** *1 1/4* **Riflessione**[43] 6730 2-9-1 **78**.................................. (p) LPKeniry 6 66
(R A Harris) *hld up in rr: swtchd rt and effrt wl over 1f out: no imp u.p fnl f* **14/1**

451 **6** *4* **Sunniva Duke (IRE)**[22] 7191 2-9-1 **78**.................................. JimCrowley 7 54
(R Hannon) *t.k.h early: hld up in last trio: rdn 2f out: no hdwy u.p wl over 1f out: wl hld fnl f* **10/3**[2]

3161 **7** *7* **Misty Glade**[13] 7308 2-9-3 **80**.................................. (b) NickyMackay 4 35
(B J Meehan) *led: rdn over 2f out: hdd 2f out: wknd qckly: wl btn and eased ins fnl f* **9/1**

1m 12.94s (-0.76) **Going Correction** -0.075s/f (Stan) 7 Ran SP% **111.1**
Speed ratings (Par 98): **102,100,97,96,94 89,80**
toteswinger: 1&2 £1.10, 1&3 £13.60, 2&3 £6.50. CSF £22.88 CT £92.28 TOTE £6.30: £2.30, £2.80; EX 22.60.
Owner The Greek Myths **Bred** Ms G P Walker **Trained** Newmarket, Suffolk

FOCUS
A fair nursery and a race run at a scorching gallop, which resulted in a new juvenile course record. The form looks solid rated around the runner-up.

NOTEBOOK
Joe Caster ◆ wasn't best away and needed to be ridden along to stay in touch early, but he then travelled very nicely once into a rhythm. When the gap appeared for him, he took full advantage before bounding clear. A winner on turf and Polytrack last month, he had a valid excuse when unplaced here last time and can probably win again on this surface. He may well turn out under a penalty at Lingfield next week. (op 5-1 tchd 9-2)
Rocket Rob(IRE), considering he took part in the early speed duel, did well to keep on up the inside rail all the way to the line and hold on to the runner-up spot. A dual winner on Polytrack, he is 4lb higher than for his last win but still looks capable off this mark. (op 7-2 tchd 4-1 and 11-4)
Retro(IRE) travelled very smoothly behind the leaders, but didn't find as much off the bridle as had looked likely and, although he was briefly short of room a furlong out, it didn't cost him his chance of winning. (tchd 9-2)
Saif Al Fahad(IRE), around four lengths in front of the unlucky-in-running Joe Caster over course and distance last time, was 2lb worse off here. Always trapped out wide from the outside stall, he had every chance but had no more to offer once into the straight. (op 4-1)
Riflessione, up 4lb after winning a Kempton claimer last time, struggled to go the early pace and though he plugged on down the outside in the home straight, he was never a threat. (op 16-1)
Sunniva Duke(IRE), who overcame the worst draw to win a Kempton maiden on his sand debut last time, was making his nursery debut here but he did himself few favours by taking a fierce hold early and found little once in line for home. (op 4-1)
Misty Glade, up 6lb after making full use of the plum draw over the minimum trip at Kempton last time, attempted the same forcing tactics, but she almost certainly did too much too soon as she had blown herself out on reaching the home straight. Official explanation: jockey said filly ran too free (op 7-1)

7461 FREE BETS @ FREEBETS.CO.UK H'CAP 1m 2f (P)
8:20 (8:20) (Class 5) (0-70,68) 3-Y-O+ **£2,590** (£770; £385; £192) **Stalls** Low

Form RPR

2240 **1** **Don Pietro**[94] 5345 5-9-8 **68**.................................. NelsonDeSouza 3 78
(P A Blockley) *t.k.h: trckd ldrs: chsd ldr 2f out: sn rdn and ev ch: led ent fnl f: r.o wl* **7/1**

3065 **2** *1 1/4* **St Petersburg**[22] 7202 8-8-11 **57**.................................. PatCosgrave 6 64
(J R Boyle) *hld up in tch: effrt towards inner wl over 1f out: kpt on fnl f to go 2nd towards fin: unable to chal wnr* **11/2**[2]

2413 **3** *1/2* **Golden Bishop**[29] 6599 3-9-4 **68**.................................. TonyHamilton 4 74
(R A Fahey) *led: rdn and c to centre 2f out: sn hrd pressed: hdd ent fnl f: edgd rt and kpt on same pce: lost 2nd towards fin* **5/2**[1]

4553 **4** *nk* **Rising Force (IRE)**[41] 3631 5-9-3 **63**.................................. (b) AdamKirby 8 69
(J L Spearing) *hld up towards rr: stl travelling wl bhd wall of horses 2f out: hdwy over 1f out: keeping on same pce whn n.m.r ins fnl f: nvr pce to chal wnr* **11/2**[2]

3546 **5** *nk* **Artreju (GER)**[113] 4739 5-9-5 **65**.................................. GeorgeBaker 11 70
(G L Moore) *stdd after s: t.k.h: hld up in rr: swtchd rt and hdwy 3f out: chsd ldrs over 1f out: edgd lft and one pce u.p fnl f* **7/1**

0525 **6** *1* **Transmission (IRE)**[44] 6726 3-9-0 **64**.................................. TomEaves 7 67
(B Smart) *chsd ldr tl 2f out: sn rdn: keeping on same pce whn swtchd lft jst ins fnl f: wknd towards fin* **16/1**

0450 **7** *4* **Rapid City**[13] 7309 5-9-4 **67**.................................. (p) TolleyDean(3) 2 62
(A J McCabe) *stdd s: t.k.h: hld up in last pl: swtchd wd and hdwy 3f out: drvn and no imp whn rdr dropped whip over 1f out: no ch fnl f* **13/2**[3]

000 **8** *hd* **Shake On It**[21] 6908 4-9-0 **67**.................................. (t) AndreaAtzeni(7) 13 62
(M J Gingell) *t.k.h: hld up in last trio: effrt and rdn jst over 2f out: outpaced over 1f out: n.d fnl f* **33/1**

-000 **9** *1 3/4* **Fantastic Morning**[158] 3294 4-9-8 **68**.................................. JerryO'Dwyer 10 59
(F Jordan) *hld up in midfield: rdn jst over 2f out: unable qck u.p 2f out: wknd over 1f out* **50/1**

4204 **10** *dist* **Claret And Amber**[27] 7115 6-9-8 **68**.................................. EddieAhern 1 —
(Mrs S Leech) *hld up towards rr: shuffled bk to last pl over 2f out: effrt u.p on inner 2f out: keeping on same pce whn lost action jst ins fnl f and eased: dismntd after fin* **14/1**

2m 8.99s (0.39) **Going Correction** -0.075s/f (Stan)
WFA 3 from 4yo+ 4lb 10 Ran SP% **115.1**
Speed ratings (Par 103): **95,94,93,93,93 92,89,88,87,—**
toteswinger: 1&2 £4.00, 1&3 £7.80, 2&3 £3.90. CSF £44.69 CT £122.90 TOTE £10.20: £2.50, £2.20, £1.10; EX 61.10.
Owner Mighty Fine Partnership **Bred** B N And Mrs Toye **Trained** Lambourn, Berks

FOCUS
An ordinary handicap rated around the runner-up, but a notable gamble was landed.
Golden Bishop Official explanation: vet said gelding returned in a distressed state

7462 FREE POKER CHIPS @ FREEBETS.CO.UK H'CAP 1m 2f (P)
8:50 (8:51) (Class 5) (0-75,77) 3-Y-O+ **£2,590** (£770; £385; £192) **Stalls** Low

Form RPR

1102 **1** **Action Impact (ARG)**[10] 7354 4-9-4 **70**.................................. GeorgeBaker 4 81+
(G L Moore) *hld up in tch: rdn 3f out: c wd st: drvn to ld ins fnl f: in command and eased towards fin* **2/1**[2]

1400 **2** *1 3/4* **Dream Of Fortune (IRE)**[49] 6598 4-9-4 **70**.................................. (t) AdamKirby 8 78
(M G Quinlan) *hld up towards rr: rdn 3f out: hdwy u.p over 1f out: edgd lft but kpt on fnl f: snatched 2nd on line: nt able to chal wnr* **10/1**

6466 **3** *hd* **Indian Skipper (IRE)**[13] 7314 3-9-2 **72**.................................. PaulMulrennan 1 79
(M H Tompkins) *hld up wl in tch: chsd ldr over 1f out: rdn to ld ent fnl f: hdd ins fnl f: nt pce of wnr fnl 100yds* **8/1**[3]

253- **4** *3/4* **Prince Zafonic**[411] 6181 5-9-4 **70**.................................. JimCrowley 5 76
(D K Ivory) *chsd ldr: rdn 3f out: lost 2nd over 1f out: kpt chsng ldrs tl no ex u.p fnl 100yds* **10/1**

0551 **5** *1 3/4* **Remember Ramon (USA)**[10] 7364 5-9-11 **77** 6ex.................................. ChrisCatlin 6 80
(J R Gask) *racd keenly: led: rdn over 2f out: drvn and hdd ent fnl f: wknd ins fnl f: btn and eased nr fin* **13/8**[1]

3360 **6** *1 1/4* **Resplendent Ace (IRE)**[17] 7278 4-9-6 **72**.................................. JimmyQuinn 9 72
(P Howling) *hld up in last pair: rdn and effrt 2f out: no imp: eased towards fin* **16/1**

0620 **7** *2 1/4* **War Anthem**[23] 7183 4-9-6 **72**.................................. (b) PatCosgrave 7 67
(J R Boyle) *stdd after s: hld up in last pl: drvn and effrt 2f out: no hdwy: wl btn fnl f* **33/1**

3505 **8** *1* **Yankee Storm**[7] 7398 3-9-5 **75**.................................. JohnEgan 2 71
(P W D'Arcy) *chsd ldrs: rdn 3f out: wknd u.p ent fnl f: eased wl ins fnl f* **16/1**

34-0 **9** *3/4* **Mount Usher**[9] 5512 6-8-10 **69**.................................. (b[1]) AndreaAtzeni(7) 3 61
(M J Gingell) *dwlt: early reminders: racd in last trio: drvn and effrt on inner 2f out: nvr trbld ldrs* **66/1**

2m 6.28s (-2.32) **Going Correction** -0.075s/f (Stan)
WFA 3 from 4yo+ 4lb 9 Ran SP% **116.9**
Speed ratings (Par 103): **106,104,104,103,102 101,99,98,98**
toteswinger: 1&2 £9.30, 1&3 £8.90, 2&3 £10.30. CSF £23.04 CT £135.23 TOTE £3.50: £1.10, £2.40, £2.20; EX 20.20.
Owner T Bowley **Bred** Santa Maria De Araras **Trained** Woodingdean, E Sussex

FOCUS
Another ordinary handicap, though the winning time was 2.71 seconds faster than the preceding contest. The second and third set the level and the form looks solid.

7463 FREE SPORTS BETS @ FREEBETS.CO.UK MEDIAN AUCTION MAIDEN STKS 1m 2f (P)
9:20 (9:21) (Class 6) 3-5-Y-O **£2,266** (£674; £337; £168) **Stalls** Low

Form RPR

0002 **1** **Mayfair's Future**[14] 7300 3-8-10 60.................................. JimCrowley 7 64
(J R Jenkins) *trckd ldr: rdn to chal over 1f out: led ins fnl f: styd on* **3/1**[2]

0 **2** *3/4* **Kipchak (IRE)**[7] 7395 3-8-10 0.................................. EddieAhern 5 63
(C E Brittain) *racd keenly: led: rdn wl over 1f out: edgd lft u.p: hdd ins fnl f: nt qckn fnl 100yds* **9/4**[1]

400 **3** *1/2* **Sensible**[87] 5568 3-8-5 65.................................. JimmyQuinn 4 57
(H J Collingridge) *trckd ldng pair: rdn 2f out: short of room ent fnl f: swtchd rt ins fnl f: kpt on but unable to chal* **4/1**[3]

4 *11* **If You Knew Suzy**[21] 3-8-5 0.................................. (t) PaulQuinn 3 35
(G A Swinbank) *t.k.h: hld up in rr: hdwy 4f out: chsd ldng trio over 3f out: rdn over 2f out: sn struggling: wl btn fnl f* **9/4**[1]

-000 **5** *6* **Scar Tissue**[239] 1135 4-8-9 38.................................. EdwardCreighton 6 23
(E J Creighton) *dwlt: racd in last trio: rdn and struggling 3f out: wl bhd fnl 2f* **25/1**

0-5 **6** *23* **Apocalypto (IRE)**[14] 7300 4-8-7 0.................................. SPRyan(7) 2 —
(E J Creighton) *stdd s: hld up in rr: rdn and lost tch wl over 2f out: t.o* **50/1**

2m 7.80s (-0.80) **Going Correction** -0.075s/f (Stan)
WFA 3 from 4yo 4lb 6 Ran SP% **112.3**
Speed ratings (Par 101): **100,99,99,90,85 67**
toteswinger: 1&2 £2.80, 1&3 £2.70, 2&3 £1.40. CSF £10.21 TOTE £4.40: £2.70, £1.50; EX 13.30 Place 6: £20.20, Place 5: £17.36..
Owner G D I Markets Ltd **Bred** R A Fionda **Trained** Royston, Herts

FOCUS
This looked a modest and uncompetitive maiden. The winner had been well held in handicap company previously and will likely continue to struggle back in that grade off his current mark.
T/Plt: £30.60 to a £1 stake. Pool: £95,209.60. 2,268.81 winning tickets. T/Qpdt: £15.50 to a £1 stake. Pool: £6,355.70. 302.20 winning tickets. SP

7377 KEMPTON (A.W) (R-H)
Friday, November 28

OFFICIAL GOING: Standard
Wind: Moderate, half-against Weather: dry, chilly

7464 CELTIC CONTRACTORS CLAIMING STKS 5f (P)
5:50 (5:52) (Class 6) 2-Y-O **£2,047** (£604; £302) **Stalls** High

Form RPR

3024 **1** **Glamorous Spirit (IRE)**[41] 6807 2-8-6 82.................................. ChrisCatlin 5 77+
(R A Harris) *mde all: clr fr 1/2-way: rdn out: unchal* **9/2**[2]

5454 **2** *3* **Barnezet (GR)**[9] 7388 2-8-5 67.................................. PatrickHills(3) 5 68
(R Hannon) *chsd ldng pair: rdn to chse wnr wl over 1f out: no imp fnl f* **10/1**

6253 **3** *1 1/4* **Imaginary Diva**[37] 6906 2-8-1 55.................................. LukeMorris(3) 9 60
(G G Margarson) *bdly hmpd s: sn bustled along: hdwy on inner 2f out: kpt on but nvr nr wnr* **8/1**[3]

1162 **4** *1 ¾* **The Magic Of Rio**53 6540 2-8-7 90........................ AshleyMorgan(7) 3 63
(W J Haggas) *awkward leaving stalls and s.i.s: sn in midfield: rdn 2f out: kpt on same pce* **8/15**1

040 **5** *1 ¾* **Old Sarum (IRE)**9 7380 2-8-8 0........................ MarcHalford(3) 8 54
(D R C Elsworth) *wnt rt s: hld up in rr: rdn 2f out: plugged on but n.d* **14/1**

0000 **6** *2* **Brown Lentic (IRE)**36 6932 2-8-6 46........................ GregFairley 1 42
(G L Moore) *chsd wnr tl wl over 1f out: wknd fnl f* **33/1**

5030 **7** *3 ½* **Buddy Marvellous (IRE)**43 6745 2-8-0 53........................ AndreaAtzeni(7) 7 30
(R A Harris) *a bhd* **16/1**

000 **8** *1* **Diamond Til (IRE)**11 7356 2-8-1 0........................ FrancisNorton 10 21
(G L Moore) *bmpd s: t.k.h: racd in midfield: rdn and struggling 2f out: no ch after* **25/1**

58.96 secs (-1.54) **Going Correction** -0.45s/f (Stan) 8 Ran SP% **123.0**
Speed ratings (Par 94): **94,89,87,84,81 78,72,71**
toteswinger: 1&2 £6.00, 1&3 £5.10, 2&3 £4.70. CSF £51.83 TOTE £4.80: £1.10, £2.90, £2.30; EX 29.70.Glamorous Spirit was claimed by Sean Curran for £10,000.
Owner The Govin Partnership **Bred** Carlo Soria **Trained** Earlswood, Monmouths

FOCUS
An uncompetitive claimer and one that took less winning than seemed likely with the favourite disappointing. The pace was sound and this was a new all-aged track record. The second, third and sixth are the best guides to the level of the form.

NOTEBOOK
Glamorous Spirit(IRE), making her debut on the all-weather and for her new yard, faced a straightforward task with her main rival disappointing, and ran out a decisive winner after getting her own thing in front against the favoured inside rail. She is all about speed and is the type to win again on artificial surfaces. She was subsequently claimed for £10,000 by Sean Curran. (op 11-4)
Barnezet(GR) had a bit to find at the weights but, although running creditably, she again hung off a true line under pressure and is an exposed sort who has yet to win a race. The switch to modest handicaps should suit but she may not be one for maximum faith. (op 9-1)
Imaginary Diva is an exposed sort who had a stiff task at the weights but was not disgraced with the headgear left off this time after meeting a bit of trouble at the start. She will be of more interest in low-grade handicaps. Official explanation: jockey said filly was hampered on leaving stalls (tchd 10-1)
The Magic Of Rio looked to have strong claims back on sand after a short break but proved disappointing after losing a bit of ground at the start and racing three deep throughout. She is better than this and is worth another chance in similar company. (op 10-11)
Old Sarum(IRE), dropped to 5f for the first time since his debut, was soundly beaten and should be better suited by longer distances in modest handicaps. Official explanation: jockey said gelding jumped right on leaving stalls

7465 LETCHWORTH COURIERS EBF MEDIAN AUCTION MAIDEN STKS 6f (P)
6:20 (6:20) (Class 5) 2-Y-O £3,561 (£1,059; £529; £264) Stalls High

Form RPR

1 **Iasia (GR)** 2-8-12 0........................ PatCosgrave 10 71+
(Jane Chapple-Hyam) *in tch: hdwy jst over 2f out: chsd wnr and swtchd lft 1f out: qcknd to ld fnl 100yds: sn in command* **20/1**

00 **2** *1 ¾* **Tagula Night (IRE)**13 7333 2-9-3 0........................(vt1) AdamKirby 3 70
(W R Swinburn) *chsd ldr tl rdn to ld over 2f out: hung lft over 1f out: edgd rt ent fnl f: wandered u.p and hdd fnl 100yds: nt pce of wnr* **25/1**

06 **3** *¾* **Rebel City**13 7333 2-9-3 0........................ ShaneKelly 6 68
(S A Callaghan) *trckd ldrs: chsd ldr 2f out: sltly hmpd jst over 1f out: kpt on same pce fnl f* **15/8**1

4 **4** *5* **Choisharp (IRE)**18 7273 2-8-10 0........................ AndreaAtzeni(7) 2 53+
(M Botti) *chsd ldrs: gng wl over 2f out: shkn up 2f out: sn rdn and no rspnse: wl btn fnl f* **5/2**2

5 *2* **Captain Flasheart (IRE)** 2-8-12 0........................ WilliamCarson(5) 12 47
(S C Williams) *v.s.i.s: wl bhd: shkn up and hdwy on inner over 2f out: kpt on but nvr nr ldrs* **25/1**

6 *nk* **Dimander (IRE)** 2-9-3 0........................ JimCrowley 4 46
(Mrs A J Perrett) *v.s.i.s: wl bhd: c wd bnd 3f out: kpt on fnl f: nvr nr ldrs* **12/1**

7 *1 ¼* **Maswerte (IRE)** 2-9-3 0........................ ChrisCatlin 1 42
(L M Cumani) *wnt lft s and v.s.a: wl bhd: pushed along 3f out: kpt on fnl f: nvr nr ldrs* **16/1**

8 *shd* **Set Em Up Mo** 2-8-12 0........................ PaulDoe 7 37
(M J Attwater) *s.i.s: towards rr: rdn and sme hdwy on inner over 2f out: nvr gng pce to rch ldrs* **80/1**

00 **9** *nk* **Pepin (IRE)**25 7165 2-9-3 0........................ HayleyTurner 9 41
(D Haydn Jones) *s.i.s: hld up wl in rr: rdn and effrt on inner over 2f out: nvr threatened ldrs* **50/1**

04 **10** *5* **Tarruji (IRE)**50 6600 2-9-3 0........................ EddieAhern 11 26
(P W Chapple-Hyam) *led tl over 2f out: wknd rapidly wl over 1f out: wl btn and eased ins fnl f* **11/4**3

66 **11** *4* **Piccaso's Sky**15 7303 2-9-3 0........................ SteveDrowne 8 14
(A B Haynes) *racd off the pce in midfield: rdn over 3f out: wknd over 2f out: wl bhd last 2f* **100/1**

0 **12** *2 ½* **Pethers Dancer (IRE)**9 7388 2-9-3 0........................(b1) FrancisNorton 5 7
(W R Muir) *a towards rr: swtchd lft and rdn wl over 2f out: no hdwy and wl btn last 2f* **66/1**

1m 13.17s (0.07) **Going Correction** +0.075s/f (Slow) 12 Ran SP% **121.7**
Speed ratings (Par 96): **102,99,98,92,89 88,87,87,86,80 74,71**
toteswinger: 1&2 £48.50, 1&3 £23.40, 2&3 £12.80. CSF £416.14 TOTE £16.80: £5.10, £8.60, £1.20; EX 354.20.
Owner Mrs M Marinopoulos **Bred** Figaia Stud **Trained** Lambourn, Berks

FOCUS
A maiden lacking strength in depth but a decent gallop and one in which the first three, who raced in the centre, pulled clear in the closing stages. The third looks the best guide to the level.

NOTEBOOK
Iasia(GR), related to a winner in France, overcame her inexperience to make a winning debut, in the process creating a reasonable impression. Although this was not a strong maiden, she should stay 7f and is entitled to improve for this outing. (op 12-1)
Tagula Night(IRE) had been well beaten on his two previous starts but turned in a much-improved effort in the first-time visor. The step into ordinary handicaps will suit, he is in good hands and is the type to pick up a minor event on Polytrack. (op 20-1)
Rebel City has improved steadily with every start and was far from disgraced after attracting plenty of support. He shapes as though the step up to 7f will suit and is one to keep an eye on in run-of-the-mill handicaps. (op 5-2 tchd 7-4 and 11-4 in places)
Choisharp(IRE) had shown ability on his debut but, although well backed, failed to build on that effort after enjoying the run of the race. However, he may do better in handicaps as he strengthens up. (op 4-1)
Captain Flasheart(IRE), a half-brother to three winners from 5f to 1m, hinted at ability on this racecourse debut. He is entitled to improve a fair bit for this experience. (op 14-1)
Dimander(IRE) will be more of a handicap type in due course. (op 11-1)
Tarruji(IRE), who had shown ability on turf, had the run of the race on this all-weather debut and first start after a short break, but he dropped out very tamely. (op 5-2 tchd 10-3)

7466 MARSHELS OF FARNHAM H'CAP 7f (P)
6:50 (6:51) (Class 5) (0-75,75) 3-Y-O+ £2,590 (£770; £385; £192) Stalls High

Form RPR

5306 **1** **Gold Express**8 7393 5-8-12 68........................ ShaneKelly 8 78+
(P J O'Gorman) *t.k.h: trckd ldrs: hdwy between horses to ld jst over 1f out: c clr fnl 75yds* **4/1**2

0450 **2** *2 ¼* **Angaric (IRE)**32 7021 5-8-9 65........................ TomEaves 2 69
(B Smart) *t.k.h: chsd ldr tl led over 4f out: rdn over 2f out: hdd jst over 1f out: sltly outpcd by ldng pair ins fnl f: kpt on to regain 2nd on line* **8/1**

5044 **3** *nse* **Mogok Ruby**30 7077 4-9-5 75........................ HayleyTurner 3 79
(L Montague Hall) *stdd s: t.k.h: hld up in last pair: hdwy on inner jst over 2f out: pressed wnr ent fnl f: no ex fnl 100yds: lost 2nd last stride* **6/1**

2210 **4** *nk* **Maybe I Wont**42 6792 3-8-10 67........................ NeilChalmers 1 69
(Lucinda Featherstone) *t.k.h: hld up in last pair: swtchd lft and effrt jst over 2f out: kpt on u.p fnl f: nt able to chal wnr* **12/1**

0415 **5** *nse* **Tender Process (IRE)**14 7316 5-8-10 66........................(b) TonyHamilton 7 69
(R A Fahey) *bustled along briefly sn after s: sn t.k.h and hld up in tch: rdn and unable qck 2f out: kpt on ins fnl f: nt pce to trble wnr* **5/1**3

0122 **6** *6* **Wing Play (IRE)**18 7277 3-8-13 70........................(p) TravisBlock 5 56
(H Morrison) *t.k.h: trckd ldrs on outer: rdn and unable qck wl over 1f out: wknd 1f out* **7/4**1

7 *1 ¾* **Fantosha (USA)**62 6294 3-9-0 71........................ PatCosgrave 6 52
(David Wachman, Ire) *led tl over 4f out: pressed ldr after: rdn over 2f out: drvn and wknd over 1f out* **8/1**

1m 27.09s (1.09) **Going Correction** +0.075s/f (Slow)
WFA 3 from 4yo+ 1lb 7 Ran SP% **117.2**
Speed ratings (Par 103): **96,93,93,93,92 86,84**
toteswinger: 1&2 £4.40, 1&3 £7.00, 2&3 £7.50. CSF £36.42 CT £191.79 TOTE £8.00: £3.00, £3.70; EX 43.00.
Owner N S Yong **Bred** Deerfield Farm **Trained** Newmarket, Suffolk

FOCUS
An ordinary handicap in which the slow pace meant most failed to settle and this form has a dubious look to it. The winner raced just off the inside rail late on. It has been rated around the third to his recent course and distance form.

7467 CELTIC CONTRACTORS NURSERY (DIV I) 1m (P)
7:20 (7:20) (Class 6) (0-65,65) 2-Y-O £1,619 (£481; £240; £120) Stalls High

Form RPR

4605 **1** **Noble Dictator**23 7190 2-9-4 62........................ RichardKingscote 1 64
(E F Vaughan) *dwlt: hld up towards rr: rdn and hung rt over 2f out: hrd drvn to join ldr jst over 1f out: rdr dropped whip ins fnl f: led fnl 75yds: hld on* **6/1**3

0004 **2** *hd* **Night Lily (IRE)**39 6865 2-9-4 65........................ LukeMorris(3) 12 67
(J Jay) *led briefly: sn stdd and hld up towards rr: rdn over 3f out: swtchd lft fr over 2f out: hdwy on outer over 1f out: r.o wl u.p fnl f: wnt 2nd nr fin: jst hld* **5/1**2

0004 **3** *nk* **Captain Walcot**19 7258 2-9-0 58........................(b) SteveDrowne 7 59
(R Hannon) *chsd ldrs tl bmpd and led 6f out: hdd over 4f out: led again over 2f out: hung lft u.p wl over 1f out: hdd fnl 75yds: no ex* **8/1**

0000 **4** *1 ½* **Ain't Talkin'**43 6745 2-7-11 48........................ AndreaAtzeni(7) 9 46
(M J Attwater) *bhd: c wd and rdn wl over 2f out: r.o wl fnl f: gng on fin: nt rch ldrs* **50/1**

0001 **5** *nk* **Kladester (USA)**18 7269 2-9-7 65........................(t) TomEaves 5 62
(B Smart) *in tch: bustled along fr 6f out: rdn and hdwy to chse ldrs jst over 1f out: wknd ins fnl f* **11/4**1

0600 **6** *2 ¼* **Sweet Virginia (USA)**15 7298 2-7-8 45........................ NoraLooby(7) 8 37
(K R Burke) *in tch: bmpd and hmpd 6f out: hdwy on inner over 2f out: pressed ldrs jst over 1f out: wknd ins fnl f* **50/1**

0001 **7** *shd* **True Britannia**19 7257 2-8-12 56........................ JamesDoyle 4 48
(S Kirk) *prom: led sn after s tl 6f out: styd handy: drvn jst over 2f out: wknd ins fnl f* **15/2**

0040 **8** *1 ¼* **Andean Margin (IRE)**58 6394 2-9-1 59........................ HayleyTurner 3 48
(S A Callaghan) *hld up in tch: travelling wl 3f out: rdn and sltly hmpd over 2f out: nt qckn u.p wl over 1f out: sn btn* **15/2**

000 **9** *½* **Jonnie Skull (IRE)**14 7312 2-8-3 50........................(b1) MarcHalford(3) 2 38
(D R C Elsworth) *chsd ldr tl led over 4f out: rdn and hdd over 2f out: sn hung lft and wknd* **20/1**

0000 **10** *11* **Harry Raffle**95 5365 2-9-3 61........................ GeorgeBaker 6 25
(S Kirk) *towards rr: rdn over 3f out: c wd wl over 2f out: no imp whn sltly hmpd 2f out* **16/1**

560 **11** *3 ¼* **Sley (FR)**32 7023 2-9-6 64........................ ChrisCatlin 11 21
(B J Meehan) *dwlt: t.k.h and sn in tch: bmpd 6f out: rdn over 2f out: wknd wl over 1f out* **8/1**

1m 41.69s (1.89) **Going Correction** +0.075s/f (Slow) 11 Ran SP% **117.9**
Speed ratings (Par 94): **93,92,92,91,90 88,88,87,86,75 72**
toteswinger: 1&2 £8.90, 1&3 £7.00, 2&3 £8.30. CSF £35.64 CT £247.59 TOTE £9.60: £2.80, £2.00, £3.10; EX 36.60.
Owner C J Murfitt **Bred** C J Murfitt **Trained** Newmarket, Suffolk

FOCUS
The first division of an ordinary nursery. The pace was only fair in the first half of the contest and the field fanned across the track in the straight. The winner was fully entitled to win off this mark.

NOTEBOOK
Noble Dictator, given the way things have been panning out at this course in recent weeks, probably deserves a bit of extra credit for winning this from the widest draw after racing three deep throughout. He showed a decent attitude, despite again carrying his head a shade high, should not be going up too much for this and is lightly raced enough to be open to a little more progress. (tchd 13-2)
Night Lily(IRE), upped to this trip for the first time, ended up towards the stands rail, despite a high draw. This was an improved effort but she did not look the most straightforward of rides and she has little margin for error from this mark. (op 6-1 tchd 9-2)
Captain Walcot had the run of the race and again ran creditably with the blinkers refitted. The return to 7f may help but he may continue to look vulnerable against the more progressive or better handicapped types in this grade. (op 7-1)
Ain't Talkin' turned in his best effort to date and left the impression that the step up to 1m2f would suit.
Kladester(USA) was found out from this 10lb higher mark after winning on the slower Fibresand surface last time. He may fare better returned to that surface. (op 7-2)

Sweet Virginia(USA) was not disgraced on this second all-weather start but did not really show enough to suggest she will be of interest in a similar event next time. (op 40-1)

7468 CELTIC CONTRACTORS NURSERY (DIV II) 1m (P)
7:50 (7:50) (Class 6) (0-65,65) 2-Y-O **£1,619** (£481; £240; £120) **Stalls** High

Form RPR

0022 **1** **Highland River**[19] 7258 2-9-2 **60**........ GeorgeBaker 8 62
(D R C Elsworth) *taken down early: t.k.h: prom: rdn and ev ch over 1f out: led fnl 100yds: styd on wl* **2/1**[1]

6043 **2** ¾ **Artesium**[51] 6573 2-8-10 **54**........ TonyHamilton 1 54
(R A Fahey) *t.k.h: hld up in tch towards rr: swtchd rt and gd hdwy jst over 2f out: ev ch 1f out: pressed wnr but unable qck fnl 100yds* **10/1**

0404 **3** hd **Lujeanie**[16] 7281 2-9-4 **62**........ JimCrowley 2 62
(D K Ivory) *stdd and dropped in bhd after s: rdn wl over 2f out: swtchd rt and gd hdwy on inner over 2f out: kpt on wl fnl f: wnt 3rd fnl 100yds: nt quite rch ldng pair* **12/1**

3043 **4** 1 **Imperial Skylight**[11] 7361 2-8-8 **57**........ MCGeran(5) 5 55
(M R Channon) *hld up wl in tch: rdn and effrt on outer over 2f out: led over 1f out: hdd fnl 100yds wknd towards fin* **8/1**

003 **5** 1 **Transfered (IRE)**[80] 5778 2-8-4 **48**........ NeilChalmers 7 44
(Lucinda Featherstone) *hld up in tch towards rr: swtchd rt and hdwy on inner over 2f out: ev ch ent fnl f: wknd fnl 100yds* **25/1**

204 **6** 1¾ **Swiss Art (IRE)**[25] 7165 2-9-7 **65**........(p) SteveDrowne 9 57
(R A Harris) *t.k.h: chsd ldr: rdn to ld 2f out: sn hdd and hung lft: wknd jst ins fnl f* **9/1**

0005 **7** ¾ **Daily Planet (IRE)**[18] 7269 2-8-1 **45**........ FrancisNorton 10 35
(B W Duke) *t.k.h: hld up in tch: swtchd lft and rdn 2f out: kpt on same pce after* **50/1**

51 **8** shd **Hawkspring (IRE)**[16] 7283 2-8-13 **60**........(t) TolleyDean(3) 11 50+
(S Parr) *in tch: rdn and unable qck over 2f out: keeping on same pce whn n.m.r over 1f out: plugged on same pce fnl f* **10/3**[2]

050 **9** hd **Impressionist Art (USA)**[63] 6240 2-9-7 **65**........ HayleyTurner 12 54
(B J Meehan) *racd keenly: led: rdn over 2f out: hdd 2f out: wknd u.p ent fnl f* **15/2**[3]

040 **10** 1¾ **Amazing Blue Sky**[59] 6359 2-9-3 **61**........ ChrisCatlin 6 47
(E J O'Neill) *stdd after s: t.k.h and hld up in rr: effrt on outer 3f out: nvr gng pce to threaten ldrs* **12/1**

000 **11** 12 **Merry May**[38] 6879 2-8-1 **45**........ JimmyQuinn 3 4
(R Hannon) *t.k.h: in tch on outer: rdn over 2f out: sn wknd: no ch and eased ins fnl f* **33/1**

1m 42.11s (2.31) **Going Correction** +0.075s/f (Slow) 11 Ran SP% **122.5**
Speed ratings (Par 94): **91,90,90,89,88 86,85,85,85,83 71**
toteswinger: 1&2 £7.10, 1&3 £8.30, 2&3 £26.30. CSF £24.43 CT £207.88 TOTE £2.30: £1.10, £3.20, £3.20; EX 32.40.
Owner J Wotherspoon **Bred** John Wotherspoon **Trained** Newmarket, Suffolk

FOCUS
The second division of an ordinary nursery but a carbon copy of the first in that the early pace was steady, the field fanned across the track passing the intersection and the winner raced in the centre.

NOTEBOOK
Highland River has improved with every outing on sand and showed a willing attitude to get off the mark. He is unlikely to be going up much for this and should continue to run well. (op 5-2 tchd 11-4)
Artesium, having only his third run for his current yard, did not fail through lack of stamina - in a moderately run race at least - on his first run over 1m. He is in good hands and is likely to be placed to best effect. (op 8-1)
Lujeanie ◆ is unexposed and again shaped better than the bare result. He fared best of those to come from off the pace, will be suited by a more truly run race and is one to keep an eye on. (op 9-1)
Imperial Skylight ran creditably after being well placed but he is an inconsistent and exposed maiden who would not be one to take too short a price about next time. (op 11-1)
Transfered(IRE) was not disgraced upped in trip for this handicap debut. Her yard has winners on sand and she may be capable of a little better.
Swiss Art(IRE), making his handicap debut and tried in cheekpieces, had the run of the race but also had his limitations exposed from a stiff-looking mark. Official explanation: jockey said gelding hung left (op 6-1)
Hawkspring(IRE), a winner on Fibresand last time, attracted support on this nursery debut and first run for his in-form yard, but he failed to build on that win returned to Polytrack. The slower surface may suit best. (op 6-1)

7469 PACIFIC INSPIRATION H'CAP 1m (P)
8:20 (8:21) (Class 6) (0-50,50) 3-Y-O+ **£2,047** (£604; £302) **Stalls** High

Form RPR

0500 **1** **Copper King**[151] 3567 4-8-12 **50**........ ChrisCatlin 12 60
(Miss Tor Sturgis) *led for 1f: stdd and hld up in midfield after: hdwy and nt clr run over 2f out: sn swtchd lft and forced way out: rdn to ld over 1f out: a holding on after* **7/2**[1]

4600 **2** ½ **King Of The Beers (USA)**[25] 7169 4-8-5 **50**........(p) AndreaAtzeni(7) 14 59
(R A Harris) *in tch tl shuffled bk grad after 1f: bhd 1/2-way: gd hdwy on inner 2f out: styd on wl to chse wnr ins fnl f: nvr quite getting to wnr* **7/1**[3]

230 **3** 2½ **Moorside Diamond**[24] 7180 4-8-12 **50**........(b) GrahamGibbons 1 53
(A D Brown) *chsd ldrs: rdn and hdwy to ld 2f out: hdd over 1f out: one pce and lost 2nd ins fnl f* **14/1**

6030 **4** 1 **Play Up Pompey**[19] 7261 6-8-11 **49**........ JimCrowley 4 50
(J J Bridger) *in tch: rdn 3f out: chsd ldrs u.p over 1f out: kpt on same pce fnl f* **8/1**

0600 **5** nse **Battling Lil (IRE)**[47] 6681 4-8-11 **49**........ AdamKirby 13 50
(J L Spearing) *in tch in midfield tl hmpd and lost pl over 4f out: gd hdwy towards inner over 2f out: chsd ldrs u.p over 1f out: no ex ins fnl f* **20/1**

00-0 **6** 1 **The Tinker Man**[3] 7441 4-8-12 **50**........ HayleyTurner 3 48
(M D I Usher) *stdd after s: hld up bhd: rdn and effrt over 2f out: kpt on u.p fr over 1f out but nvr gng pce to rch ldrs* **9/1**

60/0 **7** nk **Samson Quest**[64] 6228 6-8-11 **49**........ TomEaves 5 47
(B Smart) *s.i.s: towards rr: pushed along 4f out: rdn and effrt over 2f out: no imp u.p fnl f* **11/2**[2]

0-00 **8** ½ **Tarkamara (IRE)**[63] 6251 4-8-12 **50**........ ShaneKelly 8 46
(P F I Cole) *t.k.h: hld up in tch: swtchd out off rail and hdwy wl over 2f out: pushed wd over 2f out: no imp fr over 1f out* **16/1**

0006 **9** 1¼ **Welcome Releaf**[16] 7287 5-8-9 **50**........(p) MarcHalford(3) 6 44
(P Leech) *chsd ldrs tl led after 1f: rdn and hdd 2f out: wknd qckly fnl f* **17/2**

2005 **10** 1½ **Franksalot (IRE)**[32] 7022 8-8-12 **50**........(p) PatrickMathers 9 40
(I W McInnes) *hld up bhd: swtchd lft and rdn over 2f out: nvr trbld ldrs* **10/1**

0600 **11** 3¼ **Ma Ridge**[32] 7026 4-8-10 **48**........ GregFairley 2 31
(T D McCarthy) *chsd ldr: ev ch and drvn over 2f out: wknd wl over 1f out* **20/1**

0/10 **12** 2½ **Cordage (IRE)**[34] 4811 6-8-11 **49**........(v) LPKeniry 11 26
(M F Harris) *in tch in midfield: rdn and lost pl 4f out: wl btn and eased over 1f out* **20/1**

1600 **13** 5 **Pembo**[6] 7423 3-8-10 **50**........ SteveDrowne 7 15
(R A Harris) *chsd ldrs: rdn and struggling jst over 2f out: btn and eased ent fnl f: lame* **14/1**

1m 40.95s (1.15) **Going Correction** +0.075s/f (Slow)
WFA 3 from 4yo+ 2lb 13 Ran SP% **124.3**
Speed ratings (Par 101): **97,96,94,93,92 91,91,91,89,88 85,82,77**
toteswinger: 1&2 £6.00, 1&3 £8.80, 2&3 £9.70. CSF £27.56 CT £312.25 TOTE £3.50: £2.30, £2.30, £3.40; EX 20.70.
Owner Paul Reason **Bred** Miss A V Hill **Trained** Lambourn, Berks
■ Stewards' Enquiry : Andrea Atzeni four-day ban: used whip with excessive frequency (Dec 12-15)

FOCUS
A low-grade handicap featuring out of form and inconsistent types. The pace was only fair and the winner raced in the centre in the straight before edging towards the inside rail late on. It has been rated around the third and fourth to their recent best.
Pembo Official explanation: vet said gelding was lame in front

7470 CELTIC CONTRACTORS H'CAP 7f (P)
8:50 (8:52) (Class 3) (0-90,90) 3-Y-O+
£7,477 (£2,239; £1,119; £560; £279; £140) **Stalls** High

Form RPR

4006 **1** **Resplendent Nova**[15] 7299 6-8-6 **77**........ JimmyQuinn 5 87
(P Howling) *rrd s and slowly away: hld up wl bhd: stl last over 2f out: rapid hdwy over 1f out: led fnl 100yds: r.o wl* **16/1**

2661 **2** ½ **Orpenindeed (IRE)**[15] 7297 5-8-9 **87**........(tp) AndreaAtzeni(7) 9 96+
(M Botti) *led: hrd pressed and rdn over 2f out: battled on gamely u.p tl hdd and no ex fnl 100yds* **4/1**[2]

6000 **3** ½ **Aeroplane**[34] 6975 5-9-5 **90**........ HayleyTurner 6 97
(S A Callaghan) *stdd and dropped in bhd after s: swtchd out lft fr over 2f out: in the clr and hdwy to press ldrs ent fnl f: unable qck fnl 100yds* **14/1**

0045 **4** ¾ **Silver Wind**[15] 7297 3-8-3 **78**........(b) LukeMorris(3) 2 82
(P D Evans) *outpcd towards rr: rdn wl over 3f out: hdwy u.p. 2f out: chsd along and keeping on whn nt clr run and swtchd rt wl ins fnl f: unable to chal* **25/1**

2546 **5** ¾ **Swift Gift**[6] 7418 3-9-1 **87**........ ShaneKelly 11 89
(B J Meehan) *chsd ldrs: effrt u.p over 2f out: ev ch over 1f out: wknd fnl 100yds* **5/1**[3]

-003 **6** 2½ **Perfect Act**[9] 7386 3-8-8 **80**........ SteveDrowne 4 76
(C G Cox) *s.i.s: swtchd rt after s: wl bhd: hdwy u.p over 2f out: no imp ins fnl f* **12/1**

3420 **7** nk **Dingaan (IRE)**[14] 7313 5-9-0 **85**........(v) LPKeniry 12 81
(A M Balding) *hld up in midfield: hdwy 3f out: chsd ldrs and rdn over 1f out: fnd little: wknd fnl f* **12/1**

6101 **8** 3¾ **Bellomi (IRE)**[98] 5248 3-9-4 **90**........ EddieAhern 10 75
(Miss Gay Kelleway) *stdd s: hld up wl off the pce: pushed along and no hdwy over 2f out: nvr trbld ldrs* **20/1**

3411 **9** 2¼ **Mister Ross**[32] 7027 3-8-8 **80**........ FergusSweeney 13 58
(G L Moore) *trckd ldrs: effrt and rdn on inner 2f out: sn hung rt: wknd qckly ent fnl f* **15/8**[1]

-306 **10** ¾ **Carnivore**[140] 3928 6-8-8 **79**........ TomEaves 14 56
(T D Barron) *stdd s: hld up bhd: rdn and hld hd awkwardly over 2f out: n.d* **14/1**

3133 **11** 5 **Dvinsky (USA)**[9] 7384 7-8-10 **81** ow1........(b) IanMongan 1 45
(P Howling) *pressed ldr: c wd and rdn wl over 2f out: wknd 2f out* **20/1**

3030 **12** 12 **King's Caprice**[29] 7101 7-8-11 **82**........(t) TravisBlock 7 14
(J A Geake) *restless stalls: chsd ldrs: rdn 4f out: struggling 3f out: wl bhd and eased fnl f* **33/1**

1m 24.76s (-1.24) **Going Correction** +0.075s/f (Slow)
WFA 3 from 5yo+ 1lb 12 Ran SP% **122.4**
Speed ratings (Par 107): **110,109,108,108,107 104,103,99,97,96 90,76**
toteswinger: 1&2 £23.40, 1&3 £27.80, 2&3 £18.60. CSF £77.88 CT £952.88 TOTE £29.00: £3.20, £1.80, £3.80; EX 91.70.
Owner The Oh So Sharp Racing Partnership **Bred** A Turner **Trained** Newmarket, Suffolk
■ Stewards' Enquiry : Andrea Atzeni three-day ban: used whip with excessive frequency (Dec 16-18)

FOCUS
The best quality event of the evening but a race in which the favourite proved disappointing. The pace was sound throughout and, as with several other races on this card, the principals raced down the centre in the straight. The fourth and fifth set the level, and the form looks solid for the grade.

NOTEBOOK
Resplendent Nova, who has slipped in the weights, proved suited by the strong gallop back in trip and confirmed he retains plenty of ability. The race panned out ideally for him and it remains to be seen whether things will fall into place as well from a higher mark next time.
Orpenindeed(IRE) ◆, back in a handicap, shaped better than the bare form as he fared best of those who raced up with the strong gallop. He is capable of picking up a similar event over this trip when allowed an uncontested lead. (op 13-2)
Aeroplane has struggled in handicaps since his last win on turf in 2006 but he caught the eye with the way he went through the race. He did not find as much as seemed likely when asked for an effort, though, and has little room for manoeuvre from this mark. (tchd 16-1)
Silver Wind, a dual turf winner, ran creditably on only this fourth all-weather start. He may not be the easiest of rides but there will be easier opportunities on sand this winter.
Swift Gift attracted support and was far from disgraced after chasing the decent gallop throughout. He is a consistent sort who should continue to give a good account. (op 6-1 tchd 13-2)
Perfect Act was not disgraced, but she will have to jump off better than she did here if she is to win in similar company on sand. Official explanation: jockey said filly missed the break (op 10-1 tchd 14-1)
Mister Ross was the one progressive horse in the field but he proved a disappointment after racing keenly behind the strong pace over this shorter trip. He is in very good hands and is not one to write off yet, though. Official explanation: jockey said gelding hung right (op 2-1 tchd 9-4)
King's Caprice Official explanation: vet said gelding was stiff behind

7471 EVENTMASTERS.CO.UK OFFICIAL HOSPITALITY AT TWICKENHAM H'CAP 6f (P)
9:20 (9:24) (Class 6) (0-65,65) 3-Y-O+ **£2,047** (£604; £302) **Stalls** High

Form RPR

1006 **1** **Littledodayno (IRE)**[16] 7292 5-8-13 **60**........ FrancisNorton 7 70+
(M Wigham) *hld up bhd: swtchd rt and gd hdwy on inner over 2f out: led fnl 100yds: r.o strly* **5/1**[3]

0600 **2** ¾ **Ever Cheerful**[42] 6774 7-9-0 **61**..........(p) SteveDrowne 5 69
(A B Haynes) *t.k.h: hld up in tch: effrt jst over 2f out: kpt on u.p fnl f: wnt 2nd nr fin* **40/1**

0041 **3** *nk* **Back In The Red (IRE)**[11] 7357 4-8-10 **64** 6ex..........(b) AndreaAtzeni(7) 6 71
(R A Harris) *sn drvn along to go handy: led over 4f out: rdn 2f out: hdd fnl 100yds: no ex: lost 2nd towards fin* **2/1**[1]

4050 **4** ½ **Mistress Cooper**[90] 5510 3-8-13 **60**.......... ChrisCatlin 8 65
(W J Musson) *hld up bhd: c wd over 2f out: hdwy 2f out: chsd ldrs jst ins fnl f: no imp fnl 50yds* **33/1**

400 **5** *1* **After The Show**[24] 7182 7-9-4 **65**.......... JimCrowley 2 67+
(Rae Guest) *stdd and dropped in bhd after s: t.k.h: hld up in rr: hdwy: n.m.r and swtchd rt 2f out: chsd ldrs u.p and nt clr run ins fnl f: swtchd lft: kpt on: nvr able to chal* **14/1**

0006 **6** 1¼ **Spoof Master (IRE)**[13] 7346 4-9-1 **62**.......... AdamKirby 12 60
(C R Dore) *led tl over 4f out: chsd ldr after: rdn and chal 2f out: wknd ins fnl f* **8/1**

0-54 **7** 2½ **Polish World (USA)**[21] 7226 4-9-0 **61**.......... GregFairley 9 51
(T J Etherington) *chsd ldrs: rdn and hung rt 2f out: wknd ent fnl f* **6/1**

022 **8** ½ **Blue Charm**[6] 7416 4-8-13 **60**.......... LPKeniry 1 48
(S Kirk) *racd in midfield: rdn and unable qck over 2f out: nt trble ldrs after* **7/2**[2]

3406 **9** ¾ **Peopleton Brook**[15] 7295 6-9-2 **63**..........(t) GeorgeBaker 4 49
(B G Powell) *hld up in midfield: hdwy and nt clr run jst over 2f out: sn swtchd lft and rdn: wknd ent fnl f* **14/1**

5250 **10** *nse* **Thoughtsofstardom**[16] 7286 5-8-6 **60**.......... TobyAtkinson(7) 11 46
(P S McEntee) *awkward s: trckd ldrs: shkn up and effrt on inner 2f out: fdd fnl f* **20/1**

1300 **11** 3¾ **Commander Wish**[28] 7118 5-9-4 **65**..........(p) NeilChalmers 3 39
(Lucinda Featherstone) *chsd ldrs: rdn and struggling over 2f out: sn wknd: wl bhd fnl f* **25/1**

0500 **12** *nk* **Royal Acclamation (IRE)**[14] 7320 3-8-13 **60**.......... PaulMulrennan 10 33
(G A Harker) *hmpd s: a bhd* **14/1**

1m 12.89s (-0.21) **Going Correction** +0.075s/f (Slow) **12** Ran SP% **131.6**
Speed ratings (Par 101): **104,103,102,101,100 98,95,94,93,93 88,88**
toteswinger: 1&2 £20.10, 1&3 £3.00, 2&3 £42.50. CSF £213.22 CT £549.77 TOTE £7.10: £2.50, £4.10, £1.60; EX 332.30 Place 6 £276.25, Place 5 £92.07..
Owner John Williams P'Ship Have Ago Syndicate **Bred** Lodge Park Stud **Trained** Newmarket, Suffolk

FOCUS
An ordinary handicap in which the pace was sound, and the winner raced against the inside rail in the straight. It looks solid enough form for the grade rated around the third and fourth.
T/Plt: £500.40 to a £1 stake. Pool: £92,827.54. 135.41 winning tickets. T/Qpdt: £60.50 to a £1 stake. Pool: £9,348.18. 114.20 winning tickets. SP

7433 LINGFIELD (L-H)
Friday, November 28

OFFICIAL GOING: Standard
Wind: Almost nil Weather: Rain

7472 PA SERVICES AT EVENTIMAGE.TV NURSERY (DIV I) 7f (P)
12:20 (12:23) (Class 5) (0-75,81) 2-Y-O **£2,914** (£867; £433; £216) **Stalls** Low

Form RPR

2600 **1** **Song Of Praise**[39] 6865 2-8-3 **57**.......... JimmyQuinn 10 58
(M Blanshard) *t.k.h early: trckd ldrs: effrt on outer over 1f out: rdn and r.o fnl f to ld last strides* **50/1**

4300 **2** *hd* **Dream Date (IRE)**[15] 7306 2-8-11 **65**..........(t) MichaelHills 9 66
(W J Haggas) *dwlt: rcvrd to trck ldng pair: effrt to ld over 1f out: styd on fnl f: hdd last strides* **11/2**[3]

061 **3** *1* **Cool Art (IRE)**[9] 7389 2-9-6 **81** 6ex..........(b) AndreaAtzeni(7) 6 79+
(S A Callaghan) *t.k.h: hld up in 7th in slowly run r: effrt over 1f out: rdn and r.o wl to take 3rd nr fin: too much to do* **5/2**[1]

3634 **4** ¾ **Our Day Will Come**[19] 7259 2-9-5 **73**.......... EddieAhern 5 69
(R Hannon) *trckd ldng trio: effrt 2f out: cl enough 1f out: one pce* **7/1**

0010 **5** 1½ **It's A Game (USA)**[15] 7306 2-9-5 **73**.......... SteveDrowne 8 65
(J H M Gosden) *led: set v modest pce to 2f out: hdd and nt qckn over 1f out: fdd* **14/1**

404 **6** *hd* **Rocoppelia (USA)**[113] 4778 2-8-10 **64**.......... JimCrowley 3 56
(Mrs A J Perrett) *pressed ldr to wl over 1f out: grad outpcd* **9/2**[2]

5400 **7** ½ **Common Diva**[15] 7306 2-9-3 **71**.......... PatCosgrave 4 62
(A J McCabe) *hld up in midfield on inner: rdn 2f out: outpcd over 1f out: plugged on* **16/1**

065 **8** *1* **Art Fund (USA)**[37] 6894 2-8-12 **66**.......... FergusSweeney 2 54
(G L Moore) *hld up in last pair in slowly run r: outpcd wl over 1f out: no ch after* **12/1**

6540 **9** ½ **Quick Single (USA)**[15] 7306 2-9-2 **70**.......... GeorgeBaker 7 57
(D R C Elsworth) *stdd s: hld up in last: shkn up and no rspnse wl over 1f out* **11/2**[3]

1m 27.48s (2.68) **Going Correction** +0.05s/f (Slow) **9** Ran SP% **112.2**
Speed ratings (Par 96): **86,85,84,83,82 81,81,80,79**
toteswinger: 1&2 £23.80, 1&3 £17.30, 2&3 £8.50. CSF £296.30 CT £969.07 TOTE £96.40: £11.70, £2.20, £1.50; EX 259.90 TRIFECTA Not won..
Owner Tom Wellman **Bred** Whitsbury Manor Stud **Trained** Upper Lambourn, Berks

FOCUS
This looked the weaker of the two divisions; there was a modest gallop which only increased going into the final bend. The third and fourth help set the level.

NOTEBOOK
Song Of Praise had been well beaten on her only previous attempt on Polytrack, and even on turf her overall profile was very ordinary - hence the big price. However, she had been dropped a long way by the Handicapper in her last three races and that, combined with the longer trip and return to this surface, both of which seemed to suit her well, was just enough to get her home near the line.
Dream Date(IRE) was only just run out of it despite missing the break and pulling too hard. She had done reasonably well on previous Polytrack outings, and is good enough to find a similar race off this sort of mark. (op 8-1 tchd 5-1)
Cool Art(IRE), winner of a claimer here last time, was carrying a 6lb penalty back in nursery company. He tried to come from some way back in a modestly run race and, when pulled wide to challenge in the straight, he began to hang and was always arriving too late. The blinkers worked first time, but did not look as effective here, though he would have been better suited by a stronger tempo. (op 11-4 tchd 9-4)
Our Day Will Come continues to chase home the leaders without winning, suggesting that this mark is just beyond her.
It's A Game(USA) had the run of the race out in front but gave the impression that 6f suits her better at present. (op 10-1 tchd 9-1 and 16-1)

7473 HINDLEAP WALK (S) STKS 1m 4f (P)
12:50 (12:51) (Class 6) 3-Y-O+ **£1,978** (£584; £292) **Stalls** Low

Form RPR

1400 **1** **Wind Flow**[34] 6985 4-9-11 70..........(b) CatherineGannon 12 59
(C A Dwyer) *led 4f: pressed ldr: led over 2f out: kicked on over 1f out: hld on wl* **5/1**[3]

5460 **2** *1* **Sleepy Mountain**[16] 7293 4-8-13 53.......... AndreaAtzeni(7) 13 52
(A Middleton) *t.k.h early: trckd ldrs: effrt over 2f out: disp 2nd 1f out: kpt on but a hld* **7/1**

0000 **3** *nk* **Turner's Touch**[32] 7009 6-9-4 59..........(b) JemmaMarshall(7) 15 56
(G L Moore) *stdd s: hld up in last trio: stl wl in rr 2f out: promising prog on outer jst over 1f out: hanging and ref to go through w effrt* **16/1**

50S0 **4** *nk* **Ben Bacchus (IRE)**[44] 4924 6-9-11 45.......... ChrisCatlin 4 56
(P W Hiatt) *trckd ldng pair: effrt on inner 2f out: disp 2nd over 1f out: one pce ins fnl f* **16/1**

0056 **5** ½ **Summer Bounty**[14] 7322 12-9-6 46.......... PaulFitzsimons 8 50
(F Jordan) *hld up in rr: stdy prog over 2f out: chsd ldrs over 1f out: kpt on same pce* **33/1**

0400 **6** *nk* **Obrigado (USA)**[73] 5994 8-9-11 68..........(t) GeorgeBaker 6 55
(G L Moore) *stdd s: hld up in last trio: prog on wd outside 3f out: rdn to chse ldrs over 1f out: hanging lft and nt qckn* **7/2**[2]

4050 **7** *4* **Kames Park (IRE)**[149] 3613 6-9-6 74.......... JamesO'Reilly(5) 1 48
(I W McInnes) *s.s: hld up in rr: sme prog on inner 2f out: no imp on ldrs 1f out: fdd* **10/3**[1]

5560 **8** 1¼ **Danish Monarch**[34] 6228 7-9-6 47.......... FergusSweeney 11 41
(David Pinder) *hld up in rr: prog on outer over 3f out: chsd ldrs over 2f out: wknd over 1f out* **66/1**

0400 **9** ½ **Tenement (IRE)**[22] 7217 4-9-6 47..........(p) AmirQuinn 7 41
(Jamie Poulton) *cl up: rdn over 3f out: steadily wknd fnl 2f* **12/1**

1000 **10** *1* **Ericarrow (IRE)**[25] 6747 3-9-0 52..........(t) LPKeniry 2 39
(M F Harris) *hld up in midfield on inner: lost pl and struggling over 2f out* **50/1**

0000 **11** ¾ **Competitor**[153] 3482 7-9-11 52..........(v) IanMongan 10 43
(J Akehurst) *pressed ldr: led after 4f out over 2f out: wknd over 1f out* **25/1**

5450 **12** 3½ **Missie Baileys**[102] 5148 6-9-1 45..........(p) TGMcLaughlin 16 27
(Mrs L J Mongan) *towards rr: rdn and brief effrt on outer over 3f out: wknd over 2f out* **16/1**

0000 **13** ½ **Lord Laing (USA)**[115] 4701 5-9-6 38.......... JimmyQuinn 3 31
(H J Collingridge) *nvr beyond midfield: rdn over 3f out: wknd over 2f out* **16/1**

14 *14* **Brahms And Mist (FR)**[33] 8-9-6 0.......... FrankieMcDonald 14 9
(D J S Ffrench Davis) *s.s: hld up in last trio: wknd over 2f out: t.o* **66/1**

2m 32.28s (-0.72) **Going Correction** +0.05s/f (Slow) **14** Ran SP% **117.4**
WFA 3 from 4yo+ 6lb
Speed ratings (Par 101): **104,103,103,102,102 102,99,98,98,97 97,95,94,85**
toteswinger: 1&2 £12.50, 1&3 £10.60, 2&3 £11.90. CSF £37.50 TOTE £6.20: £2.60, £3.70, £3.80; EX 34.00 TRIFECTA Not won..There was no bid for the winner.
Owner Super Six Partnership **Bred** Lord Halifax **Trained** Burrough Green, Cambs

FOCUS
A competitive seller, the winner having landed three non-selling handicaps during 2008 as well as a claimer. Those filling the principal places came from both ends of the field, indicating a fair result. The fourth and fifth are the best guide to the level of the form.
Brahms And Mist(FR) Official explanation: jockey said gelding never travelled

7474 GALLEONS LAP MAIDEN STKS 1m 2f (P)
1:20 (1:22) (Class 5) 3-Y-O **£2,729** (£806; £403) **Stalls** Low

Form RPR

02 **1** **Spouk**[13] 7344 3-8-12 0.......... ChrisCatlin 1 66+
(L M Cumani) *trckd ldng pair: wnt 2nd over 2f out: drvn to ld jst ins fnl f: jst hld on* **7/4**[2]

0 **2** *shd* **Bantu**[9] 7387 3-8-12 0..........(v[1]) JimCrowley 10 66+
(J H M Gosden) *hld up in last: sme prog 3f out but stl only 7th whn rdn 2f out: styd on strly over 1f out: wnt 2nd and clsd on wnr fin: too much to do* **25/1**

025 **3** 1¼ **Blessing (USA)**[60] 6345 3-8-12 76.......... ShaneKelly 4 64
(J Noseda) *led: rdn and kpt on fr 2f out: hdd and one pce jst ins fnl f* **9/2**[3]

2424 **4** 1½ **Special Reserve (IRE)**[35] 6949 3-9-3 79..........(p) EddieAhern 8 66
(R Hannon) *hld up in rr: prog over 3f out: rdn to chse ldng pair over 1f out: no imp: one pce after* **5/4**[1]

0 **5** 1¾ **Resentful Angel**[105] 5047 3-8-12 0.......... PaulEddery 7 57
(Pat Eddery) *chsd ldr to over 2f out: grad fdd over 1f out* **33/1**

00 **6** 1¾ **Yvonne Evelyn (USA)**[13] 7344 3-8-12 0.......... SteveDrowne 3 54
(J R Gask) *mostly midfield on inner: rdn and in tch 2f out: fdd* **50/1**

03 **7** 1¾ **Roleplay (IRE)**[8] 7395 3-8-9 0..........(b) LukeMorris(3) 6 50
(J M P Eustace) *chsd ldrs: rdn and in tch 2f out: wknd over 1f out* **16/1**

0000 **8** ½ **Rettorical Lad**[120] 4553 3-9-3 60.......... FrancisNorton 5 54
(Jamie Poulton) *hld up in midfield: lost pl 3f out: sn struggling and off the pce: plugged on* **50/1**

0 **9** ½ **Fashion Week**[13] 7344 3-9-3 0.......... GregFairley 9 53
(M Johnston) *pushed along early in last pair: struggling in same pl oover 3f out: plugged on* **33/1**

10 *28* **Classic Dancer** 3-8-12 0.......... FrankieMcDonald 2 —
(Jane Chapple-Hyam) *a towards rr: wknd 4f out: t.o* **66/1**

2m 4.99s (-1.61) **Going Correction** +0.05s/f (Slow) **10** Ran SP% **120.0**
Speed ratings (Par 102): **108,107,106,105,104 102,101,101,100,78**
toteswinger: 1&2 £12.50, 1&3 £1.80, 2&3 £14.80. CSF £51.38 TOTE £3.00: £1.50, £4.10, £1.60; EX 38.70 Trifecta £168.70 Part won. Pool: £227.98 - 0.85 winning units..
Owner Fittocks Stud **Bred** Fittocks Stud **Trained** Newmarket, Suffolk

FOCUS
The first four home are all from good families, so in theory this could be decent form, but they are unlikely to live up to their pedigrees and price tags. They went a medium gallop, with the leader going for home three furlongs out. The performances of the sixth and eighth limit the value of the form.

7475 PA SERVICES AT EVENTIMAGE.TV NURSERY (DIV II) 7f (P)
1:55 (1:56) (Class 5) (0-75,74) 2-Y-O **£2,914** (£867; £433; £216) **Stalls** Low

Form RPR

0523 **1** **Trigger McCann**[31] 7044 2-9-0 **67**.......... LPKeniry 10 70
(J S Moore) *hld up: prog on outer 1/2-way: clsd on ldrs 2f out: drvn to ld ins fnl f: kpt on* **20/1**

326 **2** ½ **Auld Arty (FR)**[80] 5785 2-9-6 **73** ShaneKelly 8 75
(T G Mills) *mde most: drvn and edgd rt over 1f out: hdd ins fnl f: kpt on* **6/1**[3]

5405 **3** ½ **Bartica (IRE)**[18] 7273 2-8-11 **64** EddieAhern 4 67+
(R Hannon) *t.k.h early: hld up: reminders after 3f: drvn and prog 2f out: clsng whn swtchd ins and rn into trble 100yds out: nt rcvr* **14/1**

050 **4** 1 **Musigny (USA)**[30] 7080 2-8-11 **64** MichaelHills 2 62
(W Jarvis) *hld up towards rr: gng strly 3f out: rdn wl over 1f out: keeping on but hld whn bmpd nr fin* **8/1**

006 **5** shd **Mr Willis**[158] 3315 2-8-5 **58** MartinDwyer 3 58+
(J R Best) *hld up in rr: pushed along in rr: no prog tl jst over 1f out: checked ins fnl f: kpt on* **9/2**[2]

5421 **6** ¾ **Belated Silver (IRE)**[15] 7306 2-9-7 **74** RichardKingscote 5 70
(Tom Dascombe) *sn trckd ldng pair: rdn on inner 2f out: cl up jst over 1f out: sn btn* **2/1**[1]

4562 **7** 1 ¾ **Officer Mor (USA)**[11] 7361 2-8-12 **65** DarrenWilliams 9 57
(K R Burke) *sn pressed ldr: swtchd lft over 1f out: wknd fnl f* **25/1**

361 **8** 1 ¾ **Takeover Bid (USA)**[25] 7170 2-9-3 **70** GregFairley 1 57
(M Johnston) *s.i.s: a in last trio: rdn 3f out: no prog* **8/1**

021 **9** nk **Dynamo Dane (IRE)**[20] 7240 2-9-5 **72** JimCrowley 7 58
(J G Given) *chsd ldrs: rdn 3f out: lost pl 2f out: n.d after* **12/1**

5434 **10** nk **Jaslyn (IRE)**[15] 7298 2-7-13 **52** ow1 JimmyQuinn 6 38
(J R Weymes) *mostly last: detached over 2f out: n.d after* **33/1**

1m 25.48s (0.68) **Going Correction** +0.05s/f (Slow) **10** Ran SP% **113.9**
Speed ratings (Par 96): **98,97,96,95,95 94,92,90,90,90**
toteswinger: 1&2 £27.00, 1&3 £23.10, 2&3 £43.10. CSF £129.98 CT £1794.58 TOTE £26.20: £6.30, £2.50, £4.20; EX 220.80 TRIFECTA Not won..
Owner Mrs Trisha Laughton **Bred** Bottisham Heath Stud **Trained** Upper Lambourn, Berks

FOCUS
A stronger-looking line-up than division one and, not surprisingly, two seconds faster, though the pace was just a routine one.

NOTEBOOK
Trigger McCann, appreciating the extra furlong, made it a winning debut in nursery company against some useful opponents at this level. He has arrived in handicaps on a fair mark and should improve a bit for the experience of coming home in front.
Auld Arty(FR) flopped in his last turf race, but he had excuses that day and his previous form was solid. Reverting to front-running tactics here, he made a creditable all-weather debut and looks to be on a realistic mark as he bids for compensation. (op 13-2 tchd 8-1)
Bartica(IRE) ◆ improved for the switch to nursery company and longer trip. Switched inside entering the last furlong, he was unlucky to run into trouble, forcing Ahern to stop riding, but he came home well and should be on the short-list for a similar event next time. (op 25-1)
Musigny(USA), who had twice run over an extended 1m on turf, would have finished a bit closer but for being carried left inside the final furlong, though he would still have been fourth. However, this was a satisfactory nursery debut which proved that he acts on this surface. (op 7-1 tchd 6-1)
Mr Willis ◆ had been running in sprints in his qualifying races, but he clearly needs at least 7f. Stretching out really well near the finish, this strong, scopey sort looks an improver and it would be no surprise to see him winning soon. (op 11-2)
Belated Silver(IRE) failed to repeat his recent win here following a 5lb rise, but the track often appears to be slower on the inside rail in the Lingfield home straight and that may have counted against him. (op 5-2 tchd 13-8)

7476 RACING + EVERY SATURDAY ONLY 90P CONDITIONS STKS 7f (P)
2:30 (2:31) (Class 3) 2-Y-O **£6,799** (£2,023; £1,011; £505) **Stalls** Low

Form RPR

6 **1** **Global**[14] 7312 2-9-0 0 SteveDrowne 3 80
(R Hannon) *mde all: set v stdy pce tl kicked on jst over 2f out: drvn and pressed fnl f: styd on wl* **8/1**

1 **2** ¾ **Lexlenos (IRE)**[11] 7356 2-8-9 0 MarcHalford(3) 4 77
(D R C Elsworth) *dwlt: hld up in last: prog to chse wnr 2f out: tried to chal fnl f: kpt on but a hld* **7/2**[2]

3223 **3** 3 **Invincible Heart (GR)**[13] 7334 2-9-0 **87** PatCosgrave 2 71
(Jane Chapple-Hyam) *t.k.h early: hld up in 3rd: effrt 2f out: sn rdn and nt qckn* **4/5**[1]

0 **4** 2 **Cognac Boy (USA)**[171] 2903 2-9-0 0 EddieAhern 5 66
(R Hannon) *chsd wnr tl pce lifted jst over 2f out: sn btn* **4/1**[3]

1m 28.98s (4.18) **Going Correction** +0.05s/f (Slow) **4** Ran SP% **108.9**
Speed ratings (Par 100): **78,77,73,71**
CSF £32.31 TOTE £9.30; EX 26.00.
Owner A J Ilsley & G Battocchi **Bred** Lt-Col And Mrs R Bromley Gardner **Trained** East Everleigh, Wilts

FOCUS
Disappointing in numbers, though Invincible Heart had done well in six previous races, suggesting that the quality was sound enough for the prize money. However, they went no gallop and that probably favoured the all-the-way winner.

NOTEBOOK
Global had his own way out in front, and the dash for home early in the straight proved to be the winning move. Though it would be easy to deduce that he was flattered by the way the race was run, he did it with panache and, as this was only his second run, he should not be underestimated. Connections have a high opinion of him and may now put him away for the winter. (tchd 9-1)
Lexlenos(IRE) sat last while the winner was dictating a modest tempo, and her late effort was never happening quickly enough. However, she clearly stays 7f well and a stronger gallop would suit her running style much better. (op 11-4 tchd 5-2)
Invincible Heart(GR) had been running over 6f, and it remains to be seen whether this extra furlong is what he wants, since this was a muddling race and he was not able to use his proven early speed. Though probably beaten by better horses anyway, he is capable of winning a maiden, with handicaps an obvious alternative, but he is becoming expensive to follow. (op 8-1, tchd 10-11 in a place)
Cognac Boy(USA) had not run since his debut in June. Though finishing last, he was not given a hard time when beaten and will be more at home in handicaps after one more run. (op 8-1)

7477 NEW CHAPEL H'CAP 6f (P)
3:05 (3:06) (Class 4) (0-85,87) 3-Y-O+ **£4,727** (£1,406; £702; £351) **Stalls** Low

Form RPR

6201 **1** **Internationaldebut (IRE)**[9] 7390 3-9-6 **87** 6ex AdamKirby 7 104+
(S Parr) *hld up in rr on inner: had to wait for opening tl over 1f out: pushed along and ready prog after: led fnl 75yds: won w smething in hand* **5/2**[1]

0 **2** 1 **The Game**[104] 5102 3-8-13 **80** RichardKingscote 5 90
(Tom Dascombe) *led: drvn 2f out: kpt on wl but hdd and outpcd fnl 75yds* **9/1**

0023 **3** ¾ **Even Bolder**[2] 7456 5-8-13 **80** StephenCarson 1 88
(E A Wheeler) *cl up on inner: rdn to chse ldr over 1f out to ins fnl f: one pce* **8/1**[3]

0521 **4** 1 **Resplendent Alpha**[14] 7315 4-8-11 **78** JimmyQuinn 8 83
(P Howling) *stdd s: hld up in last: stl there 2f out: prog on inner over 1f out: styd on wl enoughh fnl f but no ch to rch ldrs* **8/1**[3]

6526 **5** shd **Temple Of Thebes (IRE)**[24] 7181 3-9-4 **85** TGMcLaughlin 3 89+
(E A L Dunlop) *t.k.h early: hld up bhd ldrs: grad lost pl and in last pair 2f out: shkn up over 1f out: r.o fnl f: no ch of chalng* **16/1**

5660 **6** 1 ¼ **Woodcote (IRE)**[16] 7290 6-8-9 **76** (t) LPKeniry 12 75
(P R Chamings) *t.k.h early: prom on outer: chsd ldr 2f out to over 1f out: wknd ins fnl f* **25/1**

626 **7** shd **Mambo Spirit (IRE)**[16] 7290 4-8-12 **79** JimCrowley 4 78
(J G Given) *hld up towards rr: rdn 2f out: no prog tl kpt on fnl f: n.d* **10/1**

0000 **8** shd **Buxton**[9] 7390 4-8-12 **79** (t) FergusSweeney 11 77
(R Ingram) *hld up in rr: prog on outer wl over 2f out: drvn and nt qckn over 1f out: kpt on again fnl 100yds* **12/1**

2000 **9** 1 ½ **Halsion Chancer**[22] 7215 4-9-1 **82** SteveDrowne 9 75
(J R Best) *prom on outer: rdn over 2f out: nt qckn over 1f out: wknd* **5/1**[2]

0305 **10** 5 **Tia Mia**[46] 6699 3-9-2 **83** (p) ShaneKelly 6 60
(M Botti) *chsd ldrs to over 2f out: sn wknd* **9/1**

0200 **11** 1 ¾ **Harbour Blues**[31] 7047 3-8-13 **80** (t) CatherineGannon 10 52
(A W Carroll) *pressed ldr to 2f out: wknd rapidly* **33/1**

1m 10.33s (-1.57) **Going Correction** +0.05s/f (Slow) course record **11** Ran SP% **116.9**
Speed ratings (Par 105): **112,110,109,108,108 105,105,105,103,96 94**
toteswinger: 1&2 £7.50, 1&3 £4.40, 2&3 £16.80. CSF £25.44 CT £162.84 TOTE £2.80: £1.90, £4.10, £1.90; EX 46.50 Trifecta £184.20 Pool: £455.54 - 1.83 winning units..
Owner W McKay, J Barton **Bred** Ennistown Stud **Trained** Bawtry, S Yorks

FOCUS
A decent turnout for the money, and won by a progressive type who has now won three of his races on sand. He is beginning to look very useful, and should win again. It has been rated positively around the third.

7478 HORLEY H'CAP 5f (P)
3:35 (3:35) (Class 5) (0-70,67) 3-Y-O+ **£2,729** (£806; £403) **Stalls** High

Form RPR

1 **Step It Up (IRE)**[37] 6915 4-9-1 **64** PatCosgrave 8 73
(J R Boyle) *hld up in last pair: wound up on wd outside for effrt 2f out: styd on strly fr over 1f out to ld last 75yds* **5/1**[2]

0013 **2** ¾ **Bluebok**[9] 7377 7-8-9 **63** (bt) JackDean(5) 4 69
(J M Bradley) *t.k.h: w ldr: narrow ld fr 2f out tl hdd and outpcd last 75yds* **5/1**[2]

6530 **3** hd **Matterofact (IRE)**[18] 7276 5-8-10 **62** TolleyDean(3) 1 67
(M S Saunders) *narrow ld to 2f out: w ldr after: one pce last 75yds* **13/2**

3000 **4** ¾ **Cosmic Destiny (IRE)**[36] 6925 6-9-2 **65** LPKeniry 2 69+
(E F Vaughan) *dwlt: t.k.h early: hld up in last pair: gng wl 2f out: effrt and nt clr run over 1f out: prog ent fnl f: keeping on whn out of room nr fin* **6/1**[3]

0000 **5** ½ **Magic Glade**[13] 7346 9-8-4 **60** AndrewHeffernan(7) 6 61
(Peter Grayson) *w ldrs to 2f out: nt qckn u.p over 1f out: kpt on again ins fnl f* **16/1**

002 **6** 2 ¼ **Mayoman (IRE)**[13] 7346 3-9-4 **67** EddieAhern 3 60
(M Mullineaux) *dwlt: hld up in rr: prog 1/2-way: drvn to chse ldrs over 1f out: wknd ins fnl f* **9/2**[1]

0/5 **7** 2 ¾ **Meancog (IRE)**[13] 7346 4-8-10 **62** LukeMorris(3) 9 45
(J S Moore) *racd wd: w ldrs to 2f out: wknd over 1f out* **10/1**

0020 **8** nk **Gleaming Spirit (IRE)**[14] 7323 4-8-13 **62** (v) AdamKirby 5 44
(Peter Grayson) *chsd ldrs on inner: lost pl 2f out: struggling after* **8/1**

5-00 **9** 1 ¼ **Gifted Gamble**[21] 7225 6-8-9 **65** (b) AndreaAtzeni(7) 10 42
(Peter Grayson) *in tch on outer: drvn over 2f out: no prog over 1f out: btn after* **20/1**

000 **10** 2 **Blakeshall Diamond**[9] 7377 3-8-13 **62** SteveDrowne 7 32
(K G Wingrove) *hld up towards rr: no prog over 1f out: wknd* **25/1**

58.95 secs (0.15) **Going Correction** +0.05s/f (Slow) **10** Ran SP% **113.8**
Speed ratings (Par 103): **100,98,98,97,96 92,88,88,86,82**
toteswinger: 1&2 £4.00, 1&3 £6.90, 2&3 £6.30. CSF £29.44 CT £166.36 TOTE £4.80: £2.00, £2.00, £2.20; EX 32.40 Trifecta £271.20 Pool: £659.87 - 1.80 winning units. Place 6: £1,015.31 Place 5: £488.58.
Owner Fools On Stools Partnership **Bred** David Fitzgerald **Trained** Epsom, Surrey

FOCUS
A typical low-grade sprint, with two confirmed front-runners making it a solid pace. The winner has moved from Ireland to Britain to avoid being ballotted out because of his rating, and could be ahead of the Handicapper. The form looks solid rated around the runner-up.
T/Plt: £1,259.00 to a £1 stake. Pool: £53,206.41. 30.85 winning tickets. T/Qpdt: £367.70 to a £1 stake. Pool: £4,274.10. 8.60 winning tickets. JN

7486 - (Foreign Racing) - See Raceform Interactive

7449 SAINT-CLOUD (L-H)
Friday, November 28

OFFICIAL GOING: Heavy

7487a PRIX BELLE DE NUIT (LISTED RACE) (F&M) 1m 4f 110y
12:35 (12:41) 3-Y-O+ **£19,118** (£7,647; £5,735; £3,824; £1,912)

RPR

1 **Believe Me (IRE)**[56] 6465 4-9-4 TJarnet 16 99
(A De Royer-Dupre, France)

2 1 ½ **Saturnine (IRE)**[63] 6264 3-8-8 J-BEyquem 13 94
(N Clement, France)

3 2 **Fast Lane Lili**[6] 5-8-0 JAuge 3 75
(F Doumen, France)

4 ½ **Neve Lieve (IRE)**[35] 6948 3-8-8 GBenoist 6 90
(M Botti) *racd in 2nd: led narrowly 2 1/2f out to 2f out: kpt on at one pce once hdd* **74/1**[3]

5 hd **Wingstar (IRE)**[6] 4-9-0 THuet 11 88
(Robert Collet, France)

6 1 ½ **Canzonetta (FR)**[40] 5-9-0 DBonilla 8 86
(F-X de Chevigny, France)

7 nse **La Tournesol (GER)** 3-8-8 FilipMinarik 19 87
(P Schiergen, Germany)

8 3 **Silk Affair (IRE)**[29] 7100 3-8-8 MickyFenton 9 82
(M G Quinlan) *hld up in rr: 17th st: rdn 2 1/2f out: kpt on steadily u.str.p* **42/1**[2]

9 3 **Golden Era**[35] 3-8-8 DBoeuf 1 77
(H-A Pantall, France)

10 1 **Audebelle (FR)**[25] 7171 3-8-8 GMasure 20 76
(Y De Nicolay, France)

0 **Pretty Demanding (IRE)**[19] 7045 4-9-0 JO'Dwyer 12 —
(M G Quinlan) *pushed along to ld after 1f: rdn 3f out: hdd 2 1/2f out: wknd and eased* **42/1**[2]

0 **Silver Mitzva (IRE)**[29] 7100 4-9-0 ....(b) WMongil 14 —
(M Botti) *midfield on outside: lost pl wl over 3f out: rdn and btn in last ent st* 32/1[1]

0 **Pokettas (FR)**[446] 4-9-0 .... JLBorrego 15 —
(C Alonso Pena, Spain)

0 **Folle Allure (FR)**[17] 7348 3-8-13 .... IMendizabal 7 —
(J-C Rouget, France)

0 **Cosmic Fire (FR)**[42] 3-8-8 ....(b) MaximeFoulon 10 —
(D Sepulchre, France)

0 **Lumiere Astrale (FR)**[137] 4040 3-8-8 .... TFarina 18 —
(A Fabre, France)

0 **Maine Rose**[49] 3-8-8 .... RonanThomas 5 —
(J-M Beguigne, France)

0 **Epic Similie**[17] 7348 3-8-8 .... GToupel 2 —
(H-A Pantall, France)

0 **Montagne Lointaine (IRE)**[52] 6567 3-8-8 ....(b) ACrastus 4 —
(E Lellouche, France)

3m 0.30s (180.30)
WFA 3 from 4yo+ 6lb 19 Ran SP% **9.0**
PARI-MUTUEL: WIN 6.10; PL 2.60, 2.90, 3.80; DF 42.50.
Owner M Parrish **Bred** Skymarc Farm Inc **Trained** Chantilly, France

NOTEBOOK
Neve Lieve(IRE) was not at all disgraced on this step up in class over a trip short of her best.
Silk Affair(IRE), pulled up at Lingfield last time, never got involved at any stage. She was keeping on late though and ran her race in the face of yet another stiff task.

7464 KEMPTON (A.W) (R-H)

Saturday, November 29

OFFICIAL GOING: Standard
Wind: Medium, behind Weather: Cold, overcast, spells of rain

7489 BET HENNESSY GOLD CUP - BETDAQ MEDIAN AUCTION MAIDEN STKS 1m 4f (P)

2:15 (2:15) (Class 5) 3-5-Y-0 £2,590 (£770; £385; £192) **Stalls** Centre

Form RPR

4443 1 **Capstan**[72] 6060 3-9-3 68 .... GeorgeBaker 2 67+
(G L Moore) *stdd s: hld up in tch: jnd ldrs over 2f out: shkn up to ld over 1f out: clr fnl f: easily* 1/1[1]

4332 2 3 1/2 **Locum**[12] 7364 3-9-3 65 .... PaulMulrennan 7 61
(M H Tompkins) *chsd ldr tl over 6f out: in tch after: rdn and effrt on inner 2f out: outpcd by wnr over 1f out: wnt 2nd fnl 100yds* 9/4[2]

2202 3 nk **Eureka Moment**[16] 7296 3-8-12 67 ....(b[1]) EddieAhern 3 56
(E A L Dunlop) *chsd ldrs tl wnt 2nd over 6f out: ev ch and rdn 2f out: sn outpcd by wnr: lost 2nd fnl 100yds* 4/1[3]

6 4 5 **Jayyid (IRE)**[8] 7403 3-9-3 0 .... HayleyTurner 1 53
(C E Brittain) *sn led: rdn and rn green over 2f out: hdd over 1f out: sn outpcd and wl btn* 14/1

5 1 1/4 **A Valley Away (IRE)** 4-9-4 0 .... FrankieMcDonald 5 46
(Jane Chapple-Hyam) *hld up in tch in last pl: rdn over 2f out: sn outpcd: wl btn fnl f* 33/1

0060 6 3 **Peas 'n Beans (IRE)**[8] 7401 5-9-9 43 .... ShaneKelly 6 46
(T Keddy) *hld up in tch: rdn over 2f out: sn outpcd: wl btn fnl f* 66/1

2m 38.01s (3.51) **Going Correction** +0.10s/f (Slow)
WFA 3 from 4yo+ 6lb 6 Ran SP% **111.9**
Speed ratings (Par 103): **92,89,89,86,85 83**
toteswinger: 1&2 £1.40, 1&3 £1.40, 2&3 £1.70. CSF £3.45 TOTE £1.90: £1.50, £1.60; EX 3.70.
Owner J Daniels **Bred** Aston House Stud **Trained** Woodingdean, E Sussex

FOCUS
Very ordinary maiden form based on the proximity of the sixth.

7490 BET MULTIPLES - BETDAQ H'CAP 7f (P)

2:50 (2:51) (Class 6) (0-65,67) 3-Y-0+ £2,047 (£604; £302) **Stalls** High

Form RPR

6-64 1 **To Be Or Not To Be**[14] 7344 3-8-9 **59** .... LukeMorris(3) 8 73+
(John Berry) *hld up in tch: sltly hmpd and swtchd rt over 2f out: hdwy u.p 2f out: str run to chse ldr ins fnl f: led wl ins fnl f: r.o wl* 28/1

220 2 nk **Blue Charm**[1] 7471 4-9-2 **62** .... GeorgeBaker 7 73
(S Kirk) *stdd s: hld up in midfield: hdwy over 2f out: chsd ldr over 1f out: led ent fnl f: hdd and no ex wl ins fnl f* 4/1[2]

6263 3 1 1/2 **Azure Mist**[8] 7403 3-9-4 **65** .... PaulMulrennan 9 71
(M H Tompkins) *led: clr and rdn over 2f out: drvn and hdd ent fnl f: one pce after* 16/1

2040 4 1 1/4 **Castano**[19] 7277 4-9-2 **65** ....(p) JamesMillman(3) 10 69
(B R Millman) *hld up bhd: hdwy over 2f out: rdn and r.o fr over 1f out: wnt 4th ins fnl f: nt rch ldrs* 15/2

6002 5 3/4 **Daring Dream (GER)**[12] 7359 3-8-13 **60** .... JimCrowley 11 62
(A P Jarvis) *sn pushed up to chse ldr: rdn over 2f out: lost 2nd over 1f out: wknd jst ins fnl f* 8/1

20-2 6 1 1/4 **Ede's Dot Com (IRE)**[174] 2860 4-9-3 **63** .... IanMongan 3 61
(P M Phelan) *in tch: rdn and unable qck over 2f out: kpt on u.p fnl f: nvr pce to trble ldrs* 16/1

0021 7 hd **Salt Of The Earth (IRE)**[12] 7359 3-9-6 **67** .... HayleyTurner 5 64
(T G Mills) *chsd ldrs: rdn over 3f out: edgd lft u.p over 2f out: kpt on same pce fnl 2f* 11/2[3]

301 8 3/4 **Epidaurian King (IRE)**[31] 7076 5-9-4 **64** ....(v) DarrenWilliams 4 60
(D Shaw) *stdd and dropped in bhd after s: effrt on inner 2f out: nvr trbld ldrs* 15/2

0003 9 3/4 **Mr Garston**[12] 7359 5-9-5 **65** ....(t) PatCosgrave 14 59
(J R Boyle) *chsd ldrs: pushed along over 3f out: drvn over 1f out: wknd fnl f* 7/2[1]

0000 10 1/2 **Silidan**[12] 7358 5-8-12 **58** .... FergusSweeney 13 50
(G L Moore) *stdd s: hld up in rr: nvr trbld ldrs* 12/1

6650 11 1 **Sweet Kiss (USA)**[24] 7194 3-8-13 **60** .... CatherineGannon 6 49
(M J Attwater) *racd on outer in midfield: effrt and rdn 3f out: wknd jst over 2f out: eased ins fnl f* 33/1

6005 12 1/2 **Registrar**[32] 7055 6-9-0 **60** ....(p) JohnEgan 12 48
(Mrs C A Dunnett) *hld up in rr: nvr a factor* 14/1

1m 25.95s (-0.05) **Going Correction** +0.10s/f (Slow)
WFA 3 from 4yo+ 1lb 12 Ran SP% **124.8**
Speed ratings (Par 101): **104,103,101,100,99 98,98,97,96,95 94,94**
toteswinger: 1&2 £22.40, 1&3 £53.00, 2&3 £11.30. CSF £144.25 CT £1928.48 TOTE £38.70: £7.90, £1.20, £5.00; EX 272.50.
Owner W Thomas **Bred** J M Greetham **Trained** Newmarket, Suffolk

FOCUS
A low-grade handicap featuring mainly exposed sorts, but that comment does not apply to the winner. The form looks solid for the grade, with the runner-up and third rated to their recent best.
Sweet Kiss(USA) Official explanation: jockey said filly never travelled
Registrar Official explanation: jockey said gelding was unsuited by the surface

7491 BETDAQ.CO.UK WILD FLOWER STKS (LISTED RACE) 1m 4f (P)

3:25 (3:26) (Class 1) 3-Y-O+

£22,708 (£8,608; £4,308; £2,148; £1,076; £540) **Stalls** Centre

Form RPR

0446 1 **Dansant**[24] 7193 4-9-8 109 .... EddieAhern 5 108
(G A Butler) *stdd s: hld up in midfield: hdwy over 3f out: chsd ldr gng wl 2f out: rdn to ld jst over 1f out: r.o strly* 5/1[2]

4351 2 1 3/4 **Les Fazzani (IRE)**[21] 7242 4-9-3 107 .... NCallan 11 100
(K A Ryan) *led tl over 8f out: chsd ldng pair after: effrt to ld over 2f out: rdn and hung bdly lft fr 2f out: hdd over 1f out: kpt on same pce* 5/1[2]

1201 3 1/2 **Tropical Strait (IRE)**[21] 7244 5-9-6 103 .... FergusSweeney 9 102
(D W P Arbuthnot) *in tch in midfield: rdn and hdwy over 2f out: chsd ldng pair ent fnl f: kpt on to press for 2nd but no ch w wnr* 9/2[1]

2030 4 1 1/2 **Encircled**[21] 7242 4-9-1 76 .... AdamKirby 6 95
(D Haydn Jones) *stdd s: hld up bhd: hdwy on inner jst over 2f out: kpt on same pce u.p fnl f* 100/1

0130 5 5 **Philatelist (USA)**[7] 7420 4-9-6 106 .... ShaneKelly 8 92
(M A Jarvis) *hld up towards rr: hdwy over 2f out: chsd ldng pair over 1f out tl ent fnl f: wknd* 5/1[2]

1601 6 3/4 **Mischief Making (USA)**[30] 7100 3-8-11 100 .... ChrisCatlin 2 88
(E A L Dunlop) *stdd s: hld up in rr: effrt on outer over 2f out: no imp over 1f out: nvr nr ldrs* 16/1

4100 7 2 **Celtic Spirit (IRE)**[21] 7244 5-9-6 92 .... GeorgeBaker 10 88
(G L Moore) *hld up towards rr: n.m.r and shuffled bk over 2f out: shkn up 2f out: no hdwy* 14/1

2-63 8 4 **Kahara**[21] 7242 4-9-1 93 .... HayleyTurner 7 76
(L M Cumani) *chsd ldr tl led over 8f out: hdd over 3f out: rdn over 2f out: sn wknd* 10/1

5343 9 nk **Scintillo**[24] 7193 3-9-0 109 ....(b) SteveDrowne 4 81
(R Hannon) *t.k.h: hld up in tch in midfield: rdn to chse ldng pair briefly 2f out: wknd fnl f* 8/1[3]

0110 10 3/4 **Night Crescendo (USA)**[21] 7244 5-9-6 94 ....(p) JimCrowley 3 80
(Mrs A J Perrett) *prom: chsd ldr over 8f out tl led over 3f out: rdn and hdd over 2f out: wknd qckly 2f out* 14/1

0201 11 2 1/4 **Young Mick**[33] 7017 6-9-6 105 ....(v) JimmyQuinn 1 76
(G G Margarson) *hld up in midfield on outer: pushed along and lost pl over 3f out: bhd and rdn over 2f out: sn hung rt and no rspnse* 10/1

2m 32.95s (-1.55) **Going Correction** +0.10s/f (Slow)
WFA 3 from 4yo+ 6lb 11 Ran SP% **117.7**
Speed ratings (Par 111): **109,107,107,106,103 102,101,98,98,97 96**
toteswinger: 1&2 £6.60, 1&3 £4.80, 2&3 £4.90. CSF £30.27 TOTE £5.70: £2.20, £2.40, £1.90; EX 28.60.
Owner Mrs Barbara M Keller **Bred** Mrs Cino Del Duca **Trained** Newmarket, Suffolk

FOCUS
A solid-looking Listed contest. The fourth casts some doubt over the worth of the form, but she has been rated as improving 9lb on her previous best.

NOTEBOOK
Dansant did not look as if he was at the top of his game here last time but he proved a different horse this time. He travelled impressively with Eddie Ahern still motionless when the horse threw down his challenge over a furlong out. Despite conceding weight all round, he picked up well in the final furlong to score emphatically and repeat his victory in this race a year ago. Connections are mulling over a trip to Dubai for the carnival, or staying here and targeting something like the Winter Derby. (tchd 9-2 and 11-2)
Les Fazzani(IRE) came here in great form having won a fillies' Listed event at Doncaster last month and she seems equally effective on this surface. Although tackling colts this time, she again ran a fine race despite hanging over to the stands' rail in the straight. Once straightened up she stayed on well in the final furlong and she clearly has the ability to win a race like this on Polytrack. (op 11-2 tchd 9-2)
Tropical Strait(IRE), the November Handicap winner, did not have the clearest of passages but he was not unlucky, he just lacked the instant acceleration shown by the winner. He got going late in the day and he'd have been seen to better effect if they had gone a stronger pace early. He remains progressive. (op 5-1 tchd 6-1)
Encircled seems to have run way above her level given she was clear of the remainder in fourth despite being rated just 76.
Philatelist(USA) led home the remainder but he was again not at his best. (op 11-2)
Mischief Making(USA) stayed on well from a long way off the pace and will be seen to much better effect given a stiffer test of stamina or a stronger pace. (op 12-1)
Scintillo Official explanation: jockey said colt ran too free

7492 BETDAQ.CO.UK HYDE STKS (LISTED RACE) 1m (P)

4:00 (4:01) (Class 1) 3-Y-O+

£22,708 (£8,608; £4,308; £2,148; £1,076; £540) **Stalls** High

Form RPR

0-02 1 **Mac Love**[10] 7381 7-9-2 99 .... MickyFenton 4 109
(Stef Liddiard) *stdd after s: hld up wl bhd: stl plenty to do over 2f out: plld out wd and str run over 1f out: chal ins fnl f: r.o wl to ld towards fin* 16/1

0021 2 hd **Commander Cave (USA)**[15] 7313 3-9-0 103 .... EddieAhern 7 108
(R Hannon) *in tch in midfield: hdwy over 2f out: led 2f out: sn rdn: hrd pressed ins fnl f: hdd and no ex towards fin* 11/2[2]

0160 3 3 1/4 **Tis Mighty (IRE)**[15] 7328 5-8-11 0 .... EJMcNamara 11 96
(P J Prendergast, Ire) *hld up in tch in midfield: swtchd sharply rt and effrt on inner jst over 2f out: chsd ldng pair ins fnl f: no imp fnl 100yds* 25/1

-360 4 1 **Classic Legend**[43] 6781 3-8-9 90 .... IanMongan 6 93
(B J Meehan) *towards rr: swtchd rt and gd hdwy towards inner jst over 2f out: chsd ldrs over 1f out: kpt on same pce fnl f* 25/1

1 5 1/2 **Il Grande Maurizio (IRE)**[38] 6911 4-9-2 0 ....(t) CColombi 9 101+
(Frank Sheridan) *hld up in tch in midfield: nt clr run over 2f out: bdly hmpd and lost pl 2f out: rallied fnl f: nvr able to chal* 7/1

3241 6 1 **Little White Lie (IRE)**[24] 7201 4-9-2 104 .... JimCrowley 3 96
(J R Jenkins) *chsd ldrs: rdn over 2f out: unable qck u.p 2f out: kpt on same pce after* 13/2[3]

0531 7 nk **Confuchias (IRE)**[10] 7381 4-9-2 105 .... DarrenWilliams 14 95
(K R Burke) *trckd ldrs: gng wl over 2f out: chsd ldr 2f out: sn drvn and unable qck: wknd fnl f* 8/1

6000 8 1 **Capricorn Run (USA)**[7] 7418 5-9-2 95 ....(p) AdamKirby 13 93
(A J McCabe) *v.s.a: pushed along and hdwy into midfield 5f out: rdn and lost pl over 2f out: wl btn fnl 2f* 33/1

4610 **9** *nse* **Orchard Supreme**[7] 7420 5-9-2 100 .... SteveDrowne 5 92
(R Hannon) *stdd after s: hld up towards rr: swtchd lft and hdwy over 2f out: chsd ldrs over 1f out: wknd qckly ent fnl f* **20/1**

2141 **10** *5* **Mahadee (IRE)**[16] 7299 3-9-0 90 ....(b) NCallan 10 80
(C E Brittain) *chsd ldrs: rdn over 2f out: wknd over 1f out: wl btn and eased wl ins fnl f* **16/1**

0055 **11** *2 ¼* **Al Muheer (IRE)**[10] 7381 3-9-0 94 ....(p) HayleyTurner 1 75+
(C E Brittain) *stdd s: hld up in rr: effrt towards inner whn bdly hmpd and snatched up over 1f out: no ch after* **25/1**

0432 **12** *11* **Kylayne**[15] 7328 3-8-9 100 .... JohnEgan 8 44
(P W D'Arcy) *w ldr tl led wl over 2f out: rdn and hdd 2f out: wkng whn hmpd sn after: wl btn and eased ins fnl f* **16/1**

0402 **13** *3 ¾* **General Eliott (IRE)**[28] 7147 3-9-0 109 .... ShaneKelly 12 41
(P F I Cole) *led narrowly on inner tl wl over 2f out: wkng whn hmpd 2f out: heavily eased ins fnl f* **7/4**[1]

1526 **14** *28* **Mr Lambros**[10] 7381 7-9-2 92 ....(vt) GeorgeBaker 2 —
(Miss Gay Kelleway) *racd on outer: pressed ldrs: rdn over 2f out: wkng whn bdly hmpd jst over 2f out: virtually p.u fnl f* **33/1**

1m 37.52s (-2.28) **Going Correction** +0.10s/f (Slow)
WFA 3 from 4yo+ 2lb **14** Ran SP% **128.5**
Speed ratings (Par 111): **115,114,111,110,110 109,108,107,107,102 100,89,85,57**
toteswinger: 1&2 £14.60, 1&3 £123.60, 2&3 £48.30. CSF £100.14 TOTE £18.20: £4.20, £2.00, £9.30; EX 145.50.
Owner Vimal Khosla **Bred** Kingwood Bloodstock **Trained** Great Shefford, Berks

FOCUS
This was run at a furious pace and the picture changed dramatically in the final two furlongs as the pace collapsed and those held up began to take over. The form looks sound with the third and fourth good guides to the level.

NOTEBOOK
Mac Love was ridden with terrific patience by Micky Fenton, who was clearly at pains to hold his mount up until the last possible minute. Still virtually last two furlongs out, he was pulled out and asked to go through the gears, which he did, in very impressive fashion. This was his first success since 2004, and his first over this trip, but his new connections appear to have revitalised him and this was a rattling good performance. (op 20-1)
Commander Cave(USA) was having his first run in this company having worked his way up the handicap ranks and he emerges from this with tremendous credit, staying on well having taken over entering the final furlong. He is still progressing. (tchd 9-2)
Tis Mighty(IRE) kept on well up the inside rail without showing any great change of pace and she tends to struggle in this company. (tchd 33-1)
Classic Legend shaped with more encouragement back in trip and tackling this surface for the first time.
Il Grande Maurizio(IRE) ◆, who did not have a clear passage in the straight, was forced to switch to the inside, from which point he stayed on really strongly. This was just his second start in this country having won eight races in Italy and he showed when winning a good handicap here last month that he is a quality performer on this surface. He looks one to keep on the right side. (op 8-1 tchd 9-1)
Mahadee(IRE) Official explanation: jockey said colt was hampered
Kylayne Official explanation: jockey said filly suffered interference in running
General Eliott(IRE), having his first taste of Polytrack, proved to be very disappointing after being prominent early. Official explanation: jockey said colt suffered interference in running and lost its action (op 9-4 tchd 11-4 in a place and 5-2 in places)
Mr Lambros Official explanation: jockey said gelding never travelled

7493 BETDAQ THE BETTING EXCHANGE H'CAP 1m 4f (P)
4:30 (4:31) (Class 3) (0-90,88) 3-Y-0+
£7,477 (£2,239; £1,119; £560; £279; £140) **Stalls** Centre

Form RPR

5140 **1** **Paktolos (FR)**[64] 5249 5-9-10 88 ....(b) FergusSweeney 7 100
(A King) *stdd and dropped in bhd after s: hld up in last pair: c wd over 2f out: rdn and hdwy over 1f out: 5th ent fnl f: r.o strly to ld fnl 50yds* **20/1**

521 **2** *1* **Scarab (IRE)**[25] 7174 3-8-6 76 .... JohnEgan 10 86+
(M Johnston) *chsd ldrs: wnt 2nd and chsd over 4f out: led wl over 2f out: sn rdn: clr over 1f out: edgd lft u.p fnl f: hdd and no ex fnl 50yds* **9/4**[1]

1652 **3** *½* **Lochiel**[22] 7230 4-8-13 77 .... EddieAhern 8 86
(G A Swinbank) *taken down early: chsd ldrs: drvn to chse ldr 2f out: kpt on u.p but nvr quite pce to chal* **9/2**[2]

3111 **4** *¾* **Stand Guard**[12] 7354 4-8-9 78 .... AndreaAtzeni(5) 1 86
(P Howling) *hld up in last trio: hdwy over 3f out: chsd ldrs and hrd rdn over 1f out: kpt on but nvr quite pce to rch ldrs* **11/2**[3]

0001 **5** *4* **Awatuki (IRE)**[9] 7398 5-9-5 83 .... PatCosgrave 6 85
(J R Boyle) *hld up in rr: hdwy 3f out: chsd ldrs and drvn over 1f out: wknd ent fnl f* **12/1**

6156 **6** *6* **Judgethemoment (USA)**[63] 6286 3-9-3 87 .... IanMongan 5 79
(Jane Chapple-Hyam) *led for 2f: chsd ldr after tl over 4f out: rdn over 3f out: struggling over 2f out: no ch fnl 2f* **16/1**

0551 **7** *½* **Ellmau**[41] 6839 3-9-2 86 .... ChrisCatlin 2 77
(E J O'Neill) *awkward leaving stalls: sn pushed up to chse ldr: led after 2f: clr 8f out tl reduced advantage over 4f out: hdd wl over 2f out: wknd u.p 2f out* **15/2**

1202 **8** *8* **Cupid's Glory**[51] 6599 6-9-6 84 .... GeorgeBaker 9 62
(G L Moore) *racd in midfield: hdwy 4f out: chsd ldrs on inner and rdn over 2f out: wknd qckly over 1f out* **13/2**

0636 **9** *7* **Red Wine**[16] 7301 9-8-6 75 .... EJMcNamara(5) 3 42
(A J McCabe) *s.i.s: hld up bhd: nvr trbld ldrs: wl btn and eased fnl f* **33/1**

2503 **10** *18* **Indicible (FR)**[33] 7025 4-9-4 82 .... TravisBlock 4 20
(A King) *racd on outer in midfield: rdn and struggling over 3f out: wl bhd fnl 2f: t.o* **11/1**

2m 33.11s (-1.39) **Going Correction** +0.10s/f (Slow)
WFA 3 from 4yo+ 6lb **10** Ran SP% **119.0**
Speed ratings (Par 107): **108,107,107,106,103 99,99,94,89,77**
toteswinger: 1&2 £8.80, 1&3 £17.30, 2&3 £3.30. CSF £66.48 CT £252.59 TOTE £22.50: £5.40, £1.40, £1.60; EX 99.00.
Owner P Finnegan **Bred** Stilvi Compania **Trained** Barbury Castle, Wilts

FOCUS
Strong-looking handicap form which has been rated on the positive side. It should throw up a few winners.

NOTEBOOK
Paktolos(FR) came from a long way back to win. He was hanging to his right early in the straight but, once switched to the outside, he really found his stride. He was motoring as the leaders were wilting, and that enabled him to get on top in the final strides. He is dependent on a strong pace, which is why his record is quite patchy.
Scarab(IRE) is lightly raced and improving quickly, and this was a very good effort given he chased a strong pace and was asked to go on turning for home. He understandably got tired in the closing stages but he could be a well-handicapped horse. (op 5-2 tchd 11-4 in places)
Lochiel just could not reel in Scarab having chased him for the final couple of furlongs and, although still fairly unexposed himself, he does not seem to do very much in a hurry. (op 7-1 tchd 8-1)
Stand Guard made his effort over a furlong out and kept on well enough given he's been doing all of his winning over 1m2f, but it looks like the handicapper may be closing in on him now. (op 5-1)

7494 BET PREMIER LEAGUE FOOTBALL - BETDAQ H'CAP (DIV I) 1m (P)
5:00 (5:01) (Class 5) (0-70,70) 3-Y-0+ **£2,266** (£674; £337; £168) **Stalls** High

Form RPR

0306 **1** **Dinner Date**[30] 7094 6-8-12 62 .... ShaneKelly 4 72
(T Keddy) *hld up in tch in rr: swtchd rt and qcknd smartly to ld wl over 1f out: a holding rivals fnl f: rdn out* **14/1**

4006 **2** *1 ¼* **Trafalgar Square**[12] 7360 6-9-1 65 .... JimCrowley 9 72
(M J Attwater) *dwlt: sn trcking ldng pair: gng wl whn nt clr run briefly and swtchd rt 2f out: sn chsng wnr: hrd drvn and no imp fnl f* **4/1**[1]

3004 **3** *1 ½* **Aphrodisia**[14] 7342 4-9-2 66 .... GeorgeBaker 6 70
(S C Williams) *hld up in tch in midfield: swtchd rt and hdwy 2f out: chsd ldng pair jst over 1f out: no imp fnl 100yds* **6/1**[2]

0043 **4** *1 ¾* **Restless Genius (IRE)**[12] 7360 3-9-3 69 ....(t) SteveDrowne 5 69
(A M Balding) *hld up in tch towards rr: swtchd lft and rdn over 2f out: carried sltly lft 2f out: kpt on same pce fnl f* **4/1**[1]

5000 **5** *nk* **Danski**[15] 7309 5-9-3 67 ....(p) IanMongan 11 66
(Mrs L J Mongan) *led: rdn and hung lft jst over 2f out: sn hdd: kpt on same pce u.p after* **16/1**

64 **6** *1 ½* **Watson's Bay**[12] 7360 3-8-8 67 .... RossAtkinson(7) 8 63
(Miss Tor Sturgis) *t.k.h: hld up wl in tch: rdn and effrt over 2f out: carried sltly lft 2f out: plugged on same pce* **7/1**[3]

5550 **7** *¾* **Murrin (IRE)**[16] 7302 4-9-6 70 .... TravisBlock 1 64
(T G Mills) *t.k.h: hld up in midfield on outer: swtchd lft and effrt over 2f out: carried sltly lft 2f out: no imp fr over 1f out* **8/1**

0123 **8** *2* **Margot Mine (IRE)**[30] 7088 3-8-4 56 oh4 ....(b) FrancisNorton 2 48
(J S Moore) *t.k.h: chsd ldr: rdn over 2f out: hung lft u.p jst over 2f out: wknd ent fnl f: btn whn short of room and eased wl ins fnl f* **16/1**

2002 **9** *33* **Maximus Aurelius (IRE)**[8] 7405 3-9-1 70 .... LukeMorris(3) 7 —
(J Jay) *hld up in tch in rr: c wd and effrt wl over 2f out: no hdwy 2f out: virtually p.u ins fnl f* **4/1**[1]

400 **10** *22* **Charlie Bear**[33] 7021 7-8-6 56 oh11 .... SimonWhitworth 10 —
(Miss Z C Davison) *virtually ref to r: a t.o* **40/1**

1m 39.33s (-0.47) **Going Correction** +0.10s/f (Slow)
WFA 3 from 4yo+ 2lb **10** Ran SP% **118.8**
Speed ratings (Par 103): **106,104,103,101,101 99,98,96,63,41**
toteswinger: 1&2 £14.40, 1&3 £13.00, 2&3 £6.60. CSF £70.68 CT £393.48 TOTE £15.80: £4.20, £2.30, £2.10; EX 65.70.
Owner Mrs H Keddy **Bred** J M Greetham **Trained** Newmarket, Suffolk

FOCUS
Sound form to an ordinary handicap, with the winner a course specialist, and the runner-up and third rated close to their recent all-weather marks.
Maximus Aurelius(IRE) Official explanation: trainer said colt had a breathing problem

7495 BET PREMIER LEAGUE FOOTBALL - BETDAQ H'CAP (DIV II) 1m (P)
5:30 (5:30) (Class 5) (0-70,70) 3-Y-0+ **£2,266** (£674; £337; £168) **Stalls** High

Form RPR

3500 **1** **Millfield (IRE)**[15] 7315 5-9-6 70 .... GeorgeBaker 9 79
(P R Chamings) *mounted on crse: taken down early: s.i.s: hld up in last trio: plld out jst over 2f out: rdn to ld 1f out: r.o wl: in command fnl 50yds* **3/1**[2]

0612 **2** *1 ¼* **Follow The Flag (IRE)**[3] 7457 4-8-12 67 ....(p) EJMcNamara(5) 3 74
(A J McCabe) *trckd ldrs: hdwy to chal 2f out: ev ch and rdn 1f out: kpt on but nt pce of wnr fnl 100yds* **9/4**[1]

5655 **3** *nk* **Ballora (FR)**[14] 7342 3-9-2 68 .... JamesDoyle 10 73
(S Kirk) *trckd ldrs on inner: rdn and ev ch over 1f out: nt pce of wnr fnl 100yds: kpt on* **8/1**

0430 **4** *½* **Master Pegasus**[12] 7360 5-9-0 64 .... PatCosgrave 6 69
(J R Boyle) *led: hrd pressed and rdn 2f out: hdd 1f out: kpt on same pce u.p ins fnl f* **5/1**[3]

0004 **5** *nk* **Burnbrake**[33] 7027 3-8-12 67 .... JamesMillman(3) 8 70
(L Montague Hall) *hld up in wl in tch in midfield: shkn up 2f out: chsd ldrs ent fnl frong: kpt on but nvr quite pce to chal* **16/1**

0036 **6** *nse* **My Shadow**[16] 7307 3-9-2 68 .... IanMongan 7 71
(S Dow) *taken down early: hld up in midfield: rdn and hdwy over 2f out: ev ch u.p ent fnl f: wknd ins fnl f* **17/2**

5000 **7** *2 ½* **Inquisitress**[10] 7392 4-8-3 56 oh3 .... MarcHalford(3) 2 54
(J J Bridger) *stdd and dropped in bhd after s: hld up in last pair: hdwy over 2f out: chsd ldrs over 1f out: sn outpcd and no imp fnl f* **25/1**

0000 **8** *1 ¾* **Billy One Punch**[12] 7360 6-8-10 60 .... DarrenWilliams 4 54
(D Shaw) *stdd after s: t.k.h: hld up in last pair: nvr trbld ldrs* **20/1**

2-03 **9** *5* **Certain Justice (USA)**[33] 7027 10-9-3 67 .... MickyFenton 5 50
(Stef Liddiard) *t.k.h: chsd ldr tl 2f out: sn wknd* **10/1**

1m 41.5s (1.70) **Going Correction** +0.10s/f (Slow)
WFA 3 from 4yo+ 2lb **9** Ran SP% **117.7**
Speed ratings (Par 103): **95,93,93,92,92 92,90,88,83**
toteswinger: 1&2 £2.90, 1&3 £6.70, 2&3 £5.60. CSF £10.40 CT £48.71 TOTE £3.90: £1.60, £1.20, £3.20; EX 8.00.
Owner Inhurst Players **Bred** Limestone Stud **Trained** Baughurst, Hants

FOCUS
Master Pegasus was allowed an easy lead in front and the pace was very steady, which didn't help Certain Justice, who pulled his chance away in the first couple of furlongs. There was something of a bunch finish and the winner has been rated back to something like his best.

7496 TRY BETDAQ FOR AN EXCHANGE H'CAP 1m 2f (P)
6:00 (6:01) (Class 2) (0-100,99) 3-Y-0+
£11,215 (£3,358; £1,679; £840; £419; £210) **Stalls** High

Form RPR

2211 **1** **Suits Me**[17] 7291 5-9-6 97 .... MickyFenton 7 106
(T P Tate) *mde all: jnd and rdn 2f out: forged ahd ent fnl f: styd on gamely* **6/1**[3]

1064 **2** *1 ½* **Mafeking (UAE)**[23] 7208 4-8-9 86 .... SteveDrowne 8 92
(M R Hoad) *chsd ldng pair: effrt to join wnr 2f out: sn rdn: unable qck over 1f out: kpt on same pce after* **33/1**

0302 **3** *¾* **Moynahan (USA)**[15] 7313 3-9-3 98 .... ShaneKelly 11 103
(P F I Cole) *chsd ldrs: rdn and unable qck 2f out: kpt on u.p fnl f: wnt 3rd last stride: nvr gng pce to chal wnr* **4/1**[1]

4613 **4** *shd* **Press The Button (GER)**[8] 7404 5-9-1 92 .... PatCosgrave 5 96
(J R Boyle) *chsd ldrs: hdwy to join wnr 2f out: hung rt and unable qck over 1f out: drvn and no ex ins fnl f: lost 3rd last stride* **9/2**[2]

0066 **5** *½* **Hinton Admiral**[23] 7215 4-8-3 85 oh1 .... EJMcNamara(5) 3 88+
(R A Fahey) *stdd s: hld up towards rr: hdwy 6f out: rdn and unable qck 2f out: styd on wl fnl f: nvr gng pce to rch ldrs* **8/1**

4200 **6** ¾ **Big Robert**[21] 7244 4-9-8 **99** .... JimCrowley 10 101+
(K R Burke) *stdd s: hld up in last pl: stl gng wl over 2f out: swtchd lft wl over 1f out: rdn and styd on fr over 1f out: nvr trbld ldrs* **7/1**

1100 **7** 1 **Art Man**[68] 6171 5-8-12 **89** .... FergusSweeney 9 89
(G L Moore) *stdd s: hld up in last pair: hdwy over 2f out: rdn and little rspnse 2f out: kpt on fnl f but nvr pce to rch ldrs* **6/1**[3]

5000 **8** 9 **Allanit (GER)**[35] 6984 4-8-13 **90** .... EddieAhern 6 72
(A P Stringer) *hld up towards rr: lost tch 2f out* **20/1**

0006 **9** 1 ¾ **Profit's Reality (IRE)**[8] 7404 6-8-10 **87** ....(b[1]) IanMongan 4 65
(M J Attwater) *t.k.h: chsd ldr: rdn over 2f out: short of room and snatched up jst over 2f out: sn wknd* **16/1**

0640 **10** 3 ¾ **Scartozz**[43] 6772 6-8-8 **90** ....(b) AndreaAtzeni(5) 1 61
(M Botti) *t.k.h: chsd ldrs: rdn and struggling whn jostled 2f out: wl btn after* **10/1**

3600 **11** 4 ½ **Scamperdale**[7] 7420 6-8-3 **87** .... BillyCray(7) 2 49
(B P J Baugh) *dwlt: racd on outer: sn bustled up to r in midfield: rdn over 4f out: wl bhd fnl 2f* **14/1**

2m 4.86s (-3.14) **Going Correction** -0.075s/f (Stan)
WFA 3 from 4yo+ 4lb **11** Ran SP% **119.7**
Speed ratings (Par 109): **109,107,107,107,106 106,105,98,96,93 90**
toteswinger: 1&2 £16.10, 1&3 £4.30, 2&3 £15.60. CSF £185.07 CT £893.87 TOTE £6.60: £2.40, £7.30, £1.70; EX 168.00 Place 6: £139.97, Place 5: £121.16..
Owner D E Cook **Bred** R S A Urquhart **Trained** Tadcaster, N Yorks

FOCUS
A solid handicap run at a good pace. It has been rated around the third and fourth.

NOTEBOOK
Suits Me did this the hard way, making all the running and showing a terrific attitude to keep on strongly up the straight after looking as though he was about to be pounced on turning for home. The sharp nature of this 1m2f course suits horses who like to race close to the pace and Suits Me is a rock-solid performer when allowed to dictate, despite being edged up another 5lb for dead-heating at Wolverhampton last time. (op 5-1 tchd 9-2)
Mafeking(UAE) bounced right back to form after three poor efforts, but he could not get to grips with the winner in the straight despite having been bang in contention turning for home.
Moynahan(USA) saved ground by racing against the rail throughout and he stayed on well from off the pace to snatch third. (op 9-2 tchd 5-1)
Press The Button(GER) had every chance turning for home but could not sustain his effort. (tchd 5-1)
Big Robert, who was well backed, was far too far off the pace and, although he put in some good late work, he would have needed a pair of wings to land a blow. (op 8-1 tchd 13-2)
Allanit(GER) Official explanation: jockey said gelding hung right in home straight
Profit's Reality(IRE) Official explanation: jockey said gelding suffered interference in running
T/Plt: £393.90 to a £1 stake. Pool: £82,233.78. 152.39 winning tickets. T/Qpdt: £68.50 to a £1 stake. Pool: £4,999.96. 54.00 winning tickets. SP

7451 **WOLVERHAMPTON (A.W)** (L-H)
Saturday, November 29

OFFICIAL GOING: Standard
Wind: Nil Weather: Very foggy

7497 ABBA TRIBUTE NIGHT H'CAP (DIV I) 7f 32y(P)
6:20 (6:21) (Class 6) (0-55,59) 3-Y-O+ **£2,047** (£604; £302) **Stalls** High

Form RPR

4646 **1** **Marmooq**[48] 6681 5-8-10 **51** .... GrahamGibbons 7 62
(M J Attwater) *in mid-div 4f out: 4th st: in ld wl ins fnl f: drvn out* **8/1**[3]

0646 **2** ¾ **Thabaat**[10] 7383 4-8-7 **53** ....(b) MCGeran(5) 2 62
(J M Bradley) *dwlt: in rr 4f out: hdwy and c wd st: r.o to take 2nd last strides* **9/1**

0/14 **3** nk **Wakita (IRE)**[17] 7287 5-8-13 **54** ....(t) JerryO'Dwyer 5 62
(Aidan Anthony Howard, Ire) *mid-div 4f out: 7th st: rdn and ev ch wl ins fnl f: nt qckn* **10/3**[1]

0046 **4** 4 **Karate Queen**[29] 7112 3-8-10 **52** .... LPKeniry 3 49
(A M Balding) *prom 4f out: 2nd and ev ch st: wknd towards fin* **14/1**

0006 **5** 1 **Motu (IRE)**[10] 7382 7-9-0 **55** ....(b) HayleyTurner 1 50
(I W McInnes) *prom 4f out: n.m.r briefly 2f out: 3rd st: wknd towards fin* **10/1**

5500 **6** 1 ¼ **Mr Burton**[42] 6821 4-9-0 **55** ....(p) GregFairley 12 46
(M Mullineaux) *chsd ldr 4f out: led over 2f out: wknd ins fnl f* **28/1**

0650 **7** nse **Imperial Echo (USA)**[23] 7206 7-8-11 **55** .... TolleyDean(3) 6 46
(P Howling) *towards rr 4f out: n.d* **10/1**

-003 **8** ½ **Athboy Auction**[108] 4988 3-8-9 **51** .... JimmyQuinn 10 41
(H J Collingridge) *s.i.s: towards rr 4f out: n.d* **16/1**

3351 **9** ¾ **City For Conquest (IRE)**[11] 7375 5-8-6 **54** .... StacyRenwick(7) 4 42
(John A Harris) *in rr 4f out: nvr nr ldrs* **12/1**

3601 **10** 4 **Samurai Warrior**[12] 7363 3-9-3 **59** ....(p) TomEaves 11 36
(P D Evans) *in tch whn rdn over 3f out: 6th st: wknd over 1f out* **7/2**[2]

1400 **11** 3 **Mujahope**[125] 4450 3-8-9 **51** ....(v) AndrewElliott 8 20
(C J Teague) *towards rr whn pushed along over 3f out* **12/1**

0-00 **12** 12 **Whistleupthewind**[15] 7316 5-8-11 **52** ....(b) DaleGibson 9 —
(J M P Eustace) *in ld 4f out: hdd over 2f out: 5th and wkng st* **33/1**

1m 30.53s (0.93) **Going Correction** +0.125s/f (Slow)
WFA 3 from 4yo+ 1lb **12** Ran SP% **118.9**
Speed ratings (Par 101): **99,98,97,93,92 90,90,90,89,84 81,67**
toteswinger: 1&2 £15.90, 1&3 £3.90, 2&3 £9.80. CSF £78.41 CT £294.96 TOTE £8.10: £2.40, £3.20, £1.50; EX 50.60.
Owner The Attwater Partnership **Bred** Matthews Breeding And Racing Ltd **Trained** Epsom, Surrey

FOCUS
Thick fog made for poor visibility in this low-grade opener, with the runners out of sight from 6f out to the 4f pole, and again from a furlong and a half out until the last 100 yards or so. The form is sound with the first three clear.

7498 BOOK NOW FOR BOXING DAY MAIDEN STKS 7f 32y(P)
6:50 (6:51) (Class 5) 2-Y-O **£3,238** (£722; £722; £240) **Stalls** High

Form RPR

53 **1** **Pressing Matters (IRE)**[47] 6702 2-9-3 0 .... JimmyQuinn 8 72+
(M Botti) *prom 4f out: 3rd st: in ld ins fnl f: drvn out* **7/4**[1]

2 1 **Saptapadi (IRE)** 2-9-3 0 .... DaleGibson 7 70
(Sir Michael Stoute) *chsd ldr 4f out: rdn and 2nd st: sn ev ch: nt qckn cl home* **7/1**[3]

2 dht **Racketeer (IRE)** 2-9-3 0 .... NickyMackay 1 70
(J H M Gosden) *prom 4f out: 4th st: r.o ins fnl f: jnd 2nd post* **7/2**[2]

0 **4** 2 ¾ **Miskin Flyer**[61] 6327 2-8-12 0 .... CatherineGannon 4 58
(B Palling) *mid-div 4f out: rdn over 2f out: 5th st: kpt on same pce ins fnl f* **66/1**

6 **5** ½ **Chic Shanique (USA)**[14] 7341 2-8-12 0 .... RichardKingscote 2 57
(Tom Dascombe) *led early: stl in ld 4f out: rdn and hdd wl over 1f out: one pce* **16/1**

6 ½ **Wellesley** 2-9-3 0 .... AdamKirby 9 60+
(W R Swinburn) *hld up in rr 4f out: nvr trbld ldrs* **12/1**

04 **7** ¾ **Ask Dan (IRE)**[46] 6715 2-9-3 0 .... TomEaves 10 59
(B Smart) *mid-div 4f out: 6th st: no hdwy* **11/1**

8 ½ **Angelo Poliziano** 2-9-3 0 .... PaulMulrennan 6 57
(Mrs A Duffield) *hld up towards rr 4f out: n.d* **22/1**

9 ¾ **Munjum** 2-9-3 0 .... HayleyTurner 5 55
(L M Cumani) *s.i.s: hld up in rr 4f out* **7/1**[3]

0 **10** 1 ¼ **Pyrus Time (IRE)**[176] 2769 2-9-3 0 .... LPKeniry 12 52
(J S Moore) *hld up towards rr 4f out: 7th st* **33/1**

11 21 **Champagne Aerial (IRE)**[29] 7119 2-8-12 0 .... JerryO'Dwyer 3 —
(Aidan Anthony Howard, Ire) *hld up towards rr 4f out: rdn over 2f out: sn struggling: t.o* **40/1**

0 **12** 14 **Avrilo**[10] 7388 2-8-5 0 .... JakePayne(7) 11 —
(M S Saunders) *wl bhd 4f out: t.o* **100/1**

1m 31.88s (2.28) **Going Correction** +0.125s/f (Slow) **12** Ran SP% **117.7**
Speed ratings (Par 96): **91,89,89,86,86 85,84,84,83,81 57,41**
PL: Racketeer £1.80, Saptapadi £3.20; EX: PM-R £4.50, PM-S £9.50; CSF: PM-R £3.54, PM-S £6.89. toteswinger: 1&2 (Racketeer) £2.70, 1&2 (Saptapadi) £5.30, 2&3 £6.40. TOTE £2.70: £1.20.
Owner Giuliano Manfredini **Bred** Lady Legard **Trained** Newmarket, Suffolk

FOCUS
Similarly restricted visibility for this fairly ordinary maiden, run just over a second slower than the earlier 46-55 handicap for older horses.

NOTEBOOK
Pressing Matters(IRE) had been sold out of Ed McMahon's yard for 13,000gns since finishing third at Windsor on his second start and he got off the mark on his Polytrack debut. Asserting inside the last, he was suited by the extra furlong. (op 9-4 tchd 13-8)
Saptapadi(IRE) ◆ is a full brother to this year's Queen's Vase winner Patkai, out of an unraced half-sister to the high-class Islington and Greek Dance. He shaped with plenty of promise, always racing prominently, and is sure to go one better before long, probably over a bit further. (op 13-2 tchd 10-1)
Racketeer(IRE) ◆ is a half-brother to that fine filly Attraction, winner of the 1,000 Guineas and several other Group 1 prizes in 2004. He finished well to claim a share of second and, sure to improve for the experience, looks a ready-made maiden winner. (op 13-2 tchd 10-1)
Miskin Flyer showed little on her turf debut at Bath and this was a step in the right direction. (op 50-1)
Chic Shanique(USA) showed up for a long way and may do even better once handicapped. (op 14-1)
Wellesley stayed on from the rear of the field for sixth and is likely to improve on this. (op 14-1 tchd 16-1)

7499 WOLVERHAMPTON-RACECOURSE.CO.UK CLAIMING STKS 1m 5f 194y(P)
7:20 (7:22) (Class 6) 3-Y-O+ **£3,070** (£906; £453) **Stalls** Low

Form RPR

-301 **1** **La Estrella (USA)**[17] 7280 5-9-13 **80** .... LPKeniry 8 93
(D E Cantillon) *hld up and bhd: hdwy over 3f out: 2nd st in ld ins fnl f: styd on wl* **4/1**[3]

0404 **2** 4 **Salute (IRE)**[36] 6957 9-9-5 **74** .... HayleyTurner 2 80
(P G Murphy) *prom after 2f: wnt 2nd over 7f out: led over 2f out: 2nd ins fnl f: one pce* **3/1**[1]

2-05 **3** ½ **Heathyards Pride**[114] 4771 8-9-7 **83** .... GrahamGibbons 11 81
(R Hollinshead) *hld up in rr after 2f: pushed along and hdwy 3f out: 5th st: one pce ins fnl f* **7/2**[2]

0500 **4** 4 **Birkside**[8] 7404 5-9-13 **86** .... PaulMulrennan 10 81
(K A Ryan) *mid-div after 2f: hdwy over 3f out: 4th st: wknd ins fnl f* **5/1**

-104 **5** 11 **Clear Sailing**[7] 7423 5-8-11 **76** ....(p) ChrisCatlin 3 50
(George Baker) *in ld after 2f: hdd over 2f out: 3rd st: wknd over 1f out* **11/2**

0110 **6** 14 **Zalkani (IRE)**[56] 6493 8-9-3 **58** .... JerryO'Dwyer 4 36
(J Pearce) *hld up towards rr after 2f: rdn and hdwy over 3f out: wknd over 2f out: 6th st* **25/1**

0000 **7** 4 ½ **Tykie Two**[15] 7322 4-8-3 **47** ....(b[1]) DeanHeslop(5) 1 21
(S Wynne) *prom after 2f: rdn and wknd over 3f out* **66/1**

1566 **8** ½ **Atlantic Gamble (IRE)**[12] 7355 8-8-13 **55** ....(p) AndrewElliott 9 25
(K R Burke) *chsd ldr after 2f: lost 2nd over 7f out: rdn and wknd over 3f out* **33/1**

5050 **9** 9 **Don Jose (USA)**[93] 5415 5-9-11 **43** ....[1] RichardKingscote 5 25
(N J Vaughan) *mid-div after 2f: no ch over 2f out: eased over 1f out* **40/1**

2550 **10** 33 **Gifted Heir (IRE)**[248] 1032 4-8-12 **50** .... BMcHugh(7) 6 —
(A Bailey) *t.k.h towards rr after 2f: wl bhd over 3f out: sn eased: t.o* **33/1**

0221 **11** 59 **Ricci De Mare**[32] 7050 3-7-13 **55** .... DuranFentiman(3) 7 —
(G J Smith) *mid-div after 2f: virtually p.u ins fnl f* **25/1**

3m 5.28s (-0.72) **Going Correction** +0.125s/f (Slow)
WFA 3 from 4yo+ 8lb **11** Ran SP% **116.8**
Speed ratings (Par 101): **107,104,104,102,95 87,85,85,79,61 27**
toteswinger: 1&2 £3.50, 1&3 £3.60, 2&3 £2.40. CSF £15.19 TOTE £5.50: £2.00, £1.30, £1.60; EX 19.50.
Owner Mrs J Hart C Lynas & M Freedman **Bred** Five Horses Ltd And Theatrical Syndicate **Trained** Newmarket, Suffolk

FOCUS
Not a bad claimer, with the better horses finishing clear. The form seems sound enough.
Gifted Heir(IRE) Official explanation: jockey said colt hung right-handed
Ricci De Mare Official explanation: jockey said filly hung right-handed

7500 SPONSOR A RACE BY CALLING 01902 390009 (S) STKS 1m 141y(P)
7:50 (7:51) (Class 6) 3-Y-O+ **£1,978** (£584; £292) **Stalls** Low

Form RPR

4161 **1** **Barkass (UAE)**[11] 7373 4-9-5 **69** .... GeorgeBaker 5 74
(B Ellison) *hld up in mid-div: hdwy on ins over 3f out: led 1f out: drvn out* **5/6**[1]

2 nk **Keepsgettingbetter (IRE)** 3-8-11 0 .... AndrewElliott 3 69
(K R Burke) *led 1f: chsd ldr: rdn to ld over 2f out: hdd 1f out: r.o* **50/1**

1653 **3** 2 ½ **Kingsholm**[15] 7309 6-9-5 **63** .... JimmyQuinn 7 68
(N Wilson) *hld up towards rr: hdwy on ins 3f out: hrd rdn and no ex towards fin* **4/1**[2]

0350 **4** ½ **Putra Laju (IRE)**[14] 7345 4-8-11 **58** ....(p) PatrickHills(3) 10 62
(J W Hills) *s.i.s: hld up and bhd: hdwy over 2f out: one pce fnl f* **8/1**[3]

5 nk **Broughtons Silk** 3-8-6 0 .... ChrisCatlin 4 56
(W J Musson) *t.k.h in rr: hdwy whn swtchd rt wl over 1f out: swtchd lft ins fnl f: one pce* **40/1**

0040 **6** 1 **Semah Harold**[33] 7018 3-8-11 52..........................(v) GrahamGibbons 13 59
(E S McMahon) *s.i.s: hld up towards rr: hdwy over 1f out: nvr trbld ldrs* **12/1**

6040 **7** 1 1/2 **Climate (IRE)**[7] 7423 9-9-5 55..........................(p) TomEaves 9 60
(P D Evans) *hld up in tch: no hdwy fnl 2f* **12/1**

3640 **8** 1 **Roundthetwist (IRE)**[12] 7358 3-8-4 55.................. DeclanCannon(7) 11 53
(K R Burke) *prom: rdn and ev ch over 2f out: wknd fnl f* **40/1**

6033 **9** 1 1/4 **Tallest Peak (USA)**[89] 5574 3-8-11 53.................. VinceSlattery 2 50
(M G Quinlan) *prom: rdn over 2f out: wknd over 1f out* **16/1**

10 23 **All About Jack**[16] 4-9-0 0..........................(p) FrankieMcDonald 8 —
(G A Ham) *s.i.s: a in rr: lost tch over 3f out: t.o* **80/1**

-200 **11** nk **Seta Pura**[70] 6137 3-8-6 63.................. HayleyTurner 12 —
(R Ford) *hld up in tch: lost pl 4f out: sn bhd: t.o fnl 2f* **25/1**

0000 **12** 13 **Orchestrator (IRE)**[8] 7399 4-8-7 52..........................(t) TobyAtkinson(7) 1 —
(W Clay) *plld hrd: led after 1f: sn clr: hdd over 2f out: wknd qckly: t.o* **100/1**

1m 51.8s (1.30) **Going Correction** +0.125s/f (Slow)
WFA 3 from 4yo+ 3lb 12 Ran SP% **119.8**
Speed ratings (Par 101): **99,98,96,96,95 94,93,92,91,71 70,59**
toteswinger: 1&2 £17.10, 1&3 £1.30, 2&3 £12.50. CSF £78.41 TOTE £2.00: £1.20, £7.60, £1.20; EX 58.60.There was no bid for the winner. Keepsgettingbetter was claimed by Mr J. R. Gask for £6,000.
Owner W P Smith **Bred** Darley **Trained** Norton, N Yorks

FOCUS
The winner and third are decent sotrts for the lowly grade. The form is a bit muddling but has been rated to something like face value around the winner.

7501 FLORENCE GRUBB 60TH BIRTHDAY MAIDEN STKS 5f 20y(P)
8:20 (8:22) (Class 5) 2-Y-O **£3,238** (£963; £481; £240) **Stalls** Low

Form RPR

1 **Stash** 2-9-3 0.................. GrahamGibbons 3 78+
(R Hollinshead) *a.p: led 1f out: rdn and r.o wl* **16/1**

0652 **2** 2 3/4 **Romantic Queen**[23] 7205 2-8-12 65.................. ChrisCatlin 2 63
(E A L Dunlop) *led 1f: w ldr: led 2f out to 1f out: no ex wl ins fnl f* **11/8**[1]

20 **3** nk **La Verte Rue (USA)**[47] 6696 2-8-12 0.................. ShaneKelly 5 62+
(J A Osborne) *mid-div: hdwy over 1f out: r.o to take 3rd wl ins fnl f* **3/1**[2]

0305 **4** 3 **Chimbonda**[7] 7417 2-9-3 63..........................(t) AdamKirby 4 56
(S Parr) *chsd ldrs: rdn wl over 1f out: one pce* **5/1**[3]

2402 **5** shd **Dedante**[17] 7279 2-8-7 64..........................(b) JamesO'Reilly(5) 13 51
(D K Ivory) *led after 1f: hdd 2f out: wknd fnl f* **7/1**

0 **6** 1/2 **Green Onions**[89] 5578 2-8-12 0.................. GabrielHannon(5) 8 54
(D J S Ffrench Davis) *hld up and bhd: hdwy on outside wl over 1f out: no further prog fnl f* **40/1**

0 **7** 1 1/4 **Kina Jazz**[29] 7104 2-8-5 0.................. TobyAtkinson(7) 10 44
(M E Rimmer) *towards rr: rdn wl over 1f out: n.d* **100/1**

060 **8** shd **Meydan Style (USA)**[25] 7179 2-9-0 47.................. TolleyDean(3) 9 49
(J Balding) *chsd ldrs tl wknd over 2f out* **50/1**

9 1 1/2 **Theta Wave (USA)** 2-9-3 0.................. LPKeniry 6 44
(J R Gask) *s.i.s: sn chsng ldrs: wknd wl over 1f out* **25/1**

0 **10** 2 **Yes She Can Can**[57] 6434 2-8-5 0.................. AndrewHeffernan(7) 11 32
(Peter Grayson) *swtchd lft after 1f: a towards rr* **100/1**

11 5 **Iron Max (IRE)** 2-9-0 0.................. LukeMorris(3) 7 19
(N J Vaughan) *s.s: bmpd after 1f: a in rr* **16/1**

6000 **12** 23 **Neo's Mate (IRE)**[64] 6244 2-8-5 49.................. KrishGundowry(7) 1 —
(Paul Green) *n.m.r on ins sn after s: sn bhd: t.o* **50/1**

63.07 secs (0.77) **Going Correction** +0.125s/f (Slow) 12 Ran SP% **120.2**
Speed ratings (Par 96): **98,93,93,88,88 87,85,85,82,79 71,34**
toteswinger: 1&2 £2.80, 1&3 £2.70, 2&3 £1.60. CSF £38.37 TOTE £10.20: £3.30, £1.30, £1.60; EX 61.60.
Owner R Hollinshead **Bred** Reg Hollinshead **Trained** Upper Longdon, Staffs
■ Stewards' Enquiry : Andrew Heffernan two-day ban: careless riding (Dec 13-14)

FOCUS
A moderate sprint maiden.

NOTEBOOK
Stash made a taking debut, tracking the leading pair into the straight before going on to score in nice style. A half-sister to multiple sprint winner Tartatartufata out of a triple 5f-6f winner, he is bred for speed and should win more races in the right grade for his vastly experienced trainer. (op 14-1 tchd 12-1)
Romantic Queen, who was also runner-up on her nursery debut last time, had not run over the minimum distance before. She was always up with the speed but was put in her place by the winner late on. (op 5-4 tchd 6-4)
La Verte Rue(USA) was reverting to Polytrack having finished second on it on her debut and did not appear best suited by this drop back to 5f. (op 4-1 tchd 11-4)
Chimbonda was tried in a tongue tie and stayed on late against the rail, but he is not progressing and his best trip is still open to conjecture. (op 6-1 tchd 13-2 and 9-2)
Dedante showed up for a long way, but is well and truly exposed now. (op 17-2 tchd 9-1)

7502 WOLVERHAMPTON-RACECOURSE.CO.UK H'CAP 1m 1f 103y(P)
8:50 (8:50) (Class 4) (0-85,84) 3-Y-O+ **£5,180** (£1,541; £770; £384) **Stalls** Low

Form RPR

0336 **1** **Supercast (IRE)**[44] 6758 5-8-5 71.................. LukeMorris(3) 4 82
(N J Vaughan) *led: hdd over 7f out: prom: led 2f out: drvn out* **7/2**[1]

1004 **2** 1 1/2 **Just Bond (IRE)**[17] 7291 6-9-3 83.................. DuranFentiman(3) 1 91
(G R Oldroyd) *hld up in rr: hdwy 2f out: 5th st: c to stands' rail fr over 1f out: rdn and r.o one pce ins fnl f* **7/2**[1]

0602 **3** nk **Folio (IRE)**[9] 7398 8-8-8 71.................. ChrisCatlin 3 78
(W J Musson) *hld up: hdwy over 2f out: 4th st: kpt on same pce ins fnl f* **5/1**[3]

5-05 **4** 3 1/4 **Saltagioo (ITY)**[29] 7116 4-9-2 84.................. AndreaAtzeni(5) 2 84
(M Botti) *s.s: hld up: in ld over 3f out: rdn and hdd 2f out: 2nd st: wknd ins fnl f* **9/2**[2]

2040 **5** 4 1/2 **Kildare Sun (IRE)**[152] 3557 6-8-11 74.................. PaulMulrennan 7 65
(J Mackie) *prom: rdn 2f out: 3rd st: wknd fnl f* **14/1**

6111 **6** 17 **Bavarian Nordic (USA)**[32] 7046 3-8-12 81.................. AndrewMullen(3) 6 36
(Mrs A Duffield) *w ldr: 2nd whn rdn over 3f out: 6th and wkng st* **6/1**

4040 **7** nk **Dragon Slayer (IRE)**[12] 7364 6-8-7 70 oh3.................. HayleyTurner 5 25
(John A Harris) *led over 7f out: wknd over 3f out: last st* **15/2**

2m 1.83s (0.13) **Going Correction** +0.125s/f (Slow)
WFA 3 from 4yo+ 3lb 7 Ran SP% **112.0**
Speed ratings (Par 105): **104,102,102,99,95 80,80**
toteswinger: 1&2 £22.40, 1&3 £22.40, 2&3 £1.10. CSF £15.09 CT £58.74 TOTE £5.40: £2.70, £3.10; EX 15.00.
Owner Betfair Club ROA **Bred** J Egan, J Corcoran And J Judd **Trained** Hampton, Cheshire

FOCUS
A decent handicap run at a fair pace. Straightforward form.

7503 ABBA TRIBUTE NIGHT H'CAP (DIV II) 7f 32y(P)
9:20 (9:20) (Class 6) (0-55,57) 3-Y-O+ **£2,047** (£604; £302) **Stalls** High

Form RPR

0405 **1** **Guildenstern (IRE)**[10] 7383 6-8-13 54.................. JimmyQuinn 11 62
(P Howling) *in rr over 3f out: last st: rdn and str run to ld last stride* **15/2**

0200 **2** hd **Harrison's Flyer (IRE)**[20] 7255 7-8-6 52..........................(p) MCGeran(5) 2 59
(J M Bradley) *mid-div over 3f out: 6th st: led wl ins fnl f: hdd last stride* **20/1**

2001 **3** shd **Piccolo Diamante (USA)**[10] 7382 4-9-0 55..........................(t) AdamKirby 6 62
(S Parr) *s.i.s: in rr over 3f out: 9th st: rdn and r.o wl ins fnl f* **7/1**

0030 **4** nk **Tri Chara (IRE)**[17] 7287 4-8-12 53..........................(p) GrahamGibbons 8 59
(R Hollinshead) *prom over 3f out: 4th st: nt clr run wl over 1f out: ev ch wl ins fnl f: r.o* **5/1**[3]

0112 **5** nk **Megalo Maniac**[10] 7382 5-8-9 57..........................(v[1]) BMcHugh(7) 12 63
(R A Fahey) *prom over 3f out: rdn over 2f out: 3rd st: in ld ins fnl f: sn hdd: kpt on* **9/2**[2]

0050 **6** 3/4 **Franksalot (IRE)**[1] 7469 8-8-9 50..........................(b) PatrickMathers 9 54
(I W McInnes) *hld up in rr over 3f out: 10th st: r.o ins fnl f: nt rch ldrs* **20/1**

0 **7** 1 **Coughlans Locke (IRE)**[45] 6735 5-8-11 52.................. ShaneKelly 10 53
(Kieran P Cotter, Ire) *in tch over 3f out: 5th st: no ex towards fin* **11/1**

0663 **8** 3 **Jilly Why (IRE)**[4] 7444 7-9-0 55..........................(b) ChrisCatlin 4 48
(Paul Green) *in rr over 3f out: rdn over 2f out: 8th st: n.d* **4/1**[1]

550 **9** 3/4 **Rightcar Lewis**[7] 7414 3-8-3 52.................. AndrewHeffernan(7) 1 43
(Peter Grayson) *mid-div and rdn over 3f out: 7th st: no hdwy* **25/1**

0035 **10** 7 **Sion Hill (IRE)**[17] 7287 7-8-11 55..........................(p) DuranFentiman(3) 3 27
(John A Harris) *w ldr: 2nd st: rdn over 1f out: sn wknd* **7/1**

0000 **11** 9 **Daddy Cool**[16] 7295 4-8-4 50.................. JackDean(5) 5 —
(W G M Turner) *led: stl in ld over 3f out: wknd 1f out* **50/1**

0000 **P** **Curly Brown**[15] 7321 3-8-10 52..........................(v[1]) NeilChalmers 7 —
(A Bailey) *s.i.s: p.u 5f out: broke leg: dead* **33/1**

1m 30.42s (0.82) **Going Correction** +0.125s/f (Slow)
WFA 3 from 4yo+ 1lb 12 Ran SP% **118.2**
Speed ratings (Par 101): **100,99,99,99,98 98,96,93,92,84 74,—**
toteswinger: 1&2 £9.10, 1&3 £1.70, 2&3 £26.40. CSF £152.55 CT £1114.71 TOTE £8.10: £2.00, £3.00, £2.30; EX 147.50 Place 6 £4.64, Place 5 £2.35.
Owner David Andrew Brown **Bred** Peter E Daly **Trained** Newmarket, Suffolk

FOCUS
A moderate second division of the sprint which saw a bunched finish. The form looks sound for the grade.
T/Plt: £11.50 to a £1 stake. Pool: £107,520.96. 6,810.15 winning tickets. T/Qpdt: £4.40 to a £1 stake. Pool: £6,674.66. 1,098.26 winning tickets. KH

7489 KEMPTON (A.W) (R-H)
Sunday, November 30

OFFICIAL GOING: Standard
Wind: Fresh, half against Weather: Rain

7504 TFM NETWORKS MEDIAN AUCTION MAIDEN STKS 1m 1f (P)
2:10 (2:12) (Class 5) 3-5-Y-O **£3,238** (£963; £481; £240) **Stalls** High

Form RPR

-R **1** **L'Hirondelle (IRE)**[79] 5864 4-9-6.................. PaulDoe 5 74+
(M J Attwater) *broke wl: mde all: rdn wl clr over 1f out: heavily eased fnl 50yds* **5/1**[3]

0 **2** 6 **Sestet**[48] 6705 3-8-12.................. NickyMackay 6 53
(S Dow) *t.k.h: prom: outpcd 2f out: kpt on to take 2nd fnl 50yds* **10/1**

4330 **3** 1/2 **Sir Ike (IRE)**[27] 7166 3-9-3 61..........................(t) FergusSweeney 7 57
(W S Kittow) *t.k.h in 5th: rdn over 2f out: styd on to chse easy wnr ins fnl f: lost 2nd fnl 50yds* **5/4**[1]

4 1 **Russian Angel**[10] 4-9-1.................. JimCrowley 2 50
(Jean-Rene Auvray) *chsd wnr: drvn along over 2f out: sn outpcd* **12/1**

4463 **5** 3/4 **Time To Play**[17] 7300 3-9-0 65.................. MarcHalford(3) 3 53
(T T Clement) *hld up: hdwy into 4th 6f out: effrt and v wd st: sn btn* **5/2**[2]

-000 **6** 5 **Kara Tau**[11] 7383 3-9-3 53..........................(v[1]) MickyFenton 4 42
(Stef Liddiard) *in tch tl wknd 4f out: drvn along and bhd fnl 3f* **12/1**

0060 **7** 1 1/4 **Little Rococoa**[11] 7379 3-9-3 35..........................(t) JamesDoyle 1 39
(R J Price) *wnt lft s: a bhd: rdn and no ch fnl 3f* **33/1**

300 **8** 6 **Flying Free**[48] 6707 3-9-3 41.................. AdamKirby 8 26
(J Ryan) *stdd in rr s: rdn and no ch fnl 3f* **50/1**

1m 57.88s (117.88)
WFA 3 from 4yo 3lb 8 Ran SP% **119.1**
toteswinger: 1&2 £10.60, 1&3 £2.40, 2&3 £4.50. CSF £55.33 TOTE £7.20: £2.10, £2.70, £1.10; EX 54.40.
Owner Canisbay Bloodstock **Bred** Gainsborough Stud Management Ltd **Trained** Epsom, Surrey

FOCUS
There cannot have been too many worse maidens run around this course, so even though the winner was hugely impressive having had the run of things out in front, the form looks very suspect indeed.
Time To Play Official explanation: jockey said gelding hung left

7505 TFM NETWORKS NURSERY 1m 1f (P)
2:45 (2:47) (Class 5) (0-70,70) 2-Y-O **£2,590** (£770; £385; £192) **Stalls** High

Form RPR

6654 **1** **Herschel (IRE)**[25] 7190 2-9-4 67.................. GeorgeBaker 6 77+
(G L Moore) *mde all: rdn 3 l clr over 1f out: styd on* **3/1**[1]

4041 **2** 3 1/4 **Supernoverre (IRE)**[13] 7353 2-9-7 70.................. JimCrowley 14 71
(Mrs A J Perrett) *chsd ldrs: rdn over 2f out: wnt 2nd over 1f out: no imp* **11/2**[2]

046 **3** 2 1/4 **Merton Lad**[34] 7023 2-9-4 67.................. ShaneKelly 2 64
(T G Mills) *chsd wnr: rdn over 3f out: wknd and lost 2nd over 1f out* **12/1**

2462 **4** nk **Celtic Commitment**[17] 7298 2-9-6 69.................. LPKeniry 4 65
(R Hannon) *chsd ldrs: hrd rdn 3f out: one pce fnl 2f* **10/1**

000 **5** 2 1/2 **Play To Win (IRE)**[44] 6778 2-9-0 63.................. HayleyTurner 13 54+
(D R C Elsworth) *mid-div: rdn over 3f out: styd on same pce: nvr able to chal* **6/1**[3]

2005 **6** 2 1/2 **Fongoli**[30] 7117 2-8-7 56.................. GregFairley 8 42
(B G Powell) *hld up in 5th: rdn 4f out: sn outpcd* **33/1**

020 **7** 2 3/4 **Hollow Green (IRE)**[21] 7258 2-8-3 57..........................(v[1]) AndreaAtzeni(5) 3 37
(P D Evans) *hld up towards rr: rdn over 3f out: n.d* **25/1**

0052 **8** 1/2 **Lucky Punt**[13] 7353 2-8-9 58 ow1.................. MichaelHills 7 37
(B G Powell) *s.s: in rr tl hdwy and in tch over 5f out: rdn and wknd 3f out* **14/1**

5220 **9** 1 ¼ **Caster Sugar (USA)**[48] 6700 2-9-6 69 ChrisCatlin 5 45
(L M Cumani) *towards rr: rdn over 3f out: nvr trbld ldrs* **10/1**
0204 **10** ½ **Protiva**[11] 7389 2-9-0 63 DarrenWilliams 1 38
(A P Jarvis) *t.k.h in 6th: drvn along 4f out: sn wknd* **40/1**
0002 **11** 1 ½ **Winterbrook King**[21] 7257 2-8-12 61 SteveDrowne 9 33
(J R Best) *rdn along after 3f: a bhd* **16/1**
050 **12** nk **Paddythefish (USA)**[13] 7353 2-8-11 60 (v[1]) FergusSweeney 12 31
(K R Burke) *t.k.h towards rr: rdn 4f out: sn struggling* **20/1**
053 **13** 4 ½ **Candilejas**[36] 6986 2-9-3 66 JimmyQuinn 11 28
(D J Coakley) *last most of way: rdn 5f out: no ch fnl 3f* **6/1**[3]

1m 55.83s (115.83) **13 Ran SP% 121.4**
toteswinger: 1&2 £5.30, 1&3 £8.80, 2&3 £12.10. CSF £17.97 CT £184.91 TOTE £4.50: £2.00, £2.00, £3.30; EX 23.90.
Owner Mrs M Findlay **Bred** Mount Coote Stud And M Johnston **Trained** Woodingdean, E Sussex

FOCUS
Quite a competitive nursery and solid form for this type of contest. Several of these looked likely to improve for the switch to handicap company and/or the longer trip, but very few ever got into it and the front four had pulled a long way clear even before reaching the short home straight. The winning time was over two seconds quicker than the opening maiden.

NOTEBOOK
Herschel(IRE), who was well backed when fourth on his sand debut here last time, was well supported again. Bred to be suited by this longer trip, he was sent straight into the lead and, once sent for home off the final bend, the result wasn't in doubt. He is likely to progress again and should make up into a nice middle-distance handicapper next term. (tchd 7-2)
Supernoverre(IRE), well drawn when winning a claimer here last time, was well berthed again over this shorter trip and soon took a handy position. He came off the bridle passing the two-furlong pole and, although he plugged on to finish a clear second, he was never a threat to the winner. Despite his victory here last time, he didn't look entirely at home around this tight circuit and may have a bit more to offer on a more galloping track. (op 6-1)
Merton Lad, up in trip and making his handicap debut after showing a little ability in three maidens, was another to race handily throughout, and although he came off the bridle a fair way out, he kept on right to the line. He may still have some improvement left and there should be a small race in him. (op 10-1)
Celtic Commitment, trying his longest trip to date, was always in a good position and was another to plug on after coming off the bridle on the home bend. He should be able to win a race, though he lacks the scope of a couple of those that finished ahead of him.
Play To Win(IRE), making his sand and handicap debut after showing a little ability in three maidens at the top tracks, is bred to relish this longer trip. He travelled well enough in the pack, but got caught out when the leading quartet kicked for home off the home bend and all he could do after was stay on at one pace. He is another that probably has more to offer on a more galloping track. (op 5-1)
Lucky Punt was 4lb better off with Supernoverre for a length defeat here last time, but after missing the break he was then forced to make up ground on the wide outside and those exertions eventually took their toll.
Candilejas Official explanation: jockey said filly never travelled

7506 REGISTER NOW @ BETDAQPOKER.CO.UK CLAIMING STKS 1m 3f (P)
3:15 (3:19) (Class 6) 3-Y-O £2,047 (£604; £302) **Stalls** High

Form RPR
0151 **1** **Sabre Light**[21] 7260 3-9-5 70 (p) JimmyQuinn 5 78
(J Pearce) *chsd tearaway ldrs: hdwy on bit to ld jst over 2f out: hrd rdn over 1f out: hld on narrowly u.p* **5/4**[1]
6050 **2** shd **Taken (IRE)**[30] 7111 3-9-3 67 (p) HayleyTurner 12 76
(Miss Gay Kelleway) *hld up wl off the pce: smooth hdwy over 3f out: str chal fnl f: inched clsr: nt quite get up* **9/2**[3]
6326 **3** 7 **Mystic Art (IRE)**[13] 7354 3-8-13 64 SteveDrowne 4 59
(C R Egerton) *prom in chsng gp: wnt 2nd over 3f out: chal over 2f out: sn rdn: wknd 1f out* **7/2**[2]
0340 **4** 10 **Shayera**[48] 6703 3-8-7 66 AndreaAtzeni(5) 9 40
(B R Johnson) *outpcd and bhd: rdn 5f out: sme hdwy into midfield over 2f out: kpt on past btn rivals: n.d* **10/1**
-43 **5** ½ **Piermarini**[258] 919 3-9-3 70 JamieMoriarty 1 45
(P T Midgley) *mid-div: rdn and struggling to hold pl over 3f out: kpt on same pce in st* **16/1**
00 **6** 2 ¼ **Amber Moon**[15] 7344 3-8-12 0 ShaneKelly 3 35
(J A Osborne) *chsd ldrs: drvn along fr 7f out: wknd 2f out* **33/1**
2366 **7** 2 ¾ **Threestoneburn (USA)**[21] 7260 3-8-5 48 ChrisCatlin 11 24
(J R Boyle) *chsd ldrs: rdn over 3f out: struggling to hold pl whn n.m.r over 2f out: n.d after* **18/1**
8 7 **Pic White (BEL)**[12] 3-8-11 55 FergusSweeney 13 17
(G L Moore) *outpcd towards rr: rdn and wd st: nvr a factor* **25/1**
0255 **9** 4 ½ **Rosy Dawn**[21] 7260 3-8-3 47 MarcHalford(3) 8 4
(J J Bridger) *rdn to ld after 2f and sn 7 l clr at fast pce: wknd and hdd jst over 2f out* **25/1**
0500 **10** 8 **Haydens Mark**[21] 7260 3-9-3 65 (p) MickyFenton 2 —
(D G Bridgwater) *rdn to ld 2f: chsd tearaway ldr after tl over 3f out: sn wknd* **20/1**
5000 **11** 1 ½ **What's For Tea**[57] 5086 3-8-10 58 (p) RichardKingscote 7 —
(P Butler) *outpcd and bhd: rdn and no ch fnl 4f* **50/1**
0606 **12** 2 ½ **Veras Joy**[11] 7379 3-8-10 34 (p) LPKeniry 6 —
(Miss Z C Davison) *dwlt: a outpcd and wl bhd* **100/1**
0152 **13** 11 **Coole Dodger (IRE)**[21] 4569 3-8-13 73 JimCrowley 10 —
(M Sheppard) *outpcd in midfield: dropped to rr over 4f out: no ch after* **10/1**

2m 20.52s (-1.38) **Going Correction** +0.10s/f (Slow) **13 Ran SP% 132.5**
Speed ratings (Par 98): **109,108,103,96,96 94,92,87,84,78 77,75,67**
toteswinger: 1&2 £2.70, 1&3 £2.90, 2&3 £5.60. CSF £7.40 TOTE £2.30: £1.10, £2.10, £1.80; EX 11.00.
Owner Fran O'Brien **Bred** D J And Mrs Deer **Trained** Newmarket, Suffolk
■ Stewards' Enquiry : Hayley Turner caution: used whip with excessive frequency.

FOCUS
A moderate claimer in which very few came into it in any sort of form. It has been rated around the first two.

7507 CAWLEY TWINS LIFETIME IN RACING H'CAP 1m (P)
3:45 (3:48) (Class 5) (0-75,77) 3-Y-O+ £3,238 (£963; £481; £240) **Stalls** High

Form RPR
4226 **1** **Randama Bay (IRE)**[24] 7211 3-8-13 70 CatherineGannon 14 81
(I A Wood) *disp ld: led over 4f out: hrd rdn 2f out: drew clr fnl f* **20/1**
0005 **2** 2 ¾ **Moonlight Man**[4] 7457 7-9-6 75 (t) LPKeniry 9 80
(C R Dore) *chsd ldrs: rdn to chse wnr 2f out: outpcd fnl f* **6/1**[2]
5302 **3** hd **Ocean Legend (IRE)**[12] 7374 3-9-6 77 AdamKirby 3 82
(Miss J Feilden) *mid-div: rdn to chse ldrs 2f out: styd on same pce* **6/1**[2]
1005 **4** 2 **Bilberry**[30] 7111 3-8-10 67 (t) ChrisCatlin 10 67
(S C Williams) *t.k.h in midfield: hdwy to chse ldrs 2f out: one pce appr fnl f* **7/1**

0000 **5** 1 ¼ **Super Frank (IRE)**[17] 7299 5-9-6 75 IanMongan 1 72
(J Akehurst) *hld up towards rr: promising hdwy whn nt clr run over 2f out: rdn and no imp over 1f out* **33/1**
3036 **6** 1 **Will He Wish**[20] 7278 12-9-1 75 (b) AndreaAtzeni(5) 12 70
(S Gollings) *towards rr: drvn along and sme hdwy 2f out: no imp* **13/2**[3]
1031 **7** 1 ¼ **Tous Les Deux**[25] 7194 5-9-2 71 GeorgeBaker 6 63
(G L Moore) *stdd in rr: mod effrt on outside 2f out: n.d* **7/2**[1]
1100 **8** 1 **Geoffdaw**[18] 7290 3-9-4 75 JamesDoyle 13 65
(P D Evans) *t.k.h in last pl: pushed along 3f out: sme hdwy fnl f* **16/1**
5500 **9** 1 **Elk Trail (IRE)**[37] 6949 3-8-12 69 MickyFenton 11 56
(Mrs P Sly) *in tch on outer: rdn 3f out: wkng whn hung rt over 2f out* **16/1**
1053 **10** ½ **Pippbrook Gold**[17] 7307 3-9-1 72 FergusSweeney 8 58
(J R Boyle) *disp ld tl over 4f out: wknd over 1f out* **11/1**
4310 **11** 1 ½ **Pension Policy (USA)**[38] 6936 3-9-1 72 SteveDrowne 7 55
(R Charlton) *prom tl wknd over 2f out* **8/1**
4665 **12** 1 **Purus (IRE)**[20] 7277 6-9-2 74 (p) LukeMorris(3) 5 54
(R A Teal) *t.k.h on outer: prom tl wknd 2f out* **12/1**

1m 39.94s (0.14) **Going Correction** +0.10s/f (Slow)
WFA 3 from 5yo+ 2lb **12 Ran SP% 123.2**
Speed ratings (Par 103): **103,100,100,98,96 95,94,93,92,92 90,89**
toteswinger: 1&2 £34.30, 1&3 £22.30, 2&3 £11.30. CSF £141.06 CT £844.81 TOTE £34.90: £5.50, £2.60, £1.90; EX 204.10.
Owner Neardown Stables **Bred** Kilnamoragh Stud And Paul Towell **Trained** Upper Lambourn, Berks

FOCUS
A modest handicap, but quite a competitive one. However, the early pace was only ordinary and the winner was best placed throughout in front.
Elk Trail(IRE) Official explanation: jockey said gelding reared on leaving stalls

7508 BET MULTIPLES - BETDAQ H'CAP (DIV I) 6f (P)
4:15 (4:18) (Class 6) (0-55,57) 3-Y-O+ £1,706 (£503; £252) **Stalls** High

Form RPR
0004 **1** **Kaystar Ridge**[13] 7357 3-8-11 54 (bt) JamesO'Reilly(5) 3 62
(D K Ivory) *chsd ldrs: effrt 2f out: drvn to chal ins fnl f: got up fnl 25yds* **16/1**
554 **2** shd **Duke Of Milan (IRE)**[25] 7196 5-9-0 52 MichaelHills 6 60
(G C Bravery) *hld up in rr: rapid hdwy to ld jst ins fnl f: hrd rdn and kpt on: hdd fnl 25yds* **7/1**
2002 **3** 1 ¼ **Welsh Opera**[13] 7362 3-9-0 57 (t) WilliamCarson(5) 8 59
(S C Williams) *hld up in midfield: hdwy 2f out: rdn to press ldrs over 1f out: one pce ins fnl f* **9/2**[2]
5000 **4** nse **Mind Alert**[8] 7416 7-9-1 53 (v) DarrenWilliams 2 55+
(D Shaw) *stdd s and taken to ins rail: hld up in rr: hmpd and last over 1f out: rallied and r.o strly fnl f* **22/1**
0-02 **5** ¾ **Sarah's Art (IRE)**[39] 6907 5-9-2 54 MickyFenton 4 54
(Stef Liddiard) *in tch: rdn and nt clr run over 1f out: swtchd rt ins fnl f: r.o* **8/1**
2436 **6** nk **Reigning Monarch (USA)**[5] 7444 5-9-0 52 LPKeniry 7 51
(Miss Z C Davison) *t.k.h: prom: disp ld 2f out tl jst ins fnl f: no ex* **11/2**[3]
0003 **7** hd **Mr Rev**[4] 7453 5-8-7 50 (p) MCGeran(5) 10 48
(J M Bradley) *dwlt: hld up in rr: squeezed through on far rail fr 2f out: nvr rchd ldrs* **10/1**
3556 **8** ¾ **The Little Fizzer (IRE)**[43] 6823 3-9-0 52 FergusSweeney 5 48
(P D Evans) *mid-div: struggling to hold pl 2f out: kpt on fnl f* **12/1**
005 **9** ½ **Loyal Royal (IRE)**[8] 7414 5-8-9 52 (b) JackDean(5) 11 46
(J M Bradley) *plld hrd: chsd ldrs: rdn over 2f out: wknd over 1f out* **14/1**
0060 **10** ½ **Caustic Wit (IRE)**[5] 7444 10-8-5 50 (p) JakePayne(7) 1 42
(M S Saunders) *w ldrs on outer tl wknd jst over 1f out* **50/1**
0522 **11** 1 ½ **Bountiful Bay**[11] 7377 3-9-3 55 (t) HayleyTurner 9 43
(B J Meehan) *led: jnd and disp ld fr 2f out tl jst ins fnl f: wknd qckly* **9/4**[1]

1m 13.82s (0.72) **Going Correction** +0.10s/f (Slow) **11 Ran SP% 123.6**
Speed ratings (Par 101): **99,98,96,96,95 95,94,93,93,92 90**
toteswinger: 1&2 £26.10, 1&3 £20.20, 2&3 £7.80. CSF £130.02 CT £614.94 TOTE £23.70: £4.80, £2.20, £1.80; EX 209.10.
Owner Mrs J A Cornwell and David G Owen **Bred** Mrs J A Cornwell **Trained** Radlett, Herts

FOCUS
A moderate handicap in which the early pace was steady. It has been rated around the third to her recent maiden form.
Mind Alert Official explanation: jockey said gelding was denied a clear run
Sarah's Art(IRE) Official explanation: jockey said gelding was denied a clear run

7509 BET MULTIPLES - BETDAQ H'CAP (DIV II) 6f (P)
4:45 (4:47) (Class 6) (0-55,55) 3-Y-O+ £1,706 (£503; £252) **Stalls** High

Form RPR
05 **1** **Bold Diva**[32] 7072 3-9-0 52 (v) HayleyTurner 12 63
(A W Carroll) *bhd: hdwy over 2f out: wnt 2 l 2nd over 1f out: styd on u.p to ld fnl strides* **14/1**
4005 **2** hd **Tamino (IRE)**[73] 6046 5-9-0 52 (t) JimmyQuinn 10 62
(P Howling) *led: rdn 2 l ahd over 1f out: tired fnl 100yds: ct fnl strides* **5/1**[2]
0450 **3** 2 ¼ **Shaded Edge**[31] 7102 4-8-12 50 (p) JimCrowley 6 53
(D W P Arbuthnot) *chsd ldrs: pushed along 3f out: hrd rdn over 1f out: one pce* **11/4**[1]
4052 **4** ¾ **Tadlil**[12] 7369 6-8-7 50 (v) MCGeran(5) 3 50
(J M Bradley) *in tch: effrt over 2f out: 6th and no imp whn nt clr run 1f out: swtchd lft ins fnl f: styd on* **10/1**
2603 **5** 1 **Charlotte Grey**[12] 7369 4-8-11 49 FrancisNorton 9 46
(P J McBride) *chsd ldrs: rdn over 2f out: no ex over 1f out* **16/1**
0030 **6** ¾ **Willhewiz**[5] 7444 8-9-1 53 ShaneKelly 7 48
(W M Brisbourne) *chsd ldrs tl hrd rdn and wknd over 1f out* **8/1**
3043 **7** 1 ½ **Afton View (IRE)**[8] 7414 3-9-0 55 (t) TolleyDean(3) 4 45
(S Parr) *towards rr: effrt and hrd rdn 2f out: nt pce to trble ldrs* **6/1**[3]
0 **8** 3 ¼ **Baileys Brazilian**[17] 7297 3-9-3 55 PaulEddery 8 35
(C A Dwyer) *mid-div: rdn over 2f out: wknd over 1f out* **50/1**
3044 **9** 2 ¼ **Overstayed (IRE)**[11] 7383 5-9-2 54 NeilChalmers 1 26
(A Bailey) *in rr on outer: rdn and n.d fnl 3f* **6/1**[3]
0031 **10** shd **Kindallachan**[25] 7195 5-9-2 54 (p) MichaelHills 5 26
(G C Bravery) *sn rdn along in rr: n.d fnl 3f* **7/1**
0026 **11** 9 **Calabaza**[25] 7196 6-8-10 48 PaulDoe 2 —
(M J Attwater) *chsd ldrs on outer: wknd 3f out* **12/1**

1m 13.54s (0.44) **Going Correction** +0.10s/f (Slow) **11 Ran SP% 126.8**
Speed ratings (Par 101): **101,100,97,96,95 94,92,88,85,84 72**
toteswinger: 1&2 £15.20, 1&3 £11.50, 2&3 £4.70. CSF £89.14 CT £265.70 TOTE £17.70: £4.10, £2.60, £1.50; EX 63.10.
Owner Mrs P Izamis **Bred** Peter Balding **Trained** Cropthorne, Worcs

FOCUS
Another moderate handicap, but although the early pace was much stronger than in the first division the winning time was only 0.28 seconds faster. The form looks a bit more solid, though, rated around the runner-up.

7510 **BET PREMIER LEAGUE FOOTBALL - BETDAQ H'CAP** **7f (P)**
5:15 (5:17) (Class 5) (0-70,70) 3-Y-O+ **£3,238** (£963; £481; £240) **Stalls** High

Form				RPR
4015	1		**Sofia's Star**[41] 6867 3-9-5 **70** JimCrowley 5 (S Dow) *hld up in rr: nt clr run 2f out: swtchd outside and hdwy over 1f out: styd on u.p to ld nr fin* **14/1**	80+
121	2	½	**Sendreni (FR)**[45] 6749 4-9-3 **67** ChrisCatlin 12 (M Wigham) *trckd ldrs gng wl: nt clr run 2f out: swtchd rt over 1f out: led ins fnl f: hrd rdn and kpt on: hdd nr fin* **5/2**[1]	77+
0005	3	1	**Networker**[17] 7307 5-9-5 **69** JimmyQuinn 9 (P J McBride) *stdd s and swtchd to ins rail: sn in midfield: hdwy to ld over 1f out: hung lft and sn hdd: one pce* **6/1**[3]	76
5006	4	1 ¾	**Divertimenti (IRE)**[28] 7153 4-9-4 **68** (p) LPKeniry 10 (C R Dore) *hld up in midfield: smooth hdwy 2f out: led briefly 1f out: no ex ins fnl f* **16/1**	71
1360	5	½	**Inside Story (IRE)**[57] 6491 6-9-2 **66** (b) FrankieMcDonald 2 (C R Dore) *dwlt: bhd: rdn 3f out: styd on appr fnl f: nvr nrr* **16/1**	67
5046	6	2	**Kensington (IRE)**[13] 7359 7-8-13 **63** (p) JamesDoyle 11 (P D Evans) *chsd ldrs: hrd rdn 2f out: sn outpcd* **6/1**[3]	59
0040	7	1 ½	**Shes Minnie**[15] 7346 5-9-3 **67** FergusSweeney 7 (J G M O'Shea) *in rr of midfield: rdn 2f out: nt pce to chal* **33/1**	59
2140	8	1 ¼	**Our Blessing (IRE)**[32] 7077 4-9-1 **65** DarrenWilliams 8 (A P Jarvis) *chsd ldrs: chal over 2f out: wknd wl over 1f out* **10/1**	53
5523	9	½	**Whitbarrow (IRE)**[18] 7286 9-9-2 **69** (p) JamesMillman[(3)] 13 (B R Millman) *w ldr tl over 2f out: sn wknd* **10/1**	56
6600	10	1	**Mythical Charm**[13] 7354 9-8-3 **56** oh8 ow1 (t) MarcHalford[(3)] 3 (J J Bridger) *towards rr: rdn 3f out: n.d after* **50/1**	40
3062	11	shd	**Dawson Creek (IRE)**[13] 7358 4-9-2 **66** (t) MichaelHills 14 (B Gubby) *slt ld tl wknd qckly over 1f out* **7/2**[2]	50
0005	12	1	**Lend A Grand (IRE)**[46] 6738 4-9-4 **68** TravisBlock 6 (Miss Jo Crowley) *drvn along early and sn in tch: wknd over 2f out* **14/1**	49

1m 26.55s (0.55) **Going Correction** +0.10s/f (Slow)
WFA 3 from 4yo+ 1lb 12 Ran SP% **127.5**
Speed ratings (Par 103): **100,99,98,96,95 93,91,90,89,88 88,87**
toteswinger: 1&2 £11.30, 1&3 £17.90, 2&3 £5.00. CSF £52.72 CT £254.62 TOTE £23.80: £4.10, £1.80, £2.80; EX 97.40 Place 6 £ 59.12, Place 5 £ 38.34.
Owner P Jacobs, N Scandrett, W J Taylor **Bred** Bearstone Stud **Trained** Epsom, Surrey

FOCUS
An ordinary handicap run at a solid pace. The form looks sound rated around the runner-up as improving another 5lb.
T/Jkpt: Not won. T/Plt: £111.20 to a £1 stake. Pool: £85,174.00. 558.69 winning tickets. T/Qpdt: £62.00 to a £1 stake. Pool: £6,461.86. 77.10 winning tickets. LM

TOKYO (L-H)
Sunday, November 30

OFFICIAL GOING: Firm

7511a **JAPAN CUP (GRADE 1) (TURF)** **1m 4f**
6:20 (6:21) 3-Y-O+
£1,141,577 (£454,645; £285,781; £170,879; £112,420; £78,694)

			RPR
1		**Screen Hero (JPN)**[21] 4-9-0 MDemuro 16 (Y Shikato, Japan) *a cl up: 5th 5f out: cl 7th on outside st: rdn and hdwy wl over 1f out: led 150yds out: drvn out* **40/1**	120
2	½	**Deep Sky (JPN)**[28] 3-8-10 HShii 9 (Mitsugi Kon, Japan) *mid-div on outside st: gd hdwy 2f out: chsd wnr last 150yds: r.o wl* **24/10**[1]	121
3	¾	**Vodka (JPN)**[28] 4-8-10 YIwata 4 (Katsuhiko Sumii, Japan) *led 1f: settled in 3rd: 4th st: outpcd over 2f out: rallied over 1f out: ev ch briefly 1f out: r.o same pce* **27/10**[2]	114
4	hd	**Matsurida Gogh (JPN)**[63] 5-9-0 MEbina 13 (S Kunieda, Japan) *sn racing in 4th: 3rd st: led wl over 1f out to 150yds out: r.o* **7/1**	117
5	nk	**Oken Bruce Lee (JPN)**[35] 3-8-10 HUchida 1 (H Otonashi, Japan) *a wl in tch: 6th st: hdwy over 2f out: rdn over 1f out: kpt on wl fnl f* **63/10**	119
6	1 ¼	**Meisho Samson (JPN)**[56] 6522 5-9-0 MIshibashi 2 (S Takahashi, Japan) *a wl in tch: 5th st on ins: hrd rdn to go 3rd 2f out: r.o one pce* **11/2**[3]	115
7	nk	**Never Bouchon (JPN)**[21] 5-9-0 NYokoyama 7 (M Ito, Japan) *led after 1f tl hdd wl over 1f out: kpt on* **111/1**	115
8	¾	**Asakusa Kings (JPN)**[28] 4-9-0 C-PLemaire 15 (R Okubo, Japan) *a mid-div: kpt on one pce fnl 2f* **119/10**	113
9	nse	**Purple Moon (IRE)**[42] 6854 5-9-0 JamieSpencer 6 (L M Cumani) *sme prog in mid-div 5f out: hrd rdn over 1f out: nvr a factor* **54/1**	113
10	½	**Toho Alan (JPN)**[49] 5-9-0 SFujita 8 (H Fujiwara, Japan) *mid-div: one pce fnl 2f* **33/1**	112
11	nk	**Osumi Grass One (JPN)**[28] 6-9-0 YKawada 10 (Y Arakawa, Japan) *a in rr* **58/1**	112
12	nk	**Admire Monarch (JPN)**[28] 7-9-0 KAndo 17 (H Matsuda, Japan) *a towards rr* **118/1**	111
13	1 ¼	**Sixties Icon**[36] 6993 5-9-0 JMurtagh 11 (J Noseda) *a towards rr* **50/1**	109
14	1 ½	**Papal Bull**[56] 6522 5-9-0 RyanMoore 14 (Sir Michael Stoute) *towards rr: trying to cl on ins st: sn drvn: btn over 1f out* **25/1**	107
15	nk	**Tosen Captain (JPN)**[28] 4-9-0 OPeslier 3 (Katsuhiko Sumii, Japan) *a in rr: last st* **98/1**	107
16	½	**Daiwa Wild Boar (JPN)**[35] 3-8-10 HKitamura 5 (Hiroyuki Uehara, Japan) *mid-div tl wknd appr st* **126/1**	108
17	3	**Cosmo Bulk (JPN)**[196] 2234 7-9-0 MMatsuoka 18 (K Tabe, Japan) *sn pressing ldr: 2nd st: wknd over 2f out* **107/1**	101

2m 25.5s
WFA 3 from 4yo+ 6lb 17 Ran SP% **124.9**
(including 100 yen stakes): WIN 4100; PL 710, 130, 140; DF 7620; SF25160.
Owner Teruya Yoshida **Bred** Shadai Farm **Trained** Japan

FOCUS
A top-class field was assembled, including a strong-looking European raiding party, but the race was ruined as a truly great spectacle by a lack of any early pace. This did not suit many in the race, not least all three of the English-trained participants.

NOTEBOOK
Screen Hero(JPN) had won a handicap last time and looked to have plenty to find. He was perfectly placed to strike when the race finally got serious, however, and was always doing enough when in front. He will be lucky steal a similar contest in the future, despite his admirable attitude.
Deep Sky(JPN), this year's Japanese Derby winner, was ridden from off the gallop, as is usual, and came with his customary sweep around the outside. However, he lacked the speed to get past the winner and could never inch his way past.
Vodka(JPN) ran a strange race, as she was pulling double as they started to swing into the home straight, but got caught flat-footed before running on again. The lack of pace should have suited her, so her dramatic win in the Tenno Sho (Autumn) may just have left a mark.
Purple Moon(IRE) fared the best of the European raiders, but was never seriously in the hunt, largely due to the lack of early pace.
Sixties Icon really does need a proper test at this trip and he was again not anywhere near his best.
Papal Bull tried to close on the inside rail, but his reponse when put under pressure was limited. He was another who would have enjoyed a more truly-run race.

[7497] WOLVERHAMPTON (A.W) (L-H)
Monday, December 1

OFFICIAL GOING: Standard
Wind: Light becoming moderate across Weather: Fine and cold

7512 **STAY AT WOLVERHAMPTON HOLIDAY INN H'CAP (FOR AMATEUR RIDERS)** **1m 5f 194y(P)**
2:10 (2:10) (Class 6) (0-65,65) 3-Y-O+ **£2,307** (£709; £354) **Stalls** Low

Form				RPR
4020	1		**Snowberry Hill (USA)**[12] 7385 5-10-6 **55** MrJPFeatherstone[(5)] 12 (Lucinda Featherstone) *t.k.h: a.p: led over 3f out: clr over 2f out: hrd rdn wl over 1f out: edgd rt ins fnl f: drvn out* **8/1**	62
	2	2 ¼	**Jubilant Note (IRE)**[63] 6349 6-11-0 **65** (v[1]) MrDJByrne[(7)] 6 (Michael David Murphy, Ire) *hld up towards rr: hdwy 4f out: chsd wnr over 2f out tl hung lft wl over 1f out: styd on to retake 2nd cl home* **9/2**[1]	68
224-	3	nk	**Dovedon Hero**[649] 515 8-10-12 **63** MrSMcBride[(7)] 10 (P J McBride) *hld up in rr: hdwy over 3f out: chsd wnr wl over 1f out: styd on one pce: lost 2nd cl home* **20/1**	66
	4	nse	**Daytime Dreamer (IRE)**[72] 6145 4-11-6 **64** (t) MrPRoche 13 (Conor O'Dwyer, Ire) *hld up in mid-div: hdwy over 3f out: rdn over 2f out: swtchd lft wl over 1f out: styd on one pce fnl f* **25/1**	67
0135	5	2 ¼	**Stravita**[10] 7401 4-10-7 **56** (p) MrStephenHarrison[(5)] 7 (R Hollinshead) *hld up in mid-div: lost pl over 3f out: rdn and styd on fnl 2f: nt trble ldrs* **11/2**[2]	56+
0003	6	½	**Turner's Touch**[3] 7473 6-10-10 **59** (b) MissHayleyMoore[(5)] 5 (G L Moore) *s.i.s: hld up in rr: hdwy on outside over 2f out: rdn over 1f out: one pce* **9/1**	58
0634	7	11	**Blue Hills**[10] 7401 7-11-2 **60** (b) MrsMarieKing 2 (P W Hiatt) *t.k.h: led 4f: prom tl wknd wl over 1f out* **7/1**[3]	44
-005	8	¾	**Intensifier (IRE)**[17] 7322 4-10-1 **50** MissSallyRandell[(5)] 3 (D L Williams) *t.k.h: prom tl wknd 4f out* **14/1**	33
456-	9	1 ½	**Birthday Star (IRE)**[350] 7172 6-10-6 **50** MrSWalker 8 (A G Juckes) *a towards rr* **12/1**	31
3342	10	1 ¼	**York Cliff**[21] 7265 10-10-10 **57** MrBenBrisbourne[(3)] 4 (W M Brisbourne) *s.i.s: sn hld up in mid-div: lost pl 7f out: bhd fnl 5f* **8/1**	36
1301	11	1 ¼	**Cumbrian Knight (IRE)**[21] 7265 10-11-1 **62** MissNJefferson[(3)] 9 (J M Jefferson) *s.i.s: hdwy on outside after 2f: led after 4f: hdd 5f out: wknd over 3f out* **8/1**	39
1-00	12	23	**Zelos (IRE)**[12] 7385 4-11-4 **65** (bt) MrMJJSmith[(3)] 11 (D G Bridgwater) *t.k.h: w ldrs: led 5f out tl over 3f out: sn rdn: wknd over 2f out* **40/1**	10

3m 9.47s (3.47) **Going Correction** +0.125s/f (Slow)
WFA 3 from 4yo+ 7lb 12 Ran SP% **114.8**
Speed ratings (Par 101): **95,93,93,93,92 91,85,85,84,83 82,69**
toteswinger: 1&2 £4.40, 1&3 £48.20, 2&3 £19.20. CSF £41.41 CT £697.37 TOTE £9.90: £3.20, £1.70, £8.30; EX 64.50 TRIFECTA Not won..
Owner J Roundtree **Bred** Russell S Fisher And Joe Sagginario **Trained** Atlow, Derbyshire

FOCUS
Due to sub-zero temperatures the track was power-harrowed to three or four inches after Saturday evening's fixture, then reinstated and worked with the Gallop Master before racing began. Mainly exposed performers in this run-of-the-mill handicap. An ordinary gallop increased around halfway and the enterprisingly ridden winner came down the centre in the straight. His form may be underestimated but this was a bit of a messy race.

7513 **WOLVERHAMPTON-RACECOURSE.CO.UK (S) STKS** **7f 32y(P)**
2:40 (2:42) (Class 6) 3-Y-O+ **£1,978** (£584; £292) **Stalls** High

Form				RPR
4103	1		**Singleb (IRE)**[35] 7018 4-9-9 60 (p) GeorgeBaker 8 (G L Moore) *hld up in tch: rdn to ld ins fnl f: r.o* **5/2**[1]	74
6000	2	hd	**Valentino Swing (IRE)**[14] 7359 5-9-3 58 (b) AdamKirby 9 (Miss T Spearing) *s.s: in rr: swtchd rt over 2f out: hdwy wl over 1f out: rdn and ev ch wl ins fnl f: r.o* **14/1**	67
3130	3	1 ¾	**Kannon**[14] 7359 3-9-4 65 DarrenWilliams 7 (Miss M E Rowland) *chsd ldr: led jst over 2f out: sn rdn: hdd ins fnl f: no ex towards fin* **12/1**	63
4-00	4	1 ¼	**Barnaby Rudge (IRE)**[48] 6716 3-9-3 70 (t) TGMcLaughlin 4 (Jane Chapple-Hyam) *hld up in mid-div: rdn and hdwy 2f out: wandered over 1f out: edgd lft ins fnl f: one pce* **17/2**[3]	59
0630	5	1 ¾	**Mountain Pass (USA)**[61] 6396 6-9-9 55 (p) NCallan 12 (B J Llewellyn) *hld up towards rr: hdwy 2f out: sn rdn: one pce fnl f* **10/1**	60
2550	6	1 ¼	**Sylvias Grove**[35] 7018 3-8-12 65 TomEaves 2 (B Smart) *prom: pushed along over 3f out: rdn over 1f out: wknd ins fnl f* **14/1**	46
0030	7	3	**Ten Pole Tudor**[14] 7358 3-9-3 64 ChrisCatlin 11 (R A Harris) *stdd s: in rr: hrd rdn wl over 1f out: nvr nr ldrs* **18/1**	43
0100	8	1 ¾	**Lopinot (IRE)**[89] 5604 5-9-9 64 (p) VinceSlattery 3 (M R Bosley) *hld up towards rr: rdn 3f out: no rspnse* **18/1**	44
6350	9	¾	**Cap St Jean (IRE)**[14] 7363 4-9-2 57 (p) DavidKenny[(7)] 10 (R Hollinshead) *s.i.s: swtchd lft sn after s: a bhd* **28/1**	42
-300	9	dht	**Shepherds Warning (IRE)**[10] 7405 3-8-12 65 (v[1]) RichardKingscote 1 (N J Vaughan) *led: rdn and hdd jst over 2f out: wknd over 1f out* **14/1**	31

0003 **11** *nk* **Lytton**14 7363 3-9-3 70 .... MickyFenton 6 35
(R Ford) *hld up in mid-div: hdwy on outside over 2f out: c wd st: wknd wl over 1f out* **10/3**2

0000 **12** *27* **Hit The Roof**14 7367 3-9-9 61 .... PatCosgrave 5 —
(J G Given) *hld up in tch: rdn and wknd over 3f out* **50/1**

1m 30.31s (0.71) **Going Correction** +0.125s/f (Slow) **12 Ran SP% 114.9**
Speed ratings (Par 101): **100,99,97,96,94 92,89,87,86,86 86,55**
toteswinger: 1&2 £7.10, 1&3 £8.20, 2&3 £15.10. CSF £38.16 TOTE £2.90: £1.20, £3.50, £3.40; EX 41.20 Trifecta £257.20 Part won. Pool: £347.70 - 0.51 winning units..There was no bid for the winner.
Owner R A Green **Bred** Spratstown Stud Gm **Trained** Woodingdean, E Sussex

FOCUS
A decent seller in which the pace was reasonable throughout. The winner and second raced in the centre in the straight and the form is solid for the grade, with a personal best from the winner .

7514 BOOK TICKETS ONLINE NURSERY (DIV I) 1m 141y(P)
3:10 (3:11) (Class 6) (0-65,64) 2-Y-0 **£2,729** (£806; £403) **Stalls** Low

Form RPR

6004 **1** **Dream Huntress**52 6632 2-9-0 57 .... NCallan 12 61
(B J Meehan) *s.i.s: sn hld up in tch: led over 1f out: r.o wl* **15/2**2

510 **2** *2 1/2* **Hawkspring (IRE)**3 7468 2-9-3 60 ....(tp) AdamKirby 4 59
(S Parr) *bmpd s: hld up in mid-div: hdwy on ins 2f out: swtchd rt jst over 1f out: kpt on u.p to take 2nd wl ins fnl f* **5/1**1

4043 **3** *hd* **Orphaned Annie**29 7148 2-9-2 59 .... GeorgeBaker 5 57+
(B Ellison) *hmpd s: hld up and bhd: hdwy over 2f out: rdn fnl f: kpt on* **5/1**1

0042 **4** *1 3/4* **Betws Y Coed (IRE)**9 7425 2-8-9 52 ....(p) MickyFenton 8 47
(A Bailey) *hld up: hdwy 6f out: led 2f out: rdn and hdd over 1f out: no ex towards fin* **12/1**

0044 **5** *2* **Barbeito**13 7370 2-8-0 50 ....(v) BillyCray(7) 9 40
(D J S Ffrench Davis) *a.p: rdn fnl f: fdd towards fin* **20/1**

0060 **6** *1/2* **Black Attack (IRE)**76 5988 2-9-5 62 .... PaulMulrennan 11 51
(Paul Green) *chsd ldr: led 3f out: rdn and hdd 2f out: wknd ins fnl f* **33/1**

000 **7** *2* **Canmoss (USA)**33 7080 2-9-7 64 .... ChrisCatlin 1 49+
(E J O'Neill) *mid-div whn n.m.r on ins and lost pl after 1f: nvr nr ldrs* **15/2**2

0000 **8** *1 1/4* **Alderbed**13 7372 2-8-7 50 ....(v) EdwardCreighton 7 33
(George Baker) *hld up and bhd: hdwy over 5f out: wknd wl over 1f out* **33/1**

066 **9** *1/2* **Thaumatology (USA)**16 7332 2-9-1 63 .... AndreaAtzeni(5) 3 45
(M Botti) *wnt rt s: hld up in mid-div: bhd fnl 3f* **5/1**1

0005 **10** *1* **Vien (IRE)**12 7391 2-8-13 56 .... EddieAhern 6 35
(R Hannon) *hld up in tch: wknd over 2f out* **8/1**3

040 **11** *2* **Telling Stories (IRE)**16 7341 2-9-1 58 .... GregFairley 2 33+
(M Johnston) *mid-div whn n.m.r and lost pl after 1f: a bhd* **15/2**2

0003 **12** *12* **Cool Sonata (IRE)**21 7269 2-8-2 45 .... FrancisNorton 10 —
(M Brittain) *led: hdd 3f out: wknd qckly 2f out* **25/1**

1m 53.52s (3.02) **Going Correction** +0.125s/f (Slow) **12 Ran SP% 118.6**
Speed ratings (Par 94): **91,88,88,87,85 84,83,81,81,80 78,68**
toteswinger: 1&2 £5.10, 1&3 £6.70, 2&3 £3.90. CSF £42.87 CT £209.92 TOTE £10.60: £3.00, £2.10, £2.40; EX 50.10 Trifecta £127.80 Pool: £214.18 - 1.24 winning units..
Owner Longview Stud & Bloodstock Ltd **Bred** Wyck Hall Stud Ltd **Trained** Manton, Wilts

FOCUS
Division one of a modest nursery that contained only one previous (selling) winner. The gallop was fair and the winner again raced in the centre in the straight. She is rated back to her best and the form looks reliable, if lowly.

NOTEBOOK
Dream Huntress had shown patchy form on turf and Polytrack but turned in an improved effort. This was not much of a race but she may be capable of a little better. (op 5-1)
Hawkspring(IRE), from a yard among the winners, proved a shade disappointing on his recent Polytrack debut at Kempton but fared better with the cheekpieces fitted. He handles Fibresand and may be able to pick up another low-grade event this winter. (op 7-1)
Orphaned Annie turned in an improved effort on this all-weather debut, despite edging into the whip. She handles Fibresand and the way she raced here coupled with her pedigree suggests a further step up in trip could suit. Official explanation: jockey said filly missed the break (op 7-1)
Betws Y Coed(IRE), returned to a handicap, had the run of the race and finished a similar distance behind Hawkspring as she had in a Southwell seller. She should continue to run well, but will have to improve to win a handicap from this mark. (op 10-1)
Barbeito, upped in trip and returned to Polytrack, was not disgraced back in a handicap after having the run of the race but she is likely to remain vulnerable in this type of event. (op 16-1)
Black Attack(IRE), making his all-weather debut, failed to get home on this first run since September and first beyond sprint distances. Official explanation: jockey said colt hung right-handed
Canmoss(USA) Official explanation: jockey said colt suffered interference on first bend
Thaumatology(USA) from an in-form yard, had shown ability at a modest level in maidens and attracted support on her nursery debut but proved disappointing. She was reported to have lost her front left shoe. Official explanation: vet said filly lost front left shoe (op 11-2 tchd 6-1)

7515 DINE IN THE HORIZONS RESTAURANT H'CAP 2m 119y(P)
3:40 (3:41) (Class 5) (0-75,74) 3-Y-0+ **£3,238** (£963; £481; £240) **Stalls** Low

Form RPR

1202 **1** **Master At Arms**38 6957 5-9-6 74 .... AndreaAtzeni(5) 9 85
(Daniel Mark Loughnane, Ire) *hld up towards rr: hdwy on outside over 3f out: rdn 2f out: led wl ins fnl f: styd on* **6/1**3

6-12 **2** *3/4* **Bank On Benny**4 7459 6-9-9 72 ....(tp) FrancisNorton 2 82
(P W D'Arcy) *t.k.h: a.p: led over 4f out: rdn over 2f out: edgd rt 1f out: hdd wl ins fnl f: jst hld on for 2nd* **10/3**2

0341 **3** *shd* **L'Homme De Nuit (GER)**10 7400 4-9-2 65 ....(p) GeorgeBaker 8 75+
(G L Moore) *hld up in rr: hdwy over 2f out: rdn wl over 1f out: styd on wl towards fin: jst failed to take 2nd* **15/2**

434 **4** *hd* **Dayia (IRE)**18 7304 4-9-6 69 .... JimmyQuinn 1 79
(J Pearce) *hld up in tch: wnt 2nd over 3f out: swtchd lft 1f out: hrd rdn: styd on* **5/2**1

1100 **5** *3* **Swords**14 7364 6-9-2 65 .... TomEaves 4 71
(R E Peacock) *t.k.h in tch: rdn over 2f out: nt qckn whn swtchd rt wl ins fnl f* **22/1**

2143 **6** *9* **Victory Quest (IRE)**14 7366 8-9-5 68 ....(v) ChrisCatlin 6 63
(Mrs S Lamyman) *hld up in tch: wknd over 3f out* **28/1**

0006 **7** *nk* **Calculating (IRE)**38 6957 4-9-8 71 .... HayleyTurner 5 66
(M D I Usher) *hld up towards rr: pushed along 4f out: short-lived effrt on outside over 2f out* **11/1**

0020 **8** *7* **Inchpast**14 7366 7-9-8 71 ....(b) PaulMulrennan 11 57
(M H Tompkins) *in rr: rdn 7f out: nvr nr ldrs* **14/1**

/000 **9** *26* **Mikado**38 6948 7-9-10 73 ....(p) JamieMoriarty 10 28
(Jonjo O'Neill) *hld up in mid-div: bhd fnl 4f* **50/1**

33 **10** *8* **Augustus John (IRE)**10 7400 5-9-5 68 ....(t) NCallan 12 14
(S Parr) *led: hdd over 4f out: wknd qckly wl over 2f out* **10/1**

3153 **11** *11* **Sir Sandicliffe (IRE)**10 7401 4-9-3 66 .... TGMcLaughlin 7 —
(W M Brisbourne) *hld up in mid-div: bhd fnl 4f* **20/1**

1404 **12** *23* **Spider Silk**32 7091 3-9-3 74 .... ShaneKelly 3 —
(W Jarvis) *chsd ldr tl over 4f out: sn wknd: t.o* **20/1**

0/5- **13** *6* **Roman Villa (USA)**15 3704 6-9-3 66 ....(t) EddieAhern 13 —
(M Sheppard) *v rel to r: a in rr: t.o fnl 5f* **28/1**

3m 42.1s (0.30) **Going Correction** +0.125s/f (Slow)
WFA 3 from 4yo+ 8lb **13 Ran SP% 124.5**
Speed ratings (Par 103): **104,103,103,103,102 97,97,94,82,78 73,62,59**
toteswinger: 1&2 £5.10, 1&3 £6.70, 2&3 £3.90. CSF £24.97 CT £159.67 TOTE £6.60: £2.40, £1.60, £2.70; EX 28.20 Trifecta £72.20 Pool: £257.88 - 2.64 winning units..
Owner F Purcell **Bred** Fittocks Stud **Trained** Trim, Co Meath

FOCUS
A reasonable handicap in which the pace was fair. The winner raced just off the centre of the straight and the first five pulled clear. Sound form and a race worth being positive about.
L'Homme De Nuit(GER) Official explanation: jockey said gelding was denied a clear run

7516 HOTEL & CONFERENCING AT WOLVERHAMPTON H'CAP (DIV I) 1m 1f 103y(P)
4:10 (4:10) (Class 6) (0-55,55) 3-Y-0+ **£2,047** (£604; £302) **Stalls** Low

Form RPR

0004 **1** **Pab Special (IRE)**12 7392 5-8-12 53 .... AdamKirby 7 66
(B R Johnson) *hld up in tch: led 2f out: rdn over 1f out: drvn out* **8/1**

0252 **2** *1/2* **Royal Encore**16 7345 4-8-12 53 .... EddieAhern 11 65
(J R Fanshawe) *hld up towards rr: hdwy on outside over 2f out: c wd st: rdn over 1f out: edgd lft and r.o wl ins fnl f: nt rch wnr* **4/1**1

0000 **3** *1* **Moment Of Clarity**16 7345 6-8-11 52 ....(p) TomEaves 1 62+
(R C Guest) *hld up and bhd: hdwy wl over 1f out: rdn and kpt on ins fnl f* **14/1**

5006 **4** *3* **Barathea Dreams (IRE)**25 7217 7-8-13 54 .... LPKeniry 9 58
(J S Moore) *hld up in mid-div: hdwy 2f out: rdn over 1f out: one pce* **8/1**

0200 **5** *2 3/4* **Thornaby Green**30 7132 7-8-9 55 .... DeanHeslop(5) 6 53
(T D Barron) *led: rdn and hdd 2f out: wknd fnl f* **18/1**

6220 **6** *1 1/2* **Parkview Love (USA)**13 5154 7-8-11 52 ....(v) PatCosgrave 13 47
(J G Given) *hld up in tch: rdn and weakeend over 1f out* **14/1**

5303 **7** *hd* **Casablanca Minx (IRE)**115 4807 5-8-11 52 .... NCallan 12 46
(Miss Gay Kelleway) *hld up in rr: pushed along over 2f out: hung lft over 1f out: n.d* **10/1**

4000 **8** *2 3/4* **All You Need (IRE)**16 7340 4-8-12 53 .... GrahamGibbons 3 41
(R Hollinshead) *rrd and s.v.s: in rr: rdn over 2f out: n.d* **15/2**

026 **9** *1 1/4* **Ardent Prince**31 7114 5-8-8 52 .... TolleyDean(3) 4 38
(A J McCabe) *stdd s: hld up in rr: rdn over 3f out: no rspnse* **11/1**

0030 **10** *2* **Kansas Gold**105 5157 5-8-11 52 .... PaulMulrennan 10 34
(J Mackie) *prom: chsd ldr 7f out tl rdn over 2f out: wknd wl over 1f out* **22/1**

2125 **11** *3* **Classic Blue (IRE)**26 7189 4-9-0 55 .... TGMcLaughlin 2 30
(Ian Williams) *hld up in mid-div: hdwy on ins over 2f out: rdn and wknd over 1f out* **6/1**2

0021 **12** *6* **Darley Star**39 6930 3-8-10 53 .... ChrisCatlin 5 16
(R A Harris) *chsd ldr over 2f: prom tl wknd over 3f out* **13/2**3

2m 1.78s (0.08) **Going Correction** +0.125s/f (Slow)
WFA 3 from 4yo+ 2lb **12 Ran SP% 122.0**
Speed ratings (Par 101): **104,103,102,100,97 96,96,93,92,90 88,82**
toteswinger: 1&2 £9.10, 1&3 £26.90, 2&3 £19.80. CSF £41.18 CT £456.15 TOTE £10.60: £3.60, £1.80, £5.40; EX 74.50 Trifecta £263.10 Part won. Pool: £355.67 - 0.10 winning units..
Owner T Dempsey **Bred** Ballyhane Stud **Trained** Ashtead, Surrey

FOCUS
A tightly knit handicap in which the pace was fair. The winner ended up centre to far side in the straight. Solid form, which should work out.
All You Need(IRE) Official explanation: jockey said gelding reared as stalls opened

7517 RINGSIDE CONFERENCE SUITE H'CAP 5f 20y(P)
4:40 (4:40) (Class 6) (0-65,65) 3-Y-0+ **£2,388** (£705; £352) **Stalls** Low

Form RPR

0004 **1** **Cosmic Destiny (IRE)**3 7478 6-9-4 65 .... RichardKingscote 1 79
(E F Vaughan) *hld up and bhd: hdwy 1f out: qcknd to ld wl ins fnl f: pushed out* **4/1**2

2061 **2** *1 1/4* **Ryedane (IRE)**24 7231 6-8-12 62 ....(b) DuranFentiman(3) 2 72
(T D Easterby) *hld up in mid-div: hdwy on ins wl over 1f out: sn rdn: kpt on to take 2nd wl ins fnl f* **7/2**1

0505 **3** *1 1/4* **Joss Stick**12 7377 3-8-11 58 .... ChrisCatlin 6 63
(R A Harris) *stdd s: hld up in rr: hdwy on outside wl over 1f out: kpt on towards fin* **18/1**

0132 **4** *nk* **Bluebok**3 7478 7-8-11 63 ....(bt) JackDean(5) 8 67
(J M Bradley) *t.k.h: a.p: led over 1f out: hdd and no ex wl ins fnl f* **6/1**3

2520 **5** *hd* **Metal Guru**34 7043 4-9-3 64 ....(p) NCallan 9 67
(R Hollinshead) *hld up in mid-div: hdwy 2f out: rdn and nt qckn fnl f* **8/1**

1234 **6** *3/4* **Spirit Of Coniston**24 7218 5-8-5 59 .... PaulPickard(7) 7 60
(P T Midgley) *led: hdd over 1f out: fdd towards fin* **12/1**

0041 **7** *hd* **Top Bid**26 7197 4-8-13 60 ....(b) PaulMulrennan 5 60
(T D Easterby) *prom: n.m.r ins fnl f: one pce* **7/1**

4001 **8** *1* **Fizzlephut (IRE)**18 7295 6-8-13 60 .... PaulFitzsimons 3 56
(Miss J R Tooth) *w ldr: rdn and ev ch over 1f out: wknd wl ins fnl f* **20/1**

4206 **9** *1* **Nickel Silver**17 7323 3-9-4 65 .... TomEaves 4 58+
(B Smart) *hld up in mid-div: n.m.r and lost pl 3f out: n.d after* **6/1**3

2106 **10** *3 1/2* **Ronnie Howe**129 4385 4-9-2 63 .... PaulEddery 13 43
(S R Bowring) *s.i.s: sn prom: wknd wl over 1f out* **33/1**

62.36 secs (0.06) **Going Correction** +0.125s/f (Slow) **10 Ran SP% 115.1**
Speed ratings (Par 101): **104,102,100,99,99 98,97,96,94,88**
toteswinger: 1&2 £5.60, 1&3 £16.20, 2&3 £16.10. CSF £18.14 CT £228.15 TOTE £5.70: £1.90, £1.50, £4.10; EX 20.00 Trifecta £230.50 Part won. Pool: £311.53 - 0.10 winning units..
Owner A M Pickering **Bred** The Cruelle People **Trained** Newmarket, Suffolk

FOCUS
Another ordinary handicap in which the pace was sound throughout and those held up came to the fore late on. The winner raced centre-to-far side in the straight and recorded a slight personal best. Sound form overall.
Spirit Of Coniston Official explanation: jockey said gelding hung left-handed
Ronnie Howe Official explanation: jockey said gelding moved poorly throughout

7518 HOTEL & CONFERENCING AT WOLVERHAMPTON H'CAP (DIV II) 1m 1f 103y(P)
5:10 (5:10) (Class 6) (0-55,55) 3-Y-0+ **£2,047** (£604; £302) **Stalls** Low

Form RPR

0400 **1** **Climate (IRE)**2 7500 9-9-0 55 ....(p) NCallan 3 63
(P D Evans) *hld up in mid-div: hdwy over 2f out: led jst ins fnl f: jst hld on* **4/1**2

0420 **2** *nse* **King Of Connacht**[14] 7354 5-8-12 **53**............................(p) AdamKirby 9 61
(M Wellings) *hld up towards rr: hdwy wl over 1f out: hrd rdn and r.o wl towards fin: jst failed* **17/2**

6420 **3** *½* **Noah Jameel**[89] 5611 6-8-12 **53**.. LPKeniry 12 60
(A G Newcombe) *hld up towards rr: rdn and hdwy on outside over 1f out: r.o wl towards fin* **8/1**[3]

6053 **4** *1* **Landikhaya (IRE)**[12] 7392 3-8-12 **55**..............................(p) ChrisCatlin 10 60
(D K Ivory) *a.p: wnt 2nd over 6f out: led 3f out: hrd rdn and hdd jst ins fnl f: nt qckn* **17/2**

5000 **5** *4* **Bailieborough (IRE)**[31] 6657 9-8-11 **52**.............................. TomEaves 2 49
(B Ellison) *hld up towards rr: rdn and hdwy over 1f out: nvr trbld ldrs* **14/1**

0252 **6** *1 ¼* **Moyoko (IRE)**[16] 7340 5-8-8 **54**................................... AndreaAtzeni(5) 5 48
(M Salaman) *hld up in mid-div: hdwy on outside over 2f out: rdn over 1f out: wknd ins fnl f* **2/1**[1]

40- **7** *1* **Lady Aspen (IRE)**[446] 5330 5-8-11 **52**......................... TGMcLaughlin 8 44
(Ian Williams) *t.k.h early: prom: rdn over 2f out: wknd wl over 1f out* **14/1**

5026 **8** *1 ¼* **Eternal Optimist (IRE)**[14] 7367 3-8-12 **55**.................... FrancisNorton 6 44
(Paul Green) *chsd ldr 3f: prom: wnt 2nd again briefly over 2f out: sn rdn: wknd ins fnl f* **11/1**

0600 **9** *½* **Red Current**[19] 7287 4-8-11 **52**.. ShaneKelly 4 40+
(R A Harris) *hld up in mid-div: gng wl whn hmpd on ins jst over 2f out: n.d after* **20/1**

050 **10** *½* **Jayarbee (IRE)**[22] 7256 3-8-12 **55**................................(v[1]) JimmyQuinn 1 42
(P J McBride) *hld up in tch: rdn over 2f out: sn wknd* **28/1**

60 **11** *¾* **Jonquille (IRE)**[69] 6189 3-8-11 **54**................................ MickyFenton 11 39
(R Ford) *a in rr* **50/1**

00-0 **12** *8* **Timewatch**[27] 7184 3-8-6 **54**..(v) JackDean(5) 13 23
(Miss J E Foster) *led: rdn and hdd 3f out: wknd 2f out* **66/1**

0600 **13** *¾* **This Ones For Pat (USA)**[12] 7383 3-8-10 **53**..............(t) TonyCulhane 7 20
(S Parr) *stdd s: a in rr* **10/1**

2m 3.28s (1.58) **Going Correction** +0.125s/f (Slow)
WFA 3 from 4yo+ 2lb **68** Ran SP% **127.9**
Speed ratings (Par 101): **97,96,96,95,92 90,90,88,88,88 87,80,79**
toteswinger: 1&2 £9.70, 1&3 £10.30, 2&3 £12.40. CSF £39.95 CT £274.27 TOTE £5.30: £2.20, £2.40, £2.60; EX 46.20 Trifecta £330.30 Pool: £468.69 - 1.05 winning units..
Owner J E Abbey **Bred** Mrs A Naughton **Trained** Pandy, Monmouths

FOCUS
Another tightly knit division of this modest handicap in which the pace was only fair and the first four pulled clear. The winner made his ground against the inside rail in the straight. Modest form, the winner only needing to match his recent plating efforts.
This Ones For Pat(USA) Official explanation: jockey said gelding moved poorly throughout

7519 BOOK TICKETS ONLINE NURSERY (DIV II) 1m 141y(P)
5:40 (5:40) (Class 6) (0-65,64) 2-Y-O **£2,729** (£806; £403) **Stalls** Low

Form RPR

6631 **1** **Hold The Bucks (USA)**[9] 7415 2-9-6 **63**.............................. LPKeniry 6 65
(J S Moore) *hld up in tch: led 1f out: drvn out* **7/2**[1]

010 **2** *1* **Captain Cavendish (IRE)**[21] 7269 2-9-2 **59**..............(b) MickyFenton 1 59
(A Bailey) *led: rdn over 2f out: hdd 1f out: edgd rt ins fnl f: kpt on* **18/1**

1450 **3** *½* **Barcode**[14] 7353 2-8-10 **53**.. FrancisNorton 7 52
(R Hannon) *hld up towards rr: hdwy over 1f out: rdn and kpt on ins fnl f* **12/1**

0400 **4** *½* **Shaker Style (USA)**[38] 6954 2-9-7 **64**...................(v[1]) GrahamGibbons 9 62
(J D Bethell) *chsd ldr: rdn over 2f out: lost 2nd wl over 1f out: carried rt ins fnl f: nt qckn* **9/2**[2]

6443 **5** *1 ¼* **Nimmy's Special**[35] 7016 2-9-5 **62**................................ EddieAhern 2 57
(M Mullineaux) *hld up and bhd: nt clr run over 2f out: swtchd rt ent st: kpt on ins fnl f: nvr nr to chal* **7/1**

0005 **6** *nk* **Ba Globetrotter**[14] 7353 2-8-7 **50**............................ CatherineGannon 8 45
(M R Channon) *hld up in tch: rdn 3f out: one pce whn carried rt ins fnl f* **16/1**

0654 **7** *1 ¼* **Premier Krug (IRE)**[45] 6787 2-8-13 **56**................................ NCallan 10 49+
(P D Evans) *hld up in rr: swtchd rt over 2f out: sltly hmpd over 1f out: nvr trbld ldrs* **8/1**

4602 **8** *½* **Kristopher James (IRE)**[21] 7269 2-9-3 **60**................ TGMcLaughlin 11 55+
(W M Brisbourne) *hld up in mid-div: rdn and hung lft fr wl over 1f out: eased whn btn ins fnl f* **15/2**

0600 **9** *8* **Moon Warrior**[13] 7370 2-7-10 **46** ow1.................. AndrewHeffernan(7) 3 20
(C Smith) *hld up in mid-div: bhd fnl 2f* **66/1**

604 **10** *7* **Fruitful Job (IRE)**[33] 7079 2-8-8 **51**..............................(p) ChrisCatlin 4 10
(A G Newcombe) *a in rr: no ch fnl 2f* **17/2**

0200 **11** *3* **Raise All In (IRE)**[45] 6787 2-9-0 **57**................................ JimmyQuinn 5 10
(N Wilson) *prom tl wknd wl over 1f out* **11/2**[3]

1m 52.55s (2.05) **Going Correction** +0.125s/f (Slow) **40** Ran SP% **122.0**
Speed ratings (Par 94): **95,94,93,93,92 91,90,90,83,76 74**
toteswinger: 1&2 £14.20, 1&3 £12.00, 2&3 £27.20. CSF £72.95 CT £715.72 TOTE £5.20: £1.50, £6.50, £4.20; EX 81.30 TRIFECTA Not won. Place 6: £73.04 Place 5: £28.17.
Owner E Moore & J S Moore **Bred** David E Hager Ii **Trained** Upper Lambourn, Berks

FOCUS
Division two of this low-grade nursery. The pace was only fair and the winner was another to race in the centre. The winner showed marginally improved form.

NOTEBOOK
Hold The Bucks(USA) ran as well as he ever has when winning a seller on his previous start and he showed a decent attitude to justify the market support back in a handicap. This was not much of a race but he is a consistent sort who should continue to give a good account. (op 6-1)
Captain Cavendish(IRE), a 7f selling winner in blinkers at this course, was well beaten in a visor on Fibresand on his previous start but had the run of the race and fared better back on Polytrack with the blinkers refitted. He is lightly raced enough to be open to a little improvement. (op 12-1 tchd 25-1)
Barcode has yet to win on artificial surfaces but ran creditably, shaping as though the return to a longer trip would be in her favour. (op 10-1)
Shaker Style(USA) attracted support and was not disgraced with the first-time visor replacing the blinkers, despite not looking the most straightforward under pressure. (op 6-1)
Nimmy's Special was set a fair bit to do in a race run at just an ordinary gallop, but was far from disgraced, shaping as though an even stiffer test of stamina would suit. (op 5-1)
Ba Globetrotter was well placed given the way this race panned out but, while not totally disgraced, is not the most reliable and has yet to win a race. (op 14-1)
T/Jkpt: Not won. T/Plt: £177.20 to a £1 stake. Pool: £83,344.12. 343.27 winning tickets. T/Qpdt: £19.00 to a £1 stake. Pool: £7,261.20. 281.70 winning tickets. KH

7472 LINGFIELD (L-H)
Tuesday, December 2

OFFICIAL GOING: Standard
Wind: Moderate, behind Weather: Cloudy, cold

7520 BET AT LADBROKES.COM AMATEUR RIDERS' H'CAP 2m (P)
12:30 (12:30) (Class 6) (0-60,59) 3-Y-O+ **£1,911** (£588; £294) **Stalls** Low

Form RPR

6515 **1** **Wyeth**[25] 6672 4-11-2 **59**.......................................(p) MrJoshuaMoore(5) 3 70+
(G L Moore) *hld up bhd ldrs: prog to go 2nd over 3f out: led 2f out: sn rdn clr* **11/4**[1]

6000 **2** *4 ½* **Cragganmore Creek**[22] 7265 5-10-3 **46**........................ MrBMMorris(5) 9 51
(D Morris) *racd wd towards rr: bmpd along fr 5f out: prog fr 3f out: styd on to take 2nd last 75yds* **14/1**

5065 **3** *1* **Go On Ahead (IRE)**[22] 7265 8-11-0 **52**..................(b[1]) MrsMRoberts 12 56
(M J Coombe) *led at slow pce to 7f out: sn led again and set more reasonable gallop: hdd 2f out: one pce* **5/1**[2]

0000 **4** *1 ¼* **Restart (IRE)**[26] 7216 7-10-2 **45**............................ MrJPFeatherstone(5) 14 48
(Lucinda Featherstone) *t.k.h: hld up bhd ldrs: outpcd 3f out: effrt 2f out: keeping on to press plcd horses whn short of room last 50yds* **15/2**

0400 **5** *1 ¾* **Corlough Mountain**[13] 7385 4-10-7 **52**........................ MissMBryant(7) 7 52
(P Butler) *hld up towards rr: outpcd 3f out: bmpd along and kpt on fnl 2f: n.d* **25/1**

0626 **6** *1* **Flame Creek (IRE)**[6] 7455 12-11-6 **58**.............................. MrPRoche 11 57
(E J Creighton) *hld up in midfield effrt 3f out but already outpcd: kpt on same pce after* **11/2**[3]

05-0 **7** *shd* **Festival Dreams**[46] 3022 3-10-3 **52**.............................. MrRMahon(3) 10 51
(Miss J S Davis) *racd wd: pressed ldrs: rdn 3f out: sn outpcd: plugged on* **25/1**

0030 **8** *2 ¼* **Prince Of Medina**[11] 7400 5-10-0 **45**...................(t) MissKFerguson(5) 2 41
(J R Best) *hld up in last: lft bhd fr over 3f out: modest prog fr over 1f out: no ch* **8/1**

0500 **9** *hd* **I Certainly May**[29] 5269 3-10-0 **53** ow5...................... MrAlexBarlow(7) 5 49
(S Dow) *hld up in last trio: wl outpcd 3f out: modest late prog* **40/1**

6000 **10** *1* **Highly Regal (IRE)**[9] 6436 3-10-1 **54**....................(t) MrAdamWest(7) 1 49
(R A Teal) *awkward s: hld up wl in rr: outpcd fr 3f out: no ch after* **33/1**

5000 **11** *1* **Ronsard (IRE)**[12] 7285 6-10-2 **45**..................(p) MissIsabelTompsett(5) 8 39
(P D Evans) *hld up towards rr: outpcd 3f out: no ch after* **25/1**

5250 **12** *3 ¾* **Blushing Hilary (IRE)**[6] 7455 5-11-1 **53**..............(b) MrMatthewSmith 6 42
(Mrs S J Humphrey) *pressed ldng pair: led briefly 7f out: rdn 4f out: wknd over 2f out* **16/1**

6-00 **13** *5* **Miss Habershon**[13] 7392 4-10-4 **49**........................ MrRGHenderson(7) 4 32
(Nick Mitchell) *t.k.h: hld up in midfield on inner: lost pl fr 3f out* **33/1**

0000 **14** *hd* **Finished Article (IRE)**[26] 7216 11-10-7 **45**...................... MrSWalker 13 28
(Mrs D Thomas) *t.k.h: trckd ldr to 7f out: rdn 4f out: sn wknd* **14/1**

3m 34.04s (8.34) **Going Correction** 0.0s/f (Stan)
WFA 3 from 4yo+ 8lb **14** Ran SP% **120.7**
Speed ratings (Par 101): **79,76,76,75,74 74,74,73,72,72 71,70,67,67**
toteswinger: 1&2 £9.10, 1&3 £3.20, 2&3 £17.40. CSF £40.81 CT £190.16 TOTE £3.00: £1.50, £4.30, £1.90; EX 28.30 Trifecta £80.40 Part won. Pool: £108.67 - 0.42 winning tickets..
Owner D R Hunnisett **Bred** Lael Stables **Trained** Woodingdean, E Sussex

■ Stewards' Enquiry : Mrs M Roberts caution: careless riding
Mr B M Morris caution: careless riding
Mr R G Henderson caution: used whip when out of contention

FOCUS
This very moderate handicap, confined to amateur riders, was run at a very slow early pace and most of the field failed to settle as a result. The race should be treated as being suspect overall although the form makes a fair bit of sense on paper.

7521 FRED & RON GIBSON MEMORIAL H'CAP (DIV I) 6f (P)
1:00 (1:01) (Class 6) (0-60,60) 3-Y-O+ **£1,706** (£503; £252) **Stalls** Low

Form RPR

4503 **1** **Shaded Edge**[2] 7509 4-8-8 **50**..(p) MartinDwyer 3 59
(D W P Arbuthnot) *trckd ldrs: pushed along 1/2-way: prog 2f out: wnt 2nd over 1f out: rdn to cl and ld last 100yds: idled but a holding on* **15/8**[1]

3300 **2** *nk* **Bollin Franny**[27] 7196 4-8-6 **48**................................... RichardThomas 7 56
(J E Long) *led after 2f: kicked on over 2f out: hdd and hld last 100yds* **9/1**

0050 **3** *2* **Loyal Royal (IRE)**[2] 7508 5-8-5 **52**..............................(b) JackDean(5) 11 54
(J M Bradley) *restrained s: v keen and hld up in last: prog over 2f out: urged along and styd on wl to take 3rd ins fnl f: gaining at fin* **16/1**

0130 **4** *¾* **Simpsons Gamble (IRE)**[15] 7357 5-9-2 **58**..............(p) GeorgeBaker 12 57
(R A Teal) *hld up wl in rr and racd wd: swtchd to inner and stl in last trio over 2f out: prog wl over 1f out: styd on fnl f: nrst fin* **13/2**[3]

1040 **5** *¾* **Tyrannosaurus Rex (IRE)**[18] 7323 4-9-4 **60**.................... AdamKirby 1 57
(D Shaw) *hld up towards rr: prog over 2f out: tried to cl over 1f out but nt qckn: kpt on* **9/2**[2]

6064 **6** *2* **Azygous**[13] 7377 5-9-3 **59**.. DaneO'Neill 4 49
(J Akehurst) *prom: rdn bef 1/2-way: wnt 2nd over 2f out to over 1f out: wknd rapidly fnl f* **8/1**

2000 **7** *2 ½* **Forever Changes**[10] 7416 3-8-13 **55**.............................. HayleyTurner 5 37
(L Montague Hall) *led 2f: chsd ldr to over 2f out: wknd rapidly on inner over 1f out* **25/1**

1300 **8** *hd* **Scruffy Skip (IRE)**[13] 7383 3-8-11 **53**.......................... JerryO'Dwyer 10 35
(Mrs C A Dunnett) *sharp reminder sn after s: a in rr: struggling 2f out* **20/1**

2000 **9** *hd* **Myriola**[20] 7288 3-8-4 **46** oh1.. JimmyQuinn 6 27
(S Gollings) *chsd ldrs: rdn over 2f out: wknd wl over 1f out* **25/1**

0456 **10** *nk* **Miracle Baby**[92] 5582 6-8-4 **46**... ChrisCatlin 9 26
(J A Geake) *racd wd in midfield: lost grnd bnd 2f out: sn wknd* **14/1**

0050 **11** *¾* **Professor Malone**[13] 7378 3-8-7 **49** oh1 ow3........... EdwardCreighton 8 27
(J C Tuck) *stdd s: hld up in last: urged along over 2f out: no prog* **50/1**

5006 **12** *¾* **Acclimate**[151] 3686 3-8-9 **51**.. SteveDrowne 2 26
(W S Kittow) *settled in midfield: pushed along over 2f out: sn lost pl* **25/1**

1m 10.84s (-1.06) **Going Correction** 0.0s/f (Stan) **12** Ran SP% **118.2**
Speed ratings (Par 101): **107,106,103,102,101 99,95,95,95,95 94,93**
toteswinger: 1&2 £4.30, 1&3 £12.00, 2&3 £33.60. CSF £17.93 CT £216.38 TOTE £2.50: £1.20, £3.40, £5.80; EX 25.50 Trifecta £132.10 Part won. Pool: £178.62 - 0.42 winning tickets..
Owner P M Claydon **Bred** Lady Whent **Trained** Compton, Berks

FOCUS
A very ordinary sprint handicap. It was a particularly quick winning time for the class of race and considering the early pace looked average that points to the track riding a deal faster than is often the case. The form is straightforward.

7522 FRED & RON GIBSON MEMORIAL H'CAP (DIV II) 6f (P)
1:30 (1:36) (Class 6) (0-60,60) 3-Y-0+ £1,706 (£503; £252) Stalls Low

Form RPR

05 1 **Lost All Alone**^{92} 5582 4-8-2 **47**........................ MarcHalford(3) 8 58
(D M Simcock) *unco-operative bef ent stalls: mde virtually all: clr w one chalr 1/2-way: drvn clr over 1f out: flashed tail: hld on* 6/1^{3}

0320 2 ½ **Fantasy Fighter (IRE)**^{18} 7320 3-8-4 **46** oh1........................ JimmyQuinn 11 55
(J J Quinn) *hld up in rr: plenty to do 2f out: gd prog jst over 1f out: r.o to take 2nd wl ins fnl f: clsng at fin* 10/1

5560 3 1 **The Little Fizzer (IRE)**^{2} 7508 3-8-10 **52**........................ JamesDoyle 1 58
(P D Evans) *pressed wnr: clr of rest by 1/2-way: btn off over 1f out: lost 2nd wl ins fnl f* 13/2

3563 4 1 ¾ **What Katie Did (IRE)**^{10} 7416 3-8-13 **60**........................(p) JackDean(5) 7 61
(J M Bradley) *trckd ldrs: drvn to go 3rd over 1f out but nt on terms w ldng pair: one pce after* 4/1^{2}

5232 5 1 **Muktasb (USA)**^{10} 7414 7-9-3 **59**........................(v) AdamKirby 10 56
(D Shaw) *hld up towards rr: plenty to do 2f out: shkn up over 1f out: kpt on steadily but no ch* 7/4^{1}

3000 6 ½ **Gone'N'Dunnett (IRE)**^{14} 7369 9-8-1 **46** oh1........................(v) LukeMorris(3) 3 42
(Mrs C A Dunnett) *chsd ldng pair: drvn bef 1/2-way: wknd over 1f out* 16/1

6300 7 1 ¾ **Briannsta (IRE)**^{13} 7378 6-8-8 **50**........................ RichardThomas 6 40
(J E Long) *sn drvn in midfield: nvr on terms w ldrs: one pce fnl 2f* 14/1

0304 8 2 **Taboor (IRE)**^{54} 6595 10-8-7 **49**........................ HayleyTurner 9 33
(R M H Cowell) *hld up in last trio: nvr on terms w ldrs: no real prog fnl 2f* 14/1

510 9 hd **Now You See Me**^{80} 5884 4-9-0 **56**........................ ChrisCatlin 12 39
(D Flood) *ref to go to post tl dismntd and led to s: hld up in last trio and t.k.h early: nvr a factor* 14/1

0450 10 ½ **Telephonist**^{13} 7379 3-8-5 **47** ow1........................ MartinDwyer 2 29
(J R Best) *chsd ldrs: outpcd 1/2-way: wknd over 1f out: broke down fin: dead* 16/1

0-0 11 1 ½ **Nimbelle (IRE)**^{18} 7327 3-8-12 **54**........................ EdwardCreighton 4 31
(J C Tuck) *stdd s: sn drvn: a in last trio* 40/1

1m 10.76s (-1.14) **Going Correction** 0.0s/f (Stan) 11 Ran SP% 127.3
Speed ratings (Par 101): **107,106,105,102,101 100,98,95,95,94 92**
toteswinger: 1&2 £8.20, 1&3 £7.70, 2&3 £13.30. CSF £70.43 CT £424.86 TOTE £8.20: £2.90, £2.70, £3.00; EX 81.80 TRIFECTA Not won..
Owner Tick Tock Partnership **Bred** B Whitehouse **Trained** Newmarket, Suffolk

FOCUS
They went a solid early pace in this second division of the sprint handicap and so it was surprising that it proved hard to make up ground from behind, indicating that the track was riding quick. The form looks sound enough.

7523 PLAY POKER AT LADBROKES.COM NOVICE STKS 6f (P)
2:00 (2:03) (Class 4) 2-Y-0 £3,885 (£1,156; £577; £288) Stalls Low

Form RPR

01 1 **Rulesn'Regulations**^{29} 7168 2-9-2 85........................ JimmyQuinn 3 90+
(M Salaman) *trckd ldng pair: got through to take 2nd jst over 2f out: pushed into ld over 1f out: grad drew away fnl f* 8/11^{1}

3221 2 1 ½ **Satwa Street (IRE)**^{19} 7303 2-9-2 85........................ HayleyTurner 4 85
(D M Simcock) *led: drvn and hdd over 1f out: kpt on wl but readily outpointed fnl f* 7/2^{2}

5020 3 5 **Head Down**^{18} 7311 2-8-12 83........................ DaneO'Neill 5 66
(R Hannon) *reminder over 4f out: nvr gng wl: brief effrt and in tch over 2f out: sn lft bhd* 4/1^{3}

4 1 **Kheskianto (IRE)**^{65} 2-8-7 0........................ MartinDwyer 2 58
(M Botti) *settled in last: effrt over 2f out: sn lft wl bhd* 11/1

0120 5 10 **Lady Master**^{59} 6469 2-8-9 74........................ JamesDoyle 6 30
(Ms J S Doyle) *pressed ldr to jst over 2f out: wknd rapidly* 16/1

1m 11.3s (-0.60) **Going Correction** 0.0s/f (Stan) 2y crse rec 5 Ran SP% 114.3
Speed ratings (Par 98): **104,102,95,94,80**
toteswinger: 1&2 £3.10. CSF £3.87 TOTE £1.70: £1.10, £1.50; EX 3.70.
Owner M Salaman **Bred** Marshalla Salaman **Trained** Baydon, Wilts

FOCUS
A fair little novice event, run at a sound pace and the form looks solid. The winner built on his Wolverhampton form.

NOTEBOOK
Rulesn'Regulations had comfortably beaten Satwa Street on his all-weather bow at Wolverhampton last month and he confirmed that form on identical terms with a straightforward display over the extra furlong. He moved best of all throughout the race and, likely to stay a bit further next year, looks a very useful three-year-old in the making. (op Evens, tchd 21-20 in a place)
Satwa Street(IRE) had won nicely at the track last time but, while he finished closer to the winner than was the case on his penultimate outing, he was always being held by that rival in the final furlong. He got the extra furlong well enough and there will be other days for him. (op 11-4)
Head Down struggled to go the early pace and, after recovering to join the leaders turning in, he was unable to raise his game from the top of the home straight. He is struggling to find his best trip at present and has been handicapped on the form of his decent Newmarket second back in June. He has not progressed since then so is hard to place. (tchd 9-2)
Kheskianto(IRE) was making her British debut having been placed on five of her six career starts in Italy. She did not shape without some ability and may benefit for a return to further, but the fact she is entered for a claimer at Kempton strongly suggests she is only modest. (op 16-1 tchd 10-1)
Lady Master, returning from a 59-day break, was well beaten on this debut for new connections and now looks flattered by an official mark of 74. A drop back in trip should suit ideally, however. Official explanation: jockey said filly hung right (op 12-1 tchd 20-1)

7524 PLAY POKER AT LADBROKES.COM NURSERY 1m (P)
2:30 (2:30) (Class 5) (0-75,74) 2-Y-0 £2,729 (£806; £403) Stalls High

Form RPR

600 1 **Thin Red Line (IRE)**^{17} 7333 2-9-5 **72**........................ JamieSpencer 2 78+
(E A L Dunlop) *mde all: set modest pce tl qcknd 3f out: drvn and edgd rt 1f out: maintained gallop to the fin* 2/1^{2}

0502 2 ¾ **Clerk's Choice (IRE)**^{36} 7016 2-9-0 **67**........................ HayleyTurner 1 71+
(W Jarvis) *t.k.h early: mostly trckd wnr: rdn 2f out: styd on but nvr able to bridge the gap fnl f* 15/8^{1}

033 3 6 **Colangnik (USA)**^{23} 7259 2-9-7 **74**........................ SteveDrowne 5 65
(J R Best) *cl up: outpcd and shkn up wl over 1f out: n.d after* 9/2^{3}

000 4 nk **Dicey Affair**^{33} 7097 2-9-1 **68**........................ GeorgeBaker 6 58
(G L Moore) *hld up in 5th: clsd over 2f out: sn outpcd and shkn up: no ch after* 8/1

040 5 4 ½ **Nicky Nutjob (GER)**^{34} 7069 2-8-13 **66**........................ JimmyQuinn 7 46
(J Pearce) *hld up in last: outpcd and pushed along wl over 2f out: no ch after* 14/1

4605 6 1 ½ **Voulez Vous**^{19} 7298 2-9-1 **68**........................ ChrisCatlin 4 45
(E J O'Neill) *plld hrd: hld up in 4th: effrt on outer over 2f out: sn wknd rapidly* 12/1

1m 40.44s (2.24) **Going Correction** 0.0s/f (Stan) 6 Ran SP% 111.8
Speed ratings (Par 96): **88,87,81,80,76 74**
toteswinger: 1&2 £1.50, 1&3 £2.00, 2&3 £1.70. CSF £6.10 TOTE £2.60: £1.60, £1.20; EX 6.80.
Owner Byculla Thoroughbreds **Bred** Peter Jones And G G Jones **Trained** Newmarket, Suffolk

FOCUS
The first pair came clear in this modest nursery and their form could be underestimated. The winner set a stop-start gallop.

NOTEBOOK
Thin Red Line(IRE) got off the mark at the fourth attempt on his nursery bow. He was allowed to dictate the pace from the off and his rider got the fractions spot on, so he has to rate as somewhat flattered. That said, this looks his best trip and he is entitled to some further progression in this sphere. Official explanation: trainer's rep said, regarding running, that the colt's previous run was disappointing and this time had been able to dominate over a longer trip (op 3-1)
Clerk's Choice(IRE), 2lb higher, had finished fast over 7f at Leicester on his last outing and looked an improver on this step up in trip. He got caught out when the winner kicked for home, however, and was always being held inside the final furlong. A truly run race over this distance should suit ideally and there are races to be won with him, but he will likely go up a few pounds again. (op 2-1 tchd 7-4)
Colangnik(USA) hit a flat spot before keeping on again and is another who was likely found out by the uneven pace. She looks to have begun life in handicaps on no more than a fair mark, but is too lightly-raced to be writing off as her stable is also going through a quiet spell. (op 3-1, tchd 5-1 in places)
Dicey Affair was another possible improver for the step up in trip and switch to a nursery. She proved one-paced down the home straight and perhaps a strongly-run race back over 7f is what she ideally requires at present. (op 6-1 tchd 10-1)
Nicky Nutjob(GER) was always out the back on this first run for new connections, but he would not have enjoyed the uneven pace on this drop in trip. (op 12-1 tchd 16-1)
Voulez Vous again looked tricky and needs further respite from the handicapper on this display. (tchd 16-1)

7525 PLAY BINGO AT LADBROKES.COM H'CAP 1m (P)
3:00 (3:01) (Class 4) (0-80,80) 3-Y-0+ £4,727 (£1,406; £702; £351) Stalls High

Form RPR

0011 1 **Titan Triumph**^{19} 7302 4-9-2 **76**........................(t) GeorgeBaker 6 83+
(W J Knight) *hld up in last: smooth prog on outer over 2f out: shkn up to ld 1f out: narrow advantage after: rdn out nr fin* 6/5^{1}

6020 2 nk **Premier Danseur (IRE)**^{12} 7398 3-9-5 **80**........................ JamieSpencer 7 86
(M Johnston) *led: kicked on fr 3f out: hrd rdn 2f out: hdd 1f out: styd on wl but a jst hld* 9/2^{2}

0400 3 2 ½ **Wavertree Warrior (IRE)**^{19} 7307 6-8-10 **73**........................(b) LukeMorris(3) 4 73
(N P Littmoden) *mostly chsd ldr to 2f out: rdn whn n.m.r over 1f out: kpt on same pce after* 7/1^{3}

6005 4 shd **Twilight Star (IRE)**^{13} 7390 4-9-2 **76**........................ DaneO'Neill 2 76
(R A Teal) *s.i.s: sn taking t.k.h bhd ldrs: effrt whn n.m.r and swtchd lft over 1f out: kpt on same pce after* 8/1

4300 5 1 ½ **Hucking Hero (IRE)**^{18} 7314 3-9-2 **77**........................ SteveDrowne 1 74
(J R Best) *t.k.h early: hld up bhd ldrs: rdn wl over 2f out: effrt over 1f out: nt pce to threaten* 12/1

06 6 1 **Indian Diva (IRE)**^{51} 6684 3-9-4 **79**........................(t) NelsonDeSouza 5 73
(P A Blockley) *t.k.h early: hld up in rr: rdn over 2f out on inner: effrt over 1f out: no imp* 25/1

-002 7 ½ **Imprimis Tagula (IRE)**^{35} 7047 4-9-3 **77**........................(v) JimmyQuinn 3 70
(A Bailey) *t.k.h early: hld up: nudged by wnr jst over 2f out: outpcd whn rdn over 1f out: no imp* 8/1

3460 8 ½ **Hallingdal (UAE)**^{13} 7390 3-9-0 **75**........................ JamesDoyle 8 67
(Ms J S Doyle) *hld up: prog on outer 5f out: wnt 2nd and drvn 2f out: wknd over 1f out* 10/1

1m 38.11s (-0.09) **Going Correction** 0.0s/f (Stan)
WFA 3 from 4yo+ 1lb 8 Ran SP% 119.0
Speed ratings (Par 105): **100,99,97,97,95 94,94,93**
toteswinger: 1&2 £2.00, 1&3 £4.30, 2&3 £7.50. CSF £7.15 CT £27.83 TOTE £2.00: £1.10, £1.90, £2.40; EX 7.90 Trifecta £70.60 Pool: £756.32 - 7.92 winning tickets..
Owner Canisbay Bloodstock **Bred** Hesmonds Stud Ltd **Trained** Patching, W Sussex
■ Stewards' Enquiry : Jamie Spencer three-day ban: careless riding (Dec 16-18)

FOCUS
This was not a bad handicap and it was run at a fair pace. The form looks sound with the first pair pulling clear.

7526 PLAY CASINO AT LADBROKES.COM H'CAP 1m 2f (P)
3:30 (3:31) (Class 4) (0-80,78) 3-Y-0+ £4,727 (£1,406; £702; £351) Stalls Low

Form RPR

3001 1 **Wellington Square**^{23} 7256 3-9-3 **77**........................ GeorgeBaker 9 86+
(H Morrison) *hld up in midfield: prog on outer over 2f out: clsd over 1f out: drvn to ld ins fnl f: hld on wl* 5/1^{1}

6530 2 ½ **Emperor Court (IRE)**^{54} 6599 4-9-7 **78**........................ SteveDrowne 3 86
(P J Makin) *mde most: drvn and hrd pressed fr 2f out: hdd ins fnl f: kpt on wl* 13/2^{3}

2650 3 nk **Summer Winds**^{18} 7314 3-8-13 **73**........................ HayleyTurner 7 80
(T G Mills) *hld up towards rr: prog on inner over 2f out: hrd rdn and clsd on ldrs fnl f: a jst hld* 8/1

6524 4 hd **Risque Heights**^{8} 7440 4-8-4 **64** oh1........................ LukeMorris(3) 1 71
(J R Boyle) *s.s: hld up wl in rr: effrt and prog jst over 2f out: clsng grad on ldrs wh clr run 50yds out* 15/2

0203 5 ¾ **Hold The Gold (IRE)**^{6} 7457 3-9-0 **74**........................ ChrisCatlin 4 79+
(E J O'Neill) *dwlt: hld up in last: stl there 3f out: effrt whn rn into trble 2f out: swtchd to inner: drvn and styd on fnl f: nvr able to chal* 6/1^{2}

3052 6 ½ **Trifti**^{33} 7096 7-9-1 **72**........................ TravisBlock 10 76
(Miss Jo Crowley) *hld up in rr on outer: effrt over 2f out: hanging and nt qckn wl over 1f out: styd on ins fnl f: nrst fin* 14/1

5004 7 ¾ **Prince Of Light (IRE)**^{12} 7398 5-9-7 **78**........................ JamieSpencer 5 81
(M Johnston) *trckd ldr: rdn over 2f out: nt qckn jst over 1f out and sn lost pl* 15/2

0364 8 ¾ **Run For Ede'S**^{19} 7307 4-8-3 **65**........................(p) JackDean(5) 2 66
(P M Phelan) *t.k.h: trckd ldng pair: stl racd keenly 3f out: rdn wl over 1f out: fizzled out tamely* 16/1

0240 9 1 ¼ **Palmerin**^{8} 7439 3-9-4 **78**........................ DaneO'Neill 6 77
(R Hannon) *wl in tch: effrt to chse ldng trio over 2f out: rdn and fnd nil over 1f out: sn lost pl* 11/1

3056 10 11 **Red Birr (IRE)**^{32} 7116 7-9-4 **75**........................(t) MartinDwyer 8 52
(P R Webber) *trckd ldrs: rdn and wknd rapidly over 2f out: t.o* 16/1

11 2 ¾ **Vial De Kerdec (FR)**[277] 5-8-13 **70**.......... NelsonDeSouza 12 41
(M Bradstock) *in tch on outer: pushed along 4f out: wknd 3f out: t.o* **66/1**

0132 12 nk **Star Choice**[36] 7010 3-8-5 **65**.......... JimmyQuinn 11 35
(J Pearce) *pushed along in rr early: nvr gng that wl: rdn and dropped to last wl over 2f out: t.o* **5/1**[1]

2m 5.74s (-0.86) **Going Correction** 0.0s/f (Stan)
WFA 3 from 4yo+ 3lb 12 Ran SP% **123.9**
Speed ratings (Par 105): **103,102,102,102,101 101,100,100,99,90 88,87**
toteswinger: 1&2 £10.10, 1&3 £12.70, 2&3 £22.90. CSF £38.76 CT £265.31 TOTE £4.00: £1.10, £3.00, £4.00; EX 53.30 Trifecta £213.40 Part won. Pool: £288.49 - 0.42 winning tickets. Place 6 £12.57, Place 5 £7.08.
Owner Roger Barby & Sir T Cassel **Bred** J A Peat **Trained** East Ilsley, Berks
■ Stewards' Enquiry : Jamie Spencer matter referred having served 26-days ban in 12mths; careless riding.
Luke Morris two-day ban: careless riding (Dec 16-17)

FOCUS
An open handicap, run at just a steady pace and resulting in something of a sprint finish. The form is a bit messy but the winner can rate higher.
Red Birr(IRE) Official explanation: jockey said gelding had no more to give
T/Jkpt: £2,135.80 to a £1 stake. Pool: £48,132.36. 16.00 winning tickets. T/Plt: £46.50 to a £1 stake. Pool: £50,344.36. 790.00 winning tickets. T/Qpdt: £17.50 to a £1 stake. Pool: £3,965.98. 167.40 winning tickets. JN

7441 SOUTHWELL (L-H)
Tuesday, December 2

OFFICIAL GOING: Standard
Wind: Light, across Weather: Dry and fine

7527 PLAY GOLF AT SOUTHWELL GOLF CLUB MAIDEN STKS (DIV I) 5f (F)
11:50 (11:53) (Class 5) 3-Y-O+ **£2,388** (£705; £352) **Stalls** High

Form RPR

6362 1 **Spic 'n Span**[7] 7444 3-8-12 55.......... (b) AndreaAtzeni(5) 6 69
(R A Harris) *mde all: clr over 2f out: edgd lft ins fnl f: unchal* **7/4**[1]

0632 2 6 **North South Divide (IRE)**[6] 7453 4-8-10 69.....(p) AndrewHeffernan(7) 9 47
(Peter Grayson) *hld up in tch: hdwy 2f out: sn rdn and kpt on ins fnl f: no ch w wnr* **11/2**[3]

0-0 3 ¾ **Silk Gallery (USA)**[46] 6791 3-8-12 0.......... (t) PatCosgrave 3 39
(E J Alston) *sn chsng wnr: rdn along 2f out: drvn over 1f out: lost 2nd wl ins fnl f* **15/2**

000 4 1 ¾ **The Cube**[20] 7292 4-9-0 42.......... TolleyDean(3) 11 38
(J Balding) *chsd ldrs: rdn along 2f out: sn drvn and kpt on same pce* **28/1**

4454 5 1 ¼ **Bilboa**[6] 7453 3-8-12 47.......... (p) MCGeran(5) 13 34
(J M Bradley) *dwlt: swtchd lft after s and hld up: hdwy 1/2-way: rdn and in tch whn hung bdly lft wl over 1f out: sn no imp* **18/1**

34 6 1 ¾ **Maid Of Ailsa (USA)**[26] 7213 3-8-12 0.......... TonyCulhane 8 22
(W J Haggas) *chsd ldrs: rdn along 1/2-way: nvr a factor* **2/1**[2]

0-2 7 nk **Kilvickeon (IRE)**[311] 319 4-9-3 45.......... LPKeniry 4 26
(Peter Grayson) *prom: rdn along over 2f out and sn wknd* **20/1**

0 8 11 **Mickys Mate**[18] 7321 3-9-3 0.......... PaulMulrennan 2 —
(A Crook) *chsd ldrs on outer: rdn along over 2f out and sn wknd* **40/1**

03-0 9 6 **Comic Tales**[45] 6822 7-9-3 45.......... DarrenWilliams 7 —
(M Mullineaux) *sn outpcd and a in rr* **50/1**

606- 10 1 ½ **The Brat**[390] 6730 4-8-12 37.......... (p) JamieMoriarty 12 —
(Miss Tracy Waggott) *a in rr* **150/1**

60.04 secs (0.34) **Going Correction** +0.15s/f (Slow) 10 Ran SP% **115.4**
Speed ratings (Par 103): **103,93,92,89,87 84,84,66,56,54**
toteswinger: 1&2 £2.40, 1&3 £3.90, 2&3 £9.60. CSF £11.23 TOTE £2.80: £1.20, £1.40, £2.70; EX 11.90.
Owner Mrs Ruth M Serrell **Bred** C A Cyzer **Trained** Earlswood, Monmouths
■ Stewards' Enquiry : M C Geran one-day ban: careless riding (Dec 16)

FOCUS
On paper, just four appeared to have a serious chance, but this weak maiden soon became a one-horse race. The winner is rated back to something like his best.
Bilboa Official explanation: jockey said gelding hung left

7528 PLAY GOLF AT SOUTHWELL GOLF CLUB MAIDEN STKS (DIV II) 5f (F)
12:20 (12:20) (Class 5) 3-Y-O+ **£2,388** (£705; £352) **Stalls** High

Form RPR

6520 1 **Admiral Bond (IRE)**[11] 7399 3-9-0 62.......... (p) DuranFentiman(3) 2 60+
(G R Oldroyd) *sn outpcd and rdn along towards rr: hdwy over 2f out: styd on to ld ins fnl f* **9/4**[1]

0604 2 1 ½ **Summer Rose**[110] 5015 3-8-12 40.......... (b[1]) ShaneKelly 1 50
(R M H Cowell) *chsd ldrs: hdwy 1/2-way: rdn to ld 1 1/2f out: drvn and edgd rt ent fnl f: sn hdd and kpt on same pce* **10/1**

0005 3 1 **Monte Cassino (IRE)**[18] 7323 3-9-3 60.......... TGMcLaughlin 6 51+
(J O'Reilly) *dwlt and sltly hmpd s: sn rdn along towards rr: hdwy over 2f out: swtchd lft and drvn over 1f out: kpt on ins fnl f: nrst fin* **11/2**[2]

040 4 ¾ **Bahamian Ballad**[50] 6707 3-8-12 44.......... (v) GrahamGibbons 8 43
(J D Bethell) *prom: rdn 2f out and ev ch tl drvn and one pce ent fnl f* **8/1**[3]

4520 5 3 ½ **Gelert (IRE)**[61] 6405 3-9-3 45.......... (b) PatrickMathers 5 36
(Peter Grayson) *led: rdn along 2f out: hdd 1 1/2f out: drvn and wknd appr fnl f* **17/2**

0000 6 shd **Solemn**[35] 7049 3-8-12 45.......... (b) MCGeran(5) 12 35
(J M Bradley) *s.i.s and towards rr: rdn along and hdwy wl over 1f out: nvr nr ldrs* **50/1**

300 7 1 ¼ **Steel Mask (IRE)**[199] 2187 3-9-3 53.......... MickyFenton 7 31
(M Brittain) *dwlt and sn pushed along: hdwy and in tch 1/2-way: rdn to chse ldrs wl over 1f out: sn wknd and eased ins fnl f* **14/1**

0640 8 1 ¼ **Stoneacre Chris (USA)**[14] 7369 3-8-5 46.......... AndrewHeffernan(7) 10 21
(Peter Grayson) *nvr bttr than midfield* **28/1**

5440 9 ½ **Rathmolyon**[17] 7346 3-8-12 58.......... (v[1]) FrancisNorton 13 20
(D Haydn Jones) *nvr nr ldrs* **9/1**

5000 10 1 ¼ **Firewalker**[46] 6791 3-8-12 50.......... PaulEddery 4 15
(P T Dalton) *prom: rdn along 1/2-way: sn wknd* **25/1**

0- 11 3 ½ **Jazzing About (USA)**[591] 1150 3-9-3 0.......... JamieMoriarty 9 7
(P T Midgley) *s.i.s: a in rr* **25/1**

2053 12 ½ **Princess Charlmane (IRE)**[112] 4950 5-8-12 47.......... (t) GregFairley 11 1
(C J Teague) *chsd ldrs: rdn along 2f out and sn wknd* **12/1**

0 13 3 ½ **Take That**[73] 6114 3-9-3 0.......... TonyCulhane 3 —
(S P Griffiths) *in tch on outer: rdn along 2f out and sn wknd* **33/1**

60.95 secs (1.25) **Going Correction** +0.15s/f (Slow) 13 Ran SP% **117.3**
Speed ratings (Par 103): **96,93,92,90,85 85,83,81,80,78 72,71,66**
toteswinger: 1&2 £6.70, 1&3 £3.40, 2&3 £5.90. CSF £23.34 TOTE £3.00: £1.10, £2.70, £2.40; EX 33.00.
Owner R C Bond **Bred** David Ryan **Trained** Brawby, N Yorks

FOCUS
Division two of this poor maiden and the weaker race, run in a slow time. The winner probably did not have to match his recent handicap form.
Steel Mask(IRE) Official explanation: trainer's rep said colt had a breathing problem

7529 MEMBERSHIP AT SOUTHWELL GOLF CLUB CLAIMING STKS 5f (F)
12:50 (12:50) (Class 6) 3-Y-O+ **£2,047** (£604; £302) **Stalls** High

Form RPR

6030 1 **She's Our Beauty (IRE)**[61] 6405 5-8-2 44.......... (p) FrankieMcDonald 3 58
(S T Mason) *prom: effrt 2f out: rdn over 1f out: led ins fnl f: drvn out* **33/1**

1005 2 1 ¼ **Dubai To Barnsley**[54] 6595 3-8-4 48.......... AndrewHeffernan(7) 4 63
(Garry Moss) *midfield: hdwy wl over 1f out: sn rdn and kpt on ins fnl f* **50/1**

0030 3 1 **Calmdownmate (IRE)**[34] 7066 3-8-9 70.......... DarrenWilliams 7 57
(K R Burke) *a.p: effrt and ev ch 2f out: sn rdn and kpt on same pce ins fnl f* **7/1**[3]

1024 4 shd **Came Back (IRE)**[13] 7378 5-9-3 92.......... NCallan 6 65
(K A Ryan) *led: rdn along 2f out: drvn over 1f out: hdd ins fnl f: wknd* **6/5**[1]

0440 5 3 ½ **Overstayed (IRE)**[2] 7509 5-8-9 54.......... (v[1]) NeilChalmers 8 44
(A Bailey) *sn rdn along towards rr: hdwy u.p 2f out: drvn and hung lft over 1f out: kpt on ins fnl f* **14/1**

0660 6 1 **Efistorm**[13] 7384 7-9-5 75.......... PatCosgrave 1 50
(C R Dore) *prom on wd outside: rdn along wl over 1f out: drvn and hung lft appr fnl f: sn wknd* **4/1**[2]

1033 7 hd **Tanley**[19] 7295 3-8-10 56.......... (p) WilliamCarson(5) 2 46
(J F Coupland) *prom: rdn along 2f out: sn wknd* **12/1**

5603 8 2 **Obe One**[25] 7218 8-8-11 52.......... FrancisNorton 10 34
(A Berry) *a towards rr* **16/1**

0430 9 3 **Ducal Regancy Red**[112] 4950 4-8-3 46.......... DuranFentiman(3) 5 19
(C J Teague) *cl up: rdn along 1/2-way: sn wknd* **40/1**

0600 10 ¾ **River Gleam (IRE)**[98] 5374 3-8-1 38.......... (v) DeclanCannon(7) 14 18
(A P Jarvis) *wnt lft and hmpd s: a towards rr* **100/1**

000- 11 4 ½ **Simplified**[41] 789 5-7-11 43.......... (t) AndreaAtzeni(5) 9 —
(M C Chapman) *sn outpcd and a in rr* **150/1**

2500 12 1 ¼ **Ben**[161] 3346 3-8-13 59.......... (e[1]) LPKeniry 11 2
(P G Murphy) *a towards rr* **50/1**

6400 13 7 **Rightcar Hull (IRE)**[196] 2268 3-8-4 40 ow2.......... PatrickMathers 13 —
(Peter Grayson) *hmpd s: a in rr* **150/1**

0061 P **Godfrey Street**[28] 7176 5-9-7 74.......... (b) GregFairley 12 —
(A G Newcombe) *wnt rt and hmpd s: sn chsng ldrs: shkn up and wknd qckly wl over 1f out: p.u ins fnl f* **15/2**

60.00 secs (0.30) **Going Correction** +0.15s/f (Slow) 14 Ran SP% **121.6**
Speed ratings (Par 101): **103,101,99,99,93 92,91,88,83,82 75,73,62,—**
toteswinger: 1&2 £90.80, 1&3 £19.40, 2&3 £44.70. CSF £1125.32 TOTE £26.20: £5.10, £9.10, £2.10; EX 554.30.
Owner The Mason Racing Partnership I **Bred** R N Auld **Trained** Castle Bytham, Lincs

FOCUS
A surprise outcome to this claimer, and the form looks pretty dubious with the four that stood out at the weights all a fair way below their best. The winner is the best guide to the form and is rated back to her best.
Godfrey Street Official explanation: jockey said gelding felt wrong behind; vet said gelding lost a front shoe

7530 SOUTHWELL-RACECOURSE.CO.UK (S) STKS 6f (F)
1:20 (1:21) (Class 6) 2-Y-O **£2,047** (£604; £302) **Stalls** Low

Form RPR

2660 1 **Glan Lady (IRE)**[35] 7052 2-8-6 50.......... (b[1]) TolleyDean(3) 5 56
(J L Spearing) *hld up in tch: gd hdwy on inner 2f out: led 2f out: rdn clr appr fnl f: easily* **13/2**[3]

0006 2 3 ¾ **That Boy Ronaldo**[14] 7370 2-8-9 48.......... FrancisNorton 9 45
(A Berry) *chsd ldrs: rdn along over 2f out: styd on u.p fr over 1f out: kpt on ins fnl f: no ch w wnr* **20/1**

1554 3 4 ½ **Bold Account (IRE)**[31] 7130 2-9-6 69.......... DarrenWilliams 12 42
(K R Burke) *cl up: effrt and ev ch 2f out: sn rdn and one pce appr fnl f* **10/11**[1]

005 4 ½ **No Quarter Given (IRE)**[59] 6489 2-9-0 43.......... TonyHamilton 4 35
(Mrs A Duffield) *t.k.h: chsd ldrs: effrt and ch whn n.m.r wl over 1f out: sn rdn and one pce* **16/1**

0044 5 ¾ **Dontforgeturshovel**[18] 7319 2-9-0 46.......... (v) TGMcLaughlin 8 33
(J Pearce) *hld up: hdwy 2f out: sn rdn and no imp fnl f* **8/1**

0500 6 1 ¼ **Dawn Wee**[22] 7269 2-8-6 48.......... (v[1]) DuranFentiman(3) 1 24
(G R Oldroyd) *prom on inner: rdn along and ev ch over 2f out: grad wknd* **33/1**

0300 7 3 **French Forest**[172] 3008 2-8-4 46.......... MCGeran(5) 6 15
(M Brittain) *a towards rr* **16/1**

0335 8 11 **Courageous Nature (IRE)**[7] 7443 2-9-6 55.......... (be) PatCosgrave 11 —
(A J McCabe) *led: rdn along and hdd 2f out: sn wknd* **5/1**[2]

0 9 13 **Jerry's Agent (IRE)**[29] 7165 2-9-0 0.......... PaulMulrennan 10 —
(J Balding) *t.k.h: chsd ldrs on outer: rdn along 1/2-way: sn wknd* **33/1**

2050 10 9 **Inn Swinger (IRE)**[140] 4063 2-8-6 45 ow2.......... WilliamCarson(5) 3 —
(W G M Turner) *s.i.s: a bhd* **40/1**

1m 18.71s (2.21) **Going Correction** +0.075s/f (Slow) 10 Ran SP% **118.3**
Speed ratings (Par 94): **88,83,77,76,75 73,69,55,37,25**
toteswinger: 1&2 £8.00, 1&3 £4.00, 2&3 £6.20. CSF £128.93 TOTE £9.00: £1.80, £3.60, £1.20; EX 170.10.There was no bid for the winner.
Owner Leonard Kinsella **Bred** William Flood **Trained** Kinnersley, Worcs

FOCUS
A very ordinary selling race which took little winning. Weak form, rated around the runner-up.

NOTEBOOK
Glan Lady(IRE) was blinkered for the first time. She stuck towards the far side in the home straight, was out on her own coming to the final furlong and was able to take things easily in the end. This was only her sixth start and now she has broken her duck, there may be even better to come this winter. (op 6-1 tchd 8-1)
That Boy Ronaldo, strangely named for a filly, was well beaten over farther here last time, but stayed on from off the pace to finish clear second best. This was only her second sound effort in 13 starts and whether she will reproduce it next time remains to be seen. (op 16-1)
Bold Account(IRE), 8lb in hand of the winner on official ratings, had the worst of the draw and was unable to dominate. (op 11-10 tchd 5-6)
No Quarter Given(IRE), stepping up in trip on only his fourth start, settled better and ran easily his best race to date. (op 20-1)
Dontforgeturshovel, who usually runs over farther, lacked the pace to take a hand. (op 17-2 tchd 9-1)
Courageous Nature(IRE), drawn one from the outside, made the running but dropped right away when headed. (tchd 6-1)
Jerry's Agent(IRE) Official explanation: jockey said gelding hung right

Inn Swinger(IRE) Official explanation: jockey said filly missed the break

7531 CALL 01636 814481 TO SPONSOR A RACE NURSERY 7f (F)
1:50 (1:53) (Class 6) (0-65,65) 2-Y-0 £2,047 (£604; £302) Stalls Low

Form RPR
6550 1 **Kingaroo (IRE)**69 6214 2-8-2 52 AndrewHeffernan(7) 11 57
(Garry Moss) *towards rr: gd hdwy on inner 2f out: sn rdn: drvn and styd on ins fnl f to ld last 50yds* **16/1**
6312 2 *nk* **Rio Cobolo (IRE)**14 7372 2-9-3 60 (v) ShaneKelly 10 64
(Paul Green) *trckd ldrs: hdwy 3f out: led 2f out and sn rdn: drvn and edgd rt ent fnl f: hdd and no ex last 50yds* **5/1**1
4021 3 *2 1/4* **Captain Kallis (IRE)**22 7268 2-9-7 64 FrankieMcDonald 14 63
(D J S Ffrench Davis) *led: rdn along and hdd 2f out: drvn and rallied to have ev ch ent fnl f: sn one pce* **15/2**
0001 4 *2 1/4* **Monte Mayor Eagle**18 7319 2-9-0 57 (b) NCallan 4 50
(D Haydn Jones) *trckd ldrs: effrt 2f out and sn rdn: drvn and one pce appr fnl f* **11/1**
4511 5 *nk* **Kinigi (IRE)**7 7443 2-9-3 65 6ex AndreaAtzeni(5) 13 57
(R A Harris) *in tch: hdwy on outer over 2f out: rdn to chse ldrs over 1f out: drvn and hung lft ent fnl f: sn btn* **7/1**3
0634 6 *2 1/4* **Oisin's Boy**14 7372 2-9-4 61 PatCosgrave 12 48
(J R Boyle) *chsd ldrs: rdn along 2f out: drvn over 1f out and sn no imp* **6/1**2
066 7 *1 3/4* **Katie Higgins**14 7372 2-8-6 49 (b) CatherineGannon 6 31
(J L Spearing) *midfield: hdwy to chse ldrs 2f out: sn rdn and no imp appr fnl f* **20/1**
U464 8 *3 1/4* **Chantilly Dancer (IRE)**56 6547 2-9-3 60 FrancisNorton 9 34
(M Quinn) *a in rr* **22/1**
0001 9 *hd* **Top Flight Splash**20 7281 2-8-12 55 DaleGibson 8 29
(Mrs G S Rees) *cl up: rdn along wl over 2f out: sn drvn and wknd* **14/1**
0432 10 *3/4* **Le Petit Vigier**22 7266 2-8-7 50 (t) GregFairley 2 22
(P Beaumont) *chsd ldrs on inner: rdn along 3f out and sn wknd* **5/1**1
06 11 *1* **Fuaigh Mor (IRE)**138 4101 2-9-0 57 (p) MickyFenton 3 26
(A Bailey) *prom: rdn along bef 1/2-way: sn lost pl and bhd* **20/1**
0051 12 *hd* **Miss Xu Xia**14 7370 2-8-8 54 (p) DuranFentiman(3) 5 23
(G R Oldroyd) *a towards rr* **20/1**
5300 13 *13* **Jessica Mary (IRE)**14 7372 2-8-9 52 PaulMulrennan 7 —
(B Smart) *a in rr: bhd fr 1/2-way* **16/1**
2000 14 *5* **Meydan Groove**20 7281 2-9-2 59 GrahamGibbons 1 —
(R Johnson) *s.i.s: a bhd* **22/1**

1m 32.9s (2.60) **Going Correction** +0.075s/f (Slow) 14 Ran SP% **121.6**
Speed ratings (Par 94): **88,87,85,82,82 79,77,73,73,72 71,71,56,50**
toteswinger: 1&2 £47.10, 1&3 £59.50, 2&3 £7.20. CSF £86.97 CT £496.37 TOTE £24.80: £5.70, £2.40, £3.00; EX 271.00.
Owner Brooklands Racing **Bred** Kevin Walsh **Trained** Loughborough, Leics
■ Stewards' Enquiry : Frankie McDonald five-day ban: careless riding (Dec 16-20)

FOCUS
A low-grade nursery but the form looks solid and should hold up round here in the coming months.

NOTEBOOK
Kingaroo(IRE) had been dropped 3lb after failing to see a mile out on his nursery debut at Redcar in September and gelded in the meantime. Perhaps significantly, he stuck to the far side in the home straight and did just enough in the end. (op 28-1)
Rio Cobolo(IRE), who had a double-figure draw, has shown much-improved form since being fitted with a visor. After taking a narrow advantage, to his credit he fought back all the way to the line and, if anything, proved suited by the step up to 7f. (tchd 6-1)
Captain Kallis(IRE), who had the worst of the draw, was inclined to run with the choke out. He took them along but did not see out the extra furlong anywhere near as well as the first two. (op 8-1 tchd 7-1)
Monte Mayor Eagle, hoisted 10lb after her win in selling company here when blinkered for the first time, found this much tougher. (op 17-2 tchd 12-1)
Kinigi(IRE), penalised for her hard-fought win in a claimer here last week, was another drawn on the outside. She did not help her cause by persisting in hanging right. (op 11-2 tchd 5-1 and 15-2)
Oisin's Boy, awkward to load, didn't improve for the step up in trip. (op 10-1)
Le Petit Vigier, bidding to give her jumps trainer his first Flat success, had an inside draw but was soon driven along and lacked the pace to hold on to a good pitch exiting the back stretch. (op 7-1)
Miss Xu Xia Official explanation: stewards subsequently noted filly was hampered early on
Meydan Groove Official explanation: jockey said filly missed the break and was never going

7532 HOSPITALITY AT SOUTHWELL RACECOURSE H'CAP 1m (F)
2:20 (2:21) (Class 6) (0-65,65) 3-Y-0+ £2,047 (£604; £302) Stalls Low

Form RPR
0050 1 **Rub Of The Relic (IRE)**17 7085 3-8-4 51 oh1 (v1) FrankieMcDonald 3 62
(P T Midgley) *mde all: rdn 2f out: jnd and drvn appr fnl f: kpt on gamely towards fin* **33/1**
1125 2 *1* **The Grey One (IRE)**7 7441 5-8-10 61 (p) MCGeran(5) 11 70
(J M Bradley) *towards rr: stdy hdwy 3f out: rdn to chal appr fnl f and ev ch tl drvn and no ex last 75yds* **8/1**
3532 3 *5* **West End Lad**20 7284 5-9-3 63 (b) FrancisNorton 4 61
(S R Bowring) *trckd ldrs on inner: hdwy over 2f out: sn rdn: drvn wl over 1f out and one pce ent fnl f* **11/4**1
-340 4 *1 1/2* **Prize Fighter (IRE)**27 7202 6-9-0 65 (b) SladeO'Hara(5) 10 59
(A Berry) *in tch: smooth hdwy 3f out: chsd ldrs 2f out: sn rdn and kpt on same pce* **8/1**
2341 5 *3* **Having A Ball**22 7267 4-9-2 62 ShaneKelly 7 49
(P D Cundell) *towards rr: hdwy on wd outside 2f out: sn rdn and kpt on ins fnl f: nrst fin* **7/1**3
0000 6 *6* **So Sublime**22 7270 3-8-0 52 (t) AndreaAtzeni(5) 5 25
(M C Chapman) *trckd ldrs: hdwy to chse wnr wl over 2f out: drvn wl over 1f out and grad wknd* **66/1**
31-3 7 *1* **Ridgeway Jazz**335 20 3-8-4 51 CatherineGannon 6 22
(M D I Usher) *towards rr tl sme hdwy fnl 2f: nvr a factor* **28/1**
03-0 8 *shd* **World Of Choice (USA)**18 7317 3-9-1 62 DaleGibson 8 33
(M W Easterby) *dwlt and towards rr tl sme late hdwy* **40/1**
0031 9 *4 1/2* **Provost**61 6409 4-9-1 61 PaulMulrennan 2 21
(M W Easterby) *s.i.s: a towards rr* **10/1**
0042 10 *1/2* **Captain Royale (IRE)**14 7373 3-9-1 62 NCallan 12 21
(Miss Tracy Waggott) *midfield: hdwy to chse ldrs 3f out: sn rdn and wknd fnl 2f* **10/1**
11 *1* **Soviet Trooper (IRE)**43 6871 4-8-5 51 oh1 GregFairley 13 8
(Liam McAteer, Ire) *chsd ldrs on outer: rdn along over 3f out and sn wknd* **12/1**
0133 12 *11* **Josr's Magic (IRE)**33 7096 4-9-1 61 PatCosgrave 1 —
(H J Collingridge) *midfield on inner: rdn along 3f out: sn wknd* **9/2**2
00-3 13 *nk* **Daggerman**18 7321 3-8-13 60 GrahamGibbons 9 —
(P A Blockley) *cl up: rdn along 3f out and sn wknd* **25/1**
0640 14 *49* **Zach's Harmoney (USA)**119 4710 4-9-4 64 TonyCulhane 14 —
(Miss M E Rowland) *chsd ldrs: rdn along 1/2-way and sn wknd* **33/1**

1m 43.4s (-0.30) **Going Correction** +0.075s/f (Slow)
WFA 3 from 4yo+ 1lb 14 Ran SP% **122.6**
Speed ratings (Par 101): **104,103,98,96,93 87,86,86,81,81 80,69,69,20**
toteswinger: 1&2 £76.30, 1&3 £35.70, 2&3 £11.70. CSF £272.39 CT £1009.46 TOTE £63.00: £14.30, £3.20, £1.90; EX 459.30.
Owner O R Dukes **Bred** M J Wiley **Trained** Westow, N Yorks

FOCUS
A low-grade handicap run in an ordinary time. The runner-up looks the best guide to the form.
Having A Ball Official explanation: jockey said gelding never travelled

7533 BOOK YOUR TICKETS ON LINE AT SOUTHWELL-RACECOURSE.CO.UK H'CAP 7f (F)
2:50 (2:50) (Class 6) (0-62,62) 3-Y-0+ £2,047 (£604; £302) Stalls Low

Form RPR
2202 1 **Blue Charm**3 7490 4-9-2 62 LPKeniry 13 75
(S Kirk) *prom: trckd ldr 1/2-way: rdn to ld 1 1/2f out: drvn out* **4/1**2
0304 2 *1 3/4* **Orpenella**30 7153 3-9-0 60 (b1) NCallan 9 68
(K A Ryan) *led: rdn along and qcknd over 2f out: hdd 1 1/2f out: sn drvn and kpt on same pce* **8/1**
0032 3 *2 1/2* **Solicitude**13 7383 5-8-12 58 (p) PatCosgrave 10 60
(D Haydn Jones) *towards rr: gd hdwy on outer 3f out: rdn 2f out: styd on ins fnl f: nrst fin* **12/1**
0242 4 *3/4* **Betteras Bertie**18 7316 5-8-9 55 ow2 MickyFenton 11 55
(M Brittain) *s.i.s and bhd: gd hdwy 1/2-way: rdn to chse ldng pair over 1f out: sn drvn and one pce* **11/2**3
0634 5 *3* **Louisiade (IRE)**7 7441 7-8-9 60 (p) AndreaAtzeni(5) 6 51
(M C Chapman) *in tch: hdwy to chse ldrs wl over 2f out: sn rdn and no imp* **7/2**1
4365 6 *7* **Sheriff's Silk**73 6132 4-9-0 60 (b) PaulEddery 4 33
(G D Blake) *prom: rdn along to chse ldng pair 3f out: drvn over 2f out and sn wknd* **9/1**
0056 7 *2 1/4* **Magical Song**7 7442 3-8-7 53 ow1 GrahamGibbons 7 19
(P A Blockley) *towards rr: rdn along and sme hdwy over 2f out: nvr a factor* **9/1**
0020 8 *1 1/4* **Optical Illusion (USA)**18 7320 4-8-9 55 (p) TonyHamilton 8 18
(R A Fahey) *chsd ldrs: rdn along 3f out: sn drvn and wknd* **16/1**
0000 9 *2* **August Gale (USA)**29 7166 3-8-11 57 DaleGibson 3 15
(G P Kelly) *cl up on inner: rdn along 1/2-way and sn wknd* **50/1**
5051 10 *nk* **Isabella's Fancy**44 6836 3-8-3 52 (b1) DuranFentiman(3) 1 9
(A G Newcombe) *towards rr fr 1/2-way* **16/1**
0500 11 *shd* **Hunt The Bottle (IRE)**73 6132 3-9-0 60 (be1) GregFairley 2 17
(M Mullineaux) *s.i.s and sn rdn along into midfield: drvn 1/2-way and sn wknd* **25/1**
1044 12 *1/2* **Don Picolo**265 853 3-8-8 59 ow4 (b) GabrielHannon(5) 12 14
(P A Blockley) *a in rr* **25/1**
0436 13 *1* **Feeling Fresh (IRE)**20 7288 3-9-1 61 FrancisNorton 5 14
(Paul Green) *a bhd* **16/1**
000U 14 *21* **Sir Douglas**18 7316 5-8-11 57 (t) PaulMulrennan 14 —
(M A Barnes) *in tch on outer: rdn along and hung bdly rt home turn: sn bhd and heavily eased fnl 2f* **40/1**

1m 30.0s (-0.30) **Going Correction** +0.075s/f (Slow) 14 Ran SP% **126.1**
Speed ratings (Par 101): **104,102,99,98,94 86,84,82,80,80 80,79,78,54**
toteswinger: 1&2 £7.90, 1&3 £8.40, 2&3 £16.60. CSF £36.91 CT £370.25 TOTE £4.40: £2.30, £2.90, £3.20; EX 34.10.
Owner Sylvester Kirk **Bred** Mrs R Pease **Trained** Upper Lambourn, Berks

FOCUS
Another low-grade handicap but the pick of the round-course times (hand-timed). The winner was back close to his old form.
August Gale(USA) Official explanation: trainer's rep said gelding had a breathing problem
Isabella's Fancy Official explanation: jockey said filly hung left
Sir Douglas Official explanation: jockey said gelding hung right

7534 SOUTHWELL-RACECOURSE.CO.UK H'CAP 6f (F)
3:20 (3:22) (Class 5) (0-75,75) 3-Y-0+ £2,729 (£806; £403) Stalls Low

Form RPR
5022 1 **Charles Parnell (IRE)**7 7448 5-9-2 73 DaleGibson 12 83+
(M Dods) *in tch: hdwy to chse ldng pair over 2f out: rdn over 1f out: styd on strly ins fnl f to ld last 40yds* **3/1**1
0300 2 *1 1/4* **Westwood**7 7448 3-8-11 68 ow1 NCallan 1 74
(D Haydn Jones) *cl up on inner: led after 2f: hdd 1/2-way: cl up and drvn over 1f out: rallied to ld again ins fnl f: hdd and nt qckn last 40yds* **22/1**
0040 3 *nse* **First Order**13 7384 7-8-13 75 (v) AnnStokell(5) 4 81
(Miss A Stokell) *cl up: led 1/2-way: rdn wl over 1f out: drvn and hdd ins fnl f: kpt on u.p* **28/1**
1412 4 *6* **Cool Sands (IRE)**20 7286 6-9-1 72 (v) PatCosgrave 5 59
(J G Given) *in rr and rdn along 1/2-way: hdwy 2f out: swtchd rt and rdn wl over 1f out: no imp* **3/1**1
00 5 *3 3/4* **Milton Of Campsie**158 3442 3-8-11 71 TolleyDean(3) 10 46
(S Parr) *stdd s and hld up in rr: hdwy over 2f out: rdn wl over 1f out: kpt on: nvr nr ldrs* **14/1**
50-0 6 *1 1/2* **Betty Burke**11 7406 3-8-5 62 oh3 ow1 (t) GregFairley 7 32
(Liam McAteer, Ire) *chsd ldrs: rdn along and outpcd 1/2-way: plugged on u.p fnl 2f* **33/1**
414 7 *2 1/4* **Hurricane Harriet**31 7143 3-9-2 73 ShaneKelly 3 36
(R M H Cowell) *in tch: rdn along 1/2-way: drvn over 2f out and sn wknd* **15/2**3
1220 8 *3/4* **Bold Marc (IRE)**19 7299 6-9-4 75 DarrenWilliams 2 35
(K R Burke) *led 2f: rdn along 1/2-way and sn wknd* **4/1**2
436 9 *1 1/2* **Cheap Street**15 7358 4-8-8 65 ow1 PaulMulrennan 6 20
(J G Portman) *a towards rr* **8/1**
2100 10 *2 1/4* **To Bubbles**89 5638 3-8-6 63 FrancisNorton 9 11
(A G Newcombe) *a in rr* **18/1**
5160 11 *1 1/2* **Owed**138 4107 6-8-3 63 (t) DuranFentiman(3) 11 6
(R Bastiman) *chsd ldrs: rdn along 1/2-way: sn drvn and wknd* **20/1**
12 *2 1/2* **Babel**78 5981 3-8-13 70 SimonWhitworth 13 5
(M Wigham) *chsd ldrs on outer: rdn along 1/2-way: sn wknd* **16/1**
0000 13 *4* **Count Cougar (USA)**7 7448 8-8-8 65 TonyCulhane 8 —
(S P Griffiths) *chsd ldrs: rdn along 1/2-way: sn wknd* **25/1**

1m 16.29s (-0.21) **Going Correction** +0.075s/f (Slow) 13 Ran SP% **130.0**
Speed ratings (Par 103): **104,102,102,94,89 87,84,83,81,78 76,72,67**
toteswinger: 1&2 £17.60, 1&3 £26.40, 2&3 £41.80. CSF £83.89 CT £1697.98 TOTE £3.80: £1.40, £5.90, £8.10; EX 63.00 Place 6 £105.37, Place 5 £67.37.
Owner C A Lynch **Bred** R And Mrs R Hodgins **Trained** Denton, Co Durham

FOCUS
A much stronger handicap, this 61-75 event was run at a very strong pace. Not the easiest form to pin down and it might be underrated, but it is doubtful if the winner had to match his previous strong run over course and distance.
Hurricane Harriet Official explanation: jockey said filly never travelled
T/Plt: £488.70 to a £1 stake. Pool: £46,628.96. 69.65 winning tickets. T/Qpdt: £308.10 to a £1 stake. Pool: £3,497.44. 8.40 winning tickets. JR

7504 KEMPTON (A.W) (R-H)
Wednesday, December 3

OFFICIAL GOING: Standard
Wind: nil Weather: frosty

7535 WEATHERBYS ALL WEATHER "HANDS AND HEELS" APPRENTICE SERIES H'CAP 1m (P)
6:20 (6:21) (Class 6) (0-50,50) 3-Y-O+ **£2,047** (£604; £151; £151) **Stalls** High

Form RPR
5050 **1** **Double Valentine**[14] 7382 5-8-11 **50** .... DebraEngland(3) 1 62
(R Ingram) *hld up in rr: rapid hdwy on ins over 2f out to ld wl over 1f out: sn clr: easily* **20/1**
4100 **2** *4* **Bye Baby Bunting**[28] 7196 3-8-9 **49** .... TobyAtkinson(3) 12 52
(B R Johnson) *sn in rr: stl plenty to do over 2f out: rapid hdwy sn after and r.o to go 2nd wl ins fnl f but no ch w easy wnr* **16/1**
-456 **3** *½* **Ocean Pride (IRE)**[192] 460 5-8-11 **50** ....(b) JamesRogers(3) 14 52
(L Wells) *chsd ldrs: rdn and styd on same pce fr over 1f out* **16/1**
P600 **3** *dht* **Wooden King (IRE)**[14] 7382 3-8-10 **50** .... RyanClark(3) 5 52
(P D Evans) *led: rdn 2f out: hdd and outpcd wl over 1f out* **10/1**
6002 **5** *shd* **King Of The Beers (USA)**[5] 7469 4-8-9 **50** ....(p) SPRyan(5) 8 52
(R A Harris) *in tch: rdn and kpt on fnl 2f: styd on cl home* **2/1**[1]
000 **6** *shd* **Buck Cannon (IRE)**[212] 1855 3-8-13 **50** .... CharlesEddery 10 51+
(P M Phelan) *in rr: rdn and hdwy fr 2f out: styd on wl fnl f: gng on cl home but no ch w wnr* **12/1**
006- **7** *3 ½* **Running Buck (USA)**[441] 5534 3-8-10 **50** .... NatashaEaton(3) 7 43
(A Bailey) *chsd ldrs: rdn 2f out: wknd fnl f* **20/1**
0030 **8** *¾* **Frosty's Gift**[42] 6913 4-8-7 **48** .... GemmaElford(5) 11 40
(J C Fox) *in rr: stl wl bhd 2f out: swtchd rt and rapid fnl f: fin wl* **12/1**
0000 **9** *1* **Alabama Spirit (USA)**[19] 7316 3-8-10 **50** .... AntiocoMurgia(3) 4 39
(P Howling) *chsd ldrs: rdn over 2f out: wknd fnl f* **33/1**
505 **10** *¾* **Pop Music (IRE)**[14] 7392 5-8-11 **50** ....(v) BradleyRoper(3) 13 38
(Ms J S Doyle) *in tch: hdwy over 2f out: wknd over 1f out* **5/1**[2]
5200 **11** *1* **Too Grand**[14] 7392 3-8-13 **50** .... PNolan 2 35
(J J Bridger) *outpcd most of way* **14/1**
0000 **12** *nk* **Balerno**[41] 6930 9-8-7 **48** ....(p) KierenFox(5) 9 33
(Mrs L J Mongan) *a towards rr* **13/2**[3]
6000 **13** *4 ½* **Beck**[33] 7114 4-8-9 **48** .... MatthewLawson(3) 3 22
(W M Brisbourne) *chsd ldrs on outside 5f* **16/1**
31-0 **14** *2 ½* **Kassuta**[15] 6729 4-8-11 **50** ....(v) CareyWilliamson(3) 6 19
(M J Gingell) *chsd ldrs over 5f* **25/1**
1m 40.79s (0.99) **Going Correction** 0.0s/f (Stan)
WFA 3 from 4yo+ 1lb 14 Ran SP% **128.4**
Speed ratings (Par 101): **95,91,90,90,90 90,86,86,85,84 83,83,78,76**PL: Double Valentine £5.20, Bye Baby Bunting £5.70, Ocean Pride £1.90, Wooden King £1.80. TRICAST: DV-BBB-OP £2,675.30; DV-BBB-WK: £1,750.01. toteswinger: DV&BBB: £24.50, DV&OP: £30.20, DV&WK £14.00, BBB&OP £19.00, BBB&WK: £17.90. CSF £315.27 TOTE £24.90, £027, £Owner, £Ellangowan Racing PartnersBred Ellangowan Racing Partners Trifecta £Trained Epsom, Surrey.
FOCUS
A moderate hands and heels apprentice race and a handicap virtually in name only, with the runners separated by a mere 2lb. the form, rated around the placed horses, is sound but weak.

7536 KEMPTON.CO.UK MEDIAN AUCTION MAIDEN STKS 7f (P)
6:50 (6:51) (Class 5) 3-5-Y-O **£3,238** (£963; £481; £240) **Stalls** High

Form RPR
0452 **1** **Balata**[19] 7321 3-9-3 65 .... TGMcLaughlin 12 68
(B R Millman) *t.k.h early: hld up in mid-div: gd hdwy fr 2f out to ld appr fnl f: drvn and styd on strly ins fnl f* **7/1**
0604 **2** *1 ¾* **King's Colour**[16] 7358 3-9-3 60 .... FergusSweeney 6 63
(B R Johnson) *in tch: hdwy fr 2f out: drvn to chal 1f out: outpcd by wnr ins fnl f but styd on wl for clr 2nd* **10/3**[1]
04 **3** *3* **Cabopino (IRE)**[16] 7362 3-8-12 0 .... JamieSpencer 8 50
(K R Burke) *led 1f: styd chsng ldr tl led again over 2f out: sn rdn: hdd appr fnl f: sn btn* **6/1**[3]
50 **4** *1* **Another Try (IRE)**[29] 7178 3-9-3 0 .... DarrenWilliams 9 52
(A P Jarvis) *t.k.h early: chsd ldrs: rdn over 2f out: sn one pce* **13/2**
0 **5** *½* **Elisiario (IRE)**[85] 5786 3-9-3 0 .... PatCosgrave 3 51
(J R Boyle) *in rr: rdn and hdwy fr 2f out: kpt on ins fnl f* **50/1**
6300 **6** *½* **Lady Fas (IRE)**[19] 7320 5-8-12 45 .... HayleyTurner 5 45
(A W Carroll) *in rr: sme hdwy whn hmpd ins fnl 2f: styd on again fnl f: nt a danger* **25/1**
0043 **7** *½* **Billy Hot Rocks (IRE)**[106] 5166 3-9-3 59 .... NCallan 7 48
(Miss Gay Kelleway) *t.k.h: chsd ldrs: rdn over 2f out: wknd over 1f out* **6/1**[3]
0023 **8** *1 ½* **Welsh Opera**[3] 7508 3-8-7 57 ....(t) WilliamCarson(5) 11 39
(S C Williams) *pressed ldrs: drvn to chal appr fnl 2f: wknd appr fnl f* **9/2**[2]
4/05 **9** *2 ¼* **Prix Masque (IRE)**[16] 7362 4-9-3 52 .... RichardThomas 13 38
(Christian Wroe) *mid-div: rdn and sme prog over 2f out: hung rt and wknd appr fnl f* **25/1**
3000 **10** *½* **Flying Free**[3] 7504 3-9-3 41 .... ChrisCatlin 10 37
(J Ryan) *rdr blinded as hood removed s and slowly away: a in rr* **50/1**
200 **11** *½* **Titus Gent**[35] 7074 3-9-3 62 .... MickyFenton 14 35
(J Ryan) *bhd most of way* **25/1**
12 *1 ¼* **Wardy's Wonder (IRE)**[171] 3068 3-8-12 66 .... JamesDoyle 1 27
(P D Evans) *broke wl: led after 1f: hdd over 2f out: sn wknd* **10/1**
13 *hd* **Shortwall Lady (IRE)** 3-8-9 0 .... TolleyDean(3) 4 26
(J L Spearing) *a in rr* **33/1**
0-56 **14** *28* **Apocalypto (IRE)**[6] 7463 4-9-3 0 .... EdwardCreighton 2 —
(E J Creighton) *chsd ldrs 4f* **66/1**
1m 26.23s (0.23) **Going Correction** 0.0s/f (Stan) 14 Ran SP% **124.6**
Speed ratings (Par 103): **98,96,92,91,90 90,89,88,85,84 84,82,82,50**
toteswinger: 1&2 £5.90, 1&3 £10.50, 2&3 £5.70. CSF £29.89 TOTE £9.40: £2.50, £1.50, £2.40; EX 42.90.
Owner The Links Partnership **Bred** Charlock Farm Stud **Trained** Kentisbeare, Devon

FOCUS
A modest event run at a fair pace and the form is sound enough rated around the first two.

7537 DIGIBET.COM CLAIMING STKS 6f (P)
7:20 (7:21) (Class 6) 2-Y-O **£2,047** (£604; £302) **Stalls** High

Form RPR
001 **1** **Smokey Ryder**[35] 7065 2-8-11 76 .... FergusSweeney 2 77
(G L Moore) *sn chsng ldr: slt ld ins fnl 3f: styd on wl to assert fnl f: readily* **15/8**[1]
0402 **2** *2* **Sonhador**[14] 7388 2-8-8 70 .... StephenCarson 11 68
(P Winkworth) *chsd ldrs: drvn to chal ins fnl 3f: stl ev ch u.p over 1f out: outpcd by wnr ins fnl f* **3/1**[2]
1550 **3** *4* **Fangfoss Girls**[19] 7308 2-8-2 69 .... JimmyQuinn 1 55+
(D M Simcock) *s.i.s: swtchd rt to rail after 1f: hdwy fr 2f out: styd on to go n.d 3rd ins fnl f* **7/1**
0450 **4** *1 ¼* **Lois Darlin (IRE)**[39] 6986 2-8-2 49 ....(b) FrankieMcDonald 10 46
(R A Harris) *led tl: hdd ins fnl 3f: n.m.r and hung lft sn after: wknd over 1f out* **25/1**
0604 **5** *2 ¾* **River Style (IRE)**[29] 7179 2-8-6 56 .... RichardThomas 4 42
(A P Jarvis) *chsd ldrs: rdn 3f out: wknd 2f out* **33/1**
0000 **6** *½* **Emerald Lass**[51] 6701 2-8-5 42 ow1 .... MartinDwyer 8 40
(D J Coakley) *outpcd most of way: sme mod late prog* **50/1**
5005 **7** *1 ¾* **Royal Raider**[19] 7308 2-8-4 71 .... GregFairley 7 33
(P D Evans) *in tch: chsd ldrs and rdn 3f out: one pce whn n.m.r 2f out and sn wknd* **4/1**[3]
6353 **8** *1* **Skruton (IRE)**[23] 7275 2-8-1 62 ....(p) NicolPolli(5) 9 32
(M G Quinlan) *in rr whn hmpd on rails after 1f: nvr in contention after* **8/1**
005 **9** *5* **Betoula**[155] 3584 2-8-4 46 .... HayleyTurner 3 15
(Mrs A L M King) *sn outpcd* **28/1**
00 **10** *3 ¼* **Outdroad**[16] 7356 2-8-7 0 .... CatherineGannon 12 9
(P M Phelan) *in rr whn hmpd after 1f: a wl bhd* **66/1**
1m 12.67s (-0.43) **Going Correction** 0.0s/f (Stan) 10 Ran SP% **117.1**
Speed ratings (Par 94): **102,99,94,92,88 88,85,84,77,73**
toteswinger: 1&2 £1.90, 1&3 £4.20, 2&3 £4.40. CSF £7.21 TOTE £3.00: £1.20, £1.20, £2.10; EX 8.70.Fangfoss Girls was claimed by L Wells for £6,000. Sonhador was claimed by G Prodromou for £7,000.
Owner Pleasure Palace Racing **Bred** Jeremy Hinds **Trained** Woodingdean, E Sussex
■ Stewards' Enquiry : Jimmy Quinn four-day ban: careless riding (Dec 17- 20)
FOCUS
A fair claimer and solid form. It was run at a frantic pace and the first two pulled clear, both running to their marks.
NOTEBOOK
Smokey Ryder landed a gamble and accounted for a subsequent winner dropped to this grade at Great Leighs last time. She had to work hard to get a prominent position from stall two but showed a sustained burst in the straight and won with a bit in hand. She may not have much room to manoeuvre off a mark of 76 when switched back to handicaps but has a strong will and her shrewd trainer should be able to find some more opportunities for her. (op 7-4 tchd 2-1)
Sonhador has had a few chances and his form has been a bit up and down but he ran up to his best when second to the 83-rated Swiss Diva at Lingfield last time and put in another commendable effort behind a rival with a 6lb higher rating here. He seems to have plenty of tactical speed at this trip, is possibly best ridden just behind the pace and should be able to get off the mark. (op 11-4 tchd 5-2)
Fangfoss Girls never got into it after a typically slow start but did do best of the hold-up horses and saw out the trip quite well on her first try at 6f. (tchd 8-1)
Lois Darlin(IRE) did fairly well to plug on after setting the blistering pace but she is 0-8, has an official rating of 49 and does not appeal as one to follow. (op 22-1)

7538 DIGIBET NURSERY 7f (P)
7:50 (7:52) (Class 4) (0-85,78) 2-Y-O **£3,885** (£1,156; £577; £288) **Stalls** High

Form RPR
52 **1** **Efficiency**[24] 7259 2-9-5 **76** .... LPKeniry 6 81+
(M Blanshard) *in tch: rdn and gd hdwy 2f out to ld appr fnl f: kpt on strly* **12/1**
6003 **2** *2* **Grand Honour (IRE)**[11] 7426 2-9-7 **78** .... JimmyQuinn 1 78
(P Howling) *s.i.s: in rr: gd hdwy over 2f out: chal over 1f out: styd on but nt pce of wnr ins fnl f* **9/1**
1004 **3** *1 ¾* **Aladdin's Lamp (IRE)**[11] 7426 2-8-10 **67** .... GregFairley 9 63
(M Johnston) *chsd ldr: rdn over 2f out: styd on same pce appr fnl f* **9/2**[2]
14 **4** *1* **Casual Style**[19] 7308 2-9-1 **72** .... JamieSpencer 8 65
(D E Pipe) *chsd ldrs 2f out: one pce fnl f* **9/4**[1]
1032 **5** *hd* **Rio Royale (IRE)**[14] 7389 2-9-7 **78** .... MartinDwyer 2 73+
(Mrs A J Perrett) *s.i.s: in rr: rdn and hdwy 2f out: kpt on but nvr in contention* **8/1**
603 **6** *hd* **All Spin (IRE)**[14] 7388 2-8-11 **68** .... NCallan 5 60
(A P Jarvis) *t.k.h: sn led: hdd & wknd appr fnl f* **20/1**
1332 **7** *nse* **Ray Of Joy**[20] 7306 2-9-5 **76** .... HayleyTurner 7 68
(J R Jenkins) *chsd ldrs: rdn over 2f out: outpcd fnl f* **6/1**[3]
4516 **8** *5* **Sunniva Duke (IRE)**[6] 7460 2-9-7 **78** .... EddieAhern 3 58
(R Hannon) *rdn 3f out: a bhd* **8/1**
063 **9** *½* **Captain Carey**[23] 7273 2-8-10 **67** .... VinceSlattery 4 45
(M S Saunders) *t.k.h: in tch on outside whn rdn 3f out: sn wknd* **8/1**
1m 26.36s (0.36) **Going Correction** 0.0s/f (Stan) 9 Ran SP% **119.0**
Speed ratings (Par 98): **97,94,92,91,91 91,91,85,84**
toteswinger: 1&2 £7.60, 1&3 £19.00, 2&3 £8.90. CSF £117.65 CT £570.17 TOTE £15.10: £2.90, £3.30, £1.90; EX 92.90.
Owner The First Timers **Bred** Minster Enterprises Ltd **Trained** Upper Lambourn, Berks
FOCUS
A competitive race but the early pace was steady. The winner is improving and there could be more to come.
NOTEBOOK
Efficiency almost sprang a 33-1 surprise in a 1m maiden at the course last time. She had a tough-looking mark of 76 on her nursery debut but proved her last run to be no fluke, showing a decisive turn of speed to swoop wide off the steady pace and win in good style. Further improvement looks likely from this progressive filly, who should be able to win more races. (tchd 10-1)
Grand Honour(IRE) had to wait a while to find a gap but burst through on the far rail in the closing stages and managed to confirm recent form with Aladdin's Lamp. He would have been suited by a stronger pace but did well to finish second. He is 5lb lower than his last winning mark and could be poised to strike soon. (op 11-1)
Aladdin's Lamp(IRE) was backed in from 9/1. He raced just behind the steady pace but was bustled along early in the straight and could not find the necessary gears to pose a strong threat. (op 9-1)
Casual Style, who took a strong hold and had to negotiate some traffic problems, had every chance and could not raise her game in the closing stages. She should do better off a stronger pace next time. (op 2-1)

Rio Royale(IRE) was staying on powerfully when a gap suddenly closed and ran better than his finishing position suggests. (op 10-1)

7539 DIGIBET CASINO H'CAP 1m 4f (P)
8:20 (8:20) (Class 4) (0-80,80) 3-Y-0 £5,180 (£1,541; £770; £384) Stalls Centre

Form RPR
1200 1 **Cape Colony**[64] 6355 3-9-0 **76** EddieAhern 6 83
(R Hannon) *chsd ldrs in 3rd: wnt 2nd 3f out: led ins fnl 2f: hld on wl thrght fnl f* **10/1**
4-02 2 ½ **Wine 'n Dine**[14] 7387 3-8-10 **72** FergusSweeney 4 78+
(G L Moore) *in rr: gd hdwy over 2f out whn edging rt: styd on to press wnr jst ins fnl f: no ex fnl 100yds* **15/8**[1]
1133 3 ¾ **Graylyn Ruby (FR)**[16] 7364 3-8-11 **73** NCallan 5 78
(J Jay) *in tch: rdn to chse ldrs over 1f out: styd on ins fnl f* **4/1**[3]
5162 4 4 **Bushy Dell (IRE)**[34] 7091 3-8-7 **74** AmyBaker(5) 7 73
(Miss J Feilden) *led: rdn 4f out: hdd ins fnl 2f: wknd fnl f* **5/1**
-006 5 hd **Silver Regent (USA)**[13] 7398 3-9-0 **76** MartinDwyer 2 74
(Mrs A J Perrett) *chsd ldrs: rdn over 2f out: wknd over 1f out* **7/2**[2]
6000 6 1 ½ **Lady Sorcerer**[14] 7385 3-8-4 **66** oh5 ChrisCatlin 3 62
(A P Jarvis) *bhd: hdwy 4f out: drvn and effrt to chse ldrs over 2f out: wknd fnl f* **33/1**
0-44 7 28 **Barawin (IRE)**[26] 7230 3-9-4 **80** FrancisNorton 1 31
(K R Burke) *sn chsng ldr: rdn and wknd 3f out* **16/1**

2m 33.19s (-1.31) **Going Correction** 0.0s/f (Stan) 7 Ran SP% **111.6**
Speed ratings (Par 104): **104,103,103,100,100 99,80**
toteswinger: 1&2 £3.30, 1&3 £6.70, 2&3 £1.70. CSF £27.82 TOTE £5.70: £2.90, £2.00; EX 20.50.
Owner P D Merritt **Bred** Allan Merritt **Trained** East Everleigh, Wilts

FOCUS
This was run at a reasonable pace and the form looks pretty solid.
Barawin(IRE) Official explanation: vet said filly had a breathing problem

7540 BOOK KEMPTON TICKETS ON 0844 579 3008 H'CAP 6f (P)
8:50 (8:52) (Class 5) (0-70,70) 3-Y-0+ £2,590 (£770; £385; £96; £96) Stalls High

Form RPR
1130 1 **Musical Script (USA)**[16] 7358 5-8-11 **63** (b) NCallan 7 79
(Mouse Hamilton-Fairley) *in rr: drvn and hdwy on ins to ld jst ins fnl 2f: kpt on strly fnl f* **6/1**[3]
6304 2 3 **Lekita**[11] 7428 3-8-13 **70** AndreaAtzeni(5) 4 76
(W R Swinburn) *in rr: hdwy and hung lft over 1f out: swtchd rt and r.o fnl f to chse wnr cl home but nvr any ch* **13/2**
2253 3 1 ½ **Shakespeare's Son**[29] 7182 3-9-1 **70** DuranFentiman(3) 3 72
(H J Evans) *in rr rdn and hdwy over 2f out: chsd wnr ins fnl f but no ch: lost 2nd cl home* **14/1**
436 4 1 ¾ **C'Mon You Irons (IRE)**[19] 7315 3-9-3 **69** JimmyQuinn 12 65
(M R Hoad) *chsd ldrs: ev ch 2f out: wknd ins fnl f* **7/1**
1400 4 dht **Our Blessing (IRE)**[3] 7510 4-8-13 **65** DarrenWilliams 10 61
(A P Jarvis) *led tl hdd ins fnl 2f and hung lft and btn over 1f out* **7/2**[1]
3465 6 ¾ **Replicator**[96] 5467 3-9-3 **69** MartinDwyer 8 63
(Pat Eddery) *chsd ldr: rdn and ev ch 2f out: hung lft and btn over 1f out* **13/2**
0620 7 nk **Gwilym (GER)**[26] 7225 5-8-13 **65** HayleyTurner 5 58
(D Haydn Jones) *in tch: rdn 3f out: no ch* **12/1**
0205 8 1 ½ **Interactive (IRE)**[9] 7435 5-9-1 **67** AlanDaly 9 55
(Andrew Turnell) *chsd ldrs over 3f* **10/1**
4144 9 1 ¼ **Pegasus Dancer (FR)**[27] 7206 4-8-12 **64** VinceSlattery 6 48
(R H York) *a in rr* **25/1**

1m 11.78s (-1.32) **Going Correction** 0.0s/f (Stan) 9 Ran SP% **121.2**
Speed ratings (Par 103): **108,104,102,99,99 98,98,96,94**
toteswinger: 1&2 £4.30, 1&3 £9.90, 2&3 £7.70. CSF £34.27 CT £324.94 TOTE £4.80: £2.00, £2.50, £2.20; EX 32.60.
Owner The Composers **Bred** Juddmonte Farms Inc **Trained** Bramshill, Hants
■ Stewards' Enquiry : Darren Williams three-day ban: failed to ride out for 4th place

FOCUS
A fair handicap run at a sound gallop and the winner recorded another persoanl best.
Replicator Official explanation: jockey said gelding hung-left

7541 BOOK NOW FOR BOXING DAY CLASSIFIED STKS 7f (P)
9:20 (9:23) (Class 6) 3-Y-0+ £2,047 (£604; £302) Stalls High

Form RPR
0000 1 **Tuxedo**[34] 7088 3-9-0 40 TGMcLaughlin 12 60
(P W Hiatt) *hld up in rr: gd hdwy on ins 2f out: styd on u.p to ld fnl 30yds* **25/1**
4506 2 ¾ **Eleanor Eloise (USA)**[9] 7437 4-8-9 52 AndreaAtzeni(5) 10 58
(J R Gask) *chsd ldrs: rdn to chal 1f out: slt ld fnl 100yds: ct fnl 30yds* **9/2**[3]
0464 3 ¾ **Karate Queen**[4] 7497 3-9-0 52 LPKeniry 1 56
(A M Balding) *chsd ldrs: slt ld over 1f out: hdd and no ex fnl 100yds* **14/1**
0043 4 1 ¾ **Apache Dawn**[44] 6768 4-9-0 52 StephenCarson 14 51
(G L Moore) *in rr: hdwy over 2f out: styd on fnl f but nvr gng pce to rch ldrs* **7/2**[1]
000 5 shd **Just Jimmy (IRE)**[16] 7363 3-9-0 53 NCallan 6 51
(P D Evans) *chsd ldr: drvn to chal fr over 2f out and stl ev ch appr fnl f: wknd ins fnl f* **14/1**
0400 6 2 **Follow Your Spirit**[9] 7436 3-9-0 49 (p) CatherineGannon 3 48
(B Palling) *sn led: rdn and styd on whn chal fr over 2f out: hdd over 1f out and sn wknd* **33/1**
0500 7 ½ **Copperwood**[103] 5218 3-9-0 53 FergusSweeney 9 44
(M Blanshard) *in tch: rdn and hdwy over 2f out: styd on but nvr gng pce to rch ldrs* **7/1**
3420 8 hd **Complete Frontline (GER)**[52] 6685 3-9-0 55 (v[1]) DarrenWilliams 11 44
(K R Burke) *towards rr: hdwy over 2f out: kpt on but nvr gng pce to rch ldrs* **4/1**[2]
0030 9 1 **Langham House**[14] 7382 3-9-0 51 (v[1]) HayleyTurner 13 41
(J R Jenkins) *in rr: mod prog fnl f* **12/1**
0-00 10 2 **Bourbon Balistic**[21] 7292 3-9-0 50 PatCosgrave 8 36
(Mrs A Duffield) *s.i.s: a towards rr* **20/1**
0065 11 3 **Faintly Hopeful**[28] 7195 3-9-0 49 EddieAhern 7 27
(R A Teal) *in tch: rdn 3f out: wknd fr 2f out* **16/1**
P006 12 4 ½ **Rough Rock (IRE)**[36] 7055 3-9-0 55 ChrisCatlin 4 15
(G Prodromou) *mid-div: rdn and effrt 3f oit: sn wknd* **14/1**
0060 13 nse **Blue Savannah (FR)**[11] 7423 3-8-7 47 (v[1]) StacyRenwick(7) 2 15
(G J Smith) *chsd ldrs 4f* **25/1**
6360 14 8 **Ginger Minx (IRE)**[77] 6015 3-9-0 47 RichardKingscote 5 —
(N J Vaughan) *s.i.s: in rr: sme hdwy 3f out: sn wknd* **33/1**

1m 26.3s (0.30) **Going Correction** 0.0s/f (Stan) 14 Ran SP% **124.8**
Speed ratings (Par 101): **98,97,96,94,94 91,91,91,89,87 84,79,79,69**
toteswinger: 1&2 £33.70, 1&3 £99.00, 2&3 £15.00. CSF £132.52 TOTE £28.80: £8.00, £2.60, £2.90; EX 179.50 Place 6: £404.68, Place 5: £50.12..
Owner Phil Kelly **Bred** Gainsborough Stud Management Ltd **Trained** Hook Norton, Oxon

FOCUS
The runners in this low-grade contest had managed just four wins between them in a total of 143 starts. The form is therefore unlikely to prove worth very much but appears sound enough rated around those in the frame behind the winner.
Tuxedo Official explanation: trainer said, regarding the apparent improvement in form, that the gelding hung right last time and was better suited to the right handed course and shorter trip
Faintly Hopeful Official explanation: jockey said gelding was denied a clear run
Ginger Minx(IRE) Official explanation: jockey said filly stumbled on leaving the stalls
T/Jkpt: Not won. T/Plt: £509.40 to a £1 stake. Pool: £93,571.15. 134.07 winning tickets. T/Qpdt: £25.10 to a £1 stake. Pool: £10,206.21. 299.75 winning tickets. ST

7458 GREAT LEIGHS (A.W) (L-H)
Thursday, December 4

OFFICIAL GOING: Standard
Wind: modest across Weather: dry, chilly

7542 DENGIE MARSHES NURSERY (DIV I) 6f (P)
6:20 (6:20) (Class 6) (0-65,65) 2-Y-0 £2,719 (£809; £404; £202) Stalls Low

Form RPR
005 1 **Newlyn Art**[15] 7388 2-9-4 **62** GeorgeBaker 6 78+
(D R C Elsworth) *hld up in midfield on inner: swtchd off rail and hdwy over 2f out: chal over 1f out: rdn to ld ins fnl f: pushed clr: readily* **15/8**[1]
2533 2 2 ¾ **Imaginary Diva**[6] 7464 2-8-11 **55** DaneO'Neill 1 60
(G G Margarson) *t.k.h: trckd ldrs: rdn to ld over 1f out: hdd ins fnl f: no ch w wnr after* **4/1**[2]
3034 3 1 ¼ **Clerical (USA)**[8] 7454 2-8-7 **56** (p) AndreaAtzeni(5) 2 57
(M J Gingell) *chsd ldr: rdn and ev ch over 1f out: kpt on same pce fnl f* **8/1**
006 4 2 ½ **Golden Pool (IRE)**[17] 7356 2-9-0 **58** HayleyTurner 8 52
(S A Callaghan) *t.k.h: hld up in midfield: rdn and unable qck 2f out: plugged on to go 4th ins fnl f: nvr pce to rch ldrs* **14/1**
0400 5 1 ¼ **Equinity**[21] 7306 2-9-2 **60** JimmyQuinn 3 50
(J Pearce) *led: rdn and hdd over 1f out: wknd fnl f* **8/1**
000 6 3 ¼ **Halaak (USA)**[90] 5673 2-8-2 **46** ChrisCatlin 5 26
(D M Simcock) *s.i.s: bhd: rdn over 3f out: nvr trbld ldrs* **14/1**
0455 7 2 ½ **Speak The Truth (IRE)**[140] 4101 2-9-3 **61** PatCosgrave 10 34
(J R Boyle) *stdd and dropped in after s: towards rr: rdn and outpcd over 2f out: n.d* **14/1**
2260 8 2 ½ **Blackwater Fort (USA)**[20] 7308 2-9-7 **65** (v[1]) JimCrowley 9 30
(J Gallagher) *a bhd: rdn and struggling 3f out: nvr a factor* **13/2**[3]
0030 9 1 ¾ **Tobizzy**[48] 6770 2-8-5 **49** ow1 MartinDwyer 7 9
(J R Jenkins) *t.k.h: hld up in midfield on outer: rdn and struggling over 2f out: no ch fnl 2f* **28/1**
0006 10 5 **Emerald Lass**[1] 7537 2-8-1 **45** CatherineGannon 4 —
(D J Coakley) *t.k.h: chsd ldrs: rdn and struggling over 2f out: wl bhd over 1f out* **33/1**

1m 13.43s (-0.27) **Going Correction** +0.05s/f (Slow) 10 Ran SP% **116.7**
Speed ratings (Par 94): **103,99,97,94,92 88,85,81,79,72**
toteswinger: 1&2 £4.30, 1&3 £13.10, 2&3 £5.10. CSF £9.00 CT £49.57 TOTE £2.60: £1.50, £1.60, £1.80; EX 9.90.
Owner Matthew Green **Bred** Park Farm Racing & C M Oakshott **Trained** Newmarket, Suffolk

FOCUS
A very weak nursery, run at a fair pace, and not that many got into it. The winner looked well in after running with promise last time and has the potential to do better over 7f.

NOTEBOOK
Newlyn Art ◆, who was an eyecatcher behind a long odds-on stable companion on his third outing at Lingfield last time, was making his nursery debut. Dropped in off the pace early by George Baker, he travelled into the race very nicely and, once switched out wide in order to make his effort, found more than enough. This wasn't a great race, but he still showed some signs of greenness so further improvement is very possible and his trainer believes he will get further.
Official explanation: trainer said, regarding apparent improvement in form, that the colt shows little at home it would appear to be improving with experience, this being its fourth run and appeared suited by the sharp track. (op 9-4 tchd 5-2)
Imaginary Diva, who is more exposed than the winner, travelled well behind the leaders and had every chance, but once the favourite was unleashed there was little she could do about it. She is already due to go up 6lb after splitting much higher-rated rivals in a Kempton claimer last time which will obviously make life tougher, but she may be helped by a return to the minimum trip. (op 7-2)
Clerical(USA), who has twice run well here before, hugged the inside rail throughout and posted another fair effort at this venue, but he still looks to be on a stiff mark. (op 15-2 tchd 7-1)
Golden Pool(IRE), who ran much her best race to date on her third outing last time, was making her nursery debut and was noted making some late headway from off the pace. She may still have a bit more improvement left in her. (op 8-1)
Equinity, back in trip after failing to stay 7f on her nursery debut last time, attracted market support and took the field along for a long way, but she didn't get home. (op 12-1)

7543 DENGIE MARSHES NURSERY (DIV II) 6f (P)
6:50 (6:50) (Class 6) (0-65,63) 2-Y-0 £2,719 (£809; £404; £202) Stalls Low

Form RPR
4002 1 **Spiritual Art**[57] 6579 2-9-2 **58** HayleyTurner 4 70+
(S A Callaghan) *a gng wl: trckd ldrs: shkn up to ld wl over 1f out: sn pushed clr: easily* **1/1**[1]
0061 2 4 ½ **Deckchair**[17] 7361 2-9-1 **57** (v) FrancisNorton 6 55
(H J Collingridge) *hld up in midfield: hdwy over 2f out: chsd wnr over 1f out: kpt on u.p but no ch w wnr fnl f* **4/1**[2]
003 3 1 ¼ **Lady Gem**[22] 7279 2-8-9 **51** PaulMulrennan 3 45
(D H Brown) *chsd ldr: carried wd and lost pl briefly wl over 1f out: kpt on u.p but no ch w wnr fnl f* **8/1**
0450 4 nk **Silver Salsa**[43] 6906 2-8-13 **55** ChrisCatlin 7 48
(J R Jenkins) *bhd: hdwy and rdn wl over 1f out: disp 3rd ins fnl f: kpt on: nvr nr wnr* **14/1**
004 5 ½ **Honorable Endeavor**[92] 5599 2-8-13 **55** LPKeniry 2 46
(E F Vaughan) *dwlt: bhd: hdwy jst over 2f out: rdn over 1f out: sn no imp* **8/1**
2655 6 ½ **Raimond Ridge (IRE)**[118] 4816 2-9-2 **63** MCGeran(5) 9 53
(M R Channon) *dwlt: hld up towards rr: hdwy over 2f out: carried rt wl over 1f out: sn rdn: plugged on same pce: nvr nr wnr* **7/1**[3]

The Form Book, Raceform Ltd, Compton, RG20 6NL

000 **7** 4½ **Calypso Prince**[12] 7415 2-8-5 **47**................................(v) MartinDwyer 10 23
(M D I Usher) *sn bustled along in midfield on outer: rdn 1/2-way: bhd and eased ins fnl f* **28/1**

6000 **8** 4 **Lonsdale Lad**[9] 7443 2-8-3 **45**.......................................(b[1]) JimmyQuinn 1 —
(R C Guest) *led: rdn and edgd rt wl over 1f out: sn hdd & wknd: wl bhd and eased ins fnl f* **25/1**

1m 14.19s (0.49) **Going Correction** +0.05s/f (Slow) **8** Ran SP% **118.7**
Speed ratings (Par 94): **98,92,90,89,89 88,82,77**
toteswinger: 1&2 £2.90, 1&3 £3.10, 2&3 £11.30. CSF £5.46 CT £21.36 TOTE £2.50: £1.30, £1.20, £2.10; EX 6.90.
Owner Matthew Green & M Tabor **Bred** R Haim **Trained** Newmarket, Suffolk

FOCUS
Another weak nursery but solid enough form for the grade. The early pace was fair with the first-time blinkered Lonsdale Lad going off at a rate of knots, but the winning time was 0.76 seconds slower than the first division.

NOTEBOOK
Spiritual Art ◆ was always travelling like a dream behind the leaders and after the front pair swung wide off the final bend, she powered her way up the inside to win easily. She had been raised just 1lb for finishing runner-up on her nursery debut at Nottingham last time and can expect a much bigger rise for this, but she won so easily that she can defy a penalty before being put away. (op 11-8 tchd 6-4 in places)
Deckchair, who hung in front when winning a Wolverhampton claimer last time, was making her nursery debut and she sat on the tail of the favourite throughout. Although she didn't fold when put under pressure and battled on well to hold on to second, she found the winner far too classy. (op 7-2)
Lady Gem, third behind a couple of much higher-rated rivals in a Southwell maiden last time, was back up to a more suitable trip on this nursery debut and attracted market support. Handy from the start, she wasn't done many favours when the tiring leader Lonsdale Lad hung into her soon after turning for home, so she probably did well to keep on for third. (op 12-1)
Silver Salsa, racing beyond the minimum trip for the first time and edging down the weights, stayed on from the back of the field up the home straight but was never going to get anywhere near the winner. (op 20-1)
Honorable Endeavor, who showed a little ability in three turf maidens, was trying his shortest trip to date on this sand and nursery debut. He was another to stay on late tight against the inside rail and shaped as though a return to further is required. (tchd 15-2)
Lonsdale Lad Official explanation: jockey said gelding hung right

7544 MAPLIN SANDS APPRENTICE H'CAP 6f (P)
7:20 (7:20) (Class 5) (0-75,72) 3-Y-0+ **£3,238** (£963; £481; £240) **Stalls** Low

Form RPR

4146 **1** **Milne Bay (IRE)**[17] 7357 3-8-5 **58** oh2.............................(t) MarcHalford 2 67
(D M Simcock) *trckd ldng pair: rdn and effrt wl over 1f out: sn ev ch: led ins fnl f: r.o wl* **9/4**[1]

2 **2** 1 **Compton Classic**[48] 6774 6-8-0 **58** oh1.....................(p) AndreaAtzeni(5) 4 64
(J R Boyle) *t.k.h: chsd ldrs: rdn and ev ch over 1f out: chsd wnr ins fnl f: no ex fnl 100yds* **4/1**[3]

000 **3** 1½ **Leading Edge (IRE)**[58] 6556 3-8-12 **68**............................ MCGeran(3) 1 69
(M R Channon) *led: rdn over 1f out: hdd ins fnl f: wknd fnl 50yds* **20/1**

0430 **4** 1¼ **Asian Power (IRE)**[9] 7448 3-9-0 **72**.......................... AshleyMorgan(5) 3 69
(P J O'Gorman) *t.k.h: hld up in tch: rdn and effrt wl over 1f out: kpt on same pce fr over 1f out* **9/2**

0030 **5** ½ **Royal Envoy (IRE)**[20] 7315 5-9-5 **72**........................... TolleyDean 5 68
(P Howling) *awkward leaving stalls and s.i.s: bhd: rdn and c wd 2f out: kpt on but nvr rchd ldrs* **7/1**

064 **6** 1 **This Ones For Eddy**[12] 7416 3-8-6 **59**.....................(b[1]) DuranFentiman 7 51
(S Parr) *dwlt: sn in tch on outer: rdn 2f out: edgd lft u.p over 1f out: no hdwy fnl f* **11/4**[2]

1m 13.57s (-0.13) **Going Correction** +0.05s/f (Slow) **6** Ran SP% **112.9**
Speed ratings (Par 103): **102,100,98,97,96 95**
toteswinger: 1&2 £1.20, 1&3 £0, 2&3 £4.30. CSF £11.73 TOTE £5.90: £1.80, £4.30; EX 9.80.
Owner DXB Bloodstock Ltd **Bred** Michael Boland **Trained** Newmarket, Suffolk

FOCUS
A moderate apprentice handicap dominated by those that raced handily. It has been rated through the runner-up to his latest Kempton effort.

7545 POTTON ISLAND H'CAP 1m 5f 66y(P)
7:50 (7:50) (Class 5) (0-70,70) 3-Y-0+ **£3,238** (£722; £722; £240) **Stalls** Low

Form RPR

1 **1** **Weybridge Light**[21] 7296 3-8-10 **62**...........................(b) JamieSpencer 10 71
(Eoin Griffin, Ire) *mde all at stdy pce: rdn and wnt 2 l clr jst over 2f out: a holding on after: rdn out* **5/2**[1]

3200 **2** 1¾ **Vinces**[36] 7071 4-9-2 **62**.. HayleyTurner 2 68
(T D McCarthy) *t.k.h: chsd wnr tl over 9f out: rdn to chse wnr again jst over 2f out: kpt on but nvr able to chal wnr* **25/1**

4213 **2** dht **Azabu Juban (IRE)**[9] 7447 3-9-1 **67**.................................. ChrisCatlin 9 73
(J Jay) *hld up wl in tch: rdn to chse ldng pair wl over 1f out: kpt on u.p fnl f: nt pce to rch wnr* **11/2**

045 **4** 1¼ **Euroceleb (IRE)**[21] 7304 3-9-1 **67**......................... EdwardCreighton 6 72
(H Morrison) *hung lft thrght: t.k.h: in tch tl lost pl 4f out: hld hd awkwardly but hdwy over 1f out: chsd ldrs 1f out: keeping on same pce whn n.m.r towards fin* **16/1**

-450 **5** 3¾ **Highest Esteem**[15] 7385 4-9-5 **65**.............................(p) GeorgeBaker 5 64
(G L Moore) *stdd s: hld up towards rr: hdwy on outer over 2f out: sn rdn: edgd rt and no hdwy ent fnl f* **10/3**[2]

5000 **6** 1 **Moon Mix (FR)**[17] 6007 5-9-10 **70**................................ JimCrowley 1 67
(J R Jenkins) *stdd s: hld up in last pl: hdwy on outer 2f out: drvn over 1f out: no imp fnl f* **33/1**

0210 **7** ¾ **Dubai Ace (USA)**[196] 630 7-8-11 **62**........................ AndreaAtzeni(5) 3 58
(A M Hales) *hld up in last trio: rdn and outpcd wl over 3f out: plugged on fnl f: n.d* **20/1**

330 **8** 1¼ **Augustus John (IRE)**[3] 7515 5-9-5 **68**..................(e[1]) TolleyDean(3) 4 62
(S Parr) *t.k.h: hld up in last trio: hdwy on outer over 5f out: chsd ldrs and rdn over 3f out: wknd u.p wl over 1f out* **12/1**

0-41 **9** 1¼ **Incarnation (IRE)**[21] 7300 3-9-3 **69**............................. DaneO'Neill 8 61
(L M Cumani) *dwlt: sn chsng ldrs: wnt 2nd over 9f out tl jst over 2f out: sn edgd lft and wknd* **5/1**[3]

0542 **10** 7 **Top Tiger**[13] 7401 4-9-3 **63**.. PaulMulrennan 7 45
(M H Tompkins) *t.k.h: hld up in midfield: rdn over 3f out: wknd over 2f out: eased ins fnl f* **8/1**

2m 55.68s (2.08) **Going Correction** +0.05s/f (Slow)
WFA 3 from 4yo+ 6lb **10** Ran SP% **119.9**
Speed ratings (Par 103): **95,93,93,93,90 90,89,89,88,83**
toteswinger: 1&V £30.50, 1&AJ £3.00, V&AJ £21.20. TOTE £4.10: £1.30 TRIFECTA 2nd Pl: V 4.50, AJ 2.50; Ex: WL-V 32.40, WL-AJ 10.90; CSF: WL-V 37.38, WL-AJ 8.36; TC: WL-V-AJ 164.20; WL-AJ-V 142.58.
Owner Weybridge Group Limited **Bred** Hascombe And Valiant Studs **Trained** Slieverue, Co. Kilkenny

FOCUS
A fair staying handicap, but spoilt by a pedestrian early pace which caused several to pull, and it also played into the hands of the winner. It has been rated around the third to his All-Weather form from the autumn, and the fourth to her maiden form.
Euroceleb(IRE) Official explanation: jockey said filly hung badly left
Top Tiger Official explanation: jockey said gelding ran too keen

7546 VIRLEY CHANNEL MAIDEN FILLIES' STKS 6f (P)
8:20 (8:20) (Class 4) 2-Y-0 **£5,180** (£1,541; £770; £384) **Stalls** Low

Form RPR

1 **Chantilly Pearl (USA)** 2-9-0 0.............................. PatCosgrave 2 72
(J G Given) *s.i.s: sn in midfield: shkn up over 2f out: nt clr run swtchd rt over 1f out: rdn to ld ins fnl f: r.o wl* **28/1**

2 1¼ **Twenty Score** 2-9-0 0.. PaulFitzsimons 3 69
(Miss J R Tooth) *chsd ldrs: led wl over 1f out: rdn over 1f out: hdd ins fnl f: one pce fnl 100yds* **66/1**

4025 **3** ½ **Granny McPhee**[33] 7140 2-9-0 77.................................. MickyFenton 9 67+
(A Bailey) *in tch in midfield: rdn and effrt wl over 1f out: kpt on u.p to chse ldng pair ins fnl f: styd on* **4/1**[2]

4 2¾ **Little Calla (IRE)** 2-9-0 0.. TGMcLaughlin 7 59+
(E A L Dunlop) *s.i.s: hld up towards rr: hdwy 3f out: chsng ldrs and nt clr run over 1f out: swtchd rt jst over 1f out: kpt on fnl f: unable to chal ldrs* **20/1**

5 ½ **One Cool Mission (IRE)** 2-9-0 0........................... RichardKingscote 6 57+
(Tom Dascombe) *s.i.s: bhd: hdwy on outer over 1f out: kpt on fnl f and gng on fin nvr trbld ldrs* **20/1**

0 **6** nk **Lady Vivien**[73] 6158 2-9-0 0.................................... PaulMulrennan 10 56
(D H Brown) *in tch in midfield on outer: rdn 2f out: wknd ent fnl f* **33/1**

02 **7** nk **Timeless Dream**[48] 6785 2-9-0 0.................................. JamieSpencer 8 55
(P W Chapple-Hyam) *chsd ldrs: rdn over 2f out: ev ch and drvn wl over 1f out: wknd jst ins fnl f* **8/13**[1]

8 2¾ **Yellow River (USA)**[60] 2-9-0 0....................................... HayleyTurner 11 47
(S A Callaghan) *hld up towards rr: nt clr run and hmpd wl over 1f out: n.d after* **20/1**

60 **9** 2½ **Downstream**[35] 7095 2-9-0 0....................................(b[1]) MartinDwyer 1 40
(D M Simcock) *led tl hdd wl over 1f out: sn rdn: wknd qckly over 1f out* **33/1**

10 22 **Field Fantasy** 2-9-0 0... NeilChalmers 4 —
(Garry Moss) *v.s.a: rn green in rr thrght: t.o* **66/1**

4202 **11** 3 **Miss Hollybell**[129] 4486 2-9-0 76.................................. JimCrowley 5 —
(J Gallagher) *chsd ldr tl jst over 2f out: sn wknd: wl bhd and eased ins fnl f: t.o* **6/1**[3]

1m 13.73s (0.03) **Going Correction** +0.05s/f (Slow) **11** Ran SP% **122.8**
Speed ratings (Par 95): **101,99,98,95,94 93,93,89,86,57 53**
toteswinger: 1&2 £14.30, 1&3 £13.00, 2&3 £7.80. CSF £1150.11 TOTE £22.90: £4.60, £33.60, £1.10; EX 642.70.
Owner Mrs B E Wilkinson **Bred** Marguerite Clifford **Trained** Willoughton, Lincs

FOCUS
An ordinary fillies' maiden on paper and the leaders may have gone off too quick as none of the trio that helped force the early pace figured in the finish. It has been rated more in line with the time than the uneven profile of the third.

NOTEBOOK
Chantilly Pearl(USA) ◆, a $40,000 half-sister to two winners in the US, missed the break, and her chances of getting involved looked slim at that stage. Despite looking green, though, she got stronger as the race progressed, and, with the leaders falling in a hole, she came home very strongly to score. She can surely go on to better things. (op 20-1)
Twenty Score, who cost just £400, ran a massive race at huge odds and, after having hugged the inside rail throughout, she looked like causing a shock until the winner pounced. She has a future judged on this performance and may turn out again at Lingfield on Sunday.
Granny McPhee, who has already shown enough to suggest she has the ability to win a race like this, was dropping back in trip. Never far away, she kept staying on and may be worth a try in a nursery back over further. (op 10-3)
Little Calla(IRE) ◆, a 145,000euros filly out of a useful performer at up to 1m, was another to stay on nicely after missing the break and she may also benefit from stepping up in trip.
One Cool Mission(IRE) ◆, a 45,000euros half-sister to a dual winning juvenile in France, was yet another to miss the break, and she deserves plenty of credit for finishing where she did as she was forced to make her effort very wide. Better can be expected. (op 18-1)
Lady Vivien, not seen since finishing a tailed-off last of seven on her Hamilton debut in September, wasn't disgraced as she was also trapped out wide early and raced with the choke out. (op 20-1)
Timeless Dream couldn't get to the front early and, despite plenty of assistance from the saddle rounding the home turn, the writing was soon on the wall. The Redcar maiden she finished runner-up in last time hasn't worked out and this might be as good as she is. Official explanation: jockey said filly moved poorly and hung very badly right (op 10-11 tchd Evens in places)
Miss Hollybell Official explanation: vet said filly returned in a distressed state

7547 COLNE POINT (S) STKS 1m (P)
8:50 (8:51) (Class 6) 2-Y-0 **£2,590** (£770; £385; £192) **Stalls** Centre

Form RPR

0302 **1** **Shadow Bay (IRE)**[16] 7370 2-9-3 67.......................... RichardKingscote 13 69
(Tom Dascombe) *chsd ldr: clr of remainder over 2f out: drvn wl over 1f out: led ent fnl f: styd on* **4/1**[2]

0000 **2** 1¼ **Jonnie Skull (IRE)**[6] 7467 2-8-9 50............................(b) MarcHalford(3) 5 61
(D R C Elsworth) *led: clr over 2f out: drvn over 1f out: hdd ent fnl f: kpt on same pce u.p after* **40/1**

034 **3** ½ **Precocious Air (IRE)**[12] 7425 2-8-8 65 ow1........................ ShaneKelly 3 56
(J A Osborne) *hld up in midfield: rdn and hdwy 3f out: chsd ldng pair ins fnl f: kpt on u.p but nvr gng to rch ldng pair* **8/1**[3]

00 **4** 2 **Madam'X**[35] 7097 2-8-7 0... LPKeniry 11 51+
(P F I Cole) *bhd: rdn over 4f out: stl wl bhd 2f out: hdwy and squeezed between horses over 1f out: r.o wl fnl f: nt rch ldrs* **50/1**

065 **5** 2¼ **Alimarr (IRE)**[19] 7337 2-8-7 70.. JamieSpencer 4 46
(B J Meehan) *chsd ldng pair: rdn and unable qck over 2f out: no imp on ldng pair ffr wl over 1f out: lost 2 pls fnl f* **11/8**[1]

0434 **6** ½ **Imperial Skylight**[6] 7468 2-8-7 57................................... MCGeran(5) 8 49+
(M R Channon) *hld up in midfield: nt clr run and shuffled bk 3f out: plugged on u.p over 1f out: nvr threatened ldrs* **12/1**

0 **7** 1½ **Sicilian Warrior (USA)**[17] 7356 2-8-12 0........................ NelsonDeSouza 12 46
(P F I Cole) *hld up towards rr: rdn over 3f out: nvr gng pce to rch ldrs* **16/1**

0102 **8** 1¼ **Captain Cavendish (IRE)**[3] 7519 2-9-3 59.................(b) MickyFenton 7 48
(A Bailey) *s.i.s: in rr: hdwy u.p 3f out: c wd 2f out: hung lft and no hdwy over 1f out* **10/1**

45 **9** 1½ **Mullitovermaurice**[16] 7371 2-8-12 0............................... PatCosgrave 10 40
(J G Given) *s.i.s: a towards rr: nvr trbld ldrs* **16/1**

0445 **10** *3 ½* **Barbeito**[3] 7514 2-8-2 50 .... AndreaAtzeni(5) 6 27+
(D J S Ffrench Davis) *in tch in midfield: rdn and struggling 3f out: wl bhd and eased ins fnl f* **25/1**
6430 **11** *10* **Calley Ho**[70] 6223 2-8-10 69 .... KristinStubbs(7) 1 15
(Mrs L Stubbs) *hld up in midfield on inner: hdwy over 3f out: bmpd along and wknd wl over 1f out* **12/1**
0030 **12** *2* **Admiring Glances**[12] 7415 2-8-7 50 ....(b[1]) JimmyQuinn 14 —
(J Pearce) *chsd ldrs: rdn over 3f out: struggling over 2f out: wl btn fnl 2f: eased ins fnl f* **33/1**
5000 **13** *14* **Against The Rules**[17] 7353 2-8-7 52 ....(p) MarkFlynn(5) 15 —
(Miss Gay Kelleway) *prom on outer tl rdn and lost pl qckly wl over 3f out: t.o fr 2f out* **25/1**
0500 **14** *12* **Paddythefish (USA)**[4] 7505 2-8-12 60 .... FergusSweeney 9 —
(K R Burke) *s.i.s: reminders sn after s: a bhd: eased fnl f: t.o* **20/1**

1m 41.56s (1.66) **Going Correction** +0.05s/f (Slow) **14** Ran SP% **129.3**
Speed ratings (Par 94): **93,91,91,89,87 86,85,83,82,78 68,66,52,40**
toteswinger: 1&2 £17.30, 1&3 £8.60, 2&3 £40.60. CSF £178.11 TOTE £6.20: £3.60, £17.10, £2.70; EX 243.80.There was no bid for the winner. Alimarr was claimed by S. Parr for £10,000.
Owner ONEWAY Partners **Bred** Thomas Cahalan & Sophie Hayley **Trained** Lambourn, Berks

FOCUS
A moderate seller in which the front pair were at the sharp end throughout. It has been rated around the winner to his All-Weather best.

NOTEBOOK
Shadow Bay(IRE), a dual winner on turf, had finished well beaten in his only previous try over this trip but it was a different story in this moderate contest. Stalking the leader throughout, he found what was necessary when asked to go and win his race and was well on top at the finish. (tchd 7-2)
Jonnie Skull(IRE), well beaten in four outings in better company, made a bold bid to make every yard and it looked as though he would take some catching until the winner pounced. He appeared to face an impossible task at the weights and, although it can be dangerous to take form at this level at face value, it will be a surprise if he can't win a race like this. (op 33-1)
Precocious Air(IRE), not disgraced in a maiden and a claimer at Wolverhampton in her last two starts, was one of those most favoured by these weights. She stayed on all the way up the home straight, but could never quite get on terms with the front pair. (op 15-2 tchd 9-1)
Madam'X, who was just about last on the home bend and then ran into traffic over a furlong from home, made up a lot of late ground. She had been beaten a long way in both of her previous starts, but on this evidence she may be worth a try over further in similar company. Official explanation: two-day ban: careless riding (Dec 18-19) (tchd 66-1)
Alimarr(IRE), dropping in class after running her best race so far in a course-and-distance maiden last month, was comfortably best in on official ratings and was always in a good position just behind the leaders, but when eventually put under pressure she tended to put her head to one side and found nothing. She has plenty of questions to answer now. (op 15-8 tchd 2-1 in places)
Captain Cavendish(IRE) Official explanation: caution: careless riding.

7548 FOULNESS ISLAND H'CAP — 1m (P)
9:20 (9:20) (Class 5) (0-70,68) 3-Y-0+ **£3,238** (£963; £481; £240) **Stalls** Centre

Form RPR
0345 **1** **Fine Ruler (IRE)**[17] 7358 4-8-13 **61** .... VinceSlattery 2 66
(M R Bosley) *hld up in last pl: hdwy ent fnl f: rdn and r.o wl to ld wl ins fnl f* **7/1**
2633 **2** *nk* **Azure Mist**[5] 7490 3-9-2 **65** .... PaulMulrennan 5 69
(M H Tompkins) *led: hrd pressed and rdn wl over 1f out: kpt on gamely tl hdd and no ex wl ins fnl f* **4/1[2]**
2006 **3** *shd* **Onenightinlisbon (IRE)**[21] 7302 4-9-3 **65** .... PatCosgrave 3 69
(J R Boyle) *chsd ldrs: rdn wl over 2f out: ev ch u.p ins fnl f: unable qck cl home* **10/1**
5100 **4** *nk* **All In The Red (IRE)**[51] 6716 3-9-4 **67** .... JimCrowley 1 70
(B N Pollock) *hld up towards rr: rdn 2f out: hdwy ent fnl f: ev ch ins fnl f: kpt on* **12/1**
0401 **5** *shd* **Tobar Suil Lady (IRE)**[17] 7358 3-9-3 **66** .... DaneO'Neill 7 69
(J L Spearing) *hld up in last trio: rdn wl over 2f out: effrt u.p on outer 2f out: hdwy 1f out: kpt on but nt quite pce to rch ldrs* **9/2[3]**
0030 **6** *1 ¾* **Haasem (USA)**[21] 7307 5-9-3 **65** .... GeorgeBaker 8 64
(J R Jenkins) *stdd s and dropped in bhd: hdwy 2f out: rdn and chsd ldrs over 1f out: wknd ins fnl f* **5/2[1]**
3050 **7** *1 ½* **Bermacha**[12] 7419 3-9-5 **68** .... MartinDwyer 10 63
(W R Muir) *chsd ldr tl 3f out: rdn over 2f out: styd chsng ldrs tl wknd jst ins fnl f* **7/1**
0000 **8** *1* **Billy One Punch**[5] 7495 6-8-12 **60** .... TonyCulhane 4 53
(D Shaw) *trckd ldrs: wnt 2nd gng wl 3f out: rdn wl over 1f out: nt qckn over 1f out: wknd ins fnl f* **16/1**

1m 40.88s (0.98) **Going Correction** +0.05s/f (Slow)
WFA 3 from 4yo+ 1lb **8** Ran SP% **114.4**
Speed ratings (Par 103): **97,96,96,96,96 94,92,91**
toteswinger: 1&2 £6.40, 1&3 £16.80, 2&3 £3.10. CSF £35.11 CT £280.32 TOTE £8.20: £3.10, £1.90, £3.50; EX 43.50.
Owner Mrs Jean M O'Connor **Bred** Gainsborough Stud Management Ltd **Trained** Lockeridge, Wilts

FOCUS
An average handicap in which the pace was ordinary. All eight horses were within a length or so of each other in a line across the track passing the furlong pole and the fact that the front five finished in a heap suggests the form is questionable.
T/Plt: £58.90 to a £1 stake. Pool: £101,013.22. 1,251.28 winning tickets. T/Qpdt: £44.40 to a £1 stake. Pool: £7,441.59. 123.80 winning tickets. SP

6921 DEAUVILLE (R-H)
Thursday, December 4

OFFICIAL GOING: Standard

7549a PRIX SANGUINE (FILLIES) (ALL-WEATHER) — 7f 110y
10:50 (10:52) 2-Y-0 **£12,500** (£5,000; £3,750; £2,500; £1,250)

RPR
1 **Seradim**[40] 6982 2-9-0 .... SPasquier —
(P F I Cole) *in tch on outside: 2nd of main gp bhd clr ldr ent st: hrd rdn 2f out: styd on dourly to ld post* **26/10[1]**
2 *shd* **Peach Pearl**[51] 2-8-8 .... GMasure(6) —
(Y De Nicolay, France)
3 *1 ½* **Lutece Eria (FR)**[13] 7430 2-9-0 .... ARoussel —
(C Diard, France)
4 *2 ½* **La Big (GER)** 2-8-7 .... —
(Mario Hofer, Germany)
5 *1 ½* **Genuine Lauren (USA)**[104] 2-9-0 .... —
(J-C Rouget, France)
6 *½* **Cordoba (GER)**[39] 7006 2-9-0 ....(b) —
(H Steinmetz, Germany)
6 *dht* **Etty's Diary (IRE)** 2-8-7 .... —
(S Wattel, France)
8 *¾* **Mary's Precedent (FR)** 2-8-7 .... —
(C Lerner, France)
9 *5* **Olga D'Or (USA)**[104] 2-8-11 .... —
(R Gibson, France)
10 *1 ½* **Land Of Wilkes (USA)**[36] 7086 2-8-8 ....(b)(6) —
(D Sepulchre, France)
0 **Tante Dora (FR)**[30] 2-8-11 .... —
(F-X de Chevigny, France)
0 **Berlinetta (FR)**[24] 2-8-11 .... —
(F-X de Chevigny, France)
0 **Like A Storm (IRE)**[12] 2-8-8 .... (3) —
(Y Fouin, France)
0 **Centdixhuit (USA)** 2-8-5 .... (6) —
(F-X de Chevigny, France)
0 **Wayra (GER)** 2-9-0 .... —
(R Rohne, Germany)

1m 28.9s (88.90) **15** Ran SP% **27.8**
PARI-MUTUEL: WIN 3.60; PL 1.60, 1.80, 2.20; DF 8.00.
Owner The Fairy Story Partnership **Bred** Deepwood Farm Stud **Trained** Whatcombe, Oxon

NOTEBOOK
Seradim, fourth in a Listed race at Newbury on her last start, was running on sand for the first time. Her stamina saw her through here, and this half-sister to Saddler's Quest looks sure to get middle distances next year.

7551a PRIX DE VILLEPELEE (ALL-WEATHER) — 1m 1f 110y
2:35 (3:04) 3-Y-0 **£10,294** (£4,118; £3,088; £2,059; £1,029)

RPR
1 **Rockette (FR)**[29] 7203 3-8-9 .... JBensimon(6) —
(Y De Nicolay, France)
2 *¾* **Bellamy Prince (GER)**[50] 3-9-4 .... AlexisBadel —
(Peter Scotton, Germany)
3 *2* **Taverny**[54] 6664 3-9-4 .... RMarchelli —
(S Wattel, France)
4 *4* **Macellya (FR)**[138] 3-8-8 .... —
(X Nakkachdji, France)
5 *nse* **Sterope (FR)**[119] 4762 3-8-9 .... (6) —
(D Sepulchre, France)
6 *shd* **Burdlaz (IRE)**[29] 3-9-4 .... —
(E Libaud, France)
7 *½* **Elbrus (USA)**[34] 3-9-4 .... —
(P Bary, France)
8 *¾* **Orient Celebrity**[174] 3018 3-8-8 .... —
(Mlle S-V Tarrou, France)
9 *hd* **In My Heart (GER)**[196] 3-8-9 ow1 .... —
(H Steinmetz, Germany)
10 *¾* **Royale Again (FR)**[34] 3-9-1 .... —
(J De Roualle, France)
0 **Traphalgar (IRE)**[145] 3969 3-8-11 .... SPasquier —
(P F I Cole) *racd in 4th: pushed along to chse clr ldr 2 1/2f out: wknd 1 1/2f out* **5/2[1]**
0 **Golden Giant (USA)**[20] 3-8-12 .... (6) —
(R Chotard, France)
0 **Musical Swing (FR)**[97] 3-8-2 .... (6) —
(F-X de Chevigny, France)
0 **Indran (FR)**[231] 3-8-11 .... —
(C Baillet, France)
0 **Koenigsberg (USA)**[54] 6664 3-9-4 .... —
(N Clement, France)
0 **Lasos (FR)**[93] 3-9-4 .... —
(D Sicaud, France)
0 **Good Dance (FR)** 3-8-8 .... —
(Mlle A Poirsin, France)
0 **Twin Prince (IRE)** 3-8-5 .... (6) —
(J-M Lefebvre, France)

1m 56.5s (116.50) **18** Ran SP% **28.6**
PARI-MUTUEL: WIN 7.90; PL 2.80, 7.00, 2.20; DF 92.10.
Owner Mme H Devin **Bred** Mme H Devin **Trained** France

NOTEBOOK
Traphalgar(IRE), off the track since July, has an official mark on the All-Weather of 93 and won at this track this time last year, but he failed to run anywhere near his best on this return.

7520 LINGFIELD (L-H)
Friday, December 5

OFFICIAL GOING: Standard
Wind: modest across Weather: cloudy, bright spells, dry

7552 BET AT LADBROKES.COM MAIDEN STKS (DIV I) — 1m (P)
12:10 (12:11) (Class 5) 2-Y-0 **£2,388** (£705; £352) **Stalls** High

Form RPR
242 **1** **Kings Destiny**[20] 7336 2-9-3 79 .... NCallan 5 84+
(M A Jarvis) *trckd ldrs: gng wl on inner over 2f out: gap opened and rdn to ld jst ins fnl f: sn clr: easily* **10/11[1]**
06 **2** *2 ¾* **Mellow Mixture**[20] 7343 2-9-3 0 .... DaneO'Neill 9 78
(R Hannon) *dwlt: in tch in midfield: rdn to chse ldng trio over 2f out: r.o fnl f: snatched 2nd last stride: no ch w wnr* **50/1**
6 **3** *shd* **Wee Sonny (IRE)**[20] 7336 2-9-3 0 .... RichardKingscote 7 78+
(Tom Dascombe) *w ldr: ev ch and rdn jst over 2f out: chsd wnr ins fnl f: no imp: lost 2nd last stride* **20/1**
6 **4** *½* **Love Pegasus (USA)**[55] 6655 2-9-3 0 .... JamieSpencer 8 77
(M Johnston) *led: qcknd 3f out: rdn over 1f out: hdd jst ins fnl f: no ch w wnr after: lost 2 pls ins fnl f* **9/1[3]**
02 **5** *2* **Barwell Bridge**[15] 7397 2-9-3 0 .... GeorgeBaker 3 72
(S Kirk) *hld up in tch: rdn and nt qckn over 2f out: kpt on but no imp fr over 1f out* **2/1[2]**
6 *7* **Albaasha (IRE)** 2-9-3 0 .... RyanMoore 1 57
(Sir Michael Stoute) *s.i.s: sn detached in last pl and pushed along: clsd and in tch 4f out: rdn and struggling 3f out: sn bhd* **12/1**

The Form Book, Raceform Ltd, Compton, RG20 6NL

7 1 **Crazy Colours** 2-9-3 0 FrankieMcDonald 6 55
(Jane Chapple-Hyam) *dwlt: in tch in rr: rdn and struggling 3f out: no ch fnl 2f* **66/1**

6 8 1 **Abulharith**35 7105 2-9-3 0 ChrisCatlin 4 52
(P W Chapple-Hyam) *dwlt: sn in tch in midfield: rdn and wknd over 2f out: wl bhd fnl f* **16/1**

1m 36.76s (-1.44) **Going Correction** -0.10s/f (Stan) **8** Ran SP% **117.5**
Speed ratings (Par 96): **103,100,100,99,97 90,89,88**
toteswinger: 1&2 £11.40, 1&3 £8.00, 2&3 £23.10. CSF £66.95 TOTE £2.30: £1.10, £21.10, £4.40; EX 85.10 Trifecta £141.60 Part won. Pool: £191.36, 0.87 winning units..
Owner Dennis Yardy **Bred** D A Yardy **Trained** Newmarket, Suffolk

FOCUS
An ordinary juvenile maiden, but the winning time was 1.38 seconds faster than the second division.

NOTEBOOK
Kings Destiny had been a beaten favourite on both his starts since finishing runner-up at Nottingham on his debut. However, he had not been doing much wrong, including when again second over this trip at Great Leighs on his latest start, and he found this a suitable opportunity to get off the mark. Forced to make his move towards the often unfavoured inside rail, he was fortunate to get a gap, but he soon put the result beyond doubt. He should improve for a step up to 1m2f-plus in time and should make a nice three-year-old. (op Evens, tchd 11-10 in places)
Mellow Mixture never threatened the winner but this form was still a big improvement on his first two efforts. He looks good enough to make his mark in handicaps, with further improvement likely. (op 66-1)
Wee Sonny(IRE), who ran green when behind today's winner first time up at Great Leighs, knew his job better but could not sustain his effort after racing a little keenly through the early stages. He gives the impression he can improve again. (op 25-1)
Love Pegasus(USA) set off in front but did not convince with his head carriage and was comfortably held. Official explanation: jockey said colt hung right throughout (tchd 17-2 and 10-1)
Barwell Bridge seemed to race a little keenly under restraint and was never involved. He might be able to do better now he has the option of handicaps. (op 5-2)
Albaasha(IRE), a 220,000gns purchase, out of a 1m2f winner, ran extremely green throughout. (op 8-1)

7553 BET AT LADBROKES.COM CLAIMING STKS 1m 2f (P)
12:40 (12:45) (Class 6) 3-Y-O+ **£1,978** (£584; £292) **Stalls** Low

Form RPR
1511 1 **Sabre Light**5 7506 3-9-5 70 (p) JerryO'Dwyer 4 79
(J Pearce) *hld up in midfield: plld out and hdwy over 2f out: chsd ldrs and rdn over 1f out: led and edgd lft fnl 100yds: r.o wl* **5/1**3

3603 2 1 **Zero Cool (USA)**51 6738 4-9-4 77 GeorgeBaker 12 73
(G L Moore) *trckd ldrs: rdn to chse ldr over 2f out: ev ch 2f out: kpt on same pce ins fnl f: wnt 2nd last stride* **15/8**1

2130 3 shd **Nawamees (IRE)**42 6950 10-9-8 77 (p) NCallan 1 76
(P D Evans) *chsd ldr tl rdn to ld over 2f out: hdd and no ex fnl 100yds: lost 2nd last stride* **10/3**2

4500 4 hd **Rapid City**8 7461 5-8-12 67 (p) JamesDoyle 8 67
(A J McCabe) *taken down early: stdd s: t.k.h: hld up towards rr: hdwy over 2f out: chsd ldrs and drvn over 1f out: keeping on same pce whn nt clr run towards fin* **5/1**3

0600 5 5 **Royal Choir**99 5429 4-8-4 44 AndreaAtzeni(5) 6 53
(H E Haynes) *t.k.h: hld up towards rr: rdn and effrt on outer over 2f out: kpt on u.p but nvr trbld ldrs* **66/1**

5445 6 1 **Golden Brown (IRE)**35 7114 4-8-8 47 (tp) NeilChalmers 5 50
(David Pinder) *hld up towards rr: rdn and effrt over 2f out: kpt on same pce u.p fr over 1f out* **14/1**

5500 7 1 **Gifted Heir (IRE)**6 7499 4-9-2 50 (b1) MickyFenton 3 56
(A Bailey) *t.k.h: trckd ldrs: rdn and nt qcknd jst over 2f out: no ch w ldrs fnl f* **33/1**

0005 8 2 1/2 **Muffett's Dream**37 7071 4-8-3 47 CatherineGannon 2 38
(J J Bridger) *sn bustled up to ld: stdd pce 8f out: rdn and hdd over 2f out: wknd u.p over 1f out* **40/1**

0000 9 3 **Cavalry Guard (USA)**16 7392 4-8-10 49 (b1) HayleyTurner 9 39
(T D McCarthy) *t.k.h: hld up in midfield: rdn over 2f out: no imp whn nt clr run over 1f out: n.d* **50/1**

1500 10 2 3/4 **Royal Straight**18 7354 3-9-3 65 JimCrowley 7 44
(B N Pollock) *t.k.h: hld up in midfield: rdn over 2f out: sn unable qck and no imp* **12/1**

0600 11 2 3/4 **Our Glenard**29 7216 9-8-8 34 RichardThomas 11 26
(J E Long) *a in last pair: rdn and lost tch wl over 2f out* **100/1**

60 12 16 **Sweet Demerara**265 909 4-8-7 0 ChrisCatlin 10 —
(P Butler) *uns rdr bef s: a bhd: drvn and lost tch qckly over 3f out* **100/1**

2m 5.92s (-0.68) **Going Correction** -0.10s/f (Stan)
WFA 3 from 4yo+ 3lb **12** Ran SP% **116.4**
Speed ratings (Par 101): **98,97,97,96,92 92,91,89,86,84 82,69**
toteswinger: 1&2 £3.10, 1&3 £14.10, 2&3 £2.00. CSF £14.17 TOTE £3.40: £2.00, £1.20, £1.50; EX 13.70 Trifecta £19.90 Pool: £258.46, 9.60 winning units..
Owner Fran O'Brien **Bred** D J And Mrs Deer **Trained** Newmarket, Suffolk
■ Stewards' Enquiry : Jerry O'Dwyer one-day ban: careless riding (Dec 19)

FOCUS
A reasonable claimer, and the first four, although well bunched at the line, finished a long way clear of the remainder. They went a good gallop early but the pace slowed noticeably at halfway. The proximity of the fifth and sixth limits the form.
Rapid City Official explanation: jockey said gelding was denied a clear run
Our Glenard Official explanation: Veterinary Officer said that on inspection after the race gelding had been struck into

7554 BET AT LADBROKES.COM MAIDEN STKS (DIV II) 1m (P)
1:15 (1:16) (Class 5) 2-Y-O **£2,388** (£705; £352) **Stalls** High

Form RPR
1 **Premier Banker (IRE)** 2-9-3 0 ShaneKelly 5 82+
(J Noseda) *dwlt: hld up in tch in rr: hdwy over 2f out: rdn and chsd ldr over 1f out: r.o wl to ld wl ins fnl f* **16/1**

52 2 1 1/4 **Formula (USA)**11 7438 2-9-3 0 DaneO'Neill 2 77
(R Hannon) *led at stdy pce: rdn and qcknd 2f out: clr over 1f out: drvn ins fnl f: hdd wl ins fnl f: sn btn* **2/5**1

3 3/4 **Dukes Art** 2-9-3 0 HayleyTurner 8 75+
(J A R Toller) *stdd after s: hld up in last pl: hdwy over 2f out: chsd ldng pair 1f out: kpt on* **25/1**

4 3 1/4 **Green Dynasty (IRE)** 2-9-3 0 JamieSpencer 6 68
(M Johnston) *w ldr: rdn and unable qck jst over 2f out: wknd over 1f out* **8/1**3

5 2 1/2 **Thefillyfromepsom** 2-8-12 0 IanMongan 3 58
(P M Phelan) *stdd after s: hld up in tch in rr: rdn and unable qck over 2f out: kpt on steadily fnl f: nvr trbld ldrs* **100/1**

0233 6 3/4 **Charlie Smirke (USA)**22 7298 2-9-3 70 (b1) GeorgeBaker 10 61
(G L Moore) *chsd ldrs on outer: rdn jst over 2f out: wknd qckly over 1f out* **7/1**2

7 1/2 **Bickersten** 2-9-3 0 EdwardCreighton 9 60
(M R Channon) *hld up towards rr on outer: rdn and outpcd over 2f out: no ch fnl 2f* **100/1**

8 9 **Persuasive Power (USA)**49 6797 2-9-3 0 JimCrowley 4 40
(Andrew Oliver, Ire) *in tch: rdn 4f out: struggling over 3f out: wl bhd fnl 2f* **50/1**

9 nk **Lipi** 2-9-3 0 RyanMoore 1 39
(Sir Michael Stoute) *in tch: rdn over 4f out: lost pl over 3f out: wl bhd fnl 2f* **16/1**

1m 38.14s (-0.06) **Going Correction** -0.10s/f (Stan) **39** Ran SP% **114.6**
Speed ratings (Par 96): **96,94,94,90,88 87,87,78,77**
toteswinger: 1&2 £2.40, 1&3 £28.30, 2&3 £7.90. CSF £22.89 TOTE £20.90: £3.10, £1.02, £5.50; EX 31.10 TRIFECTA Not won..
Owner J Browne **Bred** D G Hardisty Bloodstock **Trained** Newmarket, Suffolk

FOCUS
The favourite ran below form and the winning time was over a second slower than the first division.

NOTEBOOK
Premier Banker(IRE), a 50,000gns purchase, was very easy to back but he was ultimately a cosy winner. It remains to be seen exactly what he achieved, as the winning time was 1.38 seconds slower than the first division, and it's also worth noting that he displayed a pronounced knee action. However, he is expected to stay further and is likely to be given a break now. (op 14-1)
Formula(USA) had appeared to post a big effort in defeat when runner-up to a potentially smart Mark Johnston colt in a maiden run in a quick time over this course and distance 11 days earlier, and he was strongly supported at odds on, but he found one too good. While on the face of it this seems disappointing, a number of factors probably contributed to his defeat. He was forced to make his own running (rarely ideal at this track), and the race may have come too soon. Also, the way he opened up a lead of around two or three lengths in just a matter of strides at the top of the straight suggests his natural speed may be seen to better effect over shorter. (op 1-2, tchd 8-15 and 4-7 in places)
Dukes Art, a 20,000gns half-brother to a 7f juvenile winner, stuck on nicely for pressure and this was a pleasing debut. (op 33-1)
Green Dynasty(IRE), a half-brother to a winner over 1m4f-1m5f, looked in need of the experience and should do better in time when stepped up in trip. (op 15-2 tchd 10-1)
Thefillyfromepsom made a satisfactory debut.
Charlie Smirke(USA), fitted with blinkers for the first time, having looked wayward at Great Leighs on his previous start, is not progressing. (op 13-2)
Lipi, just like his stablemate in the first division, seemed very inexperienced and is going to want 1m4f-plus in time. (op 14-1 tchd 20-1)

7555 PLAY BINGO AT LADBROKES.COM NURSERY 6f (P)
1:50 (1:50) (Class 5) (0-85,90) 2-Y-O **£3,885** (£1,156; £577; £288) **Stalls** Low

Form RPR
232 1 **Noverre To Go (IRE)**57 6601 2-9-5 82 (t) RichardKingscote 3 86+
(Tom Dascombe) *mde all: shkn up and qcknd over 2f out: hung lft over 1f out: rn green and wandered ins fnl f: pushed clr fnl 100yds* **11/8**1

420 2 2 1/4 **Dakota Hills**66 6362 2-8-9 72 LPKeniry 4 69
(J R Best) *w wnr: rdn and qcknd over 2f out: ev ch after tl no ex and btn fnl 100yds* **9/1**

662 3 1/2 **Diamond Twister (USA)**18 7356 2-8-8 71 ow1 SteveDrowne 1 67+
(J R Best) *stdd s: t.k.h: trckd ldrs: rdn over 2f out: outpcd bnd 2f out: kpt on u.p fnl f: nvr pce to chal wnr* **7/2**3

1251 4 2 **Joe Caster**8 7460 2-9-8 90 6ex AndreaAtzeni(5) 2 80
(J M P Eustace) *stdd s: t.k.h: hld up in tch: rdn over 2f out: c wd and outpcd bnd 2f out: kpt on but nvr gng pce to chal ldrs* **7/4**2

1m 14.05s (2.15) **Going Correction** -0.10s/f (Stan) **4** Ran SP% **110.7**
Speed ratings (Par 96): **81,78,77,74**
CSF £12.28 TOTE £2.30; EX 12.10.
Owner John Duddy **Bred** Gestut Gorlsdorf **Trained** Lambourn, Berks

FOCUS
Only four runners, but the winner looks better than this grade.

NOTEBOOK
Noverre To Go(IRE) ◆ looks quite useful and it's easy to see why he was entered in some nice races earlier in the year. Not for the first time, he wandered around under pressure and edged away from the whip, suggesting he either has his own ideas or is still green, but he obviously has plenty of ability. He was forced to make much of his own running, which was not ideal, but he impressed with the way he quickened from the front at the top of the straight and he always looked to be doing enough, despite his waywardness. He gives the impression he can do even better when getting a lead in a bigger field and he should be capable of competing off much higher marks next year. Although his dam was a 1m2f winner, he looks to have loads of speed. (op 13-8)
Dakota Hills, returning from a two-month break, had his chance but looked to be beaten by quite a nice type. (tchd 10-1)
Diamond Twister(USA), a stablemate of the runner-up, struggled to land a telling blow on this nursery bow. (op 4-1)
Joe Caster came into this in good form but he ruined his chance by racing keenly. (op 13-8 tchd 15-8)

7556 PLAY CASINO AT LADBROKES.COM H'CAP 1m (P)
2:25 (2:25) (Class 3) (0-95,94) 3-Y-O+ **£7,641** (£2,273; £1,136; £567) **Stalls** High

Form RPR
2011 1 **Internationaldebut (IRE)**7 7477 3-9-2 92 6ex AdamKirby 11 101+
(S Parr) *stdd and dropped in bhd after s: hld up in rr: stl last 2f out: gd hdwy towards inner over 1f out: r.o wl to ld last stride* **6/4**1

1103 2 shd **Prince Of Thebes (IRE)**11 7439 7-8-5 80 PaulDoe 6 89
(M J Attwater) *chsd ldrs: rdn to chal 2f out: drvn to ld ins fnl f: edgd lft fnl 100yds: hdd last stride* **14/1**

2100 3 1 1/4 **Gallantry**11 7439 6-8-10 85 TGMcLaughlin 2 91
(P Howling) *chsd ldrs: rdn to chse ldng pair 2f out: pressed ldrs ins fnl f: one pce fnl 100yds* **16/1**

3036 4 1/2 **Flipando (IRE)**27 7245 7-9-0 89 JamieSpencer 8 94
(T D Barron) *t.k.h: hld up in rr: hdwy on outer bnd 2f out: rdn and edgd lft fr over 1f out: r.o to go 4th nr fin: nt rch ldrs* **13/2**2

2214 5 nk **Visions Of Johanna (USA)**112 5051 3-8-8 84 ow1 ShaneKelly 4 88
(J Noseda) *led: rdn wl over 1f out: hdd ins fnl f: disputing 3rd and btn whn short of room and hmpd wl ins fnl f* **8/1**

0415 6 1 1/2 **Nezami (IRE)**103 5313 3-8-12 88 NCallan 7 89
(J Akehurst) *s.i.s: sn in tch in midfield: rdn and hdwy over 1f out: keeping on same pce and btn whn nt clr run and eased fnl 50yds* **16/1**

0004 7 3 3/4 **Evident Pride (USA)**20 7339 5-9-1 90 DaneO'Neill 3 82
(B R Johnson) *t.k.h: hld up in tch in rr: rdn and brief effrt over 1f out: sn no imp* **16/1**

0202 8 1 **Premier Danseur (IRE)**3 7525 3-8-4 80 GregFairley 10 70
(M Johnston) *chsd ldrs: rdn over 2f out: wknd u.p over 1f out* **7/1**3

020 **9** 2 1/4 **Baylini**[57] 6605 4-9-5 **94** .... JamesDoyle 9 79
(Ms J S Doyle) *in tch on outer: rdn and effrt over 2f out: lost pl bnd 2f out: no imp after* **25/1**

54-0 **10** *nk* **Soccerjackpot (USA)**[202] 2210 4-8-8 **83** ow1.......... SteveDrowne 1 67
(C G Cox) *dwlt: sn in tch on inner: rdn over 2f out: wknd over 1f out: wl hld and eased ins fnl f* **10/1**

1m 35.21s (-2.99) **Going Correction** -0.10s/f (Stan) course record
WFA 3 from 4yo+ 1lb **10** Ran SP% **114.2**
Speed ratings (Par 107): **110,109,108,108,107 106,102,101,99,99**
toteswinger: 1&2 £7.00, 1&3 £8.50, 2&3 £29.80. CSF £24.32 CT £249.73 TOTE £2.50: £1.30, £3.90, £3.10; EX 22.60 Trifecta £272.30 Part won. Pool: £368.09, 0.74 winning units..
Owner W McKay, J Barton **Bred** Ennistown Stud **Trained** Bawtry, S Yorks

FOCUS
A good handicap and solid form for the grade, with the runner-up rated to this year's best form and the third, fourth and fifth close to their marks.

NOTEBOOK
Internationaldebut(IRE) completed the hat-trick following wins over 6f and 7f around here and looks better than the narrow winning margin suggests. Held up as usual, he had to wait for a gap at the top of the straight before making his move towards the inside, but his rider always looked confident he would get there. This fine, big horse has the scope to improve further and is versatile with regards to trip. (op 15-8 tchd 2-1)
Prince Of Thebes(IRE), who had run well over course and distance last time, put up a cracking effort in defeat, just being pegged back after edging left late on. (op 10-1)
Gallantry was slightly short of room late on but he was held at the time. He might be worth dropping back to 7f. (op 9-1)
Flipando(IRE), keen out the back early, crept into contention rounding the final bend but was taken very wide and got going too late. (op 8-1)
Visions Of Johanna(USA) ◆, returning after 112 days off, looked to be intimidated by the runner-up late on, although he was in trouble at the time. He is lightly raced and can improve on this form. (op 6-1)
Soccerjackpot(USA) Official explanation: Veterinary Officer said that on examination after the race gelding was lame behind

7557 PLAY POKER AT LADBROKES.COM H'CAP 7f (P)
3:00 (3:00) (Class 5) (0-75,75) 3-Y-0+ **£2,729** (£806; £403) **Stalls** Low

Form RPR

2042 **1** **I Confess**[11] 7436 3-8-10 **67**.......... (b) NCallan 7 77
(P D Evans) *mde virtually all: hdd over 2f out: sn led again: rdn clr 1f out: r.o wl: eased towards fin* **4/1**[1]

-201 **2** 2 1/2 **Everybody Knows**[185] 2695 3-9-4 **75**.......... TravisBlock 13 78
(Miss Jo Crowley) *chsd ldrs on outer: led over 2f out: sn hdd: drvn and outpcd by wnr 1f out: no ch w wnr fnl f: kpt on to hold 2nd* **12/1**

1005 **3** *hd* **Danish Art (IRE)**[53] 6695 3-9-3 **74**.......... JamieSpencer 3 76
(J A R Toller) *chsd ldr tl over 2f out: sn rdn: kpt on u.p but no ch w wnr fnl f* **11/2**[2]

0200 **4** *nse* **Russian Reel**[16] 7384 3-9-1 **75**.......... (t) AlanCreighton(3) 6 77
(E J Creighton) *chsd ldrs: rdn over 2f out: unable qck u.p wl over 1f out: kpt on but no ch w wnr fnl f* **33/1**

2352 **5** *hd* **Carmenero (GER)**[16] 7390 5-9-3 **74**.......... HayleyTurner 8 76+
(W R Muir) *t.k.h: hld up in rr: nt clr run wl over 1f out: r.o fnl f: nvr able to chal* **4/1**[1]

0052 **6** 1/2 **Cornus**[27] 7239 6-9-4 **75**.......... (be) JamesDoyle 9 75
(A J McCabe) *hld up in tch: rdn and effrt u.p 2f out: one pce and no imp fnl f* **13/2**[3]

0300 **7** 1/2 **Napoletano (GER)**[67] 6336 7-8-11 **68**.......... (p) IanMongan 2 67
(S Dow) *t.k.h: hld up towards rr: effrt and rdn over 1f out: kpt on but nvr trbld ldrs* **14/1**

6200 **8** *nk* **Ivory Lace**[13] 7419 7-9-2 **73**.......... (p) JimCrowley 5 71
(S Woodman) *hld up towards rr: effrt and rdn over 1f out: nvr trbld ldrs* **16/1**

2105 **9** 3/4 **Trimlestown (IRE)**[16] 7378 5-8-12 **69**.......... DaneO'Neill 1 65
(P D Evans) *awkward leaving stalls and slowly away: sn in midfield: no hdwy u.p fnl 2f* **12/1**

1136 **10** 2 1/2 **Fiefdom (IRE)**[16] 7390 6-9-4 **75**.......... PatrickMathers 11 65
(I W McInnes) *hld up in midfield: rdn 3f out: wd bnd 2f out: no imp fnl f* **10/1**

5000 **11** 1 1/4 **Pha Mai Blue**[49] 6771 3-9-2 **73**.......... PatCosgrave 4 59
(J R Boyle) *stdd after s: hld up in rr: nvr a factor* **14/1**

0500 **12** 8 **Ike Quebec (FR)**[120] 4777 3-9-1 **72**.......... SteveDrowne 10 37
(J R Boyle) *a bhd: lost tch over 2f out: wl bhd and eased fnl f* **20/1**

1m 23.85s (-0.95) **Going Correction** -0.10s/f (Stan) **12** Ran SP% **120.1**
Speed ratings (Par 103): **101,98,97,97,97 97,96,96,95,92 91,81**
toteswinger: 1&2 £12.50, 1&3 £5.60, 2&3 £16.20. CSF £54.49 CT £274.71 TOTE £4.60: £1.80, £3.70, £2.30; EX 40.60 Trifecta £313.20 Part won. Pool: £423.32, 0.64 winning units..
Owner Jim Ennis **Bred** Gestut Sohrenhof **Trained** Pandy, Monmouths

FOCUS
Those who raced prominently were at an advantage and this is ordinary handicap form. They finished in a bunch behind the winner. The form looks modest rated around the runner-up and third.

7558 BETTER PRICES, BIGGER WINS AT LADBROKES.COM H'CAP 1m 4f (P)
3:30 (3:30) (Class 4) (0-85,83) 3-Y-0+ **£4,727** (£1,406; £702; £351) **Stalls** Low

Form RPR

6500 **1** **Aegean Prince**[21] 7314 4-9-0 **76**.......... RyanMoore 3 86
(R Hannon) *hld up in last pl: pushed along wl over 3f out: swtchd rt wl over 1f out: rdn to ld ins fnl f: forged clr fnl 100yds* **11/2**[3]

03-1 **2** 2 1/4 **Alsadaa (USA)**[34] 6243 5-8-13 **75**.......... IanMongan 2 81
(Mrs L J Mongan) *chsd ldr tl led over 7f out: rdn over 2f out: hdd ins fnl f: kpt on same pce* **4/1**[2]

5212 **3** 3/4 **Scarab (IRE)**[6] 7493 3-8-9 **76**.......... JamieSpencer 1 81
(M Johnston) *chsd ldng pair tl wnt 2nd over 4f out: rdn and pressed ldr jst over 2f out: no ex ins fnl f* **5/6**[1]

-165 **4** 1 1/4 **Sam Lord**[21] 7314 4-9-7 **83**.......... DaneO'Neill 5 86
(A King) *hld up in last pair: rdn wl over 2f out: sltly hmpd wl over 1f out: kpt on same pce fnl f* **7/1**

0001 **5** 2 1/4 **Sign Of The Cross**[21] 7309 4-9-2 **78**.......... GeorgeBaker 4 78
(G L Moore) *t.k.h: led tl over 7f out: chsd ldr tl over 4f out: rdn 2f out: wknd ent fnl f* **11/1**

2m 29.99s (-3.01) **Going Correction** -0.10s/f (Stan)
WFA 3 from 4yo+ 5lb **5** Ran SP% **110.8**
Speed ratings (Par 105): **106,104,104,103,101**
CSF £26.63 TOTE £8.60: £3.10, £1.70; EX 32.30 Place 6: £14.06, Place 5: £7.37..
Owner Theobalds Stud **Bred** Theobalds Stud **Trained** East Everleigh, Wilts

FOCUS
An ordinary handicap for the grade but sound enough form rated around the runner-up.
T/Plt: £41.70 to a £1 stake. Pool: £40,559.42. 709.78 winning tickets. T/Qpdt: £18.90 to a £1 stake. Pool: £3,261.84. 127.70 winning tickets. SP

7512 WOLVERHAMPTON (A.W) (L-H)
Friday, December 5

OFFICIAL GOING: Standard
Wind: Fresh behind changing to fresh across from race 3 onwards Weather: Raining

7559 WOLVERHAMPTON HOLIDAY INN APPRENTICE H'CAP 1m 1f 103y(P)
6:50 (6:50) (Class 6) (0-65,64) 3-Y-0+ **£2,729** (£806; £403) **Stalls** Low

Form RPR

0005 **1** **Bailieborough (IRE)**[4] 7518 9-8-9 **52**.......... LanceBetts 13 60
(B Ellison) *a.p: led over 2f out: rdn over 1f out: styd on* **18/1**

1604 **2** 1/2 **Prince Golan (IRE)**[18] 7368 4-8-13 **61**.......... (p) AlexEdwards(5) 2 68
(J W Unett) *chsd ldrs: rdn over 1f out: edgd lft: styd on* **14/1**

000 **3** 1 **Mooted (UAE)**[17] 7374 3-9-5 **64**.......... BMcHugh 10 69
(Miss J A Camacho) *chsd ldrs: rdn over 1f out: edgd lft ins fnl f: kpt on* **28/1**

5011 **4** 3 **Salerosa (IRE)**[10] 7441 3-8-13 **63** 6ex.......... SamuelDrury(5) 12 62
(Mrs A Duffield) *led over 8f out: hdd 4f out: rdn and ev ch 2f out: no ex fnl f* **10/1**

4644 **5** 3/4 **Sir Liam (USA)**[121] 4722 4-8-10 **53**.......... RossAtkinson 6 50
(Tom Dascombe) *hld up: hdwy 2f out: sn rdn: no ex fnl f* **2/1**[1]

0010 **6** 1/2 **Stark Contrast (USA)**[14] 7405 4-9-0 **64**.......... SeanPalmer(7) 7 60
(M D I Usher) *hld up: hdwy over 2f out: rdn over 1f out: no ex fnl f* **12/1**

3030 **7** 4 **Casablanca Minx (IRE)**[4] 7516 5-8-9 **52**.......... (b) KylieManser 9 40
(Miss Gay Kelleway) *hld up: rdn and hung lft over 1f out: nvr trbld ldrs* **14/1**

8 8 **The Bodhran Beat (IRE)**[14] 7412 4-8-7 **50** oh5.......... DeclanCannon 8 21
(P J Rothwell, Ire) *chsd ldrs: nt clr run 3f out: wknd over 2f* **80/1**

5-66 **9** *shd* **Whodunit (UAE)**[26] 7261 4-8-7 **50** oh2.......... AshleyMorgan 3 21
(P W Hiatt) *chsd ldrs: led 4f out: hdd over 2f out: wknd over 1f out* **7/1**[3]

4006 **10** 1 **Jimmy Dean**[36] 7088 3-8-5 **50** oh5.......... (t) DeanHeslop 11 18
(M Wellings) *hld up: rdn over 3f out: a in rr* **66/1**

4001 **11** 5 **Climate (IRE)**[4] 7518 9-9-4 **61** 6ex.......... (p) AndreaAtzeni 1 19
(P D Evans) *led 1f: chsd ldrs: rdn over 2f out: sn wknd* **3/1**[2]

6-24 **12** 16 **Clifton Four (USA)**[35] 1203 3-8-13 **63**.......... AnthonyBetts(5) 5 —
(P J Rothwell, Ire) *s.i.s: outpcd* **25/1**

2m 2.21s (0.51) **Going Correction** +0.075s/f (Slow)
WFA 3 from 4yo+ 2lb **12** Ran SP% **116.2**
Speed ratings (Par 101): **100,99,98,96,95 94,91,84,84,83 78,64**
toteswinger: 1&2 £9.50, 1&3 £63.40, 2&3 £44.30. CSF £236.31 CT £6836.76 TOTE £27.40: £4.80, £5.40, £12.40; EX 217.90.
Owner Kristian Strangeway **Bred** Churchtown Stud **Trained** Norton, N Yorks

FOCUS
A modest handicap in which the pace was only fair and the two market leaders disappointed. The principals raced close to the inside rail in the straight. The form has been rated around the placed horses but is not solid

7560 BOOK TICKETS ONLINE CLAIMING STKS 1m 141y(P)
7:20 (7:20) (Class 6) 3-Y-0+ **£2,729** (£806; £403) **Stalls** Low

Form RPR

1004 **1** **Red Somerset (USA)**[39] 7019 5-9-7 86.......... MCGeran(5) 12 91
(R J Hodges) *hld up: hdwy 3f out: led over 1f out: r.o* **4/1**[3]

1440 **2** 1 3/4 **Boundless Prospect (USA)**[72] 6215 9-8-1 64.......... PatrickDonaghy(5) 5 67
(P D Evans) *hld up: hdwy over 1f out: r.o: nt rch wnr* **28/1**

0431 **3** 1 1/2 **Electric Warrior (IRE)**[15] 7396 5-9-8 85.......... JimCrowley 2 80
(K R Burke) *chsd ldrs: rdn and ev ch 1f out: no ex ins fnl f* **2/1**[1]

4252 **4** 2 1/2 **Obezyana (USA)**[15] 7396 6-9-12 72.......... (p) FrancisNorton 10 78
(A Bailey) *prom: rdn whn hmpd wl over 1f out: no ex fnl f* **12/1**

260 **5** 2 **Ardent Prince**[4] 7516 5-8-8 52.......... (p) LPKeniry 6 55
(A J McCabe) *s.s: hld up: r.o ins fnl f: nrst fin* **33/1**

0020 **6** *nse* **Imprimis Tagula (IRE)**[3] 7525 4-9-12 77.......... (v) JimmyQuinn 9 73
(A Bailey) *chsd ldrs: led 6f out: hdd 3f out: rdn and ev ch 2f out: wknd ins fnl f* **18/1**

02- **7** 1 **High Profit (IRE)**[15] 816 4-9-2 0.......... (p) StephenCarson 8 61
(C J Mann) *hld up: rdn over 2f out: nvr trbld ldrs* **33/1**

031 **8** 1 3/4 **Avertis**[17] 7374 3-9-1 80.......... (t) AndreaAtzeni(5) 3 63
(M Botti) *led: hdd 6f out: led again 3f out: rdn and hdd over 1f out: wknd ins fnl f* **7/2**[2]

/1-0 **9** *nk* **Xtra Torrential (USA)**[112] 5051 6-9-10 90.......... MartinDwyer 1 64
(D M Simcock) *hld up in tch: rdn over 3f out: wknd over 1f out* **9/1**

0000 **10** 1 **Marino Prince (FR)**[62] 6492 3-9-0 48.......... GregFairley 7 54
(T Wall) *chsd ldrs tl rdn and wknd over 2f out* **100/1**

0000 **11** *11* **Copperbottomed (IRE)**[21] 7317 3-8-1 50 ow4.......... (e) DeclanCannon(7) 4 22
(P G Murphy) *pushed along early in rr: rdn over 2f out: sn wknd* **40/1**

1m 50.04s (-0.46) **Going Correction** +0.075s/f (Slow)
WFA 3 from 4yo+ 2lb **11** Ran SP% **111.3**
Speed ratings (Par 101): **105,103,102,99,98 98,97,95,95,94 84**
toteswinger: 1&2 £23.90, 1&3 £2.90, 2&3 £12.80 CSF £112.82 TOTE £3.90: £2.40, £5.30, £1.02; EX 96.90.Red Somerset was the subject of a friendly claim.
Owner R J Hodges **Bred** Haras D'Etreham **Trained** Charlton Mackrell, Somerset

FOCUS
A wide range of ability on show and a couple of the market leaders proved disappointing to varying degrees. The pace was just fair and the winner raced up the centre in the straight. The form looks solid rated around the fourth to his recent handicap form.

7561 HOTEL & CONFERENCING MAIDEN FILLIES' STKS 7f 32y(P)
7:50 (7:53) (Class 5) 2-Y-0 **£3,238** (£963; £481; £240) **Stalls** High

Form RPR

4 **1** **Ajara (IRE)**[14] 7402 2-9-0 0.......... GregFairley 10 69
(N J Vaughan) *chsd ldr tl led over 2f out: rdn and edgd rt over 1f out: styd on* **9/1**

5 **2** *nk* **Volochkova (USA)**[20] 7341 2-9-0 0.......... EddieAhern 2 68
(J R Fanshawe) *chsd ldrs: rdn over 1f out: styd on* **11/2**[2]

64 **3** 2 1/2 **Passage To India (IRE)**[20] 7341 2-9-0 0.......... PaulFitzsimons 1 62
(J A Osborne) *chsd ldrs: rdn over 1f out: styd on same pce ins fnl f* **11/1**

4 3/4 **Opera Wings** 2-9-0 0.......... HayleyTurner 5 60+
(Sir Michael Stoute) *s.s: outpcd: hdwy over 2f out: r.o: nt rch ldrs* **7/1**[3]

02 **5** 2 1/2 **Rag And Bone (CAN)**[20] 7332 2-9-0 0.......... JamieSpencer 3 54
(B J Meehan) *led: rdn and hdd over 2f out: wknd fnl f* **1/1**[1]

6 6 **Anasy (USA)** 2-9-0 0.......... MartinDwyer 11 39
(D M Simcock) *s.s: outpcd: styd on ins fnl f: nrst fin* **22/1**

0 **7** 1 **Tuppenny Piece**[16] 7380 2-9-0 0.......... AdamKirby 6 37
(W R Swinburn) *sn pushed along: a in rr* **16/1**

The Form Book, Raceform Ltd, Compton, RG20 6NL

8 ½ **Lovely Steps (USA)** 2-8-7 0 ChrisHough(7) 12 36
(D M Simcock) *dwlt: outpcd* **50/1**
5 **9** 6 **Floods Of Tears**[126] 4593 2-9-0 0 IanMongan 9 21
(D Flood) *mid-div: rdn 1/2-way: wknd over 2f out* **20/1**
0 **10** 17 **Spin Sister**[21] 7312 2-9-0 0 JimCrowley 8 —
(J Gallagher) *prom: hung rt fr 1/2-way: sn wknd* **80/1**
P **False Modesty** 2-9-0 0 ChrisCatlin 7 —
(George Baker) *s.i.s: sn outpcd: t.o whn p.u fnl 3f* **28/1**
1m 30.85s (1.25) **Going Correction** +0.075s/f (Slow) **11** Ran SP% **117.9**
Speed ratings (Par 93): **95,94,91,90,88 81,80,79,72,53** —
toteswinger: 1&2 £8.40, 1&3 £15.50, 2&3 £10.70 CSF £54.77 TOTE £13.10: £1.90, £1.90, £2.90; EX 56.70.
Owner Butt Scholes **Bred** Rozelle Bloodstock **Trained** Hampton, Cheshire

FOCUS
A maiden lacking much in the way of depth and one in which the market leader was a long way below her best. The pace was ordinary and the first two raced in the centre in the straight.

NOTEBOOK
Ajara(IRE) took advantage of the below-par run of the market leader when showing improved form to win in workmanlike fashion. She should stay 1m and may do better in run-of-the-mill handicaps. (op 7-1 tchd 11-1)
Volochkova(USA) bettered the form of her debut over this course and distance last month and, while she is likely to remain vulnerable to the better types in this grade, she should pick up an ordinary event once handicapped. (tchd 5-1 and 6-1)
Passage To India(IRE) had finished just in front of Volochkova over course and distance last time but failed to confirm placings with that rival. However, she was far from disgraced and is another who will appreciate the step into modest handicaps. (op 14-1 tchd 16-1)
Opera Wings, an 80,000gns first foal of a half-sister to the very smart Bankable, was fitted with a blanket and proved reluctant to load on this debut. She showed her inexperience in the race, too, but did shape with a degree of promise and she should be able to build on this assuming her temperament holds up. (op 11-2)
Rag And Bone(CAN) looked to have strong claims judging on her previous effort but proved a big disappointment, despite being allowed to do her own thing in front. She looks one to tread carefully with at skinny odds. Official explanation: jockey said the filly ran flat (op 6-4)
Anasy(USA), a $175,000 purchase who took the eye on pedigree, was too inexperienced to do herself justice on this debut but did hint at ability and is entitled to improve for the outing. (op 16-1)
Spin Sister Official explanation: jockey said filly hung badly right handed throughout
False Modesty Official explanation: Veterinary Officer said filly pulled up lame

7562 ENJOY EVENING RACING H'CAP 5f 20y(P)
8:20 (8:20) (Class 5) (0-75,75) 3-Y-O+ **£3,885** (£1,156; £577; £288) **Stalls** Low

Form RPR
0000 **1** **Canadian Danehill (IRE)**[16] 7384 6-9-4 **75** (p) EddieAhern 1 86
(R M H Cowell) *chsd ldrs: rdn to ld ins fnl f: r.o* **6/1**[3]
0403 **2** ½ **First Order**[3] 7534 7-8-13 **75** (v) AnnStokell(5) 3 84
(Miss A Stokell) *rdr slow to remove hood: dwlt: hdwy over 1f out: rdn ins fnl f: r.o* **13/2**
1220 **3** 1 **Figaro Flyer (IRE)**[25] 7276 5-8-13 **70** IanMongan 9 75
(P Howling) *wnt rt s: hld up: hdwy over 1f out: shkn up and edgd lft ins fnl f: r.o: nt rch ldrs* **12/1**
0022 **4** 1 **Cayman Fox**[25] 7276 3-9-0 **71** TomEaves 4 73
(James Moffatt) *led: rdn: edgd rt and hdd ins fnl f: no etxra* **8/1**
6024 **5** nk **Steel City Boy (IRE)**[31] 7182 5-8-13 **70** JimCrowley 6 71
(D Shaw) *s.i.s: hld up: nt clr run 2f out: sn rdn: styd on: nt trble ldrs* **4/1**[2]
0020 **6** 1 **Monsieur Reynard**[45] 6880 3-8-4 **66** ow1 MCGeran(5) 8 63
(J M Bradley) *trckd ldrs: rdn over 1f out: styd on same pce fnl f* **22/1**
0013 **7** 3 **Fast Freddie**[15] 7393 4-9-2 **73** AdamKirby 2 59
(S Parr) *chsd ldrs: wnt 2nd 1/2-way tl rdn and edgd rt over 1f out: wknd ins fnl f* **2/1**[1]
3000 **8** 2 **Ten Down**[15] 7393 3-8-11 **68** FrancisNorton 5 47
(M Quinn) *chsd ldr tl rdn 1/2-way: wknd over 1f out* **20/1**
9 16 **Just For Mary**[238] 1317 4-9-2 **73** JamieSpencer 7 —
(P J Rothwell, Ire) *sn outpcd* **16/1**
61.90 secs (-0.40) **Going Correction** +0.075s/f (Slow) **9** Ran SP% **114.7**
Speed ratings (Par 103): **106,105,103,102,101 99,95,91,66**
toteswinger: 1&2 £31.50, 1&3 £43.10, 2&3 £10.50 CSF £44.30 CT £455.47 TOTE £7.30: £2.60, £2.40, £3.60; EX 32.10.
Owner T W Morley **Bred** Skymarc Farm Inc And Dr A J O'Reilly **Trained** Six Mile Bottom, Cambs

FOCUS
Exposed performers in this ordinary sprint handicap. The pace was sound throughout and the principals again raced up the centre in the straight. The form looks solid for the grade.
Canadian Danehill(IRE) Official explanation: trainer said, regarding the apparent improvement in form, gelding settled better and was suited by the draw

7563 DINE IN THE HORIZONS RESTAURANT H'CAP 1m 4f 50y(P)
8:50 (8:50) (Class 5) (0-75,75) 3-Y-O+ **£3,885** (£1,156; £577; £288) **Stalls** Low

Form RPR
53-0 **1** **Nobelix (IRE)**[39] 7025 6-9-9 **75** MartinDwyer 3 86
(J R Gask) *mde all: pushed clr 3f out: rdn out* **9/1**
60-1 **2** 3 **Little Carmela**[18] 7355 4-8-8 **65** WilliamCarson(5) 1 71
(S C Williams) *chsd ldrs: rdn 3f out: chsd wnr fnl f: no imp* **6/1**
0004 **3** hd **William's Way**[16] 7385 6-9-0 **66** JimCrowley 5 72+
(I A Wood) *s.s: hld up: nt clr run 2f out: swtchd rt over 1f out: r.o wl ins fnl f: nrst fin* **13/2**
2542 **4** 1½ **Potentiale (IRE)**[16] 7385 4-9-5 **71** (p) EddieAhern 6 74
(J W Hills) *hld up in tch: rdn over 1f out: styd on same pce* **7/2**[2]
3234 **5** nse **Penang Cinta**[41] 6983 5-8-7 **64** (p) AndreaAtzeni(5) 2 67
(P D Evans) *chsd wnr: rdn over 2f out: eased whn btn ins fnl f* **11/4**[1]
2022 **6** 5 **Arts Guild (USA)**[22] 7304 3-9-4 **75** (p) ChrisCatlin 7 70
(W J Musson) *hld up: racd keenly: rdn over 2f out: hung lft over 1f out: nt run on* **9/2**[3]
0500 **7** 2¾ **Kames Park (IRE)**[7] 7473 6-9-3 **74** PBradley(5) 8 65
(I W McInnes) *s.s: hld up: rdn over 2f out: wknd fnl f* **25/1**
2m 45.31s (4.21) **Going Correction** +0.075s/f (Slow)
WFA 3 from 4yo+ 5lb **7** Ran SP% **108.5**
Speed ratings (Par 103): **88,86,85,84,84 81,79**
toteswinger: 1&2 £22.50, 1&3 £22.50, 2&3 £5.00. CSF £54.70 CT £336.30 TOTE £17.50: £5.70, £1.90; EX 55.60.
Owner Resurrection Partners **Bred** Horst Rapp And Dieter Burkle **Trained** Sutton Veny, Wilts
■ Stewards' Enquiry : Andrea Atzeni four-day ban: dropped hands and lost fourth place (Dec 19-22)

FOCUS
Another ordinary handicap in which the winner was allowed to do his own thing in front. The form has been rated around the third but does not look entirely reliable. The winner raced centre to far side in the straight.

7564 WOLVERHAMPTON-RACECOURSE.CO.UK H'CAP 1m 141y(P)
9:20 (9:20) (Class 4) (0-85,83) 3-Y-O+ **£5,677** (£1,699; £849; £424; £211) **Stalls** Low

Form RPR
0031 **1** **Spinning**[25] 7278 5-8-13 **76** (b) TomEaves 2 85
(T D Barron) *hld up: hdwy over 1f out: rdn to ld ins fnl f: r.o* **9/2**[2]
6122 **2** ½ **Follow The Flag (IRE)**[6] 7495 4-8-6 **69** oh2 (p) JimmyQuinn 6 77
(A J McCabe) *chsd ldrs: rdn 3f out: led over 1f out: sn edgd rt: hdd ins fnl f: r.o u.p* **5/1**[3]
1633 **3** ¾ **Jawaab (IRE)**[25] 7278 4-8-13 **76** MartinDwyer 3 82
(W R Muir) *chsd ldrs: rdn over 1f out: styd on* **7/2**[1]
0042 **4** ¾ **Just Bond (IRE)**[6] 7502 6-9-3 **83** DuranFentiman(3) 4 88
(G R Oldroyd) *hld up: hdwy over 1f out: sn rdn and hung rt: styd on* **9/2**[2]
0000 **5** nk **Silver Hotspur**[25] 7278 4-8-12 **75** LPKeniry 1 79
(C R Dore) *hld up: nt clr run over 1f out: r.o ins fnl f: nvr nrr* **12/1**
0041 **6** 1 **Direct Debit (IRE)**[13] 7423 5-9-3 **80** AdamKirby 9 82
(M Wellings) *prom: rdn over 1f out: styd on same pce ins fnl f* **10/1**
2302 **7** 2¼ **Murfreesboro**[13] 7423 5-9-6 **83** (v) FrancisNorton 7 79
(D Shaw) *hld up: rdn over 1f out: nt trble ldrs* **12/1**
005 **8** 3½ **The Kiddykid (IRE)**[11] 7439 8-9-6 **83** TGMcLaughlin 8 71
(P D Evans) *led: rdn and hdd 2f out: wknd and eased fnl f* **9/1**
0100 **9** 4 **Bee Stinger**[229] 1502 6-9-4 **81** (v) JimCrowley 5 60
(I A Wood) *chsd ldr tl led 2f out: sn rdn and hdd: wknd fnl f* **18/1**
1m 50.69s (0.19) **Going Correction** +0.075s/f (Slow) **9** Ran SP% **115.0**
Speed ratings (Par 105): **102,101,100,100,99 99,97,93,90**
toteswinger: 1&2 £1.80, 1&3 £18.90, 2&3 £4.20 CSF £27.15 CT £87.64 TOTE £6.70: £2.20, £2.30, £2.40; EX 11.80 Place 6 £3,289.03, Place 5 £194.14..
Owner Mrs J Hazell **Bred** Cheveley Park Stud **Trained** Maunby, N Yorks

FOCUS
A fair handicap run at a reasonable gallop and the form looks sound enough rated around the second and third. The winner raced towards the centre but the entire field fanned across the track in the straight.
T/Plt: £7,314.60 to a £1 stake. Pool £103,207.00 - 10.30 winning tickets. T/Qpdt: £182.40 to a £1 stake. Pool £11,956.06 - 48.50 winning tickets. CR

7568 - 7572a (Foreign Racing) - See Raceform Interactive

7542 GREAT LEIGHS (A.W) (L-H)
Saturday, December 6

OFFICIAL GOING: Standard
Wind: Moderate, half-against Weather: bright and chilly

7573 FREE BETS @ FREEBETS.CO.UK H'CAP 1m 5f 66y(P)
1:55 (1:55) (Class 6) (0-60,59) 3-Y-O+ **£2,266** (£674; £337; £168) **Stalls** Centre

Form RPR
3002 **1** **Lapina (IRE)**[14] 7427 4-9-7 **56** (b) JamieSpencer 7 67
(A Middleton) *t.k.h: hld up in midfield on inner: hdwy to trck ldrs over 2f out: qcknd to ld over 1f out: edgd lft but sn rdn clr: eased nr fin* **10/3**[1]
0443 **2** 5 **Generous Star**[10] 7455 5-9-9 **58** JimmyQuinn 2 62
(J Pearce) *chsd ldng pair: rdn and ev ch over 1f out: outpcd by wnr ent fnl f: kpt on same pce* **9/1**
00-3 **3** shd **North Walk (IRE)**[34] 3687 5-9-5 **54** (p) FergusSweeney 6 57
(Tim Vaughan) *trckd ldrs: rdn to chse ldr over 2f out: ev ch over 1f out: outpcd by wnr ent fnl f: kpt on same pce* **9/2**[2]
4344 **4** 2½ **Sabancaya**[18] 7376 3-9-1 **56** MickyFenton 11 56
(Mrs P Sly) *hld up in tch in midfield: rdn over 2f out: c wd st: plugged on u.p to go 4th ins fnl f: nvr threatened ldrs* **11/1**
6200 **5** nk **Bienheureux**[53] 6727 7-9-4 **53** (t) NCallan 8 52
(Miss Gay Kelleway) *in tch: nt clr run briefly and swtchd rt over 2f out: rdn and outpcd wl over 1f out: wl hld fnl f* **14/1**
002 **6** nk **Dontpaytheferryman (USA)**[17] 7379 3-9-0 **55** (t) TGMcLaughlin 9 54
(P D Evans) *t.k.h: hld up towards rr: rdn and hdwy wl over 2f out: no imp fr over 1f out: nvr nr ldrs* **8/1**[3]
2103 **7** 2½ **Little Richard (IRE)**[33] 7169 9-9-10 **59** (p) AdamKirby 12 54
(M Wellings) *in tch: rdn wl over 2f out: chsd ldrs and drvn 2f out: wknd over 1f out* **12/1**
4500 **8** ½ **Touch Of Style (IRE)**[18] 7376 4-9-10 **59** (e) PatCosgrave 10 53
(J R Boyle) *stdd and dropped in bhd after s: t.k.h: hld up bhd: rdn and effrt 3f out: drvn over 1f out: nvr nr ldrs* **16/1**
0650 **9** ½ **Jemiliah**[44] 6928 3-8-13 **54** DaneO'Neill 13 47
(B G Powell) *stdd and dropped in bhd after s: hld up in rr: sme hdwy fnl f: nvr trbld ldrs* **20/1**
055- **10** nk **Kanonkop**[13] 3083 4-8-8 **48** AndreaAtzeni(5) 4 41
(M J Gingell) *rrd s: a bhd: rdn 5f out: nvr nr ldrs* **40/1**
4060 **11** 2 **Vanquisher (IRE)**[11] 7447 4-9-5 **54** StephenDonohoe 5 44
(Ian Williams) *chsd ldr: rdn to ld 3f out: hdd over 1f out: sn wknd u.p* **14/1**
000/ **12** 1¾ **Goblin**[890] 1672 7-9-8 **57** ChrisCatlin 3 44
(D E Cantillon) *stdd s: t.k.h: struggling over 3f out: wl btn after* **20/1**
0260 **13** 1½ **Oberlin (USA)**[11] 7447 3-9-2 **57** (b[1]) TonyCulhane 1 42
(T Keddy) *led tl rdn and hdd 3f out: wknd u.p wl over 1f out* **20/1**
3-50 **14** 26 **Sovereign Spirit (IRE)**[9] 6577 6-9-10 **59** JimCrowley 14 5
(C Gordon) *t.k.h: hld up in rr: rdn and struggling 4f out: wl bhd and eased fnl f: t.o* **20/1**
2m 54.46s (0.86) **Going Correction** 0.0s/f (Stan)
WFA 3 from 4yo+ 6lb **14** Ran SP% **119.1**
Speed ratings (Par 101): **97,93,93,92,92 91,90,90,89,89 88,87,86,70**
toteswinger: 1&2 £3.70, 1&3 £10.70, 2&3 £9.00. CSF £29.65 CT £138.72 TOTE £3.80: £1.70, £3.90, £2.50; EX 25.00 Trifecta £144.60 Part won. Pool £195.47 - 0.53 winning units..
Owner R J Matthews **Bred** W Maxwell Ervine **Trained** Granborough, Bucks

FOCUS
A very moderate staying handicap and modest form rated around the placed horses.
Little Richard(IRE) Official explanation: jockey said gelding hung right

7574 FREE SOCCER BETS @ FREEBETS.CO.UK MAIDEN AUCTION STKS 5f (P)
2:30 (2:31) (Class 5) 2-Y-O **£2,590** (£770; £385; £192) **Stalls** Centre

Form RPR
0532 **1** **Desert Strike**[32] 7179 2-8-11 70 NelsonDeSouza 9 73
(P F I Cole) *chsd ldrs tl lft 2nd over 3f out: ev ch over 1f out: drvn to ld fnl 100yds: styd on wl* **11/2**[3]

35 **2** ¾ **Bobs Dreamflight**[19] 7356 2-8-9 0........ ChrisCatlin 2 71+
(D K Ivory) *in tch: chsng ldrs and n.m.r jst ins fnl f: sn swtchd rt: r.o to go 2nd towards fin: unable to rch wnr* **9/4**[1]

4542 **3** 1 **Barnezet (GR)**[8] 7464 2-8-7 68........ PatrickHills(3) 7 66
(R Hannon) *chsd ldng pair tl lft in ld over 3f out: hrd pressed and rdn over 1f out: hdd fnl 100yds: no ex* **7/1**

4 ½ **Desert Bump** 2-8-8 0........ LPKeniry 5 62+
(E F Vaughan) *s.i.s: bhd: hdwy 2f out: styng on whn swtchd lft ins fnl f: gng on fin: nt rch ldrs* **20/1**

50 **5** hd **Silky Way (GR)**[68] 6327 2-8-6 0........ JimmyQuinn 4 59
(P R Chamings) *in tch in midfield: hdwy over 2f out: kpt on ins fnl f: nt pce to chal ldrs* **20/1**

5223 **6** 2 **Bees River (IRE)**[29] 7219 2-8-10 65........ NCallan 10 56
(A P Jarvis) *wnt rt s: sn chsng ldr: carried wd and dropped to 3rd over 3f out: rdn over 1f out: wknd ins fnl f* **6/1**

7 1¾ **Brynfa Boy** 2-8-11 0........ DarryllHolland 3 51+
(P W D'Arcy) *rn green in rr: c wd 2f out: edgd lft over 1f out: kpt on fnl f but nvr nr ldrs* **17/2**

0342 **8** 5 **Our Wee Girl (IRE)**[10] 7452 2-8-8 70........ JamieSpencer 6 30
(S Kirk) *led tl hung bdly rt bnd over 3f out: sn hdd: in tch after: rdn and wknd over 1f out: eased ins fnl f* **7/2**[2]

06 **9** 5 **Contradiktive (IRE)**[14] 7417 2-8-11 0........ PatCosgrave 8 15
(J R Boyle) *sn bhd: rn wd and drvn over 3f out: sn wl bhd* **66/1**

60.68 secs (0.48) **Going Correction** 0.0s/f (Stan) **9** Ran SP% **116.7**
Speed ratings (Par 96): **96,94,93,92,92 88,86,78,70**
toteswinger: 1&2 £7.50, 1&3 £6.10, 2&3 £5.50. CSF £18.11 TOTE £7.20: £2.00, £1.50, £3.00; EX 22.30 Trifecta £141.20 Pool £465.60 - 2.44 winning units..
Owner P F I Cole Ltd **Bred** Mrs Mary Rowlands **Trained** Whatcombe, Oxon

FOCUS
A modest sprint maiden.

NOTEBOOK
Desert Strike, runner-up over 6f on Fibresand last time, proved suited by the drop in trip and just did enough to get off the mark at the fifth attempt. This was a reasonable effort considering he was poorly drawn, but he was arguably a touch fortunate to hold off the extremely well-backed Bobs Dreamflight. (op 5-1)
Bobs Dreamflight ◆ looked a little unlucky as he was further back than ideal after being slow to find his stride and just got going too late having had to switch in the straight. His debut third at Sandown in the summer has been well advertised, and he should be good enough to win a similar race if connections so choose, but the handicap route will surely be tempting if he gets a mark of around 70. (op 9-2)
Barnezet(GR), having her ninth start, ran her race and this looks as good as she is. (op 5-1)
Desert Bump, a 17,000gns purchase, out of a 1m winner, gradually got the idea and finished nicely on her debut. This was a pleasing debut and she is open to improvement, particularly when stepped up in trip, but the fact she was also entered in a claimer tempers enthusiasm a touch. (op 25-1 tchd 16-1)
Silky Way(GR) is with a yard that can do well with sprinters and she should step up on this now she is qualified for a handicap mark.
Bees River(IRE) Official explanation: jockey said filly lost her action in the last 50yds; Veterinary Officer said the filly finished lame
Our Wee Girl(IRE) proved virtually impossible to steer around the bend and did not convince with her action in the straight. Official explanation: jockey said filly hung right throughout (op 3-1 tchd 11-4)

7575 FREE BETTING @ FREEBETS.CO.UK NURSERY 5f (P)
3:00 (3:01) (Class 4) (0-85,81) 2-Y-O **£4,209** (£1,252; £625; £312) **Stalls** Centre

Form RPR

0113 **1** **Rainbow Seeker**[21] 7335 2-9-4 78........(b) JamieSpencer 9 88+
(W J Haggas) *hld up in last pair: gd hdwy over 1f out: pushed into ld ins fnl f: sn clr: comf* **5/2**[2]

510 **2** 2¼ **Moscow Eight (IRE)**[56] 6644 2-9-7 81........ ChrisCatlin 7 80
(E J O'Neill) *stdd and dropped in bhd after s: plld hrd in rr: hdwy ent fnl f: r.o to go 2nd nr fin: no ch w wnr* **2/1**[1]

356 **3** hd **Love You Louis**[21] 7334 2-9-3 77........(v) JimCrowley 6 75
(J R Jenkins) *led at gd pce: rdn and edgd lft over 1f out: hdd ins fnl f: no ch w wnr after: lost 2nd nr fin* **18/1**

4201 **4** 1½ **Sharpener (IRE)**[14] 7417 2-8-11 71........ DaneO'Neill 2 64
(R Hannon) *hmpd s: racd in midfield: rdn and hdwy to chse ldrs over 2f out: edgd lft and one pce ent fnl f* **7/1**[3]

3633 **5** nk **Agnes Love**[36] 7113 2-8-1 61........ JimmyQuinn 1 53
(J Akehurst) *chsd ldr: rdn wl over 1f out: wknd jst ins fnl f* **8/1**

5660 **6** 1¼ **Chambers (IRE)**[10] 7454 2-7-12 58........ NickyMackay 10 45
(M Johnston) *in tch in midfield: rdn and struggling over 2f out: no imp fr over 1f out* **20/1**

0442 **7** 1¼ **Sweet Applause (IRE)**[36] 7113 2-9-2 76........ NCallan 8 59
(A P Jarvis) *chsd ldrs: rdn and unable qck over 1f out: eased whn btn ins fnl f* **8/1**

400 **8** nk **Ruby Tallulah**[21] 7335 2-8-13 73........ LPKeniry 3 55
(C R Dore) *bmpd s: sn in tch: rdn 2f out: wknd ent fnl f* **14/1**

5426 **9** 4½ **Sally's Dilemma**[22] 7308 2-8-4 69........(t) JackDean(5) 4 35
(W G M Turner) *racd in midfield: rdn 1/2-way: drvn and dropped to rr 2f out: n.d after* **20/1**

60.26 secs (0.06) **Going Correction** 0.0s/f (Stan) **9** Ran SP% **118.1**
Speed ratings (Par 98): **99,95,95,92,92 90,88,87,80**
toteswinger: 1&2 £5.10, 1&3 £7.60, 2&3 £8.00. CSF £8.13 CT £67.68 TOTE £3.30: £1.40, £1.40, £3.80; EX 10.20 Trifecta £95.00 Pool £432.98 - 3.37 winning units..
Owner Dwayne Woods **Bred** Brook Stud Bloodstock Ltd **Trained** Newmarket, Suffolk

FOCUS
Just a fair nursery in which the pace was very strong, resulting in a juvenile course record, and the first two home were well behind early.

NOTEBOOK
Rainbow Seeker ◆ won with loads in hand and looks capable of rating a fair bit higher. He did not get the runs of things when a beaten favourite over 6f here last time, but he proved well suited by the strong pace and comfortably made up the required ground when getting a run towards the inside early in the straight. He wears blinkers and gives the impression he might not be totally straightforward, but he is significantly better than his current rating of 78 and will be dangerous in some decent sprints when he has a strong pace to chase. (tchd 2-1 and 11-4 in places)
Moscow Eight(IRE), well beaten in a Group 3 at Ascot after winning his maiden on the Polytrack at Lingfield, raced keenly under restraint early on and could only follow the winner through in the straight. He has plenty of ability, but will need to learn to settle before he can really progress. (op 9-4 tchd 5-2)
Love You Louis ◆ deserves credit as he set a scorching pace, yet was only passed by a couple of decent rivals. His natural speed should see him wins handicaps. (op 16-1)
Sharpener(IRE) looked a touch flattered by her recent Lingfield maiden success and this was tougher. (tchd 8-1)
Agnes Love will be better off in a lower grade (op 9-1 tchd 10-1)
Sweet Applause(IRE) Official explanation: jockey said filly moved very poorly
Ruby Tallulah ◆ was by no means given a hard time in the straight and is one to keep an eye on. (op 16-1)

7576 FREE BETTING EXCHANGE BETS @ FREEBETS.CO.UK H'CAP 6f (P)
3:30 (3:30) (Class 2) (0-100,102) 3-Y+ **£11,354** (£3,398; £1,699; £849; £423) **Stalls** Centre

Form RPR

2333 **1** **Lone Wolfe**[16] 7394 4-8-0 87........ AndreaAtzeni(5) 7 97
(Jane Chapple-Hyam) *led for 1f: chsd ldr tl led again wl over 1f out: edgd lft but styd on wl fnl f* **6/1**[3]

3132 **2** 1 **Diriculous**[45] 6903 4-9-4 100........ NCallan 5 107
(T G Mills) *trckd ldrs: rdn and edging lft over 1f out: chsd wnr ins fnl f: kpt on same pce* **13/8**[1]

5034 **3** ½ **Matsunosuke**[19] 7365 6-8-8 90........ DarryllHolland 8 95+
(A B Coogan) *stdd after s: hld up in last pl: hdwy over 1f out: r.o fnl f: wnt 3rd nr fin: nt rch ldrs* **12/1**

1424 **4** ½ **Beat The Bell**[14] 7418 3-8-5 92........ NicolPolli(5) 1 96
(A Bailey) *chsd ldrs: pressed wnr and rdn over 1f out: kpt on same pce fnl 100yds* **7/2**[2]

002 **5** hd **Biniou (IRE)**[16] 7394 5-8-8 90........ EddieAhern 2 93
(R M H Cowell) *dwlt: sn in midfield: c wd and rdn 2f out: kpt on ins fnl f: nvr rchd ldrs* **15/2**

0031 **6** 2¾ **Fyodor (IRE)**[16] 7394 7-9-6 102........ LPKeniry 3 96
(C R Dore) *t.k.h: hld up in last trio: shkn up over 1f out: kpt on same pce and nvr trbld ldrs* **7/1**

1500 **7** ¾ **Vhujon (IRE)**[19] 7365 3-8-4 86........ SimonWhitworth 6 78
(P D Evans) *stdd after s: hld up in last pair: n.d* **25/1**

4502 **8** 6 **Maltese Falcon**[14] 7421 8-9-3 99........(t) NelsonDeSouza 4 72
(P F I Cole) *chsd ldr tl led after 1f: hdd wl over 1f out: sn wknd* **12/1**

1m 12.03s (-1.67) **Going Correction** 0.0s/f (Stan) **8** Ran SP% **118.1**
Speed ratings (Par 109): **111,109,109,108,108 104,103,95**
toteswinger: 1&2 £17.70, 1&3 not won, 2&3 £4.30. CSF £16.78 CT £116.81 TOTE £7.10: £1.40, £1.60, £2.80; EX 29.70 Trifecta £352.40 Pool £585.86 - 1.23 winning units..
Owner Gordon Li **Bred** P T Tellwright **Trained** Lambourn, Berks

FOCUS
A good sprint handicap run at a good gallop and solid form.

NOTEBOOK
Lone Wolfe, who had been running some decent races in defeat lately, enjoyed the run of the things just in behind early leader Maltese Falcon and stayed on best to reverse recent course and distance placings with Fyodor and Biniou. He's clearly very useful, but everything went his way this time, and his rider's 5lb claim was also a big help. (op 11-2)
Diriculous travelled well to a point and touched 1.55 in-running, but he edged left and found one too good on the day. He was short of room near the line, but it made no difference to the result. His trainer expressed concerns beforehand that the track might have been riding a little quicker than ideal and that may well have been his undoing. (op 15-8 tchd 2-1)
Matsunosuke stayed on from last to grab third, but he was never quite getting there and this extended his losing run to 22 races. (op 11-1)
Beat The Bell has progressed into a very decent type, but the Handicapper might just have him now. (op 9-2)
Biniou(IRE) continues to prove hard to win with. (op 8-1 tchd 9-1)
Fyodor(IRE) was another to trade short in-running, but he needs to get there on the bridle and he found little when forced to come under pressure. (op 13-2 tchd 6-1)
Maltese Falcon is probably best watched until returned to Lingfield. (op 9-1)

7577 FREE BETS ONLINE @ FREEBETS.CO.UK MAIDEN FILLIES' STKS (DIV I) 1m (P)
4:00 (4:02) (Class 5) 2-Y-O **£2,590** (£770; £385; £192) **Stalls** Centre

Form RPR

5 **1** **Faldal**[21] 7332 2-9-0 0........ RichardKingscote 2 80+
(Tom Dascombe) *mde all: rdn wl over 1f out: clr ent fnl f: rdn out: easily* **7/2**[2]

0 **2** 4½ **Luckier (IRE)**[21] 7341 2-9-0 0........ LPKeniry 6 70
(S Kirk) *hld up in tch in midfield: hdwy to chse ldng pair over 2f out: rdn and no hdwy over 1f out: wnt 2nd fnl 100yds: no ch w wnr* **16/1**

2 **3** 1¼ **Aurora Sky (IRE)**[22] 7312 2-9-0 0........ NCallan 8 67
(J Akehurst) *t.k.h: chsd wnr: rdn over 1f out: btn ent fnl f: lost 2nd fnl 100yds* **1/1**[1]

00 **4** 2 **Eurotanz (IRE)**[12] 7434 2-9-0 0........ TravisBlock 5 63
(H Morrison) *in tch in midfield: rdn and effrt on outer 3f out: sn outpcd by ldrs: wnt modest 4th over 2f out: plugged on but nvr nr ldrs* **14/1**[3]

0 **5** 9 **Tattercoats (FR)**[17] 7380 2-8-11 0........ MarcHalford(3) 4 43
(D M Simcock) *s.i.s: bhd: nvr nr ldrs* **33/1**

00 **6** shd **Ballade De La Mer**[24] 7282 2-9-0 0........ AdamKirby 3 43
(A J McCabe) *towards rr: reminder 5f out: lost tch over 3f out: wl bhd after* **33/1**

0 **7** 2¼ **Peace In Paradise (IRE)**[35] 7141 2-9-0 0........ GregFairley 1 38
(J A R Toller) *s.i.s: in tch tl rdn and struggling over 3f out: wl bhd fnl 2f* **20/1**

0 **8** ½ **Seminal Moment**[21] 7341 2-9-0 0........ PatCosgrave 7 37
(J G Given) *rn green: chsd ldrs: rdn and wknd qckly 3f out: wl bhd fnl 2f* **20/1**

4 **9** nk **Port De La Ponche**[124] 4692 2-9-0 0........ NelsonDeSouza 9 36
(P F I Cole) *in tch: chsd ldrs and rdn over 2f out: sn wknd: wl btn fnl 2f: eased ins fnl f* **7/2**[2]

1m 40.89s (0.99) **Going Correction** 0.0s/f (Stan) **9** Ran SP% **122.4**
Speed ratings (Par 93): **95,90,89,87,78 78,75,75,75**
toteswinger: 1&2 £13.60, 1&3 £2.40, 2&3 £5.00. CSF £54.87 TOTE £4.70: £1.10, £4.00, £1.10; EX 57.60 Trifecta £195.60 Pool £639.95 - 2.42 winning units..
Owner Mrs Bernadette Quinn **Bred** Mr & Mrs J Quinn **Trained** Lambourn, Berks

FOCUS
A weak fillies' maiden.

NOTEBOOK
Faldal ◆ improved on the form she showed when fifth in a similar race over this course and distance on her British debut. Just like last time, she was inclined to look around a bit and carry her head a touch high, but she basically just still seems very babyish. Although this wasn't much of a race, she could be quite useful if she matures as one would hope. (op 4-1)
Luckier(IRE) stepped up significantly on the form she showed when beaten a long way over 7f on her debut at Wolverhampton, but it would probably be unwise to get carried away. (op 14-1)
Aurora Sky(IRE) was well below the form she showed when runner-up over 7f on her debut at Kempton. She did not get home after racing keenly early, and a drop back in trip should suit, but it remains to be seen if she can progress. (op 13-8)

The Form Book, Raceform Ltd, Compton, RG20 6NL

Eurotanz(IRE) looks pretty limited, but she now has the option of handicaps. (op 12-1)

7578 FREE BETS ONLINE @ FREEBETS.CO.UK MAIDEN FILLIES' STKS (DIV II) 1m (P)
4:30 (4:32) (Class 5) 2-Y-O **£2,590** (£770; £385; £192) **Stalls** Centre

Form RPR
43 **1** **Three Ducks**[17] 7380 2-9-0 0 DaneO'Neill 4 70+
(L M Cumani) *mde all: rdn and drew clr over 1f out: in command fnl f: eased towards fin* **11/8**[1]
44 **2** 1 1/4 **Moonbeam Dancer (USA)**[14] 7424 2-9-0 0 StephenDonohoe 2 66
(D M Simcock) *in tch in midfield: rdn 3f out: hdwy u.p 2f out: chsd wnr and edgd rt ent fnl f: kpt on but nvr threatened wnr* **15/2**
3 2 **Rapid Light** 2-9-0 0 TGMcLaughlin 8 62+
(E A L Dunlop) *in tch in midfield: rdn and outpcd over 2f out: rallied u.p over 1f out: wnt 3rd ins fnl f: kpt on* **20/1**
4 3 **Better In Time (USA)** 2-9-0 0 FrankieMcDonald 7 55
(Jane Chapple-Hyam) *chsd ldrs on outer: rdn 2f out: wknd ent fnl f* **20/1**
5 3/4 **Queens Flight** 2-9-0 0 DarryllHolland 5 54
(J Noseda) *chsd wnr: rdn over 1f out: lost 2nd ent fnl f: wknd* **3/1**[2]
6 1 3/4 **Beat Faster** 2-9-0 0 PatCosgrave 3 50
(J G Given) *v.s.a: rn green: towards rr: rdn and outpcd over 3f out: n.d after* **25/1**
7 1 1/4 **Miss Christophene (IRE)** 2-9-0 0 JimmyQuinn 10 47
(Mrs S Lamyman) *a bhd: lost tch wl over 2f out: nvr trbld ldrs* **66/1**
8 3/4 **Gaelic Rose (IRE)** 2-9-0 0 JamieSpencer 1 45
(S Kirk) *chsd ldrs tl and dropped out qckly over 3f out: wl bhd fnl 2f* **11/1**
9 2 1/4 **Hallingdal Blue (UAE)** 2-9-0 0 EddieAhern 9 40
(H R A Cecil) *in tch: rdn and hld hd high over 2f out: sn wknd: wl bhd wl over 1f out* **11/2**[3]
10 *shd* **Arabian Silk (IRE)** 2-8-7 0 ChrisHough(7) 6 40
(D M Simcock) *a bhd: lost tch over 3f out: wl bhd fnl 2f* **33/1**

1m 41.4s (1.50) **Going Correction** 0.0s/f (Stan) 33 Ran SP% **120.4**
Speed ratings (Par 93): **92,90,88,85,85 83,82,81,79,78**
toteswinger: 1&2 £3.50, 1&3 £14.90, 2&3 £11.40. CSF £12.21 TOTE £2.90: £1.10, £2.60, £5.00; EX 11.00 Trifecta £163.50 Pool £848.76 - 3.84 winning units..
Owner Mrs James Wigan **Bred** Mrs James Wigan **Trained** Newmarket, Suffolk

FOCUS
More strength in depth than the first division, but still just an ordinary fillies' maiden.

NOTEBOOK
Three Ducks was a shade disappointing when only third over 7f at Kempton (joint favourite) last time, but she proved well suited by this step up to 1m and comfortably got off the mark at the third attempt. Things are likely to be tougher from now on, but she might be open to more improvement next year. (op 13-8 tchd 5-4 & 7-4 in a place)
Moonbeam Dancer(USA) ran her race, but she was basically beaten by a better filly on the day. She now has the option of handicaps. (op 8-1 tchd 7-1)
Rapid Light, a 26,000gns purchase, kept on from off the pace and this was a respectable debut. She ran to just a modest level, but is entitled to improve. (op 16-1)
Better In Time(USA), a $13,000 purchase, showed ability on her debut.
Queens Flight, who is out of a 1m-1m3f winner, although she didn't see her race out after appearing to get tired. (op 4-1)
Hallingdal Blue(UAE), a 15,000gns purchase, out of a 5f winner, showed ability to a point, but she looked a horrible ride and seemed to absolutely hate the kickback. Even though this was her debut, she looks one to have reservations about. (op 5-1)

7579 FREE ONLINE SPORTS BETTING @ FREEBETS.CO.UK H'CAP 1m 2f (P)
5:00 (5:02) (Class 2) (0-100,103) 3-Y-O+
£11,215 (£3,358; £1,679; £840; £419; £210) **Stalls** Centre

Form RPR
2111 **1** **Suits Me**[7] 7496 5-9-10 103 MickyFenton 4 112
(T P Tate) *mde all: rdn 2 l clr jst over 1f out: pushed out and kpt on wl: a holding rivals after* **3/1**[1]
2 1/2 **Bon Spiel**[90] 4-8-9 88 DaneO'Neill 3 96
(L M Cumani) *hld up in tch: rdn 3f out: hdwy u.p over 1f out: chsd wnr ins fnl f: kpt on but nvr gng to rch wnr* **6/1**
2006 **3** 1 1/4 **Big Robert**[7] 7496 4-9-5 98 FergusSweeney 1 104
(K R Burke) *dwlt: hld up in last pl: c wd and effrt 2f out: kpt on u.p to go 3rd ins fnl f: nvr able to chal wnr* **4/1**[3]
3023 **4** 1 **Moynahan (USA)**[7] 7496 3-9-2 98 JamieSpencer 6 102
(P F I Cole) *in tch: rdn to chse ldng pair 2f out: wknd ins fnl f* **10/3**[2]
0642 **5** 3/4 **Mafeking (UAE)**[7] 7496 4-8-8 87 JimCrowley 5 89
(M R Hoad) *t.k.h: chsd wnr rdn and unable qck over 1f out: lost 2nd ins fnl f: wknd fnl 100yds* **7/1**
0053 **6** 2 1/2 **Kayak (SAF)**[22] 7313 6-8-8 87 (b) StephenDonohoe 2 84
(D M Simcock) *chsd ldrs: rdn wl over 2f out: wknd u.p jst ins fnl f* **14/1**
1000 **7** 4 **Art Man**[7] 7496 5-8-8 87 EddieAhern 7 76
(G L Moore) *in tch: rdn over 2f out: wknd and hung lft over 1f out: no ch fnl f* **13/2**

2m 6.80s (-1.80) **Going Correction** 0.0s/f (Stan)
WFA 3 from 4yo+ 3lb 7 Ran SP% **114.9**
Speed ratings (Par 109): **107,106,105,104,104 102,99**
toteswinger: 1&2 £4.80, 1&3 £3.60, 2&3 £24.00. CSF £21.47 TOTE £4.50: £1.40, £4.60; EX 11.60.
Owner D E Cook **Bred** R S A Urquhart **Trained** Tadcaster, N Yorks
■ Stewards' Enquiry : Dane O'Neill one-day ban: using whip down the shoulder in forehand position (Dec 20)

FOCUS
A very good handicap but the winner was allowed to set just an ordinary pace. The form appears sound enough.

NOTEBOOK
Suits Me was very much allowed his own way in the lead and needed just hands-and-heels riding to hold off Bon Speil and complete the four-timer, confirming recent Kempton form with four of today's rivals. In defying a mark of 103 this rates as a career best, and he will probably have to switch to either conditions races or Listed company at some point. While there are a few opportunities in Britain for this type of horse during the course of the winter, his connections will surely have to consider chasing much bigger prizes on synthetic surfaces in the States. On a slightly different point, he continues to boost the form of the highly promising Expresso Star, who was the last horse to beat him and did so by three lengths. (op 7-2 tchd 4-1 in a place)
Bon Spiel ◆, a triple winner in Italy, ran a fine race on his British debut after three months off. Like most of these he probably would have preferred a stronger gallop, but he kept on nicely for pressure. He could progress into a very useful type for his new trainer. (op 8-1)
Big Robert would have preferred a stronger end-to-end gallop and he didn't run badly considering, reversing recent Kempton form with Mafeking and Moynahan. (op 5-1)
Moynahan(USA) is proving tricky to win with this year, but this was still a respectable effort in defeat. (op 3-1 tchd 7-2)
Mafeking(UAE) could not build on his recent Kempton second to today's winner. (op 6-1 tchd 11-2)

7580 PREMIERSHIP FOOTBALL BETS @ FREEBETS.CO.UK H'CAP 1m 2f (P)
5:30 (5:32) (Class 5) (0-70,73) 3-Y-O+ **£2,590** (£770; £385; £192) **Stalls** Centre

Form RPR
2232 **1** **Vine Street (IRE)**[21] 7342 3-8-13 65 DarryllHolland 2 76+
(M A Jarvis) *mde all: rdn wl over 1f out: styd on wl fnl f* **3/1**[1]
40-6 **2** 1 1/4 **Musashi (IRE)**[17] 7387 3-9-1 67 JohnEgan 5 75
(Jane Chapple-Hyam) *t.k.h: hld up in tch: rdn to chse wnr over 1f out: no imp fnl 100yds* **16/1**
4105 **3** 1 1/2 **Mr Napoleon (IRE)**[23] 7301 6-9-6 69 GeorgeBaker 3 74
(G L Moore) *hld up in last pl: hdwy on outer over 3f out: drvn over 1f out: swtchd lft jst ins fnl f: kpt on to go 3rd ins fnl f: nt pce to chal ldrs* **11/2**
6033 **4** 1 **Rehabilitation**[19] 7354 3-9-4 70 (p) AdamKirby 1 73
(W R Swinburn) *t.k.h: chsd wnr tl 7f out and again 3f out tl over 1f out: wknd ins fnl f* **4/1**[3]
0004 **5** 1/2 **New Beginning (IRE)**[19] 7364 4-9-6 69 JimmyQuinn 6 71
(Mrs S Lamyman) *stdd s and hld up in last trio: rdn and hdwy on inner 2f out: kpt on same pce u.p fnl f* **16/1**
0012 **6** 1 1/2 **Lord Theo**[12] 7440 4-9-4 67 JamesDoyle 4 66
(N P Littmoden) *hld up in tch: effrt u.p on outer 2f out: chsd ldrs over 1f out: wknd jst ins fnl f* **10/3**[2]
4206 **7** 20 **Wrighty Almighty (IRE)**[22] 7309 6-9-5 68 (t) JimCrowley 7 27
(P R Chamings) *stdd and dropped in bhd after s: rdn and no rspnse over 2f out: wl bhd over 1f out* **10/1**
2401 **8** 1 3/4 **Don Pietro**[9] 7461 5-9-10 73 NelsonDeSouza 8 29
(P A Blockley) *plld hrd: chsd wnr 7f out: rdn and wknd qckly 3f out: wl bhd and eased fnl f* **6/1**

2m 7.06s (-1.54) **Going Correction** 0.0s/f (Stan)
WFA 3 from 4yo+ 3lb 8 Ran SP% **118.6**
Speed ratings (Par 103): **106,105,103,103,102 101,85,84**
toteswinger: 1&2 £6.80, 1&3 £4.80, 2&3 £16.20. CSF £52.68 CT £257.76 TOTE £4.10: £1.30, £6.50, £2.40; EX 53.50 Trifecta £345.80 Pool £808.64 - 1.73 winning units. Place 6 £8.04, Place 5 £4.80..
Owner Sheikh Ahmed Al Maktoum **Bred** Darley **Trained** Newmarket, Suffolk

FOCUS
A modest handicap and the form looks solid rated around the third and fourth.
T/Plt: £7.30 to a £1 stake. Pool: £51,485.03. 5,111.66 winning tickets. T/Qpdt: £3.50 to a £1 stake. Pool: £3,558.92. 745.46 winning tickets. SP

7559 WOLVERHAMPTON (A.W) (L-H)
Saturday, December 6

OFFICIAL GOING: Standard
Wind: Almost nil Weather: Fine

7581 HORSE BETTING WITH FREEBETS.CO.UK H'CAP (DIV I) 1m 141y(P)
6:20 (6:21) (Class 6) (0-58,58) 3-Y-O+ **£2,047** (£604; £302) **Stalls** Low

Form RPR
000/ **1** **Alf Tupper**[22] 7331 5-8-6 46 StephenCarson 7 56+
(Adrian McGuinness, Ire) *s.i.s: hld up: plenty to do turning for home: hdwy over 1f out: rdn to ld ins fnl f: r.o wl* **7/1**[3]
0653 **2** 1 1/2 **Lujano**[21] 7345 3-9-2 58 PaulMulrennan 5 65
(Ollie Pears) *led: rdn clr and edgd rt over 1f out: hdd ins fnl f: styd on same pce* **7/1**[3]
2640 **3** 3/4 **Turkish Sultan (IRE)**[22] 7322 5-8-3 48 (p) MCGeran(5) 9 53
(J M Bradley) *hld up: hdwy over 1f out: r.o* **10/1**
2420 **4** 1/2 **Manchestermaverick (USA)**[19] 7358 3-9-2 58 SteveDrowne 2 62
(H Morrison) *a.p: rdn over 3f out: chsd ldr 2f out: styd on same pce fnl f* **10/3**[1]
0650 **5** 3/4 **Machinate (USA)**[11] 7442 6-8-13 56 DuranFentiman(3) 8 58
(W M Brisbourne) *sn pushed along in rr: last 2 1/2f out: r.o ins fnl f: nrst fin* **20/1**
3464 **6** *nk* **Convivial Spirit**[12] 7437 4-9-0 57 (t) TolleyDean(3) 3 59
(E F Vaughan) *s.i.s: hld up: r.o ins fnl f: nrst fin* **7/2**[2]
0056 **7** 1/2 **Tapas Lad (IRE)**[18] 7373 3-8-3 52 (v) StacyRenwick(7) 4 53
(G J Smith) *hld up in tch: rdn over 1f out: no ex fnl f* **16/1**
250 **8** 1 1/4 **Snow Dancer (IRE)**[97] 5543 4-9-3 57 JamieMoriarty 11 55
(H A McWilliams) *sn pushed along in rr: rdn over 1f out: n.d* **22/1**
2010 **9** 1 1/4 **Malinsa Blue (IRE)**[21] 7345 6-8-11 58 (p) LanceBetts(7) 6 53
(B Ellison) *mid-div: racd keenly: hdwy over 3f out: rdn and hung lft over 2f out: wknd fnl f* **16/1**
0000 **10** 3 1/4 **Chalentina**[68] 6335 5-8-6 46 oh1 RichardThomas 1 33
(J E Long) *prom: rdn over 3f out: wknd over 1f out* **33/1**
-600 **11** 4 **Beresford Lady**[22] 7322 4-8-6 46 oh1 FrancisNorton 10 24
(A D Brown) *chsd ldrs: rdn over 2f out: wknd fnl f* **80/1**
0500 **12** 1 3/4 **Dynamo Dave (USA)**[12] 7437 3-8-8 50 MartinDwyer 13 24
(M D I Usher) *chsd ldr tl rdn over 2f out: wknd over 1f out: eased* **25/1**
0265 **13** 12 **Lucky Character**[96] 5574 3-8-5 47 (t) ChrisCatlin 12 —
(N J Vaughan) *hld up: effrt over 3f out: wknd over 2f out* **14/1**

1m 50.66s (0.16) **Going Correction** -0.025s/f (Stan)
WFA 3 from 4yo+ 2lb 13 Ran SP% **115.0**
Speed ratings (Par 101): **98,96,96,95,94 94,94,93,91,89 85,83,73**
toteswinger: 1&2 £13.60, 1&3 £13.60, 2&3 £13.60 CSF £49.57 CT £490.02 TOTE £9.90: £3.00, £3.40, £2.20; EX 90.20.
Owner Curb Your Enthusiasm Syndicate **Bred** L A C Ashby Newhall Estate Farm **Trained** Lusk, Co Dublin

FOCUS
A low-grade handicap but one run at a sound pace throughout and the form appears solid enough. The winner ended up towards the inside rail.

7582 FREE BETS WITH FREEBETS.CO.UK (S) STKS 5f 216y(P)
6:50 (6:50) (Class 6) 3-4-Y-O **£2,729** (£806; £403) **Stalls** Low

Form RPR
413 **1** **Back In The Red (IRE)**[8] 7471 4-9-6 65 (b) ChrisCatlin 7 70
(R A Harris) *sn pushed along to chse ldr: led over 2f out: drvn out* **9/4**[1]
0360 **2** 2 1/4 **Hollywood George**[18] 7375 4-8-11 45 (p) DuranFentiman(3) 3 57
(Miss M E Rowland) *s.i.s: hld up: hdwy over 1f out: r.o to go 2nd nr fin: no ch w wnr* **14/1**
5503 **3** *nk* **Our Acquaintance**[22] 7323 3-9-0 63 (b) SteveDrowne 5 56
(W R Muir) *a.p: chsd wnr 2f out: sn rdn and edgd rt: styd on same pce fnl f* **5/1**[3]

04 **4** *2 1/2* **Fraizer (IRE)**78 6094 4-9-0 47 .... StephenCarson 2 46
(Adrian McGuinness, Ire) *sn pushed along in rr: hdwy 4f out: rdn over 2f out: hung lft over 1f out: styd on same pce* **16/1**

6035 **5** *3/4* **Charlotte Grey**6 7509 4-8-9 49 .... FrancisNorton 1 39
(P J McBride) *chsd ldrs: rdn over 2f out: styng on same pce whn nt clr run over 1f out* **8/1**

4000 **6** *2 3/4* **Nordic Light (USA)**31 7195 4-8-9 47 ....(b) MCGeran(5) 12 35
(J M Bradley) *chsd ldrs: outpcd 4f out: rdn over 2f out: n.d after* **33/1**

204 **7** *7* **Punching**21 7346 4-9-6 68 ....(b) MartinDwyer 4 18
(Miss Gay Kelleway) *sn led: hdd over 2f out: wknd wl over 1f out* **11/4[2]**

0 **8** *1 1/4* **Wardy's Wonder (IRE)**3 7536 3-8-9 66 .... TomEaves 8 3
(P D Evans) *s.i.s: hld up: rdn over 2f out: sn wknd* **17/2**

1m 14.95s (-0.05) **Going Correction** -0.025s/f (Stan) **8** Ran SP% **111.2**
Speed ratings (Par 101): **99,96,95,92,91 87,78,76**
toteswinger: 1&2 £6.50, 1&3 £4.10, 2&3 not won. CSF £32.73 TOTE £3.70: £1.60, £2.50, £2.10; EX 44.40.There was no bid for the winner

Owner Mrs Ruth M Serrell **Bred** Mrs Rachanee Butler **Trained** Earlswood, Monmouths

■ Stewards' Enquiry : Duran Fentiman caution: used whip without giving mount time to respond

FOCUS
A depleted field with five non-runners and a race where the second favourite disappointed. The pace was sound throughout and the winner raced against the inside rail in the straight, so the form could prove reasonable.

7583 ONLINE BETTING WITH FREEBETS.CO.UK MAIDEN STKS 1m 4f 50y(P)
7:20 (7:20) (Class 5) 3-Y-0+ £2,729 (£806; £403) Stalls Low

Form RPR

5 **1** **Cape Express (IRE)**17 7387 3-9-3 0 .... NCallan 5 83+
(M A Jarvis) *a.p: chsd ldr 8f out: hmpd and lost 2 pls over 6f out: wnt 2nd again over 5f out: led 3f out: edgd rt ins fnl f: drvn out* **11/10[1]**

/56 **2** *1 3/4* **Desert Vision**14 7423 4-9-8 0 ....(t) PaulMulrennan 7 80
(M W Easterby) *hld up in tch: racd keenly: chsd wnr over 2f out: sn rdn and ev ch: edgd rt ins fnl f: styd on same pce* **9/2[2]**

3 *7* **Castaneous (IRE)**8 7486 4-9-8 0 ....(b) StephenCarson 10 69
(P J Rothwell, Ire) *hld up: styd on appr fnl f: nvr nrr* **33/1**

0 **4** *1 1/4* **Sarando**229 1526 3-9-3 0 .... SteveDrowne 11 67
(R Charlton) *hld up: hdwy 4f out: rdn over 2f out: sn outpcd* **8/1**

5 *nk* **Tampa Boy (IRE)**24 6-9-8 0 .... FrancisNorton 9 66+
(M F Harris) *s.s: in rr: styd on u.p fr over 1f out: nvr nrr* **50/1**

0425 **6** *6* **Crazy About You (IRE)**45 6896 3-8-12 68 .... ChrisCatlin 2 52
(B W Hills) *chsd ldrs: lft in ld over 6f out: rdn and hdd 3f out: wknd wl over 1f out* **5/1[3]**

7 *2 1/2* **Dasher Reilly (USA)**6 3832 7-9-8 0 .... NeilChalmers 3 53
(A Sadik) *s.s: rdn over 2f out: n.d* **80/1**

00 **8** *13* **Seconditis**27 6470 3-9-3 0 .... CatherineGannon 6 32
(Mrs N S Evans) *sn drvn to ld: hung rt and hdd over 6f out: rdn and wknd over 3f out* **150/1**

4 **9** *1 3/4* **Starburst**160 3530 3-8-12 0 .... LPKeniry 12 24
(A M Balding) *racd keenly: trckd ldr 4f: remained handy tl rdn over 3f out: wknd over 2f out: eased* **8/1**

0 **10** *36* **Brave Optimist (IRE)**77 6114 3-8-12 0 .... TomEaves 1 —
(Paul Green) *hld up: rdn over 4f out: sn wknd* **50/1**

00 **11** *71* **Carr On Fire (USA)**119 4877 3-9-0 0 .... DuranFentiman(3) 4 —
(W M Brisbourne) *mid-div: rdn over 6f out: wknd over 5f out* **150/1**

2m 40.65s (-0.45) **Going Correction** -0.025s/f (Stan)
WFA 3 from 4yo+ 5lb **11** Ran SP% **114.1**
Speed ratings (Par 103): **100,98,94,93,93 89,87,78,77,53 6**
toteswinger: 1&2 £1.70, 1&3 £20.10, 2&3 £20.10 CSF £5.81 TOTE £2.50: £1.40, £1.40, £7.70; EX 8.00.

Owner A D Spence **Bred** March Thoroughbreds **Trained** Newmarket, Suffolk

FOCUS
A maiden lacking strength and one run at an ordinary gallop. Winner and second, who pulled clear of the remainder, raced in the centre in the straight with the latter the best guide to the form.

Dasher Reilly(USA) Official explanation: jockey said gelding missed the break
Starburst Official explanation: jockey said filly lost its action

7584 BET ONLINE WITH FREEBETS.CO.UK H'CAP 5f 20y(P)
7:50 (7:50) (Class 4) (0-85,85) 3-Y-0+ £5,180 (£1,541; £770; £384) Stalls Low

Form RPR

5221 **1** **Doubtful Sound (USA)**14 7428 4-8-7 79 ....(p) AndreaAtzeni(5) 9 96+
(R Hollinshead) *chsd ldrs: led over 1f out: r.o wl: readily* **7/2[2]**

2015 **2** *3* **Sands Crooner (IRE)**16 7393 5-8-11 78 ....(v) PaulMulrennan 10 84
(J G Given) *hld up: hdwy over 1f out: nt clr run 1f out: rdn and hung lft ins fnl f: r.o wl towards fin: no ch w wnr* **16/1**

5351 **3** *3/4* **Yungaburra (IRE)**10 7456 4-9-0 84 ....(t) TolleyDean(3) 7 87
(S Parr) *chsd ldrs: rdn over 1f out: sn hung lft: styd on* **3/1[1]**

3165 **4** *nk* **The Tatling (IRE)**10 7456 11-8-7 79 .... JackDean(5) 6 84+
(J M Bradley) *hld up: hdwy: nt clr run and hmpd 1f out: r.o wl towards fin: nvr able to chal* **12/1**

0466 **5** *2 1/4* **Bertoliver**19 7365 4-9-4 85 .... RichardKingscote 5 79
(Tom Dascombe) *chsd ldr: led wl over 1f out: sn rdn and hdd: no ex ins fnl f* **7/2[2]**

6000 **6** *1 3/4* **Almaty Express**19 7365 6-8-6 80 ....(b) BMcHugh(7) 2 68
(J R Weymes) *chsd ldrs: rdn 1/2-way: wknd fnl f* **16/1**

3150 **7** *shd* **Memphis Man**28 7239 5-8-13 80 .... VinceSlattery 1 67
(P D Evans) *s.i.s: outpcd: nvr nrr* **12/1**

2231 **8** *1* **Harry Up**24 7290 7-9-4 85 ....(p) NCallan 11 69
(K A Ryan) *sn pushed along to ld: rdn and hdd over 1f out: wknd ins fnl f* **11/2[3]**

0 **9** *6* **Just For Mary**1 7562 4-8-6 73 ....(b) StephenCarson 4 35
(P J Rothwell, Ire) *s.s: outpcd* **33/1**

60.95 secs (-1.35) **Going Correction** -0.025s/f (Stan) **9** Ran SP% **114.9**
Speed ratings (Par 105): **109,104,103,102,98 96,95,94,84**
toteswinger: 1&2 £9.50, 1&3 £5.60, 2&3 £6.90 CSF £56.95 CT £186.36 TOTE £5.10: £2.00, £3.60, £1.30; EX 60.10.

Owner Phil Pye **Bred** Millsec, Ltd **Trained** Upper Longdon, Staffs

FOCUS
A fair handicap in which the strong pace resulted in a time just outside the course record. The winner raced centre to far side in the straight.

The Tatling(IRE) Official explanation: jockey said gelding was denied a clear run

Harry Up Official explanation: jockey said gelding had no more to give

7585 HORSE BETTING WITH FREEBETS.CO.UK H'CAP (DIV II) 1m 141y(P)
8:20 (8:21) (Class 6) (0-58,58) 3-Y-0+ £2,047 (£604; £302) Stalls Low

Form RPR

0605 **1** **Royal Island (IRE)**34 7153 6-9-3 57 .... VinceSlattery 13 74+
(M G Quinlan) *stdd and swtchd lft sn after s: hld up: hdwy over 2f out: rdn to ld wl over 1f out: sn hung lft and clr: eased towards fin* **2/1[1]**

0001 **2** *2 1/4* **Gramm**21 7345 5-9-3 57 .... PaulMulrennan 12 66
(M W Easterby) *hld up: hdwy over 3f out: rdn to chse wnr over 1f out: edgd lft: styd on same pce fnl f* **5/2[2]**

2020 **3** *1 3/4* **Rowan Lodge (IRE)**21 7340 6-9-4 58 ....(b) JamieMoriarty 10 63
(Ollie Pears) *mid-div: hmpd over 3f out: hdwy u.p over 1f out: nt trble ldrs* **7/1[3]**

0000 **4** *1 3/4* **Beck**3 7535 4-8-5 48 .... DuranFentiman(3) 9 49
(W M Brisbourne) *a.p: rdn over 1f out: edgd lft and no ex fnl f* **25/1**

6000 **5** *5* **Red Current**5 7518 4-8-12 52 .... LPKeniry 1 41
(R A Harris) *prom: rdn over 3f out: wknd over 1f out* **12/1**

0000 **6** *1 3/4* **Kabis Amigos**24 7287 6-8-5 50 ....(tp) AndreaAtzeni(5) 4 35
(S T Mason) *led: rdn and hdd wl over 1f out: wknd fnl f* **9/1**

5406 **7** *1 1/4* **Imperial Djay (IRE)**22 7321 3-8-9 58 .... StacyRenwick(7) 7 41
(G J Smith) *chsd ldrs: rdn over 2f out: wknd over 1f out* **20/1**

-620 **8** *3 3/4* **Sharps Gold**150 3845 3-9-2 58 ....(t) ChrisCatlin 8 32
(D Morris) *hld up: racd keenly: rdn and wknd over 1f out* **33/1**

4300 **9** *3* **Pajada**112 5090 4-8-6 46 oh1 .... MartinDwyer 11 13
(M D I Usher) *prom: chsd ldr over 5f out: rdn over 2f out: hmpd and wknd wl over 1f out* **33/1**

4454 **10** *2* **Norwegian**236 1374 7-8-7 47 .... StephenDonohoe 2 9
(Ian Williams) *hld up: a in rr: rdn over 3f out: sn wknd* **12/1**

0000 **11** *4 1/2* **Autograph Hunter**18 7373 4-7-13 46 oh1 ....(b) AndrewHeffernan(7) 5 —
(Peter Grayson) *s.s: rdn 1/2-way: a in rr* **33/1**

000- **12** *11* **Millennium Storm (GER)**391 6775 3-8-4 46 oh1 ....(t) FrancisNorton 3 —
(M F Harris) *chsd ldr 3f: wkng whn n.m.r over 3f out* **50/1**

1m 49.85s (-0.65) **Going Correction** -0.025s/f (Stan)
WFA 3 from 4yo+ 2lb **12** Ran SP% **119.2**
Speed ratings (Par 101): **101,99,97,95,91 89,88,85,82,81 77,67**
toteswinger: 1&2 £1.10, 1&3 £5.80, 2&3 £5.50 CSF £6.33 CT £29.08 TOTE £3.00: £1.40, £1.30, £2.50; EX 7.80.

Owner M T Neville **Bred** Mrs Bill O'Neill **Trained** Newmarket, Suffolk

FOCUS
A modest handicap in which the sound pace favoured the hold up horses. The winner ended up towards the inside rail in the closing stages and the first four pulled clear, so the form looks sound enough rated around the placed horses.

7586 FREE BETTING AT FREEBETS.CO.UK H'CAP 7f 32y(P)
8:50 (8:52) (Class 5) (0-70,69) 3-Y-0+ £3,238 (£963; £481; £240) Stalls High

Form RPR

1 **Spiritina (IRE)**64 6454 3-9-3 68 .... RPCleary 3 84+
(Noel Lawlor, Ire) *hld up in tch: rdn to ld and edgd lft 1f out: r.o u.p* **5/1[3]**

212 **2** *1 1/2* **Sendreni (FR)**6 7510 4-9-2 67 .... ChrisCatlin 10 79
(M Wigham) *chsd ldrs: rdn and ev ch whn bmpd 1f out: styd on same pce* **13/8[1]**

3216 **3** *shd* **Siren Sound**29 7225 3-9-4 69 .... SteveDrowne 5 81
(H Morrison) *chsd ldr: led over 1f out: sn rdn: hdd 1f out: styd on same pce* **4/1[2]**

4551 **4** *6* **Another Genepi (USA)**22 7317 5-9-2 67 ....(b) EdwardCreighton 1 63
(E J Creighton) *trckd ldrs: racd keenly: rdn over 1f out: sn wknd* **10/1**

0466 **5** *1/2* **Kensington (IRE)**6 7510 7-8-12 63 ....(p) StephenDonohoe 2 57
(P D Evans) *led: rdn and hdd over 1f out: sn wknd* **10/1**

2104 **6** *2* **Maybe I Wont**8 7466 3-9-2 67 .... TGMcLaughlin 12 56
(Lucinda Featherstone) *hld up: rdn over 2f out: sn wknd* **18/1**

1026 **7** *shd* **Chosen Forever**50 6792 3-8-11 65 .... DuranFentiman(3) 9 54
(G R Oldroyd) *hld up: rdn over 3f out: n.d* **9/1**

6000 **8** *2 1/2* **Elliwan**15 7405 3-8-10 61 .... DaleGibson 7 43
(M W Easterby) *dwlt: outpcd* **20/1**

0P00 **9** *1 3/4* **Haroldini (IRE)**110 5156 6-9-2 67 ....(p) PaulMulrennan 11 44
(J Balding) *hld up: effrt over 2f out: sn wknd* **66/1**

-000 **10** *shd* **No Page (IRE)**14 7428 3-8-8 62 ....(b1) TolleyDean(3) 4 39
(J L Spearing) *hld up: rdn over 2f out: sn wknd* **50/1**

1m 28.84s (-0.76) **Going Correction** -0.025s/f (Stan) **10** Ran SP% **116.4**
Speed ratings (Par 103): **103,101,101,94,93 91,91,88,86,86**
toteswinger: 1&2 £1.80, 1&3 £15.70, 2&3 £1.10 CSF £13.29 CT £36.56 TOTE £4.20: £2.10, £1.50, £1.40; EX 14.80.

Owner Martin Nolan **Bred** Martin Nolan **Trained** Rathangan, Co Kildare

FOCUS
An ordinary handicap in which the pace was fair and the first three, who pulled clear, raced in or towards the centre in the straight, suggesting the form is worth rating positively.

7587 FOOTBALL BETTING WITH FREEBETS.CO.UK H'CAP 2m 119y(P)
9:20 (9:21) (Class 6) (0-65,60) 3-Y-0+ £2,388 (£705; £352) Stalls Low

Form RPR

0220 **1** **Zuwaar**15 7400 3-9-5 59 ....(t) StephenDonohoe 4 70
(Ian Williams) *hld up: hdwy over 3f out: rdn to ld over 1f out: hung lft: styd on* **7/2[2]**

2511 **2** *2* **Irish Ballad**15 7401 6-9-8 54 .... NickyMackay 2 63
(S Dow) *chsd ldrs: led over 2f out: rdn and hdd over 1f out: styd on same pce ins fnl f* **2/1[1]**

0000 **3** *1 1/4* **Daraiym (IRE)**19 7368 3-8-10 50 ow2 .... TomEaves 5 58
(Paul Green) *hld up: hdwy over 3f out: rdn over 2f out: styd on* **25/1**

4006 **4** *1* **Rare Coincidence**15 7285 7-9-9 55 ....(p) ChrisCatlin 9 61
(R F Fisher) *hld up: hdwy over 9f out: led 8f out: rdn and hdd over 2f out: no ex fnl f* **14/1**

0004 **5** *3* **Restart (IRE)**4 7520 7-8-13 45 ....(p) TGMcLaughlin 11 48
(Lucinda Featherstone) *sn pushed along in rr: hdwy 1/2-way: sn rdn: btn whn eased wl ins fnl f* **17/2**

1655 **6** *nk* **Foreign King (USA)**15 7400 4-9-12 58 .... LPKeniry 3 60
(J W Mullins) *prom: rdn over 6f out: styd on same pce fnl 2f* **10/1**

145/ **7** *11* **Silvaani (USA)**739 6630 10-8-13 45 .... NeilChalmers 6 34
(B Forsey) *hld up: hdwy 3f out: sn rdn and wknd* **33/1**

0040 **8** *21* **Tapaellya (IRE)**24 7285 4-8-13 45 .... RichardThomas 12 9
(J E Long) *prom: lost pl over 9f out: hdwy over 5f out: rdn and wknd over 2f out* **33/1**

5066 **9** *6* **Champagne Shadow (IRE)**15 7400 7-9-6 52 ....(p) JerryO'Dwyer 7 9
(J Pearce) *hld up: rdn over 4f out: a in rr: eased fnl 2f* **17/2**

The Form Book, Raceform Ltd, Compton, RG20 6NL

6340 **10** *10* **Blue Hills**[5] 7512 7-9-9 **60**............(v) WilliamCarson(5) 13 5
(P W Hiatt) *chsd ldr after 2f: led over 9f out: hdd 8f out: rdn and wknd over 3f out* **8/1**[3]

0000 **11** *6* **Ericarrow (IRE)**[8] 7473 3-8-6 **46**............(vt[1]) FrancisNorton 8 —
(M F Harris) *chsd ldrs: rdn over 6f out: wknd over 4f out* **33/1**

0 **12** *dist* **The Bodhran Beat (IRE)**[1] 7559 4-8-13 **45**.........(b[1]) StephenCarson 10 —
(P J Rothwell, Ire) *led: hdd over 9f out: wknd over 6f out: t.o fnl 4f* **50/1**

3m 39.98s (-1.82) **Going Correction** -0.025s/f (Stan)
WFA 3 from 4yo+ 8lb 12 Ran SP% **118.1**
Speed ratings (Par 101): **103,102,101,101,99 99,94,84,81,76 74,—**
toteswinger: 1&2 £4.60, 1&3 £22.90, 2&3 £22.90 CSF £10.25 CT £150.85 TOTE £5.70: £1.70, £1.40, £9.80; EX 12.80 Place 6 £12.16, Place 5 £3.21..
Owner Dr Marwan Koukash **Bred** Shadwell Estate Company Limited **Trained** Portway, Worcs

FOCUS
A moderate handicap but one run at a decent gallop throughout and solid form rated around the first two. The principals again came down the centre in the straight.
Zuwaar Official explanation: trainer said, regarding the apparent improvement in form, that gelding had benefited from re-application of a tongue strap
Champagne Shadow(IRE) Official explanation: trainer said gelding didn't eat up after race
The Bodhran Beat(IRE) Official explanation: jockey said gelding had a breathing problem
T/Plt: £11.30 to a £1 stake. Pool: £106,658.74. 6,859.29 winning tickets. T/Qpdt: £2.70 to a £1 stake. Pool: £7,950.98. 2,164.12 winning tickets. CR

7588 - 7597a (Foreign Racing) - See Raceform Interactive

7552 LINGFIELD (L-H)

Sunday, December 7

OFFICIAL GOING: Standard
Wind: Nil. Weather: bright, chilly

7589 PLAY CORAL AT CORAL.CO.UK APPRENTICE H'CAP 5f (P)
12:00 (12:00) (Class 6) (0-60,59) 3-Y-0+ **£2,047** (£604; £302) **Stalls** High

Form RPR

2500 **1** **Thoughtsofstardom**[9] 7471 5-9-4 **58**............ LukeMorris 5 67
(P S McEntee) *stdd after s: t.k.h: trckd ldrs: chal on bit ent fnl f: rdn to ld jst ins fnl f: r.o wl* **7/2**[2]

5053 **2** *½* **Joss Stick**[6] 7517 3-8-13 **58**............ AndreaAtzeni(5) 3 65
(R A Harris) *taken down early: in tch: lost pl bnd 2f out: rallied u.p over 1f out: chsd wnr ins fnl f: hld fnl 50yds* **7/4**[1]

-025 **3** *¾* **Sarah's Art (IRE)**[7] 7508 5-9-0 **54**............ TolleyDean 4 59
(Stef Liddiard) *racd in last trio: hdwy on inner over 1f out: ev ch ent fnl f: one pce fnl 100yds* **4/1**[3]

5000 **4** *2 ½* **Ben**[5] 7529 3-9-5 **59**............(v) TravisBlock 6 55
(P G Murphy) *stdd after s: hld up in last trio: rdn jst over 2f out: hdwy over 1f out: kpt on to go 4th nr fin: nvr rchd ldrs* **33/1**

4003 **5** *shd* **Triskaidekaphobia**[22] 7346 5-8-12 **57**............(t) RossAtkinson(5) 8 52
(Miss J R Tooth) *chsd ldrs: rdn 2f out: wknd ent fnl f* **8/1**

0064 **6** *½* **Our Fugitive (IRE)**[15] 7414 6-8-12 **57**............(v) JemmaMarshall(5) 2 50
(C Gordon) *w ldr: rdn and hld hd high and hanging over 1f out: stl ev ch 1f out: nt run on and btn fnl f* **11/2**

0000 **7** *¾* **A Wish For You**[25] 7286 3-9-1 **58**............(b) JamesO'Reilly(3) 9 49
(D K Ivory) *s.i.s: hld up in last trio: rdn and effrt over 1f out: nvr gng pce to threaten ldrs* **12/1**

00 **8** *¾* **Baileys Brazilian**[7] 7509 3-8-10 **55**............ MatthewDavies(5) 1 43
(C A Dwyer) *led narrowly: rdn wl over 1f out: hdd jst ins fnl f: wknd qckly* **66/1**

58.60 secs (-0.20) **Going Correction** -0.125s/f (Stan) 8 Ran SP% **117.2**
Speed ratings (Par 101): **96,95,94,90,89 89,87,86**
toteswinger: 1&2 £2.10, 1&3 £3.10, 2&3 £2.30 CSF £10.34 CT £25.08 TOTE £4.20: £1.40, £1.20, £1.60; EX 12.00 Trifecta £16.30 Pool £234.86 - 10.63 winning units..
Owner Eventmaker Racehorses **Bred** B Bargh **Trained** Newmarket, Suffolk

FOCUS
A modest handicap run at a steady pace but straightforward form rated around the first four.

7590 CORAL PLAY BLACKJACK IN SHOP H'CAP (DIV I) 1m 2f (P)
12:30 (12:30) (Class 6) (0-60,63) 3-Y-0+ **£1,706** (£503; £252) **Stalls** Low

Form RPR

0631 **1** **Can Can Star**[13] 7440 5-9-10 **63**............ ShaneKelly 5 74
(A W Carroll) *hld up in midfield: hdwy gng wl over 2f out: chsd ldr over 1f out: pushed into ld ins fnl f: cleverly* **7/2**[2]

0513 **2** *hd* **Siena Star (IRE)**[13] 7440 10-9-7 **60**............ MickyFenton 1 71
(Stef Liddiard) *chsd ldr tl led 4f out: rdn over 2f out: hdd ins fnl f: unable qck u.p fnl 100yds* **4/1**[3]

-326 **3** *2 ½* **Barton Sands (IRE)**[277] 794 11-9-3 **56**............(t) JimCrowley 7 62
(Andrew Reid) *hld up in last trio: rdn and effrt over 2f out: chsd ldng pair ins fnl f: no imp* **16/1**

4 *1 ¾* **Sea Cliff (IRE)**[54] 5520 4-8-7 **46** oh1............ MartinDwyer 2 49
(Jonjo O'Neill) *chsd ldrs: pushed along 4f out: drvn to chse ldng pair jst over 2f out: wknd ent fnl f* **9/4**[1]

6022 **5** *½* **Torrens (IRE)**[20] 7355 6-9-5 **58**............(t) JamesDoyle 6 60
(P D Evans) *in tch: chsd ldr wl over 2f out: drvn and ev ch jst over 2f out: c centre 2f out: wknd ent fnl f* **4/1**[3]

5005 **6** *1* **Fateful Attraction**[38] 7089 5-9-0 **53**............(bt) PaulDoe 8 53
(I A Wood) *s.i.s: bhd: nt clr run briefly over 2f out: sn rdn: nvr gng pce to threaten ldrs* **14/1**

1060 **7** *¾* **Space Pirate**[64] 6492 3-8-11 **53**............(p) JimmyQuinn 11 51
(J Pearce) *stdd after s: bhd: rdn and effrt over 2f out: nvr threatened ldrs* **20/1**

035- **8** *13* **Sahara Prince (IRE)**[42] 5497 8-8-7 **46** oh1............ FrancisNorton 10 18
(K A Morgan) *led tl 4f out: wknd qckly wl over 2f out: wl bhd fnl f* **50/1**

535 **9** *25* **Superior Duchess**[23] 7321 3-9-1 **57**............ FrankieMcDonald 9 —
(Jane Chapple-Hyam) *s.i.s: sn in midfield on outer: rdn over 3f out: wl bhd 2f out: eased fnl f: t.o* **33/1**

2m 3.64s (-2.96) **Going Correction** -0.125s/f (Stan)
WFA 3 from 4yo+ 3lb 9 Ran SP% **115.2**
Speed ratings (Par 101): **106,105,103,102,102 101,100,90,70**
toteswinger: 1&2 £3.20, 1&3 £9.90, 2&3 £9.80 CSF £17.53 CT £195.45 TOTE £4.70: £1.60, £1.40, £3.90; EX 14.30 Trifecta £199.00 Part won. Pool £269.04 - 0.73 winning units..
Owner K F Coleman **Bred** A W And I Robinson **Trained** Cropthorne, Worcs

FOCUS
A moderate handicap run at a fair pace and by far the faster of the two divisions. The first two were close to recent course form.

7591 CORAL.CO.UK H'CAP 1m (P)
1:00 (1:01) (Class 6) (0-60,60) 3-Y-0+ **£2,047** (£604; £302) **Stalls** High

Form RPR

2300 **1** **Star Strider**[69] 6336 4-9-5 **60**............ GeorgeBaker 7 70
(Miss Gay Kelleway) *stdd s: hld up bhd: hdwy on outer jst over 2f out: rdn over 1f out: edgd lft and led fnl 100yds: sn in command* **6/1**

3364 **2** *2 ¼* **Yakama (IRE)**[28] 7256 3-9-1 **57**............(b) LPKeniry 6 62
(Mrs C A Dunnett) *t.k.h: hld up in midfield: hdwy 2f out: rdn to ld ent fnl f: hdd fnl 100yds: nt pce of wnr* **16/1**

6001 **3** *¾* **General Feeling (IRE)**[18] 7392 7-9-5 **60**............ MartinDwyer 9 63
(S T Mason) *in tch on outer: rdn jst over 2f out: chsng ldrs and carried lft ins fnl f: wnt 3rd wl ins fnl f: kpt on* **8/1**

0265 **4** *1* **Mrs Jefferson (IRE)**[20] 7363 3-9-1 **57**............ PatCosgrave 10 58
(J G Portman) *in tch: drvn and effrt over 1f out: kpt on fnl f: nvr quite gng pce to chal ldrs* **25/1**

5450 **5** *½* **Upstairs**[13] 7437 4-8-12 **56**............ MarcHalford(3) 4 56
(D R C Elsworth) *trckd ldrs: n.m.r briefly 2f out: sn pressing ldrs and rdn: hung lft and nt qckn over 1f out: kpt on same pce ins fnl f* **11/2**[3]

5004 **6** *shd* **Aegean Pride**[13] 7436 3-9-2 **58**............ RyanMoore 12 58
(R Hannon) *chsd ldrs: wnt 2nd 5f out: rdn to ld 2f out: hdd ent fnl f: wknd fnl 100yds* **10/3**[1]

6355 **7** *nk* **Norcroft**[13] 7433 6-9-2 **57**............ ChrisCatlin 5 56
(Mrs C A Dunnett) *t.k.h: hld up in midfield: rdn 2f out: chsng ldrs and keeping on same pce whn short of room and hmpd ins fnl f: nvr able to chal* **12/1**

0013 **8** *½* **Piccolo Diamante (USA)**[8] 7503 4-9-1 **56**............(t) AdamKirby 8 56
(S Parr) *taken down early: t.k.h: hld up towards rr: hdwy on outer 3f out: rdn over 2f out: chsng ldrs and keeping on same pce whn hmpd and snatched up ins fnl f: eased after* **5/1**[2]

0100 **9** *½* **Tilsworth Charlie**[13] 7433 5-9-2 **57**............(b) StephenDonohoe 1 54
(J R Jenkins) *hld up in last trio: rdn and effrt 2f out: kpt on but nvr trbld ldrs* **33/1**

4320 **10** *1 ¾* **Over To You Bert**[199] 2337 9-8-13 **59**............ WilliamCarson(5) 11 52
(R J Hodges) *led tl rdn and hdd 2f out: wknd u.p jst over 1f out* **14/1**

0660 **11** *1 ½* **Lancaster Lad (IRE)**[52] 6746 3-9-1 **57**............(p) DaneO'Neill 2 46
(A B Haynes) *dwlt: hld in last pair: rdn and unable qckn jst over 2f out: nvr nr ldrs* **33/1**

2220 **12** *1 ¼* **Under Fire (IRE)**[20] 7354 5-8-12 **60**............ JemmaMarshall(7) 3 46
(A W Carroll) *racd in midfield on inner: rdn over 2f out: no hdwy* **16/1**

1m 37.19s (-1.01) **Going Correction** -0.125s/f (Stan)
WFA 3 from 4yo+ 1lb 12 Ran SP% **116.4**
Speed ratings (Par 101): **100,97,97,96,95 95,95,94,94,92 90,89**
toteswinger: 1&2 £33.90, 1&3 £5.00, 2&3 £27.10 CSF £93.81 CT £767.26 TOTE £6.70: £2.50, £6.40, £3.10; EX 235.20 TRIFECTA Not won..
Owner Holistic Racing Ltd **Bred** Snailwell Stud Co Ltd **Trained** Exning, Suffolk

FOCUS
A moderate race, but the winner did particularly well to come from last place given the modest tempo. The form is not that solid with the third the best guide.
Piccolo Diamante(USA) Official explanation: jockey said gelding suffered interference in running

7592 CORAL BET BY PHONE 0800 242 232 H'CAP 6f (P)
1:30 (1:32) (Class 4) (0-80,82) 3-Y-0+ **£5,180** (£1,541; £770; £384) **Stalls** Low

Form RPR

02 **1** **The Game**[9] 7477 3-9-6 **82**............ RichardKingscote 1 98+
(Tom Dascombe) *taken down early: mde all: clr over 2f out: in n.d after: unchal* **5/2**[1]

4540 **2** *4* **He's A Humbug (IRE)**[11] 7456 4-8-10 **77** ow1.......(p) JamesO'Reilly(5) 4 77
(J O'Reilly) *racd off the pce in midfield: rdn and hdwy on inner jst over 2f out: kpt on to chse wnr fnl 100yds: no ch* **16/1**

1330 **3** *½* **Dvinsky (USA)**[9] 7470 7-9-4 **80**............(b) JimmyQuinn 3 79
(P Howling) *chsd wnr for 1f: styd chsng ldrs: drvn wl over 1f out: chsd wnr again ins fnl f: no imp: lost 2nd fnl 100yds* **8/1**[3]

0602 **4** *hd* **Autumn Blades (IRE)**[44] 6952 3-9-0 **76**............ JimCrowley 8 74
(A Bailey) *stdd s: hld up wl bhd: hdwy on outer 2f out: r.o wl fnl f: nvr nr wnr* **8/1**[3]

5 *½* **Secret Dubai (IRE)**[77] 3-8-9 **76**............(t) AndreaAtzeni(5) 5 72
(M Botti) *racd wl off the pce in midfield: styd on u.p fnl f: nvr nr wnr* **16/1**

5001 **6** *½* **River Thames**[15] 7414 5-8-6 **68**............ MartinDwyer 11 63
(K A Ryan) *restless stalls: bhd: pushed along 3f out: styd on u.p fnl f: nvr nr wnr* **4/1**[2]

0000 **7** *nk* **Count Ceprano (IRE)**[51] 6771 4-9-3 **79**............ LPKeniry 6 73
(C R Dore) *dwlt: bhd: rdn and hdwy over 2f out: drvn and kpt on fnl f: nvr nr wnr* **8/1**[3]

2514 **8** *1* **Brandywell Boy (IRE)**[13] 7435 5-8-11 **73**............ ChrisCatlin 7 64
(D J S Ffrench Davis) *bhd: rdn on inner 2f out: n.d* **10/1**

-050 **9** *¾* **Shustraya**[18] 7390 4-9-3 **79**............ EddieAhern 2 67
(P J Makin) *chsd wnr for 1f: chsd ldrs after tl rdn to chse clr wnr again over 2f out: edgd rt 2f out: no imp: lost 2nd ins fnl f: wknd rapidly* **16/1**

540- **10** *18* **Luscious Lips**[420] 6195 3-8-10 **72**............ DaneO'Neill 9 3
(B Gubby) *dashed up to chse wnr after 1f tl over 2f out: wknd rapidly wl over 1f out: eased fnl f: t.o* **66/1**

626 **P** **Parisian Gift (IRE)**[44] 6952 3-9-3 **79**............ GeorgeBaker 10 —
(J R Gask) *a wl off the pce in rr: eased and p.u 2f out: dismntd* **9/1**

69.91 secs (-1.99) **Going Correction** -0.125s/f (Stan) course record 11 Ran SP% **120.1**
Speed ratings (Par 105): **108,102,102,101,101 100,100,98,97,73 —**
toteswinger: 1&2 £13.70, 1&3 £5.00, 2&3 £26.60 CSF £47.55 CT £252.16 TOTE £3.60: £1.50, £6.20, £3.00; EX 68.30 Trifecta £241.90 Part won. Pool £327.02 - 0.43 winning units..
Owner M Khan X2 **Bred** Aston House Stud **Trained** Lambourn, Berks

FOCUS
A fair race of its type for the track, with the winner making all at a good gallop. The form looks solid for the grade.
Parisian Gift(IRE) Official explanation: jockey said gelding lost its action and was subsequently pulled up

7593 WATCH RACING UK LIVE AT CORAL.CO.UK MAIDEN STKS 7f (P)
2:00 (2:03) (Class 5) 2-Y-0 **£2,729** (£806; £403) **Stalls** Low

Form RPR

52 **1** **Yellow Printer**[34] 7165 2-9-3 **0**............ RichardKingscote 7 76
(Tom Dascombe) *mde all: pressed and rdn over 1f out: kpt on wl and a holding rival fnl 100yds* **6/4**[1]

63 **2** ½ **Cabernet Sauvignon**[10] 7458 2-9-3 0 .... EddieAhern 4 75+
(J W Hills) *t.k.h: trckd ldrs: sltly hmpd jst over 2f out: chsd wnr 2f out: drvn and ev ch over 1f out: hld and no imp fnl 100yds* **2/1**[2]

0 **3** nk **Joannadarc (USA)**[13] 7438 2-8-12 0 .... PatCosgrave 10 69
(S A Callaghan) *in tch in midfield: hdwy over 2f out: rdn over 1f out: kpt on wl u.p to go 3rd wl ins fnl f: nvr quite getting to ldng pair* **66/1**

4 1 ½ **Aqwaas (USA)** 2-8-12 0 .... RyanMoore 9 65
(Sir Michael Stoute) *dwlt: sn in tch: rdn 2f out: swtchd rt over 1f out: chsd ldng pair ent fnl f: kpt on same pce* **9/2**[3]

2 **5** 3 **Twenty Score**[3] 7546 2-8-12 0 .... PaulFitzsimons 13 58
(Miss J R Tooth) *chsd ldng pair on outer: drvn 2f out: wknd u.p ent fnl f* **20/1**

04 **6** 1 ¼ **Cognac Boy (USA)**[9] 7476 2-9-3 0 .... JimCrowley 3 60
(R Hannon) *wnt lft s: chsd ldr tl 2f out: sn drvn: wknd u.p jst over 1f out* **20/1**

0 **7** ½ **Transformer (IRE)**[22] 7336 2-9-3 0 .... PaulDoe 6 58
(W J Knight) *racd off the pce in midfield: rdn wl over 2f out: kpt on but no imp* **33/1**

8 nse **Scene Two** 2-9-3 0 .... DaneO'Neill 8 60+
(L M Cumani) *wl bhd: pushed along early: hdwy over 1f out: styd on fnl f: nvr nr ldrs* **25/1**

9 1 **Haljaferia (UAE)** 2-9-0 0 .... MarcHalford(3) 11 56
(D R C Elsworth) *s.i.s: a bhd: c v wd bnd 2f out: plugged on steadily fnl f: nvr nr ldrs* **33/1**

0 **10** 4 ½ **Die Haard**[22] 7333 2-9-3 0 .... GeorgeBaker 14 45
(J R Gask) *racd off the pce in midfield: nvr a factor* **25/1**

11 nk **Saute** 2-9-3 0 .... AdamKirby 1 44
(W R Swinburn) *hmpd s and slowly away: rn green and sn rdn along in rr: nvr a factor* **25/1**

12 ½ **Flirty (IRE)** 2-8-12 0 .... ChrisCatlin 5 38
(Rae Guest) *v.s.a: a wl bhd* **50/1**

0 **13** 11 **Dulce Domum**[13] 7434 2-8-5 0 .... PNolan(7) 12 10
(A B Haynes) *v awkward s and v.s.a: a wl bhd: t.o fnl 2f* **100/1**

14 7 **Cool Madam** 2-8-12 0 .... JamesDoyle 2 —
(D Flood) *sltly hmpd: in tch in midfield: rdn over 4f out: lost pl over 3f out: wl bhd fnl 2f: t.o* **100/1**

1m 24.55s (-0.25) **Going Correction** -0.125s/f (Stan) **14** Ran SP% **123.9**
Speed ratings (Par 96): **96,95,95,93,89 88,87,87,86,81 81,80,68,60**
toteswinger: 1&2 £2.10, 1&3 £45.60, 2&3 £55.80 CSF £4.05 TOTE £2.70: £1.50, £1.70, £11.30; EX 6.60 Trifecta £194.00 Pool £393.42 - 1.50 winning units..
Owner Findlay & Bloom **Bred** Stowell Park Stud **Trained** Lambourn, Berks

FOCUS
For the second race running, a front-runner held sway in a race run at a good gallop, though many of those that were left behind from the word go were either seriously lacking in early pace, or will be seen to better effect in handicaps later in their careers. The form is rated around the first two.

NOTEBOOK
Yellow Printer had looked ready to win in his previous race and he kept on with great determination when challenged in the straight. His trainer believes he is not the sort of horse ever to win by a wide margin, but expects him to make up into a nice three-year-old and with that in mind will now give him a break. (op 2-1)
Cabernet Sauvignon, who has run well in maidens on turf as well as Polytrack, stays 7f well and ought to win soon. His debut on turf suggested he could make up into a fair handicapper next year, and he continues to progress. (op 11-4)
Joannadarc(USA), defying her odds, stepped up on her debut in a manner which suggests she should find a race. Dropped back from 1m, this daughter of Johannesburg from a good US family saw it out really well and the longer trip should not be a problem if she reverts to it. (op 50-1)
Aqwaas(USA), a Diesis filly, has some classy types in the family but her dam was unplaced in her only race. Probably no stable star, though capable of winning a run-of-the-mill maiden and then make her mark in routine handicaps, she should not be overrated on the basis of this debut performance. (op 11-2 tchd 6-1)
Twenty Score showed more early pace than most even though she was drawn wide, and now needs just one more run to qualify for a handicap mark. (op 14-1)
Cognac Boy(USA) ran himself into the ground trying to chase the speedy winner but showed enough to give him a better chance in handicaps. (op 14-1)
Transformer(IRE), a Trans Island half-brother to four good winners up to 1m, ran a bit better than he had first time out and should step up on this in handicaps after one more run.
Scene Two, a 35,000gns Act One half-brother to seven winners up to middle distances, began to pick up when it was too late and should do better over longer trips as he matures. (op 16-1)
Haljaferia(UAE), a gelded son of Halling, has winners in the family up to 1m5f. He put in a fair first effort considering he was stuck wide throughout and looks capable of improvement in the long run. (op 25-1 tchd 20-1)

7594 PLAY CORAL SLOTS IN SHOP AND ONLINE H'CAP 7f (P)
2:30 (2:32) (Class 2) (0-100,97) 3-Y-0+
£15,577 (£4,665; £2,332; £1,167; £582; £292) **Stalls** Low

Form RPR

0035 **1** **Bazroy (IRE)**[38] 7101 4-8-9 **88** ....(b) StephenDonohoe 3 98
(P D Evans) *hld up towards rr: hdwy 3f out: swtchd rt over 1f out: drvn and r.o wl fnl f to ld last stride* **16/1**

0012 **2** shd **Markab**[15] 7418 5-9-4 **97** .... PatCosgrave 1 107
(K A Morgan) *led for 1f: chsd ldrs after: shkn up over 2f out: rdn to ld again wl over 1f out: battled on gamely fnl f: hdd last stride* **7/2**[2]

4000 **3** hd **Whistledownwind**[36] 7146 3-9-4 **97** .... ShaneKelly 9 106
(J Noseda) *dropped in bhd after s: rdn jst over 2f out: c wd st: str run u.p ins fnl f: nt quite rch ldng pair* **15/2**

4244 **4** 2 **Beat The Bell**[1] 7576 3-8-8 **92** .... NicolPolli(5) 5 96
(A Bailey) *prom: chsd ldr over 4f out: ev ch over 1f out tl no ex u.p fnl 100yds* **10/1**

3440 **5** nk **Ebraam (USA)**[15] 7418 5-9-4 **97** .... IanMongan 7 100
(P Howling) *t.k.h: hld up wl in tch: rdn wl over 1f out: drvn 1f out: nt qckn and no imp ins fnl f* **16/1**

2056 **6** 3 **Decameron (USA)**[71] 6276 3-8-8 **87** .... RyanMoore 8 82
(Sir Michael Stoute) *hld up towards rr: rdn and effrt over 2f out: drvn and c wd bnd 2f out: no hdwy* **9/4**[1]

0315 **7** 1 **My Gacho (IRE)**[15] 7418 6-8-13 **92** ....(b) DarryllHolland 4 84
(M Johnston) *chsd ldr tl led after 1f: rdn and hdd wl over 1f out: bmpd over 1f out: wknd ent fnl f* **9/2**[3]

0000 **8** 5 **Capricorn Run (USA)**[8] 7492 5-8-13 **92** ....(b) AdamKirby 6 71
(A J McCabe) *rel to r and lost many l s: sn rdn along: clsd and in tch 4f out: wknd over 2f out* **10/1**

1010 **9** hd **Bellomi (IRE)**[9] 7470 3-8-9 **88** ....(p) EddieAhern 2 66
(Miss Gay Kelleway) *hld up towards rr rdn over 2f out: sn struggling: no ch fnl f* **33/1**

1m 22.52s (-2.28) **Going Correction** -0.125s/f (Stan) course record **9** Ran SP% **115.8**
Speed ratings (Par 109): **108,107,107,105,105 101,100,94,94**
toteswinger: 1&2 £8.50, 1&3 £20.40, 2&3 £6.60 CSF £71.70 CT £469.19 TOTE £15.80: £4.30, £1.50, £2.90; EX 18.30 Trifecta £440.70 Part won. Pool £595.66 - 0.10 winning units..
Owner Barry McCabe **Bred** P D Savill **Trained** Pandy, Monmouths
■ Stewards' Enquiry : Darryll Holland two-day ban: failed to ride out for 6th place (Dec 21-22)

FOCUS
A valuable race run at a good gallop. The runner-up improved on recent form with the third close to his best.

NOTEBOOK
Bazroy(IRE) peaked just after Christmas a year ago, and seems to be returning to his best just a little earlier this time round. Though only just scrambling home, it was an excellent effort to beat these smart opponents, with his trainer reporting that he had been well suited by the generous early pace. (op 8-1)
Markab has now put in three fine efforts over this course and distance in the last month. While he continues to creep up the weights, those performances suggest he is still improving and he will remain a tough opponent in similar contests round here. (op 3-1)
Whistledownwind ◆ has been running in high-quality races over a variety of trips on turf, with mixed results, but had not run at 7f since his juvenile debut. He took a while to get going but, on finding his stride in the straight, he rattled home and only just failed. He looks likely to develop into a significant player in the top Polytrack races at 1m plus and, since he stays at least 1m2f, that opens up some interesting opportunities. (op 10-1 tchd 11-1)
Beat The Bell, running for the second day running, put in a brave effort but again gave the impression that 7f stretches him a little. (op 11-1)
Ebraam(USA) does stay this distance but has been mainly campaigned at 6f and that is probably his best trip. (op 14-1)
Decameron(USA) ideally needs farther and would not be without a chance over 1m on Polytrack judged on his first two attempts on the surface. (op 3-1 tchd 10-3 in places)
My Gacho(IRE) is finding life tougher off this higher mark. Soon setting a good gallop, he merely set the race up for his opponents. (op 15-2)
Capricorn Run(USA) went off at an extraordinarily short price for a horse who had thrown away his previous four races at the start, something which he managed to do yet again here. (op 8-1 tchd 15-2)

7595 CORAL ON CHANNEL 4 TELETEXT PAGE 611 H'CAP 1m 4f (P)
3:00 (3:00) (Class 3) (0-95,93) 3-Y-0+ **£9,066** (£2,697; £1,348; £673) **Stalls** Low

Form RPR

3035 **1** **Grande Caiman (IRE)**[37] 7110 4-9-7 **93** ....(b) RyanMoore 6 102+
(R Hannon) *mde all: dictated stdy gallop: hrd pressed and rdn over 2f out: forged ahd ent fnl f: styd on wl* **13/8**[1]

5354 **2** 2 ¾ **Slip**[16] 7404 3-8-8 **85** .... MartinDwyer 8 90
(J R Boyle) *disp 2nd pl tl jnd wnr 3f out: rdn over 1f out: nt pce of wnr ent fnl f: hld on for 2nd* **11/2**[3]

04P **3** ½ **King's Head (IRE)**[16] 7404 5-9-7 **93** ....(p) GeorgeBaker 4 97
(G L Moore) *stdd s: hld up in last pl: shkn up 4f out: drvn over 2f out: styd on u.p fnl f: wnt 3rd wl ins fnl f: nvr nr wnr* **14/1**

3316 **4** ¾ **Aypeeyes (IRE)**[34] 6129 4-8-10 **82** ....(v) DaneO'Neill 2 85
(A King) *t.k.h: disp 2nd tl lost pl 3f out: rdn to chse ldrs u.p over 1f out: swtchd rt ins fnl f: no imp after* **8/1**

5200 **5** 2 ½ **Basra (IRE)**[31] 7215 5-8-10 **82** .... TravisBlock 7 81
(Miss Jo Crowley) *t.k.h: hld up in last pair: rdn and unable qck over 2f out: wknd over 1f out* **9/1**

0122 **6** 3 **War Of The Roses (IRE)**[41] 7025 5-8-12 **84** .... PaulMulrennan 1 78
(R Brotherton) *hld up in tch: rdn over 2f out: drvn and unable qckn 2f out: btn ent fnl f* **2/1**[2]

2m 31.83s (-1.17) **Going Correction** -0.125s/f (Stan)
WFA 3 from 4yo+ 5lb **6** Ran SP% **114.6**
Speed ratings (Par 107): **98,96,95,95,93 91**
toteswinger: 1&2 £2.70, 1&3 £3.70, 2&3 £6.00 CSF £11.47 CT £91.09 TOTE £2.90: £2.20, £3.10; EX 12.80 Trifecta £77.60 Pool £346.24 - 3.30 winning units..
Owner I A N Wight **Bred** Sweet Retreat Syndicate **Trained** East Everleigh, Wilts

FOCUS
The winner had the run of the race, dictating a steady tempo, but he is very effective round here and this effort should not be underestimated. Those in the frame behind the winner were pretty close to their marks.

NOTEBOOK
Grande Caiman(IRE) has been campaigned at longer trips on turf, but 1m4f suits him well on Polytrack and the return to sand paid dividends, just as the market suggested. Though useful on grass, he is several pounds more effective on this surface and - though the Handicapper is aware of that - the manner in which he saw off his opponents here suggests he is better than ever. (op 5-2)
Slip, expected to be fitter for his recent outing after a short break, ran his best race to date on Polytrack and on this evidence is capable of winning a race on the surface. However, to date he has not been quite good enough to succeed off this mark. (tchd 6-1)
King's Head(IRE), who runs more often over hurdles these days, was pulled up on the Flat last time after losing his action but showed he had suffered no long-term ill-effect. However, he picked up too late from the rear and looks worth trying over an extra furlong or two. (op 10-1 tchd 16-1)
Aypeeyes(IRE) looks too high in the weights since winning at Newbury in August, but connections have the option of reverting to hurdles. (op 15-2 tchd 17-2)
Basra(IRE)'s recent efforts over this trip and 7f have confirmed that his best distance is probably 1m2f. (op 12-1 tchd 14-1)
War Of The Roses(IRE) had a harder task at the weights than while showing good form round here when last seen in the autumn. Although he has yet to prove he can win off this higher mark, he can surely do better than this. Official explanation: jockey said gelding hung right throughout (op 7-4 tchd 13-8)

7596 CORAL PLAY BLACKJACK IN SHOP H'CAP (DIV II) 1m 2f (P)
3:30 (3:31) (Class 6) (0-60,60) 3-Y-0+ **£1,706** (£503; £252) **Stalls** Low

Form RPR

-310 **1** **Saucy**[22] 7342 7-9-0 **53** .... RichardKingscote 10 61
(Tom Dascombe) *hld up in midfield: swtchd to outer wl over 3f out: hdwy to join ldrs over 2f out: sn rdn to ld and qcknd clr: 5l ld 1f out: pushed out fnl f: eased nr fin* **9/2**[3]

102 **2** 1 **Old Romney**[32] 7189 4-9-7 **60** ....(b) FrancisNorton 3 66
(M Wigham) *plld hrd: trckd ldrs: n.m.r and shuffled bk over 2f out: chsd clr wnr wl over 1f out: kpt on but nvr able to chal* **9/4**[1]

13-0 **3** ½ **Majehar**[31] 7217 6-9-6 **59** .... DaneO'Neill 1 64+
(A G Newcombe) *hld up in midfield: hmpd and shuffled bk over 3f out: hdwy and swtchd rt wl over 1f out: wnt 3rd ins fnl f: clsng fin but nvr able to chal* **3/1**[2]

5000 **4** 1 ¾ **Sceilin (IRE)**[25] 7287 4-8-11 **50** ....(t) LPKeniry 4 52
(J Mackie) *hld up towards rr: swtchd to outer and rdn 3f out: chsd ldng pair u.p over 1f out: kpt on u.p but nvr gng pce to rch wnr* **16/1**

2046 **5** 6 **Tabulate**[22] 7342 5-9-2 **55** .... JimmyQuinn 6 45
(P Howling) *hld up in rr: hdwy on inner 2f: nvr able to chal* **9/2**[3]

2550 **6** hd **Rosy Dawn**[7] 7506 3-8-5 **47** .... CatherineGannon 2 36
(J J Bridger) *led tl rdn and hdd over 2f out: immediately outpcd by wnr: no ch fnl f* **28/1**

050 **7** 1 1/2 **Pop Music (IRE)**[4] 7535 5-8-11 **50**................................(v) JamesDoyle 8 36
(Ms J S Doyle) *hld up bhd: rdn and sme hdwy over 1f out: nvr trbld ldrs* **12/1**

0030 **8** 4 **Brave Quest (IRE)**[8] 3614 4-9-5 **58**................................(b[1]) IanMongan 11 36
(Mrs L J Mongan) *chsd ldrs: wnt 2nd wl over 3f out: jnd ldr over 2f out: sn rdn and outpcd: no ch fnl f* **18/1**

000 **9** 3/4 **Bad Moon Rising**[39] 7072 3-8-6 **48**................................(p) ChrisCatlin 9 25
(J Akehurst) *t.k.h: hld up in tch: chsd ldrs and rdn over 2f out: sn outpcd and wl btn* **33/1**

630 **10** 3/4 **Beckenham's Secret**[17] 6740 4-8-7 **46** oh1................(v[1]) MartinDwyer 7 21
(A W Carroll) *t.k.h: in tch: rdn and wkng whn short of room over 2f out: sn wl btn* **25/1**

5000 **11** 2 1/4 **Susiedil (IRE)**[28] 4679 7-8-7 **46** oh1......................(tp) FrankieMcDonald 5 17
(S T Mason) *chsd ldr tl wl over 3f out: sn lost pl: wl bhd fnl 2f* **66/1**

2m 5.03s (-1.57) **Going Correction** -0.125s/f (Stan)
WFA 3 from 4yo+ 3lb **11 Ran SP% 122.7**
Speed ratings (Par 101): **101,100,99,98,93 93,92,89,88,87 86**
toteswinger: 1&2 £3.60, 1&3 £3.50, 2&3 £3.00 CSF £15.29 CT £36.60 TOTE £6.50: £1.60, £1.70, £1.40; EX 19.90 Trifecta £62.80 Pool £1,035.69 - 12.19 winning units. Place 6 £88.03, Place 5 £70.50..
Owner Mrs Bernadette Quinn **Bred** Wyck Hall Stud Ltd **Trained** Lambourn, Berks

FOCUS
A weak race overall, and a slower time than division one, but quite a taking performance by the winner, who travelled keenly and settled the race in a couple of strides when shooting five lengths clear around the home turn. It completed a treble for her in-form trainer and jockey and the first two are rated close to theitr marks.
Tabulate Official explanation: jockey said mare was denied a clear run
T/Plt: £31.60 to a £1 stake. Pool: £91,916.36. 2,118.95 winning tickets. T/Qpdt: £14.80 to a £1 stake. Pool: £10,244.90. 510.30 winning tickets. SP

7347 TOULOUSE
Sunday, December 7

OFFICIAL GOING: Heavy

7598a PRIX MAX SICARD - 14E ETAPE DU DEFI DU GALOP (LISTED RACE) 1m 4f
1:30 (1:33) 3-Y-0+ **£220,569** (£8,824; £6,618; £4,412; £2,206)

RPR
1 **Mondovino (FR)**[16] 5-9-0 .... CStefan 12 101
(Rod Collet, France)
2 3/4 **Blue Bresil (FR)**[22] 7352 3-9-2 .... SRuis 4 107
(L Larrigade, France)
3 1 **Latin Mood (FR)**[15] 7429 5-9-3 .... SPasquier 6 101
(P Demercastel, France)
4 2 1/2 **Lady Deauville (FR)**[21] 7350 3-8-13 .... HayleyTurner 13 98
(P A Blockley) *trckd ldr: hrd rdn and trying to chal 1f out: hung lft u.p 120yds out: wknd clsng stages* **13/1**[1]
5 2 1/2 **Court Canibal**[16] 3-9-2 .... TJarnet 7 97
(M Delzangles, France)
6 dist **Go For Gold Mine (FR)**[35] 3-8-9 .... CNora 1 —
(L Larrigade, France)
7 8 **Elasos (FR)**[22] 7352 6-9-3 .... DBonilla 8 —
(D Sepulchre, France)
8 nk **Cristobal (USA)**[61] 6569 4-9-0 .... FBlondel 11 —
(J-C Rouget, France)
9 dist **Rento (FR)**[59] 6612 5-9-3 .... F-XBertras 5 —
(W Walton, France)
10 dist **Maitresse (FR)**[15] 5-8-10 .... RonanThomas 9 —
(N Bertran De Balanda, France)
11 **Sassoaloro (GER)**[16] 4-9-0 .... AlexisBadel 10 —
(H Blume, Germany)
12 **Quam Celerrime**[179] 2953 3-8-9 .... J-BEyquem 2 —
(P A Blockley) *mid-div: bhd fr 1/2-way: t.o fnl 2f* **91/1**[2]

2m 44.06s (11.76)
WFA 3 from 4yo+ 5lb **12 Ran SP% 8.2**
PARI-MUTUEL (including one euro stakes): WIN 16.40; PL 3.20, 4.80,1.40; DF 104.80.
Owner Ecurie Foret Jaune **Bred** Haras Du Mezeray **Trained** France

NOTEBOOK
Lady Deauville(FR), who has a good record at a similar level on soft ground, appeared to have every chance but did not quite get home over this longer trip.
Quam Celerrime, having his first outing since June and taking a big step up in trip, never figured and finished up well beaten.

7589 LINGFIELD (L-H)
Monday, December 8

OFFICIAL GOING: Standard
Wind: Moderate, behind Weather: Fine

7599 CROWBOROUGH H'CAP (DIV I) 1m 2f (P)
12:30 (12:30) (Class 6) (0-52,52) 3-Y-0+ **£1,706** (£503; £252) **Stalls** Low

Form RPR
0304 **1** **Play Up Pompey**[10] 7469 6-8-12 **48**................................ RichardKingscote 7 56
(J J Bridger) *dwlt: sn in midfield: last of ldng gp over 2f out: stdy prog after: shkn up and styd on to ld ins fnl f: sn clr* **4/1**[1]

0560 **2** 3 **Tapas Lad (IRE)**[2] 7581 3-8-6 **52**................................(v) StacyRenwick(7) 8 54
(G J Smith) *trckd ldrs: smooth prog to chal 3f out: chsd ldr after: rdn to ld jst over 1f out: hdd and brushed aside ins fnl f* **10/1**

0000 **3** 3/4 **Jarvo**[61] 6570 7-8-13 **49**................................(v) PatrickMathers 6 50+
(I W McInnes) *hld up in tch: rdn 4f out: effrt whn hmpd wl over 2f out: tried again u.p on inner over 1f out: kpt on: snatched 3rd nr fin* **25/1**

0300 **4** nk **Casablanca Minx (IRE)**[3] 7559 5-9-2 **52**................................(v) HayleyTurner 11 52
(Miss Gay Kelleway) *chsd ldrs: rdn over 3f out: nt qckn u.p 2f out: plugged on* **6/1**[3]

0060 **5** nk **Aston Boy**[42] 7010 3-8-7 **46** oh1................................ JimmyQuinn 5 45
(M Blanshard) *hld up towards rr: reminder 5f out: lost tch w ldrs over 3f out: effrt wl over 1f out but nt qckn: styd on last 150yds* **8/1**

0000 **6** 1 **Competitor**[10] 7473 7-8-12 **48**................................(vt) IanMongan 3 45
(J Akehurst) *hld up in rr: rdn over 4f out: sn lost tch w ldng gp: kpt on fr over 1f out: n.d* **11/2**[2]

6240 **7** 1 **Flash Of Fire (USA)**[54] 6728 3-8-11 **50**................................(b) JimCrowley 10 45
(P R Chamings) *chsd clr ldr: clsd to ld 3f out: hdd jst over 1f out: wknd* **4/1**[1]

000 **8** 2 3/4 **Deep Waters (IRE)**[29] 7256 3-8-7 **46** oh1................................ NickyMackay 4 36
(S Dow) *chsd clr ldng pair: pushed along over 4f out: stl 3rd over 1f out: sn wknd* **40/1**

00-0 **9** 1 **Lunar Limelight**[23] 7340 3-8-13 **52**................................ TravisBlock 2 40
(P J Makin) *stdd s: hld up in last trio: rdn and wl off the pce over 3f out: no ch after* **20/1**

0000 **10** 1 1/2 **Bold Phoenix (IRE)**[34] 7180 7-8-10 **46**................................(b) JerryO'Dwyer 13 31
(Miss Amy Weaver) *nvr gng wl: rdn in last pair 5f out: sn lost tch* **20/1**

0000 **11** 4 **Aura**[24] 7310 3-8-8 **47** oh1 ow1................................(bt[1]) EddieAhern 14 24
(H J L Dunlop) *stdd s: hld up wl in rr: stl gng wl enough 4f out: wknd tamely 3f out* **33/1**

000 **12** 1 1/2 **Fantasy Crusader**[53] 6753 9-8-10 **46** oh1................................ MickyFenton 12 20
(R M H Cowell) *racd wd: hld up in midfield: rdn and struggling over 4f out: no ch after* **16/1**

000- **13** 8 **Grand Court (IRE)**[504] 3803 5-8-3 **46** oh1................(p) MatthewDavies(7) 1 4
(George Baker) *racd v freely: led and clr: wknd and hdd 3f out: t.o* **16/1**

2m 5.15s (-1.45) **Going Correction** -0.15s/f (Stan)
WFA 3 from 4yo+ 3lb **13 Ran SP% 120.4**
Speed ratings (Par 101): **99,96,96,95,95 94,93,91,90,89 86,85,78**
toteswinger: 1&2 £7.30, 1&3 £24.10, 2&3 £51.20. CSF £42.09 CT £900.73 TOTE £4.00: £1.60, £6.80, £9.30; EX 46.30 TRIFECTA Not won..
Owner double-r-racing.com **Bred** M Pollitt **Trained** Liphook, Hants
■ Stewards' Enquiry : Jim Crowley one-day ban: failed to ride to draw (Dec 22)

FOCUS
A modest event, with none of the runners having finished better than fourth on their previous outing. The winner is rated to a similar level as when winning in 2007 but the form is weak.

7600 MARSH GREEN (S) STKS 6f (P)
1:00 (1:00) (Class 6) 2-Y-0 **£1,978** (£584; £292) **Stalls** Low

Form RPR
5055 **1** **Elusive Ronnie (IRE)**[19] 7389 2-8-11 51................(p) DarryllHolland 12 60
(R A Teal) *pressed ldr: upsides fr over 1f out: nosed ahd nr fin* **9/1**

2524 **2** hd **Readily**[21] 7361 2-8-6 57................................ RichardKingscote 7 54
(J G Portman) *wl away: led: hrd pressed fr 2f out: narrowly hdd nr fin* **13/8**[1]

0050 **3** 1 1/2 **Cavendish Road (IRE)**[12] 7454 2-9-2 57................(bt) MartinDwyer 1 60
(W R Muir) *chsd ldng pair: rdn and nt qckn 2f out: one pce and no imp after* **15/2**[3]

030 **4** 1 1/4 **Turn To Dreams**[21] 7361 2-8-6 52................................ PaulDoe 3 46
(P D Evans) *pushed up to go prom but snatched up after 1f and dropped to rr: effrt on inner over 1f out: one pce fnl f* **12/1**

6000 **5** 2 **Lady Mulligan**[12] 7451 2-8-6 55................................ JimmyQuinn 9 40
(M Blanshard) *trckd ldrs on outer: gng wl 1/2-way: rdn and nt qckn 2f out* **12/1**

0050 **6** nse **Royal Raider**[5] 7537 2-8-11 71................................ JamesDoyle 5 45
(P D Evans) *nvr bttr than midfield: no prog u.p fnl 2f* **15/2**[3]

04 **7** 1/2 **Fitz**[26] 7279 2-8-6 0................................ AndreaAtzeni(5) 8 44+
(M Salaman) *sn in rr: u.p and hanging wl over 1f out and nt clr run: fnlly styd on fnl 100yds: no ch* **10/1**

0050 **8** 3/4 **Tartan Turban (IRE)**[21] 7361 2-9-2 57................................ RichardSmith 4 46
(R Hannon) *pushed up to go prom but out of room after 1f and dropped bk to last: nvr on terms after: brief effrt over 1f out* **11/2**[2]

6004 **9** 4 **Wigan Pier**[25] 7303 2-7-13 48................................(e) BillyCray(7) 6 24
(M D Squance) *trckd ldrs: gng wl 1/2-way: rdn and fnd nil 2f out: wknd* **25/1**

1m 11.94s (0.04) **Going Correction** -0.15s/f (Stan) **9 Ran SP% 115.3**
Speed ratings (Par 94): **93,92,90,89,86 86,85,84,79**
toteswinger: 1&2 £3.00, 1&3 £8.70, 2&3 £3.60. CSF £23.99 TOTE £8.50: £2.70, £1.10, £2.20; EX 27.10 TRIFECTA Not won..There was no bid for the winner.
Owner The Ginger Group **Bred** The Ginger Group **Trained** Ashtead, Surrey

FOCUS
A weak race and limited form. The early pace was fairly steady and nothing got into it from behind.

NOTEBOOK
Elusive Ronnie(IRE) slugged it out up front with Readily and did well to overcome a wide draw and prevail close home. He has looked an awkward customer at times, but he responded well to reapplied cheekpieces and showed a gritty attitude to get off the mark at the 11th attempt. (op 12-1)
Readily had been more consistent than most of her rivals and had strong form claims. It is hard to knock her effort under usual forcing tactics and she should be able to win a similar race, but it is a slight worry that she has failed to take advantage of a few obvious opportunities in nine career starts. (op 2-1tchd 9-4 in a place)
Cavendish Road(IRE) has not done much since winning a 7f Brighton seller in August and never really threatened here, but he ran creditably considering the tough task he faced at the weights. (op 13-2 tchd 5-1)
Turn To Dreams kept battling and would have been suited by a stronger pace, but her form has been very up and down in 12 starts and she is not certain to improve on this placing next time.
Lady Mulligan had gone the wrong way since being placed at Bath on her second start but did a bit better here, staying on late off the sedate pace. (op 14-1)
Royal Raider held the highest official rating of 71 but was weak in the market and did not look entirely willing when pressure was applied. (op 9-2)
Wigan Pier Official explanation: trainer said filly was in season

7601 EVENT IMAGE FOR PHOTO FINISH CLAIMING STKS 7f (P)
1:30 (1:31) (Class 6) 3-Y-0+ **£1,978** (£584; £292) **Stalls** Low

Form RPR
4313 **1** **Electric Warrior (IRE)**[3] 7560 5-9-4 85................................ JimCrowley 6 80
(K R Burke) *hld up in midfield: smooth prog on outer over 2f out: led jst over 1f out: drvn fnl f: jst hld on* **13/8**[2]

6523 **2** shd **Desert Dreamer (IRE)**[14] 7436 7-9-0 80................ RichardKingscote 8 76
(Tom Dascombe) *hld up in rr: prog wl over 1f out: shkn up to chse wnr fnl f: clsd grad: needed one more stride* **4/5**[1]

0034 **3** 3 1/4 **Nikki Bea (IRE)**[14] 7433 5-8-7 53................................ PaulDoe 2 60
(Jamie Poulton) *trckd ldng pair: effrt 2f out: disp 2nd ent fnl f: sn outpcd* **33/1**

0506 **4** 1/2 **Very Well Red**[24] 7320 5-8-7 46................................(b[1]) MartinDwyer 7 59
(P W Hiatt) *t.k.h early: trckd ldng pair: wnt 2nd over 2f out: led briefly over 1f out: sn outpcd* **40/1**

1230 **5** 3/4 **Makshoof (IRE)**[19] 7378 4-9-2 80................................ DarryllHolland 5 66
(K A Ryan) *dwlt: hld up in last pair: sme prog 2f out but nvr on terms: outpcd fnl f* **13/2**[3]

2566 **6** 3 1/2 **Little Knickers**[54] 6736 3-8-7 65 ow1................(b) EdwardCreighton 4 48
(E J Creighton) *mostly midfield: rdn and effrt wl over 1f out: wknd fnl f* **28/1**

0065 **7** 1 ½ **Motu (IRE)**[9] 7497 7-8-9 53............(b) HayleyTurner 3 45
(I W McInnes) *w ldr: led over 2f out to over 1f out: wknd rapidly fnl f* **100/1**

0201 **8** 3 ¼ **Comrade Cotton**[14] 7433 4-9-0 55............(v) AdamKirby 9 42
(J Ryan) *dwlt: hld up in last pair: rdn over 2f out: sn struggling* **20/1**

6000 **9** 7 **Ma Ridge**[10] 7469 4-8-6 45............(p) AndreaAtzeni(5) 1 20
(T D McCarthy) *narrow ld to over 2f out: wknd rapidly: t.o* **100/1**

-000 **10** 5 **Mairead's Boy (IRE)**[90] 5787 3-8-6 53............ MarcHalford(3) 10 4
(J L Spearing) *nvr gng wl: struggling u.p bef 1/2-way: t.o* **66/1**

1m 22.96s (-1.84) **Going Correction** -0.15s/f (Stan) course record **10** Ran SP% **124.0**
Speed ratings (Par 101): **104,103,100,99,98 94,93,89,81,75**
toteswinger: 1&2 £1.60, 1&3 £8.30, 2&3 £6.80. CSF £3.35 TOTE £2.40: £1.10, £1.10, £5.90; EX 4.20 Trifecta £66.90 Pool: £538.17 - 5.95 winning units..
Owner Market Avenue Racing Club Ltd **Bred** Limestone Stud **Trained** Middleham Moor, N Yorks

FOCUS
A reasonable claimer, with four of the runners having a BHA rating between 79 and 85. The pace was not particularly strong but the first two fought out a thrilling finish and were clear of the rest. The moderate third looks the best guide to the true level.
Makshoof(IRE) Official explanation: jockey said gelding missed the break

7602 THREE BRIDGES MEDIAN AUCTION MAIDEN STKS 1m (P)
2:00 (2:01) (Class 6) 2-Y-O **£2,047** (£604; £302) **Stalls** High

Form RPR

3 **1** **December Draw (IRE)**[23] 7336 2-9-3 0............ ShaneKelly 3 75+
(W J Knight) *trckd ldrs: briefly looked in trble whn shkn up in 4th over 2f out: picked up and r.o to ld 1f out: sn clr* **8/15**[1]

2 3 ¼ **Dover Street Art (IRE)** 2-9-3 0............ HayleyTurner 7 68+
(D R C Elsworth) *s.s: hld up towards rr: nt clr run 3f out: prog 2f out: green whn shkn up over 1f out: styd on wl to take 2nd nr fin* **7/1**[2]

0503 **3** ¾ **Darwin's Dragon**[24] 7318 2-9-3 72............ NelsonDeSouza 12 66
(P F I Cole) *trckd ldng pair: wnt 2nd 3f out: tried to chal jst over 1f out: sn outpcd: kpt on* **11/1**[3]

00 **4** nk **Cayman Sky**[23] 7336 2-9-0 0............(b) PatrickHills(3) 4 65
(R Hannon) *chsd ldng pair: rdn in 3rd over 2f out: tried to cl 1f out: sn outpcd: kpt on* **25/1**

46 **5** shd **Ymir**[19] 7380 2-9-3 0............ PaulDoe 5 65
(M J Attwater) *pressed ldr: led over 3f out: kicked on 2f out: hdd 1f out: no ch w wnr after: lost 3 pls nr fin* **20/1**

6 1 ¼ **Fromthebeginning** 2-9-0 0............ MarcHalford(3) 6 62+
(D R C Elsworth) *s.v.s: mostly in last trio and rn green: sme prog 2f out: hanging but kpt on encouragingly fnl f* **16/1**

7 4 ½ **Marlos Moment** 2-9-3 0............ AdamKirby 8 52
(W R Swinburn) *nt wl away but sn in midfield: green and outpcd fr 3f out: n.d after* **20/1**

4 **8** 2 ½ **Where You Will**[46] 6923 2-8-12 0............ JerryO'Dwyer 2 42
(S W Hall) *chsd ldrs: drvn in 5th wl over 2f out: sn btn* **25/1**

05 **9** 3 **Vodka Shot (USA)**[16] 7425 2-8-5 0............ MalinHolmberg(7) 9 35
(M L W Bell) *racd wd in midfield: nudged along and steadily lost grnd fnl 2f* **33/1**

10 hd **Cluny** 2-8-12 0............ EddieAhern 11 35
(J R Fanshawe) *dwlt: hld up in last pair: gng wl enough but stl there 3f out and wl bhd: nt clr run briefly over 2f out: nudged along and kpt on steadily fnl f* **16/1**

11 1 **Jeronimo Joe** 2-8-10 0............ PNolan(7) 10 38
(A B Haynes) *u.p in rr over 3f out: sn bhd* **66/1**

12 30 **Rental Roy** 2-9-3 0............ MichaelHills 1 —
(Mrs P Townsley) *dwlt: rousted up on inner to ld: hdd over 3f out: wknd v rapidly: t.o* **50/1**

1m 37.59s (-0.61) **Going Correction** -0.15s/f (Stan) 12 Ran SP% **121.4**
Speed ratings (Par 94): **97,93,93,92,92 91,86,84,81,81 80,50**
toteswinger: 1&2 £2.50, 1&3 £2.70, 2&3 £4.80. CSF £4.03 TOTE £1.50: £1.10, £1.70, £2.70; EX 4.90 Trifecta £11.20 Pool: £313.22 - 20.58 winning units..
Owner Brook House **Bred** Wardstown Stud Ltd **Trained** Patching, W Sussex
■ Stewards' Enquiry : Malin Holmberg ten-day ban: breach of Rule 158 (failed to make sufficient effort) (Dec 22-23, 26-31, Jan 1-2)

FOCUS
An uncompetitive maiden and difficult to rate higher through those in the frame behind the winner, but the race should produce winners.

NOTEBOOK
December Draw(IRE) shaped with a huge amount of promise when third from a poor draw in a strong-looking 1m Great Leighs maiden last month. That form had been franked by the runner-up winning in good style next time and he set a clear standard here. He made quite hard work of it and looked in a bit of trouble coming down the hill into the turn but stayed on in determined fashion and eventually won going away. (op 1-2 tchd 4-9 and 4-7, 8-13 in a place)
Dover Street Art(IRE) ◆, who cost 35,000gns and is out of a Lingfield Oaks Trial winner, was the eyecatcher of the race. He was backed form 10-1 to 7-1 and flashed home to snatch second. He will be suited by a stiffer test in time but this was a promising debut and he should not have much trouble winning a similar event this winter. (op 10-1)
Darwin's Dragon seems to be learning to settle better and ran a solid race stepped back up to 1m behind two less exposed rivals. (op 8-1)
Cayman Sky was a long way behind December Draw at 33-1 last time, but managed to trim the gap a bit with second-time blinkers appearing to have a positive effect.
Ymir was given a positive ride and travelled with a bit more fluency than he has on two previous starts. He may have kicked on too early in the straight but did well to keep grinding away and probably posted his best effort stepped up to this trip for the first time.
Fromthebeginning was slowly away and ran very green on his debut, but should improve significantly for the experience. (op 20-1 tchd 22-1)
Marlos Moment, who is a half-brother to nine winners, should do better in time. (op 25-1)
Vodka Shot(USA) Official explanation: jockey said, regarding running and riding, that her orders were to jump out in mid-division, and to finish as close as she could, adding that the filly started to hang in home straight; trainer's rep confirmed but said trainer was disappointed that the filly was taken so wide and possibly didn't ask for sufficient effort in home straight.

7603 ALEX LAWRENCE MEMORIAL H'CAP 1m (P)
2:30 (2:30) (Class 5) (0-75,75) 3-Y-O+ **£2,729** (£806; £403) **Stalls** High

Form RPR

0062 **1** **Trafalgar Square**[9] 7494 6-8-13 68............ JimCrowley 3 80
(M J Attwater) *hld up rt bhd ldrs: effrt over 1f out: r.o to ld fnl 150yds: drvn clr* **11/4**[2]

3000 **2** 2 **Napoletano (GER)**[3] 7557 7-8-13 68............ NickyMackay 2 75
(S Dow) *t.k.h early: hld up bhd ldrs: tended to run-in snatches fr 1/2-way: effrt to chal 1f out: outpcd by wnr fnl 150yds* **10/1**

441 **3** 1 ¼ **Lyceana**[18] 7395 3-9-4 74............ DarryllHolland 6 78
(M A Jarvis) *hld up towards rr in steadily run r: effrt over 1f out: pushed along firmly and styd on to take 3rd nr fin* **2/1**[1]

0000 **4** ½ **Pegasus Again (USA)**[19] 7386 3-9-2 72............(p) HayleyTurner 7 75
(T G Mills) *pressed ldrs: rdn 3f out: stl cl enough 1f out: outpcd* **9/1**[3]

455 **5** shd **Kidlat**[143] 4161 3-9-5 75............(t) MichaelHills 8 78
(B G Powell) *stdd s fr wd draw: hld up in rr: effrt and rdn 3f out: nt qckn 2f out: kpt on fnl f* **10/1**

0004 **6** ¾ **Straight And Level (CAN)**[25] 7302 3-8-13 69............ TravisBlock 9 70
(Miss Jo Crowley) *hld up towards rr in steadily run r: rdn over 2f out: nvr pce to threaten ldrs* **14/1**

2210 **7** hd **Bridge Of Fermoy (IRE)**[224] 1685 3-9-0 75............(bt) MarkFlynn(5) 5 76
(Miss Gay Kelleway) *t.k.h early: w ldr: drvn ahd over 1f out: hdd & wknd fnl 150yds* **16/1**

5050 **8** ½ **Yankee Storm**[11] 7462 3-9-4 74............(p) ShaneKelly 10 73
(P W D'Arcy) *hld up in last pair in steadily run r: stl there over 1f out: pushed along and nvr nr ldrs* **12/1**

-030 **9** 1 ¼ **Certain Justice (USA)**[9] 7495 10-8-11 66............ MickyFenton 4 63
(Stef Liddiard) *t.k.h early: hld up in last pair: outpcd over 2f out: no ch after* **33/1**

3400 **10** 4 ½ **Paradise Dancer (IRE)**[16] 7419 4-9-4 73............ IanMongan 1 59
(J A R Toller) *t.k.h early: led at mod pce: upped the tempo 3f out: hdd & wknd rapidly over 1f out* **12/1**

1m 37.24s (-0.96) **Going Correction** -0.15s/f (Stan)
WFA 3 from 4yo+ 1lb 10 Ran SP% **119.1**
Speed ratings (Par 103): **98,96,94,94,94 93,93,92,91,86**
toteswinger: 1&2 £7.50, 1&3 £1.90, 2&3 £6.60. CSF £31.49 CT £67.18 TOTE £3.90: £1.70, £2.50, £1.80; EX 35.40 Trifecta £82.80 Pool: £295.53 - 2.64 winning units..
Owner Canisbay Bloodstock **Bred** Matthews Breeding And Racing Ltd **Trained** Epsom, Surrey

FOCUS
A fair handicap run at a reasonable pace and the form makes sense at face value.
Lyceana Official explanation: jockey said filly missed the break

7604 FOREST ROW H'CAP 1m 4f (P)
3:00 (3:00) (Class 5) (0-70,67) 3-Y-O **£2,729** (£806; £403) **Stalls** Low

Form RPR

054 **1** **Antillia**[19] 7387 3-8-13 62............ EddieAhern 6 76
(C F Wall) *hld up in 4th: effrt to chse ldr wl over 1f out: sustained chal on inner fnl f: led fnl 50yds* **4/1**[3]

2111 **2** ½ **Epsom Salts**[19] 7385 3-8-9 63............ JackDean(5) 7 76
(P M Phelan) *trckd ldr: led jst over 2f out: drvn over 1f out: collared fnl 50yds* **9/4**[1]

0661 **3** 4 ½ **Tropical Tradition (IRE)**[24] 7310 3-8-12 61............ MartinDwyer 2 67+
(D W P Arbuthnot) *hld up in 5th: swtchd to inner over 2f out and nt clr run after: drvn and one pce over 1f out* **4/1**[3]

3322 **4** 12 **Locum**[9] 7489 3-9-2 65............ PaulMulrennan 5 52
(M H Tompkins) *led at decent pce: stdd 1/2-way: hdd & wknd tamely jst over 2f out* **13/2**

0000 **5** 16 **Rettorical Lad**[10] 7474 3-8-11 60............ JimCrowley 4 21
(Jamie Poulton) *chsd ldng pair to over 3f out: wknd rapidly: t.o* **50/1**

0502 **P** **Taken (IRE)**[8] 7506 3-9-4 67............(p) HayleyTurner 1 —
(Miss Gay Kelleway) *hld up in last: lost action and p.u 5f out* **3/1**[2]

2m 30.02s (-2.98) **Going Correction** -0.15s/f (Stan) 6 Ran SP% **111.1**
Speed ratings (Par 102): **103,102,99,91,81** —
toteswinger: 1&2 £2.00, 1&3 £3.60, 2&3 £2.00. CSF £13.13 TOTE £5.20: £2.40, £1.90; EX 19.70.
Owner Ali Saeed **Bred** The Kingwood Partnership **Trained** Newmarket, Suffolk

FOCUS
A competitive event, with four of the runners having won or finished runner-up on their previous outing. The form looks sound.

7605 CROWBOROUGH H'CAP (DIV II) 1m 2f (P)
3:30 (3:31) (Class 6) (0-52,52) 3-Y-O+ **£1,706** (£503; £252) **Stalls** Low

Form RPR

-660 **1** **Whodunit (UAE)**[3] 7559 4-8-12 48............(b) ShaneKelly 13 56
(P W Hiatt) *mde all: set stop-s pce: kicked clr fr 2f out as rest got in each other's way: in n.d after despite dwindling advantage nr fin* **11/1**

3453 **2** 1 ¼ **Marie Tempest**[53] 6753 3-8-10 49............ FergusSweeney 8 54
(M R Bosley) *hld up in midfield: prog wl over 2f out: drvn to chse wnr over 1f out: clsd fnl f but no ch to chal* **7/2**[2]

1440 **3** ½ **Dazzling Begum**[24] 7310 3-8-13 52............ JimmyQuinn 3 56+
(J Pearce) *trckd ldrs: rdn over 2f out: styd on fr over 1f out to take 3rd ins fnl f: clsng fin but no ch* **11/2**[3]

0000 **4** 1 ½ **Inquisitress**[9] 7495 4-9-2 52............ JimCrowley 11 53+
(J J Bridger) *dwlt: hld up in last trio: stl there 2f out but gng wl: pushed along over 1f out: single reminder ins fnl f: r.o last 100yds* **16/1**

500 **5** nk **Pop Music (IRE)**[1] 7596 5-9-0 50............(p) JamesDoyle 10 50
(Ms J S Doyle) *prom: wnt 2nd over 3f out: hanging and looked reluctant over 2f out: lost 2nd over 1f out: one pce* **17/2**

4 **6** nse **Sea Cliff (IRE)**[1] 7590 4-8-10 46 oh1............ MartinDwyer 4 46
(Jonjo O'Neill) *j. path after 100yds: a in midfield: rdn over 2f out: kpt on same pce: n.d* **10/3**[1]

4605 **7** nk **Has To Be Abacus (IRE)**[98] 5577 3-8-9 48............ EddieAhern 6 48+
(A B Haynes) *hld up in rr: pushed along over 1f out: styd on steadily fnl f: nvr nr ldrs* **9/1**

1500 **8** 1 ¾ **Maddy**[46] 6929 3-8-6 52............(p) MatthewDavies(7) 7 48
(George Baker) *racd wd towards rr: outpcd fr 2f out: no imp after* **18/1**

0-50 **9** shd **Airedale Lad (IRE)**[51] 2395 7-8-10 46 oh1............ HayleyTurner 9 42
(C Gordon) *prom: rdn whn bmpd on inner over 2f out: wknd over 1f out* **40/1**

0-00 **10** 1 ¾ **Ella Y Rossa**[328] 171 4-8-13 49............(p) AdamKirby 12 42
(C R Dore) *stdd s: hld up in last pair: rdn and no imp on ldrs over 1f out: wknd nr fin* **14/1**

000 **11** 8 **Gun For Sale (USA)**[18] 7395 3-8-11 50............ TravisBlock 5 27
(P J Makin) *plld hrd: sn trckd ldr: lost 2nd over 3f out: cl up whn bmpd on inner over 2f out: wknd rapidly* **25/1**

P000 **12** 2 ¾ **Herrbee (IRE)**[183] 2861 3-8-4 46 oh1............ MarcHalford(3) 2 17
(J L Spearing) *a towards rr: wknd over 2f out: t.o* **20/1**

2m 5.75s (-0.85) **Going Correction** -0.15s/f (Stan)
WFA 3 from 4yo+ 3lb 41 Ran SP% **118.4**
Speed ratings (Par 101): **97,96,95,94,94 94,93,92,92,91 84,82**
toteswinger: 1&2 £13.10, 1&3 £13.80, 2&3 £4.20. CSF £48.22 CT £241.88 TOTE £14.70: £3.60, £1.60, £2.30; EX 76.40 Trifecta £195.90 Part won. Pool: £264.83 - 0.10 winning units. Place 6: £7.90 Place 5: £2.53.
Owner J W Hedges **Bred** Darley **Trained** Hook Norton, Oxon

FOCUS
An ordinary handicap in which the placed horses are close to their marks.
Pop Music(IRE) Official explanation: jockey said gelding hung left
Sea Cliff(IRE) Official explanation: jockey said gelding jumped path shortly after start and never travelled thereafter
Gun For Sale(USA) Official explanation: jockey said gelding hung left

T/Plt: £5.30 to a £1 stake. Pool: £50,530.72. 6,865.73 winning tickets. T/Qpdt: £2.20 to a £1 stake. Pool: £3,854.23. 1,242.97 winning tickets. JN

7581 WOLVERHAMPTON (A.W) (L-H)

Monday, December 8

OFFICIAL GOING: Standard

Wind: Almost nil Weather: Raining after 2.40

7606 STAY AT THE WOLVERHAMPTON HOLIDAY INN AMATEUR RIDERS' H'CAP 1m 1f 103y(P)

2:10 (2:10) (Class 5) (0-75,90) 3-Y-0+ **£3,123** (£968; £484; £242) **Stalls** Low

Form RPR

6110 **1** **Hucking Heat (IRE)**[21] 7354 4-10-13 **67**....................(p) MrLeeNewnes 2 86
(R Hollinshead) *hld up in mid-div: hdwy over 3f out: led jst over 1f out: clr ins fnl f: easily* **8/1**

1045 **2** *7* **Strike Force**[19] 7385 4-10-4 **63**.............................. MissALHutchinson(5) 1 67
(K F Clutterbuck) *hld up in mid-div: hdwy on outside over 2f out: styd on to take 2nd last strides: no ch w wnr* **8/1**

0230 **3** *hd* **Morbick**[12] 7457 4-11-1 **72**.............................. MrBenBrisbourne(3) 6 76
(W M Brisbourne) *hld up in tch: led over 2f out: sn rdn: hdd jst over 1f out: sn btn: lost 2nd last strides* **7/2**[2]

2032 **4** *1 3/4* **My Mirasol**[64] 6090 4-10-10 **64**..(p) MrSWalker 9 64
(D E Cantillon) *w ldr: led over 4f out tl over 2f out: sn rdn: one pce fnl f* **10/3**[1]

1040 **5** *2 1/4* **New Star (UAE)**[26] 7291 4-11-2 **75**.......................... MrHarryChalloner(5) 4 71
(W M Brisbourne) *hld up in tch: hrd rdn wl over 1f out: no hdwy* **8/1**

2261 **6** *1 1/4* **Randama Bay (IRE)**[8] 7507 3-10-13 **76** 6ex.................... MrCMartin(7) 7 69
(I A Wood) *prom: rdn over 2f out: wknd wl over 1f out* **8/1**

0000 **7** *1/2* **Monfils Monfils (USA)**[34] 7183 6-10-9 **70**.................... MrATBrook(7) 13 62
(A J McCabe) *hld up towards rr: rdn over 2f out: nvr trbld ldrs* **33/1**

/0-0 **8** *2* **Barodine**[12] 6899 5-10-8 **67**..(t) MrIPopham(5) 10 55
(R J Hodges) *hld up in tch: wknd wl over 1f out* **33/1**

1300 **9** *2 3/4* **Home**[19] 7385 3-10-2 **65**.. MissLGray(7) 8 47
(C Gordon) *sn wl bhd* **50/1**

0000 **10** *3 3/4* **Jord (IRE)**[58] 6663 4-10-7 **66**.. MissABevan(5) 3 40
(A J McCabe) *led: hdd over 4f out: wknd over 3f out* **50/1**

2025 **11** *2 1/2* **Mustajed**[40] 7064 7-11-0 **73**.. MrPMillman(5) 5 42
(B R Millman) *s.v.s: sn wl bhd* **11/2**[3]

2301 **12** *11* **Laish Ya Hajar (IRE)**[11] 4371 4-10-10 **71**.................... MrBBrackenbury(7) 11 17
(P R Webber) *prom tl wknd over 3f out* **20/1**

600/ **13** *15* **Nostradamus (USA)**[1541] 4529 9-12-1 **90** ow15........ MrMMcCarthy(7) 12 4
(K J Burke) *sn wl bhd: lost tch 6f out* **150/1**

2m 1.79s (0.09) **Going Correction** +0.10s/f (Slow)
WFA 3 from 4yo+ 2lb **13 Ran SP% 120.4**
Speed ratings (Par 103): **103,96,96,95,93 91,91,89,87,83 81,71,58**
toteswinger: 1&2 £13.30, 1&3 £8.10, 2&3 £3.50. CSF £67.32 CT £269.49 TOTE £9.50: £2.90, £2.60, £2.20; EX 65.70.
Owner Ed Weetman (haulage & Storage) Ltd **Bred** Thomas J Reid **Trained** Upper Longdon, Staffs

FOCUS
This handicap for amateur riders was run at a frantic early pace and produced an easy winner. The form is rated around the runner-up.

7607 WOLVERHAMPTON-RACECOURSE.CO.UK CLAIMING STKS 1m 141y(P)

2:40 (2:41) (Class 6) 2-Y-0 **£3,070** (£906; £453) **Stalls** Low

Form RPR

2055 **1** **Autumn Morning (IRE)**[21] 7361 2-8-0 52 ow3...... PatrickDonaghy(5) 12 57
(P D Evans) *t.k.h towards rr: hdwy over 2f out: sn rdn: r.o to ld wl ins fnl f* **28/1**

06 **2** *1/2* **Gwerthybyd**[12] 7452 2-8-2 0.. CatherineGannon 2 53+
(B Palling) *t.k.h in mid-div: gd hdwy on outside over 2f out: led wl over 1f out: sn rdn: hdd wl ins fnl f* **40/1**

00 **3** *4* **Peintre D'Argent (IRE)**[23] 7337 2-9-0 0.......................... SteveDrowne 9 57+
(H Morrison) *s.i.s: hld up in rr: hdwy 2f out: r.o to take 3rd ins fnl f: nt trble ldng pair* **20/1**

6540 **4** *2 1/4* **Premier Krug (IRE)**[7] 7519 2-7-13 56.......................... LukeMorris(3) 11 40
(P D Evans) *hld up towards rr: pushed along whn nt clr run 4f out: sn swtchd rt: rdn over 2f out: styd on fnl f: nvr nrr* **6/1**[3]

0000 **5** *1/2* **Alderbed**[7] 7514 2-8-7 50..(b[1]) LPKeniry 5 44
(George Baker) *hld up and bhd: hdwy on ins over 2f out: rdn and one pce fnl f* **33/1**

6460 **6** *3/4* **Give (IRE)**[21] 7353 2-8-2 54..(p) FrankieMcDonald 6 37
(R A Harris) *hld up in tch: rdn over 2f out: wknd ins fnl f* **20/1**

3260 **7** *nse* **Rose Of Coma (IRE)**[13] 7443 2-8-4 59..........................(p) GregFairley 10 39
(Miss Gay Kelleway) *prom: wnt 2nd 6f out: ev ch over 2f out: sn rdn: wknd ins fnl f* **8/1**

1032 **8** *3/4* **Jonah's Cruising (IRE)**[16] 7415 2-8-3 61.......................... ChrisCatlin 4 37
(J R Boyle) *hld up in tch: rdn jst over 1f out: wknd ins fnl f* **13/8**[1]

0400 **9** *1 1/2* **Telling Stories (IRE)**[7] 7514 2-7-7 58.......................... MatthewLawson(7) 8 30
(M Johnston) *s.i.s: in rr: pushed along 7f out: rdn over 3f out: n.d* **20/1**

2040 **10** *2 3/4* **Protiva**[8] 7505 2-8-10 63..(v) DaneO'Neill 7 35
(A P Jarvis) *sn led: hdd wl over 1f out: sn rdn and wknd* **12/1**

0050 **11** *2* **Daily Planet (IRE)**[10] 7468 2-8-0 40..............................(p) AmyScott(7) 13 27
(B W Duke) *hld up in mid-div: wknd over 2f out* **100/1**

0563 **12** *6* **Dougie Peel**[16] 7425 2-8-7 58..(p) FrancisNorton 3 15
(K A Ryan) *led early: prom: rdn over 2f out: wknd wl over 1f out* **7/2**[2]

0000 **13** *4 1/2* **Four Green Fields (IRE)**[28] 7266 2-7-9 40..................(p) AmyBaker(5) 1 —
(B W Duke) *hld up in tch: lost pl 5f out: rdn and struggling over 3f out* **40/1**

1m 52.09s (1.59) **Going Correction** +0.10s/f (Slow) **13 Ran SP% 119.9**
Speed ratings (Par 94): **96,95,92,90,89 88,88,88,86,84 82,77,73**
toteswinger: 1&2 £44.70, 1&3 £44.70, 2&3 £44.70. CSF £816.78 TOTE £31.40: £5.90, £7.30, £7.10; EX 823.10.Peintre d'Argent was claimed by A. Black for £12000.
Owner Mrs Sally Edwards **Bred** Jim McCartan **Trained** Pandy, Monmouths

FOCUS
There was a solid pace in this juvenile claimer and the first pair came clear. The form looks weak despite the first two going clear.

NOTEBOOK
Autumn Morning(IRE), whose stable won the race last year, knuckled down gamely from the furlong marker and just did enough to get up. This was her first outing beyond 6f and she evidently stays well, which was greatly highlighted by her refusal to settle early on. She is only moderate, but it should be noted that her rider carried 3lb overweight and there could be more to come after this career-first success. (op 25-1)
Gwerthybyd, up in trip, was produced wide around the home turn with a strong run and held every chance, but was just run out of it late on. She has now found her level and a slightly more patient ride over this distance can see her go one better. (op 33-1)
Peintre D'Argent(IRE) ◆ showed her first worthwhile form on this drop in class and showed more than enough to suggest she can be found a winning turn when faced with a stiffer test, something her pedigree firmly backs up. (tchd 22-1)
Premier Krug(IRE) ran in snatches and once again got going all too late in the day. She is not one for win-only purposes, but does help to put this form into perspective. (op 11-2 tchd 13-2)
Jonah's Cruising(IRE) did not get the best of passages into the home straight, but her response when in the clear was very limited. (op 6-4 tchd 7-4)

7608 DINE IN THE HORIZONS RESTAURANT (S) STKS 1m 4f 50y(P)

3:10 (3:11) (Class 6) 3-Y-0+ **£2,047** (£604; £302) **Stalls** Low

Form RPR

1615 **1** **Bridgewater Boys**[24] 7309 7-9-8 70..............................(b) GeorgeBaker 5 68
(G L Moore) *hld up in rr: hdwy over 2f out: rdn to ld ins fnl f: r.o* **8/13**[1]

0225 **2** *1/2* **Torrens (IRE)**[1] 7590 6-8-13 58..............................(t) PatrickDonaghy(5) 3 63
(P D Evans) *hld up towards rr: hdwy 3f out: led over 1f out: rdn and hdd ins fnl f: kpt on* **6/1**[3]

4602 **3** *7* **Sleepy Mountain**[10] 7473 4-9-4 50.............................. DaneO'Neill 8 52
(A Middleton) *t.k.h: a.p: wnt 2nd 3f out: rdn and ev ch wl over 1f out: wknd ins fnl f* **11/2**[2]

0565 **4** *1 1/4* **Summer Bounty**[10] 7473 12-9-4 46.............................. PaulFitzsimons 2 50
(F Jordan) *s.i.s: hld up in rr: hdwy on ins over 2f out: rdn wl over 1f out: wknd ins fnl f* **28/1**

5660 **5** *3/4* **Atlantic Gamble (IRE)**[9] 7499 8-9-1 52..............(p) DeclanCannon(7) 12 53
(K R Burke) *t.k.h: w ldr: led over 5f out tl over 1f out: wknd ins fnl f* **33/1**

3420 **6** *1/2* **York Cliff**[7] 7512 10-9-8 57.. LiamJones 6 52
(W M Brisbourne) *hld up in mid-div: hdwy over 5f out: rdn over 2f out: wknd wl over 1f out* **16/1**

0650 **7** *5* **Bond Casino**[17] 7400 4-8-10 40..............................(v[1]) DuranFentiman(3) 1 35
(G R Oldroyd) *hld up in mid-div: lost pl over 3f out: n.d after* **20/1**

0446 **8** *1* **Starcross Maid**[144] 4123 6-9-3 49.............................. VinceSlattery 9 37
(A G Juckes) *hld up towards rr: hdwy over 4f out: wknd wl over 1f out* **50/1**

0060 **9** *17* **Jimmy Dean**[3] 7559 3-8-13 42..(t) NeilChalmers 11 11
(M Wellings) *hld up in mid-div: wknd 3f out* **100/1**

P0-0 **10** *3 1/2* **I'm Agenius**[28] 7265 5-8-8 40.............................. GabrielHannon(5) 10 —
(P A Blockley) *hld up in tch: chsd ldr 5f out to 3f out: wknd qckly* **100/1**

0 **11** *32* **All About Jack**[9] 7500 4-9-4 0..............................(v[1]) FrankieMcDonald 4 —
(G A Ham) *led: hdd over 5f out: wknd over 4f out: t.o fnl 2f* **200/1**

2m 44.31s (3.21) **Going Correction** +0.10s/f (Slow)
WFA 3 from 4yo+ 5lb **11 Ran SP% 113.1**
Speed ratings (Par 101): **93,92,88,87,86 86,83,82,71,68 47**
toteswinger: 1&2 £2.30, 1&3 £2.20, 2&3 £3.10. CSF £3.97 TOTE £1.50: £1.10, £2.20, £1.30; EX 6.40.There was no bid for the winner.
Owner Matthew Green & Richard Green **Bred** Southill Stud **Trained** Woodingdean, E Sussex

FOCUS
The first pair came clear in this ordinary seller but did not need to run to their best and the third and fourth set the level to their latest marks.
York Cliff Official explanation: jockey said gelding lost its action

7609 RACING ALL YEAR ROUND MAIDEN STKS 1m 141y(P)

3:40 (3:40) (Class 5) 3-Y-0+ **£3,238** (£963; £481; £240) **Stalls** Low

Form RPR

53 **1** **Supaverdi (USA)**[23] 7344 3-8-12 0.............................. SteveDrowne 7 69+
(H Morrison) *hld up and bhd: hdwy 3f out: led over 1f out: sn rdn: clr ins fnl f: eased towards fin* **7/4**[2]

60 **2** *3 1/2* **Focail Eile**[17] 7403 3-9-3 0.. GrahamGibbons 6 66
(E S McMahon) *a.p: pushed along over 3f out: rdn wl over 1f out: wnt 2nd ins fnl f: no ch w wnr* **25/1**

6 **3** *1 1/4* **Celtic Gold (USA)**[18] 7395 4-9-5 0.............................. ChrisCatlin 1 63
(Andrew Turnell) *hld up in rr: hdwy on ins over 2f out: styd on to take 3rd towards fin* **22/1**

00 **4** *1 1/4* **Fashion Week**[10] 7474 3-9-3 0.. GregFairley 2 60
(M Johnston) *led: rdn 3f out: hdd over 1f out: fdd wl ins fnl f* **16/1**[3]

3 **5** *1 1/2* **Annabelle's Charm (IRE)**[19] 7387 3-8-12 0.......................... DaneO'Neill 9 52
(L M Cumani) *bhd: sn hung rt: rdn over 3f out: nvr trbld ldrs* **5/6**[1]

3303 **6** *1 1/2* **Sir Ike (IRE)**[8] 7504 3-9-3 61..(t) LPKeniry 3 53
(W S Kittow) *w ldr: chal 2f out: sn rdn: wknd ins fnl f* **16/1**[3]

-000 **7** *9* **Northgate Lodge (USA)**[52] 6791 3-9-3 45.......................... FrancisNorton 8 32
(M Brittain) *prom tl wknd over 2f out* **100/1**

8 *10* **Lido Shuffle** 3-9-3 0.. VinceSlattery 5 9
(M R Bosley) *prom tl wknd over 3f out* **66/1**

1m 51.56s (1.06) **Going Correction** +0.10s/f (Slow)
WFA 3 from 4yo 2lb **8 Ran SP% 113.4**
Speed ratings (Par 103): **99,95,94,93,92 91,83,74**
toteswinger: 1&2 £9.00, 1&3 £5.20, 2&3 £18.30. CSF £45.11 TOTE £2.40: £1.10, £5.90, £4.60; EX 55.60.
Owner Ben & Sir Martyn Arbib **Bred** Arbib Bloodstock Partnership **Trained** East Ilsley, Berks

FOCUS
A modest maiden which ultimately took little winning and with doubts over the placed horses the fourth is the best guide to the level.
Annabelle's Charm(IRE) Official explanation: jockey said filly hung badly right-handed

7610 HOTEL & CONFERENCING AT WOLVERHAMPTON H'CAP 1m 141y(P)

4:10 (4:10) (Class 5) (0-75,73) 3-Y-0+ **£3,885** (£1,156; £577; £288) **Stalls** Low

Form RPR

0200 **1** **Theonebox (USA)**[33] 7202 3-9-0 **72**.............................. LukeMorris(3) 11 86
(N J Vaughan) *hld up and bhd: hdwy on outside 2f out: rdn over 1f out: hung lft ins fnl f: sustained chal to ld cl home* **11/1**

2206 **2** *hd* **Outlandish**[40] 6607 5-9-5 **72**.. ChrisCatlin 6 86
(Andrew Turnell) *hld up in tch: led jst over 1f out: rdn and carried lft ins fnl f: hdd cl home* **6/1**[3]

4431 **3** *3* **Ours (IRE)**[21] 7368 5-9-3 **70**..(p) StephenDonohoe 12 77
(John A Harris) *hld up and bhd: swtchd rt and hdwy cl home: hung lft ins fnl f: one pce* **13/2**

0000 **4** *3/4* **Ninth House (USA)**[35] 7167 6-9-0 **67**.............................. LiamJones 8 72
(Mrs R A Carr) *hld up in mid-div: ev ch 1f out: rdn and one pce whn rdr dropped reins ins fnl f* **28/1**

0364 **5** *3 1/4* **Harvest Warrior**[12] 7457 6-8-13 **69**.............................. DuranFentiman(3) 9 67
(T D Easterby) *s.s: in rr: hrd rdn wl over 1f out: sme late prog: nvr nr ldrs* **12/1**

0304 **6** *nk* **Cat Whistle**[16] 7419 3-9-0 **69**.. TonyHamilton 4 66
(R A Fahey) *hld up in mid-div: nt clr run on ins over 2f out: hdwy over 1f out: sn rdn: wknd ins fnl f* **9/2**[2]

4304 **7** *1 3/4* **Master Pegasus**[9] 7495 5-8-10 **63**.............................. SteveDrowne 1 56
(J R Boyle) *wnt rt s: led after 1f: rdn and hdd jst over 1f out: wknd ins fnl f* **4/1**[1]

0052 **8** 2 1/4 **Moonlight Man**[8] 7507 7-9-6 **73**..........(t) LPKeniry 7 61
(C R Dore) *prom early: hld up: hdwy 5f out: ev ch over 2f out: wknd over 1f out* **4/1**[1]

3043 **9** 1 3/4 **Coleorton Dancer**[28] 7277 6-8-10 **63**.......... TomEaves 2 47
(K A Ryan) *sltly hmpd s: t.k.h: prom tl wknd 1f out* **10/1**

0-00 **10** 9 **Redeemed**[179] 2976 3-8-13 **68**..........(t) FrancisNorton 3 31
(M Brittain) *t.k.h: chsd ldr to 3f out: wknd 2f out* **66/1**

1m 50.26s (-0.24) **Going Correction** +0.10s/f (Slow)
WFA 3 from 5yo+ 2lb **10** Ran SP% **115.9**
Speed ratings (Par 103): **105,104,102,101,98 98,96,94,93,85**
toteswinger: 1&2 £14.20, 1&3 £13.50, 2&3 £8.20. CSF £75.09 CT £482.09 TOTE £14.80: £3.50, £2.30, £2.30; EX 104.80.
Owner The Straight Batters **Bred** Normandy Farm Llc & Nancy K Polk **Trained** Hampton, Cheshire
■ Stewards' Enquiry : Chris Catlin caution: careless riding
Luke Morris caution: careless riding.

FOCUS
A fair handicap for the class and the form is worth treating fairly positively.
Moonlight Man Official explanation: vet said gelding returned lame

7611 ENJOY EVENING RACING AT WOLVERHAMPTON H'CAP 5f 216y(P)
4:40 (4:40) (Class 5) (0-70,74) 3-Y-0+ **£3,885** (£1,156; £577; £288) **Stalls** Low

Form RPR

6-02 **1** **Richelieu**[17] 7399 6-9-1 **67**.......... TonyCulhane 4 76+
(J J Lambe, Ire) *in rr: pushed along 4f out: hdwy on ins over 1f out: sn rdn: led wl ins fnl f: drvn out* **15/2**

0014 **2** 1 1/4 **Incomparable**[13] 7448 3-9-4 **70**..........(p) StephenDonohoe 11 75
(A J McCabe) *chsd ldr: led over 4f out: rdn wl over 1f out: hdd wl ins fnl f: jst hld on for 2nd* **16/1**

121 **3** shd **River Kirov (IRE)**[16] 7416 5-8-10 **62**.......... ChrisCatlin 5 67+
(M Wigham) *plld hrd towards rr: hdwy 2f out: rdn and r.o wl towards fin: jst failed to take 2nd* **5/2**[1]

-314 **4** 1 1/2 **Radiator Rooney (IRE)**[141] 4231 5-9-1 **67**..........(v) GeorgeBaker 13 67+
(Patrick Morris, Ire) *plld hrd towards rr: rdn over 1f out: r.o ins fnl f: nrst fin* **16/1**

5342 **5** shd **Liberty Ship**[24] 7323 3-8-12 **64**..........(t) GrahamGibbons 3 64
(J D Bethell) *hld up in tch: swtchd lft wl over 1f out: rdn and nt qckn ins fnl f* **11/2**[3]

0612 **6** 1 **Ryedane (IRE)**[7] 7517 6-8-7 **62**..........(b) DuranFentiman(3) 9 59
(T D Easterby) *t.k.h in mid-div: hdwy over 2f out: no imp fnl f* **7/2**[2]

5025 **7** 1 3/4 **Dualagi**[21] 7359 4-8-10 **62**.......... VinceSlattery 2 53
(M R Bosley) *t.k.h towards rr: rdn over 1f out: swtchd lft ins fnl f: n.d* **25/1**

4040 **8** 2 1/2 **Maryolini**[70] 6340 3-9-1 **70**.......... LukeMorris 6 53
(N J Vaughan) *prom: rdn wl over 1f out: wknd ins fnl f* **15/2**

0506 **9** 3/4 **Choisette**[12] 7456 3-9-0 **66**.......... TomEaves 8 47
(B Smart) *led over 1f: chsd ldr tl over 2f out: rdn over 1f out: wknd ins fnl f* **20/1**

4510 **10** 4 1/2 **Hart Of Gold**[19] 7378 4-8-13 **65**..........(p) LPKeniry 7 31
(R A Harris) *plld hrd: prom tl wknd over 2f out* **14/1**

1m 15.21s (0.21) **Going Correction** +0.10s/f (Slow) **10** Ran SP% **116.7**
Speed ratings (Par 103): **102,100,100,98,98 96,94,91,90,84**
toteswinger: 1&2 £19.50, 1&3 £4.70, 2&3 £9.50. CSF £119.59 CT £393.54 TOTE £8.40: £2.30, £5.00, £1.40; EX 129.50 Place 6: £1, 811.10 Place 5: £735.96.
Owner Orchard County Syndicate **Bred** Darley **Trained** Dungannon, Co. Tyrone
■ Stewards' Enquiry : Graham Gibbons six-day ban: failed to ride out for 4th place (Dec 26-31)

FOCUS
A modest sprint, run at a decent early pace with the winner back to something like last year's form.
Ryedane(IRE) Official explanation: jockey said gelding ran too freely
Maryolini Official explanation: jockey said filly was struck into
T/Plt: £11,680.60 to a £1 stake. Pool: £68,643.95. 4.29 winning tickets. T/Qpdt: £20.80 to a £1 stake. Pool: £7,264.61. 258.10 winning tickets. KH

7527 SOUTHWELL (L-H)
Tuesday, December 9

OFFICIAL GOING: Standard
Wind: Light behind Weather: Bright and dry

7612 SOUTHWELL-RACECOURSE.CO.UK NURSERY 5f (F)
12:00 (12:02) (Class 6) (0-75,73) 2-Y-0 **£2,047** (£604; £302) **Stalls** High

Form RPR

3122 **1** **Rio Cobolo (IRE)**[7] 7531 2-8-8 **60**..........(v) ChrisCatlin 2 64
(Paul Green) *chsd ldrs: effrt 2f out and sn rdn: styd on u.p to ld ins fnl f* **13/8**[1]

0402 **2** 3/4 **Bold Rose**[34] 7199 2-8-6 **58**.......... HayleyTurner 6 59
(M D I Usher) *towards rr and sn pushed along: hdwy 1/2-way: rdn to ld over 1f out: drvn and hdd ins fnl f: one pce* **4/1**[3]

3054 **3** 1 1/4 **Chimbonda**[10] 7501 2-8-8 **63**.......... TolleyDean(3) 3 60
(S Parr) *cl up: rdn along 2f out and ev ch tl drvn and one pce ins fnl f* **14/1**

6404 **4** 1 1/2 **Africa's Star (IRE)**[17] 7417 2-8-13 **65**.......... DarryllHolland 7 56+
(M A Jarvis) *hld up in tch: hdwy to chse ldrs over 2f out: rdn wl over 1f out: no imp* **16/1**

2221 **5** 3 1/2 **Silent Wonder**[27] 7279 2-9-7 **73**..........(p) EddieAhern 8 52
(R M H Cowell) *cl up: led after 1f: rdn along over 2f out: hdd over 1f out and sn wknd* **7/2**[2]

0456 **6** 1/2 **Lucky Dan (IRE)**[13] 7454 2-8-10 **62**.......... PaulMulrennan 1 39
(Paul Green) *wnt lft s: sn chsng ldrs: rdn along over 2f out and sn wknd* **7/1**

3005 **7** 3 **Fasliyanne (IRE)**[13] 7451 2-8-8 **60**.......... FrancisNorton 5 26
(K A Ryan) *led 1f: cl up tl rdn along over 2f out and sn wknd* **16/1**

0005 **8** 6 **Rocket Ruby**[27] 7279 2-7-10 **51** oh2 ow1..........(v[1]) DuranFentiman(3) 4 —
(D Shaw) *s.i.s: a in rr* **66/1**

59.72 secs (0.02) **Going Correction** -0.075s/f (Stan) **8** Ran SP% **112.7**
Speed ratings (Par 94): **96,94,92,90,84 84,79,69**
toteswinger: 1&2 £1.70, 1&3 £5.70, 2&3 £9.40. CSF £7.98 CT £63.37 TOTE £2.60: £1.10, £1.80, £3.40; EX 6.80 Trifecta £81.70 Pool: £206.49 - 1.87 winning units..
Owner The Keely Gang **Bred** Yvonne & Gerard Kennedy **Trained** Lydiate, Merseyside

FOCUS
A modest nursery and, as is usually the case, those drawn out towards the centre of the track were at an advantage. The form looks solid but limited.

NOTEBOOK
Rio Cobolo(IRE), who has twice run well over further here since winning a nursery over this trip on turf early last month, was all the rage in the market beforehand. Despite fly-jumping exiting the stalls, he was soon in touch and although he tended to hang over to the far rail under pressure late on, he was always doing enough. He is likely to turn out again here over 6f on Friday and connections believe he is even better suited by that trip. (op 9-4)
Bold Rose, weighted to reverse last month's Nottingham running with Rio Cobolo, couldn't quite manage it on this different surface, but she gave herself every chance down the middle of the track and went down fighting. She is yet to win, but can surely find a race like this. (op 5-1 tchd 11-2)
Chimbonda helped force the pace from the start and kept on battling until overhauled late on. He managed to reverse last month's Lingfield running with Africa's Star, but he does look pretty exposed now. (op 9-1)
Africa's Star(IRE) soon found herself racing closest to the stands' rail and was always struggling to make an impact. She is becoming very disappointing. (op 9-1)
Silent Wonder, long odds-on winner of a moderate maiden over course and distance last time, was up there early having been switched to race down the centre from the rails draw, but he was soon on the retreat and found this much tougher. Official explanation: jockey said colt ran flat (op 3-1 tchd 4-1)

7613 MEMBERSHIP AT SOUTHWELL GOLF CLUB H'CAP 1m 3f (F)
12:30 (12:30) (Class 6) (0-65,65) 3-Y-0+ **£2,047** (£604; £302) **Stalls** Low

Form RPR

3005 **1** **Karmest**[27] 7284 4-9-5 **64**.......... GrahamGibbons 4 78
(A D Brown) *hld up in tch: smooth hdwy to trck ldrs over 4f out: effrt over 2f out: led wl over 1f out and sn rdn clr: styd on* **9/2**[2]

3001 **2** 3 3/4 **Fortunella**[25] 7322 3-8-5 **54**.......... ChrisCatlin 8 61
(Miss Gay Kelleway) *trckd ldrs: hdwy 4f out: cl up 3f out: rdn to chse wnr over 1f out: sn drvn and no imp* **11/2**

5256 **3** 3 1/4 **Transmission (IRE)**[12] 7461 3-8-13 **62**.......... TomEaves 6 64
(B Smart) *prom: cl up 1/2-way: rdn 3f out: led briefly over 2f out: drvn and hdd wl over 1f out: sn one pce* **4/1**[1]

0000 **4** 2 3/4 **Tykie Two**[10] 7499 4-8-1 **51** oh6..........(b) DeanHeslop(5) 5 48
(S Wynne) *led: rdn along over 3f out: drvn and hdd over 2f out: sn wknd* **25/1**

50 **5** 2 1/2 **Man Of Gwent (UAE)**[34] 7202 4-9-6 **65**.......... JamesDoyle 10 58
(P D Evans) *trckd ldrs on outer: hdwy 5f out: rdn along 3f out: sn drvn and btn* **4/1**[1]

0050 **6** 3/4 **King's Icon (IRE)**[30] 7261 3-8-2 **51**.......... FrancisNorton 7 42
(M Wigham) *hld up towards rr: hdwy 5f out: rdn along 3f out: sn drvn and nvr a factor* **11/2**

0000 **7** 3 **Lawyer To World**[84] 6005 4-8-6 **51** oh6..........(p) JimmyQuinn 1 37
(Mrs C A Dunnett) *chsd ldrs: rdn along over 4f out: wknd over 3f out* **66/1**

0604 **8** nk **Classical Rhythm (IRE)**[21] 7374 3-8-2 **56**..........(b) AndreaAtzeni(5) 9 42
(J R Boyle) *hld up towards rr: hdwy and in tch over 5f out: rdn along over 3f out: sn btn* **5/1**[3]

3000 **9** 12 **Bobering**[171] 3258 8-8-6 **51** oh6.......... CatherineGannon 2 16
(B P J Baugh) *a in rr* **66/1**

4040 **10** 19 **Bed Fellow (IRE)**[14] 7442 4-8-3 **51** oh2.......... DuranFentiman(3) 3 —
(Paul Murphy) *prom: rdn along and lost pl 1/2-way: sn outpcd* **25/1**

2m 27.17s (-0.83) **Going Correction** -0.20s/f (Stan)
WFA 3 from 4yo+ 4lb **10** Ran SP% **116.3**
Speed ratings (Par 101): **95,92,89,87,86 85,83,83,74,60**
toteswinger: 1&2 £3.40, 1&3 £4.10, 2&3 £3.00. CSF £28.48 CT £106.42 TOTE £6.60: £1.60, £1.20, £2.00; EX 18.70 Trifecta £107.50 Pool: £145.30 - 0.50 winning units..
Owner David Logan **Bred** Charles B B Booth **Trained** Pickering, York

FOCUS
A modest handicap, in which it was crucial to race close to the pace and nothing got into it from behind. The form is not that solid with the placed horses the best guide.
Man Of Gwent(UAE) Official explanation: trainer said, regarding running, that the gelding was unsuited by the fibresand.

7614 SOUTHWELL-RACECOURSE.CO.UK H'CAP 5f (F)
1:00 (1:05) (Class 3) (0-95,95) 3-Y-0+ **£7,771** (£2,312; £1,155; £577) **Stalls** High

Form RPR

0500 **1** **Turn On The Style**[34] 7192 6-9-7 **95**..........(b) PaulMulrennan 8 107
(J Balding) *reluctant and led to s: qckly away: mde all: rdn over 1f out: kpt on strly* **12/1**

0343 **2** 2 **Matsunosuke**[3] 7576 6-9-2 **90**.......... DarryllHolland 2 95
(A B Coogan) *hld up in midfield: hdwy 2f out: sn rdn: chsd wnr ins fnl f: no imp* **10/3**[1]

4550 **3** 1 **Pawan (IRE)**[20] 7381 8-8-5 **84** ow1..........(b) AnnStokell(5) 6 85
(Miss A Stokell) *hmpd s and towards rr: hdwy wl over 1f out: sn rdn and kpt on u.p ins fnl f* **11/1**

314 **4** hd **Garlogs**[13] 7456 5-8-2 **76**.......... HayleyTurner 10 76
(R Hollinshead) *trckd ldrs: hdwy to chse wnr 1/2-way: rdn along wl over 1f out: drvn ent fnl f and wknd* **13/2**[3]

2040 **5** nk **Soopacal (IRE)**[22] 7365 3-9-0 **88**.......... TomEaves 1 87
(B Smart) *chsd ldrs on outer: effrt 2f: sn rdn and wknd ent fnl f* **10/1**

3000 **6** 2 1/4 **Tartatartufata**[19] 7394 6-8-5 **79**..........(v) ChrisCatlin 9 70
(J G Given) *chsd ldrs: rdn along 2f out: sn btn* **18/1**

6025 **7** 1 1/4 **Luscivious**[22] 7365 4-8-11 **85**..........(b) StephenDonohoe 3 72
(A J McCabe) *hmpd s: a towards rr* **7/1**

5402 **8** 1 1/4 **He's A Humbug (IRE)**[2] 7592 4-8-2 **76**..........(p) PaulQuinn 11 58
(J O'Reilly) *chsd ldrs on outer: rdn along over 2f out and sn wknd* **16/1**

3513 **9** 1/2 **Yungaburra (IRE)**[3] 7584 4-8-11 **85** ow1..........(bt) AdamKirby 4 66
(S Parr) *wnt rt and sltly hmpd s: nvr nr ldrs* **11/2**[2]

0114 **10** 3 3/4 **Irish Pearl (IRE)**[19] 7394 3-9-7 **95**.......... FergusSweeney 7 62
(K R Burke) *chsd wnr: rdn along 1/2-way: drvn wl over 1f out and wknd qckly* **11/2**[2]

58.65 secs (-1.05) **Going Correction** -0.075s/f (Stan) **10** Ran SP% **115.9**
Speed ratings (Par 107): **105,101,100,99,99 95,93,91,91,85**
toteswinger: 1&2 £8.60, 1&3 £22.90, 2&3 £9.90. CSF £51.61 CT £473.41 TOTE £11.70: £3.60, £1.40, £2.80; EX 74.20 TRIFECTA Not won..
Owner The Haydock Badgeholders **Bred** J And Mrs Bowtell **Trained** Scrooby, Notts

FOCUS
A decent sprint handicap run at a furious pace and, although the draw didn't seem to be significant, the principals all ended up racing centre to far side. The placed horses set a reasonably solid standard.

NOTEBOOK
Turn On The Style had to be walked to the start, but came back rather quicker. Off the same mark as when last successful on sand, but unplaced in three previous tries over this course and distance, he was soon blazing his way down the middle of the track in front and it was obvious from some way out that nothing was going to get near him. Future plans for him remain fluid. (op 10-1 tchd 9-1)
Matsunosuke, currently well handicapped on his best form but without a win in over a year, was well drawn and after travelling well in the middle of the field, eventually emerged from the pack to chase the winner home, but never caused him any concern. This was only his second start on Fibresand and he has been placed in both. (op 4-1)
Pawan(IRE), not seen for 20 days, which is a lengthy layoff for him, was having his 25th outing of the year and ran his usual sort of race, staying on late to snatch third without ever looking like winning. (op 12-1 tchd 14-1)

Garlogs, a standing dish over this straight 5f, had an awkward, high draw to overcome, but he gradually edged to his left throughout the contest which eventually saw him try and challenge on the inside of the winner, so at least he was given every chance and just wasn't quite good enough on the day. (op 11-2 tchd 7-1)
Soopacal(IRE), having his first try here and still 10lb higher than for his last win, ran a creditable race from his decent draw and this should have put him spot on. (op 14-1)
Tartatartufata, who has a decent record over this course and distance, hasn't been at her best in three starts fort her current yard since returning from a break in October. Forced to switch right after losing her place at halfway, she then found herself racing closest to the stands' rail so wasn't completely disgraced under the circumstances. (op 16-1 tchd 14-1)
Irish Pearl(IRE), unbeaten in two previous starts here albeit over 6f, dropped right out after showing good early pace and although still 7lb higher than for her last win, this was still too bad to be true. Official explanation: jockey said filly lost its action (op 5-1 tchd 6-1)

7615 HOSPITALITY AT SOUTHWELL RACECOURSE H'CAP (DIV I) 6f (F)
1:30 (1:31) (Class 6) (0-60,60) 3-Y-O+ **£1,706** (£503; £252) **Stalls** Low

Form RPR
2000 **1** **Swallow Forest**[14] 7444 3-8-3 **50**.....................(b) DeanHeslop(5) 3 66
(T D Barron) *towards rr: pushed along 1/2-way: gd hdwy on inner 2f out: rdn over 1f out: styd on u.p ins fnl f to ld fnl 100yds: sn clr* **25/1**
3002 **2** 2¾ **Westwood**[7] 7534 3-9-4 **60**..................... HayleyTurner 7 68
(D Haydn Jones) *a.p: effrt 2f out: rdn to chal over 1f out: drvn to ld briefly ins fnl f: hdd and no ex fnl 100yds* **9/4**[1]
3060 **3** 1¼ **Hamaasy**[30] 7255 7-8-11 **56**..................... KevinGhunowa(3) 10 60
(R A Harris) *chsd ldrs: hdwy 1/2-way: rdn wl over 1f out: drvn and kpt on same pce ins fnl f* **11/2**[3]
0061 **4** hd **The Geester**[14] 7444 4-9-1 **57**.....................(b) PaulEddery 11 60
(S R Bowring) *prom on outer: led over 4f out: rdn wl over 1f out: drvn and hdd ins fnl f: wknd towards fin* **5/1**[2]
5050 **5** shd **Everything**[76] 6219 3-9-2 **58**..................... JamieMoriarty 2 61
(P T Midgley) *midfield: hdwy wl over 2f out: rdn to chse ldrs over 1f out: drvn and one pce ins fnl f* **33/1**
5603 **6** 1½ **The Little Fizzer (IRE)**[7] 7522 3-8-10 **52**..................... JamesDoyle 8 50
(P D Evans) *nvr bttr than midfield* **15/2**
03 **7** 4½ **Double Carpet (IRE)**[21] 7375 5-7-13 **46** oh1..................... AndreaAtzeni(5) 13 29
(G Woodward) *dwlt: midfield tl hdwy over 2f out: rdn to chse ldrs wl over 1f out: drvn and wknd appr last* **8/1**
3000 **8** hd **Scruffy Skip (IRE)**[7] 7521 3-8-11 **53**.....................(b) TGMcLaughlin 5 36
(Mrs C A Dunnett) *midfield: rdn along wl over 2f out: n.d* **33/1**
0524 **9** 5 **Tadlil**[9] 7509 6-8-3 **50**.....................(v) MCGeran(5) 14 17
(J M Bradley) *chsd ldrs on wd outside: effrt wl over 2f out: sn rdn and btn* **17/2**
0306 **10** 2¼ **Woqoodd**[132] 4542 4-8-13 **55**..................... DarrenWilliams 1 15
(D Shaw) *led on inner: hdd over 4f out: cl up tl rdn over 2f out and sn wknd* **16/1**
00-0 **11** ¾ **Sandies Choice**[203] 2268 3-8-4 **46** oh1.....................(b[1]) FrancisNorton 9 3
(M Brittain) *a bhd* **80/1**
5111 **12** 6 **Soba Jones**[291] 655 11-8-13 **58**..................... TolleyDean(5) 6 —
(J Balding) *t.k.h: hld up in tch: rdn along 1/2-way: sn wknd* **16/1**
4300 **13** 6 **Ducal Regancy Red**[7] 7529 4-8-1 **46**..................... DuranFentiman(3) 4 —
(C J Teague) *cl up: rdn along wl over 2f out: sn drvn and wknd* **80/1**

1m 15.21s (-1.29) **Going Correction** -0.20s/f (Stan) **13** Ran SP% **120.2**
Speed ratings (Par 101): **100,96,94,94,94 92,86,86,79,76 75,67,59**
toteswinger: 1&2 £20.00, 1&3 £41.60, 2&3 £4.20. CSF £79.85 CT £390.52 TOTE £41.10: £10.10, £1.80, £2.10; EX 188.40 TRIFECTA Not won..
Owner Laurence O'Kane **Bred** Foreneish Bloodstock **Trained** Maunby, N Yorks

FOCUS
A moderate sprint handicap and the slowest of the three over the trip on the day, but the form looks fair for the grade.

7616 CALL 01636 814481 TO SPONSOR A RACE CLAIMING STKS 6f (F)
2:00 (2:01) (Class 6) 3-Y-O+ **£1,978** (£584; £292) **Stalls** Low

Form RPR
0244 **1** **Came Back (IRE)**[7] 7529 5-8-10 **92**..................... DarrylIHolland 7 88+
(K A Ryan) *mde all: pushed clr over 1f out: easily* **10/11**[1]
0303 **2** 3¾ **Calmdownmate (IRE)**[7] 7529 3-8-8 **70**..................... DarrenWilliams 8 72
(K R Burke) *a chsng wnr: effrt over 2f out and sn rdn: drvn over 1f and no imp ins fnl f* **4/1**[2]
0613 **3** 4 **Bazguy**[20] 7378 3-8-7 **72**.....................(b) JamesO'Reilly(5) 10 63
(J O'Reilly) *chsd ldng pair: rdn along 2f out: sn drvn and one pce* **5/1**[3]
0350 **4** 3½ **Red Cape (FR)**[160] 3601 5-9-4 **83**.....................(b) LiamJones 5 58
(Mrs R A Carr) *trckd ldrs: effrt over 2f out: sn rdn and btn* **8/1**
4000 **5** ½ **Obe Royal**[68] 6411 4-8-10 **60**.....................(b) JamesDoyle 1 48
(P D Evans) *a in rr* **12/1**
0-00 **6** 4½ **Sultan Of The Sand**[176] 1453 3-8-8 **38**..................... FrankieMcDonald 4 32
(C C Bealby) *chsd ldrs: rdn along 1/2-way: sn wknd* **100/1**
-560 **7** 1¼ **Swallow Senora (IRE)**[187] 2491 6-7-11 **39**..................... AndreaAtzeni(5) 3 22
(M C Chapman) *a bhd* **80/1**

1m 14.43s (-2.07) **Going Correction** -0.20s/f (Stan) **7** Ran SP% **110.1**
Speed ratings (Par 101): **105,100,94,90,89 83,81**
.Came Back was claimed by J. R. Gask for £8,000. \n\x\x
Owner Mrs Ger O'Driscoll **Bred** Yeomanstown Stud **Trained** Hambleton, N Yorks

FOCUS
An uncompetitive claimer with the usual wide range of abilities and the race went just as the market suggested it would. the runner-up sets the level but the proximity of the sixth and seventh limits it.
Red Cape(FR) Official explanation: jockey said gelding hung left

7617 PLAY GOLF AT SOUTHWELL GOLF CLUB H'CAP 1m 6f (F)
2:30 (2:31) (Class 5) (0-75,74) 3-Y-O+ **£2,729** (£806; £403) **Stalls** Low

Form RPR
0504 **1** **Simple Jim (FR)**[27] 7285 4-8-9 **55** oh3..................... GrahamGibbons 8 63
(A D Brown) *hld up in rr: gd hdwy over 3f out: rdn to chal 2f out: sn led and hung lft 1f out: kpt on* **9/1**
0060 **2** 1 **Calculating (IRE)**[8] 7515 4-9-11 **71**..................... HayleyTurner 1 78
(M D I Usher) *chsd ldrs on inner: rdn along over 4f out: drvn and outpcd over 2f out: swtchd rt and rallied ent fnl f: styd on strly towards fin* **11/2**[3]
1436 **3** hd **Victory Quest (IRE)**[8] 7515 8-9-8 **68**.....................(v) ChrisCatlin 5 74
(Mrs S Lamyman) *chsd ldr: effrt 4f out: rdn along 3f out: drvn and outpcd 2f out: rallied wl u.p ins fnl f* **7/1**
-416 **4** nk **Dart**[22] 7366 4-9-7 **67**..................... AdamKirby 3 73
(J R Fanshawe) *a.p: effrt and cl up 3f out: sn rdn and ev ch tl drvn and n.m.r 1f out: no ex ins fnl f* **4/1**[2]
6 **5** hd **El Diego (IRE)**[26] 7304 4-9-12 **72**..................... DarrylIHolland 2 78
(J R Gask) *led: pushed along 4f out: rdn and qcknd 3f out: hdd wl over 1f out and sn drvn: n.m.r ins fnl f: no ex towards fin* **9/1**
-122 **6** 9 **Pertemps Networks**[14] 7447 4-10-0 **74**..................... DaleGibson 6 67
(M W Easterby) *trckd ldrs: effrt 4f out: pushed along over 3f out: sn rdn and btn over 2f out* **2/1**[1]
4111 **7** 5 **Zaffeu**[253] 1121 7-9-4 **64**..................... VinceSlattery 4 50
(A G Juckes) *hld up: hdwy over 4f out: rdn to chse ldrs over 3f out: sn wknd* **16/1**
6266 **8** 2¼ **Flame Creek (IRE)**[7] 7520 12-8-10 **56**..................... EdwardCreighton 7 39
(E J Creighton) *hld up: effrt over 3f out: sn rdn along and outpcd* **14/1**

3m 5.53s (-2.77) **Going Correction** -0.20s/f (Stan) **8** Ran SP% **113.8**
Speed ratings (Par 103): **99,98,98,98,98 92,90,88**
toteswinger: 1&2 £8.10, 1&3 £9.00, 2&3 £7.20. CSF £56.84 CT £367.95 TOTE £10.60: £2.60, £2.20, £2.10; EX 82.90 TRIFECTA Not won..
Owner R G Fell **Bred** Snc Haras Des Peltrais, Laurent Thibault **Trained** Pickering, York
■ Stewards' Enquiry : Graham Gibbons one-day ban: careless riding (Dec 23)

FOCUS
A fair staying handicap, but despite what appeared to be solid pace the front five finished in a heap. The third and fourth ran close to recent course form.
El Diego(IRE) ◆ Official explanation: jockey said gelding hung right in home straight

7618 HOSPITALITY AT SOUTHWELL RACECOURSE H'CAP (DIV II) 6f (F)
3:00 (3:02) (Class 6) (0-60,59) 3-Y-O+ **£1,706** (£503; £252) **Stalls** Low

Form RPR
646 **1** **This Ones For Eddy**[5] 7544 3-9-4 **59**..................... AdamKirby 7 77
(S Parr) *mde most: rdn and qcknd clr wl over 1f out: styd on strly* **7/2**[1]
5262 **2** 8 **Mister Incredible**[21] 7375 5-8-2 **48**.....................(v) MCGeran(5) 4 40
(J M Bradley) *chsd ldrs: hdwy over 2f out: rdn to chse wnr wl over 1f out: sn drvn and no imp* **7/2**[1]
0355 **3** ¾ **Foxy Jane**[127] 4686 3-8-12 **53**..................... JimmyQuinn 6 43
(M Brittain) *towards rr: hdwy 2f out: sn rdn and styd on ins fnl f: nrst fin* **20/1**
0/50 **4** 1¼ **Meancog (IRE)**[11] 7478 4-9-0 **58**..................... LukeMorris(3) 3 44
(J S Moore) *towards rr: hdwy 2f out: sn rdn and kpt on ins fnl f: nrst fin* **12/1**
0000 **5** 1 **Myriola**[7] 7521 3-8-4 **45**.....................(b[1]) HayleyTurner 2 27
(S Gollings) *cl up: rdn along 2f out: drvn and hung rt over 1f out: sn wknd* **16/1**
0064 **6** 1 **Night Prospector**[14] 7444 8-8-11 **55**.....................(b) KevinGhunowa(3) 13 34
(R A Harris) *racd wd: chsd ldrs: rdn and hdwy over 2f out: drvn wl over 1f out and grad wknd* **8/1**[3]
2001 **7** nk **Varinia (IRE)**[101] 5501 3-8-10 **51**..................... FrancisNorton 1 29
(M Brittain) *bhd: rdn along and sme hdwy on inner wl over 1f out: nt rch ldrs* **25/1**
0330 **8** 5 **Tanley**[7] 7529 3-9-1 **56**.....................(p) ChrisCatlin 8 18
(J F Coupland) *prom: rdn along over 2f out: drvn wl over 1f out and sn wknd* **6/1**[2]
0000 **9** 1 **Orchestration (IRE)**[187] 2753 7-8-4 **45**.....................(v) LiamJones 14 4
(Garry Moss) *racd wd: a towards rr* **40/1**
0005 **10** nk **Dark Champion**[29] 7270 8-8-4 **45**.....................(v) PaulQuinn 10 3
(R E Barr) *chsd ldrs: rdn along 1/2-way: sn wknd* **10/1**
0006 **11** ½ **Gone'N'Dunnett (IRE)**[7] 7522 9-8-4 **45**.....................(v) CatherineGannon 9 1
(Mrs C A Dunnett) *chsd ldrs: rdn along 1/2-way and sn wknd* **14/1**
3000 **12** shd **Nautical**[18] 7399 10-8-11 **52**..................... JerryO'Dwyer 11 8
(J R Holt) *towards rr: swtchd wd and effrt over 2f out: sn rdn and no hdwy* **25/1**
0000 **13** 7 **Firewalker**[7] 7528 3-8-9 **50**..................... TomEaves 5 —
(P T Dalton) *a outpcd in rr* **66/1**
2046 **14** 1¼ **Blakeshall Quest**[27] 7286 8-9-2 **57**.....................(b) PaulMulrennan 12 —
(R Brotherton) *chsd ldrs: hdwy over 2f out: rdn wl over 1f out and wknd qckly* **11/1**

1m 14.93s (-1.57) **Going Correction** -0.20s/f (Stan) **14** Ran SP% **123.9**
Speed ratings (Par 101): **102,91,90,88,87 86,85,78,77,77 76,76,67,65**
toteswinger: 1&2 £4.00, 1&3 £14.10, 2&3 £14.80. CSF £13.80 CT £223.60 TOTE £4.70: £1.90, £1.50, £4.90; EX 18.60 Trifecta £216.90 Part won. Pool: £293.19 - 0.43 winning units..
Owner Willie McKay **Bred** Broughton Bloodstock **Trained** Bawtry, S Yorks

FOCUS
A moderate sprint handicap run 0.72 secs slower than the first division and half a second slower than the claimer earlier in the afternoon. The winner landed a gamble and showed considerable improvement to score with the runner-up helping to set the level.
This Ones For Eddy Official explanation: trainer said, regarding apparent improvement in form, that the gelding appeared to benefit from the removal of blinkers and racing on fibresand .
Blakeshall Quest Official explanation: jockey said mare ran flat

7619 BOOK YOUR TICKETS ON LINE AT SOUTHWELL-RACECOURSE.CO.UK H'CAP 7f (F)
3:30 (3:31) (Class 6) (0-60,59) 3-Y-O+ **£2,047** (£604; £302) **Stalls** Low

Form RPR
0222 **1** **Ugenius**[15] 7437 4-9-1 **56**..................... TGMcLaughlin 1 70
(Mrs C A Dunnett) *midfield: hdwy wl over 2f out: rdn over 1f out: styd on to ld ent fnl f: drvn out* **7/1**[3]
6564 **2** ½ **Jojesse**[25] 7320 4-8-4 **45**..................... PaulQuinn 3 57
(G A Swinbank) *hld up towards rr: gd hdwy on inner over 2f out: rdn to ld wl over 1f out: drvn kpt on and hdd ent fnl f:* **12/1**
4054 **3** 2½ **Kingsmaite**[14] 7442 7-9-2 **57**.....................(b) PaulEddery 8 62
(S R Bowring) *trckd ldrs: smooth hdwy 3f out: effrt 2f out and sn ev ch tl rdn and one pce over 1f out* **13/2**[2]
4051 **4** ¾ **Guildenstern (IRE)**[10] 7503 6-9-1 **56**..................... JimmyQuinn 6 59
(P Howling) *midfield: hdwy 2f out: rdn over 1f out: kpt on ins fnl f: nrst fin* **10/1**
0100 **5** 2¾ **Bahamian Bay**[235] 1455 6-8-6 **47**..................... FrancisNorton 4 43
(M Brittain) *in tch: hdwy to chse ldrs wl over 2f out and sn rdn: drvn wl over 1f out and kpt on same pce* **22/1**
0060 **6** ¾ **Mister Benji**[150] 3951 9-8-4 **45**..................... CatherineGannon 11 39
(B P J Baugh) *led: rdn along 3f out: drvn over 2f out: hdd wl over 1f out and grad wknd* **66/1**
0002 **7** 2½ **Valentino Swing (IRE)**[8] 7513 5-9-3 **58**.....................(b) AdamKirby 2 45
(Miss T Spearing) *dwlt: sn chsng ldrs: rdn 2f out: drvn and edgd rt wl over 1f out: sn wknd* **8/1**
6010 **8** 1 **Samurai Warrior**[10] 7497 3-9-4 **59**..................... JamesDoyle 5 44
(P D Evans) *cl up on inner: rdn along over 2f out and sn wknd* **20/1**
6345 **9** 1¾ **Louisiade (IRE)**[7] 7533 7-9-4 **59**.....................(p) HayleyTurner 12 39
(M C Chapman) *cl up: rdn over 2f out and ev ch: sn drvn and grad wknd* **9/1**

0640 **10** 1 1/2 **Dasheena**[35] 7184 5-8-5 53....(be) KarenKenny(7) 14 29
(A J McCabe) *a towards rr* **20/1**

-600 **11** 3 **Flaxton (UAE)**[132] 4542 3-8-10 51.... MickyFenton 10 19
(M Brittain) *a towards rr* **50/1**

5000 **12** 2 1/4 **Northern Chorus (IRE)**[21] 7369 5-8-4 45....(v) DaleGibson 7 7
(J O'Reilly) *chsd ldrs: rdn along 3f out: sn wknd* **33/1**

6201 **13** 5 **Mrs Bun**[25] 7316 3-9-0 55....(p) DarryllHolland 9 —
(K A Ryan) *dwlt: rr and swtchd wd after 1f: a bhd* **2/1**[1]

0006 **14** 4 1/2 **So Sublime**[7] 7532 3-8-6 52....(bt[1]) AndreaAtzeni(5) 13 —
(M C Chapman) *chsd ldrs: rdn along wl over 2f out: sn wknd* **14/1**

1m 28.53s (-1.77) **Going Correction** -0.20s/f (Stan) **14** Ran SP% **124.0**
Speed ratings (Par 101): **102,101,98,97,94 93,90,89,87,86 82,80,74,69**
toteswinger: 1&2 £11.20, 1&3 £9.80, 2&3 £14.80. CSF £83.33 CT £603.16 TOTE £8.80: £2.30, £2.30, £3.30; EX 74.30 Trifecta £224.20 Part won. Pool: £303.07 - 0.53 winning units. Place 6: £33.51 Place 5: £21.54.
Owner Miss Georgia Ioannou **Bred** Three Acres Stud **Trained** Hingham, Norfolk
■ Stewards' Enquiry : T G McLaughlin one-day ban: careless riding (Dec 23)

FOCUS
A moderate handicap in which the front pair came from quite a long way back. The form looks sound enough with the first two close to previous form backed up by the third.
Mrs Bun Official explanation: jockey said filly was reluctant to race
T/Plt: £112.40 to a £1 stake. Pool: £49,185.17. 319.40 winning tickets. T/Qpdt: £44.00 to a £1 stake. Pool: £3,936.46. 66.10 winning tickets. JR

[7535] KEMPTON (A.W) (R-H)
Wednesday, December 10

OFFICIAL GOING: Standard
Wind: Moderate, half against Weather: Cold, dark

7620 BOOK NOW FOR BOXING DAY H'CAP 1m 2f (P)
6:20 (6:22) (Class 6) (0-65,65) 3-Y-O+ **£2,047** (£604; £302) **Stalls** High

Form RPR

5244 **1** **Risque Heights**[8] 7526 4-9-5 63.... DaneO'Neill 8 72
(J R Boyle) *t.k.h early: hld up towards rr: crept clsr over 2f out: squeezed through over 1f out to ld fnl 150yds: hld on wl* **7/2**[2]

0024 **2** nk **Valdan (IRE)**[23] 7354 4-9-5 63.... StephenDonohoe 9 71
(P D Evans) *hld up towards rr: prog 2f out: rdn to press wnr last 150yds: nt qckn and a jst hld* **4/1**[3]

006 **3** 2 1/4 **Yvonne Evelyn (USA)**[12] 7474 3-9-2 63.... MartinDwyer 1 67
(J R Gask) *s.s: rcvrd as rest dawdled to ld after less than 1f: kicked on over 2f out: hdd and outpcd ins fnl f* **50/1**

4023 **4** 1 1/4 **Good Effect (USA)**[23] 7355 4-9-1 59....(t) SteveDrowne 3 60
(C P Morlock) *hld up in last pair: prog on wd outside fr wl over 1f out: styd on but no ch of rching ldrs* **15/2**

0006 **5** 1 **Our Kes (IRE)**[16] 7440 6-9-4 62.... IanMongan 11 61
(P Howling) *hld up bhd ldrs: prog to dispute 2nd over 1f out: sn nt qckn u.p and btn* **7/1**

6005 **6** hd **Bombardier Wells**[16] 7436 3-9-1 62.... StephenCarson 10 61
(Eve Johnson Houghton) *led 100yds: trckd ldr after: stl disputing 2nd over 1f out: fdd* **14/1**

520- **7** hd **Gizmondo**[75] 6263 5-8-9 60.... JemmaMarshall(7) 7 58
(G L Moore) *hld up in last pair: stl there whn pce qcknd over 2f out: styd on fr over 1f out: no ch* **14/1**

3535 **8** 2 1/4 **Coral Shores**[11] 6868 3-9-2 63....(v) EdwardCreighton 6 57
(P W Hiatt) *chsd ldrs: drvn over 2f out: lost pl and btn over 1f out* **33/1**

60-0 **9** 2 1/4 **Bianca Capello**[156] 3801 3-9-2 63....(v[1]) AdamKirby 2 52
(J R Fanshawe) *led briefly after 100yds: trckd ldr: rdn and nt qckn 2f out: wknd rapidly fnl f* **40/1**

1044 **10** 3/4 **Sudden Impulse**[15] 7447 7-9-7 65.... GrahamGibbons 4 53
(A D Brown) *hld up in midfield: no prog whn rdn over 2f out: wknd rapidly fnl f* **14/1**

6200 **11** 1/2 **Sharps Gold**[4] 7585 3-8-8 58....(t) LukeMorris(3) 12 45
(D Morris) *chsd ldrs: u.p and losing pl whn snatched up 2f out: no ch after* **50/1**

5465 **12** nse **Artreju (GER)**[13] 7461 5-9-7 65.... GeorgeBaker 5 52
(G L Moore) *t.k.h: hld up and racd wd: hanging 1/2-way: effrt over 2f out: sn no prog and btn over 1f out* **3/1**[1]

2m 9.71s (1.71) **Going Correction** +0.125s/f (Slow)
WFA 3 from 4yo+ 3lb **12** Ran SP% **120.8**
Speed ratings (Par 101): **98,97,95,94,94 94,93,92,90,89 89,89**
toteswinger: 1&2 £4.20, 1&3 £33.20, 2&3 £40.00. CSF £17.95 CT £600.08 TOTE £5.00: £1.30, £2.20, £12.60; EX 22.70.
Owner Serendipity Syndicate 2006 **Bred** R Charles **Trained** Epsom, Surrey

FOCUS
A moderate handicap run at a very steady pace, but the first two still managed to pull some way clear of the rest. The form makes sense and could prove solid.
Bianca Capello Official explanation: jockey said filly ran too free
Sharps Gold Official explanation: jockey said filly was denied a clear run
Artreju(GER) Official explanation: jockey said gelding ran too free

7621 AFM SERVICES DATA CENTRE CONSTRUCTION H'CAP 5f (P)
6:50 (6:51) (Class 5) (0-75,75) 3-Y-O+ **£2,590** (£770; £385; £192) **Stalls** High

Form RPR

0540 **1** **Bookiesindex Boy**[16] 7435 4-8-12 69....(v) StephenDonohoe 9 79
(J R Jenkins) *fast away: grabbed inner and mde all: at least 2l clr over 1f out: wknd fnl 100yds: hld on* **9/1**

5001 **2** 1/2 **Thoughtsofstardom**[3] 7589 5-8-1 61 oh3.... LukeMorris(3) 11 69
(P S McEntee) *sn chsd wnr: drvn over 1f out: grad clsd ins fnl f but nt in time* **6/1**[3]

1301 **3** 3/4 **Musical Script (USA)**[7] 7540 5-8-12 69 6ex....(b) DaneO'Neill 12 74
(Mouse Hamilton-Fairley) *t.k.h early: towards rr on inner: gd run through to chse ldng pair over 1f out: clsng grad but hld whn out of room nr fin* **2/1**[1]

0266 **4** 1 1/2 **Hereford Boy**[21] 7384 4-8-13 75....(b) JamesO'Reilly(5) 3 75
(D K Ivory) *pushed along in midfield 1/2-way: outpcd sn after: styd on u.p fr over 1f out: nt pce to chal* **18/1**

0460 **5** hd **Bertie Southstreet**[81] 6131 5-8-8 65.... MartinDwyer 1 64
(J R Boyle) *wl away fr wd draw and chsd ldrs: outpcd fr wl over 1f out: no real imp after* **20/1**

1 **6** 1/2 **Step It Up (IRE)**[12] 7478 4-8-10 67.... SteveDrowne 6 64+
(J R Boyle) *stdd s and hld up wl in rr: no prog tl styd on fnl f: all too late* **9/1**

2110 **7** nse **Wreningham**[27] 7295 3-8-5 62.... JimmyQuinn 7 59
(T Keddy) *t.k.h early and prom: hanging and lost pl 1/2-way: nt qckn in midfield over 1f out* **14/1**

6606 **8** nk **Woodcote (IRE)**[12] 7477 6-9-3 74....(vt) GeorgeBaker 10 70+
(P R Chamings) *mistimed s then rrd as stalls opened: trying to rcvr whn hmpd on inner 2f out: no ch after: kpt on* **7/2**[2]

0206 **9** 1/2 **Monsieur Reynard**[5] 7562 3-8-3 65.... MCGeran(5) 4 59
(J M Bradley) *sn in last trio: struggling 2f out: kpt on fnl f but no ch* **28/1**

1050 **10** nse **Caribbean Coral**[114] 5151 9-9-4 75.... GrahamGibbons 8 69+
(A B Haynes) *sn in last trio: n.m.r bnd 2f out: styd on fnl f but r already over* **50/1**

5303 **11** 2 1/2 **Matterofact (IRE)**[12] 7478 5-8-5 62.... PaulDoe 5 47
(M S Saunders) *alwys towardsa rr: struggling wl over 1f out* **25/1**

0151 **12** 2 1/2 **Desert Opal**[21] 7377 8-8-10 67....(b) LiamJones 2 43
(C R Dore) *fast away fr wd draw and prom: steadily lost pl fr 1/2-way* **16/1**

59.48 secs (-1.02) **Going Correction** +0.125s/f (Slow) **12** Ran SP% **121.7**
Speed ratings (Par 103): **103,102,101,98,98 97,97,96,96,96 92,88**
toteswinger: 1&2 £26.60, 1&3 £5.40, 2&3 £2.20. CSF £61.33 CT £150.74 TOTE £13.00: £2.40, £2.50, £1.20; EX 88.10.
Owner Robin Stevens **Bred** D R Tucker **Trained** Royston, Herts
■ Stewards' Enquiry : Jimmy Quinn two-day ban: careless riding (Dec 26-27)

FOCUS
A competitive handicap featuring four contenders that had won on their previous start. The pace was strong but not many got into it from behind. The form is rated around the first two.
Woodcote(IRE) Official explanation: jockey said gelding reared as stalls opened
Desert Opal Official explanation: jockey said gelding never travelled

7622 DIGIBET MAIDEN AUCTION STKS 1m 2f (P)
7:20 (7:20) (Class 5) 2-Y-O **£3,238** (£963; £481; £240) **Stalls** High

Form RPR

545 **1** **Ocean's Minstrel**[43] 7054 2-8-12 72.... JerryO'Dwyer 7 75
(J Ryan) *trckd ldr: rdn to ld over 2f out: drvn over 1f out: edgd lft but hld on* **6/1**[3]

00 **2** 1/2 **Mile High Lad (USA)**[18] 7422 2-8-13 0.... DaneO'Neill 11 75+
(George Baker) *hld up in last pair: plenty to do 2f out: gd prog on outer over 1f out: styd on to take 2nd last 50yds but nt rch wnr* **50/1**

404 **3** 3/4 **Special Bond**[26] 7318 2-8-6 72.... ChrisCatlin 10 67
(J A Osborne) *hld up towards rr: brought to outer and prog 2f out: chsd wnr jst over 1f out: clsd slowly and lost 2nd fnl 50yds* **12/1**

00 **4** 6 **Litenup (IRE)**[46] 6977 2-8-5 0.... WandersonD'Avila 8 55
(A J Lidderdale) *led: rdn and hdd over 2f out: wknd over 1f out* **100/1**

5 **5** 1/2 **Liberty Beau (IRE)**[18] 7415 2-8-11 0.... HayleyTurner 12 60
(D R C Elsworth) *trckd ldrs: rdn over 2f out: grad fdd over 1f out* **16/1**

50 **6** 2 1/2 **Midnight Bay**[46] 6977 2-8-11 0.... EdwardCreighton 5 56
(M R Channon) *chsd ldrs: rdn over 4f out: lost pl and struggling after: plugged on fnl f* **8/1**

05 **7** 1/2 **Windpfeil (IRE)**[16] 7438 2-8-13 0.... NickyMackay 6 57
(J H M Gosden) *pushed along wl in rr bef 1/2-way: struggling after: modest late prog* **16/1**

5 **8** hd **Thefillyfromepsom**[5] 7554 2-8-1 0.... LukeMorris(3) 9 48
(P M Phelan) *t.k.h early: trckd ldrs: stl wl there 2f out: sn wknd* **14/1**

04 **9** 3 1/2 **Eastern Warrior**[20] 7397 2-8-11 0.... MichaelHills 1 48+
(J W Hills) *dwlt: racd on outer: prog fr rr 1/2-way: chsng ldrs over 2f out: losing pl whn squeezed out over 1f out: eased* **11/4**[2]

22 **10** 2 3/4 **Captainrisk (IRE)**[18] 7424 2-8-11 0.... JimmyQuinn 3 43+
(M Botti) *trckd ldrs: rn wd bnd after 2f: cl enough over 2f out: wknd over 1f out* **7/4**[1]

0004 **11** 3/4 **Ain't Talkin'**[12] 7467 2-8-9 47.... PaulDoe 4 40
(M J Attwater) *awkward s: a wl in rr: struggling 3f out: sn bhd* **80/1**

2m 8.20s (0.20) **Going Correction** +0.125s/f (Slow) **11** Ran SP% **118.7**
Speed ratings (Par 96): **104,103,103,98,97 95,95,95,92,90 89**
toteswinger: 1&2 £15.10, 1&3 £13.20, 2&3 £54.20. CSF £260.09 TOTE £10.30: £2.20, £7.00, £3.20; EX 427.60.
Owner Ocean Trailers Ltd **Bred** Black Horse Farm **Trained** Newmarket, Suffolk

FOCUS
A fair maiden auction event. The first three finished clear but the market leaders disappointed, so the form looks a bit dubious.

NOTEBOOK
Ocean's Minstrel had a chance on his fifth behind some potentially decent types at Yarmouth in October. The switch back to Polytrack and step up in trip have posed no problem, and he has put in gutsy performance to get off the mark on his fourth attempt. He raced just behind the pace and it looked like he might get swamped after hitting the front in the straight but he found plenty for the pressure and his willing attitude should guarantee further success in the future.
Mile High Lad(USA) produced a fast-finishing effort from well off the pace and has stepped up significantly on his two seventh-placed efforts at big prices in 7f and 8.5f all-weather maidens. This run will have a detrimental effect on his handicap mark but he does look steadily progressive and has stayed the trip really well.
Special Bond had interesting claims on her fourth at 66-1 in a reasonable 1m fillies maiden on debut but something to prove after showing regressive form in two subsequent runs. She does not look the sort who does anything very quickly but this does represent a step back in the right direction and considering her dam was a sprinter, she has seen this trip out well.
Litenup(IRE) had not shown much at huge prices in two previous runs at huge prices, but has shown some ability here. She had the run of the race, so may be a bit flattered but did still look inexperienced and could find a bit more improvement.
Eastern Warrior looked a threat turning for home but found very little and may not have stayed the trip.
Captainrisk(IRE) didn't handle the first bend very well, was in trouble before the trip became an issue and put in a very laboured effort. Official explanation: jockey said colt failed to handle bend after home straight

7623 DIGIBET.COM NURSERY 1m (P)
7:50 (7:50) (Class 4) (0-85,79) 2-Y-O **£4,094** (£1,209; £604) **Stalls** High

Form RPR

6451 **1** **Holberg (UAE)**[22] 7371 2-9-7 79.... JohnEgan 8 82+
(M Johnston) *dwlt and reminder sn after s: rchd midfield by 1/2-way: effrt over 2f out: sustained run to ld ins fnl f: hld on* **5/1**[2]

6002 **2** 1/2 **State General (IRE)**[42] 7069 2-9-0 72.... ChrisCatlin 6 74+
(Miss J Feilden) *hld up in last pair: effrt over 2f out: sn hrd rdn: r.o fr over 1f out: wnt 2nd and clsd on wnr nr fin* **8/1**

605 **3** 3/4 **Caravan Of Dreams (IRE)**[20] 7397 2-8-11 69.... MartinDwyer 10 69
(M A Jarvis) *wl away: led and keen early: gng easily over 2f out: shkn up and kpt on wl over 1f out: hdd and one pce ins fnl f* **16/1**

4233 **4** 1 1/2 **Black N Brew (USA)**[27] 7306 2-8-12 70.... LPKeniry 11 67+
(J R Best) *trckd ldng pair: effrt on inner to dispute 2nd whn nt clr run jst over 1f out: kpt on but n.d after* **10/1**

5011 **5** 1 **Doncosaque (IRE)**[18] 7425 2-9-6 **78** JimmyQuinn 3 73
(P Howling) *chsd ldr: stl 2nd ent fnl f but hld: fdd* **6/1**

001 **6** 2 **Double Act**[28] 7289 2-9-7 **79** (t) AdamKirby 1 71+
(J Noseda) *stdd s: hld up in rr: prog on inner over 2f out: nt clr run over 1f out: tryng again whn rn into trble ins fnl f: no ch* **9/1**

0221 **7** 1 ½ **Highland River**[12] 7468 2-8-6 **64** HayleyTurner 7 51
(D R C Elsworth) *t.k.h early and hld up in midfield: rdn and no prog over 2f out* **13/2**

0412 **8** 4 ½ **Blue Tango (IRE)**[21] 7391 2-9-6 **78** DarryllHolland 2 55
(Mrs A J Perrett) *chsd ldrs: rdn over 3f out: wknd over 2f out* **11/2**[3]

61 **9** 1 ¼ **Global**[12] 7476 2-8-13 **71** SteveDrowne 5 46
(R Hannon) *chsd ldrs: rdn 3f out: sn lost pl and struggling* **9/2**[1]

0040 **10** 5 **Innactualfact**[31] 7258 2-8-1 **59** ow1 FrankieMcDonald 4 23
(L A Dace) *hld up and detached in last early: nvr a factor* **66/1**

1m 40.65s (0.85) **Going Correction** +0.125s/f (Slow) **10** Ran SP% **115.4**
Speed ratings (Par 98): **100,99,98,97,96 94,92,88,87,82**
toteswinger: 1&2 £11.80, 1&3 £19.20, 2&3 £27.70. CSF £44.22 CT £594.98 TOTE £6.00: £2.00, £3.80, £3.80; EX 61.50.
Owner Sheikh Hamdan Bin Mohammed Al Maktoum **Bred** Darley **Trained** Middleham Moor, N Yorks
■ Stewards' Enquiry : Martin Dwyer two-day ban: careless riding (Dec 26-27)

FOCUS
A tight handicap involving six last-time-out winners. The runner-up confirmed recent improvement.

NOTEBOOK
Holberg(UAE) took a 7f Southwell maiden last time and has handled this surface really well on his Polytrack debut. He was under pressure and looked a bit unbalanced around the final turn but produced a sustained finishing burst in the straight and held the fast-finishing runner up. He has a good physique, a strong mind and looks a late-developing type who should be open to plenty of progress and looks one to follow in handicaps.
State General(IRE) looked an out-and-out stayer when second in a 1m2f Great Leighs maiden last time. He was backed from 14-1 to 8-1 and did really well to flash home from some way off the pace over this shorter trip. He will be suited by stepping back up in trip and should be able to win races when the emphasis is on stamina.
Caravan Of Dreams(IRE) was a bit keen and probably wasted some energy under a forcing ride but has put in a likeable effort on her handicap debut, and the half-sister to the high-class 1m4f/2m performer Royal And Regal should do better in time.
Black N Brew(USA)found himself short of room against the far rail in the final furlong and will be worth another chance next time.
Doncosaque(IRE) readily took advantage of straightforward tasks in all-weather claimers for Henry Cecil and Jeremy Gask the last twice. He had more to do on his handicap debut and has run respectably, but was vulnerable to some more progressive rivals.
Double Act also suffered a luckless run and deserves to be forgiven this.
Global Official explanation: jockey said colt hung left
Innactualfact Official explanation: jockey said filly reared as stalls opened

7624 DIGIBET CASINO MAIDEN STKS 6f (P)
8:20 (8:20) (Class 5) 3-Y-O+ **£2,590** (£770; £385; £192) **Stalls** High

Form RPR

0430 **1** **Billy Hot Rocks (IRE)**[7] 7536 3-9-3 59 (b[1]) DarryllHolland 5 67
(Miss Gay Kelleway) *taken down early: mostly in last pair: swtchd to inner and hrd rdn 2f out: sustained run u.p to ld fnl 100yds* **5/1**[3]

346 **2** ½ **Maid Of Ailsa (USA)**[8] 7527 3-8-12 0 LiamJones 9 60
(W J Haggas) *s.i.s: sn in tch: rdn and nt qckn 2f out: styd on fnl f to take 2nd fnl 50yds: a hld* **3/1**[2]

0053 **3** 1 **Monte Cassino (IRE)**[8] 7528 3-8-12 60 JamesO'Reilly(5) 7 62
(J O'Reilly) *led: kpt on whn pressed 2f out: hdd and no ex fnl 100yds* **16/1**

462 **4** 3 ½ **Celtic Spring (IRE)**[50] 6878 3-8-12 55 SteveDrowne 8 46
(J R Boyle) *sn trckd ldr: rdn over 2f out: nt qckn wl over 1f out: fdd fnl f* **2/1**[1]

6322 **5** 3 **North South Divide (IRE)**[8] 7527 4-8-10 65 (p) AndrewHeffernan(7) 1 41
(Peter Grayson) *taken down early: fractious in stalls: in tch: effrt to chse ldrs 2f out: sn no imp: fdd* **11/2**

050 **6** 1 ¼ **Prix Masque (IRE)**[7] 7536 4-9-3 52 EdwardCreighton 2 37
(Christian Wroe) *racd wd: chsd ldrs: u.p and btn over 2f out* **16/1**

6226 **7** ¾ **Gioacchino (IRE)**[72] 6334 3-9-0 56 (p) KevinGhunowa(3) 4 35
(R A Harris) *t.k.h early: pressed ldng pair tl wknd 2f out* **7/1**

6400 **8** 1 ½ **Only Hope**[22] 5070 4-8-12 41 (b) JerryO'Dwyer 3 25
(P S McEntee) *s.i.s: a in last pair: rdn and btn over 2f out* **25/1**

1m 14.43s (1.33) **Going Correction** +0.125s/f (Slow) **8** Ran SP% **118.5**
Speed ratings (Par 103): **96,95,94,89,85 83,82,80**
toteswinger: 1&2 £3.80, 1&3 £6.90, 2&3 £5.50. CSF £21.24 TOTE £5.70: £1.90, £1.10, £3.20; EX 24.20.
Owner Hinge, Searchfield & Tamburro **Bred** Russeltown Farms **Trained** Exning, Suffolk

FOCUS
A modest maiden in which most of the runners were exposed. The placed horses set the level but the form is weak.

7625 BOOK KEMPTON TICKETS ON 0844 579 3008 CLASSIFIED STKS 6f (P)
8:50 (8:50) (Class 7) 3-Y-O+ **£1,706** (£503; £252) **Stalls** High

Form RPR

4060 **1** **Greek Secret**[41] 7102 5-8-7 45 JamesO'Reilly(5) 8 58
(J O'Reilly) *hld up in last trio: plld out over 1f out: urged along and swept past rest to ld ins fnl f: sn clr* **10/1**

5460 **2** 2 ½ **Rosie Cross (IRE)**[72] 6335 4-8-12 45 (p) StephenCarson 3 50
(Eve Johnson Houghton) *rousted along to chse ldr fr wd draw: drvn to ld over 1f out: hdd and outpcd ins fnl f* **20/1**

3202 **3** ½ **Fantasy Fighter (IRE)**[8] 7522 3-8-12 45 JimmyQuinn 7 48
(J J Quinn) *most reluctant to enter stalls: settled towards rr: effrt 2f out: plugged on fr over 1f out: rdn and flashed tail fnl f: snatched 3rd on line* **11/4**[1]

3006 **4** hd **Lady Fas (IRE)**[7] 7536 5-8-12 45 HayleyTurner 5 48
(A W Carroll) *trckd ldrs: effrt to press ldr over 1f out: nt qckn ent fnl f* **20/1**

30P- **5** 1 ¼ **Aye Aye Definitely (IRE)**[33] 7233 4-8-12 45 (p) AdamKirby 11 44
(Adrian McGuinness, Ire) *mostly in midfield: effrt 2f out: n.m.r after: one pce* **8/1**

6504 **6** nse **Majestical (IRE)**[22] 7375 6-8-9 45 (b) KevinGhunowa(3) 4 44
(R A Harris) *led: drvn and hdd over 1f out: fdd ins fnl f* **14/1**

3602 **7** nse **Hollywood George**[4] 7582 4-8-9 45 (p) DuranFentiman(3) 9 43
(Miss M E Rowland) *nvr beyond midfield: nt qckn 2f out: one pce after* **5/1**[3]

8 1 ½ **Elkhart Lake (IRE)**[33] 7233 3-8-12 45 (t) ChrisCatlin 10 39+
(Adrian McGuinness, Ire) *hld up in last trio: swtchd to inner over 2f out: gng easily after but trapped bhd wall of rivals and nvr any hope* **9/2**[2]

0006 **9** nk **Sherjawy (IRE)**[22] 7375 4-8-12 45 (b) LPKeniry 12 43+
(Miss Z C Davison) *trckd ldrs: tried for run up inner 2f out: nt clr run over 1f out: lost pl ins fnl f* **7/1**

300- **10** 2 **Hephaestus**[387] 6864 4-8-12 45 StephenDonohoe 6 31
(Ian Williams) *trckd ldrs: nt qckn 2f out: grad wknd fnl f* **7/1**

0000 **11** 12 **Piccostar**[35] 7195 5-8-5 45 (b) PNolan(7) 1 —
(A B Haynes) *nvr gng wl: scrubbed along on outer after 2f: t.o* **50/1**

1m 13.8s (0.70) **Going Correction** +0.125s/f (Slow) **11** Ran SP% **124.9**
Speed ratings (Par 97): **100,96,96,95,94 94,93,91,91,88 72**
toteswinger: 1&2 £24.30, 1&3 £8.10, 2&3 £18.30. CSF £201.63 TOTE £13.60: £2.80, £4.00, £1.70; EX 170.10.
Owner The Boot & Shoe Ackworth Partnership **Bred** James Clark **Trained** Doncaster, S Yorks

FOCUS
A very moderate event, with all the runners rated 45 on the all-weather. It was a very messy race and there were plenty who found traffic problems. The form is rated around the first two.
Hollywood George Official explanation: jockey said colt was denied a clear run
Elkhart Lake(IRE) Official explanation: jockey said gelding was denied a clear run

7626 CITY & SUBURBAN PARKING H'CAP 1m 4f (P)
9:20 (9:20) (Class 6) (0-55,55) 3-Y-O+ **£2,047** (£604; £302) **Stalls** Centre

Form RPR

00 **1** **Blockley (USA)**[40] 7114 4-8-11 **48** StephenDonohoe 2 58
(Ian Williams) *trckd ldrs: rdn over 3f out: prog u.p over 2f out: led 1f out: styd on dourly* **13/2**

0034 **2** 2 ¾ **Colonel Sherman (USA)**[26] 7310 3-8-12 **54** ow2 AdamKirby 7 58
(L A Dace) *led at gd pce: breather 1/2-way: kicked on again 3f out: hdd and one pce 1f out* **9/1**

0040 **3** 1 ¼ **Fantasy Ride**[23] 7355 6-8-13 **50** TGMcLaughlin 6 54+
(J Pearce) *dwlt: hld up wl in rr: gd prog on outer fr over 2f out: wnt 3rd ent fnl f: one pce fnl 100yds* **11/1**

026 **4** 5 **Dontpaytheferryman (USA)**[4] 7573 3-8-13 **55** (t) DaneO'Neill 4 51
(P D Evans) *trckd ldng pair: rdn over 3f out: kpt on same pce fr over 2f out* **6/1**[3]

0030 **5** hd **Sir Haydn**[16] 7440 8-9-2 **53** DarryllHolland 14 48
(J R Jenkins) *mostly in midfield: pushed along 5f out: nvr pce to trble ldrs but kpt on fnl 2f* **14/1**

0465 **6** shd **Tabulate**[3] 7596 5-9-4 **55** JimmyQuinn 5 50
(P Howling) *hld up in last trio: gd prog on inner over 2f out to chse ldrs over 1f out: effrt petered out after* **8/1**

0004 **7** nk **Fenners (USA)**[18] 7427 5-9-1 **52** DaleGibson 11 47
(M W Easterby) *mostly in midfield: u.p fr 1/2-way: plugged on one pce fnl 3f* **7/2**[1]

6205 **8** 2 ¼ **Shouldntbethere (IRE)**[23] 7355 4-8-9 **53** NBazeley(7) 3 44
(Mrs P N Dutfield) *dwlt: hld up in last trio: rdn and sme prog 2f out: midfield and one pce jst over 1f out: fdd* **16/1**

5043 **9** ½ **The Little Master (IRE)**[26] 7310 4-9-4 **55** GeorgeBaker 8 45
(D R C Elsworth) *hld up wl in rr: prog arnd outer bnd over 4f out to over 3f out: no hdwy over 2f out* **5/1**[2]

-100 **10** 1 ¼ **Tiegs (IRE)**[30] 7272 6-8-10 **47** ChrisCatlin 10 35
(P W Hiatt) *hld up wl in rr: rapid prog fr 7f out to go 2nd 5f out: wknd rapidly wl over 2f out* **16/1**

0210 **11** 4 ½ **Darley Star**[9] 7516 3-8-8 **53** KevinGhunowa(3) 12 34
(R A Harris) *prom: rdn to go 2nd wl over 2f out to 2f out: wknd rapidly* **12/1**

0246 **12** 4 ½ **Silver Surprise**[49] 6909 4-9-1 **52** HayleyTurner 9 26
(J J Bridger) *nvr beyond midfield: wknd wl over 2f out: t.o* **28/1**

2m 36.13s (1.63) **Going Correction** +0.125s/f (Slow)
WFA 3 from 4yo+ 5lb **12** Ran SP% **125.5**
Speed ratings (Par 101): **99,97,96,93,92 92,92,91,90,89 86,83**
toteswinger: 1&2 £65.10, 1&3 £27.70, 2&3 £23.70. CSF £67.97 CT £652.07 TOTE £11.30: £3.60, £2.40, £4.50; EX 116.80.
Owner Ian Williams **Bred** Payson Stud Inc **Trained** Portway, Worcs

FOCUS
They went a decent pace and the field was quite well strung out in the early stage. The first three pulled well clear of the rest and the form looks sound and should be reliable.
T/Jkpt: Not won. T/Plt: £1,681.00 to a £1 stake. Pool: £119,054.62. 51.70 winning tickets. T/Qpdt: £266.60 to a £1 stake. Pool: £7,856.10. 21.80 winning tickets. JN

7612 SOUTHWELL (L-H)
Wednesday, December 10

OFFICIAL GOING: Standard
Wind: Fresh behind Weather: Fine and dry

7627 SOUTHWELL-RACECOURSE.CO.UK MAIDEN AUCTION STKS 1m (F)
12:00 (12:05) (Class 6) 2-Y-O **£2,047** (£604; £302) **Stalls** Low

Form RPR

1 **Battle Planner (USA)** 2-8-13 0 DarryllHolland 3 79+
(M Johnston) *dwlt and sn pushed along: hdwy to chse ldrs after 2f: rdn and rn green on outer 2f out: styd on to ld ent fnl f: kpt on strly* **6/1**[3]

0002 **2** 1 ½ **Confucius Captain (IRE)**[22] 7371 2-8-13 75 LiamJones 6 73
(J R Boyle) *led: rdn along wl over 2f out: drvn over 1f out: hdd ent fnl f: kpt on u.p* **10/3**[2]

5022 **3** 1 ¼ **Clerk's Choice (IRE)**[8] 7524 2-8-12 67 HayleyTurner 2 69
(W Jarvis) *in tch: smooth hdwy to trck ldrs 1/2-way: cl up 2f out: rdn over 1f out: drvn ins fnl f and one pce* **11/8**[1]

64 **4** 4 **Royal Keva (IRE)**[28] 7282 2-8-9 0 GrahamGibbons 7 57
(A D Brown) *cl up: effrt wl over 2f out: rdn and ev ch wl over 1f out: sn drvn and wknd ent fnl f* **6/1**[3]

53 **5** 10 **More Tea Vicar (IRE)**[25] 7337 2-8-7 0 TonyHamilton 1 33
(R A Fahey) *chsd ldrs: rdn along 3f out: sn drvn and wknd* **15/2**

00 **6** 11 **Cumbrian Gold (USA)**[18] 7422 2-8-13 0 TomEaves 4 15
(B Smart) *sn rdn along in rr: bhd fr 1/2-way* **66/1**

7 6 **Just Buzzin** 2-8-11 0 JamieMoriarty 5 —
(Mrs L Stubbs) *chsd ldrs: rdn along 3f out: grad wknd* **33/1**

1m 43.84s (0.14) **Going Correction** -0.075s/f (Stan) **7** Ran SP% **110.0**
Speed ratings (Par 94): **96,94,93,89,79 68,62**
toteswinger: 1&2 £3.30, 1&3 £3.30, 2&3 £1.60. CSF £24.17 TOTE £7.40: £2.90, £1.80; EX 20.40.
Owner Favourites Racing XXII **Bred** Mt Brilliant Farm Llc **Trained** Middleham Moor, N Yorks

FOCUS
This was an ordinary juvenile maiden and the winner should improve from this while the runner-up sets the standard.

NOTEBOOK
Battle Planner(USA) proved good enough to make a winning debut. He made a tardy start and needed to be ridden from an early stage, but kept responding to his rider's urgings. It was apparent nearing the final furlong he still had more in the locker and looked better the further he went. This $50,000 half-brother to a multiple winner in the US has plenty of size and scope, so should make up into a useful three-year-old. He can also be expected to enjoy stepping up in trip as he matures. (op 13-2 tchd 7-1 and 11-2)
Confucius Captain(IRE), officially rated 75, had finished second over 7f at the track last time and held every chance. He got outstayed by the winner and looks somewhat flattered by his mark, but there is little doubt he can be placed to go one better. (op 4-1)
Clerk's Choice(IRE), who was beaten by the uneven pace in a Lingfield nursery last time and he moved best of all into the home straight. He found less than looked likely when asked for his effort 2f out and this deeper surface over the trip likely found him out. (op 2-1 tchd 5-4)
Royal Keva(IRE) has now had all of his three outings over course and distance and helps to set the level of the form. He should fare better now he qualifies for a mark. (op 11-2 tchd 5-1)
More Tea Vicar(IRE) proved friendless in the betting on this Fibresand debut and was beaten at the top of the home straight. This was disappointing, but she too now qualifies for a mark and a return to Polytrack could suit her. (op 7-2 tchd 8-1)

7628 BOOK YOUR TICKETS ON LINE AT SOUTHWELL-RACECOURSE.CO.UK CLAIMING STKS 6f (F)
12:30 (12:35) (Class 6) 2-Y-O **£2,047** (£604; £302) **Stalls** Low

Form RPR
1624 **1** **The Magic Of Rio**[12] 7464 2-8-11 90 LiamJones 2 64+
(W J Haggas) *trckd ldr: hdwy over 2f out: rdn to ld over 1f out: clr ins fnl f* **4/11**[1]
5543 **2** *3 ½* **Bold Account (IRE)**[8] 7530 2-8-5 69 (p) DeclanCannon(7) 3 55
(K R Burke) *led: rdn along 2f out: drvn and hdd over 1f out: kpt on same pce* **4/1**[2]
4260 **3** *hd* **Sally's Dilemma**[4] 7575 2-8-8 69 (t) JackDean(5) 1 55
(W G M Turner) *chsd ldng pair: rdn along and outpcd over 2f out: styd on u.p ins fnl f* **10/1**[3]
4 *22* **Consequence** 2-9-7 0 LeeEnstone 4 —
(A Dickman) *s.i.s: sn rdn along: a bhd* **50/1**
1m 17.01s (0.51) **Going Correction** -0.075s/f (Stan) **4 Ran SP% 104.4**
Speed ratings (Par 94): **93,88,88,58**
CSF £1.87 TOTE £1.30; EX 1.50.Bold Account was claimed by Garry Moss for £6,000. The Magic of Rio was claimed by I W McInnes for £10,000.
Owner M Scotney/ D Asplin/ A Symonds **Bred** R F And S D Knipe **Trained** Newmarket, Suffolk
FOCUS
Just the four runners and a straightforward success for The Magic Of Rio, who was different class to his rivals.
NOTEBOOK
The Magic Of Rio had 22lb in hand of the runner-up at the weights. Considering she was beaten at odds of 8/15 at Kempton last time, was unproven over this trip and making her debut on Fibresand, she had something to prove, but there was never a moment's worry for her supporters. (op 2-5)
Bold Account(IRE) set off in front but was ultimately no match for the winner. (op 3-1)
Sally's Dilemma would have been 5lb better off with the runner-up in a handicap. (tchd 12-1)
Consequence ran green throughout. (op 25-1)

7629 SOUTHWELL-RACECOURSE.CO.UK (S) STKS 5f (F)
1:00 (1:06) (Class 6) 3-Y-O+ **£2,047** (£604; £302) **Stalls** High

Form RPR
3032 **1** **Calmdownmate (IRE)**[1] 7616 3-8-12 70 DarrenWilliams 6 70
(K R Burke) *mde most: rdn 2f out: drvn over 1f out: edgd lft ins fnl f: kpt on gamely u.p towards fin* **4/1**[2]
1302 **2** *nk* **Grimes Faith**[3] 7218 5-9-4 62 (p) DarryllHolland 2 75
(K A Ryan) *a.p: effrt 2f out: sn rdn and ev ch tl drvn ins fnl f and no ex nr fin* **15/8**[1]
2040 **3** *hd* **Punching**[4] 7582 4-8-11 68 (vt) KylieManser(7) 11 74
(Miss Gay Kelleway) *cl up: rdn and edgd lft fr over 1f out: ev ch tl drvn and no ex wl ins fnl f* **12/1**
5033 **4** *3 ½* **Our Acquaintance**[4] 7582 3-8-12 63 (b) HayleyTurner 4 56
(W R Muir) *chsd ldrs: rdn along wl over 1f out: kpt on same pce ins fnl f* **9/2**[3]
1060 **5** *¾* **Ronnie Howe**[9] 7517 4-9-4 63 (t) PaulEddery 12 59
(S R Bowring) *in tch: rdn along 2f out: kpt on appr fnl f: nrst fin* **40/1**
004 **6** *3 ¾* **The Cube**[8] 7527 4-8-12 42 (p) PaulMulrennan 3 39
(J Balding) *cl up: rdn along 2f out: grad wknd* **25/1**
3400 **7** *nk* **Ice Planet**[65] 6532 7-8-12 73 LiamJones 8 38
(Mrs R A Carr) *a towards rr* **6/1**
0 **8** *2* **Babel**[8] 7534 3-8-13 70 SimonWhitworth 1 32
(M Wigham) *wnt lft s: cl up on outer: rdn along over 2f out and sn wknd* **14/1**
5000 **9** *3* **Cape Roberto (IRE)**[23] 7358 3-8-12 52 FrancisNorton 10 20
(Jamie Poulton) *a towards rr* **22/1**
-000 **10** *5* **Minimum Fuss (IRE)**[140] 4294 4-8-5 38 ow5 DavidKenny(7) 7 2
(M C Chapman) *dwlt: sn cl up: rdn along 1/2-way and sn wknd* **150/1**
-560 **11** *½* **Apocalypto (IRE)**[7] 7536 4-8-12 35 (v1) EdwardCreighton 5 1
(E J Creighton) *sn outpcd and bhd* **150/1**
58.58 secs (-1.12) **Going Correction** -0.175s/f (Stan) **11 Ran SP% 113.6**
Speed ratings (Par 101): **101,100,100,94,93 87,86,83,78,70 70**
toteswinger: 1&2 £1.90, 1&3 £6.40, 2&3 £17.60. CSF £11.01 TOTE £5.10: £1.80, £1.10, £3.10; EX 15.30 Trifecta £158.60 Part won. Pool: £214.42 - 0.10 winning units..The winner was bought by D W Chapman for 3,750gns. Punching was claimed by C R Dore for £6,000.
Owner Mrs Maura Gittins **Bred** J Costello **Trained** Middleham Moor, N Yorks
FOCUS
A fairly competitive seller in which the first three came clear. The winner is rated close to recent form with the third to previous course handicap form.
Cape Roberto(IRE) Official explanation: jockey said gelding hung left

7630 BUY TICKETS ON LINE H'CAP 1m 4f (F)
1:30 (1:35) (Class 5) (0-70,66) 3-Y-O+ **£2,729** (£806; £403) **Stalls** Low

Form RPR
-303 **1** **Orkney (IRE)**[30] 7274 3-8-8 58 TomEaves 6 71+
(Miss J A Camacho) *trckd ldrs: smooth hdwy on inner to ld 3f out: rdn clr 2f out: styd on* **13/2**
0603 **2** *3 ¾* **Parnassian**[22] 7376 8-8-8 53 (v) RichardThomas 2 57
(J A Geake) *hld up: hdwy over 4f out: rdn to chse wnr over 2f out: drvn over 1f out and sn no imp* **17/2**
2643 **3** *3 ¼* **Night Orbit**[21] 7385 4-9-7 66 (v) ChrisCatlin 5 65
(Miss J Feilden) *hld up: pushed along and hdwy to chse ldrs 1/2-way: rdn 3f out: drvn 2f out and kpt on same pce* **10/3**[3]
0004 **4** *shd* **Hunting Haze**[30] 7265 5-8-7 52 oh7 AndrewElliott 4 51
(A Crook) *hld up in rr: hdwy 4f out: rdn along over 2f out: drvn and kpt on same pce appr fnl f* **33/1**
0-33 **5** *½* **North Walk (IRE)**[4] 7573 5-8-9 54 (p) FergusSweeney 3 52
(Tim Vaughan) *prom: rdn along 3f out: drvn 2f out and kpt on same pce* **11/4**[2]
0/10 **6** *13* **Mad Professor (IRE)**[13] 4935 5-8-13 58 (p) LPKeniry 7 35
(A M Hales) *prom: rdn along 5f out: wknd over 3f out* **12/1**
4541 **7** *2* **Three Strings (USA)**[22] 7376 5-9-2 61 (p) PaulMulrennan 1 35
(P D Niven) *led: rdn along and hdd 3f out: sn wknd* **5/2**[1]
2m 39.96s (-1.04) **Going Correction** -0.075s/f (Stan)
WFA 3 from 4yo+ 5lb **7 Ran SP% 112.8**
Speed ratings (Par 103): **100,97,95,95,94 86,84**
toteswinger: 1&2 £7.90, 1&3 £4.10, 2&3 £7.00. CSF £56.76 TOTE £7.70: £2.80, £2.20; EX 37.10.
Owner Axom (XIII) **Bred** Miss Yvonne Kennedy **Trained** Norton, N Yorks
FOCUS
A weak handicap run at a good pace with the runner-up rated to his latest course mark.
Mad Professor(IRE) Official explanation: jockey said gelding hung left throughout
Three Strings(USA) Official explanation: jockey said gelding ran flat

7631 MEMBERSHIP AT SOUTHWELL GOLF CLUB (S) STKS 7f (F)
2:00 (2:03) (Class 6) 3-Y-O+ **£1,978** (£584; £292) **Stalls** Low

Form RPR
2300 **1** **Crocodile Bay (IRE)**[18] 7423 5-8-13 68 (b1) JamesO'Reilly(5) 3 71
(John A Harris) *mde all: rdn clr over 2f out: drvn ins fnl f and kpt on* **5/2**[2]
1355 **2** *¾* **Elusive Warrior (USA)**[22] 7373 5-9-4 67 (p) JamesDoyle 7 69
(A J McCabe) *chseed wnr: rdn along and outpcd over 2f out: sn drvn and styd on u.p ins fnl f* **6/4**[1]
3500 **3** *2* **Cap St Jean (IRE)**[9] 7513 4-8-11 57 (p) DavidKenny(7) 2 63
(R Hollinshead) *s.i.s and bhd: hdwy 2f out: sn rdn and styd on appr fnl f: nrst fin* **28/1**
0544 **4** *1* **Vanatina (IRE)**[22] 7369 4-8-7 44 LiamJones 12 50
(W M Brisbourne) *chsd ldrs: rdn along 3f out: drvn 2f out and sn one pce* **20/1**
4405 **5** *2* **Overstayed (IRE)**[8] 7529 5-8-12 54 (v) NeilChalmers 10 49
(A Bailey) *chsd ldrs: rdn along 3f out: drvn 2f out and sn one pce* **18/1**
1303 **6** *3 ¾* **Kannon**[9] 7513 3-8-13 65 DarrenWilliams 6 40
(Miss M E Rowland) *in tch: hdwy to chse ldrs 3f out: rdn over 2f out and sn btn* **6/1**[3]
00-0 **7** *3* **Simplified**[8] 7529 5-8-0 43 (t) AlexEdwards(7) 11 26
(M C Chapman) *a in rr* **100/1**
8 *2 ¾* **Whiston Pat** 3-8-12 0 PaulEddery 4 23
(S R Bowring) *s.i.s: a bhd* **80/1**
0534 **9** *hd* **Landikhaya (IRE)**[9] 7518 3-9-4 55 (p) ChrisCatlin 5 29
(D K Ivory) *a in rr* **8/1**
6400 **10** *½* **Roundthetwist (IRE)**[11] 7500 3-8-12 52 (v1) AndrewElliott 1 22
(K R Burke) *midfield: rdn along 1/2-way: nvr a factor* **40/1**
11 *7* **Always Engaged** 3-8-10 0 ow3 PaulMulrennan 9 —
(J R Norton) *chsd ldrs: rdn along 3f out: sn wknd* **100/1**
0565 **12** *2 ½* **Hi Spec (IRE)**[185] 2866 5-8-13 44 (p) AdamKirby 13 —
(Miss M E Rowland) *a towards rr* **33/1**
1m 30.16s (-0.14) **Going Correction** -0.075s/f (Stan) **12 Ran SP% 116.0**
Speed ratings (Par 101): **97,96,93,92,90 86,82,79,79,78 70,67**
toteswinger: 1&2 £2.40, 1&3 £10.80, 2&3 £9.20. CSF £6.06 TOTE £4.50: £2.00, £1.10, £2.70; EX 11.70 Trifecta £23.60 Pool: £200.82 - 6.28 winning units..There was no bid for winner.
Owner Stan Wright Shaun Taylor **Bred** James And Joe Brannigan **Trained** Eastwell, Leics
FOCUS
A very weak affair in which it paid to race handily. The front two are a little better than this grade and the form is best rated through the third and fourth.
Whiston Pat Official explanation: jockey said gelding ran green
Hi Spec(IRE) Official explanation: jockey said mare never travelled

7632 PLAY GOLF AT SOUTHWELL GOLF CLUB MEDIAN AUCTION MAIDEN STKS 1m 3f (F)
2:30 (2:30) (Class 6) 3-5-Y-O **£2,047** (£604; £302) **Stalls** Low

Form RPR
-303 **1** **Red Expresso (IRE)**[22] 7373 3-9-3 62 HayleyTurner 1 66
(M L W Bell) *trckd ldrs: smooth hdwy on inner 3f out: rdn to ld 1 1/2f out: drvn and kpt on ins fnl f* **85/40**[2]
3035 **2** *2 ½* **Red Tarn**[22] 7376 3-9-3 58 TomEaves 9 62
(B Smart) *trckd ldrs: rdn along and outpcd 4f out: hdwy over 2f out: drvn and styd on to chse wnr ins fnl f: no imp towards fin* **15/8**[1]
-350 **3** *1* **Nowzdetime (IRE)**[86] 5964 3-9-3 65 AdamKirby 5 60
(M G Quinlan) *sn led: rdn along 3f out: drvn 2f out: hdd 1 1/2 out and sn one pce* **8/1**
000 **4** *4 ½* **Gulnaz**[36] 7174 3-8-12 32 GrahamGibbons 3 47
(Mrs G S Rees) *chsd ldrs: rdn along over 3f out: drvn and kpt on same pce fnl 2f* **100/1**
050 **5** *½* **Pick Of The Day (IRE)**[214] 2008 3-9-3 45 PaulMulrennan 4 52
(J G Given) *in tch: rdn along over 4f out: drvn over 3f out and sn wknd* **16/1**
5064 **6** *3 ¼* **Amwell House**[18] 7274 3-9-3 50 DarryllHolland 7 46
(J R Jenkins) *cl up: rdn along over 2f out: drvn wl over 1f out: grad wknd* **8/1**
534- **7** *3 ¼* **Bite The Boss**[429] 6051 3-9-3 0 ChrisCatlin 2 41
(E J O'Neill) *in tch: hdwy to trck ldng pair 1/2-way: rdn along 3f out: sn wknd* **7/1**[3]
0004 **8** *10* **General Tufto**[55] 6752 3-9-3 41 MickyFenton 6 24
(C Smith) *chsd ldrs on outer: rdn along 4f out: wknd 3f out* **25/1**
9 *5* **Grange Corner** 3-8-12 0 NeilChalmers 10 10
(Garry Moss) *s.i.s: a towards rr* **100/1**
000- **10** *48* **Miss Holderness**[442] 5702 3-8-12 0 PatrickMathers 8 —
(I W McInnes) *a towards rr* **100/1**
2m 27.66s (-0.34) **Going Correction** -0.075s/f (Stan) **10 Ran SP% 114.2**
Speed ratings (Par 101): **98,96,95,92,91 89,87,79,76,41**
toteswinger: 1&2 £1.90, 1&3 £4.40, 2&3 £3.30. CSF £6.26 TOTE £3.40: £1.10, £1.20, £3.00; EX 6.00 Trifecta £38.30 Pool: £255.16 - 4.92 winning units..
Owner Terry Neill **Bred** Lodge Park Stud **Trained** Newmarket, Suffolk
FOCUS
A moderate maiden and not form to dwell on with the runner-up the best guide.
Miss Holderness Official explanation: jockey said filly lost its action

7633 SOUTHWELL-RACECOURSE.CO.UK H'CAP 7f (F)
3:00 (3:02) (Class 4) (0-85,83) 3-Y-O+ **£4,857** (£1,445; £722; £360) **Stalls** Low

Form RPR
0000 **1** **Nightjar (USA)**[14] 7457 3-8-6 71 FrancisNorton 5 87
(M Johnston) *chsd ldr: swtchd lft over 2f out: rdn to ld over 1f out: drvn and kpt on strly ins fnl f* **9/1**

0061 **2** 2¾ **Resplendent Nova**[12] 7470 6-9-2 **81** .... JimmyQuinn 10 89
(P Howling) *in tch: hdwy on outer over 2f out: sn rdn and styd on ins fnl f: nrst fin* **7/1**

4440 **3** nse **Councellor (FR)**[16] 7439 6-9-3 **82** ....(t) MickyFenton 9 90
(Stef Liddiard) *chsd ldrs on outer: hdwy over 2f out: rdn and edgd lft over 1f out: sn drvn and kpt on same pce* **4/1**[1]

3300 **4** 2¾ **King's Ransom**[14] 7457 5-8-1 **73** .... MatthewDavies(7) 2 74
(S Gollings) *led: rdn along wl over 2f out: drvn and hdd over 1f out: wknd ent fnl f* **20/1**

0004 **5** 1 **Spectait**[21] 7386 6-9-1 **80** .... JamieMoriarty 8 78
(Jonjo O'Neill) *s.i.s and bhd: rdn along 1/2-way: drvn 2f out: kpt on ins fnl f: nrst fin* **14/1**

0206 **6** shd **Imprimis Tagula (IRE)**[5] 7560 4-8-12 **77** ....(b[1]) NeilChalmers 3 75
(A Bailey) *chsd ldrs: hdwy 2f out: sn rdn and kpt on same pce appr fnl f* **6/1**

6004 **7** ¾ **Xpres Maite**[52] 6842 5-9-4 **83** ....(b) PaulEddery 6 79
(S R Bowring) *cl up: rdn along 2f out: sn drvn and wknd* **9/1**

4124 **8** 3¼ **Cool Sands (IRE)**[8] 7534 6-8-7 **72** ....(v) ChrisCatlin 1 59
(J G Given) *a towards rr* **5/1**[2]

0505 **9** ½ **Kabeer**[211] 2085 10-8-11 **83** ....(t) KarenKenny(7) 4 69
(A J McCabe) *dwlt: sn in tch: effrt and rdn wl over 2f out: sn wknd* **20/1**

0042 **F** **Nastrelli (IRE)**[26] 7317 5-9-0 **82** ....(b) NeilBrown(3) 7 —
(T D Barron) *prom: rdn along over 2f out: wkng whn hmpd and fell over 1f out* **11/2**[3]

1m 27.98s (-2.32) **Going Correction** -0.075s/f (Stan) **10** Ran SP% **115.0**
Speed ratings (Par 105): **110,106,106,103,102 102,101,97,97,—**
toteswinger: 1&2 £14.60, 1&3 £13.60, 2&3 £8.30. CSF £69.59 CT £297.19 TOTE £10.20: £2.50, £2.30, £1.80; EX 91.30 Trifecta £306.50 Part won. Pool: £414.30 - 0.44 winning units..
Owner Crone Stud Farms Ltd **Bred** Derry Meeting Farm & London Thoroughbred Services **Trained** Middleham Moor, N Yorks
■ Stewards' Enquiry : Micky Fenton five-day ban: careless riding (Dec 26-30)

FOCUS
An open and eventful handicap and solid form with the placed horses close to recent efforts.

7634 HOSPITALITY AT SOUTHWELL RACECOURSE H'CAP 1m (F)
3:30 (3:30) (Class 6) (0-62,62) 3-Y-O+ **£2,047** (£604; £302) **Stalls** Low

Form RPR

022 **1** **Barataria**[15] 7442 6-8-13 **58** .... HayleyTurner 7 75+
(R Bastiman) *hld up in midfield: smooth hdwy 3f out: chal on bit over 1f out: qcknd to ld ins fnl f: easily* **5/2**[1]

4-43 **2** 3 **Mambo Sun**[15] 7441 5-9-1 **60** .... PaulMulrennan 1 65
(R Curtis) *chsd ldrs: hdwy to ld 2f out and sn rdn: drvn and hdd ins fnl f: one pce* **8/1**

2005 **3** ¾ **Thornaby Green**[9] 7516 7-8-5 **55** .... DeanHeslop(5) 8 58
(T D Barron) *towards rr: rdn along 3f out: hdwy on inner 2f out: styd on u.p ins fnl f: nrst fin* **8/1**

3042 **4** 2 **Orpenella**[8] 7533 3-9-0 **60** ....(b) DarryllHolland 11 59
(K A Ryan) *prom: effrt on outer 3f out: rdn 2f out: sn drvn and one pce* **7/2**[2]

0501 **5** 1¾ **Rub Of The Relic (IRE)**[8] 7532 3-8-10 **56** 6ex....(v) FrankieMcDonald 10 51
(P T Midgley) *towards rr and rdn along 1/2-way: styd on fnl 2f: nrst fin* **9/2**[3]

0000 **6** 2 **High Five Society**[50] 6888 4-8-5 **50** ....(bt) PaulEddery 2 40
(S R Bowring) *led: rdn along 3f out: hdd 2f out and grad wknd* **33/1**

P000 **7** 3¼ **Ten Spot (IRE)**[48] 6928 3-8-12 **58** ....(vt) MickyFenton 4 41
(Stef Liddiard) *chsd ldrs: rdn along over 2f out and sn wknd* **28/1**

-060 **8** 5 **Mister Maq**[36] 7177 5-8-5 **50** oh5 ....(b) AndrewElliott 3 21
(A Crook) *dwlt: a towards rr* **150/1**

0340 **9** ¾ **Liberty Valance (IRE)**[23] 7367 3-9-2 **62** .... LPKeniry 6 31
(S Kirk) *prom: rdn along over 2f out and sn wknd* **20/1**

0-00 **10** 1¾ **Gem Bien (USA)**[28] 7284 10-8-5 **50** oh5 ....(b) PaulQuinn 5 15
(T T Clement) *a in rr* **100/1**

0060 **11** 2¾ **Blue Empire (IRE)**[15] 7441 7-8-5 **50** ....(b[1]) FrancisNorton 9 9
(Ollie Pears) *chsd ldrs to 1/2-way: sn wknd* **20/1**

0430 **12** 2¼ **Time To Regret**[25] 7340 8-9-1 **60** ....(p) TomEaves 12 14
(I W McInnes) *a towards rr* **16/1**

1m 42.01s (-1.69) **Going Correction** -0.075s/f (Stan)
WFA 3 from 4yo+ 1lb **12** Ran SP% **114.6**
Speed ratings (Par 101): **105,102,101,99,97 95,92,87,86,84 82,79**
toteswinger: 1&2 £4.90, 1&3 £5.80, 2&3 £11.70. CSF £20.59 CT £141.23 TOTE £3.60: £1.70, £2.00, £2.70; EX 22.90 Trifecta £120.90 Pool: £429.91 - 2.63 winning units. Place 6: £66.29 Place 5: £18.57.
Owner Coal Trade Partnership **Bred** Hesmonds Stud Ltd **Trained** Cowthorpe, N Yorks

FOCUS
The leaders went off too fast in what was a moderate handicap but the time was decent and the placed horses are the best guides to the level.
T/Plt: £104.40 to a £1 stake. Pool: £49,996.16. 349.50 winning tickets. T/Qpdt: £26.20 to a £1 stake. Pool: £5,994.15. 169.30 winning tickets. JR

7549 DEAUVILLE (R-H)
Wednesday, December 10

OFFICIAL GOING: Standard

7635a PRIX PETITE ETOILE (LISTED RACE) (FILLIES) (ALL-WEATHER) 1m 1f 110y
2:05 (2:04) 3-Y-O **£20,221** (£8,088; £6,066; £4,044; £2,022)

RPR

1 **Rainbow Crossing**[118] 5038 3-8-12 .... F-XBertras 5 —
(F Rohaut, France)

2 hd **L'Etoile De Moscou**[56] 3-8-12 ....(b) TJarnet 1 —
(E Lellouche, France)

3 snk **Bergamask (USA)**[19] 7431 3-8-12 .... FVeron 8 —
(H-A Pantall, France)

4 1½ **Ragiam (ITY)**[24] 3-9-1 ....(b) DVargiu 10 —
(A & G Botti, Italy)

5 nse **Ballerina Blue (IRE)**[51] 3-8-12 .... SPasquier 3 —
(Y De Nicolay, France) *fin 6th: plcd 5th*

6 shd **Kirkinola**[19] 7431 3-8-12 .... GBenoist 11 —
(C Laffon-Parias, France) *fin 7th: plcd 6th*

7 ¾ **Tactful (IRE)**[59] 6684 3-8-12 .... RichardKingscote 13 —
(R M Beckett) *prom on outside: 3rd and pushed along st: 2nd and chalng 1 1/2f out: r.o tl no ex fnl 150yds: fin 5th: disqualified and plcd 7th* **5/1**[1]

8 snk **Myakoda (FR)**[54] 3-8-12 .... JBensimon 9 —
(Y De Nicolay, France)

9 ¾ **Wait And See (FR)**[135] 3-9-1 .... RMarchelli 2 —
(Robert Collet, France)

10 2½ **Texaline (FR)**[28] 3-8-12 .... J-BHamel 12 —
(D De Watrigant, France)

0 **Himariya (IRE)**[229] 1608 3-8-12 .... FBlondel 6 —
(J-C Rouget, France)

0 **Roscoff (IRE)**[15] 7450 3-8-12 ....(b) THuet 4 —
(Robert Collet, France)

0 **The World**[19] 7431 3-8-12 .... MGuyon 7 —
(A Fabre, France)

1m 57.8s (117.80) **13** Ran SP% **16.7**
PARI-MUTUEL (Including 1 Euro stake): WIN 6.00; PL 2.20, 3.90, 8.00; DF 34.20.
Owner Ecurie Skymarc Farm **Bred** Skymarc Farm & Castlemartin Stud **Trained** Sauvagnon, France

NOTEBOOK
Tactful(IRE), who was stepping up in trip from a mile, ran a creditable race on this big step up in class, having only won a Great Leighs handicap off 74 last time.

7573 GREAT LEIGHS (A.W) (L-H)
Thursday, December 11

OFFICIAL GOING: Standard
Wind: modest, half behind Weather: dry, very cold

7636 BELFRY APPRENTICE H'CAP (DIV I) 6f (P)
6:20 (6:22) (Class 6) (0-50,56) 3-Y-O+ **£2,266** (£674; £337; £168) **Stalls** Low

Form RPR

2023 **1** **Fantasy Fighter (IRE)**[1] 7625 3-8-8 **46** oh1 .... BMcHugh 4 55
(J J Quinn) *trckd ldrs: effrt to ld jst over 1f out: rdn and edgd lft 1f out: sn clr: comf* **10/3**[2]

0052 **2** 2¾ **Dubai To Barnsley**[9] 7529 3-8-5 **48** .... AndrewHeffernan(5) 1 48
(Garry Moss) *chsd ldrs: rdn and unable qck over 1f out: swtchd rt 1f out: styd on to chse wnr ins fnl f: no imp* **11/4**[1]

0P-5 **3** shd **Aye Aye Definitely (IRE)**[1] 7625 4-8-8 **46** oh1 ....(p) DEMullins 7 46
(Adrian McGuinness, Ire) *t.k.h: pressed ldr: rdn over 2f out: led over 1f out: sn hdd: outpcd by wnr 1f out: hld on for 2nd* **8/1**

0501 **4** 1 **Double Valentine**[8] 7535 5-9-1 **56** 6ex .... DebraEngland(3) 3 53+
(R Ingram) *s.i.s: bhd: hdwy over 1f out: kpt on fnl f: wnt 4th towards fin: nvr nr ldrs* **6/1**[3]

1000 **5** nk **Shava**[192] 2662 8-8-10 **48** .... DeclanCannon 5 44
(H J Evans) *racd in midfield: rdn wl over 1f out: kpt on fnl f: nvr pce to trble wnr* **14/1**

3000 **6** ¾ **Sazerac (USA)**[35] 7206 3-8-7 **50** .... AntiocoMurgia(5) 2 43
(P Howling) *led tl hdd over 1f out: sn rdn and outpcd by wnr: wknd fnl 100yds* **11/1**

0003 **7** 1¼ **Zeeran**[21] 7396 3-8-3 **46** oh1 .... RichardRowe(5) 9 35
(C E Brittain) *v.s.a: racd wd: hdwy into midfield 1/2-way: no hdwy fnl 2f* **18/1**

0030 **8** 1 **Mr Rev**[11] 7508 5-8-11 **49** ....(b[1]) DeanHeslop 6 35
(J M Bradley) *a bhd: lost tch over 2f out: n.d* **8/1**

2500 **9** ¾ **Our Kally**[44] 7049 3-8-2 **47** .... SeanPalmer(7) 12 31
(M D I Usher) *towards rr: rdn 2f out: nvr trbld ldrs* **40/1**

-000 **10** 6 **Viewforth**[160] 3665 10-8-3 **46** oh1 .... TobyAtkinson(5) 10 11
(M Wigham) *chsd ldrs tl over 3f out: wl bhd fnl 2f* **20/1**

0000 **11** ¾ **Stoneacre Donny (IRE)**[29] 7288 4-8-8 **46** oh1 .... AndreaAtzeni 8 8
(Peter Grayson) *in tch in midfield: lost pl over 3f out: c wd 2f out: no imp after* **33/1**

0060 **12** 1½ **Swindon Town Flyer (IRE)**[79] 6190 3-8-9 **50** .... PNolan(3) 11 7
(A B Haynes) *restless in stalls: in tch in midfield: lost pl over 3f out: sn rdn and bhd* **33/1**

1m 13.71s (0.01) **Going Correction** +0.025s/f (Slow) **12** Ran SP% **119.6**
Speed ratings (Par 101): **100,96,96,94,94 93,91,90,89,81 80,78**
toteswinger: 1&2 £6.20, 1&3 £15.70, 2&3 £14.60. CSF £12.49 CT £69.78 TOTE £4.60: £1.30, £1.50, £3.20; EX 10.20.
Owner The Fantasy Fellowship F **Bred** T C Clarke **Trained** Settrington, N Yorks
■ Stewards' Enquiry : P Nolan six-day ban: abusive behaviour (Dec 26-31)

FOCUS
A moderate handicap restricted to apprentices who had not ridden more than 25 winners, and it proved difficult to make up significant amounts of ground. The winning time was 0.22 seconds slower than the second division but the form looks sound enough, if ordinary for the grade.

7637 BELFRY APPRENTICE H'CAP (DIV II) 6f (P)
6:50 (6:54) (Class 6) (0-50,53) 3-Y-O+ **£2,266** (£674; £337; £168) **Stalls** Low

Form RPR

030 **1** **Double Carpet (IRE)**[2] 7615 5-8-8 **46** oh1 .... RossAtkinson 5 55
(G Woodward) *mde virtually all: rdn over 1f out: pushed along and kpt on wl ins fnl f* **15/2**

5240 **2** 1¼ **Tadlil**[2] 7615 6-8-12 **50** ....(b) DeanHeslop 4 55
(J M Bradley) *chsd ldrs: rdn to chse wnr over 1f out: kpt on same pce ins fnl f* **12/1**

5062 **3** ¾ **Eleanor Eloise (USA)**[8] 7541 4-8-12 **50** .... AndreaAtzeni 9 53
(J R Gask) *racd in midfield: rdn over 3f out: hdwy u.p over 1f out: styd on to go 3rd ins fnl f: nt rch ldng pair* **11/4**[2]

0 **4** 2 **Elkhart Lake (IRE)**[1] 7625 3-8-8 **46** oh1 ....(t) BMcHugh 3 42
(Adrian McGuinness, Ire) *dwlt: sn in tch: trckd ldrs 1/2-way: rdn and fnd little over 1f out: one pce fnl f* **6/4**[1]

51 **5** 3¾ **Lost All Alone**[9] 7522 4-8-10 **53** 6ex .... ChrisHough(5) 11 37+
(D M Simcock) *dropped in bhd after s: wl bhd in last trio: hdwy and nt clr run on inner 2f out: nvr nr ldrs* **6/1**[3]

0030 **6** nk **Pentandra (IRE)**[24] 7362 3-8-10 **48** .... RosieJessop 2 31
(J G Given) *pressed wnr: rdn over 2f out: wknd ent fnl f* **20/1**

0060 **7** 2 **Welcome Releaf**[13] 7469 5-8-10 **48** ....(p) AmyBaker 1 25
(P Leech) *dwlt: a struggling in rr: modest late hdwy* **14/1**

000 **8** 1¼ **One Way Ticket**[73] 6339 8-8-8 **46** oh1 ....(p) BillyCray 8 19
(J M Bradley) *t.k.h: chsd ldrs tl struggling over 2f out: wl bhd over 1f out* **28/1**

500- **9** ½ **Avery**[600] 1164 4-8-9 **47** .... JemmaMarshall 10 18
(R J Hodges) *a in rr: no ch fnl 2f* **50/1**

3520 **10** 2¼ **Little Finch (IRE)**[285] 767 3-8-9 **47** ....(p) DEMullins 7 11
(Denis P Quinn, Ire) *a towards rr: rdn 1/2-way: wl bhd fnl 2f* **16/1**

6406 **11** 4½ **James Street (IRE)**[259] 1035 5-8-3 **46** oh1 ....(v) AndrewHeffernan(5) 6 —
(Peter Grayson) *a wl bhd* **50/1**

1m 13.49s (-0.21) **Going Correction** +0.025s/f (Slow) **43** Ran SP% **125.1**
Speed ratings (Par 101): **102,100,99,96,91 91,88,86,86,83 77**
toteswinger: 1&2 £40.10, 1&3 £9.20, 2&3 £10.00. CSF £95.63 CT £319.16 TOTE £11.70: £3.60, £3.90, £1.70; EX 81.20.

Owner Mr & Mrs Bloom **Bred** Dr John Waldron **Trained** Maltby, S Yorks

FOCUS

The winning time was 0.22 seconds quicker than the first division and, once again, those who raced handy were at an advantage. The form looks sound enough rated around the placed horses.

7638 LYTHAM ST ANNES MEDIAN AUCTION MAIDEN STKS 6f (P)

7:20 (7:22) (Class 5) 2-Y-0 **£2,914** (£867; £433; £216) **Stalls** Low

Form				RPR
5	1		**Major Phil (IRE)**[26] 7333 2-9-3 0 DaneO'Neill 2 (L M Cumani) *trckd ldrs: shkn up 2f out: rdn to ld over 1f out: drvn 1f out: styd on wl* 1/1[1]	80+
5203	2	1 ¾	**Today's The Day**[23] 7371 2-8-12 70 (b[1]) DarryllHolland 7 (M A Jarvis) *led: hdd over 1f out: edgd rt u.p 1f out: one pce fnl f* 11/4[2]	70
	3	3 ¾	**Kilkenny Bay** 2-8-12 0 HayleyTurner 3 (W Jarvis) *dwlt: hld up in tch towards rr: hdwy towards inner over 1f out: chsd ldng pair 1f out: kpt on but no imp on ldng pair after* 16/1	59+
00	4	2 ¾	**Kingsgate Storm (IRE)**[177] 3105 2-9-3 0 GeorgeBaker 8 (J R Best) *t.k.h: chsd ldr over 4f out tl 2f out: rdn and unable qck over 1f out: wknd jst over 1f out* 5/1[3]	56
00	5	2 ¾	**Kina Jazz**[12] 7501 2-8-7 0 AndreaAtzeni(5) 4 (M E Rimmer) *t.k.h: chsd ldr tl over 4f out: stdd into midfield after: rdn 2f out: sn outpcd* 20/1	42
	6	¾	**Best In Class** 2-8-10 0 RossAtkinson(7) 5 (Tom Dascombe) *dwlt: rn green in rr: nvr nr ldrs* 10/1	45
	7	3 ¼	**Risky Lady (IRE)** 2-8-12 0 ChrisCatlin 6 (J Ryan) *s.i.s: in tch in midfield: rdn over 2f out: wknd wl over 1f out* 50/1	30
	8	6	**Kings On The Roof** 2-9-3 0 StephenDonohoe 1 (P Leech) *uns rdr bef s: awkward leaving stalls and v.s.a: a bhd: hung lft over 1f out* 40/1	17

1m 14.97s (1.27) **Going Correction** +0.025s/f (Slow) **8** Ran SP% **117.5**

Speed ratings (Par 96): **92,89,84,81,77 76,72,64**

toteswinger: 1&2 £2.60, 1&3 £4.90, 2&3 £5.90. CSF £3.94 TOTE £1.80: £1.50, £1.20, £4.20; EX 5.40.

Owner L Marinopoulos **Bred** Roger Macnair **Trained** Newmarket, Suffolk

FOCUS

An uncompetitive maiden run in a time over a second slower than the other juvenile maiden over this trip on the card, but the 70-rated Today's The Day sets the standard having appeared to run her race, and the winner, Major Phil, is a likeable type.

NOTEBOOK

Major Phil(IRE) had caught the eye in a reasonable maiden over course and distance first time up and confirmed that promise with a ready success. He will probably be rated in the high 70s after this and looks capable of progressing past that in time, but he is likely to be put away until next year. (op 6-5 tchd 5-4 in a place)

Today's The Day is now 0-8, but to her credit she did not give up once headed. A little race should come her way. (op 3-1)

Kilkenny Bay, a 6,000gns half-sister to two winners, Manhattan (over 6f and 1m1f) and dual middle-distance scorer Malthouse Master, made a respectable debut. She should be suited by a step up in trip. (op 20-1)

Kingsgate Storm(IRE) ran nowhere near the form he showed when eighth in the Windsor Castle at Royal Ascot when last seen in June. However, he was entitled to need the run and is now qualified for a handicap mark. (op 4-1)

Best In Class will know more next time having run green. (op 8-1 tchd 7-1)

7639 LOCH LOMOND H'CAP 1m 6f (P)

7:50 (7:51) (Class 4) (0-85,82) 3-Y-0+ **£4,857** (£1,445; £722; £360) **Stalls** Low

Form				RPR
2132	1		**Azabu Juban (IRE)**[7] 7545 3-8-6 70 LukeMorris(3) 5 (J Jay) *led tl 8f out: chsd ldrs after: rdn 3f out: drvn to ld fnl 100yds: styd on wl* 4/1[3]	79
11	2	½	**Weybridge Light**[7] 7545 3-8-0 68 6ex (b) DEMullins(7) 2 (Eoin Griffin, Ire) *chsd ldrs: wnt 2nd 7f out: led 5f out: rdn over 2f out: narrowly hdd wl over 1f out: led again 1f out: hdd and unable qck fnl 100yds* 7/4[1]	76
3562	3	1	**Baan (USA)**[20] 7400 5-8-10 64 JimmyQuinn 7 (H J Collingridge) *chsd ldr tl led after 6f tl 5f out: ev ch over 2f out: rdn to ld narrowly wl over 1f out tl hdd 1f out: no ex fnl 100yds* 12/1	71
53-4	4	½	**Prince Zafonic**[14] 7462 5-8-11 70 JamesO'Reilly(5) 6 (D K Ivory) *t.k.h: hld up in tch: dropped to rr over 5f out: hdwy on outer 3f out: kpt on u.p fnl f: nvr quite getting to ldrs* 9/2	76
1563	5	1 ¾	**Clear Reef**[14] 7459 4-9-10 78 TGMcLaughlin 3 (Jane Chapple-Hyam) *hld up in last pair: hdwy to chse ldrs over 5f out: drvn wl over 1f out: wknd jst ins fnl f* 7/1	82
0311	6	2 ¾	**Turban Heights (IRE)**[14] 7459 4-10-0 82 ChrisCatlin 1 (E J O'Neill) *hld up in last pl: swtchd ins and effrt 2f out: no imp fr over 1f out* 10/3[2]	82

3m 7.17s (3.97) **Going Correction** +0.025s/f (Slow)

WFA 3 from 4yo+ 7lb **6** Ran SP% **117.8**

Speed ratings (Par 105): **89,88,88,87,86 85**

toteswinger: 1&2 £5.30, 1&3 £3.90, 2&3 £8.50. CSF £12.21 TOTE £6.10: £3.20, £1.20; EX 14.30.

Owner David Fremel **Bred** P F Corbet **Trained** Newmarket, Suffolk

FOCUS

They went steady, resulting in a bunch finish, and the form might not be reliable although it makes sense on paper.

7640 TURNBERRY MAIDEN STKS 6f (P)

8:20 (8:21) (Class 4) 2-Y-0 **£3,885** (£1,156; £577; £288) **Stalls** Low

Form				RPR
F	1		**Geneva Geyser (GER)**[59] 6702 2-9-0 0 LukeMorris(3) 1 (J M P Eustace) *in tch on inner: rdn to chse ldr over 1f out: ev ch ent fnl f: led fnl 100yds: r.o wl* 7/1	74
6522	2	1 ¾	**Romantic Queen**[12] 7501 2-8-12 67 TGMcLaughlin 8 (E A L Dunlop) *hld up in tch towards rr: hdwy over 2f out: chsd ldrs and rdn ent fnl f: kpt on to go 2nd nr fin: unable to chal wnr* 3/1[2]	64
06	3	hd	**Green Onions**[12] 7501 2-8-12 0 GabrielHannon(5) 9 (D J S Ffrench Davis) *taken down early: t.k.h: chsd ldr tl led over 4f out: rdn over 1f out: hdd fnl 100yds: no ex: lost 2nd nr fin* 40/1	68
53	4	½	**Fantasy Gladiator**[19] 7417 2-9-3 0 MickyFenton 5 (R M H Cowell) *t.k.h: hld up in tch: effrt and edgd lft over 1f out: ev ch ent fnl f: wknd fnl 100yds* 7/2[3]	67
	5	½	**Flamsteed (IRE)** 2-9-3 0 DarryllHolland 6 (M Johnston) *rn green and racd wd thrght: chsd ldrs tl lost pl bnd over 3f out: rdn and rallied over 2f out: chsd ldrs over 1f out: styd on same pce fnl f* 9/4[1]	65
	6	8	**Private Equity (IRE)** 2-8-12 0 HayleyTurner 3 (W Jarvis) *in tch towards rr: sn pushed along: rdn over 2f out: sn wknd* 20/1	36
4022	7	shd	**Sonhador**[8] 7537 2-9-3 70 LiamJones 4 (G Prodromou) *t.k.h: led tl over 4f out: rdn and unable qck whn hmpd wl over 1f out: eased whn wl hld fnl f* 9/2	41
00	8	1 ¾	**Valid Point (IRE)**[44] 7038 2-9-3 0 StephenDonohoe 2 (Sir Mark Prescott) *a bhd: struggling and detached last fr 1/2-way* 33/1	36

1m 13.92s (0.22) **Going Correction** +0.025s/f (Slow) **8** Ran SP% **118.8**

Speed ratings (Par 98): **99,96,96,95,95 84,84,81**

toteswinger: 1&2 £10.10, 1&3 £22.50, 2&3 £38.40. CSF £28.97 TOTE £10.00: £2.20, £1.20, £6.90; EX 72.10.

Owner J C Smith **Bred** Graf And Grafin Von Stauffenberg **Trained** Newmarket, Suffolk

FOCUS

The bare form looks ordinary - the runner-up came into this rated 67 - but the winning time was over a second quicker than the other two-year-old maiden over this trip on the card and the race should produce some winners.

NOTEBOOK

Geneva Geyser(GER) had a terrible experience first time out, falling at Windsor in October after clipping heels, but he showed himself none the worse with a game success. He was a little green in the race, and his jockey described him as still weak and babyish afterwards, so there is plenty of room for improvement. A colt with size and scope, he should progress into a useful type next year, and a handicap mark likely to be somewhere in the 70s should be exploited. (tchd 15-2)

Romantic Queen did not enjoy the best of runs through in the straight, but she was by no means unlucky. (tchd 11-4)

Green Onions was given a positive ride and ran his best race yet. He now has the option of handicaps and looks capable of winning races.

Fantasy Gladiator had shown ability on his first two starts and promised to be suited by the switch to this track, having failed to handle Lingfield last time, but he ruined his chance by racing too keenly. He's now qualified for a handicap mark and should be suited by a positive ride over 5f. (tchd 10-3)

Flamsteed(IRE), a 50,000gns purchase, seemed to run extremely green throughout and could not quite get on terms in the straight. (op 7-2)

Sonhador Official explanation: jockey said colt had no more to give

7641 TROON H'CAP 6f (P)

8:50 (8:50) (Class 4) (0-85,84) 3-Y-0+ **£4,857** (£1,445; £722; £360) **Stalls** Low

Form				RPR
4032	1		**First Order**[6] 7562 7-8-4 75 (v) AnnStokell(5) 5 (Miss A Stokell) *hld up in tch: pushed along and hdwy over 1f out: led 1f out: rdn and r.o wl fnl f: eased nr fin* 7/2[2]	84
46	2	1 ½	**Epic Odyssey**[21] 7394 3-9-3 83 GeorgeBaker 3 (J R Boyle) *led tl 4f out: chsd ldr tl led again 2f out: rdn over 1f out: hdd 1f out: one pce ins fnl f* 6/1	87
6042	3	3 ½	**Southandwest (IRE)**[43] 7077 4-8-11 77 LPKeniry 4 (J S Moore) *w ldrs: ev ch and rdn jst over 2f out: wknd ent fnl f* 5/2[1]	70
5265	4	2 ¼	**Temple Of Thebes (IRE)**[13] 7477 3-9-4 84 TGMcLaughlin 7 (E A L Dunlop) *in tch on outer rdn over 1f out: drvn and wknd ent fnl f* 4/1[3]	70
02	5	hd	**Glencalvie (IRE)**[115] 5144 7-9-0 80 (p) DaneO'Neill 1 (J Akehurst) *bhd: rdn and struggling 1/2-way: n.d after* 10/1	65
4304	6	shd	**Asian Power (IRE)**[7] 7544 3-8-4 70 FrancisNorton 2 (P J O'Gorman) *w ldr tl led 4f out tl 2f out: w ldrs after tl wknd qckly 1f out* 9/2	55

1m 12.75s (-0.95) **Going Correction** +0.025s/f (Slow) **6** Ran SP% **112.4**

Speed ratings (Par 105): **107,105,100,97,97 96**

toteswinger: 1&2 £45.60, 1&3 £2.40, 2&3 £4.10. CSF £23.99 TOTE £4.80: £1.50, £4.40; EX 38.70.

Owner Ms Caron Stokell **Bred** Mrs Hazel Conroy **Trained** Brompton-on-Swale, N Yorks

FOCUS

A fair sprint handicap. They went a good pace and the winning time was the quickest of the five 6f races on the card, although that was to be expected. The winner is rated to his latest mark backed up by the runner-up.

7642 ST ANDREWS H'CAP 1m 2f (P)

9:20 (9:22) (Class 5) (0-70,71) 3-Y-0+ **£2,590** (£770; £385; £192) **Stalls** Low

Form				RPR
2321	1		**Vine Street (IRE)**[5] 7580 3-9-5 71 6ex DarryllHolland 2 (M A Jarvis) *mde all: rdn and clr 2f out: in command fnl f: eased towards fin* 4/7[1]	82+
5544	2	¾	**Teasing**[27] 7309 4-9-6 69 (v) JerryO'Dwyer 5 (J Pearce) *stdd s: hld up towards rr: rdn 3f out: drvn 2f out: styd on u.p fnl f: wnt 2nd nr fin: nvr able to chal wnr* 14/1	73
	3	½	**Special Pearl (IRE)**[52] 6874 4-9-0 63 ChrisCatlin 3 (E J O'Neill) *chsd ldrs: rdn over 3f out: chsd wnr wl over 1f out: kpt on same pce u.p after* 25/1	66
1004	4	shd	**All In The Red (IRE)**[7] 7548 3-9-1 67 GeorgeBaker 1 (B N Pollock) *in tch: swtchd rt and effrt 2f out: drvn and disp 2nd ent fnl f: kpt on same pce after* 8/1[3]	69
3061	5	4	**Dinner Date**[12] 7494 6-9-5 68 TonyCulhane 7 (T Keddy) *stdd after s: hld up in rr: hdwy on outer 3f out: rdn over 1f out: wknd jst ins fnl f* 17/2	62
6600	6	3	**Danse The Blues**[32] 7261 3-8-7 59 HayleyTurner 6 (E A L Dunlop) *chsd ldr tl wl over 1f out: wknd jst over 1f out* 16/1	47
5110	7	nse	**Kings Topic (USA)**[62] 6629 8-8-12 68 (p) PNolan(7) 8 (A B Haynes) *bustled along early: towards rr: rdn 6f out: wknd u.p 2f out* 12/1	56
1330	8	2	**Josr's Magic (IRE)**[9] 7532 4-8-9 61 LukeMorris(3) 9 (H J Collingridge) *hld up in tch: hdwy over 4f out: rdn and unable qck over 2f out: no ch fnl f* 11/2[2]	45

2m 7.86s (-0.74) **Going Correction** +0.025s/f (Slow)

WFA 3 from 4yo+ 3lb **8** Ran SP% **124.8**

Speed ratings (Par 103): **103,102,102,101,98 96,96,94**

toteswinger: 1&2 £2.10, 1&3 £8.40, 2&3 £2.80. CSF £12.86 CT £130.98 TOTE £1.70: £1.10, £4.40, £3.50; EX 11.50 Place 6: 66.54, Place 5: 48.01..

Owner Sheikh Ahmed Al Maktoum **Bred** Darley **Trained** Newmarket, Suffolk

FOCUS

The winner was gifted the lead and, although the runner-up and fourth are rated to recent marks, this is form to treat with caution.

T/Plt: £50.20 to a £1 stake. Pool: £123,169.13. 1,789.67 winning tickets. T/Qpdt: £16.10 to a £1 stake. Pool: £8,369.13. 383.45 winning tickets. SP

The Form Book, Raceform Ltd, Compton, RG20 6NL

7635 DEAUVILLE (R-H)

Thursday, December 11

OFFICIAL GOING: Standard

7643a PRIX LYPHARD (LISTED RACE) (ALL-WEATHER) 1m 1f 110y

2:05 (2:12) 3-Y-0+ **£19,118** (£7,647; £5,735; £3,824; £1,912)

RPR

1 **Without A Prayer (IRE)**[40] 7147 3-8-11 .... RichardKingscote 16 108
(R M Beckett) *hld up towards rr: hdwy on outside and 9th st: stdy prog fr wl over 1f out to ld last 50yds: r.o wl* **81/1**[1]

2 ¾ **Not Just Swing (IRE)**[88] 5954 4-9-5 .... MGuyon 15 111
(A Fabre, France)

3 *nse* **Diyakalanie (FR)**[141] 4320 4-8-9 .... AlexisBadel 2 101
(J Boisnard, France)

4 2½ **Far From Old (IRE)**[51] 5-8-12 .... YLerner 11 99
(J E Hammond, France)

5 ¾ **Ambassador (GER)**[432] 4-8-12 .... EPedroza 9 97
(P Rau, Germany)

6 ¾ **Willywell (FR)**[7] 7550 6-8-12 .... FBlondel 12 96
(J-P Gauvin, France)

7 ½ **Kocab**[43] 7087 6-9-2 .... SPasquier 7 99
(A Fabre, France)

8 *hd* **Roi (FR)**[117] 5115 7-8-12 ....(b) FCorallo 5 95
(J Rossi, France)

9 1 **Murcielago (FR)**[42] 3-9-1 .... FSpanu 17 99
(P Demercastel, France)

10 ½ **Diocleziano (USA)**[515] 3-8-11 .... CFiocchi 4 94
(R Menichetti, Italy)

11 **Tricien (FR)**[20] 4-8-12 .... RonanThomas 8 —
(L Urbano-Grajales, France)

12 **Zariyan (FR)**[375] 3989 5-8-12 .... VVion 10 —
(T Doumen, France)

13 **Like To Golf (USA)**[504] 3876 4-8-12 .... SMartin 6 —
(Mme J Bidgood, France)

14 **Torrid Hell (FR)**[38] 7171 3-8-11 .... JBensimon 3 —
(Y De Nicolay, France)

15 **Russian Desert (IRE)**[44] 7063 4-8-12 .... JAuge 18 —
(A Fabre, France)

16 **Ocareion (GER)** 4-8-12 .... HGrewe 14 —
(Andreas Lowe, Germany)

17 **Fontcia (FR)**[20] 4-8-9 .... MaximeFoulon 13 —
(D Sepulchre, France)

18 **Wysiwyg Lucky (FR)**[19] 5-8-9 .... TPiccone 1 —
(J-L Gay, France)

1m 55.8s (115.80)
WFA 3 from 4yo+ 2lb **18 Ran SP% 1.2**
PARI-MUTUEL (including one euro stakes): WIN 82.00; PL 18.50, 2.50,4.00; DF 249.70.
Owner McDonagh Murphy And Nixon **Bred** Brownstown Stud **Trained** Whitsbury, Hants

NOTEBOOK
Without A Prayer(IRE), running on sand for the first time since winning his maiden at Lingfield at two, saw the trip out well and notched his first success at Listed level. He needs decent ground on turf and this surface suited him.

7627 SOUTHWELL (L-H)

Friday, December 12

OFFICIAL GOING: Standard to slow

The track was riding slower than usual having been harrowed.
Wind: Light across Weather: Overcast

7644 CALL 01636 814481 TO SPONSOR A RACE H'CAP (DIV I) 5f (F)

11:50 (11:53) (Class 6) (0-55,61) 3-Y-0+ **£1,706** (£503; £252) **Stalls** High

Form RPR

6000 1 **This Ones For Pat (USA)**[11] 7518 3-8-13 **53** .... AdamKirby 10 62
(S Parr) *dwlt: sn drvn along: hdwy over 3f out: styd on u.p and edgd lft to ld wl ins fnl f* **16/1**

6240 2 ½ **Mystickhill (IRE)**[75] 6308 3-9-1 **55** .... PaulMulrennan 6 62
(J Balding) *chsd ldr: led 2f out: rdn: edgd lft and hdd wl ins fnl f* **25/1**

0060 3 1 **Hollow Jo**[23] 7383 8-8-10 **50** ....(v[1]) MickyFenton 3 53
(J R Jenkins) *sn outpcd: hdwy over 1f out: r.o: nt rch ldrs* **12/1**

250 4 3¼ **Egyptian Lord**[273] 883 5-8-4 **51** ....(b) AndrewHeffernan[(7)] 5 43
(Peter Grayson) *half-rrd s: hdwy over 3f out: rdn over 1f out: styd on same pce* **16/1**

00-5 5 1¾ **Desert Dust**[99] 5626 5-8-6 **46** oh1 ....(p) ChrisCatlin 11 31
(R M H Cowell) *chsd ldrs: rdn 1/2-way: styd on same pce appr fnl f* **25/1**

0005 6 *nse* **Helping Hand (IRE)**[21] 7399 3-9-0 **54** .... HayleyTurner 4 39
(R Hollinshead) *chsd ldrs: rdn 1/2-way: styd on same pce appr fnl f* **85/40**[1]

3621 7 ¾ **Spic 'n Span**[10] 7527 3-9-0 **61** 6ex ....(b) MatthewDavies[(7)] 14 44
(R A Harris) *prom: rdn 1/2-way: edgd lft and no ex fnl f* **3/1**[2]

5205 8 ¾ **Gelert (IRE)**[10] 7528 3-8-6 **46** oh1 ....(b) PatrickMathers 7 26
(Peter Grayson) *led: rdn and hdd 2f out: wknd ins fnl f* **16/1**

0005 9 *nk* **Myriola**[3] 7618 3-8-6 **46** oh1 ....(b) JimmyQuinn 9 25
(S Gollings) *prom: rdn 1/2-way: sn outpcd* **12/1**

0301 10 1 **She's Our Beauty (IRE)**[10] 7529 5-8-11 **51** 6ex...(p) FrankieMcDonald 8 26
(S T Mason) *chsd ldrs: rdn 1/2-way: wknd wl over 1f out* **11/1**[3]

6000 11 1¼ **Dancing Mystery**[51] 6907 14-8-10 **50** ....(b) LPKeniry 12 21
(E A Wheeler) *sn outpcd* **33/1**

0006 12 ½ **Nordic Light (USA)**[6] 7582 4-8-2 **47** .... MCGeran[(5)] 2 16
(J M Bradley) *chsd ldrs: lost pl over 3f out: sn bhd* **16/1**

0000 13 ¾ **Orchestration (IRE)**[3] 7618 7-8-6 **46** oh1 ....(v) LiamJones 1 12
(Garry Moss) *sn outpcd* **50/1**

61.05 secs (1.35) **Going Correction** +0.30s/f (Slow) **13 Ran SP% 116.8**
Speed ratings (Par 101): **101,100,98,93,90 90,89,88,87,86 84,83,82**
toteswinger: 1&2 £56.50, 1&3 £48.70, 2&3 £29.00. CSF £368.09 CT £5026.20 TOTE £22.80: £4.60, £5.30, £3.80; EX 1518.50 TRIFECTA Not won..
Owner Willie McKay **Bred** Mcmillin Brothers & James Devaney **Trained** Bawtry, S Yorks

FOCUS
This was a bad race no matter which way you look at it and the runner-up sets the level.

7645 BOOK YOUR TICKETS AT SOUTHWELL-RACECOURSE.CO.UK NURSERY 6f (F)

12:20 (12:22) (Class 5) (0-70,68) 2-Y-0 **£2,729** (£806; £403) **Stalls** Low

Form RPR

0021 1 **Spiritual Art**[8] 7543 2-9-3 **64** 6ex .... HayleyTurner 7 74+
(S A Callaghan) *led: hdd over 4f out: trckd ldrs: led on bit ins fnl f: shkn up and r.o: eased nr fin* **7/4**[1]

4446 2 ¾ **Abu Derby (IRE)**[122] 4956 2-9-5 **66** .... TPQueally 8 69
(J G Given) *chsd ldrs: led over 2f out: rdn over 1f out: hdd ins fnl f: styd on* **33/1**

1221 3 1¾ **Rio Cobolo (IRE)**[3] 7612 2-9-5 **66** 6ex ....(v) ChrisCatlin 9 64
(Paul Green) *unruly prior to loading: s.i.s: hdwy over 2f out: sn rdn: r.o* **9/4**[2]

203 4 *hd* **La Verte Rue (USA)**[13] 7501 2-9-6 **67** .... ShaneKelly 3 64
(J A Osborne) *edgd rt s: chsd ldrs: n.m.r and lost pl 5f out: hdwy u.p over 1f out: r.o* **12/1**

2046 5 ½ **Swiss Art (IRE)**[14] 7468 2-9-2 **63** ....(p) SteveDrowne 4 59
(R A Harris) *n.m.r s: sn pushed along in rr: rdn and edgd lft over 2f out: styd on wl ins fnl f: nt trble ldrs* **16/1**

0213 6 *nse* **Captain Kallis (IRE)**[10] 7531 2-9-3 **64** .... FrankieMcDonald 2 60
(D J S Ffrench Davis) *chsd ldrs: rdn over 2f out: styd on same pce fnl f* **9/2**[3]

6516 7 ¾ **Madison Belle**[16] 7451 2-9-7 **68** .... DarrenWilliams 6 61
(K R Burke) *chsd ldrs: rdn over 2f out: styd on same pce appr fnl f* **10/1**

0050 8 1 **Haulit**[100] 5606 2-8-6 **56** .... KevinGhunowa[(3)] 1 46
(R A Harris) *racd keenly: led and hung rt fr over 4f out: hdd over 2f out: nt clr run sn after: wknd over 1f out* **100/1**

2340 9 7 **Faraway Sound (IRE)**[25] 7361 2-9-2 **68** ....(p) PatrickDonaghy[(5)] 5 37
(P C Haslam) *s.i.s and hmpd s: outpcd* **18/1**

1m 18.22s (1.72) **Going Correction** +0.025s/f (Slow) **9 Ran SP% 117.2**
Speed ratings (Par 96): **89,88,85,85,84 84,83,82,73**
toteswinger: 1&2 £9.80, 1&3 £3.10, 2&3 £14.40. CSF £64.57 CT £139.23 TOTE £2.40: £1.10, £9.50, £1.80; EX 42.60 Trifecta £98.10 Part won. Pool: £132.70, 0.44 winning units..
Owner Matthew Green & M Tabor **Bred** R Haim **Trained** Newmarket, Suffolk

FOCUS
A modest nursery in which the winner was well in. The second and third set the level.

NOTEBOOK
Spiritual Art travelled like the best horse and, not really extended in the closing stages, was value for plenty more than the winning margin. She has improved markedly since going handicapping and she shrugged off a penalty for her Great Leighs win with considerable ease, despite this being a very different surface. She looks firmly on the upgrade and she has quickly proved herself very versatile surface-wise. (op 6-4 tchd 5-2)

Abu Derby(IRE), also making his Fibresand debut, boxed on gamely and put firmly behind him a disappointing effort on soft ground at Nottingham in August. Something may well have been amiss last time, given his subsequent absence, and this was much more like it. There are races to be won with him. (op 28-1)

Rio Cobolo(IRE) was under pressure at the top of the straight but he kept on, continuing his good record on this surface, although a 6lb rise for his 5f win here last time has left him vulnerable. (op 5-2 tchd 11-4 and 2-1)

La Verte Rue(USA) shaped as if she wants another furlong but she proved herself effective on the surface. (op 10-1)

Swiss Art(IRE) kept on up the inside, without ever really getting into contention. Official explanation: jockey said gelding hung left (op 28-1)

Captain Kallis(IRE) Official explanation: jockey said colt hung right

Haulit Official explanation: jockey said colt hung badly right throughout

7646 PLAY GOLF AT SOUTHWELL GOLF CLUB MEDIAN AUCTION MAIDEN STKS 7f (F)

12:55 (12:58) (Class 6) 2-Y-0 **£2,047** (£604; £302) **Stalls** Low

Form RPR

0022 1 **Confucius Captain (IRE)**[2] 7627 2-9-3 75 .... LiamJones 4 75+
(J R Boyle) *chsd ldr tl led 1/2-way: rdn clr fr over 1f out* **10/11**[1]

4 2 10 **Dante Deo (USA)**[24] 7371 2-8-12 0 .... TomEaves 2 54+
(T D Barron) *chsd ldrs: hmpd and lost pl 1/2-way: hdwy to go 2nd fnl f: no ch w wnr* **6/1**[3]

6200 3 ¾ **Shaws Diamond (USA)**[111] 5266 2-8-12 78 .... TGMcLaughlin 5 43+
(D Shaw) *s.i.s: sn prom: hmpd 1/2-way: rdn over 2f out: sn outpcd* **11/4**[2]

00 4 2¾ **Bold Bomber**[37] 7198 2-8-10 0 .... KrishGundowry[(7)] 7 41
(Paul Green) *hld up: hdwy over 2f out: sn rdn to chse wnr: hung lft and wknd over 1f out* **22/1**

00 5 1¼ **First Blade**[30] 7282 2-9-3 0 .... PaulEddery 6 38
(S R Bowring) *chsd ldrs: edgd lft 1/2-way: sn rdn: wkng whn nt clr run over 1f out* **66/1**

0655 6 9 **Alimarr (IRE)**[8] 7547 2-8-12 70 .... AdamKirby 3 11
(S Parr) *led to 1/2-way: sn rdn: wknd over 1f out* **6/1**[3]

6 7 4 **Becky Blue (IRE)**[135] 4536 2-8-12 0 .... LeeEnstone 1 —
(P C Haslam) *prom: rdn 1/2-way: wknd wl over 2f out* **40/1**

1m 31.02s (0.72) **Going Correction** +0.025s/f (Slow) **7 Ran SP% 115.9**
Speed ratings (Par 94): **96,84,83,80,79 68,64**
toteswinger: 1&2 £9.80, 1&3 £3.10, 2&3 £14.40. CSF £7.32 TOTE £1.60: £1.10, £3.70; EX 6.70.
Owner Albert Kwok **Bred** R P Ryan **Trained** Epsom, Surrey

FOCUS
A very modest little maiden. The winner probably only reproduced his recent best, with the other principals below form.

NOTEBOOK
Confucius Captain(IRE), who had the form in the book to win a run-of-the-mill maiden having bumped into unexposed sorts the last twice, and he made no mistake this time. Always close up, he scooted right away in the straight, going further and further clear as the race drew to a close. Typical of his sire, he is excelling on this surface and he looks the type to do well in handicaps off this sort of mark. (op 11-10)

Dante Deo(USA) can be marked up significantly because she was badly hampered on the home turn, where she dropped to the back of the field. Once straightened up for home, she stayed on well to go past everything bar the winner and, although she clearly wouldn't have won, she looks very interesting in similar company next time. (op 13-2 tchd 15-2)

Shaws Diamond(USA) did not reproduce her best form, perhaps because she did not handle the surface. (op 9-4 tchd 2-1 and 3-1)

Bold Bomber made good headway wide of the field turning in but he couldn't sustain his effort. He's now qualified for handicaps and it wouldn't be a surprise if he dropped back to 6f. (op 40-1)

7647 MEMBERSHIP AT SOUTHWELL GOLF CLUB APPRENTICE H'CAP 1m 4f (F)
1:30 (1:30) (Class 6) (0-65,65) 3-Y-O+ **£2,047** (£604; £302) **Stalls** Low

Form RPR

2540 **1** **Gayanula (USA)**[24] 7376 3-8-4 **55**.............. BMcHugh(5) 3 62
(Miss J A Camacho) *half-rrd s: hld up: hdwy over 4f out: led wl over 2f out: styd on wl* **10/1**

1005 **2** *2½* **Swords**[11] 7515 6-9-5 **65**.............. MatthewDavies(5) 4 68
(R E Peacock) *hld up: hdwy u.p over 2f out: chsd wnr over 1f out: edgd lft and styd on same pce ins fnl f* **5/6**[1]

6500 **3** *2¾* **Bond Casino**[4] 7608 4-8-10 **51** oh6..............(v) DuranFentiman 6 50
(G R Oldroyd) *chsd ldr: chal 4f out: sn rdn: styd on same pce appr fnl f* **11/1**

4440 **4** *2* **Reminiscent (IRE)**[21] 7401 9-8-5 **51** oh6..............(v) BillyCray(5) 5 46
(B P J Baugh) *chsd ldrs: led over 4f out: rdn and hdd over 2f out: wknd over 1f out* **16/1**

2000 **5** *14* **Mid Valley**[24] 7376 5-8-10 **51** oh2.............. TravisBlock 1 24
(J R Jenkins) *hld up: shkn up 5f out: rdn whn hmpd over 3f out: sn wknd* **3/1**[2]

0004 **6** *6* **Tykie Two**[3] 7613 4-8-5 **51** oh6..............(b) DeanHeslop(5) 2 14
(S Wynne) *led: rdn and hdd over 4f out: wknd over 3f out* **8/1**[3]

2m 42.57s (1.57) **Going Correction** +0.025s/f (Slow)
WFA 3 from 4yo+ 5lb **6** Ran SP% **114.0**
Speed ratings (Par 101): **95,93,91,90,80 76**
toteswinger: 1&2 £2.50, 1&3 £20.60, 2&3 £6.80. CSF £19.52 TOTE £8.50: £2.50, £1.20; EX 21.60.
Owner G B Turnbull Ltd **Bred** Jacqueline J Smith **Trained** Norton, N Yorks

FOCUS
More poor fare, this time in the shape of a 51-65 handicap in which nothing came into the race in peak form, and the pace was only modest until the home turn. This is form to have doubts about.

7648 CALL 01636 814481 TO SPONSOR A RACE H'CAP (DIV II) 5f (F)
2:05 (2:07) (Class 6) (0-55,55) 3-Y-O+ **£1,706** (£503; £252) **Stalls** High

Form RPR

6365 **1** **Lithaam (IRE)**[35] 7218 4-8-3 **48**..............(p) MCGeran(5) 6 56
(J M Bradley) *a.p: led over 1f out: rdn out* **15/2**

253 **2** *¾* **Westwood Dawn**[101] 5592 3-9-0 **54**..............(v) DarrenWilliams 10 59
(D Shaw) *sn outpcd: hdwy over 1f out: r.o* **18/1**

6630 **3** *nk* **Jilly Why (IRE)**[13] 7503 7-9-1 **55**..............(b) ChrisCatlin 7 59
(Paul Green) *chsd ldrs: led 1/2-way: rdn and hdd over 1f out: styd on* **9/2**[1]

046 **4** *1* **The Cube**[2] 7629 4-8-9 **49** oh1 ow3..............(p) PaulMulrennan 8 50
(J Balding) *chsd ldrs: rdn over 1f out: styd on same pce ins fnl f* **15/2**

6042 **5** *¾* **Summer Rose**[10] 7528 3-8-6 **46** oh1..............(b) HayleyTurner 5 44
(R M H Cowell) *chsd ldrs: rdn over 1f out: no ex ins fnl f* **6/1**[2]

00 **6** *½* **Lady Bahia (IRE)**[17] 7444 7-8-5 **52**..............(b) AndrewHeffernan(7) 9 48
(Peter Grayson) *s.i.s: outpcd: hdwy over 1f out: no ex ins fnl f* **40/1**

0404 **7** *½* **Bahamian Ballad**[10] 7528 3-8-6 **46** oh1..............(v) JimmyQuinn 3 40
(J D Bethell) *chsd ldrs: outpcd over 3f out: n.d after* **7/1**[3]

-040 **8** *¾* **Majestic Cheer**[30] 7292 4-8-12 **52** ow2.............. AdamKirby 2 44
(John A Harris) *s.i.s: sn prom: rdn 1/2-way: styd on same pce appr fnl f* **15/2**

060 **9** *½* **Berrymead**[137] 4476 3-8-6 **51**.............. AnnStokell(5) 4 41
(Miss A Stokell) *chsd ldrs: rdn 1/2-way: sn outpcd* **25/1**

4545 **10** *½* **Bilboa**[10] 7527 3-8-3 **46** oh1..............(p) LukeMorris(3) 14 34
(J M Bradley) *s.i.s: sme hdwy and hung lft over 1f out: sn wknd* **14/1**

2360 **11** *shd* **Twinned (IRE)**[189] 2802 5-8-9 **49**.............. LPKeniry 1 37
(Mike Murphy) *led to 1/2-way: wknd ins fnl f* **14/1**

0060 **12** *5* **Rough Rock (IRE)**[9] 7541 3-9-1 **55**.............. LiamJones 11 25
(G Prodromou) *mid-div: sn pushed along: hung lft and wknd 1/2-way* **25/1**

0600 **13** *7* **Great Fox (IRE)**[20] 7416 7-8-5 **50**.............. WilliamCarson(5) 12 —
(S C Williams) *mid-div: hung lft 3f out: sn wknd* **15/2**

61.11 secs (1.41) **Going Correction** +0.30s/f (Slow) **43** Ran SP% **120.8**
Speed ratings (Par 101): **100,98,98,96,95 94,93,92,91,91 90,82,71**
toteswinger: 1&2 £25.40, 1&3 £11.90, 2&3 £11.70. CSF £133.36 CT £686.64 TOTE £9.40: £2.50, £4.90, £1.50; EX 153.30 TRIFECTA Not won..
Owner JMB Racing.co.uk **Bred** Shadwell Estate Company Limited **Trained** Sedbury, Gloucs

FOCUS
A moderate handicap, and the action took place down the middle of the track. Ordinary form for the level with doubtas over its reliability.
Rough Rock(IRE) Official explanation: jockey said gelding never travelled

7649 HOSPITALITY AT SOUTHWELL RACECOURSE MAIDEN STKS 7f (F)
2:40 (2:40) (Class 5) 2-Y-O **£2,729** (£806; £403) **Stalls** Low

Form RPR

52 **1** **Fortuni (IRE)**[18] 7434 2-9-3 0.............. StephenDonohoe 3 73+
(Sir Mark Prescott) *s.i.s: sn drvn along: hdwy over 5f out: chsd ldr over 2f out: styd on u.p to ld wl ins fnl f* **4/11**[1]

00 **2** *2¼* **Thurston (IRE)**[23] 7389 2-8-12 0..............(b[1]) GabrielHannon(5) 5 66
(D J S Ffrench Davis) *led: hung rt over 4f out: rdn over 1f out: edgd rt: hdd and no ex wl ins fnl f* **125/1**

5 **3** *1* **Magical Destiny (IRE)**[28] 7318 2-9-3 0.............. TomEaves 8 64
(B Smart) *chsd ldrs: rdn over 2f out: styd on same pce appr fnl f* **7/1**[3]

00 **4** *¾* **City Bank (USA)**[67] 6539 2-9-3 0.............. DarryllHolland 6 62
(M Johnston) *prom: outpcd 1/2-way: rallied 2f out: styd on same pce fnl f* **13/2**[2]

5 *7* **Spartan Prince (USA)** 2-9-3 0.............. ShaneKelly 2 45
(T D Barron) *s.i.s: in rr whn swtchd rt over 5f out: sn outpcd: nvr dangrous* **16/1**

0606 **6** *5* **Black Attack (IRE)**[11] 7514 2-9-3 62.............. PaulMulrennan 1 32
(Paul Green) *chsd ldr tl rdn 3f out: wknd over 1f out* **25/1**

7 *7* **Beaux Yeux** 2-8-12 0.............. JamieMoriarty 7 10
(P T Midgley) *s.s: outpcd* **66/1**

1m 30.63s (0.33) **Going Correction** +0.025s/f (Slow) **7** Ran SP% **111.2**
Speed ratings (Par 96): **99,96,95,94,86 80,72**
toteswinger: 1&2 £15.80, 1&3 £1.10, 2&3 £38.60. CSF £82.91 TOTE £1.30: £1.02, £33.50; EX 91.00 Trifecta £98.40 Pool: £472.35, 3.55 winning units..
Owner Pacific International Management **Bred** Moyglare Stud Farm Ltd **Trained** Newmarket, Suffolk

FOCUS
A weak maiden. The winner can probably better this in time and the big-priced runner-up produced his first form.

NOTEBOOK
Fortuni(IRE) had an obvious chance on paper to get off the mark, but his supporters were made to sweat as the long odds-on favourite was being driven along from a very early stage by his rider. Two to three lengths down turning for home, he eventually wore down the long time leader, galloping on strongly and shaping as though he needs much further already. A very expensive purchase, he'll be seen to much better effect over middle distances next term. (op 2-5)
Thurston(IRE) appeared to have very little chance having shown next to nothing in two starts so far, but the application of blinkers had a miraculous effect. He travelled strongly in front and looked to have the favourite in trouble two furlongs out, before being collared in the final furlong. He kept on well though and connections will be delighted. (op 100-1)
Magical Destiny(IRE) once again put in a good shift in the final couple of furlongs and he's clearly got ability. (op 5-1)
City Bank(USA) could only keep on at the one pace and he looks decidedly modest at this stage, despite being bred to be much better. (op 8-1 tchd 6-1)

7650 SOUTHWELL-RACECOURSE.CO.UK H'CAP 1m (F)
3:15 (3:15) (Class 5) (0-75,75) 3-Y-O+ **£2,729** (£806; £403) **Stalls** Low

Form RPR

0211 **1** **Mozayada (USA)**[28] 7320 4-8-10 **66**.............. FrancisNorton 8 84+
(M Brittain) *led 1f: chsd ldrs: led on bit over 2f out: shkn up and r.o wl* **2/1**[1]

6000 **2** *3* **Rock Anthem (IRE)**[53] 6867 4-8-8 **64**.............. HayleyTurner 7 70
(Mike Murphy) *a.p: rdn over 2f out: chsd wnr over 1f out: styd on same pce ins fnl f* **12/1**

5204 **3** *nse* **Davenport (IRE)**[21] 7405 6-8-11 **70**..............(p) JamesMillman(3) 6 76
(B R Millman) *s.s: hld up: rdn over 3f out: hdwy over 1f out: r.o* **7/1**[3]

0005 **4** *¾* **Silver Hotspur**[7] 7564 4-9-5 **75**.............. LPKeniry 5 79
(C R Dore) *trckd ldrs: rdn over 1f out: one pce ins fnl f* **11/4**[2]

0104 **5** *3¼* **Trans Sonic**[30] 7284 5-8-12 **68**..............(b) PaulMulrennan 4 65
(A J Lockwood) *w ldrs tl rdn over 2f out: wknd over 1f out:* **14/1**

3211 **6** *hd* **Dancing Maite**[46] 7018 3-8-10 **67**.............. PaulEddery 3 63
(S R Bowring) *trckd ldrs: rdn over 3f out: wknd over 1f out* **9/1**

1044 **7** *1½* **Sularno**[38] 7184 4-8-12 **68**.............. SteveDrowne 9 61
(H Morrison) *rdn to after 1f: hdd over 2f out: wknd over 1f out* **9/1**

3004 **8** *3¼* **King's Ransom**[2] 7633 5-8-10 **73**.............. MatthewDavies(7) 1 58
(S Gollings) *prom: rdn over 3f out: wknd over 2f out* **14/1**

1553 **9** *13* **Punta Galera (IRE)**[182] 2361 5-8-5 **61**.............. ChrisCatlin 2 17
(Paul Green) *sn outpcd* **20/1**

1m 42.49s (-1.21) **Going Correction** +0.025s/f (Slow)
WFA 3 from 4yo+ 1lb **9** Ran SP% **118.3**
Speed ratings (Par 103): **107,104,103,103,99 99,98,95,82**
toteswinger: 1&2 £12.60, 1&3 £5.10, 2&3 £20.70. CSF £28.60 CT £146.29 TOTE £2.50: £1.10, £4.80, £2.60; EX 36.70 Trifecta £221.90 Part won. Pool: £299.90, 0.54 winning units. Place 6: £71.57, Place 5: £5.81..
Owner Mel Brittain **Bred** Shadwell Farm LLC **Trained** Warthill, N Yorks

FOCUS
A good race with several course specialists in opposition and the form appears reasonable rated around the placed horses.
T/Plt: £217.10 to a £1 stake. Pool: £37,489.07. 126.05 winning tickets. T/Qpdt: £3.90 to a £1 stake. Pool: £4,127.24. 774.90 winning tickets. CR

7606 WOLVERHAMPTON (A.W) (L-H)
Friday, December 12

OFFICIAL GOING: Standard
Wind: Fresh half behind Weather: Raining

7651 SATURDAY NIGHT IS CHRISTMAS PARTY NIGHT H'CAP (DIV I) 7f 32y(P)
6:20 (6:22) (Class 6) (0-65,65) 3-Y-O+ **£2,388** (£705; £352) **Stalls** High

Form RPR

4665 **1** **Kensington (IRE)**[6] 7586 7-9-2 **63**..............(v[1]) StephenDonohoe 5 78
(P D Evans) *hld up in mid-div: hdwy over 2f out: sn swtchd lft: rdn to ld over 1f out: edgd lft and drew clr ins fnl f: r.o wl* **8/1**

5440 **2** *3¾* **Vanadium**[35] 7226 6-8-13 **60**.............. AdamKirby 7 65
(G L Moore) *hld up towards rr: hdwy 2f out: rdn over 1f out: kpt on to take 2nd wl ins fnl f: no ch w wnr* **4/1**[2]

6462 **3** *½* **Thabaat**[13] 7497 4-8-3 **55**..............(b) MCGeran(5) 12 59
(J M Bradley) *hld up in tch: chal gng wl over 2f out: rdn and edgd sltly rt over 1f out: hung lft and lost 2nd wl ins fnl f: one pce* **9/1**

0310 **4** *2* **Provost**[10] 7532 4-9-0 **61**.............. DaleGibson 10 60
(M W Easterby) *in rr: styd on fnl f: nvr nrr* **33/1**

010 **5** *3* **Epidaurian King (IRE)**[13] 7490 5-9-2 **63**..............(v) DarrenWilliams 9 54
(D Shaw) *s.i.s: sn swtchd lft: hld up in rr: rdn and hdwy wl over 1f out: wknd ins fnl f* **9/1**

6 *1½* **Newpark Style (IRE)**[14] 7479 3-8-4 **51** oh6.............. RPCleary 2 37
(Emmanuel Hughes, Ire) *t.k.h: prom: ev ch over 2f out: wknd over 1f out* **33/1**

0631 **7** *½* **Royal Manor**[18] 7437 3-9-3 **64**.............. FergusSweeney 3 49
(N J Vaughan) *led: rdn and hdd over 1f out: wknd fnl f* **2/1**[1]

1125 **8** *8* **Megalo Maniac**[13] 7503 5-8-10 **57**..............(v) TonyHamilton 1 21
(R A Fahey) *prom: pushed along over 3f out: rdn whn hmpd on ins over 2f out: sn wknd* **11/2**[3]

5010 **9** *4½* **Forzarzi (IRE)**[69] 6491 4-9-4 **65**.............. DarryllHolland 8 16
(H A McWilliams) *chsd ldr: ev ch over 2f out: n.m.r wl over 1f out: sn wknd* **12/1**

5004 **10** *50* **Chookie Heiton (IRE)**[30] 7292 10-9-2 **63**.............. TomEaves 4 —
(I Semple) *hld up in mid-div: pushed along over 3f out: sn bhd: virtually p.u wl over 1f out* **11/1**

1m 29.69s (0.09) **Going Correction** +0.10s/f (Slow) **10** Ran SP% **121.7**
Speed ratings (Par 101): **103,98,98,95,92 90,90,81,75,18**
toteswinger: 1&2 £9.20, 1&3 £9.20, 2&3 £8.90. CSF £41.92 CT £307.77 TOTE £8.20: £2.50, £1.60, £2.90; EX 55.20.
Owner Derek Buckley **Bred** Mountarmstrong Stud **Trained** Pandy, Monmouths
■ Stewards' Enquiry : Stephen Donohoe four-day ban: careless riding (Dec 26-29)

FOCUS
A run-of-the-mill handicap in which two of the three market leaders disappointed but the form looks reasonable rated around the placed horses. The pace was fair and the winner raced against the inside rail in the last furlong.
Royal Manor Official explanation: jockey said trainer had no explanation for thje poor form shown
Forzarzi(IRE) Official explanation: jockey said colt was squeezed out turning for home

Chookie Heiton(IRE) Official explanation: jockey said gelding lost its action

7652 DINE IN HORIZONS CLAIMING STKS 7f 32y(P)

6:50 (6:51) (Class 6) 2-Y-O £2,729 (£806; £403) Stalls High

Form RPR

0123 **1** **Smalljohn**[17] 7443 2-8-9 74.....(v) TomEaves 3 71
(B Smart) *mde all: clr whn rdn over 1f out: r.o wl* **4/5**[1]

605 **2** *4* **Cwmni**[83] 6133 2-7-12 41..... CatherineGannon 2 50
(B Palling) *hld up towards rr: rdn and hdwy over 2f out: chsd wnr wl over 1f out: no imp* **66/1**

1020 **3** *1* **Captain Cavendish (IRE)**[8] 7547 2-8-9 59.....(b) MickyFenton 9 59
(A Bailey) *hld up towards rr: hdwy 2f out: rdn over 1f out: kpt on one pce* **16/1**

4 **4** *1 1/4* **Kheskianto (IRE)**[10] 7523 2-8-8 0..... JimmyQuinn 5 55
(M Botti) *t.k.h: a.p: rdn over 1f out: one pce* **9/2**[2]

2600 **5** *3/4* **Rose Of Coma (IRE)**[4] 7607 2-8-2 59.....(p) FrankieMcDonald 11 47+
(Miss Gay Kelleway) *s.i.s: hld up in rr: hdwy on ins whn nt clr run over 2f out tl wl over 1f out: nt rcvr* **22/1**

0000 **6** *2* **Nun Today (USA)**[33] 7258 2-7-13 53.....(b) LukeMorris(3) 1 42
(J S Moore) *prom: rdn 4f out: chsd wnr over 2f out tl wl over 1f out: wknd ins fnl f* **11/1**

5620 **7** *3 3/4* **Officer Mor (USA)**[14] 7475 2-8-13 66..... DarrenWilliams 4 44
(K R Burke) *prom: rdn over 2f out: wknd wl over 1f out* **15/2**[3]

0500 **8** *2 1/4* **Redhead (IRE)**[33] 7257 2-7-5 58..... CharlesEddery(7) 8 23
(R Hannon) *prom: rdn and edgd lft over 2f out: sn wknd: no ch whn hung lft ins fnl f* **9/1**

0060 **9** *29* **Spinning Belle (IRE)**[36] 7205 2-8-4 62..... LiamJones 10 —
(J W Hills) *hld up in mid-div: hmpd over 2f out: sn bhd and lost tch: t.o* **33/1**

4340 **10** *3 1/2* **Jaslyn (IRE)**[14] 7475 2-8-6 49..... MartinDwyer 6 —
(J R Weymes) *chsd wnr tl rdn over 2f out: sn n.m.r and wknd: lost tch wl over 1f out: t.o* **28/1**

1m 30.82s (1.22) **Going Correction** +0.10s/f (Slow) 10 Ran SP% **121.9**
Speed ratings (Par 94): **97,92,91,89,89 86,82,79,46,42**
toteswinger: 1&2 £31.60, 1&3 £8.50, 2&3 not won. CSF £102.44 TOTE £1.80: £1.10, £5.20, £3.00; EX 58.50.
Owner John Walsh & Reuben Glynn **Bred** W H R John And Partners **Trained** Hambleton, N Yorks

FOCUS
An uncompetitive claimer in which the winner did not have to improve to beat the 41-rated runner-up. The pace was only ordinary (over a second slower than the opener) and the winner raced towards the centre in the straight.

NOTEBOOK
Smalljohn, the pick of the weights, is a fair sort for this grade but did not have to improve to notch his second course and distance victory after enjoying the run of the race. He should continue to go well in this type of event. (op 5-6)
Cwmni faced a very stiff task at the weights but turned in easily her best effort after a break of nearly three months. She is lightly raced enough to be open to further improvement but may do better in low-grade handicaps. (op 50-1)
Captain Cavendish(IRE), who has run his best races at this course, had a bit to find at the weights with a couple of these and was not disgraced dropped in distance. He will be suited by the return to 1m. (op 12-1)
Kheskianto(IRE), dropped in grade, was nibbled at in the market and was not totally disgraced but she is going to have to settle better than she has done for this yard if she is to progress. (op 6-1)
Rose Of Coma(IRE), a dual 7f winner in the summer on fast ground, shaped better than the bare facts of the race suggest after missing a beat at the start and running into trouble at a crucial stage. She should be able to pick up a small contest on Polytrack. Official explanation: jockey said filly suffered interference in running

7653 SATURDAY NIGHT IS CHRISTMAS PARTY NIGHT H'CAP (DIV II) 7f 32y(P)

7:20 (7:21) (Class 6) (0-65,65) 3-Y-0+ £2,388 (£705; £352) Stalls High

Form RPR

1461 **1** **Milne Bay (IRE)**[8] 7544 3-8-9 **56**.....(t) JimmyQuinn 10 70
(D M Simcock) *hld up in mid-div: hdwy 3f out: rdn to ld jst over 1f out: edgd lft ins fnl f: r.o wl* **10/1**

1213 **2** *2 3/4* **River Kirov (IRE)**[4] 7611 5-9-1 **62**..... FrancisNorton 8 69
(M Wigham) *hld up in tch: rdn over 1f out: kpt on one pce: tk 2nd cl home* **10/3**[2]

002 **3** *nk* **Fancy Footsteps (IRE)**[33] 7256 3-9-2 **63**..... AdamKirby 4 69
(C G Cox) *w ldr: rdn and ev ch wl over 1f out: nt qckn fnl f: lost 2nd nr fin* **6/1**[3]

0203 **4** *4 1/2* **Dancing Deano (IRE)**[28] 7317 6-9-0 **64**..... RussellKennemore(3) 1 58
(R Hollinshead) *led: rdn and hdd jst over 1f out: wknd wl ins fnl f* **10/1**

2002 **5** *3 3/4* **Harrison's Flyer (IRE)**[13] 7503 7-8-1 **53**.....(p) MCGeran(5) 11 37
(J M Bradley) *hld up and bhd: sme hdwy over 2f out: rdn wl over 1f out: wkng whn edgd lft jst ins fnl f* **20/1**

030 **6** *hd* **Promise Of Love**[43] 7090 3-8-13 **60**.....(b) HayleyTurner 2 43
(Miss Amy Weaver) *s.s: hld up in rr: sme prog over 2f out: wknd wl over 1f out* **33/1**

0000 **7** *hd* **Rabbit Fighter (IRE)**[20] 7428 4-9-2 **63**.....(v) DarrenWilliams 3 46
(D Shaw) *t.k.h towards rr: rdn wl over 1f out: nvr nr ldrs* **14/1**

0430 **8** *1 3/4* **Coleorton Dancer**[4] 7610 6-9-2 **63**..... MartinDwyer 9 41
(K A Ryan) *t.k.h: prom tl wknd wl over 1f out* **7/1**

6203 **9** *1* **Takitwo**[23] 7382 5-8-7 **54**..... CatherineGannon 6 29
(P D Cundell) *a bhd* **10/1**

026 **10** *10* **Mayoman (IRE)**[14] 7478 3-9-4 **65**.....(e[1]) GeorgeBaker 7 13
(M Mullineaux) *a in rr* **14/1**

0012 **11** *1* **Gramm**[6] 7585 5-8-10 **57**..... PaulMulrennan 5 —
(M W Easterby) *hld up in tch: rdn 3f out: sn wknd: eased over 1f out* **11/4**[1]

1m 29.63s (0.03) **Going Correction** +0.10s/f (Slow) 11 Ran SP% **124.8**
Speed ratings (Par 101): **103,99,99,94,90 89,89,87,86,75 73**
toteswinger: 1&2 £9.00, 1&3 £20.60, 2&3 £36.60. CSF £46.10 CT £233.57 TOTE £12.80: £3.00, £1.50, £2.90; EX 48.30.
Owner DXB Bloodstock Ltd **Bred** Michael Boland **Trained** Newmarket, Suffolk

FOCUS
An ordinary handicap but, despite the steady early pace, the time was the quickest of the three races over this trip this evening. The winner raced in the centre in the straight and this was another step forward with the runner-up rated to this year's best.

Gramm Official explanation: jockey said gelding lost its action on final bend and hung left in straight

7654 BOOK TICKETS ONLINE MEDIAN AUCTION MAIDEN STKS 1m 1f 103y(P)

7:50 (7:50) (Class 6) 3-5-Y-O £2,388 (£705; £352) Stalls Low

Form RPR

3242 **1** **Templetuohy Max (IRE)**[32] 7274 3-9-3 60.....(v) JimmyQuinn 2 65
(J D Bethell) *hld up in tch: nt clr run and swtchd rt over 1f out: hrd rdn to ld wl ins fnl f: r.o* **10/3**[3]

2 *nk* **Magners Hill (IRE)**[14] 7486 4-9-5 0..... RPCleary 5 65
(Gerard Keane, Ire) *s.i.s: hld up and bhd: hdwy over 2f out: rdn to ld jst over 1f out: hdd wl ins fnl f* **4/6**[1]

306 **3** *nk* **The Wily Woodcock**[55] 6821 4-9-5 60..... GeorgeBaker 7 64
(G L Moore) *hld up in rr: hdwy wl over 1f out: rdn and kpt on fnl f* **3/1**[2]

0000 **4** *7* **Jordi Roper (IRE)**[126] 4810 3-9-0 49..... TolleyDean(3) 6 49
(S Parr) *hld up: sn in tch: rdn to ld wl over 1f out: sn hdd: wknd ins fnl f* **28/1**

20 **5** *3 1/4* **Charlie Allnut**[18] 7437 3-9-3 55.....(b) GrahamGibbons 1 42
(S Wynne) *chsd ldr: rdn to ld over 2f out: hdd wl over 1f out: wknd fnl f* **20/1**

4004 **6** *4 1/2* **Martingrange Lass (IRE)**[23] 7379 3-8-12 42..... AdamKirby 8 28
(S Parr) *led: rdn and hdd over 2f out: wkng whn sn n.m.r* **33/1**

2m 3.37s (1.67) **Going Correction** +0.10s/f (Slow)
WFA 3 from 4yo+ 2lb 6 Ran SP% **119.2**
Speed ratings (Par 101): **96,95,95,89,86 82**
toteswinger: 1&2 £1.20, 1&3 £1.60, 2&3 £1.60. CSF £6.38 TOTE £3.60: £1.20, £1.90; EX 9.20.
Owner Craig Monty **Bred** Jim Shanahan **Trained** Middleham Moor, N Yorks
■ Stewards' Enquiry : Tolley Dean caution: careless riding.

FOCUS
A modest maiden in which the ordinary gallop steadied after 2f. The principals raced centre to far side in the straight and the winner confirmed recent improvement.

7655 WOLVERHAMPTON-RACECOURSE.CO.UK CONDITIONS STKS 1m 141y(P)

8:20 (8:20) (Class 3) 2-Y-O £6,854 (£2,052; £1,026) Stalls Low

Form RPR

4101 **1** **Dialogue**[35] 7229 2-9-3 88..... DarryllHolland 1 89+
(M Johnston) *mde all: rdn wl over 1f out: clr fnl f: easily* **2/5**[1]

0203 **2** *5* **Head Down**[10] 7523 2-9-0 83..... DaneO'Neill 4 74+
(R Hannon) *chsd wnr: rdn over 2f out: hung lft fr over 1f out: sn btn* **9/1**[3]

2002 **3** *8* **Sign Of Approval**[35] 7227 2-9-0 80..... DarrenWilliams 3 68+
(K R Burke) *dwlt: hld up: rdn and effrt over 2f out: wknd over 1f out: eased ins fnl f* **5/2**[2]

1m 52.26s (1.76) **Going Correction** +0.10s/f (Slow) 3 Ran SP% **110.0**
Speed ratings (Par 100): **96,91,84**
CSF £4.29 TOTE £1.40; EX 2.80.
Owner Sheikh Hamdan Bin Mohammed Al Maktoum **Bred** Darley **Trained** Middleham Moor, N Yorks

FOCUS
A disappointing turnout for a fairly valuable prize in which the winner maintained his unbeaten record on Polytrack with an easy win. The pace was just fair.

NOTEBOOK
Dialogue, who had won his two previous races on Polytrack, was the pick of the weights, had the run of the race and won with a fair bit in hand. This did not tell us anything new about him but he looks the type to progress again as he strengthens up over the winter. (op 4-9)
Head Down had something to find with the winner at the weights but, while he was not beaten through lack of stamina on this first start over this trip, he does not look the most straightforward and may not be the easiest to place outside ordinary maiden company. (tchd 8-1)
Sign Of Approval looked the one most likely to give the winner a race but he proved disappointing after failing to settle in a muddling event and was beaten before stamina became an issue. While this was not his true running, he will have to show a fair bit more before he is a solid betting proposition. (tchd 9-4)

7656 COME TO THE CHRISTMAS PARTY TOMORROW H'CAP 1m 1f 103y(P)

8:50 (8:51) (Class 6) (0-60,60) 3-Y-0+ £2,388 (£705; £352) Stalls Low

Form RPR

4116 **1** **Plush**[23] 7392 5-8-13 **60**..... RossAtkinson(7) 11 69+
(Tom Dascombe) *dwlt: hld up in rr: hdwy 2f out: rdn to ld and hung lft ins fnl f: r.o wl* **4/1**[2]

5560 **2** *1 1/4* **Moscow Oznick**[39] 7166 3-9-0 **59**.....(v[1]) LukeMorris(3) 10 66
(N J Vaughan) *t.k.h towards rr: hdwy over 1f out: hung lft ins fnl f: wnt 2nd towards fin: nt rch wnr* **8/1**

3034 **3** *3/4* **Formidable Guest**[33] 7261 4-9-1 **55**..... JimmyQuinn 5 58
(J Pearce) *hld up in mid-div: hdwy over 2f out: led ent fnl f: sn rdn and hdd: no ex: fin 4th: plcd 3rd* **15/2**[3]

500 **4** *3 3/4* **Snow Dancer (IRE)**[6] 7581 4-9-3 **57**.....(p) DarryllHolland 3 53
(H A McWilliams) *hld up in tch: n.m.r over 2f out: no hdwy after: fin 5th: plcd 4th* **16/1**

5535 **5** *1/2* **Bavarica**[17] 7442 6-9-1 **58**..... RussellKennemore(3) 7 54
(Miss J Feilden) *t.k.h in mid-div: hdwy over 2f out: rdn wl over 1f out: wknd ins fnl f: fin 6th: plcd 5th* **8/1**

0064 **6** *1/2* **Barathea Dreams (IRE)**[11] 7516 7-9-0 **54**..... LPKeniry 12 49
(J S Moore) *sn chsng ldr: rdn to ld wl over 1f out: hdd ent fnl f: wknd: fin 7th: plcd 6th* **10/1**

6445 **7** *5* **The City Kid (IRE)**[18] 7440 5-9-4 **58**..... DaneO'Neill 4 42
(Miss Gay Kelleway) *prom: rdn wl over 1f out: wknd fnl f: fin 8th: plcd 7th* **15/2**[3]

040 **8** *1* **United Nations**[70] 6450 7-9-6 **60**..... TomEaves 1 42
(N Wilson) *a towards rr: fin 9th: plcd 8th* **16/1**

9 *1* **Downhill Skier (IRE)**[156] 3858 4-9-4 **58**..... LiamJones 9 38
(W M Brisbourne) *t.k.h: led: rdn over 2f out: hdd wl over 1f out: wknd fnl f: fin 10th: plcd 9th* **8/1**

3520 **10** *3 1/4* **Kirstys Lad**[17] 7442 6-9-6 **60**..... GeorgeBaker 2 33
(M Mullineaux) *hld up in mid-div: rdn and wknd over 1f out: fin 11th: plcd 10th* **7/2**[1]

4040 **11** *1 3/4* **Sir Billy Nick**[18] 7440 3-9-4 **60**..... GrahamGibbons 8 30
(S Wynne) *prom tl wknd over 2f out: fin 12th: plcd 11th* **28/1**

0- **12** *19* **Value Of Time (IRE)**[42] 7124 3-9-0 **56**..... FrancisNorton 13 —
(R Donohoe, Ire) *a in rr: lost tch fnl 4f: fin 13th: plcd 12th* **40/1**

0630 **D** *1/2* **Pelham Crescent (IRE)**[21] 7400 5-8-12 **57**..... MCGeran(5) 6 62+
(B Palling) *hld up in tch: lost pl 3f out: nt clr run over 2f out tl hdwy over 1f out: r.o ins fnl f: fin 3rd: disq: jockey failed to weigh in* **16/1**

2m 2.15s (0.45) **Going Correction** +0.10s/f (Slow)
WFA 3 from 4yo+ 2lb 13 Ran SP% **131.7**
Speed ratings (Par 101): **102,100,99,96,96 95,91,90,89,86 84,68,100**
toteswinger: 1&2 £39.60, 1&3 £7.20, 2&3 not won. CSF £40.52 CT £247.52 TOTE £6.10: £3.00, £2.70, £1.70; EX 75.10.
Owner John Reed **Bred** Cheveley Park Stud Ltd **Trained** Lambourn, Berks

■ Stewards' Enquiry : M C Geran seven-day ban: failing to weigh in (Dec 26-Jan 1)

FOCUS

A modest handicap in which the pace was soon sound and suited those held up. The form looks sound and the winner raced in the centre in the straight.

Pelham Crescent(IRE) Official explanation: jockey said gelding was denied a clear run

7657 WOLVERHAMPTON HOLIDAY INN H'CAP — 1m 4f 50y(P)

9:20 (9:20) (Class 4) (0-80,81) 3-Y-O+ — **£5,180** (£1,541; £770; £384) **Stalls** Low

Form — RPR

6523 1 **Lochiel**[13] 7493 4-9-6 **77** .... PaulMulrennan 3 — 88+
(G A Swinbank) *chsd ldr: led 2f out: rdn fnl f: styd on* — **5/2**[1]

0205 2 2 ½ **Quince (IRE)**[15] 7459 5-9-9 **80** .... (v) JimmyQuinn 6 — 86
(J Pearce) *hld up in tch: rdn 2f out: wnt 2nd ins fnl f: nt trble wnr* — **12/1**

2303 3 1 ¼ **Morbick**[4] 7606 4-8-12 **72** .... LukeMorris(3) 1 — 76
(W M Brisbourne) *hld up in rr: hdwy 3f out: sn rdn: styd on one pce ins fnl f* — **5/1**[3]

3-01 4 1 ¾ **Nobelix (IRE)**[7] 7563 6-9-10 **81** 6ex .... MartinDwyer 4 — 82
(J R Gask) *led: hdd 2f out: sn rdn: lost 2nd ins fnl f: fdd* — **5/2**[1]

1024 5 13 **Apache Fort**[15] 7459 5-9-4 **75** .... (b) TonyCulhane 5 — 55
(T Keddy) *hld up towards rr: pushed along 4f out: struggling 3f out* — **10/1**

6321 6 28 **Royal Amnesty**[42] 7116 5-9-9 **80** .... (b) TomEaves 2 — 16
(I Semple) *t.k.h in tch: rdn over 3f out: sn wknd: t.o* — **11/4**[2]

2m 42.95s (1.85) **Going Correction** +0.10s/f (Slow) — **6** Ran SP% **117.3**

Speed ratings (Par 105): **97,95,94,93,84 66**

toteswinger: 1&2 £25.60, 1&3 £24.00, 2&3 £15.30. CSF £32.52 TOTE £3.80: £1.80, £4.20; EX 35.40 Place 6 £47.57, Place 5£16.10..

Owner A Campbell **Bred** D W Barker **Trained** Melsonby, N Yorks

FOCUS

A fair handicap but one run at just an ordinary gallop. The winner edged towards the inside rail in the closing stages.

T/Plt: £69.80 to a £1 stake. Pool: £111,009.52. 1,159.51 winning tickets. T/Qpdt: £8.10 to a £1 stake. Pool: £8,678.60. 789.52 winning tickets. KH

7644 SOUTHWELL (L-H)

Saturday, December 13

OFFICIAL GOING: Standard

Wind: fresh, half against Weather: persistent rain

7658 CARLSBERG PROBABLY THE BEST H'CAP (DIV I) — 7f (F)

11:35 (11:36) (Class 6) (0-55,56) 3-Y-O+ — **£1,706** (£503; £252) **Stalls** Low

Form — RPR

532 1 **Run Free**[35] 6185 4-8-11 **50** .... LeeEnstone 4 — 60
(N Wilson) *mde all: qcknd over 3f out: hld on wl* — **6/1**

051 2 1 ¼ **Bold Diva**[13] 7509 3-9-3 **56** .... (v) HayleyTurner 7 — 62
(A W Carroll) *hld up in rr: hdwy on outer over 2f out: hung lft over 1f out: kpt on same pce ins fnl f* — **12/1**

2010 3 shd **Mrs Bun**[4] 7619 3-9-2 **55** .... (b[1]) DarryllHolland 5 — 61
(K A Ryan) *trckd ldrs: n.m.r over 2f out: hung lft and styd on same pce ins fnl f* — **5/1**[3]

2424 4 1 ¾ **Betteras Bertie**[11] 7533 5-9-0 **53** .... FrancisNorton 3 — 54
(M Brittain) *s.s: effrt on ins over 2f out: one pce whn n.m.r and swtchd rt wl ins fnl f* — **11/4**[1]

2622 5 4 ½ **Mister Incredible**[4] 7618 5-8-4 **48** .... (v) MCGeran(5) 6 — 37
(J M Bradley) *t.k.h: trckd ldrs: wknd 1f out* — **10/3**[2]

2630 6 7 **Bert's Memory**[25] 7373 4-8-4 **46** oh1 .... (b) DuranFentiman(3) 9 — 16
(J Mackie) *chsd ldrs: effrt over 3f out: wknd 2f out* — **15/2**

006 7 2 ½ **Spume (IRE)**[33] 7270 4-8-10 **52** .... TolleyDean(3) 8 — 15
(S Parr) *drvn to chse ldrs: drvn over 3f out: lost pl over 1f out: eased* — **11/2**

060 8 1 ¼ **Rose Of Torridge**[105] 5491 3-8-7 **46** oh1 .... ChrisCatlin 10 — 6
(A G Newcombe) *sn in tch on outside: outpcd over 4f out: lost pl over 2f out* — **40/1**

1m 32.93s (2.63) **Going Correction** +0.125s/f (Slow) — **8** Ran SP% **118.0**

Speed ratings (Par 101): **89,87,87,85,80 72,69,68**

toteswinger: 1&2 £7.00, 1&3 £8.10, 2&3 £5.10. CSF £75.72 CT £389.88 TOTE £7.70: £2.00, £3.80, £1.80; EX 93.10 Trifecta £215.10 Part won. Pool: £290.75, 0.45 winning units..

Owner The Run Free Partnership **Bred** Snailwell Stud Co Ltd **Trained** Flaxton, N Yorks

FOCUS

A low-grade handicap contested by infrequent winners at best. The form makes sense.

Mrs Bun Official explanation: jockey said filly hung left

7659 CARLSBERG UK NURSERY — 1m (F)

12:10 (12:11) (Class 6) (0-65,64) 2-Y-O — **£2,047** (£604; £302) **Stalls** Low

Form — RPR

000 1 **Thewaytosanjose (IRE)**[120] 5066 2-8-3 **46** .... CatherineGannon 8 — 56+
(S Kirk) *in rr-div: hdwy and swtchd lft over 2f out: edgd lft and led over 1f out: styd on strly* — **25/1**

2522 2 4 **Svindal (IRE)**[18] 7443 2-9-7 **64** .... (b) PaulMulrennan 3 — 63
(K A Ryan) *chsd ldrs: edgd rt over 2f out: wnt 2nd 1f out: no imp* — **13/2**

0432 3 ½ **Artesium**[15] 7468 2-8-13 **56** .... TonyHamilton 2 — 54
(R A Fahey) *w ldrs: led over 4f out: hdd over 1f out: kpt on same pce* — **11/2**[3]

0000 4 3 ¾ **Dark Desert**[25] 7372 2-8-4 **47** .... ChrisCatlin 6 — 37
(A G Newcombe) *prom: lost pl over 4f out: hdwy 3f out: one pce fnl 2f* — **12/1**

006 5 1 ¾ **Ed's Pride (IRE)**[183] 3008 2-8-2 **45** .... (b[1]) FrancisNorton 4 — 31
(K A Ryan) *mid-div: hmpd over 2f out: kpt on fnl f* — **20/1**

0010 6 2 **True Britannia**[15] 7467 2-8-13 **56** .... JamesDoyle 1 — 37
(S Kirk) *w ldrs: wknd over 1f out* — **25/1**

0433 7 6 **Orphaned Annie**[12] 7514 2-8-9 **59** .... LanceBetts(7) 10 — 27
(B Ellison) *in tch on outer: lost pl over 4f out* — **9/2**[1]

0035 8 nse **Transfered (IRE)**[15] 7468 2-8-5 **48** .... JimmyQuinn 12 — 16
(Lucinda Featherstone) *in rr: kpt on fnl 2f: nvr on terms* — **12/1**

040 9 1 ½ **Ask Dan (IRE)**[14] 7498 2-9-6 **63** .... TomEaves 13 — 28
(B Smart) *restless in stalls: chsd ldrs on outer: outpcd over 2f out: hung lft over 1f out* — **9/1**

0000 10 ½ **Angelsbemine**[25] 7370 2-7-9 **45** .... MatthewLawson(7) 5 — 9
(J R Norton) *led tl over 4f out: lost pl over 2f out* — **100/1**

006 11 3 **In Step**[21] 7425 2-9-0 **57** .... DarryllHolland 9 — 14
(W J Haggas) *chsd ldrs on outer: lost pl over 2f out* — **5/1**[2]

000 12 3 ½ **Mill Pond**[52] 6901 2-8-8 **51** .... AndrewElliott 11 — —
(M Johnston) *chsd ldrs on outer: lost pl over 2f out* — **12/1**

200 13 11 **Hollow Green (IRE)**[13] 7505 2-8-12 **55** .... (v) StephenDonohoe 7 — —
(P D Evans) *s.i.s: in rr: bhd fnl 2f* — **8/1**

6000 14 10 **Moon Warrior**[12] 7519 2-8-5 **48** ow3 .... PatrickMathers 14 — —
(C Smith) *in rr: bhd fnl 2f* — **100/1**

1m 46.0s (2.30) **Going Correction** +0.125s/f (Slow) — **14** Ran SP% **122.2**

Speed ratings (Par 94): **93,89,88,84,83 81,75,74,73,72 69,66,55,45**

toteswinger: 1&2 £62.40, 1&3 £41.40, 2&3 £4.30. CSF £177.19 CT £1075.77 TOTE £31.60: £7.30, £2.10, £2.60; EX 345.60 TRIFECTA Not won..

Owner Andy J Smith **Bred** Baronrath Stud **Trained** Upper Lambourn, Berks

FOCUS

A low-grade nursery, but competitive enough and they went a good gallop. Solid form despite the winner's big step up.

NOTEBOOK

Thewaytosanjose(IRE), beaten a long way in three maidens during the summer, adapted well to the Fibresand surface. Receiving weight from most of the field, she took advantage of a lowly first handicap mark which seems to have underestimated her ability. Official explanation: trainer's rep said, regarding apparent improvement in form, that the filly, having been off the course since August, has matured and strengthened. (op 33-1)

Svindal(IRE) has been in good form of late without winning, and he kept up the good work with a solid effort behind the unexposed winner. He is a fair sort for the track and deserves to get off the mark. (op 11-2 tchd 7-1)

Artesium, who has shown ability on turf and Polytrack, showed his versatility with a decent first effort on Fibresand. He is another who should break his duck in due course. (op 5-1 tchd 6-1)

Dark Desert, who needs farther than 6f on previous evidence, looked more comfortable for a long way over this extra 2f before tiring in the last 200 yards. He is worth trying over 7f. (tchd 10-1)

Ed's Pride(IRE) looked very modest in three outings on turf, and all-weather sellers are likely to be more his scene, but he made hard work of this in first-time blinkers and only plodded on past beaten rivals. Official explanation: jockey said colt suffered interference early in home straight (op 22-1 tchd 25-1)

True Britannia, who stays 1m on Polytrack, seemed to find the trip stretching her on this more testing surface. (op 20-1)

Orphaned Annie was soon in trouble but recent efforts on sand suggest she can do much better. (op 11-2 tchd 4-1)

7660 EUROPEAN BREEDERS' FUND MAIDEN STKS — 1m (F)

12:40 (12:41) (Class 5) 2-Y-O — **£3,885** (£1,156; £577; £288) **Stalls** Low

Form — RPR

2 1 **Racketeer (IRE)**[14] 7498 2-9-3 0 .... NickyMackay 3 — 80+
(J H M Gosden) *trckd ldrs: smooth hdwy over 2f out: edgd lft and led over 1f out: r.o towards fin* — **5/2**[2]

34 2 hd **Lord Chancellor (IRE)**[19] 7434 2-9-3 0 .... DarryllHolland 2 — 80+
(M Johnston) *led: qcknd 3f out: hdd over 1f out: n.m.r and edgd rt ins fnl f: no ex towards fin* — **6/4**[1]

06 3 4 **Ultimate**[21] 7424 2-9-3 0 .... TravisBlock 1 — 71
(H Morrison) *trckd ldrs: effrt 3f out: kpt on same pce appr fnl f* — **16/1**

4 4 3 ½ **Cubism**[58] 6760 2-9-3 0 .... AndrewElliott 5 — 63
(M Johnston) *s.i.s: hdwy over 3f out: outpcd over 2f out* — **4/1**[3]

53 5 ½ **Molesden Glen (IRE)**[31] 7282 2-9-3 0 .... TomEaves 4 — 62
(B Smart) *w ldrs: wknd over 1f out* — **8/1**

05 6 8 **Jhinga Palak (IRE)**[112] 5294 2-8-12 0 .... StephenDonohoe 6 — 40
(P D Evans) *in rr: lost pl over 2f out: sn bhd* — **12/1**

0 7 36 **Betsy The Best**[60] 6722 2-8-12 0 .... PaulMulrennan 7 — —
(R Bastiman) *s.i.s: sn prom on outer: drvn and outpcd over 4f out: lost pl over 3f out: sn bhd: t.o* — **100/1**

1m 45.03s (1.33) **Going Correction** +0.125s/f (Slow) — **7** Ran SP% **114.2**

Speed ratings (Par 96): **98,97,93,90,89 81,45**

toteswinger: 1&2 £2.30, 1&3 £10.80, 2&3 £5.50. CSF £6.63 TOTE £3.30: £2.00, £1.40; EX 6.70.

Owner Duke Of Roxburghe **Bred** Floors Farming **Trained** Newmarket, Suffolk

FOCUS

Two useful types fought out a close finish at the end of a race in which the runner-up had dictated an ordinary gallop.

NOTEBOOK

Racketeer(IRE), though not winning easily, was always just on top in the last 200 yards. A well-grown half-brother to 1,000 Guineas winner Attraction, he is the sort to improve with racing and should leave this form behind as he gains experience. (op 6-4)

Lord Chancellor(IRE) ◆ had run well in two maidens on turf and Polytrack, and he was unlucky to run into a rival of some potential at this level. Though short of room against the rail in the last furlong, he battled on with admirable tenacity and is well up to winning an all-weather maiden before making his mark in handicaps. (op 11-4)

Ultimate was just outclassed by the first two, but he has gradually improved in three races on a variety of surfaces and this was a sound effort. He could win a maiden, but handicaps are also an option now he is qualified. (op 10-1 tchd 20-1)

Cubism is bred to be high-class, and he showed promise in his only previous effort, which had been on turf. However, this switch to Fibresand was less impressive and connections will have to re-assess how to campaign him. (tchd 7-2)

Molesden Glen(IRE) made more impact over course and distance a month ago, but this was a better race and in any case his natural home will be handicaps from now on. (op 12-1 tchd 15-2)

7661 E.P.H. & MOELLER ELECTRIC MAIDEN STKS — 1m 4f (F)

1:15 (1:16) (Class 5) 3-4-Y-O — **£2,729** (£806; £403) **Stalls** Low

Form — RPR

2023 1 **Eureka Moment**[14] 7489 3-8-12 66 .... EddieAhern 7 — 70
(E A L Dunlop) *trckd ldrs: led 3f out: rdn clr over 1f out: eased towards fin* — **5/2**[1]

00 2 2 ¾ **Monaadi (IRE)**[231] 1621 3-9-3 0 .... GrahamGibbons 3 — 71
(R Hollinshead) *chsd ldrs: sn drvn along: styd on to take 2nd 1f out: no ch w wnr* — **8/1**

602 3 2 **Colourful Move**[18] 7446 3-9-3 60 .... HayleyTurner 6 — 67
(P G Murphy) *trckd ldrs: t.k.h: effrt 3f out: kpt on same pce fnl 2f* — **3/1**[3]

4 1 ½ **Savaronola (USA)**[104] 5085 3-9-3 75 .... TPQueally 5 — 65
(A P Stringer) *hld up in rr: hdwy over 3f out: rdn and hung rt over 1f out: one pce* — **11/4**[2]

-435 5 22 **Piermarini**[13] 7506 3-9-3 67 .... MickyFenton 1 — 30
(P T Midgley) *reminders after s: led: hdd 3f out: sn lost pl and bhd* — **14/1**

0040 6 14 **Sweet Seville (FR)**[22] 7400 4-9-3 35 .... AndrewElliott 4 — 2
(Mrs G S Rees) *hld up in rr: drvn over 5f out: lost pl over 3f out: sn bhd* — **80/1**

64 7 49 **Jayyid (IRE)**[14] 7489 3-9-3 0 .... DarryllHolland 2 — —
(C E Brittain) *trckd ldr: lost pl over 3f out: sn wl bhd and eased: hopelessly t.o* — **5/1**

2m 43.52s (2.52) **Going Correction** +0.125s/f (Slow)

WFA 3 from 4yo 5lb — **7** Ran SP% **115.9**

Speed ratings (Par 103): **96,94,92,91,77 67,35**

toteswinger: 1&2 £6.90, 1&3 £3.60, 2&3 £7.00. CSF £23.64 TOTE £3.80: £1.70, £4.20; EX 24.50.

Owner St Albans Bloodstock LLP **Bred** Pinnacle Bloodstock **Trained** Newmarket, Suffolk

The Form Book, Raceform Ltd, Compton, RG20 6NL

FOCUS
A solid tempo ensured a good test of stamina, but this was a weakly-contested event. The winner, who had been running well on Polytrack, made a winning start on this slower Fibresand surface. A cautious view has been taken of the form.
Jayyid(IRE) Official explanation: jockey said gelding had a breathing problem

7662 BOOK YOUR TICKETS AT SOUTHWELL-RACECOURSE.CO.UK CLAIMING STKS 1m (F)
1:50 (1:51) (Class 6) 3-4-Y-0 £2,047 (£604; £302) Stalls Low

Form RPR
0204 1 **Bookiebasher Babe (IRE)**[40] 7166 3-9-4 65 FrancisNorton 7 71
(M Quinn) *trckd ldrs: shkn up to ld over 2f out: styd on wl* 10/3[2]
5000 2 3 ¾ **Maddy**[5] 7605 3-7-13 52 ow1 (p) FrankieMcDonald 3 43
(George Baker) *trckd ldrs: hung bdly lft over 1f out: kpt on to take 2nd ins fnl f: no ch w wnr* 9/1
02 3 2 ¼ **Kipchak (IRE)**[16] 7463 3-9-9 0 HayleyTurner 4 62
(C E Brittain) *led rdrless to s: led: hung rt bnd 3f out: sn hdd: one pce* 7/1
0100 4 10 **Bellomi (IRE)**[6] 7594 3-9-9 88 (e[1]) EddieAhern 6 39
(Miss Gay Kelleway) *hld up in tch on outside: effrt over 2f out: sn wknd* 11/8[1]
2210 5 1 ¾ **Ricci De Mare**[9] 7499 3-8-0 55 (p) NickyMackay 5 12
(G J Smith) *sn drvn along: sn chsng ldrs: lost pl over 2f out* 16/1
0-00 6 9 **Nicada (IRE)**[332] 177 4-8-10 65 MickyFenton 2 —
(Stef Liddiard) *sn trcking ldrs: t.k.h: wknd over 2f out* 9/2[3]
0000 7 ½ **Autograph Hunter**[7] 7585 4-8-4 42 (v) PatrickMathers 1 —
(Peter Grayson) *s.i.s: hrd rdn and bhd 4f out* 33/1
1m 44.33s (0.63) **Going Correction** +0.125s/f (Slow)
WFA 3 from 4yo 1lb 7 Ran SP% **114.7**
Speed ratings (Par 101): **101,97,95,85,83 74,73**
toteswinger: 1&2 £3.20, 1&3 £1.80, 2&3 £5.50. CSF £32.60 TOTE £5.00: £2.80, £4.00; EX 23.50.
Owner J Henry, J Blake & A Newby **Bred** Minch Bloodstock And Castletown Stud **Trained** Newmarket, Suffolk
■ Stewards' Enquiry : Patrick Mathers caution: used whip when out of contention.
FOCUS
With the favourite again flopping on sand, and several others either out of form or running over the wrong trip, this was not hard to win. The winner probably only had to run to form.
Bellomi(IRE) Official explanation: jockey said gelding was unsuited by the kickback
Nicada(IRE) Official explanation: jockey said gelding had no more to give

7663 CARLSBERG PROBABLY THE BEST H'CAP (DIV II) 7f (F)
2:25 (2:25) (Class 6) (0-55,55) 3-Y-0+ £1,706 (£503; £252) Stalls Low

Form RPR
0304 1 **Tri Chara (IRE)**[14] 7503 4-9-1 54 (p) GrahamGibbons 10 68+
(R Hollinshead) *trckd ldrs: led 2f out: edgd lft and sn clr: eased towards fin* 8/1
5064 2 2 ¾ **Very Well Red**[5] 7601 5-8-7 46 (b) ChrisCatlin 7 53
(P W Hiatt) *chsd ldrs: kpt on to take 2nd ins fnl f: no ch w wnr* 5/1[2]
4053 3 1 **Outer Hebrides**[18] 7442 7-8-8 52 (v) MCGeran[(5)] 4 56
(J M Bradley) *mid-div: outpcd over 3f out: kpt on fnl 2f: styd on ins fnl f* 12/1
5642 4 ½ **Jojesse**[4] 7619 4-8-7 46 oh1 HayleyTurner 3 49
(G A Swinbank) *hld up towards rr: hdwy on ins over 2f out: kpt on same pce* 11/8[1]
4300 5 nk **Aggbag**[18] 7441 4-8-6 52 BillyCray[(7)] 5 54
(B P J Baugh) *prom: kpt on same pce fnl 2f* 11/1
5602 6 1 ¼ **Tapas Lad (IRE)**[5] 7599 3-8-8 50 (v) KevinGhunowa[(3)] 1 49
(G J Smith) *led tl 2f out: wknd ins fnl f* 10/1
0006 7 3 **Kabis Amigos**[7] 7585 6-8-11 50 ow2 (v) PaulMulrennan 6 41
(S T Mason) *chsd ldrs: wknd over 1f out* 10/1
0000 8 3 **Arrabiata**[25] 7375 3-8-7 46 oh1 (b) FrankieMcDonald 9 29
(C N Kellett) *s.i.s: nvr a factor* 66/1
3660 9 4 ½ **The Salwick Flyer (IRE)**[36] 7228 5-9-2 55 (p) TomEaves 2 25
(I Semple) *chsd ldrs: lost pl 2f out* 7/1[3]
1005 10 hd **Bahamian Bay**[4] 7619 6-8-8 47 FrancisNorton 8 17
(M Brittain) *prom on outer: outpcd over 4f out: sme hdwy over 2f out: sn wknd* 16/1
1m 30.08s (-0.22) **Going Correction** +0.125s/f (Slow) 10 Ran SP% **124.0**
Speed ratings (Par 101): **106,102,101,101,100 99,95,92,87,87**
toteswinger: 1&2 £4.70, 1&3 £4.30, 2&3 £11.40. CSF £50.95 CT £504.05 TOTE £10.00: £2.80, £2.10, £2.20; EX 75.10 Trifecta £132.70 Pool: £358.75, 2.00 winning units..
Owner The Tri Chara Partnership **Bred** High Bramley Grange Stud **Trained** Upper Longdon, Staffs
FOCUS
On paper a modest if competitive handicap, but it ended as a one-horse race and drew out a much faster time than division one. They went a decent gallop, and that seemed to suit the winner, who raced handily throughout but had to be slightly nudged along to press the leading three. Solid form, with a slight personal best from the winner.

7664 PLAY GOLF AT SOUTHWELL GOLF CLUB H'CAP 1m 4f (F)
2:55 (2:57) (Class 5) (0-75,75) 3-Y-0+ £2,729 (£806; £403) Stalls Low

Form RPR
1554 1 **Taikoo**[29] 7314 3-9-4 75 TravisBlock 3 92+
(H Morrison) *mde all: drvn wl clr over 2f out: eased towards fin* 4/5[1]
2 10 **Il Grande Ardone**[132] 3-9-3 74 (tp) JimmyQuinn 1 73
(D Flood) *hld up in last: effrt over 4f out: sn rdn: tk poor 2nd over 1f out* 11/4[2]
1214 3 hd **My Friend Fritz**[277] 847 8-9-2 68 ChrisCatlin 2 67
(P W Hiatt) *t.k.h: trckd ldrs: drvn over 3f out: one pce* 9/2[3]
0000 4 50 **Agapanthus (GER)**[29] 7314 3-9-4 75 TPQueally 4 —
(A P Stringer) *chsd wnr: drvn over 3f out: sn wknd: virtually p.u: hopelessly t.o* 16/1
2m 41.32s (0.32) **Going Correction** +0.125s/f (Slow)
WFA 3 from 8yo 5lb 4 Ran SP% **106.3**
Speed ratings (Par 103): **103,96,96,62**
CSF £3.11 TOTE £2.00; EX 4.10.
Owner Miss B Swire **Bred** Miss B Swire **Trained** East Ilsley, Berks
FOCUS
Three of these appeared to have a fighting chance beforehand, but in the event two of them need not have bothered to turn up. Taikoo won easily, but the form looks weak.

7665 SOUTHWELL-RACECOURSE.CO.UK H'CAP 1m (F)
3:30 (3:30) (Class 6) (0-65,67) 3-Y-0+ £2,047 (£604; £302) Stalls Low

Form RPR
4402 1 **Boundless Prospect (USA)**[8] 7560 9-8-13 64 PatrickDonaghy[(5)] 8 74
(P D Evans) *s.i.s: hdwy over 3f out: n.m.r over 2f out: wnt 2nd over 1f out: styd on strly to ld towards fin* 7/1
0022 2 1 ¾ **Boss Hog**[18] 7441 3-9-2 63 GrahamGibbons 3 69
(R Curtis) *led: wnt 4 l clr over 1f out: hdd towards fin* 2/1[1]
2021 3 6 **Blue Charm**[11] 7533 4-9-0 67 MatthewBirch[(7)] 7 59
(S Kirk) *trckd ldrs: t.k.h: kpt on same pce fnl 2f* 5/2[2]
0450 4 shd **Pearl Dealer (IRE)**[19] 7440 3-8-11 61 (p) LukeMorris[(3)] 4 53
(N J Vaughan) *trckd ldrs: effrt 3f out: kpt on same pce fnl 2f* 4/1[3]
3-00 5 1 ¾ **World Of Choice (USA)**[11] 7532 3-8-10 57 DaleGibson 5 45
(M W Easterby) *in rr and sn pushed along: kpt on fnl 2f: nvr trbld ldrs* 25/1
0404 6 ½ **Castano**[14] 7490 4-9-0 63 (p) JamesMillman[(3)] 1 50
(B R Millman) *s.i.s: hdwy on inner to sn trck ldrs: wknd fnl f* 8/1
1-30 7 7 **Ridgeway Jazz**[11] 7532 3-8-4 51 oh1 HayleyTurner 6 22
(M D I Usher) *chsd ldrs: wknd 2f out* 20/1
1m 42.3s (-1.40) **Going Correction** +0.125s/f (Slow)
WFA 3 from 4yo+ 1lb 7 Ran SP% **114.1**
Speed ratings (Par 101): **112,110,104,104,102 101,94**
toteswinger: 1&2 £3.90, 1&3 £2.80, 2&3 £2.00. CSF £21.38 CT £44.76 TOTE £9.60: £2.80, £2.00; EX 27.00 Trifecta £109.00 Pool: £313.98, 2.13 winning units. Place 6: £363.83, Place 5: £120.53..
Owner Diamond Racing Ltd **Bred** Mrs Edgar Scott Jr & Mrs Lawrence Macelree **Trained** Pandy, Monmouths
FOCUS
A modest contest won by an old favourite, who did well to come from behind considering the pace was was nothing out of the ordinary. Sound form.
T/Plt: £92.10 to a £1 stake. Pool: £62,052.57. 491.62 winning tickets. T/Qpdt: £14.00 to a £1 stake. Pool: £5,877.28. 310.25 winning tickets. WG

7651 WOLVERHAMPTON (A.W) (L-H)
Saturday, December 13

OFFICIAL GOING: Standard
Wind: Nil Weather: Raining for 9.20

7666 WOLVERHAMPTON HOLIDAY INN CLAIMING STKS 1m 1f 103y(P)
6:50 (6:51) (Class 5) 2-Y-0 £3,238 (£963; £481; £240) Stalls Low

Form RPR
0400 1 **Amazing Blue Sky**[15] 7468 2-8-5 58 ChrisCatlin 2 62
(E J O'Neill) *mde all: rdn over 1f out: r.o wl* 12/1
0343 2 2 ¼ **Precocious Air (IRE)**[9] 7547 2-8-8 62 ow2 ShaneKelly 12 61
(J A Osborne) *a.p: chsd wnr wl over 1f out: sn rdn and hung lft: no imp: jst hld on for 2nd* 3/1[2]
006 3 shd **Kiyari**[52] 6901 2-8-10 67 JimmyQuinn 7 63
(M Botti) *hld up towards rr: hdwy wl over 1f out: hrd rdn and r.o wl ins fnl f: jst failed to take 2nd* 11/4[1]
4000 4 1 ½ **Telling Stories (IRE)**[5] 7607 2-7-7 56 MatthewLawson[(7)] 8 50
(M Johnston) *hld up in rr: hdwy on ins wl over 1f out: kpt on towards fin: nvr nrr* 25/1
0424 5 shd **Betws Y Coed (IRE)**[12] 7514 2-7-11 52 (p) NicolPolli[(5)] 1 51
(A Bailey) *a.p: chsd wnr over 2f out tl rdn wl over 1f out: fdd ins fnl f* 15/2[3]
0520 6 hd **Lucky Punt**[13] 7505 2-8-11 57 StephenDonohoe 4 60
(B G Powell) *hld up in mid-div: rdn over 2f out: no real prog fnl f* 16/1
3 7 1 ¼ **Cafe Mystique (IRE)**[26] 7353 2-9-5 0 TomEaves 10 66
(T D Barron) *s.i.s: hld up in rr: hdwy on ins 2f out: rdn over 1f out: no further prog fnl f* 12/1
4034 8 4 **Strikemaster (IRE)**[26] 7353 2-8-8 53 PatrickHills[(3)] 11 50
(J W Hills) *hld up in rr: rdn over 3f out: c wd st: n.d* 9/1
5033 9 2 ¾ **Josiah Bartlett (IRE)**[21] 7415 2-8-11 58 LiamJones 5 45
(J W Hills) *s.i.s: sn mid-div: no hdwy fnl 2f* 10/1
004 10 2 ½ **Madam'X**[9] 7547 2-9-0 54 LPKeniry 6 43
(P F I Cole) *hld up in mid-div: rdn over 2f out: c wd st: sn bhd* 12/1
5000 11 3 ¾ **Ready To Prime**[31] 7282 2-8-5 45 ow1 MartinDwyer 9 27
(D K Ivory) *chsd wnr tl over 2f out: sn wknd* 33/1
000 12 5 **Red Eric**[120] 5041 2-8-2 42 LukeMorris[(3)] 3 18
(W M Brisbourne) *prom: lost pl bnd 7f out: bhd fnl 3f* 100/1
0040 13 2 ¾ **Noworneva**[49] 6986 2-8-7 48 StephenCarson 13 14
(S Kirk) *prom tl rdn and wknd over 2f out* 50/1
2m 1.59s (-0.11) **Going Correction** -0.05s/f (Stan) 13 Ran SP% **121.2**
Speed ratings (Par 96): **98,96,95,94,94 94,93,89,87,84 81,77,74**
toteswinger: 1&2 £12.20, 1&3 £11.20, 2&3 £2.40. CSF £47.69 TOTE £15.00: £2.90, £1.40, £2.00; EX 58.40.The winner was claimed by Mrs R. Carr for £5,000. Telling Stories was claimed by Barry Leavy for £5,000.
Owner Hong Kong Breeders Club **Bred** Hong Kong Breeders Club **Trained** Averham Park, Notts
FOCUS
A moderate claimer run at an ordinary gallop. Solid but very limited form. The winner raced against the inside rail in the straight.
NOTEBOOK
Amazing Blue Sky was easy to back but appreciated the drop in grade and step up in trip and got off the mark under a well-judged ride. Stamina looks his strong suit and he is likely to win again on sand. He was claimed for £5,000 by Ruth Carr. (op 10-1 tchd 16-1)
Precocious Air(IRE), who had a good chance at the weights, travelled strongly for a long way and ran creditably, despite edging left under pressure. While she may not be one to place maximum faith in, she has the ability to win a similar event. (op 7-2 tchd 4-1)
Kiyari was well supported and looks better than the bare form suggests in a race in which it paid to race up with the pace. A stiffer test of stamina will suit and she is capable of making amends. (op 9-2)
Telling Stories(IRE) had been well beaten on her last three starts on Polytrack but fared better. More of an end-to-end gallop would have suited but it remains to be seen whether this will be built on next time. (op 22-1)
Betws Y Coed(IRE), back in a claimer, had the run of the race and was not disgraced upped to this trip but left the impression that the return to 1m will suit. (op 9-1 tchd 10-1)
Lucky Punt was not totally disgraced given the way this race panned out but he looks fully exposed and is likely to remain vulnerable to the better types in this grade. (op 14-1)
Cafe Mystique(IRE) was noticeably easy to back but showed ability on this first run for new connections. A stiffer test of stamina will suit and he is not one to write off. (op 6-1)

7667 WOLVERHAMPTON SKIP HIRE H'CAP 1m 4f 50y(P)
7:20 (7:20) (Class 6) (0-60,65) 3-Y-0+ £2,388 (£705; £352) Stalls Low

Form RPR
1030 1 **Little Richard (IRE)**[7] 7573 9-9-4 57 (p) AdamKirby 7 65
(M Wellings) *led early: a.p: wnt 2nd over 1f out: rdn to ld ins fnl f: r.o* 7/2[2]
6003 2 1 ¾ **Kangrina**[31] 7280 6-9-3 56 DaneO'Neill 12 61
(George Baker) *sn led: hdd after 3f: chsd ldr: led over 2f out: rdn over 1f out: hdd ins fnl f: nt qckn* 8/1

0606 **3** ½ **Desert Hawk**[21] 7427 7-8-9 **51**.. LukeMorris(3) 2 55
(W M Brisbourne) *hld up in mid-div: rdn and hdwy 2f out: kpt on u.p ins fnl f* **12/1**

0600 **4** 1 ¼ **Vanquisher (IRE)**[7] 7573 4-8-11 **50**........................(p) StephenDonohoe 1 52
(Ian Williams) *hld up towards rr: hdwy over 1f out: hrd rdn and kpt on same pce ins fnl f* **6/1**[3]

6566 **5** nse **Semi Detached (IRE)**[34] 6951 5-8-12 **51**.................... GrahamGibbons 8 53
(J W Unett) *prom early: hld up in mid-div: hdwy over 2f out: sn rdn: one pce fnl f* **16/1**

0021 **6** shd **Lapina (IRE)**[7] 7573 4-9-12 **65**..(b) ShaneKelly 6 67
(A Middleton) *hld up in rr: swtchd rt and hdwy wl over 1f out: rdn and one pce ins fnl f* **15/8**[1]

2000 **7** 5 **Raquel White**[43] 7115 4-9-4 **60**................................... KevinGhunowa(3) 3 54
(J L Flint) *chsd ldr: led after 3f tl over 2f out: wknd fnl f* **14/1**

1505 **8** 3 **Itsy Bitsy**[59] 6728 6-8-8 **47**..(p) ChrisCatlin 5 36
(W J Musson) *hld up in tch: wknd wl over 1f out* **16/1**

2533 **9** ¾ **Berry Hill Lass (IRE)**[247] 1281 4-9-0 **58**.......................(p) MCGeran(5) 4 46
(J G M O'Shea) *s.i.s: hld up towards rr: short-lived effrt over 2f out* **20/1**

0-0 **10** 16 **Value Of Time (IRE)**[1] 7656 3-8-12 **56**.............................. TPQueally 10 19
(R Donohoe, Ire) *hld up towards rr: rdn over 3f out: eased whn no ch fnl f* **33/1**

/00- **11** 60 **Menkaura**[385] 6937 5-8-11 **50**.. NeilChalmers 11 —
(John R Upson) *t.k.h: hdwy after 2f: rdn and wknd over 3f out: eased whn no ch fnl 2f* **100/1**

2m 41.65s (0.55) **Going Correction** -0.05s/f (Stan)
WFA 3 from 4yo+ 5lb 11 Ran SP% **117.2**
Speed ratings (Par 101): **96,94,94,93,93 93,90,88,87,77 37**
toteswinger: 1&2 £6.40, 1&3 £8.20, 2&3 £17.40. CSF £31.11 CT £305.00 TOTE £4.70: £1.80, £2.10, £3.50; EX 39.80.
Owner Mark Wellings Racing **Bred** Rathbarry Stud **Trained** Six Ashes, Shropshire

FOCUS
A modest handicap in which the ordinary gallop suited those racing prominently. The winner came down the centre in the straight. Very ordinary form.
Raquel White Official explanation: jockey said filly ran too freely

7668 COLIN MOORE 50TH BIRTHDAY CELEBRATION H'CAP 7f 32y(P)
7:50 (7:50) (Class 5) (0-75,77) 3-Y-0+ **£3,238** (£963; £481; £240) **Stalls** High

Form RPR

3060 **1** **Carnivore**[15] 7470 6-9-4 **75**.. TomEaves 6 81+
(T D Barron) *hld up and bhd: hdwy over 1f out: swtchd rt ent fnl f: hrd rdn to ld last strides* **10/1**

0001 **2** nk **Nightjar (USA)**[3] 7633 3-9-6 **77** 6ex.............................. FrancisNorton 10 82
(M Johnston) *led: rdn and narrowly hdd over 1f out: led nr fin: hdd last strides* **10/3**[1]

421 **3** nse **Eastern Gift**[26] 7360 3-9-2 **73**.. DaneO'Neill 7 78
(R Hannon) *a.p: wnt 2nd over 5f out: rdn and slt ld over 1f out: hdd nr fin* **11/2**

3525 **4** ¾ **Carmenero (GER)**[8] 7557 5-9-3 **74**.................................. MartinDwyer 5 77
(W R Muir) *hld up in tch: rdn wl over 1f out: swtchd rt ins fnl f: kpt on* **9/2**[3]

6320 **5** nk **Caprio (IRE)**[24] 7386 3-9-1 **72**................................. RichardKingscote 9 74
(Tom Dascombe) *hld up in tch: rdn over 1f out: kpt on ins fnl f* **8/1**

2100 **6** 3 ¾ **Bridge Of Fermoy (IRE)**[5] 7603 3-9-4 **75**...................(bt) GeorgeBaker 3 67
(Miss Gay Kelleway) *chsd ldr tl over 5f out: prom: rdn over 1f out: wknd fnl f* **7/1**

0053 **7** ½ **Networker**[13] 7510 5-8-12 **69**.. JimmyQuinn 4 60
(P J McBride) *hld up in tch: n.m.r on ins over 1f out: sn rdn and btn* **4/1**[2]

000 **8** 1 ½ **Bright Falcon**[78] 6252 3-8-13 **70**.. AdamKirby 2 57
(S Parr) *hld up and bhd: struggling over 3f out: n.d after* **28/1**

R000 **9** 38 **Chrystal Venture (IRE)**[33] 7277 3-8-10 **67**..........(v[1]) StephenDonohoe 8 —
(A J McCabe) *s.i.s: bhd: rdn 3f out: struggling wl over 1f out: eased fnl f* **50/1**

1m 29.22s (-0.38) **Going Correction** -0.05s/f (Stan) 9 Ran SP% **114.8**
Speed ratings (Par 103): **100,99,99,98,98 94,93,91,48**
toteswinger: 1&2 £5.80, 1&3 £12.20, 2&3 £4.20. CSF £43.12 CT £206.51 TOTE £11.60: £3.80, £1.60, £1.80; EX 60.50.
Owner The Meat Eaters **Bred** Lord Halifax **Trained** Maunby, N Yorks
■ Stewards' Enquiry : Francis Norton five-day ban: used whip with excessive frequency (Dec 27-31)

FOCUS
A fair handicap but the pace was only fair producing a bunch finish and the winner, who came from off the pace and down the centre, looks better than the bare form.
Networker Official explanation: jockey said gelding hung left
Bright Falcon Official explanation: jockey said gelding had no more to give
Chrystal Venture(IRE) Official explanation: jockey said filly lost its action and felt wrong

7669 SPONSOR A RACE BY CALLING 01902 390009 MAIDEN STKS 7f 32y(P)
8:20 (8:23) (Class 5) 3-Y-0+ **£2,729** (£806; £403) **Stalls** High

Form RPR

6332 **1** **Azure Mist**[9] 7548 3-8-12 65.. PaulMulrennan 6 63
(M H Tompkins) *mde all: drvn out fnl f* **7/4**[1]

05 **2** ½ **Resentful Angel**[15] 7474 3-8-12 0................................ PaulFitzsimons 1 62
(Pat Eddery) *a.p: chsd wnr 2f out: sn rdn: kpt on towards fin* **14/1**

3300 **3** ¾ **Augustus John (IRE)**[9] 7545 5-9-3 65.............................. AdamKirby 7 65
(S Parr) *sn chsng wnr: rdn 3f out: lost 2nd 2f out: sn n.m.r and lost pl: styd on ins fnl f* **4/1**[3]

0 **4** nk **Metternich (USA)**[28] 7344 3-9-3 0..................................(t) NickyMackay 8 64
(J H M Gosden) *s.i.s: hld up in mid-div: hdwy on ins wl over 1f out: nt qckn ins fnl f* **9/1**

-063 **5** ¾ **Quick Off The Mark**[26] 7368 3-8-12 62.............................. TPQueally 3 57
(J G Given) *a.p: rdn wl over 1f out: swtchd lft ins fnl f: one pce* **3/1**[2]

4060 **6** 1 **Imperial Djay (IRE)**[7] 7585 3-8-10 55........................ StacyRenwick(7) 10 59
(G J Smith) *hld up and bhd: hdwy 2f out: rdn over 1f out: one pce* **50/1**

7 ¾ **Coill Glas (IRE)** 3-9-3 0.. DarryllHolland 4 57+
(W J Haggas) *sn outpcd and bhd: nrst fin* **7/1**

005 **8** 7 **Mr Skipiton (IRE)**[22] 7403 3-9-3 55............................... StephenCarson 5 39
(B J McMath) *hld up in mid-div: rdn over 2f out: sn wknd* **33/1**

5006 **9** 10 **Mr Burton**[14] 7497 4-9-3 52..(e[1]) GeorgeBaker 9 12
(M Mullineaux) *hld up in tch: wknd over 2f out* **33/1**

3-00 **10** 5 **Comic Tales**[11] 7527 7-8-10 41..(p) PNolan(7) 2 —
(M Mullineaux) *s.i.s: sn wl bhd* **100/1**

11 11 **Miss Pimpinella**[15] 4-8-12 0.. TomEaves 11 —
(W S Colthred) *dwlt: a wl bhd* **150/1**

1m 29.1s (-0.50) **Going Correction** -0.05s/f (Stan) 11 Ran SP% **120.0**
Speed ratings (Par 103): **100,99,98,98,97 96,95,87,75,70 57**
toteswinger: 1&2 £4.20, 1&3 £6.40, 2&3 £4.10. CSF £29.71 TOTE £3.40: £1.10, £2.60, £2.50; EX 29.40.
Owner David P Noblett **Bred** Worksop Manor Stud **Trained** Newmarket, Suffolk

FOCUS
A modest maiden in which the pace was reasonable. The winner raced in the centre of the course in the straight and did not need to match her recent handicap best.
Metternich(USA) Official explanation: jockey said colt hung left

7670 WOLVERHAMPTON-RACECOURSE.CO.UK H'CAP 1m 141y(P)
8:50 (8:56) (Class 4) (0-85,85) 3-Y-0+ **£5,180** (£1,541; £770; £384) **Stalls** Low

Form RPR

2023 **1** **Abbondanza (IRE)**[30] 7299 5-9-6 **85**.................................(p) TomEaves 2 93
(I Semple) *mde all: rdn over 1f out: drvn out* **5/1**[3]

3001 **2** ¾ **Star Strider**[6] 7591 4-8-6 **65** 6ex.................................... HayleyTurner 6 77
(Miss Gay Kelleway) *hld up in rr: swtchd lft and hdwy wl over 1f out: r.o ins fnl f: nt rch wnr* **12/1**

2-1 **3** ¾ **Princely Hero (IRE)**[17] 7457 4-9-4 **83**............................... JimmyQuinn 7 87
(M Botti) *hld up and bhd: hdwy on ins wl over 1f out: rdn and kpt on ins fnl f* **5/1**[3]

0424 **4** hd **Just Bond (IRE)**[8] 7564 6-9-4 **83**................................. PaulMulrennan 4 87
(G R Oldroyd) *hld up and bhd: stdy prog on ins over 3f out: rdn and nt qckn ins fnl f* **8/1**

3023 **5** ¾ **Ocean Legend (IRE)**[13] 7507 3-8-10 **77**................................ ChrisCatlin 8 79
(Miss J Feilden) *chsd wnr: rdn over 2f out: lost 2nd and no ex ins fnl f* **16/1**

6333 **6** 1 ½ **Jawaab (IRE)**[8] 7564 4-8-11 **76**.. MartinDwyer 3 75
(W R Muir) *prom: rdn over 2f out: fdd wl ins fnl f* **4/1**[2]

1222 **7** nk **Follow The Flag (IRE)**[8] 7564 4-8-3 **71** oh1...............(p) LukeMorris(3) 5 69
(A J McCabe) *hld up in mid-div: rdn over 3f out: sn lost pl: kpt on ins fnl f* **10/3**[1]

3106 **8** 3 ¼ **Justcallmehandsome**[17] 7457 6-8-7 **79**.........................(v) BillyCray(7) 9 69
(D J S Ffrench Davis) *prom: rdn over 2f out: wknd over 1f out* **16/1**

2020 **9** 56 **Premier Danseur (IRE)**[8] 7556 3-9-3 **84**.......................... DarryllHolland 1 —
(M Johnston) *mid-div: rdn 4f out: bhd 3f out: eased whn no ch fnl 2f* **8/1**

1m 48.7s (-1.80) **Going Correction** -0.05s/f (Stan)
WFA 3 from 4yo+ 2lb 9 Ran SP% **118.1**
Speed ratings (Par 105): **106,105,104,104,103 102,102,99,49**
toteswinger: 1&2 £10.50, 1&3 £9.80, 2&3 £8.20. CSF £64.22 CT £320.53 TOTE £6.20: £1.80, £3.10, £1.80; EX 55.80.
Owner Belstane Park Racing & Gordon Leckie **Bred** M Nolan **Trained** Carluke, S Lanarks
■ Ian Semple's first winner since renewing his licence.

FOCUS
A fair handicap run at a reasonable gallop. The winner raced centre to far side in the straight and the second was effectively 11lb higher than his recent win.
Premier Danseur(IRE) Official explanation: jockey said colt never travelled

7671 PARTY TIME H'CAP 5f 216y(P)
9:20 (9:21) (Class 5) (0-75,83) 3-Y-0+ **£3,238** (£963; £481; £240) **Stalls** Low

Form RPR

1050 **1** **Trimlestown (IRE)**[8] 7557 5-8-10 **67** ow1........................(p) DaneO'Neill 8 76
(P D Evans) *bhd: hdwy wl over 1f out: rdn to ld and edgd lft ins fnl f: r.o* **9/2**[3]

0001 **2** 1 ½ **Gainshare**[36] 7225 3-8-0 **62**.. DeanHeslop(5) 4 66
(Mrs R A Carr) *hld up and bhd: c wd st: rdn and hdwy 1f out: r.o ins fnl f: nt trble wnr* **11/1**

4012 **3** 1 ½ **Princess Valerina**[21] 7428 4-9-1 **72**.................................. TPQueally 9 74+
(D Haydn Jones) *hld up in tch: edgd lft and bdly hmpd wl over 1f out: hung lft and kpt on ins fnl f* **7/1**

3153 **4** ½ **Tangerine Trees**[21] 7428 3-8-8 **65** ow2............................. TomEaves 6 63
(B Smart) *chsd ldrs: rdn and sltly outpcd over 2f out: kpt on same pce fnl f* **7/1**

0321 **5** nk **First Order**[2] 7641 7-9-7 **83** 6ex.................................(v) AnnStokell(5) 3 80
(Miss A Stokell) *led: rdn and hdd ins fnl f: fdd towards fin* **2/1**[1]

0142 **6** 6 **Incomparable**[5] 7611 3-8-13 **70**..............................(p) StephenDonohoe 1 48
(A J McCabe) *chsd ldr: rdn over 2f out: lost 2nd whn edgd rt and bmpd wl over 1f out: wknd fnl f* **3/1**[2]

3 **7** 2 **Emacolali (IRE)**[154] 3981 4-8-4 **61**...................................... RPCleary 2 32
(Gerard Keane, Ire) *prom: rdn whn bdly hmpd wl over 1f out: sn wknd* **16/1**

00 **8** 6 **Just For Mary**[7] 7584 4-8-13 **70**....................................(b) HayleyTurner 7 22
(P J Rothwell, Ire) *s.i.s: outpcd* **40/1**

1m 13.95s (-1.05) **Going Correction** -0.05s/f (Stan) 8 Ran SP% **118.2**
Speed ratings (Par 103): **105,103,101,100,99 91,89,81**
toteswinger: 1&2 £5.30, 1&3 £6.30, 2&3 £6.10. CSF £53.77 CT £348.04 TOTE £6.90: £1.90, £2.70, £2.70; EX 43.00 Place 6 £125.91, Place 5 £77.55.
Owner L G Brookes **Bred** Liam Brennan **Trained** Pandy, Monmouths
■ Stewards' Enquiry : Stephen Donohoe two-day ban: careless riding (Dec 30-31)

FOCUS
An ordinary handicap but the strong gallop suited the hold-up horses. The winner, who edged to the inside rail in the closing stages, is rated to his best in the past year or so.
First Order Official explanation: jockey said gelding ran too freely
T/Plt: £91.00 to a £1 stake. Pool: £146,760.33. 1,176.21 winning tickets. T/Qpdt: £23.10 to a £1 stake. Pool: £7,499.32. 240.10 winning tickets. KH

7599 LINGFIELD (L-H)
Sunday, December 14

OFFICIAL GOING: Standard
Wind: Nil. Weather: misty, chilly

7672 RUBY HEN CELEBRATION H'CAP (DIV I) 5f (P)
12:10 (12:10) (Class 6) (0-60,60) 3-Y-0+ **£2,388** (£705; £352) **Stalls** High

Form RPR

0012 **1** **Thoughtsofstardom**[4] 7621 5-8-13 **58**............................ LukeMorris(3) 4 69
(P S McEntee) *hld up in tch: rdn and hdwy over 1f out: led ins fnl f: r.o wl* **4/5**[1]

4045 **2** 1 ½ **Night Premiere (IRE)**[27] 7357 3-8-11 **53**.........................(b[1]) PatDobbs 7 59
(R Hannon) *chsd ldrs: wnt 2nd wl over 1f out: rdn to ld 1f out: hdd ins fnl f: nt pce of wnr* **11/1**

0005 **3** 2 ¾ **Magic Glade**[16] 7478 9-9-2 **58**...(p) GeorgeBaker 1 54
(Peter Grayson) *hld up in tch: effrt to chse ldng pair over 1f out: one pce fnl f* **4/1**[3]

0300 **4** 2 ¼ **Kalligal**[59] 6750 3-8-10 **52**.. StephenCarson 2 40
(R Ingram) *chsd ldr tl wl over 1f out: wkng whn short of room sn after: no ch fnl f* **20/1**

6210 **5** 2 ¾ **Spic 'n Span**[2] 7644 3-8-11 **60**................................(b) MatthewDavies(7) 3 38
(R A Harris) *led: rdn over 2f out: hdd 1f out: wknd fnl f* **7/2**[2]

0200 **6** *6* **Gleaming Spirit (IRE)**[16] 7478 4-9-3 **59**........................(v) AdamKirby 10 15
(Peter Grayson) *s.i.s: racd wd: bhd: lost tch over 2f out* **25/1**

-000 **F** **Gifted Gamble**[16] 7478 6-9-4 **60**..............................(v[1]) LPKeniry 6 —
(Peter Grayson) *bhd: rdn and struggling whn fell heavily 3f out: dead* **50/1**

58.89 secs (0.09) **Going Correction** 0.0s/f (Stan) **7** Ran SP% **116.7**
Speed ratings (Par 101): **99,96,92,88,84 74,—**
toteswinger: 1&2 £7.10, 1&3 £1.10, 2&3 £5.10. CSF £11.53 CT £25.60 TOTE £1.90: £1.90, £3.60; EX 9.40 Trifecta £67.60 Part won. Pool £91.40 - 0.80 winning units..
Owner Eventmaker Racehorses **Bred** B Bargh **Trained** Newmarket, Suffolk

FOCUS
A modest event, weakened by three withdrawals.
Gleaming Spirit(IRE) Official explanation: jockey said gelding never travelled

7673 MICK FITZ BOOK SIGNING HERE TODAY CLAIMING STKS 5f (P)
12:40 (12:41) (Class 6) 2-Y-O **£2,047** (£604; £302) **Stalls** High

Form RPR

011 **1** **Smokey Ryder**[11] 7537 2-8-8 76.................................. FergusSweeney 4 75+
(G L Moore) *chsd ldrs: rdn and str run fnl f to ld fnl 50yds* **11/10**[1]

0241 **2** *½* **Glamorous Spirit (IRE)**[16] 7464 2-9-2 80.............................. ChrisCatlin 5 82
(S Curran) *chsd ldr: rdn 2f out: led over 1f out: hdd and no ex fnl 50yds* **2/1**[2]

5423 **3** *3½* **Barnezet (GR)**[8] 7574 2-8-9 68.. PatrickHills(3) 2 65
(R Hannon) *broke wl: sn lost pl: effrt and rdn 2f out: chsd ldr jst over 1f out tl ins fnl f: wknd fnl 100yds* **11/1**

2040 **4** *6* **River Rye (IRE)**[29] 7334 2-8-8 72.. LPKeniry 7 39
(J S Moore) *s.i.s: sn bustled along: clsd and in tch over 3f out: rdn and wknd 2f out* **16/1**

3420 **5** *1¾* **Our Wee Girl (IRE)**[8] 7574 2-8-5 70 ow1.....................(v[1]) MartinDwyer 1 30
(S Kirk) *sn led: rdn and hung lft over 1f out: sn hdd: wknd fnl f* **15/2**[3]

1205 **6** *3* **Lady Master**[12] 7523 2-8-6 72... JamesDoyle 6 20
(Ms J S Doyle) *chsd ldrs on outer: drvn jst over 2f out wknd wl over 1f out* **25/1**

58.29 secs (-0.51) **Going Correction** 0.0s/f (Stan) 2y crse rec **6** Ran SP% **110.8**
Speed ratings (Par 94): **104,103,97,88,85 80**
toteswinger: 1&2 £1.02, 1&3 £6.40, 2&3 £5.60. CSF £3.36 TOTE £1.80: £1.10, £2.20; EX 4.10.Smokey Ryder was claimed by R A Harris for £10,000. Glamorous Spirit was claimed by J Bridger for £14,000.
Owner Pleasure Palace Racing **Bred** Jeremy Hinds **Trained** Woodingdean, E Sussex

FOCUS
A decent claimer which produced an exciting finish between two runners with official ratings of 76 and 80. Solid claiming form.

NOTEBOOK
Smokey Ryder readily asserted when winning her second successive 6f Polytrack claimer last time. She had to work much harder here but found a sustained finishing effort to gain the initiative close home. She has a very willing attitude, seems best when racing just behind the pace and it would be no surprise if her shrewd trainer found some more opportunities for her. (op 5-4 tchd 11-8 and Evens and 13-8 in places)
Glamorous Spirit(IRE) ran away with a 5f Kempton claimer on her all-weather debut for a new yard last time. She changed hands after that and almost repeated the trick on her debut for another new trainer. It looked like she had made a decisive move at the furlong marker but she was just picked off in the closing stages. Official explanation: trainer said filly finished distressed (op 15-8 tchd 13-8 and 9-4)
Barnezet(GR) ran creditably considering the tricky task she faced at the weights and finished a long way clear of the fourth. She has not looked entirely straightforward in ten starts but her mark is steadily falling and she could make an impact back in minor handicaps. (op 10-1 tchd 12-1)
River Rye(IRE) has gone backwards since a couple of solid 6f Polytrack efforts off marks in the 60s in August and put in another lifeless performance here. (op 18-1)
Our Wee Girl(IRE) was a springer in the market and attacked from stall one, but she was possibly a bit revved up by a first-time visor and was a spent force early in the straight. (op 12-1 tchd 16-1 and 7-1)

7674 MARSH GREEN MAIDEN AUCTION STKS 6f (P)
1:10 (1:13) (Class 6) 2-Y-O **£2,729** (£806; £403) **Stalls** Low

Form RPR

3 **1** **Monsieur Fillioux (USA)**[23] 7402 2-8-13 0......................... AdamKirby 6 74
(J R Fanshawe) *stdd after s: t.k.h: hld up in tch: hdwy to chse ldrs over 2f out: chsd wnr over 1f out: squeezed through on rail to ld wl ins fnl f: hld on nr fin* **11/4**[2]

03 **2** *hd* **Hillside Lad**[27] 7356 2-8-12 0.. ChrisCatlin 8 72
(R M Beckett) *led: rdn 2f out: hrd pressed and bmpd ins fnl f: hdd wl ins fnl f: rallied towards fin* **2/1**[1]

0200 **3** *1¾* **Amosite**[57] 6818 2-8-4 75..(v) NickyMackay 4 59
(J R Jenkins) *chsd ldr for 2f: trckd ldng pair after tl wnt 2nd again over 2f out: rdn over 1f out: fnd little and no imp fnl f* **10/1**

4 *2¼* **Bahkov (IRE)** 2-8-12 0.. RichardKingscote 2 60
(Tom Dascombe) *rn green in midfield: rdn over 2f out: kpt on fnl f: nvr gng pce to threaten ldrs* **11/2**[3]

5 *1* **Cloudesley (IRE)** 2-8-10 0.. LPKeniry 7 55
(A M Balding) *rn green in midfield: bdly hmpd and wnt rt over 4f out: hdwy over 2f out: kpt on steadily fnl f: nt rch ldrs* **9/1**

6 *6* **Menhir Bay** 2-8-7 0 ow2.. JamesO'Reilly(5) 5 39
(D K Ivory) *in tch in midfield: rdn and struggling whn c wd bnd 2f out: n.d after* **33/1**

7 *2* **The Mumbo** 2-8-3 0.. LukeMorris(3) 9 27
(W Jarvis) *v.s.a: a wl bhd* **6/1**

00 **8** *10* **Rio Ramus (IRE)**[31] 7303 2-8-11 0.................................(b[1]) JamesDoyle 3 2
(R A Teal) *plld hrd: hld up in midfield: hdwy to chse ldr 4f out tl 2f out: wknd rapidly* **50/1**

50 **9** *6* **Floods Of Tears**[9] 7561 2-8-6 0.. PaulDoe 1 —
(D Flood) *sn outpcd in rr: wl bhd fr 1/2-way* **25/1**

1m 11.95s (0.05) **Going Correction** 0.0s/f (Stan) **9** Ran SP% **117.5**
Speed ratings (Par 94): **99,98,96,93,92 84,81,68,60**
toteswinger: 1&2 £1.10, 1&3 £5.70, 2&3 £6.70. CSF £8.71 TOTE £3.10: £1.70, £1.10, £1.80; EX 12.20 Trifecta £151.40 Pool £282.38 - 1.38 winning units..
Owner Mrs J Fanshawe **Bred** A Lynch Et Al **Trained** Newmarket, Suffolk
■ Stewards' Enquiry : Chris Catlin two-day ban: careless riding (Dec 28,29)

FOCUS
A fair maiden auction event but there was little strength in depth.

NOTEBOOK
Monsieur Fillioux(USA) had gone close at 9-1 in a 7f Wolverhampton maiden on debut last month and had decent form claims. There is some stamina in his US pedigree, so there was a slight concern about the drop in trip and there were also signs of reluctance to enter the stalls, but he eventually did the job in very pleasing style. He travelled smoothly just off the pace, had to wait a while to find a big enough gap against the far rail in the closing stages but then quickened to win with more in hand than the winning margin suggests. He has suffered from sore shins but represents a trainer who often brings his horses along steadily and he should be open to plenty of improvement, particularly when stepped back up in trip. (op 5-2 tchd 9-4 and 3-1 in places)
Hillside Lad looked like he was still learning when third in a similar event at Kempton last month. He was strongly supported, travelled sweetly in front for most of the way but was just overhauled in the closing stages. This was a much more professional performance by the son of Tobougg, who should not have much trouble winning a similar event. (op 11-4)
Amosite has done quite well to shrug off a potentially demoralising defeat in the Rockfel Stakes last time and posted her best effort for some time with a visor reapplied. She has had plenty of chances but was not far behind some useful types in the summer, and should be able to get off the mark. (op 8-1)
Bahkov(IRE) was a bit reluctant to enter the stalls and looked inexperienced during the race, but stayed on quite nicely under a considerate ride on his debut. (op 9-2 tchd 6-1)
Cloudesley(IRE) showed some promise on his first run. He is a half-brother to winners at 1m-1m4f out of a mare by the stamina influence Deploy, and should be suited by a stiffer test in time. (op 8-1 tchd 10-1)
The Mumbo was backed from 12-1 to 6-1 but was always outpaced on her debut. (op 12-1)

7675 FELBRIDGE CLAIMING STKS 6f (P)
1:40 (1:41) (Class 6) 3-Y-O+ **£2,729** (£806; £403) **Stalls** Low

Form RPR

0022 **1** **Little Edward**[25] 7378 10-9-5 85.. GeorgeBaker 3 89
(R J Hodges) *a travelling strly: trckd ldrs: plld out and hdwy wl over 1f out: upsides ldrs 1f out: nudged into ld ins fnl f: readily* **7/4**[1]

0506 **2** *2* **Don Pele (IRE)**[25] 7378 6-8-6 68.............................(b) KevinGhunowa(3) 6 73
(R A Harris) *t.k.h: hld up in midfield: rdn and hdwy over 1f out: styd on u.p to 2nd towards fin: no ch w wnr* **12/1**

001 **3** *¾* **Monkey Glas (IRE)**[20] 7436 4-9-9 91................................(v) ChrisCatlin 7 85
(J R Gask) *led tl 2f out: styd w ldr tl led again 1f out: hdd ins fnl f: no ch w wnr after: lost 2nd towards fin* **5/2**[2]

5140 **4** *hd* **Brandywell Boy (IRE)**[7] 7592 5-8-10 73............................ BillyCray(7) 4 78
(D J S Ffrench Davis) *in tch towards rr: rdn and gd hdwy on inner 2f out: ev ch 1f out tl one pce fnl 100yds* **11/1**

4155 **5** *hd* **Tender Process (IRE)**[16] 7466 5-8-3 66.........................(b) DaleGibson 5 63
(R A Fahey) *dwlt: bhd: hdwy towards inner over 1f out: nt clr run and swtchd rt ins fnl f: r.o cl home: nvr trbld wnr* **5/1**[3]

0356 **6** *nk* **Buy On The Red**[31] 7297 7-8-7 70...............................(p) MartinDwyer 2 66
(W R Muir) *w ldr tl led on inner 2f out: sn rdn: hdd 1f out: one pce ins fnl f* **9/1**

2004 **7** *3* **Russian Reel**[9] 7557 3-9-0 75...................................(t) AlanCreighton(3) 8 67
(E J Creighton) *chsd ldrs on outer: rdn struggling over 2f out: no ch fnl f* **33/1**

6133 **8** *4* **Bazguy**[5] 7616 3-8-8 72...(b) JamesO'Reilly(5) 9 50
(J O'Reilly) *prom: rdn and struggling over 2f out: no ch fnl f* **16/1**

1m 11.55s (-0.35) **Going Correction** 0.0s/f (Stan) **8** Ran SP% **116.5**
Speed ratings (Par 101): **102,99,98,98,97 97,93,88**
toteswinger: 1&2 £6.20, 1&3 £1.30, 2&3 £6.50. CSF £25.05 TOTE £2.50: £1.10, £2.50, £1.30; EX 30.70 Trifecta £123.20 Pool £166.60 - 1.00 winning unit..
Owner J W Mursell **Bred** J W Mursell **Trained** Charlton Mackrell, Somerset

FOCUS
A fair claimer.

7676 GODSTONE H'CAP 1m 4f (P)
2:10 (2:10) (Class 6) (0-50,54) 3-Y-O+ **£2,729** (£806; £403) **Stalls** Low

Form RPR

0032 **1** **Sagunt (GER)**[52] 6929 5-8-5 **49**................................... RossAtkinson(7) 8 59+
(S Curran) *hld up in rr: hdwy on outer over 3f out: chsd ldrs 2f out: led over 1f out: idled and rdn out fnl f* **5/1**[1]

/006 **2** *¾* **Rahy's Crown (USA)**[23] 7401 5-8-9 **46**......................... FrancisNorton 14 54
(G L Moore) *hld up in rr: hdwy on outer 2f out: styd on u.p to chse wnr ins fnl f: kpt on but a hld* **5/1**[1]

6300 **3** *2* **Amwell Brave**[22] 7078 7-8-10 **47**.. JamesDoyle 11 51+
(J R Jenkins) *hld up in rr: stl plenty to do whn nt clr run jst over 2f out: n.m.r wl over 1f out: styd on wl fnl f: wnt 3rd towards fin: nt rch ldrs* **16/1**

3041 **4** *nk* **Play Up Pompey**[6] 7599 6-9-3 **54** 6ex..................... RichardKingscote 12 58
(J J Bridger) *t.k.h: hld up in midfield: lost pl and dropped to rr wl over 3f out: swtchd to outer and hdwy over 2f out: styd on u.p fnl f: nt rch ldrs* **17/2**

0-0 **5** *½* **Lytham (IRE)**[44] 7112 7-8-11 **48**....................................... VinceSlattery 13 51
(D J Wintle) *t.k.h: hld up in midfield: hdwy 4f out: chsd ldng pair over 2f out: rdn and hung lft over 1f out: one pce fnl f* **7/1**[3]

4000 **6** *¾* **Mix N Match**[56] 6019 4-8-13 **50**................................ FrankieMcDonald 15 52
(R M Stronge) *t.k.h: hld up in rr: hdwy on outer over 4f out: chsd ldr over 2f out: led 2f out: hdd over 1f out: hung lft and wknd fnl f* **50/1**

60 **7** *1½* **Amical Risks (FR)**[116] 5183 4-8-13 **50**................................ MartinDwyer 4 50
(W J Musson) *hld up in midfield: rdn and effrt over 2f out: plugged on u.p fnl f: nvr gng pce to threaten ldrs* **13/2**[2]

0S04 **8** *½* **Ben Bacchus (IRE)**[16] 7473 6-8-13 **50**................................. ChrisCatlin 7 49
(P W Hiatt) *stdd s: t.k.h: hld up towards rr: hdwy 6f out: chsd ldrs over 4f out: hung lft and wknd over 1f out* **7/1**[3]

0006 **9** *1* **Buck Cannon (IRE)**[11] 7535 3-8-5 **50**............................ LukeMorris(3) 2 47
(P M Phelan) *in tch: rdn and chsd ldrs over 3f out: wknd ent fnl f* **13/2**[2]

054 **10** *6* **Trojan Hero (IRE)**[142] 4381 3-8-4 **46**............................ SimonWhitworth 16 34
(S W Hall) *chsd ldr tl over 8f out and again 5f out: led 3f out: rdn and hdd 2f out: wknd qckly over 1f out* **33/1**

5000 **11** *6* **I Certainly May**[12] 7520 3-8-4 **46**... NickyMackay 9 24
(S Dow) *in tch tl hdwy to chse ldr over 8f out: led over 7f out tl rdn and hdd 3f out: sn struggling: wl bhd fr over 1f out* **33/1**

6B40 **12** *4* **Bollywood (IRE)**[28] 5583 5-8-13 **50**.............................. CatherineGannon 5 22
(J J Bridger) *led tl over 7f out: styd handy tl wknd qckly over 3f out: wl bhd fnl 2f* **33/1**

0003 **13** *3¾* **Shenandoah Girl**[45] 7089 5-8-6 **50**..............................(p) KylieManser(7) 1 16
(Miss Gay Kelleway) *chsd ldrs tl rdn and wknd over 2f out: wl bhd fr over 1f out* **20/1**

2m 33.39s (0.39) **Going Correction** 0.0s/f (Stan)
WFA 3 from 4yo+ 5lb **13** Ran SP% **117.0**
Speed ratings (Par 101): **98,97,96,95,95 95,94,93,93,89 85,82,79**
toteswinger: 1&2 £7.10, 1&3 £27.20, 2&3 £13.70. CSF £26.61 CT £374.67 TOTE £6.50: £1.90, £2.10, £5.10; EX 20.70 TRIFECTA Not won..
Owner Grey Fox Racing **Bred** Gestut Schlenderhan **Trained** Hatford, Oxon

FOCUS
An ordinary handicap run at a fair pace.

Play Up Pompey Official explanation: jockey said gelding ran too free

7677 PHOTO FINISH FOR CHRISTMAS GIFTS @ EVENTIMAGE.TV H'CAP 7f (P)

2:40 (2:42) (Class 5) (0-70,70) 3-Y-O+ **£3,885** (£1,156; £577; £288) **Stalls** Low

Form RPR

0102 **1** **The Cayterers**[20] 7435 6-8-13 **70** MCGeran(5) 6 80
(A W Carroll) *in tch in midfield on outer: rdn and hdwy over 1f out: led ins fnl f: r.o wl* **10/1**

0213 **2** *¾* **Blue Charm**[1] 7665 4-9-1 **67** JamesDoyle 2 75
(S Kirk) *in tch: hdwy 2f out: drvn over 1f out: pressed wnr ins fnl f: unable qck fnl 50yds* **11/4**[1]

0306 **3** *¾* **Haasem (USA)**[10] 7548 5-8-11 **63** (v[1]) StephenDonohoe 7 69
(J R Jenkins) *stdd s: hld up in rr: hdwy towards inner wl over 1f out: hrd drvn and styd on fnl f: wnt 3rd fnl 50yds: nt rch ldng pair* **16/1**

0064 **4** *hd* **Divertimenti (IRE)**[14] 7510 4-9-0 **66** (p) LPKeniry 4 71
(C R Dore) *in tch in midfield: rdn wl over 1f out: kpt on u.p fnl f: nvr quite gng pce to rch ldrs* **10/1**

0113 **5** *1 ¼* **Charming Escort**[20] 7433 4-8-6 **58** MartinDwyer 9 60
(T T Clement) *chsd ldrs tl wnt 2nd 4f out: ev ch and drvn 2f out: led 1f out: sn hdd: wknd fnl 50yds* **8/1**

/23- **6** *nk* **Carlowsantana (IRE)**[11] 6964 5-8-11 **68** (b[1]) BACurtis(5) 11 69
(Adrian Sexton, Ire) *stdd s: hld up in rr: drvn over 2f out: little hdwy tl styd u.p fnl f: nt rch ldrs* **33/1**

0000 **7** *½* **Shake On It**[17] 7461 4-8-8 **65** (vt[1]) WilliamCarson(5) 1 65
(M J Gingell) *s.i.s: bhd: hdwy towards inner jst over 1f out: kpt on fnl f: nvr trbld ldrs* **40/1**

6002 **8** *nk* **Surwaki (USA)**[20] 7433 6-8-8 **60** TomEaves 10 59
(R M H Cowell) *t.k.h: chsd ldr tl 4f out: styd handy: rdn whn hmpd and nt clr run and swtchd rt over 1f out: wknd ins fnl f* **14/1**

0005 **9** *1 ½* **Danski**[15] 7494 5-8-13 **65** (v[1]) IanMongan 14 60
(Mrs L J Mongan) *led: rdn over 2f out: drvn and hung lft over 1f out: hdd 1f out: sn wknd* **9/1**

0130 **10** *nse* **Strabinios King**[161] 3757 4-9-0 **66** FrancisNorton 5 61+
(M Wigham) *t.k.h: hld up towards rr on inner: nt clr run fr wl over 1f out: no ch* **6/1**[2]

6060 **11** *¾* **Cativo Cavallino**[20] 7435 5-9-1 **67** RichardThomas 8 60
(J E Long) *chsd ldrs: drvn over 2f out: wknd qckly ent fnl f* **11/1**

364 **12** *hd* **C'Mon You Irons (IRE)**[11] 7540 3-9-1 **67** GeorgeBaker 13 59
(M R Hoad) *t.k.h: racd on outer in midfield: rdn and lost pl over 2f out: n.d after* **7/1**[3]

0400 **13** *36* **Flying Goose (IRE)**[18] 7457 4-8-13 **65** (p) ChrisCatlin 3 —
(R A Harris) *v.s.a and lost many l s: a t.o* **12/1**

1m 24.65s (-0.15) **Going Correction** 0.0s/f (Stan) **13** Ran SP% **126.7**
Speed ratings (Par 103): **100,99,98,98,96 96,95,95,93,93 92,92,51**
toteswinger: 1&2 £8.70, 1&3 £40.70, 2&3 £18.00. CSF £39.83 CT £466.30 TOTE £11.30: £3.80, £1.20, £5.90; EX 34.80 TRIFECTA Not won..
Owner R D Willis and M C Watts **Bred** Acrum Lodge Stud **Trained** Cropthorne, Worcs
■ Stewards' Enquiry : B A Curtis two-day ban: used whip with excessive force and frequency (Dec 28,29)

FOCUS
A fair handicap.
Strabinios King ◆ Official explanation: jockey said gelding was denied a clear run
Flying Goose(IRE) Official explanation: jockey said gelding missed the break

7678 COLEMANS HATCH CLASSIFIED STKS 1m (P)

3:10 (3:12) (Class 7) 3-Y-O+ **£2,183** (£644; £322) **Stalls** High

Form RPR

000 **1** **Tarkamara (IRE)**[16] 7469 4-9-0 45 LPKeniry 12 51
(P F I Cole) *in tch: hdwy to press ldr over 1f out: rdn to ld ins fnl f: r.o wl* **10/1**

0600 **2** *¾* **Poppy Dean (IRE)**[53] 6913 3-8-13 45 JamesDoyle 4 49
(J G Portman) *t.k.h: trckd ldng pair: drvn over 1f out: kpt on same pce u.p to go 2nd towards fin* **20/1**

6005 **3** *½* **Royal Choir**[9] 7553 4-9-5 50 ChrisCatlin 7 53
(H E Haynes) *t.k.h: hld up in midfield: hdwy over 2f out: chsd ldrs and rdn over 1f out: kpt on u.p: nvr quite gng pce to rch ldrs* **9/1**

4602 **4** *hd* **Rosie Cross (IRE)**[4] 7625 4-9-0 45 (p) StephenCarson 8 48
(Eve Johnson Houghton) *chsd ldr: upsides gng wl over 2f out: led 2f out: sn rdn: hdd jst ins fnl f: no ex: wknd and lost 2 pls towards fin* **3/1**[2]

0000 **5** *½* **Ma Ridge**[6] 7601 4-9-0 45 AdamKirby 11 46
(T D McCarthy) *stdd after s and dropped in bhd: rdn and hdwy over 2f out: chsd ldrs u.p 1f out: kpt on* **25/1**

0/00 **6** *shd* **Samson Quest**[16] 7469 6-9-0 45 TomEaves 9 46
(B Smart) *s.i.s: t.k.h: hld up in rr: gd hdwy towards inner over 1f out: no imp fnl 75yds* **11/4**[1]

6300 **7** *1 ½* **Beckenham's Secret**[7] 7596 4-8-9 45 MCGeran(5) 10 43
(A W Carroll) *t.k.h: hld up towards rr on outer rdn and effrt wl over 1f out: kpt on ins fnl f but nvr gng pce to rch ldrs* **6/1**[3]

0064 **8** *1 ½* **Lady Fas (IRE)**[4] 7625 5-9-0 45 CatherineGannon 5 39
(A W Carroll) *stdd s: t.k.h: hld up towards rr: effrt on outer 2f out: kpt on but nvr trbld ldrs* **9/1**

3030 **9** *2 ½* **Kinsman (IRE)**[256] 1142 11-8-11 45 (p) LukeMorris(3) 3 34
(T D McCarthy) *sn bustled up into midfield: drvn and unable qck 2f out: wknd over 1f out* **16/1**

600 **10** *hd* **Captain Sirus (FR)**[21] 7385 5-9-0 45 (p) RichardKingscote 6 33
(P Butler) *led: jnd and rdn over 2f out: hdd 2f out: wknd over 1f out: eased whn btn fnl f* **66/1**

5000 **11** *4 ½* **Jellytot (USA)**[30] 7316 5-8-9 45 JamesO'Reilly(5) 1 23
(J O'Reilly) *s.i.s: sn in tch in midfield: drvn and lost pl over 2f out: no ch fnl 2f* **12/1**

0000 **12** *13* **Little Firecracker**[26] 7373 3-8-10 45 DuranFentiman(3) 2 —
(Miss M E Rowland) *v.s.a and lost many l s: a wl bhd* **33/1**

1m 38.7s (0.50) **Going Correction** 0.0s/f (Stan)
WFA 3 from 4yo+ 1lb **12** Ran SP% **121.7**
Speed ratings (Par 97): **97,96,95,95,95 94,93,91,89,89 84,71**
toteswinger: 1&2 £31.70, 1&3 £22.50, 2&3 £37.60. CSF £200.08 TOTE £13.50: £3.80, £7.60, £3.20; EX 245.80 TRIFECTA Not won..
Owner A H Robinson **Bred** R N Auld **Trained** Whatcombe, Oxon

FOCUS
A modest event. It was run at a decent pace but they finished in a heap and the form looks dubious.
Beckenham's Secret Official explanation: jockey said gelding hung right
Lady Fas(IRE) Official explanation: jockey said mare ran too free

Little Firecracker Official explanation: jockey said filly missed the break

7679 RUBY HEN CELEBRATION H'CAP (DIV II) 5f (P)

3:40 (3:40) (Class 6) (0-60,60) 3-Y-O+ **£2,388** (£705; £352) **Stalls** High

Form RPR

0646 **1** **Azygous**[12] 7521 5-9-1 **57** AdamKirby 4 62
(J Akehurst) *racd in midfield: plld out and effrt over 1f out: rdn to ld fnl 100yds: edgd lft towards fin: jst hld on* **9/2**[2]

0060 **2** *nse* **Scarlet Oak**[45] 7090 4-9-2 **58** (p) ChrisCatlin 6 63
(A M Hales) *racd in midfield: c wd and lost pl bnd 2f out: str run fnl f: wnt 2nd and edgd lft towards fin: jst hld* **16/1**

0533 **3** *nk* **Monte Cassino (IRE)**[4] 7624 3-8-13 **60** JamesO'Reilly(5) 9 64
(J O'Reilly) *s.i.s: sn outpcd in last pl: rdn and hdwy on inner over 1f out: wnt 3rd wl ins fnl f: nt quite rch ldng pair* **11/2**[3]

5105 **4** *½* **Hurricane Coast**[20] 7437 9-9-1 **57** (b) TonyCulhane 1 59+
(D Flood) *dwlt: hld up in last trio: hdwy 2f out: chsd ldrs whn hit on nose by rivals whip ins fnl f: kpt on* **8/1**

0066 **5** *nk* **Spoof Master (IRE)**[16] 7471 4-9-4 **60** (p) LPKeniry 5 61
(C R Dore) *led narrowly tl rdn and hdd 2f out: led again jst ins fnl f: no ex towards fin* **13/2**

300 **6** *1 ¼* **Rightcar Dominic**[38] 7213 3-8-10 **52** PatrickMathers 8 49
(Peter Grayson) *s.i.s: sn rdn along: towards rr: hrd drvn wl over 1f out: plugged on fnl f: nvr trbld ldrs* **28/1**

0532 **7** *¾* **Joss Stick**[7] 7589 3-8-13 **58** (p) KevinGhunowa(3) 2 52
(R A Harris) *pressed ldr tl led on inner 2f out: sn hrd rdn: hdd jst ins fnl f: wknd fnl 100yds* **5/4**[1]

5442 **8** *¾* **Stoneacre Pat (IRE)**[92] 5911 3-8-11 **53** JamesDoyle 10 44
(Peter Grayson) *pressed ldrs on outer: ev ch and rdn 2f out: hrd drvn over 1f out: wknd ins fnl f* **16/1**

59.55 secs (0.75) **Going Correction** 0.0s/f (Stan) **8** Ran SP% **117.7**
Speed ratings (Par 101): **94,93,93,92,92 90,88,87**
toteswinger: 1&2 £9.70, 1&3 £8.00, 2&3 £14.90. CSF £72.97 CT £411.20 TOTE £5.20: £1.50, £4.00; EX 99.50 TRIFECTA Not won. Place 6 £9.34, Place 5 £6.11..
Owner The Grass Is Greener Partnership V **Bred** Mrs R D Peacock **Trained** Epsom, Surrey

FOCUS
A low-grade handicap that produced a very tight finish.
T/Jkpt: £987.40 to a £1 stake. Pool: £34,768.95. 25 winning tickets. T/Plt: £6.40 to a £1 stake. Pool: £58,572.20. 6,656.56 winning tickets. T/Qpdt: £4.00 to a £1 stake. Pool: £5,449.20. 999.10 winning tickets. SP

1666 SHA TIN (R-H)

Sunday, December 14

OFFICIAL GOING: Good
The jockeys reported that the ground was riding much faster than the official ground description indicates.

7682a CATHAY PACIFIC HONG KONG VASE (GROUP 1) 1m 4f

6:00 (6:01) 3-Y-O+
£514,175 (£198,454; £90,206; £51,546; £29,639; £18,041)

RPR

1 **Doctor Dino (FR)**[71] 6506 6-9-0 OPeslier 12 120
(R Gibson, France) *last to bef 1/2-way: 9th st: styd on strly towards outside to ld on line* **13/10**[1]

2 *shd* **Purple Moon (IRE)**[14] 7511 5-9-0 JamieSpencer 6 120
(L M Cumani) *cl up: wnt 2nd bef 1/2-way: 3rd 4f out: 2nd st: led narrowly over 1 1/2f out: hld on gamely u.str.p tl hdd on line* **73/10**[3]

3 *hd* **Jaguar Mail (JPN)**[35] 4-9-0 MJKinane 2 120
(N Hori, Japan) *towards rr: 10th on outside ent st: styd on fnl 2f: nrst fin* **29/10**[2]

4 *¾* **The Bogberry (USA)**[71] 6499 3-8-9 CSoumillon 5 118
(A De Royer-Dupre, France) *in tch: 4th st towards ins: kpt on steadily fnl 2f to take 4th on line* **16/1**

5 *shd* **Packing Winner (NZ)**[28] 6-9-0 DWhyte 7 118
(L Ho, Hong Kong) *set slow pce: narrowly hdd over 1 1/2f out: kpt on gamely u.p: lost 4th on line* **18/1**

6 *¾* **Buccellati**[50] 6980 4-9-0 (v) WilliamBuick 11 117
(A M Balding) *towards rr early: 6th and swtchd outside ent st: styd on at same pce* **22/1**

7 *1 ¼* **Muhannak (IRE)**[50] 6993 4-9-0 PJSmullen 4 115
(R M Beckett) *hld up: 7th st: sn rdn and one pce* **21/1**

8 *1* **Ambitious General (AUS)**[28] 5-9-0 (t) ESaint-Martin 8 113
(D Hall, Hong Kong) *in rr: 11th and carried wdst of all ent st: nvr a factor* **39/1**

9 *½* **Douro Valley (AUS)**[29] 7-9-0 (b) DBeadman 13 113
(Danny O'Brien, Australia) *in tch: 5th st: sn rdn and one pce* **14/1**

10 *2* **Poseidon Adventure (IRE)**[56] 6854 5-9-0 (b) ASuborics 3 109
(W Figge, Germany) *cl up early: dropped bk to last 3f out: n.d after* **39/1**

11 *2 ¾* **Mourilyan (IRE)**[71] 6506 4-9-0 (v) RyanMoore 1 105
(H J Brown, South Africa) *plld hrd in 3rd: 8th st: sn rdn and nt qckn* **38/1**

12 *1 ½* **Mores Wells**[48] 7034 4-9-0 (t) DPMcDonogh 10 103
(Kevin Prendergast, Ire) *in tch tl dropped to rr 3f out: 12th and btn ent st* **37/1**

13 *3 ¼* **Jackpot Delight (NZ)**[28] 5-9-0 (b) GMosse 9 97
(C Fownes, Hong Kong) *racd keenly on outside: towards rr early: hdwy to go 2nd 4f out: 3rd st: sn wknd* **22/1**

2m 29.14s (0.94)
WFA 3 from 4yo+ 5lb **13** Ran SP% **122.4**
(including HK$10 stake): WIN 23.00, PL 12.00, 23.00, 15.50; DF 126.50.
Owner J Martinez Salmean **Bred** Ecurie Pelder **Trained** Lamorlaye, France
■ Stewards' Enquiry : C Soumillon three-day ban: careless riding

FOCUS
This had a truly international flavour to it, as England, Ireland, America, Japan, France, Germany and Hong Kong all had representatives. The early pace did not seem particularly strong, which in turn appeared to produce a sprint to the line. However, that should not detract from what was a tremendous spectacle and a tremendous finish.

NOTEBOOK
Doctor Dino(FR), despite running moderately last time in Canada, when his trainer thought the horse had an off day, repeated his win of 12 months ago, but only just. He appeared to have quite a bit of ground to make up with a furlong to go, but slowly and surely he made inroads on the leader and got there just in time. Plenty of credit must go to his trainer, who has handled this globetrotter superbly.

The Form Book, Raceform Ltd, Compton, RG20 6NL

Purple Moon(IRE) is just about one of the unluckiest big-race performers about. He was mugged in last year's Melbourne Cup, did not get the gallop he needed in the Japan Cup last time and had victory snatched away from him almost in the last stride of this. Fitted with earplugs, he made a decisive move early in the straight and failed by the narrowest of margins to hang on. Connections are considering their next move, but a trip to Dubai for their Festival period must be high on the agenda.

Jaguar Mail(JPN), who attracted plenty of market support, had some good recent form lines with Screen Hero, the winner of the Japan Cup. Successful in more than half his previous races in Japan, he came down the home stretch alongside Doctor Dino but could not quite match the winner's pace.

The Bogberry(USA), having his second start since leaving Aidan O'Brien for Alain De Royer-Dupre, was close up turning in and kept battling away under seriously strong pressure. The quick ground would have been something new to him, so this can be rated a decent effort. The jockey is confident his horse will do well in France next season.

Buccellati was improving when last seen in England and confirmed that he is a horse going in the right direction. He was far from disgraced on his first try at the highest level but looked a shade one-paced inside the final two furlongs. He should give his trainer plenty of options next season.

Muhannak(IRE) had something to prove back on turf, after a wonderful run of form on an All-Weather surface, and did himself proud. His jockey was inclined to believe that the horse was not up to this standard but, in fairness to his mount, he was on the heels of those who fought out the finish and was a bit tight for room late on.

Poseidon Adventure(IRE) Official explanation: vet said horse lost its right hind plate

Mourilyan(IRE), wearing a visor for the first time, was outpaced on the home bend and never featured. He would have wanted a stronger pace to follow.

Mores Wells had been disappointing when last seen in Ireland and rarely looked like doing any better in this contest. He lost his place rounding the home bend and was allowed to come home in his own time. The rider thought the ground was the main problem.

7683a CATHAY PACIFIC HONG KONG SPRINT (GROUP 1) — 6f

6:40 (6:41) 3-Y-0+

£440,722 (£170,103; £77,320; £43,814; £25,773; £15,464)

RPR

1 **Inspiration (AUS)**[21] 5-9-0 ....(t) DBeadman 9 119
(J Moore, Hong Kong) *racd in 7th: hdwy towards outside to ld 120yds out: drvn out* **67/1**

2 *nk* **Green Birdie (NZ)**[21] 5-9-0 .... ODoleuze 5 118
(C Fownes, Hong Kong) *towards rr: 8th st: styd on strly down outside fr over 1f out: nrst fin* **71/10**

3 *nk* **Apache Cat (AUS)**[15] 6-9-0 ....(b) CBrown 2 117
(Greg Eurell, Australia) *in tch: 5th st: rdn and looked btn over 1f out: styd on again fnl 200yds* **9/10[1]**

4 *3/4* **Enthused (NZ)**[21] 5-9-0 .... DWhyte 13 115
(J Size, Hong Kong) *racd in 2nd: led 1f out to 120yds out: one pce* **11/2[3]**

5 *nk* **Sunny Power (AUS)**[21] 6-9-0 .... BPrebble 12 114
(K W Lui, Hong Kong) *in rr tl hdwy against ins rail over 1f out: kpt on* **49/10[2]**

6 *shd* **Marchand D'Or (FR)**[70] 6518 5-9-0 .... DBonilla 4 114
(F Head, France) *trckd ldrs: 5th st: tried to switch outside but forced bk in 2f out: sn rdn: edgd rt over 1f out: kpt on at same pce* **9/1**

7 *1/2* **Mythical Flight (SAF)**[225] 5-9-0 .... KShea 8 112
(S Tarry, South Africa) *led to 1f out: one pce* **31/1**

8 *1 1/4* **Laurel Guerreiro (JPN)**[21] 4-9-0 ....(t) HShii 3 108
(Mitsugi Kon, Japan) *cl up: 3rd st: one pce fnl 1 1/2f* **28/1**

9 *shd* **Tosho Courage (JPN)**[28] 6-9-0 .... KIkezoe 10 108
(Kaneo Ikezoe, Japan) *racd in 12th: nvr a factor* **100/1**

10 *1/2* **Abbadjinn (GER)**[14] 4-9-0 .... THellier 7 107
(P Rau, Germany) *racd in 9th: nvr a factor* **64/1**

11 *3 1/4* **Nightlign (NZ)**[49] 4-9-0 .... GMosse 11 97
(A Lee, Hong Kong) *a in rr* **44/1**

12 *3/4* **Moorhouse Lad**[70] 6518 5-9-0 .... JimCrowley 1 95
(B Smart) *prom on ins: 4th st: wknd under 2f out* **100/1**

13 *3 1/2* **Waikato (NZ)**[30] 5-9-0 ....(b) JSaimee 6 84
(L Laxon, Singapore) *wd thrght: in midfield tl lost pl 2 1/2f out* **65/1**

68.68 secs (68.68) **13 Ran SP% 122.6**

WIN 679.00; PL 136.00, 18.50, 11.50; DF 2449.50.

Owner Mr & Mrs Hui Sai Fun **Bred** Arrowfield Pastoral Pty Ltd & D K L & J M Raphael **Trained** Hong Kong

FOCUS

The best two horses in the race, Apache Cat and Marchand D'Or, were not quite at their best, and the form is not as good as one might expect for a race like this. The early pace was not frantic by any means.

NOTEBOOK

Inspiration(AUS) had finished only seventh when behind three of today's rivals in a course-and-distance trial on his latest start, and he had yet to prove he was up to this level, but he produced a much-improved performance to run out a surprise winner. He was almost impossible to fancy beforehand, and his trainer even admitted afterwards he felt he was just making up the numbers, but he maintained the unblemished record in this contest of Australian-breds, who have now won all ten runnings. The winner has clearly improved into a high-class sprinter but it would probably be unwise to rate this performance too highly, with the 'big two' below form, and everything went his way under a good ride.

Green Birdie(NZ) had finished in front of Inspiration over course and distance last time, but he was unable to confirm the form after that one got first run. He had to switch into the clear in the straight and probably would have preferred a stronger pace. The plan is to step him up to a mile for his next start.

Apache Cat(AUS), the Australian champion sprinter, earned a shot at this when returning to form with a close second to Takeover Target two weeks earlier. He was backed off the boards on the on-course pool but did not get the run of things. He tends to hit a flat spot in his races, and that proved his undoing on this occasion as he lost a good position just off the lead towards the inside when coming under pressure turning in. He was forced to switch wide, but still found himself hemmed in as the winner produced a better kick over a furlong out, and he finally got going all too late. He is another who would have preferred a stronger pace from the start. Official explanation: vet said gelding lost its left hind plate

Enthused(NZ) had beaten the winner and runner-up in a trial for this over course and distance on his previous start, but he enjoyed a better trip on that occasion than he did today. He raced wider than ideal, with stall 13 no help, and was also a little keen.

Sunny Power(AUS) had also beaten both Inspiration and Green Birdie last time, but he was slowly away (not for the first time) from a poor draw and would have preferred a more searching pace. He kept on towards the inside rail but was never getting there.

Marchand D'Or(FR) is the best Europe has to offer over this trip, and he is a better horse now than when sixth in this race last year, but the result was the same. Although he did not enjoy the best of runs in the straight, the quick ground was more of a problem and his jockey felt this was one race too many in a long season.

Mythical Flight(SAF), a leading South African sprinter, took them along early and ran well considering he had been off since May and seems best suited by the minimum trip.

Moorhouse Lad looks best suited by the minimum trip.

7684a CATHAY PACIFIC HONG KONG MILE (GROUP 1) — 1m

7:50 (7:51) 3-Y-0+

£587,629 (£226,804; £103,093; £58,634; £34,149; £20,619)

RPR

1 **Good Ba Ba (USA)**[21] 6-9-0 ....(t) CSoumillon 7 125+
(A Schutz, Hong Kong) *racd in 9th: swtchd outside 1 1/2f out: sn rdn: str run to ld 130yds out: edgd rt: r.o wl* **34/10[2]**

2 *2 1/2* **Able One (NZ)**[21] 6-9-0 .... DBeadman 5 118
(J Moore, Hong Kong) *racd in 5th or 6th: 5th st: rdn to go 2nd over 1f out: nt pce of wnr but styd on to regain 2nd fnl 100yds* **17/1**

3 *3/4* **Egyptian Ra (NZ)**[21] 7-9-0 ....(t) FCoetzee 13 116
(A S Cruz, Hong Kong) *set str pce: hdd 130yds out: one pce* **83/10[3]**

4 *nk* **Spirito Del Vento (FR)**[71] 6498 5-9-0 .... OPeslier 9 116
(J-M Beguigne, France) *in rr: 12th st: str run down outside fr over 1f out to take 4th on line* **65/1**

5 *nk* **Super Hornet (JPN)**[21] 5-9-0 .... YFujioka 2 115
(Y Yahagi, Japan) *racd in 10th: 11th st: kpt on clsng stages but nvr a factor* **9/1**

6 *shd* **Armada (NZ)**[21] 7-9-0 .... DWhyte 4 115
(J Size, Hong Kong) *racd in 7th: rdn and hdwy towards outside over 1 1/2f out: one pce fnl f* **11/10[1]**

7 *2* **Joy And Fun (NZ)**[21] 5-9-0 .... WCMarwing 14 110
(D Cruz, Hong Kong) *racd in 3rd: rdn and one pce fr under 2f out* **88/1**

8 *3/4* **Major Cadeaux**[57] 6814 4-9-0 .... RichardHughes 1 108
(R Hannon) *racd in 4th or 5th: 6th st: sn rdn and one pce* **100/1**

9 *shd* **Kip Deville (USA)**[50] 6996 5-9-0 ....(t) CVelasquez 12 108
(Richard Dutrow Jr, U.S.A) *cl up on outside: rn wd on fnl turn and 8th st: n.d after* **10/1**

10 *1* **Pressing (IRE)**[35] 7262 5-9-0 .... NCallan 11 106
(M A Jarvis) *racd in 5th or 6th: 4th st: sn rdn and nt qckn* **27/1**

11 *1* **Natagora (FR)**[71] 6496 3-8-9 .... C-PLemaire 10 100
(P Bary, France) *racd in 2nd: rdn over 2f out: sn btn* **14/1**

12 *1/2* **Awesome Gem (USA)**[50] 6996 5-9-0 ....(vt) GKGomez 3 102
(Craig Dollase, U.S.A) *a in rr* **100/1**

13 *1* **Laa Rayb (USA)**[57] 6814 4-9-0 .... RoystonFfrench 8 100
(M Johnston) *sn pushed along towards rr: 10th st: nvr a factor* **100/1**

14 *1 1/4* **Bullish Cash (NZ)**[63] 6-9-0 ....(t) MJKinane 6 97
(A S Cruz, Hong Kong) *last virtually thrght* **31/1**

1m 32.71s (-1.99)

WFA 3 from 4yo+ 1lb **14 Ran SP% 124.7**

WIN 44.50; PL 15.50, 49.00, 25.00; DF 370.00 (Course record).

Owner John Yuen Se Kit **Bred** Haras Santa Maria De Araras **Trained** Hong Kong

FOCUS

This looked very competitive beforehand, and the overall standard seemed well up to Group 1 level.

NOTEBOOK

Good Ba Ba(USA) was in a league of his own, producing a stunning performance to lower the course record. Settled in around mid-division by Christophe Soumillon, who replaced regular rider Olivier Doleuze, he travelled kindly throughout and produced an exceptional turn of foot when eased into the clear around a furlong and a half out. He had not been at his best in two runs since returning from a break, including when behind Egyptian Ra in a course-and-distance trial, but his connections were confident he was as good as ever, particularly after an impressive workout under his big-race jockey during the week, and they were proved right in no uncertain terms. He is clearly one of the best milers in the world, and we are likely to see plenty more of him as he is a gelding and no stud duties await. He could stay in Hong Kong to target the same sort of races he won following his success in this last season, but the Dubai Duty Free at Nad Al Sheba was mentioned as a possible target and it would be great if he turned up.

Able One(NZ) had run well to be fourth on his return from a break in the trial for the Hong Kong Sprint and that form worked out very well on the day. He travelled nicely for a long way and had his chance but the winner was too good.

Egyptian Ra(NZ) had beaten today's winner more than four lengths (getting 5lb) when producing a terrific front-running display in a trial for this, although Good Ba Ba was obviously not at his best that day. Here, he overcame stall 13 to lead and got his own way, but he could not sustain his effort late on, having helped set a track-record pace.

Spirito Del Vento(FR) improved on his sixth in this last year. He was well behind at the top of the straight, having not really travelled, but he finished strongly to take fourth.

Super Hornet(JPN) was another who was further back than ideal, having not travelled all that strongly. He got going late but, according to his rider, felt a bit lethargic.

Armada(NZ), the 2006 runner-up, was all the rage with the locals but he found little for pressure and was not at his best.

Major Cadeaux was well enough positioned but did not pick up. He looks just shy of top-notch Group 1 level and probably wants easier ground as well.

Kip Deville(USA), winner of the 2007 Breeders' Cup Mile and runner-up in the same race this year, was unproven going right-handed and he went all the way round the turn into the straight on the wrong lead. He eventually ended up extremely wide and that obviously cost him his chance.

Pressing(IRE) had won a couple of Group 2 races over this trip in recent months, but he is not top class.

Natagora(FR), this year's 1,000 Guineas winner, broke alertly and showed up to a point, but her stride quickly shortened under pressure in the straight and this was disappointing.

Laa Rayb(USA) could not muster the required pace on this first start at the top level.

7685a CATHAY PACIFIC HONG KONG CUP (GROUP 1) — 1m 2f

8:30 (8:33) 3-Y-0+

£734,536 (£283,505; £128,866; £73,454; £42,526; £25,773)

RPR

1 **Eagle Mountain**[50] 7000 4-9-0 .... KShea 5 124
(M F De Kock, South Africa) *in midfield: 7th st on outside: led 1 1/2f out: 3 l clr ins fnl f: r.o strly* **49/10[2]**

2 *1 1/4* **Balius (IRE)**[61] 5-9-0 ....(b) GMosse 13 120
(C Laffon-Parias, France) *s.s and sn pushed along: last to under 2f out: styd on strly on outside to take 2nd jst ins fnl f: no ch w wnr* **18/1**

3 *2* **Linngari (IRE)**[57] 6816 6-9-0 .... RyanMoore 12 116
(Sir Michael Stoute) *hld up in 13th: rdn towards outside 2f out: kpt on: carried rt and tk 3rd 100yds out* **51/1**

4 *3/4* **Viva Pataca**[28] 6-9-0 .... DBeadman 6 118
(J Moore, Hong Kong) *towards rr: 10th st: no room towards ins over 2f out to 1f out: styd on: carried rt clsng stages: unlucky* **30/100[1]**

5 *nk* **Bullish Luck (USA)**[28] 9-9-0 ....(b) CSoumillon 4 114
(A S Cruz, Hong Kong) *cl up early: restrained in 9th: 11th st: hdwy to dispute 2nd 1f out: lost 3rd 100yds out and edgd rt* **39/1**

6 *1 1/4* **Loup Breton (IRE)**[71] 6499 4-9-0 .... ACrastus 7 111
(E Lellouche, France) *racd in 12th: hdwy tdown outside to dispute 4th 1f out: one pce* **85/1**

7 ½ **Out Of Control (BRZ)**[50] 7000 5-9-0 ....(t) GKGomez 14 110
(Robert Frankel, U.S.A) *cl up on outside: pressed ldr over 3f out tl led jst under 2f out: hdd 1 1/2f out: btn whn hmpd 100yds out* **57/1**

8 2 **Sight Winner (NZ)**[21] 5-9-0 .... DWhyte 3 106
(J Size, Hong Kong) *cl up: 8th st: one pce fnl 2f* **21/1**

9 nk **Hawkes Bay**[28] 6-9-0 .... BPrebble 1 106
(D Hall, Hong Kong) *cl up: 6th st: rdn and unable qck 2f out* **51/1**

10 ¾ **Trincot (FR)**[71] 6499 3-8-11 .... IMendizabal 8 104
(P Demercastel, France) *prom: 3rd st: wknd over 1f out* **61/1**

11 1 ¼ **Artiste Royal (IRE)**[23] 7-9-0 ....(vt) OPeslier 2 102
(Neil Drysdale, U.S.A) *hld up: 9th st: no room on ins over 2f out to over 1f out: kpt on fnl f* **43/1**

12 1 ¾ **Viva Macau (FR)**[28] 5-9-0 ....(t) ZPurton 11 98
(J Moore, Hong Kong) *trckd ldrs: 3rd st: ev ch on ins 2f out: sn btn* **68/1**

13 17 ¾ **Estejo (GER)**[35] 7263 4-9-0 .... DPorcu 9 63
(R Rohne, Germany) *led after 2f to jst over 2f out: wknd* **100/1**

14 6 **Lush Lashes**[70] 6521 3-8-9 .... KJManning 10 49
(J S Bolger, Ire) *midfield towards outside whn hmpd after 2f: rdn on outside 2 1/2f out: 5th st: sn btn and eased* **13/1**[3]

2m 0.92s (-0.48)
WFA 3 from 4yo+ 3lb **14** Ran SP% **126.4**
WIN 59.50; PL 16.00, 27.50, 77.00; DF 308.00.
Owner Sheikh Mohammed Bin Khalifa Al Maktoum **Bred** London Thoroughbred Services Ltd **Trained** South Africa
■ Stewards' Enquiry : C Soumillon three-day ban: careless riding
G K Gomez two-day ban: careless riding
I Mendizabal four-day ban: careless riding

FOCUS
Plenty of trouble in running meant that there was an unsatisfactory finish to this top-class event, but Eagle Mountain was still a worthy winner.

NOTEBOOK
Eagle Mountain won in imperious style. Once he quickened to lead early in the home straight, the race was effectively over and Mike De Kock had claimed yet another valuable contest on the international stage. De Kock had stated prior to the off that he believed Eagle Mountain was a better horse than Archipenko, who beat Viva Pataca earlier in the year, and the trainer was proved right. A mile and a quarter looks the right trip for the horse and he should be a major player across the world next year at that sort of distance.
Balius(IRE), who was slowly away, gave vain chase to the winner inside the final furlong. Ridden by Gerald Mosse for the first time, he was getting closer as the line approached but was not in the same league as the winner on the day, especially after giving him at least a five-length start. Connections should have plenty of fun with him, and a return to Kranji for the International Cup, in which he finished a fast-finishing third this year, looks his logical spring target.
Linngari(IRE), having the final start of his career, gave his all inside the final furlong after meeting a wall of horses in front of him wherever he tried to make a challenge. It was not until far too late that the gaps opened kindly for him, but the winner had already flown.
Viva Pataca is a superstar in Hong Kong and he was forced into a very short price on course by his faithful supporters. However hugely talented the horse is, though, his racing style is completely one dimensional and his chance often depends on the breaks appearing for him. Darren Beadman will probably be having nightmares for a long time about the highly optimistic route he chose to take with his mount and, not surprisingly, he met a wall of horses in front of him when trying to get on terms. The horse passed the winning post moving easily but had no chance of getting involved at the business end of the race. It is a real shame that Viva Pataca could not get involved for the purposes of rating this race, and Beadman will no doubt come in for a lot of flack for his ride.
Bullish Luck(USA) ran above his recent efforts, on what may have been his last start. He will reach the grand age of ten in a couple of weeks and has been a class act in Hong Kong in his time.
Loup Breton(IRE) had finished behind Trincot when they met in the Prix Dollar on their last run, albeit giving away plenty of weight, but the places were reversed in clear-cut fashion here. Loup Breton stayed on quite well from off the gallop, while the three-year-old had every chance after sitting prominently throughout.
Out Of Control(BRZ) sat handy throughout and had his chance. He was already held when carved up late on by Linngari and Viva Pataca as they struggled to find a path through.
Sight Winner(NZ) endured a truly horrible passage and can be rated a lot better than his final position suggests. Every time he tried to move into a better position, the door was slammed shut in his face.
Artiste Royal(IRE) lost any chance he may have had as a result of the chaos up the home straight. His rider sat almost motionless in the last furlong and later compared the event to an apprentice race, as there was interference all over the place.
Lush Lashes appeared to get stirred up by the crowd in the stalls. She was not quickly away, lost her footing rounding the first bend, never looked to be travelling that kindly and then suffered scrimmaging in the home straight. It was a bold and admirable move by her trainer, who landed this race with Alexander Goldrun in 2004, to run her again after a tough season against just fillies and mares, but this first effort against the boys should be completely ignored on her high-class CV as she is miles better than this effort suggests. Kevin Manning eased her considerably with about a furlong to go.

7666 WOLVERHAMPTON (A.W) (L-H)
Monday, December 15

OFFICIAL GOING: Standard
Wind: Nil Weather: Cold and fine becoming misty

7686 WEATHERBYS ALL WEATHER "HANDS & HEELS" APPRENTICE SERIES H'CAP 1m 1f 103y(P)
2:15 (2:15) (Class 5) (0-75,73) 3-Y-O+ **£3,238** (£963; £481; £240) **Stalls** Low

Form RPR

6042 **1** **Prince Golan (IRE)**[10] 7559 4-8-13 **63**......................(p) AlexEdwards(3) 2 70
(J W Unett) *a.p: led wl over 1f out: pushed out* **4/1**[2]

1101 **2** hd **Hucking Heat (IRE)**[7] 7606 4-9-9 **73** 6ex..................(p) DavidKenny(3) 7 80
(R Hollinshead) *hld up in rr: stdy hdwy over 3f out: pushed along over 1f out: edgd lft and ev ch ins fnl f: kpt on* **4/5**[1]

1305 **3** 1 ½ **Summer Lodge**[19] 7455 5-8-12 **62**........................(p) KarenKenny(3) 3 65
(A J McCabe) *a.p: led over 2f out tl wl over 1f out: nt qckn ins fnl f* **7/1**

4 shd **Topenhall (IRE)**[10] 7572 7-9-2 **66**.................................. SHJames(3) 6 69
(Daniel O'Connell, Ire) *sn chsng ldr: led 5f out tl over 2f out: sn pushed along: nt qckn ins fnl f* **5/1**[3]

1100 **5** 5 **Kings Topic (USA)**[4] 7642 8-9-7 **68**.............................(p) PNolan 5 61
(A B Haynes) *nvr gng wl: a in rr: struggling over 4f out: hung rt over 1f out* **12/1**

-000 **6** 22 **Briery Blaze**[278] 858 5-8-4 **54** oh7..........................(p) AdamCarter(3) 1 1
(T Wall) *led: hdd 5f out: wknd over 3f out: t.o* **50/1**

2m 3.25s (1.55) **Going Correction** +0.10s/f (Slow) **6** Ran SP% **114.4**
Speed ratings (Par 103): **97,96,95,95,90 71**
toteswinger: 1&2 £1.70, 1&3 £2.00, 2&3 £2.00. CSF £7.86 TOTE £5.30: £2.30, £1.20; EX 8.50.
Owner M E Hughes **Bred** K Molloy **Trained** Preston, Shropshire

FOCUS
A modest 'hands and heels' apprentice handicap. The leaders seemed to go off too hard. The winner ran to his previous best with the second unable to match his recent win here.
Kings Topic(USA) Official explanation: jockey said gelding hung right throughout

7687 WOLVERHAMPTON-RACECOURSE.CO.UK (S) STKS 5f 216y(P)
2:50 (2:51) (Class 6) 2-Y-O **£2,388** (£705; £352) **Stalls** Low

Form RPR

6410 **1** **Tillers Satisfied (IRE)**[39] 7205 2-8-12 56.................... GrahamGibbons 1 58
(R Hollinshead) *hld up and bhd: hdwy on ins over 2f out: rdn to ld and edgd rt jst ins fnl f: drvn out* **13/2**

0320 **2** ½ **Forever's Girl**[19] 7454 2-8-4 57.......................... DuranFentiman(3) 2 52
(G R Oldroyd) *led 1f: a.p: rdn and ev ch ins fnl f: kpt on* **4/1**[2]

3353 **3** ½ **Kheley (IRE)**[140] 4487 2-8-7 50.. LiamJones 7 50+
(W M Brisbourne) *stdd sn after s: hld up and bhd: n.m.r over 3f out: rdn and hdwy on ins wl over 1f out: kpt on ins fnl f* **33/1**

4060 **4** 3 ¾ **Iliketoboogie**[27] 7372 2-8-7 58..................................(p) ChrisCatlin 11 39
(A J McCabe) *led after 1f: rdn and hdd jst ins fnl f: wknd towards fin* **3/1**[1]

0062 **5** 1 ¾ **That Boy Ronaldo**[13] 7530 2-8-7 50................................ FrancisNorton 12 34
(A Berry) *hld up in mid-div: lost pl over 2f out: c wd st: kpt on fnl f: nvr trbld ldrs* **25/1**

5030 **6** nk **Abhainn (IRE)**[19] 7454 2-8-12 56...........................(p) CatherineGannon 6 38
(B Palling) *prom: n.m.r over 2f out: sn wknd* **7/1**

0050 **7** nk **Cafe Fiore (IRE)**[19] 7451 2-8-11 54 ow4..................(v[1]) PaulMulrennan 3 36
(T J Pitt) *w ldrs: ev ch over 2f out: sn rdn: wknd over 1f out* **10/1**

0000 **8** nk **Harry Raffle**[17] 7467 2-8-12 56.. JamesDoyle 4 36
(S Kirk) *in rr: rdn wl over 1f out: n.d* **20/1**

0300 **9** 3 ¼ **Buddy Marvellous (IRE)**[17] 7464 2-8-9 53............. KevinGhunowa(3) 9 26+
(R A Harris) *broke wl: sn stdd and bhd: n.m.r over 3f out: n.d after* **33/1**

0506 **10** ½ **Royal Raider**[7] 7600 2-8-12 65................................(v[1]) StephenDonohoe 5 25
(P D Evans) *chsd ldrs: rdn over 2f out: wknd over 1f out* **11/2**[3]

0651 **11** 5 **Bold Ring**[68] 6572 2-8-12 59.. EdwardCreighton 8 10
(E J Creighton) *sn chsng ldrs: rdn and wknd wl over 1f out* **11/2**[3]

1m 15.76s (0.76) **Going Correction** +0.10s/f (Slow) **11** Ran SP% **125.2**
Speed ratings (Par 94): **98,97,96,91,89 88,88,88,83,83 76**
toteswinger: 1&2 £7.90, 1&3 £21.50, 2&3 £13.90. CSF £33.57 TOTE £9.40: £3.00, £2.20, £5.10; EX 44.90 TRIFECTA Not won..There was no bid for the winner.
Owner Dean Wootton **Bred** R Honniball **Trained** Upper Longdon, Staffs

FOCUS
An ordinary seller in which the leaders went too fast early and set it up for the closers.

NOTEBOOK
Tillers Satisfied(IRE), drawn in stall one, enjoyed a nice tow through the race, took the shortest route home, and stayed on well to see off Forever's Girl. The race was very much run to suit her as she is at her best challenging from off a strong pace. (op 7-1 tchd 6-1)
Forever's Girl was forced to race wide in a nursery here on her last start, but she was better drawn this time and enjoyed a better trip, following the leader through on the inside and coming to have every chance in the straight. (op 7-2 tchd 9-2)
Kheley(IRE), who had been off the track since July and was running on the all-weather for the first time, did not enjoy the clearest of runs, but she benefited from the leaders falling in a hole and ran on late for third. (op 28-1)
Iliketoboogie, dropping in grade from handicap company, had to have plenty of use made of her early to gain her favoured lead from a wide draw, and she paid for her efforts in the closing stages. (op 5-1 tchd 11-2)
That Boy Ronaldo, running on Polytrack for the first time, was stuck out wide throughout from the worst draw and ran a bit better than the bare form suggests. (op 28-1)

7688 KDS SOLUTIONS LOW VOLTAGE SWITCHGEAR MANUFACTURERS H'CAP 1m 5f 194y(P)
3:20 (3:21) (Class 6) (0-55,55) 3-Y-O+ **£2,388** (£705; £352) **Stalls** Low

Form RPR

00 **1** **Prairie Hawk (USA)**[79] 6280 3-8-2 **46** oh1...........(t) FrankieMcDonald 11 59+
(Tim Vaughan) *hld up in mid-div: hdwy 6f out: led over 2f out: styd on wl* **7/4**[1]

0050 **2** 2 ½ **Taxman (IRE)**[42] 7169 6-8-10 **47**.. LPKeniry 5 57
(A G Newcombe) *hld up in rr: hdwy 3f out: hung lft fr jst over 1f out: tk 2nd wl ins fnl f: nt trble wnr* **17/2**

0064 **3** nk **Rare Coincidence**[9] 7587 7-9-3 **54**..................................(p) ChrisCatlin 3 63
(R F Fisher) *led: hdd over 2f out: rdn jst over 1f out: lost 2nd wl ins fnl f: one pce* **4/1**[2]

0013 **4** 4 ½ **Sparkling Montjeu (IRE)**[31] 7322 3-8-10 **54**.................. DaneO'Neill 10 57
(George Baker) *a.p: wnt 2nd over 4f out: ev ch over 2f out: sn rdn: wknd fnl f* **9/1**

0432 **5** hd **Piverina (IRE)**[31] 7322 3-8-8 **52**.. TomEaves 9 55
(Miss J A Camacho) *chsd ldr tl over 4f out: rdn and wknd wl over 1f out* **8/1**

6000 **6** shd **Niqaab**[216] 2078 4-8-9 **46**.. StephenDonohoe 7 48
(W J Musson) *prom: rdn over 2f out: wknd wl over 1f out* **40/1**

7 ¾ **Hurforharmony (IRE)**[163] 3747 5-8-9 **46**............................ JamesDoyle 12 47
(Adrian McGuinness, Ire) *hld up towards rr: hdwy over 3f out: rdn 2f out: wknd fnl f* **50/1**

56-0 **8** nk **Birthday Star (IRE)**[14] 7512 6-8-10 **47**............................ VinceSlattery 8 48
(A G Juckes) *hld up in mid-div: pushed along 3f out: sn lost pl: n.d after* **33/1**

5654 **9** ¾ **Summer Bounty**[7] 7608 12-8-9 **46**.................................. PaulFitzsimons 1 46
(F Jordan) *s.i.s: hld up towards rr: swtchd lft and short-lived effrt on ins wl over 1f out* **33/1**

1355 **10** 2 ¼ **Stravita**[14] 7512 4-9-4 **55**...(p) GrahamGibbons 13 52
(R Hollinshead) *s.s: c wd st: a in rr* **5/1**[3]

3340 **11** 2 ¾ **Corrib (IRE)**[23] 7427 5-9-3 **54**.. CatherineGannon 4 47
(B Palling) *s.i.s: t.k.h in rr: rdn wl over 1f out: eased whn no ch ins fnl f* **16/1**

0600 **12** 4 ½ **Space Pirate**[8] 7590 3-8-9 **53**..................................(p) JerryO'Dwyer 2 40
(J Pearce) *hld up in mid-div: rdn over 3f out: sn bhd* **18/1**

3m 6.35s (0.35) **Going Correction** +0.10s/f (Slow)
WFA 3 from 4yo+ 7lb **12** Ran SP% **126.1**
Speed ratings (Par 101): **103,101,101,98,98 98,98,98,97,96 94,92**
toteswinger: 1&2 £9.80, 1&3 £6.30, 2&3 £6.30. CSF £18.89 CT £58.38 TOTE £3.00: £1.20, £3.70, £1.90; EX 27.00 Trifecta £387.40 Pool: £701.53 - 1.34 winning units..
Owner J Murphy **Bred** Southern Bloodstock **Trained** Aberthin, Vale of Glamorgan

FOCUS
A very moderate staying contest, but an above-average winner for the grade who has more to offer. The form looks solid.
Prairie Hawk(USA) ◆ Official explanation: trainer's rep said, regarding running, that the gelding benefited from the application of a first time tongue strap on its handicap debut.

Piverina(IRE) Official explanation: jockey said filly hung right-handed throughout

7689 KDS SOLUTIONS CHRISTMAS PARTY MAIDEN AUCTION STKS 5f 20y(P)
3:50 (3:52) (Class 6) 2-Y-O £3,070 (£906; £453) Stalls Low

Form RPR

4524 **1** **Saif Al Fahad (IRE)**[18] 7460 2-8-13 70 ChrisCatlin 11 74+
(E J O'Neill) *chsd ldrs: rdn to ld ins fnl f: r.o wl* **11/10**[1]

4 **2** 2 1/2 **Desert Bump**[9] 7574 2-8-11 0 LPKeniry 8 63+
(E F Vaughan) *mid-div: swtchd lft and hdwy whn squeezed through over 1f out: kpt on to take 2nd wl ins fnl f* **85/40**[2]

6 **3** 2 1/2 **Jolly Ranch**[35] 7273 2-8-8 0 SimonWhitworth 10 50
(A G Newcombe) *a.p: rdn wl over 1f out: one pce ins fnl f* **22/1**

066 **4** 1/2 **Wee Bizzom**[33] 7279 2-8-4 42 FrancisNorton 5 44
(A Berry) *chsd ldrs: bmpd and pushed lft over 1f out: one pce* **40/1**

00 **5** 3 **Trick Or Two**[24] 7402 2-8-13 0 JamesDoyle 2 42
(S Kirk) *w ldr: bit slipped and hung rt over 2f out: rdn to ld over 1f out: hdd ins fnl f: wknd* **25/1**

2003 **6** 3/4 **Amosite**[1] 7674 2-8-1 75 DuranFentiman(3) 6 31
(J R Jenkins) *mid-div: edgd lft over 1f out: no hdwy* **4/1**[3]

00 **7** 3 1/4 **You'relikemefrank**[33] 7279 2-8-11 0 ow2 PaulMulrennan 1 26
(J Balding) *led: hdd over 1f out: wknd ins fnl f* **33/1**

0000 **8** shd **Lonsdale Lad**[11] 7543 2-8-9 31 (b) TomEaves 9 24
(R C Guest) *a bhd* **66/1**

00 **9** nse **Yes She Can Can**[16] 7501 2-7-11 0 AndrewHeffernan(7) 4 18
(Peter Grayson) *chsd ldrs: rdn over 2f out: sn wknd* **40/1**

0 **10** 1 1/4 **Catman (IRE)**[42] 7168 2-8-6 0 PatrickMathers 7 16
(Peter Grayson) *a bhd* **66/1**

0 **11** 1 1/4 **Minibuzz**[24] 7402 2-8-11 0 DaleGibson 3 16
(Mrs G S Rees) *s.i.s: outpcd* **50/1**

62.90 secs (0.60) **Going Correction** +0.10s/f (Slow) 11 Ran SP% 120.6
Speed ratings (Par 94): **99,95,91,90,85 84,79,78,78,76 74**
toteswinger: 1&2 £1.50, 1&3 £7.60, 2&3 £9.20. CSF £3.40 TOTE £2.00: £1.10, £1.60, £3.70; EX 4.30 Trifecta £38.10 Pool: £717.58 - 13.93 winning units..
Owner Sheikh Naser Fahad Al Sabah **Bred** J Feane **Trained** Averham Park, Notts
■ Stewards' Enquiry : L P Keniry three-day ban: careless riding (Dec 29-31)

FOCUS
An uncompetitive maiden auction. The likes of the fourth govern the level but there is better to come from the front pair.

NOTEBOOK
Saif Al Fahad(IRE), drawn widest of all, had shown enough to suggest he could take this when making the frame in a couple of nurseries at Great Leighs and he assumed control inside the final furlong. It would have been closer had the runner-up not gone inside with her challenge, but he won with a bit in hand and may well continue to pay his way back in nurseries. (op 11-8)
Desert Bump, who got going too late following a slow start on her debut at Great Leighs, looked to be coming with a strong challenge when switched left and bumping with Wee Bizzom over a furlong out. She stayed on inside the final furlong, finishing a clear second, and it would have been interesting had Liam Keniry opted to come wide with his challenge. (op 9-4 tchd 5-2 and 2-1)
Jolly Ranch, never involved over 6f at the course on her debut, showed good speed on this drop in trip and ran a much-improved race. She is clearly nothing special, but has a future at the right level. (op 33-1)
Wee Bizzom, who bumped with the runner-up over a furlong out, is well exposed and ran about as well as could have been expected. Official explanation: jockey said saddle slipped (op 33-1)
Trick Or Two ran quite well considering the bit slipped through his mouth and is now qualified for a handicap mark. Official explanation: jockey said gelding hung right-handed (op 22-1)
Amosite, third at Lingfield the previous day (did not find as much as expected under pressure over 6f), had some useful form to her name earlier in the season, but she failed to reproduce the effort and may well have found the race coming too soon. (op 7-2 tchd 11-2)
You'relikemefrank Official explanation: jockey said colt hung right

7690 RINGSIDE SUITE MAIDEN STKS 1m 141y(P)
4:20 (4:20) (Class 5) 3-Y-O+ £3,885 (£1,156; £577; £288) Stalls Low

Form RPR

5/ **1** **January**[24] 7410 5-9-5 82 (t) PatCosgrave 4 84
(T M Walsh, Ire) *a.p: led over 1f out: edgd lft ins fnl f: rdn out* **5/4**[1]

2345 **2** 5 **Cheney Manor**[72] 6470 3-9-3 69 MichaelHills 5 72
(B W Hills) *chsd ldr: led jst over 2f out: rdn and hdd over 1f out: sn btn* **4/1**[3]

0 **3** 3 1/4 **Fantosha (USA)**[17] 7466 3-8-12 70 (p) DarryllHolland 2 60
(K A Ryan) *led: hdd jst over 2f out: rdn and edgd lft jst over 1f out: wknd fnl f* **4/1**[3]

0 **4** 24 **Shortwall Lady (IRE)**[12] 7536 3-8-9 0 TolleyDean(3) 7 5
(J L Spearing) *in rr: rdn over 3f out: sn struggling* **50/1**

0- **5** 28 **Triel**[218] 537 5-9-5 0 JerryO'Dwyer 6 —
(J R Holt) *s.s: hld up: rdn over 3f out: sn struggling: t.o* **150/1**

U **Son Of My Heart (USA)** 3-9-3 0 TomEaves 1 —
(P F I Cole) *stmbld and uns rdr s* **5/2**[2]

1m 51.24s (0.74) **Going Correction** +0.10s/f (Slow)
WFA 3 from 5yo 2lb 6 Ran SP% 115.6
Speed ratings (Par 103): **100,95,92,71,46** —
toteswinger: 1&2 £1.40, 1&3 £2.10, 2&3 £2.50. CSF £7.18 TOTE £2.20: £1.40, £1.40; EX 5.80.
Owner M A Ryan **Bred** Darley **Trained** Kill, Co Kildare

FOCUS
This race lost much of its interest when the newcomer, Son Of My Heart, unseated his rider on leaving the stalls, and this was a very ordinary maiden. The runner-up is a fair guide to the form.

7691 BOOK TICKETS ONLINE AT WOLVERHAMPTON-RACECOURSE.CO.UK H'CAP (DIV I) 1m 141y(P)
4:50 (4:51) (Class 6) (0-55,55) 3-Y-O+ £2,047 (£604; £302) Stalls Low

Form RPR

1040 **1** **Mr Chocolate Drop (IRE)**[30] 7340 4-8-11 49 ow1 (b) AdamKirby 11 56
(Miss M E Rowland) *t.k.h in mid-div: hdwy and swtchd lft jst over 1f out: rdn to ld wl ins fnl f: r.o* **10/1**

00/1 **2** 1 **Alf Tupper**[9] 7581 5-9-0 52 StephenCarson 3 57
(Adrian McGuinness, Ire) *hld up towards rr: hdwy over 2f out: rdn to ld jst over 2f out: hdd wl ins fnl f* **7/2**[2]

6403 **3** 3/4 **Turkish Sultan (IRE)**[9] 7581 5-8-6 49 (p) MCGeran(5) 12 52
(J M Bradley) *hld up in rr: rdn wl over 1f out: gd late prog: fin wl* **8/1**

3000 **4** 1/2 **Pajada**[9] 7585 4-8-5 46 oh1 LukeMorris(3) 9 48
(M D I Usher) *hld up in rr: rdn wl over 1f out: r.o ins fnl f: nrst fin* **80/1**

6461 **5** 3/4 **Marmooq**[16] 7497 5-9-3 55 GrahamGibbons 4 55
(M J Attwater) *hld up in tch: lost pl 4f out: rdn and hdwy wl over 1f out: kpt on ins fnl f* **5/1**[3]

0025 **6** hd **King Of The Beers (USA)**[12] 7535 4-9-0 55 (p) KevinGhunowa(3) 5 55
(R A Harris) *chsd ldrs: rdn over 2f out: one pce fnl f* **8/1**

2/0- **7** nk **Actuality**[24] 7411 6-8-10 48 (t) EddieAhern 7 47
(Patrick Martin, Ire) *hld up towards rr: hdwy 3f out: rdn 2f out: one pce fnl f* **9/4**[1]

-500 **8** nk **First In Show**[31] 7310 3-8-9 49 (t) LPKeniry 13 48
(A M Balding) *chsd ldrs: wnt 2nd 3f out: sn rdn: no ex fnl f* **12/1**

605 **9** 3/4 **Ardent Prince**[10] 7560 5-9-1 53 (p) JamesDoyle 6 50
(A J McCabe) *t.k.h: sn w ldr: led over 5f out: clr 4f out: rdn and hdd jst over 1f out: wknd wl ins fnl f* **16/1**

4500 **10** 15 **Zabeel House**[147] 4254 5-9-2 54 (p) ChrisCatlin 8 16
(John A Harris) *hld up: wknd over 2f out* **14/1**

3050 **11** 3/4 **Muncaster Castle (IRE)**[17] 7114 4-8-12 50 (b[1]) FrankieMcDonald 2 11
(R F Fisher) *led over 5f out: wknd over 2f out* **40/1**

1m 51.72s (1.22) **Going Correction** +0.10s/f (Slow)
WFA 3 from 4yo+ 2lb 11 Ran SP% 124.9
Speed ratings (Par 101): **98,97,96,96,95 95,94,94,93,80 79**
toteswinger: 1&2 £10.20, 1&3 £18.40, 2&3 £7.40. CSF £47.85 CT £314.73 TOTE £13.80: £3.30, £1.60, £2.70; EX 64.40 Trifecta £510.90 Pool: £690.46 - 0.45 winning units..
Owner Dean R Mitchell **Bred** P J Munnelly **Trained** Lower Blidworth, Notts

FOCUS
A very moderate handicap run at a strong pace, and those held up were at an advantage. There was thick fog down the back straight, which restricted viewing for a few furlongs. The bare form is very ordinary.
Muncaster Castle(IRE) Official explanation: jockey said gelding hung left-handed

7692 BOOK TICKETS ONLINE AT WOLVERHAMPTON-RACECOURSE.CO.UK H'CAP (DIV II) 1m 141y(P)
5:20 (5:23) (Class 6) (0-55,55) 3-Y-O+ £2,047 (£604; £302) Stalls Low

Form RPR

0003 **1** **Moment Of Clarity**[14] 7516 6-9-1 53 (p) GrahamGibbons 6 65
(R C Guest) *a.p: led wl over 1f out: sn rdn: edgd lft ins fnl f: r.o* **7/4**[1]

0053 **2** 1 1/2 **Thornaby Green**[5] 7634 7-8-10 53 DeanHeslop(5) 9 61
(T D Barron) *hld up in mid-div: hdwy over 3f out: kpt on to take 2nd towards fin: nt trble wnr* **9/2**[2]

0350 **3** 1 **Sion Hill (IRE)**[16] 7503 7-9-2 54 (p) ChrisCatlin 11 60
(John A Harris) *chsd ldr: led over 2f out tl wl over 1f out: rdn fnl f: no ex and lost 2nd towards fin* **18/1**

6505 **4** 3 3/4 **Machinate (USA)**[9] 7581 6-9-3 55 LiamJones 1 52
(W M Brisbourne) *hld up towards rr: hdwy over 2f out: swtchd rt wl over 1f out: one pce fnl f* **8/1**

0000 **5** 2 1/2 **All You Need (IRE)**[14] 7516 4-9-0 52 VinceSlattery 10 44
(R Hollinshead) *hld up towards rr: c wd st: sme hdwy whn hung lft jst over 1f out: nvr trbld ldrs* **7/1**[3]

5200 **6** 1/2 **Bidable**[21] 7437 4-8-7 50 MCGeran(5) 3 40+
(B Palling) *hld up in rr: shkn up and hmpd 1f out: nvr nrr* **12/1**

1002 **7** 1 3/4 **Bye Baby Bunting**[12] 7535 3-8-11 51 ow1 AdamKirby 12 37
(B R Johnson) *stdd s: hld up in rr: rdn over 2f out: n.m.r jst over 1f out: nvr nr ldrs* **10/1**

3004 **8** 1/2 **Casablanca Minx (IRE)**[7] 7599 5-8-13 51 (v) StephenDonohoe 7 36
(Miss Gay Kelleway) *hld up in rr: n.d* **10/1**

044 **9** 3 3/4 **Fraizer (IRE)**[9] 7582 4-8-9 47 StephenCarson 5 24
(Adrian McGuinness, Ire) *prom: rdn over 1f out: sn wknd* **14/1**

0650 **10** 1 1/4 **Bewdley**[102] 5652 3-8-6 46 oh1 FrancisNorton 8 20
(R E Peacock) *led: hdd over 2f out: wknd wl over 1f out* **66/1**

0600 **11** 8 **Filemot**[26] 7383 3-8-7 50 LukeMorris(3) 2 5
(John Berry) *hld up in tch: rdn 3f out: sn wknd* **25/1**

0 **12** 2 **Chiefofthemowhawks (USA)**[24] 7411 5-8-8 46 oh1 NickyMackay 13 —
(Stephen Michael Cox, Ire) *hld up in mid-div: rdn over 3f out: wknd wl over 1f out* **40/1**

0-06 **13** 1 **The Tinker Man**[17] 7469 4-8-10 48 DaneO'Neill 4 —
(M D I Usher) *a towards rr* **16/1**

1m 50.97s (0.47) **Going Correction** +0.10s/f (Slow)
WFA 3 from 4yo+ 2lb 45 Ran SP% 129.6
Speed ratings (Par 101): **101,99,98,95,93 92,91,90,87,86 79,77,76**
toteswinger: 1&2 £4.30, 1&3 £12.50, 2&3 £12.90. CSF £9.75 CT £119.70 TOTE £3.50: £1.40, £1.80, £3.30; EX 16.10 Trifecta £168.80 Pool: £456.22 - 2.00 winning units. Place 6 £30.46, Place 5 £25.69.
Owner Andrew Shedden **Bred** Lordship Stud **Trained** Carburton, Notts

FOCUS
A moderate handicap, but the time was 0.75 seconds quicker than the first division. There was thick fog in the straight, which restricted viewing somewhat. It was the stronger division and the first three are all on potentially good marks.
Bidable Official explanation: jockey said filly was denied a clear run
T/Jkpt: Not won. T/Plt: £26.50 to a £1 stake. Pool: £64,277.44. 1,768.20 winning tickets. T/Qpdt: £7.70 to a £1 stake. Pool: £5,087.10. 485.81 winning tickets. KH

7658 SOUTHWELL (L-H)
Tuesday, December 16

OFFICIAL GOING: Standard
Wind: Light across Weather: Overcast

7693 SOUTHWELL-RACECOURSE.CO.UK NURSERY 7f (F)
12:40 (12:40) (Class 6) (0-65,65) 2-Y-O £2,047 (£604; £302) Stalls Low

Form RPR

0400 **1** **Andean Margin (IRE)**[18] 7467 2-8-13 57 (b[1]) PatCosgrave 3 66+
(S A Callaghan) *s.i.s: sn pushed along to ld: rdn over 1f out: r.o* **10/1**

643 **2** 2 1/2 **Passage To India (IRE)**[11] 7561 2-9-7 65 PaulFitzsimons 9 67+
(J A Osborne) *hld up: hdwy over 2f out: rdn to chse wnr and edgd lft over 1f out: no imp ins fnl f* **13/2**[3]

000 **3** 7 **Miss Cameo (USA)**[43] 7170 2-8-6 50 HayleyTurner 10 35
(R M Whitaker) *hld up: hdwy u.p over 1f out: nt trble ldrs* **20/1**

4323 **4** 3/4 **Artesium**[3] 7659 2-8-5 56 BMcHugh(7) 11 39
(R A Fahey) *chsd ldrs: rdn over 2f out: wknd fnl f* **9/2**[2]

0500 **5** 1 **Spring Quartet**[83] 6207 2-9-4 62 PaulEddery 8 42
(Pat Eddery) *prom: rdn 1/2-way: wknd over 1f out* **20/1**

6606 **6** 1 3/4 **Chambers (IRE)**[10] 7575 2-8-10 54 GregFairley 1 30
(M Johnston) *chsd ldr: rdn over 2f out: wknd fnl furlong* **15/2**

4020 **7** 2 1/2 **Rossett Rose (IRE)**[57] 6863 2-9-4 62 FrancisNorton 4 32
(M Brittain) *chsd ldrs: rdn 1/2-way: wknd 2f out* **20/1**

0623 **8** 1 1/4 **Bulella**[28] 7372 2-8-7 58 AndrewHeffernan(7) 6 24+
(Garry Moss) *s.i.s: rdn over 2f out: a in rr* **13/2**[3]

4000 **9** nk **Terracotta Warrior**[37] 7258 2-8-7 51 (b[1]) ChrisCatlin 2 17
(J Jay) *trckd ldrs: plld hrd: wknd over 2f out* **16/1**

0015 **10** 1 3/4 **Kladester (USA)**[18] 7467 2-9-6 64 (t) PaulMulrennan 7 25
(B Smart) *s.i.s: sn mid-div: rdn 1/2-way: wknd over 2f out* **3/1**[1]

0300 **11** *13* **Admiring Glances**[12] 7547 2-8-4 **48**.................................. LiamJones 5 —
(J Pearce) *sn outpcd* **25/1**

1m 30.55s (0.25) **Going Correction** -0.10s/f (Stan) 11 Ran SP% **114.7**
Speed ratings (Par 94): **94,91,83,82,81 79,76,74,74,72 57**
toteswinger: 1&2 £20.70, 1&3 £8.50, 2&3 £43.50. CSF £67.16 CT £1302.11 TOTE £13.10: £3.00, £3.00, £3.70; EX 90.60 TRIFECTA Not won..
Owner M Tabor & Matthew Green **Bred** Epona Bloodstock Ltd **Trained** Newmarket, Suffolk

FOCUS
A modest nursery.

NOTEBOOK
Andean Margin(IRE) produced an improved effort to get off the mark at the seventh attempt in clear-cut fashion. He had not been getting home over further recently, but improved for the drop in trip and first-time blinkers, with the surface clearly in his favour as well. Given a positive ride, he responded willingly to pressure in the straight and had this in the bag over a furlong out. Connections have found his right trip, they will just have to hope the headgear continues to have the desired effect. (op 7-1 tchd 13-2)
Passage To India(IRE) had shown pretty limited ability in three runs in maiden company at Wolverhampton, but this was a reasonable effort on her nursery debut. Having raced wide for much of the way, she stayed on in the straight, but was never getting to the winner, who had something in hand. (op 6-1 tchd 7-1)
Miss Cameo(USA) was last for much of the way, but she stayed on quite well for pressure towards the inside rail in the straight. This was a respectable effort on her handicap debut, but she will probably have to show more tactical speed if she is going to win a similar race. (op 12-1)
Artesium raced wide for a lot of the way, but he seemed to have his chance. (op 3-1)
Spring Quartet showed up for much of the way but was beaten halfway up the straight. (tchd 25-1)
Chambers(IRE) probably failed to see out this trip on his first attempt over it. (op 14-1)
Kladester(USA) was 9lb higher than when winning a much weaker race over course and distance two starts back and he never really travelled after starting slowly. Official explanation: trainer's rep had no explanation for the poor form shown (op 7-2 tchd 4-1)

7694 CALL 01636 814481 TO SPONSOR A RACE (S) STKS 7f (F)
1:10 (1:10) (Class 6) 2-Y-O £1,978 (£584; £292) **Stalls** Low

Form RPR

064 **1** **Paint Splash**[21] 7443 2-8-1 0.................................. DeanHeslop(5) 4 58+
(T D Barron) *chsd ldrs: nt clr run 1/2-way: rdn to ld over 1f out: styd on wl* **6/1**[3]

0065 **2** *5* **Kneesy Earsy Nosey**[21] 7445 2-8-7 40 ow1.................. AnnStokell(5) 9 52
(Miss A Stokell) *sn pushed along in rr: n.m.r 1/2-way: hdwy over 2f out: rdn to go 2nd ins fnl f: no ch w wnr* **50/1**

3663 **3** *1 3/4* **Island Chief**[28] 7370 2-8-11 57..................................(b) ChrisCatlin 1 46
(K A Ryan) *s.i.s: rcvrd to ld 6f out: rdn: edgd rt and hdd over 1f out: no ex fnl f* **4/1**[2]

0000 **4** *1* **Herecomesbella**[145] 4337 2-8-6 47..............................(b[1]) HayleyTurner 8 39
(Stef Liddiard) *hld up: hdwy 2f out: sn rdn: no ex fnl f* **40/1**

5115 **5** *2* **Kinigi (IRE)**[14] 7531 2-8-8 61.................................. KevinGhunowa(3) 7 39
(R A Harris) *led 1f: chsd ldrs: rdn over 2f out: wknd fnl f* **1/1**[1]

5404 **6** *6* **Premier Krug (IRE)**[8] 7607 2-8-1 55.....................(v) PatrickDonaghy(5) 5 19
(P D Evans) *s.i.s: sn pushed along: a in rr* **17/2**

0625 **7** *4* **That Boy Ronaldo**[1] 7687 2-8-6 50.................................. FrancisNorton 3 9
(A Berry) *prom: rdn 1/2-way: wknd 2f out* **12/1**

4300 **8** *shd* **Calley Ho**[12] 7547 2-8-9 67.................................. KristinStubbs(7) 6 18
(Mrs L Stubbs) *s.i.s: hdwy over 4f out: wknd wl over 1f out* **12/1**

0000 **9** *2* **Moon Warrior**[3] 7659 2-8-4 36..........................(v[1]) AndrewHeffernan(7) 2 8
(C Smith) *chsd ldr: rdn 1/2-way: wknd over 2f out: eased over 1f out* **100/1**

1m 30.91s (0.61) **Going Correction** -0.10s/f (Stan) 9 Ran SP% **115.6**
Speed ratings (Par 94): **92,86,84,83,80 74,69,69,67**
toteswinger: 1&2 £19.40, 1&3 £5.40, 2&3 £12.00. CSF £242.17 TOTE £7.00: £1.90, £7.20, £1.40; EX 256.80 TRIFECTA Not won..There was no bid for the winner.
Owner Harrowgate Bloodstock Ltd **Bred** Millsec Limited **Trained** Maunby, N Yorks
■ Stewards' Enquiry : Andrew Heffernan caution: careless riding

FOCUS
A weak juvenile seller run in a time 0.36 seconds slower than the earlier 0-65 nursery.

NOTEBOOK
Paint Splash had shown very moderate form on her three previous starts, and was reported to have bled from the nose when well behind Kinigi in a course-and-distance claimer last time, but this was an improved performance. Having travelled well enough just off the lead, she lost her place when short of room rounding the bend, just as Island Chief kicked clear, but she quickly recovered the ground and ultimately pulled well clear. (op 4-1)
Kneesy Earsy Nosey came into this rated just 40. She never really travelled but kept on best of the rest. (op 33-1)
Island Chief ran a very similar race to last time, looking dangerous when kicked clear at the top of the straight, only to fail to sustain his effort. He might be worth a try over 6f, even though his breeding suggests otherwise. (op 7-2)
Herecomesbella travelled well to a point in first-time blinkers, but she could not muster the pace to pose a threat. (op 33-1)
Kinigi(IRE) was a bitter disappointment on this drop into selling company. She seemed well enough placed, but failed to pick up and looks best watched for now. (op 6-4 tchd 13-8)
That Boy Ronaldo Official explanation: jockey said filly suffered interference in running

7695 HOSPITALITY AT SOUTHWELL RACECOURSE CLAIMING STKS 1m 3f (F)
1:40 (1:40) (Class 6) 3-Y-O+ £2,047 (£604; £302) **Stalls** Low

Form RPR

3011 **1** **La Estrella (USA)**[17] 7499 5-9-7 88.................................. DaneO'Neill 13 87
(D E Cantillon) *hld up: hdwy over 3f out: rdn and hung lft fr over 2f out: led over 1f out: r.o wl: eased nr fin* **8/11**[1]

2633 **2** *6* **Elite Land**[36] 7272 5-8-13 63.................................. ChrisCatlin 7 69
(K A Ryan) *a.p: chsd ldr 8f out tl led over 3f out: rdn and hdd over 1f out: styd on same pce* **11/1**

3031 **3** *2 1/4* **Red Expresso (IRE)**[6] 7632 3-8-10 62.................................. HayleyTurner 3 66
(M L W Bell) *hld up: hdwy over 3f out: rdn over 2f out: no ex fnl f* **4/1**[2]

2230 **4** *2* **Yakimov (USA)**[32] 7309 9-9-0 82.................................. PaulMulrennan 6 63
(Ollie Pears) *awkward leaving stalls: hld up: hdwy 5f out: rdn over 3f out: wknd fnl f* **17/2**[3]

0560 **5** *nse* **Black Falcon (IRE)**[21] 7447 8-8-11 57.................................. RobertWinston 10 60
(John A Harris) *hld up: hdwy over 3f out: rdn and swtchd lft over 2f out: wknd fnl f* **33/1**

0406 **6** *4* **Semah Harold**[17] 7500 3-8-8 52..............................(v) GrahamGibbons 8 54
(E S McMahon) *chsd ldrs: nt clr run over 2f out: sn rdn: wknd over 1f out* **33/1**

0324 **7** *4* **My Mirasol**[8] 7606 4-8-13 64..............................(p) LPKeniry 5 48
(D E Cantillon) *chsd ldr: led over 9f out: rdn and hdd over 3f out: wknd 2f out* **20/1**

3003 **8** *5* **Celticello (IRE)**[19] 6472 6-9-2 73..........................(p) StephenDonohoe 11 43
(P D Evans) *s.i.s: hld up: rdn over 3f out: sn wknd* **11/1**

9 *6* **Wildbach (IRE)**[13] 6-8-11 50..................................(p) EdwardCreighton 9 27
(Miss Sheena West) *sn pushed along in rr: hdwy u.p 5f out: wknd 4f out* **33/1**

500/ **10** *15* **Tora Petcha (IRE)**[22] 5247 5-8-12 57 ow1.................. PatCosgrave 12 —
(R Hollinshead) *hld up: rdn and wknd over 3f out* **66/1**

0-U6 **11** *14* **Sir Joey**[329] 257 3-8-5 45.................................. PatrickDonaghy(5) 4 —
(B D Leavy) *chsd ldrs: rdn over 5f out: wknd over 3f out* **150/1**

00-0 **12** *3 1/4* **Que Beauty (IRE)**[7] 7376 3-7-9 40..................(b) AndrewHeffernan(7) 1 —
(R C Guest) *led: hdd over 9f out: rdn 1/2-way: sn lost pl* **150/1**

2m 26.0s (-2.00) **Going Correction** -0.10s/f (Stan)
WFA 3 from 4yo+ 4lb 12 Ran SP% **121.5**
Speed ratings (Par 101): **103,98,97,95,95 92,89,86,81,70 60,58**
.Elite Land was claimed by Mr B. Ellison for £7000. Red Expresso was claimed by \n\x\x Mr O. Pears for £8000.\n\x\x
Owner Mrs J Hart C Lynas & M Freedman **Bred** Five Horses Ltd And Theatrical Syndicate **Trained** Newmarket, Suffolk

FOCUS
A reasonable claimer but a decisive winner, who is better than this grade and did not need to match his latest form.
Wildbach(IRE) Official explanation: jockey said gelding never travelled

7696 MEMBERSHIP AT SOUTHWELL GOLF CLUB H'CAP 2m (F)
2:10 (2:11) (Class 5) (0-75,76) 3-Y-O+ £2,729 (£806; £403) **Stalls** Low

Form RPR

4363 **1** **Victory Quest (IRE)**[7] 7617 8-9-11 **65**..........................(v) RobertWinston 4 76
(Mrs S Lamyman) *chsd ldr 3f: remained handy: rdn over 2f out: styd on to ld nr fin* **7/2**[3]

1321 **2** *hd* **Azabu Juban (IRE)**[5] 7639 3-9-9 **76** 6ex.................. WilliamCarson(5) 9 87
(J Jay) *rrd at s: sn prom: led over 3f out: rdn and hung lft over 1f out: hdd nr fin* **11/4**[2]

0602 **3** *2 1/2* **Calculating (IRE)**[7] 7617 4-10-0 **68**.................................. HayleyTurner 6 76
(M D I Usher) *chsd clr ldr tl led over 3f out: sn hdd: rdn whn rdr dropped reins over 1f out: styd on same pce ins fnl f* **5/2**[1]

5041 **4** *8* **Simple Jim (FR)**[7] 7617 4-9-4 **58** 6ex.................. GrahamGibbons 5 56
(A D Brown) *hld up: rdn over 3f out: wknd 2f out* **6/1**

0460 **5** *1 1/2* **Exit To Luck (GER)**[29] 7183 7-9-10 **64**..........................(b) ChrisCatlin 8 60
(S Gollings) *hld up: hdwy over 4f out: rdn over 2f out: sn wknd* **14/1**

0400 **6** *18* **Tapaellya (IRE)**[10] 7587 4-8-9 **49** oh4......................(b) RichardThomas 3 24
(J E Long) *led and sn clr: rdn: hdd & wknd over 3f out* **50/1**

000/ **7** *2 1/2* **Heart Springs**[229] 4898 8-8-2 **49** oh3.................. MatthewCosham(7) 7 21
(Dr J R J Naylor) *s.i.s: hld up: plld hrd: rdn 6f out: wknd over 4f out* **40/1**

3512 **8** *26* **Mayadeen (IRE)**[47] 6812 6-9-3 **57**..........................(b) JamieMoriarty 2 —
(R A Fahey) *prom: hung lft and rdn over 5f out: sn wknd* **12/1**

3m 44.3s (-1.20) **Going Correction** -0.10s/f (Stan)
WFA 3 from 4yo+ 8lb 8 Ran SP% **110.5**
Speed ratings (Par 103): **99,98,97,93,92 83,82,69**
toteswinger: 1&2 £1.70, 1&3 £2.00, 2&3 £2.00. CSF £12.58 CT £25.27 TOTE £4.80: £2.00, £1.10, £1.10; EX 9.70 Trifecta £57.50 Pool: £433.83 - 5.58 winning units..
Owner P Lamyman **Bred** Miss Veronica Henley **Trained** Ruckland, Lincs
■ Stewards' Enquiry : Robert Winston one-day ban, plus three-days deferred; used whip with excessive frequency (Dec 30-31,Jan 1-2)

FOCUS
A modest staying handicap run at an even pace. The winner was back to his best form of the last couple of years, reversing recent course form with the third and fourth.
Mayadeen(IRE) Official explanation: jockey said gelding hung left

7697 PLAY GOLF AT SOUTHWELL GOLF CLUB H'CAP 5f (F)
2:40 (2:40) (Class 4) (0-85,85) 3-Y-O+ £4,857 (£1,445; £722; £360) **Stalls** High

Form RPR

1654 **1** **The Tatling (IRE)**[10] 7584 11-8-7 **79**.................................. JackDean(5) 4 91
(J M Bradley) *chsd ldrs: pushed along 1/2-way: shkn up to ld wl ins fnl f: readily* **12/1**

0000 **2** *1* **Northern Empire (IRE)**[26] 7393 5-8-4 **71** oh1.................. ChrisCatlin 1 80
(K A Ryan) *chsd ldrs: led over 3f out: rdn hung rt and hdd over 1f out: rallied to ld ins fnl f: sn hdd: styd on* **9/1**

560 **3** *nk* **Rebel Duke (IRE)**[44] 7151 4-8-13 **80**.................................. TonyHamilton 5 88
(D W Barker) *fly-leapt s: sn chsng ldrs: led over 1f out: rdn and hdd ins fnl f: styd on* **11/2**[3]

5503 **4** *1 1/4* **Pawan (IRE)**[7] 7614 8-8-11 **83**..............................(b) AnnStokell(5) 3 86
(Miss A Stokell) *led 1f: chsd ldrs: rdn 1/2-way: styd on* **6/1**

0001 **5** *1* **Canadian Danehill (IRE)**[11] 7562 6-8-12 **79**..................(p) EddieAhern 8 78
(R M H Cowell) *chsd ldrs: rdn 1/2-way: styd on same pce fnl f* **9/2**[2]

1500 **6** *2* **Memphis Man**[10] 7584 5-8-10 **77**.................................. StephenDonohoe 6 69
(P D Evans) *sn outpcd: nvr nrr* **20/1**

5000 **7** *hd* **Vhujon (IRE)**[10] 7576 3-9-4 **85**.................................. TGMcLaughlin 7 76
(P D Evans) *sn outpcd: hung lft 2f out: n.d* **16/1**

144 **8** *9* **Garlogs**[7] 7614 5-8-9 **76**.................................. HayleyTurner 2 35
(R Hollinshead) *led 4f out: sn hdd: rdn 1/2-way: wknd over 1f out* **7/4**[1]

59.36 secs (-0.34) **Going Correction** +0.075s/f (Slow) 8 Ran SP% **112.6**
Speed ratings (Par 105): **105,103,102,100,99 96,95,81**
toteswinger: 1&2 £16.10, 1&3 £10.60, 2&3 £9.70. CSF £109.35 CT £666.19 TOTE £14.80: £2.70, £2.80, £1.80; EX 141.20 Trifecta £257.50 Part won. Pool: £347.98 - 0.45 winning units..
Owner J M Bradley **Bred** Patrick J Power **Trained** Sedbury, Gloucs

FOCUS
A fair sprint handicap, but a bit of a surprise result. The winner and second have both slipped a fair way in the weights.
Pawan(IRE) Official explanation: jockey said gelding was denied a clear run
Garlogs Official explanation: jockey said gelding anticipated the start and hit its head on gates prior to opening

7698 BOOK YOUR TICKETS AT SOUTHWELL-RACECOURSE.CO.UK H'CAP 7f (F)
3:10 (3:11) (Class 6) (0-65,66) 3-Y-O+ £2,047 (£604; £302) **Stalls** Low

Form RPR

0-00 **1** **Captain Macarry (IRE)**[52] 6976 3-9-3 **64**..........................(v[1]) GregFairley 9 80
(B Smart) *led: hdd over 5f out: rdn over 1f out: rallied to ld ins fnl f: r.o wl* **22/1**

461 **2** *3* **This Ones For Eddy**[7] 7618 3-9-4 **65** 6ex.................. AdamKirby 1 73
(S Parr) *chsd ldrs: led over 5f out: rdn over 1f out: and hdd and unable qck ins fnl f* **13/8**[1]

6651 **3** *3/4* **Kensington (IRE)**[4] 7651 7-9-5 **66** 6ex..................(v) StephenDonohoe 12 72
(P D Evans) *mid-div: hdwy 4f out: rdn over 2f out: swtchd lft over 1f out: styd on* **9/2**[2]

P000 **4** *1 ¼* **Haroldini (IRE)**[10] 7586 6-9-4 **65**..............................(p) PaulMulrennan 7 68+
(J Balding) *stmbld s: sn pushed along in rr: r.o u.p ins fnl f: nt rch ldrs* **14/1**
5514 **5** *1 ¼* **Another Genepi (USA)**[10] 7586 5-9-4 **65**............(b) EdwardCreighton 3 64
(E J Creighton) *chsd ldrs: rdn over 2f out: no ex fnl f* **16/1**
0001 **6** *¾* **Swallow Forest**[7] 7615 3-8-4 **56** 6ex..................(b) DeanHeslop(5) 8 53
(T D Barron) *s.i.s: outpcd: hdwy u.p over 1f out: nt trble ldrs* **12/1**
0 **7** *3 ½* **Fandango Boy**[46] 7121 7-8-13 **60**.. DNolan 4 48
(J P Broderick, Ire) *chsd ldrs: rdn over 1f out: wknd ins fnl f* **33/1**
3450 **8** *1 ½* **Louisiade (IRE)**[7] 7619 7-8-10 **57**..............................(p) HayleyTurner 5 41
(M C Chapman) *hld up: hdwy over 3f out: sn rdn: wknd wl over 1f out* **9/1**
0221 **9** *2 ½* **Vogarth**[21] 7442 4-8-11 **61** ow1.................................. JamesMillman(3) 2 38
(B R Millman) *s.i.s: hdwy over 1f out: n.d* **6/1**[3]
3553 **10** *1 ½* **Foxy Jane**[7] 7618 3-8-6 **53**.. FrancisNorton 6 26
(M Brittain) *s.i.s: sn prom: rdn 1/2-way: wknd 2f out* **16/1**
0000 **11** *9* **Government (IRE)**[33] 7267 7-7-11 **51** oh6..............(b) AlexEdwards(7) 11 —
(M C Chapman) *mid-div: wknd 1/2-way* **100/1**
5000 **12** *12* **Herbert Crescent**[21] 7448 3-9-4 **65**.............................. JamieMoriarty 14 —
(Ollie Pears) *s.i.s: a in rr* **50/1**
1600 **13** *3 ½* **Owed**[14] 7534 6-9-0 **61**...(tp) PatCosgrave 10 —
(R Bastiman) *sn prom: rdn 1/2-way: wknd 3f out* **28/1**

1m 28.75s (-1.55) **Going Correction** -0.10s/f (Stan) **13** Ran SP% **120.4**
Speed ratings (Par 101): **104,100,99,98,96 96,92,90,87,85 75,61,57**
toteswinger: 1&2 £8.70, 1&3 £17.80, 2&3 £3.40. CSF £56.77 CT £213.19 TOTE £23.60: £5.00, £1.80, £1.70; EX 81.20 Trifecta £63.50 Pool: £671.34 - 7.82 winning units..
Owner Anthony D Gee **Bred** Humphrey Okeke **Trained** Hambleton, N Yorks

FOCUS
A modest handicap but it was a decent race for the grade run in a decent time. The form has been rated positively and should work out.
T/Plt: £115.60 to a £1 stake. Pool: £55,515.73. 350.46 winning tickets. T/Qpdt: £13.90 to a £1 stake. Pool: £4,949.18. 262.80 winning tickets. CR

7620 KEMPTON (A.W) (R-H)
Wednesday, December 17

OFFICIAL GOING: Standard
Wind: Light, across Weather: Clear

7699 EUROPEAN BREEDERS' FUND MEDIAN AUCTION MAIDEN STKS 1m (P)
6:20 (6:21) (Class 5) 2-Y-O **£3,561** (£1,059; £529; £264) **Stalls** High

Form RPR
35 **1** **Petrovsky**[32] 7336 2-9-3 0.. GregFairley 13 77+
(M Johnston) *led after 1f: mde rest: rdn 2f out: styd on steadily* **6/4**[1]
2 *¾* **Onemix** 2-8-12 0.. MichaelHills 5 70+
(B W Hills) *v.s.i.s: keen early and hld up in last trio: gd prog on inner fr 3f out: rdn and styd on to take 2nd ins fnl f: clsng on wnr fin* **25/1**
0 **3** *2 ¼* **Haljaferia (UAE)**[10] 7593 2-9-3 0..................................... GeorgeBaker 12 70
(D R C Elsworth) *stdd s: t.k.h early: hld up in rr: prog on inner over 3f out: chsd ldrs 2f out: rdn and green over 1f out: kpt on to take 3rd nr fin* **9/1**
0 **4** *¾* **Cool Hand Jake**[56] 6893 2-9-3 0..................................... TravisBlock 10 69
(P J Makin) *s.i.s but pushed up to go prom: rdn to chse wnr 3f out: urged along and nt qckn 2f out: fdd fnl f* **20/1**
062 **5** *6* **Mellow Mixture**[12] 7552 2-9-3 72.................................... RichardHughes 9 56
(R Hannon) *chsd wnr after 2f to 3f out: wknd wl over 1f out* **3/1**[2]
0 **6** *1* **Screaming Brave**[117] 5225 2-9-3 0.............................. EdwardCreighton 14 53
(M R Channon) *mostly in midfield: rdn over 2f out: wknd over 1f out* **25/1**
050 **7** *nse* **Vodka Shot (USA)**[9] 7602 2-8-12 0................................ HayleyTurner 11 48+
(M L W Bell) *prom: cl up on inner 3f out: n.m.r sn after: pushed along and grad lost pl* **25/1**
8 *1 ½* **The Age Of Anxiety (USA)**[19] 7482 2-9-3 0...................... KJManning 8 50
(Edward Lynam, Ire) *towards rr: effrt on wd outside 3f out: no prog sn after: wknd over 1f out* **10/3**[3]
0 **9** *shd* **Majd Aljazeera**[41] 7204 2-9-3 0..............................(t) StephenDonohoe 2 50
(D M Simcock) *hld up in last trio: pushed along fr over 2f out: nvr on terms* **66/1**
0 **10** *2 ¾* **Witch Of The Wave (IRE)**[26] 7402 2-8-12 0..................... SteveDrowne 6 39
(Miss J S Davis) *lost midfield pl 1/2-way: struggling in rr 3f out: n.d after* **100/1**
11 *nk* **Tiffany Lady** 2-8-7 0.. GabrielHannon(5) 7 38
(M D I Usher) *t.k.h early: hld up wl in rr: nvr a factor: bhd fnl 2f* **100/1**
12 *6* **Major Value** 2-9-3 0... AdamKirby 1 30
(C G Cox) *led 1f: rdn over 3f out: wknd rapidly over 2f out* **66/1**
0 **13** *½* **Stafford Charlie**[56] 6893 2-9-3 0................................... FergusSweeney 4 29
(J G M O'Shea) *taken down early: stdd s: plld hrd early in last pair: nvr a factor* **100/1**
14 *26* **Turnham Green** 2-9-3 0.. PaulDoe 3 —
(S Curran) *chsd ldrs on wd outside for 3f: sn lost pl: wknd 3f out: t.o* **66/1**

1m 40.83s (1.03) **Going Correction** +0.075s/f (Slow) **14** Ran SP% **121.8**
Speed ratings (Par 96): **97,96,94,93,87 86,86,84,84,81 81,75,75,49**
toteswinger: 1&2 £13.70, 1&3 £4.50, 2&3 £8.50. CSF £51.49 TOTE £2.70: £1.20, £5.80, £2.60; EX 51.20.
Owner Sheikh Hamdan Bin Mohammed Al Maktoum **Bred** Gainsborough Stud Management Ltd **Trained** Middleham Moor, N Yorks

FOCUS
A maiden lacking in strength and a race in which the second and third favourites disappointed to varying degrees but nevertheless a couple of interesting performances. The pace was on the steady side early on and the winner raced centre to far side in the straight.

NOTEBOOK
Petrovsky had shown enough, including in a race that threw up winners last time, to suggest he was a leading player from his good draw and he justified the market support to win in workmanlike fashion. He should have no problems with 1m2f and is the type to progress further. (tchd 13-8)
Onemix ◆, a half-sister to an ordinary maiden, was easy to back but shaped with plenty of encouragement after a tardy start on this debut, despite her apparent inexperience. She will be suited by 1m2f and looks capable of picking up a similar event. (tchd 33-1)
Haljaferia(UAE) was nibbled at in the market and bettered the form of his debut under mainly hands and heels riding, despite failing to keep straight in the closing stages. He is bred to stay middle distances and will be interesting when handicapped. (op 14-1)
Cool Hand Jake ◆ was nibbled in the market at big odds close to the off and shaped better than the bare form on his all-weather debut after racing three deep to the straight. He got a bit tired late on but appeals as the type to win an ordinary handicap. (op 33-1)
Mellow Mixture had shown progressive form but proved disappointing, despite having the run of the race. He has had a few chances and may remain vulnerable against the more progressive sorts in this grade. (op 5-2 tchd 10-3)
The Age Of Anxiety(USA) was well supported but failed to build on his reasonable debut effort at Dundalk. However it is too soon to be writing him off. (op 9-2)

7700 BOOK FOR BOXING DAY TODAY NURSERY 7f (P)
6:50 (6:51) (Class 6) (0-75,75) 2-Y-O **£2,047** (£604; £302) **Stalls** High

Form RPR
12 **1** **Lexlenos (IRE)**[19] 7476 2-8-13 **67**.................................... HayleyTurner 8 72+
(D R C Elsworth) *dwlt: hld up in midfield: prog on inner over 2f out: drvn ahd over 1f out and edgd lft: in command and pushed out fnl 100yds* **7/2**[1]
262 **2** *1 ½* **Auld Arty (FR)**[19] 7475 2-9-7 **75**.. ShaneKelly 12 76
(T G Mills) *led: drvn and edgd lft over 1f out: sn hdd: kpt on same pce fnl f* **6/1**[3]
0424 **3** *nk* **Five Star Junior (USA)**[57] 6879 2-9-3 **71**..................... TonyHamilton 4 71
(Mrs L Stubbs) *wl in rr: rdn and prog wl over 2f out: chsd ldrs over 1f out: kpt on same pce after* **14/1**
4053 **4** *1 ¼* **Bartica (IRE)**[19] 7475 2-8-12 **66**................................... RichardHughes 7 63
(R Hannon) *racd on outer: chsd ldrs: rdn over 2f out: cl enough after but nt qckn* **6/1**[3]
331 **5** *nse* **My Best Bet**[21] 7454 2-9-2 **70**...................................... EdwardCreighton 3 67
(M R Channon) *hld up in last pair: urged along wl over 2f out: no prog tl over 1f out: tried to cl on ldrs ins fnl f: effrt petered out fnl100yds* **4/1**[2]
6623 **6** *½* **Diamond Twister (USA)**[12] 7555 2-9-2 **70**.................... SteveDrowne 6 66
(J R Best) *towards rr on outer: rdn wl over 2f out: sn struggling: kpt on again fnl f* **8/1**
4046 **7** *¾* **Rocoppelia (USA)**[19] 7472 2-8-10 **64**............................ JimCrowley 13 58
(Mrs A J Perrett) *cl up: rdn to chal fr over 2f out to wl over 1f out: wknd fnl f* **8/1**
6040 **8** *nse* **Miss Fritton (IRE)**[57] 6886 2-9-0 **68**................................ JohnEgan 10 62
(M Botti) *chsd ldrs: rdn and nt qckn over 2f out: one pce and no real imp fr over 1f out* **16/1**
3001 **9** *3* **Ridgeway Silver**[21] 7451 2-8-8 **67**............................ GabrielHannon(5) 5 53
(M D I Usher) *s.s: a towards rr: effrt on inner 2f out: sn no prog* **40/1**
2050 **10** *½* **My Sweet Georgia (IRE)**[20] 7458 2-9-1 **69**................... PatCosgrave 14 54
(S A Callaghan) *s.s: a in last pair: rdn and no prog over 2f out* **33/1**
0504 **11** *1* **Musigny (USA)**[19] 7475 2-8-10 **64**................................... MichaelHills 9 47
(W Jarvis) *mostly chsd ldr to over 2f out: wknd wl over 1f out* **10/1**

1m 27.04s (1.04) **Going Correction** +0.075s/f (Slow) **11** Ran SP% **120.0**
Speed ratings (Par 94): **97,95,94,93,93 92,92,91,88,87 86**
toteswinger: 1&2 £5.70, 1&3 £23.10, 2&3 £49.40. CSF £25.18 CT £272.96 TOTE £3.90: £1.60, £2.00, £6.50; EX 15.50.
Owner Calypso Bloodstock & Partner **Bred** Airlie Stud **Trained** Newmarket, Suffolk

FOCUS
An ordinary but solid nursery in which the pace was again on the steady side but the winner, who edged into the centre late on, is a progressive sort and there should be more to come.

NOTEBOOK
Lexlenos(IRE) ◆ is a progressive performer who looked on a fair mark for her handicap debut and she turned in an improved effort. A stronger gallop over this trip will see her in an even better light and she's the type to win more races. (op 4-1)
Auld Arty(FR) has yet to win a race but he ran creditably from his decent draw after being allowed to set just a modest gallop. He kept responding for pressure and, although things were in his favour here, he should be able to pick up an ordinary event. (op 5-1 tchd 13-2)
Five Star Junior(USA), back in a handicap and having his first run for his new stable, may be a bit better than the bare form after faring the best of the hold up horses in a race run at a muddling gallop. He has yet to win but should find a suitable granted a stronger gallop this winter. (op 25-1)
Bartica(IRE) was closely matched with Auld Arty on recent Lingfield form and ran to a similar level after racing four deep early on. He does not seem to do anything quickly and may be worth a try over 1m. (op 4-1)
My Best Bet, 7lb higher than her Wolverhampton win, was not seen to best effect considering the way things unfolded but was anything but disgraced. A more strongly run race would suit and she is worth another chance. Official explanation: jockey said filly missed the break (op 9-2 tchd 7-2)
Diamond Twister(USA), having his first run over this trip, has had a few chances and was not disgraced but also shaped as though a stiffer overall test of stamina over this trip would have suited. (op 10-1 tchd 7-1)
My Sweet Georgia(IRE) Official explanation: jockey said filly missed the break

7701 DIGIBET MEDIAN AUCTION MAIDEN STKS 1m 3f (P)
7:20 (7:20) (Class 6) 3-5-Y-O **£2,047** (£604; £302) **Stalls** High

Form RPR
0500 **1** **Eseej (USA)**[22] 7447 3-9-3 61.. TGMcLaughlin 8 66
(P W Hiatt) *mde all: rdn and drew clr fr over 2f out: in n.d after* **5/2**[2]
0430 **2** *6* **The Little Master (IRE)**[7] 7626 4-9-7 55........................ GeorgeBaker 6 56
(D R C Elsworth) *stdd s: hld up in last: effrt over 2f out: hanging and v limited rspnse: plugged on to take 2nd ins fnl f* **2/1**[1]
4 **3** *½* **Russian Angel**[17] 7504 4-9-2 0.. JimCrowley 1 50
(Jean-Rene Auvray) *hld up in 6th: effrt on outer 3f out: chsd wnr 2f out: no imp: lost 2nd ins fnl f* **5/1**[3]
0646 **4** *8* **Amwell House**[7] 7632 3-9-3 50.. EddieAhern 7 41
(J R Jenkins) *cl up: chsd wnr 3f out to 2f out: wknd rapidly* **11/2**
00- **5** *½* **Shipboard Romance (IRE)**[30] 6693 3-8-12 47..............(t) GregFairley 4 36
(K J Burke) *chsd ldrs: rdn over 3f out: wl btn over 2f out* **16/1**
2460 **6** *1 ½* **Silver Surprise**[7] 7626 4-9-2 52...................................... DaneO'Neill 2 33
(J J Bridger) *in tch: u.p over 4f out: wknd over 2f out* **12/1**
0600 **7** *15* **Little Rococoa**[17] 7504 3-9-3 42..(t) TPQueally 3 13
(R J Price) *dwlt: sn chsd wnr: rdn over 3f out: sn wknd: t.o* **50/1**

2m 22.85s (0.95) **Going Correction** +0.075s/f (Slow)
WFA 3 from 4yo 4lb **7** Ran SP% **109.5**
Speed ratings (Par 101): **99,94,94,88,88 87,76**
toteswinger: 1&2 £1.90, 1&3 £2.90, 2&3 £1.70. CSF £7.18 TOTE £4.00: £2.50, £1.80; EX 9.60.
Owner P W Hiatt **Bred** Shadwell Farm LLC **Trained** Hook Norton, Oxon

FOCUS
A low-grade and uncompetitive maiden and one in which the pace was on the steady side and the form looks weak. The winner raced towards the inside rail in the straight.

7702 DIGIBET CASINO H'CAP 1m 3f (P)
7:50 (7:51) (Class 6) (0-60,60) 3-Y-O+ **£2,047** (£604; £302) **Stalls** High

Form RPR
0044 **1** **Sky Quest (IRE)**[30] 7355 10-8-10 **55**.............................. NathanAlison(7) 1 69
(J R Boyle) *hld up bhd ldrs: stdy prog on inner fr 3f out: led over 1f out: shuffled along and steadily drew clr* **33/1**
6445 **2** *4* **Sir Liam (USA)**[12] 7559 4-9-1 **53**............................ RichardKingscote 11 60
(Tom Dascombe) *hld up bhd ldrs: drvn over 2f out: styd on fr over 1f out to take 2nd ins fnl f: no ch w wnr* **4/1**[2]

5064 **3** 1 1/2 **Imperium**[28] 7382 7-9-3 **55**........ JimCrowley 10 59
(Jean-Rene Auvray) *stdd s: hld up in last trio: gng wl but stl there over 2f out: prog and weaved through wl over 1f out: wnt 3rd nr fin: hopeless task* **25/1**

533 **4** *nk* **Compton Falcon**[25] 7427 4-9-1 **53**........ HayleyTurner 4 57
(G A Butler) *hld up in last: rdn wl over 2f out: styd on u.p fnl 2f: no ch of rching ldrs* **8/1**

022 **5** 2 1/4 **Old Romney**[10] 7596 4-9-8 **60**........(b) RichardHughes 9 60
(M Wigham) *prom: wnt 2nd 6f out: rdn to try to cl on clr ldr over 2f out: nt qckn and sn btn: wknd ins fnl f* **15/8**[1]

0300 **6** 1/2 **Brave Quest (IRE)**[10] 7596 4-9-6 **58**........ IanMongan 12 57
(Mrs L J Mongan) *rousted along early and str reminder after 2f: chsd ldrs but nvr gng sweetly: outpcd over 2f out* **66/1**

6601 **7** 1 1/4 **Whodunit (UAE)**[9] 7605 4-9-0 **52** 6ex........(b) ShaneKelly 13 49
(P W Hiatt) *allowed soft ld: drvn clr over 3f out: c bk to field 2f out: hdd over 1f out: edgd rt and wknd ins fnl f* **12/1**

0234 **8** *shd* **Good Effect (USA)**[7] 7620 4-9-7 **59**........(t) SteveDrowne 7 56
(C P Morlock) *hld up in last trio: bustled along in last 4f out: effrt on outer over 2f out: plugged on but no hope of getting involved* **7/1**[3]

0652 **9** 1 3/4 **St Petersburg**[20] 7461 8-9-6 **58**........ PatCosgrave 8 61+
(J R Boyle) *settled towards rr on inner: hrd rdn wl over 2f out: styng on and ch of a pl whn hmpd and snatched up last 75yds* **10/1**

0400 **10** *shd* **Always Certain (USA)**[65] 6712 3-9-2 **58**........ GeorgeBaker 14 52
(P G Murphy) *chsd ldr to 6f out: steadily wknd fnl 3f* **40/1**

3504 **11** 1 3/4 **Putra Laju (IRE)**[18] 7500 4-9-5 **57**........ EddieAhern 3 48
(J W Hills) *hld up in wl in rr: effrt 3f out: sn rdn and no prog* **25/1**

0305 **12** 1 1/2 **Sir Haydn**[7] 7626 8-9-1 **53**........(v) StephenDonohoe 5 41
(J R Jenkins) *a towards rr: no prog whn rdn wl over 2f out* **33/1**

0004 **13** *10* **Inquisitress**[9] 7605 4-9-0 **52**........ TPQueally 6 23
(J J Bridger) *hld up bhd ldrs: rdn and outpcd 3f out: wknd rapidly wl over 1f out: t.o* **33/1**

066- **14** 2 1/4 **Dee Cee Elle**[34] 4843 4-9-6 **58**........(p) DaneO'Neill 2 25
(D Burchell) *settled midfield: lost pl 3f out: sn no ch: eased and t.o* **50/1**

2m 21.68s (-0.22) **Going Correction** +0.075s/f (Slow)
WFA 3 from 4yo+ 4lb **14** Ran SP% **117.6**
Speed ratings (Par 101): **103,100,99,98,97 96,95,95,94,94 93,92,84,83**
toteswinger: 1&2 £21.40, 1&3 £35.50, 2&3 £31.70. CSF £150.08 CT £3414.88 TOTE £34.30: £7.80, £1.80, £6.80; EX 278.40.
Owner M C Cook **Bred** Pendley Farm **Trained** Epsom, Surrey
■ Stewards' Enquiry : Shane Kelly two-day ban: careless riding (Dec 31, Jan 1)

FOCUS
A modest handicap in which the pace was soon reasonable and the form looks sound. The winner, who raced against the inside rail much of the way round, edged into the centre late on.

7703 DIGIBET.COM SUNBURY STKS (LISTED RACE) 7f (P)
8:20 (8:23) (Class 1) 3-Y-O+
£22,708 (£8,608; £4,308; £2,148; £1,076; £540) **Stalls** High

Form RPR

-061 **1** **Duff (IRE)**[25] 7421 5-9-4 0........ KJManning 10 116
(Edward Lynam, Ire) *mde all: kicked on over 2f out: 2 l clr over 1f out: drvn out and a holding on* **13/8**[1]

0430 **2** 1/2 **Bonus (IRE)**[28] 7381 8-9-2 104........(b) EddieAhern 6 113
(G A Butler) *hld up towards rr: gng easily whn nt clr run 2f out: pushed along and prog over 1f out: r.o wl to take 2nd fnl 50yds: clsd on wnr: too much to do* **16/1**

0116 **3** 1 1/4 **Ceremonial Jade (UAE)**[25] 7421 5-9-2 107........(t) JohnEgan 4 109
(M Botti) *wnt sltly lft s: hld up in last trio: prog on outer fr over 2f out: styd on to dispute 2nd ins fnl f: nvr able to chal* **11/1**

2501 **4** 1 1/2 **Atlantic Story (USA)**[25] 7418 6-9-2 108........(t) HayleyTurner 12 105
(M W Easterby) *prom: chsd wnr wl over 2f out: no real imp u.p after: fdd fnl 100yds* **7/2**[2]

5310 **5** 2 1/4 **Confuchias (IRE)**[18] 7492 4-9-2 105........ JimCrowley 7 99
(K R Burke) *trckd ldrs: rdn over 2f out: no imp over 1f out: fdd ins fnl f* **12/1**

-400 **6** *shd* **Finicius (USA)**[12] 7568 4-9-2 0........ FMBerry 13 99
(Eoin Griffin, Ire) *awkward s: keen early and sn in midfield: rdn over 2f out: one pce over 1f out: fdd fnl f* **14/1**

3634 **7** 1 1/4 **Red Alert Day**[28] 7381 3-9-2 101........ PatCosgrave 9 96
(S A Callaghan) *dwlt: t.k.h early: and hld up in midfield: nt qckn over 2f out: one pce and no imp after* **14/1**

0550 **8** 1 1/2 **Al Muheer (IRE)**[18] 7492 3-9-2 94........(p) RichardHughes 8 91
(C E Brittain) *hld up in last trio: rdn and no prog wl over 2f out: n.d after* **25/1**

-363 **9** 3/4 **Swiss Franc**[25] 7421 3-9-2 103........ GeorgeBaker 11 89
(D R C Elsworth) *plld hrd: hld up in midfield: effrt on inner 2f out: wknd over 1f out* **8/1**[3]

021 **10** *1* **Mac Love**[18] 7492 7-9-4 104........ MickyFenton 1 89
(Stef Liddiard) *mounted on crse: stdd s and bmpd: hld up in last: nt qckn fr over 2f out and no prog* **9/1**

0400 **11** *shd* **Salsa Steps (USA)**[25] 7421 4-8-11 90........(t) SteveDrowne 5 81
(H Morrison) *chsd wnr to wl over 2f out: wknd* **50/1**

1m 24.74s (-1.26) **Going Correction** +0.075s/f (Slow) **11** Ran SP% **122.5**
Speed ratings (Par 111): **110,109,108,106,103 103,102,100,99,98 98**
toteswinger: 1&2 £8.30, 1&3 £5.80, 2&3 £27.30. CSF £33.67 TOTE £3.00: £1.30, £4.50, £3.50; EX 33.30.
Owner Kilboy Estate **Bred** Kilboy Estate **Trained** Dunshaughlin, Co Meath

FOCUS
A good quality Listed event but another moderate gallop highlighted the benefit of racing at the head of the field. The winner raced against the inside rail in the straight and the race is rated around the placed horses.

NOTEBOOK
Duff(IRE) ◆ was conceding weight nearly all round but turned in an improved effort under a well-judged ride to maintain his unbeaten record on Polytrack. He's a smart and versatile performer, who will now be aimed at Lingfield in February. Connections are hoping for an invite to the Golden Shaheen on Dubai World Cup night but he will require a further step forward if he is to beat Diabolical and the pick of the American contingent on an unfamiliar dirt surface. (op 2-1)
Bonus(IRE) was below his best without headgear over this course and distance on his previous start but fared a good deal better with the blinkers refitted. He did well to finish as close after being held up off a muddling pace and after meeting trouble and he looks as good as ever on this evidence. (op 20-1 tchd 25-1)
Ceremonial Jade(UAE) was disappointing over 6f behind Duff at Lingfield on his previous start but showed that to be all wrong back over this longer trip. A stronger overall gallop would have suited and he is capable of picking up a race in this grade either over this trip or over 6f. (op 10-1 tchd 8-1)
Atlantic Story(USA), a prolific Polytrack winner, came here on the back of a career-best effort at Lingfield but, while anything but disgraced, failed to build on that on his first run in Listed company. A stronger overall gallop would have seen him in a better light and he is worth another chance in this grade. (tchd 9-2)
Confuchias(IRE), who won a conditions event over course and distance last month, was far from disgraced but again had his limitations exposed in a competitive Listed event. He's useful but may not be the easiest to place from here. (op 16-1)
Finicius(USA), who has won all his four races at Dundalk over a variety of distances, was fairly easy to back but was far from disgraced in this stronger grade. This was only his 13th start and he may well be capable of a bit better on Polytrack. (op 15-2 tchd 7-1)
Swiss Franc Official explanation: jockey said colt ran too free

7704 TFM NETWORKS H'CAP 1m 4f (P)
8:50 (8:54) (Class 4) (0-85,85) 3-Y-O+ **£5,180** (£1,541; £770; £384) **Stalls** Centre

Form RPR

-022 **1** **Wine 'n Dine**[14] 7539 3-8-8 **75**........ EddieAhern 4 86+
(G L Moore) *hld up in tch: covered up bhd ldrs 2f out: plld out over 1f out: drvn and r.o fnl f to ld post* **11/4**[2]

2001 **2** *nse* **Cape Colony**[14] 7539 3-9-0 **81**........ RichardHughes 5 89
(R Hannon) *trckd ldrs: effrt over 2f out: rdn to ld over 1f out: kpt on wl: hdd post* **2/1**[1]

3 1 1/4 **Choir Singer (FR)**[12] 7571 3-8-4 **71** oh1........ GregFairley 7 77
(Eoin Griffin, Ire) *hld up in tch: n.m.r over 2f out: prog on inner to chal jst over 1f out: no ex fnl 100yds* **5/1**[3]

210 **4** 3 1/2 **Drum Major (IRE)**[12] 6934 3-8-4 **71** oh1........ PaulDoe 9 71
(G L Moore) *trckd ldr: led wl over 2f out: hdd over 1f out: wknd fnl 100yds: eased* **12/1**

4324 **5** 1 3/4 **Hammer**[69] 6596 3-8-4 **71** oh2........ HayleyTurner 6 69
(R T Phillips) *hld up in rr: effrt over 2f out: nt clr run and swtchd lft: rdn and no imp over 1f out: fdd* **12/1**

0U-0 **6** 1 3/4 **Sommersturm (GER)**[136] 4-9-9 **85**........ TPQueally 2 80
(A P Stringer) *stdd s: hld up in last: effrt 3f out: shkn up and kpt on fnl 2f but nvr threatened ldrs* **50/1**

31 **7** *11* **Flying Squad (UAE)**[225] 1905 4-9-9 **85**........(t) SteveDrowne 8 62
(M F Harris) *led: urged along over 4f out: hdd wl over 2f out: wknd tamely wl over 1f out* **16/1**

1340 **8** *30* **Mutamaasek (USA)**[33] 7314 6-9-1 **77**........ RichardKingscote 1 6
(Lady Herries) *racd wd: pressed ldrs tl wknd rapidly over 3f out: t.o* **11/2**

40/ **9** *3* **Former Senator (IRE)**[835] 3062 8-8-9 **71** oh1........(t) FergusSweeney 3 —
(B R Johnson) *in tch tl wknd rapidly over 3f out: t.o* **66/1**

2m 34.45s (-0.05) **Going Correction** +0.075s/f (Slow)
WFA 3 from 4yo+ 5lb **9** Ran SP% **116.8**
Speed ratings (Par 105): **103,102,102,99,98 97,90,70,68**
toteswinger: 1&2 £1.50, 1&3 £2.90, 2&3 £2.10. CSF £8.77 CT £25.32 TOTE £3.10: £1.30, £1.40, £1.80; EX 7.00.
Owner Mrs Charles Cyzer **Bred** C A Cyzer **Trained** Woodingdean, E Sussex

FOCUS
A reasonable handicap in which the pace was only fair. The principals raced against the inside rail in the closing stages and the winner looks better than the bare form, which is rated around the third and fourth.
Mutamaasek(USA) Official explanation: jockey said gelding had no more to give

7705 TFM NETWORKS CLASSIFIED STKS 6f (P)
9:20 (9:23) (Class 6) 3-Y-O+ **£2,047** (£604; £302) **Stalls** High

Form RPR

5362 **1** **Whiskey Creek**[51] 7022 3-9-0 53........(b) TGMcLaughlin 7 63
(C A Dwyer) *mde all: 2l clr over 2f out: hrd rdn over 1f out: all out to hold on nr fin* **3/1**[2]

0230 **2** *nk* **Welsh Opera**[14] 7536 3-8-9 55........(t) WilliamCarson[(5)] 10 62
(S C Williams) *prom: chsd wnr 1/2-way: sn rdn: grad clsd fnl f but post c too sn* **5/2**[1]

0503 **3** 2 3/4 **Loyal Royal (IRE)**[15] 7521 5-8-9 52........(b) JackDean[(5)] 2 53+
(J M Bradley) *dwlt: fierce hold and hld up in last: nrly rn into bk of rivals after 2f: hrd rdn over 2f out: kpt on to take 3rd 1f out: nvr nrr* **4/1**[3]

0060 **4** 2 3/4 **Tuning Fork**[126] 4979 8-8-7 43........(e[1]) KierenFox[(7)] 6 44
(M J Attwater) *hld up: outpcd fr 1/2-way: shuffled along and modest prog over 1f out* **20/1**

3060 **5** 3/4 **Woqoodd**[6] 7615 4-9-0 55........ JimCrowley 8 42
(D Shaw) *prom 2f: sn bdly outpcd: plugged on again fnl f* **4/1**[3]

0000 **6** *shd* **Baba Ghanoush**[140] 4529 6-9-0 37........(b[1]) PaulDoe 4 42
(M J Attwater) *hld up: nvr gpoing the pce: lft bhd sn after 1/2-way* **33/1**

6 **7** 3/4 **Newpark Style (IRE)**[5] 7651 3-9-0 41........(t) SteveDrowne 9 39
(Emmanuel Hughes, Ire) *chsd wnr to 1/2-way: sn u.p: wknd fnl f* **8/1**

00 **8** *13* **Fly Time**[50] 7055 4-9-0 35........ DaneO'Neill 3 —
(D Burchell) *racd wd: prom over 2f: sn struggling: t.o* **33/1**

1m 13.29s (0.19) **Going Correction** +0.075s/f (Slow) **8** Ran SP% **115.3**
Speed ratings (Par 101): **101,100,96,93,92 92,91,73**
toteswinger: 1&2 £2.00, 1&3 £3.80, 2&3 £3.70. CSF £10.82 TOTE £3.60: £1.50, £1.60, £1.60; EX 7.20 Place 6: £ 38.50 Place 5: £18.59 .
Owner Mrs L Wheeler **Bred** R J H West **Trained** Burrough Green, Cambs

FOCUS
A low-grade event featuring several unreliable sorts but the form looks reasonable. The pace was sound and the winner hugged the inside rail in the straight, so the form looks reasonable rated around the placed horses.
Loyal Royal(IRE) Official explanation: jockey said gelding ran too free
T/Plt: £52.30 to a £1 stake. Pool: £105,810.00. 1,475.96 winning tickets. T/Qpdt: £12.40 to a £1 stake. Pool: £7,919.68. 469.30 winning tickets. JN

7672 LINGFIELD (L-H)
Wednesday, December 17

OFFICIAL GOING: Standard
Wind: Moderate, against Weather: Sunny

7706 PHOTO FINISH FOR CHRISTMAS GIFTS @ EVENTIMAGE.TV H'CAP (DIV I) 6f (P)
12:00 (12:02) (Class 6) (0-55,55) 3-Y-O+ **£1,706** (£503; £252) **Stalls** Low

Form RPR

1 **Mister Thatcher (IRE)**[19] 7479 4-8-5 **46**........(t) HayleyTurner 9 61+
(Annette McMahon, Ire) *chsd ldrs: led over 1f out: rdn clr: readily* **10/1**

0004 **2** 1 3/4 **Mind Alert**[17] 7508 7-8-12 **53**........(v) JamesDoyle 12 62
(D Shaw) *stdd s and swtchd to ins rail: bhd: gd hdwy over 1f out: r.o up to take 2nd ins fnl f* **17/2**

0000 **3** *1* **Grizedale (IRE)**[23] 7433 9-8-11 **52**........(tp) PaulDoe 10 58
(M J Attwater) *towards rr: rdn and hdwy over 1f out: r.o* **14/1**

5031 **4** ¾ **Shaded Edge**[15] 7521 4-8-13 **54**....(p) MartinDwyer 11 58+
(D W P Arbuthnot) *sn pshd along: bhd and wd: hrd rdn and gd hdwy fr over 1f out: nrst fin* **5/2**[1]

5444 **5** nk **Vanatina (IRE)**[7] 7631 4-8-5 **46** oh1.... LiamJones 5 49
(W M Brisbourne) *in tch: effrt over 2f out: styd on same pce* **11/1**

0052 **6** ¾ **Tamino (IRE)**[17] 7509 5-9-0 **55**....(t) IanMongan 2 55
(P Howling) *pressed ldrs tl wknd fnl f* **5/1**[2]

4060 **7** nk **Evenstorm (USA)**[103] 5684 3-8-10 **51**.... ChrisCatlin 7 50
(B Gubby) *outpcd in rr: wl bhd fr 1/2-way: styd on wl fnl f* **12/1**

0300 **8** 1¾ **Mr Rev**[6] 7636 5-8-7 **51** ow2....(b) KevinGhunowa(3) 8 45
(J M Bradley) *sn rdn along in rr of midfield: nvr a factor* **14/1**

0000 **9** 1½ **Daddy Cool**[18] 7503 4-8-5 **46** oh1....(b[1]) CatherineGannon 3 35
(W G M Turner) *led tl wknd qckly over 1f out* **50/1**

0253 **10** 3¾ **Sarah's Art (IRE)**[10] 7589 5-8-13 **54**.... MickyFenton 4 31
(Stef Liddiard) *held up in midfield: n.m.r on rail from 2f out: hmpd over 1f out: n.d after* **7/1**[3]

-100 **11** 5 **Takaamul**[293] 728 5-8-12 **53**.... PatCosgrave 1 14
(K A Morgan) *chsd ldrs over 3f* **20/1**

5000 **12** 4½ **Hawaii Prince**[79] 6339 4-8-5 **46** oh1.... NickyMackay 6 —
(S T Mason) *pressed ldr tl wknd ins fnl 2f* **50/1**

1m 11.0s (-0.90) **Going Correction** -0.10s/f (Stan) **12** Ran SP% **115.4**
Speed ratings (Par 101): **102,99,98,97,96 95,95,93,91,86 79,73**
toteswinger: 1&2 £15.70, 1&3 £20.30, 2&3 £15.70. CSF £88.40 CT £810.37 TOTE £8.60: £3.30, £3.70, £4.10; EX 62.00 Trifecta £196.10 Part won. Pool: £265.05 - 0.65 winning units..
Owner Mister Thatcher Syndicate **Bred** Miss Annette McMahon **Trained** Crecora, Co Limerick
■ Stewards' Enquiry : Pat Cosgrave one-day ban: careless riding (Dec 31)

FOCUS
A pretty open low-grade handicap but it was run at a decent clip and there was a fair amount to take out of it.
Sarah's Art(IRE) Official explanation: jockey said gelding was hampered in running
Hawaii Prince Official explanation: jockey said gelding lost its action

7707 THE HOLLY AND THE IVY CLAIMING STKS — 1m 2f (P)
12:30 (12:32) (Class 6) 3-Y-O+ **£1,978** (£584; £292) **Stalls** Low

Form RPR

5004 **1** **Rapid City**[12] 7553 5-8-12 65....(p) JamesDoyle 11 70
(A J McCabe) *stdd in rr s: hdwy on outer 5f out: led 2f out and wd on home turn: rdn clr 1f out: styd on wl* **4/1**[3]

2006 **2** 3¼ **Daring Racer (GER)**[55] 6927 5-8-8 54....(p) PaulDoe 9 60
(Mrs L J Mongan) *chsd ldrs: sltly outpcd over 2f out: rallied to chse wnr fnl f: one pce* **25/1**

6032 **3** 1 **Zero Cool (USA)**[12] 7553 4-9-2 77.... GeorgeBaker 13 66
(G L Moore) *in tch: drvn to chse ldrs 2f out: nt qckn fnl f* **2/1**[1]

4000 **4** ¾ **Tenement (IRE)**[19] 7473 4-8-8 45.... FrancisNorton 10 56
(Jamie Poulton) *dropped out towards rr wl off the pce: pshd along 5f out: rdn and r.o wl fr over 1f out: gng on at fin* **25/1**

5111 **5** ¾ **Sabre Light**[12] 7553 3-9-5 77....(p) JerryO'Dwyer 2 69+
(J Pearce) *sn last and wl off the pce: on and off bridle early: c bk onto bridle but nt clr run fr 3f out: swtchd to rail and blocked over 1f out: weaved through: fin wl* **7/2**[2]

0020 **6** nse **Bye Baby Bunting**[2] 7692 3-8-4 50.... HayleyTurner 3 53
(B R Johnson) *towards rr: rdn over 2f out: hdwy over 1f out: no imp fnl f* **16/1**

2000 **7** ½ **Too Grand**[14] 7535 3-8-5 48 ow3....(v) NeilChalmers 8 53
(J J Bridger) *bhd: rdn 4f out: styd on fnl f* **66/1**

0005 **8** 1½ **Red Current**[11] 7585 4-8-7 49 ow1.... KevinGhunowa(3) 7 52
(R A Harris) *chsd ldrs tl hrd rdn and wknd jst over 1f out* **66/1**

1303 **9** shd **Nawamees (IRE)**[12] 7553 10-9-8 75....(p) NCallan 14 64
(P D Evans) *sn rdn up to press ldr: slt ld 8f out tl 5f out: led 3f out tl 2f out: wknd over 1f out* **13/2**

0050 **10** 2¼ **Muffett's Dream**[12] 7553 4-8-3 45.... CatherineGannon 12 41
(J J Bridger) *prom on outer: rdn 5f out: wknd over 3f out* **66/1**

5000 **11** ½ **Gifted Heir (IRE)**[12] 7553 4-8-1 50....(b) NatashaEaton(7) 4 45
(A Bailey) *hld up towards rr: pushed along and n.d fnl 3f* **66/1**

0056 **12** 1¼ **Bombardier Wells**[7] 7620 3-8-7 62....(p) StephenCarson 5 44
(Eve Johnson Houghton) *led 2f: w ldr tl led again 5f out: hdd 3f out: wknd wl over 1f out* **10/1**

0000 **13** ½ **Highly Regal (IRE)**[15] 7520 3-8-5 50....(tp) ChrisCatlin 1 41
(R A Teal) *mid-div: hrd rdn 3f out: sn wknd* **66/1**

2m 4.61s (-1.99) **Going Correction** -0.10s/f (Stan)
WFA 3 from 4yo+ 3lb **13** Ran SP% **119.0**
Speed ratings (Par 101): **103,100,99,99,98 98,97,96,96,94 94,93,93**
toteswinger: 1&2 £24.90, 1&3 £3.30, 2&3 £21.70. CSF £104.70 TOTE £5.40: £1.70, £7.20, £1.40; EX 152.00 TRIFECTA Not won..
Owner Mrs M J McCabe **Bred** Juddmonte Farms Ltd **Trained** Babworth, Notts

FOCUS
Just run-of-the-mill claiming form.
Sabre Light ◆ Official explanation: jockey said, regarding running and riding, that his orders were to sit-mid-division, get the gelding to travel and make the best way home, stating that he had to ride the gelding to get to start, adding it was struggling to lay up and kept niggling, it was short of room, with weakening horses, turn into straight and did his best to get into a gap when it opened up; trainer confirmed but he was disappointed with the gelding's performance.
Muffett's Dream Official explanation: jockey said filly hung right

7708 EUROPEAN BREEDERS' FUND MAIDEN FILLIES' STKS — 7f (P)
1:00 (1:02) (Class 5) 2-Y-O **£3,561** (£1,059; £529; £264) **Stalls** Low

Form RPR

02 **1** **Luckier (IRE)**[11] 7577 2-9-0 0.... GeorgeBaker 1 73
(S Kirk) *chsd ldrs: rdn to ld 1f out: sn in command* **6/1**[3]

45 **2** 2¾ **Leelu**[38] 7259 2-9-0 0.... MartinDwyer 2 66
(D W P Arbuthnot) *led: hrd rdn and hdd 1f out: nt qckn* **8/1**

3 nk **Misyaar (IRE)** 2-9-0 0.... ShaneKelly 5 65+
(M A Jarvis) *in tch: rdn to chse ldrs 2f out: kpt on same pce* **15/2**

54 **4** 1 **Princess Cagliari**[30] 7356 2-9-0 0.... PatDobbs 8 63
(R Hannon) *prom: rdn over 2f out: one pce appr fnl f* **7/1**

5 1¼ **Kamanja (UAE)** 2-9-0 0.... NCallan 10 60+
(M A Jarvis) *chsd ldrs: wd and sltly outpcd 2f out: kpt on fnl f* **7/2**[1]

6 ½ **Princess Zohra** 2-9-0 0.... TGMcLaughlin 7 59
(E A L Dunlop) *hld up in midfield on outer: rdn 3f out: styd on fnl f* **16/1**

40 **7** 1¼ **Port De La Ponche**[11] 7577 2-9-0 0.... NelsonDeSouza 6 55+
(P F I Cole) *anticipated s and hit gate: sn towards rr: hrd rdn 2f out: nvr able to chal* **20/1**

0 **8** nse **Set Em Up Mo**[19] 7465 2-9-0 0.... PaulDoe 9 55
(M J Attwater) *pressed ldr: rdn over 3f out: wknd over 1f out* **100/1**

9 nk **Tuppenny's Jeanie** 2-9-0 0.... DarryllHolland 13 55
(Rae Guest) *bhd: shkn up 3f out: styd on fnl f* **8/1**

10 hd **Mytivil (IRE)** 2-8-7 0.... RossAtkinson(7) 4 54
(Tom Dascombe) *s.s: bhd: early reminders and rn green: sme late hdwy* **33/1**

5 **11** shd **One Cool Mission (IRE)**[13] 7546 2-9-0 0.... RichardKingscote 14 54
(Tom Dascombe) *prom: rdn over 2f out: wknd over 1f out* **5/1**[2]

12 2¼ **First Spirit** 2-9-0 0.... LPKeniry 12 48
(J S Moore) *sn rdn in rr: nvr a factor* **80/1**

13 12 **Bonnie Bea** 2-9-0 0.... JerryO'Dwyer 11 18
(B I Case) *sn drvn along and bhd: no ch fnl 3f* **80/1**

1m 25.03s (0.23) **Going Correction** -0.10s/f (Stan) **13** Ran SP% **116.7**
Speed ratings (Par 93): **94,90,90,89,87 87,85,85,85,85 85,82,68**
toteswinger: 1&2 £9.80, 1&3 £6.30, 2&3 £18.10. CSF £50.39 TOTE £4.30: £2.00, £3.50, £3.40; EX 40.20 Trifecta £205.90 Pool: £375.65 - 1.35 winning units..
Owner The Hon Mrs J M Corbett & C Wright **Bred** Swordlestown Stud **Trained** Upper Lambourn, Berks

FOCUS
A weak fillies' maiden.

NOTEBOOK
Luckier(IRE) bagged a good early pitch from her low stalls position and she was always travelling best. She has improved with each start so far and picked up nicely once asked to go about her business entering the final furlong and won in comfortable fashion, although this wasn't the strongest of races. That said, she is clearly going the right way and she should progress again back up in trip. (op 7-2)
Leelu made a bold bid from the front and she plugged on well enough to hold on for second and she put behind her a slightly disappointing effort at Kempton last time. (tchd 9-1)
Misyaar(IRE) was the seemingly less fancied of Michael Jarvis's two newcomers but she fared the better, staying on well despite having looked as though she'd come on a good deal for the run. She looks capable of building on this and winning races. (op 8-1)
Princess Cagliari once again ran well in defeat and is now qualified for a mark. (op 8-1)
Kamanja(UAE) didn't have the best of trips out wide and stayed on well down the middle once she found her stride, so she too looks capable of building on this. (op 9-2 tchd 11-2)
Princess Zohra was doing all of her best work in the closing stages and she'll be seen to better effect over 1m-plus in time. (op 25-1)

7709 EUROPEAN BREEDERS' FUND MAIDEN STKS — 7f (P)
1:35 (1:38) (Class 5) 2-Y-O **£3,561** (£1,059; £529; £264) **Stalls** Low

Form RPR

2 **1** **Pezula Bay**[33] 7311 2-9-0.... ShaneKelly 10 79+
(J Noseda) *hld up in rr of midfield: gd hdwy under restraint appr fnl f: led on bit fnl 30yds: cheekily: jst prevailed* **4/9**[1]

6 **2** hd **Dimander (IRE)**[19] 7465 2-9-0.... JimCrowley 6 69+
(Mrs A J Perrett) *towards rr: drvn and hdwy on ins ent st: r.o wl to dispute ld nr fin: jst pipped* **11/1**[3]

063 **3** nk **Rebel City**[19] 7465 2-9-0 70.... HayleyTurner 12 68+
(S A Callaghan) *bhd: rdn and gd hdwy over 1f out: str run fnl f: fin wl* **5/1**[2]

65 **4** ½ **It's A Mans World**[51] 7023 2-9-0.... DaneO'Neill 9 67
(P J McBride) *prom: led 3f out: rdn over 2 l clr 2f out: hrd pressed fnl f: hdd fnl 30yds* **20/1**

6 **5** 1¼ **Wellesley**[18] 7498 2-9-0.... AdamKirby 7 64
(W R Swinburn) *chsd ldrs: effrt 2f out: one pce fnl f* **14/1**

6 ½ **Sky High Kid (IRE)** 2-9-0.... EdwardCreighton 1 62
(M R Channon) *chsd ldrs: rdn 2f out: hung lft and briefly wnt 2nd 1f out: no ex ins fnl f* **33/1**

7 2 **Symonette** 2-9-0.... GregFairley 4 57
(M Johnston) *w ldrs over 4f: wknd over 1f out* **12/1**

8 1¾ **Tropical Bachelor (IRE)** 2-9-0.... MartinDwyer 2 53
(D W P Arbuthnot) *s.s: outpcd and bhd: nvr trbld ldrs* **66/1**

9 hd **Sounds Of Jupiter (IRE)** 2-9-0.... LPKeniry 5 53
(E F Vaughan) *a towards rr: rdn and n.d fnl 2f* **33/1**

10 9 **Foxtrot Bravo (IRE)** 2-9-0.... StephenCarson 3 30+
(P Winkworth) *slt ld 4f: wknd qckly over 2f out* **50/1**

1m 25.13s (0.33) **Going Correction** -0.10s/f (Stan) **10** Ran SP% **122.7**
Speed ratings (Par 96): **94,93,93,92,91 90,88,86,86,76**
toteswinger: 1&2 £4.00, 1&3 £2.10, 2&3 £9.90. CSF £6.92 TOTE £1.40: £1.02, £2.50, £2.20; EX 7.30 Trifecta £53.60 Pool: £646.20 - 8.91 winning units..
Owner G Lansbury **Bred** Lordship Stud **Trained** Newmarket, Suffolk

FOCUS
Not a strong maiden even for the time of year.

NOTEBOOK
Pezula Bay was in a different league, despite the narrow margin of victory. Shane Kelly was still sitting motionless on the Oasis Dream colt over a furlong out, despite having some three to four lengths to make up, but his mount cruised to dispute the lead and his rider was still keen to not ask his mount for any serious effort. As Dimander and Rebel City both finished like trains either side, it could have become very embarrassing for Kelly but his mount prevailed by a head. Despite the margin of victory, the handicapper isn't easily fooled and his superiority was there for all to see, even so, he is clearly a colt with potential and it will be interesting to see what kind of race connections go for next, although they indicated afterwards that he'd probably be put away now. (op 8-13 tchd 4-6 and 8-11 in places)
Dimander(IRE) stepped up markedly on his debut, when he blew the start over 6f. Bred to be better suited by this trip, he was towards the back early but once switched to the inside in the straight, he picked up with real momentum and finished fast. He looks to be learning very quickly and is of obvious interest in similar company next time. (op 10-1 tchd 12-1)
Rebel City was dropped out from his wide draw and had plenty to do turning for home but he picked up strongly down the middle and was doing all his best work in the final furlong. He is now qualified for a mark but he's already shown more than enough to suggest he can get off the mark in maiden company. (op 7-2)
It's A Mans World kicked a couple of lengths clear turning for home and stayed on well, only to be collared in the final strides. He was the only one to feature in the finish who raced close to the pace, especially as he raced quite wide for much of the way. He's of interest now eligible for nurseries, especially if stepped back up to 1m. (tchd 14-1)
Foxtrot Bravo(IRE) Official explanation: jockey said gelding hung badly right

7710 PHOTO FINISH FOR CHRISTMAS GIFTS @ EVENTIMAGE.TV H'CAP (DIV II) — 6f (P)
2:10 (2:11) (Class 6) (0-55,55) 3-Y-O+ **£1,706** (£503; £252) **Stalls** Low

Form RPR

0231 **1** **Fantasy Fighter (IRE)**[6] 7636 3-8-7 **48**.... LPKeniry 7 57
(J J Quinn) *t.k.h in midfield: hdwy 2f out: hung lft and chsd ldr over 1f out: flashed tail: styd on to ld nr fin* **6/4**[1]

3002 **2** ½ **Bollin Franny**[15] 7521 4-8-10 **51**.... RichardThomas 10 58
(J E Long) *chsd ldr: led wl over 1f out: hrd rdn and kpt on fnl f: hdd nr fin* **3/1**[2]

0306 **3** 2 **Willhewiz**[17] 7509 8-8-11 **52**....(v) TGMcLaughlin 8 53
(W M Brisbourne) *towards rr: rdn and hdwy over 1f out: styd on fnl f* **16/1**

0000 **4** shd **One Way Ticket**[6] 7637 8-8-5 **46** oh1....(p) HayleyTurner 2 46
(J M Bradley) *chsd ldrs: rdn 2f out: kpt on same pce* **25/1**

0203 5 ¾ **Green Velvet**[57] 6878 3-8-13 **54**........................ NCallan 12 52
(P J Makin) *awkward s: towards rr: rdn 3f out: styd on fr over 1f out: nt rch ldrs* **20/1**

500 6 1 ¼ **Rightcar Lewis**[18] 7503 3-8-1 **49**....................(b[1]) AndrewHeffernan[(7)] 5 43
(Peter Grayson) *chsd ldrs tl hrd rdn and wknd over 1f out* **25/1**

0000 7 nse **Desert Light (IRE)**[35] 7288 7-8-5 **46** oh1....................(v) FrancisNorton 4 44+
(D Shaw) *hld up in rr: promising hdwy over 1f out: nt clr run ent fnl f: unable to chal* **18/1**

0646 8 hd **Night Prospector**[8] 7618 8-8-11 **55**....................(b) KevinGhunowa[(3)] 6 48
(R A Harris) *led tl wl over 1f out: sn hrd rdn and wknd* **11/1**

0403 9 1 ¾ **Charmel's Lad**[28] 7383 3-8-12 **53**....................(t) AdamKirby 11 40
(W R Swinburn) *in tch on outer: rdn and wknd 2f out* **9/1**[3]

0000 10 hd **Ishibee (IRE)**[115] 5315 4-8-5 **46** oh1....................(p) NeilChalmers 3 33
(J J Bridger) *mid-div: effrt on rail 2f out: wknd over 1f out* **20/1**

0000 11 nk **Flying Free**[14] 7536 3-8-5 **46** oh1.................... ChrisCatlin 9 32
(J Ryan) *stdd s: t.k.h early: hld up in rr: rdn and n.d fnl 2f* **66/1**

0310 12 1 **Kindallachan**[17] 7509 5-8-13 **54**....................(p) MichaelHills 1 37
(G C Bravery) *sn rdn along in rr: nvr trbld ldrs* **12/1**

1m 11.43s (-0.47) **Going Correction** -0.10s/f (Stan) 12 Ran SP% **120.9**
Speed ratings (Par 101): **99,98,95,95,94 92,92,92,90,89 89,88**
toteswinger: 1&2 £2.20, 1&3 £3.30, 2&3 £17.10. CSF £5.26 CT £52.57 TOTE £2.70: £1.10, £1.70, £5.00; EX 7.50 Trifecta £104.50 Pool: £450.67 - 3.19 winning units..
Owner The Fantasy Fellowship F **Bred** T C Clarke **Trained** Settrington, N Yorks

FOCUS
Not as strong as the first division and a slower time backs that up.

7711 ROBINSON JACKSON H'CAP 1m 4f (P)
2:45 (2:45) (Class 5) (0-75,75) 3-Y-O+ **£2,729** (£806; £403) **Stalls** Low

Form RPR

0242 1 **Valdan (IRE)**[7] 7620 4-8-11 **63**.................... StephenDonohoe 7 71
(P D Evans) *t.k.h towards rr: gd hdwy over 1f out: led ins fnl f: drvn out* **8/1**

1112 2 1 **Epsom Salts**[9] 7604 3-8-6 **63**.................... JamesDoyle 14 69+
(P M Phelan) *bhd: effrt on outer 3f out: hdwy over 1f out: pressed wnr ins fnl f: r.o* **7/4**[1]

2-10 3 1 ¼ **Long Distance (FR)**[29] 6012 3-9-1 **72**.................... RobertWinston 9 76
(J R Fanshawe) *t.k.h: sn prom on outer: rdn 2f out: one pce fnl f* **10/1**

6601 4 ½ **Garrulous (UAE)**[49] 7064 5-9-1 **67**.................... GeorgeBaker 13 70
(G L Moore) *stdd s: bhd: rdn and r.o fnl 2f: nrst fin* **15/2**[3]

13-5 5 nk **Sunset Boulevard (IRE)**[229] 1768 5-8-11 **63**.................... ChrisCatlin 3 66
(Miss Tor Sturgis) *prom: pressed ldr over 2f out: no ex fnl f* **20/1**

4001 6 nk **Wind Flow**[19] 7473 4-9-2 **68**....................(b) CatherineGannon 10 71
(C A Dwyer) *sn led: rdn 3f out: hdd & wknd ins fnl f* **14/1**

2640 7 1 **King Supreme (IRE)**[33] 7314 3-9-4 **75**....................(b) PatDobbs 8 76
(R Hannon) *mid-div: effrt 2f out: no imp* **11/1**

606 8 ¾ **Resplendent Ace (IRE)**[20] 7462 4-9-4 **70**.................... IanMongan 6 70
(P Howling) *bhd: effrt and swtchd outside over 1f out: r.o* **12/1**

2002 9 1 **Vinces**[13] 7545 4-8-10 **62**.................... HayleyTurner 1 60
(T D McCarthy) *prom tl wknd over 1f out* **12/1**

0043 10 nk **William's Way**[12] 7563 6-9-0 **66**.................... NCallan 4 64
(I A Wood) *chsd ldrs tl wknd over 1f out* **13/2**[2]

0-10 11 hd **Ardmaddy (IRE)**[196] 2715 4-8-7 **59** oh1.................... FergusSweeney 12 56
(G L Moore) *t.k.h: stdd in tch: outpcd 2f out: sn btn* **33/1**

6666 12 1 ¼ **Paint The Town Red**[49] 7070 3-9-1 **72**.................... DarryllHolland 5 67
(H J Collingridge) *towards rr: rdn over 2f out: n.d* **10/1**

5534 13 1 ¼ **Rising Force (IRE)**[20] 7461 5-8-11 **63**....................(b) LiamJones 2 56
(J L Spearing) *mid-div: rdn over 2f out: wknd over 1f out* **16/1**

2m 31.58s (-1.42) **Going Correction** -0.10s/f (Stan)
WFA 3 from 4yo+ 5lb 13 Ran SP% **134.7**
Speed ratings (Par 103): **100,99,98,98,97 97,97,96,95,95 95,94,93**
toteswinger: 1&2 £7.20, 1&3 £19.40, 2&3 £10.60. CSF £25.17 CT £161.67 TOTE £11.20: £3.00, £1.60, £4.00; EX 37.60 Trifecta £293.30 Part won. Pool: £393.37 - 0.45 winning units..
Owner D Maloney **Bred** Herbertstown Stud Ltd **Trained** Pandy, Monmouths

FOCUS
An even gallop set by Wind Flow set this up for horses held up off the pace.

7712 SEASONS GREETINGS H'CAP 1m 2f (P)
3:15 (3:17) (Class 4) (0-80,80) 3-Y-O+ **£4,727** (£1,406; £702; £351) **Stalls** Low

Form RPR

23-4 1 **Bullet Man (USA)**[27] 7395 3-8-11 **75**.................... DaneO'Neill 8 87+
(L M Cumani) *s.s: sn settled in midfield: effrt and carried wd ent st: led ins fnl f: fnd ex whn chal: readily* **8/1**[3]

2035 2 1 ¾ **Hold The Gold (IRE)**[15] 7526 3-8-11 **75**.................... ChrisCatlin 1 83
(E J O'Neill) *hld up towards rr: rdn and gd hdwy over 1f out: weaved through to press wnr ins fnl f: outpcd and hld fnl 50yds* **8/1**[3]

1021 3 1 ¼ **Action Impact (ARG)**[20] 7462 4-9-0 **75**.................... GeorgeBaker 10 81
(G L Moore) *sn stdd in rr: rdn over 2f out: gd late hdwy* **7/4**[1]

0000 4 1 ¼ **Halsion Chancer**[19] 7477 4-9-5 **80**.................... HayleyTurner 11 83
(J R Best) *led after 1f: hdd & wknd ins fnl f* **16/1**

-R1 5 1 ¾ **L'Hirondelle (IRE)**[17] 7504 4-9-4 **79**.................... PaulDoe 6 79
(M J Attwater) *prom: hung rt bnd into st: sn wknd* **14/1**

5515 6 1 ¼ **Remember Ramon (USA)**[20] 7462 5-9-3 **78**.................... SteveDrowne 7 75
(J R Gask) *t.k.h in midfield: rdn and dropped to rr 4f out: sme late hdwy* **16/1**

1000 7 nk **Bee Stinger**[12] 7564 6-9-5 **80**....................(v) CatherineGannon 2 76
(I A Wood) *chsd ldrs: rdn 3f out: wknd over 1f out* **40/1**

3300 8 nk **Cactus King**[141] 4509 5-9-4 **79**.................... IanMongan 9 75
(P M Phelan) *towards rr: hdwy over 2f out: wknd over 1f out* **20/1**

0054 9 3 ¼ **Twilight Star (IRE)**[15] 7525 4-9-0 **75**.................... DarryllHolland 4 63
(R A Teal) *hld up and bhd: rdn 2f out: nvr nr ldrs* **20/1**

3211 10 2 ¾ **Vine Street (IRE)**[6] 7642 3-8-12 **76** 6ex.................... NCallan 3 59+
(M A Jarvis) *led 1f: prom tl wknd and eased over 1f out* **5/2**[2]

11 3 **Munich (IRE)**[78] 6371 4-9-3 **78**.................... JimCrowley 5 55
(L Wells) *in tch: wknd over 3f out: sn bhd* **40/1**

1543 12 6 **Mcconnell (USA)**[146] 4335 3-9-2 **80**.................... FergusSweeney 12 45
(G L Moore) *dwlt: sn chsng ldrs: hrd rdn 3f out: sn wknd* **33/1**

2m 3.69s (-2.91) **Going Correction** -0.10s/f (Stan)
WFA 3 from 4yo+ 3lb 12 Ran SP% **122.9**
Speed ratings (Par 105): **107,105,104,103,102 101,100,100,97,95 93,88**
toteswinger: 1&2 £5.90, 1&3 £4.70, 2&3 £5.20. CSF £68.57 CT £164.83 TOTE £8.50: £1.60, £2.70, £1.30; EX 67.90 Trifecta £91.90 Pool: £758.35 - 6.10 winning units. Place 6 £60.06, Place 5 £8.47..
Owner Kevin Bailey & Ms Nicola Mahoney **Bred** Stillmeadow Farm Llc **Trained** Newmarket, Suffolk

FOCUS
A fair handicap run at a strong pace.
Twilight Star(IRE) Official explanation: jockey said gelding ran too free
Vine Street(IRE) Official explanation: trainer said, regarding running, that the filly was unable to dominate
T/Plt: £53.10 to a £1 stake. Pool: £42,331.11. 581.88 winning tickets. T/Qpdt: £3.60 to a £1 stake. Pool: £4,914.30. 992.20 winning tickets. LM

7636 GREAT LEIGHS (A.W) (L-H)
Thursday, December 18

OFFICIAL GOING: Standard
Wind: medium, behind Weather: dry

7713 STUBBS MEDIAN AUCTION MAIDEN STKS 1m 5f 66y(P)
6:50 (6:50) (Class 5) 3-5-Y-O **£2,590** (£770; £385; £192) **Stalls** Low

Form RPR

1 **Anfield Road**[33] 6348 3-9-3 70.................... TPQueally 8 74+
(L Corcoran) *hld up in midfield: hdwy over 5f out: swtchd lft over 5f out: trckd ldr 2f out: led on bit 1f out: v easily* **11/8**[1]

003 2 2 ½ **Sensible**[21] 7463 3-8-12 60.................... DarryllHolland 12 61
(H J Collingridge) *chsd ldrs: wnt 2nd over 4f out: rdn to ld 2f out: hdd 1f out: no ch w wnr* **9/2**[3]

06-3 3 6 **Bring It On Home**[13] 7379 4-9-9 58....................(b) GeorgeBaker 10 57
(G L Moore) *hld up in midfield: reminder after 5f: hdwy over 5f out: chsd ldrs and rdn wl over 2f out: wnt modest 3rd ent fnl f: no ch w ldrs* **7/2**[2]

4 4 **Flowerbud** 3-8-12 0.................... JamesDoyle 5 46
(Ms J S Doyle) *s.i.s: towards rr: hdwy over 3f out: plugged on to go modest 4th 1f out: nvr trbld ldrs* **66/1**

6060 5 2 ½ **Bonzo**[29] 7379 3-9-3 50.................... TGMcLaughlin 7 47
(P Howling) *slowly away: bhd: hdwy and rdn over 3f out: plugged on but nvr nr ldrs* **66/1**

0335 6 4 **Coco L'Escargot**[29] 7379 4-9-4 51....................(v) NickyMackay 4 36
(J R Jenkins) *t.k.h: hld up in tch: rdn over 3f out: outpcd over 2f out: no ch w ldrs after* **25/1**

5 7 1 **A Valley Away (IRE)**[19] 7489 4-9-4 0.................... JohnEgan 9 35
(Jane Chapple-Hyam) *led for 1f: chsd ldr tl led after 4f: rdn and hdd jst over 2f out: wknd qckly over 1f out* **16/1**

605- 8 4 **Evette**[403] 6775 3-8-12 45.................... HayleyTurner 3 29
(H J Collingridge) *stdd s: hld up in rr: nvr nr ldrs* **25/1**

9 4 **My Mate Granite (USA)** 4-9-9 0.................... JerryO'Dwyer 11 28
(M Wigham) *a towards rr: pushed along briefly over 7f out: rdn over 4f out: lost tch 3f out* **50/1**

34-0 10 4 ½ **Bite The Boss**[8] 7632 3-9-3 67.................... ChrisCatlin 6 21
(E J O'Neill) *sn pushed along: a towards rr: rdn and struggling 4f out* **9/1**

0 11 5 **Classic Dancer**[20] 7474 3-8-12 0.................... PatCosgrave 1 9
(Jane Chapple-Hyam) *chsd ldrs: reminder over 6f out: wkng whn hmpd over 5f out: sn wl bhd* **100/1**

4206 12 2 ¼ **Smetana**[125] 5077 3-8-10 50.................... SPRyan[(7)] 2 10
(E J Creighton) *chsd ldr tl led after 1f to 4f: chsd ldr after tl over 4f out: rdn and wknd qckly over 3f out* **14/1**

2m 54.39s (0.79) **Going Correction** +0.05s/f (Slow)
WFA 3 from 4yo 6lb 12 Ran SP% **118.7**
Speed ratings (Par 103): **99,97,93,91,89 87,86,84,81,79 75,74**
toteswinger: 1&2 £4.50, 1&3 £2.90, 2&3 £1.10. CSF £7.23 TOTE £2.80: £2.00, £1.20, £1.90; EX 12.40.
Owner The A T P Racing Partnership **Bred** Mountgrange Stud Ltd **Trained** Kingsbridge, Devon

FOCUS
A modest maiden and the winner justified his official rating but there are doubts about the placed horses.

7714 WEATHERBYS BANK NOVICE STKS 6f (P)
7:20 (7:20) (Class 4) 2-Y-O **£4,533** (£1,348; £674; £336) **Stalls** Low

Form RPR

2321 1 **Noverre To Go (IRE)**[13] 7555 2-9-2 89....................(t) RichardKingscote 4 76+
(Tom Dascombe) *t.k.h: trckd ldr: rdn jst over 2f out: ev ch over 1f out: hrd drvn to ld wl ins fnl f: r.o wl* **4/5**[1]

0051 2 nk **Newlyn Art**[14] 7542 2-9-0 72.................... HayleyTurner 1 73+
(D R C Elsworth) *disp 2nd: rdn jst over 2f out: hrd drvn and ev ch over 1f out: kpt on same pce fnl 100yds* **4/1**[3]

010 3 ¾ **Lesley's Choice**[82] 6274 2-9-9 77.................... DarryllHolland 2 80
(R Curtis) *led: rdn and qcknd over 2f out: hrd pressed ent fnl f: hdd wl ins fnl f: wknd towards fin* **25/1**

5102 4 1 ¼ **Moscow Eight (IRE)**[12] 7575 2-9-0 83.................... ChrisCatlin 3 67
(E J O'Neill) *stdd after s: hld up in last pl: rdn over 2f out: kpt on same pce u.p fr over 1f out* **11/4**[2]

1m 14.12s (0.42) **Going Correction** +0.05s/f (Slow) 4 Ran SP% **106.1**
Speed ratings (Par 98): **99,98,97,95**
CSF £4.13 TOTE £1.70; EX 6.40.
Owner John Duddy **Bred** Gestut Gorlsdorf **Trained** Lambourn, Berks

FOCUS
This novice event developed into a tactical dash from over 2f out and the first two remain capable of better.

NOTEBOOK
Noverre To Go(IRE) was good enough to win this with a bit in hand. Best in on the ratings by at least 6lb, he can still be a touch keen and was momentarily caught for pace. His rider resisted the temptation of going for everything inside the last furlong but ultimately won a shade cosily. He ran third over 7f at Goodwood in October and now he is settling, he looks capable of tackling the longer distances that his pedigree suggest. Connections now plan to rest him and will bring him back on turf, possibly over 1m. (op 10-11 tchd Evens, 11-10 in a place)
Newlyn Art comes out of this with plenty of credit. Winner of a handicap here off a mark of 62 two weeks ago, he was meeting the winner on 15lb worse terms than in a handicap but went down fighting. While certainly on the upgrade, the Handicapper may make things difficult. (op 10-3)
Lesley's Choice was given a fine ride from the front and despite hanging to the right after a couple of furlongs was driven into a decisive lead over 2f out which swung the advantage his way. He wasn't overhauled until inside the last, and having done all his best running at 5f, it may be that he is best over the minimum trip. (tchd 16-1)
Moscow Eight(IRE) was keen early and when the pace quickened he was always going to be struggling from that position. He has also done his best running over 5f. (tchd 9-4)

7715 WEATHERBYS PRINTING H'CAP 1m 6f (P)
7:50 (7:51) (Class 5) (0-75,75) 3-Y-O+ **£3,238** (£963; £481; £240) **Stalls** Low

Form RPR

4344 1 **Dayia (IRE)**[17] 7515 4-9-11 72.................... JerryO'Dwyer 3 83
(J Pearce) *trckd ldrs: rdn and effrt towards inner wl over 1f out: led 1f out: styd on wl* **6/1**[3]

3 **2** ¾ **Special Pearl (IRE)**[7] 7642 4-9-2 **63** ChrisCatlin 6 72
(E J O'Neill) *chsd ldr: rdn and ev ch over 2f out: kpt on same pce u.p ins fnl f* **9/2**[2]

5623 **3** 1¾ **Baan (USA)**[7] 7639 5-9-3 **64** JohnEgan 8 71
(H J Collingridge) *chsd ldrs: effrt and rdn over 2f out: kpt on same pce fnl f* **6/1**[3]

112 **4** nk **Weybridge Light**[7] 7639 3-9-0 **68** (b) DaneO'Neill 4 75
(Eoin Griffin, Ire) *led jnd and drvn over 2f out: hdd 1f out: no ex u.p fnl f* **2/1**[1]

5424 **5** 1½ **Potentiale (IRE)**[13] 7563 4-9-9 **70** MichaelHills 2 74
(J W Hills) *hld up wl in tch: drvn and effrt wl over 1f out: kpt on same pce fnl f* **11/1**

0-12 **6** hd **Little Carmela**[13] 7563 4-8-13 **65** WilliamCarson(5) 7 69
(S C Williams) *s.i.s: hld up towards rr: hdwy on outer over 5f out: chsd ldrs and rdn over 2f out: wknd ent fnl f* **8/1**

1333 **7** 1¼ **Graylyn Ruby (FR)**[15] 7539 3-9-4 **75** LukeMorris(3) 11 77+
(J Jay) *hld up towards rr: shuffled bk and dropped to last 4f out: drvn 3f out: plugged on fnl f but nvr pce to threaten ldrs* **7/1**

5420 **8** 1½ **Top Tiger**[14] 7545 4-9-0 **61** PaulMulrennan 9 61
(M H Tompkins) *stdd and dropped in bhd after s: effrt on inner 2f out: nvr trbld ldrs* **28/1**

2144 **9** 2¾ **Faith And Reason (USA)**[106] 4371 5-10-0 **75** TPQueally 10 72
(A P Stringer) *hld up in midfield: rdn and effrt 3f out: c wd st: no prog over 1f out* **20/1**

3335 **10** 7 **Fourth Dimension (IRE)**[111] 5465 9-9-5 **66** GeorgeBaker 1 53
(Miss T Spearing) *stdd s: hld up in rr: hdwy over 3f out: rdn and c wd st: wknd over 1f out: eased ins fnl f* **25/1**

6200 **P** **War Anthem**[21] 7462 4-9-8 **69** (b) PatCosgrave 5 —
(J R Boyle) *hld up in tch in midfield: rdn over 2f out: struggling whn lost action 2f out: sn p.u* **50/1**

3m 5.19s (1.99) **Going Correction** +0.05s/f (Slow)
WFA 3 from 4yo+ 7lb **11** Ran SP% **126.0**
Speed ratings (Par 103): **96,95,94,94,93 93,92,91,90,86** —
toteswinger: 1&2 £9.50, 1&3 £9.60, 2&3 £8.60. CSF £34.39 CT £177.28 TOTE £7.90: £2.40, £2.00, £2.20; EX 45.50.
Owner Lady Green **Bred** Shadwell Estate Company Limited **Trained** Newmarket, Suffolk

FOCUS
A fair staying handicap, the form looks pretty sound and the winner should do better.
Top Tiger Official explanation: jockey said gelding ran too keen

7716 WEATHERBYS BLOODSTOCK INSURANCE H'CAP 5f (P)
8:20 (8:27) (Class 2) (0-100,102) 3-Y-O+ **£11,656** (£3,468; £1,733; £865) **Stalls** Low

Form RPR

021 **1** **The Game**[11] 7592 3-8-6 **88** 6ex RichardKingscote 6 97
(Tom Dascombe) *chsd ldr: ev ch wl over 1f out: led wl ins fnl f: hld on gamely* **5/2**[1]

3432 **2** nk **Matsunosuke**[9] 7614 6-8-8 **90** DarryllHolland 2 98
(A B Coogan) *hld up in tch: rdn over 1f out: swtchd rt 1f out: r.o wl fnl 100yds: nt quite get to wnr* **5/2**[1]

2310 **3** nk **Harry Up**[12] 7584 7-8-4 **86** oh1 (p) ChrisCatlin 3 93
(K A Ryan) *led: hrd pressed and rdn over 1f out: hdd and no ex wl ins fnl f* **14/1**

4405 **4** ½ **Ebraam (USA)**[11] 7594 5-8-12 **97** TolleyDean(3) 1 102
(P Howling) *chsd ldrs: rdn and effrt 2f out: ev ch 1f out tl no ex fnl 50yds* **6/1**[3]

2211 **5** 3¾ **Doubtful Sound (USA)**[12] 7584 4-8-6 **88** (p) HayleyTurner 7 80
(R Hollinshead) *chsd ldrs: rdn 2f out: drvn and wknd ent fnl f* **7/2**[2]

0316 **6** ½ **Fyodor (IRE)**[12] 7576 7-9-6 **102** (v) DaneO'Neill 4 92
(C R Dore) *t.k.h: hld up in rr: rdn and effrt wl over 1f out: no hdwy over 1f out: wl hld fnl f* **8/1**

3215 **7** 1½ **First Order**[5] 7671 7-8-3 **87** 6ex ow4 (v) AnnStokell(5) 5 75
(Miss A Stokell) *hld up in tch: c wd st: rdn over 1f out: wknd ent fnl f* **16/1**

58.80 secs (-1.40) **Going Correction** +0.05s/f (Slow) **7** Ran SP% **117.3**
Speed ratings (Par 109): **113,112,112,111,105 104,102**
toteswinger: 1&2 £1.10, 1&3 £34.30, 2&3 £5.80. CSF £9.28 TOTE £3.50: £3.00, £2.00; EX 12.20.
Owner M Khan X2 **Bred** Aston House Stud **Trained** Lambourn, Berks

FOCUS
A very fast pace which resulted in a new track record by 0.45sec. The form looks solid rated around the placed horses.

NOTEBOOK
The Game was suited by the fast pace having done all his winning over 6f. He was able to sit up with the leaders which proved a big advantage, and despite racing off a 6lb higher mark that when winning at Lingfield on December 7th was always going to last home. (op 2-1 tchd 11-4, 3-1 in places)
Matsunosuke is frustrating and needs things to fall right if he is going to win. He tried to come from just off the pace which was going to be difficult despite racing off a 1lb lower mark than when last successful over this trip at Lingfield in October 2007. He was never quite going to get there despite finishing well enough. (op 9-2 tchd 5-1 in places)
Harry Up tried to make all and was only collared near the finish, but the Handicapper knows exactly what he is capable of. (op 12-1)
Ebraam(USA) got himself into the action from the home turn but was dropping back from two runs over 7f. He was never going to live with these in-form sprinters off a mark that is still 4lb higher than when last successful in February. (op 11-2)
Doubtful Sound(USA) recovered from a nudge at the start to race up with the pace, but the 9lb rise for her last win found her out. (op 9-2 tchd 10-3)

7717 WEATHERBYSSHOP.CO.UK H'CAP 1m 5f 66y(P)
8:50 (8:50) (Class 3) (0-95,99) 3-Y-O+
£7,477 (£2,239; £1,119; £560; £279; £140) **Stalls** Low

Form RPR

0351 **1** **Grande Caiman (IRE)**[11] 7595 4-10-0 **99** 6ex (b) DaneO'Neill 6 107
(R Hannon) *chsd ldr tl led 4f out: hung lft u.p over 1f out: styd on wl fnl f* **11/4**[2]

1000 **2** ½ **Celtic Spirit (IRE)**[19] 7491 5-9-7 **92** GeorgeBaker 1 99
(G L Moore) *trckd ldrs: wnt 2nd 4f out: plld out and rdn wl over 1f out: unable qck u.p fnl f* **13/8**[1]

0215 **3** 3½ **Bentley Brook (IRE)**[219] 2076 6-8-7 **83** GabrielHannon(5) 3 85
(R Curtis) *chsd ldrs: wnt 3rd 4f out: rdn and unable qck jst over 1f out: one pce fnl f* **16/1**

4P3 **4** 8 **King's Head (IRE)**[11] 7595 5-9-8 **93** (p) FergusSweeney 4 83
(G L Moore) *stdd s: hld up in last pl: pushed along 7f out: rdn and wknd wl over 2f out* **6/1**

3542 **5** 3¼ **Slip**[11] 7595 3-8-8 **85** (b[1]) RichardKingscote 7 70
(J R Boyle) *t.k.h: hld up in tch: rdn over 2f out: sn btn* **3/1**[3]

5455 **6** 6 **St Savarin (FR)**[15] 1544 7-9-3 **88** DarryllHolland 5 64
(B R Johnson) *led tl 4f out: sn lost pl: wl bhd fr over 2f out* **18/1**

151- **P** **Toparudi**[458] 5478 7-8-8 **79** oh3 LiamJones 2 —
(M H Tompkins) *stdd s: t.k.h: hld up in last pl: lost action and p.u over 3f out* **16/1**

2m 52.37s (-1.23) **Going Correction** +0.05s/f (Slow)
WFA 3 from 4yo+ 6lb **7** Ran SP% **121.1**
Speed ratings (Par 107): **105,104,102,97,95 91,**—
toteswinger: 1&2 £1.10, 1&3 £21.00, 2&3 £10.30. CSF £8.31 TOTE £4.10: £2.20, £1.50; EX 11.20.
Owner I A N Wight **Bred** Sweet Retreat Syndicate **Trained** East Everleigh, Wilts

FOCUS
A good handicap run at a sound gallop.

NOTEBOOK
Grande Caiman(IRE) had done all his winning on this surface at Lingfield but was equally at home here off a career-high winning mark of 99. Last time he made all and was right on the pace here and, having twice been successful over this distance there were no stamina doubts. With the rail to help, he was always just holding the advantage. (op 7-2)
Celtic Spirit(IRE) was well-backed to win on this step up in trip, but despite a positive ride, he lacked a decisive turn of pace when the winner stretched turning for home. His last win was over 1m4f and it may be that is as far as he wants to go. (tchd 7-4 and 2-1 in places)
Bentley Brook(IRE) five all-weather wins have come at Southwell and it looks as though that deeper surface suits him as he looked very one-paced throughout the last 2f. (op 12-1)
King's Head(IRE) may be hard to win with while he's still rated in the 90s. (op 9-1)
Slip was only two and three quarter lengths behind Grande Caiman at Lingfield last time but was a bitter disappointment. He was beaten too far out to say that he didn't stay this extra distance.
Official explanation: jockey said gelding ran too keen early on (tchd 7-2)
St Savarin(FR) Official explanation: jockey said gelding moved poorly

7718 WASH NURSERY 1m 2f (P)
9:20 (9:20) (Class 5) (0-75,72) 2-Y-O **£2,590** (£770; £385; £192) **Stalls** Low

Form RPR

0000 **1** **Canmoss (USA)**[17] 7514 2-8-11 **62** DarryllHolland 8 65
(E J O'Neill) *chsd ldr tl led 2f: mde rest: clr and idled 2f out: hrd pressed and looked vulnerable 1f out: edgd rt and fnd ex ins fnl f: in command towards fin* **14/1**

0405 **2** 1½ **Nicky Nutjob (GER)**[16] 7524 2-8-12 **63** JerryO'Dwyer 4 63
(J Pearce) *stdd s: hld up in rr: hdwy on outer 3f out: chsd ldrs over 1f out: kpt on to go 2nd nr fin: unable to chal wnr* **50/1**

005 **3** hd **Play To Win (IRE)**[18] 7505 2-8-11 **62** HayleyTurner 10 62
(D R C Elsworth) *chsd ldrs: rdn 4f out: chsd wnr over 2f out: pressed wnr ent fnl f: one pce fnl 100yds* **3/1**[2]

6311 **4** hd **Hold The Bucks (USA)**[17] 7519 2-8-13 **67** LukeMorris(3) 1 66
(J S Moore) *hld up towards rr: swtchd rt over 4f out: rdn and hdwy over 2f out: pressed wnr ent fnl f: no ex and lost 2 pls towards fin* **13/2**

0400 **5** nk **Innactualfact**[8] 7623 2-8-7 **58** RichardKingscote 3 57
(L A Dace) *stdd s: hld up in rr: rdn and hdwy over 2f out: styd on u.p fnl f: nt rch ldrs* **66/1**

0022 **6** 4 **State General (IRE)**[8] 7623 2-9-7 **72** ChrisCatlin 5 64
(Miss J Feilden) *hld up towards rr: rdn and no prog wl over 2f out: plugged on past btn horses fnl f: nvr nr ldrs* **6/4**[1]

0350 **7** 1¾ **Transfered (IRE)**[5] 7659 2-7-7 **51** oh1 ow2 AndrewHeffernan(7) 2 39
(Lucinda Featherstone) *led 2f out: chsd ldrs after: rdn 3f out: drvn and wknd wl over 1f out* **33/1**

4004 **8** 6 **Shaker Style (USA)**[17] 7519 2-8-12 **63** (v) GrahamGibbons 7 41
(J D Bethell) *hld up in midfield: rdn over 4f out: bhd fnl 2f* **16/1**

0042 **9** 2¼ **Night Lily (IRE)**[20] 7467 2-9-3 **68** LiamJones 9 42
(J Jay) *t.k.h: chsd wnr 8f out: rdn wl over 3f out: outpcd over 2f out: wknd wl over 1f out* **15/2**

4624 **10** ¾ **Celtic Commitment**[18] 7505 2-9-2 **67** PatDobbs 6 39
(R Hannon) *hld up in midfield: rdn and lost pl over 3f out: bhd fnl 2f* **6/1**[3]

2m 8.59s (-0.01) **Going Correction** +0.05s/f (Slow) **10** Ran SP% **123.3**
Speed ratings (Par 96): **102,100,100,100,100 97,95,90,89,88**
toteswinger: 1&2 £34.20, 1&3 £8.30, 2&3 £14.50. CSF £559.51 CT £2659.98 TOTE £13.60: £3.10, £7.60, £1.10; EX 208.80 Place 6: £28.02, Place 5: £24.37..
Owner David and Linda Kilburn **Bred** Tom Evans, Macon Wilmil Equines Et Al **Trained** Averham Park, Notts
■ Stewards' Enquiry : Hayley Turner three-day ban: careless riding (Jan 1-3)

FOCUS
A modest nursery and a close finish. The form is weakened by the below-par effort of the favourite and the placed horses set the standard.

NOTEBOOK
Canmoss(USA) was soon dictating, and the combination of a fine tactical ride, drop of 2lb and a step up to 1m2f was the right combination. Although driven along on the home turn and idling a little, he was well in command at the line despite a tendency to edge to the right. (op 12-1)
Nicky Nutjob(GER) ran his best race so far, all the more creditable as he was still last with just over 3f to run. However, he had stayed on over this distance at Pontefract in October and despite disappointing since, showed enough to win a race of this type, battling on well for second after coming wide. (op 33-1)
Play To Win(IRE) was ridden positively at this first attempt over 1m2f, but was treading water in the closing stages. (op 10-3 tchd 7-2)
Hold The Bucks(USA) was on a hat-trick and made things hard for himself by losing a decent early sit then had to use himself to get into contention on the home turn. For a few strides at the furlong pole it looked possible he would get to the winner, but he faded and might not have got home on this first attempt at the trip. (op 15-2 tchd 8-1)
Innactualfact ran the best race of his career and appreciated this move up in distance but was never going to continue his run through to a challenging position. (op 50-1)
State General(IRE) likes to some from off the pace but had an impossible task when he was still last with over 2f to run. He stayed on but was never holding any chance. (tchd 13-8 and 7-4 in places)
T/Plt: £85.90 to a £1 stake. Pool: £104,352.59. 886.24 winning tickets. T/Qpdt: £44.80 to a £1 stake. Pool: £7,602.27. 125.40 winning tickets. SP

7693 SOUTHWELL (L-H)
Thursday, December 18

OFFICIAL GOING: Standard
Wind: moderate 1/2 behind Weather: fine and dry but breezy

7719 BOOK YOUR TICKETS ONLINE AT SOUTHWELL-RACECOURSE.CO.UK NURSERY 5f (F)
12:30 (12:31) (Class 6) (0-65,65) 2-Y-O **£2,047** (£604; £302) **Stalls** High

Form RPR

5332 **1** **Imaginary Diva**[14] 7542 2-9-3 **61** ChrisCatlin 1 63
(G G Margarson) *chsd ldrs: led over 1f out: hld on towards fin* **10/3**[2]

4330 **2** ½ **La Capriosa**[22] 7454 2-9-1 **59** ... RobertWinston 9 59
(A J McCabe) *chsd ldrs: kpt on ins fnl f: no ex towards fin* **20/1**

0050 **3** *hd* **Rocket Ruby**[9] 7612 2-8-4 **48** ... FrancisNorton 10 47
(D Shaw) *sn outpcd towards rr: hdwy over 2f out: styd on wl fnl f* **33/1**

4022 **4** 1 ¼ **Bold Rose**[9] 7612 2-9-0 **58** ... HayleyTurner 8 53
(M D I Usher) *mid-div: outpcd over 2f out: styd on fnl f: nt rch ldrs* **5/2**[1]

0543 **5** 3 ¾ **Chimbonda**[9] 7612 2-9-2 **63** ...(bt) TolleyDean(3) 2 44
(S Parr) *t.k.h: led tl hdd & wknd over 1f out* **4/1**[3]

6556 **6** 1 **Raimond Ridge (IRE)**[14] 7543 2-8-12 **61** ... MCGeran(5) 5 39
(M R Channon) *sn outpcd and in rr: sme hdwy over 1f out: nvr nr ldrs* **11/1**

6556 **7** ½ **Alimarr (IRE)**[6] 7646 2-9-7 **65** ...(tp) AdamKirby 3 41
(S Parr) *mid-div: hung lft and outpcd over 2f out* **9/1**

5006 **8** ½ **Dawn Wee**[16] 7530 2-7-12 **45** ...(v) DuranFentiman(3) 4 19
(G R Oldroyd) *chsd ldrs: wknd over 1f out* **66/1**

1440 **9** ¾ **Key To Love (IRE)**[34] 7308 2-9-2 **60** ... NeilChalmers 7 31
(A J Chamberlain) *hmpd s: a in rr* **16/1**

2640 **10** 3 ¼ **Red Cell (IRE)**[36] 7281 2-8-13 **64** ...(b) BMcHugh(7) 6 24
(I W McInnes) *swvd rt s: a outpcd and in rr* **9/1**

59.57 secs (-0.13) **Going Correction** -0.225s/f (Stan) **10** Ran SP% **115.1**
Speed ratings (Par 94): **92,91,90,88,82 81,80,79,78,73**
toteswinger: 1&2 £7.90, 1&3 £21.00, 2&3 £41.60. CSF £68.58 CT £1900.02 TOTE £4.50: £1.40, £4.20, £7.80; EX 55.70 Trifecta £158.10 Part won. Pool: £213.66 - 0.10 winning units..
Owner Graham Lodge Partnership **Bred** Norcroft Park Stud **Trained** Newmarket, Suffolk

FOCUS
A modest nursery featuring mainly exposed sorts but solid-enough form. Although the pace was strong, very few got into a race where the first two raced in the centre throughout.

NOTEBOOK
Imaginary Diva isn't very big but she is a consistent sort who turned in an improved effort down in trip on this Fibresand debut. She should not be going up too much for this and should continue to give a good account. (op 3-1)
La Capriosa was easy to back and had been well beaten at this course on her debut, but turned in an improved effort returned to Fibresand. She is worth another try over 6f and is capable of picking up a similar event. (op 16-1)
Rocket Ruby ◆, with no headgear this time, shaped better than the bare form considering she came from off the pace and raced away from the first two from her draw. This was her best effort and she will be interesting in similar company when her stable is in better form. (op 66-1)
Bold Rose ran well over this course and distance on her previous start but, while not disgraced in terms of form, she failed to build on that after being taken off her feet and after edging towards the far side under pressure. She looks worth a try at 6f. (op 9-4)
Chimbonda, the better fancied of the yard's runners, raced with the choke out and failed to get home with the blinkers and tongue-tie re-fitted after showing plenty of dash, finishing further behind Bold Rose than on his previous start. He looks fully exposed. Official explanation: jockey said colt ran too freely (op 6-1)
Raimond Ridge(IRE) was not totally disgraced on this Fibresand debut, but left the impression that the return to 6f would be more to his liking. (op 12-1)
Alimarr(IRE) Official explanation: jockey said filly was never travelling

7720 CALL 01636 814481 TO SPONSOR A RACE MAIDEN AUCTION STKS — 7f (F)
1:00 (1:01) (Class 6) 2-Y-O **£2,047** (£604; £302) **Stalls** Low

Form RPR

04 **1** **Blaise Tower**[34] 7311 2-8-13 0 ... FergusSweeney 4 73
(G L Moore) *led tl over 4f out: chal over 2f out: sn drvn: styd on to ld fnl 100yds* **4/5**[1]

2 1 ½ **Sakheart** 2-8-0 0 ow3 ... AntiocoMurgia(7) 1 63+
(M Botti) *sn w ldr: led over 4f out: hdd and no ex ins fnl f* **25/1**

644 **3** 3 ¾ **Royal Keva (IRE)**[8] 7627 2-8-10 0 ... GrahamGibbons 6 57
(A D Brown) *chsd ldrs: one pce fnl 2f* **6/1**[3]

4 *nk* **Sixties Gift (UAE)** 2-8-6 0 ... RichardKingscote 2 52
(Rae Guest) *chsd ldrs: one pce fnl 2f* **33/1**

5 7 **Solo Choice** 2-9-2 0 ... TonyCulhane 5 45
(D Flood) *s.s: sn trcking ldrs: drvn over 3f out: lost pl over 2f out* **40/1**

02 **6** ½ **Markadam**[41] 7221 2-8-13 0 ... PaulMulrennan 7 40
(Miss S E Hall) *drvn along to chse ldrs: sn t.k.h: hung rt and wknd 2f out* **9/2**[2]

5 **7** *nk* **Watch The Master**[27] 7402 2-8-10 0 ... JerryO'Dwyer 3 37
(B I Case) *chsd ldrs: drvn over 4f out: lost pl over 1f out* **6/1**[3]

1m 29.52s (-0.78) **Going Correction** -0.225s/f (Stan) **7** Ran SP% **111.5**
Speed ratings (Par 94): **95,93,89,88,80 80,79**
toteswinger: 1&2 £6.10, 1&3 £1.60, 2&3 £7.70. CSF £25.36 TOTE £2.00: £1.70, £7.40; EX 16.60.
Owner D J Deer **Bred** D J And Mrs Deer **Trained** Woodingdean, E Sussex

FOCUS
An uncompetitive maiden in which the gallop was only fair. The first two pulled clear, the winner raced in the centre and the form looks fairly solid.

NOTEBOOK
Blaise Tower, who had the best Polytrack form on offer, was the subject of solid support and turned in his best effort to get off the mark on this Fibresand debut. He'll stay at least a mile, is in very good hands and appeals as the sort to win again. (op 5-4 tchd 6-4)
Sakheart ◆, whose dam won over 1m4f, was very easy to back but shaped with a fair degree of promise, despite edging towards the far rail on this racecourse debut. She should stay at least a mile and has the ability to pick up a similar event. (op 16-1)
Royal Keva(IRE), who attracted support in the morning but was easy to back before the off, again had his limitations exposed in this grade over this shorter trip. The return to 1m should suit but his future lies in run-of-the-mill handicaps. (op 11-4)
Sixties Gift(UAE) has plenty of stamina in her pedigree but, while she only hinted at ability on this racecourse debut (very easy to back), she is likely to fare better over middle distances once handicapped. (op 20-1)
Markadam attracted support but failed by a long chalk to reproduce his improved Musselburgh run on this all-weather debut after a short break. Official explanation: jockey said gelding hung right (op 6-1 tchd 4-1)

7721 SOUTHWELL-RACECOURSE.CO.UK MAIDEN STKS — 1m 3f (F)
1:30 (1:30) (Class 5) 3-Y-O+ **£2,729** (£806; £403) **Stalls** Low

Form RPR

1 **Take Me There**[28] 5-9-7 0 ... JimCrowley 4 71
(John Berry) *trckd ldrs: led over 2f out: drvn out* **11/4**[2]

4 **2** 2 ½ **Wing Diva (IRE)**[50] 7084 3-8-12 0 ... PaulMulrennan 1 62
(B Smart) *led: hung rt thrght: hdd over 2f out: kpt on fnl f* **12/1**

U **3** 1 **Son Of My Heart (USA)**[3] 7690 3-9-3 0 ... GeorgeBaker 7 65
(P F I Cole) *chsd ldrs: drvn 4f out: kpt on same pce fnl 2f* **9/4**[1]

04 **4** 8 **Sarando**[12] 7583 3-9-3 0 ... SteveDrowne 2 52
(R Charlton) *chsd ldrs: rdn over 2f out: wknd over 1f out* **7/2**[3]

0040 **5** 1 **General Tufto**[8] 7632 3-8-10 41 ...(b[1]) AndrewHeffernan(7) 9 50
(C Smith) *in rr: outpcd over 4f out: hdwy on ins over 2f out: edgd rt and wknd over 1f out* **100/1**

5 **6** 15 **Tampa Boy (IRE)**[12] 7583 6-9-7 0 ... FrancisNorton 6 25
(M F Harris) *prom: outpcd over 4f out: sn lost pl and bhd* **14/1**

3245 **7** 4 **Santera (IRE)**[15] 578 4-9-2 39 ... AndrewElliott 8 13
(A M Hales) *mid-div: outpcd over 4f out: sn lost pl* **22/1**

8 3 ¼ **Stockman** 4-9-7 0 ... TravisBlock 3 12
(H Morrison) *s.i.s: last and reminders after 2f: bhd fnl 5f: t.o 3f out* **6/1**

2m 24.8s (-3.20) **Going Correction** -0.225s/f (Stan)
WFA 3 from 4yo+ 4lb **8** Ran SP% **113.6**
Speed ratings (Par 103): **102,100,99,93,92 82,79,76**
toteswinger: 1&2 £7.00, 1&3 £2.90, 2&3 £5.10. CSF £34.65 TOTE £3.40: £1.10, £2.10, £1.50; EX 37.10 Trifecta £312.10 Part won. Pool: £421.77 - 0.50 winning units..
Owner Paul Devereaux **Bred** Darley **Trained** Newmarket, Suffolk

FOCUS
Another ordinary maiden, but the winner may be able to score again on sand. The gallop was only moderate and the principals raced in the centre in the straight.
Sarando Official explanation: trainer said gelding was unsuited by the fibresand

7722 PLAY GOLF AT SOUTHWELL GOLF CLUB H'CAP — 1m 4f (F)
2:00 (2:00) (Class 5) (0-70,70) 3-Y-O+ **£2,729** (£806; £403) **Stalls** Low

Form RPR

3031 **1** **Orkney (IRE)**[8] 7630 3-8-10 **64** 6ex ... PaulMulrennan 4 72
(Miss J A Camacho) *led: qcknd 8f out and over 4f out: kpt on wl fnl 2f: hld on towards fin* **9/4**[2]

/50- **2** *nk* **Mr Aitch (IRE)**[63] 4732 6-9-7 **70** ...(t) SteveDrowne 6 78
(R T Phillips) *rn in snatches: in rr: hdwy over 3f out: rdn over 2f out: hung lft and styd on fnl f* **66/1**

0051 **3** ½ **Karmest**[9] 7613 4-9-7 **70** 6ex ... GrahamGibbons 3 77
(A D Brown) *hld up: effrt over 4f out: wnt cl 2nd 2f out: no ex ins fnl f* **17/2**

0052 **4** 2 ½ **Swords**[6] 7647 6-9-2 **65** ... GeorgeBaker 1 68
(R E Peacock) *hld up: effrt over 4f out: chsng ldrs over 1f out: wknd fnl 75yds* **6/1**[3]

6032 **5** 2 ¾ **Parnassian**[8] 7630 8-8-7 **56** oh3 ...(v) RichardThomas 5 55
(J A Geake) *trckd ldrs: effrt over 3f out: hung lft and wknd appr fnl f* **16/1**

001 **6** 12 **Prairie Hawk (USA)**[3] 7688 3-8-2 **51** 6ex ...(t) ChrisCatlin 2 36
(Tim Vaughan) *trckd wnr: pushed along over 4f out: edgd rt and lost pl over 1f out* **11/10**[1]

2m 39.0s (-2.00) **Going Correction** -0.225s/f (Stan)
WFA 3 from 4yo+ 5lb **6** Ran SP% **110.6**
Speed ratings (Par 103): **97,96,96,94,92 84**
toteswinger: 1&2 £7.60, 1&3 £2.90, 2&3 £11.80. CSF £81.35 TOTE £3.90: £1.70, £7.70; EX 92.50.
Owner Axom (XIII) **Bred** Miss Yvonne Kennedy **Trained** Norton, N Yorks

FOCUS
An ordinary handicap but one that did not take as much winning as seemed likely as the well-backed favourite proved a big disappointment. The winner was allowed to dominate and raced in the centre in the straight while the placed horses set the standard.
Mr Aitch(IRE) Official explanation: jockey said gelding hung left
Parnassian Official explanation: jockey said gelding hung left
Prairie Hawk(USA) Official explanation: trainer was unable to offer any explanation for the poor performance shown

7723 MEMBERSHIP AT SOUTHWELL GOLF CLUB (S) STKS — 1m (F)
2:30 (2:32) (Class 6) 3-Y-O+ **£1,978** (£584; £292) **Stalls** Low

Form RPR

1045 **1** **Clear Sailing**[19] 7499 5-9-1 74 ...(p) ChrisCatlin 5 82
(George Baker) *led after 1f: qcknd clr 3f out: hrd rdn: unchal* **4/1**

2304 **2** 7 **Yakimov (USA)**[2] 7695 9-9-7 82 ... PaulMulrennan 9 72
(Ollie Pears) *chsd ldrs: effrt on outside over 3f out: wnt 2nd over 1f out: kpt on same pce* **9/4**[1]

4021 **3** *nk* **Boundless Prospect (USA)**[5] 7665 9-9-2 64 ... PatrickDonaghy(5) 6 71+
(P D Evans) *s.i.s: in rr and drvn along: hdwy 2f out: styd on ins fnl f* **7/2**[3]

3552 **4** *nse* **Elusive Warrior (USA)**[8] 7631 5-9-7 67 ...(p) JamesDoyle 3 71
(A J McCabe) *led 1f: trckd ldrs: t.k.h: kpt on same pce fnl 2f* **12/1**

1611 **5** 6 **Barkass (UAE)**[19] 7500 4-9-7 69 ... GeorgeBaker 4 57
(B Ellison) *prom: outpcd over 4f out: hdwy on outside over 2f out: wknd over 1f out* **11/4**[2]

5605 **6** 6 **Black Falcon (IRE)**[2] 7695 8-9-2 57 ...(b[1]) JamesO'Reilly(5) 11 43
(John A Harris) *chsd ldrs: wknd over 1f out* **25/1**

4-00 **7** 2 ¼ **Mount Usher**[21] 7462 6-8-10 66 ...(v) WilliamCarson(5) 10 32
(M J Gingell) *dwlt: hdwy to chse ldrs after 2f: wknd 2f out* **66/1**

0-36 **8** 2 ¼ **Bourbon Highball (IRE)**[33] 2037 3-9-0 58 ... LeeEnstone 2 27
(P C Haslam) *chsd ldrs: outpcd over 4f out: wknd 2f out* **100/1**

2303 **9** 6 **Moorside Diamond**[20] 7469 4-8-10 50 ...(b) GrahamGibbons 8 8
(A D Brown) *trckd ldrs: outpcd over 4f out: lost pl over 3f out* **28/1**

0000 **10** 8 **Brutus Maximus**[36] 7280 5-8-8 40 ...(b) BMcHugh(7) 1 —
(I W McInnes) *in rr: reminders 5f out: bhd fnl 3f* **200/1**

600- **11** 1 ½ **Siegfrieds Night (IRE)**[501] 3610 7-8-8 42 ... AlexEdwards(7) 7 —
(M C Chapman) *in rr: bhd fnl 5f: t.o 3f out* **200/1**

1m 40.78s (-2.92) **Going Correction** -0.225s/f (Stan)
WFA 3 from 4yo+ 1lb **11** Ran SP% **118.1**
Speed ratings (Par 101): **105,98,97,97,91 85,83,81,75,67 65**
toteswinger: 1&2 £4.60, 1&3 £6.30, 2&3 £5.00. CSF £13.27 TOTE £6.40: £1.90, £1.30, £1.90; EX 18.50 Trifecta £196.80 Pool: £428.38 - 1.61 winning units..The winner was bought by Ollie Pears for 7,000gns.
Owner Michael H Watt **Bred** Juddmonte Farms Ltd **Trained** Moreton Morrell, Warwicks

FOCUS
A mixed bag and an ordinary gallop. The winner, who raced centre to far side in the straight, won unchallenged and could rate higher.
Barkass(UAE) Official explanation: jockey said gelding was never travelling
Moorside Diamond Official explanation: jockey said filly lost its action

7724 COME RACING TOMORROW H'CAP — 1m (F)
3:00 (3:02) (Class 5) (0-75,75) 3-Y-O+ **£2,729** (£806; £403) **Stalls** Low

Form RPR

2111 **1** **Mozayada (USA)**[6] 7650 4-9-3 **72** 6ex ... FrancisNorton 2 79+
(M Brittain) *led: qcknd over 4f out: a in command: pushed out: v readily* **8/15**[1]

0151 **2** ¾ **Sofia's Star**[18] 7510 3-9-5 **75** ... JimCrowley 3 81
(S Dow) *awkward to load: dwlt: sn chsng ldrs: effrt over 3f out: wnt 2nd jst ins fnl f: kpt on same pce* **7/1**[3]

3003 **3** *nk* **Augustus John (IRE)**[5] 7669 5-8-11 **66** ow1 ...(p) AdamKirby 5 71
(S Parr) *sn trcking ldrs on outer: chal over 2f out: kpt on same pce fnl f* **7/2**[2]

The Form Book, Raceform Ltd, Compton, RG20 6NL

0200 **4** *13* **Realt Na Mara (IRE)**[66] [6706] 5-9-4 **73**.......................... SteveDrowne 1 48
(H Morrison) *chsd ldrs: drvn over 4f out: wknd over 1f out: sn eased* **10/1**

1m 41.53s (-2.17) **Going Correction** -0.225s/f (Stan)
WFA 3 from 4yo+ 1lb 4 Ran SP% **109.0**
Speed ratings (Par 103): **101,100,99,86**
CSF £4.80 TOTE £1.60; EX 3.80.
Owner Mel Brittain **Bred** Shadwell Farm LLC **Trained** Warthill, N Yorks

FOCUS
Not a strong handicap but another win from in-form Mozayada, another on this card to show the benefit of getting an uncontested lead at this course. The pace was moderate and the runner-up is rated to form backed up by the third.

7725 HOSPITALITY AT SOUTHWELL RACECOURSE H'CAP 1m (F)
3:30 (3:30) (Class 6) (0-60,65) 3-Y-O **£2,047** (£604; £302) **Stalls** Low

Form RPR
6532 **1** **Lujano**[12] [7581] 3-9-4 **60**.......................... PaulMulrennan 1 68
(Ollie Pears) *mde all: styd on u.p fnl 2f: edgd lft and hld on wl* **6/4**[1]
0004 **2** *1 1/4* **Jordi Roper (IRE)**[6] [7654] 3-8-0 **49**.......................... AndrewHeffernan(7) 2 54
(S Parr) *s.i.s: sn chsng ldrs: chal over 2f out: kpt on same pce fnl f* **11/1**
0400 **3** *3 3/4* **Sir Billy Nick**[6] [7656] 3-9-4 **60**.......................... (b[1]) LeeEnstone 6 56
(S Wynne) *s.i.s: sn chsng ldrs: effrt over 3f out: one pce fnl 2f* **8/1**
2000 **4** *3* **Broughtons Flight (IRE)**[43] [5964] 3-9-2 **58**.......................... ChrisCatlin 9 47
(W J Musson) *sn chsng ldrs on outer: drvn 3f out: fdd over 1f out* **9/1**
6006 **5** *nk* **Gambling Jack**[26] [7414] 3-8-10 **52**.......................... (t) HayleyTurner 8 41
(A W Carroll) *w wnr: effrt over 3f out: wknd over 1f out* **10/3**[2]
0200 **6** *21* **Kirkie (USA)**[27] [7403] 3-9-1 **60**.......................... TolleyDean(3) 7 —
(S Parr) *in rr: sn drvn along: hdwy on ins 3f: sn wknd: eased whn bhd ins fnl f* **5/1**[3]
2000 **7** *11* **Rich James (IRE)**[165] [3753] 3-8-4 **46** oh1.......................... AndrewElliott 3 —
(J D Bethell) *chsd ldrs: sn drvn along: reminders over 4f out: sn lost pl: bhd whn eased over 1f out* **33/1**

1m 42.22s (-1.48) **Going Correction** -0.225s/f (Stan) 7 Ran SP% **112.1**
Speed ratings (Par 98): **98,96,93,90,89 68,57**
toteswinger: 1&2 £4.20, 1&3 £3.30, 2&3 £8.60. CSF £18.72 CT £98.79 TOTE £2.20: £1.60, £4.00; EX 16.20 Trifecta £127.90 Pool: £240.33 - 1.39 winning units. Place 6: £56.85 Place 5: £10.50.
Owner David Scott and Co (Pattern Makers) Ltd **Bred** D Scott **Trained** Norton, N Yorks

FOCUS
A low-grade handicap but another modest gallop and another front-running winner, who also came down the centre. The first two pulled clear and the race is rated around them.
Kirkie(USA) Official explanation: jockey said gelding was never travelling
Rich James(IRE) Official explanation: jockey said gelding was never travelling
T/Plt: £95.70 to a £1 stake. Pool: £42,091.36. 321.07 winning tickets. T/Qpdt: £10.80 to a £1 stake. Pool: £3,661.14. 249.50 winning tickets. WG

7719 SOUTHWELL (L-H)
Friday, December 19

OFFICIAL GOING: Standard
Wind: Virtually nil Weather: Overcast and dry

7726 EUROPEAN BREEDERS' FUND MAIDEN STKS 1m (F)
12:25 (12:31) (Class 5) 2-Y-O **£3,753** (£1,108; £554) **Stalls** Low

Form RPR
006 **1** **Sky Gate (USA)**[29] [7397] 2-9-3 66.......................... (b[1]) DaneO'Neill 4 70+
(B J Meehan) *prom: led over 4f out: qcknd clr 3f out: rdn over 1f out: styd on: eased nr fin* **8/1**
0 **2** *2 1/2* **Tartan Gunna**[114] [5387] 2-9-3 0.......................... GregFairley 8 64+
(M Johnston) *s.i.s and bhd: hdwy 1/2-way: rdn to chse wnr wl over 1f out: sn drvn and no imp ins fnl f* **13/8**[1]
303 **3** *6* **Sussex Dancer (IRE)**[27] [7422] 2-8-12 74.......................... ShaneKelly 3 45
(J A Osborne) *dwlt: sn trcking ldrs: hdwy 3f out: rdn to chse wnr wl over 2f out: sn drvn and kpt on same pce* **10/3**[2]
4 *8* **Aliybee (IRE)**[14] [7566] 2-8-7 0.......................... EJMcNamara(5) 2 28
(E J O'Neill) *cl up: rdn along 3f out: drvn and one pce fnl 2f* **12/1**
5 *nk* **Manana Manana** 2-9-3 0.......................... AdamKirby 5 32
(S Parr) *trckd ldrs: hdwy to chse wnr over 3f out: rdn over 2f out: sn drvn and grad wknd* **25/1**
6 **6** *3* **Beat Faster**[13] [7578] 2-8-12 0.......................... TPQueally 1 20
(J G Given) *led over 3f: cl up untl rdn along and wknd 3f out* **12/1**
5 **7** *3 1/2* **Queens Flight**[13] [7578] 2-8-12 0.......................... DarryllHolland 6 13
(J Noseda) *t.k.h early: trckd ldrs: effrt 3f out: sn rdn along and wknd* **4/1**[3]
8 *16* **Giant Strides** 2-8-12 0.......................... StephenDonohoe 7 —
(P D Evans) *s.i.s: a bhd* **50/1**

1m 42.95s (-0.75) **Going Correction** -0.10s/f (Stan) 8 Ran SP% **113.5**
Speed ratings (Par 96): **99,96,90,82,82 79,75,59**
toteswinger: 1&2 £4.50, 1&3 £5.00, 2&3 £2.30. CSF £21.12 TOTE £8.60: £2.20, £1.30, £1.50; EX 23.50 Trifecta £122.40 Pool: 172.03 - 1.04 winning units.
Owner Atlantic Crossing **Bred** Ashleigh Stud, Frank Ramos & Jackie Ramo **Trained** Manton, Wilts

FOCUS
This was just a modest maiden and the winner may not be able to beat the runner-up again.

NOTEBOOK
Sky Gate(USA), unplaced in three previous attempts, did get a little better with each run and there was hope from his pedigree that he would handle this surface. Sporting first-time blinkers, he received an enterprising ride from O'Neill and got first run on the favourite, kicking into a clear lead off the final bend and being eased close home. He was not for catching and it will be interesting to see how/if he progresses through the winter. (op 11-1 tchd 6-1)
Tartan Gunna ◆ would have won had he not blown the start. Well supported at the head of the market, he literally walked out the stalls, giving up many lengths, and was forced to sit in behind. The winner had flown by the time he hit top gear, but he drew well clear of the remainder and this represented a big step up on his initial effort (since been gelded). Winning a similar contest should prove a formality. (op 9-4 tchd 5-2)
Sussex Dancer(IRE) gives the form a solid look. Already third in a couple of maidens, she chased the early pace and kept on down the straight, but could do nothing as the front pair ran away from her. She in turn was well ahead of the rest and will find a small race at some stage. (op 11-4 tchd 5-2)
Aliybee(IRE) kept on again to run newcomer Manana Manana out of fourth. (tchd 11-1)
Queens Flight shaped with a bit of promise when fifth at Great Leighs on her debut, but was unable to build on it, racing keenly and possibly disliking the different surface. Official explanation: jockey said filly ran too freely (op 11-4)

7727 MEMBERSHIP AT SOUTHWELL GOLF CLUB (S) STKS 6f (F)
1:00 (1:07) (Class 6) 3-Y-0+ **£1,978** (£584; £292) **Stalls** Low

Form RPR
2441 **1** **Came Back (IRE)**[10] [7616] 5-9-5 85.......................... DarryllHolland 7 69+
(J R Gask) *sn led: pushed clr over 2f out: eased ins fnl f: comf* **2/5**[1]
0603 **2** *3/4* **Hamaasy**[10] [7615] 7-9-2 56.......................... KevinGhunowa(3) 4 67
(R A Harris) *trckd ldrs: hdwy to chse wnr over 2f out and sn rdn: drvn and styd on ins fnl f: nt rch wnr* **12/1**[3]
3022 **3** *3* **Grimes Faith**[9] [7629] 5-9-5 62.......................... (p) PaulMulrennan 1 57
(K A Ryan) *towards rr: hdwy on inner 1/2-way: rdn to chse ldng pair over 1f out: kpt on u.p ins fnl f* **13/2**[2]
0005 **4** *2 3/4* **Head To Head (IRE)**[31] [7369] 4-8-12 45.......................... GrahamGibbons 12 42
(A D Brown) *chsd ldrs: rdn along wl over 2f out: sn drvn and one pce* **40/1**
3020 **5** *2 3/4* **Avoca Dancer (IRE)**[28] [7399] 5-8-9 61 ow2.......................... (e[1]) KylieManser(7) 10 37
(Miss Gay Kelleway) *in rr: hdwy wl over 2f out: sn rdn and styd on appr last: nrst fin* **14/1**
-000 **6** *1 1/4* **Redeemed**[11] [7610] 3-8-2 68.......................... MCGeran(5) 2 24
(M Brittain) *towards rr: hdwy over 2f out: sn rdn and kpt on appr last: nrst fin* **50/1**
1110 **7** *6* **Soba Jones**[10] [7615] 11-9-2 58.......................... TolleyDean(3) 6 17
(J Balding) *cl up: rdn along wl over 2f out: grad wknd* **22/1**
5600 **8** *2 1/2* **Swallow Senora (IRE)**[10] [7616] 6-8-0 39.......................... (t) AlexEdwards(7) 9 —
(M C Chapman) *chsd ldrs to 1/2-way: sn wknd* **100/1**
00 **9** *8* **Babel**[9] [7629] 3-9-0 68.......................... SimonWhitworth 5 —
(M Wigham) *prom: rdn along 1/2-way: sn wknd* **33/1**
1200 **10** *2 1/2* **Sea Salt**[66] [6724] 5-9-5 66.......................... PatCosgrave 3 —
(A J McCabe) *prom on inner: rdn along 1/2-way: sn wknd* **12/1**[3]
5600 **11** *2 1/2* **Santa Clara**[72] [6571] 3-8-4 40.......................... (b[1]) LukeMorris(3) 11 —
(P Leech) *a in rr* **100/1**

1m 15.34s (-1.16) **Going Correction** -0.10s/f (Stan) 11 Ran SP% **120.5**
Speed ratings (Par 101): **103,102,98,94,90 89,81,77,67,63 60**
toteswinger: 1&2 £3.80, 1&3 £1.80, 2&3 £5.50. CSF £6.42 TOTE £1.40: £1.02, £2.80, £1.60; EX 6.70 Trifecta £27.20 Pool: £229.75 - 6.23 winning units.The winner was sold to Ann Stokell for £7,000.
Owner Horses First Racing Limited **Bred** Yeomanstown Stud **Trained** Sutton Veny, Wilts

FOCUS
A decent seller rated around the runner-up and fourth.

7728 BILL YATES IS SIXTY TODAY NURSERY 6f (F)
1:35 (1:40) (Class 6) (0-60,60) 2-Y-O **£2,047** (£604; £302) **Stalls** Low

Form RPR
0006 **1** **Halaak (USA)**[15] [7542] 2-8-6 **45**.......................... (b[1]) GregFairley 6 49
(D M Simcock) *cl up: led over 2f out: rdn clr over 1f out: drvn and edgd lft ent fnl f: styd on* **16/1**
6230 **2** *2 1/2* **Bulella**[3] [7693] 2-8-12 **58**.......................... AndrewHeffernan(7) 7 54
(Garry Moss) *s.i.s and bhd: gd hdwy 1/2-way: rdn 2f out: styd on to chse wnr over 1f out: drvn and hung lft ent fnl f: sn no imp* **9/2**[1]
0300 **3** *1 1/2* **Sicilian Pink**[67] [6700] 2-9-7 **60**.......................... HayleyTurner 10 52
(E F Vaughan) *chsd ldrs: rdn along to chse wnr over 2f out: sn drvn and one pce fr over 1f out* **8/1**[3]
0010 **4** *4* **Top Flight Splash**[17] [7531] 2-9-0 **53**.......................... DaleGibson 4 33
(Mrs G S Rees) *chsd ldrs: effrt over 2f out: sn rdn and kpt on same pce* **7/1**[2]
6601 **5** *1 1/4* **Glan Lady (IRE)**[17] [7530] 2-9-4 **60**.......................... (b) TolleyDean(3) 8 36
(J L Spearing) *wnt lft s: sn outpcd and rdn along in rr: hdwy over 2f out: nvr rch ldrs* **9/2**[1]
0660 **6** *4 1/2* **Katie Higgins**[17] [7531] 2-8-11 **50** ow1.......................... (b) AdamKirby 1 12
(J L Spearing) *midfield: rdn along 1/2-way: nvr a factor* **14/1**
0063 **7** *1* **Senora Verde**[132] [4873] 2-8-6 **45**.......................... LiamJones 5 4
(P T Midgley) *led: rdn along and hdd over 2f out: sn hung lft and wknd* **16/1**
000 **8** *2 1/4* **Raise All In (IRE)**[18] [7519] 2-9-2 **55**.......................... PatCosgrave 9 8
(N Wilson) *prom: rdn along 1/2-way: sn wknd* **17/2**
033 **9** *2* **Lady Gem**[15] [7543] 2-8-12 **51**.......................... PaulMulrennan 11 —
(D H Brown) *cl up on outer: rdn along 1/2-way: sn wknd* **9/2**[1]
000 **10** *3 3/4* **Rebelwithoutacause (IRE)**[150] [4270] 2-9-1 **54**.......................... ChrisCatlin 3 —
(George Baker) *a towards rr* **9/1**

1m 16.79s (0.29) **Going Correction** -0.10s/f (Stan) 10 Ran SP% **117.1**
Speed ratings (Par 94): **94,90,88,83,81 75,74,71,68,63**
toteswinger: 1&2 £10.90, 1&3 £17.50, 2&3 £8.50. CSF £87.06 CT £633.36 TOTE £13.30: £3.20, £2.40, £2.80; EX 79.10 TRIFECTA Not won..
Owner Saeed Misleh **Bred** Brereton C Jones **Trained** Newmarket, Suffolk

FOCUS
This was a weak nursery.

NOTEBOOK
Halaak(USA), who made no impact on her nursery debut at Great Leighs, was trying a different surface here and the fitting of first-time blinkers clearly made a huge difference. Always prominent, she was driven to the front over two out and stayed on right the way to the line. She is only modest, but could do better again if the headgear continues to have the same effect. Official explanation: trainer's representative said, regarding the apparent improvement in form, that the filly appeared to have benefitted from wearing blinkers for the first time and racing on fibresand surface (op 17-2)
Bulella, who finished well beaten here off this mark last time, had earlier run a couple of decent races and this was more like her best form. She did well to finish second considering she was slowly away and failed to obtain a position. (op 5-1 tchd 11-2)
Sicilian Pink was being ridden along quite early and kept plodding away for pressure to claim third. (op 10-1 tchd 15-2)
Top Flight Splash, who seemed not to stay 7f at the course last time, was 4lb higher than when winning over this course and distance the time before (Bulella behind) and she ran better, but could find no extra inside the final furlong. Official explanation: jockey said filly hung left (op 8-1)
Glan Lady(IRE), easy winner of a course and distance seller this month (wore first-time blinkers), looked of obvious interest here if the headgear had the same effect, but she was slowly away and soon found herself behind. She kept on down the straight without ever threatening to get seriously involved and probably deserves another chance. (op 4-1)
Senora Verde Official explanation: jockey said filly lost its action

Lady Gem, who had a wide draw to overcome, showed good early speed, but was being scrubbed along at halfway and failed to run her race. Official explanation: jockey said filly hung right (op 4-1 tchd 5-1)

7729 SOUTHWELL-RACECOURSE.CO.UK H'CAP 1m 3f (F)
2:10 (2:10) (Class 5) (0-70,67) 3-Y-O £2,729 (£806; £403) **Stalls** Low

Form RPR

1040 1 **Benedict Spirit (IRE)**[158] 4021 3-9-3 **66**........ PaulMulrennan 6 76
(M H Tompkins) *trckd ldng pair: effrt on outer over 3f out: led over 2f out and sn rdn: drvn ent fnl f and kpt on gamely* **2/1**[1]

5401 2 1 ½ **Gayanula (USA)**[7] 7647 3-8-3 **55**........ LukeMorris(3) 3 62
(Miss J A Camacho) *trckd ldrs: rdn along over 4f out: hdwy 2f out: rdn over 1f out and ev ch tl drvn and one pce ins fnl f* **5/2**[2]

0012 3 nk **Fortunella**[10] 7613 3-8-5 **54**........ ChrisCatlin 5 60
(Miss Gay Kelleway) *cl up: led 3f out: rdn and hdd 2f out: cl up and ev ch tl drvn and one pce ent fnl f* **5/2**[2]

0044 4 16 **All In The Red (IRE)**[8] 7642 3-9-4 **67**........ JimCrowley 2 46
(B N Pollock) *trckd ldrs: effrt over 3f out: sn rdn and outpcd over 2f out* **6/1**[3]

-030 5 26 **Spinning Ridge (IRE)**[234] 1696 3-9-0 **66**........ KevinGhunowa(3) 1 —
(R A Harris) *led: rdn along 4f out: hdd 3f out: sn drvn and wknd* **20/1**

2m 27.59s (-0.41) **Going Correction** -0.10s/f (Stan) Ran SP% **109.5**
Speed ratings (Par 102): **97,95,95,84,65**
toteswinger: 1&2 £6.70. CSF £7.22 TOTE £3.00: £2.40, £1.60; EX 8.40.

Owner Mrs S Ashby **Bred** Allevamento Pian Di Neve Srl **Trained** Newmarket, Suffolk

FOCUS
A moderate handicap but fairly sound rated arounsd the placed horses.

7730 ARCHER ELECTRICAL H'CAP 6f (F)
2:45 (2:46) (Class 4) (0-80,78) 3-Y-O+ £4,857 (£1,445; £722; £360) **Stalls** Low

Form RPR

0221 1 **Charles Parnell (IRE)**[17] 7534 5-9-4 **78**........ DaleGibson 3 88
(M Dods) *midfield: hdwy over 2f out: rdn to chal over 1f out: drvn to ld ins fnl f: kpt on wl* **11/2**[3]

5062 2 shd **Don Pele (IRE)**[5] 7675 6-8-5 **68**........(b) KevinGhunowa(3) 6 78
(R A Harris) *chsd ldrs: hdwy to ld 2f out: sn rdn: drvn and hdd ins fnl f: rallied wl u.p: jst hld* **10/1**

5214 3 1 **Resplendent Alpha**[21] 7477 4-9-4 **78**........ IanMongan 7 85
(P Howling) *hld up towards rr: hdwy on outer 2f out: rdn over 1f out: drvn and ev ch ins fnl f: wknd towards fin* **7/1**

0016 4 2 ¾ **River Thames**[12] 7592 5-8-8 **68**........ PaulMulrennan 9 66
(K A Ryan) *hld up in midfield: hdwy 2f out: rdn and hung lft over 1f out: kpt on u.p ins fnl f* **9/1**

3013 5 ½ **Musical Script (USA)**[9] 7621 5-8-10 **70**........(b) DaneO'Neill 5 66+
(Mouse Hamilton-Fairley) *dwlt and towards rr: hdwy over 2f out: rdn to chse ldrs whn n.m.r over 1f out: sn drvn and no imp* **15/2**

4020 6 ½ **He's A Humbug (IRE)**[10] 7614 4-8-11 **76**........(p) JamesO'Reilly(5) 10 71
(J O'Reilly) *sn outpcd and rdn along in rr: hdwy over 2f out: styd on appr fnl f: nrst fin* **10/1**

0245 7 1 ¼ **Steel City Boy (IRE)**[14] 7562 5-8-9 **69**........ JimCrowley 4 60
(D Shaw) *cl up: led 1/2-way: rdn and hdd 2f out: sn drvn and wknd* **7/2**[1]

6513 8 1 **Kensington (IRE)**[3] 7698 7-8-1 **66** 6ex........(v) PatrickDonaghy(5) 2 54
(P D Evans) *cl up: effrt over 2f out: sn rdn and wknd wl over 1f out* **9/2**[2]

5500 9 5 **Loose Caboose (IRE)**[35] 7315 3-8-5 **72**........(p) KarenKenny(7) 1 44
(A J McCabe) *led: rdn along and hdd 1/2-way: sn wknd* **50/1**

-120 10 12 **Only A Game (IRE)**[131] 4900 3-9-4 **78**........ AdamKirby 8 11
(Miss M E Rowland) *prom: rdn along over 2f out and sn wknd* **20/1**

1m 15.76s (-0.74) **Going Correction** -0.10s/f (Stan) Ran SP% **115.00**
Speed ratings (Par 105): **100,99,98,94,94 93,91,90,83,67**
toteswinger: 1&2 £10.90, 1&3 £4.40, 2&3 £12.10. CSF £58.40 CT £389.37 TOTE £4.40: £1.50, £3.50, £3.70; EX 45.30 Trifecta £129.10 Pool: £418.92 - 2.40 winning units..

Owner C A Lynch **Bred** R And Mrs R Hodgins **Trained** Denton, Co Durham

FOCUS
Quite a competitive sprint handicap but the form looks sound enough rated around the first three.

7731 HOSPITALITY AT SOUTHWELL RACECOURSE H'CAP 1m (F)
3:20 (3:20) (Class 6) (0-65,65) 3-Y-O+ £2,047 (£604; £302) **Stalls** Low

Form RPR

6533 1 **Kingsholm**[20] 7500 6-9-4 **63**........ LeeEnstone 6 71
(N Wilson) *hld up in tch on outer: smooth hdwy 1/2-way: cl up 3f out: led 2f out: rdn and edgd lft jst ins fnl f: kpt on: comf* **13/2**[2]

5000 2 ¾ **Elk Trail (IRE)**[19] 7507 3-9-5 **65**........ MickyFenton 10 71
(Mrs P Sly) *cl up: led 3f out: rdn along and hdd 2f out: drvn and hld whn n.m.r ins fnl f: swtchd rt and r.o fnl 100yds* **8/1**[3]

221 3 2 ¼ **Barataria**[9] 7634 6-9-5 **64** 6ex........ HayleyTurner 9 65
(R Bastiman) *rr: pushed along and hdwy 3f out: rdn to chse ldrs wl over 1f out: sn drvn and no imp fnl f: tk 3rd nr fin* **1/2**[1]

4500 4 1 **Louisiade (IRE)**[3] 7698 7-8-12 **57**........(b) StephenDonohoe 4 56
(M C Chapman) *trckd ldrs: rdn and hdwy to chse ldng pair wl over 1f out: sn drvn and one pce: lost 3rd nr fin* **12/1**

0000 5 8 **Government (IRE)**[3] 7698 7-8-5 **50** oh5........ NickyMackay 2 30
(M C Chapman) *led: rdn along and hdd 3f out: drvn over 2f out and grad wknd* **50/1**

0000 6 3 ½ **Elliwan**[13] 7586 3-8-11 **57**........ DaleGibson 8 29
(M W Easterby) *dwlt: a in rr* **12/1**

0060 7 nk **Spume (IRE)**[6] 7658 4-8-7 **52**........(t) ChrisCatlin 7 24
(S Parr) *prom: rdn along 1/2-way: sn wknd* **14/1**

0006 8 hd **Fitzwarren**[47] 7152 7-8-2 **50** oh5........(p) LukeMorris(3) 1 21
(A D Brown) *prom: rdn along 1/2-way: sn wknd* **80/1**

1m 42.67s (-1.03) **Going Correction** -0.10s/f (Stan)
WFA 3 from 4yo+ 1lb Ran SP% **116.8**
Speed ratings (Par 101): **101,100,98,97,89 85,85,85**
toteswinger: 1&2 £4.00, 1&3 £2.00, 2&3 £1.90. CSF £57.76 CT £71.56 TOTE £7.00: £1.70, £1.90, £1.10; EX 47.00 Trifecta £94.60 Pool: £1068.51 - 8.35 winning tickets.

Owner Mrs N C Wilson **Bred** J C , J R And S R Hitchins **Trained** Flaxton, N Yorks

FOCUS
A moderate contest and not the result many expected, with the hot favourite running rather flat.

Barataria Official explanation: jockey said gelding ran flat

T/Plt: £27.00 to a £1 stake. Pool: £57,180.95. 1,543.39 winning tickets. T/Qpdt: £24.90 to a £1 stake. Pool: £4,634.43. 137.40 winning tickets. JR

7686 WOLVERHAMPTON (A.W) (L-H)
Friday, December 19

OFFICIAL GOING: Standard
Wind: Moderate behind Weather: Fine

7732 DINE & DANCE IN THE RINGSIDE APPRENTICE H'CAP 1m 1f 103y(P)
6:50 (6:50) (Class 6) (0-65,65) 3-Y-O+ £2,729 (£806; £403) **Stalls** Low

Form RPR

4430 1 **Cherri Fosfate**[25] 7440 4-9-2 **63**........(b) MatthewLawson(3) 11 74
(Paul W Flynn, Ire) *bhd: c wd st: rdn and hdwy over 1f out: edgd lft ins fnl f: r.o to ld cl home* **6/1**

00 2 ¾ **Fandango Boy**[3] 7698 7-9-2 **60**........ JPFahy 5 69
(J P Broderick, Ire) *hld up towards rr: hdwy over 2f out: led and edgd lft jst ins fnl f: hdd cl home* **12/1**

0051 3 2 ¾ **Bailieborough (IRE)**[14] 7559 9-8-7 **56**........ AnthonyBetts(5) 3 60
(B Ellison) *hld up in mid-div: hdwy 5f out: led wl over 2f out: rdn wl over 1f out: hdd jst ins fnl f: no ex* **17/2**

4 2 **Imco Tendence (IRE)**[14] 7569 6-9-4 **62**........(p) PNolan 10 61
(W J Burke, Ire) *hld up in tch: rdn over 1f out: one pce fnl f* **4/1**[1]

0-55 5 1 ¾ **Rigat**[334] 240 5-8-10 **59**........ PaulPickard(5) 8 55
(J S Goldie) *plld hrd early: sn towards rr: hdwy over 3f out: rdn over 1f out: wknd ins fnl f* **18/1**

0344 6 3 **Formidable Guest**[7] 7656 4-8-6 **55**........ TobyAtkinson(5) 2 44
(J Pearce) *hld up in mid-div: short-lived effrt over 2f out* **9/2**[2]

2550 7 shd **Alfredtheordinary**[22] 7166 3-8-10 **63** ow4........ AliceHaynes(7) 6 52
(M R Channon) *prom tl wknd over 2f out* **14/1**

8 5 **Sly Tiger (GER)**[29] 7121 4-9-3 **61**........ GFCarroll 1 40
(M Halford, Ire) *hld up towards rr: n.m.r on ins over 3f out: n.d after* **17/2**

2526 9 2 ½ **Moyoko (IRE)**[18] 7518 5-8-10 **54**........ NSLawes 13 28
(M Salaman) *stdd s: a in rr* **18/1**

0031 10 7 **Moment Of Clarity**[4] 7692 6-8-12 **59** 6ex........(p) KarenKenny(3) 4 18
(R C Guest) *led: hdd wl over 2f out: wknd wl over 1f out* **5/1**[3]

50-0 11 2 ¾ **Nota Liberata**[24] 7442 4-8-6 **57**........ HollyHall(7) 12 10
(Ollie Pears) *sn chsng ldr: ev ch 3f out: sn n.m.r and wknd* **66/1**

000- 12 17 **Professor Twinkle**[417] 6547 4-9-4 **65**........(b[1]) AndrewHeffernan(3) 9 —
(I W McInnes) *prom: rdn and wknd 4f out* **40/1**

2m 0.52s (-1.18) **Going Correction** +0.025s/f (Slow)
WFA 3 from 4yo+ 2lb Ran SP% **119.02**
Speed ratings (Par 101): **106,105,102,101,99 96,96,92,90,83 81,66**
toteswinger: 1&2 not won, 1&3 £2.30, 2&3 £32.90. CSF £76.41 CT £618.57 TOTE £7.80: £3.70, £4.20, £3.30; EX 119.40.

Owner Ms G O'Ferrall **Bred** The Newchange Syndicate **Trained** Colehill, Co. Longford

FOCUS
Exposed performers in this modest handicap but the form looks sound rated around the placed horses. The pace was reasonable and the winner came down the centre in the straight.

7733 RACING ALL YEAR ROUND AT WOLVERHAMPTON H'CAP 5f 20y(P)
7:20 (7:20) (Class 5) (0-75,75) 3-Y-O+ £3,885 (£1,156; £577; £288) **Stalls** Low

Form RPR

0002 1 **Northern Empire (IRE)**[3] 7697 5-8-13 **70**........ JamieSpencer 6 81
(K A Ryan) *s.i.s: hld up: hdwy wl over 1f out: rdn to ld ins fnl f: r.o* **5/2**[1]

2203 2 ¾ **Figaro Flyer (IRE)**[14] 7562 5-8-13 **70**........ IanMongan 7 78
(P Howling) *hld up: hdwy over 2f out: rdn and ev ch over 1f out: nt qckn ins fnl f* **10/3**[2]

6126 3 1 ¼ **Ryedane (IRE)**[11] 7611 6-8-3 **63**........(b) DuranFentiman(3) 1 67
(T D Easterby) *outpcd in rr: rdn and r.o ins fnl f: tk 3rd last strides* **7/1**

2060 4 hd **Nickel Silver**[18] 7517 3-8-5 **62**........ GregFairley 2 65
(B Smart) *a.p: led over 1f out: rdn and hdd ins fnl f: one pce* **16/1**

0204 5 1 ¼ **Bishopbriggs (USA)**[28] 7399 3-8-7 **67**........ TolleyDean(3) 4 65
(S Parr) *towards rr: hdwy on ins wl over 1f out: rdn and no ex ins fnl f* **20/1**

600 6 6 **Drifting Gold**[23] 7456 4-8-10 **67**........(b) AdamKirby 3 44
(C G Cox) *prom tl rdn and wknd 1f out* **18/1**

2230 7 2 ¼ **Best One**[37] 7290 4-9-1 **75**........(b) KevinGhunowa(3) 8 44
(R A Harris) *s.i.s: hdwy on outside over 2f out: wknd wl over 1f out* **9/1**

0224 8 1 ¾ **Cayman Fox**[14] 7562 3-8-13 **70**........ JimCrowley 5 32
(James Moffatt) *led: hdd over 1f out: sn wknd* **4/1**[3]

62.06 secs (-0.24) **Going Correction** +0.025s/f (Slow) Ran SP% **111.8**
Speed ratings (Par 103): **102,100,98,98,96 86,83,80**
toteswinger: 1&2 £3.20, 1&3 £1.60, 2&3 £3.80. CSF £10.35 CT £42.67 TOTE £3.00: £1.20, £1.10, £2.10; EX 8.70.

Owner Sunpak Potatoes **Bred** Denis McDonnell **Trained** Hambleton, N Yorks

FOCUS
An ordinary handicap and one run at a strong gallop so the form looks sound. The winner again came down the centre in the straight.

Bishopbriggs(USA) Official explanation: jockey said gelding hung right
Cayman Fox Official explanation: trainer said the filly injured herself leaving the stalls

7734 BOOK TICKETS ONLINE MEDIAN AUCTION MAIDEN FILLIES' STKS 5f 216y(P)
7:50 (7:52) (Class 5) 2-Y-O £2,729 (£806; £403) **Stalls** Low

Form RPR

1 **Night Affair** 2-9-0 0........ MartinDwyer 12 74+
(D W P Arbuthnot) *led early: chsd ldr: led wl over 2f out: rdn ins fnl f: r.o wl* **6/1**[3]

0 2 3 ¼ **Luckydolly (IRE)**[14] 7567 2-8-9 0........ EJMcNamara(5) 9 64
(F Costello, Ire) *plld hrd: a.p: edgd lft over 2f out: sn chsng wnr: no imp* **11/4**[1]

4504 3 5 **Lois Darlin (IRE)**[16] 7537 2-8-11 49........(b) KevinGhunowa(3) 6 49
(R A Harris) *chsd ldrs: rdn and wknd over 1f out* **14/1**

56 4 ¾ **Swiss Lake Sweetie (USA)**[99] 5838 2-8-11 0........ TolleyDean(3) 11 47
(George Baker) *chsd ldrs: rdn 2f out: wknd over 1f out* **8/1**

5 6 **Crystal Feather** 2-9-0 0........ JamieSpencer 8 29
(E F Vaughan) *s.i.s: hdwy over 2f out: wknd wl over 1f out* **4/1**[2]

55 6 1 ½ **Cindy Incidentally**[36] 7303 2-9-0 0........ DarryllHolland 5 24
(Miss Gay Kelleway) *hld up in mid-div: rdn 2f out: sn wknd* **9/1**

0 7 hd **Nairana**[23] 7452 2-9-0 0........ PatCosgrave 3 24
(J G Given) *s.i.s: towards rr: rdn and short-lived effrt over 2f out* **14/1**

003 8 7 **Gracie's Games**[23] 7452 2-9-0 58........ JimCrowley 1 3
(R J Price) *towards rr: nt clr run and swtchd rt over 2f out: n.d after* **7/1**

6000 9 2 ¼ **Valentine Bay**[46] 7170 2-9-0 48........(p) HayleyTurner 4 —
(M Mullineaux) *prom tl wknd over 2f out* **25/1**

05 **10** *nk* **Tattercoats (FR)**[13] 7577 2-9-0 0 StephenDonohoe 7 —
(D M Simcock) *a bhd* **33/1**

11 *26* **Forel** 2-9-0 0 LiamJones 2 —
(J Ryan) *s.i.s: outpcd: t.o* **50/1**

0 **12** *nk* **Risky Lady (IRE)**[8] 7638 2-9-0 0 MickyFenton 10 —
(J Ryan) *sn led: hdd wl over 2f out: sn bdly hmpd on ins: nt rcvr: t.o* **66/1**

1m 15.84s (0.84) **Going Correction** +0.025s/f (Slow) **12** Ran SP% **118.1**
Speed ratings (Par 93): **95,90,84,83,75 73,72,63,60,60 25,24**
toteswinger: 1&2 £25.60, 1&3 £25.60, 2&3 £17.80. CSF £22.15 TOTE £8.30: £2.60, £1.60, £4.70; EX 25.20.
Owner Lady Whent And Friends **Bred** Mrs C R D Wilson **Trained** Compton, Berks

FOCUS
An ordinary maiden run at an ordinary gallop and the proximity of the 49-rated third holds the form down, although it looks fairly solid. The winner raced just off the inside rail in the straight.

NOTEBOOK
Night Affair, who refused to be mounted on the course and had to be withdrawn on her intended debut at Lingfield last month, attracted support and created a fair impression in this ordinary event. She should stay 7f and is entitled to improve for the experience. (op 9-1 tchd 12-1)
Luckydolly(IRE) had been running creditably at Dundalk and she seemed to give it her best shot, despite racing keenly. She looks the best guide to this form and is capable of picking up a race but is likely to remain vulnerable to the more progressive sorts in this grade. (op 5-2 tchd 15-8)
Lois Darlin(IRE) seemed to run creditably in the face of a stiff task but her proximity confirms this form is nothing special and low-grade handicaps will provide her with the best chance of success. (op 20-1)
Swiss Lake Sweetie(USA) caught the eye on her debut but again failed to reproduce that effort after racing wide on this all-weather debut after a break. Modest handicaps will be the way forward but she will have to show more before she is a solid betting proposition. (op 7-1)
Crystal Feather, who is related to winners, showed ability after a tardy start until tiring in the straight and she is entitled to improve for the experience. (op 7-2 tchd 5-1)
Cindy Incidentally, who again had her limitations exposed upped in trip, may also improve for the step into low-grade handicaps. (op 14-1 tchd 20-1)
Risky Lady(IRE) Official explanation: jockey said filly suffered interference in running

7735 SHREDICOTE MAIDEN STKS 7f 32y(P)
8:20 (8:22) (Class 5) 2-Y-O **£2,729** (£806; £403) **Stalls** High

Form RPR

0 **1** **Scene Two**[12] 7593 2-9-3 0 JamieSpencer 10 70+
(L M Cumani) *towards rr: pushed along over 4f out: hdwy over 2f out: missed trble over 1f out: rdn to ld ins fnl f: r.o* **3/1**[3]

2 *nk* **Commandingpresence (USA)** 2-8-12 0 HayleyTurner 5 64+
(B J Meehan) *bmpd s: chsd ldrs: led over 1f out: sn rdn and hung rt: hdd ins fnl f: kpt on* **17/2**

5 **3** *4 1/2* **Appropriate (IRE)**[27] 7424 2-8-12 0 LiamJones 3 56+
(W J Haggas) *wnt rt s: plld hrd: sn led: rdn over 2f out: hdd and hmpd over 1f out: wknd ins fnl f* **11/8**[1]

0 **4** *2 1/4* **Gurteen Diamond**[34] 7341 2-8-9 0 LukeMorris(3) 11 49+
(N J Vaughan) *sn chsng ldr: rdn 2f out: bdly hmpd over 1f out: wknd ins fnl f* **66/1**

0 **5** *3 1/4* **Lovely Steps (USA)**[14] 7561 2-8-12 0 StephenDonohoe 8 40
(D M Simcock) *chsd ldrs: wknd over 3f out* **66/1**

00 **6** *6* **Cause For Applause (IRE)**[76] 6480 2-8-12 0 (v[1]) JimCrowley 4 25
(B Smart) *s.i.s: a bhd* **33/1**

6 **7** *nse* **Tillietudlem (FR)**[42] 7221 2-8-12 0 GaryBartley(5) 7 30
(J S Goldie) *bhd fnl 4f* **40/1**

8 *1* **Michael Collins (IRE)**[228] 1878 2-9-3 0 MartinDwyer 2 27
(Ms Maria Kelly, Ire) *led early: sn n.m.r on ins: hmpd after 1f: chsd ldrs: rdn 3f out: sn wknd* **11/4**[2]

9 *16* **Dependonyou** 2-8-9 0 TolleyDean(3) 9 —
(A J McCabe) *s.i.s: a in rr: t.o* **66/1**

10 *7* **Elements (IRE)** 2-8-12 0 RobertWinston 6 —
(E J Alston) *s.i.s: a in rr: t.o* **16/1**

1m 30.49s (0.89) **Going Correction** +0.025s/f (Slow) **10** Ran SP% **120.0**
Speed ratings (Par 96): **95,94,89,86,83 76,76,75,56,48**
toteswinger: 1&2 £1.70, 1&3 £4.40, 2&3 £4.70. CSF £28.48 TOTE £4.80: £1.70, £3.20, £1.10; EX 26.10.
Owner Team Spirit 2 **Bred** R E Crutchley **Trained** Newmarket, Suffolk

FOCUS
An ordinary maiden in which the two market leaders disappointed to varying degrees and the form looks messy. A reasonable gallop but a fairly rough race and the winner raced centre to far side.

NOTEBOOK
Scene Two ◆ proved easy to back and took plenty of stoking up but turned in an improved effort to get off the mark at the second attempt. He missed all the trouble late on but did win a shade cosily in the end and looks the sort to progress again, especially when upped to 1m. (op 9-4 tchd 4-1)
Commandingpresence(USA) ◆, related to several winners in the US, showed a fair level of ability on this debut and would have gone even closer had she not been denied a run at a crucial stage and not been knocked sideways when hitting the front. She looks sure to pick up a similar event. (op 15-2 tchd 6-1 and 9-1)
Appropriate(IRE), who caught the eye on her debut, attracted plenty of support, despite dropping in trip. She looks a bit better than the bare form as she failed to settle and took a hefty bump once headed. She is worth another chance back up in trip but will need to settle better if she is to progress. (tchd 13-8)
Gurteen Diamond, well beaten on her debut, had the headgear on again but fared considerably better. She looked held when taking a bump in the closing stages and may do better in ordinary handicaps in due course. (op 50-1)
Lovely Steps(USA) fared a little better than on her debut and, while likely to remain vulnerable in this grade, should do better granted a stiffer test once handicapped. (op 50-1)
Michael Collins(IRE), who showed ability at an ordinary level behind subsequent dual Group 1 winner Mastercraftsman in a race that threw up numerous winners on his debut in May, was the subject of a gamble on this first run since, but proved disappointing after meeting early trouble. He is probably worth another chance. Official explanation: jockey said colt hung out on the bend (op 9-1 tchd 5-2)

7736 SPONSOR A RACE BY CALLING 01902 390009 CLASSIFIED STKS 1m 141y(P)
8:50 (8:51) (Class 7) 3-Y-O+ **£1,364** (£403; £201) **Stalls** Low

Form RPR

5650 **1** **Hi Spec (IRE)**[9] 7631 5-9-0 44 (p) AdamKirby 10 51
(Miss M E Rowland) *s.i.s: bhd: hdwy whn nt clr run and swtchd lft ins fnl f: str run to ld post* **18/1**

00-3 **2** *shd* **Mocha Java**[64] 6752 5-8-7 43 RossAtkinson(7) 12 50
(M Salaman) *hld up in tch: led over 2f out: rdn over 1f out: hdd post* **7/1**[3]

-406 **3** *1 1/4* **Rawaabet (IRE)**[16] 6161 6-9-0 43 JimCrowley 13 47
(R Hollinshead) *s.i.s: bhd: hdwy over 2f out: rdn wl over 1f out: kpt on ins fnl f* **9/2**[2]

006 **4** *nk* **Amber Moon**[19] 7506 3-8-12 45 (b[1]) MickyFenton 1 47
(J A Osborne) *led after 1f: rdn and hdd over 2f out: kpt on same pce fnl f* **14/1**

04 **5** *3/4* **Elkhart Lake (IRE)**[8] 7637 3-8-12 45 (t) RobertWinston 5 45
(Adrian McGuinness, Ire) *mid-div: rdn and hdwy 2f out: one pce fnl f* **5/2**[1]

0004 **6** *hd* **Pajada**[4] 7691 4-9-0 43 HayleyTurner 9 45
(M D I Usher) *hld up and bhd: hdwy wl over 1f out: no ex towards fin* **15/2**

6000 **7** *hd* **Autumn Charm**[45] 7180 3-8-12 45 NeilChalmers 3 44
(Lucinda Featherstone) *hld up in tch: rdn over 2f out: one pce fnl f* **25/1**

2460 **8** *hd* **Abbeygate**[39] 7270 7-9-0 45 (p) NickyMackay 6 44
(T Keddy) *hld up in rr: hdwy over 5f out: rdn over 1f out: one pce* **8/1**

3000 **9** *9* **Poppy Red**[15] 6896 3-8-5 45 (p) AndrewHeffernan(7) 8 23
(C J Gray) *s.i.s: a in rr* **100/1**

3600 **10** *3 3/4* **Ginger Minx (IRE)**[16] 7541 3-8-9 45 LukeMorris(3) 7 14
(N J Vaughan) *led 1f: chsd ldr tl over 4f out: rdn over 2f out: wknd over 1f out* **40/1**

00 **11** *2 1/2* **Chiefofthemowhawks (USA)**[4] 7692 5-9-0 44 (p) PatCosgrave 2 9
(Stephen Michael Cox, Ire) *half-rrd s: a bhd* **20/1**

0060 **12** *7* **Honeycott (IRE)**[148] 4332 3-8-12 45 (v) DarryllHolland 4 —
(J D Bethell) *hld up in mid-div: rdn over 2f out: sn wknd* **10/1**

0000 **13** *37* **Rich James (IRE)**[1] 7725 3-8-12 44 MartinDwyer 11 —
(J D Bethell) *hld up in mid-div: lost pl and hrd rdn over 3f out: t.o* **40/1**

1m 50.98s (0.48) **Going Correction** +0.025s/f (Slow)
WFA 3 from 4yo+ 2lb **13** Ran SP% **117.6**
Speed ratings (Par 97): **98,97,96,96,95 95,95,95,87,84 81,75,42**
toteswinger: 1&2 £11.80, 1&3 £16.70, 2&3 £4.60. CSF £130.88 TOTE £21.30: £5.00, £3.50, £2.10; EX 182.60.
Owner Miss M E Rowland **Bred** Mrs Marita Rogers **Trained** Lower Blidworth, Notts
■ Stewards' Enquiry : Adam Kirby one-day ban: use of whip

FOCUS
A weak event but one run at a sound pace and the form is very limited. The winner raced towards the centre in the straight.

7737 WOLVERHAMPTON-RACECOURSE.CO.UK H'CAP 7f 32y(P)
9:20 (9:22) (Class 3) (0-95,92) 3-Y-O **£7,569** (£2,265; £1,132; £566; £282) **Stalls** High

Form RPR

4403 **1** **Councellor (FR)**[9] 7633 6-8-10 84 ow2 (t) MickyFenton 6 91
(Stef Liddiard) *hld up in mid-div: hdwy over 2f out: led wl ins fnl f: r.o* **7/1**

0003 **2** *1/2* **Aeroplane**[21] 7470 5-9-3 91 JamieSpencer 1 97
(S A Callaghan) *hld up in mid-div: hdwy 2f out: chal over 1f out: kpt on ins fnl f* **5/2**[1]

3153 **3** *nk* **Willkandoo (USA)**[27] 7423 3-8-8 82 StephenDonohoe 7 87
(D M Simcock) *a.p: rdn to ld over 1f out: hdd wl ins fnl f: nt qckn* **12/1**

1003 **4** *3/4* **Gallantry**[14] 7556 6-8-11 85 TGMcLaughlin 4 88
(P Howling) *a.p: rdn and ev ch wl over 1f out: nt qckn ins fnl f* **6/1**[3]

1000 **5** *nk* **The Jostler**[48] 7146 3-8-9 83 MartinDwyer 9 85
(B W Hills) *in rr: hdwy on ins over 1f out: nvr able to chal* **25/1**

0121 **6** *shd* **Mister New York (USA)**[25] 7439 3-8-11 85 JimCrowley 8 88+
(Noel T Chance) *hld up and bhd: rdn whn nt clr run fr wl over 1f out tl r.o ins fnl f: n.m.r cl home* **10/3**[2]

0303 **7** *2* **Methaaly (IRE)**[83] 6278 5-8-9 83 LiamJones 3 79
(M Mullineaux) *hld up and bhd: hdwy whn swtchd lft over 1f out: no further prog ins fnl f* **25/1**

5260 **8** *10* **Mr Lambros**[20] 7492 7-9-4 92 (vt) DarryllHolland 2 61
(Miss Gay Kelleway) *led early: chsd ldr: led over 2f out: rdn and hdd over 1f out: sn wknd* **8/1**

0036 **9** *4* **Perfect Act**[21] 7470 3-8-4 78 HayleyTurner 5 37
(C G Cox) *sn led: hdd over 2f out: wknd wl over 1f out* **8/1**

1m 28.95s (-0.65) **Going Correction** +0.025s/f (Slow) **9** Ran SP% **116.0**
Speed ratings (Par 107): **104,103,103,102,101 101,99,88,83**
toteswinger: 1&2 £7.90, 1&3 £7.00, 2&3 £4.30. CSF £24.99 CT £206.07 TOTE £9.00: £2.30, £1.30, £4.30; EX 35.10 Place 6 £84.40, Place 5 £15.12..
Owner ownaracehorse.co.uk **Bred** Janus Bloodstock & Pontchartrain Stud **Trained** Great Shefford, Berks

FOCUS
The feature race of the night and a valuable prize but one comprising exposed performers. The pace was sound and the principals raced in the centre in the straight and the form looks solid enough with the winner, third and fourth reproducing previous course form.

NOTEBOOK
Councellor(FR) had slipped to a fair mark, proved suited by the decent gallop and did enough to win his fourth race at this track, despite his rider posting overweight. Things panned out well for him here but he is a largely consistent sort who handles Fibresand and should continue to go well after reassessment. (op 8-1)
Aeroplane once again travelled like the best horse in the race but again found less than expected once asked for an effort. He has more than enough ability to win a race of this nature and may be worth a try in headgear but does not look one to be taking too short a price about. (op 2-1 tchd 11-4)
Willkandoo(USA) had the cheekpieces left off for the return to handicap company and he ran creditably to fare the best of the prominent racers. He has little margin for error from this mark but is a reliable type who should continue to give a good account. (op 14-1 tchd 16-1)
Gallantry, returning to his optimum distance, got a good tow into the race and ran well with no excuses. A truly run race over this trip are his requirements but he is vulnerable to the better handicapped or more progressive sorts from his mark. (op 11-2)
The Jostler, who raced away from the main action in the straight, ran creditably on this first run at this track but his lack of consistency means he would not be certain to build on this next time. (op 33-1)
Mister New York(USA), up in the weights and in grade, was far from disgraced after being short of room in the closing stages. He looked fourth best here and this regular winner and reliable sort should continue to run well up to 1m. (op 5-1 tchd 3-1)
T/Plt: £69.60 to a £1 stake. Pool: £114,884.42. 1,203.97 winning tickets. T/Qpdt: £10.10 to a £1 stake. Pool: £9,026.31. 657.40 winning tickets. KH

7706 LINGFIELD (L-H)
Saturday, December 20

OFFICIAL GOING: Standard
Wind: Fresh, half-behind Weather: Cloudy

7738 PHOTO FINISH FOR CHRISTMAS GIFTS @ EVENTIMAGE.TV (S) STKS 6f (P)
12:25 (12:29) (Class 6) 2-Y-O **£1,978** (£584; £292) **Stalls** Low

Form RPR

0650 **1** **Art Fund (USA)**[22] 7472 2-8-11 63 FergusSweeney 8 64+
(G L Moore) *chsd ldng trio: rdn over 2f out: brought wd in st: r.o fnl f to ld last 75yds: won gng away* **7/2**[2]

0551 **2** 1 1/4 **Elusive Ronnie (IRE)**[12] 7600 2-8-11 57......................(p) JimCrowley 10 60
(R A Teal) *chsd ldr: rdn over 2f out: grad clsd fnl f: upsides 100yds out: sn outpcd* **13/2**

6200 **3** 1 1/4 **Officer Mor (USA)**[8] 7652 2-9-2 63..................................(b[1]) NCallan 12 62+
(K R Burke) *led and tk fierce hold: wd bnd 2f out: hrd rdn over 1f out: wknd and hdd last 75yds* **11/2**

0002 **4** 1 **Jonnie Skull (IRE)**[16] 7547 2-8-11 59..........................(b) HayleyTurner 3 54
(D R C Elsworth) *chsd ldr: rdn over 2f out: tried to chal on inner over 1f out: fdd fnl f* **3/1**[1]

0 **5** 1 3/4 **Mandhooma**[58] 6933 2-8-6 0.. ChrisCatlin 1 43
(P W Hiatt) *hld up towards rr: wl off the pce sn after 1/2-way: nudged along and styd on takingly fr over 1f out: do bttr* **16/1**

4205 **6** hd **Our Wee Girl (IRE)**[6] 7673 2-8-7 70 ow1........................ JamieSpencer 7 44
(S Kirk) *wnt lft s and bmpd rival: mostly in midfield: outpcd sn after 1/2-way: hanging bdly over 1f out: r.o ins fnl f* **9/2**[3]

7 3 1/2 **Flying River (IRE)** 2-7-13 0.. RossAtkinson(7) 4 32
(Tom Dascombe) *awkward s: pushed along in last pair after 2f: sn wl adrift of ldrs: styd on fnl f* **20/1**

0000 **8** 3 1/4 **Harry Raffle**[5] 7687 2-8-11 56..(b[1]) LPKeniry 5 27
(S Kirk) *sn in midfield: outpcd fr 1/2-way: wknd over 1f out* **20/1**

0 **9** 1 1/4 **Rental Roy**[12] 7602 2-8-11 0.. AdamKirby 6 24
(Mrs P Townsley) *dwlt and bmpd sn after s: t.k.h early: hld up in midfield: outpcd 1/2-way: wknd over 1f out* **66/1**

3000 **10** 10 **Claphands**[28] 7415 2-8-6 55..(tp) PaulDoe 11 —
(M A Allen) *dwlt and reminder sn after s: a in last pair and nvr gng wl: t.o* **50/1**

1m 11.93s (0.03) **Going Correction** -0.15s/f (Stan) **10** Ran SP% **113.0**
Speed ratings (Par 94): **93,91,89,88,86 85,81,76,75,61**
toteswinger: 1&2 £2.90, 1&3 £5.70, 2&3 £4.30. CSF £24.38 TOTE £4.80: £1.80, £1.80, £2.00; EX 28.20 TRIFECTA Not won..There was no bid for the winner.
Owner R A Green **Bred** Candyland Farm **Trained** Woodingdean, E Sussex

FOCUS
A seller of reasonable quality; the principals had some previous form to their names and the pace was respectable for the grade and the form looks solid enough.

NOTEBOOK
Art Fund(USA) had shown ability in four races including a nursery, so was an obvious contender dropped to this level. The return to 6f suited him well, but the way he finished suggests he can do better than on his only previous attempt at 7f if returned to the longer trip. (tchd 3-1)
Elusive Ronnie(IRE), winner of a seller here last time, ran another sound race and looks very much at home in this company, with the cheekpieces continuing to have a positive effect. (op 5-1 tchd 7-1)
Officer Mor(USA) did well to make the running from the outside stall and battled on well in first-time blinkers. Though he has been largely disappointing since winning at Beverley in May, the drop in class and application of headgear seemed to spark something of a revival. (op 8-1 tchd 5-1)
Jonnie Skull(IRE) has also done better since being dropped to sellers, though he was short of a finishing kick in the final furlong and would be suited by a return to 7f or 1m. (op 4-1)
Mandhooma left John Gosden's stable for just 1,000gns after finishing last of 12 at Great Leighs in October, but on this evidence she is not a hopeless cause by any means. Staying on steadily from well off the pace, she should make her mark in modest company if continuing to progress. (op 20-1)
Our Wee Girl(IRE) is failing to live up to her early promise, and her recent Polytrack form does not inspire confidence. (op 7-2)

7739 CARLSBERG UK NOVICE STKS 7f (P)
1:00 (1:00) (Class 5) 2-Y-O **£3,885** (£1,156; £577) **Stalls** Low

Form RPR

51 **1** **Sonning Gate**[26] 7434 2-9-5 81.. GeorgeBaker 2 87+
(D R C Elsworth) *t.k.h early: trckd ldr 1f: lft in 2nd again 2f out: cruised into ld over 1f out: comf* **2/5**[1]

5160 **2** 2 3/4 **Sunniva Duke (IRE)**[17] 7538 2-9-2 76........................ RichardHughes 1 75
(R Hannon) *fast away: led: reminders whn pressed over 3f out: hdd over 1f out: no ch w wnr after* **9/1**[3]

0023 **3** 1 1/2 **Sign Of Approval**[8] 7655 2-8-12 80......................................(v[1]) NCallan 4 67
(K R Burke) *t.k.h early: trckd ldr after 1f: upsides fr over 3f out tl hung bdly rt bnd 2f out and threw away all ch* **3/1**[2]

1m 24.87s (0.07) **Going Correction** -0.15s/f (Stan) **3** Ran SP% **106.4**
Speed ratings (Par 96): **93,89,88**
CSF £4.01 TOTE £1.30; EX 2.10.
Owner A Heaney **Bred** Sunley Stud **Trained** Newmarket, Suffolk

FOCUS
Uncompetitive fare, with the runner-up soon dictating a weak tempo and the odds-on winner proving far too good. A difficult race to gauge accurately.

NOTEBOOK
Sonning Gate had a simple task but the manner of success confirmed his potential. Showing that he is as home over 7f as he has been at 1m, he left the runner-up standing with Baker barely moving and will go on to much better things in the New Year. He returned with a cut on a hind leg, having been struck into during the race, but it is not expected to be a long-term issue. (op 4-9 tchd 1-2 in places)
Sunniva Duke(IRE) had things his own way in front, and Hughes is a master in such situations, but when it came to the crunch he was quickly outclassed. He has been too high in the weights in recent nurseries, so may have to wait his turn. (op 10-1 tchd 14-1)
Sign Of Approval is not going the right way at present and the application of a visor failed to turn turn things round. His chance ended when he cornered into the straight, and he does not look one to have much faith in for the time being. (op 11-4 tchd 9-4)

7740 CARLSBERG, PROBABLY THE BEST CONDITIONS STKS 1m (P)
1:35 (1:35) (Class 3) 3-Y-O+ **£7,641** (£2,273; £1,136; £567) **Stalls** Low

Form RPR

4342 **1** **Banknote**[35] 7339 6-8-12 98.. FrancisNorton 5 98
(A M Balding) *tended to run in snatches: hld up tl trckd ldrs 3f out: wnt 3rd wl over 1f out: hanging lft and nt look keen: cajoled along to cl and fnd enough to ld last 50yds* **9/4**[1]

3000 **2** hd **Philario (IRE)**[28] 7421 3-8-11 97.................................... FergusSweeney 10 97
(K R Burke) *racd wd: pressed ldng pair: wnt 2nd over 2f out: rdn to ld over 1f out: worn down last 50yds* **7/1**

0231 **3** 2 1/4 **Abbondanza (IRE)**[7] 7670 5-9-3 85..............................(p) PaulMulrennan 4 97
(I Semple) *pressed ldr: led 3f out: drvn and hdd over 1f out: outpcd fnl f* **5/1**[3]

0-60 **4** 2 1/2 **Lady Jane Digby**[84] 6266 3-8-6 90.................................... GregFairley 2 81
(M Johnston) *hld up in tch: effrt whn trapped bhd wkng rival 2f out and lost grnd: hrd rdn and kpt on* **16/1**

6100 **5** 1/2 **Orchard Supreme**[21] 7492 5-9-5 99.............................. RichardHughes 8 92
(R Hannon) *hld up in last: sme prog over 2f out: shkn up and nt qckn over 1f out: kpt on same pce* **3/1**[2]

2616 **6** 4 **Randama Bay (IRE)**[12] 7606 3-8-11 75................................ CatherineGannon 6 76
(I A Wood) *steadily lost early pl and pushed along in rr 1/2-way: struggling over 2f out: no ch after* **33/1**

0000 **7** 3 1/4 **Bee Stinger**[3] 7712 6-8-12 80..(v) AdamKirby 3 68
(I A Wood) *t.k.h early: hld up: pushed along over 3f out: struggling in last over 2f out* **8/1**

003- **8** 2 3/4 **Count Trevisio (IRE)**[504] 4167 5-8-12 94.................................. NCallan 1 62
(J R Gask) *led to 3f out: wknd 2f out* **12/1**

1m 35.1s (-3.10) **Going Correction** -0.15s/f (Stan) course record
WFA 3 from 5yo+ 1lb **8** Ran SP% **112.6**
Speed ratings (Par 107): **109,108,106,104,103 99,96,93**
toteswinger: 1&2 £4.40, 1&3 £3.90, 2&3 £4.70. CSF £18.00 TOTE £2.50: £1.10, £2.40, £1.80; EX 21.30 Trifecta £150.50 Pool: £223.74 - 1.50 winning units.
Owner The Queen **Bred** Exors Of The Late Queen Elizabeth **Trained** Kingsclere, Hants
■ Stewards' Enquiry : Francis Norton one-day ban: excessive use of whip (Jan 3)

FOCUS
A good-quality turnout bordering on Listed class, but the pace was no better than medium until it stepped up 3f from home. The form looks relatively ordinary for the grade.

NOTEBOOK
Banknote, just best-in on official figures, scraped home in the end and not without giving his supporters some anxious moments. Trying to hang in behind the two leaders when asked for his effort, he had to be re-organised by Norton, who cajoled him to the front close home without use of the whip. He will now take his chance in Dubai. (op 7-4 tchd 5-2)
Philario(IRE), theoretically only a pound behind the winner on these terms, went extremely close over a longer distance than usual. He has been struggling in decent sprint company of late and looks more of a miler these days. (op 9-1)
Abbondanza(IRE) ran well at the weights on his first visit to the track. However, he has put in some good performances at other Polytrack venues and remains in top form on the surface. (tchd 9-2)
Lady Jane Digby has been disappointing since winning on her juvenile debut. Off the track for three months, she put in a fair first run on the all-weather, but it was no more than that and she must improve to justify her current mark if returned to handicaps. (op 12-1 tchd 11-1)
Orchard Supreme is on a testing mark in handicaps at present and conceding weight to these rivals was also a stiff task. He could have done with a stronger gallop, but he just about ran his race and showed enough to keep his supporters onside. (op 7-2)

7741 QUEBEC STKS (LISTED RACE) 1m 2f (P)
2:05 (2:05) (Class 1) 3-Y-O+
£22,708 (£8,608; £4,308; £2,148; £1,076; £540) **Stalls** Low

Form RPR

4461 **1** **Dansant**[21] 7491 4-9-5 114.. EddieAhern 5 116
(G A Butler) *hld up in last pair: pushed along and prog on outer fr 3f out: brought wd in st: rdn to ld ent fnl f: sn wl on top* **9/4**[1]

1111 **2** 2 1/2 **Suits Me**[14] 7579 5-9-3 108.. MickyFenton 3 109
(T P Tate) *trckd ldr: led 2f out and gng strly: rdn and hdd ent fnl f: sn outpcd* **7/1**

2 **3** 2 1/4 **Bon Spiel**[14] 7579 4-9-3 90.. JamieSpencer 6 105
(L M Cumani) *chsd ldrs: rdn over 3f out: tried to cl over 1f out: kpt on same pce* **14/1**

5224 **4** 1/2 **Re Barolo (IRE)**[28] 7420 5-9-3 109..............................(t) JohnEgan 2 104+
(M Botti) *hld up in 5th: wnt for run up inner over 3f out but no room and snatched up: renewed effrt over 1f out: kpt on one pce* **3/1**[2]

3430 **5** 3 3/4 **Scintillo**[21] 7491 3-9-0 109..(b) RichardHughes 7 96
(R Hannon) *led to 2f out: wknd fnl f* **5/1**[3]

6000 **6** shd **Grand Passion (IRE)**[28] 7420 8-9-3 104.............................. GeorgeBaker 4 96
(C F Wall) *hld up in last pair: outpcd fr 3f out: nvr on terms after* **12/1**

0023 **7** 23 **Harvest Queen (IRE)**[28] 7420 5-8-12 102................................ NCallan 1 45
(P J Makin) *hmpd after 100yds: trckd ldrs: wknd over 2f out: virtually p.u* **7/1**

2m 1.63s (-4.97) **Going Correction** -0.15s/f (Stan) course record
WFA 3 from 4yo+ 3lb **7** Ran SP% **111.8**
Speed ratings (Par 111): **113,111,109,108,105 105,87**
toteswinger: 1&2 £1.90, 1&3 £5.00, 2&3 £4.00. CSF £17.61 TOTE £3.70: £1.80, £3.10; EX 16.80.
Owner Mrs Barbara M Keller **Bred** Mrs Cino Del Duca **Trained** Newmarket, Suffolk
■ Stewards' Enquiry : Richard Hughes one-day ban: careless riding (Jan 3)

FOCUS
A solid gallop in this Listed event helped set up a track record. The winner is rated back to his best with the runner-up a shade off.

NOTEBOOK
Dansant was the one to beat on official figures, and his Kempton win a month ago showed he was back to his best. He has now won five times on Polytrack, including the Winter Derby Trial here in February. Effective at 1m2f and 1m4f, he is one of the stars of the winter season and is now likely to head to Dubai for the Maktoum Challenge series, and then to the USA.
Suits Me, still improving and in great recent form on Polytrack, looked set to land his fifth successive victory when taking the lead around the final bend but the winner wore him down the final furlong. He has gone so far up the weights that Listed races are now his natural level, and he looks well at home in this grade. (op 9-2)
Bon Spiel had a lot to do on these terms, having been beaten by the runner-up at Great Leighs despite receiving 15lb. In the circumstances, it was a fine effort which suggests that this Italian import is still on the upgrade, though placing him may cause a few problems if he is harshly re-assessed. (op 12-1 tchd 9-1)
Re Barolo(IRE) was hampered on the inside rail just as the race was beginning to develop, which left him with too much to do against these classy opponents. He remains a very useful performer on Polytrack and deserves to pick up a decent prize. (op 7-2)
Scintillo was the subject of a morning gamble but it went astray as he was comfortably swamped in the home straight. He continues to be disappointing on the whole. (op 6-1)
Grand Passion(IRE), who was Geoff Wragg's last-ever runner here a month ago, remains well below his form of previous seasons. (op 16-1)
Harvest Queen(IRE) Official explanation: jockey said mare suffered interference in running

7742 DECK THE HALLS H'CAP 1m 2f (P)
2:40 (2:40) (Class 5) (0-70,70) 3-Y-O+ **£2,729** (£806; £403) **Stalls** Low

Form RPR

2441 **1** **Risque Heights**[10] 7620 4-9-6 69.................................... GeorgeBaker 7 81
(J R Boyle) *dwlt: hld up in last trio: prog to go 4th over 2f out: chsd ldr jst over 1f out: rdn and r.o wl to ld last 75yds* **7/2**[1]

3101 **2** 1/2 **Saucy**[13] 7596 7-8-11 60.................................... RichardKingscote 4 71
(Tom Dascombe) *trckd ldng pair: gng strly 2f out: squeezed through to ld over 1f out: rdr dropped whip sn after: r.o fnl f: hdd last 75yds* **6/1**

3 3 3/4 **Sinntaran (IRE)**[50] 7123 4-8-13 62.................................... RPCleary 1 65
(M Halford, Ire) *t.k.h early: pressed ldr: upsides over 2f out to over 1f out: outpcd fnl f* **4/1**[2]

6515 **4** 2 **Ministerofinterior**[33] 7354 3-8-5 57.................................... ChrisCatlin 6 56
(G L Moore) *pushed along in midfield and nvr gng that wl: outpcd u.p 2f out: plugged on* **5/1**[3]

241- **5** *nk* **Cinematic (IRE)**[408] 6738 5-9-7 **70** PatCosgrave 9 68
(J R Boyle) *hld up in last: effrt on wd outside over 2f out: hanging and nt qckn over 1f out: pushed along and kpt on fnl f* **10/1**

0050 **6** *1½* **Lend A Grand (IRE)**[20] 7510 4-9-3 **66** TravisBlock 3 61
(Miss Jo Crowley) *trckd ldrs: pushed along over 3f out: struggling over 2f out: brief effrt on inner over 1f out: wknd* **20/1**

0414 **7** *hd* **Play Up Pompey**[6] 7676 6-8-7 **56** FrancisNorton 2 51
(J J Bridger) *hld up in rr: rdn over 3f out: struggling over 2f out* **14/1**

0126 **8** *¾* **Lord Theo**[14] 7580 4-9-4 **67** JamesDoyle 5 61
(N P Littmoden) *t.k.h early: mde most: rdn over 2f out: hdd & wknd over 1f out* **7/1**

0620 **9** *10* **Dawson Creek (IRE)**[20] 7510 4-9-2 **65** NCallan 8 39
(B Gubby) *t.k.h and racd on outer: trckd ldrs: rdn over 3f out: wknd 2f out: eased* **17/2**

2m 4.90s (-1.70) **Going Correction** -0.15s/f (Stan)
WFA 3 from 4yo+ 3lb **9** Ran SP% **116.7**
Speed ratings (Par 103): **100,99,96,95,94 93,93,92,84**
toteswinger: 1&2 £9.40, 1&3 £8.60, 2&3 £10.90. CSF £25.03 CT £87.61 TOTE £4.20: £1.90, £1.70, £1.10; EX 12.00 Trifecta £46.20 Pool: £318.49 - 5.10 - winning units.
Owner Serendipity Syndicate 2006 **Bred** R Charles **Trained** Epsom, Surrey

FOCUS
They went a fair gallop early on and, though the pace slackened somewhat after 3f, the front-runners quickened things up again fully 4f from home. The form looks sound enough rated around the third and fourth to recent marks.

7743 GOOD KING WENCESLAS H'CAP 5f (P)
3:20 (3:20) (Class 5) (0-70,73) 3-Y-0+ £2,729 (£806; £403) Stalls High

Form RPR

0121 **1** **Thoughtsofstardom**[6] 7672 5-9-0 **69** 6ex LukeMorris(3) 6 81
(P S McEntee) *trckd ldrs: wnt 3rd 2f out: urged along to ld 1f out: wl in command after* **4/1**[2]

005 **2** *2* **After The Show**[22] 7471 7-8-13 **65** JimCrowley 1 69
(Rae Guest) *missed break: settled in last trio: effrt on inner wl over 1f out: drvn and r.o to take 2nd last 50yds* **7/2**[1]

4656 **3** *½* **Replicator**[17] 7540 3-9-1 **67** (b[1]) PaulEddery 7 70
(Pat Eddery) *awkward s: hanging rt bnd after 1f: off the pce in midfield: hrd rdn and styd on fnl f to snatch 3rd last stride* **12/1**

1324 **4** *shd* **Bluebok**[19] 7517 7-8-6 **63** (bt) JackDean(5) 2 65
(J M Bradley) *t.k.h early: w ldr 1f: trcking after: cl up over 1f out: hrd rdn and nt qckn* **17/2**

0000 **5** *nse* **Ten Down**[15] 7562 3-8-12 **64** FrancisNorton 3 66
(M Quinn) *mde most tl hdd 1f out: no ch w wnr after: wknd and lost pls nr fin* **10/1**

5401 **6** *¾* **Bookiesindex Boy**[10] 7621 4-9-7 **73** (v) StephenDonohoe 5 72
(J R Jenkins) *w ldr after 1f: upsides jst over 1f out: weakene3d* **8/1**[3]

6461 **7** *¾* **Azygous**[6] 7679 5-8-11 **63** 6ex AdamKirby 4 60
(J Akehurst) *nvr bttr than midfield: plugged on fr over 1f out but no imp on ldrs* **9/1**

16 **8** *hd* **Step It Up (IRE)**[10] 7621 4-9-1 **67** PatCosgrave 9 63
(J R Boyle) *pushed along towards rr and off the pce: drvn and kpt on fr over 1f out: nt pce to threaten* **7/2**[1]

1510 **9** *3¼* **Desert Opal**[10] 7621 8-9-1 **67** (b) LiamJones 8 51
(C R Dore) *missed break: a last and struggling* **14/1**

58.08 secs (-0.72) **Going Correction** -0.15s/f (Stan) **9** Ran SP% **119.5**
Speed ratings (Par 103): **99,95,95,94,94 93,92,92,86**
toteswinger: 1&2 £9.40, 1&3 £8.60, 2&3 £10.90. CSF £19.18 CT £158.33 TOTE £6.10: £1.80, £2.10, £1.80; EX 32.40 Trifecta £329.40 Part won. Pool: £445.23 - 0.10 winning units. Place 6 £22.04, Place 5 £7.16..
Owner Eventmaker Racehorses **Bred** B Bargh **Trained** Newmarket, Suffolk

FOCUS
Run at a strong pace, with two front-runners taking one another on, and producing a winner who is in the form of his life. The form looks sound enough although some of these are not the most solid performers.
Desert Opal Official explanation: jockey said gelding suffered interference on leaving the stalls
T/Plt: £16.40 to a £1 stake. Pool: £44,771.08. 1,990.09 winning tickets. T/Qpdt: £5.30 to a £1 stake. Pool: £3,103.93. 433.30 winning tickets. JN

[7732] WOLVERHAMPTON (A.W) (L-H)
Saturday, December 20

OFFICIAL GOING: Standard to fast
Wind: Moderate, behind Weather: Fine

7744 WOLVERHAMPTON-RACECOURSE.CO.UK CLAIMING STKS 1m 4f 50y(P)
6:20 (6:20) (Class 6) 3-Y-0+ £2,388 (£705; £352) Stalls Low

Form RPR

-053 **1** **Heathyards Pride**[21] 7499 8-9-2 80 GrahamGibbons 3 78
(R Hollinshead) *hld up: hdwy over 2f out: led over 1f out: clr ins fnl f: readily* **11/8**[1]

6151 **2** *5* **Bridgewater Boys**[12] 7608 7-9-6 68 (b) GeorgeBaker 4 74
(G L Moore) *hld up in rr: nt clr run over 2f out: swtchd rt whn rdn and hdwy wl over 1f out: wnt 2nd ins fnl f: no ch w wnr* **8/1**

600- **3** *2* **Corriolanus (GER)**[434] 6172 8-9-0 85 FrancisNorton 5 65
(A M Balding) *t.k.h in tch: nt clr run fr over 3f out tl wl over 1f out: sn pushed along: kpt on same pce to take 3rd towards fin* **9/2**[2]

2252 **4** *½* **Torrens (IRE)**[12] 7608 6-8-5 58 (t) PatrickDonaghy(5) 8 60
(P D Evans) *hld up and bhd: hdwy on outside over 2f out: rdn over 1f out: one pce fnl f* **9/1**

3030 **5** *2¾* **Nawamees (IRE)**[3] 7707 10-9-10 75 (p) TGMcLaughlin 6 70
(P D Evans) *chsd ldr 4f: prom: rdn over 2f out: wknd ins fnl f* **13/2**[3]

0250 **6** *2* **Mustajed**[12] 7606 7-9-1 73 (v) JamesMillman(3) 12 60
(B R Millman) *s.s: sn prom: led over 4f out: rdn over 2f out: hdd over 1f out: wknd fnl f* **8/1**

5000 **7** *15* **Kames Park (IRE)**[15] 7563 6-8-12 68 (b) PaulMulrennan 10 30
(I W McInnes) *hmpd s: plld hrd early: sn mid-div: hdwy over 3f out: wknd 2f out* **20/1**

0000 **8** *7* **Ten Spot (IRE)**[10] 7634 3-8-2 55 (vt) NickyMackay 11 14
(Stef Liddiard) *t.k.h in tch: pushed along whn n.m.r over 2f out: sn wknd* **100/1**

0 **9** *4½* **Dasher Reilly (USA)**[2] 7583 7-9-4 0 (b[1]) NeilChalmers 9 18
(A Sadik) *hdwy to chse ldr after 4f: rdn and lost 2nd over 5f out: wknd 4f out* **150/1**

2451 **10** *½* **Buscador (USA)**[266] 1086 9-9-2 64 RichardKingscote 7 15
(W M Brisbourne) *broke wl: led: sn clr: hdd over 4f out: rdn 3f out: wknd 2f out* **25/1**

11 *8* **Cosmic String (IRE)**[37] 3254 6-8-10 65 (b) ChrisCatlin 1 —
(Dr R D P Newland) *s.i.s: in rr: lost tch 4f out* **80/1**

2m 39.36s (-1.74) **Going Correction** -0.05s/f (Stan)
WFA 3 from 6yo+ 5lb **11** Ran SP% **117.3**
Speed ratings (Par 101): **103,99,98,98,96 94,84,80,77,76 71**
toteswinger: 1&2 £4.50, 1&3 £2.60, 2&3 £8.10. CSF £12.78 TOTE £2.70: £1.30, £1.70, £1.60; EX 10.40.
Owner L A Morgan **Bred** L A Morgan **Trained** Upper Longdon, Staffs
■ Stewards' Enquiry : T G McLaughlin £140 fine: failed to arrive in time to weigh out

FOCUS
A decent claimer with the winner not needing to run to his best to score.
Ten Spot(IRE) Official explanation: jockey said filly ran too freely

7745 JOHN HOLLOWOOD CHRISTMAS CLASSIC H'CAP (DIV I) 5f 216y(P)
6:50 (6:51) (Class 6) (0-60,64) 3-Y-0+ £2,047 (£604; £302) Stalls Low

Form RPR

301 **1** **Double Carpet (IRE)**[9] 7637 5-8-1 **50** RossAtkinson(7) 5 71
(G Woodward) *sn led: clr 2f out: rdn over 1f out: r.o wl* **8/1**

3041 **2** *6* **Tri Chara (IRE)**[7] 7663 4-9-8 **64** (p) GrahamGibbons 12 66
(R Hollinshead) *a.p: rdn wl over 1f out: chsd wnr and edgd lft ent fnl f: no imp* **3/1**[1]

2406 **3** *1* **Elusive Dreams (USA)**[26] 7433 4-9-0 **56** TGMcLaughlin 3 55
(P Howling) *hld up in mid-div: rdn over 2f out: styd on to take 3rd towards fin* **10/3**[2]

5634 **4** *½* **What Katie Did (IRE)**[18] 7522 3-8-13 **60** (p) MCGeran(5) 11 57
(J M Bradley) *t.k.h in tch: rdn over 1f out: one pce* **17/2**

0-11 **5** *hd* **Ask Jenny (IRE)**[22] 7479 6-9-3 **59** LPKeniry 4 55
(Patrick Morris, Ire) *a.p: rdn over 1f out: one pce* **14/1**

3063 **6** *nse* **Willhewiz**[3] 7710 8-8-7 **52** (v) DuranFentiman(3) 8 48
(W M Brisbourne) *led early: chsd ldr: rdn over 1f out: lost 2nd ent fnl f: wknd* **10/1**

1054 **7** *½* **Hurricane Coast**[6] 7679 9-9-1 **57** (b) TonyCulhane 1 52
(D Flood) *hld up and bhd: c wd st: sme late prog: nvr nrr* **12/1**

3010 **8** *1¼* **Namu**[33] 7357 5-9-2 **58** (p) ChrisCatlin 7 49
(Miss T Spearing) *hld up in rr: nrst fin* **16/1**

2325 **9** *hd* **Muktasb (USA)**[18] 7522 7-9-2 **58** (v) AdamKirby 6 48
(D Shaw) *hld up in mid-div: rdn over 1f out: eased whn btn ins fnl f* **13/2**[3]

0130 **10** *2½* **Piccolo Diamante (USA)**[13] 7591 4-8-11 **56** TolleyDean(3) 13 38
(S Parr) *hld up and bhd: pushed along 3f out: rdn wl over 1f out: no rspnse* **16/1**

5000 **11** *4* **Our Kally**[9] 7636 3-7-11 **46** oh1 SeanPalmer(7) 2 15
(M D I Usher) *a towards rr* **66/1**

0050 **12** *shd* **Fish Called Johnny**[32] 7375 4-8-6 **48** FrancisNorton 10 17
(A Berry) *bhd fnl 3f* **28/1**

1m 14.07s (-0.93) **Going Correction** -0.05s/f (Stan) **12** Ran SP% **123.2**
Speed ratings (Par 101): **104,96,94,94,93 93,93,91,91,87 82,82**
toteswinger: 1&2 £5.90, 1&3 £5.60, 2&3 £3.70. CSF £33.45 CT £101.58 TOTE £10.10: £2.80, £1.50, £2.10; EX 45.10.
Owner Mr & Mrs Bloom **Bred** Dr John Waldron **Trained** Maltby, S Yorks
■ Stewards' Enquiry : Ross Atkinson one-day ban: used whip when gelding was clearly winning

FOCUS
A moderate sprint handicap and form to treat with some caution, as Double Carpet, who was unchallenged in front, gradually increased the pace to draw well clear. The winning time was 0.40 seconds quicker than the second division and the race is rated at face value.

7746 STAY AT THE WOLVERHAMPTON HOLIDAY INN H'CAP (DIV II) 5f 216y(P)
7:20 (7:21) (Class 6) (0-60,60) 3-Y-0+ £2,047 (£604; £302) Stalls Low

Form RPR

1 **1** **Mister Thatcher (IRE)**[3] 7706 4-8-10 **52** 6ex (t) HayleyTurner 6 65
(Annette McMahon, Ire) *mde all: rdn fnl f: r.o wl* **1/1**[1]

2530 **2** *1¾* **Sarah's Art (IRE)**[3] 7706 5-8-12 **54** MickyFenton 8 61
(Stef Liddiard) *hld up in mid-div: hdwy over 2f out: rdn fnl f: tk 2nd cl home: nt trble wnr* **8/1**

4325 **3** *1* **Monte Major (IRE)**[28] 7416 7-9-0 **56** (v) DarrenWilliams 5 60
(D Shaw) *broke wl: a.p: chsd wnr over 2f out tl rdn wl over 1f out: one pce ins fnl f* **13/2**[2]

0001 **4** *nk* **This Ones For Pat (USA)**[8] 7644 3-9-2 **58** AdamKirby 11 61
(S Parr) *hld up in rr: hdwy on ins wl over 1f out: rdn and kpt on ins fnl f* **14/1**

3621 **5** *shd* **Whiskey Creek**[3] 7705 3-9-3 **59** 6ex (b) TGMcLaughlin 1 62
(C A Dwyer) *w wnr: rdn over 1f out: no ex and lost 2nd cl home* **13/2**[2]

2402 **6** *nk* **Tadlil**[9] 7637 6-8-3 **50** (v) MCGeran(5) 3 52
(J M Bradley) *hld up towards rr: rdn over 1f out: nvr nr to chal* **15/2**[3]

6020 **7** *3* **Hollywood George**[10] 7625 4-8-4 **49** (p) DuranFentiman(3) 7 41
(Miss M E Rowland) *hld up towards rr: nvr trbld ldrs* **22/1**

0614 **8** *1* **The Geester**[11] 7615 4-9-1 **57** (b) PaulEddery 2 46
(S R Bowring) *plld hrd in tch: wknd fnl f* **10/1**

4445 **9** *1¼* **Vanatina (IRE)**[3] 7706 4-8-4 **46** oh1 LiamJones 13 31
(W M Brisbourne) *mid-div: rdn and wknd over 2f out* **22/1**

200 **10** *1¼* **Diminuto**[38] 7292 4-8-13 **58** LukeMorris(3) 10 39
(M D I Usher) *prom: rdn over 2f out: wknd wl over 1f out* **33/1**

5000 **11** *8* **Dynamo Dave (USA)**[14] 7581 3-8-4 **46** oh1 ChrisCatlin 9 2
(M D I Usher) *a towards rr* **66/1**

1m 14.47s (-0.53) **Going Correction** -0.05s/f (Stan) **11** Ran SP% **128.4**
Speed ratings (Par 101): **101,98,97,96,96 96,92,91,89,87 77**
toteswinger: 1&2 £2.90, 1&3 £3.80, 2&3 £11.00. CSF £10.79 CT £43.21 TOTE £2.10: £1.20, £1.70, £2.60; EX 14.20.
Owner Mister Thatcher Syndicate **Bred** Miss Annette McMahon **Trained** Crecora, Co Limerick

FOCUS
A moderate sprint handicap run in a time 0.40 seconds slower than the first division but solid enough for the grade with the four immediately behind the winner close to their marks.

7747 WOLVERHAMPTON-RACECOURSE.CO.UK H'CAP 1m 5f 194y(P)
7:50 (7:51) (Class 4) (0-85,83) 3-Y-0+ **£5,046** (£1,510; £755; £377; £188) Stalls Low

Form RPR

3 **1** **Choir Singer (FR)**[3] 7704 3-8-8 **70** GregFairley 6 77
(Eoin Griffin, Ire) *chsd ldr: led over 2f out: rdn over 1f out: edgd lft jst ins fnl f: drvn out* **3/1**[1]

5231 **2** *nk* **Lochiel**[8] 7657 4-10-0 **83** PaulMulrennan 8 89
(G A Swinbank) *hld up: sn in tch: rdn over 1f out: styd on u.p ins fnl f: tk 2nd towards fin* **7/2**[2]

00/0 **3** *½* **Davorin (JPN)**[7] 7486 7-9-7 **76** (tp) RPCleary 4 81
(M Halford, Ire) *hld up: hdwy on ins over 3f out: rdn over 1f out: nt qckn cl home* **11/1**

4042 **4** *1* **Salute (IRE)**[21] 7499 9-9-4 **73** SteveDrowne 3 77
(P G Murphy) *led: rdn and hdd over 2f out: one pce ins fnl f* **4/1**[3]

2021 **5** ½ **Master At Arms**[19] 7515 5-9-5 **79** PatrickDonaghy(5) 7 82
(Daniel Mark Loughnane, Ire) *hld up in rr: rdn 3f out: nvr able to chal* **9/2**

063/ **6** 5 **Noubian (USA)**[41] 7062 6-9-2 **76** EJMcNamara(5) 1 72
(E McNamara, Ire) *hld up: stdy prog over 6f out: rdn wl over 1f out: sn wknd* **9/2**

3m 3.89s (-2.11) **Going Correction** -0.05s/f (Stan)
WFA 3 from 4yo+ 7lb **6** Ran SP% **111.9**
Speed ratings (Par 105): **104,103,103,102,102 99**
toteswinger: 1&2 £2.20, 1&3 £4.70, 2&3 £5.90. CSF £13.62 CT £96.74 TOTE £4.20: £2.50, £1.90; EX 15.50.
Owner Ten Up Syndicate **Bred** Greenhill Farm Ltd **Trained** Slieverue, Co. Kilkenny

FOCUS
A fair staying handicap on paper, but they went an ordinary pace, resulting in the field still being well bunched leaving the back straight on the final circuit, and it developed into a bit of a dash to the line. Four of the six runners were trained in Ireland and the form is rather muddling.

7748 ENJOY CHRISTMAS PARTY NIGHT H'CAP 7f 32y(P)
8:20 (8:20) (Class 5) (0-75,75) 3-Y-0+ **£3,238** (£963; £481; £240) **Stalls** High

Form RPR

-641 **1** **To Be Or Not To Be**[21] 7490 3-8-4 **64** LukeMorris(3) 4 73+
(John Berry) *hld up in tch: rdn and wnt 2nd wl over 1f out: led ins fnl f: r.o wl* **5/2**[1]

4060 **2** 1 **Alqaahir (USA)**[15] 7572 6-8-5 **62** LiamJones 2 69
(Patrick Morris, Ire) *hld up in mid-div: hdwy on ins over 3f out: r.o to take 2nd towards fin* **10/1**

4 **3** ½ **Imco Tendence (IRE)**[1] 7732 6-8-5 **62**(p) NickyMackay 3 67
(W J Burke, Ire) *hld up in rr: rdn over 1f out: r.o wl to take 3rd last strides* **10/3**[2]

3205 **4** ½ **Caprio (IRE)**[7] 7668 3-9-1 **72** RichardKingscote 7 76
(Tom Dascombe) *led over 2f: w ldr: led over 2f out: rdn wl over 1f out: hdd and no ex ins fnl f* **11/2**

-021 **5** 2¼ **Richelieu**[12] 7611 6-9-0 **71** TonyCulhane 6 69
(J J Lambe, Ire) *hld up towards rr: rdn and short-lived effrt jst over 1f out* **7/1**

0501 **6** 1¾ **Trimlestown (IRE)**[7] 7671 5-9-1 **72**(p) StephenDonohoe 9 65
(P D Evans) *hld up towards rr: rdn over 1f out: no rspnse* **7/2**[3]

1046 **7** 3¼ **Maybe I Wont**[14] 7586 3-8-8 **65** NeilChalmers 1 49
(Lucinda Featherstone) *t.k.h: w ldr: led 4f out tl over 2f out: rdn and wknd over 1f out* **20/1**

0040 **8** 8 **Russian Reel**[6] 7675 3-9-1 **75**(tp) AlanCreighton(3) 8 38
(E J Creighton) *prom tl rdn and wknd wl over 1f out* **33/1**

1m 29.08s (-0.52) **Going Correction** -0.05s/f (Stan) **8** Ran SP% **118.6**
Speed ratings (Par 103): **100,98,98,97,95 93,89,80**
toteswinger: 1&2 £6.20, 1&3 £7.50, 2&3 £27.70. CSF £30.01 CT £86.38 TOTE £4.20: £1.70, £5.10, £1.20; EX 47.00.
Owner W Thomas **Bred** J M Greetham **Trained** Newmarket, Suffolk

FOCUS
A modest handicap run at an even pace and the form is ordinary with the winner not appearing to need to improve to score.

7749 DINE & DANCE IN THE RINGSIDE MEDIAN AUCTION MAIDEN STKS 1m 1f 103y(P)
8:50 (8:52) (Class 6) 3-5-Y-0 **£2,388** (£705; £352) **Stalls** Low

Form RPR

1 **Rambling Dancer (IRE)**[15] 7569 4-9-5 54 WJLee 3 60+
(Mrs Valerie Keatley, Ire) *chsd ldr tl over 6f out: prom: shkn up to ld ins fnl f: rdn out* **85/40**[2]

56 **2** 1½ **That'll Do Nicely (IRE)**[35] 7344 5-9-5 0 PaulMulrennan 8 57
(N G Richards) *hld up in tch: wnt 2nd over 6f out: led over 2f out: rdn and edgd rt jst over 1f out: hdd ins fnl f: nt qckn* **9/2**[3]

-005 **3** 5 **Glamoroso (IRE)**[19] 7174 3-9-3 27 ChrisCatlin 6 47?
(A Kirtley) *in rr: rdn and struggling wl over 1f out: tk 3rd nr fin* **50/1**

3063 **4** nk **The Wily Woodcock**[8] 7654 4-9-5 60 GeorgeBaker 4 46
(G L Moore) *t.k.h: set stdy pce: hdd over 2f out: rdn over 1f out: wknd ins fnl f: lost 3rd nr fin* **6/4**[1]

2m 7.51s (5.81) **Going Correction** -0.05s/f (Stan)
WFA 3 from 4yo+ 2lb **4** Ran SP% **92.1**
Speed ratings (Par 101): **72,70,66,65**
toteswinger: 1&2 £5.70. CSF £7.60 TOTE £2.50; EX 8.00.
Owner Common Sense Partnership **Bred** Albert Conneally **Trained** The Curragh, Co Kildare

FOCUS
A terrible maiden, in which the winner came into the race rated 54, and the third home had a mark of just 27, which clearly limits the form. They went no pace early.

7750 DINE IN THE HORIZONS RESTAURANT H'CAP 1m 141y(P)
9:20 (9:20) (Class 4) (0-80,79) 3-Y-0+ **£5,459** (£1,612; £806) **Stalls** Low

Form RPR

0621 **1** **Hyde Lea Flyer**[29] 7405 3-8-10 **71** GrahamGibbons 10 80+
(E S McMahon) *hld up in tch: swtchd rt jst over 2f out: led jst over 1f out: hrd rdn ins fnl f: jst hld on* **9/4**[1]

161 **2** nse **Plush**[8] 7656 5-7-13 **65** oh1 RossAtkinson(7) 4 74+
(Tom Dascombe) *stdd s: hld up in rr: hdwy over 2f out: rdn over 1f out: r.o ins fnl f: jst failed* **3/1**[2]

0311 **3** nk **Spinning**[15] 7564 5-9-6 **79**(b) GeorgeBaker 8 87
(T D Barron) *s.i.s: hld up towards rr: hdwy over 2f out: rdn and ev ch fnl f: r.o* **9/4**[1]

1150 **4** 2½ **Rebellious Spirit**[238] 1630 5-9-6 **79** JamesDoyle 7 81
(S Curran) *a.p: rdn and ev ch wl over 1f out: no ex wl ins fnl f* **14/1**

5 2¼ **Atlas Peak (IRE)**[62] 6848 3-8-4 **65** oh5 RPCleary 1 62
(M Halford, Ire) *prom: rdn 2f out: wknd ins fnl f* **40/1**

0040 **6** ¾ **Prince Of Light (IRE)**[18] 7526 5-9-4 **77** GregFairley 2 72
(M Johnston) *w ldr: led over 3f out: rdn over 2f out: hdd jst over 1f out: wknd ins fnl f* **13/2**[3]

0106 **7** 14 **Stark Contrast (USA)**[15] 7559 4-8-3 **65** oh2 LukeMorris(3) 9 28
(M D I Usher) *hld up towards rr: n.m.r over 3f out: sn struggling* **16/1**

000 **8** 1¾ **Ignition**[35] 6654 6-8-6 **65** oh20 ChrisCatlin 5 24
(A Kirtley) *led: hdd over 3f out: wknd over 2f out* **100/1**

105- **9** 4 **Salaasa (USA)**[17] 3936 4-8-9 **73** EJMcNamara(5) 3 23
(E McNamara, Ire) *hld up in mid-div: rdn and bhd 3f out: eased whn no ch over 1f out* **33/1**

1m 48.68s (-1.82) **Going Correction** -0.05s/f (Stan)
WFA 3 from 4yo+ 2lb **9** Ran SP% **118.8**
Speed ratings (Par 105): **106,105,105,103,101 100,88,86,83**
toteswinger: 1&2 £7.50, 1&3 £3.00, 2&3 £1.50. CSF £9.50 CT £16.70 TOTE £4.10: £1.40, £1.50, £1.10; EX 11.00 Place 6 £15.77, Place 5 £11.50..
Owner Kemmel Partnership **Bred** Hesmonds Stud Ltd **Trained** Lichfield, Staffs

FOCUS
A fair handicap run at a sound pace and the form looks solid.
T/Plt: £80.80 to a £1 stake. Pool: £124,303.62. 1,121.75 winning tickets. T/Qpdt: £30.40 to a £1 stake. Pool: £7,477.96. 181.50 winning tickets. KH

7588 HOLLYWOOD PARK (L-H)
Saturday, December 20

OFFICIAL GOING: Fast

7751a CASHCALL FUTURITY (GRADE 1) (CUSHION TRACK) 1m 110y(D)
12:05 (12:11) 2-Y-O **£201,005** (£75,377; £50,251; £25,126; £15,075; £10,050)

RPR

1 **Pioneerof The Nile (USA)**[56] 6997 2-8-9 GKGomez 5 115
(Bob Baffert, U.S.A) **14/10**[1]

2 nse **I Want Revenge (USA)**[133] 2-8-9 JTalamo 7 115
(Jeff Mullins, U.S.A) **13/2**[3]

3 1½ **Chocolate Candy (USA)**[42] 2-8-9 RBejarano 6 112
(Jerry Hollendorfer, U.S.A) **71/10**

4 2 **Bittel Road (USA)**[21] 2-8-9 MESmith 10 108
(Todd Pletcher, U.S.A) **72/10**

5 1½ **Azul Leon (USA)**[27] 2-8-9 JRosario 1 105
(Doug O'Neill, U.S.A) **52/10**[2]

6 nse **Axel Foley (USA)**[66] 6737 2-8-9 MCBaze 4 105
(J R Best) *missed break and behind, 10th straight, stayed on but never a threat* **238/10**

7 ¾ **Mark S The Cooler (USA)**[42] 2-8-9 MGarcia 12 103
(Doug O'Neill, U.S.A) **755/10**

8 ¾ **Hype (USA)**[21] 2-8-9 (b) ASolis 3 102
(Todd Pletcher, U.S.A) **245/10**

9 ¾ **Frumious (USA)** 2-8-9 VEspinoza 9 100
(Jeff Bonde, U.S.A) **209/10**

10 2¼ **J P Jammer (USA)**[42] 2-8-9 AGryder 2 96
(Rafael Becerra, U.S.A) **42/1**

11 ¾ **Ventana (USA)**[27] 2-8-9 CNakatani 8 94
(Bob Baffert, U.S.A) **131/10**

1m 41.95s (-0.04) **11** Ran SP% **118.9**
PARI-MUTUEL (Including $2 stake): WIN 4.80; PL (1-2) 3.40, 6.20;SHOW (1-2-3) 2.60, 4.40, 4.40; DF 20.00.
Owner Zayat Stables LLC **Bred** Zayat Stables Llc **Trained** USA

7713 GREAT LEIGHS (A.W) (L-H)
Sunday, December 21

OFFICIAL GOING: Standard
Wind: Fresh, half-behind Weather: bright

7752 REINDEER H'CAP 1m 2f (P)
2:15 (2:15) (Class 5) (0-75,75) 3-Y-0 **£2,914** (£867; £433; £216) **Stalls** Low

Form RPR

5523 **1** **Bluejain**[31] 7398 3-9-4 **75** JamieSpencer 4 84
(Miss Gay Kelleway) *stdd s: hld up in tch in last pl: hdwy to trck ldrs and swtchd lft 2f out rdn to ld ent fnl f: r.o wl* **9/4**[2]

6503 **2** ½ **Summer Winds**[19] 7526 3-9-3 **74** HayleyTurner 2 82
(T G Mills) *hld up in tch: chsd ldr and carried rt 2f out: pressed wnr u.p 1f out: unable qck and a hld after* **2/1**[1]

0-62 **3** 3¼ **Musashi (IRE)**[15] 7580 3-8-11 **68** JohnEgan 3 70
(Jane Chapple-Hyam) *set stdy gallop: c centre and rdn 2f out: hdd ent fnl f: sn outpcd* **11/4**[3]

-410 **4** 9 **Incarnation (IRE)**[17] 7545 3-8-11 **68** DaneO'Neill 6 52
(L M Cumani) *chsd ldr: rdn over 2f out: carried wd ent st: sn drvn and wknd* **5/1**

3145 **5** 17 **Tiger's Rocket (IRE)**[234] 1750 3-8-11 **68** ChrisCatlin 5 18
(S Gollings) *hld up in last pair: rdn and lost tch over 3f out: t.o* **20/1**

2m 9.22s (0.62) **Going Correction** +0.075s/f (Slow) **5** Ran SP% **112.2**
Speed ratings (Par 102): **100,99,97,89,76**
toteswinger: 1&2 £3.90. CSF £7.34 TOTE £3.10: £1.90, £1.70; EX 7.40.
Owner Countrywide Classics Limited **Bred** David Sugars And Bob Parker **Trained** Exning, Suffolk

FOCUS
An ordinary handicap and not particularly competitive. The pace was only steady and the form is a bit muddling.

7753 SANTA H'CAP 1m 2f (P)
2:50 (2:51) (Class 4) (0-85,85) 3-Y-0+ **£4,857** (£1,445; £722; £360) **Stalls** Low

Form RPR

6023 **1** **Folio (IRE)**[22] 7502 8-8-7 **71** ChrisCatlin 3 78
(W J Musson) *hld up in last trio: hdwy over 2f out: gd hdwy over 1f out: r.o wl to ld wl ins fnl f* **13/2**[3]

-054 **2** hd **Saltagioo (ITY)**[22] 7502 4-9-5 **83**(t) JohnEgan 1 90
(M Botti) *chsd ldrs: rdn jst over 2f out: ev ch ins fnl f: no ex wl ins fnl f* **14/1**

1114 **3** ½ **Stand Guard**[22] 7493 4-9-0 **78** IanMongan 4 84
(P Howling) *hld up in midfield: hdwy 5f out: led 3f out: 2 l clr and rdn jst over 2f out: edgd rt ins fnl f: hdd and no ex wl ins fnl f* **2/1**[2]

0060 **4** 1¾ **Profit's Reality (IRE)**[22] 7496 6-9-7 **85** JimCrowley 2 88
(M J Attwater) *awkward s: hld up bhd: hdwy 4f out: chsd ldrs and swtchd lft over 1f out: kpt on same pce fnl f* **20/1**

0011 **5** nk **Wellington Square**[19] 7526 3-9-0 **81** GeorgeBaker 5 83
(H Morrison) *hld up in last trio: hdwy over 4f out: chsd ldr and rdn over 2f out: keeping on same pce whn hmpd jst ins fnl f: no imp after* **5/4**[1]

0-00 **6** 30 **Andorn (GER)**[31] 7398 4-8-11 **75** TPQueally 7 17
(A P Stringer) *chsd ldr tl led briefly over 3f out: sn rdn and wknd: t.o* **25/1**

2003 **7** 20 **Invasian (IRE)**[63] 6839 7-9-2 **80** MickyFenton 6 —
(P W D'Arcy) *dwlt: sn pushed up to ld and clr: reduced advantage 5f out: rdn and hdd over 3f out: sn wknd: t.o* **10/1**

2m 7.69s (-0.91) **Going Correction** +0.075s/f (Slow)
WFA 3 from 4yo+ 3lb **7** Ran SP% **115.5**
Speed ratings (Par 105): **106,105,105,104,103 79,63**
toteswinger: 1&2 £6.60, 1&3 £2.50, 2&3 £4.20. CSF £88.06 TOTE £8.50: £2.90, £9.70; EX 68.20.
Owner Goodey and Broughton **Bred** Lord Rothschild **Trained** Newmarket, Suffolk

The Form Book, Raceform Ltd, Compton, RG20 6NL

■ Stewards' Enquiry : Chris Catlin two-day ban: used whip with excessive force (Jan 4-5)

FOCUS

A fair handicap run at a reasonable pace. The time was around a second and a half faster than the earlier three-year-olds' handicap and the form looks solid.

7754 CHRISTMAS PUDDING MAIDEN AUCTION STKS 1m (P)

3:20 (3:20) (Class 4) 2-Y-O **£4,533** (£1,348; £674; £336) **Stalls** Centre

Form RPR

403 **1** **Kaolak (USA)**[31] 7397 2-8-9 78 ChrisCatlin 6 82+
(J Ryan) *mde all: clr 6f out: rdn and styd on wl fr over 1f out: unchal* **5/2**[2]

2 *4* **One Slick Chick (IRE)** 2-8-6 0 JohnEgan 2 70
(M Botti) *s.i.s: pushed along over 3f out: hdwy on inner over 1f out: wnt 2nd and edgd rt jst ins fnl f: nvr trbld wnr* **16/1**

4 **3** *shd* **Better In Time (USA)**[15] 7578 2-7-12 0 RossAtkinson(7) 1 69
(Jane Chapple-Hyam) *hld up in midfield: rdn over 3f out: swtchd rt and hdwy 2f out: edgd lft u.p jst over 1f out: kpt on but nvr nr wnr* **10/1**

6 **4** *2 1/4* **Fromthebeginning**[13] 7602 2-8-13 0 MartinDwyer 9 72
(D R C Elsworth) *stdd after s: t.k.h: hld up in last pair: rdn over 3f out: edgd lft over 1f out: plugged on fnl f: n.d* **6/4**[1]

535 **5** *1* **More Tea Vicar (IRE)**[11] 7627 2-8-7 70 PaulHanagan 3 64
(R A Fahey) *chsd ldrs: rdn and unable qck over 2f out: wknd and edgd rt jst over 1f out* **16/1**

020 **6** *1 1/4* **Indian Tonic (IRE)**[78] 6473 2-8-8 81 HayleyTurner 4 62
(W Jarvis) *chsd wnr: rdn over 2f out: no imp on wnr: lost 2nd jst ins fnl f: wknd* **7/2**[3]

55 **7** *3* **Liberty Beau (IRE)**[11] 7622 2-8-11 0 DaneO'Neill 5 58
(D R C Elsworth) *t.k.h: hld up towards rr: hdwy over 3f out: chsd ldng pair and rdn over 2f out: wkng whn short of room jst over 1f out* **12/1**

1m 40.68s (0.78) **Going Correction** +0.075s/f (Slow) **7 Ran SP% 119.3**

Speed ratings (Par 98): **99,95,94,92,91 90,87**

toteswinger: 1&2 £8.50, 1&3 £3.20, 2&3 £13.20. CSF £42.10 TOTE £4.60: £2.90, £3.50; EX 71.80 Trifecta £98.80 Part won. Pool £133.59 - 0.67 winning units..

Owner Simon Kerr **Bred** And Mrs Robert Courtney Sr Et Al **Trained** Newmarket, Suffolk

FOCUS

Just a modest maiden in which the winner set a good pace.

NOTEBOOK

Kaolak(USA) had started slowly in his first three outings, but he was well away here and made virtually all. Quickly going several lengths ahead, he wound things up from the three-furlong pole and stayed on strongly for an emphatic win. A very tall, scopey individual, there will be more improvement in him when he strengthens into his frame. This looks his trip. (op 7-2)

One Slick Chick(IRE) made an encouraging debut. She was a little outpaced in rear through the first part of the race, but began to pick up down the inside in the home stretch and ran on for second place, if never near the all-the-way winner. She will have learned from this. (op 14-1)

Better In Time(USA) was fourth in a race of this nature here on her debut and probably ran to a similar level, staying on towards the outside and just missing out on second spot. (op 8-1 tchd 7-1)

Fromthebeginning had been clueless at Lingfield on his debut before running on pleasingly late on. This time he was dropped in from his wide draw, failing to settle properly, and had been relegated to last place by the home turn. He did stay on in the straight after being switched towards the inside, but was never a threat. He still has some learning to do. (op 13-8 tchd 7-4)

More Tea Vicar(IRE) did not really improve for this return to Polytrack and again ran below her official mark of 70. (op 11-1)

Indian Tonic(IRE) was last seen finishing in midfield behind the ill-fated Tiger Eye in a valuable Newmarket sales race. Chasing the winner but unable to make any impression, she was under pressure before the straight and weakened out of second spot at the furlong pole. (op 4-1 tchd 11-2)

Liberty Beau(IRE) raced prominently but was on the retreat when slightly hampered in the straight. He is now qualified for handicaps.

7755 MINCE PIE H'CAP 1m (P)

3:50 (3:51) (Class 2) (0-100,96) 3-Y-O+

£12,462 (£3,732; £1,866; £934; £466; £234) **Stalls** Centre

Form RPR

0364 **1** **Flipando (IRE)**[16] 7556 7-8-13 89 JamieSpencer 3 99
(T D Barron) *hld up wl bhd: stl plenty to do over 2f out: hdwy and swtchd rt over 1f out: drvn and r.o wl to chal ins fnl f: led and edgd lft towards fin* **15/8**[1]

0041 **2** *nk* **Red Somerset (USA)**[16] 7560 5-8-5 86 MCGeran(5) 1 96
(R J Hodges) *in tch: chsd ldng pair over 2f out: rdn to chse ldr over 1f out: drvn and ev ch whn squeezed ins fnl f: kpt on* **9/2**[2]

0016 **3** *1* **Samarinda (USA)**[37] 7313 5-9-4 94 MickyFenton 10 101
(Mrs P Sly) *led for 2f: chsd ldr after tl rdn to ld over 1f out: edgd rt ins fnl f: hdd and no ex towards fin* **12/1**

1216 **4** *6* **Mister New York (USA)**[2] 7737 3-8-8 85 JimCrowley 9 78+
(Noel T Chance) *stdd after s: hld up bhd: c wd and rdn jst over 2f out: styd on fnl f: nvr nr ldrs* **6/1**[3]

0665 **5** *1 1/4* **Hinton Admiral**[22] 7496 4-8-8 84 (p) PaulHanagan 8 75
(R A Fahey) *pushed along early: hdwy to ld 6f out: rdn over 2f out: hdd over 1f out: wknd ent fnl f* **13/2**

3150 **6** *nk* **My Gacho (IRE)**[14] 7594 6-9-1 91 (b) GregFairley 2 81
(M Johnston) *towards rr: rdn and effrt on inner jst over 2f out: no imp* **7/1**

0612 **7** *2 1/4* **Resplendent Nova**[11] 7633 6-8-5 81 ChrisCatlin 5 66
(P Howling) *chsd ldrs early: steadily lost pl: no ch fnl 2f* **10/1**

260 **8** *11* **Lancetto (FR)**[91] 3-9-5 96 FergusSweeney 6 55
(K R Burke) *t.k.h: chsd ldrs: rdn over 2f out: sn struggling: wl btn over 1f out* **25/1**

6440 **9** *2 3/4* **Ballinteni**[142] 4587 6-8-12 91 DuranFentiman(3) 7 44
(T D Easterby) *towards rr: rdn over 3f out: bhd fnl 2f* **20/1**

134- **10** *15* **Aviso (GER)**[217] 4-9-5 95 TPQueally 4 14
(A P Stringer) *stdd s: t.k.h: sn plld way up into midfield: rdn and wknd over 2f out: t.o* **33/1**

1m 38.65s (-1.25) **Going Correction** +0.075s/f (Slow)

WFA 3 from 4yo+ 1lb **10 Ran SP% 121.4**

Speed ratings (Par 109): **109,108,107,101,100 100,97,86,84,69**

toteswinger: 1&2 £6.80, 1&3 £8.10, 2&3 £16.20. CSF £10.35 CT £84.16 TOTE £3.40: £1.50, £1.40, £6.30; EX 13.90 Trifecta £229.40 Part won. Pool £310.10 - 0.67 winning units..

Owner Mrs J Hazell **Bred** Denis McDonnell **Trained** Maunby, N Yorks

■ Stewards' Enquiry : Jamie Spencer caution: careless riding

Micky Fenton one-day ban: careless riding (Jan 4)

FOCUS

A valuable and well-contested handicap run at a strong gallop and good, solid form. The first three came close together late on and the result stood following an inquiry

NOTEBOOK

Flipando(IRE) had not won since Redcar's Zetland Gold Cup in May 2007 and had been described by his trainer as a professional loser, but he ended the drought with a last-gasp win. Sharper for his recent first run on Polytrack, he was held up at the back and brought with a well-timed run to lead in the last few strides. A strongly run race at this trip suits him. (op 5-2 tchd 11-4)

Red Somerset(USA) won a good claimer at Wolverhampton last time, form boosted by wins for the placed horses, and he was bidding to maintain an unbeaten record on this surface. He went very close, but could not quite force his head in front and did not have much room in which to manoeuvre between the winner and third in the last 50 yards.This was a good effort. (op 5-1)

Samarinda(USA) was ridden much more positively than usual and got past the pacesetter in the straight, but could not quite hold on. This was a good first run at this venue and he finished clear of the rest. (op 11-1)

Mister New York(USA), badly drawn at Wolverhampton on Friday night, stayed on quite well from the rear without being able to get involved. (op 11-2)

Hinton Admiral recovered from a sluggish start to lead, but his exertions told in the straight. This was a respectable effort with the cheekpieces back on, but he is without a win since taking a Listed event at Lingfield for Mark Johnston in the spring of his three-year-old season. He has become well handicapped. (op 6-1 tchd 7-1)

My Gacho(IRE) had never run at a trip this far and gave himself little chance of staying by taking a keen tug early. (op 10-1)

Resplendent Nova had been in good heart but has not shown his form in three visits now. (op 8-1)

Lancetto(FR) had high-class form in Germany and cost current connections 120,000gns, but was well beaten under top weight on this sand debut. He probably needs a bit further.

Ballinteni was last seen in action at Glorious Goodwood when trained by Gay Kelleway and he was well beaten on his debut for this yard following his break. (op 16-1)

Aviso(GER) won last season's German 2000 Guineas (Group 2) but has not been at his best this year and there was not much encouragement to be gleaned from this British debut. (op 22-1)

7756 MISTLETOE H'CAP 6f (P)

4:20 (4:20) (Class 3) (0-90,91) 3-Y-O+

£7,477 (£2,239; £1,119; £560; £279; £140) **Stalls** Low

Form RPR

4322 **1** **Matsunosuke**[3] 7716 6-9-4 90 TPQueally 4 100
(A B Coogan) *hld up in rr on inner: hdwy on rail 2f out: pushed along over 1f out: led fnl 100yds: pushed out* **5/2**[1]

3303 **2** *3/4* **Dvinsky (USA)**[14] 7592 7-8-7 79 (b) PaulDoe 1 87
(P Howling) *chsd ldrs: rdn over 2f out: chsd ldr over 1f out: ev ch ins fnl f: nt pce of wnr fnl 100yds* **11/1**

3331 **3** *nk* **Lone Wolfe**[15] 7576 4-8-11 90 RossAtkinson(7) 2 97
(Jane Chapple-Hyam) *chsd ldr tl led jst over 2f out: rdn over 1f out: drvn ins fnl f: hdd fnl 100yds: no ex* **3/1**[3]

0221 **4** *2* **Little Edward**[7] 7675 10-9-5 91 6ex GeorgeBaker 6 92
(R J Hodges) *stdd s: hld up in rr: hdwy over 3f out: rdn and effrt wl over 1f out: kpt on same pce fnl f* **7/1**

4500 **5** *4* **Fromsong (IRE)**[199] 2760 10-8-8 85 JamesO'Reilly(5) 3 73
(D K Ivory) *dwlt: sn chsng ldrs: rdn over 2f out: wknd jst over 1f out* **25/1**

6060 **6** *3 3/4* **Silver Prelude**[194] 2906 7-8-7 79 ChrisCatlin 5 55
(S C Williams) *led tl jst over 2f out: rdn and wknd qckly jst over 1f out* **28/1**

3210 **7** *nse* **Dazzling Bay**[25] 7456 8-8-5 80 (b) DuranFentiman(3) 7 56
(T D Easterby) *towards rr: rdn and no prog over 2f out: nvr nr ldrs* **8/1**

0501 **8** *3 1/2* **Ingleby Arch (USA)**[26] 7448 5-8-7 79 JamieSpencer 9 43
(T D Barron) *chsd ldrs: rdn 3f out: drvn and struggling over 2f out: no ch fr over 1f out* **11/4**[2]

0002 **9** *1 3/4* **Bo McGinty (IRE)**[113] 5493 7-8-11 83 (b) PaulHanagan 10 42
(R A Fahey) *racd wd: a bhd: lost tch over 2f out* **20/1**

1m 12.44s (-1.26) **Going Correction** +0.075s/f (Slow) **9 Ran SP% 124.2**

Speed ratings (Par 107): **111,110,109,106,101 96,96,91,89**

toteswinger: 1&2 £7.90, 1&3 £2.60, 2&3 £9.00. CSF £32.78 CT £90.91 TOTE £3.80: £1.30, £3.40, £1.60; EX 40.00 Trifecta £344.80 Part won. Pool £466.00 - 0.90 winning units..

Owner A B Coogan **Bred** R Coogan **Trained** Soham, Cambs

■ Stewards' Enquiry : Paul Doe caution: use of whip

FOCUS

A decent sprint handicap and solid enough rated around the placed horses.

NOTEBOOK

Matsunosuke gained reward for his consistency. He was held up under a patient ride before improving up the inside rail in the straight and winning a shade cosily. He is just as effective at 5f but a rise in the weights for this victory will take him out of this grade. (op 11-4 tchd 3-1)

Dvinsky(USA) is another with a consistent overall profile and he ran his race again, holding every chance but never quite able to force his head in front under pressure. (op 9-1)

Lone Wolfe had Matsunosuke behind in third when scoring over course and distance recently, but went up 6lb for that. He got to the front in the straight but could not hold off the challengers in the last half-furlong. (tchd 10-3)

Little Edward, with a 6lb penalty for his claiming win at Wolverhampton, ran on from the rear without getting to the principals. (op 13-2 tchd 6-1)

Fromsong(IRE) had not run since June and this was a pleasing return to action. (op 40-1)

Silver Prelude, who has left Dean Ivory's yard since his latest appearance in June, showed his customary pace but is more effective over the minimum trip. (op 25-1)

Ingleby Arch(USA), put up 6lb for his Southwell win, was in trouble from a relatively early stage and he has yet to show he likes this venue. Official explanation: jockey said gelding moved poorly throughout (op 7-2 tchd 4-1)

7757 TURKEY MAIDEN STKS 1m (P)

4:50 (4:54) (Class 5) 3-4-Y-O **£3,238** (£963; £481; £240) **Stalls** Centre

Form RPR

25 **1** **Fosool (IRE)**[31] 7395 3-8-12 0 JamieSpencer 5 67+
(W J Haggas) *hld up in midfield: hdwy over 2f out: rdn to ld over 1f out: edgd lft but r.o wl fnl f: comf* **3/1**[1]

05 **2** *2* **Elisiario (IRE)**[18] 7536 3-9-3 0 PatCosgrave 12 67
(J R Boyle) *dropped in after s: t.k.h: hld up in midfield: swtchd lft and hdwy wl over 1f out: chsd wnr jst ins fnl f: r.o but no imp on wnr* **25/1**

4 **3** *3* **Light The Light (IRE)**[108] 5627 3-8-12 0 JimCrowley 4 55
(Rae Guest) *t.k.h: chsd ldrs: rdn and unable qck over 1f out: plugged on to go 3rd ins fnl f* **22/1**

2 **4** *1/2* **Keepsgettingbetter (IRE)**[22] 7500 3-9-3 0 ChrisCatlin 3 59
(J R Gask) *led: hrd pressed and rdn over 2f out: hdd over 1f out: plugged on same pce fnl f* **7/1**[3]

5 *3 1/4* **Lucky Dancer** 3-9-3 0 GeorgeBaker 10 52+
(D R C Elsworth) *v.s.a: bhd: rdn over 2f out: hdwy and hanging lft over 1f out: nvr nr ldrs* **11/1**

0030 **6** *nk* **Athboy Auction**[22] 7497 3-8-12 50 HayleyTurner 7 46
(H J Collingridge) *chsd ldr: upsides and rdn over 2f out: edgd rt and hdd over 1f out: wknd fnl f* **25/1**

7 *1 1/4* **Waldorf (IRE)** 3-9-3 0 MartinDwyer 11 48+
(W R Muir) *hld up in midfield: rdn and unable qck over 2f out: wl hld fr over 1f out* **7/2**[2]

8 *2 3/4* **Oxus (IRE)** 3-9-3 0 FergusSweeney 1 42
(B R Johnson) *s.i.s: a towards rr: rdn over 2f out: no hdwy and wl btn over 1f out* **66/1**

9 2 ½ **Buail Isteach (IRE)** 3-8-12 0.. MickyFenton 2 31
(E J Creighton) *s.i.s: t.k.h and sn chsng ldrs: rdn 3f out: wknd qckly over 1f out* **25/1**

10 2 ½ **Forced Opinion (USA)**[26] 3-9-3 0.. TPQueally 8 30
(K A Morgan) *stdd s: plld hrd and m green in rr: effrt on outer over 2f out: wknd wl over 1f out* **100/1**

11 6 **Lukatara (USA)**[26] 3-9-3 0.. EdwardCreighton 6 17
(Miss Sheena West) *s.i.s: a bhd: rdn and toiling over 3f out: t.o* **80/1**

1m 41.87s (1.97) **Going Correction** +0.075s/f (Slow) **11** Ran SP% **87.7**
Speed ratings (Par 103): **93,91,88,87,84 83,82,79,77,74 68**
toteswinger: 1&2 £12.40, 1&3 £7.30, 2&3 £19.50. CSF £39.53 TOTE £2.90: £1.10, £4.90, £4.30; EX 45.90 Trifecta £58.40 Part won. Pool £78.95 - 0.20 winning units..
Owner Ms Nicola Mahoney **Bred** Corduff Stud & J Corcorcan **Trained** Newmarket, Suffolk

FOCUS
A very modest maiden which took even less winning after the well-backed Boss Hog, who would have been favourite, was withdrawn after getting down in the stalls and not form to be positive about.
T/Jkpt: £2,622.70 to a £1 stake. Pool: £132,986.53. 36.00 winning tickets. T/Plt: £90.60 to a £1 stake. Pool: £87,162.77. 701.82 winning tickets. T/Qpdt: £13.40 to a £1 stake. Pool: £6,146.62. 336.96 winning tickets. SP

7699 KEMPTON (A.W) (R-H)
Monday, December 22

OFFICIAL GOING: Standard
Wind: Moderate, across Weather: Cloudy

7758 BETDAQ THE BETTING EXCHANGE H'CAP — 1m 2f (P)
2:20 (2:21) (Class 5) (0-75,74) 3-Y-0+ **£3,238** (£963; £481; £240) **Stalls** High

Form RPR

05 1 **Man Of Gwent (UAE)**[13] 7613 4-8-10 **63**.. JamesDoyle 2 69
(P D Evans) *stdd s: hld up in last trio: rdn over 2f out: prog on outer over 1f out: sustained effrt fnl f to ld post* **6/1**

0366 2 shd **Will He Wish**[22] 7507 12-9-5 **72**..(b) PatCosgrave 3 78
(S Gollings) *trckd ldng pair: rdn wl over 1f out: sustained effrt to ld nr fin: hdd fnl stride* **25/1**

3361 3 nk **Supercast (IRE)**[23] 7502 5-9-4 **74**.. LukeMorris(3) 1 79
(N J Vaughan) *trckd ldr: pushed up to chal 4f out: drvn and fnlly led jst over 1f out: hdd nr fin* **11/2[3]**

0054 4 nse **Silver Hotspur**[10] 7650 4-9-7 **74**.. LiamJones 10 79
(C R Dore) *hld up in 5th: trckd ldng pair over 1f out gng best of all: urged along to chal fnl f: styd on but outpcd nr fin* **16/1**

443 5 ½ **Parson's Punch**[43] 7256 3-8-12 **68**.. MartinDwyer 4 72
(P D Cundell) *led at mod pce: pressed fr 4f out: narrowly hdd jst over 1f out: kpt pressing tl no ex nr fin* **4/1[1]**

0105 6 1 ¼ **Epidaurian King (IRE)**[10] 7651 5-8-9 **62**.. NickyMackay 5 64
(D Shaw) *s.s: hld up in last in modly run r: effrt wl over 1f out: styd on: no ch of rching ldrs* **20/1**

3005 7 hd **Hucking Hero (IRE)**[20] 7525 3-9-4 **74**.. GeorgeBaker 7 75
(J R Best) *unco-operative to post: stdd s: hld up in last pair in modly run r: effrt on inner over 1f out: kpt on but no ch to rch ldrs* **7/1**

4002 8 hd **Dream Of Fortune (IRE)**[25] 7462 4-9-4 **71**..(t) AdamKirby 11 72
(M G Quinlan) *hld up in 8th in modly run r: effrt over 1f out: reminders and kpt on ent fnl f: nvr on terms* **9/2[2]**

2020 9 nk **Key Decision (IRE)**[17] 7568 4-8-12 **70**..(t) MHarley(5) 8 70
(Shaun Harley, Ire) *hld up in midfield: rdn on outer over 2f out: in tch over 1f out: one pce and no prog after* **14/1**

1-05 10 ¾ **King's Majesty (IRE)**[36] 6659 6-8-13 **66**.. AndrewElliott 6 65
(A M Hales) *hld up in midfield: rdn on outer over 2f out: lost pl and struggling over 1f out* **15/2**

5020 11 1 ½ **Hilbre Court (USA)**[58] 6989 3-9-2 **72**.. HayleyTurner 9 68
(B P J Baugh) *t.k.h: trckd ldng pair: rdn and cl up over 1f out: sn wknd* **10/1**

2m 9.45s (1.45) **Going Correction** +0.225s/f (Slow)
WFA 3 from 4yo+ 3lb **11** Ran SP% **122.4**
Speed ratings (Par 103): **103,102,102,102,102 101,101,100,100,100 98**
toteswinger: 1&2 £32.30, 1&3 £7.00, 2&3 £17.40. CSF £149.47 CT £886.55 TOTE £6.50: £1.70, £9.20, £1.60; EX 104.20.
Owner L G Brookes **Bred** And Mrs K J Mercer **Trained** Pandy, Monmouths

FOCUS
A blanket finish with only one length separating the first five home. The early pace was ordinary, though it increased a bit going into the back straight and they were soon strung out by 15 lengths.

7759 BETDAQ.CO.UK MEDIAN AUCTION MAIDEN STKS — 7f (P)
2:50 (2:51) (Class 6) 3-5-Y-0 **£2,047** (£604; £302) **Stalls** High

Form RPR

0300 1 **Langham House**[19] 7541 3-9-3 49.. NickyMackay 3 59
(J R Jenkins) *t.k.h early: prom: wnt 2nd 1/2-way: led over 2f out and kicked on: drvn out and hld on wl* **20/1**

3353 2 ¾ **Dark Camellia**[35] 7358 3-8-12 62..(t) JamesDoyle 4 52
(H J L Dunlop) *hld up in last: smooth prog on outer fr over 2f out but plenty to do: wnt 2nd ent fnl f: hrd rdn to cl on wnr: no imp last 50yds* **13/8[1]**

2000 3 1 ¾ **Waterloo Dock**[53] 7102 3-9-3 50.. PatCosgrave 8 52
(M Quinn) *chsd ldr to 1/2-way: rdn over 2f out: kpt on to dispute 2nd 1f out: one pce after* **12/1[3]**

3642 4 hd **Yakama (IRE)**[15] 7591 3-9-3 59..(b) HayleyTurner 5 52
(Mrs C A Dunnett) *stdd s: hld up in last pair: rdn and prog on outer over 2f out: disp 2nd 1f out: one pce after* **13/8[1]**

5 ¾ **The Staffy (IRE)** 3-9-0 0.. LukeMorris(3) 9 50
(N J Vaughan) *s.i.s: rcvrd to chse ldrs on inner: lost pl whn rdn 2f out: plugged on again fnl f* **7/1[2]**

0/ 6 1 **Fluntas (IRE)**[595] 1551 5-8-12 0..(t) MHarley(5) 1 47
(Shaun Harley, Ire) *fast away fr outside draw: led to over 2f out: steadily wknd over 1f out* **14/1**

0055 7 1 ¾ **Bobal Girl**[62] 6883 3-8-7 50 ow2.. HollyHall(7) 6 39
(M D Squance) *hld up in rr: urged along on inner over 2f out: trying to cl on ldrs but no real ch whn m short of room 1f out* **25/1**

0400 8 1 ¾ **Szaba**[56] 7022 3-8-12 48.. AdamKirby 2 33
(J Akehurst) *in tch: pushed along over 3f out: lost pl over 2f out: struggling after* **18/1**

1m 27.87s (1.87) **Going Correction** +0.175s/f (Slow) **8** Ran SP% **116.9**
Speed ratings (Par 101): **96,95,93,92,92 90,88,86**
toteswinger: 1&2 £4.80, 1&3 £12.70, 2&3 £5.40. CSF £54.37 TOTE £17.80: £3.20, £1.10, £3.60; EX 70.90.
Owner Nick Hodge **Bred** N R Hodge **Trained** Royston, Herts

FOCUS
A poor maiden, but they went a fair gallop, with prominent runners and hold-up horses alike filling the first four places.
Szaba Official explanation: jockey said filly had no more to give

7760 BET KING GEORGE VI CHASE - BETDAQ CLAIMING STKS — 7f (P)
3:20 (3:22) (Class 6) 2-Y-0 **£2,047** (£604; £302) **Stalls** High

Form RPR

0106 1 **True Britannia**[9] 7659 2-8-2 55..(v[1]) NickyMackay 5 55
(S Kirk) *hld up in midfield: produced on outer and prog to ld jst over 1f out: edgd rt fnl f: styd on wl* **16/1**

046 2 1 ¾ **Cognac Boy (USA)**[15] 7593 2-8-8 65.. PatrickHills(3) 10 60
(R Hannon) *prom: rdn on inner over 2f out: chal wl over 1f out: kpt on same pce u.p fnl f* **7/1**

5231 3 shd **Trigger McCann**[24] 7475 2-9-3 71.. LPKeniry 6 65
(J S Moore) *t.k.h early: hld up in rr: gng easily 2f out: nt clr run sn after: hrd rdn and styd on ins fnl f to take 3rd last stride* **13/2**

04 4 hd **Turn To Dreams**[14] 7600 2-8-2 47.. LiamJones 4 50
(P D Evans) *hld up in rr: rdn and prog on outer fr over 2f out: tried to cl 1f out: kpt on same pce* **33/1**

3432 5 shd **Precocious Air (IRE)**[9] 7666 2-8-3 62.. FrancisNorton 7 51
(J A Osborne) *t.k.h early: cl up: chal 2f out: nt qckn and hld 1f out: nt clr run ins fnl f* **5/2[1]**

0054 6 hd **Pansy Potter**[110] 5606 2-8-11 61.. MartinDwyer 1 58
(B J Meehan) *t.k.h early: trckd ldrs: rdn over 2f out and nt qckn: kpt on same pce after* **14/1**

00 7 nk **Sicilian Warrior (USA)**[18] 7547 2-8-9 0..(t) NelsonDeSouza 2 55
(P F I Cole) *awkward ride in last: plld out and drvn over 2f out: no hdwy tl over 1f out: kpt on: nvr able to chal* **25/1**

2603 8 ¾ **Sally's Dilemma**[12] 7628 2-8-3 65..(t) LukeMorris(3) 3 51
(W G M Turner) *stdd s but keen in last pair: effrt on inner over 2f out: tried to cl over 1f out: one pce* **20/1**

4000 9 ½ **Common Diva**[24] 7472 2-8-3 69.. HayleyTurner 9 46
(A J McCabe) *led: tried to kick over 2f out: hdd jst over 1f out: wkng whn squeezed out ins fnl f* **3/1[2]**

102 10 8 **Hawkspring (IRE)**[21] 7514 2-8-13 60..(t) AdamKirby 8 36
(S Parr) *pressed ldr: rdn over 2f out: losing pl whn squeezed out over 1f out: eased* **5/1[3]**

1m 27.76s (1.76) **Going Correction** +0.175s/f (Slow) **10** Ran SP% **120.2**
Speed ratings (Par 94): **96,94,93,93,93 93,92,92,91,82**
toteswinger: 1&2 £20.80, 1&3 £13.70, 2&3 £6.30. CSF £124.09 TOTE £22.40: £6.10, £3.20, £1.50; EX 149.60.
Owner T R Lock **Bred** Cleaboy Farms Co **Trained** Upper Lambourn, Berks
■ Stewards' Enquiry : Nicky Mackay two-day ban: careless riding (Jan 5-6)

FOCUS
The early tempo was weak, with several runners getting in one another's way, and they only reached full racing pace early in the straight.

NOTEBOOK
True Britannia looks better suited by Polytrack than Fibresand, and the first-time visor brought her back to the form that had won her a nursery here last month. She is effective at this trip and 1m, but her tendency to lug right-handed in the home straight was not endearing and it needs to be seen whether the headgear will continue to work. (op 10-1)
Cognac Boy(USA) has shown minor ability in three previous races and this drop to a claimer shows that he is going to prove expensive, having changed hands for 140,000gns earlier this year. However, he is lightly raced and may yet succeed at this level. Official explanation: jockey said colt hung left (op 15-2 tchd 17-2)
Trigger McCann can be rated a little better than his placing suggests, since he had to wait to find a run while the winner was sailing past the field out wide. He is a useful all-weather performer at a modest level and should find more opportunities. (op 4-1)
Turn To Dreams, who has been running over 6f, was one of the first off the bridle but she never stopped staying on and is worth another try at this longer trip, or even 1m. (op 25-1 tchd 50-1)
Precocious Air(IRE) has been close up without winning in modest company over 7f and 1m, but is not without hope if kept to sellers and claimers. (op 7-2 tchd 9-4)
Common Diva, best-in at the weights, reverted to the front-running tactics that had been employed for her only victory. However, she was already beaten when tightened up inside the final furlong and is not really firing at present. (op 5-1 tchd 13-2)
Hawkspring(IRE) Official explanation: jockey said colt hung left

7761 TRY BETDAQ FOR AN EXCHANGE H'CAP — 1m 4f (P)
3:50 (3:52) (Class 6) (0-65,65) 3-Y-0 **£2,047** (£604; £302) **Stalls** Centre

Form RPR

3444 1 **Mission Control (IRE)**[137] 4762 3-9-4 **65**.. PatCosgrave 8 76
(J R Boyle) *hld up in 6th: lost pl sltly over 2f out: rdn and decisive move to ld over 1f out: styd on wl fnl f* **9/2[3]**

0651 2 2 **Berry Baby (IRE)**[49] 7169 3-9-0 **61**.. HayleyTurner 2 69
(G A Butler) *t.k.h early: hld up in last: effrt on wd outside over 2f out: styd on but nvr quite pce to chal: drvn to take 2nd last strides* **5/2[1]**

264 3 hd **Dontpaytheferryman (USA)**[4] 7626 3-8-1 **51**..(t) LukeMorris(3) 1 59
(P D Evans) *hld up in 7th: prog 3f out: rdn to ld jst over 2f out: hdd over 1f out: one pce after: lost 2nd last strides* **6/1**

4114 4 1 ½ **Bluebell Ridge (IRE)**[31] 7400 3-9-3 **64**.. MartinDwyer 6 69
(D W P Arbuthnot) *hld up in 5th: trcking ldrs over 2f out: sn rdn and nt qckn: one pce after* **11/4[2]**

0021 5 3 ¾ **Mayfair's Future**[25] 7463 3-9-1 **62**.. NickyMackay 9 61
(J R Jenkins) *trckd ldng trio: rdn and effrt to chal over 2f out: wknd over 1f out* **11/1**

3444 6 ½ **Sabancaya**[16] 7573 3-8-0 **54**.. CharlotteKerton(7) 3 52
(Mrs P Sly) *dwlt and pushed up to go 3rd: chsd ldr 3f out: upsides over 2f out: bmpd along and wknd wl over 1f out* **11/1**

3404 7 10 **Shayera**[22] 7506 3-9-1 **62**..(p) AdamKirby 7 44
(B R Johnson) *hld up in last pair: rdn and no rspnse wl over 2f out: btn after: t.o* **7/1**

20R6 8 hd **Bella Medici**[62] 6883 3-9-1 **62**.. LPKeniry 5 44
(P G Murphy) *trckd ldr to 3f out: sn lost pl u.p: t.o* **33/1**

5506 9 4 ½ **Rosy Dawn**[15] 7596 3-8-4 **51** oh6.. LiamJones 4 26
(J J Bridger) *led to jst over 2f out: wknd rapidly: t.o* **25/1**

2m 36.12s (1.62) **Going Correction** +0.175s/f (Slow) **9** Ran SP% **123.7**
Speed ratings (Par 98): **101,99,99,98,96 95,89,88,85**
toteswinger: 1&2 £4.00, 1&3 £6.10, 2&3 £3.90. CSF £17.48 CT £71.47 TOTE £5.80: £1.70, £1.60, £2.50; EX 17.20.
Owner M Khan X2 **Bred** Darley **Trained** Epsom, Surrey

FOCUS
The tempo appeared to be just a routine one until the pace-making Rosy Dawn quickened it up entering the straight, but it did not inconvenience the hold-up performers, who filled the first three places.

7762 BET PREMIER LEAGUE FOOTBALL - BETDAQ H'CAP 6f (P)
4:20 (4:25) (Class 5) (0-70,70) 3-Y-O+ £3,238 (£963; £481; £120; £120) Stalls High

Form RPR
0135 1 **Musical Script (USA)**[3] 7730 5-9-4 70 ....(b) LPKeniry 11 79
(Mouse Hamilton-Fairley) *hld up in 5th: squeezed through over 1f out: led ins fnl f: kpt on gamely u.str.p* 5/2[1]
6403 2 ¾ **Forest Dane**[28] 7435 8-9-4 70 .... GeorgeBaker 3 77
(Mrs N Smith) *dropped in fr wd draw and hld up in last trio: rdn and prog on outer fr 2f out: styd on fnl f to snatch 2nd on line* 6/1[2]
3046 3 shd **Asian Power (IRE)**[11] 7641 3-9-1 67 .... ShaneKelly 5 74
(P J O'Gorman) *hld up in midfield on inner: prog over 1f out: jnd wnr ins fnl f: upsides tl no ex last 50yds: lost 2nd on post* 15/2
0061 4 nk **Littledodayno (IRE)**[24] 7471 5-8-12 64 .... FrancisNorton 4 70
(M Wigham) *hld up in midfield: rdn over 2f out: effrt u.p over 1f out: styd on ins fnl f: nvr quite able to chal* 14/1
0100 4 dht **Namu**[2] 7745 5-8-6 58 ....(p) LiamJones 9 64
(Miss T Spearing) *hld up in midfield: effrt towards outer 2f out: drvn and styd on fnl f: nvr quite able to chal* 16/1
6310 6 shd **Royal Manor**[10] 7651 3-8-12 64 .... FergusSweeney 8 69
(N J Vaughan) *trckd ldng trio: prog over 2f out: led over 1f out tl ins fnl f: one pce last 100yds* 10/1
0602 7 1¼ **Scarlet Oak**[8] 7679 4-8-6 58 ....(p) ChrisCatlin 7 59
(A M Hales) *hld up in abt 9th: rdn and sme prog 2f out: chsng ldrs 1f out: no imp after: fdd* 16/1
0000 8 ¾ **Decider (USA)**[201] 2710 5-8-7 62 .... KevinGhunowa(3) 1 61
(R A Harris) *led to over 1f out: wknd ins fnl f* 50/1
512 9 nse **Bold Diva**[9] 7658 3-8-4 56 ....(v) HayleyTurner 6 55
(A W Carroll) *hld up in last: ambitious effrt up inner over 2f out: nt clr run briefly over 1f out: pushed along and no hdwy fnl f* 20/1
3144 10 1 **Radiator Rooney (IRE)**[14] 7611 5-9-1 67 ....(v) PatCosgrave 10 63
(Patrick Morris, Ire) *mostly pressed ldr to over 2f out: sn lost pl and btn* 7/1[3]
2533 11 1½ **Shakespeare's Son**[19] 7540 3-9-1 70 .... DuranFentiman(3) 12 61
(H J Evans) *pressed ldng pair: losing pl whn squeezed out over 1f out* 10/1
3313 12 ¾ **Efisio Princess**[27] 7448 5-8-12 64 .... RichardThomas 2 52
(J E Long) *a in last trio: struggling u.p over 2f out* 8/1
1m 12.88s (-0.22) **Going Correction** +0.175s/f (Slow) **12** Ran SP% **121.6**
Speed ratings (Par 103): **108,107,106,106,106 106,104,103,103,102 100,99**
toteswinger: 1&2 £4.70, 1&3 £7.50, 2&3 £11.60. CSF £17.09 CT £104.32 TOTE £3.10: £1.20, £2.40, £2.80; EX 22.10.
Owner The Composers **Bred** Juddmonte Farms Inc **Trained** Bramshill, Hants
■ Stewards' Enquiry : L P Keniry one-day ban: careless riding (Jan 5)
FOCUS
A good gallop paved the way for the hold-up horses, the winner amongst them.

7763 BETDAQ.CO.UK H'CAP (DIV I) 7f (P)
4:50 (4:54) (Class 5) (0-70,70) 3-Y-O+ £2,914 (£867; £433; £216) Stalls High

Form RPR
0001 1 **Tuxedo**[19] 7541 3-8-1 56 oh2 .... LukeMorris(3) 1 67
(P W Hiatt) *stdd s: fierce hold in 7th: urged along over 2f out: picked up on wd outside over 1f out: r.o to ld last 75yds* 9/1
6-02 2 ½ **Ravi River (IRE)**[240] 1636 4-9-4 70 .... RichardKingscote 7 80
(Tom Dascombe) *trckd ldng trio: effrt on outer 2f out: rdn to ld ins fnl f: hdd and jst outpcd last 75yds* 15/8[1]
0210 3 1½ **Salt Of The Earth (IRE)**[23] 7490 3-9-1 67 .... HayleyTurner 2 73
(T G Mills) *led: steadily increased pce fr over 2f out: kpt on fr over 1f out: hdd and outpcd ins fnl f* 15/2
1135 4 1 **Charming Escort**[8] 7677 4-8-1 58 .... MCGeran(5) 8 61
(T T Clement) *heavily restrained s: hld up in 5th on inner: effrt over 2f out: kpt on over 1f out but nvr pce to threaten* 3/1[2]
0030 5 nk **Mr Garston**[23] 7490 5-8-13 65 ....(t) PatCosgrave 9 67
(J R Boyle) *trckd ldng pair: rdn over 2f out: sn lost pl: tried to cl u.str.p jst over 1f out: sn outpcd* 4/1[3]
0305 6 1¼ **Royal Envoy (IRE)**[18] 7544 5-9-1 70 .... TolleyDean(3) 4 69
(P Howling) *stdd s: t.k.h and hld up in last pair: urged along and no prog over 2f out: fnlly styd on jst over 1f out: nrst fin* 10/1
4301 7 nse **Billy Hot Rocks (IRE)**[12] 7624 3-8-10 62 ....(b) LiamJones 3 61
(Miss Gay Kelleway) *t.k.h: hld up in 6th: rdn over 2f out: cl enough over 1f out: wknd ins fnl f* 14/1
5001 8 1¾ **Copper King**[24] 7469 4-8-4 56 .... ChrisCatlin 6 50
(Miss Tor Sturgis) *t.k.h: pressed ldr to over 1f out: wknd* 12/1
5000 9 2 **Ike Quebec (FR)**[17] 7557 3-9-2 68 .... TGMcLaughlin 5 57
(J R Boyle) *hld up and sn in last pair: shkn up and no prog over 2f out* 33/1
1m 27.49s (1.49) **Going Correction** +0.175s/f (Slow) **9** Ran SP% **127.9**
Speed ratings (Par 103): **98,97,95,94,94 92,92,90,88**
toteswinger: 1&2 £6.30, 1&3 £8.30, 2&3 £5.10. CSF £29.27 CT £146.97 TOTE £15.60: £3.20, £1.80, £2.30; EX 53.00.
Owner Phil Kelly **Bred** Gainsborough Stud Management Ltd **Trained** Hook Norton, Oxon
FOCUS
The pace was modest, so the winner did well to come from third-last.
Billy Hot Rocks(IRE) Official explanation: jockey said gelding hung right

7764 BETDAQ.CO.UK H'CAP (DIV II) 7f (P)
5:20 (5:20) (Class 5) (0-70,70) 3-Y-O+ £2,914 (£867; £433; £216) Stalls High

Form RPR
0602 1 **Alqaahir (USA)**[2] 7748 6-8-10 62 .... LiamJones 9 71
(Patrick Morris, Ire) *trckd ldng trio: smooth prog 2f out: pushed into ld 1f out: hrd pressed fnl f but hld on wout rdr using whip* 5/2[1]
4521 2 hd **Balata**[19] 7536 3-8-13 65 .... TGMcLaughlin 8 73
(B R Millman) *hld up in 8th: prog on inner over 2f out: chal over 1f out: pressed wnr fnl f: a jst hld* 9/2[3]
2221 3 1¼ **Ugenius**[13] 7619 4-8-9 61 .... HayleyTurner 3 66
(Mrs C A Dunnett) *trckd ldng pair: smooth prog to ld 2f out: sn pressed: hdd 1f out: one pce fnl f* 6/1
2132 4 2 **Blue Charm**[8] 7677 4-9-1 67 .... LPKeniry 7 66
(S Kirk) *hld up in 6th: clsd on ldrs 2f out: nt qckn wl over 1f out: one pce after* 11/4[2]
1000 5 2½ **Landucci**[54] 7068 7-9-1 70 ....(b[1]) PatrickHills(3) 5 62
(J W Hills) *hld up in 5th: cruised up to chal over 2f out: sn rdn and nt qckn: tried to cl again over 1f out: wknd fnl f* 14/1
5014 6 ½ **Double Valentine**[11] 7636 5-8-2 61 ow2 .... DebraEngland(7) 6 52
(R Ingram) *hld up in last pair: effrt over 2f out but no real impact: plld wdr and plugged on fnl f* 16/1
3462 7 1½ **Maid Of Ailsa (USA)**[12] 7624 3-8-4 56 .... ChrisCatlin 2 43
(W J Haggas) *pressed ldr to over 2f out: stl nrly upsides wl over 1f out: wknd tamely* 11/1
0000 8 4 **Pha Mai Blue**[17] 7557 3-9-4 70 .... PatCosgrave 4 46
(J R Boyle) *stdd s: hld up last: detached and struggling 3f out: nvr a factor* 20/1
1000 9 2 **Tilsworth Charlie**[15] 7591 5-8-4 56 oh1 ....(b) NickyMackay 1 27
(J R Jenkins) *settled in 7th: pushed along over 2f out and no prog: sn btn* 25/1
1640 10 shd **Certifiable**[310] 587 7-8-5 57 oh8 ow1 .... PaulDoe 10 28
(Miss Z C Davison) *led at decent pce to 2f out: wknd rapidly* 33/1
1m 26.29s (0.29) **Going Correction** +0.175s/f (Slow) **28** Ran SP% **120.1**
Speed ratings (Par 103): **105,104,103,101,98 97,95,91,89,88**
toteswinger: 1&2 £5.40, 1&3 £7.30, 2&3 £6.30. CSF £14.25 CT £63.93 TOTE £3.70: £1.30, £2.00, £2.30; EX 20.90 Place 6: £180.24, Place 5: £40.15..
Owner Leslie Laverty **Bred** Shadwell Farm LLC **Trained** Ruanbeg, Co. Kildare
FOCUS
A much better gallop than division one, a returning a faster time.
T/Plt: £111.90 to a £1 stake. Pool: £65,040.83. 424.02 winning tickets. T/Qpdt: £22.10 to a £1 stake. Pool: £6,684.64. 223.50 winning tickets. JN

7738 LINGFIELD (L-H)
Monday, December 22

OFFICIAL GOING: Standard
Wind: medium, across Weather: overcast

7765 EVENT IMAGE FOR PHOTO FINISH APPRENTICE H'CAP (DIV I) 7f (P)
12:30 (12:31) (Class 6) (0-55,55) 3-Y-O+ £2,047 (£604; £302) Stalls Low

Form RPR
0000 1 **Cavalry Guard (USA)**[17] 7553 4-8-5 46 ....(b) AmyBaker 9 54
(T D McCarthy) *led tl rdn and hdd over 1f out: rallied gamely to ld again fnl 50yds* 12/1
2010 2 ½ **Comrade Cotton**[14] 7601 4-8-11 55 ....(p) DebraEngland(3) 3 62
(J Ryan) *trckd ldrs: rdn and effrt over 1f out: pressed ldrs ins fnl f: kpt on to go 2nd nr fin* 6/1[2]
0003 3 nk **Grizedale (IRE)**[5] 7706 9-8-4 52 ....(tp) KierenFox(7) 7 58
(M J Attwater) *t.k.h early: hld up in midfield: pushed along and hdwy over 2f out: led ins fnl f: nt run on and hdd fnl 50yds: lost 2nd nr fin* 6/1[2]
-02 4 1½ **Victory Spirit**[52] 7114 4-8-11 52 .... BMcHugh 6 54
(I Semple) *taken down early: hld up in tch: plld out and rdn wl over 1f out: plugged on same pce fnl f* 4/1[1]
0430 5 1½ **Afton View (IRE)**[22] 7509 3-8-13 54 ....(p) AshleyMorgan 1 52
(S Parr) *s.i.s: hdwy to chse ldr after 1f: rdn to ld over 1f out: hdd and wknd ins fnl f* 10/1[3]
0506 6 ½ **Silver Spruce**[194] 2941 3-8-2 50 ....(be) MarieLequarre(7) 2 47
(D Flood) *s.i.s: hld up in midfield: rdn and outpcd over 2f out: kpt on fnl f: nvr pce to rch ldrs* 50/1
0506 7 ½ **Franksalot (IRE)**[23] 7503 8-8-4 50 ....(b) AndrewHeffernan(5) 12 45
(I W McInnes) *racd wd tl 1/2-way: t.k.h: hld up in midfield: rdn over 1f out: kpt on but nvr pce to trble ldrs* 16/1
0343 8 ½ **Nikki Bea (IRE)**[14] 7601 5-8-12 53 .... KylieManser 10 47
(Jamie Poulton) *chsd ldrs: pushed along 3f out: rdn and kpt on same pce fr over 1f out* 4/1[1]
000 9 ½ **Bad Moon Rising**[15] 7596 3-8-0 46 oh1 ....(p) NathanAlison(5) 11 39
(J Akehurst) *racd wd: chsd ldrs: rdn and wknd wl over 1f out* 33/1
66/0 10 hd **Black Draft**[116] 5427 6-8-5 46 oh1 .... BillyCray 4 38
(B Forsey) *hld up in rr: rdn and effrt 2f out: nvr trbld ldrs* 100/1
0000 11 1¾ **Spanish Ace**[47] 7195 7-8-7 48 .... DeanHeslop 8 35
(J M Bradley) *a bhd: nvr trbld ldrs* 25/1
0000 12 4½ **Silidan**[23] 7490 5-9-0 55 .... JemmaMarshall 5 30
(G L Moore) *led to s: v.s.a: racd freely: hdwy into midfield 5f out: wknd 3f out: bhd whn wd bnd 2f out* 6/1[2]
1m 24.58s (-0.22) **Going Correction** -0.05s/f (Stan) **12** Ran SP% **115.3**
Speed ratings (Par 101): **99,98,98,96,94 94,93,92,92,92 90,85**
toteswinger: 1&2 £32.90, 1&3 £32.70, 2&3 £8.00. CSF £78.28 CT £488.05 TOTE £14.40: £5.70, £2.30, £1.80; EX 146.80 TRIFECTA Not won..
Owner Inside Track Racing Club **Bred** W G Lyster Iii **Trained** Godstone, Surrey
FOCUS
Moderate form for this apprentice handicap, and it was a messy race. There was no pace on through the first couple of furlongs, before the gallop noticeably increased. The time was 0.83secs slower than the second division.

7766 EVENT IMAGE FOR PHOTO FINISH APPRENTICE H'CAP (DIV II) 7f (P)
1:00 (1:00) (Class 6) (0-55,55) 3-Y-O+ £2,047 (£604; £302) Stalls Low

Form RPR
4505 1 **Upstairs**[15] 7591 4-8-13 54 .... AmyBaker 3 68
(D R C Elsworth) *hld up in rr: hdwy jst over 2f out: gd hdwy to ld jst ins fnl f: r.o wl* 11/4[1]
0400 2 2 **Torquemada (IRE)**[28] 7437 7-8-5 53 ....(t) KierenFox(7) 8 61
(M J Attwater) *hld up towards rr: hdwy over 3f out: chsd ldrs and rdn 2f out: chsd wnr ins fnl f: r.o but no imp on wnr* 16/1
0042 3 1¾ **Jordi Roper (IRE)**[4] 7725 3-8-3 49 ....(t) AndrewHeffernan(5) 4 53
(S Parr) *chsd ldrs: rdn and effrt on inner 2f out: pressed ldrs ent fnl f: sn outpcd by wnr* 7/1
0642 4 ½ **Very Well Red**[9] 7663 5-8-9 50 ....(b) RossAtkinson 10 52
(P W Hiatt) *led for 1f: chsd ldr after: ev ch and rdn wl over 1f out: one pce fnl f* 7/2[3]
4623 5 ½ **Thabaat**[10] 7651 4-9-0 55 ....(b) DeanHeslop 12 56
(J M Bradley) *dwlt: racd wd: towards rr: hdwy over 4f out: jnd ldrs over 2f out: sn rdn: kpt on same pce fr over 1f out* 10/3[2]
6000 6 nse **Great Fox (IRE)**[10] 7648 7-8-6 47 .... AshleyMorgan 2 48
(S C Williams) *taken down early: chsd ldr tl led after 1f: rdn and hdd jst ins fnl f: wknd* 33/1
0520 7 1 **Straight Face (IRE)**[126] 5157 4-8-12 53 ....(b) KylieManser 9 51
(Miss Gay Kelleway) *t.k.h: chsd ldrs: rdn and unable qck 2f out: no ch w ldrs after* 10/1

6000 **8** *nk* **Halsion Challenge**[102] 5832 3-8-2 **46** oh1..........................(t) PNolan[(3)] 1 43
(J R Best) *hld up towards rr: rdn over 2f out: kpt on but nvr pce to trble ldrs* **25/1**

00-0 **9** *1 3/4* **Grand Court (IRE)**[14] 7599 5-8-5 **46** oh1.................. MatthewDavies 5 39
(George Baker) *a bhd: rdn over 4f out: nvr nr ldrs* **66/1**

0650 **10** *2 1/4* **Motu (IRE)**[14] 7601 7-8-11 **52**.......................(v) BMcHugh 6 39
(I W McInnes) *chsd ldrs: rdn over 3f out: lost pl over 2f out: no ch fr wl over 1f out* **12/1**

1m 23.75s (-1.05) **Going Correction** -0.05s/f (Stan) **43** Ran SP% **115.4**
Speed ratings (Par 101): **104,101,99,99,98 98,97,97,95,92**
toteswinger: 1&2 £12.60, 1&3 £5.30, 2&3 £15.80. CSF £47.36 CT £281.28 TOTE £3.90: £1.80, £3.40, £2.50; EX 58.10 Trifecta £273.70 Part won. Pool: £369.92 - 0.47 winning units..
Owner D R C Elsworth **Bred** Miss C Tagart **Trained** Newmarket, Suffolk

FOCUS
They went a good pace and the winning time was 0.83secs quicker than the first division.
Thabaat Official explanation: jockey said gelding hung right

7767 EDENBRIDGE MAIDEN AUCTION STKS 7f (P)
1:30 (1:32) (Class 6) 2-Y-O **£2,388** (£705; £352) **Stalls** Low

Form RPR

46 **1** **Zim Ho**[38] 7311 2-8-10 0 ow1.................................. DaneO'Neill 4 67
(J Akehurst) *t.k.h: chsd ldr tl rdn to ld 2f out: clr ins fnl f: a holding on* **5/2**[1]

2 *nk* **Premier Angel (USA)** 2-8-9 0.................................. JohnEgan 2 65
(Jane Chapple-Hyam) *s.i.s: sn pushed up and in tch: rdn over 2f out: chsd wnr ins fnl f: gaining towards fin* **8/1**

2034 **3** *1 1/2* **La Verte Rue (USA)**[10] 7645 2-8-9 67.......................... ShaneKelly 9 62
(J A Osborne) *broke wl but sn stdd and in rr: rdn over 4f out: bhd over 2f out: hdwy u.p over 1f out: styd on wl u.p fnl f to go 3rd wl ins fnl f: nt rch ldrs* **4/1**[3]

00 **4** *hd* **Lucky Fortune (IRE)**[25] 7458 2-8-10 0.................... MickyFenton 8 62
(Miss Amy Weaver) *racd in midfield: rdn over 2f out: unabe to qckn over 2f out: styd on wl u.p fnl f: wnt 4th wl ins fnl f* **66/1**

5 *1* **Lady Micklegate (USA)** 2-8-7 0 ow1....................... SteveDrowne 7 57
(J R Best) *s.i.s: t.k.h early: hld up in midfield: rdn over 2f out: kpt on same pce fr over 1f out* **11/1**

6 *1/2* **Hatman Jack (IRE)** 2-8-11 0.................................. MichaelHills 6 59
(B G Powell) *s.i.s: hld up towards rr: effrt on inner over 1f out: kpt on fnl f: nvr trbld ldrs* **5/1**

6344 **7** *1* **Our Day Will Come**[24] 7472 2-8-7 73.......................... ChrisCatlin 1 53
(R Hannon) *led tl hdd 2f out: sn rdn: lost 2nd ins fnl f: wknd qckly fnl 75yds* **3/1**[2]

8 *3/4* **Esteem Lord** 2-8-9 0.. FrancisNorton 3 53
(Jamie Poulton) *s.i.s: in rr and pushed along: kpt on fr over 1f out: nvr trbld ldrs* **40/1**

03P4 **9** *2 1/2* **Danzadil (IRE)**[26] 7451 2-8-9 62 ow1....................... RobertWinston 5 47
(R A Teal) *t.k.h: chsd ldrs: rdn over 2f out: wknd wl over 1f out* **8/1**

1m 25.14s (0.34) **Going Correction** -0.05s/f (Stan) **9** Ran SP% **124.7**
Speed ratings (Par 94): **96,95,93,93,92 92,90,90,87**
toteswinger: 1&2 £7.30, 1&3 £3.30, 2&3 £9.40. CSF £25.88 TOTE £3.60: £1.30, £2.60, £1.80; EX 30.00 Trifecta £62.90 Pool: £692.80 - 8.15 winning units..
Owner Green Pastures Farm **Bred** Green Pastures Farm **Trained** Epsom, Surrey

FOCUS
A modest juvenile maiden.

NOTEBOOK
Zim Ho improved slightly on the form he showed on his first two starts and justified market support. Just as on his previous start, he got noticeably warm, and he again raced keenly, but showed he has plenty of ability. There was a lot to like about the way he picked up for pressure, despite having been denied the early lead, but he will surely need to become more relaxed if he is going to continue to progress. He is likely to be given a break now. (op 7-1)
Premier Angel(USA), a $65,000 purchase, out of a dual winner at 5f-6f in the US, shaped nicely on her debut. She ran on well in the closing stages having briefly been outpaced turning into the straight and she can improve for the experience. (op 14-1)
La Verte Rue(USA) came off the bridle a long way out but she plugged on to take a respectable third. Some headgear might sharpen her up. (op 5-1)
Lucky Fortune(IRE) had shown little on her first two starts over 6f, but this was more encouraging. She might improve again for a further step up in trip and now has the option of handicaps.
Lady Micklegate(USA), a $30,000 purchase, out of a multiple winner in the US, was too keen for her own good on this racecourse debut. (op 8-1 tchd 15-2)
Hatman Jack(IRE), a half-brother to multiple sprint winner Compton Banker, was well backed in the morning but never really got competitive. He was stuck towards the inside for most of the way after starting slowly, which was not ideal, and he should improve a fair bit for the run. (op 7-2)
Our Day Will Come made much of the running before dropping out and was nowhere near her official mark of 73. (op 5-2 tchd 9-2)

7768 ASHDOWN FOREST CLAIMING STKS 6f (P)
2:00 (2:01) (Class 6) 3-Y-O+ **£2,047** (£604; £302) **Stalls** Low

Form RPR

4213 **1** **Mutamared (USA)**[39] 7297 8-9-0 84.............................. NCallan 3 85
(K A Ryan) *mounted on crse: t.k.h: chsd ldr tl rdn to ld wl over 1f out: r.o wl fnl f* **13/8**[1]

5232 **2** *nk* **Desert Dreamer (IRE)**[14] 7601 7-8-9 77............... RichardKingscote 2 79
(Tom Dascombe) *mounted on crse: chsd ldrs: rdn over 2f out: disp 2nd 1f out: kpt on fnl f 50yds* **15/8**[2]

3166 **3** *nk* **Fyodor (IRE)**[4] 7716 7-9-5 102.................................. LPKeniry 5 88
(C R Dore) *taken down early: dropped in after s: plld hrd: hld up in rr: hdwy 2f out: disp 2nd 1f out: rdn and one pce ins fnl f* **11/4**[3]

6060 **4** *2 1/4* **Woodcote (IRE)**[12] 7621 6-9-0 74...................(vt) FrancisNorton 4 76
(P R Chamings) *t.k.h: led: hdd wl over 1f out: sn rdn wknd ins fnl f* **10/1**

0000 **5** *5* **Ishibee (IRE)**[5] 7710 4-8-1 43 ow2.................(p) FrankieMcDonald 1 47?
(J J Bridger) *racd in last pair: rdn and outpcd 2f out: wl hld fnl f* **66/1**

1m 11.06s (-0.84) **Going Correction** -0.05s/f (Stan) **5** Ran SP% **110.1**
Speed ratings (Par 101): **103,102,102,99,92**
CSF £5.01 TOTE £2.90: £1.30, £2.00; EX 4.80.
Owner Errigal Racing **Bred** E J Hudson Jr, Irrevocable Trust & Kilroy T'Bred **Trained** Hambleton, N Yorks

FOCUS
A very good claimer on paper, but the worry was a potential lack of pace and the tempo was indeed ordinary.

7769 POWER 2000 MAIDEN STKS 6f (P)
2:30 (2:32) (Class 5) 2-Y-O **£2,729** (£806; £201; £201) **Stalls** Low

Form RPR

352 **1** **Bobs Dreamflight**[16] 7574 2-9-3 71.............................. ChrisCatlin 4 74
(D K Ivory) *in tch: swtchd lft over 1f out: rdn ent fnl f: r.o wl to ld towards fin* **9/4**[1]

2 *1/2* **Theatre Street (IRE)** 2-8-12 0.................................. ShaneKelly 1 68
(J Noseda) *chsd ldrs: hdwy and rdn 2f out: led ins fnl f: drvn and hdd towards fin* **8/1**

532 **3** *nk* **Comadoir (IRE)**[66] 6770 2-9-3 80.............................. TravisBlock 8 72
(Miss Jo Crowley) *w ldr tl rdn to ld jst over 2f out: drvn wl over 1f out: hdd ins fnl f: no ex towards fin* **3/1**[2]

2032 **3** *dht* **Today's The Day**[11] 7638 2-8-12 70.........................(b) NCallan 3 67
(M A Jarvis) *broke wl: led: hdd and rdn jst over 2f out: ev ch u.p fr over 1f out: no ex fnl 100yds* **5/1**

0 **5** *1 1/4* **Maswerte (IRE)**[24] 7465 2-9-3 0.............................. DaneO'Neill 7 68
(L M Cumani) *s.i.s: t.k.h: hld up towards rr: hdwy and rdn jst over 2f out: hung lft over 1f out: kpt on steadily fnl f: nt rch ldrs* **4/1**[3]

6 *1 3/4* **Dance And Dance (IRE)** 2-9-3 0.......................... FergusSweeney 9 63
(E F Vaughan) *awkward s and s.i.s: t.k.h and sn chsng ldrs: rdn and outpcd over 1f out: kpt on same pce fnl f* **33/1**

7 *2 1/4* **Freeing** 2-8-12 0.. SteveDrowne 2 51
(J A R Toller) *s.i.s: hld up towards rr: rdn over 3f out: struggling over 2f out: no ch after* **20/1**

00 **8** *8* **Sparks Alive**[62] 6885 2-8-7 0.............................. AmyBaker[(5)] 5 27
(D R C Elsworth) *sn pushed along and outpcd in rr: lost tch 1/2-way* **66/1**

000 **9** *hd* **Valid Point (IRE)**[11] 7640 2-9-3 0...................... StephenDonohoe 6 31
(Sir Mark Prescott) *s.i.s: sn rdn and outpcd in last pl* **66/1**

1m 12.1s (0.20) **Going Correction** -0.05s/f (Stan) **9** Ran SP% **114.2**
Speed ratings (Par 96): **96,95,94,94,93 90,87,77,77**PL: Bob's Dreamflight £1.10, Theatre Street £2.60, Comadoir £0.90, Today's the Day £0.70. toteswinger: 1&2 £5.60, BD&C £1.30, BD&TTD £1.30, TS&C £3.20, TS&TTD £3.40. CSF £20.19 TOTE £3.10; EX 24.00 TRIFECTA Pool: £815.10. With Comadoir: £227 Owner.

FOCUS
An ordinary but competitive sprint maiden.

NOTEBOOK
Bobs Dreamflight ◆ had run with encouragement on all three of his previous starts, including when slightly unlucky over 5f at Great Leighs on his latest outing, and he found this a suitable opportunity to get off the mark. He looks better than the bare result, as he lost his place just after halfway and was forced to switch towards the often unfavoured inside rail in the straight, although at the same time it's fair to say the runner-up is open to a good deal of improvement. The winner's handicap mark of 71 is likely to be revised considering he had something to find at the weights with a couple of these, and that will make things tougher, but he gives the impression we have yet to see the best of him. (op 7-2)
Theatre Street(IRE), the first foal of a 7f winner at three, was easy to back but showed a fair amount of ability on her racecourse debut. She was only given a couple of smacks with the whip very late on and can improve plenty. (op 6-1 tchd 5-1 and 10-1)
Today's The Day looked in real trouble when headed turning into the straight, but she ran on again near the finish. Her last two runs now have suggested she could be worth another try over 7f. (op 5-2 tchd 7-2)
Comadoir(IRE) was given every chance and he ran a respectable race, but he was below his official mark of 80. (op 5-2 tchd 7-2)
Maswerte(IRE) again showed ability but he ruined his chance by hanging left in the straight. A horse with a bit of size, he should do better in time, probably when stepped up in trip on a more galloping track. Official explanation: jockey said colt hung left (op 8-1 tchd 7-2)

7770 THREE BRIDGES H'CAP 2m (P)
3:00 (3:06) (Class 4) (0-85,87) 3-Y-O+ **£4,857** (£1,445; £722; £360) **Stalls** Low

Form RPR

2110 **1** **Greenwich Village**[86] 6272 5-9-2 **73**........................ ShaneKelly 2 82
(W J Knight) *chsd ldr tl 10f out: in tch: rdn over 2f out: ev ch 1f out: r.o wl u.p to ld on post* **4/1**[3]

1122 **2** *nse* **Epsom Salts**[5] 7711 3-8-1 **66**.............................. PaulHanagan 7 75
(P M Phelan) *t.k.h: hld up in tch: dropped to rr over 8f out: hdwy and squeezed between horses over 2f out: drvn to ld jst ins fnl f: hdd on post* **9/4**[1]

3212 **3** *1* **Azabu Juban (IRE)**[6] 7696 3-8-3 **73**................... WilliamCarson[(5)] 3 81
(J Jay) *chsd ldrs: rdn to ld jst over 2f out: drvn over 1f out: hdd jst ins fnl f: kpt on same pce fnl 100yds* **3/1**[2]

0660 **4** *3 1/2* **Greenwich Meantime**[86] 6288 8-10-0 **85**.................. DaneO'Neill 5 89
(A King) *hld up in last trio: rdn 4f out: outpcd wl over 2f out: plugged on fnl f: nvr trbld ldrs* **12/1**

5 **5** *3* **Rock Soleil**[31] 7404 4-10-2 **87**.............................. NCallan 1 87
(Jane Chapple-Hyam) *led at stdy gallop tl hdd 9f out: chsd ldrs after tl led again 3f out: sn rdn: hdd jst over 2f out: ev ch 1f out: wknd fnl f* **10/1**

3-44 **6** *hd* **Prince Zafonic**[11] 7639 5-8-12 **69**.............................. JohnEgan 8 69
(D K Ivory) *t.k.h: chsd ldrs tl wnt 2nd over 6f out: led 4f out: hdd and rdn 3f out: wkng whn jostled over 2f out* **7/1**

3116 **7** *4* **Turban Heights (IRE)**[11] 7639 4-9-10 **81**.................. ChrisCatlin 4 76
(E J O'Neill) *uns rdr bef s: stdd after s: t.k.h: hld up in rr tl swtchd rt and hdwy over 10f out: led 9f out tl 4f out: rdn and wknd over 2f out* **14/1**

4-24 **8** *5* **Colophony (USA)**[30] 5676 8-8-2 **66**................... DeclanCannon[(7)] 6 55
(K A Morgan) *dwlt: bustled along early: t.k.h after 2f: hld up in midfield: rdn and struggling over 4f out: wl bhd fnl 2f* **25/1**

3m 24.28s (-1.42) **Going Correction** -0.05s/f (Stan)
WFA 3 from 4yo+ 8lb **8** Ran SP% **115.6**
Speed ratings (Par 105): **101,100,100,98,97 97,95,92**
toteswinger: 1&2 £2.70, 1&3 £3.40, 2&3 £2.70. CSF £13.61 CT £30.14 TOTE £4.90: £1.40, £1.40, £1.80; EX 14.60 Trifecta £65.10 Pool: £703.46 - 7.99 winning units..
Owner Ecurie Franglaise **Bred** Cotswold Stud **Trained** Patching, W Sussex

FOCUS
A fair staying handicap run at an ordinary pace.
Prince Zafonic Official explanation: jockey said gelding hung both ways

7771 FOREST ROW H'CAP 1m (P)
3:30 (3:34) (Class 5) (0-70,70) 3-Y-O+ **£3,070** (£906; £453) **Stalls** High

Form RPR

0005 **1** **Young Bertie**[35] 7360 5-8-13 **64**.......................(v) TravisBlock 7 72
(H Morrison) *t.k.h: hld up in midfield: rdn and nt qckn 3f out: stl plenty to do over 1f out: str run u.p fnl f to ld nr fnish* **5/1**[2]

0420 **2** *nk* **Moon Crystal**[35] 7360 3-9-0 **66**....................(t) TGMcLaughlin 3 73
(E A L Dunlop) *t.k.h: chsd ldrs: rdn 2f out: squeezed between horses to ld wl ins fnl f: hdd towards fin* **12/1**

3100 **3** *nk* **Pension Policy (USA)**[22] 7507 3-9-4 **70**..............(v[1]) SteveDrowne 4 76
(R Charlton) *chsd ldrs: hdwy to join ldr over 2f out: drvn over 1f out: edgd lft and led jst ins fnl f: hdd wl ins fnl f: no ex towards fin* **8/1**

0046 **4** *1/2* **Straight And Level (CAN)**[14] 7603 3-9-3 **69**...........(v[1]) DaneO'Neill 2 74
(Miss Jo Crowley) *chsd ldr tl led wl over 2f out: drvn 2f out: hdd jst ins fnl f: kpt on same pce fnl 100yds* **12/1**

0002 **5** *nk* **Napoletano (GER)**[14] 7603 7-9-4 **69**.....................(p) NCallan 6 73
(S Dow) *t.k.h: hld up in midfield on inner: nt clr run jst over 2f out: rdn and hdwy over 1f out: kpt on fnl f but nt rch ldrs* **9/2**[1]

5500 **6** *hd* **Murrin (IRE)**[23] 7494 4-9-3 **68**.................. FrankieMcDonald 10 72
(T G Mills) *stdd and swtchd lft after s: t.k.h: hld up in rr: plld out over 2f out: kpt on fnl f: nt rch ldrs* **11/2**[3]

3046 **7** *2* **Cat Whistle**[14] 7610 3-9-2 **68**.................. PaulHanagan 11 67
(R A Fahey) *t.k.h: hld up in rr: rdn and effrt on outer 2f out: kpt on fnl f: nvr rchd ldrs* **9/2**[1]

2006 **8** *¾* **Tevez**[52] 7115 3-9-1 **67**.................. MickyFenton 1 65
(Miss Amy Weaver) *led: rdn 3f out: sn hdd: wknd over 1f out* **25/1**

0063 **9** *1 ¼* **Onenightinlisbon (IRE)**[18] 7548 4-8-7 **65**.................. NathanAlison(7) 9 60
(J R Boyle) *a towards rr: rdn over 1f out: nvr threatened ldrs* **7/1**

0000 **10** *½* **Shake On It**[8] 7677 4-8-9 **65**..................(vt) WilliamCarson(5) 12 59
(M J Gingell) *stdd s: t.k.h: hld up towards rr: hdwy on outer over 4f out: chsd ldrs and rdn over 2f out: wknd over 1f out* **25/1**

0500 **11** *2 ½* **Bermacha**[18] 7548 3-8-13 **65**.................. StephenDonohoe 5 53
(W R Muir) *dwlt: sn chsng ldrs: rdn over 3f out: wknd over 2f out* **20/1**

1m 37.74s (-0.46) **Going Correction** -0.05s/f (Stan)
WFA 3 from 4yo+ 1lb **11** Ran SP% **119.9**
Speed ratings (Par 103): **100,99,99,98,98 98,96,95,94,93 91**
toteswinger: 1&2 £9.10, 1&3 £10.20, 2&3 £13.70. CSF £62.93 CT £474.03 TOTE £5.80: £1.70, £4.10, £3.80; EX 68.50 Trifecta £467.40 Part won. Pool: £631.69 - 0.40 winning units. Place 6: £15.51, Place 5: £3.97..
Owner M T Bevan **Bred** Red House Stud **Trained** East Ilsley, Berks
■ Stewards' Enquiry : N Callan one-day ban, plus four days deferred, careless riding (Jan 5-9)

FOCUS
A modest handicap and a rather messy race, as there was no pace on for much of the way, and the first six finished in a bit of a heap.
T/Plt: £31.10 to a £1 stake. Pool: £55,479.10. 1,302.23 winning tickets. T/Qpdt: £3.70 to a £1 stake. Pool: £6,303.09. 1,234.78 winning tickets. SP

7726 SOUTHWELL (L-H)
Tuesday, December 23

OFFICIAL GOING: Standard
Wind: Light across Weather: Overcast

7772 BOOK YOUR TICKETS ON LINE AT SOUTHWELL-RACECOURSE.CO.UK H'CAP (DIV I) 7f (F)
12:00 (12:00) (Class 6) (0-60,60) 3-Y-O+ **£1,706** (£503; £252) **Stalls** Low

Form RPR

321 **1** **Run Free**[10] 7658 4-8-11 **53**.................. LeeEnstone 8 64
(N Wilson) *chsd ldrs: pushed along 1/2-way: led 2f out: sn rdn and hung lft: styd on* **5/1**[2]

0543 **2** *2* **Kingsmaite**[14] 7619 7-9-1 **57**..................(b) PaulEddery 5 63
(S R Bowring) *sn led: rdn and hdd 2f out: styd on same pce ins fnl f* **9/2**[1]

5004 **3** *1 ¼* **Louisiade (IRE)**[4] 7731 7-9-1 **57**..................(b) PatrickMathers 10 59
(M C Chapman) *hld up: hdwy over 2f out: sn rdn: styd on u.p* **17/2**[3]

0514 **4** *hd* **Guildenstern (IRE)**[14] 7619 6-9-0 **56**.................. IanMongan 4 58
(P Howling) *hld up: hdwy u.p 2f out: styd on* **9/2**[1]

0420 **5** *½* **Captain Royale (IRE)**[21] 7532 3-9-4 **60**..................(p) GregFairley 7 60
(Miss Tracy Waggott) *chsd ldr: ev ch 2f out: sn rdn: no ex ins fnl f* **16/1**

0606 **6** *nk* **Mister Benji**[14] 7619 9-8-4 **46** oh1..................(p) AndrewElliott 9 46
(B P J Baugh) *chsd ldrs: rdn over 2f out: hung lft over 1f out: styd on same pce fnl f* **16/1**

/030 **7** *¾* **Capped For Victory (USA)**[233] 1822 7-8-9 **51** ow1.... RobertWinston 3 49
(G A Swinbank) *s.i.s: hld up: rdn 1/2-way: hdwy over 2f out: no ex ins fnl f* **10/1**

0606 **8** *5* **Imperial Djay (IRE)**[10] 7669 3-9-1 **60**.................. KevinGhunowa(3) 11 44
(G J Smith) *s.i.s: sn mid-div: hdwy 1/2-way: rdn and wknd 2f out* **25/1**

6000 **9** *27* **Beresford Lady**[17] 7581 4-8-1 **46** oh1.................. LukeMorris(3) 2 —
(A D Brown) *prom: rdn and edgd lft 1/2-way: sn wknd* **100/1**

6424 **10** *6* **Very Well Red**[1] 7766 5-8-9 **51** ow1..................(b) DarrenWilliams 1 —
(P W Hiatt) *sn pushed along and prom: lost pl whn hmpd 1/2-way: sn bhd: eased over 1f out* **9/2**[1]

4400 **11** *2* **Crafty Fox**[139] 4748 5-8-4 **46** oh1..................(v) ChrisCatlin 6 —
(John A Harris) *s.i.s: sn outpcd* **10/1**

1m 29.49s (-0.81) **Going Correction** -0.10s/f (Stan) **11** Ran SP% **116.5**
Speed ratings (Par 101): **100,97,96,96,95 95,94,88,57,50 48**
toteswinger: 1&2 £5.00, 1&3 £11.10, 2&3 £9.30. CSF £27.49 CT £191.53 TOTE £5.60: £2.20, £1.60, £2.50; EX 30.60 Trifecta £40.10 Pool: £175.66, 3.24 winning units..
Owner The Run Free Partnership **Bred** Snailwell Stud Co Ltd **Trained** Flaxton, N Yorks

FOCUS
Ordinary handicap form, and the slower of the two divisions by 0.45sec.

7773 CALL 01636 814481 TO SPONSOR A RACE MAIDEN STKS 7f (F)
12:30 (12:31) (Class 5) 2-Y-O **£3,070** (£906; £453) **Stalls** Low

Form RPR

1 **Trueblue Wizard (IRE)** 2-9-3 0.................. MartinDwyer 7 71+
(W R Muir) *chsd ldrs: led 1/2-way: rdn and edgd rt ins fnl f: r.o: eased nr fin* **6/1**[3]

5 **2** *2 ¾* **Manana Manana**[4] 7726 2-9-3 0.................. RobertWinston 9 62
(S Parr) *a.p: hung rt 1/2-way: rdn to chse wnr over 2f out: no ex wl ins fnl f* **20/1**

5 **3** *1* **Solo Choice**[5] 7720 2-9-3 0.................. TonyCulhane 8 60
(D Flood) *prom: rdn 1/2-way: outpcd over 2f out: rallied over 1f out: styd on* **40/1**

03 **4** *hd* **Joannadarc (USA)**[16] 7593 2-8-12 0.................. PatCosgrave 4 54
(S A Callaghan) *sn pushed along and prom: outpcd over 2f out: rallied over 1f out: styd on* **5/6**[1]

0 **5** *3* **Tinshu (IRE)**[31] 7424 2-8-12 0.................. ChrisCatlin 3 47
(D Haydn Jones) *sn outpcd: swtchd wd after 1f: hdwy and hung lft over 1f out: nt trble ldrs* **20/1**

60 **6** *6* **King's Chorister**[84] 6359 2-9-3 0..................(e[1]) HayleyTurner 1 37
(Miss Gay Kelleway) *sn pushed along in rr: rdn over 2f out: sn wknd* **10/1**

7 *4 ½* **Badge Of Honour** 2-9-3 0.................. GregFairley 6 25
(M Johnston) *chsd ldr tl led 5f out: hdd 1/2-way: rdn over 2f out: sn hung lft and wknd* **10/3**[2]

4 **8** *15* **Consequence**[13] 7628 2-9-3 0.................. LeeEnstone 2 —
(A Dickman) *s.s: outpcd* **150/1**

0000 **9** *¾* **Lonsdale Lad**[8] 7689 2-8-12 31..................(b) JamesO'Reilly(5) 5 —
(R C Guest) *sn rdn to ld: hdd 5f out: wknd 1/2-way* **200/1**

1m 29.64s (-0.66) **Going Correction** -0.10s/f (Stan) **9** Ran SP% **114.1**
Speed ratings (Par 96): **99,95,94,94,91 84,79,61,61**
toteswinger: 1&2 £6.30, 1&3 £16.20, 2&3 £12.90. CSF £106.32 TOTE £8.00: £1.50, £2.60, £4.80; EX 67.50 Trifecta £462.10 Part won. Pool: £624.55, 0.97 winning units..
Owner M J Caddy **Bred** Keatly Overseas Ltd **Trained** Lambourn, Berks

FOCUS
Modest maiden form.

NOTEBOOK
Trueblue Wizard(IRE), a fifth foal and a half-brother to four winners, is a rangy, well-made individual. He knew his job and was always doing more than enough to withstand his only serious challenger. He has quite a pounding action and this surface suited him. He should make a fair handicapper at three. (op 5-1)
Manana Manana improved significantly on his debut effort here just four days earlier. He can improve again and go one better in a modest maiden. (op 18-1)
Solo Choice, well beaten on his debut here five days earlier, stayed on really well late in the day to snatch third spot and can improve again. (op 33-1)
Joannadarc(USA), third in a fair maiden at Lingfield, had easily the best credentials of those that had run, but she was soon making hard work of it and never really threatened to pull it off. Polytrack obviously suits her a lot better than the Fibresand surface here. (tchd Evens)
Tinshu(IRE), backed at long odds, was soon adrift. A stocky type she kept in the closing stages and looks capable of further improvement. (op 33-1 tchd 18-1)
Badge Of Honour, a short-backed leggy newcomer, dropped right out in the final two furlongs. He is almost certainly capable of much better. (op 4-1 tchd 3-1)

7774 CALL 01636 814481 TO SPONSOR A RACE H'CAP (DIV I) 5f (F)
1:00 (1:00) (Class 6) (0-60,60) 3-Y-O+ **£1,706** (£503; £252) **Stalls** High

Form RPR

0014 **1** **This Ones For Pat (USA)**[3] 7746 3-9-2 **58**..................(p) RobertWinston 5 67
(S Parr) *chsd ldr: rdn 1/2-way: led over 1f out: hung lft ins fnl f: r.o* **13/8**[1]

6225 **2** *1* **Mister Incredible**[10] 7658 5-8-9 **51** ow3..................(v) DarrenWilliams 3 56
(J M Bradley) *a.p: rdn 1/2-way: ev ch over 1f out: styd on* **9/2**[2]

0060 **3** *nk* **Sherjawy (IRE)**[13] 7625 4-8-4 **46** oh1..................(b) SimonWhitworth 4 50
(Miss Z C Davison) *sn outpcd: hdwy over 1f out: r.o* **16/1**

3600 **4** *1 ¼* **Twinned (IRE)**[11] 7648 5-8-6 **48**..................(b) FrankieMcDonald 2 48
(Mike Murphy) *sn led: rdn: hung lft and hdd over 1f out: styd on* **12/1**

0540 **5** *¾* **Hurricane Coast**[3] 7745 9-9-1 **57**..................(b) TonyCulhane 7 54
(D Flood) *dwlt and hmpd s: outpcd: hdwy u.p over 1f out: nt rch ldrs* **6/1**[3]

6303 **6** *hd* **Jilly Why (IRE)**[11] 7648 7-8-13 **55**..................(b) NeilChalmers 6 51
(Paul Green) *edgd rt s: chsd ldrs: rdn 1/2-way: no ex fnl f* **7/1**

0010 **7** *2 ¾* **Fizzlephut (IRE)**[22] 7517 6-9-3 **59**.................. PaulFitzsimons 9 46
(Miss J R Tooth) *chsd ldrs: rdn 1/2-way: wknd ins fnl f* **16/1**

0306 **8** *hd* **Promise Of Love**[11] 7653 3-8-13 **55**..................(b) PaulEddery 1 41
(Miss Amy Weaver) *racd alone towards far side: in rr: rdn and hung rt 1/2-way: n.d* **28/1**

04 **9** *¾* **Egyptian Lord**[11] 7644 5-8-8 **50**..................(b) PatrickMathers 11 33
(Peter Grayson) *prom: rdn and hung rt fr 1/2-way: wknd over 1f out* **14/1**

006 **10** *8* **Walragnek**[46] 7231 4-9-1 **57**.................. VinceSlattery 8 11
(J G M O'Shea) *s.s: outpcd* **20/1**

0-40 **11** *4* **Orphan Boy**[319] 486 3-8-1 **46** oh1.................. DominicFox(3) 10 —
(H J Collingridge) *sn outpcd* **150/1**

1000 **12** *10* **Flying Indian**[176] 3564 3-9-4 **60**..................(b[1]) JerryO'Dwyer 12 —
(J Balding) *free to post: s.i.s: outpcd fnl 3f* **50/1**

58.60 secs (-1.10) **Going Correction** -0.15s/f (Stan) **12** Ran SP% **120.0**
Speed ratings (Par 101): **102,100,99,97,96 96,92,91,90,77 71,55**
toteswinger: 1&2 £2.60, 1&3 £9.30, 2&3 £12.60. CSF £8.30 CT £88.95 TOTE £2.50: £1.30, £1.40, £5.80; EX 11.30 Trifecta £106.90 Pool: £582.49, 4.03 winning units..
Owner Willie McKay **Bred** Mcmillin Brothers & James Devaney **Trained** Bawtry, S Yorks

FOCUS
The quicker of the two divisions by 0.3sec, and the winner landed a gamble.

7775 MEMBERSHIP AT SOUTHWELL GOLF CLUB H'CAP 1m 6f (F)
1:30 (1:30) (Class 5) (0-70,68) 3-Y-O+ **£4,094** (£1,209; £604) **Stalls** Low

Form RPR

50/0 **1** **Amron Hill**[31] 7427 5-8-6 **48**.................. AndreaAtzeni(5) 2 56
(R Hollinshead) *n.m.r s: sn led: rdn and hung rt 2f out: edgd lft fnl f: styd on gamely* **16/1**

2600 **2** *¾* **Oberlin (USA)**[17] 7573 3-8-11 **55**.................. NickyMackay 3 62
(T Keddy) *chsd ldrs: rdn over 3f out: styd on* **33/1**

0123 **3** *1* **Fortunella**[4] 7729 3-8-11 **55**..................(p) ChrisCatlin 7 61
(Miss Gay Kelleway) *trckd ldrs: rdn over 3f out: unable qck ins fnl f* **7/2**[2]

6235 **4** *2* **Dusk**[67] 6775 3-9-10 **68**..................(b) DaneO'Neill 8 71
(Mrs S J Humphrey) *a.p: rdn over 1f out: no ex ins fnl f* **8/1**

5161 **5** *nk* **Coda Agency**[24] 6740 5-10-0 **65**.................. MartinDwyer 1 67
(D W P Arbuthnot) *chsd ldr tl rdn over 4f out: sn outpcd: styd on ins fnl f* **5/4**[1]

0313 **6** *21* **Red Expresso (IRE)**[7] 7695 3-9-6 **64**.................. PaulMulrennan 5 37
(Ollie Pears) *sn pushed along in rr: hdwy after 3f: reminders over 5f: rdn and wknd over 3f out: t.o* **15/2**[3]

-000 **7** *44* **Gouranga**[190] 5-8-2 **46** oh1..................(b) JakePayne(7) 6 —
(A W Carroll) *s.i.s: a in rr: bhd fr 5f: t.o* **100/1**

0003 **8** *½* **Daraiym (IRE)**[17] 7587 3-8-6 **50**.................. HayleyTurner 4 —
(Paul Green) *hld up: rdn over 7f out: wknd 5f out: t.o* **8/1**

6604 **9** *2 ¼* **Very Green (FR)**[26] 5752 6-8-10 **47**..................(tp) RobertWinston 9 —
(Mrs A L M King) *s.i.s: hld up: rdn and wknd over 4f out: t.o* **16/1**

3m 7.98s (-0.32) **Going Correction** -0.10s/f (Stan)
WFA 3 from 5yo+ 7lb **9** Ran SP% **116.3**
Speed ratings (Par 103): **96,95,95,93,93 81,56,56,54**
toteswinger: 1&2 £32.20, 1&3 £12.70, 2&3 £17.40. CSF £422.37 CT £2260.22 TOTE £14.60: £2.50, £6.50, £1.30; EX 457.30 TRIFECTA Not won..
Owner Geoff Lloyd **Bred** R Hollinshead **Trained** Upper Longdon, Staffs

FOCUS
The top weight was rated 5lb below the race ceiling in this moderate heat.

7776 KYLKENNY H'CAP 1m 4f (F)
2:00 (2:01) (Class 6) (0-60,57) 3-Y-O+ **£2,047** (£604; £302) **Stalls** Low

Form RPR

3550 **1** **Stravita**[8] 7688 4-9-2 **55**..................(p) AndreaAtzeni(5) 9 68
(R Hollinshead) *hld up: hdwy 7f out: led over 2f out: sn rdn: hung rt fr over 1f out: styd on wl* **13/2**

4403 **2** *3 ¼* **Dazzling Begum**[15] 7605 3-8-13 **52**.................. JerryO'Dwyer 11 60
(J Pearce) *hld up: hdwy over 7f out: rdn over 2f out: styng on same pce whn hung rt ins fnl f* **9/2**[3]

3 *3 ¾* **Pinewood Legend (IRE)**[79] 6446 6-8-11 **45**..........(b) PaulMulrennan 4 47
(P D Niven) *hld up in tch: rdn and ev ch over 2f out: hung lft over 1f out: no ex fnl f* **9/2**[3]

6122 **4** *6* **Ba Dreamflight**[43] 7272 3-9-3 **56**.................. ChrisCatlin 10 48
(H Morrison) *mid-div: sn pushed along: hdwy 4f: rdn over 4f out: wknd over 1f out* **11/4**[1]

0032 **5** *1 ¼* **Kangrina**[10] 7667 6-9-9 **57**.................. DaneO'Neill 1 47
(George Baker) *chsd ldr tl led over 4f out: rdn and hdd over 2f out: wknd over 1f out* **3/1**[2]

5003 **6** 1 1/4 **Bond Casino**[11] 7647 4-8-10 **47**....................(v) DuranFentiman(3) 7 35
(G R Oldroyd) *chsd ldrs: drvn along after 2f: wknd over 3f out* **14/1**

4000 **7** 17 **Charlie Bear**[24] 7494 7-8-11 **45**.................... SimonWhitworth 6 6
(Miss Z C Davison) *s.s: a wl bhd: t.o* **66/1**

0-00 **8** 12 **Que Beauty (IRE)**[7] 7695 3-7-13 **45**.................... AndrewHeffernan(5) 5 —
(R C Guest) *a in rr: rdn and lost tch fr over 5f out: t.o* **100/1**

0046 **9** 10 **Tykie Two**[11] 7647 4-8-11 **45**....................(b) RobertWinston 3 —
(S Wynne) *chsd ldrs: rdn over 5f out: sn wknd: t.o* **25/1**

0060 **10** 3 3/4 **So Sublime**[14] 7619 3-8-9 **48**....................(bt) GregFairley 8 —
(M C Chapman) *led: rdn and hdd over 4f out: sn wknd: t.o* **40/1**

2660 **11** 15 **Vintage Quest**[297] 770 6-8-12 **46** ow1.................... VinceSlattery 2 —
(D Burchell) *sn outpcd: rdn 7f out: wkng whn hung lft 5f out: t.o* **66/1**

2m 38.28s (-2.72) **Going Correction** -0.10s/f (Stan)
WFA 3 from 4yo+ 5lb **11** Ran SP% **118.3**
Speed ratings (Par 101): **105,102,100,96,95 94,83,75,68,66 56**
toteswinger: 1&2 £8.20, 1&3 £8.80, 2&3 £5.00. CSF £35.24 CT £147.60 TOTE £8.60: £2.70, £2.00, £2.00; EX 52.90 Trifecta £601.00 Part won. Pool: £812.25, 0.97 winning units..
Owner E Bennion **Bred** Eric Bennion And Miss Sarah Hollinshead **Trained** Upper Longdon, Staffs

FOCUS
They went off very fast here and by the final turn there were just five still in serious contention.

7777 HOSPITALITY AT SOUTHWELL RACECOURSE H'CAP — 1m 3f (F)
2:30 (2:31) (Class 4) (0-80,80) 3-Y-O+ **£6,476** (£1,927; £963; £481) **Stalls** Low

Form RPR

4060 **1** **Robby Bobby**[29] 7439 3-9-4 **80**.................... GregFairley 3 95+
(M Johnston) *led over 4f: chsd ldrs: rdn to ld and hung lft over 1f out: sn clr: eased ins fnl f* **2/1**[2]

2043 **2** 3 1/4 **Davenport (IRE)**[11] 7650 6-8-12 **70**....................(p) DaneO'Neill 6 74
(B R Millman) *hld up: hdwy over 3f out: rdn to chse wnr over 1f out: sn outpcd* **10/3**[3]

0440 **3** 4 **Sudden Impulse**[13] 7620 7-8-3 **66** oh4.................... PatrickDonaghy(5) 2 63
(A D Brown) *chsd ldrs: rdn over 4f out: led over 2f out: hdd over 1f out: wknd fnl f* **20/1**

40-5 **4** 3 1/4 **Drawback (IRE)**[30] 7150 5-8-13 **74**.................... LukeMorris(3) 5 66
(Heather Dalton) *chsd ldr over 4f: remained handy: rdn over 3f out: bmpd over 2f out: wknd over 1f out* **8/1**

1102 **5** 1 1/4 **Opera Writer (IRE)**[48] 7202 5-8-7 **70**....................(p) AndreaAtzeni(5) 1 60
(R Hollinshead) *trckd ldrs: racd keenly: pushed along and lost pl 5f out: rdn over 3f out: wknd 2f out* **7/4**[1]

5050 **6** 22 **Kabeer**[13] 7633 10-9-1 **80**....................(t) KarenKenny(7) 4 32
(A J McCabe) *hld up in tch: led over 6f out: rdn and hdd over 2f out: sn wknd: t.o* **28/1**

2m 26.85s (-1.15) **Going Correction** -0.10s/f (Stan)
WFA 3 from 5yo+ 4lb **6** Ran SP% **112.1**
Speed ratings (Par 105): **100,97,94,92,91 75**
toteswinger: 1&2 £2.10, 1&3 £5.00, 2&3 £3.10. CSF £9.08 TOTE £2.90: £1.60, £1.80; EX 10.40.
Owner C M , B J & R F Batterham Ii **Bred** Highclere Stud **Trained** Middleham Moor, N Yorks

FOCUS
They went a very steady gallop here until Kabeer seemed to take charge soon after the halfway mark.

7778 CALL 01636 814481 TO SPONSOR A RACE H'CAP (DIV II) — 5f (F)
3:00 (3:00) (Class 6) (0-60,59) 3-Y-O+ **£1,706** (£503; £252) **Stalls** High

Form RPR

100 **1** **Now You See Me**[21] 7522 4-9-0 **55**.................... TonyCulhane 2 63
(D Flood) *chsd ldrs: n.m.r over 3f out: rdn to ld wl ins fnl f* **8/1**

3651 **2** nk **Lithaam (IRE)**[11] 7648 4-8-11 **52**....................(p) NeilChalmers 3 59
(J M Bradley) *w ldr: led over 3f out: rdn over 1f out: hdd wl ins fnl f* **4/1**[2]

006 **3** 3 **Lady Bahia (IRE)**[11] 7648 7-8-9 **50**....................(b) PatrickMathers 5 46
(Peter Grayson) *s.s: outpcd: hdwy u.p over 1f out: no imp ins fnl f* **14/1**

2402 **4** 3/4 **Mystickhill (IRE)**[11] 7644 3-9-3 **58**.................... JerryO'Dwyer 1 52
(J Balding) *trckd ldrs: rdn over 1f out: wknd ins fnl f* **11/4**[1]

0000 **5** 1 1/4 **Firewalker**[14] 7618 3-8-4 **45**....................(b[1]) FrankieMcDonald 4 34
(P T Dalton) *chsd ldrs: rdn 1/2-way: wknd fnl f* **66/1**

0600 **6** 1 1/2 **Berrymead**[11] 7648 3-8-5 **51** ow3.................... AnnStokell(5) 10 35
(Miss A Stokell) *dwlt: sn drvn along in rr: sme hdwy over 1f out: wknd ins fnl f* **28/1**

0605 **7** 3/4 **Ronnie Howe**[13] 7629 4-9-2 **57**....................(t) PaulEddery 6 38
(S R Bowring) *led: hdd over 3f out: sn rdn: wknd over 1f out* **7/1**

0405 **8** 3 1/2 **Tyrannosaurus Rex (IRE)**[21] 7521 4-9-3 **58**....................(v) DarrenWilliams 9 26
(D Shaw) *prom: edgd rt over 4f out: rdn and wknd wl over 1f out* **5/1**[3]

0000 **9** 4 1/2 **Viewforth**[12] 7636 10-8-4 **45**....................(b) SimonWhitworth 8 —
(M Wigham) *chsd ldrs: lost pl over 3f out: sn bhd* **20/1**

1300 **10** 6 **Piccolo Diamante (USA)**[3] 7745 4-9-1 **56**....................(t) RobertWinston 11 —
(S Parr) *s.i.s: in rr whn hmpd over 4f out: sn bhd: eased fnl f* **5/1**[3]

58.90 secs (-0.80) **Going Correction** -0.15s/f (Stan) **10** Ran SP% **120.0**
Speed ratings (Par 101): **100,99,94,93,91 89,87,82,75,65**
toteswinger: 1&2 £8.40, 1&3 £20.70, 2&3 £11.30. CSF £40.58 CT £452.83 TOTE £12.20: £3.60, £1.70, £4.00; EX 61.30 Trifecta £334.70 Pool: £877.61, 1.94 winning units..
Owner S W Lang **Bred** Gainsborough Stud Management Ltd **Trained** Wollerton, Shropshire

FOCUS
Moderate handicap form and the slower of the two divisions by 0.3sec.

7779 BOOK YOUR TICKETS ON LINE AT SOUTHWELL-RACECOURSE.CO.UK H'CAP (DIV II) — 7f (F)
3:30 (3:30) (Class 6) (0-60,60) 3-Y-O+ **£1,706** (£503; £252) **Stalls** Low

Form RPR

3550 **1** **Norcroft**[16] 7591 6-9-0 **56**....................(p) VinceSlattery 2 66
(Mrs C A Dunnett) *s.i.s: sn prom: rdn to ld over 1f out: styd on gamely* **11/1**

4450 **2** hd **The City Kid (IRE)**[11] 7656 5-9-1 **57**.................... DaneO'Neill 8 67
(Miss Gay Kelleway) *hld up: hdwy over 2f out: rdn and ev ch fr over 1f out: styd on* **9/2**[2]

3104 **3** 2 3/4 **Provost**[11] 7651 4-9-4 **60**.................... DaleGibson 6 62
(M W Easterby) *s.i.s: hdwy over 5f out: lost pl 4f out: hdwy over 1f out: styd on* **12/1**

0260 **4** 3 **Eternal Optimist (IRE)**[22] 7518 3-8-11 **53**.................... PaulMulrennan 10 47
(Paul Green) *led: rdn and hdd over 1f out: wknd ins fnl f* **20/1**

0-22 **5** 1/2 **Hennessy Island (USA)**[243] 1592 3-9-2 **58**.................... HayleyTurner 4 51
(T G Mills) *hld up: hung rt fnl 3f: n.m.r over 2f out: sn rdn: nt trble ldrs* **6/5**[1]

06-0 **6** 1 1/2 **Running Buck (USA)**[20] 7535 3-8-3 **50**....................(b) AndreaAtzeni(5) 5 39
(A Bailey) *prom: rdn over 2f out: wknd over 1f out* **10/1**

0005 **7** 1 1/4 **Government (IRE)**[4] 7731 7-8-5 **47** oh1 ow1.................... GregFairley 9 32
(M C Chapman) *chsd ldrs: rdn 1/2-way: wknd 2f out* **20/1**

0533 **8** 1 1/4 **Outer Hebrides**[10] 7663 7-8-5 **52**....................(v) MCGeran(5) 1 34
(J M Bradley) *chsd ldrs: rdn over 2f out: wknd over 1f out* **7/1**[3]

0400 **9** 6 **Majestic Cheer**[11] 7648 4-8-7 **49**.................... ChrisCatlin 3 15
(John A Harris) *chsd ldr: rdn over 2f out: sn wknd* **16/1**

6060 **10** 15 **Fan Club**[105] 5770 4-8-4 **46** oh1....................(b) LiamJones 7 —
(Mrs R A Carr) *mid-div: rdn 1/2-way: sn wknd* **33/1**

1m 29.04s (-1.26) **Going Correction** -0.10s/f (Stan) **10** Ran SP% **119.6**
Speed ratings (Par 101): **103,102,99,96,95 93,92,91,84,67**
toteswinger: 1&2 £7.80, 1&3 £10.20, 2&3 £7.80. CSF £60.03 CT £632.27 TOTE £12.30: £3.10, £1.70, £3.10; EX 55.20 Trifecta £862.30 Part won. Pool: £1,165.32, 0.70 winning units. Place 6: £287.30, Place 5: £136.26..
Owner The Star Seekers **Bred** Norcroft Park Stud **Trained** Hingham, Norfolk

FOCUS
Another moderate event but it was run in a time 0.45sec quicker than the first division.
T/Jkpt: Not won. T/Plt: £980.40 to a £1 stake. Pool: £71,159.62. 52.98 winning tickets. T/Qpdt: £39.00 to a £1 stake. Pool: £8,082.46. 153.30 winning tickets. CR

7744 WOLVERHAMPTON (A.W) (L-H)
Friday, December 26

OFFICIAL GOING: Standard
Wind: Light half-against Weather: Sunny and cold

7780 CHRISTMAS PUDDING CLAIMING STKS (DIV I) — 7f 32y(P)
1:05 (1:05) (Class 6) 3-Y-O+ **£2,388** (£705; £352) **Stalls** High

Form RPR

2034 **1** **Dancing Deano (IRE)**[14] 7653 6-8-10 63 ow2.... RussellKennemore(3) 5 68
(R Hollinshead) *a.p: wnt 2nd over 4f out: led over 2f out: rdn and hung rt fr wl over 1f out: drvn out* **17/2**

013 **2** 2 3/4 **Monkey Glas (IRE)**[12] 7675 4-9-5 91....................(v) ChrisCatlin 4 66
(J R Gask) *wnt lft s: led early: chsd ldr tl over 4f out: swtchd lft jst over 1f out: rallied and wnt 2nd ins fnl f: nt trble wnr* **7/4**[1]

1031 **3** 1/2 **Singleb (IRE)**[25] 7513 4-8-11 65.................... HayleyTurner 3 57
(Miss Gay Kelleway) *carried lft s: hld up and bhd: n.m.r wl over 1f out: sn rdn: hdwy ent fnl f: kpt on same pce* **9/2**[3]

3020 **4** shd **Murfreesboro**[21] 7564 5-9-5 80....................(v) AdamKirby 1 65
(D Shaw) *carried lft s: bhd: hdwy and squeezed through 1f out: rdn and kpt on one pce ins fnl f* **9/4**[2]

0060 **5** 1 1/4 **Kabis Amigos**[13] 7663 6-8-7 45....................(b[1]) GregFairley 2 49
(S T Mason) *hmpd s: sn hld up in mid-div: rdn and hdwy on ins whn bmpd 1f out: no ex* **25/1**

0600 **6** 2 3/4 **Jimmy Dean**[18] 7608 3-8-11 37....................(tp) PaulFitzsimons 6 46
(M Wellings) *mid-div: hdwy over 3f out: rdn and chsd wnr 2f out tl wknd ins fnl f* **100/1**

4000 **7** 1 1/4 **Ice Planet**[16] 7629 7-8-5 70.................... LiamJones 7 37
(Mrs R A Carr) *c wd st: a bhd* **16/1**

0100 **8** 1/2 **Samurai Warrior**[17] 7619 3-8-8 58 ow1.................... JamesDoyle 9 38
(P D Evans) *hld up in tch: rdn wl over 1f out: wknd ins fnl f* **28/1**

3001 **9** 13 **Crocodile Bay (IRE)**[16] 7631 5-8-10 68 ow2....(b) JamesO'Reilly(5) 10 10
(John A Harris) *sn led: clr over 5f out: hdd over 2f out: wknd wl over 1f out* **12/1**

1m 28.94s (-0.66) **Going Correction** +0.025s/f (Slow) **9** Ran SP% **117.7**
Speed ratings (Par 101): **104,100,100,100,98 95,94,93,78**
toteswinger: 1&2 £9.70, 1&3 £4.80, 2&3 £2.30. CSF £24.04 TOTE £9.50: £2.00, £1.50, £1.80; EX 34.90 Trifecta £99.50 Part won. Pool £134.46 - 0.10 winning units..
Owner Ron Wood **Bred** Mrs Olivia Farrell **Trained** Upper Longdon, Staffs

FOCUS
An ordinary claimer in which only a few appeared to hold a realistic chance at the weights and the early pace was frantic.

7781 SPONSOR A RACE IN 2009 NOVICE STKS — 1m 141y(P)
1:35 (1:35) (Class 5) 2-Y-O **£3,885** (£1,156; £577; £288) **Stalls** Low

Form RPR

1 **1** **Premier Banker (IRE)**[21] 7554 2-9-5 0.................... ShaneKelly 1 90+
(J Noseda) *chsd ldr: led over 3f out: clr over 2f out: easily* **1/12**[1]

606 **2** 13 **King's Chorister**[3] 7773 2-8-12 0....................(e) HayleyTurner 2 55
(Miss Gay Kelleway) *led: hdd over 3f out: sn rdn and no ch w wnr: wknd over 1f out* **16/1**[2]

3 1 1/4 **Fire Me Gun** 2-8-4 0 ow1.................... LiamJones 4 45
(M Mullineaux) *hld up: pushed along and struggling over 3f out: hung lft ins fnl f* **18/1**[3]

4 6 **Key Of Fortune (IRE)**[190] 3184 2-8-7 0.................... ChrisCatlin 3 35
(Jennie Candlish) *hld up in last: short-lived effrt 5f out: toiling over 3f out* **33/1**

1m 51.16s (0.66) **Going Correction** +0.025s/f (Slow) **4** Ran SP% **106.4**
Speed ratings (Par 96): **98,86,85,80**
CSF £2.28 TOTE £1.10; EX 2.00.
Owner J Browne **Bred** D G Hardisty Bloodstock **Trained** Newmarket, Suffolk

FOCUS
As uncompetitive an event as you could imagine.

NOTEBOOK
Premier Banker(IRE), who beat a long odds-on shot on his Lingfield debut three weeks earlier, duly followed up as a 1-12 shot should, but at least Shane Kelly pushed him right out after he had taken over in front entering the last half-mile to help educate him. This obviously told us nothing new about him, but he remains a colt of potential. (op 1-14)
King's Chorister tried to make a race of it and set a reasonable early pace, but he was outclassed when the favourite loomed large. At least his earlier earlier exertions didn't cost him second place and he may be worth switching to handicaps now.
Fire Me Gun, a half-sister to a winning juvenile sprinter, was off the bridle early before plugging on but it's hard to say what she achieved. (op 16-1 tchd 20-1)
Key Of Fortune(IRE), who had not been seen since finishing well beaten on her debut at Fairyhouse in June, was always toiling on this debut for her new yard. (op 22-1 tchd 20-1 and 40-1)

7782 CHRISTMAS PUDDING CLAIMING STKS (DIV II) — 7f 32y(P)
2:05 (2:06) (Class 6) 3-Y-O+ **£2,388** (£705; £352) **Stalls** High

Form RPR

-314 **1** **Smirfys Systems**[303] 718 9-8-7 53.................... GregFairley 3 64
(E S McMahon) *mde all: rdn jst over 1f out: drvn out* **8/1**

0400 **2** 1 1/4 **Mystic Roll**[34] 7423 5-8-0 53.................... AndreaAtzeni(5) 7 59
(Jane Chapple-Hyam) *chsd wnr: rdn over 2f out: r.o same pce ins fnl f* **12/1**

5145 **3** 1 3/4 **Another Genepi (USA)**[10] 7698 5-8-1 65....(b) DuranFentiman(3) 2 53
(E J Creighton) *s.i.s: hdwy on ins over 2f out: rdn and kpt on one pce fnl f* **11/2**[3]

0005 **4** *hd* **Obe Royal**[17] 7616 4-8-8 58..........(b) LukeMorris(3) 6 60
(P D Evans) *t.k.h in tch: rdn over 2f out: one pce ins fnl f* **15/2**

3504 **5** *½* **Red Cape (FR)**[17] 7616 5-9-5 75..........(b) LiamJones 8 66
(Mrs R A Carr) *hld up and bhd: hdwy over 2f out: rdn and one pce fnl f* **9/1**

1324 **6** *1½* **Blue Charm**[4] 7764 4-8-9 67.......... JamesDoyle 4 52
(S Kirk) *a.p: hrd rdn 2f out: wknd ins fnl f* **11/8**[1]

2305 **7** *½* **Makshoof (IRE)**[18] 7601 4-9-1 79.......... PaulMulrennan 9 57
(K A Ryan) *hld up in mid-div: hung rt bnd 3f out: c wd st: sn bhd* **7/2**[2]

-030 **8** *¾* **Bungie**[36] 3139 4-8-7 40..........(b) HayleyTurner 5 47
(Jennie Candlish) *s.i.s: a bhd* **40/1**

0000 **9** *2¼* **Mean Machine (IRE)**[16] 6824 6-9-1 43.......... ChrisCatlin 1 49
(D Flood) *a in rr* **28/1**

1m 30.37s (0.77) **Going Correction** +0.025s/f (Slow) **9** Ran SP% **126.2**
Speed ratings (Par 101): **96,94,92,92,91 90,89,88,86**
toteswinger: 1&2 £11.50, 1&3 £16.00, 2&3 £12.60. CSF £107.28 TOTE £8.80: £2.40, £2.50, £2.50; EX 198.40 TRIFECTA Not won..
Owner Mrs Dian Plant **Bred** Gerard Bingham **Trained** Lichfield, Staffs

FOCUS
Another ordinary claimer, but in contrast to the first division they went no pace early and the winning time was 1.43 seconds slower.

7783 WOLVERHAMPTON-RACECOURSE.CO.UK MAIDEN STKS 7f 32y(P)
2:35 (2:36) (Class 5) 2-Y-O **£3,561** (£1,059; £529; £264) **Stalls** High

Form RPR

22 **1** **Miss Beat (IRE)**[34] 7422 2-8-12 0.......... ShaneKelly 6 67
(B J Meehan) *mde all: edgd rt wl over 1f out: hrd rdn fnl f: r.o* **8/11**[1]

3002 **2** *½* **Dream Date (IRE)**[28] 7472 2-8-9 67.......... GilmarPereira(3) 7 66
(W J Haggas) *chsd wnr: swtchd lft wl over 1f out: rdn and ev ch ins fnl f: nt qckn* **9/2**[2]

00 **3** *2¼* **Cousin Charlie**[37] 7380 2-9-3 0.......... GeorgeBaker 2 65
(S Kirk) *a.p: rdn and one pce ins fnl f* **14/1**

0 **4** *¾* **Giant Strides**[7] 7726 2-8-12 0.......... JamesDoyle 3 59
(P D Evans) *hld up in tch: pushed along and outpcd 2f out: styd on towards fin* **40/1**

5 *3¾* **Echo Dancer** 2-9-3 0.......... HayleyTurner 4 54
(S A Callaghan) *a bhd* **5/1**[3]

6 *4½* **Divinatore** 2-9-3 0.......... AdamKirby 1 43
(D Haydn Jones) *swvd bdly lft s and rel to r: a in rr* **10/1**

00 **7** *3¾* **Die Haard**[19] 7593 2-9-3 0.......... ChrisCatlin 5 34
(J R Gask) *hld up in tch: wknd 3f out* **16/1**

1m 30.31s (0.71) **Going Correction** +0.025s/f (Slow) **7** Ran SP% **116.8**
Speed ratings (Par 96): **96,95,92,92,87 82,78**
toteswinger: 1&2 £1.10, 1&3 £7.30, 2&3 £26.00. CSF £4.63 TOTE £1.70: £1.40, £2.00; EX 5.10.
Owner Coleman Bloodstock Limited **Bred** Michael Woodlock & Seamus Kennedy **Trained** Manton, Wilts

FOCUS
An uncompetitive maiden.

NOTEBOOK
Miss Beat(IRE) had finished runner-up in her first two starts, including when beaten at odds-on over a longer trip here last time, but was allowed to stride on over this shorter distance. She quickened from the front off the home bend, but although she was inclined to carry her head rather high in the straight, she managed to keep on finding what was required. (op 5-6, tchd 10-11 in places)
Dream Date(IRE), by far the most experienced in the field and back in maiden company after three outings in nurseries, always had the favourite in her sights and was given another chance when her rival appeared to be thinking about out starting up the straight, but she then was always being held. Her official rating of 67 provides the benchmark to the form and though she is looking exposed, she should be able to find a small race on Polytrack at some point. (op 5-2)
Cousin Charlie, who had beaten a total of three rivals after starting slowly in his two previous outings, was always in about the same place and this was a much better effort, albeit in a modest race. He now qualifies for handicaps. (op 20-1 tchd 10-1)
Giant Strides, a long way last of eight on her Southwell debut seven days earlier, ran better this time but may not come into her own until qualifying for a mark. (op 50-1 tchd 25-1)
Echo Dancer, a 50,000gns half-brother to three winners at up to 1m4f out of a triple winner at up to 1m, never got involved and may need more time. (op 9-1)
Divinatore can be forgiven this debut effort as he dived violently left exiting the stalls and forfeited a huge amount of ground. (op 9-1)

7784 MERRY CHRISTMAS NURSERY 1m 141y(P)
3:15 (3:15) (Class 4) (0-85,79) 2-Y-O **£5,046** (£1,510; £755; £377; £188) **Stalls** Low

Form RPR

0115 **1** **Doncosaque (IRE)**[16] 7623 2-9-5 77.......... IanMongan 4 81
(P Howling) *hld up: hdwy 2f out: rdn to ld ins fnl f: r.o wl* **8/1**

0016 **2** *2½* **Double Act**[16] 7623 2-9-7 79..........(t) ShaneKelly 5 78
(J Noseda) *hld up and bhd: hdwy 3f out: rdn to ld briefly ins fnl f: nt qckn* **10/3**[1]

025 **3** *nse* **Barwell Bridge**[21] 7552 2-9-5 77.......... GeorgeBaker 8 76
(S Kirk) *hld up in tch: wnt 2nd 3f out: ev ch over 1f out: rdn and nt qckn ins fnl f* **10/3**[1]

4001 **4** *1½* **Amazing Blue Sky**[13] 7666 2-8-5 63.......... LiamJones 1 58
(Mrs R A Carr) *led: rdn and hdd ins fnl f: no ex towards fin* **14/1**

004 **5** *1½* **City Bank (USA)**[14] 7649 2-8-8 66.......... GregFairley 6 58
(M Johnston) *chsd ldr tl rdn 3f out: wknd wl over 1f out* **8/1**

6432 **6** *2* **Passage To India (IRE)**[10] 7693 2-8-7 65.......... PaulFitzsimons 3 53
(J A Osborne) *hld up: short-lived effrt 2f out* **7/2**[2]

004 **7** *1¼* **Big Nige (IRE)**[34] 7422 2-9-0 72.......... JerryO'Dwyer 7 58
(J Pearce) *hld up in rr: c wd and rdn st: no rspnse* **20/1**

6053 **8** *8* **Caravan Of Dreams (IRE)**[16] 7623 2-9-0 72.......... ChrisCatlin 2 41
(M A Jarvis) *prom tl wknd over 2f out* **11/2**[3]

1m 50.57s (0.07) **Going Correction** +0.025s/f (Slow) **8** Ran SP% **117.4**
Speed ratings (Par 98): **100,97,97,96,95 93,92,85**
toteswinger: 1&2 £4.90, 1&3 £5.60, 2&3 £4.20. CSF £35.85 CT £109.28 TOTE £10.00: £2.80, £1.50, £1.60; EX 41.40 Trifecta £133.30 Pool £347.76 - 1.93 winning units..
Owner Jo Hearn **Bred** Ammerland Verwaltung Gmbh **Trained** Newmarket, Suffolk

FOCUS
An ordinary nursery, but the pace was solid enough despite there being four in a line across the track a furlong out and the time was 0.59 seconds faster than the long odds-on Premier Banker took in the earlier novice event.

NOTEBOOK
Doncosaque(IRE) ◆, winner of two claimers last month, including one very easily over this course and distance, had been well held on his nursery debut at Kempton last time, but he seemed much happier back here and he produced a smart turn of foot to seal it after being switched out wide off the home bend. He obviously likes this track and couldn't be discounted back here even after the inevitable rise. (op 7-1)
Double Act, who did not enjoy the run of the race on his nursery debut at Kempton last time when behind Doncasaque, had previously won his maiden here. Held up early, he made a wide sweeping move around the outside starting the home bend and had every chance, but he had no answer to the winner's turn of foot. (op 7-2 tchd 11-4)
Barwell Bridge, making his handicap debut on this fourth outing after showing ability in maidens, was another to be produced from off the pace to hold every chance and he still has a bit of scope. (op 4-1 tchd 9-2)
Amazing Blue Sky, snapped up by current connections after making all to win a claimer over an extra furlong here last time, attempted the same tactics and battled on well when challenged, but he may need a return to further. (op 17-2)
City Bank(USA), making his nursery debut after showing some ability in three maidens on turf and Fibresand, was up with the pace early but he was having to be niggled along to maintain his position at halfway and was eventually made to look one-paced. (op 17-2 tchd 10-1)
Passage To India(IRE), steadily improving with each outing and very well backed here, seemed to travel well enough off the pace but when asked to go and pick up the leaders off the final bend, the response was very limited. (op 13-2)
Caravan Of Dreams(IRE), who had both Doncosaque and Double Act behind her when third on her nursery debut at Kempton last time, seemed to be in a great position just behind the leaders early but she folded very tamely over the last couple of furlongs and this was most disappointing. (op 9-2 tchd 6-1)

7785 WOLVERHAMPTON-RACECOURSE.CO.UK H'CAP 1m 4f 50y(P)
3:45 (3:45) (Class 4) (0-85,85) 3-Y-O+ **£6,308** (£1,888; £944; £472; £235) **Stalls** Low

Form RPR

5635 **1** **Clear Reef**[15] 7639 4-8-8 77.......... AndreaAtzeni(5) 4 87
(Jane Chapple-Hyam) *t.k.h in tch: rdn and wnt 2nd 2f out: led ins fnl f: edgd lft: r.o wl* **4/1**[3]

2123 **2** *2¼* **Scarab (IRE)**[21] 7558 3-8-8 77.......... GregFairley 5 83
(M Johnston) *led early: chsd ldr: led over 2f out: rdn over 1f out: hdd ins fnl f: nt qckn* **6/4**[1]

1012 **3** *nk* **Hucking Heat (IRE)**[11] 7686 4-9-0 78..........(p) HayleyTurner 2 84
(R Hollinshead) *hld up in rr: hdwy over 2f out: rdn and nt qckn fnl f* **10/3**[2]

1025 **4** *3¾* **Opera Writer (IRE)**[3] 7777 5-8-0 71 oh1..........(p) AlexEdwards(7) 3 71
(R Hollinshead) *hld up in rr: hdwy 6f out: wknd wl over 1f out* **8/1**

2052 **5** *1* **Quince (IRE)**[14] 7657 5-9-2 80..........(v) JerryO'Dwyer 6 78
(J Pearce) *hld up in tch: rdn 4f out: sn wknd* **5/1**

0 **6** *9* **Boo**[44] 7291 6-9-7 85.......... RichardKingscote 7 69
(J W Unett) *sn led: hdd over 2f out: sn rdn: wknd over 1f out* **10/1**

2m 40.46s (-0.64) **Going Correction** +0.025s/f (Slow)
WFA 3 from 4yo+ 5lb **6** Ran SP% **119.9**
Speed ratings (Par 105): **103,101,101,98,98 92**
toteswinger: 1&2 £3.00, 1&3 £4.20, 2&3 £1.50. CSF £11.38 TOTE £5.80: £2.70, £1.60; EX 15.90.
Owner Chapple-Hyam Tegel Ward **Bred** Hesmonds Stud Ltd **Trained** Lambourn, Berks

FOCUS
Not a bad middle-distance handicap, but the early pace was only ordinary and this was a race of changing fortunes.

7786 HOLLY & IVY H'CAP 1m 1f 103y(P)
4:15 (4:15) (Class 5) (0-70,70) 3-Y-O+ **£3,885** (£1,156; £577; £288) **Stalls** Low

Form RPR

0635 **1** **Quick Off The Mark**[13] 7669 3-8-7 61.......... RichardKingscote 8 68
(J G Given) *mde all: clr 2f out: sn rdn: jst hld on* **14/1**

051 **2** *hd* **Man Of Gwent (UAE)**[4] 7758 4-9-3 69 6ex.......... JamesDoyle 11 76
(P D Evans) *hld up in mid-div: lost pl over 4f out: pushed along over 3f out: c wd st: hrd rdn and hdwy over 1f out: r.o ins fnl f: jst failed* **9/4**[1]

0421 **3** *nk* **Prince Golan (IRE)**[11] 7686 4-8-4 63..........(p) AlexEdwards(7) 7 69
(J W Unett) *plld hrd in rr: hdwy over 6f out: edgd lft over 1f out: r.o ins fnl f* **15/2**[3]

0004 **4** *1* **Ninth House (USA)**[18] 7610 6-9-0 66.......... LiamJones 1 70
(Mrs R A Carr) *chsd wnr to 6f out: prom: wnt 2nd again 2f out: rdn over 1f out: nt qckn wl ins fnl f* **10/1**

5442 **5** *½* **Teasing**[15] 7642 4-9-4 70..........(p) JerryO'Dwyer 9 73
(J Pearce) *hld up in rr: hdwy over 6f out: rdn over 2f out: kpt on one pce ins fnl f* **17/2**

2421 **6** *nse* **Templetuohy Max (IRE)**[14] 7654 3-8-9 63..........(v) ChrisCatlin 5 66
(J D Bethell) *t.k.h: prom: lost pl over 5f out: rdn and hdwy 1f out: no ex towards fin* **10/1**

3451 **7** *1¼* **Fine Ruler (IRE)**[22] 7548 4-8-10 62.......... VinceSlattery 6 62
(M R Bosley) *plld hrd in tch: lost pl over 6f out: hdwy on ins over 2f out: sn rdn: fdd wl ins fnl f* **18/1**

602 **8** *2¼* **Focail Eile**[18] 7609 3-8-9 63.......... GregFairley 12 58
(E S McMahon) *hld up in mid-div: hdwy over 6f out: wknd wl over 1f out* **15/2**[3]

1312 **9** *6* **Top Seed (IRE)**[195] 3029 7-9-1 67.......... IanMongan 4 50
(Ian Williams) *hld up in rr: no ch fnl 3f* **14/1**

2040 **10** *2* **Lunar Promise (IRE)**[42] 7309 6-8-10 65.......... RussellKennemore(3) 2 44
(Ian Williams) *a bhd* **10/3**[2]

2m 5.07s (3.37) **Going Correction** +0.025s/f (Slow)
WFA 3 from 4yo+ 2lb **10** Ran SP% **124.7**
Speed ratings (Par 103): **86,85,85,84,84 84,83,81,75,73**
toteswinger: 1&2 £26.60, 1&3 £3.50, 2&3 £6.70. CSF £48.95 CT £274.17 TOTE £14.10: £5.10, £1.10, £1.70; EX 81.70 Trifecta £375.20 Pool £699.76 - 1.38 winning units.Place 6 £14.68, Place 5 £9.25..
Owner Peter Onslow & Ian Henderson **Bred** Gainsborough Stud Management Ltd **Trained** Willoughton, Lincs

FOCUS
Probably the most competitive race on the card, but spoiled by a moderate early pace, which caused several to pull hard and this developed into a rather messy contest. Again this race was won by the horse able to get an uncontested lead in a moderately run race.
T/Plt: £22.30 to a £1 stake. Pool: £34,889.43. 1,139.02 winning tickets. T/Qpdt: £15.30 to a £1 stake. Pool: £1,967.35. 94.60 winning tickets. KH

7752 GREAT LEIGHS (A.W) (L-H)
Saturday, December 27

OFFICIAL GOING: Standard
Wind: Moderate behind Weather: Fine

7787 RACING ON THE 29TH H'CAP 1m 5f 66y(P)
6:50 (6:51) (Class 6) (0-60,60) 3-Y-O+ **£2,590** (£770; £385; £192) **Stalls** Low

Form RPR

0600 **1** **Spume (IRE)**[8] 7731 4-8-10 48..........(t) AdamKirby 10 57
(S Parr) *hld up: swtchd lft and hdwy over 1f out: led ins fnl f: shkn up and r.o wl* **16/1**

4432 **2** 2¼ **Generous Star**[21] 7573 5-9-5 **57** .... GeorgeBaker 7 63
(J Pearce) *hld up: rdn and hdwy over 3f out: hung lft fr over 1f out: styd on same pce ins fnl f* **7/4**[1]

S040 **3** *hd* **Ben Bacchus (IRE)**[13] 7676 6-8-10 **48** .... TGMcLaughlin 9 53
(P W Hiatt) *chsd ldr tl led over 2f out: sn rdn: hdd and unable qck ins fnl f* **8/1**

6004 **4** 1¾ **Vanquisher (IRE)**[14] 7667 4-8-11 **49** ....(p) JimCrowley 5 52
(Ian Williams) *hld up: hdwy over 2f out: rdn over 1f out: no ex ins fnl f* **11/2**[3]

000/ **5** *nk* **Wester Lodge (IRE)**[723] 6256 6-9-2 **57** .... LukeMorris(3) 4 59
(J M P Eustace) *prom: rdn over 3f out: sn outpcd: styd on ins fnl f* **20/1**

2005 **6** ¾ **Bienheureux**[21] 7573 7-8-13 **51** ....(t) ChrisCatlin 6 52
(Miss Gay Kelleway) *hld up: hdwy over 5f out: rdn over 1f out: no ex ins fnl f* **9/2**[2]

00/0 **7** 3½ **Goblin**[21] 7573 7-9-2 **54** .... IanMongan 3 50
(D E Cantillon) *s.i.s: hld up: rdn over 1f out: n.d* **11/1**

2000 **8** 2¾ **Satindra (IRE)**[18] 7355 4-8-13 **51** ....(tp) LPKeniry 8 43
(C R Dore) *sn led: rdn and hdd over 2f out: hung lft over 1f out: wknd fnl f* **20/1**

0605 **9** 2¾ **Bonzo**[9] 7713 3-8-4 **48** .... LiamJones 2 36
(P Howling) *prom: pushed along over 4f out: rdn over 2f out: sn wknd* **10/1**

0000 **10** 2½ **Me Fein**[32] 7447 4-9-8 **60** .... TPQueally 1 44
(A P Stringer) *chsd ldrs: rdn over 2f out: wknd over 1f out: hung rt ins fnl f* **14/1**

2m 55.5s (1.90) **Going Correction** +0.125s/f (Slow)
WFA 3 from 4yo+ 6lb **10** Ran SP% **120.5**
Speed ratings (Par 101): **99,97,97,96,96 95,93,91,90,88**
toteswinger: 1&2 £10.10, 1&3 £0.00, 2&3 £15.00. CSF £45.86 CT £253.44 TOTE £15.00: £4.70, £1.10, £3.10; EX 92.40.
Owner Willie McKay **Bred** Ballymacoll Stud Farm Ltd **Trained** Bawtry, S Yorks

FOCUS
Largely exposed types in this modest handicap and, although the gallop was only fair, three of the first four home came from off the pace. The winner raced against the inside rail in the straight.

7788 EAGLE CLAIMING STKS 6f (P)
7:20 (7:20) (Class 5) 2-Y-O **£3,561** (£1,059; £529; £264) **Stalls** Low

Form RPR

1223 **1** **Gone Hunting**[59] 7065 2-8-11 84........(t) JackDean(5) 1 77+
(W G M Turner) *chsd ldrs: wnt 2nd over 2f out: swtchd rt over 1f out: rdn to ld ins fnl f: r.o: eased towards fin* **4/5**[1]

5503 **2** 1½ **Fangfoss Girls**[24] 7537 2-8-2 67........ ChrisCatlin 2 56
(L Wells) *led: rdn and edgd rt over 1f out: hdd and unable qck ins fnl f* **11/2**[3]

6241 **3** 4½ **The Magic Of Rio**[17] 7628 2-8-3 90........ AndrewHeffernan(7) 5 50
(Peter Grayson) *trckd ldrs: plld hrd: rdn over 1f out: wknd ins fnl f* **9/4**[2]

05 **4** ½ **Mandhooma**[7] 7738 2-8-3 0........ LukeMorris(3) 3 45
(P W Hiatt) *chsd ldr tl rdn over 2f out: wknd ins fnl f* **16/1**

0300 **5** ¾ **Sorrel Ridge (IRE)**[43] 7319 2-8-2 46........(tp) NicolPolli(5) 4 43
(M G Quinlan) *s.i.s: hld up: plld hrd: rdn over 1f out: wknd ins fnl f* **33/1**

1m 15.05s (1.35) **Going Correction** +0.125s/f (Slow) **5** Ran SP% **110.5**
Speed ratings (Par 96): **96,94,88,87,86**
CSF £5.86 TOTE £1.90: £1.10, £2.70; EX 6.00.
Owner E A Brook **Bred** Norman Court Stud **Trained** Sigwells, Somerset

FOCUS
An uncompetitive claimer weakened by the below-par show of the second favourite. The pace was fair and the winner raced just off the inside rail in the closing stages. He did not have to be at his best to score.

NOTEBOOK
Gone Hunting, tried in a tongue-tie, is a reliable type who did not have to improve to notch his third win of the year and justify the market support. He is a fair sort for this grade, has a good attitude and should continue to give a good account. (op 11-10 tchd 5-4 in a place)
Fangfoss Girls had the run of the race and ran creditably on this first run for her new yard. She may be able to pick up a small event, but is likely to remain vulnerable to the better types in this grade. (op 9-2)
The Magic Of Rio was the pick on official ratings but proved a disappointment after failing to settle on this first run for a yard that has been struggling for winners. She is better than this, but looks one to have reservations about at present. (op 7-4)
Mandhooma had a stiff task at the weights and had her limitations exposed. She may do better in modest handicaps over further. (op 20-1)
Sorrel Ridge(IRE), an inconsistent maiden, had a stiff task on these terms and was soundly beaten in the first time tongue-tie and cheekpieces.

7789 SWAN NURSERY 1m (P)
7:50 (7:50) (Class 6) (0-60,67) 2-Y-O **£2,638** (£785; £392; £196) **Stalls** Centre

Form RPR

060 **1** **Trusted Venture (USA)**[40] 7356 2-9-3 **56** .... GeorgeBaker 6 58
(J R Best) *trckd ldrs: racd keenly: led and edgd lft fr over 1f out: drvn out* **14/1**

4001 **2** *nk* **Andean Margin (IRE)**[11] 7693 2-10-0 **67** ....(b) PatCosgrave 8 68
(S A Callaghan) *hld up: racd keenly: rdn hdwy over 3f out: shkn up over 1f out: hrd rdn and hung lft ins fnl f: r.o* **7/2**[1]

0551 **3** ¾ **Autumn Morning (IRE)**[19] 7607 2-9-0 **58** .... PatrickDonaghy(5) 2 58+
(P D Evans) *s.s: hld up: hdwy 2f out: hmpd over 1f out: rdn and ev ch ins fnl f: no ex towards fin* **8/1**

020 **4** 1 **Hawkspring (IRE)**[5] 7760 2-9-7 **60** .... AdamKirby 12 57+
(S Parr) *hld up: hdwy: hung lft and nt clr run over 1f out: sn rdn: nt rch ldrs* **6/1**

0000 **5** 1½ **Fleur De'Lion (IRE)**[51] 7212 2-8-13 **52** .... RichardKingscote 10 46
(S Kirk) *hld up: rdn over 2f out: hung lft and r.o ins fnl f: nvr nrr* **14/1**

0652 **6** ½ **Kneesy Earsy Nosey**[11] 7694 2-8-10 **54** .... AnnStokell(5) 3 47+
(Miss A Stokell) *chsd ldrs: rdn and nt clr run over 1f out: no ex fnl f* **16/1**

0001 **7** ½ **Thewaytosanjose (IRE)**[14] 7659 2-9-2 **55** .... LPKeniry 9 47
(S Kirk) *hld up: rdn and hung lft fr over 1f out: nvr nrr* **4/1**[2]

0000 **8** *shd* **Viking Rock (IRE)**[48] 7258 2-8-10 **56** .... RossAtkinson(5) 4 48+
(M Salaman) *led: rdn and hdd whn hmpd over 1f out: wknd ins fnl f* **20/1**

4640 **9** 1¼ **Chantilly Dancer (IRE)**[25] 7531 2-8-13 **57** .... JackDean(5) 7 46+
(M Quinn) *prom: outpcd over 3f out: nt clr run and dropped in rr over 2f out: wkng whn nt clr run ins fnl f* **25/1**

4245 **10** ½ **Betws Y Coed (IRE)**[14] 7666 2-8-13 **52** ....(p) NeilChalmers 5 40
(A Bailey) *s.i.s: sn pushed along and prom: rdn over 2f out: wknd fnl f* **14/1**

3003 **11** 2½ **Sicilian Pink**[8] 7728 2-9-6 **59** .... JimCrowley 1 41
(E F Vaughan) *chsd ldr: rdn and ev ch over 1f out: wknd ins fnl f* **9/2**[3]

1m 42.6s (2.70) **Going Correction** +0.125s/f (Slow) **11** Ran SP% **120.3**
Speed ratings (Par 94): **91,90,89,88,87 86,86,86,85,84 82**
toteswinger: 1&2 £13.90, 1&3 £14.90, 2&3 £4.10. CSF £64.07 CT £441.00 TOTE £16.30: £6.50, £2.10, £1.60; EX 102.60.
Owner New Venture Racing **Bred** Yates Thoroughbreds **Trained** Hucking, Kent

FOCUS
An ordinary event run at a fair pace and rated around the third. The winner raced centre to far side in the straight.

NOTEBOOK
Trusted Venture(USA) ◆ had hinted at ability on his second start but turned in an improved effort on this handicap debut on this first run over this trip, despite going freely to post. He showed his inexperience under pressure and may well be capable of better. (op 12-1)
Andean Margin(IRE), upped 10lb for his Southwell win when fitted with blinkers, ran at least as well back up in trip and switched to Polytrack. He should be able to win a race on this surface. (tchd 4-1 in a place)
Autumn Morning(IRE), who won a claimer on her previous start, lost more ground at the start than she was eventually beaten and turned in her best effort yet. She is the type to win more races for this yard. (op 13-2)
Hawkspring(IRE) had been well beaten on his previous start but showed that to be all wrong with the tongue-tie left off. A stronger overall gallop would have seen him to better effect and he is lightly raced enough to be open to further progress. (op 8-1 tchd 11-2)
Fleur De'Lion(IRE), an inconsistent maiden, was far from disgraced after racing wide throughout. This trip seemed to suit, but it remains to be seen whether it will be built on next time. (tchd 16-1)
Kneesy Earsy Nosey had been raised 14lb after a seemingly improved effort in a Fibresand seller last time, but had her limitations exposed on this Polytrack debut back in a nursery. (op 14-1)
Thewaytosanjose(IRE), 9lb higher than her Southwell victory, proved disappointing back on Polytrack and she just wanted to hang left under pressure. The return to the slower surface at Southwell should suit.

7790 GREATLEIGHS.COM APPRENTICE H'CAP 1m (P)
8:20 (8:20) (Class 6) (0-65,65) 3-Y-O+ **£2,590** (£770; £385; £192) **Stalls** Centre

Form RPR

6042 **1** **King's Colour**[24] 7536 3-8-12 **60** .... AndrewHeffernan(3) 2 74
(B R Johnson) *sn led: qcknd clr over 2f out: rdn out* **2/1**[1]

0-0 **2** 3 **Lady Aspen (IRE)**[26] 7518 5-8-3 **52** .... AlexEdwards(5) 5 59
(Ian Williams) *led early: chsd ldrs: rdn to chse wnr 2f out: no imp fnl f* **8/1**

3321 **3** *hd* **Azure Mist**[14] 7669 3-9-1 **65** .... ThomasBubb(5) 6 71
(M H Tompkins) *hld up in tch: rdn over 1f out: hung lft: styd on same pce* **5/2**[2]

0102 **4** 1 **Comrade Cotton**[5] 7765 4-8-11 **55** ....(p) DebraEngland 7 59
(J Ryan) *hld up: swtchd lft sn after s: pushed along 1/2-way: styd on fnl f: n.d* **13/2**[3]

0000 **5** 7 **Wahoo Sam (USA)**[108] 5799 8-8-9 **58** .... RyanClark(5) 3 46
(P D Evans) *prom: chsd wnner 6f out tl rdn 2f out: wknd fnl f* **13/2**[3]

0050 **6** 1¼ **Bury Treasure (IRE)**[107] 5815 3-9-3 **65** ....(p) MatthewLawson(3) 4 50
(Miss Gay Kelleway) *prom: hmpd and outpcd 6f out: n.d after* **11/1**

1000 **7** 6 **Lopinot (IRE)**[26] 7513 5-8-9 **60** ....(p) GemmaElford(7) 1 31
(M R Bosley) *chsd wnr 2f: remained handy tl rdn over 2f out: sn wknd* **20/1**

1m 39.89s (-0.01) **Going Correction** +0.125s/f (Slow)
WFA 3 from 4yo+ 1lb **7** Ran SP% **112.8**
Speed ratings (Par 101): **105,102,101,100,93 92,86**
toteswinger: 1&2 £4.50, 1&3 £1.10, 2&3 £3.70. CSF £18.09 TOTE £2.90: £1.50, £5.30; EX 20.40.
Owner Tann Racing **Bred** Cheveley Park Stud Ltd **Trained** Ashtead, Surrey

FOCUS
A run-of-the-mill handicap in which the pace was just ordinary. The winner raced against the inside rail in the straight.

7791 RECOVERY H'CAP 1m 2f (P)
8:50 (8:50) (Class 4) (0-80,76) 3-Y-O+ **£5,504** (£1,637; £818; £408) **Stalls** Low

Form RPR

0020 **1** **Dream Of Fortune (IRE)**[5] 7758 4-9-2 **71** ....(t) AdamKirby 4 81
(M G Quinlan) *hld up and bhd: hdwy over 2f out: rdn over 1f out: hung lft and led ins fnl f: r.o: eased nr fin* **3/1**[2]

4413 **2** ¾ **Lyceana**[19] 7603 3-9-1 **73** .... ChrisCatlin 1 82
(M A Jarvis) *chsd ldr 8f out: led over 1f out: sn rdn: hdd ins fnl f: styd on same pce* **4/1**[3]

0213 **3** 6 **Action Impact (ARG)**[10] 7712 4-9-6 **75** .... GeorgeBaker 3 72
(G L Moore) *hld up: hdwy over 4f out: rdn over 2f out: edgd lft over 1f out: wknd fnl f* **11/8**[1]

0015 **4** ½ **Sign Of The Cross**[22] 7558 4-9-7 **76** .... FergusSweeney 5 72
(G L Moore) *led after 1f: rdn over 2f out: hdd over 1f out: wknd ins fnl f* **8/1**

0 **5** 4½ **Munich (IRE)**[10] 7712 4-9-5 **74** .... JimCrowley 2 61
(L Wells) *led 1f: chsd ldrs: lost pl 4f out: wknd over 2f out* **20/1**

2421 **6** *hd* **Valdan (IRE)**[10] 7711 4-8-9 **69** .... PatrickDonaghy(5) 6 55
(P D Evans) *hld up: plld hrd: hdwy 4f out: rdn over 2f out: wknd over 1f out* **11/2**

2m 8.04s (-0.56) **Going Correction** +0.125s/f (Slow)
WFA 3 from 4yo 3lb **6** Ran SP% **118.4**
Speed ratings (Par 105): **107,106,101,101,97 97**
toteswinger: 1&2 £7.80, 1&3 £2.10, 2&3 £1.10. CSF £16.34 TOTE £4.70: £2.60, £2.90; EX 18.80.
Owner N J Jones **Bred** Newborough Stud **Trained** Newmarket, Suffolk

FOCUS
A decent gallop to this fair handicap and the first two pulled clear of the disappointing market leader. The winner ended up against the inside rail.

7792 NEW HOLLAND H'CAP 1m 2f (P)
9:20 (9:21) (Class 6) (0-50,50) 3-Y-O+ **£2,590** (£770; £385; £192) **Stalls** Low

Form RPR

00-0 **1** **Northern Dune (IRE)**[307] 695 4-8-11 **47** .... TPQueally 1 56
(A P Stringer) *hld up: hdwy over 1f out: rdn to ld wl ins fnl f: r.o* **14/1**

0500 **2** ¾ **Jayarbee (IRE)**[26] 7518 3-8-6 **50** .... AndreaAtzeni(5) 9 57
(P J McBride) *hld up: rdn over 1f out: edgd lft and r.o ins fnl f* **20/1**

0001 **3** ¾ **Tarkamara (IRE)**[13] 7678 4-8-12 **48** .... LPKeniry 3 54
(P F I Cole) *trckd ldrs: racd keenly: led and edgd rt over 1f out: rdn and hdd wl ins fnl f* **8/1**[3]

4532 **4** 1½ **Marie Tempest**[19] 7605 3-8-10 **49** .... FergusSweeney 13 52
(M R Bosley) *chsd ldrs: rdn and hung lft fr over 1f out: sn ev ch: no ex wl ins fnl f* **3/1**[1]

0003 **5** ¾ **Jarvo**[19] 7599 7-9-0 **50**........(v) PatrickMathers 6 51
(I W McInnes) *prom: nt clr run and lost pl 8f out: hdwy over 4f out: hrd rdn fnl f: styd on same pce* **10/1**

0002 **6** ½ **Maddy**[14] 7662 3-8-10 **49**........(p) FrankieMcDonald 2 49
(George Baker) *hld up: hdwy and n.m.r over 1f out: sn rdn: styd on same pce ins fnl f* **10/1**

0000 **7** ¾ **Gifted Heir (IRE)**[10] 7707 4-8-11 **47**........(b) NeilChalmers 12 46
(A Bailey) *hld up: rdn on outer over 2f out: edgd lft and styd on ins fnl f: nt trble ldrs* **16/1**

4563 **8** 1 **Ocean Pride (IRE)**[24] 7535 5-9-0 **50**........(p) JimCrowley 11 47
(L Wells) *hld up: hdwy over 4f out: rdn over 1f out: hung lft and wknd ins fnl f* **10/1**

4456 **9** nk **Golden Brown (IRE)**[22] 7553 4-8-11 **47**........(tp) ChrisCatlin 5 43
(David Pinder) *hld up: rdn over 1f out: n.d* **11/1**

6665 **10** 4½ **Split The Wind (USA)**[51] 7217 4-8-12 **48**........ EdwardCreighton 4 35
(Miss Sheena West) *led: rdn and hdd over 1f out: wknd ins fnl f* **10/3**[2]

0006 **11** 3¼ **Competitor**[19] 7599 7-8-10 **46**........(v) IanMongan 7 26
(J Akehurst) *chsd ldr: rdn over 2f out: wknd fnl f* **10/1**

0440 **12** 5 **Capania (IRE)**[294] 841 4-8-12 **48**........ PaulFitzsimons 8 18
(E G Bevan) *chsd ldrs: rdn over 3f out: wknd over 2f out: eased ins fnl f* **33/1**

-000 **13** 8 **Ella Y Rossa**[19] 7605 4-8-10 **46**........(b[1]) LiamJones 10 —
(C R Dore) *s.i.s: sn prom: rdn over 2f out: sn wknd* **20/1**

2m 9.48s (0.88) **Going Correction** +0.125s/f (Slow)
WFA 3 from 4yo+ 3lb **13 Ran SP% 128.9**
Speed ratings (Par 101): **101,100,99,98,98 97,97,96,95,92 89,85,79**
toteswinger: 1&2 £41.40, 1&3 £41.40, 2&3 £20.70. CSF £283.74 CT £2418.50 TOTE £19.70: £6.90, £8.20, £2.40; EX 162.60 Place 6: £215.87 Place 5: £109.55.
Owner Curley Leisure **Bred** Derek Iceton **Trained** Newmarket, Suffolk

FOCUS
A low-grade handicap in which the pace was decent. The winner and second both came from off the pace and up the centre of the track.
T/Plt: £178.50 to a £1 stake. Pool: £95,051.67. 388.71 winning tickets. T/Qpdt: £53.30 to a £1 stake. Pool: £6,106.88. 84.68 winning tickets. CR

7772 SOUTHWELL (L-H)
Saturday, December 27

OFFICIAL GOING: Standard
Wind: Light, across Weather: Overcast and cold

7793 HOSPITALITY AT SOUTHWELL RACECOURSE CLAIMING STKS 5f (F)
12:10 (12:10) (Class 6) 3-Y-0+ **£2,047** (£604; £302) **Stalls** High

Form RPR

1663 **1** **Fyodor (IRE)**[5] 7768 7-9-9 100........ LPKeniry 10 86
(C R Dore) *dwlt: hld up in tch: smooth hdwy 2f out: rdn and qcknd to ld ins fnl f: edgd lft and kpt on* **5/2**[1]

0404 **2** ½ **Colorus (IRE)**[43] 7323 5-8-3 62........(p) AndreaAtzeni(5) 7 69
(W J H Ratcliffe) *prom: effrt 2f out: rdn to ld over 1f out: drvn and hdd ins fnl f: edgd rt and kpt on* **8/1**

0 **3** ¾ **Rocketball (IRE)**[70] 6830 3-8-3 56........(v[1]) LiamJones 3 62
(Patrick Morris, Ire) *sn led: rdn along and hdd over 1f out: drvn and hld whn n.m.r ins fnl f: one pce* **18/1**

3253 **4** hd **Monte Major (IRE)**[7] 7746 7-8-0 56........(v) LukeMorris(3) 14 61
(D Shaw) *midfield: hdwy 2f out: sn rdn and styd on ins fnl f: nrst fin* **18/1**

0321 **5** 1½ **Calmdownmate (IRE)**[17] 7629 3-8-0 65........ DanielleMcCreery(5) 6 58
(Mrs R A Carr) *chsd ldrs: rdn along and sltly outpcd over 2f out: styd on u.p fnl f* **4/1**[3]

5130 **6** ¾ **Yungaburra (IRE)**[18] 7614 4-9-7 84........(t) AdamKirby 2 71
(S Parr) *chsd ldrs on wd outside: rdn along wl over 1f out: grad wknd* **7/2**[2]

0054 **7** ½ **Head To Head (IRE)**[8] 7727 4-8-1 45 ow3........ PatrickDonaghy(5) 5 54
(A D Brown) *wnt lft s: sn rdn along and outpcd towards rr: swtchd lft and rdn 2f out: styd on ins fnl f: nrst fin* **66/1**

045 **8** ¾ **Alugat (IRE)**[32] 7444 5-7-11 52 ow1........(p) RosieJessop(7) 13 49
(Mrs A Duffield) *chsd ldrs: rdn along wl over 1f out: grad wknd* **20/1**

3010 **9** 1¾ **She's Our Beauty (IRE)**[15] 7644 5-8-0 45 ow2....(p) FrankieMcDonald 8 39
(S T Mason) *cl up: rdn along 1/2-way and sn wknd* **25/1**

000- **10** 1½ **Mumaathel (IRE)**[397] 6946 5-9-3 60........ ShaneKelly 1 51
(W R Muir) *chsd ldrs: rdn along over 2f out and sn wknd* **9/1**

0522 **11** 3 **Dubai To Barnsley**[16] 7636 3-7-10 49........ AndrewHeffernan(7) 12 26
(Garry Moss) *hmpd s: in tch: rdn along 2f out and sn wknd* **20/1**

3510 **12** 1¼ **City For Conquest (IRE)**[28] 7497 5-8-2 54 ow2........ ChrisCatlin 4 20
(John A Harris) *dwlt and bmpd s: a in rr* **25/1**

3000 **13** 1¾ **Ducal Regancy Red**[18] 7615 4-7-13 43........ DuranFentiman(3) 11 14
(C J Teague) *wnt rt s: chsd ldrs: rdn along 1/2-way and sn wknd* **100/1**

60.24 secs (0.54) **Going Correction** +0.20s/f (Slow) **13 Ran SP% 122.1**
Speed ratings (Par 101): **103,102,101,100,98 97,96,95,92,89 85,83,80**
toteswinger: 1&2 £4.10, 1&3 £16.10, 2&3 £35.50. CSF £21.97 TOTE £2.90: £1.70, £3.20, £3.60; EX 21.10 Trifecta £79.00 Pool: £226.60 - 2.12 winning units..
Owner Liam Breslin **Bred** E J Banks And D I Scott **Trained** West Pinchbeck, Lincs

FOCUS
An interesting little claimer.

7794 SOUTHWELL-RACECOURSE.CO.UK NURSERY 6f (F)
12:40 (12:40) (Class 5) (0-75,70) 2-Y-0 **£2,729** (£806; £403) **Stalls** Low

Form RPR

62 **1** **Hellbender (IRE)**[31] 7454 2-8-13 **62**........ RichardKingscote 2 63
(S Kirk) *chsd ldrs: rdn along wl over 2f out: drvn over 1f out: hung rt ins fnl f: styd on wl u.p to ld last 50yds* **9/4**[1]

4462 **2** nk **Abu Derby (IRE)**[15] 7645 2-9-7 **70**........ TPQueally 7 70
(J G Given) *cl up: led 1/2-way: shkn up over 1f out: drvn ins fnl f: hdd and no ex last 50yds* **9/2**[3]

505 **3** 1 **Diamond Surprise**[52] 7198 2-8-8 **62**........ GabrielHannon(5) 5 59
(R Curtis) *chsd ldng pair: rdn along and outpcd 2f out: styd on u.p ins fnl f: nrst fin* **20/1**

605 **4** ½ **Chocolicious (IRE)**[61] 7015 2-9-4 **67**........ PaulMulrennan 1 63
(B Smart) *t.k.h: led to 1/2-way: cl up tl drvn and one pce ent fnl f* **7/1**

3202 **5** ½ **Forever's Girl**[12] 7687 2-8-2 **54**........ DuranFentiman(3) 6 48
(G R Oldroyd) *chsd ldrs: hdwy 2f out: rdn and ch over 1f out: sn drvn and wknd ins fnl f* **8/1**

4101 **6** 2 **Tillers Satisfied (IRE)**[12] 7687 2-8-7 **61**........ AndreaAtzeni(5) 4 49
(R Hollinshead) *t.k.h: hld up in tch: effrt and hdwy on outer 2f out: sn rdn and no imp appr fnl f* **11/2**

2213 **7** 5 **Rio Cobolo (IRE)**[15] 7645 2-9-3 **66**........(v) ChrisCatlin 3 39
(Paul Green) *t.k.h: hld up in rr: effrt 2f out: sn rdn and no hdwy* **7/2**[2]

1m 17.26s (0.76) **Going Correction** -0.05s/f (Stan) **7 Ran SP% 114.9**
Speed ratings (Par 96): **92,91,90,89,88 86,79**
toteswinger: 1&2 £4.00, 1&3 £13.50, 2&3 £14.50. CSF £12.83 TOTE £3.90: £2.60; EX 7.00.
Owner Norman Ormiston **Bred** James Lombard **Trained** Upper Lambourn, Berks

FOCUS
A modest nursery in which the top weight was rated 5lb below the ceiling for the race.

NOTEBOOK
Hellbender(IRE) had run quite well on his handicap debut at Wolverhampton last month, and was well backed ahead of this Fibresand debut. The slower surface brought about further improvement and, having been under pressure turning in, he galloped on strongly to score. There should be more to come from him. (op 3-1)
Abu Derby(IRE) was going best of all as they swung into the straight and a furlong and a half out Tom Queally was looking over his shoulder as though it was a question of 'how far?', but there was less in the tank than he realised and the winner saw it out that bit stronger. He is likely to drop back to 5f for his next start. (op 7-2)
Diamond Surprise, making her handicap and all-weather debuts, did not settle through the early stages would not have helped her chances. She did not run too badly in the circumstances. (op 22-1)
Chocolicious(IRE), another turning out in a handicap and on sand for the first time, made the early running and is entitled to come on for this first run in two months. (op 13-2 tchd 6-1)
Forever's Girl reversed recent Wolverhampton form with Tillers Satisfied, but both found this competition tougher than the plating-class opposition they encountered there.

7795 CALL 01636 814481 TO SPONSOR A RACE (S) STKS 5f (F)
1:15 (1:16) (Class 6) 2-Y-0 **£1,978** (£584; £292) **Stalls** High

Form RPR

005 **1** **Trick Or Two**[12] 7689 2-8-12 50........ LPKeniry 1 68
(S Kirk) *cl up on outer: effrt to ld 2f out: rdn clr ent fnl f: styd on strly* **16/1**

3302 **2** 3½ **La Capriosa**[9] 7719 2-8-2 60........ AndreaAtzeni(5) 12 51
(A J McCabe) *trckd ldrs: hdwy 2f out and sn chsng wnr: rdn and hung lft appr fnl f and sn no imp* **9/4**[1]

5242 **3** 1 **Readily**[19] 7600 2-8-7 52........ RichardKingscote 4 47
(J G Portman) *wnt rt s: cl up: rdn along and lost pl after 2f: swtchd lft and drvn over 1f out: kpt on ins fnl f* **3/1**[2]

2460 **4** ½ **Sills Vincero**[114] 5647 2-8-7 65........ HayleyTurner 6 45
(D Shaw) *squeezed out s and bhd tl styd on appr fnl f: nrst fin* **13/2**

5 ½ **Pinball (IRE)**[88] 6365 2-8-7 0........ LiamJones 5 43
(Patrick Morris, Ire) *wnt rt s: cl up: led 1/2-way: rdn and hdd 2f out: sn drvn and wknd appr fnl f* **9/2**[3]

0004 **6** ½ **Dancing Wave**[101] 6009 2-8-2 45........ AmyBaker(5) 2 42
(M C Chapman) *prom: rdn along 1/2-way and sn wknd* **20/1**

0054 **7** ½ **No Quarter Given (IRE)**[25] 7530 2-8-12 43........ PatCosgrave 10 45
(Mrs A Duffield) *cl up: rdn along whn n.m.r 2f out and sn wknd* **33/1**

5435 **8** 1½ **Chimbonda**[9] 7719 2-8-12 63........ AdamKirby 7 39
(S Parr) *led: rdn along and hdd 1/2-way: drvn and edgd rt 2f out: sn wknd* **6/1**

000 **9** 8 **Minenotyours (IRE)**[125] 5316 2-8-12 48........ ChrisCatlin 3 11
(D E Cantillon) *a in rr: rdn along and outpcd fr 1/2-way* **25/1**

61.61 secs (1.91) **Going Correction** +0.20s/f (Slow) **9 Ran SP% 119.0**
Speed ratings (Par 94): **92,86,84,84,83 82,81,79,66**
toteswinger: 1&2 £12.40, 1&3 £10.50, 2&3 £2.50. CSF £52.86 TOTE £21.70: £1.60; EX 95.80 Trifecta £136.60 Pool: £203.17 - 1.10 winning units..The winner was sold to D W Chapman for 6,500gns.
Owner Fairway Racing **Bred** Jeremy Green And Sons **Trained** Upper Lambourn, Berks

FOCUS
An ordinary seller.

NOTEBOOK
Trick Or Two, who had an excuse last time and came into the race very unexposed, had the best draw on paper, although the whole field raced towards the stands' side. Having travelled well towards the front, he kept on really well to win by a clear margin, and the switch to Fibresand clearly suited him. He should be able to hold his own in slightly better company on this evidence, a view presumably taken by David Chapman, who picked him up in the subsequent auction.\n\x\x He should be able to hold his own in slightly better company on this evidence, a view presumably taken by David Chapman, who picked him up in the subsequent auction. (op 14-1)
La Capriosa looked the one to beat on her recent course-and-distance second, but had work to do from stall 12. Racing next to the unfavoured stands' rail, she kept on out of the pack to take second, but the winner had gone beyond recall. (tchd 11-4)
Readily, who is fairly consistent and stays 6f, was keeping on at the finish. (op 7-2 tchd 11-4)
Sills Vincero was the unlucky horse of the race. Having her first run for Derek Shaw, she was officially best in at the weights, but she was squeezed out at the start and was struggling in behind in the early stages, getting a load of kickback in her face. She then found her path partially blocked as she tried to stay on inside the final furlong and a half. She shaped a bit better than her finishing position suggests. (op 6-1)
Pinball(IRE) showed good early speed, but did not really see her race out. (op 11-1)

7796 MEMBERSHIP AT SOUTHWELL GOLF CLUB H'CAP 1m (F)
1:50 (1:50) (Class 5) (0-75,75) 3-Y-0+ **£2,729** (£806; £403) **Stalls** Low

Form RPR

0544 **1** **Silver Hotspur**[5] 7758 4-9-5 **74**........ LiamJones 5 90
(C R Dore) *trckd ldrs: hdwy on bit and cl up 2f out: led appr fnl f: shkn up and sn qcknd clr* **7/2**[2]

-001 **2** 2¾ **Captain Macarry (IRE)**[11] 7698 3-9-4 **74**........(v) GregFairley 6 84
(B Smart) *cl up: led wl over 2f out: jnd and rdn 2f out: drvn and hdd appr fnl f: kpt on same pce* **9/4**[1]

5331 **3** 3¼ **Kingsholm**[8] 7731 6-8-13 **68**........ LeeEnstone 1 71
(N Wilson) *trckd ldrs on inner: effrt 3f out: rdn over 2f out: sn drvn and one pce fr wl over 1f out* **11/2**[3]

2012 **4** 1¾ **Everybody Knows**[22] 7557 3-9-5 **75**........ TravisBlock 3 74
(Miss Jo Crowley) *led: rdn along 3f out: sn hdd: drvn 2f out and grad wknd* **10/1**

0004 **5** ¾ **Haroldini (IRE)**[11] 7698 6-8-10 **65**........(p) PaulMulrennan 4 62
(J Balding) *hld up in rr: hdwy over 2f out: sn rdn and no imp* **8/1**

4313 **6** 1¾ **Ours (IRE)**[19] 7610 5-9-1 **70**........(p) ChrisCatlin 7 63
(John A Harris) *hld up: effrt over 2f out: sn rdn and no hdwy* **6/1**

0434 **7** 4½ **Restless Genius (IRE)**[28] 7494 3-8-13 **69**........(t) TPQueally 2 51
(B Ellison) *plld hrd: chsd ldrs: rdn over 2f out and sn wknd* **8/1**

1m 42.42s (-1.28) **Going Correction** -0.05s/f (Stan)
WFA 3 from 4yo+ 1lb **7 Ran SP% 114.0**
Speed ratings (Par 103): **104,101,98,96,95 93,89**
toteswinger: 1&2 £3.00, 1&3 £7.30, 2&3 £3.20. CSF £11.75 TOTE £4.30: £1.20; EX 15.70.
Owner Patrick Wilmott **Bred** Theobalds Stud **Trained** West Pinchbeck, Lincs

FOCUS
They did not go much of an early gallop in this modest handicap and plenty of the runners raced keenly.

7797 PLAY GOLF AT SOUTHWELL GOLF CLUB H'CAP 1m 4f (F)
2:25 (2:25) (Class 5) (0-75,75) 3-Y-O+ £2,729 (£806; £403) Stalls Low

Form RPR
2 **1** **Il Grande Ardone**[14] 7664 3-8-13 **74**...(tp) AndreaAtzeni(5) 9 85
(F Sheridan) *hld up in tch: hdwy 4f out: effrt over 2f out: rdn to ld wl over 1f out and sn jnd: drvn ins fnl f and kpt on gamely* **13/2**[3]
3343 **2** *shd* **Rawdon (IRE)**[15] 6726 7-9-5 **70**...(vt) HayleyTurner 4 81
(M L W Bell) *trckd ldrs: smooth hdwy 3f out: chal on bit over 1f out: rdn and ev ch tl no ex nr fin* **7/1**
2506 **3** *5* **Mustajed**[7] 7744 7-9-2 **70**...(v) JamesMillman(3) 2 73
(B R Millman) *hld up towards rr: hdwy 3f out: rdn to chse ldrs 2f out: drvn and kpt on fnl f* **12/1**
0513 **4** *2* **Karmest**[9] 7722 4-9-2 **72**... PatrickDonaghy(5) 10 71
(A D Brown) *trckd ldrs: smooth hdwy on outer 4f out: led 3f out: rdn and hdd wl over1f out: sn drvn and wknd* **10/1**
0231 **5** *1 ½* **Eureka Moment**[14] 7661 3-8-11 **67**... TGMcLaughlin 1 64
(E A L Dunlop) *hld up: hdwy on inner over 3f out: rdn over 2f out: sn drvn and no imp* **10/1**
6360 **6** *4 ½* **Red Wine**[28] 7493 9-8-12 **70**... KarenKenny(7) 7 60
(A J McCabe) *hld up and bhd: hdwy over 2f out: sn rdn and no imp* **20/1**
3053 **7** *shd* **Summer Lodge**[12] 7686 5-8-10 **61**...(p) PatCosgrave 8 51
(A J McCabe) *cl up: led over 7f out: rdn along over 4f out: hdd 3f out and sn wknd* **8/1**
0321 **8** *3* **Brave Mave**[32] 7447 3-9-5 **75**... SteveDrowne 5 60
(W Jarvis) *led 31/2f: cl up on inner: rdn along over 4f out: wknd 3f out* **7/4**[1]
5510 **9** *37* **Hill Billy Rock (IRE)**[219] 2332 5-9-5 **70**... RobertWinston 6 —
(G A Swinbank) *cl up: rdn along over 5f out: wknd 4f out: sn bhd and eased* **5/1**[2]
0004 **10** *9* **Agapanthus (GER)**[14] 7664 3-8-12 **68**...(p) TPQueally 3 —
(A P Stringer) *towards rr: hdwy on outer to chse ldrs 1/2-way: rdn along over 4f out: sn wknd and eased* **33/1**

2m 39.44s (-1.56) **Going Correction** -0.05s/f (Stan)
WFA 3 from 4yo+ 5lb **10** Ran SP% **123.6**
Speed ratings (Par 103): **103,102,99,98,97 94,94,92,67,61**
toteswinger: 1&2 £7.80, 1&3 £22.70, 2&3 £18.50. CSF £54.74 CT £548.98 TOTE £8.30: £4.30; EX 86.30 TRIFECTA Not won..
Owner Frank Sheridan **Bred** Shortgrove Manor Stud **Trained** Newbold Pacey, Warwicks

FOCUS
A fair middle-distance handicap.

7798 BOOK YOUR TICKETS ON LINE AT SOUTHWELL-RACECOURSE.CO.UK MAIDEN STKS 6f (F)
2:55 (2:55) (Class 5) 3-Y-O+ £2,729 (£806; £403) Stalls Low

Form RPR
1 **Triple Axel (IRE)**[50] 7233 4-8-12 57... ShaneKelly 3 64
(J Noseda) *chsd ldng pair: hdwy on outer over 2f out: chal wl over 1f out: rdn to ld over 1f out: kpt on* **7/4**[1]
0033 **2** *2 ¼* **Augustus John (IRE)**[9] 7724 5-9-3 67...(p) AdamKirby 2 62
(S Parr) *trckd ldrs: hdwy over 2f out and sn rdn: drvn over 1f out: kpt on same pce ins fnl f* **7/4**[1]
0 **3** *¾* **Nizhoni (USA)**[198] 2966 3-8-12 0... PaulMulrennan 6 54
(B Smart) *cl up: led 1/2-way: rdn over 2f out: edgd lft wl over 1f out: drvn and hdd appr fnl f: one pce* **13/2**[2]
4 *2 ¾* **Circle Dance (IRE)**[70] 6828 3-9-3 68...(v[1]) DarrenWilliams 5 51
(D Shaw) *t.k.h: led: pushed along and hdd 1/2-way: sn rdn: drvn 2f out and grad wknd* **7/1**[3]
20 **5** *12* **Naias (IRE)**[164] 4076 3-8-12 0... TonyHamilton 4 7
(R A Fahey) *in tch: rdn along 1/2-way: sn wknd* **12/1**
P **6** *10* **Redlynch**[153] 4461 3-9-0 0... TolleyDean(3) 7 —
(S Parr) *dwlt and wnt rt: sn outpcd and a bhd* **28/1**
000 **7** *2* **Foolish Optimist**[40] 7362 3-8-6 30 ow1...(t) KrishGundowry(7) 1 —
(Paul Green) *chsd ldrs on inner: rdn along 1/2-way: sn wknd* **50/1**

1m 16.14s (-0.36) **Going Correction** -0.05s/f (Stan) **7** Ran SP% **111.7**
Speed ratings (Par 103): **100,97,96,92,76 63,60**
toteswinger: 1&2 £1.50, 1&3 £3.40, 2&3 £3.00. CSF £4.45 TOTE £3.60: £1.50; EX 5.70 Trifecta £38.50 Pool: £400.65 - 7.70 winning units..
Owner Mrs Paul Shanahan **Bred** Forenaghts Stud **Trained** Newmarket, Suffolk

FOCUS
A poor maiden.

7799 SOUTHWELL-RACECOURSE.CO.UK H'CAP 1m (F)
3:30 (3:31) (Class 6) (0-60,64) 3-Y-O+ £2,047 (£604; £302) Stalls Low

Form RPR
0400 **1** **United Nations**[15] 7656 7-9-2 **57**...(b) LeeEnstone 5 73
(N Wilson) *chsd ldrs: hdwy on outer over 2f out: rdn to ld wl over 1f out: clr ent fnl f* **14/1**
5015 **2** *4 ½* **Rub Of The Relic (IRE)**[17] 7634 3-9-1 **57**...(v) FrankieMcDonald 2 62
(P T Midgley) *chsd ldrs: rdn along and outpcd 2f out: swtchd lft and drvn over 1f out: kpt on ins fnl f: no ch w wnr* **9/1**
4432 **3** *1* **Mambo Sun**[17] 7634 5-9-5 **60**... RobertWinston 4 63
(R Curtis) *cl up: effrt over 2f out: sn rdn and ev ch tl drvn and one pce over 1f out* **9/2**[2]
2563 **4** *hd* **Transmission (IRE)**[18] 7613 3-9-4 **60**... PaulMulrennan 1 63
(B Smart) *led: rdn along 3f out: drvn 2f out: sn hdd and kpt on same pce* **6/1**[3]
0405 **5** *½* **General Tufto**[9] 7721 3-7-11 **46**...(b) AndrewHeffernan(7) 10 47
(C Smith) *midfield: hdwy and in tch over 2f out: sn rdn: drvn wl over 1f out: kpt on ins fnl f* **33/1**
0560 **6** *hd* **Magical Song**[25] 7533 3-8-6 **53** ow3...(p) GabrielHannon(5) 11 54
(R Curtis) *cl up: effrt over 2f out: sn rdn and ev ch tl drvn and wknd wl over 1f out* **20/1**
5003 **7** *1 ¾* **Cap St Jean (IRE)**[17] 7631 4-9-3 **58**...(p) HayleyTurner 3 55
(R Hollinshead) *dwlt and towards rr: rdn along and sme hdwy over 2f out: nvr nr ldrs* **7/1**
0141 **8** *2 ¾* **This Ones For Pat (USA)**[4] 7774 3-9-8 **64** 6ex... AdamKirby 12 55
(S Parr) *stdd s and plld hrd: hld up towards rr: effrt and rdn 3f out: n.d* **4/1**[1]
2210 **9** *2 ¼* **Vogarth**[11] 7698 4-9-2 **60**... JamesMillman(3) 9 45
(B R Millman) *s.i.s: a in rr* **7/1**
4066 **10** *1 ½* **Semah Harold**[11] 7695 3-8-7 **54** ow2...(v) JamesO'Reilly(5) 14 36
(E S McMahon) *chsd ldrs: rdn along 3f out: drvn over 2f out and sn wknd* **11/1**
4000 **11** *9* **Mujahope**[28] 7497 3-8-8 **50**... AndrewElliott 8 11
(C J Teague) *a in rr* **40/1**
1100 **12** *11* **Top Jaro (FR)**[39] 7374 5-8-13 **57**... DuranFentiman(3) 13 —
(Mrs R A Carr) *s.i.s: a in rr* **25/1**
001 **13** *nk* **Drumalee Lass (IRE)**[14] 4207 3-8-10 **52**... PatCosgrave 6 —
(P M Mooney, Ire) *chsd ldrs: rdn along over 3f out: sn wknd* **16/1**
0423 **P** **Jordi Roper (IRE)**[5] 7766 3-8-6 **51**... TolleyDean(3) 7 —
(S Parr) *midfield: lost action and bhd after 1f: sn p.u* **9/1**

1m 41.97s (-1.73) **Going Correction** -0.05s/f (Stan)
WFA 3 from 4yo+ 1lb **14** Ran SP% **132.3**
Speed ratings (Par 101): **106,101,100,100,99 99,97,95,92,91 82,71,71,—**
toteswinger: 1&2 £33.20, 1&3 £20.50, 2&3 £10.90. CSF £142.70 CT £514.27 TOTE £25.00: £5.90, £4.20, £1.80; EX 236.20 TRIFECTA Not won. Place 6 £27.93, Place 5 £12.48.
Owner Beverley Embassy Syndicate **Bred** Cyril Humphris **Trained** Flaxton, N Yorks

FOCUS
A competitive handicap.
T/Plt: £51.70 to a £1 stake. Pool: £42,408.90. 598.17 winning tickets. T/Qpdt: £15.10 to a £1 stake. Pool: £2,726.50. 133.20 winning tickets. JR

7765 LINGFIELD (L-H)
Sunday, December 28

OFFICIAL GOING: Standard
Wind: Light, half-against Weather: Sunny, cold

7800 GLAD TIDINGS H'CAP (DIV I) 1m 2f (P)
12:15 (12:15) (Class 6) (0-65,67) 3-Y-O+ £2,047 (£604; £302) Stalls Low

Form RPR
3446 **1** **Formidable Guest**[9] 7732 4-8-10 **54**... TGMcLaughlin 6 61
(J Pearce) *t.k.h early: hld up in 8th: sweeping run on wd outside 2f out to ld jst over 1f out: sn 2 l clr: drvn out fin* **8/1**
5356 **2** *¾* **Bavarica**[16] 7656 6-8-8 **57**... AmyBaker(5) 8 62
(Miss J Feilden) *stdd s: fierce hold in last: stl there and t.k.h 2f out: rn into trble jst over 1f out: plld wd and r.o wl to take 2nd last 75yds: gaining on wnr fin* **8/1**
0041 **3** *2* **Rapid City**[11] 7707 5-9-9 **67**...(p) JamesDoyle 7 68
(A J McCabe) *hld up bhd ldrs: nt clr run or much room over 1f out: sn outpcd: styd on fnl f to take 3rd last stride* **2/1**[1]
5200 **4** *nse* **Gizmondo**[18] 7620 5-9-2 **60**... GeorgeBaker 10 61
(G L Moore) *racd wd: in tch: effrt to press ldrs 2f out: upsides jst over 1f out: sn outpcd* **7/1**[3]
0010 **5** *1* **Climate (IRE)**[23] 7559 9-8-9 **58**...(p) PatrickDonaghy(5) 1 57
(P D Evans) *trckd ldrs on inner: effrt to chal and upsides over 1f out: sn rdn and nt qckn* **33/1**
052 **6** *nk* **Resentful Angel**[15] 7669 3-9-3 **64**... PaulEddery 9 62
(Pat Eddery) *led: hrd pressed over 3f out: rdn over 2f out: hdd jst over 1f out: wl outpcd after* **11/4**[2]
0040 **7** *1* **Inquisitress**[11] 7702 4-8-7 **51** oh1... NeilChalmers 3 47
(J J Bridger) *hld up in last trio on inner: trapped bhd rivals w rdr motionless thrght fnl 2f* **40/1**
0004 **8** *shd* **Sceilin (IRE)**[21] 7596 4-8-7 **51** oh3...(t) NickyMackay 2 47
(J Mackie) *trckd ldr: chal over 3f out: nt qckn over 2f out: lost pl over 1f out* **16/1**
0452 **9** *3 ½* **Strike Force**[20] 7606 4-8-12 **63**... RossAtkinson(7) 5 52
(K F Clutterbuck) *chsd ldng pair to over 2f out: lost pl qckly and sn btn* **8/1**

2m 6.06s (-0.54) **Going Correction** -0.025s/f (Stan)
WFA 3 from 4yo+ 3lb **9** Ran SP% **117.1**
Speed ratings (Par 101): **101,100,98,98,97 97,96,96,94**
toteswinger: 1&2 £7.60, 1&3 £4.80, 2&3 £4.70. CSF £71.00 CT £178.10 TOTE £10.60: £2.40, £3.00, £1.20; EX 54.00 Trifecta £119.70 Part won. Pool: £161.84 - 0.50 winning units..
Owner Macniler Racing Partnership **Bred** Kingwood Bloodstock **Trained** Newmarket, Suffolk

FOCUS
Not a breakneck gallop, but a fair pace for the track, which resulted in hold-up horses arriving from the rear to fill the first two places.

7801 HAPPY NEW YEAR APPRENTICE CLAIMING STKS 1m (P)
12:45 (12:46) (Class 6) 3-Y-O+ £2,047 (£604; £302) Stalls High

Form RPR
4310 **1** **Smokey Rye**[45] 7302 3-8-2 70... JemmaMarshall(3) 9 59
(G L Moore) *hld up towards rr: prog on outer fr over 3f out: clsd on ldrs over 1f out gng wl: kidded along and led ins fnl f* **11/8**[1]
1024 **2** *1* **Comrade Cotton**[1] 7790 4-8-10 55...(p) RosieJessop(3) 4 64
(J Ryan) *s.i.s: rcvrd to chse ldrs: rdn over 2f out: styd on to chal 1f out: kpt on* **7/1**
1000 **3** *¾* **Samurai Warrior**[2] 7780 3-8-11 58... AndreaAtzeni 7 61
(P D Evans) *led: pressed and hrd rdn 2f out: hdd and one pce ins fnl f* **9/2**[2]
0210 **4** *¾* **Northern Desert (IRE)**[286] 914 9-8-10 65...(p) RossAtkinson(3) 5 61
(S Curran) *pressed ldr: chal fr 2f out: upsides 1f out: wknd last 100yds* **6/1**[3]
0542 **5** *1 ½* **Magic Warrior**[134] 5087 8-8-9 59... CharlesEddery(5) 6 58
(J C Fox) *wl in tch: effrt over 2f out: kpt on same pce and nvr on terms w ldrs* **10/1**
640 **6** *4 ½* **Jayyid (IRE)**[15] 7661 3-8-5 0...(t) DebraEngland(5) 10 45
(C E Brittain) *hld up in 11th: lft bhd fr over 3f out: shkn up and carried hd unattractively fnl 2f: passed wkng rivals* **33/1**
1006 **7** *1 ¼* **Bridge Of Fermoy (IRE)**[15] 7668 3-9-2 72...(bt) KylieManser(3) 8 51
(Miss Gay Kelleway) *trckd ldng pair tl: steadily wknd fr over 2f out* **7/1**
6400 **8** *1 ½* **Dasheena**[19] 7619 5-8-0 50...(be) KarenKenny(7) 2 34
(A J McCabe) *hld up in rr: prog to latch on to bk of ldng gp 3f out: wknd 2f out* **25/1**
6000 **9** *1 ¾* **Mythical Charm**[28] 7510 9-8-6 45...(t) JackDean 12 29
(J J Bridger) *racd wd: hld up bhd ldrs: rdn and wknd over 2f out* **40/1**
0060 **10** *1* **Tagula Sands (IRE)**[162] 4181 4-9-0 43... PatrickDonaghy 1 35
(J C Fox) *stdd s: hld up in detached last: snatched up 3f out whn already wl off the pce: no ch after* **100/1**
0000 **11** *2 ¾* **Little Cee (IRE)**[10] 4806 3-8-2 47...(b[1]) DeanHeslop(3) 11 21
(N J Hawke) *reluctant to go to post: stdd s: plld hrd and hld up in rr: rdn sn after 1/2-way: struggling fnl 3f* **150/1**

The Form Book, Raceform Ltd, Compton, RG20 6NL

600 12 27 **Sweet Demerara**[23] 7553 4-8-3 0..................................(p) AmyBaker(3) 3 —
(P Butler) *prom to 1/2-way: wknd rapidly: t.o* **200/1**

1m 37.38s (-0.82) **Going Correction** -0.025s/f (Stan)
WFA 3 from 4yo+ 1lb **12** Ran SP% **120.0**
Speed ratings (Par 101): **103,102,101,100,99 94,93,91,90,89 86,59**
toteswinger: 1&2 £3.50, 1&3 £2.30, 2&3 £7.60. CSF £11.60 TOTE £2.30: £1.60, £2.30, £1.50; EX 14.70 Trifecta £28.80 Pool: £228.29 - 5.86 winning units..Smokey Rye was claimed by George Baker for £5,000.
Owner Darrell Hinds Susan Bell Pat Butcher **Bred** Jeremy Hinds **Trained** Lower Beeding, W Sussex

FOCUS
The pace steadied noticeably after a furlong and did not pick up again until over two furlongs from home.

7802 FOREST ROW MAIDEN STKS 5f (P)
1:15 (1:16) (Class 5) 2-Y-0 **£2,729** (£806; £403) **Stalls** High

Form RPR
032 1 **Hillside Lad**[14] 7674 2-9-3 72.. GeorgeBaker 7 69+
(R M Beckett) *chsd ldr after 100yds: rdn to ld 1f out: sn in command: drvn out nr fin* **4/5**[1]
460 2 1 3/4 **Edith's Boy (IRE)**[106] 5904 2-9-3 60.................................. IanMongan 8 62
(S Dow) *t.k.h early and hanging rt: hld up bhd ldrs: effrt over 1f out: shkn up to chse wnr ins fnl f: fnd little and no imp* **16/1**
06 3 1 **Lady Vivien**[24] 7546 2-8-12 0.. PaulMulrennan 4 53
(D H Brown) *sn trckd ldrs: trying to cl on inner whn nt clr run 1f out: styd on again last 100yds* **16/1**
4 hd **Acrosstheuniverse (USA)** 2-8-12 0.................................. TPQueally 2 54+
(J R Gask) *hld up in last trio: hung rt and green bnd 2f out: shkn up over 1f out: styd on encouragingly fnl f* **20/1**
063 5 hd **Green Onions**[17] 7640 2-8-12 70.................................. GabrielHannon(5) 5 57
(D J S Ffrench Davis) *led after 100yds: rdn 2f out: hanging lft and hdd 1f out: fdd* **13/2**[3]
6 6 1 1/4 **Menhir Bay**[14] 7674 2-9-3 0.. SteveDrowne 6 52
(D K Ivory) *pushed along towards rr after 2f: effrt to chse ldrs 2f out: sn no imp* **40/1**
52 7 3 1/4 **Manana Manana**[5] 7773 2-9-3 0.. AdamKirby 10 41
(S Parr) *outpcd in last pair: nvr on terms* **4/1**[2]
8 5 **Countrywide Jaime (IRE)** 2-8-7 0.............................. AndreaAtzeni(5) 9 18
(S A Callaghan) *stdd s: hld up in last and sn wl bhd: no ch whn hmpd 1f out* **16/1**
00 9 1 1/4 **Risky Lady (IRE)**[9] 7734 2-8-12 0..................................(v[1]) HayleyTurner 3 13
(J Ryan) *led 100yds: chsd ldrs tl wknd 2f out: no ch whn hung lft 1f out* **50/1**

59.44 secs (0.64) **Going Correction** -0.025s/f (Stan) **9** Ran SP% **115.7**
Speed ratings (Par 96): **93,90,88,88,87 85,80,72,70**
toteswinger: 1&2 £4.20, 1&3 £4.90, 2&3 £19.00. CSF £16.27 TOTE £1.80: £1.10, £3.20, £3.60; EX 16.60 Trifecta £163.60 Pool: £316.18 - 1.43 winning units..
Owner P Hickey **Bred** B Whitehouse **Trained** Whitsbury, Hants

FOCUS
They were soon going a respectable gallop, though not 5f handicap tempo, and prominent runners filled the first two places. The runner-up is probably the best guide to the level of the form.

NOTEBOOK
Hillside Lad has been threatening to win a maiden and impressed in the way he chased the pace and finished the job off readily when asked. He handled the drop to 5f professionally and should do well in handicaps at this trip and 6f as long as he is fairly assessed. (op 10-11)
Edith's Boy(IRE), stuck wide all the way, put in an improved effort following a break. Though still showing his relative inexperience here, he is probably good enough to win a typical Polytrack maiden, but handicaps are an even more attractive alternative. (op 22-1)
Lady Vivien has stepped up steadily in three performances to date. She handled the drop in trip, but kept on well and a return to 6f should be no problem.
Acrosstheuniverse(USA), who fetched 48,000gns at the breeze-ups, took a while to pick up but was running on encouragingly at the finish. She can build on this debut and should be suited by an extra furlong. (op 16-1)
Green Onions was in front early on for the second race running, but may have done too much over this shorter trip. The tactics are worth repeating at 6f if a little more can be saved for the finish. (op 9-2)
Menhir Bay will have more chance when qualified for handicaps, though 5f looks too sharp for him. (op 33-1)
Manana Manana could not handle the drop to 5f, and needs to be returned to a longer trip. (op 6-1)

7803 AULD LANG SYNE H'CAP 7f (P)
1:45 (1:45) (Class 6) (0-65,65) 3-Y-0+ **£2,388** (£705; £352) **Stalls** Low

Form RPR
4615 1 **Marmooq**[13] 7691 5-8-9 56 ow1.. IanMongan 14 67
(M J Attwater) *racd wd: in tch: prog over 2f out: hrd rdn to ld 1f out: drvn out* **14/1**
0314 2 1 1/4 **Shaded Edge**[11] 7706 4-8-7 54......................................(p) HayleyTurner 3 62
(D W P Arbuthnot) *hld up in midfield: prog to trck ldrs 2f out: nt clr run over 1f out: r.o fnl f to snatch 2nd last stride* **9/2**[2]
0020 3 nse **Surwaki (USA)**[14] 7677 6-8-8 60.................................(p) AndreaAtzeni(5) 5 67
(R M H Cowell) *hld 1f: trckd ldr: urged along fr 3f out: led 2f out: hdd and nt qckn 1f out: lost 2nd last stride* **8/1**
2132 4 shd **River Kirov (IRE)**[16] 7653 5-9-1 62.................................. JimCrowley 7 69
(M Wigham) *hld up in rr: smooth prog to trck ldrs over 1f out: trapped bhd rivals gng easily: stormed home fnl 100yds* **3/1**[1]
3063 5 1/2 **Haasem (USA)**[14] 7677 5-9-2 63....................................(v) GeorgeBaker 2 69
(J R Jenkins) *hld up in rr: prog to trck ldrs over 2f out: nt clr run and swtchd rt 1f out: r.o: nt rch ldrs* **7/1**[3]
6002 6 1 1/4 **Ever Cheerful**[30] 7471 7-9-2 63.....................................(p) SteveDrowne 12 65
(A B Haynes) *led after 1f: drvn and hdd 2f out: wknd ins fnl f* **14/1**
4620 7 nk **Maid Of Ailsa (USA)**[6] 7764 3-8-9 56...............................(b[1]) LiamJones 11 58
(W J Haggas) *settled wl in rr: only 12th 2f out: rdn and styd on fr over 1f out: no ch* **14/1**
3400 8 1/2 **Liberty Valance (IRE)**[18] 7634 3-8-11 58...............................(t) LPKeniry 1 58
(S Kirk) *trckd ldrs: effrt on inner 2f out: hrd rdn and cl up over 1f out: wknd ins fnl f* **9/1**
4402 9 shd **Vanadium**[16] 7651 6-8-13 60.. TPQueally 4 60
(G L Moore) *t.k.h early: hld up and racd on outer: in tch over 2f out: lost pl wl over 1f out: n.d after: plugged on* **10/1**
5666 10 hd **Little Knickers**[20] 7601 3-9-1 62.................................. EdwardCreighton 13 62
(E J Creighton) *hld up in last trio: struggling over 2f out: plugged on fnl f* **25/1**
1020 11 1 **Batchworth Blaise**[39] 7392 5-8-7 54.................................. JamesDoyle 6 51
(E A Wheeler) *s.s: last and detached to over 2f out: plugged on fnl f* **25/1**
3200 12 1/2 **Over To You Bert**[21] 7591 9-8-6 58.................................. LukeMorris(3) 10 53
(R J Hodges) *pressed ldng pair: u.p fr 3f out: wknd wl over 1f out* **16/1**

0146 13 1/2 **Double Valentine**[6] 7764 5-8-5 59.................................. DebraEngland(7) 8 53
(R Ingram) *chsd ldrs: lost pl 1/2-way: struggling in rr 2f out* **33/1**

1m 23.94s (-0.86) **Going Correction** -0.025s/f (Stan) **13** Ran SP% **122.4**
Speed ratings (Par 101): **103,101,101,101,100 99,99,98,98,98 97,96,95**
toteswinger: 1&2 £13.10, 1&3 £35.50, 2&3 £11.60. CSF £76.34 CT £576.13 TOTE £14.70: £3.60, £2.00, £3.00; EX 87.60 Trifecta £179.30 Part won. Pool: £242.31 - 0.20 winning units..
Owner The Attwater Partnership **Bred** Matthews Breeding And Racing Ltd **Trained** Epsom, Surrey

FOCUS
A decent gallop, but there were plenty in contention in the straight, with the favourite failing to find a run until it was too late.

7804 DIDCOT 60TH H'CAP 7f (P)
2:15 (2:15) (Class 2) (0-100,107) 3-Y-0+ **£11,656** (£3,468; £1,733; £865) **Stalls** Low

Form RPR
0032 1 **Aeroplane**[9] 7737 5-8-10 92.. HayleyTurner 2 101+
(S A Callaghan) *stdd s: hld up in last: wnt 4th over 2f out: shuffled along over 1f out: sn tk off and cruised through to ld fnl 50yds* **15/8**[1]
4156 2 3/4 **Nezami (IRE)**[23] 7556 3-7-13 86.................................. AndreaAtzeni(5) 4 93
(J Akehurst) *led: kicked on over 2f out: hrd rdn over 1f out: hdd and brushed aside last 50yds* **9/2**[3]
0034 3 1 **Gallantry**[9] 7737 6-8-1 86 oh1.................................. DuranFentiman(3) 1 90
(P Howling) *trckd ldrs: disp 2nd fr 3f out: drvn over 1f out: kpt on same pce* **7/2**[2]
3131 4 1 3/4 **Electric Warrior (IRE)**[20] 7601 5-7-11 86 oh4............ RossAtkinson(7) 6 85
(K R Burke) *tk v t.k.h on outer: disp 2nd fr 3f out: nt qckn over 1f out: fdd* **9/2**[3]
1454 5 11 **Naomh Geileis (USA)**[442] 6170 3-9-1 97.............................. GregFairley 5 67
(M Johnston) *chsd ldr to 3f out: sn wknd and bhd* **6/1**

1m 24.13s (-0.67) **Going Correction** -0.025s/f (Stan) **5** Ran SP% **107.7**
Speed ratings (Par 109): **102,101,100,98,85**
toteswinger: 1&2 £9.60. CSF £9.94 TOTE £2.60: £1.20, £2.40; EX 12.80.
Owner Saleh Al Homaizi & Imad Al Sagar **Bred** C R Mason **Trained** Newmarket, Suffolk

FOCUS
The pace was steady for two furlongs but then increased a bit, though it was nothing out of the ordinary.

NOTEBOOK
Aeroplane had been impossible to win with for over a year, but Turner rode him beautifully and produced a perfectly timed late run, a strategy which appears to suit him ideally. Though his overall record is frustrating, his record on the all-weather is hard to knock and he is undoubtedly handicapped to win more races during the winter if he continues to put his best foot forward. (op 7-4 tchd 9-4)
Nezami(IRE) is on a stiff mark at present, so this was a solid effort. He was held up when winning at Leicester in August, but seemed happy enough with the switch back to front-running until the winner sailed past and left him standing. (op 5-1 tchd 11-2 and 4-1)
Gallantry continues to perform with credit off this sort of mark without being quite good enough to win. (op 10-3 tchd 4-1)
Electric Warrior(IRE)'s recent form has been in claimers. However, he is on an attractive mark at present if he can return to the level of his form early this year. (tchd 7-2)

7805 HOGMANAY H'CAP 6f (P)
2:45 (2:45) (Class 2) (0-100,101) 3-Y-0+ **£11,656** (£3,468; £1,733; £865) **Stalls** Low

Form RPR
5001 1 **Turn On The Style**[19] 7614 6-9-5 101..............................(b) PaulMulrennan 5 112
(J Balding) *led: rdn and hdd jst over 2f out: kpt on wl fr over 1f out: drvn ahd again last 100yds* **15/8**[1]
4054 2 3/4 **Ebraam (USA)**[10] 7716 5-8-11 96.................................. TolleyDean(3) 1 105
(P Howling) *t.k.h early and hld up in last pair: effrt and got through on inner to ld jst over 2f out: rdn over 1f out: worn down last 100yds* **7/2**[2]
3221 3 1 1/2 **Matsunosuke**[7] 7756 6-9-2 98 6ex.. TPQueally 4 102
(A B Coogan) *stdd s: t.k.h and hld up in last pair: effrt and wdst of all bnd 2f out: nt qckn over 1f out: kpt on* **15/8**[1]
462 4 1 3/4 **Epic Odyssey**[17] 7641 3-7-13 86 oh3.................................. AndreaAtzeni(5) 2 84
(J R Boyle) *trckd wnr: upsides over 2f out: nt qckn and btn over 1f out* **4/1**[3]

1m 11.04s (-0.86) **Going Correction** -0.025s/f (Stan) **4** Ran SP% **111.8**
Speed ratings (Par 109): **104,103,101,98**
toteswinger: 1&2 £5.90. CSF £8.76 TOTE £2.50; EX 6.70.
Owner The Haydock Badgeholders **Bred** J And Mrs Bowtell **Trained** Scrooby, Notts

FOCUS
Short on numbers, and an ordinary tempo for a decent-quality sprint.

NOTEBOOK
Turn On The Style is a useful handicap sprinter under any conditions, but he excels around this track. He has now won on four of his six visits, and the way he battled to get back on top confirmed that he is right back in form. He has had a relatively light year after picking up a minor injury in Dubai last winter, and he may return there for another crack at some valuable prizes, although connections are tempted to wait until 2010 when the new track opens there. If he stays at home he can be placed to advantage again. (tchd 7-4 and 2-1)
Ebraam(USA) found a dream run on the inside turning for home but that meant he had to fight out the finish against the rail, where the surface is usually a little slower. He does not win as often as one of his ability should, but he gave the winner a good race until forced to concede close home. (op 9-4)
Matsunosuke did his best under a 6lb penalty, but previous form suggested it was always likely to test him, and the fact that he raced so wide did not help. However, he would have appreciated a stronger gallop. (op 11-4)
Epic Odyssey had looked as if she might find a race off this mark in her previous race, but these opponents were significantly stronger and he will do better in a slightly lower class of handicap. (op 6-1 tchd 7-2)

7806 LARCH HILL H'CAP 1m 5f (P)
3:15 (3:15) (Class 6) (0-60,60) 3-Y-0+ **£2,047** (£604; £302) **Stalls** Low

Form RPR
1106 1 **Zalkani (IRE)**[29] 7499 8-9-4 56.. PatCosgrave 8 65
(J Pearce) *hld up towards rr: stdy prog over 3f out: cajoled along to take 2nd 1f out: styd on to catch faltering ldr last strides* **20/1**
0342 2 3/4 **Colonel Sherman (USA)**[18] 7626 3-8-10 54.............................. AdamKirby 4 62
(L A Dace) *led and sn clr: 20 l ahd 1/2-way: stl 8 l clr 2f out: tired fnl f: hdd last strides* **17/2**
0605 3 1 **Terminate (GER)**[36] 7427 6-8-12 50.................................. JimCrowley 11 56
(Ian Williams) *stdd s: plld hrd early and hld up wl in rr: stdy prog 3f out but stl plenty to do: rdn over 1f out: styd on wl: nrst fin* **8/1**
5112 4 1/2 **Irish Ballad**[22] 7587 6-9-3 55.. NickyMackay 14 61
(S Dow) *prom in chsng gp: chsd clr ldr over 3f out: no real imp: one pce and lost 2nd 1f out* **11/2**[2]
2524 4 dht **Torrens (IRE)**[8] 7744 6-8-13 56..............................(t) PatrickDonaghy(5) 2 62
(P D Evans) *t.k.h early: hld up in last trio: prog fr 3f out: drvn and styd on fr over 1f out: nrst fin* **12/1**

0062 **6** 1 ½ **Rahy's Crown (USA)**[14] 7676 5-8-11 **49**.................... FergusSweeney 6 52
(G L Moore) *hld up in midfield: stdy prog fr over 3f out: effrt to dispute 2nd 1f out: wknd* **7/2**[1]

3003 **7** 3 ¾ **Amwell Brave**[14] 7676 7-8-11 **49**.................................. JamesDoyle 13 47
(J R Jenkins) *hld up in midfield: effrt u.p 3f out: no real prog over 1f out* **14/1**

0321 **8** 1 ¾ **Sagunt (GER)**[14] 7676 5-8-10 **55**........................ RossAtkinson(7) 9 50
(S Curran) *hld up wl in rr: prog on wd outside over 3f out: wd bnd 2f out: sn no prog* **6/1**[3]

0653 **9** 1 **Go On Ahead (IRE)**[26] 7520 8-8-6 **51**......................(b) RichardRowe(7) 5 45
(M J Coombe) *prom in chsng gp: rdn on inner over 4f out: lost pl over 3f out: struggling in rr over 2f out* **12/1**

4005 **10** 2 ¼ **Corlough Mountain**[26] 7520 4-8-12 **50**.................... RichardKingscote 1 40
(P Butler) *t.k.h early: mostly chsd clr ldr to over 3f out: steadily wknd* **20/1**

0000 **11** 16 **Prince Charlemagne (IRE)**[44] 7309 5-9-2 **54**.............. GeorgeBaker 3 20
(G L Moore) *hld up in rr: no prog 3f out: sn wknd: t.o* **8/1**

0000 **12** 3 ½ **Deep Waters (IRE)**[20] 7599 3-7-13 **46** oh1...................... LukeMorris(3) 7 7
(S Dow) *t.k.h: disp 2nd bhd clr ldr to over 4f out: sn wknd: t.o* **66/1**

2100 **13** 5 **Dubai Ace (USA)**[24] 7545 7-9-8 **60**.................................. LPKeniry 12 14
(A M Hales) *prom in chsng gp: rdn 5f out: wknd over 3f out: t.o* **16/1**

2m 44.72s (-1.28) **Going Correction** -0.025s/f (Stan)
WFA 3 from 4yo+ 6lb **13** Ran SP% **123.6**
Speed ratings (Par 101): **102,101,100,100,100 99,97,96,95,94 84,82,79**
toteswinger: 1&2 £56.30, 1&3 £46.00, 2&3 £13.40. CSF £184.07 CT £1501.73 TOTE £26.00: £5.70, £2.90, £3.30; EX 303.60 TRIFECTA Not won..
Owner Mrs Lisa Matthews **Bred** His Highness The Aga Khan's Studs S C **Trained** Newmarket, Suffolk

FOCUS
A bizarre-looking race, with the runner-up soon racing 20 lengths clear and only being run out of it near the finish.

7807 GLAD TIDINGS H'CAP (DIV II) 1m 2f (P)
3:45 (3:45) (Class 6) (0-65,64) 3-Y-0+ **£2,047** (£604; £302) **Stalls Low**

Form RPR

0053 **1** **Royal Choir**[14] 7678 4-8-5 **50**.................................. LukeMorris(3) 4 60
(H E Haynes) *settled in midfield: in rr of main gp and rdn over 2f out: prog over 1f out on outer: hanging but drvn to ld ins fnl f* **16/1**

1303 **2** ¾ **Majehar**[21] 7596 6-9-3 **59**... SteveDrowne 2 67
(A G Newcombe) *hld up in midfield: nt clr run twice arnd 2f out: prog jst over 1f out: r.o to take 2nd nr fin: nt rch wnr* **9/4**[1]

4650 **3** 1 **Artreju (GER)**[18] 7620 5-9-7 **63**.................................. GeorgeBaker 9 69
(G L Moore) *stdd s: hld up in last: stdy prog on outer over 2f out: shkn up to ld jst over 1f out: hanging lft and fnd nil: hdd and btn ins fnl f* **13/2**[3]

6430 **4** 1 ½ **Flam**[60] 7071 3-9-0 **64**.. AndreaAtzeni(5) 10 67
(A M Hales) *pushed up fr wd draw to dispute ld: def advantage 2f out: hdd and one pce over 1f out* **8/1**

5132 **5** *hd* **Siena Star (IRE)**[21] 7590 10-9-6 **62**............................... TPQueally 7 65
(Stef Liddiard) *in tch: prog to trck ldrs 1/2-way: cl up 3f out: rdn to ld over 1f out: sn hdd and outpcd* **3/1**[2]

0013 **6** *hd* **General Feeling (IRE)**[21] 7591 7-9-4 **60**........................ HayleyTurner 8 62
(S T Mason) *hld up in rr: trapped on inner in 9th 2f out: eased out 1f out and styd on: no ch* **17/2**

5000 **7** ¾ **Touch Of Style (IRE)**[22] 7573 4-9-1 **57**......................(v[1]) PatCosgrave 6 58
(J R Boyle) *trckd ldng pair: cl up over 1f out: sn nt qckn: wknd ins fnl f* **9/1**

000 **8** ¾ **Drumhallagh (IRE)**[439] 6246 3-8-13 **58**.................... RichardKingscote 3 57
(Tom Dascombe) *hld up in last pair: dropped to last and pushed along 3f out: no ch whn carried rt fnl f: plugged on* **16/1**

5340 **9** *nk* **Landikhaya (IRE)**[18] 7631 3-8-9 **54**............................(p) GregFairley 1 53
(D K Ivory) *trckd ldrs: cl up 2f out: n.m.r over 1f out: wknd fnl f* **20/1**

5060 **10** 2 **Rosy Dawn**[6] 7761 3-8-4 **49** oh4.............................. FrankieMcDonald 5 44
(J J Bridger) *disp ld to 2f out: wkng on inner whn snatched up 1f out* **40/1**

2m 5.46s (-1.14) **Going Correction** -0.025s/f (Stan)
WFA 3 from 4yo+ 3lb **10** Ran SP% **119.7**
Speed ratings (Par 101): **103,102,101,100,100 100,99,98,98,97**
toteswinger: 1&2 £8.00, 1&3 £16.40, 2&3 £4.60. CSF £53.59 CT £273.11 TOTE £20.70: £4.80, £1.50, £2.50; EX 80.30 Trifecta £291.50 Pool: £752.48 - 1.91 winning units. Place 6 £38.11, Place 5 £19.06..
Owner The Reddown High Explosive Partnership **Bred** Easton Park Stud **Trained** Highworth, Wilts
■ Stewards' Enquiry : Hayley Turner two-day ban: careless riding (Jan 11-12)

FOCUS
A good gallop set the race up for the come-from-behind performers, with the race changing dramatically in the home straight. The time was faster than division one, but not significantly so.
T/Plt: £35.40 to a £1 stake. Pool: £51,350.65. 1,057.38 winning tickets. T/Qpdt: £17.40 to a £1 stake. Pool: £3,619.50. 153.80 winning tickets. JN

7787

GREAT LEIGHS (A.W) (L-H)

Monday, December 29

OFFICIAL GOING: Standard
Wind: modest, half against Weather: overcast, dry

7808 WHISKY H'CAP (DIV I) 6f (P)
12:55 (12:55) (Class 6) (0-55,55) 3-Y-0+ **£1,942** (£578; £288; £144) **Stalls Low**

Form RPR

0056 **1** **Helping Hand (IRE)**[17] 7644 3-8-8 **52**........................ AndreaAtzeni(5) 10 68
(R Hollinshead) *mde all: grad crossed over to rail: rdn clr over 2f out: styd on wl* **13/2**[3]

2311 **2** 1 ¼ **Fantasy Fighter (IRE)**[12] 7710 3-8-7 **53**....................... BMcHugh(7) 5 65
(J J Quinn) *dwlt: racd in midfield: swtchd rt and effrt over 2f out: chsd clr wnr over 1f out: hung lft but clsd on wnr tl no imp fnl 100yds* **11/4**[1]

0042 **3** 2 **Mind Alert**[12] 7706 7-9-2 **55**...............................(v) DarrenWilliams 1 61
(D Shaw) *stdd s: hld up in rr: stdy hdwy over 3f out: drvn over 1f out: r.o to go 3rd fnl 100yds: nvr nr ldng pair* **7/1**

6000 **4** 2 ¼ **Bateleur**[145] 4746 4-9-1 **54**...................................... EdwardCreighton 8 53
(M R Channon) *racd in midfield: pushed along over 4f out: hdwy to chse ldng pair over 2f out: wnt 2nd 2f out tl over 1f out: kpt on same pce* **12/1**

6006 **5** ½ **Berrymead**[6] 7778 3-8-5 **49** ow1.................................. AnnStokell(5) 2 46
(Miss A Stokell) *sn pushed along to chse ldrs: outpcd whn hit rail 3f out: plugged on same pce fr over 1f out* **40/1**

0603 **6** ¾ **Hollow Jo**[17] 7644 8-8-11 **50**...............................(v) NickyMackay 3 45
(J R Jenkins) *chsd ldrs: rdn and unable qck over 2f out: no ch w ldrs fnl f* **6/1**[2]

542 **7** *nse* **Duke Of Milan (IRE)**[29] 7508 5-9-1 **54**........................ MichaelHills 11 49
(G C Bravery) *stdd after s: hld up in rr: sme hdwy u.p over 1f out: nvr trbld ldrs* **13/2**[3]

0060 **8** *nk* **Gone'N'Dunnett (IRE)**[20] 7618 9-8-7 **46** oh1.................(v) GregFairley 7 40
(Mrs C A Dunnett) *dwlt: sn pushed along in rr: nvr nr ldrs* **16/1**

532 **9** 1 **Westwood Dawn**[17] 7648 3-9-2 **55**.........................(v) TGMcLaughlin 9 45
(D Shaw) *hld up in last trio: rdn and no hdwy 2f out: no ch whn n.m.r wl ins fnl f* **8/1**

0000 **10** 1 ½ **Honest Value (IRE)**[68] 6907 3-8-8 **47**.....................(p) RichardThomas 13 33
(Mrs L C Jewell) *t.k.h: chsd wnr tl 2f out: sn wknd* **50/1**

0260 **11** 1 ¾ **Calabaza**[29] 7509 6-8-7 **46** oh1.................................(p) JimCrowley 4 26
(M J Attwater) *t.k.h: chsd ldrs: rdn and struggling over 2f out: bhd fnl f: burst blood vessel* **12/1**

1m 13.45s (-0.25) **Going Correction** +0.075s/f (Slow) **11** Ran SP% **116.9**
Speed ratings (Par 101): **104,102,99,96,96 95,94,94,93,91 88**
toteswinger: 1&2 £5.20, 1&3 £11.50, 2&3 £3.60. CSF £24.48 CT £133.61 TOTE £8.70: £2.80, £1.70, £2.00; EX 30.60 Trifecta £106.20 Part won. Pool of £143.54 - 0.60 winning units..
Owner N Chapman **Bred** P F Mulholland **Trained** Upper Longdon, Staffs

FOCUS
A modest handicap run at a fair gallop, but those held up were at a disadvantage. The winner raced close to the inside rail throughout.

7809 WHISKY H'CAP (DIV II) 6f (P)
1:30 (1:30) (Class 6) (0-55,55) 3-Y-0+ **£1,942** (£578; £288; £144) **Stalls Low**

Form RPR

3043 **1** **Perlachy**[108] 5871 4-8-12 **54**...................................(v) LukeMorris(3) 6 63
(D Shaw) *t.k.h: hld up in tch: hdwy wl over 1f out: led and edgd lft ins fnl f: r.o wl* **3/1**[1]

2302 **2** ¾ **Welsh Opera**[12] 7705 3-9-2 **55**...................................... LiamJones 3 62
(S C Williams) *chsd ldng pair: rdn to chal on inner over 1f out: ev ch 1f out: kpt on same pce fnl 100yds* **8/1**

0526 **3** 1 ¼ **Tamino (IRE)**[12] 7706 5-9-2 **55**................................(t) IanMongan 8 58
(P Howling) *led: rdn 2f out: hrd pressed and drvn over 1f out: hdd ins fnl f: no ex fnl 100yds* **6/1**[2]

005 **4** *hd* **Just Jimmy (IRE)**[26] 7541 3-8-11 **50**............................ JamesDoyle 7 52
(P D Evans) *racd in midfield: rdn and unable qck wl over 2f out: kpt on u.p ins fnl f* **7/1**[3]

3604 **5** 1 **Davids Mark**[54] 7195 8-8-7 **51**.............................. AndreaAtzeni(5) 9 50
(J R Jenkins) *chsd ldr: rdn and ev ch over 1f out tl wknd ins fnl f* **15/2**

4366 **6** *hd* **Reigning Monarch (USA)**[29] 7508 5-8-11 **50**............... SimonWhitworth 5 49
(Miss Z C Davison) *in tch in midfield: rdn over 2f out: kpt on same pce fr over 1f out* **12/1**

0000 **7** ½ **Desert Light (IRE)**[12] 7710 7-8-7 **46** oh1....................(v) JimCrowley 12 43
(D Shaw) *dropped in bhd after s: sme late hdwy u.p: nvr trbld ldrs* **16/1**

000 **8** *nk* **Ignition**[9] 7750 6-8-7 **46** oh1.. GregFairley 2 42
(A Kirtley) *sn pushed along in rr: rdn wl over 2f out: sme hdwy whn swtchd lft ent fnl f: nvr trbld ldrs* **40/1**

0601 **9** *nk* **Greek Secret**[19] 7625 5-8-10 **54** ow2........................ JamesO'Reilly(5) 4 49
(J O'Reilly) *t.k.h: hld up in rr: rdn over 2f out: swtchd rt over 1f out: nt clr run jst ins fnl f: nvr able to chal* **9/1**

4305 **10** *shd* **Afton View (IRE)**[7] 7765 3-9-1 **54**.............................. HayleyTurner 11 49
(S Parr) *hld up in rr: c wd and rdn wl over 1f out: kpt on but nvr trbld ldrs* **8/1**

11 2 **Donard Lodge (IRE)**[52] 7233 3-9-0 **53**..................(t) PaulMulrennan 10 41
(J Balding) *chsd ldrs: drvn over 2f out: wknd over 1f out* **12/1**

000 **12** 3 ¼ **Baileys Brazilian**[22] 7589 3-8-9 **48**............................... PaulEddery 1 26
(C A Dwyer) *chsd ldrs on inner: rdn jst over 2f out: wknd u.p over 1f out* **40/1**

1m 14.13s (0.43) **Going Correction** +0.075s/f (Slow) **12** Ran SP% **121.9**
Speed ratings (Par 101): **100,99,97,97,95 95,94,94,94,93 91,86**
toteswinger: 1&2 £6.50, 1&3 £8.00, 2&3 £6.50. CSF £27.92 CT £141.25 TOTE £5.30: £1.80, £2.80, £2.60; EX 24.70 Trifecta £34.20 Pool of £97. 06 - 2.10 winning units..
Owner Mrs N Macauley **Bred** J James **Trained** Danethorpe, Notts

FOCUS
Division two of a modest sprint handicap. The pace was reasonable and the prominent racers again held an edge. The winner raced centre to far side in the straight.

7810 MANNINGTREE MAIDEN STKS 6f (P)
2:00 (2:01) (Class 5) 2-Y-0 **£2,590** (£770; £385; £192) **Stalls Low**

Form RPR

6 **1** **Sky High Kid (IRE)**[12] 7709 2-9-3 0............................ TonyCulhane 3 65+
(M R Channon) *t.k.h: w ldr: led wl over 1f out: sn rdn: drvn ins fnl f: a jst holding on* **15/8**[1]

6 **2** *hd* **Princess Zohra**[12] 7708 2-8-12 0............................... HayleyTurner 6 59
(E A L Dunlop) *dwlt: t.k.h: hld up in tch: rdn and effrt wl over 1f out: drvn 1f out chsd wnr ins fnl f: clsng towards fin: nvr quite getting to wnr* **9/2**[2]

5043 **3** 1 ½ **Lois Darlin (IRE)**[10] 7734 2-8-9 54.......................(p) KevinGhunowa(3) 4 55
(R A Harris) *set stdy gallop: rdn over 2f out: hdd wl over 1f out: kpt on u.p: lost 2nd ins fnl f: one pce* **17/2**

4 **4** 1 ¼ **Little Calla (IRE)**[25] 7546 2-8-12 0......................... TGMcLaughlin 5 51
(E A L Dunlop) *s.i.s: plld hrd: hld up in last pair: rdn and effrt over 1f out: kpt on same pce fnl f* **15/8**[1]

0000 **5** 1 ¾ **Jack's House (IRE)**[37] 7425 2-8-12 51....................(t) AndreaAtzeni(5) 8 51
(Jane Chapple-Hyam) *t.k.h: trckd ldng pair: rdn wl over 1f out: hung lft and wknd ent fnl f* **8/1**[3]

0 **6** 7 **Kings On The Roof**[18] 7638 2-9-3 0.......................... FrankieMcDonald 2 30
(P Leech) *fly-jmpd s and s.i.s: rn green and a bhd: lost tch 2f out* **50/1**

1m 16.2s (2.50) **Going Correction** +0.075s/f (Slow) **6** Ran SP% **111.3**
Speed ratings (Par 96): **86,85,83,82,79 70**
toteswinger: 1&2 £2.10, 1&3 £2.30, 2&3 £4.30. CSF £10.67 TOTE £2.80: £1.70, £2.00; EX 10.20 Trifecta £58.40 Pool of £456.86 - 5.78 winning units..
Owner Box 41 **Bred** Paget Bloodstock **Trained** West Ilsley, Berks

FOCUS
An uncompetitive maiden in which the pace was steady and this bare form does not look reliable. The winner raced centre to far side in the straight.

NOTEBOOK
Sky High Kid(IRE), who had shown ability over 7f on his debut, was ideally placed considering the way this race panned out and probably did not have to improve too much to get off the mark over this shorter trip. This form is nothing special but he is entitled to progress again. (op 2-1 tchd 9-4)
Princess Zohra was nibbled at in the market and turned in a better effort, despite dropping in distance. A much stiffer overall test of stamina is going to see her in a more favourable light and she should be able to pick up a race on Polytrack. (op 11-2 tchd 6-1)
Lois Darlin(IRE), an exposed 54-rated performer who had the cheekpieces back on to replace blinkers, was allowed to do her own thing in front and looks flattered by her proximity. She is likely to remain vulnerable in this grade. (op 12-1 tchd 8-1)

Little Calla(IRE) had shaped encouragingly over this course and distance on her debut but was not seen to best effect dropped out in this steadily run race. The step up to 7f and a stronger gallop will suit and she is likely to leave this bare form behind in due course. Her rider reported she had run too freely. (op 11-8 tchd 5-4 and 2-1)

Jack's House(IRE), with the tongue-tie refitted, failed to settle and again had his limitations firmly exposed. Modest handicaps will provide his best chance of success but he'll have to show a bit more before he's a betting proposition. (op 12-1)

7811 CHAMPAGNE H'CAP 6f (P)

2:35 (2:35) (Class 5) (0-75,75) 3-Y-O+ **£2,590** (£770; £385; £192) **Stalls** Low

Form				RPR
0003	1		**Leading Edge (IRE)**[25] 7544 3-8-10 **67**........................ TonyCulhane 9 *(M R Channon) t.k.h: chsd ldr tl 4f out: styd handy: wnt 2nd again over 1f out: rdn to ld ins fnl f: drvn out* **12/1**	74
3034	2	nk	**Wotashirtfull (IRE)**[123] 5417 3-9-4 **75**.........................(p) PaulMulrennan 7 *(K A Ryan) led: rdn wl over 1f out: hrd rdn and hdd ins fnl f: unable qck towards fin* **12/1**	81
2200	3	nk	**War And Peace (IRE)**[91] 6340 4-9-1 **72**........................ FrankieMcDonald 3 *(Jane Chapple-Hyam) t.k.h: hld up in rr: rdn and c wd 2f out: r.o wl ins fnl f: nt quite rch ldng pair* **11/2**[3]	77
1404	4	1	**Brandywell Boy (IRE)**[15] 7675 5-8-9 **73**........................ BillyCray[(7)] 8 *(D J S Ffrench Davis) dwlt: sn bustled along: hdwy on outer over 3f out: chsd ldrs over 1f out: kpt on same pce fnl f* **10/1**	75
5	5	½	**Secret Dubai (IRE)**[22] 7592 3-8-13 **75**........................(t) AndreaAtzeni[(5)] 1 *(M Botti) in tch in midfield tl lost pl and dropped to last trio over 4f out: rdn over 2f out: drvn over 1f out: styd on fnl f: nvr pce to rch ldrs* **2/1**[1]	75
1000	6	½	**Geoffdaw**[29] 7507 3-9-3 **74**........................(v) JamesDoyle 2 *(P D Evans) s.i.s: rdn 3f out: drvn and edgd out rt over 1f out: kpt on: nvr rchd ldrs* **4/1**[2]	73
0460	7	nk	**Maybe I Wont**[9] 7748 3-8-6 **63**........................ NeilChalmers 5 *(Lucinda Featherstone) chsd ldrs on inner: rdn and effrt wl over 1f out: no imp fnl f* **20/1**	61
0622	8	nse	**Don Pele (IRE)**[10] 7730 6-8-11 **71**........................(b) KevinGhunowa[(3)] 4 *(R A Harris) t.k.h: hld up in tch: rdn 2f out: hrd drvn and nt qckn ent fnl f: wknd ins fnl f* **4/1**[2]	69
136	9	1¾	**Jane's Payoff (IRE)**[192] 3224 3-8-10 **67**........................ RichardThomas 6 *(Mrs L C Jewell) t.k.h: chsd ldrs: wnt 2nd 4f out tl over 1f out: wknd qckly ent fnl f* **25/1**	59

1m 14.18s (0.48) **Going Correction** +0.075s/f (Slow) **9** Ran SP% **121.8**

Speed ratings (Par 103): **99,98,98,96,96 95,95,95,92**

toteswinger: 1&2 £14.90, 1&3 £13.90, 2&3 £17.90. CSF £152.44 CT £899.78 TOTE £11.20: £3.10, £2.70, £1.60; EX 45.80 Trifecta £164.50 Pool of £435.76 - 1.96 winning units..

Owner M Channon **Bred** Rathasker Stud **Trained** West Ilsley, Berks

FOCUS

A run-of-the-mill handicap in which the three market leaders disappointed. The winner raced towards the centre and this was another contest that suited the prominent racers.

7812 MILDEN MAIDEN STKS 1m (P)

3:05 (3:05) (Class 5) 2-Y-O **£2,590** (£770; £385; £192) **Stalls** Centre

Form				RPR
2	1		**Dover Street Art (IRE)**[21] 7602 2-9-3 0........................ HayleyTurner 2 *(D R C Elsworth) trckd ldng pair: chsd ldr wl over 1f out: sn ev ch: rdn to ld ins fnl f: pushed out* **4/5**[1]	82+
02	2	1½	**Tartan Gunna**[10] 7726 2-9-3 0........................ GregFairley 1 *(M Johnston) dwlt: sn led: rdn and clr w wnr over 1f out: hdd ins fnl f: nt pce of wnr* **11/8**[2]	79+
0	3	7	**Sounds Of Jupiter (IRE)**[12] 7709 2-9-3 0........................ GeorgeBaker 3 *(E F Vaughan) chsd ldr: rdn over 2f out: lost 2nd wl over 1f out: no ch w ldng pair fnl f* **15/2**[3]	63
6	4	1¼	**Maison D'Or**[35] 7438 2-9-3 0........................ RobertHavlin 5 *(R Ingram) hld up in midfield: rdn and effrt wl over 1f out: sn outpcd and no ch w ldrs fnl f: wnt modest 4th towards fin* **33/1**	61
	5	½	**Toll Road** 2-8-12 0........................ TGMcLaughlin 9 *(E A L Dunlop) a towards rr: rdn over 2f out: no ch w ldrs fnl f* **11/1**	54
0	6	1	**Philmack Dot Com**[44] 7336 2-9-3 0........................ TPQueally 8 *(Miss Amy Weaver) hld up in midfield: rdn and outpcd wl over 1f out: no ch w ldrs fnl f* **33/1**	57
0	7	1¼	**Crazy Colours**[24] 7552 2-9-3 0........................(p) FrankieMcDonald 6 *(Jane Chapple-Hyam) s.i.s: rn green and a bhd: rdn over 2f out: lost tch wl over 1f out* **25/1**	55
0	8	13	**Art Discovery (IRE)**[47] 7282 2-8-10 0........................ ThomasBubb[(7)] 7 *(M H Tompkins) s.i.s: alway last: lost tch 3f out: t.o fnl f* **50/1**	26

1m 40.57s (0.67) **Going Correction** +0.075s/f (Slow) **8** Ran SP% **129.4**

Speed ratings (Par 96): **99,97,90,89,88 87,86,73**

toteswinger: 1&2 £1.30, 1&3 £2.50, 2&3 £2.90. CSF £2.52 TOTE £2.00: £1.10, £1.20, £1.40; EX 3.20 Trifecta £9.10 Pool of £822.50 - 66.38 winning units..

Owner Matthew Green **Bred** Aylesfield Farms Stud Ltd **Trained** Newmarket, Suffolk

FOCUS

Little strength in depth but a race in which the two market leaders (who raced towards the inside rail) pulled clear in the straight. The pace was fair and the winner looks a decent prospect with the runner-up clear of the rest and also a fair sort.

NOTEBOOK

Dover Street Art(IRE) ◆, who was well supported, fully confirmed the promise shown on his debut and needed only to be pushed out to register a fluent success after racing keenly. He looks the type to progress over further and, although he is unlikely to be overfaced before next spring, appeals strongly as the sort to win more races. (op 11-10 tchd 6-5)

Tartan Gunna ◆, was much better out of the stalls than he had been on his previous two starts and he turned in an improved display. He pulled clear of the remainder, should have no problems staying 1m2f and is sure to win a race. (op 13-8)

Sounds Of Jupiter(IRE), who hinted at ability over 7f on his debut, was nibbled at in the market but had his limitations exposed against a couple of potentially fair sorts. However, he was far from disgraced and will be of more interest once handicapped. (op 10-1)

Maison D'Or again showed ability at an ordinary level and should do better over further in ordinary handicaps in due course.

Toll Road, a half-sister to triple Group 3 winner at up to middle distances Mores Wells, was relatively easy to back and showed only a moderate level of ability on this racecourse debut. She is entitled to improve for the experience, though. (tchd 12-1)

Philmack Dot Com hinted at ability on this second start but is likely to remain vulnerable in this type of event. (tchd 40-1)

7813 NEW YEAR H'CAP 1m (P)

3:40 (3:41) (Class 3) (0-95,86) 3-Y-O+

£7,477 (£2,239; £1,119; £560; £279; £140) **Stalls** Centre

Form				RPR
0412	1		**Red Somerset (USA)**[8] 7755 5-9-5 **86**........................ GeorgeBaker 3 *(R J Hodges) mde all: rdn jst over 2f out: drvn and edgd rt ent fnl f: styd on wl* **4/5**[1]	94
5231	2	¾	**Bluejain**[8] 7752 3-8-13 **81** 6ex........................ HayleyTurner 5 *(Miss Gay Kelleway) t.k.h: sn chsng wnr: rdn wl over 1f out: drvn ent fnl f: unable qck and a hld after* **7/1**[3]	87
0000	3	½	**Art Man**[23] 7579 5-9-4 **85**........................ FergusSweeney 4 *(G L Moore) s.i.s: hld up in last pl: rdn and effrt over 1f out: drvn jst ins fnl f: wnt 3rd towards fin: nt rch ldng pair* **11/1**	90
0235	4	hd	**Ocean Legend (IRE)**[16] 7670 3-8-9 **77**........................ LiamJones 2 *(Miss J Feilden) in tch in last pair: rdn over 2f out: hdwy over 1f out: disp 3rd ins fnl f: kpt on same pce fnl 100yds* **12/1**	81
0621	5	¾	**Trafalgar Square**[21] 7603 6-8-7 **74**........................ JimCrowley 1 *(M J Attwater) t.k.h: trckd ldng pair: drvn and effrt on inner over 1f out: unable qck fnl f: lost 2 pls fnl 100yds* **5/1**[2]	77
213	6	1¾	**Princely Hero (IRE)**[16] 7670 4-8-11 **83**........................ AndreaAtzeni[(5)] 6 *(M Botti) t.k.h: hld up in tch: rdn 2f out: wknd u.p 1f out* **5/1**[2]	82

1m 40.26s (0.36) **Going Correction** +0.075s/f (Slow)

WFA 3 from 4yo+ 1lb **6** Ran SP% **117.4**

Speed ratings (Par 107): **101,100,99,99,98 97**

toteswinger: 1&2 £2.20, 1&3 £3.80, 2&3 £8.00. CSF £7.81 TOTE £2.00: £1.30, £2.70; EX 7.40.

Owner R J Hodges **Bred** Haras D'Etreham **Trained** Charlton Mackrell, Somerset

FOCUS

Exposed sorts in this fair handicap, but a modest gallop means the bare form is not entirely reliable. Winner and second raced centre in the straight.

NOTEBOOK

Red Somerset(USA) was able to race from the same mark as on his latest close second to Flipando over this course and distance and George Baker ensured the cards were stacked in his favour with a perfectly judged ride from the front. He's a gutsy sort and regular winner who should continue to give it his best shot. (op 11-8, tchd 6-4 in a place)

Bluejain, under a penalty for his recent 1m2f victory at this course, was ideally placed, given the way this race panned out, and ran creditably back in distance. He will not mind the return to further and should be able to win again on Polytrack. (op 6-1)

Art Man looks a bit better than the bare form as he missed the break and was held up in a race run at just a modest gallop. A stronger pace back over 1m2f will suit and he is one to keep an eye on now he has slipped to a fair mark. (op 10-1)

Ocean Legend(IRE) is another that would have been suited by a stronger gallop but, for all his consistency, he's been beaten in all 12 of his starts in handicap company. (op 14-1)

Trafalgar Square, up 6lb for his Lingfield success, was not disgraced but had his limitations exposed in this stronger event. (tchd 9-2 and 11-2)

Princely Hero(IRE) proved disappointing, even though he would have preferred a more end-to-end gallop. (op 4-1)

7814 NEW YEAR AT GREAT LEIGHS H'CAP 1m 2f (P)

4:10 (4:11) (Class 3) (0-95,92) 3-Y-O+

£7,477 (£2,239; £1,119; £560; £279; £140) **Stalls** Low

Form				RPR
0060	1		**Sgt Schultz (IRE)**[38] 7404 5-9-0 **88**........................ LukeMorris[(3)] 4 *(J S Moore) hld up in tch: hdwy to trck ldng pair 2f out: rdn to ld over 1f out: clr 1f out: comf* **12/1**	99
1102	2	4	**Australia Day (IRE)**[67] 6238 5-9-7 **92**........................ MartinDwyer 2 *(P R Webber) mounted on crse: taken down early: fly-jmpd s and s.i.s: led after 1f: hung rt on bnds: hdd over 2f out: 3rd and btn whn hit on nose by rivals whip over 1f out: wnt 2nd ins fnl f: no ch w wnr* **11/8**[1]	95
0601	3	¾	**Robby Bobby**[6] 7777 3-8-12 **86** 6ex........................ GregFairley 5 *(M Johnston) led for 1f: chsd ldr after tl led again over 2f out: rdn and hdd over 1f out: no ch w wnr: lost 2nd ins fnl f* **6/4**[2]	88
6425	4	1	**Mafeking (UAE)**[23] 7579 4-9-1 **86**........................ AndrewElliott 3 *(M R Hoad) hld up in tch: rdn jst over 2f out: no ch w wnr fnl f: plugged on* **12/1**	86
0200	5	3¾	**Baylini**[24] 7556 4-9-6 **91**........................ JamesDoyle 1 *(Ms J S Doyle) t.k.h: hld up in tch: rdn over 2f out: drvn and edgd rt over 1f out: sn outpcd and no ch fnl f* **20/1**	83
2020	6	43	**Cupid's Glory**[30] 7493 6-8-12 **83**........................ FergusSweeney 6 *(G L Moore) s.i.s: hld up in last pl: rdn and no reponse wl over 1f out: virtually p.u fnl f* **9/2**[3]	—

2m 6.60s (-2.00) **Going Correction** +0.075s/f (Slow)

WFA 3 from 4yo+ 3lb **6** Ran SP% **120.4**

Speed ratings (Par 107): **111,107,107,106,103 69**

toteswinger: 1&2 £4.80, 1&3 £5.30, 2&3 £1.40. CSF £31.62 TOTE £15.90: £4.40, £1.40; EX 38.20.

Owner Jim Barnes **Bred** Frank Dunne **Trained** Upper Lambourn, Berks

FOCUS

A decent handicap run at an ordinary pace, and a race in which the two market leaders proved a shade disappointing. The winner raced towards the centre in the straight.

NOTEBOOK

Sgt Schultz(IRE) had been well beaten since his last win in March but was back on a fair mark and took advantage of a couple of below-par performances from the market leaders when returning to his best over this shorter trip. Life is going to be tougher in competitive company after reassessment.

Australia Day(IRE) was well supported on only this second all-weather start and was not disgraced in terms of form but he is going to have to step up on this level if he is to win a decent handicap on sand from his current mark of 92. (op 7-4 tchd 2-1 and 5-4)

Robby Bobby won a lesser handicap in good style at Southwell last week but failed to build on that under a penalty on this quicker surface over this slightly shorter trip. That slower surface and middle distances may suit best but there may not be too many opportunities for one of his rating at Southwell in the coming weeks. (op 9-4)

Mafeking(UAE), who was easy to back, was far from disgraced but a handicap mark of 86 offers precious little margin for error, especially in races that feature well-handicapped or progressive types. (op 8-1)

Baylini's form since her last win has been very patchy and she was again below her best returned to this longer trip after enjoying the run of the race. She will have to show a fair bit more before she is a solid betting proposition. (op 14-1)

Cupid's Glory, well beaten over 1m4f on his previous start, again proved a big disappointment, hanging badly and eased when his chance had clearly gone. He looks one to tread carefully with at present. (op 4-1)

7815 MULLED WINE CLASSIFIED STKS 1m 2f (P)
4:40 (4:42) (Class 7) 3-Y-0+ £1,706 (£503; £252) Stalls Low

Form RPR

4400 1 **Chalice Welcome**[65] 1562 5-8-12 43 HayleyTurner 7 51
(N B King) *hld up towards rr: gd hdwy on inner 2f out: rdn to ld ent 1f out: sn clr: pushed out* 10/1[3]

2466 2 2 ¾ **Jiminor Mack**[55] 7174 5-8-7 42 (p) AndreaAtzeni(5) 3 46
(W J H Ratcliffe) *s.i.s: in tch in midfield: rdn 4f out: hdwy u.p and edgd out rt over 1f out: chsd wnr jst ins fnl f: kpt on but no imp* 10/1[3]

0316 3 2 ½ **Itsawindup**[232] 930 4-8-12 44 (t) EdwardCreighton 11 41
(Miss Sheena West) *hld up in midfield: rdn and effrt over 2f out: edgd lft u.p over 1f out: styd on to go 3rd ins fnl f: no ch w wnr* 9/2[2]

0000 4 1 ¼ **Autumn Charm**[10] 7736 3-8-9 45 LiamJones 9 38
(Lucinda Featherstone) *hld up towards rr: hdwy on outer over 2f out: kpt on fnl f: nvr nr ldrs* 16/1

0053 5 1 ¼ **Glamoroso (IRE)**[9] 7749 3-8-10 45 ow1 PaulMulrennan 8 37
(A Kirtley) *led for 1f: chsd ldr after tl rdn to ld over 1f out: hdd ent fnl f: wknd* 20/1

0046 6 hd **Martingrange Lass (IRE)**[17] 7654 3-8-7 40 ow1 TolleyDean(3) 6 36
(S Parr) *stdd after s: hld up towards rr: rdn and effrt over 3f out: kpt on fnl f: nvr nr ldrs* 28/1

4500 7 hd **Missie Baileys**[31] 7473 6-8-12 42 (p) IanMongan 1 35
(Mrs L J Mongan) *chsd ldrs: swtchd rt and rdn over 2f out: drvn and wknd over 1f out* 10/1[3]

4063 8 2 ¾ **Rawaabet (IRE)**[10] 7736 6-8-12 45 JimCrowley 4 29
(R Hollinshead) *in tch: rdn over 4f out: drvn and struggling over 2f out: wl btn over 1f out* 1/1[1]

0350 9 ¾ **Sahara Prince (IRE)**[22] 7590 8-8-12 42 (p) PatCosgrave 2 28
(K A Morgan) *awkward and s.i.s: hdwy to ld after 1f: rdn and hdd over 1f out: wknd qckly fnl f* 16/1

660 10 33 **Veronicas Way**[11] 7267 3-8-5 40 ow1 JamesO'Reilly(5) 12 —
(G J Smith) *t.k.h: chsd ldrs tl wknd qckly over 2f out: t.o and eased fnl f* 66/1

0000 11 51 **Bold Phoenix (IRE)**[21] 7599 7-8-12 43 (bt) TPQueally 10 —
(Miss Amy Weaver) *dropped in bhd after s: a last: rdn 5f out: lost tch 3f out: t.o and virtually p.u fr over 1f out* 20/1

2m 9.35s (0.75) **Going Correction** +0.075s/f (Slow)
WFA 3 from 4yo+ 3lb 11 Ran SP% 121.7
Speed ratings (Par 97): **100,97,95,94,93 93,93,91,90,64 23**
toteswinger: 1&2 £14.50, 1&3 £10.90, 2&3 £8.40. CSF £104.10 TOTE £12.00: £2.60, £2.50, £2.70; EX 99.40 Trifecta £421.80 Part won. Pool of £570.08 - 0.10 winning units..
Owner The Dyball Partnership **Bred** The Dyball Partnership **Trained** Newmarket, Suffolk

FOCUS
A low-grade event run at a fair gallop. The winner raced towards the inside rail in the straight.
T/Plt: £31.50 to a £1 stake. Pool: £62,462.61. 1,443.10 winning tickets. T/Qpdt: £10.80 to a £1 stake. Pool: £4,308.98. 293.30 winning tickets. SP

7800 LINGFIELD (L-H)
Tuesday, December 30

OFFICIAL GOING: Standard
Wind: Almost Nil Weather: Sunny, crisp

7816 WILLIAM HILL JANUARY SALE - BETTER ODDS! CLAIMING STKS 1m 2f (P)
12:20 (12:20) (Class 6) 3-Y-0+ £1,978 (£584; £292) Stalls Low

Form RPR

1512 1 **Bridgewater Boys**[10] 7744 7-8-7 70 (b) FergusSweeney 3 69
(G L Moore) *dwlt: sn chsd ldr: rdn 3f out and looked hld: styd on doughtily to ld ins fnl f* 11/4[2]

2630 2 ¾ **Acropolis (IRE)**[52] 7244 7-9-0 93 (v) PaulMulrennan 4 75
(I Semple) *awkward s but sn led and set decent pce: gng best over 2f out: rdn and fnd nil over 1f out: hdd ins fnl f* 5/6[1]

0105 3 2 ¾ **Climate (IRE)**[2] 7800 9-8-8 58 (p) JamesDoyle 6 63
(P D Evans) *chsd ldng pair after 4f: rdn and nt qckn over 2f out: kpt on same pce after* 14/1

4006 4 4 ½ **Obrigado (USA)**[32] 7473 8-8-7 66 (t) HayleyTurner 1 53
(G L Moore) *hld up: wnt 4th 1/2-way: rdn on outer 3f out: no imp and wl hld after: wknd fnl f* 11/2[3]

6600 5 1 **Lancaster Lad (IRE)**[23] 7591 3-8-11 54 (p) SteveDrowne 2 58
(A B Haynes) *hld up in last: pushed along and no prog over 3f out: no ch after* 66/1

0004 6 hd **Tenement (IRE)**[13] 7707 4-8-7 52 SimonWhitworth 5 51
(Jamie Poulton) *chsd ldng pair 4f: sn dropped to last pair: struggling over 2f out* 16/1

2m 4.21s (-2.39) **Going Correction** -0.075s/f (Stan)
WFA 3 from 4yo+ 3lb 6 Ran SP% 110.6
Speed ratings (Par 101): **106,105,103,99,98 98**
toteswinger: 1&2 £1.40, 1&3 £2.30, 2&3 £2.40. CSF £5.23 TOTE £3.20: £1.20, £1.40; EX 5.30.Bridgewater Boys was claimed by P. D. Evans for £5,000.
Owner R A Green **Bred** Southill Stud **Trained** Lower Beeding, W Sussex

FOCUS
A weak claimer that only concerned the two with the highest official ratings.

7817 ZENDRILL SCAFFOLDING H'CAP (DIV I) 7f (P)
12:50 (12:51) (Class 6) (0-52,52) 3-Y-0+ £1,706 (£503; £252) Stalls Low

Form RPR

6003 1 **Wooden King (IRE)**[27] 7535 3-8-12 **50** JamesDoyle 2 58
(P D Evans) *chsd ldng pair: flat out to hold position after 3f: drvn and kpt on fr over 1f out to ld ins fnl f* 12/1

0605 2 ½ **Kabis Amigos**[4] 7780 6-8-8 **46** oh1 (b) GregFairley 6 53
(S T Mason) *t.k.h early: led: drvn 2f out: hdd and one pce ins fnl f: jst hld on for 2nd* 5/1[2]

5060 3 nk **Franksalot (IRE)**[8] 7765 8-8-12 **50** (b) PatrickMathers 7 56
(I W McInnes) *s.i.s: hld up in last pair: rdn over 2f out: prog over 1f out: styd on wl to take 3rd last strides* 16/1

0033 4 ½ **Grizedale (IRE)**[8] 7765 9-9-0 **52** (tp) PaulDoe 3 57
(M J Attwater) *t.k.h early: trckd ldng quartet: rdn over 2f out: kpt on to dispute 2nd ins fnl f: nt qckn* 11/2[3]

5000 5 ¾ **Copperwood**[27] 7541 3-8-12 **50** DaneO'Neill 12 53
(M Blanshard) *trckd ldng trio: rdn over 2f out: nt qckn over 1f out: one pce after* 4/1[1]

0065 6 nk **Gambling Jack**[12] 7725 3-8-11 **49** (bt[1]) ShaneKelly 9 51
(A W Carroll) *chsd ldr: rdn wl over 2f out: fdd fnl f* 7/1

2/00 7 ½ **Actuality**[15] 7691 6-8-10 **48** (t) PaulMulrennan 4 49
(J Balding) *towards rr: taken to outer and effrt 3f out but no rspnse: kpt on fnl f: nrst fin* 5/1[2]

0000 8 1 ½ **Halsion Challenge**[8] 7766 3-8-8 **46** oh1 (t) SteveDrowne 1 43
(J R Best) *dwlt: sn rchd midfield on inner: no prog over 2f out: n.d after* 16/1

0000 9 ½ **I Certainly May**[16] 7676 3-8-8 **46** oh1 (p) NickyMackay 8 41
(S Dow) *detached in last and u.p over 4f out: virtually t.o 3f out: plugged on* 20/1

0000 10 2 **Balerno**[27] 7535 9-8-9 **47** ow1 IanMongan 10 37
(Mrs L J Mongan) *towards rr: effrt on inner wl over 1f out but nvr rchd ldrs: wknd fnl f* 14/1

3000 11 2 ½ **Briannsta (IRE)**[28] 7522 6-8-10 **48** RichardThomas 5 31
(J E Long) *chsd ldrs: u.p and struggling wl over 2f out: wknd over 1f out* 25/1

3004 12 nse **Kalligal**[16] 7672 3-8-12 **50** RobertHavlin 11 33
(R Ingram) *taken down early: stdd s: hld up in last trio: taken to outer and no prog 1/2-way: no ch after* 20/1

1m 23.55s (-1.25) **Going Correction** -0.075s/f (Stan) 12 Ran SP% 120.7
Speed ratings (Par 101): **104,103,103,102,101 101,100,99,98,96 93,93**
toteswinger: 1&2 £5.70, 1&3 £25.70, 2&3 £14.90. CSF £70.36 CT £998.22 TOTE £11.30: £3.30, £2.10, £3.50; EX 79.90 TRIFECTA Not won..
Owner Hitchcock & King **Bred** Terence E Connelly **Trained** Pandy, Monmouths

FOCUS
With a ratings band of 46 to 52 this was a selling handicap in everything but name.

7818 ZENDRILL SCAFFOLDING H'CAP (DIV II) 7f (P)
1:20 (1:20) (Class 6) (0-52,52) 3-Y-0+ £1,706 (£503; £252) Stalls Low

Form RPR

5033 1 **Loyal Royal (IRE)**[13] 7705 5-8-9 **52** (b) JackDean(5) 12 61
(J M Bradley) *stdd s fr wd draw: fierce hold in last pair: plenty to do over 2f out: gd prog on outer over 1f out: drvn and styd on to ld last strides* 9/2[2]

0001 2 shd **Cavalry Guard (USA)**[8] 7765 4-8-3 **46** (b) AmyBaker(5) 3 54
(T D McCarthy) *led and keen early: urged along fr 2f out: holding rivals ent fnl f: hdd last strides* 4/1[1]

0005 3 2 ¾ **Ishibee (IRE)**[8] 7768 4-8-8 **46** oh1 (p) NeilChalmers 10 47
(J J Bridger) *prom: rdn 2f out: disp 2nd over 1f out: kpt on but outpcd ins fnl f* 16/1

0000 4 nse **King Of Cadeaux (IRE)**[62] 5421 3-8-6 **49** (p) GabrielHannon(5) 7 50
(M A Magnusson) *led 1f: chsd ldr and styd on inner: hld ent fnl f: one pce* 8/1

4000 5 ¾ **Roundthetwist (IRE)**[20] 7631 3-8-5 **50** (p) DeclanCannon(7) 6 49
(K R Burke) *s.i.s: sn midfield: nt qckn and struggling wl over 2f out: styd on fnl f: no threat* 8/1

506 6 hd **Prix Masque (IRE)**[20] 7624 4-8-12 **50** EdwardCreighton 2 48
(Christian Wroe) *hld up in last pair: rdn and stl there 2f out: styd on fnl f: nrst fin* 14/1

5000 7 nse **First In Show**[15] 7691 3-8-10 **48** (t) MartinDwyer 5 46
(A M Balding) *pushed along in midfield after 3f: effrt to chse ldrs 2f out: disp 2nd u.p jst over 1f out: fdd* 9/2[2]

0600 8 ¾ **Evenstorm (USA)**[13] 7706 3-8-11 **49** GregFairley 4 45
(B Gubby) *t.k.h early and hld up in midfield: effrt wl over 1f out: no real imp on ldrs* 6/1[3]

0604 9 2 ¼ **Tuning Fork**[13] 7705 8-8-1 **46** oh1 (e) KierenFox(7) 1 36
(M J Attwater) *t.k.h in midfield: effrt on inner over 2f out: sn shkn up and no real prog* 12/1

0000 10 nse **Chalentina**[24] 7581 5-8-8 **46** oh1 RichardThomas 11 36
(J E Long) *prom on outer: disp 2nd over 2f out: wknd over 1f out* 20/1

6/00 11 8 **Black Draft**[8] 7765 6-8-1 **46** oh1 BillyCray(7) 8 14
(B Forsey) *t.k.h early: hld up and wd: sddle slipped 1/2-way and no ch after* 33/1

1m 24.64s (-0.16) **Going Correction** -0.075s/f (Stan) 36 Ran SP% 120.8
Speed ratings (Par 101): **97,96,93,93,92 92,92,91,89,89 79**
toteswinger: 1&2 £3.00, 1&3 £9.30, 2&3 £14.80. CSF £23.57 CT £276.36 TOTE £4.80: £2.10, £1.10, £6.20; EX 19.30 Trifecta £175.90 Part won. Pool of £237.81 - 0.49 winning units..
Owner JMB Racing.co.uk **Bred** J F Tuthill **Trained** Sedbury, Gloucs

FOCUS
A terrible wins to run ratio for the runners in this poor event with just nine successes coming from a combined 180 starts.

7819 MALCOLM EVERETT SEMI-RETIREMENT (S) STKS 6f (P)
1:55 (1:55) (Class 6) 3-Y-0+ £1,978 (£584; £292) Stalls Low

Form RPR

3640 1 **C'Mon You Irons (IRE)**[16] 7677 3-9-0 65 JimCrowley 4 70
(M R Hoad) *chsd ldr: drvn 2f out: looked hld tl styd on wl fnl 100yds to ld last strides* 4/1[3]

4131 2 nk **Back In The Red (IRE)**[24] 7582 4-9-3 65 (b) KevinGhunowa(3) 1 75
(R A Harris) *led: drvn over 1f out: kpt on wl and looked to be holding on fnl f: hdd last strides* 7/2[2]

3100 3 nk **One More Round (USA)**[39] 7399 10-9-6 74 (b) JamesDoyle 6 74
(P D Evans) *stdd s: hld up in last pair: gd prog on wd outside wl over 1f out: clsd on ldng pair fnl f: nvr quite got there* 5/2[1]

3010 4 3 **Billy Hot Rocks (IRE)**[8] 7763 3-9-6 62 (b) DaneO'Neill 2 64
(Miss Gay Kelleway) *s.i.s: sn in midfield: rdn 2f out: nt qckn over 1f out: no ch w ldrs after* 7/1

3030 5 hd **Mafaheem**[36] 7435 6-9-6 68 (b) RobertHavlin 3 64
(A B Haynes) *chsd ldrs: pushed along fr 1/2-way: no imp u.p over 1f out: wl hld after* 12/1

1000 6 1 ¼ **Angel Voices (IRE)**[41] 7378 5-8-8 65 (p) DeclanCannon(7) 7 55
(K R Burke) *pressed ldng pair and racd wd: rdn 2f out: nt qckn over 1f out: fdd* 16/1

0050 7 1 ½ **Danski**[16] 7677 5-9-0 63 (v) IanMongan 8 49
(Mrs L J Mongan) *s.i.s: in tch in midfield: rdn 2f out: hanging bdly lft over 1f out and sn btn* 9/2

0060 8 6 **Acclimate**[28] 7521 3-8-9 49 (v[1]) FergusSweeney 5 25
(W S Kittow) *t.k.h early: hld up in last pair: shkn up and wknd rapidly over 1f out* 50/1

1m 11.35s (-0.55) **Going Correction** -0.075s/f (Stan) 8 Ran SP% 117.0
Speed ratings (Par 101): **100,99,99,95,94 93,91,83**
toteswinger: 1&2 £3.70, 1&3 £3.30, 2&3 £2.10. CSF £18.93 TOTE £5.50: £2.10, £1.20, £1.10; EX 22.00 Trifecta £51.80 Pool of £642.09 - 9.17 winning units..The winner was bought in for £3,600 guineas
Owner Fortunes Always Hiding Partnership **Bred** Airlie Stud **Trained** Lewes, E Sussex
■ Stewards' Enquiry : James Doyle one-day ban: improper riding (Jan 14)

Kevin Ghunowa three-day ban: improper riding (Jan 13-15)

FOCUS
A tight seller won by the only horse not wearing any headgear.

7820 WILLIAM HILL JANUARY SALE NOW ON! NURSERY 6f (P)
2:30 (2:30) (Class 4) (0-85,90) 2-Y-O £3,885 (£1,156; £577; £288) Stalls Low

Form	Pos	Dist	Horse / Details	RPR
0512	1		**Newlyn Art**[12] 7714 2-8-9 **72** HayleyTurner 9 (D R C Elsworth) *wl away fr wd draw: w ldr: pushed into ld over 1f out: shkn up and r.o wl fnl f* **5/4**[1]	81+
3563	2	2½	**Love You Louis**[24] 7575 2-9-0 **77** (p) SimonWhitworth 4 (J R Jenkins) *t.k.h: trckd ldng pair: rdn to chse wnr jst ins fnl f: styd on but sn no ch* **25/1**	75
2231	3	1	**Gone Hunting**[3] 7788 2-9-8 **90** 6ex (t) JackDean(5) 6 (W G M Turner) *racd wdst of all: chsd ldrs: lost grnd bnd 2f out: rdn and r.o to take 3rd ins fnl f* **11/1**	85
5321	4	1¾	**Desert Strike**[24] 7574 2-8-11 **74** JimCrowley 5 (P F I Cole) *led to over 1f out: wknd fnl f* **7/1**[3]	64
0032	5	¾	**Grand Honour (IRE)**[27] 7538 2-9-2 **79** IanMongan 1 (P Howling) *nvr bttr than midfield: outpcd fr 2f out: n.d after* **10/1**	67
431	6	nk	**Fesko**[84] 6545 2-9-1 **78** GregFairley 2 (M Johnston) *settled in rr: last 2f out: pushed along on inner and kpt on steadily fnl f: nvr nr ldrs* **4/1**[2]	65
015	7	¾	**Riflessione**[33] 7460 2-8-10 **76** (p) KevinGhunowa(3) 7 (R A Harris) *t.k.h early: trckd ldrs: rdn and grad lost pl fr 2f out* **8/1**	60
004	8	¾	**Kingsgate Storm (IRE)**[19] 7638 2-9-3 **80** GeorgeBaker 8 (J R Best) *stdd s: hld up in last: c wd and reminder 2f out: shuffled along and nvr nr ldrs after* **11/1**	62
1610	9	1¼	**Misty Glade**[33] 7460 2-9-3 **80** DaneO'Neill 3 (Miss Amy Weaver) *stdd s: hld up in abt 6th: outpcd 2f out: no ch whn rdn over 1f out* **20/1**	58

1m 11.51s (-0.39) **Going Correction** -0.075s/f (Stan) **9 Ran SP% 122.4**
Speed ratings (Par 98): **99,95,94,92,91 90,89,88,86**
toteswinger: 1&2 £11.90, 1&3 £3.80, 2&3 £19.00. CSF £43.26 CT £271.48 TOTE £2.10: £1.40, £7.00, £2.40; EX 53.60 Trifecta £166.80 Pool of £771.28 - 3.42 winning units..
Owner Matthew Green **Bred** Park Farm Racing & C M Oakshott **Trained** Newmarket, Suffolk

FOCUS
A decent contest that was won with some authority and the form looks solid rated around the placed horses.

NOTEBOOK
Newlyn Art, 10lb higher than his last victory, is clearly improving as he was 15lb wrong when a close second to Noverre To Go in a four-runner conditions race at the same course 12 days ago and was off the same rating here. When the handicapper looks at that run and this win, he might make a stern adjustment. (op 6-4 tchd 6-5 and 7-4 in a place)
Love You Louis makes things very hard for himself and rider by running free and was still tanking over two furlongs out. He did well to stay on for second without ever looking likely to trouble the easy winner, and despite being tried over shorter, this looks the right distance. (op 28-1 tchd 33-1)
Gone Hunting was moving out of claiming company but may have to go back into it to win again. He tried hard enough but 90 looks a stiff-enough mark for him. (op 8-1 tchd 12-1)
Desert Strike, in a handicap for the first time, likes to race prominently but the exertions told once the winner swept by and he faded badly in the final half furlong. He will need to conserve energy if he is to figure in handicaps. (op 11-2 tchd 5-1)
Grand Honour(IRE) was held towards the rear and never looked a threat after making an effort on the inside from two furlongs out. This was too sharp and a move back to longer distances might be prudent. (tchd 11-1 and 12-1 in places)
Fesko should have been suited by this move up to 6f but never got into the action after being held towards the rear early. (op 9-2 tchd 5-1)
Kingsgate Storm(IRE), in a handicap for the first time, never got competitive and is probably better than he showed in this. (op 14-1 tchd 16-1)

7821 BEATRICE WESTBROOK H'CAP 1m (P)
3:05 (3:06) (Class 4) (0-85,84) 3-Y-O+ £4,727 (£1,406; £702; £351) Stalls High

Form	Pos	Dist	Horse / Details	RPR
0111	1		**Titan Triumph**[28] 7525 4-9-3 **82** (t) JimCrowley 8 (W J Knight) *heavily restrained into last sn after s: sweeping prog on wd outside 2f out to go 2nd over 1f out: led jst ins fnl f: styd on* **10/3**[1]	91
0310	2	1	**Tous Les Deux**[30] 7507 5-8-6 **71** SimonWhitworth 10 (G L Moore) *t.k.h early: led at mod pce but uncontested: wound it up fr over 2f out: hdd jst ins fnl f: outpcd but kpt on* **16/1**	78
0002	3	½	**Jake The Snake (IRE)**[43] 7360 7-8-3 **73** AmyBaker(5) 7 (A W Carroll) *a cl up: urged along and styd on fr wl over 1f out but a jst lacked pce to chal* **7/1**	79
5063	4	½	**Totally Focussed (IRE)**[54] 7211 3-8-12 **78** IanMongan 6 (S Dow) *t.k.h early: hld up bhd ldrs: cruising over 2f out: nt clr run 2f out tl ent fnl f: shuffled along and appeared to fin w plenty lft* **6/1**	82
3044	5	¾	**Dichoh**[36] 7439 5-9-2 **81** MartinDwyer 3 (M A Jarvis) *hld up in midfield on inner: pushed along wl over 2f out: effrt over 1f out: sn outpcd* **7/2**[2]	84
2510	6	2¼	**Sotik Star (IRE)**[95] 6250 5-8-12 **77** PatCosgrave 4 (K A Morgan) *dwlt: a in rr: rdn and no prog wl over 1f out* **20/1**	75
4240	7	2¼	**Mataram (USA)**[209] 2711 5-9-2 **81** RobertHavlin 2 (W Jarvis) *dwlt: hld up in rr: shkn up and no prog wl over 1f out* **9/1**	73
0012	8	shd	**Star Strider**[17] 7670 4-8-8 **73** HayleyTurner 5 (Miss Gay Kelleway) *dwlt: t.k.h and sn prom on outer: chsd ldng pair 2f out: wknd over 1f out* **5/1**[3]	65
200	9	shd	**Alpes Maritimes**[36] 7439 4-9-5 **84** GeorgeBaker 9 (G L Moore) *t.k.h early: chsd ldr to over 1f out: wknd rapidly* **12/1**	76

1m 37.43s (-0.77) **Going Correction** -0.075s/f (Stan)
WFA 3 from 4yo+ 1lb **9 Ran SP% 117.1**
Speed ratings (Par 105): **100,99,98,98,97 95,92,92,92**
toteswinger: 1&2 £10.70, 1&3 £5.40, 2&3 £14.80. CSF £57.07 CT £355.67 TOTE £4.40: £1.40, £5.80, £1.90; EX 74.50 Trifecta £95.10 Pool of £703.51 - 5.47 winning units..
Owner Canisbay Bloodstock **Bred** Hesmonds Stud Ltd **Trained** Patching, W Sussex

FOCUS
A strong-looking handicap.

7822 WILLIAM HILL JANUARY SALE - WHY BET ELSEWHERE? MAIDEN STKS 1m 2f (P)
3:35 (3:35) (Class 5) 3-Y-O £2,729 (£806; £403) Stalls Low

Form	Pos	Dist	Horse / Details	RPR
00	1		**Planetary Motion (USA)**[64] 7026 3-9-3 0 GregFairley 6 (M Johnston) *mde all: hrd pressed fr 2f out: hld on wl thrght fnl f* **11/1**	74
04	2	½	**Confederate**[87] 6470 3-9-3 0 DaneO'Neill 8 (George Baker) *dwlt: sn rcvrd to trck wnr: chal jst over 2f out: persistently jst hld off thrght fnl f* **15/8**[1]	73
40	3	4½	**Starburst**[24] 7583 3-8-12 0 MartinDwyer 3 (A M Balding) *chsd ldng pair: steadily outpcd fr 2f out: kpt on* **11/1**	59
3500	4	2½	**Filun**[118] 5605 3-9-3 69 IanMongan 1 (A Middleton) *wl in tch: rdn over 2f out: sn outpcd by ldng pair: plugged on* **20/1**	59
0	5	hd	**Forced Opinion (USA)**[9] 7757 3-9-3 0 PatCosgrave 5 (K A Morgan) *stdd s: hld up in last pair: stl there and lft bhd over 2f out: shuffled along and kpt on steadily* **66/1**	59
5	6	1½	**Lucky Dancer**[9] 7757 3-9-3 0 GeorgeBaker 9 (D R C Elsworth) *stdd s: hld up in last pair: prog on wd outside 3f out: easily outpcd 2f out: no ch after* **2/1**[2]	56
03	7	3¾	**Fantosha (USA)**[15] 7690 3-8-12 65 JimCrowley 4 (K A Ryan) *trckd ldng pair: rdn over 2f out: steadily wknd fnl 2f* **11/2**[3]	43
05	8	½	**Romantic Retreat**[200] 2989 3-8-12 0 FergusSweeney 7 (G L Moore) *hld up in midfield: rdn and wknd 2f out* **17/2**	42
	9	9	**Jolies Dee**[13] 3-8-12 0 JamesDoyle 2 (J R Jenkins) *in tch: u.p and dropped to last over 2f out: t.o* **33/1**	24

2m 5.89s (-0.71) **Going Correction** -0.075s/f (Stan) **9 Ran SP% 119.9**
Speed ratings (Par 102): **99,98,95,93,92 91,88,88,81**
toteswinger: 1&2 £6.00, 1&3 £12.60, 2&3 £6.80. CSF £32.91 TOTE £10.50: £4.40, £1.30, £3.90; EX 50.50 Trifecta £499.90 Pool of £1,054.00 - 1.56 winning units..
Owner Sheikh Hamdan Bin Mohammed Al Maktoum **Bred** Mellon Patch, Inc **Trained** Middleham Moor, N Yorks

FOCUS
Two had this race to themselves after two furlongs. The pace was not that quick early.
T/Jkpt: Not won. T/Plt: £29.90 to a £1 stake. Pool: £78,077.00. 1,901.76 winning tickets. T/Qpdt: £5.00 to a £1 stake. Pool: £6,605.14. 965.88 winning tickets. JN

7780 WOLVERHAMPTON (A.W) (L-H)
Tuesday, December 30

OFFICIAL GOING: Standard
Wind: Nil Weather: Fine and cold

7823 PLAY POKER AT LADBROKES.COM MAIDEN AUCTION STKS 7f 32y(P)
6:20 (6:22) (Class 6) 2-Y-O £2,729 (£806; £403) Stalls High

Form	Pos	Dist	Horse / Details	RPR
4	1		**Emeebee**[85] 6534 2-8-12 0 ChrisCatlin 1 (W J Musson) *t.k.h: sn settled in mid-div: hdwy over 1f out: rdn to ld wl ins fnl f: r.o* **7/2**[2]	73
2	2	1	**Sakheart**[12] 7720 2-8-2 0 ow5 AntiocoMurgia(7) 10 (M Botti) *a.p: led jst over 1f out: hdd and nt qckn wl ins fnl f: jst hld on for 2nd* **13/2**[3]	68
0	3	shd	**Mytivil (IRE)**[13] 7708 2-8-6 0 RichardKingscote 7 (Tom Dascombe) *s.i.s: hld up and bhd: hdwy over 1f out: r.o ins fnl f: jst failed to take 2nd* **20/1**	64
602	4	2¼	**Why Nee Amy**[39] 7402 2-8-4 67 LiamJones 9 (Miss Gay Kelleway) *a.p: ev ch jst over 1f out: one pce ins fnl f* **7/1**	57
5	5	nk	**Cloudesley (IRE)**[16] 7674 2-8-11 0 NeilChalmers 4 (A M Balding) *hld up in tch: rdn and one pce ins fnl f* **14/1**	63
0253	6	1¾	**Granny McPhee**[26] 7546 2-8-1 74 NicolPolli(5) 12 (A Bailey) *t.k.h: sn w ldr: led 2f out: rdn and hdd jst over 1f out: wknd wl ins fnl f* **3/1**[1]	54
	7	5	**Esteem Dancer** 2-8-13 0 TPQueally 8 (J G Given) *hld up: hdwy over 5f out: wknd 2f out* **40/1**	49
	8	2½	**Sally's Swansong** 2-8-1 0 DuranFentiman(3) 6 (M Wellings) *s.s: hung lft wl over 1f out: a in rr* **100/1**	33
0	9	1¼	**Missed Mondays**[39] 7402 2-8-4 0 FrankieMcDonald 3 (A Berry) *led: hdd 2f out: rdn and wkng whn hung lft jst over 1f out* **8/1**	30
3	10	1¾	**Kilkenny Bay**[19] 7638 2-8-6 0 HayleyTurner 5 (W Jarvis) *s.i.s: hld up towards rr: no imp whn n.m.r on ins jst over 1f out* **7/2**[2]	28+
	11	4½	**Cruise Control** 2-8-6 0 LukeMorris(3) 11 (R J Price) *s.s: hung bdly rt bnd wl over 2f out: a in rr* **40/1**	20

1m 31.15s (1.55) **Going Correction** +0.10s/f (Slow) **11 Ran SP% 123.7**
Speed ratings (Par 94): **95,93,93,91,90 88,83,80,78,76 71**
toteswinger: 1&2 £22.80, 1&3 £4.60, 2&3 not won. CSF £27.45 TOTE £7.40: £3.50, £2.90, £6.60; EX 52.00.
Owner Broughton Thermal Insulation **Bred** Broughton Bloodstock **Trained** Newmarket, Suffolk

FOCUS
A modest maiden auction event, but several runners did have some kind of form chance and there were two major market movers. The form is not that solid but could be better than this.

NOTEBOOK
Emeebee was the subject of a late gamble that shortened his price from 12-1 to 7-2. He travelled comfortably behind the leaders, was switched wide in the straight and swept into the lead to win with something in hand on his second start. This represents a significant step forward from his promising debut at Warwick in October. The scopey, gelded son of Medicean has clearly been doing some good work at home and should go on to better things. (op 10-1 tchd 12-1)
Sakheart finished clear of the rest when giving a fair start a run for his money at Southwell on her debut this month. She travelled smoothly for a long way switched to Polytrack and posted an improved effort but could not cope with the market springer. (op 11-2 tchd 5-1)
Mytivil(IRE) ◆ looked a bit shell-shocked before getting the hang of things late on her debut this month. There was cause for concern when she sat down in the stalls before this race but she eventually got up, caught the eye staying on strongly from off the pace in the closing stages and seems to have learned a lot from her initial experience. (op 16-1)
Why Nee Amy had left her previous form behind when an unlucky second last time. She had solid form claims and every chance, but could not find an extra gear when she needed it. (op 7-2)
Cloudesley(IRE) never quite got close enough to land a blow but stayed on steadily and confirmed his debut promise. He is a half-brother to some middle-distance winners and should be more strongly competitive over a stiffer test. (op 11-1)
Granny McPhee set the standard on her defeat by a nose over 7f at Chester in September. She got a good early position from stall 12 but was a bit keen and the gamble that shortened her price from 13-2 to 3-1 was derailed early in the straight. (op 13-2 tchd 5-2)

7824 BET AT LADBROKES.COM CLAIMING STKS 1m 141y(P)
6:50 (6:52) (Class 6) 2-Y-O £3,070 (£906; £453) Stalls Low

Form	Pos	Dist	Horse / Details	RPR
450	1		**Mullitovermaurice**[26] 7547 2-8-3 58 HayleyTurner 9 (J G Given) *sn chsng ldr: led over 2f out: rdn over 1f out: sn hung rt: drvn out* **7/1**	59
2450	2	nk	**Betws Y Coed (IRE)**[3] 7789 2-7-7 52 (p) NicolPolli(5) 4 (A Bailey) *hld up and bhd: rdn and hdwy on ins over 2f out: ev ch wl ins fnl f: kpt on* **17/2**	53
1061	3	hd	**True Britannia**[8] 7760 2-8-0 55 (v) NickyMackay 3 (S Kirk) *led early: a.p: rdn and ev ch wl ins fnl f: kpt on* **4/1**[3]	55

0000 **4** ½ **Common Diva**[8] 7760 2-7-13 69 .... LukeMorris(3) 11 56
(A J McCabe) *s.i.s: hld up and bhd: pushed along over 3f out: hung rt bnd wl over 2f out: hung lft 1f out: gd late hdwy: fin wl* **14/1**

0014 **5** nk **Amazing Blue Sky**[4] 7784 2-8-9 63 .... LiamJones 8 62
(Mrs R A Carr) *t.k.h: a.p: rdn and outpcd over 2f out: rallied towards fin* **2/1**[1]

4043 **6** 2½ **Special Bond**[20] 7622 2-8-9 68 ow1 .... ShaneKelly 10 59+
(J A Osborne) *hld up in tch: chal 2f out: rdn and hung lft over 1f out: hmpd ent fnl f: wknd towards fin* **11/4**[2]

400 **7** 4½ **Port De La Ponche**[13] 7708 2-9-2 64 .... ChrisCatlin 5 55
(P F I Cole) *s.i.s: pushed along over 3f out: a bhd* **18/1**

0000 **8** 14 **Red Eric**[17] 7666 2-8-3 35 .... PaulQuinn 6 12
(W M Brisbourne) *sn led: hdd over 2f out: sn wknd* **100/1**

006 **9** 4½ **Ballade De La Mer**[24] 7577 2-7-9 47 .... DuranFentiman(3) 2 —
(A J McCabe) *bhd: rdn over 3f out: sn struggling* **40/1**

1m 52.39s (1.89) **Going Correction** +0.10s/f (Slow) **9** Ran SP% **118.4**
Speed ratings (Par 94): **95,94,94,94,93 91,87,75,71**
toteswinger: 1&2 £23.10, 1&3 £9.30, 2&3 £11.50. CSF £66.40 TOTE £9.00: £2.60, £2.70, £2.10; EX 75.80.True Britannia was claimed by Gary Martin for £6,000.
Owner Joseph Hogan **Bred** Joseph Hogan **Trained** Willoughton, Lincs
■ Hayley Turner became the first woman jockey to ride 100 domestic winners in a season in Britain.

FOCUS
A modest claimer, most of the runners held official ratings between 52 and 69. The placed horses help set a weak level of form.

NOTEBOOK
Mullitovermaurice travelled sweetly into the lead approaching the turn, stuck on gamely, despite veering sharply to the right, and just managed to hold on. The slightly stiffer test and switch to more positive tactics seemed to rekindle his interest on his fourth start. (op 17-2 tchd 10-1)
Betws Y Coed(IRE) had seemed to be going off the boil recently but put in a commendable effort turned out quickly after a modest run in a nursery at Great Leighs three days earlier. It is hard to know if she will repeat this form next time but she may be able to get off the mark in a similar race or in a minor handicap off a current mark of 52. (op 10-1 tchd 11-1 and 8-1)
True Britannia had won two of her last four and was entered on a decent weight here. She stayed on steadily, responded positively to a second-time visor and saw the trip out well. (op 7-2 tchd 9-2)
Common Diva, a 6f maiden winner in the summer, had not been the same force since, and she took a while to get going but eventually stayed on strongly. The step up to an extended 1m seemed to encourage an improved effort. (op 12-1 tchd 16-1)
Amazing Blue Sky attracted a flood of money but took a strong grip, went a bit in snatches and was in serious trouble at an early stage before rallying late. (op 4-1)
Special Bond ran much better than the finishing position suggests. She was hampered by the winner when challenging at the furlong pole, but was under pressure and carrying her head a bit awkwardly at the time, so it is hard to rate her as an unlucky loser. (op 2-1 tchd 7-2)

7825 BET AT LADBROKES ON 0800 777 888 NURSERY — 5f 20y(P)
7:20 (7:20) (Class 5) (0-75,73) 2-Y-O £3,238 (£963; £481; £240) Stalls Low

Form RPR

3321 **1** **Imaginary Diva**[12] 7719 2-8-12 64 .... ChrisCatlin 3 66+
(G G Margarson) *hld up in tch: led jst ins fnl f: drvn out* **5/4**[1]

4566 **2** ¾ **Lucky Dan (IRE)**[21] 7612 2-8-10 62 ow2 .... PaulMulrennan 5 61
(Paul Green) *hld up in tch: pushed along 3f out: rdn and hung lft over 1f out: r.o ins fnl f: tk 2nd cl home: nt rch wnr* **12/1**

0500 **3** ¾ **Cafe Fiore (IRE)**[15] 7687 2-7-5 50 .... (b[1]) MatthewLawson(7) 4 47
(T J Pitt) *t.k.h: w ldr: led jst over 2f out: rdn wl over 1f out: hdd jst ins fnl f: nt qckn: lost 2nd cl home* **14/1**

2003 **4** 1½ **Officer Mor (USA)**[10] 7738 2-8-9 61 .... (b) DarrenWilliams 1 52
(K R Burke) *led: hdd jst over 2f out: rdn wl over 1f out: wknd ins fnl f* **7/4**[2]

0410 **5** 6 **The Cuckoo**[87] 6469 2-9-7 73 .... PatCosgrave 2 43
(M Quinn) *hld up in tch: wknd fnl f* **13/2**[3]

63.68 secs (1.38) **Going Correction** +0.10s/f (Slow) **5** Ran SP% **108.5**
Speed ratings (Par 96): **92,90,89,87,77**
toteswinger: 1&2 £2.70. CSF £15.29 TOTE £1.80: £1.10, £5.10; EX 11.60.
Owner Graham Lodge Partnership **Bred** Norcroft Park Stud **Trained** Newmarket, Suffolk

FOCUS
A modest-looking nursery with the winner on of few on the upgrade.

NOTEBOOK
Imaginary Diva finally got off the mark when winning a nursery against some exposed sorts on her Fibresand debut last time and overcame the potential perils of a small-field tactical affair to follow up off a 3lb higher mark in professional style. She did not have a great deal in hand but should not receive much punishment for this win and may be able to strike again. (op 6-4 tchd 13-8 and 11-10)
Lucky Dan(IRE) was the first in trouble but eventually picked up and did well to get as close to the winner as he did. He is fairly treated and should be suited by an extra furlong but his lack of tactical pace could continue to make things tricky. (op 17-2 tchd 8-1 and 14-1)
Cafe Fiore(IRE) had shown little worthwhile form so far but seemed to be galvanized by the drop back to 5f with a visor swapped for blinkers. She raced enthusiastically up with the pace and kept on quite well after being headed at the furlong pole. (op 12-1 tchd 22-1)
Officer Mor(USA) has taken a fierce grip over 6f and shaped like this drop in trip would suit. He set off in front but started to struggle around the home turn and put in a very disappointing effort. It is possible that the beneficial effect of blinkers has quickly dissolved. (op 11-4)
The Cuckoo was very weak in the market on his debut for a new yard after 87 days off. He sat just behind the pace but found very little when asked for an effort. He may have needed the run but will have some questions to answer next time. (op 10-3)

7826 BETTER PRICES, BIGGER WINS AT LADBROKES.COM H'CAP — 5f 20y(P)
7:50 (7:50) (Class 4) (0-85,85) 3-Y-O+ £5,046 (£1,510; £755; £377; £188) Stalls Low

Form RPR

41 **1** **Ivory Silk**[40] 7393 3-8-13 80 .... (b) ChrisCatlin 1 91
(J R Gask) *hld up in mid-div: hdwy wl over 1f out: led ins fnl f: hrd rdn: r.o* **9/2**[2]

2214 **2** ½ **Little Edward**[9] 7756 10-9-4 85 .... GeorgeBaker 2 94
(R J Hodges) *a.p: ev ch 1f out: r.o: jst hld on for 2nd* **4/1**[1]

0021 **3** shd **Northern Empire (IRE)**[11] 7733 5-8-7 74 .... HayleyTurner 4 83
(K A Ryan) *hld up towards rr: hung rt bnd over 2f out: rdn and hdwy 1f out: r.o: jst failed to take 2nd* **4/1**[1]

0015 **4** ½ **Canadian Danehill (IRE)**[14] 7697 6-8-12 79 .... (p) ShaneKelly 9 86
(R M H Cowell) *w ldr: led over 1f out: rdn and hdd ins fnl f: nt qckn* **14/1**

6541 **5** 1 **The Tatling (IRE)**[14] 7697 11-8-11 83 .... JackDean(5) 6 86
(J M Bradley) *hld up in mid-div: kpt on same pce ins fnl f* **5/1**[3]

2045 **6** 1¼ **Bishopbriggs (USA)**[11] 7733 3-8-4 71 oh6 .... (tp) LiamJones 5 70
(S Parr) *prom tl: wknd wl over 1f out* **22/1**

0152 **7** ½ **Sands Crooner (IRE)**[24] 7584 5-8-11 78 .... (v) TPQueally 8 75
(J G Given) *s.i.s: towards rr: rdn and hdwy on ins over 1f out: wknd wl ins fnl f* **8/1**

0000 **8** 3¼ **Vhujon (IRE)**[14] 7697 3-9-3 84 .... TGMcLaughlin 7 69
(P D Evans) *in rr: struggling whn rn wd ent st* **16/1**

0006 **9** 1¾ **Almaty Express**[24] 7584 6-8-10 77 .... (b) JimCrowley 3 56
(J R Weymes) *led: hdd over 1f out: wknd ins fnl f* **9/1**

61.50 secs (-0.80) **Going Correction** +0.10s/f (Slow) **9** Ran SP% **112.9**
Speed ratings (Par 105): **110,109,109,108,106 104,103,98,95**
toteswinger: 1&2 £2.70, 1&3 £1.90, 2&3 £5.00. CSF £22.26 CT £76.31 TOTE £6.30: £2.20, £1.90, £1.40; EX 24.60.
Owner Richard L Page **Bred** K T Ivory **Trained** Sutton Veny, Wilts

FOCUS
A competitive handicap involving three last-time-out winners. It was run at a strong pace and produced an exciting finish.

7827 PLAY BINGO AT LADBROKES.COM H'CAP — 2m 119y(P)
8:20 (8:20) (Class 5) (0-70,68) 3-Y-O+ £3,154 (£944; £472; £236; £117) Stalls Low

Form RPR

2201 **1** **Zuwaar**[24] 7587 3-9-5 64 .... (t) JimCrowley 9 73
(Ian Williams) *hld up in rr: smooth prog on outside over 3f out: led and hung lft fr over 1f out: styd on* **7/2**[1]

3350 **2** 1½ **Squirtle (IRE)**[34] 7455 5-9-5 59 .... LukeMorris(3) 5 66
(W M Brisbourne) *hld up towards rr: hdwy over 3f out: rdn over 1f out: wnt 2nd ins fnl f: carried lft: nt qckn* **20/1**

6001 **3** 1 **Spume (IRE)**[3] 7787 4-9-3 54 6ex .... (t) AdamKirby 4 60
(S Parr) *hld up in rr: hdwy over 2f out: rdn jst over 1f out: hld whn n.m.r on ins towards fin* **7/1**

0030 **4** 2¼ **Daraiym (IRE)**[7] 7775 3-8-5 50 .... RichardKingscote 1 53
(Paul Green) *hld up in mid-div: rdn over 2f out: hdwy whn edgd lft jst over 1f out: nt rch ldrs* **25/1**

1055 **5** 2¼ **Dramatic Solo**[47] 7296 3-9-9 68 .... (b) AndrewElliott 7 69
(K R Burke) *a.p: led wl over 3f out tl jst over 2f out: sn rdn: wknd ins fnl f* **17/2**

0201 **6** hd **Snowberry Hill (USA)**[29] 7512 5-9-6 57 .... NeilChalmers 6 57
(Lucinda Featherstone) *hld up in mid-div: hdwy 5f out: led jst over 2f out: rdn and hdd over 1f out: wknd ins fnl f* **8/1**

4 **7** 3¼ **Daytime Dreamer (IRE)**[29] 7512 4-9-13 64 .... (t) ShaneKelly 2 60
(Conor O'Dwyer, Ire) *hld up in tch: rdn over 2f out: wknd wl over 1f out: hung lft ins fnl f* **6/1**[2]

0650 **8** 11 **Synonymy**[34] 7455 5-8-9 46 oh1 .... (b) HayleyTurner 11 29
(M Blanshard) *hld up towards rr: no ch fnl 3f* **20/1**

6124 **9** 4 **Pseudonym (IRE)**[18] 7455 6-10-0 65 .... (t) SteveDrowne 8 43
(M F Harris) *led after 1f: hdd wl over 3f out: rdn and wkng whn n.m.r on ins over 2f out* **14/1**

32 **10** hd **Special Pearl (IRE)**[12] 7715 4-10-0 65 .... ChrisCatlin 10 43
(E J O'Neill) *sn chsng ldr: wknd over 3f out: fin lame* **13/2**[3]

0-01 **11** 4½ **Amron Hill**[7] 7775 5-9-0 54 6ex .... RussellKennemore(3) 3 27
(R Hollinshead) *led 1f: prom tl rdn and wknd over 3f out* **13/2**[3]

3m 42.83s (1.03) **Going Correction** +0.10s/f (Slow)
WFA 3 from 4yo+ 8lb **11** Ran SP% **117.3**
Speed ratings (Par 103): **101,100,99,98,97 97,96,90,89,88 86**
toteswinger: 1&2 £29.10, 1&3 £10.40, 2&3 £29.10. CSF £81.24 CT £471.05 TOTE £4.50: £1.60, £5.30, £4.00; EX 66.40.
Owner Dr Marwan Koukash **Bred** Shadwell Estate Company Limited **Trained** Portway, Worcs
■ Stewards' Enquiry : Jim Crowley two-day ban: careless riding (Jan 13-14)

FOCUS
A fair handicap involving several in-form runners and a vibrant market. The early pace was steady.

7828 PLAY POKER AT LADBROKES.COM H'CAP — 5f 216y(P)
8:50 (8:50) (Class 4) (0-85,84) 3-Y-O+ £5,046 (£1,510; £755; £377; £188) Stalls Low

Form RPR

3032 **1** **Dvinsky (USA)**[9] 7756 7-8-13 79 .... (b) PaulDoe 8 88
(P Howling) *pushed along to sn ld: hung lft fnl f: r.o* **6/1**

034 **2** nk **Silvanus (IRE)**[40] 7393 3-8-6 72 .... ChrisCatlin 1 80
(I Semple) *t.k.h in rr: hdwy ins fnl f: r.o: nt rch wnr* **9/2**[3]

1306 **3** ½ **Yungaburra (IRE)**[3] 7793 4-9-4 84 .... (bt) AdamKirby 3 90
(S Parr) *s.i.s: hld up: hdwy wl over 1f out: wnt 2nd ins fnl f: rdn and nt qckn* **5/2**[2]

4 hd **Mrs Penny (AUS)**[295] 4-9-0 80 .... SteveDrowne 4 86
(J R Gask) *hld up: hdwy on outside over 2f out: rdn jst over 1f out: kpt on ins fnl f* **10/1**

5006 **5** 1 **Memphis Man**[14] 7697 5-8-4 75 .... PatrickDonaghy(5) 7 78
(P D Evans) *t.k.h: prom: rdn and btn over 1f out* **14/1**

6022 **6** ½ **Ravi River (IRE)**[8] 7763 4-8-4 70 .... RichardKingscote 6 71
(Tom Dascombe) *led early: chsd wnr: rdn over 1f out: wknd ins fnl f* **15/8**[1]

1m 15.97s (0.97) **Going Correction** +0.10s/f (Slow) **6** Ran SP% **111.6**
Speed ratings (Par 105): **97,96,95,95,94 93**
toteswinger: 1&2 £1.90, 1&3 £11.30, 2&3 £4.40. CSF £31.91 CT £82.36 TOTE £4.50: £2.60, £2.40; EX 18.20.
Owner Richard Berenson **Bred** Eclipse Bloodstock & Tipperary Bloodstock **Trained** Newmarket, Suffolk

FOCUS
A reasonable handicap but the pace was muddling and the hold-up horses looked at a disadvantage, so the form may not work out.

7829 BET AT LADBROKES.COM H'CAP — 7f 32y(P)
9:20 (9:21) (Class 5) (0-70,70) 3-Y-O+ £3,238 (£963; £481; £240) Stalls High

Form RPR

5212 **1** **Balata**[8] 7764 3-8-13 65 .... TGMcLaughlin 4 75
(B R Millman) *hld up in mid-div: hdwy over 1f out: rdn to ld last strides* **7/2**[1]

5130 **2** hd **Kensington (IRE)**[11] 7730 7-8-13 70 .... PatrickDonaghy(5) 7 79
(P D Evans) *hld up in mid-div: hdwy on outside 2f out: led over 1f out: sn hung lft: hdd last strides* **20/1**

1300 **3** nk **Strabinios King**[16] 7677 4-9-0 66 .... JimCrowley 6 74
(M Wigham) *n.m.r s: hld up in rr: hdwy on outside over 1f out: rdn and edgd lft ins fnl f: r.o* **6/1**

612 **4** 2¾ **This Ones For Eddy**[14] 7698 3-9-4 70 .... AdamKirby 5 71
(S Parr) *hld up in rr: hdwy 1f out: rdn and kpt on one pce ins fnl f* **9/2**[2]

2301 **5** ½ **A Big Sky Brewing (USA)**[101] 6132 4-8-12 69 .... (b) DeanHeslop(5) 10 68
(T D Barron) *sn led: hdd over 5f out: prom: rdn over 1f out: one pce* **9/1**

2610 **6** shd **Romantic Verse**[75] 6749 3-9-2 68 .... ShaneKelly 8 67
(E S McMahon) *hld up in tch: hung lft over 1f out: rdn and no ex ins fnl f* **16/1**

4000 **7** ¾ **Liberty Valance (IRE)**[2] 7803 3-8-6 58 .... (t) RichardKingscote 2 55
(S Kirk) *hld up in rr: hdwy on ins whn nt clr run 1f out: nt rcvr* **7/1**

4 **8** *3 ½* **Topenhall (IRE)**[15] 7686 7-8-13 **65**........................ PatCosgrave 12 53
(Daniel O'Connell, Ire) *t.k.h: led over 5f out tl over 2f out: hrd rdn over 1f out: wknd fnl f* **11/1**

0412 **9** *3* **Tri Chara (IRE)**[10] 7745 4-8-12 **64**........................(p) HayleyTurner 9 44
(R Hollinshead) *plld hrd: prom tl wknd wl over 1f out* **11/2**[3]

0012 **10** *1* **Gainshare**[17] 7671 3-8-11 **63**........................ LiamJones 11 40
(Mrs R A Carr) *plld hrd: sn prom: led over 2f out tl over 1f out: sn wknd* **20/1**

0040 **11** *½* **Chookie Heiton (IRE)**[18] 7651 10-8-10 **62**................ PaulMulrennan 1 38
(I Semple) *led early: lost pl over 4f out: hdwy wl over 1f out: nt clr run ent fnl f: nt rcvr* **33/1**

1m 29.31s (-0.29) **Going Correction** +0.10s/f (Slow) 11 Ran SP% **119.3**
Speed ratings (Par 103): **105,104,104,101,100 100,99,95,92,91 90**
toteswinger: 1&2 £22.10, 1&3 £5.00, 2&3 £16.00. CSF £79.92 CT £415.77 TOTE £5.10: £1.50, £7.90, £3.20; EX 111.50 Place 6: £207.54, Place 5: £64.49..
Owner The Links Partnership **Bred** Charlock Farm Stud **Trained** Kentisbeare, Devon

FOCUS
The early pace was only moderate, but the first three pulled clear of the rest and the form could be reliable.
T/Plt: £128.90 to a £1 stake. Pool: £130,196.00. 737.22 winning tickets. T/Qpdt: £13.70 to a £1 stake. Pool: £10,169.07. 547.05 winning tickets. KH

7816 LINGFIELD (L-H)
Wednesday, December 31

OFFICIAL GOING: Standard
Wind: Light, against Weather: Dull

7830 WILLIAM HILL JANUARY SALE - WHY BET ELSEWHERE? MEDIAN AUCTION MAIDEN STKS 7f (P)
12:00 (12:00) (Class 6) 2-Y-O **£2,047** (£604; £302) **Stalls** Low

Form RPR

62 **1** **Dimander (IRE)**[14] 7709 2-9-3 0........................ JimCrowley 9 72+
(Mrs A J Perrett) *prom: rdn 3f out: drvn to ld fnl 100yds: hld on a shade comf* **13/8**[1]

05 **2** *nk* **Maswerte (IRE)**[9] 7769 2-9-3 0........................ DaneO'Neill 7 71
(L M Cumani) *chsd ldrs: led over 1f out: hdd and hld by wnr fnl 100yds* **7/2**[2]

0323 **3** *2* **Today's The Day**[9] 7769 2-8-12 70........................(b) NCallan 5 61
(M A Jarvis) *s.s: sn in rr of main gp: hdwy to chse ldng pair 1f out: one pce ins fnl f* **5/1**

4043 **4** *¾* **Lujeanie**[33] 7468 2-9-3 64........................(p) GeorgeBaker 2 64
(D K Ivory) *sn w ldr: led after 2f: hdd over 1f out: hung rt and faltered: sn btn: kpt on again fnl 100yds* **14/1**

0 **5** *2 ¾* **Bickersten**[26] 7554 2-9-3 0........................ TonyCulhane 4 58
(M R Channon) *outpcd and bhd: pushed along and styd on fnl 2f: nvr nrr* **16/1**

0 **6** *2* **Mrs Slocombe (IRE)**[155] 4513 2-8-12 0........................ IanMongan 8 48
(J Akehurst) *in tch tl wknd and hung lft ent st* **22/1**

6 **7** *5* **Jaq's Sister**[132] 5200 2-8-12 0........................ AdamKirby 1 35
(M Blanshard) *s.i.s: outpcd and detached last: nvr a factor* **66/1**

6 **8** *½* **Hatman Jack (IRE)**[9] 7767 2-9-3 0........................ MichaelHills 3 39
(B G Powell) *led 2f: prom tl wknd ent st* **9/2**[3]

0 **9** *13* **Dependonyou**[12] 7735 2-8-12 0........................(p) JamesDoyle 6 —
(A J McCabe) *in tch on rail: rdn and wknd over 3f out: wl bhd whn eased fnl f* **100/1**

1m 24.35s (-0.45) **Going Correction** -0.075s/f (Stan) 9 Ran SP% **114.5**
Speed ratings (Par 94): **99,98,96,95,92 90,84,83,68**
toteswinger: 1&2 £2.90, 1&3 £2.20, 2&3 £4.00. CSF £7.17 TOTE £2.60: £1.20, £1.40, £1.70; EX 8.50 Trifecta £27.80 Pool of £645.96 - 27.80 winning units..
Owner Lady Clague **Bred** Newberry Stud Company **Trained** Pulborough, W Sussex

FOCUS
With a couple of big-name stables represented and the highest-rated horse having an official rating of 70, this was probably not a bad maiden for the time of the year and the fourth helps set the level with the winner likley to do better.

NOTEBOOK
Dimander(IRE) showed plenty of promise on his debut in November and then went very close to getting off the mark over this course and distance last time just before Christmas. His jockey rushed him up early to get prominent but space became limited rounding the final bend. However, a parting Moses would have been proud of opened up for him entering the home straight and, after being made to knuckle down, he did just enough to gain victory. A lazy looking type, he will be put away now and brought back for races at about a mile on turf. (op 9-4)
Maswerte(IRE) was a place behind Dimander on his debut and built on that effort with a fair effort next time, despite hanging under pressure, when a place behind Today's The Day. Close up throughout from a handy draw, he hit the front just over a furlong out but could not resist the late thrust of the winner. He also seems sure to benefit from a stiffer test.
Today's The Day has continually found it difficult to get her head in front and was stepping back up in trip after a couple of attempts at 6f. Very slowly away, she did not always get the best of runs, but it is probably fair to presume that she will usually find a way to get beaten, as she hardly looked to be trying her hardest under pressure. (op 9-2 tchd 11-2)
Lujeanie, taking a drop in trip, caught the eye on his last couple of starts but was largely ignored in the betting for this. Cheekpieces were fitted for this run, but he shied away from the inside rail turning in when in front and then hung into the middle of the course inside the final furlong when given a slap by his rider. (op 12-1 tchd 10-1)
Bickersten ◆, who attracted market support, ran green in the early stages, but he caught the eye inside the final two furlongs under considerate riding - his jockey reported he hung right. If he is progressing mentally for his experiences on the course, it should not be long before he goes much closer. (op 33-1)
Mrs Slocombe(IRE) ran one good race for previous connections in Ireland, but was thrashed on both her other outings. She ran with some promise in this until being outpaced off the final bend. One would imagine her shrewd connections will find the right opportunities for her. (op 20-1)
Jaq's Sister
Hatman Jack(IRE) attracted market support on his debut last week but never looked like landing the money after starting slowly. Punters were not so keen this time, as he drifted before the off, and after being prominent early he dropped away quickly under pressure. (op 10-3)

7831 WILLIAM HILL JANUARY SALE - BONUSES GALORE! (S) STKS 1m 4f (P)
12:30 (12:30) (Class 6) 3-Y-O+ **£1,978** (£584; £292) **Stalls** Low

Form RPR

0016 **1** **Wind Flow**[14] 7711 4-9-8 68........................(b) CatherineGannon 3 59
(C A Dwyer) *mde all: rdn over 2f out: hld on wl u.p fnl f* **2/1**[1]

0000 **2** *1 ½* **Poppy Red**[12] 7736 3-8-1 42........................(p) AndrewHeffernan(7) 6 48
(C J Gray) *chsd wnr 2f: prom: rdn to dispute 2nd fnl f: kpt on* **100/1**

0305 **3** *nse* **Nawamees (IRE)**[11] 7744 10-9-8 73........................(p) NCallan 8 57
(P D Evans) *chsd ldrs: drvn to dispute 2nd fnl f: kpt on* **2/1**[1]

2050 **4** *nse* **Shouldntbethere (IRE)**[21] 7626 4-8-11 51........................ NBazeley(7) 4 53
(Mrs P N Dutfield) *hld up and bhd: hdwy 2f out: rdn and r.o appr fnl f: nrst fin* **33/1**

0064 **5** *1 ¾* **Obrigado (USA)**[1] 7816 8-9-8 66........................(t) GeorgeBaker 10 54
(G L Moore) *stdd s: hld up in last: hdwy on outside 3f out: rdn and edgd lft over 1f out: styd on: nvr finding enough* **8/1**[2]

0060 **6** *nse* **Competitor**[4] 7792 7-9-8 46........................(b) DaneO'Neill 9 54
(J Akehurst) *hdwy to chse wnr after 2f: hrd rdn and wknd 1f out* **33/1**

0056 **7** *hd* **Fateful Attraction**[24] 7590 5-8-13 50........................(b) PaulDoe 7 45
(I A Wood) *dwlt: t.k.h towards rr: effrt over 2f out: styd on same pce: nvr able to chal* **16/1**

0036 **8** *½* **Turner's Touch**[30] 7512 6-9-1 56........................(b) JemmaMarshall(7) 1 53
(G L Moore) *hld up towards rr: hdwy on rail and in tch over 1f out: hrd rdn and no ex ins fnl f* **16/1**

1000 **9** *5* **Crispian (IRE)**[34] 7085 4-9-8 56........................(t) FergusSweeney 5 45
(Jamie Snowden) *mid-div: rdn 3f out: sn outpcd* **22/1**

0062 **10** *4* **Daring Racer (GER)**[14] 7707 5-9-4 55........................(p) IanMongan 11 34
(Mrs L J Mongan) *in tch: wnt 3rd over 3f out: wknd 2f out* **9/1**[3]

0660 **11** *hd* **Champagne Shadow (IRE)**[25] 7587 7-9-8 50................(p) ChrisCatlin 2 38
(J Pearce) *chsd ldrs tl wknd over 4f out* **10/1**

2m 33.66s (0.66) **Going Correction** -0.075s/f (Stan)
WFA 3 from 4yo+ 5lb 11 Ran SP% **119.9**
Speed ratings (Par 101): **94,93,92,92,91 91,91,91,87,85 85**
toteswinger: 1&2 £38.20, 1&3 £2.00, 2&3 £35.50. CSF £323.12 TOTE £2.90: £1.20, £12.90, £1.50; EX 402.00 TRIFECTA Not won..There was no bid for the winner.
Owner Super Six Partnership **Bred** Lord Halifax **Trained** Burrough Green, Cambs

FOCUS
Plenty of old characters in this seller, in which the winner was allowed to set his own, fairly steady pace. Nothing got into the race from the rear and the form should be treated with some caution.

7832 WILLIAM HILL JANUARY SALE - ENHANCED FAVOURITES! NURSERY (DIV I) 7f (P)
1:00 (1:01) (Class 6) (0-60,60) 2-Y-O **£1,706** (£503; £252) **Stalls** Low

Form RPR

6035 **1** **Cut And Thrust (IRE)**[43] 7372 2-9-7 **60**........................(p) NCallan 10 72+
(M A Jarvis) *in tch: effrt over 2f out: led 1f out: rdn clr* **7/2**[2]

4346 **2** *2 ¾* **Imperial Skylight**[27] 7547 2-9-4 **57**........................ TonyCulhane 6 61
(M R Channon) *hld up in midfield: effrt over 2f out: wnt 3rd and hung lft over 1f out: styd on to take 2nd ins fnl f* **4/1**[3]

5504 **3** *1 ¾* **Itsher**[52] 7257 2-9-3 **56**........................ JimCrowley 8 56
(S C Williams) *led over 2f: led over 2f out tl 1f out: no ex* **13/2**

5666 **4** *3* **Flawless Diamond (IRE)**[63] 7065 2-8-12 **54**..............(p) LukeMorris(3) 1 46
(J S Moore) *dwlt: sn in midfield: rdn and outpcd 2f out: kpt on fnl f* **16/1**

043 **5** *nk* **Captain Walcot**[33] 7467 2-9-7 **60**........................(b) GeorgeBaker 3 51
(R Hannon) *trckd ldrs on rail: outpcd 2f out: sn btn* **11/4**[1]

5005 **6** *¾* **Tricky Trev (USA)**[42] 7454 2-9-6 **59**........................(b) PaulDoe 4 49
(S Curran) *chsd ldrs tl hrd rdn and wknd over 1f out* **8/1**

44 **7** *2* **Turn To Dreams**[9] 7760 2-8-8 **47**........................ LiamJones 11 32
(P D Evans) *towards rr: pushed along over 3f out: n.d* **14/1**

000 **8** *¾* **Ma Patrice**[37] 7434 2-8-11 **50**........................ AdamKirby 9 33
(T D McCarthy) *hld up and bhd: pushed along over 2f out: nvr trbld ldrs* **66/1**

5000 **9** *1 ½* **Redhead (IRE)**[19] 7652 2-9-2 **55**........................(b[1]) DaneO'Neill 2 34
(R Hannon) *sn chsng ldr: led over 4f out tl over 2f out: sn wknd* **16/1**

0500 **10** *2 ½* **Indian Blade (IRE)**[39] 7425 2-8-7 **46**........................(v[1]) HayleyTurner 5 19
(M D I Usher) *nvr gng wl: a bhd* **33/1**

0300 **11** *18* **Tobizzy**[27] 7542 2-8-6 **45**........................ NickyMackay 7 —
(J R Jenkins) *prom to 1/2-way: sn lost pl* **66/1**

1m 24.14s (-0.66) **Going Correction** -0.075s/f (Stan) 11 Ran SP% **117.7**
Speed ratings (Par 94): **100,96,94,91,91 90,87,87,85,82 61**
toteswinger: 1&2 £5.20, 1&3 £6.10, 2&3 £9.80. CSF £17.84 CT £86.86 TOTE £4.20: £2.00, £1.40, £2.80; EX 26.00 Trifecta £134.10 Pool of £427.69 - 2.36 winning units..
Owner A D Spence **Bred** Bloomsbury Stud **Trained** Newmarket, Suffolk

FOCUS
The first division of the nursery looked a tricky affair to sort out. Most of them came into the race at the top of their game, such as that was, so the form should be fairly reliable at this level and is worth being positive about. The time was more than two seconds quicker than the second division.

NOTEBOOK
Cut And Thrust(IRE), whose last two runs had been on Fibresand, only had one piece of form that saw him go remotely close to winning before and was very weak in the market. However, that did not prevent him from winning in good style after receiving a perfect ride. One would imagine that the rise in the weights he will get for landing this race is going to be tough for him to overcome. (op 11-4 tchd 5-2 and 4-1)
Imperial Skylight, who had plenty of experience behind him and was well backed just before the off, sat just behind a wall of horses early, going strongly. He followed the winner through off the final bend but showed no acceleration and could not close down the gap. He might be better served by being closer to the pace next time. (op 7-1 tchd 8-1)
Itsher had shown promise on all of her previous starts and once again ran well. She was in front as the field turned in but did not stay there for long, as the first two swept past her well over a furlong out. Under strong pressure, she stayed on resolutely to finish a clear third. (op 7-1)
Flawless Diamond(IRE) finished well but had absolutely no chance of being involved in the finish from her starting point on the inside rail as she was behind horses over two furlongs out. It is impossible to know whether the first-time cheekpieces had any effect. (op 18-1 tchd 20-1)
Captain Walcot, dropped in trip, had improved since having blinkers fitted and may have gone much closer if a gap had opened up down the inside rail when he needed one. However, that was never likely to happen and the jockey was forced to wait until pulling his mount outwards, losing valuable ground in the process. The response by the horse was virtually zero when he was asked to quicken and he never got involved. (op 3-1 tchd 10-3 and 5-2)
Tricky Trev(USA) ran quite well in first-time blinkers last time and was moved up in trip for this. He ran his race but did not seem obviously suited by the extra furlong. (op 15-2 tchd 7-1)
Redhead(IRE) was never in the race and his jockey reported it was because the filly did not face the blinkers early. (tchd 18-1, tchd 20-1 in a place)

7833 WILLIAM HILL JANUARY SALE - ENHANCED FAVOURITES! NURSERY (DIV II) 7f (P)
1:30 (1:32) (Class 6) (0-60,60) 2-Y-O **£1,706** (£503; £252) **Stalls** Low

Form RPR

0065 **1** **Mr Willis**[33] 7475 2-9-5 **58**........................ SteveDrowne 1 63+
(J R Best) *trckd ldrs: rdn to ld 1f out: r.o wl: readily* **11/10**[1]

6001 **2** *1 ½* **Song Of Praise**[33] 7472 2-9-7 **60**........................ DaneO'Neill 7 61
(M Blanshard) *t.k.h: in tch: effrt and wd st: styd on to take 2nd ins fnl f* **13/2**

0612 **3** *¾* **Deckchair**[27] 7543 2-8-13 **57**........................(v) AmyBaker(5) 10 56
(H J Collingridge) *hld up towards rr: rdn and r.o fnl 2f: nrst fin* **11/2**[3]

0006 **4** *¾* **Nun Today (USA)**[19] 7652 2-8-8 **50**........................(p) LukeMorris(3) 6 48
(J S Moore) *led over 1f: w ldr: led 2f out tl 1f out: no ex* **12/1**

Admiral Sandhoe (USA) *Mrs A J Perrett* 77
2 ch c Diesis—Dancing Sea (USA) (Storm Cat (USA))
4184[6] 4720[5] 4974[3] 5459[3] 6198[3] 6892[5]

Admiral Savannah (IRE) *T D Easterby* 51
4 b g Dilshaan—Valmarana (USA) (Danzig Connection (USA))
6550[8]

Admirals Way *C N Kellett* a61 65
3 ch g Observatory(USA) —Dockage (CAN) (Riverman (USA))
595[8] 797[7] 876[2] 1120[4] 1315[11] 1743[6] 2126[2] (2549) 3031[2] 3442[7] 4061[6] 4524[3] 4920[4] 5312[2] 5836[5] 6116[4] 6685[6]

Admiral Troy *M D I Usher* a43
3 b c Umistim—Troia (IRE) (Last Tycoon)
645[7] 820[7] 953[8]

Admire Aura (JPN) *H Matsuda* 120
4 b h Agnes Tachyon(JPN) —Biwa Heidi (JPN) (Caerleon (USA))
1090a[9]

Admire Monarch (JPN) *H Matsuda* 122
7 b h Dream Well(FR) —Split The Night (JPN) (Tony Bin)
7511a[12]

Admiring Glances *J Pearce* a46 50
2 b f Green Tune(USA) —Follow The Girl (FR) (Saumarez)
6559[9] 6884[8] 7164[3] 7415[8] 7547[12] 7693[11]

Adolfina (GER) *W Figge* 104
3 b f Sholokhov(IRE) —Akilinda (FR) (Monsun (GER))
(5737a) 7350a[4]

Adorabella (IRE) *A King* a71 77
5 b m Revoque(IRE) —Febrile (USA) (Trempolino (USA))
2641[4] 3311[2] 3843[6] 4183[3] 4568[5] (5232) 5476[4] 6203[5]

Adored (IRE) *A P O'Brien* 111
3 b f Galileo(IRE) —Sudden Hope (FR) (Darshaan)
(2113a) 2792[15] 4006a[6] 5952a[5] ◆ 6495a[12]

Adorn *J Noseda* a85 104
2 b f Kyllachy—Red Tiara (USA) (Mr Prospector (USA))
5271[4] ◆ (5673) ◆ 6441[4]

Adozen Dreams *G R Oldroyd* a54 62
2 b f Monsieur Bond(IRE) —Chicago Bond (USA) (Real Quiet (USA))
1324[6] 3005[7] 3437[4] (3788) 4558[5] 5834[6] 6350[12] 7113[4] 7361[10]

Adragon (ITY) *L Mariani* 94
2 b c Denon(USA) —Ambiziosa (IRE) (Bluebird (USA))
7253a[4]

A Dream Come True *D K Ivory* a68 64
3 b f Where Or When(IRE) —Katy Ivory (IRE) (Night Shift (USA))
419[5] (547) ◆ (665) 5146[5] 5472[11]

Adriano (USA) *H Graham Motion* a102 102
3 ch c A.P. Indy(USA) —Gold Canyon (USA) (Mr Prospector (USA))
1820a[19]

Adriatic *Michael Mulvany* a69 70
8 ch g Bahamian Bounty—Veuve Hoornaert (IRE) (Standaan (FR))
6366a[27]

Advanced *K A Ryan* a96 119
5 b g Night Shift(USA) —Wonderful World (GER) (Dashing Blade)
959[13] 1420[5] 1986[5] 2580[4] 3722[2] 5259[2] 6104[13] 6304[14] 6903[7] 7245[14] 7325a[4]

Adversity *Sir Michael Stoute* a80 98
3 b c Oasis Dream—Tuxford Hideaway (Cawston's Clown)
1524[2] 1923[5] 3039[8] (3475) 4553[8] 5495[6]

Advertise *A M Balding* 74
2 b g Passing Glance—Averami (Averti (IRE))
2324[6] ◆ (5364) 5791[14]

Advice *S Seemar* a77 96
7 b g Seeking The Gold(USA) —Anna Palariva (IRE) (Caerleon (USA))
739a[5] 818a[11]

Advice (USA) *Todd Pletcher* a92
2 bb c Chapel Royal(USA) —Word O' Wisdom (USA) (Hennessy (USA))
6503a[9]

Advisor (FR) *M L W Bell* 72
2 gr c Anabaa(USA) —Armilina (FR) (Linamix (FR))
6580[6] 7080[5]

Aegean Dancer *B Smart* a105 102
6 b g Piccolo—Aegean Flame (Anshan)
5[4] ◆ 2129[10] 2390[2] 4240[6] 4445[13] 6290[12] 6653[13] 6971[16] 7151[7]

Aegean Pride *R Hannon* a62 62
3 b f Sakhee(USA) —Aegean Dream (IRE) (Royal Academy (USA))
4277[12] 5023[3] 5608[5] 6356[10] 6867[9] 7436[4] 7591[6]

Aegean Prince *R Hannon* a86 86
4 b g Dr Fong(USA) —Dizzydaisy (Sharpo)
1682[8] 1874[2] 2153[6] 2540[5] 2895[3] 3449[3] (3802) 4155[6] 4645[5] 5699[7] 7314[9] (7558)

Aegean Warning *K A Ryan* a62 63
2 b c Reset(AUS) —Aegean Blue (Warning)
2746[6] 3055[3] 3411[12] 4079[3] 4340[6] 4733[5] 5870[7] 6343[3]

Aerach (USA) *J S Bolger* a59 65
2 ch f Speightstown(USA) —Rhiana (USA) (Runaway Groom (CAN))
4804a[5]

Aeroplane *S A Callaghan* a101 99
5 b h Danehill Dancer(IRE) —Anita At Dawn (IRE) (Anita's Prince)
1420[10] 1989[3] 3247[15] 4059[6] 5095[9] 6484[8] 6975[8] 7470[3] 7737[2] (7804)

Aestival *Sir Mark Prescott* a46 28
2 b g Falbrav(IRE) —Summer Night (Nashwan (USA))
6051[15] 6407[6] 6879[9]

Affair (FR) *P Rau* 86
3 b f Montjeu(IRE) —Amicella (Laroche (GER))
4675a[14]

Affirmatively *A W Carroll* a69 68
3 b f Diktat—Circlet (Lion Cavern (USA))
355[3] 538[5] 899[5] 1671[10] 1867[7] 5617[10] 6190[12] 6679[10] 7195[6] 7416[11]

Affluent *R Charlton* 74
2 b f Oasis Dream—Valencia (Kenmare (FR))
(7082)

Affrettando (IRE) *J A R Toller* a67 65
4 b g Danetime(IRE) —Trading Aces (Be My Chief (USA))
1491[3] 3116[7] 4081[11] 5755[3] 6211[8]

Aflaam (IRE) *J H M Gosden* 86
3 b c Dubai Destination(USA) —Arjuzah (IRE) (Ahonoora)
4161[3] (4606)

Afram Blue *W J Knight* a79 70
3 b g Fraam—Tup Tim (Emperor Jones (USA))
1868[6] 2276[9] 2974[13] 4731[7] 5086[5] 5576[4] 5994[8] (6400) 6719[8] 7009[4]

Afrashad (USA) *Saeed Bin Suroor* a96
6 ch h Smoke Glacken(USA) —Flo White (USA) (Whitesburg (USA))
814a[15]

African Appeal (SAF) *M F De Kock* 112
7 b g Model Man(SAF) —Kentucky Lass (SAF) (Kentucky Slew (USA))
474a[5] ◆ 671a[7] 818a[16]

African Art (USA) *B J Meehan* 66
2 ch c Johannesburg(USA) —Perovskia (USA) (Stravinsky (USA))
7106[4]

African Blues *D J S Ffrench Davis* 41
5 ch g College Chapel—Pearl Dawn (IRE) (Jareer (USA))
1533[8] ◆

African Pursuits (USA) *Jamie Poulton* a51 68
4 b g Johannesburg(USA) —Woodland Orchid (IRE) (Woodman (USA))
1932[5] 2365[5] (2932) 3344[4]

African Rose *Mme C Head-Maarek* 116
3 ch f Observatory(USA) —New Orchid (USA) (Quest For Fame)
3357a[4] 4915a[2] (5891) 6496a[7]

African Skies *K A Ryan* 100
2 b f Johannesburg(USA) —Rababah (USA) (Woodman (USA))
2627[2] ◆ 3192[4] ◆ (4403) 5272[6] 6519a[12]

Africa's Star (IRE) *M A Jarvis* a56 67
2 br f Johannesburg(USA) —Grable (IRE) (Sadler's Wells (USA))
2160[6] 3495[4] 4337[8] 7417[4] 7612[4]

After The Show *Rae Guest* a73 80
7 b g Royal Applause—Tango Teaser (Shareef Dancer (USA))
187[3] 459[5] 746[5] 875[7] (994) (1189) (1366) 1739[3] 2166[4] 2644[7] 7182[9] 7471[5] ◆ 7743[2] ◆

Afton View (IRE) *S Parr* a64 64
3 gr g Clodovil(IRE) —Moonlight Partner (IRE) (Red Sunset)
321[5] 785[5] 803[8] 980[5] 2189[11] 3952[7] 4107[12] 4702[2] 4952[3] 5223[7] 7255[4] 7414[3] 7509[7] 7765[5] 7809[10]

Again (IRE) *David Wachman* 110
2 b f Danehill Dancer(IRE) —Cumbres (FR) (Kahyasi)
(5132a) (5549a) 6519a[14]

Against The Grain *L Lungo* 104
5 b g Pivotal—Oh Hebe (IRE) (Night Shift (USA))
(1069) 3491[4] 3758[5] (6069) 7243[2]

Against The Rules *Miss Gay Kelleway* a47 55
2 b g Diktat—Bella Bellisimo (IRE) (Alzao (USA))
4199[12] 4421[5] 4827[12] 5606[7] 7353[12] 7547[13]

Agapanthus (GER) *A P Stringer* a78 88
3 b g Tiger Hill(IRE) —Astilbe (GER) (Monsun (GER))
3074a[8] 3773a[16] 6698[12] 7025[11] 7314[13] 7664[4] 7797[10]

Ageebah *C E Brittain* a58 64
2 b f Acclamation—Flag (Selkirk (USA))
4088[6] ◆ 4692[5] 5640[10] 6697[5]

Agente Parmigiano (IRE) *G A Butler* a79 87
2 ch c Captain Rio—Kama's Wheel (Magic Ring (IRE))
1983[2] 2541[6] (2979) 3522[5] 4822[4] 6082[7]

Agente Romano (USA) *G A Butler* a72 72
3 br c Street Cry(IRE) —Dixie Bay (USA) (Dixieland Band (USA))
1410[3] 1746[9] 2151[15] 6129[2] 6379[3]

Agent Stone (IRE) *D Nicholls* 62
2 ch g Night Shift(USA) —Just One Smile (IRE) (Desert Prince (IRE))
4289[7] 4740[3] 4960[5]

Age Of Aquarius (IRE) *A P O'Brien* a82 110
2 b c Galileo(IRE) —Clara Bow (FR) (Top Ville)
7294a[4]

Age Of Chivalry (IRE) *John M Oxx* 106
3 b f Invincible Spirit(IRE) —Aravonian (Night Shift (USA))
1495a[7] (2738a) 3619a[2] 4467a[4] 5130a[6]

Age Of Couture *W Jarvis* 50
2 ch f Hold That Tiger(USA) —Three Wishes (Sadler's Wells (USA))
5535[6] 6187[8]

Age Of Magic (USA) *M Johnston* a49
2 b f Rahy(USA) —Avitrix (USA) (Storm Bird (CAN))
4740[12] 5590[5]

Age Of Miracles (IRE) *G A Ham* a41 47
3 b g Carrowkeel(IRE) —Busking (So Factual (USA))
2772[8] 3521[8] 3823[6] 5218[12] 5912[12]

Age Of Reason (UAE) *M Johnston* a95 106
3 b g Halling(USA) —Time Changes (USA) (Danzig (USA))
(217) ◆ 2408[3] 3196[11] 3877[11] 4552[4] 4856[8]

Aggbag *B P J Baugh* a61 41
4 b g Fath(USA) —Emaura (Dominion)
(32) 214[6] 432[4] (521) 724[3] 861[6] 1209[4] 1371[3] 1780[8] 7441[7] 7663[5]

Aggi Mac *L R James* a12 16
7 b m Defacto(USA) —Giffoine (Timeless Times (USA))
282[11] 657[8] 7446[10]

Agglestone Rock *W G M Turner* a63 60
3 b g Josr Algarhoud(IRE) —Royalty (IRE) (Fairy King (USA))
705[5] 820[4] 1034[3] 1364[4]

Aggravation *D R C Elsworth* a72 78
6 b g Sure Blade(USA) —Confection (Formidable (USA))
1729[8] 2203[3] 2373[9] 2897[5] 3090[3] 3457[4] 4162[19] 4567[2] 4946[8]

Agnes Love *J Akehurst* a63 27
2 gr f Piccolo—Erracht (Emarati (USA))
1385[8] 1955[9] 2479[12] 3032[10] 4942[5] (5567) 5680[3] 5933[6] 6469[3] 7113[3] 7575[5]

Agon Eyes (USA) *D J Coakley* a50 47
3 b f Stravinsky(USA) —Dixie Eyes Blazing (USA) (Gone West (USA))
1186[11] 2753[9]

Ahla Wasahl *D M Simcock* a78 93
2 br f Dubai Destination(USA) —In Full Cry (USA) (Seattle Slew (USA))
2821[5] (3373) ◆ 3851[3] 4868[13] 6473[6] 7144[11]

Ahlawy (IRE) *M W Easterby* a76 86
5 gr g Green Desert(USA) —On Call (Alleged (USA))
1072[13] 1613[6] 1793[5] 2155[12] 2784[5] 3006[5] 4244[6] 6134[3] 6450[3] 6629[2] 6862[3]

Ahoy (IRE) *David Wachman* 80
4 b h Danehill Dancer(IRE) —Alessia (GER) (Warning)
3531a[7]

Aiboa (IRE) *L Urbano-Grajales* 97
2 ch f King Charlemagne(USA) —Spirit of Hope (IRE) (Danehill Dancer (IRE))
7185a[3]

Aigle De Mer (IRE) *B J Meehan* a39
2 ch f Hawk Wing(USA) —Waratah (IRE) (Entrepreneur)
6682[11] 7097[11]

Ai Hawa (IRE) *Eamon Tyrrell* a54 38
5 b m Indian Danehill(IRE) —Arabian Princess (Taufan (USA))
151[6]

Ailsa Craig (IRE) *R Hannon* 60
2 b f Chevalier(IRE) —Sharplaw Destiny (IRE) (Petardia)
5584[5] ◆ 6013[6] 6198[7]

Ailton (GER) *Carmen Bocskai* 79
4 b g Fly To The Stars—Aznavour (GER) (Lagunas)
423a[2] 605a[10]

Aim *J R Jenkins* a53 56
3 b c Weetman's Weigh(IRE) —Ballet On Ice (FR) (Fijar Tango (FR))
1166[13]

Aim To Achieve (IRE) *B W Hills* 45
2 b f Galileo(IRE) —Sabander Bay (USA) (Lear Fan (USA))
6945[15]

Ainama (IRE) *M Wigham* a58 90
4 b g Desert Prince(IRE) —Gilah (IRE) (Saddlers' Hall (IRE))
1719[14] 1947[3] ◆ 2107[8] 2599[10] 3044[9] 3925[15] (4645) 5199[2] (5498) ◆

Aine (IRE) *T Stack* 100
3 ch f Danehill Dancer(IRE) —Antinnaz (IRE) (Thatching)
2606[2] 3532a[12] 6315a[10] 6514a[2]

Aine's Delight (IRE) *Andrew Turnell* a18 22
2 b f King's Best(USA) —Gentle Thoughts (Darshaan)
5214[12] 6166[13]

Ainia *D M Simcock* a52 80
3 b f Alhaarth(IRE) —Vayavaig (Damister (USA))
2079[5] 2560[4] 3796[2] 4708[2] 6027[4] 6605[5] 6896[2]

Ain't Talkin' *M J Attwater* a46 52
2 ch c Zaha(CAN) —Royal Ivy (Mujtahid (USA))
2562[10] 3001[11] 4184[12] 6572[11] 6745[12] 7467[4] 7622[11] 7833[8]

Air Bag (FR) *Mme C Barande-Barbe* a77 103
4 b m Poliglote—Avrilana (FR) (Deep Roots)
1108a[6] 5113a[5]

Air Chief *H J L Dunlop* a69 76
3 ch g Dr Fong(USA) —Fly For Fame (Shaadi (USA))
(1128) (1530) 1696[5] 2302[8] 2665[12] 3836[9] 4179[2] 5759[2] 6028[12] 6542[5] 6678[3]

Airedale Lad (IRE) *C Gordon* a42 43
7 b g Charnwood Forest(IRE) —Tamarsiya (USA) (Shahrastani (USA))
1895[5] 2395[7] 7605[9]

Airman (IRE) *B P J Baugh* a68 68
5 b g Danehill(USA) —Jiving (Generous (IRE))
526[8] 4409[9] 6364[13]

Ajaan *H R A Cecil* 108
4 br h Machiavellian(USA) —Alakananda (Hernando (FR))
(1812) (2202) ◆ 3250[5] 3743[7] 5229[18] 7244[11]

Ajara (IRE) *N J Vaughan* a69
2 b f Elusive City(USA) —My-Lorraine (IRE) (Mac's Imp (USA))
7402[4] (7561)

Ajhar (USA) *M P Tregoning* a109 108
4 b g Diesis—Min Alhawa (USA) (Riverman (USA))
1468[11] (5677) 6303[3] 7193[4] 7420[6]

Ajigolo *M R Channon* a104 102
5 ch h Piccolo—Ajig Dancer (Niniski (USA))
(593) 836[9] 925[2] 1079[4] 1346[5] 1689[5] 1917[8] 2195[6] (2426) 3647[8] 4145[8] 4437[14] 4586[5] 4687[9] 5109[20]

Ajjaadd (USA) *Saeed Bin Suroor* a78 64
2 b c Elusive Quality(USA) —Millstream (USA) (Dayjur (USA))
4199[6] 7098[4] 7214[3]

Ajsaam *Kevin Prendergast* 18
2 ch c Pivotal—Ulfah (USA) (Danzig (USA))
3509a[16]

Akarem *K R Burke* a82 107
7 b h Kingmambo(USA) —Spirit Of Tara (IRE) (Sadler's Wells (USA))
2599[2] 2939[7] 3490[4] 3942[11] 5054[5] 5853[10]

Akarshan (IRE) *Evan Williams* 73
3 b g Intikhab(USA) —Akdara (IRE) (Sadler's Wells (USA))
2449[2] 3473[5]

Akbabend *M Johnston* a71 80
2 b c Refuse To Bend(IRE) —Akdariya (IRE) (Shirley Heights)
6535[7] 6778[4] 7069[3]

Akhenaten *M R Channon* 96
2 b c High Chaparral(IRE) —Lady Adnil (IRE) (Stravinsky (USA))
5093[6] 5641[3] (5882) 6428[4] 6648[5] 6717[4]

Akiem (IRE) *Andreas Lowe* 96
3 b c Kutub(IRE) —Anacapri (FR) (Anabaa (USA))
3074a[3] 3773a[13] 5137a[3] 6148a[6]

Akimbo (USA) *James Leavy* a77 89
7 b g Kingmambo(USA) —All At Sea (USA) (Riverman (USA))
4003a[17]

Akmal *J L Dunlop* 77
2 ch g Selkirk(USA) —Ayun (USA) (Swain (IRE))
6026[9] 6384[6] 6777[7]

Akona Matata (USA) *Doug Watson* a100 100
6 b h Seeking The Gold(USA) —Oh What A Dance (USA) (Nijinsky (CAN))
382a[2] 563a[7]

Akrisrun (IRE) *D K Weld* 87
2 b c Danehill Dancer(IRE) —Labrusca (Grand Lodge (USA))
6317a[10]

Akua'Ba (IRE) *J S Bolger* a90 101
4 b m Sadler's Wells(USA) —Ghana (IRE) (Lahib (USA))
1105a[14] 2420a[10] 2740a[2] 2961a[6] 4467a[3]

Alaazo (USA) *William Mott* a99
3 bb c A.P. Indy(USA) —Atelier (USA) (Deputy Minister (CAN))
4678a[4]

Alabama Spirit (USA) *P Howling* a64 67
3 bb f Dixie Union(USA) —Appealing Spirit (USA) (Valid Appeal (USA))
12[7] (154) 333[2] 480[5] 714[4] 1475[6] 1738[5] 2676[14] 3086[13] 7072[9] 7316[11] 7535[9]

Alabaster Flatley (IRE) *J R Jenkins*
3 ch c Spinning World(USA) —Lady In The Night (IRE) (Royal Academy (USA))
6566[11]

Alabjar *J R Jenkins* a11 42
3 b c High Estate—Princess Lieven (Royal Palace)
3326[10] 3870[7] 5377[8]

Alacity (IRE) *N Bycroft* 32
2 b f Elusive City(USA) —Minamala (IRE) (Desert King (IRE))
6481[12] 6722[11]

Aladdin's Lamp (IRE) *M Johnston* a69 65
2 b c Cape Cross(IRE) —Luminata (IRE) (Indian Ridge)
4530[3] 4847[3] 5497[5] 5960[2] (6207) 6525[11] 6954[10] 7426[4] 7538[3]

Alamanni (USA) *E Borromeo* 107
4 bb m Elusive Quality(USA) —Altamura (USA) (El Gran Senor (USA))
4212a[7] 6521a[9] 7348a[7]

Alamgiyr (IRE) *Ms Joanna Morgan* 73
5 b g Kalanisi(IRE) —Alaiyda (USA) (Shahrastani (USA))
4511a[6]

Alanbrooke *M Johnston* 69
2 gr c Hernando(FR) —Alouette (Darshaan)
6026[5] (6580)

Alan Devonshire *M H Tompkins* 101
3 br g Mtoto—Missed Again (High Top)
1992[4] 2829[13] 3880[4] 4505[6] 6476[21] 6670[7]

Alannah (IRE) *Mrs P N Dutfield* a38 14
3 b f Alhaarth(IRE) —Aljeeza (Halling (USA))
1251[8] 4564[12]

Al Aqabah (IRE) *B Gubby* a73 50
3 ch f Redback—Snow Eagle (IRE) (Polar Falcon (USA))
1930[9]

Alarazi (IRE) *John M Oxx* 110
4 b g Spectrum(IRE) —Alaya (IRE) (Ela-Mana-Mou)
1105a[4] 1353a[2] 1882a[2] 3983a[5] 5135a[2]

Al Asayl Rose (USA) *H J L Dunlop* 51
3 ch f Awesome Again(CAN) —Eden (USA) (Holy Bull (USA))
5182[5] 5750[9] 6705[13]

Alasil (USA) *R J Price* a67 72
8 bb g Swain(IRE) —Asl (USA) (Caro)
219[7]

Alaska River (GER) *P Schiergen* 112
4 b h Anabaa(USA) —Ariosta (GER) (Scenic)
3752a[7] 4912a[9] 7005a[11]

Alasoun (IRE) *Evan Williams* 56
5 b g Kalanisi(IRE) —Alasana (IRE) (Darshaan)
(2914)

Alayala (IRE) *M Johnston* 48
2 b f Cape Cross(IRE) —Lady's Secret (IRE) (Alzao (USA))
2821[11]

Alazeyab (USA) *M A Jarvis* 93
2 b c El Prado(IRE) —Itnab (Green Desert (USA))
5468[6] (6117) 6647[3]

Al Azy (IRE) *J L Dunlop* 71
3 b c Nayef(USA) —Nasheed (USA) (Riverman (USA))
1173[3] 1516[4] 2244[13] 3004[13]

Albaasha (IRE) *Sir Michael Stoute* a57
2 ch c Lemon Drop Kid(USA) —Cozy Maria (USA) (Cozzene (USA))
7552[6]

Albabilia (IRE) *C E Brittain* 102
3 b f King's Best(USA) —Sonachan (IRE) (Darshaan)
745a[9] 1401[11]

Albaher *J L Dunlop* 80
2 b c Oasis Dream—Dance Sequence (USA) (Mr Prospector (USA))
(4446)

Albahri (FR) *M Delzangles* 105
3 b g Bahri(USA) —Alharir (USA) (Zafonic (USA))
3074a[5]

Albaqaa *R A Fahey* 92
3 ch g Medicean—Basbousate Nadia (Wolfhound (USA))
(991) 1428[2] (1576) 2819[4] 3919[10] 4783[5] 5257[2] 5858[5] (6276) 6646[12]

Albaraari *Sir Michael Stoute* a68 74
3 b f Green Desert(USA) —Brigitta (IRE) (Sadler's Wells (USA))
1930[8] 3272[5] 3761[3]

Albarouche *M A Jarvis* a84 85
3 b f Sadler's Wells(USA) —Alakananda (Hernando (FR))
1599[3] 2454[7] *(3133)* 4160[8] 4984[2] *5683[3]* 6542[12]

Albaseet (IRE) *M P Tregoning* a73 71
2 b g Desert Style(IRE) —Double Eight (IRE) (Common Grounds)
4980[4] 5929[6] 6531[4] *7191[2] 7417[2]*

Albertine Rose *W R Muir* a72 87
2 gr f Namid—Barathiki (Barathea (IRE))
5147[3] 5584[7] *6089[2]* 6863[2] 7107[3] *(7273)*

Alberts Story (USA) *R A Fahey* a62 62
4 b g Tale Of The Cat(USA) —Hazino (USA) (Hazaam (USA))
1953[8] 2274[3] 2662[14] 3226[8] 3814[9] 4458[11] *6955[3]*

Albertus Maximus (USA) *Vladimir Cerin* a121
4 b h Albert The Great(USA) —Chasethewildwind (USA) (Forty Niner (USA))
(6995a)

Albinus *A M Balding* 59
7 gr g Selkirk(USA) —Alouette (Darshaan)
1841[8]

Albisola (IRE) *Robert Collet* 116
3 b f Montjeu(IRE) —Mahalia (IRE) (Danehill (USA))
2237a[5] 2651a[3] 4657a[4] 5331a[3] (7037a)

Alcalde *M Johnston* 83
2 b c Hernando(FR) —Alexandrine (IRE) (Nashwan (USA))
(5812) (6561)

Alcimedes *P W Chapple-Hyam* a71 61
3 b g Domedriver(IRE) —Allegra (Niniski (USA))
225[4] 434[4]

Al Cobra (IRE) *M A Jarvis* a45 58
3 b f Sadler's Wells(USA) —Marienbad (FR) (Darshaan)
2291[11]

Alderbed *George Baker* a44 46
2 b g Bahri(USA) —Tanasie (Cadeaux Genereux)
2893[7] 4480[9] 4890[14] *7372[11] 7514[8] 7607[5]*

Aldermoor (USA) *S C Williams* 96
2 b c Tale Of The Cat(USA) —Notting Hill (BRZ) (Jules (USA))
(4289) 4685[2] (6274)

Aleagueoftheirown (IRE) *David Wachman* 101
4 b m Danehill Dancer(IRE) —Golden Coral (USA) (Slew O'Gold (USA))
2738a[5] 3619a[6] 3982a[7] 4467a[2] ◆ 5922a[5] 6315a[5]

Aleatricis *Sir Mark Prescott* a31 78
3 bg g Kingmambo(USA) —Alba Stella (Nashwan (USA))
2247[5] 2719[5] (3580) (4019) (4147) (4281) (4334) 5146[2]

Alecia (IRE) *B G Powell* a51 67
4 gr m Keltos(FR) —Ahliyat (USA) (Irish River (FR))
3562[10]

Alectrona (FR) *J R Best* 52
2 b f Invincible Spirit(IRE) —Dom Pennion (Dominion)
2497[6]

Alekhine (IRE) *J W Unett* a65 68
7 b g Soviet Star(USA) —Alriyaah (Shareef Dancer (USA))
559[9] 4936[13]

Alendha (GER) *T Clout* 92
5 b m Lend A Hand—Alster (GER) (Esclavo (FR))
5113a[0]

Aleron (IRE) *J J Quinn* a14 69
10 b g Sadler's Wells(USA) —High Hawk (Shirley Heights)
1137[3] 1779[5] 2701[4] 5385[3]

Alessandro Volta *A P O'Brien* 119
3 b c Montjeu(IRE) —Ventura Highway (Machiavellian (USA))
1509a[4] (1992) 2829[6] 3535a[4] 4042a[6] 5892[10] 7188a[20]

Aleutian *F Nass* a105 91
8 gr g Zafonic(USA) —Baked Alaska (Green Desert (USA))
493a[2] 667a[2] 817a[9]

Alexa (GER) *H J Groschel* 93
4 b m Areion(GER) —Arween (Armistice Day)
5334a[8] 6323a[4] 6852a[5]

Alexander Castle (USA) *K A Ryan* 107
3 b g Lemon Drop Kid(USA) —Palapa (USA) (Storm Cat (USA))
1421[5] 2032a[14] 5856[4] 6120[20]

Alexander Gulch (USA) *K A Ryan* a60 83
2 b c Thunder Gulch(USA) —Lovely Later (USA) (Green Dancer (USA))
3663[7] (4740) *7445[3]*

Alexander Guru *M Blanshard* a69 65
4 ch g Ishiguru(USA) —Superspring (Superlative)
(128) 300[5] 430[8] 811[5] 1301[3] *1605[3] 1853[2] 2715[2]* 3347[5] *4078[4] 4343[12] 6825[4]* 7076[7] 7367[5]

Alexander Huricane (IRE) *K A Ryan* a93 81
4 b g Danetime(IRE) —Alpine Lady (IRE) (Tirol)
(319) (522) 528[2] (782) ◆ *846[2]* 1309[2] ◆ 2005[3] 2773[6] 3668[3] 4218[2] (4736) 5390[7] 6314[6] *(6663) (6952)*

Alexander Loyalty (IRE) *J Noseda* 63
2 b f Invincible Spirit(IRE) —Nassma (IRE) (Sadler's Wells (USA))
5929[7]

Alexander Newstalk (IRE) *S A Callaghan* a22 34
2 b f Choisir(AUS) —National Ballet (Shareef Dancer (USA))
4634[9] 4980[10]

Alexandros *Saeed Bin Suroor* 113
3 ch c Kingmambo(USA) —Arlette (IRE) (King Of Kings (IRE))
1943[4] 2788[2] 3102[7] 4622[2] 5095[7] 5856[3] (6670) 7147[3]

Alexia Rose (IRE) *A Berry* a39 45
6 b m Mujadil(USA) —Meursault (IRE) (Salt Dome (USA))
562[6] 3255[11] 3582[RR] (Dead)

Alfathaa *W J Haggas* 105
3 b g Nayef(USA) —Arctic Char (Polar Falcon (USA))
1808[13] 3156[6] 3880[2] 4622[8] 6123[6]

Alfie Flits *G A Swinbank* a96 115
6 b g Machiavellian(USA) —Elhilmeya (IRE) (Unfuwain (USA))
1655a[3] 2169[6] 3295[3] 3721[8] 6106[4]

Alfie Lee (IRE) *D A Nolan* a3 50
11 ch g Case Law—Nordic Living (IRE) (Nordico (USA))
1772[8] 1827[10] 2145[11] 2248[7] 2576[4] 2843[12] 3212[3] 4950[7]

Alfie Noakes *Mrs A J Perrett* a71 81
6 b g Groom Dancer(USA) —Crimson Rosella (Polar Falcon (USA))
1473[11] 1877[6] 2414[4] 3060[4] 3917[6] 4299[2] 4892[5] *5376[5] 6210[5]* 6403[10] 6983[9]

Alfie Tupper (IRE) *J R Boyle* a78 71
5 ch g Soviet Star(USA) —Walnut Lady (Forzando)
240[2] 504[7] 682[2] 811[4] 4267[P] (4568) 4791[7] *5209[6] (6134) 6452[4] (6826)* 6989[3]

Alfredtheordinary *M R Channon* a65 58
3 b g Hunting Lion(IRE) —Solmorin (Fraam)
920[6] 1163[5] 2208[13] 2451[14] *2805[3]* 3065[14] *5378[11]* 6541[2] *6685[2]* 7050[5] *7070[5] 7166[7] 7732[7]*

Alfresco *I A Wood* a101 84
4 b g Mtoto—Maureena (IRE) (Grand Lodge (USA))
124[2] 218[5] 336[3] (594) 680[2] 834[8] 906[11] 1365[8] 2013[8] 2308[6] 2619[8] 2837[2] 3093[4] 3363[4] 4528[9] 4865[2] 5091[2] 5532[2] 5695[12] 6340[7] 6625[11]

Alf Tupper *Adrian McGuinness* a57 48
5 b g Atraf—Silvery (Petong)
(7581) 7691[2]

Algarade *Sir Mark Prescott* a86 94
4 b m Green Desert(USA) —Alexandrine (IRE) (Nashwan (USA))
(3163) ◆ (3433) 3751a[7] 4520[12] *5569[10]*

Algharb *A Manuel* a97 93
6 bb g Mujahid(USA) —Actress (Known Fact (USA))
290a[2] *473a[11] 670a[11]*

Al Gillani (IRE) *J R Boyle* a85 22
3 b g Monashee Mountain(USA) —Whisper Dawn (IRE) (Fasliyev (USA))
923[5] 2756[7] 3268[10] *4090[2]* 4793[11] *(5627) (5801) (6225)* ◆

Alhaban (IRE) *Kevin Prendergast* 107
2 gr c Verglas(IRE) —Anne Tudor (IRE) (Anabaa (USA))
3534a[2] 4465a[5] 6317a[12]

Alhabeeb (IRE) *Kevin Prendergast* a87 99
3 b g Alhaarth(IRE) —Elfaslah (IRE) (Green Desert (USA))
1497a[7] 4512a[9]

Alhaque (USA) *P W Chapple-Hyam* 83
2 ch c Galileo(IRE) —Safeen (USA) (Storm Cat (USA))
6084[2] 6425[2] 6777[5]

Alibar's Surprise (IRE) *A Berry* 51
2 b f Masterful(USA) —Go Likecrazy (Dowsing (USA))
5383[4]

Ali Bruce *M R Hoad* a49 45
8 b g Cadeaux Genereux—Actualite (Polish Precedent (USA))
938[12] 1534[3]

Alicante *Sir Mark Prescott* 52
2 gr f Pivotal—Alba Stella (Nashwan (USA))
6110[9] 6244[6] 6555[8]

Aliceaneileen (IRE) *Patrick J Flynn* a36 54
3 b f Indian Danehill(IRE) —Stylish Icon (USA) (Royal Academy (USA))
4613a[5]

Ali D *G Woodward* a51 36
10 b g Alhijaz—Doppio (Dublin Taxi)
80[10]

Aligned *A W Carroll* 9
2 br f Singspiel(IRE) —Align (Petong)
6665[9]

Alimarr (IRE) *S Parr* a65 55
2 ch f Noverre(USA) —Tiger Desert (GER) (Desert King (IRE))
6559[10] 6884[6] *7337[5] 7547[5] 7646[6] 7719[7]*

Alisar (IRE) *E J Creighton* a44 92
8 b g Entrepreneur—Aliya (IRE) (Darshaan)
638[7]

Alix Road (FR) *Mme M Bollack-Badel* 103
5 gr m Linamix(FR) —Life On The Road (IRE) (Persian Heights)
4914a[6] 5332a[8] 5623a[2] 6495a[8] 7037a[8]

Aliybee (IRE) *E J O'Neill* a56
2 b f Barathea(IRE) —Aliyshan (IRE) (Darshaan)
7726[4]

Alkhafif *E A L Dunlop* 78
2 b c Royal Applause—My First Romance (Danehill (USA))
(2411)

Al Khaleej (IRE) *E A L Dunlop* a107 112
4 b g Sakhee(USA) —Mood Swings (IRE) (Shirley Heights)
(1566) ◆ 1982[2]

Alkyoni (IRE) *Jane Chapple-Hyam* 43
3 b f High Chaparral(IRE) —Alanis (Warning)
2763[8] 3094[10] 6248[6]

All About Jack *G A Ham*
4 b g Cigar—Dorothea Sharp (IRE) (Foxhound (USA))
7500[10] 7608[11]

All About You (IRE) *R Charlton* 86
2 b c Mind Games—Expectation (IRE) (Night Shift (USA))
6072[2] (6702)

Allahor *D J S Ffrench Davis* a43 65
3 br g Rock City—Miss Puci (Puissance)
1216[8] 6560[11] *7089[8]*

All Angel *Miss Amy Weaver* a39 56
2 b f Lend A Hand—Opera Babe (IRE) (Kahyasi)
4088[8] (4487) 4827[10] *6573[8]*

Allanit (GER) *A P Stringer* a72 103
4 b g Tiger Hill(IRE) —Astilbe (GER) (Monsun (GER))
3306a[5] 5528a[10] 6649[9] 6984[13] *7496[8]*

All Annalena (IRE) *Andreas Lowe*
2 b f Dubai Destination(USA) —Alla Prima (IRE) (In The Wings)
7006a[6]

Allegretto (IRE) *Sir Michael Stoute* 115
5 ch m Galileo(IRE) —Alleluia (Caerleon (USA))
2542[8] 3154[4] 5243[4] (5826) 7008a[2]

Alleviate (IRE) *Sir Mark Prescott* a86 91
4 br m Indian Ridge—Alleluia (Caerleon (USA))
(2076) (2525) ◆ 3307a[4] 4911a[4] 5625a[9]

Allexes (IRE) *J R Boyle* 30
2 bb f Exceed And Excel(AUS) —Lizanne (USA) (Theatrical)
5860[8] 6601[7]

Allez Frank (GER) *A E Jones* a57
7 b g Macanal(USA) —Agua Clara (GER) (Roi Dagobert)
4932[3] 6136[11]

Allez Melina *Mouse Hamilton-Fairley* a48
7 b m Cloudings(IRE) —Theme Arena (Tragic Role (USA))
317[7] 435[9] 524[5] 754[10] 778[10] 930[14]

Allformary *B Smart* 73
2 b f Tobougg(IRE) —Bollin Rita (Rambo Dancer (CAN))
6381[2] (6722)

All For You (IRE) *D R Lanigan* a62
2 b f High Chaparral(IRE) —Quatre Saisons (FR) (Homme De Loi (IRE))
7380[5]

All Guns Firing (IRE) *M A Jarvis* 74
2 b g High Chaparral(IRE) —Lili Cup (FR) (Fabulous Dancer (USA))
6720[7] 6977[3]

Allicansayis Wow (USA) *J S Bolger* a98 96
3 b f Street Cry(IRE) —Crown Of Jewels (USA) (Half A Year (USA))
1199a[2] 2113a[4] 4007a[13]

Allied Powers (IRE) *M L W Bell* a70 102
3 b c Invincible Spirit(IRE) —Always Friendly (High Line)
867[3] 1059[6] 1614[3] (1731) (1919) ◆ (2151) ◆ 3719[4] 4784[3] 5830[2] (6041) 6646[11]

All In The Red (IRE) *B N Pollock* a75 75
3 ch g Redback—Light-Flight (IRE) (Brief Truce (USA))
1162[6] ◆ 1453[2] *(1581)* 2429[4] *2705[3]* 5162[2] *5345[2]* 5841[5] (6173) *6433[7]* 6716[12] *7548[4] 7642[4] 7729[4]*

Allium (IRE) *B W Hills* a52 34
3 ch f Namid—Top Of The Form (IRE) (Masterclass (USA))
412[3] 634[3] 734[4] 2774[8]

All Lit Up *A King* a56 56
3 b g Fantastic Light(USA) —Maiden Aunt (IRE) (Distant Relative)
2280[8] 2719[4] *3566[3]* 4334[3] 4564[7]

Alloro *D W Thompson* a50 51
4 ch g Auction House(USA) —Minette (Bishop Of Cashel)
1587[5]

All Speedy (FR) *Mlle S-V Tarrou* 97
2 b f Pyramus(USA) —Alpina (GER) (Lavirco (GER))
7186a[5]

All Spin (IRE) *A P Jarvis* a65 69
2 ch g Spinning World(USA) —Mad Annie (USA) (Anabaa (USA))
3049[10] 3895[10] 5286[4] 6246[2] *6732[6] 7273[7] 7388[3] 7538[6]*

All That And More (IRE) *Doug Watson* a69 59
6 ch g Unfuwain(USA) —Ideal Lady (IRE) (Seattle Slew (USA))
204a[11]

All The Aces (IRE) *M A Jarvis* a79 109
3 b c Spartacus(IRE) —Lili Cup (FR) (Fabulous Dancer (USA))
(1618) 1922[2] 3193[4]

Alltheclews *B J McMath* a28 10
3 b g Zindabad(FR) —Burton Gold (Master Willie)
4620[13] *5477[6]*

All The Good (IRE) *Saeed Bin Suroor* a106 118
5 ch h Diesis—Zarara (USA) (Manila (USA))
4444[4] 4844[9] (5229) (6835a)

All The Nines (IRE) *Miss V Haigh* 23
2 b f Elusive City(USA) —Sagaing (Machiavellian (USA))
6788[11]

All The Winds (GER) *A Wohler* 89
3 ch c Samum(GER) —All Our Luck (GER) (Spectrum (IRE))
3074a[9] 5529a[6]

All You Need (IRE) *R Hollinshead* a76 72
4 b g Iron Mask(USA) —Choice Pickings (IRE) (Among Men (USA))
2005[12] *2263[6]* 2806[5] *3329[2]* 3825[3] 4125[9] *4934[10] 5474[4] 5709[12]* 6334[10] *7340[7] 7516[8]* 7692[5]

Almajd (IRE) *Sir Michael Stoute* a69 98
3 b c Marju(IRE) —Irish Valley (USA) (Irish River (FR))
3396[4] 6073[6]

Alma Mater *Sir Mark Prescott* a74 100
5 b m Sadler's Wells(USA) —Alouette (Darshaan)
6517a[5] 7429a[0]

Almaram (USA) *D Selvaratnam* a100 94
8 b h A.P. Indy(USA) —Beraysim (Lion Cavern (USA))
378a[6] (473a) 563a[2] 648a[9]

Al Marmoom (USA) *Saeed Bin Suroor* 84
2 b c Medaglia D'Oro(USA) —Lady Laika (USA) (Gone West (USA))
6122[6] 6715 [2] (7054)

Almass (IRE) *Kevin Prendergast* a74 113
3 b f Elnadim(USA) —Harmless Albatross (Pas De Seul)
(7157a)

Almaty Express *J R Weymes* a93 62
6 b g Almaty(IRE) —Express Girl (Sylvan Express)
(29) ◆ *(126) 359[3] 580[8] (699) 840[3] 1033[3] 1195[3] 1582[3]* 1908[9] *2292[5]* (2501) 3320[6] 7066[9] 7290[10] 7365[9] 7584[6] 7826[9]

Almazar *J L Dunlop* a57 50
2 b g Green Desert(USA) —Zaqrah (USA) (Silver Hawk (USA))
4199[10] *5996[7]* 6553[7]

Almiqdaad *M A Jarvis* 98
2 b c Haafhd—Etizaaz (USA) (Diesis)
4360[4] (5068) 6267[5]

Al Mogeer (IRE) *P J McBride* 23
3 b g Montjeu(IRE) —Jumbo Delight (IRE) (Don't Forget Me)
4085[10] 5163[11] 5322[10]

Almonafis (IRE) *Sir Michael Stoute* 74
3 gr c Sadler's Wells(USA) —Sulaalah (IRE) (Darshaan)
3654[3] 4124[4] 4689[4] 5182[4] 6584[3]

Almora Guru *W M Brisbourne* a52 60
4 b m Ishiguru(USA) —Princess Almora (Pivotal)
4491[8] *5157[9]*

Almost Married (IRE) *J S Goldie* a54 65
4 b g Indian Ridge—Shining Hour (USA) (Red Ransom (USA))
9804 3759[9] 4013[7] (4846) 5392[8] 6039[2] 6159[3] 6411[6]

Al Moulatham *R Ford* a68 77
9 b g Rainbow Quest(USA) —High Standard (Kris)
283[9]

Almoutaz (USA) *B W Hills* a53 87
3 bb c Kingmambo(USA) —Dessert (USA) (Storm Cat (USA))
1441[10] 2425[6] 3592[2] 4206[7] 6194[2] *6900[11]*

Almoutezah (USA) *M A Jarvis* 64
3 br f Storm Cat(USA) —Probable Colony (USA) (Pleasant Colony (USA))
2413[10]

Almowj *G H Jones* a41 30
5 b g Fasliyev(USA) —Tiriana (Common Grounds)
862[6] 1031[9] 1636[4] 1895[7]

Al Mugtareb (IRE) *M Johnston* a69 64
2 b c Acclamation—Billie Bailey (USA) (Mister Baileys)
4598[4] 6062[5] *6910[3]*

Al Muheer (IRE) *C E Brittain* a96 104
3 b c Diktat—Dominion Rose (USA) (Spinning World (USA))
3635[2] 3919[16] 4404[5] 4842[2] 5275[16] 5495[8] 6269[25] *7192[5] 7381[5] 7492[11] 7703[8]*

Al Mukaala (IRE) *C E Brittain* a53 66
2 ch c Cadeaux Genereux—Crescent Moon (Mr Prospector (USA))
3495[8] 4108[4] 4510[5] *5671[8] 6223[7]* 7052[9]

Almuraad (IRE) *Doug Watson* a88 106
7 b h Machiavellian(USA) —Wellspring (IRE) (Caerleon (USA))
205a[8] 384a[3] 474a[2] 745a[4] 818a[10]

Almutawaazin *M P Tregoning*
2 b g Nayef(USA) —Crown Water (USA) (Chief's Crown (USA))
6977[17]

Alnadana (IRE) *A De Royer-Dupre* 107
3 gr f Danehill Dancer(IRE) —Alnamara (FR) (Linamix (FR))
5738a[3]

Alnitak (USA) *B Olsen* 97
7 br h Nureyev(USA) —Very True (USA) (Proud Truth (USA))
2708a[9] 4676a[5] 5958a[5]

Alnwick *P D Cundell* a74 78
4 b g Kylian(USA) —Cebwob (Rock City)
(212) ◆ *588[3] 793[2] 880[6] 1856[2]* (3179) 3685[4] (4193)

Alocin (IRE) *W A Murphy* a31 64
5 b g Titus Livius(FR) —Poker Dice (Primo Dominie)
3532a[15] *7453[5]*

Alone He Stands (IRE) *J C Hayden* a86 89
8 b g Flying Spur(AUS) —Millennium Tale (FR) (Distant Relative)
1103a[4] 1497a[14] 3532a[16] 5550a[7] 5731a[13]

Along The Nile *K G Reveley* 83
6 b g Desert Prince(IRE) —Golden Fortune (Forzando)
6582[14] 6862[11]

Alonso De Guzman (IRE) *J R Boyle* a81 80
4 b g Dockside(USA) —Addaya (IRE) (Persian Bold)
104[2] (196) 1768[2] 2304[4] *2804[4] 3613[5]* 4200[2] (4592) 4817[2] *7064[2] 7301[2]*

Alpacco (IRE) *L Kelp* a91 105
6 b g Desert King(IRE) —Albertville (GER) (Top Ville)
294a[10] 379a[12] 669a[2] 739a[2] 818a[8] 2708a[14] 4676a[10] 5335a[11] 5958a[8]

Alpes Maritimes *G L Moore* a92 82
4 b g Danehill Dancer(IRE) —Miss Riviera (Kris)
315[2] 1719[11] *7439[12] 7821[9]*

Alphabeth *M R Channon* a64 66
2 b f Hunting Lion(IRE) —Bold Gem (Never So Bold)
995[7] *1177[5]* (2004) 3910[2] (3961) 4143[2] 4175[6] 4648[4] 5043[4] *(5473) 5866[4] 6350[11]*

Alpha Tauri (USA) *H R A Cecil* a53 63
2 b c Aldebaran(USA) —Seven Moons (JPN) (Sunday Silence (USA))
6423[6] 6714[6]

Alpine Rose (FR) *J-C Rouget* 105
3 gr f Linamix(FR) —Fragrant Hill (Shirley Heights)
5039a[3] 7348a[5]

Alqaahir (USA) *Patrick Morris* a71 76
6 b h Swain(IRE) —Crafty Example (USA) (Crafty Prospector (USA))
2735[2] 3227[4] 3664[8] 4876[6] 5419[6] *7748[2] (7764)*

Alqaffay (IRE) *Saeed Bin Suroor* a76
3 b c King's Best(USA) —Spirit Of Tara (IRE) (Sadler's Wells (USA))
6047[10] 6470[3]

Al Qasi (IRE) *P W Chapple-Hyam* a85 120
5 b h Elnadim(USA) —Delisha (Salse (USA))
1619[2] 2193[8] 3982a[2] 4506[7] 5095[2] 5893[3] 7157a[3]

Al Qeddaaf (IRE) *W J Haggas* 65
2 b g Alhaarth(IRE) —Just Special (Cadeaux Genereux)
6776[14] 7240[2]

Al Rayanah *G Prodromou* a60 57
5 b m Almushtarak(IRE) —Desert Bloom (FR) (Last Tycoon)
1029[4] 1258[2] 1606[9] 1705[3] 2003[10] (4282) 4479[3] 4797[6] 5161[3] 5318[4] 6036[6] 6255[2] 6888[11] 7261[13]

Alright Chuck *P W Hiatt* 24
4 b g Petoski—Snowline (Bay Express)
3688[10] 3810[8] 4249[13] 5427[11] 6175[10] 7387[10]

Al Sabaheya *C E Brittain* 81
2 b f Kheleyf(USA) —Baalbek (Barathea (IRE))
(5165) 6076[3]

Alsace Lorraine (IRE) *J R Fanshawe* 72
3 b f Giant's Causeway(USA) —Mer De Corail (IRE) (Sadler's Wells (USA))
2955[2] 4161[4] 6530[6]

Alsadaa (USA) *Mrs L J Mongan* a81 77
5 b g Kingmambo(USA) —Aljawza (USA) (Riverman (USA))
(6243) 7558[2]

Alsadeek (IRE) *J L Dunlop* 78
3 b g Fasliyev(USA) —Khulan (USA) (Bahri (USA))
1971[5] 2883[5] 3282[8] 3731[5]

Alsahil (USA) *M P Tregoning* a72
2 ch c Diesis—Tayibah (IRE) (Sadler's Wells (USA))
7312[3]

Al Samha (USA) *M Johnston* a75 78
3 b c Elusive Quality(USA) —Dubian (High Line)
(837) ◆ 1875[6] 2464[8] 3031[4] 3599[5]

Al Sayed *Miss D Mountain* 43
2 b c Tobougg(IRE) —Wrong Bride (Reprimand)
6600[8]

Alseraaj (USA) *Ian Williams* 71
3 ch f El Prado(IRE) —Barzah (IRE) (Darshaan)
1423[8] 2015[8] 2956[5] 4300[12] 4663[7] 4814[5] 5198[12]

Al Shemali *Saeed Bin Suroor* 113
4 ch h Medicean—Bathilde (IRE) (Generous (IRE))
(296a) 1990[3] 2797[4] 4192[9] 5694[12]

Alta Fedelta *V Caruso* 41
2 b f Oasis Dream—Infiel (Luge)
6891a[7]

Alta Luna (FR) *J-C Rouget* 89
2 b f Fasliyev(USA) —Lunatoria (IRE) (Vettori (IRE))
7103a[9]

Altamira *E Lellouche* a79 106
4 ch m Peintre Celebre(USA) —Arlesienne (IRE) (Alzao (USA))
5332a[6] 6498a[7]

Al Tamooh (IRE) *J L Dunlop* 78
2 b f Dalakhani(IRE) —Claxon (Caerleon (USA))
4643[6] ◆ 5640[4] 6081[4]

Altenburg (FR) *Mrs N Smith* a75 70
6 b g Sadler's Wells(USA) —Anna Of Saxony (Ela-Mana-Mou)
1267[10]

Alternative *Jorge Romero* 85
4 ch h Dr Fong(USA) —Oatey (Master Willie)
5113a[U]

Alternative Choice (USA) *N P Littmoden* a62
2 b c Grand Slam(USA) —Northern Fleet (USA) (Afleet (CAN))
6375[8] 7011[8]

Altilhar (USA) *G L Moore* a86 83
5 b g Dynaformer(USA) —Al Desima (Emperor Jones (USA))
96[4]

Altimatum (USA) *P F I Cole* 64
2 ch c Rahy(USA) —Aldiza (USA) (Storm Cat (USA))
6443[6] 6978[15]

Altitude *Sir Mark Prescott* a78 83
3 gr f Green Desert(USA) —Alouette (Darshaan)
3227[3] (3688) ◆ 4021[9] 4699[2] 5199[11]

Alto Singer (IRE) *B R Millman* 61
3 b f Alhaarth(IRE) —Sonatina (Distant Relative)
3801[4] 4277[11] 5026[6] 5749[7]

Altos Reales *D Shaw* a62 42
4 b m Mark Of Esteem(IRE) —Karsiyaka (IRE) (Kahyasi)
118[6] (451) 664[3] 841[8] 1266[8] 1639[4]

Alto Vertigo *P C Haslam* a71 55
5 b g Averti(IRE) —Singer On The Roof (Chief Singer)
15[4] (49) 235[11]

Alucica *D Shaw* a62 50
5 b m Celtic Swing—Acicula (IRE) (Night Shift (USA))
571[5] 624[4] 711[6] (898) 1142[4] 1313[5] 2670[7] 3026[7] 3567[9] (3839) 4168[9] 7076[3] 7194[7] 7433[9]

Alugat (IRE) *Mrs A Duffield* a57 41
5 b g Tagula(IRE) —Notley Park (Wolfhound (USA))
2448[11] 3112[16] 6823[4] 7444[5] 7793[8]

Alutando (IRE) *B Palling* 61
3 b f Lend A Hand—Mystic Oak (IRE) (Waajib)
1964[7] 2772[9] 3379[12] 3605[15]

Alvee (IRE) *J R Fanshawe* a66 63
3 br f Key Of Luck(USA) —Alleluia (Caerleon (USA))
5231[6] 5750[4] 6168[3]

Alwaabel *J L Dunlop* a16 82
3 b c Green Desert(USA) —Etizaaz (USA) (Diesis)
1295[2] 5104[2]

Alwaary (USA) *J H M Gosden* a72 82
2 b c Dynaformer(USA) —Tabrir (IRE) (Unfuwain (USA))
5672[3] ◆ (6057)

Alwajeeha (USA) *Kiaran McLaughlin* 113
3 b f Dixieland Band(USA) —Ridaa (USA) (Seattle Slew (USA))
5745a[6]

Al Wasef (USA) *M Johnston* 73
3 b c Danzig(USA) —Widady (USA) (Gone West (USA))
1429[2] 2571[8] 3051[4] 3548[6]

Always A Rock (IRE) *M Johnston* a85 92
3 b c Rock Of Gibraltar(IRE) —Rachelle (IRE) (Mark Of Esteem (IRE))
662[3] ◆ 909[2] ◆ (1410) ◆ (2575) (4197) ◆ 4404[8] 4553[15] 5207[11] 5635[15] 6352[5] 6976[9]

Always Attractive (IRE) *M Johnston* a30 40
3 ch f King's Best(USA) —Fife (IRE) (Lomond (USA))
135[9]

Always Beautiful (USA) *David Wachman* 97
3 b f Kingmambo(USA) —Diali (USA) (Dayjur (USA))
3070a[5] 4100a[11] 4833a[15]

Always Best *R Allan* a59 62
4 b g Best Of The Bests(IRE) —Come To The Point (Pursuit Of Love)
3204[8] 4142[9] 4556[9] 4947[3] (5415) 5637[6] 6727[12] 7042[12]

Always Bold (IRE) *M Johnston* a93 94
3 ch g King's Best(USA) —Tarakana (USA) (Shahrastani (USA))
58[3] 674[2] (758) 1618[8] 2310[8] (4146) ◆ (4426) 4519[12] 5249[6] 5423[3] 5940[3] (6154) 6288[7] 6646[13] 6817[13]

Always Brave *M Johnston* a76 72
3 ch g Danehill Dancer(IRE) —Digge Park (USA) (Capote (USA))
1208[9] (1448) 1622[2] 2288[2] 2496[9] 3004[12] 3366[11] 4015[4] 4248[5] 4633[6] 4991[4] 5388[2] 5971[3] 6161[4] 6825[5]

Always Certain (USA) *P G Murphy* a68 70
3 ch g Giant's Causeway(USA) —Mining Missharriet (USA) (Mining (USA))
413[2] 936[4] 1306[7] 2261[9] (2907) 3436[7] 3886[8] 4244[9] 5630[4] 6210[10] 6712[8] 7702[10]

Always Cruising (USA) *M Johnston* a71 76
3 b g Fusaichi Pegasus(USA) —Mrs Marcos (USA) (Private Account (USA))
961[13] 1114[2] 2847[4] 3711[3] 3911[5] 4501[2]

Always Engaged *J R Norton*
3 b f Compton Place—Good Standing (USA) (Distant View (USA))
7631[11]

Always Gunner *J O'Reilly*
2 b g Mujahid(USA) —Westcourt Ruby (Petong)
3055[12] 6837[10]

Always Optimistic *M Mullineaux*
5 b g Puissance—Glorious Aragon (Aragon)
2929[12]

Always Ready *C E Brittain* a85 83
3 ch c Best Of The Bests(IRE) —Tahara (IRE) (Caerleon (USA))
(926) 1074[5] 1686[5] 4423[6] 5102[5] 5425[6] 6194[3] 6420[7] 6734[13]

Always Rocking (FR) *G D Blake* a43 53
2 ch f Rock Of Gibraltar(IRE) —Darzana (IRE) (Ashkalani (IRE))
5571[8] 6391[9]

Always The Groom (IRE) *Patrick J Flynn* 77
6 br g Darshaan—Kyka (USA) (Blushing John (USA))
4003a[10]

Always There (IRE) *R Hannon* 66
2 b f Bachelor Duke(USA) —Ansariya (USA) (Shahrastani (USA))
3632[7] 4980[2] 5214[10] 5838[5] 7016[11]

Always The Sun *P Leech* a44
2 b f Intikhab(USA) —Dane Dancing (IRE) (Danehill (USA))
6755[6] 7289[8] 7458[11]

Al Wujood (IRE) *D M Simcock* 55
2 gr c Orpen(USA) —Man Eater (Mark Of Esteem (IRE))
5158[14] 5364[9]

Alyarf (USA) *B W Hills* 96
2 b c Dixie Union(USA) —Tabheej (IRE) (Mujtahid (USA))
3895[7] (6246) ◆

Alyseve *Mrs C A Dunnett* a19 18
3 b f Averti(IRE) —Leen (Distant Relative)
6047[13] 6393[14] 7026[12]

Alystar (IRE) *P F I Cole* 17
2 ch f Rock Of Gibraltar(IRE) —Arpege (IRE) (Sadler's Wells (USA))
7141[16]

Alzaroof (USA) *E A L Dunlop* a56 65
3 b f Kingmambo(USA) —Ranin (Unfuwain (USA))
1964[6] 2971[6] 3611[8] 4282[8] 4825[6] 6048[10]

Amaakin (USA) *P W Chapple-Hyam* 67
3 b c Gone West(USA) —Pink Coral (IRE) (Sadler's Wells (USA))
2197[5] 4871[8] 5278[13]

Amaldi (ITY) *A Renzoni* 98
3 b c Blu Air Force(IRE) —Lan Fei (ITY) (Love The Groom (USA))
1513a[6]

Amanda Carter *R A Fahey* 89
4 b m Tobougg(IRE) —Al Guswa (Shernazar)
1394[9] (2185) 2376[2] 3059[10] (3673) 3864[6] (4419) 6238[5] 6974[9]

Amanda's Lad (IRE) *M C Chapman* a10 61
8 b g Danetime(IRE) —Art Duo (Artaius (USA))
4073[11] 4294[7] 4476[10] 4691[12]

Amanjena *A M Balding* a86 96
3 b f Beat Hollow—Placement (Kris)
961[10] (1412) 1991[6] 3124[11] 3527[2] (6238)

Amarama (IRE) *David P Myerscough* 96
3 br f Fraam—Amarapura (FR) (Common Grounds)
5550a[2]

Amaranda (IRE) *David Wachman* 85
3 b f Fasliyev(USA) —Top Table (Shirley Heights)
2024a[9]

Amaretto Venture *R Johnson* 34
4 b m Tobougg(IRE) —CC Canova (Millkom)
5361[12]

Amarillo Slim (IRE) *S Curran* a37 36
4 b g Danehill Dancer(IRE) —Jungle Story (IRE) (Alzao (USA))
526[11] 843[10]

Amarula Ridge (IRE) *Niall Madden* a64 67
7 b g Indian Ridge—Mail Boat (Formidable (USA))
4799a[6]

Amatara (IRE) *B G Powell* a24 40
2 b f Indian Haven—Mother's Hope (IRE) (Idris (IRE))
3632[13] 5782[4] 6016[12] 6555[10]

Amazing Blue Sky *Mrs R A Carr* a62 51
2 b c Barathea(IRE) —Azure Lake (USA) (Lac Ouimet (USA))
3568[10] 5590[4] 6359[11] 7468[10] (7666) 7784[4] 7824[5]

Amazing Day *John A Harris* a48 61
3 b g Averti(IRE) —Daynabee (Common Grounds)
486[7] 597[8]

Amazing King (IRE) *P A Kirby* a68 57
4 b g King Charlemagne(USA) —Kraemer (USA) (Lyphard (USA))
4048[10] 4503[4] (7427)

Amazing Spirit *Miss V Haigh* a38 34
3 ch f Hawk Wing(USA) —Free Spirit (IRE) (Caerleon (USA))
306[7] 393[5] 547[6] 665[9] 864[6]

Amazing Star (IRE) *M Halford* a86 81
3 b c Soviet Star(USA) —Sadika (IRE) (Bahhare (USA))
3155[13] 6242[8] 6625[4] 6900[3]

Amazing Toto *Miss Diana Weeden*
3 b g Mtoto—Star Princess (Up And At 'Em)
6566[12]

Amba *Joss Saville* 19
2 ch f Hold That Tiger(USA) —Gal Gloria (PR) (Tralos (USA))
5256[11]

Ambassador (GER) *P Rau* a97 103
4 b h Acatenango(GER) —After Eight Blues (CAN) (Bold Ruckus (USA))
7643a[5]

Amber Bamber *D Haydn Jones* 36
3 b f Piccolo—Martha P Perkins (IRE) (Fayruz)
3379[11] 5049[7] 5749[8] 6328[12]

Amber May *J P L Ewart*
5 b m Mark Of Esteem(IRE) —June Brilly (IRE) (Fayruz)
634[12] 980[9]

Amber Moon *J A Osborne* a47
3 ch f Singspiel(IRE) —Merewood (USA) (Woodman (USA))
837[9] 7344[10] 7506[6] 7736[4]

Amber Queen (IRE) *B W Hills* 89
3 ch f Cadeaux Genereux—Our Queen Of Kings (Arazi (USA))
2198[8] (3977) 4818[5] 5841[3] 6981[5] (7143)

Amber Ridge *B P J Baugh* a40 54
3 b g Tumbleweed Ridge—Amber Brown (Thowra (FR))
998[9] 1315[10] 2549[11] 3333[10] 5457[8] 6530[10]

Amber Sunset *J Jay* a60 78
2 b f Monsieur Bond(IRE) —Quantum Lady (Mujadil (USA))
2306[4] ◆ 2691[10] 2944[4] 3734[3] 4297[2] 5567[4] 6240[8] (6535) (6809) 6924[4] 7241[14]

Ambitious General (AUS) *D Hall* 113
5 b h General Nediym(AUS) —Lake Lagoda (AUS) (Military Plume (NZ))
7682a[8]

Ambitious Genes (IRE) *J W Hills* a70 46
4 ch m Grand Lodge(USA) —Doula (USA) (Gone West (USA))
540[9] 963[11] 1929[7]

Ambrix (IRE) *M R Channon* a61 44
3 br f Xaar—Amber Tide (IRE) (Pursuit Of Love)
595[6] 645[4] 772[4] 918[9] 4253[11] 4806[7]

Ambrose Princess (IRE) *R A Harris* a60 63
3 b f Chevalier(IRE) —Mark One (Mark Of Esteem (IRE))
3314[9] (3605) (4165) 4326[7] 4722[2] 5169[2] 5399[2] 5489[5] 6719[3] 7260[3]

Ambrosiano *Miss E C Lavelle* a68 77
4 b g Averti(IRE) —Secret Circle (Magic Ring (IRE))
5800[13] 5994[9] 6380[9] 6825[8]

Ameeq (USA) *G L Moore* a90 84
6 bb g Silver Hawk(USA) —Haniya (IRE) (Caerleon (USA))
5900[14] 6243[12]

Amen To That (IRE) *R M Beckett* a10
2 b f Acclamation—In Time (Generous (IRE))
1762[8]

Americain (USA) *A Fabre* 107
3 b c Dynaformer(USA) —America (IRE) (Arazi (USA))
4042a[11] 4959a[2] 5685a[2]

American Art (IRE) *B W Hills* a90 88
3 b g Statue Of Liberty(USA) —Peshawar (Persian Bold)
(178) ◆ 1806[8] 2405[12] 3745[2] 4392[2] 4790[6] 5682[13]

American Madness (USA) *M G Quinlan* a65 54
3 bb c Johannesburg(USA) —Nasty Little Star (USA) (Nasty And Bold (USA))
4620[10] 4871[10] 5182[6] 6227[3] 6741[7]

Amerigo (IRE) *M A Jarvis* 94
3 gr g Daylami(IRE) —Geminiani (IRE) (King Of Kings (IRE))
(1690) (2310) ◆ 3196[2]

Amethyst Dawn (IRE) *T D Easterby* 77
2 ro f Act One—A L'Aube (IRE) (Selkirk (USA))
4109[8] 4394[3] ◆ (5256) 5791[5] 6946[13]

Amhooj *M P Tregoning* a76 67
3 br f Green Desert(USA) —Harayir (USA) (Gulch (USA))
1854[3] 2920[7] 3611[2] 4342[2] 7304[3]

Am I Blue *H J L Dunlop* 55
2 b f Dubai Destination(USA) —Seal Indigo (IRE) (Glenstal (USA))
6893[6]

Amicable Terms *Rae Guest* a52 85
3 b f Royal Applause—Friendly Finance (Auction Ring (USA))
1499[7] 2067[6] 2704[3] (2915) (3421) 3656[3] 4086[2] (4326) ◆ (4409) 4607[2] 5075[4] 5536[6] 6241[13]

Amical Risks (FR) *W J Musson* a65 63
4 bl g Take Risks(FR) —Miss High (FR) (Concorde Jr (USA))
128[5] 451[2] 559[6] 963[4] 1280[6] 2483[6] 4690[6] 5183[7] 7676[7]

Amicus *D K Ivory* a52
3 br f Xaar—Kartuzy (JPN) (Polish Precedent (USA))
1586[8] 1938[14] 6728[11] 7089[7]

Amicus Meus (IRE) *A Bailey* 86
4 b h Danehill Dancer(IRE) —Top Brex (FR) (Top Ville)
(3438) ◆ 4831[2] ◆ 5067[4] (5419) ◆ 6105[7]

Amie Magnificent (IRE) *P Winkworth* a55 54
3 b f Mujahid(USA) —Darbela (IRE) (Doyoun)
1959[10]

Amir El Jabal (FR) *D E Pipe* 21
5 b g Enrique—Premonitary Dream (FR) (Exit To Nowhere (USA))
2476[8]

Amir Pasha (UAE) *W R Swinburn* a58 58
3 br g Halling(USA) —Clarinda (IRE) (Lomond (USA))
2681[14] 3043[6] 4124[7] 5154[6] 5537[8] 6708[3]

Amjad *Miss Kate Milligan* 20
11 ch g Cadeaux Genereux—Babita (Habitat)
4879[7]

Amnesty *L A Dace* a51 47
9 ch g Salse(USA) —Amaranthus (Shirley Heights)
455[2] 585[5] 695[9] 930[10]

Amongst Amigos (IRE) *C Moore* a54 37
7 b g Imperial Ballet(IRE) —Red Lory (Bay Express)
1313[9]

Amorachy *K A Ryan* a21 68
2 b g Kyllachy—Mi Amor (IRE) (Alzao (USA))
1377[5] 1770[5] 2281[3] 4628[5] 6247[13] 6661[9]

Amosite *J R Jenkins* a64 75
2 b f Central Park(IRE) —Waterline Dancer (IRE) (Danehill Dancer (IRE))
957[17] 1177[4] 1413[9] 1961[2] 2253[3] 3123[13] 3734[6] 4705[7] 5461[2] 6172[17] 6818[15] 7674[3] 7689[6]

Amouretta *T T Clement* a40 47
3 b f Daylami(IRE) —Allumette (Rainbow Quest (USA))
2015[11] 4750[10] 5269[10] 7149[6]

Amour Propre *H Candy* 108
2 ch c Paris House—Miss Prim (Case Law)
2759[7] (3417) ◆ (4323) (6644) ◆

Amphibalus (IRE) *D K Ivory* a45
3 gr g Daylami(IRE) —Dramatically (USA) (Theatrical)
903[13] 1272[7] 1586[12]

Amron Hill *R Hollinshead* a56 35
5 b g Polar Prince(IRE) —Maradata (IRE) (Shardari)
7427[9] (7775) 7827[11]

Amwell Brave *J R Jenkins* a69 89
7 b g Pyramus(USA) —Passage Creeping (IRE) (Persian Bold)
91[9] 332[3] 533[3] 720[6] 1206[3] 1459[4] 2290[3] 3820[6] 4275[3] 6729[8] 7078[8] 7676[3] 7806[7]

Amwell House *J R Jenkins* a53 52
3 gr g Auction House(USA) —Amwell Star (USA) (Silver Buck (USA))
2984[7] 3421[6] 3873[3] 4564[5] 5077[7] 6678[6] 7274[4] 7632[6] 7701[4]

Amyann (IRE) *J R Holt* a58 44
3 b f Indian Lodge(IRE) —Moral Certainty (USA) (Seeking The Gold (USA))
74[8] 1870[14] 4368[8] 4702[6] 5471[4] 6530[9]

Amylee (IRE) *C G Cox* 84
3 b f Danehill Dancer(IRE) —Igreja (ARG) (Southern Halo (USA))
1302[2] 1946[5] 2196[4] 2761[6] 3325[10] 3977[5] 5580[6] 6124[10] 6566[2]

Amy's Mercdes *N Bycroft* 9
4 ch m Defacto(USA) —Efipetite (Efisio)
3796[6] 4378[8] 6217[15]

Ana Americana (FR) *P Demercastel* 102
2 b f American Post—Ana Marie (FR) (Anabaa (USA))
5301a[2] 5987a[4] 6519a[8]

Anaasheed *J L Dunlop* a53 37
2 b f Cape Cross(IRE) —Kahalah (IRE) (Darshaan)
3913[12] 5570[6] 6165[7]

Anabaa's Creation (IRE) *A De Royer-Dupre* 112
4 b m Anabaa(USA) —Premiere Creation (FR) (Green Tune (USA))
6612a[2]

Anabaa's Secret (IRE) *J A Osborne* a54 49
3 bb g Anabaa Blue—Rizo Amoro (USA) (Fit To Fight (USA))
184[4] 325[3] 439[3] 644[6]

Anacaona (IRE) *R Hannon* a41 58
2 ch f Distant Music(USA) —Tarrara (UAE) (Lammtarra (USA))
1413[11] (3091) 3670[8] 4706[2] 5581[9] 6414[9] 6572[9] 6906[10]

Anacarde (FR) *J-C Rouget* 101
3 b c Anabaa Blue—Genuine (FR) (Generous (IRE))
1887a[6]

Anacreon (IRE) *J H M Gosden* 58
2 b c Dansili—Anbella (FR) (Common Grounds)
7106[8]

Anak Nakal (USA) *Nicholas Zito* a106
3 bb c Victory Gallop(CAN) —Misk (USA) (Quiet American (USA))
1820a[7] 2858a[3]

Anani (USA) *S Seemar* a101 72
8 ch g Miswaki(USA) —Mystery Rays (USA) (Nijinsky (CAN))
296a[12]

Anasy (USA) *D M Simcock* a39
2 b f Gone West(USA) —Blue Moon (FR) (Lomitas)
7561[6]

An Carrig *K R Burke* 32
2 b c Peintre Celebre(USA) —Inchberry (Barathea (IRE))
2521[4] (Dead)

Ancien Regime (IRE) *M A Jarvis* 113
3 b c King's Best(USA) —Sadalsud (IRE) (Shaadi (USA))
1834[6] (2410) ◆ 3047[3] (3739) 5891[6]

Ancient Cross *M W Easterby* a69 76
4 b g Machiavellian(USA) —Magna Graecia (IRE) (Warning)
1139[2] 1490[5] 1815[4] 2535[4] 3050[4] 3454[2] ◆ 4538[2] 5390[3] 6043[8]

Ancient Egypt *Annelie Larsson* a87 43
6 b g Singspiel(IRE) —Nekhbet (Artaius (USA))
2233a[7]

Ancient Lights *H R A Cecil* 89
3 b c High Chaparral(IRE) —Fascinating Hill (FR) (Danehill (USA))
(2370) ◆ 4122[3]

Andaman Sunset *G Wragg* a77 84
3 b c Red Ransom(USA) —Miss Amanpuri (Alzao (USA))
1149[4] 1379[5] 4194[8] 5185[6] (6049) 6537[4]

Andean Margin (IRE) *S A Callaghan* a68 62
2 b c Giant's Causeway(USA) —Spiritual Air (Royal Applause)
4600[5] 5404[11] 5842[8] 6214[4] 6394[13] 7467[8] (7693) 7789[2]

Andhaar *E A L Dunlop* a73 74
2 bb g Bahri(USA) —Deraasaat (Nashwan (USA))
3001[6] 4062[3] 4728[2] 5165[7] 6058[4]

Andorn (GER) *A P Stringer* a51 103
4 b h Monsun(GER) —Anthyllis (GER) (Lycius (USA))
6908[9] 7398[8] 7753[6]

Andorran (GER) *A Bailey* a54 54
5 b g Lando(GER) —Adora (GER) (Danehill (USA))
171[2] 345[10] 2755[6]

Andrasta *A Berry* a58 71
3 b f Bertolini(USA) —Real Popcorn (IRE) (Jareer (USA))
17[7] 38[6] 237[7] 279[3] 444[DSQ] 977[3] 1611[7] 2141[7] 2661[11] 2747[3] 3217[6] 3434[2] 3577[8] 3753[4] 4163[6] 4242[3] 4450[3] 4686[4] 4852[6] (5393) 5417[2] 5714[7] 6150[7] 6308[5] 6765[9]

Andronikos *P F I Cole* a95 80
6 ch h Dr Fong(USA) —Arctic Air (Polar Falcon (USA))
226[7] 442[5] 1278[5] 1617[9]

Anduril *I W McInnes* a61 59
7 ch g Kris—Attribute (Warning)
219[5] 323[10] (465) 640[6] 844[4] 1064[8] 1116[8] 1776[9] 1902[6] 3593[2] 4065[5] 4797[7] 4919[3] 5420[8] 5538[9] 6570[8] 6693[6] 6912[8]

Anfield Dream *J R Jenkins* a81 32
6 b g Lujain(USA) —Fifth Emerald (Formidable (USA))
54[10]

Anfield Road *L Corcoran* a74 75
3 ch g Dr Fong(USA) —Mackenzie's Friend (Selkirk (USA))
(7713)

Anfield Star (IRE) *G M Lyons* 59
2 b c Celtic Swing—Shenkara (IRE) (Night Shift (USA))
6317a[18]

Angaric (IRE) *B Smart* a79 78
5 ch g Pivotal—Grannys Reluctance (IRE) (Anita's Prince)
2007[3] 2400[11] 2818[4] 3281[7] 4239[4] 4736[5] 7021[13] 7466[2]

Angela Tee (IRE) *T D Easterby* 25
2 b f Redback—First Fling (IRE) (Last Tycoon)
2217[11] 2887[10] 3334[10]

Angel De Madrid (CHI) *Rune Haugen* 100
7 ch g More Royal(USA) —Labrada (CHI) (Laguardia (USA))
5335a[9]

Angel Dragon (GER) *P Schiergen* 99
3 b f Royal Dragon(USA) —Abazzia (GER) (Acatenango (GER))
7350a[5]

Angelofthenorth *C J Teague* 53
6 b m Tomba—Dark Kristal (IRE) (Gorytus (USA))
1827[7] 2040[7] (2248) 2576[3] 2928[5] 3212[4]

Angelo Minny (FR) *A Fabre* 101
3 b c Red Ransom(USA) —Bielska (USA) (Deposit Ticket (USA))
5927a[5] 6921a[2]

Angelo Poliziano *Mrs A Duffield* a57
2 ch g Medicean—Helen Sharp (Pivotal)
7498[8]

Angel Rock (IRE) *M Botti* a86 89
3 b c Rock Of Gibraltar(IRE) —Nomothetis (IRE) (Law Society (USA))
(3654) 4160[9] (5018) ◆ 6021[4] 6424[11] (7083)

Angelsbemine *J R Norton* a9 30
2 b f Almaty(IRE) —Undercover Girl (IRE) (Barathea (IRE))
5384[9] 5959[16] 7044[7] 7370[8] 7659[10]

Angels Quest *A W Carroll* a48 63
3 b f Piccolo—Tamara (Marju (IRE))
885[7] 4124[8] 4484[4] 5291[2]

Angels Story (IRE) *J S Bolger* 96
3 b f Galileo(IRE) —Love Excelling (FR) (Polish Precedent (USA))
3805a[13]

Angel Voices (IRE) *K R Burke* a73 73
5 b m Tagula(IRE) —Lithe Spirit (IRE) (Dancing Dissident (USA))
56[2] (90) 245[5] 574[2] 628[3] 887[8] 1204[4] 4013[5] 4749[4] (4967) 5455[8] 6650[15] 7378[9] 7819[6]

Angharad *K R Burke* a35
3 b f Danehill Dancer(IRE) —Hot Tin Roof (IRE) (Thatching)
65[5]

Angle Of Attack (IRE) *A D Brown* a74 83
3 b g Acclamation—Travel Spot Girl (Primo Dominie)
4700[11] (4971) 5222[12] 5417[3] 5886[3] 6232[5] 6881[5] 7081[11]

Anglezarke (IRE) *T D Easterby* 103
2 br f Acclamation—Welsh Mist (Damister (USA))
(1425) 3625[4] (4434) 5244[6] 5852[2] 6068[5] 6644[4]

Angliana (USA) *Gary Contessa* a101
6 ch h Giants Causeway—Pratella (USA) (Jade Hunter (USA))
6373a[8]

Angus Newz *M Quinn* a79 96
5 ch m Compton Place—Hickleton Lady (IRE) (Kala Shikari)
1157[3] 1346[2] 2219[3] 2426[12] 2993[6] (3370) (3460) 3948[3] 4198[7] 4660[7] 5310[5] (5781) (5884) 6430[3] 6782[11] 7243[16]

Anice Stellato (IRE) *R M Beckett* 81
2 br f Dalakhani(IRE) —Summer Spice (IRE) (Key Of Luck (USA))
(5240) ◆

Animator *P F I Cole* a78 76
3 b g Act One—Robsart (IRE) (Robellino (USA))
(1244) 1618[4] 2045[10] 4571[6] (5146) 6129[8] 6400[3]

Anisakis (FR) *N Clement* a88 91
4 b g Kaldounevees(FR) —Julna (FR) (Zieten (USA))
5113a[2]

Anjella (GER) *J Hirschberger*
2 ch f Monsun(GER) —Attilia (GER) (Tiger Hill (IRE))
7006a[4] 7264a[3]

Anjuna (USA) *J H M Gosden* a39 50
2 bb f El Corredor(USA) —Red Dot (USA) (Diesis)
3027[9] 3558[5] 4425[6] 4956[4] 5937[7] 6696[10]

Anmar (USA) *Saeed Bin Suroor* 98
2 ch c Rahy(USA) —Ranin (Unfuwain (USA))
(5468) ◆ 5898[2] 6648[7]

Annabelle's Charm (IRE) *L M Cumani* a67
3 ch f Indian Ridge—Kylemore (IRE) (Sadler's Wells (USA))
7387[3] 7609[5]

Anna Ivanovna *J R Fanshawe*
2 ch f Selkirk(USA) —Ice Palace (Polar Falcon (USA))
7259[P]

Anna Lane *G A Swinbank* a12 28
3 b f Vettori(IRE) —Cranachan (Selkirk (USA))
2929[8] 3338[5] 4379[8] 6843[7]

Annaliesse (IRE) *R A Fahey* 71
3 ch f Rock Of Gibraltar(IRE) —Oh So Well (IRE) (Sadler's Wells (USA))
2699[6] 3127[4] 3667[6]

Anna Pavlova *R A Fahey* 114
5 b m Danehill Dancer(IRE) —Wheeler's Wonder (IRE) (Sure Blade (USA))
2791[8] 3511a[3] (3720) ◆ 3878[6] 4914a[5]

Annapolis *M Johnston* 75
2 b c Anabaa(USA) —Pennyghael (UAE) (Pennekamp (USA))
3651[3] ◆ 4169[3] 4425[2] 5043[5]

Annapurna Sunrise (IRE) *Eamon Tyrrell* a58 58
4 b m Monashee Mountain(USA) —Gloriette (Petoski)
716[3] 869[9]

Annawanna *S Wynne* a2
4 b m Ziggy's Dancer(USA) —Veni Vici (IRE) (Namaqualand (USA))
1410[8] 2500[10] 2571[11]

Annemasse *R A Fahey* a93 103
4 b g Anabaa(USA) —Statua (IRE) (Statoblest)
960[9] 2132[4] 2789[13]

Anne Of Kiev (IRE) *J H M Gosden* a87 68
3 b f Oasis Dream—Top Flight Queen (Mark Of Esteem (IRE))
5205[2] 6192[2] (6633) 6990[2] ◆

Annes Rocket (IRE) *J C Fox* a67 66
3 b c Fasliyev(USA) —Aguilas Perla (IRE) (Indian Ridge)
178[5] 364[6] 2760[13] 3564[7] 4278[4] 5088[11]

Annibale Caro *Grant Tuer* a58 79
6 b g Mtoto—Isabella Gonzaga (Rock Hopper)
1702[3] (1890) (2286) (2364) ◆ 2579[3] 3814[2] 4015[2] 4419[9]

Annie Skates (USA) *Jane Chapple-Hyam* a77 99
3 ch f Mr Greeley(USA) —Vivalita (USA) (Deputy Minister (CAN))
1470[8] 2305[2] 2975[3] 3807a[11] 6266[17] 6718[6]

Anosti *K A Ryan* a77 90
3 b f Act One—Apennina (USA) (Gulch (USA))
1401[13] 1623[6] 1999[10] 3141[5] 3554[10] 4083[5] 4745[2] 5998[2] 6340[14]

Another Bottle (IRE) *J J Quinn* 80
7 b g Cape Cross(IRE) —Aster Aweke (IRE) (Alzao (USA))
1016[8] 1481[12] 2218[5]

Anotherbottleteddy *I W McInnes* 35
2 b f Lend A Hand—Lv Girl (IRE) (Mukaddamah (USA))
5304[7] 6581[10]

Another Decree *M Dods* 72
3 b c Diktat—Akhira (Emperor Jones (USA))
1817[10] (2380) 4329[6]

Another Echo *W Storey* 22
2 b f Bahamian Bounty—Blue Nile (IRE) (Bluebird (USA))
2746[8] 4896[10]

Another Genepi (USA) *E J Creighton* a83 68
5 br m Stravinsky(USA) —Dawn Aurora (USA) (Night Shift (USA))
15[3] (155) 367[2] 576[4] 639[2] 783[2] (839) (856) 899[9] 949[4] 5594[13] 6448[4] 7118[5] 7152[5] (7317) 7586[4] 7698[5] 7782[3]

Another Luke (IRE) *T J Etherington* a47 61
2 b c Captain Rio—Belalzao (IRE) (Alzao (USA))
957[12] 1220[4] 1390[4] 3411[11] 4079[9] 4292[6]

Another Moment *G A Swinbank* 90
4 b g Sakhee(USA) —Taqreem (IRE) (Nashwan (USA))
(5042) 6113[2] ◆

Another Socket *E S McMahon* a74 74
3 b f Overbury(IRE) —Elsocko (Swing Easy (USA))
1707[4] ◆ 2122[3] 2896[7] 3462[9] 3811[3] 6011[17] 6658[3] 7276[10]

Another Try (IRE) *A P Jarvis* a63
3 b g Spinning World(USA) —Mad Annie (USA) (Anabaa (USA))
6935[5] 7178[8] 7536[4]

Another World (GER) *W Hickst* 101
5 b m Night Shift(USA) —Arsila (IRE) (Tirol)
(2879a)

Ans Bach *D Selvaratnam* a106 97
5 b g Green Desert(USA) —Bezzaaf (Machiavellian (USA))
205a[4] 384a[9] 668a[6]

An Scaribh *Mrs L C Jewell* a70 71
3 br g Where Or When(IRE) —Wadenhoe (IRE) (Persian Bold)
(1119) 1527[10] 1678[5] (2080) 2495[2] (2894) 3327[12]

Ansells Pride (IRE) *B Smart* a78 91
5 b g King Charlemagne(USA) —Accounting (Sillery (USA))
852[2] ◆ (1308) ◆ 1910[17] (2334) ◆ 2913[2] 3122[15]

An Tadh (IRE) *G M Lyons* a104 111
5 b g Halling(USA) —Tithcar (Cadeaux Genereux)
829a[9] (1198a) 1783a[6] 2417a[6] 2685a[4] 3532a[19] 4223a[12]

Anthemion (IRE) *Mrs J C McGregor* a48 61
11 ch g Night Shift(USA) —New Sensitive (Wattlefield)
2523[9] 2749[5] 3082[2] 3789[3] 4018[7] 4148[6]

Anthill *I A Wood* a70 69
4 b m Slickly(FR) —Baddi Heights (FR) (Shirley Heights)
899[2] 1153[4] 1565[5] 2533[11] 4084[2] (4727) 5088[4]

Anthology *B Smart* 82
2 b c Haafhd—Annapurna (IRE) (Brief Truce (USA))
5857[11] (6655)

Antigua Sunrise (IRE) *R A Fahey* 67
2 b f Noverre(USA) —Staff Approved (Teenoso (USA))
3976[5] 4380[5] 5882[8] 6110[5] 6809[2]

Antillia *C F Wall* a76 53
3 b f Red Ransom(USA) —Milly Of The Vally (Caerleon (USA))
6393[8] 6705[5] 7387[4] (7604) ◆

Antinea *P Bary* 85
2 b f Royal Applause—Wish (Danehill (USA))
3749a[5]

Antinori (IRE) *W R Swinburn* a68 79
2 b g Fasliyev(USA) —Albavilla (Spectrum (IRE))
5996[4] ◆ 6539[2] ◆ 6892[2]

Antiquities *A Fabre* 105
3 ch f Kaldounevees(FR) —Historian (IRE) (Pennekamp (USA))
1760a[2] 2743a[2] 7037a[11]

Anton Chekhov *W Hickst* 108
4 b h Montjeu(IRE) —By Charter (Shirley Heights)
2346a[7] 3540a[6] 4232a[6] 6325a[6]

Antonym (USA) *Mario Hofer* 98
4 b m Bahri(USA) —Annaba (IRE) (In The Wings)
4233a[7] 6852a[7]

Anyaar (IRE) *F Head* 95
2 br f Green Desert(USA) —Petit Calva (FR) (Desert King (IRE))
3749a[6] 5850a[5]

Any Given Day (IRE) *D M Simcock* a65 87
3 gr g Clodovil(IRE) —Five Of Wands (Caerleon (USA))
1389[8] 2043[3] (2340) ◆ 3380[3] (4448) 5249[5] (6195) ◆

Any Luck (IRE) *I W McInnes*
2 b g Key Of Luck(USA) —Zingari (Groom Dancer (USA))
5041[11] 5357[7]

Anything Once (USA) *D Carroll* a51 54
5 b g Elusive Quality(USA) —Bushy's Pride (USA) (Hagley's Reward (USA))
69[5]

Aoibhinn *Patrick J Flynn* a43 44
2 b f Green Desert(USA) —Khalkissa (USA) (Diesis)
5438a[7]

A One (IRE) *H J Manners* a43 55
9 b g Alzao(USA) —Anita's Contessa (IRE) (Anita's Prince)
3422[9] 4052[13] 4428[9] 4691[3] 4910[3] (5148) 5489[8] 5912[8]

Apache Cat (AUS) *Greg Eurell* 124
6 ch g Lion Cavern(USA) —Tennessee Blaze (AUS) (Whiskey Road (USA))
7683a[3]

Apache Dawn *G L Moore* a89 89
4 ch g Pursuit Of Love—Taza (Persian Bold)
314[7] 717[7] 910[10] 1049[2] 1143[6] 1670[2] 2329[9] 4707[8] 5166[14] 5748[4] 6768[3] 7541[4]

Apache Fort *T Keddy* a78 75
5 b g Desert Prince(IRE) —Apogee (Shirley Heights)
(1151) 1482[10] (1768) 2304[6] 3220[6] 3375[4] 3884[6] 4592[3] 4771[19] 5576[5] (6129) 6279[3] 6626[6] 6898[14] (6985) 7230[7] 7314[2] 7459[4] 7657[5]

Apache Nation (IRE) *M Dods* a42 68
5 b g Fruits Of Love(USA) —Rachel Green (IRE) (Case Law)
1160[11] 1578[5] ◆ 1966[8] 2662[3] 3175[10] 3755[8] 4168[4] 4679[4] 4851[5] 5420[2] 5538[10] (6408) 6827[11]

Apache Point (IRE) *N Tinkler* a11 55
11 ch g Indian Ridge—Ausherra (USA) (Diesis)
4541[8] 4919[7] 5303[6] 6162[13]

Apache Ridge (IRE) *K A Ryan* 66
2 ch c Indian Ridge—Seraphina (IRE) (Pips Pride)
6246[3]

A P Arrow (USA) *Todd Pletcher* a117
6 ch h A.P. Indy(USA) —Garimpeiro (USA) (Mr Prospector (USA))
1092a[4] 5558a[4] 6373a[7]

A P Cardinal (USA) *Cam Gambolati* a64
2 gr c A.P. Indy(USA) —Smok'n Frolic (USA) (Smoke Glacken (USA))
6501a[9]

Aphorism *J R Fanshawe* a73 83
5 b m Halling(USA) —Applecross (Glint Of Gold)
1472[11] 2888[2] (3296)

Aphrodisia *S C Williams* a70 82
4 b m Sakhee(USA) —Aegean Dream (IRE) (Royal Academy (USA))
317[2] 545[3] 736[6] 1127[8] (1644) 1932[2] 2483[4] (3272) 3500[3] 4189[10] 4520[11] 7342[4] 7494[3]

Aphrodite's Rock *Miss Gay Kelleway* 47
2 ch f Falbrav(IRE) —Comtesse Noire (CAN) (Woodman (USA))
7104[9]

Apocalypto (IRE) *E J Creighton* a32
4 b g Auction House(USA) —Scared (Royal Academy (USA))
7300[5] 7463[6] 7536[14] 7629[11]

Apollo Shark (IRE) *J Howard Johnson* 78
3 ch g Spartacus(IRE) —Shot Of Redemption (Shirley Heights)
3048[8] 4206[10] 4608[5] 5400[7] (6219) 6792[7]

Apollo Star (GER) *Lenka Horakova* 117
6 ch g Devil River Peek(USA) —Arwina (GER) (Windwurf (GER))
(6692a)

Apotheosis *W R Swinburn* 62
3 ch c Dr Fong(USA) —Carradale (Pursuit Of Love)
4194[6] 4929[4]

Appalachian Trail (IRE) *Miss L A Perratt* a102 116
7 b g Indian Ridge—Karinski (USA) (Palace Music (USA))
294a[9] 666a[5] 959[10] 1619[5] (1989) 2607[3] 3498[4] 4459[4] 5586[4] 6104[25]

Appel Au Maitre (FR) *Wido Neuroth* 104
4 ch h Starborough—Rotina (FR) (Crystal Glitters (USA))
1662a[8] 2708a[2] (5335a) (5958a) 6324a[6]

Applaude *G A Swinbank* 80
3 b g Royal Applause—Flossy (Efisio)
2786[2] ◆ 3629[10] 3854[8] 4560[6] 5504[2] 5888[4] 6487[2] 6762[4]

Applause (IRE) *J Noseda* a79
2 b f Danehill Dancer(IRE) —Sniffle (IRE) (Shernazar)
5674[3] ◆ 6622[2]

Apple Blossom (IRE) *G Wragg* a60 79
4 b m Danehill Dancer(IRE) —Silk (IRE) (Machiavellian (USA))
1287[4]

Apple Charlotte *H R A Cecil* 80
2 b f Royal Applause—Maid Of Camelot (Caerleon (USA))
(7140) ◆

Applehays *W G M Turner* 11
2 b f Fleetwood(IRE) —Child Star (FR) (Bellypha)
2338[8] 3092[9]

Apple Martini (USA) *Chris Block* 87
3 ch f Giant's Causeway(USA) —Crafty Oak (USA) (Crafty Prospector (USA))
5744a[9]

Apple Pie Order (IRE) *R J Hodges* a24 63
3 b f Namid—Apple Sauce (Prince Sabo)
2341[10] 2620[4] 3000[6] 3381[4] 3960[11] 4584[3] 4865[8] 5751[7] 5998[9]

Applesnap (IRE) *Miss Amy Weaver* a76 76
3 b f Clodovil(IRE) —Apple Brandy (USA) (Cox's Ridge (USA))
1715[6] 2077[3] 2428[10] (2983) 3271[10] 3653[7] 4341[7] 4696[7] 5142[6] (5629) 6046[8] 6634[8] 7055[14]

Appointment *Mrs L J Mongan* a64 52
3 ch f Where Or When(IRE) —Shoshone (Be My Chief (USA))
2603[8] 2997[12] 3562[14] 4527[8] 5429[3]

Appraisal *R Hannon* 78
2 ch c Mark Of Esteem(IRE) —Anytime Baby (Bairn (USA))
3682[8] 4625[8] 5811[2] (6197) 6426[8] 6673[12]

Appropriate (IRE) *W J Haggas* a61
2 b f Montjeu(IRE) —Novelette (Darshaan)
7424[5] ◆ 7735[3]

Approved *M W Easterby* 38
2 br f Makbul—Emma Amour (Emarati (USA))
2035[12] 2671[6] 2910[11]

Apres Ski (IRE) *J F Coupland* a50 52
5 b g Orpen(USA) —Miss Kinabalu (Shirley Heights)
1449[13] 1700[4] 2087[9] 2375[11] 3175[13] 3662[11] 4073[10] 4476[4] 4903[3] 5454[6] 5916[11]

April Fool *J A Geake* a76 70
4 ch g Pivotal—Palace Affair (Pursuit Of Love)
1954[6] 2640[4] (3037) 3360[3] 4390[9] 6211[3] 6544[2] (7077) 7194[3] 7390[9]

April Pride *James Cassidy* 98
2 b f Falbrav(IRE) —Hasta (USA) (Theatrical)
(1263) 1838[2] 2147[2] 3192[5] 3681[2] 4403[4] 5266[3] 6966a[11]

April's Daughter *B R Millman* 60
3 b f Kyllachy—April Stock (Beveled (USA))
1965[6] 2681[4] ◆ 3530[8] 4572[7] 5232[7]

April's Quest (IRE) *David Pinder* a41 43
3 ch f Spectrum(IRE) —Coastal Jewel (IRE) (Kris)
1533[14]

April The Second *R J Price* a46 56
4 b g Tomba—Little Kenny (Warning)
999[5] 1266[6]

Apro Lunare (IRE) *Laura Grizzetti* 93
2 b c Orpen(USA) —My Filly (FR) (Last Tycoon)
7163a[10]

Apsara *G M Moore* 65
7 br m Groom Dancer(USA) —Ayodhya (IRE) (Astronef)
2467[11] 2849[9] 3642[3] 4220[5] 4879[10]

Apt (IRE) *David Wachman* 75
2 b f Danetime(IRE) —Sheila Blige (Zamindar (USA))
6319a[19]

Apt Son (USA) *Francis Ennis* a70 89
3 b g Aptitude(USA) —Jungle Sun (USA) (Private Terms (USA))
645[3]

Aqlaam *W J Haggas* 119
3 b c Oasis Dream—Bourbonella (Rainbow Quest (USA))
(2198) ◆ (3119) ◆

Aqmaar *E Charpy* a95 95
4 b h Green Desert(USA) —Hureya (USA) (Woodman (USA))
379a[11] 473a[9]

Aqua Pura (GER) *A P Stringer* a56 53
9 b g Acatenango(GER) —Actraphane (Shareef Dancer (USA))
67[7] 179[2] 322[3] 1017[11] 1459[5] 1726[6]

Aquarian Dancer *Jedd O'Keeffe* a48 51
3 b f Mujahid(USA) —Admonish (Warning)
1479[4] 1912[6] 2704[6] 3816[4]

Aquino (URU) *Doug Watson* a96
4 ch h First American(USA) —Perla Fighter (BRZ) (Irish Fighter (USA))
292a[3] 567a[9] 813a[6]

Aqwaal (IRE) *E A L Dunlop* 75
2 b c Red Ransom(USA) —Mubkera (IRE) (Nashwan (USA))
4826[10] 5578[3] (5901)

Aqwaas (USA) *Sir Michael Stoute* a65
2 ch f Diesis—Jinaan (USA) (Mr Prospector (USA))
7593[4]

Arabesque Dancer *M Botti* a60
3 b f Dubai Destination(USA) —Seven Of Nine (IRE) (Alzao (USA))
288[4] 325[2] 644[4] 1251[4]

Arabian Art (USA) *H R A Cecil* a70 83
3 br f E Dubai(USA) —Slamya (USA) (Seattle Slew (USA))
1372[5] 2038[2] (3177) ◆ 3782[3] (4333) 4595[8] 6174[4] 7109[2]

Arabian Flame (IRE) *M R Channon* 81
2 b c King's Best(USA) —Frappe (IRE) (Inchinor)
4151[3] ◆ 4600[3]

Arabian Gleam *J Noseda* a89 119
4 b h Kyllachy—Gleam Of Light (IRE) (Danehill (USA))
2193[5] 3100[8] 4506[6] 5095[4] (5893)

Arabian Mirage *B J Meehan* a83 73
2 b f Oasis Dream—Bathilde (IRE) (Generous (IRE))
6030[12] 7141[4] (7341)

Arabian Moon (IRE) *R Brotherton* 47
12 ch g Barathea(IRE) —Excellent Alibi (USA) (Exceller (USA))
4366[6]

Arabian Moonlight *E F Vaughan* 44
2 b f Barathea(IRE) —Ludynosa (USA) (Cadeaux Genereux)
5240[13]

Arabian Prince (USA) *Doug Watson* a100 86
5 b g Fusaichi Pegasus(USA) —Add (USA) (Spectacular Bid (USA))
203a[5] 477a[7] 565a[6]

Arabian Silk (IRE) *D M Simcock* a40
2 b f Barathea(IRE) —Anthyllis (IRE) (Night Shift (USA))
7578[10]

Arabian Spirit *E A L Dunlop* a96 94
3 b c Oasis Dream—Royal Flame (IRE) (Royal Academy (USA))
1934[5] 2481[2] 2705[5] (3904) ◆ 4345[2] 4983[3] 5580[2] 6170[2] (6467)

Arabian Sun *M J Attwater* a68 64
4 b g Singspiel(IRE) —Bright Halo (IRE) (Bigstone (IRE))
544[6] 754[7] 1052[4] 1246[9] 1726[3] (2643) 3377[8] 4105[9] 4935[11] 5367[12] 5917[10] 6594[5]

Arachnophobia (IRE) *Pat Eddery* a65 60
2 b g Redback—La Mata (IRE) (Danehill Dancer (IRE))
2759[9] 5784[5] 6389[3] ◆ 6865[8] (7205)

Arazan (IRE) *John M Oxx* 115
2 b c Anabaa(USA) —Asmara (USA) (Lear Fan (USA))
(5296a) 5946a[3]

Arcadia's Angle (USA) *P Bary* 109
3 bb c Aldebaran(USA) —Diane's Birthday (USA) (With Approval (CAN))
1361a[4] (2875a) 4010a[14] 5138a[6]

Arc Bleu (GER) *A J Martin* a85 99
7 ch g Monsagem(USA) —Antala (FR) (Antheus (USA))
(3490) ◆ 4493a[3] 6510a[8] 6817[2]

Arc De Triomphe (GER) *D Fechner* 106
6 b h Big Shuffle(USA) —Alepha (Celestial Storm (USA))
3243a[10]

Arcetri (IRE) *K A Ryan* a51 58
3 b f Galileo(IRE) —Shewillifshewants (IRE) (Alzao (USA))
918[8] 1592[5] 2282[9] 2750[8]

Arch *A M Crow* 27
5 ch g Arkadian Hero(USA) —Loriner's Lass (Saddlers' Hall (IRE))
1825[5] 2735[7]

Arch Event *J M Bradley* a22
3 ch f Umistim—Arch Angel (IRE) (Archway (IRE))
6707[12] 7026[13]

Archie Rice (USA) *W Jarvis* 91
2 b c Arch(USA) —Gold Bowl (USA) (Seeking The Gold (USA))
4394[5] (6080) ◆ 6644[6]

Archilini *M Sheppard* a62 60
3 b c Bertolini(USA) —Dizzy Knight (Distant Relative)
2824[8] 3526[6] 3960[9] 4106[5] 4370[10] 4580[7] 4808[8]

Archimboldo (USA) *T Wall* a64 62
5 ch g Woodman(USA) —Awesome Strike (USA) (Theatrical)
701[6] 778[7] 1408[4] 3697[4] 4935[10] 5367[13]

Archipenko (USA) *M F De Kock* 122
4 b h Kingmambo(USA) —Bound (USA) (Nijinsky (CAN))
472a[10] (651a) 1090a[3] (1666a) (3940) 4889a[2]

Archirondel *B P J Baugh* a35 52
10 b g Bin Ajwaad(IRE) —Penang Rose (NZ) (Kingdom Bay (NZ))
373[7] 578[10] 771[9]

Archmani (USA) *G M Lyons* a74 65
3 b f Arch(USA) —Latifah (USA) (Allen's Prospect (USA))
4494a[7]

Arch Rebel (USA) *Noel Meade* a95 115
7 b g Arch(USA) —Sheba's Step (USA) (Alysheba (USA))
2432a[5] 5136a[5] 5729a[4] 5921a[6] 6261a[6]

Arch Swing (USA) *John M Oxx* 115
4 b m Arch(USA) —Gold Pattern (USA) (Slew O'Gold (USA))
2420a[4]

Arcola (IRE) *D M Simcock* a59 48
2 ch f Nayef(USA) —Ashbilya (USA) (Nureyev (USA))
6391[10] ◆ 7093[6]

Arctic Cape *M Johnston* 87
3 b g Cape Cross(IRE) —Arctic Air (Polar Falcon (USA))
1595[4] 1806[11] 2953[8] 3627[9] 4158[4] 4404[7] 5069[2] 5863[8]

Arctic Desert *Miss Gay Kelleway* a76 69
8 b g Desert Prince(IRE) —Thamud (IRE) (Lahib (USA))
24[4] (101) (250) 373[3] 577[4] 607[3] 753[3] (868) 914[9] 1055[5] 2069[6] 3501[5] (3822) (4129) 4386[6] 4529[8] (Dead)

Arctic Freedom (USA) *E A L Dunlop* a68 72
2 bb f War Chant(USA) —Polar Bird (Thatching)
3456[2] 7333[3]

Ardalan (IRE) *Paul Nolan* 70
5 b g Sinndar(IRE) —Asmara (USA) (Lear Fan (USA))
4493a[16]

Ardent Prince *A J McCabe* a59 60
5 b g Polar Prince(IRE) —Anthem Flight (USA) (Fly So Free (USA))
2870[13] 3182[8] 3569[2] 4031[2] 4268[7] 4540[2] 4898[14] 6768[10] 6955[2] 7114[6] 7516[9] 7560[5] 7691[9]

Ard Fheis (IRE) *J S Bolger* 89
3 b f Lil's Boy(USA) —Affianced (IRE) (Erins Isle)
5550a[18] 6689a[17]

Ardglass (IRE) *Mrs P Townsley* a16 57
6 b g Danehill Dancer(IRE) —Leggagh Lady (IRE) (Doubletour (USA))
1281[4] 1562[13]

Ardkilly Belle (IRE) *Ruaidhri Joseph Tierney* 9
3 ch f Spartacus(IRE) —Wensum Dancer (Shareef Dancer (USA))
3133[14]

Ardmaddy (IRE) *G L Moore* a63 57
4 b g Generous(IRE) —Yazmin (IRE) (Green Desert (USA))
(485) 2715[8] 7711[11]

Are Can (USA) *J S Wainwright* 55
2 bb c Arch(USA) —Golden Show (USA) (Theatrical)
3495[9] 4616[7]

Arena's Dream (USA) *J R Boyle* a71 73
4 rg g Aljabr(USA) —Witching Well (IRE) (Night Shift (USA))
518 542[4] 631[3]

Ares Choix *P C Haslam* 92
2 b f Choisir(AUS) —Ares Vallis (IRE) (Caerleon (USA))
1961[6] (2485) 3192[6] 4403[6] 5112a[3] 6102[5]

Areutherepeg (IRE) *H Rogers* a66 58
2 b f Desert Style(IRE) —Schonbein (IRE) (Persian Heights)
6320a[16]

Arfajah (IRE) *Kevin Prendergast* a81 88
2 b f Invincible Spirit(IRE) —Banadiyka (IRE) (Darshaan)
5438a[4] 5924a[5] 6507a[3]

Arfinnit (IRE) *Mrs A L M King* a66 63
7 b g College Chapel—Tidal Reach (USA) (Kris S (USA))
(13) 165[4] 270[4] 515[9] 964[10] 1534[9] 2010[7] 2706[6] 3033[2] 3316[3] (3346) 3783[4] 4273[9] 5610[5] 6204[6] 6419[10] 7022[8] 7835[6]

Arganil (USA) *K A Ryan* a100 89
3 ch g Langfuhr(CAN) —Sherona (USA) (Mr Greeley (USA))
5366[4] (5561) (6011) 6232[6] (7066) (7365) ◆

Argentine (IRE) *L Lungo* a53 79
4 b g Fasliyev(USA) —Teller (ARG) (Southern Halo (USA))
1309[5] 1952[10] 2444[14] 3080[14] 4846[3] 5392[11] 7288[3]

Ariadnes Filly (IRE) *Mrs A J Perrett* a64 62
2 b f Xaar—Christaleni (Zilzal (USA))
5640[7] 6620[6]

Ariege (USA) *Robert Frankel* a113 106
3 bb f Doneraile Court(USA) —Kostroma (Caerleon (USA))
5745a[3]

Arikinui *K R Burke* 38
3 b f Noverre(USA) —Off The Blocks (Salse (USA))
5361[8] 6660[11]

Aristi (IRE) *Evan Williams* a47 54
7 b m Dr Fong(USA) —Edessa (IRE) (Tirol)
188[3] 322[5] 661[12]

Aristocrat *A P O'Brien* 102
2 b c Galileo(IRE) —Silver Colours (USA) (Silver Hawk (USA))
7158a[3]

Arizona John (IRE) *John M Oxx* a66 86
3 b g Rahy(USA) —Preseli (IRE) (Caerleon (USA))
826a[8]

Arkadina (IRE) *David Wachman* 100
4 b m Danehill(USA) —Cumbres (FR) (Kahyasi)
1353a[5] 2113a[6] 3805a[2] 4833a[3]

Arkando (IRE) *K R Burke* a51 45
3 b f Mull Of Kintyre(USA) —Arjan (IRE) (Paris House)
2577[7] (486) 629[7] 780[9] 835[4] 4686[14]

Arlanda (GER) *S Smrczek*
7 br m Lando(GER) —Artemis (GER) (Lagunas)
5115a[0]

Arlene Phillips *R Hannon* 51
2 ch f Groom Dancer(USA) —Careful Dancer (Gorytus (USA))
5643[12] 6358[7]

Armada (NZ) *J Size* 121
7 ch g Twokay(IRE) —Dance In Time (NZ) (Red Tempo (NZ))
7684a[6]

Armure *M A Jarvis* a94 93
3 gr f Dalakhani(IRE) —Bombazine (IRE) (Generous (IRE))
(3611) 5249[7] (5699) ◆ (6171) 6819[6] 7100[8]

Army Of Angels (IRE) *Saeed Bin Suroor* 114
6 ch g King's Best(USA) —Angelic Sounds (IRE) (The Noble Player (USA))
3946[3] 4330[2]

Arniecoco *Miss J R Gibney* a59
3 b g Dr Fong(USA) —Groovy (Shareef Dancer (USA))
897[6] 1054[4] 1343[3] ◆ 1586[3] 3483[7]

Aromatherapy *H R A Cecil* a88 94
3 b f Oasis Dream—Fragrant View (USA) (Distant View (USA))
(1721) (2532) 5273[3] 6283[6] 7146[11]

Aromatic *J H M Gosden* 67
2 b f Medicean—Red Garland (Selkirk (USA))
6081[5] ◆

Aroundthebay *H J L Dunlop* a74 74
2 b f Diktat—Bayleaf (Efisio)
6358[2] (6770)

Arqaam *Doug Watson* a94 108
4 b h Machiavellian(USA) —Khams-Alhawas (IRE) (Marju (IRE))
565a[5] 742a[4]

Arrabiata *C N Kellett* a51 35
3 b f Piccolo—Paperweight (In The Wings)
505[4] 700[6] 873[10] 3086[8] 4531[8] 5203[9] 7375[10] 7663[8]

Arrewig Lissome (USA) *A M Balding* a51 51
3 b g Black Tie Affair—Lissome (USA) (Lear Fan (USA))
1173[6]

Arriva La Diva *J J Quinn*
2 ch f Needwood Blade—Hillside Girl (IRE) (Tagula (IRE))
3707[8]

Arrogance *G L Moore* a64 63
2 b g Josr Algarhoud(IRE) —Rise 'n Shine (Night Shift (USA))
4274[14] 5165[6] 5609[4] 6223[10]

Art Connoisseur (IRE) *M L W Bell* 113
2 b c Lucky Story(USA) —Withorwithoutyou (IRE) (Danehill (USA))
(1168) ◆ (1399) ◆ (3103) ◆ 4465a[2] 5226[8]

Art Correspondent (IRE) *G L Moore* 67
2 ch c Choisir(AUS) —Tip Tap Toe (USA) (Pleasant Tap (USA))
4020[4] 4346[4] (Dead)

Art Currency (USA) *M J Wallace* a60 81
3 bb c Street Cry(IRE) —Lady In Silver (USA) (Silver Hawk (USA))
(2269) 3263[5]

Art Discovery (IRE) *M H Tompkins* a26
2 br g Indian Haven—Lady Cinders (IRE) (Dance Of Life (USA))
7282[11] 7812[8]

Artesium *R A Fahey* a54 47
2 ch g Haafhd—Multicolour (Rainbow Quest (USA))
3170[4] 3568[6] 4289[9] 6406[4] 6573[3] 7468[2] 7659[3] 7693[4]

Arteus *G G Margarson* 37
2 b c Fantastic Light(USA) —Enchanted (Magic Ring (IRE))
5158[10] 5500[13] 5905[P]

Art Exhibition (IRE) *J Noseda* a68
3 ch g Captain Rio—Miss Dilletante (Primo Dominie)
590[10] 748[10] 1343[2] 1586[2] (1710)

Art Fund (USA) *G L Moore* a64 50
2 b g Speightstown(USA) —Kew Garden (USA) (Seattle Slew (USA))
5628[7] 6575[6] 6894[5] 7472[8] (7738)

Art Gallery *G L Moore* a42 39
4 ch g Indian Ridge—Party Doll (Be My Guest (USA))
1694[8] 2070[8] 2352[7]

Art Historian (IRE) *E G Bevan* a63 53
5 b g Barathea(IRE) —Radhwa (FR) (Shining Steel)
144[10] 323[11] 1025[9]

Arthurian (IRE) *J Jay* 40
3 b g Daylami(IRE) —Kiltubber (IRE) (Sadler's Wells (USA))
1539[7] 1931[8]

Arthurs Dream (IRE) *A W Carroll* a51 51
6 b g Desert Prince(IRE) —Blueprint (USA) (Shadeed (USA))
140[6] 215[2] 303[4] 415[3] 507[2] 578[4] 770[3] 821[2]

Arthur's Edge *B Palling* a82 62
4 b g Diktat—Bright Edge (Danehill Dancer (IRE))
(21) 177[2] (1604) ◆ 2262[8]

Arthur's Girl *G Wragg* a86 104
3 b f Hernando(FR) —Maid Of Camelot (Caerleon (USA))
1444[3] (2123) 3153[2] 4196[4] 7193[9]

Article *T D Easterby* a50
3 b g Mujahid(USA) —Zamarra (Clantime)
441[4] 616[5] (Dead)

Article Rare (USA) *E Lellouche* 105
2 gr f El Prado(IRE) —Action Francaise (USA) (Nureyev (USA))
5301a[4] 5987a[2] (6891a)

Artie Bucco (DEN) *Wido Neuroth*
3 ch g Funambule(USA) —Alamea (IRE) (Ela-Mana-Mou)
4918a[6]

Artie Hot (USA) *Nicholas Gonzalez* a103 103
4 b g Black Minnaloushe(USA) —Dyrce (USA) (Sandpit (BRZ))
2472a[4]

Artimino *J R Fanshawe* a106 106
4 b g Medicean—Palatial (Green Desert (USA))
2595[3] ◆ 3921[14] 4405[12] 6468[2] 6947[12]

Artiste Royal (IRE) *Neil Drysdale* 116
7 b h Danehill(USA) —Agathe (USA) (Manila (USA))
7685a[11]

Artistic License (IRE) *M R Channon* a89 80
3 b f Chevalier(IRE) —Alexander Eliott (IRE) (Night Shift (USA))
967[3] 1066[3] 1819[17] 3918[10] 4615[3] 4773[2] 4988[2] (5142) 5346[7] (5936) ◆ 6160[3] 6699[8]

Artistic Light *W R Muir* a63 51
3 ch f Fantastic Light(USA) —Artisia (IRE) (Peintre Celebre (USA))
2805[7] 3667[4] 4810[6] 5429[8] 5787[5] 6912[13]

Art Man *G L Moore* a93 75
5 b g Dansili—Persuasion (Batshoof)
(22) (185) 409[2] 692[5] (927) (1935) (2531) ◆ 3684[9] 6171[7] 7496[7] 7579[7] 7813[3]

Art Market (CAN) *Miss Jo Crowley* a71 68
5 ch g Giant's Causeway(USA) —Fantasy Lake (USA) (Salt Lake (USA))
1112[4] 1585[5] 1725[4] 2101[6] ◆ 3036[10] 4910[4]

Art Martial (FR) *A De Royer-Dupre* 102
4 ch g Monsun(GER) —Veiled Wings (FR) (Priolo (USA))
1663a[11]

Art Modern (IRE) *G L Moore* a78 84
6 ch g Giant's Causeway(USA) —Sinead (USA) (Irish River (FR))
735[7]

Art Of Being (IRE) *M C Chapman* a38 25
4 ch g Selkirk(USA) —Gloriously Bright (USA) (Nureyev (USA))
481[7] 553[5] 788[7] 1700[6] 2207[12] 4023[10]

Art Preview (USA) *G L Moore* a89
2 bb c Strong Hope(USA) —Elle Est Revenue (IRE) (Night Shift (USA))
(3315) ◆ 4822[2]

Art Princess (USA) *B W Hills* 96
2 ch f Officer(USA) —Rhumb Line (USA) (Mr Greeley (USA))
1419[2] (1961) 3192[7] 3851[2] 5642[5] 5827[20] 6441[12] 6644[8] 7107[8]

Artreju (GER) *G L Moore* a70 76
5 ch g Perugino(USA) —Art Of Easter (GER) (Dashing Blade)
150[6] 406[4] ◆ 1932[12] (2374) 3132[3] 3800[5] 4309[4] 4739[6] 7461[5] 7620[12] 7807[3]

Arts Guild (USA) *W J Musson* a81 83
3 b c Theatrical—Gilded Edge (Cadeaux Genereux)
748[4] 1467[3] 3275[4] 5032[2] 6704[11] 6762[2] 7304[2] 7563[6]

Artsu *M Dods* a78 82
3 b g Bahamian Bounty—War Shanty (Warrshan (USA))
1113[5] 1524[12] 1875[4] 2714[12] 3458[5] (3999) 4595[5] 4854[11] 5358[4] 5962[4] 6556[2] 6724[3] 7222[3]

Art Trend (IRE) *P W Chapple-Hyam* 83
3 b g Hawk Wing(USA) —Skiphall (Halling (USA))
1221[2] 1446[3] 2191[4] (2779)

Arturius (IRE) *R A Harris* a71 30
6 b g Anabaa(USA) —Steeple (Selkirk (USA))
423a[11] 605a[0] 914[2] 1349[3] 1604[8] 1898[10] 4807[9]

Art Value *M Wigham* a65 73
3 ch g Barathea(IRE) —Empty Purse (Pennine Walk)
2161[16] 6004[8] 6433[12] 6716[17]

Arty Crafty (USA) *Sir Mark Prescott* a54
2 b f Arch(USA) —Princess Kris (Kris)
6910[11] 7095[8] 7289[9]

Artzola (IRE) *C A Horgan* a58 50
8 b m Alzao(USA) —Polistatic (Free State)
1807 ◆ 541[4] 7161[1] 1562[3] 2755[7] 3025[5] 4704[5] 5869[5]

Arushore (IRE) *R Hannon* 68
2 b c Kyllachy—Cutting Reef (IRE) (Kris)
2796[7] 3645[3] 4788[8] 5460[4] 5747[4] 6412[11] (6924)

Asaint Needs Brass (USA) *R M Beckett* a84 83
2 bb c Lion Hearted(USA) —British Columbia (Selkirk (USA))
(1078) 1399[7] (2713) 3105[25] 4190[16] 5422[4]

Asakusa *M Johnston* 26
2 b f Royal Applause—Kiss And Don'Tell (USA) (Rahy (USA))
6858[12]

Asakusa Kings (JPN) *R Okubo* 121
4 b h White Muzzle—Croupier Star (JPN) (Sunday Silence (USA))
7511a[8]

Asateer (IRE) *B W Hills* 76
2 b c Alhaarth(IRE) —Catatonic (Zafonic (USA))
4625[4] ◆ 5066[4]

Ascalon *Pat Eddery* 107
4 ch h Galileo(IRE) —Leaping Flame (USA) (Trempolino (USA))
1473[8] 2152[2] 2591[5] (5100) ◆ (6272)

Ascendant *Sir Mark Prescott* a69 72
2 ch g Medicean—Ascendancy (Sadler's Wells (USA))
5572[5] ◆ 5811[3] 6135[3]

Ascot Fayre *Miss Gay Kelleway*
2 gr f Daggers Drawn(USA) —T G's Girl (Selkirk (USA))
6682[12]

Ascot Lime *Sir Michael Stoute* a97 90
3 ch c Pivotal—Hector's Girl (Hector Protector (USA))
1573[5] 2954[5] 4130[2] (4790) ◆ 5677[2] 6649[6]

Aseena (IRE) *Thomas Demeaulte* 92
2 gr f Verglas(IRE) —Pop Alliance (IRE) (Entrepreneur)
7430a[11]

Asfurah's Dream (IRE) *M P Tregoning* a67 88
3 b f Nayef(USA) —Asfurah (USA) (Dayjur (USA))
(3205) 4520[3] 5311[7]
Ashantee (GER) *M Rulec* 102
3 ch f Areion(GER) —Api Sa (IRE) (Zinaad)
3705a[2] (5329a) 6148a[4]
Ashapoo (USA) *Anthony Mitchell*
2 ch f Petitionville(USA) —Royal Deception (USA) (Sovereign Dancer (USA))
6613a[7]
Ashby (IRE) *Niall Moran* a64 57
5 b m Galileo(IRE) —Ashkirk (Selkirk (USA))
4799a[5]
Ashbys Dance *M Botti*
3 b f Danehill Dancer(IRE) —Ashford Castle (USA) (Bates Motel (USA))
3177[P] (Dead)
Ashdown Express (IRE) *W J Knight* a93 109
9 ch g Ashkalani(IRE) —Indian Express (Indian Ridge)
3063[3] 3504[5] 3921[12] 4624[14] 5347[7] 5899[5] 6624[8]
Ashes (IRE) *K R Burke* a72 69
6 b m General Monash(USA) —Wakayi (Persian Bold)
86[6]
Ashleigh Anderson (FR) *Eamon Tyrrell* a48 62
4 b m Black Minnaloushe(USA) —Miswakette (USA) (Miswaki (USA))
861[7]
Ashmolian (IRE) *Miss Z C Davison* a56 55
5 b g Grand Lodge(USA) —Animatrice (USA) (Alleged (USA))
303[8] 330[7] 438[4] 778[3] 1281[6] 1538[2] 3250[11] 4087[6] 5367[14] 6060[12]
Ashram (IRE) *J W Hills* a84 113
2 ch c Indian Haven—Tara's Girl (IRE) (Fayruz)
(5066) 5696[2] (6428) ◆ 6815[6]
Ashton Heights *Miss Gay Kelleway* a7 12
3 b g Kyllachy—Silver Elite (Forzando)
5160[12] 6003[13] 7395[10]
Ashwell Rose *J R Jenkins* a46 63
6 b m Anabaa(USA) —Finicia (USA) (Miswaki (USA))
1692[4] 2091[5] 5232[10]
Ashwinder (IRE) *B J Meehan* a44 55
2 b c Bahri(USA) —Ecco Mi (IRE) (Priolo (USA))
4530[6] 4827[3] 5184[9] 5614[4] 6059[8] 6343[7]
Asian Classic (IRE) *R Charlton* 59
3 b g Montjeu(IRE) —Yafoul (USA) (Torrential (USA))
1172[6] 1526[11] 1896[8] 3022[6]
Asian Lady *R Charlton* a67 68
3 br f Kyllachy—Prancing (Prince Sabo)
1215[3] 1529[3] ◆ 2102[5] 2946[5] 3442[8] 4413[4] 5142[7]
Asian Power (IRE) *P J O'Gorman* a77 76
3 ch g Bertolini(USA) —Cynara (Imp Society (USA))
364[4] (538) 756[10] 924[3] 967[5] 1167[2] 1584[3] 1995[2] 6169[3] 6420[9] 6624[7] 6881[4] 7315[3] 7448[9] 7544[4] 7641[6] 7762[3]
Asian Tale (IRE) *A B Haynes* 73
2 b f Namid—Literary (Woodman (USA))
1515[3] 2035[7] (2459) 2859[3] 5228[6] 6666[3] 6886[8]
Asiatic Boy (ARG) *M F De Kock* a121 121
5 b h Not For Sale(ARG) —S. S. Asiatic (USA) (Polish Navy (USA))
(295a) 815a[3] 1092a[2]
Ask *Sir Michael Stoute* 124
5 b h Sadler's Wells(USA) —Request (Rainbow Quest (USA))
(1596) 3121[5] 4406[5] 6522a[6] 6980[7]
Askar Tau (FR) *M P Tregoning* a106 98
3 b c Montjeu(IRE) —Autriche (IRE) (Acatenango (GER))
2449[10] 3393[2] ◆ (3671) (4573) ◆ (4751) (5249) ◆ (5940) ◆ 6817[4]
Ask Dan (IRE) *B Smart* a59 59
2 b g Refuse To Bend(IRE) —Bush Cat (USA) (Kingmambo (USA))
6481[13] 6715 [4] 7498[7] 7659[9]
Ask Jenny (IRE) *Patrick Morris* a59 59
6 b m Marju(IRE) —Waltzing Matilda (Mujtahid (USA))
(50) (386) 7745[5]
Ask Nicely *W R Muir* a47 58
3 b f Red Ransom(USA) —Oiselina (FR) (Linamix (FR))
2681[8] 3297[5] 3688[6] 4280[4] 4722[8] 5710[4] 6111[3] 6747[6]
Ask No More *J Ryan* a58 30
5 b g Pyramus(USA) —Nordesta (IRE) (Nordico (USA))
100[5] 254[6] 693[7]
Ask The Butler *L M Cumani* 108
4 b g Dansili—Heronetta (Halling (USA))
(2369) ◆ 3045[4] (4422) (5508) 6120[6] ◆ 6476[8]
Asmodea *D J Coakley* a58 46
3 b f Dr Fong(USA) —Latina (IRE) (King's Theatre (IRE))
416[10] 748[8] 1147[7] 1412[11] 2244[8] 2639[9] 6716[8]
Aspectus (IRE) *A Fabre* 112
5 ch h Spectrum(IRE) —Anna Thea (IRE) (Turfkonig (GER))
912a[3] 1240a[5] 4320a[6]
Aspendale (IRE) *D Carroll* 27
3 b g Docksider(USA) —Ambria (ITY) (Final Straw)
3338[7] 3712[9] 4378[6]
Aspen Darlin (IRE) *A Bailey* 109
2 b f Indian Haven—Manuka Magic (IRE) (Key Of Luck (USA))
(1385) 1914[2] 2167[3] 2497[3] 3192[8] 5055[5] (5448) (6102) 6441[2] 6818[2]
Aspirational (IRE) *B Palling*
2 ch c Rainbow Quest(USA) —Londonnetdotcom (IRE) (Night Shift (USA))
7200[17]
Aspro Mavro (IRE) *J H M Gosden* 65
2 b c Spartacus(IRE) —Alexia Reveuse (IRE) (Dr Devious (IRE))
6425[7]
Asrar *Miss Lucinda V Russell* 43
6 b m King's Theatre(IRE) —Zandaka (FR) (Doyoun)
982[9] 1304[6] 2752[7] 3216[3] 3545[5] 4947[6] 5415[3] 5559[8]
Assafair (FR) *Mme C Dufreche* 97
3 gr c Charge D'Affaires—Assaranxa (FR) (Linamix (FR))
6148a[7]
Assail *H Morrison* a72
2 b c Bertolini(USA) —Roofer (IRE) (Barathea (IRE))
7282[2] ◆
Assam (GER) *Carmen Bocskai* a92 96
6 b h Big Shuffle(USA) —Arbarine (GER) (Aspros (GER))
421a[7] 603a[3]
Assent (IRE) *B R Millman* 64
2 b f Kheleyf(USA) —Villafranca (IRE) (In The Wings)
5147[9] 5584[4] 6244[5] 6579[4] 6865[7]
Asserting *A G Foster* 52
2 b f Reset(AUS) —Appelone (Emperor Jones (USA))
4014[8] 5219[2] 6037[4] 6381[12]
Assertive *R Hannon* 117
5 ch h Bold Edge—Tart And A Half (Distant Relative)
1420[2] (2106) 3247[14] 3922[8] 4915a[16] 5891[2] 6304[7] 6645[8]
Asset (IRE) *Saeed Bin Suroor* a105 121
5 b g Marju(IRE) —Snow Peak (Arazi (USA))
5899[2] 6285[2] ◆
Astania *P W D'Arcy* a55 72
3 b f Shahrastani(USA) —So Ambitious (Teenoso (USA))
2956[9] 3799[13] 7401[10]
Aston (USA) *R C Guest* a30
8 b g Bahri(USA) —Halholah (USA) (Secreto (USA))
461[8] 661[10]
Aston Boy *M Blanshard* a45 50
3 ch g Dr Fong(USA) —Hectic Tina (Hector Protector (USA))
4249[10] 4929[9] 5653[7] 6374[6] 7010[12] 7599[5]
Aston Lad *Micky Hammond* 52
7 b g Bijou D'Inde—Fishki (Niniski (USA))
1892[4] 6550[4] 7042[4]
Astorygoeswithit *G C Bravery* a57 42
5 b g Foxhound(USA) —La Belle Mystere (Lycius (USA))
79[5] 189[7] 370[2] 554[8] 596[9]
Astroangel *M H Tompkins* a69 68
4 b m Groom Dancer(USA) —Nutmeg (IRE) (Lake Coniston (IRE))
2070[4] 3218[11] 4053[4] 4540[8] 4806[3] 5604[5] 6036[3]
Astrobrava *M H Tompkins* a55 42
2 ch f Falbrav(IRE) —Nutmeg (IRE) (Lake Coniston (IRE))
6392[13] 6745[8] 7332[9]
Astrodiva *M H Tompkins* 66
2 b f Where Or When(IRE) —Astromancer (USA) (Silver Hawk (USA))
6887[5]
Astrodome *Sir Mark Prescott* a69 74
3 b g Domedriver(IRE) —Alexandrine (IRE) (Nashwan (USA))
2273[9] 2984[3] 3781[6] 4247[5] (4630) (4972) 6092[5] 6740[3]
Astrodonna *M H Tompkins* a64 80
3 ch f Carnival Dancer—Mega (IRE) (Petardia)
1540[4] 2161[2] 3002[5] 3442[2] 3849[5] 4539[5] 5580[4] 6027[6] 6417[4] 6976[6]
Astroleo *M H Tompkins* a48 40
2 ch g Groom Dancer(USA) —Astrolove (IRE) (Bigstone (IRE))
1736[6] 3372[9] 3645[6] 5006[7]
Astrolibra *M H Tompkins* a56 61
4 b m Sakhee(USA) —Optimistic (Reprimand)
2072[2] 2353[3] (2863) 3113[2] 3448[2] 3657[4] 4054[4] (5321) 6050[13] 6364[5]
Astrologie (FR) *A Fabre* 109
3 ch f Polish Precedent(USA) —Quest For Ladies (Rainbow Quest (USA))
5039a[5] (5597a) 6495a[4]
Astronomer Royal (USA) *A P O'Brien* 119
4 b h Danzig(USA) —Sheepscot (USA) (Easy Goer (USA))
2193[11] (2417a) 3247[7] 3922[4] ◆ 4915a[5] 5891[14]
Astronomical Odds (USA) *J J Lambe* a43 18
5 b g Miswaki(USA) —Perfectly Polish (USA) (Polish Numbers (USA))
3759[11] 4849[8]
Aswaaq (IRE) *J L Dunlop* 71
2 b f Peintre Celebre(USA) —Hureya (USA) (Woodman (USA))
6559[5]
Atabaas Allure (FR) *M Johnston* a81 70
2 b f Alhaarth(IRE) —Atabaa (FR) (Anabaa (USA))
4109[5] 4788[2] 5387[8] (6087) (6756)
Atabaas Pride *M Johnston* a80 80
3 b g Pivotal—Atabaa (FR) (Anabaa (USA))
966[3] 1576[3] 2842[3] 3709[4] 5390[10] 6491[3] 6663[11] 6936[4]
At A Great Rate (USA) *H R A Cecil* 62
2 b f Arch(USA) —Glia (USA) (A.P. Indy (USA))
7141[8]
Atalia (GER) *Mario Hofer* 97
3 ch f Sholokhov(IRE) —Anna Kalinka (GER) (Lion Cavern (USA))
5334a[3]
Ateeb *M Johnston* a63 52
2 b c Red Ransom(USA) —Design Perfection (USA) (Diesis)
6213[6] 6621[6]
A Teen *P Howling* a49 49
10 ch g Presidium—Very Good (Noalto)
75[5] 120[4] 621[7] 877[2] 922[8] 1053[6]
Ateesh *L M Cumani* 53
3 ch c Medicean—Diana Panagaea (Polar Falcon (USA))
3051[6] 3629[8]
Atephobia *K R Burke* a69 65
3 bb c Auction House(USA) —Seren Teg (Timeless Times (USA))
93[2] (222)
Athania (IRE) *A P Jarvis* a76 70
2 ch f Fath(USA) —Xania (Mujtahid (USA))
3837[8] (5022) (5422) ◆ 6477[9]
Athanor (FR) *F Head* a103 108
6 ch g Ashkalani(IRE) —Leariva (USA) (Irish River (FR))
2876a[2] 3357a[6] 5555a[2]
Athboy Auction *H J Collingridge* a60 64
3 b f Auction House(USA) —Thabeh (Shareef Dancer (USA))
4163[13] 4615[11] 4988[3] 7497[8] 7757[6]
Atheer Dubai (IRE) *E F Vaughan* a73 88
3 b c Dubai Destination(USA) —Atheer (USA) (Lear Fan (USA))
608[3] 909[5] 1057[7] 1113[3] 2189[7] 3442[11] 4284[12] 6336[11] (7213)
Athenian Way (IRE) *J R Fanshawe* a83 105
4 b m Barathea(IRE) —Grecian Bride (IRE) (Groom Dancer (USA))
1544[6]
Athlumney Lad (IRE) *Noel Meade* 84
9 b g Mujadil(USA) —Simouna (Ela-Mana-Mou)
4493a[7]
Ath Tiomain (IRE) *D J S Ffrench Davis* a20 47
5 b g Night Shift(USA) —Broken Spirit (IRE) (Slip Anchor)
916[8] 3361[11]
Atlantic Air (FR) *A De Mieulle* 115
6 gr h Kaldounevees(FR) —Beg Meil (FR) (Tel Quel (FR))
5114a[8]
Atlantic Beach *R A Fahey* 75
3 ch g Kyllachy—Amused (Prince Sabo)
1139[6] 1519[4] (1971) 2407[3] 3202[6]
Atlantic Dancer (GER) *A Schennach* 86
5 b h Starborough—Arousal (GER) (Goofalik (USA))
421a[2] (603a)
Atlantic Gamble (IRE) *K R Burke* a67 65
8 b g Darnay—Full Traceability (IRE) (Ron's Victory (USA))
18[4] 129[9] 682[5] (822) 859[5] 1020[6] 7355[6] 7499[8] 7608[5]
Atlantic Racer (GER) *M Rulec* 60
3 b c Big Shuffle(USA) —Appena La (IRE) (Tirol)
6744a[7]
Atlantic Sport (USA) *M R Channon* 109
3 b c Machiavellian(USA) —Shy Lady (FR) (Kaldoun (FR))
(3635) 4153[2] 4622[3] (5840)
Atlantic Story (USA) *M W Easterby* a115 96
6 bb g Stormy Atlantic(USA) —Story Book Girl (USA) (Siberian Express (USA))
138[4] 336[4] 594[4] (679) (904) 2172[2] 5831[5] 6269[27] (7418) ◆ 7703[4]
Atlas Peak (IRE) *M Halford* a62 41
3 b g Namid—My Delilah (IRE) (Last Tycoon)
7750[5]
Atomic Winner (IRE) *A King* 72
4 b m Poliglote—Freedom Flame (Darshaan)
2920[8] 3650[5]
Atoned (USA) *Todd Pletcher* a102
3 bb c Repent(USA) —Amidst (USA) (Icecapade (USA))
4678a[6]
Attacca *J R Weymes* a59 59
7 b g Piccolo—Jubilee Place (IRE) (Prince Sabo)
792[3] 861[11] 1775[12] 3079[11] 3211[3] 3789[9] 4605[7] 4951[8] 6680[9]
Attainable *Mrs A J Perrett* a68 37
2 bb f Kalanisi(IRE) —Balleta (USA) (Lyphard (USA))
5753[6] 6205[2]
Atteme Bomb *S Curran* 39
3 b f Fraam—Atemme (Up And At 'Em)
3692[8] 4298[4] 4707[7]
At The Money *J M P Eustace* a68 74
5 b g Robellino(USA) —Coh Sho No (Old Vic)
405[5] 1017[2] 1518[3] 2076[10] (2567) 2888[3] 6672[4] 6861[9]
Attilius (BRZ) *E Charpy* a90 90
6 b h Dodge(USA) —Favorite Blass (BRZ) (Tokatee (USA))
378a[10] 492a[5]
Atullia (GER) *T Clout* 89
3 b f Tertullian(USA) —A Prisa (GER) (Royal Solo (IRE))
7450a[8]
Aturo (FR) *C Sprengel* 101
4 br h Big Shuffle(USA) —Avanti Adda (GER) (Law Society (USA))
7005a[4]
Auchroisk (SWE) *L Reutersklold Jr* a95
5 b m Nicolotte—Fernet-Branca (SWE) (Diligo (FR))
4917a[2]
Auction Belle *P A Blockley* 48
3 b f Auction House(USA) —Island Colony (USA) (Pleasant Colony (USA))
5117[5]
Auctioniki *B Palling*
2 ch f Auction House(USA) —Cashiki (IRE) (Case Law)
7164[10]
Audebelle (FR) *Y De Nicolay* a85 90
3 gr f Ange Gabriel(FR) —Fiddlesticks (FR) (Never So Bold)
7487a[10]
Audemar (IRE) *E F Vaughan* a76
2 ch c Exceed And Excel(AUS) —Bathe In Light (USA) (Sunshine Forever (USA))
5572[2] (6755)
Auenmoon (GER) *P Monteith* 25
7 ch g Monsun(GER) —Auenlady (GER) (Big Shuffle (USA))
5563[6] (Dead)
Auentime (GER) *U Ostmann* 100
3 b f Dashing Blade—Aruba (GER) (Big Shuffle (USA))
3073a[4] 3705a[7] 4675a[7] 5737a[7]
Auenwunder (GER) *Frau K Haustein*
2 ch f Seattle Dancer(USA) —Aruba (GER) (Big Shuffle (USA))
7006a[8]
Augmentation *P W D'Arcy* a53 50
3 br g Dansili—Moulin Rouge (Shareef Dancer (USA))
2079[6] 2982[4] 3221[9] 6492[5]
Augusta Gold (USA) *B J Meehan* a68 66
2 bb c Medaglia D'Oro(USA) —Golden Gorse (USA) (His Majesty (USA))
6025[6] 6731[8] 7011[3]
August Days (IRE) *R M Beckett* a46 57
2 ch f Noverre(USA) —Vitesse (IRE) (Royal Academy (USA))
1838[6] 2458[7] 3378[10] 4387[3] 4764[3] (5287) 5475[8]
August Gale (USA) *G P Kelly* a83 66
3 b g Storm Cat(USA) —Lady Bonanza (USA) (Seeking The Gold (USA))
796[2] ◆ 1295[11] 1601[3] 2532[2] 2929[3] 3200[2] 3641[8] 5968[12] 6352[7] 6659[8] 6989[13] 7166[11] 7533[9]
Augustus John (IRE) *S Parr* a74 79
5 gr g Danehill(USA) —Rizerie (FR) (Highest Honor (FR))
4111[8] 4902[7] 5454[7] 7064[3] 7400[3] 7515[10] 7545[8] 7669[3] 7724[3] 7798[2]
Aula *E A L Dunlop* a59 48
2 gr f Linamix(FR) —Doomna (IRE) (Machiavellian (USA))
4870[16] 5788[8] 6081[10]
Auld Arty (FR) *T G Mills* a76 73
2 bb g Dansili—Provisoire (USA) (Gone West (USA))
2592[5] ◆ 3274[3] 4926[2] 5785[6] 7475[2] 7700[2]
Auntie Mame *D J Coakley* a68 68
4 b m Diktat—Mother Molly (USA) (Irish River (FR))
(2097) (2770) 3163[5] 4485[2] 5476[3] 6400[2] 7078[4] 7342[7]
Aunt Nicola *M L W Bell* a71 85
2 b f Reel Buddy(USA) —Night Gypsy (Mind Games)
2702[2] (3207) 3496[3]
Aura *H J L Dunlop* a39 47
3 b f Barathea(IRE) —Finger Of Light (Green Desert (USA))
1965[8] 2500[8] 5019[8] 6032[7] 6753[9] 7310[13] 7599[11]
Aura Of Calm (IRE) *Ronald O'Leary* a43 63
6 ch g Grand Lodge(USA) —Perils Of Joy (IRE) (Rainbow Quest (USA))
5476[11] 6708[9]
Aureate *B Ellison* a79 93
4 ch g Jade Robbery(USA) —Anne D'Autriche (IRE) (Rainbow Quest (USA))
1018[4] 1137[2] 1472[8] 1947[5] 2830[3] 3045[10]
Aurora Sky (IRE) *J Akehurst* a70
2 gr f Hawk Wing(USA) —To The Skies (USA) (Sky Classic (CAN))
7312[2] 7577[3]
Aurorian (IRE) *R Hannon* a87 87
2 b c Fantastic Light(USA) —Aurelia (Rainbow Quest (USA))
5314[10] (5578) ◆ 6075[4] 6466[2] 6779[6]
Ausonius *L M Cumani* 46
2 b c Kyllachy—Baileys Silver (USA) (Marlin (USA))
6029[11] 6552[7]
Aussie Blue (IRE) *R M Whitaker* a62 69
4 b g Bahamian Bounty—Luanshya (First Trump)
990[9] 1520[7] 2375[2] 2787[4] 3229[5] (3557) 4172[12] 4650[7] 4878[8] 6215[7] 6353[3] 7167[6]
Austintatious (USA) *B J Meehan* a75 89
3 ch g Distorted Humor(USA) —Fancy Ruler (USA) (Half A Year (USA))
(1854) 2403[11]
Australia Day (IRE) *P R Webber* a95 99
5 gr g Key Of Luck(USA) —Atalina (FR) (Linamix (FR))
357[7] 2897[3] 3090[4] (3561) (4350) 5508[7] 6238[2] 7814[2]
Autograph Hunter *Peter Grayson* a58 38
4 b g Tobougg(IRE) —Kalindi (Efisio)
125[9] 251[8] 420[8] 2949[9] 3691[3] 3789[6] 4181[2] 4824[10] 6208[11] 6729[12] 7373[10] 7585[11] 7662[7]
Autre Gemme (IRE) *A & G Botti*
2 ch c Masterful(USA) —Ailleacht Nadurtha (ITY) (Barathea (IRE))
2745a[2]
Autumn Blades (IRE) *A Bailey* a82 80
3 ch g Daggers Drawn(USA) —September Tide (IRE) (Thatching)
163[2] 355[2] 514[2] 1995[4] (3445) (4083) 4408[3] 4893[5] 5697[11] 6242[6] 6695[10] 6952[2] 7592[4]
Autumn Charm *Lucinda Featherstone* a60 50
3 ch f Reel Buddy(USA) —Eurolink Cafe (Grand Lodge (USA))
30[4] (81) 156[2] 3667[5] 4049[8] 5407[6] 6162[11] 6560[8] 7180[13] 7736[7] 7815[4]
Autumn Morning (IRE) *P D Evans* a58 38
2 b f Danetime(IRE) —Soviet Maid (IRE) (Soviet Star (USA))
4692[14] 5022[10] 6489[2] 7113[12] 7199[5] 7361[5] (7607) 7789[3]
Ava Gee *B De Haan* 63
3 br f Averti(IRE) —Spring Sunrise (Robellino (USA))
3023[14]
A Valley Away (IRE) *Jane Chapple-Hyam* a46
4 ch m City On A Hill(USA) —Sharkiyah (IRE) (Polish Precedent (USA))
7489[5] 7713[7]
Avanguardia (GER) *Y De Nicolay* 100
3 b f Choisir(AUS) —Anthurium (GER) (Hector Protector (USA))
3243a[5]

Avanti Polonia (GER) *F Head* 110
4 br m Polish Precedent(USA) —Alisa (GER) (Daun (GER))
1713a[4] 2553a[5] 4041a[10] (4914a) 5557a[8] 5954a[6] 6324a[7]

Avant Premiere (USA) *C Boutin* 71
3 b f Vindication(USA) —Committed Actress (USA) (Theatrical)
6744a[8]

Ava's World (IRE) *Peter Grayson* a63 82
4 b m Desert Prince(IRE) —Taibhseach (USA) (Secreto (USA))
142[7] 255[4] 297[6]

Avatea (IRE) *A Berry*
3 b f Orpen(USA) —Nousaiyra (IRE) (Be My Guest (USA))
6114[15] 6791[18]

Ave *Sir Michael Stoute* a84 85
2 b f Danehill Dancer(IRE) —Anna Amalia (IRE) (In The Wings)
5643[4] ◆ (6166) 6439[9]

Avening *Eve Johnson Houghton* a43 73
8 br g Averti(IRE) —Dependable (Formidable (USA))
6200[8] 6377[7] 7012[12]

Aven Mac (IRE) *N Bycroft* 48
2 ch f Indian Haven—Anamara (IRE) (Fairy King (USA))
3277[9] 3792[10] 4921[9] 5771[4] 6014[8] 6214[2] 6524[10]

Averoo *M D Squance* a67 73
3 br g Averti(IRE) —Roo (Rudimentary (USA))
966[9] 1297[15] 1572[9] 2161[6] 2549[5] 3030[4] ◆ (3441) 3678[3] 4329[9]

Avertis *M Botti* a82 82
3 b g Averti(IRE) —Double Stake (USA) (Kokand (USA))
(3116) 3407[3] 4130[9] 4731[12] 6598[14] 7167[3] (7374) 7560[8]

Avertitop *R Hannon* a68 77
3 b g Averti(IRE) —Lucayan Belle (Cadeaux Genereux)
1899[9] 2664[3]

Avertuoso *B Smart* a77 89
4 b g Averti(IRE) —First Musical (First Trump)
2212[5] 2489[6] 2938[5] 4171[4] 4418[9] 4962[9] 6651[10]

Avery *R J Hodges* a18 62
4 gr g Averti(IRE) —Bandanna (Bandmaster (USA))
7637[9]

Avian Flew *J A Pickering* a38 48
3 b f Averti(IRE) —Ice Bird (Polar Falcon (USA))
486[4] 780[10] 1169[7] 3692[9]

Aviso (GER) *A P Stringer* a14 108
4 b g Tertullian(USA) —Akasma (GER) (Windwurf (GER))
7755[10]

Avitus *Micky Hammond* 37
2 rg g Monsieur Bond(IRE) —Top (Shirley Heights)
6230[13] 6789[11] 7038[11]

Avoca Dancer (IRE) *Miss Gay Kelleway* a69 65
5 ch m Compton Place—Kashra (IRE) (Dancing Dissident (USA))
174[2] (264) 469[2] 625[3] (858) 898[3] ◆ 5474[8] (5601) 5801[3] 6889[12] 7090[2] 7399[11] 7727[5]

Avoir Choisi (IRE) *P W Chapple-Hyam* 64
2 ch c Choisir(AUS) —Dolara (IRE) (Dolphin Street (FR))
7051[4]

Avoncreek *B P J Baugh* a45 58
4 b g Tipsy Creek(USA) —Avondale Girl (IRE) (Case Law)
46[2] 232[5] 469[4] 642[7] 972[9] 1453[9] (2511) 3638[10] 4327[13] 6357[7] 6889[6]

Avonlini *B P J Baugh*
2 b f Bertolini(USA) —Avondale Girl (IRE) (Case Law)
1610[7] 2357[8] 6273[10]

Avontuur (FR) *Mrs R A Carr* a62 70
6 ch g Kabool—Ipoh (FR) (Funambule (USA))
168[10] (255) 347[3] 466[4] 576[9] 681[3] (766) 990[4] 1061[2] 1191[6] 1338[5] 1634[3] 2009[4] 2444[3] 2751[13] 2891[7] (3079) 3339[7] 3713[2] 3825[7] 4174[8] 4453[9] 4951[6] 5392[2] 6219[3] (6411) 6724[7] 6889[3] 7055[4]

Avrilo *M S Saunders* a10
2 ch f Piccolo—Arctic High (Polar Falcon (USA))
7388[10] 7498[12]

Awaken *Miss Tracy Waggott* 57
7 b m Zafonic(USA) —Dawna (Polish Precedent (USA))
2365[10] 3077[9] 3644[8]

Awash (USA) *D Broad* a54 56
6 ch g Coronado's Quest(USA) —All At Sea (USA) (Riverman (USA))
3606[5]

Awatuki (IRE) *J R Boyle* a88 60
5 b g Distant Music(USA) —Itkan (IRE) (Marju (IRE))
626[5] 927[2] 3375[9] 6607[9] 7025[7] (7398) 7493[5]

Awesome Gem (USA) *Craig Dollase* a116 114
5 ch g Awesome Again(CAN) —Piano (USA) (Pentelicus (USA))
6996a[6] 7684a[12]

Awesome Light (IRE) *W R Muir* a64 32
3 bb c Catcher In The Rye(IRE) —Stardance (USA) (Rahy (USA))
163[7] 343[4] 595[4] 698[5] 3166[6] 3730[7]

Awfeyaa *W J Haggas* a80 67
2 ch f Haafhd—Aspen Leaves (USA) (Woodman (USA))
6030[9] 6360[4] (7097)

Awinnersgame (IRE) *J Noseda* 108
2 b c Kyllachy—Polish Descent (IRE) (Danehill (USA))
2134[2] (2569) 3103[6] 4187[3] (4600) (5827) ◆ 6317a[6]

A Wish For You *D K Ivory* a70 68
3 ch f Tumbleweed Ridge—Peperonata (IRE) (Cyrano De Bergerac)
199[3] 324[4] 4693[10] 5346[9] 6864[11] 7286[7] 7589[7]

Axel Foley (USA) *J R Best* a105
2 bb c Officer(USA) —Morganza (USA) (Clever Trick (USA))
5996[3] (6737) ◆ 7751a[6]

Axinit (GER) *E J Creighton* a30 5
8 gr g Linamix(FR) —Assia (IRE) (Royal Academy (USA))
4935[9] 6606[15]

Axiom *L M Cumani* a85 98
4 ch h Pivotal—Exhibitor (USA) (Royal Academy (USA))
(2787) ◆ 3627[7] 4509[5] 6130[11] (7019) ◆ 7245[5]

Axxos (GER) *P Schiergen* 110
4 b h Monsun(GER) —Acerbis (GER) (Rainbow Quest (USA))
(1667a) 2230a[8] 3053a[6] 4470a[9]

Aye Aye Definitely (IRE) *Adrian McGuinness* a55 71
4 b m Danetime(IRE) —Taispeain (IRE) (Petorius)
7625[5] 7636[3]

Aye Aye Digby (IRE) *H Candy* 92
3 b g Captain Rio—Jane Digby (IRE) (Magical Strike (USA))
1441[9] (1999) 2967[5] 3222[2] 4553[5] 5096[4] 5470[12] 5897[5] 6239[7] 6783[5] 7239[14]

Aypeeyes (IRE) *A King* a85 86
4 b g King Charlemagne(USA) —Habaza (IRE) (Shernazar)
(1963) 2153[8] 2822[4] 4078[3] 4645[3] (5092) 6129[6] 7595[4]

Ayrpassionata *Miss L A Perratt* 36
3 ch f Where Or When(IRE) —Least Said (USA) (Trempolino (USA))
2246[6] 3130[6]

Ayrus (USA) *B J Meehan* a60 76
2 bb c Dixie Union(USA) —Miss Brickyard (USA) (A.P. Indy (USA))
4199[5] 5462[8] 6025[7] 6597[7] 6924[10]

Ay Tay Tate (IRE) *I W McInnes* 69
2 b c Catcher In The Rye(IRE) —Vintage Belle (IRE) (Waajib)
2134[6] 2592[3] ◆ 3107[12] 4740[4] 5632[11] 5895[7] 6524[6]

Azabara *A Fabre* 106
3 ch f Pivotal—Danella (FR) (Highest Honor (FR))
2033a[5] (2902a) 3775a[5]

Azabu Juban (IRE) *J Jay* a87 69
3 b f Catcher In The Rye(IRE) —Snipe Victory (IRE) (Old Vic)
657[3] 903[10] 961[4] 1119[2] (7274) 7447[3] 7545[2] (7639) 7696[2] 7770[3]

Azalee (GER) *J Hirschberger* 94
3 b f Lando(GER) —Anthyllis (GER) (Lycius (USA))
4675a[11]

Azarole (IRE) *Jane Chapple-Hyam* a101 102
7 b g Alzao(USA) —Cashew (Sharrood (USA))
205a[3] 382a[12] 960[17] 3946[6] 5208[6]

Azeer (USA) *P W Chapple-Hyam* 88
3 ch c Giant's Causeway(USA) —Touch Of Love (USA) (Alydar (USA))
1379[10] 2189[10] 3031[11]

Aziz (IRE) *Miss D Mountain* a40 49
2 b c Catcher In The Rye(IRE) —Imposition (UAE) (Be My Guest (USA))
5246[17] 6581[7] 6760[11] 7079[6] 7282[9]

Azul Leon (USA) *Doug O'Neill* a107
2 b c Lion Heart(USA) —Quick Blue (CAN) (Cure The Blues (USA))
6997a[9] 7751a[5]

Azure Mist *M H Tompkins* a71 69
3 ch f Bahamian Bounty—Inquirendo (USA) (Roberto (USA))
1575[5] 2118[15] 3117[6] 4260[3] 4797[2] 5568[2] 6049[3] 6332[2] 6712[6] 6935[2] 7178[6] 7403[3] 7490[3] 7548[2] (7669) 7790[3]

Azwa *E A L Dunlop* a71 68
2 b f Haafhd—Shahaamah (IRE) (Red Ransom (USA))
2306[5] 3373[5] 3959[2] 4729[8] (5680) 6023[4] 6769[8]

Azygous *J Akehurst* a70 80
5 ch g Foxhound(USA) —Flag (Selkirk (USA))
1037[2] 1242[3] 1997[16] 2330[4] 2710[3] 2881[4] 3159[6] 4812[2] 5187[4] 5645[6] (6190) 6339[11] 6750[6] 7092[9] 7206[6] 7377[4] 7521[6] (7679) 7743[7]

Azzaamm *C A Dwyer* 45
3 b g Green Desert(USA) —Tarfshi (Mtoto)
2279[6] 2823[7] 3268[12] 4056[8] 4684[11] 5167[14]

Baaher (USA) *T J Pitt* a71 32
4 b g War Chant(USA) —Raajiya (USA) (Gulch (USA))
837[7] 991[7] 1521[11] 3211[12] 4390[12]

Baan (USA) *H J Collingridge* a74 81
5 ch g Diesis—Madaen (USA) (Nureyev (USA))
68[3] 185[5] 5321[6] 7400[2] 7639[3] 7715[3]

Baariq *P W Chapple-Hyam* 79
2 b c Royal Applause—Second Of May (Lion Cavern (USA))
5099[7] 6083[2] ◆ (6359)

Baba Ghanoush *M J Attwater* a50 11
6 ch m Zaha(CAN) —Vrennan (Suave Dancer (USA))
209[12] 389[7] 535[7] 2355[13] 4268[10] 4529[7] 7705[6]

Bab Al Salam (USA) *Saeed Bin Suroor* a78
2 b c Seeking The Gold(USA) —Encandiladora (ARG) (Equalize (USA))
(6620)

Babel *M Wigham* a69 72
3 b f Xaar—Day Star (Dayjur (USA))
7534[12] 7629[8] 7727[9]

Babieca (USA) *A B Haynes* a55 36
4 gr g Tactical Cat(USA) —Secret Mountain (USA) (Mt. Livermore (USA))
659[6] 1083[5] 1383[12] 1521[9] 1626[5] 4181[9] 6185[11]

Babilu *A G Newcombe* a74 61
3 ch f Lomitas—Creeking (Persian Bold)
4689[3] 5155[2] 6662[7]

Babodana *M H Tompkins* a100 106
8 ch h Bahamian Bounty—Daanat Nawal (Machiavellian (USA))
960[3] 1326[3] 1631[6] 2600[3] 5896[11] 7147[10]

Baby Houseman *J H M Gosden* a5 96
3 b f Oasis Dream—Photogenic (Midyan (USA))
(2307) ◆ 3500[2] 6911[13]

Baby Is Here (IRE) *D J S Ffrench Davis* a21 42
2 b f Namid—Attymon Lill (IRE) (Marju (IRE))
1866[8] 6392[12] 6696[11]

Baby Josr *I A Wood* a55 52
2 b g Josr Algarhoud(IRE) —Bella Helena (Balidar)
4973[8] 5431[8] 5959[11] 6572[3] 6924[12]

Baby Princess (BRZ) *J W Hills* a34 11
4 b m Crimson Tide(IRE) —Shareef Princess (Shareef Dancer (USA))
201a[12] 496a[11] 3163[7] 5291[12] 6380[12]

Baby Rock *C F Wall* 72
3 b g Selkirk(USA) —Vanishing Point (USA) (Caller I.D. (USA))
4301[4] 5160[3] 5636[14] 6003[2] 6543[11]

Baby Special *C G Cox* 28
2 b f Needwood Blade—Bollin Victoria (Jalmood (USA))
2011[8] 2309[7] 3670[14]

Baby Strange *D Shaw* a91 105
4 gr h Superior Premium—The Manx Touch (IRE) (Petardia)
677[9] 832[9] 925[7] 1071[14] 1300[2] 1571[6] 1809[4] (2195) 2426[4] 3489[5] 3973[6] 4145[2] ◆ 4586[2] 5109[10] 6104[26] 6468[8]

Baby Wood (FR) *S Loeuillet* 102
2 b c Elnadim(USA) —Talkata (IRE) (Suave Dancer (USA))
5330a[14] 6642a[7]

Backbord (GER) *Mrs L Wadham* 91
6 b g Platini(GER) —Bukowina (GER) (Windwurf (GER))
2202[7] 2609[8]

Back In The Red (IRE) *R A Harris* a77 79
4 ch g Redback—Fureur De Vivre (IRE) (Bluebird (USA))
3352[9] 4370[5] 4535[5] 4958[4] 5709[6] 6024[2] 6204[3] ◆ 6357[10] 6711[7] 7231[4] (7357) 7471[3] (7582) 7819[2]

Backlash *A W Carroll* a48 41
7 b m Fraam—Mezza Luna (Distant Relative)
125[4] 269[7] 377[7] 544[5] 3901[5]

Backseat Rhythm (USA) *Patrick L Reynolds* a106 110
3 b f El Corredor(USA) —Kiss A Miss (USA) (Kissin Kris (USA))
3807a[7] (5164a) (5745a)

Badalona *M L W Bell* 84
3 b f Cape Cross(IRE) —Badawi (USA) (Diesis)
1930[2] 3109[4] 3944[2] 4970[2]

Badaria (FR) *E Charpy* a89 93
3 b f Almutawakel—Green Maid (USA) (Green Dancer (USA))
201a[5] 496a[10]

Bad Baron (IRE) *Eve Johnson Houghton* a60 67
2 ch g Lomitas—Dyna Flyer (USA) (Marquetry (USA))
4296[4] 4769[4] 5678[8]

Bad Beat *V Smith* a75 86
2 ch c Beat Hollow—Judiam (Primo Dominie)
957[13] (1118) 1399[8] 2204[4] 3245[6] 3924[3] 4600[2]

Bad Boy Al (IRE) *N J Vaughan* 66
4 b g Cape Cross(IRE) —Ladycromby (IRE) (Lycius (USA))
2361[2] 2752[3] 3589[6]

Baddam *Ian Williams* 111
6 b g Mujahid(USA) —Aude La Belle (FR) (Ela-Mana-Mou)
1717[5] 2609[7] 3104[9] 3250[9] (4516) 5854[9] 6527[4] 6817[30]

Badge Of Honour *M Johnston* a25
2 ch c Storming Home—Loch Katrine (Selkirk (USA))
7773[7]

Badger Or Bust (IRE) *Liam Roche* a86 98
3 b c Orpen(USA) —Peace Dividend (IRE) (Alzao (USA))
1356a[4] 3155[27]

Badiat Alzaman (IRE) *D M Simcock* a72 66
2 b f Zamindar(USA) —Fair Weather (IRE) (Marju (IRE))
5241[8] 6167[4] 7097[4]

Bad Moon Rising *J Akehurst* a57 51
3 ch g Piccolo—Janette Parkes (Pursuit Of Love)
60[9] 3678[16] 4278[13] 7072[8] 7596[9] 7765[9]

Ba Dreamflight *H Morrison* a59 58
3 b g Noverre(USA) —Aunt Tate (Tate Gallery (USA))
325[9] 1186[4] 1553[6] 2552[4] 3763[4] 4481[8] 4978[4] 5537[3] 6584[6] (6753) 7085[2] 7272[2] 7776[4]

Badtanman *Peter Grayson* a25
2 ch c Primo Valentino(IRE) —Pearls (Mon Tresor)
4634[10] 6133[9] 6489[11]

Badweia (USA) *J L Dunlop* 81
3 b f Kingmambo(USA) —Alshadiyah (USA) (Danzig (USA))
1445[4] 1964[4] (2620) ◆ 3849[6] 5073[2] 5580[3] 6027[9] (6387) 6981[13]

Bagber *H J L Dunlop* 74
2 b c Diktat—Torcross (Vettori (IRE))
4150[4] 5227[5] 5754[3]

Bagenalstown (IRE) *M Wellings* a19 35
3 b g Fath(USA) —Rhapsani (IRE) (Persian Bold)
2571[10] 3065[11] 3731[9] 4043[6] 4298[7] 4990[8]

Baggio (IRE) *Charles O'Brien* a97 102
7 b g Foxhound(USA) —Starring Role (IRE) (Glenstal (USA))
4004a[13] 5731a[17] 6510a[7] 6963a[6] 7325a[6]

Ba Globetrotter *M R Channon* a49 53
2 ch g Needwood Blade—Generous Share (Cadeaux Genereux)
2702[7] 2916[9] 3140[9] 3444[12] 4666[7] 4827[9] 5041[5] 5460[12] 5909[2] 6059[7] 6343[8] 7257[11] 7353[5] 7519[6]

Bahama Baileys *M Johnston* 75
3 ch g Bahamian Bounty—Baileys Silver (USA) (Marlin (USA))
1952[14] 2268[4] 2463[17] 3581[7]

Bahamarama (IRE) *R A Harris* a60 50
3 ch f Bahamian Bounty—Cole Slaw (Absalom)
38[3] 154[6] 467[2] 780[6] 917[3] (1081) 1257[3] 1560[6] 1635[6] 2803[3] 3330[5]

Bahamian Babe *M L W Bell* a78 93
2 ch f Bahamian Bounty—Baby Bunting (Wolfhound (USA))
(1183) ◆ (1447) (2167) 3123[10] 4190[4] 4648[3] 5852[11] 6644[5]

Bahamian Ballad *J D Bethell* a43 68
3 ch f Bahamian Bounty—Record Time (Clantime)
1795[5] 2399[5] 3202[5] 4236[8] 4615[4] 6707[11] 7528[4] 7648[7]

Bahamian Ballet *E S McMahon* a83 91
6 ch g Bahamian Bounty—Plie (Superlative)
1908[7] 2359[4] 3009[16] 3520[2] ◆ 4103[2] 4668[8] 6006[7] 6486[12]

Bahamian Bay *M Brittain* a53 17
6 b m Bahamian Bounty—Moly (Inchinor)
642[2] 718[8] (808) 877[7] 1455[11] 7619[5] 7663[10]

Bahamian Bliss *J A R Toller* a67
3 b f Bahamian Bounty—Fragrance (Mtoto)
608[5] 885[2] 1709[2] (3847) 5142[5] 5998[3] 6880[10]

Bahamian Blue (IRE) *P G Murphy* a55 63
3 ch g Touch Of The Blues(FR) —Cattiva (ITY) (Lomond (USA))
1193[7] 1696[13] 2126[3] 3183[10] 3406[9] 4056[6] 4806[12] 5533[10]

Bahamian Ceilidh *B R Millman* 77
2 ch f Bahamian Bounty—Crofters Ceilidh (Scottish Reel)
1610[4] 2253[4] (3032) 3961[2] 4434[5] 6274[13] 6666[8]

Bahamian Duke *K R Burke* a54 66
5 ch g Bahamian Bounty—Madame Sisu (Emarati (USA))
21[9] 4385[4] 4653[14] (Dead)

Bahamian Kid *R Hollinshead* a76 73
3 b c Bahamian Bounty—Barachois Princess (USA) (Barachois (CAN))
1298[5] 1808[14] 2380[2] 2976[14] 3731[2] (6254) 6634[4] 6952[8] 7428[8]

Bahamian Lad *R Hollinshead* a75 75
3 b g Bahamian Bounty—Danehill Princess (IRE) (Danehill (USA))
130[7] (505) 756[7]

Bahamian Princess *R Hollinshead* a56 52
3 ch f Bahamian Bounty—Cutlass Princess (USA) (Cutlass (USA))
1019[10] 1311[7] (1709) 4770[7] 5307[6] 6088[11]

Baharah (USA) *G A Butler* a111 115
4 b m Elusive Quality(USA) —Bahr (Generous (IRE))
(308) ◆ 418[2] 1087a[14] (1981) ◆ 2827[5] ◆ 3120[13] (4361) 5730a[9] 6814[11] (7099) 7420[2]

Bahar Shumaal (IRE) *C E Brittain* a103 98
6 b h Dubai Millennium—High Spirited (Shirley Heights)
1076[5] 1212[4] 1633[3] 1920[4] 2545[7] (3167) 3503[5] 3740[14] 4853[10] (5569) 6033[8]

Baheeya *C E Brittain* 41
2 ch f Almutawakel—My American Beauty (Wolfhound (USA))
3349[11]

Bahhmirage (IRE) *C N Kellett* a58 54
5 ch m Bahhare(USA) —Border Mirage (Selkirk (USA))
76[8] 219[9] 249[5] 401[4] (507) (691) (770) 1505[12] 1776[10]

Bahia Breeze *Rae Guest* 109
6 b m Mister Baileys—Ring Of Love (Magic Ring (IRE))
1631[8] 2827[8] 4007a[8] 4855[2] 5332a[4] 7037a[7]

Bahiano (IRE) *C E Brittain* a89 94
7 ch g Barathea(IRE) —Trystero (Shareef Dancer (USA))
227[6] 680[5] 833[4] 1723[6] 3319[7] 4744[8] 6695[12] 7143[2] 7386[8]

Bahia Palace *M D I Usher* a41 26
3 b f Zamindar(USA) —Inya Lake (Whittingham (IRE))
1051[7] 1274[6] 1603[5] 2801[6]

Bahkov (IRE) *Tom Dascombe* a60
2 ch c Bahamian Bounty—Petrikov (IRE) (In The Wings)
7674[4]

Bahrain Storm (IRE) *Patrick J Flynn* a89 100
5 b g Bahhare(USA) —Dance Up A Storm (USA) (Storm Bird (CAN))
3250[8]

Baila Me (GER) *W Baltromei* 110
3 b f Samum(GER) —Bandeira (GER) (Law Society (USA))
(3073a) 4675a[3] 5952a[9] (6324a)

Bailey (IRE) *B J Meehan* a79 80
3 ch g Captain Rio—Baileys Cream (Mister Baileys)
1336[3] 3270[8] 3502[3]

Baileys Benchmark *M E Sowersby* a35 52
3 ch f Mark Of Esteem(IRE) —Estrelinha (Sadler's Wells (USA))
694[9] 4689[8] 5380[2] 6583[9]

Baileys Best *M F Harris* 59
6 b g Mister Baileys—Miss Rimex (IRE) (Ezzoud (IRE))
3698[8]

Baileys Brazilian *C A Dwyer* a43
3 ch f Captain Rio—Pico (Piccolo)
7297[8] 7509[8] 7589[8] 7809[12] 7835[8]

Baileys Cacao (IRE) *R Hannon* 105
2 b f Invincible Spirit(IRE) —Baileys Cream (Mister Baileys)
(2253) 3123[7] (3496) 5549a[6] 6319a[2] 6818[4]

Baileys Outshine *J G Given* a76 76
4 ch m Inchinor—Red Ryding Hood (Wolfhound (USA))
(113) 427[8] 580[9] 726[3] 1373[2] 2159[10] 2676[11] 3212[6] 3565[9]

Baileys Red *J G Given* a48 48
2 b g Diktat—Red Ryding Hood (Wolfhound (USA))
4256[6] 5304[5] 5870[6]

Bailieborough (IRE) *B Ellison* a83 94
9 b g Charnwood Forest(IRE) —Sherannda (USA) (Trempolino (USA))
1217[7] 1613[9] 2107[10] 2487[2] 2927[15] 3054[5] 3229[7] 6136[8] 6657[11] 7518[5] (7559) 7732[3]

Bain Douche (BRZ) *R Colombo* a54 70
4 b h Know Heights(IRE) —Uaiasol (USA) (Choctaw Ridge (USA))
292a[14] 474a[11] 650a[10]

Bainisteoir *S Kirk* a50 65
3 b g Tobougg(IRE) —Peruvian Jade (Petong)
2047[11] 2563[8] 2982[12] 3845[7] 4026[2] 4498[7] 4722[11] 5020[9] 5216[8]

Baizically (IRE) *George Baker* a94 94
5 ch g Galileo(IRE) —Baize (Efisio)
2264[8] 3167[5] 4104[12] 4895[8]

Bajan Parkes *E J Alston* 92
5 bb g Zafonic(USA) —My Melody Parkes (Teenoso (USA))
1947[12] (2447) 2939[10] 2970[8] 4662[8] 5391[2] 5858[13] 6288[9]

Bajan Pride *R A Fahey* a78 85
4 b g Selkirk(USA) —Spry (Suave Dancer (USA))
1308[5] 1910[9] 2220[9]

Bajan Tryst (USA) *K A Ryan* a70 77
2 bb c Speightstown(USA) —Garden Secrets (USA) (Time For A Change (USA))
5500[2] 6062[3] 6575[3]

Bakers Boy *J E Long* a17 34
4 ch g Tipsy Creek(USA) —Unparalleled (Primo Dominie)
1535[14] 3445[4] 4412[9] 5533[11]

Balaagha (USA) *M A Jarvis* 70
2 b f Mr Greeley(USA) —Echo Echo Echo (USA) (Eastern Echo (USA))
6776[5]

Balais Folly (FR) *B Palling* a54 53
3 ch g Act One—Bhima (Polar Falcon (USA))
20[7] 1553[3] 1871[8] 2475[6] 3166[4] 3264[4] 3692[5] 4026[3] 4366[12] 5215[3] 5710[6] 6562[5] 6747[5] 6927[8]

Balakar (IRE) *J J Lambe* 67
12 b g Doyoun—Balaniya (USA) (Diesis)
4848[4]

Balakiref *M Dods* a61 86
9 b g Royal Applause—Pluck (Never So Bold)
1327[12] 1818[11] 2484[6] 2535[8] 3454[5] ◆ 3626[14] 3713[5] (3998) 5991[9] 6043[6] 6724[6] 7131[4] 7239[8]

Balata *B R Millman* a75 70
3 b g Averti(IRE) —Manila Selection (USA) (Manila (USA))
1167[6] 1781[8] 2429[14] 2991[4] 4090[5] 7321[2] (7536) 7764[2] (7829)

Baldemar *K R Burke* 91
3 b g Namid—Keen Melody (USA) (Sharpen Up)
1623[2] 1999[2] 3047[15] 3723[5] 4416[6] (5358) 5930[5] 6676[4]

Balerno *Mrs L J Mongan* a57 58
9 b g Machiavellian(USA) —Balabina (USA) (Nijinsky (CAN))
32[5] 121[3] 247[6] 937[8] 1248[2] 1455[4] (1687) 2003[9] 3034[8] 3588[13] 6335[8] 6693[7] 6930[7] 7535[12] 7817[10]

Balios (GER) *A Wohler* 97
3 ch c Tertullian(USA) —Brighella (GER) (Lomitas)
1514a[5] 2066a[4] 2875a[8] 3515a[7]

Balius (IRE) *C Laffon-Parias* a104 120
5 b h Mujahid(USA) —Akhla (USA) (Nashwan (USA))
912a[2] 1240a[4] 1666a[2] 2234a[3] 7685a[2]

Baliyana (IRE) *John M Oxx* 92
2 gr f Dalakhani(IRE) —Balanka (IRE) (Alzao (USA))
5132a[5] 6318a[10]

Balkan Knight *D R C Elsworth* 114
8 b g Selkirk(USA) —Crown Of Light (Mtoto)
1829[7] 2192[4] 2542[2] 3743[6] 5094[7] 5646[3] 5854[2] 6306[2] 6820[6]

Ballade De La Mer *A J McCabe* a43
2 b f Ishiguru(USA) —Riviere Rouge (Forzando)
6988[7] 7282[10] 7577[6] 7824[9]

Balladeuse (FR) *A Fabre* 113
3 b f Singspiel(IRE) —Featherquest (Rainbow Quest (USA))
2650a[3] 5597a[3] (6495a)

Balladiene (IRE) *M H Tompkins* a57 69
2 b f Noverre(USA) —Kinnego (IRE) (Sri Pekan (USA))
2117[7] 2691[4] 3135[6] 4373[7] (6059) 6394[7] 6886[3]

Ballad Maker (IRE) *Mrs S J Humphrey* a70 60
4 b g Marju(IRE) —Cappella (IRE) (College Chapel)
2753[10] 3160[8] 3844[12]

Ballantrae (IRE) *M L W Bell* 93
2 b f Diktat—Badawi (USA) (Diesis)
(3869) 4868[9] (5791) ◆ 6439[10]

Ballarina *E J Alston* 16
2 b f Compton Place—Miss Uluwatu (IRE) (Night Shift (USA))
957[18] 3259[10] 3470[5]

Ballerina Blue (IRE) *Y De Nicolay* a74 95
3 b f High Chaparral(IRE) —Delicieuse Lady (Trempolino (USA))
1760a[4] 2743a[5] 6664a[10] 7635a[5]

Ballet Boy (IRE) *Charles O'Brien* a91 85
4 b g Sadler's Wells(USA) —Happy Landing (FR) (Homing)
4493a[18]

Ballet Dancer (IRE) *M A Jarvis* a66 69
2 b f Refuse To Bend(IRE) —Showlady (USA) (Theatrical)
6945[3] ◆ 7337[4]

Ballinteni *T D Easterby* a95 100
6 b h Machiavellian(USA) —Silabteni (USA) (Nureyev (USA))
929[2] 1180[6] (1970) 2325[4] 2545[4] 3122[6] 3503[4] 4443[4] 4587[14] 7755[9]

Ballisodare *P W Chapple-Hyam* 64
3 b g Elusive Quality(USA) —River Jig (USA) (Irish River (FR))
1446[6]

Ballochroy (IRE) *B W Hills* 88
3 b c Mull Of Kintyre(USA) —Shonara's Way (Slip Anchor)
1171[2] ◆ 1424[5] 1919[7] 5098[3] 6079[5] (6542)

Ballora (FR) *S Kirk* a77 79
3 ro f Kendor(FR) —Vodka (FR) (Ali-Royal (IRE))
4300[8] 4976[3] 5428[7] 5605[7] 5888[2] 6450[5] 6605[6] 6771[5] 7342[5] 7495[3]

Ballpoint (IRE) *E Libaud* 86
3 b f Oasis Dream—Gold Script (FR) (Script Ohio (USA))
6744a[2]

Ballyalla *R Hannon* 81
2 b f Mind Games—Molly Brown (Rudimentary (USA))
3913[9] (4149) 5642[9] 6426[5]

Ballybunion (IRE) *B J Llewellyn* a55 63
9 ch g Entrepreneur—Clarentia (Ballad Rock)
1370[10]

Ballycroy Boy (IRE) *A Bailey* a77 52
3 b g Captain Rio—Royal Baldini (USA) (Green Dancer (USA))
(38) 170[3] 339[3] 619[3] (635) 1339[2] 7048[5] 7317[8] 7448[8]

Ballygologue (IRE) *T Stack* a31 85
3 b f Montjeu(IRE) —Admiring (USA) (Woodman (USA))
4003a[7]

Ballyhealy Lady *D K Ivory* a43 45
3 b f Tobougg(IRE) —Amal (Top Ville)
298[5] 583[6] 714[10]

Ballyvourney (IRE) *M Halford* 41
3 b g Traditionally(USA) —Wild Bluebell (IRE) (Bluebird (USA))
3861a[11] (Dead)

Balnagore *J L Dunlop* 76
4 bb h Tobougg(IRE) —Bogus Mix (IRE) (Linamix (FR))
2619[9] 3003[6] ◆ 3518[7] 3914[8] 4829[2] 5583[10] 5935[5]

Balor (FR) *M Weiss* 101
5 ch g Hernando(FR) —Visions On Space (IRE) (Lure (USA))
(423a) 605a[6]

Balthazaar's Gift (IRE) *L M Cumani* 119
5 b h Xaar—Thats Your Opinion (Last Tycoon)
1420[14] 2106[8] (2680) 3247[10] 4188[3] 4915a[9] 5275[2] 5891[12] 6304[10] 6645[7] 6814[4]

Baltimore Jack (IRE) *M W Easterby* a64 84
4 b g Night Shift(USA) —Itsibitsi (IRE) (Brief Truce (USA))
2158[8] 3050[17] 3477[7] 3834[4] 4245[4] 4293[6] 4537[2] 5450[8] 6090[5] 6628[4]

Banana Man (AUS) *Michael Kent* 97
5 b g Desert King(IRE) —Chinju (AUS) (Kaapstad (NZ))
6922a[8]

Bandama (IRE) *Mrs A J Perrett* a104 99
5 b h Green Desert(USA) —Orinoco (IRE) (Darshaan)
2830[2] 3209[5] 3896[4] 4422[2] 4642[4] 6238[8] 6479[7] (6784) 7404[8]

Bandanaman (IRE) *G A Swinbank* 76
2 b g Danehill Dancer(IRE) —Band Of Angels (IRE) (Alzao (USA))
4921[2] 6014[5] 6292[4] 6524[12]

Banda Sea (IRE) *P J Makin* a54 60
2 b c Tagula(IRE) —Non Ultra (USA) (Peintre Celebre (USA))
4973[7] 6000[8] 6412[8]

Banderella (IRE) *W Hickst* 88
4 b m Diktat—Baskama (GER) (Surumu (GER))
2347a[8]

Bandits Pistol (NZ) *M Madgwick* a49 42
8 gr g Foxbay(NZ) —Copasetic (NZ) (One Pound Sterling)
207[6] 332[8] 611[9] 1109[4] 1694[4] 2353[13]

Bandoran *J R Holt* 3
3 ch g Band On The Run—Breezy Day (Day Is Done)
3338[9] 4461[9] 7178[12] 7400[13]

Banjo Bandit (IRE) *J S Moore* a64 35
3 b c Mujadil(USA) —Common Cause (Polish Patriot (USA))
(23) ◆ 184[3]

Banjo Patterson *M G Quinlan* a64 60
6 b h Green Desert(USA) —Rumpipumpy (Shirley Heights)
1500[5] ◆ 2087[10] 2978[11] 3422[6] 4162[18] 5166[2] 5533[8]

Bankable (IRE) *L M Cumani* 123
4 b h Medicean—Dance To The Top (Sadler's Wells (USA))
(1719) ◆ (2600) ◆ 3122[5] 4192[2] 5265[2] ◆ 5932[2] 6440[2] 6780[2] 7147[6]

Banknote *A M Balding* a103 110
6 b h Zafonic(USA) —Brand (Shareef Dancer (USA))
2044[4] 3503[3] 6670[4] 7339[2] (7740)

Bank On Benny *P W D'Arcy* a82 64
6 b g Benny The Dip(USA) —Green Danube (USA) (Irish River (FR))
(7366) ◆ 7459[2] 7515[2]

Bannaby (FR) *M Delcher Sanchez* 115
5 ch h Dyhim Diamond(IRE) —Trelakari (FR) (Lashkari)
5956a[2] (6497a) 7008a[4]

Banquet (IRE) *T D Walford* 61
3 ch g Dr Fong(USA) —Barbera (Barathea (IRE))
2847[7] 3666[4] 4247[7] 4879[9] (5399)

Bansha (IRE) *A Bailey* a59 47
2 b g Indian Haven—Cha Cha (IRE) (Charnwood Forest (IRE))
6581[9] 6778[11] 7079[7]

Bantu *J H M Gosden* a66
3 bb f Cape Cross(IRE) —Lalindi (IRE) (Cadeaux Genereux)
7387[8] 7474[2]

Banus Flyer (IRE) *N Tinkler* 35
3 ro g Distant Music(USA) —Gracious Gretclo (Common Grounds)
2187[15] 2488[13]

Baraari (USA) *J L Dunlop* 74
3 bb f Nayef(USA) —Reem Al Barari (USA) (Storm Cat (USA))
2015[2] ◆ 2862[4]

Barashi *J Howard Johnson* 27
3 b g King's Best(USA) —Maid To Dance (Pyramus (USA))
3402[8] 4075[8]

Barataria *R Bastiman* a75 62
6 ch g Barathea(IRE) —Aethra (USA) (Trempolino (USA))
2009[6] ◆ 3593[8] 4168[3] 5538[11] 7270[2] 7442[2] (7634) 7731[3]

Barathea Dreams (IRE) *J S Moore* a61 71
7 b g Barathea(IRE) —Deyaajeer (USA) (Dayjur (USA))
2617[8] 2795[2] 3036[6] 4048[8] (4710) 5458[5] 5639[12] 6396[8] 7217[6] 7516[4] 7656[6]

Barawin (IRE) *K R Burke* a81 79
3 ch f Hawk Wing(USA) —Cosabawn (IRE) (Barathea (IRE))
1730[4] 7230[4] 7539[7]

Barbar *Eve Johnson Houghton* a49 58
5 b g Anabaa(USA) —Prends Ca (IRE) (Reprimand)
1145[11] 2010[8] 2478[10]

Barbarian *B W Hills* a68 64
2 b c Noverre(USA) —Love In The Mist (USA) (Silver Hawk (USA))
6246[4] 6714[7] 7170[2]

Barbaricus (AUS) *Danny O'Brien* 114
4 gr g Lion Hunter(AUS) —Light Of Erin (AUS) (Palace Music (USA))
6835a[3] 7188a[19]

Barbary Boy (FR) *M L W Bell* 79
3 b c Rock Of Gibraltar(IRE) —Don't Worry Me (IRE) (Dancing Dissident (USA))
(3712) 4787[3] 5028[5] 6024[3]

Barbecue Eddie (USA) *Brian Koriner* a112
4 b g Stormy Atlantic(USA) —The Green Owl (USA) (Carson City (USA))
1089a[4]

Barbee (IRE) *E A L Dunlop* a59 77
2 ch f Night Shift(USA) —Barbizou (FR) (Selkirk (USA))
1722[3] 2117[3] (2534) 3496[7] 4640[6] 5204[10] 6172[9] 6477[12]

Barbeito *D J S Ffrench Davis* a41 39
2 b f Zaha(CAN) —Tinta (Robellino (USA))
6158[6] 6574[8] 7079[11] 7266[4] 7370[4] 7514[5] 7547[10]

Barbirolli *W M Brisbourne* a54 70
6 b g Machiavellian(USA) —Blushing Barada (USA) (Blushing Groom (FR))
1528[10] 2286[4] 2512[4] 2884[3] 3084[3] 3698[3] 3912[5] 4155[4] 4630[6] 5869[3]

Barbossa *A J McCabe* a32
3 ch g Bahamian Bounty—Marjurita (IRE) (Marju (IRE))
845[7] 1489[4]

Barcode *R Hannon* a52 58
2 b f Tobougg(IRE) —Truly Madly Deeply (Most Welcome)
2011[10] 3348[7] 3674[11] 4079[12] 4827[7] (5488) 6573[4] 7257[5] 7353[7] 7519[3]

Barcola (USA) *Mark Hennig* a105
5 ch h Old Trieste(USA) —Myrtle Beach (USA) (Kingmambo (USA))
1087a[12]

Bargouzine (USA) *A Fabre* 94
2 b f Stravinsky(USA) —Bailonguera (ARG) (Southern Halo (USA))
3052a[2] 3774a[4] 4673a[4]

Bari Bay *R M Beckett* a42
2 b f Bahri(USA) —Sea Nymph (IRE) (Spectrum (IRE))
6877[7]

Barkass (UAE) *B Ellison* a72 77
4 b g Halling(USA) —Areydha (Cadeaux Genereux)
4162[15] 5561[4] (6385) 6899[6] (7373) (7500) 7723[5]

Barley Bree (IRE) *Mrs A Duffield* 40
3 ch f Danehill Dancer(IRE) —Aunty Mary (Common Grounds)
5636[7]

Barley Moon *T Keddy* a26 39
4 b m Vettori(IRE) —Trojan Desert (Troy)
1687[12] 2933[10] 3371[11] 4261[6] 4599[7] 4820[6] 5105[9] 5322[11]

Barliffey (IRE) *D J Coakley* a78 78
3 b g Bahri(USA) —Kildare Lady (IRE) (Indian Ridge)
2079[3] 2714[5] 3312[4] 4104[8] 4571[2] 6256[3] (6956)

Barman (USA) *M Mullineaux* 62
9 ch g Atticus(USA) —Blue Tip (FR) (Tip Moss (FR))
3176[10]

Barnabas (IRE) *C P Donoghue* a57 68
4 b g Gold Away(IRE) —Seattle Star (USA) (Seeking The Gold (USA))
4799a[7]

Barnaby Rudge (IRE) *Jane Chapple-Hyam* a82 81
3 b c Danetime(IRE) —Gild (IRE) (Caerleon (USA))
6471[13] 6716[16] 7513[4]

Barnbrook Empire (IRE) *L A Dace* a46 47
6 b m Second Empire(IRE) —Home Comforts (Most Welcome)
455[4] 575[7] 776[3] 1181[11]

Barney McGrew (IRE) *M Dods* a101 103
5 b g Mark Of Esteem(IRE) —Success Story (Sharrood (USA))
1300[11] 1809[14] 2172[13] (2538) 3451[10] 4145[4] ◆ 4624[24] 5503[10] 6289[2] 6911[5] 7245[2]

Barnezet (GR) *R Hannon* a68 68
2 b f Invincible Spirit(IRE) —Le Meridien (IRE) (Magical Wonder (USA))
3092[5] 3323[6] 4480[2] 4786[5] 6327[4] 6540[5] 7388[4] 7464[2] 7574[3] 7673[3]

Barodine *R J Hodges* a55 36
5 ch g Barathea(IRE) —Granted (FR) (Cadeaux Genereux)
6899[10] 7606[8]

Baron De'L (IRE) *Edward P Harty* a76 102
5 ch g In The Wings—Lightstorm (IRE) (Darshaan)
1353a[6]

Baron Otto (IRE) *W J Haggas* 71
2 b g Anabaa(USA) —Marie Laurencin (Peintre Celebre (USA))
6122[5] 6535[4]

Baronovici (IRE) *D W Barker* 73
3 b g Namid—Allegrina (IRE) (Barathea (IRE))
1328[6] 1484[11] 1819[9] 1988[12] 3416[8] 3833[6] 5397[9] 6150[2] 6382[13]

Baron's Court *M Johnston* a77 69
3 ch c Pivotal—Grafin (USA) (Miswaki (USA))
(265) 2842[2] 3039[10]

Barons Spy (IRE) *R J Price* a84 94
7 b g Danzero(AUS) —Princess Accord (USA) (D'Accord (USA))
(2644) 3040[4] (3435) 4177[4] 4661[9] 5368[4] 5897[8] 6277[8] 6670[5] 7019[11]

Barood (IRE) *M R Channon* 61
2 b g Xaar—Radiant Energy (IRE) (Spectrum (IRE))
5459[4] 5811[6]

Barraland *M R Channon* a70 77
3 b g Compton Place—Dance Land (IRE) (Nordance (USA))
798[3] (977) 1484[16] 2258[6] 2570[7] 2896[4] 3256[5] 3811[4] 4325[2] 4584[4] 4904[5] (5531) 5902[4] 6232[13] 6486[9] 6765[5]

Barrashot *M J McGrath*
3 ch g Barathea(IRE) —Highland Shot (Selkirk (USA))
3762[4]

Barricado (FR) *R Charlton* a69 78
3 b g Anabaa(USA) —Aube D'Irlande (FR) (Selkirk (USA))
1380[2] ◆ 1855[2] 2974[4] 4104[3] 4582[3] 5491[5]

Barring Decree (IRE) *E J O'Neill* a64 89
3 b f Dalakhani(IRE) —Barring Order (IRE) (Barathea (IRE))
903[6] 1279[4] (2015) 3018a[5]

Barry Island *D R C Elsworth* a65 64
9 b g Turtle Island(IRE) —Pine Ridge (High Top)
57[5] 546[6] 1049[9] 1692[6] 2060[4] 2513[4] 2949[8] 4156[9] 5008[12] 5631[4]

Barshiba (IRE) *D R C Elsworth* a84 112
4 ch m Barathea(IRE) —Dashiba (Dashing Blade)
1807[3] 2193[7] 2827[9] 3120[6] 3940[2] 4361[2] 4674a[6] 5506[4] 6475[6] (6781)

Bartercard (USA) *Stef Liddiard* a76 74
7 b g Sir Cat(USA) —Pure Misk (Rainbow Quest (USA))
772[3] 909[6] 1125[4] 1450[P] (1591) 2085[2] 2293[9] 2837[10] (2917) 3376[13] 3648[7] 4129[4] 4481[3] 4789[6] 4991[3] ◆ 5161[14]

Bartica (IRE) *R Hannon* a67 63
2 b c Tagula(IRE) —More Risk (IRE) (Fayruz)
4926[4] 5609[5] 6072[4] 6863[10] 7273[5] 7475[3] ◆ 7700[4]

Barton Sands (IRE) *Andrew Reid* a63 58
11 b g Tenby—Hetty Green (Bay Express)
133[3] 352[2] 794[6] 7590[3]

Barwell Bridge *S Kirk* a77 62
2 b c Red Ransom(USA) —Sentimental Value (USA) (Diesis)
2324[7] ◆ 7397[2] ◆ 7552[5] 7784[3]

Basalt (IRE) *T J Pitt* a91 86
4 b g Rock Of Gibraltar(IRE) —Sniffle (IRE) (Shernazar)
(435) ◆ (510) ◆ 588[6] 1947[7] 2168[11] 2628[2] 3104[6] 3250[16] 5887[3]

Basaltico (IRE) *A & G Botti* 113
4 b h Shantou(USA) —Sfilza (Indian Ridge)
6325a[2] 7263a[5]

Basanti (USA) *B W Hills* a35 75
3 ch f Galileo(IRE) —Ozone Friendly (USA) (Green Forest (USA))
2716[3] 3133[11] 4821[5] ◆ 5814[4] (6331) 7070[10]

Bashkirov *A P O'Brien* a76 115
3 ch c Galileo(IRE) —Tina Heights (Shirley Heights)
2829[15] 3535a[6] 4042a[9] 5892[9] 6324a[9]

Basinet *J J Quinn* a61 54
10 b g Alzao(USA) —Valiancy (Grundy)
989[4] 1391[3] 2274[14]

Basko De Zarautz (ARG) *Saeed Bin Suroor* a70
4 ch h Engrillado(ARG) —Lady Lode (ARG) (Lode (USA))
292a[6] 650a[15]

Basque Beauty *W J Haggas* 96
3 b f Nayef(USA) —River Cara (USA) (Irish River (FR))
(4447) 4977[7] 6034[12] 6266[11]

Basra (IRE) *Miss Jo Crowley* a94 90
5 b g Soviet Star(USA) —Azra (IRE) (Danehill (USA))
409[3] 678[6] 962[6] (1502) 1935[3] 2711[5] 3676[5] 4276[2] 5910[11] 7215[7] 7595[5]

Bassinet (USA) *J A R Toller* a80 80
4 b m Stravinsky(USA) —Berceau (USA) (Alleged (USA))
390[4] 736[5] ◆ 941[3] 1151[3] 1563[3] 2241[2] 2558[2] (3220) 3925[5] 4771[13] 7314[3] 7459[7]

Bastakiya (IRE) *J H M Gosden* a90 97
3 ch f Dubai Destination(USA) —Ting A Folie (ARG) (Careafolie)
3460[3] 6430[2] 6782[3]

Batchworth Blaise *E A Wheeler* a56 60
5 b g Little Jim—Batchworth Dancer (Ballacashtal (CAN))
176[3] 516[12] 624[5] 711[5] 898[5] 1269[9] (2355) 3218[5] 3563[3] 4053[2] 4414[11] 4772[9] (5267) 5604[7] 6396[2] 7392[11] 7803[11]

Bateleur *M R Channon* a72 78
4 b g Fraam—Search Party (Rainbow Quest (USA))
1872[7] 2205[5] 2484[4] 2923[7] 3352[13] 4051[6] 4125[12] 4605[9] 4746[8] 7808[4]

Bathwick Breeze *D E Pipe* a63 63
4 ch g Sugarfoot—She's A Breeze (Crofthall)
4704[8]

Bathwick Icon (IRE) *A B Haynes* 53
3 b f Xaar—Greek Icon (Thatching)
3524[9] 4338[10]

Bathwick Man *D E Pipe* 62
3 b g Mark Of Esteem(IRE) —Local Abbey (IRE) (Primo Dominie)
1899[8] 3004[14] 3524[11] 4278[7]

Bathwick Minstrel *A B Haynes* a36 40
3 br f Singspiel(IRE) —Polenta (IRE) (Sunday Silence (USA))
3362[6] 3894[13] 4302[6] 7310[12]

Bathwick Penny *A B Haynes*
4 b m Peintre Celebre(USA) —La Riveraine (USA) (Riverman (USA))
1690[6]

Bathwick Pursuit *A M Balding* a58
2 b c Pursuit Of Love—Society Rose (Saddlers' Hall (IRE))
7397[8]

Battle *H Morrison* a62 69
2 gr g Compton Place—Molly Moon (IRE) (Primo Dominie)
6077[5] 6531[3] 6879[5]

Battle Hero *Sir Michael Stoute*
2 b c Red Ransom(USA) —Appointed One (USA) (Danzig (USA))
6759[9]

Battle Of Hastings *M L W Bell* 83
2 b g Royal Applause—Subya (Night Shift (USA))
2663[4] 3485[6] 3707[6] (4828) (5895)

Battle Paint (USA) *J H M Gosden* 115
4 b h Tale Of The Cat(USA) —Black Speck (USA) (Arch (USA))
(4617) ◆ 5275[11] 5738a[10]

Battle Planner (USA) *M Johnston* a79
2 b c War Chant(USA) —The Administrator (USA) (Afleet (CAN))
(7627)

Battle Royal (IRE) *B Smart* 61
2 b c Refuse To Bend(IRE) —Style Of Life (USA) (The Minstrel (CAN))
4968[4] 6480[5]

Battling Lil (IRE) *J L Spearing* a50 56
4 b m Daggers Drawn(USA) —Salva (Grand Lodge (USA))
1869[9] 2509[9] 2955[6] 3757[10] 6681[11] 7469[5]

Bauer (IRE) *L M Cumani* a47 114
5 gr h Halling(USA) —Dali's Grey (Linamix (FR))
1468[9] 1944[8] 4508[2] 5229[7] (6922a) 7188a[2]

Bauhaus Bourbon (USA) *P F I Cole* a73 60
3 gr f Behrens(USA) —Southern Tradition (USA) (Family Doctor (USA))
3325[9] 3737[4] 4183[6] 4727[2] 5119[10] 5915[5] 6417[9] 7194[6]

Baunagain (IRE) *M J Wallace* a84 85
3 b g No Excuse Needed—Manuka Honey (Mystiko (USA))
705[3] (855) 1066[4] 1277[2] (1934) ◆ 2674[5] 2883[3] 4831[5] 5067[5] 5594[4] 6169[7]

Bavarian Nordic (USA) *Mrs A Duffield* a86 81
3 b c Barathea(IRE) —Dubai Diamond (Octagonal (NZ))
1579[10] 2464[4] 2675[9] 3716[6] 4017[4] 5888[6] (6216) (6726) (7046) 7502[6]

Bavarica *Miss J Feilden* a72 79
6 b m Dansili—Blue Gentian (USA) (Known Fact (USA))
1676[3] 2078[4] 2374[10] 2978[4] 3163[2] 3422[4] 4371[2] 4739[4] 4945[3] 5512[5] 6090[7] 6395[5] 7094[5] 7342[3] 7442[5] 7656[5] 7800[2] ◆

Bawaardi (IRE) *J H M Gosden* 77
2 b c Acclamation—Global Trend (Bluebird (USA))
4446[2]

Baybshambles (IRE) *R E Barr* 76
4 b g Compton Admiral—Payvashooz (Ballacashtal (CAN))
(1431) 1827[3] (2270) 2596[6] 3405[3] (3594) 4218[7] 5719[2] 6218[12]

Baycat (IRE) *J G Portman* 90
2 b g One Cool Cat(USA) —Greta D'Argent (IRE) (Great Commotion (USA))
(1439) (1714) 3152[11] 4517[10] 4908[6]

Bay Hawk *B G Powell* a74 71
6 b g Alhaarth(IRE) —Fleeting Vision (IRE) (Vision (USA))
2617[3]

Baylaw Star *I W McInnes* a47 79
7 b g Case Law—Caisson (Shaadi (USA))
7491[4] 2806[11] 3201[7] 3662[10] 4479[7] 4961[9] 5420[9]

Baylini *Ms J S Doyle* a102 91
4 gr m Bertolini(USA) —Bay Of Plenty (FR) (Octagonal (NZ))
(97) 185[4] 592[2] ◆ 678[3] 906[7] 3088[6] 5033[6] 5536[4] 6078[10] 6346[2] 6605[13] 7556[9] 7814[5]

Baynes Cross (IRE) *Ms Joanna Morgan* a85 81
5 b g Namid—Flying Clouds (Batshoof)
829a[2]

Bay Swallow (IRE) *Patrick J Flynn* 55
2 b f Daylami(IRE) —Starlight Smile (USA) (Green Dancer (USA))
5549a[12]

Baytown Blaze *P S McEntee* a76 74
3 ch f Zaha(CAN) —Lightning Blaze (Cosmonaut)
59[2] (243) 470[4] 798[5] 1852[2] 1911[5] 2068[6] 3462[11] 4074[7]

Baytown Paikea *W G M Turner* a56 59
4 b m Primo Valentino(IRE) —Mystical Song (Mystiko (USA))
440[9] 558[5]

Bazart *K R Burke* a76 98
6 b g Highest Honor(FR) —Summer Exhibition (Royal Academy (USA))
591[6] 735[6] 838[7] 1340[3] 2006[2] 2585[2] 3045[3] 3368[9]

Bazergan (IRE) *C E Brittain* a96 103
3 b c Machiavellian(USA) —Lunda (IRE) (Soviet Star (USA))
(5463) 6276[9] 6625[3]

Bazguy *J O'Reilly* a77 69
3 b g Josr Algarhoud(IRE) —Ewenny (Warrshan (USA))
1781[9] 1995[5] 2570[8] 2945[7] 4056[3] (4271) 4765[3] (5050) 5346[3] 6448[10] 7013[6] (7206) 7378[3] 7616[3] 7675[8]

Bazroy (IRE) *P D Evans* a106 88
4 b g Soviet Star(USA) —Kunucu (IRE) (Bluebird (USA))
26[2] ◆ 313[4] (329) (417) (456) 594[12] 836[6] 904[8] 2595[12] 3680[8] 3973[8] 4201[11] 4437[9] 4608[2] 4831[8] 5096[11] 5681[7] 5906[11] 6402[10] 6911[3] 7101[5] (7594)

Beach Bound (IRE) *D K Weld* a60 70
5 b g Grand Lodge(USA) —South Of Heaven (IRE) (Fairy King (USA))
4514a[10]

Beach Bunny (IRE) *Kevin Prendergast* a70 102
3 b f High Chaparral(IRE) —Miss Hawai (FR) (Peintre Celebre (USA))
1847a[4] 3070a[2] 3511a[4] 4007a[7] (5547a) 5920a[2] 6298a[5]

Beacon Lodge (IRE) *C G Cox* 106
3 b c Clodovil(IRE) —Royal House (FR) (Royal Academy (USA))
1471[6] 2605[4]

Bea Menace (USA) *P F I Cole* a61 67
2 b f Mizzen Mast(USA) —Questonia (Rainbow Quest (USA))
6245[2] 6534[3] 6877[4]

Beamon (USA) *Miss D Mountain* a35
2 b g Sky Mesa(USA) —Not A Solution (USA) (Grand Slam (USA))
7283[7]

Beamsley Beacon *Miss Tracy Waggott* a55 52
7 ch g Wolfhound(USA) —Petindia (Petong)
857[6] 1025[8]

Bear Bottom *W J Musson* a59
4 b g Imperial Ballet(IRE) —Pigeon Hole (Green Desert (USA))
10[5] 143[8] 1747[7] 2870[8]

Bear Now (USA) *Reade Baker* a114
4 bb m Tiznow(USA) —Controlled (USA) (In Excess I (IRE))
6969a[8]

Beat Faster *J G Given* a50
2 b f Beat Hollow—Supersonic (Shirley Heights)
7578[6] 7726[6]

Beat Seven *Miss Gay Kelleway* 104
2 ch f Beat Hollow—Twenty Seven (IRE) (Efisio)
1419[4] (1680) 3123[11] 3924[4] 4348[2] 4868[8] 6268[4]

Beat The Bell *A Bailey* a99 75
3 b c Beat All(USA) —Bella Beguine (Komaite (USA))
1215[7] 2966[4] 3282[5] ◆ (3434) 3811[6] 4258[2] 4595[12] 5028[2] (6420) (6634) (6902) 7151[4] 7192[2] 7418[4] 7576[4] 7594[4]

Beat Up *P R Chamings* 68
2 b g Beat Hollow—Whitgift Rose (Polar Falcon (USA))
5579[3] 6412[9] 7105[9]

Beaubrav *P W D'Arcy* a54 54
2 b c Falbrav(IRE) —Wavy Up (IRE) (Brustolon)
3001[9] 5578[6] 6597[13]

Beauchamp Turbo *N Wilson* a12
6 ch g Pharly(FR) —Compton Astoria (USA) (Lion Cavern (USA))
31[7] 377[11]

Beauchamp Viceroy *G A Butler* a96 95
4 ch g Compton Admiral—Compton Astoria (USA) (Lion Cavern (USA))
1765[5] 2195[10] 2711[4] 3398[7] 5051[5] 5569[4] 6120[8]

Beauchamp Viking *S C Burrough* a45 55
4 b g Compton Admiral—Beauchamp Jade (Kalaglow)
6018[8]

Beauchamp Warrior *G A Butler* a61 64
3 b c Compton Admiral—Beauchamp Buzz (High Top)
1696[15] 4455[3] 5087[13]

Beauchamp Wizard *G A Butler* a77 73
3 b c Compton Admiral—Compton Astoria (USA) (Lion Cavern (USA))
4454[2] ◆ (5049)

Beauchamp Wonder *G A Butler* a61 63
3 b f Compton Admiral—Beauchamp Jade (Kalaglow)
3035[2] 3350[4] 6331[3]

Beauchamp Xenia *H Candy* 59
2 b f Compton Admiral—Beauchamp Jade (Kalaglow)
7141[10]

Beauchamp Xiara *H Candy* 58
2 b f Compton Admiral—Beauchamp Buzz (High Top)
7140[10]

Beau Fighter *C F Wall* a50 65
3 b g Tobougg(IRE) —Belle De Jour (Exit To Nowhere (USA))
2046[8] 2528[11] 2885[4] ◆

Beau Jazz *W De Best-Turner* a33 31
7 br g Merdon Melody—Ichor (Primo Dominie)
5433[10] 6225[6]

Beaujeu (IRE) *M Johnston* a11
3 ch c Singspiel(IRE) —Baya (USA) (Nureyev (USA))
3688[9]

Beaumont Boy *A G Foster* 54
4 b g Foxhound(USA) —Play The Game (Mummy's Game)
214[9] 2747[4] 3211[5] 3789[4] 5389[11] 5636[6] 6546[12]

Beauthea (IRE) *H Rogers* 84
2 b f Barathea(IRE) —Beau Cheval (IRE) (Spectrum (IRE))
3534a[5] 5132a[4] 5549a[7] 6318a[11]

Beautiful Breeze (IRE) *M Johnston* 76
2 ch g Tobougg(IRE) —Khayrat (IRE) (Polar Falcon (USA))
4536[3] (4960) 5447[5] 5791[16] 6112[5]

Beautiful Dreamer *Sir Michael Stoute* 25
3 br f Red Ransom(USA) —Flight Of Fancy (Sadler's Wells (USA))
2669[9]

Beautiful Filly *D M Simcock* a62
2 b f Oasis Dream—Royal Alchemist (USA) (Royal Academy (USA))
5835[7] 6697[3]

Beautiful Lady (IRE) *P F I Cole* a67 74
3 b f Peintre Celebre(USA) —Puteri Wentworth (Sadler's Wells (USA))
1176[2] 1542[4] 3611[5] 4326[3] (4607) 4859[12] 5406[7] 6703[13] 7149[8]

Beau Torero (FR) *B N Pollock* a49
10 gr g True Brave(USA) —Brave Lola (FR) (Dom Pasquini (FR))
6729[5]

Beau Vengerov (IRE) *D Smaga* a80 94
4 b h Danehill(USA) —Arpege (IRE) (Sadler's Wells (USA))
5115a[7]

Beaux Yeux *P T Midgley* a10
2 b f Cadeaux Genereux—Cloud Hill (Danehill (USA))
7649[7]

Beaver Patrol (IRE) *Eve Johnson Houghton* a109 109
6 ch g Tagula(IRE) —Erne Project (IRE) (Project Manager)
472a[3] 649a[3] 741a[4] 1809[13] 2106[12] 2426[10] 3248[2] 3504[8] 4624[15] 5095[3] 5586[3] 6073[8]

Becausewecan (USA) *M Johnston* a75 73
2 b c Giant's Causeway(USA) —Belle Sultane (USA) (Seattle Slew (USA))
2730[2] ◆ 3254[7] 4176[3] 4874[5] 5632[3] 5895[11] 6101[8] 6970[11] (7130) (7298)

Becher *A De Mieulle* a96 104
4 b h Vettori(IRE) —Hidden Meaning (Cadeaux Genereux)
5115a[0]

Beck *W M Brisbourne* a59 49
4 ch g Cadeaux Genereux—River Cara (USA) (Irish River (FR))
3431[12] 4597[5] 5157[6] 6408[10] 6693[11] 7114[7] 7535[13] 7585[4]

Beckenham's Secret *A W Carroll* a51 59
4 b g Foxhound(USA) —Berliese (IRE) (High Estate)
164[5] 401[9] 3025[2] 3361[7] 3657[9] 4322[6] 5489[3] 6740[9] 7596[10] 7678[7]

Beckermet (IRE) *R F Fisher* a88 114
6 b g Second Empire(IRE) —Razida (IRE) (Last Tycoon)
291a[4] 497a[8] 649a[8] 745a[3] 815a[8] 1420[13] 1619[4] 1989[5] 2106[3] 2607[6] 3063[8] 3488[3] 3946[2] 4188[11]

Becky Blue (IRE) *P C Haslam* 39
2 b f Pyrus(USA) —Amoras (IRE) (Hamas (IRE))
4536[6] 7646[7]

Becky Quick (IRE) *Bruce Hellier*
3 b f Fantastic Light(USA) —Private Bluff (USA) (Pine Bluff (USA))
3955[8]

Becomes You *M Delzangles* a81 101
2 ch f Lomitas—Joyeuse Entree (Kendor (FR))
6855a[3]

Bed Fellow (IRE) *Paul Murphy* a65 79
4 b g Trans Island—Moonlight Partner (IRE) (Red Sunset)
622[5] 1049[6] 1771[8] 2220[6] 2795[17] 3142[4] 3399[12] 4048[16] 5559[11] 6189[4] 6396[11] 6727[4] 6950[18] 7132[4] 7442[9] 7613[10]

Bedizen *Mrs P Sly* 79
5 b g Fantastic Light(USA) —Barboukh (Night Shift (USA))
1742[3] 2373[17] 3029[8]

Bedloe's Island (IRE) *R C Guest* a31 54
3 b g Statue Of Liberty(USA) —Scenaria (IRE) (Scenic)
4301[10] 5160[6] 6822[8]

Bedouin Blue (IRE) *P C Haslam* a71 66
5 b g Desert Style(IRE) —Society Fair (FR) (Always Fair (USA))
(989) 1184[2]

Bee Bounty *J G Portman*
2 b f Bahamian Bounty—Sharena (IRE) (Kahyasi)
7415[12]

Beech Games *F Jordan* a68 55
4 b g Mind Games—Dane Dancing (IRE) (Danehill (USA))
88[3] 180[2] 239[4] 2513[6] 3025[7] 3321[8] 4704[11]

Beechside (IRE) *W A Murphy* a23 53
4 b m Orpen(USA) —Tokurama (IRE) (Mtoto)
857[8] 987[10]

Beech View (IRE) *John Joseph Murphy* 46
3 b f Desert Prince(IRE) —Karakapa (FR) (Subotica (FR))
3861a[15]

Bees River (IRE) *A P Jarvis* a63 73
3 ch f Acclamation—Notley Park (Wolfhound (USA))
2186[3] 2581[U] 6037[5] 6578[2] 6932[2] 7219[3] 7574[6]

Bee Sting *W R Swinburn* a96 93
4 b g Selkirk(USA) —Desert Lynx (IRE) (Green Desert (USA))
1473[10] (4642) 5279[16] 5843[6] 6479[5] ◆ 6698[3]

Bee Stinger *I A Wood* a88 89
6 b g Almaty(IRE) —Nest Egg (Prince Sabo)
(274) 357[5] 592[5] 692[2] 910[7] (1065) 1335[14] 1502[7] 7564[9] 7712[7] 7740[7]

Beethoven (USA) *John T Ward Jr* a105
2 b c Sky Mesa(USA) —Moonlight Sonata (USA) (Carson City (USA))
6502a[3]

Beetuna (IRE) *B Smart* a78 76
3 b g Statue Of Liberty(USA) —High Atlas (Shirley Heights)
812a[9] 2674[12] 4606[4] 5965[6] 6088[3] 6712[4] 6821[2] (7115)

Be Fantastic (IRE) *G M Lyons* a82 71
3 ch g Fantastic Light(USA) —Be Decisive (Diesis)
4494a[5] 6366a[28]

Before You Go (IRE) *Saeed Bin Suroor* a96 106
5 b g Sadler's Wells(USA) —Here On Earth (USA) (Mr Prospector (USA))
381a[8] (477a) 673a[7]

Befortyfour *M A Jarvis* a102 109
3 b g Kyllachy—Ivania (First Trump)
(1255) ◆ (2529) ◆ (3028) 3273[2] 4957[3]

Be Free *Sir Mark Prescott* a62 45
3 b f Selkirk(USA) —Showdown (Darshaan)
65[6] 172[2] 350[3] 5868[11] 6337[9]

Beggars End (USA) *E F Vaughan* a60 65
3 rg g Mizzen Mast(USA) —Hasardeuse (USA) (Distant View (USA))
3333[4] 4066[4] 6032[13]

Bel Air Sizzle (USA) *Barry Abrams* 106
3 bb f Unusual Heat(USA) —Bel Air Belle (USA) (Runaway Groom (CAN))
3807a[3] 5744a[10]

Belated Silver (IRE) *Tom Dascombe* a73 68
2 rg g Clodovil(IRE) —Premier Place (USA) (Out Of Place (USA))
4579[8] 6359[5] 6578[4] 7052[2] (7306) 7475[6]

Bel Cantor *W J H Ratcliffe* a80 95
5 b h Largesse—Palmstead Belle (IRE) (Wolfhound (USA))
342[2] ◆ (466) 801[3] 824[6] 1300[5] 1430[3] 1891[8] 2698[3] 3050[5] 3111[3] 3477[8] 3973[5] (4460) 4854[2] (5503) 6069[4] 6289[8] 6947[14]

Belclare (IRE) *Tracey Collins* a59 83
3 gr f Verglas(IRE) —Vital Laser (USA) (Seeking The Gold (USA))
6845a[8]

Believe Me (IRE) *A De Royer-Dupre* 108
4 ch m In The Wings—Golden Wings (USA) (Devil's Bag (USA))
1713a[3] 2553a[3] 4914a[3] (7487a)

Belinda Rose (IRE) *J G Given* a47 53
4 b m Namid—Barathiki (Barathea (IRE))
7180[14]

Bella Amica (GER) *Frau Marion Rotering* 93
3 b f Black Sam Bellamy(IRE) —Bennetta (FR) (Top Ville)
4675a[12]

Bellalatino (IRE) *Norma Twomey* a54 54
3 b f Modigliani(USA) —Quaver (USA) (The Minstrel (CAN))
3611[14] 5379[13]

Bella Marie *L R James* 47
5 b m Kasakov—Onemoretime (Timeless Times (USA))
189[11]

Bella Medici *P G Murphy* a44 68
3 ch f Medicean—Missouri (Charnwood Forest (IRE))
3813[8] (4280) 4646[8] 4796[2] 6129[7] 6403[RR] 6883[6] 7761[8]

Bellamy Prince (GER) *Peter Scotton* 89
3 ch c Black Sam Bellamy(IRE) —Bukett (GER) (Turfkonig (GER))
7551a[2]

Bella Olympia *A J McCabe* a13 22
2 b f Groom Dancer(USA) —Cephalonia (Slip Anchor)
2821[14] 3568[9] 4109[11] 7117[11]

Bella Rowena *A M Balding* 70
2 b f Kyllachy—Luxurious (USA) (Lyphard (USA))
2614[6] 4554[4] 5584[6]

Bellas Chicas (IRE) *P T Midgley* a3 49
3 ch f Captain Rio—Persian Light (IRE) (Persian Heights)
767[10] 993[4] 1187[5] 1754[6] 2040[8]

Bella's Story *J S Goldie* 53
2 b f Lucky Story(USA) —Harrken Heights (IRE) (Belmez (USA))
3254[6] 3754[4] 4014[6] 5414[4]

Belle Allure (IRE) *R Pritchard-Gordon* 109
3 ch f Numerous(USA) —Mare Aux Fees (Kenmare (FR))
(1664a) 2877a[8] 5331a[6] 6498a[4]

Belle Bellino (FR) *R M Beckett* 65
3 b f Robellino(USA) —Hoh Chi Min (Efisio)
2127[4] 2922[5] 3381[7] (5749) 6564[10]

Belle Choisir *B Smart* a6 13
2 ch f Choisir(AUS) —Beausite (Grand Lodge (USA))
6764[10] 7319[10]

Belle Des Airs (IRE) *R M Beckett* 81
2 ch f Dr Fong(USA) —Belle Reine (King Of Kings (IRE))
2124[6] (4534) 5228[2] 5855[10]

Belle Et Celebre (FR) *A De Royer-Dupre* 110
3 b f Peintre Celebre(USA) —Rotina (FR) (Crystal Glitters (USA))
(2237a) 2877a[11] 6148a[5] 6854a[4]

Belle Isnarde (IRE) *V Caruso* 100
3 b f Desert Prince(IRE) —Attitre (FR) (Mtoto)
3076a[9]

Belle Jeanne (FR) *C Ferland* 94
2 b f Diableneyev(USA) —Ashley River (Ashkalani (IRE))
5300a[6]

Belle Noverre (IRE) *J S Bolger* a79 82
4 b m Noverre(USA) —Belle Etoile (FR) (Lead On Time (USA))
3531a[11]

Belleshee Banshee (IRE) *Peter Casey* a18 32
3 ch f Monashee Mountain(USA) —Annabel Lee (UAE) (Halling (USA))
3861a[8]

Belle's Ridge *Timothy Doyle* a77 91
4 ch h Tumbleweed Ridge—Alton Belle (Blakeney)
4576a[8]

Belliflore (FR) *Mlle S-V Tarrou* a77 110
4 gr m Verglas(IRE) —Truffle (IRE) (Ezzoud (IRE))
2637a[2] 3357a[7] 4915a[3] 5738a[5] 7187a[11]

Bell Island *Lady Herries* a78 91
4 b g Dansili—Thermal Spring (Zafonic (USA))
1563[4] (2862) 3802[9] 4200[5] 5017[6] 5999[4] 6243[14]

Bellomi (IRE) *Miss Gay Kelleway* a75 94
3 gr g Lemon Drop Kid(USA) —Reina Blanca (Darshaan)
1834[10] 2405[6] (2794) 3155[24] (5248) 7470[8] 7549[9] 7662[4] 7837[8]

Belotto (IRE) *R Charlton* a79 87
3 b f Peintre Celebre(USA) —Bel (Darshaan)
1444[6] 2197[3] 3362[3] (5231) 5683[5] 6195[4] (6605)

Belpasso (IRE) *A Selvaratnam* a82 72
5 ch g Danehill Dancer(IRE) —Beltisaal (FR) (Belmez (USA))
566a[5]

Beltanus (GER) *F Willenbrock* 106
4 ch h Tertullian(USA) —Brighella (GER) (Lomitas)
3515a[5]

Ben *P G Murphy* a73 73
3 b g Bertolini(USA) —Bold Byzantium (Bold Arrangement)
612[4] 777[7] 928[3] (1162) 1707[8] 2068[2] 2602[5] 2864[9] 3346[11] 7529[12] 7589[4]

Ben Ami *Miss J R Gibney* a79 66
3 ch g Pivotal—Darya (USA) (Gulch (USA))
1283[2] 2197[6] 2612[3] 3393[8] 4976[5] 5532[6] (6048) 6422[2] (6599)

Benandonner (USA) *R A Fahey* a98 106
5 ch g Giant's Causeway(USA) —Cape Verdi (IRE) (Caerleon (USA))
958[2] (1133) ◆ 1469[2] 2133[2] 3413[6] 3974[8] 4512a[12] 5508[9] 6103[3]

Benayoun *B J Llewellyn* a57 57
4 b h Inchinor—Sosumi (Be My Chief (USA))
68[8] 305[4] 521[9] 631[5] 788[3]

Ben Bacchus (IRE) *P W Hiatt* a56 33
6 b g Bahhare(USA) —Bodfaridistinction (IRE) (Distinctly North (USA))
585[7] 606[2] (751) 843[3] 999[15] 1206[5] 1562[11] 4295 [S] 4924[7] 7473[4] 7676[8] 7787[3]

Benbaun (IRE) *M J Wallace* 124
7 b g Stravinsky(USA) —Escape To Victory (Salse (USA))
2652a[5] 3101[7] 3533a[2] 3922[10] 5245[5] 5793[6] 6315a[3]

Ben Chorley *D R Lanigan* a23 98
4 gr g Inchinor—Arantxa (Sharpo)
(1520) (2619) (3173)

Bencoolen (IRE) *R Charlton* a54 92
3 b g Daylami(IRE) —Jakarta (IRE) (Machiavellian (USA))
1524[5] 1875[5] 2425[5] (3649) 4621[13] 5682[12] (6446)

Beneath The Trees (USA) *J A Osborne* a46 29
3 b c Forestry(USA) —Arabis (USA) (Deputy Minister (CAN))
712[5] 820[8]

Benedetto *Mrs A J Perrett* a73 80
3 b c Fasliyev(USA) —Inchyre (Shirley Heights)
(1060) 1216[3] 1622[5] 2563[3] 2945[10] 3571[3] (3893) 4306[10] (4413) 5185[8] 5580[7] 5841[7] 6124[6] 6417[6] 6554[7] 6749[2] 6936[2]

Benedict Spirit (IRE) *M H Tompkins* a76 69
3 b c Invincible Spirit(IRE) —Kathy Caerleon (IRE) (Caerleon (USA))
221[4] (350) 1746[7] 2173[4] 4021[10] (7729)

Beneking *D Burchell* a66 61
8 bb g Wizard King—Gagajulu (Al Hareb (USA))
56[10]

Benellino *R M Stronge* a29 47
5 b g Robellino(USA) —Benjarong (Sharpo)
517[10]

Benetti (IRE) *M R Channon* 44
2 ch g Kheleyf(USA) —Assigh Lady (IRE) (Great Commotion (USA))
2979[10] 3358[8] 3570[4] 4257[3] 4827[8]

Benfleet Boy *B G Powell* a54 83
4 gr g Fasliyev(USA) —Nicely (IRE) (Bustino)
(1126) 3612[10] 4131[4] 4627[3] 6028[9] 6250[12] 6675[10] 6983[2]

Benhavis *J L Dunlop* 78
3 b g Lomitas—Northern Goddess (Night Shift (USA))
1348[4] 5309[7] 6704[12]

Benhego *S C Williams* a77 76
3 ch g Act One—Sadaka (USA) (Kingmambo (USA))
1344[5] 1748[8] 2455[8] 3327[7] (4067) ◆ 4573[6] 5322[2] (5406) ◆ 5938[10] 6329[5] 6790[11]

Benitez Bond *G R Oldroyd* 35
3 ch g Bahamian Bounty—Triple Tricks (IRE) (Royal Academy (USA))
7084[6]

Benllech *D M Simcock* a102 62
4 b g Lujain(USA) —Four Legs Good (IRE) (Be My Guest (USA))
(94) (312) 503[2] (574) 824[2] (925) 3394[5] (5681) (7192)

Bennelong *R M Beckett* 81
2 b g Bahamian Bounty—Bundle Up (USA) (Miner's Mark (USA))
6077[3] ◆ 6677[3]

Bennie Blue (SAF) *M F De Kock* a95 95
6 ch h Rich Man's Gold(USA) —Biloxi Blue (SAF) (Al Mufti (USA))
202a[4] 380a[2] 568a[4]

Benny The Bull (USA) *Richard Dutrow Jr* a120
5 bb h Lucky Lionel(USA) —Comet Cat (USA) (Birdonthewire (USA))
(1089a)

Benny The Bus *J R Weymes* a64 47
6 b g Komaite(USA) —Amy Leigh (IRE) (Imperial Frontier (USA))
3826[9] 4073[8] 4476[8]

Ben's Dream (IRE) *A M Balding* 72
2 br g Kyllachy—Kelso Magic (USA) (Distant View (USA))
4510[8] 5988[4] 6389[2] ◆ 6865[2]

Bens Georgie (IRE) *D K Ivory* a62 73
6 ch m Opening Verse(USA) —Peperonata (IRE) (Cyrano De Bergerac)
54[9] 235[7] 375[2] 571[3] 749[10] 2806[10] 3329[8] 3825[8]

Bentley *J G Given* a69 62
4 b g Piccolo—April Lee (Superpower)
71[2] ◆ 142[2] 191[2] 370[5] 515[10] 581[8] 690[4] 774[6] 971[3] 1028[2] 1185[2] 1378[7] 1706[4] 3034[2] (3329) 3569[4] 3826[3] 4746[2] 5610[11] 6132[11] 7118[3]

Bentley Brook (IRE) *R Curtis* a90 51
6 ch g Singspiel(IRE) —Gay Bentley (USA) (Riverman (USA))
159[2] 260[3] (443) 450[3] (638) 838[8] 1026[2] (1904) 2076[5] 7717[3]

Bentong (IRE) *P F I Cole* a92 108
5 b g Anabaa(USA) —Miss Party Line (USA) (Phone Trick (USA))
(1346) 1765[6] 3248[6] 3722[3] 4624[LFT] 4840[RR]

Benwilt Breeze (IRE) *G M Lyons* a105 107
6 b g Mujadil(USA) —Image Of Truce (IRE) (Brief Truce (USA))
1495a[8] 3532a[14]

Benyw (IRE) *J G Given*
2 b f Noverre(USA) —Abington Angel (Machiavellian (USA))
6109[10]

Beraimi (IRE) *M A Jarvis* a58 75
2 b c Alhaarth(IRE) —Akrmina (Zafonic (USA))
4062[8] 4570[2] 5678[9]

Berbatov *Paul Green* a58 51
4 b g Alhaarth(IRE) —Neptunalia (Slip Anchor)
771[6] 1408[11]

Berbice (IRE) *R Hannon* a93 105
3 gr g Acclamation—Pearl Bright (FR) (Kaldoun (FR))
1400[9] 2530[3] 3197[24] 3905[7] 4153[5] 4522[5] 4842[6] 5270[6] 6239[5]

Bere Davis (FR) *P D Evans* a61 82
3 gr g Verglas(IRE) —Zerelda (Exhibitioner)
1074[9] 1899[2] 2189[3] 3251[6] 3641[4] 3969[5] 4206[5] 4682[4] 5185[2] 5492[6] 6554[8]

Beresford Lady *A D Brown* a47 48
4 b m Presidium—Coney Hills (Beverley Boy)
6726[6] 6956[10] 7322[10] 7581[11] 7772[9]

Beret Rouge (IRE) *A De Royer-Dupre* 103
3 gr c Red Ransom(USA) —Bernimixa (FR) (Linamix (FR))
3191a[9]

Bergamask (USA) *H-A Pantall* 89
3 ch f Kingmambo(USA) —Adonesque (IRE) (Sadler's Wells (USA))
7431a[7] 7635a[3]

Bergonzi (IRE) *J Howard Johnson* a78 91
4 ch g Indian Ridge—Lady Windley (Baillamont (USA))
2168[9] 3929[9]

Berkeley Castle (USA) *E F Vaughan* 54
4 b g Mizzen Mast(USA) —Bristol Channel (Generous (IRE))
3457[11] 3965[8] 5163[12]

Berlinetta (FR) *F-X de Chevigny* 64
2 b f Xaar—Lamballe (USA) (Woodman (USA))
7549a[0]

Bermacha *W R Muir* a74 69
3 ch f Bertolini(USA) —Machaera (Machiavellian (USA))
1381[3] 1685[8] 2118[5] 7419[11] 7548[7] 7771[11]

Bermondsey Bob (IRE) *J L Spearing* a12 75
2 b g Trans Island—Tread Softly (IRE) (Roi Danzig (USA))
3968[12] 4905[11] (5459) 6002[7] 6603[6] 6987[11]

Bermuda Rye (IRE) *M Delzangles* 109
3 b c Cape Cross(IRE) —Alleluia Tree (IRE) (Royal Academy (USA))
1376a[6] 2032a[8] 4719a[4] 7162a[4]

Bernie The Bolt (IRE) *A M Balding* a54 29
2 br g Milan—Chaparral Lady (IRE) (Broken Hearted)
7200[10] 7397[10]

Berriedale *Mrs A Duffield* 34
2 ch f Fraam—Carradale (Pursuit Of Love)
4213[11] 6789[10]

Berry Baby (IRE) *G A Butler* a69 63
3 b f Rainbow Quest(USA) —Inchberry (Barathea (IRE))
2833[5] 3351[2] ◆ 4527[7] 5105[6] 6529[5] (7169) 7761[2]

Berry Hill Lass (IRE) *J G M O'Shea* a60 61
4 b m Alhaarth(IRE) —Gold Mist (Darshaan)
132[2] 248[5] 575[3] 1281[3] 7667[9]

Berrymead *Miss A Stokell* a49 63
3 br f Killer Instinct—Mill End Quest (King's Signet (USA))
(1187) 1548[8] 3416[10] 3960[6] 4476[7] 7648[9] 7778[6] 7808[5]

Berrynarbor *A G Newcombe* a62 59
3 b f Tobougg(IRE) —River Art (USA) (Irish River (FR))
156[4] 3692[2] 4669[3] 5216[6]

Berry Pomeroy *A G Newcombe*
3 ch c Fantastic Light(USA) —Compton Emerald (IRE) (Bluebird (USA))
1896[11] 3604[14]

Bertbrand *D Flood* a75 77
3 b g Bertolini(USA) —Mi Amor (IRE) (Alzao (USA))
(17) 364[7] 538[4] 1852[4] 2127[10] 2983[5] (3330) 3587[7] 3946[9] 4030[8] 4693[9] 6011[11] 6448[7] 6634[9] 6821[11]

Bertha *J A Osborne* a33
3 b f Bertolini(USA) —Thea (USA) (Marju (IRE))
2084[5] 2803[6]

Berti *J Pearce* 47
2 gr c Bertolini(USA) —Incatinka (Inca Chief (USA))
6720[13] 7105[14]

Bertie Boo *B Smart* 52
3 b g Where Or When(IRE) —Lucy Boo (Singspiel (IRE))
2847[10] 5042[9] 5505[9] 6226[12]

Bertie Smalls *M H Tompkins* a54 52
2 b g Xaar—Largo (IRE) (Selkirk (USA))
5184[8] 5678[10] 6165[8]

Bertie Southstreet *J R Boyle* a78 78
5 bb g Bertolini(USA) —Salvezza (IRE) (Superpower)
274[5] 314[4] 636[6] 729[7] 2087[8] 2692[5] (3352) 3585[4] 4025[5] 4555[9] 4981[4] 5467[6] 6131[11] 7621[5] 7834[2]

Bertie Swift *J Gallagher* a68 59
4 b g Bertolini(USA) —Hollybell (Beveled (USA))
964[2] 1541[8] 2484[5] 3169[5] 3733[9] 5050[4] 6063[12]

Bertie Vista *T D Easterby* 66
3 b g Bertolini(USA) —Off Camera (Efisio)
1298[7] 1795[4] 1971[3] 2466[3] 3144[6] 3416[11] 4702[5] 4877[3] 6116[2] 6792[3] 7040[3]

Bertoliver *Tom Dascombe* a94 101
4 b g Bertolini(USA) —Calcavella (Pursuit Of Love)
1420[19] (1917) 2129[3] 2626[17] 3948[10] 4445[6] 6468[7] 6669[4] 7151[6] 7365[6] 7584[5]

Bertranicus (FR) *L Urbano-Grajales* a111 110
5 br g Take Risks(FR) —L'Etoile La Lune (IRE) (Groom Dancer (USA))
3357a[5]

Bert's Memory *J Mackie* a55 59
4 b m Bertolini(USA) —Meg's Memory (IRE) (Superlative)
(1025) 1578[7] 2670[2] 2988[6] 7270[3] 7373[12] 7658[6]

Besi *A Berry* a51 45
6 b g Lavirco(GER) —Brangane (IRE) (Anita's Prince)
433[5] 559[8] 613[6] 989[7] 2776[6] 3083[6] 3399[10]

Be Smart (USA) *D Wayne Lukas* a103
2 ch f Smarty Jones(USA) —Eishin Bridle (USA) (Unbridled (USA))
6967a[12]

Bespoke Boy *P C Haslam* a23 97
3 b g Acclamation—Milly Fleur (Primo Dominie)
1484[9] 1623[10] 1925[11] 4875[12] 7040[6] 7276[12]

Bessemer (JPN) *Miss M E Rowland* a68 62
7 b g Carnegie(IRE) —Chalna (IRE) (Darshaan)
2003[8] 2870[2]

Bessie Lou (IRE) *K A Ryan* 73
2 b f Montjeu(IRE) —Almond Mousse (FR) (Exit To Nowhere (USA))
6291[4] 6565[4]

Bessie Smith (IRE) *D R Gandolfo* 43
5 ch m Almutawakel—Rajaura (IRE) (Storm Bird (CAN))
513[8]

Best Bidder (USA) *R A Fahey* 72
2 b f Mr Greeley(USA) —Party Stripes (USA) (Candy Stripes (USA))
5882[5] 6319a[15] 6760[10]

Best In Class *Tom Dascombe* a45
2 gr c Best Of The Bests(IRE) —Third Party (Terimon)
7638[6]

Best Joking (GER) *W Hefter* 99
3 ch f Big Shuffle(USA) —Bergwelt (GER) (Solarstern (FR))
4881a[3]

Best Lead *Ian Emmerson* a58 52
9 b g Distant Relative—Bestemor (Selkirk (USA))
2036[6] 2248[4] 3212[10]

Bestofthem (USA) *Miss D Mountain* a75 87
3 bb c Stormin Fever(USA) —Mambo Mistress (USA) (Kingmambo (USA))
6440[15]

Best One *R A Harris* a78 85
4 ch g Best Of The Bests(IRE) —Nasaieb (IRE) (Fairy King (USA))
26[8] 275[4] 609[4] 731[3] (1035) ◆ (2351) ◆ 2906[2] 3127[4] 3868[3] 4106[4] 5861[2] 6174[2] 6623[3] 7290[7] 7733[7]

Best Prospect (IRE) *M Dods* a74 99
6 b g Orpen(USA) —Bright Prospect (USA) (Miswaki (USA))
(1072) 1569[12] 2218[8] 5772[8] 6041[4] 6536[7] (7056)

Best Selection *Mrs L J Mongan* a71 71
4 ch m Inchinor—Manila Selection (USA) (Manila (USA))
449[4] 881[6] 1052[3] 1181[2] 1538[4] 4029[4] 4343[3] 4935[4] 6019[4] 6882[5]

Best Suited *J J Quinn* 62
3 b f Averti(IRE) —Scarlett Holly (Red Sunset)
1819[8] 2159[8] 2661[15] 3139[9] 4207[15]

Best Warning *J Ryan* a9 47
4 br m Best Of The Bests(IRE) —Just Warning (Warning)
3377[12]

Be Superior *J Balding* a2
3 b f Superior Premium—Miss Tun (Komaite (USA))
4388[11]

Beth *Andrew Oliver* 82
2 ch f Deportivo—Nashira (Prince Sabo)
5132a[6]

Bethanys Boy (IRE) *A M Hales* a65 56
7 ch g Docksider(USA) —Daymoon (USA) (Dayjur (USA))
373[2] 481[2] 611[3] 794[4] 863[3] 1562[4] 1679[3] (Dead)

Bethie *R Brotherton* 55
2 b f Bold Edge—Baytown Rhapsody (Emperor Jones (USA))
1385[4] 1866[9] 2608[7] 3178[4] 4101[7]

Bet Noir (IRE) *W R Swinburn* a62 65
3 b f King's Best(USA) —Ivowen (USA) (Theatrical)
3326[6] 5231[4] 5803[9] ◆ 6044[3] 6529[9] 6703[14]

Betonart *R M Beckett* a43 54
3 b f Tamure(IRE) —Heather Honey (Insan (USA))
1709[6] 2480[4] 2756[13] 3314[3] 3763[3]

Betoula *Mrs A L M King* a38
2 ch f Bertolini(USA) —Pab's Choice (Telsmoss)
1866[10] 2709[9] 3584[5] 7537[9]

Betsy The Best *R Bastiman* 16
2 ch f Best Of The Bests(IRE) —Dusty's Darling (Doyoun)
6722[10] 7660[7]

Betteras Bertie *M Brittain* a59 49
5 gr g Paris House—Suffolk Girl (Statoblest)
2487[5] 2697[7] 3814[7] 4168[8] 7180[2] 7267[4] 7316[2] 7533[4] 7658[4]

Better Hand (IRE) *M R Channon* 95
3 b c Montjeu(IRE) —Silly Game (IRE) (Bigstone (IRE))
1443[6] 1810[3] 2194[13] 2425[4] 3157[11] 3875[5] (Dead)

Better In Heaven *H J L Dunlop* a40 60
3 b c Zamindar(USA) —Peace (Sadler's Wells (USA))
1695[5] 2047[7] 3206[10] 4524[10] 5087[12] 5961[7]

Better In Time (USA) *Jane Chapple-Hyam* a68
2 b f City Place(USA) —Ineda Doll (USA) (Langfuhr (CAN))
7578[4] 7754[3]

Better Talk Now (USA) *H Graham Motion* 121
9 bb g Talkin Man(CAN) —Bendita (USA) (Baldski (USA))
1091a[9] 3995a[3] 7000a[8]

Bett's Spirit (IRE) *M J Grassick* a82 96
3 b f Invincible Spirit(IRE) —Hi Bettina (Henbit (USA))
6315a[12]

Betty Burke *Liam McAteer* a62 67
3 b f Choisir(AUS) —Island Lover (IRE) (Turtle Island (IRE))
6043[7] 7534[6]

Bettys Touch *W J Musson* 55
3 b f Lujain(USA) —Fadaki Hawaki (USA) (Vice Regent (CAN))
2549[10] 4207[13] 4533[9]

Between Dreams *Miss E C Lavelle*
5 br m Silver Wizard(USA) —I Have A Dream (SWE) (Mango Express)
2717[10]

Betws Y Coed (IRE) *A Bailey* a53 48
2 br f Indian Haven—Tommys Queen (IRE) (Ali-Royal (IRE))
1610[DSQ] 2887[6] 4870[15] 6787[14] 7266[8] 7283[4] 7425[2] 7514[4] 7666[5] 7789[10] 7824[2]

Beverly Hill Billy *A King* a81 82
4 b g Primo Valentino(IRE) —Miss Beverley (Beveled (USA))
3561[2] 4131[7] 4565[3] 4894[11]

Bewdley *R E Peacock* a39 58
3 b f Best Of The Bests(IRE) —Garota De Ipanema (FR) (Al Nasr (FR))
1478[15] 2670[10] 2988[10] 3359[6] 4298[5] 5652[7] 7692[10]

Beyond Our Reach (IRE) *T Stack* 103
2 ch f Danehill Dancer(IRE) —Bluebell Wood (IRE) (Bluebird (USA))
5549a[3] 6441[9] 6966a[12]

Bianca Capello *J R Fanshawe* a52 57
3 b f Medicean—Totom (Mtoto)
3801[7] 7620[9]

Bianca Maria *T D Easterby* 24
2 b f Bertolini(USA) —Dominelle (Domynsky)
2035[14]

Bickersten *M R Channon* a60
2 ch g Piccolo—Niseem (USA) (Hennessy (USA))
7554[7] 7830[5] ◆

Bidable *B Palling* a48 66
4 b m Auction House(USA) —Dubitable (Formidable (USA))
1160[15] 1898[9] 2097[13] 3383[8] 4368[5] 6560[2] 6928[9] 7437[8] 7692[6]

Bid Art (IRE) *A M Balding* a65 65
3 b g Hawk Wing(USA) —Crystal Theatre (IRE) (King's Theatre (IRE))
1479[8] 1958[7] 2244[6]

Bid For Glory *H J Collingridge* a95 98
4 ch h Auction House(USA) —Woodland Steps (Bold Owl)
1427[3] 1812[5] 2593[5] 3398[5] 4191[P] 4867[8] 5635[8] 6035[4] ◆ 6482[23]

Bid For Gold *Jedd O'Keeffe* 76
4 b g Auction House(USA) —Gold And Blue (IRE) (Bluebird (USA))
992[15] 1217[11] 1450[9] 1826[8] 2846[3] (2891) 3454[7] 4174[3] 4736[3] 4875[3] (5455) 6164[7] 6724[12]

Bid To Dance *K A Morgan* a31 43
2 b f Auction House(USA) —Westmead Tango (Pursuit Of Love)
4986[3] 6931[10] 7164[7]

Bid To The Beat *H J Collingridge* a54 54
3 b c Auction House(USA) —Sophies Symphony (Merdon Melody)
2259[6] 3694[4] 4524[12] 6048[15] (Dead)

Bienheureux *Miss Gay Kelleway* a61 69
7 b g Bien Bien(USA) —Rochea (Rock City)
91[8] 224[5] 330[6] 575[4] 675[9] 793[4] 843[6] 1505[4] (1643) 2071[4] (2423) 2558[4] 2908[10] 3900[4] 4155[5] 4811[4] 5183[5] 5583[6] 5833[2] 6019[9] 6727[10] 7573[5] 7787[6]

Bigalos Bandit *D Nicholls* a80 89
6 ch g Compton Place—Move Darling (Rock City)
1325[10] 2828[18]

Bigalo's Banjo *L A Mullaney* a26 51
5 bb g Fraam—Polly Particular (Beveled (USA))
2806[12] 3172[5] 4903[11]

Bigalo's Magic (UAE) *E J O'Neill* a61 67
3 ch g Halling(USA) —Roseate (USA) (Mt. Livermore (USA))
2785[8] 3436[3] 3711[10]

Bigalo's Star (IRE) *L A Mullaney* a40 66
2 b g Xaar—Toi Toi (IRE) (In The Wings)
5825[5] 6466[6] 6789[4]

Big Apple Boy (IRE) *Jedd O'Keeffe* 81
2 b c Statue Of Liberty(USA) —Go For Grace (IRE) (Shalford (IRE))
4169[4] (6229) ◆ 6525[3]

Big Boom *M J Wallace* a38
3 ch g Cadeaux Genereux—Kastaway (Distant Relative)
706[8] 1027[5] 1255[5] 1581[7]

Big Booster (USA) *Mike Mitchell* a114 112
7 b g Accelerator(USA) —Waterside (USA) (Topsider (USA))
6993a[3]

Big Bound (USA) *J H M Gosden* 79
2 b c Grand Slam(USA) —Golden Cat (USA) (Storm Cat (USA))
6292[2] ◆ 6759[4]

Big Brown (USA) *Richard Dutrow Jr* a128 120
3 b c Boundary(USA) —Mien (USA) (Nureyev (USA))
(1820a) (2215a) 2858a[9] (4678a) (5928a)

Bigfanofthat (IRE) *K R Burke* 78
3 b g Rock Of Gibraltar(IRE) —Miss Salsa (USA) (Unbridled (USA))
1297[11] 5863[9] 6041[7]

Big Monologue (IRE) *H-A Pantall* 93
3 br f Testa Rossa(AUS) —Baracoa (SWI) (Llandaff (USA))
6852a[4]

Big Nige (IRE) *J Pearce* a69 56
2 br c Mull Of Kintyre(USA) —Queen's Quest (Rainbow Quest (USA))
6715 [14] 7106[9] 7422[4] 7784[7]

Big Noise *Dr J D Scargill* a96 94
4 b h Lake Coniston(IRE) —Mitsubishi Video (IRE) (Doulab (USA))
2371[3] 2818[12] 4405[7] ◆ 4869[4] 5405[2] 6269[20]

Bon News (IRE) *B Smart* 70
4 ch m Spectrum(IRE) —Princess Nutley (IRE) (Mujtahid (USA))
3481[7] 4117[9] 5634[10]

Bonnie Bea *B I Case* a18
2 b f Royal Applause—Boojum (Mujtahid (USA))
7708[13]

Bonnie Charlie *R Hannon* 108
2 ch c Intikhab(USA) —Scottish Exile (IRE) (Ashkalani (IRE))
(1363) 4507[2] 5244[2] (5794) 6713a[3] 6979[2] ◆

Bonnie Prince Blue *B W Hills* a90 91
5 ch g Tipsy Creek(USA) —Heart So Blue (Dilum (USA))
(85) 259[6] 442[7] (1278) 1617[11] 2195[9] 3998[8] 4854[6] 5831[9] 6532[7] 6925[7]

Bonny Bright Eyes *Miss Kate Milligan* a24 52
3 b f Barathea(IRE) —Moonlight (IRE) (Night Shift (USA))
2488[8] 2779[3] 4075[3] 4498[4] 7376[14]

Bonny Rose *M Johnston* 73
3 ch f Zaha(CAN) —Marina Park (Local Suitor (USA))
1524[11] 2378[3] 3109[7] 3725[3]

Bonny's Babe *G D Blake* a47 54
3 b f City On A Hill(USA) —Ashtree Belle (Up And At 'Em)
1187[7] 1271[10] 4125[16]

Bon Spiel *L M Cumani* a105 83
4 b h Singspiel(IRE) —L'Affaire Monique (Machiavellian (USA))
7579[2] ◆ 7741[3]

Bon Ton Roulet *R Hannon* a64 50
3 ch f Hawk Wing(USA) —Evangeline (Sadler's Wells (USA))
52[4] 221[7] 547[5] 803[6] 1163[9] 1364[8] 2639[5] ◆ 3524[4] 4569[4] 5815[7] 6913[5]

Bonus (IRE) *G A Butler* a115 96
8 b g Cadeaux Genereux—Khamseh (Thatching)
(137) 226[3] 337[2] 677[3] 832[4] 1809[21] 6285[11] 6903[4] 7192[3] 7381[8] 7703[2]

Bonzo *P Howling* a54 21
3 b g Where Or When(IRE) —Making Memories (IRE) (Alzao (USA))
1563[8] 2090[6] 3035[9] 6226[6] 7379[7] 7713[5] 7787[9]

Boo *J W Unett* a95 69
6 b g Namaqualand(USA) —Violet (IRE) (Mukaddamah (USA))
1711[2] 2335[9] 2904[8] 7291[10] 7785[6]

Boogie Board *Garry Moss* a50 40
4 b m Tobougg(IRE) —Royal Gift (Cadeaux Genereux)
4479[11] 4891[10]

Boogie Dancer *H S Howe* a65 68
4 b m Tobougg(IRE) —Bolero (Rainbow Quest (USA))
53[4]

Boogie Magic *R W Price* a29 51
8 b m Wizard King—Dalby Dancer (Bustiki)
160[10] (Dead)

Bookiebasher Babe (IRE) *M Quinn* a71 72
3 b f Orpen(USA) —Jay Gee (IRE) (Second Set (IRE))
(281) 464[5] (785) 1161[3] 1637[2] 2118[12] 2288[4] 4795[7] 5317[10] 5836[13] 6437[2] 6712[9] 7166[4] (7662)

Bookiesindex Boy *J R Jenkins* a79 78
4 bb g Piccolo—United Passion (Emarati (USA))
(1033) 1378[4] 1582[6] 2292[7] 2551[8] 4064[8] 5187[3] 6190[2] 6990[9] 7182[5] 7276[4] 7435[8] (7621) 7743[6]

Bookish *Jamie Poulton* a75 61
3 b f Dubai Destination(USA) —Daybook (IRE) (Daylami (IRE))
(102) ◆ 355[4] 975[5] 2622[11] 2930[4] 3210[8] 3345[6] 3874[7] 4862[12]

Book Of Facts (FR) *S W Hall* a80 46
4 ch g Machiavellian(USA) —Historian (IRE) (Pennekamp (USA))
613[7]

Book Of Music (IRE) *Saeed Bin Suroor* 111
5 b g Sadler's Wells(USA) —Novelette (Darshaan)
(293a) 491a[6] 740a[4] 5288[8]

Boomtown *M Johnston* a80 69
3 b g Fantastic Light(USA) —Ville D'Amore (USA) (Irish River (FR))
20[5] (116) 184[2] (225) 360[2]

Bootleg *D Nicholls*
2 b g Bahamian Bounty—Asbo (Abou Zouz (USA))
6065[6]

Boot 'n Toot *M Sheppard* a84 73
7 b m Mtoto—Raspberry Sauce (Niniski (USA))
4691[11]

Boot Strap Bill *Miss J R Tooth* a34 62
3 ch g Timeless Times(USA) —Nuthatch (IRE) (Thatching)
1642[12] 1897[11]

Booyah (USA) *Jerry Fanning* a103 91
4 b h Running Stag(USA) —Coral Necklace (USA) (Conquistador Cielo (USA))
6993a[8]

Boppys Dancer *P T Midgley* a55 55
5 b g Clan Of Roses—Dancing Mary (Sri Pekan (USA))
654[8]

Boppys Diamond *P T Midgley* 32
4 b m Clan Of Roses—Dancing Mary (Sri Pekan (USA))
1222[9] 1550[11]

Boppys Pride *P T Midgley* a57 58
6 ch h Clan Of Roses—Joara (FR) (Radetzky)
77[6] 143[7] 251[3] 352[4] 4458[10] 4813[11] 6162[9] 6235[5] 6408[3] 6585[5] 7132[6] 7270[12]

Borasco (USA) *T D Barron* a67 89
3 ch f Stormy Atlantic(USA) —Seek (USA) (Devil's Bag (USA))
2911[10] (3416) (4875) 5635[5]

Border Artist *J Pearce* a59 65
9 ch g Selkirk(USA) —Aunt Tate (Tate Gallery (USA))
1248[6] 1602[6] 2355[6] 2861[5] 3034[11] 3501[10] 4052[4] 5533[4] 6335[14] 6751[6]

Border Defence (IRE) *P A Blockley* a53 57
3 bb g Princely Heir(IRE) —Dakhira (Emperor Jones (USA))
1364[10]

Border Edge *J J Bridger* a71 65
10 b g Beveled(USA) —Seymour Ann (Krayyan)
164[4] 328[3] 537[9] 2353[8] 3090[13]

Border Fox *L Lungo* 59
5 b g Foxhound(USA) —Vado Via (Ardross)
2360[11] 2571[5] 2847[9] 3755[13]

Borderlescott *R Bastiman* a105 121
6 b g Compton Place—Jeewan (Touching Wood (USA))
(1772) 2404[2] 3063[2] 3948[2] 4624[3] (5245) 6518a[3] (6963a)

Border Maid *E A L Dunlop* a45 56
2 b f Falbrav(IRE) —Madame Maxine (USA) (Dayjur (USA))
6080[11] 6555[11] 6770[9] 7338[6]

Border Music *A M Balding* a113 102
7 b g Selkirk(USA) —Mara River (Efisio)
1985[2] 3197[4]

Border Owl (IRE) *R Hannon* a85 81
3 b g Selkirk(USA) —Nightbird (IRE) (Night Shift (USA))
1896[10] 2302[3] 2714[4] 3325[3] 3969[3] (4484) 5098[5] 6467[3] 6675[4]

Border Patrol *R Charlton* 75
2 b c Selkirk(USA) —Ffestiniog (IRE) (Efisio)
6602[3] ◆

Border Tale *James Moffatt* a69 44
8 b g Selkirk(USA) —Likely Story (IRE) (Night Shift (USA))
4630[9]

Bordes Lane *A M Balding* a26
3 b g Olden Times—Rimba (USA) (Dayjur (USA))
2528[13]

Borehan *D Selvaratnam* a99 40
5 b g Agnes World(USA) —Crime Ofthecentury (Pharly (FR))
497a[10] 670a[10]

Boris De Deauville (IRE) *S Wattel* 118
5 b h Soviet Star(USA) —Logjam (IRE) (Royal Academy (USA))
1240a[3] 2238a[5] 3053a[3] 4320a[3] (5114a) 6499a[4] 7162a[12]

Born To Be King (USA) *A P O'Brien* 87
2 b c Storm Cat(USA) —Quarter Moon (IRE) (Sadler's Wells (USA))
3509a[8]

Born Tobouggie (GER) *H R A Cecil* a93 100
3 b f Tobougg(IRE) —Braissim (Dancing Brave (USA))
(1379) 1730[2] 2412[6] ◆ (4694) 5425[3] 6034[13] (6718) 7099[5]

Born To Frill *Miss L C Siddall*
3 b f Muhtarram(USA) —Superfrills (Superpower)
3452[9]

Born To Rock (IRE) *J T Gorman* 80
2 b c Statue Of Liberty(USA) —Daziyra (IRE) (Doyoun)
6317a[15]

Born West (USA) *N B King* a70 71
4 b g Gone West(USA) —Admirer (USA) (Private Terms (USA))
7042[13]

Borodinsky *R E Barr* a42 69
7 b g Magic Ring(IRE) —Valldemosa (Music Boy)
1826[10] 2597[16] 3281[5] 3593[15] 3755[14]

Borrowdale *J A Osborne* a71 64
3 b g Royal Applause—Night Mirage (USA) (Silver Hawk (USA))
1149[10] 1215[8] 1311[4] 1870[9] (2833) 3483[2] 4054[6] 4564[2] 5698[2] 6022[3] 6421[7] 6824[4]

Borzoi Maestro *D G Bridgwater* a63 61
7 ch g Wolfhound(USA) —Ashkernazy (IRE) (Salt Dome (USA))
100[6] 254[13] 297[3] 440[10]

Bosamcliff (IRE) *A B Haynes* a62 69
3 b f Daylami(IRE) —L'Animee (Green Tune (USA))
2454[6] 3483[11] 4810[2] (5388) 5803[10] 5815[4] 6703[6]

Boscobel *Saeed Bin Suroor* a100 116
4 ch g Halling(USA) —Dunnes River (USA) (Danzig (USA))
476a[7] 740a[7]

Boss Hog *R Curtis* a69 42
3 b g Key Of Luck(USA) —Dania (GER) (Night Shift (USA))
261[4] 529[3] 867[8] 1396[7] 1897[7] ◆ 2451[10] 7267[2] 7441[2] 7665[2]

Boston Lodge *Doug Watson* a111 84
8 ch g Grand Lodge(USA) —Ffestiniog (IRE) (Efisio)
204a[15] 815a[14]

Bosun Breese *P W D'Arcy* a65 89
3 b g Bahamian Bounty—Nellie Melba (Hurricane Sky (AUS))
1597[8] 1852[6] 2258[2] ◆ 2843[13] 3028[7] 3273[6] 3696[4] (4347) 4591[10] 6650[2]

Botanical (USA) *E Charpy* a102 96
7 b g Seeking The Gold(USA) —Satin Flower (USA) (Shadeed (USA))
295a[6] 497a[3] 666a[10] 814a[11]

Botham (USA) *J S Goldie* a58 61
4 bb g Cryptoclearance(USA) —Oval (USA) (Kris S (USA))
283[6] 2523[7] (2936) 3079[3] 3129[3] 3582[5] 4018[9] 4117[8] 4915[5] 5389[4] 5970[3] 6310[5] 6409[4]

Bothar Brugha (IRE) *J G M O'Shea* a53 46
4 b g Alexius(IRE) —Denise's Stride (IRE) (Fumo Di Londra (IRE))
143[5] 369[6] 513[5] 1895[8] 2456[4] 3344[6]

Bothy *R M Beckett* 82
2 ch c Pivotal—Villa Carlotta (Rainbow Quest (USA))
6604[2]

Boucheron *R A Fahey* 83
3 b f Galileo(IRE) —Rainbow Lyrics (IRE) (Rainbow Quest (USA))
3297[3] (3813) 4435[5] 4784[8]

Bouggie Daize *C G Cox* 69
2 b f Tobougg(IRE) —Milly's Lass (Mind Games)
2618[5] ◆ 3674[2] 4593[4] 5511[9] ◆ 6240[5]

Bouggler *Miss J A Camacho* 63
3 b g Tobougg(IRE) —Rush Hour (IRE) (Night Shift (USA))
1397[2] 2495[3] 2985[7] 4247[3] (4735) 6386[3]

Bouguereau *P W Chapple-Hyam* 111
3 b c Alhaarth(IRE) —Blessed Honour (Ahonoora)
(1014) 1443[2] 2028a[7] 2829[9] 3875[3] 4505[4]

Boule Masquee *David P Myerscough* a69 84
4 ch m Compton Place—Burqa (Nashwan (USA))
5884[11] 7325a[9]

Boulevin (IRE) *R J Price* a38 52
8 bb g Perugino(USA) —Samika (IRE) (Bikala)
215[3] 1369[7]

Boundless (NZ) *Stephen McKee* 108
4 ch m Van Nistelrooy(USA) —Nothing Less (NZ) (Star Way)
6835a[11] 7188a[15]

Boundless Applause *I A Wood* 34
2 b f Royal Applause—Liberty Bound (Primo Dominie)
5459[10] 6327[14]

Boundless Prospect (USA) *P D Evans* a74 84
9 b g Boundary(USA) —Cape (USA) (Mr Prospector (USA))
51[5] 331[6] 512[3] 716[13] (864) 992[5] ◆ (1301) 2250[4] (2667) 3230[4] 5961[4] 6215[8] 7560[2] (7665) 7723[3]

Bountiful Bay *B J Meehan* a63 51
3 b f Bahamian Bounty—My Preference (Reference Point)
2257[11] 2560[11] 3629[11] 5026[7] 6681[5] 7196[2] 7377[2] 7508[11]

Bounty Box *C F Wall* 82
2 b f Bahamian Bounty—Bible Box (IRE) (Bin Ajwaad (IRE))
4792[3] ◆ 6080[4] (7015)

Bounty Reef *P D Evans* a33 56
2 b f Bahamian Bounty—Shaieef (IRE) (Shareef Dancer (USA))
3798[5] 4027[9] 4062[7] 4337[11] 5778[2] (6214) 6561[4] 7257[13]

Bourbon Balistic *Mrs A Duffield* a40 61
3 ch g Piccolo—Last Ambition (IRE) (Cadeaux Genereux)
6219[8] 7292[9] 7541[10]

Bourbon Highball (IRE) *P C Haslam* a27 61
3 b g Catcher In The Rye(IRE) —Be Exciting (IRE) (Be My Guest (USA))
1823[3] 2037[6] 7723[8]

Bourn Fair *P J McBride* a56 34
2 ch f Systematic—Astelia (Sabrehill (USA))
6884[9] 7209[7] 7337[9]

Bournonville *M Wigham* a47 31
5 b g Machiavellian(USA) —Amellnaa (IRE) (Sadler's Wells (USA))
2374[8] 4371[8]

Bourse (IRE) *A G Foster* 72
3 b g Dubai Destination(USA) —Quarter Note (USA) (Danehill (USA))
980[6] 1306[4] ◆ 1558[8] (2247) 2496[3] ◆ 2840[12] 3494[8] 3790[3] 4241[3] 4455[6] 4952[4] 5221[6] (7224)

Bouvardia *H R A Cecil* 84
2 b f Oasis Dream—Arabesque (Zafonic (USA))
4870[2] ◆ 5640[2] (6030) 6533[7]

Bovered (IRE) *A Berry* a16 20
4 b m Fayruz—Lucky Pick (Auction Ring (USA))
19[6] 289[11] 2491[13]

Bowder Stone (IRE) *M H Tompkins* 86
3 b c Rock Of Gibraltar(IRE) —Ghita (IRE) (Zilzal (USA))
1295[3] 1579[2] 2002[3] 2427[5] 3494[3] 3911[2] (4663) 4906[3] 5858[16] 6276[3] 6704[6]

Bowl Of Cherries *I A Wood* a58 44
5 b g Vettori(IRE) —Desert Nomad (Green Desert (USA))
1148[5] 1262[6] 1282[4] 2870[9] 3265[10]

Boxhall (IRE) *N Wilson* a63 72
6 b g Grand Lodge(USA) —March Hare (Groom Dancer (USA))
3010[11] 4817[5] 5396[10] 5869[7]

Box Office *M Johnston* 83
2 b c Storming Home—Dream Ticket (USA) (Danzig (USA))
6158[2] 6407[3] (6715)

Boy Blue *D W Barker* 86
3 b c Observatory(USA) —Rowan Flower (IRE) (Ashkalani (IRE))
1297[10] 1923[4] 3494[6] (4017) 4783[8] 5635[16]

Boy Dancer (IRE) *J J Quinn* a60 65
5 ch g Danehill Dancer(IRE) —Mary Gabry (IRE) (Kris)
109[7] 749[6] 991[6] 2009[8] (2662) 3082[4] 3557[6] 4215[3] (4537) 4850[3] 6216[9]

Boy On A Swing (USA) *J A Osborne* a75 6
3 ch c Hold That Tiger(USA) —Balancoire (USA) (Diesis)
416[9] 500[2] ◆ 570[4] 837[4] (919) 1543[11] 2310[10] 3566[5]

Boy Racer (IRE) *M Johnston* a67 67
3 br c Singspiel(IRE) —Gombay Girl (USA) (Woodman (USA))
310[3] 1690[5] 2207[13] 3555[10]

Boz *L M Cumani* a99 90
4 gr h Grand Lodge(USA) —Dali's Grey (Linamix (FR))
1273[3] (1744) 2076[8] 2591[8] (3864) 4742[14] 5423[5] 6171[8] (6698)

Bozeman Trail *P F I Cole* a61 64
3 b g Averti(IRE) —Crystal Power (USA) (Pleasant Colony (USA))
2043[10] 2480[10] 2917[14]

Brabazon (IRE) *Barry Potts* 62
5 b g In The Wings—Azure Lake (USA) (Lac Ouimet (USA))
988[12]

Brace Of Doves *D W Whillans* a55 54
6 b g Bahamian Bounty—Overcome (Belmez (USA))
5968[13]

Braddock (IRE) *S Donohoe* a77 85
5 b g Pivotal—Sedna (FR) (Bering)
1103a[7] 4576a[10] 6928[5]

Brad's Luck (IRE) *M Blanshard* 61
2 ch g Lucky Story(USA) —Seymour (IRE) (Eagle Eyed (USA))
4890[10] 5225[10] 6292[6]

Brae Hill (IRE) *M L W Bell* 87
2 b g Fath(USA) —Auriga (Belmez (USA))
2117[2] (2458) 3105[12] 3879[3] 5286[2] 5827[3] 6483[9]

Bragging Rights (IRE) *K A Ryan* 64
2 b c Xaar—Graceful Air (IRE) (Danzero (AUS))
1948[3] 2657[6]

Brahms And Mist (FR) *D J S Ffrench Davis* a9
8 b g River Mist(USA) —Strabit (Stradavinsky)
7473[14]

Braille *T D Walford* 71
3 b g Bahamian Bounty—Branston Gem (So Factual (USA))
2966[15] 3282[7] 3438[4] 3868[11] (4216)

Braishfield Lass *B G Powell* a49 46
2 b f Superior Premium—Time To Tell (Keen)
5147[15] 5570[10] 6330[9] 6892[7] 7283[5] 7415[6]

Brakey Hill (USA) *B J Meehan* a57
3 gr c Forest Wildcat(USA) —Divine Angel (USA) (Matty G (USA))
2834[9] 6888[13]

Bramalea *B W Duke* a73 61
3 b f Whitmore's Conn(USA) —Aster (IRE) (Danehill (USA))
2612[7] 2954[8] ◆ 3333[5] 5119[5] 5218[3] (5378) 5712[10] 6048[6] 6332[U] (6821) 7166[9] 7360[12]

Bramantino (IRE) *T A K Cuthbert* a47 42
8 b g Perugino(USA) —Headrest (Habitat)
3176[7] 3399[5] 3756[11] 4848[13]

Bramaputra (IRE) *B R Millman* 90
3 b f Choisir(AUS) —Bayalika (IRE) (Selkirk (USA))
1445[2] 1715[2] ◆ (2571) 2975[6]

Bramcote Lorne *R C Guest* a57 61
5 b g Josr Algarhoud(IRE) —Dreamtime Quest (Blakeney)
300[3] 517[4] 769[3] 822[6] 1152[5] 1776[2] 3029[7] 3226[5] 4173[6]

Brandane (IRE) *R A Fahey* a58 67
3 br g Danehill Dancer(IRE) —Oumaldaaya (USA) (Nureyev (USA))
2488[6] 3126[5] 3717[11] 4044[7] 6162[6] (6693) (7132) ◆

Brandywell Boy (IRE) *D J S Ffrench Davis* a78 74
5 b g Danetime(IRE) —Alexander Eliott (IRE) (Night Shift (USA))
55[5] 2923[8] 3352[3] 3868[15] 4668[2] 4944[4] 5046[4] 5206[6] 6131[3] 6357[2] 7013[2] 7066[5] (7378) 7435[4] 7592[8] 7675[4] 7811[4]

Branston Tiger *Ian Emmerson* a71 76
9 b g Mark Of Esteem(IRE) —Tuxford Hideaway (Cawston's Clown)
2081[10]

Brasingaman Hifive *Mrs G S Rees* 84
3 b f High Estate—Our Miss Florence (Carlitin)
2333[6] 3263[7] 4300[5] (4818) 5635[2] 6249[7] 6482[15]

Brass Damask (USA) *A Fabre* 92
3 b f Lemon Drop Kid(USA) —Blush Damask (USA) (Green Dancer (USA))
6568a[6]

Brassini *B R Millman* a63 98
3 bg g Bertolini(USA) —Silver Spell (Aragon)
1284[5] 1597[4] (1995) ◆ 2410[9] 2998[3] 3744[3] 4158[2] (4312) 4983[3] 5862[7] 6277[4] 6676[2] 6947[17]

Brastar Jelois (FR) *R Hollinshead* a67 68
5 b m True Brave(USA) —Star Angels (FR) (Ski Chief (USA))
999[7] 1310[3] 1679[8] 1890[6]

Brathay (IRE) *Ian Williams* a29 38
4 b g Sadler's Wells(USA) —Love Everlasting (Pursuit Of Love)
2779[7] 3687[9] 5230[7] 5993[17] 7078[11]

Bravalto *B Smart* 60
2 b c Falbrav(IRE) —Bunty Boo (Noalto)
7020[9] 7240[6]

Brave Boogie *H J L Dunlop* a35 59
3 ch f Tobougg(IRE) —Be Brave (FR) (Green Forest (USA))
758[7] 919[8] 1173[4] 1397[6] 2997[11] 4247[2] 5613[9] 6022[12]

Brave Bugsy (IRE) *A M Balding* a60 66
5 b g Mujadil(USA) —Advancing (IRE) (Ela-Mana-Mou)
545[4] 758[4] 823[3] 1856[10] (2245) 2888[6] 4105[4] 4652[4] 5613[7]

Brave Falcon (IRE) *Leo J Temple* a91 78
4 b g Fasliyev(USA) —Don't Care (IRE) (Nordico (USA))
4004a[11] 6963a[5]

Brave Hawk *M A Jarvis* a78 81
3 b c Hawk Wing(USA) —Triomphale (USA) (Nureyev (USA))
265[6] 500[7] 705[2] 920[2] 1082[2] 2311[4] 2974[5] (3325) 3560[2] 4927[5] 5862[10]

Braveheart Move (IRE) *Sir Mark Prescott* a77 34
2 b c Cape Cross(IRE) —Token Gesture (IRE) (Alzao (USA))
6029[10] (6253)

Brave Hiawatha (FR) *G J Smith* a10 46
6 b g Dansili—Alexandrie (USA) (Val De L'Orne (FR))
1391[16]

Brave Knave (IRE) *B De Haan* 43
3 b c Averti(IRE) —Recall (IRE) (Revoque (IRE))
4124[11] 5182[9] 5652[6]

Bravely (IRE) *T D Easterby* 89
4 b g Rock Of Gibraltar(IRE) —Raghida (IRE) (Nordico (USA))
6215[16] 6724[11] 7175[3] ◆

Brave Mave *W Jarvis* a83 71
3 gr f Daylami(IRE) —Baalbek (Barathea (IRE))
1381[6] 3841[8] 4427[7] 4795[2] 5291[9] 5964[10] 6741[10] 6898[3] 7183[2] (7447) 7797[8]

Brave Optimist (IRE) *Paul Green* 34
3 b f Diktat—Maine Lobster (USA) (Woodman (USA))
6114[8] 7583[10]

Brave Prospector *P W Chapple-Hyam* 108
3 b c Oasis Dream—Simply Times (USA) (Dodge (USA))
1068^{9} 1400^{11} 2410^{4} (3047) ◆ 3488^{9} 4660^{8} 6121^{13}

Brave Quest (IRE) *Mrs L J Mongan* a57 67
4 b g Indian Danehill(IRE) —Mill Rainbow (FR) (Rainbow Quest (USA))
1932^{9} 2561^{7} 2884^{3} 3614^{11} 7596^{8} 7702^{6}

Brave Tin Soldier (USA) *M F De Kock* a90 104
4 b h Storm Cat(USA) —Bless (USA) (Mr Prospector (USA))
649a^{9} 815a^{6} 1087a^{8}

Brave Victory (USA) *Nicholas Zito* a88
2 b c Lion Heart(USA) —I'm In Celebration (USA) (Copelan (USA))
6501a^{7}

Bravo Echo *J H M Gosden* 85
2 b c Oasis Dream—Bold Empress (USA) (Diesis)
6084^{7} ◆ (6714) 6979^{11}

Brazilian Art *P W Chapple-Hyam* 79
2 ch c Captain Rio—Little Greenbird (Ardkinglass)
2893^{12} 4734^{2} 5158^{2} (5753) 6344^{3} 6970^{12}

Brazilian Brush (IRE) *H Morrison* a71 76
3 ch g Captain Rio—Ejder (IRE) (Indian Ridge)
1995^{7} (2602) 2864^{3} 3000^{8} 4025^{11} 4904^{7} 5401^{8} 6046^{10} 6433^{4} (6680)

Breach Of Peace (USA) *R Charlton* 61
2 b f Royal Academy(USA) —Hasardeuse (USA) (Distant View (USA))
4643^{8}

Breadstick *H Morrison* a70 51
2 br f Diktat—Poilane (Kris)
5640^{9} 6682^{3} 7093^{5}

Breaker Morant (IRE) *J G Burns* a75 66
6 b g Montjeu(IRE) —Arcade (Rousillon (USA))
128^{2} 809^{2}

Breakevie (IRE) *R A Fahey* 51
2 b f Mull Of Kintyre(USA) —Skehana (IRE) (Mukaddamah (USA))
6545^{3} 7082^{7}

Break Out *J M Bradley* a40 48
4 b h Kayf Tara—Clifton Girl (Van Der Linden (FR))
3312^{7} 3901^{8} 4055^{9}

Break Water Edison (USA) *John C Kimmel* a96
2 b c Lemon Drop Kid(USA) —August Storm (USA) (Storm Creek (USA))
6501a^{8}

Brean Dot Com (IRE) *Mrs P N Dutfield* a60 36
4 b g Desert Sun—Anna Elise (IRE) (Nucleon (USA))
1906^{13} 2355^{10}

Breathe *R T Phillips* a42 56
3 b f Dansili—Starfan (USA) (Lear Fan (USA))
706^{7} 873^{11}

Breezy Heights (IRE) *Miss Tor Sturgis* a28 54
6 b m Petorius—Royal Golden (IRE) (Digamist (USA))
1031^{11}

Brenin Taran *D M Simcock* a79 79
2 gr c Lujain(USA) —Silver Chime (Robellino (USA))
1399^{4} ◆ 1640^{2} (2054) 6769^{5}

Brenthurst (USA) *J Noseda* a74 62
2 b c Johannesburg(USA) —Kitra (USA) (Woodman (USA))
5099^{6} 6620^{4}

Brer Rabbit *B W Hills* a61 58
2 b f Invincible Spirit(IRE) —Red Rabbit (Suave Dancer (USA))
3378^{7} 4020^{10} 4926^{9} 7258^{3}

Bretwalda (IRE) *P T Midgley* 58
5 b g Imperial Ballet(IRE) —Prime Time Girl (Primo Dominie)
1307^{5} 1579^{8} 2009^{9} 3281^{11} 3643^{7}

Brexca (IRE) *C G Cox* a78 80
3 b g Diktat—Hemaca (Distinctly North (USA))
1695^{2} 2046^{3} 2948^{5} 3737^{3} 4303^{2} 4581^{2} 6018^{3} 6378^{4}

Briannsta (IRE) *J E Long* a61 80
6 b g Bluebird(USA) —Nacote (IRE) (Mtoto)
819^{8} 964^{8} 1641^{7} 2897^{13} 3266^{6} 6063^{3} 6334^{14} 7378^{11} 7522^{7} 7817^{11}

Bridge Of Fermoy (IRE) *Miss Gay Kelleway* a76 60
3 b c Danetime(IRE) —Banco Solo (Distant Relative)
12^{4} (266) 589^{3} (712) (820) 900^{4} (1034) 1245^{2} 1407^{2} (1487) 1685^{12} 7603^{7} 7668^{6} 7801^{7}

Bridgewater Boys *G L Moore* a74 72
7 b g Atraf—Dunloe (IRE) (Shaadi (USA))
(57) (300) (1056) 1296^{4} 2558^{3} (3482) 4254^{6} (7096) 7309^{5} (7608) 7744^{2} (7816)

Brief Candle *W R Swinburn* a77 82
2 br f Diktat—Bright Hope (IRE) (Danehill (USA))
4080^{3} ◆ 4554^{11} (5469) ◆ 6268^{8}

Brief Encounter (IRE) *A M Balding* a74 81
2 bb g Pyrus(USA) —Just One Look (Barathea (IRE))
4126^{3} 5628^{2} (6327)

Brief Goodbye *John Berry* 84
8 b g Slip Anchor—Queen Of Silk (IRE) (Brief Truce (USA))
(1877) 2414^{2} 3044^{4} 3900^{7} 4426^{3} 5092^{12} 6329^{7}

Brierty (IRE) *D Carroll* a75 82
2 b f Statue Of Liberty(USA) —Bridelina (FR) (Linamix (FR))
1627^{7} (2011) 5960^{11} (6223) 6477^{2}

Briery Blaze *T Wall* a54 58
5 b m Dansili—Sabonis (USA) (The Minstrel (CAN))
338^{9} 560^{9} 858^{11} 7686^{6}

Briery Lane (IRE) *J M Bradley* a54 67
7 ch g Tagula(IRE) —Branston Berry (IRE) (Mukaddamah (USA))
1312^{8} 1476^{4} 1634^{6} 1865^{9} 2881^{8} 2934^{4}

Brigadore *J G Given* a50 70
9 b g Magic Ring(IRE) —Music Mistress (IRE) (Classic Music (USA))
2448^{10} 2891^{5} 3079^{4} 3834^{11} 4327^{12} 4535^{7} 4609^{9} 6679^{7}

Brigadore (USA) *Ian Williams* a59 68
5 rg g Sandpit(BRZ) —Mersey I (Crystal Palace (FR))
1052^{8} 1164^{5} 1533^{7} 1694^{3}

Bright Enough *E J O'Neill* a79 59
2 b f Fantastic Light(USA) —Good Enough (FR) (Mukaddamah (USA))
3869^{6} 4339^{6} 4776^{2} (5606) 5747^{6} 6376^{6}

Bright Falcon *S Parr* a57 74
3 ch g Hawk Wing(USA) —Cream Tease (Pursuit Of Love)
1171^{5} 2819^{13} 4900^{9} 5858^{15} 6052^{14} 6252^{9} 7668^{8}

Bright Sparky (GER) *M W Easterby* a52 31
5 ch g Dashing Blade—Braissim (Dancing Brave (USA))
69^{4} 152^{2} 287^{6}

Bright Sun (IRE) *N Tinkler* a26 70
7 b g Desert Sun—Kealbra Lady (Petong)
1963^{13} 2365^{15} 2487^{6} 2957^{9} 3226^{7} 3666^{7} 4217^{4} 4537^{6} 5003^{8} 5869^{9}

Bright Wire (IRE) *M L W Bell* 26
2 b g Elusive City(USA) —Alinga (IRE) (King's Theatre (IRE))
5099^{10} 5649^{9}

Brigydon (IRE) *J R Fanshawe* a66 70
5 b g Fasliyev(USA) —Creme Caramel (USA) (Septieme Ciel (USA))
6736^{8} 7048^{3} 7374^{5}

Brilliana *D R Lanigan* 63
2 b f Danehill Dancer(IRE) —Streak Of Silver (USA) (Dynaformer (USA))
6565^{6}

Bring It On Home *G L Moore* a58 69
4 b g Beat Hollow—Dernier Cri (Slip Anchor)
7379^{3} 7713^{3}

Brisant (GER) *M Trybuhl* 112
6 br g Goofalik(USA) —Beresina (Surumu (GER))
1662a^{9} 2346a^{3} 4041a^{4} 4911a^{5} 5625a^{2} 6517a^{4} 7008a^{11}

Briseida *P Schiergen* 109
3 ch f Pivotal—Party Doll (Be My Guest (USA))
(2655a) 3852^{5} 4674a^{7} 5596a^{8}

Britannic *C Von Der Recke* 106
5 ch g Rainbow Quest(USA) —Anka Britannia (USA) (Irish River (FR))
423a^{4} 605a^{12}

Britomart (AUS) *Rick Hore-Lacy* 90
5 b m Zabeel(NZ) —Marshow (AUS) (Marscay (AUS))
6922a^{14}

Broad Cairn *R Charlton* 77
2 b g Green Desert(USA) —Celtic Cross (Selkirk (USA))
4150^{2} ◆

Broad Town Girl *Mrs H Sweeting* a36
5 b m Woodborough(USA) —Fortunes Course (IRE) (Crash Course)
236^{5} 392^{10} 804^{10}

Broken Applause (IRE) *R A Fahey* 102
3 br f Acclamation—Pink Cashmere (IRE) (Polar Falcon (USA))
2000^{9} 2666^{7} 5795^{9} 6105^{4}

Broken Moon *J R Fanshawe* a73 79
3 gr f Galileo(IRE) —Bedazzling (IRE) (Darshaan)
2257^{10} 3057^{4} 3843^{4} 4344^{4} (5163) 5698^{6} 6390^{5}

Bronte's Hope *M P Tregoning* a58
4 ch m Gorse—General Jane (Be My Chief (USA))
5915^{13} 6209^{8} 7102^{7} 7414^{11}

Bronze Cannon (USA) *J H M Gosden* a110 112
3 bb c Lemon Drop Kid(USA) —Victoria Cross (IRE) (Mark Of Esteem (IRE))
(1424) ◆ (2425) 3193^{7} 7145^{3} 7420^{5}

Bronze Dancer (IRE) *B Storey* 76
6 b g Entrepreneur—Scrimshaw (Selkirk (USA))
105^{7} 1892^{10} 3642^{9}

Brooklyn Spirit *C G Cox*
2 ch g Cadeaux Genereux—Serengeti Bride (USA) (Lion Cavern (USA))
6978^{16}

Brooksby *R Hannon* a73 68
2 b f Diktat—Lovely Lyca (Night Shift (USA))
4149^{13} 4905^{3} 5584^{3} ◆ 6082^{6} ◆ 6700^{6} 7073^{3} (7190)

Broomfield Buddy *D W Barker*
2 b f Reel Buddy(USA) —Tancred Arms (Clantime)
6109^{12} 6785^{13}

Brother Barry (USA) *G A Swinbank* 65
3 bb g Forestry(USA) —Saratoga Sugar (USA) (Gone West (USA))
1403^{8} ◆ 2199^{13} 3271^{13} 4329^{7} 6385^{9} 6792^{11}

Broughton Beck (IRE) *R F Fisher* a56
2 ch g Distant Music(USA) —Mauras Pride (IRE) (Cadeaux Genereux)
7282^{6} 7422^{8}

Broughtons Dream *W J Musson* a43
2 b f Kyllachy—Broughton Bounty (Bahamian Bounty)
7207^{4}

Broughtons Flight (IRE) *W J Musson* a67 67
3 ch f Hawk Wing(USA) —Aldburgh (Bluebird (USA))
2429^{12} 3095^{13} 3667^{2} 4152^{10} 4524^{13} 5964^{13} 7725^{4}

Broughtons Paradis (IRE) *W J Musson* a48 35
2 b f Royal Applause—Amankila (IRE) (Revoque (IRE))
5271^{10} 5835^{8} 6240^{25}

Broughtons Silk *W J Musson* a54
3 b f Medicean—Soviet Cry (Soviet Star (USA))
7500^{5}

Brouhaha *B J McMath* a64 67
4 b g Bahhare(USA) —Top Of The Morning (Keen)
1528^{12} 2003^{2} 2597^{3} 3034^{3} 3839^{2} 4168^{2} 4797^{4} 5069^{10}

Brown Lentic (IRE) *G L Moore* a42 40
2 b c Invincible Spirit(IRE) —Indienne (IRE) (Indian Ridge)
5860^{9} 6341^{8} 6677^{8} 6932^{10} 7464^{6}

Bruges (IRE) *David P Myerscough* 102
3 b c Marju(IRE) —Liege (IRE) (Night Shift (USA))
1879a^{5} 4223a^{8}

Bruki (IRE) *M Botti* a67 65
3 b f Captain Rio—Coup De Coeur (IRE) (Kahyasi)
4342^{13} 4796^{3} 5077^{3} 5322^{6} 6754^{2}

Brunel (IRE) *E Charpy* a52 114
7 b h Marju(IRE) —Castlerahan (IRE) (Thatching)
205a^{11}

Brunelleschi *P L Gilligan* a52 84
5 ch g Bertolini(USA) —Petrovna (IRE) (Petardia)
2205^{7} (3271) 3898^{10} 4375^{7} 4831^{11} 5067^{7} 5247^{13} 5600^{12} 6340^{12} 7302^{10}

Brunston *R Charlton* 66
2 gr c High Chaparral(IRE) —Molly Mello (GER) (Big Shuffle (USA))
6604^{9} 6977^{9}

Brushing *M H Tompkins* 32
2 ch f Medicean—Seasonal Blossom (IRE) (Fairy King (USA))
6030^{14}

Brut *D W Barker* a58 76
6 b g Mind Games—Champenoise (Forzando)
596^{10} 994^{12} 1431^{3} 1624^{17} (1893) 1997^{13} 2583^{13} 2777^{5} 3129^{7} 3401^{7} 3594^{6}

Bruton Street (USA) *J H M Gosden* 65
2 bb c Dynaformer(USA) —Fit For A Queen (USA) (Fit To Fight (USA))
6720^{10}

Brutus Maximus *I W McInnes* a17 37
5 b h Sir Harry Lewis(USA) —Horton Lady (Midyan (USA))
989^{11} 1391^{5} 2456^{7} 3182^{10} 5303^{9} 7280^{7} 7723^{10}

Brynfa Boy *P W D'Arcy* a51
2 b c Namid—Funny Girl (IRE) (Darshaan)
7574^{7}

Brynris *Mrs G S Rees* a32 11
4 gr g Perryston View—Isle Of Mull (Elmaamul (USA))
214^{8} 249^{10} 523^{10}

Buachaill Dona (IRE) *D Nicholls* a38 110
5 b g Namid—Serious Contender (IRE) (Tenby)
378a^{13} 492a^{3} 668a^{5} 1917^{5} 2172^{10} (3451) 4624^{10} 5890^{21}

Buail Isteach (IRE) *E J Creighton* a31
3 b f Acclamation—Its All Eurs (IRE) (Barathea (IRE))
7757^{9}

Bubbles Darling *M R Bosley*
3 b f Bertolini(USA) —Tattinger (Prince Sabo)
2664^{10}

Bubbly Baby *T D Easterby* 61
2 ch f Bahamian Bounty—Encore Du Cristal (USA) (Quiet American (USA))
2909^{11} 4499^{7} 4965^{4} 5384^{4} 5855^{14} 6547^{11}

Bubses Boy *M L W Bell* 47
2 ch g Needwood Blade—Welcome Home (Most Welcome)
4734^{8} 5158^{12} 5753^{4}

Buccellati *A M Balding* 117
4 ch h Soviet Star(USA) —Susi Wong (IRE) (Selkirk (USA))
2543^{8} 3195^{4} ◆ 3721^{5} ◆ (4363) 5741a^{4} (6444) (6980) 7682a^{6}

Bucintoro (IRE) *J E Hammond* 107
4 b h Galileo(IRE) —Dear Girl (IRE) (Fairy King (USA))
2653a^{7} 6237a^{8}

Buck Cannon (IRE) *P M Phelan* a52
3 b g High Chaparral(IRE) —Folgore (USA) (Irish River (FR))
1054^{7} 1367^{14} 1855^{8} 7535^{6} 7676^{9}

Buckers Beauty (IRE) *P D Evans* a23 59
2 b f Viking Ruler(AUS) —Kingpin Delight (Emarati (USA))
2569^{7} 3669^{8} 4907^{5} 5184^{12} 5294a^{9} 5606^{10} 6787^{12}

Buckle Up *D K Ivory* a24 34
2 ch g Primo Valentino(IRE) —Ambitious (Ardkinglass)
1078^{8} 1523^{9} 6341^{13}

Buddha O' Neil *M R Channon* 44
2 b g Superior Premium—Girl Band (IRE) (Bluebird (USA))
5227^{13} 5812^{10} 6709^{11}

Buddhist Monk *Sir Mark Prescott* a79 92
3 b g Dr Fong(USA) —Circle Of Light (Anshan)
2546^{2} ◆ 3161^{5} 4116^{2} 4941^{2} 5453^{2} (6018) 6288^{2} 6646^{17}

Buddy Holly *Pat Eddery* a44 84
3 b g Reel Buddy(USA) —Night Symphonie (Cloudings (IRE))
796^{9} (1479) (1696) 2564^{2} (3004) 3745^{9} 4688^{3} 5098^{4} 6078^{4} 7056^{5}

Buddy Marvellous (IRE) *R A Harris* a30 57
2 ch c Redback—La Paola (IRE) (Common Grounds)
1523^{6} 2011^{5} 3967^{5} 4827^{13} 5488^{3} 6745^{11} 7464^{7} 7687^{9}

Buds Dilemma *W M Brisbourne* a19 50
4 b m Anabaa(USA) —Lady Thynn (FR) (Crystal Glitters (USA))
1626^{4} 1968^{7}

Buenos Dias (IRE) *E Lellouche* 105
3 b c Peintre Celebre(USA) —Buenos Aires (IRE) (Rainbow Quest (USA))
(5529a) 6854a^{5}

Bufera (IRE) *Robert Collet* 103
2 b f King's Best(USA) —Mahalia (IRE) (Danehill (USA))
6891a^{3} 7185a^{4}

Buffalo Man (CAN) *Cam Gambolati* a103 110
4 b h El Prado(IRE) —Perfect Six (USA) (Saratoga Six (USA))
6504a^{10}

Bugsy's Boy *George Baker* a73 77
4 b g Double Trigger(IRE) —Bugsy's Sister (Aragon)
14^{9} 283^{8} (754) (1017) 1267^{2} 2135^{12} 6672^{9} 6861^{4}

Bukit Tinggi (IRE) *M A Jarvis* a70 94
4 b g Peintre Celebre(USA) —Puteri Wentworth (Sadler's Wells (USA))
1798^{2} ◆ (2332) ◆ (2628) ◆ 3104^{4} 3490^{14}

Bulberry Hill *R W Price* a67 45
7 b g Makbul—Hurtleberry (IRE) (Tirol)
436^{4} 695^{7} 4775^{8}

Bulella *Garry Moss* a56 46
2 b f Makbul—Bella Tutrice (IRE) (Woodborough (USA))
3005^{8} 6110^{11} 6389^{8} 7205^{6} 7281^{2} 7372^{3} 7693^{8} 7728^{2}

Bullet Man (USA) *L M Cumani* a87 73
3 br c Mr Greeley(USA) —Silk Tapestry (USA) (Tank's Prospect (USA))
7395^{4} (7712)

Bullish Cash (NZ) *A S Cruz* 113
6 b g Howbaddouwantit(USA) —La Mafia (NZ) (Phizam (NZ))
1666a^{9} 7684a^{14}

Bullish Luck (USA) *A S Cruz* a114 118
9 b g Royal Academy(USA) —Wild Vintage (USA) (Alysheba (USA))
1090a^{13} 7685a^{5}

Bull Market (IRE) *Ian Williams* a80 84
5 b g Danehill(USA) —Paper Moon (IRE) (Lake Coniston (IRE))
(1164) 1612^{7} 1793^{9} (2361) 2904^{3} (2970) 3673^{4} 4111^{10} 4532^{6} 4662^{11}

Bulwark (IRE) *Ian Williams* a107 111
6 b g Montjeu(IRE) —Bulaxie (Bustino)
(1916) 3250^{4} 4551^{7} 5854^{5} 6817^{29}

Bundle Up *P D Evans* a57 58
5 b m Diktat—Bundle (Cadeaux Genereux)
2949^{5} 3265^{7} 4026^{8} 4250^{2} (4722) 6252^{4} 6421^{P}

Bungie *Jennie Candlish* a48 35
4 gr g Forzando—Sweet Whisper (Petong)
596^{8} 2748^{3} 3139^{11} 7782^{8}

Bunny Hug *T D Easterby* 47
3 b f Royal Applause—White Rabbit (Zilzal (USA))
1519^{9} 3552^{9}

Bun Penny *G M Moore* 36
2 ch f Bertolini(USA) —Mint Royale (IRE) (Cadeaux Genereux)
4237^{6} 6110^{10} 6788^{12}

Bunsen Burner (IRE) *J S Bolger* a90 92
3 ch c Lil's Boy(USA) —Aeraiocht (IRE) (Tenby)
3532a^{22} 6845a^{15}

Bunty Malenoir *Mrs C A Dunnett* a38 38
3 b f Silver Patriarch(IRE) —Captivating (IRE) (Wolfhound (USA))
1721^{11} 2552^{12} 3841^{11} 4796^{7} 4991^{9} 5322^{8}

Burdlaz (IRE) *E Libaud* 86
3 ch c Indian Ridge—Babalu (IRE) (Doyoun)
7551a^{6}

Bureaucrat *P J Hobbs* 96
6 b g Machiavellian(USA) —Lajna (Be My Guest (USA))
(2830) 4444^{9} 5229^{16}

Burgundy *R A Teal* a76 76
11 b g Lycius(USA) —Decant (Rousillon (USA))
139^{5} 728^{3}

Burgundy Ice (USA) *Saeed Bin Suroor* 82
2 rg f Storm Cat(USA) —Cara Rafaela (USA) (Quiet American (USA))
(6559) 7144^{12}

Burma Rock (IRE) *L M Cumani* 67
2 b c Danehill Dancer(IRE) —Burmese Princess (USA) (King Of Kings (IRE))
4792^{9} 6031^{2} 6553^{2}

Burnbank (IRE) *P Bowen* a72 75
5 ch g Danehill Dancer(IRE) —Roseau (Nashwan (USA))
2361^{6}

Burnbrake *L Montague Hall* a71 74
3 b g Mujahid(USA) —Duena (Grand Lodge (USA))
1748^{7} (2429) 3039^{4} 3855^{11} 5104^{7} 6242^{10} 7027^{4} 7495^{5}

Burning Flute *B J Meehan* 87
2 ch c Piccolo—Fiamma Royale (IRE) (Fumo Di Londra (IRE))
2098^{3} 2324^{4} (2769) 3105^{19} (4297) 5244^{18} 5496^{5} 6483^{21}

Burning Incense (IRE) *M Dods* a82 102
5 b g Namid—Night Scent (IRE) (Scenic)
1071^{4} 2595^{8} 3489^{6} 4854^{3} 6069^{19} 6289^{6} 6710^{9} 7239^{21}

Burnley (IRE) *Mrs A L M King* a17 40
5 b g Distant Music(USA) —Dance Ahead (Shareef Dancer (USA))
14^{13} 242^{12}

Burn The Breeze (IRE) *H R A Cecil* 85
3 b f Beat Hollow—Madiyla (Darshaan)
(1444) 1919^{3} 2975^{7} 4790^{4}

Burnt Oak (UAE) *C W Fairhurst* a60 75
6 b g Timber Country(USA) —Anaam (Caerleon (USA))
2822^{11} 3414^{3} 4178^{6} 4652^{3} 5853^{7} 6054^{10} 6606^{3} 6948^{15}

Burnwynd Boy *Miss L A Perratt* 106
3 b g Tobougg(IRE) —Cadeau Speciale (Cadeaux Genereux)
1949^{2} 2403^{12} 3488^{3} 4660^{10} 6104^{27} 6153^{3} 6484^{16}

Burriscarra *Eamon Tyrrell* a70 69
3 b f Mujahid(USA) —Cressida (Polish Precedent (USA))
136^{8} 2889^{6}

Burry Green *R Hannon* 47
3 b f Averti(IRE) —Taylor Green (USA) (Green Dancer (USA))
1695^{8} 2123^{14} 3342^{3}

Bury Treasure (IRE) *Miss Gay Kelleway* a69 59
3 ch g Choisir(AUS) —Future Treasure (Habitat)
102^{3} (321) 527^{2} 2047^{6} 4061^{8} 4332^{11} 5167^{5} 5815^{8} 7790^{6}

Buscador (USA) *W M Brisbourne* a69 50
9 ch g Crafty Prospector(USA) —Fairway Flag (USA) (Fairway Phantom (USA))
(143) 219^{2} (231) 323^{3} 559^{4} 646^{3} (682) 771^{2} 859^{4} 1044^{5} (1086) 7744^{10}

Bushman *D M Simcock* a82 110
4 gr g Maria's Mon(USA) —Housa Dancer (FR) (Fabulous Dancer (USA))
1082^{3} ◆ (1526) ◆ (2545) ◆ 3683^{2} 6106^{7}

Carmenero (GER) *W R Muir* a81 80
5 b g Barathea(IRE) —Claire Fraser (USA) (Gone West (USA))
2722[2] 3087[4] 3599[8] 3761[6] 4345[5] 5156[7] 5345[4] 6380[2] 6695[3] 7302[5] 7390[2] 7557[5] 7668[4]
Carmine Rock *R Hollinshead* a51 50
3 ch f Arkadian Hero(USA) —Cloudy Reef (Cragador)
1674[3] 3686[3] 3818[6] 5395[4] 5832[13]
Carmond (GER) *B G Powell* 79
4 ch g Kornado—Cachira (GER) (Windwurf (GER))
4193[5] 5054[8]
Carnaby Haggerston (IRE) *K A Ryan* 83
2 gr c Invincible Spirit(IRE) —Romanylei (IRE) (Blues Traveller (IRE))
2608[2] 3005[3] 3707[3] (4143) ◆ 4594[3] 6118[16] 6717[3] 6972[10]
Carniolan *W R Swinburn* 100
3 b g Royal Applause—Dancing Feather (Suave Dancer (USA))
2279[2] 2918[2] (3897) ◆ (4158) 5795[4]
Carnival Dream *H A McWilliams* a50 65
3 b f Carnival Dancer—Reach The Wind (USA) (Relaunch (USA))
257[4] 1306[8] 2399[7]
Carnivore *T D Barron* a86 85
6 ch g Zafonic(USA) —Ermine (IRE) (Cadeaux Genereux)
2818[3] ◆ 3197[26] 3928[6] 7470[10] (7668) ◆
Caro George (USA) *R Charlton* a55 69
3 bb f Distant View(USA) —Gossamer (USA) (Seattle Slew (USA))
1669[4] 2455[2] 2772[5] 5790[4] 7256[6]
Carole Os (IRE) *S W Hall* a48 64
3 b f Catcher In The Rye(IRE) —Kuda Chantik (IRE) (Lashkari)
3180[7] 3845[13]
Carpe Diem (DEN) *L Reuterskiold Jr*
3 b g Richard Of York—Laser Show (IRE) (Wassl)
4918a[4]
Carpe Diem *W J Haggas* 58
3 b g Stravinsky(USA) —Spare That Tree (USA) (Woodman (USA))
1068[6] 2380[6] 2981[9] 4044[9] 6336[5]
Carriage Trail (USA) *Claude McGaughey III* a114 104
5 b m Giant's Causeway(USA) —Manoa (USA) (Seeking The Gold (USA))
(6523a) 6969a[4]
Carribean Sunset (IRE) *D K Weld* 113
3 b f Danehill Dancer(IRE) —Bonheur (IRE) (Royal Academy (USA))
(1230a) (2024a) 2433a[3] 3194[3] 3807a[4] (5134a) 5730a[8] 6298a[9]
Carrimion *T H Caldwell* 25
2 b g Lucky Owners(NZ) —Cap It If You Can (IRE) (Capitano)
6944[15] 7424[11]
Carr On Fire (USA) *W M Brisbourne* 37
3 bb g Hook And Ladder(USA) —Escarrgot (USA) (Carr De Naskra (USA))
1894[7] 4877[10] 7583[11]
Carry On Cleo *A Berry* a60 56
3 ch f First Trump—Classy Cleo (IRE) (Mujadil (USA))
20[8] 156[7] 424[4] 527[4] 589[5] 665[8] 1364[3] (1407) 1614[6] 3314[10] (3791) 3996[4] 4165[7] 4629[7] 4680[4] 5380[4] 5968[9] 6040[5] 6654[7]
Carry On Ellie (IRE) *J G Given* 38
3 b f Fasliyev(USA) —Dinka Raja (USA) (Woodman (USA))
2981[15]
Carson's Spirit (USA) *W S Kittow* a73 78
4 ch g Carson City(USA) —Pascarina (FR) (Exit To Nowhere (USA))
6537[5]
Carte Diamond (USA) *B Ellison* 109
7 ch g Theatrical—Liteup My Life (USA) (Green Dancer (USA))
1070[3] 1944[3] 3490[13] 3721[RR] 4585[11] 5229[8] 5885[2] 6820[9] 7244[10]
Carte D'Oro (IRE) *P W Chapple-Hyam* 36
2 b f Medaglia D'Oro(USA) —Prospectress (USA) (Mining (USA))
6778[10]
Carter *W M Brisbourne* a60 45
2 b g Reset(AUS) —Cameo Role (GER) (Acatenango (GER))
3107[6] 6451[4] 6988[5]
Cartimandua *E S McMahon* 111
4 b m Medicean—Agrippina (Timeless Times (USA))
(2000) 2738a[3] 3927[9] 5275[10]
Cartography (IRE) *R Bouresly* a2 107
7 b h Zafonic(USA) —Sans Escale (USA) (Diesis)
290a[10] 378a[14]
Cartoon *M A Jarvis* 53
2 br f Danehill Dancer(IRE) —Elfin Laughter (Alzao (USA))
7140[14]
Carved Emerald *R Gibson* a86 61
3 b f Pivotal—Emerald Peace (IRE) (Green Desert (USA))
3870[5] 7450a[13]
Carygali (IRE) *John Joseph Murphy* 46
2 b f Catcher In The Rye(IRE) —Gas Light (IRE) (Victory Note (USA))
2686a[8]
Casablanca Minx (IRE) *Miss Gay Kelleway* a68 60
5 br m Desert Story(IRE) —Conspire (IRE) (Turtle Island (IRE))
21[6] 44[5] 117[4] 426[4] 490[2] 577[3] 685[4] 736[8] 841[4] 872[5] 915[2] (1032) 1374[6] 1406[3] 1486[7] 1842[6] 2097[10] 2930[7] 3023[9] 3648[2] 3822[2] 4031[5] 4386[3] 4635[7] 4807[3] 7516[7] 7559[7] 7599[4] 7692[8]
Casa Catalina (IRE) *M Johnston* a44 80
3 b f King's Best(USA) —Ruacana Falls (USA) (Storm Bird (CAN))
2109[11] 3048[3] 3433[7] 4419[10]

Cascata (IRE) *L M Cumani* a73
2 b f Montjeu(IRE) —Leaping Water (Sure Blade (USA))
(7332)
Casela Park (IRE) *S Kirk* a68 40
3 ch g Elnadim(USA) —Taormina (IRE) (Ela-Mana-Mou)
5023[7] 5268[4] 5627[3] (6251) 6631[7] 6746[14]
Casey's On Call (USA) *Wayne Catalano* a74
2 b c Gimmeawink(USA) —Silver Tear (USA) (Silver Buck (USA))
(6502a)
Cashed Up *P Winkworth* 66
2 b g Baryshnikov(AUS) —Aunt Hilda (Distant Relative)
2796[8] 3444[6] (4050) 4706[9]
Cashel Bay (USA) *Luke Comer* a42 55
10 b g Nureyev(USA) —Madame Premier (USA) (Raja Baba (USA))
1105a[19]
Cash In The Attic *M R Channon* a29 60
2 b f Auction House(USA) —Aziz Presenting (IRE) (Charnwood Forest (IRE))
3603[9] 4050[3] 4734[3] 4980[5] 5363[8] 5567[9] 6572[12] 7452[8]
Cashleen (USA) *K A Ryan* 68
2 ch f Lemon Drop Kid(USA) —Radu Cool (USA) (Carnivalay (USA))
(6245) 6982[9]
Cashmere Jack *K G Reveley* 9
3 b g Daylami(IRE) —Cashmere (Barathea (IRE))
6055[15]
Cash On (IRE) *Karen George* a71 65
6 ch g Spectrum(IRE) —Lady Lucre (IRE) (Last Tycoon)
5476[6] 6252[3] 6606[16] 6985[11]
Casilda (IRE) *W J Knight* 95
3 b f Cape Cross(IRE) —Koniya (IRE) (Doyoun)
1525[5] (2328) (2920) 3633[4] 4582[2] 5311[2]
Casino Drive (USA) *Kazuo Fujisawa* a120
3 ch c Mineshaft(USA) —Better Than Honour (USA) (Deputy Minister (CAN))
7001a[12]
Casino Night *R Johnson* a66 74
3 ch f Night Shift(USA) —Come Fly With Me (Bluebird (USA))
918[10] (1912) 2041[5] 2367[3] 2575[3] 2842[4] 3183[12] 3578[4] 3790[5] 3958[2] 4241[8] (5224) (5565) 6155[5] 6387[4] 6718[5] (7111) 7166[12]
Casla Beag (IRE) *B Palling* a6 57
3 b f Acclamation—Carna (IRE) (Anita's Prince)
243[5] 397[8] 2474[9] 2771[7]
Cassie's Choice (IRE) *B Smart* 68
4 b m Fath(USA) —Esteraad (IRE) (Cadeaux Genereux)
2039[4] (2399) 2751[7]
Cassique Lady (IRE) *T Stack* a85 89
3 b f Langfuhr(CAN) —Palacoona (FR) (Last Tycoon)
6261a[9]
Castaneous (IRE) *P J Rothwell* a69
4 b g Lahib(USA) —Witchy Native (IRE) (Be My Native (USA))
7583[3]
Castano *B R Millman* a69 74
4 br g Makbul—Royal Orchid (IRE) (Shalford (IRE))
3313[9] 3966[2] 4186[6] 4710[6] (4979) 5088[3] 5267[4] 5779[2] 6177[8] 7021[4] 7277[7] 7490[4] 7666[6]
Caster Sugar (USA) *L M Cumani* a45 68
2 b f Cozzene(USA) —Only Royale (IRE) (Caerleon (USA))
4337[4] 4896[5] 5534[2] 6231[2] 6700[9] 7505[9]
Castiglione (FR) *D Fechner* 93
3 b g Marju(IRE) —Chupa (FR) (Kendor (FR))
6064a[0]
Casting Couch (IRE) *B W Hills* a49 57
2 b f Royal Applause—Mcqueenie (IRE) (Danehill (USA))
2769[4] ◆ 3610[5]
Castle Bar Sling (USA) *T J O'Mara* 85
3 b c Diesis—Lady Of The Woods (USA) (Woodman (USA))
5550a[12]
Castleburg *G L Moore* a54 47
2 b f Johannesburg(USA) —Castellina (USA) (Danzig Connection (USA))
6077[8] 6575[7] 6910[10]
Castlebury (IRE) *G A Swinbank* 71
3 b g Spartacus(IRE) —La Vie En Rouge (IRE) (College Chapel)
1295[9] 1452[4] 2014[3] 2367[2] 3737[5] 4115[3] 4455[5]
Castle Durrow (IRE) *Seamus Fahey* a42 7
4 b m Strike Out(IRE) —Marylin Park (IRE) (Kendor (FR))
375[11]
Castle Frome (IRE) *A E Price* a49
9 b g Spectrum(IRE) —Vendimia (Dominion)
238[6] 322[7] 377[3] 654[6] 770[4] 862[4] 1031[4] 1192[2] 1310[5]
Castlemaine *R Hannon* 9
2 br f Hernando(FR) —Stormont Castle (USA) (Irish River (FR))
6552[10] 6893[12]
Castle Myth (USA) *B Ellison* 55
2 bb g Johannesburg(USA) —Castlemania (CAN) (Bold Ruckus (USA))
3492[4] 4415[12] 5106[10]
Castles In The Air *Pat Eddery* a72 77
3 b c Oasis Dream—Dance Parade (USA) (Gone West (USA))
1297[14] (2407) 3050[10] 3499[3] 4121[7] 4743[13]
Casual Affair *J D Bethell* a83 79
5 b g Golden Snake(USA) —Fontaine Lady (Millfontaine)
(344) ◆ 540[6] 838[2] 981[3] 1299[2] 1998[3] 2822[6] (4699) 5376[3] 5940[7]
Casual Conquest (IRE) *D K Weld* 119
3 b c Hernando(FR) —Lady Luck (IRE) (Kris)
(2023a) ◆ 2829[3] 3535a[2]

Casual Garcia *Sir Mark Prescott* a56 80
3 gr g Hernando(FR) —Frosty Welcome (USA) (With Approval (CAN))
2468[14] (3264) 3574[6] (4564) (4775)
Casual Style *D E Pipe* a69 72
2 ch f Bahamian Bounty—Artistry (Night Shift (USA))
(3830) 7308[4] 7538[4]
Catamarca (USA) *J H M Gosden* a72
2 b f Seeking The Gold(USA) —Sunray Superstar (Nashwan (USA))
6682[4] 7093[2]
Cat Belling (IRE) *R Bouresly* a77 86
8 br m Catrail(USA) —Lute And Lyre (IRE) (The Noble Player (USA))
200a[3] 475a[8]
Cat By The Tale (USA) *David Wachman* a84 87
5 b f Tale Of The Cat(USA) —St Clair Ridge (IRE) (Indian Ridge)
7235a[5]
Catch A Fire (FR) *C Scandella* 33
3 b c Loup Solitaire(USA) —Spring Of Passion (FR) (Zieten (USA))
385a[6]
Catching The Light (USA) *H R A Cecil* a62 14
3 bb f Fantastic Light(USA) —Cat Ali (USA) (Storm Cat (USA))
2291[2] 2973[9]
Categorical *K G Reveley* a69 73
5 b g Diktat—Zibet (Kris)
1304[3] 6790[6] 7128[7]
Catenaccio (IRE) *P Winkworth* a53 24
2 b c Spartacus(IRE) —Montessori (Akarad (FR))
2754[8] 3392[6] 5461[10] 6343[11]
Cathedral Walk (USA) *K R Burke* a77 75
3 ch c Johannesburg(USA) —Hilarity (USA) (Kingmambo (USA))
595[2] 826a[3] 1448[4] 3709[2] 4621[11] 5202[8] 5799[6]
Catherines Cafe (IRE) *A C Whillans* a58 60
5 b m Mull Of Kintyre(USA) —Wisecrack (IRE) (Lucky Guest)
4683[14] 5415[9] 6161[8]
Catholic Hill (USA) *B J Meehan* a66 58
3 rg c Pleasant Tap(USA) —Celestial Bliss (USA) (Relaunch (USA))
2119[7] 2763[9] 3094[11] 4281[3] 5868[5] (6374) 6868[6]
Catigo (USA) *Sir Michael Stoute* 57
2 b f Giant's Causeway(USA) —Onaga (USA) (Mr Prospector (USA))
6776[7]
Cativo *B R Millman* 19
2 b f Deportivo—Catriona (Bustino)
6360[11]
Cativo Cavallino *J E Long* a84 81
5 ch g Bertolini(USA) —Sea Isle (Selkirk (USA))
887[5] 1146[5] 1567[4] 2058[2] 2679[11] 3317[6] 4058[4] 4865[3] 5144[3] 5789[6] 6194[7] 6695[6] 7435[10] 7677[11]
Cat Junior (USA) *B J Meehan* 117
3 bb c Storm Cat(USA) —Luna Wells (IRE) (Sadler's Wells (USA))
2121[6] 3102[4] 4010a[4] 5276[9] 6123[2] 6814[2]
Catman (IRE) *Peter Grayson* a16
2 b f Namid—Rihana (IRE) (Priolo (USA))
7168[10] 7689[10]
Cat Patrol *H J L Dunlop* a76 67
2 b f One Cool Cat(USA) —Ambrosine (Nashwan (USA))
2835[12] 4634[2] ◆ 5055[6] (5431) 5937[2] 6769[9]
Catskill Mountain (IRE) *P W Chapple-Hyam* 93
2 b g One Cool Cat(USA) —Catch The Moon (IRE) (Peintre Celebre (USA))
(7104) ◆
Cat Whistle *R A Fahey* a74 79
3 b f Dansili—Mighty Flyer (IRE) (Mujtahid (USA))
2405[11] 3554[4] 3849[8] 4440[11] 4900[4] 5273[6] ◆ 6043[12] 6380[3] 7077[7] 7419[4] 7610[6] 7771[7]
Caudillo (GER) *Dr A Bolte* 113
5 b h Acatenango(GER) —Corsita (Top Ville)
(2346a) 4041a[2] 5333a[5] 6497a[9]
Caught In Paradise (IRE) *D W Thompson* 59
3 b g Catcher In The Rye(IRE) —Paradis (Bijou D'Inde)
1558[7] 2041[15] 2268[9] 3139[7] 3406[7] 3715[2] 3791[4] 4381[5] 4680[8] 5399[10]
Caught On Camera *M L W Bell* a57 40
2 b f Red Ransom(USA) —Colorsnap (Shirley Heights)
5147[12] 6166[7] 6682[9]
Cause For Applause (IRE) *B Smart* a25 36
2 b f Royal Applause—Polyandry (IRE) (Pennekamp (USA))
6109[11] 6480[11] 7735[6]
Causeway King (USA) *M Johnston* a61 68
2 ch g Giant's Causeway(USA) —A P Petal (USA) (A.P. Indy (USA))
5469[9] ◆ 6031[7] 6423[5]
Caustic Wit (IRE) *M S Saunders* a68 74
10 b g Cadeaux Genereux—Baldemosa (FR) (Lead On Time (USA))
1872[11] 2128[11] 2242[6] (2350) 2679[8] 2798[2] 3024[7] 3363[8] 3608[5] 3872[4] 5601[6] 5817[7] 6895[10] 7225[10] 7255[12] 7399[6] 7444[10] 7508[10]
Cavallini (USA) *G L Moore* a78 74
6 bb g Bianconi(USA) —Taylor Park (USA) (Sir Gaylord)
28[8] (1181) 1744[2] 1933[3] (4526)
Cavallo Di Ferro (IRE) *M J Gingell* a62 57
4 b g Iron Mask(USA) —Lacinia (Groom Dancer (USA))
1481[0] 517[9] 851[6] 1109[9]
Cavalry Guard (USA) *T D McCarthy* a70 52
4 ch g Officer(USA) —Leeward City (USA) (Carson City (USA))
175[3] 265[10] 609[8] 888[6] 2243[14] 2533[13] 2561[12] 6889[10] 7076[14] 7392[9] 7553[9] (7765) 7818[2]
Cave Lion (USA) *J H M Gosden* a93 85
3 b c Storm Cat(USA) —Loving Kindness (USA) (Seattle Slew (USA))
2834[4] (3326) ◆ 4571[3] (5350) 5675[3] 6467[12]

Cavendish *J M P Eustace* a69 77
4 b g Pursuit Of Love—Bathwick Babe (IRE) (Sri Pekan (USA))
3301[3] 771[8] (1459) (1892) 2051[6] 2849[2] 3832[3] 4193[3] 4516[16]
Cavendish Road (IRE) *W R Muir* a60 70
2 b c Bachelor Duke(USA) —Gronchi Rosa (IRE) (Nashwan (USA))
2916[5] 3408[2] 4169[8] (4769) 5511[13] 6362[12] 6954[12] 7338[5] 7454[8] 7600[3]
Cavera (USA) *A M Balding* 90
2 b f Not For Love(USA) —Spelling (USA) (Alphabet Soup (USA))
4973[2] ◆ 5487[2] 5827[4]
Cavitie *E J Creighton* a46
2 b g Teofilio(IRE) —Kirriemuir (Lochnager)
5904[11] 6381[11] 7388[7]
Cavorting *B Bo* a36 94
6 ch g Polar Falcon(USA) —Prancing (Prince Sabo)
2232a[10]
Cawdor (IRE) *H Candy* 75
2 b c Kyllachy—Dim Ots (Alhijaz)
3798[3] 4480[4] 5860[2]
Cayman Breeze *J M Bradley* a60 59
8 b g Danzig(USA) —Lady Thynn (FR) (Crystal Glitters (USA))
161[0] 46[7] 119[3] 713[6] 877[8] 922[5]
Cayman Calypso (IRE) *Mrs P Sly* a45
7 ro g Danehill Dancer(IRE) —Warthill Whispers (Grey Desire)
374[7]
Cayman Fox *James Moffatt* a77 74
3 ch f Cayman Kai(IRE) —Kalarram (Muhtarram (USA))
5991[11] 6486[7] 6822[2] ◆ 7276[2] 7562[4] 7733[8]
Cayman Sky *R Hannon* a65 33
2 b c Fantastic Light(USA) —Comme Ca (Cyrano De Bergerac)
4665[12] 7336[7] 7602[4]
Cecilia's Lass *D H Brown* 55
2 b f Dr Fong(USA) —Russian Dance (USA) (Nureyev (USA))
9951[1] 1610[3] 1961[9] (Dead)
Cecily *Sir Mark Prescott* 74
2 b f Oasis Dream—Odette (Pursuit Of Love)
2479[7] ◆ (3085)
Cecina Marina *Mrs K Walton* 46
5 b m Sugarfoot—Chasetown Cailin (Suave Dancer (USA))
2731[4] 3335[5] 3602[4] 4503[15] 4899[2] 5308[11] 6215[11]
Cedar Mountain (IRE) *Neil Drysdale* a106 110
5 b g Galileo(IRE) —Ventura (IRE) (Spectrum (IRE))
6993a[6]
Ceduna Roadhouse (IRE) *A M Crow* 44
3 b f Fraam—Countess Miletrian (IRE) (Barathea (IRE))
1556[7] 1951[7] 2750[13] 3213[7] 4019[7] 5540[7]
Cee Bargara *J A Osborne* a94 99
3 b g Acclamation—Balsamita (FR) (Midyan (USA))
(687a) 905[8]
Ceili Mor (IRE) *M Johnston* a57 55
3 ch f Kyllachy—Octagleam (Octagonal (NZ))
3452[6] 3977[6] 4378[2] 5087[11] 6492[3] 6735[13]
Ceist Eile (IRE) *J S Bolger* 77
2 b f Noverre(USA) —Sharafanya (IRE) (Zafonic (USA))
3466a[8] 5132a[7] 6319a[11]
Ceka Dancer (IRE) *E J O'Neill* a75 73
3 ch f Danehill Dancer(IRE) —Tidal Reach (USA) (Kris S (USA))
3402[3] 3841[4] 4170[4] (4737)
Celebrissime (IRE) *F Head* 105
3 ch c Peintre Celebre(USA) —Ring Beaune (USA) (Bering)
1887a[6] 5555a[4]
Celeb Style (IRE) *Paul Green* a37 51
4 b m Tagula(IRE) —Lovely Me (IRE) (Vision (USA))
4653[12]
Celestial Dream (IRE) *A M Balding* a57 57
2 b f Oasis Dream—Lochangel (Night Shift (USA))
6894[4] 7207[3]
Cellarmaster (IRE) *Mark Gillard* a43
7 ch g Alhaarth(IRE) —Cheeky Weeky (Cadeaux Genereux)
2832[9]
Celt *L M Cumani* a56 87
3 b c Selkirk(USA) —Puce (Darshaan)
1684[4] ◆ 2151[4] 2840[7] ◆ 3459[2] ◆ 4205[3] (5182) 6196[3] 6542[4]
Celtic Change (IRE) *M Dods* a73 86
4 br g Celtic Swing—Changi (IRE) (Lear Fan (USA))
1217[3] ◆ 1473[12] 2582[3] 3493[5] 3864[5] 4111[4] 4876[7] 7278[5]
Celtic Charlie (FR) *P M Phelan* a64 19
3 ch c Until Sundown(USA) —India Regalona (USA) (Dehere (USA))
2563[12] 4333[5] 5574[12]
Celtic Commitment *R Hannon* a67 61
2 gb c Mull Of Kintyre(USA) —Grey Again (Unfuwain (USA))
3798[10] 4126[8] 6165[2] 6745[4] 7190[6] 7298[2] 7505[4] 7718[10]
Celtic Dane (IRE) *Kevin Prendergast* a80 102
4 b g Danetime(IRE) —Quelle Celtique (FR) (Tel Quel (FR))
1105a[8] 3531a[5] (4512a) 5550a[6]
Celtic Dragon *Mrs A J Perrett* a83 78
3 b c Fantastic Light(USA) —Zanzibar (IRE) (In The Wings)
1695[9] (2327) 2948[2] 3459[8] 5464[6] 5938[6] 6202[4]
Celticello (IRE) *P D Evans* a74 83
6 bb g Celtic Swing—Viola Royale (IRE) (Royal Academy (USA))
(2476) 2784[6] 2990[4] 3311[4] 3474[3] 3884[7] 4930[2] 5059[3] 5092[14] 5900[9] 6472[3] 7695[8]

Celtic Gold (USA) *Andrew Turnell* a63
4 b g Elusive Quality(USA) —Fortune (IRE) (Night Shift (USA))
7395[6] 7609[3]

Celtic Jazz (IRE) *A J McCabe*
5 b m Lil's Boy(USA) —Just Jazzy (Prince Tenderfoot (USA))
5710[8]

Celtic Lynn (IRE) *M Dods* 78
3 br f Celtic Swing—Sheryl Lynn (Miller's Mate)
1453[3] (1795) 3369[4] 3883[11] 4875[2] ◆ 6043[11]

Celtic Mill *D W Barker* a107 110
10 b g Celtic Swing—Madam Millie (Milford)
1483[6] 1986[7]

Celtic Rebel (IRE) *S A Callaghan* a57 45
2 b g Bahri(USA) —Farjah (IRE) (Charnwood Forest (IRE))
5316[6] 5905[9] 6389[9] 6906[2] 7113[6] 7205[3] 7451[10]

Celtic Slipper (IRE) *R M Beckett* 106
3 b f Anabaa(USA) —Celtic Silhouette (FR) (Celtic Swing)
2305[7]

Celtic Spirit (IRE) *G L Moore* a100 96
5 ch g Pivotal—Cavernista (Lion Cavern (USA))
1180[4] (1544) 1812[11] 7244[15] 7491[7] 7717[2]

Celtic Spring (IRE) *J R Boyle* a61 52
3 b f Celtic Swing—Spring Clean (FR) (Danehill (USA))
2620[10] 3268[5] 3847[4] 5186[6] 6878[2] 7624[4]

Celtic Spur (IRE) *A M Balding* a84
2 b c Celtic Swing—Kart Star (IRE) (Soviet Star (USA))
3372[2] ◆ (5016) ◆ (Dead)

Celtic Step *P D Niven* a81 84
4 br g Selkirk(USA) —Inchiri (Sadler's Wells (USA))
342[3] 456[8] 2007[2] 2672[2] 3006[11] 3716[2]

Celtic Strand (IRE) *T P Tate* a59 80
3 b g Celtic Swing—Mur Taasha (USA) (Riverman (USA))
2539[2] 4206[11] 4500[9] 6235[2] 6950[6]

Celtic Sultan (IRE) *T P Tate* 108
4 b g Celtic Swing—Farjah (IRE) (Charnwood Forest (IRE))
(1942) 2580[5] 3197[7] 3740[15] 5495[12] 6269[26] 6947[18] 7245[17]

Celtie Rod (IRE) *X Nakkachdji* 91
4 b h Dansili—Lady Golconda (FR) (Kendor (FR))
5113a[4]

Censored *Sir Michael Stoute* 81
3 b f Pivotal—Confidante (USA) (Dayjur (USA))
2119[6] 4620[2] (5031) 5865[11] 6605[10]

Centdixhuit (USA) *F-X de Chevigny*
2 b f Vindication(USA) —Look Of The Lynx (USA) (Forest Wildcat (USA))
7549a[0]

Centenary (IRE) *D E Cantillon* a48 58
4 b g Traditionally(USA) —Catherinofaragon (USA) (Chief's Crown (USA))
1913[8] 3732[7] 4490[4] 4879[6]

Centenerola (USA) *B W Hills* a38 85
3 b f Century City(IRE) —Lady Angharad (IRE) (Tenby)
1068[3] (1302) 1448[10] 2196[18] 4082[9] 6124[12] 6734[12]

Centennial (IRE) *J H M Gosden* 114
3 gr c Dalakhani(IRE) —Lurina (IRE) (Lure (USA))
(1632) 2131[4] 3535a[8] 4042a[8] (5263) 5953a[3] 6494a[3]

Central Station (IRE) *D K Weld* 105
3 ch c Indian Ridge—Token Gesture (IRE) (Alzao (USA))
2435a[3] 3156[7] 5550a[15]

Centreboard (USA) *Mrs L Williamson* a26 47
4 rg m Mizzen Mast(USA) —Corsini (Machiavellian (USA))
4949[9]

Cerebus *A J McCabe* a84 78
6 b m Wolfhound(USA) —Bring On The Choir (Chief Singer)
173[3] (349) 431[3] 850[4] (1021) 1134[3] 1261[3] 1386[5] 1500[3] 1796[10] (2077) 2293[5] 2504[9] 4944[3] 5594[6]

Ceremonial Jade (UAE) *M Botti* a113 98
5 b g Jade Robbery(USA) —Talah (Danehill (USA))
677[2] 904[4] 1079[2] (1765) 3504[12] (4059) (6285) 7421[6] 7703[3]

Cerito *M R Channon* 91
2 ch c Bahamian Bounty—Pascali (Compton Place)
(2098) 3152[6] 3634[6] 4685[3] 5294a[12] (5969) 6483[19]

Certain Justice (USA) *Stef Liddiard* a74 76
10 gr g Lit De Justice(USA) —Pure Misk (Rainbow Quest (USA))
5101[9] 7027[3] 7495[9] 7603[9]

Certain Promise (USA) *Sir Michael Stoute* a42 81
3 b f El Prado(IRE) —Shining Bright (Rainbow Quest (USA))
1444[8] 3762[2] (4533) (4795) 5910[12]

Certifiable *Miss Z C Davison* a54 37
7 b g Deploy—Gentle Irony (Mazilier (USA))
(164) 267[6] 402[4] 587[8] 7764[10]

Cesare *J R Fanshawe* a95 123
7 b g Machiavellian(USA) —Tromond (Lomond (USA))
(1716) 2193[4] 3100[4] 3940[3]

C'Est La Guerre (NZ) *John D Sadler* 119
4 b g Shinko King(IRE) —La Magnifique (NZ) (Kampala)
7188a[3]

Cha Cha Cha *K A Ryan* a87 88
4 b m Efisio—Shall We Dance (Rambo Dancer (CAN))
111[3] 192[3] (979) 1069[3] 1308[3] 1774[3] 2284[2] (2947) 3138[2] 3548[3] 4110[3] 5071[9] 6069[26]

Chadwell Spring (IRE) *Miss J Feilden* a62 51
2 b f Statue Of Liberty(USA) —Cresalin (Coquelin (USA))
3869[8] 5066[11] 6282[2] 6886[6]

Chaenomeles (USA) *M Johnston* a63 57
3 bb f Fusaichi Pegasus(USA) —Eliza (USA) (Mt. Livermore (USA))
1575[6] 2208[16] 2659[2] 3081[9] 3578[7]

Chalentina *J E Long* a55 59
5 b m Primo Valentino(IRE) —Chantilly Myth (Sri Pekan (USA))
2055[8] 4414[9] 4825[10] 6335[11] 7581[10] 7818[10]

Chalice Welcome *N B King* a51 38
5 b g Most Welcome—Blue Peru (IRE) (Perugino (USA))
1562[7] (7815)

Chalk Hill Blue *Eve Johnson Houghton* a51 65
2 b f Reset(AUS) —Golubitsa (IRE) (Bluebird (USA))
4337[7] 5364[2] 6205[6]

Challenging (UAE) *R D E Woodhouse* 53
2 b f Halling(USA) —Small Change (IRE) (Danzig (USA))
6234[8] 6808[6] 7220[2]

Challow Hills (USA) *B W Hills* a59 72
3 ch f Woodman(USA) —Cascassi (USA) (Nijinsky (CAN))
419[9] (1870) 2244[4] 2451[2] 3221[10] 3672[8] 5149[5] 5964[4] 6544[7]

Chamara (GER) *P Schiergen* 80
3 b f Key Of Luck(USA) —Chaguaramas (IRE) (Mujadil (USA))
5334a[6]

Chambers (IRE) *M Johnston* a56 65
2 b g Green Desert(USA) —Court Lane (USA) (Machiavellian (USA))
5905[5] 6109[2] 6701[5] 6953[6] 7219[6] 7454[10] 7575[6] 7693[6]

Chaminka (FR) *Mme N Rossio* 61
3 br f Marathon(USA) —Fusee Francaise (FR) (Anabaa (USA))
6742a[0]

Champagne Aerial (IRE) *Aidan Anthony Howard* 19
2 b f Night Shift(USA) —Song Of The Sea (Bering)
7498[11]

Champagne Dancer *P D Evans* a36 51
3 ch g Lomitas—Rosewood Belle (USA) (Woodman (USA))
5961[5] 6374[8] 6594[8]

Champagne Fizz (IRE) *Miss Jo Crowley* a45 67
2 gr f King Charlemagne(USA) —Silver Moon (Environment Friend)
4430[3] 5227[3] 5642[13] 6087[6]

Champagne Future *W R Swinburn* 44
2 b f Compton Place—Jade Pet (Petong)
2324[13]

Champagne Lawn (USA) *T D Barron* a23 54
3 gr f Aljabr(USA) —Quality Gift (Last Tycoon)
634[6] 2084[10] 2823[3] 3217[8] 3816[12] 3958[3] 4241[5] 4381[13]

Champagne Leader *A B Haynes* a3 30
2 b f Monsieur Bond(IRE) —Delicious (Dominion)
1384[8] 2548[5] 2720[6]

Champagne Shadow (IRE) *J Pearce* a83 71
7 b g Kahyasi—Moet (IRE) (Mac's Imp (USA))
(129) 388[3] (455) 682[3] 869[7] 1408[5] 6740[8] 7169[6] 7400[6] 7587[9] 7831[11]

Champagne Sue *D W Barker* 29
4 ch m Foxhound(USA) —Pigeon (Casteddu)
2399[10] 3600[7] 5044[9]

Champain Sands (IRE) *E J Alston* a61 74
9 b g Green Desert(USA) —Grecian Bride (IRE) (Groom Dancer (USA))
1891[9] 2445[2] 2841[3] 3087[7] 3599[10] 4650[5] 4744[3] 6186[8] 6250[11] 6951[5]

Champion Girl (IRE) *D Haydn Jones* a40 66
2 b f Captain Rio—Sea Of Serenity (USA) (Conquistador Cielo (USA))
5147[11] 6166[14] 6552[2] 6954[11]

Championship Point (IRE) *M R Channon* 118
5 b h Lomitas—Flying Squaw (Be My Chief (USA))
477a[12] 669a[5] 739a[8] (1427) 1596[4] (1921) 3974[13] 4504[8] 4855[5] 5276[6] 5932[6] 6980[6]

Champion's Time (GER) *M Rulec* 84
3 ch f Bertolini(USA) —Courtly Times (Machiavellian (USA))
6742a[10]

Champs Elysees *Robert Frankel* a117 116
5 b h Danehill(USA) —Hasili (IRE) (Kahyasi)
6506a[3] 7001a[8]

Change Alley (USA) *A Al Raihe* a86 41
3 b c Elusive Quality(USA) —Fortune (IRE) (Night Shift (USA))
292a[9] 567a[10] 812a[4]

Change The World (IRE) *J-C Rouget* 112
3 b c Sakhee(USA) —Mrs Seek (Unfuwain (USA))
4042a[5] 5302a[8]

Changing Skies (IRE) *B J Meehan* 111
3 b f Sadler's Wells(USA) —Magnificient Style (USA) (Silver Hawk (USA))
1444[2] 1915[3] 3153[6] (4124) 4657a[2] 5331a[5] 6567a[3]

Channel Crossing *S Wynne* a42 73
7 b g Deploy—Wave Dancer (Dance In Time (CAN))
1890[10] 2667[2] 3550[7] (4299) 4892[2] 5305[3] 5563[3] 6154[8]

Chanrossa (IRE) *E A L Dunlop* 33
2 b f Galileo(IRE) —Palacoona (FR) (Last Tycoon)
6391[11]

Chantal Sally (AUS) *J Symons & Sheila Laxon* 97
6 b m Johan Cruyff—Sell The Ark (AUS) (Ark Regal (NZ))
6922a[9]

Chanteuse De Rue (IRE) *M Johnston* a51 51
3 b f Street Cry(IRE) —Mt Morna (USA) (Mt. Livermore (USA))
1115[6] (1343) 1478[13] 1950[4] 2273[5] 2750[7]

Chanthea (IRE) *H Rogers* a53 61
2 b f Barathea(IRE) —Chantelle (IRE) (Lake Coniston (IRE))
6320a[15]

Chantilly Dancer (IRE) *M Quinn* a46 60
2 b f Danehill Dancer(IRE) —Antiguan Jane (Shirley Heights)
3158[7] 3848[U] 4747[4] 6008[6] 6547[4] 7531[8] 7789[9]

Chantilly Pearl (USA) *J G Given* a72
2 bb f Smart Strike(CAN) —Cataballerina (USA) (Tabasco Cat (USA))
(7546) ◆

Chantilly Tiffany *E A L Dunlop* a98 108
4 ch m Pivotal—Gaily Royal (IRE) (Royal Academy (USA))
1331[2] 1801[5] 2890[4] 4424[7] 4841[2] (5334a) 5829[2] (7005a)

Chantra (GER) *P Rau* 103
4 rg m Lando(GER) —Chalkidiki (GER) (Nebos (GER))
2347a[7] 3357a[2] 4590[8]

Chaplinesque (USA) *A Selvaratnam* a60
9 ch g Mt. Livermore(USA) —Silent City (USA) (Carson City (USA))
378a[12] 566a[11]

Chapter (IRE) *Mrs A L M King* a48 57
6 ch g Sinndar(IRE) —Web Of Intrigue (Machiavellian (USA))
(2072) 2884[5] 3084[7] 3657[6] 4261[10] 5450[6] 6421[RR]

Chapter And Verse (IRE) *B W Hills* 78
2 gr c One Cool Cat(USA) —Beautiful Hill (IRE) (Danehill (USA))
6072[9] 6412[2] 6944[6]

Charging Indian (IRE) *M R Channon* 73
2 b c Chevalier(IRE) —Kathy Tolfa (IRE) (Sri Pekan (USA))
(2696)

Charismatic Charli (IRE) *P W D'Arcy* a59 59
2 b g King Charlemagne(USA) —Emly Express (IRE) (High Estate)
2331[5] 3219[9] 4296[12] 5914[4]

Charismatic Lady *G G Margarson* 46
2 ch f Bertolini(USA) —Norcroft Lady (Mujtahid (USA))
4337[10]

Charles Darwin (IRE) *M Blanshard* a54 93
5 ch g Tagula(IRE) —Seymour (IRE) (Eagle Eyed (USA))
1300[16] (2188) 2644[5] 3477[9] 3898[8] 4341[10] 4831[9] 5648[2] 5991[2] 6200[14] 6556[4] 7315[9]

Charles Dickens (IRE) *M Johnston* 29
2 b c Cape Cross(IRE) —Carry On Katie (USA) (Fasliyev (USA))
4647[6]

Charles Parnell (IRE) *M Dods* a88 82
5 b g Elnadim(USA) —Titania (Fairy King (USA))
1818[4] 2188[4] 2583[4] 2892[12] 3724[6] 3868[4] 4246[7] 4736[2] 5419[5] 6066[5] 6388[5] 6724[5] 6859[7] 7055[2] 7448[2] (7534) (7730)

Charlevoix (IRE) *C F Wall* a74 78
3 b f King Charlemagne(USA) —Cayman Sound (Turtle Island (IRE))
(2041) (3656) 3874[4] 5019[4] 5964[11]

Charlie Allnut *S Wynne* a42 58
3 b g Desert Style(IRE) —Queen Of Africa (USA) (Peintre Celebre (USA))
1795[6] 2187[12] 2966[5] 4018[5] 4683[4] 6173[2] 7437[11] 7654[5]

Charlie Be (IRE) *Mrs P N Dutfield* a47 57
3 ch g King Charlemagne(USA) —Miriana (IRE) (Bluebird (USA))
1533[10] 1694[7] 2611[10] 3359[5] 4165[5] 4707[9]

Charlie Bear *Miss Z C Davison* a50 46
7 ch h Bahamian Bounty—Abi (Chief's Crown (USA))
101[11] 220[7] 328[10] 401[2] 693[6] 5088[8] 5318[6] 6560[4] 6928[13] 7021[8] 7494[10] 7776[7]

Charlie Chan *Mrs R A Carr* a5
7 gr g Paris House—Vindictive Lady (USA) (Foolish Pleasure (USA))
66[7] 172[7] 432[8]

Charlie Delta *J G M O'Shea* a66 78
5 b g Pennekamp(USA) —Papita (IRE) (Law Society (USA))
2128[4] (2337) 2923[2] (3501) 3904[5] 6125[10] 6402[3] 6734[10]

Charlie Farnsbarns (IRE) *B J Meehan* 117
4 b h Cape Cross(IRE) —Lafleur (IRE) (Grand Lodge (USA))
(2133) 2543[5] 6476[13] 6670[2] (6780)

Charlie Green (IRE) *Paul Green* a33 35
3 b g Traditionally(USA) —Saninka (IRE) (Doyoun)
141[9] 803[10] 2954[12] 7446[9]

Charlie Smirke (USA) *G L Moore* a68 62
2 b c Gulch(USA) —Two Altazano (USA) (Manzotti (USA))
5468[11] 6000[2] 6375[3] 7298[3] 7554[6]

Charlie Tiger (USA) *C G Cox* 86
2 ch c Hold That Tiger(USA) —Fairy Dancer (USA) (Nijinsky (CAN))
2324[14] 6085[2]

Charlie Tipple *T D Easterby* 87
4 b g Diktat—Swing Of The Tide (Sri Pekan (USA))
1327[3] 1612[4] 1910[5] 2220[5] 2499[5] 3108[10] 3366[3] 4206[8] (4876) 5635[6] 6041[5] (6482)

Charlie Tokyo (IRE) *R A Fahey* a99 106
5 b g Trans Island—Ellistown Lady (IRE) (Red Sunset)
834[10] 906[12] 1076[4] 1427[4] 2789[11] 3046[11] 3974[6] 4856[9] 5382[11]

Charlotte Bronte *David Wachman* 95
3 b f Danehill Dancer(IRE) —Speak Softly To Me (USA) (Ogygian (USA))
2024a[6]

Charlottebutterfly *P J McBride* a61 50
8 b m Millkom—Tee Gee Jay (Northern Tempest (USA))
234[6] 579[7] (795) 938[8]

Charlotte Grey *P J McBride* a67 64
4 gr m Wizard King—Great Intent (Aragon)
167[2] (254) 469[7] 2802[3] 3033[7] 4064[4] 4285[8] 4749[6] 5007[6] 5101[4] 5832[2] 5916[6] 6733[10] 7369[3] 7509[5] 7582[5]

Charlotte Ki (FR) *M Boutin* 78
2 ch f Sin Kiang(FR) —Autarcie (FR) (Ski Chief (USA))
1886a[5]

Charlotte Point (USA) *P F I Cole* a77 60
2 b f Distorted Humor(USA) —Skygusty (USA) (Skywalker (USA))
6392[6] 6620[3] 6901[2] (7093)

Charlotte Vale *Micky Hammond* 82
7 ch m Pivotal—Drying Grass Moon (Be My Chief (USA))
1020[3] 1299[5] (2379) 2839[4] 3110[2] 3368[11]

Charly's Rose *P C Haslam* 28
2 b f Makbul—Parkside Prospect (Piccolo)
2980[6] 3225[6] 4203[16]

Charmel's Lad *W R Swinburn* a62 64
3 ch g Compton Place—Fittonia (FR) (Ashkalani (IRE))
1315[5] 1743[5] 3525[11] 4777[9] 5421[4] 6334[15] 7383[3] 7710[9]

Charming Ballet (IRE) *G L Moore* a53 68
5 b g Imperial Ballet(IRE) —Some Merit (Midyan (USA))
883[6] 1455[8] 2355[11] 3033[9]

Charming Escort *T T Clement* a62 45
4 ch g Rossini(USA) —Iktizawa (Entrepreneur)
4644[5] 5790[8] (6735) (7072) 7433[3] 7677[5] 7763[4]

Charming Tale (USA) *B J Meehan* a56 59
3 b f Kingmambo(USA) —Crystal Crossing (IRE) (Royal Academy (USA))
1525[12] 2566[9] 3183[2] 3524[3] 4061[5] 5574[10] 6679[5] 7345[8]

Charm School *J H M Gosden* a85 101
3 b g Dubai Destination(USA) —Eve (Rainbow Quest (USA))
(1073) ◆ 1598[2] 6625[8] 7019[3] 7245[3]

Chart Express *P Howling* a45 34
4 b g Robellino(USA) —Emerald Angel (IRE) (In The Wings)
242[11] 471[9] 776[7] 1041[7]

Chartist *R Hannon* a76 93
3 ch g Choisir(AUS) —Sareb (FR) (Indian Ridge)
1075[5] 1404[8] 1597[2] 1945[2] 3273[7] 4591[12] 5930[7] 6354[12] 6557[5]

Chart Oak *P Howling* a57
5 b g Robellino(USA) —Emerald Angel (IRE) (In The Wings)
197[4] 377[10] 471[4] 715[2] (776)

Chasing Amy *M G Quinlan* a65 59
2 b f Namid—Inspiring (IRE) (Anabaa (USA))
4562[3] 5158[5] 5431[2] 7205[11]

Chasing Memories (IRE) *A M Hales* a51 62
2 b f Pursuit Of Love—Resemblance (State Diplomacy (USA))
341[4] 362[3] 516[P] 1248[7] 2070[10]

Chatanoogachoochoo *G A Swinbank* 64
3 ch f Piccolo—Taza (Persian Bold)
3130[4] 4161[10] 5445[3] 5965[10]

Chateauneuf (IRE) *B W Hills* 53
2 b f Marju(IRE) —Night Eyes (IRE) (Night Shift (USA))
6077[9] 6358[6]

Chatshow (USA) *A W Carroll* a74 79
7 br g Distant View(USA) —Galanty Show (Danehill (USA))
45[4] 106[3] 213[2] 241[3] 466[2] (515) 536[4] 615[2] 681[7] 896[5] 994[3] 1338[2] 1522[5] 1634[8]

Chatterszaha *C Drew* a64 56
2 ch f Zaha(CAN) —Chatter's Princess (Cadeaux Genereux)
4425[4] 4931[5] 5835[4] 6223[12] 6933[7]

Chausson Dore (IRE) *A Fabre*
2 b f Hawk Wing(USA) —Don't Worry Me (IRE) (Dancing Dissident (USA))
7430a[6]

Cheam Forever (USA) *R Charlton* a69 54
2 b g Exchange Rate(USA) —Many Charms (USA) (St Jovite (USA))
5344[3] 5996[8] 7104[8]

Cheap Street *J G Portman* a59 79
4 ch g Compton Place—Anneliina (Cadeaux Genereux)
1368[3] 1683[9] 2679[5] 3797[10] 5233[4] 6706[3] 7358[6] 7534[9] 7834[9]

Cheap Thrills *J A Osborne* a64
2 ch f Bertolini(USA) —Licence To Thrill (Wolfhound (USA))
1762[7] 4634[3]

Che Castagna *Tom Dascombe* a36
2 ch f Bahamian Bounty—Mana Pools (IRE) (Brief Truce (USA))
6697[12] 6931[13]

Checkit (IRE) *R Bouresly* a62 94
8 br h Mukaddamah(USA) —Collected (IRE) (Taufan (USA))
474a[10] 492a[7]

Checklow (USA) *J Noseda* a55 90
3 b g Street Cry(IRE) —Comstock Queen (USA) (Silver Hawk (USA))
1398[3] ◆ (1684) ◆ 4618[4] 5573[11]

Check Up (IRE) *J L Flint* a40 62
7 b g Frimaire—Melons Lady (IRE) (The Noble Player (USA))
3844[2] (4250) 4704[2] 5058[7] 5611[12] 5917[7] 6668[6] 7427[10]

Cheeky Chilli *A J McCabe* a36 58
3 b f Olden Times—Promissory (Caerleon (USA))
2084[6] 2500[5] 2786[5] 3690[11] 4043[4] 4271[4] 4531[5]

Cheeky Download (IRE) *E A L Dunlop* a61 70
3 b f Fasliyev(USA) —Glam Rock (Nashwan (USA))
1684[5] 4166[3] 5182[3] 6168[4] 6991[12]

Cheeky Try (USA) *G Prodromou* a57 55
3 ch g Rahy(USA) —Touch Of Truth (USA) (Storm Cat (USA))
1743[9] 2089[5] 2549[16]

Cheers For Thea (IRE) *T D Easterby* 60
3 gr f Distant Music(USA) —Popiplu (USA) (Cozzene (USA))
1429[6] 1814[11] 2008[5] 2659[9] (4173) 4738[2]

Cheery Cat (USA) *D W Barker* a53 68
4 bb g Catienus(USA) —Olinka (USA) (Wolfhound (USA))
990[19] (1952) 2400[7] 2751[8] 2968[7] 3404[4] 3591[5] 4174[5] 4453[6] 4700[5] 5198[F]

Chelsea Girl *C G Cox* a76 69
3 b f Kyllachy—Ghassanah (Pas De Seul)
1836[3] 2279[3] 2898[5] 5749[4] 6192[3] (6658) 6880[9] 6990[3]

Cheney Manor *B W Hills* a73 64
3 b g Piccolo—One For Philip (Blushing Flame (USA))
1601[6] 1854[6] 3180[6] ◆ 4484[2] 4860[3] 5568[4] 6470[5] 7690[2]

Cheonmado (USA) *J R Gask* a56 64
4 ch g Miswaki(USA) —Academie Royale (IRE) (Royal Academy (USA))
275[10] 879[8] 1116[3] 1266[12] 4863[11]

Cherished Song *M G Quinlan* a56 53
3 b f Mark Of Esteem(IRE) —Waseyla (IRE) (Sri Pekan (USA))
195[6] 462[3] 597[6] 3330[7] 3605[5] 4298[10] 4794[3]

Cherish The Moment (IRE) *B W Hills* 68
2 b c Galileo(IRE) —Belleclaire (IRE) (Bigstone (IRE))
6977[6] ◆

Cherokee Star *C C Bealby* a49 70
3 br g Primo Valentino(IRE) —Me Cherokee (Persian Bold)
2573[2] 3297[4] 3835[4] 6018[10]

Cherries On Top (IRE) *I A Wood* a42 36
3 ch g Elnadim(USA) —Easy Going (Hamas (IRE))
1215[9] 2240[6] 2918[9] 4725[8] 5679[5]

Cherri Fosfate *Paul W Flynn* a74 75
4 b g Mujahid(USA) —Compradore (Mujtahid (USA))
(1626) 1673[7] (1968) 2335[2] 2697[4] 2927[4] 4899[3] 7440[8] (7732)

Cherry Belle (IRE) *P D Evans* a46 58
2 b f Red Ransom(USA) —Pondicherry (USA) (Sir Wimborne (USA))
2275[6] 2980[5] (3225) 3706[8] 4063[3] 4387[7] 4604[2] 5041[6] 5747[3] 6059[5] 6343[2] 6694[6] 7079[5]

Cherrytree Ella (IRE) *K R Burke*
3 b f Clodovil(IRE) —Music Khan (Music Boy)
1302[10]

Cheshire Prince *W M Brisbourne* 91
4 br g Desert Prince(IRE) —Bundle Up (USA) (Miner's Mark (USA))
1388[6] 2155[3] 2585[10] 2904[6] 3258[2] 3474[2] (3947) (4662) 4856[3] 5494[B] 5885[6] 6238[7] 6536[8]

Cheshire Rose *T D Barron* a54 70
3 ch f Bertolini(USA) —Merch Rhyd-Y-Grug (Sabrehill (USA))
2602[2] 3455[5] 4000[7] 4216[4] (4852) 5417[6] 5902[2] 6218[13] 6765[6] 7456[8]

Chesterton (IRE) *John Joseph Murphy* a57 60
3 bb c Namid—Beguine (USA) (Green Dancer (USA))
4613a[10]

Chevaliers Dream (IRE) *T D Easterby* a53 38
3 b g Chevalier(IRE) —Danny's Miracle (Superlative)
867[7] 953[4] 1139[10] 1912[15] 2915[13]

Cheveley Flyer *J Pearce* a45 55
5 ch g Forzando—Cavern Breeze (Lion Cavern (USA))
541[8]

Cheveton *R J Price* a96 102
4 ch g Most Welcome—Attribute (Warning)
1082[8] 1311[2] 1674[4] 2261[4] 2644[3] 2773[2] ◆ (3042) (3724) (3945) (4668) (5206) 5890[5] 6653[2] 6971[13]

Chevie (IRE) *T Hogan* a82 95
3 b g Chevalier(IRE) —Omanah (USA) (Kayrawan (USA))
1233a[6] 3531a[17] 4512a[7]

Cheviot (USA) *M A Jarvis* a77 84
2 b g Rahy(USA) —Camlet (Green Desert (USA))
5271[9] (5572) ◆ 6118[4] 6540[4]

Cheviot Red *Miss Tracy Waggott* a19 59
3 b f Red Ransom(USA) —Cheviot Hills (USA) (Gulch (USA))
1423[14] 2043[12] 2946[11] 4739[10]

Chevron (IRE) *C Leck* 69
5 b g Medicean—Lishaway (FR) (Polish Precedent (USA))
2234a[15]

Cheyenne Star (IRE) *Ms F M Crowley* a106 112
5 b m Mujahid(USA) —Charita (IRE) (Lycius (USA))
1880a[10] 2420a[3] (3619a) 4590[2] 5730a[10] 6689a[16]

Chia (IRE) *D Haydn Jones* a72 66
5 ch m Ashkalani(IRE) —Motley (Rainbow Quest (USA))
(117) 196[5] 340[3] 1048[7] 2097[9] 3089[5]

Chiberta King *A M Balding* 63
2 b g King's Best(USA) —Glam Rock (Nashwan (USA))
3682[9] 4151[9] 5641[6]

Chicago Cop (IRE) *D Nicholls* 83
2 b g Fasliyev(USA) —Sassari (IRE) (Darshaan)
(2584) 4374[6]

Chicken George (IRE) *M F Harris* 78
4 ch g Observatory(USA) —Missing (Singspiel (IRE))
992[11] ◆ 1771[5] 2406[7] 3229[3] 3563[7] 4650[11] 6050[6]

Chicken Momo *K R Burke* a67 51
2 b g Pyrus(USA) —Italian Affair (Fumo Di Londra (IRE))
1889[5] 3215[3] 4986[4] 5541[2] (6573) ◆

Chicken Soup *S Parr* a106 89
6 br g Dansili—Radiancy (IRE) (Mujtahid (USA))
2158[7] 2397[6]

Chicory Cottage *G L Moore*
2 b c Tumbleweed Ridge—Blooming Lucky (IRE) (Lucky Guest)
5784[10] 6333[9]

Chic Retreat (USA) *M L W Bell* a26 34
2 b f Elusive Quality(USA) —Saraa Ree (USA) (Caro)
5535[8] 7341[11]

Chic Shanique (USA) *Tom Dascombe* a57
2 bb f Dynaformer(USA) —Toll Order (USA) (Loup Sauvage (USA))
7341[6] 7498[5]

Chief Editor *M A Jarvis* a99 112
4 b g Tomba—Princess Zara (Reprimand)
1325[2] (1571) ◆ 4957[2] 5551a[6] 5890[13] (6289) ◆ 7243[3]

Chief Eric *B I Case* 67
3 gr c Slickly(FR) —Last Romance (IRE) (Last Tycoon)
997[5] 1467[13]

Chief Exec *J R Gask* a81 65
6 br g Zafonic(USA) —Shot At Love (IRE) (Last Tycoon)
452[9] (755) 819[4] 1084[4] 1604[2] 1842[13] 2010[10] 7277[6]

Chiefofthemowhawks (USA) *Stephen Michael Cox* a52 62
5 b g Giant's Causeway(USA) —Devine Beauty (USA) (Mr Prospector (USA))
1602[8] 7692[12] 7736[11]

Chief Red Cloud (USA) *K R Burke* 48
2 bb g Cherokee Run(USA) —Pertuisane (Zamindar (USA))
4014[7] 5825[7]

Chiff Chaff *C R Dore* a64 64
4 b m Mtoto—Hen Harrier (Polar Falcon (USA))
77[8] 171[6] 287[5] 374[2] 461[7] 544[3] 3377[11] 3589[7] 3871[3] 4391[3] (4490) 4924[6] 5322[5] (5385) 5613[2] 5917[9] 6115[7]

Chifong *J Akehurst* 43
2 ch f Dr Fong(USA) —Chiasso (USA) (Woodman (USA))
4480[8]

Chilly Filly (IRE) *M Johnston* 74
2 b f Montjeu(IRE) —Chill Seeking (USA) (Theatrical)
4921[4] ◆ 5256[3] 5771[2] 6231[3] 6857[9]

Chiltai (IRE) *J J Bridger* a26 13
7 b h Taipan(IRE) —Chilling (Chilibang)
1567[6] 1641[12]

Chimbonda *S Parr* a60 69
2 ch c Dr Fong(USA) —Ambonnay (Ashkalani (IRE))
3417[5] 4456[4] 4923[4] 5363[11] 7113[10] 7240[3] 7306[9] 7417[5] 7501[4] 7612[3] 7719[5] 7795[8]

Chimes At Midnight (USA) *Luke Comer* a52 65
11 b h Danzig(USA) —Surely Georgies (USA) (Alleged (USA))
(585) 716[8]

China Cherub *S Dow* a93 94
5 ch m Inchinor—Ashlinn (IRE) (Ashkalani (IRE))
26[12] 1928[6] 2339[3] 2773[4] 3093[2] 3418[3] 3587[8] 4051[3] 4483[6] 4831[7] 5170[7]

China Pink *Sir Mark Prescott* a42 65
3 b f Oasis Dream—Red Bouquet (Reference Point)
4260[4] ◆ 4607[4] (4796) ◆ 5077[9] 5758[2] 6155[2] 6934[8]

Chinchon (IRE) *C Laffon-Parias* 114
3 b c Marju(IRE) —Jarama (IRE) (Hector Protector (USA))
2654a[5] 4473a[3] 5302a[4] 6237a[3]

Chinese Mandarin (USA) *E Van Doorn* a93 94
5 ch h Kingmambo(USA) —Rose Gypsy (Green Desert (USA))
(4676a)

Chinese Profit *G C Bravery* 58
3 b g Acclamation—Tancholo (So Factual (USA))
6192[8] 7111[12]

Chinese Temple (IRE) *M G Quinlan* a81 79
3 b c Choisir(AUS) —Savage (IRE) (Polish Patriot (USA))
136[3] 376[5] 737[3] 3418[9] 3811[7] 4595[11] 5531[6]

Chinese White (IRE) *D K Weld* 114
3 gr f Dalakhani(IRE) —Chiang Mai (IRE) (Sadler's Wells (USA))
(1847a) 2792[9] 4006a[4] 4833a[12]

Chinkara *Doug Watson* a95 95
8 ch g Desert Prince(IRE) —You Make Me Real (USA) (Give Me Strength (USA))
380a[9] 568a[10] 650a[14]

Chintz (IRE) *David Wachman* 106
2 b f Danehill Dancer(IRE) —Gold Dodger (USA) (Slew O'Gold (USA))
3466a[2] 4095a[2] (6318a)

Chin Wag (IRE) *J S Goldie* a76 69
4 b g Iron Mask(USA) —Sweet Chat (IRE) (Common Grounds)
990[5] ◆ 1450[10] 2444[10] 2672[3] (3201) 3557[10] 3755[2] 3957[4] 4537[5] 4849[2] 4969[5] 5390[9] 5564[11] 6786[8]

Chioroscuro *J L Dunlop* 65
3 gr g Act One—Colorspin (FR) (High Top)
3521[5] 4581[5] 5463[7] (Dead)

Chip N Pin *T D Easterby* 57
4 b m Erhaab(USA) —Vallauris (Faustus (USA))
1892[6] 2286[8]

Chipolini (IRE) *D Carroll* 59
2 b g Bertolini(USA) —Chimere (FR) (Soviet Lad (USA))
2443[7] 2657[7] 2924[3] 6014[10] 6547[6]

Chiracahua (IRE) *P Butler* a10 46
6 ch g Desert Prince(IRE) —Irish Celebrity (USA) (Irish River (FR))
713[8]

Chirango (FR) *P Demercastel* 99
3 gr c Chicastenango(FR) —European Style (FR) (Ezzoud (IRE))
1239a[6] 2064a[5] 5529a[2] 6921a[6]

Chivola (IRE) *B Smart* a71 73
3 b g Invincible Spirit(IRE) —Boudica (IRE) (Alhaarth (IRE))
19[2] (114) 977[7] 1484[15]

Chjimes (IRE) *C R Dore* a81 88
4 b g Fath(USA) —Radiance (IRE) (Thatching)
359[5] 427[3] 574[3] 801[6] 1023[6] 1327[6] 1630[11] 1954[4] 3138[3] (3317) 3842[4] 4030[3] (4307) 4944[7] 5433[8] 5936[6] 6356[14] 6952[7] 7225[5] (7435)

Chock Dee (FR) *X Betron* 80
3 b c Cardoun(FR) —Cometina (FR) (Arctic Tern (USA))
549a[3]

Choco Express (DEN) *O Larsen* a50
5 b m Richard Of York—Boss Lady (IRE) (Last Tycoon)
4917a[7]

Chocolate Candy (USA) *Jerry Hollendorfer* a112
2 b c Candy Ride(ARG) —Crownette (USA) (Seattle Slew (USA))
7751a[3]

Chocolate Caramel (USA) *R A Fahey* a91 89
6 b g Storm Creek(USA) —Sandhill (BRZ) (Baynoun)
(1583) 2202[10] (2623) 3045[7] 3480[6] (4046) 4439[2]

Chocolicious (IRE) *B Smart* a64 66
2 bb f Captain Rio—Queenfisher (Scottish Reel)
6051[6] ◆ 6245[7] 7015[5] 7794[4]

Choir Singer (FR) *Eoin Griffin* a77 70
3 b g Fantastic Light(USA) —Seductrice (USA) (Kingmambo (USA))
7704[3] (7747)

Choiseau (IRE) *Pat Eddery* 84
3 b g Choisir(AUS) —Little Linnet (Be My Guest (USA))
1960[2] (2981)

Choisette *B Smart* a70 73
3 b f Choisir(AUS) —Final Pursuit (Pursuit Of Love)
2676[8] 3080[9] (3665) 4216[10] 5007[5] 6011[8] 7456[6] 7611[9]

Choisharp (IRE) *M Botti* a62
2 b c Choisir(AUS) —Ballea Queen (IRE) (College Chapel)
7273[4] 7465[4]

Choisky (IRE) *R Bouresly* a70 61
3 b c Choisir(AUS) —Vinicky (USA) (Kingmambo (USA))
292a[13] 567a[13] 812a[5]

Chookie Hamilton *Miss L A Perratt* a76 67
4 ch g Compton Place—Lady Of Windsor (IRE) (Woods Of Windsor (USA))
(3550) 4457[5] 4850[2] 4972[4] 5543[2] (5971) 6657[3] 7230[6]

Chookie Heiton (IRE) *I Semple* a65 79
10 br g Fumo Di Londra(IRE) —Royal Wolff (Prince Tenderfoot (USA))
3956[5] 4393[9] 6232[11] 7292[4] 7651[10] 7829[11]

Choose Me (IRE) *Kevin Prendergast* a85 92
2 ch f Choisir(AUS) —Hecuba (Hector Protector (USA))
(5294a) 6318a[8]

Choose Your Moment *P C Haslam* 108
3 b c Choisir(AUS) —Time Will Show (FR) (Exit To Nowhere (USA))
1441[8] ◆ 2819[2] 3880[3] 4122[2] (4459)

Chopastair (FR) *T Lemer* a110 111
7 b g Astair(FR) —Very Sol (FR) (Solicitor (FR))
1108a[5] 4212a[3] (6612a) 7162a[7]

Choral Festival *Sir Mark Prescott* a71 75
2 b f Pivotal—Choirgirl (Unfuwain (USA))
5048[10] 5256[2] 5590[2]

Choral Service *W J Haggas* 55
2 ch g Pivotal—Choir Mistress (Chief Singer)
7054[12]

Choreography *Jim Best* a48 86
5 ch g Medicean—Stark Ballet (USA) (Nureyev (USA))
2337[12] (2933) 3033[3] (3345) 3653[9] (4723) 5207[14]

Chosen Forever *G R Oldroyd* a69 66
3 b g Choisir(AUS) —Forever Bond (Danetime (IRE))
(3867) 4875[10] 6628[2] 6792[6] 7586[7]

Chosen One (IRE) *B Smart* 68
3 ch g Choisir(AUS) —Copious (IRE) (Generous (IRE))
4877[5] (5395) (6150) ◆ 7040[8]

Chosen Son (IRE) *P J O'Gorman* a69
2 bb g Kheleyf(USA) —Choice Pickings (IRE) (Among Men (USA))
5609[6] 5939[8] 6932[3] 7308[3]

Chris Corsa *J R Weymes* a5 59
5 b g Mark Of Esteem(IRE) —Risque Lady (Kenmare (FR))
2[6]

Christalini *J C Fox* a57 58
4 b g Bertolini(USA) —Jay Tee (IRE) (Charnwood Forest (IRE))
219[4] 606[8] 915[8] 3675[5]

Christian Bendix *P Howling* a58 41
6 ch g Presidium—Very Good (Noalto)
11[14]

Christophers Quest *A W Carroll* a69 68
3 b c Forzando—Kaprisky (IRE) (Red Sunset)
936[2] 1149[3] 1467[15] 2429[3] 3221[6] 5218[9]

Chrystal Venture (IRE) *A J McCabe* a74 69
3 ch f Barathea(IRE) —Ukraine Venture (Slip Anchor)
(1216) 1426[19] 2039[RR] 2189[8] 2705[8] 7277[12] 7668[9]

Churchills Victory (IRE) *W Jarvis* a55 71
2 b g Danehill Dancer(IRE) —Kingsridge (IRE) (King's Theatre (IRE))
2951[5] 3408[3] 4861[7]

Church Service (USA) *Mike Mitchell* a112 112
5 b g Pulpit(USA) —To Be Approved (USA) (With Approval (CAN))
6993a[2]

Churchtown Star (IRE) *P Budds* 42
4 b g Welsh Lion(IRE) —Laura Ellen (IRE) (River Falls)
3861a[12]

Ciao (USA) *Frank J Kirby* 106
4 b m Lear Fan(USA) —Ciao For Now (USA) (Nureyev (USA))
4888a[8]

Cicerole (FR) *J-C Rouget* 107
4 ch m Barathea(IRE) —Uryale (FR) (Kendor (FR))
2827[2] 4888a[6]

Ciel Rouge (FR) *J-C Rouget* 103
2 b f Red Ransom(USA) —Raisonnable (Common Grounds)
6891a[2]

Cigalas *B W Hills* 83
3 ch g Selkirk(USA) —Langoustine (AUS) (Danehill (USA))
3694[5] (5366) 6242[15]

Cihangir (IRE) *D K Weld* a70 78
3 br g Fasliyev(USA) —Toujours Irish (USA) (Irish River (FR))
6366a[13]

Ciloster (ITY) *R Betti* 49
2 b c Colossus(IRE) —Mugnaga (IRE) (Catrail (USA))
4441a[8]

Cima De Triomphe (IRE) *B Grizzetti* 119
3 b c Galileo(IRE) —Sopran Londa (IRE) (Danehill (USA))
(2028a) 4042a[7] 6522a[9] 7263a[11]

Cindy Incidentally *Miss Gay Kelleway* a43
2 ch f Shinko Forest(IRE) —Bayrami (Emarati (USA))
6183[5] 7303[5] 7734[6]

Cinematic (IRE) *J R Boyle* a77 82
5 b g Bahhare(USA) —Eastern Star (IRE) (Sri Pekan (USA))
7742[5] ◆

Cinerama (IRE) *M P Tregoning* a61 65
3 b f Machiavellian(USA) —Disco Volante (Sadler's Wells (USA))
1440[6] 2449[7] 3221[8] 3636[5] (6332) 6821[10]

Cinnamon Hill *Eve Johnson Houghton* a76 69
4 ch m Compton Place—Cajole (IRE) (Barathea (IRE))
(1178) ◆ 1368[11] 1858[4] 2457[6] 3317[7] 3506[15] 4862[8] 6338[3] 6749[8]

Cinq Cinq (FR) *J P Sabatino* 102
3 b c Volochine(IRE) —Saaria (FR) (Sarhoob (USA))
3191a[6] 5529a[7]

Circadian Rhythm *S C Williams* a64 57
3 br f Lujain(USA) —Maristax (Reprimand)
244[5] 3801[8] 4255[6] 4796[8] 5318[2] (5379) (5575) 5631[2] 6049[11] 6227[4] 6746[10]

Circle Dance (IRE) *D Shaw* a51 74
3 bb g Namid—Rivana (Green Desert (USA))
7798[4]

Circuit Dancer (IRE) *D Nicholls* a73 80
8 b g Mujadil(USA) —Trysinger (IRE) (Try My Best (USA))
983[6] 1451[9] 1624[11] 2005[8] 2444[5] 2583[10] 2843[2] ◆ 3042[3] 3255[2] 3477[4] 4239[11]

Circus Clown (IRE) *Miss L A Perratt* 60
3 b g Vettori(IRE) —Comic (IRE) (Be My Chief (USA))
2847[6] 3402[5] 4116[4] 4859[9] 6386[5]

Circus Polka (USA) *W M Brisbourne* a75
4 br g Stravinsky(USA) —Far Wiser (USA) (Private Terms (USA))
103[4] 250[4] 768[4] 861[5] 915[7] 1064[6]

Citizenship *Pat Eddery* 76
2 b c Beat Hollow—Three More (USA) (Sanglamore (USA))
3853[8] 4658[6] 6481[10]

Citron Presse (USA) *J H M Gosden* a67 67
3 bb f Lemon Drop Kid(USA) —Cozy Maria (USA) (Cozzene (USA))
2800[7] 3318[6] 3801[5] 4259[4] 4607[5] 5611[2] 6337[2]

City Bank (USA) *M Johnston* a62 55
2 ch g Rahy(USA) —Lucrative (USA) (Seeking The Gold (USA))
6230[7] 6539[12] 7649[4] 7784[5]

City Bonus (IRE) *J H M Gosden* 77
3 b c Cadeaux Genereux—Ellebanna (Tina's Pet)
(1429)

City Dancer (IRE) *Miss S Collins* a86 80
2 b f Elusive City(USA) —Calypso Dancer (FR) (Celtic Swing)
6320a[2] (6507a)

City Diamond *P J Makin* a76 46
2 b c Lujain(USA) —Gem (Most Welcome)
2916[8] ◆ (3821) ◆

City For Conquest (IRE) *John A Harris* a57 56
5 b m City On A Hill(USA) —Northern Life (IRE) (Distinctly North (USA))
1185[13] 2748[9] 3405[12] 3565[3] 3783[2] 4107[4] (4308) 4462[3] 4858[4] 5007[3] 6419[6] 6890[3] 7022[3] 7049[5] (7375) 7497[9] 7793[12]

City Leader (IRE) *B J Meehan* 114
3 gr c Fasliyev(USA) —Kanmary (FR) (Kenmare (FR))
1421[6] (2303) 3193[6] 4473a[2] 5302a[3] 5953a[4] 6816[10]

City Of The Kings (IRE) *G A Harker* a83 94
3 b c Cape Cross(IRE) —Prima Volta (Primo Dominie)
1600[11] 3134[5] ◆ (3458) 3877[6] ◆ 4417[4] 6526[7] 6783[15]

Cityscape *R Charlton* 112
2 ch c Selkirk(USA) —Tantina (USA) (Distant View (USA))
5068[2] (5641) ◆ 6267[2] ◆

City Stable (IRE) *Sir Michael Stoute* a86 80
3 b g Machiavellian(USA) —Rainbow City (IRE) (Rainbow Quest (USA))
1618[7] 5042[2] (5376) ◆ 5938[8]

City Style (USA) *Cheryl Asmussen* 108
2 ch g City Zip(USA) —Brattothecore (CAN) (Katahaula County (CAN))
6998a[4]

City Well *M Johnston* a73
5 b g Sadler's Wells(USA) —City Dance (USA) (Seattle Slew (USA))
4200[9]

Ci Vediamo (IRE) *R M Beckett* 65
3 b f Polish Precedent(USA) —Vitesse (IRE) (Royal Academy (USA))
1525[10] 2449[11] 3061[3] 4708[9] 5291[5]

Civitas Filius (USA) *D M Simcock* a58 61
3 ch c Proud Citizen(USA) —Saltinella (USA) (Salt Lake (USA))
2681[7] 3894[9] 4695[10] 5803[12] 6049[7] 6685[7]

C Karma (USA) *Gregory De Gannes* a90 102
2 bb f Exchange Rate(USA) —C B Carm (USA) (Slick (USA))
6966a[8]

Claire Et Bleu (FR) *Mme M Bollack-Badel* 105
4 b m Anabaa Blue—Clarte Du Soir (FR) (Kaldoun (FR))
912a[4] 1713a[2] 2553a[8] 6612a[8]

Claphands *M A Allen* a51 57
2 b f Royal Applause—Social Storm (USA) (Future Storm (USA))
2821^{7} 3437^{7} 3821^{5} 4525^{7} 5567^{3} 6906^{7} 7212^{9} 7415^{9} 7738^{10}

Clare Park *H J Manners*
4 ch m Kier Park(IRE) —Shafayif (Ela-Mana-Mou)
5477^{7}

Claret And Amber *Mrs S Leech* a81 74
6 b g Forzando—Artistic Licence (High Top)
34^{3} ◆ 357^{2} 531^{7} 2334^{8} 2578^{3} (2658) 3142^{RR} 4451^{3} 4878^{3} 5708^{5} 6491^{2} 6629^{9} 6663^{4} 6826^{2} 6841^{8} 7115^{4} 7461^{10} (Dead)

Clarricien (IRE) *Patrick Griffin* a37 76
4 br g Key Of Luck(USA) —Tango Two Thousand (IRE) (Sri Pekan (USA))
4655a^{18}

Class Attraction (IRE) *J E Hammond* a83 98
4 b m Act One—She's All Class (USA) (Rahy (USA))
7348a^{13}

Classically (IRE) *R Charlton* 85
2 b c Indian Haven—Specifically (USA) (Sky Classic (CAN))
6978^{2} ◆

Classical Rhythm (IRE) *J R Boyle* a60 68
3 ch g Traditionally(USA) —Golden Angel (USA) (Slew O'Gold (USA))
(1540) 2043^{8} 2695^{3} 3745^{7} 3886^{4} 4344^{7} 6049^{8} 6437^{6} 6905^{10} 7374^{4} 7613^{8}

Classic Blade (IRE) *Tom Dascombe* 107
2 b c Daggers Drawn(USA) —Queen Bodicea (IRE) (Revoque (IRE))
1616^{4} (2783) (3522) (3876) 5330a^{9} 6442^{5}

Classic Blue (IRE) *Ian Williams* a60 43
4 b m Tagula(IRE) —Palace Blue (IRE) (Dara Monarch)
145^{2} 287^{2} (387) 1562^{5} 3025^{10} 6228^{2} (6570) 7094^{2} 7189^{5} 7516^{11}

Classic Contours (USA) *G A Swinbank* 67
2 b g Najran(USA) —What's Up Kittycat (USA) (Tabasco Cat (USA))
3078^{7} 4213^{7} 4697^{2} 5632^{6}

Classic Dancer *Jane Chapple-Hyam* a9
3 b f Groom Dancer(USA) —Versatility (Teenoso (USA))
7474^{10} 7713^{11}

Classic Descent *P J Makin* a77 90
3 b c Auction House(USA) —Polish Descent (IRE) (Danehill (USA))
(2427) 2819^{8}

Classic Encounter (IRE) *D M Simcock* a96 96
5 b g Lujain(USA) —Licence To Thrill (Wolfhound (USA))
866^{3} ◆ 1689^{7} 2211^{9} 2326^{7} 3594^{9} 4291^{7} 4693^{7} 6449^{8} 6823^{9}

Classic Hall (IRE) *J Akehurst* a40 47
5 b m Saddlers' Hall(IRE) —Classic Mix (IRE) (Classic Secret (USA))
365^{10} 1564^{9} 1694^{2} 2731^{7} 3844^{6} 4811^{10}

Classic Lass *Rae Guest* a11 73
3 b f Dr Fong(USA) —Cool Storm (IRE) (Rainbow Quest (USA))
4283^{2} 5471^{6} 6047^{14}

Classic Legend *B J Meehan* a93 93
3 b f Galileo(IRE) —Lady Lahar (Fraam)
6034^{3} ◆ 6241^{6} 6781^{7} 7492^{4}

Classic Port (FR) *M Wigham* a103 100
4 gr h Slickly(FR) —Portella (GER) (Protektor (GER))
834^{4} ◆ 960^{20} 2044^{6} 3040^{11}

Classic Punch (IRE) *D R C Elsworth* 114
5 b g Mozart(IRE) —Rum Cay (USA) (Our Native (USA))
1980^{7} 2543^{13} 3497^{4} 3942^{14} 6444^{2} 6820^{7} 7017^{4}

Classic Remark (IRE) *H J L Dunlop* a70 107
3 b f Dr Fong(USA) —Claxon (Caerleon (USA))
1440^{4} ◆ 1991^{5} 2612^{2} (3415) 4623^{6} 5331a^{9} 6781^{9} 7242^{2}

Classic Summer (GER) *M Trybuhl*
2 ch f Pentire—Classic Queen (GER) (Greinton)
7006a^{9}

Classic Swain (USA) *A Fabre* 97
3 ch c Swain(IRE) —Affirm Miss (USA) (Sky Classic (CAN))
4880a^{5} 5685a^{6}

Classic Vintage (USA) *Mrs A J Perrett* 87
2 b c El Prado(IRE) —Cellars Shiraz (USA) (Kissin Kris (USA))
5468^{12} (5842) (6665)

Class Is Class (IRE) *Sir Michael Stoute* 76
2 b c Montjeu(IRE) —Hector's Girl (Hector Protector (USA))
6720^{9} 7200^{2}

Classy Affair *D Morris* a51 40
4 b m Swain(IRE) —Egoli (USA) (Seeking The Gold (USA))
3328^{4} 3654^{9} 4182^{7} 4664^{9} 5020^{16} 6032^{10} 7256^{7}

Classy-Lady (BRZ) *H J Brown* a69 95
4 b m Fahim—Hiparca (BRZ) (Troyanos (BRZ))
200a^{6} 475a^{3} 672a^{5} 744a^{6}

Classy Landlady (CAN) *Michael J Doyle* 85
4 ch m Sky Classic(CAN) —Side View (USA) (Stage Door Johnny (USA))
6505a^{9}

Classy Wonder (USA) *Larry Lay*
2 u c (USA) — (USA) (Carson City (USA))
6502a^{9}

Claws *A J Lidderdale* a61 61
5 b m Marju(IRE) —Paws (IRE) (Brief Truce (USA))
32^{8}

Clear Call *R J Hodges* a19
3 b f Bandmaster(USA) —Distant Call (Distant Relative)
222^{7} 424^{7}

Clear Daylight *J R Best* a58 63
3 b c Daylami(IRE) —Barbara Frietchie (IRE) (Try My Best (USA))
4637^{7} 4964^{7}

Cleard For Action *J R Weymes* 18
2 b g Daggers Drawn(USA) —Aimee's Delight (Robellino (USA))
2845^{9} 3707^{11} 5539^{9}

Clear Hand *B R Millman* a53 41
2 b g Lend A Hand—Miss Maisey (IRE) (Entrepreneur)
4636^{8} 5996^{9} 6397^{10}

Clearing House *E A L Dunlop* a59
3 ch c Zamindar(USA) —Easy Option (IRE) (Prince Sabo)
1252^{8} 1504^{6} 1669^{6}

Clearly Foxy (USA) *Mark Casse* a92 114
3 b f Volponi(USA) —Sermon (USA) (Pulpit (USA))
3807a^{3}

Clear Pond (USA) *George R Arnold II* 93
3 bb f Dynaformer(USA) —Kelly Pond (USA) ((USA))
5744a^{3}

Clear Reef *Jane Chapple-Hyam* a91 83
4 b h Hernando(FR) —Trinity Reef (Bustino)
(3) ◆ 159^{5} 638^{2} 981^{5} 3044^{10} 3104^{14} 3630^{7} (4652) 4866^{5} 5376^{6} 7459^{3} 7639^{5} (7785)

Clear Sailing *George Baker* a82 82
5 b g Selkirk(USA) —Welsh Autumn (Tenby)
(4953) 5858^{17} 7423^{4} 7499^{5} (7723)

Cleaver *Lady Herries* a82 86
7 ch g Kris—Much Too Risky (Bustino)
962^{5} 2076^{3} (2621) 3375^{3} 4178^{7} 5900^{2} 6948^{14}

Clelt Di San Jore (IRE) *L D'Auria* 96
3 gr c Celtic Swing—Claw (IRE) (Law Society (USA))
2028a^{17}

Clerical (USA) *M J Gingell* a58 47
2 b g Yes It's True(USA) —Clerical Etoile (ARG) (The Watcher (USA))
2424^{8} 3055^{7} 3651^{10} 4828^{8} 5834^{3} 6414^{8} 6755^{3} 7454^{4} 7542^{3}

Clerk's Choice (IRE) *W Jarvis* a71 66
2 b g Bachelor Duke(USA) —Credit Crunch (IRE) (Caerleon (USA))
2979^{9} 5431^{5} 6443^{8} 7016^{2} 7524^{2} 7627^{3}

Cleveland *R Hollinshead* a73 57
6 b g Pennekamp(USA) —Clerio (Soviet Star (USA))
42^{8} 109^{3} (191) 278^{5} 460^{3} 599^{2} 868^{3} 1642^{6} 1865^{10} 3779^{3} 4808^{3} 5601^{13}

Clever Millie (USA) *John E Kiely* 75
4 b m Cape Canaveral(USA) —Fateful (USA) (Topsider (USA))
6689a^{14}

Clewer *A B Haynes* a56 28
4 b m Bahamian Bounty—Polisonne (Polish Precedent (USA))
2934^{7} 3360^{12}

Clifton Dancer *Tom Dascombe* 98
3 b f Fraam—Crofters Ceilidh (Scottish Reel)
1441^{5} (2196) (3420) 4590^{6} 5644^{8}

Clifton Four (USA) *P J Rothwell* a62 72
3 b f Forest Wildcat(USA) —Black Truffle (USA) (Mt. Livermore (USA))
772^{2} 1203^{4} 7559^{12}

Climate (IRE) *P D Evans* a69 36
9 ch g Catrail(USA) —Burishki (Chilibang)
101^{2} 176^{6} 209^{6} 341^{5} (611) ◆ (724) 809^{6} 916^{2} 938^{7} 1083^{2} (1192) (1369) 2477^{9} 2943^{6} 7167^{7} 7363^{4} 7423^{8} 7500^{7} (7518) 7559^{11} 7800^{5} 7816^{3}

Climate Change (USA) *Miss Venetia Williams* 81
6 ch g Langfuhr(CAN) —Summer Mist (USA) (Miswaki (USA))
2599^{8} 3044^{8} 3917^{4}

Climaxtackledotcom *M W Easterby* a6 71
3 b g Bahri(USA) —La Danseuse (Groom Dancer (USA))
1781^{3} 5595^{10}

Clinging Vine (USA) *R Hannon* a59
2 bb f Fusaichi Pegasus(USA) —Nemea (USA) (The Minstrel (CAN))
6166^{6} 7332^{10}

Clipperdown (IRE) *E J Creighton* a69 110
7 b g Green Desert(USA) —Maroussie (FR) (Saumarez)
960^{16} 1503^{5} 2132^{6} 3167^{7}

Clipper Hoy *Mrs H Sweeting* a58 23
6 ch g Bahamian Bounty—Indian Flag (IRE) (Indian Ridge)
1706^{8}

Clodazone (IRE) *M G Quinlan* a40
2 b f Clodovil(IRE) —Allspice (Alzao (USA))
4199^{13} 5571^{9} 7370^{10}

Clodoline *P F I Cole* a58 19
2 b f Clodovil(IRE) —Esquiline (USA) (Gone West (USA))
5673^{9} 6358^{11} 7095^{7}

Close Alliance (USA) *J H M Gosden* a82
2 b c Gone West(USA) —Shoogle (USA) (A.P. Indy (USA))
(6597) ◆

Closeout (USA) *Thomas F Proctor* 105
3 b f Repriced(USA) —Deep Discount (USA) (Relaunch (USA))
(5744a)

Closertobelieving *D R C Elsworth* a72 97
3 b c Xaar—Glorious (Nashwan (USA))
1417^{8} 1748^{4} 2119^{4} 2678^{8} (3095) 3800^{4} 4984^{3} (5502) (5858) 6445^{3} 6984^{10}

Cloudesley (IRE) *A M Balding* a63
2 b g Trans Island—Decatur (Deploy)
7674^{5} 7823^{5}

Cloudy's Knight (USA) *Frank J Kirby* 121
8 ch g Lord Avie(USA) —Cloudy Spot (USA) (Solar City (USA))
4889a^{7}

Cloudy Start *H R A Cecil* 90
2 b c Oasis Dream—Set Fair (USA) (Alleged (USA))
3853^{7} ◆ 4625^{3} 6057^{2} (6480)

Clovis *N P Mulholland* a71 78
3 b g Kingmambo(USA) —Darling Flame (USA) (Capote (USA))
454^{4} 982^{3} 3970^{9} 4582^{4} 4766^{3} 4978^{10} 5428^{10} 6210^{8} 6403^{9}

Clowance *R Charlton* 106
3 b f Montjeu(IRE) —Freni (GER) (Sternkoenig (IRE))
(1440) (2149) 2792^{4}

Clowance House *R Charlton* 84
2 ch c Galileo(IRE) —Corsican Sunset (USA) (Thunder Gulch (USA))
6397^{4} 6978^{3}

Cluain Fhada (USA) *J S Bolger* a59 65
2 b f Fusaichi Pegasus(USA) —Butterfly Blue (IRE) (Sadler's Wells (USA))
4513a^{4}

Club Captain (USA) *T D McCarthy* a50 41
5 b g Red Ransom(USA) —Really Fancy (USA) (In Reality (USA))
11^{5} 147^{2} 401^{13} 693^{6} 1269^{3} 2513^{14} 2949^{13} 3162^{14}

Club Tahiti *R Charlton* 87
2 b f Hernando(FR) —Freni (GER) (Sternkoenig (IRE))
(6600) 6982^{11}

Clueless *A J McCabe* 90
6 b g Royal Applause—Pure (Slip Anchor)
3368^{5} 3864^{8} 4111^{7} 4299^{8} 4701^{8} 4963^{6} 5637^{13}

Clumber Place *R C Guest* 69
2 ch f Compton Place—Inquirendo (USA) (Roberto (USA))
(1515)

Cluny *J R Fanshawe* a35
2 b f Celtic Swing—Muschana (Deploy)
7602^{10}

C'Mon You Irons (IRE) *M R Hoad* a73 82
3 b g Orpen(USA) —Laissez Faire (IRE) (Tagula (IRE))
1837^{3} 2410^{12} 2598^{6} 2998^{8} 4864^{9} 5403^{4} 7013^{3} 7315^{6} 7540^{4} 7677^{12} (7819)

Cnocan Gold (IRE) *D K Weld* 78
2 b f Danehill Dancer(IRE) —Gold Script (FR) (Script Ohio (USA))
6319a^{13}

Coach And Four (USA) *S A Callaghan* a52 71
3 bl c Storm Cat(USA) —Tacha (USA) (Mr Prospector (USA))
2786^{8} 3117^{5} 4086^{8} 4524^{11}

Coachhouse Lady (USA) *K A Ryan* a52 80
3 b f Rahy(USA) —Secret Advice (USA) (Secreto (USA))
2190^{5} 4300^{3} 4893^{8} 5273^{7} 6053^{8} 6765^{13}

Coal Play (USA) *Nicholas Zito* a113
3 b c Mineshaft(USA) —Wiscasset (USA) (Kris S (USA))
4678a^{2}

Coastal Breeze *A J Chamberlain* a44
3 b g Fasliyev(USA) —Classic Design (Busted)
264^{6} 535^{9}

Coastal Path *A Fabre* 119
4 b h Halling(USA) —Coraline (Sadler's Wells (USA))
(1663a) (2236a) 3154^{3} 5333a^{3}

Cobalt Blue (USA) *S Seemar* a106
4 ch h Golden Missile(USA) —Prado Star (IRE) (El Prado (IRE))
1089a^{12}

Cobbold Point *S W Hall* a33 36
3 b g Tipsy Creek(USA) —Mofeyda (IRE) (Mtoto)
1251^{5} 1741^{7} 2259^{13} 3844^{10} 4794^{8}

Cobo Bay *K A Ryan* a83 104
3 b c Primo Valentino(IRE) —Fisher Island (IRE) (Sri Pekan (USA))
(1428) 1595^{3} 2825^{8} 4153^{7} 4869^{6} 5360^{3} 5795^{5}

Cobos *M G Quinlan* a64
2 b f Royal Applause—Darya (USA) (Gulch (USA))
5240^{17} 6901^{5} 7227^{5}

Cocabana *J G Portman* a67 72
3 b f Captain Rio—Hiraeth (Petong)
(59)

Cocktail Party (IRE) *J W Hills* a50 62
2 b f Acclamation—Irish Moss (USA) (Irish River (FR))
2011^{4} 4251^{8} 4634^{8} 4925^{5} 5933^{2} (6579) 6865^{6} 7199^{4}

Cocoa Beach (CHI) *Saeed Bin Suroor* a121 118
4 bb m Doneraile Court(USA) —Visionera (CHI) (Edgy Diplomat (USA))
201a^{2} (496a) (744a) 1088a^{3} 6969a^{2}

Cocodrail (IRE) *F & L Brogi* a87 105
7 b h Croco Rouge(IRE) —Seattle Jey (ITY) (Seattle Dancer (USA))
2027a^{7}

Coco L'Escargot *J R Jenkins* a41 56
4 b m Slip Anchor—Dafne (Nashwan (USA))
878^{5} 1382^{9} 1542^{5} 2354^{6} 4477^{12} 4599^{3} 6806^{3} 7379^{5} 7713^{6}

Coconut Moon *D Flood* a77 86
6 b m Bahamian Bounty—Lunar Ridge (Indian Ridge)
1021^{4} 1451^{8} 2210^{9} 2359^{7} 2906^{5} (3585) 3948^{6} 4103^{6} 5867^{11} 5884^{9} 6418^{9} 6823^{10}

Coconut Shy *G Prodromou* a33 89
2 b f Bahamian Bounty—Lets Be Fair (Efisio)
2508^{2} 3584^{6} 3959^{5} (5158) (5363) 5852^{8} 6102^{6} 6644^{18} 7107^{11}

Cocopalm (FR) *M Delzangles* 94
3 gr f Linamix(FR) —Caribbeandriftwood (USA) (Woodman (USA))
6323a^{7}

Coda Agency *D W P Arbuthnot* a71 55
5 b g Agnes World(USA) —The Frog Lady (IRE) (Al Hareb (USA))
(654) 789^{3} (1052) 1337^{5} (1856) 2567^{6} (6740) ◆ 7775^{5}

Co Dependent (USA) *J A Osborne* a69 41
2 ch c Cozzene(USA) —Glowing Breeze (USA) (Southern Halo (USA))
2916^{14} 6375^{7} 7073^{6}

Code Violation *Jean-Rene Auvray* a55 50
3 gr f Silver Patriarch(IRE) —Lady High Sheriff (IRE) (Lancastrian)
570^{6} 1176^{6} 2716^{8} 3483^{8} 5752^{5} (Dead)

Coeur Brule (FR) *J R Gask* a49
2 b g Polish Summer—Sally's Cry (FR) (Freedom Cry)
6879^{8} 7289^{7}

Coeur Courageux (FR) *G L Moore* a86 78
6 b g Xaar—Linoise (FR) (Caerwent)
1936^{8} 2329^{8} 2722^{6} ◆ 2930^{8}

Coeur De Lionne (IRE) *E A L Dunlop* a106 91
4 b g Invincible Spirit(IRE) —Lionne (Darshaan)
296a^{8} 381a^{10} ◆ 652a^{7} 3249^{16} 4844^{10} 7208^{3}

Coffee Cup (IRE) *G A Swinbank* 61
3 b f Royal Academy(USA) —Christel Flame (Darshaan)
1448^{13} 3081^{12}

Coffee In Bed (USA) *Kelly Breen* a91
2 b f Toccet(USA) —Grace Bay (USA) (Waquoit (USA))
6500a^{5}

Cognac Boy (USA) *R Hannon* a63 41
2 bb c Hennessy(USA) —City Sleeper (USA) (Carson City (USA))
2903^{9} 7476^{4} 7593^{6} 7760^{2}

Coiled Spring *Mrs A J Perrett* 82
2 b c Observatory(USA) —Balmy (Zafonic (USA))
6085^{3} 6539^{6} 6777^{4}

Coill Glas (IRE) *W J Haggas* a57
3 b g Green Desert(USA) —Forest Express (AUS) (Kaaptive Edition (NZ))
7669^{7}

Coin Of The Realm (IRE) *E A L Dunlop* a78 86
3 b c Galileo(IRE) —Common Knowledge (Rainbow Quest (USA))
1382^{12} 1728^{4} 2668^{3} 3802^{2} (4302) 4662^{4} 5349^{9}

Coka (IRE) *Miss D Mountain* 23
2 ch f Nayef(USA) —Raydaniya (IRE) (In The Wings)
6081^{16}

Colangnik (USA) *J R Best* a73 44
2 b f Sky Classic(CAN) —Rainbow Strike (USA) (Smart Strike (CAN))
2821^{12} 7023^{3} 7259^{3} 7524^{3}

Cold Mountain (IRE) *J W Mullins* 51
6 b g Inchinor—Streak Of Silver (USA) (Dynaformer (USA))
5027^{7}

Cold Quest (USA) *Miss L A Perratt* a86 98
4 b g Seeking The Gold(USA) —Polaire (IRE) (Polish Patriot (USA))
6667^{2} 7244^{21}

Cold Turkey *G L Moore* a99 98
8 bb g Polar Falcon(USA) —South Rock (Rock City)
96^{3} 315^{8} ◆ (428) 757^{7}

Coleorton Choice *K A Ryan* 84
2 ch c Choisir(AUS) —Tayovullin (IRE) (Shalford (IRE))
1967^{5} 3178^{3} 3590^{8} 4857^{3} (5381) (6067)

Coleorton Dagger *J R Holt* a25
4 ch m Daggers Drawn(USA) —Tayovullin (IRE) (Shalford (IRE))
65^{11}

Coleorton Dancer *K A Ryan* a81 79
6 ch g Danehill Dancer(IRE) —Tayovullin (IRE) (Shalford (IRE))
85^{3} 194^{6} 636^{4} 1485^{10} 1624^{4} 1952^{5} 2751^{6} 3129^{4} 3713^{4} 3890^{3} 5634^{3} 6218^{17} 7118^{4} 7277^{3} 7610^{9} 7653^{8}

Colin Staite *R Brotherton* 21
2 b g Superior Premium—Downclose Duchess (King's Signet (USA))
2458^{9} 3358^{12} 3902^{5} 7165^{9}

Coliseum *Sir Michael Stoute* 43
3 ch c Medicean—Fearless Revival (Cozzene (USA))
3654^{7} 4695^{11}

Collateral *J A Geake* a7
5 ch m Groom Dancer(USA) —Cugina (Distant Relative)
22^{6}

Collateral Damage (IRE) *T D Easterby* a84 93
5 b g Orpen(USA) —Jay Gee (IRE) (Second Set (IRE))
(1016) 1816^{5} 1910^{13} 2218^{4} 3413^{5} 3627^{4} 4204^{6} 4876^{5} 5360^{4}

Collection (IRE) *W J Haggas* 113
3 b c Peintre Celebre(USA) —Lasting Chance (USA) (American Chance (USA))
1297^{6} ◆ (2109) ◆ (3156) ◆ 4473a^{5} 5742a^{5}

College Land Boy *A Kirtley* 55
4 b g Cois Na Tine(IRE) —Welcome Lu (Most Welcome)
1221^{7} 2250^{6} 2463^{6} 2662^{12} 2846^{12} 3226^{6} 3602^{9} 4217^{9} 5637^{14}

College Queen *S Gollings* a39 41
10 b m Lugana Beach—Eccentric Dancer (Rambo Dancer (CAN))
119^{7} 189^{9} 254^{10}

College Scholar (GER) *Liam McAteer* a65 89
4 ch g Dr Fong(USA) —Colina (GER) (Caerleon (USA))
1103a^{12} 3532a^{6} 4004a^{5} 6105^{3}

Collegiate (USA) *Mark Hennig* a88
2 b f Saarland(USA) —La Sorbonne (ARG) (Southern Halo (USA))
6500a^{8}

Colleoni (IRE) *G A Butler* a64 57
3 b g Sadler's Wells(USA) —Francfurter (Legend Of France (USA))
52^{8} 396^{4} 2259^{7} 4646^{4} 6374^{2} 6905^{6}

Collette's Choice *R A Fahey* a41 71
5 b m Royal Applause—Brilliance (Cadeaux Genereux)
1559^{2} 2006^{3} 2107^{3} 2585^{5} 3007^{7} 3729^{6} 4220^{3} 4556^{4}

Colloquial *H Candy* a90 101
7 b g Classic Cliche(IRE) —Celia Brady (Last Tycoon)
1841^{7} 2609^{2} ◆ 4362^{3} 6061^{10}

Collow (GER) *M Weiss* 104
8 b g Lando(GER) —Conga (Robellino (USA))
423a^{8} 605a^{3}
Colmar Magic (IRE) *Miss D Mountain* a39 56
3 b f Dixie Union(USA) —On View (USA) (Distant View (USA))
4391^{3}
Colombard (IRE) *J G Burns* a78 60
3 b g Almutawakel—Searching Star (Rainbow Quest (USA))
6510a^{9}
Colombey (FR) *K Borgel* 58
3 b c Bering—Collegiale (FR) (Sillery (USA))
385a^{5}
Colonel Flay *Mrs P N Dutfield* a68 79
4 ch g Danehill Dancer(IRE) —Bobbie Dee (Blakeney)
(1779) 1998^{6} 2921^{2} 3900^{5} 4432^{3} (5465) 6403^{6}
Colonel John (USA) *Eoin Harty* a126
3 b c Tiznow(USA) —Sweet Damsel (USA) (Turkoman (USA))
1820a^{6} 7001a^{6}
Colonel Sherman (USA) *L A Dace* a62 45
3 bb c Mr Greeley(USA) —Spankin 'n Fannin (USA) (Lear Fan (USA))
5636^{12} 6345^{10} 6883^{3} 7310^{4} 7626^{2} 7806^{2}
Colony (IRE) *Sir Michael Stoute* 99
3 b c Statue Of Liberty(USA) —Funoon (IRE) (Kris)
(1600) ◆ 2194^{3} (3157) ◆ 4519^{11}
Colophony (USA) *K A Morgan* a70
8 ch g Distant View(USA) —Private Line (USA) (Private Account (USA))
3321^{2} 5676^{4} 7770^{8}
Colorado Blue (IRE) *C E Longsdon* 79
3 ch g Nayef(USA) —Colouring (IRE) (Catrail (USA))
1265^{3} 1684^{3} 2151^{7} 2665^{5} 3384^{6} (3737) 4350^{5} 5199^{8} 6400^{13}
Colorado Rapid (IRE) *Saeed Bin Suroor* a84 103
4 b g Barathea(IRE) —Rafting (IRE) (Darshaan)
205a^{6} 495a^{3} ◆
Colorado Springs *W Jarvis* a65 56
3 b f Olden Times—Engulfed (USA) (Gulch (USA))
2090^{3} 2984^{9} 3393^{7} (3844) 4165^{3} 4750^{5}
Coloratura (IRE) *E A L Dunlop* a57 57
3 b f Cape Cross(IRE) —Elauyun (IRE) (Muhtarram (USA))
1115^{7} 1637^{4} 3397^{11}
Colorus (IRE) *W J H Ratcliffe* a69 85
5 b g Night Shift(USA) —Duck Over (Warning)
1431^{5} 1624^{3} 1893^{9} 2270^{3} 2583^{7} 3112^{2} 3665^{5} 3868^{2} 4385^{5} 4462^{8} 5044^{3} 5260^{13} 6766^{4} 7043^{11} 7323^{4} 7793^{2}
Coloso *P D Cundell* a64 11
4 ch g Compton Place—Nashville Blues (IRE) (Try My Best (USA))
175^{6} ◆ 448^{4} ◆ 1058^{7} 1209^{12}
Colourful Move *P G Murphy* a69 54
3 b c Rainbow Quest(USA) —Flit (USA) (Lyphard (USA))
3654^{6} 5612^{7} 7446^{2} 7661^{3}
Colour Of Money *S A Callaghan* 46
3 br g Kyllachy—Euridice (IRE) (Woodman (USA))
1737^{9} 1951^{8} 2824^{7}
Colour Trooper (IRE) *P Winkworth* a67 75
3 ch g Traditionally(USA) —Viola Royale (IRE) (Royal Academy (USA))
1926^{12} 5463^{5} (5790) 6256^{9} 6738^{12}
Colourways (IRE) *Mrs A J Perrett* 92
3 b f Singspiel(IRE) —Chartres (IRE) (Danehill (USA))
2716^{7} (3350) 4667^{9} (6416)
Colton *J M P Eustace* a79 60
5 b g Zilzal(USA) —Picot (Piccolo)
2884^{9} 3655^{5} 4261^{4} 5650^{3}
Colwyn Bay (IRE) *R M Stronge* a65 70
6 b g Sadler's Wells(USA) —Stolen Tear (FR) (Cadeaux Genereux)
2888^{8} 3377^{9}
Comadoir (IRE) *Miss Jo Crowley* a79 78
2 ch c Medecis—Hymn Of The Dawn (USA) (Phone Trick (USA))
5615^{5} 5905^{3} 6770^{2} 7769^{3}
Comanche Trail (FR) *R M Whitaker* a20
2 b c American Post—Rainbird (Rainbow Quest (USA))
1078^{9}
Comandante Xara (BRZ) *A Selvaratnam* a97 54
5 gr h Bonapartiste(FR) —Massabielle (BRZ) (Executioner (USA))
473a^{15} 738a^{10}
Combat Zone (IRE) *Saeed Bin Suroor* 78
2 b g Refuse To Bend(IRE) —Zeiting (IRE) (Zieten (USA))
3853^{6} ◆ 4311^{2} 4890^{3}
Come And Go (UAE) *G A Swinbank* 81
2 b g Halling(USA) —Woven Silk (USA) (Danzig (USA))
3364^{7} 4289^{3} (4815) 5359^{4} 5791^{7}
Comeback Queen *S Kirk* a88 91
3 gb f Nayef(USA) —Miss Universe (IRE) (Warning)
1332^{2} 2105^{7} 3124^{6} 3415^{7} 3742^{8}
Comeintothespace (IRE) *K J Burke* a20 53
6 b g Tagula(IRE) —Playa Del Sol (IRE) (Alzao (USA))
5917^{11}
Come On Buckers (IRE) *E J Creighton* a60 61
2 ch g Fath(USA) —Deerussa (IRE) (Jareer (USA))
1168^{4} 1324^{4} (2450) 2980^{3} 3091^{2} 3652^{2} 5294a^{19} 6632^{12} 7164^{8} 7451^{2}
Come On Jonny (IRE) *R M Beckett* 96
6 b g Desert King(IRE) —Idle Fancy (Mujtahid (USA))
1070^{4} 1841^{9} 2830^{9} 3505^{2} ◆ 3925^{10} 5894^{11}
Come On Molly *R Brotherton*
4 b m Dreams End—Quakeress (IRE) (Brief Truce (USA))
837^{12} 1172^{14} 1372^{9}
Come On Nellie (IRE) *J G M O'Shea* 41
4 b m Diktat—Bauci (IRE) (Desert King (IRE))
3733^{7} 4322^{11} 4806^{6}

Come On Toby *Miss Amy Weaver* 30
2 b c Piccolo—Fleeting Moon (Fleetwood (IRE))
4024^{13} 4256^{13} 6438^{12}
Come Out Fighting *P A Blockley* a100 101
5 b h Bertolini(USA) —Ulysses Daughter (IRE) (College Chapel)
(226) 3337^{7} 677^{10} 836^{10} 1393^{3}
Come What July (IRE) *D Shaw* a56 44
7 b g Indian Rocket—Persian Sally (IRE) (Persian Bold)
125^{8} 161^{3} 303^{7} 400^{5} 499^{5} 585^{3} 751^{5}
Comghaire (IRE) *P D Evans* 52
2 b f Acclamation—All Of Yesterday (IRE) (Second Empire (IRE))
2450^{3} ◆ 2910^{8} 3815^{P} (Dead)
Comic Tales *M Mullineaux* a27 34
7 b g Mind Games—Glorious Aragon (Aragon)
6822^{10} 7527^{9} 7669^{10}
Coming Back *J H M Gosden* 65
2 ch f Fantastic Light(USA) —Return (USA) (Sadler's Wells (USA))
7141^{6}
Commander Cave (USA) *R Hannon* a108 103
3 bb c Tale Of The Cat(USA) —Royal Shyness (Royal Academy (USA))
(796) ◆ (1208) ◆ (1595) 2403^{2} 3155^{16} 5313^{10} 6283^{7} 7101^{2} (7313) 7492^{2}
Commander Wish *Lucinda Featherstone* a67 75
5 ch g Arkadian Hero(USA) —Flighty Dancer (Pivotal)
86^{4} 304^{2} 1634^{4} 1997^{9} 2511^{2} 3665^{3} (4047) (4743) 4981^{3} 6880^{12} 7118^{10} 7471^{11}
Commandingpresence (USA) *B J Meehan* a64
2 bb f Thunder Gulch(USA) —Sehra (USA) (Silver Hawk (USA))
7735^{2} ◆
Command Marshal (FR) *M J Scudamore* 79
5 b g Commands(AUS) —Marsakara (IRE) (Turtle Island (IRE))
1798^{3} 2012^{2} 2332^{9} 3179^{6} 3950^{2} 4662^{7} 4866^{P} 5199^{10}
Commendation *J H M Gosden* a53
2 b f Royal Applause—Ring Of Love (Magic Ring (IRE))
6166^{9}
Commit To Memory *Andrew Oliver* a78 75
3 br g Best Of The Bests(IRE) —Simonida (IRE) (Royal Academy (USA))
6657^{12}
Common Diva *A J McCabe* a66 72
2 ch f Auction House(USA) —Vida (IRE) (Wolfhound (USA))
2035^{8} 2534^{3} (2887) 3625^{5} 4297^{4} 6987^{9} 7306^{8} 7472^{7} 7760^{9} 7824^{4}
Common Market *A Peraino* 64
2 b f Compton Place—Common Consent (IRE) (Common Grounds)
5951a^{5}
Common Purpose (USA) *Jane Chapple-Hyam* a76 77
4 b g Elusive Quality(USA) —Kithira (Danehill (USA))
246^{3} ◆ 447^{3}
Common Sense (SWE) *B Bo*
3 ch c Pennekamp(USA) —By The Book (IRE) (Definite Article)
4918a^{14}
Communique (USA) *George R Arnold II* 110
4 b m Smart Strike(CAN) —Martinique (USA) (Pleasant Colony (USA))
4888a^{2}
Competitor *J Akehurst* a67 39
7 b g Danzero(AUS) —Ceanothus (IRE) (Bluebird (USA))
352^{9} (569) 631^{2} (935) 1210^{6} 1694^{9} 2353^{15} 2832^{10} 3265^{8} 3482^{9} 7473^{11} 7599^{6} 7792^{11} 7831^{6}
Complete Frontline (GER) *K R Burke* a60 61
3 ch g Tertullian(USA) —Carola Rouge (Arazi (USA))
590^{3} 777^{10} 1306^{9} 1819^{4} 2660^{5} 2911^{9} 3717^{3} 4413^{3} 5161^{4} 5575^{2} 6685^{9} 7541^{8}
Completo (IRE) *F Castro* a92 50
5 b g Mull Of Kintyre(USA) —Bold Avril (IRE) (Persian Bold)
(2232a) 5957a^{13}
Compton Blue *R Hannon* 64
2 b c Compton Place—Blue Goddess (IRE) (Blues Traveller (IRE))
6600^{5} 6863^{11} 7105^{5}
Compton Charlie *J G Portman* a52 64
4 b g Compton Place—Tell Tale Fox (Tel Quel (FR))
(1281) 1913^{5} 2694^{2} 3347^{4} 4275^{2} 4930^{5} 5802^{9} 6668^{4}
Compton Classic *J R Boyle* a77 82
6 b g Compton Place—Ayr Classic (Local Suitor (USA))
(45) 165^{7} 386^{2} 939^{4} 1061^{7} 4025^{13} 4478^{14} 6774^{2} 7544^{2}
Compton Commander *E W Tuer* a62 45
10 ch g Barathea(IRE) —Triode (USA) (Sharpen Up)
1892^{7} 3279^{9} 3399^{6} 3863^{8} 4924^{12}
Compton Court *John G Carr* a69 62
6 b g Compton Place—Loriner's Lass (Saddlers' Hall (IRE))
(6824)
Compton Dragon (USA) *W M Brisbourne* a62 67
9 ch g Woodman(USA) —Vilikaia (USA) (Nureyev (USA))
2908^{9} 5199^{6} 5637^{3}
Compton Express *Jamie Poulton* a53 46
5 gr m Compton Place—Jilly Woo (Environment Friend)
269^{9} 585^{10} 794^{8}
Compton Falcon *G A Butler* a69 73
4 ch g Peintre Celebre(USA) —Lesgor (USA) (Irish River (FR))
1039^{2} 1583^{4} 2100^{6} 4193^{6} 5163^{5} 5833^{4} 6421^{5} 7217^{3} 7427^{3} 7702^{4}

Compton Ford *M Dods* a38 56
2 ch g Compton Place—Coffee Time (IRE) (Efisio)
1220^{8} 2462^{6} 3547^{5} 4243^{4} (5541) 6350^{6} 6579^{12}
Compton Lad *D A Nolan* a11 46
5 b g Compton Place—Kintara (Cyrano De Bergerac)
2283^{8} 3784^{8} 4013^{11}
Compton Rose *H Candy* 69
3 ch f Compton Place—Benjarong (Sharpo)
1737^{3} 2341^{4} 5902^{3} 6204^{5} 6418^{8} 6706^{12}
Compton's Eleven *M R Channon* a88 92
7 gr g Compton Place—Princess Tara (Prince Sabo)
1430^{5} 1617^{10} 2013^{4} 2163^{2} 2339^{9} (2818) 3040^{6} 3222^{9} 4407^{11} 4854^{13} 5096^{8} 5589^{2} 5897^{10} 6125^{7} 6676^{7} 7101^{3} 7239^{13} 7386^{7}
Comptonspirit *B P J Baugh* a66 73
4 ch m Compton Place—Croeso Cynnes (Most Welcome)
987^{5} 1373^{4} 1997^{4} 2356^{2} 2596^{2} 3352^{2} 3868^{6} (4462) 4958^{5} 5867^{6} 6232^{7} 6388^{6} 6658^{4}
Compulsion *Pat Eddery* a60 51
5 br m Bertolini(USA) —Comme Ca (Cyrano De Bergerac)
584^{3} 749^{5} 937^{10} 1150^{6} 2866^{13} 4052^{9} 4707^{5} 5166^{5}
Comrade Cotton *J Ryan* a64 66
4 b g Royal Applause—Cutpurse Moll (Green Desert (USA))
4862^{11} 5474^{11} 6419^{4} 6693^{3} 6890^{5} 6951^{7} 7053^{2} 7270^{7} (7433) 7601^{8} 7765^{2} 7790^{4} 7801^{2}
Conakry *M R Channon* 50
2 ch g Imperial Dancer—Ajig Dancer (Niniski (USA))
3603^{14} 3902^{4} 4120^{4} 4604^{8} 5357^{6}
Conceal *R Bouresly* a81 103
10 b g Cadeaux Genereux—Mystery Play (IRE) (Sadler's Wells (USA))
291a^{6} 472a^{12} 497a^{9} 566a^{6}
Concentric *A Fabre* 102
4 b m Sadler's Wells(USA) —Apogee (Shirley Heights)
1713a^{7}
Conclave (IRE) *Adrian Sexton* a54 61
4 b m Key Of Luck(USA) —Dathuil (IRE) (Royal Academy (USA))
3^{4} 39^{4}
Conclusive *R M Beckett*
2 b g Selkirk(USA) —Never A Doubt (Night Shift (USA))
6602^{14}
Conduit (IRE) *Sir Michael Stoute* a79 127
3 ch c Dalakhani(IRE) —Well Head (IRE) (Sadler's Wells (USA))
1600^{3} ◆ (2825) 3193^{2} ◆ (4505) (5892) (7000a)
Confederate *George Baker* a73 39
3 b g Red Ransom(USA) —Grain Of Gold (Mr Prospector (USA))
1417^{9} 6470^{4} 7822^{2}
Conference Call *P Bary* 108
3 b f Anabaa(USA) —Phone West (USA) (Gone West (USA))
1360a^{2} 2033a^{11}
Confide (IRE) *John C McConnell* 69
6 ch g Namid—Confidential (Generous (IRE))
6366a^{10}
Confide In Me *G A Butler* a58 50
4 b g Medicean—Confidante (USA) (Dayjur (USA))
3628^{7} 4349^{14} 5157^{3} 6255^{9}
Confidentiality (IRE) *M Wigham* a88 83
4 b m Desert Style(IRE) —Confidential (Generous (IRE))
309^{4} 314^{3} 390^{2} 692^{4}
Confident Warrior (IRE) *J Pearce* 50
3 b g Viking Ruler(AUS) —Fluent (Polar Falcon (USA))
2427^{8} 2981^{7}
Confirm (IRE) *H Rogers* a45 63
4 b m In The Wings—Ashkirk (Selkirk (USA))
5873a^{7}
Confront *Sir Michael Stoute* a95 112
3 b g Nayef(USA) —Contiguous (USA) (Danzig (USA))
1471^{5} 5941^{4}
Confuchias (IRE) *K R Burke* a109 114
4 b h Cape Cross(IRE) —Schust Madame (IRE) (Second Set (IRE))
1619^{6} 2680^{4} ◆ 3488^{6} 3982a^{9} 4624^{20} 5109^{5} 6104^{3} (7381) 7492^{7} 7703^{5}
Confucius Captain (IRE) *J R Boyle* a75 74
2 b g Captain Rio—Dry Lightning (Shareef Dancer (USA))
5756^{3} 6025^{5} 6375^{11} 6717^{8} 7051^{9} 7371^{2} 7627^{2} (7646)
Congenial *J R Fanshawe* a18 53
2 b f Kyllachy—Peace (Sadler's Wells (USA))
4339^{9} 5754^{6} 6565^{12}
Congregation *J H M Gosden* a61 42
2 b c Cape Cross(IRE) —Have Faith (IRE) (Machiavellian (USA))
3274^{5} 3568^{5}
Congrio Dorado (USA) *C Von Der Recke* 42
6 b g Real Quiet(USA) —Cox Girl (USA) (Cox's Ridge (USA))
604a^{4}
Coniston Reload *M W Easterby* 23
2 ch g Reset(AUS) —Possessive Lady (Dara Monarch)
2845^{8} 4921^{11} 6187^{10}
Coniston Wood *M W Easterby* a45 45
2 b f Needwood Blade—Litewska (IRE) (Mujadil (USA))
3689^{6} 4474^{7} 5072^{7}
Conjecture *R Bastiman* a46 70
6 b g Danzig(USA) —Golden Opinion (USA) (Slew O'Gold (USA))
1827^{9} 2337^{7} 2936^{4} (3759) 4047^{6} 4293^{9} (6334) 7218^{7}
Connessa (IRE) *V Valiani* 99
4 b m Invincible Spirit(IRE) —Corbetta (IRE) (Polar Falcon (USA))
2438a^{9}

Connie Mac (IRE) *Andrew Oliver* a72 96
2 b f Elusive City(USA) —Strange Destiny (Mujadil (USA))
3123^{3} 6320a^{3}
Connor's Choice *Andrew Turnell* a78 78
3 b g Bertolini(USA) —Susan's Dowry (Efisio)
1763^{2} 2276^{12} 2976^{4} 3298^{6} 4083^{9} 4773^{7} 5616^{11} 6088^{10} 6681^{9} (6878) 7416^{6}
Conquest (IRE) *W J Haggas* a112 114
4 b g Invincible Spirit(IRE) —Aguinaga (IRE) (Machiavellian (USA))
(907) 1442^{8} 1831^{10} 2129^{7} 2598^{5} 3248^{13} 3504^{7} 3905^{11} (4624) 5109^{4} 6269^{18} (6645)
Conquisto *C G Cox* 95
3 ch g Hernando(FR) —Seal Indigo (IRE) (Glenstal (USA))
1381^{2} ◆ (1614) 2665^{8} 4790^{2} 5257^{6} 5843^{8} 6763^{4}
Conrendelo (IRE) *Adrian Sexton* 38
6 b m Blue Ocean(USA) —Comgren (IRE) (Common Grounds)
1025^{13}
Conroy (USA) *A Selvaratnam* a75 16
10 ch g Gone West(USA) —Crystal Gazing (USA) (El Gran Senor (USA))
378a^{4} 814a^{14}
Consequence *A Dickman*
2 bg g Paris House—Scrutinize (IRE) (Selkirk (USA))
7628^{4} 7773^{8}
Consequence (USA) *Claude McGaughey III* 101
2 ch f El Prado(IRE) —Educated Risk (USA) (Mr Prospector (USA))
6966a^{6}
Constant Cheers (IRE) *W R Swinburn* a78 87
5 b g Royal Applause—Juno Marlowe (IRE) (Danehill (USA))
1853^{5} (3089) (3631) 4078^{5} 6203^{6}
Consular *E Charpy* a99 87
6 br g Singspiel(IRE) —Language Of Love (Rock City)
202a^{6} 380a^{8} 568a^{5} 673a^{6}
Consulate (IRE) *D K Weld* a72 105
4 b h Rock Of Gibraltar(IRE) —Soha (USA) (Dancing Brave (USA))
5136a^{8}
Contat (GER) *P Vovcenko* 106
5 br h Diktat—Conga (Robellino (USA))
3515a^{3} 4912a^{2} 5553a^{6}
Contemplate *Dr J D Scargill*
2 ch f Compton Place—Billie Blue (Ballad Rock)
5784^{9}
Contemplation *G A Swinbank* a67 62
5 b g Sunday Silence(USA) —Wood Vine (USA) (Woodman (USA))
2274^{8} 2568^{5} 2940^{6} 3077^{6} 3593^{14}
Contented (IRE) *Mrs L C Jewell* a66 63
6 b g Orpen(USA) —Joyfullness (USA) (Dixieland Band (USA))
327^{2} 515^{5} (749) 879^{11} 2798^{5} 3383^{5} 4414^{10} 5088^{9} 5315^{9}
Contentious (IRE) *D M Simcock* a64 54
4 b m Danetime(IRE) —Serious Contender (IRE) (Tenby)
1373^{5} 2088^{7} (Dead)
Contessina (IRE) *P F I Cole* a67 47
3 ch f Medicean—Queen's Music (USA) (Dixieland Band (USA))
(12) 225^{8} 366^{3}
Contest (IRE) *David Wachman* a103 108
4 b h Danehill Dancer(IRE) —Mala Mala (IRE) (Brief Truce (USA))
(1783a) 2685a^{9} 3533a^{7} 4223a^{7} 5922a^{7}
Continent *D Nicholls* a83 95
11 ch g Lake Coniston(IRE) —Krisia (Kris)
3009^{19}
Contrada *R Charlton* a59 70
3 b c Medicean—Trounce (Barathea (IRE))
1125^{6} 1535^{9} 2977^{11} 4086^{11} (6337) 6436^{3} 6703^{11}
Contradiktive (IRE) *J R Boyle* a33
2 b g Diktat—Additive (USA) (Devil's Bag (USA))
7356^{9} 7417^{6} 7574^{9}
Contra Mundum (USA) *B G Powell* a78 58
5 ch g Giant's Causeway(USA) —Speak Softly To Me (USA) (Ogygian (USA))
(171) (282) (303) 368^{2} 540^{12} 2278^{5}
Contretemps (USA) *Saeed Bin Suroor* a42 73
2 bb c Street Cry(IRE) —Awaamir (Green Desert (USA))
5246^{5} 5901^{8} 7069^{11}
Control Zone (IRE) *B J Meehan* 101
2 ch c Daggers Drawn(USA) —Blusienka (IRE) (Blues Traveller (IRE))
(6122) ◆ 6428^{2}
Controvento (IRE) *Eamon Tyrrell* a39 71
6 b m Midhish—La Maya (IRE) (Scenic)
349^{6} 1103a^{10} 3532a^{21}
Convallaria (FR) *G Wragg* a64 64
5 b m Cape Cross(IRE) —Scarlet Davis (FR) (Ti King (FR))
209^{2} 356^{8} 703^{2} 1032^{8} 1853^{9} 3265^{12} (4825) 5317^{8} 7076^{8} (7383)
Converti *H J Manners* a57 56
4 b g Averti(IRE) —Conquestadora (Hernando (FR))
3084^{10} 3328^{5} 3698^{7} 4023^{4} 4250^{3} 4485^{5} 4691^{4} 5148^{9}
Convince (USA) *J M Bradley* a48 61
7 ch g Mt. Livermore(USA) —Conical (Zafonic (USA))
1642^{11} 2069^{9} 2917^{8} 3662^{12} 4102^{6}
Convivial Spirit *E F Vaughan* a72 64
4 b g Lake Coniston(IRE) —Ruby Princess (IRE) (Mac's Imp (USA))
4074° ◆ 448^{2} 819^{5} 1112^{7} 3764^{6} 4261^{9} 5712^{3} 6422^{4} 7012^{6} 7437^{4} 7581^{6}
Cook's Endeavour (USA) *K A Ryan* 82
2 b c Gone West(USA) —Weekend In London (USA) (Belong To Me (USA))
2134^{8} 4164^{3} (4530) 5791^{3} 6305^{8}

Cool Art (IRE) *S A Callaghan* a79 71
2 b c One Cool Cat(USA) —Fee Faw Fum (IRE) (Great Commotion (USA))
1832[5] (2086) 5242[8] (5997) 6426[26] 7335[6] (7389) 7472[3]

Cool Coal Man (USA) *Nicholas Zito* a116
3 b c Mineshaft(USA) —Coral Sea (USA) (Rubiano (USA))
1820a[15] 4678a[3]

Cool Ebony *P J Makin* 83
5 br g Erhaab(USA) —Monawara (IRE) (Namaqualand (USA))
(2101) 3478[6] 4104[3] 6177[3] 6363[7] 6899[7]

Coole Dodger (IRE) *M Sheppard* a65 75
3 ch g Where Or When(IRE) —Shining High (Shirley Heights)
266[2] 403[4] 712[7] 897[5] 1124[4] 1407[4] (1622) 2451[7] 2678[10] 3039[9] (3525) 3799[5] 4569[2] 7506[13]

Cool Fashion (IRE) *Ollie Pears* a46 43
3 b f Orpen(USA) —Fun Fashion (IRE) (Polish Patriot (USA))
487[5] 2661[7] 3283[9] 4028[8] 4686[7] 5501[7] 6173[8] 6822[6]

Cool Hand Jake *P J Makin* a69 57
2 b c Storming Home—Monawara (IRE) (Namaqualand (USA))
6893[8] 7699[4] ◆

Cool Isle *P Howling* a56 45
5 b m Polar Prince(IRE) —Fisher Island (IRE) (Sri Pekan (USA))
83[5] 145[5] 377[5] 776[6]

Cool Judgement (IRE) *M A Jarvis* 100
3 b g Peintre Celebre(USA) —Sadinga (IRE) (Sadler's Wells (USA))
(1805) 2665[2] 3925[3] 5494[3] ◆ 5853[8] 6646[6]

Cool Libby (IRE) *A B Haynes* a30 54
2 br f One Cool Cat(USA) —Cosabawn (IRE) (Barathea (IRE))
6893[7] 7380[14]

Cool Madam *D Flood*
2 b f Ishiguru(USA) —Face The Judge (USA) (Benny The Dip (USA))
7593[14]

Cool Sands (IRE) *J G Given* a78 56
6 b g Trans Island—Shalerina (USA) (Shalford (IRE))
4[4] 150[2] 275[5] 359[4] 442[4] 539[10] 964[5] 1153[6] 1261[4] 1455[7] 1703[4] 2662[13] 2927[14] 3175[9] (4478) 5629[9] 5709[9] 6356[4] (6773) 7048[4] (7152) 7286[2] 7534[4] 7633[8]

Cool Sonata (IRE) *M Brittain* a37 45
2 b f One Cool Cat(USA) —Sonatina (Distant Relative)
1889[2] 2217[8] 2443[6] 3008[10] 4045[10] 5632[8] 7269[3] 7514[12]

Cool Strike (UAE) *A M Balding* a65 61
2 b g Halling(USA) —Velour (Mtoto)
5754[5] 6451[2] 7073[8]

Cool Tarifa (IRE) *J G Burns* a77 81
2 b f One Cool Cat(USA) —Tarafiya (USA) (Trempolino (USA))
2686a[5] 3466a[5]

Cool The Heels (IRE) *J S Moore* a58 59
3 b g Catcher In The Rye(IRE) —Alinea (USA) (Kingmambo (USA))
5146[6]

Cooper Island Kid (USA) *P W D'Arcy* a42 62
2 bb g Arch(USA) —Raven Quiver (USA) (Old Trieste (USA))
5939[12] 6423[9] 7106[7]

Copperbeech (IRE) *A Fabre* 107
2 b f Red Ransom(USA) —Aynthia (USA) (Zafonic (USA))
6519a[3]

Copperbottomed (IRE) *P G Murphy* a69 61
3 ch g Redback—Stoneware (Bigstone (IRE))
81[2] 108[3] 403[3] (462) 572[3] 635[2] (845) (1117) 1536[2] 2099[9] (2803) 3330[2] 4056[5] 4476[13] 6377[8] 6628[9] 7018[14] 7317[11] 7560[11]

Copper Dock (IRE) *T G McCourt* a83 82
4 b g Docksider(USA) —Sundown (Polish Precedent (USA))
6963a[8]

Copper King *Miss Tor Sturgis* a67 80
4 ch g Ishiguru(USA) —Dorissio (IRE) (Efisio)
148[4] 302[2] 407[5] 576[12] 879[9] 1280[9] 1705[5] 3037[7] 3567[10] (7469) 7763[8]

Copperwood *M Blanshard* a61 74
3 ch g Bahamian Bounty—Sophielu (Rudimentary (USA))
500[6] 777[6] 1277[7] 1958[6] 4081[7] 4524[5] 4863[9] 5218[7] 7541[7] 7817[5]

Coral Creek (IRE) *M J Grassick* a73 73
4 b m Invincible Spirit(IRE) —Antapoura (IRE) (Bustino)
6629[6]

Coral Point (IRE) *S Kirk* a38
2 ch c Hawkeye(IRE) —Green Crystal (Green Dancer (USA))
3821[9] 4304[10] 5022[11] 6135[9] 7425[9]

Coral Shores *P W Hiatt* a57 68
3 b f Carnival Dancer—Leading Role (Cadeaux Genereux)
184[6] 325[6] 439[2] 556[2] 657[2] (704) 865[2] 940[6] 1034[7] 1938[4] 2288[7] 3166[2] (3551) 4254[5] 4964[3] 5308[5] 5815[3] 6050[5] 6235[3] 6868[5] 7620[8]

Corconte (FR) *R Avial Lopez* 98
3 b c Sagacity(FR) —Joie De Rose (FR) (Procida (USA))
6612a[7]

Cordage (IRE) *M F Harris* a26 54
6 ch g Dr Fong(USA) —Flagship (Rainbow Quest (USA))
(3025) 4811[12] 7469[12]

Cordell (IRE) *R Hannon* a98 76
3 b c Fasliyev(USA) —Urgele (FR) (Zafonic (USA))
902[3] (966)

Cordoba (GER) *H Steinmetz*
2 b f Tiger Hill(IRE) —Chato's Girl (GER) (Chato (USA))
7006a[12] 7549a[6]

Corking (IRE) *J L Flint* a37 59
3 b f Montjeu(IRE) —Scanno's Choice (IRE) (Pennine Walk)
2716[5] 4173[10] 5215[2] 5868[12] 6719[2] 6897[3]

Corlough Mountain *P Butler* a74 74
4 ch g Inchinor—Two Step (Mujtahid (USA))
63[6] 452[7] 609[7] 1038[4] 1954[9] 2557[3] 2861[2] 3966[6] 4186[3] ◆ 4414[13] 4865[7] 5458[8] 6209[7] 6396[4] 6719[11] 7385[9] 7520[5] 7806[10]

Cormorant Wharf (IRE) *T E Powell* a74 74
8 b g Alzao(USA) —Mercy Bien (IRE) (Be My Guest (USA))
1932[8] 2561[5] 4819[7] 5512[12]

Cornerstone *S C Williams* a58 58
4 ch g Pivotal—Splice (Sharpo)
235[5] 446[6] 663[6] 1160[16] 1578[14] 2837[5] 3034[4] 3501[3] 3842[6]

Cornish Castle (USA) *H R A Cecil* 61
2 ch c Mizzen Mast(USA) —Rouwaki (USA) (Miswaki (USA))
5246[9] 6085[12]

Cornish Rose (IRE) *M H Tompkins* 71
2 b f Kheleyf(USA) —Kiva (Indian Ridge)
2160[5] (3432) 3910[3] 4589[10] 6082[4] 6700[4]

Cornus *A J McCabe* a86 87
6 ch g Inchinor—Demerger (USA) (Distant View (USA))
85[5] 313[3] 456[3] 532[7] 618[4] 824[7] 1069[2] 1327[10] 1430[14] 1617[3] 1796[5] 2188[3] 2535[7] 2818[6] 3054[6] 3626[12] 4218[5] 4375[2] 4831[3] 5067[6] 5247[7] 6278[9] 6724[8] 7143[5] 7239[2] 7557[6] 7837[5]

Coronado's Gold (USA) *B Ellison* a40 63
7 ch g Coronado's Quest(USA) —Debit My Account (USA) (Classic Account (USA))
989[2] 1296[6] 1482[6] 1892[2] 2252[5] 2467[12] 5559[6] 6115[10] 6550[2] 6812[7]

Coronet Of A Baron (USA) *Eoin Harty* a108 108
2 ch c Pure Prize(USA) —Time For A Crown (USA) (Time For A Change (USA))
6998a[3]

Corran Ard (IRE) *Evan Williams* 89
7 b g Imperial Ballet(IRE) —Beeper The Great (USA) (Whadjathink (USA))
4191[8] 5054[6]

Corredor Sun (USA) *Carl Llewellyn* a45 62
2 b g El Corredor(USA) —Cozzie Maxine (USA) (Cozzene (USA))
3372[10] 4788[9] 6330[5]

Corrib (IRE) *B Palling* a61 72
5 b m Lahib(USA) —Montana Miss (IRE) (Earl Of Barking (IRE))
128[9] 5059[8] 5712[6] 6136[3] 6538[3] 6882[4] 7427[7] 7688[11]

Corridor Creeper (FR) *J M Bradley* a64 105
11 ch g Polish Precedent(USA) —Sonia Rose (USA) (Superbity (USA))
1366[4] 1537[2] 1802[10] 5648[4] 5861[12] 6006[11] 6225[5] 6448[11]

Corriolanus (GER) *A M Balding* a65 101
8 b g Zamindar(USA) —Caesarea (GER) (Generous (IRE))
7744[3]

Corrybrough *H Candy* 114
3 ch c Kyllachy—Calamanco (Clantime)
(1597) ◆ (2498) ◆ (3041) ◆ 4188[2] 4881a[5] 5891[4]

Corso Palladio (IRE) *B P J Baugh* 60
6 b g Montjeu(IRE) —Falafil (FR) (Fabulous Dancer (USA))
5993[9] 6606[11]

Corton Charlemagne (IRE) *Rae Guest* a66
2 b f King Charlemagne(USA) —Teller (ARG) (Southern Halo (USA))
5939[2] 6434[3] 6770[8] 7205[4]

Corum (IRE) *Mrs K Waldron* a89 88
5 b g Galileo(IRE) —Vallee Des Reves (USA) (Kingmambo (USA))
1080[6] 1998[9] 2264[6] 2952[10] 3891[4]

Coseadrom (IRE) *C Von Der Recke* a63 82
6 b g Almutawakel—Madam Lightfoot (USA) (Vice Regent (CAN))
(421a) 603a[8]

Cosimo *Sir Michael Stoute* a72 36
2 ch g Medicean—Flight Soundly (IRE) (Caerleon (USA))
7051[12] 7209[2]

Cosimo Primo *J A Geake* a47 13
4 b g Medicean—Cugina (Distant Relative)
1528[14]

Cosmea *A King* a51 83
3 b f Compton Place—St James's Antigua (IRE) (Law Society (USA))
2563[7] 3206[2] (3562) ◆ (4152) ◆ 4621[2] 5464[4] 6127[7]

Cosmic Destiny (IRE) *E F Vaughan* a79 76
6 b m Soviet Star(USA) —Cruelle (USA) (Irish River (FR))
840[2] 1646[7] 2102[11] 2351[3] 3575[2] 3695[3] 4563[4] 4809[3] 5401[3] 6006[10] 6131[13] 6925[8] 7478[4] (7517)

Cosmic Fire (FR) *D Sepulchre* 102
3 gr f Dalakhani(IRE) —Burning Sunset (Caerleon (USA))
5039a[6] 7487a[0]

Cosmic Messenger (FR) *L A Dace* a22 11
5 ch g Septieme Ciel(USA) —Bonnie And Howard (USA) (Fly So Free (USA))
5583[11] 6022[11]

Cosmic String (IRE) *Dr R D P Newland* 84
6 ch g In The Wings—Continuous (IRE) (Darshaan)
7744[11]

Cosmic Sun *R A Fahey* 81
2 b g Helissio(FR) —Cosmic Case (Casteddu)
3140[8] 3590[2] 4394[2] 4960[2] 5497[2] 5895[8] 6101[2] 6655[4]

Cosmo Bulk (JPN) *K Tabe* 114
7 b h Zagreb(USA) —Iseno Tosho (JPN) (Tosho Boy (JPN))
2234a[6] 7511a[17]

Cosmodrome (USA) *L M Cumani* a88 103
4 b m Bahri(USA) —Space Time (FR) (Bering)
1331[5] 1807[6] 3088[2] 4667[8] 4977[8]

Cosmopolitan *J H M Gosden* 89
3 ch f Cadeaux Genereux—Parisian Elegance (Zilzal (USA))
2566[DSQ] 6981[3] ◆

Cossack Prince *Mrs L J Mongan* a78 73
3 b g Dubai Destination(USA) —Danemere (IRE) (Danehill (USA))
1600[10] 2151[14] 3095[8] 3421[4] 3697[2] 4067[7] 5169[5] 6248[3] 6594[2] (7078)

Costa Lotta *E A L Dunlop* 61
2 b f Statue Of Liberty(USA) —Costa Balena (CHI) (Great Regent (CAN))
3032[7] 4149[9] 4692[7] 6118[15]

Cost Analysis (IRE) *Mrs P Ford* a37
6 ch g Grand Lodge(USA) —Flower Girl (Pharly (FR))
684[11]

Cote D'Argent *L Lungo* 55
5 b g Lujain(USA) —In The Groove (Night Shift (USA))
1520[8] 6862[10]

Cotes D'Armor (FR) *H-A Pantall* 89
2 ch f Numerous(USA) —Macotte (FR) (Nicolotte)
5486a[5]

Cotswolds *M Johnston* 41
3 br g Green Desert(USA) —Valley Of Gold (FR) (Shirley Heights)
6566[8]

Cottage Club (IRE) *N Clement* 46
3 b f Singspiel(IRE) —Quatre Saisons (FR) (Homme De Loi (IRE))
6742a[9]

Cottam Grange *M W Easterby* a17 39
8 b g River Falls—Karminski (Pitskelly)
3335[9] 4924[9]

Cotton Eyed Joe (IRE) *G A Swinbank* a78 85
7 b g Indian Rocket—Cwm Deri (IRE) (Alzao (USA))
981[9] 1340[4] (1589) 1824[3] (2822) 3368[4] 4178[8] 4742[5] 6313[3] 6838[5]

Cottonmouth (IRE) *A & G Botti* 99
4 b m Noverre(USA) —Nafzira (IRE) (Darshaan)
2438a[2]

Cotton N Silk *T D Easterby* 19
2 b f Mujahid(USA) —Bollin Janet (Sheikh Albadou)
2362[10] 3005[9] 3830[6]

Cotton Reel *P F I Cole* a53 77
3 b g Cape Cross(IRE) —Cotton House (IRE) (Mujadil (USA))
1855[6] 4195[6] 4349[6] 4777[10] 5616[13]

Coughlans Locke (IRE) *Kieran P Cotter* a53 60
5 b g All My Dreams(IRE) —Inniu (IRE) (Tirol)
6735[7] 7503[7]

Councellor (FR) *Stef Liddiard* a94 80
6 b g Gilded Time(USA) —Sudden Storm Bird (USA) (Storm Bird (CAN))
594[7] 832[7] 1045[5] 1211[4] 1335[7] 1857[5] 2083[3] (2329) 2860[3] 2995[4] 6710[4] 7313[4] 7439[8] 7633[3] (7737)

Count Almaviva (USA) *K A Ryan* a61 72
2 ch c Rossini(USA) —Mimi Kat (USA) (Storm Cat (USA))
1118[3] 1303[2] 4923[3] 5451[2] 5960[9] 6732[9]

Countback (FR) *A W Carroll* a52 16
9 b g Anabaa(USA) —Count Me Out (FR) (Kaldoun (FR))
36[2] 152[6] 499[4]

Count Ceprano (IRE) *C R Dore* a88 89
4 b g Desert Prince(IRE) —Camerlata (Common Grounds)
245[3] 302[3] 429[5] (609) 717[3] 775[2] 969[2] ◆ 1084[2] (1409) ◆ 1857[7] 1982[6] 2308[2] ◆ 2995[5] 3197[15] 3317[2] 3840[4] 4104[5] (4627) 4723[4] 5207[9] 5675[7] 6120[16] 6771[10] 7592[7]

Count Cougar (USA) *S P Griffiths* a80 19
8 b g Sir Cat(USA) —Gold Script (USA) (Seeking The Gold (USA))
1134[6] 1261[8] 1901[8] 7323[11] 7448[11] 7534[13]

Countdown *M D Squance* a89 92
6 ch g Pivotal—Quiz Time (Efisio)
1481[12] 1815[9] 2158[3] 2818[8] 3367[9] 3599[3] 3928[5] 4417[2] 5419[7] 6478[5] (6734) 7313[7]

Counterclaim *H-A Pantall* a75 95
3 ch f Pivotal—Dusty Answer (Zafonic (USA))
3076a[2] 5329a[5] 6691a[8]

Countess Zara (IRE) *A M Balding* a49 65
2 b f Xaar—Lochridge (Indian Ridge)
4974[9] 6016[8] 6399[3] 6655[5] 7190[10]

Counting House (IRE) *J A B Old* a68 85
5 ch g King's Best(USA) —Inforapenny (Deploy)
6210[12]

Count Of Tuscany (USA) *Mrs A J Perrett* 68
2 b c Arch(USA) —Corsini (Machiavellian (USA))
7106[3]

Count On Guest *G G Margarson* 63
2 ch g Fantastic Light(USA) —Countess Guest (IRE) (Spectrum (IRE))
4256[12] 4488[4]

Count Paris (USA) *M Johnston* 75
2 ch c Pivotal—Dearly (Rahy (USA))
4510[6] 5053[7] 5499[3] (5785) (6149) ◆ 6533[3] 6970[4] 7241[9]

Countrywide Belle *J L Flint*
5 b m Josr Algarhoud(IRE) —Dancing Bluebell (IRE) (Bluebird (USA))
37[P] (Dead)

Countrywide City (IRE) *P W Chapple-Hyam* a64 75
2 b c Elusive City(USA) —Handy Station (IRE) (Desert Style (IRE))
2117[4] 2909[2] (3178) 3470[2] 3908[3] 6525[12] 6739[5]

Countrywide Comet (IRE) *P Howling* a62 60
3 b g Desert Style(IRE) —Darzao (IRE) (Alzao (USA))
154[5] 797[6] 1081[4]

Countrywide Jaime (IRE) *S A Callaghan* a18
2 b f Danetime(IRE) —Naraina (IRE) (Desert Story (IRE))
7802[8]

Countrywide Luck *B N Pollock* a31 77
7 b g Inchinor—Thelma (Blakeney)
1405[9] 1702[7]

Count Trevisio (IRE) *J R Gask* a62 108
5 b g Danehill(USA) —Stylish (Anshan)
7740[8]

County Crystal *T D Easterby* 39
3 b g Mujahid(USA) —Cumbrian Crystal (Mind Games)
5261[10]

County Kerry (UAE) *Jean-Rene Auvray* a54 33
4 b m Jade Robbery(USA) —Limerick Belle (IRE) (Roi Danzig (USA))
624[10] 881[12]

Coup D'Etat *R A Harris* a52 79
6 b g Diktat—Megdale (IRE) (Waajib)
1900[14] 2101[12] 2477[7] 2642[4] 2992[8] 3360[11] 3607[7] 4168[10] 4707[6] 4808[10] 5429[9] 6335[9]

Coup De Torchon (FR) *J A Osborne* a29 56
3 b f Namid—Tashtiyana (IRE) (Doyoun)
2084[7] 3180[4] 3333[9] 4770[3] 5574[13]

Courageous (IRE) *B Smart* 101
2 ch c Refuse To Bend(IRE) —Bella Bella (IRE) (Sri Pekan (USA))
(4213) 5093[5] 5825[2] 6973[5]

Courageous Duke (USA) *Doug Watson* a31 89
9 b g Spinning World(USA) —Araadh (USA) (Blushing Groom (FR))
477a[10] 669a[8]

Courageous Nature (IRE) *A J McCabe* a62 55
2 b g Invincible Spirit(IRE) —Special Park (USA) (Trempolino (USA))
2146[11] 2601[8] 3020[6] 5363[5] (5614) 5997[6] 6281[9] 6489[4] 6574[5] 7205[7] 7281[3] 7319[3] 7443[5] 7530[8]

Courageuse (FR) *E Lellouche* a77 90
3 gr f Linamix(FR) —Lavandou (Sadler's Wells (USA))
1760a[5] 2743a[7]

Court Approval (IRE) *T G Mills* a75 76
2 b c Royal Applause—Nayzak (USA) (Silver Hawk (USA))
1983[3] 3105[18] 4020[2] 4525[9] 4905[4] 5466[12] (5904) 6023[2] 6281[8]

Court Canibal *M Delzangles* 105
3 b c Montjeu(IRE) —Pas D'Heure (IRE) (Arazi (USA))
1239a[2] 1887a[5] 6517a[3] 6921a[5] 7598a[5]

Court Judgement (IRE) *T D Easterby*
2 b c Diktat—Sharpe's Lady (Prince Des Coeurs (USA))
2657[10]

Court Of Appeal *B Ellison* a64 71
11 ch g Bering—Hiawatha's Song (USA) (Chief's Crown (USA))
1184[3] (1305) 1890[5] 2395[3] 2623[6] 2776[3] 3176[3] 3589[3] 4556[8] 5003[2] 5396[5] 6115[4] 6309[2] 6806[7]

Court Vision (USA) *William Mott* a111 110
3 b c Gulch(USA) —Weekend Storm (USA) (Storm Bird (CAN))
1820a[13]

Cousin Charlie *S Kirk* a65 28
2 b c Choisir(AUS) —Michelle Ma Belle (IRE) (Shareef Dancer (USA))
6604[14] 7380[12] 7783[3]

Cove Mountain (IRE) *M G Rimell* a44 51
6 br m Indian Danehill(IRE) —Nordic Pride (Horage)
7[10]

Cover Drive (USA) *Christian Wroe* a74 61
5 br g Giant's Causeway(USA) —Woodland Orchid (IRE) (Woodman (USA))
4789[7] 5639[9] 6577[6] 7078[5] 7440[9]

Covert Ambition *Saeed Bin Suroor* 101
3 ch c Singspiel(IRE) —Super Tassa (IRE) (Lahib (USA))
(6762)

Covert Mission *P D Evans* a66 61
5 b m Overbury(IRE) —Peg's Permission (Ra Nova)
6596[7] (7039) 7169[2] 7272[8]

Cowboy Cal (USA) *Todd Pletcher* a114 110
3 bb c Giant's Causeway(USA) —Texas Tammy (USA) (Seeking The Gold (USA))
1820a[9]

Cow Girl (IRE) *Miss Gay Kelleway* a58 67
4 b m King's Best(USA) —Reveuse De Jour (IRE) (Sadler's Wells (USA))
48[2] 123[7] 338[7] 375[9] 521[7] 4383[11] 4793[5] 4806[5]

Coyote Creek *E F Vaughan* 91
4 b g Zilzal(USA) —High Barn (Shirley Heights)
1458[4] 2153[3] (2591) 3505[7] 5100[4] 6061[6] 6479[8]

Cozy Tiger (USA) *W J Musson* a76 70
3 gr g Hold That Tiger(USA) —Cozelia (USA) (Cozzene (USA))
1748[12] 5361[6] 5964[7] 6703[4] ◆

Crackdown (IRE) *M Johnston* 88
2 b c Refuse To Bend(IRE) —Whitefoot (Be My Chief (USA))
2951[3] 4199[2] ◆ 4954[3] 5825[6] (6176)

Crackentorp *G L Moore* a93 79
3 b g Generous(IRE) —Raspberry Sauce (Niniski (USA))
4349[3] (4860) (5682) ◆

Cracking Nick (IRE) *W R Swinburn* a70 70
3 b g Cape Cross(IRE) —Enrich (USA) (Dynaformer (USA))
1110[4] 1548[3] 2122[8] 2991[11] 3506[12] 4186[10] 5015[7] 5601[10] 6716[7]

Craft (FR) *B J Meehan* a42 13
2 b c Numerous(USA) —Anyone For Tennis (IRE) (Night Shift (USA))
2944[9] 3331[9] 3645[10] 5314[18]

Crafty Dealer (IRE) *J W Hills* a65
3 b g Intikhab(USA) —Lizanne (USA) (Theatrical)
543[2] 5049[4] 5426[5] 6091[5]

Crafty Fox *John A Harris* a53 58
5 b g Foxhound(USA) —Surrealist (ITY) (Night Shift (USA))
1116[10] 2463[16] 2866[4] 3371[4] 4026[10] 4748[7] 7772[11]

Craggamore Creek *D Morris* a61 31
5 b g Tipsy Creek(USA) —Polish Abbey (Polish Precedent (USA))
(37) 76[3] (438) 1121[6] 2053[7] 5593[11] 7265[10] 7520[2]

Craigstown *Saeed Bin Suroor* 94
3 b c Cape Cross(IRE)—Craigmill (Slip Anchor)
3043^{2} (3521) 4448^{4} (5098) 5202^{5}

Cranworth Blaze *T J Etherington* a49 46
4 b m Diktat—Julietta Mia (USA) (Woodman (USA))
2008^{12} 2966^{7} 3786^{4} 4877^{6} 6045^{5} 6224^{2} 6595^{8} 7196^{12}

Crataegus *H Candy* a49 67
3 b g Gorse—Dove Tree (FR) (Charnwood Forest (IRE))
3818^{3} 4301^{7} 4709^{3} 5267^{2} ◆ 5755^{7} 6338^{11}

Crazy About You (IRE) *B W Hills* a52 71
3 b f Montjeu(IRE)—Touch Of Magic (IRE) (Brief Truce (USA))
1367^{3} 2197^{13} 5864^{4} 6748^{2} 6896^{5} 7583^{6}

Crazy Bear (IRE) *K J Burke* a69 53
5 ch m King Charlemagne(USA)—Specifiedrisk (IRE) (Turtle Island (IRE))
970^{7}

Crazy Colours *Jane Chapple-Hyam* a55
2 ch c Dalakhani(IRE)—Eternity Ring (Alzao (USA))
7552^{7} 7812^{7}

Creachadoir (IRE) *Saeed Bin Suroor* 124
4 b h King's Best(USA)—Sadima (IRE) (Sadler's Wells (USA))
1090a^{8} (2193)

Creative (IRE) *M H Tompkins* 68
3 b g Acclamation—Pride Of Pendle (Grey Desire)
2047^{9} 2429^{8} 2982^{9} 3886^{15} 4793^{8} 5045^{7}

Credential *John A Harris* a55 58
6 b h Dansili—Sabria (USA) (Miswaki (USA))
(3657) 3965^{4} 4485^{8} 5321^{3} 5961^{12} 6930^{8}

Credit Swap *L M Cumani* a84 84
3 b g Diktat—Locharia (Wolfhound (USA))
2919^{2} (3268) 5273^{8} 5962^{3} 6194^{5} 6734^{2}

Creme Brulee *P T Dalton* a61 53
5 b m College Chapel—Balinsky (IRE) (Skyliner)
106^{5}

Creshendo *R M Beckett* 72
2 b c Kyllachy—Dry Wit (IRE) (Desert Prince (IRE))
(2562)

Crete (IRE) *W J Haggas* a93 98
6 b g Montjeu(IRE)—Paesanella (Seattle Song (USA))
(3003) ◆ 3929^{10} 4191^{5} 5423^{4} 6061^{2} 6646^{19} 6784^{6}

Crewezando *P D Evans* a37 66
2 b g Forzando—Aunt Susan (Distant Relative)
1425^{5} 1778^{5} 1924^{9} 2459^{2} 2671^{12} 3091^{9}

Cribnote (USA) *Richard Violette Jr* a103
2 ch c Read The Footnotes(USA)—Totebook (USA) (Notebook (USA))
6501a^{3}

Crime Scene (IRE) *Saeed Bin Suroor* 115
5 b g Royal Applause—Crime (USA) (Gulch (USA))
816a^{6} 4585^{12} 5885^{4}

Crimson And Gold *L Reuterskiold Jr* a92 98
6 b g Singspiel(IRE)—Rosia (IRE) (Mr Prospector (USA))
2708a^{10}

Crimson Fern (IRE) *M S Saunders* a69 102
4 ch m Titus Livius(FR)—Crimada (IRE) (Mukaddamah (USA))
87^{4} 181^{2} (270) ◆ (338) 488^{4} 1312^{7} 2102^{10} (2330) ◆ 2583^{2} (2760) 3062^{3} (3680) (3943) ◆ 4550^{8} 4840^{5} 5509^{2} 5899^{3} 6429^{7}

Crimson Flame (IRE) *G F Bridgwater* a48 73
5 b g Celtic Swing—Wish List (IRE) (Mujadil (USA))
862^{10}

Crimson King (IRE) *R W Price* a89
7 ch g Pivotal—Always Happy (Sharrood (USA))
43^{2} 532^{5} 1500^{4}

Crimson Mitre *J Jay* a46 68
3 b c Bishop Of Cashel—Pink Champagne (Cosmonaut)
1140^{4} (1549) 1962^{14} 3393^{12}

Crimsonwing (IRE) *A M Hales* a54 56
3 b f Vettori(IRE)—Crimson Topaz (Hernando (FR))
2559^{7} 4053^{10} 4810^{4} 6436^{5} 7274^{7}

Cripsey Brook *K G Reveley* 83
10 ch g Lycius(USA)—Duwon (IRE) (Polish Precedent (USA))
6216^{5} 6395^{9} 6727^{14}

Crispian (IRE) *Jamie Snowden* a55 54
4 b g Hernando(FR)—Continuous (IRE) (Darshaan)
(545) 6252^{8} 6396^{14} 7085^{7} 7831^{9}

Cristal Clear (IRE) *T D Easterby* 90
3 gr f Clodovil(IRE)—Spring To Light (USA) (Blushing Groom (FR))
1623^{9} 2104^{10} 3794^{2} 4416^{5} 5795^{11} 6053^{6} 6484^{9}

Cristal Island (IRE) *Thomas Mullins* a77 95
2 ch f Trans Island—Cristalita (IRE) (Entrepreneur)
5546a^{3} 6320a^{4} 6637a^{8}

Cristobal (USA) *J-C Rouget* 107
4 br h Aptitude(USA)—Balenciaga (USA) (Gulch (USA))
4880a^{3} 5926a^{3} 7598a^{8}

Criterion *Ian Williams* 81
3 b g Dr Fong(USA)—Film Script (Unfuwain (USA))
1367^{2} (1814) 2310^{2} 3471^{4} 4784^{9}

Critical Acclaim *J H M Gosden* a78 85
3 b f Peintre Celebre(USA)—High Praise (USA) (Quest For Fame)
(6168) 7108^{5}

Critical Stage (IRE) *J D Frost* a70 59
9 b g King's Theatre(IRE)—Zandaka (FR) (Doyoun)
388^{2} 551^{4} 2715^{3} 3377^{5}

Crocodile Bay (IRE) *John A Harris* a81 93
5 b g Spectrum(IRE)—Shenkara (IRE) (Night Shift (USA))
1067^{6} (2271) 2535^{2} 2733^{8} 2969^{6} 3122^{18} 3491^{13} 4559^{2} 6215^{4} 6482^{19} 6736^{10} 6841^{3} 7048^{2} 7115^{3} 7277^{9} 7423^{9} (7631) 7780^{9}

Crocus Rose *H J L Dunlop* 40
2 b f Royal Applause—Crodelle (IRE) (Formidable (USA))
7200^{8}

Croeso Bach *J L Spearing* 66
4 b m Bertolini(USA)—Croeso-I-Cymru (Welsh Captain)
(2934) (3783) 4106^{8} 5171^{4} 6339^{14}

Croeso Cusan *J L Spearing* 67
3 b f Diktat—Croeso Croeso (Most Welcome)
1960^{13} 2279^{4} 2774^{10} 3314^{6} 4049^{4} 5167^{3} (5816) 6746^{2}

Croi Mo Ri (IRE) *P D Deegan* a91 97
3 b g Monashee Mountain(USA)—Wide Meadow (Zafonic (USA))
1356a^{2} 1783a^{7} 2793^{3} 3532a^{7}

Crooked Throw (IRE) *C F Swan* a89 108
9 bb g Anshan—Mary's View (IRE) (Phardante (FR))
829a^{7} (1105a) 1355a^{4} 3536a^{9} 3983a^{6} 4512a^{13} 6516a^{8}

Crosby Jemma *J R Weymes* 48
4 ch m Lomitas—Gino's Spirits (Perugino (USA))
2365^{8} 2523^{6} 2940^{5} 3360^{10}

Crossbow Creek *M G Rimell* a90 89
10 b g Lugana Beach—Roxy River (Ardross)
409^{5} 927^{6} 1502^{9} 1799^{3} (2585) 3060^{9} 3480^{3} 5569^{12} 6272^{10} 6472^{6}

Cross Fell (USA) *J R Boyle* a85 79
3 b c Cherokee Run(USA)—Campsie Fells (UAE) (Indian Ridge)
136^{7} (489) 756^{3} 2794^{7} 3273^{8}

Crossharbour *A Fabre* 119
4 b h Zamindar(USA)—Docklands (USA) (Theatrical)
(3053a) 4212a^{6} 5114a^{2} 5954a^{5} (6854a)

Crossing *William J Fitzpatrick* a97 106
7 b m Cape Cross(IRE)—Piney River (Pharly (FR))
672a^{6} 745a^{7} 4007a^{11} 5547a^{6} 7328a^{3}

Crossing Bridges *T D Barron* a32 16
3 ch f Dr Fong(USA)—Pontressina (USA) (St Jovite (USA))
1894^{10} 2929^{10}

Cross Of Lorraine (IRE) *C Grant* a72 72
5 b g Pivotal—My-Lorraine (IRE) (Mac's Imp (USA))
1826^{3} 2751^{12} 3454^{16} 5392^{9}

Cross Section (USA) *E F Vaughan* a71
2 bb f Cape Cross(IRE)—Demure (Machiavellian (USA))
6737^{2} ◆

Crosstar *M Botti* a77 24
3 b c Cape Cross(IRE)—Pie High (Salse (USA))
1208^{3} 1381^{10} 1745^{8} (Dead)

Cross The Line (IRE) *A P Jarvis* a88 86
7 b g Cape Cross(IRE)—Baalbek (Barathea (IRE))
1335^{5} 1502^{6} 1857^{10} 3006^{7} 3612^{6} 4364^{5} 5350^{10} 6867^{8}

Crowded House *B J Meehan* a93 121
2 ch c Rainbow Quest(USA)—Wiener Wald (USA) (Woodman (USA))
5246^{10} (5672) ◆ 6474^{2} (6973) ◆

Crown Affair (IRE) *J W Hills* 39
2 b f Royal Applause—Alyousufeya (IRE) (Kingmambo (USA))
4149^{14} 4562^{P}

Crown Choice *W R Swinburn* 77
3 b g King's Best(USA)—Belle Allemande (CAN) (Royal Academy (USA))
1417^{3} 1926^{8}

Crown The Chief (USA) *Helen Pitts*
2 u c (USA) — (USA) (Carson City (USA))
6502a^{6}

Crow's Nest Lad *J O'Reilly* a63 68
4 b g Komaite(USA)—Miss Fit (IRE) (Hamas (IRE))
190^{7} 1192^{4} 1258^{8} 1578^{15}

Crow Wood *J J Quinn* a100 74
9 b g Halling(USA)—Play With Me (IRE) (Alzao (USA))
4662^{9} 5391^{7} (Dead)

Cruel Sea (USA) *B W Hills* 92
3 gr f Mizzen Mast(USA)—Storm Dove (USA) (Storm Bird (CAN))
1833^{2} 2105^{6} 3124^{15} 5120^{5} 6034^{14}

Cruikadyke *P F I Cole* 93
2 b c Kyllachy—Shoshone (Be My Chief (USA))
(4438) 6317a^{8} 6779^{5}

Cruise Control *R J Price* a20
2 b c Piccolo—Urban Dancer (IRE) (Generous (IRE))
7823^{11}

Cruise Director *Ian Williams* a85 89
8 b g Zilzal(USA)—Briggsmaid (Elegant Air)
962^{11} 1613^{4} 1947^{2} 2153^{13} 3045^{11} 3630^{6} 4299^{6} 5183^{4} 5900^{11}

Crusoe's Return *L M Cumani* a79 81
3 b c Selkirk(USA)—Colorsnap (Shirley Heights)
2370^{5} 3094^{2} 4695^{5} 5505^{3} 6470^{2} (6748)

Crux *R E Barr* a40 57
6 b g Pivotal—Penny Dip (Cadeaux Genereux)
1138^{8}

Cry For The Moon (USA) *Mrs A J Perrett* 72
2 b c Street Cry(IRE)—Kafaf (USA) (Zilzal (USA))
5246^{8} 6026^{7} 6398^{3}

Crying Aloud (USA) *P A Blockley* a93 82
3 bb f Street Cry(IRE)—Angelic Deed (USA) (Alydeed (CAN))
(1132) ◆ 1401^{14} (5594) 5990^{7} 6532^{12}

Cry Of Freedom (USA) *M Johnston* 100
2 b g Street Cry(IRE)—Tustarta (USA) (Trempolino (USA))
(4311) (5093) 5507^{8} 6474^{16} 6979^{10}

Cryptic Clue (USA) *Mrs R A Carr* a43 47
4 b g Cryptoclearance(USA)—Nidd (USA) (Known Fact (USA))
189^{10} 371^{7} 1674^{9} 2491^{4} 2869^{8} 2936^{15} 3139^{16} 3231^{11}

Cryptonite Diamond (USA) *W R Swinburn* a48 62
3 ch f Hennessy(USA)—Cryptotoo (USA) (Cryptoclearance (USA))
2549^{8} 3395^{7} (4725)

Crystal Capella *Sir Michael Stoute* a75 107
3 b f Cape Cross(IRE)—Crystal Star (Mark Of Esteem (IRE))
1964^{2} (2536) (4435) (5311) (6241) (6819) ◆

Crystal Crown (IRE) *David Wachman* a60 70
4 b g Grand Lodge(USA)—Top Crystal (IRE) (Sadler's Wells (USA))
7374^{3}

Crystal Feather *E F Vaughan* a29
2 ch f Monsieur Bond(IRE)—Prince's Feather (IRE) (Cadeaux Genereux)
7734^{5}

Crystal Gazer (FR) *R Hannon* a88 82
4 b m Elnadim(USA)—Chrysalu (Distant Relative)
733^{3} 925^{5} 2565^{8} 2679^{6} 3138^{7}

Crystallize *A B Haynes* a50 62
2 b g Bertolini(USA)—Adamas (IRE) (Fairy King (USA))
3519^{8} 4184^{14} 5812^{3} 6632^{5}

Crystal Moments *E A L Dunlop* a86 82
2 b f Haafhd—Celestial Choir (Celestial Storm (USA))
(2309) 3865^{4} (4525) (5153) 6240^{19}

Crystal Prince *C E Longsdon* a68 77
4 b g Marju(IRE)—Crystal Ring (IRE) (Kris)
1963^{4} 2335^{10} 4299^{4} 5630^{5}

Crystal Rock (IRE) *B W Hills* 84
3 br g Rock Of Gibraltar(IRE)—State Crystal (IRE) (High Estate)
1918^{5} 3326^{2} (5505) 5865^{3} 6784^{10}

Crystal Spirit (IRE) *Enda Kelly* a64 69
3 b f Noverre(USA)—Voyage Of Dreams (USA) (Riverman (USA))
698^{2} 1082^{6}

Crystany (IRE) *E A L Dunlop* a94 98
3 b f Green Desert(USA)—Crystal Music (USA) (Nureyev (USA))
1404^{4} ◆ 2000^{2} 2606^{3} 3041^{4} 5347^{6} 5884^{6} 6271^{4}

C. S. Silk (USA) *Dale Romans* a105
2 bb f Medaglia D'Oro(USA)—Remember The Day (USA) (Settlement Day (USA))
6967a^{7}

Cuban Missile *R Charlton* a78 83
3 b g Danehill Dancer(IRE)—Lady Salsa (IRE) (Gone West (USA))
1811^{10} 2819^{11} 3134^{7}

Cuban Rhythm (USA) *R Charlton* 67
3 b f Kingmambo(USA)—Kournakova (IRE) (Sadler's Wells (USA))
2681^{3} 2973^{8} 4344^{11}

Cubism *M Johnston* a63 67
2 b c Sulamani(IRE)—Diagonale (IRE) (Darshaan)
6760^{4} 7660^{4}

Cuilaphuca (IRE) *Tracey Collins* 93
4 b m Danetime(IRE)—Run Bonnie (Runnett)
1497a^{15} 3532a^{11} 7157a^{10}

Cuis Ghaire (IRE) *J S Bolger* 105
2 b f Galileo(IRE)—Scribonia (IRE) (Danehill (USA))
(2686a) ◆ (3192) ◆ 4353a^{2} 5132a^{8}

Culloden (UAE) *J H M Gosden* 66
3 ch g Selkirk(USA)—Last Resort (Lahib (USA))
4620^{6} (Dead)

Cullybackey (IRE) *G A Swinbank* 52
3 ch f Golan(IRE)—Leitrim Lodge (IRE) (Classic Music (USA))
4877^{8} 5636^{3} 6114^{6} 6275^{11}

Cumae (USA) *J Pearce* a39 51
4 b m King Cugat(USA)—Jubilee Walk (Generous (IRE))
83^{6} 1109^{6} (1694) 1776^{8} 2640^{11} 3025^{12}

Cumana Bay *R Hannon* a69 70
2 b f Dansili—Mayaro Bay (Robellino (USA))
5643^{6} (5860) 6732^{4} 7306^{5}

Cumbrian Gold (USA) *B Smart* a42
2 ch g Gilded Time(USA)—Brackenber (USA) (Lycius (USA))
7343^{12} 7422^{10} 7627^{6}

Cumbrian Knight (IRE) *J M Jefferson* a68 53
10 b g Presenting—Crashrun (Crash Course)
(36) 779^{3} 6824^{9} (7265) 7512^{11}

Cupid's Glory *G L Moore* a89 88
6 b g Pursuit Of Love—Doctor's Glory (USA) (Elmaamul (USA))
423a^{6} 605a^{2} 2799^{5} 3376^{10} 4820^{2} (5630) ◆ 6078^{2} 6346^{14} 6759^{2} 7493^{8} 7814^{6}

Curacao *Mrs A J Perrett* a66 69
2 b g Sakhee(USA)—Bourbonella (Rainbow Quest (USA))
6000^{6} 6412^{6} 6737^{6} ◆

Curio *R M Whitaker* a55 58
3 b f Captain Rio—Luanshya (First Trump)
993^{7} 1897^{5} 2287^{6} 2928^{6} 4207^{11} 4686^{3}

Curlin (USA) *Steven Asmussen* a131 118
4 ch h Smart Strike(CAN)—Sherriff's Deputy (USA) (Deputy Minister (CAN))
(742a) (1092a) 3995a^{2} (5558a) (6373a) 7001a^{4}

Curly Brown *A Bailey* a43 40
3 b g Lujain(USA)—Shearwater (Shareef Dancer (USA))
5076^{8} 5786^{8} 6707^{8} 7321^{7} 7503^{P}

Currency *J M Bradley* a39 70
11 b g Sri Pekan(USA)—On Tiptoes (Shareef Dancer (USA))
2010^{6} 2255^{12} 2950^{9} (3021) 3446^{5} 3559^{12} 6733^{8} 6895^{12} 7196^{7}

Curtail (IRE) *Miss L A Perratt* a93 91
5 b g Namid—Nipitinthebud (USA) (Night Shift (USA))
836^{4} ◆ 2538^{12} 2938^{6} 3489^{13} 4239^{5} 5542^{7} 6164^{4}

Curtain Call (FR) *L M Cumani* 115
3 b c Sadler's Wells(USA)—Apsara (FR) (Darshaan)
(1570) ◆ 2829^{10} 3535a^{5} 4042a^{10}

Curtain Up *M W Easterby* a34 45
2 b g Act One—Better Still (IRE) (Glenstal (USA))
3689^{10} 5590^{14} 6787^{10}

Curzon Prince (IRE) *C F Wall* a90 99
4 b h Mujadil(USA)—Smooth Spirit (USA) (Alydar (USA))
218^{2} 1473^{3} (1711) ◆ 2531^{4} 3398^{8} (5033) 6307^{2} 6984^{5}

Custard Cream Kid (IRE) *R A Fahey* 66
2 b g Statue Of Liberty(USA)—Diniesque (Rainbow Quest (USA))
2217^{3} 2746^{3} 4214^{8} 4733^{11} 5447^{4} 6247^{9}

Custody (IRE) *Sir Michael Stoute* a81 73
2 b g Fusaichi Pegasus(USA)—Shahtoush (IRE) (Alzao (USA))
2796^{6} 5672^{2} 6234^{2} 6723^{2} 7098^{2}

Customary Chorus (IRE) *D K Weld* 75
3 br f Linamix(FR)—Magical Cliche (USA) (Affirmed (USA))
6689a^{7}

Cut And Thrust (IRE) *M A Jarvis* a72 53
2 b g Haafhd—Ego (Green Desert (USA))
5672^{6} 6165^{6} 6539^{7} 7266^{3} 7372^{5} (7832)

Cute Ass (IRE) *K R Burke* 102
3 b f Fath(USA)—John's Ballad (IRE) (Ballad Rock)
4159^{2} 4550^{9} 5509^{15} 5890^{20} 6289^{5} 6653^{14}

Cutter *M Gasparini* 96
3 f Singspiel(IRE)—China (Royal Academy (USA))
3076a^{13}

Cut The Cackle (IRE) *P Winkworth* 84
2 b f Danetime(IRE)—Alexander Anapolis (IRE) (Spectrum (IRE))
(4786) 5642^{11} (6540)

Cutting Comments *M Dods* 74
2 b c Acclamation—Razor Sharp (Bering)
1727^{2} 2584^{6} 3170^{2} (3788) 4594^{8} 4816^{3} 5277^{11} 5632^{4} 6656^{6}

Cwmni *B Palling* a50 30
2 b f Auction House(USA)—Sontime (Son Pardo)
4764^{6} 5866^{8} 6133^{5} 7652^{2}

Cwm Rhondda (USA) *P W Chapple-Hyam* 61
3 b f Gulch(USA)—Frayne (USA) (Red Ransom (USA))
3275^{8} 3894^{8} 4620^{8} 5322^{9} 5815^{2} 6337^{5}

Cybersnow (USA) *Barry Potts* a77 59
4 ch g Royal Anthem(USA)—Storm Dove (USA) (Storm Bird (CAN))
823^{2} 981^{12} 4655a^{13}

Cyborg *D R C Elsworth* a59 77
4 ch g Halling(USA)—Ciboure (Norwick (USA))
1931^{6} 2291^{6} 2847^{3} 4200^{8}

Cyflymder (IRE) *J G Given* 78
2 b g Mujadil(USA)—Nashwan Star (IRE) (Nashwan (USA))
4169^{10} 4616^{4} (5200) 6082^{9} 6525^{9}

Cyfrwys (IRE) *B Palling* a52 52
7 b m Foxhound(USA)—Divine Elegance (IRE) (College Chapel)
16^{6} 33^{9} 870^{4} 1053^{9} 1550^{3} 2917^{11} 2988^{3} 3608^{11}

Cygnet *L M Cumani* 80
2 b c Dansili—Ballet Princess (Muhtarram (USA))
5469^{10} (6760)

Cymbal (IRE) *H-A Pantall* 98
3 b f Singspiel(IRE)—Valdara (Darshaan)
1664a^{4} 5623a^{5} 7348a^{6}

Cyril The Squirrel *Karen George* a51
4 b g Cyrano De Bergerac—All Done (Northern State (USA))
31^{4} 273^{2} 499^{3} 695^{12}

Daanaat (IRE) *M R Channon* 54
2 b f Kheleyf(USA)—Belle Argentine (FR) (Fijar Tango (FR))
2206^{9} 3254^{5} 3959^{14}

Daarth *B W Duke* 9
3 b g Alhaarth(IRE)—Glamorous Girl (IRE) (Darshaan)
2191^{13} 2668^{14} 3362^{7} 6541^{15}

Daaweitza *B Ellison* a82 94
5 ch g Daawe(USA)—Chichen Itza (Shareef Dancer (USA))
992^{18} 1217^{6} 1630^{7} (1891) 2158^{4} (2397) (2905) 3491^{10} 3946^{7} 4407^{6} 4661^{13} 5446^{8} 6130^{4} 6431^{3} 7041^{9}

Dabbers Chief (USA) *B W Hills* 88
2 b c Broken Vow(USA)—Grey Matter (USA) (Housebuster (USA))
1439^{5} (2608) 3105^{20} 3634^{3} 5226^{11} 5827^{10} 6428^{6}

Dabbers Ridge (IRE) *B W Hills* 109
6 b h Indian Ridge—Much Commended (Most Welcome)
(1387) 1982^{21} 2580^{6} 3197^{22} 3921^{18} 5446^{11} 6104^{15} 6975^{10}

Da Bomber (IRE) *J W Unett* 58
3 b c Tagula(IRE)—Talahari (IRE) (Roi Danzig (USA))
2455^{5}

Da Bookie (IRE) *Jean-Rene Auvray* a59 70
8 b g Woods Of Windsor(USA)—Hurgill Lady (Emarati (USA))
795^{4} 1207^{8} 1670^{6}

Daddy Cool *W G M Turner* a35 82
4 b g Kyllachy—Addicted To Love (Touching Wood (USA))
3269^{7} 4064^{9} 5050^{7} 7231^{11} 7295^{11} 7503^{11} 7706^{9}

Daddy's Boy *Mrs A J Perrett* a12 65
3 ch g Selkirk(USA)—Narva (Nashwan (USA))
1467^{14} 1871^{10} 2340^{7} 2984^{8} 3483^{12}

Daddy's Gift (IRE) *R Hannon* a75 81
2 b f Trans Island—Lady Corduff (IRE) (Titus Livius (FR))
1680^{3} 2042^{3} (2754) 3924^{7} 4340^{3} 4589^{6} 5785^{3} (6193) 6414^{3} 6970^{8} 7241^{7}

Dado Mush *T T Clement* a79 57
5 b g Almushtarak(IRE)—Princess Of Spain (King Of Spain)
(68) 351^{3} (2083) 2289^{2} 2531^{9} 3167^{6} 3725^{8} 6841^{13} 7374^{6}

Dafaroun (IRE) *M A Molloy* a67 68
7 b g Royal Applause—Dafayna (Habitat)
6366a^{5}

Daffodil Walk (IRE) *P D Deegan* a81 81
2 b f Captain Rio—Majestic Launch (Lear Fan (USA))
2686a[7]

Daggerman *P A Blockley* a55 36
3 ch g Daggers Drawn(USA) —Another Mans Cause (FR) (Highest Honor (FR))
7321[3] 7532[13]

Dagua Briza (IRE) *J W Mullins* a16 35
3 b f Dilshaan—First Encounter (IRE) (Alzao (USA))
4342[14] 4821[12]

Dahama *C E Brittain* 65
2 b f Green Desert(USA) —Darling Flame (USA) (Capote (USA))
4643[9] 6360[5] 6785[12]

Daheeya *M R Channon* 75
2 gr f Daylami(IRE) —Kind Regards (IRE) (Unfuwain (USA))
2368[3] ◆ 2618[11] (4328)

Daily Double *R Hannon* a63 60
2 gr g Needwood Blade—Coffee To Go (Environment Friend)
3798[7] 4480[5] *4728[5] 5671[4] 6017[9] 6207[9]* 6924[9]

Daily Planet (IRE) *B W Duke* a35 42
2 ch c Titus Livius(FR) —Flattering News (USA) (Pleasant Colony (USA))
2146[12] 3645[7] 4570[11] 5314[11] 5747[8] 6086[9] *7269[5] 7468[7] 7607[11]*

Daisy Moses (IRE) *D Nicholls* 74
2 br f Mull Of Kintyre(USA) —Starring (FR) (Ashkalani (IRE))
(1794) 3192[14]

Daisy Nook *S Kirk* a38 49
3 b f Domedriver(IRE) —Kilbride (Selkirk (USA))
2639[6] ◆ 3359[7]

Daiwa Wild Boar (JPN) *Hiroyuki Uehara* 108
3 b c Agnes Tachyon(JPN) —Seigniorage (USA) (Nureyev (USA))
7511a[16]

Dakiyah (IRE) *Mrs L J Mongan* a86 89
4 b m Observatory(USA) —Dararyina (IRE) (Shirley Heights)
502[7] 692[7] 1273[2] 1458[2] 1877[4] 2540[2] (2799)

Dakota Hills *J R Best* a69 72
2 ch c Danehill Dancer(IRE) —Karla June (Unfuwain (USA))
4270[2] 4411[4] *5904[2]* 6362[11] *7555[2]*

Dakota Rain (IRE) *Jennie Candlish* 88
6 br g Indian Ridge—Mill Rainbow (FR) (Rainbow Quest (USA))
1174[10] 1451[6] 1818[16] 2445[9] 3169[8] 3713[9] 4535[4] 5779[5] 6219[17] 6382[10]

Dakota Two (IRE) *R A Fahey*
2 b f Frenchmans Bay(FR) —Dakota Sioux (IRE) (College Chapel)
3976[10] 4536[10] 4897[10]

Dalarossie *E J Alston* a61 67
3 br g Kyllachy—Damalis (IRE) (Mukaddamah (USA))
1155[8] *1635[3]* ◆ 1769[7] 2287[11] 4242[4] (4686) 5201[6] 5393[5] 6308[7] *7288[9]*

Dalayla (IRE) *J W Mullins*
4 gr m Midhish—Polocracy (IRE) (Aristocracy)
3133[12]

Dalepak Flyer (IRE) *G D Blake* a53 59
2 ch c Noverre(USA) —Hartstown House (IRE) (Primo Dominie)
2709[5] 3358[4] 3798[8] 4185[8]

Dalesway *J G Given* 48
2 b c Muhtarram(USA) —Si Si Si (Lomitas)
6234[6] 6580[9]

Dalghar (FR) *A De Royer-Dupre* 106
2 b c Anabaa(USA) —Daltawa (IRE) (Miswaki (USA))
7186a[2]

Dalhaan (USA) *J L Dunlop* 91
3 b c Fusaichi Pegasus(USA) —Khazayin (USA) (Bahri (USA))
1446[5] 1931[2] ◆ 2669[5] (3297) 4351[6] 6079[16]

Dalkey Girl (IRE) *M Botti* a72 92
3 ch f Raise A Grand(IRE) —Tosca (Be My Guest (USA))
137[6] 496a[6] 744a[8] 1595[8] 1811[8] 2231a[16] 3272[9] 5291[6] *5800[14]*

Dalla Finestra *C F Wall* 55
3 ch f Bahamian Bounty—Spinning Mouse (Bustino)
1795[7] 2546[7] 3452[7] 4793[4] 6004[7]

Dallool *John Queally* a32 39
7 b g Unfuwain(USA) —Sardonic (Kris)
1497a[16]

Dalpuiri (USA) *Charles Coakley* 17
2 b f Doneraile Court(USA) —Kara's Heart (USA) (American Legion (USA))
4513a[12]

Dalradian (IRE) *W J Knight* a73 65
2 b c Dansili—Aethra (USA) (Trempolino (USA))
4151[7] 4974[6] *5615[4]* 6083[8]

Daltaban (FR) *Miss E C Lavelle* 85
4 ch g Rainbow Quest(USA) —Daltaiyma (IRE) (Doyoun)
2599[11] 3104[17] *5699[12]*

Da Luego (IRE) *Patrick Allen* a25 39
4 b g Bahamian Bounty—Jelba (Pursuit Of Love)
642[9]

Daly Daly (FR) *R Laplanche* 103
4 gr m Medaaly—Dame Phanie (FR) (Kaldoun (FR))
4320a[4]

Damaniyat Girl (USA) *W J Haggas* a79 74
2 ch f Elusive Quality(USA) —Dabaweyaa (Shareef Dancer (USA))
6244[2] ◆ *(6696)*

Damascus Gold *Miss Z C Davison* 61
4 b h Thowra(FR) —Damasquiner (Casteddu)
1173[5] 1539[4] 2153[14]

Damassin *Eve Johnson Houghton* a48 60
2 b f Bertolini(USA) —Queen Linear (USA) (Polish Navy (USA))
2916[3] ◆ 3348[9] 4905[7] *5432[10] 5904[8]* 6240[21]

Dam D'Augy (FR) *Mlle S-V Tarrou* a84 92
3 ch f Bernebeau(FR) —Cardamome (FR) (Cardoun (FR))
6064a[2] 6743a[3]

Dametime (IRE) *Daniel Mark Loughnane* 74
2 b f Danetime(IRE) —Fee Eria (FR) (Always Fair (USA))
5459[6]

Damhsoir (IRE) *H S Howe* a52 48
4 b m Invincible Spirit(IRE) —Ceide Dancer (IRE) (Alzao (USA))
2644[8] 2836[7] 4273[2]

Damien (IRE) *B W Hills* 109
2 gr c Namid—Miss Shaan (FR) (Darshaan)
(4480) 5244[4] 5827[2] ◆ 6119[4] 6713a[7]

Damika (IRE) *R M Whitaker* a97 111
5 ch g Namid—Emly Express (IRE) (High Estate)
1300[4] 1517[2] 1809[2] 2172[7] 3489[3] ◆ (3722) 3921[6] 4660[2] 5275[5] 5840[4] *6285[6]* 6484[4] 6783[11]

Damini (USA) *Sir Michael Stoute* a58 75
2 b f Seeking The Gold(USA) —Dalisay (IRE) (Sadler's Wells (USA))
5048[9] 5535[2] 6392[5] 6970[14]

Damselfly *M Johnston* a53 51
2 b f Dr Fong(USA) —Mazarine Blue (Bellypha)
2627[6] 3364[11] *7023[11] 7306[13]*

Danae *H Candy* 90
3 br f Dansili—Pervenche (Latest Model)
(1423) 2666[2] 6981[12]

Danak (IRE) *Doug Watson* 118
5 br h Pivotal—Daniysha (IRE) (Doyoun)
651a[6]

Danamight (IRE) *J L Dunlop* a65 68
3 gr f Danetime(IRE) —Nuit Chaud (USA) (Woodman (USA))
1622[10] 2047[4] 2982[5] 3322[2] 4173[7] 4819[6] 5472[4] 6028[11] 6868[3]

Dance And Dance (IRE) *E F Vaughan* a63
2 b c Royal Applause—Caldy Dancer (IRE) (Soviet Star (USA))
7769[6]

Dance Card *A G Foster* 17
3 b f Cape Cross(IRE) —Dance On (Caerleon (USA))
6791[13]

Dance Club (IRE) *W Jarvis* a35 66
2 b f Fasliyev(USA) —Two Clubs (First Trump)
2479[6] ◆ *5430[8]* 6559[6] 7052[6]

Dance Easily *J L Dunlop* 39
3 b f Dansili—Crystal Flite (IRE) (Darshaan)
1186[7] 2468[7] 2985[8]

Dance Hall Diva *M D I Usher* 45
6 b m Zaha(CAN) —Eastwell Star (Saddlers' Hall (IRE))
1621[9] 2643[13]

Dance In Style *A Crook* a18 21
7 b m Desert Style(IRE) —Loves To Dance (FR) (Sadler's Wells (USA))
2391[7] 2523[13] *2866[7]* 4142[11] *7184[10]*

Dancelectic (IRE) *D R Lanigan* a22
2 b c Barathea(IRE) —Sheer Spirit (IRE) (Caerleon (USA))
7011[13] 7204[10] 7343[11]

Dancer In Demand (IRE) *Sir Michael Stoute* 75
3 ch g Danehill Dancer(IRE) —Sought Out (IRE) (Rainbow Quest (USA))
2191[3] ◆ 3637[8]

Dancer's Legacy *E A L Dunlop* a67 80
3 ch c Nayef(USA) —Blond Moment (USA) (Affirmed (USA))
1540[5] (2002) *2532[5]* 3325[7] 4603[10] *5052[8] 6695[13]*

Dance Sauvage *C W Thornton* 58
5 ch g Groom Dancer(USA) —Peace Dance (Bikala)
1304[5] ◆ 2467[F] 3279[10] 3545[3] 3863[5] 4556[7]

Dance Society *T D Easterby* 53
2 b g Mull Of Kintyre(USA) —Gracious Imp (USA) (Imp Society (USA))
5771[7] 6014[7] 6187[14]

Dance The Star (USA) *D M Simcock* a92 76
3 bb c Dynaformer(USA) —Dance The Slew (USA) (Slew City Slew (USA))
1272[3] ◆ 2669[12] (3530) *(4303)* ◆ *5573[8] (6472) 6630[3]*

Dancewiththestars (USA) *Miss J Feilden* a45 55
4 b m Cryptoclearance(USA) —Sir Harry's Waltz (IRE) (Sir Harry Lewis (USA))
1184[10]

Dan Chillingworth (IRE) *J R Fanshawe* a85 78
3 b c Indian Ridge—Shizao (IRE) (Alzao (USA))
2620[5] 3893[5] *4478[2]* 4989[3] *5346[2]* ◆ *5713[4] (6356) (6841)*

Dancing Abbie (USA) *M L W Bell* a91 95
3 ch f Theatrical—Sicy D'Alsace (FR) (Sicyos (USA))
(1042) ◆ 1915[9] *2505[2]* 3076a[3] 4196[5] (5336a) 6691a[9]

Dancing Bear *C Roberts* a5 48
7 b g Groom Dancer(USA) —Sickle Moon (Shirley Heights)
2245[5] 3059[6]

Dancing Belle *J A R Toller* 46
3 b f Fasliyev(USA) —May Ball (Cadeaux Genereux)
3177[6] 3916[7] 4987[10]

Dancing Deano (IRE) *R Hollinshead* a75 62
6 b g Second Empire(IRE) —Ultimate Beat (USA) (Go And Go)
115[3] 1780[4] *(2703) 3691[8] 4386[4] 4934[3] 5156[6] 5478[9] 6132[2] 7153[7]* 7317[3] 7653[4] (7780)

Dancing Delta *W R Muir* a32 36
2 ch f Delta Dancer—Picolette (Piccolo)
3558[7] *3821[11] 5614[6]* 6059[12]

Dancing Dik *Mrs A J Perrett* a73 70
3 b g Diktat—Maureena (IRE) (Grand Lodge (USA))
1530[4] 2045[4] 2468[9] 2997[8] (3327) *3614[2]* 3873[5] 4485[9] 4646[5] 5169[4] 5537[2] *5803[4]* 6129[9] 6703[7]

Dancing Duo *D Shaw* a62 56
4 b m Groom Dancer(USA) —Affaire Royale (IRE) (Royal Academy (USA))
56[8] 209[11] 349[3] 465[3] 555[4] 663[9] 749[13] 856[5] 938[9] 5317[2] 5871[8] 6208[7] 7112[3]

Dancing Ellie *P M Phelan* 45
3 b f Where Or When(IRE) —Eleonor Sympson (Cadeaux Genereux)
1279[7] 1876[11] 5269[15]

Dancing Forever (USA) *Claude McGaughey III* 119
5 ch h Rahy(USA) —Dancinginmydreams (USA) (Seeking The Gold (USA))
7000a[3]

Dancing Jest (IRE) *Rae Guest* a19 66
4 b m Averti(IRE) —Mezzanine (Sadler's Wells (USA))
2070[5] 3361[4] 3655[2] 4065[3]

Dancing Lyra *R A Fahey* a71 83
7 b g Alzao(USA) —Badaayer (USA) (Silver Hawk (USA))
697[5] 1217[10]

Dancing Maite *S R Bowring* a68 73
3 ch g Ballet Master(USA) —Ace Maite (Komaite (USA))
70[3] 1912[7] 2041[2] *2260[2]* 4121[12] 4329[3] 4615[7] 5397[4] 6188[3] *6707[2] (6843)* (7018) *7650[6]*

Dancing Marabout (IRE) *C R Egerton* a75 64
3 ch g Danehill Dancer(IRE) —Bluebell Wood (IRE) (Bluebird (USA))
1868[9] 2564[11] 3095[14] 4485[7] 6562[9]

Dancing Moonlight (IRE) *Mrs N Macauley* a25 13
6 b m Danehill Dancer(IRE) —Silver Moon (Environment Friend)
634[13] 753[7]

Dancing Mystery *E A Wheeler* a74 68
14 b g Beveled(USA) —Batchworth Dancer (Ballacashtal (CAN))
84[6] 301[5] 1901[7] 2934[5] 3405[5] 3575[6] 4107[10] 6204[14] *6907[11] 7644[11]*

Dancing Rhythm *M S Saunders* a25 11
3 b g Piccolo—Will You Dance (Shareef Dancer (USA))
4484[8] 5023[10] *6660[10]*

Dancing Storm *W S Kittow* a56 71
5 b m Trans Island—Stormswell (Persian Bold)
1898[2] (2477) 3023[4] 3903[3] 4428[5] 5119[6] 5935[6] 6544[3]

Dancing Sword *D Burchell* a43 67
3 b g Groom Dancer(USA) —Kristina (Kris)
1477[3] 1741[3] 2785[13] *7009[8]*

Dancing Wave *M C Chapman* a42 61
2 b f Baryshnikov(AUS) —Wavet (Pursuit Of Love)
995[5] *1118[4]* 1384[2] 4024[14] 4434[12] 5066[12] 5715[10] 6009[4] *7795[6]*

Dancing Welcome *J M Bradley* 30
2 b f Kyllachy—Highland Gait (Most Welcome)
1866[6] 2011[9]

Dancing Wizard *C G Cox* a58
4 ch g Dancing Spree(USA) —Magic Legs (Reprimand)
447[5] 643[4]

Dancourt (IRE) *Sir Michael Stoute* a69 51
2 b g Cadeaux Genereux—Stage Struck (IRE) (Sadler's Wells (USA))
6714[11] *7165[3] 7333[4]*

Dandaad (NZ) *Bart Cummings* 87
5 ch g Istidaad(USA) —Lets Dance (NZ) (Dance Floor (USA))
6922a[15]

Danderdandan *P T Midgley* a20 29
2 b c Fraam—Heneseys Leg (Sure Blade (USA))
5107[5] 5304[11] 5715[6] 6406[6] *7044[6]*

Dandy Erin (IRE) *J A Osborne* a82 84
3 b c Danehill Dancer(IRE) —Sanctuary Line (IRE) (Lake Coniston (IRE))
2109[5]

Dandygrey Russett (IRE) *D L Williams* a66
7 gr m Singspiel(IRE) —Christian Church (IRE) (Linamix (FR))
(3328) (Dead)

Dandy Man (IRE) *Saeed Bin Suroor* 122
5 b h Mozart(IRE) —Lady Alexander (IRE) (Night Shift (USA))
2404[10] 3101[4] 4550[3] 5245[7] 6518a[12]

Dane Blue (IRE) *S J Treacy* 88
6 ch m Danehill Dancer(IRE) —Palace Blue (IRE) (Dara Monarch)
5550a[10] 6298a[14] 6516a[7]

Danehill Destiny *W J Haggas* 100
2 b f Danehill Dancer(IRE) —Comeraincomeshine (IRE) (Night Shift (USA))
(1419) ◆ (2677) 3123[17] 5272[4] ◆ 5852[4] 6102[3] 6441[15]

Danehill Folly (IRE) *M D I Usher* a18
5 b g Danehill Dancer(IRE) —Theorique (IRE) (Theatrical)
3347[13] 4055[10]

Danehill Music (IRE) *David Wachman* 106
5 b m Danehill Dancer(IRE) —Tuesday Morning (Sadler's Wells (USA))
1104a[8] 1847a[6] 3536a[8] 4007a[15]

Danehill Silver *B Storey* a52 63
4 b g Silver Patriarch(IRE) —Danehill Princess (IRE) (Danehill (USA))
51[11] 3756[14]

Danehillsundance (IRE) *S Parr* a91 99
4 b h Danehill Dancer(IRE) —Rosie's Guest (IRE) (Be My Guest (USA))
834[6] 2334[2] ◆ 2595[7] 3261[9] 4649[8] 5470[4] 6307[5] *6710[8]* 7019[8] *7386[10]*

Danelor (IRE) *D Shaw* a57 42
10 b g Danehill(USA) —Formulate (Reform)
77[7]

Danesman *G L Moore* a33 66
3 ch g Danehill Dancer(IRE) —Gaily Grecian (IRE) (Ela-Mana-Mou)
1382[5] 2207[6] *5608[12]* 6868[10]

Dane's World (IRE) *R Hannon* 50
2 b f Danehill Dancer(IRE) —Khamseh (Thatching)
4521[13] 6117[13]

Danetime Lord (IRE) *J R Gask* a89 62
5 b g Danetime(IRE) —Seven Sisters (USA) (Shadeed (USA))
233[4] 456[4] 536[2] (807) 1055[2] 1211[13] 4186[11] *5144[14]*

Danetime Panther (IRE) *P F I Cole* a79 78
4 b g Danetime(IRE) —Annotate (Groom Dancer (USA))
3840[5] 4364[3] 4627[5] 5033[4] 5312[11] *5675[2]* 6346[4] 6721[3] *7009[7]*

Danidh Dubai (IRE) *M R Channon* 95
2 b f Noverre(USA) —Dani Ridge (IRE) (Indian Ridge)
1419[9] (1987) 3192[3] ◆ 4403[9] 6102[7] 6439[13] 6860[4]

Daniel Defoe (USA) *Sir Michael Stoute* 61
2 ch c Smart Strike(CAN) —Dear Daughter (Polish Precedent (USA))
7054[10]

Daniella *Rae Guest* a88 90
6 b m Dansili—Break Point (Reference Point)
1993[9] 2426[11]

Daniel O'Donnell *S C Williams* a24
6 b h Komaite(USA) —Light Slippers (IRE) (Ela-Mana-Mou)
326[5] 598[7]

Daniel Thomas (IRE) *Mrs A L M King* a79 85
6 b g Dansili—Last Look (Rainbow Quest (USA))
1182[2] 1565[6] ◆ *(1954)* (2487) 2795[4] 3664[7] 4364[8] *5800[6]* 6363[4] *6738[2] 7014[8]*

Dani's Girl (IRE) *P A Fahy* a76 100
5 bb m Second Empire(IRE) —Quench The Lamp (IRE) (Glow (USA))
1847a[8] 2420a[9] *7328a[14]*

Danish Art (IRE) *J A R Toller* a76 77
3 b c Danehill Dancer(IRE) —Lady Ounavarra (IRE) (Simply Great (FR))
2981[3] (3499) 4158[7] *6169[8] 6695[5] 7557[3]*

Danish Monarch *David Pinder* a53 56
7 b g Great Dane(IRE) —Moly (Inchinor)
2795[12] *3588[10]* 3844[3] 4322[5] 4722[13] 5059[5] 5429[5] *5787[6] 6228[15] 7473[8]*

Danish Rebel (IRE) *G A Charlton* a49 79
4 b g Danetime(IRE) —Wheatsheaf Lady (IRE) (Red Sunset)
1970[6] 3110[4] 3785[4]

Danjet (IRE) *P D Evans* a39 67
5 bl m Danehill Dancer(IRE) —Jet Lock (USA) (Crafty Prospector (USA))
(3608) ◆ *3842[11]* 4370[12] 4696[3] 4767[9]

Danjoe *R Brotherton* a53 38
4 ch g Forzando—Baytown Rhapsody (Emperor Jones (USA))
3312[8]

Dannios *L M Cumani* a65 57
2 b c Tobougg(IRE) —Fleuve D'Or (IRE) (Last Tycoon)
4778[3] *5430[3] 5939[10]*

Dansant *G A Butler* a116 113
4 b h Dansili—La Balagna (Kris)
(678) 1091a[16] 2543[10] 4585[4] *5348[4] 7193[6] (7491) (7741)*

Danse De Sioux (IRE) *M Madgwick* a26 36
3 ch f Frenchmans Bay(FR) —Purty Dancer (IRE) (Foxhound (USA))
1965[9] 2772[11] 6345[11] *7072[10]*

Danse The Blues *E A L Dunlop* a65 67
3 br f Dansili—Dixie D'Oats (Alhijaz)
1526[9] 6393[6] *6741[6]* 6868[11] *7261[8] 7642[6]*

Danseuse Volante (IRE) *J W Hills* 78
3 ch f Danehill Dancer(IRE) —Termania (IRE) (Shirley Heights)
1958[2] ◆ 2622[7] 3064[2] 3636[6]

Dansili Dancer *C G Cox* a105 108
6 b g Dansili—Magic Slipper (Habitat)
2168[12] 4444[6] 5288[6] 5646[5] *6286[3]* 6646[5]

Dansilver *D J Wintle* a57 67
4 b g Dansili—Silver Gyre (IRE) (Silver Hawk (USA))
(1551) 2012[6] 2245[DSQ] 3179[5] 4704[9]

Danski *Mrs L J Mongan* a87 81
5 b g Dansili—Manila Selection (USA) (Manila (USA))
1335[4] 1532[5] 2152[12] 3090[12] *7309[11] 7494[5] 7677[9] 7819[7]*

Dante Deo (USA) *T D Barron* a54
2 b f Proud Citizen(USA) —Best Feature (USA) (El Gran Senor (USA))
7371[4] 7646[2]

Dante's Diamond (IRE) *R Lee* a64 64
6 b g Orpen(USA) —Flower From Heaven (Baptism)
682[4]

Dan Tucker *Jim Best* a75 74
4 b g Dansili—Shapely (USA) (Alleged (USA))
1482[7] 2006[6] 2365[2] ◆ 2568[3] 3010[5] 3450[4] 3814[3] (4295) 4458[5] 4690[5] 5563[4] 6050[4] 6216[12] 6806[2] *7071[4]*

Dan Tucket *B Olsen* a58 92
3 b c Dansili—Fanfare (Deploy)
4676a[3] 5335a[8]

Danum Dancer *N Bycroft* 87
4 ch h Allied Forces(USA) —Branston Dancer (Rudimentary (USA))
1485[12]

Danzadil (IRE) *R A Teal* a56 62
2 b f Mujadil(USA) —Changari (USA) (Gulch (USA))
3378[5] 4521[9] 4926[3] 5511[P] *7451[4] 7767[9]*

Danzatrice *C W Thornton* 73
6 b m Tamure(IRE) —Miss Petronella (Petoski)
1304[2] 1773[2] (1972) 2577[2] 2734[2] 3276[4] 3414[5] 4046[3] 4452[4] 4963[3] (5540) 5967[6] 6313[5] 6672[8]

Danzig Fox *M Mullineaux* a57 65
3 b c Foxhound(USA) —Via Dolorosa (Chaddleworth (IRE))
1925[8] 2490[14] 3475[4] 3907[3] 4661[11] 5198[10] *5709[10] 7228[10] 7399[8]*

Danzili Bay *A W Carroll* a67 71
6 b h Dansili—Lady Bankes (IRE) (Alzao (USA))
2036[7] 2474[4] (2923) 3169[6] 4327[3] 5091[8] *6225[4]*

Daraahem (IRE) *B W Hills* 99
3 ch g Act One—Shamah (Unfuwain (USA))
1398[2] (1918) ◆ 3157[13] 3719[3] (4784) 6817[17]

Dara Diva (IRE) *W J Haggas* a56
3 bb f Barathea(IRE) —Dananira (High Top)
135[6] 350[7] 396[5] 644[2]

Daraiym (IRE) *Paul Green* a58 65
3 b g Peintre Celebre(USA) —Dararita (IRE) (Halo (USA))
1615[4] 1918[7] 2360[10] 2907[8] 3671[13] *7368[9] 7587[3] 7775[8] 7827[4]*

Daraybad (FR) *A Crook* 23
6 b g Octagonal(NZ) —Daraydala (IRE) (Royal Academy (USA))
5563[7]

Darcey *R A Fahey* 77
2 ch f Noverre(USA) —Firozi (Forzando)
5499[5] (6109) 6533[5]

Darcy's Pride (IRE) *D W Barker* 76
4 bb m Danetime(IRE) —Cox's Ridge (IRE) (Indian Ridge)
987[9] 1997[6] 2159[5] 2676[10] 2777[2] 3080[6] 3454[11] 3665[12] 4293[2] 4561[9] 5398[10] 5634[11]

Daredevil Dan *M H Tompkins* 44
2 b g Golden Snake(USA) —Tiempo (King Of Spain)
6085[16]

Dareh (IRE) *Saeed Bin Suroor* a67 61
2 b f Invincible Spirit(IRE) —Delage (Bellypha)
6555[3] *6933[3] 7227[3]*

Dareios (GER) *G J Smith* 43
3 ch g Numerous(USA) —Desert Chiara (USA) (Desert King (IRE))
4122[4] *4477[13] 5379[14]* 5651[11]

Darenjan (IRE) *John Joseph Hanlon* 75
5 b g Alhaarth(IRE) —Darariyna (IRE) (Shirley Heights)
4003a[6] 4511a[4]

Dar Es Salaam *J S Goldie* 84
4 ch g King's Best(USA) —Place De L'Opera (Sadler's Wells (USA))
2970[3] 3493[12] 4015[3] 4331[3] 5391[5] 5843[2] (6078) 6657[6] 6950[4]

Daressalam (GER) *W Hickst* 96
3 b c Singspiel(IRE) —Desidera (IRE) (Shaadi (USA))
3074a[4]

Darfen (IRE) *J L Flint* 46
5 b g Darnay—Miss Horage (IRE) (Horage)
5117[6]

Darfour *J S Goldie* 77
4 b g Inchinor—Gai Bulga (Kris)
2524[5] 2942[4] 3257[4] 3453[3] 4219[6] 4540[5] 4851[6]

Darghan (IRE) *W J Musson* a52 66
8 b g Air Express(IRE) —Darsannda (IRE) (Kahyasi)
3347[8]

Dariena (FR) *A De Royer-Dupre* 60
3 b f Highest Honor(FR) —Darinska (IRE) (Zilzal (USA))
3775a[7]

Daring Affair *R A Harris* a73 84
7 b m Bien Bien(USA) —Daring Destiny (Daring March)
122[2] 422a[4] 604a[2] (Dead)

Daring Dream (GER) *A P Jarvis* a67 74
3 ch c Big Shuffle(USA) —Daring Action (Arazi (USA))
1448[14] 4489[4] 4829[7] 5458[10] 6042[6] 6108[8] *6771[11] 7359[2] 7490[5]*

Daring Racer (GER) *Mrs L J Mongan* a70 68
5 ch g Big Shuffle(USA) —Daring Action (Arazi (USA))
2886[3] 3631[5] 4275[6] 4775[2] *5676[9] 6740[11]* 6927[6] *7707[2] 7831[10]*

Darjina (FR) *A De Royer-Dupre* 124
4 b m Zamindar(USA) —Darinska (IRE) (Zilzal (USA))
1090a[2] ◆ 2238a[2] 3100[2] 4674a[2] 5740a[2] 6475[2]

Dark Camellia *H J L Dunlop* a66 53
3 b f Olden Times—Miss Mirror (Magic Mirror)
1669[2] 2342[8] *2756[3] 6571[3] 7074[5] 7358[3] 7759[2]*

Dark Champion *R E Barr* a43 68
8 b g Abou Zouz(USA) —Hazy Kay (IRE) (Treasure Kay)
1485[4] 2005[4] ◆ 2444[11] 2777[3] 3111[8] 3601[3] 4047[7] 4293[8] 4703[10] 6382[12] 6546[10] *7270[5] 7618[10]*

Dark Charm (FR) *R A Fahey* a67 75
9 b g Anabaa(USA) —Wardara (Sharpo)
1369[3] 1704[5] 2394[9] 2568[12] 2940[11]

Dark Desert *A G Newcombe* a37 44
2 b c Best Of The Bests(IRE) —Dune Safari (IRE) (Key Of Luck (USA))
4274[9] 4815[9] 5488[7] *7372[8] 7659[4]*

Dark Echoes *Jedd O'Keeffe* 61
2 bl c Diktat—Calamanco (Clantime)
4815[4] 5277[9] 6051[12]

Dark Energy *M J Scudamore* 77
4 br g Observatory(USA) —Waterfowl Creek (IRE) (Be My Guest (USA))
3884[5] 4193[11] 4592[4]

Dark Humour (IRE) *D K Weld* a83 81
2 b c Bahri(USA) —Idilic Calm (IRE) (Indian Ridge)
6474[P] (Dead)

Dark Islander (IRE) *J W Hills* a112 112
5 b h Singspiel(IRE) —Lamanka Lass (USA) (Woodman (USA))
384a[5] ◆ 651a[5] *(1767)* 2214a[2] 3248[22]

Dark Lane *T D Barron* 78
2 b g Namid—Corps De Ballet (IRE) (Fasliyev (USA))
4647[3] 4923[5] (5277) 6247[2]

Dark Mischief *H Candy* 85
2 b c Namid—Syrian Queen (Slip Anchor)
(2893) 6972[5]

Dark Missile *A M Balding* a93 113
5 b m Night Shift(USA) —Exorcet (FR) (Selkirk (USA))
1420[3] 1698[2] 2606[5] 3247[9] 4188[10] 4840[4] 6304[9] 6645[11]

Dark Moment *A Dickman* 63
2 gr g Spartacus(IRE) —Dim Ofan (Petong)
3107[7] 3411[8] 4214[10] 4733[6] 5632[12]

Darknstormy *J R Weymes*
2 b g Kyllachy—Indian Gift (Cadeaux Genereux)
3277[11] 3706[10]

Dark Oasis *K A Ryan* a60 53
2 b g Dubai Destination(USA) —Silent Waters (Polish Precedent (USA))
2592[12] 3277[7] 4072[7] *5591[2] 5914[5]*

Dark Parade (ARG) *G L Moore* a73 68
7 b g Parade Marshal(USA) —Charming Dart (ARG) (D'Accord (USA))
27[6] 272[6]

Dark Planet *D W Thompson* a66 56
5 ch g Singspiel(IRE) —Warning Shadows (IRE) (Cadeaux Genereux)
5776[2] 7132[2] 7177[6]

Dark Prospect *M A Jarvis* a84 86
3 b g Nayef(USA) —Miss Mirasol (Sheikh Albadou)
2056[5] 2678[3] 3263[3] 3573[2] *(5605)* 6033[2] *6424[2]* 7056[2]

Dark Queen *D Carroll* a31 43
3 b f Bertolini(USA) —Abstone Queen (Presidium)
1635[11] 1777[6]

Dark Ranger *T J Pitt* a42 48
2 bb c Where Or When(IRE) —Dark Raider (IRE) (Definite Article)
4304[9] 4747[8] 5753[8] *6572[8] 7372[13]*

Darksideofthemoon (IRE) *N J Gifford* a73 75
6 b g Accordion—Supreme Valentine (IRE) (Supreme Leader)
3637[4] *4302[4]* (4821) *5376[7]*

Dark Society *A W Carroll* a32 50
10 b g Imp Society(USA) —No Candles Tonight (Star Appeal)
44[7] 197[6]

Dark Tara *R A Fahey* 75
3 br f Diktat—Karisal (IRE) (Persian Bold)
5714[8]

Dark Velvet (IRE) *E J Alston* 63
2 b f Statue Of Liberty(USA) —Lovingit (IRE) (Fasliyev (USA))
3125[7] 3949[7] 4202[6]

Darley Star *R A Harris* a59 62
3 gr f King's Best(USA) —Amellnaa (IRE) (Sadler's Wells (USA))
1115[9] 2496[5] 3117[7] *3483[9]* 4772[7] 5167[7] *6753[2] (6930) 7516[12] 7626[11]*

Darley Sun (IRE) *D M Simcock* 71
2 b c Tiger Hill(IRE) —Sagamartha (Rainbow Quest (USA))
5857[10] 6330[4] 7142[7]

Dar Re Mi *J H M Gosden* 117
3 b f Singspiel(IRE) —Darara (Top Ville)
(1599) 2105[3] 3543a[3] (4196) (5039a) 5243[2] 5952a[2] 6495a[3]

Dart *J R Fanshawe* a78 68
4 br m Diktat—Eilean Shona (Suave Dancer (USA))
7045[4] (7271) 7366[6] 7617[4]

D'Artagnans Dream *G D Blake* a48 67
2 b g Cyrano De Bergerac—Kairine (IRE) (Kahyasi)
4861[10] 5227[8] *5672[8]* 6394[6]

Darwin's Dragon *P F I Cole* a66 66
2 ch c Royal Dragon(USA) —Darwinia (GER) (Acatenango (GER))
6085[8] *6253[5] 6737[9]* ◆ *7318[3] 7602[3]*

Dash Back (USA) *Kevin Prendergast* a55 79
3 b f Sahm(USA) —Nadwah (USA) (Shadeed (USA))
1230a[5]

Dasheena *A J McCabe* a77 61
5 b m Magic Ring(IRE) —Sweet And Lucky (Lucky Wednesday)
72[3] 850[3] 949[3] 1260[3] 1591[2] 2005[13] 2263[10] 2457[5] *3826[8] 5474[6] 6353[4]* 7184[9] 7619[10] 7801[8]

Dasher Reilly (USA) *A Sadik* a53 5
7 b g Ghazi(USA) —Kutira (USA) (Dixieland Band (USA))
7583[7] 7744[9]

Dashing Daniel *N J Vaughan* a47
3 gr g Zamindar(USA) —Etienne Lady (IRE) (Imperial Frontier (USA))
6254[6] 6660[7]

Dash Of Grey (IRE) *Ruaidhri Joseph Tierney* a71 69
9 gr g Simply Great(FR) —Donna Katrina (Kings Lake (USA))
793[3]

Da' Tara (USA) *Nicholas Zito* a115
3 br c Tiznow(USA) —Torchera (USA) (Pirate's Bounty (USA))
(2858a)

Dauberval (IRE) *S Kirk* a77 94
3 b g Noverre(USA) —Just In Love (FR) (Highest Honor (FR))
3396[3] 4552[13] 5449[3] *5938[7]* 6542[6] 6949[8]

Davana *W J H Ratcliffe*
2 b f Primo Valentino(IRE) —Bombay Sapphire (Be My Chief (USA))
2909[12] 3334[9] 4647[9]

Davenport (IRE) *B R Millman* a76 85
6 b g Bold Fact(USA) —Semence D'Or (FR) (Kaldoun (FR))
962[13] 1532[4] (1932) 2476[5] 2897[12] 3311[5] *3824[2]* 4309[9] *7405[4] 7650[3] 7777[2]*

Dave's Revenge (USA) *R Hess Jr* a111
2 bb f The Cliff's Edge(USA) —Midnite Deelite (USA) (Afternoon Deelites (USA))
6967a[4]

Davidia (IRE) *D W Thompson* a60 64
5 b g Barathea(IRE) —Green Life (Green Desert (USA))
2[3] 83[3] 229[4] 507[6]

David Lloyd George *S W James*
3 b g Auction House(USA) —Sharp Decision (Greensmith)
2427[9]

Davidoff (GER) *P Schiergen* 106
4 b h Montjeu(IRE) —Dapprima (GER) (Shareef Dancer (USA))
383a[10] 669a[7] 912a[5] 1667a[5] 7350a[6]

David's Cavalier *R Hollinshead* a61 62
4 b g Beat All(USA) —Foxtrot Pie (Shernazar)
999[10] 1159[10] *1679[2]* ◆ 1913[6] *2290[13] 2707[7]*

Davids Mark *J R Jenkins* a60 52
8 b g Polar Prince(IRE) —Star Of Flanders (Puissance)
121[4] (247) 625[4] 1275[3] 1687[6] *6733[7] 7195[4] 7809[5]*

Davids Matador *Eve Johnson Houghton* 70
2 b c Dansili—Mousseline (USA) (Barathea (IRE))
4150[12] 4973[5] 6398[4]

Davorin (JPN) *M Halford* a81 90
7 br h Warning—Arvola (Sadler's Wells (USA))
4493a[9] *7747[3]*

Dawn At Sea *Mrs K Waldron* a45 51
6 b m Slip Anchor—Finger Of Light (Green Desert (USA))
5232[4] 6668[12]

Dawn Dew (GER) *P Schiergen* 100
3 gr f Montjeu(IRE) —Dawn Dane (FR) (Danehill (USA))
4675a[6] 5329a[3] 6156a[7]

Dawnhill (GER) *J R Fanshawe* 70
4 b g Tiger Hill(IRE) —Dateline (GER) (Surumu (GER))
2954[4]

Dawn Mystery *Rae Guest* a48 54
4 gr m Daylami(IRE) —Frustration (Salse (USA))
1643[12] 2512[2] 2694[7]

Dawn Sky *D R Lanigan* a89 89
4 b g Fantastic Light(USA) —Zacheta (Polish Precedent (USA))
1874[3] *2264[2]* 3461[4] 4146[6] *5699[11]*

Dawn Wee *G R Oldroyd* a26 50
2 ch f Monsieur Bond(IRE) —Kanisfluh (Pivotal)
6578[8] 6788[5] *6953[8] 7269[8] 7530[6] 7719[8]*

Dawn Wind *I A Wood* a58 45
3 b f Vettori(IRE) —Topper (IRE) (Priolo (USA))
644[7] 940[7] 1147[10] 1478[10] 1553[8] 2247[9] 2552[11] 3065[10] 3906[U] 4491[4] 4991[8] 5318[7] 6331[6] *6753[8]*

Dawson Creek (IRE) *B Gubby* a71 49
4 ch g Titus Livius(FR) —Particular Friend (Cadeaux Genereux)
356[2] 453[2] 708[2] 938[2] 1152[4] (4862) 5915[3] 6422[15] 7027[6] 7358[2] 7510[11] 7742[9]

Day By Day *B J Meehan* a70 102
4 ch m Kyllachy—Dayville (USA) (Dayjur (USA))
1698[6] 2000[3] 2685a[2] 3243a[4] 3739[10] 3948[9] 5275[14] 6429[8]

Dayia (IRE) *J Pearce* a83 67
4 br m Act One—Masharik (IRE) (Caerleon (USA))
6413[4] *6596[3]* ◆ *7304[4]* ◆ *7515[4] (7715)*

Day In Dubai *J J Bridger* a22 54
2 b f Dubai Destination(USA) —Pazzazz (IRE) (Green Desert (USA))
4974[10] 6072[6] *7011[12]*

Daylami Dreams *T P Tate* a78 84
4 gr g Daylami(IRE) —Kite Mark (Mark Of Esteem (IRE))
2157[2] 2628[5] 3276[2] (4200) 4516[6]

Daylumney (IRE) *E J O'Neill* a73 62
2 gr f Daylami(IRE) —Athlumney Lady (Lycius (USA))
5534[3] *5870[2] (7117)*

Days Of Pleasure (IRE) *J A Osborne* a67
3 b g Fraam—Altizaf (Zafonic (USA))
483[5] 529[5] 662[2] 773[3] (953) 1245[3] 1487[7]

Daytime Dreamer (IRE) *Conor O'Dwyer* a67 70
4 b g Diktat—Tuppenny (Salse (USA))
7512[4] 7827[7]

Daytona (IRE) *Dan L Hendricks* a85 118
4 ch g Indian Ridge—Kyka (USA) (Blushing John (USA))
6996a[10]

Day To Remember *J J Quinn* a72 77
7 gr g Daylami(IRE) —Miss Universe (IRE) (Warning)
2822[9]

Day Trip (IRE) *B J Meehan* a55 66
3 gr g Daylami(IRE) —Mount Street (IRE) (Pennekamp (USA))
2612[9] 3043[4] 3573[4] 4281[6]

Dazed And Amazed *R Hannon* a102 98
4 b g Averti(IRE) —Amazed (Clantime)
1442[7] 1802[4] 1985[4] 2195[7] 2760[12] 3646[10] 5233[7] 6200[7] (6328) *6699[3]*

Dazinski *M H Tompkins* 68
2 ch g Sulamani(IRE) —Shuheb (Nashwan (USA))
3495[7] (4256) 5460[6] 6086[5]

Dazzel *D R Lanigan* 50
2 ch f Polish Precedent(USA) —English Harbour (Sabrehill (USA))
5534[9] 6197[11]

Dazzler Mac *N Bycroft* a48 48
7 b g Komaite(USA) —Stilvella (Camden Town)
66[9]

Dazzling Bay *T D Easterby* a85 56
8 b g Mind Games—Adorable Cherub (USA) (Halo (USA))
2698[7] 3111[9] *7092[3] 7225[2] (7384) 7456[11] 7756[7]*

Dazzling Begum *J Pearce* a62 55
3 br f Okawango(USA) —Dream On Me (Prince Sabo)
6004[4] (6562) *6757[4]* 7050[4] *7310[7] 7605[3] 7776[2]*

Dazzling Dust (IRE) *W G M Turner* a27 50
2 b c Tagula(IRE) —Dusty Dazzler (IRE) (Titus Livius (FR))
1263[6] 1480[4] 1574[2] 2004[3] 2450[7] 3309[3] 3570[3] *6489[10]*

Dazzling Light (UAE) *R Charlton* a69 75
3 bb f Halling(USA) —Crown Of Light (Mtoto)
2971[3] ◆ *3637[2] 4302[3]* ◆ 5042[4]

Dea Caelestis (FR) *H R A Cecil* a56 71
3 b f Dream Well(FR) —Gwydion (USA) (Raise A Cup (USA))
2885[3] *3161[6] 4061[12]* 4427[3] 4796[6]

Deacon Blue (FR) *F Rohaut* a76 83
3 ch c Anabaa Blue—Kansas (Kahyasi)
6744a[3]

Dead Cat Bounce (IRE) *J A Osborne* a46
2 b c Mujadil(USA) —Where's Charlotte (Sure Blade (USA))
7164[4]

Deadline (UAE) *P T Midgley* a74 74
4 ch g Machiavellian(USA) —Time Changes (USA) (Danzig (USA))
973[9] 2007[10] 2375[10] 4540[16]

Deadly Encounter (IRE) *R A Fahey* 86
2 br g Lend A Hand—Cautious Joe (First Trump)
(1907) ◆ 2838[5] 4374[5] 4857[10] 5381[9]

Deadly Secret (USA) *R A Fahey* 96
2 b c Johannesburg(USA) —Lypink (USA) (Lyphard (USA))
(2937) 3920[5] 5107[2] ◆ 5827[9] 6483[11]

Deadly Silence (USA) *Dr J D Scargill* a86 88
3 b c Diesis—Mill Guineas (USA) (Salse (USA))
1621[3] *(2291)* ◆ 3048[5] 4448[5] *6355[9]*

Deal Clincher *P Winkworth* a72 65
2 b f Reset(AUS) —Princess Of Garda (Komaite (USA))
2253[6] 2638[6] *3373[2] 4079[11]* 5165[5] 6362[4] 6761[6]

Deal Flipper *P Winkworth* a69 69
3 b f Xaar—Zibet (Kris)
2976[13] 3487[7] 4102[11] *(4943) 5346[10]* 5601[11] 6173[4] *6433[3] 6736[4]*

Dealmaker Frank (USA) *Niall Moran* a44 72
3 b g Diesis—Armourette (USA) (Rahy (USA))
826a[13] 4613a[7]

Dean Iarracht (IRE) *M Dods* 68
2 b g Danetime(IRE) —Sirdhana (Selkirk (USA))
3726[2] 4203[2] 5416[3] 6112[9] 6545[5]

Dearest Trickski (USA) *John W Sadler* a115
4 b m Proudest Romeo(USA) —Trickski (USA) (Peteski (CAN))
6965a[11]

Dear Maurice *E A L Dunlop* a66 91
4 b g Indian Ridge—Shamaiel (IRE) (Lycius (USA))
1926[7] 2360[6] (2897) ◆ (3090) 3800[6] *5207[10]* 5903[8]

Dear Will *J R Fanshawe* a53 9
3 br g Mark Of Esteem(IRE) —Sweet Wilhelmina (Indian Ridge)
163[4] 1166[9] 1870[11] 2552[10]

Deauville Vision (IRE) *M Halford* 109
5 b m Danehill Dancer(IRE) —Alexia Reveuse (IRE) (Dr Devious (IRE))
1104a[3] 1353a[4] 4007a[9] 5134a[3] 5547a[2] 5920a[4] 6298a[11]

Debbys Boy *Miss Gay Kelleway* 59
2 gr g Bertolini(USA) —Zilkha (Petong)
1736[8] 2054[5] 2980[2] 3706[2] 4290[2]

Debdene Bank (IRE) *Mrs Mary Hambro* a64 69
5 b m Pivotal—Nedaarah (Reference Point)
2257[7] *5995[5]* 6446[6]

Debonnaire *M Johnston* a74 79
3 b f Anabaa(USA) —Ultra Finesse (USA) (Rahy (USA))
1688[DSQ] 2196[12] 3270[12] 3636[9] 5317[2] (6311)

Debord (FR) *Jamie Poulton* a45 67
5 ch g Sendawar(IRE) —Partie De Dames (USA) (Bering)
7216[13]

Debussy (IRE) *J H M Gosden* a66
2 b c Diesis—Opera Comique (FR) (Singspiel (IRE))
7289[4]

Decameron (USA) *Sir Michael Stoute* a87 96
3 br c Theatrical—Morning Pride (IRE) (Machiavellian (USA))
2056[3] 2509[2] (3051) 4197[2] 4853[7] *5908[5]* 6276[6] *7594[6]*

December *Sir Michael Stoute* 44
2 b c Oasis Dream—Winter Solstice (Unfuwain (USA))
5469[14]

December Draw (IRE) *W J Knight* a84
2 br g Medecis—New York (IRE) (Danzero (AUS))
7336[3] (7602)

Dechiper (IRE) *R Johnson* a35 71
6 bb g Almutawakel—Safiya (USA) (Riverman (USA))
1217[13] 1822[3] (2365) 2848[8] 3450[5] 3814[4] 4419[3] 4735[2] 5396[9] 5564[6] 6385[6] 6726[7]

Decider (USA) *R A Harris* a77 59
5 ch g High Yield(USA) —Nikita Moon (USA) (Secret Hello (USA))
625[2] (718) (846) 971[5] 1242[5] 1646[11] 1997[15] 2478[14] *2710[11] 7762[8]*

Decision *C G Cox* 77
2 b c Royal Applause—Corinium (IRE) (Turtle Island (IRE))
5053[8] 6397[3] 6720[5] 7080[3]

Deckchair *H J Collingridge* a56 46
2 b f Monsieur Bond(IRE) —Silver Sun (Green Desert (USA))
5241[13] *6016[11] 6432[8] 6709[6] (7361) 7543[2] 7833[3]*

Declaration Of War (IRE) *P W Chapple-Hyam* 111
3 b c Okawango(USA) —Date Mate (USA) (Thorn Dance (USA))
1421[7] 5932[8]

Decorum (USA) *J H M Gosden* a77 47
2 b c Dynaformer(USA) —Shy Greeting (ARG) (Shy Tom (USA))
6604[13] *7069[6] 7336[4]* ◆

Dedante *D K Ivory* a64 66
2 br f One Cool Cat(USA) —Cloridja (Indian Ridge)
1111[5] 1341[2] 1762[3] ◆ 2903[2] 3485[4] *3846[7] 7279[2] 7501[5]*

Dedicate *R Charlton* a50 70
3 b f Beat Hollow—Total Devotion (Desert Prince (IRE))
2123[5] 2669[4] 4985[9] *6044[8]*

Dedo (IRE) *Kevin Prendergast* a90 94
3 b g Modigliani(USA) —Scant (FR) (Septieme Ciel (USA))
1495a[6] 5731a[8] 6845a[3]

Dee Cee Elle *D Burchell* a25 73
4 b m Groom Dancer(USA) —Missouri (Charnwood Forest (IRE))
7702^{14}

Dee Jay Wells *D W Thompson* 68
4 b g Ishiguru(USA) —Stravaig (IRE) (Sadler's Wells (USA))
1449^{8} 1822^{8}

Deep River Bay (USA) *P W Chapple-Hyam* a67
4 b g Dixieland Band(USA) —For All You Do (USA) (Seeking The Gold (USA))
1701^{2}

Deep Sky (JPN) *Mitsugi Kon* 121
3 b c Agnes Tachyon(JPN) —Abi (Chief's Crown (USA))
7511a^{2}

Deep Waters (IRE) *S Dow* a36 38
3 b g Bahri(USA) —Keithara (IRE) (Entrepreneur)
1526^{14} 1926^{16} 7256^{10} 7599^{8} 7806^{12}

Deep Winter *R A Fahey* a64 88
3 ch f Pivotal—Russian Snows (IRE) (Sadler's Wells (USA))
1019^{4} ◆ 2038^{10} 2380^{7} (3397) (3578) (4455) ◆ 4621^{10} (5391) 6276^{4} 6667^{3}

Deer Daylami (IRE) *M R Channon* a73 78
3 gr c Daylami(IRE) —Abbeville (Highest Honor (FR))
727^{3} 1446^{7} 4116^{3} (4762) 5698^{5}

Deer Lake (IRE) *J Noseda* a37 27
3 b g King's Best(USA) —Atlantic Desire (IRE) (Ela-Mana-Mou)
2571^{9} 5587^{5} 6470^{9}

Deer Park Lord *D A Nolan*
4 b g Compton Admiral—Pretty Average (Skyliner)
1825^{7} 1951^{11} 2747^{11} 3577^{9} 3953^{11}

De Facto *J H M Gosden* a59 64
3 ch c Medicean—Ascendancy (Sadler's Wells (USA))
1418^{8} 1854^{5} 2413^{8} 3095^{12} 3421^{5}

Defaillance (IRE) *M Gasparini* 101
3 b f Marju(IRE) —Difesa Indiana (IRE) (High Estate)
2231a^{12} 3076a^{18}

Defectivedetective *Dr J D Scargill* 27
4 b g Terimon—Afterthought (Petoski)
5148^{14} 6032^{9}

Defector (IRE) *W R Muir* a69 70
2 b c Fasliyev(USA) —Rich Dancer (Halling (USA))
3323^{4} ◆ 4027^{3} 5277^{2} 6002^{5}

Defi (IRE) *D A Nolan* a75 71
6 b g Rainbow Quest(USA) —Danse Classique (IRE) (Night Shift (USA))
408^{3} 978^{6} 2250^{7} 2749^{10} 6162^{12} 7132^{7} 7224^{11}

Defies Logic *J G Given* 55
3 ch g Domedriver(IRE) —Khandahar (Zamindar (USA))
1573^{10} 2208^{3} 2915^{12} 4044^{4} 4332^{5} 4738^{5} 5505^{6} 5837^{12}

Definightly *R Charlton* 94
2 bb c Diktat—Perfect Night (Danzig Connection (USA))
4164^{5} 5053^{2} ◆ (5784) ◆ 6118^{2} ◆ (6970) 7430a^{14}

Definite Honey *A B Haynes* 25
2 ch f Baryshnikov(AUS) —By Definition (IRE) (Definite Article)
3358^{9} 5214^{15} 6333^{8}

Defnikov *A B Haynes* a46 14
3 gr g Baryshnikov(AUS) —By Definition (IRE) (Definite Article)
2864^{8} 3605^{14}

Deira Dubai *B W Hills* a72 70
3 b f Green Desert(USA) —Aspen Leaves (USA) (Woodman (USA))
1946^{8} 3379^{2} 3870^{3} (4538) 6380^{10}

Delegator *B J Meehan* 114
2 b c Dansili—Indian Love Bird (Efisio)
4826^{2} ◆ (5246) ◆ 6815^{5}

Delerios *J R Best* a35 35
3 b c Statue Of Liberty(USA) —Littleton Elbereth (Polish Precedent (USA))
1737^{10} 1957^{12} 7304^{8}

Delightful Kiss (USA) *Pete D Anderson* a113 92
4 rg g Kissin Kris(USA) —Deputy's Delight (USA) (French Deputy (USA))
6993a^{4}

Dellini (IRE) *M R Channon* 88
3 b f Green Desert(USA) —Belle Genius (USA) (Beau Genius (CAN))
3124^{7} 3971^{6}

Del Mar Sunset *W J Haggas* a83 86
9 b g Unfuwain(USA) —City Of Angels (Woodman (USA))
3003^{9} 3337^{5} 3736^{3} 4276^{8} 4565^{2} 4771^{3} 5209^{2} 6599^{6} 6989^{5} 7116^{3}

Delta Diva (USA) *P F I Cole* a69 73
3 b f Victory Gallop(CAN) —Tjinouska (USA) (Cozzene (USA))
4300^{4} 5291^{11}

Delude (IRE) *R Bouresly* a90 76
10 ch g Be My Guest(USA) —Deceive (Machiavellian (USA))
476a^{6} 493a^{4} 817a^{11}

Delvita (FR) *J-V Toux* 90
4 gr m Pinmix(FR) —Very Very Nice (IRE) (Soviet Star (USA))
6568a^{7}

Demand *W J Haggas* 55
2 b f Red Ransom(USA) —Coy (IRE) (Danehill (USA))
4740^{8} 5534^{8} 6553^{11}

Dematraf (IRE) *P D Evans* a44 69
6 gr m Atraf—Demolition Jo (Petong)
349^{5} 466^{7} (Dead)

Demeanour (USA) *E A L Dunlop* 71
2 ch f Giant's Causeway(USA) —Akuna Bay (USA) (Mr Prospector (USA))
4149^{4} ◆ 4897^{3} 6081^{9}

Democrate *A Fabre* a86 113
3 gr c Dalakhani(IRE) —Aiglonne (USA) (Silver Hawk (USA))
(1887a) 2654a^{18}

Demolition *N Wilson* a75 84
4 ch g Starborough—Movie Star (IRE) (Barathea (IRE))
1520^{5} 2155^{4} 2591^{2} 3143^{2} (4688) 5858^{8} 6233^{6} 7025^{10}

Demonious *R Pritchard-Gordon* a82 87
9 ch g Dr Devious(IRE) —Born Gold (USA) (Blushing Groom (FR))
604a^{6}

Demure Princess *W G M Turner* a34 60
3 b f Tamure(IRE) —Princess Penny (King's Signet (USA))
2549^{12} 4298^{6} 5215^{8} 5787^{10}

Denanto (IRE) *P A Fahy* a21 62
4 ch m Shinko Forest(IRE) —Sakanda (IRE) (Vayrann)
5873a^{11}

Denbera Dancer (USA) *M Johnston* a87 77
4 b h Danehill(USA) —Monevassia (USA) (Mr Prospector (USA))
95^{3} 134^{4} 357^{3} (531) 791^{2} 888^{4} 1016^{9}

Dendor *D W Barker* 63
4 b g Warningford—Dolphin Dancer (Dolphin Street (FR))
4683^{2}

Denis Of Cork (USA) *David M Carroll* a113
3 b c Harlan's Holiday(USA) —Unbridled Girl (USA) (Unbridled (USA))
1820a^{3} 2858a^{2}

Denomination (USA) *Mme C Head-Maarek* 96
2 b f Smart Strike(CAN) —Dreamlike (USA) (Storm Cat (USA))
5139a^{2} 5987a^{3} 6519a^{10} 7185a^{5}

Den's Boy *J R Boyle* a35 2
3 b g Josr Algarhoud(IRE) —Den's-Joy (Archway (IRE))
135^{8} 223^{8} 454^{7}

Den's Gift (IRE) *C G Cox* a87 90
4 rg g City On A Hill(USA) —Romanylei (IRE) (Blues Traveller (IRE))
26^{3} 417^{3} 1174^{4} 1532^{3} 2013^{3} 3167^{2} 3855^{2} 4509^{12} 6130^{2} 6675^{7} 7439^{6}

Denton Diva *M Dods* a66 63
2 b f Tobougg(IRE) —Seeking Utopia (Wolfhound (USA))
4921^{3} 5539^{3} 6381^{4} 6988^{8} (7179)

Deo Gratias (POL) *Carl Llewellyn*
8 b g Enjoy Plan(USA) —Dea (POL) (Canadian Winter (CAN))
4365^{15} 4691^{13}

Deo Valente (IRE) *B J Meehan* a67 84
3 b g Dubai Destination(USA) —Pack Ice (USA) (Wekiva Springs (USA))
2199^{3} 3002^{8} 6771^{8} 6888^{2}

Dependonyou *A J McCabe*
2 br f Makbul—Deep End (USA) (Lord Avie (USA))
7735^{9} 7830^{9}

Deposer (IRE) *J R Best* a98 90
2 b c Kheleyf(USA) —Bezant (IRE) (Zamindar (USA))
3417^{2} ◆ (3848) 5226^{6} 5693^{6} 6503a^{4}

Depraux (IRE) *G M Moore* a25 66
5 br g Generous(IRE) —Happy Memories (IRE) (Thatching)
3884^{9} 4592^{2} 4817^{3} 5396^{12} 7293^{12}

Derbaas (USA) *E A L Dunlop* 99
2 b c Seeking The Gold(USA) —Sultana (USA) (Storm Cat (USA))
3853^{4} ◆ (4360) 5462^{3} 6428^{3}

Derison (USA) *P Van De Poele* 109
6 b g Miesque's Son(USA) —Devolli (Saumarez)
2034a^{3} 4881a^{6} 5556a^{7} 5955a^{4} 6568a^{4}

Derricks Dotty *N J Vaughan* a64 69
4 br g Beat All(USA) —Pass The Rose (IRE) (Thatching)
3431^{5} (3757) 3951^{14} 4813^{12}

Derringbay (IRE) *M H Tompkins* a50
2 b g Mull Of Kintyre(USA) —Rustle In The Wind (Barathea (IRE))
6552^{13} 6737^{10}

Der Rosenkavalier (IRE) *A M Balding* a36
2 gr g Captain Rio—Brooks Masquerade (Absalom)
3331^{7}

Desdamona (IRE) *A Berry* 20
2 b f Desert Style(IRE) —Tattymulmona Queen (USA) (Royal Academy (USA))
6785^{10} 7126^{5}

Desert Ben (IRE) *Peter Casey* a57 68
5 b g Desert Prince(IRE) —Benefits Galore (IRE) (Brief Truce (USA))
6366a^{22}

Desert Bump *E F Vaughan* a63
2 b f Medicean—Greenfly (Green Desert (USA))
7574^{4} 7689^{2}

Desert Chill (USA) *Saeed Bin Suroor* a97 95
3 b f Red Ransom(USA) —Storm Song (USA) (Summer Squall (USA))
1965^{2} 2717^{3} 2994^{2} (3762) (4300) 5038a^{7} 6323a^{5} 7099^{4}

Desert Clover (USA) *P F I Cole* a76 76
3 bb c Mutakddim(USA) —Booly (USA) (Apalachee (USA))
975^{6} 1426^{5} 1688^{4} 1988^{14} 2761^{5} 3376^{11} 5170^{8} 5607^{5}

Desert Code (USA) *David Hofmans* a112 120
4 ch h E Dubai(USA) —Chatta Code (USA) (Lost Code (USA))
(6994a)

Desert Creek (IRE) *Sir Michael Stoute* 84
2 ch c Refuse To Bend(IRE) —Flagship (Rainbow Quest (USA))
6702^{2} ◆ (7051) ◆

Desert Destiny *C Grant* a86 70
8 b g Desert Prince(IRE) —High Savannah (Rousillon (USA))
5968^{3} 6312^{5} 6551^{12}

Desert Diplomat (IRE) *A B Aziz* a63
7 br g Machiavellian(USA) —Desert Beauty (IRE) (Green Desert (USA))
670a^{9}

Desert Dreamer (IRE) *Tom Dascombe* a87 79
7 b g Green Desert(USA) —Follow That Dream (Darshaan)
26^{10} 210^{3} 329^{6} 429^{2} (775) 870^{2} (1055) (1143) 1211^{11} 1588^{4} 1996^{3} 2203^{6} 2693^{5} 2917^{2} 7436^{5} 7601^{2} 7768^{2}

Desert Dust *R M H Cowell* a31 48
5 b g Vettori(IRE) —Dust (Green Desert (USA))
5626^{5} 7644^{5}

Deserted Dane (USA) *G A Swinbank* a81 91
4 b h Elusive Quality(USA) —Desertion (IRE) (Danehill (USA))
1818^{3} 2212^{3} 2583^{6} 3009^{11} 3370^{8} 4291^{F} (Dead)

Desert Fairy *P W D'Arcy* a47 13
2 b f Tobougg(IRE) —Regal Fairy (IRE) (Desert King (IRE))
4080^{8} 6391^{12} 6682^{10}

Desert Falls *R M Whitaker* a86 69
2 b g Pyrus(USA) —Sally Traffic (River Falls)
2217^{5} 2392^{3} 4045^{3} 4734^{4} 5633^{3} (5905) (6281) 6575^{4}

Desert Fever *B W Hills* 57
2 b c Dubai Destination(USA) —Gaijin (Caerleon (USA))
4510^{9}

Desert Hawk *W M Brisbourne* a58 61
7 b g Cape Cross(IRE) —Milling (IRE) (In The Wings)
999^{11} 1692^{7} 1776^{4} 2513^{7} 3113^{3} 3657^{7} 3732^{6} (4936) 5020^{5} 5450^{2} 5583^{4} 6538^{8} 6786^{6} 7039^{9} 7427^{6} 7667^{3}

Desert Hunter (IRE) *Micky Hammond* a54 55
5 b g Desert Story(IRE) —She-Wolff (IRE) (Pips Pride)
562^{3} 681^{2} 858^{7} 933^{9} 2463^{2} 2936^{7} 3079^{10} 3582^{7} 4961^{10} 7375^{11}

Desert Icon (IRE) *W J Knight* 78
2 b c Desert Style(IRE) —Gilded Vanity (IRE) (Indian Ridge)
3219^{4} (3798) ◆ 4588^{P}

Desert Kiss *W R Swinburn* 70
3 b f Cape Cross(IRE) —Kiss And Don'Tell (USA) (Rahy (USA))
5278^{8} 6345^{3} 6705^{2}

Desert Lark *G A Swinbank* 44
3 b c Sakhee(USA) —Oyster Catcher (IRE) (Bluebird (USA))
1556^{8}

Desert Leader (IRE) *W M Brisbourne* a75 55
7 b g Green Desert(USA) —Za Aamah (USA) (Mr Prospector (USA))
104^{5} 1639^{7} 2804^{7}

Desert Light (IRE) *D Shaw* a63 43
7 b g Desert Sun—Nacote (IRE) (Mtoto)
29^{7} 181^{4} 270^{6} 391^{4} 515^{7} 581^{9} 718^{6} 884^{4} (933) 1145^{10} 1275^{8} 2075^{14} 7195^{11} 7288^{11} 7710^{7} 7809^{7}

Desert Lord *K A Ryan* a101 117
8 b g Green Desert(USA) —Red Carnival (USA) (Mr Prospector (USA))
1772^{2} 2404^{3} 2652a^{12} 3533a^{3} 4550^{11} 5245^{9} 5793^{8}

Desert Love (IRE) *M Ciciarelli*
2 ch f Desert Prince(IRE) —Personal Love (USA) (Diesis)
2744a^{2}

Desert Lover (IRE) *R J Price* a61 62
6 b g Desert Prince(IRE) —Crystal Flute (Lycius (USA))
334^{4} 236^{8} 289^{2} 362^{5} 530^{7} 684^{2} 808^{5}

Desert Maze (IRE) *J Wade* 38
4 ch g Desert Sun—Allzi (USA) (Zilzal (USA))
2008^{13}

Desert Mile (IRE) *Edward Lynam* a80 75
5 b m Desert Style(IRE) —Maiskaya (IRE) (Mark Of Esteem (IRE))
6511a^{3}

Desert Ocean (IRE) *G Collet* a81 93
4 b g Desert Sun—Skerray (Soviet Star (USA))
(5113a)

Desert Opal *C R Dore* a79 80
8 ch g Cadeaux Genereux—Nullarbor (Green Desert (USA))
286^{3} 459^{6} 580^{4} 699^{5} 840^{6} 1378^{6} 2710^{4} 3724^{7} 4025^{6} 4154^{6} 5046^{5} 5260^{14} (5626) 7295^{5} (7377) 7621^{12} 7743^{9}

Desert Phantom (USA) *D M Simcock* 98
2 b c Arch(USA) —Junkinthetrunk (USA) (Top Account (USA))
(3997) (4908) ◆ (5359) 6520a^{5}

Desert Pride *W S Kittow* a65 70
3 b g Desert Style(IRE) —Dalu (IRE) (Dancing Brave (USA))
3268^{2} 3847^{2} 4431^{7} 5315^{8} 5867^{10}

Desert Rat (IRE) *Micky Hammond* a26 67
4 b g Desert Sun—Virtue Rewarded (IRE) (Darshaan)
3175^{11} 3602^{11} 3963^{8} 4031^{9} 4541^{9}

Desert Realm (IRE) *A Al Raihe* a87 87
5 b g Desert Prince(IRE) —Fawaayid (USA) (Vaguely Noble)
294a^{11} 474a^{13}

Desert Sea (IRE) *D W P Arbuthnot* a96 99
5 b g Desert Sun—Sea Of Time (USA) (Gilded Time (USA))
(3044) ◆ 3490^{15} 4843^{6} 5940^{2} 6272^{6}

Desert Soul *R H York* a61 62
4 b g Fantastic Light(USA) —Jalousie (IRE) (Barathea (IRE))
91^{13} 212^{8}

Desert Star (ITY) *S Benedetti*
2 b f Desert Prince(IRE) —Imatea (IRE) (Primo Dominie)
2744a^{10}

Desert Streak (FR) *H J L Dunlop* a62 48
2 b c Green Desert(USA) —Niner's Home (USA) (Forty Niner (USA))
6776^{11} 7098^{8}

Desert Strike *P F I Cole* a73 70
2 b c Bertolini(USA) —Mary Jane (Tina's Pet)
5904^{10} 6434^{5} 6863^{3} 7179^{2} (7574) 7820^{4}

Desert Sunset *M Johnston* 70
2 ch f Dubai Destination(USA) —Racina (Bluebird (USA))
2357^{4} 3292^{2} 3895^{P}

Desert Thistle (IRE) *H J L Dunlop* a55 75
3 b c Tamarisk(IRE) —Taajreh (IRE) (Mtoto)
4984^{6} 5428^{6} 5758^{3} 6558^{5} 6905^{7}

Desert Tommy *A Sadik* a19
7 b g Desert King(IRE) —Flambera (FR) (Akarad (FR))
661^{8}

Desert Vision *M W Easterby* a80
4 b g Alhaarth(IRE) —Fragrant Oasis (USA) (Rahy (USA))
7344^{5} 7423^{6} 7583^{2}

Desiderio *R Hannon* a67 78
3 b c Oasis Dream—Pleasuring (Good Times (ITY))
714^{8} 797^{4} 900^{3} ◆ 1115^{2} (1166) 1389^{9} (1958) 2161^{4} 2695^{9} 3407^{2} 3525^{4} 4429^{3} 4766^{2} (6888)

Desire To Excel (IRE) *P F I Cole* 76
2 b g Desert Style(IRE) —Sanpala (Sanglamore (USA))
1832^{3} 2124^{5} 2458^{4} 3444^{8}

Desperate Dan *A B Haynes* a87 77
7 b g Danzero(AUS) —Alzianah (Alzao (USA))
1190^{3} (1489) 1646^{3} 2050^{4} 2351^{4} 2474^{3} 2551^{2} 2923^{3} 3269^{2} 3520^{4} 4102^{3} (4324) (5121) 5319^{6} 5861^{11} (6045) 6328^{2} 6750^{3} 6881^{8}

Destare *J E Pease* 99
3 b f Desert Prince(IRE) —Contare (Shirley Heights)
2033a^{14}

Destiny Quest (USA) *L M Cumani* 72
2 b g Proud Citizen(USA) —Sunset Service (USA) (Deputy Minister (CAN))
5271^{11} 5753^{3}

Destinys Dream (IRE) *D W Barker* 71
3 b f Mull Of Kintyre(USA) —Dream Of Jenny (Caerleon (USA))
3369^{6} 3866^{4} 4392^{5} 4680^{5}

Detonator (IRE) *M Johnston* a107 99
3 b g Fantastic Light(USA) —Narwala (Darshaan)
3294^{3} 4205^{2} ◆ 4351^{2} 4519^{10} (5938) 6171^{4}

Deuce *Eve Johnson Houghton* a64 55
2 ch f Where Or When(IRE) —Justbetweenfriends (USA) (Diesis)
5227^{10} 5870^{4}

Devilfishpoker Com *R C Guest* a48 51
4 ch g Dr Fong(USA) —Midnight Allure (Aragon)
36^{3} 83^{2}

Devil To Pay *J L Dunlop* 64
2 b c Red Ransom(USA) —My Way (IRE) (Marju (IRE))
5022^{6} 6122^{10} 6714^{9}

Devinius (IRE) *G A Swinbank* 66
3 ch f Choisir(AUS) —Vampress (IRE) (Marju (IRE))
1073^{3} 1817^{3} 3282^{10} 3672^{5} 4163^{5} (4920) 5362^{6}

Devon Diva *M Hill* a51
2 b f Systematic—General Jane (Be My Chief (USA))
7452^{5}

Devon Flame *R J Hodges* a67 35
9 b g Whittingham(IRE) —UAE Flame (IRE) (Polish Precedent (USA))
211^{7} 515^{11} 681^{9}

Devotion To Duty (IRE) *B W Hills* 51
2 b c Montjeu(IRE) —Charmante (USA) (Alydar (USA))
6083^{12}

Deyas Dream *A M Balding* a67 76
2 b f Clodovil(IRE) —Dream On Deya (IRE) (Dolphin Street (FR))
2618^{4} 3207^{5} 3837^{3} 5855^{11} 6172^{4} 7306^{6}

De Zephyr (FR) *Robert Collet* a90 91
6 b h Zieten(USA) —Lyceta (Shirley Heights)
5115a^{8}

Dhahab (USA) *C E Brittain* 57
3 b f Kingmambo(USA) —Lucky Rainbow (USA) (Rainbow Quest (USA))
1445^{9} 1971^{4} 2500^{6} 2991^{17} 3665^{14} 4333^{2} 4777^{6}

Dhaka Dazzle *M F Harris* a48 48
3 b g Josr Algarhoud(IRE) —Magical Flute (Piccolo)
589^{6} 597^{7} 4810^{14}

Dhania (IRE) *R A Teal* a70
2 b g Gulch(USA) —Novograd (USA) (Gentlemen (ARG))
7380^{4}

Dhaular Dhar (IRE) *J S Goldie* a93 108
6 b h Indian Ridge—Pescara (IRE) (Common Grounds)
960^{15} 1218^{5} 1942^{8} (2595) 3197^{2} 3921^{10} 4405^{2} 4587^{16} 5109^{11} 6104^{14} 6269^{4} 6304^{13} 6947^{4} 7245^{9}

Dhehdaah *Mrs P Sly* a78 75
7 b g Alhaarth(IRE) —Carina Clare (Slip Anchor)
1337^{6} 7064^{7}

Dhhamaan (IRE) *Mrs R A Carr* a79 70
3 b g Dilshaan—Safe Care (IRE) (Caerleon (USA))
25^{3} 376^{4} (732) (932) (1063) (1203) 1339^{4} 1576^{6} 4329^{5} 4649^{11} 4920^{7} 5397^{10} 5965^{14} 6792^{14} 7277^{11}

Diabolical (USA) *Saeed Bin Suroor* a119 119
5 ch h Artax(USA) —Bonnie Byerly (USA) (Dayjur (USA))
295a^{4} (814a) 1089a^{7} 3247^{16} 3922^{6} 4915a^{5} 5891^{7} 6304^{2} 6994a^{2}

Diacaro *H Blume* a41 94
3 b c Alhaarth(IRE) —Diacada (GER) (Cadeaux Genereux)
2880a^{7}

Diademas (USA) *M J Gingell* a70 70
3 bb c Grand Slam(USA) —Kona Kat (USA) (Mountain Cat (USA))
70^{2} 170^{2} ◆ 307^{3} 582^{2} 635^{3} 952^{2} 1155^{12} 1257^{4} 1414^{2} 1777^{4} 3021^{11} 3224^{3} 3765^{7} 4163^{11} 4830^{5} 5592^{9} 6004^{11} 6204^{7} 6418^{4} 6907^{9}

Diagora (FR) *Robert Collet* 57
3 ch f Highest Honor(FR) —Dzinigane (FR) (Exit To Nowhere (USA))
6742a^{7}

Dialect *Mrs A J Perrett* a74 74
2 b f Diktat—Welsh Autumn (Tenby)
6910[9] 7140[3] (7380)

Dialogue *M Johnston* a89 84
2 b c Singspiel(IRE) —Zonda (Fabulous Dancer (USA))
4625[5] 5068[4] (5996) 6946[8] (7229) (7655)

Diamantgottin (GER) *P Rau* 98
3 b f Fantastic Light(USA) —Dunnellon (Shareef Dancer (USA))
2065a[4]

Diamond Blade *T D Easterby*
2 ch c Needwood Blade—Branston Gem (So Factual (USA))
957[19]

Diamond Daisy (IRE) *Mrs A Duffield* 58
2 b f Elnadim(USA) —Charlotte's Dancer (Kris)
6051[3] 6548[6] 6785[7]

Diamond Heist *M P Tregoning* a34 55
2 ch g Domedriver(IRE) —Carenage (IRE) (Alzao (USA))
2150[9] 2562[9] 6197[9] 6330[6] 6694[9]

Diamond Hurricane (IRE) *M Wellings* a46 46
4 b g Mujadil(USA) —Christoph's Girl (Efisio)
2463[18] 3033[15]

Diamond Jo (IRE) *Mrs L Williamson* 36
2 b f Johannesburg(USA) —Still As Sweet (IRE) (Fairy King (USA))
6722[7] 7117[12]

Diamond Josh *M Mullineaux* a47 62
6 ch g Primo Dominie—Exit (Exbourne (USA))
16[11]

Diamond Key (IRE) *Eoin Doyle* a80 56
4 b m Key Of Luck(USA) —Aljeeza (Halling (USA))
4511a[20]

Diamond Quest (SAF) *A M Balding* 111
7 b g Saumarez—Discover Diamonds (AUS) (Marscay (AUS))
495a[10] 669a[3] 816a[9] 3154[8] 4585[10] 5289[8]

Diamond Royal (IRE) *E A L Dunlop* 74
3 b f Red Ransom(USA) —Gaily Royal (IRE) (Royal Academy (USA))
1525[6] 1965[5] 2496[10] 3081[10]

Diamond Seeker *V Smith* a46 36
3 ch f Erhaab(USA) —Slavonic Dance (Muhtarram (USA))
424[6]

Diamond Stripes (USA) *Richard Dutrow Jr* a115
5 rg g Notebook(USA) —Romantic Summer (USA) (On To Glory (USA))
(1087a)

Diamond Surprise *R Curtis* a60 59
2 b f Mark Of Esteem(IRE) —Lucky Dip (Tirol)
6013[5] 6273[7] 7198[5] 7794[3]

Diamond Til (IRE) *G L Moore* a53
2 b f Invincible Spirit(IRE) —A'Bunadh (USA) (Diesis)
6697[9] 7095[13] 7356[11] 7464[8]

Diamond Twister (USA) *J R Best* a71 59
2 b c Omega Code(USA) —King's Pact (USA) (Slewacide (USA))
6342[6] 6863[6] 7356[2] 7555[3] 7700[6]

Diamond Tycoon (USA) *B J Meehan* a84 110
4 b h Johannesburg(USA) —Palacoona (FR) (Last Tycoon)
1077[8] 1989[2] 2580[7] 3122[7] 3921[8]

Diamond World *C A Horgan* a47 58
5 b m Agnes World(USA) —In A Twinkling (IRE) (Brief Truce (USA))
174[7]

Diamond Yas (IRE) *H R A Cecil* a83 86
3 b f Mull Of Kintyre(USA) —Balgren (IRE) (Ballad Rock)
(1869) 3002[2] 5405[4] 5759[4] 6027[2] 6528[8]

Diane's Choice *Miss Gay Kelleway* a92 91
5 ch m Komaite(USA) —Ramajana (USA) (Shadeed (USA))
162[6] 411[9] 2501[8] 2828[19] 3042[9] 3271[9] (3575) 4051[8] 4555[15] 4767[2] (5319) 5467[9] 5751[3] 6006[4] 6131[17] 6650[9]

Diapason (IRE) *Tom Dascombe* 66
2 b f Mull Of Kintyre(USA) —Suaad (IRE) (Fools Holme (USA))
6531[5] 6702[4]

Dice (IRE) *L M Cumani* 68
2 b c Kalanisi(IRE) —Rain Dancer (IRE) (Sadler's Wells (USA))
5158[7] 5784[3]

Dicey Affair *G L Moore* a66 40
2 b f Medicean—Lucky Dice (Perugino (USA))
5535[11] 6600[7] 7097[7] 7524[4]

Dichoh *M A Jarvis* a89 16
5 b g Diktat—Hoh Dancer (Indian Ridge)
280[5] 910[2] 1335[3] 1545[8] 7215[4] 7439[4] 7821[5]

Dickens (GER) *H Blume* 113
5 b h Kallisto(GER) —Desidera (IRE) (Shaadi (USA))
1662a[2] 3075a[4] 3540a[7] 4585[6] 5741a[3] 6324a[4]

Dickensian (IRE) *E Charpy* 99
2 br h Xaar—Cappella (IRE) (College Chapel)
294a[8] 495a[12]

Dickie Deano *J M Bradley* a39
4 b g Sooty Tern—Chez Bonito (IRE) (Persian Bold)
5148[15]

Dickie Le Davoir *John A Harris* a79 93
4 b g Kyllachy—Downeaster Alexa (USA) (Red Ryder (USA))
(64) 190[4] 346[2] 460[2] (536) 643[2] 801[2] 1023[2] 1084[3] 1278[6] 1588[6] 1901[6] 2293[7] 2703[6] (2747) 2891[2] (3169) 3728[8] (3812) 3956[4] 3998[7] 4171[7] 4460[7] 5222[5] 5345[12] 5594[9] 5861[6] 6069[12] 6486[18]

Dickie Valentine *M R Bosley* a52 49
3 b g Diktat—Passionelle (Nashwan (USA))
333[6] 597[3] 853[2] 976[10] 1130[6] 5148[8] 5787[8] 6747[8]

Dicksons Delight (USA) *D K Ivory* 27
2 b g Black Mambo(USA) —Another Episode (USA) (Out Of Place (USA))
4728[13] 5225[16] 6133[11]

Didactic *A J McCabe* a49 48
4 b g Diktat—Scene (IRE) (Scenic)
66[8] 282[10]

Didana (IRE) *M G Quinlan* a66 60
3 br f Diktat—Daanat Nawal (Machiavellian (USA))
1161[13] 1364[9] 1937[4]

Diddums *W J Haggas* a78 78
2 b g Royal Applause—Sahara Shade (USA) (Shadeed (USA))
4027[2] ◆ (4616) 5274[4] 6426[11] 6987[2]

Didntcomeback *M S Saunders* a41 46
3 b g Oasis Dream—Latin Beauty (IRE) (Sadler's Wells (USA))
2099[7] 3502[9] 3870[6]

Diego Rivera *P J Makin* a69 72
3 b c Orpen(USA) —Manuka Too (IRE) (First Trump)
2198[9] 2919[7] 3916[2] 4388[2] 4782[5] 5268[2] 7360[10]

Die Haard *J R Gask* a60
2 ch g Haafhd—Decision Maid (USA) (Diesis)
7333[8] 7593[10] 7783[7]

Diesis Of Cloyne (USA) *K R Burke* 64
2 ch f Diesis—Venus (USA) (Atticus (USA))
4697[4] 5256[6] 6291[8]

Different Opinion (IRE) *A Peraino* 84
3 ch f Noverre(USA) —Mainstream Opinion (IRE) (Indian Ridge)
1659a[9]

Dig Deep (IRE) *J J Quinn* a104 96
6 b g Entrepreneur—Diamond Quest (Rainbow Quest (USA))
2398[6] 2778[8] 3228[5] 3451[6] 3708[10] 4171[8] 4445[10] 4928[9] 6278[14] 6859[2]

Diggeratt (USA) *R A Fahey* 77
2 rg f Maria's Mon(USA) —Miss Exhilaration (USA) (Gulch (USA))
3734[5] (4169) 4628[2] ◆ 5228[9]

Digger Derek (IRE) *R A Fahey* a52 73
2 b c Key Of Luck(USA) —Carson Dancer (USA) (Carson City (USA))
3597[3] 4072[5] 4474[4] 5006[2] 5274[13] 6112[4] (6549) (6761)

Digit *B Smart* a23 62
2 ch f Reel Buddy(USA) —Compact Disc (IRE) (Royal Academy (USA))
2887[7] 3125[2] 3669[4] 3908[5] 4328[5] 5041[3] 5560[2] 5966[2] (6787) 7451[8]

Digital *M R Channon* a80 85
11 ch g Safawan—Heavenly Goddess (Soviet Star (USA))
1047[2] (1268) 1386[8] 1802[3] 1908[3] 2644[4] 2773[3] 3042[8] 3520[3] 3881[10] 3945[2] 4555[18] 4981[6] 5751[6] 6164[2]

Digital Dish (IRE) *Eamon Tyrrell* a51 61
3 b f Fayruz—Lyrical Vision (IRE) (Vision (USA))
1964[11] 4715a[12]

Diglett (IRE) *L Riccardi* 95
2 b f One Cool Cat(USA) —Rich Gift (Cadeaux Genereux)
5951a[9]

Dijeerr (USA) *Saeed Bin Suroor* 113
4 b h Danzig(USA) —Sharp Minister (CAN) (Deputy Minister (CAN))
379a[2] 671a[2] 743a[2] (4644) 5840[2] 6484[14] 7147[4]

Diksie Dancer *K A Ryan* a69 67
4 br m Diktat—Careful Dancer (Gorytus (USA))
1416[5]

Diktalina *W R Muir* a66 37
2 b f Diktat—Oiselina (FR) (Linamix (FR))
5643[11] 6432[6] 7023[7]

Diktaram *J R Weymes* a33
2 b g Diktat—Aries (GER) (Big Shuffle (USA))
7424[10]

Diktatorial *J Howard Johnson* a87 82
6 br g Diktat—Reason To Dance (Damister (USA))
2658[7] 4217[5] 4541[4]

Diktatorship (IRE) *Jennie Candlish* a65 50
5 b g Diktat—Polka Dancer (Dancing Brave (USA))
4477[4] 5993[6]

Diktat Tempo *I A Wood* a45 26
3 b f Diktat—Upping The Tempo (Dunbeath (USA))
5086[7] 5377[5] 5799[11] 6716[14]

Dillenda *T D Easterby* 58
2 bb f Lend A Hand—Samadilla (IRE) (Mujadil (USA))
6013[7] 6245[6] 6811[2]

Dilmoun (IRE) *Mrs A M Thorpe* a38 11
6 b g Darshaan—Mannakea (USA) (Fairy King (USA))
622[4]

Dilwin (IRE) *P R Webber* a58 61
4 b g Dilshaan—Welsh Harp (Mtoto)
3037[6]

Dimander (IRE) *Mrs A J Perrett* a72
2 ch c Namid—Red Liason (IRE) (Selkirk (USA))
7465[6] 7709[2] (7830)

Dimashq *P T Midgley* a33 61
6 b m Mtoto—Agwaas (IRE) (Rainbow Quest (USA))
3335[3] 4457[3] (4556) 4947[5] 5917[6]

Dimenticata (IRE) *Kevin Prendergast* a94 111
4 b m Danetime(IRE) —Non Dimenticar Me (IRE) (Don't Forget Me)
1880a[9] 2420a[8] 3619a[3] (4223a) 4467a[6] 6689a[11] 7328a[6]

Diminuto *M D I Usher* a80 78
4 b m Iron Mask(USA) —Thicket (Wolfhound (USA))
84[2] 359[6] 482[3] 676[7] 1047[5] 1268[5] 1285[4] 1677[5] 2102[7] 2292[6] 2616[6] 3363[10] (3825) 4103[5] 4767[6] 5026[5] 5610[10] 6564[2] 6840[9] 7292[8] 7746[10]

Dimmi Di Su (IRE) *G Miliani* 91
3 b c Desert Prince(IRE) —Gin Rosa (Lion Cavern (USA))
1513a[11]

Dinarius *D E Pipe* a67 59
3 b g Bertolini(USA) —Ambassadress (USA) (Alleged (USA))
1119[3] 5931[3]

Dingaan (IRE) *A M Balding* a93 93
5 b g Tagula(IRE) —Boughtbyphone (Warning)
1800[4] 1928[10] 2371[2] 2693[2] 3898[2] 4601[3] 5030[3] 5424[4] 7215[2] 7313[10] 7470[7]

Dinner Date *T Keddy* a72 65
6 ch g Groom Dancer(USA) —Misleading Lady (Warning)
51[12] (879) 1048[5] (1565) 1853[7] 2533[3] 6422[14] 7094[6] (7494) 7642[5]

Diocleziano (USA) *R Menichetti* a94 94
3 b c Barkerville(USA) —Essie's Maid (USA) (Linkage (USA))
7643a[10]

Diplomatic Dan (IRE) *E J Alston*
5 b g Imperial Ballet(IRE) —Yaqatha (IRE) (Sadler's Wells (USA))
2360[13]

Dirar (IRE) *M Halford* a87 93
3 b c King's Best(USA) —Dibiya (IRE) (Caerleon (USA))
1233a[5] 1509a[6]

Directa's Digger (IRE) *M J Scudamore* 76
4 b h Daggers Drawn(USA) —Chita Rivera (Chief Singer)
67[11] 2245[2] (2572) 3007[2] (3083) (3216) 4516[8] 4955[5]

Direct Debit (IRE) *M Wellings* a84 91
5 b g Dansili—Dimple (Fairy King (USA))
6431[7] 6841[12] 7278[4] (7423) 7564[6]

Director's Chair *Miss J Feilden* a66 69
3 b g Catcher In The Rye(IRE) —Capegulch (USA) (Gulch (USA))
748[5] 1130[3] 1549[2] 2090[2] 2528[8] 3614[8] (4260) 6049[5] 6379[7] 6712[10]

Directorship *P R Chamings* 74
2 br c Diktat—Away To Me (Exit To Nowhere (USA))
5842[7] 6602[4]

Diriculous *T G Mills* a107 94
4 b g Diktat—Sheila's Secret (IRE) (Bluebird (USA))
(109) ◆ 191[5] (729) 1146[2] ◆ (1261) 1683[3] (2293) ◆ 2760[5] 3374[9] (4058) 4928[3] (5424) 5681[3] 6903[2] 7576[2]

Dirtybirdie *M Halford* a57 57
3 b f Diktat—Khalafiya (Darshaan)
4613a[4]

Discanti (IRE) *T D Easterby* a47 81
3 ch g Distant Music(USA) —Gertie Laurie (Lomond (USA))
1548[4] (2287) 2570[3] ◆ (3256) ◆ 4074[3]

Dispatch Box *W Jarvis* 52
4 b h Dansili—Division Bell (Warning)
2561[8]

Dispol Bertie *P T Midgley* 30
2 b c Bertolini(USA) —Perfect Poppy (Shareef Dancer (USA))
1907[8] 2216[7]

Dispol Diva *P T Midgley* 55
2 b f Deportivo—Kingston Rose (GER) (Robellino (USA))
1425[6] (1574) 3008[11] 3225[3] 3706[6] 5006[4] 5774[3] 6214[3] 6394[3]

Dispol Grand (IRE) *P T Midgley* a69 66
2 b g Raise A Grand(IRE) —Hever Rosina (Efisio)
1967[7] 2909[7] 3365[7] 3788[4] (4948) ◆ 5306[4] 6350[2] 6579[3] 7219[4]

Dispol Isle (IRE) *T D Barron* a65 78
6 gr m Trans Island—Pictina (Petong)
(1729) 2007[6] 2672[5] 3214[4] 3552[3] 3892[4] 4219[5] (4245) 4650[9] 4744[4]

Dispol Kintie (IRE) *P T Midgley* 39
2 b f Mull Of Kintyre(USA) —Jet Lock (USA) (Crafty Prospector (USA))
3411[13] 3792[6] 4203[10] 4604[11]

Dispol Kylie (IRE) *P T Midgley* 84
2 b f Kheleyf(USA) —Professional Mom (USA) (Spinning World (USA))
(1324) (1813) 2167[9] 2838[6] (4648) 4948[3] 6068[8] 6656[8]

Dispol Mulofky (IRE) *P T Midgley* a57 56
2 b f Mull Of Kintyre(USA) —Jungle Story (IRE) (Alzao (USA))
1118[2] 1303[5] 1627[3] 2217[7] 2865[6] 3815[4] 4243[6]

Dispol Toba *P T Midgley* 35
2 ch f Tobougg(IRE) —Skiddaw Bird (Bold Owl)
995[10] 1889[3] 2206[7] 2910[6] 3106[6] 3830[5] 4257[4]

Distalino (FR) *F Doumen* 101
5 b g Poliglote—Distale (USA) (Trempolino (USA))
1888a[4]

Distant Diamond (IRE) *W R Swinburn* a66 50
3 b g Distant Music(USA) —La Belle Katherine (USA) (Lyphard (USA))
1622[P]

Distant Memories (IRE) *T P Tate* 80
2 b g Falbrav(IRE) —Amathia (IRE) (Darshaan)
6789[6] (7126)

Distant Noble *R Brotherton* a44 54
3 b g Carnival Dancer—Fly In Style (Hernando (FR))
279[5] 853[3] 950[6] 1603[7]

Distant Piper (IRE) *Adrian McGuinness* a71 79
5 b m Distant Music(USA) —Pipers Pool (IRE) (Mtoto)
5873a[6] 7342[9] 7367[3]

Distant Pleasure *M Dods* 65
4 b m Diktat—Our Pleasure (IRE) (Lake Coniston (IRE))
1520[6] 2597[7] 2957[13] 3755[10] (4683) 5420[3] 6409[2] 7131[2]

Distant Rainbow (IRE) *M Brittain*
3 ch g Distant Music(USA) —Marain (IRE) (Marju (IRE))
4378[7] 4877[13] 6530[12]

Distant Rock *D Carroll* a46 60
3 b f Distant Music(USA) —Chaffinch (USA) (Lear Fan (USA))
2660[7] 3213[8] 4952[9] 5714[6] 6040[4] 6217[3] 6485[9]

Distant Star (FR) *W Neuroth* 64
3 ch f Highest Honor(FR) —Distant Lover (Distant Relative)
5336a[7]

Distant Sun (USA) *Miss L A Perratt* a89 80
4 b g Distant View(USA) —The Great Flora (USA) (Unaccounted For (USA))
(194) (580) 824[3] 1033[2] 1481[9] 2210[12] 2538[8] 2938[9] 3203[4]

Distant Vision (IRE) *H A McWilliams* a38 45
5 br m Distant Music(USA) —Najeyba (Indian Ridge)
2248[3] 3112[5] 3404[6] 4118[10] 5452[3] 6159[11]

Distinction (IRE) *Sir Michael Stoute* 116
9 b g Danehill(USA) —Ivy Leaf (IRE) (Nureyev (USA))
1717[3] 3250[2] (3743) 4551[4] 6306[5] 6820[5]

Distinctive Image (USA) *R Hollinshead* a83 68
3 b c Mineshaft(USA) —Dock Leaf (USA) (Woodman (USA))
5780[2] (6280) 7211[4]

Distinctive Spirit (IRE) *K A Ryan* 64
2 b g Elusive City(USA) —Prince's Passion (Brief Truce (USA))
5416[5] 5959[7] 6229[10] 6858[6]

Distinctly Game *K A Ryan* a90 88
6 b g Mind Games—Distinctly Blu (IRE) (Distinctly North (USA))
(210) ◆ 482[4] 836[3] 925[3] 1195[5] 1517[6] 2358[6] 3394[3] 4058[9] 7384[4]

Distinctlythebest *F Watson* 18
8 b g Distinctly North(USA) —Euphyllia (Superpower)
3230[12]

Ditto Ditto *D R Lanigan* a70 17
2 b g Mark Of Esteem(IRE) —City Gambler (Rock City)
5158[15] 5609[7] 6351[2] (6661) 7306[4] ◆ (Dead)

Ditzy Diva *Jean-Rene Auvray* 24
2 b f Imperial Dancer—Runs In The Family (Distant Relative)
4728[14] 6581[12]

Dium Mac *N Bycroft* 83
7 b g Presidium—Efipetite (Efisio)
2379[4] 3294[7]

Divertimenti (IRE) *C R Dore* a83 71
4 b g Green Desert(USA) —Ballet Shoes (IRE) (Ela-Mana-Mou)
233[2] 342[5] 503[4] 729[11] 850[2] (1084) 1409[9] 2083[6] 4121[11] 5345[5] 5697[12] 6627[8] 7153[6] 7510[4] 7677[4]

Divinatore *D Haydn Jones* a43
2 b c Sakhee(USA) —Divina Mia (Dowsing (USA))
7783[6]

Divine Jury (SAF) *M F De Kock* 110
5 b h Jallad(USA) —Divine Nymph (SAF) (Al Mufti (USA))
294a[2] 743a[3]

Divine Love (IRE) *T Wall* a69 58
4 b m Barathea(IRE) —Darling (Darshaan)
36[10] 220[4] 323[9] 490[6] 578[6] 661[9] 779[6] 869[8]

Divine Park (USA) *Kiaran McLaughlin* a118 54
4 b h Chester House(USA) —High In The Park (USA) (Ascot Knight (CAN))
5558a[6]

Divine Power *R M Beckett* a65 82
3 b f Kyllachy—Tiriana (Common Grounds)
(1836) 2481[11] (3918) 4983[7] 5185[5] 6124[11] 6981[17]

Divine Spirit *M Dods* a61 89
7 b g Foxhound(USA) —Vocation (IRE) (Royal Academy (USA))
3009[15] 3370[10] 3708[7] 4171[14] 4418[6] ◆ 4743[5] ◆ (4962) 5542[11] 6066[7] 6859[8]

Divine White *P Bowen* a56 57
5 ch m College Chapel—Snowy Mantle (Siberian Express (USA))
6751[9]

Divinshki (IRE) *Irene J Monaghan* a39 21
8 ch g Desert Prince(IRE) —Blushing Minstrel (IRE) (Nicholas (USA))
877[9] 898[10]

Divvys Dream *P Beaumont* 16
6 gr g Environment Friend—Oriel Dream (Oats)
3227[8]

Dixey *M A Jarvis* a92 92
3 br f Diktat—Hoh Dancer (Indian Ridge)
1806[13] (2666)

Dixie Dean (USA) *Sir Michael Stoute* 58
3 b g Dynaformer(USA) —Dear Daughter (Polish Precedent (USA))
2681[13] 3094[8] 3573[5] 4573[8] 4796[5] 5537[7]

Dixigold (FR) *Carmen Bocskai* 85
7 ch g Gold Away(IRE) —Dixiella (FR) (Fabulous Dancer (USA))
422a[6] 604a[5]

Diyakalanie (FR) *J Boisnard* a101 113
4 b m Ashkalani(IRE) —Diyawara (IRE) (Doyoun)
1713a[6] 4320a[5] 7643a[3]

Diyla (IRE) *M Flannery* 63
5 b m Bahhare(USA) —Deylviyna (IRE) (Doyoun)
4655a[14]

Djalalabad (FR) *Mrs C A Dunnett* a59 61
4 b m King's Best(USA) —Daraydala (IRE) (Royal Academy (USA))
1160[17] 1505[11] 1644[11] 2055[4] 2355[9] 2550[8] 2983[8] 3268[6] 3653[8] 3842[3] 4825[7] 5161[13] 5317[5] 5797[9] (5916) 6036[14]

Django (SWE) *Caroline Stromberg* a55 96
5 b g Acatenango(GER) —Praeriens Drottning (SWE) (Elmaamul (USA))
4676a[4]

Django Reinhardt *J R Gask* a59
2 b g Tobougg(IRE) —Alexander Ballet (Mind Games)
6770[7]

Dnata Flyer (USA) *M Johnston* a67 67
3 b c Mr Greeley(USA) —Regal Miss Copelan (USA) (Copelan (USA))
1139[5] ◆ 1298[11] 1581[2] 1952[8] 2366[8] (3213) 3453[6] 3655[6]

D'Nurse (IRE) *R Hannon* 61
2 br f Catcher In The Rye(IRE) —Summerhill (Habitat)
4339[11] 4665[3] 5461[8] 6865[15] (Dead)

Do As I Say *T D Easterby* 68
3 b g Diktat—Antonia's Choice (Music Boy)
3144[5] 3712[13] 4216[12]

Do Be Brave (IRE) *G D Blake* a58
2 ch g Kheleyf(USA) —Fear Not (IRE) (Alzao (USA))
4728[3] 6552[11]

Dobravany (IRE) *Adrian McGuinness* a41 76
4 b g Danehill Dancer(IRE) —Eadaoin (USA) (King Of Kings (IRE))
4799a^{12}

Doc Jones (IRE) *P D Evans* 68
2 ch g Docksider(USA) —Quick Return (Polish Precedent (USA))
1873^{2}

Docksil *B Grizzetti* a40 99
4 b m Docksider(USA) —Simil (USA) (Apalachee (USA))
1659a^{3} 7349a^{8}

Docofthebay (IRE) *J A Osborne* a103 113
4 ch h Docksider(USA) —Baize (Efisio)
2133^{4} 2465^{4} 3122^{2} 3197^{13} 5265^{5} 5941^{2} 6476^{26}

Doctor Crane (USA) *J H M Gosden* a83 93
2 b c Doneraile Court(USA) —Sharons Song (USA) (Badger Land (USA))
(3476) (4187) 4402 ^{5} 5462^{7} 6284^{6}

Doctor Delta *M Brittain* a34 46
3 b c Dr Fong(USA) —Delta Tempo (IRE) (Bluebird (USA))
2221^{12} 2735^{4} 4689^{9} 5362^{7} 7180^{11}

Doctor Dino (FR) *R Gibson* 121
6 ch h Muhtathir—Logica (IRE) (Priolo (USA))
1091a^{3} (2653a) 3542a^{3} 5557a^{2} 6506a^{5} (7682a)

Doctor Fremantle *Sir Michael Stoute* 116
3 b c Sadler's Wells(USA) —Summer Breeze (Rainbow Quest (USA))
1424^{2} ◆ (1922) 2829^{4} 4042a^{4} 5892^{8}

Doctor Hilary *A B Haynes* a83 62
6 b g Mujahid(USA) —Agony Aunt (Formidable (USA))
378a^{11} 5206^{4} 5936^{9} 6328^{4} 6680^{11} 7315^{10}

Doctor Kris *M Ciciarelli*
2 ch c Dr Fong(USA) —Bluebelle (Generous (IRE))
2745a^{4}

Doctor Ned *Miss Sheena West* a49 52
4 b g Bahamian Bounty—Sangra (USA) (El Gran Senor (USA))
445^{12} 535^{3} 607^{6} 713^{5} 877^{4} 922^{9} 1053^{8} 1411^{6}

Doctor Parkes *E F Vaughan* 80
2 b c Diktat—Lucky Parkes (Full Extent (USA))
3895^{3} 4346^{2} 5158^{4} (5394)

Doctor Robert *Tom Dascombe* a64 79
3 b g Sakhee(USA) —Please (Kris)
2342^{6} 2974^{12}

Doctor's Cave *K O Cunningham-Brown* a80 61
6 b g Night Shift(USA) —Periquitum (Dilum (USA))
1703^{10} 2933^{12} 3383^{10} 3567^{8} 3691^{12}

Dodaa (USA) *N Wilson* a81 61
5 b g Dayjur(USA) —Ra'A (USA) (Diesis)
(100) (206) 318^{3} 488^{6} (641) (774) 971^{2} (1037) 1185^{3} (2050) 2906^{7}

Dohasa (IRE) *G M Lyons* a113 107
3 b g Bold Fact(USA) —Zara's Birthday (IRE) (Waajib)
3047^{6} 3850^{4} 6315a^{U}

Dolcetto (IRE) *J R Fanshawe* a67 64
3 b f Danehill Dancer(IRE) —Rutledge (IRE) (Entrepreneur)
1721^{5} 2509^{5} 3629^{7}

Dollar Chick (IRE) *Noel Meade* a93 85
4 b m Dansili—Dollar Bird (IRE) (Kris)
6261a^{14} 6689a^{18}

Dollarsmile (USA) *Sir Michael Stoute* 73
3 b c Elusive Quality(USA) —Mamlakah (IRE) (Unfuwain (USA))
4349^{4}

Dolly No Hair *D W Barker* 67
3 ch g Reel Buddy(USA) —Champagne Grandy (Vaigly Great)
1452^{11} 1751^{3} 2366^{2} 2891^{12} 3280^{9} 3717^{10} 6219^{18} 6560^{13}

Dolly Penrose *M R Channon* 87
3 b f Hernando(FR) —Mistinguett (IRE) (Doyoun)
1444^{4} 1840^{3} 2207^{2} 2336^{4} 2997^{2} (3930) 4351^{7} 4866^{2} 6527^{5}

Dolly Royal (IRE) *K A Ryan* 28
3 b f Val Royal(FR) —Roos Rose (IRE) (Grand Lodge (USA))
4877^{7} 5361^{10}

Dolphin Jo (AUS) *Terry & Karina O'Sullivan* 111
6 b g Dolphin Street(FR) —High Rent (AUS) (Belligerent (AUS))
6835a^{15}

Dome Blonde *W J Musson* a15
3 ch f Domedriver(IRE) —Proud Titania (IRE) (Fairy King (USA))
1251^{9}

Domenico (IRE) *J R Jenkins* a53 59
10 b g Sadler's Wells(USA) —Russian Ballet (USA) (Nijinsky (CAN))
166^{7}

Dome Rocket *W J Knight* a79 78
2 b g Domedriver(IRE) —Sea Ridge (Slip Anchor)
6674^{2} ◆ 7080^{2} ◆ 7343^{2}

Domesday (UAE) *W G Harrison* a51 53
7 b g Cape Cross(IRE) —Deceive (Machiavellian (USA))
1775^{13} 2866^{14} 5389^{7}

Domingues *Edward Lynam* 106
3 b c Danetime(IRE) —Lindfield Belle (IRE) (Fairy King (USA))
6315a^{11} 6514a^{7} 6845a^{16}

Dona Alba (IRE) *J L Dunlop* 96
3 b f Peintre Celebre(USA) —Fantastic Fantasy (IRE) (Lahib (USA))
1600^{9} (2665) 3877^{5} 4552^{12}

Donard Lodge (IRE) *J Balding* a60 40
3 b f Elnadim(USA) —Knockatotaun (Spectrum (IRE))
7809^{11}

Donatessa (GER) *C J Mann* 91
5 b m Sternkoenig(IRE) —Donadea (GER) (Dashing Blade)
2073^{P}

Donativum *J H M Gosden* 113
2 ro g Cadeaux Genereux—Miss Universe (IRE) (Warning)
2150^{4} 2663^{2} 3105^{7} (5316) (6474) (6998a)

Doncaster Rover (USA) *S Parr* 101
2 b c War Chant(USA) —Rebridled Dreams (USA) (Unbridled's Song (USA))
957^{2} ◆ (1914) 5852^{6} 6713a^{5}

Doncosaque (IRE) *P Howling* a82 68
2 b c Xaar—Darabela (IRE) (Desert King (IRE))
4776^{4} 5404^{6} 6135^{2} 6524^{5} 7054^{7} (7338) (7425) 7623^{5} (7784) ◆

Donegal (USA) *A M Balding* a92 113
3 b g Menifee(USA) —Vickey's Echo (CAN) (Clever Trick (USA))
1922^{5} 3196^{8} (3875) 4505^{2} ◆ 5094^{3} 5685a^{5}

Don Jose (USA) *N J Vaughan* a41 52
5 bb g Dynaformer(USA) —Panthera (USA) (Storm Cat (USA))
374^{11} 2572^{13} 2849^{7} 3059^{4} 3756^{7} 3950^{5} 4220^{13} 4592^{5} 5415^{10} 7499^{9}

Don Julio A (ARG) *N F Glynn* a69 77
4 gr h Salt Lake(USA) —Secret Lady (USA) (Runaway Groom (CAN))
6431^{6} 7235a^{8}

Donna's Double *Karen McLintock* a14 38
13 ch g Weldnaas(USA) —Shadha (Shirley Heights)
989^{9} 1305^{8} 2578^{7} 3131^{10}

Dono Da Raia (BRZ) *Saeed Bin Suroor* 106
6 ch h Hibernian Rhapsody(IRE) —Outra Arumba (BRZ) (Henri Le Balafre (FR))
293a^{11} 652a^{10}

Don Pasquale *J T Stimpson* a55 59
6 br g Zafonic(USA) —Bedazzling (IRE) (Darshaan)
77^{2} 251^{6} 299^{6} 769^{5} 2513^{8} (4503) 4936^{8}

Don Pele (IRE) *R A Harris* a78 90
6 b g Monashee Mountain(USA) —Big Fandango (Bigstone (IRE))
1278^{8} 2760^{10} 3093^{6} 4103^{4} 4563^{7} 5121^{2} ◆ 5315^{7} 5751^{2} 5861^{3} 6131^{14} 6200^{5} 6402^{15} 7378^{6} 7675^{2} 7730^{2} 7811^{8}

Don Picolo *P A Blockley* a59 39
3 b g Bertolini(USA) —Baby Come Back (IRE) (Fayruz)
1415 222^{3} 257^{3} (534) 623^{7} 845^{4} 853^{4} 7533^{12}

Don Pietro *P A Blockley* a77 80
5 b g Bertolini(USA) —Silver Spell (Aragon)
443^{7} (1486) 2101^{5} 2642^{10} 4001^{3} 4390^{2} 4710^{4} 5345^{11} (7461) 7580^{8}

Don Renato (CHI) *Stephane Chevalier* a109
5 ch h Edgy Diplomat(USA) —Tabla Redonda (CHI) (Braka (USA))
1087a^{3}

Dont Call Me Derek *M A Allen* a50 72
7 b g Sri Pekan(USA) —Cultural Role (Night Shift (USA))
268^{8}

Dont Cross Tina (IRE) *Seamus Fahey* 73
4 b m Cape Cross(IRE) —El Tina (Unfuwain (USA))
1497a^{13} 3531a^{18}

Dontellempike *J Gallagher* 18
3 b g Superior Premium—Hi-Hannah (Red Sunset)
5814^{6}

Don't Forget Faith (USA) *C G Cox* a82 100
3 b f Victory Gallop(CAN) —Contredance (USA) (Danzig (USA))
1470^{6} 1833^{3} 2305^{4} 2743a^{8} 5311^{10} 6266^{4} 7099^{11}

Dontforgeturshovel *J Pearce* a43 30
2 b c Josr Algarhoud(IRE) —Peggys Rose (IRE) (Shalford (IRE))
5271^{14} 5754^{9} 6343^{10} 7269^{4} 7319^{4} 7530^{5}

Don't Go On (IRE) *P D Evans*
2 b f Pyrus(USA) —Valmarana (USA) (Danzig Connection (USA))
3815^{10}

Don't Panic (IRE) *P W Chapple-Hyam* 114
4 ch g Fath(USA) —Torrmana (IRE) (Ela-Mana-Mou)
(958) ◆ 1326^{2} 1716^{2} 2788^{4} 6476^{20} 7147^{RR}

Dontpaytheferryman (USA) *P D Evans* a59 59
3 ch g Wiseman's Ferry(USA) —Expletive Deleted (USA) (Dr Blum (USA))
5261^{11} 7367^{8} 7379^{2} 7573^{6} 7626^{4} 7761^{3}

Don't Stop Me Now (IRE) *J W Hills* a64 60
3 b f Catcher In The Rye(IRE) —Persian Flower (Persian Heights)
1563^{7} 2046^{7} 2528^{10} 3566^{2} (4057)

Dont Tell Josie (IRE) *Miss Maura McGuinness* a63 67
4 b m Beckett(IRE) —Jalwa (USA) (Northern Jove (CAN))
4514a^{11}

Don't Tell Sue *D W P Arbuthnot* a71 62
5 ch g Bold Edge—Opopmil (IRE) (Pips Pride)
427^{2} 729^{12} 939^{6} 3352^{14}

Dookus (IRE) *Robert Collet*
3 gr f Linamix(FR) —Pharaoh's Delight (Fairy King (USA))
6064a^{0}

Doon Haymer (IRE) *Miss L A Perratt* 85
3 b g Barathea(IRE) —Mutige (Warning)
1297^{13} 2142^{6} 3048^{7} 3494^{7} 4017^{3} 4179^{4} 4663^{5} 5224^{2} 6162^{10} 6726^{9}

Doonigan (IRE) *Tim Vaughan* a47 51
4 b g Val Royal(FR) —Music In My Life (IRE) (Law Society (USA))
6550^{14}

Doran's Lodge (IRE) *M R Channon* a29 43
2 ch c Generous(IRE) —Outo'Theblue (IRE) (Grand Lodge (USA))
5678^{11} 6199^{12}

Doremifasollatido (USA) *James Jerkens* a106
2 bb f Bernstein(USA) —Consider It Done (USA) (Green Dancer (USA))
6967a^{10}

Doriana (FR) *A De Royer-Dupre* 101
2 gr f Kendor(FR) —Urgence (FR) (Snurge)
(7103a) (7430a)

Doric Dream *B Smart* a50 59
3 ch f Ishiguru(USA) —Generous Share (Cadeaux Genereux)
343^{7} 4018^{13}

Doric Echo *B Smart* 78
2 b g Bertolini(USA) —Latour (Sri Pekan (USA))
2909^{4} 4169^{5} 4456^{3} 6149^{3} (6406) 7241^{5}

Doric Lady *J A R Toller* a68 82
3 b f Kyllachy—Tanasie (Cadeaux Genereux)
1737^{4} 2122^{10} 2836^{5} 3571^{7} (6003) 6564^{3} (7055)

Dorn Dancer (IRE) *D W Barker* 80
6 b m Danehill Dancer(IRE) —Appledorn (Doulab (USA))
987^{3} 1015^{3} (1378) 1485^{3} 1561^{3} 1818^{2} 2005^{5} 2781^{6} (3260) 3554^{6} 3883^{3} 4016^{2} 4239^{6} 4736^{7}

Do The Deal (IRE) *J J Quinn* 71
2 ch f Halling(USA) —Cairns (UAE) (Cadeaux Genereux)
6273^{3} 6808^{3}

Dot's Delight *K J Burke* a58 58
4 b m Golden Snake(USA) —Hotel California (IRE) (Last Tycoon)
299^{9} 513^{3} (552) 710^{3} 787^{4} 851^{3} 930^{4}

Dotty's Brother *Mrs A Duffield* a56 50
2 ch g Forzando—Colonel's Daughter (Colonel Collins (USA))
1220^{5} 1341^{3} 5394^{13} 6051^{11} 6732^{7} 7113^{11}

Dotty's Daughter *B Storey* a55 46
4 ch m Forzando—Colonel's Daughter (Colonel Collins (USA))
50^{7} 100^{8} 363^{10} 562^{5} 3212^{12}

Double Act *J Noseda* a79 60
2 br g Where Or When(IRE) —Secret Flame (Machiavellian (USA))
5578^{9} 6701^{7} (7289) 7623^{6} 7784^{2}

Double Banded (IRE) *J L Dunlop* a73 97
4 b g Mark Of Esteem(IRE) —Bronzewing (Beldale Flutter (USA))
(1568) 1916^{4} 3490^{12} 4508^{8} 6061^{8} 6288^{6} 6652^{3}

Double Bill (USA) *P F I Cole* a79 74
4 bb g Mr Greeley(USA) —Salty Perfume (USA) (Salt Lake (USA))
1415^{6} 1677^{3} 1901^{2} 2205^{8} 6137^{8} 6864^{12}

Double Carpet (IRE) *G Woodward* a71 65
5 b g Lahib(USA) —Cupid Miss (Anita's Prince)
990^{8} 1485^{5} 1827^{5} 4903^{10} 6178^{15} 7375^{3} 7615^{7} (7637) (7745)

Double Deputy (IRE) *E W Tuer* 67
7 b g Sadler's Wells(USA) —Janaat (Kris)
1972^{8}

Double Duty (IRE) *B J Meehan* a53 61
3 b f Danehill Dancer(IRE) —Taking Liberties (IRE) (Royal Academy (USA))
2971^{8} 3628^{11} 5836^{10} 6735^{9}

Double Ex (IRE) *T Stack* a71 88
2 b c Exceed And Excel(AUS) —Mikara (FR) (Midyan (USA))
6317a^{9}

Double On Red *J M P Eustace* a56 75
3 br f Red Ransom(USA) —Rosy Outlook (USA) (Trempolino (USA))
1161^{8} 1389^{5} 1696^{3} 2052^{5} 2376^{5} 3690^{3} 3918^{9}

Double R *A B Haynes* a10
3 b f Fraam—Bint Albadou (IRE) (Green Desert (USA))
1539^{12}

Double Rubble (USA) *J Noseda* 72
2 b c Dixieland Band(USA) —Gracious Assault (USA) (Glitterman (USA))
5859^{7} 6425^{8} 6926^{4}

Double Spectre (IRE) *Jean-Rene Auvray* a63 74
6 b g Spectrum(IRE) —Phantom Ring (Magic Ring (IRE))
51^{9} 207^{9} 2640^{2} ◆ (2921) 3347^{3} ◆ 4432^{8} 4771^{14} 6243^{7} 6607^{11}

Double Valentine *R Ingram* a62 47
5 ch m Primo Valentino(IRE) —Charlottevalentina (IRE) (Perugino (USA))
151^{3} (174) 264^{3} 402^{2} (571) 937^{5} 1038^{5} 1145^{6} 1253^{5} 2758^{9} 3266^{5} 7382^{13} (7535) 7636^{4} 7764^{6} 7803^{13}

Doubloon *J Gallagher* a28 24
3 b g Umistim—Glistening Silver (Puissance)
2055^{14}

Doubnov (FR) *Saeed Bin Suroor* a94 104
5 gr g Linamix(FR) —Karmitycia (FR) (Last Tycoon)
381a^{2} 652a^{3} 740a^{2}

Doubtful Sound (USA) *R Hollinshead* a96 69
4 b g Diesis—Roam Free (USA) (Unbridled (USA))
4^{6} 213^{5} (307) 459^{4} 482^{6} (800) 1040^{2} 1190^{4} 1997^{10} 2255^{5} (2547) 2664^{2} 3352^{7} 5091^{4} 5708^{2} 6225^{2} (6448) 6634^{5} 7206^{2} 7393^{2} (7428) (7584) 7716^{5}

Doughnut *R Hannon* 93
2 b f Acclamation—Pure Speculation (Salse (USA))
(1122) 1927^{3} 2167^{4} 3020^{2} 3528^{4} (3908) 4190^{12} 6274^{2} 6644^{7}

Dougie Peel *K A Ryan* a60 63
2 b g Diktat—Omission (Green Desert (USA))
1425^{7} 3754^{6} 4203^{3} (4290) 4604^{3} (5041) (5909) 6857^{11} 7275^{5} 7353^{6} 7425^{3} 7607^{12}

Douro Valley (AUS) *Danny O'Brien* 117
7 b g Encosta De Lago(AUS) —Opaque (AUS) (Lord Seymour)
6835a^{13} 7682a^{9}

Douze Points (IRE) *Joseph G Murphy* a76 84
2 b c Redback—Grade A Star (IRE) (Alzao (USA))
3509a^{2} 5438a^{8}

Dove Cottage (IRE) *W S Kittow* a65 83
6 b g Great Commotion(USA) —Pooka (Dominion)
1388^{2} (1929) 2304^{7} 3802^{4} 4771^{15} 5370^{7}

Dovedon Angel *Miss Gay Kelleway* 37
2 b f Winged Love(IRE) —Alexander Star (IRE) (Inzar (USA))
7140^{16}

Dovedon Hero *P J McBride* a66 79
8 ch g Millkom—Hot Topic (IRE) (Desse Zenny (USA))
7512^{3}

Dove Mews *M L W Bell* 81
2 b f Namid—Flying Fulmar (Bahamian Bounty)
(3456) 4374^{3} 5228^{4} 5855^{13} 6533^{2}

Dover Street Art (IRE) *D R C Elsworth* a82
2 br c Alhaarth(IRE) —Santa Sophia (IRE) (Linamix (FR))
7602^{2} ◆ (7812) ◆

Dovetail (IRE) *V Smith* a60
3 b f Acclamation—Daniella Drive (USA) (Shelter Half (USA))
172^{4}

Dowlleh *T T Clement* a71 76
4 b g Noverre(USA) —Al Persian (IRE) (Persian Bold)
4934^{8} 5816^{9}

Downhiller (IRE) *J L Dunlop* a99 103
3 ch c Alhaarth(IRE) —Ski For Gold (Shirley Heights)
(1172) 1618^{3} 2310^{4} (3633) 4205^{6} 5349^{4} 5938^{3} 6272^{2}

Downhill Skier (IRE) *W M Brisbourne* a38 64
4 ch g Danehill Dancer(IRE) —Duchy Of Cornwall (USA) (The Minstrel (CAN))
7656^{9}

Downing Street (IRE) *Jennie Candlish* 83
7 b g Sadler's Wells(USA) —Photographie (USA) (Trempolino (USA))
3884^{4} 4516^{9} 6817^{24}

Downstream *D M Simcock* a53 39
2 b f Marju(IRE) —Sister Moonshine (FR) (Piccolo)
6677^{6} 7095^{9} 7546^{9}

Drachenfels *K A Ryan* a12 54
2 b g Mind Games—Its Another Gift (Primo Dominie)
2035^{13} 2388^{5} 2783^{9} 4659^{7} 4874^{8} 6906^{11}

Dragon Dancer *G Wragg* a66 116
5 b h Sadler's Wells(USA) —Alakananda (Hernando (FR))
1829^{10} 2797^{6}

Dragon Days (GER) *P Schiergen* 91
3 b f Royal Dragon(USA) —Djidda (GER) (Lando (GER))
6852a^{8}

Dragon Flame (IRE) *M Quinn* 72
5 b g Tagula(IRE) —Noble Rocket (Reprimand)
(1454) 2166^{3} 2511^{7} (6766) 7081^{5}

Dragon Fly (GER) *Frau Jutta Mayer* 112
6 ch g Acatenango(GER) —Diana's Quest (IRE) (Rainbow Quest (USA))
2346a^{4} 5625a^{8}

Dragon Lady (IRE) *M Halford* 77
3 ch f Danehill Dancer(IRE) —Born Beautiful (USA) (Silver Deputy (CAN))
5873a^{9}

Dragon Slayer (IRE) *John A Harris* a82 83
6 ch g Night Shift(USA) —Arandora Star (USA) (Sagace (FR))
409^{7} 3257^{5} 3736^{7} (3965) 4156^{F} 4565^{5} 4953^{3} (5512) 6033^{4} 6243^{13} 7056^{4} 7364^{7} 7502^{7}

Dramatic Solo *K R Burke* a69 76
3 ch f Nayef(USA) —Just Dreams (Salse (USA))
1042^{6} 1614^{4} 2173^{5} 2985^{2} 3459^{3} (4382) 6127^{8} 6991^{5} 7296^{5} 7827^{5}

Dramatic Turn *Mme J Bidgood* 64
4 b m Pivotal—Eveningperformance (Night Shift (USA))
4881a^{0}

Drawback (IRE) *Heather Dalton* a77 77
5 b g Daggers Drawn(USA) —Sacred Heart (IRE) (Catrail (USA))
7150^{5} 7777^{4}

Drawn At Dawn (IRE) *C Boutin* 69
2 b f Daggers Drawn(USA) —Brigher (IRE) (Priolo (USA))
5300a^{8}

Drawn Gold *R Hollinshead* a61 72
4 b g Daggers Drawn(USA) —Gold Belt (IRE) (Bellypha)
2375^{3} ◆ 2904^{2} 3947^{7} 4532^{3} 6056^{4} 6721^{5} 7364^{6}

Drayton (IRE) *M F De Kock* a86 111
4 bb g Danetime(IRE) —Exponent (USA) (Exbourne (USA))
378a^{3} 497a^{5} 666a^{4} 814a^{6}

Dr Brass *H J L Dunlop* a73 81
3 b c Dr Fong(USA) —Tropical Heights (FR) (Shirley Heights)
1526^{7} 2197^{7} 3161^{4} 4179^{3} (5118) 5759^{6} 6626^{7}

Dr Dream (IRE) *J G M O'Shea* a57 50
4 b g Dr Fong(USA) —Only In Dreams (Polar Falcon (USA))
273^{3} 4023^{13}

Dream Bee *E A L Dunlop* a51 57
3 b f Oasis Dream—Chief Bee (Chief's Crown (USA))
1959^{8} 2273^{6}

Dream City (IRE) *M P Tregoning* a61 64
2 b f Elusive City(USA) —On View (USA) (Distant View (USA))
1762^{6} 2638^{8} 3114^{4} (Dead)

Dreamcoat *J H M Gosden* 51
2 ch c Pivotal—Follow A Dream (USA) (Gone West (USA))
6778^{9}

Dream Date (IRE) *W J Haggas* a66 44
2 b f Oasis Dream—Femme Fatale (Fairy King (USA))
5147^{10} 5673^{4} 5835^{3} 6477^{11} 7306^{7} 7472^{2} 7783^{2}

Dream Day *R Hannon* a77 97
3 b f Oasis Dream—Capistrano Day (USA) (Diesis)
1470^{2} 2033a^{12} 2793^{4} 5829^{10} 6718^{2} 7099^{12}

Dream Desert (IRE) *M R Channon* a85 93
3 ch c Elnadim(USA) —Bravo Dancer (Acatenango (GER))
(645) (1043) 1424^{3} ◆ 3157^{4} ◆

Dream Eater (IRE) *A M Balding* a79 113
3 gr c Night Shift(USA) —Kapria (FR) (Simon Du Desert (FR))
1808^{5} 3119^{3}

Dream Empress (USA) *Kenneth McPeeka* 115 84
2 b f Bernstein(USA) —Chinese Empress (USA) (Nijinsky (CAN))
6967a^{2}

Dream Esteem *E J O'Neill* a53 66
3 b f Mark Of Esteem(IRE) —City Of Angels (Woodman (USA))
2528^{7} 2847^{2} 3130^{3} 3835^{3} 4607^{10}

Dream Express (IRE) *M Dods* a76 78
3 b g Fasliyev(USA) —Lothlorien (USA) (Woodman (USA))
1556[4] (2261) 2674[3] (3831) 4682[3] 5397[3] 6314[11] 6813[8]

Dream Forest (IRE) *P W Hiatt* a58 33
5 b g Raise A Grand(IRE) —Theresa Green (IRE) (Charnwood Forest (IRE))
485[8] 613[5] 750[3] 938[11] 1606[5] 2290[8] 2667[9]

Dream Huntress *B J Meehan* a61 60
2 ch f Dubai Destination(USA) —Dream Lady (Benny The Dip (USA))
3632[9] 4337[6] 5241[11] 5606[11] 6632[4] (7514)

Dream Impact (USA) *L Riccardi* a93 108
7 b h Royal Academy(USA) —One Fit Cat (USA) (Storm Cat (USA))
2029a[11] 7349a[12]

Dreaming Of Anna (USA) *Wayne Catalano* a116 113
4 ch m Rahy(USA) —Justenuffheart (USA) (Broad Brush (USA))
4888a[4]

Dreaming Of Liz (USA) *Wayne Catalano* a97 85
3 gr f El Prado(IRE) —Silver Maiden (USA) (Silver Buck (USA))
5744a[11]

Dream In Waiting *P F I Cole* 83
2 b f Oasis Dream—Lady In Waiting (Kylian (USA))
3437[5] 3913[4] 4380[3] (5855) 6477[4] 7144[9]

Dream Lodge (IRE) *J G Given* a103 103
4 ch h Grand Lodge(USA) —Secret Dream (IRE) (Zafonic (USA))
336[7] 502[2] 678[4] 906[8] 958[21] 1942[3] 2789[14] 3122[11] (4330) 4459[2] 5495[14] 5941[6] 6476[9]

Dream Of Fortune (IRE) *M G Quinlan* a81 78
4 b g Danehill Dancer(IRE) —Tootling (IRE) (Pennine Walk)
963[8] 1039[6] (1725) 2373[4] 2897[8] 6598[10] 7462[2] 7758[8] (7791)

Dream Of Mine *Saeed Bin Suroor* a67 38
2 bg f Tobougg(IRE) —Night Haven (Night Shift (USA))
5158[8] 5673[2] 6089[3] 6488[7]

Dream Of Olwyn (IRE) *J G Given* a65 69
3 b f Nayef(USA) —Jam (IRE) (Arazi (USA))
3628[8] 4166[7] 4461[2] 4920[5] 5378[3] 5836[8] 6530[5] 6862[2] (7085) 7202[6]

Dreamonandon (IRE) *G A Swinbank* 60
2 b g Val Royal(FR) —Boley Lass (IRE) (Archway (IRE))
5716[6] 6110[6] 6383[6]

Dream Rainbow *N Nevin* a66 72
3 b c Oasis Dream—Bint Zamayem (IRE) (Rainbow Quest (USA))
772[6]

Dream Rush (USA) *William Phipps* a116
4 bb m Wild Rush(USA) —Turbo Dream (USA) (Unbridled (USA))
6965a[12]

Dream Sea *M R Channon* a66 76
3 b f Barathea(IRE) —Countess Sybil (IRE) (Dr Devious (IRE))
931[2] 1176[3] 2052[9] 2695[5] 3127[3] 3525[7] 3717[5]

Dreams Jewel *C Roberts* a67 60
8 b g Dreams End—Jewel Of The Nile (Glenstal (USA))
(600) 722[4] (778) 954[2] 1017[4] 1551[10] 1824[9] 2245[11]

Dreamtheimpossible (USA) *David Wachman* 104
2 b f Giant's Causeway(USA) —Spain (USA) (Thunder Gulch (USA))
(5924a) 6268[3]

Dream Theme *D Nicholls* a80 96
5 b g Distant Music(USA) —Xaymara (USA) (Sanglamore (USA))
2172[5] ◆ 2426[13] 4405[11] 4586[9] 5495[10] 5991[5] 6069[9] 6278[13]

Dreamwalk (IRE) *R M Beckett* 77
2 b g Bahri(USA) —Celtic Silhouette (FR) (Celtic Swing)
3519[2] ◆ 4150[3] 4788[6] 6085[7]

Dream Win *Sir Michael Stoute* 75
2 b c Oasis Dream—Wince (Selkirk (USA))
6944[5] ◆

Dresden Doll (USA) *M L W Bell* a64 77
3 ch f Elusive Quality(USA) —Crimson Conquest (USA) (Diesis)
3031[6] 4090[9] 4696[5] 6053[5] 7055[7] 7292[11]

Dressed To Dance (IRE) *P D Evans* a70 93
4 b m Namid—Costume Drama (USA) (Alleged (USA))
856[7] 990[12] 1752[7] (2040) (2255) 2679[3] 2781[5] (3093) (3363) (3506) 3898[7] 4460[2] 4601[8] 4841[9] 5424[10] 5936[13] 6864[3] 6981[4]

Dress Rehearsal (IRE) *David Wachman* 94
3 b f Galileo(IRE) —Sassenach (IRE) (Night Shift (USA))
3720[6]

Dress To Impress (IRE) *G A Butler* a79 75
4 b h Fasliyev(USA) —Dress Code (IRE) (Barathea (IRE))
162[3] 301[4] (627)

Dr Faustus (IRE) *Sir Michael Stoute* 105
3 gr c Sadler's Wells(USA) —Requesting (Rainbow Quest (USA))
(1811) ◆ 3156[9] 3877[12] 4552[11] 5894[6]

Drift Ice (SAF) *M F De Kock* a100 101
7 b g Western Winter(USA) —Donya (SAF) (Elliodor (FR))
(290a) 472a[7] (563a) 815a[13] 1089a[8]

Drifting Gold *C G Cox* a81 74
4 ch m Bold Edge—Driftholme (Safawan)
187[6] (359) 699[6] 1033[6] 3024[6] 4313[8] 7456[10] 7733[6]

Drill Sergeant *M Johnston* 109
3 br g Rock Of Gibraltar(IRE) —Dolydille (IRE) (Dolphin Street (FR))
(1221) 1570[2] 1811[5] 2408[4] 3157[5] 3684[8] 4552[3] 4856[2] (5257) 5830[9] 6302[3] 6646[3] 6921a[3]

Driven (IRE) *Mrs A J Perrett* 68
3 b g Domedriver(IRE) —Wonderful World (GER) (Dashing Blade)
2342[9] 2976[5] 3525[6]

Driven Snow *N P Littmoden* a65 62
3 ch f Choisir(AUS) —Thermal Spring (Zafonic (USA))
416[5] 2566[4] 3023[10] 3845[12] 7053[4]

Driving Snow *Kevin Prendergast* 99
2 gr c Verglas(IRE) —Dazzling Dancer (Nashwan (USA))
4804a[3] 5296a[4]

Drizzi (IRE) *P T Midgley* a71 72
7 b g Night Shift(USA) —Woopi Gold (IRE) (Last Tycoon)
3328[2]

Dr Jameson (IRE) *R A Fahey* 77
2 b g Orpen(USA) —Touraneena (Robellino (USA))
4536[2] ◆ 5225[3] 5989[3] ◆ 6534[2] 6946[4]

Dr Knock (IRE) *Michael McElhone* 72
10 b g Dr Devious(IRE) —Fuchsia Belle (Vision (USA))
4799a[10]

Dr Light (IRE) *M A Peill* a53 56
4 b g Medicean—Allumette (Rainbow Quest (USA))
2001[11] 2957[4] 3131[11] 3588[7] 4173[9]

Dr Livingstone (IRE) *C R Egerton* a68 92
3 b g Dr Fong(USA) —Radhwa (FR) (Shining Steel)
1381[4] (1839) 2311[11] (5865) ◆ 6667[7] 7056[3]

Dr McFab *Miss Tor Sturgis* a72 70
4 ch g Dr Fong(USA) —Barbera (Barathea (IRE))
2476[9] 2978[12] 3347[11] 4155[8]

Drombeg Dawn (IRE) *A J McNamara* 51
2 b f Orpen(USA) —Dawn's Sharp Shot (IRE) (Son Of Sharp Shot (IRE))
4513a[9]

Drombeg Pride (IRE) *G P Enright* 43
4 b g High Account(USA) —Proserpina (Most Welcome)
2694[9] 3344[7] 3780[8]

Drop The Hammer *T P Tate* 67
2 b f Lucky Story(USA) —Paperweight (In The Wings)
6722[2] 7200[15]

Dr Sharp (IRE) *T P Tate* 85
8 ch g Dr Devious(IRE) —Stoned Imaculate (IRE) (Durgam (USA))
1625[4] 2609[6] 3414[8] 5498[2] 5718[7] 6071[2] 6606[12]

Dr Smart (IRE) *B Smart* 76
2 b c Dr Fong(USA) —All Glory (Alzao (USA))
2592[4] ◆ 3245[8] 4616[3]

Dr Synn *M J Attwater* a67 70
7 br g Danzero(AUS) —Our Shirley (Shirley Heights)
2615[5] 2995[12] 3839[6] 4863[3] 4910[6] 5267[8] (5797) 7076[13] 7359[12]

Drumadoon Bay (IRE) *G A Swinbank* 56
4 b h Marju(IRE) —Mythical Creek (USA) (Pleasant Tap (USA))
5361[9] 6015[4]

Drumalee Lass (IRE) *P M Mooney* 62
3 b f Quws—Grange Clare (IRE) (Bijou D'Inde)
7799[13]

Drumbeat (IRE) *A P O'Brien* 112
2 b c Montjeu(IRE) —Maskaya (IRE) (Machiavellian (USA))
5296a[5] 5946a[5] 6317a[4] 7294a[2]

Drum Dance (IRE) *M Hill* a60 56
6 b g Namid—Socialite (IRE) (Alzao (USA))
516[8] 584[5]

Drum Dragon *M H Tompkins* 67
2 b f Beat Hollow—Qilin (IRE) (Second Set (IRE))
6531[9] 6885[4]

Drumfire (IRE) *M Johnston* 111
4 b h Danehill Dancer(IRE) —Witch Of Fife (USA) (Lear Fan (USA))
1457[3] 1716[3] 4644[2] (5070) 5289[6] 5932[3] 6499a[6] 6780[8] 7145[4]

Drumhallagh (IRE) *Tom Dascombe* a57 60
3 b g Barathea(IRE) —Nashua Song (IRE) (Kahyasi)
7807[8]

Drum Major (IRE) *G L Moore* a71 67
3 b c Sadler's Wells(USA) —Phantom Gold (Machiavellian (USA))
1684[9] 2612[4] 3058[10] 3745[5] 4790[8] 5428[12] 5931[2] (6596) 6934[10] 7704[4]

Drumming Party (USA) *J R Boyle* a64 74
6 bb g War Chant(USA) —Santaria (USA) (Star De Naskra (USA))
(4273) 4765[2] (5171)

Drunken Sailor (IRE) *Paul W Flynn* a75 79
3 b g Tendulkar(USA) —Ronni Pancake (Mujadil (USA))
4494a[2] 5550a[11]

Drusus (IRE) *John C McConnell* a39
2 b c Statue Of Liberty(USA) —Babaraja (Dancing Spree (USA))
6320a[29]

Dr Valentine (FR) *S Kirk* a68 71
2 ch g Dr Fong(USA) —Red Roses Story (FR) (Pink (FR))
5798[9] 6359[4] 6731[7]

Dr Wintringham (IRE) *J S Moore* a68 59
2 b f Monsieur Bond(IRE) —Shirley Collins (Robellino (USA))
1078[4] 1177[3] 1419[8]

Dry Speedfit (IRE) *Micky Hammond* a72 93
3 b g Desert Style(IRE) —Annmary Girl (Zafonic (USA))
3396[5] 3723[11] 4731[9] 5185[7] 5605[8] 6001[5] 6215[10] 6541[8] 7267[10] 7373[RR]

Duaisbhanna (IRE) *J S Bolger* 91
2 ch f Rock Of Gibraltar(IRE) —Ovazione (Seeking The Gold (USA))
5294a[7]

Dualagi *M R Bosley* a67 71
4 b m Royal Applause—Lady Melbourne (IRE) (Indian Ridge)
994[4] ◆ 1368[5] (2102) ◆ 2616[4] 3026[6] 4025[9] 4313[11] 5026[2] 5315[5] 6209[5] 6564[9] 7255[2] 7359[5] 7611[7]

Duar Mapel (USA) *G D Blake* a75 29
2 b c Lemon Drop Kid(USA) —Pitchacurve (USA) (Defrere (USA))
4826[17] 5590[8] 6731[3]

Dubai (IRE) *P Schiergen*
2 b f Galileo(IRE) —Dapprima (GER) (Shareef Dancer (USA))
7006a[5]

Dubai Ace (USA) *A M Hales* a71 70
7 b g Lear Fan(USA) —Arsaan (USA) (Nureyev (USA))
14[7] 272[2] (544) 630[8] 7545[7] 7806[13]

Dubai Crest *Mrs A J Perrett* a70 80
2 b c Dubai Destination(USA) —On The Brink (Mind Games)
3968[7] 4311[7] 4570[4] 5511[6] (5914) ◆ 6394[2] 6700[3] 6857[2]

Dubai Diva *C F Wall* a61 43
2 b f Dubai Destination(USA) —Marine City (JPN) (Carnegie (IRE))
6887[10] 7117[7] 7337[7]

Dubai Dynamo *P F I Cole* a90 99
3 b g Kyllachy—Miss Mercy (IRE) (Law Society (USA))
1834[5] ◆ 2104[7] 2594[7] 3155[4] 3744[9] 5313[6] 5907[7] 6283[9]

Dubai Echo (USA) *Sir Michael Stoute* 64
2 bb g Mr Greeley(USA) —Entendu (USA) (Diesis)
6084[10] 6581[4]

Dubai Hills *B Smart* 82
2 b c Dubai Destination(USA) —Hill Welcome (Most Welcome)
2951[9] 3492[2] (5989) 6970[9]

Dubai Honor *Doug Watson* a104 73
9 gr h Highest Honor(FR) —Lovely Noor (USA) (Fappiano (USA))
202a[12] 568a[11]

Dubai Legend *D M Simcock* a61 78
2 ch f Cadeaux Genereux—Royal Future (IRE) (Royal Academy (USA))
4080[7] 4692[2] ◆ 5673[5] 6473[7]

Dubai Meydan (IRE) *Miss Gay Kelleway* a64 85
3 b g High Chaparral(IRE) —Miss Golden Sands (Kris)
1701[4] (1894) 2794[2] 3270[6] 3897[5] 4089[5] 5858[P]

Dubai Petal (IRE) *J S Moore* a56 77
3 b f Dubai Destination(USA) —Out Of Egypt (USA) (Red Ransom (USA))
1297[5] 1395[2] (1681) 2564[4] 2977[5] 3327[5] 3962[2] 4762[3] 5216[2] 6107[7] 6529[8]

Dubai Power *C E Brittain* a88 84
3 b f Cadeaux Genereux—Garmoucheh (USA) (Silver Hawk (USA))
1270[2] 1688[2] (2341) ◆ 2606[7] 2998[10] 3647[9] (4082) 4424[9] 5644[7] 6053[9]

Dubai Princess (IRE) *J A Osborne* a82 98
3 b f Dubai Destination(USA) —Blue Iris (Petong)
2000[4] 2498[6] 3047[11] (3273) 4586[17] 5509[16]

Dubai Samurai *J W Hills* a58 79
3 b c Dubai Destination(USA) —Eishin Eleuthera (IRE) (Sadler's Wells (USA))
2191[5] 2564[12] 4372[4] 4820[9] 5803[11] 6396[9]

Dubai's Gazal *M R Channon* 78
2 b f Fraam—Dakhla Oasis (IRE) (Night Shift (USA))
2357[3] (2638) 3412[5] 4185[3] 5228[13]

Dubai Shadow (IRE) *C E Brittain* a57 58
4 b m Cape Cross(IRE) —Farista (USA) (Alleged (USA))
1562[12] 1938[3] 2510[13] 3036[5] 3657[5] 4055[5] 5427[5]

Dubai Storming *E A L Dunlop*
2 b g Storming Home—Tropical Breeze (IRE) (Kris)
4728[12]

Dubai's Touch *M Johnston* a109 112
4 b h Dr Fong(USA) —Noble Peregrine (Lomond (USA))
678[2] 906[4] 1326[7] 1989[8] 3122[17] 3740[4] 4330[3] 4587[3] ◆ 5265[4] 6287[6] 6476[15]

Dubai's Wonder (IRE) *B W Hills* a73 68
3 b c Galileo(IRE) —Sena Desert (Green Desert (USA))
674[3] 1059[4] 2573[5] 4859[6] 5963[5] 6413[8]

Dubai To Barnsley *Garry Moss* a61 51
3 b g Superior Premium—Oakwell Ace (Clantime)
2546[8] 3144[7] 3600[3] 4125[11] 4615[6] 5074[12] (5307) 5770[11] 6405[11] 6595[5] 7529[2] 7636[2] 7793[11]

Dubai Tsunami *E A L Dunlop* 30
2 gr f Fantastic Light(USA) —Citrine Spirit (IRE) (Soviet Star (USA))
2160[7] 2554[5]

Dubburg (USA) *W J Musson* a57 69
3 ch g Johannesburg(USA) —Plaisir Des Yeux (FR) (Funambule (USA))
3286a[5] 6989[11]

Ducal Damsel *J R Weymes*
3 b f Best Of The Bests(IRE) —Lucky Thing (Green Desert (USA))
980[10] 1221[8]

Ducal Pip Squeak *A B Haynes* a38 67
4 b m Bertolini(USA) —Creeking (Persian Bold)
3481[10] 3825[11] 4806[10] 5318[5]

Ducal Regancy Duke *C J Teague* 56
4 gr g Bertolini(USA) —Fun Run (USA) (Skip Away (USA))
1674[11] 2912[3] 3227[7] 3599[13] 4148[5] 4689[12] 4924[11]

Ducal Regancy Red *C J Teague* a57 44
4 ch m Bertolini(USA) —One For Jeannie (Clantime)
598[3] 634[2] (725) 857[3] 987[12] 1185[6] 1455[12] 2802[4] 4144[3] 4950[10] 7529[9] 7615[13] 7793[13]

Duchess Of Doom (IRE) *B W Hills* 47
2 b f Exceed And Excel(AUS) —Tallahassee Spirit (THA) (Presidential (USA))
2618[13] 3323[11] 3584[8]

Duck Scary (IRE) *T J O'Mara* a68 70
4 b g Tagula(IRE) —Play The Queen (IRE) (King Of Clubs)
5873a[2]

Dudley Docker (IRE) *C R Dore* a84 75
6 b g Victory Note(USA) —Nordic Abu (IRE) (Nordico (USA))
26[9] 233[3] 314[6] ◆ 351[2] 463[2] 618[3] 833[5] (910) 1335[15] (1552) 1815[11] 2400[6] 7837[7]

Duellant (IRE) *P Schiergen* 106
3 bb c Dashing Blade—Dapprima (GER) (Shareef Dancer (USA))
3074a[6] 5624a[3] 6461a[5] 6992a[8]

Duff (IRE) *Edward Lynam* a116 117
5 b g Spinning World(USA) —Shining Prospect (Lycius (USA))
6496a[8] 6814[6] (7421) ◆ (7703) ◆

Duke Of Aquitaine (USA) *P F I Cole* a72 72
2 ch c Lion Heart(USA) —Waterwild (USA) (River Special (USA))
1523[5] 2146[3] 2663[6] 3372[3] 3924[9] 4729[7] 5460[11] 6281[7] 6574[6]

Duke Of Marmalade (IRE) *A P O'Brien* a116 130
4 b h Danehill(USA) —Love Me True (USA) (Kingmambo (USA))
(1665a) (2432a) ◆ (3121) (4406) (5276) 6522a[7] 7001a[9]

Duke Of Milan (IRE) *G C Bravery* a60 59
5 ch g Desert Prince(IRE) —Abyat (USA) (Shadeed (USA))
790[9] 883[4] (1145) 1254[3] 2936[3] 3316[9] 4064[5] 4186[5] 7196[4] 7508[2] 7808[7]

Duke Of Normandy (IRE) *M Johnston* a62 48
2 gr c Refuse To Bend(IRE) —Marie De Bayeux (FR) (Turgeon (USA))
6480[8] 6737[7]

Duke Of Touraine (IRE) *P C Haslam* a71 81
3 gr g Linamix(FR) —Miss Mission (IRE) (Second Empire (IRE))
366[4] (1396) (1575)

Dukes Art *J A R Toller* a75
2 b c Bachelor Duke(USA) —Creme Caramel (USA) (Septieme Ciel (USA))
7554[3]

Duke's Emerald *J A R Toller* a56
2 br g Bachelor Duke(USA) —Complication (Compton Place)
5798[10] 6876[8] 7170[6]

Dul Ar An Ol (IRE) *Peter Henley* a74 81
7 b g Perugino(USA) —Sprint For Gold (USA) (Slew O'Gold (USA))
1105a[6] 4576a[7] 5550a[20]

Dulce Domum *A B Haynes* a44
2 b f Dansili—Enclave (USA) (Woodman (USA))
7434[9] 7593[13]

Dulcie *M H Tompkins* 75
2 b f Hernando(FR) —Dulcinea (Selkirk (USA))
6081[8] (6674)

Dunaskin (IRE) *B Ellison* a98 110
8 b g Bahhare(USA) —Mirwara (IRE) (Darshaan)
1629[2] 2625[10] 3295[2] 3721[7] 3974[5] 6106[5] 7150[2] 7244[4]

Duncan *J L Dunlop* 103
3 b c Dalakhani(IRE) —Dolores (Danehill (USA))
4161[2] 4695[2] (6055) ◆ 6444[6] 7145[7]

Dundry *G L Moore* a74 86
7 b g Bin Ajwaad(IRE) —China's Pearl (Shirley Heights)
6898[15] 7314[7]

Dunedin Star *J H M Gosden* 55
3 b f Cape Cross(IRE) —Midnight Line (USA) (Kris S (USA))
1440[7]

Duneen Dream (USA) *W J Musson* a60 54
3 ch g Hennessy(USA) —T N T Red (USA) (Explosive Red (CAN))
(20) 288[3] 665[6] 1586[7] 1871[7] 2475[13] 3183[3] 3524[6]

Dunelight (IRE) *C G Cox* 113
5 ch h Desert Sun—Badee'A (IRE) (Marju (IRE))
2044[2] 2788[7] (3503) 4506[3]

Dunes Queen (USA) *M R Channon* 66
2 b f Elusive Quality(USA) —Queen's Logic (IRE) (Grand Lodge (USA))
6600[3]

Dungleddy Star *J M Bradley*
3 ch f Hazaaf(USA) —Art Nouveau (Cyrano De Bergerac)
3963[11] 4484[9] 4707[12] 5215[11]

Dunkerque (FR) *Mme C Head-Maarek* 104
3 b c Highest Honor(FR) —Dissertation (FR) (Sillery (USA))
(6743a) 7187a[3]

Dunmore Dodger (IRE) *R A Fahey* a69
3 b c Tagula(IRE) —Decrescendo (IRE) (Polish Precedent (USA))
65[9] (Dead)

Dunn Deal (IRE) *J Balding* a46 59
8 b g Revoque(IRE) —Buddy And Soda (IRE) (Imperial Frontier (USA))
440[7]

Dunn'o (IRE) *C G Cox* 89
3 b g Cape Cross(IRE) —Indian Express (Indian Ridge)
(1529) ◆ 1837[9] 3324[2] 3723[2] 4252[5] (4983) 5273[4] 5795[6] 6242[2]

Duntulm *H Candy* a52 105
3 b g Sakhee(USA) —Not Before Time (IRE) (Polish Precedent (USA))
1265[2] (1806) ◆ 2403[6] (3919) 4622[5] 5896[7]

Duratwill *M W Easterby* 19
2 b f Fantastic Light(USA) —Silvernus (Machiavellian (USA))
6013[13] 6234[7]

Durgan *C G Cox* 68
2 b c Dansili—Peryllys (Warning)
5468[8] 6117[6]

Duriana (DEN) *A McLaren*
3 b f Academy Award(IRE) —Elms Schooldays (Emarati (USA))
4918a[15]

Dushstorm (IRE) *R J Price* a75 52
7 b g Dushyantor(USA) —Between The Winds (USA) (Diesis)
(24) ◆ 148[6] (408) 1049[3] (1286) (1411) 1668[2] 1935[8] 2262[7] 2722[8] 3036[7] 3321[9] 4026[6] 4748[10] 6364[7] 6727[13] 6955[5] 7112[2] 7340[11] 7368[7]

Dusk *Mrs S J Humphrey* a71 71
3 b g Fantastic Light(USA) —Dark Veil (USA) (Gulch (USA))
1389[6] 2342[3] ◆ 3095[6] 4086[3] 4811[3] 5803[6] ◆ 6049[2] 6378[3] 6775[5] 7775[4]

Dustoori *E A L Dunlop* a67 92
4 b h In The Wings—Elfaslah (IRE) (Green Desert (USA))
3003[4] 3375[7]

Dustry (IRE) *R Hannon* 75
2 b c Chevalier(IRE) —Church Mice (IRE) (Petardia)
5053[9] (5959) 6603[8]

Dusty Moon *W J Knight* a82 73
3 ch f Dr Fong(USA) —Dust Dancer (Suave Dancer (USA))
1524[9] 1930[7] 2505[6] 3351[8] 4082[6]

Duty Doctor *S Kirk* a67 69
3 ch f Dr Fong(USA) —Duty Paid (IRE) (Barathea (IRE))
1372[7] 1671[2] 3918[8] 4278[3] 4806[4] 5218[5] (6660) (6928)

Duty Free (IRE) *C R Egerton* a78 91
4 b g Rock Of Gibraltar(IRE) —Photographie (USA) (Trempolino (USA))
2591[7] 3104[8] 4046[12] 5423[12]

Dvinsky (USA) *P Howling* a88 81
7 b g Stravinsky(USA) —Festive Season (USA) (Lypheor)
55[10] 165[6] 334[4] 429[3] (539) 775[4] 901[2] (1153) 1415[3] 1567[2] 2058[4] 3374[2] 3615[4] 4058[6] (4341) 4944[6] 5206[5] 5424[5] 5789[8] 6420[3] (6699) 7077[3] 7384[3] 7470[11] 7592[3] 7756[2] (7828)

Dwilano (GER) *T Satra* 102
5 ch h Silvano(GER) —Dwings (IRE) (In The Wings)
1237a[2] 1888a[5] 2440a[6] 5528a[6] 6461a[6]

Dynaforce (USA) *William Mott* 115
5 b m Dynaformer(USA) —Aletta Maria (USA) (Diesis)
6968a[8]

Dynamic Saint (USA) *Doug Watson* a104 78
5 b g Sweetsouthernsaint(USA) —Le Nat (USA) (Dynaformer (USA))
296a[11] 568a[2] 650a[3] 817a[5]

Dynamo Dancer (IRE) *G M Lyons* a105 103
5 ch g Danehill Dancer(IRE) —Imperial Graf (USA) (Blushing John (USA))
3531a[16] (Dead)

Dynamo Dane (IRE) *J G Given* a61 69
2 b c Danehill Dancer(IRE) —Takrice (Cadeaux Genereux)
6389[12] 6755[2] (7240) 7475[9]

Dynamo Dave (USA) *M D I Usher* a60 35
3 b g Distorted Humor(USA) —Nothing Special (CAN) (Tejabo (CAN))
1149[6] 1685[U] 2805[12] 2988[5] 6683[11] 7437[10] 7581[12] 7746[11]

Dzesmin (POL) *R A Fahey* a81 89
6 b g Professional(IRE) —Dzakarta (POL) (Aprizzo (IRE))
1473[5] 2107[7] 2830[11] 4299[5] (5199) 5853[5] 6288[5]

Ea (USA) *Saeed Bin Suroor* 115
4 br g Dynaformer(USA) —Enthused (USA) (Seeking The Gold (USA))
379a[8] 669a[10]

Eager To Bow (IRE) *P R Chamings* 50
2 b g Acclamation—Tullawadgeen (IRE) (Sinndar (IRE))
4367[6] 5929[9] 6553[8]

Eagle Mountain *M F De Kock* 124
4 b h Rock Of Gibraltar(IRE) —Masskana (IRE) (Darshaan)
(6440) 7000a[2] (7685a)

Eagle Nebula *B R Johnson* a70 62
4 ch g Observatory(USA) —Tarocchi (USA) (Affirmed (USA))
134[6] 265[4] 590[7] 2943[2] 3371[5] 4081[6] 5230[3] ◆ 5802[4]

Eagles Call (USA) *P W Chapple-Hyam* a68 67
2 ch c Johannesburg(USA) —Golden Flyer (FR) (Machiavellian (USA))
2275[3] 4792[8] 5628[4] 6023[8]

Earl Compton (IRE) *Stef Liddiard* a60 51
4 b g Compton Place—Noble Story (Last Tycoon)
19[5] 45[3] 114[2] 142[3] (263) 581[5] 690[7] 726[5] 774[3] 800[4] 846[F] (Dead)

Earl Kraul (IRE) *P A Blockley* a64 57
5 b g Imperial Ballet(IRE) —Bu Hagab (IRE) (Royal Academy (USA))
(10) 180[3] 352[12] 526[2] 728[7] 1280[5] 1644[4] (Dead)

Earl's Court *E Charpy* 87
6 b h King's Best(USA) —Reine Wells (IRE) (Sadler's Wells (USA))
384a[10]

Earlsmedic *S C Williams* a66 88
3 ch g Dr Fong(USA) —Area Girl (Jareer (USA))
1535[8] 2449[5] 3416[5] 3757[2] 4180[5] (4632) (5067) (5247) 5831[10] 6278[7]

Easibet Dot Net *Miss L A Perratt* a64 58
8 gr g Atraf—Silvery (Petong)
374[5] 754[6] 1062[3] 1304[4] 2252[2] 2579[6] 2752[6] 3216[2] 3545[7]

Easily Naimd *D Shaw* a29
4 b g Namid—It's So Easy (Shaadi (USA))
441[7] 514[7] 598[8] 774[8] 914[11]

East Coast Girl (IRE) *S W Hall* a51 53
3 ch f Captain Rio—Toledana (IRE) (Sure Blade (USA))
112[4] 614[2] 6681[12] 7213[5] 7444[7]

East Drive (IRE) *M A Jarvis* 77
3 b g Invincible Spirit(IRE) —You Rang Here (USA) (Dehere (USA))
1467[8] (1803) 2794[5] ◆ 3270[10] (Dead)

Eastern Anthem (IRE) *Saeed Bin Suroor* 114
4 b h Singspiel(IRE) —Kazzia (GER) (Zinaad)
2797[2] 3975[3] (4376) 5094[6]

Eastern Emperor *W R Swinburn* a72 78
4 ch g Halling(USA) —B Beautiful (IRE) (Be My Guest (USA))
2897[7] ◆ 3208[7] (3563) 4121[9] 4723[11] 5492[8] 5863[2] 6363[3]

Eastern Empire *J W Hills* a53 44
2 b g Dubai Destination(USA) —Possessive Artiste (Shareef Dancer (USA))
6117[14] 6621[7]

Eastern Gift *R Hannon* a79 95
3 ch g Cadeaux Genereux—Dahshah (Mujtahid (USA))
1333[8] 1923[11] 5470[11] 5697[8] 5841[4] 6242[13] 6695[10] 7068[4] 7307[2] (7360) 7668[3]

Eastern Hills *M Johnston* a69 80
3 b c Dubai Destination(USA) —Rainbow Mountain (Rainbow Quest (USA))
543[4] ◆ 727[7] 1556[2] 2189[9] (2761)

Eastern Pride *P A Blockley* a29 52
3 b f Fraam—Granuaile O'Malley (IRE) (Mark Of Esteem (IRE))
1964[12] 5142[9]

Eastern Princess *G H Yardley* a47 52
4 b m Almutawakel—Silvereine (FR) (Bering)
153[4] 522[8] 1259[7] 3361[12] 3604[12]

Eastern Romance *K A Ryan* 107
3 b f Oasis Dream—Ocean Grove (IRE) (Fairy King (USA))
1659a[2] 2738a[2] 3252[4] 3927[6] (Dead)

Eastern Warrior *J W Hills* a65 66
2 ch g Barathea(IRE) —Shakalaka Baby (Nashwan (USA))
6604[8] 7397[4] ◆ 7622[9]

Easy Sundae (IRE) *J E Pease* 92
2 b f Diableneyev(USA) —Sundae Girl (USA) (Green Dancer (USA))
5486a[4]

Easy Target (FR) *B Smart* 102
3 ch c Danehill Dancer(IRE) —Aiming (Highest Honor (FR))
2580[3] (4153) 4459[3] 6073[5] 6484[6] 7201[2]

Easy Wonder (GER) *I A Wood* a68 71
3 b f Royal Dragon(USA) —Emy Coasting (USA) (El Gran Senor (USA))
458[4] 619[6] 899[13] 1060[7] 1274[3] 1475[7] 1743[7] 1958[5] 2102[4] 2452[4] 2935[4] 3086[5] 3765[3] 3783[5] 4773[4] 5162[6] 6419[9]

Eau Good *M C Chapman* a86 89
4 ch g Cadeaux Genereux—Girl's Best Friend (Nicolotte)
1327[5] 1683[6]

Eau Sauvage *M J Attwater* a13
4 ch m Lake Coniston(IRE) —Mo Stopher (Sharpo)
391[8] 772[10] 2756[12] 3484[9] 5568[8]

Ebadiyan (IRE) *John M Oxx* a87 100
3 gr g Daylami(IRE) —Ebatana (IRE) (Rainbow Quest (USA))
3196[12] 4100a[4]

Ebert *R A Fahey* a71 95
5 b g Polish Precedent(USA) —Fanfare (Deploy)
1016[6] 7083[6]

Ebiayn (FR) *M A Jarvis* 73
2 b c Monsun(GER) —Drei (USA) (Lyphard (USA))
6759[3]

Ebn Malk (IRE) *M A Jarvis* a80 89
3 ch c King's Best(USA) —Auntie Maureen (IRE) (Roi Danzig (USA))
2360[4] (2700) 4731[4] (5032) 5470[3] 5695[13]

Eborbrav *T D Easterby*
2 b g Falbrav(IRE) —Eboracum (IRE) (Alzao (USA))
3277[12]

Ebraam (USA) *P Howling* a105 99
5 b g Red Ransom(USA) —Futuh (USA) (Diesis)
226[2] (411) 593[3] 677[6] 1483[3] 1917[3] 2598[4] 3881[3] 4445[24] 5109[19] 5347[2] 6468[3] 6903[4] 7192[4] 7418[7] 7594[5] 7716[4] 7805[2]

Echo Dancer *S A Callaghan* a54
2 br c Danehill Dancer(IRE) —Entail (USA) (Riverman (USA))
7783[5]

Echoes Rock (GER) *A Fabre* 109
5 ch g Tiger Hill(IRE) —Evening Breeze (GER) (Surumu (GER))
5555a[5]

Echo Forest *J R Best* a41 44
2 b g Mark Of Esteem(IRE) —Engulfed (USA) (Gulch (USA))
6000[11] 6333[5] 6737[12]

Ecoute Moi (IRE) *A & G Botti* 99
3 gr f Almutawakel—Entraque (FR) (Linamix (FR))
2231a[7]

Ecume Du Jour (FR) *F Rohaut* a73 85
3 b f Hawk Wing(USA) —Dibenoise (FR) (Kendor (FR))
7450a[14]

E'Cusson *M A Jarvis* a51
3 b f Singspiel(IRE) —Indian Love Bird (Efisio)
221[6]

Edas *J J Quinn* a71 69
6 b h Celtic Swing—Eden (IRE) (Polish Precedent (USA))
3143[7] 3947[9] 4966[2] 5456[2] 5971[7] 6551[4]

Eddie Boy *M L W Bell* a52 68
2 b g Tobougg(IRE) —Maristax (Reprimand)
5227[9] 6187[3] 7011[6]

Eddie Dowling *M R Channon* a54 65
3 b g High Chaparral(IRE) —Dans Delight (Machiavellian (USA))
1446[8] 1814[5] 2280[5] 2785[7] 3671[10] 4247[13] 4410[4] 5269[7] 6386[7] 6728[3] 6929[4]

Eddie Jock (IRE) *Saeed Bin Suroor* a111 114
4 ch g Almutawakel—Al Euro (FR) (Mujtahid (USA))
494a[3] (5941) 6440[7] 7208[2]

Eddystone (IRE) *Mrs L C Jewell* a47 42
4 ch g Fantastic Light(USA) —Far Reaching (USA) (Distant View (USA))
39[9] 134[5] 545[7] 2694[8] 3321[10] 3377[10]

Eden Park *M Dods* a56 31
2 ch f Tobougg(IRE) —Aegean Flame (Anshan)
1907[3] 2865[4] 4384[7]

Ede's Dot Com (IRE) *P M Phelan* a68 66
4 b g Trans Island—Kilkee Bay (IRE) (Case Law)
2860[2] 7490[6]

Edgbaston (IRE) *M Johnston*
3 ch g Pivotal—Pure Spin (USA) (Machiavellian (USA))
1701[9]

Edge Closer *R Hannon* a111 117
4 b h Bold Edge—Blue Goddess (IRE) (Blues Traveller (IRE))
(1079) ◆ 1765[2] 2680[6] (3063) 3248[27] 4188[5] 4624[13] (5275) 6304[11]

Edge End *R A Farrant* a61 61
4 ch g Bold Edge—Rag Time Belle (Raga Navarro (ITY))
1966[9] 2242[12] 2930[10] 3346[9] 3847[3] 4186[9] 4307[8]

Edgefour (IRE) *B I Case* a38 53
4 b m King's Best(USA) —Highshaan (Pistolet Bleu (IRE))
1207[10] 1638[4]

Edge Of Gold *B Palling* 79
3 ch f Choisir(AUS) —Beveled Edge (Beveled (USA))
1698[5] 2196[6] 2644[10]

Edge Of Light *B Palling* 93
3 b f Xaar—Bright Edge (Danehill Dancer (IRE))
1470[5] 1718[7] 3905[4] 4153[6]

Edgeworth (IRE) *B G Powell* a59 58
2 b g Pyrus(USA) —Credibility (Komaite (USA))
4579[3] 5213[7] 6000[5] 6673[11]

Edie Superstar (USA) *M A Magnusson* a72 62
3 b f Forestry(USA) —Just Out (USA) (Forty Niner (USA))
2102[12] 2452[8] 2946[10] (5141) 6209[2] 6658[9] 7377[9]

Edin Burgher (FR) *T T Clement* a51 46
7 br g Hamas(IRE) —Jaljuli (Jalmood (USA))
82[9] 264[7] 516[5] 621[9]

Edith's Boy (IRE) *S Dow* a62
2 ch c Trans Island—My Ramona (Alhijaz)
3315[4] 5430[6] 5904[7] 7802[2]

Edmondstown Lass (IRE) *R A Fahey* a75 78
3 b f Imperial Ballet(IRE) —Fleetwood Fancy (Taufan (USA))
6791[5] 7074[9] 7321[8]

Ed's Pride (IRE) *K A Ryan* a31 33
2 b c Catcher In The Rye(IRE) —Queenliness (Exit To Nowhere (USA))
2362[11] 2746[9] 3008[6] 7659[5]

Efficiency *M Blanshard* a81 51
2 b f Efisio—Trounce (Barathea (IRE))
3610[9] 5812[5] 7259[2] (7538)

Effigy *H Candy* a80 80
4 b g Efisio—Hymne D'Amour (USA) (Dixieland Band (USA))
1383[2] 1732[6] 2722[4] 3090[6] 3914[7] 4162[3] 4789[2] (5639) (6056) ◆ 6598[3] 6899[4]

Effingham (IRE) *N J Vaughan* 72
3 br g Celtic Swing—Deemeh (IRE) (Brief Truce (USA))
1685[13] 6385[5] 7405[11]

Effort *M Johnston* a86 97
2 ch g Dr Fong(USA) —Party Doll (Be My Guest (USA))
(2443) ◆ 2775[2] 3105[4] 3876[7] 4507[8] 5496[3] 6193[3] 6426[16] 7024[3]

Effortless *B W Hills* 62
3 ch f Beat Hollow—Xaymara (USA) (Sanglamore (USA))
1418[7]

Efidium *N Bycroft* a54 73
10 b g Presidium—Efipetite (Efisio)
1752[3] 2007[16] 2658[2] 3082[8] 3643[2] (4219) 4440[12] 5303[2] 6215[2] 6482[20]

Efisio Princess *J E Long* a73 66
5 br m Efisio—Hardiprincess (Keen)
2511[9] 3042[10] 5091[3] 7055[3] (7286) ◆ 7448[3] 7762[12]

Efistorm *C R Dore* a85 95
7 b g Efisio—Abundance (Cadeaux Genereux)
3009[10] 3451[12] 3945[3] (4171) 4437[4] 4601[6] 4928[7] 5906[8] 6354[4] 6650[11] 6859[9] 7047[6] 7176[6] 7384[10] 7529[6]

Egerton (GER) *P Rau* 118
7 b h Groom Dancer(USA) —Enrica (Niniski (USA))
1237a[7] 2440a[2] (3540a) 4470a[5]

Eglevski (IRE) *J L Dunlop* 93
4 b g Danehill Dancer(IRE) —Ski For Gold (Shirley Heights)
1072[9] 1473[2] 1970[10] 2784[2] 4867[6] 5382[5] 5843[4] 6536[5]

Egon (USA) *F Reuterskiold*
3 b c Tactical Cat(USA) —Maple Creek (USA) (Forty Niner (USA))
4918a[8]

Egypt *A P O'Brien* 76
2 b c Dansili—Royal Flame (IRE) (Royal Academy (USA))
3534a[6] 6815[13]

Egyptian Lord *Peter Grayson* a77 57
5 ch g Bold Edge—Calypso Lady (IRE) (Priolo (USA))
29[8] 191[8] 372[2] ◆ 437[5] 883[7] 7644[4] 7774[9] 7836[7]

Egyptian Ra (NZ) *A S Cruz* 116
7 ch g Woodborough(USA) —Egyptian Queen (NZ) (Karioi Lad (AUS))
7684a[3]

Eight Belles (USA) *J Larry Jones* a114
3 rg f Unbridled's Song(USA) —Away (USA) (Dixieland Band (USA))
1820a[2] (Dead)

Eightdaysaweek *S Kirk* 41
2 b f Montjeu(IRE) —Figlette (Darshaan)
3674[14] 5022[8]

Eight Up (IRE) *Michael David Murphy* 86
5 b g Old Vic—Square Up (IRE) (Up And At 'Em)
4511a[11]

Eighty Twenty *M W Easterby* 2
3 b f Diktat—Stonegrave (Selkirk (USA))
1478[14] 2486[9]

Eijaaz (IRE) *G A Harker* 69
7 b g Green Desert(USA) —Kismah (Machiavellian (USA))
1890[3] (2395) (2957) 4244[4] 4331[4] 5971[10] 6216[7] 6551[2] 6812[3] (7177)

Eilean Eeve *A J McCabe* a24 62
2 bb f And Beyond(IRE) —Yeveed (IRE) (Wassl)
1324[2] 1377[3] 1727[8] 2217[9] 2592[10] 5774[9] 6350[8] 6573[11]

Einstein (BRZ) *Helen Pitts* a119 119
6 b h Spend A Buck(USA) —Gay Charm (BRZ) (Ghadeer (FR))
4889a[5]

Eisteddfod *P F I Cole* a111 111
7 ch g Cadeaux Genereux—Ffestiniog (IRE) (Efisio)
1619[3] 2680[9] 3635[5] 4660[12] 5347[8] 5897[6]

Eiswind *P Schiergen* 103
4 b h Monsun(GER) —Eiszeit (GER) (Java Gold (USA))
1237a[4] 1662a[5] 5625a[3]

Ejeed (USA) *J H M Gosden* a57 64
3 b g Rahy(USA) —Lahan (Unfuwain (USA))
1573[12] 1855[5] 2982[8]

Ekhtiaar *A Al Raihe* a94 101
4 b g Elmaamul(USA) —Divina Mia (Dowsing (USA))
647a[6]

Eko Arabian Night (DEN) *Anja Runoe* 80
6 b h Final Appearance(IRE) —Stolga (FR) (Baillamont (USA))
4676a[11]

Ekrajeu (ITY) *Gianfranco Verricelli*
2 b c Ekraar(USA) —Helenjeu (Montjeu (IRE))
2745a[9]

Ekta *S Botti* 78
4 b m Danehill Dancer(IRE) —Switch Blade (IRE) (Robellino (USA))
1659a[10]

Ektimaal *E A L Dunlop* a98 91
5 ch g Bahamian Bounty—Secret Circle (Magic Ring (IRE))
227[3] 679[5]

Elaala (USA) *B D Leavy* a57 47
6 ch m Aljabr(USA) —Nufuth (USA) (Nureyev (USA))
(7285) 7455[11]

Ela Aleka Mou *Miss D Mountain* a48 29
4 ch m Tobougg(IRE) —Miss Grimm (USA) (Irish River (FR))
43[5] 208[5] 558[4] 1189[10] 2547[7] 3159[4] 3779[7]

Ela Gorrie Mou *T T Clement* 42
2 b f Mujahid(USA) —Real Flame (Cyrano De Bergerac)
6081[12] 6438[11]

Elaine's Folly *P C Haslam* 56
2 b f Bahamian Bounty—Marionetta (USA) (Nijinsky (CAN))
2035[5] (2910) 3576[4] 4604[6] 4873[6]

Ela Mario (CYP) *Mrs H Sweeting*
4 ch g Ela-Aristokrati(IRE) —Forgotten Times (USA) (Nabeel Dancer (USA))
524[9]

Elasos (FR) *D Sepulchre* 110
6 b h Pythios(IRE) —Shikasta (IRE) (Kris)
912a[6] 5114a[7] 6612a[6] 7598a[7]

Elba (GER) *C Von Der Recke* 82
3 b f Hawk Wing(USA) —Elisha (GER) (Konigsstuhl (GER))
5737a[5]

Elbistan (IRE) *Evan Williams* 66
3 ch g Peintre Celebre(USA) —Elasouna (IRE) (Rainbow Quest (USA))
3473[3]

El Bobby (IRE) *J R Weymes* 66
2 ch g City On A Hill(USA) —Newtown Breeze (IRE) (Forest Wind (USA))
1749[8] 2035[2] 2462[9] 3140[7] 4449[5] 4874[10] 5394[11] 5541[4] 5966[8]

El Bosque (IRE) *B R Millman* a64 106
4 b g Elnadim(USA) —In The Woods (You And I (USA))
1334[10] 4928[10] 5681[9] 5930[9] (Dead)

Elbrus (USA) *P Bary* 86
3 b c Giant's Causeway(USA) —Timi (Alzao (USA))
7551a[7]

El Capitan (FR) *Miss Gay Kelleway* a61 64
5 b g Danehill Dancer(IRE) —Fille Dansante (IRE) (Dancing Dissident (USA))
844[13] 915[9]

El Coto *J R Holt* a89 91
8 b g Forzando—Thatcherella (Thatching)
258[8] 526[10] 1902[7] 2003[11]

El Dececy (USA) *S Parr* a85 93
4 b g Seeking The Gold(USA) —Ashraakat (USA) (Danzig (USA))
2185[3] 2393[3] 2749[2] 3116[3] (3422) (3738) (3957) 4111[11] 4876[8] 5564[10] 5831[6] 6170[5] 6352[8] 6810[7]

El Dee (IRE) *D Carroll* a46 37
5 b g Brave Act—Go Flightline (IRE) (Common Grounds)
145[4] 283[2] 461[5] 3589[9]

Eldest (IRE) *V Caruso* 104
3 ch c Indian Ridge—Lara's Shock (IRE) (Caerleon (USA))
1513a[3] 7253a[14]

Eldfote (SWE) *E Van Doorn* a94 86
5 br g Mujahid(USA) —Ellamore (Funambule (USA))
2233a[4]

El Diego (IRE) *J R Gask* a82 70
4 b g Sadler's Wells(USA) —Goncharova (USA) (Gone West (USA))
7304[6] 7617[5] ◆

Eldorado Days (IRE) *K R Burke* a67 73
2 b c Elusive City(USA) —Blue Daze (Danzero (AUS))
2281[4] 3005[4] 3547[2] 6525[8] 6769[10] 6931[5]

El Dottore *A W Carroll* a14 63
4 b g Dr Fong(USA) —Edouna (FR) (Doyoun)
2100[11] 6175[7] 6668[13] 6768[7]

El Duende (USA) *W Jarvis* a69 68
3 bb c Elusive Quality(USA) —Brianda (IRE) (Alzao (USA))
1403[5] 1745[3] 2695[4] 3004[9]

Everyman *A W Carroll* a64 57
4 gr g Act One—Maid To Dance (Pyramus (USA))
2978[7] 3901[2] 4254[8] 5145[2] 5427[3] (5631) 5912[2] 6395[10]

Everymanforhimself (IRE) *K A Ryan* a86 101
4 b h Fasliyev(USA) —Luisa Demon (IRE) (Barathea (IRE))
2426[3] 2626[2] 3009[4] (3336) 4145[9] 5424[6] 6289[14]

Everynight (IRE) *M Botti* 69
2 b c Rock Of Gibraltar(IRE) —Rasana (Royal Academy (USA))
7200[4] ◆

Every Second *E S McMahon* 83
2 b g Kyllachy—Pendulum (Pursuit Of Love)
1693[2] 2042[2] 3005[2] (3470)

Everything *P T Midgley* a61 73
3 bl f Namid—Flight Sequence (Polar Falcon (USA))
1019[2] 1452[3] 1817[5] (3144) 3298[9] 3999[5] 5358[8] 5714[5] 6219[13] 7615[5]

Every Whisper (IRE) *Mrs A J Perrett* a58 26
3 b f High Chaparral(IRE) —Heavenly Whisper (IRE) (Halling (USA))
903[7] 4342[10] 4909[10]

Evette *H J Collingridge* a43 39
3 b f Loup Solitaire(USA) —La Scarlet (FR) (Highest Honor (FR))
7713[8]

Evianne *P W Hiatt* a23 42
4 b m Lugana Beach—Folk Dance (USA) (Bertrando (USA))
3328[8] 4123[7] 4698[8] 5215[9] 5604[6]

Evident Pride (USA) *B R Johnson* a102 89
5 b g Chester House(USA) —Proud Fact (USA) (Known Fact (USA))
138[2] 906[9] 3249[19] 4528[11] 7339[4] 7556[7]

Evita Argentina (USA) *John W Sadler* a107
2 ch f Candy Ride(ARG) —Jealous Wildcat (USA) (Forest Wildcat (USA))
6967a[9]

Excape (IRE) *D R C Elsworth* 89
3 b g Cape Cross(IRE) —Viscaria (IRE) (Barathea (IRE))
1622[13] (2043) ◆ (2272) 2665[3] (3459) ◆

Exceedingly Good (IRE) *B Smart* 66
2 ch f Exceed And Excel(AUS) —Ikan (IRE) (Sri Pekan (USA))
3027[6] ◆ 3437[3] 4289[8] 5043[3]

Excelente (IRE) *Mrs John Harrington* a93 74
2 b f Exceed And Excel(AUS) —Annaletta (Belmez (USA))
3466a[6] 6637a[2]

Excelerate (IRE) *Edward Lynam* 108
5 b g Mujadil(USA) —Perle D'Irlande (FR) (Top Ville)
1355a[7] 2026a[3] 2961a[5]

Excellent Show *B Smart* 85
2 ch f Exceed And Excel(AUS) —Quiz Show (Primo Dominie)
2206[2] ◆ (2574) 3123[16]

Excellerator (IRE) *George Baker* a74 96
2 ch f Exceed And Excel(AUS) —Amsicora (Cadeaux Genereux)
(2865) 3865[3] 4403[3] 5448[2] 6426[10]

Excelsior Academy *B J Meehan* a69 69
2 b g Montjeu(IRE) —Birthday Suit (IRE) (Daylami (IRE))
5068[10] 5404[2] 6135[4] 6330[2] 6700[10]

Exceptional Art *P W Chapple-Hyam* 92
2 ch c Exceed And Excel(AUS) —Only In Dreams (Polar Falcon (USA))
(4926) 5330a[12]

Excitable (IRE) *Miss V Haigh* 52
2 b f Exceed And Excel(AUS) —Kalwada (USA) (Roberto (USA))
2186[9] 2462[10] 5959[12] 6389[6] 6579[9]

Exclamation *B J Meehan* a89 97
3 br g Acclamation—Summer Siren (FR) (Saint Cyrien (FR))
1400[6] 5347[12]

Excusez Moi (USA) *C E Brittain* a114 111
6 b g Fusaichi Pegasus(USA) —Jiving (Generous (IRE))
(677) 907[4] ◆ 1420[18] 2607[8] 3504[9] 4188[6] 4405[4] 5095[8] 5586[5] 6285[7]

Exhibition (IRE) *S A Callaghan* 100
3 b c Invincible Spirit(IRE) —Moonbi Ridge (IRE) (Definite Article)
1949[4] 2409[4] 5102[12] 6239[15]

Exit Smiling *P T Midgley* a76 94
6 ch g Dr Fong(USA) —Away To Me (Exit To Nowhere (USA))
(659) 805[2] (1217) 1590[6] (2733) 3972[9] 4500[4] 4876[2] 5360[14] 5772[2] 6482[9]

Exit Strategy (IRE) *R A Harris* a51 70
4 b g Cadeaux Genereux—Black Belt Shopper (IRE) (Desert Prince (IRE))
1254[7] 2337[5] 2474[2] 2798[8] 3313[14] (4639) 5090[2] 5601[7] 6895[4] 7196[8]

Exit To Luck (GER) *S Gollings* a79 52
7 b g Exit To Nowhere(USA) —Emy Coasting (USA) (El Gran Senor (USA))
3[5] (533) (658) 847[3] 854[2] 1589[7] 1904[4] 6838[6] 7183[8] 7696[5]

Exopuntia *R M Whitaker* 38
2 b f Sure Blade(USA) —Opuntia (Rousillon (USA))
6010[9] 6531[11]

Expediter *H Candy* a54 54
3 b f Bahamian Bounty—Iris May (Brief Truce (USA))
1215[6] 1672[9] 2260[7] 3395[10]

Expensive Art (IRE) *S A Callaghan* a88 84
4 b m Cape Cross(IRE) —Walnut Lady (Forzando)
1285[2] (1488) ◆ 1858[2] (2058) 2398[8] 3601[5] 4341[2] 4601[4] (4944)

Expensive Dinner *E F Vaughan*
2 ch f Dr Fong(USA) —Reservation (IRE) (Common Grounds)
5066[15]

Explosive Fox (IRE) *S Curran* a51 66
7 gr g Foxhound(USA) —Grise Mine (FR) (Crystal Palace (FR))
212[9] 585[11]

Exponential (IRE) *J M Bradley* a21 72
6 b g Namid—Exponent (USA) (Exbourne (USA))
1534[8] 2350[8] 2474[5] 2881[9]

Expresso Star (USA) *J H M Gosden* 104
3 b c War Chant(USA) —Caffe Latte (IRE) (Seattle Dancer (USA))
1957[2] ◆ 2413[4] 5491[2] (6163) ◆ (6582) ◆ (6763)

Express Wish *J Noseda* a77 111
4 b h Danehill Dancer(IRE) —Waffle On (Chief Singer)
2426[2] 4437[3] 4586[11] (5586) 6814[5]

External Force (IRE) *S A Callaghan* 37
3 b g Danehill Dancer(IRE) —Fille De Joie (IRE) (Royal Academy (USA))
4161[12] 5603[5] 5748[14]

Extraterrestrial *R A Fahey* a97 101
4 b g Mind Games—Expectation (IRE) (Night Shift (USA))
1071[16] 1481[2] (1816) 1942[2] 3122[10] 3974[10] 4587[11] 4853[4] 5495[3] 6269[21] 6307[4] 6772[2]

Extremely So *P J McBride* a57 53
2 ch f Kyllachy—Antigua (Selkirk (USA))
2835[9] 3408[4] 3821[4] 5606[3] 5914[8]

Extreme Measures *Saeed Bin Suroor* a36 79
5 b g Montjeu(IRE) —Fade (Persepolis (FR))
493a[15]

Extreme North (USA) *Miss V Haigh* a65 62
3 b g Stravinsky(USA) —North Dream (USA) (Unbridled's Song (USA))
146[5] 354[4] 538[3] 714[2] 882[4] 1519[8] 1635[8] 2122[5] 2287[5] 2490[6] 3217[7] 4787[5] 5028[7] 5510[12]

Extreme Pleasure (IRE) *W J Knight* a63 64
3 b f High Chaparral(IRE) —Height Of Passion (Shirley Heights)
4342[11] 5117[3] 5750[3] 7216[11] 7455[13]

Eye For The Girls *M R Channon*
2 ch g Bertolini(USA) —Aunt Ruby (USA) (Rubiano (USA))
6923[9]

Eyes Like A Hawk (IRE) *Tom Dascombe* 41
2 bb f Diktat—Mexican Hawk (USA) (Silver Hawk (USA))
4534[7]

Eyesore *R C Guest* a8
2 b f Reel Buddy(USA) —Segretezza (IRE) (Perugino (USA))
5500[11] 6051[17] 7319[9]

Eyes To The Right (IRE) *D Burchell* a24
9 ch g Eagle Eyed(USA) —Capable Kate (IRE) (Alzao (USA))
577[6] 771[10]

Ezdeyaad (USA) *G A Swinbank* 88
4 b g Lemon Drop Kid(USA) —August Storm (USA) (Storm Creek (USA))
2008[7] 2360[5] 2846[5] (3229) 3443[4] 4417[5] 5717[3] 6052[2] 6482[22]

Ezdiyaad (IRE) *M P Tregoning* a61 106
4 b h Galileo(IRE) —Wijdan (USA) (Mr Prospector (USA))
(1473) ◆ (2593) ◆ 3249[11] 3974[3] 4856[5] 6444[4]

Ezima (IRE) *J S Bolger* a100 109
4 b m Sadler's Wells(USA) —Ezilla (IRE) (Darshaan)
1882a[5] 3720[2] 4833a[4] 6495a[7]

Fabia (IRE) *David Wachman* 80
3 b f Sadler's Wells(USA) —En Garde (USA) (Irish River (FR))
4100a[8]

Fabreze *P J Makin* a96 94
3 ch c Choisir(AUS) —Impulsive Decision (IRE) (Nomination)
(1960) 2526[3] 2998[2] ◆ (3838)

Fabuleux Cherie *W R Muir* a70 65
3 b f Noverre(USA) —Ashover Amber (Green Desert (USA))
3609[3] 5046[8] 5346[8] 6131[16] 6204[13] 6711[10]

Fabulous Strike (USA) *Todd M Beattie* a122 105
5 bb g Smart Strike(CAN) —Fabulous Find (USA) (Lost Code (USA))
6999a[5]

Factotum *L M Cumani* a97 92
4 b h Sadler's Wells(USA) —Gift Of The Night (USA) (Slewpy (USA))
1382[14] 1690[3] 2336[2] 3058[4] 4178[3] (5963) (6630)

Fadansil *J Wade* 55
5 b g Dansili—Fatah Flare (USA) (Alydar (USA))
3077[10] 3335[8] 3863[14]

Fade To Grey (IRE) *S Lycett* a57 34
4 gr g Aljabr(USA) —Aly McBear (USA) (Alydeed (CAN))
(166) 1246[5]

Fagedaboutit Sal (USA) *Luis Carvajal Jr* 105
5 rg h Yarrow Brae(USA) —Stardust Love (USA) (Wolf Power (SAF))
5928a[5]

Faintly Hopeful *R A Teal* a51 45
3 b g Marju(IRE) —Twilight Patrol (Robellino (USA))
5023[11] 5786[7] 6192[6] 7195[5] 7541[11]

Fair Along (GER) *P J Hobbs* a67 101
6 b g Alkalde(GER) —Fairy Tango (FR) (Acatenango (GER))
1916[9]

Fairbanks (USA) *Todd Pletcher* a116
5 b h Giant's Causeway(USA) —Alaska Queen (CAN) (Time For A Change (USA))
7001a[10]

Fair Breeze (GER) *Mario Hofer* 110
5 bb m Silvano(GER) —Fairwind (GER) (Andrang (GER))
(1713a) (2553a) 4470a[3] 5332a[2] 6156a[2] 6521a[14]

Fairdonna *Seamus Fahey* a64 67
5 ch m Bertolini(USA) —Shamrock Fair (IRE) (Shavian)
375[5] 395[6]

Fair Fact (IRE) *M Brittain* 12
3 br f Bold Fact(USA) —Daisy Dancer (IRE) (Distinctly North (USA))
1452[12] 2038[14]

Fairfield Flame (GER) *D R C Elsworth* a59 76
3 b f Oasis Dream—Fantastic Flame (IRE) (Generous (IRE))
500[5] 748[7] 903[8] 1575[4] (1962) 2310[3] 2985[4] 4067[5] 4646[2]

Fairfield Princess *M S Saunders* a79 67
4 b m Inchinor—Cool Question (Polar Falcon (USA))
187[7] 620[7] (2710) 3486[5] 3585[9]

Fair Gale *S Kirk* a82 90
3 b g Storming Home—Triple Green (Green Desert (USA))
2151[9] 2665[10] 3384[4] 3824[3] (4344) (4582) 4906[5] (5464) 6238[3] 6866[3]

Fairly Honest *P W Hiatt* a53 71
4 b g Alhaarth(IRE) —Miller's Melody (Chief Singer)
1350[3] 1644[7] 2053[11] 3343[2] 3572[2] 4054[2] 4322[3] 5166[11] 5575[5] 5787[3] 6032[3] 6719[9] 6927[10]

Fairmile *Saeed Bin Suroor* a100 117
6 b g Spectrum(IRE) —Juno Marlowe (IRE) (Danehill (USA))
3885[2]

Fair Sailing (IRE) *J W Hills* a58 52
4 ch m Docksider(USA) —Fair Of The Furze (Ela-Mana-Mou)
2055[7] 3025[6] 3569[10]

Fairson (TUR) *K Ozturk* a107
5 b h Royal Abjar(USA) —Fair Tail (TUR) (Cossack Guard (USA))
5743a[2]

Fair Spin *Micky Hammond* 54
8 ch g Pivotal—Frankie Fair (IRE) (Red Sunset)
1017[9] 2734[4] 3863[7]

Fairybook (USA) *H-A Pantall* 68
3 b f El Prado(IRE) —Maiden Tower (Groom Dancer (USA))
6744a[9]

Fairy Efisio *B Grizzetti* 102
3 b f Efisio—Fairy Sensazione (Fairy King (USA))
2231a[3] 3076a[19]

Fairy Festival (IRE) *J S Moore* a59 52
4 b m Montjeu(IRE) —Escape To Victory (Salse (USA))
1142[2] 1565[9] 1747[11] 2510[14]

Fairy Flow (IRE) *Ms Joanna Morgan* a43 84
4 b m King Charlemagne(USA) —Fairy Express (IRE) (Fayruz)
7325a[14]

Fairyville (IRE) *John Joseph Murphy* a52 59
3 b f Orpen(USA) —Catchy (Atticus (USA))
7297[4]

Faith And Reason (USA) *A P Stringer* a72 73
5 b g Sunday Silence(USA) —Sheer Reason (USA) (Danzig (USA))
2957[5] 3182[2] (4054) 4275[4] 4371[4] 7715[9]

Faithful Ruler (USA) *R A Fahey* a77 61
4 bb g Elusive Quality(USA) —Fancy Ruler (USA) (Half A Year (USA))
149[3] 258[2] 452[4] 5915[9] (6827) 7224[8]

Fajita *M G Quinlan* a51 65
2 b c Lahib(USA) —La Fija (USA) (Dixieland Band (USA))
3158[5] 5579[5] 6008[5] 6574[7]

Fajr (IRE) *Miss Gay Kelleway* a115 110
6 b g Green Desert(USA) —Ta Rib (USA) (Mr Prospector (USA))
(227) 308[4] 678[8] 960[18] 2530[6] 2789[10] 3122[28] 6783[16] 7418[10]

Falbrina (IRE) *M Brittain*
2 ch f Falbrav(IRE) —Haniya (IRE) (Caerleon (USA))
1392[6]

Falcativ *L M Cumani* a94 78
3 b c Falbrav(IRE) —Frottola (Muhtarram (USA))
2199[11] 4620[5] ◆ 5472[3] ◆ (6379) (7025) ◆

Falco (USA) *C Laffon-Parias* 122
3 b c Pivotal—Icelips (USA) (Unbridled (USA))
(2032a) 3102[5] 4010a[9]

Falcolnry (IRE) *J R Fanshawe* 84
3 b f Hawk Wing(USA) —Fear And Greed (IRE) (Brief Truce (USA))
2196[8] 3039[3] ◆ 4189[9] 5071[12] 6027[10]

Falcon Flyer *J R Best* a52 45
4 br m Cape Cross(IRE) —Green Danube (USA) (Irish River (FR))
8[8] 89[2] 123[8] 356[10] 4414[15] 4774[12]

Faldal *Tom Dascombe* a80 50
2 br f Falbrav(IRE) —Tidal (Bin Ajwaad (IRE))
7332[5] (7577) ◆

Falimar *C W Fairhurst* a59 64
4 b m Fasliyev(USA) —Mar Blue (FR) (Marju (IRE))
8631[1] 1025[12] 2286[12] 4295[7]

Fallen In Love *J L Dunlop* 73
2 b f Galileo(IRE) —Fallen Star (Brief Truce (USA))
4157[5] 5640[3] (6291)

Falmassim *Miss J A Camacho* a23 65
5 b g Mozart(IRE) —Scostes (Cadeaux Genereux)
1455[6] 1966[5] 2748[4] 2983[6] 3340[5] 3638[9]

False Modesty *George Baker*
2 b f Falbrav(IRE) —Heather Mix (Linamix (FR))
7561[P] (Dead)

Falun (GER) *A Trybuhl*
2 ch c Pentire—Fortunata (GER) (Daun (GER))
6853a[6]

Fame And Glory *A P O'Brien* 113
2 b c Montjeu(IRE) —Gryada (Shirley Heights)
(7294a)

Familiar Territory *Saeed Bin Suroor* a110 112
5 br h Cape Cross(IRE) —Forever Fine (USA) (Sunshine Forever (USA))
202a[2] (568a) 742a[2] 5743a[3] 6287[3]

Famous Name *D K Weld* 122
3 b c Dansili—Fame At Last (USA) (Quest For Fame)
(1232a) ◆ 2654a[2] 5729a[2] 6498a[3]

Fan Club *Mrs R A Carr* a81 77
4 ch g Zamindar(USA) —Starfan (USA) (Lear Fan (USA))
1188[12] 1776[11] 2523[12] 3211[9] 3789[5] 3834[6] 4542[12] 4609[6] 5770[9] 7779[10]

Fancy Feathers (IRE) *David Marnane* a73 75
4 ch m Redback—Idle Fancy (Mujtahid (USA))
2284[3] 4467a[11]

Fancy Footsteps (IRE) *C G Cox* a69 63
3 gr f Noverre(USA) —Fancy Intense (Peintre Celebre (USA))
1869[7] 2560[7] 7256[2] 7653[3] ◆

Fancy Woman *C N Kellett* 32
4 b m Sakhee(USA) —Fancy Wrap (Kris)
6168[7] 6584[10]

Fandango Boy *J P Broderick* a69 66
7 b g Victory Note(USA) —Dancing Chimes (London Bells (CAN))
6366a[20] 7698[7] 7732[2]

Fanditha (IRE) *R Hannon* 79
2 ch f Danehill Dancer(IRE) —Splendid (IRE) (Mujtahid (USA))
4665[5] 5097[6] (5640) 6319a[10]

Fangfoss Girls *L Wells* a69 58
2 ch f Monsieur Bond(IRE) —Bond Shakira (Daggers Drawn (USA))
(1480) (2049) ◆ 5680[5] 6469[5] 7308[8] 7537[3] 7788[2]

Fanjura (IRE) *J Noseda* 103
3 b g Marju(IRE) —Accelerating (USA) (Lear Fan (USA))
(1418) 2121[5] 6440[14] 6780[11]

Fantadot *D J S Ffrench Davis* a54
3 b g Fantastic Light(USA) —Bardot (Efisio)
1957[16]

Fantasia *L M Cumani* 111
2 b f Sadler's Wells(USA) —Blue Symphony (Darshaan)
(3923) ◆ (5266) ◆ 6268[2]

Fantasies (IRE) *Garry Moss*
2 b f Fantastic Light(USA) —Lottie Dundass (Polar Falcon (USA))
2865[9]

Fantastica (GER) *Frau K Haustein* 72
5 b m Big Shuffle(USA) —Fatal Attraction (GER) (Czaravich (USA))
3243a[9]

Fantastic Dubai (USA) *M R Channon* 56
2 b c Storm Cat(USA) —Shy Lady (FR) (Kaldoun (FR))
6601[5]

Fantastic Fred (IRE) *J A Osborne* a47 16
2 br g Fantastic Light(USA) —Luxury Launch (USA) (Seeking The Gold (USA))
4027[8] 4305[7] 5599[6]

Fantastic Lass *R A Fahey* a50 61
3 b f Fantastic Light(USA) —Shaanara (IRE) (Darshaan)
1186[2] ◆ (1478) 1678[3] 3057[7] 3671[6] 4564[11] 5388[4] 6175[4] 6529[7]

Fantastic Morning *F Jordan* a58 83
4 ch g Fantastic Light(USA) —Gombay Girl (USA) (Woodman (USA))
1072[15] 2895[7] 3294[9] 7461[9]

Fantasy Believer *J J Quinn* 101
10 b g Sure Blade(USA) —Delicious (Dominion)
1325[6] 1809[24] 3680[11] 3973[12] 4375[5] 4687[7] 5067[11]

Fantasy Crusader *R M H Cowell* a58 56
9 ch g Beveled(USA) —Cranfield Charger (Northern State (USA))
2943[9] 4053[9] 4267[5] 4371[5] 4721[4] 4819[2] 5168[3] 5427[9] 5912[10] 6753[14] 7599[12]

Fantasy Explorer *J J Quinn* a71 94
5 b g Compton Place—Zinzi (Song)
1571[9] 2359[2] 2626[8] 3009[8] 4240[11] 4445[17] 5250[2] 5796[13] (6125) 6290[2] 6971[2]

Fantasy Fighter (IRE) *J J Quinn* a65 39
3 b g Danetime(IRE) —Lady Montekin (Montekin)
1817[13] 3395[6] ◆ 3753[7] 4242[6] 4684[15] 4702[9] 6224[3] 6751[2] 7320[8] 7522[2] 7625[3] (7636) (7710) 7808[2]

Fantasy Gladiator *R M H Cowell* a67
2 b g Ishiguru(USA) —Fancier Bit (Lion Cavern (USA))
7268[5] 7417[3] ◆ 7640[4]

Fantasy Legend (IRE) *A M Hales* a47 26
5 ch g Beckett(IRE) —Sianiski (Niniski (USA))
269[6] 545[8]

Fantasy Parkes *K Bishop* a79 87
4 ch m Fantastic Light(USA) —My Melody Parkes (Teenoso (USA))
2039[2] 2406[8] 2968[11] 4901[4] 5639[8] 6211[13]

Fantasy Princess (USA) *G A Butler* a82 80
3 ch f Johannesburg(USA) —Fantasy (Cadeaux Genereux)
3636[4] 4189[8] 4872[3] 5536[2] 5910[2] 6599[10]

Fantasy Ride *J Pearce* a71 61
6 b g Bahhare(USA) —Grand Splendour (Shirley Heights)
(31) 320[2] 4991[5] 5833[8] 6007[11] 6538[9] 7089[4] 7355[8] 7626[3]

Fantino *J Mackie* 66
2 b c Shinko Forest(IRE) —Illustre Inconnue (USA) (Septieme Ciel (USA))
4497[6]

Fantoche (BRZ) *Mrs John Harrington* a93 85
6 ch g Roi Normand(USA) —Diet Lark (BRZ) (Roy (USA))
4003a[5] 4493a[4]

Fantosha (USA) *K A Ryan* a63 69
3 b f Johannesburg(USA) —Montage (USA) (Alydar (USA))
7466[7] 7690[3] 7822[7]

Faraday (IRE) *N P Mulholland* a59 60
5 b g Montjeu(IRE) —Fureau (GER) (Ferdinand (USA))
578[2] 693[3] 930[2] (1031) 2353[7] 3732[2] 4704[10] 6189[12] 7114[10]

Faraway Bay *E J O'Neill* 43
3 b f Diktat—Faraway Lass (Distant Relative)
3058[11] 3297[7] 3556[7]

Faraway Flower (USA) *B W Hills* 96
2 b f Distant View(USA) —Silver Star (Zafonic (USA))
(3437) ◆ 5266[6] 5794[2] 6441[6]

Faraway Sound (IRE) *P C Haslam* a50 75
2 b g Distant Music(USA) —Queen Consort (Diesis)
1425^{3} 2362^{2} 2657^{5} (3215) 4434^{2} 4558^{3} 5159^{4} 7361^{7} 7645^{9}

Fardi (IRE) *K W Hogg* 13
6 b g Green Desert(USA) —Shuruk (Cadeaux Genereux)
1305^{11} 2286^{11} 2395^{9} 2776^{9} 3718^{14}

Fareeha *B R Johnson* a59 61
3 b f King's Best(USA) —Shatarah (Gulch (USA))
712^{9} 5145^{10} 5429^{4} 5787^{7} 5813^{6}

Fareer *E A L Dunlop* 87
2 ch c Bahamian Bounty—Songsheet (Dominion)
2324^{3} ◆ (3055) 3924^{2}

Farefield Lodge (IRE) *C G Cox* a69 76
4 b g Indian Lodge(IRE) —Fieldfare (Selkirk (USA))
1015^{8} 1541^{5} 1900^{3} 2550^{3}

Far From Old (IRE) *J E Hammond* a99 101
5 b h Vettori(IRE) —Jabali (FR) (Shirley Heights)
3490^{9} 7643a^{4}

Far Gone *M L W Bell* a72 68
3 b f Diktat—Fairy Jackie (IRE) (Fairy King (USA))
6543^{8} 7206^{8}

Farinelli *Mrs John Harrington* a100 100
5 br g Selkirk(USA) —Melodica (Machiavellian (USA))
7235a^{14}

Farleigh *A M Balding* a62
2 b f Trans Island—Medway (IRE) (Shernazar)
6375^{2}

Farley Star *R Charlton* a88 98
4 b m Alzao(USA) —Girl Of My Dreams (IRE) (Marju (IRE))
1211^{3} 1545^{7} (2457) (2969) 3740^{12} 4189^{5} 4520^{4} ◆ 5311^{4} 6034^{7}

Farne Island *Micky Hammond* a62 62
5 ch g Arkadian Hero(USA) —Holy Island (Deploy)
1953^{7} 2365^{9} 2662^{6} 3082^{9} 3579^{6} 4215^{8} 4540^{9}

Farouge (FR) *Yvonne Durant* 74
7 gr h Croco Rouge(IRE) —Fablimixa (FR) (Linamix (FR))
5958a^{10}

Farrel (IRE) *B Grizzetti* 106
3 b c Fruits Of Love(USA) —Folcungi (IRE) (Mukaddamah (USA))
1513a^{5} 2028a^{4} 3356a^{3} 4010a^{8} 7262a^{3}

Farriers Gate *T Keddy* a12 27
2 ch f Lomitas—Mountain Stream (FR) (Vettori (IRE))
2709^{10} 3114^{10}

Far Seeking *A G Juckes* a62 58
4 b h Distant Music(USA) —House Hunting (Zafonic (USA))
48^{5} 176^{8} 530^{4} 1083^{6} 4322^{10}

Farsighted *J M P Eustace* 72
3 b f Where Or When(IRE) —Classic Vision (Classic Cliche (IRE))
1381^{8} 2118^{17} 2985^{9} 4477^{11} 5161^{16}

Far Song (IRE) *A M Balding* a54 35
3 ch f Distant Music(USA) —Charlene Lacy (IRE) (Pips Pride)
9^{5} 298^{8}

Farthermost (IRE) *R Hannon* a77 85
3 ch g Fath(USA) —Matila (IRE) (Persian Bold)
1336^{6} 1685^{6} 2127^{2} 2756^{4} 2991^{2} (3313) 3506^{2} 4408^{11} 6699^{7} 6864^{8}

Fasalee (IRE) *A P Jarvis* a60 63
3 b f Fasliyev(USA) —Monalee Lass (IRE) (Mujtahid (USA))
1413^{8} 1987^{8} 2783^{6} 3693^{3} 4079^{5} 4666^{3}

Fascinatin Rhythm *M R Channon* a69 77
4 br m Fantastic Light(USA) —Marguerite De Vine (Zilzal (USA))
1472^{10} 2125^{4} 3143^{3} 3523^{5} 3718^{5} 3785^{3}

Fashion Accessory *M Appleby* 2
4 b m Muthahb(IRE) —Queen Of Fashion (IRE) (Barathea (IRE))
197^{9}

Fashion Icon (USA) *T D Barron* 53
2 ch f Van Nistelrooy(USA) —Los Altos (USA) (Robin Des Pins (USA))
1627^{8} 3670^{7} 4499^{5} 4965^{6}

Fashion Week *M Johnston* a60
3 gr g Linamix(FR) —Picture Princess (Sadler's Wells (USA))
7344^{11} 7474^{9} 7609^{4}

Fasliyanne (IRE) *K A Ryan* a45 66
2 b f Fasliyev(USA) —Happy Memories (IRE) (Thatching)
1419^{6} 1627^{4} 2054^{3} 6764^{8} 7113^{7} 7451^{5} 7612^{7}

Fastella (IRE) *G A Butler* a71
3 b f Fasliyev(USA) —Ela Athena (Ezzoud (IRE))
965^{7} 6345^{P}

Fast Feet *K A Ryan* a75 89
3 b g Statue Of Liberty(USA) —Landowska (USA) (Langfuhr (CAN))
470^{3} 2771^{2} 3434^{3} 4028^{2} 4686^{15}

Fast Freddie *S Parr* a79 67
4 b g Agnes World(USA) —Bella Chica (IRE) (Bigstone (IRE))
(746) ◆ 840^{8} 1047^{6} 2511^{4} 2551^{9} 3171^{6} 3404^{7} 3668^{5} 4107^{5} 4703^{2} 5867^{2} 6190^{4} 6339^{9} 6895^{9} (7346) 7393^{3} 7562^{7}

Fast Lane Lili *F Doumen* a75 81
5 b m Fasliyev(USA) —Mercedes (GER) (Nebos (GER))
7487a^{3}

Fastmambo (USA) *F Head* 102
5 b g Kingmambo(USA) —Slow Down (USA) (Seattle Slew (USA))
3053a^{4}

Fastnet Storm (IRE) *T P Tate* 81
2 br g Rock Of Gibraltar(IRE) —Dreams (Rainbow Quest (USA))
2592^{7} (3334) 4373^{5} 5006^{5} 6086^{2} (6857)

Fastrac Boy *J R Best* a57 56
5 b g Bold Edge—Nesyred (IRE) (Paris House)
86^{8} 121^{7} 690^{10} 774^{4} 883^{9} 2881^{2} 3346^{3} 3575^{3} 7836^{9}

Fast Ruler (NZ) *Tony Vasil* 90
4 br g Viking Ruler(AUS) —Miss Priority (NZ) (Kaapstad (NZ))
6922a^{13}

Fatal Bullet (USA) *Reade Baker* a120 66
3 b g Red Bullet(USA) —Sararegal (CAN) (Regal Classic (CAN))
6999a^{2}

Fat Boy (IRE) *P W Chapple-Hyam* a77 116
3 ch c Choisir(AUS) —Gold Shift (USA) (Night Shift (USA))
1400^{2} (2148) (2605) 3247^{11} 3922^{9} 4550^{5}

Fat Chance *Rae Guest* 52
2 gr f Linamix(FR) —Hymenee (USA) (Chief's Crown (USA))
6885^{5}

Fateful Attraction *I A Wood* a73 47
5 b m Mujahid(USA) —Heavens Above (FR) (Pistolet Bleu (IRE))
51^{3} 316^{8} 546^{8} 1528^{16} 3036^{11} 3361^{6} 4054^{7} 4390^{5} 4722^{6} 5802^{5} 6019^{10} 6775^{7} 7089^{5} 7590^{6} 7831^{7}

Fateh Field (USA) *Saeed Bin Suroor* 104
3 b c Distorted Humor(USA) —Too Cool To Fool (USA) (Foolish Pleasure (USA))
2121^{3} 2580^{2} 3155^{21} 4153^{4}

Fathayer (USA) *P Paciello* 101
3 ch c Volponi(USA) —Bright Generation (IRE) (Rainbow Quest (USA))
2028a^{8}

Father Time *H R A Cecil* a86
2 b c Dansili—Clepsydra (Sadler's Wells (USA))
(7336) ◆

Fathey (IRE) *R A Fahey* 73
2 ch g Fath(USA) —Christoph's Girl (Efisio)
(1948) 3663^{8} 4594^{7} 5451^{5} 6067^{4} 6426^{12}

Fathom Five (IRE) *B Smart* 108
4 b g Fath(USA) —Ambria (ITY) (Final Straw)
1772^{3} 2828^{6} 3451^{5} 4840^{2} 5551a^{4} 5890^{6} 6653^{15} 6947^{15}

Fathsta (IRE) *S Kirk* a85 101
3 b g Fath(USA) —Kilbride Lass (IRE) (Lahib (USA))
(253) 489^{5} 723^{2} 975^{2} (1167) 1404^{5} 1837^{2} 1925^{2} (2104) 2793^{2} 3047^{14} 3155^{8} 3919^{19} 4197^{4} 4404^{6} 4553^{6} 5313^{3} 5446^{10} 5495^{7} 5795^{3} 6277^{2} 6576^{9}

Fathtastic (IRE) *Miss V Haigh* 22
2 b g Fath(USA) —Majesty's Dancer (IRE) (Danehill Dancer (IRE))
2671^{11} 3670^{10}

Fault *R Charlton* a74 84
2 b c Bahamian Bounty—Trundley Wood (Wassl)
(1873) 2254^{4} (4101) 4626^{9} 4942^{7} 5466^{3} 6426^{14} 6540^{3}

Favouring (IRE) *M C Chapman* a57 58
6 ch g Fayruz—Peace Dividend (IRE) (Alzao (USA))
168^{8} 256^{4} 365^{6} 528^{5}

Favourite Girl (IRE) *T D Easterby* 103
2 b f Refuse To Bend(IRE) —Zuccini Wind (IRE) (Revoque (IRE))
1390^{3} 2462^{4} 2783^{2} (3078) 3663^{3} 4190^{15} (4857) 5359^{2} 6102^{10} 6483^{2} 6972^{6}

Favours Brave *J H M Gosden* 67
2 b c Galileo(IRE) —Tuning (Rainbow Quest (USA))
6425^{6} ◆

Fawaz *Mrs C A Dunnett* a41 7
2 b c Mujahid(USA) —Ruwaya (USA) (Red Ransom (USA))
3689^{8} 4747^{9} 5158^{16}

Faylan (FR) *C Baillet* 96
2 b c Indian Rocket—Siran (FR) (R B Chesne)
5300a^{3}

Fay Street (USA) *K J Condon* a85 83
3 b g Street Cry(IRE) —Annoconnor (USA) (Nureyev (USA))
826a^{2}

Fazbee (IRE) *P W D'Arcy* a87 85
2 b f Fasliyev(USA) —Kelpie (IRE) (Kahyasi)
1680^{2} ◆ 2167^{5} 2541^{4} (4488) 4868^{12} (5375) 5937^{3}

Feared In Flight (IRE) *B W Hills* 109
3 b g Hawk Wing(USA) —Solar Crystal (IRE) (Alzao (USA))
1632^{3} 1922^{4} 3156^{11} 3877^{16} 5830^{4} 6476^{14}

Fearless Warrior *J L Dunlop* 73
3 br g Erhaab(USA) —Princess Genista (Ile De Bourbon (USA))
1839^{8} 2280^{6} 3962^{5} 4646^{7} (5537) (5758) 6012^{8} 6898^{10}

Feasible *J G Portman* a67 69
3 ch g Efisio—Zoena (Emarati (USA))
1057^{6} 1622^{8} 2047^{3} 2678^{6} 3525^{9} 3799^{12} 4524^{2} 5616^{3} 6211^{7} 7194^{11}

Featherlight *Jamie Poulton* a77 74
4 b m Fantastic Light(USA) —Feathers Flying (IRE) (Royal Applause)
27^{8} 880^{4} 1052^{2} 1337^{3} 6606^{2}

Featherweight (IRE) *B W Hills* a73 78
2 ch f Fantastic Light(USA) —Dancing Feather (Suave Dancer (USA))
5788^{3} 6081^{3} 6674^{5} 7438^{3}

Feelin Foxy *J G Given* a81 81
4 b m Foxhound(USA) —Charlie Girl (Puissance)
(987) 1178^{3} 1755^{3} 2000^{11} 2489^{7} 2892^{9} 3260^{5} 3883^{7} 4385^{3} 4563^{2} 5401^{11} 6218^{4} 6388^{10} 7081^{8}

Feeling (IRE) *T T Clement* a14 75
4 b g Sadler's Wells(USA) —La Pitie (USA) (Devil's Bag (USA))
3181^{9} 3947^{13} 4451^{10} 4664^{14} 6753^{11}

Feeling Fab (FR) *M Johnston* a84 91
2 b f Refuse To Bend(IRE) —Les Planches (Tropular)
4380^{2} 4697^{3} (5788) 6076^{4} (6477)

Feeling Fresh (IRE) *Paul Green* a66 71
3 b c Xaar—Oh'Cecilia (IRE) (Scenic)
1024 ◆ 3626^{10} (4595) 4684^{4} 5198^{14} 6219^{4} 6765^{7} 7040^{4} 7152^{3} 7288^{6} 7533^{13}

Feeling Peckish (USA) *M C Chapman* a43 41
4 ch g Point Given(USA) —Sunday Bazaar (USA) (Nureyev (USA))
39^{8} 169^{2} 345^{5} 1551^{11} 1814^{12} 4899^{4}

Feeling Pretty *C Smith* 5
3 b f Auction House(USA) —Lunalux (Emarati (USA))
614^{5} 780^{11} 1777^{8} 2823^{12} 4523^{9}

Feeling Proud (USA) *Jane Chapple-Hyam* a68 74
3 b f More Than Ready(USA) —Proud Heart (IRE) (Caerleon (USA))
756^{9} 1412^{12}

Feeling Stylish (IRE) *N Tinkler* 48
2 b f Desert Style(IRE) —No Hard Feelings (IRE) (Alzao (USA))
4394^{9} 5072^{4} 5384^{6} 6214^{17}

Feelin Irie (IRE) *M J Gingell* a59 67
5 b g Key Of Luck(USA) —Charlotte's Dancer (Kris)
844^{11} 1109^{8}

Feels All Right (IRE) *A Fabre* 111
2 b c Danehill Dancer(IRE) —Zagreb Flyer (Old Vic)
7294a^{3}

Feet Of Fury *W M Brisbourne* a56 51
2 b f Deportivo—Fury Dance (USA) (Cryptoclearance (USA))
6601^{6} 6988^{4}

Feisty Royale *M Johnston* a68 80
3 b f Royal Applause—Hawait Al Barr (Green Desert (USA))
1336^{10} 2405^{10} 2674^{10} 3109^{5} 3716^{4} 3957^{2} 4179^{5} 4500^{6} 5108^{2} 5502^{5} 5936^{8} 6160^{2} 6925^{3}

Felday *H Morrison* 84
2 b c Bahamian Bounty—Monaiya (Shareef Dancer (USA))
4151^{8} (5225) 6474^{13} 6946^{6}

Felicia *S C Williams* a58 58
3 b f Diktat—Gracia (Linamix (FR))
700^{4} 6036^{8} 6685^{4} ◆ 7088^{4} 7217^{10} 7345^{6} 7367^{4}

Fell Pack *J J Quinn* 46
4 b g Lake Coniston(IRE) —All On (Dunbeath (USA))
4378^{4} 4689^{11} 5361^{7}

Fenice (IRE) *S Seemar* a92 91
5 gr g Woodman(USA) —Venize (IRE) (Kaldoun (FR))
477a^{11}

Fenners (USA) *M W Easterby* a69 69
5 ch g Pleasant Tap(USA) —Legal Opinion (IRE) (Polish Precedent (USA))
47^{2} 344^{5} 675^{7} 778^{6} 2364^{5} (2804) 3176^{5} 4331^{5} 4966^{9} 5476^{8} 6189^{7} 6493^{9} 7169^{11} 7427^{4} 7626^{7}

Fen Spirit (IRE) *J H M Gosden* a78 75
2 b f Invincible Spirit(IRE) —Irinatinvidio (Rudimentary (USA))
4870^{4} 5570^{4} 6030^{3} 6696^{2} (7207)

Ferneley (IRE) *Francis Ennis* 108
4 b h Ishiguru(USA) —Amber Tide (IRE) (Pursuit Of Love)
1882a^{7} (2026a) 2740a^{3}

Fern House (IRE) *Bruce Hellier* a54 59
6 b g Xaar—Certain Impression (USA) (Forli (ARG))
142^{8} 153^{8} 2748^{10} 3080^{7} 3789^{2} 4118^{5} 4813^{8} 6153^{6} 6310^{8}

Fervent *J M Bradley* a42 53
4 b g Kyllachy—Romancing (Dr Devious (IRE))
1275^{9} 2070^{12} 3733^{11} 5749^{10}

Fervent Prince *H Morrison* a88 102
3 b g Averti(IRE) —Maria Theresa (Primo Dominie)
(1546) ◆ 1923^{2} (2405) ◆ 3155^{20} 3850^{14} 4553^{4} (5470) 6283^{8}

Fesko *M Johnston* a65 80
2 b f Shinko Forest(IRE) —Young Sue (Local Suitor (USA))
6051^{4} ◆ 6244^{3} (6545) 7820^{6}

Festero (GER) *C Von Der Recke*
5 ch g Silvano(GER) —Freni (GER) (Sternkoenig (IRE))
604a^{9}

Festival Dreams *Miss J S Davis* a51 54
3 ch g Largesse—Bright Spangle (IRE) (General Monash (USA))
3022^{7} 7520^{7}

Festivale (IRE) *J L Dunlop* 101
3 b f Invincible Spirit(IRE) —Cephalonie (USA) (Kris S (USA))
1401^{3} 2170^{3} (3124)

Festival Princess (IRE) *M Halford* 86
3 b f Barathea(IRE) —Uliana (USA) (Darshaan)
4006a^{13} 5550a^{13}

Festoso (IRE) *H J L Dunlop* 104
3 b f Diesis—Garah (Ajdal (USA))
5829^{3} ◆ 6475^{9}

Feudal (IRE) *M Johnston* 57
2 b c Xaar—Noble Rose (IRE) (Caerleon (USA))
6923^{5}

Fever *M W Easterby* a79 89
4 b g Dr Fong(USA) —Follow Flanders (Pursuit Of Love)
1067^{7} 1612^{6} 1909^{8} 2787^{6} 3493^{10} 3716^{9} 3996^{6} 4878^{4} 5456^{4} 5971^{8} 6248^{4}

Fictional *E J O'Neill* a71 102
7 b h Fraam—Manon Lescaut (Then Again)
679^{12}

Fiddlers Creek (IRE) *R Allan* a62 63
9 b g Danehill(USA) —Mythical Creek (USA) (Pleasant Tap (USA))
1405^{4}

Fiddlers Ford (IRE) *T Keddy* a61 61
7 b g Sadler's Wells(USA) —Old Domesday Book (High Top)
1856^{9} 3137^{6} 3377^{4} 4526^{2}

Fiefdom (IRE) *I W McInnes* a91 89
6 br g Singspiel(IRE) —Chiquita Linda (IRE) (Mujadil (USA))
1335^{10} 1630^{8} 2007^{14} 2087^{5} 2925^{2} 2969^{8} 3214^{2} 3664^{6} 4284^{6} (5144) (5789) 6627^{3} 7390^{6} 7557^{10}

Fielder (IRE) *J G Portman* 18
3 b g Catcher In The Rye(IRE) —Miss Garuda (Persian Bold)
1549^{9} 2454^{11}

Field Fantasy *Garry Moss*
2 ch f Bold Edge—Princess Carranita (IRE) (Desert Sun)
7546^{10}

Fieriness (IRE) *Saeed Bin Suroor* 58
2 ch g Pivotal—Fairy Contessa (IRE) (Fairy King (USA))
5579^{7}

Fiery Lad (IRE) *G M Lyons* a104 91
3 b g Mull Of Kintyre(USA) —Forget Paris (IRE) (Broken Hearted)
3875^{7} 6261a^{3} (7235a)

Fiesta Lady (ARG) *Saeed Bin Suroor* a102
4 br m Southern Halo(USA) —Fiereze (ARG) (Political Ambition (USA))
(201a) ◆ 496a^{2} 744a^{9}

Fifer (IRE) *R A Fahey* 35
2 b f Soviet Star(USA) —Fife (IRE) (Lomond (USA))
6788^{10} 7126^{6}

Fifteen Love (USA) *R Charlton* a98 111
3 bb c Point Given(USA) —Nidd (USA) (Known Fact (USA))
1441^{12} (3155) ◆ 3740^{5} (4587) 5742a^{8} 6476^{25}

Fifth Amendment *A Berry* 69
2 ch g Presidium—Lady Magician (Lord Bud)
6545^{9} 7038^{2}

Fifth Zak *S R Bowring* a47 41
4 b g Best Of The Bests(IRE) —Zakuska (Zafonic (USA))
369^{3} 524^{8} 843^{5}

Fifty (IRE) *R Hannon* a67 78
3 b f Fasliyev(USA) —Amethyst (IRE) (Sadler's Wells (USA))
(1835) 2428^{8} 3064^{3} 3487^{6} 3918^{6} 4252^{12}

Fifty Cents *R Charlton* 86
4 ch g Diesis—Solaia (USA) (Miswaki (USA))
1174^{3}

Figaro Flyer (IRE) *P Howling* a78 79
5 b g Mozart(IRE) —Ellway Star (IRE) (Night Shift (USA))
72^{5} 194^{5} 446^{4} 576^{5} 766^{6} 782^{2} 964^{4} 1268^{6} 1488^{5} (1901) 2292^{2} 2950^{2} ◆ 7276^{8} 7562^{3} 7733^{2}

Fight Club (GER) *R Brotherton* 102
7 b h Lavirco(GER) —Flaming Song (IRE) (Darshaan)
2543^{7} 3122^{29} 3683^{6}

Fikrah *Kevin Prendergast* a55 86
3 ch f Medicean—Justbetweenfriends (USA) (Diesis)
2024a^{7}

Filemot *John Berry* a45 64
3 ch f Largesse—Hickleton Lady (IRE) (Kala Shikari)
1737^{2} 2981^{12} 3447^{5} 4272^{8} 6766^{6} 7182^{13} 7383^{8} 7692^{11}

Filigree Lace (USA) *Sir Michael Stoute* 71
3 ch f Seeking The Gold(USA) —Yafill (USA) (Nureyev (USA))
2257^{4} 3338^{2} 3849^{13} 6275^{2}

Filios (IRE) *Saeed Bin Suroor* a31 103
4 b h Kutub(IRE) —Karlinaxa (Linamix (FR))
381a^{13} 4844^{4} 5830^{7}

Filligree (IRE) *Rae Guest* a60 91
3 b f Kyllachy—Clunie (Inchinor)
1672^{3} 1897^{2} ◆ 2452^{5} (2935) (3118) 3280^{4} (4773) 5510^{4} 6402^{2}

Film Festival (USA) *B Ellison* a72 84
5 ch g Diesis—To Act (USA) (Roberto (USA))
1970^{4} 2582^{9} 7150^{7}

Film Maker (IRE) *B J Meehan* a96 92
3 b c Danetime(IRE) —Alexander Anapolis (IRE) (Spectrum (IRE))
2198^{6} (2466) 2793^{5} 4601^{4} 5270^{9} (5403) ◆ 5681^{8} 6239^{8}

Film Queen (IRE) *Mrs L J Mongan* a56 54
4 bb m Desert Style(IRE) —Filmgame (IRE) (Be My Guest (USA))
265^{8} 413^{4} 590^{2} 708^{9} 885^{10} 1049^{5} 1209^{5} 1533^{4} 1938^{16} 2597^{11} 2861^{6} 3265^{11} 4182^{4} 5148^{10}

Film Set (USA) *Saeed Bin Suroor* a84 89
2 bb c Johar(USA) —Dippers (USA) (Polish Numbers (USA))
6230^{2} ◆ (6601) 7075^{3}

Filun *A Middleton* a59 67
3 b g Montjeu(IRE) —Sispre (FR) (Master Willie)
2191^{7} 2669^{8} 3637^{3} 4382^{5} 4984^{8} 5605^{9} 7822^{4}

Final Dynasty *Mrs G S Rees* a71 98
4 b m Komaite(USA) —Malcesine (IRE) (Auction Ring (USA))
6810^{14}

Finalmente *S A Callaghan* a106 112
6 b g Kahyasi—Sudden Spirit (FR) (Esprit Du Nord (USA))
(2542) 3154^{10} 3743^{4} 5333a^{9} 5854^{8}

Final Rhapsody *J A Geake* a64 39
2 b f Royal Applause—Rivers Rhapsody (Dominion)
5214^{9} 6327^{12} 6696^{6} 7308^{2}

Final Salute *B Smart* 71
2 b c Royal Applause—Wildwood Flower (Distant Relative)
3170^{6} 4438^{5} 6229^{3} (6865) 7241^{4}

Final Tune (IRE) *Miss M E Rowland* a81 79
5 ch g Grand Lodge(USA) —Jackie's Opera (FR) (Indian Ridge)
860^{6} 1065^{6}

Final Verse *M Salaman* a95 109
5 b g Mark Of Esteem(IRE) —Tamassos (Dance In Time (CAN))
203a^{7} 384a^{13} 743a^{6} 2044^{5} 2600^{9} 3122^{19} 4188^{9} 4687^{10} (6490) 6772^{5} 7146^{2} 7291^{3}

Final Victory *A M Balding* 69
2 ch c Generous(IRE) —Persian Victory (IRE) (Persian Bold)
6604^{5}

Financial Times (USA) *Stef Liddiard* a90 72
6 b g Awesome Again(CAN) —Investabull (USA) (Holy Bull (USA))
162^{4} 580^{2} 676^{4} (824) 887^{2} 925^{6} 1617^{8} 2188^{8}

Find Me (USA) *L Lungo* a67 34
4 ch g Point Given(USA) —Island Jamboree (USA) (Explodent (USA))
1219^{9} 1521^{7} 7132^{12}

Fine Edge *H E Haynes*
7 ch m Keen—Cap That (Derek H)
4366^{14}

Fine Ruler (IRE) *M R Bosley* a75 70
4 b g King's Best(USA) —Bint Alajwaad (IRE) (Fairy King (USA))
48^{6} (446) ◆ 683^{6} 819^{6} 1038^{6} 1153^{5} 1491^{8} 6631^{3} 7194^{4} 7358^{5} (7548) 7786^{7}

Fine Tolerance *J R Boyle* a42
2 b f Bertolini(USA) —Sashay (Bishop Of Cashel)
7207^{8} 7311^{10}

Finicius (USA) *Eoin Griffin* a108 106
4 b g Officer(USA) —Glorious Linda (FR) (Le Glorieux)
1783a^{4} 2417a^{8} 6285^{10} 7703^{6}

Finished Article (IRE) *Mrs D Thomas* a48 54
11 b g Indian Ridge—Summer Fashion (Moorestyle)
1246^{14} 2051^{9} 2245^{14} 7071^{7} 7216^{8} 7520^{14}

Finjaan *M P Tregoning* 117
2 b c Royal Applause—Alhufoof (USA) (Dayjur (USA))
(1832) 2541^{2} (4507) 6442^{9} 6815^{3}

Finmore Queen (USA) *J R Fanshawe* a86 72
3 ch f Grand Slam(USA) —Slew City Slicker (USA) (Slew City Slew (USA))
52^{2} 2328^{6} 3672^{3} (4183) 5209^{8}

Finnegan McCool *R M Beckett* a5 89
2 b g Efisio—Royal Jade (Last Tycoon)
1804^{3} 2338^{4} (3092) 3677^{2} 4190^{14} 4626^{6} 6118^{7} 6769^{11}

Finnegans Rainbow *M C Chapman* a44 46
6 ch g Spectrum(IRE) —Fairy Story (IRE) (Persian Bold)
188^{4} 2207^{10} 3176^{9} 3589^{12}

Finney Hill *H Candy* 78
3 b f Mark Of Esteem(IRE) —Ringing Hill (Charnwood Forest (IRE))
1525^{9} 3854^{4} 4166^{4}

Finsburra (USA) *Eoin Griffin* a77 79
3 br g Sky Mesa(USA) —Wood Of Binn (USA) (Woodman (USA))
6510a^{10}

Finsbury *J S Goldie* a65 76
5 gr g Observatory(USA) —Carmela Owen (Owington)
1645^{7} 2556^{4} ◆ 2992^{5} 3383^{9} (5101) 5455^{5} 5965^{12} 6631^{6} 7218^{8} 7292^{5}

Finsceal Beo (IRE) *J S Bolger* 120
4 ch m Mr Greeley(USA) —Musical Treat (IRE) (Royal Academy (USA))
1090a^{5} ◆ 2432a^{2} 3100^{3} 3511a^{9} 3852^{7} 5547a^{3}

Fin Vin De Leu (GER) *M Johnston* a75
2 b g Dr Fong(USA) —Fairy Queen (IRE) (Fairy King (USA))
5870^{3} ◆ 6282^{5} 6731^{4} 7073^{2}

Fiona Fox *J Balding* a57 48
4 b m Foxhound(USA) —First Play (Primo Dominie)
65^{12} 634^{11} 2036^{12} 2491^{16}

Firebet (IRE) *Mrs A Duffield* 85
2 b c Dubai Destination(USA) —Dancing Prize (IRE) (Sadler's Wells (USA))
(3364) 4187^{4} (5883) 6549^{4}

Fire In Cairo (IRE) *P C Haslam* a55 55
4 b m Barathea(IRE) —Ibiza (GER) (Linamix (FR))
1913^{7} 2290^{10} 2731^{8}

Fire King *J A Geake* 19
2 b g Falbrav(IRE) —Dancing Fire (USA) (Dayjur (USA))
6117^{18} 6398^{8} 7080^{13}

Fire Me Gun *M Mullineaux* a45
2 b f Reel Buddy(USA) —Manderina (Mind Games)
7781^{3}

Firenza Bond *G R Oldroyd* 79
3 b g Captain Rio—Bond Stasia (IRE) (Mukaddamah (USA))
1484^{8} 2570^{6} 4000^{6} 4074^{6} 5044^{7}

Fireside *P W Chapple-Hyam* 92
3 b c Dr Fong(USA) —Al Hasnaa (Zafonic (USA))
1808^{15}

Firespin (USA) *M Botti* a58 31
3 ch f Luhuk(USA) —Happy Numbers (USA) (Polish Numbers (USA))
706^{3} 923^{3} 1162^{4} 1475^{8} 2074^{2} 2757^{6}

Firestorm (IRE) *C W Fairhurst* 54
4 b g Celtic Swing—National Ballet (Shareef Dancer (USA))
2735^{6} 3083^{5} 3279^{11} 3589^{14} 4501^{8} 4924^{8}

Firestreak *R Hannon* 105
3 b g Green Desert(USA) —Flash Of Gold (Darshaan)
2189^{2} 3744^{2} ◆ (4522)

Fire Up The Band *A Berry* a92 87
9 b g Prince Sabo—Green Supreme (Primo Dominie)
(1022) (1190) 1393^{5} 1588^{3} 1917^{9} 2906^{12} 3212^{2} 3784^{2} 4114^{3} 4950^{2} 5044^{5} 5719^{5} 5886^{7} 6184^{7} 7129^{3} 7176^{9} 7218^{9}

Firewalker *P T Dalton* a59 66
3 b f Bertolini(USA) —Crystal Canyon (Efisio)
199^{5} 397^{5} 2159^{12} 6633^{8} 6791^{15} 7528^{10} 7618^{13} 7778^{5}

First Avenue *M A Jarvis* 96
3 b c Montjeu(IRE) —Marciala (IRE) (Machiavellian (USA))
2256^{3} 2825^{3} 3633^{2} 4021^{2} 5199^{3} (6536) 7244^{6}

First Blade *S R Bowring* a42
2 ch c Needwood Blade—Antonias Melody (Rambo Dancer (CAN))
6837^{9} 7282^{8} 7646^{5}

First Buddy *G A Swinbank* a72 103
4 ch g Rock Of Gibraltar(IRE) —Dance Treat (USA) (Nureyev (USA))
962^{2} (1613) (1771) ◆ 2465^{9} 3278^{5}

First Choice (IRE) *K A Ryan* a69 67
2 b f Choisir(AUS) —Ardent Lady (Alhaarth (IRE))
2865^{5} 3085^{5} 3598^{6} (4557) 5204^{5} 5834^{2} 6507a^{4}

First City *D M Simcock* 85
2 b f Diktat—City Maiden (USA) (Carson City (USA))
(3792) 4781^{3}

First Coming *B J McMath* 53
4 ch g Best Of The Bests(IRE) —Arriving (Most Welcome)
1741^{4}

First Defence (USA) *Robert Frankel* a118 104
4 b h Unbridled's Song(USA) —Honest Lady (USA) (Seattle Slew (USA))
6999a^{8}

First Friend (IRE) *M Hill* a71 62
7 b g Mark Of Esteem(IRE) —Bustira (Busted)
588^{8}

First Frost *M J Gingell* a39 13
4 ch m Atraf—Bless (Beveled (USA))
193^{9} 277^{7}

First Hand *M W Easterby* a18
2 b f Act One—Strong Hand (First Trump)
7443^{7}

First In Command (IRE) *Daniel Mark Loughnane* a22 90
3 b g Captain Rio—Queen Sigi (IRE) (Fairy King (USA))
3608^{2} 4494a^{10} 5490^{2} 6845a^{11}

First In Show *A M Balding* a49 42
3 b f Zamindar(USA) —Rose Show (Belmez (USA))
6206^{5} 6571^{7} 7310^{10} 7691^{8} 7818^{7}

First Look (FR) *P Monteith* 77
8 b g Acatenango(GER) —First Class (GER) (Bustino)
1824^{5} 6410^{2} 6861^{5} 7128^{3}

First Order *Miss A Stokell* a92 91
7 b g Primo Dominie—Unconditional Love (IRE) (Polish Patriot (USA))
411^{4} 983^{3} 1195^{6} 1969^{4} 2211^{8} 2398^{4} 2843^{7} 3594^{4} 4218^{3} (4418) 5542^{12} 6449^{5} 6651^{13} 7066^{8} 7201^{4} 7384^{8} 7534^{3} 7562^{2} (7641) 7671^{5} 7716^{7}

First Passage (USA) *B J Meehan* 39
2 bb f Giant's Causeway(USA) —Win's Fair Lady (USA) (Dehere (USA))
5240^{15}

First Queen *L M Cumani* a68 60
2 b f Rock Of Gibraltar(IRE) —Orange Blossom (IRE) (Sadler's Wells (USA))
3456^{9} 4109^{10} 5788^{5} ◆ 6376^{3} 6954^{4}

First Service (IRE) *R Charlton* 62
2 ch c Intikhab(USA) —Princess Sceptre (Cadeaux Genereux)
6944^{9}

First Spirit *J S Moore* a48
2 ch f First Trump—Flaming Spirt (Blushing Flame (USA))
7708^{12}

First Stream (GER) *Mario Hofer* 114
4 ch h Lomitas—First Class (GER) (Bustino)
1662a^{6} 2653a^{5} 4041a^{8} 5137a^{4}

First Swallow *R A Fahey* 64
3 ch g Bahamian Bounty—Promise Fulfilled (USA) (Bet Twice (USA))
2786^{10} 3144^{4} 3712^{5} 4453^{8} (5261) 6218^{10} 6724^{10}

First Time (GER) *Karin Suter* 103
5 br m Silvano(GER) —First Wings (IRE) (In The Wings)
423a^{7} (605a)

First To Call *P J Makin* a88 83
4 ch g First Trump—Scarlett Holly (Red Sunset)
1131^{3} 1473^{13}

First Tracks (IRE) *J W Hills* a49 48
3 b g Oasis Dream—Housekeeper (IRE) (Common Grounds)
1763^{8} 2198^{15} 2620^{13} 4431^{9} 5157^{4} 5748^{12} 6470^{8} 6912^{5}

First Trim (IRE) *B J Meehan* a78 81
3 b g Acclamation—Spanker (Suave Dancer (USA))
1995^{10} 3000^{3} (3224) 4127^{6} 4591^{7} 5056^{8} 6449^{4}

First Valentini *N Bycroft* 51
4 b m Bertolini(USA) —Oscietra (Robellino (USA))
1452^{15} 1754^{7} 2036^{9} 2463^{5} 4651^{6} 4961^{6}

Firth Of Fifth (IRE) *Tom Dascombe* a70 103
2 b c Traditionally(USA) —Wish List (IRE) (Mujadil (USA))
1214^{2} 1413^{3} 1714^{2} 3049^{3} (3267) (3920) 4517^{7} 6267^{8}

Fisadara *B W Hills* 56
2 b f Nayef(USA) —Success Story (Sharrood (USA))
7141^{11}

Fish Called Johnny *A Berry* a55 76
4 b g Kyllachy—Clare Celeste (Coquelin (USA))
138^{7} 255^{8} 6486^{19} 7197^{5} 7375^{8} 7745^{12}

Fisher Hill (USA) *K A Ryan* a65 38
2 ch c Cozzene(USA) —Song Of The Sea (USA) (Hennessy (USA))
3372^{5} 3939^{6} 5143^{4} 6376^{9}

Fishforcompliments *R A Fahey* a92 103
4 b h Royal Applause—Flyfisher (USA) (Riverman (USA))
1218^{2} 1828^{8} 1982^{7} 2595^{9} 3046^{4} 3974^{14} 4587^{8} 4845^{8} 5368^{3} 6103^{8} 6476^{27}

Fistral *P D Niven* a43 53
4 b g Piccolo—Fayre Holly (IRE) (Fayruz)
189^{6} 3131^{2} ◆ (3602) 4238^{5}

Fitolini *Mrs G S Rees* a69 60
3 ch f Bertolini(USA) —Miss Fit (IRE) (Hamas (IRE))
2506^{RR} 2660^{16}

Fits Of Giggles (IRE) *J G Given* a65 69
3 b f Cape Cross(IRE) —Itsibitsi (IRE) (Brief Truce (USA))
3057^{10}

Fit The Cove (IRE) *H Rogers* a88 87
8 b g Balla Cove—Fit The Halo (Dance In Time (CAN))
1103a^{11} 1497a^{11} 4576a^{14} 5731a^{11}

Fitz *M Salaman* a44
2 b c Mind Games—Timoko (Dancing Spree (USA))
6932^{11} 7279^{4} 7600^{7}

Fitz Flyer (IRE) *D H Brown* 88
2 b c Acclamation—Starry Night (Sheikh Albadou)
3663^{2} 4237^{2} ◆ 5244^{5} 5794^{4} 6894^{3}

Fitzolini *A D Brown* 70
2 b g Bertolini(USA) —Coney Hills (Beverley Boy)
1727^{3} 2035^{11} 2845^{5} 3078^{6} 3714^{4} 4681^{2} (5043) 5381^{4} 5883^{4} 6549^{11}

Fitzroy Crossing (USA) *M Johnston* a70 89
3 gr g Cozzene(USA) —Jaded Lady (USA) (Afleet (CAN))
1811^{7} 2825^{11} 3261^{7} 4017^{6} 4489^{6} 5472^{2} ◆ 5910^{8} 6599^{9}

Fitzwarren *A D Brown* a39 41
7 b g Presidium—Coney Hills (Beverley Boy)
4246^{12} 4700^{10} 5634^{13} 6356^{8} 6952^{9} 7152^{6} 7731^{8}

Fiulin *M Botti* a94 111
3 ch c Galileo(IRE) —Fafinta (IRE) (Indian Ridge)
961^{2} (1330) ◆ 2201^{2} 3157^{9} 5573^{7} (6061) 6427^{2} 6820^{3}

Fiume *G Prodromou* 73
3 ch c Medicean—River Abouali (Bluebird (USA))
1526^{8} 2043^{11} ◆ 2603^{3} 4427^{9} 5042^{13}

Fiumicino (NZ) *John Hawkes* 107
5 b g Zabeel(NZ) —Latte (NZ) (Maroof (USA))
6835a^{17}

Fiuntas (IRE) *Shaun Harley* a47 55
5 b g Lil's Boy(USA) —Scarpetta (USA) (Seattle Dancer (USA))
7759^{6}

Fivefootnumberone (IRE) *J J Quinn* 84
2 b g Acclamation—Longueville Legend (IRE) (Cajun Cadet)
1924^{3} (2331) ◆ 2826^{7} 3663^{5} 3978^{2} 4874^{7} 5969^{2} 6656^{3}

Fiveonthreeforjd *W J H Ratcliffe*
3 br g Compton Admiral—Patrician Fox (IRE) (Nicolotte)
6114^{12}

Five Star Junior (USA) *Mrs L Stubbs* a71 49
2 b g Five Star Day(USA) —Sir Harriett (USA) (Sir Harry Lewis (USA))
4321^{3} 4778^{10} 6434^{4} 6732^{2} 6879^{4} 7700^{3}

Five Two *Gavin Patrick Cromwell* a72 76
5 ch g Mark Of Esteem(IRE) —Queen's Gallery (USA) (Forty Niner (USA))
4514a^{13} (6662) 7230^{3} 7364^{5}

Five Wishes *M Dods* 67
4 b m Bahamian Bounty—Due West (Inchinor)
1188^{5} 1752^{5} 2009^{2} 2285^{6} 2658^{4} 3662^{2} 3963^{4} (4629) (4969) 5454^{3} 6862^{5} 7202^{11}

Fizzlephut (IRE) *Miss J R Tooth* a74 74
6 b g Indian Rocket—Cladantom (IRE) (High Estate)
113^{4} 286^{6} 359^{7} 620^{8} 746^{7} 786^{4} 875^{8} 7231^{8} (7295) 7517^{8} 7774^{7}

Fizzy Friend *J R Weymes* 27
2 ch f Reel Buddy(USA) —Champenoise (Forzando)
1907^{7} 4213^{10} 4734^{13} 6788^{13} (Dead)

Fizzy Lover *T D Easterby* 11
3 b f Kyllachy—In Love Again (IRE) (Prince Rupert (FR))
1019^{14} 1971^{9}

Flagstone (USA) *Ian Williams* a46 57
4 ch g Distant View(USA) —Navarene (USA) (Known Fact (USA))
1307^{3} 1482^{11} 7368^{8}

Flam *A M Hales* a68 75
3 b f Singspiel(IRE) —Delauncy (Machiavellian (USA))
2862^{3} 3729^{2} 4170^{5} 4532^{4} 5428^{5} 6060^{6} 6226^{4} 6775^{3} 7071^{9} 7807^{4}

Flamboyant Red (IRE) *Miss Gay Kelleway* 31
2 ch g Redback—Flamboyant (Danzero (AUS))
4636^{10} 5066^{10} 5316^{8} 5530^{10}

Flame Creek (IRE) *E J Creighton* a81 79
12 b g Shardari—Sheila's Pet (IRE) (Welsh Term)
118^{4} (272) 405^{7} 638^{3} 793^{5} 963^{5} 1136^{5} (1472) 1798^{5} 2135^{11} 2621^{9} 5934^{10} 6740^{10} 7265^{6} 7285^{2} 7455^{6} 7520^{6} 7617^{8}

Flamed Amazement *L Lungo* 65
4 b g Hernando(FR) —Alligram (USA) (Alysheba (USA))
982^{4} 1221^{5} 1773^{5} 5540^{4} 5967^{10}

Flamenco Prince *Patrick O Brady* a61 69
4 b g Royal Applause—Iberian Dancer (CAN) (El Gran Senor (USA))
4655a^{10}

Flame Of Hestia (IRE) *J R Fanshawe* 56
2 ch f Giant's Causeway(USA) —Ellen (IRE) (Machiavellian (USA))
7140^{12}

Flame Of Ireland (IRE) *M J Grassick* 81
2 b f Fasliyev(USA) —Grenouillere (USA) (Alysheba (USA))
7107^{10}

Flamestone *A E Price* a45 52
4 b g Piccolo—Renee (Wolfhound (USA))
2456^{7} 3733^{2} 4378^{5} 4653^{17} 4891^{8}

Flaming Cat (IRE) *F Watson* 49
5 bb g Orpen(USA) —Brave Cat (IRE) (Catrail (USA))
1025^{14}

Flamingo Fantasy (GER) *W Hickst* 69
3 ch c Fantastic Light(USA) —Flamingo Road (GER) (Acatenango (GER))
6517a^{6}

Flamingo Land (GER) *A P Stringer*
4 ch g Monsun(GER) —Flamingo Road (GER) (Acatenango (GER))
657^{9}

Flamingo Rainbow (GER) *H Rogers* a75 69
6 ch g Rainbow Quest(USA) —Flamingo Road (GER) (Acatenango (GER))
4511a^{14}

Flaming Ruby *N Tinkler* 43
2 b f Hunting Lion(IRE) —Floral Spark (Forzando)
1749^{9} 5633^{8} 6010^{10} 6764^{12}

Flaming Slew (USA) *Niall M O'Callaghan* a90
3 b f Slew City Slew(USA) —Flaming Faith (USA) (Marquetry (USA))
4235a^{3}

Flamsteed (IRE) *M Johnston* a65
2 b c Clodovil(IRE) —Nautical Gem (IRE) (Alhaarth (IRE))
7640^{5}

Flannel (IRE) *J R Fanshawe* a58
2 gr g Clodovil(IRE) —La Captive (IRE) (Selkirk (USA))
7023^{10}

Flapper (IRE) *J W Hills* a58 49
2 b f Selkirk(USA) —Pure Spin (USA) (Machiavellian (USA))
6978^{13} 7332^{7}

Flashgun (USA) *M G Quinlan* a49 60
2 b c Lemon Drop Kid(USA) —Tolltally Light (USA) (Majestic Light (USA))
4780^{9} 5314^{5} 5842^{10} 6376^{8} 7190^{12}

Flash Harry *M G Quinlan* a44 52
4 ch g Fantastic Light(USA) —Woodyousmileforme (USA) (Woodman (USA))
129^{5} 322^{9}

Flashing Colour (GER) *J Hirschberger* 104
4 b m Pivotal—Flashing Green (Green Desert (USA))
2347a^{2} 3623a^{2} 4233a^{6} 5334a^{9}

Flashmans Papers *J R Best* a100 104
2 b c Exceed And Excel(AUS) —Franglais (GER) (Lion Cavern (USA))
1523^{3} 1851^{3} (3105) 3152^{4} 4507^{6} 5245^{13} 5693^{5} 6503a^{8}

Flash McGahon (IRE) *John M Oxx* a97 100
4 b g Namid—Astuti (IRE) (Waajib)
1198a^{3} 3532a^{9} 4004a^{7} 4223a^{4}

Flash Of Colour *Mrs A J Perrett* a81 74
3 b g Averti(IRE) —Big Pink (IRE) (Bigstone (IRE))
58^{4} 1059^{2} ◆ (1205) 1543^{7} 1962^{5} 3586^{4} 4303^{3}

Flash Of Fire (USA) *P R Chamings* a45 57
3 b g Fantastic Light(USA) —Mistle Thrush (USA) (Storm Bird (CAN))
1731^{6} 2475^{5} 2984^{4} 3393^{13} 3873^{6} 4990^{2} 5320^{4} 6728^{8} 7599^{7}

Flashy Beau (IRE) *A J Martin* 80
8 ch g Fumo Di Londra(IRE) —Flash Donna (USA) (Well Decorated (USA))
4493a^{17}

Flashy Max *Jedd O'Keeffe* a50 55
3 b g Primo Valentino(IRE) —Be Practical (Tragic Role (USA))
1912^{4} 2247^{4} 3738^{5} (4049) (4115) 6492^{7} 6955^{10}

Flashy Photon *H Candy* 79
3 b g Compton Place—Showboat (USA) (Theatrical)
1426^{13} 2460^{4}

Flavour *A W Carroll* 31
2 b f Lujain(USA) —Forum (Lion Cavern (USA))
6193^{6} 6360^{10} 7015^{15}

Flawed Genius *Sir Michael Stoute* a20 102
3 b g Fasliyev(USA) —Talented (Bustino)
1806^{2} 2403^{4} ◆ 3155^{6} 3919^{11} 4522^{4} 5425^{7}

Flawless Diamond (IRE) *J S Moore* a57 59
2 ch f Indian Haven—Mystery Hill (USA) (Danehill (USA))
1838^{7} 2146^{8} 3207^{9} 4340^{10} (4823) 5294a^{10} 5581^{7} 6223^{5} 6343^{6} 6572^{6} 7065^{6} 7832^{4}

Flaxton (UAE) *M Brittain* a19 46
3 b c Halling(USA) —Yasmeen Valley (USA) (Danzig Connection (USA))
2008^{6} 2208^{12} 4542^{8} 7619^{11}

Fleeting Shadow (IRE) *A Al Raihe* a91 107
4 b h Danehill(USA) —Rain Flower (IRE) (Indian Ridge)
205a^{7} 382a^{10} 473a^{12} 673a^{9} 816a^{10}

Fleeting Spirit (IRE) *J Noseda* 123
3 b f Invincible Spirit(IRE) —Millennium Tale (FR) (Distant Relative)
(2404) 3101^{3} 6518a^{5} 6994a^{4}

Fleeting Star (USA) *J Noseda* a80 60
2 rg f Exchange Rate(USA) —Disperse A Star (USA) (Dispersal (USA))
2627^{8} (5430)

Fleetway (IRE) *F Watson* 8
3 ch f Fleetwood(IRE) —Eponine (Sharpo)
3227^{9} 6111^{8}

Fleetwood Flame *W M Brisbourne* 17
3 ch f Fleetwood(IRE) —Barden Lady (Presidium)
5445^{5}

Flemish Art (IRE) *R A Harris* a60
3 b c Marju(IRE) —Danalia (IRE) (Danehill (USA))
354^{6} 543^{5} 780^{4} 1063^{5} 1603^{8} 2099^{12}

Fleur De'Lion (IRE) *S Kirk* a46 53
2 ch f Lion Heart(USA) —Viburnum (USA) (El Gran Senor (USA))
3913^{11} 4251^{7} 4905^{9} 5364^{8} 6432^{10} 6933^{10} 7212^{7} 7789^{5}

Fleur De Lis *M L W Bell* 38
2 ch f Nayef(USA) —Melodist (USA) (The Minstrel (CAN))
4157^{14}

Fleur De Montjeu (IRE) *W R Swinburn* a47 56
3 b f Montjeu(IRE) —Dancing Sensation (USA) (Faliraki)
2833^{10} 4721^{8} 5379^{4} 6596^{5}

Fleuret *M D Squance* 87
4 bb m Diktat—Forthwith (Midyan (USA))
1683^{4} 1993^{8} 2339^{5} 2995^{3} 3272^{11} 6200^{9}

Fleurissimo *J L Dunlop* 77
2 ch f Dr Fong(USA) —Agnus (IRE) (In The Wings)
6559^{8} 7141^{3}

Fleuron *D R C Elsworth* a44
2 bb f Diktat—Forthwith (Midyan (USA))
5835^{11}

Fleurs De Censier *D M Simcock* a52 49
3 b f Vettori(IRE) —April Lee (USA) (Lyphard (USA))
1741^{6} 2363^{5} 3035^{5} 4259^{9} 5813^{3} 6447^{4} 6747^{3}

Flex *D J Murphy* a12 47
3 b g Averti(IRE) —Floppie Disk (Magic Ring (IRE))
279^{6}

Flexible Friend (IRE) *B J Llewellyn* 71
4 b h Danehill(USA) —Ripple Of Pride (IRE) (Sadler's Wells (USA))
4366^{13}

Fligane (FR) *Mlle S-V Tarrou* a61 70
3 ch f Bering—Flight Night (Night Shift (USA))
6742a[3]

Flight Dream (FR) *M G Quinlan* a62 64
5 gr g Highest Honor(FR) —Flight Night (Night Shift (USA))
22[5] 107[2] 317[3] 545[5] 811[6] 1280[2] 1534[6] 2001[12] 2374[9]

Flight Of Fashion (IRE) *Dr J D Scargill* a25 52
3 ch f Hawk Wing(USA) —Fashion (Bin Ajwaad (IRE))
4195[5] 5031[4] 5278[11] 7072[11]

Flight Plan *R A Fahey* a85 84
3 ch g Best Of The Bests(IRE) —Cyclone Connie (Dr Devious (IRE))
1297[9] 1623[7] 2141[8] 2480[3] 3108[7] 3406[6] 3733[4] 4684[5] (Dead)

Flight To Quality *M Johnston* 74
3 ch c Where Or When(IRE) —Southern Psychic (USA) (Alwasmi (USA))
1686[8] 3899[6] 4206[9] 4688[5]

Flintlock (IRE) *J H M Gosden* a17 71
2 b g Oasis Dream—Finity (USA) (Diesis)
3219[6] 3682[4] 4658[2] 6002[4] (6341) 6666[9] 6987[10]

Flipacoin *S Dow* a19 28
3 b f Josr Algarhoud(IRE) —Eclectic (Emarati (USA))
3061[14] 3502[7] 3847[9]

Flipando (IRE) *T D Barron* a99 106
7 b g Sri Pekan(USA) —Magic Touch (Fairy King (USA))
1816[11] 2595[4] ◆ 3122[16] 3413[4] 3740[6] 4417[6] 4587[9] 5897[4] 6269[14] 6478[3] 6783[9] 7146[3] 7245[6] 7556[4] (7755)

Flirty (IRE) *Rae Guest* a38
2 b f Lujain(USA) —Fifth Edition (Rock Hopper)
7593[12]

Flodden Field *P W Chapple-Hyam* a49 42
2 ch c Selkirk(USA) —Sister Bluebird (Bluebird (USA))
7200[9] 7336[10]

Flog It *T D Easterby* 23
2 b g Auction House(USA) —Petinata (Petong)
1392[4] 2783[8] 4169[14] 4873[9] (Dead)

Floodlight Fantasy *Dr R D P Newland* a63 60
5 b g Fantastic Light(USA) —Glamadour (IRE) (Sanglamore (USA))
215[6] 468[7] 1350[2] (1562) ◆ 1606[3] 1853[3] 2001[10] 2715[4] 3606[4] 5003[10] 5710[5] 6570[6] 6729[7]

Floodlit *J H M Gosden* a71
2 b f Fantastic Light(USA) —Westerly Air (USA) (Gone West (USA))
(4339)

Floods Of Tears *D Flood* a21 62
2 br f Lucky Story(USA) —Lady Natilda (First Trump)
4593[5] ◆ 7561[9] 7674[9]

Floor Show *E S McMahon* 73
2 ch c Bahamian Bounty—Dancing Spirit (IRE) (Ahonoora)
4530[5] 5461[6] (6212)

Flop (IRE) *M Brittain* 55
3 b f Fraam—Confidential (Generous (IRE))
2956[11] 4607[8]

Florado (GER) *T Potters* 95
5 br h Dashing Blade—Florilla (GER) (Big Shuffle (USA))
2214a[7] 4912a[8]

Floral Pegasus (AUS) *A S Cruz* 120
5 b h Fusaichi Pegasus(USA) —Crown Crest (Mill Reef (USA))
1090a[7]

Flora Trevelyan *W R Swinburn* a82
2 b f Cape Cross(IRE) —Why So Silent (Mill Reef (USA))
7341[2] ◆

Florentia *Sir Mark Prescott* a59 73
2 ch f Medicean—Area Girl (Jareer (USA))
4786[4] 5004[2] 5628[5]

Florentino *C W Thornton* a45 53
4 b m Efisio—Sirene Bleu Marine (USA) (Secreto (USA))
3718[3] 4848[9] 5993[14] 7285[7]

Flores Sea (USA) *T D Barron* a77 79
4 ch g Luhuk(USA) —Perceptive (USA) (Capote (USA))
72[4] (111) 2005[16] 3203[2] 4440[7] 4602[3] 4951[3] 6314[9]

Floristry *Saeed Bin Suroor* 107
3 b f Fasliyev(USA) —Zaeema (Zafonic (USA))
4617[5] 5275[15] 5829[7]

Flower *W J Haggas* a90 73
3 ch f Zamindar(USA) —Time For Tea (IRE) (Imperial Frontier (USA))
2052[4] 2549[3] 2922[2] 3442[3] 3727[2]

Flower Appeal *M W Easterby* 44
3 br f Diktat—Flower O'Cannie (IRE) (Mujadil (USA))
1478[5] 1592[9]

Flowerbud *Ms J S Doyle* a46
3 b f Fantastic Light(USA) —Maidment (Insan (USA))
7713[4]

Flower Song *J Gallagher* a27 58
3 b f Act One—Sweet Pea (Persian Bold)
2603[10] 3841[12]

Flowerwood (IRE) *M G Quinlan* a43
2 ch f Needwood Blade—Fauna (IRE) (Taufan (USA))
6205[10] 7148[7]

Flowing Cape (IRE) *R Hollinshead* 89
3 b g Cape Cross(IRE) —Jet Lock (USA) (Crafty Prospector (USA))
2405[7] ◆ 2624[6]

Fluoree (FR) *D W Thompson* a10 19
4 bb m Xaar—Floridene (FR) (Saumarez)
1222[12] 1372[8] 1894[9] 2536[8] 2929[11]

Flure De Leise (IRE) *Eamon Tyrrell* a83 97
3 br f Viking Ruler(AUS) —Creme De Menthe (FR) (Green Tune (USA))
1965[3] 2975[4] 3705a[9] 7099[10]

Flute Magic *W S Kittow* 73
2 b g Piccolo—Overcome (Belmez (USA))
2098[8] 3267[2] 6198[8]

Fly Butterfly *B J Meehan* a29 50
2 ch f Bahamian Bounty—Aconite (Primo Dominie)
3632[12] 4149[18] 5277[7] 5937[9]

Fly By Magic (IRE) *Patrick Carey* a81 85
4 b m Indian Rocket—Travel Tricks (IRE) (Presidium)
1495a[9] 2685a[10] 4004a[18] 7325a[8]

Fly By Nelly *H Morrison* a57 61
2 b f Compton Place—Dancing Nelly (Shareef Dancer (USA))
6341[11] 6701[4] 7191[8]

Fly Free *M L W Bell* a81 93
4 b m Halling(USA) —Gipsy Moth (Efisio)
1131[6] 1935[5] 2262[10]

Flying Applause *S R Bowring* a70 82
3 b g Royal Applause—Mrs Gray (Red Sunset)
2976[7] 3449[2] 3607[5] 4276[7] (4481) 5472[9] 6416[6] 7317[6]

Flying Bantam (IRE) *R A Fahey* a66 78
7 b g Fayruz—Natural Pearl (Petong)
1708[2] 2085[3] 2389[3] 2925[4] (3203) 3928[8] 4460[9] 4951[4] 5594[7] 6043[10] 6736[7] 7206[7] 7317[10]

Flying Clarets (IRE) *R A Fahey* a92 115
5 b m Titus Livius(FR) —Sheryl Lynn (Miller's Mate)
(1018) 1199a[4] 2130[3] 2890[2] (3403) (3974) 4395[4] 4855[4] 5792[3]

Flying Cloud (USA) *B J Meehan* 46
2 ch f Giant's Causeway(USA) —St Francis Wood (USA) (Irish River (FR))
7141[13]

Flying Flute *H Candy* 60
3 b g Piccolo—Fledge (Botanic (USA))
2187[11] 2620[11] 2918[7] 4979[4] 5218[8] 5786[5] 6178[3] 6560[5]

Flying Free *J Ryan* a40 28
3 b g Bertolini(USA) —Fly Like The Wind (Cyrano De Bergerac)
4638[3] 5160[14] 6707[13] 7504[8] 7536[10] 7710[11]

Flying Goose (IRE) *R A Harris* a86 84
4 ch g Danehill Dancer(IRE) —Top Of The Form (IRE) (Masterclass (USA))
2339[6] 2693[7] 3728[5] 4586[16] 4809[6] 5144[10] 6671[7] 6749[4] 7360[8] 7457[10] 7677[13]

Flying Grey (IRE) *Tim Vaughan* a57 63
4 gr g Desert Prince(IRE) —Grey Goddess (Godswalk (USA))
(4704) 5651[8]

Flying Indian *J Balding* a61 65
3 ch f Hawk Wing(USA) —Poppadam (Salse (USA))
1699[2] ◆ (2099) 2490[11] 2850[8] 3564[11] 7774[12]

Flying Lady (IRE) *M R Channon* 79
2 b f Hawk Wing(USA) —Lady Nessa (USA) (Al Nasr (FR))
2887[4] 3245[5] 3674[7] 4187[6] 5960[6] 6394[5] 6857[5]

Flying River (IRE) *Tom Dascombe* a32
2 b f Bachelor Duke(USA) —Suzuran (Generous (IRE))
7738[7]

Flying Seasons *B R Millman* a45 53
3 b g Elnadim(USA) —Silvereine (FR) (Bering)
265[12] 2099[8] 2771[4] 3330[6] 3605[6] 4301[5] 5268[3] 5684[P] (Dead)

Flying Silks (IRE) *J R Gask* a64
2 b g Barathea(IRE) —Future Flight (Polar Falcon (USA))
6770[6] 7191[6]

Flying Sommelier (USA) *T D Barron* a61 64
3 b g Dixieland Band(USA) —Charming Lauren (USA) (Meadowlake (USA))
616[2] 1139[3] 1556[9] 3202[7] 3790[7] 4207[9] 4538[5]

Flying Spirit (IRE) *G L Moore* a41 76
9 b g Flying Spur(AUS) —All Laughter (Vision (USA))
6594[6]

Flying Squad (UAE) *M F Harris* a83
4 b g Jade Robbery(USA) —Sandova (IRE) (Green Desert (USA))
1701[3] (1905) 7704[7]

Flying Time *M R Channon* a70 70
3 b f Mark Of Esteem(IRE) —Seagreen (IRE) (Green Desert (USA))
1395[3] 1959[3] 2244[9] 3293[2] 3552[10]

Flying Valentino *G A Swinbank* a18 83
4 b m Primo Valentino(IRE) —Flying Romance (IRE) (Flying Spur (AUS))
1826[6] 2400[10] 2781[4] (3082) (3552) 4583[5] 5207[15]

Fly In Johnny (IRE) *M R Hoad* a64 68
3 b g Fasliyev(USA) —Goodness Gracious (IRE) (Green Desert (USA))
706[5] 796[6] 924[5] 2277[2] 2480[2] 2721[6] 2753[6] 3359[2] 4053[14] 4569[5] 5166[13] 5684[13] 6541[13] 7088[8]

Flyit (IRE) *M R Channon* a66 71
2 b g King's Best(USA) —Tee Cee (Lion Cavern (USA))
2937[5] 3358[2] 3651[5] 5274[14] 5997[5] 6414[5] 6787[2]

Fly Kiss *C E Brittain* a65 82
3 b f Arkadian Hero(USA) —Kiss Me Kate (Aragon)
2190[4] 2532[8] 2993[4] 3487[3] 4408[5] 4773[3] 5142[3] 5600[4] 6356[13]

Fly Me To The Moon (FR) *C Boutin*
3 ch f Trempolino(USA) —Finagonal (FR) (Octagonal (NZ))
6742a[0]

Fly Society (DEN) *S Jensen* 95
7 b h Flyinfact(FR) —Pollenca (IRE) (Law Society (USA))
2708a[3] 5335a[7]

Fly Time *D Burchell* a43 51
4 b m Fraam—Kissing Time (Lugana Beach)
191[13] 318[9] 856[6] 972[7] 1259[4] 1529[11] 3128[6] 5941[8] 6339[12] 7155[12] 7705[8]

Fly With The Stars (USA) *E J O'Neill* a62 79
3 ch g Fusaichi Pegasus(USA) —Forest Key (USA) (Green Forest (USA))
2488[9] 7446[3]

Focail Eile *E S McMahon* a66
3 b g Noverre(USA) —Glittering Image (IRE) (Sadler's Wells (USA))
1311[6] 7403[7] 7609[2] 7786[8]

Fol Hollow (IRE) *D Nicholls* a72 101
3 b g Monashee Mountain(USA) —Constance Do (Risk Me (FR))
1404[3] 1597[11] 2410[14] 3909[5] 4591[5] 5542[6] 6290[10] 6651[3] 6810[5] 6971[3] 7151[9]

Folio (IRE) *W J Musson* a86 85
8 b g Perugino(USA) —Bayleaf (Efisio)
1072[12] 1273[4] (1585) 1828[11] 2531[5] 3003[12] 3461[7] 3800[2] 4131[9] 4688[8] 5910[7] 6424[6] 6721[8] 7398[2] 7502[3] (7753)

Folk Opera (IRE) *Saeed Bin Suroor* a76 113
4 ch m Singspiel(IRE) —Skiphall (Halling (USA))
(2103) (2402) 3720[4] 4196[2] 4549[2] (5332a) 5952a[8] (6505a) 6968a[9]

Folle Allure (FR) *J-C Rouget* 102
3 b f Poliglote—Irish Arms (FR) (Irish River (FR))
2650a[4] 7348a[3] 7487a[0]

Fol Liam *Ian Williams* 81
2 b g Observatory(USA) —Tide Of Fortune (Soviet Star (USA))
(3670) (4108) 4594[2] 5791[12]

Following Wind *K A Ryan* 38
2 ch f Reel Buddy(USA) —Cyclone Flyer (College Chapel)
4734[11] 5384[8] 6244[12]

Follow On *M A Barnes* a72 58
6 b h Barathea(IRE) —Handora (IRE) (Hernando (FR))
1052[7] 3718[4]

Follow The Band *R Hannon* a54 59
3 b c Prince Sabo—Pea Green (Try My Best (USA))
3916[11] 4278[5] 4772[12] 5790[6] 6571[12] 6746[13]

Follow The Buzz *M Wellings* a18 42
4 b g Enjoy The Buzz—Moody Madam (Man Among Men (IRE))
2667[10] 3604[6] 4429[6] 6912[14]

Follow The Colours (IRE) *J W Hills* a65 66
5 b g Rainbow Quest(USA) —Gardenia (IRE) (Sadler's Wells (USA))
1853[4] 2640[10] 2886[4] 3518[2] 4309[10]

Follow The Flag (IRE) *A J McCabe* a77 75
4 ch g Traditionally(USA) —Iktidar (Green Desert (USA))
(181) 407[3] (576) 755[2] 1058[3] 2615[4] 3208[2] 3563[2] 4875[7] 5635[10] 6178[11] 6634[10] 7090[6] (7367) 7457[2] 7495[2] 7564[2] 7670[7]

Follow The Sun (IRE) *Ronald O'Leary* 62
4 br g Tertullian(USA) —Sun Mate (IRE) (Miller's Mate)
(4902) 5456[7] 6726[4]

Follow Your Spirit *B Palling* a53 53
4 b g Compton Place—Ymlaen (IRE) (Desert Prince (IRE))
1051[5] 1870[5] 2451[8] 2922[8] 5797[4] 7018[12] 7436[7] 7541[6]

Folly Lodge *G Wragg* a91 93
4 ch m Grand Lodge(USA) —Marika (Marju (IRE))
1331[4] 1801[6] 2505[4] 2890[5] 4110[8] 6605[8] 6981[8] ◆

Folsomprisonblues (IRE) *E J O'Neill* 78
2 br c Mull Of Kintyre(USA) —Prosaic Star (IRE) (Common Grounds)
(2362) ◆ 6979[13]

Fonda (USA) *J R Fanshawe* 42
3 rg f Quiet American(USA) —Laiyl (IRE) (Nureyev (USA))
1869[5]

Fondant Fancy *H J L Dunlop* 47
2 b f Falbrav(IRE) —Foodbroker Fancy (IRE) (Halling (USA))
6776[10]

Fondled *J R Fanshawe* 96
4 b m Selkirk(USA) —Embraced (Pursuit Of Love)
(2200) ◆ 2890[7]

Fondness *B G Powell* a56 72
5 ch m Dr Fong(USA) —Island Story (Shirley Heights)
710[4]

Fongoli *B G Powell* a52 57
2 b f Dr Fong(USA) —Darmagi (IRE) (Desert King (IRE))
5534[6] 5782[2] 6358[9] 6924[7] 7117[5] 7505[6]

Fong's Alibi *J S Moore* 69
2 b f Dr Fong(USA) —Alchemy (IRE) (Sadler's Wells (USA))
2618[12] 3267[3] 3674[3] 4589[11] 5294a[8] 6086[7]

Fongs Gazelle *M Johnston* a86 89
4 b m Dr Fong(USA) —Greensand (Green Desert (USA))
1502[10] 2059[3] 2505[3] 2820[5] 4111[6] 4520[9] 4627[8] 5092[9] 6626[4] 6950[12]

Fontcia (FR) *D Sepulchre* a89 103
4 b m Enrique—Fontaine Guerard (FR) (Homme De Loi (IRE))
1888a[7] 5115a[0] 7643a[17]

Fonthill Road (IRE) *R A Fahey* a77 110
8 ch g Royal Abjar(USA) —Hannah Huxtable (IRE) (Master Willie)
5259[6] 6104[12]

Foolish Lad (AUS) *Shane Oxlade* 101
8 ch g Blevic(AUS) —Persian Express (AUS) (Persian Heights)
6922a[16]

Foolish Optimist *Paul Green* a20
3 b f Cadeaux Genereux—Shallow Ground (IRE) (Common Grounds)
6114[13] 7344[12] 7362[10] 7798[7]

Fools Gold *G D Blake* a82 38
3 b g Ishiguru(USA) —Sally Green (IRE) (Common Grounds)
848[4] 1166[2] (2705) 2922[12] 3838[7] 4696[8] 6356[2] 7048[8]

Fool's Wildcat (USA) *B J Meehan* a90 94
3 b g Forest Wildcat(USA) —Nine Flags (USA) (Forty Niner (USA))
1333[4] 4160[7] 4509[14] 5279[10] 5682[9] 6035[13] 6528[6]

Forbidden (IRE) *Daniel Mark Loughnane* a66 49
5 ch g Singspiel(IRE) —Fragrant Oasis (USA) (Rahy (USA))
234[2] 448[3]

Forced Opinion (USA) *K A Morgan* a59
3 gr c Distant View(USA) —Kinetic Force (USA) (Holy Bull (USA))
7757[10] 7822[5]

Forced Upon Us *P J McBride* a70 58
4 ch g Allied Forces(USA) —Zing (Zilzal (USA))
1209[2] 1687[7] 1954[7] (2806) 3316[2] 3615[5] 4284[8] 5610[8] 7206[13] 7363[10]

Force Group (IRE) *M H Tompkins* a59 84
4 b g Invincible Spirit(IRE) —Spicebird (IRE) (Ela-Mana-Mou)
(1521) (1732) 6079[7] 6607[4] 6862[4] 6898[2]

Force Tradition (IRE) *M H Tompkins* a57 47
3 ch g Traditionally(USA) —Kind Of Loving (Diesis)
1367[7] 1994[6] 2291[7] 6748[7] 6934[12]

Foreign Edition (IRE) *Miss J A Camacho* a58 61
6 b g Anabaa(USA) —Palacegate Episode (IRE) (Drumalis)
1207[14] 2365[6] 3113[11] (Dead)

Foreign King (USA) *J W Mullins* a64 66
4 b g Kingmambo(USA) —Foreign Aid (USA) (Danzig (USA))
406[8] 546[5] 3137[4] (3344) 3448[6] 4087[5] 7400[5] 7587[6]

Foreign Music (FR) *H J Groschel* 101
4 b m Tiger Hill(IRE) —Foreign Affair (GER) (Goofalik (USA))
2879a[5] 3751a[2] 5625a[7] 6691a[6]

Foreign Rhythm (IRE) *N Tinkler* 76
3 ch f Distant Music(USA) —Happy Talk (IRE) (Hamas (IRE))
1795[9] 2268[5] 2661[12] 3283[6] 3712[2] (3955) 4216[8] 4397[6] 4782[8] 5307[4] 5501[4] 6159[8] 7018[11]

For Eileen *D Burchell* a50 33
4 b m Dinar(USA) —Dreams Of Zena (Dreams End)
303[10] 401[12]

Forel *J Ryan*
2 b f Forzando—Polar Peak (Polar Falcon (USA))
7734[11]

Foreland Sands (IRE) *Mrs L Williamson* a58 40
4 b g Desert Sun—Penrose (IRE) (Wolfhound (USA))
2259[10] 2550[12]

Foresight *Mrs A J Perrett* a52 74
3 ch c Observatory(USA) —Avoidance (USA) (Cryptoclearance (USA))
1741[5] 4057[3] 5216[9]

Forest Dane *Mrs N Smith* a88 88
8 b g Danetime(IRE) —Forest Maid (Thatching)
1211[8] 1500[8] 1928[9] 2371[8] 6125[6] 6402[4] ◆ 6734[7] 7435[3] ◆ 7762[2] ◆

Forest Storm *J S Bolger* 96
2 ch f Galileo(IRE) —Quiet Storm (IRE) (Desert Prince (IRE))
5924a[2] 7029a[6]

Forever Changes *L Montague Hall* a58
3 gr f Bertolini(USA) —Days Of Grace (Wolfhound (USA))
1178[5] 1672[2] 2074[7] 5186[12] 7416[8] 7521[7]

Forever's Girl *G R Oldroyd* a53 48
2 b f Monsieur Bond(IRE) —Forever Bond (Danetime (IRE))
3815[3] 4557[4] 4897[4] 5715[9] 6953[3] 7319[2] 7454[7] 7687[2] 7794[5]

Forever Together (USA) *Jonathan Sheppard* a110 119
4 rg m Belong To Me(USA) —Constant Companion (USA) (Relaunch (USA))
(6968a)

Forfeiter (USA) *C Gordon* a57 42
6 ch g Petionville(USA) —Picabo (USA) (Wild Again (USA))
1280[8] 1673[8]

Forget It *R Hannon* a71 65
3 b c Galileo(IRE) —Queens Way (FR) (Zafonic (USA))
1467[11] 1684[8] 2327[5] 4829[10] 6403[5] 6740[2] 6897[2] 7216[10]

Forgotten Dreams (IRE) *H J L Dunlop* 47
2 b f Olden Times—Jawaher (IRE) (Dancing Brave (USA))
6473[14] 6788[7]

For Joy *J-M Beguigne* 96
3 ch f Singspiel(IRE) —Fine And Mellow (FR) (Lando (GER))
5597a[5]

For Life (IRE) *J E Long* a79 78
6 b g Bachir(IRE) —Zest (USA) (Zilzal (USA))
1537[5] 6435[4]

Formation (USA) *E A L Dunlop* a89 91
3 ch g Van Nistelrooy(USA) —Miss Valedictorian (USA) (With Approval (CAN))
966[2] 1074[4] 2302[2] (2889) 3896[5] 4694[5] 5209[3] 5695[3] 6431[5] 6625[6] 6704[3]

Formax (FR) *M P Tregoning* 96
6 gr g Marathon(USA) —Fortuna (FR) (Kaldoun (FR))
1469[14] 1799[2] 2308[5] (2599) 3209[3] 4508[5] 4844[3] 5229[6]

Former Senator (IRE) *B R Johnson* 82
8 b g Sadler's Wells(USA) —Elegance In Design (Habitat)
7704[9]

Formidable Guest *J Pearce* a62 25
4 b m Dilshaan—Fizzy Treat (Efisio)
10[3] 143[3] (1673) 2513[11] 3036[8] 3588[3] 4635[5] 5087[9] (5802) 6019[3] 6882[10] 7071[3] 7261[4] 7656[3] 7732[6] (7800)

Formula (USA) *R Hannon* a83 62
2 bb c Stormin Fever(USA) —Misty Gallop (USA) (Victory Gallop (CAN))
7104[5] 7438[2] ◆ 7554[2]

For Pro (GER) *G Martin* 65
3 ch c Protektor(GER) —Forlea (GER) (Lead On Time (USA))
549a[4]

Forrest Flyer (IRE) *Miss L A Perratt* 63
4 b g Daylami(IRE) —Gerante (USA) (Private Account (USA))
1773[4] 2157[4] 2849[3] (3198) 3399[2] 3756[3] 4238[8] 4848[12] 5543[3] 5971[2]

Forrest Star *Miss L A Perratt* a42 61
3 ch f Fraam—Starfleet (Inchinor)
1222[8] 1951[4] 3213[2] 3786[3] 4632[2] 6308[4] 7288[8]

Forster Island *M Blanshard* a45 57
2 b g Bertolini(USA) —Lihou Island (Beveled (USA))
1693[8] 2011[7] 3267[7] 3888[5] 4340[7] 4933[5] 5314[14]

Forsyte Saga *M Johnston* a80 78
3 br f Machiavellian(USA) —First Of Many (Darshaan)
527[7] 785[2] 920[4] (1140) (1678) 2151[13]

Fort Amhurst (IRE) *M W Easterby* a68 79
4 ch g Halling(USA) —Soft Breeze (Zafonic (USA))
2103[10] 2582[16] 3006[10] 3261[10] 5478[4] 6056[8] 6134[13] 6452[3] 6827[8]

Fort Churchill (IRE) *B Ellison* a71 94
7 b g Barathea(IRE) —Brisighella (IRE) (Al Hareb (USA))
2465[13] 2830[12] 3493[11] 3947[10] 4627[10] 4739[5] (5583) 5900[12] 6243[6]

Forte Dei Marmi *L M Cumani* a64 70
2 b c Selkirk(USA) —Frangy (Sadler's Wells (USA))
4826[9] 5404[7] 6029[4]

Forthefirstime *John M Oxx* a56 98
3 ch f Dr Fong(USA) —Gazebo (Cadeaux Genereux)
2738a[6] 3619a[11] 4467a[10]

Forthe Millionkiss (GER) *Uwe Ostmann* 115
4 bb h Dashing Blade—Forever Nice (GER) (Greinton)
4233a[2] (4916a) 5740a[8] 6322a[3] 6692a[7]

Forthright *B G Powell* a81 90
7 b g Cadeaux Genereux—Forthwith (Midyan (USA))
6079[9] 6472[4]

Fortuitous (IRE) *I W McInnes* a43 13
4 ch g Tobougg(IRE) —Shallop (Salse (USA))
524[7] 823[6]

Fortunate Bid (IRE) *B W Hills* a55 69
2 ch g Modigliani(USA) —Mystery Bid (Auction Ring (USA))
5431[9] 5784[4] 6701[3]

Fortunate Isle (USA) *R A Fahey* a91 95
6 ch g Swain(IRE) —Isla Del Rey (USA) (Nureyev (USA))
958[12] 6215[15] 6582[13]

Fortune City (UAE) *Saeed Bin Suroor* a76 82
3 ch g Rahy(USA) —Annaba (IRE) (In The Wings)
3894[6] 4302[2] 4821[2] (5612) 5900[7]

Fortune In Faith (USA) *C G Cox* a65 58
2 bb f Grand Slam(USA) —Setting (USA) (Exclusive Native (USA))
4786[6] 5628[3] 5904[6] 6414[14] 6932[9]

Fortunella *Miss Gay Kelleway* a61 48
3 b f Polish Precedent(USA) —Hazy Heights (Shirley Heights)
2156[3] 3133[10] 3555[12] (7322) 7613[2] 7729[3] 7775[3]

Fortune Point (IRE) *A W Carroll* a51 23
10 ch g Cadeaux Genereux—Mountains Of Mist (IRE) (Shirley Heights)
8[2] 147[10] 161[6] 512[7] 691[5]

Fortunes Maid (IRE) *M H Tompkins* a43 39
3 b f Raise A Grand(IRE) —Where's The Money (Lochnager)
135[10] 223[7] 1553[11] 2089[4] 2352[10] 3166[5] 4023[12] 4750[9]

Fortuni (IRE) *Sir Mark Prescott* a73
2 b c Montjeu(IRE) —Desert Ease (IRE) (Green Desert (USA))
7312[5] 7434[2] ◆ (7649)

Forty Hablador (ARG) *A Manuel* a79 63
7 b g Roar(USA) —La Charlatana (ARG) (Kasteel (FR))
204a[12]

Forty Thirty (IRE) *M R Channon* a67 69
2 b g Poliglote—Ciena (FR) (Gold Away (IRE))
5641[4] 6151[2] 6524[11] 6789[5] 7069[5]

Forward Feline (IRE) *B Palling* a70 75
2 b f One Cool Cat(USA) —Ymlaen (IRE) (Desert Prince (IRE))
1866[2] 2253[5] 2473[2] ◆ 3882[5] 5097[2] 5461[3] 5929[3] 6488[2] 6603[5]

Forzando Bloom *R A Harris* a14 30
2 ch c Forzando—Siouxtabul (Makbul)
1555[4] 1778[8] 2049[7] 2450[5] 3091[7] 3309[6] 3726[4]

Forzarzi (IRE) *H A McWilliams* a63 63
4 b h Forzando—Zarzi (IRE) (Suave Dancer (USA))
3129[2] 3454[9] 3713[7] 4172[14] 4632[5] 5538[14] (6091) 6491[7] 7651[9]

Fosool (IRE) *W J Haggas* a67 75
3 b f Pivotal—Lady's Secret (IRE) (Alzao (USA))
1379[2] ◆ 7395[5] (7757)

Fossgate *J D Bethell* a60 79
7 ch g Halling(USA) —Peryllys (Warning)
664[8] 701[4] 963[15] 2957[6] (3666) ◆ 4501[4] (4690) 4966[4] 5967[8] 6721[14] 7078[6]

Foundation Room (IRE) *A M Balding* 86
2 ch f Saffron Walden(FR) —Bellagio Princess (Kris)
(1838) 2541[3] 5827[12] 6240[6]

Foundry Condor (JPN) *S Takahashi* 103
5 b h El Condor Pasa(USA) —Masako Chan (JPN) (Sunday Silence (USA))
6498a[6]

Fountains Abbey (USA) *Sir Michael Stoute* 82
3 ch f Giant's Causeway(USA) —Dream Bay (USA) (Mr Prospector (USA))
2198[7] 2560[3] (3801) 4694[3] 5536[3]

Four Green Fields (IRE) *B W Duke* a31 34
2 b f Captain Rio—Zara Whetei (IRE) (Lomond (USA))
1680[14] 2614[9] 3135[9] 4982[7] 7266[7] 7607[13]

Four Miracles *M H Tompkins* a64 88
4 b m Vettori(IRE) —North Kildare (USA) (Northjet)
1998[2] 2202[9] (3007) 3480[2] (4439) 6272[12] 6817[10]

Fourpenny Lane *Ms Joanna Morgan* a101 101
3 b f Efisio—Makara (Lion Cavern (USA))
4223a[9] 5731a[14] 7325a[3]

Foursquare Flyer (IRE) *T J Pitt* a43 73
6 ch g Tagula(IRE) —Isla (IRE) (Turtle Island (IRE))
617[5] 6708[8] 6838[11] 7340[12]

Four Star General (IRE) *A P O'Brien* 79
2 b c Danehill Dancer(IRE) —Teslemi (USA) (Ogygian (USA))
2134[7]

Four Tel *N J Vaughan* a74 56
4 gr g Vettori(IRE) —Etienne Lady (IRE) (Imperial Frontier (USA))
683[5]

Fourth Dimension (IRE) *Miss T Spearing* a53 76
9 b g Entrepreneur—Isle Of Spice (USA) (Diesis)
1299[4] 2091[3] 2952[5] 3802[3] 4067[3] 5183[3] 5465[5] 7715[10]

Four Winds *M L W Bell* 100
2 b c Red Ransom(USA) —Fairy Godmother (Fairy King (USA))
5246[3] (6026) ◆ 6648[3]

Foxhaven *P R Chamings* 111
6 ch h Unfuwain(USA) —Dancing Mirage (IRE) (Machiavellian (USA))
4585[8] ◆ 5288[5] (5885)

Foxtrot Alpha (IRE) *P Winkworth* 72
2 b f Desert Prince(IRE) —Imelda (USA) (Manila (USA))
(2835) ◆ 3192[12] 4925[3]

Foxtrot Bravo (IRE) *P Winkworth* a31
2 b g Noverre(USA) —Standcorrected (Shareef Dancer (USA))
7709[10]

Foxtrot Charlie *P Winkworth* a34 69
2 b g Lucky Story(USA) —Holy Smoke (Statoblest)
4728[10] 5314[9] 6026[8] 6886[4]

Foxxy *J R Norton* a51 51
4 b m Foxhound(USA) —Fisher Island (IRE) (Sri Pekan (USA))
1892[5] 2467[9] 2849[12] 3863[12] 6185[8]

Foxy Diplomat *R Dickin* a54 33
4 b g Foxhound(USA) —Diplomatist (Dominion)
3604[9] 4707[13]

Foxy Jane *M Brittain* a43 53
3 b f Lujain(USA) —Foxy Alpha (IRE) (Foxhound (USA))
486[5] 1139[11] 2268[3] 3638[5] 4686[5] 7618[3] 7698[10]

Foxy Music *E J Alston* a45 85
4 b g Foxhound(USA) —Primum Tempus (Primo Dominie)
2906[4] 3370[4] 3948[4] 4962[8] 5493[12] 6651[2] 6859[4]

Fraaedd (USA) *M A Jarvis*
3 b g Empire Maker(USA) —Agama (USA) (Nureyev (USA))
1621[15]

Fraamington *M R Channon* a39 46
3 b g Fraam—Patandon Girl (IRE) (Night Shift (USA))
2803[7] 3030[15] 3118[4] 3359[10] 3605[10] 4324[14]

Fragrancy (IRE) *M A Jarvis* a85 106
4 ch m Singspiel(IRE) —Zibet (Kris)
1981[3] 2465[2] 3120[8] 4189[2] 4644[4] (6233) 6781[2] 7099[9]

Fraizer (IRE) *Adrian McGuinness* a46 48
4 b g City On A Hill(USA) —She's Our Lady (IRE) (Scenic)
642[8] 684[4] 7582[4] 7692[9]

Frame And Cover *Miss J S Davis* a40 49
2 b f Carnival Dancer—Fly In Style (Hernando (FR))
3309[9] 3726[3] 4120[2] 4534[4] 4764[4] 5473[6] 7257[7] 7443[10]

Franali (IRE) *R F Fisher* 42
2 b f Kheleyf(USA) —Christeningpresent (IRE) (Cadeaux Genereux)
3597[8] 4213[9] 4847[7] 7425[11]

Francesca D'Gorgio (USA) *J Noseda* 98
3 b f Proud Citizen(USA) —Betty's Solutions (USA) (Eltish (USA))
1830[15] 6005[3] 6271[3] 6484[13]

Francescas Boy (IRE) *P D Niven* a39 46
5 b g Titus Livius(FR) —Mica Male (ITY) (Law Society (USA))
322[11]

Francesco (FR) *Mrs L B Normile* 90
4 gr g Kaldounevees(FR) —Mount Gable (Head For Heights)
6652[7] 7128[9]

Francesco *J R Weymes* a56 55
4 ch g Vettori(IRE) —Violet (IRE) (Mukaddamah (USA))
787[7]

Franchesca's Gold *B R Millman* a53 49
2 b f Monsieur Bond(IRE) —Anita Marie (IRE) (Anita's Prince)
3027[8] 3959[10] 4411[5] 5475[3] 6009[5] 6489[6]

Francis *Niels Petersen* 79
10 b g Emperor Jones(USA) —Bint Damascus (USA) (Damascus (USA))
5957a[11]

Francis Walsingham (IRE) *J R Fanshawe* 63
2 b c Invincible Spirit(IRE) —Web Of Intrigue (Machiavellian (USA))
6944[8]

Frank Crow *J S Goldie* 79
5 b g Josr Algarhoud(IRE) —Belle De Nuit (IRE) (Statoblest)
979[6] 1308[7] 2749[11] 3214[3]

Frankly Fantastic *Jean-Rene Auvray* 6
4 gr g Fantastic Light(USA) —Fracassina (Rusticaro (FR))
5117[7] 6226[13]

Franksalot (IRE) *I W McInnes* a61 76
8 ch g Desert Story(IRE) —Rosie's Guest (IRE) (Be My Guest (USA))
916[4] 1209[3] ◆ 1641[4] 2285[8] 2936[8] 3034[10] 3593[9] 5575[7] 5604[2] 6255[10] 6693[10] 7022[5] 7469[10] 7503[6] 7765[7] 7817[3]

Frank Sonata *M G Quinlan* a81 102
7 b g Opening Verse(USA) —Megdale (IRE) (Waajib)
1158[4] 1717[6] 2503[6] 3505[11]

Frank's Quest (IRE) *A B Haynes* a51 60
8 b g Mujadil(USA) —Questuary (IRE) (Rainbow Quest (USA))
99[8] (147) 249[6] 711[9]

Frank Street *Eve Johnson Houghton* 78
2 ch g Fraam—Pudding Lane (IRE) (College Chapel)
4482[3] 4974[2] ◆ 5530[5]

Franky'N'Jonny *G J Smith* a47 47
5 b m Groom Dancer(USA) —Bron Hilda (IRE) (Namaqualand (USA))
804[8] 821[10]

Fr Dominic (USA) *R M Beckett* a66 86
3 bb g Arch(USA) —Collodia (USA) (Leo Castelli (USA))
2544[6] 4060[7] 6346[13]

Freddie Bolt *F Watson*
2 b c Diktat—Birjand (Green Desert (USA))
6383[12]

Frederick Ozanam (IRE) *B J Meehan* 63
4 b g Traditionally(USA) —Sudden Hope (FR) (Darshaan)
2604[5] 3040[12]

Fredo (IRE) *Ian Williams* 20
4 ch g Lomitas—Felina (GER) (Acatenango (GER))
6403[11]

Free Agent *R Hannon* 98
2 b c Dr Fong(USA) —Film Script (Unfuwain (USA))
(2663) (3245) ◆

Freedom Fire (IRE) *J M P Eustace* 36
2 b g Alhaarth(IRE) —Feel Free (IRE) (Generous (IRE))
6600[9]

Freedom Flying *Joss Saville* 31
5 b m Kalanisi(IRE) —Free Spirit (IRE) (Caerleon (USA))
1382[11]

Freedom Rings (USA) *David Donk* a82 100
2 ch f Proud Citizen(USA) —Dana's Wedding (USA) (Compliance (USA))
6966a[9]

Freedom Song *R Charlton* a69 69
3 b f Singspiel(IRE) —Girl Of My Dreams (IRE) (Marju (IRE))
4253[7] ◆ 6741[14] 7364[9]

Free Falling *L M Cumani* a59 53
2 ch f Selkirk(USA) —Free Flying (Groom Dancer (USA))
4870[13] 5240[11] 7397[7]

Freeing *J A R Toller* a51
2 b f Dansili—Sweeping (Indian King (USA))
7769[7]

Freeloader (IRE) *R A Fahey* a88 84
8 b g Revoque(IRE) —Indian Sand (Indian King (USA))
309[5] 592[7] 1067[4] 6108[4]

Freemusic (IRE) *L Riccardi* 111
4 b h Celtic Swing—Favignana (GER) (Grand Lodge (USA))
2230a[3] 3053a[5] 7263a[7]

Free Offer *J L Dunlop* 92
4 b m Generous(IRE) —Proserpine (Robellino (USA))
1828[9] 3046[5] 3433[4] 4520[6] 5536[5] 6446[3]

Freepressionist *R A Teal* a72 30
2 ch f Compton Place—Sophielu (Rudimentary (USA))
6555[7] 6876[2] 7095[12] 7273[2] (7452)

Free Thinker *P W D'Arcy* a79 71
2 ch c Generous(IRE) —Polish Sprite (Danzig Connection (USA))
5068[5] 5678[2] 6423[3] 7229[2] 7422[9]

Free To Choose (IRE) *A P Jarvis* a7 32
2 br g Statue Of Liberty(USA) —For Freedom (IRE) (King Of Kings (IRE))
1399[12] 2783[7] 3693[5] 5021[11] 5614[8]

Free Tussy (ARG) *G L Moore* a79 48
4 b h Freelancer(USA) —Perlada (ARG) (Cipayo (ARG))
292a[8] 567a[11] 3398[10] 4443[6] 5681[10] 5908[14] 6336[12] 7359[13]

Fregate Island (IRE) *A G Newcombe* a88 90
5 gr g Daylami(IRE) —Briery (IRE) (Salse (USA))
97[7] 331[2] 450[2] (622) 1877[2] 2577[4] 3209[2] 4200[3] 5423[2] (6361)

Fremen (USA) *D Nicholls* a73 104
8 ch g Rahy(USA) —Northern Trick (USA) (Northern Dancer (CAN))
205a[10] 384a[4] 495a[9] 960[8] 1105a[23] 1497a[5] 2218[7] 3972[13] 5503[7] 5968[2] 6103[4] 6312[3] 6771[2]

French Art *D R C Elsworth* 88
3 ch c Peintre Celebre(USA) —Orange Sunset (IRE) (Roanoke (USA))
1467[2] 1926[11] 2509[3] 3628[2] 4929[2] (5150)

French Beret (CAN) *Mark Frostad* 107
5 b g Broad Brush(USA) —Misty Mission (USA) (Miswaki (USA))
2472a[3] 6504a[7]

French Forest *M Brittain* a17 48
2 ch f Shinko Forest(IRE) —Paris Mist (Paris House)
1627[11] 2004[8] 2216[3] 2671[7] 3008[12] 7530[7]

French Riviera *Sir Michael Stoute* a70 82
3 b g Montjeu(IRE) —Arietta's Way (IRE) (Darshaan)
1526[3] 3530[5] 5117[2] 5630[8] 6542[8]

Fresca (IRE) *P J Prendergast* 53
2 br f Monashee Mountain(USA) —Gouache (IRE) (Key Of Luck (USA))
3509a[6]

Fresh Mint (IRE) *M J Wallace* a81 53
4 b m Sadler's Wells(USA) —Valley Of Song (Caerleon (USA))
(47) (132) 428[3]

Freudian Slip *S Curran* a66 65
3 b f Ishiguru(USA) —Perle D'Azur (Mind Games)
523[9]

Fricoteiro (ARG) *Niels Petersen* 84
5 ch h Lode(USA) —Fricote (USA) (Ogygian (USA))
5958a[3]

Friendly King *George Baker* a61
4 b g King's Best(USA) —Asfurah (USA) (Dayjur (USA))
2291[5]

Friends Hope *P A Blockley* a80 83
7 ch m Docksider(USA) —Stygian (USA) (Irish River (FR))
47[6] (978) 1305[3] 1697[3] 2097[2] 2423[2] 2453[3] (3311) 3403[4] 4152[8] 5118[6]

Frill A Minute *Miss L C Siddall* 30
4 b m Lake Coniston(IRE) —Superfrills (Superpower)
2399[9] 3260[13] 4454[5] 5636[15] 6836[10] 7178[10]

Frimley's Matterry *R E Barr* 51
8 b g Bluegrass Prince(IRE) —Lonely Street (Frimley Park)
1752[8] 2040[13]

Frisbee *C J Teague* a64 78
4 b m Efisio—Flying Carpet (Barathea (IRE))
598[2] 3818[2] (4207)

Frivolous (IRE) *J H M Gosden* a82 88
3 b f Green Desert(USA) —Sweet Folly (IRE) (Singspiel (IRE))
(1050) 1332[5] 3420[5]

Frognal (IRE) *B J Meehan* a81 91
2 b g Kheleyf(USA) —Shannon Dore (IRE) (Turtle Island (IRE))
4126[4] 4510[3] 5244[3] (5609) 6483[6] 7109[6]

Frogs' Gift (IRE) *G M Moore* 49
6 gr m Danehill Dancer(IRE) —Warthill Whispers (Grey Desire)
1579[12]

Froissee *S A Callaghan* a81 88
4 b m Polish Precedent(USA) —Crinkle (IRE) (Distant Relative)
1630[5] 1910[3] (2163) 2389[4] 4841[3] 5405[9]

Fromsong (IRE) *D K Ivory* a94 83
10 b g Fayruz—Lindas Delight (Batshoof)
187[2] (301) (503) 676[2] 925[4] 1956[5] 2504[8] 2760[7] 7756[5]

Fromthebeginning *D R C Elsworth* a71
2 b c Lomitas—Zacchera (Zamindar (USA))
7602[6] 7754[4]

Frontline Girl (IRE) *K R Burke* 70
2 b f Fath(USA) —Ellistown Lady (IRE) (Red Sunset)
3976[2] 4593[7] 6037[2]

Frontline In Focus (IRE) *K J Burke* a63 86
4 ch m Daggers Drawn(USA) —Christan (IRE) (Al Hareb (USA))
1676[4]

Front Rank (IRE) *Mrs Dianne Sayer* a72 61
8 b g Sadler's Wells(USA) —Alignment (IRE) (Alzao (USA))
(3399) 5559[5] 6727[7]

Frosted *J H M Gosden* 60
2 ch f Dr Fong(USA) —Arctic Air (Polar Falcon (USA))
7140[7]

Frosty Secret (USA) *M F De Kock* a105
4 bb h Put It Back(USA) —Secret From Above (USA) (Great Above (USA))
204a[3] 473a[2] (670a) 814a[9]

Frosty's Gift *J C Fox* a46 38
4 ch m Bold Edge—Coughlan's Gift (Alnasr Alwasheek)
2341[14] 2917[10] 3177[9] 6206[3] 6913[12] 7535[8]

Frozen Fire (GER) *A P O'Brien* 123
3 b c Montjeu(IRE) —Flamingo Sea (USA) (Woodman (USA))
2131[2] ◆ 2829[11] (3535a) 5892[7]

Fruitful Job (IRE) *A G Newcombe* a14 51
2 ch g Indian Haven—Poscimur (IRE) (Prince Rupert (FR))
5488[6] 6574[12] 7079[4] 7519[10]

Frumious (USA) *Jeff Bonde* a100
2 b c Grindstone(USA) —Eternal Legend (USA) (Gold Legend (USA))
7751a[9]

Fuaigh Mor (IRE) *A Bailey* a26 73
2 ch f Dubai Destination(USA) —Marl (Lycius (USA))
(1384) 1813[4] 2204[6] 3625[7] 4101[6] 7531[11]

Fuel Cell (IRE) *I W McInnes* a59 38
7 b g Desert Style(IRE) —Tappen Zee (Sandhurst Prince)
193[8] 4966[8]

Fuente Apache (IRE) *R Feligioni* 80
3 b f Hawk Wing(USA) —Szabo (IRE) (Anabaa (USA))
2439a[8]

Fuisse (FR) *Mme C Head-Maarek* 105
2 br c Green Tune(USA) —Funny Feerie (FR) (Sillery (USA))
6642a[2] 7163a[4]

Fujin Dancer (FR) *R A Fahey* a76 80
3 ch c Storming Home—Badaayer (USA) (Silver Hawk (USA))
848[3] (1193) 2109[4] 2464[7] 3579[2] 3911[4]

Fujisan *Yvonne Durant* a57 90
4 b g Fuji Kiseki(JPN) —Appreciation (IRE) (Caerleon (USA))
5957a[6]

Fulford *M Brittain* a65 62
3 ch g Elmaamul(USA) —Last Impression (Imp Society (USA))
17[6] (65) 154[3] (237) 756[5] 1306[6] 1819[3] 2490[4] 2660[15] 4236[5] 4609[10]

Fulham Broadway (IRE) *E F Vaughan* a75 70
2 ch c Exceed And Excel(AUS) —Lomalou (IRE) (Lightning Dealer)
6327[3] (6953)

Fullandby (IRE) *T J Etherington* a106 111
6 b g Monashee Mountain(USA) —Ivory Turner (Efisio)
1442[3] 1809[3] 2404[8] 3248[17] 4240[2] ◆ 5109[7] 5259[3] 5890[8] 6121[12] (6184) 6468[4] 6653[8]

Fullback (IRE) *J S Moore* a96
2 ch c Redback—Feet Of Flame (USA) (Theatrical)
4304[2] 4861[2] 5143[2] 5711[2] (6135) 6284[2]

Full Blue *S C Williams* 49
2 gb f Falbrav(IRE) —Miss University (USA) (Beau Genius (CAN))
6080[14] 7015[12]

Full House (IRE) *P R Webber* a71 98
9 br g King's Theatre(IRE) —Nirvavita (FR) (Highest Honor (FR))
1916[P] 6272[P]

Full Marks *J Noseda* a67 85
3 b f Dansili—Flying Wanda (Alzao (USA))
2717[4] 4342[5]

Full Of Gold (FR) *Mme C Head-Maarek* 107
3 ch c Gold Away(IRE) —Funny Feerie (FR) (Sillery (USA))
(1239a) 1887a[4] 2654a[20] 5953a[7] 6237a[2] 6816[6]

Full Of Love (IRE) *B W Hills* 57
2 b f Hawk Wing(USA) —Charmingly (USA) (King Of Kings (IRE))
7140[11]

Full Of Nature *K A Ryan* 78
2 ch f Monsieur Bond(IRE) —Secret Circle (Magic Ring (IRE))
(2160) 2826[6] 3412[4] 5244[12] 5791[13]

Full Snow Moon (USA) *J-C Rouget* a77 93
2 b f Vindication(USA) —Netherland (ARG) (Roy (USA))
5300a[4]

Full Speed (GER) *G A Swinbank* 89
3 b g Sholokhov(IRE) —Flagny (FR) (Kaldoun (FR))
1330[3] 1753[2] (2173) 3719[5] 4565[7] 6974[4]

Full Toss *R Hannon* 98
2 b g Nayef(USA) —Spinning Top (Alzao (USA))
3968[2] 4625[2] (5497) 6075[2]

Full Victory (IRE) *R A Farrant* a85 89
6 b g Imperial Ballet(IRE) —Full Traceability (IRE) (Ron's Victory (USA))
1365[4] 1532[2] (1910) ◆ 2083[4] 2619[6] 2762[6] 3367[15] 3887[5] 4276[10] 4723[16] 4927[6] 6250[10] 6544[6]

Fully Funded (USA) *Mme C Head-Maarek* a81 98
3 b c Aptitude(USA) —Fully Invested (USA) (Irish River (FR))
7429a[3]

Fulminant (IRE) *Karin Suter* 101
7 b g Big Shuffle(USA) —Flagny (FR) (Kaldoun (FR))
421a[5] 603a[5]

Ful Of Grace (IRE) *D E Pipe* 56
4 b m Marju(IRE) —Mitawa (IRE) (Alhaarth (IRE))
2641[6]

Fulvio (USA) *P Howling* a49 21
8 b g Sword Dance—One Tuff Gal (USA) (Lac Ouimet (USA))
6061[6]

Funatfuntasia *Ms Joanna Morgan* a87 81
4 b g Dansili—Guntakal (IRE) (Night Shift (USA))
4576a[18] 6510a[3]

Funfair Wane *D Nicholls* a61 74
9 b g Unfuwain(USA) —Ivory Bride (Domynsky)
1190[2] 1893[7] 2248[5] (2576) 2892[13]

Fun In The Sun *A B Haynes* a58 57
4 b g Piccolo—Caught In The Rain (Spectrum (IRE))
621[2] (877) 922[3] 1248[5] 1687[10] 2070[6] 2355[5] 2917[7] 3446[7] 4052[2] 4746[7] 5748[3] 6693[2] 7382[7]

Funky Town (IRE) *Grant Tuer* 45
6 b g Anshan—Dance Rhythm (IRE) (Dancing Dissident (USA))
2395[6] 2776[8] 2914[4] 3602[5]

Funseeker (UAE) *Jamie Poulton* a64 69
3 bb f Halling(USA) —Silversword (FR) (Highest Honor (FR))
419[10] 2327[7] 3393[10] 6060[13] 6436[10]

Fun Thai *A J Chamberlain* a36 46
4 ch m Fraam—Thailand (Lycius (USA))
216[5] 242[13] 530[10]

Furious Belle (IRE) *P W Chapple-Hyam* a71 74
2 ch f Rock Of Gibraltar(IRE) —Belsay (Belmez (USA))
6062[2] 6360[7] 6901[3]

Furmigadelagiusta *K R Burke* a95 105
4 ch h Galileo(IRE) —Sispre (FR) (Master Willie)
1070[2] 2168[4] 3249[5] ◆

Furnace (IRE) *M L W Bell* a91 100
4 b g Green Desert(USA) —Lyrical Dance (USA) (Lear Fan (USA))
4089[3] 5207[6] (5495) (6269) 6783[6]

Fusili (IRE) *N P Littmoden* a92 96
5 ch m Silvano(GER) —Flunder (Nebos (GER))
97[3] 138[5] 315[6] 409[4] 591[2] ◆ 908[8] 1329[6]

Fustaan (IRE) *A G Newcombe* a48 67
4 b m Royal Applause—Alhufoof (USA) (Dayjur (USA))
89[6] 173[6]

Future Deal *C A Horgan* a53 60
7 b m First Trump—Katyushka (IRE) (Soviet Star (USA))
(11) 164[7]

Future Gem *A Dickman* 42
2 b f Bertolini(USA) —Georgianna (IRE) (Petardia)
4045[11] 4536[8] 4923[10] 5541[3] 5715[4] 6009[3]

Futurity *Eve Johnson Houghton* a24 57
3 ch f Lomitas—Forthwith (Midyan (USA))
2994[8] 3801[6] 4941[4]

Fu Wa (USA) *M W Easterby* a53 23
3 ch f Distant View(USA) —Fire And Shade (USA) (Shadeed (USA))
262[8]

Fuzzy Cat *T D Barron* 48
2 b g Nayef(USA) —Curfew (Marju (IRE))
6723[6]

Fyelehk (IRE) *B R Millman* a44 51
2 b g Kheleyf(USA) —Opalescent (IRE) (Polish Precedent (USA))
1168[5] 2709[8] 3735[5] 5277[13]

Fyodor (IRE) *C R Dore* a107 101
7 b g Fasliyev(USA) —Royale Figurine (IRE) (Dominion Royale)
5[7] 337[3] ◆ 411[6] 593[4] 679[9] 836[2] 866[5] 1300[14] 1571[8] 1689[3] 2129[9] (2401) 2626[11] 3336[6] 4445[22] 5509[7] 6290[8] 7365[3] (7394) 7576[6] 7716[6] 7768[3] (7793)

Fyodorovich (USA) *J S Wainwright* 76
3 b c Stravinsky(USA) —Omnia (USA) (Green Dancer (USA))
1623[11] 2674[14]

Gabier *G L Moore* a82 88
5 b g Galileo(IRE) —Contare (Shirley Heights)
1984[7] 6472[2]

Gaborone *J R Gask* 45
2 ch f Imperial Dancer—Canadian Capers (Ballacashtal (CAN))
1480[2] 3726[5]

Gaelic Chief (IRE) *A P O'Brien* 80
2 b c Hawk Wing(USA) —Kloonlara (IRE) (Green Desert (USA))
6317a[14]

Gaelic Dancer (IRE) *J G Given* a68 66
3 b c Fasliyev(USA) —Touch And Love (IRE) (Green Desert (USA))
4730[5] 5076[5] 5278[10] 5888[8]

Gaelic Princess *A G Newcombe* a84 88
8 b m Cois Na Tine(IRE) —Berenice (ITY) (Marouble)
218[4]

Gaelic Rose (IRE) *S Kirk* a45
2 b f King Charlemagne(USA) —Harry's Irish Rose (USA) (Sir Harry Lewis (USA))
7578[8]

Ga Ga *M W Easterby*
2 b f Baryshnikov(AUS) —Spring Dew (FR) (Starborough)
2485[9] 3106[10]

Gagnoa (IRE) *A Fabre* 115
3 b f Sadler's Wells(USA) —Gwynn (IRE) (Darshaan)
(1323a) 2237a[2] 2877a[2] 4006a[3] 5952a[7] 6495a[9]

Gaia Prince (USA) *Mrs A J Perrett* 75
3 bb g Forestry(USA) —Castlebrook (USA) (Montbrook (USA))
1684[2] 2197[4] 2996[9]

Gaily Noble (IRE) *A B Haynes* a78
2 b c One Cool Cat(USA) —Dream Genie (Puissance)
7073[4] 7380[2]

Gainful (USA) *D Smaga* 85
2 b f Gone West(USA) —Fully Invested (USA) (Irish River (FR))
6891a[6]

Gainsborough's Art (IRE) *D R C Elsworth* a63 51
3 ch g Desert Prince(IRE) —Cathy Garcia (IRE) (Be My Guest (USA))
2119[8] 2509[13] 3458[6] 4298[3]

Gainsbury (GER) *P Vovcenko* 99
4 ch g Dashing Blade—Glorissima (GER) (Second Set (IRE))
2214a[5]

Gainshare *Mrs R A Carr* a72 68
3 b g Lend A Hand—Red Shareef (Marju (IRE))
1819[5] 1988[15] 3298[2] 3833[5] 4236[4] 4615[13] 5617[9] 6088[9] (7225) 7671[2] 7829[10]

Gaitskell *Miss J S Davis* a50 72
3 b c Auction House(USA) —Lady-Love (Pursuit Of Love)
4298[13]

Gala Casino Star (IRE) *R A Fahey* a89 91
3 ch g Dr Fong(USA) —Abir (Soviet Star (USA))
1622[11] (2037) (2539) ◆ 2840[10] (3709) (4392) 4876[12] 5907[5] 6249[8] 6482[18]

Galactic Star *Sir Michael Stoute* a105 115
5 ch h Galileo(IRE) —Balisada (Kris)
1829[3] 2653a[8] 4585[2] 5694[6] 6303[4]

Gala Evening *J A B Old* a99 73
6 b g Daylami(IRE) —Balleta (USA) (Lyphard (USA))
(1337) (1547) 7110[6]

Galaktea (IRE) *C Laffon-Parias* a61 93
3 br f Statue Of Liberty(USA) —Granadilla (Zafonic (USA))
6064a[8] 6743a[5]

Gal Aloud (USA) *R Hannon* 82
2 b f War Chant(USA) —Shining Jewel (USA) (Gulch (USA))
2160[4] 2821[2] 3207[3] 3924[6] (5274) 6240[12] 6477[3]

Gala Sunday (USA) *M W Easterby* a52 67
9 b g Lear Fan(USA) —Sunday Bazaar (USA) (Nureyev (USA))
1159[15] 1394[10] 1729[9] 2001[15] 2617[2] 3551[2] 3711[5] 4048[4] 4503[2]

Galaxie Des Sables (FR) *Mme N Rossio* a80 86
4 b m Marchand De Sable(USA) —Kruguy Dancer (FR) (Groom Dancer (USA))
7005a[12]

Galaxy Stars *R A Teal* a72
4 b g Golden Snake(USA) —Moly (Inchinor)
536[7]

Galeota (IRE) *R Hannon* a80 112
6 b g Mujadil(USA) —Refined (IRE) (Statoblest)
1809[23] 2106[10] 2417a[4] 2712[9] (5793) 6121[14] 6285[12] 6645[12] 7243[17]

Galient (IRE) *N J Henderson* a97 90
5 b g Galileo(IRE) —Endorsement (Warning)
3104[12]

Galistic (IRE) *Patrick J Flynn* 103
5 ch m Galileo(IRE) —Mockery (Nashwan (USA))
3070a[6] 4100a[2] 4493a[13] 6689a[9]

Gallagher *B J Meehan* 115
2 ch c Bahamian Bounty—Roo (Rudimentary (USA))
2150[6] (3603) ◆ 4588[2] 5330a[2] 6119[2] 6442[4]

Gallantian (IRE) *A Fleming* a60 29
6 gr g Turtle Island(IRE) —Galletina (IRE) (Persian Heights)
212[3]

Gallantry *P Howling* a96 92
6 b g Green Desert(USA) —Gay Gallanta (USA) (Woodman (USA))
336[2] 594[2] 904[2] 1045[3] 1218[12] 1481[15] 1942[11] 2339[10] 2905[2] (3087) 3646[11] 4060[6] 4405[14] 4602[2] 5207[13] 5908[8] 6170[6] 6710[2] (7101) 7215[8] 7439[10] 7556[3] 7737[4] 7804[3]

Gallant Son (USA) *Frank Lucarelli* a110
2 bb c Malabar Gold(USA) —Explicitly (CAN) (Exploit (USA))
6997a[7]

Gallego *R J Price* a62 73
6 br g Danzero(AUS) —Shafir (IRE) (Shaadi (USA))
2770[7] 3089[6] 3361[3] 3736[9] 4001[6] (4428) 4664[2] 5008[5] 5370[6] (6028) 6395[12] 6671[13]

Gallery Girl (IRE) *T D Easterby* a85 93
5 ch m Namid—September Tide (IRE) (Thatching)
1755[2] 2082[5] 2219[4] 2583[15] 4962[3] 5503[13] 6174[3] 6650[13] 6859[15]

Galley Slave (IRE) *M C Chapman* a62 60
3 b g Spartacus(IRE) —Cimeterre (IRE) (Arazi (USA))
70[6] 112[7] 444[5] 2549[15] 3551[11]

Gallic Charm (IRE) *D R C Elsworth* a81 72
3 b f Key Of Luck(USA) —Kimash (IRE) (Woodman (USA))
(416) (737) ◆ 1208[5] 1730[3] 2190[6]

Gallileo Figaro (USA) *N B King* a79 74
5 b m Galileo(IRE) —Temperence Gift (USA) (Kingmambo (USA))
1017[3] 1080[4] 6606[14] 6861[6]

Gallopin (NZ) *Danny O'Brien* 109
5 ch g Pins(AUS) —Carla Rossi (NZ) (Spectacular Spy (USA))
7188a[P]

Galloway Mac *M A Barnes* 23
8 ch g Environment Friend—Docklands (On Your Mark)
4420[7] 4735[7]

Galpin Junior (USA) *B J Meehan* 103
2 ch c Hennessy(USA) —Reluctant Diva (Sadler's Wells (USA))
4274[3] (4778) 6442[7] 6815[11]

Galucci (IRE) *Miss D Mountain* 72
2 gr g Verglas(IRE) —Aeraiocht (IRE) (Tenby)
6425[15]

Gambling Jack *A W Carroll* a51 61
3 b g First Trump—Star Of Flanders (Puissance)
3180[5] 3916[6] 5610[12] 6357[8] 7414[6] 7725[5] 7817[6]

Game Hunt *J H M Gosden* 62
3 b c Oasis Dream—Moment (Nashwan (USA))
1068[4] 1295[6] 1835[7]

Game Lad *T D Easterby* a61 96
6 b g Mind Games—Catch Me (Rudimentary (USA))
2595[11] 3491[3] 3928[4] 4417[9] 4875[11] (6105) 6783[14] 7041[12]

Game Lady *I A Wood* a67 68
4 b m Mind Games—Highland Gait (Most Welcome)
901[5] 939[5] 1154[6] 1488[4] 2242[9] 2474[7] (3559) 3779[5] 4580[8] (5090) 5374[5] (6063) 6377[4] 6774[4]

Game Park (USA) *J R Fanshawe* a75 78
3 ch g Elusive Quality(USA) —Carefree Cheetah (USA) (Trempolino (USA))
1781[4] 2161[3] 2714[6] 3457[5] 5800[11] 6712[5]

Game Roseanna *W M Brisbourne* a47 59
2 b f Mind Games—Rosy Sunset (IRE) (Red Sunset)
3625[8] 4658[3] 5256[9] 6632[7] 7016[15]

Gamesters Lady *W M Brisbourne* a70 70
5 br m Almushtarak(IRE) —Tycoon Tina (Tina's Pet)
1697[4] 2241[5] 2908[2] 3176[4]

Gamila (USA) *Saeed Bin Suroor* 70
2 bb f Dynaformer(USA) —Leggy Lou (IRE) (Mujadil (USA))
(4562)

Gan Amhras (IRE) *J S Bolger* 101
2 b c Galileo(IRE) —All's Forgotten (USA) (Darshaan)
6317a[2]

Gandolfini (IRE) *H Rogers* a62 69
5 b g Rossini(USA) —Persian Myth (Persian Bold)
6366a[14]

Gang Show (IRE) *W J Musson* a66 60
3 b g Desert Prince(IRE) —Terry Jean (FR) (Hero's Honor (USA))
500[3] 748[3] 6001[4] 6417[14] 6868[13]

Ganymede *Mark Gillard* a62 61
7 gr g Daylami(IRE) —Germane (Distant Relative)
3137[13] 4275[10] (Dead)

Gap Princess (IRE) *R A Fahey* a76 76
4 b m Noverre(USA) —Safe Care (IRE) (Caerleon (USA))
987[8] 1952[6] ◆ (2444) 2747[2] 3026[2] (3599) 4016[5] 6314[2] 6734[3] 6952[4]

Garafena *B G Powell* a69 67
5 b m Golden Snake(USA) —Eclipsing (IRE) (Baillamont (USA))
1273[5] 2012[7] 2682[8] 3311[3] 3631[8] 5087[6] 5611[3] 6019[11] 6395[8]

Garden City (FR) *Y De Nicolay* 101
3 b f Majorien—Green Delight (IRE) (Green Desert (USA))
2034a[7] 4881a[10]

Garden Party *Jane Chapple-Hyam* a80 73
4 b g Green Desert(USA) —Tempting Prospect (Shirley Heights)
(311) 452[3] 752[4] 2373[15] 2615[9] 3181[2] 4081[10] 4946[10] 6336[8]

Gargano (IRE) *M Johnston* 65
3 b c Galileo(IRE) —Tudor Loom (Sallust)
5453[5] 7084[3]

Garibaldi (GER) *N Wilson* a54 61
6 ch g Acatenango(GER) —Guanhumara (Caerleon (USA))
3226[4] 3814[11] 4541[3] 4898[11] 6136[5]

Garland *R Hannon* a53 67
3 ch f Hawk Wing(USA) —Al Persian (IRE) (Persian Bold)
1444[9] 2118[8] 3023[3] 3314[7] 3583[8]

Garlogs *R Hollinshead* a84 67
5 b g Hunting Lion(IRE) —Fading (Pharly (FR))
(142) 304[4] (596) (786) 1378[3] (2292) 7456[4] 7614[4] 7697[8]

Garnica (FR) *D Nicholls* 117
5 gr h Linamix(FR) —Gueridia (IRE) (Night Shift (USA))
2106[16] (2637a) 3982a[8] 4915a[14] 5738a[6]

Garra Molly (IRE) *G A Swinbank* 70
3 b f Nayef(USA) —Aminata (Glenstal (USA))
3479[4] 4116[5] 6055[6] 6529[3] 6790[3] 7042[10]

Garrulous (UAE) *G L Moore* a73 51
5 b g Lomitas—Friendly (USA) (Lear Fan (USA))
450[6] 4978[6] 6740[7] (7064) 7711[4]

Garrya *B P J Baugh* a33 45
4 ch g Mark Of Esteem(IRE) —Sherkova (USA) (State Dinner (USA))
1205[6]

Garstang *Peter Grayson* a77 79
5 ch g Atraf—Approved Quality (IRE) (Persian Heights)
1079[6] 1366[7] 2082[8] 3320[8] 4025[10] 4743[8] 5433[6] 5709[3] 6209[10]

Gasat (IRE) *Sabastiano Deledda*
7 b h Marju(IRE) —Pechenga (Nureyev (USA))
6985[10]

Gaspar Van Wittel (USA) *S A Callaghan* a98 101
3 bb c Danehill Dancer(IRE) —Akuna Bay (USA) (Mr Prospector (USA))
1333[2] 1797[2] 2121[4] 2408[5] 2544[5] 3396[2]

Gassal *J R Boyle* a68 70
2 b f Oasis Dream—Hasten (USA) (Lear Fan (USA))
2140[3] 2691[3] 3292[10] 4079[2] 4340[5] 5909[6] (6133)

Gassin (FR) *J Bertran De Balanda* a82 79
5 b g Anabaa(USA) —Golden Sea (FR) (Saint Cyrien (FR))
7429a[8]

Gassin *G Wragg* a63 55
2 b c Selkirk(USA) —Miss Riviera Golf (Hernando (FR))
6031[5] 6597[6]

Gatecrasher *G F Bridgwater* a57 45
5 gr g Silver Patriarch(IRE) —Girl At The Gate (Formidable (USA))
2053[6]

Gavanello *M C Chapman* a33 18
5 bb g Diktat—Possessive Artiste (Shareef Dancer (USA))
36[5] 169[4] 348[5] 3589[16]

Gavi *W R Swinburn* 59
2 b c Danehill Dancer(IRE) —Lydia Maria (Dancing Brave (USA))
6084[12]

Gayanula (USA) *Miss J A Camacho* a66
3 b f Yonaguska(USA) —Betamillion Bock (USA) (Bet Twice (USA))
172[3] 464[2] 784[5] 7149[4] 7376[13] (7647) 7729[2]

Gayego (USA) *Paulo H Lobo* a118
3 bb c Gilded Time(USA) —Devils Lake (USA) (Lost Code (USA))
1820a[17] 2215a[11]

Gazboolou *David Pinder* a78 80
4 b g Royal Applause—Warning Star (Warning)
1365[7] 2101[10] 2992[4] 3266[4] 4081[3] 4268[4] 4946[3] (5915) (6380) 6738[11]

Gee Ceffyl Bach *John A Harris* a52 62
4 b m Josr Algarhoud(IRE) —Miletrian Cares (IRE) (Hamas (IRE))
375[7] 663[8] 1687[5] 2662[7] (2846) 3229[8] 4172[13] 4746[4] 5161[9] 5318[12] 6178[8] 6888[3] 7053[5]

Gee Dee Nen *Jim Best* a85 98
5 b g Mister Baileys—Special Beat (Bustino)
1984[5] (2609) 3490[5] 3942[8] (4843) 6817[32]

Gee Gina *P T Midgley* 30
2 b f Hunting Lion(IRE) —La Thuile (Statoblest)
3707[5] 4499[10] 4921[10]

Geestring (IRE) *R Hannon* a69 77
3 b f Diktat—Change Of Heart (IRE) (Revoque (IRE))
1412[4] 1930[3] 2196[15] 2564[10] 2956[6] 3507[12]

Geezers Colours *K R Burke* a93 79
3 b g Fraam—Konica (Desert King (IRE))
(136) 905[3] 1213[5] 1333[5] 2104[11] 2794[8]

Gelert (IRE) *Peter Grayson* a46 51
3 b c Acclamation—Game Leader (IRE) (Mukaddamah (USA))
412[9] 734[5] 1255[4] 1560[5] 2661[4] 3395[13] 3953[5] 4450[5] 4686[2] 5452[4] 5770[5] 6159[2] 6405[9] 7528[5] 7644[8]

Gem Bien (USA) *T T Clement* a15 15
10 b g Bien Bien(USA) —Eastern Gem (USA) (Jade Hunter (USA))
5961[10] 7284[7] 7634[10]

Gemini Jive (IRE) *M G Quinlan* a45 63
2 ch f Namid—Pearl Bright (FR) (Kaldoun (FR))
3055[11] 3456[8] 3735[3] 4956[5] 5567[6] 6573[10]

Gems Star *J J Quinn* 47
2 b g Elmaamul(USA) —Slipperose (Persepolis (FR))
2696[8] 3590[10] 4169[13]

Gemswick Park (USA) *Thomas Albertrani* a100
2 ch f Speightstown(USA) —Queen's Park (USA) (Relaunch (USA))
6500a[3]

General Blucher (IRE) *P W Chapple-Hyam* a74
3 br g Marju(IRE) —Restiv Star (FR) (Soviet Star (USA))
(610) 1057[8] (Dead)

General Eliott (IRE) *P F I Cole* a41 113
3 b g Rock Of Gibraltar(IRE) —Marlene-D (Selkirk (USA))
(1598) ◆ 2032a[13] 6440[4] ◆ 6780[7] 7147[2] 7492[13]

General Feeling (IRE) *S T Mason* a63 58
7 b g General Monash(USA) —Kamadara (IRE) (Kahyasi)
(284) 550[6] 724[6] (872) 1032[6] 1729[13] 2003[12] 2274[13] 2597[5] ◆ 3281[8] 3567[4] 4031[6] 4386[9] 4961[12] (7392) 7591[3] 7807[6]

General Flumpa *Miss Tor Sturgis* a59 63
7 b g Vettori(IRE) —Macca Luna (IRE) (Kahyasi)
999[3] 1281[7] 1929[9] 2513[12] 3084[9] 3182[9] 4048[15] 5321[8] 5489[10] 5653[11]

General Knowledge (USA) *G D Blake* a87 87
5 ch g Diesis—Reams Of Verse (USA) (Nureyev (USA))
1314[4] 1590[5] 1954[10] 3780[9]

General Quarters (USA) *Thomas R McCarthy*
2 gr c Sky Mesa(USA) — (USA) (Cure The Blues (USA))
6502a[4]

General Ting (IRE) *Sir Mark Prescott* a78 80
3 b c Daylami(IRE) —Luana (Shaadi (USA))
2948[3] (3962) ◆ 4432[2] *5017[2]*

General Tufto *C Smith* a50 65
3 b g Fantastic Light(USA) —Miss Pinkerton (Danehill (USA))
1128[5] 3327[9] 4247[12] 4698[5] 6032[8] 6185[10] 6562[10] *6752[4]* *7632[8]* *7721[5]* *7799[5]*

General Zhukov *J M P Eustace* 49
2 b g Largesse—Hickleton Lady (IRE) (Kala Shikari)
5158[6]

Generous Boy *T D Easterby* 53
3 b g Fantastic Light(USA) —Supersonic (Shirley Heights)
1516[9] 2273[10]

Generous Gift (FR) *Mme M Bollack-Badel* 50
3 bl f Kabool—Hokhmah (Pennekamp (USA))
6742a[0]

Generous Jem *G G Margarson* a82 91
5 b m Generous(IRE) —Top Jem (Damister (USA))
1812[7] 4196[9] 4426[5] 4699[4] 4771[7] *5376[4]* 6061[9]

Generous Lad (IRE) *A B Haynes* a77 76
5 b g Generous(IRE) —Tudor Loom (Sallust)
97[4] *735[4]* *886[4]* *921[4]* 2071[5] 2921[10] *5576[6]* *6577[4]* *6882[2]* *7189[3]* 7355[7]

Generous Star *J Pearce* a63
5 ch g Generous(IRE) —Elegant Dance (Statoblest)
6226[9] *6596[9]* *6909[4]* *7296[4]* *7455[3]* *7573[2]* *7787[2]*

Generous Thought *P Howling* 105
3 b c Cadeaux Genereux—Rosie's Posy (IRE) (Suave Dancer (USA))
1441[2] ◆ 2104[2] 3119[7] (3880)

Geneva Geyser (GER) *J M P Eustace* a74
2 b c One Cool Cat(USA) —Genevra (IRE) (Danehill (USA))
6702[F] *(7640)*

Genipabu (IRE) *M G Quinlan* 37
2 b f Danetime(IRE) —Missish (Mummy's Pet)
6894[7] 7198[6]

Genki (IRE) *R Charlton* a53 106
4 ch g Shinko Forest(IRE) —Emma's Star (ITY) (Darshaan)
1517[4] 1809[8]

Gentle Guru *R T Phillips* 92
4 b m Ishiguru(USA) —Soft Touch (IRE) (Petorius)
2995[8] 4022[6] 4483[2] 4981[2] (5187) (5233) 5884[8]

Gentle On My Mind (IRE) *A P O'Brien* 97
3 b f Sadler's Wells(USA) —Ezilla (IRE) (Darshaan)
4006a[10] 4833a[14]

Genuine Lauren (USA) *J-C Rouget* a68 77
2 b f Elusive Quality(USA) —Charming Lauren (USA) (Meadowlake (USA))
7549a[5]

Geoffdaw *P D Evans* a79 68
3 b g Vettori(IRE) —Talighta (USA) (Barathea (IRE))
457[6] 1584[8] 4478[8] 4745[4] *(5346)* *(5617)* *5936[7]* *7290[11]* *7507[8]* *7811[6]*

Geojimali *J S Goldie* a82 89
6 ch g Compton Place—Harrken Heights (IRE) (Belmez (USA))
983[5] (1796) 2538[7] 2938[10] 3056[9] (3489) 3998[4] 4687[6] 5542[13] 6069[14] 6105[6] 6651[7] 7129[5] 7239[7]

Geordie Dancer (IRE) *A Berry* a46 46
6 b g Dansili—Awtaar (USA) (Lyphard (USA))
167[7] *285[5]* *(558)* *641[7]* 1827[8] 2145[10] 2751[14] 4849[5] 5562[4] *7369[14]*

Geordie Girl *R C Guest* a34 66
3 b f Tobougg(IRE) —Chiltern Court (USA) (Topsider (USA))
2002[10] 2670[11] 4741[10] 6215[17] (Dead)

Geordieland (FR) *J A Osborne* a96 119
7 gr h Johann Quatz(FR) —Aerdee (FR) (Highest Honor (FR))
(2169) 3154[2] 5094[5]

Georgebernardshaw (IRE) *A P O'Brien* a81 113
3 b c Danehill Dancer(IRE) —Khamseh (Thatching)
(1356a) 2032a[10] 3119[14] 3982a[3] 5130a[2]

George Henson (IRE) *Garry Moss* a60 21
4 bb g Desert Style(IRE) —Alexandria (IRE) (Irish River (FR))
88[6] *(188)* *332[7]* *388[4]* *436[2]* 1136[13] *1310[4]* 1459[12] *2707[13]* *2867[10]* 5003[11]

George Rex (USA) *B J Meehan* 69
2 bb g Johannesburg(USA) —Royal Linkage (USA) (Linkage (USA))
6072[5] 6438[4] *6910[14]*

George The Best (IRE) *Micky Hammond* a28 69
7 b g Imperial Ballet(IRE) —En Retard (IRE) (Petardia)
64[9] *232[8]* *562[7]* *684[8]*

George The Second *Miss Tor Sturgis* a80 70
5 b g Josr Algarhoud(IRE) —Pink Champagne (Cosmonaut)
427[7] *887[7]* *1037[6]* *1191[8]* 2337[13] 2478[11] 5817[8] *6419[2]* *6681[8]* *7090[10]*

Georgie Bee *D Carroll* 46
2 b f Ishiguru(USA) —Light Of Aragon (Aragon)
6010[8] 6229[6]

Georgie The Fourth (IRE) *George Baker* a70 66
3 b f Cadeaux Genereux—Septembers Hawk (IRE) (Machiavellian (USA))
265[3] *1042[4]* 1397[3] 1962[7] 3322[12]

Gerika (FR) *A & G Botti* 93
3 f Galileo(IRE) —Green Tern (ITY) (Miswaki Tern (USA))
3076a[5]

Gertie (IRE) *E J Creighton* a46 44
4 b m Redback—Rosalia (USA) (Red Ransom (USA))
471[7]

Gesseem (IRE) *M Johnston* 42
2 b c Indian Ridge—Castellane (FR) (Danehill (USA))
6151[7] 6552[8]

Gesture *E Russo* 102
6 b g Bahri(USA) —Stark Ballet (USA) (Nureyev (USA))
(2029a) 3938a[7] 7253a[2] 7349a[4]

Getaway (GER) *A Fabre* 125
5 b h Monsun(GER) —Guernica (Unfuwain (USA))
(1829) ◆ 2791[5] 3542a[5] (5557a) 6522a[8] 7008a[8]

Getcarter *R Hannon* 67
2 b c Fasliyev(USA) —Pourquoi Pas (IRE) (Nordico (USA))
6443[3] ◆ 6776[6] 7240[5]

Get Funky (USA) *John W Sadler* a52 117
5 bb h Straight Man(USA) —Miss Popularity (USA) (Storm Bird (CAN))
6994a[9]

Getrah *C Grant* 75
4 ch g Barathea(IRE) —Sahara Shade (USA) (Shadeed (USA))
1449[4] 2007[7] 2220[7] 3450[10] 4701[5] 4899[6] 6152[3] 6217[9]

Get Serious (USA) *Patrick B McBurney* a90 100
4 ch h City Zip(USA) —Java Gal (USA) (Java Gold (USA))
5928a[7]

Get Up Jude (AUS) *Diane Poidevin-Laine* 101
4 bb g Res Judicata—Minsk Square (AUS) (Red Tony (IRE))
6922a[11]

Ghaayer *M P Tregoning* 7
2 b c Nayef(USA) —Valthea (FR) (Antheus (USA))
2150[13]

Ghafeer (USA) *B Ellison* a44 73
4 b g War Chant(USA) —Hasheema (IRE) (Darshaan)
990[18] (1135) 1449[15] 2537[2] 3082[10] 3640[4] 4629[2] *6132[9]*

Ghaidaa (IRE) *M A Jarvis* 105
3 b f Cape Cross(IRE) —Midway Lady (USA) (Alleged (USA))
2123[2] ◆ (2973) 3415[6] 4520[5] 5506[3] 6266[3] ◆ 6718[3]

Ghaill Force *P Butler* a45 15
6 b g Piccolo—Coir 'A' Ghaill (Jalmood (USA))
14[8] *166[8]* *606[12]*

Ghanaati (USA) *B W Hills* a86
2 b f Giant's Causeway(USA) —Sarayir (USA) (Mr Prospector (USA))
6166[3] *(7011)*

Gharir (IRE) *E Charpy* a98 108
6 gr h Machiavellian(USA) —Summer Sonnet (Baillamont (USA))
203a[6] 383a[2] 671a[RR] 743a[RR]

Gheed (IRE) *Saeed Bin Suroor* 53
3 b f Cape Cross(IRE) —Hareer (Anabaa (USA))
4651[5]

Ghimaar *D K Weld* a73 102
3 b g Dubai Destination(USA) —Charlecote (IRE) (Caerleon (USA))
3157[8]

Ghizlaan (USA) *M Johnston* 51
3 b f Seeking The Gold(USA) —Golden Ballet (USA) (Moscow Ballet (USA))
3556[6] 5445[6]

Ghost Dancer *L M Cumani* a71 80
4 ch h Danehill Dancer(IRE) —Reservation (IRE) (Common Grounds)
5492[12] (6177) *6598[8]* *6989[6]*

Ghostmilk (IRE) *P D Deegan* a70 94
4 b m Golan(IRE) —Thermopylae (Tenby)
4467a[7] 6271[11]

Ghufa (IRE) *E A L Dunlop* a65 63
4 b g Sakhee(USA) —Hawriyah (USA) (Dayjur (USA))
2509[8] 3262[4] 3628[6] 4797[3] 5262[4] 6007[5] ◆ *6577[3]*

Giadiniera *C F Wall* 36
3 b f Bahri(USA) —Rose Des Andes (IRE) (Royal Academy (USA))
1869[13] 2307[7] 6345[9] (Dead)

Giant Love (USA) *M Johnston* a52 83
3 ch c Giant's Causeway(USA) —Morning Devotion (USA) (Affirmed (USA))
1424[9] 2539[4] 3263[2] 3366[12] 3855[4] ◆ 4204[7] 4423[4] 4894[5] 5370[5] 5900[13] (6551) 6726[12] *6839[6]*

Giant Moon (USA) *Richard Schosberg* a106
3 b c Giant's Causeway(USA) —Moonlightandbeauty (USA) (Capote (USA))
2215a[8]

Giant Slalom *T G McCourt* a80 88
4 b g Tomba—Fallara (FR) (Tropular)
829a[11] 1105a[22]

Giant Star (USA) *J S Goldie* 54
5 b g Giant's Causeway(USA) —Vogue Star (ARG) (Ringaro (USA))
982[7]

Giant Strides *P D Evans* a59
2 b f Xaar—Brandish (Warning)
7726[8] *7783[4]*

Gibb River (IRE) *P W Chapple-Hyam* 81
2 ch c Mr Greeley(USA) —Laurentine (USA) (Private Account (USA))
6122[8] 6973[13]

Gibraltar Applied (IRE) *F & L Camici* 80
3 ch c Rock Of Gibraltar(IRE) —Warranty Applied (USA) (Monteverdi)
2028a[12]

Gibson Square (USA) *S C Williams*
2 b g Gilded Time(USA) —Beyond The Fence (USA) (Grand Slam (USA))
6062[12] 6383[11]

Giddywell *R Hollinshead* a57 58
4 b m Ishiguru(USA) —Understudy (In The Wings)
2290[5] *2707[4]* 3182[4] 4048[3] 5308[7] 5653[4] 5776[4] 6719[5] 7085[5]

Gifted Flame *Miss A Stokell* a55 59
9 b g Revoque(IRE) —Little Lady Leah (USA) (Shareef Dancer (USA))
15[6] *155[3]* *328[14]* 2782[12] 2861[8]

Gifted Gamble *Peter Grayson* a42 97
6 b g Mind Games—Its Another Gift (Primo Dominie)
6490[12] *7225[12]* *7478[9]* *7672[F]* (Dead)

Gifted Heir (IRE) *A Bailey* a61 61
4 b h Princely Heir(IRE) —Inzar Lady (IRE) (Inzar (USA))
115[6] *(229)* *330[3]* *341[2]* *485[3]* *646[2]* *686[5]* *841[5]* *1032[9]* 7499[10] 7553[7] 7707[11] 7792[7]

Gifted Leader (USA) *Pat Eddery* 71
3 b c Diesis—Zaghruta (USA) (Gone West (USA))
2955[4] ◆ 3810[5] 6584[5]

Gift Horse *D Nicholls* a85 99
8 ch g Cadeaux Genereux—Careful Dancer (Gorytus (USA))
1071[7] 1809[19] 2831[3] 3728[6] 4586[7] 5067[3] ◆ 5247[5] 5556[2] 5831[2] 6069[18] *6490[2]* *6680[4]*

Giganticus (USA) *B W Hills* 109
5 ch g Giant's Causeway(USA) —Shy Princess (USA) (Irish River (FR))
1982[17] 2595[5] ◆ 3197[20] 3921[5] 4405[3] 6269[7] 6783[10]

Gilbertian *R M Beckett* 66
2 br g Sakhee(USA) —Fudge (Polar Falcon (USA))
2769[9] 3358[14] 4815[3] 5785[8]

Gilded Cove *R Hollinshead* a70 73
8 b h Polar Prince(IRE) —Cloudy Reef (Cragador)
235[6] *576[11]* *806[2]* 1015[7] *2263[4]* 4858[6] *5474[3]*

Gilded Youth *G F Bridgwater* a68 73
4 b g Gorse—Nisha (Nishapour (FR))
1174[6] 1450[7] 1900[9] *2703[8]* 5198[7] *5708[11]* 6178[17] 6364[14] 6546[14]

Gilt Edge Girl *C G Cox* 72
2 ch f Monsieur Bond(IRE) —Tahara (IRE) (Caerleon (USA))
6051[2] 6764[3] 7015[3]

Gimme Some Lovin (IRE) *D W P Arbuthnot* a69 64
4 b m Desert Style(IRE) —Licence To Thrill (Wolfhound (USA))
275[2] *426[3]* *576[2]* *775[9]* *899[4]* *1153[7]* *1253[6]*

Gimmy (IRE) *B Grizzetti* 111
4 b g Lomitas—Pursuit Of Life (Pursuit Of Love)
(2027a) 3075a[3] 6325a[4] 7263a[10]

Ginger Minx (IRE) *N J Vaughan* a55
3 ch f Raise A Grand(IRE) —Glenmalure (IRE) (Night Shift (USA))
396[6] *702[3]* *5574[6]* 6015[14] *7541[14]* *7736[10]*

Ginger Pop *G G Margarson* a65 25
4 ch g Mark Of Esteem(IRE) —Norcroft Lady (Mujtahid (USA))
432[6]

Ginger Princess (IRE) *Oliver McKiernan* a74 74
6 b m Pistolet Bleu(IRE) —Palm Lake (IRE) (Spectrum (IRE))
(75) ◆ *347[2]* 1105a[15] 1497a[4]

Ginger Punch (USA) *Robert Frankel* a123
5 ch m Awesome Again(CAN) —Nappelon (CAN) (Bold Revenue (CAN))
6969a[6]

Gingham *L M Cumani* 77
3 gr f Barathea(IRE) —Sianema (Persian Bold)
2123[4] 2956[3] 3573[P]

Ginobili (IRE) *R Hannon* 96
2 b c Fasliyev(USA) —Imperial Graf (USA) (Blushing John (USA))
(4126) 4908[3] 5487[4] 6193[2] 6401[3] 6644[11]

Ginos Destination *M Botti* 46
3 ch f Dubai Destination(USA) —Gino's Spirits (Perugino (USA))
2716[9]

Ginostra *S Wattel* a77 95
3 b f Oasis Dream—Graceful Bering (USA) (Bering)
1712a[7] 6064a[4]

Gioacchino (IRE) *R A Harris* a35 60
3 b g Rossini(USA) —Gareyba (IRE) (Fairy King (USA))
1135[3] 2480[9] 3268[4] 3678[6] 5395[2] 5749[2] 6334[6] *7624[7]*

Giocita (GER) *Andreas Lowe* 84
3 b f Kornado—Giovanella (IRE) (Common Grounds)
2655a[9] 6323a[16]

Giordana (IRE) *P Vovcenko* 76
2 b f Exceed And Excel(AUS) —Faraway Lady (Alzao (USA))
6713a[8]

Giovanni D'Oro (IRE) *Miss M E Rowland* a47 56
4 b g Johannesburg(USA) —Maddie G (USA) (Blush Rambler (USA))
872[10] *1262[14]* *1705[9]* 2055[9]

Gipson Dessert (USA) *J-C Rouget* 104
3 bb f Orientate(USA) —Gypsy Hollow (USA) (Dixieland Band (USA))
1360a[5] 3938a[5] 4590[13]

Girl Of Pangaea (GER) *E A L Dunlop* a68
3 b f Soviet Star(USA) —Genevra (IRE) (Danehill (USA))
5790[2] *6091[9]* *7178[5]*

Girolamo (USA) *Kiaran McLaughlin* a94
2 br c A.P. Indy(USA) —Get Lucky (USA) (Mr Prospector (USA))
6501a[6]

Girouette (IRE) *Tracey Collins* a90 95
3 br f Pivotal—Vassiana (FR) (Anabaa (USA))
7157a[2]

Gist (IRE) *W J Martin* a95 95
5 b m Namid—Ali Dreamer (IRE) (Ali-Royal (IRE))
6315a[4] 6689a[13] *7328a[8]*

Gitano Hernando *M Botti* a87 74
2 ch c Hernando(FR) —Gino's Spirits (Perugino (USA))
6581[6] 6926[2] *(7343)* ◆

Give (IRE) *R A Harris* a43 58
2 b f High Chaparral(IRE) —Generous Gesture (IRE) (Fasliyev (USA))
2916[6] ◆ 3349[9] 3923[6] 4925[4] 6086[6] *7353[9]* *7607[6]*

Give Her A Whirl *G A Swinbank* a20 40
4 b m Pursuit Of Love—Peggy Spencer (Formidable (USA))
1867[11] 2285[11] 2491[10] *2706[8]*

Given A Choice (IRE) *J Pearce* a89 79
6 b g Trans Island—Miss Audimar (USA) (Mr. Leader (USA))
(104) *196[3]* *252[2]* *(449)* *622[2]* *750[2]* *860[4]* *1048[9]* *(1256)* ◆ 1793[7] *2073[2]* 3649[6] 4156[3] 4751[4] 4953[4] 5913[6] 6450[7]

Giverny (IRE) *J Noseda* 40
2 b f Invincible Spirit(IRE) —Masakira (IRE) (Royal Academy (USA))
4482[5] 4692[10]

Give Us A Song (USA) *J S Moore* a66 29
2 bb c Songandaprayer(USA) —Mama G (USA) (Prospector's Bid (USA))
3848[6] 4616[8] *6282[3]* *6756[6]* *(6988)*

Gizmondo *G L Moore* a61 65
5 ch g Lomitas—India Atlanta (Ahonoora)
7620[7] *7800[4]*

Glamis Castle (USA) *C F Swan* a72 73
5 b g Selkirk(USA) —Fairy Godmother (Fairy King (USA))
4511a[3]

Glamoroso (IRE) *A Kirtley* a47 20
3 b g Mull Of Kintyre(USA) —Tuneful (Pivotal)
6725[7] 7042[11] 7174[5] *7749[3]* *7815[5]*

Glamorous Spirit (IRE) *S Curran* a82 82
2 b f Invincible Spirit(IRE) —Glamorous Air (IRE) (Air Express (IRE))
(1983) ◆ 2147[3] 3123[15] 6183[2] 6807[4] *(7464)* *7673[2]*

Glan Lady (IRE) *J L Spearing* a58 61
2 b f Court Cave(IRE) —Vanished (IRE) (Fayruz)
5364[5] 5715[2] *6133[6]* 6787[6] 7052[8] *(7530)* *7728[5]*

Glass Harmonium (IRE) *Sir Michael Stoute* 80
2 gr c Verglas(IRE) —Spring Symphony (IRE) (Darshaan)
5468[7] ◆ (6031)

Glasshoughton *M Dods* 89
5 b g Dansili—Roseum (Lahib (USA))
1393[4] 1908[2] 2760[3] 3370[7] 3812[8] 4218[4] 4831[4] 5067[8] 5455[6] 5861[5] 6069[13] 6532[4] 6724[4] 7129[4]

Gleaming Spirit (IRE) *Peter Grayson* a68 77
4 b g Mujadil(USA) —Gleam (Green Desert (USA))
901[9] *1047[4]* *1541[3]* 1739[5] 3352[10] *3819[4]* (4064) 4327[14] *5046[10]* 6039[7] 6864[13] 7176[2] *7323[10]* *7478[8]* 7672[6]

Glencal *H Morrison* a71 72
4 ch m Compton Place—Raindrop (Primo Dominie)
(1842) 1996[5] 3064[4] 3892[7] (4368) 4770[4] 6178[2] *6738[6]*

Glencalvie (IRE) *J Akehurst* a85 82
7 ch g Grand Lodge(USA) —Top Of The Form (IRE) (Masterclass (USA))
1456[7] 1996[12] *(2722)* *3317[3]* *3840[13]* *5144[2]* *7641[5]* *7837[10]*

Glenconnor Lad (IRE) *David P Myerscough* a65 66
3 ch g Elnadim(USA) —Charlotte's Dancer (Kris)
5873a[10]

Glenisland *Mrs L Williamson* 52
4 br m Diktat—Glider (IRE) (Silver Kite (USA))
3810[9] 5380[6]

Glenlini *J S Goldie* 46
2 b f Bertolini(USA) —Glenhurich (IRE) (Sri Pekan (USA))
1770[6]

Glenluji *J S Goldie* 64
3 b g Lujain(USA) —Glenhurich (IRE) (Sri Pekan (USA))
2576[8]

Glen Molly (IRE) *B W Hills* 77
2 b f Danetime(IRE) —Sonorous (IRE) (Ashkalani (IRE))
4665[2] (5097)

Glenmuir (IRE) *Adrian McGuinness* a46 74
5 b g Josr Algarhoud(IRE) —Beryl (Bering)
4514a[9]

Glen Nevis (USA) *Saeed Bin Suroor* a48 104
4 bb h Gulch(USA) —Beating The Buzz (IRE) (Bluebird (USA))
384a[2] 495a[6] (673a)

Glenridding *J G Given* a76 80
4 b g Averti(IRE) —Appelone (Emperor Jones (USA))
44[2] *(240)* *(361)* *509[2]* 2787[7] 3108[5] 3563[11] 3951[2] (4605) 4813[2] *5156[4]* *6020[6]* *6452[5]* 6989[4]

Glenveagh (IRE) *K A Ryan* a29 60
3 b g Catcher In The Rye(IRE) —Limone (IRE) (Catrail (USA))
3953[3] *4272[7]* (4684) 5457[7] 6004[10]

Glimpse Of Light (IRE) *A M Balding* a65
2 b f Passing Glance—Sankaty Light (USA) (Summer Squall (USA))
6089[5] *6488[3]*

Glistening *Michael Moroney* 92
6 b h Sadler's Wells(USA) —Shining Water (Kalaglow)
6922a[12]

Glitter Baby (IRE) *P F Cashman* 96
5 b m Danehill Dancer(IRE) —Gifts Galore (IRE) (Darshaan)
4833a[11]

Glittering Prize (UAE) *M Johnston* a70 70
3 bb f Cadeaux Genereux—Tanami (Green Desert (USA))
136[9]

Glitz (IRE) *George Baker* a54 55
3 b f Hawk Wing(USA) —Lunar Lustre (IRE) (Desert Prince (IRE))
9978 *1270[8]* 1525[14] 2694[3] 2915[10] 5318[14] 5653[13]

Global *R Hannon* a77
2 ch c Bahamian Bounty—Tuppenny Blue (Pennekamp (USA))
7312[6] *(7476)* *7623[9]*

Global City (IRE) *Saeed Bin Suroor* a93 80
2 b c Exceed And Excel(AUS) —Victory Peak (Shirley Heights)
3707[2] (4279) 4507[9] 6274[6] *(6739)*

Global Glory (IRE) *J A R Toller* 29
3 ch g Spinning World(USA) —Crimson Glory (Lycius (USA))
3180[8] 3445[5] 4194[9] 4796[11]

Global Rose (GER) *Frau K Haustein* 90
3 b f Big Shuffle(USA) —Goonda (Darshaan)
2655a[8]

Global Traffic *D Shaw* a70 68
4 br g Generous(IRE) —Eyes Wide Open (Fraam)
78[3] *198[7]* *(481)* *602[3]* *686[4]* *788[4]* *851[4]* *934[5]*

Globus (GER) *U Ostmann*
2 ch c Areion(GER) —Globuli (GER) (Surako (GER))
(6853a)

Gloria De Campeao (BRZ) *P Bary* a117 102
5 b h Impression(ARG) —Audacity (BRZ) (Clackson (BRZ))
204a[2] 650a[2] 817a[2] 1092a[8] 5115a[3] 6499a[8]

Glorious Dreams (USA) *T J Pitt* a72 17
2 bb f Honour And Glory(USA) —Crissy Aya (USA) (Saros)
(2048) 2497[10] 3105[23]

Glorious Gift (IRE) *P W Chapple-Hyam* 91
3 b c Elnadim(USA) —Queen Of Arabia (USA) (Wild Again (USA))
1125[2] (1380) ◆ 2412[3] 3325[2] 4160[3]

Gloucester *M J Scudamore* a77 77
5 b g Montjeu(IRE) —Birdlip (USA) (Sanglamore (USA))
309[8] 5887[7]

Glowing (IRE) *Charles O'Brien* a77 85
3 b f Dansili—Brightest (Rainbow Quest (USA))
3070a[10] 5547a[7]

Glowing Dawn (IRE) *Miss J S Davis* a30
6 b m Definite Article—Alizee (IRE) (College Chapel)
161[7]

Glowing Praise *E S McMahon* 74
2 ch c Fantastic Light(USA) —Beading (Polish Precedent (USA))
6080[5] ◆ (6534)

Gluteus Maximus (IRE) *A P O'Brien* a95 101
2 br c Statue Of Liberty(USA) —Skidmore Girl (USA) (Vaguely Noble)
5296a[6] 5546a[6] 6317a[7] 6637a[3] 7029a[3]

Go Amwell *J R Jenkins* a59 64
5 b g Kayf Tara—Daarat Alayaam (IRE) (Reference Point)
1518[2] 2567[4] 3296[3] 4105[4] (5934) 6672[11]

Goathemala (GER) *P Schiergen* 108
3 b f Black Sam Bellamy(IRE) —Global World (GER) (Big Shuffle (USA))
3073a[3] 3705a[4] 4657a[6] 5329a[2] (6691a)

Go Between (USA) *William Mott* a123 111
5 ch h Point Given(USA) —Mediation (IRE) (Caerleon (USA))
7001a[5]

Goblin *D E Cantillon* a50
7 b g Atraf—Forest Fantasy (Rambo Dancer (CAN))
7573[12] 7787[7]

Godfrey Street *A G Newcombe* a88 88
5 ch g Compton Place—Tahara (IRE) (Caerleon (USA))
84[4] (278) (482) 593[7] 866[9] 4668[11] 6557[6] (7176) 7529[P]

Go East (GER) *V Valiani* 98
4 ch m Highest Honor(FR) —Golden Time (GER) (Surumu (GER))
2027a[8] 2438a[5]

Go For Gold Mine (FR) *L Larrigade* 93
3 b g Goldneyev(USA) —Rudbeckia (FR) (High Estate)
7598a[6]

Go Free *J G M O'Shea* a56 43
7 gr g Easycall—Miss Traxdata (Absalom)
1267[9]

Go Go Green (IRE) *S Parr* a79 85
2 b c Acclamation—Preponderance (IRE) (Cyrano De Bergerac)
1794[3] 2186[5] 4289[4] (5451) 5791[8] (6525) (6666) 7075[4]

Going For Gold *R Charlton* 55
2 b f Barathea(IRE) —Flash Of Gold (Darshaan)
6604[10] 6977[12]

Going Going Gone *Tom Dascombe* a8 6
2 b g Auction House(USA) —Queen Of Scotland (IRE) (Mujadil (USA))
4926[10] 5277[16] 6694[13]

Going Time (USA) *M Johnston* a57 59
2 b f Forestry(USA) —Grub's Dancer (USA) (Grub (USA))
1948[5] 2746[2] 4157[10] 5006[10] 5432[11] 6017[5]

Gold Again (USA) *W R Swinburn* a60 54
3 b f Touch Gold(USA) —Miss Insync (USA) (Miswaki (USA))
5608[6] 5995[7] 6543[5]

Goldan Jess (IRE) *A W Carroll* a49 36
4 b g Golan(IRE) —Bendis (GER) (Danehill (USA))
1017[6] 1890[9] 3631[7]

Gold Blossom (IRE) *David Wachman* 46
2 ch f Danehill Dancer(IRE) —Lovely Blossom (FR) (Spinning World (USA))
3509a[9]

Gold Cup One (FR) *Mme N Rossio* 46
3 br f Tremendo(IRE) —Titillate (FR) (Caerwent)
6742a[0]

Golddigging (IRE) *J G Portman* a38 24
3 b f Acclamation—On The Make (IRE) (Entrepreneur)
1059[8] 2894[5] 3264[5]

Golden Alchemist *M D I Usher* a66 57
5 ch g Woodborough(USA) —Pure Gold (Dilum (USA))
2617[6] 3347[6]

Golden Arrow (IRE) *E Charpy* a108 104
5 b h Danehill(USA) —Cheal Rose (IRE) (Dr Devious (IRE))
204a[6] 564a[2] 745a[5] 1087a[13]

Golden Bishop *R A Fahey* a73 72
3 ch g Medicean—Hen Harrier (Polar Falcon (USA))
1172[10] 1748[10] 2509[10] 2984[2] ◆ 3555[5] 4281[2] 4796[4] (5320) 6599[3] 7461[3]

Golden Brown (IRE) *David Pinder* a63 64
4 b g Kyllachy—Sand Grouse (USA) (Arctic Tern (USA))
1406[7] 1853[12] 2243[9] 2722[9] 3162[11] 3963[7] 4182[3] 5020[13] 5145[3] 5631[6] 5912[5] 6753[4] 6913[4] 7114[5] 7553[6] 7792[9]

Golden Dagger (IRE) *K A Ryan* 89
4 ch m Daggers Drawn(USA) —Santarene (IRE) (Scenic)
1072[14] 2784[8] 3551[7] 3832[5] 4170[6]

Golden Dane (IRE) *C R Dore* a66 61
3 b g Danetime(IRE) —Golden Charm (IRE) (Common Grounds)
444[4] 612[6] 714[7] 917[2] 993[3] 1141[7] 1315[2] 1635[2] (Dead)

Golden Desert (IRE) *T G Mills* a94 95
4 b g Desert Prince(IRE) —Jules (IRE) (Danehill (USA))
1278[10] 2013[5] 2329[2] 2995[2] 3087[3] 3898[3] (4407) 5405[8] 6269[5] 6478[8]

Golden Destiny (IRE) *P J Makin* a47 78
2 ch f Captain Rio—Dear Catch (IRE) (Bluebird (USA))
3348[8] 3848[5] (4907) 5363[2] 5647[3] 6240[3] 6603[7]

Golden Dixie (USA) *R A Harris* a98 101
9 ch g Dixieland Band(USA) —Beyrouth (USA) (Alleged (USA))
1985[9] 2326[5] 3472[6] 3647[7] 3898[6] 4201[6] 4445[21] 4586[15] 5151[9] 5796[7] 6006[6] 6402[9]

Golden Eagle *Sir Michael Stoute* 26
2 b c Montjeu(IRE) —Grain Of Gold (Mr Prospector (USA))
7054[14]

Golden Era *H-A Pantall* 78
3 b f Machiavellian(USA) —Ahead (Shirley Heights)
7487a[9]

Golden Feather *O Sherwood* 82
6 ch g Dr Fong(USA) —Idolize (Polish Precedent (USA))
3561[8]

Golden Flight (IRE) *J W Hills* a56 61
2 ch g Hawk Wing(USA) —Cassilis (IRE) (Persian Bold)
6197[7] 6620[10]

Golden Games (IRE) *J L Dunlop* 58
2 b f Montjeu(IRE) —Ski For Gold (Shirley Heights)
4643[12] 5535[4] 6565[9]

Golden Giant (USA) *R Chotard* 88
3 gr g Giant's Causeway(USA) —Orellana (USA) (With Approval (CAN))
7551a[0]

Golden Hare (IRE) *Aidan Anthony Howard* a47 56
7 ch g Bahhare(USA) —Ela's Gold (IRE) (Ela-Mana-Mou)
7293[8]

Golden Horus (USA) *P J O'Gorman* a54 52
3 ch g Buddha(USA) —Sunburst (Gone West (USA))
4194[10] 4412[5] 5407[9]

Golden Joker (IRE) *A Renzoni* 87
4 ch h Shinko Forest(IRE) —Westside Girl (USA) (Way West (FR))
2029a[6]

Golden Kiss *Paul Murphy* 9
2 b f Golden Snake(USA) —Kiss Me Again (IRE) (Cyrano De Bergerac)
7220[5]

Golden Liberty (IRE) *A Peraino* 91
3 br f Statue Of Liberty(USA) —Blue Crystal (IRE) (Lure (USA))
2231a[19]

Golden Metalimo (IRE) *F Castro* a88
3 gr c Verglas(IRE) —Terracotta Hut (IRE) (Habitat)
4918a[3]

Golden Penny *H Morrison* a80 78
3 b g Xaar—Dog Rose (SAF) (Fort Wood (USA))
(1130) 1685[5] ◆ 2043[4] 2288[3] 3266[2] 3799[2] (4731) 5350[9] 6841[4]

Golden Pool (IRE) *S A Callaghan* a56 15
2 b f Danetime(IRE) —Miss Megs (IRE) (Croco Rouge (IRE))
6776[15] 7170[9] 7356[6] 7542[4]

Golden Prospect *J W Hills* a79 74
4 b g Lujain(USA) —Petonellajill (Petong)
177[7] (506) 1084[5] 1630[6] 2152[10] 2897[9] 3181[5] 3738[4] 4789[9] 4934[5]

Golden Rosie (IRE) *B W Hills* 77
2 ch f Exceed And Excel(AUS) —Kelsey Rose (Most Welcome)
2479[5] ◆ (2821) 4119[6] 4626[5] 5855[16]

Golden Spectrum (IRE) *R A Harris* a69 60
9 ch g Spectrum(IRE) —Plessaya (USA) (Nureyev (USA))
395[7] 560[7] 703[6] 724[11] 916[5] 1109[7] 1694[11] 1895[12] 2861[10]

Golden Square *A W Carroll* a65 49
6 ch g Tomba—Cherish Me (Polar Falcon (USA))
11[7] (123) 236[7] 389[6] 516[10] 711[8] 898[11] 3360[13]

Golden Stream (IRE) *Sir Michael Stoute* 94
2 b f Sadler's Wells(USA) —Phantom Gold (Machiavellian (USA))
(5241) ◆ 6268[5]

Golden Sword *A P O'Brien* 85
2 b c High Chaparral(IRE) —Sitara (Salse (USA))
5857[5]

Golden Titus (IRE) *A Renzoni* 118
4 ch h Titus Livius(FR) —Oraplata (USA) (Silver Hawk (USA))
1667a[2] 2230a[4] 2656a[7]

Golden Tokyo (IRE) *T Stack* a59 70
3 b g Danetime(IRE) —Oraplata (USA) (Silver Hawk (USA))
4613a[2]

Golden Wave (IRE) *D M Simcock* a68 62
4 b m Green Desert(USA) —Gold Bust (Nashwan (USA))
2078[3]

Gold Express *P J O'Gorman* a78 75
5 b g Observatory(USA) —Vanishing Point (USA) (Caller I.D. (USA))
5467[4] 6131[5] 6388[3] 6650[14] 7393[6] (7466)

Goldhill Fair *W G M Turner* a39 41
3 gr g Bertolini(USA) —May Queen Megan (Petorius)
6032[11] 6374[13]

Goldikova (IRE) *F Head* 125
3 b f Anabaa(USA) —Born Gold (USA) (Blushing Groom (FR))
2033a[2] 2877a[3] (3775a) (4674a) (5740a) (6996a)

Gold Plus (IRE) *M Bebbu*
2 b c Kalanisi(IRE) —Streets Of Gold (USA) (Saratoga Six (USA))
2745a[8]

Gold Prospect *M L W Bell* a89 81
4 bb g Rainbow Quest(USA) —Grain Of Gold (Mr Prospector (USA))
1076[9] (1314) ◆ 1711[4] 2531[7] 2970[5] 3474[4] 3996[5] 4568[11] 5156[5] 5699[10] 6659[3]

Goldrenched (IRE) *M L W Bell* a57 68
3 b f Montjeu(IRE) —Sundrenched (IRE) (Desert King (IRE))
1382[10] 1621[12] 2291[4] (6386) 6897[8]

Goldsmeadow *O Brennan*
9 b g Thowra(FR) —Fanny Adams (Nicholas Bill)
2867[P]

Gold Sovereign (IRE) *Saeed Bin Suroor* a91 105
4 b g King's Best(USA) —Sassenach (IRE) (Night Shift (USA))
(2913) 4845[4] 5896[2] 6307[3] 6984[3] 7146[16]

Goldstar Dancer (IRE) *K M Prendergast* a29 12
6 b g General Monash(USA) —Ravensdale Rose (IRE) (Henbit (USA))
3025[13]

Goldvil (IRE) *B J Meehan* 63
2 b c Clodovil(IRE) —Desert Bride (USA) (Key To The Kingdom (USA))
2999[7] ◆ 4024[3]

Goliaths Boy (IRE) *R A Fahey* 91
2 ch g Medecis—Green Belt (FR) (Tirol)
6229[2] ◆ 6655[3] (6811) 7449a[4]

Golly (IRE) *D L Williams* a20
12 b g Toulon—Tor-Na-Grena (Torus)
3328[9]

Golondrina *T J Fitzgerald* 39
3 b f Superior Premium—Portacasa (Robellino (USA))
3823[11] 6393[9] 6725[6] 7401[12]

Go Lovely Rose (IRE) *Robert Collet* 96
2 b f Pivotal—Side Of Paradise (IRE) (Sadler's Wells (USA))
6519a[6]

Gomarhoom *M Johnston*
2 b f Dansili—Tenuous (Generous (IRE))
7221[7]

Go Nani Go *B Smart* 82
2 b c Kyllachy—Go Between (Daggers Drawn (USA))
(1770) ◆ 2377[4] 2775[3] 5969[4]

Gone Astray (USA) *Claude McGaughey III* a99
2 bb c Dixie Union(USA) —Illicit (USA) (Mr Prospector (USA))
6501a[4]

Gone Fast (USA) *D M Simcock* a68 90
3 ch f Gone West(USA) —Abita (USA) (Dynaformer (USA))
1401[10] 2666[6] 3849[11] 5071[11] 6021[7]

Gone Hunting *W G M Turner* a85 81
2 b g Hunting Lion(IRE) —Arasong (Aragon)
1078[6] (1214) 1447[2] 2154[5] 4323[3] 4822[5] 5153[2] (5866) 6281[2] 6931[2] 7065[3] (7788) 7820[3]

Gone'N'Dunnett (IRE) *Mrs C A Dunnett* a58 58
9 b g Petardia—Skerries Bell (Taufan (USA))
4[5] 370[6] 437[6] 625[5] 1455[10] 1906[5] (2075) 2511[5] 2869[6] 3159[7] 3575[5] 4125[U] 4258[4] 4749[7] 5152[3] 6842[11] 7055[10] 7369[10] 7522[6] 7618[11] 7808[8]

Gone Theatrical (USA) *Austin Smith* 92
3 b f Theatrical—Cumulate (USA) (Gone West (USA))
5744a[6]

Gongidas *Saeed Bin Suroor* a91 97
4 b h Big Shuffle(USA) —Gonfalon (Slip Anchor)
382a[3] 564a[11]

Good Again *G A Butler* a74 79
2 ch f Dubai Destination(USA) —Good Girl (IRE) (College Chapel)
3135[2] ◆ (4359) 6305[3]

Good And Lucky (USA) *Josie Carroll* a88 96
5 bb g Wild Rush(USA) —Shannon's Innocent (USA) (Accused (USA))
2472a[11]

Good Ba Ba (USA) *A Schutz* 125
6 b g Lear Fan(USA) —Elle Meme (USA) (Zilzal (USA))
(7684a)

Good Buy Dubai (USA) *J R Best* a51 53
2 gr g Essence Of Dubai(USA) —Sofisticada (USA) (Northern Jove (CAN))
3315[5] 4480[7] 4776[8]

Goodbye *G A Swinbank* 94
4 ch m Efisio—Blow Me A Kiss (Kris)
1612[2] 1815[2] 2013[6] 3261[4] 3369[5] 5635[12] 6053[3] 6311[5]

Goodbye Cash (IRE) *P D Evans* a78 79
4 b m Danetime(IRE) —Jellybeen (IRE) (Petardia)
64[2] 210[7] 346[4] 539[7] 618[5] 783[3] 839[5] 1204[3] 1485[6] 1561[7] 1842[14] 2866[9]

Goodbye Mr Bond *E J Alston* a62 96
8 b g Elmaamul(USA) —Fifth Emerald (Formidable (USA))
1910[8] 2220[4] (3006) 3261[2] 3855[10] 4661[6] 6249[9] 6654[6]

Good Bye My Friend (FR) *N Clement* 97
2 b c Kendor(FR) —The Wise Lady (FR) (Ganges (USA))
7103a[4] 7430a[8]

Good Cause (IRE) *Mrs S Lamyman* a48 62
7 b g Simply Great(FR) —Smashing Pet (Mummy's Pet)
68[6] 368[5] 461[10] 1184[6] 1296[11] 2667[6]

Good Dance (FR) *Mlle A Poirsin*
3 b f Bad As I Wanna Be(IRE) —Val Dancer (FR) (Fabulous Dancer (USA))
7551a[0]

Good Effect (USA) *C P Morlock* a70 78
4 ch g Woodman(USA) —River Dreams (USA) (Riverman (USA))
2152[9] 2682[3] 2921[9] 3561[4] 4131[8] 4820[7] 5183[2] 6022[7] 6538[4] 6882[7] 7071[2] 7355[3] 7620[4] 7702[8]

Goodenough Magic *Andrew Turnell* 41
2 b f Lend A Hand—Rekindled Flame (IRE) (Kings Lake (USA))
2638[15] 3378[11] 4321[4] 5363[10] 6191[8]

Good For Her *J L Dunlop* a50 70
2 b f Rock Of Gibraltar(IRE) —Tyranny (Machiavellian (USA))
5673[6] 6360[2]

Good Gorsoon (USA) *B W Hills* a82 94
3 b c Stravinsky(USA) —Alwaysinbloom (USA) (Unbridled (USA))
1597[10] ◆ 1925[3] (2258) 3047[4] 3850[13] 4591[6] 5509[11]

Good Humoured *Sir Mark Prescott* a62
2 b g Rock Of Gibraltar(IRE) —Humouresque (Pivotal)
7268[2]

Good Investment *Miss Tracy Waggott* a43 53
6 b g Silver Patriarch(IRE) —Bundled Up (USA) (Sharpen Up)
171[9]

Goodison Glory (IRE) *R A Fahey* a79 79
2 br c Tout Seul(IRE) —Thorbella (Deploy)
6770[4] (7172) ◆ (7391)

Good News Too *D K Ivory* a22
3 ch f Tomba—Think It Over (IRE) (Bijou D'Inde)
1144[10] 1603[9]

Goodnight Dick (IRE) *Paul Murphy* a30 50
8 bb g Luso—Morning Susan (Status Seeker)
7446[8]

Good Operator (USA) *D K Weld* 76
2 bb c Johannesburg(USA) —Najiya (Nashwan (USA))
6317a[17]

Good Queen Best *B De Haan* 46
2 b f Best Of The Bests(IRE) —Spring Sunrise (Robellino (USA))
2835[11] 4534[6] 6392[14]

Goodwood Spirit *J M Bradley* a44 64
6 b g Fraam—Rechanit (IRE) (Local Suitor (USA))
1269[11] 1642[5] 2933[9] 2988[12] 4807[11]

Goodwood Starlight (IRE) *J L Dunlop* a94 97
3 br g Mtoto—Starring (FR) (Ashkalani (IRE))
1424[13] 2302[4] (2996) (3896) 4519[9] 5569[5] 6195[3] 6563[10]

Googoobarabajagal (IRE) *W S Kittow* 56
2 b g Almutawakel—Shamah (Unfuwain (USA))
5022[5] 5753[9] 6893[11]

Go On Ahead (IRE) *M J Coombe* a59 63
8 b g Namaqualand(USA) —Charm The Stars (Roi Danzig (USA))
2832[5] 3637[5] 5117[4] 5676[5] 6329[9] 6882[6] 7265[5] 7520[3] 7806[9]

Goose Bay (GER) *P Schiergen* 104
3 b f Groom Dancer(USA) —Golden Time (GER) (Surumu (GER))
(3076a) 7037a[14]

Goose Green (IRE) *R J Hodges* a67 68
4 b g Invincible Spirit(IRE) —Narbayda (IRE) (Kahyasi)
1645[5] 2128[12] 2642[5] 2992[6] 3383[7] 4306[5] 4414[12] 4707[4] 5871[12] 6693[9] 6912[9] 7114[9]

Gordonsville *J S Goldie* a81 86
5 b g Generous(IRE) —Kimba (USA) (Kris S (USA))
981[7] 1299[8] 2168[7] 2939[2] ◆ 3253[5] 3785[2] 4146[2] 5563[2] 6107[4] 6313[2] 6652[2] 7223[2]

Gordy Bee (USA) *G D Blake* 72
2 b c More Than Ready(USA) —Honoria (USA) (Danzig (USA))
4826[6]

Gore Hill (IRE) *K R Burke* a19
2 ch g Exceed And Excel(AUS) —Eschasse (USA) (Zilzal (USA))
6548[9] 6953[10]

Go Tech *T D Easterby* a89 86
8 b g Gothenberg(IRE) —Bollin Sophie (Efisio)
4688[9]

Got Flash (FR) *E J O'Neill* a46
2 b g Xaar—Wild Flush (USA) (Pine Bluff (USA))
4728[6] 5404[14]

Gouranga *A W Carroll* a42 11
5 b m Robellino(USA) —Hymne D'Amour (USA) (Dixieland Band (USA))
1521[10] 3178 1266[10] 7775[7]

Govenor Eliott (IRE) *M Johnston* a45 69
3 ch g Rock Of Gibraltar(IRE) —Lac Dessert (USA) (Lac Ouimet (USA))
5069[12] 5390[11] 5802[13] 6374[9]

Government (IRE) *M C Chapman* a53 53
7 b g Great Dane(IRE) —Hidden Agenda (FR) (Machiavellian (USA))
42[9] 75[2] (189) 367[4] 550[9] 792[10] 1906[12] 2703[9] 3691[9] 7267[7] 7698[11] 7731[5] 7779[7]

Gower Belle *W R Muir* a69 65
3 b f Fantastic Light(USA) —Polish Belle (Polish Precedent (USA))
1958[9] 3314[8] 3727[7] 4779[3] 5141[9] 6173[3] 6716[6]

Gower Song *D R C Elsworth* a94 111
5 b m Singspiel(IRE) —Gleaming Water (Kalaglow)
381a[6] 565a[2] 672a[4] (816a) 1091a[7] 1468[6] 1829[5]

Gower Valentine *D Nicholls* 80
2 b f Primo Valentino(IRE) —Mania (IRE) (Danehill (USA))
1749[5] 2035[3] 3292[6] (4521) 6240[9]

Gracechurch (IRE) *R J Hodges* a58 67
5 b g Marju(IRE) —Saffron Crocus (Shareef Dancer (USA))
1266[2] 1644[5] 1932[13] 2640[3] 2770[3] 4409[2] (4721) 5168[2] 5427[2] 5783[7]

Graceful Descent (FR) *R A Fahey* a74 72
3 b f Hawk Wing(USA) —Itab (USA) (Dayjur (USA))
3493[6] 3930[4] 5040[5] 6012[4] 6862[13] 7183[4]

Gracie's Games *R J Price* a54 29
2 b f Mind Games—Little Kenny (Warning)
7015[11] 7240[11] 7452[3] 7734[8]

Gracie's Gift (IRE) *A G Newcombe* a52 67
6 b g Imperial Ballet(IRE) —Settle Petal (IRE) (Roi Danzig (USA))
1188[11] 2010[4] ◆ 2706[10] 4813[4] 5458[7] 6913[6]

Gracious Girl (IRE) *Enda Kelly* a75 72
3 b f Invincible Spirit(IRE) —Supportive (IRE) (Nashamaa)
721^{3}

Grafty Green (IRE) *W M Brisbourne* a54 56
5 b g Green Desert(USA) —Banafsajee (USA) (Pleasant Colony (USA))
2001^{16} 2365^{16} 3025^{14} 4123^{9} 4490^{8} 5710^{7}

Grail Knight *Miss Gay Kelleway* a37
3 ch g Carnival Dancer—Nashkova (Nashwan (USA))
310^{6}

Gramm *M W Easterby* a66 24
5 b g Fraam—Beacon Silver (Belmez (USA))
1218^{14} 1301^{6} 1815^{13} 2672^{9} 3329^{10} (7345) 7585^{2} 7653^{11}

Granakey (IRE) *M Wigham* a63
5 b m Key Of Luck(USA) —Grand Morning (IRE) (King Of Clubs)
13^{9} 3162^{13}

Granary *H Candy* a65 85
4 b m Singspiel(IRE) —All Grain (Polish Precedent (USA))
(95) 1520^{2} 2165^{4} 2718^{4} 3293^{4} 4022^{4} 5119^{4} (5779) (6554) 6981^{16}

Granary Girl *J Pearce* a60 59
6 b m Kingsinger(IRE) —Highland Blue (Never So Bold)
77^{3} 161^{4} 373^{4} 606^{3} 822^{3} (934) 1148^{7} 1405^{3} 1692^{12} 2353^{4} 2863^{8} 3113^{6} (3448) 4259^{2} (4599) 5476^{7} 6775^{6}

Grandad Bill (IRE) *J S Goldie* a47 73
5 ch g Intikhab(USA) —Matikanehanafubuki (IRE) (Caerleon (USA))
1406^{6} 2523^{4} 2940^{7} 3204^{2} ◆ 3450^{3} 3755^{7} 4630^{4} (4850) 5420^{4} 6108^{2} (6657) 7128^{5}

Grand Adventure (USA) *Mark Frostad* 101
2 bb c Grand Slam(USA) —Val Marie (USA) (Coronado's Quest (USA))
6998a^{10}

Grand Art (IRE) *J Howard Johnson* a49 81
4 b g Raise A Grand(IRE) —Mulberry River (IRE) (Bluebird (USA))
2249^{3} 2577^{5} 6312^{7}

Grand Assault *G C Bravery* a58 18
5 b g Mujahid(USA) —As Mustard (Keen)
87^{3} 327^{4} 453^{7} 3034^{15} 4084^{12}

Grand Aurora (IRE) *Paul W Flynn* a66 56
4 ch m Grand Lodge(USA) —Oriane (Nashwan (USA))
7078^{2}

Grand Corniche (IRE) *A J Martin* 75
5 b g Machiavellian(USA) —Karri Valley (USA) (Storm Bird (CAN))
4655a^{17}

Grand Court (IRE) *George Baker* a39 53
5 b m Grand Lodge(USA) —Nice One Clare (IRE) (Mukaddamah (USA))
7599^{13} 7766^{9}

Grand Couturier *Robert Ribaudo* 123
5 b h Grand Lodge(USA) —Lady Elgar (IRE) (Sadler's Wells (USA))
3995a^{6} 7000a^{11}

Grand Cru *John Joseph Murphy* a9 60
3 b g Bahri(USA) —Sharp Top (Sharpo)
7078^{10}

Grand Diamond (IRE) *J S Goldie* a68 71
4 b g Grand Lodge(USA) —Winona (IRE) (Alzao (USA))
1822^{11} 2285^{2} 2597^{12} 3211^{4} (3789) 4949^{6} 5965^{3} 6628^{3} 7224^{4}

Grand Ducal (IRE) *A P O'Brien* 97
2 b c Danehill Dancer(IRE) —Mood Swings (IRE) (Shirley Heights)
3920^{4} 5296a^{3}

Grande Annee (USA) *J Noseda* 94
3 b f Gone West(USA) —Bollinger (AUS) (Dehere (USA))
1957^{3} ◆ (2786) (4423) (5290) 6128^{4}

Grande Caiman (IRE) *R Hannon* a107 95
4 ch h Grand Lodge(USA) —Sweet Retreat (Indian Ridge)
757^{3} 908^{2} 1544^{3} 2202^{6} 3505^{8} 3925^{12} 4843^{3} 5054^{9} 6272^{3} 7110^{5} (7595) (7717)

Grand Fleet *M Johnston* a81 81
3 b g Green Desert(USA) —Janaat (Kris)
253^{2} 926^{4}

Grand Hombre (USA) *R Bouresly* a80 92
8 bb g Grand Slam(USA) —Santona (CHI) (Winning (USA))
647a^{5} 818a^{13}

Grand Honour (IRE) *P Howling* a82 76
2 gr c Verglas(IRE) —Rosy Dudley (IRE) (Grand Lodge (USA))
1078^{5} (1341) 1714^{4} 2108^{4} 2826^{8} (4079) 4402^{6} 6426^{20} 6756^{7} 7426^{3} 7538^{2} 7820^{5}

Grand Opera (IRE) *J Howard Johnson* a84 84
5 b g City On A Hill(USA) —Victoria's Secret (IRE) (Law Society (USA))
990^{2} 1138^{6} 2445^{8} 3643^{4} (4453)

Grand Palace (IRE) *D Shaw* a72 39
5 b g Grand Lodge(USA) —Pocket Book (IRE) (Reference Point)
72^{2} 241^{7} (370) 554^{3} 786^{5} 3819^{13} 6658^{8} 6840^{7} 7182^{2} (7292) 7435^{12}

Grand Passion (IRE) *C F Wall* a109 108
8 b g Grand Lodge(USA) —Lovers' Parlour (Beldale Flutter (USA))
678^{10} 906^{5} 1077^{6} 2465^{11} 7145^{9} 7420^{9} 7741^{6}

Grand Plan (USA) *J A Osborne* a57 44
2 b f Grand Slam(USA) —Easabeau Fille (USA) (Capote (USA))
1111^{2} 1214^{4} 3889^{3} 5567^{11}

Grand Show *W R Swinburn* a96 86
6 b g Efisio—Christine Daae (Sadler's Wells (USA))
329^{11}

Grand Stitch (USA) *P A Blockley* 68
2 bb g Grand Slam(USA) —Lil Sister Stich (USA) (Seattle Bound (USA))
2424^{5} 3170^{3}

Grand Strategy (IRE) *M A Jarvis* a87 61
3 bb c Singspiel(IRE) —Game Plan (Darshaan)
(52) (376) 1043^{3} 1424^{12}

Grand Symphony *B I Case* a51 69
4 ch m Zamindar(USA) —Gitane (FR) (Grand Lodge (USA))
4825^{11} 5168^{7} 5577^{8}

Grand Value (USA) *R Ford* a52 63
3 b f Grand Slam(USA) —Privyet Nadya (USA) (Cure The Blues (USA))
1306^{2} 1558^{6} 4560^{3} 6437^{12} 6955^{7}

Grand View *J R Weymes* a51 37
12 ch g Grand Lodge(USA) —Hemline (Sharpo)
254^{11}

Grand Vista *H J Brown* a52 104
4 b h Danehill(USA) —Revealing (Halling (USA))
290a^{5} 472a^{6} 666a^{2} 738a^{3} 814a^{16}

Grand Vizier (IRE) *C F Wall* a91 78
4 b g Desert Style(IRE) —Distant Decree (USA) (Distant View (USA))
(1936) (2550) 2897^{6} ◆ 3887^{3} 5207^{8} (5675) 6035^{9} 6625^{7}

Grange Corner *Garry Moss* a10
3 ch f First Trump—Blennerville (IRE) (General View)
7632^{9}

Granny McPhee *A Bailey* a67 80
2 b f Bahri(USA) —Allumette (Rainbow Quest (USA))
5711^{4} 6030^{11} 6273^{2} 7140^{5} 7546^{3} 7823^{6}

Granski (IRE) *R Hannon* 70
2 b g Alhaarth(IRE) —Purple Haze (IRE) (Spectrum (IRE))
3968^{6} 4311^{4} 4982^{2} 5511^{8} 6305^{9} 6865^{9}

Granston (IRE) *J D Bethell* a99 92
7 gr g Revoque(IRE) —Gracious Gretclo (Common Grounds)
417^{8} 531^{6} (962) 1473^{6} 1970^{3} 2582^{6} 3046^{3} 4111^{9} 4618^{2} 6233^{4} 6763^{9}

Grantley Adams *Saeed Bin Suroor* a86 109
5 b g Dansili—Noble Peregrine (Lomond (USA))
492a^{9} 738a^{8}

Grapes Of Wrath (UAE) *M Johnston* a51
3 ch f Halling(USA) —Muscadel (Nashwan (USA))
439^{5}

Graphite Halo (USA) *Charles Simon*
2 gr f Mizzen Mast(USA) —Belle Boyd (USA) (Jolie's Halo (USA))
6613a^{9}

Grasp *G L Moore* a62 48
6 b g Kayf Tara—Circe (Main Reef)
14^{10} 2245^{9}

Gravitas *Saeed Bin Suroor* a110 114
5 ch h Mark Of Esteem(IRE) —Bombazine (IRE) (Generous (IRE))
293a^{2} (491a) 816a^{4} 1091a^{12} 5348^{2} 5741a^{6} 6444^{5} 7193^{7}

Gravitation *W Jarvis* 108
3 b f Galileo(IRE) —Guaranda (Acatenango (GER))
1444^{5} 2164^{4} (2669) 3196^{3} 3875^{2} (4549) 5826^{4}

Graycliffe (IRE) *R A Fahey* 60
2 gr c Val Royal(FR) —Popiplu (USA) (Cozzene (USA))
4213^{4} 5882^{10} 6384^{5} 6865^{5}

Graylyn Ruby (FR) *J Jay* a78 70
3 b c Limnos(JPN) —Nandi (IRE) (Mujadil (USA))
1186^{3} 1553^{2} 1731^{4} 2495^{5} 3671^{8} 4281^{4} (6436) (6775) 7091^{3} 7364^{3} 7539^{3} 7715^{7}

Gray Mountain (USA) *Miss Lucinda V Russell* 42
5 rg g Lasting Approval(USA) —Cuando Quiere (USA) (Affirmed (USA))
3253^{6}

Graysland *W G M Turner* 8
2 bl f Silver Patriarch(IRE) —Celtic Island (Celtic Swing)
2349^{5} 3760^{4} 6330^{10}

Graze On And On *J J Quinn* 33
3 ch f Elmaamul(USA) —Laena (Roman Warrior)
1817^{12} 3126^{13}

Grazeon Gold Blend *J J Quinn* 85
5 ch g Paris House—Thalya (Crofthall)
1908^{11} 2698^{5} 3056^{8} 3812^{2} (4117) 4460^{3} 4687^{3} 5222^{2} 5455^{4} 5831^{4} 7041^{3} 7175^{7}

Great Art (IRE) *P W Chapple-Hyam* 83
2 b c One Cool Cat(USA) —Passe Passe (USA) (Lear Fan (USA))
2146^{2} ◆

Great As Gold (IRE) *B Ellison* a59 85
9 b g Goldmark(USA) —Great Land (USA) (Friend's Choice (USA))
1017^{5} 1518^{7} 2135^{10} 2888^{9} 3296^{8} 3414^{9}

Great Bounder (CAN) *J R Best* a61
2 bb g Mr Greeley(USA) —Jo Zak (USA) (Vilzak (USA))
6737^{11} 7204^{6} 7434^{6} ◆

Great Charm (IRE) *M L W Bell* a82 95
3 b g Orpen(USA) —Briery (IRE) (Salse (USA))
1161^{9} (1587) (1781) 2141^{3} ◆ (2732) 3141^{2} (3723) 3850^{7} 4687^{4} 5831^{11} 6239^{3} 6947^{9}

Great Charter (USA) *M Johnston* 47
2 b g Proud Citizen(USA) —Tom's Cat (USA) (Storm Cat (USA))
2362^{7} 3055^{9} 6811^{3}

Great Destination *B Smart* a37 45
3 b g Dubai Destination(USA) —Bella Chica (IRE) (Bigstone (IRE))
529^{7} 1556^{5} 3144^{8}

Great Fox (IRE) *S C Williams* a49 47
7 b h Foxhound(USA) —Good Enough (IRE) (Simply Great (FR))
6204^{11} 7092^{6} 7295^{7} 7416^{9} 7648^{13} 7766^{6}

Great Future *J R Holt* 45
3 ch f Fantastic Light(USA) —Silvernus (Machiavellian (USA))
1477^{7} 2719^{9} 2989^{7} 6168^{6}

Great Hawk (USA) *Sir Michael Stoute* a111 106
5 b h El Prado(IRE) —Laser Hawk (USA) (Silver Hawk (USA))
906^{3} 1077^{4}

Great Hunter (USA) *Doug O'Neill* a112
4 bb h Aptitude(USA) —Zenith (USA) (Roy (USA))
1092a^{5}

Great Knight (IRE) *W J Haggas* a67 67
3 b g Acclamation—Wild Vintage (USA) (Alysheba (USA))
1311^{3} ◆ 1817^{2} 2067^{2} 3144^{2} 3447^{2} 4538^{6} 5616^{8} 6660^{6} 6956^{9}

Great Man (FR) *K M Prendergast* a56 48
7 b g Bering—Great Connection (USA) (Dayjur (USA))
4365^{9} 4936^{7} 5651^{12} 6693^{13}

Great Plains *E Charpy* a93 101
6 b h Halling(USA) —West Dakota (USA) (Gone West (USA))
293a^{6} 565a^{7} 650a^{9}

Great Rumpuscat (USA) *A P O'Brien* 95
3 b c Storm Cat(USA) —Monevassia (USA) (Mr Prospector (USA))
1421^{10} 2417a^{7} 4004a^{16}

Great View (IRE) *Mrs A L M King* a65 79
9 b g Great Commotion(USA) —Tara View (IRE) (Wassl)
1181^{8} 1538^{7} 2012^{4} 2423^{5} (3901) 4343^{4} 4690^{4} 5369^{3} 5651^{5} 5993^{12} 6983^{7}

Great War Eagle (USA) *David Wachman* a100 105
3 br c Storm Cat(USA) —Cash Run (USA) (Seeking The Gold (USA))
1879a^{2} 2961a^{2}

Great Western (USA) *P F I Cole* a51 18
2 bb c Gone West(USA) —Pleasant Temper (USA) (Storm Cat (USA))
6602^{11} 7069^{8} 7204^{8}

Grecian Dancer *Charles O'Brien* a88 109
5 b m Dansili—Pizzicato (Statoblest)
1355a^{8} 1880a^{5} (2420a) 3120^{3}

Greco Tom (ARG) *Rune Haugen*
4 ch h Shy Tom(USA) —Forty Gregaria (ARG) (Roar (USA))
3489^{14}

Greek Easter (IRE) *David P Myerscough* a85 58
5 b m Namid—Easter Heroine (IRE) (Exactly Sharp (USA))
315^{7}

Greek Envoy *T P Tate* 109
4 br g Diktat—South Shore (Caerleon (USA))
1629^{4} ◆ 3721^{12} 3975^{5} 4856^{12} 5894^{9} 7244^{12}

Greek Mythology (USA) *A P O'Brien* 86
3 b c Mr Greeley(USA) —Tell Me Now (USA) (A.P. Indy (USA))
1232a^{4} (Dead)

Greek Renaissance (IRE) *Saeed Bin Suroor* a108 119
5 b h Machiavellian(USA) —Athene (IRE) (Rousillon (USA))
3488^{7} 4059^{2}

Greek Secret *J O'Reilly* a58 64
5 b g Josr Algarhoud(IRE) —Mazurkanova (Song)
1561^{9} 2448^{9} 2950^{3} 3638^{4} 4327^{7} 4653^{6} 7102^{10} (7625) 7809^{9}

Greek Theatre (USA) *P S McEntee* a67 64
3 ch g Smoke Glacken(USA) —Theatre Flight (USA) (Theatrical)
225^{5} 4732^{8} 6754^{5} (7088)

Greek Well (IRE) *Saeed Bin Suroor* 99
5 b g Sadler's Wells(USA) —Hellenic (Darshaan)
477a^{6} 4867^{10}

Green Agenda *M Johnston* 47
2 b g Anabaa(USA) —Capistrano Day (USA) (Diesis)
6212^{7} 6474^{22} 6944^{12}

Greenbank Destiny *W J H Ratcliffe*
2 b f Tobougg(IRE) —Sea Isle (Selkirk (USA))
7221^{8}

Greenbelt *G M Moore* a73 34
7 b g Desert Prince(IRE) —Emerald (USA) (El Gran Senor (USA))
6812^{13}

Green Beret (IRE) *J H M Gosden* 83
2 b g Fayruz—Grandel (Owington)
2893^{2} 3219^{3} (3889)

Green Birdie (NZ) *C Fownes* 118
5 b g Catbird(AUS) —Mrs Squillionaire (AUS) (Last Tycoon)
7683a^{2}

Green Coast (IRE) *Doug Watson* a105 95
5 b h Green Desert(USA) —Oriental Fashion (IRE) (Marju (IRE))
473a^{4} (647a) 815a^{7} 1087a^{9}

Green Diamond *M Johnston* a76 80
3 b g Green Desert(USA) —Balisada (Kris)
2333^{4} 2699^{9} 3402^{4} 4219^{13} 4946^{2} 5595^{6} 6177^{10} 6380^{5} 6826^{7}

Green Dynasty (IRE) *M Johnston* a68
2 ch c Giant's Causeway(USA) —Rose Gypsy (Green Desert (USA))
7554^{4}

Green Endeavour (CAN) *Mrs A J Perrett* a48 21
2 b g Forestry(USA) —Zuri Ridge (USA) (Cox's Ridge (USA))
6977^{16} 7209^{8} 7438^{9}

Greenisland (IRE) *H Morrison* a76 77
2 b f Fasliyev(USA) —Green Castle (IRE) (Indian Ridge)
5240^{3} ◆ 6622^{3} (7259)

Green Lagonda (AUS) *J G Given* a70 70
6 gr g Crown Jester(AUS) —Fidelis (AUS) (John's Hope (AUS))
1624^{2} 1997^{14} 2356^{5} 2710^{7} 3281^{3} 3559^{3}

Green Lyons (IRE) *Neil Drysdale* 103
4 b m Green Desert(USA) —Spinnette (IRE) (Spinning World (USA))
6505a^{8}

Green Manalishi *K A Ryan* a97 113
7 b g Green Desert(USA) —Silca-Cisa (Hallgate)
2401^{6} 2712^{3} (3948) (4660) 6121^{8} 6518a^{13}

Green Oasis (USA) *E J O'Neill* a84 93
3 b f Green Desert(USA) —Class Kris (USA) (Kris S (USA))
7381^{7}

Green Onions *D J S Ffrench Davis* a68 16
2 b g Royal Applause—Tremiere (FR) (Anabaa (USA))
5578^{11} 7501^{6} 7640^{3} 7802^{5}

Green Park (IRE) *R A Fahey* a89 98
5 b g Shinko Forest(IRE) —Danccini (IRE) (Dancing Dissident (USA))
1071^{15} 1325^{4} ◆ 1917^{2} 2129^{11} 2626^{18} 3451^{14} 4171^{9} 4240^{10} 4962^{2} (5886) 6069^{15} 6354^{3} 6651^{6} 6971^{19}

Green Passion (USA) *M Johnston*
2 bb c Forestry(USA) —Date Stone (USA) (Forty Niner (USA))
4415^{15}

Green Pirate *C R Dore* a67 52
6 b g Bahamian Bounty—Verdura (Green Desert (USA))
15^{7} 235^{4} (305) 508^{6} 542^{3} 576^{3} (783) 1061^{6} 1455^{13} 2263^{7} 2806^{8} 3037^{5} 3265^{4} 3588^{9} 3822^{5} 4182^{6} 4479^{8}

Green Poppy *Eve Johnson Houghton* 63
2 b f Green Desert(USA) —Vimy Ridge (FR) (Indian Ridge)
3020^{4} ◆ 3417^{3} 4279^{2} 4925^{6} 6172^{11}

Greensward *B J Meehan* 83
2 b c Green Desert(USA) —Frizzante (Efisio)
4151^{5} ◆ (5099) 6970^{3} ◆

Green Tango (FR) *P Van De Poele* a82 106
5 ch h Majorien—Miss Bonfosse (FR) (Hard Leaf (FR))
4496a^{4} 5333a^{6} 6497a^{10} 7429a^{4}

Green Tobasco *M J P O'Brien* a96 70
5 b g Green Desert(USA) —Hyperspectra (Rainbow Quest (USA))
1105a^{25} 4512a^{10} 6261a^{5}

Green Velvet *P J Makin* a54
3 b f Iron Mask(USA) —Scarlett Ribbon (Most Welcome)
4523^{7} 5679^{2} 6224^{7} 6878^{3} 7710^{5}

Green Wadi *M R Channon* a78 88
3 b g Dansili—Peryllys (Warning)
909^{4} 1923^{10} 2488^{3} 3004^{8} (3362)

Greenwich Meantime *A King* a89 101
8 b g Royal Academy(USA) —Shirley Valentine (Shirley Heights)
1916^{11} 2609^{5} 4362^{2} 4843^{8} 5494^{6} 5940^{6} 6288^{8} 7770^{4}

Greenwich Village *W J Knight* a82 71
5 b g Mtoto—D'Azy (Persian Bold)
2423^{6} 2921^{3} 3321^{3} 3606^{2} (4410) (5017) 6272^{11} (7770)

Green Wonder (GER) *D M Simcock* a36 27
3 b f Big Shuffle(USA) —Green Water (Suave Dancer (USA))
3035^{8} 4909^{8} 5652^{11}

Greenwood *P G Murphy* a71 63
10 ch g Emarati(USA) —Charnwood Queen (Cadeaux Genereux)
933^{4} 1145^{5} 1313^{4} 1865^{7}

Gremlin *A King* 87
4 b g Mujahid(USA) —Fairy Free (Rousillon (USA))
5279^{14} 5843^{10} 6346^{6}

Grenadia (USA) *J-C Rouget* a77 100
3 b f Thunder Gulch(USA) —Great Lady Slew (USA) (Seattle Slew (USA))
2743a^{4}

Grenane (IRE) *Mrs A Malzard* a63 62
5 b g Princely Heir(IRE) —Another Rainbow (IRE) (Rainbows For Life (CAN))
342^{9} 509^{5} 724^{10} 1064^{2} 1207^{7} 1605^{6} 5002a^{8}

Grethel (IRE) *A Berry* a35 65
4 b m Fruits Of Love(USA) —Stay Sharpe (USA) (Sharpen Up)
1394^{11} 1577^{6} 1822^{10} 2284^{5} 2568^{6} 2662^{11} (3127) 3258^{3} 3552^{5} 3755^{11} 3996^{3} 4015^{8} 4458^{7} (4596) 4785^{8} 5221^{3} 5564^{8} 6152^{6} 6215^{9} 6786^{7} 7131^{3} 7342^{12}

Grey Boy (GER) *A W Carroll* a79 76
7 gr g Medaaly—Grey Perri (Siberian Express (USA))
1522^{10} 1872^{3} 2087^{11} 2550^{5} 3501^{9} 4053^{5} (4414) 5101^{6} 5915^{6} (6211) 6671^{3} 6899^{5}

Grey Command (USA) *M Brittain* 74
3 gr c Daylami(IRE) —Shmoose (IRE) (Caerleon (USA))
1068^{11} 1295^{7} 2008^{3} 2221^{4} 4112^{2} 4332^{6} 4737^{2} 5449^{7} 6188^{9}

Greyfriars Abbey *M Johnston* a66 89
4 b g Fasliyev(USA) —Mysistra (FR) (Machiavellian (USA))
(1580) 1691^{6}

Greyfriarsblessing (IRE) *M Johnston* 59
3 bb f Hawk Wing(USA) —Royal Bounty (IRE) (Generous (IRE))
1628^{6} 1918^{8} 5031^{2} 5391^{10} (Dead)

Grey Ghost *E F Vaughan* a32
2 gr c Linamix(FR) —Isla Azul (IRE) (Machiavellian (USA))
6135^{12} 6694^{11}

Grey Granite (IRE) *W Jarvis* 70
2 gr c Dalakhani(IRE) —Royal Ballerina (IRE) (Sadler's Wells (USA))
7054^{6}

Grey Gurkha *I W McInnes* a61 60
7 gr h Kasakov—Royal Rebeka (Grey Desire)
140^{2} 234^{4} 537^{5} 708^{7} 749^{7} ◆ 1142^{10} 1533^{2} 1578^{11} 2009^{13} 2510^{10}

Greylami (IRE) *T G Mills* a83 92
3 gr g Daylami(IRE) —Silent Crystal (USA) (Diesis)
(727) ◆ 1043^{4} 1543^{3} 2996^{7} 3745^{3} ◆ 4621^{3} 5759^{3} (6202) 6784^{5}

Grey Light (IRE) *L Lungo* a56 64
4 b g Namid—Flying Clouds (Batshoof)
559^{10}

Grey Outlook *Miss L A Perratt* 68
5 ch m Observatory(USA) —Grey Galava (Generous (IRE))
1304^{8} 1773^{6}

Grey Rhythm (IRE) *Timothy Doyle* a58 74
4 gr g Danetime(IRE) —Krayyalei (IRE) (Krayyan)
6510a^{14}

Greystoke Prince *W R Swinburn* a78 58
3 gr g Diktat—Grey Princess (IRE) (Common Grounds)
918^{2} (1274) 4083^{2} 5052^{2} 5600^{13} 6020^{9}

Grey Vision *M Brittain* a37 51
5 gr m Grey Desire—Brief Star (IRE) (Brief Truce (USA))
406 768[5] 1391[11] 2463[15]
Grezie *L A Dace* a47 44
6 gr m Mark Of Esteem(IRE) —Lozzie (Siberian Express (USA))
392[9] 621[2] 713[3] 808[4] 922[6] 3033[5]
Grimes Faith *K A Ryan* a79 79
5 b g Woodborough(USA) —Emma Grimes (IRE) (Nordico (USA))
(106) 213[4] (346) 386[2] 599[3] 729[6] 800[2] 839[2] 951[6] 1015[15] 1190[5] 4047[9] 4327[4] 4846[8] 5709[7] (6039) 6310[3] 6382[8] 7218[2] 7629[2] 7727[3]
Gris De Gris (IRE) *A De Royer-Dupre* a109 115
4 gr h Slickly(FR) —Deesse Grise (FR) (Lead On Time (USA))
1108a[2] (1761a) 2656a[3] 5742a[7] 7162a[2]
Grisham *Michael John Phillips* 88
10 b g Emarati(USA) —Shibui (Shirley Heights)
4576a[12]
Grissom (IRE) *A Berry* 70
2 b c Desert Prince(IRE) —Misty Peak (IRE) (Sri Pekan (USA))
5416[6] 5988[7] 6407[4] 6656[4] 7038[4] 7130[3] (7219)
Gris Tendre (FR) *J-C Rouget* a93 105
3 gr c Slickly(FR) —Tendre Pensee (FR) (Mujadil (USA))
2875a[7]
Grit (IRE) *M R Channon* a28 70
3 gr g Clodovil(IRE) —Lisa's Pride (IRE) (Pips Pride)
1467[18] 1926[15] 2056[9] 2639[11] (2922) ◆ 3126[3] 3790[2] 4044[3] 4180[8] 4629[6] (4680) 4990[3] 5378[16] 5965[5] (6042) 6162[8]
Grizebeck (IRE) *R F Fisher* a66 88
6 b g Trans Island—Premier Amour (Salmon Leap (USA))
436[5] 664[4] 720[3] 778[2] (869) 988[3] (1136) (1304) (1518)
Grizedale (IRE) *M J Attwater* a64 83
9 ch g Lake Coniston(IRE) —Zabeta (Diesis)
2203[8] 2615[8] 2995[10] 3383[4] 3842[2] 4084[4] 4727[4] 5088[12] 6679[2] 7090[12] 7254[8] 7358[10] 7433[7] 7706[3] 7765[3] 7817[4]
Grooms Affection *A M Hales* a61 88
8 b g Groom Dancer(USA) —Love And Affection (USA) (Exclusive Era (USA))
1639[6]
Gross Prophet *Tom Dascombe* a88 89
3 b g Lujain(USA) —Done And Dusted (IRE) (Up And At 'Em)
1375 926[6] 1075[8] 1336[9] 1546[11] 1868[11] 2276[11] 2710[10] 4030[2] 4125[10] 4641[3] (4910) 5309[3] 6242[7] 6528[2] (6908)
Groundhog Day *J Balding* a14 21
4 b m Mind Games—Millie's Lady (IRE) (Common Grounds)
2823[9] 3177[11] 3712[14] 4107[15] 4563[9] 5007[9] 6224[8]
Ground Patrol *N R Mitchell* a57 18
7 b g Ashkalani(IRE) —Good Grounds (USA) (Alleged (USA))
935[4] 1673[5] 2755[11] 4664[13]
Group Captain *H J Collingridge* a104 116
6 b g Dr Fong(USA) —Alusha (Soviet Star (USA))
3497[5] 5894[12] 6646[16] 7244[8]
Group Leader (IRE) *J R Jenkins* 18
2 ch g Noverre(USA) —Stem The Tide (USA) (Proud Truth (USA))
4598[6] 6509[9]
Group Therapy *J A Osborne* a72 98
3 ch g Choisir(AUS) —Licence To Thrill (Wolfhound (USA))
2712[10]
Grudge *D W Barker* 74
3 b g Timeless Times(USA) —Envy (IRE) (Paris House)
2171[6] 2396[3] 2850[4] 3217[2] 3455[6] 3811[8] 4216[2] 4922[2] (5201) 5796[15] 6218[11]
Gtaab *E A L Dunlop* a67 64
2 b c Cape Cross(IRE) —Nabadhaat (USA) (Mr Prospector (USA))
5468[13] 5842[6] 6423[4]
Guadalcanal (USA) *Frederick J Seitz* a78 95
3 b c Graeme Hall(USA) —Bessette (USA) (Quest For Fame (USA))
2858a[7]
Guadaloup *M Brittain* a58 56
6 ch m Loup Sauvage(USA) —Rash (Pursuit Of Love)
32[4] ◆ 82[3] 168[5] 371[4] 521[3] (663) 861[8] 1024[7] 1188[10] 2672[8]
Guardia (GER) *A Fabre* 107
4 ch m Monsun(GER) —Guernica (Unfuwain (USA))
2553a[7] 5332a[5]
Guardian Of Truth (IRE) *G L Moore* a80 79
4 ch g Barathea(IRE) —Zarara (USA) (Manila (USA))
758[2] 5092[3] 5677[10] 6413[5] (Dead)
Guerande (IRE) *A De Royer-Dupre* 42
2 b f Diesis—Gracefully (IRE) (Orpen (USA))
7449a[7]
Guerilla (AUS) *R C Guest* a38 42
8 bb g Octagonal(NZ) —Partisan (AUS) (Canny Lad (AUS))
5913[12]
Guertino (IRE) *B Smart* a79 94
3 ch g Choisir(AUS) —Isana (JPN) (Sunday Silence (USA))
566a[7] 3228[4] 3812[9] 4416[2]
Guest Connections *D Nicholls* a91 84
5 b g Zafonic(USA) —Llyn Gwynant (Persian Bold)
1138[10] 2040[4] 2255[2] 2547[2] 3050[6] 3172[2] 3591[11] (4114) (4144) 4555[12] 4743[6] (5044) 5400[10]
Guestofthenation (USA) *M Johnston* a67 85
2 bb c Gulch(USA) —French Flag (Darshaan)
5404[5] (5716) 6038[2] 7067[7]
Guga (IRE) *George Baker* 59
2 b c Rock Of Gibraltar(IRE) —Attitre (FR) (Mtoto)
6674[9]

Guilded Warrior *W S Kittow* a96 94
5 b g Mujahid(USA) —Pearly River (Elegant Air)
1174[2] 1566[2] 1982[5] 2905[3] 3529[2] 3972[3] 4661[5] 5313[8] (6277) 6902[12]
Guildenstern (IRE) *P Howling* a67 83
6 b g Danetime(IRE) —Lyphard Abu (IRE) (Lyphard's Special (USA))
71[4] 327[6] (516) 663[5] 1145[2] 1371[4] 1780[2] 2597[15] 2806[2] 3329[4] 3839[8] 4084[2] ◆ 5144[12] 5610[4] 5801[9] 7383[5] (7503) 7619[4] 7772[4]
Guilin (IRE) *P F I Cole* a33 40
2 b f Giant's Causeway(USA) —Chantress (Peintre Celebre (USA))
4643[13] 5570[9] 6081[18]
Guillotine (NZ) *David Hayes* 114
4 gr h Montjeu(IRE) —Refused The Dance (NZ) (Defensive Play (USA))
6835a[14]
Guilt *K J Burke* a42 28
8 b g Mark Of Esteem(IRE) —Guillem (USA) (Nijinsky (CAN))
710[5] 2795[11]
Gulch's Rose (USA) *J Noseda* a68 67
3 b f Gulch(USA) —England's Rose (USA) (Nureyev (USA))
1054[3] 2536[4] 3762[3] 4284[3] ◆ 5616[2] 6336[5]
Gulf Coast *T D Walford* a65 69
3 ch g Dubai Destination(USA) —Lloc (Absalom)
2208[7] 2496[4] 3551[4] 3711[2] (4048) 4503[5] 4966[7] 6551[7]
Gulf Express (USA) *Sir Michael Stoute* a83 111
4 b h Langfuhr(CAN) —Wassifa (Sure Blade (USA))
1828[14] 2103[7] 3249[18] 3684[2] (4504) 5289[4]
Gulf President *M R Channon* 60
2 b c Polish Precedent(USA) —Gay Minette (IRE) (Peintre Celebre (USA))
3926[5]
Gulf Stream Lady (IRE) *B W Hills* 70
3 ch f Cadeaux Genereux—Aoife (IRE) (Thatching)
1423[6] 1946[7] 2786[4] 3262[3]
Gull Wing (IRE) *M L W Bell* a64 106
4 ch m In The Wings—Maycocks Bay (Muhtarram (USA))
(1158) 2144[5] 3975[2] 4667[10] 5826[RR]
Gulnaz *Mrs G S Rees* a47 5
3 b f Tobougg(IRE) —Hymn Book (IRE) (Darshaan)
3262[8] 6956[7] 7174[8] 7632[4]
Gunavira (IRE) *D K Weld* 65
3 b c Green Desert(USA) —Balade Russe (USA) (Gone West (USA))
3861a[5] 4494a[9]
Gunfighter (IRE) *R Johnson* a82 92
5 ch g Machiavellian(USA) —Reunion (IRE) (Be My Guest (USA))
1069[10] 2538[3] 2938[LFT] 3812[RR] 4417[RR]
Gun For Sale (USA) *P J Makin* a44 27
3 b g Quiet American(USA) —Do The Hustle (USA) (Known Fact (USA))
2918[8] 4195[9] 7395[8] 7605[11]
Gunnadoit (USA) *M L W Bell* a66 62
3 bb g Almutawakel—Gharam (USA) (Green Dancer (USA))
976[4] ◆ 1147[2] ◆ (1350) 2280[10] 2868[4] 3483[4]
Gunner Fly (IRE) *R A Fahey* a65 48
3 b c Noverre(USA) —Anne-Lise (Inchinor)
3662[6] (Dead)
Gunner's View *R H York* a65 73
4 ch h Medicean—Stark Ballet (USA) (Nureyev (USA))
3266[9]
Gun Salute (USA) *Doug Watson* 107
6 b h Military(USA) —Hail Roberta (USA) (Roberto (USA))
494a[5] 673a[8]
Gurteen Diamond *N J Vaughan* a49
2 b f Kyllachy—Precious (Danehill (USA))
7341[8] 7735[4]
Guto *W J H Ratcliffe* a72 91
5 b g Foxhound(USA) —Mujadilly (Mujadil (USA))
370[7] (479) 620[2] 786[6] 1022[4] 1129[3] 1451[2] 1818[6] 2444[15] 2596[12] 3405[8] 3577[5] 4047[14] (4703) 5074[9] 5201[7] 5398[11] 6159[5] (6382) 6546[5] 7043[10] (7182)
Guyno (NZ) *Lou Luciani* 109
5 br g O'Reilly(NZ) —River Century (NZ) (Centaine (AUS))
6922a[5] 7188a[12]
Gwerthybyd *B Palling* a53 20
2 b f Auction House(USA) —Minette (Bishop Of Cashel)
7015[13] 7452[6] 7607[2]
Gwilym (GER) *D Haydn Jones* a69 81
5 b h Agnes World(USA) —Glady Rose (GER) (Surumu (GER))
1522[12] 1928[11] 2968[10] 3042[5] 3352[11] 5250[14] 6634[6] 7118[2] 7225[8] 7540[7]
Gyr (IRE) *J L Dunlop* 85
2 ch c Pivotal—Rafha (Kris)
2796[4] (4510) 6474[12] 6717[5]
Gyration (IRE) *G A Swinbank* a47 46
4 ch g Spinning World(USA) —Tomori (USA) (Royal Academy (USA))
611[8] 808[3]
Haadeej (USA) *C Boutin* a87 81
3 ch c Stravinsky(USA) —Tamgeed (USA) (Woodman (USA))
6744a[5]
Haafhds Delight (IRE) *W M Brisbourne* a7 35
2 b f Haafhd—Twitcher's Delight (Polar Falcon (USA))
4027[11] 6273[9] 6665[8]
Haafhd Time (IRE) *Tom Dascombe* 53
2 b f Haafhd—Amusing Time (IRE) (Sadler's Wells (USA))
3348[11]
Haaf Ok *M Halford* a80 82
2 b f Haafhd—Chilly Start (IRE) (Caerleon (USA))
5924a[6] 6637a[7]

Haajes *S Parr* a45 101
4 ch g Indian Ridge—Imelda (USA) (Manila (USA))
3868[14] 4478[12] 4958[7] (5398) 5566[4] 5796[12] (6164) 6340[2] (6486) ◆ (6557) 6650[7] 6810[4] 6971[10] 7245[13]
Haakima (USA) *C E Brittain* 87
2 bb f Dixieland Band(USA) —Be Fair (BRZ) (Fast Gold (USA))
5240[7] 6013[3] 6818[11]
Haamesh (IRE) *J S Wainwright* 58
4 ch g Noverre(USA) —Royal Fizz (IRE) (Royal Academy (USA))
3867[5]
Haarth Sovereign (IRE) *W R Swinburn* a85 84
4 b g Alhaarth(IRE) —Summer Queen (Robellino (USA))
(1048) 1502[4] 2152[3] 3003[14] 3925[6] 4771[4] 5349[6] 5992[3] 6361[2] 6948[7]
Haasem (USA) *J R Jenkins* a69 74
5 b g Seeking The Gold(USA) —Thawakib (IRE) (Sadler's Wells (USA))
1645[2] 2510[2] 3116[2] 4162[7] 4895[7] 5458[9] 6336[3] 7307[9] 7548[6] 7677[3] 7803[5]
Haashed (USA) *M Johnston* a90
2 ch c Mr Greeley(USA) —Guerre Et Paix (USA) (Soviet Star (USA))
(7438) ◆
Haatef (USA) *Kevin Prendergast* 116
4 b h Danzig(USA) —Sayedat Alhadh (USA) (Mr Prospector (USA))
2106[5]
Haatmey *N Wilson* a63 48
6 b g Josr Algarhoud(IRE) —Raneen Alwatar (Sadler's Wells (USA))
14[3] 212[7] 664[7] 869[2] 988[4] 1136[6]
Habbie Heights *R Bastiman* 56
3 b f Josr Algarhoud(IRE) —Hello Hobson'S (IRE) (Fayruz)
2466[5] 3081[6] 3790[8]
Habitual Dancer *Jedd O'Keeffe* a10 42
7 b g Groom Dancer(USA) —Pomorie (IRE) (Be My Guest (USA))
954[6]
Habshan (USA) *C F Wall* a87 92
8 ch g Swain(IRE) —Cambara (Dancing Brave (USA))
1719[4] 2057[6] 3054[4] (3855) 4509[10] 6431[4]
Hadaf (IRE) *M P Tregoning* a87 94
3 b c Fasliyev(USA) —Elhida (IRE) (Mujtahid (USA))
1404[11] 1945[5] 2998[7] (3462) 5206[10] 6239[9]
Hada Men (USA) *M P Tregoning* a69 80
3 b g Dynaformer(USA) —Catchy (USA) (Storm Cat (USA))
6092[4] 6403[2]
Hadron Collider (FR) *R Hannon* a76 74
3 ch c Dubai Destination(USA) —Liver De Saron (USA) (Mt. Livermore (USA))
1272[5] 1696[4] 2045[8] 2310[6] 2997[7] (3614) 3970[3] 4432[4] 5027[3] 5465[2] 5698[8] 6403[8]
Haigh Hall *T D Easterby* 84
2 ch f Kyllachy—Miss Meltemi (IRE) (Miswaki Tern (USA))
(2206) ◆ 2497[5]
Hail Caesar (IRE) *A P O'Brien* 107
2 gr c Montjeu(IRE) —Alabastrine (Green Desert (USA))
6316a[5] 7294a[6]
Hail Promenader (IRE) *B W Hills* 78
2 b c Acclamation—Tribal Rite (Be My Native (USA))
2759[4] 3358[3] 5860[3] (6481)
Hajoum (IRE) *Saeed Bin Suroor* 74
2 b c Exceed And Excel(AUS) —Blue Iris (Petong)
3976[4] ◆ 4792[2]
Halaak (USA) *D M Simcock* a51 33
2 br f Harlan's Holiday(USA) —Henderson Band (USA) (Chimes Band (USA))
2821[13] 3584[9] 5673[7] 7542[6] (7728)
Hala Bek (IRE) *Saeed Bin Suroor* 115
5 b h Halling(USA) —Place De L'Opera (Sadler's Wells (USA))
(3885) ◆
Halaziya (IRE) *M Halford* a72 64
2 b f Danehill Dancer(IRE) —Halawanda (IRE) (Ashkalani (IRE))
3509a[3]
Haldibari (IRE) *A King* 48
4 b g Kahyasi—Haladiya (IRE) (Darshaan)
1382[7]
Half A Crown (IRE) *D W Barker* 55
5 b c Compton Place—Penny Ha'Penny (Bishop Of Cashel)
2786[9] 5110[3] 5636[4] 6792[19]
Half A Tsar (IRE) *Mark Gillard* a55 54
4 b g Soviet Star(USA) —Villarica (IRE) (Fairy King (USA))
2721[3] 3021[5] 3316[10] 3559[6] 3779[8] 4273[12]
Halfway House *M L W Bell* 60
2 b g Dubai Destination(USA) —Zanzibar (IRE) (In The Wings)
6438[8] 6760[5] 7051[8]
Halfway To Heaven (IRE) *A P O'Brien* 118
3 gr f Pivotal—Cassandra Go (IRE) (Indian Ridge)
1230a[2] ◆ 2033a[3] (2433a) (4623) 5730a[3] (6475) 6968a[7]
Halicarnassus (IRE) *M R Channon* a78 117
4 b h Cape Cross(IRE) —Launch Time (USA) (Relaunch (USA))
565a[4] 740a[5] 816a[11] 1422[7] 2432a[4] 3195[5] 4192[10] 4436[4] 5276[5] 5694[10] 6074[9] 6780[14]
Haljaferia (UAE) *D R C Elsworth* a70
2 ch g Halling(USA) —Melisendra (FR) (Highest Honor (FR))
7593[9] 7699[3]
Halkin (USA) *F Nass* a97
6 br h Chester House(USA) —Estala (Be My Guest (USA))
564a[3] 650a[4] 815a[4] 1087a[10]
Halla San *R A Fahey* 100
6 b g Halling(USA) —St Radegund (Green Desert (USA))
1916[10] 2202[2] 3490[2] 4493a[11]

Hall Hee (IRE) *M P Tregoning* a89 80
3 br f Invincible Spirit(IRE) —Lionne (Darshaan)
2994[3] ◆ 3854[6] (5491) 6311[2] (6900)
Hallhoo (IRE) *D Selvaratnam* a60 97
6 gr g Indian Ridge—Nuit Chaud (USA) (Woodman (USA))
477a[2] 673a[4]
Hallie's Comet (IRE) *A Kinsella* a79 97
2 b f One Cool Cat(USA) —Secretariat's Tap (USA) (Pleasant Tap (USA))
6318a[3]
Hallingdal (UAE) *Ms J S Doyle* a85 77
3 b f Halling(USA) —Saik (USA) (Riverman (USA))
3607[3] 4669[8] 5032[4] 5675[5] (5800) 6471[3] ◆ 6627[4] ◆ 7014[6] 7390[10] 7525[8]
Hallingdal Blue (UAE) *H R A Cecil* a40
2 b f Halling(USA) —Blue Melody (USA) (Dayjur (USA))
7578[9]
Halling Machine (UAE) *A Feligioni* 52
2 ch c Halling(USA) —Laughsome (Be My Guest (USA))
2745a[3]
Hallings Overture (USA) *C A Horgan* a62 2
9 b g Halling(USA) —Sonata (Polish Precedent (USA))
795[12] 4635[8] (5020) 5489[11] 6019[8] 6930[6]
Halliwell House *J H M Gosden* 59
2 ch f Selkirk(USA) —Dusty Answer (Zafonic (USA))
7141[9]
Hallys Goal (IRE) *M Mullineaux*
6 b g Fourstars Allstar(USA) —Glenties (Furry Glen)
5963[9]
Halong Bay (FR) *N Clement* a55 87
3 b f Montjeu(IRE) —Lorigane (Singspiel (IRE))
7450a[6]
Halsion Challenge *J R Best* a43 46
3 b g King's Best(USA) —Zaynah (IRE) (Kahyasi)
3780[6] 4260[8] 4409[7] 5832[9] 7766[8] 7817[8]
Halsion Chancer *J R Best* a92 58
4 br g Atraf—Lucky Dip (Tirol)
(26) ◆ 456[6] (676) 2831[10] 3093[10] 3320[9] 4341[4] 4944[8] 5681[2] 5936[11] 6576[8] 7215[9] 7477[9] 7712[4]
Halton Castle *G M Moore* 47
3 ch g Zamindar(USA) —Chilly Start (IRE) (Caerleon (USA))
2912[6] 3578[8]
Hamaasy *R A Harris* a70 53
7 b g Machiavellian(USA) —Sakha (Wolfhound (USA))
1040[11] (1588) 2050[6] 4476[3] 5709[11] 6377[6] 7255[9] 7615[3] 7727[2]
Hamalka (IRE) *B W Hills* a60 69
3 br f Alhaarth(IRE) —Night Owl (Night Shift (USA))
311[5] 727[6] 4909[4] 5445[2] (6275) 6758[8]
Hambledon Hill *R Hannon* 73
2 ch c Selkirk(USA) —Dominica (Alhaarth (IRE))
4150[7] 4788[4] 5469[11] 5960[4] 6344[6]
Hameildaeme *S C Williams* 63
2 b f Storming Home—Sweet Cando (IRE) (Royal Applause)
2253[7] 3032[3] 3754[2] 4769[2] 5365[2] 5785[5] 6858[3] 7016[7]
Hamish McGonagall *T D Easterby* 105
3 b g Namid—Anatase (Danehill (USA))
1484[2] ◆ (2171) 3047[12] 3451[2] ◆ (3909) 4240[14] 5890[15] (6653) 6971[14]
Hammadi (IRE) *K A Ryan* a102 102
3 b c Red Ransom(USA) —Ruby Affair (IRE) (Night Shift (USA))
1075[3] 2034a[8] 2498[2] 3041[8] 4617[7] 5890[19]
Hammer *R T Phillips* a70 75
3 b g Beat Hollow—Tranquil Moon (Deploy)
4730[9] 5047[4] 5587[3] 6126[2] 6596[4] 7704[5]
Hammer Of The Gods (IRE) *G C Bravery* a82 40
8 ch g Tagula(IRE) —Bhama (FR) (Habitat)
(1040) 1191[3] 1865[6] 2501[4] 3394[4] 4058[7] 4944[9] 5629[3] 5867[5] ◆ 6773[6] 7834[10]
Hampton Court *M Johnston* a59 46
3 ch g King's Best(USA) —Rafting (IRE) (Darshaan)
1205[3]
Hamsat Elqamar *J H M Gosden* 75
3 b f Nayef(USA) —Moon's Whisper (USA) (Storm Cat (USA))
1840[5] 2164[6] 2985[5] 4067[4] (5269)
Hanbrin Bhoy (IRE) *R Dickin* a73 50
4 b g Cape Cross(IRE) —Sea Of Stone (USA) (Sanglamore (USA))
246[5] (357)
Handbags At Dawn (IRE) *S Kirk* a35
3 b f Clodovil(IRE) —Questing Star (Rainbow Quest (USA))
1050[7] 1243[9] 1603[10]
Handcuff *J Gallagher* a58 58
2 br c Lend A Hand—Peruvian Jade (Petong)
1118[5] 4027[7] 4270[3] 5614[3] 6017[8] 6666[6] 7024[4]
Handful Of Magic *Tom Dascombe* a50 55
2 b f Lend A Hand—Just Magic (Beveled (USA))
3837[9] 4321[2] 4747[5] 6414[12] 6573[6] 6931[9]
Hando *Christian Wroe* a66 99
4 b h Hernando(FR) —Featherquest (Rainbow Quest (USA))
380a[14] 477a[8]
Hand Painted *P J Makin* 70
2 b c Lend A Hand—Scarlett Holly (Red Sunset)
3603[4] ◆ 4050[4] 6863[5]
Handsinthemist (IRE) *P T Midgley* a48 52
3 b f Lend A Hand—Hollow Haze (USA) (Woodman (USA))
1155[10] 1769[4] 2287[3] 2661[10] 3283[3] 3526[2] 4216[13] 5307[8] 5911[3] 6308[10]
Handsome Cross (IRE) *Mrs A Duffield* a80 94
7 b g Cape Cross(IRE) —Snap Crackle Pop (IRE) (Statoblest)
3336[5] ◆ 3787[3] 5250[11]
Handsome Falcon *R A Fahey* 79
4 b g Kyllachy—Bonne Etoile (Diesis)
979[5] 1450[8] 1908[8] (2535) 2818[11] 3453[4] 4245[2] 4875[5] 5258[2] (5390) 6186[6]

Handsome Maestro (IRE) *D Smaga* 101
2 b c Dansili—Graceful Bering (USA) (Bering)
6855a[5]

Hanella (IRE) *S C Williams* 88
5 b m Galileo(IRE) —Strutting (IRE) (Ela-Mana-Mou)
1980[9] 2402[9] 2625[11] 3295[4]

Hannicean *M A Jarvis* a52 78
4 ch g Medicean—Hannah's Music (Music Boy)
2373[3] ◆ 2764[2] 3457[3] 4167[3] 4829[6]

Hanoverian Baron *John M Oxx* a85 92
3 b g Green Desert(USA) —Josh's Pearl (IRE) (Sadler's Wells (USA))
1879a[4]

Hansinger (IRE) *B I Case* a81 81
3 b g Namid—Whistfilly (First Trump)
573[2] 966[5] 1546[4]

Hansomelle (IRE) *Miss Sheena West* a66 90
6 b m Titus Livius(FR) —Handsome Anna (IRE) (Bigstone (IRE))
750[6] 935[6] 1109[3] 1345[6] 1996[10] 2795[18]

Hansomis (IRE) *B Mactaggart* 60
4 b m Titus Livius(FR) —Handsome Anna (IRE) (Bigstone (IRE))
2159[4] 2751[10] 3260[4] 3452[5] 3757[3] 4018[2] 4383[9] 4851[9] 6409[6] 6791[4] 7129[6]

Hanta Yo (IRE) *J R Gask* a48
2 ch g Alhaarth(IRE) —Tekindia (FR) (Indian Ridge)
6434[6]

Haoin An Bothar (IRE) *Adrian Sexton* a59 44
4 b g Bishop Of Cashel—Drefflane Ann (IRE) (Petorius)
37[3] 1606[6] (Dead)

Hapi *S C Williams* a39 33
3 b g Groom Dancer(USA) —Nekhbet (Artaius (USA))
1417[10] 1748[13] 2084[9] 2803[5] 3139[17] 3406[5]

Happy And Glorious (IRE) *J W Hills* 35
2 ch f Refuse To Bend(IRE) —Wondrous Joy (Machiavellian (USA))
5097[13]

Happy Anniversary (IRE) *Miss V Haigh* a52 81
2 b f Intikhab(USA) —Happy Story (IRE) (Bigstone (IRE))
1680[12] 2217[2] 2362[3] 4475[3] 4956[2] (5416) 5855[2]

Happy As Larry (USA) *J S Moore* a83 74
6 bb g Yes It's True(USA) —Don't Be Blue (USA) (Henbane (USA))
21[3] 63[5] 196[6] 1112[5] 1486[2] 3132[8] 4268[5] ◆ 4390[6] (Dead)

Happy Boy (BRZ) *Saeed Bin Suroor* a117 112
5 gr h Ski Champ(USA) —Ultra Maresca (BRZ) (Filago (USA))
(204a) 2543[9] 3246[7] 4192[4] 5743a[6] 6287[7]

Happy Day (IRE) *David Wachman* 9
2 b c Danehill Dancer(IRE) —In The Limelight (IRE) (Sadler's Wells (USA))
6474[23]

Happy Forever (FR) *M Botti* a79 79
2 b f Dr Fong(USA) —Happyanunoit (NZ) (Yachtie (AUS))
3837[4] (5214) (6469) 7107[7]

Happy Larry *Andrew Oliver* a58 47
2 b g Mujahid(USA) —Elm Dust (Elmaamul (USA))
3509a[11] (Dead)

Happy Runner (BRZ) *P Nickel Filho* a103 88
5 b h Romarin(BRZ) —Miss Klairon (BRZ) (Turville (FR))
(205a) 473a[14] 649a[7]

Hapsburg (FR) *E Libaud* 108
4 b m Anabaa(USA) —Magical Hawk (USA) (Silver Hawk (USA))
1713a[5] 2553a[4] (4320a) 5332a[3] 6499a[7]

Haqeeaq (USA) *Sir Michael Stoute* 63
3 br f Storm Cat(USA) —Happily Unbridled (USA) (Unbridled (USA))
1965[4]

Haradasun (AUS) *A P O'Brien* 123
5 b h Fusaichi Pegasus(USA) —Circles Of Gold (AUS) (Marscay (AUS))
2193[6] (3100)

Harald Bluetooth (IRE) *J R Fanshawe* 87
3 b c Danetime(IRE) —Goldthroat (IRE) (Zafonic (USA))
(3275) (3915) 4641[8]

Harare *R J Price* a83 83
7 b g Bahhare(USA) —Springs Eternal (Salse (USA))
833[10] 1030[3] 1409[3] 1532[8] 2013[10] 2262[9] 2373[10] 3054[3] 3738[3] (3951) 4602[6] 5156[11] 5863[6] 6134[9]

Harbore (FR) *E Lellouche* 110
4 b g Raintrap—Harmonique (FR) (Exit To Nowhere (USA))
5956a[DSQ] 6497a[8]

Harbour Blues *A W Carroll* a79 92
3 ch c Best Of The Bests(IRE) —Lady Georgia (Arazi (USA))
136[6] (339) 1426[4] 1764[4] (1988) 4058[8] 4687[2] 4854[9] 7047[9] 7477[11]

Harcas (IRE) *M Todhunter* 57
6 b g Priolo(USA) —Genetta (Green Desert (USA))
3545[6]

Hardanger (IRE) *T J Fitzgerald* 64
3 b c Halling(USA) —Naughty Nell (Danehill Dancer (IRE))
2380[3] 2966[9] 3438[7]

Hardcase *M Quinn* a40
3 b c Hunting Lion(IRE) —Nordesta (IRE) (Nordico (USA))
721[6] 917[9]

Hard Luck Story *Miss L A Perratt* 69
2 bb g Lucky Story(USA) —Howards Heroine (IRE) (Danehill Dancer (IRE))
5387[6] 6151[3] 6384[2] 7126[3]

Hard Rock City (USA) *M J Grassick* 111
8 b g Danzig(USA) —All The Moves (USA) (A.P. Indy (USA))
1105a[18] 3982a[6] 6516a[3]

Hard Top (IRE) *H J Brown* 107
6 b g Darshaan—Well Head (IRE) (Sadler's Wells (USA))
293a[8] 381a[5] 652a[2] (740a)

Hard To Resist (IRE) *P R Webber* 22
3 br g Statue Of Liberty(USA) —Kelpie (IRE) (Kahyasi)
4695[13] 5182[11] 5612[9]

Hark Forrard *Miss J E Foster*
2 b g Muhtarram(USA) —Lady Rock (Mistertopogigo (IRE))
3689[12]

Harlech Castle *P F I Cole* a94 87
3 b c Royal Applause—Ffestiniog (IRE) (Efisio)
1806[10] 2412[10] 3270[9] 4252[4] ◆ 4595[7] 5490[8] 6340[4] (6765) (7040) ◆ 7181[2] 7394[9]

Harlem Madness (IRE) *M Massimi Jr* 77
3 b f Fath(USA) —Rosalia (USA) (Red Ransom (USA))
2231a[10]

Harlem Shuffle (UAE) *M Johnston* a72 68
3 br f Halling(USA) —Badraan (USA) (Danzig (USA))
1685[9] 2911[14] 3552[7]

Harlequinn Danseur (IRE) *G L Moore* a45 55
3 b g Noverre(USA) —Nassma (IRE) (Sadler's Wells (USA))
1968[8] 2463[11] 3126[7] 3555[13] 4810[12] 5377[7]

Harlestone Gold *J L Dunlop* 60
3 b g Golden Snake(USA) —Harlestone Lady (Shaamit (IRE))
1539[2] 5931[5]

Harlestone Snake *J L Dunlop* 62
2 b g Golden Snake(USA) —Harlestone Lady (Shaamit (IRE))
4788[5] 6085[9] 6720[11]

Harley Fern *P J McBride* a20 5
2 b f Primo Valentino(IRE) —Its All Relative (Distant Relative)
6166[12] 6565[14]

Haroldini (IRE) *J Balding* a75 35
6 b g Orpen(USA) —Ciubanga (IRE) (Arazi (USA))
(42) ◆ 190[3] (258) 601[5] 3108[11] 4168[P] 4542[16] 5156[12] 7586[9] 7698[4] 7796[5]

Harputlu Gaggos (TUR) *R Tasdemir* a113
4 b h Royal Abjar(USA) —Beneklikiz (TUR) (Play Boy (TUR))
(5743a)

Harquahala (IRE) *T G Mills* a41 24
2 b f High Chaparral(IRE) —Distant Valley (Distant Relative)
4080[9] 4521[11]

Harriers Call (IRE) *J C Hayden* a55 75
3 b f Atraf—Bow Harrier (IRE) (Sri Pekan (USA))
6366a[2]

Harriet's Girl *K R Burke* 75
2 ch f Choisir(AUS) —Harriet (IRE) (Grand Lodge (USA))
2206[5] 2485[2] (3292) 3496[6] 5381[7] 6118[10]

Harrison George (IRE) *R A Fahey* a73 95
3 b c Danetime(IRE) —Dry Lightning (Shareef Dancer (USA))
1068[2] (2187) 2624[3] (3050) (3928) 4586[6] ◆ 5795[2] 6069[2]

Harrison's Flyer (IRE) *J M Bradley* a59 76
7 b g Imperial Ballet(IRE) —Smart Pet (Petong)
1268[7] 1646[9] 1997[5] 2242[8] 2330[5] 2478[5] 2881[7] 3313[8] 3520[5] 3724[5] 3872[3] 4125[2] 4370[9] 4535[9] 4812[4] 5121[7] 5751[8] 6895[2] 7197[7] 7255[7] 7503[2] 7653[5]

Harrison's Star *G M Moore* 49
3 gr g Erhaab(USA) —Gentle Gypsy (Junius (USA))
1429[7] 2926[4] 3671[14] 4247[6]

Harryana To *B J McMath* 52
3 ch f Compton Place—Harryana (Efisio)
2981[14] 3419[4] 4195[3] 4793[13] 5755[12]

Harry Gee *G Wragg* a82 79
3 b g Averti(IRE) —Mentro (IRE) (Entrepreneur)
136[5] ◆ 632[3] 799[6] 1600[7] 2699[4] 3561[6] 4128[4] 4983[6] 6734[5]

Harry Patch *M A Jarvis* 86
2 b g Lujain(USA) —Hoh Dancer (Indian Ridge)
(6764) (7241) ◆

Harry Raffle *S Kirk* a36 59
2 bb g Observatory(USA) —Encore My Love (Royal Applause)
4665[16] 5021[7] 5225[11] 5365[8] 7467[10] 7687[8] 7738[8]

Harry The Hawk *T D Walford* 76
4 b g Pursuit Of Love—Elora Gorge (IRE) (High Estate)
(1394) 1620[3] 2585[3] 3368[14] 6726[2] 6983[13]

Harry Tricker *G L Moore* a71 97
4 b g Hernando(FR) —Katy Nowaitee (Komaite (USA))
6061[11]

Harry Up *K A Ryan* a93 91
7 ch g Piccolo—Faraway Lass (Distant Relative)
45[2] 301[2] 580[7] (726) (1195) 1956[7] 2212[10] 3172[3] 4114[2] 4294[4] 5206[2] 6045[2] 6823[3] (7290) 7584[8] 7716[3]

Hart House *C J Gray* 24
2 b f Mull Of Kintyre(USA) —Mystic Beauty (IRE) (Alzao (USA))
5989[12] 6665[10] 6892[11]

Harting Hill *M P Tregoning* a55 52
3 b g Mujahid(USA) —Mossy Rose (King Of Spain)
2994[10] 3484[7] 4061[9] 4732[3] 5428[13] 6735[3] 7217[11]

Hartley *J D Bethell* 90
2 b g Lucky Story(USA) —Arctic Song (Charnwood Forest (IRE))
4415[9] (6110) 6972[8]

Hart Of Gold *R A Harris* a73 81
4 b g Foxhound(USA) —Bullion (Sabrehill (USA))
16[4] 421a[6] 603a[4] 782[4] 1145[4] 1268[3] (1561) 1842[5] 2798[6] 3169[3] 4154[3] 4370[4] 4535[12] 5171[2] 5315[3] 6750[4] 6864[5] (7254) 7378[8] 7611[10]

Hartshead *G A Swinbank* a84 94
9 b g Machiavellian(USA) —Zalitzine (USA) (Zilzal (USA))
1910[11] 2397[5] ◆ 2913[3] 3367[8] 3716[5] 4167[4] 4440[2] 4567[5] 6052[9] 6482[11]

Hartshead Flyer (IRE) *M J Wallace* a27
2 b g Modigliani(USA) —Along Came Molly (Dr Fong (USA))
1183[4] 6574[11]

Harts In Mo Shun (IRE) *A Berry* a51 46
4 b g Spectrum(IRE) —Offshoot (Zafonic (USA))
239[5]

Harvest Joy (IRE) *J Gallagher* a55 80
4 b m Daggers Drawn(USA) —Windomen (IRE) (Forest Wind (USA))
(1349) 1620[7] 2453[7] 2682[5] 3322[11] 4065[4] 4814[4]

Harvest Queen (IRE) *P J Makin* a107 110
5 ch m Spinning World(USA) —Royal Bounty (IRE) (Generous (IRE))
1807[2] 3120[10] 6475[8] 7099[2] 7420[3] 7741[7]

Harvest Song (IRE) *Sir Michael Stoute* 26
2 b c Sadler's Wells(USA) —La Mouline (IRE) (Nashwan (USA))
7200[12]

Harvest Warrior *T D Easterby* a72 85
6 gr g Mujahid(USA) —Lammastide (Martinmas)
5382[8] 5773[5] 6250[5] 6950[8] 7083[3] 7224[6] 7457[4] 7610[5]

Harveys Spirit (IRE) *S Curran* a51 62
3 ch f Rossini(USA) —Ex-Imager (Exhibitioner)
1855[7] 4564[10] 5611[9]

Harwalla (IRE) *M Johnston* 98
2 b c Desert Style(IRE) —Senebrova (Warning)
1474[2] ◆ 1770[2] (2217) 2838[2] 3103[16] 4190[6] 5244[10] 5827[17] 6483[9]

Hasanka (IRE) *John M Oxx* 109
4 b m Kalanisi(IRE) —Hasainiya (IRE) (Top Ville)
1882a[4] 3513a[5] 4833a[2] 5921a[5]

Hasanpour (IRE) *K J Burke* 76
8 b g Dr Devious(IRE) —Hasainiya (IRE) (Top Ville)
3250[14]

Hashbrown (GER) *C Sprengel* 99
4 b m Big Shuffle(USA) —Haraplata (GER) (Platini (GER))
2347a[5] 6323a[12]

Hassadin *A B Haynes* a64 53
2 ch g Reset(AUS) —Crocolat (Croco Rouge (IRE))
3267[12] 4861[4] 5909[3] 6330[7] 7353[10]

Has To Be Abacus (IRE) *A B Haynes* a54 48
3 br c Indian Lodge(IRE) —No Way (IRE) (Rainbows For Life (CAN))
704[6] 2611[4] 3264[6] 4182[8] 5577[5] 7605[7]

Hasty Lady *K A Ryan* a65 68
3 b f Dubai Destination(USA) —Hasten (USA) (Lear Fan (USA))
1302[4] 1867[10] 2699[7] 2946[8] (3640) 4115[2] 4332[9] 4919[6] 5377[2] 5638[6] 6048[13]

Hasty Retreat *E A L Dunlop* a65 76
3 br g King's Best(USA) —Madame Maxine (USA) (Dayjur (USA))
1367[9] (2367) ◆ 3116[5] 3612[8]

Hatch A Plan (IRE) *Mouse Hamilton-Fairley* a66 70
7 b g Vettori(IRE) —Fast Chick (Henbit (USA))
(44) 207[4] 526[9] 697[7] 3347[7] 4155[3] 4481[7] 4936[5] 5611[8] 6228[5] 6570[9] 6753[6]

Hatchet Man *P Winkworth* 62
2 ch g Needwood Blade—Mayfair (Green Desert (USA))
1693[12] 2324[12] 2859[5] 5488[4] 6207[14] 6787[7]

Hatman Jack (IRE) *B G Powell* a61
2 ch g Bahamian Bounty—Mary Hinge (Dowsing (USA))
7767[6] 7830[8]

Hattan (IRE) *C E Brittain* a116 116
6 ch h Halling(USA) —Luana (Shaadi (USA))
(906) 1596[2] 2230a[7] 2543[12] 3121[9] 4855[7] 5288[3] (5694) 6286[4]

Hatter's Way *R A Farrant* a30
3 ch f Compton Place—Fine Fettle (Final Straw)
748[13] 823[8] 1042[8] 1533[15]

Hatton Flight *A M Balding* a92 91
4 b g Kahyasi—Platonic (Zafonic (USA))
970[4] (1639) (2304) ◆ (3110) (3900) 4444[10] 6171[5] 6302[8]

Hat Trick Man *D Burchell*
7 gr g Daylami(IRE) —Silver Kristal (Kris)
541[11]

Haughton Hope *G Woodward* a35 38
5 b g Daawe(USA) —Kandymal (IRE) (Prince Of Birds (USA))
282[12]

Haulage Lady (IRE) *Karen McLintock* 65
2 b f Xaar—Blue Mantle (IRE) (Barathea (IRE))
3411[15] 4897[2] 5539[5] 5859[11] 6722[4]

Haulit *R A Harris* a46 55
2 b c Fraam—Amazing Bay (Mazilier (USA))
2473[8] 2987[8] 3417[9] 5116[5] 5606[12] 7645[8]

Havanavich *S Kirk* a65 70
3 b g Xaar—Queen Of Havana (USA) (King Of Kings (IRE))
1243[7] 2342[7] 3095[10] 3845[10] 4978[8] 5407[4] (5912) 6049[9] 6374[4] 6747[7]

Haven't A Clue *Sir Mark Prescott* a81 77
2 b f Red Ransom(USA) —Cool Question (Polar Falcon (USA))
2357[6] (2691) 2987[6] 3924[10] (4389) 4933[4] 5560[4]

Haveyouwonyet *L A Dace*
3 b f Hazaaf(USA) —Phar To Comfy (IRE) (Phardante (FR))
1840[9]

Having A Ball *P D Cundell* a69 54
4 b g Mark Of Esteem(IRE) —All Smiles (Halling (USA))
168[4] 328[2] 465[2] 587[5] 844[2] (1142) 1565[10] 1898[11] 5653[12] 6353[2] 6560[3] 7076[4] (7267) 7532[5]

Hawaana (IRE) *Eve Johnson Houghton* a77 79
3 b g Bahri(USA) —Congress (IRE) (Dancing Brave (USA))
1595[7] 2104[13] 3031[8] 5290[4] 5863[4] 6202[8] 6416[5] 6867[2] 7167[2]

Hawaass (USA) *M Johnston* 96
3 b c Seeking The Gold(USA) —Sheroog (USA) (Shareef Dancer (USA))
(3461) ◆

Hawaii Prince *S T Mason* a47 70
4 b g Primo Valentino(IRE) —Bollin Rita (Rambo Dancer (CAN))
113[5] 286[8] 370[8] 1624[14] 1997[2] 2145[3] 2596[8] 3112[18] 3401[6] 3594[5] 3868[16] 5398[15] 6339[16] 7706[12]

Hawa Khana (IRE) *N P Littmoden* a63 59
3 br f Indian Danehill(IRE) —Anearlybird (USA) (Sheikh Albadou)
81[3] 195[2] 335[2] (439) 534[2] 556[6] 704[10] 3407[9] 3817[6] 4386[8] 5684[6]

Hawkes Bay *D Hall* 110
6 b h Vettori(IRE) —Nordico Princess (Nordico (USA))
7685a[9]

Hawk Eyed Lady (IRE) *J A Osborne* a68 71
3 b f Hawk Wing(USA) —Danccini (IRE) (Dancing Dissident (USA))
2757[8] 3314[11] 4163[10] 4639[10] (5186) 5531[4] 5902[5]

Hawkeyethenoo (IRE) *M W Easterby* a45 56
2 b c Hawk Wing(USA) —Stardance (USA) (Rahy (USA))
4415[7] 5106[11] 5989[5] 6632[6]

Hawk Flight (IRE) *W R Muir* a75 75
3 b c Hawk Wing(USA) —Rapid Action (USA) (Quest For Fame)
1265[5] ◆ 2678[11] 3004[10] 3845[2] 4179[7] 5105[4] 5814[2] 6416[2] 6748[4] 6991[3]

Hawk Gold (IRE) *P Butler* a36 40
4 ch g Tendulkar(USA) —Heiress Of Meath (IRE) (Imperial Frontier (USA))
1563[9] 6719[12]

Hawk House *B W Hills* a62 66
3 gr g Alhaarth(IRE) —Arinaga (Warning)
610[3] 2564[9] 3004[5] 3886[3] 4332[3] 4721[2] 5780[3] 6378[9]

Hawk Island (IRE) *G Wragg* a65 83
3 b c Hawk Wing(USA) —Crimphill (IRE) (Sadler's Wells (USA))
1573[2] 2199[2]

Hawkit (USA) *P Monteith* a72 78
7 b g Silver Hawk(USA) —Hey Ghaz (USA) (Ghazi (USA))
2155[14] 2524[6] 3257[3] 3493[2] 3579[3] 3957[7] 4633[5] 4850[8] 4972[6] 6040[7]

Hawkleaf Flier (IRE) *T D Easterby* 52
2 b f Hawk Wing(USA) —Flyleaf (FR) (Persian Bold)
6013[8] 6212[4] 6381[6]

Hawk Mountain (UAE) *J J Quinn* 72
3 b g Halling(USA) —Friendly (USA) (Lear Fan (USA))
2700[6] 3555[3] (5077) ◆ 5637[2] 6529[2]

Hawksbury Heights *J J Lambe* 35
6 ch g Nashwan(USA) —Gentle Dame (Kris)
4848[8]

Hawk's Eye *E F Vaughan* a42 62
2 br g Hawk Wing(USA) —Inchiri (Sadler's Wells (USA))
5929[8] 6341[4] 7268[4]

Hawkspring (IRE) *S Parr* a59
2 b c Hawk Wing(USA) —Katavi (USA) (Stravinsky (USA))
7170[5] (7283) 7468[8] 7514[2] 7760[10] 7789[4]

Hawkspur (IRE) *R Hannon* 70
2 b c Hawk Wing(USA) —Lyric Fantasy (IRE) (Tate Gallery (USA))
2769[10] 4024[2] 4346[5] 4659[4] 4975[4] 6002[6]

Hawkstar Express (IRE) *J R Boyle* a50 56
3 b g Hawk Wing(USA) —Band Of Angels (IRE) (Alzao (USA))
1994[7] 2694[5] 2984[13] 3873[10] 5994[12] 6228[6] 6753[12]

Hawridge King *W S Kittow* a65 87
6 b g Erhaab(USA) —Sadaka (USA) (Kingmambo (USA))
1531[5] 1877[7] 2332[3] (3523) 4314[3] 5498[3] 6361[5] 6898[11]

Hawridge Prince *B R Millman* 107
8 b g Polar Falcon(USA) —Zahwa (Cadeaux Genereux)
1158[6] 1841[4] 3104[16] 5646[2]

Hawridge Star (IRE) *W S Kittow* a42 73
6 b g Alzao(USA) —Serenity (Selkirk (USA))
(5993)

Haydens Mark *D G Bridgwater* a83 64
3 b g Efisio—Lady In Colour (IRE) (Cadeaux Genereux)
(633) ◆ 1746[6] (1937) 4528[12] 6175[5] 6626[12] 7260[7] 7506[10]

Haydock Express (IRE) *Peter Grayson* a52
4 gr g Keltos(FR) —Blusienka (IRE) (Blues Traveller (IRE))
88[10]

Hay Fever (IRE) *Eve Johnson Houghton* a50 76
2 b g Namid—Allergy (Alzao (USA))
1413[7] 1736[2] 2554[2] 2987[2] ◆ 3888[2] 4367[2]

Hayley's Flower (IRE) *J C Fox* a57 45
4 b m Night Shift(USA) —Plastiqueuse (USA) (Quest For Fame)
122[5] 161[2] 299[11] 1938[6]

Hayley's Girl *S W James* a41 46
2 b f Deportivo—Eurolink Artemis (Common Grounds)
3456[15] 6282[8] 6559[7] 6776[12] 7097[10]

Hayley's Pearl *Mrs P Ford* a46
9 b m Nomadic Way(USA) —Pacific Girl (IRE) (Emmson)
144[5] 252[4] 490[5]

Hazelrigg (IRE) *T D Easterby* 83
3 b g Namid—Emma's Star (ITY) (Darshaan)
(1453) 1819[10] ◆ 3499[6] 4595[3] 5358[5]

Hazelwood Ridge (IRE) *James Bernard McCabe* a62 62
5 b g Mozart(IRE) —Aguilas Perla (IRE) (Indian Ridge)
6366a[9]

Hazeymm (IRE) *D Selvaratnam* a65 104
5 b g Marju(IRE) —Shimna (Mr Prospector (USA))
296a[3] 495a[4] 669a[9]

Hazy Dancer *M P Tregoning* a71
2 b f Oasis Dream—Shadow Dancing (Unfuwain (USA))
(6622) ◆

Hazytoo *S A Callaghan* a76 76
4 ch g Sakhee(USA) —Shukran (Hamas (IRE))
(1154) 1900[15] 2373[7] 2550[7] *2947[9]* 3653[6] *(4306)* *4946[9]*

Hazzard County (USA) *D M Simcock* a95 87
4 ch h Grand Slam(USA) —Sweet Lexy May (USA) (Danzig (USA))
1334[5] *1723[2]* 2905[8] *4089[2]* 4407[4] *5207[3]*

Headache *B W Duke* a57 53
3 b c Cape Cross(IRE) —Romantic Myth (Mind Games)
2786[12] 2994[9] 4278[11] *5684[2]* *6735[5]*

Head Down *R Hannon* a74 83
2 b c Acclamation—Creese (USA) (Diesis)
2146[5] 2562[8] 3219[2] *7311[8]* *7523[3]* *7655[2]*

Headford View (IRE) *James Halpin* a89 71
4 b m Bold Fact(USA) —Headfort Rose (IRE) (Desert Style (IRE))
4514a[6]

Heading East (IRE) *K A Ryan* 70
2 ch g Dubai Destination(USA) —Nausicaa (USA) (Diesis)
4214[5] 4497[4] 5304[3]

Headline Act *J H M Gosden* 79
2 ch c Dalakhani(IRE) —Daring Miss (Sadler's Wells (USA))
5859[3] ◆ 6199[2] (6926)

Head Of The River (IRE) *Daniel Mark Loughnane* 87
4 b g Galileo(IRE) —Vignelaure (IRE) (Royal Academy (USA))
1105a[10]

Head On (FR) *Mme C Head-Maarek* a74 74
3 ch f Smart Strike(CAN) —Heritiere (AUS) (Anabaa (USA))
7450a[11]

Head To Head (IRE) *A D Brown* a54 56
4 gr g Mull Of Kintyre(USA) —Shoka (FR) (Kaldoun (FR))
2703[10] 3953[9] 5044[2] 5501[10] 5770[7] *7323[7]* *7369[5]* *7727[4]* *7793[7]*

Head To Kerry (IRE) *D J S Ffrench Davis* a46 31
8 b g Eagle Eyed(USA) —The Poachers Lady (IRE) (Salmon Leap (USA))
5653[6]

Heart Alone (BRZ) *S Seemar* a5 65
7 b g Music Prospector(USA) —Sylicon Purple (BRZ) (Purple Mountain (USA))
205a[P] 492a[12]

Hearthstead Maison (IRE) *M Johnston* a107 117
4 b h Peintre Celebre(USA) —Pieds De Plume (FR) (Seattle Slew (USA))
4192[3] 4436[6] *5348[3]* *5743a[7]* (6201)

Heart Of Dubai (USA) *C E Brittain* a69 54
3 b c Outofthebox(USA) —Diablo's Blend (USA) (Diablo (USA))
1957[13] *2528[6]* *(3035)* 3641[7] *4344[8]* *6379[9]*

Heart Of Fire (IRE) *Kevin Prendergast* 98
2 b c Mujadil(USA) —Heart's Desire (IRE) (Royal Applause)
4005a[6] 5294a[2]

Heart Of Tuscany *W J Knight* a58 52
2 b f Falbrav(IRE) —Zarma (FR) (Machiavellian (USA))
5643[7] *6205[4]*

Heartsanddiamonds *A W Carroll* 40
4 ch m First Trump—La Volta (Komaite (USA))
1382[12] 1896[7] 2449[12] 3084[11] 3738[9]

Heartsease *J G Portman* a23 60
2 b f Pursuit Of Love—Balsamita (FR) (Midyan (USA))
2638[12] 3869[7] 4692[6] *5432[12]*

Heart Shaped (USA) *A P O'Brien* 110
2 ch f Storm Cat(USA) —Twenty Eight Carat (USA) (Alydar (USA))
3123[14] 3851[4] 6441[5] 6966a[2]

Heart Springs *Dr J R J Naylor* a21 54
8 b m Parthian Springs—Metannee (The Brianstan)
7696[7]

Heathyards Pride *R Hollinshead* a89 84
8 b g Polar Prince(IRE) —Heathyards Lady (USA) (Mining (USA))
3864[7] 4771[5] *7499[3]* *(7744)*

Heaven *P J Makin* a73 79
3 ch f Reel Buddy(USA) —Wedgewood Star (Bishop Of Cashel)
2102[3] ◆ 2774[2] *3332[2]* (3526) (4106) 4787[6] 5510[6] *6623[9]*

Heaven Knows *W J Haggas* a99 102
5 ch g Halling(USA) —Rambling Rose (Cadeaux Genereux)
1018[3] 1569[3] 1828[10] *3398[4]* 3974[9] 6233[2] (6649)

Heaven Knows When (IRE) *B W Hills* a45 50
2 b f Dansili—Change Partners (IRE) (Hernando (FR))
3610[6] 4827[4] 5778[10]

Heavenli Gift *S W Hall*
2 b f Bertolini(USA) —Heavenly Waters (Celestial Storm (USA))
6764[13]

Heavenly Encounter *K R Burke* a28
3 b f Lujain(USA) —Inchcoonan (Emperor Jones (USA))
38[4] *393[6]* *635[5]* 5457[11]

Heavenly Saint *R J Price* a58 58
3 b f Bertolini(USA) —Heavenly Glow (Shavian)
4669[11] 5119[14]

Heavenly Vision (USA) *Bob Baffert* a90
2 rg f Forestry(USA) —Holy Bubbette (USA) (Holy Bull (USA))
6500a[6]

Heaven Or Hell (IRE) *P D Evans* a21 63
2 b g Jammaal—Adjasalma (USA) (Lear Fan (USA))
(1264) 1384[3] 1480[8] 2450[2] 2671[3] 3008[7] 4119[8] 4203[4] *4475[4]* 5778[5]

Heaven Sent *Sir Michael Stoute* a103 115
5 ch m Pivotal—Heavenly Ray (USA) (Rahy (USA))
(1331) (1807) 3120[2] ◆ 3852[3] 4623[4] 6475[5]

Heaven's Gates *K A Ryan* a59 53
4 ch g Most Welcome—Arcady (Slip Anchor)
220[9]

Heavens Walk *P J Makin* a78 65
7 ch g Compton Place—Ghost Dancing (Lion Cavern (USA))
4324[9]

Hebridean (IRE) *A P O'Brien* 115
3 b g Bach(IRE) —Delphinium (IRE) (Dr Massini (IRE))
1232a[3] 1509a[2] (2435a) 3193[9] 4505[3] 6816[9]

Hector's House *M Dods* 70
2 b g Tobougg(IRE) —Thrasher (Hector Protector (USA))
6008[4] 6381[3] 6808[4]

Heidi Hi *J R Turner* a5 48
4 b m High Estate—Alwal (Pharly (FR))
1135[8]

Height Of Esteem *W M Brisbourne* a47 41
5 b g Mark Of Esteem(IRE) —Biscay (Unfuwain (USA))
4559[5] 4961[14] 5770[15]

Height Of Spirits *T D McCarthy* a47 52
6 b g Unfuwain(USA) —Kimono (IRE) (Machiavellian (USA))
242[5] *392[7]* *5577[7]*

Heights Of Golan *T J O'Mara* a71 61
4 br g Golan(IRE) —Nemesia (Mill Reef (USA))
4655a[9]

Hekaaya (IRE) *M P Tregoning* a53 35
2 b f Kheleyf(USA) —Victoria Regia (IRE) (Lomond (USA))
6072[10] 6600[11] *6879[6]*

Helene Mascot (IRE) *A S Cruz* a74 116
4 b h Peintre Celebre(USA) —Razana (IRE) (Kahyasi)
1666a[8]

Heliodor (USA) *R Hannon* 84
2 b c Scrimshaw(USA) —Playing Footsie (USA) (Valiant Nature (USA))
1523[2] ◆ 1832[4] 2972[6] 3941[2] 4974[4] 5244[11] 5585[4] 5827[13] (6199) 6561[2] (7142)

Hellbender (IRE) *S Kirk* a64 60
2 ch c Exceed And Excel(AUS) —Desert Rose (Green Desert (USA))
2601[7] 4274[10] 4665[14] 6531[6] *7454[2]* *(7794)*

Hellfire Bay *J Mackie* a63 56
3 b c Diktat—Composition (Wolfhound (USA))
158[3] *527[8]* *572[4]* 3407[6] 3886[14] *6712[12]*

Hello Broadway (USA) *Barclay Tagg* a97
2 ch c Broken Vow(USA) —Nightstorm (USA) (Storm Cat (USA))
6501a[5]

Hello Bunclody (IRE) *J S Bolger* 60
2 b f Galileo(IRE) —Rosa Delle Alpi (USA) (Royal Applause)
5549a[11]

Hello Man (IRE) *Eamon Tyrrell* a89 72
5 b g Princely Heir(IRE) —Mignon (Midyan (USA))
210[6] *707[7]*

Hello Morning (FR) *Mme C Head-Maarek* 116
3 gr c Poliglote—Hello Molly (FR) (Sillery (USA))
1361a[3] 2032a[5] 2654a[6] 3191a[5] 4473a[7] 5555a[6]

Hellzapoppin *D R Lanigan* a15 65
3 b c Mtoto—Pure (Slip Anchor)
2370[6] 3058[5] *3393[11]*

Helping Hand (IRE) *R Hollinshead* a68 69
3 b g Lend A Hand—Cardinal Press (Sharrood (USA))
74[5] *(261)* *489[6]* 1277[9] 1548[10] 2122[2] 2570[10] 3441[7] 4047[8] 6765[8] *7231[9]* *7399[5]* *7644[6]* (7808)

Helpmeronda *S A Callaghan* a50 61
2 b f Medicean—Lady Donatella (Last Tycoon)
3923[5] 4199[7] 4720[4] *5153[4]* 7052[10]

Hel's Angel (IRE) *Mrs A Duffield* 68
2 b f Pyrus(USA) —Any Dream (IRE) (Shernazar)
2657[3] 3277[3] 5539[2] 6008[3]

Helvetio *Micky Hammond* a18 72
6 b g Theatrical—Personal Love (USA) (Diesis)
1017[8] 1482[14]

Henderson Park *A G Foster* 92
2 ch c Bertolini(USA) —Armada Grove (Fleetwood (IRE))
4214[3] 5387[2] 6655[2] (6946)

Hendersyde (USA) *W R Swinburn* a77 83
3 ch c Giant's Causeway(USA) —Cimmaron Lady (USA) (Grand Slam (USA))
2612[5] 3094[5] 3573[3] *4344[3]* (4985) 6390[2]

Hennalaine (IRE) *Miss J S Davis* a59 37
3 b f Lujain(USA) —Daralaka (IRE) (The Minstrel (CAN))
3446[6] *6878[11]* 7018[16]

Hennessy Island (USA) *T G Mills* a61
3 ch g Hennessy(USA) —Heavenly Dawn (USA) (Holy Bull (USA))
656[2] ◆ *1592[2]* *7779[5]*

Henry James (IRE) *M Botti* a58 64
3 b c Iron Mask(USA) —Izibi (FR) (Saint Cyrien (FR))
225[7] *366[6]* *1034[5]*

Henrythenavigator (USA) *A P O'Brien* a125 128
3 br c Kingmambo(USA) —Sequoyah (IRE) (Sadler's Wells (USA))
(1808) ◆ (2418a) (3102) (4518) 5740a[5] 6270[2] *7001a[2]*

Hepburn Bell (IRE) *J R Fanshawe* a79 78
3 ch f Intikhab(USA) —Borsalino (USA) (Trempolino (USA))
1270[3] ◆ (1579) 2665[6] 4152[3] 5024[5] 5305[5] *6989[2]*

Hephaestus *Ian Williams* a52 67
4 b g Piccolo—Fragrant Cloud (Zilzal (USA))
7625[10]

Herakles (GER) *M Mullineaux* 59
7 b g Lagunas—Haraka (FR) (Kahyasi)
3258[8] 3756[10] 4972[5]

Herawati *T D Easterby* 18
2 b g Celtic Swing—Lady Of Jakarta (USA) (Procida (USA))
4780[12]

Herbert Crescent *Ollie Pears* a62 75
3 b g Averti(IRE) —With Distinction (Zafonic (USA))
5873a[5] *6511a[7]* *7277[10]* *7448[10]* *7698[12]*

Her Courtesy (IRE) *Jarlath P Fahey* a49 73
4 b m Fath(USA) —Wings Awarded (Shareef Dancer (USA))
4799a[3]

Herculaneum *M Johnston* 17
3 b g Rainbow Quest(USA) —Magna Graecia (IRE) (Warning)
3168[6] (Dead)

Here And How *M H Tompkins* a40 42
3 b f Where Or When(IRE) —Qilin (IRE) (Second Set (IRE))
4298[12] 4891[11] 6024[10]

Herecomesbella *Stef Liddiard* a44 27
2 b f Lujain(USA) —Blushing Belle (Local Suitor (USA))
1987[12] 2324[16] 3032[9] *3610[7]* 4337[12] *7694[4]*

Here Comes Danny *M Wigham* 31
2 b c Kyllachy—Clarice Orsini (Common Grounds)
7104[12]

Hereford Boy *D K Ivory* a84 87
4 ch g Tomba—Grown At Rowan (Gabitat)
1146[4] 1366[2] (1537) *2082[4]* 2644[9] 2828[11] *3320[3]* 3945[5] 4668[5] 5151[6] *6623[8]* *6881[2]* 7081[6] *7384[6]* *7621[4]*

Heritage Coast (USA) *Sir Michael Stoute* a74 84
3 b f Dynaformer(USA) —Bristol Channel (Generous (IRE))
1527[2] 3004[2] 3813[3]

Hermione's Magic *P J McBride* a71
2 ch f Systematic—Eleonor Sympson (Cadeaux Genereux)
(6488)

Hermoun (FR) *X Nakkachdji* 93
2 b c Septieme Ciel(USA) —Hermine (FR) (Kaldoun (FR))
7449a[3]

Her Name Is Rio (IRE) *Mrs S Lamyman* a57 68
3 ch f Captain Rio—L'Harmonie (USA) (Bering)
38[7] *(108)* *156[5]* *534[5]* *1117[5]* 1391[10] 1912[14] 2664[9] 2926[10] 6004[13]

Hernando Cortes *D McCain Jnr* 75
4 b h Sadler's Wells(USA) —Houseproud (USA) (Riverman (USA))
3473[6]

Hernando Royal *Dr R D P Newland* a90 96
5 b g Hernando(FR) —Louis' Queen (IRE) (Tragic Role (USA))
6288[11] 6817[11]

Hernando's Boy *K G Reveley* 74
7 b g Hernando(FR) —Leave At Dawn (Slip Anchor)
1137[4] 1559[P] 6790[12] 7177[5]

Heroes *J R Boyle* a84 95
4 b g Diktat—Wars (IRE) (Green Desert (USA))
1469[15] 1719[10] 3855[5] *5018[5]* 5588[2] *6598[5]* *7291[7]* *7457[11]*

Hero Heart *Jane Chapple-Hyam* a48 26
3 ch c Kyllachy—Rainy Day Song (Persian Bold)
146[9] *439[6]* 1124[7] *1339[3]* *1487[5]* 2463[10]

Heroic Fool *Miss Z C Davison* 39
3 ch c Arkadian Hero(USA) —Casarabonela (Magic Ring (IRE))
1123[14] 1536[4] 5749[12] 6003[15] 6192[11]

Heroic Lad *A B Haynes* a39 48
3 ch g Arkadian Hero(USA) —Erith's Chill Wind (Be My Chief (USA))
1549[6] 2454[12] *2612[10]* 3524[14] 4707[11]

Heron (IRE) *M R Hoad* a63 45
3 b g Invincible Spirit(IRE) —Alexander Express (IRE) (Sri Pekan (USA))
498[6] *780[3]* *917[4]* *1120[6]* *1370[6]* *1635[7]* 3872[5] 4336[4] 4725[13] 5186[11] 5533[13]

Heron Bay *G Wragg* a103 103
4 b h Hernando(FR) —Wiener Wald (USA) (Woodman (USA))
1076[8] 1629[5] 2202[4] 2625[7] 5264[5]

Heros Reward (USA) *Dale Capuano* 114
6 bb g Partner's Hero(USA) —Lifes Passage (USA) (Caveat (USA))
6994a[5]

Herrbee (IRE) *J L Spearing* a52 53
3 b g Mark Of Esteem(IRE) —Reematna (Sabrehill (USA))
265[11] *335[4]* *623[8]* *797[8]* *1051[11]* *1251[2]* 1364[P] *1586[9]* *2611[9]* 2861[9] *7605[12]*

Herrera (IRE) *R A Fahey* 69
3 b f High Chaparral(IRE) —Silk (IRE) (Machiavellian (USA))
2221[10] 2536[2] 3058[2] 3710[4] 4382[3] 4859[10]

Herring Senior (IRE) *P F I Cole* a63 65
2 bb c Kheleyf(USA) —Karenaragon (Aragon)
2117[6] 2584[7] 3254[3] 4185[6] 4776[6] *5473[3]* *6207[5]* *6694[4]*

Herschel (IRE) *G L Moore* a77 67
2 br c Dr Fong(USA) —Rafting (IRE) (Darshaan)
5469[12] 5812[6] 6197[6] 6673[5] *7190[4]* *(7505)*

He's A Humbug (IRE) *J O'Reilly* a82 91
4 b g Tagula(IRE) —Acidanthera (Alzao (USA))
1300[13] 1818[9] 2583[3] 3050[8] 3370[2] (3708) 4418[5] 4962[11] 5503[12] 5796[6] 6092[3] *6623[4]* 6859[5] *7317[4]* *7456[7]* *7592[2]* 7614[8] 7730[6]

He's Got Rhythm (IRE) *David Marnane* a79 82
3 b g Invincible Spirit(IRE) —Kathy Jet (USA) (Singspiel (IRE))
2283[2] *7325a[10]*

Hesketh (IRE) *R M Beckett* a36 54
2 b c Nayef(USA) —Agony Aunt (Formidable (USA))
4296[10] 4665[8] *5672[13]* 6394[10]

He's Mine Too *D G Bridgwater* a73 69
4 b g Indian Ridge—Screen Idol (IRE) (Sadler's Wells (USA))
240[6] *1605[5]* 2483[7] 2795[16] *4529[5]*

Hessian (IRE) *M D Squance* a78 73
4 b m Barathea(IRE) —Red Letter (Sri Pekan (USA))
910[6] *969[12]* *(1253)* *1604[4]* 1809[16] 2329[5] 2457[2] 2670[9] 2993[9] *5789[12]* 6125[19] *6880[7]* *7027[2]* 7307[8] 7386[5]

Hester Brook (IRE) *J G M O'Shea* a47 57
4 b m Soviet Star(USA) —Keen To Please (Keen)
400[8] *513[4]* *1269[7]* 2456[2] 2932[2] 3344[2] 3786[2] 4023[2] (4322) 4797[10] 4953[6]

Hettie Hubble *T D Easterby* 60
2 ch f Dr Fong(USA) —White Rabbit (Zilzal (USA))
4380[6] 4896[9] 6229[8]

Heureux (USA) *J Howard Johnson* 77
5 b h Stravinsky(USA) —Storm West (USA) (Gone West (USA))
2251[5] 3108[3] 4117[4] 4605[2]

Hevelius *W R Swinburn* 91
3 b c Polish Precedent(USA) —Sharp Terms (Kris)
2994[6] (3810)

Hey Byrn (USA) *Edward Plesa Jr* a103
3 b c Put It Back(USA) —Restraining Order (USA) (Skip Trial (USA))
2215a[7]

Hey Presto *R Rowe* a51 40
8 b g Piccolo—Upping The Tempo (Dunbeath (USA))
267[4] *392[6]* *(1269)* *1747[13]* *3371[10]*

Hey Up Dad *M Dods* 73
2 b g Fantastic Light(USA) —Spanish Quest (Rainbow Quest (USA))
4593[3] (6065)

Heywood *D Nicholls* a64 97
4 b g Tobougg(IRE) —Owdbetts (IRE) (High Estate)
958[13] 1174[9] 1942[7] 2358[2] (2778) 2905[7] 5446[2] 6277[12]

H Harrison (IRE) *I W McInnes* a68 91
8 b g Eagle Eyed(USA) —Penrose (IRE) (Wolfhound (USA))
1146[9] *1409[6]* *1604[7]* *1708[4]* 2397[4] 2778[2] 3087[6] 3203[6] 3435[7] 3646[8] 4174[4] 4460[5] *4862[2]* 5144[5] 5400[11] 5600[2] 6132[10] 6314[8] 7012[10]

Hiawatha (IRE) *A M Hales* a54 69
9 b g Danehill(USA) —Hi Bettina (Henbit (USA))
125[5] *695[2]* *934[14]*

Hibou De Nuit (IRE) *J R Boyle*
3 b g Night Shift(USA) —Mrs Pertemps (Ashkalani (IRE))
965[8] 1125[13]

Hi Calypso (IRE) *Sir Michael Stoute* 111
4 b m In The Wings—Threefold (USA) (Gulch (USA))
3246[9] 4549[7] 5333a[4]

Hiccups *M Dods* 89
8 b g Polar Prince(IRE) —Simmie's Special (Precocious)
1069[5] 1450[4] 1891[2] 3087[8] 3591[4] 3599[4] 5717[2] 7041[8]

Hi Dancer *P C Haslam* a58 63
5 b g Medicean—Sea Music (Inchinor)
1776[6] 2364[4] 2467[2] 3279[7] 6786[9]

Hidden Brief *M A Jarvis* 69
2 b f Barathea(IRE) —Hazaradjat (IRE) (Darshaan)
7054[4] ◆

Hieroglyph *M Johnston* a76 77
3 b f Green Desert(USA) —Mighty Isis (USA) (Pleasant Colony (USA))
25[4] *281[2]* *(366)*

Hi Fling *B J Meehan* 66
2 b c Oasis Dream—Crafty Buzz (USA) (Crafty Prospector (USA))
6029[7] 6778[6]

Higgy's Boy (IRE) *R Hannon* a76 96
3 b c Choisir(AUS) —Pagan Rhythm (USA) (Joanie's Chief (USA))
1244[4] *1543[2]* 1839[2] 2256[6] 2996[4] 3527[7] 4021[6] (4276) 4906[2] 5759[5] 6078[11] (6346) 6542[3]

Higha (FR) *P Demercastel* 97
2 b f Vettori(IRE) —High Mecene (FR) (Highest Honor (FR))
4472a[7] 5486a[2] 6520a[6] 7185a[6]

High Alert *J Noseda* a77 89
2 b c Kyllachy—Haste (Halling (USA))
(4304) 4968[2] 5585[2] 5791[6] 6474[11] (6717)

Highams Park (IRE) *J G Portman* 12
2 ch f Redback—Miss Caoimhe (IRE) (Barathea (IRE))
3674[16] *6016[13]*

High Class Problem (IRE) *D C O'Brien* a66 71
5 b g Mozart(IRE) —Sarah-Clare (Reach)
(176) 2758[8] *3162[10]* *7194[12]*

High Coincidence *Andrew Turnell* a49 39
3 bb g Diktat—Our Pleasure (IRE) (Lake Coniston (IRE))
2279[5] 3268[11] 3694[9] *5837[5]* *6374[5]* *6685[8]*

High Command *M W Easterby* a38 49
5 b g Galileo(IRE) —Final Shot (Dalsaan)
2623[10] *2867[7]* 3673[5] *4477[10]*

High Country (IRE) *Micky Hammond* a41 93
8 b g Danehill(USA) —Dance Date (IRE) (Sadler's Wells (USA))
770[6] *930[12]*

High Court Drama (IRE) *P D Deegan* a94 84
3 b c Theatrical—Mountain Law (USA) (Mountain Cat (USA))
(826a) *7235a[13]*

High Curragh *K A Ryan* a70 93
5 b g Pursuit Of Love—Pretty Poppy (Song)
1071[2] 1517[9] 2210[2] 2698[6] 3228[7] 3477[2] 3812[11] 4240[9] 4854[10] 5503[8] 6066[2] *7047[7]* 7239[20]

High Dee Jay (IRE) *A King* 51
3 b g High Chaparral(IRE) —Brogan's Well (IRE) (Caerleon (USA))
4334[9]

Highest Esteem *G L Moore* a74 55
4 b g Mark Of Esteem(IRE) —For More (FR) (Sanglamore (USA))
224[4] *406[5]* *7385[8]* *7545[5]*

High Five Society *S R Bowring* a64 58
4 b g Compton Admiral—Sarah Madeline (Pelder (IRE))
770[2] (804) (862) 1371[9] 4785[4] 5779[10] 6189[13] 6716[9] 6888[9] *7634[6]* ◆

High Heeled (IRE) *B W Hills* a79 85
2 b f High Chaparral(IRE) —Uncharted Haven (Turtle Island (IRE))
4157[2] 4554[6] *(5571)* ◆ 6319a[6]

High Lady *C R Egerton* 25
3 b f Pivotal—Ballerina Suprema (IRE) (Sadler's Wells (USA))
3094[13]

Highland Burn *D R C Elsworth* a66 47
2 gr f Indian Creek—Jilly Woo (Environment Friend)
5643[8] 6081[11] *6622[7]* 6857[16]

Highland Daughter (IRE) *C G Cox* 96
3 b f Kyllachy—Raysiza (IRE) (Alzao (USA))
1401[8] 1718[5] 2594[6] 3420[4] 3849[10] 5644[5]

Highland Flight *J S O Arthur* 38
10 gr m Missed Flight—In The Highlands (Petong)
(5002a)

Highland Glen *Sir Michael Stoute* 66
2 b c Montjeu(IRE) —Daring Aim (Daylami (IRE))
6778[7]

Highland Harvest *D R C Elsworth* a82 85
4 b h Averti(IRE) —Bee One (IRE) (Catrail (USA))
(314) 509 [3] (548) 910[4] 1365[3]

Highland Homestead *M R Hoad* a69 66
3 b g Makbul—Highland Rossie (Pablond)
1265[6] ◆ 1685[10] *3690[2]* 4086[6] *4477[7]* 4978[5] 5748[10] (6541) *(6754) 6882[8] 7216[6]*

Highland Laddie *C R Egerton* 72
3 ch g Lomitas—Sirena (GER) (Tejano (USA))
1556[6] 3459[6] 4077[8]

Highland Legacy *M L W Bell* 100
4 ch g Selkirk(USA) —Generous Lady (Generous (IRE))
(1625) ◆ 1916[5] 3490[18] 4843[7]

Highland Love *J T Stimpson* a60 72
3 b g Fruits Of Love(USA) —Diabaig (Precocious)
1161[4] 1575[2] 2272[4] 2785[14] (3436) 4244[2] (4964) 5502[4] 6487[4] 7202[3]

Highland Relish *George Baker* 10
3 b g Kyllachy—Branston Jewel (IRE) (Prince Sabo)
7084[8] *7317[14]*

Highland River *D R C Elsworth* a62 49
2 b g Indian Creek—Bee One (IRE) (Catrail (USA))
4826[12] 5158[13] 6085[15] *6573[2] 7258[2] (7468) 7623[7]*

Highland Song (IRE) *R F Fisher* a50 59
5 ch g Fayruz—Rose 'n Reason (IRE) (Reasonable (FR))
372[5] 437[3] 558[2] 719[5] 871[6] 1827[2] 3546[10] *7112[9]*

Highlands Skye *L Montague Hall* a12
4 b m Diktat—Manhattan Sunset (USA) (El Gran Senor (USA))
715[5]

Highland Starlight (USA) *C G Cox* a67
2 ch f Dixieland Band(USA) —Fran's Flash (USA) (Star De Naskra (USA))
6167[11] 6622[5]

Highland Storm *J G Given* a58 78
2 b c Storming Home—Real Emotion (USA) (El Prado (IRE))
3331[3] 3926[2] 4625[6] (5242) 5895[16] 6058[8] 6474[19]

Highland Venture (IRE) *D R C Elsworth* a32
3 b f Averti(IRE) —Bee One (IRE) (Catrail (USA))
1050[8]

Highland Warrior *P T Midgley* a50 88
9 b g Makbul—Highland Rowena (Royben)
994[5] 1386[3] 1451[3] ◆ 1624[9] 2583[12] 2760[2] 3171[3] 3370[5] (3784) (4950) (5260) 6066[4] 6164[3] 7081[10] 7222[4] *7323[9]*

Highly Acclaimed *Mrs A Duffield* 43
2 b f Acclamation—Ebba (Elmaamul (USA))
5219[3]

Highly Regal (IRE) *R A Teal* a61 57
3 b g High Chaparral(IRE) —Regal Portrait (IRE) (Royal Academy (USA))
2613[2] 2984[6] 4086[12] *5611[13] 6436[11] 7520[10] 7707[13]*

High Maintenance (FR) *A Fabre* 105
4 gr m Highest Honor(FR) —Fabulous Hostess (USA) (Fabulous Dancer (USA))
1663a[7] 4496a[2] 5956a[3] 7037a[5] 7429a[5]

High 'n Dry (IRE) *M A Allen* a75 75
4 ch m Halling(USA) —Sisal (IRE) (Danehill (USA))
463[5] 639[4] 806[4] ◆ *(938)* ◆ *1030[7] 1253[2] 1954[3]* 2457[4] *3036[3]* 4568[10] *4946[5]* 5458[13]

High Office *R A Fahey* a71 71
3 b g High Chaparral(IRE) —White House (Pursuit Of Love)
5387[3] 6213[2] ◆ *7073[5]*

High Plains (FR) *R Hannon* a67 69
3 ch c Golan(IRE) —Perusha (USA) (Southern Halo (USA))
1216[6] 1572[4] *2261[11]* 2917[15]

High Point (IRE) *G P Enright* a81 76
10 b g Ela-Mana-Mou—Top Lady (IRE) (Shirley Heights)
630[5] 880[8] 1856[7] 2091[4]

High Profit (IRE) *C J Mann* a61
4 ch g Selkirk(USA) —Spot Prize (USA) (Seattle Dancer (USA))
7560[7]

High Queen (IRE) *T Stack* 79
2 b f High Chaparral(IRE) —Lucky Achievement (USA) (St Jovite (USA))
4804a[RR]

High Reach *J G M O'Shea* a61 83
8 b g Royal Applause—Lady Of Limerick (IRE) (Thatching)
106[2] (167) 655[3] 1275[3] 2242[3] 2478[7] 3021[6] 3559[2] 3784[4] 4118[3] (4336) 4765[6] 4958[8]

High Ridge *J M Bradley* a78 73
9 ch g Indian Ridge—Change For A Buck (USA) (Time For A Change (USA))
2950[13] 3313[16] 3363[6] 4102[10]

High Rock (IRE) *J-C Rouget* 116
3 ch c Rock Of Gibraltar(IRE) —Hint Of Silver (USA) (Alysheba (USA))
(1362a) ◆ 2654a[4]

High Shanamara *P T Midgley*
3 b f High Estate—Shanamara (IRE) (Shernazar)
4651[11] 4877[11] 6055[16]

High Society Girl (IRE) *T D Easterby* 21
2 b f Key Of Luck(USA) —Touch And Love (IRE) (Green Desert (USA))
4328[10] 4780[13]

High Standing (USA) *S A Callaghan* a87 92
4 bb g High Yield(USA) —Nena Maka (Selkirk (USA))
(2276) 3270[2] *4060[2]*

High Tensile *J G Given* 24
2 b f Diktat—Shifty Mouse (Night Shift (USA))
6381[7] 6789[20]

High Voltage *Mrs J L Le Brocq* 73
7 ch g Wolfhound(USA) —Real Emotion (USA) (El Prado (IRE))
5002a[3]

Highway (IRE) *F Castro* a94 75
5 b g King's Theatre(IRE) —Havinia (Habitat)
2233a[4] 2708a[11]

Highway Magic (IRE) *A P Jarvis* a37 66
2 ch c Rainbow Quest(USA) —Adultress (IRE) (Ela-Mana-Mou)
2972[16] 4062[5] 6777[8] *7209[10]*

High Window (IRE) *G P Kelly* a47 65
8 b g King's Theatre(IRE) —Kayradja (IRE) (Last Tycoon)
153[2] 254[5] 371[6] 2491[3] 3231[9] 3638[3] 4653[4] 4898[12]

Hi Hopes *T G Mills* a55
3 ch g Where Or When(IRE) —Chelsea (USA) (Miswaki (USA))
1243[5]

Hilbre Court (USA) *B P J Baugh* a87 75
3 br g Doneraile Court(USA) —Glasgow's Gold (USA) (Seeking The Gold (USA))
799[7] 3134[4] 3527[10] 3911[7] *4181[DSQ]* 4429[2] *4528[3] 4731[3] 5209[7] (5377) 5607[4]* 6283[5] 6452[9] 6659[2] 6989[10] 7758[11]

Hilbre Point (USA) *B J Meehan* 47
2 b c Giant's Causeway(USA) —Lady Carla (Caerleon (USA))
7106[10]

Hill Billy Rock (IRE) *G A Swinbank* a51 78
6 b g Halling(USA) —Polska (USA) (Danzig (USA))
1219[5] 1482[5] (1773) 2332[7] *7797[9]*

Hill Cloud *W M Brisbourne* a50 40
6 gr g Cloudings(IRE) —Hill Farm Dancer (Gunner B)
4879[11] 5752[11]

Hill Cross (IRE) *Mrs A Duffield* 59
2 b g Barathea(IRE) —Darayna (IRE) (Shernazar)
2845[6] 3411[10] 6480[12] 7016[17]

Hill Fairy *J Morrison* 65
6 ch m Monsun(GER) —Homing Instinct (Arctic Tern (USA))
(4655a)

Hill Of Clare (IRE) *G H Jones* a17 44
6 gr m Daylami(IRE) —Sarah-Clare (Reach)
822[10] 1896[5] 3419[6] 4123[10] 4365[7]

Hill Of Lujain *Ian Williams* a64 67
4 b g Lujain(USA) —Cinder Hills (Deploy)
334[8]

Hillside Lad *R M Beckett* a72
2 b g Tobougg(IRE) —Cumbrian Concerto (Petong)
7191[9] 7356[3] 7674[2] (7802)

Hills Of Aran *W K Goldsworthy* 53
6 b g Sadler's Wells(USA) —Danefair (Danehill (USA))
6203[10] 6606[9]

Hilltop Artistry *S W James* a29 44
2 b c Polish Precedent(USA) —Hilltop (Absalom)
6029[9] 6438[9] *7098[12]*

Hilltop Legacy *S W James* a9 19
5 b m Danzig Connection(USA) —Hilltop (Absalom)
5608[13] 6003[11]

Himalya (IRE) *J Noseda* 106
2 b c Danehill Dancer(IRE) —Lady Miletrian (IRE) (Barathea (IRE))
(2592) ◆ 3103[4] ◆

Himariya (IRE) *J-C Rouget* 90
3 b f Marju(IRE) —Hariya (IRE) (Shernazar)
7635a[0]

Hindford Oak Sioux *Mrs L Williamson* 62
2 b f Green Card(USA) —Sharp Susy (Beveled (USA))
6013[10] 6273[5]

Hindu Kush (IRE) *A P O'Brien* 110
3 b c Sadler's Wells(USA) —Tambora (Darshaan)
1233a[4] 2023a[4] 3535a[10] 5892[4] 6324a[8] 6494a[5]

Hint Of Honey *A G Newcombe* a37
2 ch f King Charlemagne(USA) —Jugendliebe (IRE) (Persian Bold)
7275[7]

Hinton Admiral *R A Fahey* a88 106
4 b g Spectrum(IRE) —Shawanni (Shareef Dancer (USA))
959[14] 1483[4] 1809[22] 2172[3] 2595[2] 3197[23] 3921[16] 4624[18] 5109[13] 5495[11] 6277[7] *6911[6] 7215[6] 7496[5] 7755[5]*

Hip *E A L Dunlop* a75 89
3 b f Pivotal—Hypnotize (Machiavellian (USA))
2196[9] 3272[3] 3852[10] *6471[9]*

Hip Hip Hooray *L A Dace* a61 65
3 ch f Monsieur Bond(IRE) —Birthday Belle (Lycius (USA))
2048[6] 2865[2] 3652[3] (4925) 5228[5] *6207[2]* 6761[4] 7016[8]

Hippodrome (IRE) *G L Moore* a66 74
6 b g Montjeu(IRE) —Moon Diamond (Unfuwain (USA))
3613[8]

Hippolytus *J J Quinn* 72
3 ch g Observatory(USA) —Pasithea (IRE) (Celtic Swing)
1751[2] 2269[3] 3628[3] 4180[4] 4737[3]

His Greatness (USA) *Marco P Salazar* a95
2 ch c Honour And Glory(USA) —Klair Alley (USA) (Well Decorated (USA))
6503a[6]

Hi Shinko *B R Millman* 75
2 b g Shinko Forest(IRE) —Up Front (IRE) (Up And At 'Em)
2916[10] 3417[7] 4907[2] 5459[2] 5959[2] 6426[15]

Hi Spec (IRE) *Miss M E Rowland* a51 49
5 b m Spectrum(IRE) —Queen Of Fibres (IRE) (Scenic)
236[3] 365[9] (684) 1064[4] 1313[10] 1700[5] 1906[6] 2866[5] 7631[12] (7736)

Hiss And Boo *P Howling* a50
3 ch g Starborough—Royal Lady (IRE) (Royal Academy (USA))
163[6] 514[6] 1937[7] 2611[12] 3115[7]

Historical Giant (USA) *E F Vaughan* a46 57
3 ch g Giant's Causeway(USA) —Onima (USA) (Jade Hunter (USA))
5366[6] 6566[10] *7010[8]*

Historic Place (USA) *J A Geake* a56 56
2 b g Dynaformer(USA) —Captive Island (Northfields (USA))
3820[5] 4391[10] 4935[8] 5367[6] 5752[3] 5993[5] 6861[10]

History Lesson *R Hannon* a84 77
2 ch c Golan(IRE) —Once Upon A Time (Teenoso (USA))
5053[6] 6122[2] *6731[2]*

History Prize (IRE) *A G Newcombe* a47
5 b g Celtic Swing—Menominee (Soviet Star (USA))
678 377[8]

Hitchens (IRE) *G L Moore* a104 111
3 b c Acclamation—Royal Fizz (IRE) (Royal Academy (USA))
(3504) 4405[17] 4624[11] 6269[19] *6903[3]*

Hitches Dubai (BRZ) *D Nicholls* 27
3 ch c A Good Reason(BRZ) —Orquidea Vermelha (BRZ) (Lucence (USA))
6791[9]

Hits Only Cash *J Pearce* a73 70
6 b g Inchinor—Persian Blue (Persian Bold)
506[5] 685[5] 1368[10] *1605[2]* 2087[7] 2510[3] *3371[8]* 3903[6] 4489[5] 5088[2] 5755[8] 6056[6] 6544[10] *6825[12]*

Hits Only Jude (IRE) *P A Blockley* a89 83
5 gr g Bold Fact(USA) —Grey Goddess (Godswalk (USA))
(256) ◆ *(347) 362[2] (636) 833[3]* 1278[4] 1891[5] 2679[10]

Hits Only Time *P A Blockley* a55 52
3 ch g Bertolini(USA) —South Wind (Tina's Pet)
556[4] 2991[6] ◆ 5307[9]

Hits Only Vic (USA) *D Carroll* a43 100
4 b g Lemon Drop Kid(USA) —Royal Family (USA) (Private Terms (USA))
2286[5] 2364[2] (2701) (3059) (3143) 3368[2] 3832[2] 4046[2] (5992) (6410) 6817[14] 7244[5]

Hit The Roof *J G Given* a73 69
3 b g Auction House(USA) —Rave On (ITY) (Barathea (IRE))
52[6] 135[4] (572) 723[8] 820[9] 900[9] 7367[9] *7513[12]*

Hit The Switch *R A Fahey* a53 70
2 b g Reset(AUS) —Scenic Venture (IRE) (Desert King (IRE))
5798[6] (6158) 6525[10]

Hla Tun (USA) *W R Swinburn* a57 47
3 b g Johannesburg(USA) —Sophie (USA) (Pulpit (USA))
796[8] 1247[7] 1592[3] 2639[8] *3397[7]* 4531[7] *5152[7]*

Hoar Frost *M R Channon* a48 57
3 b f Fraam—Natalie Jay (Ballacashtal (CAN))
773[6] 919[10] 2197[11] 2719[10] (2941) 3580[8] 4147[2] 4564[3] *5833[7]* 6111[4] 6541[5] 6747[9] (6883) *7010[7]*

Hobby *R M Beckett* 100
3 b f Robellino(USA) —Wydah (Suave Dancer (USA))
2149[3] 3153[3] 5329a[4] 6241[8]

Hoboob (USA) *J L Dunlop* 49
2 ch f Seeking The Gold(USA) —Bint Salsabil (USA) (Nashwan (USA))
4870[12]

Hobson *Eve Johnson Houghton* a76 76
3 b g Choisir(AUS) —Educating Rita (Emarati (USA))
1110[2] 1584[9] 1995[9] 2690[5] 3363[13] 4154[10] 4333[3] 5639[4] 6746[4] *7226[11]*

Hogmaneigh (IRE) *S C Williams* a72 112
5 b g Namid—Magical Peace (IRE) (Magical Wonder (USA))
1442[5] 1809[6] 2828[4] 5109[8] (5890) 6104[17] 6514a[3] 6653[4]

Hoh Hoh Hoh *R J Price* a63 111
6 ch g Piccolo—Nesting (Thatching)
959[15] 1157[2] 1831[6] 1986[6] 3504[2] 3948[7] 4188[8] 4624[21] (5509) 5890[17]

Hoh Mike (IRE) *M L W Bell* 115
4 ch h Intikhab(USA) —Magical Peace (IRE) (Magical Wonder (USA))
2106[5] 2680[5] 3101[5] 3739[3] 4159[6] 5259[7] 6005[2] 6429[9]

Hoh Wotanite *R Hollinshead* a90 82
5 ch h Stravinsky(USA) —West One (Gone West (USA))
958[20] *1711[5]* 1920[6] 2334[5] 2595[14] (Dead)

Holamo (IRE) *M Botti* a59 73
2 br f Montjeu(IRE) —Holy Nola (USA) (Silver Deputy (CAN))
5571[6] 6291[3] 6887[3]

Holbeck Ghyll (IRE) *A M Balding* a97 99
6 ch g Titus Livius(FR) —Crimada (IRE) (Mukaddamah (USA))
(1047) (1415) ◆ 2195[2] (2828)

Holberg (UAE) *M Johnston* a82 75
2 ch c Halling(USA) —Sweet Willa (USA) (Assert)
5500[6] 5859[4] 6602[5] *(7371) (7623)*

Holden Caulfield (IRE) *Mouse Hamilton-Fairley* a51 51
3 b g Catcher In The Rye(IRE) —God Speed Her (Pas De Seul)
1193[6] 1533[6] *2259[2]* 2639[4] 2915[8]

Holden Eagle *A G Newcombe* 79
3 b c Catcher In The Rye(IRE) —Bird Of Prey (IRE) (Last Tycoon)
2919[6] 3629[4] ◆ 4818[2] 5491[8] 6950[3]

Hold Fire *A W Carroll* a56 4
4 b m Lear Spear(USA) —Kahyasi Moll (IRE) (Brief Truce (USA))
727[10] 931[8] 1144[9] 2003[13]

Hold Me Love Me (IRE) *A P O'Brien* 97
3 b f Sadler's Wells(USA) —Jude (Darshaan)
3805a[10] 4100a[5] 4833a[5] 5826[3] 6494a[7]

Hold That Call (USA) *A J Chamberlain* a56 67
3 ch g Hold That Tiger(USA) —Rainbow Master (USA) (Entropy (USA))
125 403[5] 523[5] 1187[6] 1533[16] 2935[7] *4523[6] 4943[6] 5406[P]*

Hold The Bucks (USA) *J S Moore* a66 57
2 b g Hold That Tiger(USA) —Buck's Lady (USA) (Alleged (USA))
3091[8] 3225[2] 3706[3] *4340[2]* 5006[9] 5460[8] *5606[2] 5914[6] 7257[6] 7338[3] (7415) (7519)* 7718[4]

Hold The Gold (IRE) *E J O'Neill* a84 75
3 b c Danehill Dancer(IRE) —Ashkirk (Selkirk (USA))
3251[9] *6467[7] 6757[8] 7116[2] 7291[9] 7457[3] 7526[5] 7712[2]*

Hold The Star *E F Vaughan* a56
2 b f Red Ransom(USA) —Sydney Star (Machiavellian (USA))
6167[8]

Holiday Cocktail *J J Quinn* a69 81
6 b g Mister Baileys—Bermuda Lily (Dunbeath (USA))
1159[14] 1729[3] 2375[8] 2697[8] (3226) 3551[3] (3814) 4015[7] (4458) (4739) 5040[3] 6113[7]

Hollander (IRE) *D J Coakley* a84
3 b g Fasliyev(USA) —Pietra Dura (Cadeaux Genereux)
(1490)

Hollins *Micky Hammond* 74
4 b g Lost Soldier(USA) —Cutting Reef (IRE) (Kris)
2363[2] 2735[3] 3835[2] 5042[5] 5718[10]

Hollow Dream (IRE) *R A Harris* a40
3 b f Beat Hollow—Sarah's Dream (IRE) (Lion Cavern (USA))
195[7]

Hollow Green (IRE) *P D Evans* a41 60
2 b f Beat Hollow—Three Greens (Niniski (USA))
2253[8] 3603[11] 4604[4] 5041[4] (5778) 6214[8] *6632[10]* 7079[2] *7258[11] 7505[7] 7659[13]*

Hollow Jo *J R Jenkins* a75 54
8 b g Most Welcome—Sir Hollow (USA) (Sir Ivor (USA))
275[8] 515[6] (620) 746[3] 901[3] 1242[6] 1541[10] 2947[11] 3371[7] 3506[8] 4084[9] 5401[9] 6774[7] 7255[6] 7383[7] 7644[3] 7808[6]

Hollow Point (IRE) *P T Midgley* a61
3 b g Cherokee Run(USA) —Squeak (Selkirk (USA))
321[3] 458[6] 1057[10] 1487[8] 1626[12]

Holly Cleugh *J R Fanshawe* 54
3 ch f Compton Place—True Precision (Presidium)
2341[6] 2824[4] 4301[6]

Holly Golightley *K A Ryan* a60 60
3 b f Choisir(AUS) —Breakfast Bay (IRE) (Charnwood Forest (IRE))
112[2]

Holly Hawk (IRE) *Kevin F O'Donnell* 75
3 br f Dubai Destination(USA) —Kardashina (FR) (Darshaan)
5550a[9]

Hollywood George *Miss M E Rowland* a57 55
4 b h Royal Applause—Aunt Tate (Tate Gallery (USA))
901[11] 1491[10] 1966[11] 2597[6] *2806[4]* 3201[14] 4414[2] 4863[7] *6251[10] 6419[8] 6912[12] 7049[3]* 7316[6] 7375[9] 7582[2] 7625[7] 7746[7]

Holocene (USA) *P Bary* a87 114
4 bb h Lemon Drop Kid(USA) —Witching Hour (FR) (Fairy King (USA))
1761a[5] 2876a[9] 5555a[3] 6498a[8]

Holst (IRE) *T D Easterby* 30
2 b c Distant Music(USA) —Classic Ring (IRE) (Auction Ring (USA))
1392[7] 3107[9] 3706[11] 4203[11]

Holyfield Warrior (IRE) *I A Wood* a55 28
4 b g Princely Heir(IRE) —Perugino Lady (IRE) (Perugino (USA))
341[3] (542)

Holyrood *Sir Michael Stoute* 80
2 b g Falbrav(IRE) —White Palace (Shirley Heights)
3853[4] ◆ 4625[7] 6117[3] ◆

Holy Storm (IRE) *Eve Johnson Houghton* 48
3 b g Mujahid(USA) —Slupia (IRE) (Indian Ridge)
1586[11] 1871[12]

Home *C Gordon* a73 71
3 b g Domedriver(IRE) —Swahili (IRE) (Kendor (FR))
(73) (156) 266[3] 712[4] (865) 1034[2] 1364[7] *1678[4] (2080)* 4664[3] 5504[7] *7385[10] 7606[9]*

Home Before Dark *R M Whitaker* a39 49
2 b g Bertolini(USA) —Compton Girl (Compton Place)
4169[7] 5106[4] 6010[7] *6281[11] 6573[9]*

Homebound (USA) *J-C Rouget* 99
2 b f Dixie Union(USA) —Black Speck (USA) (Arch (USA))
(5486a) 6891a[4]

Home Call (USA) *C Von Der Recke* 99
6 b h Chester House(USA) —Call Account (USA) (Private Account (USA))
605a[11]

Hometown *J H M Gosden* a69 69
2 b f Storming Home—Nazoo (IRE) (Nijinsky (CAN))
6205[5] 6884[2] *(7282)*

Honduras (SWI) *G L Moore* a92 95
7 gr g Daylami(IRE) —High Mare (FR) (Highest Honor (FR))
569[4]

Honestly (USA) *B J Meehan* a36
2 b f Yes It's True(USA) —Sweetheart (USA) (Mr Prospector (USA))
5835[15]

Honest Quality (USA) *H R A Cecil* 98
2 b f Elusive Quality(USA) —Honest Lady (USA) (Seattle Slew (USA))
2160[3] (2627) (4348) 6982[6]

Honest Value (IRE) *Mrs L C Jewell* a57 56
3 b g Chevalier(IRE) —Sensimelia (IRE) (Inzar (USA))
514[5] 767[2] 928[2] 1162[5] 2074[9] 5911[10] 6419[13] 6907[10] 7808[10]

Honest Yankee (USA) *Mrs L C Jewell* a23 32
3 ch g Yankee Gentleman(USA) —Tresor (USA) (Pleasant Tap (USA))
547[7] 674[8] 1166[14]

Honeycott (IRE) *J D Bethell* 49
3 ch f King's Best(USA) —Kingsridge (IRE) (King's Theatre (IRE))
2208[15] 2915[9] 3644[6] 4332[7] 7736[12]

Honey Monster (IRE) *A J McCabe* a89 85
3 ch g Choisir(AUS) —Caribbean Escape (Pivotal)
1204[2] (1339) 2945[3] (3136) (3394) 3723[4] 3850[11] 4341[5]

Honeypot Splenda *H S Howe*
3 sk f Stetsen—Balfour Lady (Absalom)
5750[11]

Hongkong Superstar (USA) *Jeffrey D Thornbury*
2 u c (USA) — (USA) (Carson City (USA))
6502a[7]

Honimiere (IRE) *G A Swinbank* 70
2 b f Fasliyev(USA) —Sugar (Hernando (FR))
1770[4] 2534[4] 6013[4]

Honkey Tonk Tony (IRE) *Luke Comer* a55 78
3 b c On The Ridge(IRE) —Lisa's Girl (IRE) (Distinctly North (USA))
823[5]

Honky Tonk Sally *M L W Bell* a76 83
3 b f Dansili—Flower Girl (Pharly (FR))
1332[8] 2532[9]

Honolulu (IRE) *A P O'Brien* 121
4 b h Montjeu(IRE) —Cerulean Sky (IRE) (Darshaan)
2169[4] (3250) 4551[6] (5854) 7188a[21]

Honorable Endeavor *E F Vaughan* a46 50
2 b g Law Society(USA) —Lilac Dance (Fabulous Dancer (USA))
3267[13] 5165[8] 5599[4] 7543[5]

Honorable Love *M Dods* 80
4 ch m Highest Honor(FR) —Everlasting Love (Pursuit Of Love)
(1329) 5391[8] 6293[8]

Honoria (IRE) *A P O'Brien* 106
3 b f Sadler's Wells(USA) —Tedarshana (Darshaan)
3805a[3] 4006a[9] 4833a[6] 5952a[12] 6495a[11]

Honour Devil (ARG) *M F De Kock* a121
4 b h Honour And Glory(USA) —Diamond Fitz (ARG) (Fitzcarraldo (ARG))
(292a) (567a) ◆ 813a[2] (1088a)

Honoured Guest (IRE) *A P O'Brien* 113
4 b h Danehill(USA) —Wind Silence (USA) (A.P. Indy (USA))
1355a[9] 2106[11] 3100[11] 5740a[10] 6270[6]

Honours Stride (IRE) *Sir Michael Stoute* a47 69
2 b f Red Ransom(USA) —Dance Parade (USA) (Gone West (USA))
5788[11] 6360[3]

Hopeful Purchase (IRE) *J R Gask* a83 58
5 ch g Grand Lodge(USA) —Funoon (IRE) (Kris)
1857[11] 5290[8] 5789[3] 6170[9] 6490[11] 6736[11] 7009[12]

Hope Junior (USA) *B J Meehan* a19 19
2 rg g Strong Hope(USA) —L'Amour Toujours (USA) (Blushing Groom (FR))
6604[15] 7312[13]

Hopes And Fears (IRE) *J-C Rouget* a93 105
3 b c Captain Rio—Saibhreas (IRE) (Last Tycoon)
4473a[8] 5927a[3]

Hora *Sir Mark Prescott* a79 63
4 b m Hernando(FR) —Applecross (Glint Of Gold)
(283) ◆ 345[3]

Horatio Carter *K A Ryan* 84
3 b g Bahamian Bounty—Jitterbug (IRE) (Marju (IRE))
1297[16] 1556[12] 3280[7] (3717) 4453[3] (4682) 4951[2] 5717[9]

Hornpipe *M Hill* a65 73
6 b g Danehill(USA) —Dance Sequence (USA) (Mr Prospector (USA))
518[8] 585[12]

Horseford Hill *D R C Elsworth* a85 90
4 b g In The Wings—Love Of Silver (USA) (Arctic Tern (USA))
3060[2] ◆ 3925[8] 5249[9] 5699[6] ◆ 6361[8]

Horsley Warrior *E S McMahon* 60
2 b c Alhaarth(IRE) —Polish Lake (Polish Precedent (USA))
6580[3] ◆

Hosanna *B J Meehan* a67 54
2 b f Oasis Dream—Rada's Daughter (Robellino (USA))
2160[8] 3456[12] 4157[15] 5535[5] 5937[5] 6730[2]

Hostess (USA) *J H Bond* 109
5 bb m Chester House(USA) —Charge Daffaires (USA) (Vice Regent (CAN))
6505a[7]

Host Nation *Miss Venetia Williams* 111
5 b g Grand Lodge(USA) —Hunt The Sun (Rainbow Quest (USA))
6820[4]

Hot Bertie *Peter Grayson* a51 55
3 b g Bertolini(USA) —Desert Dawn (Belfort (FR))
855[3] 953[5] 1073[9] 1674[6] (2268) 5141[8]

Hot Diamond *P J Hobbs* a62 89
4 b g Desert Prince(IRE) —Panna (Polish Precedent (USA))
2202[5]

Hotel Du Cap *G Wragg* a92 103
5 br h Grand Lodge(USA) —Miss Riviera Golf (Hernando (FR))
1619[8] 5070[7] 6073[14]

Hotel Felix *Miss Gay Kelleway* 43
3 ch g Best Of The Bests(IRE) —Jaljuli (Jalmood (USA))
1549[7] 2926[8]

Hot Fudge (SWE) *L Reuterskiold Jr* 80
5 ch m Lomitas—Christian Church (IRE) (Linamix (FR))
4676a[6] 5336a[2]

Hotham *N Wilson* a85 90
5 b g Komaite(USA) —Malcesine (IRE) (Auction Ring (USA))
2356[6] 3050[3] 3601[6] 3973[7] 4171[2] 4246[4] 4854[5] 5222[11] 5796[8] (6066) 6232[3] 6449[2] (6651) 6810[9] 6971[7] 7222[8]

Hot Marta *L Reuterskiold Jr*
3 b f Hernando(FR) —Seditieuse (IRE) (Night Shift (USA))
4918a[10]

Hotstufanthensome (USA) *Teresa Pompay* 105
8 b g Awesome Again(CAN) —Don't Read My Lips (USA) (Turkoman)
5928a[6]

Houdella *B P J Baugh*
2 b f Josr Algarhoud(IRE) —Norbella (Nordico (USA))
4923[11]

Houghton (IRE) *Sir Michael Stoute* a76 74
3 b c Sadler's Wells(USA) —Love And Affection (USA) (Exclusive Era (USA))
1446[4] 4372[3] 5963[3] (6226) 6630[6]

Houri (IRE) *J T Stimpson* a59 79
3 b f Alhaarth(IRE) —Witching Hour (IRE) (Alzao (USA))
1695[10] 2043[6] (2956) ◆ 3421[2] 4669[2] 5428[4] 6028[8] 6379[8] 6991[6] 7447[12]

House *L M Cumani* a78 98
3 b c Elusive Quality(USA) —Eurolink Raindance (IRE) (Alzao (USA))
(3031) ◆ 4553[2]

House Martin *C R Dore* a35 60
6 bb m Spectrum(IRE) —Guignol (IRE) (Anita's Prince)
769[9] 821[9]

House Of Bourbon (IRE) *C F Swan* a61 46
5 ch g Rainbow Quest(USA) —Her Ladyship (Polish Precedent (USA))
4493a[19]

House Of Lords (USA) *M L W Bell* a80 81
3 bb g Doneraile Court(USA) —Farrfesheena (USA) (Rahy (USA))
(974) ◆ 1543[5] 2412[4] ◆ 4906[7] 5472[8] 6256[7]

House Of Tudor *David Pinder* a15 66
3 b g Medicean—Wrong Bride (Reprimand)
1527[9] 1962[13] 3206[11] 4086[10] 4334[8] 5379[8] 5748[11] 6541[14]

Houston Dynimo (IRE) *Kevin Prendergast* a70 90
3 b c Rock Of Gibraltar(IRE) —Quiet Mouse (USA) (Quiet American (USA))
1233a[3]

Hovman (DEN) *Ms C Erichsen* a85 95
9 ch g Kateb(IRE) —Skee The Feen (Viking (USA))
5335a[12]

Howard *J L Dunlop* 72
2 ch c Haafhd—Dolores (Danehill (USA))
3495[6] 4150[5] 6292[7]

Howards Dream (IRE) *D A Nolan*
10 b g King's Theatre(IRE) —Keiko (Generous (IRE))
1824[12]

Howards Hope *Miss L A Perratt* a59 60
3 ch g Kyllachy—Howards Heroine (IRE) (Danehill Dancer (IRE))
3790[6] 4115[8] 4241[9] 4680[6] 5388[6] 5565[8]

Howards Prince *D A Nolan* a6 48
5 gr g Bertolini(USA) —Grey Princess (IRE) (Common Grounds)
1826[11] 2145[12] 2576[6] 3128[7] 3212[7] 3784[5] 4144[4] 4846[6] 4967[4] 5220[4] 5452[7] 6153[7] 6310[10]

Howards Tipple *Miss L A Perratt* a66 73
4 b g Diktat—Grey Princess (IRE) (Common Grounds)
(581) ◆ 806[9] 1826[7] 2145[7] 2748[5] 3255[9] 3404[3] (3577) 3956[3] 4114[5] 4561[4] 4846[12] 4971[7] 6159[4] 6405[10]

Howards Way *Miss L A Perratt* 62
3 b g Bertolini(USA) —Love Quest (Pursuit Of Love)
1951[5] ◆ 2466[7] 5392[12]

Howdigo *J R Best* a78 95
3 b c Tobougg(IRE) —Woodrising (Nomination)
3002[6] 3325[8] (4021) 4519[3] 5843[3] 6079[2]

Howe's Jack (IRE) *M C Chapman* a33 42
3 b g Fasliyev(USA) —Berenique (IRE) (Bering)
1684[11] 2080[6] 2894[4] 3730[6] 4023[11] 4498[5]

How's She Cuttin' (IRE) *T D Barron* a99 94
5 ch m Shinko Forest(IRE) —Magic Annemarie (IRE) (Dancing Dissident (USA))
1571[5] ◆ 2626[10] 3252[3] 3451[4] 4004a[3] 4240[7] 6651[5] 6782[7] (7151) 7421[4]

Hucking Harkness *J R Best* a63 63
3 ch c Dr Fong(USA) —Dalaauna (Cadeaux Genereux)
2823[4] 4306[13] 4637[9] 4777[4] (5755) 6036[13] 6554[10] 6878[10]

Hucking Harmony (IRE) *J R Best* a54 62
3 b f Spartacus(IRE) —Gute (IRE) (Petardia)
3269[5] 3447[7] 4307[11] 4793[12] 5679[6] 6224[10]

Hucking Harrier (IRE) *J R Best* a38
3 ch g Hawk Wing(USA) —Dangerous Mind (IRE) (Platini (GER))
221[8] 354[7]

Hucking Heat (IRE) *R Hollinshead* a86 67
4 b g Desert Sun—Vltava (IRE) (Sri Pekan (USA))
(40) 302[5] 331[4] 433[3] 449[2] (637) 658[4] 1296[5] (1605) 2097[12] (2568) 2908[3] 3551[17] 3965[3] 4309[7] 4710[5] 5783[5] 6134[6] (6395) (6825) 7354[9] (7606) 7686[2] 7785[3]

Hucking Heist *J R Best* 74
4 b g Desert Style(IRE) —Oriental Queen (GER) (Big Shuffle (USA))
3529[7] 6758[10]

Hucking Hero (IRE) *J R Best* a77 64
3 b c Iron Mask(USA) —Selkirk Flyer (Selkirk (USA))
(25) 457[4] 573[4] 799[3] 6949[17] 7314[12] 7525[5] 7758[7]

Hucking Hill (IRE) *J R Best* a77 52
4 ch g City On A Hill(USA) —Con Dancer (Shareef Dancer (USA))
55[6] 94[3] 150[5] 165[3] 334[5] 404[5] 729[4] 1853[11] 3374[4] 4186[8] 4307[5]

Hue *B Ellison* a64 82
7 ch g Peintre Celebre(USA) —Quandary (USA) (Blushing Groom (FR))
(988) ◆ 1136[3] 1984[2] 2839[3] 3368[8] 6817[8]

Huggle *P Leech* a48 62
5 b g Groom Dancer(USA) —Perle De Sagesse (Namaqualand (USA))
552[2] 654[5] 930[8] 1246[12]

Hugs Destiny (IRE) *M A Barnes* a64 64
7 b g Victory Note(USA) —Embracing (Reference Point)
988[14] 1137[7] 1340[6] 2051[2] 2286[3] 2447[5] 2579[2] 2908[8] 3083[3] 3414[7] 3756[4] 4295[4] 5040[4] 5869[6]

Hujum (IRE) *J E Hammond* a85 103
4 b h Rock Of Gibraltar(IRE) —Clara Bow (FR) (Top Ville)
2876a[4]

Hukba (IRE) *E A L Dunlop* 81
2 b f Anabaa(USA) —Banaadir (USA) (Diesis)
6559[2] ◆

Hula Ballew *M Dods* 86
8 ch m Weldnaas(USA) —Ballon (Persian Bold)
1449[3] 1729[2] ◆ 2445[3] (2672) 3109[3] 3366[4] (4206) 4649[5] 4970[5] 6052[15] 6311[4]

Hula Hula *Miss D Mountain* a34 19
3 ch f Cadeaux Genereux—Eurolink Sundance (Night Shift (USA))
265[13]

Hula King (GER) *B J Meehan* a86 75
2 b c Green Tune(USA) —Hula Queen (USA) (Irish River (FR))
5271[7] ◆ 6085[4] (6423)

Human Touch *G A Butler* a21 36
3 b f Oasis Dream—Seltitude (IRE) (Fairy King (USA))
6822[11]

Humble Opinion *B J Meehan* a75 95
6 br g Singspiel(IRE) —For More (FR) (Sanglamore (USA))
1633[2] 1828[5] (2582)

Humbolt (IRE) *M Weiss*
8 gr h Ashkalani(IRE) —Midnight Angel (Machiavellian (USA))
421a[8]

Hum Cat (IRE) *J S Moore* a67 58
2 br c One Cool Cat(USA) —Jojeema (Barathea (IRE))
3358[5] 3895[9] 4367[5] 5432[4] 6087[9] (6694) 6924[8]

Humungous (IRE) *C R Egerton* a87 111
5 ch g Giant's Causeway(USA) —Doula (USA) (Gone West (USA))
1982[12] 3122[8] 3684[5] 4191[4] (4443) 4504[11] 5288[7] 5694[11]

Hunch *Garry Moss* a31 15
2 b c Tobougg(IRE) —Swellegant (Midyan (USA))
2548[7] 3106[8] 3815[7] 4257[5] 5774[12]

Hundonette *R M H Cowell* a31 39
3 b f Carnival Dancer—Captiva (Darshaan)
2427[7] 2756[9] 2981[13] 4125[15] 4797[9]

Hungry For More *M R Hoad* a8 32
4 b g Silver Patriarch(IRE) —Plaything (High Top)
2528[P] 2885[10] 4123[14] 6018[11]

Huntdown (USA) *J H M Gosden* 109
2 ch c Elusive Quality(USA) —Infinite Spirit (USA) (Maria's Mon (USA))
5271[2] ◆ (6072) 6442[3] ◆ 6815[8]

Hunters' Glen (USA) *Doug Watson* a88 97
5 b h Bahri(USA) —Hedera (USA) (Woodman (USA))
380a[15]

Hunter Street *R Menichetti* 26
5 b h Compton Place—Sewards Folly (Rudimentary (USA))
7187a[12]

Hunterview *M A Jarvis* 77
2 ch g Reset(AUS) —Mount Elbrus (Barathea (IRE))
5777[3] (6187) 6946[11]

Hunting Country *M Johnston* a89 96
3 b c Cape Cross(IRE) —Steeple (Selkirk (USA))
2143[4] ◆ 2488[2] 3094[4] (3736) (4191) 4350[3] 4552[10] 5279[9] 6974[3] 7150[3]

Hunting Haze *A Crook* a51 56
5 b g Foxhound(USA) —Second Affair (IRE) (Pursuit Of Love)
657[7] 863[8] 1679[9] 3399[7] 7265[4] 7630[4]

Hunt The Bottle (IRE) *M Mullineaux* a58 74
3 b c Bertolini(USA) —Zanoubia (USA) (Our Emblem (USA))
1546[9] 1988[7] 2407[5] 3270[13] 3626[5] 4782[7] 6132[7] 7533[11]

Hurakan (IRE) *Mrs A J Perrett* a74 78
2 gr g Daylami(IRE) —Gothic Dream (IRE) (Nashwan (USA))
5227[11] (5678) 6344[2]

Hurforharmony (IRE) *Adrian McGuinness* a47 51
5 b m Orpen(USA) —Zolba (IRE) (Classic Secret (USA))
7688[7]

Hurlingham *M W Easterby* a77 87
4 b g Halling(USA) —Society (IRE) (Barathea (IRE))
1910[15] 2582[14] 2969[4] 3795[2] 4204[5] (4785) (5563) 6154[3] 6410[3] 7150[6]

Hurricane Coast *D Flood* a64 74
9 b g Hurricane Sky(AUS) —Tread Carefully (Sharpo)
4031[7] 5871[10] 6208[6] ◆ 6570[4] 6693[5] (6733) 7357[7] 7437[5] 7679[4] 7745[7] 7774[5]

Hurricane Harriet *R M H Cowell* a36 77
3 b f Bertolini(USA) —Cold Blow (Posse (USA))
1454[7] 2427[6] 4125[4] (4793) (4988) ◆ 5319[4] (6564) 7143[4] 7534[7]

Hurricane Hen *P D Evans* a82 72
3 ch g Compton Place—Peyto Princess (Bold Arrangement)
9[2] 228[5] 324[2] ◆ 498[2] 800[3] (917) (3565) (4028) 4272[2]

Hurricane Hymnbook (USA) *B J Meehan* a82 104
3 b g Pulpit(USA) —April Squall (USA) (Summer Squall (USA))
1875[2] ◆ 3155[19] 5208[9] 5942[7]

Hurricane James (IRE) *E Charpy* a79 84
6 bb h Night Shift(USA) —Ginger Candy (USA) (Hilal (IRE))
379a[14]

Hurricane Spirit (IRE) *J R Best* a106 97
4 b h Invincible Spirit(IRE) —Gale Warning (IRE) (Last Tycoon)
472a[9] 666a[6] 741a[9] 1619[7] 2598[3] 3647[4] 3973[11]

Hurricane Thomas (IRE) *R E Barr* a75 77
4 b g Celtic Swing—Viola Royale (IRE) (Royal Academy (USA))
3711[9] 4220[10] 4537[8] 5559[9] 6189[5] 6727[5] 6786[11]

Hurstpierpoint (IRE) *M G Rimell* a62 59
3 b f Night Shift(USA) —Double Gamble (Ela-Mana-Mou)
1306[11] 1912[2] 2486[2] 2801[5] 4326[10] 4910[8]

Hustle (IRE) *R Hannon* a91 91
3 ch c Choisir(AUS) —Granny Kelly (USA) (Irish River (FR))
(1113) 1441[13] 2532[4] 3038[2] 3382[3] 5279[13] 5682[2] 6238[9]

Huxaar *Mrs L Stubbs* 72
2 b g Xaar—Green Song (FR) (Green Tune (USA))
3055[10] 4780[6] 5304[2] 5716[3] (5771) 6101[6]

Huzzah (IRE) *B W Hills* a89 105
3 b c Acclamation—Borders Belle (IRE) (Pursuit Of Love)
(1441) (1923) 2403[10] 3919[6] 4587[5] 5896[3] 6476[12]

Hyades (USA) *H R A Cecil* 84
2 bb c Aldebaran(USA) —Lingerie (Shirley Heights)
6777[2] ◆

Hyde Lea Flyer *E S McMahon* a80 74
3 b c Hernando(FR) —Sea Ridge (Slip Anchor)
1750[4] 2161[7] 3004[15] 6450[6] 6712[2] (7405) (7750) ◆

Hydrant *P W Chapple-Hyam* 68
2 b c Haafhd—Spring (Sadler's Wells (USA))
4151[6] 5468[10]

Hydrophonic *R A Fahey* a41 63
3 ch f Golden Snake(USA) —Lambast (Relkino)
2929[4] 3333[6] 4379[2] 4737[4] 5203[3]

Hype (USA) *Todd Pletcher* a102 87
2 b c More Than Ready(USA) —Western Woman (USA) (West By West (USA))
7751a[8]

Hypnosis *D W Barker* a79 90
5 b m Mind Games—Salacious (Sallust)
1755[4] 2489[9] 3708[4] (4291) 4631[2] 5793[4] 6290[13] 6651[15]

Hypnotic *D Nicholls* a33 60
6 ch g Lomitas—Hypnotize (Machiavellian (USA))
2533[14] 2968[6] ◆ 3366[15] 5389[5]

Hypnotic Gaze (IRE) *C G Cox* 48
2 b c Chevalier(IRE) —Red Trance (IRE) (Soviet Star (USA))
5022[7] 6122[16]

Hypnotist (UAE) *C E Brittain* 59
2 b c Halling(USA) —Poised (USA) (Rahy (USA))
4421[4]

Hypocrisy *D Carroll* a79 56
5 b m Bertolini(USA) —Glensara (Petoski)
506[4] 683[2]

Hystericalady (USA) *Jerry Hollendorfer* a118
5 ch m Distorted Humor(USA) —Sacramentada (CHI) (Northair (USA))
6969a[5]

Hysterical Lady *D Nicholls* 71
2 b f Choisir(AUS) —Royal Mistress (Fasliyev (USA))
2443[2] ◆ 3598[4]

Hythe Bay *J R Jenkins* a70 69
4 b m Auction House(USA) —Ellway Queen (USA) (Bahri (USA))
29[6] 150[3] 165[8] 786[8]

Iachimo *K R Burke* 47
2 ch g Sakhee(USA) —Latin Review (IRE) (Titus Livius (FR))
3735[8] 5860[7] 6578[6]

Iamagrey (IRE) *C J Down* a60 65
3 gr f Clodovil(IRE) —Xania (Mujtahid (USA))
2922[16] 3906[6] 4580[9] 6328[11]

I Am The Best *D M Simcock* a75 92
2 ch c King's Best(USA) —Needles And Pins (IRE) (Fasliyev (USA))
2204[2] ◆ 2713[3] 3103[7] ◆ 3876[5] 5021[6] 5609[2]

Ianapourna (GER) *J Hirschberger* 86
3 b f Dai Jin—Iora (GER) (Konigsstuhl (GER))
4675a[16] 5329a[9]

Iasia (GR) *Jane Chapple-Hyam* a71
2 b f One Cool Cat(USA) —Alanis (Warning)
(7465)

Ibbetson (USA) *W R Swinburn* a71 65
3 bb g Street Cry(IRE) —Object Of Virtue (USA) (Partner's Hero (USA))
6055[9] 6583[6] 7395[2]

Ibn Khaldun (USA) *Saeed Bin Suroor* 116
2 ch c Dubai Destination(USA) —Gossamer (Sadler's Wells (USA))
1808[10]

Ibn Qutaiba (USA) *Saeed Bin Suroor* 71
3 b c Dynaformer(USA) —Ministrada (USA) (Deputy Minister (CAN))
3094[7]

Ibrox (IRE) *A D Brown* 64
3 b g Mujahid(USA) —Ling Lane (Slip Anchor)
6042[3] 6529[6]

Icabad Crane (USA) *H Graham Motion* a103
3 bb c Jump Start(USA) —Adorahy (USA) (Rahy (USA))
2215a[3] 2858a[8]

Icannshift (IRE) *T M Jones* a54 64
8 b g Night Shift(USA) —Cannikin (IRE) (Lahib (USA))
9991[4] 1538[5] 2884[8] 3448[3] 4275[8] 5183[12]

Icansingarainbow *R Hollinshead* a58 51
4 b g Rainbow High—Carole's Choir (Primo Dominie)
2012[9] 2572[10] 3182[7]

Ice And Fire *J T Stimpson* a61 69
9 b g Cadeaux Genereux—Tanz (IRE) (Sadler's Wells (USA))
36[4] 283[4]

Ice Bellini *Miss Gay Kelleway* a68 58
3 ch f Erhaab(USA) —Peach Sorbet (IRE) (Spectrum (IRE))
1423[16] 1876[14] 6374[10] (6725) (7149) 7285[3] 7376[9]

Ice Bound (IRE) *J C Hayden* a41 63
2 gr c Verglas(IRE) —Mubadalah (USA) (Dumaani (USA))
6320a[24]

Ice Chariot (AUS) *Ron Maund* 110
6 b g Semipalatinsk(USA) —Snow Chariot (AUS) (Chariot (AUS))
6835a[8] 7188a[11]

Ice Lad (NZ) *R Brotherton* a13
9 br g Woodbury Lad(USA) —Ice Queen (NZ) (Dorchester (FR))
2867[9]

Icelandic *Frank Sheridan* 112
6 b h Selkirk(USA) —Icicle (Polar Falcon (USA))
(5368) 5840[3] 6484[3] (7243)

Iceman George *D Morris* a67 68
4 b g Beat Hollow—Diebiedale (Dominion)
1692[9] 1904[6] 2374[2] 2978[3] 3655[8] 4371[11] 4739[8]

Ice Planet *Mrs R A Carr* a81 98
7 b g Polar Falcon(USA) —Preference (Efisio)
1300[9] 1517[12] 1796[8] 2501[5] 3370[11] 4393[7] 5222[3] 5886[4] 6066[8] 6532[9] 7629[7] 7780[7]

Ice Queen (IRE) *A P O'Brien* a69 118
3 b f Danehill Dancer(IRE) —Wadud (Nashwan (USA))
1104a[6] 1991[4] 2792[16] (3070a) 3511a[6] 4006a[2] 5952a[11] 6495a[10]

I Certainly May *S Dow* a62 64
3 b g Royal Applause—Deep Ravine (USA) (Gulch (USA))
58[8] 325[4] 547[4] 940[5] 1147[14] 2931[5] 5169[7] 5269[11] 7520[9] 7676[11] 7817[9]

Icesolator (IRE) *R Hannon* 101
2 b g One Cool Cat(USA) —Zinnia (Zilzal (USA))
1399[9] (1804) (1927) (2541) 3103[13] 4507[10] 6119[7]

I Confess *P D Evans* a77 80
3 br g Fantastic Light(USA) —Vadsagreya (FR) (Linamix (FR))
2449[6] 2906[8] 3256[3] 3475[6] 3728[4] 4408[6] 5056[7] 5697[13] 6178[4] (6433) 6736[2] 6976[11] 7277[4] 7436[2] (7557) 7837[2] ◆

Icon Project (USA) *B J Meehan* 106
3 bb f Empire Maker(USA) —La Gueriere (USA) (Lord At War (ARG))
1599[2] (2336) 3153[4] 4196[3] 5597a[7]

Icy Cool (IRE) *J Noseda* a63 68
3 b c Galileo(IRE) —Epping (Charnwood Forest (IRE))
6470[6] 6762[5] ◆

Idealist (GER) *A P Stringer* 108
6 b h Tiger Hill(IRE) —I Go Bye (GER) (Don't Forget Me)
7396[4]

Ideal World (USA) *A Fabre* 116
3 b c Kingmambo(USA) —Banks Hill (Danehill (USA))
4473a[4] 5953a[2]

Identity *E J O'Neill* a55 67
2 ch f Reel Buddy(USA) —Kind Of Shy (Kind Of Hush)
3792[4] 4169[2] 4593[9] 5591[6] 5966[11] 6406[3] 6730[8]

Idesia (IRE) *W R Swinburn* a74 72
4 b m Green Desert(USA) —Indaba (IRE) (Indian Ridge)
1372[4] ◆ 1963[11] 2718[2] 4081[4] 5069[9] 6671[2] 7277[8]

Idiot Proof (USA) *Clifford Sise Jr* a115 112
4 b h Benchmark(USA) —Perfectly Pretty (USA) (Bertrando (USA))
1089a[2] 6994a[13]

Idle Court *Bruce Hellier*
3 b f Mind Games—Change Of Image (Spectrum (IRE))
3955[7] 4451[15] 5395[10]

Idle Power (IRE) *J R Boyle* a82 90
10 b g Common Grounds—Idle Fancy (Mujtahid (USA))
1537[4] 1800[3] (2565) 2831[5] 4928[5] 5270[10] 6676[5] 7143[9]

Idle Tears *J H M Gosden* 58
2 ch f Selkirk(USA) —Land Of Dreams (Cadeaux Genereux)
7140[9]

Idolino (GER) *J Hirschberger* 101
3 b c Tertullian(USA) —I Go Bye (GER) (Don't Forget Me)
2880a[3] 6322a[11] 7005a[7]

Idonea (CAN) *Mario Hofer* 97
3 ch f Swain(IRE) —Ivastar (CAN) (Alwasmi (USA))
2065a[9]

Ifatfirst (IRE) *J S Goldie* a65 55
5 b g Grand Lodge(USA) —Gaily Grecian (IRE) (Ela-Mana-Mou)
5543[7] 6657[7]

I Feel Fine *A Kirtley* 44
5 ch m Minster Son—Jendorcet (Grey Ghost I)
3227[11] 3479[7] 3810[6] 4537[10] 6015[9]

If Paradise *M Halford* a70 93
7 b g Compton Place—Sunley Stars (Sallust)
6366a[21]

If You Knew Suzy *G A Swinbank* a35
3 b f Efisio—Sioux (Kris)
7463[4]

Igneous *K R Burke* a30 48
2 ch g Lucky Story(USA) —Double Top (IRE) (Thatching)
3199[4] 4027[10] 4847[6] 5632[17] 6059[6]

Ignition *A Kirtley* a42 64
6 ch m Rock City—Fire Sprite (Mummy's Game)
3593[13] 4219[17] 4596[7] 5968[8] 6654[8] 7750[8] 7809[8]

Ignotus *G A Swinbank* 45
6 b g Vitus—Linns Heir (Leading Counsel (USA))
5963[6]

Igor Protti *Saeed Bin Suroor* a104 105
6 b h Opening Verse(USA) —La Busona (IRE) (Broken Hearted)
(380a) 667a[3] 817a[6] 5208[2] 6123[5] 7201[3]

Igotim *J Gallagher* a44 19
2 b c Umistim—Glistening Silver (Puissance)
4907[11] 5431[11] 6062[11]

Igoyougo *P T Midgley* 51
2 b c Millkom—Club Oasis (Forzando)
9578 2775[7] 6051[7] 6548[5]

Iguacu *J L Spearing* 54
4 b g Desert Prince(IRE) —Gay Gallanta (USA) (Woodman (USA))
1900[13] 2242[13] 2477[8] 3033[17]

Iguazu Falls (USA) *Saeed Bin Suroor* a90 109
3 ch c Pivotal—Anna Palariva (IRE) (Caerleon (USA))
1797[3] 2544[2] (2793) ◆ 3197[27] 4912a[7] 6073[7]

Iide Kenshin (JPN) *Mitsugi Kon* a92
3 b c Thunder Gulch(USA) —Heavenly Advice (USA) (Theatrical)
1088a[8]

Ike Quebec (FR) *J R Boyle* a78 69
3 ch g Dr Fong(USA) —Avezia (FR) (Night Shift (USA))
(582) 967[4] 1584[7] 1875[8] 2311[9] 3653[5] 4083[12] 4777[8] 7557[12] 7763[9]

Il Castagno (IRE) *B Smart* a42 89
5 ch g Night Shift(USA) —Cartesian (Shirley Heights)
1774[2] ◆ 2158[2] 3548[7]

Il Divo (GER) *A Wohler* 100
3 b c Dashing Blade—Independent Miss (GER) (Polar Falcon (USA))
2880a[2] 3773a[10] 6461a[6]

Ile Royale *B R Johnson* a60 60
3 b f Royal Applause—Island Destiny (Kris)
931[4] 1166[8] 1870[12] 2721[8] 3345[7] 4181[8] 4414[16]

Il Grande Ardone *F Sheridan* a85
3 b c Dr Fong(USA) —Bombalarina (IRE) (Barathea (IRE))
7664[2] (7797)

Il Grande Maurizio (IRE) *Frank Sheridan* a106
4 b h King Charlemagne(USA) —Ciubanga (IRE) (Arazi (USA))
(6911) 7492[5] ◆

Ilie Nastase (FR) *R Gibson* a98 100
4 b g Royal Applause—Flying Diva (Chief Singer)
5115a[2]

Iliketoboogie *A J McCabe* a60
2 ch f Tobougg(IRE) —Marjurita (IRE) (Marju (IRE))
3331[8] 3689[4] 6697[8] 6933[6] 7372[7] 7687[4]

I'll Do It Today *J M Jefferson* a60 63
7 b g Mtoto—Knayton Lass (Presidium)
345[9]

Illusion *J H M Gosden* a78 96
3 b f Anabaa(USA) —Fantasize (Groom Dancer (USA))
1721[3] (2257) 2819[7] 3124[2] 3742[3] 4590[11] 6271[8]

Illusionary *J G Portman* 43
3 b g Observatory(USA) —Tease (IRE) (Green Desert (USA))
1186[9] 2894[6] 3692[6] 4807[10] 6206[10]

Illustrious Blue *W J Knight* a113 113
5 bb h Dansili—Gipsy Moth (Efisio)
491a[2] 740a[6] 816a[8] 1077[2] 1596[5] 2708a[7] 3195[7] 4504[10] 4587[7] 5070[8] 5694[2] 6074[7] 7193[5]

I Lost My Choo (USA) *Philip M Serpe* 99
3 b f Western Expression(USA) —Fairy Queen (USA) (Tom Rolfe (USA))
5164a[5]

Il Ranzani (ITY) *V Toccolini*
2 b c Tenby—Perfect Desire (USA) (Green Forest (USA))
2745a[7]

Ilviz (FR) *Ollie Pears* a57 58
6 gr g Medaaly—Move The Mouse (IRE) (Foxhound (USA))
485[6] 1184[5]

Il Warrd (IRE) *Saeed Bin Suroor* a108 114
3 b c Pivotal—Demure (Machiavellian (USA))
(1333) ◆ 2032a[12] 3119[2] 4506[4] 5095[5] 6073[2] (6484) 6814[13]

Imaam *J L Dunlop* 79
2 ch c Pivotal—Khulood (USA) (Storm Cat (USA))
3495[2] 4151[2] 5578[2] 6229[4]

I'm Agenius *P A Blockley* a35 43
5 br m Killer Instinct—I'm Sophie (IRE) (Shalford (IRE))
7265[12] 7608[10]

Imaginary Diva *G G Margarson* a66 54
2 b f Lend A Hand—Distant Diva (Distant Relative)
3558[6] 3778[4] 4705[3] 5204[6] 5394[6] 5475[2] 6579[5] 6906[3] 7464[3] 7542[2] (7719) (7825)

I'm Aimee *Mrs J L Le Brocq* 34
6 ch m Timeless Times(USA) —Marfen (Lochnager)
5002a[5]

Imco Tendence (IRE) *W J Burke* a67 70
6 b g Fasliyev(USA) —Treasure Hope (IRE) (Treasure Kay)
7732[4] 7748[3]

Imminent Victory *R M H Cowell* a52
5 b g Benny The Dip(USA) —Brave Vanessa (USA) (Private Account (USA))
179[6]

Im Ova Ere Dad (IRE) *D E Cantillon* a90 87
5 b g Second Empire(IRE) —Eurolink Profile (Prince Sabo)
2087[4] (2795) ◆ 2978[5]

Impeller (IRE) *Jane Chapple-Hyam* a103 103
9 ch g Polish Precedent(USA) —Almaaseh (IRE) (Dancing Brave (USA))
202a[3] ◆ 380a[13] 477a[9] 1077[7] 2103[6] 2503[3] (Dead)

Imperial Amber *Karen George* a56
6 ch m Emperor Fountain—Bambolona (Bustino)
507[4] 750[4] (821) 935[7] 1041[5]

Imperial Angel (IRE) *D Carroll* 55
2 gr f Tagula(IRE) —New Deal (Rainbow Quest (USA))
3334[8] 4380[7] 4697[6]

Imperial Decree *John Berry* 71
3 b f Diktat—Docklands Princess (IRE) (Desert Prince (IRE))
1738[6] 2429[17] 4326[8]

Imperial Djay (IRE) *G J Smith* a64 67
3 b g Dilshaan—Slayjay (IRE) (Mujtahid (USA))
1556[3] 1894[4] 2380[13] 2674[9] 3564[4] 3831[5] 4076[4] 4686[7] 7321[6] 7585[7] 7669[6] 7772[8]

Imperial Echo (USA) *P Howling* a77 91
7 b g Labeeb—Regal Baby (USA) (Northern Baby (CAN))
442[8] 594[11] 833[8] 994[8] (1485) 1891[6] 2358[7] 4928[8] 5247[15] 5779[7] 6046[11] 6490[7] 6774[6] 7012[5] 7206[10] 7497[7]

Imperial Guest *G G Margarson* 98
2 ch c Imperial Dancer—Princess Speedfit (FR) (Desert Prince (IRE))
1873[4] (2507) 3245[9] 4828[5] (5286) 5756[4] 6305[11] 6426[3] (6972)

Imperialista (BRZ) *Saeed Bin Suroor* a106
5 b h Voando Baixo(BRZ) —Zarumba Bis (BRZ) (Be My Chief (USA))
204a[7] 493a[3] 648a[3] 742a[5]

Imperial Lucky (IRE) *M J Wallace* a72 64
5 b m Desert Story(IRE) —Irina (IRE) (Polar Falcon (USA))
(3034) 3345[3] 3834[3] 4282[6] 4770[5] (6628) 6821[5]

Imperial Quest *E J Alston* 59
4 ch m Rainbow Quest(USA) —Imperial Bailiwick (IRE) (Imperial Frontier (USA))
5110[6] 5389[10]

Imperial Skylight *M R Channon* a64 64
2 gr g Imperial Dancer—Sky Light Dreams (Dreams To Reality (USA))
1078[3] 1263[4] 1851[8] 4589[8] 5165[4] 5414[3] 6087[8] 6547[3] 6603[13] 6906[4] 7361[3] 7468[4] 7547[6] 7832[2]

Imperial Star (IRE) *Saeed Bin Suroor* a114 114
5 br h Fantastic Light(USA) —Out West (USA) (Gone West (USA))
476a[3] 673a[2] 816a[7] 5070[6]

Imperial Sword *T D Barron* a56 68
5 b g Danehill Dancer(IRE) —Hajat (Mujtahid (USA))
109[4] 256[13] 639[5] 790[4] 1024[6] 1455[2] 1687[3] (1865) 2751[9] 3582[2] 3757[9] 3789[7] 3952[2] 4846[2] 5392[4] 6219[2] 6411[5]

Imperium *Jean-Rene Auvray* a65 68
7 b g Imperial Ballet(IRE) —Partenza (USA) (Red Ransom (USA))
149[5] 276[2] 407[7] 453[4] 708[3] 879[4] 1154[3] 1996[6] 2128[6] 2355[3] 2758[12] 4529[8] 4772[8] 5267[3] 5801[5] 6178[12] 7102[6] 7382[4] 7702[3]

Impero *G F Bridgwater*
10 b g Emperor Jones(USA) —Fight Right (FR) (Crystal Glitters (USA))
471[8]

Impetious *Eamon Tyrrell* 99
4 b m Inchinor—Kauri (USA) (Woodman (USA))
202a[16] 475a[9] 672a[8] 1807[5] 2890[8] 3623a[5] 4512a[17]

Implication *E A L Dunlop* 43
2 b f Pivotal—Insinuation (IRE) (Danehill (USA))
4870[14]

Important News *M Johnston* 58
3 b g Royal Applause—Kissing Time (Lugana Beach)
2380[11] 2673[9] 3200[3] ◆ 3592[7]

Importer (IRE) *W R Muir* a70 70
2 b c Efisio—Dwingeloo (IRE) (Dancing Dissident (USA))
3848[4] 4905[6] 6197[3] 6412[7] 6924[3] 6988[2]

Imposing *Sir Michael Stoute* 84
2 b c Danehill Dancer(IRE) —On Fair Stage (IRE) (Sadler's Wells (USA))
5777[2] ◆ (6292) 6474[14]

Impossible Dream (IRE) *A Kinsella* a63 93
4 b h Indian Danehill(IRE) —Recoleta (USA) (Wild Again (USA))
5731a[15] 6315a[7] 6845a[7]

Impostor (IRE) *R A Harris* a45 77
5 b g In The Wings—Princess Caraboo (IRE) (Alzao (USA))
118[5] 212[11]

Impressible *E J Alston* a52 64
2 b f Oasis Dream—Imperial Bailiwick (IRE) (Imperial Frontier (USA))
2903[4] 3598[5] 4202[7] 4659[5] 5004[5] 5834[8] (6788)

Impressionist Art (USA) *B J Meehan* a54 61
2 ch f Giant's Causeway(USA) —Chalamont (IRE) (Kris)
4157[12] 5534[5] 6240[24] 7468[9]

Imprimis Tagula (IRE) *A Bailey* a82 83
4 b g Tagula(IRE) —Strelitzia (IRE) (Bluebird (USA))
3394[7] 6842[10] 7047[2] ◆ 7525[7] 7560[6] 7633[6]

Impromptu *P G Murphy* a73 83
4 b g Mujadil(USA) —Pie In The Sky (Bishop Of Cashel)
887[6] 1146[7] 1683[P]

Improper (USA) *Mouse Hamilton-Fairley* 42
2 b g Northern Afleet(USA) —Bare It Properly (USA) (Proper Reality (USA))
6702[8]

I'm Sensational *H R A Cecil* 79
3 b f Selkirk(USA) —Ego (Green Desert (USA))
3275[5] 5278[3] (5786)

Incanto Dream *C Lerner* 115
4 ch h Galileo(IRE) —Atlantic Blue (USA) (Nureyev (USA))
1663a[4] 1888a[2] (4041a) 5956a[6] 6497a[2]

Incarnation (IRE) *L M Cumani* a70 61
3 b f Samum(GER) —River Patrol (Rousillon (USA))
5155[4] (7300) 7545[9] 7752[4]

Inca Slew (IRE) *P C Haslam* 49
2 ch g City On A Hill(USA) —Con Dancer (Shareef Dancer (USA))
2459[3] 2910[7] 3225[4]

Inca Soldier (FR) *R C Guest* a66 69
5 br g Intikhab(USA) —Chrysalu (Distant Relative)
506[8] 581[2] 766[5] 801[5] 1485[7] 1775[7] 2251[10] 4903[14]

Incendo *J R Fanshawe* 68
2 ch g King's Best(USA) —Kindle (Selkirk (USA))
6083[10] 6552[3] 7054[8]

In Chambers *M Delzangles* 107
3 b c Oasis Dream—Cas Royaux (USA) (Woodman (USA))
2096a[2] 3356a[2] 4473a[6] 5742a[6] 6322a[5]

Inch High *J S Goldie* 54
10 ch g Inchinor—Harrken Heights (IRE) (Belmez (USA))
3204[3] 3756[6] 4238[3]

Inchloch *Miss C Dyson* a89 86
6 ch g Inchinor—Lake Pleasant (IRE) (Elegant Air)
1072[5] 1472[4] 1998[8] 2623[2] 6950[11]

Inch Lodge *Miss D Mountain* a81 66
6 ch h Grand Lodge(USA) —Legaya (Shirley Heights)
450[5] 626[7] 1409[7] 1692[11] (2512) 3089[7] 3824[7] 6662[4] 6985[6] 7376[6] 7447[8]

Inchnadamph *T J Fitzgerald* a53 93
8 b g Inchinor—Pelf (USA) (Al Nasr (FR))
1568[9] 1916[7] 3490[10] 4439[3]

Inchpast *M H Tompkins* a84 80
7 ch g Inchinor—Victor Ludorum (Rainbow Quest (USA))
2135[8] 2628[11] 4200[6] 4314[4] 4516[2] 6054[15] 6329[8] 6817[9] 7271[2] 7366[8] 7515[8]

Inchwood (IRE) *M A Jarvis* a93 100
3 b f Dubai Destination(USA) —Inchiri (Sadler's Wells (USA))
(2164) 2977[2] ◆ (3586) ◆ 5111[2] 6127[3] (6866) (Dead)

Incline (IRE) *R McGlinchey* a102 105
9 b g Danehill(USA) —Shalwar Kameez (IRE) (Sadler's Wells (USA))
829a[10] 1105a[26] 4512a[8] 5968[5] ◆ 6490[10]

Incomparable *A J McCabe* a75 79
3 ch g Compton Place—Indian Silk (IRE) (Dolphin Street (FR))
1167[5] 1484[10] 2732[6] 6627[11] 6990[7] 7182[7] (7323) 7448[4] 7611[2] ◆ 7671[6]

Inconspicuous Miss (USA) *George Baker* a66
2 bb f War Chant(USA) —Orissa (USA) (Devil's Bag (USA))
6986[5] 7179[3] (7402)

Incy Wincy *J M Bradley* 14
2 b g Zahran(IRE) —Miss Money Spider (IRE) (Statoblest)
2882[4] 3670[15] 4203[12]

Indecision *M W Easterby* a50 58
3 b g Muhtarram(USA) —Emma Amour (Emarati (USA))
704 534[3] 845[5] 1117[4] 1391[7] 1823[4] 2080[4] 3335[11]

In Decorum *J A Geake* a41 51
3 gr f Averti(IRE) —Decorous (IRE) (Runnett)
23[9] 2946[12] 3065[9] 3611[13] 5269[12]

In Deep *Mrs P N Dutfield* a46 45
7 b m Deploy—Bobbie Dee (Blakeney)
37[6]

Indiana Fox *B G Powell* 55
5 b m Foxhound(USA) —Ridgewood Ruby (IRE) (Indian Ridge)
6583[8] 6748[9] 6896[8]

Indiana Gal (IRE) *Patrick Martin* a89 102
3 b f Intikhab(USA) —Genial Jenny (IRE) (Danehill (USA))
1104a[5] 1847a[3] 2024a[3] 4007a[3]

Indian Art (IRE) *R Hannon* a66 87
2 b c Choisir(AUS) —Eastern Ember (Indian King (USA))
1851[4] (2324) 2826[2] 3553[3] 5244[8] 5615[7] 5827[11] 6717[2]

Indian Blade (IRE) *M D I Usher* a27 57
2 ch g Daggers Drawn(USA) —Belle Bijou (Midyan (USA))
2098[9] 3267[5] 3603[12] 4373[8] 4475[5] 6535[11] 7425[8] 7832[10]

Indian Blessing (USA) *Bob Baffert* a117
3 bb f Indian Charlie(USA) —Shameful (USA) (Flying Chevron (USA))
6965a[2]

Indian Choice (USA) *P Bary* a92 111
4 b g With Approval(CAN) —Cheyenne Dream (Dancing Brave (USA))
6237a[7]

Indian Daffodil (IRE) *J-C Rouget* 109
3 b c Hernando(FR) —Danseuse Indienne (IRE) (Danehill (USA))
(3356a) 4212a[5] 6612a[3]

Indian Days *J G Given* 104
3 ch c Daylami(IRE) —Cap Coz (IRE) (Indian Ridge)
1614[2] 2109[2] (2464) 3157[7] 3877[3] (4552) ◆ 5932[5] 6120[3] 6476[10]

Indian Diva (IRE) *P A Blockley* a80 83
3 b f Indian Danehill(IRE) —Katherine Gorge (USA) (Hansel (USA))
(1868) 2196[16] 6271[13] 6684[6] 7525[6]

Indian Edge *B Palling* a62 79
7 ch g Indian Rocket—Beveled Edge (Beveled (USA))
1605[4] 1900[5] 2477[6] 2642[12] 3903[7] 4710[8] 6821[12]

Indian Fiesta (IRE) *B G Powell* 42
2 b c Indian Danehill(IRE) —San Jovita (CAN) (St Jovite (USA))
2592[14] 3444[11]

Indian Groom (IRE) *J Howard Johnson* 79
3 gr g High Chaparral(IRE) —Taatof (IRE) (Lahib (USA))
2207[3] 3297[6]
Indian Haze (IRE) *Daniel Mark Loughnane* a37 33
2 bb f Indian Haven—Hollow Haze (USA) (Woodman (USA))
4513a[11]
Indian Lady (IRE) *Mrs A L M King* a36 45
5 b m Namid—Lady Eberspacher (IRE) (Royal Abjar (USA))
1416[7] 1865[13] 2474[13] 3559[9] 4324[4] 4580[4] 4812[6] 6328[10]
Indian Ocean (IRE) *A P O'Brien* 94
2 b c Montjeu(IRE) —Dance Desire (IRE) (Caerleon (USA))
5946a[4] 6973[10]
Indian Pace (IRE) *John E Kiely* 84
7 ch g Indian Ridge—Blend Of Pace (IRE) (Sadler's Wells (USA))
1105a[9] 4003a[3] 4493a[5]
Indian's Feather (IRE) *N Tinkler* a80 81
7 ch m Indian Ridge—Mashmoum (Lycius (USA))
850[6] (949) 1287[5] 1590[3] 1903[3] 2289[8] 2672[12]
Indian Skipper (IRE) *M H Tompkins* a79 76
3 b g Indian Danehill(IRE) —Rosy Lydgate (Last Tycoon)
(1054) ◆ 1421[8] 5104[5] 5865[6] 6528[4] 6949[6] 7314[6] 7462[3]
Indian Star (GER) *P D Evans* a61
10 br g Sternkoenig(IRE) —Indian Night (GER) (Windwurf (GER))
182[4] 348[3] 394[3] 682[6] 754[5]
Indian Tonic (IRE) *W Jarvis* a61 76
2 b f Tiger Hill(IRE) —Wellspring (IRE) (Caerleon (USA))
5431[7] 6176[2] 6473[12] 7754[6]
Indian Trail *D Nicholls* a93 112
8 ch g Indian Ridge—Take Heart (Electric)
290a[6] 492a[4] 666a[7] 1420[12] 1986[4] 2401[8] 2626[6] 3248[24] 4445[14] 4624[19] 6104[23] 6653[12] 6810[12] 6971[8]
Indicible (FR) *A King* a91 83
4 ch g Dyhim Diamond(IRE) —Caslon (FR) (Deep Roots)
1935[2] 2152[5] 6763[7] 7025[3] 7493[10]
Indigo Belle (IRE) *Mrs A Duffield* 20
2 b f Mull Of Kintyre(USA) —Frances Canty (USA) (Lear Fan (USA))
6187[12] 6789[12]
Indigo Blue (FR) *J-P Gallorini* 103
3 b g Night Shift(USA) —Eye Witness (IRE) (Don't Forget Me)
1376a[3]
Indonesia *T D Walford* a68 82
6 ch g Lomitas—Idraak (Kris)
2628[3]
Indonesian Idol (IRE) *B Smart*
2 b c Exceed And Excel(AUS) —Jakarta (IRE) (Machiavellian (USA))
3707[10]
Indran (FR) *C Baillet* 82
3 b c Indian Rocket—Siran (FR) (R B Chesne)
7551a[0]
Industrial Star (IRE) *Micky Hammond* 74
7 ch g Singspiel(IRE) —Faribole (IRE) (Esprit Du Nord (USA))
2734[3] 3480[5] 4652[5] 5385[10]
Indy Driver *J R Fanshawe* a79 71
3 ch g Domedriver(IRE) —Condoleezza (USA) (Cozzene (USA))
1504[2] 1817[4] 2699[5] 3612[4] ◆ 4481[5] 5595[2] 6363[6] 6571[5] 6956[2]
Infallible *J H M Gosden* 112
3 b f Pivotal—Irresistible (Cadeaux Genereux)
(1401) 1830[4] 3194[2] ◆ 3852[2] 4506[5]
Infamous Angel *R Hannon* 105
2 b f Exceed And Excel(AUS) —Evangeline (Sadler's Wells (USA))
2618[6] ◆ (3019) 4190[2] (5272) 6441[7]
Infinite Charm (IRE) *M J P O'Brien* a84 72
5 ch g Peintre Celebre(USA) —Tenue D'Amour (FR) (Pursuit Of Love)
829a[8] 1103a[8]
Infinite Patience *J S Moore* a15 65
3 bb f High Chaparral(IRE) —Idma (Midyan (USA))
1161[14] 2127[3] 2452[7] 2922[11] 3381[10] 4052[8] 4298[8]
Infinity Bond *G R Oldroyd* a56 67
3 b g Forzando—Bond Girl (Magic Ring (IRE))
1304[4] 1751[7] 2187[4] 2911[13] 3280[6] ◆ (3786) 4560[4]
Infiraad *B W Hills* 75
2 ch c Haafhd—Razzle (IRE) (Green Desert (USA))
6438[3]
Inflagrantedelicto (USA) *Mrs R A Carr* a63 18
4 ch g Gentlemen(ARG) —Imprudent Love (USA) (Foolish Pleasure (USA))
80[12] 215[6] 436[9]
Inflammable *Sir Mark Prescott* a70 70
2 b f Montjeu(IRE) —Flame Valley (USA) (Gulch (USA))
5672[9] 6837[2] ◆ 7126[2]
Ingleby Arch (USA) *T D Barron* a95 98
5 b g Arch(USA) —Inca Dove (USA) (Mr Prospector (USA))
(442) 1071[6] 1517[5] 1689[6] 2538[6] 2938[7] 3489[7] 3812[6] 4218[8] 5222[9] 5594[5] 6842[8] (7448) 7756[8]
Ingleby Hill (IRE) *Micky Hammond* a51 50
4 b g Averti(IRE) —Living Daylights (IRE) (Night Shift (USA))
862[5] 1626[9]
Ingleby Princess *T D Barron* 78
4 br m Bold Edge—Bob's Princess (Bob's Return (IRE))
1826[2] ◆ 2205[6] 2444[6] 2928[3] 3050[15] (3404) 3728[3] 4016[4] 4858[8] 5455[3] 6160[4] 6564[6] 6813[6]
Ingleby Star (IRE) *T D Barron* a67 78
3 b g Fath(USA) —Rosy Scintilla (IRE) (Thatching)
4563[10] 4950[6] 5393[7] (6218) 6308[8]
Inheritor (IRE) *B Smart* 81
2 b g Kheleyf(USA) —Miss Devious (IRE) (Dr Devious (IRE))
3078[4] 3334[2] 4072[2] (4497) 5791[11] 6549[6]
In Her Shoes *B J Meehan* 57
2 ch f Pivotal—Ebaraya (IRE) (Sadler's Wells (USA))
6244[9] 6565[8] 6887[8]
Inhibition *A M Balding* 65
2 br f Nayef(USA) —Spurned (USA) (Robellino (USA))
6081[6] ◆
Inis Boffin *S Kirk* 43
2 b f Danehill Dancer(IRE) —Windmill (Ezzoud (IRE))
5240[16] 5640[13] 6240[26]
Inis Ceithleann (IRE) *Peter Casey* a49 72
4 b m Desert Sun—Sylvella (Lear Fan (USA))
4799a[9]
Inka Dancer (IRE) *B Palling* a64 70
6 ch m Intikhab(USA) —Grannys Reluctance (IRE) (Anita's Prince)
165[9] 5871[9] 6357[6] 6749[10]
Ink Spot *M L W Bell* a69 90
3 b g Diktat—Good Girl (IRE) (College Chapel)
1194[2] 1426[2] 1988[8] (2481) 3270[5] 3928[2] 4167[2] 5419[3] 6070[3]
Inkster (AUS) *Mick Price* 102
4 b m Umatilla(NZ) —Delgara (AUS) (Delgado (USA))
6922a[10]
Ink Stone (IRE) *Jane Chapple-Hyam* 27
3 b g Rock Of Gibraltar(IRE) —Pithara (GR) (Never So Bold)
4709[7]
In My Heart (GER) *H Steinmetz*
3 bb f Tiger Hill(IRE) — (USA) (Quest For Fame (USA))
7551a[9]
Innactualfact *L A Dace* a57 58
2 b f Lujain(USA) —Alzianah (Alzao (USA))
2146[6] 2614[3] 3373[8] 5585[8] 7052[4] 7258[14] 7623[10] 7718[5]
Inner Voice (USA) *J J Lambe* a4 57
5 gr g Cozzene(USA) —Miss Henderson Co (USA) (Silver Hawk (USA))
3756[2]
Inn For The Dancer *J C Fox* a54 38
6 b g Groom Dancer(USA) —Lady Joyce (FR) (Galetto (FR))
330[4]
Inn Swinger (IRE) *W G M Turner* a46 26
2 b f Makbul—Sheik'n Swing (Celtic Swing)
2459[6] 2720[2] 3309[8] 3815[5] 4063[8] 7530[10]
Inontime (IRE) *Jean-Rene Auvray* a59 41
3 ch f Golan(IRE) —Phantom Ring (Magic Ring (IRE))
74[2] 484[2] 974[6] 1222[11] 2052[11] 2861[7] 7442[7]
Inourthoughts (IRE) *Francis Ennis* a79 101
4 b m Desert Style(IRE) —Inourhearts (IRE) (Pips Pride)
2685a[11]
Inquest *Mrs A J Perrett* a44 75
3 b g Rainbow Quest(USA) —Katy Nowaitee (Komaite (USA))
4695[7] 5558[7] 5864[2] 6748[3] 7260[9]
Inquisitive Look *P W Chapple-Hyam* 84
3 b f Montjeu(IRE) —Whassup (FR) (Midyan (USA))
2668[2] ◆ 2989[3] (4909) 5737a[4]
Inquisitress *J J Bridger* a66 55
4 b m Hernando(FR) —Caribbean Star (Soviet Star (USA))
3839[4] 4414[3] (4529) 6338[5] 7012[7] 7076[11] 7392[12] 7495[7] 7605[4] ◆ 7702[13] 7800[7]
Insaaf *W J Haggas* 96
3 b f Averti(IRE) —Molly Brown (Rudimentary (USA))
1834[7] 2170[7] 3124[10] 3849[3] (4970) 7242[4]
In Seclusion (USA) *A Fabre* 93
3 gr c Cozzene(USA) —Be Exclusive (IRE) (Be My Guest (USA))
2096a[5]
In Secret *J L Dunlop* 41
2 b f Dalakhani(IRE) —Conspiracy (Rudimentary (USA))
5643[10]
Inside Knowledge (USA) *Mrs A J Perrett* a46 57
2 rg g Mizzen Mast(USA) —Kithira (Danehill (USA))
1873[5] 2754[6]
Inside Story (IRE) *C R Dore* a76 82
6 b g Rossini(USA) —Sliding (Formidable (USA))
133[2] 512[4] 768[2] 992[9] 2487[3] 2672[6] 3077[3] 3643[3] 4172[7] (4597) 4969[3] 6215[6] 6491[9] 7510[5] ◆ 7834[7]
Insiyaabi (USA) *J G Burns* a75 85
4 b h Aljabr(USA) —Elle Seule (USA) (Exclusive Native (USA))
1497a[10] 3532a[20]
Inspainagain (USA) *T D Barron* 79
4 ch g Miswaki(USA) —Counter Cat (USA) (Hennessy (USA))
2843[10] 3080[11] 3787[9] (3931) 4418[8] 5719[7] 5861[9] 6164[11]
Inspector (TUR) *U Bekmezci* 117
4 b h Bin Ajwaad(IRE) —Pandora (GER) (Platini (GER))
(5741a)
Inspector Clouseau (IRE) *T P Tate* a60 81
3 gr g Daylami(IRE) —Claustra (FR) (Green Desert (USA))
2209[2] 3048[2] 3641[5] 4419[4] 6113[5] 6698[9]
Inspiration (AUS) *J Moore* 119
5 ch g Flying Spur(AUS) —La Bamba (AUS) (Last Tycoon)
(7683a)
Inspirina (IRE) *R Ford* a75 80
4 b g Invincible Spirit(IRE) —La Stellina (IRE) (Marju (IRE))
361[2] (513) 701[2] (1388) 1947[4] 2332[2] 3010[4] 3368[6] 5498[8] 5992[5] 7064[8]
Instalment *R Hannon* 102
2 b g Cape Cross(IRE) —New Assembly (IRE) (Machiavellian (USA))
(2146) ◆ 3103[14] 4517[6] 5507[7] 6399[2]
Instant Recall (IRE) *M Al Muhairi* a96 103
7 ch g Indian Ridge—Happy Memories (IRE) (Thatching)
379a[6] (474a) ◆ 649a[10] (741a)
In Step *W J Haggas* a53 56
2 b f Montjeu(IRE) —Heart's Harmony (Blushing Groom (FR))
6887[7] 7343[7] 7425[6] 7659[11]
Institute *Sir Michael Stoute* 76
3 ch c Pivotal—Constitute (USA) (Gone West (USA))
4249[11] 5491[6]
Instructor *C A Mulhall* a88 87
7 ch g Groom Dancer(USA) —Doctor's Glory (USA) (Elmaamul (USA))
1970[9] 2220[10] 2591[9]
In Summation (USA) *Christophe Clement* a117 106
5 bb h Put It Back(USA) —Fiesta Baby (USA) (Dayjur (USA))
6999a[4]
Insured *A J McCabe* a46 41
3 ch g Intikhab(USA) —Self Assured (IRE) (Ahonoora)
1490[7] 1905[5]
Intabih (USA) *C E Brittain* a89 65
3 bb c More Than Ready(USA) —Lookaway Dixieland (USA) (Dixieland Band (USA))
5278[5] 5864[6] 6047[3] 6422[3] (6712) (6905) 7291[5]
Intangaroo (USA) *Gary Sherlock* a114
4 br m Orientate(USA) —Tasso's Magic Roo (USA) (Tasso (USA))
6965a[6]
Intavac Boy *S P Griffiths* a61 65
7 ch g Emperor Fountain—Altaia (FR) (Sicyos (USA))
1394[12] 3010[10] 3602[8]
Integral (GER) *P Rau* 83
4 b h Lando(GER) —Incenza (GER) (Local Suitor (USA))
6156a[6] 6692a[9]
Integration *Miss M E Rowland* a44 44
8 b g Piccolo—Discrimination (Efisio)
36[6] 238[7]
Integria *J M P Eustace* a63 69
2 b g Intikhab(USA) —Alegria (Night Shift (USA))
6701[8] 7051[3] 7289[5]
Intense *B W Hills* 84
2 b f Dansili—Modesta (IRE) (Sadler's Wells (USA))
4521[2] ◆ (5643) 6439[11]
Intense Focus (USA) *J S Bolger* 118
2 b c Giant's Causeway(USA) —Daneleta (IRE) (Danehill (USA))
3103[2] ◆ 3534a[3] 4005a[5] 5946a[6] 6317a[3] 6520a[3] (6815)
Intensifier (IRE) *D L Williams* a61 56
4 b g Sinndar(IRE) —Licorne (Sadler's Wells (USA))
6364[10] 6668[8] 7322[5] 7512[8]
Interactive (IRE) *Andrew Turnell* a75 68
5 b g King's Best(USA) —Forentia (Formidable (USA))
334[9] 608[4] 777[2] 1036[3] 1312[4] 1541[6] 5639[11] 6338[10] 6706[2] 6890[7] 7435[5] 7540[8]
Interchange (IRE) *J R Fanshawe* 89
3 b f Montjeu(IRE) —Key Change (IRE) (Darshaan)
3894[4] ◆ (4871) 6415[4] 7108[2] 7242[5]
Interchoice Star *K G Wingrove* a31 36
3 b g Josr Algarhoud(IRE) —Blakeshall Girl (Piccolo)
5366[8] 5627[7] 6254[9]
Intercom *H R A Cecil* 71
3 b c Dansili—Dialing Tone (USA) (Distant View (USA))
2763[6] 3654[11] 4124[9]
Interest (USA) *T D Barron* a39 41
4 ch g Banker's Gold(USA) —Princess Kris (Kris)
69[9] 83[4] 215[8]
Internationaldebut (IRE) *S Parr* a104 91
3 b g High Chaparral(IRE) —Whisper Light (IRE) (Caerleon (USA))
961[3] 1221[3] 1524[6] 2109[10] 3051[3] 4121[3] (4301) (6452) 6663[6] 6976[2] 7239[10] (7390) ◆ (7477) ◆ (7556)
Intersky Charm (USA) *R M Whitaker* a86 80
4 ch g Lure(USA) —Catala (USA) (Northern Park (USA))
(192) 280[4] 531[2] 962[15] 2220[3] 2582[11] 3142[2] 3478[5] 3947[12] 4111[5] 5382[4] 5773[9] 5910[4] 6352[6]
Intersky Melody (USA) *E J Creighton* a68 62
3 b g Sky Mesa(USA) —Mayan Maiden (USA) (Lyphard (USA))
1161[15] 1516[5] 2273[3] 2915[6] (3230) 5380[3] 6217[8] 7310[9]
Intersky Sports (USA) *Miss C Dyson* a69 63
4 gr g Chester House(USA) —Nightlong (Night Shift (USA))
431[4] 569[5] 3698[12]
Inter Vision (USA) *A Dickman* a96 102
8 b g Cryptoclearance(USA) —Fateful (USA) (Topsider (USA))
1393[10] 1796[14] 2210[4] (2398) (2489) 2538[5] 5503[6] 5890[10] 6104[24]
Inthawain *M R Channon* 68
2 b f Bertolini(USA) —Ambassadress (USA) (Alleged (USA))
4202[8] 4579[6] 5394[3] 5838[4] 6809[6]
In The Light *Sir Michael Stoute* a97 108
4 br m Inchinor—Exclusive Approval (USA) (With Approval (CAN))
4977[5] 5506[10] 6781[3] 7099[6]
In The Moment *W G M Turner* 30
2 ch f Baryshnikov(AUS) —Grace Bankes (Efisio)
1264[5] 1555[3] 2548[4] 2882[3]
In The Mood (IRE) *W Jarvis* 69
2 ch f Hawk Wing(USA) —Grecian Glory (IRE) (Zafonic (USA))
6030[8] 6319a[18]
Intikama (IRE) *M H Tompkins* 74
2 ch f Intikhab(USA) —Really Gifted (IRE) (Cadeaux Genereux)
4792[5] 5838[3] 6110[3]
Into Action *Mrs Marjorie Fife* a66 68
4 b g Sendawar(IRE) —Syrian Dancer (IRE) (Groom Dancer (USA))
988[9] 1136[14] 3589[15] 3822[12]
Into My Arms *M S Saunders* a23
2 gr f Kyllachy—True Love (Robellino (USA))
2769[11] 3584[7] 3968[10]
Into The Light *E S McMahon* a69 65
3 b g Fantastic Light(USA) —Boadicea's Chariot (Commanche Run)
2380[9] 2954[7] 3629[5] 4173[5] 6092[2] 6708[2] 7366[11]
In Toto *M Wigham* a48 42
3 b g Intikhab(USA) —Motto (FR) (Mtoto)
1581[4] 2823[8] 3447[6] 3893[7] 4796[9]
In Transit (IRE) *M R Channon* a80 80
2 b c Trans Island—Meranie Girl (IRE) (Mujadil (USA))
2054[4] 2324[2] (2554) 2713[2] 2859[3] 2987[3] 3553[5] 4119[9] 4626[10] 5242[5] 5747[7] 6376[5] 6694[3] 6946[7]
Intrepid Jack *H Morrison* a102 115
6 b h Compton Place—Maria Theresa (Primo Dominie)
2401[2] 3248[10] ◆ 3739[7] (4188) 4915a[13] 5553a[4] 6304[8] 6645[10]
Intrepid Lady (IRE) *J C Tuck* 56
2 br f Namid—Hard To Lay (IRE) (Dolphin Street (FR))
4149[17] 4534[8] 4764[2] 5581[4] 7451[12]
Invasian (IRE) *P W D'Arcy* a96 93
7 ch g Desert Prince(IRE) —Jarrayan (Machiavellian (USA))
61[4] 410[8] 1812[9] 2120[3] 2531[8] 3250[15] 4200[4] 4645[2] 5100[8] 5677[9] 6839[3] 7753[7]
Inventing Paradise *J D Bethell* 42
2 ch f Bahamian Bounty—Phi Beta Kappa (USA) (Diesis)
3078[8]
Invention (USA) *Miss E C Lavelle* a89 88
5 b g Lear Fan(USA) —Carya (USA) (Northern Dancer (CAN))
1719[15] 1799[7] 2153[12] 6671[10]
Inventor (IRE) *B J Meehan* a103 102
3 b g Alzao(USA) —Magnificent Bell (IRE) (Octagonal (NZ))
(2256) 2610[6] (3719) 4784[7] 5573[2] 6171[2] 6646[4]
Investor (IRE) *G Martin* a95 81
9 b g Marju(IRE) —Shine On Me (Machiavellian (USA))
421a[10]
Invincible Ash (IRE) *M Halford* a95 79
3 b f Invincible Spirit(IRE) —Fully Fashioned (IRE) (Brief Truce (USA))
6963a[2]
Invincible Brave (IRE) *R A Fahey* a21 29
2 b c Invincible Spirit(IRE) —Recall (IRE) (Revoque (IRE))
7079[9] 7275[10]
Invincible Force (IRE) *Paul Green* a100 101
4 b g Invincible Spirit(IRE) —Highly Respected (IRE) (High Estate)
1917[10] 2211[6] 2401[3] 3931[2] 4445[7] 4660[4] 4957[5] 5990[2] 6290[7] 7151[12] (7245)
Invincible Heart (GR) *Jane Chapple-Hyam* a85 88
2 b c Invincible Spirit(IRE) —Flamingo Bay (IRE) (Catrail (USA))
4826[4] 5271[5] 5794[3] ◆ 6077[2] 6776[2] 7334[3] 7476[3]
Invincible Joe (IRE) *G M Lyons* a56 85
3 b g Invincible Spirit(IRE) —Abbey Park (USA) (Known Fact (USA))
826a[10] 3286a[2]
Invincible Lad (IRE) *E J Alston* a90 73
4 b g Invincible Spirit(IRE) —Lady Ellen (Horage)
(700) 1189[6] 2009[12] 3080[5] (3581) (4013) 4563[3] 5796[9] 6039[9] (6840) ◆ (6990)
Invincible Rose (IRE) *M E Sowersby* a24 45
3 b f Invincible Spirit(IRE) —Yorkshire Rose (IRE) (Sadler's Wells (USA))
534[6] 4207[5] 5303[10]
Invisible Man *J H M Gosden* a71
2 ch c Elusive Quality(USA) —Eternal Reve (USA) (Diesis)
7209[3]
Inwaan (IRE) *P R Webber* a53 66
5 b g King's Best(USA) —Balaabel (USA) (Sadler's Wells (USA))
2075[7] 2355[12] 3446[4] 4793[6]
In With A Shout *J G Given* a5
3 b f Choisir(AUS) —Shouting The Odds (IRE) (Victory Note (USA))
7213[9] 7362[11]
Inwood (IRE) *Paul Magnier* a80 82
5 b g Bluebird(USA) —Hardshan (IRE) (Warrshan (USA))
1497a[3] 4576a[9] 6511a[8]
Inxile (IRE) *D Nicholls* 110
3 b g Fayruz—Grandel (Owington)
1170[2] 1712a[3] 2498[3] 3041[2] ◆ 4240[3] ◆ (4881a) 5556a[2]
Io (IRE) *J L Dunlop* a55 56
3 b f King's Best(USA) —Callisto (IRE) (Darshaan)
1147[5] 1527[7] 1962[9] 2475[2] 2931[6]
Iolith (GER) *A Fabre* 96
3 b c Monsun(GER) —Indian Jewel (GER) (Local Suitor (USA))
6664a[0]
Iorek Byrnison *D Nicholls* a55 50
2 ch c Auction House(USA) —Thicket (Wolfhound (USA))
3365[10] 3815[2] 4965[5] 5591[3] 6787[8] 7370[5]
Ipdipdoo (IRE) *R Hollinshead* 14
2 b f Beckett(IRE) —Lady Charlotte (Night Shift (USA))
5959[15]
Iraschko *J L Spearing* 36
3 b f Bertolini(USA) —Bright Future (FR) (Akarad (FR))
3262[6] 3894[12] 4695[15]

Ireland Dancer (IRE) *P M Phelan* a55 9
4 ch g Trans Island—Come Dancing (Suave Dancer (USA))
2755^{13} 4054^{10}
Ireland's Call (IRE) *Peter Casey* a88 97
7 gr g King's Theatre(IRE) —Tarikhana (Mouktar)
5731a^{18}
Irish Artist (FR) *R Hannon* a78 71
3 b c Orpen(USA) —Anchusa (IRE) (Nashwan (USA))
900^{2} ◆ *(1082)* (Dead)
Irish Ballad *S Dow* a63 56
6 b g Singspiel(IRE) —Auenlust (GER) (Surumu (GER))
1148^{9} *1562*^{9} 4055^{2} 4275^{12} 4811^{11} *5676*^{3} *5917*^{2} *6740*^{5} *(7216)* *(7401)* *7587*^{2} 7806^{4}
Irish Bay (IRE) *Luke Comer* 52
5 b g Brief Passing(IRE) —Echo Bay (IRE) (Barry's Run (IRE))
6543^{7} 6705^{12}
Irish Brooke (IRE) *B Smart*
3 ch f Night Shift(USA) —Away With The Wind (Irish River (FR))
2283^{10}
Irish Cape *Mrs N Smith* a50
5 br m Cape Cross(IRE) —Praglia (IRE) (Darshaan)
95^{6} *175*^{9}
Irish Conection (IRE) *Thomas McLaughlin* a51 35
5 b g Bold Fact(USA) —Trojan Girl (IRE) (Up And At 'Em)
1259^{3} 2751^{15}
Irish Joe (USA) *T D Barron* a24 15
2 rg c Brahms(USA) —Morning Pearl (CAN) (Morning Bob (USA))
3821^{10} 4604^{9}
Irish Legend (IRE) *C Roberts* 52
8 b g Sadler's Wells(USA) —Wedding Bouquet (Kings Lake (USA))
5367^{7}
Irish Mayhem (USA) *B J Meehan* a108 87
3 bb c Woodman(USA) —Adventurous Di (USA) (Private Account (USA))
1424^{6} (1686) 2412^{7} 3325^{5} 4783^{9} *(5207)* *(5907)*
Irish Music (IRE) *A P Jarvis* a73 60
3 b g Namid—Kelly's Tune (Alhaarth (IRE))
796^{3} *965*^{2} *1414*^{3} 1737^{5} 2490^{9}
Irish Pearl (IRE) *K R Burke* a104 89
3 b f Statue Of Liberty(USA) —Helen Wells (IRE) (Sadler's Wells (USA))
1170^{3} 2148^{4} 3794^{5} 4416^{7} 4962^{6} 5757^{2} 5962^{11} 6651^{12} *(7047)* *(7181)* *7394*^{4} *7614*^{10}
Irish Quest (IRE) *M A Jarvis* a64 87
4 b g Galileo(IRE) —No Quest (IRE) (Rainbow Quest (USA))
1337^{8} 2414^{6} 3044^{5} *3613*^{9} 4751^{2} *5376*^{9} 6054^{11} 6361^{7}
Irish Saint (IRE) *T J Pitt* a60 29
2 ch g Kheleyf(USA) —Tarifana (IRE) (Dr Devious (IRE))
6187^{9} 6808^{9} *7343*^{5}
Irish Whispers (IRE) *B G Powell* a60 53
5 b g Marju(IRE) —Muneera (USA) (Green Dancer (USA))
4105^{7} 5183^{11}
Iron Cross (IRE) *Sir Mark Prescott* a50 46
3 b g Cape Cross(IRE) —Alithini (IRE) (Darshaan)
2340^{13} *3483*^{10} *4477*^{6} 4859^{13} *5593*^{13}
Iron Man Of Mersey (FR) *A W Carroll* 41
2 b c Poliglote—Miss Echo (Chief Singer)
7106^{12}
Iron Max (IRE) *N J Vaughan* a19
2 b g Iron Mask(USA) —Starisa (IRE) (College Chapel)
7501^{11}
Iron Out (USA) *R Hollinshead* 59
2 b c Straight Man(USA) —Fit Fighter (USA) (Fit To Fight (USA))
4296^{7}
Iron Pearl *J Ryan* a57 51
4 b m Iron Mask(USA) —Fast Tempo (IRE) (Statoblest)
167^{6} *327*^{11} *392*^{11} *445*^{10}
Irony (IRE) *A M Balding* a81 91
9 gr g Mujadil(USA) —Cidaris (IRE) (Persian Bold)
3904^{2} (4121) ◆ 4602^{4} *5051*^{8} 5290^{5} *6576*^{12}
Irving Place *R A Fahey* 78
3 ch g Compton Place—Prince's Feather (IRE) (Cadeaux Genereux)
1426^{7} 1925^{6} 2967^{7} 3416^{4} 3723^{13} 4236^{3} 4450^{4} 6357^{11} 6792^{17}
Isa'Af (IRE) *P W Hiatt* a57 78
9 b g Darshaan—Shauna's Honey (IRE) (Danehill (USA))
67^{5} *(152)* *179*^{7} *394*^{5}
Isabella Grey *K A Ryan* 86
2 gr f Choisir(AUS) —Karsiyaka (IRE) (Kahyasi)
3259^{5} (3625) 4348^{8}
Isabella Romee (IRE) *Jane Chapple-Hyam* a49 61
2 gr f Bahri(USA) —Silver Clasp (IRE) (Linamix (FR))
2614^{5} 4184^{8} 5097^{8} *5591*^{7} 6214^{13} *6931*^{6}
Isabella's Fancy *A G Newcombe* a57 45
3 br f Captain Rio—Princess Of Spain (King Of Spain)
1453^{8} 1795^{8} 2546^{5} *3397*^{5} 4044^{10} 5652^{5} *(6836)* *7533*^{10}
Isabelonabicycle *A M Balding* a68
3 b f Helissio(FR) —Santa Isobel (Nashwan (USA))
6018^{2} *6909*^{3}
Isanous (FR) *J-C Rouget* a90 97
3 gr f Zamindar(USA) —Douceur Creole (FR) (Highest Honor (FR))
5556a^{6}
Isent She Rich (IRE) *David P Myerscough* 70
3 ch f Dubai Destination(USA) —Rahika Rose (Unfuwain (USA))
6487^{11}
Ishe Mac *N Bycroft* 76
2 b f Ishiguru(USA) —Zacinta (USA) (Hawkster (USA))
2887^{9} 3140^{2} 4202^{3} 4874^{2} 6525^{7}
Ishetoo *A Dickman* 103
4 b g Ishiguru(USA) —Ticcatoo (IRE) (Dolphin Street (FR))
2211^{2} ◆ 2626^{3} 3056^{5} 3451^{9} 3973^{4} (5542) 6104^{21} 6653^{7} 6947^{10}
Ishiadancer *E J Alston* a65 64
3 b f Ishiguru(USA) —Abaklea (IRE) (Doyoun)
5203^{4} 5561^{5} *6254*^{2} 6792^{5} *7226*^{6} *7403*^{4}
Ishibee (IRE) *J J Bridger* a61 61
4 b m Ishiguru(USA) —Beauty (IRE) (Alzao (USA))
13^{5} *263*^{7} *327*^{9} 2622^{14} 4273^{7} 4779^{7} 4979^{7} 5315^{10} *7710*^{10} *7768*^{5} *7818*^{3}
Ishiquick *T D Easterby* 20
2 b f Ishiguru(USA) —Adaptable (Groom Dancer (USA))
3140^{11} 3707^{9} 5715^{11} (Dead)
Is It Me (USA) *A W Carroll* a57 79
5 ch g Sky Classic(CAN) —Thea (GER) (Surumu (GER))
118^{3} *268*^{7} 2482^{5} 2908^{5} 3220^{5} 3650^{3} 4410^{3} 5465^{8} *5917*^{8} 6672^{15}
Is It Time (IRE) *Mrs P N Dutfield* a66 57
4 b m Danetime(IRE) —Ishaam (Selkirk (USA))
13^{6} *86*^{7} *191*^{11} *1145*^{3} *(1285)* *1541*^{4} 2102^{8} *7834*^{11}
Island Breeze (IRE) *Andrew Oliver* a71 59
2 b f Trans Island—Dame Laura (IRE) (Royal Academy (USA))
6637a^{10}
Island Chief *K A Ryan* a54 64
2 b c Reel Buddy(USA) —Fisher Island (IRE) (Sri Pekan (USA))
4921^{6} 5387^{4} 6065^{3} *7067*^{6} *7275*^{6} *7370*^{3} *7694*^{3}
Island Home *J E Pease* 71
2 b f Act One—Island Race (Common Grounds)
3749a^{8}
Island King (IRE) *R Bastiman* a38 41
5 br g Turtle Island(IRE) —Love Of Paris (Trojan Fen)
69^{8} *377*^{6}
Island Music (IRE) *J J Quinn* 70
3 b f Mujahid(USA) —Ischia (Lion Cavern (USA))
(2039) 2575^{5} 3109^{6} 3717^{4} 4219^{4} 4741^{7} 6216^{4} 7224^{3}
Island Sunset (IRE) *W R Muir* a70
2 ch f Trans Island—Islandagore (IRE) (Indian Ridge)
(6986)
Island Treasure *H Morrison* a63 64
3 b c Cadeaux Genereux—Gallivant (Danehill (USA))
2834^{10} 3326^{7} 4195^{4} 4637^{3} 5755^{9} 6396^{3} 6746^{6} *6936*^{3}
Island Vista *M A Jarvis* a72 90
3 b f Montjeu(IRE) —Colorvista (Shirley Heights) (4695) 6241^{7} 7108^{9}
Isle Of Capri *R Hannon* 78
3 b f Cape Cross(IRE) —Zenith (Shirley Heights)
2198^{19} 2800^{5} 3061^{4} 4112^{4} (4485) 6202^{6}
Is Mise An Ri (IRE) *Emmanuel Hughes* a42
6 br g General Monash(USA) —Mystic Shadow (IRE) (Mtoto)
100^{3} *119*^{6}
Isobel Rose (IRE) *J L Spearing* a67 38
4 b m Royal Applause—Total Love (Cadeaux Genereux)
16^{9} *(445)*
Isphahan *A M Balding* a71 96
5 b g Diktat—Waltzing Star (IRE) (Danehill (USA))
1900^{4} 2128^{2} (2992) 3218^{2} (3383) 4284^{4} (4789) 5470^{2} 6250^{2} (6307)
Istead Rise (IRE) *P A Blockley* a56 49
4 b g Mull Of Kintyre(USA) —Tommys Queen (IRE) (Ali-Royal (IRE))
387^{5} *533*^{7}
Istibian (IRE) *Mrs H Sweeting* a49 50
4 b g Sakhee(USA) —Cap Coz (IRE) (Indian Ridge)
1280^{13}
Istiqdaam *J H M Gosden* 81
3 b g Pivotal—Auspicious (Shirley Heights)
3262^{2}
Istria (USA) *R M Beckett* a62 40
3 b f Zavata(USA) —Estri (USA) (Conquistador Cielo (USA))
1957^{11} 2622^{13} *3397*^{12}
Itainteasybeingme *J R Boyle* a58 56
2 ch c Lucky Story(USA) —Concubine (IRE) (Danehill (USA))
4480^{14} 4778^{5} 5089^{4} 6191^{2} *6572*^{2} 6924^{6}
Italian Goddess *M L W Bell* a49 66
3 ch f Medicean—Little Italy (IRE) (Common Grounds)
1397^{5} *2052*^{7} 2559^{2} 3874^{3} 4669^{12} 5108^{6} *6227*^{8}
Italian Romance *J W Unett* a79 45
5 b g Medicean—Polish Romance (USA) (Danzig (USA))
185^{7} 4167^{7}
Italstar (IRE) *Miss D Mountain* a45
4 ch m Galileo(IRE) —Jorghinia (FR) (Seattle Slew (USA))
1611^{0} *2691*^{3}
Ithbaat (USA) *J H M Gosden* 77
2 bb c Arch(USA) —Annul (USA) (Conquistador Cielo (USA))
5469^{4} ◆
Ithinkbest *Sir Michael Stoute* 60
2 b g King's Best(USA) —Monturani (IRE) (Indian Ridge)
7105^{7}
Itlaaq *J L Dunlop* 72
2 b c Alhaarth(IRE) —Hathrah (IRE) (Linamix (FR))
4570^{12} 4982^{5} 5901^{4} 6857^{8}
Itmaybeyou (NZ) *B Dean* 33
6 b g Howbaddouwantit(USA) —Julie's Sailboat (USA) (Naevus (USA))
2234a^{16}
It's A Date *A King* a13 82
3 b g Kyllachy—By Arrangement (IRE) (Bold Arrangement)
(2191) 2665^{7} 3380^{6} 4021^{5} 4573^{5} *5406*^{6} 6012^{3} 6607^{2}
It's A Dream (FR) *M W Easterby* a79 82
5 b g Kaldounevees(FR) —Bahia Mar (USA) (Arctic Tern (USA))
872^{6} *1491*^{4} 2274^{4} (2749) ◆ 3478^{2} 3738^{2} 4219^{11} *4934*^{6} *6090*^{3} 6485^{6} *6826*^{3} *(6989)*
It's A Game (USA) *J H M Gosden* a72 39
2 b f Forestry(USA) —Gotablush (Nashwan (USA))
4251^{13} 4643^{14} *(6697)* *7306*^{10} *7472*^{5}
Itsagroom (SWE) *Vanja Sandrup*
3 b c Itsabrahma—Saucy Girl (FR) (Taufan (USA))
4918a^{7}
Its Alice *Peter Grayson* 5
2 bl f Needwood Blade—Zamyatina (IRE) (Danehill Dancer (IRE))
6089^{11} *6489*^{12} 6764^{11}
It's A Mans World *P J McBride* a68 69
2 b c Kyllachy—Exhibitor (USA) (Royal Academy (USA))
6085^{6} *7023*^{5} *7709*^{4}
Itsawindup *Miss Sheena West* a50 20
4 b g Elnadim(USA) —Topwinder (USA) (Topsider (USA))
691^{3} *(715)* *930*^{6} *7815*^{3}
It's Dubai Dolly *A J Lidderdale* a69 72
2 ch f Dubai Destination(USA) —Betrothal (IRE) (Groom Dancer (USA))
5147^{8} 5650^{2} *6432*^{4} 7142^{3}
It's Early Days *W R Muir* 5
3 ch g Singspiel(IRE) —Exultate Jubilate (USA) (With Approval (CAN))
5117^{8}
It's Gino (GER) *P Vovcenko* 126
5 b h Perugino(USA) —Imelda (GER) (Lomitas)
(2440a) 3540a^{2} 4232a^{3} 5736a^{3} 6522a^{3}
Itsher *S C Williams* a56 55
2 br f Diktat—Shararah (Machiavellian (USA))
4488^{5} 4776^{5} 5530^{8} *7257*^{4} *7832*^{3}
Itshim *S C Williams* 11
2 b g Ishiguru(USA) —Sumitra (Tragic Role (USA))
5287^{5} 5530^{11} 5753^{10} 6085^{17}
It's Josr *I A Wood* a65 61
3 b g Josr Algarhoud(IRE) —It's So Easy (Shaadi (USA))
900^{7} *1057*^{9} 2695^{8} *3483*^{13} 4664^{7} 5167^{12} (5218) *6353*^{5}
It's Me Again *E J O'Neill* 16
2 b g Bahri(USA) —Evening Charm (IRE) (Bering)
5304^{9}
Its Moon (IRE) *T D Walford* 76
4 b m Tobougg(IRE) —Shallat (IRE) (Pennekamp (USA))
2006^{4} 2423^{3} 2572^{5} 3624^{5} 4652^{6} 5637^{8} 5967^{2} 6313^{7} 7039^{10}
It's My Day (IRE) *Jane Chapple-Hyam* a66 72
3 ch g Soviet Star(USA) —Ezana (Ela-Mana-Mou)
1543^{6} 2045^{2} 2785^{11}
It's No Problem (IRE) *Mrs N S Evans* a58 58
4 b m Averti(IRE) —Polar Rock (Polar Falcon (USA))
(1895) 3631^{4} 5653^{10}
It's Toast (IRE) *R M Beckett* 70
2 b f Diktat—Kapria (FR) (Simon Du Desert (FR))
3456^{11} 3913^{6} (4705) 5855^{5} 6477^{10} 6809^{7}
Itsy Bitsy *W J Musson* a47 51
6 b m Danzig Connection(USA) —Cos I Do (IRE) (Double Schwartz)
166^{13} *613*^{4} *1262*^{11} (4261) 4599^{5} *6228*^{12} *6728*^{5} *7667*^{8}
Ivan Ivan (USA) *Megan Morrison*
2 u c (USA) — (USA) (Chief's Crown (USA))
6502a^{11}
Ivan Poddubny *A Shavuyev* 61
2 b c Sadler's Wells(USA) —Be Glad (Selkirk (USA))
6855a^{6}
Ivestar (IRE) *D Nicholls* a49 76
3 b g Fraam—Hazardous (Night Shift (USA))
1130^{4} 1428^{3} 1753^{4}
Ivona *Saeed Bin Suroor* a44
3 b f Indian Ridge—Mot Juste (Mtoto)
3133^{9}
Ivor Novello (IRE) *G A Swinbank* 25
2 b c Noverre(USA) —Pearly Brooks (Efisio)
3055^{8} 4176^{9}
Ivory Lace *S Woodman* a88 94
7 b m Atraf—Miriam (Forzando)
2371^{6} 2762^{9} 3210^{7} 3944^{4} 4509^{4} 4723^{8} 4841^{6} 5311^{9} *5683*^{6} 6307^{6} *6627*^{2} *7302*^{11} *7419*^{7} *7557*^{8}
Ivory's Icon (IRE) *Miss Jo Crowley* a45
2 gr g Catcher In The Rye(IRE) —Ivory's Promise (Pursuit Of Love)
4305^{8} *7069*^{12}
Ivory Silk *J R Gask* a91 73
3 b f Diktat—Ivory's Joy (Tina's Pet)
1144^{3} ◆ 1423^{9} *1763*^{10} ◆ 2976^{8} 3381^{2} 3727^{4} 4252^{3} 4987^{2} *(5402)* 6402^{5} *6680*^{4} *(7393)* *(7826)*
Ivy Creek (USA) *G Wragg* 115
5 b h Gulch(USA) —Ivy Leaf (IRE) (Nureyev (USA))
1468^{4} 1980^{P} (Dead)
I Want Revenge (USA) *Jeff Mullins* a115
2 b c Stephen Got Even(USA) —Meguial (ARG) (Roy (USA))
7751a^{2}
Izanagi (USA) *J E Hammond* a81 98
3 b c A.P. Indy(USA) —Insight (FR) (Sadler's Wells (USA))
385a^{4}
Izzibizzi *E A L Dunlop* a81 86
3 b f Medicean—Sleave Silk (IRE) (Unfuwain (USA))
5786^{3} *(6571)* (6981) *7210*^{4} *7419*^{12}
Izzi Mill (USA) *D R C Elsworth* a69 71
2 rg f Lemon Drop Kid(USA) —Lets Get Cozzy (USA) (Cozzene (USA))
2951^{4} 3346^{5} 6776^{4} *7097*^{6}
Izzy Lou (IRE) *K A Ryan* 71
2 ch f Spinning World(USA) —High Spot (Shirley Heights)
4896^{2} 5256^{5}
Jaadull *M Johnston* 88
3 b g Dubai Destination(USA) —Saafeya (IRE) (Sadler's Wells (USA))
(6530) 6866^{2}
Jaassey *J S Wainwright* a49 38
5 b g Josr Algarhoud(IRE) —Saaryeh (Royal Academy (USA))
189^{4} *365*^{5} *844*^{3} 2040^{10} 2463^{8} 3662^{9}
Jabal Tariq *B W Hills* 90
3 ch c Rock Of Gibraltar(IRE) —Sueboog (IRE) (Darshaan)
(1628) 2194^{9} (3174) 4205^{4} 5111^{4}
Jabraan (USA) *Mrs R A Carr* a42 42
6 b g Aljabr(USA) —Miss Zafonic (FR) (Zafonic (USA))
615^{5} *719*^{6} *786*^{7} *846*^{8} *871*^{5} *1705*^{6} 2491^{6} *2869*^{9} 2936^{14} 3231^{10}
Jacaranda (IRE) *B R Millman* 68
8 ch g Bahhare(USA) —Near Miracle (Be My Guest (USA))
2097^{6} 2640^{7}
Jachol (IRE) *W J Haggas* 49
2 b g Bachelor Duke(USA) —Restiv Star (FR) (Soviet Star (USA))
7020^{11} 7104^{10} 7240^{12}
Jack Cool (IRE) *P W Chapple-Hyam* 55
2 b c One Cool Cat(USA) —Rachrush (IRE) (Sadler's Wells (USA))
5246^{12}
Jack Dawkins (USA) *H R A Cecil* a101 101
3 b c Fantastic Light(USA) —Do The Mambo (USA) (Kingmambo (USA))
6526^{3} 7145^{10} *7339*^{3}
Jackday (IRE) *T D Easterby* 61
3 b g Daylami(IRE) —Magic Lady (IRE) (Bigstone (IRE))
2496^{8} 3555^{6} 4077^{4} (4247) 4735^{4} 5385^{11}
Jack Got Even (USA) *D M Simcock* a52 76
3 ch c Stephen Got Even(USA) —Nara (USA) (Green Forest (USA))
1587^{4}
Jackie Kiely *R Brotherton* a79 73
7 ch g Vettori(IRE) —Fudge (Polar Falcon (USA))
78^{2} *159*^{4} *(368)* *1026*^{4} *1131*^{2} *1589*^{3} *1904*^{3} 4156^{5} 4458^{3} 4739^{3} 5783^{11} 6662^{6} 7046^{5} 7183^{6}
Jack Jicaro *Mrs L Williamson* 44
2 b g Mind Games—Makeover (Priolo (USA))
2903^{10} 3199^{5} 4986^{6}
Jack Junior (USA) *B J Meehan* a102 110
4 bb g Songandaprayer(USA) —Ra Hydee (USA) (Rahy (USA))
(3262) 3740^{10} 4330^{4} *5208*^{5} *5941*^{3} *6287*^{10}
Jackpot Delight (NZ) *C Fownes* 120
5 gr g Danasinga(AUS) —Principation (NZ) (Prince Echo)
7682a^{13}
Jack Rackham *B Smart* a77 93
4 ch g Kyllachy—Hill Welcome (Most Welcome)
3009^{17} 3336^{12} 5796^{14} 6859^{13} 7239^{18}
Jack Rio (IRE) *Michael McElhone* 72
3 gr f Captain Rio—Order Of Success (USA) (With Approval (CAN))
4494a^{6}
Jack Rolfe *G L Moore* a89 81
6 b g Polish Precedent(USA) —Haboobti (Habitat)
105^{2} *268*^{2} *(405)* *630*^{4}
Jack's A Guest (IRE) *Miss Jane Thomas* 37
3 br g Expelled(USA) —Jennifers Guest (IRE) (Be My Guest (USA))
4715a^{9}
Jack's House (IRE) *Jane Chapple-Hyam* a51 24
2 b c Danetime(IRE) —Groupetime (USA) (Gilded Time (USA))
5866^{7} 7079^{10} *7318*^{9} *7425*^{7} *7810*^{5}
Jack Sullivan (USA) *G A Butler* a116 105
7 ch g Belong To Me(USA) —Provisions (USA) (Devil's Bag (USA))
62^{2} *204a*^{13} *476a*^{4} *(680)* *(832)* 1767^{4}
Jacobite Prince (IRE) *M H Tompkins* 68
2 b g Chevalier(IRE) —Kind Gesture (IRE) (Alzao (USA))
3651^{9} 4199^{11} 4960^{4} 6112^{8}
Jaconet (USA) *T D Barron* a43 76
3 ch f Hussonet(USA) —Radiant Rocket (USA) (Peteski (CAN))
1454^{4} 2490^{7} 2660^{12} (3139) (3753) 4242^{2} (4397) 4922^{5}
Jadaara *M Johnston* a75 84
3 b f Red Ransom(USA) —Berasyim (Lion Cavern (USA))
3134^{10} 3649^{3} 5100^{3} 5773^{7} 6898^{4} *7305*^{5}
Jadalee (IRE) *G A Butler* a82 77
5 b g Desert Prince(IRE) —Lionne (Darshaan)
1944^{10} 3249^{17} 4362^{7} *5423*^{9} 6078^{9} *6424*^{4} ◆
Jadan (IRE) *E J Alston* 60
7 b g Imperial Ballet(IRE) —Sports Post Lady (IRE) (M Double M (USA))
5452^{10} 6039^{6} 6310^{7} 6382^{14}
Jafaru *G A Butler* a69 70
4 b g Silver Hawk(USA) —Rafha (Kris)
1620^{2} 1824^{4} 2567^{10} *3321*^{6} 4067^{6} *4343*^{9} 5148^{4}
Jafra (IRE) *R M Whitaker* 68
3 ch g Choisir(AUS) —Polish Saga (Polish Patriot (USA))
1396^{3} 2041^{3} 3221^{7} 3886^{9} (4244) 4688^{6} 6485^{5} (6806)
Jagger *G A Butler* a94 94
8 gr g Linamix(FR) —Sweetness Herself (Unfuwain (USA))
626^{3} *838*^{5} *1547*^{3} *3375*^{2} 4627^{7} 5054^{3} *(5423)* 6061^{5} 6288^{3}
Jago (SWI) *A M Hales* a72
5 b g Brief Truce(USA) —Jariyah (USA) (It's The One (USA))
675^{2} *(802)*
Jagodin (IRE) *L Reuterskiold Jr* a73 87
8 b g Be My Guest(USA) —Native Joy (IRE) (Be My Native (USA))
4676a^{7} 5958a^{6}
Jaguar Mail (JPN) *N Hori* 120
4 b h Jungle Pocket(JPN) —Haya Beni Komachi (JPN) (Sunday Silence (USA))
7682a^{3}

Jajoleen (IRE) *P A Blockley* a13 47
5 ch m Titus Livius(FR) —Radeda (IRE) (Great Commotion (USA))
145^{8}

Jakam (IRE) *E J O'Neill* a48 46
3 b g Diktat—Key Virtue (USA) (Atticus (USA))
1556^{11} 1894^{8} 2915^{7} 3791^{7} 4298^{9}

Jakeini (IRE) *E S McMahon* a18 68
5 b g Rossini(USA) —Talita Kumi (IRE) (High Estate)
1191^{7} 1378^{2} 1997^{8} 2777^{11} 3112^{15} 4462^{11} 5398^{9} 6405^{2} 7197^{2}

Jake The Snake (IRE) *A W Carroll* a84 85
7 ch g Intikhab(USA) —Tilbrook (IRE) (Don't Forget Me)
(1146) ◆ 1857^{6} ◆ 2203^{2} 2619^{12} 3905^{6} 4393^{3} 5144^{6} 6125^{8} 6695^{14} 7077^{8} 7360^{2} 7821^{3}

Jalamid (IRE) *M A Barnes* a47 61
6 b g Danehill(USA) —Vignelaure (IRE) (Royal Academy (USA))
1605^{7} 1747^{10} 2158^{10} 2535^{12} 3131^{4} 3602^{10}

Jalandy (IRE) *S Curran* a47 43
5 b m Desert Millennium(IRE) —Jaldini (IRE) (Darshaan)
76^{6}

Jalil (USA) *Saeed Bin Suroor* a120 87
4 bb h Storm Cat(USA) —Tranquility Lake (USA) (Rahy (USA))
(493a) (650a) (817a) 1092a^{7}

Jalmira (IRE) *C F Swan* a105 110
7 b m Danehill Dancer(IRE) —Jaldini (IRE) (Darshaan)
1104a^{4} 2420a^{7} 2740a^{4} 3536a^{5} 4007a^{2} 4512a^{3} 5332a^{9} 5920a^{5} 6298a^{4} (7328a)

Jal Music *R A Harris* a66 66
3 ch g Ishiguru(USA) —Musica (Primo Dominie)
311^{4} 483^{2} 700^{2} 848^{5} 1603^{3} (1777) 2255^{9} 2864^{4} 3559^{10} 3779^{6} 4324^{5} 5166^{4} 6173^{7} 6716^{5}

Jalons Bridewell *M Quinn* a70 56
3 b g Compton Place—Inflation (Primo Dominie)
146^{4} 271^{2} 441^{2} 629^{3} 721^{2} 855^{4} 2122^{9} 2864^{7} 3332^{4} 3686^{13} 4523^{5} 5141^{7} 6433^{9}

Jamboretta (IRE) *Sir Michael Stoute* 100
4 b m Danehill(USA) —Jiving (Generous (IRE))
(1633) 1981^{5} 2827^{7} 3415^{5} 6266^{10}

James Dean (IRE) *P F I Cole* a74 65
3 b c Clodovil(IRE) —Karenaragon (Aragon)
1601^{4} 1854^{7} 2480^{5} 2721^{5}

James Junior *D Carroll* 40
2 ch g Tobougg(IRE) —Celts Dawn (Celtic Swing)
5394^{10} 5633^{10} 6008^{9}

James Pollard (IRE) *D R C Elsworth* a64 54
3 ch g Indian Ridge—Manuetti (IRE) (Sadler's Wells (USA))
4929^{10} 5608^{8} 5995^{11} 6437^{7} ◆ 6741^{3} 7111^{7}

James Street (IRE) *Peter Grayson* a52 77
5 b g Fruits Of Love(USA) —Humble Mission (Shack (USA))
33^{7} 120^{10} 254^{4} 445^{6} 696^{4} 972^{11} 1035^{6} 7637^{11}

Jamieson Gold (IRE) *Miss L A Perratt* a59 94
5 b g Desert Style(IRE) —Princess Of Zurich (IRE) (Law Society (USA))
259^{8} 833^{11} 979^{4} 1218^{6} 2158^{5} 2841^{6} 3453^{5} 4419^{2} ◆ 5221^{4} 5418^{2} 6070^{9} 6487^{10} 7131^{7} 7224^{7}

Jamindar (IRE) *A Lyon* 98
3 b c Zamindar(USA) —Balachova (FR) (Kaldoun (FR))
6664a^{6}

Ja Myford *P T Midgley* a59 59
4 b g Auction House(USA) —Daleside Ladybird (Tolomeo)
1679^{6} 1968^{3} 2364^{14}

Jane Blue (FR) *C Ferland* 104
3 b c Indian Rocket—Rastella (FR) (Funambule (USA))
6064a^{7} 6743a^{10}

Jane Of Arc (FR) *J S Goldie* 57
4 ch m Trempolino(USA) —Aerleon Jane (Caerleon (USA))
2523^{11} 2752^{4} 3131^{3} 3550^{2} 3756^{9} 4220^{4} 4630^{3} 5559^{7} 5968^{4} 6185^{6} (6309) 6806^{8}

Jane's Payoff (IRE) *Mrs L C Jewell* a69 63
3 b f Danetime(IRE) —Alimony (IRE) (Groom Dancer (USA))
9^{3} 146^{3} (1635) 2602^{3} 3224^{6} 7811^{9}

Janet's Delight *S Curran* a56 55
3 b f Erhaab(USA) —Ishona (Selkirk (USA))
2260^{4} 4278^{10} 5575^{4}

Janina *B W Hills* 94
3 b f Namid—Lady Dominatrix (IRE) (Danehill Dancer (IRE))
3849^{9} 5310^{4}

Janshe Gold *J G Portman* a43 57
3 ch f Bertolini(USA) —Rekindled Flame (IRE) (Kings Lake (USA))
1525^{8} 1869^{10} 2528^{12} 3845^{11}

January *T M Walsh* a84 58
5 gr g Daylami(IRE) —Noushkey (Polish Precedent (USA))
(7690)

Ja One (IRE) *B W Hills* 58
2 b f Acclamation—Special Dancer (Shareef Dancer (USA))
4554^{12} 5640^{8} 6565^{7}

Japan (GER) *D Smaga* a71 96
3 gr f Key Royal(GER) —Jeanine (GER) (Neshad (USA))
(7450a)

Japura (USA) *T J Pitt* a37 69
4 ch g Giant's Causeway(USA) —Exchange Place (USA) (Affirmed (USA))
7362^{9} 7403^{8}

Jaq's Sister *M Blanshard* a35
2 b f Bertolini(USA) —Polly Golightly (Weldnaas (USA))
5200^{6} 7830^{7}

Jardines Bazaar *Martin Brassil* 54
4 b g Halling(USA) —Alumisiyah (USA) (Danzig (USA))
6071^{7}

Jargelle (IRE) *W J Haggas* 100
2 b f Kheleyf(USA) —Winter Tern (USA) (Arctic Tern (USA))
3085^{3} (3735) (4190) 4507^{3} 6441^{13}

Jarrah Bay *J G M O'Shea* a46 50
2 b f Mark Of Esteem(IRE) —Wannaplantatree (Niniski (USA))
4973^{6} 6016^{9} 7015^{14}

Jarvo *I W McInnes* a58 58
7 b g Pursuit Of Love—Pinkie Rose (FR) (Kenmare (FR))
143^{6} 220^{3} (251) 541^{5} (769) 1692^{10} (2513) 2957^{11} 3732^{P} 4066^{6} 4215^{7} 4797^{11} 5802^{11} 6570^{13} 7599^{3} 7792^{5}

Jaser *P W Chapple-Hyam* a68 97
3 ch c Alhaarth(IRE) —Waafiah (Anabaa (USA))
(1161) ◆ (1381) ◆ 2403^{3} 3155^{23} 5360^{13} 6763^{3}

Jaslyn (IRE) *J R Weymes* a46 46
2 bb f Pyrus(USA) —Ruby Julie (Clantime)
2534^{9} 3259^{6} 4449^{4} 4873^{5} 5473^{4} 7220^{3} 7298^{4} 7475^{10} 7652^{10}

Jasmines Hero (USA) *A Manuel* a73 66
3 b c War Chant(USA) —Ryn (USA) (Mr Prospector (USA))
292a^{7}

Jasoora *M P Tregoning* a58
3 b f Mark Of Esteem(IRE) —Kotdiji (Mtoto)
2977^{13}

Jasper Cliff *Mark Gillard*
2 b g Lucky Owners(NZ) —Catmint (Piccolo)
2893^{15} 5022^{12}

Jastaanhi *B N Pollock* a39 59
3 b f Superior Premium—Cavern Breeze (Lion Cavern (USA))
397^{7} 614^{3} 767^{6} 917^{7} 5074^{15}

Jatman *Mrs L Stubbs* 80
2 b g Choisir(AUS) —Partenza (USA) (Red Ransom (USA))
4847^{8} 5416^{2} ◆ 6426^{28}

Jaubertie *W G M Turner* 47
2 b f Bertolini(USA) —Jucinda (Midyan (USA))
5782^{3} 6133^{10} 7079^{8}

Jawaab (IRE) *W R Muir* a82 79
4 ch g King's Best(USA) —Canis Star (Wolfhound (USA))
1719^{8} 2406^{4} 4162^{6} (6363) 6721^{6} 7068^{3} 7278^{3} 7564^{3} 7670^{6}

Jawad (IRE) *Ms Joanna Morgan* a77 90
7 b g Kahyasi—Mystic Charm (Nashwan (USA))
3104^{7}

Jayanjay *B R Johnson* a61 72
9 b g Piccolo—Morica (Moorestyle)
1646^{6} 2075^{5} 2350^{2} 3033^{10} 3346^{6} 4025^{7} 4693^{5} (4812) 5171^{7} 5817^{5} 6190^{5} 7022^{4} 7195^{2}

Jayarbee (IRE) *P J McBride* a57 65
3 b f Prince Sabo—Spirito Libro (USA) (Lear Fan (USA))
3823^{8} 5864^{5} 7256^{8} 7518^{10} 7792^{2}

Jay Gee Wigmo *A W Carroll* a30 53
3 b g First Trump—Queen Of Shannon (IRE) (Nordico (USA))
2559^{9} 3022^{8} 3893^{6} 4369^{3} 5684^{9} 6332^{7}

Jayne Dean *A Crook* 14
4 b m Rock City—Otterington Girl (Noble Patriarch)
1301^{5} 1626^{8} 2395^{8} 3640^{9}

Jay Peg (SAF) *H J Brown* 123
5 b h Camden Park(USA) —Laptop Lady (SAF) (Al Mufti (USA))
383a^{6} 671a^{3} 818a^{2} (1090a) (2234a)

Jays Secret (IRE) *H Rogers* a73 52
2 b f Celtic Swing—Lorraine's Secret (IRE) (Desert King (IRE))
4513a^{8}

Jayyid (IRE) *C E Brittain* a53
3 b g Daylami(IRE) —Mellow Jazz (Lycius (USA))
7403^{6} 7489^{4} 7661^{7} 7801^{6}

Jazacosta (USA) *Mrs A J Perrett* 81
2 ch c Dixieland Band(USA) —Dance With Del (USA) (Sword Dance)
1832^{6} 2150^{3} 3001^{2} (3164) 4589^{3} 5242^{3} 5585^{7} 6086^{4}

Jazenio *K A Ryan* a61 61
3 b f Auenadler(GER) —Jade Chequer (Green Desert (USA))
271^{3} 487^{2} 721^{4} 1019^{9} (1169) 1558^{11} 1754^{4}

Jazrawy *D Carroll* a83 59
6 b g Dansili—Dalila Di Mare (IRE) (Bob Back (USA))
344^{9} 847^{5}

Jazzing About (USA) *P T Midgley* a7 39
3 bb g Dixie Union(USA) —Erstwhile (USA) (Arts And Letters (USA))
7528^{11}

Jazz Jam *P F I Cole* a89 100
3 ch f Pivotal—Applaud (USA) (Rahy (USA))
(1332) 2305^{5} 3124^{14} 3971^{4} 4520^{2} 5744a^{8}

Jazz Police *R Hannon* a82 90
2 b c Beat Hollow—Tease (IRE) (Green Desert (USA))
(3274) ◆ 5093^{3} 5889^{6} 6466^{4}

Jazz Romance (IRE) *D Shaw* a26
3 ch f Choisir(AUS) —Music In My Life (IRE) (Law Society (USA))
141^{11} 257^{8}

Jazz Stick (IRE) *D A Nolan* 60
3 ch c Choisir(AUS) —Basin Street Blues (IRE) (Dolphin Street (FR))
6150^{10}

Jazzy (ARG) *Mark Hennig* a99 99
6 b m Mutakddim(USA) —Jollie Fille (ARG) (Southern Halo (USA))
6965a^{8}

Jebel Ali (IRE) *B Gubby* a80 64
5 b g Fruits Of Love(USA) —Assertive Lass (USA) (Assert)
1932^{15} 2682^{6} 3003^{13} (3836) 4081^{5} 4829^{9}

Jebel Tara *C E Brittain* a62 97
3 b g Diktat—Chantilly (FR) (Sanglamore (USA))
2530^{7} 3039^{7} 3475^{9} 4341^{9} 5104^{3} 5273^{10} 6020^{11} 7206^{11}

Jedburgh *J L Dunlop* a73 99
7 b h Selkirk(USA) —Conspiracy (Rudimentary (USA))
1857^{8} 2371^{5} 3197^{3} 4405^{19}

Jedediah *A M Balding* 105
3 b g Hernando(FR) —Penelewey (Groom Dancer (USA))
1595^{6} 2403^{8} ◆ 3155^{6} (3877)

Jedi *Sir Michael Stoute* 78
2 ch c Pivotal—Threefold (USA) (Gulch (USA))
6425^{10} 6760^{3} (7080) ◆

Jeer (IRE) *E A L Dunlop* a86 96
4 ch g Selkirk(USA) —Purring (USA) (Mountain Cat (USA))
1180^{5} 1473^{4} 1793^{2} (2120) 2369^{2} 3045^{5} 3684^{4} 4191^{11} 4642^{5} 5569^{7} 6129^{3} 6582^{3}

Jelly Mo *J W Hills* a70 66
3 b f Royal Applause—Flawless (Warning)
1637^{5} 2118^{7} 2956^{8} 3322^{7} 4054^{8} 4774^{10} (5787) 6492^{8}

Jellytot (USA) *J O'Reilly* a41 64
5 b m Minardi(USA) —Dounine (Kaldoun (FR))
2866^{8} 3079^{16} 3340^{7} 3662^{7} 4542^{3} 4961^{5} 7048^{7} 7184^{11} 7316^{10} 7678^{11}

Jember Red *B Smart* a46 33
5 b m Polish Precedent(USA) —Arabellajill (Aragon)
79^{6}

Jemiliah *B G Powell* a60 59
3 b f Dubai Destination(USA) —Cape Cod (IRE) (Unfuwain (USA))
547^{3} 976^{5} 1938^{2} 2451^{16} 2984^{10} (3524) 4259^{6} 4721^{3} 5602^{9} 6227^{6} 6746^{5} 6928^{12} 7573^{9}

Jemima's Art *M W Easterby* a39 57
3 bb f Fantastic Light(USA) —Subya (Night Shift (USA))
644^{5} 2468^{4} 2750^{2} 3580^{4} 4173^{8} (4738) 4964^{4} 5308^{8} 5776^{8} 6015^{8}

Jeninsky (USA) *Rae Guest* a83 88
3 ch f Stravinsky(USA) —Don't Ruffle Me (USA) (Pine Bluff (USA))
1332^{7} 2170^{5} 2605^{6} 3222^{7} 3850^{12} 4983^{2} 5841^{2} 6532^{6} 6911^{7}

Jennie Jerome (IRE) *L M Cumani* a79 81
3 br f Pivotal—Colourfast (IRE) (Spectrum (IRE))
2307^{4} 4194^{3} (5162) 5964^{3} 7083^{4} 7419^{5}

Jennifer's Dream (IRE) *K A Ryan* a47 78
3 b f Statue Of Liberty(USA) —Elara (USA) (Spinning World (USA))
2747^{5} 4271^{3} 4891^{6}

Jenny Soba *Lucinda Featherstone* a52 68
5 b m Observatory(USA) —Majalis (Mujadil (USA))
238^{3} 2245^{6} 3863^{4} 4879^{8} (5308) 5593^{5} (5653) 5776^{12} 6161^{2} 6538^{2} 6983^{11} 7085^{9} 7202^{12}

Jentris Girl (IRE) *A C Whillans* 57
4 b m Golan(IRE) —Carranza (IRE) (Lead On Time (USA))
2290^{14} 3756^{13}

Jeremiah (IRE) *J G Portman* a60 72
2 ch g Captain Rio—Miss Garuda (Persian Bold)
3323^{10} 3848^{3} 4274^{2} 5294a^{11} 6118^{12}

Jeronimo Joe *A B Haynes* a38
2 ch c Primo Valentino(IRE) —Yanomami (USA) (Slew O'Gold (USA))
7602^{11}

Jerry Hamilton (USA) *M Johnston* a71 46
3 bb g Cherokee Run(USA) —Helsinki (Machiavellian (USA))
2014^{11} 3117^{13} 3591^{12} 3822^{10}

Jerry's Agent (IRE) *J Balding*
2 b g Imperial Ballet(IRE) —Agent Scully (IRE) (Simply Great (FR))
7165^{8} 7530^{9}

Jesse James (IRE) *J H M Gosden* 78
2 b c King's Best(USA) —Julie Jalouse (USA) (Kris S (USA))
6944^{7} 7105^{2}

Jessica Mary (IRE) *B Smart* a38 56
2 b f Lucky Story(USA) —Hopping Higgins (IRE) (Brief Truce (USA))
3292^{9} 3792^{5} 5715^{3} 5966^{7} 7372^{9} 7531^{13}

Jessicas Girl *Eamon Tyrrell* a28 56
2 b f Domedriver(IRE) —Sulitelma (USA) (The Minstrel (CAN))
1961^{8}

Jessica Wigmo *A W Carroll* a63 50
5 b m Bahamian Bounty—Queen Of Shannon (IRE) (Nordico (USA))
99^{2} 176^{2} (276) 402^{6} (624) 937^{9} (1209) 1565^{3} 2128^{13} 2670^{4} 3023^{11} 3481^{4} 4084^{8} 4863^{5}

Jessy Jones *R Brotherton* 36
2 b f Largesse—Polar Storm (IRE) (Law Society (USA))
5213^{9} 6089^{12} 6534^{8}

Jet D'Eau (FR) *R Pritchard-Gordon* 93
2 b f Numerous(USA) —La Fontainiere (IRE) (Kaldoun (FR))
3192^{10} 5300a^{5} 5987a^{5}

Jet Express (SAF) *A Al Raihe* a100 107
6 b g Jet Master(SAF) —Outback Romance (SAF) (Sharp Romance (USA))
204a^{8} 379a^{4} 671a^{5} 742a^{3} 815a^{5} 1087a^{7}

Jethro Bodine (IRE) *W J H Ratcliffe* 54
2 b g Fath(USA) —John's Ballad (IRE) (Ballad Rock)
1794^{6} 2216^{2} 2909^{8} 3639^{5} 3830^{3} 4948^{6}

Jethro Wheeler *E J Creighton* a22
5 b g Marju(IRE) —Panorama (Shirley Heights)
6596^{11}

Jet Past (SAF) *S Seemar* a88 99
6 b m Jet Master(SAF) —Rather Rich (NZ) (Star Way)
200a^{7} 475a^{7} 672a^{10}

Jetta Joy (IRE) *Mrs A Duffield* a60 41
3 b f Hawk Wing(USA) —Woopi Gold (IRE) (Last Tycoon)
2468^{11} 6115^{6} 7045^{3} 7285^{5}

Jettymarc (IRE) *Tracey Collins* 78
3 b c Indian Danehill(IRE) —Leinster Mills (IRE) (Doyoun)
3861a^{3}

Jeu De Roseau (IRE) *A P Stringer* a57 77
4 b g Montjeu(IRE) —Roseau (Nashwan (USA))
159^{6} 436^{8}

Jeunesse (IRE) *R M Beckett* a53
2 gr f King's Best(USA) —Crepe Ginger (IRE) (Sadler's Wells (USA))
6731^{11}

Jeunopse (IRE) *B Smart* 55
2 b f Hawk Wing(USA) —Innocence (Unfuwain (USA))
6788^{4} ◆

Jevington Star (IRE) *B Ellison* a40 48
3 ch g Noverre(USA) —Khalisiyn (Shakapour)
1343^{7} 1626^{3} 1968^{4} 2247^{6} 2463^{3} 3139^{3} 3213^{4} 3715^{4} 4043^{5} 4542^{9}

Jewelled Dagger (IRE) *Miss L A Perratt* a63 98
4 b g Daggers Drawn(USA) —Cappadoce (IRE) (General Monash (USA))
1970^{2} 2218^{2} 2465^{10} 3046^{9} 4618^{6} 6654^{2} 7019^{13} 7245^{8}

Jewelled Reef (IRE) *Eve Johnson Houghton* 61
2 b f Marju(IRE) —Aqaba (Lake Coniston (IRE))
3323^{7} 4251^{6} 5534^{4} 6240^{23}

Jhinga Palak (IRE) *P D Evans* a40 70
2 b f Fath(USA) —Livius Lady (IRE) (Titus Livius (FR))
2638^{11} 5294a^{5} 7660^{6}

Jibboom (USA) *Robert Frankel* a108
4 rg m Mizzen Mast(USA) —Palisade (USA) (Gone West (USA))
6523a^{7}

Jiggalong *G G Margarson* 34
2 ch f Mark Of Esteem(IRE) —Kalamansi (IRE) (Sadler's Wells (USA))
3735^{7} 5530^{9}

Jiggs Coz (CAN) *Sid Attard* a100 95
4 rg h Cozzene(USA) —Young Brodie (CAN) (Broad Brush (USA))
2472a^{9}

Jiggy Spriggy (IRE) *H J Collingridge* a34 47
5 b m King Charlemagne(USA) —Amneris (IRE) (Alzao (USA))
6208^{12} 6752^{10} (Dead)

Jill Dawson (IRE) *John Berry* a70 67
5 b m Mull Of Kintyre(USA) —Dream Of Jenny (Caerleon (USA))
1954^{2} 2718^{6} 3561^{10} 4081^{12} 4789^{10}

Jillolini *T D Easterby* 12
2 bg f Bertolini(USA) —Someone's Angel (USA) (Runaway Groom (CAN))
1627^{9}

Jilly Why (IRE) *Paul Green* a70 84
7 b m Mujadil(USA) —Ruwy (Soviet Star (USA))
596^{4} 699^{3} 806^{10} (1185) 1488^{6} (1997) (2212) 2359^{8} 2666^{8} 2906^{10} 4407^{12} 5073^{7} 5493^{9} 5886^{8} 6218^{6} 7182^{6} 7444^{3} 7503^{8} 7648^{3} 7774^{6}

Jiminor Mack *W J H Ratcliffe* a46 51
5 bl m Little Jim—Copper Trader (Faustus (USA))
1579^{7} 2782^{3} 3732^{10} 4048^{9} 5262^{2} 5308^{4} 5776^{6} 7174^{6} 7815^{2}

Jim Martin *Miss L A Perratt* a72 79
3 b g Auction House(USA) —Folly Finnesse (Joligeneration)
632^{6} 2747^{7} 3251^{10} 3592^{8} 5544^{9} (6040) 6493^{7} 6657^{10}

Jimmy Dean *M Wellings* a46 49
3 b g Ishiguru(USA) —Sister Sal (Bairn (USA))
2055^{10} 2259^{12} 3330^{8} 3559^{13} 4531^{4} 6173^{11} 6752^{7} 7088^{6} 7559^{10} 7608^{9} 7780^{6}

Jimmy Styles *C G Cox* 101
4 ch g Inchinor—Inya Lake (Whittingham (IRE))
(1985) 2195^{5}

Jimmy The Guesser *N P Littmoden* a90 70
5 ch g Piccolo—Brush Away (Ahonoora)
1195^{7} 1368^{9} 1683^{11} 2205^{4} 2892^{10} 3506^{9}

Jimwasright (IRE) *P D Evans* 43
2 b g Iron Mask(USA) —Our Little Law (IRE) (Law Society (USA))
3603^{8} 4764^{5} 5778^{7}

Jimwil (IRE) *M Dods* 72
2 b g One Cool Cat(USA) —Vulnerable (Hector Protector (USA))
2186^{6} 2783^{3} 3254^{2} 3754^{3} 4292^{5} 6247^{7} 6857^{12}

Joannadarc (USA) *S A Callaghan* a69
2 ch f Johannesburg(USA) —Game Player (USA) (Drumalis)
7438^{7} 7593^{3} 7773^{4}

Jobe (USA) *K A Ryan* 103
2 b c Johannesburg(USA) —Bello Cielo (USA) (Conquistador Cielo (USA))
4237^{3} (4847) ◆ 5226^{3} ◆ 6442^{8} 6979^{6}

Jobekani (IRE) *Mrs L Williamson* a60 58
2 b c Tagula(IRE) —Lyca Ballerina (Marju (IRE))
2569^{5} 3125^{5} 4593^{8} 4956^{8} 6087^{5} 6632^{3} 6986^{7}

Jo'Burg (USA) *Mrs A J Perrett* a75 99
4 b g Johannesburg(USA) —La Martina (Atraf)
2565^{4} 3167^{4} 3915^{8} 4310^{3} 5350^{7} 6028^{5} 6758^{7} 6908^{4}

Jocheski (IRE) *A G Newcombe* a65 63
4 b g Mull Of Kintyre(USA) —Ludovica (Bustino)
7085^{4}

Jockser (IRE) *J W Mullins* a48 65
7 b g Desert Story(IRE) —Pupa Fiorini (ITY) (Indian Ridge)
6403^{12}

Jodhpur *A Fabre* a82 96
4 ch h Pivotal—Khumbla Mela (IRE) (Hero's Honor (USA))
2876a^{10}

Joe Caster *J M P Eustace* a88 84
2 b c Makbul—Oedipus Regina (Fraam)
1168^{2} 4279^{3} (6578) (6987) ◆ 7173^{2} 7335^{5} (7460) ◆ 7555^{4}

Joe Jo Star *B P J Baugh* a57 50
6 b g Piccolo—Zagreb Flyer (Old Vic)
(468) (578) 686^{6} 841^{6} 1032^{7} 1528^{9} 5912^{3} ◆ 6570^{3}

Joe Rich *Mrs L C Jewell* a43 38
4 b g Piccolo—Lady Lacey (Kampala)
183^{6} 445^{8} 713^{7} 877^{12} 1162^{7} 1347^{6} 3445^{7}

Johannes (IRE) *R A Fahey* a75 86
5 b g Mozart(IRE) —Blue Sirocco (Bluebird (USA))
2210[3] 2538[10] 3336[3] 3647[5] 4555[8] 6125[4] 6859[6] 7222[10] 7386[6]

Johar Jamal (IRE) *P D Deegan* a76 84
3 b f Chevalier(IRE) —Miss Barcelona (IRE) (Mac's Imp (USA))
1404[9] 6510a[11]

John Dillon (IRE) *P C Haslam* a59 69
4 ch g Traditionally(USA) —Matikanehanafubuki (IRE) (Caerleon (USA))
963[13] 1159[11] 3711[8] 4299[7]

John Keats *J S Goldie* a53 86
5 b g Bertolini(USA) —Nightingale (Night Shift (USA))
2005[18] 2968[3] (3111) 3255[5] (3477) 3626[3] 3812[3] 4239[10] 4608[4] 5067[2] 5247[11] 6066[10] 7222[11]

Johnmanderville *K R Burke* 78
2 b g Kheleyf(USA) —Lady's Walk (IRE) (Charnwood Forest (IRE))
1474[7] 1616[3] 1907[2] (3576) 3809[4] (6082) ◆ 6305[5]

Johnny Friendly *K R Burke* a65 68
3 b g Auction House(USA) —Quantum Lady (Mujadil (USA))
(797) 918[3] 1060[2] 3578[3] 4115[6] 4702[3] 5258[4] 5616[12]

Johnny McGurk *M E Rimmer* a43 53
3 b g Mtoto—Blorenge (Prince Sabo)
3161[12] 5160[7] 5426[8] 6004[5] 6707[7] 6878[12]

Johnny Rook (GER) *E A L Dunlop* a54 68
2 b c Dashing Blade—Just Zoud (Ezzoud (IRE))
2150[2] 3245[11] 4050[2] 4305[6] 6761[14] 7190[9] 7389[7]

John Potts *B P J Baugh* a59 32
3 b g Josr Algarhoud(IRE) —Crown City (USA) (Coronado's Quest (USA))
141[8] 321[4] 527[5] 665[2] 803[2] 976[9] 4332[12] 5477[4] 6216[13] 7115[10] 7274[5]

Johnston's Glory (IRE) *E J Alston* a66 71
4 b m Desert Sun—Clos De Tart (IRE) (Indian Ridge)
328[5] 375[4] 560[8] 837[5] 1024[10] 1951[3] 2283[5] 2448[7] 2966[10] (3953) (4293) (4542)

Johnstown Lad (IRE) *Niall Moran* a96 92
4 b g Invincible Spirit(IRE) —Pretext (Polish Precedent (USA))
411[2] 1198a[4] 6624[10] 6676[8]

John Terry (IRE) *Mrs A J Perrett* a100 98
5 b g Grand Lodge(USA) —Kardashina (FR) (Darshaan)
(410) 908[4] 1076[3] 1212[7] 2830[13] 3505[3] 4444[15] 4516[14] 6784[3]

John Veale (USA) *J S Bolger* 59
2 b c Strong Hope(USA) —Soccory (USA) (Tricky Creek (USA))
3509a[14]

Joinedupwriting *R M Whitaker* a46 77
3 b g Desert Style(IRE) —Ink Pot (USA) (Green Dancer (USA))
1576[4] 1899[7] 2378[5] 3641[3] 4663[4] 5362[5] 6528[9] 6905[8]

Joint Agency (IRE) *N Wilson* a34 36
3 b f Captain Rio—Prima Marta (Primo Dominie)
2966[16] 3139[13] 3565[11]

Join Up *W R Swinburn* a56 55
2 b g Green Desert(USA) —Rise (Polar Falcon (USA))
2951[11] 3603[7] 4164[10] 4729[6] 5581[8] 6573[5]

Jojesse *G A Swinbank* a57 59
4 ch g Compton Place—Jodeeka (Fraam)
82[6] 2869[5] 3546[8] 4561[6] 5452[5] 5970[6] 7320[4] 7619[2] ◆ 7663[4]

Joleahs Star (IRE) *Paul Nolan* a41 16
4 b m Definite Article—Joleah (IRE) (Ela-Mana-Mou)
1562[6]

Jolie Fleur *D E Cantillon* a36 35
3 b f Josr Algarhoud(IRE) —Jenny Rocket (Minster Son)
4195[8] 5318[15]

Jolies Dee *J R Jenkins* a24
3 br f Diktat—Jolies Eaux (Shirley Heights)
7822[9]

Joli Haven (IRE) *W G M Turner* a33 45
2 ch f Indian Haven—Game Leader (IRE) (Mukaddamah (USA))
995[6] 1111[6]

Jollyhockeysticks *M R Channon* a74 77
3 b f Fantastic Light(USA) —Between The Sticks (Pharly (FR))
966[4] ◆ 1244[3] 1839[10] 2118[4] 2700[2] 3221[3] 3578[2] 3906[3] 4082[4] 4724[4] 5119[2] 5218[2] (5836) 6048[5] 6332[3] 6683[7] 6936[5]

Jolly Ranch *A G Newcombe* a50
2 gr f Compton Place—How Do I Know (Petong)
7273[6] 7689[3]

Jollys Joy *K F Clutterbuck* a12
4 b m Averti(IRE) —Nest Egg (Prince Sabo)
22[7] 447[6]

Jolly Tipsy *S W Hall* a19 20
3 ch f Tipsy Creek(USA) —Busy (IRE) (In The Wings)
3166[11]

Jomelamin *M Sheppard* a16 41
6 gr m Silver Patriarch(IRE) —Jomel Amou (IRE) (Ela-Mana-Mou)
4105[6] 4811[7] 6740[12]

Jomus *L Montague Hall* a59 59
7 b g Soviet Star(USA) —Oatey (Master Willie)
164[2] 267[2] 328[6] 517[3] 611[4] 728[8] (1207) (Dead)

Jonah's Cruising (IRE) *J R Boyle* a60 21
2 b f Barathea(IRE) —Rivana (Green Desert (USA))
5835[14] (6574) 7079[12] 7283[3] 7415[2] 7607[8]

Jonnie Skull (IRE) *D R C Elsworth* a61 19
2 b g Pyrus(USA) —Sovereign Touch (IRE) (Pennine Walk)
6701[12] 7011[10] 7312[10] 7467[9] 7547[2] 7738[4]

Jonny Ebeneezer *D Flood* a46 66
9 b g Hurricane Sky(AUS) —Leap Of Faith (IRE) (Northiam (USA))
3724[10] 3868[5] 4186[2] 4393[6] 4639[7] 4696[6] 5817[9] 5970[9] 6232[12] 6895[15]

Jonny Lesters Hair (IRE) *T D Easterby* a68 81
3 b g Danetime(IRE) —Jupiter Inlet (IRE) (Jupiter Island)
1426[6] (1817) 2189[5] 2674[7] 3141[8] 4682[5] 5258[3] 5397[2] (6186) 6471[7] 7041[5]

Jonquil (IRE) *Doug Watson* a93
6 ch h Machiavellian(USA) —Jumilla (USA) (El Gran Senor (USA))
202a[10] 648a[8]

Jonquille (IRE) *R Ford* a39 50
3 ch f Rock Of Gibraltar(IRE) —Moonlight Wish (IRE) (Peintre Celebre (USA))
5203[6] 6189[9] 7518[11]

Jontobel *Jedd O'Keeffe* 32
3 b g Tobougg(IRE) —Belinda (Mizoram (USA))
1628[F] 2221[14] 3297[9] 4112[10] 4785[11]

Jools *D K Ivory* a66 70
10 b g Cadeaux Genereux—Madame Crecy (USA) (Al Nasr (FR))
56[4]

Jord (IRE) *A J McCabe* a82 58
4 b m Trans Island—Arcevia (IRE) (Archway (IRE))
21[2] 192[6] 752[6] 852[4] 949[2] 1160[6] 1585[3] 1903[2] 2289[5] 2531[10] 4390[10] 5594[10] 6663[12] 7606[10]

Jordans Elect *P Monteith* a24 66
8 ch g Fleetwood(IRE) —Cal Norma's Lady (IRE) (Lyphard's Special (USA))
1822[13]

Jordan's Light (USA) *P Monteith* a77 68
5 rg g Aljabr(USA) —Western Friend (USA) (Gone West (USA))
2524[8] 2848[7] 3198[4] 3756[8] 3954[4] 6161[7]

Jordan Strada (ITY) *A Renzoni* 48
4 br h Glen Jordan—Strada Facendo (Final Straw)
7349a[11]

Jordaura *W R Swinburn* a68 66
2 br c Primo Valentino(IRE) —Christina's Dream (Spectrum (IRE))
6342[3] 6770[3] 7191[3]

Jordi Roper (IRE) *S Parr* a54 54
3 ch g Traditionally(USA) —Xema (Danehill (USA))
1379[11] 2187[9] 2380[10] 3958[7] 4653[11] 4810[13] 7654[4] 7725[2] 7766[3] 7799[P]

Josama *R Bastiman* a23 18
4 br m Desert Sun—Edge Of Darkness (Vaigly Great)
483[9] 804[11] 1135[9] 1259[8] 1519[13]

Jose Bove *R Dickin* a44 32
6 ch g So Factual(USA) —Dark Sirona (Pitskelly)
5491[7]

Joseph Henry *D Nicholls* 99
6 b g Mujadil(USA) —Iris May (Brief Truce (USA))
1796[2] ◆ 1942[4] 2831[9] 3489[10] 4586[3] 4854[4] 5109[9] 5503[4] 5831[3] 6069[3] 6289[12]

Josephine Malines *Mrs A Duffield* a16 78
4 b m Inchinor—Alrisha (IRE) (Persian Bold)
2536[5] 3077[8] 3662[5] (3963) 5318[13] 6015[3] 6927[4] 7267[12]

Josh *K A Ryan* a86 72
6 b g Josr Algarhoud(IRE) —Charlie Girl (Puissance)
75[6]

Joshua *D E Cantillon* a45
3 b g Josr Algarhoud(IRE) —Magic Flute (Magic Ring (IRE))
154[4] 7265[9]

Joshua's Gold (IRE) *D Carroll* a64 74
7 b g Sesaro(USA) —Lady Of The Night (IRE) (Night Shift (USA))
1159[12] 1383[9] 2365[7] 3211[2] 3599[7] 3755[9] 4813[6] 4949[4] 5712[9] 6116[8] (Dead)

Joshua's Princess *John M Oxx* a77 92
4 b m Danehill(USA) —Josh's Pearl (IRE) (Sadler's Wells (USA))
3619a[9] 4007a[14] 6261a[13]

Josh You Are *M Wigham* a76 64
5 b g Josr Algarhoud(IRE) —Cibenze (Owington)
(710) 754[3] 886[2] 3160[3] 3276[6] 3756[5]

Josiah Bartlett (IRE) *J W Hills* a60 59
2 b c Invincible Spirit(IRE) —Princess Caraboo (IRE) (Alzao (USA))
1851[10] 2324[9] 3259[8] 3846[6] 4933[2] 5460[13] 5606[5] 6720[12] 7257[3] 7415[3] 7666[9]

Josr's Magic (IRE) *H J Collingridge* a72 63
4 b g Josr Algarhoud(IRE) —Just The Trick (USA) (Phone Trick (USA))
10[12] 125[7] 352[3] (430) 611[7] 938[4] 1160[10] (1374) 1725[2] 3457[7] 3914[10] 4162[16] 4936[4] 5145[5] 5407[3] 5802[7] (6353) 6882[3] 7096[3] 7532[12] 7642[8]

Joss Stick *R A Harris* a71 65
3 b g Josr Algarhoud(IRE) —Queen's College (IRE) (College Chapel)
(1414) 1707[9] 4154[8] 4325[3] 5046[7] 5645[5] 6045[8] 7377[5] 7517[3] 7589[2] 7679[7]

Joy And Fun (NZ) *D Cruz* 114
5 b g Cullen(AUS) —Gin Player (NZ) (Defensive Play (USA))
7684a[7]

Joy And Pain *M J Attwater* a67 68
7 b g Pursuit Of Love—Ice Chocolate (USA) (Icecapade (USA))
(453) 609[3] (708) 879[10] 1038[2] 1182[4] 3615[6] 4306[4] 4862[13]

Joyeaux *L R James* a71 74
6 b m Mark Of Esteem(IRE) —Divine Secret (Hernando (FR))
5775[6] 6131[10] 6232[8] 6564[8] 6766[3] 6890[2] (7043) 7182[8] 7218[10]

J P Jammer (USA) *Rafael Becerra* a96
2 ch c Old Topper(USA) —Word Puzzle (USA) (Ghazi (USA))
7751a[10]

J'Ray (USA) *Todd Pletcher* a99 108
5 ch m Distant View(USA) —Bubbling Heights (FR) (Darshaan)
6505a[4]

Jubilant Note (IRE) *Michael David Murphy* a68 69
6 b g Sadler's Wells(USA) —Hint Of Humour (USA) (Woodman (USA))
7512[2]

Jubilee Juggins (IRE) *N P Littmoden* a59 70
2 b c Clodovil(IRE) —Alleged Touch (USA) (Alleged (USA))
3848[9] 4270[4] 4634[6] 4942[6] 5647[2] (5933) 6023[3] 6603[12] 7361[9]

Jucebabe *J L Spearing* a17 64
5 b m Zilzal(USA) —Jucea (Bluebird (USA))
3363[11] 4106[6] 4273[8] 4812[5] 5074[13] 5626[10]

Juce Of Hearts *John R Upson* 46
4 b g Zilzal(USA) —Jucea (Bluebird (USA))
3361[10] 4461[RR]

Judd Street *Eve Johnson Houghton* a97 111
6 b g Compton Place—Pudding Lane (IRE) (College Chapel)
1831[8] 2404[7] 2712[6] 3504[10] 3943[8] 5275[13] 5906[5] 6121[5] (6290) 6429[5]

Judge 'n Jury *R A Harris* a81 114
4 ch g Pivotal—Cyclone Connie (Dr Devious (IRE))
354[3] (498) 676[6] 699[4] (1386) 1624[12] 2760[4] 3363[7] 4313[2] 4668[3] (4981) 5151[2] (5796) ◆ 6354[5] (6650) ◆ (6810) (6971) ◆ 7243[4]

Judgethemoment (USA) *Jane Chapple-Hyam* a84 91
3 br c Judge T C(USA) —Rachael Tennessee (USA) (Matsadoon (USA))
(1283) 2201[5] 2675[10] 3196[6] (3685) 4351[5] 6286[6] 7493[6]

Juicy Couture (IRE) *Charles O'Brien* 53
3 ch f Namid—Canaan (IRE) (Alhaarth (IRE))
6366a[10]

Jukebox Jury (IRE) *M Johnston* 114
2 gr c Montjeu(IRE) —Mare Aux Fees (Kenmare (FR))
(4625) 5139a[4] 5739a[3] (6267) 6973[2]

Julian Joachim (USA) *D Shaw* a49 53
4 b g Officer(USA) —Seeking The Jewel (USA) (Seeking The Gold (USA))
516[11] 587[7] 728[10] 898[9]

Julie Mill (IRE) *P G Murphy* 23
2 b f Apprehension—Ann's Mill (Pelder (IRE))
3821[12] 5022[9] 6534[9]

Julius Caesar (GER) *P Schiergen*
2 b c Monsun(GER) —Juvena (GER) (Platini (GER))
7264a[4]

Jul's Lad (IRE) *Paul Green* 70
2 b c Modigliani(USA) —Woodenitbenice (USA) (Nasty And Bold (USA))
3669[7] 4176[11] 5364[6] 5989[8]

July Days (IRE) *David Marnane* a73 51
2 b f Exceed And Excel(AUS) —Tocade (IRE) (Kenmare (FR))
5294a[15]

July Jasmine (USA) *Sir Michael Stoute* 80
2 b f Empire Maker(USA) —Camanoe (USA) (Gone West (USA))
(6565)

Jumaana (IRE) *J L Dunlop* 66
2 b f Selkirk(USA) —Weqaar (USA) (Red Ransom (USA))
6084[5] ◆ 6565[13]

Jumbajukiba *Mrs John Harrington* 115
5 b g Barathea(IRE) —Danseuse Du Soir (IRE) (Thatching)
(1355a) 1882a[8] 3536a[2] (3982a) 4915a[11] 5134a[5] (5944a) 6516a[2]

Jump For You (FR) *H Rogers* 101
6 b g Montjeu(IRE) —Polly's Wika (USA) (Miswaki (USA))
4493a[10]

Jumpin Johnnie *M Mullineaux* a36 37
3 ch g Compton Place—Trump Street (First Trump)
5223[6]

Junction Line *M Al Muhairi* a96
10 b g Indian Ridge—Nassma (IRE) (Sadler's Wells (USA))
378a[15]

Jun Fan (USA) *B Ellison* a61 64
6 br g Artax(USA) —Ringside Lady (NZ) (Clay Hero (AUS))
(1338) 1634[11] 2448[2] 2777[8] 3340[2] ◆ 3454[12] 4047[3] ◆ 4107[3] 4293[7] 4703[7] 6251[6] 6546[11] 6823[7]

Jung (USA) *J R Gask*
2 bb c Stroll(USA) —Witching Well (IRE) (Night Shift (USA))
6488[11]

Jungle Lion *P A Kirby* 16
10 ch g Lion Cavern(USA) —Star Ridge (USA) (Storm Bird (CAN))
3820[11] 4295[6]

Juniper Berry (IRE) *John Joseph Murphy* 88
3 b f Galileo(IRE) —Lucky Achievement (USA) (St Jovite (USA))
1847a[9] 4833a[9]

Juniper Girl (IRE) *M L W Bell* 104
5 b m Revoque(IRE) —Shajara (FR) (Kendor (FR))
5646[4] 5854[4]

Jupiter Pluvius (USA) *A P O'Brien* 107
3 b c Johannesburg(USA) —Saratoga Honey (USA) (Boundary (USA))
2418a[4] 3119[6]

Just A Dancer (IRE) *B W Hills* a29 76
3 b f Choisir(AUS) —New Foundation (IRE) (College Chapel)
1834[11] 2258[10] 2690[7] 3324[8] 3893[4] 4268[9] 4988[8]

Just Bond (IRE) *G R Oldroyd* a93 88
6 b g Namid—Give Warning (IRE) (Warning)
1970[7] 2406[2] 2672[4] 3006[2] 3229[2] 3278[3] 4104[10] 4649[2] 4876[14] 5908[7] (6250) 6482[10] 7116[8] 7291[4] 7502[2] 7564[4] 7670[4]

Just Buzzin *Mrs L Stubbs*
2 b g Kyllachy—Smoke Signal (IRE) (College Chapel)
7627[7]

Justcallmehandsome *D J S Ffrench Davis* a84 53
6 ch g Handsome Ridge—Pearl Dawn (IRE) (Jareer (USA))
80[3] (140) (234) ◆ 284[4] 525[3] (660) 730[5] (1030) 1532[7] 1936[3] (2262) 7278[7] 7457[6] 7670[8]

Just Chrissie *G Fierro* 12
4 b m Classic Cliche(IRE) —Marsh Marigold (Tina's Pet)
1173[7]

Just Crystal *B P J Baugh* a47 33
4 b m Polar Prince(IRE) —Grandads Dream (Never So Bold)
33[10]

Just Dan *R Hollinshead* a53 43
2 b g Best Of The Bests(IRE) —Scapavia (FR) (Alzao (USA))
7080[10] 7343[9] 7424[7]

Just Dennis *D G Bridgwater* a48
4 b g Superior Premium—Sweets (IRE) (Persian Heights)
919[6]

Just Dust *M W Easterby* a56 87
4 b g Makbul—Dusty Bankes (Greensmith)
516[4] 587[6]

Just Five (IRE) *M Dods* 56
2 b g Olmodavor(USA) —Wildsplash (USA) (Deputy Minister (CAN))
1967[11] 2965[3] 3706[U] 4203[7] 4290[3] 5966[5] 6214[5]

Just For Mary *P J Rothwell* a73 72
4 b g Groom Dancer(USA) —Summer Dance (Sadler's Wells (USA))
7562[9] 7584[9] 7671[8]

Just Intersky (USA) *H J Collingridge* a69 62
5 gr g Distant View(USA) —Hexane (FR) (Kendor (FR))
27[4] 139[2] (248) 1165[7] 1411[3] 1554[4] 1853[6] 2456[3] 3220[4] 4526[5] 4829[3] 5105[5] 6019[2]

Just Jimmy (IRE) *P D Evans* a63 64
3 b g Ashkalani(IRE) —Berkeley Hall (Saddlers' Hall (IRE))
998[8] 1635[5] ◆ (1897) 2260[5] 3030[12] 3825[4] 3960[3] 4369[5] 5162[3] 5474[7] 6716[10] 7363[7] 7541[5] 7809[4]

Just Joey *J R Weymes* a53 85
4 b m Averti(IRE) —Fly South (Polar Falcon (USA))
987[13] 1818[15] 2159[11] (2448) 2928[4] 3080[3] 3363[2] 3575[4] 4016[6] 4246[5] 4462[7] 4502[5] 6711[6] 7231[10] 7295[8]

Just Josie *G L Moore*
2 b f Josr Algarhoud(IRE) —Spatham Rose (Environment Friend)
6553[12]

Just Kenko *N J Vaughan* a48
3 ch g Primo Valentino(IRE) —Coffee To Go (Environment Friend)
158[6] 360[5] 645[5]

Just Like A Woman *M L W Bell* a72 89
3 b f Observatory(USA) —Always On My Mind (Distant Relative)
1057[5] 1546[6] 2976[2] 3210[2] 3849[2] 4110[4] 5071[6] (5644) 6981[2] 7450a[4]

Just Like Ivy (CAN) *Patrick Martin* a30 68
3 b f Street Cry(IRE) —Celtic Craft (USA) (Danehill (USA))
4715a[5]

Just Like Silk (USA) *G A Butler* a58 69
2 b c Elusive Quality(USA) —Ocean Silk (USA) (Dynaformer (USA))
6084[6] 6597[9]

Just Lille (IRE) *Mrs A Duffield* 96
5 b m Mull Of Kintyre(USA) —Tamasriya (IRE) (Doyoun)
2220[2] (2499) 3627[2] 4191[12] 5279[12]

Just Mossie *W G M Turner* a63 34
3 ch g Ishiguru(USA) —Marinsky (USA) (Diesis)
73[2] 195[3] 432[7] 6492[2] 6741[12]

Just Mustard (USA) *G A Butler* 65
2 rg c Johannesburg(USA) —After All (IRE) (Desert Story (IRE))
6443[5]

Just 'N' Casey (IRE) *Tim Vaughan* 4
5 b g Marignan(USA) —De-Veers Currie (IRE) (Glenstal (USA))
3844[11]

Just Olive *G Fierro*
7 ch m Double Trigger(IRE) —My Home (Homing)
1172[13]

Justonefortheroad *N J Vaughan* 67
2 b c Domedriver(IRE) —Lavinia's Grace (USA) (Green Desert (USA))
4213[3] 4815[6]

Just Oscar (GER) *W M Brisbourne* a58 68
4 b g Surako(GER) —Jade Chequer (Green Desert (USA))
1029[11] 1687[9] 2782[9] 3422[3] 3431[2] 3951[6] 4168[6] 4428[8] 6255[12] 6570[14] 7178[7]

Just Puddie *W G M Turner* a40 48
3 b f Piccolo—Miss Laetitia (IRE) (Entitled)
845[8] 1081[5] 1370[9] 1536[5]

Just Rob *R Hollinshead* 85
3 b g Robellino(USA) —Scapavia (FR) (Alzao (USA))
1573[4] ◆ 1899[5] 2272[2] 2699[2] 3996[2] (5202)

Just Sam (IRE) *D W Barker* a61 62
3 b f Mull Of Kintyre(USA) —Strawberry Sands (Lugana Beach)
1558[2] 1870[2] 2208[2] 2833[3] 3126[12] 3692[4] 3730[3] 3791[3] 4043[2] 4702[11] 5544[8] 6217[4] 6562[7]

Just Sort It *W Jarvis* 80
3 b g Averti(IRE) —Lady Kris (IRE) (Kris)
2276[8] 2945[11] 4051[10]

Just Spike *B P J Baugh* a59 63
5 ch g Cayman Kai(IRE) —Grandads Dream (Never So Bold)
87[7] 718[5] 1029[10] (4535) 4749[3] 6890[11] 7118[8]

Just The Lady *D Nicholls* a64 72
2 b f Ishiguru(USA) —Just Run (IRE) (Runnett)
1122[3] 1303[3] 1762[5] 1914[5] (2720) (2924) 3788[3] 4558[4] 5475[4] (6009) 6274[3] 6769[12]

Just Two Numbers *W Jarvis* a45 83
4 b g Bahamian Bounty—Khadino (Relkino)
1682[13] 3003[3] 4131[6] 5100[6] 6839[8]

Just Waz (USA) *R M Whitaker* a53 65
6 ch g Woodman(USA) —Just Tops (USA) (Topsider (USA))
283[3] 600[6] 988[7] 1551[8] 1892[3] 2467[5] 7285[8]

Juzilla (IRE) *W R Swinburn* a72 55
4 b m Marju(IRE) —Mizillablack (IRE) (Eagle Eyed (USA))
407[6] 685[2] ◆ 1085[2] 1406[5] 3816[3] 4529[2]

Kaada *C E Brittain* a35 46
2 b f Fasliyev(USA) —Kyda (USA) (Gulch (USA))
3348[14] 3645[4] 4861[11] 5242[12] 6931[12]

Kaateb (IRE) *W J Haggas* a89 101
5 b g Alhaarth(IRE) —Muhaba (USA) (Mr Prospector (USA))
2120[2] 3294[2] (3684) 4443[2] 5508[P] (Dead)

Kaballero (GER) *S Gollings* a75 73
7 ch g Lomitas—Keniana (IRE) (Sharpo)
1719[9] 2203[11] 2533[9] (3583) 4081[2] 4529[F]

Kabeer *A J McCabe* a98 47
10 ch g Unfuwain(USA) —Ta Rib (USA) (Mr Prospector (USA))
6[2] (259) 442[2] 532[3] 679[11] 757[10] 1133[5] 1723[7] 2085[5] 7633[9] 7777[6]

Kabis Amigos *S T Mason* a56 76
6 ch g Nashwan(USA) —River Saint (USA) (Irish River (FR))
979[3] 1138[13] 1450[13] 2289[3] ◆ 2445[10] 2658[6] 3567[11] 4540[18] 4736[10] 6116[15] 7287[8] 7585[6] ◆ 7663[7] 7780[5] 7817[2]

Kabougg *P A Blockley* a30
2 b f Tobougg(IRE) —Karameg (IRE) (Danehill (USA))
4387[8] 6187[13]

Kadia *P T Midgley* a48 49
5 ch m Arkadian Hero(USA) —Soba Up (Persian Heights)
1258[6] 1559[11] 1752[4] 2463[7] 3175[14] 3795[7]

Kadouchski (FR) *John Berry* a58 58
4 b g Ski Chief(USA) —Douchka (FR) (Fijar Tango (FR))
234[5] 406[9] 708[10] 863[4] 2884[11] 3820[14] 5912[4] 6228[16]

Kafuu (IRE) *S A Callaghan* a88 94
4 b h Danehill Dancer(IRE) —Nausicaa (USA) (Diesis)
2262[2] 2619[5] (3646) ◆ 4269[4] 5446[9] 6478[12]

Kahara *L M Cumani* a76 93
4 b m Sadler's Wells(USA) —Kithanga (IRE) (Darshaan)
6127[6] 7242[3] 7491[8]

Kaichou (IRE) *B J Meehan* 15
4 b m Peintre Celebre(USA) —Lipica (IRE) (Night Shift (USA))
3813[12] 4057[P]

Kaijai (IRE) *Mrs L C Jewell*
2 b f Trans Island—Consultant Stylist (IRE) (Desert Style (IRE))
6205[14]

Kaikoura *G D Blake* a36 40
2 br f High Chaparral(IRE) —Landowska (USA) (Langfuhr (CAN))
4251[9] 5572[9]

Kai Mer (IRE) *Miss J A Camacho* a23 31
3 b f Captain Rio—No Shame (Formidable (USA))
1132[5] 1453[7] 1795[11]

Kaiser Willie (IRE) *B W Duke* 45
2 b c Xaar—Miss Bellbird (IRE) (Danehill (USA))
4187[7] 6122[13] 6715 [10]

Kalahari Gold (IRE) *A M Balding* 117
3 ch g Trans Island—Neat Shilling (IRE) (Bob Back (USA))
(2919) 3897[4] (4641) (4869) ◆ (6073)

Kalasam *M W Easterby* a82 77
4 ch g Noverre(USA) —Spring Sixpence (Dowsing (USA))
1482[15] 1732[7] 2585[11] 3054[8] 4371[9] 5040[2] 5993[7] 6243[9] 6395[4]

Kal Barg *M A Jarvis* a77 101
3 b c Medicean—Persian Air (Persian Bold)
1441[6] 2405[2] ◆ 3222[4] 4197[3] 5425[8] (6249)

Kaldoun Kingdom (IRE) *R A Fahey* a47 101
3 b c King's Best(USA) —Bint Kaldoun (IRE) (Kaldoun (FR))
1404[2] ◆ 2104[12] 3850[16] 3973[2] 4842[3] ◆ 6069[21] 6947[2] 7109[4]

Kalhan Sands (IRE) *G A Swinbank* a80 82
3 b g Okawango(USA) —Night Spirit (IRE) (Night Shift (USA))
136[4] 376[6] 1328[4] 1911[6] 3050[18]

Kalidaha (IRE) *John M Oxx* a94 93
3 ch f Cadeaux Genereux—Kalimanta (IRE) (Lake Coniston (IRE))
6689a[2] 7328a[5]

Kalinka Malinka (IRE) *D K Weld* a80 73
3 b f Pivotal—Hoh Dear (IRE) (Sri Pekan (USA))
6511a[9]

Kalligal *R Ingram* a54 73
3 br f Kyllachy—Anytime Baby (Bairn (USA))
1277[8] 1699[5] 2896[3] 3526[3] 4308[8] 5028[3] 5201[9] 5817[3] 6388[13] 6750[8] 7672[4] 7817[12]

Kalokairi (IRE) *J L Dunlop* a55 63
3 b f Galileo(IRE) —Naziriya (FR) (Darshaan)
1478[4] 1871[3] 2468[8] 3624[9] 4859[5] 5269[5] 5613[6] 6022[9] 6436[7]

Kaloni (IRE) *Mrs P Sly* a76 43
2 b f Kalanisi(IRE) —Santarene (IRE) (Scenic)
5029[5] 5571[3] 6016[2] 6756[5]

Kamado *Edward Lynam* 99
2 b c Kyllachy—Palacegate Episode (IRE) (Drumalis)
4005a[3] ◆ 5546a[5]

Kamal *W R Muir* a64 42
3 ch g Bahamian Bounty—Star Tulip (Night Shift (USA))
178[6] 419[8] 480[6] 767[7] 835[2] 876[3] 1051[3]

Kamanda Laugh *K A Ryan* a89 84
7 ch g Most Welcome—Kamada (USA) (Blushing Groom (FR))
1138[12]

Kama Night (IRE) *G A Swinbank* 51
3 b g Night Shift(USA) —Kamalame (USA) (Souvenir Copy (USA))
4454[3]

Kamanja (UAE) *M A Jarvis* a60
2 b f Red Ransom(USA) —Nasmatt (Danehill (USA))
7708[5]

Kames Park (IRE) *I W McInnes* a93 93
6 b g Desert Sun—Persian Sally (IRE) (Persian Bold)
410[5] 757[9] (859) 968[6] 1137[8] 2185[2] 2249[4] 2585[8] 2822[5] 3613[10] 7473[7] 7563[7] 7744[7]

Kammaan *M A Jarvis* 72
2 b f Diktat—Qasirah (IRE) (Machiavellian (USA))
4534[2]

Kamsin (GER) *P Schiergen* 119
3 br c Samum(GER) —Kapitol (GER) (Winged Love (IRE))
(1850a) 2880a[4] (3773a) (5137a) (5736a) 6522a[11]

Kandahar Run *H R A Cecil* 116
3 gr c Rock Of Gibraltar(IRE) —Kenmist (Kenmare (FR))
1402[2] (1810) 2829[14] 4010a[5]

Kandidate *C E Brittain* a111 116
6 b h Kabool—Valleyrose (IRE) (Royal Academy (USA))
476a[2] 817a[U] (1077) 1422[8] 3683[3] 3940[7] 5348[6]

Kangrina *George Baker* a65 67
6 b m Acatenango(GER) —Kirona (Robellino (USA))
2353[2] 3089[8] 3657[2] 4267[3] 5478[5] 6395[6] 6882[9] ◆ 7039[13] 7280[3] 7667[2] 7776[5]

Kanisorn (SWE) *Mike Hammond* a73 26
6 b g Be My Chief(USA) —American Pay Day (USA) (Cryptoclearance (USA))
(83) 260[9] 348[2] 533[2] 600[2] 754[8] 787[2] 1184[12] 1702[2] 2867[5] 3137[12] 5593[12]

Kannie Annie *T J Pitt*
2 ch f Cayman Kai(IRE) —Minskip Miss (Lucky Wednesday)
2206[11] 6229[12] 6722[13]

Kannon *Miss M E Rowland* a63 69
3 b f Kyllachy—Violet (IRE) (Mukaddamah (USA))
1535[6] 1926[14] 2622[8] 2898[2] 3395[4] 3678[8] (4338) 4770[2] 4825[3] (6746) 6928[3] 7359[9] 7513[3] 7631[6]

Kanonkop *M J Gingell* a50 50
4 b m Observatory(USA) —Camcorder (Nashwan (USA))
7573[10]

Kanpai (IRE) *J G M O'Shea* 68
6 br g Trans Island—David's Star (Welsh Saint)
6054[2] ◆ 6606[10]

Kansai Spirit (IRE) *J H M Gosden* a81 78
2 ch c Sinndar(IRE) —Daanat Nawal (Machiavellian (USA))
6084[8] 6425[4] 7204[2]

Kansas Gold *J Mackie* a72 65
5 b g Alhaarth(IRE) —Star Tulip (Night Shift (USA))
128[6] 2243[11] 3569[8] 4567[3] 5157[12] 7516[10]

Kaolak (USA) *J Ryan* a81 74
2 bb c Action This Day(USA) —Cerita (USA) (Magesterial (USA))
5246[4] 7054[9] 7397[3] (7754)

Kapellmeister (IRE) *M S Saunders* a43 2
5 b g Mozart(IRE) —March Hare (Groom Dancer (USA))
5118[7] 5576[8]

Kapowee *W J Musson* 43
2 b f Groom Dancer(USA) —Trevorsninepoints (Jester)
2924[5] 3959[8] 4257[2] 4827[11] 6059[15]

Kappalyn (IRE) *R Hannon* 46
3 b f Marju(IRE) —Miss Tardy (JPN) (Lammtarra (USA))
4277[10] 4709[5] 5023[8] 5755[6]

Kapsiliat (IRE) *J Noseda* 57
2 b f Cape Cross(IRE) —Kootenay (IRE) (Selkirk (USA))
4359[5]

Karaburan (GER) *P Monteith* 37
4 ch g Samum(GER) —Kimora (GER) (Dashing Blade)
978[10] 1305[9] 6309[9]

Karashar (IRE) *Evan Williams* 67
3 b g Kalanisi(IRE) —Karaliyfa (IRE) (Kahyasi)
1539[6] 2454[4]

Kara Tau *Stef Liddiard* a56 55
3 b g Efisio—Donna Anna (Be My Chief (USA))
5160[13] 7026[7] 7383[11] 7504[6]

Karate Queen *A M Balding* a57 51
3 b f King's Best(USA) —Black Belt Shopper (IRE) (Desert Prince (IRE))
1637[6] 2922[14] 3524[8] 6735[4] 7112[6] 7497[4] 7541[3]

Kardyls Hope (IRE) *Jarlath P Fahey* a34 68
2 b f Fath(USA) —Elite Hope (USA) (Moment Of Hope (USA))
6320a[6]

Kareemah (IRE) *J E Hammond* 105
3 ch f Peintre Celebre(USA) —Rahayeb (Arazi (USA))
5039a[7] (6567a) 7348a[9]

Karelian (USA) *George R Arnold II* 111
6 b g Bertrando(USA) —Leaning Tower (USA) (Theatrical)
6504a[5]

Kargan (IRE) *A G Foster* a62 65
3 b g Intikhab(USA) —Karkiyla (IRE) (Darshaan)
1073[2] 2429[13] 2750[5] 4738[6] 5224[8] 6042[9] 6951[2]

Karibu Blue *C F Wall*
4 b m Most Welcome—Lazybird Blue (IRE) (Bluebird (USA))
3823[12] 5652[12]

Karky Schultz (GER) *J M P Eustace* a66 68
3 gr g Diktat—Kazoo (Shareef Dancer (USA))
1743[3] 2429[15] 2891[10] 3799[11] 5421[9] 6004[9]

Karlani (IRE) *G A Swinbank* 71
5 br g Fantastic Light(USA) —Karliyka (IRE) (Last Tycoon)
5543[5] 6115[9] 6550[13]

Karlu (GER) *John C McConnell* a72 79
6 ch g Big Shuffle(USA) —Krim (GER) (Lagunas)
4655a[P]

Karma Llama (IRE) *George Baker* a55 67
4 b m Intikhab(USA) —Ustka (Lomond (USA))
792[4] 872[3] 1064[12] (Dead)

Karmei *R Curtis* a51 61
3 b g Royal Applause—Lafite (Robellino (USA))
629[6] 918[7] 2639[3] 2930[3] 3343[4] 7189[13] 7385[15]

Karmest *A D Brown* a78 73
4 ch m Best Of The Bests(IRE) —Karmafair (IRE) (Always Fair (USA))
(69) (277) 368[3] (613) 771[3] 963[6] 1219[6] 1394[4] (1577) 2453[6] 6487[3] 6726[8] 7046[7] 7284[5] (7613) 7722[3] 7797[4]

Karnak (IRE) *J H Scott* 46
6 b g Sadler's Wells(USA) —Aspen Leaves (USA) (Woodman (USA))
3861a[13]

Karoush (USA) *P W Chapple-Hyam* 82
3 b c Gone West(USA) —Victorica (USA) (Exbourne (USA))
2198[3] 2673[2]

Karramalu (IRE) *Daniel Mark Loughnane* a14 51
7 b m Entrepreneur—Bold Feather (Persian Bold)
4936[10]

Kasaa Ed *M Johnston* 66
2 b f Marju(IRE) —Muwajaha (Night Shift (USA))
6565[5]

Kasbah Bliss (FR) *F Doumen* a78 114
6 b g Kahyasi—Marital Bliss (FR) (Double Bed (FR))
(5956a) 6497a[4]

Kasban *Jane Chapple-Hyam* 81
4 b g Kingmambo(USA) —Ebaraya (IRE) (Sadler's Wells (USA))
2153[10] 2621[4] (3276) 4193[7] 4516[12]

Kashimin (IRE) *G A Swinbank* 84
3 b c Kyllachy—Oh So Misty (Teenoso (USA))
1404[13] 3056[12] 3626[2] 3999[4] 4682[2] 4875[9]

Kashmina *Miss Sheena West* a67 69
3 ch f Dr Fong(USA) —Lady Melbourne (IRE) (Indian Ridge)
1247[2] ◆ 1412[5] 2002[5] 2563[5] 3023[6] 6437[5]

Kashoof *J L Dunlop* 84
3 b f Green Desert(USA) —Khulood (USA) (Storm Cat (USA))
1999[8] 3028[8]

Kassuta *M J Gingell* a62 57
4 b m Kyllachy—Happy Omen (Warning)
6729[11] 7535[14]

Kasthari (IRE) *J D Bethell* a69 102
9 gr g Vettori(IRE) —Karliyka (IRE) (Last Tycoon)
1568[10] 1916[13] 3975[7] 4439[4] 5423[10] 5718[4] 6272[9] 6817[22]

Kasumi *H Morrison* a87 109
5 ch m Inchinor—Raindrop (Primo Dominie)
1981[2] ◆ (2284) (2890) 3852[8] 4361[3]

Kate The Great *M J Wallace* a76 75
2 b f Xaar—Ros The Boss (IRE) (Danehill (USA))
(1177) 1813[6] 2507[3] 3105[22] 3846[2] 4768[2] 5204[4]

Kathanikki Girl (IRE) *Mrs L Williamson* a14
2 b f Tagula(IRE) —Tenalist (IRE) (Tenby)
6661[8] 6988[11]

Katie Boo (IRE) *A Berry* a54 84
6 br m Namid—Misty Peak (IRE) (Sri Pekan (USA))
2938[8] 3370[9] 3554[3] 3713[8] 4016[3] 4117[3] 4383[5] (4631) 4858[3] 4971[2] 5222[7]

Katie Coniston *Dr J R J Naylor* a38 37
4 b m Lake Coniston(IRE) —Lycius Touch (Lycius (USA))
24[8]

Katie Girl *Mrs G S Rees* 23
2 b f Makbul—Katie Komaite (Komaite (USA))
5633[12] 5989[11] 6808[10]

Katie Higgins *J L Spearing* a43 52
2 b f Spartacus(IRE) —Smooth Technology (IRE) (Astronef)
3754[5] 5754[10] 6600[10] 7281[6] 7372[6] 7531[7] 7728[6]

Katie Kingfisher *M E Rimmer* a46 42
4 b m Fraam—Sonic Sapphire (Royal Academy (USA))
37[4] 438[14] 606[15] 7265[11]

Katie Lawson (IRE) *D Haydn Jones* a51 38
5 b m Xaar—Idle Chat (USA) (Assert)
40[3]

Katie's Biscuit *Ian Emmerson* 34
6 b m Cayman Kai(IRE) —Peppers (IRE) (Bluebird (USA))
2038[13] 2250[9]

Katimont (IRE) *B W Hills* 87
3 b f Montjeu(IRE) —Katiyfa (Auction Ring (USA))
(1525) 2149[5]

Katiypour (IRE) *B R Johnson* a91 65
11 ch g Be My Guest(USA) —Katiyfa (Auction Ring (USA))
57[3] (389)

Katiyra (IRE) *John M Oxx* 117
3 b f Peintre Celebre(USA) —Katiykha (IRE) (Darshaan)
2024a[2] ◆ 2792[3] 4006a[5] (5920a) 6521a[3]

Kattar *D M Simcock* a65 54
2 ch c Singspiel(IRE) —Lady Zonda (Lion Cavern (USA))
5246[13] 7209[6] 7438[4] ◆

Katy Kitten (UAE) *G L Moore* a49 49
3 b f Halling(USA) —Fatinat Al Melouk (USA) (Belong To Me (USA))
3205[5] 3611[10] 5471[5] 5912[9] 6337[12]

Kavachi (IRE) *G L Moore* a67 94
5 b g Cadeaux Genereux—Answered Prayer (Green Desert (USA))
1473[9] (1742) (2152) 2582[4] 3122[4] 3740[9] 4509[9]

Kavatcha (FR) *Miss Tor Sturgis* a17 41
5 gr g Nikos—Kaleigh's Jovite (USA) (St Jovite (USA))
3530[11] 3894[11] 4302[10]

Kawagino (IRE) *J W Mullins* 76
8 b g Perugino(USA) —Sharakawa (IRE) (Darshaan)
6672[2]

Kayaba *C Laffon-Parias* 101
3 b f Anabaa(USA) —Senkaya (FR) (Valanour (IRE))
2033a[10] 2902a[3]

Kayak (SAF) *D M Simcock* a99 87
6 b g Western Winter(USA) —Donya (SAF) (Elliodor (FR))
380a[12] 493a[6] 667a[4] 2711[3] 3505[12] 4363[5] 5569[9] 6033[9] 6625[5] 7313[3] 7579[6]

Kayceebee *R M Beckett* a47 55
2 b g Cyrano De Bergerac—Twice Upon A Time (Primo Dominie)
3323[13] 4020[5] 4905[10] 6572[7] 6906[6]

Kay Es Jay (FR) *B W Hills* a79 98
3 b f Xaar—Angel Rose (IRE) (Definite Article)
1332[9] 1715[3] 2666[3] 3420[6] 4424[6] 4522[6] 5644[2] 6277[3] ◆ 6981[14]

Kayf Aramis *Miss Venetia Williams* a66 79
6 b g Kayf Tara—Ara (Birthright)
2135[4] 2628[4] 3250[10]

Kayfiar (USA) *P F I Cole* a60 64
2 ch c Lion Heart(USA) —Ivor Jewel (USA) (Sir Ivor (USA))
4150[10] 4890[5] 5404[8]

Kayflaa (IRE) *T D Walford* a68 51
3 b f Dubai Destination(USA) —Arhaaff (IRE) (Danehill (USA))
1042[2] 1348[3] 2037[9] 2982[14] 5308[9] 6015[7] 6485[11] 7012[13]

Kay Gee Be (IRE) *W Jarvis* a100 99
4 b g Fasliyev(USA) —Pursuit Of Truth (USA) (Irish River (FR))
1545[2] 1723[5] 3398[6] 4845[3] 6249[10] 6975[6] 7313[9]

Kaymich Perfecto *R M Whitaker* a59 59
8 b g Sheikh Albadou—Manhattan Diamond (Primo Dominie)
2672[10] 3229[6] 4219[3] 4540[12] 6215[14]

Kaystar Ridge *D K Ivory* a65 42
3 b g Tumbleweed Ridge—Kayartis (Kaytu)
60[8] 146[8] 6543[12] 7076[12] 7357[4] (7508)

Kay Tee Jo (IRE) *Peter Grayson*
3 br f High Chaparral(IRE) —Kariyh (USA) (Shadeed (USA))
543[12]

Kay Two (IRE) *R J Price* a87 94
6 ch g Monashee Mountain(USA) —Tricky (Song)
3472[5] (3881) 4240[16] 6354[6] 6651[4] (6859) 6971[5] 7290[4]

Kazakstan *Mrs L C Jewell* a50 59
4 b g Kyllachy—Niseem (USA) (Hennessy (USA))
87[5] 245[7] 516[13] 607[8]

Kazbow (IRE) *L M Cumani* 38
2 b c Rainbow Quest(USA) —Kasota (IRE) (Alzao (USA))
6581[11] 7200[16]

Keagles (ITY) *J E Long* a41 32
5 b m Indian Danehill(IRE) —Athens Belle (IRE) (Groom Dancer (USA))
88[9]

Keel (IRE) *C R Dore* a66 56
5 br g Carrowkeel(IRE) —First Degree (Sabrehill (USA))
6356[5] ◆ 6663[8] 6826[5] 7094[3] 7183[10]

Keelung (USA) *R Ford* 83
7 b g Lear Fan(USA) —Miss Universal (IRE) (Lycius (USA))
3296[6] (3891) (3950) 4516[5] 5887[6]

Keenes Day (FR) *M Johnston* a96 76
3 gr g Daylami(IRE) —Key Academy (Royal Academy (USA))
5111[5] 5698[3] ◆ 6390[7] (6838) (6957) 7404[9]

Keen Eye *W J Knight* 49
3 b f Nayef(USA) —Mexican Hawk (USA) (Silver Hawk (USA))
1599[11] (Dead)

Keen Look (IRE) *Gerard Keane* a79 87
9 b g Key Of Luck(USA) —Killone Lady (IRE) (High Estate)
6511a[11]

Keen Rabbit *Micky Hammond* a25 18
2 b f Keen—Arella Rabbit (Presidium)
2965[6] 3106[7] 4203[15] 4387[9]

Keeparryappy (IRE) *K R Burke* a50 64
3 b g Fath(USA) —Coppelia (IRE) (Mac's Imp (USA))
1315[9] 2260[9] 3231[12]

Keep Dancing (IRE) *A M Balding* 69
2 ch f Distant Music(USA) —Miss Indigo (Indian Ridge)
5784[2] 6245[3]

Keep Discovering (IRE) *M Johnston* a93 101
3 b g Oasis Dream—Side Of Paradise (IRE) (Sadler's Wells (USA))
1113[4] 1441[3] (1745) ◆ 2104[9] 2794[11] 3897[2] 4553[9] (5030) (5446) 5795[7]

Keepers Knight (IRE) *W Clay* a9 6
7 b g Sri Pekan(USA) —Keepers Dawn (IRE) (Alzao (USA))
2867[12] (Dead)

Keep Icy Calm (IRE) *M F De Kock* a64
2 br f One Cool Cat(USA) —Alazima (USA) (Riverman (USA))
7458[5]

Keepsgettingbetter (IRE) *J R Gask* a67
3 b g Modigliani(USA) —Adua (IRE) (Kenmare (FR))
7500[2] 7757[4]

Keeptheboatafloat (USA) *K R Burke* a90 90
2 b g Fusaichi Pegasus(USA) —The Perfect Life (IRE) (Try My Best (USA))
2584[11] (3170) 3553[2] 5693[10] 6176[4]

Keep Your Distance *P J McBride* a57 64
4 b g Distant Music(USA) —Queen G (USA) (Matty G (USA))
6422[5] 6751[3] 6930[3] 7287[12]

Keidas (FR) *C F Wall* a73 76
4 b m Lomitas—Kahina (GER) (Warning)
736[3] 1039[7]

Keiser Blue *P C Haslam*
2 ch g Loup Sauvage(USA) —Sea Idol (IRE) (Astronef)
1555[6]

Keisha Kayleigh (IRE) *B Ellison* a68 80
5 b m Almutawakel—Awtaar (USA) (Lyphard (USA))
1394[6] (1822) 2284[4] 2697[2] (3450) 4111[2] 4419[7] 4970[6] 5564[7]

Kelamon *M D I Usher* a77 83
4 b g Keltos(FR) —Faraway Moon (Distant Relative)
463[4] 554[5] 636[3] 755[4] (819) 1522[3] 1800[5] 2085[4] 2679[7] (3797) 4025[2] ◆ (4154) ◆ 4478[10] 4928[4] 5233[5] 5648[12] (6402)

Kellies Boost (IRE) *G A Swinbank* 57
2 b f Invincible Spirit(IRE) —Misaayef (USA) (Swain (IRE))
4681[5] 6212[3] 6545[6]

Kelowna (IRE) *J L Dunlop* 90
3 ch f Pivotal—Kootenay (IRE) (Selkirk (USA))
1423[10] (1926) 2902a[5] 3742[11]

Kempsey *J J Bridger* a67 55
6 ch g Wolfhound(USA) —Mockingbird (Sharpo)
149[8] 312[3] 414[2] 515[3] 620[4] 746[3] 875[10] 939[2] 1037[8] 1522[13] 1646[12] 2255[10] 2837[11] 3966[5] 4154[4] 5315[4] 5582[9] 5626[11] 5916[9]

Kenland (IRE) *S W Hall*
3 br g Lend A Hand—Ferghana Ma (Mtoto)
529[11]

Kenmore *I W McInnes* 88
6 b g Compton Place—Watheeqah (USA) (Topsider (USA))
1069[4] 1327[13] (2036) 2255[11] 2950[12] 3033[4] 3404[2]

Kennington *Mrs C A Dunnett* a74 59
8 ch g Compton Place—Mim (Midyan (USA))
191[4] 437[2] 596[5] 1865[4]

Kennyboy *P G Murphy* a46 49
3 b g Apprehension—Eastbury Rose (Beveled (USA))
1621[14] 2454[9] 3637[9] 5913[10] 6594[12]

Ken's Girl *W S Kittow* a64 69
4 ch m Ishiguru(USA) —There's Two (IRE) (Ashkalani (IRE))
1522[11] 2128[7] 3208[9] 3892[2] 4708[4] (6560) 7021[7]

Kensington (IRE) *P D Evans* a79 80
7 b g Cape Cross(IRE) —March Star (IRE) (Mac's Imp (USA))
235[3] 506[2] (555) (683) 755[10] (1368) 1552[4] 1683[8] 2615[3] 2693[6] 3093[8] 3607[4] 4104[6] 4407[14] 4895[3] 5779[6] 6554[5] 6826[9] 7286[4] 7359[6] 7510[6] 7586[5] (7651) ◆ 7698[3] 7730[8] 7829[2]

Kensington Oval *Sir Michael Stoute* 88
3 b g Sadler's Wells(USA) —Request (Rainbow Quest (USA))
(2763) ◆ 3156[14] 6302[11]

Kentavr's Dream *P Howling* a47 23
5 b m Robellino(USA) —Very Good (Noalto)
7300[4]

Kentish Dream *S A Callaghan* a71 82
2 b c Oasis Dream—Danella (FR) (Highest Honor (FR))
3879[2] ◆ (4184) 4685[4] 5615[6]

Kenton Street *J A R Toller* a69 69
3 ch g Compton Place—Western Applause (Royal Applause)
1960[14] 3502[4] 4258[5] 6192[4] 6543[3] 7074[4]

Kentucky Bear (USA) *Reade Baker* a111 65
3 ch c Mr Greeley(USA) —Tate (USA) (Afleet (CAN))
2215a[6]

Kentucky Beauty (FR) *T Lerner* 87
3 b f Orpen(USA) —Cruelle (USA) (Irish River (FR))
6064a[0]

Kentucky Boy (IRE) *Jedd O'Keeffe* a48 65
4 b g Distant Music(USA) —Delta Town (USA) (Sanglamore (USA))
5385[4] 6054[12]

Kentucky Bullet (USA) *A G Newcombe* a50 56
12 b g Housebuster(USA) —Exactly So (Caro)
171[5] 613[2] 1262[8]

Kenz (FR) *C Baillet* 81
2 b f Indian Rocket—Manettia (FR) (Midyan (USA))
3774a[3] 4472a[6]

Keon (IRE) *R Hollinshead* a60 60
6 b g Rossini(USA) —Lonely Brook (USA) (El Gran Senor (USA))
32[9] 168[6] 804[2] 862[2] 972[3] 1025[2]

Kerashan (IRE) *A Al Raihe* a94 84
6 b g Sinndar(IRE) —Kerataka (IRE) (Doyoun)
381a[7] 493a[12]

Kerayasi (FR) *G L Moore* a67 71
6 b g Kahyasi—Good Blend (FR) (Darshaan)
(6577) 6983[5]

Kerry's Blade (IRE) *Micky Hammond* 49
6 ch g Daggers Drawn(USA) —Treasure (IRE) (Treasure Kay)
2914[2] 4220[14]

Kerrys Requiem (IRE) *M R Channon* 96
2 b f King's Best(USA) —Moonlight Wish (IRE) (Peintre Celebre (USA))
1866[4] 2306[3] 2838[3] ◆ 3020[3] (3528) 3851[7] 5055[2] 5642[6] 5852[10]

Kersivay *W R Swinburn* a76 70
2 b g Royal Applause—Lochmaddy (Selkirk (USA))
4184[15] 4720[3] 5649[7] 6087[3]

Kessraa (IRE) *M R Channon* a37 9
2 b c Kheleyf(USA) —Safe Care (IRE) (Caerleon (USA))
5344[11] 6539[13]

Kestrel Cross (IRE) *L M Cumani* a19 73
6 b g Cape Cross(IRE) —Lady Rachel (IRE) (Priolo (USA))
2762[10] 3461[8] 6035[11]

Ketter (BRZ) *R Bouresly* a78
7 ch g Much Better(BRZ) —Diana-Bela (BRZ) (Empire Day (BRZ))
564a[10]

Kevkat (IRE) *Eoin Griffin* a95 101
7 br g Dushyantor(USA) —Diamond Display (IRE) (Shardari)
6261a[7]

Key Decision (IRE) *Shaun Harley* a70 80
4 br g Key Of Luck(USA) —Adalya (IRE) (Darshaan)
991[5] 1382[8] 1814[2] 2249[8] 2447[2] 3368[15] 7758[9]

Key News (IRE) *M A Jarvis* a66
3 br f Halling(USA) —Belle Argentine (FR) (Fijar Tango (FR))
350[2] 867[4] 1410[6]

Key Of Fortune (IRE) *Jennie Candlish* a35 40
2 b f Key Of Luck(USA) —Alaynia (IRE) (Hamas (IRE))
7781[4]

Key Partners (IRE) *P A Blockley* a64 64
7 b g Key Of Luck(USA) —Teacher Preacher (IRE) (Taufan (USA))
91[12] 449[3] 617[4] 658[2] (1702) 2100[9] 2707[9] 3328[7]

Keypit *W R Swinburn* a37
2 b c Key Of Luck(USA) —Meadow Pipit (CAN) (Meadowlake (USA))
7336[14]

Key Signature *Pat Eddery* a77 83
2 b f Dansili—Musical Key (Key Of Luck (USA))
3349[5] 3913[2] (5048) 5511[2] 6673[4]

Keys Of Cyprus *D Nicholls* 86
6 ch g Deploy—Krisia (Kris)
4605[13] (5045) 5634[6] (5965) (6043) 6537[6] 6813[2]

Key To Caius (IRE) *R F Fisher*
5 b g Shinko Forest(IRE) —Alpine Lady (IRE) (Tirol)
4698[9] 5042[11]

Key To Love (IRE) *A J Chamberlain* a64 69
2 b f Key Of Luck(USA) —Ski For Me (IRE) (Barathea (IRE))
3837[6] 4339[5] 4705[2] 5200[3] 5671[5] (6191) 6730[4] 6931[4] 7308[9] 7719[9]

Key To Pleasure (GER) *Mario Hofer* 109
8 b h Sharp Prod(USA) —Key To Love (FR) (Alzao (USA))
2214a[9] 3752a[6] 4912a[6] 7005a[3]

K'Gari (USA) *B Ellison* 29
2 ch g Fusaichi Pegasus(USA) —To Act (USA) (Roberto (USA))
4415[10] 4968[6]

Khadija *R Dickin* a23
7 ch m Kadastrof(FR) —Dark Sirona (Pitskelly)
152[7]

Khandaar (IRE) *Werner Glanz* 26
3 b f Xaar—Khaydariya (IRE) (Akarad (FR))
5737a[8]

Khan Tengri (IRE) *M P Tregoning* 77
2 gr g Sadler's Wells(USA) —Ela Athena (Ezzoud (IRE))
4625[13] 4788[3] 5842[3]

Khateeb (IRE) *M A Jarvis* a92 109
3 b c King's Best(USA) —Choc Ice (IRE) (Kahyasi)
1418[2] (1855) 2544[4] 3156[4] ◆ 4552[15] 5070[3]

Khayar (IRE) *M H Tompkins* 53
2 b c Refuse To Bend(IRE) —Khatela (IRE) (Shernazar)
6944[10]

Khazina (USA) *C E Brittain* 66
3 bb f Kingmambo(USA) —Easy Now (USA) (Danzig (USA))
(1019) 1297[12] 2039[5] 2378[7] 3381[6] 4282[4] 4637[6] 5088[6] 6353[13]

Kheley (IRE) *W M Brisbourne* a50 51
2 b f Kheleyf(USA) —Namesake (Nashwan (USA))
1384[6] 1574[3] 2004[6] 2508[3] 3091[3] 3225[5] 4487[3] 7687[3]

Kheleyf's Silver (IRE) *B Smart* 73
2 b f Kheleyf(USA) —Silver Arrow (USA) (Shadeed (USA))
4734[6] 5394[2] 6548[2] (6863)

Kheskianto (IRE) *M Botti* a57 83
2 b f Kheleyf(USA) —Gently (IRE) (Darshaan)
7523[4] 7652[4]

Kheylide (IRE) *Miss V Haigh* a77 66
2 ch g Kheleyf(USA) —Jayzdoll (IRE) (Stravinsky (USA))
2657[9] 2893[10] 3140[3] 3392[3] (3846) 4143[5] 4434[10] 4857[8]

Khor Dubai (IRE) *Saeed Bin Suroor* a101 100
2 b c Kheleyf(USA) —Dievotchkina (IRE) (Bluebird (USA))
2608[3] 3105[9] (3651) (4185) ◆ 4588[8] 5693[4] 6119[6] 6483[4] (7109)

Kiama Bay (IRE) *J J Quinn* 54
2 b g Fraam—La Panthere (USA) (Pine Bluff (USA))
6109[6] ◆ 6545[8] 7038[6]

Kibitzer *J W Hills* a69
3 b c Diesis—Kitza (IRE) (Danehill (USA))
130[2] ◆ 662[4] 936[3]

Kick And Prance *G L Moore* a45 63
5 ch g Groom Dancer(USA) —Unerring (Unfuwain (USA))
1052[9] (Dead)

Kidlat *B G Powell* a78 76
3 b c Cape Cross(IRE) —Arruhan (IRE) (Mujtahid (USA))
2509[4] 3227[5] 4161[5] 7603[5]

Kidson (USA) *George Baker* a23 37
2 bb c Lemon Drop Kid(USA) —Solo (USA) (Halo (USA))
3968[8] 4890[13] 5590[10]

Kielty's Folly *B P J Baugh* a45 45
4 gr g Weet-A-Minute(IRE) —Three Sweeties (Cruise Missile)
769[7] 4414[5] 4898[3] 5420[5]

Kiho *Eve Johnson Houghton* 69
3 b g Dashing Blade—Krim (GER) (Lagunas)
1467[9] 1994[2] 2907[4] 4112[5] 5216[7]

Kijani (IRE) *M R Channon* 7
3 b g Green Desert(USA) —Sweet Times (Riverman (USA))
3521[7] 3963[9]

Kijivu *A J Lidderdale* a48 53
3 gr f Erhaab(USA) —Alsiba (Northfields (USA))
885[9] 974[7] 2191[10] 2468[12] 2611[2] 3562[6] 5077[8] 5931[6] 6753[13]

Kildare Sun (IRE) *J Mackie* a79 79
6 b g Desert Sun—Megan's Dream (IRE) (Fayruz)
531[5] 659[4] (809) 860[2] 1520[12] 2262[4] 3557[7] 7502[5]

Kilkenny Bay *W Jarvis* a59
2 b f Tobougg(IRE) —Miss Arizona (IRE) (Sure Blade (USA))
7638[3] 7823[10]

Killcara Boy *H Candy* a50 86
3 b f Tobougg(IRE) —Barakat (Bustino)
(1840) 2256[4] 3380[5] 4130[3] (4619) 5464[3] 6079[6]

Killena Boy (IRE) *W Jarvis* a93 98
6 b g Imperial Ballet(IRE) —Habaza (IRE) (Shernazar)
4269[3] 5051[7] 5843[7]

Killer Class *J S Goldie* 70
3 ch f Kyllachy—Class Wan (Safawan)
(993) (1141) (1475) 1560[3] 2287[7] 2527[3] 2676[2] 3080[8] 3256[2] 3455[3] 4000[8] 4852[3] 5393[4] (5417) 6039[5] 6066[6] 7081[12] 7222[12]

Killinan (IRE) *G M Lyons* a85 82
4 b m Danehill Dancer(IRE) —Kill The Crab (IRE) (Petorius)
6510a[6]

Killmarnock *R A Teal* a51 56
2 b g King's Best(USA) —Noodle Soup (USA) (Alphabet Soup (USA))
2796[5] 3372[7] 5314[17] 5811[4] 6926[9]

Killyea *R A Harris* a35
2 b f Bertolini(USA) —Real Popcorn (IRE) (Jareer (USA))
4321[8] 4474[9] 5475[9]

Kilmagner (IRE) *William Coleman O'Brien* a63 67
2 b g Night Shift(USA) —Jalopy (Jalmood (USA))
3509a[5]

Kilmeena Magic *J C Fox* a52 47
6 b m Fumo Di Londra(IRE) —Kilmeena Lady (Inca Chief (USA))
269[2] 415[6] 5020[12]

Kilometre Neuf (FR) *F Doumen* a105 105
5 b h Double Bed(FR) —Mary Astor (FR) (Groom Dancer (USA))
5113a[7]

Kilsyth (IRE) *S Parr* a17 58
2 b f Marju(IRE) —Easter Song (USA) (Rubiano (USA))
4921[12] 4965[8] 5219[5] 6291[9] 6761[11] 6953[9]

Kiltycross (IRE) *M Halford* 57
3 b g Cape Cross(IRE) —Solar Attraction (IRE) (Salt Dome (USA))
4613a[15]

Kilvickeon (IRE) *Peter Grayson* a49 49
4 b g Daggers Drawn(USA) —Queen Of Sweden (IRE) (Solid Illusion (USA))
319[2] 7527[7]

Kimberley Downs (USA) *M Johnston* a80
2 gr c Giant's Causeway(USA) —Fountain Lake (USA) (Vigors (USA))
7209[4] (7422)

Kimbolton *H R A Cecil* a57 65
3 b f Helissio(FR) —Kyle Rhea (In The Wings)
1638[3] 2207[5] 3484[4] 4607[6] 6044[9]

Kimoe Warrior *M Mullineaux* a19
10 ch g Royal Abjar(USA) —Thewaari (USA) (Eskimo (USA))
471[6]

Kimono My House *J G Given* a81 71
4 ch m Dr Fong(USA) —Roselyn (Efisio)
2274[15] 2597[18] 3569[9] (3816) 4168[5] (4479) (4797) ◆ 5161[6] (5783) 6050[12] 6841[5] (7184) 7284[3] (Dead)

Kina Jazz *M E Rimmer* a44
2 b f Kyllachy—Tapas En Bal (FR) (Mille Balles (FR))
7104[13] 7501[7] 7638[5]

Kindallachan *G C Bravery* a64 45
5 b m Magic Ring(IRE) —Moore Stylish (Moorestyle)
3585[6] 4285[7] 4825[12] 6419[7] 6681[3] (7195) 7509[10] 7710[12]

Kind Heart *Sir Mark Prescott* a77
2 b f Red Ransom(USA) —Portorosa (USA) (Irish River (FR))
6933[2] 7207[2] (7445)

Kindkintyre (IRE) *R A Fahey* a51
4 b g Mull Of Kintyre(USA) —Sweet Nature (IRE) (Classic Secret (USA))
33[5] 236[9]

Kindlelight Blue (IRE) *N P Littmoden* a80 71
4 gr g Golan(IRE) —Kalimar (IRE) (Bigstone (IRE))
(28) 185[3] 591[4] 2784[9] 3947[11] 4162[17]

Kinfayre Boy *K W Hogg*
6 b g Grey Eagle—Amber Gambler (ITY) (Nijin (USA))
988[11]

King After *J R Best* a63 56
6 b g Bahamian Bounty—Child Star (FR) (Bellypha)
139[3] 275[3] 316[5] 356[5] 430[7] 453[6] 3037[8] 4946[7] 5145[9] 5407[8] 6228[10]

King And King (AUS) *D Koh* 102
8 b g Celestial Dancer(IRE) —Merriang Road (AUS) (Persian Heights)
2234a[12]

Kingaroo (IRE) *Garry Moss* a57 60
2 b g King Charlemagne(USA) —Lady Naomi (USA) (Distant View (USA))
3008[8] 3597[7] 3706[4] 5304[6] 5716[5] 5771[5] 6214[18] (7531)

King Bathwick (IRE) *B R Millman* a60 67
3 b g Golan(IRE) —Princess Sabaah (IRE) (Desert King (IRE))
1389[3] 1696[2] 2244[10] 2763[7] 3206[7]

King Canute (IRE) *E F Vaughan* a55 59
4 b g Danehill(USA) —Mona Stella (USA) (Nureyev (USA))
5020[2] 6374[12]

King Charles *E A L Dunlop* a88 105
4 b g King's Best(USA) —Charlecote (IRE) (Caerleon (USA))
384a[8] 673a[3] 1828[3] 2103[5] 3249[3] 3721[6] 5508[12] 6649[7]

King Columbo (IRE) *Miss J Feilden* a86 86
3 ch g King Charlemagne(USA) —Columbian Sand (IRE) (Salmon Leap (USA))
2714[2] ◆ 3745[10] 4128[6] 5209[10] 6542[11] 7111[3]

Kingdom Of Fife *Sir Michael Stoute* 90
3 b g Kingmambo(USA) —Fairy Godmother (Fairy King (USA))
2786[7] 3326[3] 3911[6] (4984) (5472) 6033[3] ◆ 6563[3]

Kingdom Of Heaven (IRE) *M J Gingell*
3 b f Heron Island(IRE) —Heavenly Hill (Nomadic Way (USA))
3762[5]

King Fingal (IRE) *J J Quinn* 85
3 b g King's Best(USA) —Llia (Shirley Heights)
1556[10] 2008[2] 2488[4] 3229[4] (3592) 4539[6] 6482[12] (6862)

King Hafhafah *I A Wood* a87 82
3 ch g King Charlemagne(USA) —Hafhafah (Shirley Heights)
905[5] 1213[8] 2953[6] 3458[4] 3907[5] 4731[5] (Dead)

King Harson *J D Bethell* a66 83
9 b g Greensmith—Safari Park (Absalom)
1138[4] 1450[6] 1891[7] 2400[8] 2846[8] 4605[8] 5045[4]

King Jock (USA) *R J Osborne* a82 112
7 bb g Ghazi(USA) —Glen Kate (Glenstal (USA))
205a[5] 383a[5] 495a[2] 743a[7] 1761a[7] (2656a) 2876a[6] 3357a[8] 5596a[7]

King Kenny *S Parr* a78 79
3 ch c Lomitas—Salanka (IRE) (Persian Heights)
1380[3] 1728[5] 2046[4] 2173[6] (3402) 4128[8] 4392[6] 4745[3] ◆ 4951[7] 5713[5] 6188[5] 6256[4] 6744a[4]

Kingly (IRE) *John Joseph Murphy* 36
3 b c King's Best(USA) —Fantazia (Zafonic (USA))
7310[11]

King Of Cadeaux (IRE) *M A Magnusson* a54 40
3 br g Cadeaux Genereux—Purple Haze (IRE) (Spectrum (IRE))
(1672) 2549[7] 3030[8] 3395[9] 5167[10] 5421[11] 7818[4]

King Of Charm (IRE) *M Hill* a53 42
5 ch g King Charlemagne(USA) —Pumpona (USA) (Sharpen Up)
119[8] 174[3] (297) 414[5] 522[5] 2097[8]

King Of Connacht *M Wellings* a61 64
5 b g Polish Precedent(USA) —Lady Melbourne (IRE) (Indian Ridge)
67[10] 999[12] 1280[4] 1528[4] (1776) 2957[12] 3113[4] 3347[10] 3914[3] 4261[3] 4568[3] 4785[9] 6364[4] 6930[2] 7354[7] 7518[2]

King Of Defence *M A Jarvis* 61
2 ch g Kyllachy—Duena (Grand Lodge (USA))
4982[8] 6714[8] 7051[11]

King Of Diamonds *Norma Twomey* a57 24
7 b g Mtoto—Capricious Lass (Corvaro (USA))
91[10] 207[7] 332[6] 1207[13] 4365[13]

King Of Dixie (USA) *W J Knight* a101 115
4 ch h Kingmambo(USA) —Dixie Accent (USA) (Dixieland Band (USA))
(175) ◆ (1211) ◆ 1982[3] ◆ (2580) 3498[2] 4506[8]

King Of Knight (IRE) *G Prodromou* a61 39
7 gr g Orpen(USA) —Peace Melody (IRE) (Classic Music (USA))
1031[5]

King Of Legend (IRE) *A G Foster* a63 63
4 b h King Charlemagne(USA) —Last Quarry (Handsome Sailor)
48[3] 216[4] (508) 703[3] 2597[8] 3201[12] 4949[5]

King Of Pentacles *H Morrison* 65
3 b c King's Best(USA) —Maid To Perfection (Sadler's Wells (USA))
1695[6] 1994[3] 2340[3] 4334[4] 5269[6]

King Of Rhythm (IRE) *D Carroll* a66 81
5 b g Imperial Ballet(IRE) —Sharadja (IRE) (Doyoun)
1383[5] 1963[2] 2165[2] 3006[13] 3257[2] 3711[6] 4244[3] 4650[2] 4895[9] 6186[7] 6598[12] 6813[9] 6989[8]

King Of Rome (IRE) *A P O'Brien* 112
3 b c Montjeu(IRE) —Amizette (USA) (Forty Niner (USA))
1509a[5] 1992[2] 2829[12] 3156[3] 3773a[6] (4356a) (5135a) 5732a[8] 5953a[5] 6324a[3]

King Of Sparta (USA) *T J Fitzgerald* a45 38
3 b c Van Nistelrooy(USA) —Selling Sunshine (USA) (Danzig (USA))
2269[8] 2929[9] 3419[5] 5378[7] 6753[P]

King Of Swords (IRE) *N Tinkler* a54 94
4 b g Desert Prince(IRE) —Okey Dorey (IRE) (Lake Coniston (IRE))
1796[6] ◆ 2212[2] 2489[10] 3009[12] 3336[14] 4385[10] 4743[11] 5719[3] (5970) 6011[6] 6388[7] 6486[5] 6840[5] 7081[4]

King Of Sydney (USA) *Mario Hofer* 107
2 b c Diesis—Padmore (USA) (French Deputy (USA))
6855a[2] 7294a[8]

King Of The Beers (USA) *R A Harris* a59 54
4 rg g Silver Deputy(CAN) —Pracer (USA) (Lyphard (USA))
778[12] 2100[4] 2482[6] 6022[13] 7169[7] 7469[2] 7535[5] 7691[6]

King Of The Moors (USA) *T D Barron* a65 81
5 b g King Of Kings(IRE) —Araza (USA) (Arazi (USA))
660[6] 852[6] 992[12] 1217[14] 1449[12] 1822[2] 1953[5] 2749[6] 2841[4] 3175[7] 3579[7] 4537[7] 4898[6] (4949) (5564) 5773[8] 6152[4] 6485[7]

Kingoftheswingers (IRE) *K J Burke* a55 54
4 b g Barathea(IRE) —Milly's Song (Millfontaine)
284[3] 305[2] 695[5] 1704[4]

King Of Wands *J L Dunlop* 74
2 b c Galileo(IRE) —Maid To Treasure (IRE) (Rainbow Quest (USA))
4826[8] 5842[4] ◆ 6199[3]

King Of Westphalia (USA) *A P O'Brien* a85 92
3 b c Kingmambo(USA) —Quarter Moon (IRE) (Sadler's Wells (USA))
4356a[4] 5135a[5] 5944a[6] 6261a[10]

King Olav (UAE) *M A Jarvis* a82 85
3 ch g Halling(USA) —Karamzin (USA) (Nureyev (USA))
2763[3] ◆ (5047) 5858[3] 6582[P]

King Orchisios (IRE) *K A Ryan* a93 103
5 ch g Tagula(IRE) —Wildflower (Namaqualand (USA))
677[11] 907[9] 1071[3] 1442[4] 1917[P] (Dead)

King O'The Gypsies (IRE) *R Charlton* 96
3 b c Sadler's Wells(USA) —Love For Ever (IRE) (Darshaan)
1398[4] ◆ 3854[3] ◆ 4372[2] (5117) 6563[5]

King Quantas (IRE) *B Bo* 90
10 b h Danehill(USA) —Palacegate Episode (IRE) (Drumalis)
5957a[8]

King's Account (USA) *S Gollings* a54 57
6 ch g King Of Kings(IRE) —Fighting Countess (USA) (Ringside (USA))
1898[14] 3113[8]

Kings Ace (IRE) *A P Jarvis* 58
2 b g King's Best(USA) —Full Cream (USA) (Hennessy (USA))
4446[5] 4665[4] 5461[9] 6247[10] 6579[6]

King's Alchemist *M D I Usher* 62
3 b g Slickly(FR) —Pure Gold (Dilum (USA))
1379[6] ◆ 1695[7] 2161[14] 2603[4] 3206[14] 3671[11] 4112[8] 4428[6]

King's Apostle (IRE) *W J Haggas* a89 116
4 b h King's Best(USA) —Politesse (USA) (Barathea (IRE))
1809[5] 3248[3] ◆ 4405[15] 4624[2] 5275[7] (6304)

King's Bastion (IRE) *M L W Bell* a66 90
4 b g Royal Applause—Aunty Mary (Common Grounds)
1327[2] 2163[5] (2203) 2818[2] 3197[18] 4407[7] 5096[3] 5446[6] 5897[9] 6783[12]

King's Caprice *J A Geake* a98 92
7 ch g Pursuit Of Love—Palace Street (USA) (Secreto (USA))
2163[4] 3905[5] 4375[3] 5096[9] 5930[3] 7101[8] 7470[12]

King's Charm (FR) *J Noseda* 80
3 b c King's Best(USA) —On Fair Stage (IRE) (Sadler's Wells (USA))
1417[4] ◆ 2119[P] (Dead)

King's Chorister *Miss Gay Kelleway* a61 60
2 ch g King's Best(USA) —Chorist (Pivotal)
5996[6] 6359[9] 7773[6] 7781[2]

Kings College Boy *R A Fahey* a56 74
8 b g College Chapel—The Kings Daughter (Indian King (USA))
840[10] 1015[14] 1309[6] 1624[15] 2145[8] 2448[5] 2748[7] 2892[5] (3080) (3340) 3401[2] 3581[3] 4047[4] 4114[4] 4743[3] 5201[3] 5260[7] 6131[12] 6382[2] 6840[12] 7043[13] 7176[7]

King's Colour *B R Johnson* a74 60
3 b g King's Best(USA) —Red Garland (Selkirk (USA))
4302[9] 6345[6] 6705[7] 7358[4] 7536[2] (7790)

Kings Confession (IRE) *D Carroll* a57 35
5 b g Danetime(IRE) —Night Rhapsody (IRE) (Mujtahid (USA))
104[4]

King's Counsel (IRE) *B Smart* 49
2 ch g Refuse To Bend(IRE) —Nesaah's Princess (Sinndar (IRE))
3277[6] 4150[11] 5304[4] 6214[15]

Kingsdalemillenium (IRE) *W M Roper* 60
3 b f Hawk Wing(USA) —Jinsiyah (USA) (Housebuster (USA))
4715a[15]

Kingsdale Ocean (IRE) *D K Weld* a97 96
5 b g Blue Ocean(USA) —Madmosel John (IRE) (Martin John)
1103a[5] 3532a[5] 4004a[4]

Kingsdale Orion (IRE) *B Ellison* 99
4 bb g Intikhab(USA) —Jinsiyah (USA) (Housebuster (USA))
1469[6] 1828[12] 2789[7] (3413) 3972[4] 5005[3] 5382[10] 5772[6] 7083[5] 7127[2] 7239[9]

Kings Destiny *M A Jarvis* a84 82
2 b g Dubai Destination(USA) —Jalousie (IRE) (Barathea (IRE))
6581[2] 6978[4] 7336[2] (7552)

King's Envoy (USA) *Mrs J C McGregor* a11 37
9 b g Royal Academy(USA) —Island Of Silver (USA) (Forty Niner (USA))
2252[6]

King's Event (USA) *Sir Michael Stoute* a92 93
4 b h Dynaformer(USA) —Magic Of Love (Magic Ring (IRE))
4363[3] 4856[10] 5569[2] 6698[6]

King's Fable (USA) *Karen George* a68 65
5 b g Lear Fan(USA) —Fairy Fable (IRE) (Fairy King (USA))
31[3] 387[3] (664) 716[6] 881[4] (1044) 1408[9] 1583[3] 2012[3] 2804[3] 3523[7] 4391[8]

Kingsgate Castle *J R Best* a71 58
3 b c Kyllachy—Ella Lamees (Statoblest)
60[3] (271) 457[5] 6435[7] 6706[9] 6880[3]

Kingsgate Native (IRE) *J R Best* 123
3 b c Mujadil(USA) —Native Force (IRE) (Indian Ridge)
3101[10] (3247) 3922[5] 5245[3]

Kingsgate Storm (IRE) *J R Best* a62 80
2 gr c Mujadil(USA) —In The Highlands (Petong)
2709[11] 3105[8] ◆ 7638[4] 7820[8]

King's Head (IRE) *G L Moore* a97 98
5 b g King's Best(USA) —Ustka (Lomond (USA))
315[11] 2830[4] 7404[P] 7595[3] 7717[4]

Kingshill Prince *W J Musson* 63
2 b g Mark Of Esteem(IRE) —Trefoil (FR) (Blakeney)
6535[5] 7240[4]

Kingship (USA) *Charles Dickey* 103
5 b h King Cugat(USA) —Artistry (USA) (Theatrical)
6504a[11]

Kingship Spirit (IRE) *J Noseda* 94
2 b g Invincible Spirit(IRE) —Jupiter Inlet (IRE) (Jupiter Island)
2411[3] 2999[2] 5271[3] 6010[2] (6426) 6979[8]

Kingsholm *N Wilson* a82 67
6 ch g Selkirk(USA) —Putuna (Generous (IRE))
697[6] 992[14] 2007[9] 2391[4] 2510[7] 3175[8] 3732[4] 3822[8] 5871[6] (6189) (6255) 6364[6] 6985[5] 7309[3] 7500[3] (7731) 7796[3]

Kings House *M W Easterby* a47 47
2 b c Mujahid(USA) —High Petergate (IRE) (Mujadil (USA))
1183[3] 1390[5] 2004[5] 2581[5] 2965[4] 3788[6]

King's Icon (IRE) *M Wigham* a74 78
3 b g King's Best(USA) —Pink Sovietstaia (FR) (Soviet Star (USA))
1336[5] 1688[3] 2302[11] 2976[10] 5595[8] 6188[4] 6629[12] 6825[10] 7115[5] 7261[10] 7613[6]

King's Jester (IRE) *J J Lambe* a25 71
6 b g King's Best(USA) —Scent Of Success (USA) (Quiet American (USA))
7401[11]

King's Kazeem *B W Hills* 73
3 b f King's Best(USA) —Kazeem (Darshaan)
2123[7]

King's La Mont (IRE) *Mrs A J Perrett* a68 74
2 b c King's Best(USA) —La Leuze (IRE) (Caerleon (USA))
4570[9] 5184[4] 6731[6]

Kings Maiden (IRE) *James Moffatt* 43
5 b m King's Theatre(IRE) —Maidenhair (IRE) (Darshaan)
4701[4] 5042[12] 5453[3]

Kingsmaite *S R Bowring* a68 58
7 b g Komaite(USA) —Antonias Melody (Rambo Dancer (CAN))
42[7] 189[2] 236[2] 256[5] 365[4] 1588[2] (1675) 1966[3] (2081) (2263) 2950[4] 3567[7] 7286[5] 7442[4] 7619[3] 7772[2]

King's Majesty (IRE) *A M Hales* a72 79
6 b g King's Best(USA) —Tiavanita (USA) (J O Tobin (USA))
6134[8] 6659[5] 7758[10]

Kings On The Roof *P Leech* a30
2 b c King Charlemagne(USA) —Stylish Clare (IRE) (Desert Style (IRE))
7638[8] 7810[6]

Kings Point (IRE) *D Nicholls* a89 99
7 b h Fasliyev(USA) —Rahika Rose (Unfuwain (USA))
2905[4] (3548) 3855[6] 4509[8] 5207[7] 5446[3] (5717) 6105[2] 6277[5]

Kings Quay *J J Quinn* a95 88
6 b h Montjeu(IRE) —Glen Rosie (IRE) (Mujtahid (USA))
757[5] 962[14] (5005) 5858[6] 6120[17] 6667[10]

King's Ransom *S Gollings* a82 73
5 b g Daylami(IRE) —Luana (Shaadi (USA))
192[2] 601[3] (646) (730) 789[7] (1112) 1256[3] 2262[3] 7299[9] 7457[9] 7633[4] 7650[8]

King's Road *John Joseph Murphy* 71
3 ch c King's Best(USA) —Saphire (College Chapel)
(4715a)

King's Sabre *W R Muir* a43 80
2 ch g King's Best(USA) —Lightsabre (Polar Falcon (USA))
5615[8] 6117[2] 6474[21]

King's Siren (IRE) *A M Balding* a72 64
2 b f King's Best(USA) —Blue Siren (Bluebird (USA))
6358[4] ◆ 6601[4] (7095)

King's Song (IRE) *Sir Michael Stoute* 66
2 ch c Indian Ridge—Alleluia (Caerleon (USA))
6715[5] 6977[8]

King's Starlet *H Morrison* 76
2 b f King's Best(USA) —Brightest Star (Unfuwain (USA))
5241[6] ◆ 6473[13]

Kings Story (IRE) *Mrs S Leech* a60 68
4 b g Royal Applause—Poppy Carew (IRE) (Danehill (USA))
1151[7]

Kings Topic (USA) *A B Haynes* a77 53
8 ch g Kingmambo(USA) —Topicount (USA) (Private Account (USA))
1039[3] 1152[2] 1210[2] 1505[2] 1673[2] 1853[8] 3265[5] 4267[2] 5087[5] (5145) (5407) 6629[11] 7642[7] 7686[5]

Kings Troop *H R A Cecil* 84
2 ch c Bertolini(USA) —Glorious Colours (Spectrum (IRE))
2086[5] 2951[6] (3888) ◆ 4828[2] 6082[14] 6946[16]

Kingstyle (IRE) *M Brittain* 52
3 b g King Charlemagne(USA) —Stylish Clare (IRE) (Desert Style (IRE))
1187[3] 2282[6]

King Supreme (IRE) *R Hannon* a82 86
3 b c King's Best(USA) —Oregon Trail (USA) (Gone West (USA))
1163[6] 1364[2] 1681[3] 2045[3] 2340[2] 3022[2] 4254[2] (4771) 5699[5] 6196[2] 6479[6] 6866[4] 7314[10] 7711[7]

Kingswinford (IRE) *P D Evans* a47 85
2 b g Noverre(USA) —Berenica (IRE) (College Chapel)
1263[3] 1474[4] 2042[4] 2392[2] ◆ 2473[4] 2987[4] 3105[15] 3670[4] 4389[5] 4659[6] 4905[2] (5228) 6533[4] (6603) 6972[9] 7241[2]

King's Wonder *W R Muir* a93 88
3 ch g King's Best(USA) —Signs And Wonders (Danehill (USA))
1490[3] 1806[7] 4252[6] 4553[10] 4976[4] 5052[3] 5140[2] 5713[2] (6020) 6200[2] 6576[11]

Kingvati (FR) *S Wattel* a84 93
6 b g Alamo Bay(USA) —Vatipan (FR) (Trepan (FR))
5115a[6]

Kinigi (IRE) *R A Harris* a57 54
2 gr f Verglas(IRE) —Kamalame (USA) (Souvenir Copy (USA))
5777[5] 6488[4] 6858[5] (7266) (7443) 7531[5] 7694[5]

Kinlochard *Eve Johnson Houghton* 49
3 b f Efisio—Rainbow D'Beaute (Rainbow Quest (USA))
5057[5] 5666[6] 6768[9]

Kinnego Bay (IRE) *B W Hills* a69 76
3 ch g Hennessy(USA) —New Music (USA) (Prospector's Music (USA))
1875[7] 3275[6] 4269[7] (4777) 5713[8] 6554[2] 6749[5]

Kinout (IRE) *K A Ryan* a78 74
3 b g Invincible Spirit(IRE) —Kinn (FR) (Suave Dancer (USA))
977[2] (1066) 1484[7] 1852[3] 2529[6] 3136[6] 3581[4] 3833[3] 4074[4] 5592[6] 6150[5] 6658[11] 7359[11]

Kinrande (IRE) *P J Makin* a71 88
6 b g Sri Pekan(USA) —Pipers Pool (IRE) (Mtoto)
4276[9] ◆

Kinsman (IRE) *T D McCarthy* a52 34
11 b g Distant Relative—Besito (Wassl)
99[5] 164[3] 328[11] 711[3] 1142[7] 7678[9]

Kinsya *M H Tompkins* a98 103
5 ch g Mister Baileys—Kimono (IRE) (Machiavellian (USA))
3885[5] 4504[9] 4845[6] 5360[10] 5903[3] 6233[3] 6667[4] 6984[6] 7146[5] 7291[8]

Kintyres Promise (IRE) *Mrs N Macauley*
4 gr m Mull Of Kintyre(USA) —Ivory's Promise (Pursuit Of Love)
1709[8]

Kiowa Princess *M Dods* 38
3 ch f Compton Place—Sunley Stars (Sallust)
1560[13] 2463[19]

Kipchak (IRE) *C E Brittain* a63
3 bb g Soviet Star(USA) —Khawafi (Kris)
7395[7] 7463[2] 7662[3]

Kip Deville (USA) *Richard Dutrow Jr* a107 122
5 rg h Kipling(USA) —Klondike Kaytie (USA) (Encino (USA))
6996a[2] 7684a[3]

Kiribati King (IRE) *M R Channon* a62 84
3 b g Kalanisi(IRE) —Everlasting (Desert King (IRE))
1140[2] ◆ (1397) 1962[4] 2310[7] 2985[3] 3471[2] 3962[3] 4426[4] (4859) (5651) (6054) 6390[3]

Kirkby's Treasure *A Berry* a50 70
10 gr g Mind Games—Gem Of Gold (Jellaby)
990[11] 1449[11] 2251[8] 2658[8] 4683[13] 4949[3] 5538[12] 6116[7] 6408[8] 7132[9]

Kirkhammerton (IRE) *J T Stimpson* a62 48
6 ch g Grand Lodge(USA) —Nawara (Welsh Pageant)
231[5] 788[5]

Kirkie (USA) *S Parr* a68 27
3 bb g Gulch(USA) —Saleela (USA) (Nureyev (USA))
158[4] 261[2] 867[5] 3117[11] 3339[9] 4972[7] 5154[13] 7226[2] 7345[5] 7367[8] 7403[9] 7725[6]

Kirkinola *C Laffon-Parias* 98
3 b f Selkirk(USA) —Spinola (FR) (Spinning World (USA))
7431a[5] 7635a[6]

Kirklees (IRE) *Saeed Bin Suroor* 119
4 b h Jade Robbery(USA) —Moyesii (USA) (Diesis)
6780[3] 7145[2]

Kirk Michael *H Candy* a94 82
4 b g Selkirk(USA) —Pervenche (Latest Model)
6911[8]

Kirkson *P W Chapple-Hyam*
2 ch g Selkirk(USA) —Viva Maria (Hernando (FR))
7106[14]

Kirstys Lad *M Mullineaux* a65 53
6 b g Lake Coniston(IRE) —Killick (Slip Anchor)
4679[12] 5008[8] 5198[9] 5478[6] 5871[5] 6189[8] (6955) 7226[3] 7345[5] 7367[2] 7442[10] 7656[10]

Kiss A Prince *D K Ivory* 1
2 b g Fraam—Prancing (Prince Sabo)
6863[14]

Kiss Chase (IRE) *J S Goldie* a20 65
4 br g Val Royal(FR) —Zurarah (Siberian Express (USA))
6786[14] 7287[11]

Kissi Kissi *Garry Moss* a41 43
5 b m Paris House—Miss Whittingham (IRE) (Fayruz)
50[9] 87[6] 254[12] 469[6] 7286[11]

Kissing The Camera *J Noseda* 88
2 b f Galileo(IRE) —Hoh Dear (IRE) (Sri Pekan (USA))
(2368) ◆ 4403[8] 4868[5] 6473[10]

Kiss Me Hardy *J D Bethell* 10
3 b f Storming Home—Hunters Of Brora (IRE) (Sharpo)
4651[10] 6393[16] 6725[8]

Kiss N Run *Andrew Oliver* 68
3 b c Averti(IRE) —Honeytrap (FR) (Primo Dominie)
3286a[4]

Kiss The Kid (USA) *Amy Tarrant* a108 108
5 bb h Lemon Drop Kid(USA) —Black Tie Kiss (USA) (Danzig (USA))
5928a[9]

Kitaj *J-C Rouget* 97
3 br c Sakhee(USA) —Jumairah Sunset (Be My Guest (USA))
4719a[8]

Kitchen Sink (IRE) *Jean-Rene Auvray* a65 62
6 ch g Bold Fact(USA) —Voodoo Rocket (Lycius (USA))
153[9]

Kite Wood (IRE) *M A Jarvis* 108
2 b c Galileo(IRE) —Kite Mark (Mark Of Esteem (IRE))
4890[2] ◆ (5857) (6648)

Kitto Katsu *D J Coakley* a58 48
4 b m Ishiguru(USA) —Zacinta (USA) (Hawkster (USA))
694[5] 878[2] 1344[6] 2010[13] 2806[9]

Kitty Allen *M Botti* a55 45
2 br f One Cool Cat(USA) —Aly McBe (USA) (Alydeed (CAN))
2709[4] 3114[7] 3584[2] 4270[5] 7451[7]

Kitty Hawk Miss (IRE) *J S Bolger* a54 95
3 b f Galileo(IRE) —Sandrella (IRE) (Darshaan)
7235a[10]

Kitty Matcham (IRE) *A P O'Brien* 105
3 b f Rock Of Gibraltar(IRE) —Imagine (IRE) (Sadler's Wells (USA))
1830[9] ◆ 2433a[10] 2877a[12] 3153[8] 5134a[4]

Kiwi Bay *M Dods* a88 89
3 b g Mujahid(USA) —Bay Of Plenty (FR) (Octagonal (NZ))
1381[9] 1988[5] 2481[3] (2911) 3928[13] 4539[4] 4893[4] 5104[8] 6710[3] 6976[5] 7239[5]

Kiwi Moon *B Smart* 70
2 b c Nayef(USA) —Mauri Moon (Green Desert (USA))
6292[8] 6714[5] (7221)

Kiwi Princess *M Brittain* a46 55
3 b f Vettori(IRE) —The Kings Daughter (Indian King (USA))
527[6] 2490[12] 3549[6] 6707[10]

Kiyari *M Botti* a64 36
2 b f Key Of Luck(USA) —Ashford Castle (USA) (Bates Motel (USA))
5650[8] 6622[9] 6901[6] 7666[3]

Kladester (USA) *B Smart* a63 47
2 ch g Van Nistelrooy(USA) —Longing To Dance (USA) (Nureyev (USA))
3107[8] 4415[11] 6008[7] (7269) ◆ 7467[5] 7693[10]

Klarity *J Pearce* a46 69
3 b f Acclamation—Clarice Orsini (Common Grounds)
1475[10] 2660[3] 2991[13] 3395[12] (3733) 4073[5] 4808[5] 6173[10] 6680[7]

Klassy (IRE) *Bryan F Murphy* 72
6 br g Kahyasi—Edelora (IRE) (Doyoun)
4003a[16]

Klynch *B J Meehan* a92 80
2 b g Kyllachy—Inchcoonan (Emperor Jones (USA))
1439[6] 1523[4] 2338[2] (2709) 3152[7] 3663[6] 3941[4] 4594[5] (4729) 5244[14] 5693[8] 6118[11] 6281[4] 6533[8]

Knavesmire (IRE) *M Brittain* 90
2 b f One Cool Cat(USA) —Caribbean Escape (Pivotal)
957[3] ◆ 1220[3] (1749) 2167[6] (2497)

Kneesy Earsy Nosey *Miss A Stokell* a52 52
2 ch f Compton Place—Evie Hone (IRE) (Royal Academy (USA))
1480[6] (2216) 2671[5] 3008[9] 3706[5] 5006[8] 5715[8] 6059[9] 7319[6] 7445[5] 7694[2] 7789[6]

Knickyknackienoo *T T Clement* a31 39
7 b g Bin Ajwaad(IRE) —Ring Fence (Polar Falcon (USA))
1931[11] 2557[5] 2930[9]

Knight Valliant *J Howard Johnson* 54
5 bl g Dansili—Aristocratique (Cadeaux Genereux)
2752[9]

Knock Three Times (IRE) *M L W Bell* a34 21
2 b f Hernando(FR) —Tawoos (FR) (Rainbow Quest (USA))
7054[13] 7259[11] 7353[11]

Knot In Wood (IRE) *R A Fahey* a114 110
6 b g Shinko Forest(IRE) —Notley Park (Wolfhound (USA))
959[9] 1198a[2] 1517[10] 1809[7] ◆ 2401[5] 3248[4] 3722[4] (4145) 4624[6] 5109[14] 5891[13] 6104[4] (6153) (6468)

Know No Fear *J J Quinn* a70 80
3 b g Primo Valentino(IRE) —Alustar (Emarati (USA))
2171[9] 2570[5] ◆ (4074) 4397[4] 5796[17]

Know The Law *D R C Elsworth* a85 79
4 b g Danehill Dancer(IRE) —Mackenzie's Friend (Selkirk (USA))
2372[8] 2895[5] 3802[5] 4131[3] 4791[4] 5910[5] 6129[4]

Kocab *A Fabre* a110 114
6 b h Unfuwain(USA) —Space Quest (Rainbow Quest (USA))
1092a[11] 4320a[2] 7643a[7]

Kochanski (IRE) *M Johnston* 31
2 ch f King's Best(USA) —Ascot Cyclone (USA) (Rahy (USA))
4897[6]

Koenigsberg (USA) *N Clement* 94
3 b c Danzig(USA) —Mariensky (USA) (Gulch (USA))
6664a[9] 7551a[0]

Kofi *Karen George* a47
6 br g Emperor Fountain—La Vie En Primrose (Henbit (USA))
552[3] 661[5] 776[P] 1405[5] 2643[12]

Kokawango (FR) *M Roussel* 96
2 b c Okawango(USA) —Matakana (FR) (Green Tune (USA))
7103a[7]

Kokkokila *Lady Herries* a61 72
4 b m Robellino(USA) —Meant To Be (Morston (FR))
1564[8] 1929[2] (3084) 3917[3] 5027[4] 5613[3] (6606) 7293[6]

Kokkola (IRE) *V Valiani* 91
3 b f Daylami(IRE) —Sidelined (IRE) (In The Wings)
2439a[7]

Komreyev Star *R E Peacock* a60 52
6 b g Komaite(USA) —L'Ancressaan (Dalsaan)
(193) 287[7] (601) 2870[7] 2904[7] 3431[9] 4001[5] 5712[7] 6353[12]

Kong Moon (FR) *H-A Pantall* 85
3 b f Hernando(FR) —Russian Rose (IRE) (Soviet Lad (USA))
3018a[7]

Konig Concorde (GER) *C Sprengel* 106
3 b c Big Shuffle(USA) —Kaiserin (GER) (Ile De Bourbon (USA))
1376a[5] 2066a[2] 3515a[4] 4916a[2] 6322a[7]

Konig Turf (GER) *C Sprengel* 113
6 b h Big Shuffle(USA) —Kaiserin (GER) (Ile De Bourbon (USA))
(1108a)

Konka (USA) *E F Vaughan* 12
2 ch f Johannesburg(USA) —Defining Style (USA) (Out Of Place (USA))
2150[12] 4870[17] 6010[12]

Kool Katie *Mrs G S Rees* a61 55
3 b f Millkom—Katie Komaite (Komaite (USA))
74[4] 487[4] 2002[9] 2333[9] 2805[5] 3081[8] 4207[8] 4684[10] 6409[9]

Koraleva Tectona (IRE) *Pat Eddery* a61 79
3 b f Fasliyev(USA) —Miss Teak (USA) (Woodman (USA))
997[3] 1622[3] 2118[3] 2429[7] (3298) 3678[7] 4745[6] (5589)

Korty *W J Musson* a51 34
4 b g Averti(IRE) —Promissory (Caerleon (USA))
123[10] 468[11] 795[6] 1207[12]

Kosama *M R Channon* 40
2 b f Xaar—Petomi (Presidium)
2916[15] 3091[10] 3652[4] 4063[4] 4290[5]

Kosciusko *J D Frost* 30
7 b m Sea Raven(IRE) —Impetuous Lady (USA) (Imp Society (USA))
2988[8] 4366[10]

Kossack *L M Cumani* 98
3 b c Sadler's Wells(USA) —Kithanga (IRE) (Darshaan)
2370[4] ◆ 2763[5] ◆ 4124[2] ◆ (4689) 6061[3] 6563[9]

Kostar *C G Cox* a96 109
7 ch g Komaite(USA) —Black And Amber (Weldnaas (USA))
677[7] 1420[15] 2172[14]

Kotsi (IRE) *E F Vaughan* 104
3 b f Nayef(USA) —Ingozi (Warning)
2149[2] 2975[8] 6034[10] 6266[15]

Kouloura (IRE) *M Botti* a68 69
2 ch f Redback—Negria (IRE) (Al Hareb (USA))
5227[2] 6016[4] 7095[4]

Krakatau (FR) *D J Wintle* a62 35
4 b g Noverre(USA) —Tomanivi (Caerleon (USA))
80[2] 209[8] 352[10] 560[3] 861[12] 1032[5] 1282[8] 1562[8]

Krasavitsa *J L Dunlop* 5
3 b f Fasliyev(USA) —Desert Alchemy (IRE) (Green Desert (USA))
1445[10] 1957[15]

Krasivi's Boy (USA) *G L Moore* a53 48
6 bb g Swain(IRE) —Krasivi (USA) (Nijinsky (CAN))
606[10]

Krataios (FR) *C Laffon-Parias* 109
8 b g Sabrehill(USA) —Loxandra (Last Tycoon)
1761a[4]

Kris Kin Line (IRE) *Sir Michael Stoute* 63
2 ch c Kris Kin(USA) —Shell Garland (USA) (Sadler's Wells (USA))
6893[5]

Krismick (IRE) *G A Ham* a20
4 b m Orpen(USA) —Untold (Final Straw)
273[5]

Krisnando *G L Moore* a53 62
3 b f Hernando(FR) —Kris Mundi (Kris)
1696[7] 2342[4] 2695[7] 2997[9] (Dead)

Kristal Glory (IRE) *J L Dunlop* a41 57
3 ch c Night Shift(USA) —Kristal's Paradise (IRE) (Bluebird (USA))
1479[12] 2833[12]

Kristiansand *P Monteith* 59
8 b g Halling(USA) —Zonda (Fabulous Dancer (USA))
2157[RR] 2849[6] 5967[RR] (Dead)

Kristopher James (IRE) *W M Brisbourne* a56 62
2 ch g Spartacus(IRE) —Ela Alethia (Kris)
4658[4] 6451[6] 6986[8] 7269[2] 7519[8]

Kritzia *H R A Cecil* a73 59
3 gr f Daylami(IRE) —Katrina (IRE) (Ela-Mana-Mou)
3611[6] 4057[2] 4871[7] 5163[4] (5833) 6060[7] 6934[11]

Krugerrand (USA) *W J Musson* a80 81
9 ch g Gulch(USA) —Nasers Pride (USA) (Al Nasr (FR))
747[7] 962[8] 1682[5] 2540[6] 2895[6] (4829) 5105[8] 5783[4] 6108[6] 7009[3]

Kryptonite (IRE) *J W Hills* a68 61
3 b c Kris Kin(USA) —Brockton Saga (IRE) (Perugino (USA))
116[3] 325[5] (784) 1530[11] 1962[12] 2894[2] 3335[4] 3824[4]

Kuanyao (IRE) *P J Makin* a40 47
2 b g American Post—Nullarbor (Green Desert (USA))
6702[6] 7098[9]

Kudu Country (IRE) *T P Tate* 77
2 gr g Captain Rio—Nirvavita (FR) (Highest Honor (FR))
3107[3] 4415[4] (6187) 6946[12]

Kunte Kinteh *D Nicholls* a69 69
4 b g Indian Lodge(IRE) —Summer Siren (FR) (Saint Cyrien (FR))
1450[12] 2005[14] 2550[2] 2782[8] 3211[7] 3599[11] 4327[9]

Kuriyama (IRE) *M H Tompkins* 61
3 ch g Raise A Grand(IRE) —Gobolino (Don)
961[12] 1403[9] 2273[7] 2868[6] 4564[8] 6111[5] 6541[10]

Kurtiniadis (IRE) *S Kulak* 112
5 b h Mujahid(USA) —Fiddler's Moll (IRE) (Dr Devious (IRE))
5742a[4]

Kutanga (USA) *R M H Cowell* a48
2 bb f Deputy Commander(USA) —Greyciousness (USA) (Miswaki (USA))
5431[10] 6089[7] 6432[12]

Kuwinda *M R Channon* a18
2 b f Hunting Lion(IRE) —Gayane (Nureyev (USA))
1341[5] 2450[6]

Kwitara (GER) *P Monteith*
4 b m Acatenango(GER) —Kirona (Robellino (USA))
2579[7] 2844[P]

Kyber *J S Goldie* a28 66
7 ch g First Trump—Mahbob Dancer (FR) (Groom Dancer (USA))
988[8] 2579[4] (2844) 3198[5] (3545) 3756[12] 4238[2] 4556[5] (4947) 5540[3] 5967[4] 6313[6] 6790[10] 7293[10]

Kylayne *P W D'Arcy* a99 98
3 b f Kyllachy—Penmayne (Inchinor)
1401[2] 1993[3] 3420[3] 4059[8] 5829[6] 6271[16] 6718[4] 7099[3] 7328a[2] 7492[12]

Kyle (IRE) *C R Dore* a88 87
4 ch g Kyllachy—Staylily (IRE) (Grand Lodge (USA))
969[4] 1174[7] 1683[7] 2339[7] (2679) 2923[6] (4765) 5936[12]

Kyleene *J Noseda* a65 55
2 b f Kyllachy—Mrs Nash (Night Shift (USA))
6084[11] 6696[5]

Kyle Of Bute *J L Dunlop* a47 59
2 ch c Kyllachy—Blinding Mission (IRE) (Marju (IRE))
2972[13] 3682[7] 4296[8] 5671[9] 6223[9] 6924[5]

Kyles Prince (IRE) *V Smith* a86 75
6 b g In The Wings—Comprehension (USA) (Diesis)
3482[7]

Kylkenny *H Morrison* a81 60
13 b g Kylian(USA) —Fashion Flow (Balidar)
260[8] 638[4] 847[2] 1020[4] 1131[4] 1589[5] 2617[7] 3551[10] 4267[6] 6577[12] (7272)

Kyllachy Star *R A Fahey* 80
2 b c Kyllachy—Jaljuli (Jalmood (USA))
3078[2] 3411[3] 4394[6] 4626[8] 5200[2] (6037) 6426[9]

Kyllachy Storm *R J Hodges* a52 69
4 b g Kyllachy—Social Storm (USA) (Future Storm (USA))
1642[2] 1865[2] 2478[2] 2798[3] 2991[5] 3316[8] 4154[7] 5121[4] (5315) 6334[2] (6895) 7118[7]

Kyllis *B Smart* a65 64
3 b f Kyllachy—Princess Latifa (Wolfhound (USA))
1132[4] 1558[3] 1952[13] 3081[7] 3831[6] 4684[6]

Kyllorien *B W Hills* 33
2 b f Kyllachy—Lorien Hill (IRE) (Danehill (USA))
1385[6]

Kyniska (IRE) *Tracey Collins* 107
3 b f Choisir(AUS) —Lunadine (FR) (Bering)
5130a[3] 5922a[8]

Kyrie Eleison (IRE) *R Hannon* a68 73
3 b g Kalanisi(IRE) —Peratus (IRE) (Mujadil (USA))
(773) 1530[2] 1805[3] 2244[3] 3095[4] (3384)

Kyzer Chief *R E Barr* 66
3 b g Rouvres(FR) —Payvashooz (Ballacashtal (CAN))
1141[5] 1560[2] 2396[2] 2850[2] 3283[2] 3600[6] 4216[3]

Laa Baas (IRE) *M A Jarvis* a34 57
3 b f Green Desert(USA) —Baaderah (IRE) (Cadeaux Genereux)
2038[6] 2981[6] 3332[10]

La Adelita (IRE) *M L W Bell* 92
3 b f Anabaa(USA) —Aiming (Highest Honor (FR))
5097[5] (5650) 6002[2] 7144[7]

Laahig *G A Butler* a83 89
2 ch c Medicean—Aunt Tate (Tate Gallery (USA))
(3365) 4374[2] 5143[3] 6176[3] 6860[3]

Laa Rayb (USA) *M Johnston* a87 117
4 b g Storm Cat(USA) —Society Lady (USA) (Mr Prospector (USA))
1828[6] 1982[U] (2218) 2600[6] 3197[5] (4405) 5025[2] (5555a) 5893[7] 6322a[2] 6814[3] 7684a[13]

La Bamba (GER) *A Wohler* 77
4 b m Samum(GER) —Loja (GER) (Spectrum (IRE))
2879a[8]

La Belle Joannie *S Curran* a53 49
3 b f Lujain(USA) —Sea Clover (IRE) (Ela-Mana-Mou)
523[6]

La Big (GER) *Mario Hofer*
2 b f Big Shuffle(USA) —La Blue (GER) (Bluebird (USA))
7549a[4]

Labisa (IRE) *H Morrison* a62 53
2 b f High Chaparral(IRE) —Damiana (IRE) (Thatching)
5241[16] 6945[12] 7117[2]

La Blue Hill *J De Roualle* 76
4 b m Tiger Hill(IRE) —La Blue (GER) (Bluebird (USA))
6323a[13]

La Boum (GER) *Robert Collet* a92 106
5 br m Monsun(GER) —La Bouche (GER) (In The Wings)
1713a[9] 2553a[2] 4320a[8] 6495a[6] 7037a[6] (7348a)

La Brigitte *A J McCabe* a75 84
2 ch f Tobougg(IRE) —Bardot (Efisio)
1778[3] 1961[7] (2702) 3663[4] (4175) 4434[7] (4874) 5855[4] 6068[4] 6102[9] 6533[6]

Lac A Dancer (IRE) *G M Lyons* a64 87
2 b f Danehill Dancer(IRE) —Lac Dessert (USA) (Lac Ouimet (USA))
4095a[4] 4353a[4]

La Capriosa *A J McCabe* a61 46
2 ch f Kyllachy—La Caprice (USA) (Housebuster (USA))
6351[9] 6764[6] 6932[4] 7168[3] 7303[3] 7454[11] 7719[2] 7795[2]

Lachafinna (IRE) *D Carroll* 50
3 b f Invincible Spirit(IRE) —Hasbaat (Sabrehill (USA))
5361[4] 5636[8] 6015[13]

La Chicaluna *J G Given* a74 83
3 ch f Cadeaux Genereux—Crescent Moon (Mr Prospector (USA))
2333[11] 2674[2] 3141[6] 3907[2] 4300[9] 5052[5] 5714[9] 6137[9] 6356[11]

La Columbina *R Hannon* a70 80
3 ch f Carnival Dancer—Darshay (FR) (Darshaan)
2151[6] 2920[4] 3351[6] 4130[7] 4669[6] (5086) (5230)

La Cortezana *P G Murphy* a36
4 ch m Piccolo—Blushing Belle (Local Suitor (USA))
1119[5]

La Coveta (IRE) *B J Meehan* 84
3 b f Marju(IRE) —Colourful Cast (IRE) (Nashwan (USA))
3272[6] (3636) 4022[7] 4189[4] 4433[4]

Lacy Sunday (USA) *A Trybuhl* 81
2 b f King's Best(USA) —Lungta (USA) (Storm Cat (USA))
5686a[5]

La Dawa *A Wohler*
2 b f Dansili—La Salina (GER) (Singspiel (IRE))
7006a[7]

Laddies Poker Two (IRE) *J Noseda* a85 107
3 gr f Choisir(AUS) —Break Of Day (USA) (Favorite Trick (USA))
(244) ◆ 5071[3] ◆ (6239) ◆ 6782[6]

La De Two (IRE) *B W Hills* 86
2 ch c Galileo(IRE) —Firecrest (IRE) (Darshaan)
5857[2] ◆

Ladies Best *B Ellison* a81 104
4 b g King's Best(USA) —Lady Of The Lake (Caerleon (USA))
1766[5] 2103[8] 2790[2] 4444[13] 5894[7] 6302[5] 6649[8] 7244[9]

La Diosa (IRE) *W J Haggas* a55 71
2 b f Dansili—El Divino (IRE) (Halling (USA))
4296[9] 5314[3] 6539[4] 6954[8]

Ladouce (FR) *Robert Collet* 90
2 b f Ski Chief(USA) —Veliana (FR) (Vettori (IRE))
5330a[8] 5850a[6] 6713a[9]

Lady Amberlini *P D Evans* a66 43
3 ch f Bertolini(USA) —Deco Lady (Wolfhound (USA))
9[6] 175[5] 416[4] 595[3] 694[7] 2002[11] 2781[12] 2946[2] 4727[8] 4825[9]

Lady Amy *Miss Amy Weaver* a14
3 b f Fleetwood(IRE) —Hartest Rose (Komaite (USA))
3818[7] 4298[11]

Lady Angelica *Dr J D Scargill* a41 47
2 ch f Piccolo—Fine Frenzy (IRE) (Great Commotion (USA))
4199[9] 4486[5] 5375[5] 6240[27] 7258[12]

Lady Aoy (IRE) *D J Wintle*
2 ch f Indian Haven—Dane's Lady (IRE) (Danehill (USA))
3085[10] 3603[16]

Lady Aquitaine (USA) *B J Meehan* a97 97
3 gr f El Prado(IRE) —Chalamont (IRE) (Kris)
3420[7] 3742[10] 4424[4] 5071[4]

Lady Asheena *J Jay* a52
3 gr f Daylami(IRE) —Star Profile (IRE) (Sadler's Wells (USA))
7344[8]

Lady Aspen (IRE) *Ian Williams* a59 80
5 b m Elnadim(USA) —Misty Peak (IRE) (Sri Pekan (USA))
7518[7] 7790[2]

Lady Avenger (IRE) *J M P Eustace* a88 94
3 ch f Namid—Shioda (USA) (Bahri (USA))
1597[7] 2529[4] 3028[9] 5906[12] 6354[13]

Lady Aviator *T D Easterby* a15 30
3 b f Averti(IRE) —Flying Carpet (Barathea (IRE))
953[9] 1452[10] 2287[13] 2661[13] 2928[9] 3686[12]

Lady Bahia (IRE) *Peter Grayson* a61 57
7 b m Orpen(USA) —Do The Right Thing (Busted)
2050[3] 2356[8] 2710[8] 2836[6] 4308[3] 6711[12] 7444[12] 7648[6] 7778[3] 7835[5]

Lady Benjamin *P C Haslam* a58 75
3 b f Spinning World(USA) —Fresh Look (IRE) (Alzao (USA))
1819[11] 2141[5] 2674[6] 3416[7] 4542[5] 5045[9] 6219[11]

Lady Bower *Miss M E Rowland* a57 62
3 b f Bertolini(USA) —Noble Water (FR) (Noblequest (FR))
38[8] 7012[14]

Lady Brora *A M Balding* a80 79
3 b f Dashing Blade—Tweed Mill (Selkirk (USA))
3161[7] 4277[8] (5426) 6256[2] 6605[4]

Lady Carollina *Rae Guest* 73
3 b f Bertolini(USA) —Carollan (IRE) (Marju (IRE))
1960[8] 3177[2] ◆ (3727) (3960) 4535[F] (Dead)

Lady Charlemagne *N P Littmoden* a50 11
3 b f King Charlemagne(USA) —Prospering (Prince Sabo)
5603[7] 7072[7]

Lady Cottingham *R Hannon* a66
2 b f Dr Fong(USA) —Mystify (Batshoof)
3135[4] (3610)

Lady Deauville (FR) *P A Blockley* 113
3 gr f Fasliyev(USA) —Mercalle (FR) (Kaldoun (FR))
1470[3] 1830[12] 2651a[4] 4657a[5] (4977) (5120) 5932[4] (6106) 6521a[13] 6664a[2] 7037a[12] (7350a) 7598a[4]

Lady Dedlock *Jamie Poulton* a67 84
4 b m Josr Algarhoud(IRE) —Ideal Candidate (Celestial Storm (USA))
(1246) 2567[2] 4087[2] 4516[7] (4866)

Lady Dinsdale (IRE) *T Keddy* 41
2 b f Refuse To Bend(IRE) —Lady Digby (IRE) (Petorius)
3651[11] 4562[5]

Lady Docker (IRE) *H J L Dunlop* a58 38
3 ch f Docksider(USA) —Copper Creek (Habitat)
1912[11]

Lady Drac (IRE) *B W Hills* a64 71
2 gr f Hawk Wing(USA) —Cause Celebre (IRE) (Peintre Celebre (USA))
6076[9] 6731[5]

Lady Dunhill (IRE) *J S Goldie* 46
2 br f High Chaparral(IRE) —Ribbon Glade (UAE) (Zafonic (USA))
4847[5] 5387[13] 6655[12] 6785[8]

Lady Fantasie *Mrs A Duffield* 51
2 b f Fasliyev(USA) —Andilisa (Danehill (USA))
1303[6] 2140[4] 2574[3] 2965[2] 3215[2] 3830[2] 4120[3] 6009[16]

Lady Fas (IRE) *A W Carroll* a50 50
5 b m Fasliyev(USA) —Lady Sheriff (Taufan (USA))
114[5] 247[9] 297[5] 562[8] 634[10] 3608[9] 3695[5] ◆ 4207[7] 4535[6] 4779[6] 5090[3] 7013[7] 7320[11] 7536[6] 7625[4] 7678[8]

Lady Fire (USA) *M Dods* 21
3 br f Kafwain(USA) —Lamsat Al Hob (Lion Cavern (USA))
2156[6]

Lady Firecracker (IRE) *J R Best* a51 59
4 b m Almutawakel—Dazzling Fire (IRE) (Bluebird (USA))
10[10] 88[7] 161[8] 197[7] 400[10] 518[4] 693[4] 804[5] 877[11] 2056[10] 2352[11]

Lady Florence *A B Coogan* a49 52
3 gr f Bollin Eric—Silver Fan (Lear Fan (USA))
953[6] ◆ 1147[11] 1379[7] 1871[11] 1938[5] 2552[6] 3161[10] 3395[8] 4028[9] 5167[2] 6913[7]

Lady Francesca *W R Muir* 83
2 b f Montjeu(IRE) —Purring (USA) (Mountain Cat (USA))
5365[3] 6473[8] 7144[10]

Lady Friend *J W Hills* a80 81
6 gr m Environment Friend—Lady Prunella (IRE) (Supreme Leader)
1329[3] ◆ 1730[5] 4945[6] 6415[7] 6983[6] 7202[10]

Lady Gem *D H Brown* a46 50
2 b f Captain Rio—Cosmic Song (Cosmonaut)
5633[5] 5989[4] 6110[8] 6988[10] 7279[3] 7543[3] 7728[9]

Lady Gloria *J G Given* a88 113
4 b m Diktat—Tara Moon (Pivotal)
1801[2] 2600[2] (2827) 3852[9] 5730a[7] (5932) 6521a[5]

Lady Grace (IRE) *W J Haggas* a89 108
4 b m Orpen(USA) —Lady Taufan (IRE) (Taufan (USA))
959[7] 1355a[6] (3040) 3488[10] 3927[2]

Lady Grantley *M W Easterby* a18 45
3 ch f Bertolini(USA) —South Shore (Caerleon (USA))
3479[8] 4019[4] 4498[3] 4698[7]

Lady Hestia (USA) *M P Tregoning* a49
3 b f Belong To Me(USA) —Awtaan (USA) (Arazi (USA))
6571[7] 6896[9] 7256[9]

Lady Hopeful (IRE) *Peter Grayson* a49 54
6 b m Lend A Hand—Treble Term (Lion Cavern (USA))
50[3] 206[3] 297[2] 562[4] 725[4] 871[2] 1489[5] 2050[5]

Lady In Chief *Miss J A Camacho* 51
3 ch f Fantastic Light(USA) —Risque Lady (Kenmare (FR))
1222[5] 1553[13] 2926[6] 3580[10] 6111[6]

Lady Jane Digby *M Johnston* a81 98
3 b f Oasis Dream—Scandalette (Niniski (USA))
5120[6] 6266[16] 7740[4]

Lady Jinks *R J Hodges* a50 64
3 ch f Kirkwall—Art Deco Lady (Master Willie)
1710[6] 2080[9] 2611[5] 3065[4] 3264[3] 3692[3] (4023) 4564[9] 4722[7] (5215) 5868[9]

Lady Kent (IRE) *Timothy Doyle* a78 58
2 b f Danetime(IRE) —Winning Note (IRE) (Victory Note (USA))
4513a[7]

Lady Killer Queen *D Carroll* 57
4 b m Killer Instinct—Princess Of War (Warrshan (USA))
1382[6] 2006[7] 4457[6] 4924[3] 5385[15] 5637[10] 6185[4] 6309[5]

Lady Kingston *K R Burke* 15
2 ch f Kyllachy—Ash Moon (IRE) (General Monash (USA))
1156[3]

Lady Llanover *P D Evans* 45
8 ch m Halling(USA) —Francia (Legend Of France (USA))
4123[4]

Lady Longcroft *J Pearce* 61
3 ch f Tobougg(IRE) —Top Of The Morning (Keen)
1344[2]

Lady Lorins *Andrew Turnell* a43 43
4 ch m Tomba—Charleigh Keary (Sulaafah (USA))
1865[11] 2556[8] 3844[8] 4181[5] 4932[8] 5577[9]

Lady Lu *P F I Cole* a46 45
2 b f Lujain(USA) —Noble Story (Last Tycoon)
4692[8] 6089[8] 6621[9]

Lady Lucinda *C N Kellett* a7 23
7 b m Muhtarram(USA) —Lady Phyl (Northiam (USA))
120[13] 249[11] 821[11]

Lady Marguerite *M P Tregoning* 55
3 b f Dubai Destination(USA) —Shimaal (Sadler's Wells (USA))
3205[6] 3637[6] 4620[9]

Lady Marian (GER) *W Baltromei* 123
3 b f Nayef(USA) —La Felicita (Shareef Dancer (USA))
(3705a) 4675a[2] (5331a) (6521a) ◆

Lady Marmelade (ITY) *D Ducci* a82 95
5 b m Diktat—Ridge Reef (IRE) (Indian Ridge)
1659a[6] 2029a[8] 7349a[13]

Lady Marquet (IRE) *Jarlath P Fahey* 50
3 b f Atraf—Marqueterie (USA) (Well Decorated (USA))
4715a[13]

Lady Master *Ms J S Doyle* a68 74
2 b f Kheleyf(USA) —Syzygy (IRE) (Entrepreneur)
3734[8] (4411) 5466[2] ◆ 6469[10] 7523[5] 7673[6] (Dead)

Lady Maya *Dr J R J Naylor* a36 52
3 br f Prince Sabo—Monte Mayor Lady (IRE) (Brief Truce (USA))
2341[9] 3065[12] 4336[7] 4807[8] 5215[5]

Lady MB (FR) *J De Roualle* 82
3 b f Golan(IRE) —Blaine (USA) (Lyphard's Wish (FR))
7431a[13]

Lady Meg (IRE) *B Palling* 25
2 b f Spartacus(IRE) —Carna (IRE) (Anita's Prince)
4367[8] 6892[10]

Lady Micklegate (USA) *J R Best* a59
2 b f Johar(USA) —Crimson Native (USA) (The Name's Jimmy (USA))
7767[5]

Lady Mulligan *M Blanshard* a40 63
2 b f Compton Place—Plumeria (Revoque (IRE))
2916[13] 5213[3] 5784[6] 6414[11] 7205[9] 7451[9] 7600[5]

Lady Norlela *R Hannon* a33 44
2 b f Reset(AUS) —Lady Netbetsports (IRE) (In The Wings)
2479[9] 4080[11] 4705[5] 6923[6]

Lady Petrus *H J L Dunlop* a53 54
3 b f Oasis Dream—Odalisque (IRE) (Machiavellian (USA))
1621[7] 2244[11] 2719[7] 4774[4] 5837[14]

Lady Pickpocket *F P Murtagh* a55 49
4 b m Benny The Dip(USA) —Circe (Main Reef)
1136[15] 2051[12]

Lady Pilot *Jim Best* a74 62
6 b m Dansili—Mighty Flyer (IRE) (Mujtahid (USA))
1551[3] (7455)

Lady Rangali (IRE) *Mrs A Duffield* 90
3 b f Danehill Dancer(IRE) —Promising Lady (Thunder Gulch (USA))
2819[3] 3369[2]

Lady Ruler (IRE) *Thomas Cleary* 66
2 b f Viking Ruler(AUS) —Lady Pennekamp (IRE) (Pennekamp (USA))
4513a[3]

Lady Rusty (IRE) *P Winkworth* 73
2 gr f Verglas(IRE) —Patteness (FR) (General Holme (USA))
4692[3] ◆ (5584) 6344[4]

Lady Salama *K R Burke* 66
2 b f Fasliyev(USA) —Change Of Heart (IRE) (Revoque (IRE))
2627[7] 3432[3] 4658[5] (5219) 5451[6] 6809[5]

Lady Sandicliffe (IRE) *Miss Jo Crowley* a65 65
3 b f Noverre(USA) —Tigava (USA) (Machiavellian (USA))
98[4] 184[8] 1051[P] (Dead)

Lady Selkirk *R Charlton* 55
3 ch f Selkirk(USA) —Hyde Hall (Barathea (IRE))
2566[7] *3483[14]*

Lady Silca *A D Smith*
3 b f Silca Blanka(IRE) —Lady Glyde (Inchinor)
2126[11]

Lady Siro (GER) *W Hickst* 97
3 bb f Auenadler(GER) —Lady Lilac (GER) (Konigsstuhl (GER))
3073a[5]

Lady's Law *Rae Guest* a48 57
5 b m Diktat—Snugfit Annie (Midyan (USA))
1[3] 229[3]

Lady Sorcerer *A P Jarvis* a70 79
3 b f Diktat—Silk Law (IRE) (Barathea (IRE))
966[10] 1336[7] 1930[6] 2464[6] 2785[4] 3459[9] *3841[3]* 4646[3] (5027) 6107[6] *6934[9] 7211[7] 7385[14]* 7539[6]

Lady Special (IRE) *C G Cox* 46
3 b f Namid—Crevelli (IRE) (Dolphin Street (FR))
2328[14] 4166[10] 4909[12]

Lady Sprinter (USA) *Juan J Reviriego* a102
4 b m Orientate(USA) —Passionate Player (USA) (Dixieland Band (USA))
6965a[9]

Lady Suffragette (IRE) *John Berry* a45 28
5 b m Mull Of Kintyre(USA) —Miss Senate (IRE) (Alzao (USA))
3657[8]

Lady Traill *G L Moore* a56 53
4 b m Barathea(IRE) —Halska (Unfuwain (USA))
6060[9]

Lady Trish *J R Fanshawe* a44
2 b f Red Ransom(USA) —Artifice (Green Desert (USA))
7311[9]

Lady Valentino *M Dods* a48 58
4 b m Primo Valentino(IRE) —Mystery Night (FR) (Fairy King (USA))
1577[3] 2523[2] 3201[5] 5776[11] 6217[2] 6485[4] *6768[4]*

Lady Vibeeka *Mrs H Sweeting* a62 67
3 b f Josr Algarhoud(IRE) —Indian Flag (IRE) (Indian Ridge)
487[3] 612[7] 1414[6] 1635[10] 3526[7]

Lady Vivien *D H Brown* a56 5
3 b f Kyllachy—Elsie Plunkett (Mind Games)
6158[7] *7546[6] 7802[3]*

Lady Zabeen (IRE) *D M Simcock* 71
3 b f Singspiel(IRE) —Britannia House (USA) (Diesis)
2920[13] 3481[9]

Lady Zena *M W Easterby* 37
2 b f Mind Games—Alustar (Emarati (USA))
5500[10] 6383[10] 6858[11]

La Estrella (USA) *D E Cantillon* a93 92
5 b g Theatrical—Princess Ellen (Tirol)
735[3] 5423[8] (7280) (7499) (7695)

La Famiglia *H Candy* a50 72
3 ch f Tobougg(IRE) —Sea Isle (Selkirk (USA))
3061[7] 3379[10] *5019[7]* 6036[4] 6334[7] (6890)

La Fortalesa (IRE) *K A Ryan* 64
3 b g Rock Of Gibraltar(IRE) —Another Legend (USA) (Lyphard's Wish (FR))
2360[8] 2673[6] 3416[6] 4952[5]

La Fresca *Mme M Bollack-Badel* 99
3 b f Peintre Celebre(USA) —Lanaba (IRE) (Anabaa (USA))
1323a[5]

Lagan Handout *Dr J R J Naylor* 57
2 gr g Lend A Hand—Due To Me (Compton Place)
9574 1263[5] 1640[4] 2098[7] 2508[4]

Lagavulin (IRE) *Miss E C Lavelle* a59 60
4 b g Marju(IRE) —Anna Kareena (IRE) (Charnwood Forest (IRE))
4821[8] *6226[5]* 6413[6] (Dead)

La Gifted *M R Channon* 22
2 b f Fraam—Aileen's Gift (IRE) (Rainbow Quest (USA))
6030[15]

Lago D'Orta (IRE) *D Nicholls* 75
8 ch g Bahhare(USA) —Maelalong (IRE) (Maelstrom Lake)
978[11] 989[13]

La Guancha *D A Nolan* 60
3 b f Timeless Times(USA) —Westcourt Ruby (Petong)
1769[10] 2287[12] 2576[5] 3128[5] 3217[9] 3784[7] 4632[8] 4852[U]

Laguna Salada (IRE) *R Feligioni* 94
2 b f Invincible Spirit(IRE) —Flying Flag (IRE) (Entrepreneur (USA))
7449a[8]

Lahaleeb (IRE) *M R Channon* 112
2 b f Redback—Flames (Blushing Flame (USA))
3444[5] 3869[9] 4337[5] (4666) ◆ (4733) 5266[4] ◆ 5828[3] 6318a[2] (6818)

Laish Ya Hajar (IRE) *P R Webber* a64 76
4 ch g Grand Lodge(USA) —Ya Hajar (Lycius (USA))
2243[12] 2795[6] (3182) 3422[2] 3780[3] 4254[11] (4371) *7606[12]*

Lake Chini (IRE) *M W Easterby* a81 80
6 b g Raise A Grand(IRE) —Where's The Money (Lochnager)
1015[6] 3454[13] 3787[5] 5392[13] (5719) (5775) 6039[3] 6486[6] 6766[11]

Lake Kalamalka (IRE) *J L Dunlop* 63
2 b f Dr Fong(USA) —Lady Of The Lake (Caerleon (USA))
3913[13] 4554[9] 5240[8] 6058[9]

Lakeman (IRE) *B Ellison* 81
2 b g Tillerman—Bishop's Lake (Lake Coniston (IRE))
3411[4] (3976) 4628[3] 5107[3] 5585[6] 5883[2] 6549[2] 7241[12]

Lake Nayasa *H Morrison* 37
3 b f Nayef(USA) —Lady Of The Lake (Caerleon (USA))
2668[12] 2989[6]

Lake Poet (IRE) *C E Brittain* a83 108
5 ch h Galileo(IRE) —Lyric (Lycius (USA))
293a[7] 381a[14] 477a[5] 652a[5]

Lake Sabina *E S McMahon* a72 70
3 b f Diktat—Telori (Muhtarram (USA))
1988[11] 2460[5] 3111[4] 4207[4] 4987[5] *5402[2]* 6219[9] *6448[5]*

Lake Windermere (IRE) *J H M Gosden* a79 71
3 b f Oasis Dream—Spinnette (IRE) (Spinning World (USA))
3452[3] (4195) *6695[2] 7077[12]*

Lambda (USA) *Sir Michael Stoute* 79
3 b f Empire Maker(USA) —South Of Saturn (USA) (Seattle Slew (USA))
2123[12] 3061[2] 3866[5] (5471)

Lambency (IRE) *J S Goldie* a50 61
5 b m Daylami(IRE) —Triomphale (USA) (Nureyev (USA))
9874 1309[7] 1561[6] 2009[7] 2159[2] 2448[8] 2748[6] 2936[2] 3260[8] 3638[7] 3759[5] 4118[7] 4383[2] 4609[5] 4653[8] 5970[2] 6310[4] 7218[6] 7288[5]

Lambourn Genie (UAE) *Tom Dascombe* a59 4
2 b c Halling(USA) —Mystery Play (IRE) (Sadler's Wells (USA))
5227[15] *6876[9] 7191[10]*

Lambrini Lace (IRE) *Mrs L Williamson* a60 65
3 b f Namid—Feather 'n Lace (IRE) (Green Desert (USA))
(2774) 3668[8] 4325[7] 4767[10] 5201[5] 5970[10] 6411[2] *7118[11]*

Lamentation *M Gasparini* 100
4 ch m Singspiel(IRE) —Dark Veil (USA) (Gulch (USA))
2438a[4]

L'Amico Steve (BRZ) *A Cintra Pereira* 103
5 b h Spend A Buck(USA) —All For Love (BRZ) (Ghadeer (FR))
381a[12] 652a[8]

Lamistrelle (IRE) *R Bouresly* a8 60
3 b f Barathea(IRE) —Samriah (IRE) (Wassl)
201a[13]

Lana's Charm *P J Makin* 42
2 b f Lend A Hand—Eljariha (Unfuwain (USA))
4579[7] 6894[6]

Lancaster Lad (IRE) *A B Haynes* a58 63
3 b c Piccolo—Ruby Julie (Clantime)
98[6] 704[5] 1251[3] 1553[14] 2089[3] 2352[9] (3359) (3572) 4053[12] (4278) 4413[7] 4724[6] 6332[6] 6746[9] *7591[11] 7816[5]*

Lancetto (FR) *K R Burke* a55 102
3 b c Dubai Destination(USA) —Lanciana (IRE) (Acatenango (GER))
1850a[2] 2880a[6] 4473a[10] *7755[8]*

Landed Gent (IRE) *Miss V Haigh* a40 16
3 b g Kyllachy—Land Ahead (USA) (Distant View (USA))
597[5] (Dead)

Land Hawk (IRE) *J Pearce* 70
2 br c Trans Island—Heike (Glenstal (USA))
5649[5] ◆ 6057[5] 6438[6] 6886[5]

Landikhaya (IRE) *D K Ivory* a65 72
3 ch g Kris Kin(USA) —Montana Lady (IRE) (Be My Guest (USA))
1082[5] 1364[5] 1527[5] 2045[11] 2639[13] (3166) 3799[6] 4086[13] 4280[5] *7392[3] 7518[4] 7631[9] 7807[9]*

Land 'n Stars *Jamie Poulton* a91 104
8 b g Mtoto—Uncharted Waters (Celestial Storm (USA))
5646[6] 6306[7] 6817[25]

Land Of Wilkes (USA) *D Sepulchre* 78
2 ch f Diesis—Aqua Galinte (USA) (Kris S (USA))
7549a[10]

Landucci *J W Hills* a84 75
7 b g Averti(IRE) —Divina Luna (Dowsing (USA))
53[3] 313[7] (643) 807[5] 1143[5] 2917[4] 3345[5] *4268[6] (5345) 6020[12]* 6490[8] 7068[7] 7764[5]

Lan Force (ITY) *A Renzoni* 96
2 b f Blu Air Force(IRE) —Lan Fei (ITY) (Love The Groom (USA))
5951a[2] 7430a[13]

Langham House *J R Jenkins* a59 63
3 ch g Best Of The Bests(IRE) —Dafne (Nashwan (USA))
2047[12] 2429[18] *6049[14] 7072[3] 7382[9] 7541[9] (7759)*

Langkawi Breeze (IRE) *T J O'Mara* 44
3 b g Bahri(USA) —Zelah (IRE) (Alzao (USA))
3861a[16]

Lang Shining (IRE) *Sir Michael Stoute* 110
4 ch h Dr Fong(USA) —Dragnet (IRE) (Rainbow Quest (USA))
(1469) ◆ 2132[2] 3122[21] 3740[8] 4587[18] 5508[2] 6476[18] 7145[6]

Langs Lash (IRE) *M G Quinlan* 107
2 b f Noverre(USA) —Temple Street (IRE) (Machiavellian (USA))
(1736) 2167[2] (3123) 5272[3] 6441[11]

Lanterns Of Gold *G A Swinbank* 71
3 b f Fantastic Light(USA) —Reason To Dance (Damister (USA))
2272[8]

La Nuage *T J Etherington*
4 gr m Tobougg(IRE) —Cole Slaw (Absalom)
435[10]

Laokoon (GER) *Mario Hofer* a81 91
3 b c Areion(GER) —Little Movie Star (Risk Me (FR))
6743a[8]

La Peinture (GER) *W Hickst* 80
3 ch f Peintre Celebre(USA) —La Capilla (Machiavellian (USA))
3073a[8]

Lapina (IRE) *A Middleton* a70 71
4 ch m Fath(USA) —Alpina (USA) (El Prado (IRE))
1127[5] 1929[4] (2952) 3276[5] 3697[3] 4775[3] 5465[10] 6672[10] *7427[2] (7573) 7667[6]*

Lap Of Honour (IRE) *Jennie Candlish* a63 90
4 b g Danehill Dancer(IRE) —Kingsridge (IRE) (King's Theatre (IRE))
958[18] 1481[10] 1612[10] 2406[9] 2818[10] 3165[2] 3599[12] 4219[18] 4650[10] 5991[4] 6385[4] ◆ (6724)

Lap Of The Gods *Miss Z C Davison* a35 39
4 b g Fleetwood(IRE) —Casarabonela (Magic Ring (IRE))
5752[7]

Laraffelle (GR) *E A L Dunlop* a44 55
2 ch f Bertolini(USA) —Holgera (GER) (Winged Love (IRE))
4692[12] 5184[7] *5570[8]* 6059[16]

Laragh (USA) *John Terranova II* a89 108
2 rg f Tapit(USA) —Rose Of Summer (USA) (El Prado (IRE))
6966a[3]

Lara's Girl *S Wynne*
6 b m Tipsy Creek(USA) —Joe's Dancer (Shareef Dancer (USA))
4711[1]

Larella (GER) *P Rau* 94
3 br f Anabaa(USA) —Laurella (Acatenango (GER))
3073a[6] 4675a[10]

Largem *Jane Chapple-Hyam* a53
2 b g Largesse—Jem's Law (Contract Law (USA))
5590[7]

Larkham (USA) *R M Beckett* 75
2 bb g Action This Day(USA) —La Sarto (USA) (Cormorant (USA))
5099[3] ◆ 6080[9] 6359[3]

La Rochette *P W Chapple-Hyam* a36 47
3 b f Rock Of Gibraltar(IRE) —Soolaimon (IRE) (Shareef Dancer (USA))
3350[8] *4302[7]* 5076[7] *5379[11]*

L'Art Du Silence (IRE) *J R Boyle* a69 25
3 b g Xaar—Without Words (Lion Cavern (USA))
1674[8] 2506[6] 3690[12] 7433[10]

La Sarrazine (FR) *J R Fanshawe* a63 96
3 b f Medicean—Fulcrum (Pivotal)
1748[5] 2199[4] (2566) (3796) 4791[3] (5108) ◆ 6034[11] (6984)

Lascelles *J A Osborne* a66
4 b h Halling(USA) —Poppy's Song (Owington)
216[2] 435[7] 716[4] 881[7] 1044[6]

Lasos (FR) *D Sicaud* 79
3 b c Miesque's Son(USA) —Erivia (FR) (Kendor (FR))
7551a[0]

Lassarina (IRE) *B W Hills* 98
2 b f Sakhee(USA) —Kalanda (Desert King (IRE))
(6076) 6818[7]

Lassie Goes West (IRE) *E J Creighton* 17
3 b f The West(USA) —Go Lassie Go (IRE) (Turtle Island (IRE))
3166[9] 3605[11] 4899[P]

Lasso The Moon *M R Channon* 82
2 b c Sadler's Wells(USA) —Hotelgenie Dot Com (Selkirk (USA))
6602[2] ◆ 6892[4]

Last Angel (IRE) *M Wigham* a45 43
3 b f King Charlemagne(USA) —Magdalene (FR) (College Chapel)
709[4] 873[3] 950[3] 4165[8] 4280[8] 4794[2]

Lastbustowoodstock (IRE) *J A Osborne* a22
2 gr g Kheleyf(USA) —Strelitzia (IRE) (Bluebird (USA))
4304[11] 6133[7]

Last Chance Dance *Andrew Oliver* a64 59
4 ch m Best Of The Bests(IRE) —Real Emotion (USA) (El Prado (IRE))
239[7]

Last Emperor *John Joseph Murphy* a44 57
3 ch g Hawk Wing(USA) —Clara Vale (IRE) (In The Wings)
7071[6] 7296[8]

Last Of The Line *H J L Dunlop* a78 56
3 b c Efisio—Dance By Night (Northfields (USA))
1057[2] 1333[7] 1899[10] *2714[8]* 3266[8] *4345[4] 5052[6] 5345[9] 5617[4] 5867[9]* 6338[8] 6895[13]

Lastroarofdtiger (USA) *K R Burke* a63
2 b c Cherokee Run(USA) —Innocent Affair (IRE) (Night Shift (USA))
6910[7]

Last Sovereign *Jane Chapple-Hyam* a79 81
4 b h Pivotal—Zayala (Royal Applause)
246[2] ◆ 2619[3] 3090[7] *3840[11]* 4603[3] (5069)

Last Three Minutes (IRE) *E A L Dunlop* 89
3 b g Val Royal(FR) —Circe's Isle (Be My Guest (USA))
(4255) 4876[3] 5279[7] 5862[6] 6242[11]

La Sylvia (IRE) *Desmond McDonogh* a76 84
3 b f Oasis Dream—Hawas (Mujtahid (USA))
4004a[6]

La Tee (USA) *Mark Glatt* a97 100
4 b m Broken Vow(USA) —Ashcreek (USA) (Stalwart (USA))
6965a[10]

Latency (ARG) *J B Udaondo* a89 109
7 bb h Slew Gin Fizz(USA) —Latencia (ARG) (El Asesor (ARG))
817a[8] 1091a[11]

Laterly (IRE) *T P Tate* 102
3 b g Tiger Hill(IRE) —La Candela (GER) (Alzao (USA))
1753[3] 2173[2] (2675) 3719[2] (4205) ◆ 5853[12] 6445[4]

Latif (USA) *Paul Green* a62 61
7 b g Red Ransom(USA) —Awaamir (Green Desert (USA))
525[4] 601[6] 701[7] 811[9] 996[3] *1032[4] 1374[3]* 2003[7] 2274[6] 2572[12] 4172[11]

Latimer House (IRE) *Dr J D Scargill* a46 36
3 ch f Observatory(USA) —Tramonto (Sri Pekan (USA))
2552[8] 2984[12] 4280[6] 4990[7]

Latin Lad *R Hannon* a97 101
3 b c Hernando(FR) —Decision Maid (USA) (Diesis)
1333[3] 1632[6] 1943[7] 3156[13] 3919[18] 4552[9] 6128[6] 6542[10]

Latin Mood (FR) *P Demercastel* 107
5 b h Acatenango(GER) —Baranciaga (USA) (Bering)
1663a[9] (7429a) 7598a[3]

Latino Magic (IRE) *D K Weld* a74 100
8 ch h Lion Cavern(USA) —Tansy (Shareef Dancer (USA))
384a[6] *563a[9]* 743a[8]

Latin Scholar (IRE) *A King* a65 79
3 ch g Titus Livius(FR) —Crimada (IRE) (Mukaddamah (USA))
2047[10] 2451[3] 3095[2] 3384[7] (4254) 5118[4] 6202[9]

Latin Tinge (USA) *P F I Cole* a84 87
2 rg f King Cugat(USA) —Southern Tradition (USA) (Family Doctor (USA))
5225[2] ◆ 5828[7] *(6205)* 7142[4]

La Tizona (IRE) *R Charlton* a53 76
2 b c Alhaarth(IRE) —Rosse (Kris)
6000[9] 6412[4] ◆ 6720[4]

La Tournesol (GER) *P Schiergen* 87
3 ch f Samum(GER) —La Bouche (GER) (In The Wings)
7487a[7]

La Troupe (IRE) *J H M Gosden* a32 71
3 b f King's Best(USA) —Passe Passe (USA) (Lear Fan (USA))
2560[6] 2971[7] 3322[5] 4572[4] *6378[8] 6712[11]*

Laudatory *W R Swinburn* a74
2 b g Royal Applause—Copy-Cat (Lion Cavern (USA))
7011[2] (7311)

Laughing Game *A M Hales* a57 41
4 b m Classic Cliche(IRE) —Ground Game (Gildoran)
2755[8] 4029[11]

Laughter (IRE) *Sir Michael Stoute* 87
3 b f Sadler's Wells(USA) —Smashing Review (USA) (Pleasant Tap (USA))
1915[7]

Lauras Joy (IRE) *G P Enright* 38
5 b m Lear Spear(USA) —Atisayin (USA) (Al Nasr (FR))
3559[7] 4052[11] 5533[6] 6024[9]

Laurel Creek (IRE) *M J Grassick* a77 63
3 b c Sakura Laurel(JPN) —Eastern Sky (AUS) (Danehill (USA))
6630[2] (7293) ◆

Laureldean (IRE) *Michael Cunningham* 78
10 b g Shernazar—Power Run (Deep Run)
4655a[15]

Laureldean Dream (USA) *P W Chapple-Hyam* a67 64
3 b f Stravinsky(USA) —Classy Women (USA) (Relaunch (USA))
3177[3] 3977[7] 4987[4] *5617[6] 7362[6]*

Laureldean Gale (USA) *Saeed Bin Suroor* a88 112
3 bb f Grand Slam(USA) —Ravnina (USA) (Nureyev (USA))
1830[13]

Laurel Guerreiro (JPN) *Mitsugi Kon* 117
4 b h King Halo(JPN) —Big Tenby (JPN) (Tenby)
7683a[8]

Laurentian Lad *Rae Guest* a51 49
4 ch h Medicean—Cup Of Kindness (USA) (Secretariat (USA))
909[10] 1206[7] 1459[13]

Laurie Grove (IRE) *T G Mills* a85 68
2 b c Danehill Dancer(IRE) —Fragrant (Cadeaux Genereux)
6474[17] *(7204)*

Lauro *Miss J A Camacho* a62 68
8 b m Mukaddamah(USA) —Lapu-Lapu (Prince Sabo)
949[5] 1391[9] 1577[4] 3077[2] (4215)

Lauro (GER) *A Wohler* 107
5 b h Monsun(GER) —Laurencia (Shirley Heights)
6506a[8]

Lautenspielerin (GER) *Frau Marion Rotering*
2 br f Areion(GER) —Lutte Marie (GER) (Frontal)
5686a[4] 7006a[10]

Lavana (GER) *Werner Glanz* 88
5 br m Silvano(GER) —Lady Lilac (GER) (Konigsstuhl (GER))
3751a[5]

Lavande *M J Wallace* a61 62
3 b f Tipsy Creek(USA) —Skara Brae (Inchinor)
3600[9] *4388[4]* 4793[9]

Lavarone (ARG) *H J Brown* a82 81
5 ch g Sekari—Siusi (ARG) (Engrillado (ARG))
473a[6]

La Varrosa *J D Frost* a52 18
3 b f Josr Algarhoud(IRE) —Ebony Anne (IRE) (Danetime (IRE))
92[6] 3605[12]

Lava Steps (USA) *P F I Cole* a66 56
2 b c Giant's Causeway(USA) —Miznah (IRE) (Sadler's Wells (USA))
6199[7] 6604[11] *7209[5]*

La Vecchia Scuola (IRE) *J S Goldie* a39 95
4 b m Mull Of Kintyre(USA) —Force Divine (FR) (L'Emigrant (USA))
2447[3] (2752) ◆ 2939[3] 3368[7] (3630) 3942[2] 4516[10] 4843[5] 5853[3]

Lavender And Lace *T Keddy* a63 43
3 b f Barathea(IRE) —Summertime Legacy (Darshaan)
1073[12] 2118[6] 3057[13] 3459[11] 4260[11] 4774[9] 5318[9] *7321[9]*

Lavender Girl *P Winkworth* a43 29
2 b f Lucky Owners(NZ) —Lavender Dancer (Tragic Role (USA))
3309^{4} 4387^{5} 4823^{7}

La Verte Rue (USA) *J A Osborne* a64 65
2 b f Johannesburg(USA) —Settling In (USA) (Green Desert (USA))
6327^{2} 6696^{7} 7501^{3} 7645^{4} 7767^{3}

Law And Order *Miss J R Tooth* a46 62
2 b g Lear Spear(USA) —Sarcita (Primo Dominie)
5225^{9} 5905^{7} 6342^{11}

Lawdy Miss Clawdy *D W P Arbuthnot* a50 49
4 ch m Bold Edge—Long Tall Sally (IRE) (Danehill Dancer (IRE))
142^{5} 264^{4} 392^{4} 535^{6} 884^{7} 1150^{5} 1254^{4}

Law Lord *Saeed Bin Suroor* 109
4 br g Diktat—First (Highest Honor (FR))
472a^{2} 668a^{3} 745a^{6} 5368^{6} 6005^{5}

Law Maker *A Bailey* a71 56
8 b g Case Law—Bo' Babbity (Strong Gale)
1338^{9} 2263^{12} 2802^{8} 4653^{18}

Law Of The Jungle (IRE) *David Wachman* 74
2 b f Catcher In The Rye(IRE) —Haut Volee (Top Ville)
6319a^{14}

Law Of The Land (IRE) *B W Duke* a63 64
4 b g Trans Island—Bella's Dream (IRE) (Case Law)
164^{8}

Lawton *Miss J R Tooth* a68 63
3 b g Lear Spear(USA) —First Veil (Primo Dominie)
698^{4} 974^{4} 1685^{7} 2451^{11} 4061^{4} (5616) 6020^{3}

Lawyers Choice *Pat Eddery* a83 62
4 b m Namid—Finger Of Light (Green Desert (USA))
417^{6} 733^{2} 910^{3} 5018^{8} 5350^{12}

Lawyer To World *Mrs C A Dunnett* a48 52
4 gr g Marju(IRE) —Legal Steps (IRE) (Law Society (USA))
1459^{15} 1643^{9} 3863^{11} 4123^{11} 5247^{17} 6005^{7} 7613^{7}

Lay Down Darling *N Tinkler* 9
3 b f Presidium—Scoffera (Scottish Reel)
1754^{8} 2466^{10}

Layer Cake *J W Hills* a76 65
2 b c Monsieur Bond(IRE) —Blue Indigo (FR) (Pistolet Bleu (IRE))
4360^{5} 4931^{2} 5497^{4} 6305^{12}

Lay The Cash (USA) *B G Powell* a66 39
4 ch g Include(USA) —Shanade (USA) (Sentimental Slew (USA))
352^{11} 881^{13} 1052^{11} 1206^{6} 1408^{10} 2352^{6} 2557^{4}

La Zarza *S C Williams* a28
3 b f Domedriver(IRE) —La Fazenda (Warning)
909^{11} 1125^{9} 2126^{9}

Lazeyma *M A Jarvis* a49 60
3 b f Fantastic Light(USA) —Zahrat Dubai (Unfuwain (USA))
4871^{5} 5155^{9} 6378^{5} 6909^{5}

Lazio (GER) *F G Hand* a93 88
7 b g Dashing Blade—Leontine (GER) (Selkirk (USA))
4003a^{18}

Lazy Days *D R C Elsworth* 95
3 ch g Bahamian Bounty—Vivianna (Indian Ridge)
(2056) 2819^{5} ◆ 3155^{5} ◆ 3877^{8} 4404^{4} ◆

Leadenhall Lass (IRE) *P M Phelan* a71 75
2 ch f Monsieur Bond(IRE) —Zest (USA) (Zilzal (USA))
(4482) 5375^{3} 6240^{16}

Lead Home (IRE) *B J Meehan* a36
2 b f Dansili—Lead Note (USA) (Nijinsky (CAN))
6737^{13}

Leading Edge (IRE) *M R Channon* a79 79
3 gr f Clodovil(IRE) —Ja Ganhou (Midyan (USA))
1155^{9} 1548^{2} 1738^{2} 2014^{5} 2141^{2} 2428^{6} 2757^{2} 2976^{11} 3202^{2} 3636^{7} (4329) 4631^{5} 4864^{8} 5101^{16} 5490^{10} 6340^{10} 6556^{7} 7544^{3} (7811)

Leaf Hollow *M Madgwick* 26
2 ch f Beat Hollow—Lauren (GER) (Lightning (FR))
1680^{16} 1955^{10} 3267^{11}

League Champion (USA) *R Bouresly* a98 61
5 b g Rahy(USA) —Meiosis (USA) (Danzig (USA))
378a^{P} 668a^{8} 741a^{10}

Leahurst (IRE) *J Noseda* 57
2 gr g Verglas(IRE) —Badee'A (IRE) (Marju (IRE))
4792^{7}

Leamington (USA) *M Johnston* a87 41
3 b f Pleasant Tap(USA) —Muneefa (USA) (Storm Cat (USA))
12^{2} (131) (434) 1919^{9} 3586^{3}

Leandros (FR) *G M Lyons* a101 88
3 br g Invincible Spirit(IRE) —Logjam (IRE) (Royal Academy (USA))
6510a^{2}

Learo Dochais (USA) *M J Wallace* a74
2 b c Mutakddim(USA) —Brush With The Law (USA) (Broad Brush (USA))
3821^{2} 5344^{5}

Lease Of Life (USA) *B W Hills* 94
3 b c Cozzene(USA) —Kinema (USA) (Graustark)
6393^{4} ◆ (6705) ◆ 7146^{17}

Leaving Alone (BRZ) *Doug Watson* a86 81
5 b g Vettori(IRE) —Que Normand (BRZ) (Roi Normand (USA))
380a^{5}

Le Baron Jenney (ITY) *L Riccardi* 16
3 gr c College Chapel—Beverly Pepper (Love The Groom (USA))
1712a^{8}

Le Big (GER) *U Stoltefuss* 97
4 b h Big Shuffle(USA) —La Luganese (IRE) (Surumu (GER))
7005a^{8}

Le Brocquy *M G Quinlan* a33 87
3 b g Pursuit Of Love—Catawba (Mill Reef (USA))
(3223) ◆ 3930^{2} 5938^{11} 6563^{12}

Le Cadre Noir (IRE) *D K Weld* 110
4 b h Danetime(IRE) —Rinass (IRE) (Indian Ridge)
2029a^{4} 3533a^{4} 4004a^{2} 4223a^{6} (6315a)

Lecanvey *R A Fahey* 69
3 b g Where Or When(IRE) —Catch The Flame (USA) (Storm Bird (CAN))
4494a^{8} 5504^{9}

Leceile (USA) *W J Haggas* a61
2 bb f Forest Camp(USA) —Summerwood (USA) (Boston Harbor (USA))
7289^{6} 7434^{3}

Lechero (IRE) *John A Harris* a49 16
3 ch g Millkom—Lovely Ali (IRE) (Dunbeath (USA))
439^{8} 462^{4} 6173^{16} 6584^{9} 6836^{7} 7053^{6}

Le Chiffre (IRE) *Miss Sheena West* a77 67
6 br g Celtic Swing—Implicit View (Persian Bold)
3090^{11} 3567^{2} 3822^{3} 4052^{6} (4386) 4727^{10} (4961) 5303^{5} 5533^{5} (5708) 5799^{3} 6211^{4} (6422) 6598^{2}

Le Citadel (USA) *P D Deegan* a76 92
3 b g Stravinsky(USA) —Halholah (USA) (Secreto (USA))
5731a^{16}

Le Corvee (IRE) *A W Carroll* a73 81
6 b g Rossini(USA) —Elupa (IRE) (Mtoto)
28^{9} 320^{7} 3606^{14} 4371^{6}

Ledgerwood *A J Chamberlain* a64 62
3 b g Royal Applause—Skies Are Blue (Unfuwain (USA))
(98) 321^{6} 820^{2} 1115^{5} 1407^{5} (2089) 2352^{5} 2833^{11} 2932^{6} 4275^{13} 5429^{13}

Ledicea *P Rau* 99
4 ch m Medicean—Lacatena (GER) (Acatenango (GER))
2347a^{3} 3623a^{8}

Leelu *D W P Arbuthnot* a66
2 b f Largesse—Strat's Quest (Nicholas (USA))
6737^{4} ◆ 7259^{5} 7708^{2}

Lee Miller (IRE) *L M Cumani* 84
3 ch f Danehill Dancer(IRE) —Brianza (USA) (Thunder Gulch (USA))
2257^{3} ◆ 2800^{2} (3556) 4520^{8} 5504^{3} 6027^{5} 6605^{7}

Left Hand Drive *B W Duke* a31 41
5 b g Erhaab(USA) —Eyelet (IRE) (Satco (FR))
3137^{11}

Leftontheshelf (IRE) *J L Spearing* a87 80
2 ch f Namid—Corryvreckan (IRE) (Night Shift (USA))
3735^{2} (4486) 5204^{3} 5487^{3} 6281^{3} 7065^{4}

Legal Eagle (IRE) *J H M Gosden* a73 84
3 b g Invincible Spirit(IRE) —Lupulina (CAN) (Saratoga Six (USA))
1925^{4} 2732^{5} 5433^{9}

Legal Legacy *M Dods* 57
2 ch g Beat Hollow—Dans Delight (Machiavellian (USA))
6230^{14} 6723^{5} 7038^{5}

Legal Set (IRE) *Miss A Stokell* a51 64
12 gr g Second Set(IRE) —Tiffany's Case (IRE) (Thatching)
3759^{8}

Legendary Guest *D W Barker* 76
3 b g Bahamian Bounty—Legend Of Aragon (Aragon)
1306^{12} (1548) ◆ 1988^{9} 2141^{4} 2490^{8} 2526^{4} 3280^{8} 3601^{4} 4329^{2} 4450^{7} 4700^{8}

Legend Erry (IRE) *Jane Chapple-Hyam* a87 80
4 b g Act One—Azure Lake (USA) (Lac Ouimet (USA))
(67) (169) 268^{5} 1337^{2} 1472^{5} 3104^{15}

Legerete (USA) *A Fabre* 116
4 b m Rahy(USA) —Sea Hill (USA) (Seattle Slew (USA))
1713a^{11}

Legion D'Honneur (UAE) *L Lungo* 79
3 b g Halling(USA) —Renowned (IRE) (Darshaan)
1307^{4} (1950)

Legislate *B W Hills* 82
2 b c Dansili—Shining Water (Kalaglow)
6117^{8} 6778^{3}

Legislation *J H M Gosden* a92 86
3 b c Oasis Dream—Kite Mark (Mark Of Esteem (IRE))
1074^{8} 1524^{4} 1746^{5} 2302^{5} 3038^{4} 4010a^{15} 4539^{3} (5209) 5682^{8}

Le Grand Amour (IRE) *B W Hills* 75
2 b f Montjeu(IRE) —L'Amour (USA) (Gone West (USA))
3349^{8} 3913^{8} (5782) 6561^{3}

Leg Spinner (IRE) *A J Martin* 107
7 b g Intikhab(USA) —Road Harbour (USA) (Rodrigo De Triano (USA))
6817^{5}

Le Havre (IRE) *J-C Rouget* 103
2 b c Noverre(USA) —Marie Rheinberg (GER) (Surako (GER))
7163a^{7}

Leitmotif (USA) *J L Dunlop* a23 66
3 rg c Linamix(FR) —First Melody (Vettori (IRE))
1839^{11} 2340^{14} 2785^{9} 3962^{8} 4879^{5} 6728^{10}

Lekezia (IRE) *J W Hills* a25 39
3 b f Fasliyev(USA) —Etaaq (IRE) (Sadler's Wells (USA))
2834^{11} 3177^{10} 3694^{7} 4429^{7} 5218^{10} 5631^{15} 6913^{13}

Lekin Sedona (IRE) *Joss Saville* a50 49
3 ch g Namid—Abrahamsdotter (IRE) (College Chapel)
1257^{6} 2287^{10} (Dead)

Lekita *W R Swinburn* a76 77
3 b f Kyllachy—Tender Moment (IRE) (Caerleon (USA))
2620^{6} (3502) 4300^{6} 4731^{6} 5149^{3} 5800^{7} 7428^{4} 7540^{2}

Lella Beya *S Kirk* a60 45
3 b f Diktat—Seamstress (IRE) (Barathea (IRE))
141^{10}

Le Miracle (GER) *W Baltromei* 115
7 bb g Monsun(GER) —L'Heure Bleue (IRE) (Kendor (FR))
1663a^{6} 2236a^{4} 3154^{9} 6497a^{6} 7008a^{7}

Lemon Dash *L A Mullaney* a44 44
2 b f Paris House—Icenaslice (IRE) (Fayruz)
3949^{9} 4681^{4} 5475^{7} 6009^{9} 7279^{8}

Lemonesse (USA) *H R A Cecil* a75 71
3 b f Lemon Drop Kid(USA) —Policy Setter (USA) (Deputy Minister (CAN))
2291^{12} 3168^{2} 3688^{3} 4342^{4} 4821^{9} 6790^{7}

Lemon N Sugar (USA) *J Noseda* a77 60
3 b f Lemon Drop Kid(USA) —Altos De Chavon (USA) (Polish Numbers (USA))
6705^{8} 7026^{2}

Lemon Silk (IRE) *D E Pipe* a57 70
4 ch g Barathea(IRE) —Bois De Citron (USA) (Woodman (USA))
5183^{6}

Lend A Grand (IRE) *Miss Jo Crowley* a81 81
4 br g Lend A Hand—Grand Madam (Grand Lodge (USA))
2262^{6} 3367^{11} 3840^{10} 5789^{9} 6738^{5} 7510^{12} 7742^{6}

Lend A Light *I W McInnes* a51 55
2 b c Lend A Hand—No Candles Tonight (Star Appeal)
6580^{7} 7343^{10} 7424^{9}

Leni Riefenstahl (IRE) *Mario Hofer* 93
3 b f Mull Of Kintyre(USA) —Rofan (USA) (Cozzene (USA))
5329a^{10}

Lennie Briscoe (IRE) *S Kirk* 71
2 b c Rock Of Gibraltar(IRE) —Tammany Hall (IRE) (Petorius)
6539^{8} 6978^{7}

Lenouska (IRE) *J W Hills* a8 54
3 b f Montjeu(IRE) —Crystal City (Kris)
3206^{16} 3730^{4} 4280^{7} 5148^{12}

Leocorno (IRE) *Sir Michael Stoute* 80
2 br f Pivotal—Highland Gift (IRE) (Generous (IRE))
(6945) ◆

Leonard Charles *C R Dore* a76 52
4 b g Best Of The Bests(IRE) —Iris May (Brief Truce (USA))
3339^{12} 3733^{13} 4031^{11}

Leonardo's Friend *B G Powell* a34 87
5 b g Polish Precedent(USA) —Glider (IRE) (Silver Kite (USA))
6594^{10} 6824^{10}

Leonid Glow *M Dods* 82
3 b f Hunting Lion(IRE) —On Till Morning (IRE) (Never So Bold)
1019^{5} 1452^{5} 2038^{4} 2399^{2} (3086) 3298^{3} 3717^{2} (4236) 4595^{4}

Leopold (SLO) *D W Thompson* 16
7 b g Solarstern(FR) —Lucera (GER) (Orofino (GER))
6550^{11}

Leo's Girl (IRE) *D Carroll* a39 26
3 b f Viking Ruler(AUS) —Space Travel (Dancing Dissident (USA))
5710^{10}

Leo's Pride (IRE) *D K Weld* a73 87
3 ch c Medicean—Alpine Park (IRE) (Barathea (IRE))
826a^{4}

Leo's Starlet (IRE) *A De Royer-Dupre* a83 108
3 ch f Galileo(IRE) —Premiere Creation (FR) (Green Tune (USA))
(1760a) ◆ 2877a^{9} 3543a^{2} 6495a^{5}

Le Petit Vigier *P Beaumont* a49 46
2 b f Groom Dancer(USA) —Fallujah (Dr Fong (USA))
5256^{12} 6008^{10} 6811^{4} 7172^{3} 7266^{2} 7531^{10}

Lepido (ITY) *L M Cumani* 92
4 b g Montjeu(IRE) —Luv Is For Sharing (USA) (Miswaki (USA))
2168^{15} 2593^{4} 3209^{6}

Leprechaun's Gold (IRE) *B J Llewellyn* a62 56
4 ch g Spectrum(IRE) —Ashirah (USA) (Housebuster (USA))
1694^{6} 2731^{3} 4023^{8} 4250^{11}

Leptis Magna *R H York* a55 82
4 ch g Danehill Dancer(IRE) —Dark Eyed Lady (IRE) (Exhibitioner)
1682^{14} 2373^{18} 2897^{10} 3383^{6} 4429^{4} (4748) 5008^{2} 5198^{3} 6211^{11} 6544^{8}

Le Reve Royal *G R Oldroyd* a44 66
2 ch f Monsieur Bond(IRE) —Bond Royale (Piccolo)
5004^{3} 5835^{10} 6481^{6}

Les Allues (IRE) *H S Howe* a43 43
3 b f Chevalier(IRE) —Cwm Deri (IRE) (Alzao (USA))
3359^{9} 4326^{12} 5748^{13} 6331^{8}

Les Arcs (USA) *S Parr* a113 98
8 bb g Arch(USA) —La Sarto (USA) (Cormorant (USA))
3722^{11}

Les Fazzani (IRE) *K A Ryan* a100 109
4 b m Intikhab(USA) —Massada (Most Welcome)
1713a^{10} 4007a^{U} 4667^{4} 5311^{3} 7100^{5} (7242) 7491^{2}

Lesley's Choice *R Curtis* a80 76
2 b g Lucky Story(USA) —Wathbat Mtoto (Mtoto)
2011^{2} ◆ 2473^{3} ◆ 3603^{6} (4474) 4857^{6} 5680^{7} (6023) 6274^{11} 7714^{3}

Leslingtaylor (IRE) *J J Quinn* 82
6 b g Orpen(USA) —Rite Of Spring (Niniski (USA))
4742^{9} 5199^{5}

Lessing (FR) *R Gibson* a99 106
3 b f Orpen(USA) —Lady Morgane (IRE) (Medaaly)
1360a^{3} 2033a^{9} 5038a^{5}

Lessing (IRE) *O Pessi* 67
3 b c Almutawakel—Liszewska (IRE) (Desert King (IRE))
2028a^{14}

Lesson In Humility (IRE) *K R Burke* 110
3 b f Mujadil(USA) —Vanity (IRE) (Thatching)
1597^{5} 2171^{2} (2594) ◆ 3420^{2} (4437) (5899) 6304^{6}

Lethal *R A Fahey* a90 93
5 ch g Nashwan(USA) —Ipanema Beach (Lion Cavern (USA))
5^{8} 329^{4} 456^{7} 707^{5} ◆ 839^{4} 1134^{2} ◆ 1261^{2} 1588^{5} 2040^{2} 3128^{4} 3567^{5} 3626^{11} (4073) 4700^{4} 5400^{6}

Lethal Glaze (IRE) *R Hannon* 77
2 gr g Verglas(IRE) —Sticky Green (Lion Cavern (USA))
4151^{13} 4510^{10} 5022^{4} (5585) (6394)

Let It Be *K G Reveley* a57 78
7 ch m Entrepreneur—Noble Dane (IRE) (Danehill (USA))
1890^{8} 2467^{10} 2849^{4} 3279^{3} 3642^{5} 3863^{2} (4220) (4452) (4963) (5396) 6313^{4} 6527^{9} 6790^{8}

Let Me Pass (USA) *Jane Chapple-Hyam* a37 55
3 b f Kafwain(USA) —Sabeline (IRE) (Caerleon (USA))
1721^{9} 2971^{10} 3350^{7} 4564^{13} (Dead)

L'Etoile De Moscou *E Lellouche* 92
3 b f Peintre Celebre(USA) —L'Etoile De Mer (FR) (Caerleon (USA))
5597a^{8} 7635a^{2}

Le Toreador *K A Ryan* a83 82
3 ch g Piccolo—Peggy Spencer (Formidable (USA))
1611^{9} 2396^{4} (3231) (3609) (3811) 4787^{4} 6449^{6} 7222^{2}

Let's Rock (GER) *P Rau* 92
3 br c Dashing Blade—Les Intimes (IRE) (Be My Guest (USA))
1514a^{4}

Lets Roll *C W Thornton* 96
7 b g Tamure(IRE) —Miss Petronella (Petoski)
1568^{13} 1798^{9} 5858^{11} 6107^{8} 6657^{2} 6948^{11} 7223^{6}

Lettre Spirituelle *J E Pease* a94 76
3 b f Invincible Spirit(IRE) —Epistole (IRE) (Alzao (USA))
1712a^{5}

Leulahleulahlay *M Johnston* a63
2 ch c Dr Fong(USA) —Fidelio's Miracle (USA) (Mountain Cat (USA))
6165^{5}

Levera *A King* a113 110
5 b g Groom Dancer(USA) —Prancing (Prince Sabo)
2044^{7} 2580^{8} 3885^{4} 4192^{7} 4504^{16}

Levitation (IRE) *W S Kittow* 34
2 b f Vettori(IRE) —Uplifting (Magic Ring (IRE))
5225^{15}

Lewis Lloyd (IRE) *R E Barr* a49 62
5 b g Indian Lodge(IRE) —Sandy Fitzgerald (IRE) (Last Tycoon)
(2463) 2846^{13} 3281^{2} 3593^{10} 3755^{12} 4217^{12} 6217^{13}

Lewis Michael (USA) *Wayne Catalano* a119 105
5 b h Rahy(USA) —Justenuffheart (USA) (Broad Brush (USA))
6995a^{7}

Lexlenos (IRE) *D R C Elsworth* a74
2 ch f Intikhab(USA) —Blazing Glory (IRE) (Glow (USA))
(7356) 7476^{2} (7700) ◆

Leyte Gulf (USA) *C C Bealby* a68 61
5 b g Cozzene(USA) —Gabacha (USA) (Woodman (USA))
443^{5} 954^{4} 1121^{2} 1559^{3} 1933^{2} 2572^{9} 3137^{2} 3377^{2} 3613^{3} 6538^{7} 7045^{10}

L'Hirondelle (IRE) *M J Attwater* a79
4 b g Anabaa(USA) —Auratum (USA) (Carson City (USA))
5864^{RR} (7504) 7712^{5}

L'Homme De Nuit (GER) *G L Moore* a75 60
4 b g Samum(GER) —La Bouche (GER) (In The Wings)
1682^{10} 2153^{15} 3321^{11} 3614^{3} 7216^{4} (7400) 7515^{3}

Liang Kay (GER) *U Ostmann* 113
3 b c Dai Jin—Linton Bay (GER) (Funambule (USA))
(1514a) 2066a^{3} (3074a) 3773a^{4} (5624a) 6499a^{5}

Liani (IRE) *J R Norton* a51 49
3 b f Modigliani(USA) —Well Wisher (USA) (Sanglamore (USA))
237^{8}

Lia Rumma (ITY) *F Folco* 98
3 ch f Monashee Mountain(USA) —Scuola Romana (IRE) (Rudimentary (USA))
2231a^{18}

Libel Law *M A Jarvis* 65
2 ch c Kingmambo(USA) —Innuendo (IRE) (Caerleon (USA))
7105^{4} ◆

Liberally (IRE) *B J Meehan* a53 81
3 b f Statue Of Liberty(USA) —Specifically (USA) (Sky Classic (CAN))
2955^{7} 3133^{7} 3629^{2} 4253^{6} (5119) (5428)

Liberate *P J Hobbs* a88 93
5 ch g Lomitas—Eversince (USA) (Foolish Pleasure (USA))
3104^{3} 6817^{7}

Liberation (IRE) *M Johnston* 104
2 b c Refuse To Bend(IRE) —Mosaique Bleue (Shirley Heights)
5468^{3} ◆ (5811) (6305) 6474^{4}

Liberation Spirit (USA) *J Noseda* a82 86
3 b c Gone West(USA) —Katherine Seymour (Green Desert (USA))
1748^{2} ◆ 2360^{2} ◆ 2994^{4} (4194) 4641^{5} 5247^{12} 6627^{5}

Libero Mercato (IRE) *A & G Botti* 94
3 b c Golan(IRE) —Afto (USA) (Relaunch (USA))
2028a^{16}

Libertador (FR) *J-M Capitte* 105
4 b h Slickly(FR) —Dancing Fan (USA) (Lear Fan (USA))
5926a^{5}

Liberty Beau (IRE) *D R C Elsworth* a60
2 b g Statue Of Liberty(USA) —La Shalak (IRE) (Shalford (IRE))
7415^{5} ◆ 7622^{5} 7754^{7}

Liberty Belle (IRE) *J R Best* a61 82
3 bb f Statue Of Liberty(USA) —Enaya (Caerleon (USA))
1995^{11} (2690) 3000^{9} 3224^{8} 4375^{6} 4749^{8} 5151^{7} 6554^{11} 6880^{8}

Liberty Diamond *K R Burke* 73
2 br f Needwood Blade—Take Liberties (Warning)
4734[5] 5989[2] 6407[2]

Liberty Estelle (IRE) *G A Swinbank*
2 gr f Statue Of Liberty(USA) —Bella Estella (GER) (Sternkoenig (IRE))
6381[U] 6722[12]

Liberty Key (IRE) *T P Tate* 35
3 b g Statue Of Liberty(USA) —Key To Win (Lead On Time (USA))
2700[5]

Liberty Lodge (IRE) *G A Swinbank* 19
2 b g Statue Of Liberty(USA) —Lady Justice (Compton Place)
4681[6]

Liberty Seeker (FR) *John A Harris* a36 74
9 ch g Machiavellian(USA) —Samara (IRE) (Polish Patriot (USA))
485[9] 602[8] 7376[12]

Liberty Ship *J D Bethell* a66 74
3 b g Statue Of Liberty(USA) —Flag (Selkirk (USA))
918[5] 6791[3] 7043[4] 7323[2] 7611[5]

Liberty To Rock (IRE) *J T Gorman* 71
2 b c Statue Of Liberty(USA) —Polynesian Goddess (IRE) (Salmon Leap (USA))
6320a[27]

Liberty Trail (IRE) *Miss L A Perratt* 70
2 b g Statue Of Liberty(USA) —Karinski (USA) (Palace Music (USA))
3754[7] 4014[2] 6037[6]

Libertytyne *S Kirk* a48
3 br f Statue Of Liberty(USA) —Coffee Time (IRE) (Efisio)
1740[11]

Liberty Valance (IRE) *S Kirk* a79 67
3 b g Statue Of Liberty(USA) —Tabdea (USA) (Topsider (USA))
(413) 538[2] 2481[9] 2883[6] 3136[5] 3609[4] 4090[7] ◆ 4531[3] 4943[4] 7367[7] 7634[9] 7803[8] 7829[7] ◆

Libor (IRE) *L M Cumani* a82 56
5 b h Lend A Hand—America Lontana (FR) (King's Theatre (IRE))
3228[8]

Libre *F Jordan* a72 69
8 b g Bahamian Bounty—Premier Blues (FR) (Law Society (USA))
973[5] 1160[13] 1406[9] 1898[3] 2510[4] 2957[7] 3089[4] (3903) 4215[6] 4710[2] 5161[2] 6363[12] 6671[6] 6821[7]

Lidana (IRE) *John M Oxx* a80 70
3 b f King's Best(USA) —Lidakiya (IRE) (Kahyasi)
6511a[4]

Lido Shuffle *M R Bosley* a9
3 ch g Band On The Run—June The Eighth (IRE) (Lake Coniston (IRE))
7609[8]

Liebermann (GER) *D K Weld* 99
2 bb c Big Shuffle(USA) —La Ola (GER) (Dashing Blade)
7029a[4]

Lieutenant Pigeon *G D Blake* a80 73
3 ch g Captain Rio—Blue Velvet (Formidable (USA))
(849) ◆ (924) 1426[8] 2555[2] 3136[2] 3696[6] 3890[6] 6420[8] 6695[9] 7435[7]

Life's A Whirl *Mrs C A Dunnett* a51 65
6 b m Machiavellian(USA) —Spinning Top (Alzao (USA))
2057[5] 2510[11] 3116[4] 3501[6] 4065[6] ◆ 4282[10] 5161[7] (5318)

Lifetime Endeavour *R E Barr* 33
4 b g Aragon—Musical Star (Music Boy)
5110[12] 5395[7] 5636[10]

Light Dubai (IRE) *M R Channon* 67
2 b f Fantastic Light(USA) —Seeking A Way (USA) (Seeking The Gold (USA))
5240[6]

Light From Mars *B R Millman* 88
3 gr g Fantastic Light(USA) —Hylandra (USA) (Bering)
1573[3] 2449[3] (3312) (4128) 4790[7] 6130[6]

Light Green (BRZ) *A De Royer-Dupre* a100 112
4 b h Blush Rambler(USA) —Star Procida (USA) (Procida (USA))
672a[3] 1088a[4] 4212a[8] 5114a[4] 5954a[3] 6521a[6] 7037a[2]

Light Hearted *J Noseda* a85 85
3 b f Green Desert(USA) —Gay Gallanta (USA) (Woodman (USA))
1423[11] (2067) 2594[4] 4591[8] 6169[5] 6699[6]

Lighting Shadow *N Wilson* 4
3 b g Captain Rio—Bonny Ruan (So Factual (USA))
3338[8] 4378[10] 4689[14]

Light It Up (IRE) *M Halford* a74 67
2 b f Elusive City(USA) —Fabuco (IRE) (Mujadil (USA))
6319a[20]

Lightning Squall (USA) *M Botti* a67 51
3 b c Rahy(USA) —The Franchise (USA) (Deputy Minister (CAN))
2198[14] 2509[16] 3396[6] 4061[10] 6685[10]

Light Sea (IRE) *M R Channon* 61
3 ch f King's Best(USA) —Bint Al Balad (IRE) (Ahonoora)
1440[9] 1840[10] 4564[4] 5077[10] 5399[P]

Light Sleeper *P W Chapple-Hyam* 75
2 b c Kyllachy—Snoozy (Cadeaux Genereux)
5649[2]

Lights Of Vegas *S Kirk* a53 71
4 b g Traditionally(USA) —Catch The Lights (Deploy)
3311[8] 5157[10] 5916[4] 6208[5] 6570[5] 6912[10] 7112[5] 7373[4]

Light The Fire (IRE) *B J Meehan* 98
2 b c Invincible Spirit(IRE) —Rouge Noir (USA) (Saint Ballado (CAN))
1714[5] ◆ (2275) ◆ 3105[10] (3681) 5330a[6] 6644[12]

Light The Light (IRE) *Rae Guest* a55
3 ch f King Charlemagne(USA) —Saana (IRE) (Erins Isle)
5627[4] 7757[3]

Light Vision (NZ) *Robert Smerdon* 112
5 b g Zerpour(IRE) —Switched (AUS) (Naturalism (NZ))
6922a[4]

Like A Storm (IRE) *Y Fouin*
2 b f Ultimately Lucky(IRE) —River Valentine (FR) (River Majesty (USA))
7549a[0]

Like For Like (IRE) *R J Hodges* a66 72
2 ch f Kheleyf(USA) —Just Like Annie (IRE) (Mujadil (USA))
2638[3] ◆ 2944[3] 3092[3] 3558[2] 3778[3] 3949[5] (4764) 5287[2]

Like Magic (IRE) *Patrick Martin* a85 97
2 b c Invincible Spirit(IRE) —Magic Annemarie (IRE) (Dancing Dissident (USA))
5546a[4]

Like To Golf (USA) *Mme J Bidgood* a92 55
4 bb g Bianconi(USA) —Like To Shimmy (USA) (Shimatoree (USA))
7643a[13]

Lilac Moon (GER) *N J Vaughan* a67 71
4 b m Dr Fong(USA) —Luna De Miel (Shareef Dancer (USA))
2001[9] (3588) (4331) (5105)

Lilac Wine *D J S Ffrench Davis* a54
5 ch m Dancing Spree(USA) —Stay With Me Baby (Nicholas Bill)
5913[5]

Lilburn (IRE) *J R Fanshawe* a50 74
3 b g Statue Of Liberty(USA) —Vahine (USA) (Alysheba (USA))
2509[7] 3161[9] 3886[10] 4569[3] (5161) 5964[8] 6862[14]

Lilia (GER) *Frau E Mader* 99
4 gr m Dashing Blade—Lindia (GER) (Konigsstuhl (GER))
2879a[6] (3751a) 5528a[7]

Liliaceae *D Shaw* a16
2 b f Lujain(USA) —Polytess (IRE) (Polish Patriot (USA))
4164[12] 4456[7] 4931[7] 5473[9] 5870[9]

Lille Ida *M P Tregoning* a78 63
3 br f Hawk Wing(USA) —Fur Will Fly (Petong)
1470[13] 1764[6]

Lilly Blue (IRE) *M R Channon* a64 85
2 b f Hawk Wing(USA) —Holly Blue (Bluebird (USA))
5097[10] 5898[5] 6291[6] 6682[6]

Lilly Grove *A G Foster* 45
3 b f Mtoto—Armada Grove (Fleetwood (IRE))
6163[2]

Lily Jicaro (IRE) *Mrs L Williamson* 62
2 ch f Choisir(AUS) —Mourir D'Aimer (USA) (Trempolino (USA))
6788[2] 7172[5]

Lily La Belle *A W Carroll* a47 42
4 b m King Charlemagne(USA) —Corniche Quest (IRE) (Salt Dome (USA))
48[4] 89[5] 249[3] 392[8] 553[4] 684[6] 862[9]

Lily Of The Nile (UAE) *J G Portman* 30
2 ch f Halling(USA) —Covet (Polish Precedent (USA))
5314[16] 6081[15]

Lily Waters *W M Brisbourne* 37
2 ch f Reset(AUS) —Chilly Waters (Polar Falcon (USA))
2903[8] 4149[16] 4692[11]

Limatus (GER) *P Vovcenko* 106
7 br g Law Society(USA) —Limaga (Lagunas)
(4496a) 5333a[10]

Limbo King *J R Fanshawe* a79 79
4 b g Barathea(IRE) —Ermine (IRE) (Cadeaux Genereux)
5935[2] 6626[5] 7025[5]

Limehouse (SAF) *M F De Kock* a91 81
5 b g Rich Man's Gold(USA) —Biloxi Blue (SAF) (Al Mufti (USA))
202a[9] 379a[9]

Limelight (USA) *Sir Mark Prescott* a48 58
3 gr f Dalakhani(IRE) —Last Second (IRE) (Alzao (USA))
4992[3] 5169[3] 5537[4] 6044[5] 6447[5] 6753[10]

Limonia (GER) *Mike Murphy* a60 57
6 b m Perugino(USA) —Limoges (GER) (Konigsstuhl (GER))
596[2] 790[2] 856[2] 1185[4] 1455[5] 1675[4] (2706) 2869[7] 3501[7]

Linby (IRE) *Miss Tor Sturgis* a31 57
3 b g Dr Fong(USA) —Dubious (Darshaan)
2221[11] 2847[5] 3227[6] 3886[13] 4165[4] (4498) 6374[7] 6883[9]

Linda Green *M R Channon* a72 80
7 b m Victory Note(USA) —Edge Of Darkness (Vaigly Great)
334[6] 599[6] 964[7] 1178[2] 1285[5] 1522[4] 1739[6] 2102[6] 2478[9] 3026[4] 3313[5] 3506[6] 3797[13] (4483) (4696) 4749[5] 4767[5] 5315[2] 5610[9] 6160[5] 6564[7] 6706[7] 7055[8]

Lindbergh *J Ryan* a66 71
6 b g Bold Edge—Halland Park Girl (IRE) (Primo Dominie)
516[3] (584) 690[3] 749[2] 896[3] 964[9] 1541[7] 2205[9] 2983[11]

Lindelaan (USA) *Sir Michael Stoute* a73 98
3 ch f Rahy(USA) —Crystal Symphony (USA) (Red Ransom (USA))
1946[2] ◆ (2500) 2953[2] ◆ (3560) (4189) 5506[9] 6266[7]

Linden Lime *Jamie Poulton* a76 51
6 ch m Double Trigger(IRE) —Linden Grace (USA) (Mister Baileys)
268[6] 405[6]

Linden's Lady *J R Weymes* a21 54
8 b m Compton Place—Jubilee Place (IRE) (Prince Sabo)
3764[8] 3834[9] 4683[10] 4949[7] 5045[13] 5420[11]

L'Indiscreta *B Grizzetti* 98
3 b f Desert Prince(IRE) —I Remember (IRE) (Dominion)
1659a[4] 2231a[5] 7253a[16] 7349a[5]

Lindner (GER) *W Hickst* 102
3 b c Golan(IRE) —Lindenblute (Surumu (GER))
6156a[3] 6664a[5]

Lindoro *W R Swinburn* a93 93
4 b g Marju(IRE) —Floppie (FR) (Law Society (USA))
1426[10] 1988[3] (2674) ◆ 3039[2] 3744[8] 4893[6] 6277[6] 6576[3] 6911[4]

Lindy Hop (IRE) *W R Swinburn* a63 57
2 b f Danehill Dancer(IRE) —Healing Music (FR) (Bering)
5788[6] 6273[6]

Lindy Lou *C F Wall* a61 72
4 b m Hernando(FR) —Daylight Dreams (Indian Ridge)
1959[7] 2533[7] 5163[2] 5637[4] (6007) 6662[P]

Linlithgow (IRE) *P Bowen* a46 58
4 gr g Linamix(FR) —Diarshana (GER) (Darshaan)
2245[13]

Linnet Park *J G Given* a52 62
3 b f Compton Place—Shifty Mouse (Night Shift (USA))
1475[2] 1769[5] 2823[5] 4216[15] 4686[6] 5015[3] 5421[7] 6595[9]

Linngari (IRE) *Sir Michael Stoute* a89 122
6 ch h Indian Ridge—Lidakiya (IRE) (Kahyasi)
(294a) 651a[4] 1090a[14] 3100[10] (4470a) 5742a[2] 6816[3] 7685a[3]

Lion Gate (USA) *J H M Gosden* 52
3 b c Distant View(USA) —Viviana (USA) (Nureyev (USA))
4255[5] 4695[12]

Lion Sands *L M Cumani* a111 115
4 b g Montjeu(IRE) —Puce (Darshaan)
1980[5] 2625[4] (3497) 3878[4] 4585[3] 5094[8] 5694[5] 6303[5]

Lipi *Sir Michael Stoute* a39
2 gr c Sadler's Wells(USA) —Frosty Welcome (USA) (With Approval (CAN))
7554[9]

Lipocco *R M Beckett* 112
4 br g Piccolo—Magical Dancer (IRE) (Magical Wonder (USA))
2680[2] 3248[11] 4223a[5] 5890[12] 6289[3]

Lips Arrow (GER) *Andreas Lowe* 102
3 b f Big Shuffle(USA) —Lips Plane (IRE) (Ashkalani (IRE))
1375a[6] 4912a[5]

Lisathedaddy *B G Powell* a94 88
6 br m Darnay—Erith's Chill Wind (Be My Chief (USA))
138[3] 315[5] 502[6] 927[5] 2120[4] 2505[5] 2820[6] 3729[8] 4726[8] 4945[5] 5683[RR] 6403[7] 6904[8] 7210[RR]

Lisbon Lion (IRE) *N J Vaughan* 62
3 bg g Mull Of Kintyre(USA) —Ludovica (Bustino)
2336[6] 2847[8] 3473[4] 4859[3] 5415[11]

Lisburn (IRE) *M Brittain* 81
2 ch f Bahamian Bounty—Golden Fortune (Forzando)
(1474) 1813[3] 2167[8] 2507[7] 3809[5] 3978[3] (4594) 4956[3] 5381[3] 5855[8] 6247[11] 7199[3]

Lislin *S Kirk* a49 28
2 b f Monsieur Bond(IRE) —Ferrybridge (IRE) (Mister Baileys)
1693[10] 2048[8] 3158[3] 4340[8] 4823[4]

Lista Lightning (IRE) *Kevin Prendergast* a75 76
2 b g Intikhab(USA) —Alassio (USA) (Gulch (USA))
6320a[9]

Listen (IRE) *A P O'Brien* 115
3 b f Sadler's Wells(USA) —Brigid (USA) (Irish River (FR))
5730a[5] 6475[10]

Lisvale (IRE) *David Wachman* 115
3 b c Danehill Dancer(IRE) —Farthingale (IRE) (Nashwan (USA))
2435a[2] (3536a) 3983a[4]

Litenup (IRE) *A J Lidderdale* a55 40
2 b f Trans Island—Common Cause (Polish Patriot (USA))
6166[11] 6977[14] 7622[4]

Literato (FR) *Saeed Bin Suroor* 124
4 gr h Kendor(FR) —La Cibeles (FR) (Cardoun (FR))
1090a[12] 2238a[6]

Liteup My World (USA) *B Ellison* a61
2 ch g Hennessy(USA) —Liteup My Life (USA) (Green Dancer (USA))
6253[8] 6932[6] 7333[9]

Lithaam (IRE) *J M Bradley* a61 61
4 ch g Elnadim(USA) —Elhida (IRE) (Mujtahid (USA))
971[7] 1028[9] 1370[8] 1529[10] (3447) 3668[7] 4106[11] 4285[12] 4812[7] 5074[3] 5401[7] 6418[6] 6546[3] 7022[6] 7218[5] (7648) 7778[2] (7836)

Little Angel (IRE) *Miss V Haigh* a50 42
3 br f Auction House(USA) —Green Sea (Groom Dancer (USA))
1339[5]

Little Belle (USA) *Saeed Bin Suroor* a115
3 b f A.P. Indy(USA) —Dubai Belle (USA) (Mr Prospector (USA))
4235a[2] 6523a[4]

Little Blacknumber *R Hannon* a53
2 b f Superior Premium—The Synergist (Botanic (USA))
5286[6] 7388[6] 7452[4] 7833[5]

Little Bones *J F Coupland* a53 56
3 ch f Tobougg(IRE) —City Gambler (Rock City)
1592[7] 2088[4] 2399[6] 3026[9]

Little Calla (IRE) *E A L Dunlop* a59
2 ch f Indian Ridge—Queen Of Palms (IRE) (Desert Prince (IRE))
7546[4] ◆ 7810[4]

Little Carmela *S C Williams* a70 62
4 gr m Beat Hollow—Carmela Owen (Owington)
(7355) 7563[2] 7715[6]

Little Cee (IRE) *N J Hawke* a45 53
3 b f Averti(IRE) —Rivermead (USA) (Irish River (FR))
1499[5] 1960[12] 2341[7] 2946[9] 3395[14] 4806[9] 7801[11]

Littledodayno (IRE) *M Wigham* a70 63
5 b m Mujadil(USA) —Perfect Welcome (Taufan (USA))
56[6] (391) 515[8] 539[9] 766[7] 901[4] 4542[7] 5201[2] (5474) 5709[DSQ] 6766[12] 7292[6] (7471) 7762[4]

Little Dreams (FR) *F Rossi* 93
2 b c Della Francesca(USA) —Little Anchor (FR) (Kendor (FR))
4441a[2]

Little Eden (IRE) *T D Barron* a67 59
3 b g Piccolo—Paradise Eve (Bahamian Bounty)
(1027) 1769[2]

Little Edward *R J Hodges* a96 98
10 gr g King's Signet(USA) —Cedar Lady (Telsmoss)
(3320) 3647[6] 4928[11] 5509[6] 5906[4] 6669[8] 7215[11] 7297[2] 7378[2] (7675) 7756[4] 7826[2]

Little Evie *R J Hodges* 46
3 b f First Trump—Cedar Lady (Telsmoss)
3605[16]

Little Eye (IRE) *D K Weld* a68 85
7 b g Groom Dancer(USA) —Beaming (Mtoto)
3531a[14]

Little Fighter (GER) *H Blume* 98
3 bb c Montjeu(IRE) —Lohsa (IRE) (Aragon)
3074a[2] 4232a[4]

Little Finch (IRE) *Denis P Quinn* a47 54
3 b f Acclamation—Hard To Lay (IRE) (Dolphin Street (FR))
92[2] 237[5] 298[2] 767[11] 7637[10]

Little Firecracker *Miss M E Rowland* a61 62
3 b f Cadeaux Genereux—El Hakma (Shareef Dancer (USA))
262[2] (288) 803[4] 1034[6] 4898[10] 5602[7] 6227[13] 6757[7] 7149[7] 7373[9] 7678[12]

Little Hotpotch *M J Gingell* a23 39
4 b m Erhaab(USA) —Berzoud (Ezzoud (IRE))
282[13] 4376[3] 4599[6] 5070[11]

Little Jimbob *R A Fahey* a69 83
7 b g Desert Story(IRE) —Artistic Licence (High Top)
1700[2] 2073[4] 2499[3] (3077) (3954) 4217[2] 4541[5] (Dead)

Little Knickers *E J Creighton* a71 74
3 b f Prince Sabo—Pants (Pivotal)
582[4] 712[8] 899[3] 1063[3] 1203[3] 1479[5] (1671) 1738[4] 5617[2] 5998[5] 6387[6] 6736[6] 7601[6] 7803[10]

Little Lady (GER) *Frau Nina Bach* a38 83
3 ch f Dashing Blade—Lake House (IRE) (Be My Guest (USA))
201a[11]

Little Lily Morgan *R Bastiman* a33 42
5 gr m Kayf Tara—Cool Grey (Absalom)
600[10]

Little Lovely (IRE) *A G Newcombe* a58 54
3 ch f Mizzen Mast(USA) —Copper Play (USA) (Fast Play (USA))
343[6]

Littlemisssunshine (IRE) *Tracey Collins* a63 96
3 b f Oasis Dream—Sharp Catch (IRE) (Common Grounds)
2685a[8]

Little Miss Tara (IRE) *A B Haynes* a57 66
4 b m Namid—Circled (USA) (Cozzene (USA))
10[7] 352[13] 736[7]

Little Molly (IRE) *E J Creighton* 33
3 b f Namid—Molly-O (IRE) (Dolphin Street (FR))
1601[7] 1876[13]

Little Pandora *G P Kelly* a32
4 b m Komaite(USA) —Little Talitha (Lugana Beach)
2038[15] 6254[8] 6791[17]

Little Pete (IRE) *A M Balding* a67 95
3 ch g City On A Hill(USA) —Full Traceability (IRE) (Ron's Victory (USA))
2258[3] (2570) 3028[2] 3273[3] 3472[3] 3909[3] 4445[23] 4591[2] 4842[6] 5509[9] 5930[4]

Little Richard (IRE) *M Wellings* a68 59
9 b g Alhaarth(IRE) —Intricacy (Formidable (USA))
(125) 332[4] 575[5] 675[4] 720[2] 934[2] (1062) 6577[10] 7169[3] 7573[7] (7667)

Little Rococoa *R J Price* a39 11
3 b g Killer Instinct—Little Kenny (Warning)
997[11] 1695[13] 2046[12] 6762[13] 7274[6] 7379[8] 7504[7] 7701[7]

Little Sark (IRE) *P D Evans* 48
3 b g Singspiel(IRE) —Notenqueen (GER) (Turfkonig (GER))
961[9]

Little Tokyo (USA) *J Howard Johnson* 61
2 b g Langfuhr(CAN) —Tisourturn (USA) (Rhodes (USA))
2746[4] ◆ 3364[4] 4072[3] 4733[12] 5560[3] 5966[4] 6214[11]

Littleton Aldor (IRE) *Mark Gillard* a41 47
8 b g Pennekamp(USA) —Belle Etoile (FR) (Lead On Time (USA))
282[14]

Littleton Telchar (USA) *S W Hall* a76 66
8 ch g Atticus(USA) —Miss Waikiki (USA) (Miswaki (USA))
3165[3] 3501[8] 4081[14] 4739[7] 5873a[8] 6366a[12]

Little Toto *C G Cox* a63 64
3 b c Mtoto—Moonlight Seas (Sabrehill (USA))
785[3] 1274[7] 3690[5]

Little Warrior (ITY) *B Simonaggio* 60
4 b h Della Scala(IRE) —Secretville (ITY) (Classic Secret (USA))
2029a[9]

Little White Lie (IRE) *J R Jenkins* a96 111
4 b g Orpen(USA) —Miss Informed (IRE) (Danehill (USA))
829a[6] 960[11] 1105a[17] 2545[2] (2789) (3921) 4869[3] 5313[2] 6476[4] (7201) 7492[6]

Little Wing (IRE) *J A Osborne* a93 66
3 b c Hawk Wing(USA) —Hartstown House (IRE) (Primo Dominie)
(483) ◆ (619) 723[5]

Littonfountain (IRE) *K R Burke* a55
3 b g Desert Style(IRE) —Idle Chat (USA) (Assert)
589[4] 712[6] 853[5]

Littorio (AUS) *Nigel Blackiston* 115
4 b g Bellotto(USA) —Our Centasea (AUS) (Centaine (AUS))
6835a[5] 7188a[13]

Liturgical (USA) *M A Magnusson* a79 77
2 b c Songandaprayer(USA) —Ra Hydee (USA) (Rahy (USA))
2098[6] 2458[2] 2972[4] (3277)

Lively Fling (USA) *J H M Gosden* 56
2 b c Dynaformer(USA) —Creaking Board (Night Shift (USA))
5857[8]

Liverpool Echo (FR) *Mrs K Waldron* 44
8 b g Poliglote—Miss Echo (Chief Singer)
2952[11]

Living On A Prayer *Thomas McLaughlin* a53 59
5 b m Josr Algarhoud(IRE) —Denton Lady (Inchinor)
1262[4] ◆ 2286[2] 2752[2] 2844[2]

Livvy Inn (USA) *Miss Lucinda V Russell* 59
3 ch g Woodman(USA) —London Be Good (USA) (Storm Bird (CAN))
1825[2] 1950[5] 2750[6] 3580[3] 4147[3] 4630[7]

Lizarazu (GER) *D J Wintle* a50 62
9 b g Second Set(IRE) —Lilly (GER) (Motley (USA))
289[6] 804[9] 862[8]

Lizard Island (USA) *Jane Chapple-Hyam* a94 110
3 b c Danehill Dancer(IRE) —Add (USA) (Spectacular Bid (USA))
292a[4] 812a[3] 6073[12] 6576[10]

Liz Long *P Howling* a43 44
3 b f Reel Buddy(USA) —Surrealist (ITY) (Night Shift (USA))
73[3]

Lizzie Wiggins *Mrs Marjorie Fife* a69 63
3 gr f Mujahid(USA) —Amarella (FR) (Balleroy (USA))
(1245) 1959[5] 2496[6] 3127[F] 3791[2] 4898[7] 5399[5] 6217[11] 6685[13]

Llab Nala *M R Channon* a59 54
3 gr g Tobougg(IRE) —Zilkha (Petong)
333[5] 501[2] 572[2] 732[3] 1051[4] 1166[3] 1216[4] 1912[16] 2041[18] 3397[13] 3572[6]

Loaderfun (IRE) *I W McInnes* a47 80
6 br g Danehill Dancer(IRE) —Sideloader Special (Song)
11[10] 174[5] 254[7]

Lobby *Mrs A J Perrett* a37 64
3 ch c Dr Fong(USA) —Real Trust (USA) (Danzig (USA))
3521[6] 5605[10]

Lobengula (IRE) *I W McInnes* a92 70
6 b g Spectrum(IRE) —Playwaki (USA) (Miswaki (USA))
1502[11] 1793[8] 1910[14]

Local Poet *Ollie Pears* a73 65
7 b g Robellino(USA) —Laugharne (Known Fact (USA))
155[4] 433[4] 553[2] 844[9] 1705[8] 2250[11]

Location *Mrs A J Perrett* 49
2 b f Dansili—Well Away (IRE) (Sadler's Wells (USA))
4562[4]

Loched Up *P A Blockley* a31 44
2 b c Mull Of Kintyre(USA) —Princesse Sonia (FR) (Ashkalani (IRE))
2239[3] 3821[8] 5041[7] 6059[13]

Lochiel *G A Swinbank* a89 82
4 b g Mind Games—Summerhill Special (IRE) (Roi Danzig (USA))
(1825) 2249[2] (2579) 2939[11] (3368) 5391[6] 6154[5] 7230[2] 7493[3] (7657) 7747[2]

Loch Jipp (USA) *J S Wainwright* 98
3 b f Belong To Me(USA) —Miss Keyonna (USA) (Septieme Ciel (USA))
1698[10] 2594[8] 3041[7] 3252[9] 4617[9]

Lochstar *A M Balding* a89 76
4 b g Anabaa(USA) —Lochsong (Song)
4668[10] 5936[2] 6650[5]

Loch Verdi *A M Balding* 98
5 b m Green Desert(USA) —Lochsong (Song)
5509[8] 5793[2] 6121[11]

Lock 'N' Load (IRE) *B Smart* 70
2 b f Johannesburg(USA) —Margay (IRE) (Marju (IRE))
3292[8] 4380[4] 6655[7]

Lockstone Lad (USA) *M S Saunders* 53
5 gr g Mazel Trick(USA) —Humble (USA) (Valiant Nature (USA))
3310[8] 3362[5] 3871[7]

Locum *M H Tompkins* a73 66
3 ch g Dr Fong(USA) —Exhibitor (USA) (Royal Academy (USA))
1057[3] 2043[9] 2801[2] 3436[4] 4427[6] 6337[4] 6437[3] ◆ 7070[3] 7364[2] 7489[2] 7604[4]

Lodgician (IRE) *K G Reveley* 53
6 b g Grand Lodge(USA) —Dundel (IRE) (Machiavellian (USA))
2185[11] 2849[10] 3863[9] 4220[7] 4452[2] ◆ 5385[13]

Lodi (IRE) *J Akehurst* a85 91
3 ch g Bertolini(USA) —Lady Of Leisure (USA) (Diesis)
1995[3] 2555[4] ◆ 2998[6] (3324) 4252[10] 4864[3] 5056[9] 5580[5] 6124[2] 6478[11] 6902[8] 7215[5]

Lois Darlin (IRE) *R A Harris* a55 43
2 ch f Indian Haven—Miriana (IRE) (Bluebird (USA))
995[8] 1111[3] 1680[13] 6223[11] 6343[4] 6877[5] 6986[10] 7537[4] 7734[3] 7810[3]

L'Oiseau De Feu (USA) *Mrs K Waldron* a23 60
4 b g Stravinsky(USA) —Off You Go (USA) (Seattle Slew (USA))
2001[7] 2643[3] 3179[7]

Lombok *G Wragg* 48
2 b c Hernando(FR) —Miss Rinjani (Shirley Heights)
6777[10]

Lomica *Miss J A Camacho* a29 60
2 ch f Lomitas—Ecstatic (Nashwan (USA))
5256[8] 5716[4] 6451[9]

London Bid (USA) *Sir Michael Stoute* 58
3 br f Rainbow Quest(USA) —Islington (IRE) (Sadler's Wells (USA))
3810[4] 4166[8]

London Bridge *J H M Gosden* 81
2 br c Beat Hollow—Cantanta (Top Ville)
6977[2] ◆

London Times (IRE) *M Johnston* 73
3 ch g Lomitas—Vituisa (Bering)
2668[4] 3471[5]

Lonely Star (IRE) *D R Lanigan* a49 73
2 b f Bachelor Duke(USA) —Soviet Belle (IRE) (Soviet Star (USA))
5468[5] ◆ 6167[10] 6392[3] ◆ 6674[8]

Lonesome Maverick (IRE) *Donal Kinsella* 86
4 gr g Celtic Swing—Abyat (USA) (Shadeed (USA))
4576a[5]

Lone Star (GER) *M Trybuhl* a77 88
3 ch c Kalatos(GER) —Luzelia (GER) (Stanford)
2880a[5]

Lone Wolfe *Jane Chapple-Hyam* a97 100
4 b g Foxhound(USA) —Fleet Hill (IRE) (Warrshan (USA))
3040[7] 3491[14] 4417[8] 5697[2] 6624[3] 6902[3] 7394[3] (7576) 7756[3]

Longboat Key *M Johnston* a36 77
2 b c Dr Fong(USA) —You Are The One (Unfuwain (USA))
6451[7] 6892[3]

Long Distance (FR) *J R Fanshawe* a76 72
3 bb g Storming Home—Lovers Luck (IRE) (Anabaa (USA))
(5477) ◆ 6012[7] 7711[3]

Longevity *W Jarvis* a78 69
3 b c Olden Times—Gevity (Kris)
1467[4] (2084) 2563[6] 5836[14]

Long Gone *John A Harris* a6 34
5 b m Mtoto—Absentee (Slip Anchor)
1[4] 322[12]

Longoria (IRE) *Lucinda Featherstone* a81 69
3 bb f Fasliyev(USA) —Shangri La (IRE) (Sadler's Wells (USA))
(186) (1637) ◆ 2149[7]

Long Road (USA) *Niall Madden* 58
7 b g Diesis—Tuviah (USA) (Eastern Echo (USA))
4003a[9]

Longspur *M W Easterby* a75 84
4 br g Singspiel(IRE) —Bunting (Shaadi (USA))
1569[14] 1793[6] 2107[9] 2623[5] 2822[12] 3258[5]

Longville (GER) *H J Brown* 102
4 br h Lando(GER) —La Paz (GER) (Roi Dagobert)
293a[3] 491a[5]

Longy The Lash *Paul Murphy* 20
5 b g Contract Law(USA) —Hello Hobson'S (IRE) (Fayruz)
681[10] 839[6] 915[11]

Lonsdale Lad *R C Guest* a24 20
2 b g Elusive City(USA) —Winchcombe (Danehill (USA))
1722[6] 2657[11] 5959[14] 7443[8] 7543[8] 7689[8] 7773[9]

Lookafternumberone (IRE) *J G Given* 72
2 gr c Verglas(IRE) —Septieme Face (USA) (Lit De Justice (USA))
2331[4] 2730[3] 5072[2] 5363[3] 5632[2] 5960[5] 7052[7]

Look Busy (IRE) *A Berry* 113
3 b f Danetime(IRE) —Unfortunate (Komaite (USA))
1772[4] (1945) (2390) (3252) 3927[4] (4240) 4660[6] (5259) (5551a) 5884[2] 6121[4]

Look For Value *N Tinkler* 39
2 b f Auction House(USA) —Fresh Look (IRE) (Alzao (USA))
1967[8] 2584[13] 4734[12] 5106[7] 5357[3] 5774[10]

Look Here *R M Beckett* 121
3 b f Hernando(FR) —Last Look (Rainbow Quest (USA))
1991[2] (2792) 5892[3]

Lookouthereicome *T T Clement*
7 b m Rudimentary(USA) —Sylvatica (Thatching)
4821[13]

Looks Could Kill (USA) *A B Haynes* a60 73
6 bb g Red Ransom(USA) —Mingling Glances (USA) (Woodman (USA))
1842[16] 2692[11]

Look So *R M Beckett* a90 87
4 b m Efisio—Last Look (Rainbow Quest (USA))
(1365) (1903)

Looks The Business (IRE) *W G M Turner* a69 59
7 b g Marju(IRE) —Business Centre (IRE) (Digamist (USA))
(18) 122[7] 182[3] 794[3] 859[3] 1310[2] 1668[4] 2072[3] 2353[9] 2755[3] (3321) 4811[5] 5154[8] 6882[13]

Looktheotherway (IRE) *J G M O'Shea* 58
4 br m Val Royal(FR) —Gold Stamp (Golden Act (USA))
2100[7] 2453[4] 3059[11] 3901[6]

Look To This Day *R Charlton* a46 79
3 ch f In The Wings—Yanka (USA) (Blushing John (USA))
2328[9] 3894[7] 4249[6] (5216) 6079[8] 6630[7]

Looping The Loop (USA) *J G Portman* a49 56
3 rg g Alphabet Soup(USA) —Citidance Missy (USA) (Citidancer (USA))
1252[11] 1467[17] 2046[10] 6018[5] 6421[9]

Loose Caboose (IRE) *A J McCabe* a78 68
3 b f Tagula(IRE) —Tama (IRE) (Indian Ridge)
17[4] 170[4] 364[3] 470[6] 619[2] 849[2] (952) 1484[13] (1584) 1764[2] 1934[3] 3554[11] 4900[8] 5403[5] 6623[5] 7047[8] 7315[11] 7730[9]

Loose Leaf (USA) *Kenneth McPeek* a101 86
4 b h Notebook(USA) —Claire's Smile (USA) (Carson City (USA))
5558a[5]

Looter (FR) *J L Dunlop* a59 55
3 b g Red Ransom(USA) —Water Echo (USA) (Mr Prospector (USA))
1161[7] 2613[3] 3022[5] 3763[7] 4533[5] 4807[6] 5086[6]

Lopinot (IRE) *M R Bosley* a80 77
5 br g Pursuit Of Love—La Suquet (Puissance)
34[6] 246[6] 2722[10] 3422[7] 3764[3] 4306[12] (4772) 5458[12] 5604[11] 7513[8] 7790[7]

L'Orage *M G Quinlan* a20 48
3 b f Storming Home—Rosa Canina (Bustino)
1279[5] 1549[5] 2080[5]

Lord Admiral (USA) *Charles O'Brien* a103 116
7 b h El Prado(IRE) —Lady Ilsley (USA) (Trempolino (USA))
(383a) 651a[3] (818a) 1090a[10] 2026a[2] 4356a[2] 5732a[5] 6504a[4] 6995a[8]

Lord Chancellor (IRE) *M Johnston* a80 77
2 b c King's Best(USA) —Summer Serenade (Sadler's Wells (USA))
6720[3] 7434[4] 7660[2] ◆

Lord Deevert *W G M Turner* a68 63
3 br g Averti(IRE) —Dee-Lady (Deploy)
(93) 222[2] 339[4] 2480[6] 2803[4] 3021[9] 3406[2] 3572[4] (3678) (4090) 4413[6] (6880) 7225[3] 7435[9] 7834[6]

Lord Fasliyev (IRE) *L D'Auria*
2 b c Fasliyev(USA) —Freccia D'Oro (GER) (Acatenango (GER))
2745a[5]

Lord Hill (GER) *C Zeitz* 114
4 b h Tiger Hill(IRE) —Lady Fox (GER) (Monsun (GER))
2440a[4] 3306a[7] 5528a[2] 6156a[4] 6692a[3] 7350a[3]

Lord Laing (USA) *H J Collingridge* a53 48
5 bb g Chester House(USA) —Johanna Keene (USA) (Raise A Cup (USA))
420[3] 541[7] 2353[14] 2884[7] 4029[8] 4701[9] 7473[13]

Lord Nellsson *A B Haynes* a52 54
12 b g Arctic Lord—Miss Petronella (Petoski)
152[9] 4105[13]

Lord Of Adventure (IRE) *Mrs L C Jewell* a33 37
6 b g Inzar(USA) —Highly Fashionable (IRE) (Polish Precedent (USA))
545[P]

Lord Of Dreams (IRE) *G L Moore* a69 10
6 ch g Barathea(IRE) —The Multiyorker (IRE) (Digamist (USA))
316[6] 430[5] 546[2] ◆ (631) 935[5] 1895[10]

Lord Of Esteem *J Ryan* a54 51
3 ch c Mark Of Esteem(IRE) —Lady Rockstar (Rock Hopper)
5278[14] 5407[13]

Lord Of The Dance (IRE) *J M P Eustace* a60
2 ch c Indian Haven—Maine Lobster (USA) (Woodman (USA))
7204[7]

Lord Of The Flame *W De Best-Turner* 16
2 br g Largesse—Maylan (IRE) (Lashkari)
6075[6]

Lord Of The Reins (IRE) *J G Given* a84 91
4 b g Imperial Ballet(IRE) —Waroonga (IRE) (Brief Truce (USA))
126[5] (286) 459[3] 574[6] 875[3] 994[7] ◆ (1242) (1582) ◆ 1802[2] ◆ 2501[3] 3009[3] 3336[8] ◆ 3881[6] 4201[8] 4418[2] (5250) 5796[11] 6354[11] 6650[16]

Lord Orpen (IRE) *Patrick Morris* a41 51
4 b g Orpen(USA) —Kenyane (IRE) (Kahyasi)
387[6] 415[7]

Lord Rathvinden (IRE) *Tracey Collins* 68
3 ch c Captain Rio—With Finesse (Be My Guest (USA))
4715a[6]

Lord Sandicliffe (IRE) *B W Hills* 80
3 ch c Spartacus(IRE) —Devious Miss (IRE) (Dr Devious (IRE))
1623[5] 1999[6] 3723[12] 5962[8] 6363[8]

Lord's Bidding *R Ingram* a59 64
3 b c Auction House(USA) —Lady Ploy (Deploy)
940[2] 1147[8] 1539[3] 1871[2] 2310[9] 2997[4] 3483[6]

Lord Shanakill (USA) *K R Burke* 117
2 b c Speightstown(USA) —Green Room (USA) (Theatrical)
1447[3] (2134) 3103[3] ◆ 4517[2] 5330a[3] 5852[5] (6119) 6815[2]

Lordship (IRE) *A W Carroll* a58 72
4 b g King's Best(USA) —Rahika Rose (Unfuwain (USA))
2010[9] 2478[4] ◆ 2556[3] 2693[3] 3181[8] 3366[2] 3725[7] 3903[2] 4927[7] 5168[6] 6056[14] 6178[6] 6560[7] 6585[11] 6928[4]

Lordswood (IRE) *J R Best* a60 50
4 b g Mark Of Esteem(IRE) —Dinwood (Charnwood Forest (IRE))
44[6] (99) ◆ 123[5] 176[4] (352) 546[3] 675[6] 886[5] 2053[10] 2755[10] 4267[8] 4371[10] 4748[15]

Lord Theo *N P Littmoden* a81 86
4 b g Averti(IRE) —Love You Too (Be My Chief (USA))
274[4] 509[7] 747[2] 1048[3] 1273[6] 1456[2] 1719[13] 2057[3] 2334[3] 3006[16] 4627[6] 4723[13] 5290[7] 5600[8] 6177[9] 6577[7] (7094) 7440[2] 7580[6] 7742[8]

Lorikeet *G L Moore* a79 77
9 b g Rainbow Quest(USA) —Destiny Dance (USA) (Nijinsky (CAN))
185[6] 358[6] 540[3] 710[2] 880[2] 1052[5] 1337[7] 1856[5] (Dead)

Los Gigantes (FR) *J-C Rouget* 91
2 b c Kendor(FR) —Suerte (Halling (USA))
5139a[6]

Los Nadis (GER) *P Monteith* 81
4 ch g Hernando(FR) —La Estrella (GER) (Desert King (IRE))
981[11] 4972[2] 6071[3] 7223[7]

Lost All Alone *D M Simcock* a58 49
4 b h Bertolini(USA) —Wandering Stranger (Petong)
131[0] 181[3] 255[7] 5582[5] (7522) 7637[5]

Lost In Paris (IRE) *T D Easterby* 62
2 b g Elusive City(USA) —Brazilia (Forzando)
3170[5] 5959[9] 6158[4] 6603[4] 6857[14]

Lost Soldier Three (IRE) *D Nicholls* 98
7 b g Barathea(IRE) —Donya (Mill Reef (USA))
2625[12] 3295[5] 5894[8] (6113) 6652[4]

Lough Beg (IRE) *Miss Tor Sturgis* a65 49
5 b g Close Conflict(USA) —Mia Gigi (Hard Fought)
(8) (299) 387[4] 874[4] (1206) 2512[5] 6775[10]

Lough Diver (IRE) *M H Tompkins* 80
3 gr g Act One—Spicebird (IRE) (Ela-Mana-Mou)
2669[7] 3813[4] 4871[2] (5931) 6427[6] 6948[17]

Louidor *J R Boyle* a58 75
2 b g Lujain(USA) —Simonida (IRE) (Royal Academy (USA))
4482[2] 4907[8] 5430[7]

Louie's Lad *J A Geake* 52
2 gr g Compton Place—Silver Louie (IRE) (Titus Livius (FR))
3092[6] 4274[8] 4480[10] 4975[10] 5228[14] 5933[4] 6540[7] 7082[5]

Louise Bonne (USA) *C G Cox* 5
2 bb f Yes It's True(USA) —Blushing Issue (USA) (Blushing John (USA))
4251[15]

Louisiade (IRE) *M C Chapman* a73 64
7 b g Tagula(IRE) —Titchwell Lass (Lead On Time (USA))
(66) 250[3] (367) 432[2] (553) 601[2] 639[3] 791[4] 1188[8] 1260[6] 1449[16] 2550[9] 2897[11] 3218[7] 3591[10] 4156[10] 4371[7] 4603[6] 7184[3] 7441[4] 7533[5] 7619[9] 7698[8] 7731[4] 7772[3]

Louis Seffens (USA) *G A Swinbank* 70
3 b c Elusive Quality(USA) —Miss Seffens (USA) (Dehere (USA))
1068[12] 2008[17] 6528[10]

Loulou (USA) *S A Callaghan* a59
2 ch f El Prado(IRE) —Hatoof (USA) (Irish River (FR))
5570[5] 6282[6] 6597[14] 7257[9]

Lounaos (FR) *Eoin Griffin* 89
5 b m Limnos(JPN) —Luanda (IRE) (Bigstone (IRE))
1655a[6]

Loup Breton (IRE) *E Lellouche* 118
4 b h Anabaa(USA) —Louve (USA) (Irish River (FR))
(1240a) 2238a[3] 3121[7] 5557a[7] 6499a[2] 7685a[6]

Louphole *P J Makin* a81 75
6 ch g Loup Sauvage(USA) —Goodwood Lass (IRE) (Alzao (USA))
55[4] 94[2] 329[7] 1567[5] 3506[5] 4051[2] 4341[6] 4809[4] 6046[3] (6435) 6880[6]

Loutka (FR) *A De Royer-Dupre* 99
3 b f Trempolino(USA) —Arionella (Bluebird (USA))
(3018a) 4657a[9] 7037a[13]

Love Academy *Luke Comer* a40 12
13 b g Royal Academy(USA) —Quiet Week-End (Town And Country)
821[6] 1148[P]

Love Academy (GER) *P Schiergen* 101
3 ch f Medicean—Laurencia (Shirley Heights)
2065a[2] 2655a[4]

Love And Glory (FR) *G L Moore* a65 70
3 b c Intikhab(USA) —La Splendide (FR) (Slip Anchor)
1530[6] 2045[6] (2719) 3004[6] 3586[5] 6558[4]

Love Angel (USA) *J J Bridger* a57 51
6 bb g Woodman(USA) —Omnia (USA) (Green Dancer (USA))
934[8] 1152[6] 2072[5] 2617[5] 3614[13]

Love Cat (USA) *K A Ryan* 47
3 bb g Stormin Fever(USA) —Remuda (USA) (Gilded Time (USA))
1193[8]

Love Dancing (ARG) *Saeed Bin Suroor* a77
4 br m Salt Lake(USA) —Le Midi (ARG) (Fitzcarraldo (ARG))
201a[7] 473a[8] 744a[3]

Love Empire (USA) *M Johnston* a65 47
3 b g Empire Maker(USA) —Gioconda (USA) (Nijinsky (CAN))
221[5] 547[2] 632[2] 940[3] 2750[10] 3566[4] 4147[4] 4477[8] 5593[10] 6594[4]

Love Galore (IRE) *M Johnston* 106
3 b c Galileo(IRE) —Lobmille (Mill Reef (USA))
2142[2] 2425[3] 3155[25] 3877[4] 4160[2] (4519) 5508[11] 5741a[5] 6120[13] 6444[7]

Loveinanelevator *M L W Bell* a67 74
3 ch f Dr Fong(USA) —Londonnetdotcom (IRE) (Night Shift (USA))
1270[6] 1964[8] 2429[9] ◆ 2946[3] 3481[2] (3731) 4300[7] 4795[3] 5836[9]

Love Intrigue (IRE) *A Peraino* 104
3 b f Marju(IRE) —Love Contest (IRE) (Love The Groom (USA))
(1659a) 2029a[7]

Lovelace *M Johnston* a112 118
4 b h Royal Applause—Loveleaves (Polar Falcon (USA))
832[3] 959[8] 2235a[7] 2607[7] 3197[8] (3740) 3921[2] (5596a) 5740a[7] 6504a[9]

Lovely Dream (IRE) *Patrick Morris* a39 70
3 ch f Elnadim(USA) —Bid Dancer (Spectacular Bid (USA))
6366a[29]

Lovely Lilling *P T Midgley* a13 25
3 ch f Presidium—Coney Hills (Beverley Boy)
1019[11] 2038[16] 3144[10] 3712[15] 4216[11] 5110[9] 6224[9]

Lovely Steps (USA) *D M Simcock* a40
2 bb f Gone West(USA) —Magicalmysterycat (USA) (Storm Cat (USA))
7561[8] 7735[5]

Lovely Thought *W J Haggas* 62
2 b f Dubai Destination(USA) —Fairy Flight (IRE) (Fairy King (USA))
3923[7] 4328[9] 4926[6] (7052)

Love Of Dubai (USA) *C E Brittain* a85 105
3 b f More Than Ready(USA) —Diamond Kris (USA) (Prospect Bay (CAN))
201a[6] 496a[3] 744a[2] 1332[6] 1470[12] (2231a) 2655a[3] 3194[11] 3852[11]

Loveofmylife *R M Beckett* a35 57
3 gr f Dr Fong(USA) —True Love (Robellino (USA))
1477[4] 1896[6] 2475[3] 3574[2] 4334[7] 5027[8] 6248[7]

Love On Sight *J R Boyle* a75 85
4 b m Beat Hollow—Greek Dream (USA) (Distant View (USA))
536[3] 694[6] 807[4] (896) ◆ 1146[10] 2692[2] 3210[4] 3636[8]

Love Pegasus (USA) *M Johnston* a77 61
2 bb c Fusaichi Pegasus(USA) —Take Charge Lady (USA) (Dehere (USA))
6655[6] 7552[4]

Lovers Quest (IRE) *G M Lyons* a60 72
2 b f Pyrus(USA) —Amorous Pursuits (Pursuit Of Love)
6320a^{21}

Lovespell (USA) *Ms J S Doyle* 59
3 ch f Diesis—Loose Arrow (USA) (Lyphard (USA))
2123^{13} 2454^{10} 3350^{6} 5269^{13} 5913^{13}

Love To Dance (IRE) *A P O'Brien* a74 94
3 b f Sadler's Wells(USA) —Lagrion (USA) (Diesis)
3070a^{7} 4007a^{18} 4833a^{7} 5920a^{3}

Love You Always (USA) *Jane Chapple-Hyam* a48 45
8 ch g Woodman(USA) —Encorenous (USA) (Diesis)
189^{5} 400^{4} 691^{7} 770^{11}

Love You Louis *J R Jenkins* a75 76
2 b c Mark Of Esteem(IRE) —Maddie's A Jem (Emperor Jones (USA))
1873^{3} 2424^{6} (2759) 4190^{23} 6183^{3} 6807^{5} 7334^{6} 7575^{3} ◆ 7820^{2}

Low Flyer (USA) *T D Barron* a54 63
3 rg g Runaway Groom(CAN) —To The Right (USA) (Saint Ballado (CAN))
656^{4} ◆ 2041^{7} 2911^{5} 3213^{5} 3549^{8}

Lowry's Art *R M Beckett* a52 63
3 b f Night Shift(USA) —Creme Caramel (USA) (Septieme Ciel (USA))
(998) 1271^{9}

Loyalist (SAF) *S Seemar* a71 96
7 ch g Dominion Royale—Court Belle (SAF) (Royal Prerogative)
291a^{3} 497a^{6} 666a^{3} 738a^{5} 5556a^{10}

Loyal Knight (IRE) *S Kirk* a75 75
3 ch g Choisir(AUS) —Always True (USA) (Geiger Counter (USA))
3325^{11} 3745^{8} 4332^{8} 4732^{6} 5167^{6} 6036^{10}

Loyal Royal (IRE) *J M Bradley* a68 80
5 b g King Charlemagne(USA) —Supportive (IRE) (Nashamaa)
1033^{7} 3024^{8} 3363^{3} 4103^{7} 4186^{13} 5374^{8} 6357^{13} 7414^{5} 7508^{9} 7521^{3} 7705^{3} (7818)

Luberon *M Johnston* a109 101
5 b g Fantastic Light(USA) —Luxurious (USA) (Lyphard (USA))
1180^{2} ◆ 1503^{2} (2168) 4444^{3} ◆ 4504^{17} 5508^{10} 6233^{5} 6784^{2}

Luca Brasi (FR) *F Castro* a105 48
4 b h Singspiel(IRE) —Diamond Field (USA) (Mr Prospector (USA))
2708a^{8} 5958a^{11}

Lucarno (USA) *J H M Gosden* a89 122
4 b h Dynaformer(USA) —Vignette (USA) (Diesis)
2543^{11} 3542a^{6} (3878) 4406^{7} 5736a^{5} 6506a^{8}

Lucayan Dancer *D Nicholls* a77 88
8 b g Zieten(USA) —Tittle Tattle (IRE) (Soviet Lad (USA))
962^{10} (1041) 1164^{3} 1305^{5} 1521^{2} 1732^{3} 1947^{8} 2220^{8} 2697^{5} 2904^{5} (3474) 4066^{3} (4541) (4701) 5994^{5} 6312^{8}

Lucayos *K R Burke* a96 90
5 ch g Bahamian Bounty—Indian Flag (IRE) (Indian Ridge)
137^{4} 226^{6} 337^{6} 532^{6} 707^{4} 1211^{9} 1500^{7} 1683^{2} 1928^{8} 2679^{12} 2831^{8} 3587^{6} (4700) ◆ 5222^{10} 5433^{2} 5648^{5} 5936^{3} 7384^{12}

Lucefer (IRE) *G C H Chung* a23 47
10 b g Lycius(USA) —Maharani (USA) (Red Ransom (USA))
5427^{6}

Lucerne *W J Knight* a52
2 br f One Cool Cat(USA) —Salagama (IRE) (Alzao (USA))
7380^{7} (Dead)

Lucidor (GER) *Frau E Mader* 100
5 b g Zafonic(USA) —La Felicita (Shareef Dancer (USA))
6156a^{5} 6692a^{4}

Lucies Pride (IRE) *M Halford* a62 84
3 b f Noverre(USA) —Ghassak (IRE) (Persian Bold)
6511a^{6}

Lucifer Sam (USA) *A P O'Brien* 102
3 b c Storm Cat(USA) —Rafina (USA) (Mr Prospector (USA))
1361a^{5} 2032a^{19} 3536a^{6}

Lucius Verrus (USA) *D Shaw* a68 8
8 b g Danzig(USA) —Magic Of Life (USA) (Seattle Slew (USA))
13^{7} 71^{7} 115^{2} 285^{6} 530^{3} 615^{3} 792^{6} 844^{10}

Luckette *M Brittain* 24
2 b f Lucky Story(USA) —Thea (USA) (Marju (IRE))
2134^{10} 2584^{12}

Luckier (IRE) *S Kirk* a73
2 gr f Key Of Luck(USA) —Ibiza (GER) (Linamix (FR))
7341^{7} 7577^{2} (7708)

Luck Money (IRE) *P F I Cole* 107
3 b c Indian Ridge—Dundel (IRE) (Machiavellian (USA))
2409^{9}

Luck Will Come (IRE) *H J Collingridge* a72 72
4 b m Desert Style(IRE) —Petite Maxine (Sharpo)
1867^{9} 2533^{2} (3293) 3866^{3} 4282^{3} 4572^{2} (4945) 5536^{8} 6422^{13}

Luck Wud Have It (IRE) *Patrick J Flynn* a77 85
4 b g Key Of Luck(USA) —Disregard That (IRE) (Don't Forget Me)
4514a^{7} 5873a^{4}

Lucky Art (USA) *J Howard Johnson* 85
2 b g Johannesburg(USA) —Syrian Summer (USA) (Damascus (USA))
2775^{5} 3707^{4} (4647) 6274^{8} 6807^{6}

Lucky Bid *J M Bradley* 16
2 b g Josr Algarhoud(IRE) —Double Fault (IRE) (Zieten (USA))
2916^{18} 3358^{13} 3670^{12} 4321^{10}

Lucky Buddha *Jedd O'Keeffe* 55
2 gr c Kyllachy—Heaven-Liegh-Grey (Grey Desire)
1390^{8} 1967^{10} 2462^{5}

Lucky Character *N J Vaughan* a47 42
3 b g Key Of Luck(USA) —Gay Heroine (Caerleon (USA))
310^{7} 645^{6} 1410^{9} 3030^{7} 3549^{2} 4044^{6} 5574^{5} 7581^{13}

Lucky Copy (USA) *Todd Pletcher* 98
3 ch f Unbridled's Song(USA) —Perfect Copy (USA) (Deputy Minister (CAN))
5744a^{2}

Lucky Dan (IRE) *Paul Green* a61 62
2 b g Danetime(IRE) —Katherine Gorge (USA) (Hansel (USA))
2746^{U} 4658^{9} 6764^{4} 7020^{5} 7454^{6} 7612^{6} 7825^{2}

Lucky Dance (BRZ) *A G Foster* a88 96
6 b h Mutakddim(USA) —Linda Francesa (ARG) (Equalize (USA))
379a^{7} 495a^{11} 673a^{5} 4417^{10} 4856^{7} 5360^{6} 6103^{7} 6536^{6} 6654^{4} (7146) 7245^{11}

Lucky Dancer *D R C Elsworth* a56
3 ch g Selkirk(USA) —Spot Prize (USA) (Seattle Dancer (USA))
7757^{5} 7822^{6}

Luckydolly (IRE) *F Costello* a64 58
2 ch f Daggers Drawn(USA) —Dolly Dimpler (IRE) (Nordico (USA))
6320a^{11} 7734^{2}

Lucky Find (SAF) *M F De Kock* a116 113
5 ch g Rich Man's Gold(USA) —Little Erna (SAF) (Ernani)
(203a) (476a) 817a^{3} 1092a^{6} (6287) 7147^{5}

Lucky Forteen *P W Hiatt* a31
5 b m Forzando—Grey Blade (Dashing Blade)
6091^{11} 7363^{8}

Lucky Fortune (IRE) *Miss Amy Weaver* a64
2 ch g Lucky Story(USA) —Majborah (IRE) (Entrepreneur)
7333^{11} 7458^{9} 7767^{4}

Lucky Girl (GER) *Miss A Casotti*
7 b m Monsun(GER) —Lilian (GER) (Acatenango (GER))
423a^{10}

Lucky In Love (IRE) *Mark Gillard* a1
2 b f Lucky Owners(NZ) —Into Orbit (Safawan)
5614^{9} 5866^{9}

Lucky Kyllachy (USA) *Jane Chapple-Hyam* a77 96
4 bb h Kyllachy—Intangible (USA) (Diesis)
259^{7} 1079^{5}

Lucky Larkin (IRE) *J T Gorman* a57 62
2 b c Pyrus(USA) —Lucky Bet (IRE) (Lucky Guest)
5294a^{13}

Lucky Leigh *M R Channon* 95
2 b f Piccolo—Solmorin (Fraam)
(2035) 3123^{4} 3851^{5} 4323^{2} 5055^{8}

Lucky Numbers (IRE) *Paul Green* 81
2 b c Key Of Luck(USA) —Pure Folly (IRE) (Machiavellian (USA))
3669^{3} 3949^{4} 4681^{3} (4923) 6274^{10} (7173) 7241^{3}

Lucky Punt *B G Powell* a60 55
2 ch g Auction House(USA) —Sweet Coincidence (Mujahid (USA))
1736^{4} 2098^{4} 2324^{11} 2759^{8} 5606^{6} 5914^{10} 6343^{9} 7258^{5} 7353^{2} 7505^{8} 7666^{6}

Lucky Redback (IRE) *R Hannon* 85
2 b c Redback—Bayletta (IRE) (Woodborough (USA))
2275^{2} 2458^{3} (3408) (3693) 4666^{2} 5791^{9} ◆ 6979^{12}

Lucky Score (IRE) *Mouse Hamilton-Fairley* 65
2 b f Lucky Story(USA) —Musical Score (Blushing Flame (USA))
1693^{9} 4982^{3} 5227^{7} 6700^{5}

Lucky Stream *M Brittain* 45
3 b f Tamayaz(CAN) —Call Me Lucky (Magic Ring (IRE))
1187^{8}

Lucky Strike *A Trybuhl* 112
10 br g Petong—Urania (Most Welcome)
2214a^{6}

Lucullus *M Blanshard* a70 51
3 b g Bertolini(USA) —Calcavella (Pursuit Of Love)
796^{7} (936) 3893^{8}

Lucy Brown *M W Easterby* 41
2 br f Compton Place—Harambee (IRE) (Robellino (USA))
4593^{11} 5882^{7}

Lui Rei (ITY) *A Renzoni* 111
2 b c Reinaldo(FR) —My Luigia (IRE) (High Estate)
(4472a) 5330a^{10} 7186a^{3}

Lujano *Ollie Pears* a68 65
3 b g Lujain(USA) —Latch Key Lady (USA) (Tejano (USA))
2660^{4} 3825^{9} (4381) 4920^{6} 6088^{7} 6485^{12} 6825^{6} 7166^{5} 7345^{3} 7581^{2} (7725)

Lujeanie *D K Ivory* a64 64
2 br g Lujain(USA) —Ivory's Joy (Tina's Pet)
4980^{12} 6342^{4} 6863^{7} 7281^{4} ◆ 7468^{3} ◆ 7830^{4}

Lujiana *M Brittain* a64 66
3 b f Lujain(USA) —Compact Disc (IRE) (Royal Academy (USA))
19^{3} (444) ◆ 557^{3} ◆ 1257^{2} 1475^{5} 1819^{13} 3050^{11} 3960^{8} (4107) 4242^{5} 4609^{4} 5007^{8} 5638^{8}

Lukatara (USA) *Miss Sheena West* a17
3 b g Kayrawan(USA) —Hey Winnie (USA) (Hey Big Spender (USA))
7757^{11}

Lullaby Lady *B W Hills* a64 57
3 b f Piccolo—Musetta (IRE) (Cadeaux Genereux)
1709^{4} 2118^{16} 3678^{11}

Luloah *J G M O'Shea* a46 56
5 b m Mujahid(USA) —Bangles (Chilibang)
174^{4} 440^{8} (2474) (3128) 3577^{2} 4114^{6}

Lulu's Flight (IRE) *J P Broderick* 57
2 b f Masterful(USA) —Voici Voila (Groom Dancer (USA))
4513a^{6}

Lumen (FR) *O Larsen* 100
6 gr m Verglas(IRE) —La Le Lu (FR) (Exit To Nowhere (USA))
3751a^{6} 4676a^{12} 5336a^{8}

Lumiere Astrale (FR) *A Fabre* 97
3 ch f Trempolino(USA) —Lumiere Rouge (FR) (Indian Ridge)
7487a^{0}

Lumiere Noire (FR) *R Gibson* a85 101
4 ch m Dashing Blade—Lumiere Rouge (FR) (Indian Ridge)
3243a^{7} 5556a^{8} 7005a^{6}

Luminaire (IRE) *J S Bolger* a34 80
3 b g Green Desert(USA) —Luminata (IRE) (Indian Ridge)
7325a^{13}

Luminous Eyes (IRE) *D K Weld* 102
2 ch f Bachelor Duke(USA) —Mood Indigo (IRE) (Indian Ridge)
(4095a) 6319a^{4}

Luminous Gold *C F Wall* a72 81
3 b f Fantastic Light(USA) —Nasaieb (IRE) (Fairy King (USA))
(1738) 5962^{6} 6340^{6} 6695^{7} 7055^{9}

Luna Landing *Jedd O'Keeffe* a74 85
5 ch g Allied Forces(USA) —Macca Luna (IRE) (Kahyasi)
4204^{9} 4742^{4} 6113^{3} 6657^{8}

Lunar Limelight *P J Makin* a49 53
3 b g Royal Applause—Moon Magic (Polish Precedent (USA))
7340^{13} 7599^{9}

Luna Royale (IRE) *H-A Pantall* a83 95
3 b f Royal Applause—Lunaska (FR) (Ashkalani (IRE))
1360a^{7} 2902a^{7}

Lunar Promise (IRE) *Ian Williams* a71 78
6 b g Mujadil(USA) —Lunadine (FR) (Bering)
962^{12} 1072^{6} 5033^{7} 5370^{2} 6721^{9} 6985^{4} 7309^{7} 7786^{10}

Lunar River (FR) *David Pinder* a71 66
5 b m Muhtathir—Moon Gorge (Pursuit Of Love)
1266^{4} 1577^{5} 2561^{4} 2640^{6} 2957^{2} 3265^{3} (4031) 4156^{7} 4572^{6} 5059^{4} 5478^{2} 6134^{5} 6422^{6} 6825^{2} 7342^{8}

Lunar Romance *T J Pitt* 52
2 b f Royal Applause—Witness (Efisio)
1813^{7} 3432^{4} 3792^{7} 4659^{8}

Lunatico (GER) *S C Williams* 28
3 b g Bertolini(USA) —La Playa (Shavian)
70^{8}

Lunces Lad (IRE) *M R Channon* a86 84
4 gr g Xaar—Bridelina (FR) (Linamix (FR))
1211^{6} ◆ 1566^{4} 1800^{6} 2058^{3} 2565^{5} (3024) 3418^{7} 4103^{9} 5101^{12} 6200^{6} 6650^{10}

Lunduv (IRE) *D K Weld* a92 92
3 b f Pivotal—Another Dancer (FR) (Groom Dancer (USA))
7328a^{11}

Lundy's Lane (IRE) *A M Balding* a94 106
8 b g Darshaan—Lunda (IRE) (Soviet Star (USA))
381a^{4} 5279^{5} ◆ (Dead)

Lune Rose *P Bary* 95
3 b f High Chaparral(IRE) —Lunassa (FR) (Groom Dancer (USA))
3018a^{3} 6567a^{8}

Lupe Lamora *J A Osborne* a49
2 b f Monsieur Bond(IRE) —Bond Stasia (IRE) (Mukaddamah (USA))
6089^{9} 7168^{5} 7361^{6}

Lupita (IRE) *B G Powell* 63
4 ch m Intikhab(USA) —Sarah (IRE) (Hernando (FR))
(1267) 1538^{8} 2012^{8}

Lupo Alberto (ITY) *R Santini* 97
3 b c Ekraar(USA) —La Candelora (IRE) (Be My Guest (USA))
2028a^{15}

Lura (USA) *Saeed Bin Suroor* 67
3 b f Street Cry(IRE) —Belva (USA) (Theatrical)
4166^{5}

Luscious Lips *B Gubby* a3 76
3 b f Mujahid(USA) —Zing (Zilzal (USA))
7592^{10}

Luscivious *A J McCabe* a94 93
4 ch g Kyllachy—Lloc (Absalom)
866^{6} (1393) ◆ 1571^{7} 1796^{9} (2082) 2292^{3} 3451^{11} 3881^{8} 5206^{9} 5259^{8} 5831^{19} 6069^{24} 6354^{8} 6810^{6} 6971^{15} 7151^{2} 7365^{5} 7614^{7}

Lush (IRE) *R Hannon* a72 76
3 b f Fasliyev(USA) —Our Hope (Dancing Brave (USA))
1423^{4} 1803^{4} 2328^{10} 3351^{3} 3611^{4} 4152^{9} 4669^{7} 6168^{2} 6678^{7}

Lush Lashes *J S Bolger* 121
3 b f Galileo(IRE) —Dance For Fun (Anabaa (USA))
1104a^{7} 1830^{6} ◆ (2105) 2792^{5} (3194) 4623^{2} ◆ (5243) (5730a) 6521a^{2} 7685a^{14}

Lustful (USA) *Gary G Hartlage*
2 ch f Yonaguska(USA) —Ornate (USA) (Gilded Time (USA))
6613a^{8}

Lu's Woman *M W Easterby* a4 56
3 b f Lujain(USA) —Business Woman (Primo Dominie)
1912^{12} 2288^{8}

Lutece Eria (FR) *C Diard*
2 ch f Gold Away(IRE) —Dark Mile (USA) (Woodman (USA))
7430a^{3} 7549a^{3}

Luthien (IRE) *W R Swinburn* a70
2 b f Polish Precedent(USA) —Triplemoon (USA) (Trempolino (USA))
7093^{4}

Luvmedo (IRE) *R Hannon* a20 48
2 b f One Cool Cat(USA) —Dress Code (IRE) (Barathea (IRE))
3315^{8} 5214^{5}

Luxuria (IRE) *R Hannon* a62 47
2 b f Kheleyf(USA) —Dust Flicker (Suave Dancer (USA))
2253^{9} (3584) 4119^{10}

Lyceana *M A Jarvis* a82 64
3 ch f Medicean—Wax Lyrical (Safawan)
5057^{4} ◆ 6583^{4} (7395) 7603^{3} 7791^{2} ◆

Lydia's Legacy *T J Etherington* 23
3 b f Bahamian Bounty—Lydia's Look (IRE) (Distant View (USA))
2966^{13} 3712^{8} 3955^{6}

Lyonesse *R Hannon* 49
2 b f Dr Fong(USA) —Lyna (Slip Anchor)
4024^{9} 4769^{5} 5277^{14} 5747^{5}

Lyon's Hill *M Mullineaux* 49
4 ch g Generous(IRE) —New Abbey (Sadler's Wells (USA))
1814^{10} 3950^{6}

Lyra's Daemon *W R Muir* 71
2 b f Singspiel(IRE) —Seven Of Nine (IRE) (Alzao (USA))
5640^{11} (6360)

Lyrical Girl (USA) *H J Manners* a12 26
7 b m Orpen(USA) —Lyric Theatre (USA) (Seeking The Gold (USA))
1895^{13}

Lyric Art (USA) *B Smart* 60
2 b f Red Ransom(USA) —String Quartet (IRE) (Sadler's Wells (USA))
4815^{7} 6391^{6}

Lysander's Quest (IRE) *R Ingram* a54 47
10 br g King's Theatre(IRE) —Haramayda (FR) (Doyoun)
544^{4} 1052^{10} 4410^{5} 4775^{6}

Lyster (IRE) *P D Evans* 40
9 b g Oscar(IRE) —Sea Skin (Buckskin (FR))
4821^{10}

Lytham (IRE) *D J Wintle* a56
7 b g Spectrum(IRE) —Nousaiyra (IRE) (Be My Guest (USA))
7112^{8} 7676^{5}

Lytton *R Ford* a93 88
3 b g Royal Applause—Dora Carrington (IRE) (Sri Pekan (USA))
2529^{U} 3047^{10} 3850^{19} 4375^{8} 6169^{9} 6710^{11} 7363^{3} 7513^{11}

Maadraa (IRE) *M A Jarvis* a81
3 br c Josr Algarhoud(IRE) —Del Deya (IRE) (Caerleon (USA))
416^{2} 645^{2} 837^{3} (1059)

Maahe (IRE) *R A Fahey* a13 51
3 b f Namid—Almond Flower (IRE) (Alzao (USA))
1141^{2} 2074^{8} 2661^{14} 3139^{8}

Ma Al Salamah (IRE) *C E Brittain* a51 60
3 ch f Noverre(USA) —Tres Sage (Reprimand)
1763^{5} 2376^{9} 3672^{6}

Mabait *L M Cumani* a75 74
2 b c Kyllachy—Czarna Roza (Polish Precedent (USA))
3392^{5} 4164^{4} 4530^{4} 5632^{16} (6247) 6987^{3}

Mabel (IRE) *J Mackie* 67
5 b m In The Wings—Ma N'leme Biche (USA) (Key To The Kingdom (USA))
4457^{9}

Mabuya (UAE) *P J Makin* 69
2 b c Halling(USA) —City Of Gold (IRE) (Sadler's Wells (USA))
5225^{5} 6412^{5}

Macademy Royal (USA) *P S McEntee* a68 34
5 b g Royal Academy(USA) —Garden Folly (USA) (Pine Bluff (USA))
16^{2} 285^{3} 719^{4} 726^{6} 884^{9} 2075^{13} 4285^{15}

Macarthur *A P O'Brien* 122
4 b h Montjeu(IRE) —Out West (USA) (Gone West (USA))
1353a^{7} (1944) ◆ 2791^{3} (3246) 4406^{8}

Mac Dalia *A J McCabe* a68 70
3 b f Namid—Maugwenna (Danehill (USA))
199^{6} (279) 484^{5} (614) 635^{4} 952^{5} 2074^{3} 3455^{10} 3686^{2} 4107^{6} (4272) 5401^{10} 5592^{7}

Macdillon *W S Kittow* 81
2 b g Acclamation—Dilys (Efisio)
2124^{4} (2999)

Mac Don (IRE) *Eamon Tyrrell* a64 74
4 b g Soviet Star(USA) —Sharena (IRE) (Kahyasi)
860^{7} 5105^{2}

Macedon *T P Tate* 88
5 b g Dansili—Hypnotize (Machiavellian (USA))
2158^{9}

Macellya (FR) *X Nakkachdji* 100
3 ch f Testa Rossa(AUS) —Macellum (IRE) (Machiavellian (USA))
7551a^{4}

Mac Gille Eoin *J Gallagher* a93 107
4 b h Bertolini(USA) —Peruvian Jade (Petong)
1985^{8} (2831) 3504^{4} 3943^{7} 4624^{5} 4840^{6} 5347^{9} 6289^{11} 6903^{8}

Machinate (USA) *W M Brisbourne* a72 58
6 bb g Machiavellian(USA) —Dancing Sea (USA) (Storm Cat (USA))
148^{3} (341) 395^{4} 509^{6} 685^{3} 752^{3} 914^{3} (1085) 1369^{4} 1486^{4} 5198^{13} 6134^{12} 6491^{13} 6827^{6} 7340^{5} 7442^{13} 7581^{5} 7692^{4}

Machinist (IRE) *D Nicholls* a95 106
8 br g Machiavellian(USA) —Athene (IRE) (Rousillon (USA))
291a^{5} 497a^{2} 670a^{12} 1079^{3} 1420^{11} 1986^{2} 2172^{4} 2626^{7} 2831^{12} 3248^{12} 4624^{4}

Macho Again (USA) *Dallas Stewart* a110
3 rg c Macho Uno(USA) —Go Donna Go (USA) (Wild Again (USA))
2215a^{2} 2858a^{5}

Machynleth *M Al Muhairi* a80 83
8 b g Machiavellian(USA) —Tanami (Green Desert (USA))
290a^{8}

Mac Jack (IRE) *Niall Moran* 58
2 ch c Bachelor Duke(USA) —Sandy Desert (Selkirk (USA))
6320a^{13}

Mac Love *Stef Liddiard* a109 110
7 b g Cape Cross(IRE) —My Lass (Elmaamul (USA))
6073^{15} 7381^{2} (7492) 7703^{10}

Mac's Power (IRE) *P J O'Gorman* a64
2 b c Exceed And Excel(AUS) —Easter Girl (Efisio)
5905^{4}

Mac Warren *M G Quinlan*
2 b c Falbrav(IRE) —Kanzina (Machiavellian (USA))
2745a^{13}

Mac Waterloo *M G Quinlan*
2 b f Zamindar(USA) —Least Said (USA) (Trempolino (USA))
2744a[8]

Mad About You (IRE) *D K Weld* 114
3 b f Indian Ridge—Irresistible Jewel (IRE) (Danehill (USA))
2433a[2] ◆ 3511a[2] ◆ 4006a[8] (6689a)

Madam Carwell *J G Given* a3 54
3 b f King's Best(USA) —Delirious Moment (IRE) (Kris)
3057[11] 3816[10] 4531[6]

Madame Bountiful *A King* a49 52
3 ch f Bahamian Bounty—Madame Crecy (USA) (Al Nasr (FR))
1938[8] 2639[10] 2922[17]

Madame Hoi (IRE) *M R Channon* a87 74
3 ch f Hawk Wing(USA) —Lindesberg (Doyoun)
1332[3] 1833[7] 2328[4] 2560[8] 3944[6] 5600[15] 6671[9] 6822[3] 7066[4] 7213[2] (7362)

Madame Jourdain (IRE) *N Wilson* 65
2 b f Beckett(IRE) —Cladantom (IRE) (High Estate)
1390[9] 2485[6] (2671) 2924[2] 3809[2] 4143[4] 5381[8] 6547[10]

Madame Montom (USA) *S W Hall* a36 24
3 b f French Envoy(USA) —Sticky Fingers (USA) (Crafty Prospector (USA))
2069[7]

Madame Rio (IRE) *M Mullineaux* a26 61
3 b f Captain Rio—Glenviews Purchase (IRE) (Desert Story (IRE))
9936 1453[13] 1777[7] 3436[8] 5203[8]

Madame Trop Vite (IRE) *K A Ryan* 104
2 b f Invincible Spirit(IRE) —Gladstone Street (IRE) (Waajib)
(2903) 3496[5] 3908[2] 4781[4] (5055) (5852)

Madamlily (IRE) *J J Quinn* 75
2 b f Refuse To Bend(IRE) —Rainbow Dream (Rainbow Quest (USA))
4897[5] 6013[2] (6524)

Madam President *W R Swinburn* a58 71
3 b f Royal Applause—White House (Pursuit Of Love)
4249[3] 4695[6] 6331[5] 6826[8]

Madam Vouvray *B G Powell* a67 55
4 ch m Vettori(IRE) —April Stock (Beveled (USA))
1267[4] 1538[6]

Madam'X *P F I Cole* a51 15
2 b f Xaar—Bonne Etoile (Diesis)
6811[7] 7097[9] 7547[4] 7666[10]

Madaway *C Laffon-Parias* 107
3 ch f Machiavellian(USA) —Danzigaway (USA) (Danehill (USA))
2237a[4] 2743a[3]

Madda's Force (ITY) *R Betti* 94
2 b f Blu Air Force(IRE) —Madda'sblueyes (Selkirk (USA))
4673a[3]

Maddison County *K R Burke* a11
3 b f Invincible Spirit(IRE) —Topwinder (USA) (Topsider (USA))
65[10] 195[8]

Maddy *George Baker* a63 63
3 b f Daggers Drawn(USA) —Summer Lightning (IRE) (Tamure (IRE))
1274[4] 1479[3] 1637[3] 1870[6] (3730) 4750[4] (4990) 5320[5] 5710[9] 6929[11] 7605[8] 7662[2] 7792[6]

Madge *W Storey* a25 20
6 br m Marju(IRE) —Aymara (Darshaan)
2286[9]

Madison Belle *K R Burke* a67 55
2 ch f Bahamian Bounty—Indian Flag (IRE) (Indian Ridge)
2147[5] 2338[5] 2638[10] 2987[7] 3677[8] 5937[4] 6223[6] 6987[5] (7372) 7451[6] 7645[7]

Madison Heights (IRE) *J Howard Johnson* 68
3 ch g Monashee Mountain(USA) —Stormchaser (IRE) (Titus Livius (FR))
2488[7] 3641[6] 4455[2] 6216[6] 6551[6] (Dead)

Mad Man Will (IRE) *S C Williams* a51 38
3 b g Namid—Native Queen (FR) (Desert King (IRE))
183[5] 397[6] 873[9] 998[6] 1124[6]

Mad Professor (IRE) *A M Hales* a35 66
5 b g Mull Of Kintyre(USA) —Fancy Theory (USA) (Quest For Fame)
(4365) 4935[12] 7630[6]

Mad Rush (USA) *L M Cumani* 117
4 b g Lemon Drop Kid(USA) —Revonda (IRE) (Sadler's Wells (USA))
2372[2] ◆ 3249[2] (3721) ◆ 5333a[2] 6835a[4] 7188a[7]

Mae Cigan (FR) *M Blanshard* a65 74
5 gr g Medaaly—Concert (Polar Falcon (USA))
1383[3] 1613[3] (2153) 2621[5] 3060[8] 3917[5] 4785[2] 5058[6] 5900[4] 6279[5] 6606[4] 6898[5]

Maeve (IRE) *E J Creighton* a51 45
4 b m Tomba—Boozy (Absalom)
120[11]

Mafaaz *J H M Gosden* a83 96
2 ch c Medicean—Complimentary Pass (Danehill (USA))
(5798) 6474[5]

Mafaheem *A B Haynes* a79 85
6 b g Mujahid(USA) —Legend Of Aragon (Aragon)
(16) (213) (285) 466[5] 783[4] 839[3] 2263[DSQ] 2478[8] 2547[3] (4749) 5091[6] 5392[15] 5867[3] 6634[13] 7206[3] 7435[11] 7819[5]

Mafasina (USA) *B Smart* a70 24
3 b f Orientate(USA) —Money Madam (USA) (A.P. Indy (USA))
178[3] ◆ 4016[9] 4934[9] 6090[12]

Mafeking (UAE) *M R Hoad* a93 79
4 b g Jade Robbery(USA) —Melisendra (FR) (Highest Honor (FR))
61[3] (138) 315[12] 1766[6] 7208[4] 7496[2] 7579[5] 7814[4]

Magadan (IRE) *E Lellouche* 117
3 b c High Chaparral(IRE) —Molasses (FR) (Machiavellian (USA))
2654a[11] 4042a[3]

Magadino (FR) *Mme Brigitte Renk* 107
7 b g Solon(GER) —Madeleina (FR) (Top Waltz (FR))
(4880a) 5557a[6] 6854a[8]

Magaling (IRE) *L M Cumani* 84
2 ch c Medicean—Fling (Pursuit Of Love)
3651[2] ◆ 4510[4] 5316[2] (6062) 6426[7]

Magdalene *Rae Guest* a70 73
4 ch m Act One—Three Terns (USA) (Arctic Tern (USA))
1127[4] 1383[4] 6721[10] 7202[9]

Maggie Kate *R Ingram* a66 69
3 b f Auction House(USA) —Perecapa (IRE) (Archway (IRE))
60[4] 175[8] 419[2] 629[2] 899[11] 1110[3] 1178[4] 1454[2] 1743[4] (2074) 2506[4] 3000[2] 3405[9] 4127[3] 4904[6] 5510[9]

Maggie Lou (IRE) *K A Ryan* 86
2 b f Red Ransom(USA) —Triomphale (USA) (Nureyev (USA))
(1610) 3865[2] 4441a[4] 5272[7] 6102[14]

Maghya (IRE) *W J Haggas* a94 94
3 b f Mujahid(USA) —Khaizarana (Alhaarth (IRE))
1149[2] ◆ (1669) (2118) 3109[2] (3500) 4189[6] 6266[6] 6772[4]

Magical Destiny (IRE) *B Smart* a69
2 b c Exceed And Excel(AUS) —Magic Lady (IRE) (Bigstone (IRE))
7318[5] 7649[3]

Magical Fantasy (USA) *Patrick Gallagher* a76 112
3 ch f Diesis—Kissing Gate (USA) (Easy Goer (USA))
3807a[6]

Magical Forest (USA) *Joseph DeMola* a104
3 bb c Forest Camp(USA) —Silken Magic (USA) (Naevus (USA))
4678a[7]

Magical Illusion *P D Evans* 65
2 b f Tobougg(IRE) —Magical Gift (Groom Dancer (USA))
2338[7] 2769[3] 3020[5] 3651[7] 3961[4] (4706)

Magicalmysterytour (IRE) *W J Musson* 104
5 b g Sadler's Wells(USA) —Jude (Darshaan)
(5894) 6646[7] 7244[7]

Magical Night *T D Walford* 61
2 b f Bahri(USA) —Northern Goddess (Night Shift (USA))
1627[12] 6176[5] 6789[13]

Magical Song *R Curtis* a56 56
3 ch g Forzando—Classical Song (IRE) (Fayruz)
141[6] (262) ◆ 287[7] (656) ◆ 849[6] 873[7] 998[2] 1161[10] 1870[10] 2704[5] 7442[6] 7533[7] 7799[6]

Magical Speedfit (IRE) *G G Margarson* a77 78
3 ch g Bold Fact(USA) —Magical Peace (IRE) (Magical Wonder (USA))
1123[2] 1454[6] (2068) 2460[8] 3224[4] 3462[7] 3499[4] 3782[2] 4051[7] 4127[5] 4347[7] 5531[2] 6131[15] 6232[4] 7315[4] 7393[7]

Magic Amigo *J R Jenkins* a54 77
7 ch g Zilzal(USA) —Emaline (FR) (Empery (USA))
420[2] 1282[5] 1505[3] 5020[4] 5631[8]

Magic Amour *P A Blockley* a68 60
10 ch g Sanglamore(USA) —Rakli (Warning)
440[5] (530) 615[4] 1024[4]

Magic Carpet (IRE) *David Wachman* 100
4 b m Danehill(USA) —Paper Moon (IRE) (Lake Coniston (IRE))
6298a[12]

Magic Cat *K R Burke* 101
2 b g One Cool Cat(USA) —Magic Music (IRE) (Magic Ring (IRE))
4456[2] (5383) (6068) 6644[10]

Magic Cloud *John Joseph Hanlon* a60 69
3 b g Cloudings(IRE) —Magic Orb (Primo Dominie)
4494a[15]

Magic Echo *M Dods* a88 92
4 b m Wizard King—Sunday News'N'Echo (USA) (Trempolino (USA))
1329[5] (1676) 1903[4] (2784) 3403[3] 4970[4] 5382[6] 5858[2] 6293[7]

Magic Eye (IRE) *Andreas Lowe* 98
3 b f Nayef(USA) —Much Commended (Most Welcome)
(6852a)

Magic Glade *Peter Grayson* a94 95
9 b g Magic Ring(IRE) —Ash Glade (Nashwan (USA))
5[9] 162[5] 411[7] 2828[13] 3320[5] 4555[13] 5493[11] 6990[10] 7346[7] 7478[5] 7672[3]

Magic Haze *Miss S E Hall* 54
2 b g Makbul—Turn Back (Pivotal)
4213[6] 4734[10] 6109[4]

Magic Instinct *Peter G Moody* 105
6 b g Entrepreneur—Passe Passe (USA) (Lear Fan (USA))
6922a[3]

Magic Rush *Norma Twomey* a78 83
6 b g Almaty(IRE) —Magic Legs (Reprimand)
6170[4] 6450[4]

Magic Warrior *J C Fox* a71 53
8 b g Magic Ring(IRE) —Clarista (USA) (Riva Ridge (USA))
148[5] 300[4] 451[3] 716[10] 1747[3] 2533[5] 2943[8] 3182[5] 3764[4] 5087[2] 7801[5]

Magners Hill (IRE) *Gerard Keane* a69
4 b g Desert Sun—Tropicana (IRE) (Imperial Frontier (USA))
7654[2]

Magnificience (USA) *Bruce Headley* a109
4 ch m Stormy Atlantic(USA) —Fashion Delight (USA) (Fappiano (USA))
6965a[7]

Magnitude *W J Haggas* 84
3 ch g Pivotal—Miswaki Belle (USA) (Miswaki (USA))
(997) ◆ (1688) 1923[9] 2761[4]

Magnol *J G M O'Shea* a47 52
3 gr f Tobougg(IRE) —Magnolia (Petong)
1869[15] 2894[8]

Magnus (AUS) *Peter G Moody* 122
6 b h Flying Spur(AUS) —Scandinavia (AUS) (Snippets (AUS))
2235a[2] 3101[8]

Magpie (IRE) *B G Powell* a42 54
3 br g Hawk Wing(USA) —Swilly (USA) (Irish River (FR))
4085[5] 4349[9] 4484[6] 5145[13] 5458[14] 5837[8]

Magritte (ITY) *R Menichetti* 108
3 b f Modigliani(USA) —Star Of Siligo (USA) (Saratoga Six (USA))
7349a[16]

Magroom *R J Hodges* a67 75
4 b g Compton Place—Fudge (Polar Falcon (USA))
1641[8] ◆ 2243[2] 2477[3] 3087[2] 3360[8] 4979[9] 5170[4] 5492[2] 5800[10] 6336[15]

Mahaatheer (IRE) *F Head* 101
3 b f Daylami(IRE) —Al Ihtithar (IRE) (Barathea (IRE))
7037a[10]

Mahadee (IRE) *C E Brittain* a95 82
3 br g Cape Cross(IRE) —Rafiya (Halling (USA))
918[4] 1272[4] 1543[8] 3525[10] 3763[2] (4086) 4448[6] (5595) 5836[2] (6424) 6704[4] (7299) ◆ 7492[10]

Maha Dubai (USA) *M Johnston* 71
3 b f Kingmambo(USA) —Magical Allure (USA) (General Meeting (USA))
1628[4] 2536[3] 3473[2] 4382[2] 4964[2] 6007[9] 6551[5]

Maia *Ollie Pears* 67
4 ch m Observatory(USA) —Preference (Efisio)
990[3] ◆ 1450[14] 2005[9] 2846[9] 6219[14] 6716[13]

Maiden Investor *Stef Liddiard* a54 50
5 b m Orpen(USA) —Actress (Known Fact (USA))
99[4] 151[7] 232[6] 247[3] 522[9] 641[3]

Maid For Music (IRE) *E S McMahon* 82
2 b f Dubai Destination(USA) —Green Tambourine (Green Desert (USA))
2357[2] 2887[3] (3674) 4348[6] 5462[6] 6231[5]

Maid For Sucess (FR) *Robert Collet* 70
3 b f Choisir(AUS) —Arctic Maid (IRE) (Darshaan)
6742a[0]

Maid Of Ailsa (USA) *W J Haggas* a67
3 ch f Pivotal—Chiquita (IRE) (College Chapel)
7773[3] ◆ 7213[4] 7527[6] 7624[2] 7764[7] 7803[7]

Maid Of Ale (IRE) *D J Wintle* 59
4 b m Barathea(IRE) —Borders Belle (IRE) (Pursuit Of Love)
478[8]

Maidstone Mixture (FR) *Paul Murphy* a81
3 gr c Linamix(FR) —Marie Jbeil (FR) (Double Bed (FR))
2829[16] 5892[14]

Maid To Believe *J L Dunlop* 103
4 b m Galileo(IRE) —Maid For The Hills (Indian Ridge)
1812[10] 2402[8] 2797[8]

Maiepoimai (IRE) *M Gasparini* 80
3 b f Kalanisi(IRE) —Mocassino (IRE) (Turtle Island (IRE))
3076a[10]

Maigh Eo (IRE) *D J G Murray Smith*
2 b g Elusive City(USA) —Princess Magdalena (Pennekamp (USA))
1303[8]

Maille Le Nelois (FR) *V Greco* a78 81
3 ch c Maille Pistol(FR) —Lady Come Home (FR) (Belgio (FR))
2032a[17] 3356a[7]

Maimoona (IRE) *W J Haggas* a77 93
3 ch f Pivotal—Shuruk (Cadeaux Genereux)
(1737) 2529[4] (3794) 5310[3] 6676[3]

Main Aim *Sir Michael Stoute* 108
3 b c Oasis Dream—Orford Ness (Selkirk (USA))
(2918) ◆ (3744) ◆ 4312[3] (5831) ◆ 6429[11] 7243[8]

Maine Rose *J-M Beguigne* 84
3 b f Red Ransom(USA) —Messila Rose (Darshaan)
7487a[0]

Mairead's Boy (IRE) *J L Spearing* a59 39
3 ch g Noverre(USA) —Welltold (IRE) (Danehill (USA))
98[7] 2613[13] 5787[12] 7601[10]

Maisie Mouse *S C Williams* a25
2 b f Acclamation—Maugwenna (Danehill (USA))
4905[12] 5788[13] 6709[12]

Maison Dieu *E J Alston* a61 67
5 bb g King Charlemagne(USA) —Shining Desert (IRE) (Green Desert (USA))
1602[3] 1826[4] 2285[4] 3079[9] (3255) 3582[6] 4174[9] 4903[6] 6116[13]

Maison D'Or *R Ingram* a61
2 b g Auction House(USA) —Figura (Rudimentary (USA))
7438[6] 7812[4]

Maitresse (FR) *N Bertran De Balanda* a73 82
5 b m Singspiel(IRE) —Gold Peble (FR) (Glint Of Gold)
7598a[10]

Majd Aljazeera *D M Simcock* a50
2 b c King's Best(USA) —Tegwen (USA) (Nijinsky (CAN))
7204[11] 7699[9]

Majeen *W J Haggas* 76
3 ch c Rock Of Gibraltar(IRE) —Guilty Secret (IRE) (Kris)
2333[5] 3031[5] (6345) 6949[13]

Majehar *A G Newcombe* a67 53
6 b g Marju(IRE) —Joonayh (Warning)
7217[9] 7596[3] ◆ 7807[2] ◆

Majestical (IRE) *R A Harris* a63 65
6 b g Fayruz—Haraabah (USA) (Topsider (USA))
56[7] 181[6] 270[5] 528[6] 584[7] (1150) 1670[9] 2255[8] 2547[4] 3034[7] (3779) 4476[5] 4808[9] 5090[5] 6335[6] 6733[5] 7195[10] 7375[4] 7625[6]

Majestic Blue (USA) *Kiaran McLaughlin* a96
2 br c Forestry(USA) —Cariada (USA) (Seeking The Gold (USA))
6503a[5]

Majestic Bull (USA) *E J O'Neill* a67
2 bb c Holy Bull(USA) —Croissant (USA) (Lycius (USA))
6837[4] 7148[5] 7282[5]

Majestic Cheer *John A Harris* a67 65
4 b g Royal Applause—Muwasim (USA) (Meadowlake (USA))
6766[13] 7197[4] 7292[7] 7648[8] 7779[9]

Majestic Concorde (IRE) *D K Weld* 95
5 b g Definite Article—Talina's Law (IRE) (Law Society (USA))
(4493a)

Majestic Eviction (IRE) *M Halford* a88 88
4 b m King's Theatre(IRE) —Evictress (IRE) (Sharp Victor (USA))
3805a[12]

Majestic Issue (IRE) *M Dods* a23
4 ch g Fruits Of Love(USA) —Queen's Share (Main Reef)
529[12] 698[8]

Majestic Lady (IRE) *B W Hills* 63
2 b f Royal Applause—Kiris World (Distant Relative)
5860[4] ◆ 6327[10] 6702[5]

Majestic Roi (USA) *M R Channon* 115
4 ch m Street Cry(IRE) —L'Extra Honor (USA) (Hero's Honor (USA))
1090a[15] 2193[10] 2788[5] 3120[4] 3852[6] 4623[8] 6073[4] 6271[6]

Majestic Times (IRE) *Liam McAteer* a100 100
8 b g Bluebird(USA) —Simply Times (USA) (Dodge (USA))
3532a[17] 4512a[15] 5731a[12] 6845a[4]

Major Cadeaux *R Hannon* 119
4 ch h Cadeaux Genereux—Maine Lobster (USA) (Woodman (USA))
1355a[2] (1631) (2607) 4518[3] 5138a[3] 5893[2] 6814[9] 7684a[8]

Major Eazy (IRE) *B J Meehan* a35 103
3 b g Fasliyev(USA) —Castilian Queen (USA) (Diesis)
6645[5] 6903[10]

Major Faux Pas (IRE) *O Sherwood* 71
6 b g Barathea(IRE) —Edwina (IRE) (Caerleon (USA))
122[9]

Majority (IRE) *B J Meehan* 76
3 ch g Pivotal—Renashaan (FR) (Darshaan)
3969[7] 4128[11]

Major League (USA) *W S Kittow* a55 65
6 b g Magic Cat(USA) —Quick Grey (USA) (El Prado (IRE))
1207[11] 6570[12]

Major Magpie (IRE) *M Dods* 92
6 b g Rossini(USA) —Picnic Basket (Pharly (FR))
1016[3] 1612[3] 2334[7] 3716[3] 3887[6] (4744) 5418[4] (6052) 6249[12]

Major Phil (IRE) *L M Cumani* a80
2 b c Captain Rio—Choral Sundown (Night Shift (USA))
7333[5] ◆ (7638)

Major Potential (USA) *R M H Cowell* a7 22
2 ch c Officer(USA) —Protea (USA) (Roanoke (USA))
5364[11] 6282[12]

Major Promise *G G Margarson* 63
3 b g Lomitas—Distant Diva (Distant Relative)
3813[6] 4255[7] 4581[4] 5163[9] 5758[6]

Major Value *C G Cox* a30
2 b c Tobougg(IRE) —Surrealist (ITY) (Night Shift (USA))
7699[12]

Major Wing (IRE) *W Menuet* 74
3 b c Hawk Wing(USA) —Majinskaya (FR) (Marignan (USA))
4959a[9]

Majounes Song *M Johnston* 105
4 gr m Singspiel(IRE) —Majoune (FR) (Take Risks (FR))
1921[P] (Dead)

Majuba (USA) *K A Ryan* a44 81
2 b g Johannesburg(USA) —Rumored (USA) (Royal Academy (USA))
1447[4] 1794[2] 2108[3] 4558[2] 4948[2] 5969[3] 6545[2] 6932[8]

Majuro (IRE) *K A Ryan* a101 100
4 b h Danetime(IRE) —First Fling (IRE) (Last Tycoon)
2905[9] 5503[9] 5831[12] 6103[10] (6352) ◆ 7418[3]

Maj William Martin *M Quinn*
2 ch c Ishiguru(USA) —Hagley Park (Petong)
2548[8] 3815[9] 4120[6]

Makaamen *B W Hills* 75
2 ch c Selkirk(USA) —Bird Key (Cadeaux Genereux)
6438[2]

Makaaseb (USA) *M A Jarvis* 100
3 b f Pulpit(USA) —Turn And Sparkle (USA) (Danzatore (CAN))
2170[4] 3124[12] 3742[7] 4395[3] 6034[5]

Makabul *B R Millman* a71 81
5 b g Makbul—Victoria Sioux (Ron's Victory (USA))
1368[12] 1800[8] 2242[10] 3093[3] 3797[11] 3966[9] 4324[7] 4639[6] 5090[4]

Makai *M R Hoad* a67 54
5 ch g Cayman Kai(IRE) —Young Sue (Local Suitor (USA))
1643[4] 2755[5] 3344[5] 4055[7] 4391[7] 4811[9]

Makaluna *W G M Turner* a30 50
2 b g Makbul—Easter Moon (FR) (Easter Sun)
1384[7] 2049[3] 2548[3] 2882[2] 3091[6] 3815[8] 4120[5] 4764[7]

Makaykla *E J Alston* 57
2 b f Makbul—Primum Tempus (Primo Dominie)
6578[5] 6785[3] 7015[10]

Make Amends (IRE) *R J Hodges* 69
3 b f Indian Ridge—Chill Seeking (USA) (Theatrical)
4277[7] (4709) 5119[8] 6671[14]

Make My Dream *J Gallagher* a74 80
5 b g My Best Valentine—Sandkatoon (IRE) (Archway (IRE))
3346[4] (4025) 4313[3] 4693[2] 5151[4] 5796[5] 6232[2] 6340[3] 6750[2] 7081[2] 7315[5]

Makfly *R Hollinshead* a52 80
5 b g Makbul—Flying Flip (Rolfe (USA))
76[7] 249[9]

Makhaaleb (IRE) *B W Hills* a73 74
2 b g Haafhd—Summerhill Parkes (Zafonic (USA))
3853[9] 4890[6] 6122[12] 7067[3]

Making Music *T D Easterby* 68
5 b m Makbul—Crofters Ceilidh (Scottish Reel)
3868[7] 4246[11] 4743[14] 5260[12] 6218[16]
Makshoof (IRE) *K A Ryan* a85 87
4 b g Kyllachy—Tres Sage (Reprimand)
1134[5] 1430[4] 2778[5] 3271[5] (3626) 3998[5] 5222[4] 5594[3] (5991) 6278[2] 6842[3] 7378[7] 7601[5] 7782[7]
Maktavish *R Brotherton* a51 58
9 b g Makbul—La Belle Vie (Indian King (USA))
167[4] 440[2] 562[2] 725[3] 951[5] 1185[10]
Malahem (IRE) *E Charpy* a54 92
6 b g Mark Of Esteem(IRE) —Majmu (USA) (Al Nasr (FR))
477a[14]
Malakiya (IRE) *Jonjo O'Neill* a57 71
5 b g Sadler's Wells(USA) —State Crystal (IRE) (High Estate)
5993[16]
Malapropism *M R Channon* a84 89
8 ch g Compton Place—Mrs Malaprop (Night Shift (USA))
1393[2] 1802[5] 2212[8] 2489[4] 2843[4] 3062[11] 3472[9] 3708[6] 3945[4] 4246[3] 4291[4] 4502[3] 4668[7] 5187[2] 5796[18] 6131[8] 6388[11] 6925[4]
Malayeen (AUS) *A Selvaratnam* a93
6 br h Anabaa(USA) —Wily Trick (USA) (Clever Trick (USA))
295a[3] 566a[4] 814a[8]
Malcheek (IRE) *T D Easterby* a92 96
6 br g Lend A Hand—Russland (GER) (Surumu (GER))
1481[5] 2172[6] 3056[6] 4437[15] 4687[8] 6125[15] 6314[10]
Maldivian (NZ) *Mark Kavanagh* 122
6 b g Zabeel(NZ) —Shynzi (USA) (Danzig (USA))
6835a[9]
Malguru *A G Foster* 59
4 b g Ishiguru(USA) —Vento Del Oreno (FR) (Lando (GER))
988[15] 1305[7] 2250[5] (2523) 3204[4] (4420) 4540[6]
Malibu (IRE) *A W Carroll* a45 44
7 b g Second Empire(IRE) —Tootle (Main Reef)
6708[10]
Malibu Girl (USA) *E A L Dunlop* a70 70
3 b f Malibu Moon(USA) —Gale The Queen (USA) (Dr Blum (USA))
1746[10] 3351[10] 4152[11]
Malinsa Blue (IRE) *B Ellison* a63 72
6 b m Desert Style(IRE) —Talina's Law (IRE) (Law Society (USA))
1138[11] 1520[13] 2007[5] 2375[5] 2841[5] 3293[6] 3644[3] 4215[4] 4633[2] 6395[11] (6951) 7345[10] 7581[9]
Malta (USA) *J H M Gosden* 43
3 b f Gone West(USA) —Kithira (Danehill (USA))
2981[11]
Malt Empress (IRE) *B W Duke* a52
3 b f Second Empire(IRE) —Sunset Malt (IRE) (Red Sunset)
570[U] 903[11] 1054[6] 2719[14]
Maltese Falcon *P F I Cole* a111 99
8 b g Mark Of Esteem(IRE) —Crime Ofthecentury (Pharly (FR))
411[8] 677[4] 907[5] 7192[10] 7421[2] 7576[8]
Malt Or Mash (USA) *R Hannon* a109 108
4 gr h Black Minnaloushe(USA) —Southern Tradition (USA) (Family Doctor (USA))
(968) 1468[10] 1829[6] 2192[5]
Mama Leo *J G M O'Shea* a52 57
3 ch f Forzando—Milady Lillie (IRE) (Distinctly North (USA))
108[2] 186[3] 486[6] 2126[7] 2935[8] 3605[9] 3963[10]
Mambazo *S C Williams* a82 48
6 b g Dansili—Kalindi (Efisio)
150[9] 391[2] 414[9] 488[2] 628[7] 766[3] 782[3] 875[11] 1338[6] 1634[2] 2263[2] 2710[2] 2881[5] 3615[10] 4307[6] 4824[8] 5474[12] 6045[7]
Mambo In Seattle (USA) *Neil J Howard* a125
3 b c Kingmambo(USA) —Weekend In Seattle (USA) (Seattle Slew (USA))
6373a[4]
Mambo King (DEN) *L Kelp* a78 92
6 b h Diktat—Gypsy Singer (USA) (Kingmambo (USA))
202a[14] 477a[13] 648a[5]
Mambo Light (USA) *A Wohler* 77
2 ch f Kingmambo(USA) —Piquetnol (USA) (Private Account (USA))
1419[3] 2160[2] 5686a[2] 6319a[22]
Mambo Spirit (IRE) *J G Given* a91 89
4 b g Invincible Spirit(IRE) —Mambodorga (USA) (Kingmambo (USA))
1796[7] 2359[3] ◆ 2906[3] 3708[3] 4171[11] 4555[19] 5493[6] ◆ 6623[2] ◆ 7290[6] 7477[7]
Mambo Sun *R Curtis* a65 70
5 ro g Superior Premium—The Manx Touch (IRE) (Petardia)
7270[4] 7441[3] 7634[2] ◆ 7799[3]
Mamichor *B R Johnson* a54 52
5 br g Mamalik(USA) —Ichor (Primo Dominie)
2930[6] 3588[12] 4053[13] 5166[12]
Ma Mirage (IRE) *S C Williams* a27 41
3 b f Oasis Dream—Ma N'Ieme Biche (USA) (Key To The Kingdom (USA))
1302[9] 1957[14] 2786[16] 3118[2] 3727[8] 4271[6] 4725[10] 4793[7]
Mamlakati (IRE) *R Hannon* 81
2 b f Invincible Spirit(IRE) —Elba (IRE) (Ela-Mana-Mou)
(4251) ◆ 6401[4]
Mamlook (IRE) *D E Pipe* 93
4 br g Key Of Luck(USA) —Cradle Brief (IRE) (Brief Truce (USA))
3104[2] 6817[3]
Ma Nadri *S T Mason*
3 b f Red Ransom(USA) —Frustration (Salse (USA))
4901[9] 5505[12]
Managua *M R Channon* 80
2 br c Kaldounevees(FR) —Teresa Balbi (Master Willie)
2601[5] (3001) 3920[8]
Manahej (USA) *Saeed Bin Suroor* a74
2 b c Mr Greeley(USA) —Indemnify (USA) (Cox's Ridge (USA))
7204[3]
Manalito *M R Channon* 71
3 b c High Chaparral(IRE) —Brush Strokes (Cadeaux Genereux)
3310[5] 3813[5] (Dead)
Manana Manana *S Parr* a62
2 b g Tobougg(IRE) —Midnight Allure (Aragon)
7726[5] 7773[2] 7802[7]
Man Appeal *B J Meehan* 33
3 ch f Mark Of Esteem(IRE) —Emma Peel (Emarati (USA))
3694[11] 3916[8] 4584[6]
Manassas (IRE) *B J Meehan* 97
3 b g Cape Cross(IRE) —Monnavanna (IRE) (Machiavellian (USA))
1598[5]
Manathon (FR) *A E Jones* a67 45
5 b g Marathon(USA) —Fleurissante (FR) (Legend Of France (USA))
3824[5] 4066[5]
Mancebo (GER) *R Curtis* 26
5 b g Acambaro(GER) —Marsixa (FR) (Linamix (FR))
166[12]
Manchestermaverick (USA) *H Morrison* a65 63
3 ch g Van Nistelrooy(USA) —Lydia Louise (USA) (Southern Halo (USA))
3823[4] 4076[2] ◆ 4412[2] 6836[4] 7228[2] 7358[7] 7581[4]
Manchurian *M J Wallace* a96 94
4 b g Singspiel(IRE) —Royal Passion (Ahonoora)
1500[2] 1683[12] 2358[3] (2995) 4121[4] 4489[7]
Mandalay King (IRE) *Mrs Marjorie Fife* a49 72
3 b g King's Best(USA) —Mahamuni (IRE) (Sadler's Wells (USA))
2246[4] 2704[9] 3139[4] (3638) 3753[3] (3952) ◆ (4450) ◆ 4684[2] 5714[2] 7040[5]
Mandalay Prince *W J Musson* a69 69
4 b g Tobougg(IRE) —Autumn Affair (Lugana Beach)
(287) 802[4] ◆ 1266[9] 1732[2] 2621[11] 3160[6]
Mandarin Spirit (IRE) *G C H Chung* a83 77
8 b g Primo Dominie—Lithe Spirit (IRE) (Dancing Dissident (USA))
1023[5] 1415[5] 2010[2] ◆ 2400[4] 2484[3] 3033[8] 3169[2] 3797[2] (4051) 4125[5] 4809[7] 5433[4] (5532) 5789[7] 6125[11] 6200[4] 6556[3] 6952[5]
Mandelieu (IRE) *Ollie Pears* a59 73
3 b g Acclamation—Notley Park (Wolfhound (USA))
2122[4] 2690[3] 3224[5] (3782) 5400[8] 6150[9] 6448[8]
Mandhooma *P W Hiatt* a45
2 b f Oasis Dream—Shatarah (Gulch (USA))
6933[12] 7738[5] 7788[4]
Mandobi (IRE) *D Selvaratnam* a95 104
7 ch h Mark Of Esteem(IRE) —Miss Queen (USA) (Miswaki (USA))
294a[6] 474a[14]
Mandrake Miss *C R Wilson*
4 br m Hunting Lion(IRE) —Dragons Daughter (Mandrake Major)
4901[U] 5505[13]
Mandurah (IRE) *D Nicholls* a58 79
4 b g Tagula(IRE) —Fearfully Grand (Grand Lodge (USA))
1451[14] 1624[10] 1818[10] (2356) 2596[4] 2751[4] 3171[8] (3668) 4555[3] 4743[10] ◆ 5493[10]
Maneki Neko (IRE) *E W Tuer* a75 74
6 b g Rudimentary(USA) —Ardbess (Balla Cove)
1482[2] ◆ (2006) 2939[8] 3440[7] 4244[10] 5040[6]
Manere Bay *J L Dunlop* 63
3 b f Olden Times—Madurai (Chilibang)
6345[4] 6705[4] 7084[2] ◆
Manero *J A Osborne* a66 48
2 br c Millkom—Discoed (Distinctly North (USA))
1987[7] 6620[8] 7165[P] (Dead)
Mangano *A Berry* a41 55
4 b g Mujadil(USA) —Secret Dance (Sadler's Wells (USA))
2749[12] 3082[13] 3431[11] 3757[8] 4018[12] 4503[13] 4851[7] 4919[11] 5420[7]
Mangham (IRE) *D H Brown* 101
3 b g Montjeu(IRE) —Lovisa (USA) (Gone West (USA))
(2221) 2699[3] 3641[2] 3911[3] (4783) 5360[15] (6526) 7019[2]
Mango Lady *C F Wall* a70 79
3 gr f Dalakhani(IRE) —Generous Lady (Generous (IRE))
(6126) 6626[8] 7108[8]
Mango Masher (IRE) *J L Flint* a61 60
4 ch g Danehill Dancer(IRE) —Shariyfa (FR) (Zayyani)
36[9] 198[5] 374[4] 544[8] 6228[4] 6594[11]
Mango Music *M Quinn* a70 91
5 ch m Distant Music(USA) —Eurolink Sundance (Night Shift (USA))
1253[7] (1739) (2205) 2504[6] 3271[3] (3554) 3883[6] 4198[6] 4601[9] 5250[4] 5781[2] 6053[4] 6557[3] 6925[6]
Manhattan Dream (USA) *B W Hills* 81
3 b f Statue Of Liberty(USA) —Vallee Des Reves (USA) (Kingmambo (USA))
(3419) (4539) 6124[16]
Manhattan Sunrise (USA) *G D Blake* a54
2 ch f Hold That Tiger(USA) —Sellsey (USA) (Pulpit (USA))
3689[7] 4339[7] 6910[13]
Manipura (GER) *H Steguweit* 97
3 b f Dansili—Macara (GER) (Acatenango (GER))
2065a[6] 2655a[5] 4912a[10] (6323a)
Manita (IRE) *Mario Hofer* 73
3 ch f Peintre Celebre(USA) —Mosquera (GER) (Acatenango (GER))
6323a[11]
Mannello *Jim Best* a61 59
5 b m Mamalik(USA) —Isle Of Sodor (Cyrano De Bergerac)
2664[7] (2861) 2933[5] 3034[14] (4052) 4336[2] 4808[6] 5166[6]
Mannlichen *M Johnston* a78 77
2 ch c Selkirk(USA) —Robe Chinoise (Robellino (USA))
3164[5] 4214[2] 4497[2] 6101[7] (7397)
Man Of Gwent (UAE) *P D Evans* a87 79
4 b g In The Wings—Welsh Valley (USA) (Irish River (FR))
(396) 626[2] ◆ 1568[12] 1947[6] 2582[13] 3132[4] 3836[7] 4276[3] 5290[9] 5800[8] 6177[4] ◆ 6582[12] 6900[5] 7202[14] 7613[5] (7758) 7786[2]
Man Of Letters (UAE) *M Hill* a54 26
7 b g Belong To Me(USA) —Personal Business (USA) (Private Account (USA))
973[7] 1209[9] 1780[10] 2478[12]
Manolito Montoya (IRE) *J W Hills* 71
2 b g High Chaparral(IRE) —Queens Wharf (IRE) (Ela-Mana-Mou)
5468[14] 6198[6] 6674[12]
Mansii *P J McBride* a67 79
3 b c Dr Fong(USA) —Enclave (USA) (Woodman (USA))
3812[13] 4831[10] 5049[5] 6395[13] 6889[13]
Mantadive (FR) *Mme N Rossio* a65 79
2 ch f Okawango(USA) —Missanticia (FR) (Sicyos (USA))
7430a[2]
Mantoro (GER) *Mario Hofer*
2 b c Dashing Blade—Mistic World (Monsun (GER))
7264a[2]
Manuka Bee *J Howard Johnson* 62
3 b g Xaar—Legend (Belmez (USA))
2675[11] 3640[3] 4248[4] 4738[4] 5362[8] (Dead)
Many Colours *Saeed Bin Suroor* a98 108
4 b m Green Desert(USA) —First Of Many (Darshaan)
(200a) 475a[2] 672a[2] 3120[9] 4590[14]
Manyriverstocross (IRE) *A King* 90
3 b c Cape Cross(IRE) —Alexandra S (IRE) (Sadler's Wells (USA))
1446[2] 1931[4] 2454[2] (3310) 4784[4] 5054[4] 6563[8]
Many Volumes (USA) *H R A Cecil* a119 116
4 b h Chester House(USA) —Reams Of Verse (USA) (Nureyev (USA))
1828[15] 1990[2] 2503[2] 3195[2] (3683) (5348) 5694[4] 6201[3]
Many Welcomes *B P J Baugh* a44 52
3 ch f Young Ern—Croeso Cynnes (Most Welcome)
721[5] 1019[15] 1489[3] 3283[4] 3753[6] (5457) 6409[5]
Manzila (FR) *D Nicholls* 107
5 ch m Cadeaux Genereux—Mannsara (IRE) (Royal Academy (USA))
2000[6] (2211) 2738a[10] 3252[5] 3927[5] 4467a[13] 5884[3] 6184[4] 6430[4]
Maoineach (USA) *J S Bolger* 100
2 ch f Congaree(USA) —Trepidation (USA) (Seeking The Gold (USA))
(5546a) 6519a[16]
Maori *M Johnston* 82
3 b c Singspiel(IRE) —Nawadi (Machiavellian (USA))
(3058)
Ma Patrice *T D McCarthy* a44 18
2 ch f Tumbleweed Ridge—Ma Barnicle (IRE) (Al Hareb (USA))
5578[10] 6205[9] 7434[11] 7832[8]
Maraagel (USA) *G A Ham* a50 28
5 b g Danzig(USA) —Hasnaael Reef (USA) (Seattle Slew (USA))
50[2] ◆ 535[5] 1529[9] 2474[11] 2988[16]
Maraahel (IRE) *Sir Michael Stoute* a99 120
7 b h Alzao(USA) —Nasanice (IRE) (Nashwan (USA))
1921[2] 2543[2] 3246[3] 3741[8]
Maraased *M A Jarvis* 91
3 b g Alhaarth(IRE) —Fleeting Rainbow (Rainbow Quest (USA))
1398[5] ◆ 1918[3] ◆
Marajaa (IRE) *W J Musson* a97 90
6 b g Green Desert(USA) —Ghyraan (IRE) (Cadeaux Genereux)
3855[8] 4602[5] 5290[P]
Maram (USA) *Chad C Brown* 110
2 bb f Sahm(USA) —American Dreamer (USA) (Quest For Fame (USA))
(6966a)
Maramba (USA) *Sir Michael Stoute* a67 94
3 ch f Hussonet(USA) —Coco (USA) (Storm Bird (CAN))
3124[13] 3971[3] 4520[10] 6034[9] 6763[8]
Marangu (IRE) *W Hickst*
2 b g Intikhab(USA) —Massada (Most Welcome)
7264a[6]
Maraoute Gaugain (FR) *Ron Caget*
3 br f Showbrook(IRE) —Exceptionnal Risks (FR) (Take Risks (FR))
6742a[0]
Marbled Cat (USA) *M Johnston* a68 70
2 bb c Cherokee Run(USA) —Catstar (USA) (Storm Cat (USA))
4446[3] 5099[8] 5572[4] 5997[9] 6350[4]
Marbush (IRE) *D Selvaratnam* a104 89
7 ro h Linamix(FR) —Fig Tree Drive (USA) (Miswaki (USA))
647a[2] 815a[12]
Marceau (IRE) *Patrick J Flynn* 44
3 b g Tendulkar(USA) —Pillow Talk (IRE) (Taufan (USA))
4715a[14]
Marchand D'Or (FR) *F Head* a95 126
5 gr g Marchand De Sable(USA) —Fedora (FR) (Kendor (FR))
(2652a) 3247[6] (3922) (4915a) (6518a) 7683a[6]
Marchingontogether (IRE) *D Carroll* 74
3 b f Mull Of Kintyre(USA) —Stolen Music (IRE) (Taufan (USA))
1453[4] 1795[2] 2187[7] 3694[6]
Marching Time *Sir Michael Stoute* 80
2 b c Sadler's Wells(USA) —Marching West (USA) (Gone West (USA))
4570[6] (6029) 6973[14]
March Mate *B Ellison* 61
4 b g Warningford—Daira (Daring March)
2009[14] 2365[13] 2782[2] 2940[2] 3339[2] 3834[10] 4679[9]
Marchpane *R M Beckett* a21 70
3 b f Olden Times—Ecstasy (Pursuit Of Love)
1839[12] 3322[13] 3843[8] 6049[12] 6446[7]
Marcus Crassus (IRE) *H J L Dunlop* a43 42
2 b c Spartacus(IRE) —My First Paige (IRE) (Runnett)
4304[8] 5021[10] 5753[5]
Mardood *W J Haggas* 71
3 b g Oasis Dream—Gaelic Swan (IRE) (Nashwan (USA))
2143[5] 2603[9]
Maree Basse (IRE) *J-C Rouget* a93 93
3 b f Royal Applause—Mabalane (IRE) (Danehill (USA))
7450a[3]
Margarita (IRE) *J R Fanshawe* 60
2 b f Marju(IRE) —Kalinka (IRE) (Soviet Star (USA))
6080[8]
Margot Mine (IRE) *J S Moore* a53 32
3 b f Choisir(AUS) —Delisha (Salse (USA))
5119[9] 5832[4] 6228[7] (6752) 6912[2] 7088[3] 7494[8]
Maria Antonia (IRE) *M J Gingell* a63 60
5 ch m King's Best(USA) —Annieirwin (IRE) (Perugino (USA))
(348) 438[2] 551[3] 716[7] 789[4]
Maria Di Scozia *P W Chapple-Hyam* a38 83
3 ch f Selkirk(USA) —Viva Maria (Hernando (FR))
674[5] 2164[2] 2669[2] (3168) 3962[7] (6487)
Maria Milena *M J Wallace* 40
2 b f Stravinsky(USA) —Aswhatilldois (IRE) (Blues Traveller (IRE))
1363[7] 3106[3]
Marias Buddy *Eamon Tyrrell* a55 65
3 b f Reel Buddy(USA) —Mitsuki (Puissance)
2396[7]
Marias Dream (IRE) *John A Quinn* a80 83
7 b m Desert Sun—Clifton Lass (IRE) (Up And At 'Em)
63[2] 117[2]
Mariaverdi *P G Murphy* a53 34
4 b m Diktat—Belinda (Mizoram (USA))
39[6] 231[2] 420[7] 722[5] 930[9]
Ma Ridge *T D McCarthy* a57 52
4 ch g Tumbleweed Ridge—Ma Barnicle (IRE) (Al Hareb (USA))
95[5] 402[8] 937[4] 1763[9] 2055[6] 2756[5] 4085[7] 4412[6] 6912[7] 7026[9] 7469[11] 7601[9] 7678[5]
Marie Camargo *R A Fahey* 55
3 b f Kyllachy—Wheeler's Wonder (IRE) (Sure Blade (USA))
2659[6] 3580[5]
Marie Claude *J Noseda* a46
3 b f Where Or When(IRE) —Lalique (IRE) (Lahib (USA))
135[7] 223[6] 439[10]
Marie Louise *H R A Cecil* a57 59
3 b f Helissio(FR) —Self Esteem (Suave Dancer (USA))
1621[5] 3484[5] 3835[6]
Marieschi (USA) *R F Fisher* 68
4 b g Maria's Mon(USA) —Pennygown (Rainbow Quest (USA))
1449[14] 2249[7] 3204[6] 4295[5] 6550[6]
Marie Tempest *M R Bosley* a55 49
3 b f Act One—Hakkaniyah (Machiavellian (USA))
1440[10] 2164[10] 2868[3] 3555[4] 5631[5] 6753[3] 7605[2] 7792[4]
Marikova *A B Haynes*
3 ch f Baryshnikov(AUS) —Mary Hayden (Imp Society (USA))
6541[16] 6747[10]
Marillos Proterras *Mrs A Duffield* a12 61
2 b f Fraam—Legend Of Aragon (Aragon)
6945[8] 7282[12]
Marina Of Venice (IRE) *J S Bolger* 86
2 ch f Galileo(IRE) —Dame's Violet (IRE) (Groom Dancer (USA))
4804a[4] 5549a[8] 6319a[16]
Marine Boy (IRE) *Tom Dascombe* 105
2 b g One Cool Cat(USA) —Bahamamia (Vettori (IRE))
(4665) ◆ 5226[7] 6119[5]
Marino Prince (FR) *T Wall* a70 47
3 b g Dr Fong(USA) —Hula Queen (USA) (Irish River (FR))
116[5] 217[5] 527[7] 785[8] 803[9] 1479[7] 6492[10] 7560[10]
Mariol (FR) *Robert Collet* 116
5 b g Munir—La Bastoche (IRE) (Kaldoun (FR))
291a[2] 472a[5] 649a[5] 741a[5] 2652a[8] 3243a[3] 3752a[3] (3938a) 4915a[10] 5556a[3] 5738a[4] 6518a[14] 7187a[10]
Marist Madame *T J Pitt* a48 43
4 ch m Tomba—Linda's Schoolgirl (IRE) (Grand Lodge (USA))
160[9]
Marjalina (IRE) *Kevin Prendergast* 108
3 bb f Marju(IRE) —Atalina (FR) (Linamix (FR))
(1104a) 2113a[7] 3511a[8]
Marju King (IRE) *W S Kittow* 52
2 b c Marju(IRE) —Blue Reema (IRE) (Bluebird (USA))
6122[11] 6715[12]
Marjury Daw (IRE) *J G Given* 56
2 b f Marju(IRE) —The Stick (Singspiel (IRE))
6391[8] 6945[14] 7200[13]
Markab *K A Morgan* a107 99
5 b g Green Desert(USA) —Hawafiz (Nashwan (USA))
227[7] 336[6] (969) (1218) 1469[5] 5681[4] 6269[17] 6911[12] (7215) 7418[2] 7594[2]
Markadam *Miss S E Hall* a40 60
2 b g Mark Of Esteem(IRE) —Elucidate (Elmaamul (USA))
6381[8] 7221[2] 7720[6]

Marker *J D Frost* a47 74
8 ch g Pivotal—Palace Street (USA) (Secreto (USA))
8^{12}

Market Watcher (USA) *Seamus Fahey* a58 56
7 b g Boundary(USA)—Trading (USA) (A.P. Indy (USA))
754^{9} 7293^{4} ◆

Markhesa *C F Wall* 45
2 b f Sakhee(USA)—Marciala (IRE) (Machiavellian (USA))
6031^{6}

Markington *P Bowen* a74 70
5 b g Medicean—Nemesia (Mill Reef (USA))
1998^{4} 2332^{5} 3673^{3} 4193^{10} 5993^{13}

Mark Of An Angel (IRE) *Kevin Prendergast* 87
2 ch f Mark Of Esteem(IRE)—Dream Time (Rainbow Quest (USA))
$4095a^{3}$ $4513a^{2}$

Mark Of Meydan *M Dods* 79
3 ch g Mark Of Esteem(IRE)—Rose Bounty (Polar Falcon (USA))
1519^{3} 2187^{2}

Marko Jadeo (IRE) *R A Harris* a70 77
10 b g Eagle Eyed(USA)—Fleeting Quest (Rainbow Quest (USA))
755^{9} (884) 1061^{4} 1150^{4} 1670^{5} (2721) 3021^{4} 3313^{10} 3559^{8} 4102^{7}

Mark S The Cooler (USA) *Doug O'Neill* a103
2 b g Johar(USA)—Felucca (USA) (Diesis)
$7751a^{7}$

Markyg (USA) *K R Burke* a84 89
2 bb c Fusaichi Pegasus(USA)—Spring Pitch (USA) (Storm Cat (USA))
2937^{4} 3245^{3} 3939^{4} (6731)

Marlang (CAN) *Deborah England* 108
3 b c Langfuhr(CAN)—Marienburg (CAN) (Conquistador Cielo (USA))
$6506a^{10}$

Marlena (IRE) *T D Easterby* 54
3 bb f Marju(IRE)—Red Rosie (USA) (Red Ransom (USA))
1396^{9} 1754^{10} 2486^{7}

Marlos Moment *W R Swinburn* a52
2 b c Where Or When(IRE)—Tender Moment (IRE) (Caerleon (USA))
7602^{7}

Marmooq *M J Attwater* a67 62
5 ch g Cadeaux Genereux—Portelet (Night Shift (USA))
151^{4} 305^{5} 401^{6} (518) (693) 898^{2} 1029^{3} (1275) 1602^{4} 1966^{2} 2550^{4} 3034^{6} 3501^{4} 6681^{6} (7497) 7691^{5} (7803)

Marning Star *D Nicholls* 83
3 b g Diktat—Mustique Dream (Don't Forget Me)
1448^{2} 1894^{3} (2246) 2913^{4} (3263) 3560^{3} 6070^{8}

Maromito (IRE) *R Bastiman* a53 56
11 b g Up And At 'Em—Amtico (Bairn (USA))
50^{10} 363^{7} 440^{6} 871^{10}

Maroni (IRE) *F Rohaut* 86
3 b c Oasis Dream—Miss Chryss (IRE) (Indian Ridge)
$385a^{5}$ (549a)

Marquee (IRE) *P A Blockley* a65 60
4 b g Mark Of Esteem(IRE)—Queen's Ransom (IRE) (Last Tycoon)
1406^{8} 1895^{6} 2643^{9}

Marquesa (USA) *David Wachman* a80 105
2 b f Kingmambo(USA)—Dietrich (USA) (Storm Cat (USA))
$2686a^{2}$ ◆ $5549a^{10}$ $6519a^{5}$ 6818^{13}

Marquis De Louvois (IRE) *Mrs A Duffield* a57 30
3 b g Iron Mask(USA)—Sweet Compliance (Safawan)
146^{7} 261^{7} 441^{3} 714^{9} 1051^{9} 1139^{12} 3733^{12} 4073^{12}

Marraasi (USA) *M P Tregoning* a76 67
3 ch f Rahy(USA)—Bashayer (USA) (Mr Prospector (USA))
1930^{4} ◆ 3117^{9} 3679^{3} 4183^{2} 5471^{3} 7026^{5}

Marramed *J O'Reilly* 41
3 ch f Medicean—Marrakech (IRE) (Barathea (IRE))
2221^{8} 2269^{7} 2704^{12} 2915^{11} 3166^{7}

Marsam (IRE) *M G Quinlan* a78 95
5 gr g Daylami(IRE)—Dancing Prize (IRE) (Sadler's Wells (USA))
47^{5}

Marsh Court *J W Hills* a16
5 b m Overbury(IRE)—Lady Prunella (IRE) (Supreme Leader)
4941^{5}

Marsh Side (USA) *Neil Drysdale* a103 117
5 b h Gone West(USA)—Colonial Play (USA) (Pleasant Colony (USA))
(6506a)

Marsool *M P Tregoning* 44
2 br g Key Of Luck(USA)—Chatifa (IRE) (Titus Livius (FR))
2146^{10}

Martell (GER) *P Schiergen*
2 b c Tiger Hill(IRE)—Murnau (IRE) (Rudimentary (USA))
$6853a^{5}$

Martha (IRE) *D R C Elsworth* a53
3 ch f Alhaarth(IRE)—Dominio (IRE) (Dominion)
60^{7} 498^{3} 706^{6}

Martha's Girl (USA) *D Carroll* 56
2 ch f E Dubai(USA)—Blue Stream (USA) (King Of Kings (IRE))
6580^{5} 6945^{10}

Martingrange Boy (IRE) *D J Murphy* a69
3 b g Danetime(IRE)—Coloma (JPN) (Forty Niner (USA))
17^{8}

Martingrange Lass (IRE) *S Parr* a46 49
3 b f Chevalier(IRE)—Jellybeen (IRE) (Petardia)
961^{15} 1709^{5} 1795^{13} 4420^{4} 4607^{11} 5223^{4} $6742a^{0}$ 7322^{11} 7379^{4} 7654^{6} 7815^{6}

Martyr *R Hannon* a91 60
3 b g Cape Cross(IRE)—Sudeley (Dancing Brave (USA))
131^{2} (632) 1746^{4} 3134^{6}

Marvellous Value (IRE) *M Dods* 97
3 b g Danetime(IRE)—Despondent (IRE) (Broken Hearted)
(1139) ◆ (1611) 2171^{3} 3723^{6} (4416) ◆ 5102^{6} 6069^{5}

Marvin Gardens *P S McEntee* a58 47
5 b g Largesse—En Grisaille (Mystiko (USA))
2055^{12} 4052^{5} 4284^{7} 4806^{13} 5426^{7} 6003^{9} 6752^{6} 7316^{7} (7453)

Marvo *M H Tompkins* 78
4 b g Bahamian Bounty—Mega (IRE) (Petardia)
1458^{3} 1874^{4} 3493^{13} 3947^{3} 4894^{2} 5040^{8} 5863^{3} 6035^{12} 6400^{10} 6675^{2} 6867^{7}

Mary Athena (FR) *M G Quinlan* a59 58
3 b f Barathea(IRE)—Miss Daisy (FR) (Shirley Heights)
4342^{6} 5042^{7} 5612^{3} 6226^{8} 6897^{5}

Mary Dunsmore *B J McMath* a12
4 b m Mujahid(USA)—Piroshka (Soviet Star (USA))
1252^{12} 1588^{7}

Marygate (IRE) *M Brittain* 61
2 b f Spartacus(IRE)—Thorn Tree (Zafonic (USA))
1324^{3} 1447^{9} 2206^{8} 2462^{7}

Mary Mason *Mrs A Duffield* 73
2 b f Hunting Lion(IRE)—Kalarram (Muhtarram (USA))
3590^{6} (5500) 5969^{7}

Maryolini *N J Vaughan* a79 76
3 b f Bertolini(USA)—Mary Jane (Tina's Pet)
2407^{2} 2945^{5} 3256^{4} 5493^{7} 5998^{4} 6340^{13} 7611^{8}

Maryqueenofscots (IRE) *M L W Bell* a29 75
3 b f Fantastic Light(USA)—Marie De Blois (IRE) (Barathea (IRE))
4520^{13} 5075^{5} 6215^{5} 6683^{13}

Marysedge *R Brotherton* a28 8
3 b f Bold Edge—Dekelsmary (Komaite (USA))
855^{6} 997^{10} 1777^{9} 2084^{8} 2474^{12} 3086^{12} 3605^{13} 4031^{12}

Mary's Precedent (FR) *C Lerner*
2 ch f Storming Home—Suvretta Queen (IRE) (Polish Precedent (USA))
$7549a^{8}$

Mary West (IRE) *R A Fahey* 52
2 b f Pyrus(USA)—Pivot D'Amour (Pivotal)
6230^{5} ◆ 6548^{4} 6863^{13}

Masaalek *M P Tregoning* a106 110
3 b c Green Desert(USA)—Hammiya (IRE) (Darshaan)
1403^{3} (1763) ◆ 2412^{2} ◆ 3155^{2} 3740^{3} 4587^{2} 5208^{3}

Masada (IRE) *B J Meehan* 93
3 br f Key Of Luck(USA)—Desert Bloom (IRE) (Pilsudski (IRE))
1698^{8} 2428^{7} 2998^{5} (3696) 4252^{2} 6239^{4} ◆ (6430) 6782^{8}

Masai Moon *B R Millman* a97 101
4 b g Lujain(USA)—Easy To Imagine (USA) (Cozzene (USA))
1071^{5} 1617^{4} (2085) 2545^{9} (3222) 4405^{10} 4869^{7} 5313^{4} 5930^{2} 6478^{2} 6783^{8} 7245^{16}

Masako (IRE) *W Hickst* 92
3 b f High Chaparral(IRE)—Medina (IRE) (Pennekamp (USA))
$3623a^{10}$ $6323a^{6}$ $6852a^{2}$

Masamah (IRE) *E A L Dunlop* a97 88
2 gr c Exceed And Excel(AUS)—Bethesda (Distant Relative)
(2108) (4822) 6119^{8}

Masettos Fun *M Botti* 20
3 b g Dr Fong(USA)—Macina (IRE) (Platini (GER))
3530^{6}

Mashaahed *E Charpy* 115
5 b h In The Wings—Patacake Patacake (USA) (Bahri (USA))
$671a^{4}$

Masked (IRE) *R M Beckett* a88
7 b g Soviet Star(USA)—Moon Masquerade (IRE) (Darshaan)
268^{3} ◆ 630^{3} ◆ 838^{3}

Masking Baldini (IRE) *P T Midgley* a47 43
4 b g Iron Mask(USA)—Royal Baldini (USA) (Green Dancer (USA))
1086^{4} 1304^{7}

Mask Of Conspiracy (IRE) *N Nevin* a66 65
3 b g Iron Mask(USA)—Petitesse (Petong)
777^{4}

Maslaha *R W Price* a84 50
3 b f Selkirk(USA)—Mingora (USA) (Mtoto)
633^{2} ◆ (885) 1113^{2} 2428^{9} 6035^{15}

Maslak (IRE) *P W Hiatt* a94 92
4 b g In The Wings—Jeed (IRE) (Mujtahid (USA))
(260) ◆ 358^{3} (591) (735) 1569^{16} (1947) 2372^{10} 3045^{8} 3929^{6} 4742^{7}

Mason Ette *C G Cox* a64 82
4 br m Grand Lodge(USA)—Karlaska (Lashkari)
1800^{7} 1928^{5} 2565^{3} 3064^{7}

Massams Lane *G C Bravery* a58 55
4 b g Lahib(USA)—Night Trader (USA) (Melyno)
2550^{10} 4409^{8} 6421^{13}

Massiuta (UAE) *C E Brittain* 62
3 b f Selkirk(USA)—Forget Me Not (IRE) (Danehill Dancer (IRE))
1599^{9}

Massive (IRE) *D Selvaratnam* a36 103
4 b g Marju(IRE)—Khatela (IRE) (Shernazar)
$649a^{6}$

Massive Drama (USA) *Dale Romans* a115
3 bb c Kafwain(USA)—Peyvon (USA) (Slewacide (USA))
$1088a^{9}$

Masta Plasta (IRE) *D Nicholls* a99 114
5 b g Mujadil(USA)—Silver Arrow (USA) (Shadeed (USA))
2211^{3} (2626) 2828^{5} $3243a^{2}$ (4004a) 4550^{2} $5130a^{5}$ $5551a^{2}$ (6568a) $6963a^{3}$

Master At Arms *Daniel Mark Loughnane* a85 67
5 ch g Grand Lodge(USA)—L'Ideale (USA) (Alysheba (USA))
3606^{11} (4935) ◆ 5476^{2} 5967^{7} 6957^{2} (7515) 7747^{5} ◆

Master Chef (IRE) *B Olsen* a83 96
3 b c Oasis Dream—Miss Honorine (IRE) (Highest Honor (FR))
$5957a^{5}$

Mastercraftsman (IRE) *A P O'Brien* 118
2 ch c Danehill Dancer(IRE)—Starlight Dreams (USA) (Black Tie Affair)
(3534a) ◆ (4465a) ◆ (5946a) ◆ $6520a^{4}$

Master Fong (IRE) *B W Hills* a62 81
2 b g Dr Fong(USA)—Last Cry (FR) (Peintre Celebre (USA))
4304^{5} ◆ 4625^{14} (6198) 6756^{8}

Master Kid (DEN) *B Olsen*
3 b c Academy Award(IRE)—Stolga (FR) (Baillamont (USA))
$4918a^{9}$

Master Lightfoot *W R Swinburn* a80 61
2 b c Kyllachy—Two Step (Mujtahid (USA))
4346^{6} 5430^{2} 6389^{4} 6769^{2}

Master Mahogany *R J Hodges* a80 69
7 b g Bandmaster(USA)—Impropriety (Law Society (USA))
1532^{6} 2101^{8} 2476^{3} 2642^{6} 3090^{9} 3518^{4} 4953^{2} 5118^{2} (5312) 5863^{7}

Master Marvel (IRE) *T J O'Mara* 84
7 ch g Selkirk(USA)—Insijaam (USA) (Secretariat (USA))
$1497a^{12}$

Master Nimbus *J J Quinn* a53 68
8 b g Cloudings(IRE)—Miss Charlie (Pharly (FR))
(3176) 3399^{4} 3912^{3} (4457) 4690^{3} 5305^{2}

Master Noverre (IRE) *R A Fahey* 105
2 ch g Noverre(USA)—Boston Ivy (USA) (Mark Of Esteem (IRE))
(2186) (3663) 5226^{2} 5889^{5}

Master Of Arts (USA) *Sir Mark Prescott* a104 87
3 b g Swain(IRE)—Grazia (Sharpo)
(2260) ◆ (2451) ◆ (2563) (3319) (4089) (4269)

Masterofceremonies *James Moffatt* 77
5 ch g Definite Article—Darakah (Doulab (USA))
6487^{13}

Master Of Disguise *C G Cox* 83
2 b c Kyllachy—St James's Antigua (IRE) (Law Society (USA))
2098^{2} 6426^{21} (6894)

Master Of Light *P A Blockley* 54
3 b c Bertolini(USA)—Lucky Dip (Tirol)
1960^{9} 5261^{5} ◆ 5636^{5}

Masterofthehorse (IRE) *A P O'Brien* 105
2 b c Sadler's Wells(USA)—Shouk (Shirley Heights)
$6316a^{3}$ 6973^{11}

Master O'Reilly (NZ) *Danny O'Brien* 117
6 br g O'Reilly(NZ)—Without Remorse (NZ) (Bakharoff (USA))
$6835a^{7}$ $7188a^{4}$

Master Pegasus *J R Boyle* a89 89
5 b g Lujain(USA)—Seeking Utopia (Wolfhound (USA))
315^{10} 531^{4} 1335^{13} 1585^{6} 4694^{7} 5033^{8} 5349^{10} 6599^{4} 6758^{3} 7360^{7} 7495^{4} 7610^{7}

Master Rooney (IRE) *B Smart* 87
2 bb c Cape Cross(IRE)—Wimple (USA) (Kingmambo (USA))
2937^{2} ◆ 4164^{2} 6213^{4} (7020)

Mastership (IRE) *J J Quinn* a101 102
4 ch g Best Of The Bests(IRE)—Shady Point (IRE) (Unfuwain (USA))
2172^{9} 3056^{2} 3921^{4} 4405^{9} ◆ 5347^{3} 6269^{29} 6772^{8} 7245^{12}

Master Spy *J H M Gosden* a91 86
3 br c Cape Cross(IRE)—Secret Seeker (USA) (Mr Prospector (USA))
1379^{4} (1701) ◆ 2194^{10} 3002^{4} 3745^{6} 4335^{2} 5202^{6} (Dead)

Master Wells (IRE) *J D Frost* a34 69
7 b g Sadler's Wells(USA)—Eljazzi (Artaius (USA))
3970^{4} 4526^{7}

Mastery *M Johnston* 98
2 b c Sulamani(IRE)—Moyesii (USA) (Diesis)
(6581) ◆ 6779^{3}

Mast Track (USA) *Robert Frankel* a120 110
4 b h Mizzen Mast(USA)—Nawal (FR) (Homme De Loi (IRE))
$6995a^{5}$

Maswerte (IRE) *L M Cumani* a71
2 b c Fraam—Rose Chime (IRE) (Tirol)
7465^{7} 7769^{5} 7830^{2}

Mataram (USA) *W Jarvis* a91 71
5 b g Matty G(USA)—Kalinka (USA) (Mr Prospector (USA))
97^{2} 309^{2} (409) 592^{8} 929^{4} 1502^{2} 1935^{4} 2711^{8} 7821^{7}

Mathool (IRE) *C W Thornton* 30
3 b f Alhaarth(IRE)—Mathaayl (USA) (Shadeed (USA))
1965^{11} 2468^{10} 3555^{15}

Matilda Poliport *W R Swinburn* a19
2 b f Mind Games—Poppy Carew (IRE) (Danehill (USA))
7227^{12}

Matinee Idol *Mrs S Lamyman* a45 49
5 ch m In The Wings—Bibliotheque (USA) (Woodman (USA))
282^{2} 435^{6} 551^{5} 600^{7} 637^{2} 787^{3} 1121^{7} 1551^{9} 3687^{7} 4698^{4} 5396^{11}

Matraash (USA) *M Johnston* 55
2 b c Elusive Quality(USA)—Min Alhawa (USA) (Riverman (USA))
6655^{9}

Matrix (GER) *W Baltromei* 110
7 b h Big Shuffle(USA)—Massena (GER) (Konigsstuhl (GER))
$2214a^{4}$ $3752a^{8}$

Matsunosuke *A B Coogan* a105 107
6 b g Magic Ring(IRE)—Lon Isa (Grey Desire)
907^{2} 1831^{4} 1917^{13} 2404^{12} 2626^{15} 2712^{5} 3101^{13} 3739^{9} 3943^{6} 4159^{4} 4445^{26} 5509^{4} 5906^{3} 6285^{3} 6429^{4} 6669^{5} 6902^{7} 7151^{3} 7365^{4} 7576^{3} 7614^{2} 7716^{2} (7756) 7805^{3}

Matsurida Gogh (JPN) *S Kunieda* 123
5 br h Sunday Silence(USA)—Paper Rain (USA) (Bel Bolide (USA))
$1666a^{6}$ $7511a^{4}$

Mattamia (IRE) *B R Millman* 68
2 b g Makbul—Lady Dominatrix (IRE) (Danehill Dancer (IRE))
2124^{9} 2999^{5} 4164^{8} 5103^{5}

Matterofact (IRE) *M S Saunders* a67 75
5 b m Bold Fact(USA)—Willow Dale (IRE) (Danehill (USA))
2102^{2} 2330^{3} 2836^{3} 4273^{5} 4370^{3} (4693) 4958^{2} 5121^{3} 5645^{2} (5817) 6131^{2} 6388^{2} 6658^{6} 6750^{5} 7081^{3} 7276^{11} 7478^{3} 7621^{11}

Matters At Hand (IRE) *D K Weld* a81 81
3 b g Red Ransom(USA)—Hint Of Humour (USA) (Woodman (USA))
$2023a^{5}$

Matwan (FR) *C Boutin* 93
2 b f Indian Rocket—Spain (FR) (Bering)
(4441a) $5330a^{11}$ $5850a^{7}$ 6644^{16}

Maundy Money *David Marnane* a82 97
5 b g King's Best(USA)—Royal Gift (Cadeaux Genereux)
(4514a) (4576a) $5731a^{2}$ $6845a^{6}$

Mauralakana (FR) *Christophe Clement* a89 113
5 b m Muhtathir—Jimkana (FR) (Double Bed (FR))
(4888a) $6968a^{6}$

Maverick's Magic *W G M Turner*
2 ch g Karinga Bay—Magical Day (Halling (USA))
5778^{13}

Maverin (IRE) *J Noseda* 77
2 ch c King's Best(USA)—Minerva (IRE) (Caerleon (USA))
6944^{4}

Ma Vie En Rose (IRE) *A M Balding* a47 62
3 b f Red Ransom(USA)—Stop Out (Rudimentary (USA))
2566^{10} 2918^{5} 3381^{8} 3867^{4} 4301^{3} 4638^{2}

Mawatheeq (USA) *M P Tregoning* a83 104
3 b c Danzig(USA)—Sarayir (USA) (Mr Prospector (USA))
4730^{2} (5278) ◆ (6242) ◆ 6780^{6}

Mawjaat (IRE) *J L Dunlop* 67
2 b f Sakhee(USA)—Al Durrah (USA) (Darshaan)
2835^{3} ◆ 4380^{8} 5066^{6} 5585^{5} 6761^{10}

Maxabillion (IRE) *Edward Lynam* a58 44
3 b g No Excuse Needed—Elfin Queen (IRE) (Fairy King (USA))
$826a^{12}$

Maximix *G L Moore* a70 57
5 gr g Linamix(FR)—Time Will Show (FR) (Exit To Nowhere (USA))
2245^{8}

Maximo (GER) *T G McCourt* a77 77
5 b g Orpen(USA)—Maltage (USA) (Affirmed (USA))
$4514a^{4}$ $6511a^{5}$

Maxim's (ARG) *L Reuterskiold Jr* a66 96
7 br g Lode(USA)—Mari's Ballerina (USA) (Mari's Book (USA))
$2232a^{8}$ $5957a^{4}$

Maximus Aurelius (IRE) *J Jay* a76 73
3 b c Night Shift(USA)—Dame's Violet (IRE) (Groom Dancer (USA))
1348^{2} 1540^{3} 2161^{10} 2907^{2} 3393^{15} 4156^{16} 7405^{2} 7494^{9}

Max One Two Three (IRE) *Tom Dascombe* 99
3 b f Princely Heir(IRE)—Dakota Sioux (IRE) (College Chapel)
1830^{11}

Maxwell Hawke (IRE) *P W Chapple-Hyam* 63
2 br c Rock Of Gibraltar(IRE)—Twice The Ease (Green Desert (USA))
3879^{5}

Maxwil *G L Moore* 90
3 b g Storming Home—Lady Donatella (Last Tycoon)
2151^{2} ◆ 3038^{3} 3527^{6}

Mayaalah *J H M Gosden* a72 68
2 b f Cape Cross(IRE)—Chater (Alhaarth (IRE))
5048^{5} 6167^{3} 6887^{4} 7332^{4}

Mayadeen (IRE) *R A Fahey* a57 63
6 b g King's Best(USA)—Inaaq (Lammtarra (USA))
1219^{11} 5456^{3} 6161^{5} (6728) 6812^{2} 7696^{8}

Maybach *B Bo* a99 98
7 gr h Machiavellian(USA)—Capote Line (USA) (Capote (USA))
$2233a^{2}$

Maybe Blue *Mrs L J Mongan*
2 b f Josr Algarhoud(IRE)—Rosina May (IRE) (Danehill Dancer (IRE))
1177^{6}

Maybe Grace (IRE) *Mrs John Harrington* a82 82
2 b f Hawk Wing(USA)—Close Regards (IRE) (Danehill (USA))
$6319a^{7}$

Maybe I Will (IRE) *S Dow* a70 73
3 b f Hawk Wing(USA)—Canterbury Lace (USA) (Danehill (USA))
2118^{13} (2639) (3023) 3679^{6} 4104^{11} 5149^{7} (5602) 6028^{10}

Maybe I Wont *Lucinda Featherstone* a72 72
3 b g Kyllachy—Surprise Surprise (Robellino (USA))
93^{3} 186^{2} 339^{2} (393) 6792^{8} 7466^{4} 7586^{6} 7748^{7} 7811^{7}

Maybeme *N Bycroft* 59
2 b f Lujain(USA)—Malvadilla (IRE) (Doyoun)
4896^{8} 5859^{8}

May Boy *R J Hodges*
2 br g Bandmaster(USA)—Kathies Pet (Tina's Pet)
5487^{5} 5778^{15} 6709^{10}

May Day Queen (IRE) *R Hannon* a74 86
3 b f Danetime(IRE) —Birthday Present (Cadeaux Genereux)
1837[4] 2196[13] 2276[10] 2757[10]

Mayfair's Future *J R Jenkins* a64 55
3 b c High Estate—Riva La Belle (Ron's Victory (USA))
4730[7] 4929[8] 5790[7] 6437[10] 7300[2] (7463) 7761[5]

Maylea Gold (IRE) *Mrs S C Bradburne*
5 b g Fasliyev(USA) —Clipping (Kris)
1827[14] 1951[10] 2578[9]

May Need A Spell *J G M O'Shea* a59 49
2 b g Needwood Blade—Under My Spell (Wizard King)
5431[6] 6051[8] 6488[10]

Mayoman (IRE) *M Mullineaux* a67 70
3 b c Namid—America Lontana (FR) (King's Theatre (IRE))
(2396) 3455[7] 4397[8] 5991[12] 7346[2] 7478[6] 7653[10]

Mayorstone (IRE) *B Smart* 10
2 ch f Exceed And Excel(AUS) —Coolrain Lady (IRE) (Common Grounds)
4647[8]

May Parkin (IRE) *Eamon Tyrrell* a48 1
3 b f Acclamation—Pretext (Polish Precedent (USA))
4987[12] 7074[6]

Maysarah (IRE) *G A Butler* a76 52
4 b m Green Desert(USA) —Royale (IRE) (Royal Academy (USA))
55[2]

Mays Louise *B P J Baugh* a29
4 ch m Sir Harry Lewis(USA) —Maysimp (IRE) (Mac's Imp (USA))
172[6] 289[10]

Mayta Capac (USA) *E F Vaughan* a57
2 ch c Thunder Gulch(USA) —Yvecrique (FR) (Epervier Bleu)
4728[4]

Mayweather *J-C Rouget* a100 98
3 ch c Nayef(USA) —Misplace (IRE) (Green Desert (USA))
1239a[5] 2096a[3] 2654a[17]

Mazaaya (USA) *D R Lanigan* a94 91
3 b f Cozzene(USA) —Mariamme (USA) (Verbatim (USA))
(1746) 2201[4] 3676[2] 4021[8] (4894) 5209[3] 6034[15] 6293[6]

Mazara (IRE) *J L Dunlop* 69
3 ch g Alhaarth(IRE) —Azdihaar (USA) (Mr Prospector (USA))
1840[6]

Mazaris (IRE) *L M Cumani* a72 63
3 b g Mull Of Kintyre(USA) —Kingdom Pearl (Statoblest)
4255[4] 5150[3] 5426[2] ◆ 5790[3] 6206[2] 6660[2] 6935[3]

Maze (IRE) *B Smart* 101
3 ch g Dr Fong(USA) —Aryadne (Rainbow Quest (USA))
1400[5] 2409[7] 3047[18] 3491[5] 4145[6]

Mazloma (USA) *M R Channon* 71
3 b f Kingmambo(USA) —Opera Aida (IRE) (Sadler's Wells (USA))
1222[3] 1946[6] 3205[4]

Mazzola *M R Channon* a81 82
2 b g Bertolini(USA) —Elegant Dance (Statoblest)
1693[3] 1927[4] (2349) 2507[2] 2826[5] 3470[3] 3902[2] 4434[4] (4628) 5466[11] 5866[3] 6469[6] 6769[7]

McCartney (GER) *Saeed Bin Suroor* 114
3 bb c In The Wings—Messina (GER) (Dashing Blade)
2131[6]

Mcconnell (USA) *G L Moore* a77 82
3 ch g Petionville(USA) —Warsaw Girl (IRE) (Polish Precedent (USA))
25[2] 135[3] 1839[7] (2302) 2996[5] 4130[4] 4335[3] 7712[12]

Mceldowney *M C Chapman* a44 91
6 b g Zafonic(USA) —Ayodhya (IRE) (Astronef)
5858[14] 5961[9] 6527[10] 6838[9]

Mchepple *W Storey* 50
3 b f Fleetwood(IRE) —Roleover Mania (Tragic Role (USA))
993[5] 1141[6] 1560[7] 1754[9] 3230[6] 3580[6] 3715[6] 6111[7]

Mcnairobi *P D Cundell* a89 86
5 b m Josr Algarhoud(IRE) —Bonita Bee (King Of Spain)
969[8] 1335[12]

Mcqueen (IRE) *J T Stimpson* a53 65
8 ch g Barathea(IRE) —Bibliotheque (USA) (Woodman (USA))
2572[11] 3279[2] 3642[6] 5396[8]

Meadow Cottage (IRE) *Mrs P Ford* a32
5 b g Indian Danehill(IRE) —Lady Of The Chase (IRE) (Doyoun)
396[7] 758[10] 919[11]

Meancog (IRE) *J S Moore* a54 74
4 ch m Monashee Mountain(USA) —Mislead (IRE) (Distinctly North (USA))
7346[5] 7478[7] 7618[4]

Mean Machine (IRE) *D Flood* a49 56
6 b g Idris(IRE) —Date Mate (USA) (Thorn Dance (USA))
4029[10] 4105[12] 4785[13] 5968[10] 6824[11] 7782[9]

Mean Mr Mustard (IRE) *J A Osborne* a56 41
2 b g Invincible Spirit(IRE) —White Lavender (USA) (Mt. Livermore (USA))
1955[8] 2999[9] 3315[3] 3809[8] 4389[4] 4768[8]

Measured Response *J G M O'Shea* a38 59
6 ch g Inchinor—Seal Indigo (IRE) (Glenstal (USA))
369[5] 1895[4] 2557[6]

Measurement (IRE) *R Hannon* 95
2 b c Viking Ruler(AUS) —El-Libaab (Unfuwain (USA))
2562[3] (2916) 3522[2] (3924) 5462[5] 5898[3] 6267[7]

Meathop (IRE) *R F Fisher* a44 46
4 b g Imperial Ballet(IRE) —Jacobina (Magic Ring (IRE))
663[10] 1452[P] 1951[9]

Medan (GER) *P Schiergen*
4 gr h Singspiel(IRE) —Midnight Society (USA) (Imp Society (USA))
4911a[8]

Media Hora (CHI) *F Castro* a67 24
8 ch g Somersham(USA) —Membrana (CHI) (The Great Shark (USA))
2232a[6]

Media Stars *J A Osborne* a65 41
3 gr g Green Desert(USA) —Starine (FR) (Mendocino (USA))
1855[3] 2360[9] 2695[13] 3763[5] 4182[5]

Medicea Sidera *E F Vaughan* a96 99
4 br m Medicean—Broughtons Motto (Mtoto)
1981[7] 2947[2] 3210[6] (4424) 6271[2] 6782[2]

Medici Gold *B G Powell* a34 50
3 ch f Medicean—Silence Is Golden (Danehill Dancer (IRE))
3023[8] 3524[12] 4054[9] 4326[11]

Medicine Path *P W Chapple-Hyam* a111 116
4 b h Danehill Dancer(IRE) —Indian Mystery (IRE) (Indian Ridge)
(418) (1326) ◆ 1631[7]

Medici Pearl *T D Easterby* a39 93
4 b m Medicean—In Love Again (IRE) (Prince Rupert (FR))
2375[6] (2781) (3369) 3892[5] 4661[8] (5635) (6070) ◆ 6482[3] 7245[10]

Medici Time *T D Easterby* 70
3 gr g Medicean—Pendulum (Pursuit Of Love)
1558[4] 2272[7] 2911[3] 3126[8] 6042[10] (6791) 7021[9]

Medieval Maiden *Mrs L J Mongan* a69 56
5 gr m Zaha(CAN) —Brillante (FR) (Green Dancer (USA))
132[3] 332[5] 436[6] (695) 794[2] 934[3] 1459[6] 1692[5] 2949[2] 3160[2] 3562[11] 4568[6] 5611[11] 5802[14] 6729[10] 7385[7]

Meditation *I A Wood* a82 64
6 ch m Inchinor—Trojan Desert (Troy)
28[5] 139[3] 316[3] 340[6] 546[9] 646[7] (736)

Medlock *J Noseda* 54
2 b c Johannesburg(USA) —Marcelia (Coronado's Quest (USA))
4199[8] 4890[9] 5811[7]

Meeriss (IRE) *M R Channon* a102 99
3 b c Dubai Destination(USA) —Bless The Bride (IRE) (Darshaan)
1810[2] 2142[5] 2610[9] 4197[6] 4622[7] 5257[3] 5942[2]

Meethaaq (USA) *Sir Michael Stoute* 89
3 b c Kingmambo(USA) —New Harmony (USA) (A.P. Indy (USA))
2370[2] ◆ (2668)

Meeting Of Minds *D Carroll* a50 46
4 b m Mind Games—Turn Back (Pivotal)
277[5]

Me Fein *A P Stringer* a78 5
4 gr g Desert Prince(IRE) —Attachment (USA) (Trempolino (USA))
(863) (2051) 5992[7] 6558[7] 7177[9] 7447[13] 7787[10]

Mefraas (IRE) *E A L Dunlop* 67
2 b g King's Best(USA) —Khaizarana (Alhaarth (IRE))
3274[4] 3926[3] 4394[8]

Megalala (IRE) *J J Bridger* a64 62
7 b g Petardia—Avionne (Derrylin)
(160) (242) 303[2] 541[6] 728[2] 881[5] 1148[3] 1564[5] 1644[2] 1932[6] 2561[3] 2799[3] 4275[11] (5058) 5512[8] 6775[12]

Megalo Maniac *R A Fahey* a72 62
5 b g Efisio—Sharanella (Shareef Dancer (USA))
1780[11] 2081[8] 2706[9] 3691[5] 3834[5] 5045[2] 5797[7] (7049) (7180) 7382[2] 7503[5] 7651[8]

Megasecret *R Hannon* a60 69
2 b c Falbrav(IRE) —Silver Quest (Rainbow Quest (USA))
5929[10] 6341[2] 7020[4] 7303[2] 7458[12]

Mega Steps (IRE) *Jennie Candlish* 45
4 b g Groom Dancer(USA) —Marmaga (IRE) (Shernazar)
6812[8] 7042[8]

Mega Watt (IRE) *W Jarvis* 81
3 b g Acclamation—Kilshanny (Groom Dancer (USA))
1535[2] (1899) 2311[5] 3527[4] 4021[4] 4906[6] 5865[5] 6949[5]

Meg Jicaro *Mrs L Williamson* 62
2 b f Reel Buddy(USA) —Anita In Wales (IRE) (Anita's Prince)
995[3] ◆ 1627[2] 1914[6] 2473[5] 2865[8] 6051[16] 6158[5] 6579[11] 7130[5]

Mehendi (IRE) *B J Meehan* 75
2 b g Indian Danehill(IRE) —Wedding Cake (IRE) (Groom Dancer (USA))
6604[4] 6893[2]

Meinardus (IRE) *T D Barron* a27 51
3 b g Noverre(USA) —Volte Face (Polar Falcon (USA))
634[7] 4454[4] 5110[11] 5457[5]

Meirig's Dream (IRE) *B G Powell* 58
2 b g Golan(IRE) —Women In Love (IRE) (Danehill (USA))
2042[5] 3603[15] 3968[11]

Meisho Samson (JPN) *S Takahashi* 123
5 b h Opera House—My Vivien (JPN) (Dancing Brave (USA))
6522a[10] 7511a[6]

Mejala (IRE) *J L Dunlop* 64
2 b f Red Ransom(USA) —Wissal (USA) (Woodman (USA))
5643[5] 6076[10]

Mejhar (IRE) *E J Creighton* a61 47
8 b g Desert Prince(IRE) —Factice (USA) (Known Fact (USA))
348[4]

Mekong Melody (IRE) *C G Cox* a66 88
3 b f Cape Cross(IRE) —Nini Princesse (IRE) (Niniski (USA))
748[2] ◆ 961[6] 1525[2] (1930) ◆ 2953[7] 3679[2] 4022[3] 4583[4] 5149[2] 5506[6] 6027[3] 6266[2]

Mekong Miss *J Jay* 62
2 ch f Mark Of Esteem(IRE) —Missouri (Charnwood Forest (IRE))
5650[7] 6014[3] 6473[16] 6761[15]

Melalchrist *K A Ryan* a72 91
6 b g Almaty(IRE) —Lawless Bridget (Alnasr Alwasheek)
983[13] 1393[7] 1908[5]

Melandre *M Brittain* a47 45
6 b m Lujain(USA) —Talighta (USA) (Barathea (IRE))
522[4] 641[6] 857[7] 3546[9]

Melange (USA) *P F I Cole* 49
2 b c Alphabet Soup(USA) —Garendare (Vacarme (USA))
5227[12] 6230[11]

Mel Del (IRE) *L Byrne* 27
3 b f Minardi(USA) —Parker's Cove (USA) (Woodman (USA))
3861a[7]

Melhor Impossivel (BRZ) *A Selvaratnam* a79
7 b h Fast Fingers(BRZ) —Desapercebida (BRZ) (Grammont (BRZ))
566a[13]

Melia (GR) *Jane Chapple-Hyam* 36
3 b f So Factual(USA) —Eriza (Distant Relative)
4651[9] 6566[9]

Melkatant *N Bycroft* 42
2 b f Rock City—Change Of Image (Spectrum (IRE))
6229[9] 6788[9] 7172[7]

Mellifluous (IRE) *J W Hills* a33 24
3 b f Noverre(USA) —Danestar (Danehill (USA))
1855[9] 2456[11] 3692[7]

Mellow Mixture *R Hannon* a78
2 b c Marju(IRE) —Night Owl (Night Shift (USA))
6977[18] 7343[6] 7552[2] 7699[5]

Melodramatic (IRE) *R Charlton* 102
3 b f Sadler's Wells(USA) —My Branch (Distant Relative)
1423[2] (1965) 2975[2] 3742[6] 5120[9] 6034[6]

Melody Break (USA) *A & G Botti* 101
3 b f Sunday Break(JPN) —Lycalleged (CAN) (Alleged (USA))
2231a[15] 3076a[15]

Melody Fair (IRE) *W R Muir*
3 b f Montjeu(IRE) —Manchaca (FR) (Highest Honor (FR))
4909[13]

Melt (IRE) *R Hannon* a61 61
3 b f Intikhab(USA) —Kindle (Selkirk (USA))
4368[6] 4772[5] 5574[2] 6334[12] 6564[11] 6889[2] 7256[5] 7437[3]

Me Me Me *E F Vaughan* a25
3 b g Red Ransom(USA) —Jalousie (IRE) (Barathea (IRE))
6883[8]

Memphis Man *P D Evans* a81 88
5 b g Bertolini(USA) —Something Blue (Petong)
84[3] 194[2] 278[3] 442[6] 618[2] 717[5] 824[8] 1023[3] 1138[3] 1368[4] 1430[2] 1522[9] 1872[4] 1996[4] 2406[5] 2923[5] 2992[3] 3313[7] 3797[3] 3903[5] 4030[6] 4440[5] (4858) 5121[5] 5233[2] 5400[2] 5594[8] 6842[5] 7584[7] 5991[3] 6200[3] (6340) 7239[17] 7697[6]

Men Bhavin Bradley (USA) *J Noseda* 63
2 bb c Officer(USA) —Lucky Kodi (AUS) (Thunder Gulch (USA))
6923[3]

Menestrol (FR) *D Prod'Homme* a88 106
6 ch h Dyhim Diamond(IRE) —Magaletta (FR) (Galetto (FR))
5115a[5]

Meneur (FR) *G L Moore* 71
6 gr g Septieme Ciel(USA) —Mamamia (FR) (Linamix (FR))
5465[4] ◆ 6243[11]

Menfromallover (IRE) *B N Pollock* a42 61
3 br f Statue Of Liberty(USA) —Gilding The Lily (IRE) (High Estate)
4531[9]

Menhir Bay *D K Ivory* a52
2 b g Sure Blade(USA) —Turkish Delight (Prince Sabo)
7674[6] 7802[6]

Menkaura *John R Upson* a37 79
5 b g Pivotal—Nekhbet (Artaius (USA))
7667[11]

Me No Puppet *E J Alston* a48 12
4 b m Mtoto—Puppet Play (IRE) (Broken Hearted)
249[4] 698[7] 804[6]

Mensadil *Mrs L Stubbs* 40
3 b g Mind Games—Jezadil (IRE) (Mujadil (USA))
2455[9] 3953[6] 4794[5] 5457[4] 6004[12]

Menwaal (FR) *Michael David Murphy* 96
6 b g Montjeu(IRE) —Mythical Creek (USA) (Pleasant Tap (USA))
7244[17]

Meohmy *M R Channon* a49 48
5 b m Marju(IRE) —Meshhed (USA) (Gulch (USA))
934[4] 1044[8] 1281[5] 2467[14] 3025[4] 3361[8] 4261[5] 4774[2] 5105[12] 5427[7] 5631[7]

Merchant Marine (USA) *H Allen Jerkens* a114
4 b g Tiznow(USA) —Head East (USA) (Gone West (USA))
6373a[3]

Merchant Of Dubai *G A Swinbank* a99 98
3 b c Dubai Destination(USA) —Chameleon (Green Desert (USA))
2889[3] 3673[2] 4784[10] (5967) 6154[4] (6355) ◆ (6652) 7223[5]

Mercury Chief (SAF) *A Manuel* a73 86
7 ch g London News(SAF) —Ivor's Girl (SAF) (Northern Guest (USA))
295a[9] 497a[11]

Merdaam *J L Dunlop* 48
2 ch c Dubai Destination(USA) —Faydah (USA) (Bahri (USA))
5579[9]

Meribel (USA) *Helen Pitts* a94 111
5 bb m Peaks And Valleys(USA) —Count To Six (USA) (Saratoga Six (USA))
4888a[7]

Meridian Line (IRE) *J G Portman* a54 81
3 b f Trans Island—Meranie Girl (IRE) (Mujadil (USA))
2196[17] 2773[7] 3696[5] 4102[8] 4943[3] 5217[6] 5601[3] (6024) 6564[13] 6878[4] 7254[9] 7357[11]

Merlin's Dancer *S Dow* a103 95
8 b g Magic Ring(IRE) —La Piaf (FR) (Fabulous Dancer (USA))
676[3] 907[7] 1582[4] 1956[3] 2828[2] 4555[10] 5270[8] 5906[14]

Merlins Quest *J M Bradley* a32 60
4 b g Wizard King—Wonderland (IRE) (Dolphin Street (FR))
120[12]

Merrion Tiger (IRE) *A G Foster* a59 59
3 ch g Choisir(AUS) —Akita (IRE) (Foxhound (USA))
1429[5] 1817[9] 2380[8] 3592[4] 3960[10] 4377[3] 5162[7] 7340[4]

Merry Diva *C F Wall* 73
2 b f Bahamian Bounty—Merry Rous (Rousillon (USA))
6341[6] (6885)

Merrymadcap (IRE) *M Blanshard* a79 76
6 b g Lujain(USA) —Carina Clare (Slip Anchor)
973[2] 1266[3] 1898[5] 2101[4] 2561[2] 2770[5] 4390[4] 4819[4] (5059) 5312[5] 5492[10] 5935[7]

Merrymaker *W M Brisbourne* a79 72
8 b g Machiavellian(USA) —Wild Pavane (Dancing Brave (USA))
1340[5] 2012[5] 2572[8] 2888[5] 3545[2] 3891[5] 3950[3] 4935[4] (6115) 6708[4] 7293[7]

Merry May *R Hannon* a36 30
2 b f Compton Place—Swift Dame (IRE) (Montjeu (IRE))
6077[11] 6341[10] 6879[10] 7468[11]

Merryvale Man *Miss Kariana Key* a8 17
11 b g Rudimentary(USA) —Salu (Ardross)
4947[7]

Merton Lad *T G Mills* a66 37
2 ch g Fantastic Light(USA) —Artistic Blue (USA) (Diesis)
5754[8] 6165[4] 7023[6] 7505[3]

Merveilles *Mrs John Harrington* a67 101
5 b g Vettori(IRE) —Finlaggan (Be My Chief (USA))
3250[7] 4100a[9]

Mesa Gold (USA) *David E Pate*
2 u c (USA) — (USA) (Carson City (USA))
6502a[8]

Mesbaah (IRE) *R A Fahey* a87 102
4 b g Noverre(USA) —Deyaajeer (USA) (Dayjur (USA))
1045[6] 1469[16] 2103[11] 2582[17] 3046[2] 3664[2] 3929[7] 4500[2] 5405[6] 6307[8] 6810[13] 7047[11]

Meshtri (IRE) *M A Jarvis* a81 100
3 ch c Dalakhani(IRE) —Arctic Hunt (IRE) (Bering)
1172[2] ◆ (1615) 4784[2] 5573[9] 5894[5] ◆ (6288)

Mess Around (FR) *J-C Rouget* 98
3 ro c Sagacity(FR) —Bubba Gump (IRE) (Charnwood Forest (IRE))
1362a[5]

Messiah Garvey *D Nicholls* a74 68
4 b g Lear Fan(USA) —Maid Of Camelot (Caerleon (USA))
990[7] 1188[2] 1449[6] 1775[5] 2005[10] 2891[8] 3175[5] (3662) 4073[2] 4293[11] 4919[10] 6116[12]

Messias Da Silva (USA) *J Noseda* a83 46
3 bb f Tale Of The Cat(USA) —Indy Power (USA) (A.P. Indy (USA))
2967[12] 5403[7] 5789[11] 6242[12]

Mesyaal *M R Channon* 67
2 ch c Alhaarth(IRE) —Rowaasi (Green Desert (USA))
2338[3] ◆ 2769[5] 3547[3] 4101[4] 4647[5] 4975[7] 5306[5]

Metal Guru *R Hollinshead* a70 71
4 ch m Ishiguru(USA) —Gemtastic (Tagula (IRE))
241[8] 2676[9] (2928) 3260[7] 3695[7] 4370[7] 5398[2] 6339[5] 6711[2] 7043[7] 7517[5]

Metal Madness (IRE) *M G Quinlan* 74
3 b c Acclamation—Dosha (Touching Wood (USA))
(2208) 2429[6] 2982[2] 3183[5] (4613a) 4715a[3] 6188[7]

Metaphoric (IRE) *M L W Bell* 115
4 b g Montjeu(IRE) —Virgin Hawk (USA) (Silver Hawk (USA))
3250[3] (3942) (6306)

Methaaly (IRE) *M Mullineaux* a79 89
5 b g Red Ransom(USA) —Santorini (USA) (Spinning World (USA))
241[5] 342[7] 404[8] 466[3] 782[5] (801) 994[11] 1040[6] 1191[4] 1312[2] 1488[3] 1917[11] 3435[4] 3626[13] 3956[7] (4030) (4239) (4393) ◆ 4601[2] 5493[8] 5990[3] 6069[22] 6278[3] 7737[7]

Metroland *P C Haslam* 75
2 b f Royal Applause—Chetwynd (IRE) (Exit To Nowhere (USA))
1821[3] 2140[5] 2522[2] 3078[3] (3714) (4243) 4816[6]

Metropolitan Chief *P Burgoyne* a66 63
4 b g Compton Place—Miss Up N Go (Gorytus (USA))
56[5] 749[11] 937[2] 1154[4] 1371[8] 1645[6] 2075[4] 2355[7] 3034[16]

Metropolitan Man *D M Simcock* 113
5 ch g Dr Fong(USA) —Preceder (Polish Precedent (USA))
379a[5] 745a[2] 1631[3] 2044[3] 2788[8]

Metternich (USA) *J H M Gosden* a64
3 bb c Seeking The Gold(USA) —Valentine Waltz (IRE) (Be My Guest (USA))
7344[9] 7669[4]

Mexican Pete *A King* a79 83
8 b g Atraf—Eskimo Nel (IRE) (Shy Groom (USA))
344[3]

Mexican Venture *W Jarvis* a89 82
3 b g Tobougg(IRE) —Nacho Venture (FR) (Rainbow Quest (USA))
1252[3] ◆ 1504[3] ◆ (2161) 2714[3] ◆ 3002[3] 4160[5]

Mexilhoeira *J R Gask* a37 41
4 ch m Observatory(USA) —With Music In Mind (Mind Games)
7074[10] 7363[12]

Mey Blossom *R M Whitaker* a78 92
3 ch f Captain Rio—Petra Nova (First Trump)
(1484) 1945[4] 2498[4] 2967[8] 3794[4] 4416[9] 5358[7] 6053[7] 6471[4] 6900[8] 6976[4]

Meydan City (USA) *Saeed Bin Suroor* 106
3 b c Kingmambo(USA) —Crown Of Crimson (USA) (Seattle Slew (USA))
3275[3] (3854) ◆ (4830) 5263[5] 6201[6]

Meydan Dubai (IRE) *J R Best* a72 91
3 b c Alzao(USA) —Rorkes Drift (IRE) (Royal Abjar (USA))
1806[5] ◆ 2412[8] 2794[6] 3197[9] 3527[8] 3560[6] 3899[2] 4731[10] 4927[4] 5140[4]

Meydan Groove *R Johnson* a64 69
2 b f Reset(AUS) —In The Groove (Night Shift (USA))
1680[8] 2048[5] 3135[3] (3726) 4373[3] 4828[6] 6133[2] ◆ 6761[16] 7016[10] 7281[8] 7531[14]

Meydan Princess (IRE) *J Noseda* a89 107
3 b f Choisir(AUS) —Miss Assertive (Zafonic (USA))
(1336) ◆ 1834[2] 2104[3] 3047[13] 4424[2] (6271)

Meydan Style (USA) *J Balding* a49 35
2 b c Essence Of Dubai(USA) —Polish Ruby (USA) (Polish Pro (USA))
3259[7] 3735[6] 7179[7] 7501[8]

Meyyal (USA) *B W Hills* 78
2 b c War Chant(USA) —Tamgeed (USA) (Woodman (USA))
6944[3] ◆

Mezel (USA) *S Seemar* a102 84
5 b g Grand Slam(USA) —Spankin' (USA) (A.P. Indy (USA))
384a[11] 563a[10]

Mezenah *Saeed Bin Suroor* 80
2 b f Cape Cross(IRE) —Saytarra (USA) (Seeking The Gold (USA))
6565[2] 6884[3] 7141[2]

Mezuzah *M W Easterby* a57 89
8 b g Barathea(IRE) —Mezzogiorno (Unfuwain (USA))
1069[6] 1217[8] 1327[8]

Mezzanisi (IRE) *M L W Bell* a89 90
3 b g Kalanisi(IRE) —Mezzanine (Sadler's Wells (USA))
1252[5] 2043[2] 2244[2] 2564[8] (3484) 3793[2] 4021[3] 4619[3] 5502[3] 6355[2] 6563[2]

Mezzoforte (IRE) *J S Moore* 30
2 b c One Cool Cat(USA) —Lillibits (USA) (Kingmambo (USA))
4826[16] 6342[15] 6601[8]

Mfi'Ve *B R Millman* a27 49
2 ch c Monsieur Bond(IRE) —Kastaway (Distant Relative)
4184[13] 4905[8] 5473[8] 5778[6]

Mganga *M R Channon* a63 64
3 b g Dr Fong(USA) —Hannalou (FR) (Shareef Dancer (USA))
799[5] 1128[4] 1530[9] 2045[12] 2552[5] 2915[4] 3524[2] 3799[9] 4049[5] 4115[4] 4278[2] 4810[8] 5167[8] 6036[11] 6712[7] 6746[3]

Mharadono (GER) *P Hirschberger* 108
5 b h Sharp Prod(USA) —Monalind (GER) (Park Romeo)
3515a[9] 6322a[10] 6692a[5]

Miacarla *H A McWilliams* a36 66
5 b m Forzando—Zarzi (IRE) (Suave Dancer (USA))
1309[10] 2159[6] 2448[14] 2928[7] 3080[13] 3112[4] 3260[12] (5452) 5566[5] 6164[13]

Mia Kross (IRE) *B Grizzetti* 97
5 b m Cape Cross(IRE) —Waku Waku (ITY) (Big Reef)
2438a[6]

Mia's Boy *C A Dwyer* a101 111
4 b h Pivotal—Bint Zamayem (IRE) (Rainbow Quest (USA))
(731) (805) (1067) (1456) ◆ 1723[3] (2132) ◆ 2788[6] 5896[5] 6287[5] 6476[23]

Micallef *R A Fahey* 29
3 b f Orpen(USA) —Sadler's Song (Saddlers' Hall (IRE))
2500[9] 2735[5] 3227[10]

Michael Collins (IRE) *Ms Maria Kelly* a27 57
2 b c Oasis Dream—West Virginia (IRE) (Gone West (USA))
7735[8]

Micheals Boy (IRE) *J R Boyle* a60 60
3 ch g Bertolini(USA) —Red Storm (Dancing Spree (USA))
163[3] ◆ 413[3] 3268[13] 4061[11] 4338[2] 4806[11] 5377[9] 5601[12]

Michita (USA) *J H M Gosden* 114
3 bb f Dynaformer(USA) —Thunder Kitten (USA) (Storm Cat (USA))
1470[9] (2305) 2792[7] (3153) 5243[3] 5952a[4]

Mick Is Back *G G Margarson* a57 65
4 b g Diktat—Classy Cleo (IRE) (Mujadil (USA))
258[7] 587[9] 1126[4] 1747[8] 2060[3] 2069[3] 2456[10] 2513[2] (2557) 2795[7] 3218[8] 3732[8] 4129[3] 4710[7] 5161[12] 5533[9] (5748) 6032[2] 6217[5] 6888[4] 7050[2]

Mick Jerome (IRE) *Rune Haugen* 90
7 b g Kahyasi—Acquilata (USA) (Irish River (FR))
4676a[9] (Dead)

Mickleberry (IRE) *M Brittain* a55 52
4 b m Desert Style(IRE) —Miss Indigo (Indian Ridge)
79[8] 4073[7] 5501[3] 7197[6] 7375[5]

Mickmacmagoole (IRE) *Evan Williams* 81
6 b g Sadler's Wells(USA) —Musk Lime (USA) (Private Account (USA))
1472[12]

Mick's Dancer *W R Muir* a79 57
3 b g Pivotal—La Piaf (FR) (Fabulous Dancer (USA))
1125[8] 1524[10] 3717[12] 4637[10] 5218[6] 6004[2] (6629) 6905[2] 7211[2]

Micky Mac (IRE) *T D Walford* a64 70
4 b g Lend A Hand—Gazette It Tonight (Merdon Melody)
123[6] 389[2] (559) ◆ 686[3] 3591[3] (3834) 4245[6] 6178[10] 7043[14] 7228[5]

Mickys Mate *A Crook*
3 b g Choisir(AUS) —Adept (Efisio)
7321[11] 7527[8]

Micro Chip *B G Powell*
2 b f Piccolo—Ridgewood Ruby (IRE) (Indian Ridge)
5214[14] 5535[13]

Midday *H R A Cecil* 95
2 b f Oasis Dream—Midsummer (Kingmambo (USA))
4554[7] 5241[3] (6081) ◆ 7144[4]

Middlemarch (IRE) *J S Goldie* a64 86
8 ch g Grand Lodge(USA) —Blanche Dubois (Nashwan (USA))
992[4] 1982[13] 2158[6] 2535[10] 3366[10] 4407[10] 4876[13] 5454[8] 5968[6] (6215) 6482[16] 6989[7]

Middle Of Nowhere (USA) *M A Magnusson* a35 11
3 b c Carson City(USA) —Ivy Leaf (IRE) (Nureyev (USA))
3628[10] 7304[7]

Midmaar (IRE) *M Wigham* a59 70
7 b g Cape Cross(IRE) —Khazinat El Dar (USA) (Slew O'Gold (USA))
13[3]

Mid Mon Lady (IRE) *H Rogers* a88 72
3 br f Danetime(IRE) —Shining Desert (IRE) (Green Desert (USA))
7328a[12]

Midnight Bay *M R Channon* a56 67
2 br g Domedriver(IRE) —Serriera (FR) (Highest Honor (FR))
6665[5] 6977[7] 7622[6]

Midnight Cruiser (IRE) *R Hannon* 94
2 ch c Captain Rio—Kriva (Reference Point)
4826[3] ◆ (5227) ◆ 5825[4] 6779[4] 6973[12]

Midnight Fantasy *Rae Guest* 68
2 b f Oasis Dream—Midnight Shift (IRE) (Night Shift (USA))
4202[10] 5214[8] 6555[2] 6885[3]

Midnight Fling *R Charlton* a59 71
3 b f Groom Dancer(USA) —Perfect Night (Danzig Connection (USA))
1587[3] 2757[5] 3381[9]

Midnight In May (IRE) *W R Muir* 73
2 b g Mull Of Kintyre(USA) —Birthday (IRE) (Singspiel (IRE))
6198[5] 6745[3] (6923)

Midnight Lute (USA) *Bob Baffert* a129
5 bb h Real Quiet(USA) —Candytuft (USA) (Dehere (USA))
(6999a)

Midnight Manhattan (USA) *M Halford* a45 45
2 ch f Action This Day(USA) —Lever To Heaven (IRE) (Bluebird (USA))
6319a[24]

Midnight Muse (USA) *T D Barron* 84
3 b g Swain(IRE) —Witching Hour (FR) (Fairy King (USA))
1943[8] 3251[4] 3919[13] 4539[2] 4818[3] 5862[4] (Dead)

Midnight Mystique (IRE) *T D Barron* 67
3 b f Noverre(USA) —Dark Hyacinth (IRE) (Darshaan)
1222[2] 2659[8]

Midnight Oasis *Rae Guest* a13 45
3 b f Oasis Dream—Midnight Shift (IRE) (Night Shift (USA))
3395[15] 3790[9] 4161[13] 4338[8]

Midnite Blews (IRE) *A B Haynes* a29 66
3 gr g Trans Island—Felicita (IRE) (Catrail (USA))
1123[3] 1347[4] 2099[10] (2771) 2864[5] 3021[10] 3446[3] 3765[5] 4336[6] 4580[5]

Midshipman (USA) *Bob Baffert* a118
2 ch c Unbridled's Song(USA) —Fleet Lady (USA) (Avenue Of Flags (USA))
(6997a)

Midships (USA) *Mrs A J Perrett* a98 104
3 gr c Mizzen Mast(USA) —Interim (Sadler's Wells (USA))
1600[2] 2194[2] 2825[6] 4443[3] 5573[6] (6128) 6445[2]

Midsummer Madness (IRE) *David Pinder* a49
2 b f Alhaarth(IRE) —Robalana (USA) (Wild Again (USA))
6205[8] 6682[8] 7023[12]

Mid Valley *J R Jenkins* a64 60
5 ch g Zilzal(USA) —Isabella D'Este (IRE) (Irish River (FR))
76[2] 231[4] (602) 789[2] 934[9] 1704[2] 2290[4] 2884[2] 3448[7] 4261[11] 7376[8] 7647[5]

Mid Wicket (USA) *B W Hills* 51
2 b c Strong Hope(USA) —Sunday Bazaar (USA) (Nureyev (USA))
6443[10]

Miesko (USA) *M Johnston* a73 86
3 b c Quiet American(USA) —Polish Style (USA) (Danzig (USA))
1075[7] 1484[14] 1852[7] 3263[12]

Miesque Girl (FR) *J Heloury*
2 b f Miesque's Son(USA) —Zeta Jones (FR) (Loup Solitaire (USA))
2744a[6]

Might Be Magic *P W Chapple-Hyam* a71 50
3 b g Fraam—Modelliste (Machiavellian (USA))
570[2] (698) 3737[7]

Mighty Alfred (IRE) *E A L Dunlop* 55
3 gr c Kendor(FR) —Night Shifter (IRE) (Night Shift (USA))
2673[11]

Mighty Kitchener (USA) *P Howling* a72 55
5 br g Mighty(USA) —Libeccio (NZ) (Danzatore (CAN))
3448[12] 3614[10] 4490[5] 4932[6] 7089[6]

Mighty Moon *R A Fahey* a90 86
5 gr g Daylami(IRE) —Moon Magic (Polish Precedent (USA))
1580[2] (2135) 4511a[9] 5498[5] 6817[28] 7128[2]

Mighty Mover (IRE) *B Palling* a66 47
6 ch g Bahhare(USA) —Ericeira (IRE) (Anita's Prince)
44[9] 323[7] 559[2] 686[2] 872[7] 2640[15] 4936[12] 6929[5] 7169[4] 7427[11]

Mignonette (IRE) *E A L Dunlop* a58 23
3 b f Fasliyev(USA) —Labrusca (Grand Lodge (USA))
1050[4] 1721[6] 4166[13]

Miguelight (FR) *Mme P Alexanian* a53 79
2 b c Divine Light(JPN) —Miguelina Pous (FR) (Kaid Pous (FR))
3052a[6] 4441a[9]

Mikado *Jonjo O'Neill* a28 74
7 b g Sadler's Wells(USA) —Free At Last (Shirley Heights)
5853[9] 6288[12] 6948[20] 7515[9]

Mikao (IRE) *M H Tompkins* a72 96
7 b g Tagula(IRE) —Oumaladia (IRE) (Waajib)
2372[9] 2599[9] 3925[7] 4178[5] 4662[5] 5100[7] 7046[4]

Mikhail Fokine (IRE) *A P O'Brien* a68 99
3 b c Sadler's Wells(USA) —Rain Flower (IRE) (Indian Ridge)
3513a[7] 5921a[7] 7008a[10]

Milanais (FR) *B De Watrigant* 118
2 ch c Dyhim Diamond(IRE) —Milanaise (FR) (Marignan (USA))
5330a[4] 5739a[2] 6520a[2] 7163a[6]

Milanollo *M L W Bell* a64 64
3 b f Soviet Star(USA) —Military Tune (IRE) (Nashwan (USA))
694[2] 1163[4] 2495[8] 2956[4] 3314[5] 4727[12] 6048[9]

Mileaminutemurphy *R Hannon* a57 30
3 b g Fasliyev(USA) —Shining Hour (USA) (Red Ransom (USA))
265[5] 590[4] 629[8] 732[4] 932[3] 1081[6] 2255[16]

Mile High Lad (USA) *George Baker* a75
2 bb c Sky Mesa(USA) —Thunder Warmth (USA) (Thunder Gulch (USA))
6837[7] 7422[7] 7622[2]

Miles Gloriosus (USA) *R Menichetti* a108 111
5 b h Repriced(USA) —Treasure Coast (CAN) (Foolish Pleasure (USA))
2656a[8]

Military Cross *L M Cumani* a104 104
5 b g Cape Cross(IRE) —Tipsy (Kris)
(3382) 4587[12] 6269[28]

Military Power *J W Hills* a96 97
3 b c Dubai Destination(USA) —Susun Kelapa (USA) (St Jovite (USA))
1490[2] 1926[3] (2488) (3048) ◆ 4552[2] 5942[4] 6476[19]

Mill Annie *G M Moore*
3 ch f Karinga Bay—Brookhill (GER) (Desert King (IRE))
5505[11]

Mill Beattie *G M Moore* 55
3 b f Beat All(USA) —Step On Degas (Superpower)
2488[10] 3338[4] 4076[5] 4741[11] 5362[3] 5783[10] 6562[4]

Mill Creek *Jedd O'Keeffe* 40
3 ch f Ishiguru(USA) —Hollia (Touch Boy)
2268[8] 2661[6] 3139[12] 3582[8] 4294[9] 4686[9] 5307[7]

Milldown Bay *B R Millman* 66
3 b f Bertolini(USA) —Barnacla (IRE) (Bluebird (USA))
1265[7] 1869[11] 2341[3] 3381[12] 4277[14] 6192[9] 6396[15] (Dead)

Mille Feuille (IRE) *R M Beckett* a71 72
3 b f Choisir(AUS) —Watch The Clock (Mtoto)
3694[3] 4277[2] 5049[2] (6206) 6683[4]

Millenium Sun (IRE) *E J Creighton* a33 59
4 b g Tendulkar(USA) —Millenium Love (IRE) (Great Commotion (USA))
690[12] 1135[5] 1675[14] 2069[11]

Millennium Storm (GER) *M F Harris* a50 37
3 b c Samum(GER) —Millennium Dawn (IRE) (Cadeaux Genereux)
7585[12]

Millers Saphire *K G Wingrove*
3 b f Sly—So Welcome (Weld)
195[9]

Millfield (IRE) *P R Chamings* a81 79
5 br g Elnadim(USA) —Eschasse (USA) (Zilzal (USA))
49[8] 245[2] 334[2] 775[3] (1058) 1345[5] (1645) 2101[7] 2329[6] 2722[7] 3138[5] 3761[2] (4081) 4723[14] 5350[8] 5800[3] 6491[5] 6738[9] 7315[8] (7495)

Millfields Dreams *P Leech* a72 76
9 b g Dreams End—Millfields Lady (Sayf El Arab (USA))
1488[7] 2166[2] 2205[2] 2551[4] 2644[6] 3271[11] 3313[3] (3842) 3905[2] 4555[16] 4601[7] 6125[17] 7436[9]

Millharbour (IRE) *B W Hills* 70
2 b g Nayef(USA) —My Funny Valentine (IRE) (Mukaddamah (USA))
3853[10] 7105[11]

Millie's Rock (IRE) *M J Wallace* a67 71
3 b f Rock Of Gibraltar(IRE) —Miletrian (IRE) (Marju (IRE))
1027[4] 1255[3] 2041[13] (2552) 2833[2] (3667) 3843[5] 4183[4]

Million Percent *C R Dore* a78 74
9 b g Ashkalani(IRE) —Royal Jade (Last Tycoon)
2277[3] 2753[4] 2861[4] 3371[2] 3583[6] 4084[11] 4748[9]

Milloaks (IRE) *E J Creighton*
3 b f Tamayaz(CAN) —Jaldini (IRE) (Darshaan)
1215[10] 1380[9] 1957[17]

Mill Pond *M Johnston* a43 26
2 b f King's Best(USA) —All Grain (Polish Precedent (USA))
2584[10] 5788[12] 6901[8] 7659[12]

Millville *M A Jarvis* a114 94
8 ch g Millkom—Miss Top Ville (FR) (Top Ville)
(61) 410[4] (757) 968[3] 1568[6] (7404)

Millway Beach (IRE) *Pat Eddery* 74
2 b g Diktat—Cape Cod (IRE) (Unfuwain (USA))
4151[4] 4625[12] 5459[11] 6480[7]

Milly Rose *M Blanshard* a46 57
2 br f Diktat—Milly Fleur (Primo Dominie)
2618[8] 3408[6] 4304[7]

Milne Bay (IRE) *D M Simcock* a70 10
3 b g Tagula(IRE) —Fiction (Dominion)
1669[9] 2079[7] 5574[4] (6679) 6773[4] 7357[6] (7544) (7653) ◆

Milne Graden *J Noseda* 104
4 b g Montjeu(IRE) —Glen Rosie (IRE) (Mujtahid (USA))
(1799) ◆ 4508[6] 5229[13] 5894[14]

Milord Du Bourg (FR) *K Schafflutzel*
5 br h Nombre Premier—Milady Du Bourg (FR) (Mister Sicy (FR))
422a[7]

Milton Of Campsie *S Parr* a46 69
3 ch f Medicean—La Caprice (USA) (Housebuster (USA))
1019[6] ◆ 1222[4] (2038) 2433a[11] 3442[9] 7534[5]

Miltons Choice *J M Bradley* a44 64
5 b g Diktat—Starosta (Soviet Star (USA))
(1534)

Milton's Keen *M Salaman* a59 61
5 gr g Largesse—Not A Word (Batshoof)
(267)

Mimetico (IRE) *B Grizzetti* 104
4 b m Monsun(GER) —Liza (IRE) (Lycius (USA))
(2438a) 6495a[13]

Mimicker *M W Easterby* 48
2 b f Kyllachy—Blane Water (USA) (Lomond (USA))
2004[10] 2910[2] 6212[11]

Minaash (USA) *D M Simcock* a81 18
4 b h Dixie Union(USA) —Metanoia (USA) (Seeking The Gold (USA))
1146[8] 2293[6] 2679[13] 3615[9]

Mind Alert *D Shaw* a68 41
7 b g Mind Games—Bombay Sapphire (Be My Chief (USA))
16[7] (82) (121) 211[3] 347[7] 404[2] 515[12] 628[6] 901[7] 964[3] 1154[5] 1703[7] 2263[9] 7416[10] 7508[4] 7706[2] 7808[3]

Minder *J G Portman* a57 64
2 b g Mind Games—Exotic Forest (Dominion)
2562[4] 2916[4] 3358[7] 5511[15] 6207[7]

Mind How You Go (FR) *J R Best* a73 80
10 b g Hernando(FR) —Cos I Do (IRE) (Double Schwartz)
272[4] 1744[7]

Mind That Fox *T Wall* a46 1
6 b g Mind Games—Foxie Lady (Wolfhound (USA))
100[10] 219[10]

Mine (IRE) *J D Bethell* 109
10 b h Primo Dominie—Ellebanna (Tina's Pet)
960[6] 1469[13] 1982[10] 3921[17]

Mine Behind *J R Best* a77 84
8 b g Sheikh Albadou—Arapi (IRE) (Arazi (USA))
150[8] 275[9] 312[5] 353[5] 427[4] 1739[7] 3316[4]

Minefield (USA) *Saeed Bin Suroor* a85
4 b h Silver Deputy(CAN) —Copperfield (USA) (Tricky Creek (USA))
473a[5] ◆ 648a[4]

Minenotyours (IRE) *D E Cantillon* a11 33
2 b g Tagula(IRE) —Holly Rose (Charnwood Forest (IRE))
3485[7] 4474[11] 5316[9] 7795[9]

Mineral Rights (USA) *Miss L A Perratt* a70 71
4 ch g Gulch(USA) —Long Vacation (IRE) (Thatching)
(362) 576[8] 681[4] 861[3] (1371) 1952[3] 2748[2] ◆ 3080[12] 3404[9]

Minerton Mountain *B R Millman* a55 15
3 b g Carnival Dancer—Eau Rouge (Grand Lodge (USA))
265[7] 416[12] 1835[8] 2639[15]

Mine That Bird (USA) *Richard E Mandella* a103
2 b g Birdstone(USA) —Mining My Own (USA) (Smart Strike (CAN))
6997a[12]

Mine The Balance (IRE) *H J Manners* a61 48
5 b g Desert Style(IRE) —Dia (IRE) (Astronef)
6335[15]

Ming Vase *P T Midgley* a55 55
6 b g Vettori(IRE) —Minstrel's Dance (CAN) (Pleasant Colony (USA))
640[4] (788) 989[12] 1262[2] 1702[5] 2375[9] 2870[3] 3551[8] 4172[4] 4458[9] 4878[7] 5303[3] 5631[11] 5776[3]

Minibuzz *Mrs G S Rees* a16
2 b g Superior Premium—Amy Leigh (IRE) (Imperial Frontier (USA))
7402[11] 7689[11]

Mini Mosa *J H M Gosden* a71 71
4 b m Indian Ridge—Baldemosa (FR) (Lead On Time (USA))
95[7]

Minimum Fuss (IRE) *M C Chapman* a22 57
4 b m Second Empire(IRE) —Jamis (IRE) (Be My Guest (USA))
109[8] 3733[10] 4294[8] 7629[10]

Ministerofinterior *G L Moore* a59 65
3 b g Nayef(USA) —Maureen's Hope (USA) (Northern Baby (CAN))
1994[5] 2413[9] 3095[5] 3566[6] 4281[5] (5813) 7354[5] 7742[4]

Minjim *C E Brittain* a49 45
3 b c Kyllachy—Sarabah (IRE) (Ela-Mana-Mou)
3168[7] 3656[6]

Minkowski *J Noseda* 99
5 b g Galileo(IRE) —Abitara (IRE) (Rainbow Quest (USA))
4504[12] 5229[9] 6272[4] 6948[12]

Minneapolis *A P O'Brien* a102 97
3 b c Sadler's Wells(USA) —Teggiano (IRE) (Mujtahid (USA))
2435a[7] 3102[8]

Minnie Mill *B P J Baugh* a60 53
4 b m Mind Games—Sometime Never (IRE) (College Chapel)
220[10]

Minnis Bay (CAN) *E F Vaughan* a84 81
4 b g Royal Academy(USA) —Aly's Daylite (USA) (Dayjur (USA))
1857[12] 3271[12] 3761[7] 4946[12]

Minnola *Rae Guest* 53
3 b f Royal Applause—Miss Anabaa (Anabaa (USA))
5261^{3} 5636^{11}

Minnow *S C Williams* a71 50
4 b m Averti(IRE) —Tharwa (IRE) (Last Tycoon)
86^{2} 263^{3}

Minority Report *D Nicholls* 108
8 b g Rainbow Quest(USA) —Queen Sceptre (IRE) (Fairy King (USA))
958^{19} 1218^{13} 1481^{14} 1816^{13} 2969^{3} 3142^{8} 5360^{16} 6070^{11} (6314)

Minor Vamp (IRE) *R Hannon* a62 97
2 b f Hawk Wing(USA) —Miss Champagne (FR) (Bering)
3373^{6} (3913) 4868^{3} (6319a)

Minotaurious (IRE) *K R Burke* 79
2 b f Acclamation—Bella Vie (IRE) (Sadler's Wells (USA))
2497^{8} 3598^{2} 4202^{2} 6102^{11}

Mintoe *K A Ryan* a58 63
2 b g Noverre(USA) —West One (Gone West (USA))
3049^{5} 3547^{6} 3976^{7} 5997^{8}

Minturno (USA) *Mrs A Duffield* 54
2 b c Ten Most Wanted(USA) —Panama Jane (USA) (Perrault)
6212^{5}

Minus Fifteen (IRE) *K A Ryan* a85 76
3 ch g Trans Island—Bumble (Rainbow Quest (USA))
(848) ◆ 1988^{16} 2674^{4} 3999^{3} (5052) 5697^{4} 6021^{3} 6352^{3}

Minute Limit (IRE) *J A Osborne* a73
2 b f Pivotal—Magic Cove (USA) (Kingmambo (USA))
5835^{5} 6697^{2} (6933)

Minwir (IRE) *M Quinn* a59 68
3 b g Green Desert(USA) —Elshamms (Zafonic (USA))
849^{7} 1166^{5} 1479^{11} 2549^{13} 2982^{15} (3395) 4090^{8} 5617^{8} 7109^{7} 7255^{11}

Mi Odds *Mrs N Macauley* a44 4
12 b g Sure Blade(USA) —Vado Via (Ardross)
37^{7} 77^{4} 282^{5} 438^{10} 481^{8} 4932^{10}

Miracle Baby *J A Geake* a56 50
6 b m Atraf—Musica (Primo Dominie)
2753^{2} 3608^{7} 4414^{4} 4825^{5} 5582^{6} 7521^{10}

Miracle Seeker *C G Cox* 103
3 br f Rainbow Quest(USA) —Miracle (Ezzoud (IRE))
1440^{3} (1991) 2792^{11} 3543a^{4} 4549^{3}

Miracle Steps (CAN) *Andrew Oliver* a53 57
3 b f Theatrical—Schonbrunn (CAN) (Val De L'Orne (FR))
7446^{4}

Miraculous Miss (USA) *Steven B Klesaris* a111
5 ch m Mr Greeley(USA) —No Small Miracle (USA) (Silver Deputy (CAN))
6965a^{4}

Mirageleve (FR) *Frau C Brandstatter* 87
2 b f Tobougg(IRE) —Mixture (Linamix (FR))
4441a^{3}

Miramare (GER) *A P Stringer* a99 102
4 ch m Rainbow Quest(USA) —Minaccia (GER) (Platini (GER))
968^{2} 2402^{3} 3088^{3}

Miranda's Girl (IRE) *Thomas Cleary* a79 85
3 b f Titus Livius(FR) —Ela Tina (IRE) (Ela-Mana-Mou)
(4494a) 5550a^{4} 6315a^{8} 6510a^{12}

Mirjan (IRE) *L Lungo* 96
12 b g Tenby—Mirana (IRE) (Ela-Mana-Mou)
6154^{6} 6948^{13} 7128^{8}

Mirrored *Sir Michael Stoute* a75 76
2 b c Dansili—Reflections (Sadler's Wells (USA))
4062^{6} 4600^{4} 6737^{3}

Misaro (GER) *R A Harris* a93 96
7 b g Acambaro(GER) —Misniniski (Niniski (USA))
482^{5} 707^{3} 824^{4} 1146^{3} ◆ 1195^{8} 1582^{2} 1956^{4} 2242^{2} (2906) 3269^{3} (3520) (3868) (4103) 4201^{4} 5509^{12} 5906^{6} 6121^{9} 6289^{4} 6669^{3} 6810^{8} 7192^{9}

Mis Chicaf (IRE) *D Carroll* a49 49
7 b m Prince Sabo—Champagne Season (USA) (Vaguely Noble)
1675^{10} 2578^{6} 2658^{11} 3172^{8} 4383^{10} 4542^{17} 4605^{10} 4919^{15}

Mischief Lady *E A L Dunlop* a67 61
3 b f Cape Cross(IRE) —Cruinn A Bhord (Inchinor)
2257^{8} 2834^{5} 4987^{7} 5836^{7} ◆ 6629^{5}

Mischief Making (USA) *E A L Dunlop* a99 91
3 br f Lemon Drop Kid(USA) —Fraulein (Acatenango (GER))
58^{5} 221^{2} (464) (920) ◆ (1557) 1833^{6} 2650a^{7} (7100) 7491^{6}

Misdaqeya *B W Hills* a82 93
2 br f Red Ransom(USA) —Crystal Power (USA) (Pleasant Colony (USA))
1419^{7} ◆ 2368^{2} (3135) 4868^{2} 6439^{7}

Mishrif (USA) *P W Chapple-Hyam* 94
2 bb c Arch(USA) —Peppy Priscilla (USA) (Latin American (USA))
4826^{5} (5754) 6860^{2}

Miskin Flyer *B Palling* a58 30
2 b f Lend A Hand—Sipsi Fach (Prince Sabo)
6327^{11} 7498^{4}

Misphire *M Dods* 85
5 b m Mister Baileys—Bombay Sapphire (Be My Chief (USA))
1430^{11} 2818^{5} 3260^{6} 3554^{8} (3892) 4110^{7} 5991^{7} 7129^{2} (7239)

Misplaced Fortune *N Tinkler* a47 65
3 b f Compton Place—Tide Of Fortune (Soviet Star (USA))
2187^{3} 2490^{2} 2911^{7} 3644^{5} 4112^{6} 4540^{7} 6935^{8} 7111^{2}

Miss Aoife (IRE) *C F Swan* a54 64
3 ch f Midhish—Diva La Vida (IRE) (Perugino (USA))
4494a^{13}

Miss Beat (IRE) *B J Meehan* a74 76
2 b f Beat Hollow—Bolas (Unfuwain (USA))
7140^{2} ◆ 7422^{2} (7783)

Miss Belle Eve *T M Jones* 17
2 b f Josr Algarhoud(IRE) —Waraqa (USA) (Red Ransom (USA))
995^{12} 1955^{11} 4823^{12} (Dead)

Miss Bootylishes *A B Haynes* 86
3 b f Mujahid(USA) —Moxby (Efisio)
1801^{7} 2825^{10} 3415^{8} 3971^{5} 4872^{5} 5588^{5} 5865^{10}

Miss Bouggy Wouggy *M Blanshard* a56 40
3 b f Tobougg(IRE) —Polly Golightly (Weldnaas (USA))
98^{5} 288^{9} 803^{5} 1166^{4} 1740^{5}

Miss Bronte *R Hollinshead* a60 23
3 b f Ishiguru(USA) —Gemtastic (Tagula (IRE))
114^{4} 767^{9} 917^{8} 1081^{8}

Miss Brown To You (IRE) *M L W Bell* a79 74
3 b f Fasliyev(USA) —Almaaseh (IRE) (Dancing Brave (USA))
1423^{3} 1946^{9} 2413^{6} 6896^{3} (7210) 7419^{8}

Miss Cameo (USA) *R M Whitaker* a48 47
2 b f Mizzen Mast(USA) —Angela Niner (USA) (Forty Niner (USA))
6481^{8} 6785^{11} 7170^{7} 7693^{3}

Miss Carlotta *M P Tregoning* a66
3 b f Helissio(FR) —Ninfa Of Cisterna (Polish Patriot (USA))
3484^{2} 4860^{4} 6206^{8}

Miss Chamanda (IRE) *P D Evans* 75
2 ch f Choisir(AUS) —Smandar (USA) (Sahm (USA))
1363^{2} (1523)

Miss Christophene (IRE) *Mrs S Lamyman* a47
2 b f Christophene(USA) —Lotus Flower (IRE) (Grand Lodge (USA))
7578^{7}

Miss Clarice (USA) *B J Meehan* a49 56
3 bb f Mr Greeley(USA) —Mutton Maniac (USA) (Wolf Power (SAF))
1423^{13} 3379^{5} 4349^{12} 4708^{8} 5167^{13} 6746^{12} 7340^{6}

Miss Clonyn (IRE) *Christian Wroe* a77 75
3 br f Statue Of Liberty(USA) —Second Prayer (IRE) (Singspiel (IRE))
201a^{9} 496a^{8} 744a^{5} 2800^{8} 3838^{6} 4431^{6} 5346^{11}

Miss Cracklinrosie *J R Weymes* a51 63
2 b f Tobougg(IRE) —Anatase (Danehill (USA))
5771^{3} 6151^{4} 6722^{3} 6986^{6} 7172^{2}

Miss Cruisecontrol *J R Best* a30 54
3 b f Hernando(FR) —Wenda (IRE) (Priolo (USA))
3843^{7} 4334^{6} 5003^{5} 5077^{2} 5269^{9} (6111)

Miss Curly (IRE) *Gerard Keane* a56 41
8 b m Danetime(IRE) —Little Thoughts (IRE) (Don't Forget Me)
(318) 641^{5} 681^{5}

Miss Daawe *B Ellison* a51 74
4 b m Daawe(USA) —Feiticeira (USA) (Deposit Ticket (USA))
987^{2} 2444^{7} (2676) 2780^{2} 2928^{2} 3405^{4} (3713) (4385) 4971^{6} 6486^{4} 6840^{6} ◆

Miss Deeds (IRE) *N P Littmoden* a38 34
3 b f Invincible Spirit(IRE) —Aseelah (Nashwan (USA))
298^{4} 557^{7}

Miss Devious (ITY) *J Bindi* 85
2 b f Dr Devious(IRE) —Shyam (USA) (Shadeed (USA))
2744a^{4}

Miss Double Daisy *B Smart* a38
5 ch m Compton Place—Stealthy (Kind Of Hush)
261^{8}

Missed Mondays *A Berry* a53
2 ch f Distant Music(USA) —Lilting Prose (IRE) (Indian Ridge)
7402^{7} 7823^{9}

Misselliebee *J W Hills* a2 52
3 b f Polish Precedent(USA) —Pursuit Of Peace (IRE) (Pursuit Of Love)
1854^{11} 4249^{7} 4909^{7} 5489^{14}

Miss Emma May (IRE) *D R C Elsworth* a54 80
3 b f Hawk Wing(USA) —For Example (USA) (Northern Baby (CAN))
3627^{8} 4395^{6} 5149^{6} 6027^{8} 6446^{5} 6936^{9}

Miss Eze *G Wragg* 81
2 b f Danehill Dancer(IRE) —Miss Corniche (Hernando (FR))
(6555) 7107^{6}

Miss Fancy Pants *Noel Meade* a62 83
4 gr m Act One—Sweetness Herself (Unfuwain (USA))
(4003a) 4493a^{6}

Miss Ferney *A Kirtley* 54
4 ch m Cayman Kai(IRE) —Jendorcet (Grey Ghost I)
5361^{11} 6055^{12} 6275^{6} 6786^{15}

Miss Firefly *R J Hodges* a66 70
3 b f Compton Place—Popocatepetl (FR) (Nashwan (USA))
777^{5} 1671^{7} 2099^{3} 3086^{6} 3765^{2} 4308^{2} (4325) 5171^{5} 5217^{3} 5998^{7} 6339^{7} 6711^{11}

Miss Fritton (IRE) *M Botti* a62 68
2 b f Refuse To Bend(IRE) —Golly Gosh (IRE) (Danehill (USA))
2309^{6} 3456^{7} 6245^{4} 6886^{10} 7700^{8}

Miss Galileo (IRE) *L Camici* 89
3 ch f Galileo(IRE) —Carisheba (USA) (Alysheba (USA))
2231a^{11} 3076a^{7}

Miss Gibboa (IRE) *G A Swinbank* 50
2 ch f Spartacus(IRE) —Ludovica (Bustino)
2462^{8} 4734^{9} 5633^{6}

Miss Gorica (IRE) *Ms Joanna Morgan* a101 103
4 b m Mull Of Kintyre(USA) —Allegorica (IRE) (Alzao (USA))
3532a^{3} 4467a^{5} 5130a^{7} 7328a^{13}

Miss Habershon *Nick Mitchell* a42 63
4 b m Baryshnikov(AUS) —Mighty Squaw (Indian Ridge)
7261^{9} 7392^{10} 7520^{13}

Miss Havisham (IRE) *J R Weymes* a39 56
4 b m Josr Algarhoud(IRE) —Agony Aunt (Formidable (USA))
843^{4} 1773^{7} 2364^{12} 4217^{8} 4556^{12} 4698^{6}

Miss Holderness *I W McInnes* 29
3 ch f Millkom—Miles (Selkirk (USA))
7632^{10}

Miss Hollybell *J Gallagher* 71
2 b f Umistim—Hollybell (Beveled (USA))
1385^{2} 1693^{4} 2054^{2} 3105^{11} 4486^{2} 7546^{11}

Miss Hoolie *W G M Turner* a28 39
4 b m Danehill Dancer(IRE) —Silky Dawn (IRE) (Night Shift (USA))
48^{9}

Missie Baileys *Mrs L J Mongan* a53 55
6 ch m Mister Baileys—Jilly Woo (Environment Friend)
269^{4} 1726^{5} 2832^{3} 3482^{5} 4250^{4} 4722^{5} 5148^{11} 7473^{12} 7815^{7}

Missile Dodger (USA) *R M Beckett* a91 88
2 bb c Golden Missile(USA) —Brady's Best (USA) (Wild Again (USA))
(1693) 2204^{5} 3105^{14} 3846^{3} 4525^{2} 4729^{3} 5693^{9} 6575^{8}

Mission Approved (USA) *Gary Contessa* 109
4 b h With Approval(CAN) —Fortunate Find (USA) (Fortunate Prospect (USA))
3995a^{7}

Mission Control (IRE) *J R Boyle* a76 73
3 ch g Dubai Destination(USA) —Stage Manner (In The Wings)
(803) ◆ 3206^{3} 3676^{4} 4335^{4} 4762^{4} (7761)

Missioner (USA) *M Johnston* a79 89
3 b c Rahy(USA) —Magic Mission (Machiavellian (USA))
2056^{2} (2360) 2889^{2} 3157^{14} 3877^{10} 4422^{7} 5051^{9} 5309^{8}

Mission Impossible *P C Haslam* a70 81
3 gr g Kyllachy—Eastern Lyric (Petong)
(1155) 2460^{2} 2732^{3} 5962^{9} 6486^{15}

Mission Secrete (IRE) *E Lellouche* 87
3 b f Galileo(IRE) —Miss Tahiti (IRE) (Tirol)
7429a^{9}

Missit (IRE) *B Cecil* 108
3 b f Orpen(USA) —High Spot (Shirley Heights)
3807a^{5}

Miss Jabba (IRE) *Miss J Feilden* a43 1
2 b f Bertolini(USA) —Najaaba (USA) (Bahhare (USA))
5939^{11} 6432^{9} 6858^{15}

Miss Jodarah (USA) *J R Best* a16 19
2 b f Action This Day(USA) —Suzie Diamond (USA) (Secreto (USA))
5184^{13} 6205^{13}

Miss Jolyon (USA) *M A Jarvis* a73 80
3 b f Johannesburg(USA) —Konvincha (USA) (Cormorant (USA))
1543^{9} 1959^{2} 2931^{2} 3351^{11}

Miss Kadee *P D Evans* a43 59
2 ch f Needwood Blade—Deco Lady (Wolfhound (USA))
3323^{14} 6893^{4} 7164^{6} 7283^{6} 7425^{P}

Miss Leona *J M Bradley* 28
2 b f Kyllachy—Feather Circle (IRE) (Indian Ridge)
3019^{8} 3309^{7} 3734^{10}

Miss Mactango *W M Brisbourne* 52
3 b f Fleetwood(IRE) —Miss Tango (Batshoof)
1549^{4} 1918^{6} 2156^{2} 2750^{9} 3671^{12} 5077^{4}

Miss Marauder *M Botti* a71
4 b m Mujahid(USA) —Double Stake (USA) (Kokand (USA))
(878) (1287) ◆ 2078^{7} 2483^{10}

Miss Medusa *Mrs C A Dunnett* a16
3 b f Medicean—College Night (IRE) (Night Shift (USA))
6047^{15} 6393^{15} 7026^{11}

Miss Mojito (IRE) *J W Hills* a45 37
2 ch f Lucky Story(USA) —Lamanka Lass (USA) (Woodman (USA))
1851^{7} 2306^{6} 6273^{8}

Miss Moloney (IRE) *Mrs S Lamyman* a45 47
2 b f Sesaro(USA) —Mickey Towbar (IRE) (Mujadil (USA))
2702^{5} 3140^{5} 3689^{5} 4827^{5} 6051^{14}

Miss Mujahid Times *A D Brown* a57 54
5 b m Mujahid(USA) —Stealthy Times (Timeless Times (USA))
2036^{4} 2869^{11} 3340^{12} 3789^{10}

Miss Mujanna *J Akehurst* a74 63
3 b f Mujahid(USA) —Robanna (Robellino (USA))
135^{2} 416^{3} 573^{7} (899) 1336^{4} 2196^{7} 2622^{5} 4252^{11} 7837^{4}

Miss Ocean City (USA) *Nicholas Zito* a73
2 b f Mineshaft(USA) —Madam Lagonza (USA) (Kingmambo (USA))
6500a^{9}

Miss Okaloosa *D M Simcock* a56 16
3 br f Hawk Wing(USA) —Shalimar (IRE) (Indian Ridge)
1271^{8} 1637^{7} 2898^{8} 6751^{5}

Miss Olivia *Ollie Pears* 51
3 ch f Dr Fong(USA) —Beleaguer (Rainbow Quest (USA))
1637^{U} 2208^{10} 2549^{9} 3690^{10}

Missoula (IRE) *Miss Suzy Smith* 92
5 b m Kalanisi(IRE) —Medway (IRE) (Shernazar)
1916^{14} 2609^{4} (3104) 3490^{8} 6272^{7} 6817^{12}

Missou Maiden *M H Tompkins* a46 55
2 ch f Medicean—Sosumi (Be My Chief (USA))
3651^{12} 4157^{11} 4870^{10} 5632^{15} 6555^{5} 6730^{7} 6924^{14}

Missouri (USA) *M A Barnes* a50 18
5 b g Gulch(USA) —Coco (USA) (Storm Bird (CAN))
3176^{11} (Dead)

Miss Pebbles (IRE) *R Dickin* a61 20
8 ch m Lake Coniston(IRE) —Sea Of Stone (USA) (Sanglamore (USA))
970^{6}

Miss Pelling (IRE) *B J Meehan* a69 64
3 b f Danehill Dancer(IRE) —Morningsurprice (USA) (Future Storm (USA))
3061^{8} 4166^{6} 5231^{5} (6437)

Miss Percy *I W McInnes* a35 59
4 b m Mark Of Esteem(IRE) —Anabaa's Music (Anabaa (USA))
1602^{11} 2456^{5} 2940^{12} 4217^{10}

Miss Perfectionist *S A Callaghan* a67 42
2 b f Invincible Spirit(IRE) —To The Woods (IRE) (Woodborough (USA))
6083^{13} 6933^{9} 7458^{4}

Miss Phoebe (IRE) *S Kirk* a69 69
3 b f Catcher In The Rye(IRE) —Stroke Of Six (IRE) (Woodborough (USA))
12^{6} 1685^{11} 1930^{10} 3065^{2} 3322^{8} 3874^{5} 4253^{8} 6088^{4}

Miss Pimpinella *W S Coltherd*
4 b m Bal Harbour—Adjusting (IRE) (Busted)
7669^{11}

Miss Poppy *P R Chamings* a66 69
3 b f Averti(IRE) —Pretty Poppy (Song)
2774^{6} 3447^{4} 4273^{10} 4779^{2} 5026^{4} 6334^{13}

Miss Porcia *P A Blockley* a58 54
7 ch m Inchinor—Krista (Kris)
1898^{4} 2245^{7} 2641^{2} 3025^{9} 4250^{5} 4664^{8} 5961^{8}

Miss Pusey Street *J Gallagher*
2 ch f Compton Place—Pusey Street Girl (Gildoran)
4126^{7}

Miss Puss (IRE) *David Wachman* a75 81
2 b f One Cool Cat(USA) —Love Emerald (USA) (Mister Baileys)
6319a^{8} 6637a^{9}

Miss Red Eye (IRE) *Luke Comer* 67
3 b f On The Ridge(IRE) —Wayne's Gal (IRE) (Karaar)
1230a^{8}

Miss Riviera Chic *G Wragg* a32
3 b f Cadeaux Genereux—Miss Riviera (Kris)
3061^{15} 3318^{11} 5402^{5}

Miss Rochester (IRE) *Sir Michael Stoute* 83
3 b f Montjeu(IRE) —Pilgrim's Way (USA) (Gone West (USA))
2221^{3} 2716^{4} (4669) ◆ 5024^{6} 6079^{4} 6415^{6}

Miss Scarlet *K A Ryan* 66
2 b f Red Ransom(USA) —Give Warning (IRE) (Warning)
3714^{7} 4562^{2} 5219^{4}

Miss Serena *Mrs P Sly* a72 76
3 gr f Singspiel(IRE) —Valnerina (IRE) (Caerleon (USA))
2668^{9} 3058^{7} 3556^{3} 4077^{7} 5077^{5} 5322^{7} (6022) (6421) 6861^{2}

Miss Solo *P C Haslam* a46 54
3 bb f Intikhab(USA) —American Rouge (IRE) (Grand Lodge (USA))
2041^{10}

Miss Sophisticat *W J Knight* 73
2 b f Alhaarth(IRE) —She's Classy (USA) (Boundary (USA))
3913^{5} 4554^{13} 5029^{2} 5585^{3} 6391^{2} 6665^{3}

Miss Sunshine *J S Goldie* 48
3 b f Piccolo—Rhinefield Beauty (IRE) (Shalford (IRE))
977^{5} 1769^{3} 2527^{7} 3217^{5} 3441^{6} 3753^{11} 4107^{13} 4236^{6} 4561^{7}

Miss Sure Bond (IRE) *G R Oldroyd* a57 65
5 ch m Danehill Dancer(IRE) —Desert Rose (Green Desert (USA))
143^{9} 578^{13}

Miss Taboo (IRE) *P T Midgley* a22 56
4 b m Tobougg(IRE) —Miss Croisette (Hernando (FR))
1139^{7} 1519^{5} 2500^{7} 3481^{8} 3712^{3} 4207^{3} 4542^{14} 5007^{7} 5261^{8} 5770^{6}

Miss Tango Hotel *J H M Gosden* 72
2 b f Green Desert(USA) —Inchyre (Shirley Heights)
4149^{11} 5099^{2}

Miss The Boat *A Lund* 98
6 b m Mtoto—Missed Again (High Top)
5335a^{10}

Miss Thippawan (USA) *P T Midgley* a43 44
2 bb f Street Cry(IRE) —Sheathanna (USA) (Mr. Leader (USA))
5107^{6} 5384^{10} 5904^{5} 6545^{4} 6906^{5}

Miss Tiddlypush *Miss Kariana Key*
7 gr m Defacto(USA) —Misty Rocket (Roan Rocket)
2703^{14}

Miss Tikitiboo (IRE) *E F Vaughan* a56 27
2 b f Elusive City(USA) —Sabindra (Magic Ring (IRE))
4907^{9} 5788^{10} 6016^{6} 7454^{3}

Miss Tilen *V Smith* a46 44
3 ch f Tipsy Creek(USA) —Ashleen (Chilibang)
141^{7} 262^{6} 439^{11} 665^{5} 1051^{10} 4540^{15} 4794^{7} 5162^{11}

Miss Una (IRE) *Patrick Martin* a49 76
6 b m Spectrum(IRE) —Fer De Lance (IRE) (Diesis)
5873a^{12}

Miss Understanding *J R Weymes* a47 44
3 br f Dansili—Crossed Wire (Lycius (USA))
991^{10} 1894^{6} 2008^{9} 2247^{8} 3081^{4} 3644^{7} 4115^{5} 4241^{4} 5544 ^{5} 7088^{2}

Missus Christie *Ian Williams* a60 60
2 ch f Auction House(USA) —Dazzling Quintet (Superlative)
(2965) 4108^{6} 4823^{2} 5473^{10}

Missus Molly Brown *R A Fahey* a44 51
4 b m Mind Games—Prim N Proper (Tragic Role (USA))
1185^{11} 1675^{12} 3139^{2} 5501^{5} 5770^{4} 6405^{12}

Miss Varreville (FR) *Ron Caget*
3 b f Antarctique(IRE) —Mis D'Orthe (FR) (Kadounor (FR))
6742a^{0}

Miss Wolf *G H Jones* a27 23
8 b m Wolfhound(USA) —Jussoli (Don)
490^{7} 781^{3} 915^{6}

Miss Xu Xia *G R Oldroyd* a46 37
2 b f Monsieur Bond(IRE) —Bond Girl (Magic Ring (IRE))
2569^{9} 3008^{4} 5499^{8} 5715^{12} 6009^{5} 7038^{9} 7227^{11} 7266^{5} (7370) 7531^{12}

Missycomelightly *W J H Ratcliffe* 22
5 bl m Killer Instinct—Clean Singer (Chief Singer)
1382^{13} 2735^{8} 4606^{7}

Missy Que (IRE) *W R Muir* a47 53
2 ch f Fath(USA) —Eimkar (Junius (USA))
1111[4] 1413[10] 1961[11] (2508) 4063[6] 4823[10] 6059[14]

Mista Rossa *H Morrison* a74 73
3 br g Red Ransom(USA) —Cloud Hill (Danehill (USA))
(1163) 1696[8] 2280[3] 3555[7] 4344[2] ◆ 4527[2] 6379[6] 6775[4] 7091[6]

Mister Always *D Flood* a57 51
4 b g Titus Livius(FR) —Pieta (IRE) (Perugino (USA))
151[8] 232[4] 521[8] 1135[10] 1338[13] 3725[9] 4028[10] (Dead)

Mister Arjay (USA) *B Ellison* a60 81
8 b g Mister Baileys—Crystal Stepper (USA) (Fred Astaire (USA))
1137[5] 1299[10] 1972[2] 2135[2] (2393) 2628[9] 3296[5] (3832) 4046[11] 4963[7] 5498[7]

Mister Bannon (USA) *Ms F M Crowley* a75 77
3 b g Langfuhr(CAN) —Stark Passage (USA) (Woodman (USA))
4494a[14]

Mister Benji *B P J Baugh* a54 31
9 b g Catrail(USA) —Katy-Q (IRE) (Taufan (USA))
168[3] 284[2] 465[6] 663[7] 724[5] 872[9] 1207[6] 1491[6] 1602[10] 3431[13] 3691[6] 3951[13] 7619[6] 7772[6]

Mister Bombastic (IRE) *M Dods* 61
2 ch c Monsieur Bond(IRE) —Sheen Falls (IRE) (Prince Rupert (FR))
4415[13] 5387[5] 6481[5]

Mister Completely (IRE) *Ms J S Doyle* a76 70
7 b g Princely Heir(IRE) —Blue Goose (Belmez (USA))
(118) 630[6] 880[3] 1052[6] 1337[4] 1547[5] 2567[7] 3137[5] 3377[7] 3613[2] 4087[3] 4193[9] 4526[4] 5367[2] 5613[10] 5676[8] 6672[14]

Mister Dee Bee (IRE) *B W Hills* a53 84
2 b c Orpen(USA) —Acidanthera (Alzao (USA))
3372[6] 4150[8] 5021[3] 5791[2] ◆ 6305[6]

Mister Elegant *J L Spearing* a58 61
6 b g Fraam—Risky Valentine (Risk Me (FR))
131[7] 64[5] 584[4] 790[8]

Mister Fantastic *M Dods* 68
2 ch g Green Tune(USA) —Lomapamar (Nashwan (USA))
3364[3] 4014[5]

Mister Fasliyev (IRE) *E Charpy* a91 97
6 b g Fasliyev(USA) —Carisheba (USA) (Alysheba (USA))
296a[5] 495a[13] 648a[7]

Mister Fips (IRE) *Jane Chapple-Hyam* a83 88
3 b g Chevalier(IRE) —Blue Holly (IRE) (Blues Traveller (IRE))
1404[16] 1707[5] 3172[4] 3675[2]

Mister Fizzbomb (IRE) *J S Wainwright* a62 72
5 b g Lend A Hand—Crocus (IRE) (Mister Baileys)
207[8] 2274[10] 2927[2] 3337[3] 3602[2] 4396[5] 4501[3] 5305[4] 5971[9] 6485[3] 6806[4] 7039[8]

Mister Genepi *W R Muir* 52
6 b g Mister Baileys—Ring Queen (USA) (Fairy King (USA))
3046[10] (Dead)

Mister Green (FR) *D Flood* a82 89
2 b g Green Desert(USA) —Summertime Legacy (Darshaan)
(2502) ◆ 3439[4] 4119[2] 4389[3] 5244[13] 6469[8] 6575[9]

Mister Hardy *R A Fahey* a93 91
3 b c Kyllachy—Balladonia (Primo Dominie)
1075[6] 1328[5] 1623[4] 1999[7] 2410[5] 3141[4] 3475[2] 3999[6] 4416[8] 4661[7] (5222) 5831[13] 6069[7] 6902[2] 7181[3]

Mister Incredible *J M Bradley* a56 57
5 b g Wizard King—Judiam (Primo Dominie)
46[5] 82[8] 247[7] 642[5] 696[2] 790[6] 7375[2] 7618[2] 7658[5] 7774[2]

Misterisland (IRE) *A Bailey* 46
3 b c Spectrum(IRE) —Carranita (IRE) (Anita's Prince)
1751[5] 1918[9]

Mister Jingles *R M Whitaker* a44 66
5 ch g Desert Story(IRE) —Fairy Free (Rousillon (USA))
1780[7] 2285[7] 3108[6] (3339) 4245[9] 5638[3] 7048[6] 7441[8]

Mister Laurel *R A Fahey* 81
2 b c Diktat—Balladonia (Primo Dominie)
(3400) 4108[3] 4857[9] 5827[8] 6426[24]

Mister Maq *A Crook* a21 46
5 b g Namaqualand(USA) —Nordico Princess (Nordico (USA))
4219[16] 4420[6] 7177[10] 7634[8]

Mister Marmaduke *D A Nolan* 46
7 b g Marju(IRE) —Lalique (IRE) (Lahib (USA))
2576[9] 3787[10] 3952[11] 4950[11] 5220[7] 6159[13]

Mister New York (USA) *Noel T Chance* a89 46
3 b c Forest Wildcat(USA) —Shebane (USA) (Alysheba (USA))
228[2] (457) (756) 905[9] 926[2] 5403[10] 5841[10] 6124[13] 6627[9] 7014[7] (7277) 7386[2] (7439) 7737[6] 7755[4]

Mister Pete (IRE) *W Storey* 66
5 b g Piccolo—Whistfilly (First Trump)
3176[2] (3718) 4220[6] 4924[4] 5385[12] (5559) 6115[3] 6727[3] 7042[2] 7177[2]

Mister Right (IRE) *D J S Ffrench Davis* a50 78
7 ch g Barathea(IRE) —Broken Spirit (IRE) (Slip Anchor)
1531[2] 2822[13] 3060[10] 3375[8] 5576[9]

Mister Ross *G L Moore* a84 89
3 b g Medicean—Aqualina (IRE) (King's Theatre (IRE))
4349[11] 4929[3] ◆ 5587[4] (6867) ◆ (7027) 7470[9]

Mister Standfast *J M P Eustace* a51 59
2 b g Haafhd—Off The Blocks (Salse (USA))
6375[10] 6715[9] 7051[7]

Mister Thatcher (IRE) *Annette McMahon* a65 2
4 ch g Tagula(IRE) —Thatching Craft (IRE) (Alzao (USA))
(7706) (7746) 7834[8]

Mister Tinktastic (IRE) *M Dods* 65
2 ch g Noverre(USA) —Psychic (IRE) (Alhaarth (IRE))
6383[4] 7082[3] ◆

Mister Trickster (IRE) *R Dickin* a57
7 b g Woodborough(USA) —Tinos Island (IRE) (Alzao (USA))
149[4]

Mister Wilberforce *Mrs L Williamson*
2 b c Paris House—She's A Breeze (Crofthall)
5200[5] 7080[15] 7170[10]

Mistress Cooper *W J Musson* a65 71
3 bb f Kyllachy—Litewska (IRE) (Mujadil (USA))
3026[3] 4127[4] 4408[10] 4988[5] 5510[10] 7471[4] 7834[4]

Mistress Eva *P Winkworth* 76
3 br f Diktat—Foreign Mistress (Darshaan)
2920[11] 3970[5] 4669[4] 5146[3] 5758[5] (6607) 6898[6]

Mistress Greeley (USA) *Sir Michael Stoute* 85
3 ch f Mr Greeley(USA) —My Reem (USA) (Chief's Crown (USA))
2170[6] 5273[11]

Mistress Mary *G G Margarson* a45 44
2 b f Needwood Blade—Plentitude (FR) (Ela-Mana-Mou)
2368[8] 3584[3] 3848[7] 6059[4] 6214[19] 6988[6]

Mistress Rio (IRE) *J G Given* a34 18
3 ch f Captain Rio—Bu Hagab (IRE) (Royal Academy (USA))
662[5] 950[8]

Misty Dancer *Miss Venetia Williams* 97
9 gr g Vettori(IRE) —Light Fantastic (Deploy)
2830[8]

Misty Glade *Miss Amy Weaver* a79 70
2 ch f Compton Place—Shifting Mist (Night Shift (USA))
1961[13] 2306[P] 2702[4] 3610[2] 4340[4] 4706[7] 5277[6] 5937[6] 6207[3] (6547) 6769[6] (7308) 7460[7] 7820[9]

Miswaat (KSA) *J Gardel* a100
5 b h Torrey Canyon(USA) —Seema (KSA) (Thoughtless (USA))
648a[2]

Misyaar (IRE) *M A Jarvis* a65
2 b f Dubai Destination(USA) —Saafeya (IRE) (Sadler's Wells (USA))
7708[3]

Mith Hill *Ian Williams* 84
7 b g Daylami(IRE) —Delirious Moment (IRE) (Kris)
2332[6] 3891[3] 4516[3] 5718[3] 6361[3] 6861[11]

Mitra Jaan (IRE) *W R Swinburn* a69 61
2 b f Diktat—Persian Lass (IRE) (Grand Lodge (USA))
4157[9] 5571[4] 6539[5]

Mixing *M J Attwater* a65 60
6 gr g Linamix(FR) —Tuning (Rainbow Quest (USA))
125[6] (332) 716[2] 881[3] 963[14] 1562[2] 2715[5] 2949[3] 4343[2] 4930[4] (5611) 5802[2] (6210) 6577[11] 6929[6] 7301[4]

Mix N Match *R M Stronge* a60 57
4 b g Royal Applause—South Wind (Tina's Pet)
402[3] 517[2] 587[10] 1528[15] 3265[2] 3588[4] 4635[9] 5802[10] 6019[13] 7676[6]

Miyasaki (CHI) *Rune Haugen* a91 94
6 b h Memo(CHI) —Cantame Al Oido (CHI) (Yendaka (USA))
2232a[2] 3491[9]

Mizooka *R M Beckett* a64 79
3 b f Tobougg(IRE) —Tetravella (IRE) (Groom Dancer (USA))
1208[4] 1805[4] 2342[2] 3384[2] (3970)

Moandei *R Ingram* 54
4 b m Silver Wizard(USA) —Its All Too Much (Chaddleworth (IRE))
6345[8] 6705[9]

Moatize (AUS) *Bart Cummings* 105
4 br g Danehill Dancer(IRE) —Shezabeel (NZ) (Zabeel (NZ))
6922a[2] 7188a[6]

Moayed *N P Littmoden* a77 67
9 b g Selkirk(USA) —Song Of Years (IRE) (Shareef Dancer (USA))
807[3] 896[4] 1055[4] 1369[2] 2073[3] 2753[5] 3567[6]

Mocha Java *M Salaman* a50 74
5 b g Bertolini(USA) —Coffee Cream (Common Grounds)
6752[3] 7736[2]

Mocha Java (SAF) *E F Vaughan* a86 80
6 b m National Assembly(CAN) —Mabola Plum (SAF) (Fort Wood (USA))
2000[10] 2712[7] 3504[14]

Model (USA) *Neil Drysdale* a107
4 b m Giant's Causeway(USA) —Snowfire (Machiavellian (USA))
6523a[2]

Modernist *Sir Michael Stoute* 57
3 b c Singspiel(IRE) —Helloimustbegoing (USA) (Red Ransom (USA))
1379[9] 1994[4] (Dead)

Modern Look *D Smaga* 114
3 b f Zamindar(USA) —Prophecy (IRE) (Warning)
1375a[2] 2033a[4] (2651a) 3194[10]

Modern Practice (IRE) *Miss V Haigh* a51
3 br g Modigliani(USA) —Practice (USA) (Diesis)
130[6] 6091[7] 6843[8]

Modern Verse (USA) *Jennie Candlish* a64 59
5 b g Pleasant Tap(USA) —Sandalwood (USA) (El Gran Senor (USA))
3718[13]

Moggy (IRE) *M L W Bell* a51 52
2 br f One Cool Cat(USA) —Termania (IRE) (Shirley Heights)
6565[11] 6885[6] 7095[10]

Mogok Ruby *L Montague Hall* a89 82
4 gr g Bertolini(USA) —Days Of Grace (Wolfhound (USA))
55[3] (150) 329[3] 503[3] 574[5] ◆ 1928[15] 4341[11] 5101[3] 6125[5] 6402[8] ◆ 6699[4] 7077[4] 7466[3]

Mohanad (IRE) *M R Channon* 76
2 b c Invincible Spirit(IRE) —Irish Design (IRE) (Alhaarth (IRE))
2592[6] 3049[2] 3519[3] 4214[9]

Mohathab (IRE) *J H M Gosden* 86
3 b g Cadeaux Genereux—Zeiting (IRE) (Zieten (USA))
1467[12] 1926[4] 3205[2] 5076[2]

Mohawk Ridge *M Dods* 61
2 b g Storming Home—Ipsa Loquitur (Unfuwain (USA))
6037[3] 6383[7] 6858[10]

Mohawk Star (IRE) *I A Wood* a75 52
7 ch g Indian Ridge—Searching Star (Rainbow Quest (USA))
4727[9] 5003[6] 5367[10] (5676) (5917) 6022[6] 6672[12] 6957[3] 7216[2] 7366[4]

Moheebb (IRE) *Mrs R A Carr* a63 81
4 b g Machiavellian(USA) —Rockerlong (Deploy)
992[10] 1072[3] 1217[2] 1388[3] 1613[7] 1771[2] 1910[4] 1970[8] 2733[4] 2790[9] 3716[7] 3972[5] 4204[10] 5390[2] 6070[7] (6162) ◆ 6385[3] 6482[5] 6582[9] 7224[5]

Mohtarres (USA) *D T Hughes* 67
5 b g Kingmambo(USA) —Adored Slew (USA) (Seattle Slew (USA))
4511a[8] 4655a[5]

Moiqen (IRE) *Kevin Prendergast* 103
3 b g Red Ransom(USA) —Za Aamah (USA) (Mr Prospector (USA))
1232a[2] (1509a) 2023a[3] 3193[5] 5135a[4] 5944a[5]

Mojeerr *M P Tregoning* a35 38
2 b g Royal Applause—Princess Miletrian (IRE) (Danehill (USA))
5468[16] 6000[10] 6702[9]

Mojito Royale (IRE) *Eoin Doyle* a102 96
4 b g Val Royal(FR) —Beseeching (IRE) (Hamas (IRE))
1783a[9] 4512a[18] 7235a[9]

Moksi *P W Chapple-Hyam* a68 54
3 b g Olden Times—Yasalam (IRE) (Fairy King (USA))
1252[4]

Molesden Glen (IRE) *B Smart* a69 27
2 b c Spartacus(IRE) —Sea Glen (IRE) (Glenstal (USA))
6811[5] 7282[3] ◆ 7660[5]

Mollie Blackburn *A D Brown* a35
4 b m Warningford—Riyoom (USA) (Vaguely Noble)
823[7] 1119[6] 1579[13]

Molly Ann (IRE) *T D Easterby* a67 58
3 b f Medicean—Molly Mello (GER) (Big Shuffle (USA))
261[5] 1781[7] 2376[7] 2911[8] 3282[9] (3549) 3717[6]

Mollyatti *Miss V Haigh* a72 68
3 b f Medicean—Tolyatti (Green Desert (USA))
1499[3] 1584[10] 2190[7] 2452[10] 3438[9] 4615[5] 4988[7] 5074[5] 5374[9] 5592[5] 6045[6]

Molly Max (GER) *Frau K Haustein* 108
4 ch h Big Shuffle(USA) —Molly Dancer (GER) (Shareef Dancer (USA))
2876a[7]

Molly The Witch (IRE) *M P Tregoning* a60
2 b f Rock Of Gibraltar(IRE) —Tree Peony (Woodman (USA))
5048[7] 6166[10]

Molly Two *L A Mullaney* a50 48
3 ch f Muhtarram(USA) —Rum Lass (Distant Relative)
3712[11] 5110[5] 5261[4] 5970[8] 6822[5]

Molnaya (IRE) *Jane Chapple-Hyam* a51 35
2 b c Statue Of Liberty(USA) —Minerwa (GER) (Protektor (GER))
6333[6] 6879[7] 7388[8]

Moluccella *H Morrison* a55
3 b f Marju(IRE) —Pine Needle (Kris)
1144[7] 1870[13] 2613[11] 3571[8]

Moment Of Clarity *R C Guest* a71 66
6 b g Lujain(USA) —Kicka (Shirley Heights)
104[6] 973[4] 1085[7] 2568[8] 2927[7] (3258) 3450[7] 3814[10] 4458[12] 6090[9] 6825[9] 7345[9] 7516[3] ◆ (7692) 7732[10]

Moment's Notice *R W Price* a79 91
3 ch g Beat Hollow—Figlette (Darshaan)
966[8] 1681[5] 2043[5] (2603) 3196[7] 3875[8] 5100[10]

Mo Mhuirnin (IRE) *R A Fahey* a63 71
2 b f Danetime(IRE) —Cotton Grace (IRE) (Case Law)
2696[4] 3259[9] 3598[3] 5306[2] 5904[3]

Momtic (IRE) *S Seemar* a83 20
7 ch g Shinko Forest(IRE) —Uffizi (IRE) (Royal Academy (USA))
379a[15]

Monaadema (IRE) *W J Haggas* 79
3 b f Elnadim(USA) —Suhaad (Unfuwain (USA))
2466[2] (3180) ◆

Monaadi (IRE) *R Hollinshead* a71 56
3 b g Singspiel(IRE) —Bint Albaadiya (USA) (Woodman (USA))
1398[13] 1621[13] 7661[2]

Monaazalah (IRE) *Rae Guest* a78 101
3 b f Green Desert(USA) —Karamah (Unfuwain (USA))
2967[11] 5275[17] 5899[4] 6271[12] 6782[13]

Monaco Mistress (IRE) *P C Haslam* 63
2 b f Acclamation—Bendis (GER) (Danehill (USA))
4202[9] 5004[4] 6785[5]

Monadreen Flyer (IRE) *Daniel Mark Loughnane* a82 79
3 b g Atraf—First Kiss (GER) (Night Shift (USA))
(228) 457[2]

Monahullan Prince *Gerard Keane* a64 71
7 b g Pyramus(USA) —Classic Artiste (USA) (Arctic Tern (USA))
4655a[6]

Mona Lisa (GER) *Mario Hofer* 88
3 b f Spinning World(USA) —Miss Holsten (USA) (Diesis)
5334a[5] 7450a[9]

Mon Ami (IRE) *G Di Chio* a72
6 b h Desert Story(IRE) —Claal (GER) (Alzao (USA))
(127)

Monashee Brave (IRE) *M A Allen* a63 68
5 b g Monashee Mountain(USA) —Miss Butterfield (Cure The Blues (USA))
181[7] 356[11] 460[7] 719[2] 806[12] 884[5] 1028[6] 1642[8] 7197[16]

Monasheemini (IRE) *Mrs N Macauley*
5 gr m Monashee Mountain(USA) —Ivory's Promise (Pursuit Of Love)
655[4]

Monashee Prince (IRE) *J R Best* a69 63
6 ch g Monashee Mountain(USA) —Lodema (IRE) (Lycius (USA))
165[2] 334[7] 427[5] 515[2] 628[4] 729[9] 1035[5] 2010[3] 2255[13] 2350[6] 2692[7] 3316[7] 3506[11] 3559[4]

Monashee Rock (IRE) *M Salaman* a70 76
3 b f Monashee Mountain(USA) —Polar Rock (Polar Falcon (USA))
772[7] 2622[12] (3064) 3525[12] (4369) 4789[4] 5588[4] 6242[14] 6758[5] 7009[11] 7096[5] 7342[10]

Monash Lad (IRE) *P Butler* a11 18
6 ch g General Monash(USA) —Story Time (IRE) (Mansooj)
3084[13] 3732[9]

Monba (USA) *Todd Pletcher* a114
3 gr c Maria's Mon(USA) —Hamba (USA) (Easy Goer (USA))
1820a[20]

Mon Colonel (IRE) *R Menichetti*
2 b c Tout Seul(IRE) —Lady Vicky (USA) (Cryptoclearance (USA))
2745a[6]

Monda *M Hill* a56 60
6 b m Danzig Connection(USA) —Fairey Firefly (Hallgate)
1528[3] ◆ 2642[14] 4368[2] 4813[9] 5916[3] 6208[3] 7013[5]

Mondial Jack (FR) *P D Evans* a58
9 ch g Apple Tree(FR) —Cackle (USA) (Crow (FR))
317[4] 435[5] 524[3] 778[9]

Mondo Marcio (ITY) *F Natalizi* 46
2 b c Della Scala(IRE) —Stravinskinia (USA) (Stravinsky (USA))
5951a[7]

Mondovi *N J Vaughan* a89 95
4 b m Kyllachy—Branston Fizz (Efisio)
1956[6] (2359) ◆ 3252[6] 5310[7] 5681[5]

Mondovino (FR) *Rod Collet* a88 101
5 b h Black Minnaloushe(USA) —Divinite (USA) (Alleged (USA))
(7598a)

Monetary Fund (USA) *G A Butler* 82
2 b c Montjeu(IRE) —Maddie G (USA) (Blush Rambler (USA))
4625[15] 6777[3]

Monet's Lady (IRE) *R A Fahey* a43 49
4 gr m Daylami(IRE) —Wide Range (IRE) (Spectrum (IRE))
4457[11] 4848[14]

Money Bags (SAF) *M F De Kock* a87 103
6 ch h Rich Man's Gold(USA) —Maiden Lady (SAF) (Sportsworld (USA))
384a[14] 494a[6] 673a[10]

Moneycantbuymelove (IRE) *M L W Bell* 80
2 b f Pivotal—Sabreon (Caerleon (USA))
4643[3] 5256[4] 6473[4]

Money Hills *Mrs C A Dunnett*
6 b g Vettori(IRE) —Starfida (Soviet Star (USA))
1726[P]

Money Money Money *P Winkworth* a65 49
2 b f Generous(IRE) —Shi Shi (Alnasr Alwasheek)
5048[4] 5535[7] 6199[8]

Monfils Monfils (USA) *A J McCabe* a67 83
6 b g Sahm(USA) —Sorpresa (USA) (Pleasant Tap (USA))
3824[6] 3965[5] 4244[8] 4331[2] 4699[3] (4892) 5092[5] 5858[10] 6279[8] 6626[9] 7183[9] 7606[7]

Monitor Closely (IRE) *P W Chapple-Hyam* 93
2 b c Oasis Dream—Independence (Selkirk (USA))
5857[3] ◆ 6474[6] (6977)

Monkey Glas (IRE) *J R Gask* a97 81
4 b h Mull Of Kintyre(USA) —Maura's Pet (IRE) (Prince Of Birds (USA))
(63) (124) 594[3] 680[3] 904[3] (1045) 1334[7] 4522[7] (7436) 7675[3] 7780[2]

Mon Michel (IRE) *G L Moore* 93
5 b g Montjeu(IRE) —Miniver (IRE) (Mujtahid (USA))
7017[5]

Monmouthshire *R J Price* a49 64
5 b g Singspiel(IRE) —Croeso Cariad (Most Welcome)
251[9]

Monolith *L Lungo* 91
10 b g Bigstone(IRE) —Ancara (Dancing Brave (USA))
1824[10] 6410[6] 6861[12]

Mon Petite Amour *D W P Arbuthnot* a65 63
5 b m Efisio—Food Of Love (Music Boy)
209[5] 300[2] 430[2] (490) 579[3] 736[4]

Mon Plaisir (USA) *J L Dunlop* a53 79
3 bb c Pleasant Tap(USA) —Coquine (USA) (Gone West (USA))
1572[8] (2342) ◆ 3459[4] 4771[10] 5464[9] 5999[12] 6416[8]

Monreale (GER) *G Brown* 85
4 b g Silvano(GER) —Maratea (USA) (Fast Play (USA))
5279[17] 5843[11] 6346[9]

Mons Calpe (IRE) *P F I Cole* a65 58
2 b g Rock Of Gibraltar(IRE) —Taking Liberties (IRE) (Royal Academy (USA))
2972[11] 3682[6] 6165[3] 6700[13]

Monsieur Dumas (IRE) *R Bastiman* a47 58
4 b g Iron Mask(USA) —Serenity (Selkirk (USA))
2053[8] 3201[4] 4261[12] 4540[3] 4898[9]

Monsieur Fillioux (USA) *J R Fanshawe* a74
2 ch g Hennessy(USA) —Eventually (USA) (Affirmed (USA))
7402[3] (7674)

Monsieur Jourdain (IRE) *T D Easterby* 52
2 b g Royal Applause—Palwina (FR) (Unfuwain (USA))
1324^{5} 3590^{11} 4045^{7} 4733^{9} 6214^{12}

Monsieur Kiss Kiss *G A Butler* 57
2 b c Monsieur Bond(IRE) —Known Class (USA) (Known Fact (USA))
7104^{7} 7240^{7}

Monsieur Reynard *J M Bradley* a72 82
3 ch g Compton Place—Tell Tale Fox (Tel Quel (FR))
244^{3} 975^{4} 1155^{2} 2122^{7} 2258^{5} 2570^{2} (2896) 3462^{3} 4347^{4} 4595^{9} 4854^{14} 5151^{8} 5490^{9} 5991^{8} 6448^{2} 6880^{11} 7562^{6} 7621^{9}

Montaff *M R Channon* 81
2 b c Montjeu(IRE) —Meshhed (USA) (Gulch (USA))
5842^{2} ◆ (6384)

Montagne Lointaine (IRE) *E Lellouche* 102
3 b f Numerous(USA) —Memoire (FR) (Sadler's Wells (USA))
6567a^{4} 7487a^{0}

Montalba (USA) *J Lau* a79
8 rg g Southern Halo(USA) —Time Knap (USA) (Timeless Native (USA))
382a^{7} 473a^{13} 564a^{13}

Montalegre (IRE) *A & G Botti* 105
6 b h Montjeu(IRE) —Alma Alegre (IRE) (Lahib (USA))
2027a^{2}

Montana Sky (IRE) *R A Harris* a50 61
5 b g Peintre Celebre(USA) —Catch The Lights (Deploy)
8^{11}

Montaquila *J Howard Johnson* 84
3 b g Hawk Wing(USA) —Intellectuelle (Caerleon (USA))
2209^{3} 2674^{13} 3723^{10} 4682^{8} 5358^{6}

Montbretia *H R A Cecil* 98
3 b f Montjeu(IRE) —Bayswater (Caerleon (USA))
1440^{2} (4166) 6127^{2} 6415^{3}

Mont Cervin *Ian Williams* a58 74
3 b g Sakhee(USA) —Daylight Dreams (Indian Ridge)
2056^{6} 2509^{6} (2885) 5202^{9} 6450^{10} 6663^{9} 6868^{12}

Monte Alto (IRE) *L M Cumani* 105
4 b h Danehill Dancer(IRE) —Peruvian Witch (IRE) (Perugino (USA))
2465^{3} 3195^{6} 3974^{12} 4504^{5} 6120^{7} 6784^{9}

Monte Cassino (IRE) *J O'Reilly* a64 50
3 ch g Choisir(AUS) —Saucy Maid (IRE) (Sure Blade (USA))
1429^{9} 3079^{17} 4044^{11} 4538^{4} 4702^{10} 6913^{14} 7180^{12} 7323^{5} 7528^{3} 7624^{3} 7679^{3}

Montefiore (IRE) *M Botti* a66 49
3 b c Orpen(USA) —Tokurama (IRE) (Mtoto)
712^{2} 900^{8} 1063^{4} 1245^{4}

Monte Major (IRE) *D Shaw* a75 67
7 b g Docksider(USA) —Danalia (IRE) (Danehill (USA))
539^{6} 699^{2} 840^{7} 1268^{4} 1476^{6} 2010^{11} 3565^{4} 4047^{10} 5074^{11} 5374^{2} 5626^{3} 5770^{10} 7092^{4} 7231^{3} 7295^{2} 7416^{5} 7746^{3} 7793^{4}

Monte Mayor Eagle *D Haydn Jones* a55 39
2 ch f Captain Rio—Ink Pot (USA) (Green Dancer (USA))
2638^{9} 3085^{7} 5344^{9} 6837^{8} (7319) 7531^{4}

Montemayorprincess (IRE) *D Haydn Jones* a60 57
4 b m Fath(USA) —Blonde Goddess (IRE) (Godswalk (USA))
(7) ◆ 258^{4} (916) 1258^{5} 3569^{11} 6716^{15}

Monte Pattino (USA) *C J Teague* 22
4 ch g Rahy(USA) —Jood (USA) (Nijinsky (CAN))
991^{13} 2488^{12} 2573^{11} 3279^{13} 3589^{13} 3718^{10} 4452^{5} 4947^{8}

Monteriggioni (IRE) *John Geoghegan* a102 102
6 b g Blue Ocean(USA) —Jibabit (IRE) (Waajib)
3531a^{8} 4512a^{5} 7235a^{4}

Monterrico *G Wragg* a75 77
3 b g Dubai Destination(USA) —Mezzogiorno (Unfuwain (USA))
(1114) 1839^{5} 3633^{5} 5999^{8} 6790^{4}

Montevetro *R Hannon* a55 53
3 b g Galileo(IRE) —Three Piece (Jaazeiro (USA))
1114^{5} 1367^{10} 4372^{6} 4859^{8} 6248^{8}

Montfjord (IRE) *E J O'Neill* a78 66
3 b c Montjeu(IRE) —Mythical Creek (USA) (Pleasant Tap (USA))
310^{2} 702^{2} 1615^{3} 2997^{14}

Montgomery (SWE) *B Olsen*
3 b g Mujahid(USA) —Mercurial (Highest Honor (FR))
4918a^{11}

Monthly Medal *Anthony Mullins* a86 92
5 b g Danehill Dancer(IRE) —Sovereign Abbey (IRE) (Royal Academy (USA))
1105a^{21} 6511a^{2} 6845a^{12}

Montiboli (IRE) *K A Ryan* a76 77
3 ch f Bahamian Bounty—Aunt Sadie (Pursuit Of Love)
199^{4} 480^{2} 714^{5} 952^{4} (1558) 2002^{4} (2288) 2705^{2} 2781^{3} 3592^{3} 4082^{3} 4920^{3} 5713^{6}

Montiona *R C Guest* a6
4 b g Montjoy(USA) —Lady Iona (Weldnaas (USA))
219^{11}

Montjeu's Melody (IRE) *J E Long* a66 71
4 b m Montjeu(IRE) —Pride Of Place (IRE) (Caerleon (USA))
2561^{9} 4343^{13}

Mont Joux (FR) *H Billot* 78
6 b g Montjeu(IRE) —Lune De Mai (Kenmare (FR))
7429a^{10}

Montmartre (FR) *A De Royer-Dupre* 126
3 gr c Montjeu(IRE) —Artistique (IRE) (Linamix (FR))
2654a^{15} (3191a) (4042a)

Montmartre (USA) *K A Ryan* 44
2 b g Awesome Again(CAN) —Sacre Coeur (USA) (Saint Ballado (CAN))
3400^{4} 4697^{5}

Montmorency (IRE) *Saeed Bin Suroor* 77
2 ch c Pivotal—Clear Spring (USA) (Irish River (FR))
5089^{3} 5499^{2} (5929)

Montosari *R A Teal* a72 65
9 ch g Persian Bold—Sartigila (Efisio)
405^{8} 455^{3} 1181^{10}

Montparnasse (SWE) *B Bo* 80
5 b g Richard Of York—Jezebel (SWE) (Diaghlyphard (USA))
5958a^{7}

Montpellier (IRE) *A Al Raihe* a97 95
5 bb g Montjeu(IRE) —Ring Of Esteem (Mark Of Esteem (IRE))
383a^{7} 564a^{6}

Montrachet *M L W Bell* a83 85
4 ch m Singspiel(IRE) —Riberac (Efisio)
1287^{2} ◆ 1456^{4} 1801^{9} 2619^{4} 2820^{3} 3163^{4} 4022^{5} 4596^{3} (5149) 5829^{12} 6852a^{3}

Montreal (GER) *H R A Cecil* 54
3 b f Boreal(GER) —Margie's Darling (USA) (Alydar (USA))
2164^{8} 2717^{9}

Montrose Man *B J Meehan* a71 68
4 ch g Foxhound(USA) —Don't Jump (IRE) (Entitled)
2165^{9} 2886^{6} 3258^{9} 6090^{13}

Montzando *B R Millman* a61 51
5 b g Forzando—Clashfern (Smackover)
327^{10} 535^{8} 725^{5} (871) 972^{10} 1185^{5} (1370) 1966^{14} 3565^{8} 5374^{12}

Mooakada (IRE) *J H M Gosden* 84
2 gr f Montjeu(IRE) —Sulaalah (IRE) (Darshaan)
(6778) ◆

Mood Music *Mario Hofer* a77 109
4 b g Kyllachy—Something Blue (Petong)
2034a^{2} 2652a^{11} 3243a^{8} 4881a^{2} 6568a^{3} 7187a^{7}

Moody Tunes *K R Burke* a58 91
5 b g Merdon Melody—Lady-Love (Pursuit Of Love)
833^{12} 958^{9} 1105a^{12} 1456^{6} 2619^{7} 3453^{2} 3627^{6} 3972^{11} (5221) 5635^{9} 6152^{2}

Mookhlesa *B W Hills* 80
3 bb f Marju(IRE) —Ikhlas (IRE) (Lahib (USA))
1404^{17} 2171^{8}

Moomoo *J R Weymes* a1 5
2 ch f Kheleyf(USA) —Quick Flight (Polar Falcon (USA))
3215^{4} 4474^{12}

Moonage Daydream (IRE) *T D Easterby* a61 73
3 b g Captain Rio—Thelma (Blakeney)
848^{6} 953^{2} 1139^{8} 1572^{7} (2490) 2660^{6} 3280^{5} 3960^{2} 4163^{3} 4745^{7} (4900) 5358^{9} 5634^{9}

Moonbeam Dancer (USA) *D M Simcock* a66
2 bb f Singspiel(IRE) —Shepherd's Moon (USA) (Silver Hawk (USA))
7117^{4} 7424^{4} 7578^{2}

Moon Bound (IRE) *W R Muir* a74
3 b c Observatory(USA) —Inspiring (IRE) (Anabaa (USA))
114^{3} (183) 4090^{10}

Moonburst *E A L Dunlop* a58 70
2 ch f Dalakhani(IRE) —Moon Goddess (Rainbow Quest (USA))
2368^{4} ◆ 3135^{5}

Moon Crystal *E A L Dunlop* a73
3 b f Fasliyev(USA) —Sabreon (Caerleon (USA))
748^{6} ◆ (931) 1412^{3} 1959^{4} 6422^{11} 6905^{4} 7166^{2} 7360^{9} 7771^{2}

Moon Forest (IRE) *J M Bradley* a62 60
6 br g Woodborough(USA) —Ma Bella Luna (Jalmood (USA))
1313^{8} 1641^{5} 1900^{7} 2069^{10} 2988^{7} 3662^{13}

Moonlife (IRE) *Saeed Bin Suroor* a85 104
2 b f Invincible Spirit(IRE) —Marania (IRE) (Marju (IRE))
5147^{6} (5674) 6439^{2} 6818^{5}

Moonlight Affair (IRE) *E S McMahon* 75
2 b f Distant Music(USA) —Petite Maxine (Sharpo)
3437^{2} (4593) 6172^{16}

Moonlight Angel *W R Swinburn* a70 66
3 b f Kyllachy—Far Post (USA) (Defensive Play (USA))
1050^{3} 1572^{6}

Moonlight Danceuse (IRE) *F Doumen* 86
3 ch f Bering—Stage Struck (IRE) (Sadler's Wells (USA))
7431a^{11}

Moonlight Fantasy (IRE) *Lucinda Featherstone* a65 59
5 b g Night Shift(USA) —County Girl (IRE) (Prince Rupert (FR))
316^{7} 2374^{3} 3089^{11}

Moonlight Man *C R Dore* a86 96
7 ch g Night Shift(USA) —Fleeting Rainbow (Rainbow Quest (USA))
26^{7} 314^{5} 452^{5} (509) 692^{6} 747^{4} 1065^{2} 1314^{5} 1569^{15} 1910^{10} 2200^{9} 2818^{7} 3222^{11} 3725^{4} (4248) 4723^{2} 4927^{3} 5018^{3} 5350^{2} 6598^{13} 6900^{10} 7278^{12} 7457^{5} 7507^{2} 7610^{8}

Moon Lightning (IRE) *M H Tompkins* a76 61
2 b c Desert Prince(IRE) —Moon Tango (IRE) (Last Tycoon)
3492^{7} 6359^{8} (7318)

Moonlitesilhouette (IRE) *Noel Lawlor* a62 61
3 br f Xaar—Little Pixie (USA) (Woodman (USA))
102^{5} 116^{4}

Moon Mix (FR) *J R Jenkins* a88 76
5 gr g Linamix(FR) —Cherry Moon (USA) (Quiet American (USA))
405^{2} ◆ 630^{7} 1080^{7} 1299^{11} 1691^{4} 2060^{5} 3925^{13} 4930^{10} 6007^{14} 7545^{6}

Moonquake (USA) *J H M Gosden* 98
3 bb c Mr Greeley(USA) —Beaming Meteor (USA) (Pleasant Colony (USA))
1417^{6} 1918^{2} (2847) 3157^{3} ◆ 5894^{13} 6563^{11}

Moon Quest (IRE) *Saeed Bin Suroor* a96 92
4 ch g Rainbow Quest(USA) —Midnight Line (USA) (Kris S (USA))
(3398) 4508^{13}

Moonshine Beach *P W Hiatt* a66 64
10 b g Lugana Beach—Monongelia (Welsh Pageant)
3137^{3} (3377) 3710^{5} 4391^{5} 5367^{3} 5676^{2} 5917^{3}

Moonshine Creek *P W Hiatt* a53 65
6 b g Pyramus(USA) —Monongelia (Welsh Pageant)
2100^{5} 2755^{2} (3650) 3912^{4} 4811^{6} 5369^{2} (5489) 6007^{3} 6403^{4}

Moonshine Hall (USA) *Mark Casse* 94
8 ch g Spinning World(USA) —Pink Dove (USA) (Argument (FR))
2472a^{8}

Moon Sister (IRE) *W Jarvis* 103
3 b f Cadeaux Genereux—Tanz (IRE) (Sadler's Wells (USA))
1946^{3} ◆ 2560^{5} 3351^{4} (3894) 5024^{3} (5536) 6034^{2} 6781^{10}

Moon Spray (USA) *K A Ryan* a40 51
3 ch g Malibu Moon(USA) —Sun Spray (USA) (Woodman (USA))
976^{6} 1186^{12} 1560^{9}

Moonstone *A P O'Brien* 118
3 b f Dalakhani(IRE) —Solo De Lune (IRE) (Law Society (USA))
2105^{4} ◆ 2792^{2} (4006a) 6521a^{12} 7008a^{6}

Moonstreaker *R M Whitaker* a73 70
5 b g Foxhound(USA) —Ling Lane (Slip Anchor)
1258^{3} (1578) 1953^{3} 2274^{5} (2697) 2927^{9} 3450^{9} 5564^{2} 6216^{2} 6487^{9} 7183^{3} 7447^{5}

Moonwalking *Jedd O'Keeffe* a34 78
4 b g Danehill Dancer(IRE) —Macca Luna (IRE) (Kahyasi)
1482^{12} 1904^{7} 2249^{6}

Moon Warrior *C Smith* a29 23
2 b g Yoshka—Lunalux (Emarati (USA))
1324^{7} 2392^{6} 5778^{12} 6779^{7} 7269^{6} 7319^{8} 7370^{7} 7519^{9} 7659^{14} 7694^{9}

Mooretown Lady (IRE) *H Rogers* a75 94
5 b m Montjeu(IRE) —Chaturanga (Night Shift (USA))
1353a^{8} 1880a^{7} 2420a^{2} 2432a^{6} 5922a^{6} 6689a^{8}

Moorhouse Lad *B Smart* a91 116
5 b g Bertolini(USA) —Record Time (Clantime)
3101^{11} 4550^{7} 5245^{6} 5793^{3} ◆ (6121) 6518a^{2} 7683a^{12}

Moorhouse Lass (IRE) *D Carroll* 24
2 b f Acclamation—Stella Marais (IRE) (Second Empire (IRE))
4740^{10}

Moorside Diamond *A D Brown* a53 53
4 b m Elmaamul(USA) —Dispol Diamond (Sharpo)
107^{7} 529^{10} 643^{5} 821^{3} 1025^{6} 1626^{10} 2259^{5} 2707^{10} 3963^{2} 6912^{3} 7180^{9} 7469^{3} 7723^{9}

Moosley (IRE) *C A Dwyer* a72 14
3 b g Marju(IRE) —Shauna's Honey (IRE) (Danehill (USA))
4531^{10}

Mooted (UAE) *Miss J A Camacho* a71 75
3 b g Mtoto—Assraar (Cadeaux Genereux)
1467^{6} (1876) 2714^{13} 5635^{17} 7070^{7} 7374^{7} 7559^{3}

Mooteeah (IRE) *M A Jarvis* 68
2 b f Sakhee(USA) —Cerulean Sky (IRE) (Darshaan)
5240^{5} 6565^{10}

Moothir (USA) *M Johnston* a68
3 gr c Elusive Quality(USA) —Alattrah (USA) (Shadeed (USA))
1068^{10}

Mootriba *W J Haggas* a66
2 ch f Nayef(USA) —Tarbiyah (Singspiel (IRE))
6166^{4} 6910^{5} 7338^{2}

Moral Code (IRE) *E J O'Neill* a71 51
4 ch h Danehill Dancer(IRE) —Scruple (IRE) (Catrail (USA))
529^{4} 653^{3} 868^{2}

Morbick *W M Brisbourne* a78 55
4 ch g Kyllachy—Direcvil (Top Ville)
(220) (323) ◆ 525^{2} (697) 860^{5} 973^{3} 1065^{5} 6989^{12} 7278^{2} 7405^{3} 7457^{7} 7606^{3} 7657^{3}

More Applause *Pat Eddery* 43
3 b f Royal Applause—Three More (USA) (Sanglamore (USA))
3177^{8}

Moresco *W R Swinburn* 73
2 gr c Dalakhani(IRE) —Majoune (FR) (Take Risks (FR))
6026^{4} 6720^{6}

Morestead (IRE) *B G Powell* a14 71
3 ch g Traditionally(USA) —Itsy Bitsy Betsy (USA) (Beau Genius (CAN))
1128^{6} 1681^{6} 4533^{4} 4664^{10} 5631^{12}

Mores Wells *Kevin Prendergast* 118
4 b h Sadler's Wells(USA) —Endorsement (Warning)
1882a^{3} 3513a^{2} (5136a) 5732a^{3} 5921a^{4} 7682a^{12}

More Tea Vicar (IRE) *R A Fahey* a68
2 b f Bahhare(USA) —Grand Splendour (Shirley Heights)
7165^{5} 7337^{3} 7627^{5} 7754^{5}

More Than Many (USA) *R A Fahey* 62
2 bb c More Than Ready(USA) —Slewnami (AUS) (Seattle Slew (USA))
(5106) 5632^{9}

More Time Tim (IRE) *Timothy Doyle* 69
3 b g Namid—Lady Nasrana (FR) (Al Nasr (FR))
4613a^{13}

Morghim (IRE) *E Charpy* a87 100
5 b h Machiavellian(USA) —Saleela (USA) (Nureyev (USA))
380a^{7}

Morinqua (IRE) *J G Given* a38 102
4 b m Cadeaux Genereux—Victoria Regia (IRE) (Lomond (USA))
(1698) 2000^{13} 2828^{15} 3252^{8} 4550^{12}

Mormeatmic *M W Easterby* a51 62
5 b g Orpen(USA) —Mimining (Tower Walk)
1451^{7} 1893^{12} 2270^{16} 2706^{3} 3582^{4} 4013^{3} 4703^{11} 5770^{13} 6382^{15}

Morning Calm *R Charlton* 55
2 b f Montjeu(IRE) —Tempting Prospect (Shirley Heights)
5240^{12} 6945^{11}

Morning Farewell *P W Chapple-Hyam* a76 80
4 br g Daylami(IRE) —Got To Go (Shareef Dancer (USA))
320^{4}

Morning Queen (IRE) *C G Cox* a51 42
2 b f Night Shift(USA) —Woodland Glade (Mark Of Esteem (IRE))
6327^{8} 6697^{10}

Morning Sir Alan *M J McGrath* 55
2 b c Diktat—Menhoubah (USA) (Dixieland Band (USA))
4062^{10}

Morning Smile (IRE) *Robert Collet* a46 71
2 b c Haafhd—New Story (USA) (Dynaformer (USA))
5139a^{7}

Moroccan Party *M W Easterby* a25 21
2 ch g Bertolini(USA) —Towaahi (IRE) (Caerleon (USA))
2909^{10} 3689^{11} 5560^{6}

Morocchius (USA) *Miss J A Camacho* a65 67
3 b g Black Minnaloushe(USA) —Shakespearean (USA) (Theatrical)
1448^{6} 2288^{6} 2496^{11} 3886^{16} 4524^{9} 6036^{2} 6791^{7} 7012^{3} 7226^{9}

Morotai Marauder (IRE) *M J P O'Brien* a57 62
4 b g Grand Lodge(USA) —Lumber Jill (USA) (Woodman (USA))
4514a^{14}

Morrigan (IRE) *Michael Fitzsimons* a62 59
3 b f Danetime(IRE) —Shelini (Robellino (USA))
4613a^{11}

Morristown Music (IRE) *J S Wainwright* 69
4 b m Distant Music(USA) —Tongabezi (IRE) (Shernazar)
987^{11} 1476^{9} 2676^{13} 3665^{11} 4047^{15} 5770^{3} 6382^{11} 6405^{6}

Morse (IRE) *J A Osborne* a65 62
7 b g Shinko Forest(IRE) —Auriga (Belmez (USA))
1872^{12} 2478^{6} 2798^{11} 3825^{5} ◆ 4084^{6} 4858^{2} 5091^{5} 5709^{4} ◆ 6209^{4} 6377^{2} 6773^{2} 7255^{8}

Mosaic *A Al Raihe* a98 88
6 bb h Singspiel(IRE) —Ela Romara (Ela-Mana-Mou)
202a^{7} 293a^{10} 380a^{10}

Moscow Eight (IRE) *E J O'Neill* a80 60
2 b c Elusive City(USA) —Hurricane Lily (IRE) (Ali-Royal (IRE))
5286^{5} (6434) 6644^{17} 7575^{2} 7714^{4}

Moscow Oznick *N J Vaughan* a66 63
3 bb g Auction House(USA) —Cozette (IRE) (Danehill Dancer (IRE))
343^{5} 6254^{5} 6928^{6} 7166^{8} 7656^{2}

Mosman Park (FR) *Charles O'Brien* a62 71
3 b g Barathea(IRE) —Dalannda (IRE) (Hernando (FR))
826a^{9}

Moss Likely (IRE) *M R Channon* a83 87
2 gr f Clodovil(IRE) —Lichen (Lycius (USA))
1385^{3} (1762) (2147) 3105^{16} 3681^{3} 4190^{11} 4403^{7} 6320a^{14}

Mosspaul *A C Whillans*
2 b f King Charlemagne(USA) —Vettorina (IRE) (Vettori (IRE))
1220^{7} 4873^{11}

Moss Way *W J Musson* a34 24
3 b g Zaha(CAN) —Ruwaya (USA) (Red Ransom (USA))
950^{4} 1343^{8} 1710^{8}

Most Definitely (IRE) *R M Stronge* a79 73
8 b g Definite Article—Unbidden Melody (USA) (Chieftain)
14^{4} 91^{3} 406^{3} 540^{2} 586^{3} 941^{5} 1044^{2} 1388^{5} 1929^{8}

Motafarred (IRE) *Micky Hammond* a72 83
6 ch g Machiavellian(USA) —Thurayya (Nashwan (USA))
(2375) 2445^{6} 3367^{6} 3899^{3} 4500^{5} 4744^{2} 5005^{4} 5382^{7}

Motarid (USA) *T D Walford* 84
3 gr g Maria's Mon(USA) —Saabga (USA) (Woodman (USA))
2573^{4} 3297^{2} 3813^{2} 4742^{8} 5963^{4} 6790^{2} 6948^{19}

Motarjm (USA) *H J Collingridge* a89 84
4 br g Elusive Quality(USA) —Agama (USA) (Nureyev (USA))
224^{2} 358^{5} (524) (701) (838) 1212^{3} 1691^{5} 2076^{4} 4726^{5}

Motherwell *M Brittain* 31
3 b f Tamayaz(CAN) —Mother Corrigan (IRE) (Paris House)
1222^{13} 3640^{8}

Motivated Choice *L M Cumani* a67 67
3 b f Compton Place—Makhsusah (IRE) (Darshaan)
5205^{4} 6192^{5} (6543) 7435^{6} ◆

Motive (FR) *J Howard Johnson* 92
7 ch g Machiavellian(USA) —Mistle Song (Nashwan (USA))
2839^{5}

Motor Home *A M Balding* 76
2 b g Tobougg(IRE) —Desert Dawn (Belfort (FR))
2150^{8} 2601^{3} (3107) 3439^{3} 3924^{8} 4589^{9} 5511^{12} 5895^{12}

Motu (IRE) *I W McInnes* a67 73
7 b g Desert Style(IRE) —Pink Cashmere (IRE) (Polar Falcon (USA))
2391^{6} 2925^{12} 3211^{11} 3567^{3} 3826^{4} 5712^{11} 7012^{8} 7226^{10} 7382^{6} 7497^{5} 7601^{7} 7766^{10}

Mouette (GER) *Mario Hofer* 69
3 ch f Tertullian(USA) —Montserrat (GER) (Zilzal (USA))
6323a^{14}

Mountain Cat (IRE) *W J Musson* a80 73
4 b g Red Ransom(USA) —Timewee (USA) (Romanov (IRE))
1729^{11} 2262^{11} 2619^{10} 3376^{8}

Mountain Forest (GER) *H Morrison* a45 52
2 b g Tiger Hill(IRE) —Moricana (GER) (Konigsstuhl (GER))
6398[7] 6674[13] 7209[9]

Mountain Pass (USA) *B J Llewellyn* a66 65
6 b g Stravinsky(USA) —Ribbony (USA) (Dayjur (USA))
103[6] (914) 1369[5] 2277[4] (2930) 3431[4] 4104[7] 4878[6] 5799[3] 6396[7] 7513[5]

Mountain Pride (IRE) *J L Dunlop* 90
3 b g High Chaparral(IRE) —Lioness (Lion Cavern (USA))
1443[5] 1811[9] (3002) 4509[6] 5360[11] 5903[6] 6675[5]

Mountain Ridge (IRE) *John Joseph Murphy* a57 27
2 b c Gulch(USA) —Elegant Ridge (IRE) (Indian Ridge)
7397[12]

Mountain Snow (IRE) *W P Mullins* a83 81
8 ch g Barathea(IRE) —Mountains Of Mist (IRE) (Shirley Heights)
4511a[2]

Mount Ella *J A Osborne* a18 54
2 b f Royal Applause—Hiraeth (Petong)
1680[11] 4482[6] 5673[10]

Mount Hadley (USA) *G A Butler* a68 96
4 b g Elusive Quality(USA) —Fly To The Moon (USA) (Blushing Groom (FR))
3503[6] 4528[10] 6120[19] 6598[11] 6900[6]

Mount Helicon *A Fabre* 106
3 b c Montjeu(IRE) —Model Queen (USA) (Kingmambo (USA))
1239a[4] 3191a[4] 4959a[3]

Mount Hermon (IRE) *H Morrison* a85 78
4 b g Golan(IRE) —Machudi (Bluebird (USA))
1335[8] 2369[4] 3003[7] 3970[6] (4268) ◆ 4723[9] 5018[2] 5207[4] 5908[11]

Mount Lavinia (IRE) *R M Beckett* a89 86
3 b f Montjeu(IRE) —Havinia (Habitat)
1172[8] 2340[4] (3022) 3671[4] (4432) 6127[9] (6403) 7100[7]

Mount Nelson *A P O'Brien* 123
4 b h Rock Of Gibraltar(IRE) —Independence (Selkirk (USA))
1882a[6] 2876a[3] 3100[5] (3741) 4889a[3]

Mount Pleasure (USA) *Christian Wroe* a87 100
3 ch c Mt. Livermore(USA) —Private Beach (USA) (Unaccounted For (USA))
5025[8] 5897[12] 6239[17]

Mount Usher *M J Gingell* a61 77
6 br g Polar Falcon(USA) —Division Bell (Warning)
5512[11] 7462[9] 7723[7]

Mourayan (IRE) *John M Oxx* 107
2 b c Alhaarth(IRE) —Mouramara (IRE) (Kahyasi)
6316a[2] (7158a)

Mourilyan (IRE) *H J Brown* a107 117
4 b h Desert Prince(IRE) —Mouramara (IRE) (Kahyasi)
(381a) ◆ (652a) 816a[2] 1091a[8] 2234a[8] 5694[3] ◆ 6506a[6] 7682a[11]

Mouse White *H Candy* a40 54
3 gr g Auction House(USA) —Petinata (Petong)
1380[6] 1695[12] 2084[4] 2805[11] 3730[2] 4332[10] 5230[6] 5607[6]

Mousse Au Chocolat (USA) *J-C Rouget* 107
3 br f Hennessy(USA) —Muskoka Dawn (USA) (Miswaki (USA))
1360a[4] 2651a[2]

Mousy Mousy (IRE) *T D Easterby* a10 46
2 b f One Cool Cat(USA) —Leopard Creek (Weldnaas (USA))
1627[10] 4647[7] 4923[9] 6350[10] 6579[7]

Moverra (IRE) *M J Gingell* a52 59
4 ch m Noverre(USA) —Muneera (USA) (Green Dancer (USA))
718[9] 1687[2] 2009[11] 3034[9] 3201[6] 5797[5] 6208[8] 6418[10]

Moves Goodenough *Andrew Turnell* a70 84
5 ch g Woodborough(USA) —Rekindled Flame (IRE) (Kings Lake (USA))
1842[2] 2243[7] 3383[3] 3583[4] 4053[6] 4772[4] (6396) (6585) (6899)

Movie Mogul *M L W Bell* a57 57
4 bb m Sakhee(USA) —Norfolk Lavender (CAN) (Ascot Knight (CAN))
22[4]

Moville (IRE) *B W Hills* 79
3 b g Alhaarth(IRE) —No Sugar Baby (FR) (Crystal Glitters (USA))
2955[3] 3223[3] 4695[4] (5587) 6203[9] 6704[9]

Moving Story *M E Sowersby* 48
5 b g Desert Story(IRE) —Arianna Aldini (Habitat)
3230[8]

Moyenne Corniche *G Wragg* 107
3 ch c Selkirk(USA) —Miss Corniche (Hernando (FR))
(1467) ◆ 2121[2] 2875a[5] 4192[11] 4622[4] 5856[2] 6440[12]

Moynahan (USA) *P F I Cole* a103 103
3 ch c Johannesburg(USA) —Lakab (USA) (Manila (USA))
1808[6] 3156[15] 6440[10] 6670[3] 7146[7] 7313[2] 7496[3] 7579[4]

Moyoko (IRE) *M Salaman* a61 57
5 b m Mozart(IRE) —Kayoko (IRE) (Shalford (IRE))
1645[4] 2097[14] 2642[2] 2943[5] 7340[2] 7518[6] 7732[9]

Mozakhraf (USA) *K A Ryan* a73 67
6 b g Miswaki(USA) —Anakid (USA) (Danzig (USA))
64[8] 1634[12]

Mozayada (USA) *M Brittain* a84 48
4 ch m Street Cry(IRE) —Fatina (Nashwan (USA))
526[13] 1577[9] 2001[14] 2467[8] 2734[5] 2927[10] 3644[4] 4420[8] 5636[13] 7184[2] (7270) (7320) (7650) (7724)

Mr Aitch (IRE) *R T Phillips* a78 76
6 b g Soviet Star(USA) —Welsh Mist (Damister (USA))
7722[2]

Mr Aviator (USA) *R Hannon* a107 112
4 bb h Lear Fan(USA) —In Bloom (USA) (Clever Trick (USA))
(929) 1076[2] (1180) 1766[2] 2790[10] (3122) 4504[13] 6201[7] (6975) 7420[P] (Dead)

Mr Belvedere *A J Lidderdale* a49 29
7 b g Royal Applause—Alarming Motown (Warning)
401[5] 542[6] 621[10] 693[5]

Mr Bones (IRE) *J G Coogan* a80 61
6 b g Trans Island—Leaghillaun (IRE) (Turtle Island (IRE))
4511a[10]

Mr Burton *M Mullineaux* a55 64
4 gr g Thethingaboutitis(USA) —Quay Four (IRE) (Barathea (IRE))
4379[3] 5366[5] 5780[5] 6628[7] 6821[13] 7497[6] 7669[9]

Mr Cellophane *J R Jenkins* a81 77
5 ch g Pursuit Of Love—Fresh Fruit Daily (Reprimand)
539[2] 609[2] 729[10]

Mr Chocolate Drop (IRE) *Miss M E Rowland* a56 34
4 b g Danetime(IRE) —Forest Blade (IRE) (Charnwood Forest (IRE))
33[2] 66[3] 189[3] 289[3] (535) (621) 792[8] 7114[4] 7340[8] (7691)

Mr Clearview *B R Millman* a24 53
2 br g Makbul—Piccolo Cativo (Komaite (USA))
1156[4] 2562[6] 3019[6] 4933[6] 5778[4]

Mr Crystal (FR) *Micky Hammond* a41 77
4 ch g Trempolino(USA) —Iyrbila (FR) (Lashkari)
(2157) 2393[2] 2577[3] 5396[2] 6054[5] (6861)

Mr Deal *Eve Johnson Houghton* a53 46
2 b g King's Best(USA) —One Of The Family (Alzao (USA))
5143[5] 5469[13] 6199[14]

Mr Excel (IRE) *G A Ham* a82 59
5 b g Orpen(USA) —Collected (IRE) (Taufan (USA))
14[11]

Mr Fantozzi (IRE) *M Botti* a66 63
3 br g Statue Of Liberty(USA) —Indian Sand (Indian King (USA))
900[6] 1186[13] 2161[5] 2982[3] (3690) 5378[9] 6048[11] 6353[6]

Mr Flannegan *H Candy* 67
2 ch g Forzando—Star Of Flanders (Puissance)
4367[7] 4973[4] 5213[5] 5647[8] 6865[3]

Mr Forthright *J M Bradley* a51 56
4 b g Fraam—Form At Last (Formidable (USA))
1476[11] 3340[11] 3724[11] 4324[10] 5074[2] 5582[7] 6895[8] 7049[11]

Mr Freddy (IRE) *R A Fahey* 60
2 b c Intikhab(USA) —Bubble N Squeak (IRE) (Catrail (USA))
4923[8] 5988[5] 7038[7]

Mr Funshine *Mrs P N Dutfield* a62 62
3 b g Namid—Sunrise Girl (King's Signet (USA))
2240[7] 2771[5] (3686) 4025[12] 4904[4] 5592[4] 6204[9] 6895[16] 7197[10]

Mr Garston *J R Boyle* a79 91
5 b g Mull Of Kintyre(USA) —Ninfa Of Cisterna (Polish Patriot (USA))
1334[8] 3612[5] 3915[7] 4345[8] 6841[11] 7359[3] 7490[9] 7763[5]

Mr Grumble (USA) *P D Evans*
3 ch g Mr Greeley(USA) —Fumble (USA) (Deputy Minister (CAN))
5117[9]

Mr Hichens *B J Meehan* 91
3 b c Makbul—Lake Melody (Sizzling Melody)
1418[4] 1957[8] 2198[12] 2678[5] 3221[2] 3525[2] 3915[4] (4566) (5309) (5759) 5865[4] 6763[5] 7019[6]

Mr Lambros *Miss Gay Kelleway* a99 78
7 ch g Pivotal—Magical Veil (Majestic Light (USA))
(55) (233) 337[5] 679[2] 7381[6] 7492[14] 7737[8]

Mr Line (ARG) *P Shaw* 90
6 ch g Llers Fitz(ARG) —Miss Maleva (ARG) (Mirfak (ARG))
2234a[13]

Mr Loire *K G Wingrove* a67 76
4 b g Bertolini(USA) —Miss Sancerre (Last Tycoon)
121[8] 211[5] 255[2] 264[2] (363) 372[4] 445[4] 5582[8] 5832[7] 7225[11]

Mr Lu *Miss L A Perratt* a64 71
3 b g Lujain(USA) —Libretta (Highest Honor (FR))
1161[11] 1560[10] 2287[4] (4560) 5544 [2] 5965[2] 6491[6]

Mr Macattack *N J Vaughan* a68 63
3 b c Machiavellian(USA) —Aunty Rose (IRE) (Caerleon (USA))
(343) 2333[7]

Mr Magician (IRE) *W M Roper* 61
2 b c Indian Haven—Annmarie's Magic (IRE) (Flying Spur (AUS))
6320a[12]

Mr Medici (IRE) *Kevin Prendergast* a101 108
3 b c Medicean—Way For Life (GER) (Platini (GER))
1356a[5] 1879a[3] 2435a[4] 5729a[3] 6261a[2]

Mr Melodious *B W Hills* a44 12
2 ch g Green Tune(USA) —Moly (FR) (Anabaa (USA))
957[14] 2754[7] 3158[6]

Mr Mischief *M C Chapman* a73 65
8 b g Millkom—Snow Huntress (Shirley Heights)
1589[6]

Mr Napoleon (IRE) *G L Moore* a76 69
6 gr g Daylami(IRE) —Dathuil (IRE) (Royal Academy (USA))
51[4] 316[2] 888[5] 941[4] (5576) 6607[7] 7301[5] 7580[3]

Mr. Nightlinger (USA) *W Bret Calhoun* a99 122
4 b h Indian Charlie(USA) —Timely Quarrel (USA) (Time For A Change (USA))
6994a[11]

Mr Plod *Andrew Reid* a48
3 ch g Silver Patriarch(IRE) —Emily-Mou (IRE) (Cadeaux Genereux)
674[7] 902[8]

Mr Prolific *B W Hills* 51
2 b c Haafhd—Rumpipumpy (Shirley Heights)
6342[13] 6715 [8] 7105[10]

Mr Redford *N P Littmoden* 56
2 ch g Dr Fong(USA) —Skies Are Blue (Unfuwain (USA))
4425[5] 5066[7] 5316[5] 7257[14]

Mr Rev *J M Bradley* a65 42
5 b g Foxhound(USA) —Branston Berry (IRE) (Mukaddamah (USA))
245[4] 326[3] 514[3] 755[11] 923[2] 1061[5] 1641[11] 2010[14] 2991[9] 4084[10] 7453[3] 7508[7] 7636[8] 7706[8]

Mr Rio (IRE) *A P Jarvis* a16 58
3 b g Captain Rio—Amoras (IRE) (Hamas (IRE))
1971[6] 2620[9] 5627[5]

Mr Rooney (IRE) *A Berry* a59 70
5 b g Mujadil(USA) —Desert Bride (USA) (Key To The Kingdom (USA))
1015[10] 1129[4] 1893[4] 2270[2] 2448[3] 2780[5] 3112[9] 3559[5] 4294[5] (4561) 4846[9] 5220[3] 5398[6] 5970[11] 6823[5] 7231[7]

Mrs Beeton (IRE) *W R Swinburn* a66
2 b f Dansili—Eliza Acton (Shirley Heights)
6910[4]

Mrs Bun *K A Ryan* a61 52
3 b f Efisio—Card Games (First Trump)
2823[6] 3144[9] 3712[4] 4967[6] 7049[2] 7197[15] (7316) 7619[13] 7658[3]

Mrs Fox *N P Littmoden*
2 ch f Needwood Blade—Shalyah (IRE) (Shalford (IRE))
7148[11]

Mrs Jefferson (IRE) *J G Portman* a66 48
3 ch f Traditionally(USA) —Machikane Akaiito (IRE) (Persian Bold)
(694) 899[7] 1412[10] 2603[12] 3604[3] 4278[8] 5086[2] 7076[6] 7363[5] 7591[4]

Mr Skipiton (IRE) *B J McMath* a54
3 b g Statue Of Liberty(USA) —Salty Air (IRE) (Singspiel (IRE))
6660[8] 6935[9] 7403[5] 7669[8]

Mrs Kipling (IRE) *S A Callaghan* 98
2 b f Exceed And Excel(AUS) —Quinzey (JPN) (Carnegie (IRE))
2951[2] ◆ (3485) 3851[8] (5951a) 6644[3]

Mrs Lindsay (USA) *F Rohaut* 118
4 ch m Theatrical—Vole Vole Monamour (USA) (Woodman (USA))
1665a[5] 2553a[6] 4914a[4]

Mr Snowballs *R A Farrant* a43 58
2 gr g Monsieur Bond(IRE) —Swissmatic (Petong)
3798[4] 4728[7] 5959[8]

Mrs Penny (AUS) *J R Gask* a86 92
4 br m Planchet(AUS) —Respective (AUS) (Noalcoholic (FR))
7828[4]

Mrs Slocombe (IRE) *J Akehurst* a48 78
2 b f Masterful(USA) —Mrs Beatty (Cadeaux Genereux)
4513a[13] 7830[6]

Mrs Summersby (IRE) *H Morrison* a64 62
3 ch f King's Best(USA) —Kournikova (SAF) (Sportsworld (USA))
1270[7] 1958[4] 2367[6] 3314[4]

Mr Toshiwonka *D Nicholls* 69
4 b g Compton Place—Victoria (Old Vic)
3282[11] 4379[7] 4877[2] (5258) ◆ 6186[12]

Mr Udagawa *R M Beckett* a64 70
2 b g Bahamian Bounty—Untold Riches (USA) (Red Ransom (USA))
4305[5] 5314[4] 5996[5] 6673[3]

Mr Willis *J R Best* a63 51
2 b g Desert Sun—Santiburi Girl (Casteddu)
2893[8] 3092[7] 3315[6] 7475[5] ◆ (7833) ◆

Mr Wolf *D W Barker* a77 89
7 b g Wolfhound(USA) —Madam Millie (Milford)
983[9] 1300[18] 1552[5] 2005[11] 2398[5] 2892[2] 3111[6] 3812[5] 4171[3] 4462[2] 4743[7] 5400[3] 5493[3] (6232) 6634[3] 6859[3]

Mt Desert *E W Tuer* 70
6 b g Rainbow Quest(USA) —Chief Bee (Chief's Crown (USA))
1972[4] 2332[8] 2888[10] 3399[8] 6115[2]

Mt Kintyre (IRE) *M H Tompkins* 76
2 b c Mull Of Kintyre(USA) —Nihonpillow Mirai (IRE) (Zamindar (USA))
3682[5] 5901[6] 6317a[16]

Mtoto Girl *J J Bridger* a53 36
4 b m Mtoto—Shalati (FR) (High Line)
147[5] 303[6] 415[P] 518[5] 691[6] 877[6] 1053[13] 1210[5] 1350[5] 1673[6] 2561[11] 5148[13] 5429[10] 5577[4] 6378[7]

Mt Weather (IRE) *R Donohoe* a70 69
5 b g Namid—It Takes Two (IRE) (Alzao (USA))
6366a[6]

Mubaashir (IRE) *A Bianco* a95 78
4 ch h Noverre(USA) —Birdsong (IRE) (Dolphin Street (FR))
7253a[17]

Mubrook (USA) *L M Cumani* 83
3 b c Alhaarth(IRE) —Zomaradah (Deploy)
5491[4] 6055[2] 6584[2]

Much Obliged (USA) *Malcolm Pierce* 102
3 b f Kingmambo(USA) —Danka (USA) (Strawberry Road (AUS))
5164a[8] 5744a[5]

Mucho Loco (IRE) *R Curtis* a59 64
5 ch g Tagula(IRE) —Mousseux (IRE) (Jareer (USA))
11[6] 249[6] 914[6]

Much Reality (IRE) *Gordon Elliott* a40 59
6 ch g Lil's Boy(USA) —Arquette (IRE) (Darshaan)
284[7]

Mudawin (IRE) *M F Harris* a99 100
7 b g Intikhab(USA) —Fida (IRE) (Persian Heights)
3490[7] 4516[18] 4843[9] 6817[31]

Mudhish (IRE) *C E Brittain* a77 77
3 b g Lujain(USA) —Silver Satire (Dr Fong (USA))
3324[7] 4174[14] 4809[9] 4989[6] 5090[8]

Mud Monkey *B G Powell* a68 53
4 ch g Muhtarram(USA) —Tenderfoot (Be My Chief (USA))
1643[10]

Muffett's Dream *J J Bridger* a45 52
4 b m Fraam—Loveless Carla (Pursuit Of Love)
2128[14] 2353[6] 3322[9] 3518[6] 3914[6] 4254[7] 4485[10] (4819) 5024[7] 5427[10] 6768[8] 7071[5] 7553[8] 7707[10]

Muftarres (IRE) *Sir Michael Stoute* 82
3 b c Green Desert(USA) —Ghazal (USA) (Gone West (USA))
2786[6] (3282) (4584) ◆ 5056[3] 5510[5] 6532[8]

Mugeba *Miss Gay Kelleway* a49 65
7 b m Primo Dominie—Ella Lamees (Statoblest)
1126[5] 1534[4] 1867[6] 2781[13] 3789[8] 4258[7] 4746[3] 4779[4]

Mugs Game (IRE) *A J Martin*
5 b g Turtle Island(IRE) —Windfall (GER) (Konigsstuhl (GER))
7446[11]

Muhajaar (IRE) *L M Cumani* 85
3 b g Cape Cross(IRE) —Ya Hajar (Lycius (USA))
2620[2] ◆ (2966) 3723[9]

Muhannak (IRE) *R M Beckett* a112 115
4 b g Chester House(USA) —Opera (Forzando)
(2904) 3929[12] (5349) (6261a) (6993a) 7682a[7]

Muharjam *C E Brittain* a56 68
3 b c Diktat—Elsie Plunkett (Mind Games)
3161[8] 3799[3] 4112[7] 4481[9] 5868[10] 6421[14]

Muhim *C E Brittain* a60 61
2 ch c Diesis—Coolberry (USA) (Rahy (USA))
5246[16] 5672[5] 6057[7] 6394[14] 7190[11]

Mujaadel (USA) *E A L Dunlop* a88 82
3 ch g Street Cry(IRE) —Quiet Rumour (USA) (Alleged (USA))
1074[6] 2302[10] 5104[6] 6021[2] 6424[10]

Mujada *M Brittain* a52 39
3 b f Mujahid(USA) —Catriona (Bustino)
81[5] 480[4] ◆ 876[7] 1558[12] 4076[7] 4207[20] 5457[10]

Mujahope *C J Teague* a67 58
3 b g Mujahid(USA) —Speak (Barathea (IRE))
360[3] 704[8] 1034[4] 1247[6] 1407[3] ◆ 1823[5] 2041[14] 2704[4] 3030[6] 3283[5] (3600) 3686[4] 3960[12] 4450[8] 7497[11] 7799[11]

Mujamead *A W Carroll* a71 28
4 b g Mujahid(USA) —Island Mead (Pharly (FR))
166[2] (238) (322) (461)

Mujart *J A Pickering* a58 53
4 b m Mujahid(USA) —Artifact (So Factual (USA))
46[11] 100[11] 523[7]

Mujinda *M Brittain* a50 29
3 b f Mujahid(USA) —Arminda (Blakeney)
20[10] 393[4] (780) 993[8]

Mujma *S Parr* a49 68
4 gb g Indian Ridge—Farfala (FR) (Linamix (FR))
1449[17] 1779[9] 2185[12] 2394[7] 4479[2] 4903[4] 4967[8] 5152[12]

Mujobliged (IRE) *J R Best* a49 53
5 b g Mujadil(USA) —Festival Of Light (High Top)
44[3] 299[10] 352[14]

Mujood *Eve Johnson Houghton* a87 98
5 b g Mujahid(USA) —Waqood (USA) (Riverman (USA))
1278[3] 1617[5] (1800) (2057) (2389) 2604[2] 2789[8] 3122[23] 3382[4] 3840[6] 4405[13] 4522[2] 5096[6] 5270[2] 5695[16] 6005[4] 6249[11]

Mukhber *J H M Gosden* a77 92
3 br g Anabaa(USA) —Tarbiyah (Singspiel (IRE))
1297[4] ◆ 1686[4] (2311) ◆ 3919[8] 4783[7] 5425[5]

Muktasb (USA) *D Shaw* a73 52
7 b g Bahri(USA) —Maghaarb (Machiavellian (USA))
(54) (165) 312[2] 404[7] 707[6] 782[6] 4058[10] 5610[7] 6046[9] 6209[9] 7090[5] ◆ 7254[2] ◆ 7357[3] 7414[2] 7522[5] 7745[9]

Mulaazem *J Mackie* a70 75
5 b g King's Best(USA) —Harayir (USA) (Gulch (USA))
1963[9] 2335[6] 2952[7]

Mulaqat *D Selvaratnam* a97 109
5 b g Singspiel(IRE) —Atamana (IRE) (Lahib (USA))
293a[9] 491a[4] 564a[5] 650a[6]

Mulberry Lad (IRE) *S Curran* a60 41
6 b g Entrepreneur—Taisho (IRE) (Namaqualand (USA))
211[8] 270[3] 327[8] (353) 523[8] 884[8] 1035[8] 1275[5] 1642[9] 2337[14] 5797[2] (6208) ◆ 6419[11]

Mullein *R M Beckett* a82 97
3 b f Oasis Dream—Gipsy Moth (Efisio)
(965) ◆ 1988[4] 2896[6] 4595[2] (4928) ◆ 6069[16] (6532)

Mullglen *T D Easterby* 83
2 b c Mull Of Kintyre(USA) —However (IRE) (Hector Protector (USA))
1727[5] 1967[2] (2281) (3978) ◆ 4190[13]

Mulligan's Gold (IRE) *T D Easterby* a57 71
5 b g Fasliyev(USA) —Magic Lady (IRE) (Bigstone (IRE))
1893[5]

Mullionmileanhour (IRE) *J R Best* a89 98
2 b c Mull Of Kintyre(USA) —Lady Lucia (IRE) (Royal Applause)
(1413) ◆ 3105[3] ◆

Mullitovermaurice *J G Given* a61
2 ch g Pursuit Of Love—Ellovamul (Elmaamul (USA))
7170[4] 7371[5] 7547[9] (7824)

Mull Of Dubai *T P Tate* a49 102
5 b g Mull Of Kintyre(USA) —Enlisted (IRE) (Sadler's Wells (USA))
1018[6] 1569[7] (1920) 2830[14] 3929[2] 5494[4] 5853[4] 6646[18] 7244[13]

Mull Of Fire (IRE) *A Berry*
2 br g Mull Of Kintyre(USA) —Capetown Girl (Danzero (AUS))
6811[9] 7126[7]

Mull On The Run (IRE) *Michael McElhone* a78 90
4 b g Desert Sun—Clifton Lass (IRE) (Up And At 'Em)
4576a[11]

Multahab *M Wigham* a74 68
9 bb g Zafonic(USA) —Alumisiyah (USA) (Danzig (USA))
286[4] (488) 840[5] 1997[7] 2351[8] 4186[12] 4639[9] 5250[13] 5401[5] 6131[9] (6339) 7092[5]

Multakka (IRE) *M P Tregoning* a89 53
5 b g Alhaarth(IRE) —Elfaslah (IRE) (Green Desert (USA))
4509[17] *(6170) (6598)* ◆ *7313[5]*

Multicultural *D M Simcock* a75 80
5 bl g Singspiel(IRE) —Three Piece (Jaazeiro (USA))
1682[4] 2060[2] 2799[2] 3110[3] (3655)

Multidimensional (IRE) *H R A Cecil* 120
5 b h Danehill(USA) —Sacred Song (USA) (Diesis)
1422[4] 1921[4] 2791[9] 3246[2] 3741[7] (4855) 5732a[4] 6074[3]

Multiplication *R Charlton* 79
2 b f Marju(IRE) —Lunda (IRE) (Soviet Star (USA))
5241[4] ◆ 5643[3] 6240[13]

Multi Tasker *Miss J R Tooth* a57 51
2 b c Lear Spear(USA) —Lola Lola (IRE) (Piccolo)
1078[7] 1413[5] 1736[5] *2049[4] 6732[8] 7212[8] 7415[11]*

Multitude (IRE) *T D Easterby* a3 68
4 b g Mull Of Kintyre(USA) —Sea Modena (IRE) (Mac's Imp (USA))
3082[11] 3591[8] 4174[11] 4542[19]

Mumaathel (IRE) *W R Muir* a58 86
5 b g Alhaarth(IRE) —Alhufoof (USA) (Dayjur (USA))
7793[10]

Mumayeza *Sir Michael Stoute* a70 76
3 b f Indian Ridge—Nasanice (IRE) (Nashwan (USA))
3133[2] ◆ (5864)

Mumblesverve (IRE) *W Jarvis* a84 83
4 b h City On A Hill(USA) —Dolcezza (FR) (Lichine (USA))
(1504) ◆ *1936[5]* 2722[3] 3478[3] *3840[2]* 4603[2] 5030[5] *5695[9] 6841[7]*

Mummy's Lodge (IRE) *F Castro* a83
4 ch m Raise A Grand(IRE) —Mummys Best (Bustino)
4917a[4]

Mums The Best *A B Coogan* a17 16
3 ch f Best Of The Bests(IRE) —Super Sally (Superlative)
903[14] (Dead)

Munaddam (USA) *E Charpy* a22 105
6 ch g Aljabr(USA) —Etizaaz (USA) (Diesis)
741a[3] *1089a[15]*

Muncaster Castle (IRE) *R F Fisher* a57 58
4 b g Johannesburg(USA) —Eubee (FR) (Common Grounds)
560[5] 660[7] 724[7] 1953[4] 2446[5] 3201[3] 3550[3] 4848[10] 6806[5] *7114[11] 7691[11]*

Munching Mike (IRE) *K M Prendergast* a55 60
5 br g Orpen(USA) —Stargard (Polish Precedent (USA))
277[2]

Mundo's Magic *M Dods* a38 76
4 b g Foxhound(USA) —Amber's Bluff (Mind Games)
2005[7] 2444[13] 2846[7] 6116[9] *6681[7]*

Mundybash *N Clement* 107
3 b c Diktat—Cootamundra (FR) (Double Bed (FR))
4473a[9]

Munich (IRE) *L Wells* a83 78
4 b g Noverre(USA) —Mayara (IRE) (Ashkalani (IRE))
7712[11] 7791[5]

Munjum *L M Cumani* a55
2 b c Sakhee(USA) —Ann Veronica (IRE) (Sadler's Wells (USA))
7498[9]

Munlochy Bay *W S Kittow* a51 64
4 b m Karinga Bay—Meghdoot (Celestial Storm (USA))
3035[6] 3688[11] 4909[6] 5367[4] 5752[2] ◆ (6672)

Munnings (USA) *Todd Pletcher* a107
2 ch c Speightstown(USA) —La Comete (USA) (Holy Bull (USA))
6501a[2] 6997a[10]

Munsef *J L Dunlop* 115
6 b g Zafonic(USA) —Mazaya (IRE) (Sadler's Wells (USA))
1070[5] 1980[2] 4376[2] 5646[7]

Muntami (IRE) *John A Harris* a74 73
7 gr g Daylami(IRE) —Bashashah (IRE) (Kris)
600[9] 789[6] 1121[5] 2952[6] *3820[10]* 4490[6]

Muraco *A M Hales* a58 74
4 b g Bertolini(USA) —Miss Honeypenny (IRE) (Old Vic)
2623[8] 2914[6] 4811[8] *5145[12]*

Muraweg (IRE) *J H M Gosden* 68
2 b c Kheleyf(USA) —Lady Moranbon (USA) (Trempolino (USA))
3001[5]

Murcar *C G Cox* a61 74
3 ch g Medicean—In Luck (In The Wings)
8676 1014[4] (1896) ◆ 2977[10] 3671[3] 4985[3]

Murcielago (FR) *P Demercastel* a99 108
3 ch c Spinning World(USA) —So Long Girl (Selkirk (USA))
1361a[2] 2875a[4] 3356a[5] 4010a[11] *7643a[9]*

Murdoch *E S McMahon* a34 54
4 b g Mutamarkiz(IRE) —Miss Pharly (Pharly (FR))
1258[9] 1898[12] *2866[11]*

Murfreesboro *D Shaw* a98 90
5 b g Bahamian Bounty—Merry Rous (Rousillon (USA))
308[3] 834[9] 908[3] ◆ *968[5]* 1990[5] 3045[13] *5051[2]* *5405[3] 7313[8] 7423[2]* 7564[7] 7780[4]

Murhee (USA) *D R Lanigan* a54 48
2 b c Rahy(USA) —Grand Ogygia (USA) (Ogygian (USA))
4826[13] *5672[7]*

Murrays Magic (IRE) *D Nicholls* 41
2 b f Bahri(USA) —Fiina (Most Welcome)
6037[7] 6789[8] 7172[4]

Murrin (IRE) *T G Mills* a82 83
4 bb g Trans Island—Flimmering (Dancing Brave (USA))
1112[2] 1719[6] 2308[9] *2722[5] 3376[3] 3836[4]* 4603[7] *(4946) 5350[5] 5800[5]* 6346[5] *7302[9]* 7494[7] 7771[6]

Murrisk *Eamon Tyrrell* a60 55
4 ch g Groom Dancer(USA) —Food Of Love (Music Boy)
708[4] 858[10] 5157[11] 7102[11]

Musaalem (USA) *W J Haggas* 101
4 gr g Aljabr(USA) —Atyab (USA) (Mr Prospector (USA))
(2087) ◆ (3056) 4405[18] 6289[10]

Musango *Tim Vaughan* a73 57
5 b g Night Shift(USA) —Imbabala (Zafonic (USA))
574 1298 569[3] 788[6] 4275[7] *4932[7]*

Musashi (IRE) *Jane Chapple-Hyam* a77 72
3 ch c Hawk Wing(USA) —Soubrette (USA) (Opening Verse (USA))
7387[6] 7580[2] 7752[3]

Musca (IRE) *C Grant* 84
4 b g Tendulkar(USA) —Canary Bird (IRE) (Catrail (USA))
1815[3] 2445[5] 2913[6] 4001[8]

Musharahb *M Appleby* a39
3 b c Muthahb(IRE) —Naz (IRE) (Naheez (USA))
543[11] 702[4] 865[5]

Mushka (USA) *William Mott* a75 96
3 br f Empire Maker(USA) —Sluice (USA) (Seeking The Gold (USA))
5744a[7]

Mushtaaq (USA) *M A Jarvis* a74 87
3 b c Dynaformer(USA) —Siyadah (USA) (Mr Prospector (USA))
2668[5] 3168[3] 3962[4] 4821[4] *5406[3] 6226[2]* 6748[5]

Musical Affair *F Jordan* a14 51
4 b m Alflora(IRE) —Song For Jess (IRE) (Accordion)
930[13]

Musical Bar (IRE) *B W Hills* 94
3 b f Barathea(IRE) —Musical Treat (IRE) (Royal Academy (USA))
(1445) 2170[2]

Musical Beat *Miss V Haigh* a81 86
4 b g Beat Hollow—Warbler (Warning)
2818[9] 3109[8] 4110[2] 4424[5] 4602[7] (Dead)

Musical Bridge *Mrs L Williamson* a47 78
2 b c Night Shift(USA) —Carrie Pooter (Tragic Role (USA))
1263[2] 1924[6] 2462[2] 3019[3] 5989[6] 6656[2] *6987[8]*

Musical Charm (IRE) *T D Easterby* a30 66
3 b f Distant Music(USA) —Fairybird (FR) (Pampabird)
1019[12] 1396[12] 2490[13]

Musical Feud (IRE) *Jane Chapple-Hyam* a62 52
3 b c Distant Music(USA) —Family At War (USA) (Explodent (USA))
158[2]

Musical Maze *W M Brisbourne* 66
2 b f Distant Music(USA) —Maze Garden (USA) (Riverman (USA))
3008[3] 3432[2] 3869[3] 4292[4] (5006) 5747[2] 6231[4] 6761[9]

Musical Review (UAE) *G Kennedy* a28 61
5 b m Jade Robbery(USA) —Treble Clef (USA) (Danzig (USA))
5873a[3]

Musical Script (USA) *Mouse Hamilton-Fairley* a79 64
5 b g Stravinsky(USA) —Cyrillic (USA) (Irish River (FR))
413 1815 263[2] 393[3] (628) 875[6] 4639[11] 4981[7] 5171[6] *5610[3]* 5817[6] *6251[4]* 6733[2] (6907) (7012) 7228[3] 7358[11] (7540) 7621[3] 7730[5] (7762)

Musical Swing (FR) *F-X de Chevigny* a67
3 b f Kingsalsa(USA) —Sophie La Belle (FR) (Fabulous Dancer (USA))
7551a[0]

Musical Way (FR) *P Van De Poele* a109 114
6 ch m Gold Away(IRE) —Mulika (FR) (Procida (USA))
1240a[8] 1666a[7] 2234a[14]

Music Box Express *George Baker* a69 76
4 b g Tale Of The Cat(USA) —Aly McBe (USA) (Alydeed (CAN))
29[9] 191[3] 286[5] 766[2] 806[6] 1037[5] (1061) 1191[5] 1386[9] *1491[9]* 1703[5] 2263[5] 3446[2] 4324[2] 4765[7] 5074[4] (5582) 5601[4] (6357) 6377[9] 7118[9]

Music Celebre (IRE) *S Curran* a66 79
8 b g Peintre Celebre(USA) —Marwell (Habitat)
553[7]

Music In Exile (USA) *B W Hills* 57
3 ch f Diesis—Royal Occasion (USA) (El Gran Senor (USA))
1701[11]

Music In The Glen *P Leech* a19
2 ch f Kyllachy—Musica (Primo Dominie)
6360[12] *6621[10] 7417[7]*

Music Note (IRE) *Miss Gay Kelleway* a79 85
5 b g Indian Ridge—Samara Middle East (FR) (Marju (IRE))
274[7] 555[2] 791[6] 996[7]

Music Note (USA) *Saeed Bin Suroor* a122
3 b f A.P. Indy(USA) —Note Musicale (Sadler's Wells (USA))
(4235a) 6969a[3]

Music Party (USA) *M Johnston* a60
3 b f Swain(IRE) —Dance Trick (USA) (Diesis)
931[5] 1042[5]

Musigny (USA) *W Jarvis* a62 65
2 bb c Forest Wildcat(USA) —Water Rights (USA) (Kris S (USA))
6062[8] 6581[5] 7080[8] *7475[4] 7700[11]*

Muskatsturm (GER) *Shaun Harley* a2 105
9 b g Lecroix(GER) —Myrthe (GER) (Konigsstuhl (GER))
1280[7] *2290[11]* 4799a[DSQ]

Musleh (USA) *Saeed Bin Suroor* a78
2 b c Forestry(USA) —Lucifer's Stone (USA) (Horse Chestnut (SAF))
5615[2] (6621)

Mustajed *B R Millman* a87 92
7 b g Alhaarth(IRE) —Jasarah (IRE) (Green Desert (USA))
1076[6] 1473[16] 2540[3] 3060[5] 3649[4] 4131[5] 4742[11] 5092[8] *5913[2]* 6203[7] *6662[2] 7064[5] 7606[11] 7744[6] 7932[6]*

Mustamad *Miss A M Newton-Smith* a51 60
5 b g Anabaa(USA) —Nasanice (IRE) (Nashwan (USA))
2710 224[9]

Mustameet (USA) *Kevin Prendergast* 119
7 b h Sahm(USA) —Hamasah (USA) (Irish River (FR))
(2740a) 3983a[3] 4356a[3]

Mustaqer (IRE) *B W Hills* 91
3 b c Dalakhani(IRE) —Al Ihtithar (IRE) (Barathea (IRE))
5093[2] ◆ 5859[5] (6777)

Mut'Ab (USA) *C E Brittain* a90 93
3 b c Alhaarth(IRE) —Mistle Song (Nashwan (USA))
1213[7] 1632[5] (4283) *5907[8]* 6307[9] *6772[10]*

Mutabayen (USA) *A Al Raihe* a91 98
3 bb c Doneraile Court(USA) —La Frou Frou (IRE) (Night Shift (USA))
567a[7] 813a[5]

Mutadarrej (IRE) *Mrs Y Dunleavy* 88
4 ch g Fantastic Light(USA) —Najayeb (USA) (Silver Hawk (USA))
4493a[20]

Mutajarred *W J Haggas* a113 109
4 ch g Alhaarth(IRE) —Bedara (Barathea (IRE))
1457[2] *(2503)* 3974[11] 6106[2] 7145[8]

Mutakarrim *D K Weld* 106
11 ch g Mujtahid(USA) —Alyakkh (IRE) (Sadler's Wells (USA))
4003a[11]

Mutamaasek (USA) *Lady Herries* a85 68
6 bb g Swain(IRE) —Tamgeed (USA) (Woodman (USA))
(28) (224) (358) 591[3] 7025[4] 7314[14] 7704[8]

Mutamared (USA) *K A Ryan* a99 105
8 ch g Nureyev(USA) —Alydariel (USA) (Alydar (USA))
1809[9] 2172[8] 3532a[13] *5347[11] 6045[3] 6624[4]* 6864[2] *(7013) 7297[3] (7768)*

Mutamarres *Doug Watson* a94 113
5 b g Green Desert(USA) —Injaad (Machiavellian (USA))
(497a) (666a) (738a) *1089a[10]*

Mutared (IRE) *N P Littmoden* a35
10 b g Marju(IRE) —Shahaada (USA) (Private Account (USA))
1269[8]

Mutasallil (USA) *Doug Watson* a99 94
8 bb h Gone West(USA) —Min Alhawa (USA) (Riverman (USA))
381a[15] *568a[3] (667a) 817a[4]*

Mutawahej (USA) *J H M Gosden* a58 69
4 bb h Storm Cat(USA) —Serena's Tune (USA) (Mr Prospector (USA))
4349[5] 5278[6] *6047[7] 6599[12]*

Mutayam *D A Nolan* 54
8 b g Compton Place—Final Shot (Dalsaan)
1309[11] 1772[7] 1827[11] 3112[17] 3546[7] 3787[8] 4144[5] 4561[11] 4971[8]

Muthabaie (FR) *R Pritchard-Gordon* a95 90
4 ch m Muhtathir—Slew Bay (FR) (Beaudelaire (USA))
6323a[15]

Muthabara (IRE) *J L Dunlop* 109
3 b f Red Ransom(USA) —Hureya (USA) (Woodman (USA))
(1470) ◆ 1830[8] 3194[5] 4623[5] 5331a[7] 5932[6]

Mutheeb (USA) *Saeed Bin Suroor* a77
3 b c Danzig(USA) —Magicalmysterykate (USA) (Woodman (USA))
(5995) ◆

Mutually Mine (USA) *Mrs P Sly* 69
2 ch f Golden Missile(USA) —Gal Of Mine (USA) (Mining (USA))
2534[5] 3292[3] 4870[9]

Mvuto *C G Cox* a69 60
3 b f Mtoto—Cavina (Ardross)
2681[4] ◆ *5155[5] 6909[2]*

Myakoda (FR) *Y De Nicolay* 99
3 b f Trempolino(USA) —Tibbie Shiels (Deploy)
2650a[5] 3543a[5] 4657a[11] *7635a[8]*

Myanmar (IRE) *J Noseda* a68 83
3 b c Rock Of Gibraltar(IRE) —Bold As Love (Lomond (USA))
2413[5] ◆ *2834[8]* (3916) 4989[2] (5841)

My Aunt Fanny *A M Balding* a71 92
3 b f Nayef(USA) —Putuna (Generous (IRE))
1715[4] ◆ 2328[3] 2920[2] (3473) (3911) ◆ 4519[6] 5257[4] 6276[7]

My Baby Baby (USA) *Kenneth McPeek* a89 101
3 b f Bernstein(USA) —Sarah Darling (USA) (Wavering Monarch (USA))
3807a[12]

My Baby Love *J Akehurst* a9
2 b f Superior Premium—Sonneteer (IRE) (Victory Note (USA))
5996[12] 7332[P] 7438[10]

My Beautaful *Miss J S Davis* a11 19
4 ch m Classic Cliche(IRE) —Ginger Rogers (Gildoran)
5215[6] *5869[11]*

My Best Bet *M R Channon* a68 61
2 ch f Best Of The Bests(IRE) —Cibenze (Owington)
5650[5] 6158[3] *6879[3] (7454) 7700[5]*

My Best Man *B R Millman* a67 69
2 b g Forzando—Victoria Sioux (Ron's Victory (USA))
2916[12] 3603[3] 3889[2] 4367[3] 5213[12] *5997[4]* 6414[7] 6865[12]

Myboycharlie (IRE) *T Stack* 120
3 b c Danetime(IRE) —Dulceata (IRE) (Rousillon (USA))
2417a[5] 3533a[5]

Mycenean Prince (USA) *R C Guest* a47 44
5 b g Swain(IRE) —Nijinsky's Beauty (USA) (Nijinsky (CAN))
1116[7] 3545[8]

My Central (ITY) *A & G Botti* 100
4 b m Central Park(IRE) —My Luigia (IRE) (High Estate)
2438a[3]

My Chestnut Girl (USA) *H R A Cecil* 55
2 ch f Horse Chestnut(SAF) —Mien (USA) (Nureyev (USA))
6392[9]

My Choice *A P Jarvis* a34 29
2 b g Groom Dancer(USA) —Beleza (IRE) (Revoque (IRE))
4488[7] *4728[11]* 5314[15]

My Dark Rosaleen *A P O'Brien* 78
3 b f Sadler's Wells(USA) —Danilova (USA) (Lyphard (USA))
4007a[17]

My Dixie Darling (USA) *R Hannon* a39 41
2 b f Bernstein(USA) —Dixie Eyes Blazing (USA) (Gone West (USA))
4020[9] 4579[5] *6574[9] 6694[12]*

My Flame *J R Jenkins* a40 60
3 b c Cool Jazz—Suselja (IRE) (Mon Tresor)
1740[2] 2549[4] 4044[5] 5186[5] *5684[5] 6913[9] 7375[7]*

Myfrenchconnection (IRE) *P T Midgley* a72 69
4 b g Tendulkar(USA) —Papinette (IRE) (Maelstrom Lake)
2274[7] 2391[3] 2925[7] 3557[3] (4650) *6211[2] 6629[4] 6826[12]*

My Friend Fritz *P W Hiatt* a76
8 ch g Safawan—Little Scarlett (Mazilier (USA))
435[2] (551) 654[2] (789) 847[4] 7664[3]

My Gacho (IRE) *M Johnston* a99 89
6 b g Shinko Forest(IRE) —Floralia (Auction Ring (USA))
2210[13] 2938[2] ◆ 3111[7] 3401[8] (3728) ◆ 4437[8] 5503[15] 6278[10] *6576[4] (6842) 7047[10] 7215[3]* ◆ *(7386)* ◆ 7418[5] 7594[7] 7755[6]

My Girl Jode *M H Tompkins* 62
2 ch f Haafhd—Brush Strokes (Cadeaux Genereux)
6884[4] 7141[15]

My Girl Sophie (USA) *J S Bolger* a70 97
3 b f Danzig(USA) —Just Fly (USA) (Capote (USA))
1497a[2] 2738a[9] 3619a[5]

My Indy (ARG) *Saeed Bin Suroor* a101
4 br h Indygo Shiner(USA) —My Light (ARG) (Southern Halo (USA))
292a[2] 567a[3] 1088a[6]

My Jeanie (IRE) *J C Fox* a55 26
4 ch m King Charlemagne(USA) —Home Comforts (Most Welcome)
123[9]

My Kaiser Chief *W J H Ratcliffe* a58 72
3 bl g Paris House—So Tempted (So Factual (USA))
1027[6] (1452) 1819[2] 1988[10] 3050[16] 3626[7] 3928[7] 4609[8] 5638[4]

My Kingdom (IRE) *H Morrison* a38 78
2 b g King's Best(USA) —Nebraas (Green Desert (USA))
2972[12] *3372[11]* (5599) 6305[10] 6924[2]

Mykingdomforahorse *M R Channon* 69
2 b c Fantastic Light(USA) —Charlecote (IRE) (Caerleon (USA))
4636[6] 5021[4] 5314[12] 6761[2] (6886)

My Learned Friend (IRE) *A M Balding* a72 83
4 b g Marju(IRE) —Stately Princess (Robellino (USA))
1842[8] (2615) (2837) 3040[5] 3443[9] *5144[7]* 5600[5] 6554[4] *7077[5]*

My Legal Eagle (IRE) *E G Bevan* a40 51
14 b g Law Society(USA) —Majestic Nurse (On Your Mark)
3606[9] 3901[3] 4366[7] 4722[3]

My Les *J R Best* a31 4
2 b f Josr Algarhoud(IRE) —Ashantiana (Ashkalani (IRE))
4861[12] 5535[10] *6282[11]*

Mymateeric *J Pearce* a52 67
2 b g Reset(AUS) —Ewenny (Warrshan (USA))
1727[7] 2086[3] 4425[7] 5277[4] *5432[8]* 5785[4] 6058[6] 6362[8]

My Mate Granite (USA) *M Wigham* a28
4 ch g High Yield(USA) —Fellwaati (USA) (Alydar (USA))
7713[9]

My Mate Mal *B Ellison* a62 68
4 b g Daawe(USA) —Kandymal (IRE) (Prince Of Birds (USA))
9911[1] 6114[4] *6660[5] 6836[3]* (7053) *7184[7]*

My Mate Max *R Hollinshead* a79 79
3 b g Fraam—Victory Flip (IRE) (Victory Note (USA))
116[2] 1448[5] 2109[6] 2675[4] 2977[12] 3555[2] *6630[4] 6934[5]*

My Mate Pete (IRE) *Mrs L Stubbs* a78 60
3 b g Captain Rio—Lady Peculiar (CAN) (Sunshine Forever (USA))
1113[6] 1426[16] 1777[5] 2268[2] 2527[8]

My Mentor (IRE) *Sir Mark Prescott* a83
4 b g Golan(IRE) —Vanille (IRE) (Selkirk (USA))
68[2] 192[4] 546[4] 659[2] 728[5] (847) 1151[8] 1589[4] 1933[4] 2804[6] 3036[2] (3691) 4345[3] 5018[7]

My Michelle *B Palling* a70 63
7 b m Ali-Royal(IRE) —April Magic (Magic Ring (IRE))
34[5] 509 [4] 685[6]

My Mirasol *D E Cantillon* a68 65
4 ch m Primo Valentino(IRE) —Distinctly Blu (IRE) (Distinctly North (USA))
133[5] (249) 400[2] (579) 841[3] 874[3] 1032[2] 5018[10] 5577[3] 6090[2] 7606[4] 7695[7]

My Monna *Miss Sheena West* a53 42
4 b m Josr Algarhoud(IRE) —Albarsha (Mtoto)
317[5] 420[6]

My Pal Charlie (USA) *Albert Stall Jr* a116
3 b c Indian Charlie(USA) —Shahalo (USA) (Halo (USA))
6995a[4]

My Paris *Ollie Pears* a90 102
7 b g Paris House—My Desire (Grey Desire)
1816[4] 2218[3] 2582[18] 3173[3] 4206[3] 4649[7] 5418[7] 6052[7] 6487[6] 6862[17]

My Pin Up *Christian Wroe* a71 26
3 b f Forzando—Victoria Sioux (Ron's Victory (USA))
2757[9] 3064[8] *7074[11]*

My Princess Jess (USA) *Barclay Tagg* 109
3 bb f Stormy Atlantic(USA) —Jewell Of Jewels (USA) (Pleasant Colony (USA))
5745a[4]

Myriola *S Gollings* a53 62
3 ch f Captain Rio—Spaniola (IRE) (Desert King (IRE))
1560[4] 1769[9] 2928[12] 3834[8] 4542[11] 4987[9] 5307[2] 5770[12] 7178[9] 7288[7] 7521[9] 7618[5] 7644[9]

My Sacrifice (TUR) *C Kurt* 72
3 b f Always A Classic(CAN) —Lotabennit (USA) (Crafty Prospector (USA))
5742a[10]

My Shadow *S Dow* a83 83
3 b g Zamindar(USA) —Reflections (Sadler's Wells (USA))
385a[2] 549a[2] 909[7] (1115) ◆ (1247) ◆ 1524[8] 1745[4] 3319[6] 3840[12] 5800[12] 6417[10] 6683[3] 7307[6] 7495[6]

Myshkin *M A Jarvis* 23
2 b g Refuse To Bend(IRE) —Marmaga (IRE) (Shernazar)
6778[13] 7080[12]

My Spring Rose *J R Jenkins* a38 61
4 b m Lake Coniston(IRE) —Diamond Jayne (IRE) (Royal Abjar (USA))
11[12]

Mysterious Moon *Saeed Bin Suroor* 75
3 ch c Medicean—It's A Secret (Polish Precedent (USA))
6055[3]

Mystery Sail (USA) *Mrs A J Perrett* a75 75
3 b f Mizzen Mast(USA) —Questonia (Rainbow Quest (USA))
2302[7] 4571[4] 6904[6] 7305[4]

Mystery Star (IRE) *M H Tompkins* a85 89
3 ch g Kris Kin(USA) —Mystery Hill (USA) (Danehill (USA))
1424[10] 2109[3] 2464[3] 4519[8] 4790[9] 5569[8] 5682[3] 6128[7]

Mystical Ayr (IRE) *Miss L A Perratt* a17 72
6 br m Namid—Scanno's Choice (IRE) (Pennine Walk)
1030[8] 1771[4] 1953[9] 3127[6] 3579[8] 4851[4] 4949[2] 5454[4] 5564[4] 6162[5] 6408[7]

Mystical Lady (IRE) *A P O'Brien* a98 101
3 b f Halling(USA) —Lady Icarus (Rainbow Quest (USA))
2433a[12] 3619a[4] 4007a[4] 5944a[3] 6298a[7] 6689a[5]

Mystical Spirit (IRE) *J R Weymes* a37 46
2 b f Xaar—Samsung Spirit (Statoblest)
7221[3] 7445[4]

Mystic Art (IRE) *C R Egerton* a74 68
3 b g Peintre Celebre(USA) —Mystic Lure (Green Desert (USA))
2974[16] 3327[11] 3886[2] 4086[5] 4902[6] 6908[3] 7260[2] 7354[6] 7506[3]

Mystickhill (IRE) *J Balding* a65 60
3 ch f Raise A Grand(IRE) —Lady Eberspacher (IRE) (Royal Abjar (USA))
2803[10] 3332[5] 3686[10] 4216[6] 4615[2] 6224[4] 6308[11] 7644[2] 7778[4]

Mystic Lipstick (IRE) *J Heloury* 89
3 b f Kalanisi(IRE) —Art Fair (Alzao (USA))
2439a[9]

Mystic Mayfly (IRE) *Daniel Miley* 65
3 b f King Charlemagne(USA) —Vol De Reve (IRE) (Nordico (USA))
4613a[12]

Mystic Prince *B J Meehan* 69
2 b g Dubai Destination(USA) —Hazy Heights (Shirley Heights)
6602[9] 6978[8]

Mystic Roll *Jane Chapple-Hyam* a59 65
5 br g Medicean—Pain Perdu (IRE) (Waajib)
3162[2] 3839[5] 4479[12] 4635[12] 6255[4] 7317[12] 7423[7] 7782[2]

Mystic Spin (IRE) *K J Burke* a1
4 b h Tendulkar(USA) —Mystical Jumbo (Mystiko (USA))
319[4] 433[6]

Mystic Storm *B G Powell* a53 75
5 b g Medicean—Mrs Nash (Night Shift (USA))
4254[12] 4820[5] 7217[13] 7355[9]

Mystic Ways (IRE) *Traugott Stauffer*
4 b h Testa Rossa(AUS) —Metal Chimes (USA) (Chimes Band (USA))
421a[9]

Mystified (IRE) *R F Fisher* a37 54
5 b g Raise A Grand(IRE) —Sunrise (IRE) (Sri Pekan (USA))
374[9] 1972[6]

Mystik Megan *M Mullineaux*
7 gr m Wizard King—Sian's Girl (Mystiko (USA))
396[8] 758[12]

My Superstar *Sir Michael Stoute* 74
2 b f Sadler's Wells(USA) —Maddie May (USA) (Not For Love (USA))
5147[5] (5534) 6473[11]

My Sweet Baby (USA) *R Menichetti* 98
2 b f Minardi(USA) —Gmaasha (IRE) (Kris)
7185a[8]

My Sweet Georgia (IRE) *S A Callaghan* a54 76
2 b f Royal Applause—Harda Arda (USA) (Nureyev (USA))
2627[5] 3092[2] 3603[2] 5785[2] 6172[13] 7207[5] 7458[10] 7700[10]

Mytexie (FR) *M Johnston* 50
3 ch g Peintre Celebre(USA) —Texinadress (USA) (Copelan (USA))
1382[16] 2143[7] 2700[8] 3126[11]

Mythical Air (IRE) *S Lycett* 36
7 b m Magic Ring(IRE) —Legendary Dancer (Shareef Dancer (USA))
661[13]

Mythical Blue (IRE) *S C Williams* a39 75
2 b c Acclamation—Proud Myth (IRE) (Mark Of Esteem (IRE))
3309[2] 4184[5] 4497[8] (5103) (5466) 5969[8] 6281[10]

Mythical Border (USA) *J Noseda* 102
2 ch f Johannesburg(USA) —Border Dispute (USA) (Boundary (USA))
(1955) ◆ 5852[3] ◆ 6441[14]

Mythical Charm *J J Bridger* a59 64
9 b m Charnwood Forest(IRE) —Triple Tricks (IRE) (Royal Academy (USA))
56[9] 89[4] 2795[13] 3208[10] 4825[13] 5059[6] 5312[6] 7102[9] 7354[10] 7510[10] 7801[9]

Mythical Flight (SAF) *S Tarry* 112
5 ch g Jet Master(SAF) —Mythical Bird (SAF) (Harry Hotspur (SAF))
7683a[7]

Mythical Thrill *J G Given*
2 b g Alhaarth(IRE) —Mythical Girl (USA) (Gone West (USA))
6381[10] 6759[11]

Mythicism *B Smart* 70
2 b f Oasis Dream—Romantic Myth (Mind Games)
6010[6] (6785) 7241[10]

Mytivil (IRE) *Tom Dascombe* a64
2 gr f Clodovil(IRE) —Mytilene (IRE) (Soviet Star (USA))
7708[10] 7823[3] ◆

My Trip (IRE) *Kieran P Cotter* a49 55
6 bb g Midhish—Crissy (IRE) (Entitled)
3820[12]

Myttons Maid *A Bailey* a21 42
2 b f Bertolini(USA) —The In-Laws (IRE) (Be My Guest (USA))
5835[16] 6065[4] 7141[14]

My Valley (IRE) *P A Fahy* 79
6 b m Saddlers' Hall(IRE) —Marble Sound (IRE) (Be My Native (USA))
(4511a)

My Verse *M A Jarvis* a73
2 b f Exceed And Excel(AUS) —Reematna (Sabrehill (USA))
7097[3]

Naaqoos *F Head* 119
2 b c Oasis Dream—Straight Lass (IRE) (Machiavellian (USA))
5330a[5] (6520a) ◆

Nabeeda *M Brittain* a35 58
3 b g Namid—Lovellian (Machiavellian (USA))
1453[5] 1674[7] 4379[5] (5110) 5307[5] 5455[9] 6382[5] 6840[8]

Nabir (FR) *P D Niven* a60 45
8 gr g Linamix(FR) —Nabagha (FR) (Fabulous Dancer (USA))
188[2] 481[3] 602[4] 654[7] 4217[7]

Nabra *M Brittain* a50 47
4 b m Kyllachy—Muja Farewell (Mujtahid (USA))
79[7] 469[3] 783[6] 858[13] 2038[12] 2399[8] 3026[8] 4383[8] 7369[11]

Nacho Libre *M W Easterby* 100
3 b g Kyllachy—Expectation (IRE) (Night Shift (USA))
1400[4] 2793[7] 4869[11] 6239[16] 7176[8]

Nags To Riches (IRE) *J A Osborne* a68
3 b g Acclamation—Beauharnaise (FR) (Linamix (FR))
483[4] ◆ 529[2] 698[3] 3095[F] (Dead)

Naheell *M A Jarvis* a70 57
2 ch c Lomitas—Seyooll (IRE) (Danehill (USA))
6292[5] 7023[2] 7343[3]

Nahoodh (IRE) *M Johnston* 116
3 gr f Clodovil(IRE) —Mise (IRE) (Indian Ridge)
1470[10] 1830[5] ◆ 2433a[7] 3194[6] (3852) 4674a[4] 5730a[2] 6475[7] 7263a[8]

Naias (IRE) *R A Fahey* a7 45
3 ch f Namid—Sovereign Grace (IRE) (Standaan (FR))
3600[2] 4076[8] 7798[5]

Naipe Marcado (URU) *Saeed Bin Suroor* a93 86
5 ch h Timber'o(URU) —Nadinka Foss (URU) (Full Toss (ARG))
202a[15] 382a[11] 564a[14]

Nairana *J G Given* a36
2 b f Lend A Hand—Flukes (Distant Relative)
7452[7] 7734[7]

Naizak *J L Dunlop* a57 72
2 ch f Medicean—Sunny Davis (USA) (Alydar (USA))
4665[15] 6358[3] 7140[4] 7298[6]

Nakoma (IRE) *B Ellison* 54
6 b m Bahhare(USA) —Indian Imp (Indian Ridge)
5042[6]

Nala (USA) *J R Best* a33 11
2 b f Lion Heart(USA) —Miss Chit Chat (USA) (Phone Trick (USA))
4778[9] 6375[13] 6661[7]

Nala's Pride (USA) *Hugh Robertson*
2 b f Lion Heart(USA) —Erica's Dream (USA) (Two's A Plenty (USA))
6613a[3]

Naledi *J R Norton* a47 63
4 b g Indian Ridge—Red Carnation (IRE) (Polar Falcon (USA))
7[9] 168[9] 2365[12] 3796[7] 4207[10] 5779[11]

Namarian (IRE) *M E Sowersby* a39 43
4 b m Namid—Zalamera (Rambo Dancer (CAN))
3230[11]

Namaste's Wish (USA) *William Mott* 97
3 b f Pulpit(USA) —Copelan's Bid Gal (USA) (Copelan (USA))
5164a[4]

Named At Dinner *Miss Lucinda V Russell* 48
7 ch g Halling(USA) —Salanka (IRE) (Persian Heights)
3718[11]

Namibian Pink (IRE) *R H York* a55 54
4 b m Cape Cross(IRE) —Sky Pink (Warning)
1209[14] 1673[9]

Namid Reprobate (IRE) *P F I Cole* a77 86
5 br g Namid—Morning Surprise (Tragic Role (USA))
2619[11] 3090[14] 3646[9] 4129[5] 5345[14]

Namir (IRE) *D Shaw* a69 83
6 b g Namid—Danalia (IRE) (Danehill (USA))
901[10] 994[10] 1268[2] 1386[6] 1624[13] (1908) 2760[9] (2892) 3336[4] 3708[8] 4171[5] 4743[2] 4962[10] 5250[7] (6131) 6278[5] 6859[11] 6990[6]

Namroud (USA) *D Carroll* a76 91
9 b g Irish River(FR) —Top Line (FR) (Top Ville)
66[5] 101[7] 653[4]

Namu *Miss T Spearing* a64 74
5 b m Mujahid(USA) —Sheraton Heights (Deploy)
3260[10] 3695[9] 4064[3] ◆ 4327[10] 4639[3] 6063[5] 6334[11] 6357[4] 6890[9] 6895[3] 7197[11] (7255) 7357[8] 7745[8] 7762[4]

Nanosecond (USA) *S A Callaghan* a54 59
5 ch g Kingmambo(USA) —Easyngold (USA) (Slew O'Gold (USA))
179[8] 930[3] 1031[7] 1206[2] 1643[16]

Nanotech (IRE) *Jarlath P Fahey* a93 93
4 ch g Fath(USA) —Wing And A Prayer (IRE) (Shalford (IRE))
4004a[10] 5731a[4] 6845a[2] 7157a[4] 7325a[11]

Nans Best (IRE) *Liam McAteer* a70 75
4 b g Rock Of Gibraltar(IRE) —Hawas (Mujtahid (USA))
6108[5]

Nans Joy (IRE) *E J O'Neill* a92 105
4 b m In The Wings—True Joy (IRE) (Zilzal (USA))
1331[3] 1801[4] (2347a) 3120[7] 4590[7] (4841) 5120[4]

Nanton (USA) *J S Goldie* a94 99
6 rg g Spinning World(USA) —Grab The Green (USA) (Cozzene (USA))
2593[2] ◆ 4111[3] (4618) 5508[8] 6120[14] 6476[2] 6654[5] (7291)

Nanuka (IRE) *T Stack* 51
3 b f Hawk Wing(USA) —Galleta (Hernando (FR))
3861a[4]

Naomh Geileis (USA) *M Johnston* a91 94
3 ch f Grand Slam(USA) —St Aye (USA) (Nureyev (USA))
7804[5]

Napoleon Dynamite (IRE) *Miss Susan A Finn* a79 66
4 b h Danetime(IRE) —Anita's Contessa (IRE) (Anita's Prince)
6366a[4]

Napoletano (GER) *S Dow* a75 76
7 b g Soviet Star(USA) —Noble House (GER) (Siberian Express (USA))
123[2] 209[7] 356[4] 453[5] 537[4] 708[6] (937) 1154[7] (1641) 2758[3] 2860[4] 3208[5] 3383[2] (3764) 4081[8] 5144[8] 5267[10] 5600[3] 6020[7] 6336[7] 7557[7] 7603[2] 7771[5]

Narc (SAF) *M F De Kock* a92
6 ch g National Assembly(CAN) —She's No Secret (SAF) (Our Casey's Boy (USA))
1089a[9]

Narcisco (GER) *P Schiergen* 88
3 b c Fantastic Light(USA) —Nicola Bella (IRE) (Sadler's Wells (USA))
3773a[12]

Nasaq (USA) *M P Tregoning* a78 67
3 b g Gulch(USA) —Irtahal (USA) (Swain (IRE))
6762[7]

Nashharry (IRE) *R A Harris* a65 51
4 b m Ishiguru(USA) —Abbey Park (USA) (Known Fact (USA))
3839[10] 5166[10]

Nashmiah (IRE) *C E Brittain* a62 101
2 b f Elusive City(USA) —Frond (Alzao (USA))
3610[4] 4157[8] (4636) 4868[4] 5507[5] 6439[3]

Nasri *B J Meehan* 98
2 b c Kyllachy—Triple Sharp (Selkirk (USA))
4024[10] 4530[2] (5053) ◆ (6118) ◆ 6474[3] 6979[9]

Nassar (IRE) *G Prodromou* a59 56
5 b h Danehill(USA) —Regent Gold (USA) (Seeking The Gold (USA))
468[5] (1747) 2513[3] 2870[4]

Nassau Beach (IRE) *T D Easterby* 41
2 b g Bahamian Bounty—Oh'Cecilia (IRE) (Scenic)
2584[9] 3049[11]

Nastjir *M A Jarvis* 16
3 b g Nayef(USA) —Success Story (Sharrood (USA))
2669[11]

Nastrelli (IRE) *T D Barron* a86 93
5 b g Mozart(IRE) —Dawnsio (IRE) (Tate Gallery (USA))
3532a[18] 5731a[7] 6845a[9] 7181[4] 7317[2] 7633[F]

Natagora (FR) *P Bary* 117
3 gr f Divine Light(JPN) —Reinamixa (FR) (Linamix (FR))
(1375a) (1830) 2654a[3] 4674a[3] 5138a[2] 5740a[6] 6496a[2] 7684a[11]

Nathan Dee *Mrs H Sweeting* a51 55
3 ch g Guys And Dolls—Blu Air Flow (ITY) (Entrepreneur)
1166[10] 1533[11] 2559[11]

National Colour (SAF) *S Tarry* a114 116
6 gr m National Assembly(CAN) —Rainbow Cake (SAF) (Mr Eats (IRE))
3101[6] 5245[2] 6518a[10]

National Day (IRE) *D R C Elsworth* a57 54
4 b m Barathea(IRE) —Rise And Fall (Mill Reef (USA))
545[2] ◆ 727[11] 4342[9] 4930[7] 5163[7] 5802[12] 6022[10]

Native Dame (IRE) *P D Deegan* a51 33
2 b f Spartacus(IRE) —Wisecrack (IRE) (Lucky Guest)
6320a[20]

Nativity *J L Spearing* 64
2 ch f Kyllachy—Mistral's Dancer (Shareef Dancer (USA))
1866[5] 2309[4] 2835[10] 4101[2] 5363[9]

Natural Action *W Jarvis* a78 79
4 b g Diktat—Naskhi (Nashwan (USA))
1691[2] 2153[4] 2585[4] 3480[4] 4087[4] 5154[2] 5376[2]

Natural Flair (USA) *P W Chapple-Hyam* 80
2 ch f Giant's Causeway(USA) —Forest Lady (USA) (Woodman (USA))
6391[7] 6887[2]

Natural Rhythm (IRE) *Mrs R A Carr* a66 67
3 ch g Distant Music(USA) —Nationalartgallery (IRE) (Tate Gallery (USA))
281[4] 366[5] 1161[16] 1389[7] 1448[8] 1575[3] 1912[9] 2041[9] 2259[3] 2367[5] 2704[8] 3126[2] 3436[2] (3958) (4180) 4455[7] 4964[9] 5224[7] 5565[2] 5888[3] 6042[5] 6786[10]

Naughty Frida (IRE) *M Botti* a83 83
3 b f Royal Applause—Nausicaa (USA) (Diesis)
723[4] 905[10] 1546[3] (2714) 3210[2] 5071[13] 6471[8] 7210[3] 7419[9]

Naughty Girl (IRE) *John A Harris* a28 50
8 b m Dr Devious(IRE) —Mary Magdalene (Night Shift (USA))
914[8] 1116[13] 4491[9] 4748[8] 5533[3] 5776[13]

Naughty Natz *P T Midgley* 31
2 ch f Noverre(USA) —Deep Ravine (USA) (Gulch (USA))
1480[7] 2004[9] 2965[7]

Naughty Thoughts (IRE) *Tom Dascombe* a72 70
4 b m Grand Lodge(USA) —Gentle Thoughts (Darshaan)
490[4] (607) (841) 1127[3] 1697[5] (2125) 2505[8] (3010) 3562[3] 4599[4] 4751[5] 5154[10]

Nautical *J R Holt* a70 86
10 gr g Lion Cavern(USA) —Russian Royal (USA) (Nureyev (USA))
211[4] 347[4] 460[4] 479[2] (523) 581[6] 655[2] 719[3] 7182[12] 7254[12] 7399[9] 7618[12]

Navajo Joe (IRE) *B J Meehan* a87 86
3 ch c Indian Ridge—Maid Of Killeen (IRE) (Darshaan)
2571[2] (2834) 4404[11] 5682[5] 5862[8] 6526[11]

Navajo Moon (IRE) *David Wachman* 109
4 b m Danehill(USA) —Star Begonia (Sadler's Wells (USA))
1847a[7] 2420a[6] (4007a) 5920a[6] 6298a[8]

Navajo Nation (IRE) *B J Meehan* 63
2 b g Indian Haven—Kathy Desert (Green Desert (USA))
4665[9] 6031[3]

Naval Officer (USA) *J-C Rouget* 107
2 b c Tale Of The Cat(USA) —Wandering Star (USA) (Red Ransom (USA))
6147a[2] (6855a)

Naval Review (USA) *Sir Michael Stoute* 75
3 bb g Storm Cat(USA) —Arutua (USA) (Riverman (USA))
2624[7] 3002[7] 3915[5] 4158[8] 5639[7]

Navene (IRE) *C F Wall* a44 70
4 b m Desert Style(IRE) —Majudel (IRE) (Revoque (IRE))
1780[5] (2510) ◆ 3481[6] 4282[2] 4863[2] 5161[5] 6363[2]

Navy (USA) *D W P Arbuthnot* a61
2 b f Dance Master(USA) —Sea Saint (USA) (Saint Ballado (CAN))
7318[2]

Nawaadi (USA) *J H M Gosden* a73
2 ch c El Corredor(USA) —Louise's Time (USA) (Gilded Time (USA))
(6282) ◆

Nawaaff *M R Channon* a72 82
3 ch g Compton Place—Amazed (Clantime)
798[6] 975[3] 1426[9] 1819[12] 2127[7] 2555[5] 3499[5] 3960[7] 4333[4] 4684[9] 5141[3] 5421[3] 5684[8] 5911[5] 6679[8] 6733[3] 6907[3] 7013[10]

Nawaahi (IRE) *K A Morgan* a50 59
3 ch f Dubai Destination(USA) —Maraatib (IRE) (Green Desert (USA))
5203[2] 5962[12] 6741[13]

Nawamees (IRE) *P D Evans* a81 89
10 b g Darshaan—Truly Generous (IRE) (Generous (IRE))
182[2] (1310) (1668) 3045[9] (4123) 5577[2] (5961) 6607[3] 6950[14] 7553[3] 7707[9] 7744[5] 7831[3]

Nawojka (IRE) *J G Given* 53
2 gr f Daylami(IRE) —Panna (Polish Precedent (USA))
5650[3]

Nawow *P D Cundell* a84 83
8 b g Blushing Flame(USA) —Fair Test (Fair Season)
1583[2] 2076[11] 6079[15]

Nayarna *R A Fahey* 60
3 b f Nayef(USA) —Dimakya (USA) (Dayjur (USA))
2221[9] 2500[3] 3200[4] 3672[7] 4019[5] 4630[10]

Nayessence *M W Easterby* 47
2 ch g Nayef(USA) —Fragrant Oasis (USA) (Rahy (USA))
4394[10] 5716[7] 5882[F] 6230[9]

Nbhan (USA) *L M Cumani* a69 64
2 b c With Approval(CAN) —Crisp And Cool (USA) (Ogygian (USA))
6777[11] 7106[5] 7311[5]

Nchike *D Nicholls* 67
2 b g Zaha(CAN) —Tinkerbird (Music Boy)
957[10] 2217[6] 2746[7] 2910[3] 3008[14] 4604[5] 4873[2] 5041[8] 5357[2] (5715) (5966) 6549[10]

Ndola *P Butler* a57 42
9 b g Emperor Jones(USA) —Lykoa (Shirley Heights)
330[2] 420[3] 499[2] 606[5] 779[12] 914[10] 1184[9] 1562[10]

Neardown Beauty (IRE) *A J McCabe* a93 88
5 br m Bahhare(USA) —Habla Me (IRE) (Fairy King (USA))
90[2] (190) ◆ (280) ◆ (390) 594[6] 679[6] 832[6] 929[7] 4269[5] 4528[6] 4945[4] 5207[12]

Near The Front *Miss Gay Kelleway* a51 57
3 b g Compton Place—Once In My Life (IRE) (Lomond (USA))
1311[5] 1777[2] 3458[7] 3817[7] 6015[2] 6562[8] 6883[4] 7050[3]

Neat 'n Tidy *A E Jones* a27 25
4 b m Josr Algarhoud(IRE) —Raspberry Sauce (Niniski (USA))
3559[14]

Necker (FR) *M R Hoad* a14
7 b g Useful(FR) —Babouche I (FR) (Pure Flight (USA))
2832[12]

Ned Ludd (IRE) *J G Portman* 92
5 b g Montjeu(IRE) —Zanella (IRE) (Nordico (USA))
1472[3] 1984[6] 3044[7] 6606[8] 7110[3]

Needwood Lad *R A Fahey* 81
2 ch c Needwood Blade—Polish Girl (Polish Precedent (USA))
2909[3] ◆ (4734) 5381[2] 5791[15]

Nefaf (IRE) *C E Brittain* 37
3 b c Cape Cross(IRE) —Iftitan (USA) (Southern Halo (USA))
1418[9] 2509[14]
Negra Del Oro (GER) *A Lund* a49 84
5 br m Danehill Dancer(IRE) —Notenqueen (GER) (Turfkonig (GER))
5336a[6]
Nehaam *J H M Gosden* 80
2 b c Nayef(USA) —Charm The Stars (Roi Danzig (USA))
(6083) ◆
Nell's Girl (IRE) *Patrick Morris* a51 62
4 b m Fasliyev(USA) —Pipisflying (IRE) (Pips Pride)
391[5]
Nelsons Column (IRE) *G M Moore* 85
5 b g Benny The Dip(USA) —Sahara Rose (Green Desert (USA))
981[14] 1394[3] 1909[7] 2447[7] 4075[7] 4501[6] 4698[3] 5385[8]
Nelson Vettori *Miss L A Perratt* 52
4 ch h Vettori(IRE) —Eskimo Nel (IRE) (Shy Groom (USA))
1307[6] 2143[6] 3131[9] 4238[4] 4735[6]
Nemorosa *W J Haggas* a70 65
2 b f Pivotal—Anthos (GER) (Big Shuffle (USA))
6531[2] 6953[2] 7341[3]
Nemo Spirit (IRE) *W R Muir* 96
3 gr c Daylami(IRE) —La Bayadere (Sadler's Wells (USA))
1615[2] 1931[5] (2454) 3719[7] 6948[10] (7223) 7429a[6]
Neon Blue *R M Whitaker* a54 78
7 bb g Atraf—Desert Lynx (IRE) (Green Desert (USA))
1327[9] 1900[8] 2535[9] 3281[6] 3443[5] 3643[5] 4440[8] 4736[8] 4849[4] 6216[10] (6786)
Neo's Mate (IRE) *Paul Green* 42
2 br f Modigliani(USA) —Gute (IRE) (Petardia)
1610[5] 1924[7] 2206[6] 2903[11] 5363[7] 6244[11] 7501[12]
Nepotista (BRZ) *A Manuel* 104
6 b g Know Heights(IRE) —Wekilinda (BRZ) (Kenetico (BRZ))
381a[16] 652a[9]
Nera Divine (FR) *M Boutin* a82 99
3 ch f Divine Light(JPN) —Nera Zilzal (IRE) (Zilzal (USA))
1360a[6]
Nero West (FR) *Miss L A Perratt* 78
7 ch g Pelder(IRE) —West River (USA) (Gone West (USA))
1219[2] (1824) 2939[6] 3414[4] (3785) 4146[3] 5540[2] 5967[11] 7128[4]
Nesayem (IRE) *D M Simcock* a69 33
2 b f Diktat—Zibet (Kris)
5650[9] 6016[10] 6432[3]
Nesno (USA) *J D Bethell* a72 71
5 ch g Royal Academy(USA) —Cognac Lady (USA) (Olympio (USA))
2365[3] 2848[2] 3736[2] 4419[5] (5478) 6056[13] 6452[11]
Nessen Dorma (IRE) *J S Wainwright* a21 53
7 b g Entrepreneur—Goldilocks (IRE) (Caerleon (USA))
638[6] 1020[5]
Nestor Protector (IRE) *A B Haynes* a28 57
3 b g Bold Fact(USA) —Irma La Douce (IRE) (Elbio)
876[9] 1187[9] 1550[10] 2099[6] 3605[7]
Netta (IRE) *P J Makin* 58
2 b f Barathea(IRE) —Nishan (Nashwan (USA))
6117[9]
Net Value (USA) *B Smart* a24 5
2 b c Van Nistelrooy(USA) —Gritsie Girl (USA) (Boone's Mill (USA))
6789[18] 7240[15] 7371[6]
Networker *P J McBride* a81 81
5 ch g Danzig Connection(USA) —Trevorsninepoints (Jester)
2373[8] 2693[8] 3612[7] 4162[12] 7307[5] ◆ 7510[3] 7668[7]
Neuchatel (GER) *M Johnston* a80 79
2 b g Rahy(USA) —Nalani (IRE) (Sadler's Wells (USA))
6597[4] ◆ (6759) 7391[4]
Neutrino *D G Bridgwater* a64 62
6 b g Mtoto—Fair Seas (General Assembly (USA))
4691[6] 6243[15]
Neva A Mull Moment (IRE) *D Nicholls*
2 b g Mull Of Kintyre(USA) —Serious Contender (IRE) (Tenby)
6789[19]
Nevada Desert (IRE) *R M Whitaker* a85 92
8 b g Desert King(IRE) —Kayanga (Green Desert (USA))
1016[7] 1481[8] 1612[5] 2271[2] 3006[3] 3367[16] 3664[5] 4206[6] (4500) 4744[7] 5360[5] 5418[5] 5772[4] 6052[3] 6841[2]
Neve Lieve (IRE) *M Botti* a56 90
3 bb f Dubai Destination(USA) —Love Of Silver (USA) (Arctic Tern (USA))
3057[5] 3322[3] (3843) 4619[4] (4992) 5938[9] (6390) 6948[3] 7487a[4]
Never Bouchon (JPN) *M Ito* 115
5 b h Marvelous Sunday(JPN) —Pearl Necklace (Mill Reef (USA))
7511a[7]
Never Catcher (IRE) *P A Blockley* 69
3 br f Catcher In The Rye(IRE) —Never End (Alzao (USA))
997[6] (1123) 1381[5] 1867[5]
Never Cross (IRE) *M A Barnes* 2
4 b m Cape Cross(IRE) —Itsy Bitsy Betsy (USA) (Beau Genius (CAN))
1307[7] 1890[15]
Never Cry *Saeed Bin Suroor* a60
2 b f Reset(AUS) —Triple Wood (USA) (Woodman (USA))
3837[6]
Never Ending Tale *W Jarvis* a76 87
3 ch g Singspiel(IRE) —Bright Finish (USA) (Zilzal (USA))
1417[5] (2612) 3745[12] 4500[3] 5449[5] 6202[10]
Never Lose *C E Brittain* 85
2 br f Diktat—Enchanted Princess (Royal Applause)
4747[2] 5184[3] 6030[2] 6268[6]
Neveronamonday (IRE) *A Berry*
4 br m Night Shift(USA) —Appalachia (IRE) (Imperial Frontier (USA))
308[5] (Dead)
Never On Sunday (FR) *J-C Rouget* 113
3 gr c Sunday Break(JPN) —Hexane (FR) (Kendor (FR))
(6148a)
Never Pink (FR) *Ian Williams* a52 60
4 b m Poliglote—Ring Pink (USA) (Bering)
1383[10] 1620[6] 7042[9] 7272[5]
Never Retreat (USA) *Kiaran McLaughlin* a107 100
3 bb f Smart Strike(CAN) —Lisieux (USA) (Steady Growth (CAN))
4235a[5]
Never Sold Out (IRE) *J G M O'Shea* a58 53
3 ch c Captain Rio—Vicious Rosie (Dancing Spree (USA))
195[5] 1274[5] 3166[8] 3605[2] 4794[6]
Never Without Me *J F Coupland* a28 73
8 ch g Mark Of Esteem(IRE) —Festival Sister (Belmez (USA))
2293[11] 2892[6] 3171[2] 3868[12] 4125[3] 4502[4] 5260[11] 6159[12] 6310[6] 6680[10]
Nevinstown (IRE) *C Grant* a54 58
8 b g Lahib(USA) —Moon Tango (IRE) (Last Tycoon)
978[9]
Nevsky Bridge *M Todhunter* 38
6 b m Soviet Star(USA) —Pontressina (USA) (St Jovite (USA))
3718[6] 4879[4] 5415[8]
New Adventure *P F I Cole* 46
2 b c Generous(IRE) —Sari (Faustus (USA))
3645[9] 6085[14] 6745[10]
New Approach (IRE) *J S Bolger* 131
3 ch c Galileo(IRE) —Park Express (Ahonoora)
1808[2] ◆ 2418a[2] (2829) 5276[3] (5732a) (6816)
New Art (USA) *R Bouresly* a54
5 br g Gone West(USA) —Sopran Mariduff (Persian Bold)
566a[12]
New Balls Please (IRE) *P M Phelan* a56 54
3 ch g Titus Livius(FR) —Kilkee Bay (IRE) (Case Law)
2935[5] 3605[4] 4338[7] 4725[5]
New Beginning (FR) *H J L Dunlop* a66 43
2 b f Nayef(USA) —Chrysalu (Distant Relative)
6392[11] 6910[2] 7165[6]
New Beginning (IRE) *Mrs S Lamyman* a73 103
4 b g Keltos(FR) —Goldthroat (IRE) (Zafonic (USA))
757[8] 2582[15] 3007[6] 3440[2] 3925[11] 4618[5] 5773[10] 6444[11] 6974[12] 7364[4] 7580[5]
Newcastle Sam *J J Bridger* a6 35
3 b g Atraf—Ballyewry (Prince Tenderfoot (USA))
4441[3] 4978[9] 6018[13]
New England *W M Brisbourne* a70 69
6 ch g Bachir(IRE) —West Escape (Gone West (USA))
7189[P]
New Fee (GER) *Andreas Lowe* 26
4 bl m Monsun(GER) —Nillfeedir (GER) (Fabulous Dancer (USA))
3623a[11]
New Freedom (BRZ) *D R Lanigan* a101 105
7 b g Burooj—Beautiful Maria (BRZ) (Ghadeer (FR))
(378a) 814a[3] 1089a[5] 3248[9] 3722[6] ◆ 4445[25] 4840[7] 5347[10]
Newgate (UAE) *Mrs R A Carr* a60 33
4 b g Jade Robbery(USA) —Patruel (Rainbow Quest (USA))
48[10] 107[4] 216[3] 362[4] 1064[10] 1258[7] (1491) 1602[5] 2251[11] 2375[12] 2846[14] 3329[9] 3839[13]
Newgate Lodge (IRE) *M Halford* a71 95
4 b m Namid—Oh'Cecilia (IRE) (Scenic)
5731a[10]
New Guinea *Saeed Bin Suroor* a93 109
5 b g Fantastic Light(USA) —Isle Of Spice (USA) (Diesis)
293a[4] 491a[3] 652a[4] 740a[3] 5494[7] 5894[4]
New Havens *C R Egerton* 47
3 b f Indian Ridge—Lady High Havens (IRE) (Bluebird (USA))
1957[9] 2307[5] 3061[12]
New Jersey (IRE) *Doug Watson* a90 95
3 br c Statue Of Liberty(USA) —Shinkoh Rose (FR) (Warning)
567a[8] 812a[6]
Newlyn Art *D R C Elsworth* a81 63
2 ch c Compton Place—Miss Rimex (IRE) (Ezzoud (IRE))
6702[7] 6978[10] 7388[5] ◆ (7542) ◆ 7714[2] (7820)
New Minerton (IRE) *B R Millman* a38 43
3 b f Trans Island—Irish Lover (USA) (Irish River (FR))
998[10] 1166[11] 1478[12] 1897[8] 2451[15]
Newpark Spirit (IRE) *Emmanuel Hughes* a45 4
5 b g Desert Style(IRE) —Newpark Lady (IRE) (Foxhound (USA))
99[7] 120[6]
Newpark Style (IRE) *Emmanuel Hughes* a45 7
3 b g Desert Style(IRE) —Newpark Lady (IRE) (Foxhound (USA))
7651[6] 7705[7]
Newport (AUS) *Paul Perry* 110
6 gr g Encosta De Lago(AUS) —Sibelienne (Nishapour (FR))
7188a[10]
New Seeker *P F I Cole* 114
8 b g Green Desert(USA) —Ahbab (IRE) (Ajdal (USA))
2132[5] 2580[10]
New Star (UAE) *W M Brisbourne* a85 80
4 b g Green Desert(USA) —Princess Haifa (USA) (Mr Prospector (USA))
1458[5] 1947[9] 2476[4] (2617) 2970[6] 3947[2] 4633[7] 6235[4] (6450) 6950[7] 7116[4] 7291[12] 7606[5]
New Tricks *Miss L A Perratt* 51
2 b g Falbrav(IRE) —Numberonedance (USA) (Trempolino (USA))
4237[5] 5387[9] 6151[5]
New York Oscar (IRE) *A J McCabe* a88 69
4 b g Tobougg(IRE) —Special Dissident (Dancing Dissident (USA))
84[10] 1033[5] 1582[5] 2501[7] 4028[4] 4743[12]
New York Prince (IRE) *R J Osborne* a36 37
4 b g Desert Prince(IRE) —Katch Me Katie (Danehill (USA))
1254[9]
New Zealand (IRE) *A P O'Brien* a77 104
3 ch c Galileo(IRE) —Worlds Apart (Darshaan)
5921a[2]
Next Best *A Berry* a50 50
3 b f Best Of The Bests(IRE) —Lone Pine (Sesaro (USA))
993[10] 2283[12]
Next Flight (IRE) *R E Barr* 51
9 b g Woodborough(USA) —Sans Ceriph (IRE) (Thatching)
1184[11] 1551[7] 1773[8]
Next Of Kin (IRE) *Jennie Candlish* a60 71
3 b g Kris Kin(USA) —Lady Of Shalott (Kings Lake (USA))
3580[2] 4077[2] 4859[7] 6092[7]
Next Vision (IRE) *J Hirschberger* 96
2 ch c Rock Of Gibraltar(IRE) —Night Petticoat (GER) (Petoski)
6853a[2]
Nexus (IRE) *Saeed Bin Suroor* 66
3 ch c Pivotal—Bordighera (USA) (Alysheba (USA))
5505[2]
Neyraan *M Johnston* a55
3 b f Lujain(USA) —Zaynaat (Unfuwain (USA))
130[5] 306[6] 439[7]
Nezami (IRE) *J Akehurst* a93 91
3 b g Elnadim(USA) —Stands To Reason (USA) (Gulch (USA))
2405[3] 2794[9] 3744[7] 4641[4] (4893) 5313[5] 7556[6] 7804[2]
Nicada (IRE) *Stef Liddiard* a76 70
4 ch g Titus Livius(FR) —Rhapsani (IRE) (Persian Bold)
63[7] 177[12] 7662[6]
Nice Dream *C E Brittain* a64 51
3 b f Oasis Dream—Have Fun (Indian Ridge)
1302[3] 1499[2] 1581[3] 3118[6] 5617[5]
Nice Matin (USA) *J A R Toller* a70 53
3 bb f Tiznow(USA) —Quelle Affaire (USA) (Riverman (USA))
(3318) 4082[7] 4795[6] 6560[12]
Nice Time (IRE) *M H Tompkins* a69 56
2 ch f Tagula(IRE) —Nicea (IRE) (Dominion)
6887[9] 7140[13] (7337)
Nice To Know (FR) *G L Moore* a89 79
4 ch m Machiavellian(USA) —Entice (FR) (Selkirk (USA))
1335[2] 1857[4] 2993[5] 3210[5] 4407[16] 5695[6] ◆ 6170[7]
Nice Wee Girl (IRE) *S Kirk* a72 86
3 b f Clodovil(IRE) —Neat Dish (CAN) (Stalwart (USA))
17[5] 1144[4] 1271[2] (1315) ◆ (2127) 2196[5] 2428[2] 2793[6]
Nickel Silver *B Smart* a65 71
3 ro g Choisir(AUS) —Negligee (Night Shift (USA))
3712[6] 4163[8] 4397[5] 6388[4] ◆ 6765[2] 7081[9] 7323[6] 7517[9] 7733[4]
Nick's Nikita (IRE) *M Halford* 107
5 ch m Pivotal—Elaine's Honor (USA) (Chief's Crown (USA))
1655a[4] 3070a[4] 3513a[6] 4833a[10]
Nicky Nutjob (GER) *J Pearce* a63 63
2 b c Fasliyev(USA) —Natalie Too (USA) (Irish River (FR))
6117[12] 6524[4] 7069[10] 7524[5] 7718[2]
Nicokellhann (USA) *J T Gorman* 43
2 gr f Kaldounevees(FR) —Rattrapee (IRE) (Swain (IRE))
5294a[14]
Niconero (AUS) *David Hayes* 117
7 b g Danzero(AUS) —Nicola Lass (AUS) (Scenic)
1090a[11]
Nigella *E S McMahon* a79 73
5 b m Band On The Run—Yabint El Sham (Sizzling Melody)
301[6] 580[3] 840[9] 1373[3] 2676[3]
Night Affair *D W P Arbuthnot* a74
2 b f Bold Edge—Twilight Mistress (Bin Ajwaad (IRE))
(7734)
Night Crescendo (USA) *Mrs A J Perrett* a94 103
5 bb g Diesis—Night Fax (USA) (Known Fact (USA))
1569[4] 2144[4] 3249[8] 3975[10] 4508[11] 5677[4] 6120[9] (6302) (6646) 7244[19] 7491[10]
Night Dancer (IRE) *B W Hills* 10
2 b f Night Shift(USA) —Graten (IRE) (Zieten (USA))
5860[10] 6341[15]
Night Groove (IRE) *P Butler* a48 63
5 b g Night Shift(USA) —Taysala (IRE) (Akarad (FR))
1661[0] 9151[0]
Night Heart (IRE) *W Baltromei* 90
3 b f High Chaparral(IRE) —Night Year (IRE) (Jareer (USA))
5329a[8]
Night Hour (IRE) *Saeed Bin Suroor* a87 99
6 b g Entrepreneur—Witching Hour (IRE) (Alzao (USA))
493a[14] 3253[4] 3929[4] (4742) 6974[6]
Nightjar (USA) *M Johnston* a87 87
3 b c Smoke Glacken(USA) —Night Risk (USA) (Wild Again (USA))
1054[9] 1763[6] (3694) 4364[4] 4553[12] 5033[2] 5290[2] 5449[2] 6276[8] 6526[8] 7278[11] 7457[12] (7633) 7668[2]
Night Knight (IRE) *M L W Bell* 59
2 b g Bachelor Duke(USA) —Dark Albatross (USA) (Sheikh Albadou)
4616[9] 6359[10] 6714[13]
Nightlign (NZ) *A Lee* 97
4 ch h Align(AUS) —Indian Squaw (NZ) (Carolingian (AUS))
7683a[11]
Night Lily (IRE) *J Jay* a67 75
2 b f Night Shift(USA) —Kedross (IRE) (King Of Kings (IRE))
4157[4] 4870[3] 5165[10] 6002[9] 6362[10] 6865[4] 7467[2] 7718[9]
Night Of Fortune *Sir Mark Prescott* a79 85
2 b g Key Of Luck(USA) —La Nuit Rose (FR) (Rainbow Quest (USA))
2521[3] 3277[4] 3778[2] (4340) ◆ 4475[2] (5447) 5883[5]
Night Orbit *Miss J Feilden* a72 72
4 b g Observatory(USA) —Dansara (Dancing Brave (USA))
919[5] 1119[4] 2185[10] (2978) 3449[7] 3914[4] 4739[2] 5105[11] 6007[15] 6607[8] 6721[2] 6862[6] 7202[4] 7385[3] 7630[3]
Night Premiere (IRE) *R Hannon* a59 61
3 b f Night Shift(USA) —Star Studded (Cadeaux Genereux)
897[4] 965[4] 1672[6] ◆ 2260[6] 4824[9] 5617[3] 6150[3] 6435[6] 6564[4] 6890[12] 7254[4] 7357[5] 7672[2]
Night Prospector *R A Harris* a69 68
8 b g Night Shift(USA) —Pride Of My Heart (Lion Cavern (USA))
627[4] 884[2] 1035[3] 1150[8] 1370[5] 1642[3] 2050[2] 2474[6] 3021[3] 3346[5] 3565[2] 3783[3] 4102[5] 4324[3] (4580) 4765[4] 4812[3] 5171[3] 5398[4] 5645[3] 6024[6] 6204[8] 6339[6] 6711[9] 6895[14] 7377[6] 7444[4] 7618[6] 7710[8]
Night Rainbow (IRE) *Mrs S Leech* a55 47
5 ch m Night Shift(USA) —Teresita (Rainbow Quest (USA))
1966[4] 2622[15] 3177[7] 3405[11] 3608[12]
Night Robe *P D Evans* a47 49
3 b f Robellino(USA) —Camp Fire (IRE) (Lahib (USA))
38[5] 81[6] (Dead)
Night Rocket (IRE) *A M Balding* a66 76
4 b m Night Shift(USA) —Exorcet (FR) (Selkirk (USA))
3847[5] (4388) 4767[3] ◆ (5026) 5467[8] 5751[4]
Nightscape (USA) *Charles A DeMario* 88
4 ch g Mojave Moon(USA) —Northern Flair (USA) (Caveat (USA))
5928a[8]
Night Seed (IRE) *R Hannon* a72 74
2 b f Exceed And Excel(AUS) —Night Scent (IRE) (Scenic)
2608[5] (3902) 4525[3] 4925[2] 5055[7] 5866[2] 6172[12] 6730[3]
Night Skier (IRE) *J L Dunlop* a69 78
3 ch f Night Shift(USA) —Ski For Me (IRE) (Barathea (IRE))
2481[6]
Nightspot *Eve Johnson Houghton* a82 80
7 ch g Night Shift(USA) —Rash Gift (Cadeaux Genereux)
1874[6] 2335[5] 2770[2] 2990[3] 3914[5] 4721[P]
Nightstrike (IRE) *Luke Comer* a58 67
5 b m Night Shift(USA) —Come Together (Mtoto)
746[6] 875[5] 1145[7] 1747[9]
Nightswimmer (IRE) *David P Myerscough* 80
3 ch f Noverre(USA) —Buckle (IRE) (Common Grounds)
5873a[13]
Night Wolf (IRE) *S Curran* a63 63
8 gr g Indian Ridge—Nicer (IRE) (Pennine Walk)
4053[5] 5604[8]
Nijinsky Ballet (USA) *Robert Gorham* 88
3 b f Rahy(USA) —Star Of The Ballet (USA) (Nijinsky (CAN))
5744a[13]
Nijoom Dubai *M R Channon* 103
3 b f Noverre(USA) —Aileen's Gift (IRE) (Rainbow Quest (USA))
1401[6] 2033a[8] 2651a[5] 4590[9] 5829[8] 6266[14]
Nikki Bea (IRE) *Jamie Poulton* a66 64
5 ch m Titus Livius(FR) —Strong Feeling (USA) (Devil's Bag (USA))
276[5] 453[3] 571[6] 4306[8] 4825[8] 5575[3] 7433[4] 7601[3] 7765[8]
Nikolaievich (IRE) *P F I Cole* a64 66
3 b g Xaar—Seren Quest (Rainbow Quest (USA))
1342[3] 1563[6] 2043[13] (2480) 2922[9] 3525[8] 4086[4] 4427[5] 4901[2] 5603[4] 6332[4] 6746[11]
Nil Bleu (USA) *Noel T Chance* a54 63
4 b g Swain(IRE) —Nany's Affair (USA) (Colonial Affair (USA))
510[5] 722[7] 3588[11] 4250[7]
Nimbelle (IRE) *J C Tuck* a56 50
3 bb f Namid—Bellissi (IRE) (Bluebird (USA))
2287[9] 7522[11]
Nimello (USA) *A G Newcombe* a65 78
12 b g Kingmambo(USA) —Zakota (IRE) (Polish Precedent (USA))
69[2] 215[7] 617[2] (843) 2707[8] 3687[5] 5489[13]
Nimmy's Special *M Mullineaux* a57 61
2 ch f Monsieur Bond(IRE) —Mammas F-C (IRE) (Case Law)
2388[7] 4384[6] 6244[4] 6709[4] 7016[3] 7519[5]
Nina Morena (USA) *R Menichetti*
2 b f Black Minnaloushe(USA) —Soundproof (IRE) (Ela-Mana-Mou)
2744a[9]
Ninefineirishmen (IRE) *K R Burke* a54 78
3 bb g Statue Of Liberty(USA) —Tallassee (Indian Ridge)
1295[4] 1868[8] 2378[2] 2539[3] (3200) 4017[2] 4407[20] 4682[10] 5390[4] 6043[4] 6490[9]

Nine Stories (IRE) *J Howard Johnson* 89
3 b g Catcher In The Rye(IRE) —Irinatinvidio (Rudimentary (USA))
3046[6] ◆ 3494[10] (4204)

Nino Cochise (IRE) *C R Egerton* a71 70
3 b g High Chaparral(IRE) —Lady Scarlett (Woodman (USA))
1572[3] 2151[10] 2977[7] 3781[7]

Nino Zachetti (IRE) *E J Alston* 36
2 ch c Daggers Drawn(USA) —Paganina (FR) (Galetto (FR))
3714[8] 4593[12] 5539[6]

Ninth Client (USA) *D Wayne Lukas* 96
2 ch c Malibu Moon(USA) —Bird Cage (USA) (Kris S (USA))
6998a[9]

Ninth House (USA) *Mrs R A Carr* a89 64
6 b h Chester House(USA) —Ninette (USA) (Alleged (USA))
63[3] 252[3] 314[2] (429) (577) (768) (833) 910[9] 1045[4] 1545[5] 1936[6] 2703[11] 3108[8] 3478[7] 3840[8] 6452[10] 7167[9] 7610[4] 7786[4]

Niqaab *W J Musson* a63 70
4 ch m Alhaarth(IRE) —Shanty (Selkirk (USA))
39[3] 144[2] 317[6] 1206[10] 1639[9] 2078[8] 7688[6]

Nisaal (IRE) *J J Quinn* 80
3 b g Indian Ridge—Kahalah (IRE) (Darshaan)
1398[8] 2191[6] 3310[2] 3813[10] 6950[10] 7239[3] ◆

Nisbah *C E Brittain* a43 41
3 ch f Kyllachy—Amazing Bay (Mazilier (USA))
1721[10] 2549[14] 5574[11]

Niska (USA) *A Fabre* a69 69
3 b f Smart Strike(CAN) —Lady Of Talent (USA) (Siphon (BRZ))
6743a[0]

Nistle's Crunch (USA) *Kenneth McPeek* a85 105
3 b c Van Nistelrooy(USA) —Sam Eye Am (USA) (Island Whirl (USA))
4678a[5]

Niteowl Lad (IRE) *J Balding* 65
6 ch g Tagula(IRE) —Mareha (IRE) (Cadeaux Genereux)
1476[7] 2270[5] 2596[3] 3112[6] 3668[2] 4285[9] 4563[5]

Niza D'Alm (FR) *A Crook* a2 31
7 bb m Passing Sale(FR) —Bekaa II (FR) (Djarvis (FR))
778[11]

Nizhoni (USA) *B Smart* a54 36
3 ch f Mineshaft(USA) —Carinae (USA) (Nureyev (USA))
2966[11] 7798[3]

Nizhoni Dancer *C F Wall* a60 78
2 b f Bahamian Bounty—Hagwah (USA) (Dancing Brave (USA))
4792[4] 5158[3] 5430[4] (5960) 6886[2]

Noah Jameel *A G Newcombe* a60 59
6 ch g Mark Of Esteem(IRE) —Subtle One (IRE) (Polish Patriot (USA))
10[8] (541) ◆ 999[6] 1528[8] 2949[6] 4267[4] 4919[2] 5611[7] 7518[3]

Nobelix (IRE) *J R Gask* a86 92
6 gr g Linamix(FR) —Nataliana (Surumu (GER))
7025[9] (7563) 7657[4]

Nobilissima (IRE) *J L Spearing* a53 88
4 b m Orpen(USA) —Shadow Smile (IRE) (Slip Anchor)
1278[2] (1617) 1796[11] 2773[8] (5648)

Noble Artist *D H Brown* a15 37
2 b g Bertolini(USA) —Lamu Lady (IRE) (Lomond (USA))
4384[8] 5590[12] 5771[6] 6394[15]

Noble Citizen (USA) *D M Simcock* a98 93
3 b c Proud Citizen(USA) —Serene Nobility (USA) (His Majesty (USA))
1811[6] 2412[5] 3270[3] 4312[4] 4893[3] (5580) (6471) 7101[7] 7381[3]

Noble Dictator *E F Vaughan* a64 65
2 b g Diktat—Noble Desert (FR) (Green Desert (USA))
4256[4] 4747[6] 6876[7] 7190[5] (7467)

Noble Edge *Karen McLintock* a40 57
5 ch g Bold Edge—Noble Soul (Sayf El Arab (USA))
863[7] 1679[7] 2578[8] 4559[6]

Noble Heart (IRE) *T D Barron* 52
2 b f Acclamation—Toldya (Beveled (USA))
4045[8] 4921[7] 6245[8]

Noble Jack (IRE) *R Hannon* a69 84
2 b c Elusive City(USA) —Begine (IRE) (Germany (USA))
2601[2] ◆ 2972[2] 4150[6] 4626[3] 5244[7] 6737[5]

Noble Minstrel *S C Williams* a77 78
5 ch g Fantastic Light(USA) —Sweetness Herself (Unfuwain (USA))
105[4] (182)

Noble Plum (IRE) *Sir Mark Prescott* a88
4 b m King's Best(USA) —Perfect Plum (IRE) (Darshaan)
(159) 260[4] 561[5]

Noble Prince (GER) *A Fabre* 114
4 b g Montjeu(IRE) —Noble Pearl (GER) (Dashing Blade)
1888a[3] 2653a[4] 4041a[3] 5956a[5] 6497a[11]

Noble Storm (USA) *E S McMahon* 88
2 b c Yankee Gentleman(USA) —Changed Tune (USA) (Tunerup (USA))
3125[3] ◆ 3882[3] 4923[6] (5647) (6533) 6972[4]

Noche De Reyes *E J Alston* 45
3 b c Foxhound(USA) —Ashleigh Baker (IRE) (Don't Forget Me)
1894[5] 2966[14] 3958[6] 4207[17]

Nocturnal Lad (IRE) *M G Quinlan* 39
2 b c High Chaparral(IRE) —Jumbo Delight (IRE) (Don't Forget Me)
6944[13]

Noddies Way *J F Panvert* a67 71
5 b g Nomadic Way(USA) —Sharway Lady (Shareef Dancer (USA))
(1179) 2135[3] 3250[13]

Noddledoddle (IRE) *J Ryan* a46 41
4 b m Daggers Drawn(USA) —En Retard (IRE) (Petardia)
120[3] 174[8] 247[4] 326[4] 445[9] 696[7]

Nodform William *Karen McLintock* 55
6 b g Prince Sabo—Periwinkle (FR) (Perrault)
5042[8]

Nod's Star *Jim Best* a59 27
7 ch m Starborough—Barsham (Be My Guest (USA))
1246[11]

No Grouse *E J Alston* a62 74
8 b g Pursuit Of Love—Lady Joyce (FR) (Galetto (FR))
1634[10] 1775[8] (3129) 3435[3] (4018) 4327[2] 4700[2] 5708[6] 6813[13] 7021[6]

Nok Twice (IRE) *K A Ryan* a66 72
7 b g Second Empire(IRE) —Bent Al Fala (IRE) (Green Desert (USA))
(990) 1217[12] 1449[7] 1620[4] 1779[7] 2007[4] ◆ 4245[8] 4451[4] 4961[2] 6043[2] 6186[11] 6312[6] 6771[13]

Nolas Lolly (IRE) *M Botti* 98
4 gr m Lomitas—Holy Nola (USA) (Silver Deputy (CAN))
1981[6] 2879a[2] 3623a[3] 5120[8] 6034[8] 6852a[6]

Nomadic Warrior *J R Best* 40
3 b g Nomadic Way(USA) —Jesmund (Bishop Of Cashel)
4821[11]

Nom Du Jeu (NZ) *Murray Baker* 118
4 br h Montjeu(IRE) —Prized Gem (NZ) (Prized (USA))
6835a[2] 7188a[8]

Nomoreblondes *P T Midgley* a57 73
4 ch m Ishiguru(USA) —Statuette (Statoblest)
2270[8] 3080[4] 3695[2] 3868[8] 4291[2] 4561[2] 5250[8]

Non Dom (IRE) *H Morrison* a61 76
2 b c Hawk Wing(USA) —Kafayef (USA) (Secreto (USA))
6978[5] ◆ 7200[6] 7422[5]

No Nightmare (USA) *Jane Chapple-Hyam* a41 52
2 bb f Lion Heart(USA) —Attasliyah (IRE) (Marju (IRE))
4359[6] 7458[13]

Non Sucre (USA) *P A Blockley* a73 76
3 bb c Minardi(USA) —Vieille Rose (IRE) (Dancing Spree (USA))
2761[3] 3442[6] 4641[6] 4864[5]

No Nukes *P D Evans* a31 49
3 b g Where Or When(IRE) —Intellibet One (Compton Place)
3310[7]

Noodles Blue Boy *Ollie Pears* a77 72
2 b g Makbul—Dee Dee Girl (IRE) (Primo Dominie)
(4045) 5375[2] 6149[4] 6525[13]

Noordhoek Kid *C R Egerton* a73 56
2 b g Dansili—Anqood (IRE) (Elmaamul (USA))
5798[4] 6423[2] 6893[9]

No Page (IRE) *J L Spearing* a51 81
3 b f Statue Of Liberty(USA) —Esligier (IRE) (Sabrehill (USA))
5648[11] 6137[10] 7428[10] 7586[10]

No Pardon (GER) *A Trybuhl* 86
3 ch c Dashing Blade—No Merci (GER) (General Assembly (USA))
1850a[3]

Noplace For A Lady *N Tinkler* 41
3 ch f Compton Place—Pusey Street Girl (Gildoran)
2898[9]

No Point (IRE) *P A Blockley* a43 47
3 ch f Point Given(USA) —Youngus (USA) (Atticus (USA))
2099[11] 2771[6]

No Quarter Given (IRE) *Mrs A Duffield* a45 30
2 b g Elusive City(USA) —Tides (Bahamian Bounty)
5633[13] 6051[13] 6489[5] 7530[4] 7795[7]

Nora Chrissie (IRE) *Niall Moran* a74 62
6 br m Bahhare(USA) —Vino Veritas (USA) (Chief's Crown (USA))
132[5] 1199a[7]

Nora Mae (IRE) *S Kirk* 91
2 ch f Peintre Celebre(USA) —Wurfklinge (GER) (Acatenango (GER))
6122[4] ◆ (6358) 6982[5]

Norcroft *Mrs C A Dunnett* a73 63
6 b g Fasliyev(USA) —Norcroft Joy (Rock Hopper)
55[8] 1189[9] 1687[4] 1865[5] 2758[7] 2983[4] 3506[10] 3615[3] 4125[7] 4749[2] 5582[2] 6046[4] 6209[3] 6680[6] 7090[3] 7254[5] 7433[5] 7591[7] (7779)

Nordic Commander (IRE) *E A L Dunlop* a66 65
3 b c Viking Ruler(AUS) —Rising Lady (Alzao (USA))
1622[7] 2559[3] 3095[9] 3886[11] 4991[6] 6628[8]

Nordic Light (USA) *J M Bradley* a44 74
4 bb g Belong To Me(USA) —Midriff (USA) (Naevus (USA))
1366[8] 1683[13] 2242[14] 2350[3] 2798[12] 2968[9] 3313[15] 3363[14] 3733[6] 4052[15] 4808[4] 6334[4] 6895[7] 7022[12] 7195[8] 7582[6] 7644[12]

Norfolk Broads (IRE) *M Johnston* a42 74
2 b f Noverre(USA) —Dreamboat (USA) (Mr Prospector (USA))
2709[7] 3005[6] 5089[2] 5855[15] 6172[2] (6414) 6656[5]

Norman The Great *A King* a78 80
4 b g Night Shift(USA) —Encore Du Cristal (USA) (Quiet American (USA))
6667[9]

Nortburn *G M Lyons* a81 88
4 b g Tobougg(IRE) —Duxyana (IRE) (Cyrano De Bergerac)
7325a[7]

North Cape (USA) *H Candy* 60
2 b g Action This Day(USA) —Cape (USA) (Mr Prospector (USA))
5753[7] 6892[6]

North East Corner (USA) *B W Hills* 81
2 b c Giant's Causeway(USA) —Saree (Barathea (IRE))
(6084) 6428[7]

Northern Acres *D Nicholls* 55
2 b c Mtoto—Bunting (Shaadi (USA))
5882[6]

Northern Bolt *D Nicholls* a68 86
3 b g Cadeaux Genereux—Shafir (IRE) (Shaadi (USA))
1167[10] 2171[10] 4291[6] 4553[13] 5358[2] 5796[3] 6449[7]

Northern Boy (USA) *M W Easterby* a70 74
5 ch g Lure(USA) —Catala (USA) (Northern Park (USA))
49[3] 342[8] 2925[13] 3339[5] 3826[10] 4476[9] 5074[8]

Northern Chorus (IRE) *J O'Reilly* a36 65
5 ch g Distant Music(USA) —Nationalartgallery (IRE) (Tate Gallery (USA))
3112[11] 3665[8] 4703[5] 6218[14] 6546[9] 7369[8] 7619[12]

Northern Dare (IRE) *D Nicholls* a30 97
4 b g Fath(USA) —Farmers Swing (IRE) (River Falls)
1103a[3] 1809[12] 2538[4] 3532a[2] 3881[5] 4586[8] 5109[17] 5831[15] 6069[17]

Northern Desert (IRE) *S Curran* a72 61
9 b g Desert Style(IRE) —Rosie's Guest (IRE) (Be My Guest (USA))
24[2] (115) 250[7] 607[2] (753) 914[7] 7801[4]

Northern Dune (IRE) *A P Stringer* a56
4 b g Dilshaan—Zoudie (Ezzoud (IRE))
695[8] (7792)

Northern Empire (IRE) *K A Ryan* a98 100
5 ch g Namid—Bumble (Rainbow Quest (USA))
5[2] (162) 411[5] 593[2] 866[2] 2129[4] 2828[9] 3451[16] 4201[10] 4445[20] 6290[14] 6354[9] 6651[14] 6859[14] 7181[8] 7393[10] 7697[2] (7733) 7826[3] ◆

Northerner (IRE) *J O'Reilly* a53 63
5 b g Mark Of Esteem(IRE) —Ensorceleuse (FR) (Fabulous Dancer (USA))
6115[12]

Northern Fling *D Nicholls* a80 109
4 b g Mujadil(USA) —Donna Anna (Be My Chief (USA))
(1325) 2401[4] 2626[13] 3248[8] 4445[9] 4624[8] 5503[3] 5890[16] 6104[19]

Northern Flyer (GER) *J J Quinn* 52
2 b c Hawk Wing(USA) —Nachtigall (GER) (Danehill (USA))
6383[9] 6858[8]

Northern Hero (IRE) *E A L Dunlop* 42
2 b c Hawk Wing(USA) —Bona Dea (IRE) (Danehill (USA))
6080[17]

Northern Jem *G G Margarson* 87
4 b g Mark Of Esteem(IRE) —Top Jem (Damister (USA))
1456[3] 1569[9] 2369[6] 2799[6]

Northern Shore (IRE) *J O'Reilly*
2 br g Clodovil(IRE) —Distant Shore (IRE) (Jareer (USA))
2909[13] 4873[14]

Northern Spy (USA) *S Dow* a92 81
4 b g War Chant(USA) —Sunray Superstar (Nashwan (USA))
409[6] 962[7] 1067[8] 1857[2] ◆ 2308[7] 2790[6] 4528[7] 5051[10] 5349[8]

Northern Tour *P F I Cole* a69 81
2 b c Tobougg(IRE) —Swift Spring (FR) (Bluebird (USA))
957[6] ◆ (1276) (2204) 3522[3] 7229[3] 7391[6]

Northgate (IRE) *Joseph G Murphy* a97 85
3 b g Mujadil(USA) —Arcevia (IRE) (Archway (IRE))
6261a[4] 7235a[3]

Northgate Lodge (USA) *M Brittain* a32 53
3 ch g Hold That Tiger(USA) —Sabaah Elfull (Kris)
785[7] 4538[11] 6791[16] 7609[7]

Northgate Maisie *Jedd O'Keeffe* 42
3 b f Sugarfoot—Chasetown Cailin (Suave Dancer (USA))
2156[4] 2750[12] 2926[5] 3580[11] 5543[9]

North Parade *B J Meehan* 92
3 b g Nayef(USA) —Queen Sceptre (IRE) (Fairy King (USA))
1943[5] (2573) 4519[13] 5054[7] 5230[2] 6129[11] 6400[6]

Northside Prince (IRE) *G A Swinbank* 55
2 b g Desert Prince(IRE) —Spartan Girl (IRE) (Ela-Mana-Mou)
6213[8] 6655[8]

North South Divide (IRE) *Peter Grayson* a69 85
4 b g Namid—Bush Rose (Rainbow Quest (USA))
95[2] 1344[3] 1928[2] 2339[11] ◆ 2679[2] 2947[10] 3502[2] 5648[7] 6200[11] 6556[6] 7213[3] 7453[2] 7527[2] 7624[5]

Northstar Express (IRE) *J L Spearing* a46 16
5 b m Tagula(IRE) —Ramich John (Kampala)
48[7] 239[6] 401[11] 878[3] 1053[11] 1606[8] 2070[11]

Northumberland *M Johnston* a65 73
2 b c Bertolini(USA) —Cal Norma's Lady (IRE) (Lyphard's Special (USA))
2388[6] 2657[8] 3372[4] 4589[2]

North Walk (IRE) *Tim Vaughan* a57 84
5 b g Monashee Mountain(USA) —Celtic Link (IRE) (Toca Madera)
3687[3] 7573[3] 7630[5]

Northwest *A Berry* 48
3 b g Reel Buddy(USA) —Adorable Cherub (USA) (Halo (USA))
1823[6] 2142[7] 2486[6] 2941[7] 3715[5] 4043[10]

Nortune (USA) *B Smart* 70
3 b c Street Cry(IRE) —Gilded Leaf (USA) (Lyphard (USA))
(980) 1448[7] 2002[7] 5638[10]

No Rules *M H Tompkins* a54 67
3 b g Fraam—Golden Daring (IRE) (Night Shift (USA))
1252[9] 2045[9] 2340[6] 2997[6] 4859[4] 6060[5] 6386[4]

Norwegian *Ian Williams* a55 57
7 b g Halling(USA) —Chicarica (USA) (The Minstrel (CAN))
140[4] 323[4] 468[4] 508[5] 1374[4] 7585[10]

Norwegian Dancer (UAE) *E S McMahon* a66 66
2 b c Halling(USA) —Time Changes (USA) (Danzig (USA))
4921[5] 6451[3]

No Sting *W G M Turner* 13
2 b f Exit To Nowhere(USA) —Beacon Silver (Belmez (USA))
5650[10]

Nostradamus (USA) *K J Burke* a4
9 bb h Gone West(USA) —Madam North (CAN) (Halo (USA))
7606[13]

No Strings (IRE) *D K Weld* a92 84
3 ch g Diesis—First Breeze (USA) (Woodman (USA))
3531a[9] 4512a[11]

No Supper (IRE) *M G Quinlan* a55
4 ch g Inchinor—Be Thankfull (IRE) (Linamix (FR))
758[5]

Nota Bene *D R C Elsworth* a111 106
6 b g Zafonic(USA) —Dodo (IRE) (Alzao (USA))
(2530) 3248[26] 3504[6] 3722[7] 4059[5]

Nota Liberata *Ollie Pears* a10 69
4 b g Spinning World(USA) —Kyda (USA) (Gulch (USA))
7442[11] 7732[11]

Not Another Cat (USA) *K R Burke* a71 67
4 ch g Hennessy(USA) —Isle Be Loving You (USA) (Stuka (USA))
598[4] 805[3] 1030[6] 1521[12] 2940[10]

Notepad *W Jarvis* 59
3 b f King's Best(USA) —Petite Epaulette (Night Shift (USA))
855[5]

Note Perfect *M W Easterby* a54 55
3 b f Diktat—Better Still (IRE) (Glenstal (USA))
154[2] (480) 583[4] 849[3] 1187[4] 2704[7] 3686[7] 4684[13] 5307[12] (6405) 7197[12] 7444[11]

Notforloveormoney *A G Foster* 15
3 br f Kyllachy—Greenfly (Green Desert (USA))
700[7] 1019[16] 1519[12] 2576[7] 3212[13]

Nothing Likea Dame *D J Coakley* a62 66
3 ch f Bahamian Bounty—Dame Jude (Dilum (USA))
424[5]

Nothingtodeclaire *V Smith* a68 32
4 b g Tobougg(IRE) —Double Fault (IRE) (Zieten (USA))
941[10] 1725[6] ◆ 2289[7] 2707[11] 2949[4] 3614[5] 5604[12]

Nothing To Worry (IRE) *M R Channon* 30
2 b c Noverre(USA) —Rahika Rose (Unfuwain (USA))
3323[15] 5966[12]

No Time (IRE) *A J McCabe* a76 69
8 b h Danetime(IRE) —Muckross Park (Nomination)
55[9] 94[5] 1129[8] 1378[8] 1966[6] 2270[6] 2596[10] 2892[4] 2950[8]

Notional (USA) *Doug O'Neill* a118 103
4 b h In Excess I(IRE) —Truly Blessed (USA) (French Deputy (USA))
1090a[16]

Not Just Swing (IRE) *A Fabre* a111 115
4 b h King's Best(USA) —Misbegotten (IRE) (Baillamont (USA))
(1888a) 2653a[3] 3542a[7] 5954a[4] 7643a[2]

Notker (IRE) *R T Phillips* 38
2 b g King Charlemagne(USA) —Boutique (Selkirk (USA))
6715 [13]

Not My Choice (IRE) *S Parr* a88 89
3 ch g Choisir(AUS) —Northgate Raver (Absalom)
1484[12] (1925) 2390[6] 3472[8] 5831[17] 6278[6] 6743a[4] 7066[3] 7290[5] 7394[5] 7456[9]

Not Now Lewis (IRE) *F P Murtagh* a66 60
4 b g Shinko Forest(IRE) —Pearl Egg (IRE) (Mukaddamah (USA))
101[8] (328) (587) 879[3] 1049[4] 1486[5] 1968[2] 2352[4] 3162[9] 5971[11]

Notnowrosie (IRE) *A G Foster* 47
3 b f King Charlemagne(USA) —Rosie (FR) (Bering)
1307[8] 2143[8] 2941[5] 4147[5] 5637[16] 6309[10]

Notonthesamepage (USA) *Wesley A Ward* a95
2 ch c Catienus(USA) —Blue Holiday (USA) (Cure The Blues (USA))
6503a[11]

No To Trident *P D Evans* a67 82
3 b g Zilzal(USA) —Charmante Femme (Bin Ajwaad (IRE))
903[9] (961) 1171[3] 1919[5] 2610[8] 3527[5] 3800[7] 5098[6] 5230[5] 5961[2] 6175[3] 6400[8]

Not Secret *Eva Sundbye* a66 79
4 b h Largesse—Not A Word (Batshoof)
2232a[7]

Not Too Taxing *G A Ham* a67 11
4 b g Forzando—Areish (IRE) (Keen)
10[13] 269[11]

Noubian (USA) *E McNamara* a72 74
6 ch g Diesis—Beraysim (Lion Cavern (USA))
7747[6]

Nounou *Miss J E Foster* a63 60
7 b g Starborough—Watheeqah (USA) (Topsider (USA))
320[8] 2157[5] 2393[4] 7271[7] 7455[2]

Novasky (SWE) *T Gustafsson* a80 88
6 bb m Diaghlyphard(USA) —Novaux (USA) (Deploy)
4917a[5] 5336a[3]

Novastasia (IRE) *W R Swinburn* a62
2 b f Noverre(USA) —Pink Sovietstaia (FR) (Soviet Star (USA))
7095[6] 7458[7]

Novellen Lad (IRE) *E J Alston* a69 82
3 b c Noverre(USA) —Lady Ellen (Horage)
1601[5] 2008[4] (2282) ◆ (2967) 4329[4] 4900[6] 6124[15]

Noverre To Go (IRE) *Tom Dascombe* a86 81
2 ch c Noverre(USA) —Ukraine Venture (Slip Anchor)
4616[2] ◆ 6412[3] 6601[2] (7555) ◆ (7714)

Noverre To Hide (USA) *J R Best* a67 54
2 b g Noverre(USA) —Zanoubia (USA) (Our Emblem (USA))
4507[11] 4980[7] 5939[4]

Novestar (IRE) *G J Smith* a73 68
3 ch g Noverre(USA) —Star Of Cayman (IRE) (Unfuwain (USA))
195[4] 350[5] 439[9] 462[2] (597) 644[3] 865[4] 950[2] (976) 1147[3] (1186) 1397[7] 1592[6] 2613[4] (2867) 3393[3] 3566[7] (3824) 4732[7]

Novikov *J H M Gosden* a87 93
4 ch g Danehill Dancer(IRE) —Ardisia (USA) (Affirmed (USA))
1365[12] 1719[7] 2540[7] 3836[3] (4791) (6033)

Novita (FR) *P Schiergen* 97
2 b f American Post—Nouvelle Reine (GER) (Konigsstuhl (GER))
7185a[9]

Now *P Winkworth* 58
2 br f Where Or When(IRE) —Tup Tim (Emperor Jones (USA))
3207[6] 3869[11] 6539[10]

Now Again (GER) *W Hickst* 91
4 ch m Lomitas—Notre Dame (GER) (Acatenango (GER))
2879a[4] 3751a[4]

Now Forever (GER) *P Schiergen* 95
3 b f Tiger Hill(IRE) —Notre Dame (GER) (Acatenango (GER))
3623a[9] 6323a[8]

Nownownow (USA) *David Wachman* a104 109
3 b c Whywhywhy(USA) —Here And Now (FR) (Exit To Nowhere (USA))
2418a[5]

No Wonga *P D Evans* 58
3 b g Where Or When(IRE) —Fizzy Fiona (Efisio)
4249[8] 4484[7] 4709[4] 5146[4] 5653[2]

Noworneva *S Kirk* a37 51
2 ch g Where Or When(IRE) —Azula (Bluebird (USA))
1363[10] 1616[5] 2562[7] 3341[5] 3677[6] 4340[9] 6059[10] 6394[4] 6986[9] 7666[13]

No Worries Yet (IRE) *J L Spearing* 67
4 b m Orpen(USA) —Charming Victoria (IRE) (Mujadil (USA))
1997[17] 4047[13] (Dead)

Now You See Me *D Flood* a64 27
4 b m Anabaa(USA) —Bright Vision (Indian Ridge)
213[6] 305[3] 523[4] 627[2] 726[4] (857) 1028[5] (1706) 5884[10] 7522[9] (7778) 7835[3]

Nowzdetime (IRE) *M G Quinlan* a69
3 b c Statue Of Liberty(USA) —Sensitive (IRE) (Posen (USA))
570[3] 903[5] 5964[14] 7632[3]

Nubar Lady (IRE) *T Stack* a92 93
3 b f Danetime(IRE) —Sarah Stokes (IRE) (Brief Truce (USA))
3123[6] 5438a[2] 6514a[5]

Nufoudh (IRE) *Miss Tracy Waggott* 63
4 b g Key Of Luck(USA) —Limpopo (Green Desert (USA))
1578[6] 1775[11] 2040[9] 2780[6] 3175[4] 3593[6] 4559[4] 4683[12] 5045[8] 5501[9]

Nuit Sombre (IRE) *G A Harker* a45 83
8 b g Night Shift(USA) —Belair Princess (USA) (Mr Prospector (USA))
992[13] 1069[11] 1815[5] 1891[10] 2397[7] 3142[7] 3599[2] 4245[7] 4688[4] 6186[3]

Numaany (USA) *Saeed Bin Suroor* a107
3 ch c A.P. Indy(USA) —Munnaya (USA) (Nijinsky (CAN))
567a[5] ◆ 813a[3] ◆ 1088a[10]

Numero Due *G M Moore* 88
6 b g Sinndar(IRE) —Kindle (Selkirk (USA))
1427[6] 1625[5] 2135[6] (2577) 3007[4] 3832[6] 4046[4] 4439[6] 5718[5] (Dead)

Numide (FR) *G L Moore* 113
5 b g Highest Honor(FR) —Numidie (FR) (Baillamont (USA))
1944[5] 6074[8] 6980[5]

Nun Today (USA) *J S Moore* a59 54
2 b f Chapel Royal(USA) —Oldupai (USA) (Gulch (USA))
2618[10] 3207[7] 3674[10] 4063[7] (4387) 4933[3] 5591[8] 6573[7] 6709[7] 7258[7] 7652[6] 7833[4]

Nur Tau (IRE) *H Morrison* 87
4 b g Peintre Celebre(USA) —Litchfield Hills (USA) (Relaunch (USA))
1473[14] 2152[6] 2591[6] 3368[10] 4791[6]

Nusoor (IRE) *Peter Grayson* a72 76
5 b g Fasliyev(USA) —Zulfaa (USA) (Bahri (USA))
1634[5] 2145[6] 2777[6] (3269) 3486[2] 3585[3] 4064[2] (4370) 4563[6] 5250[15] 6131[7]

Nut Hand (IRE) *T D Easterby* 57
2 b g Noverre(USA) —Walnut Lady (Forzando)
5497[7] 6008[8] 6213[5]

Nutkin *J R Fanshawe* a65 85
4 gr m Act One—Cashew (Sharrood (USA))
1159[3] ◆ 1742[2] 2152[8] (3944) 4970[3] 6035[8] 7019[9]

Nyumba (IRE) *P R Chamings* 49
3 b f High Chaparral(IRE) —Barbizou (FR) (Selkirk (USA))
3133[13] 5491[9] 6584[7]

Oakbridge (IRE) *R Brotherton* a68 55
6 b g Indian Ridge—Chauncy Lane (IRE) (Sadler's Wells (USA))
68[7] 654[9] 1064[7]

Oakley Absolute *J C Fox* a56 63
6 ch g Bluegrass Prince(IRE) —Susie Oakley VII (Damsire Unregistered)
4635[11]

Oakley Heffert (IRE) *R Hannon* a81 81
4 b g Titus Livius(FR) —Daftiyna (IRE) (Darshaan)
28[3] 185[2] 525[5] 838[6] 1065[7]

Oarsman *R Charlton* a70 81
3 ch c Selkirk(USA) —Felucca (Green Desert (USA))
1125[3] 1535[5] 3696[2] 4431[2]

Oasis Breeze *T D Easterby* 86
2 b f Oasis Dream—Forever Fine (USA) (Sunshine Forever (USA))
(3027) ◆ 3634[4] 4403[13] 5642[12] 6172[6] (6807) 7107[5] 7219[2]

Oasis Davis *David Marnane* a80 81
3 b c Oasis Dream—Panarea (FR) (Highest Honor (FR))
4223a[11]

Oasis Knight (IRE) *M P Tregoning* 81
2 b c Oasis Dream—Generous Lady (Generous (IRE))
2146[13] 2972[10] 3682[3] (6086)

Oasis On Island *B Smart* a28 43
2 b c Oasis Dream—Ocean View (USA) (Gone West (USA))
6246[7] 6953[11] 7458[14]

Oasis Sun (IRE) *J R Best* a63 40
5 ch m Desert Sun—Albaiyda (IRE) (Brief Truce (USA))
31[6] 695[6] (716) 881[11] 2353[12] 2641[9] 3588[5] 3843[9] 4267[7] 5611[4] (6019) 6775[11] 7078[9]

Oasis Sunset (IRE) *David Wachman* a77 77
2 b f Oasis Dream—Sunset Cafe (IRE) (Red Sunset)
6473[9]

Oasis Wind *P F I Cole* 99
3 b c Oasis Dream—Haibah (Rainbow Quest (USA))
1170[5] 1837[8] 2410[7] 3251[8]

Oat Cuisine *M L W Bell* a88 90
4 b m Mujahid(USA) —Gazebo (Cadeaux Genereux)
1253[3] 1565[2] 1867[12] (2373) ◆ 3272[4] 3507[6] 3866[2] (4162) (5683) (6130) 6266[5] 6904[3] 7146[6]

Obe Brave *R A Fahey* a35 109
5 b g Agnes World(USA) —Pass The Rose (IRE) (Thatching)
495a[14] 668a[9] 3056[7] 3489[11] 3973[10] 4869[8] 5247[8] (5562) 6105[8] (6335) 6448[9] 6864[4]

Obe Gold *D Nicholls* a96 98
6 b g Namaqualand(USA) —Gagajulu (Al Hareb (USA))
1071[10] 1430[6] 1969[3] (2358) 2504[2] 2831[11] 3228[6] 4586[12] 5831[6] 6069[25] 6532[11]

Obe One *A Berry* a48 57
8 b g Puissance—Plum Bold (Be My Guest (USA))
161[2] 155[5] 1752[10] 2936[6] 3128[2] 3404[5] 3759[3] 3952[4] 4118[9] 4144[2] 4462[4] 4653[3] 4903[2] 5392[7] (5566) 6011[5] 6159[6] 6546[8] 7218[3] 7529[8]

Oberlin (USA) *T Keddy* a77 63
3 ch g Gone West(USA) —Balanchine (USA) (Storm Bird (CAN))
311[2] 573[3] (657) 1516[7] 2280[9] 3327[10] 3793[5] 4564[15] 7149[2] 7271[6] 7447[9] 7573[13] 7775[2]

Oberows Lady (IRE) *Adrian McGuinness* a42 39
6 b m Petorius—She's Our Lady (IRE) (Scenic)
289[4] 305[6] 642[6] 684[10]

Obe Royal *P D Evans* a77 76
4 b g Wizard King—Gagajulu (Al Hareb (USA))
(15) 49[4] 103[2] (241) 404[4] 463[3] 609[5] 729[3] 840[4] 1040[4] 1084[6] 1191[2] 1312[5] 1431[2] 2128[5] 2692[8] 2778[3] 2923[9] 2983[2] 3255[6] 3506[14] 3797[4] 3966[4] 4440[14] 5198[11] 6411[8] 7616[5] 7782[4]

Obezyana (USA) *A Bailey* a80 85
6 ch g Rahy(USA) —Polish Treaty (USA) (Danzig (USA))
1612[8] 1936[7] 2373[5] ◆ (2406) 2969[2] 3054[7] 3222[5] 4104[14] 4407[5] 4649[6] 4661[3] 5908[10] 6035[5] 6900[4] 7068[2] 7299[5] 7396[2] 7560[4]

Objeto De Arte (BRZ) *P Bary* a103 96
5 ch h Boatman(Valentino)—Adrienne (ARG) (Ocean Falls)
205a[2] 5113a[9]

Obrigado (USA) *G L Moore* a79 67
8 b g Bahri(USA) —Glorious Diamond (USA) (His Majesty (USA))
97[8] 747[9] 941[6] 1585[7] 2373[16] (3036) 3970[7] 4481[4] 5349[12] 5994[7] 7473[6] 7816[4] 7831[5]

Observatory Ridge *R Bouresly* a51 61
3 ch f Observatory(USA) —Chiasso (USA) (Woodman (USA))
201a[10]

Observatory Star (IRE) *T D Easterby* 87
5 br g Observatory(USA) —Pink Sovietstaia (FR) (Soviet Star (USA))
2733[2] 3173[2] 3367[5] 3972[12] (4649) 6052[5]

Obstructive *E J Creighton* a73 96
4 ch g Zilzal(USA) —Emily-Mou (IRE) (Cadeaux Genereux)
5906[13] 6354[14] 6736[14]

Obvious *B W Hills* a57
2 b f Falbrav(IRE) —Bright And Clear (Danehill (USA))
6167[7]

Ocareion (GER) *Andreas Lowe* a92
4 b h Areion(GER) —Ocamira (GER) (Kamiros II)
7643a[16]

O'Casey (IRE) *J G M O'Shea* a48 47
3 b g Bold Fact(USA) —Miss Scott (IRE) (Be My Guest (USA))
486[3] 623[5] 4793[14]

Occasion *G M Moore* 12
3 b f Zamindar(USA) —Set Fair (USA) (Alleged (USA))
6114[10] 6530[14]

Oceana Blue *A M Balding* a81 78
3 b f Reel Buddy(USA) —Silken Dalliance (Rambo Dancer (CAN))
419[7] (1051) ◆ 1193[3] 1671[3] (2452) 3270[4] 3849[7] 4424[3] 5071[5] 6242[4] 6684[2] 6981[6]

Oceana Gold *A M Balding* 96
4 ch g Primo Valentino(IRE) —Silken Dalliance (Rambo Dancer (CAN))
1828[2] ◆ 2200[5] 3122[20]

Ocean Avenue (IRE) *C A Horgan* a76 77
9 b g Dolphin Street(FR) —Trinity Hall (Hallgate)
27[7] 2921[12] 3614[6] 4275[5] 4485[3] 4820[8] 5465[12] 6729[4]

Ocean Blaze *B R Millman* 90
4 b m Polar Prince(IRE) —La Belle Vie (Indian King (USA))
1366[5] 1956[2] 2489[3] 2828[17] 4201[2] 4555[6] 5250[16] 6174[8]

Ocean Countess (IRE) *Miss J Feilden* 3
2 b f Storming Home—Pennycairn (Last Tycoon)
5241[17]

Ocean Glory (IRE) *Peter Grayson* a46 63
3 b g Redback—Finty (IRE) (Entrepreneur)
298[6]

Oceanic Dancer (IRE) *Mrs L Williamson* 48
2 b f Danetime(IRE) —Almasa (Faustus (USA))
6785[9] 7082[4]

Ocean Legend (IRE) *Miss J Feilden* a82 75
3 b g Night Shift(USA) —Rose Of Mooncoin (IRE) (Brief Truce (USA))
52[3] 244[2] (867) 1540[2] 3134[3] ◆ 3612[2] 3840[3] 4731[8] 5104[5] 5595[3] 6936[10] 7374[2] 7507[3] 7670[5] 7813[4]

Ocean Pride (IRE) *L Wells* a52 82
5 b g Lend A Hand—Irish Understudy (ITY) (In The Wings)
127[4] 229[5] 460[6] 7535[3] 7792[8]

Ocean Rock *C A Horgan* a59 36
7 b g Perugino(USA) —Polistatic (Free State)
451[4] 695[13] 934[10] 1246[4]

Ocean's Minstrel *J Ryan* a75 73
2 b c Pivotal—Minstrel's Dance (CAN) (Pleasant Colony (USA))
3495[5] 6375[4] 7054[5] (7622)

Ocean Transit (IRE) *W G M Turner* a74 80
3 b f Trans Island—Wings Awarded (Shareef Dancer (USA))
723[6]

Ochenvay *C J Down* a48 51
3 gr f Tobougg(IRE) —Bogus Mix (IRE) (Linamix (FR))
2772[7] 3359[3] 6331[7]

Ochre Bay *R Hollinshead* a76 72
5 b g Polar Prince(IRE) —Cloudy Reef (Cragador)
4030[5] 4934[7] 5708[9]

Oddsmaker (IRE) *M A Barnes* a61 84
7 b g Barathea(IRE) —Archipova (IRE) (Ela-Mana-Mou)
1067[3] 1625[8] 2970[7]

Odiham *Dr R D P Newland* a104 97
7 b g Deploy—Hug Me (Shareef Dancer (USA))
1568[11] 1916[8]

Oeuf A La Neige *Miss L A Perratt* a36 64
8 b g Danehill(USA) —Reine De Neige (Kris)
1822[6] 2523[3] 2749[3] 3082[7] 3591[6] 3757[5] 4118[2] ◆ 4633[8] 4736[4] 4849[3] 4967[3] 5420[10] 5538[4] 6159[9] 6409[8] 7112[11]

Ofaraby *M A Jarvis* a94 36
8 b g Sheikh Albadou—Maristax (Reprimand)
4867[9] 5569[13]

Off Hand *T D Easterby* 35
2 b f Lend A Hand—Off Camera (Efisio)
3590[13]

Officer *G L Moore* a83 88
4 b h Medicean—Appointed One (USA) (Danzig (USA))
3382[5] 4191[14] 4723[7] 5156[3] 5350[6]

Officer In Command (USA) *J S Moore* a81
2 bb c Officer(USA) —Luv To Stay N Chat (USA) (Candi's Gold (USA))
4861[3] 6253[2] 6597[3] (7073)

Officer Mor (USA) *K R Burke* a63 71
2 ch c Officer(USA) —Hot August Nights (USA) (Summer Squall (USA))
1948[2] (2388) 3105[21] 3910[4] 4628[4] 5488[5] 7212[6] 7361[2] 7475[7] 7652[7] 7738[3] 7825[4]

Offshore Anna (IRE) *J J Quinn* 86
3 bb f Marju(IRE) —Anna Kareena (IRE) (Charnwood Forest (IRE))
1019[7] 3338[3] 3796[5] 4332[2] ◆ 4607[3] (5888) (6155) 6949[7]

Off The Record *J G Given* a92 107
4 b h Desert Style(IRE) —Record Time (Clantime)
1071[12] (1809) 2404[6] 3248[16] 3739[5] 3922[12] 4624[7]

Oglumemre (TUR) *Sab Arslan* a76
3 ch c Royal Abjar(USA) —Sketch (TUR) (Ezy Koter)
5743a[4]

Ogmore Junction (IRE) *Mrs S Leech* a67 44
3 b c Catcher In The Rye(IRE) —Fairy Berry (IRE) (Fairy King (USA))
1130[2] 1389[10] 2002[8] 2288[9]

Ogre (USA) *P D Evans* a75 81
3 bb f Tale Of The Cat(USA) —Soverign Lady (USA) (Aloha Prospector (USA))
2052[3] 2486[4] (2801) (3343) (3604) (4724) 5800[9] 5994[2] (6528) 6949[11]

Ohana *N J Gifford* a17 46
5 b g Mark Of Esteem(IRE) —Subya (Night Shift (USA))
5575[9]

Oh Goodness Me *J S Bolger* 100
2 b f Galileo(IRE) —Coyote (Indian Ridge)
7158a[2]

Oh Gracious Me (IRE) *P A Blockley* a49 38
4 b h Traditionally(USA) —Classic Jenny (IRE) (Green Desert (USA))
792[7] 858[6] 1455[15]

Ohiyesa (IRE) *G M Lyons* a88 89
2 b f Noverre(USA) —Crohal Di San Jore (Saddlers' Hall (IRE))
2497[7] 6637a[5]

Oh So (IRE) *P A Blockley* a39 49
4 ch m Mark Of Esteem(IRE) —Manuetti (IRE) (Sadler's Wells (USA))
140[5] 284[6] 373[5] 578[12] 788[8]

Oh So Saucy *C F Wall* a60 85
5 b m Imperial Ballet(IRE) —Almasi (IRE) (Petorius)
(2055) (2670) 2992[2] 3653[2] (4284)

Oil Man (IRE) *P Winkworth* a48 85
2 b g Pyrus(USA) —So Precious (IRE) (Batshoof)
3372[8] 4184[2] (4776) 5511[3] ◆

Oisin's Boy *J R Boyle* a60 61
2 b g Catcher In The Rye(IRE) —Red Storm (Dancing Spree (USA))
6077[10] 6341[9] 6701[6] 7268[3] 7372[4] 7531[6]

Oi Vay Joe (IRE) *W Jarvis* a57 77
4 b g Namid—Nuit Des Temps (Sadler's Wells (USA))
850[5] 1550[4] 1996[2] 4284[5] 4863[6] 5601[5] 6890[4]

Okafranca (IRE) *W R Muir* a63 75
3 b g Okawango(USA) —Villafranca (IRE) (In The Wings)
1147[4] 1478[2] 1710[3] 2340[11] 2475[10] 3035[10] (3873) 4859[2] (5887) 6390[6]

Okba (USA) *M P Tregoning* a48
2 b f Diesis—Awtaan (USA) (Arazi (USA))
7380[10]

Oke Bay *R M Beckett* a17 48
2 b f Tobougg(IRE) —Barakat (Bustino)
6397[9] 7204[9]

Oken Bruce Lee (JPN) *H Otonashi* 119
3 b c Jungle Pocket(JPN) —Silver Joy (CAN) (Silver Deputy (CAN))
7511a[5]

Olaudah Equiano *M H Tompkins* 59
2 ch c Dubai Destination(USA) —Magongo (Be My Chief (USA))
2086[3] (Dead)

Old Etonian (UAE) *Peter Grayson* a84 47
4 ch g Jade Robbery(USA) —Favoured (Chief's Crown (USA))
95[8] 611[10] 1269[10]

Old Father Zieten *Tom Dascombe* a37 58
2 b g Zieten(USA) —Emergency Exit (FR) (Exit To Nowhere (USA))
1640[5] 1987[5] 3821[6] 4292[8] 6343[U] 6694[10]

Oldjoesaid *H Candy* a108 113
4 b g Royal Applause—Border Minstral (IRE) (Sri Pekan (USA))
(1442) ◆ 3948[5] 4445[18] 5347[5] 5890[4] 6184[3] 6903[6]

Oldrik (GER) *P J Hobbs* 77
5 b g Tannenkonig(IRE) —Onestep (GER) (Konigsstuhl (GER))
(3914) 5092[4] 6243[3]

Old Romney *M Wigham* a77 83
4 br g Halling(USA) —Zaeema (Zafonic (USA))
962[17] 1296[14] 1732[8] 2165[8] 2621[13] 2908[4] 5087[4] (5429) 6090[10] 7189[2] 7596[2] 7702[5]

Old Sarum (IRE) *D R C Elsworth* a56 26
2 b g Elusive City(USA) —Quintellina (Robellino (USA))
6764[9] 7212[4] 7380[11] 7464[5]

Old Street *R Charlton* 57
2 b g Dansili—New Abbey (Sadler's Wells (USA))
4151[11] 4890[11] 5599[5] (Dead)

Old Time Dancing *J F Panvert* a15 42
5 b m Danehill Dancer(IRE) —Rare Old Times (IRE) (Inzar (USA))
445[11] 1265[8] 1694[5] 2640[13]

Olga D'Or (USA) *R Gibson* a79 79
2 b f Medaglia D'Oro(USA) —Fasateen (USA) (Alysheba (USA))
7549a[9]

Olimpo (FR) *B R Millman* 88
7 ch g Starborough—Emily Allan (IRE) (Shirley Heights)
1877[10] 2764[6] 3368[12] 3802[8] 4123[2] 4568[2] (4820) 5369[6] 6607[16]

Ollie Fliptrik (USA) *P F I Cole* a32
3 bb c Essence Of Dubai(USA) —Etoufee (USA) (Tabasco Cat (USA))
58[10]

Ollie George (IRE) *A M Balding* a69 94
5 ch g Fruits Of Love(USA) —The Iron Lady (IRE) (Polish Patriot (USA))
1531[3] 2372[4] 3060[3] (3209) 5249[2]

Olympian Order (IRE) *G A Swinbank*
2 b g High Chaparral(IRE) —Southey (USA) (Broad Brush (USA))
5387[12]

Olympic City (BRZ) *M F De Kock* a98 88
5 b m Yagli(USA) —A Primogenita (BRZ) (Tsunami Slew (USA))
200a[2] 475a[6] 647a[7] 814a[13] 5071[10] 5569[3] 6171[6] 6536[9] 6904[7]

Olympic Dream *R A Fahey* 80
2 b c Kyllachy—Opening Ceremony (USA) (Quest For Fame)
957[15] 3364[8] 3997[2] ◆ 4438[3] 4740[2] 5244[17] 6483[20]

Olympic Glory (BRZ) *A Al Raihe* a84
4 b m Choctaw Ridge(USA) —Glorious Glory (BRZ) (Minstrel Glory (USA))
201a[3] 496a[7] 744a[10]

Olynard (IRE) *R M Beckett* a85 80
2 b g Exceed And Excel(AUS) —Reddening (Blushing Flame (USA))
4024[7] (4634) 5680[2] 6483[12]

Ommadawn (IRE) *J R Fanshawe* a70 68
4 b m Montjeu(IRE) —Bonheur (IRE) (Royal Academy (USA))
1779[6] 2482[3] 5576[3] 5999[6] 6577[2]

Omnium Duke (IRE) *J W Hills* a53 70
2 ch c Indian Haven—Please Be Good (IRE) (Prince Of Birds (USA))
5225[4] 6085[13] 6553[5] 7190[8]

Omokoroa (IRE) *M H Tompkins* a64 64
2 b g Hawkeye(IRE) —Alycus (USA) (Atticus (USA))
4747[3] 6057[8] 6731[9]

Onatopp (IRE) *T D Easterby* a51 70
4 b m Soviet Star(USA) —Blueprint (USA) (Shadeed (USA))
2007[11] 2400[5] 2925[6] 3293[5]

Once A Gulch (USA) *J Noseda* a89 86
3 bb c Gulch(USA) —Once Around (CAN) (You And I (USA))
2079[2] (4730) 5425[4] 6526[4]

Onceaponatime (IRE) *E A L Dunlop* a85 84
3 b g Invincible Spirit(IRE) —Lake Nyasa (IRE) (Lake Coniston (IRE))
1073[8] (2279) (2945) 3324[5] 5403[8] 6194[8] 6734[9]

Once More Dubai (USA) *Gianluca Bietolini* 108
3 b c E Dubai(USA) —Go Again Girl (USA) (Broad Brush (USA))
2028a[6] 7263a[3]

Once Upon A Grace (IRE) *B J Meehan* 97
4 b m Spinning World(USA) —Adamparis (Robellino (USA))
1993[5]

Onceuponatime (NZ) *D Hill* 105
4 ch h Van Nistelrooy(USA) —Scarlet Runner (NZ) (Kingdom Bay (NZ))
2234a^9

On Cue (IRE) *J M P Eustace* a44 49
2 ch f Indian Haven—On Time Arrival (USA) (Devil's Bag (USA))
6167^{14} 6534^5 7015^7

One And Gone (IRE) *Miss M E Rowland* a3 61
4 b g Machiavellian(USA) —Bright Smile (IRE) (Caerleon (USA))
31^9

Onebidkintymill (IRE) *M Mullineaux* a30 60
3 b g Mull Of Kintyre(USA) —More Risk (IRE) (Fayruz)
4076^3 4388^8 5261^6

One Called Alice *A W Carroll* a59 59
3 gr f Zilzal(USA) —Boadicea The Red (IRE) (Inchinor)
619^4 785^4 873^4 998^4 1117^2 1169^3 1603^2 2259^4 (2704) 2801^3 3166^3 3406^8 3817^2 4165^2

One Cool Kitty *M G Quinlan* 70
2 b f One Cool Cat(USA) —Exultate Jubilate (USA) (With Approval (CAN))
2979^4 3734^9 3959^3 4373^6 (5632) 6086^8 6700^{11}

One Cool Mission (IRE) *Tom Dascombe* a57
2 b f One Cool Cat(USA) —San Luis Rey (Zieten (USA))
7546^5 ◆ 7708^{11}

One Cool Pet (IRE) *P C Haslam* 7
2 ch f Compton Place—Petarga (Petong)
2485^{10} 3106^9 3670^{13}

One Cool Quest (IRE) *P A Blockley* 30
2 br c One Cool Cat(USA) —No Quest (IRE) (Rainbow Quest (USA))
3092^8 5041^{10}

Onefourseven *Lucinda Featherstone* a38
15 b g Jumbo Hirt(USA) —Dominance (Dominion)
179^5

One Great Cat (USA) *A P O'Brien* 104
3 br c Storm Cat(USA) —Blissful (USA) (Mr Prospector (USA))
1361a^7 2032a^{18} 3536a^{10}

Onemix *B W Hills* a70
2 gr f Fair Mix(IRE) —One For Philip (Blushing Flame (USA))
7699^2 ◆

Onemoreandstay *R W Price* a59 68
3 ch f Dr Fong(USA) —Subito (Darshaan)
4987^3 5160^4 5608^7 6055^4

One More Round (USA) *P D Evans* a85 98
10 b g Ghazi(USA) —Life Of The Party (USA) (Pleasant Colony (USA))
103^3 2040^3 2277^6 2721^2 (2753) (3567) 5708^3 5994^{10} 6736^3 (7288) 7358^8 7399^7 7819^3

Onenightinlisbon (IRE) *J R Boyle* a76 75
4 br m Bold Fact(USA) —Mickey Towbar (IRE) (Mujadil (USA))
90^6 177^4 274^3 426^2 548^5 1954^5 (2943) 3208^4 3507^2 4022^8 4789^8 5291^7 5915^2 6020^2 6380^{14} 7027^7 7302^6 7548^3 7771^9

One Night In May (IRE) *M Dods* 46
3 b f Choisir(AUS) —Dream Genie (Puissance)
2681^{15} 2973^{10} (3715) 4381^7 4680^9

One Night In Paris (IRE) *P D Evans* a79 61
5 bb m Danetime(IRE) —Forget Paris (IRE) (Broken Hearted)
63^4 246^4 390^3 577^2 753^5 (1083) (1636) (2456) 3604^U (Dead)

One Oak (USA) *B J Meehan* a35 59
3 b f Galileo(IRE) —Beat It (USA) (Diesis)
2191^{12} 2971^5 3611^{11}

Oneofthesedayz (IRE) *Miss V Haigh* 48
2 b f Acclamation—Thornby Park (Unfuwain (USA))
5499^{11} 5959^{10} 6229^7

One Oi *D W P Arbuthnot* a59
3 b g Bertolini(USA) —Bogus Penny (IRE) (Pennekamp (USA))
2612^8 3484^6 6206^7 7076^{10} 7392^2

One Slick Chick (IRE) *M Botti* a69
2 b f One Cool Cat(USA) —Ms Mary C (IRE) (Dolphin Street (FR))
7754^2

One To Follow *C G Cox* a72 74
4 b g Mtoto—Becalmed (Dilum (USA))
540^7 880^7 1165^2 1929^{10} 2482^2 2921^{11} 3614^7 7071^{10}

One Tou Many *C W Fairhurst* 18
3 b f Tobougg(IRE) —Reine De Thebes (FR) (Darshaan)
4461^8

One Trick Pony *B Storey* 33
5 ch g Timeless Times(USA) —Lavernock Lady (Don't Forget Me)
3784^9 4451^{14}

One Union (USA) *Richard E Mandella* 106
5 bb h Dixie Union(USA) —Onceinabluemamoon (USA) (Al Mamoon (USA))
6994a^8

On Every Street *R Bastiman* a49 55
7 b g Singspiel(IRE) —Nekhbet (Artaius (USA))
36^8 282^4 585^2 751^2 776^2 1262^{10} 1890^{11} 2467^3 2884^6

One Way Love *W G M Turner*
3 ch f Dr Fong(USA) —Pomponette (USA) (Rahy (USA))
848^8

One Way Ticket *J M Bradley* a55 76
8 ch h Pursuit Of Love—Prima Cominna (Unfuwain (USA))
690^8 774^5 883^5 2351^2 3346^{12} 3486^7 4051^{12} 4370^{11} 6339^{15} 7637^8 7710^4

Oniz Tiptoes (IRE) *J S Wainwright* 66
7 ch g Russian Revival(USA) —Edionda (IRE) (Magical Strike (USA))
1017^{12}

Only A Game (IRE) *Miss M E Rowland* a78 67
3 b g Foxhound(USA) —Compendium (Puissance)
(170) ◆ 489^2 4900^{10} 7730^{10}

Only A Grand *R Bastiman* a59 53
4 b m Cloudings(IRE) —Magic Orb (Primo Dominie)
7^5 258^6 478^2 640^3 792^2 949^6 1578^{13} 2274^{11} 2940^3 3640^5 4540^{11} 4748^{12}

Only Answer *A Fabre* 112
4 b m Green Desert(USA) —Occupandiste (IRE) (Kaldoun (FR))
(2034a) 2652a^6 3938a^3 4915a^{12} (5955a) 6994a^{14}

Only A Splash *Mrs R A Carr* a10 42
4 b g Primo Valentino(IRE) —Water Well (Sadler's Wells (USA))
1135^6 1674^{10} 1754^5 2036^{11} 2491^{11} 2936^{11} 3139^5

Only For Sue *W S Kittow* a11 54
9 ch g Pivotal—Barbary Court (Grundy)
1121^8

Only Hope *P S McEntee* a53 27
4 b m Marju(IRE) —Sellette (IRE) (Selkirk (USA))
10^{14} 125^{11} 499^6 575^6 751^6 776^4 1726^{12} 5070^{10} 7624^8

Only If I Laugh *M J Attwater* a51 45
7 ch g Piccolo—Agony Aunt (Formidable (USA))
11^3 120^5 147^3 289^5 621^6 877^3 922^4 1053^2 1269^4 2075^{12} 4414^{14} 5533^{12}

Only In Jest *J Gallagher* a53 74
3 br f Averti(IRE) —Silver Purse (Interrex (CAN))
2068^3 2551^7 2774^{11}

On Offer (IRE) *T D Easterby* 75
2 b f Clodovil(IRE) —Camassina (IRE) (Taufan (USA))
2485^3 2887^2 (3411)

On Our Way *H R A Cecil* 107
2 b c Oasis Dream—Singed (Zamindar (USA))
4184^3 ◆ (4788) 5462^2 ◆ 6267^3 (6779)

On The Edge (IRE) *John Joseph Murphy* a65 61
2 gr c Dalakhani(IRE) —Najmati (Green Desert (USA))
7214^5 7312^7

On The Feather *P Winkworth* a71 52
2 br f Josr Algarhoud(IRE) —Fotheringhay (Loup Sauvage (USA))
3378^9 ◆ 4088^4 5214^6 5997^2 6223^4

On The Map *Joss Saville* a62 57
4 b m Agnes World(USA) —Noor El Houdah (IRE) (Fayruz)
173^7 338^8 2055^{11} 2658^9 4294^{10} 6175^{11}

On The Other Hand (IRE) *C F Swan* 65
8 b g Oscar(IRE) —Coumeenoole Lady (The Parson)
4511a^{19}

Onyergo (IRE) *M A Barnes* 63
6 b g Polish Precedent(USA) —Trick (IRE) (Shirley Heights)
7039^6 7177^4

Oops Another Act *W R Swinburn* a59 42
3 rg f Act One—Oops Pettie (Machiavellian (USA))
3133^8 ◆ 4302^5 4909^5 6227^{11}

Opal Noir *Miss L A Perratt* a21 74
4 b g Lujain(USA) —Wrong Bride (Reprimand)
1952^4 2444^8 (2751) 3129^6 3581^8 4117^5 6164^{12} 6448^{12} 7018^5

Openide *B W Duke* a55 52
7 b g Key Of Luck(USA) —Eyelet (IRE) (Satco (FR))
5613^8

Opening Act *P F I Cole* a61 53
3 gr g Daylami(IRE) —Bluebelle (Generous (IRE))
1905^3 2681^{11} 3022^9

Opening Hand *Evan Williams* a38 58
3 b g Observatory(USA) —Belle Ile (USA) (Diesis)
350^6 1529^{12} 2198^{11} 2805^{10} 4365^{11}

Operachy *B R Millman* 60
3 b g Kyllachy—Sea Music (Inchinor)
1897^{12}

Opera De Luna *D Shaw* a61 65
3 ch f Singspiel(IRE) —Villa Carlotta (Rainbow Quest (USA))
3133^5 4620^{11} 4871^4 5605^6 6044^6 6390^4 6754^3 6897^6 7366^7

Opera Prince *S Kirk* a87 93
3 b g Kyllachy—Optaria (Song)
1410^2 (2014) 2460^3 ◆ 2794^4 2998^4 (5863) ◆ 6283^3 (6704)

Opera Wings *Sir Michael Stoute* a60
2 ch f Medicean—Wings Of Love (Groom Dancer (USA))
7561^4

Opera Writer (IRE) *R Hollinshead* a71 74
5 b g Rossini(USA) —Miss Flite (IRE) (Law Society (USA))
(320) 561^8 722^3 1062^2 1408^7 1933^5 2572^4 3084^6 (3698) 3900^6 4299^3 5450^9 (6364) (6538) 6948^{18} 7202^2 7777^5 7785^4

Opinion Poll (IRE) *M A Jarvis* 83
2 b c Halling(USA) —Ahead (Shirley Heights)
6085^{10} (6720) ◆

Opportunist (IRE) *Doug Watson* a103
9 b h Machiavellian(USA) —Fatefully (USA) (Private Account (USA))
382a^5 493a^7

Optical Illusion (USA) *R A Fahey* a61 70
4 b g Theatrical—Paradise River (USA) (Irish River (FR))
1029^2 1313^3 (3582) 4117^6 4736^9 5455^7 6310^{11} 6631^8 7072^2 7320^9 7533^8

Optical Seclusion (IRE) *A Berry* a56 16
5 b g Second Empire(IRE) —Theda (Mummy's Pet)
7218^{13}

Optimal Power (IRE) *Edward Lynam* 80
2 gr c Verglas(IRE) —Optimal (IRE) (Green Desert (USA))
3509a^{10}

Optimistic Alfie *B G Powell* a52 53
8 b g Afzal—Threads (Bedford (USA))
67^4 169^6

Optimum (IRE) *J T Stimpson* a52 56
6 br g King's Best(USA) —Colour Dance (Rainbow Quest (USA))
152^3 374^8

Optimus (USA) *B G Powell* a84 82
6 ch g Elnadim(USA) —Ajfan (USA) (Woodman (USA))
1532^{10} 2304^5 3523^8 3685^6 4129^2 4829^8 5069^7 5583^2 6243^4 6607^{14} 6898^{16}

Optimus Maximus (IRE) *P F I Cole* 74
3 ch c Galileo(IRE) —Morning Welcome (IRE) (Be My Guest (USA))
3094^6 3530^3 4372^5

Optional Dream (IRE) *Eamon Tyrrell* 51
3 ch f Fayruz—Optional (Prince Sabo)
2399^4

Opus Maximus (IRE) *M Johnston* a79 90
3 ch g Titus Livius(FR) —Law Review (IRE) (Case Law)
706^2 ◆ (777) ◆ 1426^{12} 1764^5 (2141) 2410^{11} 2624^4 3050^{14} 3442^4 3744^4 (4167) 4876^9 5697^6 ◆ (6035) 6249^6 6482^4

Oracle West (SAF) *M F De Kock* 120
7 b g Western Winter(USA) —Noble Prophet (SAF) (Noble Ambition (USA))
(494a) 816a^3 1091a^{13}

Orama's Ghost *M Botti* a61 74
4 b m Golan(IRE) —Orange Sunset (IRE) (Roanoke (USA))
239^2 513^2

Orangeleg *S C Williams* 34
2 b g Intikhab(USA) —Red Shareef (Marju (IRE))
3485^8 4778^8 5754^{11}

Orange Orchid (IRE) *James A Browne* 49
9 ch m Persian Bold—Broken Spirit (IRE) (Slip Anchor)
4142^4 4322^2

Orange Pip *R Hannon* 86
3 ch f Bold Edge—Opopmil (IRE) (Pips Pride)
1836^2 2341^2 (2898) 4483^8

Orange River (IRE) *J H M Gosden* 71
3 b f Cape Cross(IRE) —Simla Bibi (Indian Ridge)
2973^6 4447^4 6331^2 6868^2

Orange Square (IRE) *D W Barker* a65 48
3 br g King Charlemagne(USA) —Unaria (Prince Tenderfoot (USA))
9^4 60^5 183^3 324^3 403^2 (467) 614^4 3283^{10} 4013^9 4216^{14} 4686^{11}

Orangina Wood (GER) *A Berry* a24 44
5 b m Perugino(USA) —Orletta (GER) (Platini (GER))
1579^{11} 2283^{11} 2491^{15}

Oranmore Castle (IRE) *R A Fahey* 82
6 b g Giant's Causeway(USA) —Twice The Ease (Green Desert (USA))
1485^{15} 1617^{12} 1818^{12} 4393^{10} 4950^8 (Dead)

Oratory (IRE) *R Hannon* 91
2 b c Danehill Dancer(IRE) —Gentle Night (Zafonic (USA))
2951^8 (3519) 4187^2 5507^{10}

Orbital Orchid *W S Kittow* a56 68
3 b f Mujahid(USA) —Carati (Selkirk (USA))
1479^{10} 2015^5 2833^6 3483^5 4054^5 4326^4 4978^3 6436^9

Orbitor *M L W Bell* a75 78
2 b c Galileo(IRE) —Peacock Alley (IRE) (Salse (USA))
6084^9 ◆ 6759^2 (7069)

Orchard House (FR) *J Jay* a61 38
5 b g Medaaly—Louisa May (IRE) (Royal Abjar (USA))
345^8 436^7

Orchard Supreme *R Hannon* a107 96
5 ch g Titus Livius(FR) —Bogus Penny (IRE) (Pennekamp (USA))
227^2 906^6 958^{17} 1469^{12} 1982^{16} (2308) ◆ 2545^8 3122^9 3382^2 4509^{18} 5903^7 6478^4 6670^6 (7339) 7420^7 7492^9 7740^5

Orchestration (IRE) *Garry Moss* a48 58
7 ch g Stravinsky(USA) —Mora (IRE) (Second Set (IRE))
50^8 100^4 119^5 232^7 479^4 972^4 1455^{14} 1675^9 1906^{10} 2703^{12} 2753^{11} 7618^9 7644^{13}

Orchestrator (IRE) *W Clay* a68 69
4 b g Docksider(USA) —Summerhill (Habitat)
1876^7 2203^{10} 2556^{10} 2917^{12} 7399^{12} 7500^{12}

Orchestrion *Miss T Jackson* 63
3 ch f Piccolo—Mindomica (Dominion)
4194^4 4651^2 5205^5 6387^5 6792^{13} 7039^{11}

Order Order *H J L Dunlop* 63
2 br f Diktat—Brocheta (Hector Protector (USA))
3674^6 4149^8 4554^{10} 6240^{22} 6761^{13}

Ordinata (GER) *Frau Ira Ferentschak* 91
5 b m Silvano(GER) —Ordina (GER) (Zampano (GER))
6852a^9 7350a^7

Ordination (IRE) *B J Meehan* 84
3 ch c Fantastic Light(USA) —Seek Easy (USA) (Seeking The Gold (USA))
1690^2 (3637)

Ordnance Row *R Hannon* 117
5 b g Mark Of Esteem(IRE) —Language Of Love (Rock City)
1716^5 (2044) 2600^5 3503^2 (5025) 6073^3 6440^3 6814^{12}

Oren Ishi (IRE) *Miss M E Rowland* a43 41
4 ch m Lil's Boy(USA) —Menesiah (IRE) (Project Manager)
1588^8

Oriental Cavalier *R Hollinshead* 68
2 ch g Ishiguru(USA) —Gurleigh (IRE) (Pivotal)
5364^7 6014^6 6535^2 6857^4

Oriental Gift (FR) *H A McWilliams* 33
4 ch g Orientate(USA) —Golden Queen (USA) (Gold Fever (USA))
2246^5 2658^{12}

Oriental Girl *J A Geake* a55 68
3 b f Dr Fong(USA) —Zacchera (Zamindar (USA))
1271^5 2563^4 (3314) 4253^3 (4766) 6417^{12} 7111^{10}

Orientalist Art *P W Chapple-Hyam* a93 90
3 b g Green Desert(USA) —Pink Cristal (Dilum (USA))
(608) ◆ 1213^2 1513a^9

Oriental Rose *G M Moore* 74
2 b f Dr Fong(USA) —Sahara Rose (Green Desert (USA))
1220^6 1447^8 (4108) 4874^6 6082^{13}

Oriental Tiger (GER) *U Ostmann* 118
5 b h Tiger Hill(IRE) —Oriental Flower (GER) (Big Shuffle (USA))
(1237a) (1662a) 2440a^5 5137a^{DSQ} (Dead)

Oriental Time (GER) *U Ostmann*
2 b f Dashing Blade—Oriental Pearl (GER) (Big Shuffle (USA))
7006a^{13}

Orient Celebrity *Mlle S-V Tarrou* 89
3 b f Peintre Celebre(USA) —Graffiti Girl (IRE) (Sadler's Wells (USA))
3018a^6 7551a^8

Orion Queen (FR) *H-A Pantall* a91 74
3 b f Speedmaster(GER) —Okocha (GER) (Platini (GER))
1760a^6 3018a^9

Orion Star (FR) *H-A Pantall* 115
6 gr g Sternkoenig(IRE) —Okocha (GER) (Platini (GER))
1663a^2 2236a^2 4041a^7 6497a^3

Orizaba (IRE) *M R Channon* 112
2 b c Orpen(USA) —Jus'Chillin' (IRE) (Elbio)
(2150) ◆ 3103^5 ◆ (4517) 6267^4

Orkney (IRE) *Miss J A Camacho* a72 56
3 b g Trans Island—Bitty Mary (Be My Chief (USA))
1549^3 6991^7 7274^3 (7630) (7722)

Orlando's Tale (USA) *J R Fanshawe* a45
3 ch g Tale Of The Cat(USA) —Tell Seattle (USA) (A.P. Indy (USA))
7026^{10}

Ornella *H Morrison* a77 80
4 b m Medicean—Paradise Soul (USA) (Dynaformer (USA))
1729^{10} 2670^8 3089^3 (3780) 4055^4 4435^2 4945^2 5209^5 6127^{10}

Oronsay *B R Millman* a38 54
3 ch f Elmaamul(USA) —Glenfinlass (Lomond (USA))
3064^9 3678^{15} 4368^{10} 5023^9 5813^2 6562^3 6747^4

Orotund *T D Easterby* a46 61
4 b g Orpen(USA) —Soyalang (FR) (Alydeed (CAN))
1561^8 2081^4 2780^4 3079^5 4858^7 5392^{14}

Orpen Bid (IRE) *A M Crow* 51
3 b f Orpen(USA) —Glorious Bid (IRE) (Horage)
1817^7 2282^5 2659^{10} 3753^8 4453^7 4851^3 ◆ 4967^5 5388^5 5544 ^{10}

Orpenella *K A Ryan* a68 32
3 b f Orpen(USA) —M N L Lady (Polar Falcon (USA))
616^3 ◆ 1132^2 1452^{14} 6356^3 6792^{15} 7153^4 7533^2 7634^4

Orpen Fire (IRE) *E S McMahon* a70 82
3 b f Orpen(USA) —Feet Of Flame (USA) (Theatrical)
1867^2 2781^2 3369^3 3883^{10}

Orpenindeed (IRE) *M Botti* a96 99
5 bb g Orpen(USA) —Indian Goddess (IRE) (Indian Ridge)
1689^2 2211^4 3056^3 3647^3 4928^6 5424^2 6624^6 6902^6 (7297) 7470^2 ◆

Orpen's Art (IRE) *R McGlinchey* a77 75
3 b c Invincible Spirit(IRE) —Bells Of Ireland (UAE) (Machiavellian (USA))
(112) 243^2 444^3 (612) 714^3 (882) 1066^6 2258^8 2506^2 3224^2 3486^4 3609^2 5260^{10} 6511a^{14}

Orpen Wide (IRE) *M C Chapman* a87 93
6 b g Orpen(USA) —Melba (IRE) (Namaqualand (USA))
6^5 1816^{14}

Orphan (IRE) *G M Moore* 61
6 b g Orpen(USA) —Ballinlee (IRE) (Skyliner)
3079^8 3582^3 4018^4 4597^3 4690^7 5779^{12}

Orphan Boy *H J Collingridge* a14
3 b g Tipsy Creek(USA) —Miss Jingles (Muhtarram (USA))
108^4 486^8 7774^{11}

Orphaned Annie *B Ellison* a57 58
2 b f Lend A Hand—Great Exception (Grundy)
1515^7 2154^4 2909^9 6809^4 7148^3 7514^3 7659^7

Orphina (IRE) *B G Powell* a55 56
5 b m Orpen(USA) —Keralba (USA) (Sheikh Albadou)
999^{16} 1643^{14} 3698^6 4432^6 5027^{11}

Orpsie Boy (IRE) *N P Littmoden* a107 98
5 b g Orpen(USA) —Nordicolini (IRE) (Nordico (USA))
226^4 (337) ◆ 679^3 (836) 3504^{11} 4445^5 4624^{16} 6285^8 6429^6 6947^5 7192^6

Orsippus (USA) *M R Channon* a76 75
2 bb c Sunday Break(JPN) —Mirror Dancing (USA) (Caveat (USA))
4861^8 (5314) 5711^3

Orthodox (USA) *John Glenney* a95 100
2 b c Pulpit(USA) —Dominique's Joy (USA) (Strawberry Road (AUS))
6998a^7

Orthology (IRE) *M H Tompkins* a38 80
2 b c Kalanisi(IRE) —Al Shakoor (Barathea (IRE))
5672^{12} 6085^5 6524^2 7142^5

Oscar Silk *M R Channon* 66
2 b f Selkirk(USA) —Sciunfona (IRE) (Danehill (USA))
3348^6 4747^7

Oscar Wild *James Moffatt* 48
6 b g Tragic Role(USA) —Minster Lascar (Scallywag)
5042^{10} 5453^4 6055^8

Osiris Way *P R Chamings* a89 99
6 ch g Indian Ridge—Heady (Rousillon (USA))
(3062) 3680^3 4201^5 4586^4 4928^2 (5270) 5930^{10} (6669)

Oskari *P T Midgley* a50 2
3 b g Lear Spear(USA) —Cedar Jeneva (Muhtarram (USA))
6530^{11} 6843^3

Osolomio (IRE) *Jennie Candlish* a83 89
5 b g Singspiel(IRE) —Inanna (Persian Bold)
105[6]

Osteopathic Care (IRE) *Miss Tracy Waggott* 57
4 b g Montjeu(IRE) —Super Gift (IRE) (Darshaan)
1814[9] 2207[9] 2847[13] 3279[12] 4168[11]

Osteopathic Remedy (IRE) *M Dods* 100
4 ch g Inchinor—Dolce Vita (IRE) (Ela-Mana-Mou)
992[7] 1217[15] 1450[11] (2007) (2524) (3367) 4649[3] (5360) 6103[6] 6482[12]

Osterhase (IRE) *J E Mulhern* a88 88
9 b g Flying Spur(AUS) —Ostrusa (AUT) (Rustan (HUN))
2685a[5]

Ostinata (IRE) *B W Duke* a52 52
3 ch f Spartacus(IRE) —Poly Dancer (Suave Dancer (USA))
20[9] 665[4] 1710[7] 3614[9]

Ostland (GER) *P Schiergen* 110
3 b c Lando(GER) —Ost Tycoon (GER) (Last Tycoon)
3773a[2] 5736a[4] 6324a[5]

Osty Eria (FR) *C Diard* 85
2 b f Kingsalsa(USA) —Nashida (FR) (Kahyasi)
4441a[5]

Osumi Grass One (JPN) *Y Arakawa* 118
6 ch h Grass Wonder(USA) —Hokko Oka (JPN) (Lindo Shaver (USA))
7511a[11]

Otaared *M A Jarvis* a103 88
3 b c Storm Cat(USA) —Society Lady (USA) (Mr Prospector (USA))
1403[2] (6393) 6911[2]

Otaki (IRE) *Sir Mark Prescott* a59
4 gr m King's Best(USA) —On Call (Alleged (USA))
(179) ◆ 322[4] 544[9]

Otis May (IRE) *A W Carroll* a51 25
4 ch g Dockside(USA) —Dutosky (Doulab (USA))
5491[10] 6206[4] 6571[10]

Ottomax (GER) *Andreas Lowe* 94
3 ch c Banyumanik(IRE) —Omicenta (IRE) (Platini (GER))
6664a[0]

Oui Say Oui (IRE) *T Stack* 99
2 b f Royal Applause—Mohican Princess (Shirley Heights)
5132a[2] 6319a[5]

Ouqba *B W Hills* 107
2 b c Red Ransom(USA) —Dancing Mirage (IRE) (Machiavellian (USA))
1399[3] ◆ 1832[2] (3879) 5244[9] 5889[4] (6401) 6815[9]

Our Acquaintance *W R Muir* a73 75
3 ch g Bahamian Bounty—Lady Of Limerick (IRE) (Thatching)
1110[8] 1277[3] 1707[6] 2127[5] 4000[4] 4325[5] (4904) 5217[4] 6024[5] 6328[5] 6864[9] 7323[3] 7582[3] 7629[4]

Our Angel *Ms N M Hugo* 15
2 b f Primo Valentino(IRE) —Abaklea (IRE) (Doyoun)
4815[10]

Our Apolonia (IRE) *A Berry* 50
2 b f Intikhab(USA) —Algaira (USA) (Irish River (FR))
3432[5] 5106[2] 5539[8] 5883[6] 6809[9]

Ourbelle *Miss Tracy Waggott* 10
3 b f Bertolini(USA) —Guardienne (Hector Protector (USA))
3282[14] 3452[8] 3953[8] 4684[7] 5501[13]

Our Blessing (IRE) *A P Jarvis* a75 84
4 b g Lujain(USA) —Berenice (ITY) (Marouble)
969[7] 1415[7] 1500[6] 1928[13] 3050[9] 3675[4] 4491[3] 4664[4] 5050[3] 5629[2] 6040[8] 6680[2] (6774) 7014[4] 7077[9] 7510[8] 7540[4]

Our Bridget *C W Fairhurst* 2
2 b f Statue Of Liberty(USA) —Lamasat (USA) (Silver Hawk (USA))
4873[8] 6013[11]

Our Day Will Come *R Hannon* a72 71
2 b f Red Ransom(USA) —Dawnus (IRE) (Night Shift (USA))
3348[12] 4109[4] 4328[2] 4975[3] 5959[6] 6876[3] 7259[4] 7472[4] 7767[7]

Our Dolly *Garry Moss* a38 48
3 b f Lomitas—Amidst (Midyan (USA))
2269[9] 3694[8] 4566[3] 4794[4] 4891[9] 5379[15] 6752[9]

Our Faye *S Kirk* a81 101
5 b m College Chapel—Tamara (Marju (IRE))
1331[7] 1809[25] 2831[2] (2993) 3197[12] (3927)

Our Fugitive (IRE) *C Gordon* a73 71
6 gr g Titus Livius(FR) —Mystical Jumbo (Mystiko (USA))
2351[7] 2692[3] 2798[10] 3269[4] 3797[9] 3966[8] 4824[2] 5101[13] 5801[8] 6895[6] 7414[4] 7589[6] 7836[8]

Our Glenard *J E Long* a40 28
9 b g Royal Applause—Loucoum (FR) (Iron Duke (FR))
2755[12] 3344[8] 4409[6] 5787[9] 7216[14] 7553[11]

Our Jane *P G Murphy* a52
3 b f Apprehension—Honey Mill (Milford)
610[4] 919[12]

Our Kally *M D I Usher* a47 57
3 bb f Kyllachy—Rendition (Polish Precedent (USA))
1414[5] 1672[8] 1740[4] 2452[6] 2774[3] 3332[3] 4308[6] 4904[2] 5217[5] 5421[8] 7049[10] 7636[9] 7745[11]

Our Kes (IRE) *P Howling* a77 67
6 gr m Revoque(IRE) —Gracious Gretclo (Common Grounds)
177[9] 395[2] 430[3] 540[5] 802[3] (874) 970[3] 1266[5] 1725[3] (1853) 2078[2] 2423[4] 2957[3] 3361[2] 4183[8] 5018[9] 5350[11] 6210[13] 6629[10] 7440[6] 7620[5]

Our Lament *J G Portman* a52 54
3 ch g Compton Place—Glider (IRE) (Silver Kite (USA))
4484[5]

Our Nations *D Carroll* a47 44
3 gr g Highest Honor(FR) —Lines Of Beauty (USA) (Line In The Sand (USA))
3628[9] 4124[10] 4689[10] 6044[7] 6421[11]

Our Piccadilly (IRE) *W S Kittow* a70 75
3 b f Piccolo—Dilys (Efisio)
2196[11] 3838[8] 4483[5] 5028[6] 5490[4] (5902) 6765[4]

Ours (IRE) *John A Harris* a77 74
5 b g Mark Of Esteem(IRE) —Ellebanna (Tina's Pet)
805 2274[2] 2597[2] 2925[5] 3366[9] (4172) 4895[5] 6056[2] 6585[4] 6671[4] 7021[3] (7368) 7610[3] 7796[6]

Our Serendipity *R M Whitaker* 1
5 ch m Presidium—Berl's Gift (Prince Sabo)
7280[8]

Our Sunnie *D Nicholls* a53 65
3 b g Averti(IRE) —Barawin (FR) (Fijar Tango (FR))
977[4] 1081[3] 1117[3] 1169[2] (1754) 2268[12] 2463[14]

Our Wee Girl (IRE) *S Kirk* a60 77
2 bb f Choisir(AUS) —Zwadi (IRE) (Dockside (USA))
2309[2] ◆ 2479[2] 2826[9] 3378[3] 3908[4] 7452[2] 7574[8] 7673[5] 7738[6]

Ouster (GER) *D R C Elsworth* 92
2 b c Lomitas—Odabella's Charm (Cadeaux Genereux)
5857[8] (6398) ◆ 7142[2]

Out After Dark *C G Cox* 104
7 b g Cadeaux Genereux—Midnight Shift (IRE) (Night Shift (USA))
2565[7] 3040[8]

Outdroad *P M Phelan* a29
2 ch c Desert Sun—Loch Fyne (Ardkinglass)
7065[8] 7356[8] 7537[10]

Outer Hebrides *J M Bradley* a57 77
7 b g Efisio—Reuval (Sharpen Up)
1160[12] 1641[10] 1842[12] 2477[5] 2917[5] 3181[6] 3604[10] 4710[3] 4979[2] 6178[5] 6255[8] 6693[4] 7320[7] 7382[5] 7442[3] 7663[3] 7779[8]

Outland (IRE) *M H Tompkins* 39
2 gr g Indian Haven—Sensuality (IRE) (Idris (IRE))
5158[9] 6084[14] 6553[10]

Outlandish *Andrew Turnell* a86 73
5 b g Dr Fong(USA) —Velvet Lady (Nashwan (USA))
(317) ◆ 921[2] 970[2] 5900[10] 6607[6] 7610[2] ◆

Outlook *P T Midgley* a49 66
5 ch g Observatory(USA) —Area Girl (Jareer (USA))
752[7] 864[8]

Out Of Control (BRZ) *Robert Frankel* a44 117
5 b h Vettori(IRE) —Heavenly Dancer (BRZ) (Fitzcarraldo (ARG))
5558a[7] 7000a[5] 7685a[7]

Out Of Control (TUR) *M Yigiter* 113
5 b h Cape Cross(IRE) —Committal (USA) (Chief's Crown (USA))
5741a[2]

Out Of India *P T Dalton* a51 56
6 b m Marju(IRE) —Tide Of Fortune (Soviet Star (USA))
3964[5] 4219[14] 4535[3] 5007[4] 6251[7] 6419[5] 7021[11] 7180[6] 7369[6]

Out Of Nothing *K M Prendergast* a58 70
5 br m Perryston View—Loves To Dare (IRE) (Desert King (IRE))
1383[13] 1729[4] 4368[9] 4979[6] 5816[2] 6821[9] (7131) 7267[5]

Outofoil (IRE) *R M Beckett* 79
2 b g King's Best(USA) —Simplicity (Polish Precedent (USA))
4430[2] ◆ (4974) 7241[8]

Out Of This Way *Mrs N S Evans* a58 34
5 b g Spectrum(IRE) —Pirouette (Sadler's Wells (USA))
3606[15] 4479[10] 6583[11]

Outside Edge (IRE) *W R Swinburn* a70 73
3 b g Danetime(IRE) —Naraina (IRE) (Desert Story (IRE))
1611[5] 2127[6] 3031[7] 3442[10] 4338[4] 4865[4] 5186[4] 5616[4] 6048[3] (6336)

Overbright (IRE) *G L Moore* a49 53
2 b c Exceed And Excel(AUS) —Todi (IRE) (Spinning World (USA))
4980[6] 5572[7] 6342[14]

Overdose *S Ribarszki* 123
3 b c Starborough—Our Poppet (IRE) (Warning)
(3752a) (5553a) (7349a)

Over Ice *Karen George* a47 63
5 b m Mister Baileys—Oublier L'Ennui (FR) (Bellman (FR))
32[7] 490[3] 822[4] 1031[U]

Overrule (USA) *B Ellison* 91
4 b g Diesis—Her Own Way (USA) (Danzig (USA))
1218[6] 1481[11] 1815[6] 2905[10] 3646[7] 4162[14] 4603[8] 5199[4] 6007[2] ◆ 6243[2]

Overstayed (IRE) *A Bailey* a65 84
5 ch g Titus Livius(FR) —Look Nonchalant (IRE) (Fayruz)
304[5] 414[3] 554[7] 620[3] 681[8] 875[2] 1242[7] 1827[6] 2448[12] 4107[2] 5626[6] 6063[2] 6190[3] 6382[9] 7359[4] 7383[4] 7509[9] 7529[5] 7631[5]

Over The Tylery (IRE) *Eamon Tyrrell* 72
4 b m Swallow Flight(IRE) —Ivory Turner (Efisio)
3532a[8] 6366a[19]

Over To You Bert *R J Hodges* a66 61
9 b g Overbury(IRE) —Silvers Era (Balidar)
209[10] (402) 516[2] 587[4] 749[3] 1154[2] 2337[15] 7591[10] 7803[12]

Overturn (IRE) *W R Swinburn* 93
4 b g Barathea(IRE) —Kristal Bridge (Kris)
2762[4] 3122[12]

Overwing (IRE) *R M H Cowell* a79 77
5 b m Fasliyev(USA) —Sierva (GER) (Darshaan)
2836[4] (3026) 3260[2] 3695[4] 3883[9] (4779) 5073[3] 5532[4]

Ovthenight (IRE) *Mrs P Sly* a57 74
3 b c Noverre(USA) —Night Beauty (King Of Kings (IRE))
(1553) (2280) 2785[3] 3793[8] 5999[11]

Owain James *M Salaman* a36 39
3 ch g Dancing Spree(USA) —Jane Grey (Tragic Role (USA))
1836[8] 2126[8] 3264[8] 4810[7]

Owed *R Bastiman* a68 41
6 b g Lujain(USA) —Nightingale (Night Shift (USA))
647 346[3] 460[8] 599[4] 786[3] 846[3] 1024[3] 1338[11] 1703[3] 2081[2] 2706[5] (2869) 3819[6] 4107[14] 7534[11] 7698[13]

Oxbridge *J M Bradley* a32 60
3 ch g Tomba—Royal Passion (Ahonoora)
2555[6] ◆ 2935[6] 3441[9] 4083[11] 4278[14]

Oxus (IRE) *B R Johnson* a42
3 ch g Sinndar(IRE) —River Dancer (Irish River (FR))
7757[8]

Ozone Trustee (NZ) *G A Swinbank* 85
4 b g Montjeu(IRE) —Bold Faith (Warning)
(5453) 5858[7] 6288[13]

Pab Special (IRE) *B R Johnson* a77 81
5 b g City On A Hill(USA) —Tinos Island (IRE) (Alzao (USA))
243 542[2] ◆ 728[6] 935[3] 1565[4] 2070[3] (2352) 2863[6] 5799[8] 6882[12] 7189[10] 7392[4] (7516) ◆

Pachakutek (USA) *E F Vaughan* 72
2 ch c Giant's Causeway(USA) —Charlotte Corday (Kris)
6778[5]

Pachattack (USA) *G A Butler* 100
2 ch f Pulpit(USA) —El Laoob (USA) (Red Ransom (USA))
3001[4] ◆ (4554) 5266[9] 6439[4]

Pacific Bay (IRE) *Mrs A Duffield* a64 65
2 b f Diktat—Wild Clover (Lomitas)
2485[4] 3292[5] 3597[6] 5381[11] 6017[2]

Pacific Ocean (ARG) *Miss Z C Davison* 46
9 b g Fitzcarraldo(ARG) —Play Hard (ARG) (General (FR))
5163[8] 5322[4]

Pacific Pride *J J Quinn* 95
5 b g Compton Place—Only Yours (Aragon)
(1969) 2358[5] 2818[13] 3336[7] 4218[11] 4393[2] 4962[5] 5247[16] 6278[11]

Pacifism (UAE) *M A Jarvis* a94 93
3 ch g Halling(USA) —African Peace (USA) (Roberto (USA))
(58) ◆ 217[2] 1600[4] 6698[7]

Packers Hill (IRE) *G A Swinbank* 71
4 b g Mull Of Kintyre(USA) —Head For The Stars (IRE) (Head For Heights)
2942[5] 3366[8] 3736[5] 4219[10] 6056[5] 6312[9] (6485) 6657[4] 6862[9]

Packing Winner (NZ) *L Ho* 118
6 b g Zabeel(NZ) —Musical Note (AUS) (Marscay (AUS))
1666a[4] 7682a[5]

Paco Boy (IRE) *R Hannon* a101 127
3 b c Desert Style(IRE) —Tappen Zee (Sandhurst Prince)
(905) ◆ (1471) 2032a[7] (4506) (5095) 5740a[3] (6496a)

Pactolos Way *P R Chamings* a70 65
5 b g Docksider(USA) —Arietta's Way (IRE) (Darshaan)
430[6] 1644[6] 2070[9]

Paddy Bear *R A Fahey* 71
2 b c Piccolo—Lily Of The Guild (IRE) (Lycius (USA))
3714[3] 4113[2] 5394[4] 5633[4]

Paddy Jack *J R Weymes* a9 70
3 ch g Rambling Bear—Bayrami (Emarati (USA))
977[6] 1556[13] 2396[9] 2527[4] 3217[4] 3811[2] 3955[2] 4118[11] 4450[9] 4852[7] 5110[2] 5307[10]

Paddyntrev Bakfavs (IRE) *T D Easterby* 60
2 b g Elnadim(USA) —One For Fun (Unfuwain (USA))
3669[13] 4415[13] 6787[5]

Paddy Rielly (IRE) *P D Evans* a68 64
3 b g Catcher In The Rye(IRE) —The Veil (IRE) (Barathea (IRE))
1478[7] 1696[11] 2280[2] 2785[5] 3022[3] 4485[11] 5399[6] (5593) 6210[3] 6447[6] 6827[10] 6868[4] 6991[4]

Paddys Lad (IRE) *Francis Ennis* 69
2 b g Fath(USA) —Rosy Scintilla (IRE) (Thatching)
3509a[17]

Paddythefish (USA) *K R Burke* a61 9
2 bb c More Than Ready(USA) —Comstock Queen (USA) (Silver Hawk (USA))
5500[9] 5696[5] 7353[8] 7505[12] 7547[14]

Paddy The Pro (IRE) *Patrick Gallagher* a95 75
2 b c Exceed And Excel(AUS) —Vinicky (USA) (Kingmambo (USA))
6998a[12]

Paddywack (IRE) *Mrs R A Carr* a59 67
11 b g Bigstone(IRE) —Millie's Return (IRE) (Ballad Rock)
142[4] 285[4] 1015[16] 1431[9] 2270[13]

Pagan Belief *J A R Toller* a70 69
4 b g Fraam—Au Contraire (Groom Dancer (USA))
1910[16]

Pagan Flight (IRE) *B J Meehan* 38
2 b g Hawk Wing(USA) —Regal Darcey (IRE) (Darshaan)
6117[16] 6602[10]

Pagan Force (IRE) *Mrs A J Perrett* 64
2 b c Green Desert(USA) —Brigitta (IRE) (Sadler's Wells (USA))
2972[9] 3895[4]

Paidrin (USA) *J S Bolger* 74
2 ch f Pulpit(USA) —Sun Princessa (USA) (Pleasant Colony (USA))
6519a[13]

Painted Sky *R A Fahey* a80 66
5 ch g Rainbow Quest(USA) —Emplane (USA) (Irish River (FR))
962[9] 2155[10]

Painted Smile (IRE) *Dr J D Scargill* a41
4 b m Iron Mask(USA) —Hope And Glory (USA) (Well Decorated (USA))
3823[5]

Paint Splash *T D Barron* a58 42
2 ch f Beat Hollow—Questa Nova (Rainbow Quest (USA))
6655[10] 7318[6] 7443[4] (7694)

Paint Stripper *W Storey* 61
3 b g Prince Sabo—Passing Fancy (Grand Lodge (USA))
1558[9] 1750[7] 3753[12] 4903[12] 5565[7] 7153[8] 7175[9]

Paint The Town Red *H J Collingridge* a79 55
3 b c Mujahid(USA) —Oneforthéditch (USA) (With Approval (CAN))
2079[4] (3161) 5018[6] 5309[6] 6256[6] 7070[6] 7711[12]

Pairumani Pat (IRE) *J Pearce* a48 53
3 ch g Pairumani Star(IRE) —Golden Skiis (IRE) (Hector Protector (USA))
4250[6] 4698[2] 5148[7] 6060[10] 6447[3] 6824[6]

Pajada *M D I Usher* a48 49
4 b m Bertolini(USA) —Last Ambition (IRE) (Cadeaux Genereux)
518[10] 621[8] 711[7] 1053[7] 1269[6] 1705[4] 2474[10] 2866[12] 3445[8] 4273[4] 4580[3] 4806[8] 5090[9] 7585[9] 7691[4] 7736[6]

Paktolos (FR) *A King* a100 95
5 b g Dansili—Pithara (GR) (Never So Bold)
1212[2] 1841[5] (3060) 3505[4] 5249[10] (7493)

Palacefield (IRE) *P W Chapple-Hyam* 75
2 b c Green Desert(USA) —Multaka (USA) (Gone West (USA))
7054[3]

Palace Moon *H Morrison* 89
3 b g Fantastic Light(USA) —Palace Street (USA) (Secreto (USA))
1835[2] ◆ (4431) ◆ 7109[3] ◆

Palace Walk (FR) *B G Powell* a52 52
6 b g Sinndar(IRE) —Page Bleue (Sadler's Wells (USA))
4366[3] 5163[5]

Palacio De Amor (USA) *Myung Kwon Cho* a108
2 ch f Dixieland Band(USA) —Haitian Vacation (USA) (Petionville (USA))
6967a[13]

Palais Polaire *J A Geake* a62 60
6 ch m Polar Falcon(USA) —Palace Street (USA) (Secreto (USA))
168[2] 276[7] 402[7] 3816[8] (4770) 5755[2] 6338[2] 7102[2] 7320[5]

Palanoverre (IRE) *D J S Ffrench Davis* a49 70
4 ch m Noverre(USA) —Palavera (FR) (Bikala)
6570[10] 6929[7]

Palavicini (USA) *J L Dunlop* 94
2 b c Giant's Causeway(USA) —Cara Fantasy (IRE) (Sadler's Wells (USA))
5246[2] ◆ 6075[3] (6602)

Palazzone (IRE) *G M Lyons* a93 78
2 b g Bertolini(USA) —Genny Lim (IRE) (Barathea (IRE))
3509a[4]

Pallodio (IRE) *J E Hammond* a92 103
3 br c Medecis—Bent Al Fala (IRE) (Green Desert (USA))
(6237a)

Palm Court *A Al Raihe* a89 78
3 b g Green Desert(USA) —Amenixa (FR) (Linamix (FR))
812a[10]

Palmerin *R Hannon* a81 81
3 b c Oasis Dream—Armorique (IRE) (Top Ville)
1074[7] 2194[12] 2564[7] 2974[3] 3384[3] (3745) 4130[5] 4621[4] 4984[4] 5472[6] 6028[7] 7014[2] 7299[4] 7439[9] 7526[9]

Palme Royale (IRE) *E Lellouche* 85
2 b f Red Ransom(USA) —Palmeraie (USA) (Lear Fan (USA))
6519a[9]

Palmetto Point *H Morrison* a71 76
4 ch g Bahamian Bounty—Forum (Lion Cavern (USA))
2561[6] 2795[9] 3457[2] 4162[4] 4789[3] 5492[9] 6056[7] 6338[6] 6749[7]

Pampas (USA) *Jane Chapple-Hyam* a71 57
3 ch f Distant View(USA) —Alvernia (USA) (Alydar (USA))
1423[12]

Pampas Cat (USA) *J H M Gosden* 108
3 b c Seeking The Gold(USA) —Golden Cat (USA) (Storm Cat (USA))
(1398) ◆ 1922[3] 2408[2] 3156[10] (4122)

Panadin (IRE) *Mrs L C Jewell* 43
6 b g Desert King(IRE) —Strident Note (The Minstrel (CAN))
3446[8] 4054[11] 4250[8]

Panamar Besar (IRE) *J Howard Johnson* 29
3 b g Bahri(USA) —Paradise Blue (IRE) (Bluebird (USA))
3297[8] 4075[9]

Pansy Potter *B J Meehan* a60 56
2 b f Auction House(USA) —Ellway Queen (USA) (Bahri (USA))
4251[14] 5097[12] 5277[5] 5606[4] 7760[6]

Pantherii (USA) *P F I Cole* a60 64
3 ch f Forest Wildcat(USA) —Saraa Ree (USA) (Caro)
1247[3] 1671[6] 2757[7] 3030[3]

Papal Bull *Sir Michael Stoute* 126
5 b h Montjeu(IRE) —Mialuna (Zafonic (USA))
2791[4] 3878[2] 4406[2] 5137a[2] 6522a[12] 7511a[14]

Papa Meilland *Eve Johnson Houghton* 74
2 b c Dr Fong(USA) —Rosacara (Green Desert (USA))
4274[5] (4982) 5511[7] 6002[P] (Dead)

Paparaazi (IRE) *I W McInnes* a62 70
6 b g Victory Note(USA) —Raazi (My Generation)
3551[9] (3732) 4503[10] 5008[6] 5145[14] 5776[10] 6189[11]

Papa's Princess *J S Goldie* a17 62
4 b m Mujadil(USA) —Desert Flower (Green Desert (USA))
1406[10] 2250[2] 2578[4] 2782[7] 3127[2] 3552[4] (3755) 4142[6] 4851[2] 5538[13]

Papeete (GER) *Mrs N Smith* a69 45
7 b m Alzao(USA) —Prairie Vela (Persian Bold)
2567[8]

Paperboy *Karen George* a40
4 b g Double Trigger(IRE) —Paperweight (In The Wings)
1405[8]

Papetti (ITY) *B Grizzetti* 107
3 b c Shantou(USA) —Pasionaria (IRE) (Celtic Swing)
2028a^{3} 7263a^{4}

Papillio (IRE) *J R Fanshawe* 73
3 b g Marju(IRE) —Danish Gem (Danehill (USA))
2919^{5} 4121^{6}

Pappas Image *A J McCabe* a53
4 b g Arkadian Hero(USA) —Fair Attempt (IRE) (Try My Best (USA))
65^{3} 79^{4} 167^{3} 278^{4} 371^{3} 440^{3} 528^{3} 599^{5} 790^{7} 846^{4} 951^{3} 1906^{9}

Pappoose *H Candy* 49
3 b f Namid—Bryn (Saddlers' Hall (IRE))
6003^{6} 6192^{10} 6543^{10}

Papradon *J R Best* a70 70
4 b g Tobougg(IRE) —Salvezza (IRE) (Superpower)
2884^{12} 3588^{2} (4156) 4819^{9} 6577^{9} 6775^{2}

Papuan Prince (IRE) *S Kirk* 67
3 b g Tagula(IRE) —Pussie Willow (IRE) (Catrail (USA))
1876^{6} 2772^{3}

Papyrian *W Jarvis* 43
2 b c Oasis Dream—La Papagena (Habitat)
7104^{11}

Paquerettza (FR) *D H Brown* 64
2 ch f Dr Fong(USA) —Cover Look (SAF) (Fort Wood (USA))
1794^{4} 5882^{3} 6392^{10}

Paradise Dancer (IRE) *J A R Toller* a80 68
4 b m Danehill Dancer(IRE) —Pintada De Fresco (FR) (Marignan (USA))
(426) 548^{2} 775^{5} 1112^{3} 1742^{4} 3272^{10} 7419^{10} 7603^{10}

Paradise Island (IRE) *E A L Dunlop* a63 66
3 b f Green Desert(USA) —Meadow Pipit (CAN) (Meadowlake (USA))
2786^{11} 3318^{4} 4253^{10} 4727^{5} 5816^{3} 6889^{8}

Paradise Walk *E W Tuer* a55 73
4 b m Sakhee(USA) —Enclave (USA) (Woodman (USA))
5305^{6} 6050^{7} 6235^{6}

Paraguay (USA) *Miss V Haigh* a78 82
5 b g Pivotal—Grisonnante (FR) (Kaldoun (FR))
731^{5} (2274) (2561) 2662^{5} (3208) (3478) 3915^{2} 4162^{10} 4567^{4} 4603^{5} 6186^{4} 6352^{2}

Parasol (IRE) *Doug Watson* a81 74
9 br g Halling(USA) —Bunting (Shaadi (USA))
380a^{16}

Parc Aux Boules *John C McConnell* a71 71
7 gr g Royal Applause—Aristocratique (Cadeaux Genereux)
1198a^{5} 6366a^{17}

Parc Des Princes (USA) *A M Balding* a42 63
2 bb c Ten Most Wanted(USA) —Miss Orah (Unfuwain (USA))
4728^{8} 6333^{2} 6745^{9}

Parchment (IRE) *A J Lockwood* 63
6 ch g Singspiel(IRE) —Hannalou (FR) (Shareef Dancer (USA))
69^{11} 2395^{4} 2914^{3} 3279^{4} 3589^{8} 3666^{5} 5003^{7}

Paris Bell *T D Easterby* a28 85
6 gr g Paris House—Warning Bell (Bustino)
1430^{7} 1796^{12} 1969^{6} 2293^{10} 2778^{7} 3454^{15} 3812^{4} 3890^{4} 4239^{12} 5222^{8} 5634^{4} 6011^{9} 6219^{10} 6411^{7}

Paris Hall *I W McInnes* a25 19
3 b g Paris House—Topcliffe (Top Ville)
1453^{11} 1894^{11} 2803^{8} 3640^{11} 4541^{10}

Parisian Art (IRE) *J Noseda* a80 86
2 b c Clodovil(IRE) —Cafe Creme (IRE) (Catrail (USA))
(4421) 5507^{11} 5794^{5} 6466^{5}

Parisian Gift (IRE) *J R Gask* a75 84
3 b g Statue Of Liberty(USA) —My Micheline (Lion Cavern (USA))
2189^{6} 4284^{2} 6952^{6} 7592^{P}

Parisian Playboy *A D Brown* a16 14
8 gr g Paris House—Exordium (Exorbitant)
2394^{8}

Parisian Pyramid (IRE) *D Nicholls* 89
2 gr g Verglas(IRE) —Sharadja (IRE) (Doyoun)
3492^{3} 3670^{3} 4237^{4} (4626) ◆ 5496^{2} 6067^{3}

Park Lane *B W Hills* 77
2 b c Royal Applause—Kazeem (Darshaan)
5053^{4} ◆ 5929^{2} 6426^{13}

Park Royal (UAE) *D E Cantillon* a73 73
3 bb f Cape Cross(IRE) —Shbakni (USA) (Mr Prospector (USA))
366^{2} ◆ 748^{11} 1222^{7}

Park Run *A W Carroll* 48
3 b f Tomba—Erica Jayka (Golden Heights)
3694^{10} 4124^{12} 4249^{12} 5119^{13} 5653^{9}

Parkside Pursuit *J M Bradley* a49 51
10 b g Pursuit Of Love—Ivory Bride (Domynsky)
3021^{12}

Park's Prodigy *P C Haslam* a53 56
4 b g Desert Prince(IRE) —Up And About (Barathea (IRE))
67^{2} 3589^{2} 3718^{9}

Park Valley Prince *W R Muir* a59 44
4 ch g Noverre(USA) —Santorini (USA) (Spinning World (USA))
56^{12} 3034^{18}

Parkview Love (USA) *J G Given* a75 70
7 bb g Mister Baileys—Jerre Jo Glanville (USA) (Skywalker (USA))
55^{7} 177^{3} 274^{2} 452^{8} 506^{3} 683^{3} 755^{8} 1084^{8} 1449^{5} 1604^{5} 1708^{5} 2597^{14} 2957^{8} 3666^{6} 4477^{2} 4690^{2} 5154^{7} 7516^{6}

Parliamentary (JPN) *Mrs A L M King* 70
3 b g Diktat—Rebuff (Kris)
1265^{11}

Parnassian *J A Geake* a60 75
8 ch g Sabrehill(USA) —Delphic Way (Warning)
963^{9} 7009^{6} 7189^{7} 7376^{3} 7630^{2} 7722^{5}

Parson's Punch *P D Cundell* a72 70
3 b g Beat Hollow—Ordained (Mtoto)
416^{7} 1855^{4} 3022^{4} 7256^{3} 7758^{5}

Parthenon *M Johnston* 90
2 b c Dubai Destination(USA) —Grecian Slipper (Sadler's Wells (USA))
(5777) ◆ 6025^{4} 6946^{3} ◆

Parthenope *J A Geake* a61 54
5 gr m Namid—Twosixtythreewest (FR) (Kris)
2243^{10} 3034^{5} (3371) 3839^{12} 4727^{6} 5604^{10}

Partner (IRE) *David Marnane* 37
2 b c Indian Ridge—Oregon Trail (USA) (Gone West (USA))
3509a^{15}

Partner In Crime *C E Longsdon*
4 ch m Namid—La Sencilla (ARG) (Lookinforthebigone (USA))
1638^{5}

Partner Shift (IRE) *E A L Dunlop* a74
2 b g Night Shift(USA) —What A Picture (FR) (Peintre Celebre (USA))
7098^{6} 7289^{2}

Partners In Jazz (USA) *T D Barron* a101 105
7 gr g Jambalaya Jazz(USA) —Just About Enough (USA) (Danzig (USA))
(6) ◆ 958^{8} 1218^{9}

Party Boss *C E Brittain* a109 80
6 gr h Silver Patriarch(IRE) —Third Party (Terimon)
1045^{7} 1133^{3} 1334^{9}

Party Cat (IRE) *R Hannon* 71
2 b g One Cool Cat(USA) —Congress (IRE) (Dancing Brave (USA))
2424^{4} 2601^{4} 3895^{5} 6342^{5} 6673^{7} ◆ 6946^{9}

Party Frock *J H M Gosden* a72 69
3 b f Oasis Dream—Dance Dress (USA) (Nureyev (USA))
5057^{2} 5995^{2} 7026^{4} 7403^{2}

Party In The Park *Miss J A Camacho* a70 77
3 b g Royal Applause—Halland Park Girl (IRE) (Primo Dominie)
1277^{5} 1743^{2} 1897^{4} (2126) 2911^{2} 3717^{13} (4531) 5799^{12} 6628^{10}

Party Lover (FR) *Mme M Bollack-Badel* a75 82
3 ch f Tobougg(IRE) —Zaneton (FR) (Mtoto)
2650a^{10}

Party Palace *H S Howe* a52 50
4 b m Auction House(USA) —Lady-Love (Pursuit Of Love)
14^{6} 1181^{12} 2641^{5}

Pasar Silbano (IRE) *G M Lyons* a86 97
2 b f Elnadim(USA) —Give A Whistle (IRE) (Mujadil (USA))
3466a^{4} (6320a)

Pas De Roland *S W Hall* 2
3 b g Tipsy Creek(USA) —Agara (Young Ern)
4283^{4} 5780^{6} 6433^{13}

Passage Of Time *H R A Cecil* 115
4 bl m Dansili—Clepsydra (Sadler's Wells (USA))
1807^{4} 2543^{14} (4192) 4623^{3} 5243^{5}

Passager (FR) *Mme C Head-Maarek* a81 117
5 bb g Anabaa(USA) —Passionnee (USA) (Woodman (USA))
5893^{5} 7162a^{6}

Passage To India (IRE) *J A Osborne* a67
2 ch f Indian Ridge—Kathy College (IRE) (College Chapel)
7117^{6} 7341^{4} 7561^{3} 7693^{2} 7784^{6}

Passato (GER) *R A Harris* a60 70
4 b g Lando(GER) —Passata (FR) (Polar Falcon (USA))
21^{7} 177^{9} 526^{7} 2957^{14} 3422^{8} 3569^{12}

Pas Seule (FR) *F Head* 84
3 br f Iron Mask(USA) —Only Alone (USA) (Rahy (USA))
3775a^{6} 5740a^{11}

Passionately Royal *M Brittain* a40 49
6 b g Royal Applause—Passionelle (Nashwan (USA))
80^{11} 770^{8}

Passionforfashion (IRE) *R Hannon* a58
3 b f Fasliyev(USA) —Jiving (Generous (IRE))
1144^{6}

Passion Fruit *C W Fairhurst* a72 92
7 b m Pursuit Of Love—Reine De Thebes (FR) (Darshaan)
2039^{6} 2890^{6} 3369^{7} 3646^{6} 4110^{6} 4417^{3} ◆ 4875^{8} 5635^{13} 6186^{9} 6484^{15} 6813^{11}

Pass The Port *D Haydn Jones* a88 87
7 ch g Docksider(USA) —One Of The Family (Alzao (USA))
96^{5} 260^{5} 561^{6} 838^{4} (981) 1568^{4} (1998) 2414^{3} 3044^{DSQ} 3630^{4} 5249^{12} 6288^{4} 6630^{5} 6838^{3}

Pasta Prayer *S A Callaghan* a60 55
3 br c Bertolini(USA) —Benedicite (Lomond (USA))
1036^{7} 1149^{5} ◆ 1897^{10} 4862^{14} 5186^{3} 5421^{2} 5574^{8} 6251^{9}

Past The Point (USA) *Eoin Harty* a118
4 b h Indian Charlie(USA) —Bit Of The Bubbly (USA) (A.P. Indy (USA))
5558a^{2}

Patavellian (IRE) *R Charlton* a41 109
10 bb g Machiavellian(USA) —Alessia (Caerleon (USA))
3722^{9} 4624^{17} 5109^{6} 6104^{6} 6676^{6} 6971^{6}

Patavium Prince (IRE) *Miss Jo Crowley* a54 81
5 ch g Titus Livius(FR) —Hoyland Common (IRE) (Common Grounds)
151^{2} 327^{3} 624^{6} 795^{5} 1282^{3} 1528^{11} 2355^{2} 2933^{2} (3761) (4186) 4696^{2} (5091) 6200^{12} 7255^{10} 7416^{7} ◆

Path To Glory *Miss Z C Davison* a50 58
4 b g Makbul—Just Glory (Glory Of Dancer)
2795^{8}

Patio *David Marnane* a93 93
3 b f Beat Hollow—Maze Garden (USA) (Riverman (USA))
496a^{4} 744a^{4} 6689a^{3} 7328a^{7}

Patkai (IRE) *Sir Michael Stoute* 108
3 ch c Indian Ridge—Olympienne (IRE) (Sadler's Wells (USA))
1443^{3} 1919^{2} ◆ (2610) (3196) ◆ 5263^{4}

Patrician's Glory (USA) *Jane Chapple-Hyam* 103
2 b c Proud Citizen(USA) —Landholder (USA) (Dixieland Band (USA))
(4151) 5507^{3} 6267^{6}

Patrickswell (IRE) *Marcus Callaghan* a68 70
4 gr g Iron Mask(USA) —Gladstone Street (IRE) (Waajib)
6366a^{7}

Patronne *Sir Mark Prescott*
2 b f Domedriver(IRE) —Pat Or Else (Alzao (USA))
7273^{8}

Pat's Legacy (USA) *D Shaw* a73
2 ch g Yankee Gentleman(USA) —Sugars For Nanny (USA) (Brocco (USA))
6575^{2}

Patsymartin *M G Quinlan* a40 27
3 ch g Bertolini(USA) —Souadah (USA) (General Holme (USA))
796^{11} 2084^{11}

Pattern Mark *Ollie Pears* 43
2 b g Mark Of Esteem(IRE) —Latch Key Lady (USA) (Tejano (USA))
6213^{10} 6789^{9} 7080^{11}

Patthepainter (GER) *K R Burke* a24 56
3 ch g Alhaarth(IRE) —Picturesque (Polish Precedent (USA))
1478^{8} (2926) 3555^{11} 5868^{7}

Patxaran (IRE) *P C Haslam* 34
6 b m Revoque(IRE) —Stargard (Polish Precedent (USA))
1136^{9}

Pauline's Prince *R Hollinshead* a64 64
6 b h Polar Prince(IRE) —Etma Rose (IRE) (Fairy King (USA))
75^{4}

Paul The Carpet (UAE) *G L Moore* a53 28
3 ch g Halling(USA) —Favoured (Chief's Crown (USA))
262^{7} 464^{7} (644) 784^{4} 1350^{7} 1710^{2} 3687^{12} 5215^{10}

Pauvic (IRE) *Mrs A Duffield* a48 67
5 b g Fayruz—Turntable (IRE) (Dolphin Street (FR))
32^{11} 151^{9} 255^{5} 871^{3} 972^{8}

Paveroc *Jane Chapple-Hyam* a95 93
3 b c Royal Applause—Take Liberties (Warning)
292a^{5} 567a^{6} 813a^{4} 4407^{15} 4830^{4} 5279^{15} 6196^{6}

Pavershooz *N Wilson* 86
3 b g Bahamian Bounty—Stormswept (USA) (Storm Bird (CAN))
2187^{5} 2526^{2} ◆ (3202) ◆ (3833) ◆ 4416^{3} 4900^{5} 6239^{13} 6976^{3}

Pawan (IRE) *Miss A Stokell* a87 97
8 ch g Cadeaux Genereux—Born To Glamour (Ajdal (USA))
5^{3} 84^{8} 1677^{2} 1908^{4} 2292^{4} 2598^{2} 2831^{7} 3489^{2} (3647) 4145^{3} 4437^{7} 4617^{2} 4869^{2} 5368^{5} 5495^{9} 5897^{11} 6153^{4} 6184^{5} 6354^{2} 6842^{6} 7047^{4} 7151^{5} 7181^{5} 7381^{10} 7614^{3} 7697^{4}

Pawn In Life (IRE) *Mrs R A Carr* a49 36
10 b g Midhish—Lady-Mumtaz (Martin John)
33^{8} 193^{7} 365^{2} 465^{5} 550^{8} 792^{12} 868^{4}

Paymaster In Chief *M D I Usher* a40 63
2 b g Minardi(USA) —Allegedly (IRE) (Alhaarth (IRE))
1693^{11} 2944^{10} 3444^{7} 3888^{6} 4119^{3} 4594^{4} 4706^{4} 5228^{7} 5960^{10}

Payne Relief (IRE) *M L W Bell* a55 54
3 bb f Desert Prince(IRE) —Saffron Crocus (Shareef Dancer (USA))
1166^{6} ◆ 1586^{6} 3397^{9}

Pay Parade *T D Easterby* 55
3 b f Mujahid(USA) —Bollin Sophie (Efisio)
1452^{6} 1751^{6}

Pay Pay Pay *P D Evans* a13 57
3 ch f Reel Buddy(USA) —Marabela (IRE) (Shernazar)
1694^{12} 2611^{8}

Pay The Grey *R Hannon* a40 36
3 gr f Daylami(IRE) —Dance Clear (IRE) (Marju (IRE))
1205^{5} 2694^{10} 2894^{7} 3264^{7}

Pay Time *R E Barr* a55 67
9 ch m Timeless Times(USA) —Payvashooz (Ballacashtal (CAN))
1891^{11} 2400^{9} 2781^{10} 3108^{9} 3834^{7} 4453^{5}

Peace Concluded *B R Millman* 68
2 b f Bertolini(USA) —Effie (Royal Academy (USA))
3349^{7} 3869^{2} 6358^{5}

Peaceful Rule (USA) *D Nicholls* 69
2 b c Peace Rules(USA) —La Cat (USA) (Mr Greeley (USA))
5716^{2}

Peace In Paradise (IRE) *J A R Toller* a38 9
2 b f Dubai Destination(USA) —Paola Maria (Daylami (IRE))
7141^{17} 7577^{7}

Peace Offering (IRE) *D Nicholls* a98 115
8 b g Victory Note(USA) —Amnesty Bay (Thatching)
3739^{6} (4159) (4957) 5259^{4} (6429) 6963a^{4}

Peace Royale (GER) *A Wohler* 103
3 bb f Sholokhov(IRE) —Peace Time (GER) (Surumu (GER))
(2065a) (3623a) 4675a^{5} 5596a^{2}

Peach Pearl *Y De Nicolay* 87
2 b f Invincible Spirit(IRE) —Paix Royale (Royal Academy (USA))
7549a^{2}

Peak (IRE) *H Morrison* a40
2 b c Exceed And Excel(AUS) —Glympse (IRE) (Spectrum (IRE))
7336^{13}

Peak District (IRE) *David Wachman* 100
4 b h Danehill(USA) —Coralita (IRE) (Night Shift (USA))
1495a^{5} 2685a^{7}

Peak Seasons (IRE) *M C Chapman* a52 36
5 ch g Raise A Grand(IRE) —Teresian Girl (IRE) (Glenstal (USA))
2623^{9} 2983^{10} 3218^{9}

Peal Park *B J Meehan* a64 26
2 b f Sulamani(IRE) —Cape Siren (Warning)
6081^{14} 6682^{5}

Pearl (IRE) *I A Wood* a74 71
4 b m Daylami(IRE) —Briery (IRE) (Salse (USA))
309^{7} 1273^{8} 1547^{4} 1933^{6} 4704^{13} 5154^{11} 5611^{10} 5802^{6} 6421^{8}

Pearl Dealer (IRE) *N J Vaughan* a75 69
3 b g Marju(IRE) —Anyaas (IRE) (Green Desert (USA))
1925^{9} 2570^{9} 3626^{6} 4174^{13} 4605^{4} 7368^{5} 7440^{7} 7665^{4}

Pearl Of Esteem *J Pearce* a43 53
5 ch m Mark Of Esteem(IRE) —Ribot's Pearl (Indian Ridge)
400^{9} 637^{4}

Pearl Of Manacor (IRE) *M R Channon* 67
2 b c Danehill Dancer(IRE) —Mountain Law (USA) (Mountain Cat (USA))
4665^{10} 5053^{3}

Pearl Of Valor (USA) *Dallas Stewart* a44
2 b f Medaglia D'Oro(USA) —Madeira M'Dear (USA) (Black Tie Affair)
6613a^{5}

Pearly King (USA) *M Al Muhairi* a92 99
5 br g Kingmambo(USA) —Mother Of Pearl (IRE) (Sadler's Wells (USA))
667a^{6} 740a^{8}

Pearly Wey *C G Cox* a92 104
5 b g Lujain(USA) —Dunkellin (USA) (Irish River (FR))
2831^{6} 4201^{9} ◆ (4586) 5275^{6} 6269^{15} 6468^{6}

Peas And Carrots (DEN) *L Reuterskiold Jr* a99 97
5 b g Final Appearance(IRE) —Dominet Hope (Primo Dominie)
(2233a) (2708a) 4676a^{2} 5335a^{3} 5958a^{2}

Peas In A Pod *J R Best* a53 57
3 ch g Kyllachy—Entwine (Primo Dominie)
1247^{4} 2055^{3} 2549^{2} 2922^{3} 3395^{5} 4793^{3} 6492^{4} 6751^{10} 6888^{10}

Peas 'n Beans (IRE) *T Keddy* a46 49
5 ch g Medicean—No Sugar Baby (FR) (Crystal Glitters (USA))
585^{14} 776^{8} 4751^{6} 5321^{5} 6252^{7} 6596^{8} 6824^{7} 7296^{6} 7401^{7} 7489^{6}

Pebble Rock (IRE) *J R Jenkins* 73
3 b g Sadler's Wells(USA) —Soviet Artic (FR) (Bering)
3223^{4} 3854^{9} 6001^{7} (Dead)

Peckforton *Mrs L Williamson* a29 36
2 b f Needwood Blade—Boavista (IRE) (Fayruz)
2048^{10} 3949^{8} 4499^{11} 6109^{7} 6406^{7}

Pecoiquen (CHI) *F Castro* a93 77
7 ch g Hussonet(USA) —Tonguie (ARG) (Big Play (USA))
2233a^{10} 4676a^{13}

Pedasus (USA) *T Keddy* a76
2 b c Fusaichi Pegasus(USA) —Butterfly Cove (USA) (Storm Cat (USA))
6621^{2} ◆

Pedestrian (IRE) *W J Haggas* 30
2 b f Royal Applause—Tropical Lass (IRE) (Ballad Rock)
4486^{7} 4747^{10}

Pediment *J R Fanshawe* a86 76
5 b f Desert Prince(IRE) —White Palace (Shirley Heights)
1685^{3} ◆ 2528^{2} 2885^{2} (3841) 5699^{4} 6416^{4}

Pedra Pompas *M Gasparini* 98
4 ch h Mark Of Esteem(IRE) —Edwardian Era (Bering)
7262a^{5}

Pedregal *R A Fahey* 53
2 b g Diktat—Bella Chica (IRE) (Bigstone (IRE))
2140^{7} 2909^{5} 3669^{10}

Peedee *G R Oldroyd* 18
3 b f Elmaamul(USA) —Dispol Diamond (Sharpo)
2912^{10} 7084^{7}

Pee Jay's Dream *M W Easterby* a71 74
6 ch g Vettori(IRE) —Langtry Lady (Pas De Seul)
1299^{3} (1482) ◆ 1824^{2} 2701^{3} 3143^{8}

Peer Pressure *B R Johnson* a54 64
3 gr g Verglas(IRE) —Mystery Quest (IRE) (Rainbow Quest (USA))
1743^{12} 2255^{14} 4165^{6} 4722^{10}

Pegasus Again (USA) *T G Mills* a80 95
3 b g Fusaichi Pegasus(USA) —Chit Chatter (USA) (Lost Soldier (USA))
902^{5} 1402^{6} 4312^{7} 4790^{11} 6949^{18} 7386^{11} 7603^{4}

Pegasus Dancer (FR) *R H York* a74 76
4 b g Danehill Dancer(IRE) —Maruru (IRE) (Fairy King (USA))
113^{3} 307^{2} 460^{5} 479^{3} 4476^{12} 4950^{4} (5374) 6711^{4} 7206^{4} 7540^{9}

Pegasus Lad (USA) *M Johnston* 86
2 bb g Fusaichi Pegasus(USA) —Leo Girl (USA) (Seattle Slew (USA))
2937^{3} 3245^{7} 3939^{2} (4570) 5274^{7}

Pegasus Mondrianus (GER) *Mrs S C Bradburne* 35
8 ch g Mondrian(GER) —Pineta (GER) (Armistice Day)
5540^{6}

Pegasus Prince (USA) *Miss J A Camacho* a72 67
4 b g Fusaichi Pegasus(USA) —Avian Eden (USA) (Storm Bird (CAN))
822^{7} (1262) (1679) ◆ 2185^{8} (2707) 3083^{2} 3710^{2} 4046^{7}

Peintre D'Argent (IRE) *H Morrison* a57 52
2 ch f Peintre Celebre(USA) —Petite-D-Argent (Noalto)
6945^{13} 7337^{10} 7607^{3} ◆

Peking Prince *A M Balding* 76
2 b g Passing Glance—Brandon Princess (Waajib)
(5213)

Pelham Crescent (IRE) *B Palling* a70 64
5 ch g Giant's Causeway(USA) —Sweet Times (Riverman (USA))
395^{3} 526^{6} 646^{5} 874^{6} 5779^{8} 6090^{6} 6825^{3} 7400^{7} 7656^{DSQ}

Pelican Prince *K R Burke* 85
3 b c Fraam—Nightingale Song (Tina's Pet)
1075^{10} (Dead)

Pelican Waters (IRE) *E F Vaughan* a86 96
4 b m Key Of Luck(USA) —Orlena (USA) (Gone West (USA))
958[10] *1331[6]* 2402[6]

Peligroso (FR) *Mario Hofer*
2 ch c Trempolino(USA) —Pitpit (IRE) (Rudimentary (USA))
(7264a)

Peltre *M Brittain* 43
3 b f Bertolini(USA) —Pewter Lass (Dowsing (USA))
2466[4] 4076[10] 4538[10]

Pelvoux (FR) *Robert Collet* 94
3 b c Diktat—Thiva (USA) (Concern (USA))
(385a)

Pembo *R A Harris* a52 52
3 b g Choisir(AUS) —Focosa (ITY) (In The Wings)
(5748) *6735[6]* *6912[11]* *7423[10]* *7469[13]*

Penang Cinta *P D Evans* a68 80
5 b g Halling(USA) —Penang Pearl (FR) (Bering)
963[12] *2264[4]* 2568[4] 3226[9] 3676[3] 4254[4] 4662[3] 5118[3] 6203[2] *6493[3]* 6983[4] *7563[5]*

Penang Princess *R M Beckett* a58 69
2 bg f Act One—Pulau Pinang (IRE) (Dolphin Street (FR))
5678[6] 6674[4] ◆

Penchesco (IRE) *Pat Eddery* a71 75
3 b g Orpen(USA) —Francesca (IRE) (Perugino (USA))
1957[7] 2673[4] 3180[3] (3799) 4741[4] 5863[10] *6683[8]*

Pencil Hill (IRE) *Tracey Collins* a59 105
3 b g Acclamation—Como (USA) (Cozzene (USA))
1783a[8]

Pendragon (USA) *Mrs L B Normile* 53
5 ch g Rahy(USA) —Turning Wheel (USA) (Seeking The Gold (USA))
1890[4] 2776[2] 3954[3]

Pendulum Star *W R Swinburn* a86 72
4 gr m Observatory(USA) —Pendulum (Pursuit Of Love)
1335[9] 2013[9]

Penel (IRE) *P T Midgley* a59 61
7 b g Orpen(USA) —Jayess Elle (Sabrehill (USA))
639[8] *1116[2]* 1391[2] 2394[3] 2927[13] 3662[4] 4215[10] 4898[5] 4961[11]

Peninsula Girl (IRE) *M R Channon* 72
2 b f Cape Cross(IRE) —Rio De Jumeirah (Seeking The Gold (USA))
4149[6] 4643[2] 5147[7] 6362[6]

Peninsular War *K R Burke* 80
2 b g Deportivo—Queens Jubilee (Cayman Kai (IRE))
1770[3] 2140[2] 2522[3]

Penkinella (FR) *A Couetil* 96
5 b m Pennekamp(USA) —Pimpinella (FR) (Highest Honor (FR))
1713a[8]

Pennine Rose *A Berry* 41
2 b f Reel Buddy(USA) —Adorable Cherub (USA) (Halo (USA))
3365[11] 3792[9] 4169[12] 4557[3] 6109[9] 6548[10]

Pennybid (IRE) *C R Wilson* 40
6 b g Benny The Dip(USA) —Stamatina (Warning)
4451[13] 4878[9] 6215[12]

Pennygee *S R Bowring* a58
4 b m Bertolini(USA) —Samadilla (IRE) (Mujadil (USA))
1372[6] *1709[3]* *2261[7]* 3481[11]

Penny Island (IRE) *John A Harris* 72
6 b g Trans Island—Sparklingsovereign (Sparkler)
(1383) 1895[2] 2667[4]

Penny's Gift *R Hannon* 105
2 b f Tobougg(IRE) —Happy Lady (FR) (Cadeaux Genereux)
2124[3] ◆ (2473) (2987) 3192[2] 4190[7] 5272[2] (6240) 6818[6] (7107)

Pennyspider (IRE) *M S Saunders* a36 69
3 b f Redback—Malacca (USA) (Danzig (USA))
1144[8] *1311[11]* 1529[7] (1699) 4106[3] 4325[4] 4584[2] 4767[4] 4958[9] (5217) 5902[6]

Penperth *J M P Eustace* a69
2 b f Xaar—Penelewey (Groom Dancer (USA))
7093[3] *7337[2]*

Penrice Castle *R Hannon* a66 69
3 br f Averti(IRE) —Stormont Castle (USA) (Irish River (FR))
1178[6] *1414[4]* 1699[8] 2602[6] 3526[8] *4028[5]* 4336[3] 4580[2] *(5421)* 5582[3] 6190[6] 6418[7]

Penryn *P T Midgley* 53
5 ch g Selkirk(USA) —Camcorder (Nashwan (USA))
3006[15] 3478[8]

Pension Policy (USA) *R Charlton* a76 68
3 bb f Danzig(USA) —Domain (USA) (Kris S (USA))
5278[4] 5786[4] *5995[3]* ◆ *(6683)* 6936[7] *7507[11]* *7771[3]*

Pentacle (FR) *J-Y Beaurain* a67
3 b g Anabaa Blue—Bumble (FR) (Pistolet Bleu (IRE))
687a[5]

Pentandra (IRE) *J G Given* a53 58
3 b f Bahri(USA) —Miss Willow Bend (USA) (Willow Hour (USA))
1817[8] 2659[5] 2982[13] *3816[9]* 4381[10] *7195[3]* *7362[8]* *7637[6]*

Pentathlon (IRE) *M Johnston* a78 61
3 b g Storming Home—Nawaiet (USA) (Zilzal (USA))
867[2] 1014[5] *(1342)*

Pentatonic *L M Cumani* 99
5 b m Giant's Causeway(USA) —Fascinating Rhythm (Slip Anchor)
1812[6] 2402[4] 3415[4]

Penthouse Serenade (IRE) *M Gonnelli* 98
4 br m Val Royal(FR) —Misty Peak (IRE) (Sri Pekan (USA))
2438a[7]

Penton Hook *P Winkworth* a64 71
2 gr g Lucky Owners(NZ) —Cosmic Star (Siberian Express (USA))
2601[6] *4304[3]* 5184[2]

Penzena *W J Knight* 57
2 ch f Tobougg(IRE) —Penmayne (Inchinor)
6392[8]

Peopleton Brook *B G Powell* a62 87
6 b h Compton Place—Merch Rhyd-Y-Grug (Sabrehill (USA))
1646[10] 1997[11] 2330[7] 2351[5] 2934[6] 3340[6] 3665[7] 4106[12] 4285[10] 4370[6] *5832[3]* 6650[4] 6925[9] *7295[6]* *7471[9]*

Peper Harow (IRE) *M D I Usher* 82
2 b f Compton Place—Faraway Moon (Distant Relative)
2835[4] 3496[4] 4403[14] 4786[2] 5530[3] 5746[5] 6426[18]

Pepin (IRE) *D Haydn Jones* a41
2 ch g King Charlemagne(USA) —Consignia (IRE) (Definite Article)
6531[12] *7165[7]* *7465[9]*

Pepito Collonges (FR) *Mrs L J Mongan* a42
5 b g Brier Creek(USA) —Berceuse Collonges (FR) (Vorias (USA))
2073[6] *3137[7]*

Pepper's Ghost *Miss J Feilden* a63 66
3 gr g Act One—Mill On The Floss (Mill Reef (USA))
784[2] ◆ 1140[3] *1678[6]* 1962[3] (Dead)

Peppertree Lane (IRE) *M Johnston* 114
5 ch h Peintre Celebre(USA) —Salonrolle (IRE) (Tirol)
1717[2] 2542[4] (2797) 3513a[3] 4100a[3] 5094[10] 6517a[2]

Pequeno Dinero (IRE) *C W Fairhurst* a34 59
3 b f Iron Mask(USA) —Mrs Kanning (Distant View (USA))
1478[9] 1950[7] *2868[5]* 4077[9] 5224[6] 5565[4] 6408[9]

Perception (IRE) *R Charlton* 69
2 b f Hawk Wing(USA) —Princesse Darsha (GER) (Darshaan)
4184[4] 5535[3] 6391[5]

Percolator *P F I Cole* a70 106
2 b f Kheleyf(USA) —Coffee Cream (Common Grounds)
995[2] *(1111)* (1886a) (3052a) (3774a) 4472a[2] 5245[12]

Percy Douglas *Miss A Stokell* a39 38
8 b g Elmaamul(USA) —Qualitair Dream (Dreams To Reality (USA))
153[7] *318[8]* *363[6]* *372[6]* 1893[13] 2777[12] 3212[9] *3565[7]* 3759[7] 3784[6] 4013[12] 4950[9] 5220[6]

Percys Corismatic *J Gallagher* 65
2 b f Systematic—Corisa (IRE) (Be My Guest (USA))
995[13] 1263[8] 2306[7] 2980[4] 3760[3] 4063[5]

Percyslavenderblue *J Gallagher* 25
3 gr f Orpen(USA) —Peacock Blue (IRE) (Octagonal (NZ))
4909[11] 5814[7] 6126[6]

Perez (IRE) *W Storey* a66 49
6 b g Mujadil(USA) —Kahla (Green Desert (USA))
1305[4] 1559[9]

Perez Prado (USA) *W Jarvis* 63
3 b c Kingmambo(USA) —Marisa (USA) (Swain (IRE))
2199[7]

Perfect Act *C G Cox* a84 87
3 b f Act One—Markova's Dance (Mark Of Esteem (IRE))
1441[11] 6981[15] *7386[3]* *7470[6]* *7737[9]* *7837[6]*

Perfect Affair (USA) *R M Beckett* 68
2 b c Perfect Soul(IRE) —Caribbean Affair (USA) (Red Ransom (USA))
6397[7]

Perfect Citizen (USA) *W R Swinburn* a79 86
2 ch c Proud Citizen(USA) —Near Mint (USA) (Dehere (USA))
3001[3] ◆ 4150[9] *(4728)* 5274[2] 6082[10] 6673[6]

Perfect Class *C G Cox* a37 58
2 b f Cape Cross(IRE) —Liberty (Singspiel (IRE))
5213[6] 5860[5] 6389[10] *7113[9]*

Perfect Flight *M Blanshard* 98
3 b f Hawk Wing(USA) —Pretty Girl (IRE) (Polish Precedent (USA))
1597[6] 2258[7] 2883[7] 4127[8] (4864) (5310) (5930) 6782[9] 7243[7]

Perfect Friend *S Kirk* a67 67
2 b f Reel Buddy(USA) —Four Legs Good (IRE) (Be My Guest (USA))
5021[5] 5213[4] (5746) 6362[2] 6673[10] *6954[6]* *7190[2]*

Perfect Hand *P Bary* 87
3 ch f Barathea(IRE) —Tarocchi (USA) (Affirmed (USA))
2743a[6]

Perfect Honour (IRE) *Joss Saville*
2 ch f Exceed And Excel(AUS) —Porcelana (IRE) (Highest Honor (FR))
5384[11] *6451[10]*

Perfect Polly *J Noseda* 103
3 b f Efisio—Nashira (Prince Sabo)
(1949) (2606) 6645[9] 7243[6]

Perfect Portrait *Mrs A Malzard* 52
8 ch g Selkirk(USA) —Flawless Image (USA) (The Minstrel (CAN))
5002a[7]

Perfect Practice *C G Cox* a67 19
4 ch m Medicean—Giusina Mia (USA) (Diesis)
(89) *209[3]* *340[5]* *537[10]*

Perfect Pride (USA) *C G Cox* 80
2 b f Forest Wildcat(USA) —Kisses To Yall (USA) (Copelan (USA))
3632[8] 4149[2] (5461) 5827[15]

Perfect Shot (IRE) *J L Dunlop* 77
2 b c High Chaparral(IRE) —Zoom Lens (IRE) (Caerleon (USA))
3519[4] 4184[10] 5314[2] 6524[3]

Perfect Silence *C G Cox* 81
3 b f Dansili—Perfect Echo (Lycius (USA))
3379[4] 5057[3] (6192) (6706)

Perfect Star *C G Cox* 105
4 b m Act One—Granted (FR) (Cadeaux Genereux)
4520[7] (4845) 5120[3]

Perfect Storm *W G M Turner* a54 57
9 b g Vettori(IRE) —Gorgeous Dancer (IRE) (Nordico (USA))
129[2] *394[2]* *569[2]* *631[4]* *2832[7]*

Perfect Stride *Sir Michael Stoute* 107
3 b c Oasis Dream—First (Highest Honor (FR))
1808[12] (4404) ◆ 4622[6] 6440[11]

Perfect Treasure (IRE) *J A R Toller* a79 84
5 ch m Night Shift(USA) —Pitrizza (IRE) (Machiavellian (USA))
(2860) 3222[8] 4198[4] 4723[15] *5789[5]* *6627[6]*

Perfect Truth (IRE) *A P O'Brien* a87 87
2 ch f Galileo(IRE) —Charroux (IRE) (Darshaan)
5924a[4] 6318a[12]

Pergamon (IRE) *J H M Gosden* 80
2 b c Dalakhani(IRE) —Pinaflore (FR) (Formidable (USA))
4421[3] 4954[2]

Perihelion (IRE) *A P O'Brien* 100
3 ch f Galileo(IRE) —Medicosma (USA) (The Minstrel (CAN))
3805a[7] 4006a[11] 4100a[7] 4833a[16] 5826[2] 6819[5]

Per Incanto (USA) *J L Dunlop* 118
4 bb h Street Cry(IRE) —Pappa Reale (Indian Ridge)
1420[16]

Perks (IRE) *J L Dunlop* 114
3 b g Selkirk(USA) —Green Charter (Green Desert (USA))
(1297) 1806[3] 3155[12] 3919[7] (4856) ◆ (5792) 6106[3]

Perlachy *D Shaw* a65 71
4 b g Kyllachy—Perfect Dream (Emperor Jones (USA))
29[3] *126[3]* *165[5]* *241[3]* *391[7]* *581[7]* *681[6]* *806[13]* *971[4]* (1416) 1634[13] 3159[3] 3825[12] 5629[4] 5871[3] (7809) ◆

Permanent Way (IRE) *R Lee* a85 71
5 b g Fantastic Light(USA) —Itab (USA) (Dayjur (USA))
757[4] *1076[14]* *6659[10]*

Permesso *F & L Camici* 108
3 b c Sakhee(USA) —Persian Filly (IRE) (Persian Bold)
2028a[2] 3075a[5] 7263a[2]

Perpetually (IRE) *M Johnston* 80
2 b c Singspiel(IRE) —Set In Motion (USA) (Mr Prospector (USA))
(4394)

Persian Buddy *Jamie Poulton* a64 46
2 b g Reel Buddy(USA) —Breeze Again (USA) (Favorite Trick (USA))
5066[14] *5678[5]* 6026[10]

Persian Flyer (IRE) *J W Mullins* a46 20
3 b g Persian Brave(IRE) —Raheen Flyer (IRE) (Shalford (IRE))
1114[6] 1835[9] 2919[9]

Persian Fox (IRE) *A G Juckes* a51 58
4 b g King Charlemagne(USA) —Persian Mistress (IRE) (Persian Bold)
127[2] *214[7]* *507[3]* *769[8]* *864[5]* 1694[10] 2932[3] 4250[9] 4891[12]

Persian Khanoom (IRE) *D E Cantillon* a42
6 b m Royal Applause—Kshessinskaya (Hadeer)
133[6] *242[8]* *401[10]*

Persian Memories (IRE) *J L Dunlop* a67 72
2 br f Indian Ridge—Persian Fantasy (Persian Bold)
3349[13] 4554[3] ◆ 6273[4] *6901[4]*

Persian Peril *G A Swinbank* a83 79
4 br g Erhaab(USA) —Brush Away (Ahonoora)
3294[6] 3711[7] (3996) 4419[11] (4814) 5092[13] (5418) 6108[3] *6839[2]* *7046[2]*

Persian Sea (UAE) *M A Jarvis* 97
3 b f Dubai Destination(USA) —Polska (USA) (Danzig (USA))
1964[3] 2571[3] (3452) ◆ (4110) 5273[9] (6053) ◆

Persian Storm (GER) *A Fabre* 111
4 b g Monsun(GER) —Private Life (FR) (Bering)
1240a[6] 1761a[6]

Persian Tomcat (IRE) *Miss J Feilden* 40
2 gr g One Cool Cat(USA) —Persian Mistress (IRE) (Persian Bold)
1399[11] 2054[6] 4769[6] 5159[5]

Persian Wish (IRE) *J W Mullins* a31 56
3 b c Persian Brave(IRE) —Ottawa (IRE) (Sir Mordred)
1059[9] 1367[11] 1896[2] 2342[11] 2931[3] 3574[7] 5169[9]

Persistent (IRE) *P T Midgley* a58 36
3 b g Cape Cross(IRE) —Insistent (USA) (Diesis)
803[3] ◆ *976[3]* 1186[10] *1592[4]* 2367[12] *3687[2]*

Persistently (USA) *Claude McGaughey III* a106
2 ch f Smoke Glacken(USA) —Just Reward (USA) (Deputy Minister (CAN))
6500a[2] *6967a[5]*

Persona (IRE) *B J McMath* a65 65
6 b m Night Shift(USA) —Alonsa (IRE) (Trempolino (USA))
91[11]

Personal Choice *M Brittain* 56
3 ch f Choisir(AUS) —Bonkers (Efisio)
3549[3] *3816[11]* 4044[12] 4381[9]

Personal Power (GER) *C Von Der Recke* a95 80
5 br h Dashing Blade—Personal Hope (GER) (Great Lakes)
605a[9]

Personify *J L Flint* a57 78
6 ch g Zafonic(USA) —Dignify (IRE) (Rainbow Quest (USA))
21[8] *101[4]* *341[6]* *1083[3]* 1280[10] 1528[7] 1895[3] 2353[5] 2863[9] 3604[5] 4322[4] 4707[3] 4807[7] *5869[4]* (6228) 6927[7] 7112[10]

Persuasive Power (USA) *Andrew Oliver* a48 43
2 b c Gone West(USA) —Mill Guineas (USA) (Salse (USA))
7554[8]

Pertemps Networks *M W Easterby* a82 77
4 b g Golden Snake(USA) —Society Girl (Shavian)
(1219) ◆ *1589[2]* *7447[2]* *7617[6]*

Pertemps Power *A D Smith* a55 51
4 b g Zaha(CAN) —Peristyle (Tolomeo)
5752[8]

Peruvian Prince (USA) *R A Fahey* a71 97
6 b g Silver Hawk(USA) —Inca Dove (USA) (Mr Prospector (USA))
1569[8] 2168[14] 2582[2] 2784[4] 3294[4] 3649[5] 4396[3] 4618[7] *5994[5]* 6312[4] *6659[9]* *6985[3]*

Peruvian Style (IRE) *J M Bradley* a56 57
7 b g Desert Style(IRE) —Lady's Vision (IRE) (Vision (USA))
3021[7] 3446[9] 3559[11] 4052[12] 4102[9] 4580[10] 4808[11]

Petara Bay (IRE) *T G Mills* 112
4 b h Peintre Celebre(USA) —Magnificient Style (USA) (Silver Hawk (USA))
1468[13] 1980[3] 2543[6] 3121[8] 3878[3] 4406[6] 5264[2] 6306[6]

Petella *C W Thornton* 65
2 b f Tamure(IRE) —Miss Petronella (Petoski)
5004[9] 6245[5] 6785[6]

Peter Grimes (IRE) *H J L Dunlop* 70
2 ch c Alhaarth(IRE) —Aldburgh (Bluebird (USA))
4311[8] 5022[3] 5314[6] 6362[7]

Peter Island (FR) *J Gallagher* a83 84
5 b g Dansili—Catania (USA) (Aloma's Ruler (USA))
2351[6] 2968[4] (3418) 3506[3] 3890[2] 4809[2] *5424[8]* (6200) 6340[9] *6699[2]* 6925[5]

Peter's Gift (IRE) *K A Ryan* a68 72
2 b f Catcher In The Rye(IRE) —Eastern Blue (IRE) (Be My Guest (USA))
2821[3] 3437[6] 4202[12] *6933[4]* (7220) *7426[2]* ◆

Peter's Joy (USA) *Jean-Rene Auvray* a7
3 b g Stravinsky(USA) —Jadarah (USA) (Red Ransom (USA))
244[7]

Peter's Storm (USA) *K A Ryan* a80 75
3 ch g Van Nistelrooy(USA) —Fairy Land Flyer (USA) (Lyphard's Wish (FR))
1576[7] 1925[7] 3202[3] 3724[2] 4000[5] 4615[10] 5714[10] *6169[2]* *7448[6]*

Peter Tchaikovsky *A P O'Brien* 92
2 ch c Dansili—Abbatiale (FR) (Kaldoun (FR))
3103[9] 4005a[7] 7029a[7]

Pethers Dancer (IRE) *W R Muir* a7
2 b c Kyllachy—La Piaf (FR) (Fabulous Dancer (USA))
7388[11] *7465[12]*

Petite Denise *M W Easterby* 33
2 ch f Tobougg(IRE) —Hilwa Ya Baladi (USA) (Smoke Glacken (USA))
2216[5] 2671[8] 2924[4]

Petite Mac *N Bycroft* a27 60
8 b m Timeless Times(USA) —Petite Elite (Anfield)
2009[10] 4073[9] 4919[8]

Petite Music (IRE) *T D Easterby* a25 32
3 b f Distant Music(USA) —Petite Maxine (Sharpo)
634[8] *780[5]* *845[6]* (Dead)

Petite Rocket (IRE) *A G Foster*
2 b f Fayruz—Courtisane (Persepolis (FR))
6787[18]

Petomic (IRE) *Christian Wroe* a60
3 ch c Dubai Destination(USA) —Petomi (Presidium)
3268[14]

Petrafied (FR) *David P Myerscough* 65
2 ch f Gold Away(IRE) —Thai Rose (USA) (Gulch (USA))
5924a[7]

Petroglyph *P Bowen* 64
4 ch g Indian Ridge—Madame Dubois (Legend Of France (USA))
4349[15] 4709[9]

Petrosian *T T Clement* a49 67
4 b g Sakhee(USA) —Arabis (Arazi (USA))
443[8] 4121[13] *4386[10]* 4592[8] 4814[3] *5917[13]* 6129[10] *6424[12]*

Petrovich (USA) *R A Harris* a68 108
5 ch h Giant's Causeway(USA) —Pharma (USA) (Theatrical)
561[7]

Petrovsky *M Johnston* a77 72
2 rg c Daylami(IRE) —Russian Society (Darshaan)
7200[3] ◆ *7336[5]* *(7699)*

Petsas Pleasure *L R James* a65 69
3 b g Observatory(USA) —Swynford Pleasure (Reprimand)
6480[3] 6776[9] *7148[2]*

Pevensey (IRE) *J J Quinn* a91 102
6 b g Danehill(USA) —Champaka (IRE) (Caerleon (USA))
1569[10] 2168[2] 3249[9] 3721[4] 4444[14] 5229[4] 6302[4] 6646[2]

Pezula *R T Phillips* 22
2 b f Diktat—Mashmoum (Lycius (USA))
6759[8]

Pezula Bay *J Noseda* a80
2 b c Oasis Dream—Easy To Love (USA) (Diesis)
7311[2] *(7709)*

Pha Mai Blue *J R Boyle* a79 77
3 b g Acclamation—Queen Of Silk (IRE) (Brief Truce (USA))
1215[2] 1347[3] *(1764)* 2407[8] *2945[9]* *3587[5]* 4252[13] *6467[9]* *6771[7]* *7557[11]* *7764[8]*

Phantom Serenade (IRE) *M Dods* 47
3 b g Orpen(USA) —Phantom Rain (Rainbow Quest (USA))
1751[4] 2673[8] 2912[9] 4019[6]

Phantom Whisper *B R Millman* a91 100
5 br g Makbul—La Belle Vie (Indian King (USA))
1985[3] 2426[7] 3647[2] (3905) 4437[12] 5096[5] 5897[7] 6269[23] (6676) 7245[7]

Pharaohs Justice (USA) *N P Littmoden* a80
3 br g Kafwain(USA) —Mary Linoa (USA) (L'Emigrant (USA))
7398[10]

Pharaohs Queen (IRE) *E A L Dunlop* a65 68
3 b f Bahri(USA) —Medway (IRE) (Shernazar)
1279[3] *2052[6]* 2376[6] 5815[6] *6437[8]* *6757[5]*

Pharly Green *G P Enright*
6 ch m Pharly(FR) —Pastures Green (Monksfield)
1539[11] *1905[6]*

Pheidias (IRE) *Mrs P Sly* a52 44
4 ch g Spectrum(IRE) —Danse Grecque (IRE) (Sadler's Wells (USA))
954[5] 1136[11]

Philanthropy *K A Ryan* 96
4 ch g Generous(IRE) —Clerio (Soviet Star (USA))
1625[9] 1920[8] 2582[7] 3045[2] 4396[4]

Philario (IRE) *K R Burke* a104 106
3 ch c Captain Rio—Salva (Grand Lodge (USA))
1400[7] 3041[3] 3488[8] 7243[14] 7421[8] 7740[2]

Philatelist (USA) *M A Jarvis* a107 108
4 b h Rahy(USA) —Polent (Polish Precedent (USA))
(592) 906[10] (1076) 1596[3] 7420[8] 7491[5]

Phillipina *Sir Michael Stoute* 76
2 b f Medicean—Discerning (Darshaan)
6076[7]

Philmack Dot Com *Miss Amy Weaver* a57
2 b g Traditionally(USA) —Lilli Marlane (Sri Pekan (USA))
7336[9] 7812[6]

Phinerine *Miss J E Foster* a56 30
5 ch g Bahamian Bounty—Golden Panda (Music Boy)
16[5] 64[3] 82[2] 168[7] 256[10] 3079[12] 3340[10] 4476[11]

Phluke *Eve Johnson Houghton* a89 95
7 b g Most Welcome—Phlirty (Pharly (FR))
1566[6] (2013) 2371[7] 2397[3] 2905[6] 3376[4] 3887[4] 4694[6] 5697[15] 6035[3] 6250[13]

Phoenix Enforcer *George Baker* a32 71
2 b f Bahamian Bounty—Kythia (IRE) (Kahyasi)
4763[5] 5430[9] 6391[3] 6745[7]

Phoenix Flight (IRE) *Sir Mark Prescott* a88 63
3 b g Hawk Wing(USA) —Firecrest (IRE) (Darshaan)
6450[8] 6758[4] (7070)

Phoenix Hill (IRE) *D R Gandolfo* a63 44
6 b g Montjeu(IRE) —Cielo Vodkamartini (USA) (Conquistador Cielo (USA))
471[5] 585[8] 4029[9]

Phoenix Ice (IRE) *M J P O'Brien* a93 87
4 b g Desert Style(IRE) —Alajyal (IRE) (Kris)
5550a[21] (6510a)

Phoenix Nights (IRE) *A Berry* 41
8 b g General Monash(USA) —Beauty Appeal (USA) (Shadeed (USA))
4556[13] 4739[9]

Phoenix Tower (USA) *H R A Cecil* a80 126
4 b h Chester House(USA) —Bionic (Zafonic (USA))
(1422) 2193[2] 3121[2] 3741[2] 5276[2]

Phone Call *Mouse Hamilton-Fairley* a63 37
5 b m Anabaa(USA) —Phone West (USA) (Gone West (USA))
39[2] 248[4] 436[3] 617[3] 779[2] 1127[6]

Pianoforte (USA) *E J Alston* a68 68
6 b g Grand Slam(USA) —Far Too Loud (CAN) (No Louder (CAN))
101[3] 250[2] (373) 559[5] 753[2] 841[7] 978[3] 1301[2] 1822[4] 1953[2] 2446[6] 2524[4] (2940) 3557[4] 4172[10] 4451[5] 4898[2] 5538[7]

Piano Key *M D I Usher* a51 50
4 ch m Distant Music(USA) —Ivorine (USA) (Blushing Groom (FR))
69[3] 169[5] 277[6] 613[3] (661) 869[5] 1408[13] (Dead)

Piano Man *J C Fox* a59 62
6 b g Atraf—Pinup (Risk Me (FR))
2617[9] 2795[5] 4491[5] 4664[5] 5008[10]

Piano Sonata *B W Hills* 72
3 b f Observatory(USA) —Matinee (Sadler's Wells (USA))
1599[6] 2119[5] 2885[7]

Piaras (IRE) *Vanja Sandrup*
3 b g Fath(USA) —Tartan Lane (IRE) (Posen (USA))
4918a[12]

Piazza San Pietro *C G Cox* 84
2 ch c Compton Place—Rainbow Spectrum (FR) (Spectrum (IRE))
3603[5] 5286[3] 5777[4] 6317a[11] 6677[2] 7020[3]

Piccaso's Sky *A B Haynes* a45 38
2 b c Piccolo—Skylark (Polar Falcon (USA))
1640[6] 7303[6] 7465[11]

Piccleyes *A J McCabe* a49 56
7 b g Piccolo—Dark Eyed Lady (IRE) (Exhibitioner)
846[6] 1675[8] 1906[8]

Piccolinda *W R Muir* a67 46
2 b f Piccolo—Belinda (Mizoram (USA))
5431[4] (5939) 6865[11]

Piccolo Diamante (USA) *S Parr* a62 48
4 bb g Three Wonders(USA) —Bafooz (USA) (Clever Trick (USA))
3340[13] 4107[16] 4542[4] 5152[10] (5832) 5916[2] 7195[9] 7254[11] (7382) 7503[3] 7591[8] 7745[10] 7778[10]

Piccolo Express *B P J Baugh* 25
2 b g Piccolo—Ashfield (Zilzal (USA))
4530[8] 5497[6] 6246[8]

Piccolo Mondo *P Winkworth* a70 73
2 b c Piccolo—Oriel Girl (Beveled (USA))
4126[6] 4980[8] 6342[2] 6877[2]

Piccolo Pete *T P Tate* 61
3 b g Piccolo—Goes A Treat (IRE) (Common Grounds)
1187[2] ◆ 1548[7] 1912[13] 2463[13]

Piccolo Pride *B G Powell* a12
3 ch g Piccolo—Jaycat (IRE) (Catrail (USA))
135[12] 222[6]

Piccolo Prince *Mrs Marjorie Fife* a58 64
7 ch g Piccolo—Aegean Flame (Anshan)
167[5] 256[9]

Piccostar *A B Haynes* a57 58
5 b m Piccolo—Anneliina (Cadeaux Genereux)
121[6] 264[5] 353[4] 445[2] 625[7] (713) 883[3] 933[7] 1275[7] 3021[13] 7022[11] 7195[12] 7625[11]

Pickering *E J Alston* a65 80
4 br g Prince Sabo—On The Wagon (Then Again)
2892[3] 3724[9] 3812[12] 4743[9] 5566[7]

Pickled Again *S Dow* a43 24
4 br m Piccolo—Queen Of Tides (IRE) (Soviet Star (USA))
4412[8] 4860[7] 5429[12] 5603[9]

Pick Of The Day (IRE) *J G Given* a52 40
3 ch g Choisir(AUS) —Reveuse De Jour (IRE) (Sadler's Wells (USA))
1380[7] 1701[5] 2008[16] 7632[5]

Picobella (GER) *A Wohler* 95
3 ch f Big Shuffle(USA) —Palanda (GER) (Lando (GER))
2655a[11]

Pic Up Sticks *B G Powell* a59 88
9 gr g Piccolo—Between The Sticks (Pharly (FR))
1928[12] 2242[7] 3062[5] 3352[5] 4103[8] 4154[5] 5101[7] 5467[2] 6131[6] 6339[2] 7295[10] 7377[7]

Pic White (BEL) *G L Moore* a17
3 b c Fabulous White(FR) —A Nous Cinq (FR) (Ataxerxes (GER))
7506[8]

Piece Of My Heart *R W Price* a68 75
3 b f Fasliyev(USA) —Cultured Pearl (IRE) (Lammtarra (USA))
2077[4] 4831[13]

Pie O My (IRE) *J Jay* a53
3 gr c Nayef(USA) —Sea Drift (FR) (Warning)
310[5] ◆ 454[5] 1710[5] 2552[13] 6594[13]

Piermarini *P T Midgley* a68 76
3 b g Singspiel(IRE) —Allespagne (USA) (Trempolino (USA))
131[4] 919[3] 7506[5] 7661[5]

Pietersen (IRE) *J E Long* a73 71
4 ch g Redback—Faye (Monsanto (FR))
177[8] 506[7] 639[6] 1752[11] 4306[14] 4863[10]

Pilca (FR) *D Carroll* 45
8 ch g Pistolet Bleu(IRE) —Caricoe (Baillamont (USA))
3589[5]

Pill (IRE) *A De Royer-Dupre* 89
2 gr f Linamix(FR) —Pharmacist (IRE) (Machiavellian (USA))
6519a[15]

Pilot Light *T D Easterby* 56
2 b g Falbrav(IRE) —Bollin Jeannie (Royal Applause)
3476[4] 3926[8] 4213[8]

Pimento (IRE) *J L Dunlop* 54
3 b g Red Ransom(USA) —Souffle (Zafonic (USA))
2681[9]

Pinafore *B R Millman* a6 42
6 ch m Fleetwood(IRE) —Shi Shi (Alnasr Alwasheek)
174[9] 365[11]

Pinball (IRE) *Patrick Morris* a50 32
2 b f Namid—Luceball (IRE) (Bluebird (USA))
7795[5]

Pinch Of Salt (IRE) *A M Balding* a99 96
5 b g Hussonet(USA) —Granita (CHI) (Roy (USA))
1076[7] 1544[2] 1766[3] 2711[2] 3249[14] 4191[2] 5677[6]

Pinea (GER) *Frau Nina Bach* 94
6 br m Platini(GER) —Pleasant Touch (GER) (Windwurf (GER))
2347a[6]

Pinewood Legend (IRE) *P D Niven* a49 60
6 br g Idris(IRE) —Blue Infanta (Chief Singer)
7776[3]

Pinewood Lulu *R C Guest* a7 64
3 b f Lujain(USA) —Lucy Glitters (USA) (Cryptoclearance (USA))
3031[12] 4650[6] 5565[6]

Pinkabout (IRE) *N Nevin* a44 83
4 br m Desert Style(IRE) —Dinka Raja (USA) (Woodman (USA))
6510a[13]

Pinkalicious (IRE) *M L W Bell* a37 30
2 b f Alhaarth(IRE) —Pilgrim's Way (USA) (Gone West (USA))
6559[11] 6884[12] 7259[9] 7353[13]

Pink Candie (FR) *Y De Nicolay* 88
2 b f Fath(USA) —Lyphard's Dream (IRE) (Lyphard (USA))
3052a[4] 4441a[7]

Pinkindie (USA) *E A L Dunlop* 85
3 ch c Smart Strike(CAN) —Only Princesses (USA) (Chief's Crown (USA))
1297[3] 1811[P] (Dead)

Pink Ivory *Saeed Bin Suroor* a77
3 ch f Sakhee(USA) —Anna Of Saxony (Ela-Mana-Mou)
(6935)

Pink Salmon *Mrs L J Mongan* a37 55
4 ch m Dr Fong(USA) —West Humble (Pharly (FR))
24[9] 455[7] (Dead)

Pinnacle Point *G L Moore* a52 64
3 ch g Best Of The Bests(IRE) —Alessandra (Generous (IRE))
3206[12] 3781[3] 4334[2] 4704[7] 5169[6] 6337[6] 7010[6]

Pinpoint (IRE) *W R Swinburn* a96 116
6 b g Pivotal—Alessia (GER) (Warning)
1990[4] 2503[4] 3195[3] 3740[11] 4504[2] 5508[6] 6201[4]

Pintano *J Howard Johnson* 72
3 ch g Dr Fong(USA) —Heckle (In The Wings)
3144[3] 3831[7] 4381[3] 5501[2] 5965[11] 6791[6]

Pioneerof The Nile (USA) *Bob Baffert* a115
2 bb c Empire Maker(USA) —Star Of Goshen (USA) (Lord At War (ARG))
6503a[3] 6997a[5] (7751a)

Pipedreamer *J H M Gosden* 121
4 b h Selkirk(USA) —Follow A Dream (USA) (Gone West (USA))
1422[3] ◆ 2543[3] ◆ 3121[3] 3741[3] (4436) 5276[4] 6816[7]

Piper's Song (IRE) *B G Powell* a69 84
5 gr g Distant Music(USA) —Dane's Lane (IRE) (Danehill (USA))
2535[11] 2904[4] (3337) 3736[4] 3947[6] 4500[7] 6052[12] 7202[15] 7354[12]

Pipoldchap (CHI) *Helena Fylking* a75 73
8 bb g The Great Shark(USA) —Tiquitiquiti (CHI) (Cresta Rider (USA))
2232a[4] 5957a[12]

Pippa Greene *P F I Cole* a85 101
4 b h Galileo(IRE) —Funny Girl (IRE) (Darshaan)
2168[6] 3721[11] (4444) 5229[10] 5853[16] 6817[26]

Pippbrook Gold *J R Boyle* a78 78
3 ch g Golden Snake(USA) —Chiaro (Safawan)
1876[2] (2772) 6675[9] 7014[5] 7307[3] 7507[10]

Pips Assertive Way *A W Carroll* a38 30
7 ch m Nomadic Way(USA) —Return To Brighton (Then Again)
4322[9] 5752[10]

Piquante *M L W Bell* 75
2 b f Selkirk(USA) —China (Royal Academy (USA))
6559[4]

Piquet *G F Bridgwater* a37 67
10 br m Mind Games—Petonellajill (Petong)
365[7] 471[10] 606[11]

Piran (IRE) *Evan Williams* a53
6 b g Orpen(USA) —Dancing At Lunasa (IRE) (Dancing Dissident (USA))
664[6]

Piscean (USA) *T Keddy* a93 83
3 bb c Stravinsky(USA) —Navasha (USA) (Woodman (USA))
1707[2] ◆ 1945[3] 3273[5] 3462[4] 3794[6] (4591) 5102[10] 5206[7] 5510[7] 6402[7] (6623) 6971[9] 7066[2]

Piste *B J Meehan* a69 69
2 b f Falbrav(IRE) —Arctic Char (Polar Falcon (USA))
2253[11] 3378[8] 5097[4] 5997[10] 6469[4] 6932[5]

Pitbull *Mrs G S Rees* a66 68
5 b g Makbul—Piccolo Cativo (Komaite (USA))
1486[6] 2001[2] 2335[4] 2697[9] 3029[5] 3258[6] 3725[2] 4001[4] 4597[4] 4813[3] 6250[6] 6537[2] 6862[8] 7167[4]

Piverina (IRE) *Miss J A Camacho* a55 55
3 b f Pivotal—Alassio (USA) (Gulch (USA))
1019[8] ◆ 1912[8] 2660[10] 3081[5] 3816[6] 4241[7] 4680[3] 5308[3] ◆ 6228[9] 6719[4] 7010[3] 7322[2] 7688[5]

Pivka *Sir Michael Stoute* a87 71
3 ch f Pivotal—Ghariba (Final Straw)
4730[3] 5076[4] 5608[2] 6566[3] (7026) (7307)

Pivotal Flame *E S McMahon* 97
6 b h Pivotal—Reddening (Blushing Flame (USA))
2680[7] (Dead)

Pivotal Point *P J Makin* 106
8 b g Pivotal—True Precision (Presidium)
2680[11] 3063[7] 3504[13]

Pivotal Queen (IRE) *L M Cumani* a73 78
3 ch f Pivotal—Queen Of Norway (USA) (Woodman (USA))
(7403)

Pixie's Blue (IRE) *J H M Gosden* a69 88
3 br f Hawk Wing(USA) —Isle Of Flame (Shirley Heights)
1499[4]

Place De L'Etoile (IRE) *J E Hammond* 103
3 b f Sadler's Wells(USA) —Sweet Emotion (IRE) (Bering)
2237a[6] 7431a[8]

Place The Duchess *D W P Arbuthnot* 51
2 b f Compton Place—Barrantes (Distant Relative)
3032[6] 4705[6] 5530[7] 6023[6] 6666[7]

Plain Champagne (IRE) *Dr J R J Naylor* a35 36
6 b m Victory Note(USA) —Paddys Cocktail (IRE) (Tremblant)
2512[6] 3160[7] 3631[9]

Plaisterer *C F Wall* a58 75
3 b f Best Of The Bests(IRE) —Lumiere D'Espoir (FR) (Saumarez)
4342[8] 4860[5] 5182[2] 6703[2] 7091[5]

Plaka (FR) *W M Brisbourne* a57 57
3 gr f Verglas(IRE) —Top Speed (IRE) (Wolfhound (USA))
20[4] 288[8] 556[5] 665[7]

Plan (USA) *A P O'Brien* 113
3 ch c Storm Cat(USA) —Spain (USA) (Thunder Gulch (USA))
1808[8] 3536a[4] (3983a) 4887a[2]

Plane Painter (IRE) *M Johnston* a77 83
4 b g Orpen(USA) —Flight Sequence (Polar Falcon (USA))
1472[7] 1984[4] 2332[4] 2525[2] 3179[2]

Planetarium *M Johnston* 93
3 gr c Fantastic Light(USA) —Karsiyaka (IRE) (Kahyasi)
1557[3] 3719[9]

Planetary Motion (USA) *M Johnston* a74 27
3 gr c Gone West(USA) —Gaviola (USA) (Cozzene (USA))
6393[12] 7026[8] (7822)

Planet Paradise (IRE) *D Shaw* a46 46
3 b f Spinning World(USA) —Just Heavens Gate (Slip Anchor)
557[6] 709[5] 767[3] 876[6] 952[3] 1120[3] 1257[5] 2074[6] 2268[7] 2774[4] 3030[13] 3332[8] 3695[8]

Planet Queen *K R Burke* a29 56
3 ch f Bahamian Bounty—Ash Moon (IRE) (General Monash (USA))
2490[3] 3298[11] 3753[5] 5258[9] 5389[9] 6150[4] 6409[10] 6733[9]

Plateau *C R Dore* a77 72
9 b g Zamindar(USA) —Painted Desert (Green Desert (USA))
109[5] 353[3] 432[3] 523[3] 530[6] 858[8] 1029[8]

Platoche (IRE) *P W Chapple-Hyam* 62
3 b c Galileo(IRE) —Political Parody (USA) (Doonesbury (USA))
991[3] 1539[10] 2056[8]

Plavius (USA) *Saeed Bin Suroor* a74 74
3 bb c Danzig(USA) —Sharp Minister (CAN) (Deputy Minister (CAN))
4085[2] 4620[4] 6047[2]

Players Please (USA) *M Johnston* a92 103
4 ch g Theatrical—Miss Tobacco (USA) (Forty Niner (USA))
1076[13] 2830[15] 3249[15] 4444[7] 4508[4] 5229[17] 5894[10] 6302[6] 6479[2]

Playfellow (IRE) *M A Jarvis* a93 108
2 bb c Kheleyf(USA) —Love And Adventure (USA) (Halling (USA))
(4176) ◆ (5615) 5889[3] (6860)

Playful *R M Beckett* a83 87
5 b m Piccolo—Autumn Affair (Lugana Beach)
2219[5] 3062[2] 3680[5] 4668[6] 6699[9] 7393[9]

Playful Asset (IRE) *R M Beckett* a48 60
2 ch f Johannesburg(USA) —Twickin (USA) (Two Punch (USA))
6122[9] 7073[9]

Play It Sam *W R Swinburn* 63
2 b c Bahamian Bounty—Bombalarina (IRE) (Barathea (IRE))
6359[7] 6715 [7]

Playtotheaudience *R A Fahey* a68 57
5 b g Royal Applause—Flyfisher (USA) (Riverman (USA))
(861) (1029) 1260[4] 1604[3] 2274[9] 2806[6] 3329[7] 4503[7] 4679[7] 5008[4] (Dead)

Play To Win (IRE) *D R C Elsworth* a62 62
2 b c Singspiel(IRE) —Spot Prize (USA) (Seattle Dancer (USA))
5859[10] 6425[9] 6778[8] 7505[5] 7718[3]

Play Up Pompey *J J Bridger* a59 28
6 b g Dansili—Search For Love (FR) (Groom Dancer (USA))
10[4] 180[5] 300[6] 611[6] 795[3] 1056[3] 1152[3] 1282[7] 1643[13] 4155[7] 4568[12] 4635[4] 5631[3] 5912[6] 6728[7] 7078[3] 7261[12] 7469[4] (7599) 7676[4] 7742[7]

Playwithmyheart *T Doumen* 86
2 b f Diktat—Treasure Trove (USA) (The Minstrel (CAN))
7449a[5]

Please Sing *M R Channon* 98
2 b f Royal Applause—Persian Song (Persian Bold)
(2479) ◆ 3192[11] (3851) 5272[5] 6519a[11]

Plenilune (IRE) *M Brittain* 68
3 b c Fantastic Light(USA) —Kathleen's Dream (USA) (Last Tycoon)
1298[4] 1429[3] 1628[7] 2488[5] 2699[8] 5362[2] 6216[11] 6868[14]

Plenty Of Action (USA) *M J Wallace* a52
3 bb f Hennessy(USA) —Mary Had A Lot (USA) (Double Zeus (USA))
19[4]

Plotting *K A Ryan* a67 71
2 b f Medicean—Quite Happy (IRE) (Statoblest)
4109[2] 5241[10] (6351) 7103a[8] 7335[9]

Plumage *M Blanshard* a64 59
3 b f Royal Applause—Cask (Be My Chief (USA))
2257[12] 3061[6] 3679[5] 4368[3] 4825[2] 6088[2] 6353[7] 6746[7]

Plumania *A Fabre* 107
2 b f Anabaa(USA) —Featherquest (Rainbow Quest (USA))
6519a[4] ◆

Plum Asset (USA) *R M Beckett* a65 57
3 b f Doneraile Court(USA) —Twickin (USA) (Two Punch (USA))
1144[5] 1709[7] 2455[6] 3507[10] 5426[10] 6437[11]

Plum Pudding (IRE) *R Hannon* a97 112
5 b g Elnadim(USA) —Karayb (IRE) (Last Tycoon)
594[5] ◆ 834[2] 958[7] 1469[9] 1545[3] 1942[10] (2371) 2595[13] 3413[9] 4405[25] (6478) (6783) 6975[11]

Plush *Tom Dascombe* a74 36
5 ch g Medicean—Glorious (Nashwan (USA))
3583[9] 3951[10] 6955[4] (7287) (7340) ◆ 7392[6] (7656) 7750[2] ◆

Poaka Beck (IRE) *R F Fisher* 32
2 b c Fath(USA) —Star Of The Future (USA) (El Gran Senor (USA))
4289[10]

Pochard *J M P Eustace* a61 58
5 br m Inchinor—Pomorie (IRE) (Be My Guest (USA))
461[6] 2643[2] ◆ 3137[8]

Pocket Queens *Miss D Mountain*
2 ch f Auction House(USA) —Sweet Harriet (Hector Protector (USA))
6030[16]

Pocket's Pick (IRE) *G L Moore* 83
2 ch g Exceed And Excel(AUS) —Swizzle (Efisio)
2541[7] 2999[3] 3485[2] 4190[17] 4510[11] 4768[5] 5466[8]

Pocket Too *M Salaman* a82 76
5 b g Fleetwood(IRE) —Pocket Venus (IRE) (King's Theatre (IRE))
91[4] (198) (268) (1501) 3942[13]

Pocketwood *Jean-Rene Auvray* a72 79
6 b g Fleetwood(IRE) —Pocket Venus (IRE) (King's Theatre (IRE))
47[4] 198[3] 2153[7] 2621[2] (3917) 4892[6] (6558) 6983[3]

Poet *A P O'Brien* 99
3 b c Pivotal—Hyabella (Shirley Heights)
1402[3]

Pointillist (IRE) *R M Beckett* 61
2 b f Peintre Celebre(USA) —For Example (USA) (Northern Baby (CAN))
6398[5]

Point Of Light *Sir Mark Prescott* a45 55
2 b c Pivotal—Lighthouse (Warning)
5905[8] 6109[3] 6701[10]

Points Of View *Sir Mark Prescott* a88 84
3 b g Galileo(IRE) —On Point (Kris)
3251[5] 4918a[13] 5682[7] 6033[5] 6839[5]

Pokettas (FR) *C Alonso Pena* 61
4 br m Kaldou Star—Pocantas (FR) (Cosmopolitan (FR))
7487a[0]

Pokfulham (IRE) *A P Jarvis* a51 68
2 b g Mull Of Kintyre(USA) —Marjinal (Marju (IRE))
1447[7] 1987[9] 4488[6] 4827[2] 5460[3] 6065[2] 6877[6]

Polan (FR) *R Martin Sanchez* 97
3 ch c Golan(IRE) —Slinky (Ashkalani (IRE))
(5927a)

Polar Annie *M S Saunders* a73 83
3 b f Fraam—Willisa (Polar Falcon (USA))
3487[2] 3944[3] 4433[3] (5056) 5490[3] 6402[14]

Polar Force *Mrs C A Dunnett* a58 69
8 ch g Polar Falcon(USA) —Irish Light (USA) (Irish River (FR))
191[12] 625[6] 1185[9] (1455) 1865[12] 2075[3] 2706[7] 3033[6] 5152[9]

Polar Wind (ITY) *R Menichetti* a50 99
4 ch h Rob's Spirit(USA) —Miss Buffy (Polar Falcon (USA))
2029a[12] 7253a[12] 7349a[7]

Polenta (ITY) *F & L Camici* 95
3 b f Shantou(USA) —Mugnaga (IRE) (Catrail (USA))
3076a[16]

Police Officer *W J Musson* a48 48
3 b g Mark Of Esteem(IRE) —No Rehearsal (FR) (Baillamont (USA))
2552[9] 2926[3]

Poligold (IRE) *C Laffon-Parias* a76 80
3 b c Poliglote—Soft Gold (USA) (Gulch (USA))
4010a[16]

Polish Corridor *M Dods* 73
9 b g Danzig Connection(USA) —Possibility (Robellino (USA))
1217[5] 1613[8] 2155[8] 2787[5] 3725[5] 4015[6] 4597[2] 4898[8] 5538[5] 6786[5]

Polished *K J Burke* 35
9 ch g Danzig Connection(USA) —Glitter (FR) (Reliance II)
1184[8]

Polish Power (GER) *J S Moore* a96 96
8 br h Halling(USA) —Polish Queen (Polish Precedent (USA))
61[2] 410[6] 757[2] 908[7] (1793) (2059) 4003a[13] 4844[8] 5349[14] 6033[10] 7025[8] 7150[4]

Polish Pride *M Brittain* 89
2 b f Polish Precedent(USA) —Purple Tiger (IRE) (Rainbow Quest (USA))
(1303) 1813[2] 3978[4] 4187[5] 4640[3] (4816) ◆ 5447[10] 5855[3] 6067[2] 6483[8] 7109[5]

Polish Priory (IRE) *P D Evans* a43 64
3 b f Polish Precedent(USA) —Glenstal Priory (Glenstal (USA))
1135[2] 1487[3] 1550[13]

Polish Prize *W R Swinburn* a51 50
4 b g Polish Precedent(USA) —Forest Prize (Charnwood Forest (IRE))
(236) 392[3]

Polish Red *G G Margarson* 83
4 b g Polish Precedent(USA) —Norcroft Joy (Rock Hopper)
1568[14] 1877[9] 2682[7] 3010[8]

Polish Star *Miss L A Perratt* a27 52
4 b g Polish Precedent(USA) —Apennina (USA) (Gulch (USA))
2747[6] 3201[10] 4015[9] 4629[5] 4949[8] 5420[6] 6405[8] 6823[8]

Polish World (USA) *T J Etherington* a68 69
4 b g Danzig(USA) —Welcometotheworld (USA) (Woodman (USA))
6773[5] 7226[4] 7471[7]

Politeia (USA) *R Hannon* a70 73
3 bb f Mr Greeley(USA) —Ujane (USA) (Theatrical)
2678[2] 3322[6] 3886[5] 4527[4] 5428[3] 6703[3]

Political Matters (IRE) *T P Tate*
2 br g Diktat—Timewee (USA) (Romanov (IRE))
6008[12]

Pollish *A Berry* a40 41
2 b f Polish Precedent(USA) —Fizzy Fiona (Efisio)
4456[6] 4965[7] 5989[7] 6764[7] 7044[5] 7199[7]

Polly's Choice (IRE) *R Hannon* a63 63
2 ch f Hawk Wing(USA) —Scanno's Choice (IRE) (Pennine Walk)
3027[5] 3373[7] 3913[7] 5228[12] 6118[14] 7016[4] 7275[4] 7389[6]

Polly's Mark (IRE) *C G Cox* 73
2 b f Mark Of Esteem(IRE) —Kotdiji (Mtoto)
3913[3] 5227[4] 6291[2]

Polmaily *J Akehurst* 78
3 b g Hawk Wing(USA) —Hampton Lucy (IRE) (Anabaa (USA))
1526[5] 1918[4] 2311[8] 2918[4] 3419[2] 7143[11]

Polyanta (GER) *Markus Klug* 89
6 b m Lomitas—Pierette (GER) (Local Suitor (USA))
3751a[3]

Polychrome *John Berry* a51 54
3 b f Polish Precedent(USA) —Pantone (Spectrum (IRE))
543[7] 1125[5] 1740[3] 2208[14] 4260[9] 4564[14]

Pompeyano (IRE) *C Laffon-Parias* 101
3 b c Rainbow Quest(USA) —Lady Lodger (Be My Guest (USA))
4959a[6] 5927a[2]

Pondapie (IRE) *R M Whitaker* 73
3 b g Highest Honor(FR) —Fruhling Feuer (FR) (Green Tune (USA))
1628[3] 2173[7] 3174[4] 4173[2] 4902[9] (6185) 6529[11]

Pont Des Arts (FR) *K Schafflutzel* 100
4 b h Kingsalsa(USA) —Magic Arts (IRE) (Fairy King (USA))
5528a[5] 6992a[5]

Ponte Tresa (FR) *Y De Nicolay* 112
5 b m Sicyos(USA) —Ponte Brolla (FR) (Highest Honor (FR))
1663a[3] 2236a[3] 4041a[6] (5333a) 6497a[7]

Ponte Vecchio (IRE) *J R Boyle* a46 39
4 b g Trans Island—Gino Lady (IRE) (Perugino (USA))
99[6] 160[4] 242[3] 468[9] 715[3] 821[5]

Ponting (IRE) *R M Beckett* a53 61
2 bb g Clodovil(IRE) —Polar Lady (Polar Falcon (USA))
6341[5] 6953[5]

Pont Wood *Mrs N S Evans* a59 1
4 b g Iron Mask(USA) —Bajan Rose (Dashing Blade)
11[13]

Ponty Rossa (IRE) *T D Easterby* a78 97
4 ch m Distant Music(USA) —Danish Gem (Danehill (USA))
6153[5] 6947[11] 7245[20]

Popiel *Saeed Bin Suroor* 77
2 b c Halling(USA) —Polska (USA) (Danzig (USA))
5165[3] 5599[2] 6539[3] 6789[3]

Pop Music (IRE) *Ms J S Doyle* a70 64
5 b g Tagula(IRE) —Easy Pop (IRE) (Shernazar)
196[2] 4268[8] 4727[13] 5105[7] 5427[4] 5799[10] 6544[9] 6827[5] 7027[9] 7392[5] 7535[10] 7596[7] 7605[5]

Poppets Sweetlove *A B Haynes* 70
4 b m Foxhound(USA) —Our Poppet (IRE) (Warning)
1126[3] 2097[11] 2622[3] 4708[7] 5119[7] 5318[3] (6036) 6544[11] 6889[5]

Poppy Day *M W Easterby* 53
5 b m Bal Harbour—Snappy (First Trump)
4689[6] 4961[8] 5303[8] 5776[5] 5993[10] 6727[9]

Poppy Dean (IRE) *J G Portman* a58 58
3 ch f Night Shift(USA) —Miss Devious (IRE) (Dr Devious (IRE))
1147[12] 2719[8] 3763[6] 4326[9] 6913[10] 7678[2]

Poppy Gregg *Dr J R J Naylor* 49
3 b f Tamure(IRE) —Opalette (Sharrood (USA))
1695[11] 2123[11] 2971[9] 3562[12] 3843[10] 4366[4] 5269[8]

Poppy Red *C J Gray* a53 42
3 ch f Lear Spear(USA) —Pooka's Daughter (IRE) (Eagle Eyed (USA))
704[2] 1243[6] 1710[9] 1938[13] 2611[11] 2932[5] 3359[8] 3605[3] 4052[10] 4707[10] 6896[12] 7736[9] 7831[2]

Poppy's Rose *I W McInnes* a53 72
4 b m Diktat—Perfect Peach (Lycius (USA))
1188[4] 1449[9] 1867[3] 2039[3] 2251[3] 2968[5] 3260[3] 3481[5] 3883[5] 4174[2] 4393[5]

Porta Westfalica (IRE) *W Hickst* 99
3 ch f Noverre(USA) —Silk Point (IRE) (Barathea (IRE))
4675a[8]

Port De La Ponche *P F I Cole* a55 66
2 b f Dr Fong(USA) —Darling Harbour (USA) (Candy Stripes (USA))
4692[4] 7577[9] 7708[7] 7824[7]

Porthole (USA) *B W Hills* a82 87
3 rg c Mizzen Mast(USA) —Privity (USA) (Private Account (USA))
(2681) ◆ 3527[9] 4552[8] 5449[4] 5942[6]

Portland *K J Burke* a25 84
5 b g Zafonic(USA) —Bayswater (Caerleon (USA))
512[8]

Portodora (USA) *H R A Cecil* a79 89
3 b f Kingmambo(USA) —High Walden (USA) (El Gran Senor (USA))
1423[5] (1946) ◆ 3272[8] 4641[2] (5185) 6471[6]

Port Of Spain (USA) *A P O'Brien* 80
4 b h Danehill(USA) —Dietrich (USA) (Storm Cat (USA))
1497a[8] 3532a[10]

Porto Santana (IRE) *D Nicholls* a66 75
3 ch g Captain Rio—River Dance (GER) (Lomitas)
826a[7] 4962[13] 5501[12]

Port Quin *G Wragg* a69 77
3 ch g Dr Fong(USA) —Saphila (IRE) (Sadler's Wells (USA))
2109[12] 3134[11] 4894[10]

Port Ronan (USA) *J S Wainwright* 59
2 rg c Cozzene(USA) —Amber Token (USA) (Hennessy (USA))
2186[11] 2592[9] 3055[4] 3365[9] 4456[5] 5414[5]

Portrush Storm *D Carroll* a8 71
3 ch f Observatory(USA) —Overcast (IRE) (Caerleon (USA))
1452[9] 1737[6] 2367[4] (2659) 2907[7] 5773[11] 6629[13]

Portugal *T J Etherington* 20
3 ch f Bahamian Bounty—Swynford Elegance (Charmer)
2823[11] 3712[10] 3953[10]

Portugese Caddy (IRE) *P Winkworth* 79
2 b g Great Palm(USA) —Paintbrush (IRE) (Groom Dancer (USA))
(3323) (5756) 6193[4]

Poseidon Adventure (IRE) *W Figge* 116
5 b h Sadler's Wells(USA) —Fanny Cerrito (USA) (Gulch (USA))
1237a[8] 1662a[3] 2440a[3] 3540a[4] 4041a[11] 5557a[3] 6324a[2] 6854a[3] 7682a[10]

Positive Move (IRE) *Gerard Keane* a39 60
4 ch g Daggers Drawn(USA) —Ostjessy (IRE) (In The Wings)
320[5]

Positive Opinion *B R Millman* a31 55
2 ch f Observatory(USA) —St Edith (IRE) (Desert King (IRE))
3267[10] 3674[5] 4296[11] 4823[6] 5778[8]

Positivity *B Smart* 67
2 ch f Monsieur Bond(IRE) —Pretty Pollyanna (General Assembly (USA))
4045[2] 4499[3] 6240[14] 7015[6] 7198[4]

Poster (IRE) *L M Cumani* a94 82
2 b c Johannesburg(USA) —Whipped Queen (USA) (Kingmambo (USA))
4062[4] (4890) (5711) ◆ 6284[4]

Postman *B Smart* 62
2 b g Dr Fong(USA) —Mail The Desert (IRE) (Desert Prince (IRE))
4014[4] ◆ 4394[7] 5387[10] 7016[12]

Postmaster *R Ingram* a61 53
6 b g Dansili—Post Modern (USA) (Nureyev (USA))
123[4] 267[5] 389[3] 517[6] 795[7] 1142[5] 1207[2] 1747[6] 2943[7] 3162[3] 3588[6] 3732[3] 3839[3] 4365[5] 5020[10]

Potemkin (USA) *A King* 61
3 bb g Van Nistelrooy(USA) —Bolshoia (USA) (Moscow Ballet (USA))
2280[7] 2719[3]

Potentiale (IRE) *J W Hills* a80 80
4 ch g Singspiel(IRE) —No Frills (IRE) (Darshaan)
1963[5] 2304[2] 3010[3] 4645[7] 5512[3] 5999[2] 6243[5] 7096[4] 7385[2] 7563[4] 7715[5]

Poulaine Bleue *M L W Bell* a41 39
3 b f Bertolini(USA) —Blue Indigo (FR) (Pistolet Bleu (IRE))
1535[11] 1869[6] 2455[7] 3816[5] 4180[7]

Pouvoir Absolu *E Lellouche* 91
3 b c Sadler's Wells(USA) —Pine Chip (USA) (Nureyev (USA))
6921a[4]

Power Ballad *W J Knight* a59 63
4 ch m Titus Livius(FR) —Sea Music (Inchinor)
1287[6] 1645[8] 2722[12]

Power Elite (IRE) *K A Morgan* a48 97
8 gr g Linamix(FR) —Hawas (Mujtahid (USA))
6078[8] 6410[4] 6698[11]

Powerful Speed *L Brogi* 95
3 b f Compton Place—Gandini (Night Shift (USA))
1659a[11]

Power Of Future (GER) *Andrew Oliver* a66 96
5 ch m Definite Article—Pik Konigin (GER) (Konigsstuhl (GER))
3104[11] 4100a[6] 4493a[2]

Power Of Speech *J Gallagher*
3 b g Advise(FR) —Marsara (Never So Bold)
1741[8]

Power Player *D J Coakley* a69 48
4 br g Diktat—Royal Patron (Royal Academy (USA))
1563[5] 2414[7] 3035[7] 4819[8]

Power Politics (USA) *M Al Muhairi* a94 93
5 b h Seeking The Gold(USA) —Stormy Pick (USA) (Storm Creek (USA))
295a[10]

Power Shared (IRE) *P G Murphy* a67 71
4 gr g Kendor(FR) —Striking Pose (IRE) (Darshaan)
524[2]

Poyle Dee Dee *R M Beckett* a56 71
3 b f Oasis Dream—Poyle Fizz (Damister (USA))
3379[9] 4277[3] 5023[4] 5402[4] 6048[7] 6363[5] 6896[4]

Poyle Meg *R M Beckett* a74 79
2 b f Dansili—Lost In Lucca (Inchinor)
4251[2] ◆ 4786[3] 5461[4] 6240[7] 6696[3] 7458[2]

Practicallyperfect (IRE) *M J Wallace* a74 78
4 b m King Charlemagne(USA) —Morningsurprice (USA) (Future Storm (USA))
(2537) 3376[5]

Pragmatism *M Johnston* 77
3 b g Kingmambo(USA) —Sheer Reason (USA) (Danzig (USA))
5076[3] 6055[10]

Pragmatist *P Winkworth* a68 68
4 b m Piccolo—Shi Shi (Alnasr Alwasheek)
1867[8] (2556) 3383[12] 4825[4] 5755[10]

Prairie Hawk (USA) *Tim Vaughan* a59 61
3 bb g Hawk Wing(USA) —Lady Carla (Caerleon (USA))
5995[13] 6280[8] (7688) ◆ 7722[6]

Prairie Spirit (FR) *E Lellouche* 93
4 ch g Grape Tree Road—Prairie Runner (IRE) (Arazi (USA))
4880a[9]

Prairie Storm *A M Balding* 85
3 b g Storming Home—Last Dream (IRE) (Alzao (USA))
1526[6] 2151[5] 2564[3] 6899[2] (7202)

Praise Of Folly *P Winkworth* a47 55
2 b f Selkirk(USA) —Song Of Hope (Chief Singer)
5534[7] 6167[12]

Pravda Street *P F I Cole* a74 91
3 ch g Soviet Star(USA) —Sari (Faustus (USA))
(1125) ◆ 1441[7]

Prayer Boat (IRE) *John Joseph Murphy* a82 72
2 b c Oasis Dream—Reasonably Devout (CAN) (St Jovite (USA))
5296a[9] 7214[2] 7334[5]

Precious Boy (GER) *W Hickst* 118
3 br c Big Shuffle(USA) —Pretty Su (IRE) (Surumu (GER))
1514a[2] (2066a) (6322a)

Precious Dancer *P Bowen* a46 21
5 b g Sinndar(IRE) —Crodelle (IRE) (Formidable (USA))
2682[9]

Precious Kitten (USA) *Robert Frankel* a107 119
5 bb m Catienus(USA) —Kitten's First (USA) (Lear Fan (USA))
4888a[5] 6996a[4]

Precious Secret (IRE) *C F Wall* a57 63
2 b f Fusaichi Pegasus(USA) —Gharam (USA) (Green Dancer (USA))
7141[7] 7332[8]

Precipice *D Carroll* a65 79
3 b f Observatory(USA) —On The Brink (Mind Games)
772[5] 953[3] 1019[3] 1315[8] 1819[7]

Precision Break (USA) *P F I Cole* a93 78
3 b c Silver Deputy(CAN) —Miss Kitty Cat (USA) (Tabasco Cat (USA))
223[5] 311[6] (1539) (1871) (2785) (3566) 3793[7] 5464[5] (5698) ◆ 6355[3] (7091) (7230)

Precocious Air (IRE) *J A Osborne* a63
2 b f Redback—Wee Merkin (IRE) (Thatching)
6622[10] 7117[3] ◆ 7425[4] 7547[3] 7666[2] 7760[5]

Precocious Star (IRE) *K R Burke* a87 91
4 ch m Bold Fact(USA) —Flames (Blushing Flame (USA))
26[6] 233[8]

Predict *Sir Mark Prescott* a79 74
2 b f Oasis Dream—Procession (Zafonic (USA))
2614[2] 3027[2] (3331) 3809[7] 4942[4] 5541[6]

Predictable (IRE) *M W Easterby* 48
3 b f Traditionally(USA) —Presumed (USA) (Dynaformer (USA))
4877[12] 5361[5] 5505[7] 6015[12] 6217[6] 6806[10]

Pre Eminance (IRE) *L R James* a28 40
7 b g Peintre Celebre(USA) —Sorb Apple (IRE) (Kris)
553[6]

Prelude *W M Brisbourne* 77
7 b m Danzero(AUS) —Dancing Debut (Polar Falcon (USA))
1577[7] 2453[5] 2908[6] 3433[2] 3624[3] (3912) 4170[2] 4662[6] 5199[9] 5450[7] 6279[11]

Prema (GER) *W Hickst*
2 ch f Big Shuffle(USA) —Pretty Su (IRE) (Surumu (GER))
7006a[2]

Premier Angel (USA) *Jane Chapple-Hyam* a67
2 b f Arch(USA) —Angel Song (USA) (Reign Road (USA))
7767[2]

Premier Banker (IRE) *J Noseda* a90
2 b c Cape Cross(IRE) —Heavenly Whisper (IRE) (Halling (USA))
(7554) (7781)

Premier Class (IRE) *J S Wainwright* 56
3 b g Indian Danehill(IRE) —Shams Wa Matar (Polish Precedent (USA))
2142[8] 2468[15] 2495[9] 4049[10]

Premier Danseur (IRE) *M Johnston* a86 86
3 b c Noverre(USA) —Destiny Dance (USA) (Nijinsky (CAN))
1167[7] 1868[2] 1988[6] (2378) 3038[7] 4392[3] 5675[6] 6033[11] 7299[2] 7398[9] 7525[2] 7556[8] 7670[9]

Premier Demon (IRE) *P D Evans* a8 53
2 b f Tagula(IRE) —Luisa Demon (IRE) (Barathea (IRE))
1680[15] 1924[8] 4027[12] 4367[4] 4706[5] 5614[7]

Premiere Dan (FR) *D Allard* 19
3 b f Dananeyev(FR) —Bella Clara (FR) (Always Fair (USA))
6744a[10]

Premier Krug (IRE) *P D Evans* a56 62
2 b f Xaar—Perugia (IRE) (Perugino (USA))
1385[5] 1851[6] 2048[7] 2584[3] 2691[7] 3254[4] 3639[4] 4525[8] 5475[6] 5866[5] 6787[4] 7519[7] 7607[4] 7694[6]

Premier Lad *T D Barron* 60
2 b c Tobougg(IRE) —Al Joudha (FR) (Green Desert (USA))
6010[4] 6548[3] ◆

Premier Superstar *M H Tompkins* 53
2 ch f Bertolini(USA) —Absolve (USA) (Diesis)
3869[5] 4776[9]

Premier Yank (USA) *J A Osborne* a71 34
3 br c Johannesburg(USA) —Sallybrooke (USA) (Dehere (USA))
412[4] ◆ (634)

Premio Loco (USA) *C F Wall* a114 99
4 ch g Prized(USA) —Crazee Mental (Magic Ring (IRE))
2426[9] ◆ (4528) ◆ (5695) ◆ 6476[6]

Premium Tap (USA) *J Gardel* a128
6 b h Pleasant Tap(USA) —Premium Red (USA) (Thirty Six Red (USA))
1092a[9]

Presbyterian Nun (IRE) *J L Dunlop* 99
3 b f Daylami(IRE) —Conspiracy (Rudimentary (USA))
1424[8] 1991[3] 3076a[4] 4196[6] 4667[3] 5826[5]

Prescription *Sir Mark Prescott* a87 84
3 gr f Pivotal—Doctor's Glory (USA) (Elmaamul (USA))
4987[8] (5160) ◆ (5998) ◆ (6160) 6225[3] ◆

Present *M J Gingell* a48 53
4 ch m Generous(IRE) —Miss Picol (Exit To Nowhere (USA))
2060[6]

President Elect (IRE) *T D Barron* 75
3 b g Imperial Ballet(IRE) —Broadway Rosie (Absalom)
1484[5] ◆ 1911[7] 3282[3] 3955[5]

Preskani *Mrs N Macauley* a36 38
6 b g Sri Pekan(USA) —Lamarita (Emarati (USA))
153[5] 371[9] 792[11] 1258[4]

Pressed For Time (IRE) *E J Creighton* a63 52
2 b f Traditionally(USA) —Desert Palace (Green Desert (USA))
3178[5] 4986[2] (5475) (5834) 6017[3] 7308[10]

Pressing (IRE) *M A Jarvis* 118
5 bb h Soviet Star(USA) —Rafif (USA) (Riverman (USA))
2230a[2] 3121[4] 3940[4] 4470a[2] (5742a) (7262a) 7684a[10]

Pressing Matters (IRE) *M Botti* a72 74
2 br c Oasis Dream—Pasithea (IRE) (Celtic Swing)
6327[5] ◆ 6702[3] (7498)

Press The Button (GER) *J R Boyle* a96 92
5 b g Dansili—Play Around (IRE) (Niniski (USA))
1633[7] 2152[13] 2799[4] (3449) (3676) 4363[4] 5349[5] 6196[5] 6536[4] 7025[6] (7314) 7404[3] 7496[4]

Presto Levanter *R Hannon* 73
3 b f Rock Of Gibraltar(IRE) —Presto Vento (Air Express (IRE))
2047[8] 2563[9] 2898[3] (3030) 3381[3] 3678[5]

Presumptive (IRE) *R Charlton* a98 102
8 b g Danehill(USA) —Demure (Machiavellian (USA))
1334[4] ◆ 1982[15] 3222[3] 4405[8] 5313[11] 6576[7]

Presvis *L M Cumani* 113
4 b g Sakhee(USA) —Forest Fire (SWE) (Never So Bold)
2360[3] 2673[5] 3628[5] (4131) 4350[2] 5279[2] ◆ (6120) ◆

Pret A Porter (UAE) *P D Evans* a72 71
4 br m Jade Robbery(USA) —Velour (Mtoto)
27[3] 268[4] 510 [3] 561[3] 591[5]

Prettilini *A W Carroll* a61 62
5 ch m Bertolini(USA) —Pretiosa (IRE) (Royal Abjar (USA))
42[14] 264[10] 338[4] 445[3] 469[5] 642[3] 696[5] 858[5] 972[6] 1035[4] 1254[6] 1370[3]

Pretty Ballerina (USA) *John Joseph Murphy* a40 83
3 b f Swain(IRE) —Hawzah (Green Desert (USA))
3124[16] 3205[3]

Pretty Bonnie *A E Price* a52 87
3 b f Kyllachy—Joonayh (Warning)
2774[9] 3086[2] ◆ 3441[2] (3695) ◆ 4383[4] (4767) 5007[2] (5490) (5839) 6006[5] 6239[10]

Pretty Demanding (IRE) *M G Quinlan* a61 81
4 b m Night Shift(USA) —Absolute Glee (USA) (Kenmare (FR))
1482[4] 2361[4] 3003[10] 3220[8] 3606[8] 4259[7] 4511a[12] 4655a[8] (4799a) 6882[11] 7045[7] 7487a[0]

Pretty Miss *H Candy* 79
4 b m Averti(IRE) —Pretty Poppy (Song)
1537[3] 2166[5] 3062[4] (3486)

Pretty Officer (USA) *Rae Guest* a43 55
3 b f Deputy Commander(USA) —La Samanna (USA) (Trempolino (USA))
3065[6] 3524[5] 3780[2] 4260[6] 4810[3] 5379[6]

Pretty Orchid *G C H Chung* a43 57
3 b f Forzando—Dunloe (IRE) (Shaadi (USA))
5608[9]

Pretty Posey *J G M O'Shea* 25
4 b m Dolpour—Aegean Glory (Shareef Dancer (USA))
4322[12]

Pretty Selma *Mark Gillard* a48
4 b m Diktat—Brave Vanessa (USA) (Private Account (USA))
2881[10] 4979[11]

Pride Of India (USA) *J Noseda* a72 66
3 b c Johannesburg(USA) —How Could You (USA) (Boundary (USA))
1763[3] 5608[4] 6003[5]

Pride Of Kings *M Johnston* 74
2 b c King's Best(USA) —Aunty Mary (Common Grounds)
1714[7] 2186[10] 3334[3] (4292) 6549[3]

Pride Of Nation (IRE) *J W Hills* a92 116
6 b h Danehill Dancer(IRE) —Anita Via (IRE) (Anita's Prince)
495a[5] 745a[10] 3122[24] 4587[17] 5896[9] 6576[6] 6772[6] 7146[9]

Pride Of Northcare (IRE) *D Shaw* a77 62
4 gr g Namid—Pride Of Pendle (Grey Desire)
3826[6] 4727[11] 5395[3] (5679) 6218[5] (6711) 7092[2] 7276[6]

Prigsnov Dancer (IRE) *J O'Reilly* 85
3 ch g Namid—Brave Dance (IRE) (Kris)
1157[6] 1426[17] 2498[7] 3111[10] 6218[15]

Prima Ballerina *J G Portman* 67
4 b m Pivotal—Kirov (Darshaan)
5750[10] 6538[5]

Prima Fonteyn *Miss Sheena West* a36 36
2 ch f Imperial Dancer—Flying Wind (Forzando)
2893[13] 3373[9] 4149[15] 4666[8] 7438[8]

Prima Laurea (IRE) *J G Given* 33
2 b f Royal Applause—First Degree (Sabrehill (USA))
6245[10] 6578[7]

Prima Luce (IRE) *J S Bolger* 109
3 b f Galileo(IRE) —Ramona (Desert King (IRE))
(1880a) 2877a[10] 4006a[7] 5136a[4] 5729a[5] 5944a[2]

Prime Contender *George Baker* a82 52
6 b g Efisio—Gecko Rouge (Rousillon (USA))
2075 451[6] 3448[10]

Prime Defender *B W Hills* a105 115
4 ch h Bertolini(USA) —Arian Da (Superlative)
959[4] 1420[7] 2106[7] 2680[3] 3248[19] 3739[2] 3922[7] ◆ 4624[12] 5245[8] 5891[5] 6304[4] 6645[6]

Prime Delivery (USA) *R M H Cowell* 93
2 b c More Than Ready(USA) —Rise And Fall (USA) (Quiet American (USA))
(3590) 3876[6] 4402[3] 5107[4] 5507[9] 6815[12]

Prime Exhibit *R Charlton* 91
3 b g Selkirk(USA) —First Exhibit (Machiavellian (USA))
1424[7] ◆ 1806[4]

Prime Factor *B W Hills* a78 57
3 b g Bertolini(USA) —Medina De Rioseco (Puissance)
1834 (514) 756[4] ◆ 2529[3] 2945[2] 3626[16] 4864[7] 5346[5] 5697[10] 6356[7]

Prime Mood (IRE) *B Smart* 87
2 ch c Choisir(AUS) —There With Me (USA) (Distant View (USA))
4176[2] ◆ 4557[2] 5500[3] 5827[7] (6383) 6483[16]

Prime Number (IRE) *J Akehurst* a79 81
6 gr g King's Best(USA) —Majinskaya (FR) (Marignan (USA))
28[4] 224[6] 450[7] (747) 927[4] 1349[2] 1682[6] 2071[3] (3132) 3449[5] 4156[13] 4309[3] 4726[4] 5512[6] 6171[10] 6698[8] 7025[12]

Prime Realestate (USA) *Wayne Catalano* 101
3 ch c Prime Timber(USA) —Pretty Pretty Lady (USA) (Only Dreamin (USA))
4887a[4]

Prime Recreation *P S Felgate* a48 20
11 b g Primo Dominie—Night Transaction (Tina's Pet)
100[9] 363[11] 690[5]

Prime Spirit (IRE) *B Smart* 92
2 b c Invincible Spirit(IRE) —Turtulla (IRE) (Night Shift (USA))
(2154) 3439[2] 3920[7]

Primo Dilettante *W J Knight* a58 58
2 b g Primo Valentino(IRE) —Jezadil (IRE) (Mujadil (USA))
4776[7] 5344[6] 5812[4] 6207[12] 6892[9]

Primo Way *Miss L A Perratt* a76 76
7 b g Primo Dominie—Waypoint (Cadeaux Genereux)
3957[5] 4559[3] 4851[8] 4969[2] 5454[2] 5564[9] 6161[3]

Princability (IRE) *M R Channon* 76
2 b c King's Best(USA) —Harmonic Sound (IRE) (Grand Lodge (USA))
5901[3] 6397[6] 6674[3]

Prince Afram *R M Beckett* 68
3 b c Fraam—Miletrian Cares (IRE) (Hamas (IRE))
4301[2] 4709[2]

Prince Andjo (USA) *I W McInnes* a56 20
2 b g Van Nistelrooy(USA) —Magic Flare (USA) (Danzatore (CAN))
6253[7] 6789[17]

Prince Charlemagne (IRE) *G L Moore* a78 79
5 br g King Charlemagne(USA) —Ciubanga (IRE) (Arazi (USA))
28[6] 104[3] 504[4] 735[2] 794[5] 935[2] 1388[7] 1932[11] 2243[8] 2621[12] 3113[9] (3265) 3583[3] 4343[7] 5087[7] 5576[7] 6825[11] 7309[10] 7806[11]

Prince Desire (IRE) *Tom Dascombe* a73 77
3 b g Fasliyev(USA) —No Quest (IRE) (Rainbow Quest (USA))
1745[6] 1988[13] 2714[7] 3384[9] 4081[9] 6703[5] 6898[13]

Prince Des Neiges (FR) *M R Hoad* a57 66
5 b g Milford Track(IRE) —Miss Smith (FR) (Grand Lodge (USA))
2352[3] 2932[9]

Prince Egor (IRE) *M Dods* 73
5 b g Imperial Ballet(IRE) —Harifana (FR) (Kahyasi)
1160[2] 1520[3]

Prince Erik *D K Weld* a85 105
4 gr g Indian Ridge—Miracle (Ezzoud (IRE))
4003a[2]

Prince Evelith (GER) *J J Quinn* 86
5 b g Dashing Blade—Peace Time (GER) (Surumu (GER))
6487[7]

Prince Fasliyev *H-A Pantall* a93 104
4 b h Fasliyev(USA) —Malaisienne (FR) (Saumarez)
2637a[8] 4912a[4] 5738a[8] 7005a[5]

Prince Flori (GER) *S Smrczek* 122
5 br h Lando(GER) —Princess Liberte (GER) (Nebos (GER))
3540a[5] 4232a[5] (5528a) (6461a) 6992a[4] 7350a[2]

Prince Forever (IRE) *M A Jarvis* 105
4 b h Giant's Causeway(USA) —Routilante (IRE) (Rousillon (USA))
960[19] 1387[4] 1920[5] 2830[6] 3974[4] 4867[5] 5279[6] 6649[3]

Prince Golan (IRE) *J W Unett* a70 82
4 b g Golan(IRE) —Mohican Princess (Shirley Heights)
1520[11] 2619[2] 2846[4] 3261[6] 3725[6] 4478[7] 4858[10] (6178) 6560[6] 7021[12] 7368[4] 7559[2] (7686) 7786[3]

Prince Hamlet (IRE) *B Smart* a86 87
3 b c Fantastic Light(USA) —Hamsaat Hi Haat (USA) (Hennessy (USA))
1297[7] 2209[4] 2575[2] (2842) 4218[9] 4682[6] 6710[6]

Prince Joshua *J Jay* 21
3 b c Josr Algarhoud(IRE) —Feathers Flying (IRE) (Royal Applause)
2862[7]

Prince Kalamoun (IRE) *G A Swinbank* 99
3 ch g Desert Prince(IRE) —Grenouillere (USA) (Alysheba (USA))
980[2] 1307[2] 2366[4] (3227) (3641) 4160[4] (5449) 6120[4] ◆ 6476[22]

Princely Hero (IRE) *M Botti* a88 84
4 b g Royal Applause—Dalu (IRE) (Dancing Brave (USA))
(7457) 7670[3] 7813[6]

Princely Ted (IRE) *W Clay* a62 62
7 b g Princely Heir(IRE) —Just Out (IRE) (Bluebird (USA))
802[5] 2591[10] 2867[8] 3084[8] 3321[12] 3951[4] 4451[8] 4664[11] 4936[9]

Princelywallywogan *John A Harris* a25 73
6 b g Princely Heir(IRE) —Dublivia (Midyan (USA))
395[8] 601[7] 811[10] 1160[3] (1280) 1528[2] (2001) (2483) 2927[3] 3711[4] 3954[2] 4458[6] 5783[6]

Prince Namid *D Nicholls* a80 88
6 b g Namid—Fen Princess (IRE) (Trojan Fen)
1430[13] 2145[5] 2398[2] 2778[6] 3111[5] 3435[5] 3713[6] 6011[3] 6066[12]

Prince Noel *N Wilson* a81 70
4 b g Dr Fong(USA) —Baileys On Line (Shareef Dancer (USA))
2672[11] 3142[6] 3755[4] 4148[2] 4248[3] 4785[10] 5156[2] 6452[2] 6950[16] 7167[5]

Prince Of Charm (USA) *R A Teal* a72 73
4 ch g Mizzen Mast(USA) —Pretty Clear (USA) (Mr Prospector (USA))
51[10] 177[11] (Dead)

Prince Of Delphi *R M Beckett* a78 77
5 b g Royal Applause—Princess Athena (Ahonoora)
1153[2] 1488[2] 2242[4] 2484[2] 2837[6] 3024[2] 3506[4] 3728[7] 4051[4] 5600[14]

Prince Of Gold *Ms N M Hugo* a59 52
8 b g Polar Prince(IRE) —Gold Belt (IRE) (Bellypha)
32[10] 1029[12] 2053[5]

Prince Of Light (IRE) *M Johnston* a91 106
5 ch g Fantastic Light(USA) —Miss Queen (USA) (Miswaki (USA))
2789[12] 3197[14] 3740[13] 4060[3] ◆ 4509[15] 5858[12] 6424[5] 7019[7] 7116[7] 7398[4] 7526[7] 7750[6]

Prince Of Love (IRE) *Jedd O'Keeffe* a72 39
5 b g Fruits Of Love(USA) —Teodora (IRE) (Fairy King (USA))
2701[7] 3258[10]

Prince Of Medina *J R Best* a53 57
5 ch g Fraam—Medina De Rioseco (Puissance)
14[2] 152[5] 179[4] 374[6] (499) 575[2] 4410[6] 4775[7] 5833[10] 6421[10] 6729[3] 7400[10] 7520[8]

Prince Of Thebes (IRE) *M J Attwater* a89 93
7 b g Desert Prince(IRE) —Persian Walk (FR) (Persian Bold)
1633[6] 2013[2] 2789[9] 3382[6] 3899[7] 4269[2] 4509[7] 5018[4] 5350[4] 5470[9] 6130[12] 6598[6] (6738) (7014) 7299[8] 7439[3] 7556[2]

Prince Rhyddarch *Miss L A Perratt* 73
3 b g Josr Algarhoud(IRE) —Nova Zembla (Young Ern)
1221[4] 1825[3] 2143[9] 2750[11] (5223) 5456[5] 6155[3] (6727)

Prince Rossi (IRE) *A E Price* a57 65
4 b g Royal Applause—Miss Rossi (Artaius (USA))
235[12] 640[11] 1159[9] 1266[7] 1528[6] 2731[10]

Prince Sabaah (IRE) *R Hannon* a89 93
4 b g Spectrum(IRE) —Princess Sabaah (IRE) (Desert King (IRE))
1212[4] 1568[8] 1841[6] 2107[2] 2372[5] 3505[5] 4350[4] 4742[12] 6479[4] 6974[10]

Prince Samos (IRE) *E S McMahon* a85 90
6 b g Mujadil(USA) —Sabaniya (FR) (Lashkari)
962[16] 1771[3] 1947[11] 4001[2] 4744[5] 5961[3]

Prince's Decree *G M Moore* 60
3 br g Diktat—Rock Face (Ballad Rock)
1516[6] 2272[9] 4019[9]

Prince Shaun (IRE) *Patrick J Flynn* a99 107
3 b g Acclamation—Style Parade (USA) (Diesis)
2961a[3] 3536a[11]

Prince Siegfried (FR) *A M Balding* 109
2 b c Royal Applause—Intrum Morshaan (IRE) (Darshaan)
(3968) 5507[6] 6474[7] 7163a[2]

Princess Aimee *D Burchell* a47 47
8 b m Wizard King—Off The Air (IRE) (Taufan (USA))
1052[12]

Princess Cagliari *R Hannon* a63
2 b f Efisio—Queenie (Indian Ridge)
7191[5] 7356[4] 7708[4]

Princess Charlmane (IRE) *C J Teague* a46 48
5 b m King Charlemagne(USA) —Bint Alreeys (Polish Precedent (USA))
634[5] 790[10] 871[8] 1027[3] 1454[5] 2159[9] 2576[2] 3212[8] 3546[5] 4950[3] 7528[12]

Princess Cocoa (IRE) *R A Fahey* a82 78
5 b m Desert Sun—Daily Double (FR) (Unfuwain (USA))
344 218[3] (525) 626[4] 1041[2] 1711[3] 2271[3] 2623[4] 3337[2] 3433[6] 4244[5]

Princess Ellis *E J Alston* 95
4 ch m Compton Place—Star Cast (IRE) (In The Wings)
1386[7] 1624[16] 2212[4] (2843) ◆ 3252[2] 3472[7] 4240[4] 4291[3] 5542[2] 5793[7] 6429[3] 6651[11]

Princess Flame (GER) *B G Powell* 79
6 br m Tannenkonig(IRE) —Pacora (GER) (Lagunas)
1526[13] 1621[11] 1896[3] ◆ 2336[8] 2863[4] (3347) 5783[2] (6050) (6235)

Princess Gee *B J McMath* a63 49
3 b f Reel Buddy(USA) —Queen G (USA) (Matty G (USA))
2528[4] 3333[3] 4156[14] 5161[15]

Princess Hannah *R Hannon* a48 70
2 b f Royal Applause—Helloimustbegoing (USA) (Red Ransom (USA))
3378[4] 4554[14] (4973) 5997[11] 6240[28]

Princess India (IRE) *P Winkworth* a76 65
3 ch f Hawk Wing(USA) —Litchfield Hills (USA) (Relaunch (USA))
2196[14] 4183[5] 4930[9] 5291[10] 5803[8] 6227[2] 6437[4] (6741)

Princess Janet *A B Coogan*
2 ch f Deportivo—Idolize (Polish Precedent (USA))
6029[12] 6443[11]

Princess Lavinia *G Wragg* a71 72
5 ch m Fraam—Affaire De Coeur (Imperial Fling (USA))
1620[5] 2886[2]

Princess Livius (IRE) *P A Blockley* a66 58
3 ch f Titus Livius(FR) —Last Shaambles (IRE) (Shaamit (IRE))
2715 (487) 899[6] 2014[8] 2956[10]

Princess Lomi (IRE) *E J O'Neill* a66 75
3 b f Lomitas—Athlumney Lady (Lycius (USA))
903[3] 1477[2] 1950[2] (2495) 2977[8]

Princess Maria (USA) *R A Fahey* 48
3 b f Giant's Causeway(USA) —Passive Action (USA) (Double Negative (USA))
1912[10] 2659[4] 2984[14] 3555[16]

Princess Namid (IRE) *R A Harris* 2
3 br f Namid—Banutan (IRE) (Charnwood Forest (IRE))
6004[14] 7453[8]

Princess Of Aeneas (IRE) *R Johnson* a48 6
5 b m Beckett(IRE) —Romangoddess (IRE) (Rhoman Rule (USA))
2537[5]

Princess Petra (FR) *M Rulec* 12
4 ch m Samum(GER) —Pastell Rouge (GER) (Lomitas)
5625a[10]

Princess Rainbow (FR) *Jennie Candlish* a68 76
3 b f Raintrap—Chausseneige (FR) (Mad Captain)
5155[6] 5963[2] 6725[2]

Princess Raya *M E Rimmer* a56 50
3 gr f Act One—Tapas En Bal (FR) (Mille Balles (FR))
694[4] 1042[7] 1176[5] 3483[15] 4260[5] 4564[16] 5077[13] 5379[9]

Princess Rebecca *E F Vaughan* a52 36
2 ch f Compton Place—Sunley Stars (Sallust)
4486[6] 5835[9] 6351[6]

Princess Rhianna (IRE) *Mrs G S Rees* a59 66
3 ch f Fath(USA) —Persian Sally (IRE) (Persian Bold)
2282[4] 2781[9] 3213[6] (4044) 4180[9] (Dead)

Princess Rose Anne (IRE) *E F Vaughan* a78 72
3 ch f Danehill Dancer(IRE) —Hawksleys Jill (Mujtahid (USA))
2366[7] (2757) 6435[5] 7276[9] 7448[7]

Princess Soraya *R Dickin* 39
2 ch f Compton Place—Eurolink Cafe (Grand Lodge (USA))
6531[10]

Princess Taylor *M Botti* a77 93
4 ch m Singspiel(IRE) —Tapas En Bal (FR) (Mille Balles (FR))
2373[2] ◆ (3109) 3500[4] 4189[7] 5311[6] 6130[3] (6293) 6781[6]

Princess Valerina *D Haydn Jones* a77 87
4 ch m Beat Hollow—Heart So Blue (Dilum (USA))
3892[6] 5144[13] 5789[4] 6052[10] (6556) 7428[2] 7671[3]

Princess Zaha *A G Newcombe* a42 33
6 b m Zaha(CAN) —Otaru (IRE) (Indian Ridge)
8[7] 365[3] 5851[3] 863[9]

Princess Zhukova (IRE) *R J Price* a17
3 b f Terroir(IRE) —Miss Bussell (Sabrehill (USA))
146[11]

Princess Zohra *E A L Dunlop* a59
2 b f Royal Applause—Desert Royalty (IRE) (Alhaarth (IRE))
7708[6] 7810[2]

Prince Tamino *A Al Raihe* a95 110
5 b g Mozart(IRE) —Premiere Dance (IRE) (Loup Solitaire (USA))
(291a) 472a[4] (649a) 738a[4] 814a[7]

Prince Troy (GER) *Werner Glanz* 88
9 b h Acatenango(GER) —Princess Nana (Bellypha)
3307a[6]

Prince Tum Tum (USA) *P Howling* a32 92
8 b g Capote(USA) —La Grande Epoque (USA) (Lyphard (USA))
85[8] 7363[11]

Prince Valentine *G L Moore* a53 59
7 b g My Best Valentine—Affaire De Coeur (Imperial Fling (USA))
922[2] 1053[3] 1269[5] 2070[7] 2353[10] 2863[3] ◆ 3764[2] (4053) 4772[6] 5604[4] 6928[8]

Prince Zafonic *D K Ivory* a76 83
5 ch g Zafonic(USA) —Kite Mark (Mark Of Esteem (IRE))
7462[4] 7639[4] 7770[6]

Print (IRE) *M R Channon* 69
2 b c Exceed And Excel(AUS) —Hariya (IRE) (Shernazar)
4826[14] 6062[4]

Prinz (GER) *A Wohler* 105
4 b h Lando(GER) —Prairie Darling (Stanford)
3540a[8] 5137a[5]

Prior Warning *Miss D Mountain* a102 102
4 ch h Barathea(IRE) —Well Warned (Warning)
1420[20] 1809[15] 2426[5] 3197[28] 3881[2] 4687[5] 5424[11] 6290[9] 6669[6] 6947[16] 7146[10]

Priti Fabulous (IRE) *W J Haggas* a87 76
3 b f Invincible Spirit(IRE) —Flying Diva (Chief Singer)
1445[8] 1836[4] 2620[7] (2946) 3918[5] 4377[2] (6021) 6684[4]

Privalova (IRE) *R Pritchard-Gordon* 102
2 b f Alhaarth(IRE) —Special Lady (FR) (Kaldoun (FR))
3749a[3] 5850a[4]

Private Equity (IRE) *W Jarvis* a36
2 b f Haafhd—Profit Alert (IRE) (Alzao (USA))
7640[6]

Private Passion (IRE) *Pat Eddery* a37 52
2 b g Captain Rio—Victoria's Secret (IRE) (Law Society (USA))
6327[6] 6701[11] 7098[10]

Private Soldier *N J Vaughan* a59 34
5 gr g Dansili—Etienne Lady (IRE) (Imperial Frontier (USA))
214[3] 521[10]

Privet (IRE) *W McCreery* a71 79
3 b f Cape Cross(IRE) —Pacific Grove (Persian Bold)
6511a[12]

Prix Masque (IRE) *Christian Wroe* a48 33
4 b g Iron Mask(USA) —Prima Marta (Primo Dominie)
3268[7] 7362[5] 7536[9] 7624[6] 7818[6]

Prize Fighter (IRE) *A Berry* a74 87
6 b g Desert Sun—Papal (Selkirk (USA))
5994[3] 6826[4] 7202[8] 7532[4]

Prize Lady (NZ) *Graeme Sanders* 105
7 b m Prized(USA) —Pen Bal Lady (Mummy's Game)
7188a[17]

Prize Point *K A Ryan* 77
2 ch g Bahamian Bounty—Golden Symbol (Wolfhound (USA))
(3199) ◆ 4108[5]

Prize Spirit (USA) *Joseph G Murphy* a52 77
3 ch g Pure Prize(USA) —Corporate Spirit (USA) (Corporate Report (USA))
1495a[10]

Proclaim *M Johnston* 80
2 b c Noverre(USA) —Pescara (IRE) (Common Grounds)
4289[6] (4658) 5228[8] 6058[3]

Procrastinate (IRE) *R F Fisher* a47 52
6 ch g Rossini(USA) —May Hinton (Main Reef)
377[9] 783[7]

Professor Malone *J C Tuck* a48 29
3 ch g Ishiguru(USA) —Molly Malone (Formidable (USA))
3502[10] 3847[8] 4388[7] 5749[5] 7378[10] 7521[11]

Professor Twinkle *I W McInnes* a61 70
4 ch h Dr Fong(USA) —Shining High (Shirley Heights)
7732[12]

Proficiency *T D Walford* 59
3 gr f El Prado(IRE) —Talent Quest (IRE) (Rainbow Quest (USA))
3556[4] 5361[3] 6163[5] 7085[3]

Profitability (USA) *J H M Gosden* 71
3 b f Cherokee Run(USA) —Lucrative (USA) (Seeking The Gold (USA))
1445[6] 2918[3] (3379)

Profit's Reality (IRE) *M J Attwater* a88 96
6 br g Key Of Luck(USA) —Teacher Preacher (IRE) (Taufan (USA))
757[6] ◆ 1018[5] 3505[6] (3925) 4444[12] 4844[7] 6302[12] 6536[11] 7404[6] 7496[9] 7753[4]

Profound Beauty (IRE) *D K Weld* 110
4 b m Danehill(USA) —Diamond Trim (IRE) (Highest Honor (FR))
1353a[3] 2113a[3] 3070a[2] (4100a) 5136a[3] 7188a[5]

Profumo Affair *M L W Bell* a9 26
3 b g Oasis Dream—Affair Of State (IRE) (Tate Gallery (USA))
867[9] 997[9] 1295[10] 3126[9]

Prohibit *J H M Gosden* a108 100
3 b g Oasis Dream—Well Warned (Warning)
(1404) ◆ 1718[3] 2410[3] 2605[5] 3047[9] (6903) 7421[7]

Prohibition (IRE) *W J Haggas* 80
2 b c Danehill Dancer(IRE) —Crumpetsfortea (IRE) (Henbit (USA))
6425[13] 6714[4] (7200)

Project Dane (IRE) *L Polito* 104
4 ch h Dane Friendly—Sweet College (IRE) (College Chapel)
7262a[2]

Prolific (IRE) *R Hannon* 105
2 ch c Compton Place—Photo Flash (IRE) (Bahamian Bounty)
(2117) ◆ 2677[2] 3152[3] ◆ 3876[3] (4588) 6442[6]

Prom *M Brittain* 39
2 b f Lujain(USA) —Ball Gown (Jalmood (USA))
3959[11] 4164[9] 4604[7]

Promised Gold *J A Geake* a31 59
3 ch g Bahamian Bounty—Delphic Way (Warning)
1478[11] 4527[10] 5218[13]

Promise Maker (USA) *T D Walford* a48 60
3 b g Empire Maker(USA) —Sunday Bazaar (USA) (Nureyev (USA))
1417[7] 6114[7] 6530[8] 7189[9]

Promise Me Merlot (USA) *W Cesare*
2 u c (USA) — (USA) (Seeking The Gold (USA))
6502a[12]

Promise Of Love *Miss Amy Weaver* a77 66
3 b f Royal Applause—Beloved Visitor (USA) (Miswaki (USA))
6366a[15] 6633[3] 7090[14] 7653[6] 7774[8]

Promising Lead *Sir Michael Stoute* 117
4 b m Danehill(USA) —Arrive (Kahyasi)
(2130) ◆ (3511a) ◆

Proper (IRE) *C J Mann* a81 80
4 b g Rossini(USA) —Pardoned (IRE) (Mujadil (USA))
(1273) ◆ 1585[2] 2076[7] 3010[7] 3561[5] 3676[6] 4276[5] 4771[11]

Proper Holiday (USA) *P W Chapple-Hyam* 62
2 b c Harlan's Holiday(USA) —Proper Lassie (USA) (Topsider (USA))
6057[6] 6539[11]

Proper Tool (IRE) *R A Harris* a26 47
2 b c Orpen(USA) —Silent Star (IRE) (Ali-Royal (IRE))
1263[7] 1955[7] 6709[9]

Prophetise (USA) *J W Hills* a68 62
2 bb f Arch(USA) —Maisonette (USA) (Pulpit (USA))
3674[4] 4339[3] 5048[3]

Prophet's Star *H J L Dunlop*
3 b g Daylami(IRE) —Profit Alert (IRE) (Alzao (USA))
5963[8] 6226[11] 6659[12]

Propinquity *Liam McAteer* 92
6 b g Primo Dominie—Lydia Maria (Dancing Brave (USA))
1105a[11] 6071[5]

Proponent (IRE) *R Charlton* 104
4 b g Peintre Celebre(USA) —Pont Audemer (USA) (Chief's Crown (USA))
1469[4] (1828) ◆ 3249[6] ◆ 4504[7] 5508[5] 6120[18]

Proportional *Mme C Head-Maarek* 114
2 b f Beat Hollow—Minority (Generous (IRE))
(6519a) ◆

Prospect Court *A C Whillans* a37 83
6 ch g Pivotal—Scierpan (USA) (Sharpen Up)
1327[16] 1818[8] 2292[8] 3370[6]

Prospect Place *M A Allen* a20 85
4 b g Compton Place—Encore My Love (Royal Applause)
56[13]

Prospect Wells (FR) *A Fabre* 118
3 b c Sadler's Wells(USA) —Brooklyn's Dance (FR) (Shirley Heights)
(2064a) 2654a[8] 4042a[2] 5953a[6] 6854a[6]

Protector (SAF) *A G Foster* a94 109
7 b g Kilconnel(USA) —Mufski (SAF) (Al Mufti (USA))
4145[12] 4624[26] 5109[16] 6069[6] 6484[7] 6975[4] 7245[18]

Protiva *A P Jarvis* a62 65
2 ch f Deportivo—Prowse (USA) (King Of Kings (IRE))
3610[8] 4328[6] 4643[7] 5228[11] 5671[10] 6694[2] 7016[14] 7389[4] 7505[10] 7607[10]

Proud Boris (GER) *J Hanacek* 96
4 b h Silvano(GER) —Parista (Armistice Day)
6461a[10] 6992a[9]

Proud Catch (IRE) *J G Burns* 66
2 b c Catcher In The Rye(IRE) —Time Limit (IRE) (Alzao (USA))
3509a[13]

Proudinsky (GER) *Robert Frankel* 112
5 b h Silvano(GER) —Proudeyes (GER) (Dashing Blade)
5928a[2]

Proud Killer *J R Jenkins* a69 72
5 b g Killer Instinct—Thewaari (USA) (Eskimo (USA))
41[4] 446[8] 554[4] 1126[2] 1368[6] 1476[5] 2692[10] 4478[11] 5170[5] 5233[3]

Proud Linus (USA) *D Carroll* 92
3 b c Proud Citizen(USA) —Radcliffe Yard (USA) (Boston Harbor (USA))
2283[4] 3155[28]

Proud Times (USA) *G A Swinbank* 81
2 b g Proud Citizen(USA) —Laura's Pistolette (USA) (Big Pistol (USA))
4593[2]

Provence *B W Hills* a76 83
3 b f Averti(IRE) —Prowse (USA) (King Of Kings (IRE))
1960[6] 2966[3] (4277) 6695[4] 7077[6]

Proviso *A Fabre* 113
3 b f Dansili—Binche (USA) (Woodman (USA))
1664a[3] 2237a[3] 2877a[4] 3775a[3] 4657a[3] 6521a[7]

Provost *M W Easterby* a62 85
4 ch g Danehill Dancer(IRE) —Dixielake (IRE) (Lake Coniston (IRE))
1067[9] 1218[11] 1612[9] 1815[10] 2487[8] 2925[10] 3557[11] 6116[3] ◆ (6409) 7532[9] 7651[4] 7779[3]

Prowl *E A L Dunlop* 76
2 b f One Cool Cat(USA) —Go Supersonic (Zafonic (USA))
2479[3] ◆ 6240[17]

Prudenzia (IRE) *P Bary* 102
3 b f Dansili—Platonic (Zafonic (USA))
2650a[6] 4657a[8]

Psalm (IRE) *A P O'Brien* 114
3 b f Sadler's Wells(USA) —Litani River (USA) (Irish River (FR))
1230a[7] 2033a[6] 3194[7] 4007a[5] 5730a[6] (6516a)

Pseudonym (IRE) *M F Harris* a73 72
6 ch g Daylami(IRE) —Stage Struck (IRE) (Sadler's Wells (USA))
6054[6] (6329) 7366[2] 7455[4] 7827[9]

Psychic Star *Mrs A M Thorpe* a72 56
5 b m Diktat—Southern Psychic (USA) (Alwasmi (USA))
3604[8] 4365[6] 4710[9]

Psycho Cat *W M Brisbourne* a42 51
5 b g Hunting Lion(IRE) —Canadian Capers (Ballacashtal (CAN))
1116[14] 2374[6] 2731[2] 3131[7] 3844[7]

Psycho Killer *R M Beckett* 53
3 b f Best Of The Bests(IRE) —Kasamba (Salse (USA))
5652[4]

P'Tit Fute (FR) *F Flood* 88
7 b g Roakarad—Centadj (FR) (Tadj (FR))
4493a[12]

Public Eye *L A Dace* a44 54
7 b g Zafonic(USA) —Stardom (Known Fact (USA))
1726[14]

Public Forum *M Al Muhairi* a93 99
6 b h Rainbow Quest(USA) —Valentine Girl (Alzao (USA))
650a[13]

Puggy (IRE) *Yvonne Durant* 102
4 b m Mark Of Esteem(IRE) —Jakarta (IRE) (Machiavellian (USA))
5957a[9]

Pugilist *B J Meehan* a48 75
6 b g Fraam—Travel Mystery (Godswalk (USA))
4104[13] 5069[5] 6134[7] 6450[12] 6721[12]

Pugnacity *A Berry* a36 48
4 b m Zilzal(USA) —Attention Seeker (USA) (Exbourne (USA))
3131[12] 5262[5] 6040[6] 6185[7] 6309[11]

Pulsate *E F Vaughan* a22 47
4 ch m Inchinor—Salanka (IRE) (Persian Heights)
375[8]

Pumpkin *Sir Michael Stoute* a53
2 ch f Pivotal—Gallivant (Danehill (USA))
6696[8]

Punch Drunk *J G Given* 72
2 b f Beat Hollow—Bebe De Cham (Tragic Role (USA))
4328[8] (4897) 5895[6] 6477[8] 7052[3]

Punching *Miss Gay Kelleway* a76 74
4 b g Kyllachy—Candescent (Machiavellian (USA))
523[2] 884[6] 1035[2] 1150[2] 1370[4] (1642) (1872) 3477[3] 3819[2] 3898[4] 4258[8] 4478[4] 4809[8] 6335[7] 6418[3] 6840[2] 7055[11] 7346[4] 7582[7] 7629[3]

Punjabi *N J Henderson* a86 98
5 b g Komaite(USA) —Competa (Hernando (FR))
(2372) ◆ (2540)

Punta Galera (IRE) *Paul Green* a71 71
5 br g Zafonic(USA) —Kobalt Sea (FR) (Akarad (FR))
78[5] 526[4] 697[4] 752[5] 1086[2] (1165) 1613[5] 2006[5] 2361[3] 7650[9]

Pure Brief (IRE) *R Hollinshead* a37
11 b g Brief Truce(USA) —Epure (Bellypha)
438[8] 606[7] 779[8]

Pure Clan (USA) *Robert E Holthus* a109 116
3 ch f Pure Prize(USA) —Gather The Clan (IRE) (General Assembly (USA))
(3807a) 5745a[2] 6968a[10]

Pure Crystal *M G Quinlan* a52
2 ch f Dubai Destination(USA) —Crystal Flute (Lycius (USA))
5404[9] 5590[9] 6597[12] 7258[8]

Pure Imagination (IRE) *D Nicholls* a75 78
7 ch g Royal Academy(USA) —Ivory Bride (Domynsky)
979[2] 1126[6]

Pure Inspiration *A G Newcombe* a36 31
3 ch f Tobougg(IRE) —Blue Diamond (First Trump)
923[6] 2089[6] 3115[5] 3692[10] 5407[12]

Pure Joy *Mme C Head-Maarek* 93
2 b f Zamindar(USA) —Posteritas (USA) (Lear Fan (USA))
3749a[2]

Purely By Chance *J Pearce* a54 64
3 b f Galileo(IRE) —Sioux Chef (Be My Chief (USA))
2197[9] 2989[4] 3521[4] 5216[5] 5651[4] 6390[8] 7010[9] 7401[8]

Pure Poetry (IRE) *R Hannon* 100
2 b c Tagula(IRE) —Express Logic (Air Express (IRE))
3001[7] (3669) 4190[8] (4374) 5827[19]

Pure Rhythm *S C Williams* a48 46
2 b f Oasis Dream—Degree (Warning)
5534[10] 5905[6] 6342[7]

Pure Scandal *M W Easterby* a53 52
3 b g Barathea(IRE) —Sharena (IRE) (Kahyasi)
1186[8] 1397[4] 1913[11] 7280[6]

Pure Song *J L Dunlop* a73 73
3 b f Singspiel(IRE) —Pure Grain (Polish Precedent (USA))
1444[7] 2164[11] 3350[3] 4170[8] 5155[3] 6226[3] 6413[2]

Purissima (USA) *Sir Michael Stoute* 90
2 b f Fusaichi Pegasus(USA) —Willstar (USA) (Nureyev (USA))
(6531) 6818[10]

Purlando (GER) *H Morrison* 33
3 b g Lando(GER) —Purple Haze (GER) (Nebos (GER))
2191[15] 6762[10]

Puro (CZE) *M Weiss* 53
6 ch g Rainbows For Life(CAN) —Pulnoc (CZE) (Shy Groom (USA))
604a[3]

Purple Emperor (USA) *Saeed Bin Suroor* a58 95
4 b h Red Ransom(USA) —Checkerspot (USA) (Affirmed (USA))
202a[11] 493a[9]

Purple Moon (IRE) *L M Cumani* 120
5 ch g Galileo(IRE) —Vanishing Prairie (USA) (Alysheba (USA))
6201[5] 6854a[2] 7511a[9] 7682a[2]

Purple Ransom (IRE) *D J Wintle* a40 55
3 b g Intikhab(USA) —Brittas Blues (IRE) (Blues Traveller (IRE))
2260[8] 2805[8] 3183[13] 5748[8]

Purple Sage (IRE) *B W Hills* a74 94
2 b f Danehill Dancer(IRE) —Kylemore (IRE) (Sadler's Wells (USA))
4870[5] 5240[4] 5788[2] (6273) 6818[9] 6982[7]

Pur Star (FR) *N B King*
5 b g Lone Bid(FR) —Grive Star (FR) (Seurat)
1702[6]

Pur Sucre (FR) *R Pritchard-Gordon* a106 96
4 ch g Zamindar(USA) —Sugar (FR) (Nashwan (USA))
1077[5] 5115a[0]

Pursuit Of Glory (IRE) *David Wachman* a93 106
2 b f Fusaichi Pegasus(USA) —Sophisticat (USA) (Storm Cat (USA))
6441[3] ◆ 6967a[11]

Pursuit Of Purpose *G L Moore* 20
2 b f Dansili—Sinead (USA) (Irish River (FR))
6076[11]

Purus (IRE) *R A Teal* a87 93
6 b g Night Shift(USA) —Pariana (USA) (Bering)
904[5] 1211[10] 1982[9] 2371[4] 3222[12] 5589[5] 6194[4] 6734[6] 7143[6] 7277[5] 7507[12]

Pusey Street Lady *J Gallagher* a81 98
4 b m Averti(IRE) —Pusey Street Girl (Gildoran)
(1071) 1300[7] 1986[3] 2426[8] 3451[3] 3973[9] 4586[U]

Puskas (IRE) *J M Bradley* a54 83
5 b g King's Best(USA) —Chiquita Linda (IRE) (Mujadil (USA))
1865[3] 2330[6] 4285[4] 4903[9] 5152[8] 5374[7] 5916[8]

Put It On The Card *J S Wainwright* a66 57
4 ch r Bertolini(USA) —Madame Jones (IRE) (Lycius (USA))
66[10]

Putney Bridge (USA) *Mme C Head-Maarek* 103
3 b c Mizzen Mast(USA) —Valentine Band (USA) (Dixieland Band (USA))
1362a[7] 2096a[4] 4719a[7]

Putra Laju (IRE) *J W Hills* a73 51
4 b h Trans Island—El Corazon (IRE) (Mujadil (USA))
21[4] 274[6] 660[3] 805[4] 1085[4] 1486[3] 1932[7] 2513[9] 3822[9] 6827[3] 7194[5] 7345[7] 7500[4] 7702[11]

Putra One (IRE) *M A Jarvis* 59
2 b g Danehill Dancer(IRE) —Veronica Cooper (IRE) (Kahyasi)
6777[9] 7200[7]

Putra Square *P F I Cole* a83 87
4 b g Cadeaux Genereux—Razzle (IRE) (Green Desert (USA))
1026[3] 1256[2] 1473[15] 2120[5]

Puy D'Arnac (FR) *G A Swinbank* a70 84
5 b g Acteur Francais(USA) —Chaumeil (FR) (Mad Captain)
963[2] (1137) ◆ (1299) ◆ 1568[7] 1798[7] 6279[7] 6948[6] (7128) 7459[6]

Puzzlemaster *G G Margarson* 56
2 ch c Lomitas—Norcroft Joy (Rock Hopper)
6230[6] ◆ 6552[6]

Pyrenees (IRE) *David Wachman* a72 100
3 ch c Rock Of Gibraltar(IRE) —Belsay (Belmez (USA))
2435a[9]

Pyro (USA) *Steven Asmussen* a118
3 bb c Pulpit(USA) —Wild Vision (USA) (Wild Again (USA))
1820a[8] 6995a[6]

Pyrrha *C F Wall* 82
2 b f Pyrus(USA) —Demeter (USA) (Diesis)
2979[2] (3348) ◆ 4403[12] 6426[2]

Pyrus Time (IRE) *J S Moore* a52 28
2 b g Pyrus(USA) —Spot In Time (Mtoto)
2769[8] 7498[10]

Qaasi (USA) *M Brittain* a63 62
6 ch g Rahy(USA) —Recording (USA) (Danzig (USA))
(145) (197) 238[2] 664[5] 720[5] 771[5] 2286[7] 2701[6] 2804[5] 3589[10] 5003[4] 5456[8] 7169[8] 7322[7]

Qadar (IRE) *N P Littmoden* a101 100
6 b g Xaar—Iktidar (Green Desert (USA))
137[3] 226[8] 337[4] 679[7] 836[8] 904[6] 969[10] 1134[4]

Qalahari (IRE) *D J Coakley* 93
2 b f Bahri(USA) —Daqtora (Dr Devious (IRE))
2638[2] ◆ 3348[2] (4321) 5266[8] 6401[2] 7107[2] ◆

Qasayed (USA) *C E Brittain* a58 55
3 b f Diesis—Bright And Cheery (USA) (Event Of The Year (USA))
2971[11] 4349[7] 4770[6]

Qassas *Michael David Murphy* 71
6 b g Nashwan(USA) —Hasanat (Night Shift (USA))
4003a[8]

Qelaan (USA) *M P Tregoning* a58 66
2 b f Dynaformer(USA) —Irtahal (USA) (Swain (IRE))
5048[8] 5469[7]

Qeyaada (USA) *E A L Dunlop* a54 62
3 b f Elusive Quality(USA) —Al Desima (Emperor Jones (USA))
6047[6] 6393[7] 6762[8]

Quadrifolio *N Tinkler* 19
2 b g Key Of Luck(USA) —Berkeley Note (IRE) (Victory Note (USA))
1392[5] 1574[6] 3225[8] 4203[9] 4873[10]

Quaglino Way (GR) *P R Charnings* a70 70
4 b g Mark Of Esteem(IRE) —Pringipessa's Way (Machiavellian (USA))
2897[4] ◆ 3208[8] 3764[4] 4084[7] 4481[6] 5816[6]

Quai D'Orsay *M Johnston* 79
2 ch c Sulamani(IRE) —Entente Cordiale (USA) (Affirmed (USA))
(6151) ◆ 6648[8]

Quail Landing *M P Tregoning* a67 47
3 b f Mark Of Esteem(IRE) —Tarneem (USA) (Zilzal (USA))
2834[6] 3823[2] 4566[4] 6935[4]

Quality Street *P Butler* a79 67
6 ch m Fraam—Pusey Street Girl (Gildoran)
94[6] 275[6] 312[4] 427[6] 1842[17] 2337[11] 3316[5] 4307[9] 4824[6] 7392[7]

Quam Celerrime *P A Blockley* a76 95
3 b g Xaar—Divine Secret (Hernando (FR))
1171[6] 2953[9] 7598a[12]

Quanah Parker (IRE) *R M Whitaker* 81
2 b c Namid—Uncertain Affair (IRE) (Darshaan)
4213[5] 4847[2] (5499) 6483[17]

Quantum Leap *S Dow* a73 73
11 b g Efisio—Prejudice (Young Generation)
1038[8] 1153[3] 1565[7] 2128[9]

Quarayed (USA) *J-C Rouget* 104
3 b f Dynaformer(USA) —Golden Aster (USA) (Seeking The Gold (USA))
1323a[4] 5038a[3]

Quaroma *Jane Chapple-Hyam* a69 97
3 ch f Pivotal—Quiz Time (Efisio)
2506[5] 2896[5] 3883[2] (4258) ◆ (5073) ◆ 6064a[3] 6568a[5]

Quartz Jem (IRE) *Mme Pia Brandt* 98
4 b g Sakhee(USA) —Erinys (FR) (Kendor (FR))
4880a[6] 7429a[2]

Quatermain *B Smart* 83
2 ch c Peintre Celebre(USA) —Fancy Lady (Cadeaux Genereux)
3245[10] (4214) 4733[2] 5447[3] 5895[13] 6946[2]

Que Beauty (IRE) *R C Guest* a44 26
3 b f Val Royal(FR) —Ardbess (Balla Cove)
7376[10] 7695[12] 7776[8]

Quebec Citizen (BRZ) *M Al Muhairi* a91 59
5 b h Know Heights(IRE) —Importanza (BRZ) (Basim (USA))
493a[5] 651a[9]

Queen Althea (IRE) *Noel Meade* a81 76
4 b m Bach(IRE) —Countess Marengo (IRE) (Revoque (IRE))
4493a[8]

Queen America (FR) *Robert Collet* a77 101
2 b f American Post—Gandelia (FR) (Ganges (USA))
5301a[3] 5739a[5] 5987a[6] 6713a[6]

Queen Eleanor *J H M Gosden* a67 75
2 b f Cape Cross(IRE) —Rainbow Queen (Rainbow Quest (USA))
6622[6] ◆ 6945[2] ◆

Queen Excalibur *C Roberts* a21 61
9 ch m Sabrehill(USA) —Blue Room (Gorytus (USA))
2241[6] 2453[2] 2990[9] 3311[7] 3903[9] 4366[8]

Queen Jock (USA) *Tracey Collins* a86 90
3 bb f Repent(USA) —My Special K'S (USA) (Tabasco Cat (USA))
201a[4] 496a[9] 1230a[6] 2433a[9] 3619a[8] 6689a[12]

Queen Macha (IRE) *A M Hales* a52 20
3 b f Almutawakel—Cahermee Queen (USA) (King Of Kings (IRE))
424[3] 931[7] 1176[7] 2260[10] 2456[8]

Queen Of Burlesque (USA) *B J Meehan* a28
2 bb f Black Mambo(USA) —Berlinette (USA) (Maudlin (USA))
5798[11] 6016[14]

Queen Of Dalyan (IRE) *P C Haslam* 26
2 ch f Redback—Face The Storm (IRE) (Barathea (IRE))
1390[6] 2216[6]

Queen Of Destiny (IRE) *B Palling* a26
2 b f Superior Premium—Divine Miss-P (Safawan)
6089[10]

Queen Of France (USA) *David Wachman* a95 93
4 b m Danehill(USA) —Hidden Storm (USA) (Storm Cat (USA))
1199a[3]

Queen Of Naples *J H M Gosden* a73 104
3 b f Singspiel(IRE) —Napoleon's Sister (IRE) (Alzao (USA))
(1638) 1915[4] 2305[6] 3720[3] 4549[5] 5826[7]

Queen Of Thebes (IRE) *G L Moore* 80
2 b f Bahri(USA) —Sopran Marida (IRE) (Darshaan)
(3558) 4108[7] 5642[7] 6426[17]

Queen Sally (IRE) *J L Spearing* 70
2 b f Key Of Luck(USA) —Crystal Blue (IRE) (Bluebird (USA))
3259[3] 4176[7] 5116[3] 6172[8] 6535[10]

Queen Sensazione (IRE) *B Grizzetti* 89
2 b f King Charlemagne(USA) —Sensazione (Cadeaux Genereux)
(2744a)

Queens Fair (IRE) *Thomas Mullins* a52 62
2 b f King Charlemagne(USA) —Fun Of The Fair (Mistertopogigo (IRE))
6320a[19]

Queens Flight *J Noseda* a54
2 b f King's Best(USA) —Birdie (Alhaarth (IRE))
7578[5] 7726[7]

Queens Forester *P F I Cole* 36
2 b f Needwood Blade—Bonsai (IRE) (Woodman (USA))
3348[15] 4692[9] 6008[11]

Queens Mantle *P J Makin* a54 28
3 b f Bold Edge—Queen Shirley (IRE) (Fairy King (USA))
917[6]

Queen's Speech (IRE) *J H M Gosden* a80 78
3 b f Medicean—Jazan (IRE) (Danehill (USA))
1270[4] ◆ 1525[11] 2052[2] 2288[5] 3057[9] 4447[2] 5019[6] 5471[P] (Dead)

Queen's Treasure (IRE) *S Dow* a14 46
3 b f Bahamian Bounty—Daltak (Night Shift (USA))
59[5]

Quelle Surprise (IRE) *Tracey Collins* a50 57
2 b f Noverre(USA) —Quelle Celtique (FR) (Tel Quel (FR))
6320a[28]

Que Piensa Cat (ARG) *Saeed Bin Suroor* 59
4 ch m Easing Along(USA) —Compenetrada (ARG) (Compatible (ARG))
4660[13] 5506[12]

Querido (GER) *M Bradstock* 57
4 b h Acatenango(GER) —Quest Of Fire (FR) (Rainbow Quest (USA))
4978[7] 6177[11]

Quest For Honor *T Doumen* 106
4 gr h Highest Honor(FR) —Quest For Ladies (Rainbow Quest (USA))
1240a[7] 4880a[4] 5926a[2] 7162a[8]

Quest For Success (IRE) *R A Fahey* a85 89
3 b g Noverre(USA) —Divine Pursuit (Kris)
1999[3] 2410[10] 3141[7] 3723[14] 6532[5] 6842[9] (6976) 7041[4] (7129) ◆ 7418[8]

Quick Flash *R M Beckett*
3 b f Fantastic Light(USA) —Brief Glimpse (IRE) (Taufan (USA))
5463[10]

Quick Gourmet *A G Foster* 42
2 b f Lend A Hand—Rhiann (Anshan)
6151[6] 7221[4]

Quick Off The Mark *J G Given* a68 46
3 b f Dr Fong(USA) —Equity Princess (Warning)
6393[10] 7166[6] 7368[3] 7669[5] (7786)

Quick Release (IRE) *D M Simcock* a87 78
3 b c Red Ransom(USA) —Set The Mood (USA) (Dixie Brass (USA))
4345[6]

Quick Single (USA) *D R C Elsworth* a70 66
2 bb c Doneraile Court(USA) —Summer Strike (USA) (Smart Strike (CAN))
6080[6] 6620[5] 6858[4] 7306[12] 7472[9]

Quicks The Word *T A K Cuthbert* a28 65
8 b g Sri Pekan(USA) —Fast Tempo (IRE) (Statoblest)
2444[2] 2936[5] 3255[7] 3713[3] 4293[5] 7218[12]

Quicuyo (GER) *P Monteith* 48
5 ch g Acatenango(GER) —Quila (IRE) (Unfuwain (USA))
5415[5] 5993[8]

Quiet Elegance *E J Alston* 96
3 b f Fantastic Light(USA) —Imperial Bailiwick (IRE) (Imperial Frontier (USA))
(1170) 1401[12] 2606[10] 5884[5] 6290[3] 6651[9]

Quiet Times (IRE) *K A Ryan* a94 64
9 ch g Dolphin Street(FR) —Super Times (Sayf El Arab (USA))
41[6] 71[3]

Quijano (GER) *P Schiergen* 121
6 ch g Acatenango(GER) —Quila (IRE) (Unfuwain (USA))
816a[5] 1091a[4] 1666a[5] (3075a) 4232a[2] 6506a[9]

Quilboquet (BRZ) *L Kelp* a86 91
5 br h Jules(USA) —Greystoke (BRZ) (Tokatee (USA))
2233a[6]

Qui Moi (CAN) *J R Fanshawe* a53 80
3 bb f Swain(IRE) —Qui Bid (USA) (Spectacular Bid (USA))
1243[4] 2046[2] (2717) 4790[10] 6033[7] 6346[11]

Quince (IRE) *J Pearce* a86 90
5 b g Fruits Of Love(USA) —Where's Charlotte (Sure Blade (USA))
962[3] 1072[7] 1682[12] 2120[7] (3029) 3461[6] 3736[6] 4396[2] 4894[7] 5699[2] 6479[11] 7459[5] 7657[2] 7785[5]

Quinmaster (USA) *M Halford* a103 109
6 gr g Linamix(FR) —Sherkiya (IRE) (Goldneyev (USA))
829a[5] 7235a[7]

Quinzey's Best (IRE) *W J Knight* a50 58
3 ch f King's Best(USA) —Quinzey (JPN) (Carnegie (IRE))
1504[7] 1926[9] 2560[9] 3384[5] 3845[5] 4572[10] 5607[9] 5994[11]

Quiquillo (USA) *H R A Cecil* a60 60
2 ch f Cape Canaveral(USA) —Only Seventeen (USA) (Exploit (USA))
6166[5] 6887[6]

Quirina *J H M Gosden* 92
3 b f Red Ransom(USA) —Qirmazi (USA) (Riverman (USA))
1946[4] 2328[7] (3672) (5075) 5311[5] 6293[4] 7108[6]

Quiron (IRE) *Carmen Bocskai* a67 107
7 b g Desert King(IRE) —Quebra (GER) (Surumu (GER))
423a[3] 605a[8]

Quitit (IRE) *Mrs S A Watt* a61 73
3 b g Kalanisi(IRE) —Wattrey (Royal Academy (USA))
(7042) 7177[8]

Quito (IRE) *Mrs R A Carr* a79 108
11 b r Machiavellian(USA) —Qirmazi (USA) (Riverman (USA))
6975[5] 7243[10] 7381[9]

Quorn Master *Mrs P Ford* a47
6 b g Bal Harbour—Queen Of The Quorn (Governor General)
6659[11]

Quorum (GER) *M Al Muhairi* a92 76
5 b g Acatenango(GER) —Quest Of Fire (FR) (Rainbow Quest (USA))
382a[9] 476a[5]

Quotation *Sir Michael Stoute* a94 95
3 b f Medicean—Eloquent (Polar Falcon (USA))
2123[3] (3679) 5907[4]

Quws Vision (IRE) *Mrs L C Jewell*
5 b m Quws—Turtle Vision (IRE) (Turtle Island (IRE))
1283[5] 2255[15]

Raaeidd (IRE) *M A Jarvis* a78 59
2 b c King's Best(USA) —Bahr (Generous (IRE))
7104[6] (7312)

Rabbit Fighter (IRE) *D Shaw* a80 78
4 ch g Observatory(USA) —Furnish (Green Desert (USA))
901[8] 1015[9] (1312) 3454[6] 3724[4] 3998[2] 4341[3] 4962[7] 5260[3] 5648[6] 5861[7] 6634[11] 7077[11] 7428[7] 7653[7]

Rabeera *A M Balding* 66
3 b f Beat Hollow—Gai Bulga (Kris)
1440[8] 2716[10] 3729[4] 4259[10]

Raccoon (IRE) *Mrs R A Carr* 86
8 b g Raphane(USA) —Kunucu (IRE) (Bluebird (USA))
1997[3] 2145[4] ◆ 2551[5] 3112[3] (3546) 4064[7] 4294[2] 5398[5] 5970[7] 6310[2] 6486[2]

Racecar Rhapsody (USA) *Kenneth McPeek* a102
3 b c Tale Of The Cat(USA) —Reflect The Music (USA) (A.P. Indy (USA))
2215a[4]

Racer Forever (USA) *J H M Gosden* a111 116
5 b g Rahy(USA) —Ras Shaikh (USA) (Sheikh Albadou)
474a[4] (668a) ◆ 738a[6] 1767[2] 1989[6] 3197[11] (3498) 3921[7] 4506[9] 6285[5] 6814[14]

Racie Gracie *C A Dwyer* 55
3 gr f Dr Fong(USA) —Maxizone (FR) (Linamix (FR))
732[5]

Racinger (FR) *F Head* 116
5 b h Spectrum(IRE) —Dibenoise (FR) (Kendor (FR))
818a[14] (4212a) 5138a[7] 6270[7] 7162a[3]

Racingisdreaming (USA) *J-C Rouget* 97
2 b c Fusaichi Pegasus(USA) —Luna Wells (IRE) (Sadler's Wells (USA))
5739a[6]

Racing Stripes (IRE) *K O Cunningham-Brown* a57 61
4 ch g Night Shift(USA) —Swan Lake (IRE) (Waajib)
211[6] 263[5] 414[10] 1675[13] 2934[3] 3346[8] 3565[5] 3733[3]

Racketeer (IRE) *J H M Gosden* a80
2 b c Cape Cross(IRE) —Flirtation (Pursuit Of Love)
7498[2] ◆ (7660)

Radames (GER) *U Bosshard*
9 br g Lagunas—Royal Ascot (GER) (Pentathlon)
603a[10]

Radegund Abbey *B Smart* 64
2 b c Nayef(USA) —St Radegund (Green Desert (USA))
6151[8] 6384[3] 6760[6]

Radhakunda *S Billeri* 99
3 b f Galileo(IRE) —Nawasib (IRE) (Warning)
2439a[2] 3076a[8]

Radiator Rooney (IRE) *Patrick Morris* a70 59
5 br g Elnadim(USA) —Queen Of The May (IRE) (Nicolotte)
54[2] ◆ (404) 414[4] 7611[4] 7762[10]

Raedah (USA) *M A Jarvis* a62 80
2 b f Elusive Quality(USA) —Fatwa (IRE) (Lahib (USA))
3378[2] ◆ (4456) 6172[15] 6575[5]

Rafaan (USA) *M Johnston* 72
2 bb c Gulch(USA) —Reem Al Barari (USA) (Storm Cat (USA))
5579[2] ◆ 6029[3]

Rafferty (IRE) *S Dow* a65 58
9 ch g Lion Cavern(USA) —Badawi (USA) (Diesis)
151[11] 276[4] 429[4] 621[5] (Dead)

Raffish *M J Scudamore* a40 74
6 ch g Atraf—Valadon (High Line)
4817[6]

Raffys Rock (IRE) *S C Williams* 15
2 b g Intikhab(USA) —Sagrada (GER) (Primo Dominie)
6552[12] 7240[14]

Rafiqa (IRE) *C F Wall* 86
2 b f Mujahid(USA) —Shamara (IRE) (Spectrum (IRE))
(3882) 4781[5] 5511[14] (6058) 6240[4]

Rafta (IRE) *W G Harrison* 21
2 b f Atraf—First Kiss (GER) (Night Shift (USA))
6548[7] 6785[14]

Ragamuffin Man (IRE) *W J Knight* a80 78
3 gr g Dalakhani(IRE) —Chamela Bay (IRE) (Sadler's Wells (USA))
1424[4] 2151[8] 6678[4] 6934[3]

Rag And Bone (CAN) *B J Meehan* a68
2 bb f Street Cry(IRE) —Something Mon (USA) (Maria's Mon (USA))
6697[11] 7332[2] 7561[5]

Ragdollianna *Norma Twomey* 87
4 b m Kayf Tara—Jupiters Princess (Jupiter Island)
3362[2] 4196[7] (4581) (5369) ◆ 6241[12]

Ragged Staff (IRE) *P A Fahy* a84 92
4 b g Desert Style(IRE) —Hardshan (IRE) (Warrshan (USA))
4512a[16]

Raggle Taggle (IRE) *R M Beckett* a73 97
2 b f Tagula(IRE) —Jesting (Muhtarram (USA))
1177[2] 1474[3] 2618[2] (3114) 3681[4] 4190[9] 5112a[2] 6068[7]

Ragheed (USA) *E Charpy* a46 107
4 ch h Rahy(USA) —Highbury (USA) (Seattle Slew (USA))
495a[7] 668a[2] ◆ 738a[7]

Ragiam (ITY) *A & G Botti* 102
3 b f Martino Alonso(IRE) —My Luigia (IRE) (High Estate)
2439a[3] 3076a[6] 7635a[4]

Raging Creek (USA) *R Bouresly* a73
9 b h Storm Creek(USA) —Yardstick (USA) (Sunny Clime (USA))
566a[8]

Rahaan (USA) *C E Brittain* a40 62
3 b f Forestry(USA) —Jordanesque (USA) (Mr Prospector (USA))
3318[9] 4194[11] 5205[6]

Rahan (FR) *G Bailly* 39
2 ch c Feu A Volonte(FR) —Missyos (FR) (Sicyos (USA))
4441a[10] 5850a[8]

Rahere (IRE) *M Johnston* 68
3 ch c King's Best(USA) —Ascot Cyclone (USA) (Rahy (USA))
4566[2] 5278[7] 6049[15] 6862[16]

Rahymi (USA) *F & L Camici* 54
2 br c Rahy(USA) —Timi (Alzao (USA))
2745a[11]

Rahy's Attorney (CAN) *Ian Black* 114
4 b g Crown Attorney(CAN) —Rahy's Hope (USA) (Rahy (USA))
(2472a) 6504a[6]

Rahy's Crown (USA) *G L Moore* a54 70
5 b g Rahy(USA) —Inca Princess (USA) (Big Spruce (USA))
6136[7] 7217[14] 7401[6] 7676[2] 7806[6]

Rahzeena *R Brotherton*
2 b g Raheen(USA) —Dreams Of Zena (Dreams End)
3309[10] 5473[11] 5778[16]

Raihanah *D Shaw* a17
4 b m Dr Fong(USA) —Al Shadeedah (USA) (Nureyev (USA))
598[6] 922[10]

Raimond Ridge (IRE) *M R Channon* a53 66
2 bb g Namid—Jinsiyah (USA) (Housebuster (USA))
1122[4] 1220[2] 1363[6] 3576[5] 4816[5] 7543[6] 7719[6]

Rain And Shade *E W Tuer* a76 63
4 ch g Rainbow Quest(USA) —Coretta (IRE) (Caerleon (USA))
1909[6]

Rainbow Bay *Miss Tracy Waggott* a70 76
5 b g Komaite(USA) —Bollin Victoria (Jalmood (USA))
1997[12] 2255[6] 2664[4] 3024[4] 3169[4] 4073[4] 4293[3] 4542[2] 4700[6] 5566[2] 5817[4] 6159[10] 6251[3]

Rainbow Crossing *F Rohaut* a79 101
3 b f Cape Cross(IRE) —Rainbows For All (IRE) (Rainbows For Life (CAN))
1375a[5] 5038a[4] (7635a)

Rainbow Dancing *Mlle H Van Zuylen* 103
3 b f Rainbow Quest(USA) —Danceabout (Shareef Dancer (USA))
6567a[5] 7348a[2]

Rainbow Dash (IRE) *T G McCourt* a77 77
9 b g Rainbow Quest(USA) —High Spirited (Shirley Heights)
754[2] (3137) 4511a[18]

Rainbow Fox *R A Fahey* a70 77
4 b g Foxhound(USA) —Bollin Victoria (Jalmood (USA))
1451[11] 1952[2] 2188[2] 2751[5] 2938[3] ◆ 3454[8] 4239[3] 4605[12] 5392[3] 5965[8] 6774[8]

Rainbow Mirage (IRE) *E S McMahon* a89 92
4 b g Spectrum(IRE) —Embers Of Fame (IRE) (Sadler's Wells (USA))
1617[7] 1985[5] 2504[7] 3367[3] (3887) 4206[2] 4853[5] 5405[7] (5772) 6249[3] 6763[6]

Rainbow Seeker *W J Haggas* a88 53
2 b g Dubai Destination(USA) —Zephirine Drouhin (Desert Style (IRE))
5649[8] 6000[7] 6620[11] (6906) (7113) ◆ 7335[3] (7575) ◆

Rainbow View (USA) *J H M Gosden* 117
2 b f Dynaformer(USA) —No Matter What (USA) (Nureyev (USA))
(4157) ◆ (4868) ◆ (5828) ◆ (6268)

Rainbow Zest *W Storey* 67
5 b g Rainbow Quest(USA) —Original (Caerleon (USA))
1752[6] (2446) 2749[9]

Raincoat *J H M Gosden* 113
4 b h Barathea(IRE) —Love The Rain (Rainbow Quest (USA))
(1629) 1944[9] ◆ 2797[5] 3743[5] 4508[12]

Rain Delayed (IRE) *G M Lyons* a92
2 b g Oasis Dream—Forever Phoenix (Shareef Dancer (USA))
6507a[2]

Rain Esteem *H-A Pantall* 73
3 b f Mark Of Esteem(IRE) —Rain Lily (FR) (Priolo (USA))
6742a[8]

Rain Of Melody (IRE) *Robert Collet* 78
2 b c Night Shift(USA) —Hit The Sky (USA) (Cozzene (USA))
5139a[5]

Rain Rush (IRE) *David Marnane* a95 101
5 b g Monashee Mountain(USA) —Ewar Sunrise (Shavian)
3531a[13] (5731a) 7157a[7]

Rain Stops Play (IRE) *M Quinn* a74 84
6 b g Desert Prince(IRE) —Pinta (IRE) (Ahonoora)
1456[5] 1729[6] 2373[12] 2642[11] 3964[8] 4162[8] 4479[5] 5069[8] 5318[11] 5631[13]

Rainy Night *R Hollinshead* a55 65
2 b c Kyllachy—Rainy Day Song (Persian Bold)
3259[4] 6953[4]

Raise Again (IRE) *Mrs P N Dutfield* a54 66
5 b g Raise A Grand(IRE) —Paryiana (IRE) (Shernazar)
922[7] 1053[5]

Raise All In (IRE) *N Wilson* a65 67
2 b f Exceed And Excel(AUS) —Inforapenny (Deploy)
3412[2] 4088[3] 4337[3] 5274[12] 5614[2] 6547[7] 6787[9] 7519[11] 7728[8]

Raise A Row (IRE) *Edward P Harty* a63 74
4 ch g Raise A Grand(IRE) —Tadasna (IRE) (Thatching)
4511a[16]

Raise The Goblet (IRE) *P Hughes* a80 78
4 b g Almutawakel—Saninka (IRE) (Doyoun)
4003a[4] 4511a[17]

Raja (IRE) *F Rohaut* a90 90
3 b f Pivotal—Limpopo (Green Desert (USA))
5955a[P]

Rajam *W K Goldsworthy* 44
10 b g Sadler's Wells(USA) —Rafif (USA) (Riverman (USA))
2643[6] 6929[10]

Rajayoga *M H Tompkins* a53 54
7 ch g Kris—Optimistic (Reprimand)
1726[8] 2091[2]

Rajeh (IRE) *J L Spearing* 97
5 b g Key Of Luck(USA) —Saramacca (IRE) (Kahyasi)
2107[6] 2372[6] 3044[3] (3480) (4314) 4508[3] 5249[3] 6061[7]

Ra Junior (USA) *B J Meehan* 99
2 b c Rahy(USA) —Fantasia Girl (IRE) (Caerleon (USA))
5468[4] 6026[2] (6443) 6779[2]

Rakeekah *J S Moore* a58 64
3 b f Bahri(USA) —Amanah (USA) (Mr Prospector (USA))
899[12] 5616[14]

Ramaad *Miss D Mountain* 81
3 ch g Dr Fong(USA) —Artifice (Green Desert (USA))
1894[2] (2929) 3475[3] 6431[9]

Ramatni *M Johnston* a83 85
3 b f Green Desert(USA) —Wardat Allayl (IRE) (Mtoto)
1170[6] 1923[12] 2405[4] 2967[10]

Ramblin Bob *W J Musson* a60 68
3 b g Piccolo—Bijan (IRE) (Mukaddamah (USA))
23[4] 3224[10] 4163[9] 4535[11] 5162[10] 5832[6] 6751[11]

Rambling Dancer (IRE) *Mrs Valerie Keatley* a60 53
4 b g Imperial Ballet(IRE) —Wayfarer's Inn (IRE) (Lucky Guest)
(7749)

Rambling Light *A M Balding* a84 79
4 b g Fantastic Light(USA) —Rambler (Selkirk (USA))
1335[6] 1630[10] 2308[4] 3090[5] (3529) 4407[8] 6734[8] 7302[3] 7439[2]

Rambling Socks *S R Bowring* a56 39
5 ch m Rambling Bear—Cledeschamps (Doc Marten)
864[2] (972) 1700[3] 1780[12] 2706[4] 2869[4] 3569[13]

Rambo Honours (IRE) *P A Blockley* a43 56
4 b g Dilshaan—Rousselino (USA) (Silver Hawk (USA))
435[8]

Ramona Chase *S Kirk* a98 102
3 b g High Chaparral(IRE) —Audacieuse (Rainbow Quest (USA))
1441[4] ◆ 1811[2] 2194[4] 2825[2] 3157[10] 3877[14] 4552[6] 5677[7] 5942[3] 6276[5] 6649[2] 6984[7]

Ramonti (FR) *Saeed Bin Suroor* 125
6 b h Martino Alonso(IRE) —Fosca (USA) (El Gran Senor (USA))
3940[5]

Rampallion *E Charpy* a101 103
5 b h Daylami(IRE) —Minute Waltz (Sadler's Wells (USA))
(202a) 476a[10] 650a[11]

Rampant Ronnie (USA) *P W D'Arcy* a65 62
3 b g Honor Glide(USA) —Jalfrezi (Jalmood (USA))
1962[10] 3183[6] (3692) 4796[10] 5407[5] 5537[10]

Ramprakash *M L W Bell* a65 61
3 b g Best Of The Bests(IRE) —Missy Dancer (Shareef Dancer (USA))
608[7] 773[4] 997[7] (2613) 3004[16] 3656[5] 4344[9] 5087[8] 5611[14]

Ramvaswani (IRE) *N B King* a52 41
5 b g Spectrum(IRE) —Caesarea (GER) (Generous (IRE))
330[12]

Randama Bay (IRE) *I A Wood* a81 73
3 bb c Frenchmans Bay(FR) —Randama (Akarad (FR))
902[7] 1057[4] 1572[2] 2246[2] 7211[6] (7507) 7606[6] 7740[6]

Rangali Belle *C A Horgan* a44 61
4 b m Diktat—Dalaauna (Cadeaux Genereux)
401[14]

Rankayo Hitam (USA) *P F I Cole* a79 71
3 b c Yonaguska(USA) —Catala (USA) (Northern Park (USA))
(135) 2378[6] 2665[14] 3138[4] (4181) 5248[6] 5377[4] 5708[7] 6417[8] 6736[13]

Rann Na Cille (IRE) *P T Midgley* a67 66
4 br m Agnes World(USA) —Omanah (USA) (Kayrawan (USA))
(719) 1021[3] 1185[7] 1642[4] 2036[5] 4107[8] 4285[2] 5374[3] 5626[4] 6595[7]

Rapanui Belle *G L Moore* a44 41
2 b f Compton Place—Belle Ile (USA) (Diesis)
2999[11] 3528[6] 4088[7] 5530[6] 5746[6] 6191[7]

Rapid City *A J McCabe* a90 84
5 b g Dansili—West Dakota (USA) (Gone West (USA))
929[5] 1502[3] 2057[4] 2711[10] 3802[7] 5910[10] 6243[17] 6659[4] 7068[5] 7309[8] 7461[7] 7553[4] (7707) 7800[3]

Rapid Flow *J W Unett* a51 36
6 b g Fasliyev(USA) —Fleet River (USA) (Riverman (USA))
1029[9] 1338[4]

Rapidity *E J O'Neill* a94 59
3 b c Mind Games—Lunasa (IRE) (Don't Forget Me)
(419) ◆ (484) ◆ (527) (573) ◆

Rapid Light *E A L Dunlop* a62
2 ch f Tobougg(IRE) —La Coqueta (GER) (Kris)
7578[3]

Rapid Release (CAN) *Sir Mark Prescott* a87 84
2 ch c Action This Day(USA) —Bail Money (USA) (St Jovite (USA))
2362[6] 2554[3] 2754[2] (3760) 4292[2] 4589[12] 6756[2]

Rapid Water *A M Balding* 60
2 b c Anabaa(USA) —Lochsong (Song)
6776[8]

Raptor (GER) *K R Burke* a106 106
5 b h Auenadler(GER) —Royal Cat (Royal Academy (USA))
960[11] 1103a[2] (1457) 1989[4] 3635[6] 3982a[5] 4587[15] 5360[12] 6104[16] 6476[28]

Raquel White *J L Flint* a70 64
4 b m Robellino(USA) —Spinella (Teenoso (USA))
31[2] 586[7] 1127[7] 7115[8] 7667[7]

Rare Art *S A Callaghan* a54 70
2 b c Kyllachy—Succumb (Pursuit Of Love)
5016[4] 6578[3] 6932[7] (7198)

Rare Coincidence *R F Fisher* a73 75
7 ch g Atraf—Green Seed (IRE) (Lead On Time (USA))
(722) 779[7] 1824[11] 2252[4] 6493[8] 6708[7] 7285[6] 7587[4] 7688[3]

Rare Old Bird *J F Panvert* a16
3 b f Bertolini(USA) —Rare Old Times (IRE) (Inzar (USA))
5679[9] 6254[11] 6633[9]

Rare Ransom *D K Weld* 95
2 b f Oasis Dream—Rapid Ransom (USA) (Red Ransom (USA))
(4513a) 5132a[3] 5549a[9] 6318a[6]

Rare Ruby (IRE) *Jennie Candlish* 67
4 b m Dilshaan—Ruby Setting (Gorytus (USA))
5396[7] 6054[7] 6672[6] 6861[8]

Rasaman (IRE) *K A Ryan* a86 90
4 b g Namid—Rasana (Royal Academy (USA))
983[8] 1451[13] 2489[8] 2968[8] 3405[7] 3594[2] (3956) ◆ (4246) 4555[20] 5796[2] 6174[11] 6651[8] 6842[2] 7384[7]

Rascal In The Mix (USA) *R M Whitaker* a56
2 rg f Tapit(USA) —Ready Cat (USA) (Storm Cat (USA))
7179[5]

Rascasse *Bruce Hellier* 50
3 b g Where Or When(IRE) —Sure Flyer (IRE) (Sure Blade (USA))
2700^{7} 3262^{5} 3786^{7} 4115^{7} 4850^{9} 6150^{8} 6308^{9}

Rash Judgement *W S Kittow* 91
3 b g Mark Of Esteem(IRE) —Let Alone (Warning)
1597^{3} ◆ 2171^{5} 2967^{6} 4591^{4} 5102^{9} 5270^{4} 5795^{8} 6402^{12}

Ras Laffan *D McCain Jnr* a57 58
3 b g Vettori(IRE) —Supreme Angel (Beveled (USA))
4663^{6} 6111^{2}

Rasmani *Miss Gay Kelleway* a34 37
4 ch m Medicean—Rasmalai (Sadler's Wells (USA))
2374^{5} 2929^{7} 3218^{12} 3573^{6} *3816^{7}*

Raspoutine (USA) *E Lellouche* 102
3 b c Seeking The Gold(USA) —Rolly Polly (IRE) (Mukaddamah (USA))
4719a^{5}

Rastignano (IRE) *V Caruso* 100
3 b c Spartacus(IRE) —Ravana (GER) (Lomitas)
2028a^{10}

Rathkenny (IRE) *William Coleman O'Brien* a63 33
10 b g Standiford(USA) —Shine (Sharrood (USA))
2264^{7}

Rathlin Light (USA) *W R Swinburn* 45
2 bb f Grand Slam(USA) —Baltic Sea (CAN) (Danzig (USA))
5214^{7}

Rathmolyon *D Haydn Jones* a58 71
3 ch f Bahamian Bounty—Feather Circle (IRE) (Indian Ridge)
1529^{2} 2102^{9} 2774^{5} 3526^{4} *6633^{4} 7346^{9} 7528^{9}*

Rationale (IRE) *S C Williams* a91 89
5 b g Singspiel(IRE) —Logic (Slip Anchor)
(450) ◆ *592^{3}* 2790^{3} 3490^{17} 4191^{15} 4771^{6} *5349^{13} 5940^{4} 6626^{3}* ◆

Rattan (USA) *H R A Cecil* 93
3 ch c Royal Anthem(USA) —Rouwaki (USA) (Miswaki (USA))
(2199) 3155^{15} 3880^{5} 5470^{6}

Rava (IRE) *S Wattel* a61 92
3 b f Nayef(USA) —Lucky Date (IRE) (Halling (USA))
(6742a)

Ravel (USA) *Todd Pletcher* a99
4 bb h Fusaichi Pegasus(USA) —Let (USA) (A.P. Indy (USA))
6373a^{5}

Ravenna *J R Gask* a72 79
4 ch m Compton Place—Cultural Role (Night Shift (USA))
6078^{15}

Raven Rascal *J F Coupland* a45 19
4 b m Zaha(CAN) —Eccentric Dancer (Rambo Dancer (CAN))
193^{10} 365^{8} 653^{5}

Raven's Pass (USA) *J H M Gosden* a128 131
3 ch c Elusive Quality(USA) —Ascutney (USA) (Lord At War (ARG))
1421^{2} 1808^{4} 3102^{2} 4010a^{2} 4518^{2} (5265) ◆ (6270) *(7001a)*

Ravine Rose *B I Case* a43 40
2 b f Lomitas—Chine (Inchinor)
4823^{11} 6205^{11} 6535^{9}

Ravi River (IRE) *Tom Dascombe* a80 81
4 ch g Barathea(IRE) —Echo River (USA) (Irish River (FR))
979^{8} *1636^{2} 7763^{2}* ◆ *7828^{6}*

Rawaabet (IRE) *R Hollinshead* a48 56
6 b g Bahhare(USA) —Haddeyah (USA) (Dayjur (USA))
299^{4} 1025^{10} 6161^{6} *7736^{3} 7815^{8}*

Rawaaj *Sir Michael Stoute* a56 63
2 gr g Linamix(FR) —Inaaq (Lammtarra (USA))
2592^{16} 5579^{6} *6282^{4}*

Rawdon (IRE) *M L W Bell* a81 75
7 b g Singspiel(IRE) —Rebecca Sharp (Machiavellian (USA))
6726^{3} *7797^{2}*

Raw Silk (USA) *Thomas Albertrani* 106
3 b f Malibu Moon(USA) —Silken Sash (IRE) (Danehill (USA))
3807a^{8} 5164a^{3} 5745a^{5}

Raydan (IRE) *D R Gandolfo* a60
6 b g Danehill(USA) —Rayseka (IRE) (Dancing Brave (USA))
180^{8} 332^{9} 5869^{10}

Ray Diamond *M Madgwick* a52 52
3 ch g Medicean—Musical Twist (USA) (Woodman (USA))
335^{3} 623^{3} 2922^{13} 3524^{13} 4254^{9} *4527^{6}* 5537^{12}

Raydiya (IRE) *John M Oxx* 98
3 b f Marju(IRE) —Raydaniya (IRE) (In The Wings)
2435a^{5} (3805a) 4100a^{12} 5136a^{9}

Rayeni (IRE) *John M Oxx* 110
2 ch c Indian Ridge—Rayyana (IRE) (Rainbow Quest (USA))
(7029a)

Rayhani (USA) *M P Tregoning* a97 105
5 b g Theatrical—Bahr Alsalaam (USA) (Riverman (USA))
1503^{3} 1812^{4} 2168^{13} *3398^{3}* 4443^{5} 5279^{4} 6302^{10} *6698^{10}*

Raymi Coya (CAN) *M Botti* 99
3 b f Van Nistelrooy(USA) —Something Mon (USA) (Maria's Mon (USA))
(2170) 3194^{8} 4674a^{8} 5506^{7} 6266^{8} 6781^{11}

Ray Of Joy *J R Jenkins* a75 57
2 b f Tobougg(IRE) —Once Removed (Distant Relative)
3323^{5} 4256^{8} 4905^{5} 5581^{3} *(6017) 6223^{3} 6732^{3} 7306^{2} 7538^{7}*

Rayvin Mad (IRE) *P W Chapple-Hyam* 77
2 b c Bahamian Bounty—Poppy's Song (Owington)
1399^{6} 1616^{2} 1967^{3}

Raza Cab (IRE) *Karen George* a83 67
6 b g Intikhab(USA) —Laraissa (Machiavellian (USA))
506^{6} 643^{3} 717^{4} 819^{2}

Razzano (IRE) *A M Hales* a52 57
4 b m Fasliyev(USA) —Shewillifshewants (IRE) (Alzao (USA))
1275^{6} 1416^{3} 2069^{2} 4808^{2} 5166^{8} *5797^{10}*

Reaction *M R Channon* a69 79
2 ch g Alhaarth(IRE) —Hawas (Mujtahid (USA))
3495^{3} 4184^{7} 4636^{3} *5870^{5}* 6344^{5} (6673)

Readily *J G Portman* a55 67
2 ch f Captain Rio—Presently (Cadeaux Genereux)
1680^{4} 1961^{10} 2638^{5} 3032^{5} 3570^{2} 4243^{5} *7212^{2} 7361^{4} 7600^{2} 7795^{3}*

Ready For Battle (IRE) *C G Cox* 58
2 b g Namid—Enamoured (Groom Dancer (USA))
5225^{14} 5649^{6} 6072^{7}

Ready's Echo (USA) *Todd Pletcher* a109 97
3 bb c More Than Ready(USA) —Menekineko (USA) (Kingmambo (USA))
2858a^{3}

Ready To Crown (USA) *Andrew Turnell* a55 58
4 b m More Than Ready(USA) —Dili (USA) (Chief's Crown (USA))
524^{6} 1142^{3} 1528^{5} 2100^{3} *5837^{3} 6255^{11}*

Ready To Prime *D K Ivory* a39 23
2 ch f Primo Valentino(IRE) —Blue Topaz (IRE) (Bluebird (USA))
1722^{5} 2042^{8} 6341^{12} *7282^{7} 7666^{11}*

Ready To Rocknroll (IRE) *J T Gorman* a79 89
3 b g Statue Of Liberty(USA) —Stream (Unfuwain (USA))
5550a^{8}

Real Dandy *J G Given* a41 60
2 b g Bahamian Bounty—You Make Me Real (USA) (Give Me Strength (USA))
3997^{7} 4593^{10} 4815^{5} *5591^{9}* 7079^{14}

Real Diamond *A Dickman* 65
2 b f Bertolini(USA) —Miss Fit (IRE) (Hamas (IRE))
1749^{7} 2206^{10} 4045^{9} 5043^{2} 6788^{3} (7038)

Realism (FR) *M W Easterby* a97 92
8 b g Machiavellian(USA) —Kissing Cousin (IRE) (Danehill (USA))
6974^{11}

Really Ransom *P C Haslam* 84
3 b f Red Ransom(USA) —Really Polish (USA) (Polish Numbers (USA))
2305^{9} 4435^{7} 5075^{6}

Really Really Wish *J R Best* a74 72
3 b g Bertolini(USA) —Shanghai Lil (Petong)
4127^{9} *5046^{3}* 5493^{13} 5839^{5} 6556^{5}

Realt Na Mara (IRE) *H Morrison* a82 77
5 bb g Tagula(IRE) —Dwingeloo (IRE) (Dancing Dissident (USA))
(41) ◆ *190^{2} 636^{2}* 4313^{4} ◆ 4865^{6} 5247^{14} *5594^{2} 5867^{7}* 6706^{10} *7724^{4}*

Reballo (IRE) *J R Fanshawe* a81 67
5 b g King's Best(USA) —Lyrical Dance (USA) (Lear Fan (USA))
(452) (Dead)

Re Barolo (IRE) *M Botti* a114 106
5 b h Cape Cross(IRE) —Dalaiya (USA) (Irish River (FR))
227^{8} 679^{4} (834) 1326^{8} *(1724)* 2465^{7} (3046) 5508^{14} *5941^{5} 6287^{2}* ◆ *7193^{2} 7420^{4}* 7741^{4}

Rebecca De Winter *R Hannon* a76 83
2 b f Kyllachy—Miss Adelaide (IRE) (Alzao (USA))
1762^{2} ◆ (1924) 3123^{9} 4190^{21} *(7212)*

Rebecca's Pride (IRE) *John C McConnell* a30 40
5 b m Stravinsky(USA) —Benguela (USA) (Little Current (USA))
3952^{3} 4851^{10}

Rebel Aclaim (IRE) *P F Cashman* a57 69
3 b f Acclamation—Tribal Rite (Be My Native (USA))
4494a^{3} 6366a^{24}

Rebel City *S A Callaghan* a69 49
2 b c Elusive City(USA) —Seguro (IRE) (Indian Ridge)
4778^{7} *7333^{6} 7465^{3} 7709^{3}*

Rebel Duke (IRE) *D W Barker* a88 94
4 ch g Namid—Edwina (IRE) (Caerleon (USA))
(1129) (1309) ◆ 1451^{5} 1917^{6} *7151^{8} 7697^{3}*

Rebellion *H Graham Motion* a118 107
5 b h Mozart(IRE) —Last Resort (Lahib (USA))
6995a^{2}

Rebellious Spirit *S Curran* a85 81
5 b g Mark Of Esteem(IRE) —Robellino Miss (USA) (Robellino (USA))
40^{2} (110) 208^{2} 433^{2} (685) (728) (811) (996) 1159^{5} 1630^{9} *7750^{4}* ◆

Rebel Prince (IRE) *M G Quinlan* 45
2 b g Barathea(IRE) —Rebel Clan (IRE) (Tagula (IRE))
6234^{4}

Rebel Radio (USA) *J Howard Johnson* 28
2 ch g Came Home(USA) —Visual Art (USA) (Deputy Minister (CAN))
5499^{10} 6212^{8}

Rebel Raider (IRE) *B N Pollock* a50
9 b g Mujadil(USA) —Emily's Pride (Shirley Heights)
231^{6} (471) 585^{6} 787^{5}

Rebel Swing *W R Muir* a41 61
2 b c Robellino(USA) —Ninia (USA) (Affirmed (USA))
6977^{11} ◆ 7200^{5} *7397^{11}*

Rebelwithoutacause (IRE) *George Baker* a45 44
2 b c Redback—Christmas Kiss (Taufan (USA))
3140^{13} 3888^{8} *4270^{7} 7728^{10}*

Rebetica *H Candy* 38
2 b f Domedriver(IRE) —Hymne D'Amour (USA) (Dixieland Band (USA))
5584^{9}

Rebounding *S C Williams* 62
2 b f Reset(AUS) —In Love Again (IRE) (Prince Rupert (FR))
4256^{10} 4488^{3} 5535^{12}

Recalcitrant *S Dow* a61 61
5 b g Josr Algarhoud(IRE) —Lady Isabell (Rambo Dancer (CAN))
176^{5} 1747^{3} 2070^{2} 2642^{7} *2943^{3}* 3208^{6} *3588^{8}* 4053^{7} 4414^{7} 4721^{6} *5020^{6}*

Recapturetheglory (USA) *L Roussel Iii* a110
3 b c Cherokee Run(USA) —Cold Awakening (USA) (Dehere (USA))
1820a^{5}

Recast (AUS) *L Laxon* 118
8 ch r Thunder Gulch(USA) —Abonnement (AUS) (Marauding (NZ))
2234a^{2}

Recent Times *T D Easterby* 70
3 b f Dansili—Forever Times (So Factual (USA))
2038^{7} 2399^{3} 2824^{5} 3231^{7} 4684^{14} 5110^{10} 5395^{9}

Recession Proof (FR) *S A Callaghan* a80 73
2 ch c Rock Of Gibraltar(IRE) —Elevate (Ela-Mana-Mou)
5246^{15} 5842^{9} *6135^{5} (6632)* 6761^{3} *6954^{3}*

Recharge (IRE) *Kevin Prendergast* 104
2 b c Cape Cross(IRE) —Rebelline (IRE) (Robellino (USA))
6316a^{4}

Reclamation (IRE) *Sir Mark Prescott* a87 57
3 b f Red Ransom(USA) —Overruled (IRE) (Last Tycoon)
(2052) 3134^{2} ◆ *3586^{2}* ◆ *5573^{3} 6355^{4}*

Recoil (IRE) *R Johnson* 57
3 b c Red Ransom(USA) —Dazilyn Lady (USA) (Zilzal (USA))
6152^{7} 6485^{13}

Record Breaker (IRE) *M Johnston* 102
4 b g In The Wings—Overruled (IRE) (Last Tycoon)
(2839) 3253^{2} 3721^{9} 4508^{10} 4844^{2} 5229^{12} 5494^{5} 5853^{15} 6652^{5}

Red *R M Stronge* a66 66
4 ch m Fraam—Great Tern (Simply Great (FR))
88^{8}

Red Alert Day *S A Callaghan* a101 107
3 b c Diktat—Strike Hard (IRE) (Green Desert (USA))
1471^{3} 2409^{3} 3119^{12} 3635^{3} 3880^{6} 6975^{3} *7381^{4} 7703^{7}*

Red Amaryllis *H J L Dunlop* a61 70
3 ch f Piccolo—Passiflora (Night Shift (USA))
1271^{4} 1867^{4} 2616^{5} 3086^{9} 3727^{3} 5002a^{2} *5627^{6}*

Red And White (IRE) *M Johnston* a76 84
3 b f Red Ransom(USA) —Candice (IRE) (Caerleon (USA))
6070^{5} 6293^{5} 6704^{2} *6904^{5}*

Redarsene *S Wynne* a71 71
3 ch c Sakhee(USA) —Triple Zee (USA) (Zilzal (USA))
1479^{3} 2199^{5} *(2805) 4083^{8}* 4377^{7} *5595^{7}* 6004^{6} *7166^{3}*

Red Barnet *S W Hall* a38 52
4 ch g Tipsy Creek(USA) —Heather Valley (Clantime)
261^{6}

Red Baron Dancer *J R Boyle* a74 83
2 ch g Fraam—Reamzafonic (Grand Lodge (USA))
3106^{2} *3689^{2}* (3949) (4659)

Red Birr (IRE) *P R Webber* a82 83
7 b g Bahhare(USA) —Cappella (IRE) (College Chapel)
(3181) 4509^{11} 5033^{3} 6346^{16} 6950^{5} *7116^{6} 7526^{10}*

Red Cape (FR) *Mrs R A Carr* a86 74
5 b g Cape Cross(IRE) —Muirfield (FR) (Crystal Glitters (USA))
137^{7} 1071^{11} *1133^{6} 1334^{6}* 1796^{13} 2058^{5} 2398^{3} 2892^{11} 3050^{7} 3255^{3} 3477^{5} 3601^{7} *7616^{4} 7782^{5}*

Red Cauldron *E J O'Neill* a47 66
3 ch g Choisir(AUS) —First Musical (First Trump)
2996^{8} 3421^{7} *3817^{4}*

Red Cell (IRE) *I W McInnes* a67 64
2 b g Kheleyf(USA) —Montana Lady (IRE) (Be My Guest (USA))
1183^{2} (1889) 2392^{5} 3809^{9} 4297^{3} 4768^{3} *4942^{2} 5204^{2} 5680^{6} 5834^{4} 7281^{7} 7719^{10}*

Red Century *G D Blake*
3 ch f Captain Rio—Red Millennium (IRE) (Tagula (IRE))
2620^{15}

Redchete *C E Brittain* 29
3 b f Red Ransom(USA) —Zacheta (Polish Precedent (USA))
3061^{13}

Red China Blues (USA) *J Howard Johnson* 48
2 ch g Royal Academy(USA) —Viewy (USA) (Majestic Light (USA))
2937^{6}

Red Contact (USA) *A Dickman* a76 46
7 b g Sahm(USA) —Basma (USA) (Grey Dawn II)
258^{3} 4031^{8}

Red Current *R A Harris* a61 70
4 b m Soviet Star(USA) —Fleet Amour (USA) (Afleet (CAN))
40^{4} 2476^{7} 2978^{10} 3518^{8} 4708^{3} 5059^{2} 5312^{7} (6175) 6400^{9} 6719^{6} *6908^{7} 7287^{10} 7518^{9} 7585^{5}* 7707^{8}

Red Dagger (IRE) *T D McCarthy* a34
2 b c Daggers Drawn(USA) —Dash Of Red (Red Sunset)
6000^{12} 6539^{14} *6877^{8} 7388^{9}*

Red Delight (IRE) *R A Fahey* 60
3 b f Redback—Lindas Delight (Batshoof)
1819^{15}

Redding Colliery (USA) *Jane Chapple-Hyam* a83 30
2 rg c Mineshaft(USA) —Joop (USA) (Zilzal (USA))
4360^{7} *6597^{2} (6910)*

Red Diva *Mario Hofer* 103
4 ch m Zinaad—Royal Cat (Royal Academy (USA))
2879a^{3}

Red Dune (IRE) *M A Jarvis* 100
3 b f Red Ransom(USA) —Desert Beauty (IRE) (Green Desert (USA))
2257^{2} (2800) (3849) 4590^{4} 5829^{4} 6782^{4}

Reddy Ronnie (IRE) *D Carroll* a41 55
4 b g Redback—Daffodil Dale (IRE) (Cyrano De Bergerac)
2662^{2} ◆ 3201^{8} 3593^{5}

Redeemed *M Brittain* a57 72
3 b f Red Ransom(USA) —Pastel (Lion Cavern (USA))
2118^{14} 2976^{12} *7610^{10} 7727^{6}*

Redefine *Mrs A L M King* a29
3 ch f Bertolini(USA) —Azur (IRE) (Brief Truce (USA))
4277^{15} *4860^{8}*

Red Eric *W M Brisbourne* a18 39
2 ch g Reset(AUS) —Lady Soleas (Be My Guest (USA))
3888^{10} 4290^{7} 5041^{9} *7666^{12} 7824^{8}*

Redesignation (IRE) *R Hannon* 99
3 b c Key Of Luck(USA) —Disregard That (IRE) (Don't Forget Me)
2311^{2} ◆ 2819^{6} 3896^{2} 4642^{2} (5843) 6784^{4} 6984^{2}

Red Expresso (IRE) *Ollie Pears* a68 78
3 ch g Intikhab(USA) —Cafe Creme (IRE) (Catrail (USA))
6660^{3} 6936^{8} 7373^{3} (7632) 7695^{3} 7775^{6}

Red Fama *N Bycroft* a56 84
4 ch g Fraam—Carol Again (Kind Of Hush)
1^{2} 435^{4} 552^{5} 991^{9} 1913^{2} (4966) (5305) ◆ (5637) 5992^{2}

Redford (IRE) *M L W Bell* 108
3 b g Bahri(USA) —Ida Lupino (IRE) (Statoblest)
(2819) ◆ 3155^{14} ◆ (3491) ◆ 4405^{6} 5025^{4}

Red Gala *Sir Michael Stoute* a112 114
5 b h Sinndar(IRE) —Red Camellia (Polar Falcon (USA))
1468^{5} 1944^{4} 2625^{5} 3497^{3} (5494) *(6286)* ◆

Redhead (IRE) *R Hannon* a65 65
2 ch f Redback—Rinneen (IRE) (Bien Bien (USA))
2368^{5} *2713^{4} 3135^{7}* 3677^{4} *4079^{7}* 4666^{5} *5914^{9} 7257^{8} 7652^{8} 7832^{9}*

Red Horse (IRE) *M L W Bell* 45
2 ch g Bachelor Duke(USA) —Miss Childrey (IRE) (Dr Fong (USA))
5066^{13} 6080^{16} 6776^{13} 7240^{13}

Red Hot Pepper *A M Balding* 33
2 b f Red Ransom(USA) —Granita (CHI) (Roy (USA))
6117^{17}

Red Humour (IRE) *B W Hills* a75 56
2 bb c Elusive City(USA) —Arctic Flight (Polar Falcon (USA))
3219^{10} *(4305)* ◆ *4729^{4}* 5447^{7} 6970^{10}

Red Icon *R M Beckett* a74 79
3 b f Red Ransom(USA) —Blue Icon (Peintre Celebre (USA))
1926^{6} 2564^{13} 3057^{2} ◆ 3729^{5} 4427^{2} 4582^{5} *5913^{4}* (Dead)

Red Jade *J H M Gosden* 81
3 ch c Dubai Destination(USA) —Red Slippers (USA) (Nureyev (USA))
6393^{3} ◆ (6583)

Red Junior *B J Meehan* a68 74
2 b c Red Ransom(USA) —Island Destiny (Kris)
6026^{3} ◆ *6597^{5}* 6977^{10}

Red Kestrel (USA) *Saeed Bin Suroor* a93 83
3 ch g Swain(IRE) —The Caretaker (Caerleon (USA))
4124^{3} *(4941)* ◆

Red Kyte *K A Ryan* 82
2 br f Hawk Wing(USA) —Ruby Affair (IRE) (Night Shift (USA))
3959^{12} 4521^{7} (5004) 6240^{10} 6426^{4}

Red Lancer *D Nicholls* a68 86
7 ch g Deploy—Miss Bussell (Sabrehill (USA))
525^{7} 981^{13}

Red Lily (IRE) *J R Fanshawe* a74 72
3 b f Red Ransom(USA) —Panna (Polish Precedent (USA))
2376^{4} 2603^{2} 3793^{4} 5322^{3} 6007^{6} 6529^{4} *6905^{3} 7261^{5} (7342)*

Red Linnet *M L W Bell* a76 74
3 b f Cape Cross(IRE) —Red Conquest (Lycius (USA))
454^{2} ◆ *(674)* 1618^{6} 2045^{5} *7305^{3}*

Red Lord (AUS) *Anthony Cummings* 106
5 b g Redoute's Choice(AUS) —Dame Cath (NZ) (Zabeel (NZ))
7188a^{16}

Redlynch *S Parr*
3 b g Sinndar(IRE) —Red Azalea (Shirley Heights)
4461^{P} *7798^{6}*

Red Margarita (IRE) *D R C Elsworth* 13
2 ch f Dalakhani(IRE) —Red Bartsia (Barathea (IRE))
6760^{12}

Red Max (IRE) *T D Easterby* 58
2 b g Kheleyf(USA) —Set Trail (IRE) (Second Set (IRE))
3049^{6} 3492^{6} 4384^{5} 6112^{6} 6549^{7}

Red Merlin (IRE) *C G Cox* 79
3 ch g Soviet Star(USA) —Truly Bewitched (USA) (Affirmed (USA))
2244^{7} 2695^{2} 3004^{4} 3793^{3} 4448^{7} 5058^{3} (5814) 6202^{2} (6678)

Red Moloney (USA) *Kevin Prendergast* a99 109
4 b g Sahm(USA) —Roja (USA) (L'Enjoleur (CAN))
906^{13} (1353a) 1655a^{2} 3513a^{4} 3805a^{8} 5921a^{3}

Red Myth *Karen George*
2 ch f Arkadian Hero(USA) —Denise Best (IRE) (Goldmark (USA))
2239^{4} *4387^{10}* 5214^{16}

Redolent (IRE) *R Hannon* a93 108
3 ch c Redback—Esterlina (IRE) (Highest Honor (FR))
1213^{4} 1402^{4} (1797) (2544) 3306a^{2} 5025^{3} 5624a^{2} 6106^{8}

Redolini *W M Brisbourne*
2 b g Bertolini(USA) —Red Cloud (IRE) (Taufan (USA))
2569^{12} 4658^{10}

Red Rani *B W Duke* 1
3 ch f Whittingham(IRE) —Crystal Magic (Mazilier (USA))
3916^{9}

Red Reef *D J Coakley* a53 64
2 ch f King's Best(USA) —Rafiya (Halling (USA))
3135^{8} 4184^{9} 4720^{6} (5460)

Red River Boy *C W Fairhurst* 53
3 ch g Bahamian Bounty—Riviere Rouge (Forzando)
1795[10] 2287[8] (2661) 3283[7]

Red River Rebel *J R Norton* a50 59
10 b g Inchinor—Bidweaya (USA) (Lear Fan (USA))
2290[6]

Red Robert *J L Dunlop* a37 55
2 b c Dr Fong(USA) —Red Bug (Cadeaux Genereux)
3798[12] 4274[7] 5459[8] 5914[12] 6572[10]

Red Rock Canyon (IRE) *A P O'Brien* 118
4 b h Rock Of Gibraltar(IRE) —Imagine (IRE) (Sadler's Wells (USA))
2432a[3] 3121[11] 4406[4] 5276[7] 5732a[6] 6522a[16] 7000a[6]

Red Rock Prince (IRE) *P F I Cole* a13
3 b g Rock Of Gibraltar(IRE) —Red Bartsia (Barathea (IRE))
3094[0] 3688[8]

Red Rocks (IRE) *Mark Hennig* 125
5 bb h Galileo(IRE) —Pharmacist (IRE) (Machiavellian (USA))
(1990) 2791[6] (3995a) 7000a[10]

Red Romeo *G A Swinbank* a91 85
7 ch g Case Law—Enchanting Eve (Risk Me (FR))
(43) ◆ 259[4] 1069[12] 1327[15] 1409[2] 1774[9] 2083[5] 3203[U] 3435[6] 3928[10] 5635[3]

Red Rosanna *R Hollinshead* 70
2 b f Bertolini(USA) —Lamarita (Emarati (USA))
3178[2] ◆ 3734[4] 4176[8] 4965[2] (6051) 6274[7]

Red Rossini (IRE) *R Hannon* a74 77
2 b g Rossini(USA) —La Scala (USA) (Theatrical)
2709[2] 2999[4] (4020) 4857[4] 5103[4] 5466[10] 6274[4] 6469[7] 6666[5] 7335[7]

Red Rouge *G J Smith* 56
3 b f Celtic Swing—Red To Violet (Spectrum (IRE))
1751[9] 2156[5] 2486[3] 3115[2] 4048[14] 4298[2] 4531[11] (Dead)

Red Rudy *A W Carroll* a77 73
6 ch g Pivotal—Piroshka (Soviet Star (USA))
404[3] 539[4] 729[2] 896[2] 915[3] (1204) 2040[5] 2557[2] 2667[7]

Red Ruler (NZ) *John Sargent* 112
4 b g Viking Ruler(AUS) —Ransom Bay (USA) (Red Ransom (USA))
6835a[6]

Red Rumour (IRE) *R M Beckett* a93 92
3 b g Redback—Church Mice (IRE) (Petardia)
(1074) 1806[12] 2104[14] 5695[14] (5862) 6283[10] 7019[5]

Red Sabre *J S Moore* 44
2 ch c Deploy—Miss Bussell (Sabrehill (USA))
6122[14]

Redsensor *M Quinn* a74 74
3 b g Redback—Xtrasensory (Royal Applause)
632[7] 918[6] 2161[13] 2801[4] 3730[5] (4794) 6001[6] 6173[9] 6741[8] 7053[3] (Dead)

Redsetgo *S W Hall* 10
2 ch f Observatory(USA) —Tamani (IRE) (Unfuwain (USA))
2614[7] 3652[6]

Red Skipper (IRE) *N Wilson* 66
3 ch g Captain Rio—Speed To Lead (IRE) (Darshaan)
3298[7] 3753[10] 4241[2] 4702[8] (4952) 5224[5] 5504[5] 6042[2] 6792[4] 7111[6]

Red Somerset (USA) *R J Hodges* a96 93
5 b g Red Ransom(USA) —Bielska (USA) (Deposit Ticket (USA))
1067[5] 1365[6] 1719[3] 2152[4] 2540[8] 3529[5] 4104[2] (4364) (4927) 6130[7] 6667[8] 7019[4] (7560) 7755[2] (7813)

Red Sonja (IRE) *D Morris* a48 6
3 b f Kalanisi(IRE) —Pink Stone (FR) (Bigstone (IRE))
163[5] 416[13] 773[5] 3656[7]

Red Spider *J H M Gosden* a79 92
2 b c Red Ransom(USA) —Lane County (USA) (Rahy (USA))
(6165) 6973[9]

Red Stiletto *Rae Guest* a34 35
2 b f Red Ransom(USA) —The Blade (GER) (Sure Blade (USA))
4080[10] 6887[11]

Red Tarn *B Smart* a64 72
3 gr g Fraam—Cumbrian Melody (Petong)
2282[2] 2911[12] 3731[6] 6254[3] 6827[12] 7178[3] 7376[5] 7632[2]

Red Tulip (FR) *Mme C Head-Maarek* 74
3 ch f Bering—Silver Tulip (USA) (Silver Hawk (USA))
7450a[10]

Red Twist *H Morrison* a68 71
3 b g Red Ransom(USA) —Spinning The Yarn (Barathea (IRE))
2603[7] 3384[11] 4527[5] 5218[11]

Red Wind (IRE) *N Wilson* 27
3 ch g Tagula(IRE) —Trim (IRE) (Ela-Mana-Mou)
4379[9] 5110[13] 5501[8]

Red Wine *A J McCabe* a70 85
9 b g Hamas(IRE) —Red Bouquet (Reference Point)
91[7] 224[3] 430[4] 533[4] 675[3] 854[3] (963) (1020) 1159[7] 1299[6] 1732[4] (1798) 2107[12] 2591[3] 2822[2] 3480[7] 4146[5] 4742[6] 5092[11] 5967[3] 6107[3] 6721[11] 6948[8] ◆ 7064[6] 7177[3] 7301[6] 7493[9] 7797[6]

Redwood *B W Hills* 88
2 b c High Chaparral(IRE) —Arum Lily (USA) (Woodman (USA))
(6425) ◆

Reel Ale *P Winkworth* a63 53
2 ch c Reel Buddy(USA) —Betty Stogs (IRE) (Perugino (USA))
3267[8] 4305[4] 4778[6] 5671[6] 6017[6] 6694[5]

Reel Bluff *D W Barker* 53
2 b g Reel Buddy(USA) —Amber's Bluff (Mind Games)
1749[6] 6110[7] 6212[10] 6547[9]

Reel Buddy Blaze *T P Tate* 69
3 ch g Reel Buddy(USA) —Hope Chest (Kris)
2464[5] 3551[14] 3795[6] 4538[7] 4964[8]

Reel Buddy Star *G M Moore* 81
3 ch g Reel Buddy(USA) —So Discreet (Tragic Role (USA))
1750[6] 3263[4] 3494[4] 3887[2] 4783[3] (5504) 5772[5] 6482[7]

Reel Classy *T J Pitt* 18
3 ch f Reel Buddy(USA) —Classy Lassie (IRE) (Goldmark (USA))
3479[10] 4043[9]

Reel Cool *B Smart* 44
3 b f Reel Buddy(USA) —Waterfowl Creek (IRE) (Be My Guest (USA))
1751[10]

Reel Gift *R Hannon* a82 103
3 b f Reel Buddy(USA) —Its Another Gift (Primo Dominie)
1698[9] 2000[12] 2407[6]

Reel Hope *J R Best* 49
2 b f Reel Buddy(USA) —Compton Amber (Puissance)
3674[12] 4337[9] 5184[10]

Reeling N' Rocking (IRE) *B W Hills* a78 71
5 b m Mr Greeley(USA) —Mystic Lure (Green Desert (USA))
90[5] 692[10]

Reel Man *D K Ivory* a58 49
3 ch g Reel Buddy(USA) —Yanomami (USA) (Slew O'Gold (USA))
1060[9] 2084[3] 2805[9] 4278[15]

Reflective Glory (IRE) *J S Wainwright* a27 47
4 ch m City On A Hill(USA) —Sheznice (IRE) (Try My Best (USA))
193[12]

Refuse To Decline *D M Simcock* a33 50
2 ch f Refuse To Bend(IRE) —Oulianovsk (IRE) (Peintre Celebre (USA))
2368[6] 3349[12] 7422[11]

Regal Best (IRE) *Mrs A J Perrett* a68 86
3 b c King's Best(USA) —Carranza (IRE) (Lead On Time (USA))
(2994) 4197[5] 5862[11] 6467[10]

Regal Bird (USA) *M A Magnusson* a73 79
3 bb f Grand Slam(USA) —Storm Ring (USA) (Storm Bird (CAN))
2714[14] 3270[11] 5713[7]

Regal Curtsy *P R Chamings* a44 63
4 b m Royal Applause—Giant Nipper (Nashwan (USA))
2718[3] 3181[7] 3816[13]

Regal Dream (IRE) *J W Unett* a64 63
6 b g Namid—Lovely Me (IRE) (Vision (USA))
1578[10] 2950[11] 3951[9] 4125[8] 5816[8]

Regaleya (IRE) *H Rogers* a80 84
5 b m Mujadil(USA) —Probable (IRE) (Selkirk (USA))
3531a[15] 6510a[5]

Regal Flush *Saeed Bin Suroor* 116
4 b h Sakhee(USA) —Ruthless Rose (USA) (Conquistador Cielo (USA))
2192[2] 2625[3] 3154[6] 4551[5] (5646) 6444[8]

Regal Lyric (IRE) *T P Tate* 71
2 b g Royal Applause—Alignment (IRE) (Alzao (USA))
(6213) 6603[10] 7241[13]

Regal Parade *D Nicholls* a97 112
4 ch g Pivotal—Model Queen (USA) (Kingmambo (USA))
958[5] 1133[2] ◆ 1308[2] 1816[2] 1942[6] (3197) 3921[3] 4587[10] (6104) 6645[4]

Regal Royale *Peter Grayson* a76 74
5 b g Medicean—Regal Rose (Danehill (USA))
87[2] 121[2] (211) 414[7] 488[3] 628[8] 933[6] 1022[2] 1254[8] 1275[2] 2270[14] 2780[7] 2881[3] (3316) (3872) 4307[10] 4639[2] (4865) 5151[3] 5532[5] (5757) 6066[9] 6290[11] 6557[4]

Regal Step *R M H Cowell* 83
3 b f Royal Applause—Two Step (Mujtahid (USA))
2258[11] 3462[10] 3909[7] 4347[5] 5531[7]

Regal Veil *R W Price* a49 46
3 b f Royal Applause—Shararah (Machiavellian (USA))
(92) 237[6] 333[3] 583[2] 876[4] 1536[3] 2661[2] 2935[2] 3086[4] 3571[4] 4988[6] 5607[7] 5832[10]

Regal Wave *P F I Cole* a31
2 b f Royal Applause—Graceful Lass (Sadler's Wells (USA))
6432[11]

Regence (IRE) *Stal Darnal* a77 75
4 b m Anabaa Blue—Realy Queen (USA) (Thunder Gulch (USA))
6568a[8]

Regency Red (IRE) *W M Brisbourne* a61 61
10 ch g Dolphin Street(FR) —Future Romance (Distant Relative)
18[2]

Regeneration (IRE) *S A Callaghan* 63
2 b g Chevalier(IRE) —Cappuchino (IRE) (Roi Danzig (USA))
7106[6]

Regent's Secret (USA) *J S Goldie* a85 82
8 br g Cryptoclearance(USA) —Misty Regent (CAN) (Vice Regent (CAN))
1771[6] 1953[6] ◆ 2445[7] 2939[9] 3366[6] 3579[4] 4148[3] 4633[3] ◆ 5564[5]

Regime (IRE) *M L W Bell* 115
4 b h Golan(IRE) —Juno Madonna (IRE) (Sadler's Wells (USA))
1468[7] (1882a) 2543[4] 3121[10] 3983a[2] 5335a[6] 6074[4] 6780[13]

Regional Counsel *K J Burke* a88 85
4 b h Medicean—Regency Rose (Danehill (USA))
502[4] 908[5] 929[6]

Registrar *Mrs C A Dunnett* a60 68
6 ch g Machiavellian(USA) —Confidante (USA) (Dayjur (USA))
1476[8] 1966[12] 3033[13] 3266[3] (3653) 4284[9] (4489) 4746[6] 6125[13] 6889[7] 7055[5] 7490[12]

Rehabilitation *W R Swinburn* a76 67
3 ch c Dr Fong(USA) —Lamees (USA) (Lomond (USA))
(1194) 1546[7] 2311[10] 2974[10] 3325[6] 4061[7] 4819[3] 7354[3] ◆ 7580[4]

Rehearsal *L Lungo* a81 68
7 b g Singspiel(IRE) —Daralaka (IRE) (The Minstrel (CAN))
561[4] 981[10] 2155[11] 2867[6] 4075[5] 6309[3] 7293[9]

Reigning In Rio (IRE) *P C Haslam* 44
2 br f Captain Rio—Saibhreas (IRE) (Last Tycoon)
3277[5] 3669[11] 7318[10]

Reigning Monarch (USA) *Miss Z C Davison* a64 61
5 b g Fusaichi Pegasus(USA) —Torros Straits (USA) (Boundary (USA))
54[3] (87) 391[6] 964[6] 1534[2] 1996[9] 2692[9] 2798[4] 3033[11] 6063[9] 6595[2] 6733[4] 7196[3] 7444[6] 7508[6] 7809[6]

Reine De Coeur (IRE) *David Marnane* 66
3 b f Montjeu(IRE) —Tip Tap Toe (USA) (Pleasant Tap (USA))
4613a[16]

Reine De Violette *H R A Cecil* a64 53
3 b f Olden Times—Aissa (Dr Devious (IRE))
1380[4] ◆ 1669[3] 6254[10] 6843[4]

Relampago Plus (ARG) *B Bo* 97
8 gr g Alpha Plus(USA) —Taos Ski Valley (USA) (J O Tobin (USA))
5957a[3]

Relatively Ready (USA) *David Donk* 102
2 bb c More Than Ready(USA) —Relativa (ARG) (Parade Marshal (USA))
6998a[5]

Relative Order *J R Best* a101 104
3 b c Diktat—Aunt Ruby (USA) (Rubiano (USA))
(3270) 3919[3] 4553[3] ◆ (5273) 5907[2] 6269[2]

Relative Strength (IRE) *A M Balding* a82 79
3 ch g Kris Kin(USA) —Monalee Lass (IRE) (Mujtahid (USA))
(1543) 2948[4] 3471[3]

Reload (IRE) *Thomas Mullins* a91 91
5 b g Minardi(USA) —Rapid Action (USA) (Quest For Fame)
3531a[6] 5550a[16]

Remaadd (USA) *D Selvaratnam* a99 103
7 gr g Daylami(IRE) —Bint Albaadiya (USA) (Woodman (USA))
202a[13] 381a[3] 568a[9]

Remaah (IRE) *W J Haggas* 37
2 b c Green Desert(USA) —Utr (USA) (Mr Prospector (USA))
5578[8] 6359[13]

Remarque (IRE) *L Riccardi* 95
3 b c Marju(IRE) —Run For Me (IRE) (Danehill (USA))
1513a[8] 2029a[5] 7253a[3]

Remember Ramon (USA) *J R Gask* a80 90
5 ch g Diesis—Future Act (USA) (Known Fact (USA))
6170[8] 6599[5] 7009[5] (7364) 7462[5] 7712[6]

Reminiscent (IRE) *B P J Baugh* a50 48
9 b g Kahyasi—Eliza Orzeszkowa (IRE) (Polish Patriot (USA))
129[6] 345[6] 661[4] 869[4] 1062[4] 7401[9] 7647[4]

Renda (USA) *Juan D Arias* a97 90
2 bb f Medaglia D'Oro(USA) —Ten Carats (USA) (Capote (USA))
6966a[10]

Renege The Joker *S Regan* a35
5 b g Alflora(IRE) —Bunty (Presidium)
317[9] 3654[10] 4302[13]

Rental Roy *Mrs P Townsley* a24
2 ch c Mark Of Esteem(IRE) —Kinkajoo (Precocious)
7602[12] 7738[9]

Rento (FR) *W Walton* 106
5 gr g Medaaly—Rosalita (FR) (Nashamaa)
(5926a) 6612a[4] 7598a[9]

Repealed *H Morrison* 59
2 b c Reset(AUS) —Great Verdict (AUS) (Christmas Tree (AUS))
6745[5]

Repeat (IRE) *M Wellings* a23 7
8 ch g Night Shift(USA) —Identical (IRE) (Machiavellian (USA))
3159[8] 3608[14]

Replicator *Pat Eddery* a76 71
3 b g Mujahid(USA) —Valldemosa (Music Boy)
2127[11] 2506[3] 2945[4] 3374[6] 5467[5] 7540[6] 7743[3]

Reprieved *M C Chapman* a58 11
3 ch g Bertolini(USA) —Crystal Seas (Zamindar (USA))
1701[6] 1905[4] 2080[3] 2291[10] 2705[6] 2982[11] 3221[11] 3690[4]

Requia *H Candy* 62
3 b f Nayef(USA) —Strelitzia (SAF) (Fort Wood (USA))
1599[10] 2668[6] 3310[4] 4457[12] 5232[6] 5814[5]

Requisite *I A Wood* a76 87
3 ch f Pivotal—Chicarica (USA) (The Minstrel (CAN))
(60) (364) 2428[3] 2757[4] (3000) 3462[6] 3909[2] 4127[2] 4660[11] 4864[4] 5250[12] 5490[6] 6169[6] 6420[6] 6623[7]

Resaass (USA) *J O'Reilly* a20 46
5 bb g Seeking The Gold(USA) —Sheroog (USA) (Shareef Dancer (USA))
1296[13] 2395[5] 2914[9]

Rescue Me *R Hannon* a63 78
3 b f Red Ransom(USA) —Duchcov (Caerleon (USA))
1671[8] 2161[15] 3918[7] (4253) 4572[3] 4910[2] (5291) 5492[5] 5863[11]

Resentful Angel *Pat Eddery* a62
3 b f Danehill Dancer(IRE) —Leaping Flame (USA) (Trempolino (USA))
5047[7] 7474[5] 7669[2] 7800[6]

Residency (IRE) *M J Wallace* a36 39
2 b c Danetime(IRE) —Muckross Park (Nomination)
5572[10] 6230[10]

Resolute Defender (IRE) *J Howard Johnson* 57
3 b g Namid—Snowspin (Carwhite)
2490[15] 2780[11] 4118[8] 4683[6]

Resonate (IRE) *A G Newcombe* a79 91
10 b h Erins Isle—Petronelli (USA) (Sir Ivor (USA))
96[6] 450[4] 1531[4] 1874[8] 3045[6] 4276[4] 5935[3] 6040[2]

Resort *Sir Michael Stoute* 71
2 b f Oasis Dream—Gay Gallanta (USA) (Woodman (USA))
3456[5]

Resounding Glory (USA) *R A Fahey* 82
3 b c Honour And Glory(USA) —Resounding Grace (USA) (Thunder Gulch (USA))
2889[4] 3494[5] 4017[7] 4818[4] 5202[3] 5773[3] 6250[8]

Respite *W J Haggas* 73
2 b f Pivotal—Truce (Nashwan (USA))
3923[2] ◆

Resplendent Ace (IRE) *P Howling* a79 70
4 b h Trans Island—Persian Polly (Persian Bold)
(91) 675[8] 881[2] 1296[3] (1564) 2165[6] 2365[4] 2921[8] 4156[12] (4343) 4726[6] 5630[3] 5999[3] 6210[6] 7278[8] 7462[6] 7711[8]

Resplendent Alpha *P Howling* a86 87
4 ch g Best Of The Bests(IRE) —Sunley Scent (Wolfhound (USA))
85[4] 210[5] 313[5] 729[8] 887[4] 1146[6] 1928[4] 2203[4] 2484[7] 2837[8] 3271[2] 4375[4] (4601) 4831[6] 5067[9] 5433[5] 6125[2] (7315) 7477[4] 7730[3]

Resplendent Light *W R Muir* a69 96
3 b g Fantastic Light(USA) —Bright Halo (IRE) (Bigstone (IRE))
1543[10] 2173[3] (2840) (3380) ◆ 5529a[4] 5927a[4] 6427[4]

Resplendent Nova *P Howling* a93 82
6 b g Pivotal—Santiburi Girl (Casteddu)
679[8] 833[9] 969[3] 1334[3] 1566[3] 2203[5] 2615[7] 2947[3] 4989[4] 5697[14] 5908[9] 7299[6] (7470) 7633[2] 7755[7]

Resplendent Star (IRE) *Mrs L J Young* 37
11 b g Northern Baby(CAN) —Whitethroat (Artaius (USA))
3606[12]

Restart (IRE) *Lucinda Featherstone* a50 58
7 b g Revoque(IRE) —Stargard (Polish Precedent (USA))
2585[9] 3863[3] 5385[5] 5917[12] 6550[10] 6824[8] 7216[9] 7520[4] 7587[5]

Rest By The River *A G Newcombe* 52
2 ch f Reset(AUS) —Palace Green (IRE) (Rudimentary (USA))
4974[7] 6077[7]

Restless Genius (IRE) *B Ellison* a73 78
3 b g Captain Rio—Mainmise (USA) (Septieme Ciel (USA))
(1347) 1837[10] 5067[10] 6532[10] 7018[4] 7360[3] 7494[4] 7796[7]

Restless Knight *W S Kittow* 50
2 b g Reset(AUS) —Sleepless (Night Shift (USA))
6359[12] 6574[13]

Resurge (IRE) *J Noseda* a92 86
3 b g Danehill Dancer(IRE) —Resurgence (Polar Falcon (USA))
1926[2] ◆ (2413) 4197[7] 6900[2]

Retirement *Ms V S Lucas* a44 32
9 b g Zilzal(USA) —Adeptation (USA) (Exceller (USA))
5002a[6]

Retro (IRE) *R Hannon* a75 72
2 b c Tagula(IRE) —Cabcharge Princess (IRE) (Rambo Dancer (CAN))
4024[5] 4274[4] 5609[3] 6080[10] 6677[4] (6879) 7460[3]

Rettorical Lad *Jamie Poulton* a54 48
3 rg g Vettori(IRE) —Reciprocal (IRE) (Night Shift (USA))
1467[19] 1669[7] 2563[11] 4553[17] 7474[8] 7604[5]

Return To Paradise (USA) *Todd Pletcher* 54
3 b f El Prado(IRE) —Winner's Edge (USA) (Seeking The Gold (USA))
5744a[12]

Reve De Soleil (FR) *E J O'Neill* 103
2 ch g Dyhim Diamond(IRE) —Siro (GER) (Grand Lodge (USA))
2134[4] 2584[2] (3125) (3553) 4588[3]

Reve Lunaire (USA) *S Seemar* a78 96
5 bb g Hennessy(USA) —My Dream Castles (USA) (Woodman (USA))
568a[8]

Reverence *E J Alston* a104 111
7 ch g Mark Of Esteem(IRE) —Imperial Bailiwick (IRE) (Imperial Frontier (USA))
1157[5] 1495a[3] 1831[7] (1986) 2652a[9] 3488[5] 3722[10] 4660[3] 5891[8] 6121[10] 6468[5] 6653[9]

Reveur *M Mullineaux* a55 54
5 b m Rossini(USA) —Without Warning (IRE) (Warning)
10[9] 3037[3] 3431[3] 3951[8] 4390[7]

Reve Vert (FR) *A W Carroll* a56 49
3 b c Oasis Dream—Comme D'Habitude (USA) (Caro)
2451[9] 2922[4] 3221[5] 3964[2] 4180[6] 4777[3] 6047[8] 6752[2] 7072[6]

Revolve *Mrs L J Mongan* a66 61
8 b g Pivotal—Alpine Time (IRE) (Tirol)
122[8] 352[6] 517[7] 631[6]

Revolving World (IRE) *L R James* a39 56
5 b g Spinning World(USA) —Mannakea (USA) (Fairy King (USA))
2053[4] 2914[7] 4261[7]

Revue Princess (IRE) *T D Easterby* 71
3 b f Mull Of Kintyre(USA) —Blues Queen (Lahib (USA))
1426[15] 1611[10] (2159) 2676[12] 3455[8] 3811[9]

Reward Of Faith (IRE) *Liam Roche* a30 46
3 br g Fraam—Markskeepingfaith (IRE) (Ajraas (USA))
826a[14]

Rey Davis (IRE) *Robert Collet* a82 100
3 b c King Charlemagne(USA) —San Luis Rey (Zieten (USA))
6064a[6]

Reykon (IRE) *A Renzoni* 98
4 b h Invincible Spirit(IRE) —Realt Dhun Eibhir (Indian Ridge)
7349a[6]

Reynaldothewizard (USA) *Eoin Harty* a82
2 b c Speightstown(USA) —Holiday Runner (USA) (Meadowlake (USA))
6503a^{10}

Rhadegunda *J H M Gosden* a65 97
3 b f Pivotal—St Radegund (Green Desert (USA))
3452^{2} 3977^{2} 4253^{2} (5203) (6027) ◆ 6605^{2} 7083^{2} (7431a)

Rhapsilian *J A Geake* a66 65
4 br m Dansili—Rivers Rhapsody (Dominion)
54^{6} 1541^{2} 1872^{9} 2758^{10} 3316^{6} 4186^{4} 5610^{2} 5801^{2} 6334^{3} 6774^{3} 7255^{5}

Rhode Island Red (USA) *H J L Dunlop* a57 50
3 ch f Tale Of The Cat(USA) —Miss Sobriety (CAN) (Temperence Hill (USA))
306^{2} 556^{3} 873^{8} 1870^{4} 2559^{10} 3524^{10}

Rhuby River (IRE) *R Dickin* a43
6 b m Bahhare(USA) —Westside Flyer (Risk Me (FR))
11^{8} 147^{6} 269^{10} 400^{13}

Rhuepunzel *P F I Cole* a69 82
4 b m Elnadim(USA) —Fairy Story (IRE) (Persian Bold)
5697^{16}

Rhydian *R M Beckett*
2 ch c Monsieur Bond(IRE) —Miss Flirtatious (Piccolo)
1168^{6} 3091^{11}

Ribadesella *C Laffon-Parias* 88
2 b f Hernando(FR) —Barsine (IRE) (Danehill (USA))
3749a^{7}

Ricci De Mare *G J Smith* a58 58
3 b f Cadeaux Genereux—Procession (Zafonic (USA))
335^{7} (950) 1193^{10} 5593^{14} 6227^{9} 6562^{2} 6883^{2} (7050) 7499^{11} 7662^{5}

Richardlionheart (USA) *B Gubby* 39
2 ch g Lion Heart(USA) —Cleito (USA) (Unbridled's Song (USA))
4480^{12}

Richardthesecond (IRE) *W M Brisbourne* a62 65
3 b g Acclamation—Tahlil (Cadeaux Genereux)
1315^{6} 1635^{4} 2527^{5} 3332^{7}

Richelieu *J J Lambe* a76 80
6 b g Machiavellian(USA) —Darling Flame (USA) (Capote (USA))
6366a^{16} 7399^{2} (7611) 7748^{5}

Rich Harvest (USA) *P D Evans* a47 60
3 bb g High Yield(USA) —Mangano (USA) (Quiet American (USA))
1603^{4} (2988) 4369^{8} 4684^{3} 5045^{10} 5186^{7} 5684^{12} 6063^{8} 6328^{9}

Rich James (IRE) *J D Bethell* a49 60
3 b g Ishiguru(USA) —Mourir D'Aimer (USA) (Trempolino (USA))
70^{9} 557^{2} 780^{2} 1315^{12} 2704^{13} 3753^{13} 7725^{7} 7736^{13}

Rich Kid (IRE) *R A Harris* a73 76
3 b g Spartacus(IRE) —Sea Glen (IRE) (Glenstal (USA))
102^{2} 393^{2} 1685^{2} 1839^{6} 1899^{3} 2974^{8} 3560^{5} 3969^{4} 4533^{3} (Dead)

Richo *D H Brown* a77 77
2 ch g Bertolini(USA) —Noble Water (FR) (Noblequest (FR))
957^{11} 2217^{4} 2584^{5} (4415) 5274^{10} 6112^{3} 6549^{8} 6756^{4}

Rich Red (IRE) *R Hannon* 60
2 ch g Redback—Pink N Prosperous (IRE) (Grand Lodge (USA))
1363^{8} 1736^{7} 2275^{4} 3941^{3} 4975^{9}

Rickety Bridge (IRE) *P R Chamings* a75 62
5 ch g Elnadim(USA) —Kriva (Reference Point)
358^{7}

Ride A White Swan *D Shaw* a63 66
3 gr g Baryshnikov(AUS) —The Manx Touch (IRE) (Petardia)
1396^{5} 1781^{6} 3213^{3} 3690^{6} 3831^{2} 4118^{6} 4632^{3} 5378^{2} 5836^{12}

Ridge Boy (IRE) *Mrs John Harrington* 89
7 b g Indian Ridge—Bold Tina (IRE) (Persian Bold)
3531a^{3} 5550a^{17}

Ridge Dance *J H M Gosden* 105
3 b c Selkirk(USA) —Pearl Dance (USA) (Nureyev (USA))
1810^{4}

Ridgeway Jazz *M D I Usher* a50
3 b f Kalanisi(IRE) —Billie Holiday (Fairy King (USA))
20^{3} 7532^{7} 7665^{7}

Ridgeway Silver *M D I Usher* a65 64
2 b f Lujain(USA) —Barefooted Flyer (USA) (Fly So Free (USA))
1377^{4} 1778^{6} 2987^{5} (3677) 3941^{6} 5153^{3} 5422^{3} 5937^{8} 6666^{11} (7451) 7700^{9}

Ridge Wood Dani (IRE) *E J Alston* 84
3 b g Invincible Spirit(IRE) —Dani Ridge (IRE) (Indian Ridge)
2527^{2} 3455^{11} 4450^{2} (4787) (5510) ◆ 6859^{10}

Ridley Didley (IRE) *N Wilson* a57 48
3 b g Tagula(IRE) —Dioscorea (IRE) (Pharly (FR))
3955^{4} 4388^{10} 7836^{2}

Rievaulx World *K A Ryan* 102
2 b c Compton Place—Adhaaba (USA) (Dayjur (USA))
1924^{5} 2331^{2} 2574^{2} (3140) (3639) 4507^{4}

Riff Raff *C J Gray* a28 76
5 b m Daylami(IRE) —Rafiya (Halling (USA))
588^{7} 754^{11}

Riflessione *R A Harris* a72 76
2 ch c Captain Rio—Hilites (IRE) (Desert King (IRE))
957^{5} ◆ 1122^{2} 1363^{3} 2473^{6} 4190^{20} 4942^{3} 5213^{14} (6730) ◆ 7460^{5} 7820^{7}

Rigat *J S Goldie* a68 72
5 b g Dansili—Fudge (Polar Falcon (USA))
68^{5} 240^{5} 7732^{5} ◆

Rigged *J A Osborne* 43
2 b g Desert Sun—Emma Peel (Emarati (USA))
2011^{P} 2349^{4} 5599^{7} 5784^{7}

Riggins (IRE) *L M Cumani* a92
4 b h Cape Cross(IRE) —Rentless (Zafonic (USA))
(5405) ◆

Rightcar Dominic *Peter Grayson* a54
3 b c Kyllachy—Vallauris (Faustus (USA))
734^{3} 5608^{10} 7213^{8} 7679^{6}

Rightcar Hull (IRE) *Peter Grayson* a48 42
3 b f Fantastic Light(USA) —Verbania (IRE) (In The Wings)
343^{8} 412^{6} 505^{6} 767^{5} 882^{6} 1141^{4} 1560^{11} 2268^{13} 7529^{13}

Rightcar Lewis *Peter Grayson* a53
3 ch f Noverre(USA) —Abeyr (Unfuwain (USA))
6633^{5} 7231^{5} 7414^{10} 7503^{9} 7710^{6} 7836^{6}

Right Edge (USA) *F & L Camici*
2 b f The Cliff's Edge(USA) —Right Here (IRE) (Hector Protector (USA))
2744a^{7}

Rightful Ruler *N Wilson* a59 53
6 b g Montjoy(USA) —Lady Of The Realm (Prince Daniel (USA))
4947^{2} ◆ 5385^{7}

Right Option (IRE) *J L Flint* a75 76
4 b g Daylami(IRE) —Option (IRE) (Red Ransom (USA))
212^{2} 588^{2} 3179^{3} 3613^{4} 4193^{4} 5367^{5} (6252) 6983^{10}

Right Price *A P Jarvis*
2 b f Lujain(USA) —Bon Marche (Definite Article)
1385^{7}

Right Stuff (FR) *G L Moore* a70 78
5 bb g Dansili—Specificity (USA) (Alleged (USA))
2762^{11} 4131^{10} (4930) (5183) 5900^{5}

Right You Are (IRE) *Paul Green* a52 52
8 ch g Right Win(IRE) —Ancadia (Henbit (USA))
144^{4} 524^{4} 758^{11} 1408^{8} 4173^{3} 4501^{9} 5262^{6} 7039^{7} 7373^{13}

Riguez Dancer *P C Haslam* a63 76
4 b g Dansili—Tricoteuse (Kris)
1020^{2} 4742^{10} 5092^{10} 6054^{9}

Riley Boys (IRE) *J G Given* a70 87
7 ch g Most Welcome—Scarlett Holly (Red Sunset)
2391^{5} (2927) 3337^{4} 3664^{3} (3711) 4167^{6}

Rileyskeepingfaith *M R Channon* 101
2 b c Hunting Lion(IRE) —Keeping The Faith (IRE) (Ajraas (USA))
3895^{2} (4199) 4588^{6} 4908^{2} 5330a^{13} 6025^{2} (6399) (6647) 6979^{4}

Riley Tucker (USA) *William Mott* a103
3 bb c Harlan's Holiday(USA) —My Sweet Country (USA) (Bold Ruckus (USA))
2215a^{12}

Rimsky Korsakov (IRE) *Micky Hammond* 34
4 b g Sadler's Wells(USA) —Tedarshana (Darshaan)
5505^{8} 6055^{13}

Rindless *J F Panvert* a35
3 b f Bertolini(USA) —Streaky (IRE) (Danetime (IRE))
6633^{7} 7213^{7}

Ring Bertie *Micky Hammond* 7
3 b g Bertolini(USA) —Ring Side (IRE) (Alzao (USA))
2912^{11} 7174^{10}

Ringo Zaar *A B Haynes* a55 21
3 b g Xaar—Tomanivi (Caerleon (USA))
6892^{12} 7338^{7} 7415^{4}

Rinterval (IRE) *David Wachman* a80 91
3 ch f Desert Prince(IRE) —Interpose (Indian Ridge)
1401^{7} 1715^{5} 1801^{8} 3415^{10} 6261a^{12} 6689a^{10}

Rio Carnival (USA) *J H M Gosden* a46
2 b f Storm Cat(USA) —Zenda (Zamindar (USA))
5571^{7}

Rio Cobolo (IRE) *Paul Green* a64 57
2 b c Captain Rio—Sofistication (IRE) (Dayjur (USA))
2608^{4} 3140^{6} 3590^{12} 4175^{4} 5363^{6} 6247^{3} (7199) 7372^{2} 7531^{2} (7612) 7645^{3} 7794^{7}

Riodan (IRE) *L A Mullaney* 64
6 ch m Desert King(IRE) —Spirit Of The Nile (FR) (Generous (IRE))
3642^{7} 4046^{9} 4220^{11}

Rio De Janeiro (IRE) *Miss E C Lavelle* a74 74
7 b g Sadler's Wells(USA) —Alleged Devotion (USA) (Alleged (USA))
5934^{11}

Rio De La Plata (USA) *Saeed Bin Suroor* 118
3 ch c Rahy(USA) —Express Way (ARG) (Ahmad (ARG))
2032a^{2} 2829^{7} 4010a^{3}

Rio Del Oro (USA) *R Hannon* a17 50
2 b c Touch Gold(USA) —Diablo's Girl (USA) (Diablo (USA))
3939^{5} 4311^{6} 4636^{7} 5914^{13} 6330^{8}

Rio Gael (IRE) *M S Saunders* a30 57
2 b g Captain Rio—Palavera (FR) (Bikala)
4579^{4} 5599^{3} 7227^{9} 7443^{6}

Rio Guru (IRE) *M R Channon* a83 83
3 b f Spartacus(IRE) —Montessori (Akarad (FR))
1445^{3} 1915^{8} 3977^{4} 4255^{3} 4860^{2} (5155) 5311^{8} 5683^{2} ◆ 6127^{4} 6415^{9} 6904^{4} (7211) 7305^{2}

Rioja Ruby (IRE) *Miss Kate Milligan* 44
2 b f Redback—Bacchanalia (IRE) (Blues Traveller (IRE))
1392^{3} 2004^{4} 2671^{4} 2965^{5} 4499^{8} 4873^{7} 6009^{11}

Rioka (IRE) *R Gibson* 95
3 b f Captain Rio—Karlinaxa (Linamix (FR))
6323a^{10}

Rioliina (IRE) *J G Portman* 82
2 b f Captain Rio—Anneliina (Cadeaux Genereux)
3348^{5} (4763) 6172^{5}

Rio L'Oren (IRE) *N J Vaughan* a62 38
3 ch f Captain Rio—Princess Sofie (Efisio)
130^{3} (662) 2946^{6} 4952^{6} 5616^{6} 6048^{8}

Rio Novo *J Howard Johnson* 10
3 b g Nayef(USA) —Dead Certain (Absalom)
2779^{6}

Rio Pomba (IRE) *D Carroll* 55
2 b f Captain Rio—Lyrebird (USA) (Storm Bird (CAN))
3714^{5} 6010^{5} 6341^{14}

Rio Ramus (IRE) *R A Teal* a2
2 ch g Captain Rio—Quaeramus Seria (IRE) (Catrail (USA))
6863^{15} 7303^{7} 7674^{8}

Rio Riva *Miss J A Camacho* a100 109
6 b g Pivotal—Dixie Favor (USA) (Dixieland Band (USA))
960^{4} 1133^{4} 1569^{11} 1816^{12} 3413^{2} 5896^{8} 6103^{9}

Rio Royale (IRE) *Mrs A J Perrett* a75 78
2 b c Captain Rio—Lady Nasrana (FR) (Al Nasr (FR))
1804^{2} 2324^{5} 2554^{4} 2859^{2} (3444) 3941^{7} 6931^{3} 7389^{2} 7538^{5}

Riorun (IRE) *Ian Williams* a47 57
3 b g Captain Rio—Sulaka (Owington)
4180^{10} 4533^{11} 5379^{12}

Rio Sabotini *G A Swinbank* 56
3 ch c Captain Rio—Sabotini (Prince Sabo)
2660^{13} 3717^{9}

Rio Sands *R M Whitaker* 76
3 b g Captain Rio—Sally Traffic (River Falls)
1155^{6} 1452^{2} 1611^{2} (2283) 2732^{2} 3298^{5} 3455^{2} 4000^{3} 4397^{3} 5417^{5} 6486^{13}

Rios Boy (IRE) *T D Easterby* 9
2 ch c Captain Rio—Zalivora (IRE) (Zilzal (USA))
1727^{10} 2388^{8} 2910^{10}

Riotista (IRE) *E J O'Neill* 88
2 b f Captain Rio—Elitista (FR) (Linamix (FR))
(4499) ◆ 5055^{3} 6102^{13}

Ripple (FR) *J-C Rouget* 103
3 b c Rock Of Gibraltar(IRE) —Slipstream Queen (USA) (Conquistador Cielo (USA))
2064a^{2} 3191a^{8}

Ripples Maid *J A Geake* a96 106
5 b m Dansili—Rivers Rhapsody (Dominion)
290a^{7} 497a^{4} 649a^{2} 741a^{6} 959^{6} 1698^{4} 2000^{7} 2606^{8} 3063^{4} 3927^{8} 4198^{2}

Riptide *C F Wall*
2 b g Val Royal(FR) —Glittering Image (IRE) (Sadler's Wells (USA))
5246^{18}

Rip Van Winkle (IRE) *A P O'Brien* 114
2 b c Galileo(IRE) —Looking Back (IRE) (Stravinsky (USA))
(4353a) ◆ 6815^{7} ◆

Riqaab (IRE) *E A L Dunlop* a70 77
3 b c Peintre Celebre(USA) —Jeed (IRE) (Mujtahid (USA))
1054^{2} 1272^{6} ◆ 1805^{5} (4065) ◆ 4663^{2}

Rising Force (IRE) *J L Spearing* a72 76
5 b g Selkirk(USA) —Singing Diva (IRE) (Royal Academy (USA))
240^{3} (406) 586^{4} 2153^{5} 2394^{5} 3631^{3} 7461^{4} 7711^{13}

Rising Kheleyf (IRE) *G A Swinbank* 53
2 ch g Kheleyf(USA) —Rising Spirits (Cure The Blues (USA))
4741^{11} 5882^{9} 6109^{5} 6525^{4}

Rising Prospect *G M Moore* 82
2 ch c Traditionally(USA) —La Sylphide (Rudimentary (USA))
(3926) 4968^{3} 5895^{14} (6101) 6973^{15}

Rising Shadow (IRE) *N Wilson* a81 111
7 b g Efisio—Jouet (Reprimand)
959^{10} 1517^{7} 1809^{17} 2106^{15} (2698) 3489^{4} 3722^{5} 4145^{10} 4624^{23} 5109^{15} 6104^{7} 6484^{12} 7187a^{9}

Rising Star *J L Spearing* 50
2 ch c Medicean—Arkadia Park (IRE) (Polish Precedent (USA))
7105^{12}

Risk (IRE) *C R Egerton* a92 88
5 ch g Acatenango(GER) —Belua (GER) (Lomitas)
3045^{15}

Risk Challenge (USA) *C J Price* a33 38
6 ch g Mt. Livermore(USA) —Substance (USA) (Diesis)
2100^{10}

Risk Runner (IRE) *James Moffatt* 71
5 b g Mull Of Kintyre(USA) —Fizzygig (Efisio)
4662^{10} 6054^{8} 6551^{9}

Risky Capital *S A Callaghan* a64 39
2 b g Tobougg(IRE) —Panoramic View (Polar Falcon (USA))
6351^{3} 6787^{11} 6931^{7}

Risky Lady (IRE) *J Ryan* a30
2 b f Tamarisk(IRE) —My Croft (Crofter (USA))
7638^{7} 7734^{12} 7802^{9}

Risque Belle *E J Creighton*
2 b f Fantastic Light(USA) —Risque Lady (Kenmare (FR))
7341^{12}

Risque Heights *J R Boyle* a92 79
4 b g Mark Of Esteem(IRE) —Risque Lady (Kenmare (FR))
97^{5} 417^{7} 3561^{9} 3836^{10} 5209^{9} 6028^{6} 6544^{5} 7009^{2} 7440^{4} 7526^{4} (7620) (7742)

Ritano (IRE) *B I Case* a70 42
2 b g Kalanisi(IRE) —Sadika (IRE) (Bahhare (USA))
6199^{13} 6597^{8} 7073^{7}

Ritsi *Grant Tuer* a56 68
5 b g Marju(IRE) —Anna Comnena (IRE) (Shareef Dancer (USA))
(2734) 3414^{6} 3642^{4} 4046^{8} 4652^{8} 4924^{5}

Ritzy Wildcat (USA) *S C Williams* a64 63
2 b g Forest Wildcat(USA) —Ritzy Dame (USA) (Distorted Humor (USA))
1851^{5} 2186^{7} 2349^{2} 2826^{10}

Riva San (AUS) *Peter G Moody* 105
4 bl m Any Given Sunday(AUS) —Best River (AUS) (Best Western (AUS))
6835a^{16}

River Ardeche *P C Haslam* 78
3 b g Elnadim(USA) —Overcome (Belmez (USA))
1949^{5} 3557^{12} 4682^{12}

River Best (IRE) *V Caruso* 90
3 b f King's Best(USA) —River Hill (USA) (Danehill (USA))
2439a^{6}

River Bounty *A P Jarvis* a70 72
3 b f Bahamian Bounty—Artistic Merit (Alhaarth (IRE))
3552^{11} (3966) 4483^{3} 5026^{3} 5346^{6} 6773^{7} 7013^{11}

River Captain (IRE) *S Kirk* a57 74
2 ch c Captain Rio—Pardoned (IRE) (Mujadil (USA))
2944^{5} 3323^{12} 4570^{7} (4975) (5747) 5895^{10} 6320a^{22}

River City (IRE) *Noel T Chance* a62 70
11 b g Norwich—Shuil Na Lee (IRE) (Phardante (FR))
771^{7}

River Danube *T J Fitzgerald* a65 68
5 b g Dansili—Campaspe (Dominion)
1814^{7} 2573^{8} 5042^{3} 5887^{4} 6790^{9} 7042^{3} 7271^{3}

River Dee (IRE) *Miss Amy Weaver* 76
2 b c Almutawakel—Fiaba (Precocious)
3651^{8} (4257) 4659^{3} 4975^{2} 5447^{2} 5632^{5} 6305^{4} 6673^{7}

River Falcon *J S Goldie* a93 104
8 b g Pivotal—Pearly River (Elegant Air)
1071^{8} 1325^{3} 2129^{2} 2626^{14} 3451^{13} 4240^{5} 4437^{6} 5890^{2} 6104^{10} 6653^{5} 6971^{4}

River Gleam (IRE) *A P Jarvis* a66 66
3 b f Trans Island—Gleam (Green Desert (USA))
899^{14} 1271^{11} 1738^{7} 1968^{6} 2463^{12} 5374^{11} 7529^{10}

Riverhill (IRE) *Miss T Jackson* a35 58
5 b g Mull Of Kintyre(USA) —Thrill Seeker (IRE) (Treasure Kay)
989^{6} 2940^{4} 4451^{7} 6727^{16} 7267^{11} 7369^{9}

River Kent *Mrs A Duffield* a63 58
3 b g Fantastic Light(USA) —Ciboure (Norwick (USA))
1477^{8} 1628^{5} 2273^{2} 2926^{2} 3666^{8} 5223^{2} (5868) 6252^{2} 6493^{4} 6957^{8} 6991^{10}

River Kirov (IRE) *M Wigham* a76 88
5 b g Soviet Star(USA) —Night Shifter (IRE) (Night Shift (USA))
3728^{9} 4602^{8} 5090^{6} 5601^{8} 6679^{4} ◆ (7196) 7357^{2} (7416) ◆ 7611^{3} 7653^{2} 7803^{4} ◆ (7834) ◆

River Mint *D W Barker* 9
4 b g River Falls—Penny Mint (Mummy's Game)
4075^{10}

River Naiad *J A R Toller* a18
3 ch f Nayef(USA) —Waqood (USA) (Riverman (USA))
4161^{14} 5155^{8}

River N' Blues (IRE) *Dr J R J Naylor* a55 64
5 ch f Touch Of The Blues(FR) —Feather River (USA) (Strike The Gold (USA))
2127^{9} 2602^{4} 3086^{11} 4090^{11} 4910^{5}

River Proud (USA) *P F I Cole* 115
3 b c Proud Citizen(USA) —Da River Hoss (USA) (River Special (USA))
1421^{4} 2032a^{3} (4622) 5302a^{2} 6148a^{P} (Dead)

River Rye (IRE) *J S Moore* a72 80
2 b f Acclamation—Rye (IRE) (Charnwood Forest (IRE))
1419^{5} (2042) 2377^{3} 3470^{4} 3961^{3} 4729^{5} 5422^{2} 5855^{9} 6247^{4} 7334^{7} 7673^{4}

Riverscape (IRE) *Mrs A J Perrett* a74 81
3 ch f Peintre Celebre(USA) —Orinoco (IRE) (Darshaan)
(1279) 1527^{3} 1805^{2} 4573^{2} 4985^{4} 6203^{11}

Riverside *M Brittain* 38
3 b f Kyllachy—My Cadeaux (Cadeaux Genereux)
1073^{6} 1302^{7} 2041^{16}

River Style (IRE) *A P Jarvis* a51 47
2 b f Desert Style(IRE) —Charlene Lacy (IRE) (Pips Pride)
5487^{6} 5746^{8} 6534^{7} 6730^{6} 6931^{8} 7179^{4} 7537^{5}

River Thames *K A Ryan* a74 88
5 b g Efisio—Dashing Water (Dashing Blade)
85^{6} 1451^{3} 2760^{6} 3111^{2} 3594^{3} 4239^{9} 4608^{3} 5542^{10} 6278^{4} 6813^{5} 7041^{7} 7239^{11} (7414) ◆ 7592^{6} 7730^{4}

River Tiber *Saeed Bin Suroor* 106
5 b g Danehill(USA) —Heavenly Whisper (IRE) (Halling (USA))
(379a) 495a^{8} 743a^{9}

Riviera Red (IRE) *L Montague Hall* a51
8 b g Rainbow Quest(USA) —Banquise (IRE) (Last Tycoon)
99^{3} 299^{8}

Rivington Pike (IRE) *J J Quinn* a48 65
3 b g Catcher In The Rye(IRE) —Bean Island (USA) (Afleet (CAN))
991^{12} 2495^{7} 3393^{5} 4077^{6} 4247^{14}

Road To Hucking (GER) *J R Best* 64
3 gr g Pentire—Reine Rouge (GER) (Nebos (GER))
1526^{12} 2056^{11} 3326^{5} 3873^{9} 6868^{9}

Road To Love (IRE) *M Johnston* a94 115
5 ch g Fruits Of Love(USA) —Alpine Flair (IRE) (Tirol)
1724^{3}

Road To Recovery *D J Wintle* a46 42
4 b g Mujahid(USA) —Legend Of Aragon (Aragon)
3607^{8} 4053^{11} 4891^{4} 5748^{7}

Roaring Forte (IRE) *W J Haggas* a106 90
3 b c Cape Cross(IRE) —Descant (USA) (Nureyev (USA))
3897^{3} 4423^{2} 5309^{2} (6283)

Roar Of Applause *B J Meehan* a64 56
2 b g Royal Applause—Les Hurlants (IRE) (Barathea (IRE))
5072^{8} 5579^{8} 6062^{6} (7258)

Robbie Can Can *A W Carroll* a54 50
9 b g Robellino(USA) —Can Can Lady (Anshan)
1148^{8} 3901^{7} 4123^{13} 5148^{5}

Robbmaa (FR) *A W Carroll* a30 57
3 bl g Cape Cross(IRE) —Native Twine (Be My Native (USA))
1836^{9} 2451^{13} 3183^{11} 3604^{11} 4930^{6}

Robby Bobby *M Johnston* a95 84
3 ch c Selkirk(USA) —Dancing Mirage (IRE) (Machiavellian (USA))
1428^{4} 1806^{9} 7291^{6} 7439^{11} (7777) ◆ 7814^{3}

Robert Burns (IRE) *Miss D Mountain* 71
3 b g Invincible Spirit(IRE) —Double Red (IRE) (Thatching)
2954[3] 3275[9] 3629[3] 4283[3] 4377[9] 6762[15]

Robert The Brave *P R Webber* a82 68
4 b g Primo Valentino(IRE) —Sandicliffe (USA) (Imp Society (USA))
2369[7] 3090[10] 3258[7] 5512[9]

Robin De La Folie (FR) *James Moffatt*
6 b g Robin Des Pres(FR) —Cazeres (FR) (Goodland (FR))
4116[6]

Robin The Till *R Hannon* 62
2 ch g Bold Edge—My Dancer (IRE) (Alhaarth (IRE))
1873[6] 2150[7] 2903[5] 4579[2]

Robinzal *A W Carroll* a68 70
6 b g Zilzal(USA) —Sulitelma (USA) (The Minstrel (CAN))
351[5] 542[7] 703[4] 844[12] 898[7]

Rob Roy (USA) *Sir Michael Stoute* 118
6 bb h Lear Fan(USA) —Camanoe (USA) (Gone West (USA))
1631[2] 2193[9] 3741[5] 5276[8]

Robustian *George Baker* a93 91
5 b g Robellino(USA) —Pontressina (USA) (St Jovite (USA))
(1131) 1502[8] 1799[5] 3440[6] 6839[4] (Dead)

Rochdale *A Al Raihe* a86 99
5 ch g Bertolini(USA) —Owdbetts (IRE) (High Estate)
492a[6] 566a[10]

Rochefort (IRE) *J H M Gosden* a88 94
3 b c Red Ransom(USA) —Sombreffe (Polish Precedent (USA))
2825[3] 3877[9] 4731[2] (5104) 5695[15] 6526[9]

Rocheport *G C H Chung* a50 63
3 ch g Reel Buddy(USA) —Just A Gem (Superlative)
3738[8] 4268[11] 5141[5] 5911[8] 7180[10]

Rock Anthem (IRE) *Mike Murphy* a77 79
4 ch g Rock Of Gibraltar(IRE) —Regal Portrait (IRE) (Royal Academy (USA))
309[6] 504[5] (852) ◆ 1910[7] 2762[8] 3457[6] 5350[13] 6177[12] 6867[13] 7650[2]

Rock Art (IRE) *B J Meehan* 58
2 ch f Rock Of Gibraltar(IRE) —Lindesberg (Doyoun)
5240[9]

Rockbranglen (USA) *F Reuterskiold*
5 b g Sandpit(BRZ) —Medicine Path (USA) (Strawberry Road (AUS))
605a[7]

Rockellio (IRE) *B W Hills* 58
3 b f Rock Of Gibraltar(IRE) —Lillibits (USA) (Kingmambo (USA))
1073[5] 2717[6] 3351[9] 4992[6]

Rocker *G L Moore* a74 85
4 b g Rock Of Gibraltar(IRE) —Jessica's Dream (IRE) (Desert Style (IRE))
746[2] 875[9] 1037[3] 1646[2] 2330[2] 3346[2] 3585[7] (4313) 4586[18] 5247[10] 5467[6] 5817[2] (6388) (6750) 6925[2]

Rocketball (IRE) *Patrick Morris* a62 68
3 b g Namid—Luceball (IRE) (Bluebird (USA))
4846[7] 7793[3]

Rocket Rob (IRE) *S A Callaghan* a68 65
2 b g Danetime(IRE) —Queen Of Fibres (IRE) (Scenic)
2999[8] (3652) (4933) 5432[9] 5581[2] (5671) 7052[5] 7460[2]

Rocket Ruby *D Shaw* a47 47
2 br f Piccolo—Kitty Kitty Cancan (Warrshan (USA))
2424[7] 2865[7] 7168[9] 7279[5] 7612[8] 7719[3] ◆

Rockets 'n Rollers (IRE) *A Manuel* a75 88
8 b h Victory Note(USA) —Holly Bird (Runnett)
378a[8] 492a[8] 563a[6]

Rockette (FR) *Y De Nicolay* 94
3 ch f Ange Gabriel(FR) —Racoon (FR) (Be My Guest (USA))
(6744a) (7551a)

Rockfella *D J Coakley* a54 69
2 ch g Rock Of Gibraltar(IRE) —Afreeta (USA) (Afleet (CAN))
3372[12] 3888[4] ◆ 5213[10] 6086[3] 6376[7] 6926[5]

Rockfield Lodge (IRE) *M E Rimmer* a75 81
3 b g Stravinsky(USA) —La Belle Simone (IRE) (Grand Lodge (USA))
457[3] 756[6] 924[8] 1063[2] 1203[2] 3116[6] (3406) 3761[4] 3838[3] 4258[6] 4489[2] 4773[6] 5247[2] 6125[14] 6765[11] 7013[9]

Rockfield Rose *J A Osborne* 46
3 ch f Kyllachy—Owdbetts (IRE) (High Estate)
2307[6] 3061[9] 3268[8] 3678[13]

Rockfield Tiger (IRE) *J A Osborne* a79 74
3 b c Dubai Destination(USA) —Aljazeera (USA) (Swain (IRE))
(458) 573[5] 2714[9] 4104[9] 4429[5] 5713[3] 6256[8] 6736[9]

Rock Harmonie (FR) *Mme C Head-Maarek* 107
3 b f Rock Of Gibraltar(IRE) —Rigoureuse (USA) (Septieme Ciel (USA))
5955a[2] 6518a[6] 7187a[6]

Rock Haven (IRE) *W M Brisbourne* a59 63
6 b g Danehill Dancer(IRE) —Mahabba (USA) (Elocutionist (USA))
1350[6] 2523[8] 2795[10] 2886[9]

Rockhorse (IRE) *B Grizzetti* 92
3 ch c Rock Of Gibraltar(IRE) —Maelalong (IRE) (Maelstrom Lake)
7253a[5]

Rocking *Miss L A Perratt* 80
3 b f Oasis Dream—Council Rock (General Assembly (USA))
3256[6] 4631[7]

Rocking Laura *R Craggs*
2 b f Rock City—Distinctly Laura (IRE) (Distinctly North (USA))
3830[8]

Rockinit (IRE) *M R Channon* a33 67
2 b f Rock Of Gibraltar(IRE) —Tidal Reach (USA) (Kris S (USA))
3341[4] 3693[2] 4579[9] 5914[11] 6059[2]

Rockjumper *Mrs T J Hill* a41 57
3 br g Cape Cross(IRE) —Bronzewing (Beldale Flutter (USA))
1684[10] 2639[12] 3030[11] 4056[7] 4807[2] 5837[6] 6746[8]

Rockmaster (IRE) *G Pucciatti* 104
5 b h Galileo(IRE) —Cromac (ITY) (Machiavellian (USA))
2027a[3] 3075a[6]

Rock Me (IRE) *S A Callaghan* a34 41
3 ch g Rock Of Gibraltar(IRE) —Final Farewell (USA) (Proud Truth (USA))
4722[12] 4990[4]

Rock Moss (IRE) *J S Bolger* a91 109
3 b g Rock Of Gibraltar(IRE) —Raghida (IRE) (Nordico (USA))
(3532a) 4223a[10] 5130a[4] 5922a[2]

Rocknest Island (IRE) *P D Niven* a59 66
5 b m Bahhare(USA) —Margin Call (IRE) (Tirol)
1136[12] 1518[5] 2157[3] 2393[5] 3083[4] 4220[8] 4848[5] 5385[9] 7042[7]

Rock 'N' Roller (FR) *W R Muir* a67 82
4 bb g Sagacity(FR) —Diamond Dance (FR) (Dancehall (USA))
1026[5] (1538) 2621[7] (2888) 3296[7] 3950[7] 4963[5] 5934[2] 6606[13]

Rock Of Rochelle (USA) *A Kinsella* a89 108
3 br c Rock Of Gibraltar(IRE) —Recoleta (USA) (Wild Again (USA))
1356a[6] 2961a[8] (5922a) 6516a[4] 7005a[2]

Rock Of Tarik (IRE) *M J Grassick* a64 68
4 ch g Rock Of Gibraltar(IRE) —Molasses (FR) (Machiavellian (USA))
6366a[8]

Rock On Ciara (IRE) *D J Wintle* 38
2 b f Rock Of Gibraltar(IRE) —Secret Wells (USA) (Sadler's Wells (USA))
2479[10] 4890[12]

Rock Peak (IRE) *H Morrison* a67 76
3 b g Dalakhani(IRE) —Convenience (IRE) (Ela-Mana-Mou)
1114[4] 1367[5] 2564[6] 3327[3] 4573[3] 4985[8] 5465[7] 6775[9]

Rock Relief (IRE) *Sir Mark Prescott* a37 66
2 gr c Daylami(IRE) —Sheer Bliss (IRE) (Sadler's Wells (USA))
6187[7] 6488[8] 6923[2] ◆

Rock Soleil *Jane Chapple-Hyam* a87 93
4 b h Rock Of Gibraltar(IRE) —Hunt The Sun (Rainbow Quest (USA))
7404[5] 7770[5]

Rockson (IRE) *B W Hills* a44
2 bb f Rock Of Gibraltar(IRE) —Opera Star (IRE) (Sadler's Wells (USA))
7434[8]

Rocksy *D J Coakley* a30 65
2 b f Kyllachy—Sea Music (Inchinor)
2916[16] 3848[11] 5364[3]

Rocky Heights (IRE) *J L Dunlop* 33
2 b f Rock Of Gibraltar(IRE) —Height Of Fantasy (IRE) (Shirley Heights)
7140[17]

Rocoppelia (USA) *Mrs A J Perrett* a58 59
2 ch c Hennessy(USA) —Eternally (USA) (Timeless Moment (USA))
4024[4] 4510[7] 4778[4] 7472[6] 7700[7] 7833[6]

Rodeo *C W Thornton* 78
5 ch g Pivotal—Flossy (Efisio)
1217[16] 1520[14] 2697[10]

Rogalt (IRE) *B Smart*
2 b c Rock Of Gibraltar(IRE) —Rills (USA) (Clever Trick (USA))
6759[10]

Rohaani (USA) *Doug Watson* a95 101
6 ch h High Yield(USA) —Strawberry's Charm (USA) (Strawberry Road (AUS))
652a[6] 817a[10]

Roi (FR) *J Rossi* a95
7 bl g Octagonal(NZ) —Riziere (FR) (Groom Dancer (USA))
(5115a) 7643a[8]

Roker Park (IRE) *K R Burke* 91
3 b g Choisir(AUS) —Joyful (IRE) (Green Desert (USA))
5831[21] 6810[10] (7222)

Roleplay (IRE) *J M P Eustace* a61 39
3 b f Singspiel(IRE) —In Your Dreams (IRE) (Suave Dancer (USA))
6705[14] 7395[3] 7474[7]

Roll Em Over *A Crook* a5 25
5 b m Tamure(IRE) —Miss Petronella (Petoski)
2157[6] 2914[10]

Rolling Bag (FR) *M Roussel* 97
2 ro c Rashbag—Kiritsou (FR) (Great Palm (USA))
6642a[4]

Rolling Sea (USA) *Steven Asmussen* a106 80
5 ch m Sefapiano(USA) —Almost Sma (USA) (Cure The Blues (USA))
6523a[10]

Rollin 'n Tumblin *W Jarvis* a78
4 ch g Zaha(CAN) —Steppin Out (First Trump)
22[3] (88) 406[7] (675) (793) (880) 1179[2] 1501[6]

Roll Over Rover (IRE) *Noel Meade* 63
4 ch g Act One—Glamadour (IRE) (Sanglamore (USA))
4799a[2]

Roly Boy *R Hannon* a74 90
2 b g Dansili—Night At Sea (Night Shift (USA))
1983[4] 2826[4] (3372) 3941[5] 4589[4] 5242[2] 5895[3] 6970[13]

Romance Bere (FR) *Thomas Demeaulte* 99
3 gr f Verglas(IRE) —Kanonette (FR) (Kaldoun (FR))
7431a[9]

Romancingthestone *I A Wood* a36
2 b f Pursuit Of Love—Ruby Princess (IRE) (Mac's Imp (USA))
6877[9] 7207[6]

Roman Glory (IRE) *B J Meehan* 96
2 b g Soviet Star(USA) —Putout (Dowsing (USA))
5468[9] 6197[2] 6425[3] 6745[2] 6973[6]

Roman History (IRE) *Miss Tracy Waggott* a58 59
5 b g Titus Livius(FR) —Tetradonna (IRE) (Teenoso (USA))
1305[12] 2250[8] 2365[14] 2487[4] 3077[7] 3230[3] 4215[9] 4541[6] 6217[12] 6255[3] 6485[8] 6951[10]

Roman Maze *W M Brisbourne* a88 95
8 ch g Lycius(USA) —Maze Garden (USA) (Riverman (USA))
4661[10] 5717[7] 5908[12] 6452[8] 6826[11]

Romanoff (GER) *M Weiss* 99
5 br h Silvano(GER) —Royal Army (GER) (Pirate Army (USA))
3307a[7]

Roman Quintet (IRE) *A J McCabe* a43 73
8 ch g Titus Livius(FR) —Quintellina (Robellino (USA))
1634[9] 1966[10] 3079[6] 3405[2] 3665[4] 4653[5]

Roman Republic (FR) *M Johnston* 82
2 b c Cape Cross(IRE) —Mare Nostrum (Caerleon (USA))
6604[7] (6944)

Roman's Run (USA) *Doug Watson* a98
4 bb h Tiznow(USA) —Ensnare (USA) (Seeking The Gold (USA))
564a[9] 815a[9]

Romantic Destiny *K A Ryan* 95
3 b f Dubai Destination(USA) —My First Romance (Danehill (USA))
2038[5] 2500[2] 3452[4] (4379) 5504[6]

Romantic Interlude (IRE) *A P Jarvis* a59 15
2 b f Hawk Wing(USA) —Kissin A Lot (USA) (Kissin Kris (USA))
5048[11] 6038[4] 6682[7]

Romantic Queen *E A L Dunlop* a64 52
2 b f Medicean—Bandit Queen (Desert Prince (IRE))
3027[7] 5835[6] 6933[5] 7205[2] 7501[2] 7640[2]

Romantic Retreat *G L Moore* a42 62
3 ch f Rainbow Quest(USA) —Magical Retreat (USA) (Sir Ivor (USA))
2328[11] 2989[5] 7822[8]

Romantic Verse *E S McMahon* a69 62
3 b f Kyllachy—Romancing (Dr Devious (IRE))
2670[6] 3086[3] 3564[2] 4083[6] (6088) 6749[9] 7829[6]

Roman Villa (USA) *M Sheppard* 76
6 b g Chester House(USA) —Danzante (USA) (Danzig (USA))
7515[13]

Romany Nights (IRE) *Miss Gay Kelleway* a78 84
8 b g Night Shift(USA) —Gipsy Moth (Efisio)
4336[5] 4639[8] (4746) 5088[5] 5247[3] 5639[10] 6125[18] 6338[9]

Romany Princess (IRE) *R Hannon* a88 82
3 b f Viking Ruler(AUS) —Fag End (IRE) (Treasure Kay)
2196[3] 2481[4] 6981[11] 7390[3] (7419)

Romeo's On Fire (IRE) *G M Lyons* a88 77
4 b h Danehill(USA) —Fighting Countess (USA) (Ringside (USA))
(7325a)

Romford Car Two *Miss J Feilden* a53 50
3 b g Josr Algarhoud(IRE) —Film Buff (Midyan (USA))
1163[8] 1938[11] 2868[7]

Romiosini Way (GR) *P R Chamings* 62
3 gr f Harmonic Way—Omorfita (GR) (Wadood (USA))
3061[11] 3801[3]

Ronaldsay *R Hannon* a99 108
4 gr m Kirkwall—Crackling (Electric)
1427[5] 2130[4] 2402[5] (2820) (3088) 4196[8] 4667[2] 5288[2] 6241[3] 6781[5] 7100[3]

Rondeau (GR) *P R Chamings* a77 72
3 ch g Harmonic Way—Areti (GR) (Wadood (USA))
2756[6] 3180[2] ◆ 3799[4] 4369[4] 4637[4] 5616[9] (6209) 6706[4]

Ronnie Howe *S R Bowring* a59 72
4 b g Hunting Lion(IRE) —Arasong (Aragon)
1015[12] 1431[7] 1893[2] (2748) 3401[9] 4385[6] 7517[10] 7629[5] 7778[7]

Ronnies Girl *C J Teague*
4 b m Tobougg(IRE) —Tryptonic (FR) (Baryshnikov (AUS))
4116[7] 4454[7] 4950[12] 5261[12]

Ronsard (IRE) *P D Evans* a59 67
6 b g Spectrum(IRE) —Touche-A-Tout (IRE) (Royal Academy (USA))
36[7] 67[6] 345[4] 438[6] 606[9] 661[2] 779[11] 869[3] 1062[5] 1121[4] 1726[10] 2245[12] 2643[4] 2776[7] 4366[5] 5993[11] 7265[7] 7285[10] 7520[11]

Ron's Princess (IRE) *P C Haslam* 14
2 b f Fantastic Light(USA) —Persea (IRE) (Fasliyev (USA))
1574[5] 2671[10]

Roodolph *Eve Johnson Houghton* a81 78
4 ch g Primo Valentino(IRE) —Roo (Rudimentary (USA))
1532[9] (2060) 2499[4] 2895[2] 3029[6] 5512[4] 6028[2] 6203[4] 6721[7]

Roof Fiddle (USA) *Kevin Prendergast* 91
2 bb f Cat Thief(USA) —Woodmaven (USA) (Woodman (USA))
(4965) 5438a[3] 6318a[7]

Rookwith (IRE) *T G McCourt* a65 67
8 b g Revoque(IRE) —Resume (IRE) (Lahib (USA))
6366a[18]

Roos Abu (IRE) *John Joseph Hanlon* 45
2 br c Fasliyev(USA) —Roos Rose (IRE) (Grand Lodge (USA))
6320a[25]

Rosabee (IRE) *Miss V Haigh* 97
2 ch f No Excuse Needed—Tilbrook (IRE) (Don't Forget Me)
1515[5] 1749[3] 2357[5] (3809) (3865) (4119) 4403[2] 6441[8] 6818[12]

Rosa Del Dubai (IRE) *B Grizzetti* 103
3 b f Dubai Destination(USA) —Rosa Di Brema (ITY) (Lomitas)
(2439a)

Rosa Grace *Rae Guest* 107
3 ro f Lomitas—Night Haven (Night Shift (USA))
2305[3] ◆ (2975) 4006a[12] 5164a[2]

Rosaleen (IRE) *B J Meehan* a63 98
3 b f Cadeaux Genereux—Dark Rosaleen (IRE) (Darshaan)
1401[4] (1715) 2305[8] 3124[5] (3742) 5506[8] 6266[12]

Rosbay (IRE) *T D Easterby* 92
4 b g Desert Prince(IRE) —Dark Rosaleen (IRE) (Darshaan)
1072[4] 1580[3] 1909[2] 2582[10] 3142[5] 3493[3] 4191[3] 4742[3] 6107[5]

Rosberg (USA) *E Charpy* a107 96
7 br h A.P. Indy(USA) —Bosra Sham (USA) (Woodman (USA))
203a[3] (648a) 1087a[5]

Roscoff (IRE) *Robert Collet* a81 104
3 b f Daylami(IRE) —Traou Mad (IRE) (Barathea (IRE))
687a[3] 1375a[7] 7450a[5] 7635a[0]

Rosco Flyer (IRE) *J R Boyle* a66 57
2 b g Val Royal(FR) —Palace Soy (IRE) (Tagula (IRE))
6072[8] 6553[6] 6910[6]

Ros Cuire (IRE) *W A Murphy* a70 30
3 br c Expelled(USA) —Haven Island (IRE) (Revoque (IRE))
826a[6] 991[6] 4388[6] 5561[6]

Rose Bien *P J McBride* a65 68
6 bb m Bien Bien(USA) —Madame Bovary (Ile De Bourbon (USA))
544[10] 1165[3] 1856[4] 2135[5] 3059[2] 3276[3] 3642[2] 4516[17]

Rose Cheval (USA) *M R Channon* a60 72
2 ro f Johannesburg(USA) —La Samanna (USA) (Trempolino (USA))
2821[6] ◆ 3349[2] 4080[6]

Rose De Rita *L P Grassick* a26 36
3 b f Superior Premium—Rita's Rock Ape (Mon Tresor)
2771[3] 3565[10] 4324[11] 5749[9] 6224[6] 7453[6]

Rose Diamond (IRE) *R Charlton* 101
2 gr f Daylami(IRE) —Tante Rose (IRE) (Barathea (IRE))
2821[4] ◆ (3219) 4403[5] ◆ 5266[2] 5828[4] 6519a[7]

Rose Hill Doloise (FR) *A Bonin* 92
2 b f Marchand De Sable(USA) —Nachata (FR) (Always Fair (USA))
7103a[5] 7430a[5]

Rosemarkie *B J Llewellyn* a6 15
4 br m Diktat—Sparkling Isle (Inchinor)
6896[7]

Rosenreihe (IRE) *P Schiergen* 107
3 b f Catcher In The Rye(IRE) —Rosengeste (IRE) (Be My Guest (USA))
2065a[3] 2655a[2] 3306a[4] 4233a[5] (4675a) 6521a[10]

Rosentraub *H J L Dunlop* a64 57
3 b c Dansili—Ambrosine (Nashwan (USA))
1573[14] 3563[9]

Rose Of Coma (IRE) *Miss Gay Kelleway* a47 59
2 br f Kheleyf(USA) —Rosalia (USA) (Red Ransom (USA))
1480[3] 2004[2] 2216[4] 2671[2] (2980) (4063) 5006[3] 5460[2] 5774[6] 7443[9] 7607[7] 7652[5] 7833[10]

Rose Of Torridge *A G Newcombe* a6 26
3 ch f Zaha(CAN) —Revoke (USA) (Riverman (USA))
4277[13] 4709[6] 5491[12] 7658[8]

Rose Row *Mrs Mary Hambro* a67 72
4 gr m Act One—D'Azy (Persian Bold)
134[3] 510[2] 1165[5] (1697) 2241[3] (2682)

Rose Siog *R A Fahey* 81
3 ch f Bahamian Bounty—Madame Sisu (Emarati (USA))
1484[3] ◆ 1945[7]

Rose Street (IRE) *M A Jarvis* a94 101
4 b m Noverre(USA) —Archipova (IRE) (Ela-Mana-Mou)
4528[2] ◆ (5382) 6120[2]

Roshina (IRE) *J S Bolger* a73 72
2 b f Chevalier(IRE) —Tus Maith (IRE) (Entrepreneur)
5294a[16]

Rosie Cross (IRE) *Eve Johnson Houghton* a67 64
4 b m Cape Cross(IRE) —Professional Mom (USA) (Spinning World (USA))
86[5] 571[7] 718[7] 774[7] 4812[8] 5152[5] 5582[4] 5797[6] 6335[12] 7625[2] 7678[4]

Rosie Says No *R M H Cowell* a70 67
3 b f Catcher In The Rye(IRE) —Curlew Calling (IRE) (Pennine Walk)
(1743) 2452[2] 2757[3] 3118[5] 5629[5] 6046[6] 6564[5] 7021[2] 7320[3]

Rosies Dawn *D Carroll* a36 21
3 b f Tobougg(IRE) —Celts Dawn (Celtic Swing)
6114[9] 6633[6] 6791[12] 7049[7] 7270[11]

Rosie's Glory (USA) *M F Harris* a64 71
4 bb m More Than Ready(USA) —Cukee (USA) (Langfuhr (CAN))
320[6] 455[6] 490[8]

Rosika *Sir Michael Stoute* a67
2 b f Sakhee(USA) —Blush Rambler (IRE) (Blushing Groom (FR))
7289[3]

Rosinka (IRE) *H Graham Motion* a96 113
5 b m Soviet Star(USA) —Last Drama (IRE) (Last Tycoon)
4888a[9] 6523a[3]

Rossett Rose (IRE) *M Brittain* a32 67
2 ch f Rossini(USA) —Sabaah Elfull (Kris)
3049[12] 3792[3] 4438[4] 4816[4] 5451[4] 5632[10] 6547[2] 6863[8] 7693[7]

Rossini Byline (IRE) *J L Spearing* a49 55
3 b f Rossini(USA) —Byliny (IRE) (Archway (IRE))
354[5] 837[10] 2935[3] 3118[7] 4725[9] 7369[7]

Rossini's Dancer *R A Fahey* a60 64
3 b g Rossini(USA) —Bint Alhabib (Nashwan (USA))
634[4] 1161[6] 1396[2] ◆ 2367[10] 2842[5] 3442[5] 3717[7] 4745[8] 5008[3] 5224[3] 5544[3] 5565[3] (6015) 6585[6]

Ross Moor *Mike Murphy* a77 73
6 b g Dansili—Snipe Hall (Crofthall)
1151[4] 1585[4] 2278[4] (2764) 3003[11] 3461[3] 4078[8] 4791[8]

Rosy Alexander *S A Callaghan* a56 72
3 ch f Spartacus(IRE) —Sweet Angeline (Deploy)
5032[5] 5317[6] 6007[10]

Rosy Dawn *J J Bridger* a56 52
3 ch f Bertolini(USA) —Blushing Sunrise (USA) (Cox's Ridge (USA))
704[9] 940[9] (1251) 1530[8] 1681[7] 2719[13] 2932[7] 3524[15] 3605[8] 3844[9] 4774[6] 5232[8] 5631[10] 6337[3] 6541[11] 6729[2] 7010[5] 7260[5] 7506[9] 7596[6] 7761[9] 7807[10]

Rosy Mantle *W R Muir* a74 96
2 b f Daylami(IRE) —Dominion Rose (USA) (Spinning World (USA))
(5835) 6240[2] ◆ 6982[2] 7144[6]

Rotative *W R Swinburn* a74
3 ch f Spinning World(USA) —Kristal Bridge (Kris)
(5568) ◆ 6379[4]

Rothesay Dancer *J S Goldie* a76 77
5 b m Lujain(USA) —Rhinefield Beauty (IRE) (Shalford (IRE))
987[7] 1309[3] ◆ 1431[6] (1827) 2145[2] 2583[5] 2596[5] 2843[8] 3401[5] 3581[2] 3787[2] 3956[2] (4016) 4239[8] 4631[3] 4971[5] (5220) 5542[8] 6164[9] 6990[4] 7222[5]

Rotuma (IRE) *M Dods* a30 55
9 b g Tagula(IRE) —Cross Question (USA) (Alleged (USA))
468[8] 989[8] 3230[5] 3814[5] 4142[5] 4420[5] 6040[9]

Rough Rock (IRE) *G Prodromou* a58 70
3 ch g Rock Of Gibraltar(IRE) —Amitie Fatale (IRE) (Night Shift (USA))
2122[12] 2555[3] 2983[9] 3224[9] 3571[6] 3782[6] 4271[P] 6388[8] 6890[8] 7055[6] 7541[12] 7648[12]

Round The Cape *R Hannon* 86
3 b f Cape Cross(IRE) —Rock The Boat (Slip Anchor)
2198[2] ◆ (2560)

Roundthetwist (IRE) *K R Burke* a71 63
3 b g Okawango(USA) —Delta Town (USA) (Sanglamore (USA))
30[2] 572[5] 920[5] 1140[6] 2272[5] 2603[13] 2941[3] 4049[6] 4629[4] 7358[12] 7500[8] 7631[10] 7818[5]

Rouse The Cat (USA) *Ollie Figgins III* a106 111
4 bb g Sir Cat(USA) —Crouse Mill (USA) (Strike Gold (USA))
6994a[12]

Rovana Jowe (GER) *A Wohler* 98
5 b m Silvano(GER) —Rovana (GER) (Dashing Blade)
2347a[4]

Rowaad *A E Price* a69 72
3 ch g Compton Place—Level Pegging (IRE) (Common Grounds)
1467[20] 2276[3] 2918[6] 3438[10] 6003[14] 6357[16] 6566[7] 6792[10] 7021[10]

Rowan Dancer *J R Boyle* a56 56
3 b f Medicean—Golden Seattle (IRE) (Seattle Dancer (USA))
3397[2] 3845[3] 4572[12] 5378[15] 6541[4] 6913[8]

Rowan Lodge (IRE) *Ollie Pears* a65 69
6 ch g Indian Lodge(IRE) —Tirol Hope (IRE) (Tirol)
1160[14] (1391) 1752[9] 2667[3] 3077[4] 3230[2] 4217[6] (4451) (4878) 5712[2] 6353[10] 6827[2] 7340[9] 7585[3]

Rowan Rio *W J Haggas* a74 90
3 ch g Lomitas—Lemon Tree (USA) (Zilzal (USA))
(570) ◆ 3134[8] (3793) (5370) 6012[6] 6866[5]

Rowan River *Tom Dascombe* a64 77
4 b m Invincible Spirit(IRE) —Lemon Tree (USA) (Zilzal (USA))
1287[3] 1577[8] 3322[4] 4152[7] 7009[13]

Rowan Tiger *J R Boyle* 64
2 b g Tiger Hill(IRE) —Lemon Tree (USA) (Zilzal (USA))
6604[12] 6978[9]

Rowayton *J D Bethell* a83 76
2 bg f Lujain(USA) —Bandanna (Bandmaster (USA))
(2462) 5642[14] 6769[3] 7075[2] 7335[4]

Rowe Park *Mrs L C Jewell* a101 116
5 b g Dancing Spree(USA) —Magic Legs (Reprimand)
1831[9] 2712[8] 3739[8] 4188[12] 4550[6] 4957[4] 6121[6] 6429[10]

Royal Acclaim *M H Tompkins*
2 b f Royal Applause—Movie Queen (Danehill (USA))
3584[U]

Royal Acclamation (IRE) *G A Harker* a45 71
3 b g Acclamation—Lady Abigail (IRE) (Royal Academy (USA))
1073[7] 1161[12] 1396[11] 1558[10] (2780) 3280[2] 3831[4] 4329[8] 4700[9] 5634[12] 6219[7] 6357[5] 7040[7] 7320[12] 7471[12]

Royal Amnesty *I Semple* a84 75
5 br g Desert Prince(IRE) —Regal Peace (Known Fact (USA))
389[4] (686) 811[2] (973) ◆ 1314[3] (1953) ◆ (2249) 2839[6] 5699[3] 6450[2] (7116) 7657[6]

Royal And Regal (IRE) *M A Jarvis* 119
4 b g Sadler's Wells(USA) —Smart 'n Noble (USA) (Smarten (USA))
(1468) ◆ 2169[2] 2542[3] 5333a[7] 5854[3]

Royal Applord *K A Ryan* a74 74
3 b g Royal Applause—Known Class (USA) (Known Fact (USA))
(74) 253[3] 458[3] 1576[8] 3263[10] (4043) 4451[6] 4969[4] 5248[5] 5303[12] 6215[3] 6490[4] 7018[6] 7317[9]

Royal Arruhan *M Halford* a61 69
2 b f Royal Applause—Arruhan (IRE) (Mujtahid (USA))
6319a[17]

Royal Arthur *L A Dace* 6
2 ch c Imperial Dancer—Scenic Lady (IRE) (Scenic)
4150[13] 5812[9]

Royal Astronomer (IRE) *Lester Winters* a85 85
3 b g Soviet Star(USA) —Queen's Quest (Rainbow Quest (USA))
4512a[14]

Royal Auditon *T T Clement* a44 58
7 ch m First Trump—Loriner's Lass (Saddlers' Hall (IRE))
299[12] 585[9] 776[10] (1127) 1262[12] 2884[10] 3276[7]

Royal Avenue (IRE) *T D Easterby* 49
3 ch g Kris Kin(USA) —Flying Feet (USA) (Devil's Bag (USA))
1628[9] 2008[15] 2269[6] 3555[9]

Royal Axminster *Mrs P N Dutfield* a48 47
13 b g Alzao(USA) —Number One Spot (Reference Point)
188[5]

Royal Ballade (USA) *Thomas Albertrani*
2 b f Elusive Quality(USA) —Musical Chimes (USA) (In Excess I (IRE))
6500a[10]

Royal Bet (IRE) *Sir Michael Stoute* 46
2 b c Montjeu(IRE) —Queen Of Norway (USA) (Woodman (USA))
7106[11]

Royal Bloom (IRE) *J R Fanshawe* 38
3 b f Royal Applause—Bethesda (Distant Relative)
1535[10]

Royal Challenge *I W McInnes* a79 82
7 b g Royal Applause—Anotheranniversary (Emarati (USA))
194[4] ◆ 801[4] 1040[3] 1312[9] 1485[8] 1908[6] 2270[9] 2780[10] 2891[4] 3211[8] 3255[4] ◆ 3665[6] (4174) 4327[5] 4934[4] 5392[6] (5709) (5867) 6137[2] 6634[2] 7428[9]

Royal Choir *H E Haynes* a60 39
4 ch m King's Best(USA) —Harmonic Sound (IRE) (Grand Lodge (USA))
1565[11] 1966[13] 2513[13] 4748[6] 5166[9] 5429[7] 7553[5] 7678[3] (7807)

Royal Citadel (IRE) *Mrs L B Normile* a10 57
5 b m City On A Hill(USA) —Royal Baldini (USA) (Green Dancer (USA))
4018[14] 4142[10] 4630[8] 4850[4] 7039[14]

Royal Collection (IRE) *J Pearce* 70
2 b c Val Royal(FR) —Rachel Green (IRE) (Case Law)
6341[7] 6720[8] 7104[3]

Royal Composer (IRE) *T D Easterby* 67
5 b g Mozart(IRE) —Susun Kelapa (USA) (St Jovite (USA))
2270[4] 3665[2] 4174[7] 4393[8] 5260[5] 6219[6] ◆

Royal Confidence *B W Hills* 107
3 b f Royal Applause—Never A Doubt (Night Shift (USA))
1400[3] 1830[7] ◆ 3119[11] 3619a[10] 4590[5] (5829) 6814[10]

Royal Defence (IRE) *D Nicholls* 70
2 b c Refuse To Bend(IRE) —Alessia (GER) (Warning)
5882[2]

Royal Degree *B Smart* a64 77
3 b c Royal Applause—First Degree (Sabrehill (USA))
2966[6] 4595[10] 5261[2] 6308[3] 6822[4] 7118[6]

Royal Destination (IRE) *J Noseda* 85
3 b c Dubai Destination(USA) —Royale (IRE) (Royal Academy (USA))
2056[4] 4161[11]

Royal Diamond (IRE) *Sir Mark Prescott* a47 66
2 b g King's Best(USA) —Irresistible Jewel (IRE) (Danehill (USA))
6031[4] 6359[6] 6621[8]

Royal Dignitary (USA) *D Nicholls* a91 97
8 br g Saint Ballado(CAN) —Star Actress (USA) (Star De Naskra (USA))
1016[10] 1286[2] (1902) (2250) 2578[2] (3281) (3643) (4559)

Royale Again (FR) *J De Roualle* a83 81
3 b f Fasliyev(USA) —Royale Figurine (IRE) (Dominion Royale)
7551a[10]

Royal Embrace *D Shaw* a63 47
5 b g Bertolini(USA) —Tight Spin (High Top)
56[3] 235[9] 448[5] 537[7] 768[3] 915[4] 1083[4] 1505[13]

Royal Encore *J R Fanshawe* a65 58
4 b m Royal Applause—Footlight Fantasy (USA) (Nureyev (USA))
3438[5] 3867[3] 5205[8] 6063[7] 6338[7] 6735[2] 7076[5] 7345[2] 7516[2]

Royal Entourage *G M Lyons* a67 65
3 b g Royal Applause—Trempkate (USA) (Trempolino (USA))
3861a[9]

Royal Envoy (IRE) *P Howling* a82 86
6 b g Royal Applause—Seven Notes (Zafonic (USA))
13[2] 149[2] (334) 539[3] 775[6] (901) 1040[8] (1191) ◆ 1415[4] 1567[3] (1818) 2359[5] 5250[10] 5648[13] 5936[10] 6634[7] 6952[3] 7315[7] 7544[5] 7763[6]

Royal Executioner (USA) *P W Chapple-Hyam* 78
2 b c Royal Academy(USA) —Guillotine (USA) (Proud Truth (USA))
2916[11] 3476[2] 4415[3] 5274[3] ◆

Royal Fantasy (IRE) *N Tinkler* a84 85
5 bb m King's Best(USA) —Dreams (Rainbow Quest (USA))
586[2] ◆ 927[3] 1691[3] 2820[2] 3088[4] 4435[6] 5279[18] 5635[11]

Royal Fire (GER) *Miss A Casotti* 18
9 b h Bin Ajwaad(IRE) —Royal Future (IRE) (Royal Academy (USA))
422a[9] 604a[7]

Royal Flyer (IRE) *R A Farrant* a43
4 b g Winged Love(IRE) —Saronicos King (IRE) (King's Ride)
5477[5]

Royal Flynn *Mrs K Walton* 82
6 b g Royal Applause—Shamriyna (IRE) (Darshaan)
1613[2] 3673[6]

Royal God (USA) *F Head* 108
3 b c Royal Academy(USA) —Gold Splash (USA) (Blushing Groom (FR))
2875a[6] 4719a[2] 5738a[9] 7162a[5]

Royal Grace *T D Easterby* 63
3 b f Royal Applause—Olivia Grace (Pivotal)
2380[12] (2823) 3260[9] 4216[7] (4615)

Royal Guest *J R Jenkins* a66 55
4 b g Royal Applause—Bajan Blue (Lycius (USA))
161[9] 256[12] 328[8] 516[9] 587[11]

Royal Honor (GER) *T Vana* 73
5 b h Highest Honor(FR) —Rosolida (Niniski (USA))
422a[8]

Royal Indulgence *W M Brisbourne* a49 66
8 b g Royal Applause—Silent Indulgence (USA) (Woodman (USA))
3947[8] 4458[8] 5427[8] 6136[6]

Royal Intruder *R Hannon* a89 98
3 b c Royal Applause—Surprise Visitor (IRE) (Be My Guest (USA))
1837[6] ◆ 2529[2] 3273[4] 3850[5] 4553[7] 5102[2] 5795[14] 6676[10] 6911[10]

Royal Island (IRE) *M G Quinlan* a86 86
6 b g Trans Island—Royal House (FR) (Royal Academy (USA))
829a[4] 1105a[7] 1497a[6] 2200[4] 2504[5] 2947[8] 3317[5] 3800[9] (4707) 5345[6] 5635[4] 6125[9] 6491[11] 6663[10] 6826[6] 6989[9] 7153[5] (7585)

Royalist (IRE) *M A Jarvis* a85 88
3 b c King's Best(USA) —Nebraas (Green Desert (USA))
(1295) 1923[8] 5795[13] 6290[6] 6624[5]

Royal Jasra *E A L Dunlop* a68 78
4 b g Royal Applause—Lake Pleasant (IRE) (Elegant Air)
1935[6] 2304[11] 2895[4] 3220[9] 6210[11]

Royal Jet *M R Channon* a98 93
6 b g Royal Applause—Red Bouquet (Reference Point)
3505[9] 4191[13] 4444[5] 4742[13] 5677[3] 6171[9]

Royal Keva (IRE) *A D Brown* a68
2 b g Medecis—Karmafair (IRE) (Always Fair (USA))
7148[6] 7282[4] 7627[4] 7720[3]

Royal Lustre *Miss Tracy Waggott* a50 64
7 b g Deputy Minister(CAN) —Snow Bride (USA) (Blushing Groom (FR))
862[11] 1116[12]

Royal Manor *N J Vaughan* a70 57
3 b f King's Best(USA) —She's Classy (USA) (Boundary (USA))
6047[4] 6275[5] 6868[7] 7189[6] 7340[3] (7437) 7651[7] 7762[6]

Royal Max (IRE) *C G Cox* a45 55
2 b g Hawkeye(IRE) —Baccara (IRE) (Sri Pekan (USA))
3140[12] 3492[5] 4474[8] 5774[4] 6214[7] 7257[12]

Royal Miswaki (IRE) *Wido Neuroth* 80
4 b h Royal Academy(USA) —Driving Miswaki (USA) (Miswaki (USA))
5957a[10]

Royal Muwasim *M R Channon* 48
2 b f Reset(AUS) —Millitrix (Doyoun)
2485[5] 3125[4] 4113[3] 4487[2]

Royal Oath (USA) *J H M Gosden* a102 117
5 b h Kingmambo(USA) —Sherkiya (IRE) (Goldneyev (USA))
651a[2] 818a[5] 2472a[5]

Royal Orissa *D Haydn Jones* a63 69
6 b g Royal Applause—Ling Lane (Slip Anchor)
7[8] 147[9] 264[8]

Royal Pleasure (USA) *Jonathan Sheppard* 102
5 ch m Royal Academy(USA) —Pleasure Center (USA) (Diesis)
6505a[6]

Royal Power (IRE) *D Nicholls* a108 104
5 b h Xaar—Magic Touch (Fairy King (USA))
2133[3] 2789[6] ◆ 3122[3] 3491[11] 3921[13] 4587[13] (5208)

Royal Premier (IRE) *H J Collingridge* a63 73
5 b g King's Theatre(IRE) —Mystic Shadow (IRE) (Mtoto)
881[9] (1692) 1929[6] (2482) 3917[7] 4892[4] 5476[9] 6007[12] 6775[13]

Royal Premium *H A McWilliams* 50
2 b c Superior Premium—Royal Shepley (Royal Applause)
2443[8] 3125[8] 4203[5] 4290[4] 4734[7] 5357[4] 5414[2] 5560[5] 7266[9]

Royal Raider *P D Evans* a59 77
2 b f Piccolo—Baileys Applause (Royal Applause)
(3309) 3681[5] 4403[15] 5473[7] 7308[5] 7537[7] 7600[6] 7687[10]

Royal Rainbow *P W Hiatt* a47 42
4 ch g Rainbow Quest(USA) —Royal Future (IRE) (Royal Academy (USA))
919[7] 1296[9] 1913[9]

Royal Rock *C F Wall* a89 107
4 b g Sakhee(USA) —Vanishing Point (USA) (Caller I.D. (USA))
(1689) ◆ 2195[3]

Royal Salsa (IRE) *R A Fahey* 52
2 b f Royal Applause—Lady Salsa (IRE) (Gone West (USA))
4616[5] 5106[8] 5500[7] 6214[10]

Royal Senga *C A Horgan* a43 54
5 b m Agnes World(USA) —Katyushka (IRE) (Soviet Star (USA))
264[9]

Royal Society *M Johnston* 54
2 b c King's Best(USA) —Nawaiet (USA) (Zilzal (USA))
6065[5] 6412[10]

Royal Sovereign (IRE) *G C H Chung* a59 63
3 b g Invincible Spirit(IRE) —Ombry Girl (IRE) (Distinctly North (USA))
4806[2] 5186[8] 6433[5] 6889[14] 7102[5]

Royal Soverin *M J Wallace* a55 51
3 b g Royal Applause—Glorious Colours (Spectrum (IRE))
454[6] 610[5] 1490[6] 1938[9] 2273[11] 3264[2] 4023[3] 4750[7] 5215[4]

Royal Storm (IRE) *B R Millman* a73 86
9 b h Royal Applause—Wakayi (Persian Bold)
2101[3] (2693) 2925[11] 3443[8] 3646[3] (3675) 4121[10] 4167[5] 4744[6] 5708[8]

Royal Straight *B N Pollock* a74 66
3 ch g Halling(USA) —High Straits (Bering)
1854[4] 2302[13] 4390[8] 5086[3] 5559[5] (5994) ◆ 6741[5] 7115[9] 7354[11] 7553[10]

Royal Superlative *R M Beckett* 10
2 b f King's Best(USA) —Supereva (IRE) (Sadler's Wells (USA))
3959[13]

Royal Tartan (USA) *G L Moore* a43 27
3 b f Lemon Drop Kid(USA) —Castellina (USA) (Danzig Connection (USA))
2994[11] 3530[7] 4607[9] 7071[8]

Royal Tender (IRE) *H J Collingridge* a53 41
4 gr m Woods Of Windsor(USA) —Tender Guest (IRE) (Be My Guest (USA))
3698[9] 3871[5] 4490[9] 4599[2] 5602[8] 6018[9]

Royal Toerag *W J Knight* a42 69
2 b c Bertolini(USA) —Yesterday's Song (Shirley Heights)
5344[10] 5901[5] 6199[11]

Royal Trooper (IRE) *J G Given* 66
2 b c Hawk Wing(USA) —Strawberry Roan (IRE) (Sadler's Wells (USA))
5246[14] 5859[6] 6384[4]

Royal Vintage (SAF) *M F De Kock* a115 97
4 ch h Rich Man's Gold(USA) —Derry Wood (SAF) (Fort Wood (USA))
567a[2] (813a) 1088a[2] 6073[9] 6287[4]

Royal Willy (IRE) *W Jarvis* 71
2 b c Val Royal(FR) —Neat Dish (CAN) (Stalwart (USA))
5754[7] 6438[7] 7106[2]

Roy's Delight (IRE) *Edward P Harty* a74 70
4 b g Indian Lodge(IRE) —Allurah (IRE) (Goldmark (USA))
4514a[12]

Ruasgreyasme (USA) *W R Muir* a33 53
2 rg f Smoke Glacken(USA) —Newhall Road (USA) (Dixieland Band (USA))
3895[6] 4521[10] 4823[5] 6350[7] 7065[9]

Rubacuori (BRZ) *J M P Eustace* a81 79
4 b g Dodge(USA) —So Cosas (BRZ) (So Blue (BRZ))
3635[7] 4060[5] 4565[6] 5908[4] 6598[9]

Rubbinghousedotcom (IRE) *P M Phelan* a51
2 b g Desert Style(IRE) —Marain (IRE) (Marju (IRE))
6876[10] 7312[8]

Rubenstar (IRE) *D J G Murray Smith* a84 82
5 b g Soviet Star(USA) —Ansariya (USA) (Shahrastani (USA))
1308[4] 1900[11]

Rubilini *Miss Sheena West* a51 45
4 ch m Bertolini(USA) —Aunt Ruby (USA) (Rubiano (USA))
303[5] (365) 465[8] 478[6] 606[14] 863[6] 930[11]

Rubirosa (IRE) *M Dods* 89
3 b g Acclamation—Bendis (GER) (Danehill (USA))
1426[14] 1999[5] (2526) 2967[2] 4408[4] 5102[13] 6976[10]

Rublevka Star (USA) *J Noseda* a67 63
2 b f Elusive Quality(USA) —Al Desima (Emperor Jones (USA))
6030[6] (6932)

Rub Of The Relic (IRE) *P T Midgley* a66 75
3 b c Chevalier(IRE) —Bayletta (IRE) (Woodborough (USA))
1124[3] 1479[6] 6356[9] 6792[16] 6836[5] 7085[8] (7532) 7634[5] 7799[2]

Rubro Meridio (IRE) *I Bugattella* 24
5 b h Cadeaux Genereux—Beauty Dancer (IRE) (Alzao (USA))
7349a[14]

Ruby Best *D K Ivory* a28 41
2 b f Best Of The Bests(IRE) —Ice Bird (Polar Falcon (USA))
4980[11] 5673[8] 6342[10]

Ruby Delta *A G Juckes* a66 69
3 b g Delta Dancer—Picolette (Piccolo)
705[8] 1060[8] 1958[11] 2244[12] 3065[7] 3206[8] (5710)

Ruby Rocks *P S McEntee*
3 ch f Zaha(CAN) —Natural Grace (Zamindar (USA))
5205[7] 5402[7]

Ruby's Rainbow (IRE) *J Balding* a24 22
3 b f Fayruz—Sweet Finesse (IRE) (Revoque (IRE))
4615[14] 5501[11] 5592[10]

Ruby's Song (IRE) *J M Bradley*
2 b f Clodovil(IRE) —Gales Bridge (IRE) (Mujadil (USA))
1640[8] 2951[13] 4530[9]

Ruby Tallulah *C R Dore* a72 75
2 b f Piccolo—Tallulah Belle (Crowning Honors (CAN))
3558[4] 4411[2] 4634[4] ◆ (4942) 5103[3] 6414[4] 7241[11] 7335[8] 7575[8] ◆

Rubytwosox (IRE) *W R Muir* a56 57
3 b f Redback—Policy (Nashwan (USA))
1251[6] 1740[7]

Rudry Dragon (IRE) *P A Blockley* a78 89
4 b h Princely Heir(IRE) —Jazz Up (Cadeaux Genereux)
1131[5] 1365[5] 1682[3] 1909[3] 2599[3]

Rudry World (IRE) *M Mullineaux* a72 78
5 ch g Spinning World(USA) —Fancy Boots (IRE) (Salt Dome (USA))
2572[2] 2908[12] 3630[8] 4238[7] 4972[3] 5369[5] 5559[10] 6136[9]

Rue De Cabestan (IRE) *T G McCourt* a23 57
3 b f Orpen(USA) —Beaufort Lady (IRE) (Alhaarth (IRE))
4715a[2]

Rue Soleil *J R Weymes* a29 59
4 ch m Zaha(CAN) —Maria Cappuccini (Siberian Express (USA))
1561^{11} 1827^{13} 2676^{4} 2777^{10} 3454^{14} 4047^{16} 7375^{12}

Ruff Diamond (USA) *J R Best* a82 85
3 bb g Stormin Fever(USA) —Whalah (USA) (Dixieland Band (USA))
905^{7} 1632^{9} 2194^{14} 2840^{9} 3633^{7} 3925^{9} 4046^{10}

Ruffie (IRE) *Miss J Feilden* a71 51
5 b m Medicean—Darling Lover (USA) (Dare And Go (USA))
74 220^{2} 330^{8} (478) 579^{5} 915^{5} 1116^{9} 2795^{14} 3162^{7} 3842^{10} 5059^{9} 5312^{10}

Rule For Ever *I W McInnes* a78 70
6 br g Diktat—Tous Les Jours (USA) (Dayjur (USA))
3820^{7} 4391^{11}

Ruler Of All (IRE) *B W Hills* 58
2 b c Sadler's Wells(USA) —Shabby Chic (USA) (Red Ransom (USA))
6425^{12}

Rulesn'Regulations *M Salaman* a89 51
2 b c Forzando—Al Awaalah (Mukaddamah (USA))
4665^{7} (7168) (7523)

Ruling Reef *M R Bosley* a54 51
6 b m Diktat—Horseshoe Reef (Mill Reef (USA))
788^{2} 843^{2} 1280^{3} 1505^{9} 3448^{11}

Ruman (IRE) *M J Attwater* a77 58
6 b g Fayruz—Starway To Heaven (ITY) (Nordance (USA))
5629^{6}

Rumble Of Thunder (IRE) *D W P Arbuthnot* a77 75
2 b g Fath(USA) —Honey Storm (IRE) (Mujadil (USA))
3323^{3} ◆ 4907^{4} 5461^{5} 6058^{2} 6954^{2} 7391^{3}

Rum Jungle *H Candy* a73 87
4 b g Robellino(USA) —Anna Karietta (Precocious)
1926^{10} 3161^{3} 4121^{2} (4602) 4927^{2} 5588^{3} (6194)

Rumline *W S Kittow* a48 47
3 b f Royal Applause—Waypoint (Cadeaux Genereux)
3611^{12} 4349^{10} 4695^{14} 5378^{8} 5837^{11} 7395^{9}

Rum Raisin *John Joseph Murphy* a65 50
2 b f Invincible Spirit(IRE) —Femme Femme (USA) (Lyphard (USA))
7332^{3}

Rumramah (USA) *D M Simcock* 56
2 b f Mr Greeley(USA) —She's Vested (USA) (Boundary (USA))
6030^{10}

Runaway *R Pritchard-Gordon* 110
6 b h King's Best(USA) —Anasazi (IRE) (Sadler's Wells (USA))
1108a^{4} 2876a^{5} 5138a^{5} 6322a^{4}

Run For Ede'S *P M Phelan* a71 72
4 b m Peintre Celebre(USA) —Raincloud (Rainbow Quest (USA))
1842^{18} 2758^{5} 3583^{2} (4022) 4694^{8} 5291^{3} 6867^{6} 7307^{4} 7526^{8}

Run For The Hills *J H M Gosden* 92
2 b c Oasis Dream—Maid For The Hills (Indian Ridge)
4199^{3} ◆ 4510^{2} (6776) ◆

Run Free *N Wilson* a64 71
4 b g Agnes World(USA) —Ellie Ardensky (Slip Anchor)
42^{5} 4173^{11} 4597^{9} 5157^{5} 5710^{3} 6185^{2} (7658) (7772)

Run From Nun *John Berry* a49 39
3 b f Oasis Dream—Nunatak (USA) (Bering)
141^{3} 306^{4} 583^{5} 3395^{11} 4725^{6} 6822^{9}

Running Buck (USA) *A Bailey* a43 54
3 b c Running Stag(USA) —Dinghy (USA) (Fortunate Prospect (USA))
7535^{7} 7779^{6}

Running Home (GER) *A Wohler*
2 b c Storming Home—Roma Libera (GER) (Pharly (FR))
6853a^{4}

Running Supreme *Mrs N Smith* a35
4 b m Josr Algarhoud(IRE) —Running Glimpse (IRE) (Runnett)
183^{7} 705^{9} 1125^{10} 1499^{6} 1644^{9}

Runswick Bay *G M Moore* 84
3 b g Intikhab(USA) —Upend (Main Reef)
1428^{P}

Rupestrian *M Johnston* a65 74
2 b g Fantastic Light(USA) —Upper Strata (Shirley Heights)
6808^{7} 6977^{4} 7343^{4}

Rushing Dasher (GER) *A Wohler* a66 89
6 ch g Dashing Blade—Roma Libera (GER) (Pharly (FR))
(422a) 603a^{2}

Russet Reward *Mrs L Stubbs* 87
2 b g Bahamian Bounty—Appleacre (Polar Falcon (USA))
1303^{4} 1821^{4} 2186^{2} (2522) (3020) 3681^{7} 6644^{19}

Russian Angel *Jean-Rene Auvray* a50
4 gr m Baryshnikov(AUS) —Eventuality (Petoski)
7504^{4} 7701^{3}

Russian Art *R M Beckett* a59 56
2 b c Johannesburg(USA) —Sweet Deimos (Green Desert (USA))
2124^{8} 2999^{10} 3485^{5} 4119^{5} 5591^{4} 5914^{3} 6086^{10}

Russian Cross (IRE) *A Fabre* a89 118
3 b c Cape Cross(IRE) —Dievotchka (Dancing Brave (USA))
(5302a) 6148a^{2} 6816^{4}

Russian Desert (IRE) *A Fabre* a92 109
4 ch h Desert Prince(IRE) —Dievotchka (Dancing Brave (USA))
5114a^{6} 7643a^{15}

Russian Empress (IRE) *David P Myerscough* a80 95
4 b m Trans Island—Russian Countess (USA) (Nureyev (USA))
(1497a) 5731a^{5} 6484^{11} 7157a^{6}

Russian Empress (USA) *Sir Michael Stoute* a56 61
3 b f Kingmambo(USA) —Balistroika (USA) (Nijinsky (CAN))
2257^{9} 3318^{7} 4277^{9}

Russian Epic *M A Jarvis* a58 84
4 b g Diktat—Russian Rhapsody (Cosmonaut)
1857^{9} 2334^{4} 2762^{5} 3928^{9} (4895) 6035^{14}

Russian George (IRE) *T P Tate* a76 77
2 ch g Sendawar(IRE) —Mannsara (IRE) (Royal Academy (USA))
3821^{3} 4394^{4} 4780^{4} 6082^{2}

Russian Invader (IRE) *A King* a16 84
4 ch g Acatenango(GER) —Ukraine Venture (Slip Anchor)
6582^{11}

Russian Rave *J G Portman* 68
2 ch f Danehill Dancer(IRE) —Russian Ruby (FR) (Vettori (IRE))
3207^{4} 3632^{4} 4554^{8} 6240^{20}

Russian Reel *E J Creighton* a80 90
3 b g Reel Buddy(USA) —Charlie Girl (Puissance)
4004a^{17} 5681^{6} 6124^{14} 6435^{2} 7143^{10} 7384^{9} 7557^{4} 7675^{7} 7748^{8}

Russian Rocket (IRE) *Mrs C A Dunnett* a67 74
6 b g Indian Rocket—Soviet Girl (IRE) (Soviet Star (USA))
(951) 1185^{8} 1966^{7} 2511^{3} 2950^{5} (5319) 6006^{2} 6840^{13}

Russian Saint *T J Pitt* 33
2 b f Red Ransom(USA) —Tessara (GER) (Big Shuffle (USA))
5365^{9}

Russian Spirit *M A Jarvis* 68
2 b f Falbrav(IRE) —Russian Rhapsody (Cosmonaut)
7141^{5}

Russian Symphony (USA) *C R Egerton* a85 81
7 ch g Stravinsky(USA) —Backwoods Teacher (USA) (Woodman (USA))
26^{11} 210^{8} 2501^{2} 4154^{9} 5046^{2} 7276^{7} 7456^{2}

Russki (IRE) *D M Simcock* a109 87
4 b g Fasliyev(USA) —Rose Of Mooncoin (IRE) (Brief Truce (USA))
(1545) 1942^{9} 4528^{4} (5051) 5695^{7} (6576)

Rutba *M P Tregoning* a70 63
3 b f Act One—Elhilmeya (IRE) (Unfuwain (USA))
2885^{9} 3671^{5} 4247^{15} (5322) (5613) (6897) 7216^{3}

Ruud Revenge (USA) *Miss V Haigh* 35
2 b g Van Nistelrooy(USA) —Savannah's Revenge (USA) (West By West (USA))
3476^{6} 3888^{11}

Ruwain *P J McBride* a56 48
4 b g Lujain(USA) —Ruwaya (USA) (Red Ransom (USA))
161^{5} 1374^{7} 1747^{14} 2755^{9} 3113^{10} 3657^{3} (4267) 4491^{6} 5020^{8} 5321^{4}

Ryan (IRE) *J Hanacek* 102
5 b h Generous(IRE) —Raysiza (IRE) (Alzao (USA))
3307a^{2} 4911a^{3} 7008a^{9}

Ryan's Future (IRE) *J S Moore* a62 77
8 b h Danetime(IRE) —Era (Dalsaan)
57^{2} 999^{4} 1159^{2} (1266) 2097^{5} 2640^{5} 5783^{9} 6493^{6} 6927^{5}

Ryan's Rock *T D McCarthy* a48 33
3 b g Lujain(USA) —Diamond Jayne (IRE) (Royal Abjar (USA))
4249^{12} 4929^{11} 5086^{4}

Rydal (USA) *Miss Jo Crowley* a76 73
7 ch g Gilded Time(USA) —Tennis Partner (USA) (Northern Dancer (CAN))
4862^{5} 5492^{11} 6020^{13} 6880^{4} 7834^{5}

Rydal Mount (IRE) *W S Kittow* a80 92
5 b m Cape Cross(IRE) —Pooka (Dominion)
1522^{7} 1872^{2} 2329^{7} (2622) 2947^{6} (3210) 3994^{5}

Ryedale Ovation (IRE) *M Hill* a76 71
5 b g Royal Applause—Passe Passe (USA) (Lear Fan (USA))
(586) 1682^{11} 2476^{2} 3132^{7} 3347^{9} 3836^{5} 4365^{2} 4785^{12} 6211^{9} (7009) 7309^{2} 7405^{5}

Ryedane (IRE) *T D Easterby* a75 69
6 b g Danetime(IRE) —Miss Valediction (IRE) (Petardia)
1485^{17} 2005^{15} 2263^{8} 3546^{4} 3638^{11} 4047^{11} 4293^{4} (4653) 4903^{5} 5474^{2} 5709^{8} 7043^{6} (7231) 7517^{2} 7611^{6} 7733^{3}

Ryedon Bye *T D Easterby* 48
2 ch g Distant Music(USA) —Payphone (Anabaa (USA))
3364^{6}

Ryehill Dreamer (IRE) *T Stack* 104
2 b c Catcher In The Rye(IRE) —No Way (IRE) (Rainbows For Life (CAN))
4517^{9} 5296a^{2}

Rye Rocket *K R Burke* 45
3 b g Catcher In The Rye(IRE) —Platinum Michelle (Pivotal)
1573^{11} 2221^{13} 2779^{5} 4247^{10} 4564^{6} 6386^{8}

Saafend Geezer *A Berry* a63 53
3 ch g Kyllachy—Kindred Spirit (IRE) (Cadeaux Genereux)
1115^{3} 1247^{5} 1958^{10} 2480^{8} 2753^{7} 3549^{7} 3953^{4} 4207^{19} 4236^{7} 4632^{6} 4901^{6} 5748^{15}

Saameq (IRE) *D W Thompson* a61 52
7 b g Bahhare(USA) —Tajawuz (Kris)
(4932)

Sabana Perdida (IRE) *A De Royer-Dupre* 115
5 b m Cape Cross(IRE) —Capriola (USA) (Mr Prospector (USA))
(1993) (3120) 4674a^{5} 6270^{3}

Sabancaya *Mrs P Sly* a60 65
3 b f Nayef(USA) —Serra Negra (Kris)
1525^{7} 1721^{8} 2376^{3} 2785^{10} 3327^{4} 3562^{4} 4966^{3} 5399^{4} 7376^{4} 7573^{4} 7761^{6}

Sabirli (TUR) *C Kurt* 113
7 b h Strike The Gold(USA) —Free Trade (TUR) (Shareef Dancer (USA))
5742a^{9}

Sabi Star *J H M Gosden* 58
2 b c Green Desert(USA) —Balisada (Kris)
4311^{5}

Saborido (USA) *Mrs A J Perrett* a36 60
2 gr c Dixie Union(USA) —Alexine (ARG) (Runaway Groom (CAN))
5996^{10} 6397^{8} 6602^{7}

Sabre Light *J Pearce* a82 69
3 b g Fantastic Light(USA) —Good Grounds (USA) (Alleged (USA))
961^{7} 1140^{7} 1516^{8} (2486) 2984^{5} (3115) 3436^{5} 4066^{2} (4491) 4721^{7} 5836^{4} 6134^{2} ◆ 6424^{7} (6757) 6888^{5} (7260) (7506) (7553) 7707^{5} ◆

Sabre's Edge (IRE) *G A Ham* a30 69
7 b g Sadler's Wells(USA) —Brave Kris (IRE) (Kris)
1265^{P} (Dead)

Sacho (GER) *W Kujath* 105
10 br g Dashing Blade—She's His Guest (IRE) (Be My Guest (USA))
4881a^{4}

Sacred Flame (USA) *B J Meehan* a52 67
3 b f Rahy(USA) —Ashraakat (USA) (Danzig (USA))
2973^{5} 3611^{9} 4085^{6} 4669^{9} 5167^{15}

Sacrilege *D R C Elsworth* a77 81
3 ch g Sakhee(USA) —Idolize (Polish Precedent (USA))
58^{9} 3161^{2} (3725) 4128^{5} 5773^{6} 6528^{5}

Saddex *P Rau* 123
5 b h Sadler's Wells(USA) —Remote Romance (USA) (Irish River (FR))
1665a^{2} (2230a)

Sadeek *B Smart* 83
4 ch g Kyllachy—Miss Mercy (IRE) (Law Society (USA))
1430^{12} 2210^{5} 2535^{3} (3443) 7239^{16}

Sadler's Hill (IRE) *M J McGrath* a46 30
4 b g Sadler's Wells(USA) —Dedicated Lady (IRE) (Pennine Walk)
400^{12} 751^{4} 1726^{13}

Sadler's Kingdom (IRE) *R A Fahey* a54 96
4 b h Sadler's Wells(USA) —Artful Pleasure (USA) (Nasty And Bold (USA))
981^{8} 1472^{6} 1625^{6} 3493^{7} ◆

Sadler's Star (GER) *B G Powell* a64 84
5 b g Alwuhush(USA) —Sadlerella (IRE) (King's Theatre (IRE))
96^{10}

Safari Dancer (IRE) *Miss L A Perratt* 59
3 b g Indian Danehill(IRE) —Umlani (IRE) (Great Commotion (USA))
3126^{15} 3578^{6} 3958^{5}

Safari Guide *P Winkworth* 65
2 b g Primo Valentino(IRE) —Sabalara (IRE) (Mujadil (USA))
4907^{3} 5213^{11}

Safari Mischief *P Winkworth* a96 97
5 b g Primo Valentino(IRE) —Night Gypsy (Mind Games)
(1802) 2326^{2} 2828^{3} 3320^{2} 4445^{4} 5509^{3} (6624)

Safari Song (IRE) *B Smart* 51
2 b c War Chant(USA) —Leopard Hunt (USA) (Diesis)
6655^{11} 6944^{11}

Safari Sundowner (IRE) *P Winkworth* a89 58
4 b g Daggers Drawn(USA) —Acadelli (IRE) (Royal Academy (USA))
(356) (448) (546) ◆ 752^{2} (888) 1273^{7} 2152^{11} (2711) 3398^{9} (4078) 4726^{3} 5349^{11} 5699^{9}

Safari Sunup (IRE) *P Winkworth* a67 95
3 b g Catcher In The Rye(IRE) —Nuit Des Temps (Sadler's Wells (USA))
1600^{6} 2610^{7} 5573^{10} 6202^{3} (6667)

Safaseef (IRE) *K A Morgan* a51 55
3 b f Cadeaux Genereux—Asaafeer (USA) (Dayjur (USA))
2823^{2} 3282^{12} 4987^{6} 5261^{7} 6735^{8}

Safebreaker *N Tinkler* a80 70
3 b g Key Of Luck(USA) —Insijaam (USA) (Secretariat (USA))
157^{2} 458^{7} 920^{3} 3709^{5} 4392^{7} 4750^{6} 4990^{5} 5868^{6} 6729^{9}

Safe Investment (USA) *B N Pollock* a88 89
4 b g Gone West(USA) —Fully Invested (USA) (Irish River (FR))
53^{5} 122^{6} 388^{5} 587^{12}

Safety Investments (AUS) *J Lau* a84 91
9 br g Fuji Kiseki(JPN) —Tipsy Myar (NZ) (Dahar (USA))
380a^{6} 563a^{8} 669a^{6}

Saffron's Son (IRE) *P T Midgley* 54
2 b g Saffron Walden(FR) —Try My Rosie (Try My Best (USA))
5716^{8} 6234^{3} 6524^{9}

Safranine (IRE) *Miss A Stokell* a40 61
11 b m Dolphin Street(FR) —Webbiana (African Sky)
2010^{12} 2676^{7} 3695^{6} 4016^{8} 4462^{10} 4903^{13} 5374^{10}

Saga D'Or (FR) *F Head* 86
3 gr f Sagacity(FR) —Fedora (FR) (Kendor (FR))
1375a^{8}

Sagara (USA) *Saeed Bin Suroor* 123
4 b g Sadler's Wells(USA) —Rangoon Ruby (USA) (Kingmambo (USA))
2797^{10} 3154^{5} 3878^{5} 4551^{3} 5854^{6} 6306^{3} 6820^{2}

Sagarich (FR) *C F Swan* 72
4 gr m Sagamix(FR) —Baranciaga (USA) (Bering)
4655a^{3}

Sageburg (IRE) *A De Royer-Dupre* 123
4 gr h Johannesburg(USA) —Sage Et Jolie (Linamix (FR))
1665a^{3} (2238a) 3100^{6} 5138a^{4} 5740a^{4} 6498a^{2}

Sagunt (GER) *S Curran* a59 67
5 ch g Tertullian(USA) —Suva (GER) (Arazi (USA))
56^{11} 276^{6} 1644^{10} 2003^{14} 2782^{11} 6228^{3} 6929^{2} (7676) 7806^{8}

Sahaadi *R Hannon* a78 72
3 b f Dansili—Shardette (IRE) (Darshaan)
1899^{6} 2276^{4} 2920^{12} 3272^{7} (3615) 3883^{8} 4483^{4}

Saharan Royal *M Salaman* 65
2 b f Val Royal(FR) —Saharan Song (IRE) (Singspiel (IRE))
2769^{7} 3645^{2} 4720^{2}

Sahara Prince (IRE) *K A Morgan* a44 49
8 b g Desert King(IRE) —Chehana (Posse (USA))
7590^{8} 7815^{9}

Sahara Sphinx (USA) *M Al Muhairi* a86 74
5 ch h Giant's Causeway(USA) —Sculpture (USA) (Deputy Minister (CAN))
476a^{9}

Sahf London *G L Moore* a60 27
6 b g Vettori(IRE) —Lumiere D'Espoir (FR) (Saumarez)
(161) 299^{2} 330^{5} 695^{4} 1206^{8} 1528^{13}

Sahpresa (USA) *Rod Collet* 113
3 b f Sahm(USA) —Sorpresa (USA) (Pleasant Tap (USA))
6780^{4}

Sahrati *C E Brittain* a74 98
4 ch g In The Wings—Shimna (Mr Prospector (USA))
1026^{7} 1568^{5} 2120^{6} (3505) 4363^{6} 4844^{5} 5494^{8} 5910^{DSQ} 6210^{7} 6302^{7}

Saif Al Fahad (IRE) *E J O'Neill* a74 66
2 ch c Shinko Forest(IRE) —Golden Ciel (USA) (Septieme Ciel (USA))
3199^{2} 3882^{4} 6837^{5} 7335^{2} 7460^{4} (7689)

Sail (IRE) *A P O'Brien* 103
3 b f Sadler's Wells(USA) —Pieds De Plume (FR) (Seattle Slew (USA))
(1915) ◆ 2792^{13} 3511a^{7} 4833a^{13} 5136a^{6} 5729a^{7} 5920a^{7} 6298a^{10} 6819^{8}

Sailor King (IRE) *D K Ivory* a88 86
6 b g King's Best(USA) —Manureva (USA) (Nureyev (USA))
(313) 594^{8} 717^{6} 1174^{8} 1630^{12} 2085^{6} 3797^{12}

Sainglend *S Curran* a40 77
3 b g Galileo(IRE) —Verbal Intrigue (USA) (Dahar (USA))
1854^{9} 2256^{7} 2974^{14} 3886^{7} (6868)

Saint Arch (CAN) *M Johnston* a89 82
2 bb c Arch(USA) —Halo Silver (USA) (Silver Buck (USA))
(6553) (7214)

Saint Chapelle (IRE) *Mrs A J Perrett* 55
2 b f Noverre(USA) —Chartres (IRE) (Danehill (USA))
6978^{11}

Saint Eric (FR) *Noel T Chance* a48
6 b g Lesotho(USA) —Fearnan (Blakeney)
287^{U} 485^{5} 720^{4} 869^{6} 1062^{6}

Saintly Gaze *W R Swinburn* a67 65
3 ch g Observatory(USA) —St Edith (IRE) (Desert King (IRE))
2455^{3} 3419^{3} 4929^{7} 5836^{6}

Saint Stan (FR) *Mlle A De Clerck* 85
10 ch g College Chapel—Soon Point (FR) (Groom Dancer (USA))
3243a^{11}

Saintsylvadene *T D Walford* a7 8
3 b g First Trump—Elle Reef (Shareef Dancer (USA))
867^{10} 1014^{7} 1452^{13}

Saipan (FR) *Gerard Keane* a53
7 b g Alhaarth(IRE) —Ishtiyak (Green Desert (USA))
322^{2}

Sairaam (IRE) *J L Dunlop* 63
2 bb f Marju(IRE) —Sayedati Eljamilah (USA) (Mr Prospector (USA))
4870^{8} 6197^{5} 6926^{8}

Sakhacity *J R Jenkins* 67
3 b f Sakhee(USA) —Subtle One (IRE) (Polish Patriot (USA))
3918^{11}

Sakheart *M Botti* a68
2 b f Sakhee(USA) —Tanwir (Unfuwain (USA))
7720^{2} ◆ 7823^{2}

Sakheela *Pat Eddery* 58
3 br f Sakhee(USA) —Salinova (FR) (Linamix (FR))
5750^{6}

Sakhee's Pearl *Miss Gay Kelleway* 75
2 gr f Sakhee(USA) —Grey Pearl (Ali-Royal (IRE))
6600^{2}

Sakhee's Secret *H Morrison* 126
4 ch h Sakhee(USA) —Palace Street (USA) (Secreto (USA))
1831^{2} 3247^{17} 5245^{14}

Sakhee's Song (IRE) *D R C Elsworth* 109
4 b m Sakhee(USA) —Show Me The Money (IRE) (Mujadil (USA))
2606^{9} 3460^{5} 4159^{3} 4550^{10} 4841^{10} 5275^{9} 5829^{9}

Sakza (IRE) *M Delzangles* 96
3 b f Sakhee(USA) —Miss Sazanica (FR) (Zafonic (USA))
7431a^{4}

Salaam Dubai (AUS) *A Selvaratnam* a104 93
7 b g Secret Savings(USA) —Gulistan (AUS) (Rubiton (AUS))
295a^{2} 566a^{3} 814a^{5} 2235a^{9}

Salaasa (USA) *E McNamara* a23 89
4 ch g Swain(IRE) —Jawla (Wolfhound (USA))
7750^{9}

Salamandra (FR) *C Laffon-Parias* a66 43
3 b f Numerous(USA) —Soierie (FR) (Bering)
6742a^{0}

Salamon *P F I Cole* a46
2 gr f Montjeu(IRE) —Farfala (FR) (Linamix (FR))
7093^{7}

Salar Micol (ITY) *M Marcialis* 100
3 br f Morigi—This Is The End (IRE) (Hamas (IRE))
7349a^{9}

Salattus (GER) *G Raveneau* 94
7 b g Acatenango(GER) —Saas Fee (Top Ville)
605a^{4}

Salawat *T T Clement* a29
5 b m Tomba—Galadriel (Fairy King (USA))
461^{9} 787^{6}

Saleima (IRE) *P W Chapple-Hyam* a76 80
3 b f Rock Of Gibraltar(IRE) —Lumber Jill (USA) (Woodman (USA))
2164^{5} 2675^{5} 3479^{2} 4152^{4} 5019^{5} ◆ 5595^{4} 6049^{4}

Sale Or Return (IRE) *T D Easterby* a39 50
2 b f Fath(USA) —Kaguyahime (Distant Relative)
1515^{6} 3106^{5} 4045^{5} 4499^{9} 6009^{2} *6350^{5}* 6579^{8} 6787^{13} *7281^{5}*

Salerosa (IRE) *Mrs A Duffield* a67 58
3 b f Monashee Mountain(USA) —Sainte Gig (FR) (Saint Cyrien (FR))
1429^{4} 2269^{5} 2781^{8} *(7178) (7441) 7559^{4}*

Salgrev (IRE) *Irene J Monaghan* 49
2 gr f Verglas(IRE) —Leverick Bay (Octagonal (NZ))
4847^{4}

Salient *M J Attwater* a95 93
4 b h Fasliyev(USA) —Savannah Belle (Green Desert (USA))
1765^{3} ◆ 1982^{19} (2604) 3040^{9} *3319^{4}* 3899^{8} 4407^{13} 5030^{4} 5313^{9} 5589^{3} 5897^{2} *6625^{9} 6911^{11} 7215^{13}*

Salingers Star (IRE) *G A Swinbank* 76
3 b f Catcher In The Rye(IRE) —Head For The Stars (IRE) (Head For Heights)
5717^{8} 6188^{8}

Salisburgo (ITY) *V di Napoli* a100 101
5 b h Big Shuffle(USA) —Exy Girl (IRE) (Alzao (USA))
$7253a^{13}$

Salishan (IRE) *Adrian McGuinness* a53 77
6 ch m Namid—Lancea (IRE) (Generous (IRE))
$4467a^{9}$

Sally Bond (IRE) *T D Easterby*
2 b f Monsieur Bond(IRE) —Sally Green (IRE) (Common Grounds)
1907^{6} 2462^{11}

Sally's Dilemma *W G M Turner* a55 81
2 b f Primo Valentino(IRE) —Lake Mistassiu (Tina's Pet)
(957) 1156^{2} 1838^{5} 2147^{4} 2239^{2} *7308^{6} 7575^{9} 7628^{3} 7760^{8}*

Sally's Swansong *M Wellings* a33
2 b f Mind Games—Sister Sal (Bairn (USA))
7823^{8}

Salomo (GER) *J L Dunlop* 60
2 b c Monsun(GER) —Salka (GER) (Doyoun)
5246^{11} 5857^{6}

Saloon (USA) *S Curran* a56 72
4 b g Sadler's Wells(USA) —Fire The Groom (USA) (Blushing Groom (FR))
1172^{11} *1408^{6} 2051^{11}* 2715^{6} 5489^{P} *5611^{5}* 6364^{3} 6668^{2} 6929^{3}

Salpado (FR) *R Martin Sanchez* 100
2 b c Royal Applause—Moonbaby (FR) (Le Balafre (FR))
$7163a^{9}$

Salsa De La Tour (FR) *P Demercastel* a87 82
4 b g Kingsalsa(USA) —Ridiyla (IRE) (Akarad (FR))
$5115a^{10}$

Salsalavie (FR) *P Demercastel* 100
3 b c Fly To The Stars—Lavayssiere (FR) (Sicyos (USA))
$1362a^{2}$ $2064a^{4}$ $2654a^{12}$ $4212a^{9}$

Salsa Star (USA) *R A Fahey* 87
2 ch f Giant's Causeway(USA) —Miss Salsa (USA) (Unbridled (USA))
2377^{2} 3192^{9} 4202^{4} ◆ 6068^{3} 6483^{13}

Salsa Steps (USA) *H Morrison* a92 101
4 ch m Giant's Causeway(USA) —Dance Design (IRE) (Sadler's Wells (USA))
(1683) ◆ 1993^{4} 3927^{11} 5275^{4} 6271^{10} *7421^{9} 7703^{11}*

Salsa Time *Miss J A Camacho* 65
3 b f Hernando(FR) —Kabayil (Dancing Brave (USA))
1579^{5} 1964^{10} 2659^{3}

Saltagioo (ITY) *M Botti* a90 91
4 b h Dr Devious(IRE) —Sces (Kris)
6625^{10} 7116^{5} 7502^{4} 7753^{2}

Salt Of The Earth (IRE) *T G Mills* a76 62
3 b g Invincible Spirit(IRE) —Get The Accountant (Vettori (IRE))
60^{2} 146^{2} 354^{2} 737^{4} 2481^{10} 2555^{7} *5617^{12} 6048^{14} 7194^{2} (7359)* 7490^{7} 7763^{3}

Salt Track (ARG) *Niels Petersen* a100 94
8 br h Salt Lake(USA) —Astralisima (ARG) (Fitzcarraldo (ARG))
$204a^{5}$ $382a^{8}$ $564a^{8}$ $2233a^{3}$

Saluscraggie *R E Barr* 66
6 b m Most Welcome—Upper Caen (High Top)
1219^{8} (1559) 2701^{5} 3602^{6} 4048^{11} 4295^{2} 5040^{9} 5543^{4} 6050^{14} 6189^{10} 6812^{12}

Salute (IRE) *P G Murphy* a89 89
9 b g Muhtarram(USA) —Alasib (Siberian Express (USA))
859^{2} 981^{6} 1179^{3} 1501^{5} 2621^{5} *(3613)* 4314^{7} 4955^{4} 6622^{7} *6957^{4} 7499^{2} 7747^{4}*

Salute Him (IRE) *A J Martin* 90
5 b g Mull Of Kintyre(USA) —Living Legend (ITY) (Archway (IRE))
5229^{11}

Salute The Count (USA) *Richard Dutrow Jr* 111
8 b g Count The Time(USA) —Marie De Hesse (USA) (Iron Courage (USA))
$6994a^{6}$

Salut L'Africain (FR) *Robert Collet* a96 109
3 b c Ski Chief(USA) —Mamana (IRE) (Highest Honor (FR))
(1376a) $2032a^{11}$ $3938a^{6}$ $4719a^{9}$ $5556a^{5}$ $5738a^{7}$ $7187a^{8}$

Salut Saint Cloud *G L Moore* a79 64
7 b g Primo Dominie—Tiriana (Common Grounds)
27^{9} 224^{7} 461^{4} 544^{2} 1246^{2} 1459^{2}

Salve Germania (IRE) *W Hickst* 97
3 ch f Peintre Celebre(USA) —Salve Regina (GER) (Monsun (GER))
$3705a^{5}$ $4675a^{13}$ $5597a^{4}$ $6691a^{3}$

Salvestro *A W Carroll* a47 65
5 b g Medicean—Katy Nowaitee (Komaite (USA))
24^{5} 120^{7} 160^{6} 242^{9} 400^{11} 518^{9} 693^{9}

Salybia Bay *R Hannon* a68
2 b f Fraam—Down The Valley (Kampala)
6205^{7} 6737^{8} 7095^{5} 7259^{7}

Samahir (USA) *T T Clement* a54 55
4 b m Forest Wildcat(USA) —Saabga (USA) (Woodman (USA))
2513^{5} 3218^{4} 3814^{12} 4156^{8} 4282^{7} *6422^{9} 6753^{7} 6930^{5}* 7050^{8}

Samara Valley (IRE) *H R A Cecil* 78
2 ch f Dalakhani(IRE) —Slap Shot (IRE) (Lycius (USA))
2614^{4} (3349)

Samarinda (USA) *Mrs P Sly* a101 93
5 ch g Rahy(USA) —Munnaya (USA) (Nijinsky (CAN))
227^{4} (502) 834^{11} 958^{15} 1766^{4} 2711^{11} 3122^{25} *4528^{8} 5695^{10} (6772) 7313^{6}* 7755^{3}

Samba Mirander *C Drew* a51
2 b f Zaha(CAN) —Silent Scream (IRE) (Lahib (USA))
5404^{10}

Samba Queen (IRE) *J L Spearing* 50
2 ch f Captain Rio—Khawafi (Kris)
2638^{13} 3114^{6} 3645^{8} 4297^{5} 4986^{5} 5715^{7}

Samba School (IRE) *Kevin Prendergast* 91
2 b f Sahm(USA) —Lulua (USA) (Bahri (USA))
$6319a^{3}$

Samira Gold (FR) *L M Cumani* a98 107
4 ch m Gold Away(IRE) —Capework (USA) (El Gran Senor (USA))
3720^{9} 4549^{6} 6034^{4} *7100^{2}*

Sam Lord *A King* a86 90
4 ch g Observatory(USA) —My Mariam (Salse (USA))
(3800) 4191^{6} *7314^{5} 7558^{4}*

Sampeyre (ITY) *Laura Grizzetti* 94
3 b c Orpen(USA) —Absintina (IRE) (Bluebird (USA))
$1513a^{10}$

Sampi *Mrs A J Perrett* a67 78
2 ch f Beat Hollow—Delta (Zafonic (USA))
6016^{5} (6392)

Sampower Quin (IRE) *D Carroll* a58 66
2 b g Sampower Star—Quinolina (Shareef Dancer (USA))
5870^{8} 6253^{10} 6597^{10} 6857^{3}

Sampower Rose (IRE) *D Carroll* 62
2 b f Sampower Star—Rosebank (USA) (El Prado (IRE))
3707^{7} 4289^{5} 4740^{6} (6112)

Sam's Cross (IRE) *K R Burke* a78 86
3 b g Cape Cross(IRE) —Fancy Lady (Cadeaux Genereux)
2967^{9} 3324^{4} 4408^{8} 5397^{8} 5580^{9} *6738^{4}* ◆ *7302^{2} 7457^{8}*

Sam Sharp (USA) *H R A Cecil* 58
2 bb c Johannesburg(USA) —Caffe (USA) (Mr Prospector (USA))
3001^{8}

Sams Lass *M Mullineaux* 51
2 b f Refuse To Bend(IRE) —Dina Line (USA) (Diesis)
6785^{4}

Samson Quest *B Smart* a47
6 b g Cyrano De Bergerac—Zenita (IRE) (Zieten (USA))
6228^{13} 7469^{7} 7678^{6}

Samsons Son *J R Best* a81 91
4 b g Primo Valentino(IRE) —Santiburi Girl (Casteddu)
3800^{3} 3896^{9} 4867^{3} 5279^{3} *5677^{5}* 6120^{5} 6238^{4} 6646^{9} 6784^{8}

Sam's Secret *G A Swinbank* a69 87
6 b m Josr Algarhoud(IRE) —Twilight Time (Aragon)
1891^{4} 2190^{3} 2578^{5} 3054^{2} 3272^{2} 3403^{2}

Sams Spirit *P J McBride* a56
2 br g Diktat—Winning Girl (Green Desert (USA))
6597^{11}

Samuel *J L Dunlop* 116
4 ch h Sakhee(USA) —Dolores (Danehill (USA))
2169^{3} (2625) 3743^{2} ◆

Samuel Charles *C R Dore* a75 68
10 b g Green Desert(USA) —Hejraan (USA) (Alydar (USA))
(275) (433) 542^{5} 683^{4} 819^{7} (1109) 1670^{4} 3822^{7} 4182^{9} 4748^{4} 4919^{16} *5478^{8}*

Samurai Warrior *P D Evans* a71 60
3 br g Beat All(USA) —Ma Vie (Salse (USA))
135^{5} 310^{4} 1530^{7} 3406^{3} 4338^{6} 4891^{7} *(7363) 7497^{10} 7619^{8} 7780^{8} 7801^{3}*

San Antonio *Mrs P Sly* a96 81
8 b g Efisio—Winnebago (Kris)
1520^{9} 2697^{6} (3175) 3557^{2} (3795) 4895^{4}

Sanbuch *L M Cumani* a86 115
4 b h Tobougg(IRE) —Monte Calvo (Shirley Heights)
2202^{3} ◆ 3942^{4} (4508) 5264^{4} 6306^{4}

Sand Cat *G L Moore* a85 91
5 b g Cadeaux Genereux—Desert Lynx (IRE) (Green Desert (USA))
85^{2} 280^{3} 442^{3} 707^{2} 887^{3} ◆ 1346^{4} *1566^{8}* 4586^{14} 4981^{8} *5433^{6}* 5861^{8} 6418^{5} 6880^{5}

San Deng *Micky Hammond* a68 61
6 gr g Averti(IRE) —Miss Mirror (Magic Mirror)
1559^{6} 2364^{8} 2579^{5} 2849^{5}

Sandies Choice *M Brittain* a3 30
3 ch f Tobougg(IRE) —Nijmah (Halling (USA))
2268^{11} *7615^{11}*

Sandies Sister *M Brittain* 29
2 ch f Bertolini(USA) —Nijmah (Halling (USA))
1727^{8} 1907^{5} 2485^{7} 3008^{13} (Dead)

Sand Maiden (IRE) *T D Easterby* 54
3 ch f Desert Prince(IRE) —Maka (USA) (Diesis)
1553^{9} 2367^{9} 6015^{6}

Sandokan (GER) *Shaun Harley* 37
7 bb g Tiger Hill(IRE) —Suivez (FR) (Fioravanti (USA))
1281^{9}

San Domenico *Doug Watson* a101 103
4 b h Zamindar(USA) —Guarded (Eagle Eyed (USA))
$291a^{9}$ *$563a^{5}$* $668a^{10}$

Sandor *P J Makin* a78 75
2 ch c Fantastic Light(USA) —Crystal Star (Mark Of Esteem (IRE))
4728^{9} 5678^{3} 5996^{2} 6397^{2} *7098^{3}*

Sand Repeal (IRE) *Miss J Feilden* a71 71
6 b g Revoque(IRE) —Columbian Sand (IRE) (Salmon Leap (USA))
3^{3} 345^{2} 600^{3} 779^{10} 1136^{4} 1551^{4} 2245^{4} 3059^{5} 3448^{5} 3871^{2} 4490^{3} (4691) (5450) 5583^{5} 5993^{15}

Sandrey (IRE) *P W Chapple-Hyam* a83 92
4 b g Noverre(USA) —Boudica (IRE) (Alhaarth (IRE))
532^{4}

Sand Rose (IRE) *S Slevin* 32
3 bb f Daylami(IRE) —Sand Pigeon (Lammtarra (USA))
$3861a^{10}$

Sands Crooner (IRE) *J G Given* a84 70
5 b g Imperial Ballet(IRE) —Kurfuffle (Bluebird (USA))
29^{2} 113^{2} (187) 301^{3} 503^{6} 580^{5} 676^{5} (840) (939) 1195^{4} 2596^{13} 3112^{7} 3724^{3} ◆ 4047^{5} 4246^{10} 4703^{3} 6045^{4} *6766^{2}* ◆ 7043^{9} (7276) 7393^{5} 7584^{2} 7826^{7}

Sands Of Barra (IRE) *I W McInnes* a61 75
5 gr g Marju(IRE) —Purple Risks (FR) (Take Risks (FR))
990^{17} 1188^{3} ◆ 1450^{5} 1729^{12} 2007^{12} 2251^{2} 2891^{9} 2925^{9} 3431^{8} 3951^{5} 4018^{6} 5101^{8} 5198^{5} 5389^{3} 5538^{3} *5871^{7}* 5965^{9}

Sandwith *R Johnson* a70 81
5 ch g Perryston View—Bodfari Times (Clantime)
(1624) 2145^{9} 2843^{9} 3370^{3} (3787) 4239^{7} 4418^{4} 4700^{3} 5542^{4} 6066^{11} 6486^{10}

Sandy Par *J M Bradley* a53 62
3 ch g No Excuse Needed—Nesting (Thatching)
1155^{11} 1699^{6} 2068^{7} 4584^{5} 5074^{10}

Sandy Road (FR) *C Boutin* a52 56
3 b f Marchand De Sable(USA) —Route Des Indes (FR) (Dernier Empereur (USA))
$687a^{6}$

Sanjida (IRE) *A Fabre* 109
3 b f Polish Precedent(USA) —Sanariya (IRE) (Darshaan)
$1323a^{3}$ $1760a^{3}$ $2877a^{13}$ $6567a^{2}$

San Jose City (IRE) *D Carroll* a86 86
3 b g Clodovil(IRE) —Allspice (Alzao (USA))
1781^{2} 2333^{2} ◆ (2673) 3263^{6} 3696^{3} 4158^{5} 4682^{7} 6314^{7} *6420^{2} 6842^{7}*

Sans Frontieres (IRE) *J Noseda* 73
2 ch c Galileo(IRE) —Llia (Shirley Heights)
(5579) ◆

San Sicharia (IRE) *J-C Rouget* a85 96
3 ch f Daggers Drawn(USA) —Spinamix (Spinning World (USA))
3927^{3}

San Silvestro (IRE) *Mrs A Duffield* a59 68
3 b c Fayruz—Skehana (IRE) (Mukaddamah (USA))
3831^{3} 4248^{6} 5258^{5} ◆ 6056^{16} *6491^{8}* 6813^{7}

Santabella (FR) *B Barbier* 76
2 b f Goldneyev(USA) —Shakkaline (FR) (Homme De Loi (IRE))
$1886a^{2}$

Santa Clara *P Leech* a57 59
3 b f Night Shift(USA) —Mena (Blakeney)
74^{7} 480^{7} 1081^{7} 3446^{10} *3686^{8} 4271^{5}* 4990^{6} 5186^{9} *6571^{13} 7727^{11}*

Santando *P Bowen* a78 49
8 b g Hernando(FR) —Santarem (USA) (El Gran Senor (USA))
4817^{4}

Sant'Antonio (ITY) *A & G Botti* 96
3 b c Shantou(USA) —Nonna Rina (IRE) (Bluebird (USA))
$2028a^{13}$

Santa Teresita (USA) *Eric J Guillot* a109
4 b m Lemon Drop Kid(USA) —Sweet Gold (USA) (Gilded Time (USA))
$6969a^{7}$

Santera (IRE) *A M Hales* a49 43
4 br m Gold Away(IRE) —Sainte Gig (FR) (Saint Cyrien (FR))
145^{3} 197^{2} 377^{4} 578^{5} 7721^{7}

Santero (GER) *N Sauer* 90
3 b c Black Sam Bellamy(IRE) —Strofa (POL) (Winds Of Light (USA))
$3074a^{7}$ $3773a^{11}$

Santiago (GER) *H Blume* a113 112
6 gr h Highest Honor(FR) —Serenata (GER) (Lomitas)
$3515a^{2}$ $4470a^{6}$ *$5743a^{5}$* $7162a^{11}$

Santiago Atitlan *P Schiergen* a95 103
6 b g Stravinsky(USA) —Sylvette (USA) (Silver Hawk (USA))
$290a^{3}$

Santoriney (IRE) *D Flood* a43 24
2 ch f Indian Haven—Darsenia (IRE) (Ashkalani (IRE))
4692^{13} 6014^{9} *6694^{7}*

Sanvean (IRE) *M R Channon* 90
2 b f Danehill Dancer(IRE) —Russian Muse (FR) (Machiavellian (USA))
2627^{3} 3920^{6} 4554^{5} 4868^{10}

Sanziro (AUS) *C Fownes* 120
7 b h Danzero(AUS) —Will Fly (AUS) (Will Dancer (FR))
$2235a^{3}$

Saoirse Abu (USA) *J S Bolger* 111
3 ch f Mr Greeley(USA) —Out Too Late (USA) (Future Storm (USA))
$1230a^{3}$ 1830^{3} $2433a^{5}$

Saphira's Fire (IRE) *W R Muir* a79 98
3 b f Cape Cross(IRE) —All Our Hope (USA) (Gulch (USA))
(1372) ◆ (1833) 2792^{10} 6819^{3}

Sapiranga (GER) *Frau Marion Rotering* 90
4 ch m Acatenango(GER) —Sabanila (GER) (In The Wings)
$3307a^{3}$ $4911a^{6}$ $5625a^{6}$

Sapphire Prince (USA) *J R Best* a78 70
2 b c Read The Footnotes(USA) —Anna Jackson (USA) (Houston (USA))
2754^{5} (3392) 3920^{9} 6002^{8}

Sapphire Rose *J G Portman* a54 57
2 b f Tobougg(IRE) —Pearly River (Elegant Air)
3456^{10} 4870^{11} 5584^{8} *6207^{6}*

Saptapadi (IRE) *Sir Michael Stoute* a70
2 ch c Indian Ridge—Olympienne (IRE) (Sadler's Wells (USA))
7498^{2} ◆

Saraab (GER) *P Vovcenko* 71
6 bb g Alwuhush(USA) —Sohaila (GER) (Owington)
$4911a^{7}$

Saraba (FR) *Mrs L J Mongan* a72 70
7 gr m Soviet Star(USA) —Sarliya (IRE) (Doyoun)
(881) 1056^{5} 1564^{4} 1959^{6} 2354^{3} 2567^{11} (3322)

Sarah Park (IRE) *B J Meehan* a51 76
3 ch f Redback—Brillano (FR) (Desert King (IRE))
3314^{2} (4168) ◆ 4377^{5} 4766^{5} (6889)

Sarah's Art (IRE) *Stef Liddiard* a61 36
5 gr g City On A Hill(USA) —Treasure Bleue (IRE) (Treasure Kay)
5101^{14} *6907^{2} 7508^{5} 7589^{3} 7706^{10} 7746^{2}*

Sarah's Boy *S Dow* a40 39
3 ch g Nayef(USA) —Bella Bianca (IRE) (Barathea (IRE))
1149^{9} 1586^{10} 4085^{9}

Sarah's First *E A L Dunlop* a57 67
3 ch f Cadeaux Genereux—Band (USA) (Northern Dancer (CAN))
1247^{8} 1586^{5} 2475^{9} 2915^{5} 4260^{10}

Sarando *R Charlton* a67 62
3 b g Hernando(FR) —Dansara (Dancing Brave (USA))
1526^{10} *7583^{4} 7721^{4}*

Saranome (IRE) *R Charlton* 71
3 b g Statue Of Liberty(USA) —My Gray (FR) (Danehill (USA))
1699^{3} ◆ 1995^{8} 2991^{16} 3441^{8}

Sarasota Sunshine *N P Littmoden* 49
2 b f Oasis Dream—Never Explain (IRE) (Fairy King (USA))
6555^{12} 7020^{7} 7198^{3}

Saratee *C E Brittain* 56
3 b f Mark Of Esteem(IRE) —Salalah (Lion Cavern (USA))
4447^{7} 6357^{15}

Sardan Dansar (IRE) *Mrs A Duffield* 54
2 b f Alhaarth(IRE) —Peruvian Witch (IRE) (Perugino (USA))
3590^{9} 4072^{4} 5256^{7} 6112^{10}

Sariska *M L W Bell* 87
2 b f Pivotal—Maycocks Bay (Muhtarram (USA))
(7141) ◆

Sarissa (BRZ) *P Bary* a100 100
5 b m Music Prospector(USA) —Sylicon Purple (BRZ) (Purple Mountain (USA))
$378a^{2}$ $670a^{2}$ $814a^{4}$ $1089a^{11}$ $4881a^{7}$ $5740a^{9}$ $6568a^{2}$

Sarraaf (IRE) *Miss L A Perratt* a60 63
12 ch g Perugino(USA) —Blue Vista (IRE) (Pennine Walk)
250^{5} 2940^{8} (4142) 4633^{4} 4969^{6} 5538^{8} 6162^{4} 6409^{3} 7132^{10} *7287^{3}*

Sartorio (FR) *G Dolfi* 97
3 b c Sendawar(IRE) —Sweet Shirley (IRE) (Shirley Heights)
$2028a^{11}$

Sarwin (USA) *W J Musson* a75 59
5 rg g Holy Bull(USA) —Olive The Twist (USA) (Theatrical)
7471^{11} 1048^{8}

Sashay Queen (USA) *Sir Michael Stoute* a38
2 bb f Mr Greeley(USA) —Jack's Touch (USA) (Touch Gold (USA))
7337^{11}

Sasphee (GER) *E Kurdu* 89
4 b m Lomitas—Suanita (GER) (Big Shuffle (USA))
$5334a^{11}$

Sassoaloro (GER) *H Blume* 96
4 ch h Acatenango(GER) —Spartina (USA) (Northern Baby (CAN))
$7598a^{11}$

Satan's Circus (USA) *Christophe Clement* 115
3 br f Gone West(USA) —Delmonico Cat (USA) (Storm Cat (USA))
$2877a^{5}$ $3807a^{2}$ $5745a^{8}$

Satier (FR) *Mario Hofer* 108
3 b c Lord Of Men—Stiletta (GER) (Primo Dominie)
$3773a^{5}$ $5624a^{5}$ $6324a^{10}$

Satin Braid *D R C Elsworth* a74 71
4 b m Diktat—Beading (Polish Precedent (USA))
340^{2}

Satindra (IRE) *C R Dore* a65 53
4 b g Lil's Boy(USA) —Voronova (IRE) (Sadler's Wells (USA))
122^{2} 300^{7} 526^{12} 716^{12} 863^{2} 1086^{7} 7045^{9} 7355^{10} 7787^{8}

Satu (IRE) *David P Myerscough* a84 92
4 b g Marju(IRE) —Magic Touch (Fairy King (USA))
5830^{3}

Saturday Boy *Paul Green* a56 52
3 b c Josr Algarhoud(IRE) —Prideway (IRE) (Pips Pride)
1186^{6} 1614^{7} 2273^{4} 2750^{3} 6115^{11}

Saturnine (IRE) *N Clement* 96
3 gr f Galileo(IRE) —Katchina Quest (FR) (Highest Honor (FR))
$5597a^{6}$ $7487a^{2}$

Saturn Way (GR) *P R Chamings* a50 72
2 b c Bachelor Duke(USA) —Senseansensibility (USA) (Capote (USA))
5798^{7} (6552)

Satwa Boy *E A L Dunlop* 55
2 b c Royal Applause—Crown Of Spring (USA) (Chief's Crown (USA))
2349^{3} 2951^{12} 3798^{6} 4768^{7} 5287^{6}

Satwa Gold (USA) *E A L Dunlop* 41
2 ch c Rahy(USA) —No More Ironing (USA) (Slew O'Gold (USA))
5068^{11}

Satwa Laird *E A L Dunlop* 90
2 b c Johannesburg(USA) —Policy Setter (USA) (Deputy Minister (CAN))
4480^{3} ◆ (5072) 5791^{4} 6474^{18} 6970^{2}

Satwa Street (IRE) *D M Simcock* a84
2 br c Elusive City(USA) —Black Tribal (IRE) (Mukaddamah (USA))
2754^{9} 5939^{3} 6434^{2} 7168^{2} (7303) 7523^{2}

Satyricon *M Botti* a78 81
4 b h Dr Fong(USA) —Belladera (IRE) (Alzao (USA))
15^{5} (208) 452^{6} 730^{7} 1055^{3} 1143^{3}

Saucey Evening (USA) *H Graham Motion* a108 105
2 ch f More Than Ready(USA) —Jeweled Lady (USA) (General Meeting (USA))
$6966a^{4}$

Saucy *Tom Dascombe* a71 69
7 b m Muhtarram(USA) —So Saucy (Teenoso (USA))
6913^{3} (7217) ◆ 7342^{11} (7596) 7742^{2} ◆

Saucy Brown (IRE) *R Hannon* 90
2 b c Fasliyev(USA) —Danseuse Du Bois (USA) (Woodman (USA))
(2424) 3105^{5} 3634^{2} 4588^{9} 5852^{9} 6118^{6}

Saunders Encore *M S Saunders* a33
3 b f Piccolo—Magical Dancer (IRE) (Magical Wonder (USA))
146^{10} 222^{5}

Saunton Sands *A G Newcombe* 35
2 ch c Best Of The Bests(IRE) —Victoriet (Hamas (IRE))
1263^{9} 2098^{11} 4625^{16}

Saute *W R Swinburn* a44
2 b c Hawk Wing(USA) —Lifting (IRE) (Nordance (USA))
7593^{11}

Savannah *Luke Comer* a73 69
5 b h Sadler's Wells(USA) —La Papagena (Habitat)
588^{4} 747^{5} 880^{5} 1151^{6} 1744^{4} 2921^{5} 3160^{5} $4511a^{5}$ $5921a^{9}$

Savannah Poppy (IRE) *M L W Bell* a71 78
3 b f Statue Of Liberty(USA) —Refined (IRE) (Statoblest)
(1068) 1470^{11} 2428^{5} 3000^{12} 5073^{4} 5317^{4} 5713^{9} 6387^{2}

Savanna's Gold *G Prodromou* a37 10
4 ch m Bold Edge—Midnight Romance (Inca Chief (USA))
2546^{9} 3318^{10} 5160^{11} 5631^{14} 6836^{9}

Savarain *L M Cumani* 113
3 b c Rainbow Quest(USA) —Frangy (Sadler's Wells (USA))
1398^{6} (1931) ◆ 2303^{6} 3157^{2} ◆ 4519^{2} (6427) ◆

Savaronola (USA) *A P Stringer* a73 79
3 ch g Pulpit(USA) —Running Debate (USA) (Open Forum (USA))
7661^{4}

Save My Blushes *C G Cox* 32
2 ch c Tobougg(IRE) —American Rouge (IRE) (Grand Lodge (USA))
6977^{15}

Save The Day *M Johnston* a52 59
2 b f Dr Fong(USA) —Modelliste (Machiavellian (USA))
4521^{8} 4896^{6} 5570^{7} 6632^{9}

Savethisdanceforme (IRE) *A P O'Brien* a80 110
3 b f Danehill Dancer(IRE) —Bex (USA) (Explodent (USA))
$1104a^{2}$ 1830^{10} $2433a^{6}$ 2792^{8}

Savile's Delight (IRE) *Tom Dascombe* a78 83
9 b g Cadeaux Genereux—Across The Ice (USA) (General Holme (USA))
(153) 206^{2} 270^{2} (437) 521^{5} (554) 596^{3} 786^{2} 951^{2} 1022^{3} 1368^{2} (1522) 1739^{2} 1800^{2} 1928^{3} 2255^{3}

Saving Grace *E J Alston* 42
2 br f Lend A Hand—Damalis (IRE) (Mukaddamah (USA))
5539^{7} 6244^{8} 6580^{10}

Saviour Sand (IRE) *D R C Elsworth* a77 76
4 b g Desert Sun—Teacher Preacher (IRE) (Taufan (USA))
95^{4} 396^{2} 529^{6} (860) 973^{8} 1520^{10} 3449^{6} (4066) 6659^{7}

Saviours Spirit *T G Mills* a94 84
7 ch g Komaite(USA) —Greenway Lady (Prince Daniel (USA))
226^{10}

Savoury Gem (IRE) *P D Deegan* 46
4 b m Mull Of Kintyre(USA) —El-Libaab (Unfuwain (USA))
$4799a^{11}$

Sawpit Sunshine (IRE) *J L Spearing* 65
3 b f Mujadil(USA) —Curie Express (IRE) (Fayruz)
2014^{7} 2451^{6}

Sawtooth Mountain (USA) *A P O'Brien* 97
2 b c Johannesburg(USA) —American Jewel (USA) (Quiet American (USA))
$4804a^{2}$ $5296a^{8}$ $6316a^{6}$

Sawwaah (IRE) *D Carroll* a79 86
11 b g Marju(IRE) —Just A Mirage (Green Desert (USA))
(133) (252) 577^{5} 692^{8} (781) 989^{10} 1041^{6} 3474^{8} 3551^{15} 4075^{11}

Saxford *Mrs L Stubbs* 104
2 b g Reset(AUS) —Bint Makbul (Makbul)
957^{9} (1220) 1447^{6} 2154^{2} (3412) (3634) 4588^{4} 5226^{4} $6713a^{2}$

Sayago (GER) *C J Mann* 30
6 b g Lavirco(GER) —Sweet Virtue (USA) (Halo (USA))
2071^{6} 2770^{6}

Say Anything (IRE) *Patrick Allen* a40 48
7 b m Perugino(USA) —Dama De Noche (Rusticaro (FR))
684^{5}

Sayedati Elhasna (IRE) *J L Dunlop* 65
3 b f Alhaarth(IRE) —Sayedati Eljamilah (USA) (Mr Prospector (USA))
4300^{13} 4872^{6} 6417^{11}

Sayif (IRE) *P W Chapple-Hyam* 116
2 b c Kheleyf(USA) —Sewards Folly (Rudimentary (USA))
2254^{2} 3876^{2} ◆ 4517^{3} 6119^{3} ◆ 6442^{2} 6972^{11}

Say No Now (IRE) *D R Lanigan* a84
2 b f Refuse To Bend(IRE) —Star Studded (Cadeaux Genereux)
5674^{2} 6166^{2}

Sayrianna *M D I Usher* 20
7 br m Sayaarr(USA) —Arianna Aldini (Habitat)
2072^{6}

Sayyaaf *B W Hills* a82 78
2 ch c Alhaarth(IRE) —Almurooj (Zafonic (USA))
5469^{3} 5798^{2} (Dead)

Sayyedati Symphony (USA) *C E Brittain* 88
3 b f Gone West(USA) —Sayyedati (Shadeed (USA))
1833^{4} 2105^{8} 2717^{5} 3944^{7}

Say You Say Me *N J Vaughan* 54
2 b f Acclamation—Mindfulness (Primo Dominie)
3949^{3}

Say You Will (IRE) *Saeed Bin Suroor* a99 98
4 b m A.P. Indy(USA) —Saytarra (USA) (Seeking The Gold (USA))
$6523a^{6}$

Sazerac (USA) *P Howling* a56 24
3 b g Dixie Union(USA) —Starboard Stinger (USA) (Hennessy (USA))
441^{6} ◆ 505^{5} 590^{6} ◆ 721^{7} 882^{5} 1635^{9} 2074^{4} 5162^{9} 5684^{3} 6955^{9} 7022^{9} 7206^{9} 7636^{6}

Scamperdale *B P J Baugh* a100 78
6 br g Compton Place—Miss Up N Go (Gorytus (USA))
(34) (309) (692) 929^{3} 1180^{3} 2531^{6} 3561^{11} 7420^{10} 7496^{11}

Scania Classic *M J Scudamore* a54 60
7 gr g Thethingaboutitis(USA) —Gifted Gale (Aird Point)
5780^{4} 6226^{7} 6345^{7} 6708^{5} 6983^{8}

Scanno (IRE) *M Mullineaux* a44 59
3 b g Captain Rio—In Denial (IRE) (Maelstrom Lake)
1311^{12} 1674^{5} 2660^{11} 3907^{6} 4241^{6} 4952^{8} 5223^{5} 5453^{6}

Scarab (IRE) *M Johnston* a86 83
3 br c Machiavellian(USA) —Russian Society (Darshaan)
6280^{5} 6583^{2} (7174) ◆ 7493^{2} 7558^{3} 7785^{2}

Scaramoushca *G C Bravery* a56 6
5 gr g Most Welcome—Kinraddie (Wuzo (USA))
67^{9} 1459^{14}

Scarlet Blade *Mrs A Duffield* 40
2 b g Needwood Blade—Red Typhoon (Belfort (FR))
1390^{7} 2443^{5} 2910^{5} 3106^{4} 3706^{12} 5778^{14}

Scarlet Flyer (USA) *G L Moore* a78 82
5 b g Gilded Time(USA) —Tennis Partner (USA) (Northern Dancer (CAN))
775^{8} 1058^{2} 1182^{3} 1996^{7} 5600^{6} 6020^{5}

Scarlet Oak *A M Hales* a63 71
4 b m Zamindar(USA) —Flamenco Red (Warning)
1872^{8} 2622^{6} 3093^{5} 3615^{8} (3883) 4393^{4} ◆ 5073^{6} 5588^{7} 6671^{15} 6864^{6} 7090^{13} 7679^{2} 7762^{7}

Scarlet Royal *Mrs Marjorie Fife* 46
3 b f Red Ransom(USA) —Royal Future (IRE) (Royal Academy (USA))
2247^{P}

Scarlets *P D Evans* 54
2 b f Red Ransom(USA) —Bread Of Heaven (Machiavellian (USA))
4274^{11} 4480^{6} 5097^{15} 6406^{5}

Scarlett Heart (IRE) *S Curran* a68 68
4 b m Lujain(USA) —Scarlett Ribbon (Most Welcome)
806^{7} 1150^{3} 1642^{7} 2255^{7} 2721^{7} 2802^{6} 3559^{15}

Scarth Hill (IRE) *Mrs A Duffield* a21 53
2 ch g Selkirk(USA) —Louve Sereine (FR) (Sadler's Wells (USA))
2730^{4} 3568^{8}

Scar Tissue *E J Creighton* a53 58
4 ch m Medicean—Possessive Lady (Dara Monarch)
387^{7} 693^{10} 1135^{7} 7463^{5}

Scartozz *M Botti* a92 99
6 b g Barathea(IRE) —Amazing Bay (Mazilier (USA))
1816^{6} 3278^{2} 3413^{10} 4845^{5} 5208^{8} 5569^{6} 6249^{4} 6772^{7} 7496^{10}

Scary Movie (IRE) *D J Coakley* a69 63
3 b g Daggers Drawn(USA) —Grinning (IRE) (Bellypha)
1669^{8} 2198^{20} 2772^{4} 3333^{2} 5118^{5} 5477^{3}

Sceilin (IRE) *J Mackie* a52 63
4 b m Lil's Boy(USA) —Sharifa (IRE) (Cryptoclearance (USA))
1455^{9} 2352^{2} 3089^{2} (3361) ◆ 3644^{2} 4458^{2} 4596^{5} 5407^{11} 6951^{8} 7287^{9} 7596^{4} 7800^{8}

Scene Two *L M Cumani* a70
2 gr c Act One—Gleaming Water (Kalaglow)
7593^{8} (7735) ◆

Scenic Pass *E S McMahon* a57 74
2 br f Passing Glance—Scenic Air (Hadeer)
2909^{6} ◆ 3008^{2} (3106) 3670^{5} 3924^{5} 4079^{4} 4292^{3} 4604^{10} (4873) (5560) 6149^{2} 6406^{2}

Sceptre Rouge (IRE) *A De Royer-Dupre* 102
3 b c Red Ransom(USA) —Marque Royale (Royal Academy (USA))
$1376a^{4}$

Schelm (GER) *Ronald O'Leary* a69 69
6 b g Alwuhush(USA) —Shoba (GER) (Local Suitor (USA))
240^{4} (526) 701^{3}

Schiaparelli (GER) *Saeed Bin Suroor* 119
5 ch h Monsun(GER) —Sacarina (Old Vic)
$5954a^{2}$ ◆ $6522a^{13}$

Schinken Otto (IRE) *J M Jefferson* a61 36
7 ch g Shinko Forest(IRE) —Athassel Rose (IRE) (Reasonable (FR))
(219) (330) 438^{3} 1296^{12} 4556^{10} 7385^{6}

Schnipp Schnapp (FR) *M Swinnens*
7 b g Acatenango(GER) —Selva (IRE) (Darshaan)
$4911a^{9}$

Schopenhauer (USA) *L M Cumani* 83
3 bb c Giant's Causeway(USA) —Fine Jade (USA) (Jade Hunter (USA))
1926^{13} 2413^{3} ◆ 3223^{2}

Schutzenjunker (GER) *U Ostmann* 100
3 b c Lord Of Men—Schutzenliebe (GER) (Alkalde (GER))
$1514a^{3}$ $6461a^{9}$ $6992a^{3}$

Sciatin (IRE) *David P Myerscough* 89
5 b g Alhaarth(IRE) —Robalana (USA) (Wild Again (USA))
$1105a^{24}$

Scientific *G Prodromou* a56 54
3 b g Fraam—Lady Butler (IRE) (Puissance)
184^{5} 335^{6} 501^{4} 873^{5} 1193^{5} 2552^{3} 4281^{7} 5429^{11} 5575^{8} 6032^{12}

Scintillo *R Hannon* a108 110
3 ch c Fantastic Light(USA) —Danseuse Du Soir (IRE) (Thatching)
1421^{9} 1808^{11} 2303^{2} 4505^{5} 5263^{3} 6980^{4} 7193^{3} 7491^{9} 7741^{5}

Scorched (IRE) *J R Fanshawe* a57 21
4 ch m Desert Sun—Kappa Signey (USA) (Honor Grades (USA))
1252^{7} 4566^{7}

Scotch Bonnet (IRE) *Edward P Harty* 101
4 b m Montjeu(IRE) —Valley Of Hope (USA) (Riverman (USA))
$1655a^{5}$

Scotland Yard (UAE) *D E Pipe* a76 58
5 b g Jade Robbery(USA) —Aqraba (Polish Precedent (USA))
3060^{11}

Scots W'Hae *A Bailey* a56 36
3 b g Piccolo—Ionian Secret (Mystiko (USA))
244^{6} 413^{6} 629^{5} 873^{6} 1166^{7} 1533^{13} 5457^{6} 6595^{3} 7297^{7}

Scottish Affair *E A L Dunlop* a55 52
2 b g Selkirk(USA) —Southern Queen (Anabaa (USA))
5072^{5} 5572^{6} 5904^{9}

Scottish Colourist *M W Easterby*
2 b f Orpen(USA) —Spanish Serenade (Nashwan (USA))
4604^{12}

Scottish River (USA) *M D I Usher* a70 69
9 b g Thunder Gulch(USA) —Overbrook (Storm Cat (USA))
1853^{13} 2617^{10} 2978^{6}

Scotty's Future (IRE) *A Berry* a39 58
10 b g Namaqualand(USA) —Persian Empress (IRE) (Persian Bold)
978^{7} 1391^{12} 2394^{4} 2658^{5} 2927^{11} 3366^{14} 3551^{6} 3662^{3} 4048^{6} 4503^{11} 4679^{5} 4961^{3} 5303^{4} 5776^{U} 7132^{11} 7184^{6} 7373^{11}

Scrapper Smith (IRE) *E F Vaughan* a65 57
2 b c Choisir(AUS) —Lady Ounavarra (IRE) (Simply Great (FR))
1987^{10} 2709^{3} 3178^{6} 4185^{5} 5277^{15}

Screaming Brave *M R Channon* a53 62
2 b g Hunting Lion(IRE) —Hana Dee (Cadeaux Genereux)
5225^{8} 7699^{6}

Screen Hero (JPN) *Y Shikato* 120
4 ch h Grass Wonder(USA) —Running Heroine (JPN) (Sunday Silence (USA))
(7511a)

Scripted (USA) *C F Wall* a73 65
4 br g Theatrical—Val Gardena (CHI) (Roy (USA))
727^{5} 941^{2} ◆ 1486^{8} 2886^{8}

Scruffy (IRE) *John A Harris* 24
4 b g Second Empire(IRE) —Karakapa (FR) (Subotica (FR))
277^{9}

Scruffy Skip (IRE) *Mrs C A Dunnett* a58 64
3 b g Diktat—Capoeira (USA) (Nureyev (USA))
656^{3} 785^{9} 1553^{10} 1912^{5} 2041^{6} 2463^{9} 2704^{2} 5684^{7} 6063^{6} (6681) 7102^{3} 7316^{12} 7383^{10} 7521^{8} 7615^{8}

Scuba (IRE) *H Morrison* a66 72
6 b g Indian Danehill(IRE) —March Star (IRE) (Mac's Imp (USA))
1705^{2} 2263^{3} 2869^{12} 5801^{10}

Scuffle *R Charlton* 103
3 gr f Daylami(IRE) —Tantina (USA) (Distant View (USA))
(1964) (2953) ◆ (3971) 6484^{10}

Sculastic *J Howard Johnson* 84
5 b g Galileo(IRE) —Mutual Consent (IRE) (Reference Point)
2379^{3} 3142^{3}

Scutch Mill (IRE) *P C Haslam* a63 65
6 ch g Alhaarth(IRE) —Bumble (Rainbow Quest (USA))
1148^{6} 1578^{9} 2274^{12} 2957^{10} 7112^{7}

Sea Admiral *R Charlton* a52 77
3 b g Sinndar(IRE) —Overboard (IRE) (Rainbow Quest (USA))
1681^{4} 1962^{6} 2495^{6} (2931) (3574) 3891^{2} 4432^{5} 5698^{9}

Seabow (USA) *M Al Muhairi* a60 99
5 b h Rainbow Quest(USA) —Dream Bay (USA) (Mr Prospector (USA))
$650a^{12}$

Seachange (NZ) *Graeme Sanders* 113
6 br m Cape Cross(IRE) —Just Cruising (AUS) (Broad Reach (NZ))
$818a^{6}$ $1090a^{6}$ 3247^{12} 3852^{4}

Sea Chorus *M L W Bell* a59 79
3 b f Singspiel(IRE) —Island Race (Common Grounds)
1382^{3} ◆ 1728^{3} 2291^{3} 2785^{6} 3562^{5} (4646) 5024^{2} 5249^{11} 6415^{5} 7108^{10}

Sea Cliff (IRE) *Jonjo O'Neill* a49 36
4 b g Golan(IRE) —Prosaic Star (IRE) (Common Grounds)
7590^{4} 7605^{6}

Sea Cookie *W De Best-Turner* a44 46
4 b m Largesse—Maylan (IRE) (Lashkari)
2453^{8}

Sea Crest *M Brittain* 65
2 b f Xaar—Talah (Danehill (USA))
3005^{5} 4384^{2} 4499^{4} 5106^{5} 5384^{2} 5633^{7} 6865^{10}

Seafield Towers *D A Nolan* 57
8 ch g Compton Place—Midnight Spell (Night Shift (USA))
2748^{13} 2843^{14} 3759^{10} 3787^{4} 4013^{10} 4561^{8} 4846^{4} 4950^{5} 5220^{5} 5452^{11} 6153^{8} 6310^{13} 7218^{14}

Seaflower Reef (IRE) *A M Balding* a48 61
4 b m Robellino(USA) —Sankaty Light (USA) (Summer Squall (USA))
3163^{6}

Sea Frolic (IRE) *Jennie Candlish* a48 46
7 b m Shinko Forest(IRE) —Centre Travel (Godswalk (USA))
318^{8} 809^{9} 1975^{5}

Sea Hunter *A Al Raihe* a95 98
6 b h Lend A Hand—Ocean Grove (IRE) (Fairy King (USA))
$205a^{12}$ $295a^{5}$ $814a^{10}$

Sea Land (FR) *B Ellison* a76 64
4 ch g King's Best(USA) —Green Bonnet (IRE) (Green Desert (USA))
1309^{9} 1476^{12} 1624^{19} 2444^{12} 3593^{11}

Seal Bay (IRE) *D Smaga* 101
3 ch f Hernando(FR) —Torrealta (In The Wings)
$2650a^{8}$ $5597a^{10}$

Sealy Hill (CAN) *Mark Casse* a109 116
4 bb m Point Given(USA) —Boston Twist (USA) (Boston Harbor (USA))
$6505a^{3}$ $6968a^{2}$

Sea Map *Miss Sheena West* a62 51
6 ch g Fraam—Shehana (USA) (The Minstrel (CAN))
14^{14}

Seamus Shindig *H Candy* a83 92
6 b g Aragon—Sheesha (USA) (Shadeed (USA))
1683^{5} (1928) (2339) 3418^{5} 4341^{8} (4831) 5270^{3}

Sea Of Leaves (USA) *J H M Gosden* 88
2 b f Stormy Atlantic(USA) —Dock Leaf (USA) (Woodman (USA))
1961^{5} (3378) ◆ 3851^{6} 4403^{10}

Sea Of Marmara (USA) *A P O'Brien* 92
2 b c Johannesburg(USA) —Emmaus (USA) (Silver Deputy (CAN))
$3534a^{4}$ $4005a^{4}$ $4465a^{4}$ $5946a^{7}$ $6520a^{7}$

Seaquel *A B Haynes* 57
2 b f Kyllachy—Broughton Singer (IRE) (Common Grounds)
5365^{4} 5901^{7} 6535^{6}

Search Me *C Gordon* 48
6 ch g Danzig Connection(USA) —Elusive (Little Current (USA))
5182^{7}

Sea Rover (IRE) *M Brittain* 76
4 b h Jade Robbery(USA) —Talah (Danehill (USA))
1451^{12} 2005^{17} 2891^{14}

Sea Salt *A J McCabe* a59 78
5 b g Titus Livius(FR) —Carati (Selkirk (USA))
(1752) (4849) 5638^{2} 6178^{13} 6724^{15} 7727^{10}

Sea Sex Sun *A Fabre* 101
3 b f Desert Prince(IRE) —Asmita (Efisio)
$2231a^{13}$ $6567a^{6}$

Seasider *Sir Michael Stoute* a90 79
3 b g Zamindar(USA) —Esplanade (Danehill (USA))
2104^{8}

Seaside Retreat (USA) *Mark Casse* a107 111
5 b g King Cugat(USA) —Shes Like Rio (USA) (Boundary (USA))
$6506a^{4}$

Seasonal Cross *S Dow* a60 54
3 b f Cape Cross(IRE) —Seasonal Blossom (IRE) (Fairy King (USA))
543^{3} 885^{6} 4730^{12} 5616^{5} 6036^{7} 6357^{9}

Sea Storm (IRE) *James Moffatt* a67 76
10 b g Dolphin Street(FR) —Prime Interest (IRE) (Kings Lake (USA))
6056^{15}

Sea Swell (USA) *G A Butler* a53 22
3 b f Elusive Quality(USA) —Ocean Queen (USA) (Zilzal (USA))
5031^{5} 5995^{9} 6470^{7} 7433^{11}

Sea The Stars (IRE) *John M Oxx* 106
2 b c Cape Cross(IRE) —Urban Sea (USA) (Miswaki (USA))
(6316a)

Seattle Spy (USA) *Miss J Feilden* a37 42
5 bb g Catienus(USA) —Theyrplayinoursong (USA) (Seattle Dancer (USA))
3655^{9}

Seattle Storm (IRE) *D R C Elsworth* a72 79
3 b g Robellino(USA) —Seattle Ribbon (USA) (Seattle Dancer (USA))
1398^{10} 1686^{3} (2046) 2564^{5} 3038^{5} 3380^{4}

Seaway *J H M Gosden* 92
2 b c Dr Fong(USA) —Atlantic Destiny (IRE) (Royal Academy (USA))
1987^{2} ◆ 2592^{2} ◆ 3245^{2}

Seconditis *Mrs N S Evans* a32 18
3 b c Spinning World(USA) —Hairy Night (IRE) (Night Shift (USA))
5963^{7} 6470^{10} 7583^{8}

Second Opinion (IRE) *J M P Eustace* a55 65
3 ch f Dr Fong(USA) —Second To Go (USA) (El Prado (IRE))
1215^{5} 1475^{3} 2122^{13} 2616^{3} 2850^{6} 3833^{7} 6566^{5} 6889^{9}

Second Reef *T A K Cuthbert* a64 50
6 b g Second Empire(IRE) —Vax Lady (Millfontaine)
3257^{7} 3757^{11} 4451^{9} 4679^{11}

Second To Nun (IRE) *Jean-Rene Auvray* a50 53
2 b f Bishop Of Cashel—One For Me (Tragic Role (USA))
3869^{4} 6016^{7} 6360^{8}

Secrecy *M A Jarvis* 104
2 b g King's Best(USA) —Wink (Salse (USA))
(5825) ◆ 6305^{2}

Secret Asset (IRE) *W M Brisbourne* a96 98
3 gr g Clodovil(IRE) —Skerray (Soviet Star (USA))
1945^{6} 2498^{5} 3028^{5} 5906^{2} 6290^{4} 6669^{2} 6810^{11}

Secret Cavern (USA) *H J Evans* a37
6 b g Lion Cavern(USA) —River Dyna (USA) (Dynaformer (USA))
282[7]

Secret City (IRE) *R Bastiman* 57
2 b g City On A Hill(USA) —Secret Combe (IRE) (Mujadil (USA))
2581[3] 3114[9] 3997[5] 4874[4] 6547[5] 6858[7]

Secret Dancer (IRE) *J R Fanshawe* 93
3 b g Sadler's Wells(USA) —Discreet Brief (IRE) (Darshaan)
(2197) ◆ 3045[12] 5830[6] ◆ 6563[6]

Secret Dubai (IRE) *M Botti* a75 86
3 b c Dubai Destination(USA) —Secret Pride (Green Desert (USA))
7592[5] 7811[5]

Secret Gem (IRE) *Tom Dascombe* 66
3 b f Cape Cross(IRE) —Orlena (USA) (Gone West (USA))
1622[9] 2118[10] 3893[2] 4368[7] 4863[8] 7048[9]

Secret Getaway (USA) *Michael Stidham* a106 90
3 ch c Skip Away(USA) —Chief's Honey (USA) (Chief's Crown (USA))
4887a[8]

Secret Liaison *Garry Moss* a93 80
5 gr g Medicean—Courting (Pursuit Of Love)
124[5] 280[6] 1174[P] (Dead)

Secret Meaning *W G M Turner* a63 60
3 b f Mujahid(USA) —Hidden Meaning (Cadeaux Genereux)
797[9] (853) 1124[5] 1407[6] (1603) 2126[4] 2753[3] 3115[3]

Secret Night *C G Cox* a87 81
5 gr m Dansili—Night Haven (Night Shift (USA))
329[8] (733) 1211[5] 2457[3] 3087[5] 3636[2] 4407[2] 5101[10] 5697[9] 6684[3] 7101[4] 7419[2]

Secret Society *M L W Bell* 78
2 b c Exceed And Excel(AUS) —Shady Point (IRE) (Unfuwain (USA))
2507[6] 4778[2]

Secret Star (IRE) *R Bastiman*
2 b g Sampower Star—Fishy (Irish River (FR))
6246[10] 6787[19] 7283[9]

Secret Venue *Jedd O'Keeffe* 71
2 ch g Where Or When(IRE) —Sheila's Secret (IRE) (Bluebird (USA))
2388[2] 3055[2] 3590[3] (4384) 5244[19] 5969[6] 6656[7] 7173[4]

Secret World (IRE) *J Noseda* a95 111
5 ch g Spinning World(USA) —Classic Park (Robellino (USA))
2503[5] 3122[27]

Secundus (GER) *H Blume* 78
3 b c Daliapour(IRE) —Sly (GER) (Monsun (GER))
3773a[14]

Security Joan (IRE) *R Hannon* a49 60
2 ch f Dubai Destination(USA) —Divine Quest (Kris)
5459[5] 5674[4] 6199[9] 6330[3] 6761[8]

Sedge (USA) *P T Midgley* a77 70
8 b g Lure(USA) —First Flyer (USA) (Riverman (USA))
755[7] 1084[7] 3339[8] 4030[7] 4440[3] 4679[3] 5345[8] 6132[8] 6628[5] 6827[7] 7316[4] 7441[6]

Sedgwick *Ian Williams* a65 74
6 b g Nashwan(USA) —Imperial Bailiwick (IRE) (Imperial Frontier (USA))
1188[7] ◆

Sedna (IRE) *W T Farrell* 95
6 ch m Priolo(USA) —Delphinus (Soviet Star (USA))
4007a[16]

Seductive Witch *J Balding* a61 45
3 ch f Zamindar(USA) —Thicket (Wolfhound (USA))
23[6] 92[5] 306[5] (425) (557) 612[2] 882[2] 1110[5] 1315[7] 3332[9] 4163[7] 5015[11]

Seedless *A M Balding* a58 64
3 br f Mtoto—Unseeded (Unfuwain (USA))
1599[8] 2454[8] 3035[4] 3393[6]

Seeking Faith (USA) *C G Cox* a42
2 bb f Chapel Royal(USA) —Padrao Global (USA) (Storm Bird (CAN))
6205[12]

Seeking Star (IRE) *M R Channon* a65 91
3 b g King's Best(USA) —Firedrake (USA) (Kris S (USA))
1075[9] 1441[14] 3047[8] 3475[10]

Seeking The Star (CAN) *D M Simcock* a68 60
3 b g Seeking The Gold(USA) —Water Music (CAN) (Danzig (USA))
1216[5] 2907[9] 3117[3] 3571[5]

Seek N' Destroy (IRE) *B W Hills* 76
2 b c Exceed And Excel(AUS) —Very Nice (Daylami (IRE))
5929[5] 6426[25]

Seek The Fair Land *J R Boyle* a66 39
2 b g Noverre(USA) —Duchcov (Caerleon (USA))
5798[5] 6031[9] 6770[4]

See That Girl *P W Chapple-Hyam* 42
2 b f Hawk Wing(USA) —Hampton Lucy (IRE) (Anabaa (USA))
7140[15]

Sefroua (USA) *J-C Rouget* 101
3 b f Kingmambo(USA) —Sophisticat (USA) (Storm Cat (USA))
2902a[2] (5038a)

Segal (IRE) *J Noseda* a82 76
3 b g Cadeaux Genereux—Camcorder (Nashwan (USA))
458[2] (595) 1043[2] 1171[4] 1543[4] 1919[6]

Sehoy (USA) *J H M Gosden* 52
2 bb c Menifee(USA) —Another Storm (USA) (Gone West (USA))
4570[10]

Sehrezad (IRE) *Andreas Lowe* 111
3 b c Titus Livius(FR) —Trebles (IRE) (Kenmare (FR))
2066a[6] (3515a) 4233a[3] 5596a[3] 6322a[8]

Sekula Pata (NZ) *E J Creighton* a61 61
9 b g Pompeii Court(USA) —Torquay (NZ) (Wharf (USA))
935[9] 1286[4] 3604[13] 3844[13]

Select (IRE) *P W Chapple-Hyam* 89
2 ch f Choisir(AUS) —Intercession (Bluebird (USA))
2835[6] 3496[2] 3959[7]

Select Committee *J J Quinn* 70
3 b g Fayruz—Demolition Jo (Petong)
1155[4] 1611[8] 2490[10] 2850[7] (3455) ◆ 3811[5] 4852[4] 5307[3] 5393[2] 6011[2] 6382[3] 6766[5] 7043[3]

Select Reason (BRZ) *A Cintra Pereira* a90
4 b h A Good Reason(BRZ) —Place D'Armes (BRZ) (Fast Gold (USA))
378a[5] 473a[7] 670a[6] 812a[2]

Self Defense *Miss E C Lavelle* a111 97
11 b g Warning—Dansara (Dancing Brave (USA))
3942[12] 5094[9]

Selfish Option (IRE) *H Morrison* a71 56
3 ch c Selkirk(USA) —Pride In Me (Indian Ridge)
2509[11] 2834[7]

Selinka *R Hannon* 105
4 b m Selkirk(USA) —Lady Links (Bahamian Bounty)
2827[4] ◆ 3120[11] 4192[5] 4977[4] 5506[11]

Sell Out *G Wragg* a74 106
4 gr m Act One—Nordica (Northfields (USA))
2130[5] 3415[2] 5094[4] (5623a) 6980[3]

Selmis *V Caruso* 106
4 ch h Selkirk(USA) —Nokomis (Caerleon (USA))
1667a[3] 2230a[5] 2656a[4] 7263a[9]

Selsey *Sir Michael Stoute* 71
3 b f Selkirk(USA) —Louella (USA) (El Gran Senor (USA))
2123[10] 2800[4] 3507[3] 4572[5] 5317[7]

Semah Harold *E S McMahon* a76 77
3 b g Beat All(USA) —Semah's Dream (Gunner B)
1868[10] 2674[11] 3031[10] 3653[4] 4533[6] 5008[11] 6088[8] 6716[4] 7018[7] 7500[6] 7695[6] 7799[10]

Semi Detached (IRE) *J W Unett* a59 63
5 b g Distant Music(USA) —Relankina (IRE) (Broken Hearted)
1160[4] 2243[6] 3422[5] 6255[6] 6951[6] 7667[5]

Seminal Moment *J G Given* a37
2 b f Sakhee(USA) —Thracian (Green Desert (USA))
7341[9] 7577[8]

Seminole (IRE) *J H M Gosden* a69 77
2 ch g Indian Ridge—Mystic Tempo (USA) (El Gran Senor (USA))
3274[2] ◆ 3682[2] 4861[9] 6474[20] 6837[3]

Sempre Libera (IRE) *R T Phillips* a66
3 b f Statue Of Liberty(USA) —Lucky Oakwood (USA) (Elmaamul (USA))
243[4] 3672[9] 4307[12] 4825[14] 5749[11]

Senatorial *B W Hills* 81
2 b c Oasis Dream—Stormy Channel (USA) (Storm Cat (USA))
1399[5] 1924[4] 2663[3] (3254) 3553[4] 6082[11] 6414[2]

Sendali (FR) *J D Bethell* 57
4 b g Daliapour(IRE) —Lady Senk (FR) (Pink (FR))
2364[15] (2849) 3279[8] 3710[6] 4924[2] 5385[6] 6115[5]

Sendama (FR) *S Loeuillet* 57
2 gr f Sendawar(IRE) —Mariejordonne (FR) (Adieu Au Roi (IRE))
3749a[9]

Sendefaa (IRE) *S Lycett* a57 63
3 bb f Halling(USA) —Patruel (Rainbow Quest (USA))
2376[8] 2833[8] 4259[5] 4750[2] 5653[8] 6492[6]

Sendreni (FR) *M Wigham* a79 72
4 b g Night Shift(USA) —Sendana (FR) (Darshaan)
607[5] 1620[8] 4031[10] (5871) ◆ 6631[2] (6749) 7510[2] 7586[2]

Seneschal *A B Haynes* a75 71
7 b g Polar Falcon(USA) —Broughton Singer (IRE) (Common Grounds)
111[4] (148) 275[7] 302[4] 536[5] 731[2] 1058[5] 1345[7] 4104[15] 4306[3] 4863[4] (5166) 5267[12] 5755[5] 6335[4] 6671[12]

Senlis (IRE) *E Borromeo* 111
3 b c High Chaparral(IRE) —Senebrova (Warning) (1513a) 2028a[9] 2875a[2] 4010a[13]

Senora Lenorah *D A Nolan* 27
4 ch m Tumbleweed Ridge—Blue Diamond (First Trump)
980[8] 3200[6] 3577[7] 3952[10] 4454[6]

Senora Verde *P T Midgley* a35 37
2 ch f Bahamian Bounty—Spain (Polar Falcon (USA))
2035[15] 3292[12] 3689[9] 4290[6] 4873[3] 7728[7]

Senor Benny (USA) *M McDonagh* a108 108
9 br h Benny The Dip(USA) —Senora Tippy (USA) (El Gran Senor (USA))
1103a[9] 1495a[4] 1783a[5] 3533a[8] 4004a[9] 5922a[3] 6315a[6] (6514a) 6845a[14] 6963a[7]

Senor Berti *B Smart* 72
2 b g Bertolini(USA) —Pewter Lass (Dowsing (USA))
4536[5] 5106[6] 6481[3] (6808)

Senor Dali (IRE) *E Charpy* 108
5 ch h Peintre Celebre(USA) —Far Fetched (IRE) (Distant Relative)
383a[4] 671a[6] 818a[15]

Senorita Mirasol *K A Ryan*
2 b f Mind Games—Distinctly Blu (IRE) (Distinctly North (USA))
4027[13] 7319[11]

Senorita Parkes *E F Vaughan* a20 55
3 ch f Medicean—Lucky Parkes (Full Extent (USA))
2067[4] 5160[9] 5626[12]

Senor Mirasol *K A Ryan* a70 106
2 ch c Deportivo—Hidden Meaning (Cadeaux Genereux)
(1778) (2775) 4190[3] 4472a[3] (5438a) 5852[12]

Senor Set (GER) *D Shaw* a45 63
7 b g Second Set(IRE) —Shine Share (IRE) (El Gran Senor (USA))
1505[10] 1653[10] 2707[5] 3377[6] 3710[7] 3820[13]

Sensacion Sensual *J G Given* a43 58
2 b f Josr Algarhoud(IRE) —Charlie Girl (Puissance)
5072[3] 5384[7] 5835[13]

Sensazione World (IRE) *B Grizzetti* 99
3 b f Spinning World(USA) —Sensazione (Cadeaux Genereux)
2231a[4] 3076a[11]

Sensible *H J Collingridge* a64
3 ch f Almutawakel—Opera (Forzando)
3133[4] 4342[12] 5568[7] 7463[3] 7713[2]

Sentinelese (IRE) *Saeed Bin Suroor* 102
5 b g Cape Cross(IRE) —Savage (IRE) (Polish Patriot (USA))
(384a)

Sentry Duty (FR) *N J Henderson* 104
6 b g Kahyasi—Standing Around (FR) (Garde Royale)
1916[15]

Separate Ways (IRE) *Seamus G O'Donnell* 68
3 b g Chevalier(IRE) —Choralli (Inchinor)
4494a[4]

September Sunrise (IRE) *B McGann* a53
4 b m Mull Of Kintyre(USA) —Deep In September (IRE) (Common Grounds)
2232a[9]

Septimus (IRE) *A P O'Brien* 124
5 b h Sadler's Wells(USA) —Caladira (IRE) (Darshaan)
(3513a) ◆ (5921a) 7188a[18]

Sequillo *R Hannon* a68 72
2 b c Lucky Story(USA) —Tranquillity (Night Shift (USA))
4826[11] 5314[7] 5678[4] ◆ (6344) 6946[18]

Seradim *P F I Cole* 95
2 ch f Elnadim(USA) —Seren Devious (Dr Devious (IRE))
4521[4] (4896) 5266[7] 5642[3] 6982[4] (7549a)

Sereth (IRE) *J Hirschberger* 103
5 b g Monsun(GER) —Saderlina (IRE) (Sadler's Wells (USA))
1237a[5] 2346a[5] (3307a)

Sergeant Cecil *B R Millman* a66 119
9 ch g King's Signet(USA) —Jadidh (Touching Wood (USA))
1468[12] 2169[5] 2542[5] 4551[8]

Sergeant Pink (IRE) *S Gollings* a57 70
2 b c Fasliyev(USA) —Ring Pink (USA) (Bering)
4861[5] (5304) ◆ 5895[15] 6394[11] 6857[13]

Sergeant Sharpe *M H Tompkins* a64 65
3 ch g Cadeaux Genereux—Halcyon Daze (Halling (USA))
1364[6] 1937[3] 2894[3] 3115[4] 3873[8]

Sergeant Slipper *C Smith* a5 19
11 ch g Never So Bold—Pretty Scarce (Handsome Sailor)
371[8] 790[11]

Sericus (IRE) *W Jarvis* a38 61
2 bg c Verglas(IRE) —Cartier Bijoux (Ahonoora)
3219[11] 3651[6] 4020[6] 5274[9] 5785[7] 6931[11]

Serienhoehe (IRE) *P Schiergen*
2 b f High Chaparral(IRE) —Saldenehre (GER) (Highest Honor (FR))
(5686a) 7006a[11]

Serious Attitude (IRE) *Rae Guest* 110
2 b f Mtoto—Zameyla (IRE) (Cape Cross (IRE))
(4905) (5642) ◆ (6441)

Serious Choice (IRE) *J R Boyle* a58 76
3 b g Choisir(AUS) —Printaniere (USA) (Sovereign Dancer (USA))
1743[10] ◆ (2982) 4128[10] 5935[9] 6395[2] 6607[5]

Serious Impact (USA) *J H M Gosden* 44
3 b c Empire Maker(USA) —Diese (USA) (Diesis)
4349[13]

Sermons Mount (USA) *Mouse Hamilton-Fairley* a52 5
2 bb g Vicar(USA) —Ginny Auxier (USA) (Racing Star (USA))
6602[12] 7011[7]

Serpentaria *W P Mullins* a74 86
4 b m Golden Snake(USA) —French Spice (Cadeaux Genereux)
4493a[15]

Serva Jugum (USA) *P F I Cole* a86 98
2 bb c Fusaichi Pegasus(USA) —Shake The Yoke (Caerleon (USA))
(6466) ◆ 7163a[8]

Servenya (GER) *J Hirschberger* 90
3 bb f Dashing Blade—Slawa (GER) (Polish Precedent (USA))
3073a[7] 5329a[6]

Servoca (CAN) *B W Hills* a78 84
2 gr c El Prado(IRE) —Cinderellaslipper (USA) (Touch Gold (USA))
1399[2] ◆ 2569[2] 3152[8] 3677[3] 4373[2] 4815[2] 5905[2]

Sesenta (IRE) *W P Mullins* 82
4 b m King's Theatre(IRE) —Cincuenta (IRE) (Bob Back (USA))
4655a[2]

Sestet *S Dow* a53 46
3 b f Golden Snake(USA) —Sestina (FR) (Bering)
6705[11] 7504[2]

Seta Pura *R Ford* 68
3 b f Domedriver(IRE) —Sulitelma (USA) (The Minstrel (CAN))
3601[2] 5222[14] 6137[11] 7500[11]

Setareh *J S Wainwright* 45
4 b h King's Best(USA) —Hejraan Two (IRE) (Green Desert (USA))
3402[7]

Setareh (GER) *P Olsanik* 105
3 b c Areion(GER) —Sety's Spirit (USA) (Seattle Song (USA))
5596a[4] 7005a[10]

Set Em Up Mo *M J Attwater* a55
2 b f Reset(AUS) —Mo Stopher (Sharpo)
7465[8] 7708[8]

Set Sail (IRE) *A P O'Brien* 103
2 ch c Danehill Dancer(IRE) —Ahdaab (USA) (Rahy (USA))
4517[8] 6973[4]

Settigano (IRE) *Michael Joseph Fitzgerald* 104
5 b g Sadler's Wells(USA) —Bonita Francita (CAN) (Devil's Bag (USA))
(3531a) 4512a[6] 5550a[5]

Sevenna (FR) *H R A Cecil* a93 85
3 b f Galileo(IRE) —Silvassa (IRE) (Darshaan)
2328[12] (2971) ◆ 4351[4] 4784[5] 5938[2]

Seven No Trumps *J M Bradley* a46 57
11 ch g Pips Pride—Classic Ring (IRE) (Auction Ring (USA))
2474[8]

Sevenovus (IRE) *Peter Grayson*
3 ch c Observatory(USA) —Flaming Salsa (FR) (Salse (USA))
734[9] 3264[12]

Seven Royals (IRE) *Miss A M Newton-Smith* 62
3 b g Val Royal(FR) —Seven Notes (Zafonic (USA))
2198[18] 2620[8] ◆ 3916[4] 4194[5] 6204[12] 6560[10]

Seven Stars *M E Sowersby* 60
3 b g Dubai Destination(USA) —Galette (Caerleon (USA))
2191[8] 3043[8] 6217[10]

Seventh Cavalry (IRE) *H R A Cecil* a67 79
3 gr c No Excuse Needed—Mixwayda (FR) (Linamix (FR))
2370[3] ◆ 2763[4] 3035[3] 3894[3] 4255[2] 4606[3] 5140[3] 5426[3] 5652[2] 6091[4] 6660[4]

Seventh Hill *M Blanshard* 72
3 ch g Compton Place—Dream Baby (Master Willie)
1573[7] 2014[4] 2678[7] 3407[4] 4128[9] 4637[8] 4978[2] 5428[11] 5815[5]

Seyaadi *Miss Tracy Waggott* a15 65
6 b g Intikhab(USA) —Sioux Chef (Be My Chief (USA))
2155[13] 2483[8] 2848[4] 3226[2] 3450[6] 3957[8] 4217[3] 4419[6] 4878[5]

Sforzando *Mrs L Stubbs* a64 72
7 b m Robellino(USA) —Mory Kante (USA) (Icecapade (USA))
117[3] 340[4] 1159[8] 1482[8] 1963[6] 2335[3] 2848[5] 2978[8] 3624[10] 4259[8]

Sgt Roberts (IRE) *J S Moore* 73
2 b g Diktat—Ann's Annie (IRE) (Alzao (USA))
5578[4] 6008[2] 6539[9]

Sgt Schultz (IRE) *J S Moore* a99 85
5 b g In The Wings—Ann's Annie (IRE) (Alzao (USA))
96[2] 315[3] ◆ 410[3] ◆ 592[4] (908) 1076[11] 2168[8] 2593[6] 7404[7] (7814)

Shaama Rose (FR) *M R Channon* 66
3 gr f Verglas(IRE) —River Ballade (USA) (Irish River (FR))
2015[7] ◆ 2327[6]

Shaaridh (USA) *M Johnston* 31
2 bb f Dixieland Band(USA) —Boston Lady (USA) (Boston Harbor (USA))
6884[10]

Shabahar (IRE) *M J McGrath* a71 79
4 b g Hernando(FR) —Shara (IRE) (Kahyasi)
747[8] 1072[11] 2476[6] (2886) ◆ 3449[4] 4065[2] 4567[7] 5370[4] 5935[8] (Dead)

Shabib (USA) *B W Hills* 80
2 b c Intidab(USA) —Muklah (IRE) (Singspiel (IRE))
6080[3] 6601[3]

Shabiba (USA) *M P Tregoning* a88 101
3 b f Seeking The Gold(USA) —Misterah (Alhaarth (IRE))
1401[9] 2196[2] 3124[3] 3742[5] 4590[3] (5506) 6440[9] 7099[8]

Shabnaam *P Howling* a49 62
3 b f Diktat—Noble View (USA) (Distant View (USA))
17[9] 425[4] 597[4] 897[3] 1051[8] 1347[5] 1603[6]

Shadayid Khanum (IRE) *M P Tregoning* a27 61
3 b f Mujahid(USA) —Ashjaan (USA) (Silver Hawk (USA))
2756[11] 3342[2] 4447[5]

Shaded Edge *D W P Arbuthnot* a63 65
4 b g Bold Edge—Twilight Mistress (Bin Ajwaad (IRE))
2337[3] ◆ 2758[4] 3383[13] 4862[10] 5458[4] 6396[5] 7102[8] 7509[3] (7521) 7706[4] 7803[2]

Shadow Bay (IRE) *Tom Dascombe* a69 75
2 b g Deportivo—Champion Tipster (Pursuit Of Love)
957[16] 1214[5] 1425[4] 3677[7] (4203) (4956) 5242[9] 6574[3] 6924[11] 7370[2] (7547)

Shadow Jumper (IRE) *J T Stimpson* a54 47
7 b g Dayjur(USA) —Specifically (USA) (Sky Classic (CAN))
42[11] 79[9] 328[13] 684[7] 792[9] 1550[12]

Shadows Lengthen *M W Easterby* a51 53
2 b g Dansili—Bay Shade (USA) (Sharpen Up)
3411[14] 4045[6] 4474[6] 6214[20]

Shadowtime *Miss Tracy Waggott* a73 73
3 b c Singspiel(IRE) —Massomah (USA) (Seeking The Gold (USA))
221[3] ◆ 633[4] 1579[3] 2037[5] (2496) 3366[5] 3709[3] 5504[7] 5915[7] 6186[10]

Shady Gloom (IRE) *K A Ryan* 85
3 b c Traditionally(USA) —Last Drama (IRE) (Last Tycoon)
2143[3] 2779[2] (3130) ◆ 4619[2] 6113[6]

Shady Lady (IRE) *M Johnston* 76
2 b f Celtic Swing—Viola Royale (IRE) (Royal Academy (USA))
4780[10] (6789) 7158a[6]

Shafrons Canyon (IRE) *P M Rogers* a47 74
5 b m Lend A Hand—Carroll's Canyon (IRE) (Hatim (USA))
338[5]

Shaftesbury (IRE) *Jane Southcombe* a64 67
3 b g Lomitas—Vivid Concert (IRE) (Chief Singer)
225[3] ◆ 434[3] 1389[2] 1530[5] 1871[9] 6897[4]

Shaftesbury Avenue (USA) *J O'Reilly* a58 54
5 ch g Fusaichi Pegasus(USA) —Little Firefly (IRE) (Danehill (USA))
42[12] 1313[7] 1578[12] 1776[12] 4961[13]

Shaheer (IRE) *J Gallagher* a58 58
6 b g Shahrastani(USA) —Atmospheric Blues (IRE) (Double Schwartz)
10[6] 133[4] 299[3] 468[6] 541[10] 1282[10] 4322[8] 4722[9]

Shahin (USA) *M P Tregoning* a103 114
5 b h Kingmambo(USA) —String Quartet (IRE) (Sadler's Wells (USA))
2797[9] 3246[8] 4585[9] 5264[3] 5854[7]

Shakedown *E S McMahon* a38 69
3 b g Domedriver(IRE) —Stormy Weather (Nashwan (USA))
4378[3] 5366[2] 6003[3] 6566[4] 7362[7]

Shake On It *M J Gingell* a72 88
4 b g Lomitas—Decision Maid (USA) (Diesis)
1682[2] 2369[5] 2790[5] 3440[8] 5209[11] 6078[13] 6346[10] 6738[7] 6908[10] 7461[8] 7677[7] 7771[10]

Shaker (IRE) *M L W Bell* 96
3 b f Key Of Luck(USA) —Gravieres (FR) (Saint Estephe (FR))
1833[5] 2149[6] 3124[4] ◆ 4361[4] 5745a[7]

Shaker Style (USA) *J D Bethell* a62 66
2 ch g Gulch(USA) —Carr Shaker (USA) (Carr De Naskra (USA))
3055[6] 4214[7] 5500[4] 6112[11] 6954[7] 7519[4] 7718[8]

Shakespeare's Son *H J Evans* a75 74
3 b g Mind Games—Eastern Blue (IRE) (Be My Guest (USA))
1897[3] 2660[2] 3030[5] 3313[2] 3678[2] (5592) 5709[2] 6418[2] 6706[5] 7182[3] 7540[3] 7762[11]

Shake The Moon (GER) *A Fabre* a77 98
3 ch f Loup Solitaire(USA) —Sporades (USA) (Vaguely Noble)
5623a[4]

Shakin John *E J O'Neill* 52
2 b g Refuse To Bend(IRE) —Qudrah (IRE) (Darshaan)
6057[10] 6581[8] 6760[7]

Shakis (IRE) *Kiaran McLaughlin* a86 116
8 bb h Machiavellian(USA) —Tawaaded (IRE) (Nashwan (USA))
5928a[3] 6504a[2] 6996a[11] (Dead)

Shalamara (FR) *P Demercastel* 81
3 ch f Chicastenango(FR) —Konile (FR) (In The Wings)
6742a[5]

Shallal *P W Chapple-Hyam* 96
3 b c Cape Cross(IRE) —First Waltz (FR) (Green Dancer (USA))
1471[4] 3119[16]

Shaloo Diamond *R M Whitaker* 85
3 b g Captain Rio—Alacrity (Alzao (USA))
2037[4] 2272[3] (2699) 3493[4] 4392[4] 5257[5] 5504[4] (6188) 6949[2]

Shamali *W J Haggas* a89 81
3 ch c Selkirk(USA) —Shamaiel (IRE) (Lycius (USA))
5786[6] 6530[3] ◆ (7344) ◆

Shamayel *B W Hills* a74 83
3 b f Pivotal—Mauri Moon (Green Desert (USA))
2819[10] ◆ 3646[5] 4423[5]

Shami *Mrs R A Carr* a44
9 ch h Rainbow Quest(USA) —Bosra Sham (USA) (Woodman (USA))
863[10] 916[7] 1025[7] 1206[9]

Shampagne *P F I Cole* a100 90
2 b c Orpen(USA) —Arndilly (Robellino (USA))
1377[2] ◆ (1851) ◆ (2377) 3103[12] 3634[7] 4190[22] (4475) 5244[15] (6284) 6979[7]

Shamrock Lady (IRE) *J Gallagher* a81 76
3 b f Orpen(USA) —Shashi (IRE) (Shaadi (USA))
1868[5] 2761[9] 3064[5] 3507[7] 4022[9] (5170) 5600[9] 6554[6] (6627)

Sham Sheer *L M Cumani* a64
2 b c Cape Cross(IRE) —Viola Da Braccio (IRE) (Vettori (IRE))
6423[8] 7098[7]

Shamwari Lodge (IRE) *R Hannon* 80
2 b f Hawk Wing(USA) —Ripalong (IRE) (Revoque (IRE))
5097[7] (6244)

Shanafarahan (IRE) *T P Tate* 65
3 b g Marju(IRE) —Sedna (FR) (Bering)
2333[8] 3263[8] 3416[12] 3793[6] 4331[6] 4902[4]

Shanagolden Juan (IRE) *M R Bosley* a42
5 ch g King Charlemagne(USA) —Ida Lupino (IRE) (Statoblest)
273[4] 513[6]

Shanavaz *Mrs G S Rees* 65
2 gr f Golden Snake(USA) —Safinaz (Environment Friend)
4176[5] 4815[8] 6291[7]

Shandelight (IRE) *Mrs A Duffield* a52 63
4 b m Dilshaan—By Candlelight (IRE) (Roi Danzig (USA))
602[5] 728[11] 1044[3] 1262[5] 1551[5] (2641) 3687[6] 4075[6] 6136[10] 6728[9]

Shangani *H Candy* a60
2 b f Ishiguru(USA) —Sheesha (USA) (Shadeed (USA))
3848[2]

Shankly Bond (IRE) *Mrs L B Normile* 48
6 b g Danehill Dancer(IRE) —Fanellan (Try My Best (USA))
4848[7] 5540[5] (Dead)

Shannersburg (IRE) *E J O'Neill* 80
3 bb g Johannesburg(USA) —Shahoune (USA) (Blushing Groom (FR))
1171[7] 2209[6]

Shantina's Dream (USA) *J R Boyle* a45 57
4 b m Smoke Glacken(USA) —J'Aime Jeblis (USA) (Jeblar (USA))
89[7] 220[11]

Shanzu *H Candy* a65 81
3 b f Kyllachy—Limuru (Salse (USA))
1671[4] (3507) 4253[5] 4572[8] (5964) 6675[13]

Shape Shifter (USA) *J R Best* 40
2 ch g Performing Magic(USA) —Shot Gun Frances (USA) (Commemorate (USA))
3001[10] 4256[9] 4636[9]

Shape Up (IRE) *R Craggs* a72 80
8 b g Octagonal(NZ) —Bint Kaldoun (IRE) (Kaldoun (FR))
1026[8] (Dead)

Sharav *Eve Johnson Houghton* a59 60
2 b c Monsieur Bond(IRE) —May Light (Midyan (USA))
1363[5] 2098[5] 4126[5] 4975[6] 5277[12] 6017[4] 6207[8] 6923[7]

Sharaxia (IRE) *C F Wall* 30
2 b f Xaar—Shioda (USA) (Bahri (USA))
5099[9]

Shareholder (GER) *L Kelp* 79
4 gr g Act One—Secret Energy (USA) (Alwuhush (USA))
2708a[13]

Sharki *J H M Gosden* 53
3 ch f Indian Ridge—Blue Sirocco (Bluebird (USA))
4194[7] 6705[6] 6896[11]

Sharleez (IRE) *John M Oxx* a88 104
3 b f Marju(IRE) —Sharesha (IRE) (Ashkalani (IRE))
1880a[4] 4223a[2] 6689a[15] 7328a[9]

Sharmy (IRE) *Ian Williams* a47 61
12 b g Caerleon(USA) —Petticoat Lane (Ela-Mana-Mou)
4123[12] 4691[10] 5154[9]

Sharp Bullet (IRE) *W R Swinburn* 78
2 b c Royal Applause—Anna Frid (GER) (Big Shuffle (USA))
(4980)

Sharp Discovery *J M Bradley* 27
2 b f Needwood Blade—You Found Me (Robellino (USA))
1263[10] 1523[10] 1866[7] 2011[11] 4203[13] 4321[11]

Sharpened Edge *B Palling* 61
2 b f Exceed And Excel(AUS) —Beveled Edge (Beveled (USA))
6072[3]

Sharpener (IRE) *R Hannon* a69 72
2 b f Invincible Spirit(IRE) —Daily Double (FR) (Unfuwain (USA))
3923[3] 4149[7] 4634[5] 6555[4] 6894[2] 7308[7] (7417) 7575[4]

Sharp Indian *W J H Ratcliffe* a43 49
4 ch m Gorse—Indian Wardance (ITY) (Indian Ridge)
483[8] 1130[5] 1302[6] 1561[5] 2448[13] 2928[15] 5636[9]

Sharp Nephew *B J Meehan* a94 102
3 ch c Dr Fong(USA) —Snap Crackle Pop (IRE) (Statoblest)
(1213) 6073[10] 6440[13] 6814[15]

Sharps Gold *D Morris* a56 40
3 ch f Twice As Sharp—Toking N' Joken (IRE) (Mukaddamah (USA))
156[6] 623[2] 3845[14] 7585[8] 7620[11]

Sharp Sovereign (USA) *T D Barron* 71
2 b g Cactus Ridge(USA) —Queen Of Humor (USA) (Distorted Humor (USA))
3411[6] ◆ 4415[8] (6014) 6857[15]

Sharp Spartan (IRE) *R J Osborne* 38
2 ch c Spartacus(IRE) —College Dreamer (IRE) (College Chapel)
6320a[18]

Sharp Susan (USA) *William Mott* a87 109
4 br m Touch Gold(USA) —Winter's Gone (USA) (Dynaformer (USA))
6523a[8]

Sharp Tune (USA) *J D Frost* a26 51
6 ch g Diesis—Moonflute (USA) (The Minstrel (CAN))
305[9]

Shatter Resistant (IRE) *M D Squance* a69 69
3 b g Fath(USA) —Beech Bramble (IRE) (Cyrano De Bergerac)
928[4] 1370[2] 1672[5] 1958[8] 2122[11] 2551[6] 2864[2] 3224[7] 3332[6] 3765[6] 4159[7] 4272[6] 4523[3] 4793[10] 5015[5] 5679[3] 6224[5] 6707[4] 7022[10]

Shava *H J Evans* a56 48
8 b g Atraf—Anita Marie (IRE) (Anita's Prince)
79[3] 256[7] (392) 584[8] 1687[8] 2662[10] 7636[5]

Shavansky *C J Mann* a81 74
4 b g Rock Of Gibraltar(IRE) —Limelighting (USA) (Alleged (USA))
6079[14] (7387) 7439[7]

Shavoulin (USA) *Christian Wroe* a50 34
4 bb g Johannesburg(USA) —Hello Josephine (USA) (Take Me Out (USA))
5091[9] 5748[9]

Shaweel *M Johnston* 118
2 b c Dansili—Cooden Beach (IRE) (Peintre Celebre (USA))
2134[3] ◆ (2521) ◆ 3103[8] 3920[3] 4517[5] (5226) 5946a[2] 6815[4]

Shawnee Saga (FR) *W Baltromei* 97
3 b c Sagacity(FR) —Shawnee (GER) (Dashing Blade)
5529a[3] 6921a[8] 7429a[7]

Shaws Diamond (USA) *D Shaw* a73 81
2 ch f Ecton Park(USA) —Dear Abigail (USA) (Dehere (USA))
3331[6] 3568[2] 4348[7] 5266[10] 7646[3]

Shaydreambeliever *R A Fahey* a62 73
5 ch g Daggers Drawn(USA) —Aunt Sadie (Pursuit Of Love)
18[5] 252[5]

Shayera *B R Johnson* a44 66
3 b f Hawk Wing(USA) —Trick (IRE) (Shirley Heights)
1525[13] 4909[3] 5931[4] 6703[12] 7506[4] 7761[7]

Shaylee *T D Walford* 58
3 b f Muhtarram(USA) —Fairywings (Kris)
3629[9] 4461[6] 4680[2] (5362) 6155[6] 6529[10] 6806[6]

Shayrazan (IRE) *James Leavy* 89
7 ch g Zilzal(USA) —Shayraz (Darshaan)
1105a[16] 4576a[3] 5550a[14]

Shecher Para *H R A Cecil* 25
3 b f Clodovil(IRE) —Shaken And Stirred (Cadeaux Genereux)
2197[14] 3043[7]

Sheer Bluff (IRE) *D R C Elsworth* a75 67
3 b g Indian Ridge—Sheer Bliss (IRE) (Sadler's Wells (USA))
1746[2] 2342[5] 2532[7] 3870[2] 4161[8] 4377[4] 4745[9] 5836[11] 6396[10]

Sheer Fantastic *P C Haslam* a70 70
3 b g Fantastic Light(USA) —Sheer Bliss (USA) (Relaunch (USA))
(184) 1140[5] 1950[3] 3555[14]

She Hates Me (IRE) *E Lellouche* 96
3 b f Hawk Wing(USA) —Topira (FR) (Pistolet Bleu (IRE))
5623a[6]

Sheik'N'Knotsterd *J F Coupland* a53 60
3 ch g Zaha(CAN) —Royal Ivy (Mujtahid (USA))
2929[6] 3690[8] 4076[6] 6163[7] 6836[6] 7049[8]

Shekan Star *K G Reveley* a53 55
6 b m Sri Pekan(USA) —Celestial Welcome (Most Welcome)
5637[12] 6309[4] 6727[8]

Shela House *J H Culloty* a82 94
4 ch g Selkirk(USA) —Villa Carlotta (Rainbow Quest (USA))
1502[5] 1877[3] 2372[3] 3209[4] 4576a[15]

Shemima *A De Royer-Dupre* 106
3 gr f Dalakhani(IRE) —Shemaka (IRE) (Nishapour (FR))
5039a[2] (5685a) 6494a[2]

Shemoli *M A Jarvis* 58
2 ch g Singspiel(IRE) —Felawnah (USA) (Mr Prospector (USA))
6425[11]

Shenandoah Girl *Miss Gay Kelleway* a57 62
5 b m Almushtarak(IRE) —Thundering Papoose (Be My Chief (USA))
529[9] 694[8] 953[7] (1184) 1405[7] 1726[11] 1913[3] (2694) 3176[8] 3344[3] 3624[4] 3843[3] 4774[7] (5003) 5183[10] 5465[9] 5783[8] 6806[9] 7089[3] 7676[13]

Shepherds Warning (IRE) *N J Vaughan* a68 66
3 ch f Vettori(IRE) —Sky Red (Night Shift (USA))
393[3] 2670[12] 7405[10] 7513[9]

Sherbet Lemon *Miss J A Camacho* 28
3 b f Nayef(USA) —Travesty (IRE) (Spectrum (IRE))
2573[10] 4689[13]

Sheriffen (IRE) *Ann Michanek*
5 b g Mull Of Kintyre(USA) —Slieu Whallian (In The Wings)
2708a[4]

Sheriff's Silk *G D Blake* a70 46
4 b g Forzando—Sylhall (Sharpo)
1591[4] 2798[7] 3374[3] 3691[4] 4478[3] 5610[6] 6132[5] 7533[6]

Sherjawy (IRE) *Miss Z C Davison* a63 48
4 b g Diktat—Arruhan (IRE) (Mujtahid (USA))
247[2] (440) (696) 766[4] 933[8] 1129[6] 1476[10] 1865[8] 2075[11] 5582[10] 7375[6] 7625[9] 7774[3]

Sherman McCoy *B R Millman* 62
2 ch g Reset(AUS) —Naomi Wildman (USA) (Kingmambo (USA))
3888[7] 4636[5] 6199[6]

She's A Shaw Thing *P D Evans* a39 87
2 b f Reel Buddy(USA) —So Discreet (Tragic Role (USA))
(995) (1156) 1914[4] 3105[24] 3978[5] 6483[22] 7275[8]

Shes Billie *J G M O'Shea* 34
2 b f Auction House(USA) —Wintzig (Piccolo)
995[9] 1264[4]

Shesha Bear *W R Muir* a65 76
3 b f Tobougg(IRE) —Sunny Davis (USA) (Alydar (USA))
2328[5] 2885[5] 3384[10] 3886[6] (5168) 5602[2] 5935[4] 6758[9] 7070[9]

Shes Minnie *J G M O'Shea* a77 88
5 b m Bertolini(USA) —Wintzig (Piccolo)
1278[9] 1858[3] 2077[2] 3554[9] 3905[9] 6859[16] 7081[13] 7225[4] 7346[8] 7510[7]

She's My Outsider *A W Carroll* a78 82
6 b m Docksider(USA) —Solar Flare (IRE) (Danehill (USA))
210[4] 329[5]

She's Our Beauty (IRE) *S T Mason* a56 56
5 b m Imperial Ballet(IRE) —Eleonora D'Arborea (Prince Sabo)
100[12] 2748[12] 3759[12] 5044[6] 5452[8] 5566[3] 6405[7] (7529) 7644[10] 7793[9]

She's Our Dream *R C Guest* a26 60
3 b f Statue Of Liberty(USA) —Mainly Sunset (Red Sunset)
3868[17]

She's Our Lass (IRE) *K A Ryan* a66 87
7 b m Orpen(USA) —Sharadja (IRE) (Doyoun)
1329[2] 3729[7] (4001) 4894[4] 5100[5] 5199[7] (5773) 6040[3]

She's Our Mark *Patrick J Flynn* a101 106
4 ch m Ishiguru(USA) —Markskeepingfaith (IRE) (Ajraas (USA))
1880a[3] 2420a[5] 3511a[5] 4007a[12] 4512a[2] 5732a[7] 6298a[2]

She's So Pretty (IRE) *G L Moore* a75 68
4 ch m Grand Lodge(USA) —Plymsole (USA) (Diesis)
1643[7] 4811[2] 5058[2] 5458[6] 5583[9] (6929) (7261)

She's The Lady *E J O'Neill* a63
8 b m Unfuwain(USA) —City Of Angels (Woodman (USA))
(39) 272[7] 600[13]

She Who Dares Wins *L R James* a9 48
8 b m Atraf—Mirani (IRE) (Danehill (USA))
2491[7] 3231[5] 3638[13] 6310[12]

She Wont Wait *T M Jones* a36 45
4 b m Piccolo—Who Goes There (Wolfhound (USA))
2067[7]

Shifting Gold (IRE) *K A Ryan* a47 58
2 b g Night Shift(USA) —Gold Bust (Nashwan (USA))
2730[5] 4176[6] 4658[7] 5774[2] ◆ 6214[16] 6632[11] (7079) 7266[6]

Shifting Star (IRE) *W R Swinburn* a103 103
3 ch g Night Shift(USA) —Ahshado (Bin Ajwaad (IRE))
1764[3] 2162[4] (2998) ◆ (3898) (4842) ◆ 5347[4] 6104[20] 6947[3]

Shifty *Jedd O'Keeffe* a73 67
9 b g Night Shift(USA) —Crodelle (IRE) (Formidable (USA))
7[6] 193[5] 465[7] 553[3] 640[7] 863[5] 1025[3]

Shillelagh Slew (CAN) *Michael DePaulo* a91 95
5 bb h Chief Seattle(USA) —Frippalina (USA) (Theatrical)
2472a[6]

Shimah (USA) *Kevin Prendergast* 109
2 ch f Storm Cat(USA) —Sayedat Alhadh (USA) (Mr Prospector (USA))
(3466a) ◆ 5549a[2]

Shimoni *G L Moore* a85 87
4 b m Mark Of Esteem(IRE) —Limuru (Salse (USA))
(4726) 5024[4] 5423[6] 5900[6] (6203) 6415[8]

Shindy (FR) *J A R Toller* a74 74
3 b f Intikhab(USA) —Sheriya (USA) (Green Dancer (USA))
3318[5] 3918[3] 4583[3] (5317) 5841[9] 6491[12] 7143[7]

Shining Armour (IRE) *D K Weld* 90
3 b g Green Desert(USA) —Perfect Touch (USA) (Miswaki (USA))
6514a[6] 6845a[10]

Shining Times (IRE) *D W Barker* 50
2 br f Danetime(IRE) —Shining Desert (IRE) (Green Desert (USA))
5633[11] 6548[8] 6788[6]

Shinko's Best (IRE) *A Kleinkorres* 110
7 ch g Shinko Forest(IRE) —Sail Away (GER) (Platini (GER))
2214a[8] 3752a[4] 4912a[3]

Shipboard Romance (IRE) *K J Burke* a36 47
3 b f Captain Rio—In Other Words (IRE) (Lake Coniston (IRE))
7701[5]

Shipmaster *A King* 111
5 b g Slip Anchor—Cover Look (SAF) (Fort Wood (USA))
1158[2] (1717) 1916[P]

Shiraz (GER) *M Weiss* 81
8 br h Bigstone(IRE) —Sintenis (GER) (Polish Precedent (USA))
422a[5]

Shirley High *P Howling* a51
2 b f Forzando—Ripple Effect (Elmaamul (USA))
5939[9] 6488[6] 6661[5] 7452[10]

Shiva Adiva *Tom Dascombe* 74
2 gr f Needwood Blade—Eastern Lyric (Petong)
1680[9] 2124[2] 2618[7] 4486[3] (5116) 6240[15] 6666[12]

Shiwawa *G A Swinbank*
6 b g Halling(USA) —I Will Lead (USA) (Seattle Slew (USA))
7446[P]

Shmookh (USA) *Doug Watson* 105
4 b h Green Desert(USA) —Elrafa Ah (USA) (Storm Cat (USA))
492a[11] 668a[7]

Shogun Prince (IRE) *W Jarvis* a77 82
5 b g Shinko Forest(IRE) —Lady Of Dreams (IRE) (Prince Rupert (FR))
96[7] 344[4] 697[3] (941) (1458) 1877[5] 2784[3] 3003[8]

Shooting Party (IRE) *R Hannon* a68 75
2 b c Noverre(USA) —L-Way First (IRE) (Vision (USA))
4665[6] 5344[4] 6085[11] (6700)

Shoot Pontoon (IRE) *S A Callaghan* a57 40
3 b g Danehill Dancer(IRE) —Burmese Princess (USA) (King Of Kings (IRE))
1367[13] 2259[9] 2475[11]

Shopfitter *P T Midgley* a34 50
5 b g Sugarfoot—Madam Wurlitzer (Noble Patriarch)
65[8]

Short Affair *M Gasparini* 95
3 b f Singspiel(IRE) —L'Affaire Monique (Machiavellian (USA))
2231a[9] 3076a[14]

Short Cut *S Kirk* a34 46
2 b c Compton Place—Rush Hour (IRE) (Night Shift (USA))
2338[9] 4274[12] 4980[9] 5567[7] 5860[11]

Short N Swift *M Wellings*
2 b f Primo Valentino(IRE) —Flick Em Off (Turtle Island (IRE))
4534[9]

Short Sharp Shock *J Mackie* a59 39
2 b c Mujahid(USA) —Possibility (Robellino (USA))
6246[9] 6715 [11] 7402[6]

Shortwall Lady (IRE) *J L Spearing* a29
3 b f Court Cave(IRE) —Vanished (IRE) (Fayruz)
7536[13] 7690[4]

Shoshiba (IRE) *Mafalda Osthaus* 68
5 b m Plumbird—Magic Surprise (Bluebird (USA))
1659a[13]

Shosolosa (IRE) *R C Guest* a55 60
6 b m Dansili—Hajat (Mujtahid (USA))
220[8] 375[6] 508[3] 640[9] 724[2] 1248[4] 1406[4] 1606[2] 1747[5] (2597) 2846[10] 3293[3] 3866[7] 3964[4] 4219[9]

Shotley Mac *N Bycroft* 85
4 ch g Abou Zouz(USA) —Julie's Gift (Presidium)
2391[2] (2925) 3339[4] 3664[4] 3928[11] 4245[3] 4650[3] (4901) (5638) 6056[12] 6482[6] 6724[2] (7041) (7175) 7239[12]

Shot To Fame (USA) *S Kirk* a72 85
9 b g Quest For Fame—Exocet (USA) (Deposit Ticket (USA))
992[6] 1301[4] 1550[2] (1670) 2277[5] (3033) 3313[11] 3797[8] 4862[3] 5267[9] 6020[10] 6380[13] 6774[5] 7090[11] 7414[9]

Shouldntbethere (IRE) *Mrs P N Dutfield* a69 56
4 ch g Soviet Star(USA) —Octomone (USA) (Hennessy (USA))
208[3] 448[7] 750[5] 1049[7] 3583[7] 4635[3] 5611[6] 6728[2] 7078[7] 7355[5] 7626[8] 7831[4]

Showtime Ice *Ms Deborah J Evans* a69 55
3 b f Lujain(USA) —Rebel County (IRE) (Maelstrom Lake)
6137[6] 6707[9]

Show Winner *A M Balding* a85 87
5 b g Mtoto—Rose Show (Belmez (USA))
1682[7] 2153[2] ◆ 2599[5] 3132[2] 4078[2] 4726[2] 5843[5]

Shraayef *M Botti* a61 54
3 b f Nayef(USA) —Gorgeous Dancer (IRE) (Nordico (USA))
2717^8 3479^5 4260^7 4797^5 (5803) 6019^{12} 7355^U

Shrek (GER) *A Wohler* 112
4 b h Pelder(IRE) —Septima (GER) (Touching Wood (USA))
1662a^4 2230a^9 3306a^3 4470a^4

Shrewd Dude *Carl Llewellyn* a53 45
4 bb g Val Royal(FR) —Lily Dale (IRE) (Distinctly North (USA))
2930^5 3343^3

Shreyas (IRE) *J S Bolger* 103
3 gr f Dalakhani(IRE) —Sadima (IRE) (Sadler's Wells (USA))
(6298a) 6819^7

Shropshirelass *Norma Twomey* a52 53
5 b m Beat All(USA) —Emma-Lyne (Emarati (USA))
1207^4 5020^7

Shunkawakhan (IRE) *Miss L A Perratt* a70 65
5 b g Indian Danehill(IRE) —Special Park (USA) (Trempolino (USA))
267^3 587^2 749^4 (1064) (1406) 1775^4 2285^{12} 2806^3 3211^6 (5538) 6821^3 (7226)

Shustraya *P J Makin* a90 82
4 b m Dansili—Nimble Fan (USA) (Lear Fan (USA))
226^{11} 733^5 7390^8 7592^9

Shy *P Winkworth* a75 80
3 ch f Erhaab(USA) —Shi Shi (Alnasr Alwasheek)
1741^2 2528^3 2862^2 3327^2 3841^5 4732^4 5750^2 6413^3

Shybutwilling (IRE) *Mrs P N Dutfield* a28 13
3 ch f Best Of The Bests(IRE) —Reticent Bride (IRE) (Shy Groom (USA))
2772^{10} 5608^{11}

Shy Glance (USA) *P Monteith* a76 79
6 b g Red Ransom(USA) —Royal Shyness (Royal Academy (USA))
1822^7 2155^6 2524^3 2749^7 (3204) 3755^6 (4015) 4850^{10} 5390^6 6108^7

Shy Prophet *A J McCabe* 51
2 b g Ishiguru(USA) —Blushing Victoria (Weldnaas (USA))
6714^{12} 7148^9

Shyrl *S A Callaghan* 97
2 b f Acclamation—Finicia (USA) (Miswaki (USA))
2677^3 3123^2 ◆ (3598) ◆ 5055^4 5245^{10} 5852^7

Si Belle (IRE) *Rae Guest* a78 91
3 gr f Dalakhani(IRE) —Stunning (USA) (Nureyev (USA))
595^5 748^9 873^2 ◆ 1163^3 2340^5 (2868) (2985) 4911a^2 5625a^5

Siberian Tiger (IRE) *M R Channon* a87 107
3 b c Xaar—Flying Millie (IRE) (Flying Spur (AUS))
567a^{12} 902^4 1811^4 2303^5 2825^4 3155^{26} 4552^{14} 4830^2 (5903) 6120^{11} 6476^{24} 6649^4

Sibi Saba (USA) *Saeed Bin Suroor* a78 71
3 b f Dixieland Band(USA) —Dancing Mirage (USA) (Alleged (USA))
4249^4 4689^2 5155^{10} (7304)

Sibo Baggins (IRE) *Mrs C A Dunnett* a22 59
4 ch g Docksider(USA) —Isadora Duncan (IRE) (Sadler's Wells (USA))
1692^{14} 2055^{13} 3113^{13} 3687^{10}

Siciliando *M L W Bell* 63
2 b g Bertolini(USA) —Donna Vita (Vettori (IRE))
2979^8 3408^5 3651^4 5242^{11} 6394^9

Sicilian Pink *E F Vaughan* a54 70
2 b f Beat Hollow—Sweet Pea (Persian Bold)
2821^9 3632^{11} 4425^3 4975^8 6700^{12} 7728^3 7789^{11}

Sicilian Warrior (USA) *P F I Cole* a57
2 b c War Chant(USA) —Gravina (CAN) (Sir Ivor (USA))
7356^7 7547^7 7760^7

Sidereus (IRE) *F & L Camici* 101
4 b h Grand Lodge(USA) —Simaat (USA) (Mr Prospector (USA))
2027a^6

Sidestreet *K McAuliffe* a45
3 b g Compton Place—April Lee (Superpower)
796^{10} 897^9 6433^{10}

Siegfrieds Night (IRE) *M C Chapman* a44 54
7 ch g Night Shift(USA) —Shelbiana (USA) (Chieftain)
7723^{11}

Siena *Mrs C A Dunnett* a56 30
3 b f Lomitas—Sea Lane (Zafonic (USA))
2509^{15} 3611^7 5576^{10} 5803^{13} 6036^{15} 6735^{12}

Siena Star (IRE) *Stef Liddiard* a71 72
10 b g Brief Truce(USA) —Gooseberry Pie (Green Desert (USA))
352^5 541^3 611^2 716^5 (1152) 1282^2 1505^8 2097^7 2949^{12} 3089^{13} 3518^5 (6927) 7440^3 7590^2 7807^5

Sienna Lake (IRE) *R Hannon* a60 64
2 b f Fasliyev(USA) —Lolita's Gold (USA) (Royal Academy (USA))
1680^{10} 1961^{15} 3207^{10} 4387^2 (4827) 5460^{10} 6207^4 6730^9

Sierra Rose *P J McBride* a40 51
4 b m Auction House(USA) —Young Whip (Bold Owl)
3839^9 4261^8 4748^5

Sierras Future *Miss L A Perratt* 52
4 b g Fusaichi Pegasus(USA) —Sierra Virgen (USA) (Stack (USA))
982^8

Sight Winner (NZ) *J Size* 107
5 b h Faltaat(USA) —Kinjinette (NZ) (Kinjite (NZ))
7685a^8

Signalman *P Monteith* 61
4 b g Silver Patriarch(IRE) —Kairine (IRE) (Kahyasi)
(4238) 4556^6 4848^2 5415^2 5993^3 6727^2

Signella *P W Chapple-Hyam* a32
2 ch f Selkirk(USA) —Sarah Georgina (Persian Bold)
7097^{13}

Sign Of Approval *K R Burke* a76 80
2 b c Refuse To Bend(IRE) —Scarlet Plume (Warning)
5756^2 6119^9 6474^{15} 7227^2 7655^3 7739^3

Sign Of The Cross *G L Moore* a88 85
4 b g Mark Of Esteem(IRE) —Thea (USA) (Marju (IRE))
1874^5 2531^3 3836^8 4894^9 6352^9 (7309) 7558^5 7791^4

Signora (IRE) *M Johnston* a64 60
3 ch f Indian Ridge—Lady Catherine (Bering)
2500^3 3133^3 3731^7

Signora Frasi (IRE) *A G Newcombe* a52 74
3 b f Indian Ridge—Sheba (IRE) (Lycius (USA))
7206^{12}

Signorinasilvani (IRE) *Rod Collet*
2 ch f Trans Island—Emy's Girl (USA) (Prospect Bay (CAN))
7430a^7

Signor Panettiere *A D Brown* a59 54
7 b g Night Shift(USA) —Christmas Kiss (Taufan (USA))
318^7 1646^5 1893^6 2270^{15} 2748^8 3783^6 4324^{13} 4958^{11}

Signor Peltro *H Candy* a86 98
5 b g Bertolini(USA) —Pewter Lass (Dowsing (USA))
1481^3 2195^4 3489^{12} 3905^3 4460^4 5030^2 (5313) 5897^3 ◆ 6269^9 6783^2

Silaah *E A L Dunlop* a88 60
4 b g Mind Games—Ocean Grove (IRE) (Fairy King (USA))
6571^4 (7074) 7384^2

Silca Chiave *M R Channon* 89
4 ch m Pivotal—Silca-Cisa (Hallgate)
2666^4 3120^{12} 4424^8 5071^8 5644^4

Silca Destination *M R Channon* a69 66
3 b f Dubai Destination(USA) —Golden Silca (Inchinor)
(623) (709) 797^3 2622^{10} 3065^3 3266^7 6387^7 6417^{13} 6683^9 7027^8 7068^6

Silent Act (USA) *Mrs A J Perrett* 54
2 b f Theatrical—Vinista (USA) (Jade Hunter (USA))
7141^{12}

Silent Applause *Dr J D Scargill* a53 76
5 b g Royal Applause—Billie Blue (Ballad Rock)
2373^{14} 2886^5 3655^7 4156^2 5105^3 6007^4 6721^4 7261^7

Silent Hero *M A Jarvis* a74 78
2 b g Oasis Dream—Royal Passion (Ahonoora)
2275^7 3495^{10} 4176^4 4828^4 5242^7 (5591) 6087^2 (6362) 6970^5

Silent Master (USA) *M Johnston* a83 58
3 b c Cherokee Run(USA) —Polent (Polish Precedent (USA))
1754 608^2 (772) 5789^2 ◆ 6021^8 6314^{13}

Silent Storm *Peter Grayson* a81 75
8 ch g Zafonic(USA) —Nanda (Nashwan (USA))
6955^{11} 7375^P (Dead)

Silent Sunday (IRE) *H-A Pantall* a95 96
3 b f Testa Rossa(AUS) —Snow Lady (SWI) (Vision (USA))
1375a^4 2033a^{13} 2902a^4 7162a^{10}

Silent Treatment (IRE) *Miss Gay Kelleway* a54 62
2 ch f Captain Rio—Without Words (Lion Cavern (USA))
2473^9 3019^5 (3815) 4823^3 (4986) 5159^3 5567^5 5933^3 6350^9

Silent Valor (USA) *Todd Pletcher* a109
2 bb c Lion Heart(USA) —Few Choice Words (USA) (Valid Appeal (USA))
6997a^8

Silent Wonder *R M H Cowell* a68 73
2 b c Diktat—Silent Miracle (IRE) (Night Shift (USA))
5633^2 5988^2 6351^5 6764^2 7082^2 7198^2 (7279) 7612^5

Silidan *G L Moore* a55 55
5 b g Dansili—In Love Again (IRE) (Prince Rupert (FR))
42^{10} 781^2 1029^4 2009^5 2597^{17} 3593^7 7194^{10} 7358^9 7490^{10} 7765^{12}

Silk Affair (IRE) *M G Quinlan* 94
3 b f Barathea(IRE) —Uncertain Affair (IRE) (Darshaan)
1557^2 1915^6 2975^5 3805a^6 4006a^{14} 6427^5 7100^P 7487a^8

Silk Cotton (USA) *E A L Dunlop* a68 64
2 b f Giant's Causeway(USA) —Calico Moon (USA) (Seeking The Gold (USA))
4157^{13} 4896^4 5571^5

Silk Drum (IRE) *J Howard Johnson* 68
3 gr g Intikhab(USA) —Aneydia (IRE) (Kenmare (FR))
3366^7 4077^5 ◆

Silken Promise (USA) *W R Swinburn* 62
2 bb f Pulpit(USA) —Banksia (Marju (IRE))
6945^7

Silk Gallery (USA) *E J Alston* a36 57
3 b f Kingmambo(USA) —Moon Flower (IRE) (Sadler's Wells (USA))
6791^{10} 7527^3

Silk Hall (UAE) *D W P Arbuthnot* a87 75
3 b g Halling(USA) —Velour (Mtoto)
1839^9 2244^5 2997^3 4573^4 4985^2 5269^3 6060^4 (6708) (6934)

Silk Meadow (IRE) *B J Meehan* 63
2 b f Barathea(IRE) —Perils Of Joy (IRE) (Rainbow Quest (USA))
3625^{10} 4643^{16}

Silk Star (IRE) *Mrs L Williamson* a26
2 b f Pyrus(USA) —Silk Feather (USA) (Silver Hawk (USA))
7117^{10}

Silk Trail *Saeed Bin Suroor* a71
2 b f Dubai Destination(USA) —Satin Flower (USA) (Shadeed (USA))
7095^2

Silky Steps (IRE) *P J Makin* a67 66
3 gr f Nayef(USA) —Legal Steps (IRE) (Law Society (USA))
1958^3 3023^7 3507^{11} 3799^7 5167^{11} 6227^5 6436^2 6882^{14}

Silky Way (GR) *P R Chamings* a59 44
2 b f Harmonic Way—Flourishing Way (Sadler's Wells (USA))
4321^5 6327^7 7574^5

Sills Vincero *D Shaw* a45 68
2 b f Piccolo—Aegean Magic (Wolfhound (USA))
3114^3 3734^2 4251^4 4499^6 5647^9 7795^4

Silly Gilly (IRE) *R E Barr* a55 63
4 b m Mull Of Kintyre(USA) —Richly Deserved (IRE) (Kings Lake (USA))
856^3 987^6 1189^{11} 1906^4 2936^{12} 3175^3 3593^3 (4540) 4898^4 5538^2 6408^5

Silvaani (USA) *B Forsey* a34 56
10 gr g Dumaani(USA) —Ruby Silver (USA) (Silver Hawk (USA))
7587^7

Silvador *W R Muir* 64
2 gr c Selkirk(USA) —Dali's Grey (Linamix (FR))
6122^{15} 6715^3

Silvanus (IRE) *I Semple* a80 80
3 b g Danehill Dancer(IRE) —Mala Mala (IRE) (Brief Truce (USA))
2981^2 3438^3 (4523) 6435^8 7276^3 7393^4 7828^2

Silver Abby (IRE) *Noel Lawlor* 60
2 gr f Clodovil(IRE) —Red Titian (IRE) (Titus Livius (FR))
4513a^5

Silver Arrow (ITY) *R Menichetti* 88
3 b c Silver Wizard(USA) —Eros Love (ITY) (Love The Groom (USA))
2028a^{18}

Silver Blue (IRE) *W K Goldsworthy* a67 74
5 ch g Indian Lodge(IRE) —Silver Echo (Caerleon (USA))
356^7 507^5 587^3 711^2 795^8 844^7 1064^5 1142^8 1269^2 (2070) 2097^3 (2353) ◆ 2558^5 ◆ (2990) 3208^3 3800^8 4364^7 4791^5 6662^5 6838^8 7354^8

Silver Deal *J A Pickering* a42 42
3 b f Lujain(USA) —Deal In Facts (So Factual (USA))
279^4 467^4 6173^{15}

Silver Diamond *W Jarvis* a34 46
3 b f Josr Algarhoud(IRE) —Silvermour (Aydimour)
2756^8 3445^6

Silverfoot (USA) *Dallas Stewart* 117
8 rg g With Approval(CAN) —Northern Silver (USA) (Silver Ghost (USA))
4889a^4

Silver Frost (IRE) *Y De Nicolay* 108
2 gr c Verglas(IRE) —Hidden Silver (Anabaa (USA))
(4673a) 5330a^7 (6642a) 7163a^3

Silver Games (IRE) *M R Channon* 84
2 gr f Verglas(IRE) —Mise (IRE) (Indian Ridge)
5097^{11} (5535) 6076^5 6268^7

Silverglas (IRE) *C A Horgan* 58
2 b c Verglas(IRE) —Yellow Trumpet (Petong)
6117^{11}

Silver Guest *M R Channon* a93 97
3 br g Lujain(USA) —Ajig Dancer (Niniski (USA))
(590) 905^4 ◆

Silver Hotspur *C R Dore* a94 75
4 b g Royal Applause—Noble View (USA) (Distant View (USA))
46^3 (79) ◆ (168) 232^3 347^5 (431) 555^2 (618) 659^3 (791) (850) 1133^7 2905^{12} 3222^{10} 3319^5 5908^{13} 6576^{13} 6900^9 7278^9 7564^5 7650^4 7758^4 (7796)

Silverlord (FR) *Frau Nina Bach* a78 101
4 ch g Numerous(USA) —Silverware (FR) (Polish Precedent (USA))
296a^{10} 381a^{11}

Silver Mitzva (IRE) *M Botti* a95 95
4 b m Almutawakel—Ribblesdale (Northern Park (USA))
4667^7 5329a^7 6241^9 7100^4 7487a^0

Silver Mont (IRE) *S R Bowring* a63 57
5 b g Montjeu(IRE) —Silvernus (Machiavellian (USA))
1779^4 5593^8

Silver Pivotal (IRE) *G A Butler* a111 108
4 br m Pivotal—Silver Colours (USA) (Silver Hawk (USA))
(315) ◆ 906^2 ◆ 5289^5

Silver Prelude *S C Williams* a96 67
7 gr g Prince Sabo—Silver Blessings (Statoblest)
137^2 411^3 593^6 836^7 907^6 1366^6 1956^8 2501^6 2906^9 7756^6

Silver Print (USA) *W R Swinburn* a76 75
2 rg c Maria's Mon(USA) —Shutterbug (USA) (Deputy Minister (CAN))
3968^4 4570^3 5901^2 6376^2 6946^{17}

Silver Regent (USA) *Mrs A J Perrett* a79 87
3 b c Silver Deputy(CAN) —Alexine (ARG) (Runaway Groom (CAN))
6704^7 6949^{12} 7398^6 7539^5

Silver Rime (FR) *R Hannon* 91
3 gr c Verglas(IRE) —Severina (Darshaan)
1297^2 (1524) 2194^8 2953^3 3919^5 5862^3 6249^5

Silver Salsa *J R Jenkins* a48 52
2 b f Lujain(USA) —Tango Teaser (Shareef Dancer (USA))
3558^9 4020^8 4705^9 5530^4 6191^5 6906^8 7543^4

Silver Sceptre (IRE) *W J Musson* 39
2 b g Intikhab(USA) —Silver Pursuit (Rainbow Quest (USA))
3798^9 4024^{12} 5499^9

Silver Seeker (USA) *Miss P Robson* 69
8 gr g Seeking The Gold(USA) —Zelanda (IRE) (Night Shift (USA))
(2252) ◆ (2467) 2844^3 (3279) 4516^{13} 5396^6

Silver Shoon (IRE) *D K Weld* a79 96
2 gr f Fasliyev(USA) —Limpopo (Green Desert (USA))
3105^{13} 5546a^2

Silver Sprite *D Shaw* a55
3 gr g Best Of The Bests(IRE) —Nightingale (Night Shift (USA))
20^6 157^4 262^5 335^5 464^9

Silver Spruce *D Flood* a47 65
3 gr g First Trump—Red Typhoon (Belfort (FR))
(1364) 1731^5 2080^7 2486^5 2801^7 2941^6 7765^6

Silver Suitor (IRE) *D R C Elsworth* 102
4 gr g Swain(IRE) —Taatof (IRE) (Lahib (USA))
1812^3 ◆ (1984)

Silver Surprise *J J Bridger* a57 52
4 gr m Orpen(USA) —Dim Ofan (Petong)
1929^{11} 2354^7 3347^{12} 4343^5 4820^{10} 5027^6 5232^{11} 5676^{10} 6378^2 6728^4 6909^6 7626^{12} 7701^6

Silver Thatch *W G M Turner*
2 b f Silver Patriarch(IRE) —Native Thatch (IRE) (Thatching)
2980^7

Silver Touch (IRE) *M R Channon* 113
5 b m Dansili—Sanpala (Sanglamore (USA))
1880a^8 2607^4 3063^5 6782^{12}

Silver Tree (USA) *William Mott* a116 116
8 ch h Hennessy(USA) —Blue Begum (USA) (With Approval (CAN))
5928a^4

Silver Waters *D R C Elsworth* a68 79
3 gr g Fantastic Light(USA) —Silent Waters (Polish Precedent (USA))
416^8 ◆ 570^5 ◆ 727^2 1114^3 (1516) 1731^3 2201^3 2977^9

Silver Willow *J E Long* a50 52
3 b f Where Or When(IRE) —Silver Bubble (USA) (Silver Hawk (USA))
1504^8 2046^9 2668^{13} 6374^{11}

Silver Wind *P D Evans* a83 89
3 b g Ishiguru(USA) —My Bonus (Cyrano De Bergerac)
1328^3 1837^7 1925^5 2405^8 3904^6 (4408) 4864^2 5096^{10} 6239^{11} 6624^9 6902^4 7297^5 7470^4

Simarian (IRE) *Evan Williams* 63
3 b g Kalanisi(IRE) —Sinnariya (IRE) (Persian Bold)
1535^4 2451^5

Simawa (IRE) *John M Oxx* a94 94
3 b f Anabaa(USA) —Sinntara (IRE) (Lashkari)
1199a^5 3070a^9 3805a^4 6298a^{15}

Simba Sun (IRE) *A King* a83 83
4 b g Intikhab(USA) —Lions Den (IRE) (Desert Style (IRE))
3685^7 4314^6

Simonas (IRE) *A Wohler* 104
9 gr g Sternkoenig(IRE) —Sistadari (Shardari)
423a^9 604a^8 6992a^7

Simone Martini (IRE) *R Charlton* 69
3 b g Montjeu(IRE) —Bona Dea (IRE) (Danehill (USA))
4382^6 5098^8 5651^2

Simon Gray *R Hannon* a63 74
2 b c Act One—Shardette (IRE) (Darshaan)
6397^5 6978^6 7434^5

Simon Magus (GER) *W Hickst* 99
4 br h Golan(IRE) —S'Il Vous Plait (GER) (Dashing Blade)
5528a^9

Simple Jim (FR) *A D Brown* a66 57
4 b g Jimble(FR) —Stop The Wedding (USA) (Stop The Music (USA))
234^8 533^6 551^2 720^8 6550^5 6812^{11} 7285^4 (7617) 7696^4

Simple Rhythm *N Tinkler* a68 68
2 b f Piccolo—Easy Beat (IRE) (Orpen (USA))
1616^6 (2548) 3639^2 4434^9 (5159) 5473^2 5866^6 6732^{10} 7113^8

Simple Solution (USA) *B W Hills* a81 67
2 b f Dynaformer(USA) —Super Staff (USA) (Secretariat (USA))
4643^5 (5570) ◆

Simplex (FR) *K Schafflutzel* 17
7 b h Rainbow Quest(USA) —Russyskia (USA) (Green Dancer (USA))
423a^{12}

Simplification *R Hannon* a62 78
2 gr f Daylami(IRE) —Bella Cantata (Singspiel (IRE))
4570^5 ◆ 5241^5 5788^7

Simplified *M C Chapman* a26 43
5 b m Lend A Hand—Houston Heiress (USA) (Houston (USA))
7529^{11} 7631^7

Simply St Lucia *J R Weymes* a39 47
6 b m Charnwood Forest(IRE) —Mubadara (IRE) (Lahib (USA))
438^9 481^5 661^7

Simply The Quest *R Simpson* a22
4 br m Mtoto—Wydah (Suave Dancer (USA))
513^7

Simpsons Gamble (IRE) *R A Teal* a63 27
5 b g Tagula(IRE) —Kiva (Indian Ridge)
123^3 209^4 (326) 584^6 933^3 1145^9 (1254) 7254^3 7357^{10} 7521^4

Sina (GER) *W Hickst* 91
3 b f Trans Island—Soiree De Vienne (IRE) (Marju (IRE))
5737a^6

Sinaaf *M P Tregoning* a66 77
3 b f Nayef(USA) —Elutrah (Darshaan)
3521^3

Sinbad The Sailor *J W Hills* 75
3 b g Cape Cross(IRE) —Sinead (USA) (Irish River (FR))
2002^2 2907^3 3384^8 (4332) 4621^5 5472^7 6079^{13} 6416^7

Sinchiroka (FR) *E F Vaughan* 55
2 b c Della Francesca(USA) —Great Care (USA) (El Gran Senor (USA))
6789^7

Sin City *R A Fahey* 82
5 b g Sinndar(IRE) —Turn Of A Century (Halling (USA))
2939^4 3368^{13} 4164^4 6657^9 (Dead)

Sindajan (IRE) *A De Royer-Dupre* 90
3 b c Medicean—Sinndiya (IRE) (Pharly (FR))
4042a^{12} 5138a^8

Sindanna *A King*
4 ch m Sinndar(IRE) —Esclava (USA) (Nureyev (USA))
1542[6]

Sinead Of Aglish (IRE) *Peter Grayson* a69 74
3 ch f Captain Rio—Final Favour (IRE) (Unblest)
4028[7] 4943[5] 5531[9]

Singapore Treat (FR) *Robert Collet* a70 76
2 b f Sagacity(FR) —Desert Threat (IRE) (Desert Prince (IRE))
5486a[6]

Sing Baby Sing (USA) *Jack Bruner* a108
5 b h Unbridled's Song(USA) —Roll Over Baby (USA) (Rollin On Over (USA))
6999a[6]

Singh Street (IRE) *Donal Hassett* 53
9 gr m Dolphin Street(FR) —Singhana (IRE) (Mouktar)
4799a[8]

Singing Lion *M Dods* 11
3 b g Hunting Lion(IRE) —Arasong (Aragon)
3282[13]

Singing Poet (IRE) *E Charpy* a94 78
7 b g Singspiel(IRE) —Bright Finish (USA) (Zilzal (USA))
817a[7]

Singleb (IRE) *Miss Gay Kelleway* a74 72
4 b g Intikhab(USA) —Bubble N Squeak (IRE) (Catrail (USA))
4026[11] 4748[2] (4891) (5533) 6338[4] (6716) 6928[11] 7018[3] (7513) 7780[3]

Single Vote *H R A Cecil* 53
3 br f Pivotal—Singleton (Singspiel (IRE))
2164[7]

Sinntaran (IRE) *M Halford* a65 74
4 b g Machiavellian(USA) —Sinntara (IRE) (Lashkari)
7742[3]

Sinsational *Edward Lynam* a89 90
4 ch g Indian Ridge—Pretty Girl (IRE) (Polish Precedent (USA))
1497a[9]

Sintenis Mac (GER) *P J O'Gorman* a63 66
5 ch g Pivotal—Sintenis (GER) (Polish Precedent (USA))
1209[11] 1780[9] 2165[3] 2374[4] 2949[7] (3218) 3457[10] 3501[2] 3855[7]

Sion Hill (IRE) *John A Harris* a69 70
7 b g Desert Prince(IRE) —Mobilia (Last Tycoon)
11[4] (120) 232[2] 402[9] 521[6] 624[2] (711) 795[2] 1024[8] 1189[3] (1602) (1780) 2933[8] 3371[9] 4934[12] 5478[12] 5709[5] 6178[14] 6975[9] 7228[3] 7287[5] 7503[10] 7692[3]

Sioux Rising (IRE) *R A Fahey* 56
2 b f Danetime(IRE) —Arvika (FR) (Baillamont (USA))
5271[8]

Sir Al (IRE) *K R Burke* a80
2 ch c Desert Prince(IRE) —Shallop (Salse (USA))
5696[3] ◆

Sir Arthur (IRE) *B Ellison* 79
5 ch g Desert Prince(IRE) —Park Express (Ahonoora)
963[10]

Sir Billy Nick *S Wynne* a74 70
3 b c Bertolini(USA) —Follow Flanders (Pursuit Of Love)
965[3] (1252) 1686[6] 2161[8] 4731[11] 5052[7] 6134[4] 6422[10] 6827[4] 7440[12] 7656[11] 7725[3]

Sir Bond (IRE) *G R Oldroyd* a62 62
7 ch g Desert Sun—In Tranquility (IRE) (Shalford (IRE))
80[8] 550[3] 724[4] 872[8] 1086[8] 3281[10] 3643[6] 3822[4] 4479[4] 4919[12]

Sir Boss (IRE) *D E Cantillon* a69 73
3 b g Tagula(IRE) —Good Thought (IRE) (Mukaddamah (USA))
1960[5] (2824) 3270[7] 4478[6] 4895[6] 5458[3]

Sircozy (IRE) *S C Williams* 51
2 b g Celtic Swing—Furnish (Green Desert (USA))
6552[9] 7240[9]

Sir Don (IRE) *E S McMahon* a63 59
9 b g Lake Coniston(IRE) —New Sensitive (Wattlefield)
54[8] (372)

Sir Douglas *M A Barnes* a74 64
5 ch g Desert Sun—Daintree (IRE) (Tirol)
15[2] (103) 150[10] 342[4] 429[6] 783[8] 1143[7] 1900[12] 2753[8] 2988[15] 7316[U] 7533[14]

Sir Duke (IRE) *P W D'Arcy* a79 95
4 b g Danehill(USA) —Dimanche (IRE) (Sadler's Wells (USA))
(1505) ◆ 1564[3] (2165) (2264) ◆ 2839[2] (3440) 3900[2] (4111) 5494[F] (Dead)

Sir Edwin Landseer (USA) *Christian Wroe* a91 83
8 gr g Lit De Justice(USA) —Wildcat Blue (USA) (Cure The Blues (USA))
566a[2] 670a[5] 5270[7] 5930[6] 6676[9]

Siren Party *L M Cumani* a67 70
3 br f Pivotal—Ludynosa (USA) (Cadeaux Genereux)
2341[8] 3177[4] ◆ (4987) 5317[9] 5998[6]

Siren's Gift *A M Balding* a100 104
4 ch m Cadeaux Genereux—Blue Siren (Bluebird (USA))
2626[5] 3504[3] 3943[3] 4445[8] 4624[9] 5890[3] 6429[2] 6653[10]

Siren Sound *H Morrison* a81 67
3 br f Singspiel(IRE) —Warning Belle (Warning)
1803[3] 2566[5] 3061[5] 5402[3] 6048[2] (6631) 7225[6] 7586[3]

Sirenuse (IRE) *B Smart* 77
2 b f Exceed And Excel(AUS) —Cefira (USA) (Distant View (USA))
3590[4] ◆ (4202) 4648[2]

Sir Freddie *Lady Herries* a56 56
2 b g Fraam—Height Of Folly (Shirley Heights)
7054[11] 7336[8]

Sir Geoffrey (IRE) *A J McCabe* a82 74
2 b g Captain Rio—Disarm (IRE) (Bahamian Bounty)
2502[3] 2944[2] 3392[4] 4965[3] (5633) 5969[5] (6769)

Sir George (IRE) *P W Chapple-Hyam* a78 71
3 b g Mujadil(USA) —Torrmana (IRE) (Ela-Mana-Mou)
(1215)

Sir Gerry (USA) *J R Fanshawe* 116
3 ch c Carson City(USA) —Incredulous (FR) (Indian Ridge)
1471[7] (1718) 2652a[3] 3247[3] 3922[13] 6304[3] 6645[3]

Sir Haydn *J R Jenkins* a66 46
8 ch g Definite Article—Snowscape (Niniski (USA))
212[6] 5630[6] 6019[14] 7189[11] 7261[3] 7440[11] 7626[5] 7702[12]

Sir Ike (IRE) *W S Kittow* a67 67
3 b c Xaar—Iktidar (Green Desert (USA))
1836[6] 2991[3] 3564[6] 4412[4] 5836[3] 6417[3] 7166[13] 7504[3] 7609[6]

Sir Isaac *W J Haggas* 10
2 b g Key Of Luck(USA) —Rainbow Queen (FR) (Spectrum (IRE))
5271[15]

Sir Jake *T T Clement* a53 34
4 b h Killer Instinct—Waikiki Dancer (IRE) (General Monash (USA))
727[8] 934[7] 1262[7] 1459[9]

Sir Joey *B D Leavy* a51 51
3 ch g Forzando—Estabella (IRE) (Mujtahid (USA))
108[U] 257[6] 7695[11]

Sir John Lilley (USA) *M Johnston* a62
3 ch c Gulch(USA) —Brackish (USA) (Alleged (USA))
1504[5] 2246[8] 2735[9]

Sir Kyffin's Folly *J A Geake* 71
3 b f Dansili—Persia (IRE) (Persian Bold)
1445[5] 1965[7] 2566[8] 3918[2] 4572[9] 6124[9]

Sir Liam (USA) *Tom Dascombe* a76 69
4 b g Monarchos(USA) —Tears (USA) (Red Ransom (USA))
406[6] 546[7] 1056[6] 1182[5] 2933[7] 3218[6] 3574[4] 4055[6] 4409[4] 4722[4] 7559[5] 7702[2]

Sir Loin *P Burgoyne* a62 64
7 ch g Compton Place—Charnwood Queen (Cadeaux Genereux)
(86) 263[4] (414) 690[11]

Sir Mikeale *J Pearce* a36
5 b g Easycall—Sleep Standing (IRE) (Standaan (FR))
3371[12] 4748[14]

Sir Night (IRE) *M Hill* a16 43
8 b g Night Shift(USA) —Highly Respected (IRE) (High Estate)
171[8] 1779[8] 2643[7]

Sir Nod *Miss J A Camacho* a86 87
6 b g Tagula(IRE) —Nordan Raider (Domynsky)
2188[5] 2398[7] 3050[12] 3626[9]

Sirocco Breeze *Saeed Bin Suroor* 94
3 b c Green Desert(USA) —Baldemosa (FR) (Lead On Time (USA))
(6566) 6975[7]

Sir Rique (FR) *P J Hobbs* 53
5 b g Enrique—Fontaine Guerard (FR) (Homme De Loi (IRE))
999[8]

Sir Royal (USA) *G A Swinbank* 80
3 b c Diesis—Only Royale (IRE) (Caerleon (USA))
1379[3] 1728[2]

Sir Sandicliffe (IRE) *W M Brisbourne* a70 71
4 b g Distant Music(USA) —Desert Rose (Green Desert (USA))
2908[13] 3550[5] 3912[2] 4556[3] 4848[3] 5154[5] 5559[3] 5887[2] 6279[9] 6550[3] (6812) 7042[5] 7401[3] 7515[11]

Sir Slick (NZ) *Graeme Nicholson* 115
7 b g Volksraad—Miss Opera (NZ) (Paris Opera (AUS))
1666a[11] 2234a[5]

Sirvino *T D Barron* 71
3 b g Vettori(IRE) —Zenita (IRE) (Zieten (USA))
1579[4] 2700[4] 5505[5] 6585[2]

Sir Xaar (IRE) *B Smart* a58 97
5 bb g Xaar—Cradle Brief (IRE) (Brief Truce (USA))
2172[12] 2595[6] 3122[26] 3491[7] (4417) 5446[7] 6478[10] 7245[19]

Siryena *B I Case* a57 55
3 b f Oasis Dream—Ard Na Sighe (IRE) (Kenmare (FR))
2982[6] 3799[14] 4708[5] 5119[11] (5603) 5961[6] 6436[8]

Sister Act *J R Fanshawe* a75 87
4 b m Marju(IRE) —Kalinka (IRE) (Soviet Star (USA))
2373[13] 3376[6]

Sister Agnes (IRE) *M F Harris* 63
4 ch m Dr Fong(USA) —Nibbs Point (IRE) (Sure Blade (USA))
1267[7] 1538[3] 1856[11] 3697[7] 5651[6]

Sister Clement (IRE) *C R Egerton* a54 58
2 b f Oasis Dream—Miss Party Line (USA) (Phone Trick (USA))
2691[11] 4274[6] 4692[15] 7205[5]

Sister Moonshine *W R Muir* a60 64
3 b f Averti(IRE) —Cal Norma's Lady (IRE) (Lyphard's Special (USA))
1960[3] 2546[6] 2898[6] 6063[11]

Sistos Fascination *M Botti* a63 65
3 b g Fasliyev(USA) —Sierra Virgen (USA) (Stack (USA))
98[3] (335) 2480[7] 3648[6] 4181[4] 5377[3]

Site Sentry (IRE) *M F Harris* a65 38
5 ch g Nashwan(USA) —Balwa (USA) (Danzig (USA))
545[6] 758[6] 773[2] 1056[4] 1296[7] 3711[12] 4182[13]

Sitwell *J R Fanshawe* a53
2 b g Dr Fong(USA) —First Fantasy (Be My Chief (USA))
7380[8]

Six Of Clubs *W G M Turner*
2 ch g Bertolini(USA) —Windmill Princess (Gorytus (USA))
6199[15]

Six Of Hearts *Cecil Ross* a81 81
4 b g Pivotal—Additive (USA) (Devil's Bag (USA))
4514a[3]

Sixth Zak *S R Bowring* a49
3 br g Fantastic Light(USA) —Zakuska (Zafonic (USA))
7321[4] 7446[5]

Sixties Gift (UAE) *Rae Guest* a52
2 bb f Singspiel(IRE) —Sicily (USA) (Kris S (USA))
7720[4]

Sixties Icon *J Noseda* a108 118
5 b h Galileo(IRE) —Love Divine (Diesis)
1829[2] (2325) 3121[12] (4585) (5094) (6303) 6993a[5] 7511a[13]

Sixties Swinger (USA) *M A Jarvis* 74
2 b g Refuse To Bend(IRE) —Kardashina (FR) (Darshaan)
3939[3] ◆ 6674[7] 7080[4]

Siyabona (USA) *Saeed Bin Suroor* 74
3 b f Kingmambo(USA) —Relish (IRE) (Sadler's Wells (USA))
2971[4] 3810[3] 4447[3]

Siyasa (USA) *Saeed Bin Suroor* 82
3 ch f Rahy(USA) —Jood (USA) (Nijinsky (CAN))
2123[6] 2716[2] 2973[2] 3556[2]

Skadrak (USA) *B J Meehan* a87 94
3 ch g Forest Camp(USA) —Occhi Verdi (IRE) (Mujtahid (USA))
1601[2] 2148[3]

Skagerrak (USA) *D Smaga* 98
4 gr h Dynaformer(USA) —Si Je N'Avais Plus (IRE) (Kaldoun (FR))
2637a[6]

Skanky Biscuit *B J Meehan* 111
2 ch c Peintre Celebre(USA) —Blushing Gleam (Caerleon (USA))
(6604) 6973[3]

Skhilling Spirit *T D Barron* 103
5 b g Most Welcome—Calcavella (Pursuit Of Love)
958[6] 1218[10] 1481[4] (1774) 1982[8] 6104[5] 6269[22] (6947) 7243[15]

Skiathos Queen (IRE) *William J Fitzpatrick* 60
3 b f Exit To Nowhere(USA) —Phil's Lady (IRE) (Shalford (IRE))
3861a[14]

Skiddaw Fox *Mrs L Williamson* a7 44
4 ch h Foxhound(USA) —Stealthy Times (Timeless Times (USA))
101[9]

Skid Solo (IRE) *Mme G Rarick* a44 85
2 ch c Bahamian Bounty—Amaniy (USA) (Dayjur (USA))
1439[2] 1714[6] 3152[10] 4931[6] 6118[3] 6603[9] 7430a[12]

Skipadate (USA) *Mark Casse* a61 101
2 rg c Skip Away(USA) —Valid Approval (USA) (Valid Appeal (USA))
6998a[11]

Skipped Bail (CAN) *Eric Coatrieux* 105
5 bb g Skip Away(USA) —Striking Proposal (USA) (Smart Strike (CAN))
2472a[7]

Ski Sunday *M A Jarvis* a66 54
3 b g King's Best(USA) —Lille Hammer (Sadler's Wells (USA))
58[7] 288[2] (325) ◆ 434[2]

Skit *W M Brisbourne* 40
5 b g In The Wings—Skew (Niniski (USA))
1551[6] 2849[11]

Skruton (IRE) *M G Quinlan* a60 73
2 b f Titus Livius(FR) —Zurarah (Siberian Express (USA))
1749[4] (2614) 3496[8] 3865[6] 4768[4] 5103[6] 5647[5] 5997[7] 6414[6] 6787[3] 7016[5] 7275[3] 7537[8]

Skycap (IRE) *Saeed Bin Suroor* 82
3 ch c Dubai Destination(USA) —Flagbird (USA) (Nureyev (USA))
3654[2] 4124[5]

Sky Chart (IRE) *N J Vaughan* a50 55
4 ch g Fantastic Light(USA) —Marion Haste (IRE) (Ali-Royal (IRE))
287[3] 485[4] 2185[7] 2572[7] 3059[9] 3698[2] 3912[6]

Sky Diva (USA) *Steven B Klesaris* a112
2 ch f Sky Mesa(USA) —Swift Girl (USA) (Unbridled (USA))
(6500a) 6967a[3]

Sky Dive *L M Cumani* a87 70
3 ch c Dr Fong(USA) —Free Flying (Groom Dancer (USA))
1381[11] 1745[2] ◆ 2532[3] 6424[8]

Skye But N Ben *G A Harker* a59 64
4 b g Auction House(USA) —Island Colony (USA) (Pleasant Colony (USA))
989[5] 1160[7] 1679[4] 1890[7] 2456[6] 2731[6] 3182[3] 3230[7] 4123[3] 4541[7] 4966[5]

Sky Gate (USA) *B J Meehan* a70 35
2 b c Arch(USA) —Mista Mayberry (USA) (Touch Gold (USA))
6122[17] 6620[9] 7397[6] (7726)

Sky High Kid (IRE) *M R Channon* a65
2 b g One Cool Cat(USA) —Market Hill (IRE) (Danehill (USA))
7709[6] (7810)

Skylarker (USA) *T A K Cuthbert* 19
10 b g Sky Classic(CAN) —O My Darling (USA) (Mr Prospector (USA))
6385[10] 6786[12] 6950[17]

Skyler *J L Flint* a42
7 b g Dr Massini(IRE) —Commanche Token (IRE) (Commanche Run)
1405[6]

Sky Mystic (IRE) *J S Bolger* a62 78
2 b f Galileo(IRE) —Raghida (IRE) (Nordico (USA))
2686a[6] 3466a[7]

Sky Quest (IRE) *J R Boyle* a71 76
10 b g Spectrum(IRE) —Rose Vibert (Caerleon (USA))
1932[4] 2374[7] 2795[15] 3583[10] 4568[8] 6771[12] 6899[9] 7189[4] 7355[4] (7702)

Skyscape *Thomas Cooper* a78 84
6 b m Zafonic(USA) —Aquarelle (Kenmare (FR))
4576a[16]

Skyteam (FR) *Mme C Head-Maarek* a88 93
4 b g Anabaa(USA) —Spenderella (FR) (Common Grounds)
5113a[6]

Skywards *E Charpy* a100 92
6 b g Machiavellian(USA) —Nawaiet (USA) (Zilzal (USA))
382a[4] 473a[3] ◆ 564a[12]

Slam *B W Hills* a100 95
3 b c Beat Hollow—House Hunting (Zafonic (USA))
(2079) 3251[3] 3877[15] (5425) 5907[3] 6445[7]

Slam Dunk (USA) *G M Lyons* a96 97
3 b g Grand Slam(USA) —Deep In My Heart (USA) (Rahy (USA))
3531a[4] 6283[4]

Slant (IRE) *Eve Johnson Houghton* 80
2 b f Spinning World(USA) —Sweet Honesty (IRE) (Charnwood Forest (IRE))
4149[3] ◆ 4521[6] 5294a[4] 5640[5] 7015[2]

Slavonic Lake *I A Wood* a56 54
4 b g Lake Coniston(IRE) —Slavonic Dance (Muhtarram (USA))
166[3] 238[4]

Sleeping *M H Tompkins* 59
3 b f Mujahid(USA) —Tenpence (Bob Back (USA))
1519[11] 2199[6] 2509[12] 4795[5] 5837[13] 6175[6] 6562[11] 6888[12]

Sleeping Dragon *P A Blockley* 35
3 ch g Tobougg(IRE) —Wathbat Mtoto (Mtoto)
1367[12]

Sleepy Dreams (IRE) *David Marnane* a56 71
2 b f Invincible Spirit(IRE) —Mambodorga (USA) (Kingmambo (USA))
5438a[6]

Sleepy Hollow *H Morrison* 88
3 b g Beat Hollow—Crackling (Electric)
(2045) ◆ 2342[12] 4448[2] 5100[2] 6079[11] 6542[2] 6948[4]

Sleepy Mountain *A Middleton* a61 63
4 ch g Beat Hollow—La Sorrela (IRE) (Cadeaux Genereux)
4302[8] 4821[7] 5612[5] 6136[4] 6538[6] 7293[11] 7473[2] 7608[3]

Sleepy Valley (IRE) *A Dickman* 56
2 b f Clodovil(IRE) —Kilkee Bay (IRE) (Case Law)
4384[4] 7172[6]

Slew's Tiznow (USA) *Doug O'Neill* a110
3 bb c Tiznow(USA) —Hepatica (USA) (Slewpy (USA))
6995a[10]

Slew's Tizzy (USA) *Doug O'Neill* a110 96
4 bb h Tiznow(USA) —Hepatica (USA) (Slewpy (USA))
6995a[11]

Sley (FR) *B J Meehan* a54 65
2 ch f Lomitas—Samara (IRE) (Polish Patriot (USA))
6030[5] 6555[6] 7023[8] 7467[11]

Slickly Royal (FR) *P Demercastel* a93 95
4 bl h Slickly(FR) —Royal Bride (FR) (Garde Royale)
2876a[11] 5115a[4]

Sligo *A P O'Brien* a75 87
3 b c Sadler's Wells(USA) —Arabesque (Zafonic (USA))
1362a[4] 1943[6]

Slim Jim Phantom *J G Given* a13
3 b g Compton Place—Lyna (Slip Anchor)
6633[10]

Slip *J R Boyle* a90 90
3 b g Fraam—Niggle (Night Shift (USA))
(3065) 3325[4] (4130) ◆ 4791[2] 5573[5] 6078[3] 6667[5] 7404[4] 7595[2] 7717[5]

Slip Star *T J Etherington* a18 56
5 b m Slip Anchor—Shiny Kay (Star Appeal)
2038[8] 3079[7] (3481) 3866[6] 6419[12]

Slivovic (IRE) *J S Wainwright* 35
4 b m Fruits Of Love(USA) —Ned's Contessa (IRE) (Persian Heights)
978[8] 1391[15] 2207[8] 2731[11]

Slo Mo Shun *C Gordon* a49 52
4 b m Polish Precedent(USA) —Malvadilla (IRE) (Doyoun)
795[11]

Sloop Johnb *R A Fahey* 79
2 b g Bahamian Bounty—Soundwave (Prince Sabo)
1749[2] 2035[6] 3365[2] (4449) 4874[9] 5277[10]

Slow Escape (USA) *M Wigham* 52
4 b g Storm Creek(USA) —Amy Leigh (USA) (Sefapiano (USA))
1876[12]

Slugger O'Toole *B W Hills* a89 100
3 br g Intikhab(USA) —Haddeyah (USA) (Dayjur (USA))
1403[4] (1601) (1834) 2794[3] 3155[9] 3919[8] 4405[20] (5795) ◆ 6478[9] 6783[3]

Sly Tiger (GER) *M Halford* a40 62
4 b g Tiger Hill(IRE) —Shoah (GER) (Acatenango (GER))
7732[8]

Smalljohn *B Smart* a73 76
2 ch g Needwood Blade—My Bonus (Cyrano De Bergerac)
1214[3] 1413[6] ◆ 1693[6] 2186[4] 2569[6] (3008) 3670[2] 3978[6] 4243[2] (4604) 4733[7] (7164) 7275[2] 7443[3] (7652)

Smart Artist *S Kirk*
3 b g Zaha(CAN) —Cabaret Artiste (Shareef Dancer (USA))
1563[10] 2449[14]

Smart Coco (USA) *T Stack* 93
2 b f Smarty Jones(USA) —Djebel Amour (USA) (Mt. Livermore (USA))
6318a[5]

Smart Endeavour (USA) *W R Swinburn* 49
2 ch c Smart Strike(CAN) —Luminance (USA) (Deputy Minister (CAN))
2972[7] ◆

Smarten Die (IRE) *Frau E Mader* a101 89
5 ch h Diesis—Highest Dream (IRE) (Highest Honor (FR))
603a[7] 4881a[8] *7421*[5]

Smart Enough *M A Magnusson* a107 109
5 gr g Cadeaux Genereux—Good Enough (FR) (Mukaddamah (USA))
1326[6] *1767*[6] 2465[12] 3921[15]

Smarterthanuthink (USA) *R A Fahey* a73 71
3 b g Smart Strike(CAN) —Dance Gaily (USA) (Nureyev (USA))
2208[6] (2750) ◆ 3174[2] 4331[8] 6235[7] *6741*[2] *7070*[8]

Smart Instinct (USA) *R A Fahey* 100
4 ch g Smart Strike(CAN) —Smile N Molly (USA) (Dixieland Band (USA))
2103[4] 2465[5] 2790[4] 3249[10] 5229[19] 6479[10] 6784[P] (Dead)

Smart Pick *Mrs L Williamson* a48 56
5 ch m Piccolo—Nevita (Never So Bold)
3130[5] 3431[10] 3951[11] 4683[8] 5045[6]

Smart Tazz *H J Evans* 26
3 b g Mujahid(USA) —Katy-Q (IRE) (Taufan (USA))
5366[9] 5652[9]

Smarty Socks (IRE) *P T Midgley* a80 90
4 ch g Elnadim(USA) —Unicamp (Royal Academy (USA))
5635[14] 6056[11] (7021) *(7153)* 7239[6] *(7284)* ◆

Smash N'Grab (IRE) *J R Jenkins* a58 59
4 ch m Jade Robbery(USA) —Sallwa (IRE) (Entrepreneur)
79[11]

Smelly Cat *T D Easterby* 38
2 b f One Cool Cat(USA) —Grecian Halo (USA) (Southern Halo (USA))
3976[8] 4202[11]

Smetana *E J Creighton* a58 56
3 b g Kylian(USA) —Shimmer (Bustino)
1871[5] 2475[4] *2868*[2] 3671[7] 5077[6] *7713*[12]

Smiddy Hill *R Bastiman* a70 54
6 b m Factual(USA) —Hello Hobson'S (IRE) (Fayruz)
4285[5] 4561[3] 5319[8] 6339[10]

Smileforawhile (IRE) *K A Ryan* 69
3 b g Green Desert(USA) —Woodyousmileforme (USA) (Woodman (USA))
1819[16]

Smiling Tiger *M J Gingell*
4 b g Contract Law(USA) —Nouvelle Cuisine (Yawa)
3910

Smirfys Gold (IRE) *E S McMahon* a59 59
4 ch g Bad As I Wanna Be(IRE) —Golden Jorden (IRE) (Cadeaux Genereux)
2448[4] *2802*[2] 3340[9] 4285[3] 4703[12] *5374*[4] 6328[7]

Smirfy's Silver *E S McMahon* a31 71
4 b g Desert Prince(IRE) —Goodwood Blizzard (Inchinor)
(1620) 2165[7] 3029[3] 4156[11] 4785[5]

Smirfys Systems *E S McMahon* a64 53
9 b g Safawan—Saint Systems (Uncle Pokey)
255[3] *(469)* *718*[4] *(7782)*

Smitain *Mrs S Lamyman* 37
2 b g Lujain(USA) —Mitsuki (Puissance)
2702[6] 5394[12]

Smokejumper (GER) *Frau E Mader* 102
4 b h Big Shuffle(USA) —Shikoku (Green Desert (USA))
3515a[6]

Smoke Me A Kipper (IRE) *Mrs A Duffield* 43
2 gr f Verglas(IRE) —Anoukit (Green Desert (USA))
2887[8] 3334[7] 4072[8] 5256[13] 5774[11] 5966[9]

Smokey Oakey (IRE) *M H Tompkins* a76 113
4 b g Tendulkar(USA) —Veronica (Persian Bold)
(960) 1422[6] (2543) 4855[6] 5893[6] 7145[11]

Smokey Ryder *G L Moore* a77 71
2 ch f Bertolini(USA) —Another Secret (Efisio)
4786[7] 5214[3] (5530) 6118[8] *6469*[9] 6666[10] *(7065)* *(7537)* *(7673)*

Smokey Rye *G L Moore* a83 78
3 b f Bertolini(USA) —Another Secret (Efisio)
136[2] *178*[2] ◆ 3744[6] *4082*[8] 4312[5] *5052*[4] *5607*[3] *(6771)* *7302*[7] *(7801)*

Smokey Storm *W Jarvis* 92
2 br c One Cool Cat(USA) —Marisa (GER) (Desert Sun)
1363[4] ◆ (1640) 1927[2] (2826) 3103[15] 4588[10] 6426[23]

Smokey The Bear *Miss Sheena West* a88 27
6 ch g Fumo Di Londra(IRE) —Noble Soul (Sayf El Arab (USA))
91[2] *125*[3] *331*[3] *(388)* *(512)* *(540)* *626*[6] *678*[12] *7471*[0] 1076[12] 1411[5]

Smokin Beau *N P Littmoden* a74 78
11 b g Cigar—Beau Dada (IRE) (Pine Circle (USA))
187[4] 1582[7] *2710*[5] 4154[11] *7092*[8]

Smokin Joe *J R Best* a82 6
7 b g Cigar—Beau Dada (IRE) (Pine Circle (USA))
26[5] *357*[8] *456*[9] *747*[6] *757*[7] *1256*[6] 2355[15] *3376*[12] *4862*[9] *5915*[12] 6211[6]

Smooth Air (USA) *Bennie F Stutts Jr* a117 111
3 b c Smooth Jazz(USA) —Air France (USA) (French Deputy (USA))
1820a[11] *7001a*[7]

Smooth As Silk (IRE) *C R Egerton* 70
3 b f Danehill Dancer(IRE) —Doula (USA) (Gone West (USA))
1836[5] 2496[2] ◆ 3023[12] *5605*[12]

Smoothie (IRE) *E G Bevan* a50 55
10 gr g Definite Article—Limpopo (Green Desert (USA))
18[6] *197*[8]

Smoothly Does It *R A Fahey* a43 58
7 b g Efisio—Exotic Forest (Dominion)
69[7] *277*[4] 2364[3] 2697[3]

Smooth Operator (GER) *Mario Hofer* 112
2 b g Big Shuffle(USA) —Salzgitter (Salse (USA))
3052a[5] (6713a) (7186a)

Smooth Sovereign (IRE) *M Johnston* a63
3 ch g King's Best(USA) —Mellow Park (IRE) (In The Wings)
610[2] ◆

Smorova (IRE) *F Saggiomo* 87
3 b f Efisio—Shariba (IRE) (Bluebird (USA))
1659a[8] 2231a[8]

Smugglers Bay (IRE) *T D Easterby* 78
4 b g Celtic Swing—Princess Mood (GER) (Muhtarram (USA))
981[4] 1824[6] 6551[11]

Snaefell (IRE) *M Halford* 113
4 gr g Danehill Dancer(IRE) —Sovereign Grace (IRE) (Standaan (FR))
(1103a) (1495a) 2417a[3] 2685a[3] 3247[13] (5130a) 5551a[5] 5922a[4] 6315a[2]

Snake Catcher *M W Easterby* a32 27
3 b g Golden Snake(USA) —Search For Love (FR) (Groom Dancer (USA))
2912[8] *3333*[8] 3796[8] 4738[8] 5077[12] 5565[5]

Snake Hips *B Palling* a55 61
4 b g Golden Snake(USA) —Royal Loft (Homing)
129[3] *282*[6] *322*[10] 3310[9] 6748[6]

Snake Skin *J Gallagher* a63 66
5 ch m Golden Snake(USA) —Silken Dalliance (Rambo Dancer (CAN))
(999) 1127[2] 1697[7] 2071[2] 2354[4] *7183*[7] *7355*[11]

Snark (IRE) *Simon Earle* a82 76
5 b g Cape Cross(IRE) —Agoer (Hadeer)
2153[16] 2335[7] ◆ 2561[10] 4664[12]

Sneak Preview *E S McMahon* 98
2 ch f Monsieur Bond(IRE) —Harryana (Efisio)
3027[3] (3959) 4781[2] 5642[2] 6102[2]

Snoose Goose (USA) *McLean Robertson* 89
3 b c Aptitude(USA) —Elusive (USA) (Elmaamul (USA))
4887a[7]

Snoqualmie Boy *Jane Chapple-Hyam* a97 106
5 b g Montjeu(IRE) —Seattle Ribbon (USA) (Seattle Dancer (USA))
293a[5] 381a[9] 739a[6] *1503*[4] 2465[6] 3684[6] 3974[16]

Snoqualmie Girl (IRE) *D R C Elsworth* 102
2 b f Montjeu(IRE) —Seattle Ribbon (USA) (Seattle Dancer (USA))
3092[4] ◆ 3632[10] 4157[3] (4870) ◆ (5462) 5828[2] 6439[12]

Snow Bay *B Smart* 71
2 ch c Bahamian Bounty—Goodwood Blizzard (Inchinor)
1948[4] 3411[2] (3754)

Snowberry Hill (USA) *Lucinda Featherstone* a64 51
5 b g Woodman(USA) —Class Skipper (USA) (Skip Trial (USA))
(14) *779*[4] 1136[7] *1408*[2] *7385*[13] *(7512)* *7827*[6]

Snow Bounty *J S Moore* a59 21
3 b g Bahamian Bounty—Christmas Rose (Absalom)
413[4] *(501)* *737*[6] *1051*[6] *1203*[5] 1740[8]

Snow Bunting *Jedd O'Keeffe* a59 63
10 ch g Polar Falcon(USA) —Marl (Lycius (USA))
32[3] *115*[5] *255*[6]

Snow Dancer (IRE) *H A McWilliams* a55 72
4 b m Desert Style(IRE) —Bella Vie (IRE) (Sadler's Wells (USA))
1613[10] 2155[7] 2446[7] 2927[5] 3624[6] 4170[3] 4596[2] 4630[5] 5543[8] *7581*[8] *7656*[4]

Snowdrop Princess *W J Haggas* a71 82
3 b f Vettori(IRE) —Princess Louise (Efisio)
416[6] ◆ *(447)* ◆ *2532*[6] 3057[6] 3729[3] (4427) (4572) 5075[3] 6027[11]

Snowed Under *J D Bethell* a79 86
7 gr g Most Welcome—Snowy Mantle (Siberian Express (USA))
1388[4] (1909) 2278[3] 2784[7] 3711[11] (4532) 5370[8] 6203[12]

Snowflight *P T Midgley* a38 69
4 b g Danehill Dancer(IRE) —Sadler's Song (Saddlers' Hall (IRE))
7265[13]

Snow Key (USA) *J E Pease* a78 104
4 bb m Cozzene(USA) —Snowbowl (USA) (Northjet)
2876a[8] 3357a[3]

Snowy Indian *Sir Michael Stoute* a65 74
3 b f Indian Ridge—Snow Princess (IRE) (Ela-Mana-Mou)
3057[12] 4152[5] 4902[3] 5232[9]

Soap Wars *M Halford* a92 83
3 b g Acclamation—Gooseberry Pie (Green Desert (USA))
4004a[12] *7325a*[2]

Soapy Danger *M Johnston* a78 113
5 bb h Danzig(USA) —On A Soapbox (USA) (Mi Cielo (USA))
(1070) 1717[4] 2625[6]

Soba Jones *J Balding* a64 41
11 b g Emperor Jones(USA) —Soba (Most Secret)
64[4] *109*[6] *256*[3] *371*[5] *(528)* *(615)* *(655)* *7615*[12] *7727*[7]

Soccerjackpot (USA) *C G Cox* a67 88
4 b g Mizzen Mast(USA) —Rahbaby (USA) (Rahy (USA))
2210[11] *7556*[10]

Socceroo *S Parr* a48 63
3 b f Choisir(AUS) —Silca Boo (Efisio)
2036[10] 2661[3] 2928[10]

Social Rhythm *A C Whillans* a71 81
4 b m Beat All(USA) —Highly Sociable (Puissance)
90[3] *342*[6] *539*[5] *782*[7] 1015[11] 3079[13] 3366[13] 4215[11] 5538[6] *6951*[9] *7112*[4]

Social Spirit (IRE) *J R Weymes* 50
3 br f Auction House(USA) —Sibilant (Selkirk (USA))
1553[12] *2080*[8]

Society Music (IRE) *M Dods* 79
6 b m Almutawakel—Society Fair (FR) (Always Fair (USA))
1327[7] 1485[9] 1815[8] 2375[4] (2942) 3552[8] 3758[7] 4172[3] 4248[2] 4597[6] 4813[5] 6056[9]

Society's Chairman (CAN) *Roger L Attfield* 109
5 b h Not Impossible(IRE) —Athena's Smile (CAN) (Olympio (USA))
2472a[2] 6504a[12]

Society Venue *Jedd O'Keeffe* 75
3 b g Where Or When(IRE) —Society Rose (Saddlers' Hall (IRE))
1448[3] 2143[2] 2840[11] 3551[5] 4172[8]

Sofia's Star *S Dow* a81 82
3 bb g Lend A Hand—Charolles (Ajdal (USA))
967[6] *1167*[8] *1546*[8] *3376*[9] 4310[5] 5185[3] 5589[4] *6211*[10] (6544) 6867[5] *(7510)* *7724*[2]

Sofinella (IRE) *A W Carroll* a61 66
5 gr m Titus Livius(FR) —Mystical Jumbo (Mystiko (USA))
1378[10] 2088[3] 3695[10] 6204[4] 6418[11] *6658*[12]

Sofonisba *M L W Bell* a29 55
2 b f Rock Of Gibraltar(IRE) —Lothlorien (USA) (Woodman (USA))
6029[8] 7051[6] *7207*[7]

Soft Morning *Sir Mark Prescott* a107 107
4 b m Pivotal—Summer Night (Nashwan (USA))
3885[3] 4395[2] 4623[7] 6298a[3] *7235a*[11]

Soft Shoe Shuffle (IRE) *W R Swinburn* a96 93
3 ch f Danehill Dancer(IRE) —Why So Silent (Mill Reef (USA))
1964[5] 2560[2] ◆ (3061) 3742[9] (4906) 6128[3] *6467*[2]

Soggy Dollar *M H Tompkins* a68 71
3 ch g Bahamian Bounty—Ninia (USA) (Affirmed (USA))
2885[6] *3484*[3] 5362[9] *6741*[9] *6908*[6]

Sohcahtoa (IRE) *R Hannon* 96
2 b c Val Royal(FR) —Stroke Of Six (IRE) (Woodborough (USA))
2150[5] (2796) (4589) 5462[4] 5898[4] 6474[9]

Sohraab *H Morrison* a77 104
4 b g Erhaab(USA) —Riverine (Risk Me (FR))
(3009) 3680[7] (4201) 4445[15] 4624[25] 5509[10]

Soinlovewithyou (USA) *A P O'Brien* 82
3 b f Sadler's Wells(USA) —Love Me True (USA) (Kingmambo (USA))
1847a[11] 2433a[13]

Sokar (FR) *J Boisnard* 100
2 gr c Slickly(FR) —Mia Stella (FR) (Courtroom (FR))
(5300a) 6642a[5]

Sokoke *D A Nolan* a2 73
7 ch g Compton Place—Sally Green (IRE) (Common Grounds)
1309[12] 2283[9] 3212[11] 3581[9] 3953[7] 4632[7] 5220[8]

Solapur (GER) *A Wohler* 99
3 ch c Ekraar(USA) —Shina (GER) (Lomitas)
3773a[9]

Solar Dance (USA) *J H M Gosden* 77
3 b f Kingmambo(USA) —Solar Colony (USA) (Pleasant Colony (USA))
2973[3] 3350[2] 4871[9]

Solar Graphite (IRE) *J L Dunlop* 60
2 b g Rock Of Gibraltar(IRE) —Solar Crystal (IRE) (Alzao (USA))
4360[6] 5021[9] 6083[6]

Solaria (IRE) *E J O'Neill* a50
3 ch f Desert Prince(IRE) —Radiant Energy (IRE) (Spectrum (IRE))
424[2] *704*[7]

Solar Max (IRE) *C R Egerton* 59
3 b g Galileo(IRE) —Vanishing River (USA) (Southern Halo (USA))
2191[11] 3637[7] 4124[6]

Solar Spirit (IRE) *G A Swinbank* 86
3 b g Invincible Spirit(IRE) —Misaayef (USA) (Swain (IRE))
(1519) 2189[4] 3228[3] 3723[7] 4158[3] 4416[10] 4900[3]

Solas Alainn (IRE) *J R Fanshawe* 67
3 b g Fantastic Light(USA) —Littlepacepaddocks (IRE) (Accordion)
1477[5] 2046[5] 2668[7] *4057*[P]

Solas Na Greine (IRE) *J S Bolger* a95 89
3 b f Galileo(IRE) —Key To Coolcullen (IRE) (Royal Academy (USA))
1509a[7] 6689a[4] *7328a*[4]

Soldier Field *J S Wainwright* a61 50
4 b g Fantastic Light(USA) —Khambani (IRE) (Royal Academy (USA))
80[4] *209*[9] 2537[4]

Soldier Of Fortune (IRE) *A P O'Brien* 127
4 b h Galileo(IRE) —Affianced (IRE) (Erins Isle)
(2791) 3542a[2] 6522a[3] 7000a[4]

Soldier Soldier *J R Jenkins*
2 ch c Tobougg(IRE) —Bijan (IRE) (Mukaddamah (USA))
7106[13]

Soldiers Quest *P D Evans* a58 85
4 b g Rainbow Quest(USA) —Janaat (Kris)
1369[8] *2832*[4] *3036*[9] *3328*[6] *3482*[3] 4023[5] *4635*[13] 5148[2] *6824*[8] (Dead)

Soledad (GER) *U Stech* 81
3 b f Auenadler(GER) —Sweety (GER) (Sir Felix (FR))
2065a[8]

Soledad (IRE) *G Cherel* 103
8 b g Priolo(USA) —True (FR) (Common Grounds)
1663a[10]

Solemn *J M Bradley* a65 61
4 b g Pivotal—Pious (Bishop Of Cashel)
1311[8] 1699[4] 2991[12] 3441[10] *3819*[14] 3960[13] *5421*[12] 6192[7] *7049*[9] *7528*[6]

Solent (IRE) *J J Quinn* a96 108
6 b g Montjeu(IRE) —Stylish (Anshan)
3721[14] 3975[9] 5494[9]

Solent Ridge (IRE) *J S Moore* a91 92
3 b g Namid—Carrozzina (Vettori (IRE))
1213[6] 2066a[7] 2825[9] 3155[11] 3897[6] 5580[10] *6900*[12]

Solicitude *D Haydn Jones* a65 9
5 ch m Bertolini(USA) —Sibilant (Selkirk (USA))
42[2] ◆ *234*[3] *(375)* *571*[4] *1209*[7] *1260*[7] 2917[13] *6821*[8] *7316*[3] *7383*[2] 7533[3]

Solid Silver *K G Reveley* 61
7 gr g Pharly(FR) —Shadows Of Silver (Carwhite)
6583[7] 7174[9]

Solis *J J Quinn* 47
2 b g Josr Algarhoud(IRE) —Passiflora (Night Shift (USA))
6230[8] 7082[6]

Solis (GER) *P Monteith* 71
5 ch g In The Wings—Seringa (GER) (Acatenango (GER))
1308[8] 5418[6] 6162[3] 7224[9]

Solitary *H Candy* 72
2 b f Lahib(USA) —Bond Solitaire (Atraf)
3348[4] 4149[5] 5147[2]

Solo Act (IRE) *R A Fahey* 64
2 b f One Cool Cat(USA) —Vermillian (IRE) (Mujadil (USA))
4045[4]

Solo Attempt *M Botti* a73 83
2 b f Anabaa(USA) —Sonja's Faith (IRE) (Sharp Victor (USA))
2502[2] *(2944)* (4072) 4348[5] *5711*[5]

Solo Choice *D Flood* a60
2 b g Needwood Blade—Top Of The Class (IRE) (Rudimentary (USA))
7720[5] *7773*[3]

Solo Performer (IRE) *H Rogers* a64 50
3 ch g Distant Music(USA) —Royal Pagent (IRE) (Balinger)
4715a[11]

Solo River *P J Makin* a57 67
3 b f Averti(IRE) —Surakarta (Bin Ajwaad (IRE))
1271[6] *1672*[6] *2260*[3] *2833*[4] *3569*[6] 4054[3] 4326[2] (4810) 5602[10]

Sol Rojo *J Pearce* a71 71
6 b g Efisio—Shining Cloud (Indian Ridge)
21[5] *525*[6] *(921)* 1521[6] 1963[12] 2185[6] *2715*[9] (Dead)

Somerset Falls (UAE) *M Johnston* a53 69
3 b f Red Ransom(USA) —Dunnes River (USA) (Danzig (USA))
4379[4] 6114[2] *6452*[7] *7359*[8]

Something (IRE) *D Nicholls* a108 112
6 b g Trans Island—Persian Polly (Persian Bold)
291a[7] 2390[3] 2580[9] 3248[21] 3943[9] 4417[7] 4624[22] 5990[4]

Something Perfect (USA) *H R A Cecil* a77 72
2 b f Perfect Soul(IRE) —Lady Angharad (IRE) (Tenby)
(6016) *6466*[3] 6946[10]

Something Stupid (GER) *Mario Hofer* 79
3 b g Big Shuffle(USA) —Salzgitter (Salse (USA))
1850a[5]

Some Time Good (IRE) *M R Channon* 65
2 bg g Clodovil(IRE) —El Alma (IRE) (Goldmark (USA))
5578[7] 6199[5]

Sommersturm (GER) *A P Stringer* a80 103
4 b g Tiger Hill(IRE) —Sommernacht (GER) (Monsun (GER))
3540a[9] *7704*[6]

Sommertag (GER) *J Hirschberger* 115
5 b h Tiger Hill(IRE) —Sommernacht (GER) (Monsun (GER))
3542a[8] 5557a[5] (6992a)

Somnus *J J Quinn* 102
8 b g Pivotal—Midnight's Reward (Night Shift (USA))
4617[4] ◆ 5893[8] 6783[17]

Som Tala *M R Channon* a94 101
5 ch g Fantastic Light(USA) —One Of The Family (Alzao (USA))
1080[3] 1916[2] 3104[5] 4516[15]

Sonett *A J McCabe* a39 55
2 b f Primo Valentino(IRE) —Signs And Wonders (Danehill (USA))
2479[11] 2821[8] 3292[11] *5473*[5] 6009[12]

Soneva (USA) *Y De Nicolay* 101
2 b f Cherokee Run(USA) —Lakabi (USA) (Nureyev (USA))
(5987a)

Songmaster (USA) *A King* a68 63
5 b g Singspiel(IRE) —One Beautiful Lady (USA) (Broad Brush (USA))
727[4] 1172[5] 1929[5] 2567[9] 3084[4] 3448[4] 4105[10]

Song Of Hiawatha *A P O'Brien* 110
4 b h Sadler's Wells(USA) —Sabria (USA) (Miswaki (USA))
2791[11] 3542a[9]

Song Of Praise *M Blanshard* a61 61
2 b f Compton Place—Greensand (Green Desert (USA))
2306[8] *2944*[7] 3417[4] 4119[4] 4706[8] 5116[2] 5647[6] 6023[7] 6865[14] *(7472)* *7833*[2]

Song Of Victory (GER) *M Weiss* 64
4 b h Silvano(GER) —Song Of Hope (GER) (Monsun (GER))
422a[3]

Sonhador *G Prodromou* a68 70
2 b c Compton Place—Fayre Holly (IRE) (Fayruz)
1736[3] 1955[6] 3341[2] 4101[3] 4768[10] 6023[9] 6863[4] *7191*[7] *7388*[2] *7537*[2] *7640*[7]

Sonnengold (GER) *B J Llewellyn* 59
7 bb m Java Gold(USA) —Standing Ovation (ITY) (Law Society (USA))
2776[5] 3606[3] 3901[4] (4366) 5613[11]

Sonning Gate *D R C Elsworth* a87 72
2 b g Desert Sun—Sunley Scent (Wolfhound (USA))
6977[5] ◆ *(7434)* ◆ *(7739)*

Sonny Parkin *J Pearce* a77 83
6 b g Spinning World(USA) —No Miss Kris (USA) (Capote (USA))
1349[5] 2373[6] *2943*[4] 3218[3] (3457) 4162[11] 4422[4] 4603[4] 4829[5] 5069[4] 5759[7] 6130[9] 6446[4]

Sonny Red (IRE) *R Hannon* 112
4 b g Redback—Magic Melody (Petong)
959[2] (1157) 1420[4] 2106[17] 2680[8] 5275[12] 5899[6] 6073[13]

Sonny Sam (IRE) *M H Tompkins* a58 64
3 b g Black Sam Bellamy(IRE) —Purple Risks (FR) (Take Risks (FR))
1059[7] 2468[3] 2985[6] 4247[11] *5833*[12]

Son Of My Heart (USA) *P F I Cole* a65
3 bb c Dynaformer(USA) —Sophie My Love (USA) (Danzig (USA))
7690[U] 7721[3]

Son Of Samson (IRE) *R J Price*
7 ch g Diesis—Delilah (IRE) (Bluebird (USA))
144[9] 396[P]

Son Of The Cat (USA) *B Gubby* a90 83
2 b c Tale Of The Cat(USA) —Dixieland Gal (USA) (Dixieland Band (USA))
6000[4] (6677) 7024[2] 7334[2]

Sonoma (IRE) *B G Powell* a45 44
8 ch m Dr Devious(IRE) —Mazarine Blue (USA) (Chief's Crown (USA))
166[5] 283[10]

Soomar *T G Mills* a54
3 gr g Act One—Bint Shihama (USA) (Cadeaux Genereux)
2291[9]

Soopacal (IRE) *B Smart* a92 82
3 b g Captain Rio—Fiddes (IRE) (Alzao (USA))
(470) 1075[2] 1597[9] 1999[4] 7365[8] 7614[5]

Sophia Gardens *D W P Arbuthnot* a78 81
4 ch m Barathea(IRE) —Lovely Lyca (Night Shift (USA))
(173) (351) 431[2]

Sophie's Girl *C A Dwyer* a84 93
3 b f Bahamian Bounty—Merry Rous (Rousillon (USA))
1718[6] 2410[8] 3460[2] 3850[18] 4312[6] 5403[6] 6169[4]

Sopran Promo (IRE) *B Grizzetti* a108 108
4 b h Montjeu(IRE) —Middle Prospect (USA) (Mr Prospector (USA))
2230a[6] 2656a[6] 3075a[7] 6325a[7] 7262a[4]

Sorbiesharry (IRE) *Mrs N Macauley* a51 19
9 gr g Sorbie Tower(IRE) —Silver Moon (Environment Friend)
77[5] 160[2] 400[7] 1031[8] 1262[13] 1505[6]

Sorrel Point *H J Collingridge* a60 51
5 b h Bertolini(USA) —Lightning Princess (Puissance)
517[8] 3162[12] 3842[9] 4284[11]

Sorrel Ridge (IRE) *M G Quinlan* a43 43
2 ch g Namid—She Legged It (IRE) (Cape Cross (IRE))
1276[3] 2362[9] 5628[8] 6191[3] 6579[10] 7319[7] 7788[5]

Sorrento Moon (IRE) *G M Moore* a27 56
4 b m Tagula(IRE) —Honey For Money (IRE) (Alzao (USA))
4901[3] (5380) 6185[5]

Sortita (GER) *M A Jarvis* a61 95
3 b f Monsun(GER) —Sacarina (Old Vic)
1931[3] ◆ (4620) 5682[11] (6196)

So Serene *Charles O'Brien* a70 69
3 b f Danetime(IRE) —Kallavesi (USA) (Woodman (USA))
6511a[10]

Sosostris Pitch (FR) *P C Haslam* a49 47
3 b g Pivotal—Sonja's Faith (IRE) (Sharp Victor (USA))
1519[6] 2673[7] 3818[4] 5074[14]

So Sublime *M C Chapman* a69 45
3 b g Bertolini(USA) —Petalite (Petong)
(257) 1448[12] 1548[12] 1870[8] 2208[9] 2552[14] 3690[7] 4901[7] 7270[8] 7532[6] 7619[14] 7776[10]

Sotik Star (IRE) *K A Morgan* a75 79
5 b g Elnadim(USA) —Crystal Springs (IRE) (Kahyasi)
2406[6] 2897[2] ◆ 3915[6] 4428[2] 4789[5] (5492) 6250[7] 7821[6]

Soto *M W Easterby* a34 72
5 b g Averti(IRE) —Belle Of The Blues (IRE) (Blues Traveller (IRE))
1189[8] 1485[2] ◆ 1703[8] 2780[3] 3591[7] 4047[2] 4246[6] 4609[2] 4967[2] 5775[5] 6219[5]

Sottone *B Grizzetti* 99
2 b c Observatory(USA) —Scundes (IRE) (Barathea (IRE))
7253a[6]

Souffleur *P Bowen* 86
5 b g In The Wings—Salinova (FR) (Linamix (FR))
981[2] 5992[4] 6288[10] 6817[18]

Soul Blazer (USA) *Miss Gay Kelleway* a67 8
5 b g Honour And Glory(USA) —See You (USA) (Gulch (USA))
703[5]

Soul City (IRE) *R Hannon* 110
2 b c Elusive City(USA) —Savage (IRE) (Polish Patriot (USA))
2893[4] (3853) 4517[4] (5139a) (5739a) (6317a) 6815[10]

Soul Sista (IRE) *J L Spearing* 77
2 b f City On A Hill(USA) —Fraamtastic (Fraam)
1276[2] (1392) 2507[4] 3677[5] (3967) 4706[3] 4908[5]

Soum (GER) *A Fabre* 97
3 b c Monsun(GER) —Suivi (GER) (Darshaan)
3773a[8]

Soundbyte *J Gallagher* a73 79
3 b g Beat All(USA) —Gloaming (Celtic Swing)
1994[8] 2611[3] 3482[2] 4026[7] (4811) (5169) 6379[2] 6948[2] ◆

Sound Of Nature (USA) *H R A Cecil* 99
5 b h Chester House(USA) —Yashmak (USA) (Danzig (USA))
1469[17] 1828[7]

Sounds Of Jupiter (IRE) *E F Vaughan* a63
2 ch c Galileo(IRE) —Sena Desert (Green Desert (USA))
7709[9] 7812[3]

Sourire *Sir Mark Prescott* a95 90
3 b f Domedriver(IRE) —Summer Night (Nashwan (USA))
3849[4] (4917a) 7099[7] 7242[7]

Souter Point (USA) *R Charlton* 80
2 bb c Giant's Causeway(USA) —Wires Crossed (USA) (Caller I.D. (USA))
5468[2] ◆ 6075[5]

Souter's Sister (IRE) *R Hannon* 106
2 b f Desert Style(IRE) —Hemaca (Distinctly North (USA))
1680[7] 1955[2] 2618[3] 2759[2] (3341) 4190[19] (4640) 5266[5] 5642[4] (6439) 6818[3]

Southandwest (IRE) *J S Moore* a87 94
4 ch g Titus Livius(FR) —Cheviot Indian (IRE) (Indian Ridge)
1300[10] 1985[6] (2158) 3222[6] 3898[9] 4407[18] 5030[6] 5470[10] 6035[6] 6346[15] 6734[4] 7077[2] 7641[3] (7837)

South Cape *M R Channon* a94 97
5 b g Cape Cross(IRE) —Aunt Ruby (USA) (Rubiano (USA))
1469[10] 1982[11] 3197[6] 3899[4] 4405[5] 4661[2] 4869[10] 5446[5] (5897) 6269[10] 6576[5] 7101[6]

South Central (USA) *J Howard Johnson* 107
2 bb c Forest Camp(USA) —Brittan Lee (USA) (Forty Niner (USA))
(2657) ◆ (3152)

Southern Mistral *M Wigham* a69 59
3 b g Desert Prince(IRE) —Hyperspectra (Rainbow Quest (USA))
2161[17] 5378[14] 5803[3] 6049[10] 6685[11] 7010[13] 7310[5]

Southern Scarlet *Miss J A Camacho*
2 b f Red Ransom(USA) —Dixie Favor (USA) (Dixieland Band (USA))
2845[10]

Southoffrance (IRE) *W G M Turner* a42 27
2 b f Dr Fong(USA) —Mystery Solved (USA) (Royal Academy (USA))
3558[8] 4387[6]

South O'The Border *Miss Venetia Williams* a79 74
6 b g Wolfhound(USA) —Abbey's Gal (Efisio)
2304[10]

Southpaw Lad *J R Best* a72 85
3 b c Diktat—Ashantiana (Ashkalani (IRE))
3221[4] (4621)

South Wales *R W Price* a71 68
3 b g Sakhee(USA) —Santorini (USA) (Spinning World (USA))
52[9] 311[8] 705[10] 2552[2] 2915[2] 3655[3] (3763) (5458) 5712[4]

Southwark Newsboy (IRE) *Mrs C A Dunnett* a1 19
3 b g Chevalier(IRE) —Canoe Cove (IRE) (Grand Lodge (USA))
1194[6] 1454[9] 3118[9] 4066[8]

Southwest Star (IRE) *J S Moore* a74 60
3 b g No Excuse Needed—Christeningpresent (IRE) (Cadeaux Genereux)
(355) 419[4] (629) 924[4] 967[7] 1336[8] 1958[12] 2721[4]

Sovereign's Honour (USA) *Sir Michael Stoute* 95
3 ch f Kingmambo(USA) —Chiming (IRE) (Danehill (USA))
1599[4] 2105[5] 3153[7] 5231[3]

Sovereign Spirit (IRE) *C Gordon* a69 64
6 b g Desert Prince(IRE) —Sheer Spirit (IRE) (Caerleon (USA))
14[5] 657[13] 757[14]

Sovereignty (JPN) *D K Ivory* a73 73
6 b g King's Best(USA) —Calando (USA) (Storm Cat (USA))
151[5] (232) (327) 446[7] 576[6] 755[3] ◆ 819[3] 1085[3] 1491[2] 1605[8] 1842[4] 2337[2] 2758[11] (4084) 4696[4] 5345[13] 5629[8] 6132[6] 6631[9] 7013[8] 7090[8]

Soviet (IRE) *M Johnston* 72
3 b c Danehill Dancer(IRE) —Miss Sacha (IRE) (Last Tycoon)
2360[12] 2955[5] 3629[6] 4018[10] 4532[2] 4829[4]

Soviet Cat (IRE) *D W P Arbuthnot* 40
3 b g Soviet Star(USA) —Forest Kitten (IRE) (Marju (IRE))
3419[DSQ] 5268[5]

Soviet Palace (IRE) *K A Ryan* a81 86
4 b g Jade Robbery(USA) —Daisy Hill (Indian Ridge)
43[4] 190[6] 245[6] 783[5] 807[6]

Soviet Rhythm *G M Moore* 65
2 b f Soviet Star(USA) —Aldevonie (Green Desert (USA))
3865[5] 4202[5] ◆ 4923[7] 6230[4] 6547[8]

Soviet Sceptre (IRE) *Tim Vaughan* a54 62
7 ch g Soviet Star(USA) —Princess Sceptre (Cadeaux Genereux)
(3606) 4275[9] 4704[3] 5802[8] 6668[11]

Sovietta (IRE) *Ian Williams* a56 60
7 b m Soviet Star(USA) —La Riveraine (USA) (Riverman (USA))
438[11] 461[3] 754[4] (930) 2051[3] 2643[8] 3698[11]

Soviet Trooper (IRE) *Liam McAteer* a36 58
4 ch g Soviet Star(USA) —Akarita (IRE) (Akarad (FR))
7532[11]

Sovine (IRE) *Michael G Holden* a78 71
3 b f Xaar—Elemental (Rudimentary (USA))
(364)

So Will I *Doug Watson* a61 109
7 ch g Inchinor—Fur Will Fly (Petong)
(472a)

Soxy Doxy (IRE) *M Johnston* a51 48
3 ch f Hawk Wing(USA) —Feather Bride (IRE) (Groom Dancer (USA))
158[5] 758[3] 1163[7] 1553[7] 1950[6]

Spabreaksdotcom (IRE) *J S Wainwright*
3 b f Desert Prince(IRE) —Adirika (IRE) (Miswaki (USA))
2786[15] 3403[5] 3791[6]

Space Pirate *J Pearce* a52 62
3 b c Bahamian Bounty—Science Fiction (Starborough)
464[4] 3183[9] 3656[8] 4049[3] 4810[9] (5167) 5815[9] 6049[6] 6492[9] 7590[7] 7688[12]

Spacious *J R Fanshawe* 112
3 b f Nayef(USA) —Palatial (Green Desert (USA))
1830[2] 3194[4] (5856) 6475[4] 6781[4]

Spanish Ace *J M Bradley* a47 93
7 b g First Trump—Spanish Heart (King Of Spain)
1537[7] 2356[10] 3024[5] 3062[10] 3352[12] 3520[7] 6190[10] 6208[7] 7195[7] 7765[11]

Spanish Baron (USA) *R M H Cowell* a83 77
2 b c Dixieland Band(USA) —Spanish Harbor (USA) (Corporate Report (USA))
4027[5] 4598[2] (5089) 6739[2]

Spanish Bounty *J G Portman* a73 98
3 b g Bahamian Bounty—Spanish Gold (Vettori (IRE))
1404[15] 2162[2] 2967[3] (3850) 4842[4] 6239[18]

Spanish Conquest *Sir Mark Prescott* a75 62
4 b g Hernando(FR) —Sirena (GER) (Tejano (USA))
2252[3] 2707[12] (3820) 4391[2] 6838[4]

Spanish Cross (IRE) *D K Weld* 61
3 gr f Cape Cross(IRE) —Espana (Hernando (FR))
1847a[10] 4613a[6]

Spanish Cruise (IRE) *Andrew Turnell* a59 66
4 gr g Daylami(IRE) —Baldemara (FR) (Sanglamore (USA))
919[4] 1621[4] 2291[13]

Spanish Cygnet (USA) *Mrs A J Perrett* a81 85
2 b f El Corredor(USA) —Dixie Dos (USA) (Dixieland Band (USA))
3207[2] (4080) 4348[4] 5615[3]

Spanish Diva *S C Williams* a64 81
4 b m Singspiel(IRE) —Allespagne (USA) (Trempolino (USA))
919[2] 1205[4] 3220[7] 3507[4] 4481[2] 4691[2] 4721[5] 5450[10] 6491[4] 6629[8] 7096[6]

Spanish Don *D R C Elsworth* a83 82
10 b g Zafonic(USA) —Spanish Wells (IRE) (Sadler's Wells (USA))
3457[12] 4162[13]

Spanish Hidalgo (IRE) *J L Dunlop* 111
4 b h Night Shift(USA) —Spanish Lady (IRE) (Bering)
1158[3] 2192[3] 4496a[3] 7017[2] 7429a[0]

Spanish Moon (USA) *Sir Michael Stoute* a117 118
4 b h El Prado(IRE) —Shining Bright (Rainbow Quest (USA))
(1980) 3246[6] 4192[6] 4855[3] (5288) 6074[2] (7193)

Spares And Repairs *Mrs S Lamyman* a67 48
5 b g Robellino(USA) —Lady Blackfoot (Prince Tenderfoot (USA))
107[3] 283[7]

Sparkaway *W J Musson* a31 53
2 ch g Gold Away(IRE) —West River (USA) (Gone West (USA))
4421[8] 5066[8] 6031[10] 7258[13]

Sparkbridge (IRE) *S C Burrough* a42 56
5 b g Mull Of Kintyre(USA) —Persian Velvet (IRE) (Distinctly North (USA))
751[3]

Sparkling Crystal (IRE) *B W Hills* a71 71
2 ch f Danehill Dancer(IRE) —Crystal Curling (IRE) (Peintre Celebre (USA))
2769[2] ◆ 3373[4] 4109[3] 4666[4] 5153[6] 5671[2] 6362[5]

Sparkling Montjeu (IRE) *George Baker* a57 64
3 b f Montjeu(IRE) —Dart Board (IRE) (Darshaan)
1622[12] 2340[12] 3362[4] 3781[4] 4224[8] 5320[3] 6447[8] 6719[7] (6747) 7322[3] 7688[4]

Sparkling Silver *T J Pitt* a23
3 gr f Silver Patriarch(IRE) —Full English (Perugino (USA))
7344[13]

Sparkling Suzie *R Hannon* a62 8
2 b f Deportivo—Sparkling Jewel (Bijou D'Inde)
3085[9] 3837[5]

Sparks Alive *D R C Elsworth* a27 28
2 b f Indian Haven—Sarah-Clare (Reach)
6434[8] 6885[14] 7769[8]

Sparkwell *D Shaw* a69 37
6 b g Dansili—West Devon (USA) (Gone West (USA))
230[5] 304[3]

Sparky Vixen *C J Teague* a56 56
4 b m Mujahid(USA) —Lucy Glitters (USA) (Cryptoclearance (USA))
478[3] (550) 640[10] 872[4] 978[4] 1116[6] 1262[3] 1606[4] 1776[3] 2003[5] 2446[8] 2870[10]

Spartan Dance *J A Geake* a65 61
4 ch g Groom Dancer(USA) —Delphic Way (Warning)
5087[14]

Spartan Prince (USA) *T D Barron* a45
2 b c Mr Greeley(USA) —Yalta (USA) (Private Terms (USA))
7649[5]

Sparta Rebel (IRE) *M J Wallace* 70
2 b f Spartacus(IRE) —Safkana (IRE) (Doyoun)
2206[3] 2638[4] 3032[4]

Sparton Duke (IRE) *K A Ryan* a83 84
3 b g Xaar—Blueberry Walk (Green Desert (USA))
(146) 489[3] 1934[2] ◆ 2575[4] 2967[4] 3838[4] 4416[4] 4900[2] 5403[3] 6278[8] 6627[7]

Spate River *C F Wall* a79 85
3 b g Zaha(CAN) —Rion River (IRE) (Taufan (USA))
2056[7] 5049[3] (5713) ◆ 6177[2] (6417) ◆ 6663[7]

Spa Wells (IRE) *Barry Potts* a41 49
7 ch g Pasternak—La Tache (Namaqualand (USA))
822[8]

Speagle (IRE) *D Shaw* a85 75
6 ch g Desert Sun—Pohutakawa (FR) (Affirmed (USA))
128[7] 323[5] 602[2] (720) 802[6] 863[12]

Speak Freely *C Smith*
2 b f Domedriver(IRE) —Miss Tolerance (USA) (Mt. Livermore (USA))
7148[12]

Speak The Truth (IRE) *J R Boyle* a61 56
2 br g Statue Of Liberty(USA) —Brave Truth (IRE) (Brief Truce (USA))
2049[8] 2324[15] 2502[4] 3846[5] 4101[5] 7542[7]

Spear Thistle *Mrs N Smith* a87 17
6 ch g Selkirk(USA) —Ardisia (USA) (Affirmed (USA))
4791[9]

Special Adviser *T J Etherington* a52
2 b g Dr Fong(USA) —Dimakya (USA) (Dayjur (USA))
7402[10]

Special Bond *J A Osborne* a70 57
2 b f Monsieur Bond(IRE) —Fizzy Treat (Efisio)
6622[4] 6945[9] 7318[4] 7622[3] 7824[6]

Special Branch Ami (IRE) *C R Egerton* a57 72
3 ch g Galileo(IRE) —Helena's Paris (IRE) (Peintre Celebre (USA))
3310[3]

Special Chapter (IRE) *A B Haynes* a18
3 b f Acclamation—Literary (Woodman (USA))
7436[8]

Special Cuvee *Sir Mark Prescott* a78 56
2 b c Diktat—Iris May (Brief Truce (USA))
2663[5] 3392[2] (3689) 4525[6]

Special Day *B W Hills* 97
4 b m Fasliyev(USA) —Mustique Dream (Don't Forget Me)
1300[12] 1809[10] 2129[5] 2626[9] 3451[15] 4555[7] 5247[5]

Special Feature (IRE) *C R Egerton* a43 52
3 b g Montjeu(IRE) —Starring Role (IRE) (Glenstal (USA))
2475[8] 2694[6] 3666[9]

Special Pearl (IRE) *E J O'Neill* a72 66
4 b m Alhaarth(IRE) —Royals Special (IRE) (Caerleon (USA))
7642[3] 7715[2] 7827[10]

Special Reserve (IRE) *R Hannon* a74 83
3 b c Sadler's Wells(USA) —Ionian Sea (Slip Anchor)
1059[3] 1330[2] 1840[2] 2191[2] 2825[7] 3521[2] 3915[3] 4249[2] 5463[4] 6345[2] 6949[4] 7474[4]

Spectagula (IRE) *Thomas Cleary* 33
2 b f Tagula(IRE) —Inspectors Choice (IRE) (Spectrum (IRE))
6320a[26]

Spectait *Jonjo O'Neill* a82 75
6 b g Spectrum(IRE) —Shanghai Girl (Distant Relative)
6123[9] 6536[10] 7019[12] 7386[4] ◆ 7633[5]

Spectra (IRE) *M Rulec* 95
4 b m Spectrum(IRE) —Suenna (GER) (Lando (GER))
3751a[8]

Spectrana *Mrs A J Perrett* a55 60
3 b f Spectrum(IRE) —Anapola (GER) (Polish Precedent (USA))
1540[6] 2931[4] 3322[14] 3690[9]

Speed Dating *Sir Mark Prescott* a54 44
2 ch c Pivotal—Courting (Pursuit Of Love)
6213[7] 6383[8] 6620[12]

Speed Dial Harry (IRE) *C R Dore* a81 11
6 b g General Monash(USA) —Jacobina (Magic Ring (IRE))
68[4] 80[6] 323[6] 438[5] 602[6]

Speed Dream (IRE) *David Wachman* a67 101
4 ch h Pivotal—Copper Creek (Habitat)
4004a[14]

Speed Gifted *L M Cumani* 114
4 b h Montjeu(IRE) —Good Standing (USA) (Distant View (USA))
2797[3] ◆ 3246[4] 4041a[5] 5494[8] 6444[3]

Speed Skater (FR) *N Clement* a78 49
3 gr c Verglas(IRE) —Nidorina (IRE) (Persian Bold)
549a[7]

Speed Song *W J Haggas* 91
3 b f Fasliyev(USA) —Superstar Leo (IRE) (College Chapel)
(4127) ◆ 4347[2]

Speed Ticket *L M Cumani* a67 82
4 b h Galileo(IRE) —Kassiyra (IRE) (Kendor (FR))
(3094)

Speedy Cleaners (IRE) *R Hannon* a73
2 b f King Charlemagne(USA) —Miss Serendipity (IRE) (Key Of Luck (USA))
5571[2] 6167[2]

Speedy Dollar (USA) *M A Jarvis* a86 100
3 b g Dixie Union(USA) —Kelli's Ransom (USA) (Red Ransom (USA))
1333[6] 1806[8] 2819[12] (6005) 6239[12]

Speedy Guru *H Candy* 72
2 b f Ishiguru(USA) —Gowon (Aragon)
5459[9] 5959[3] (6858)

Speedy Sam *K R Burke* a104 97
5 b h Medicean—Warning Star (Warning)
315[4] 502[8] 592[6] 1018[7] 1314[2] 1799[6] 1874[7] (2278) 2499[2] 3046[8] 4191[9] 4627[4]

Speedy Senorita (IRE) *K R Burke* a64 79
3 b f Fayruz—Sinora Wood (IRE) (Shinko Forest (IRE))
1155[5] 1396[13] 1611[6] 2287[2] (2527) (2864) (3217) 3462[2] 5490[7] 6131[4] 6486[16] 6859[12]

Speedy Silver (FR) *H-A Pantall* 95
3 b c Kutub(IRE) —Speedgirl (FR) (Monsun (GER))
5927a[6] 6494a[8]

Spell Caster *R M Beckett* a82 89
3 ch f Bertolini(USA) —Princess Claudia (IRE) (Kahyasi)
2311[6] 2920[5] 3459[5] 4152[2] (4520) 6128[5]

Spellman *N P Littmoden* a50 42
4 ch g Dr Fong(USA) —Justbetweenfriends (USA) (Diesis)
107[5] 610[6] 758[8] 988[13] 1181[7] 1459[11] 2715[7] 3113[5]

Spence Appeal (IRE) *C Roberts* a45 46
6 b g Nicolotte—It's All Academic (IRE) (Mazaad)
2990[7] 3311[6] 4365[14]

Spence's Choice (IRE) *G P Kelly* a46 53
4 b g Desert Sun—Late Night Lady (IRE) (Mujadil (USA))
250[6] (Dead)

Spent *Mouse Hamilton-Fairley* a58 68
3 b g Averti(IRE) —Top (Shirley Heights)
2342[10] 2805[6] 3095[7] 3780[5] (4806) 5167[4] 5816[7] 6088[6] 6396[12]

Speyside (IRE) *J W Hills* a74 62
3 b g Orpen(USA) —Dandaka (Warning)
974[2] 1252[6] 1535[3] 2090[7] 2974[15] 4061[2] 5568[3] 5915[8] 6422[7] 6741[11] 6956[3]

Sphere (IRE) *J R Fanshawe* a46 77
3 b f Daylami(IRE) —Apple Town (Warning)
1014[3] 1814[8] 2716[6] 3624[2] 4751[2] 5651[3] 6596[6]

Sphinx (FR) *E W Tuer* a59 96
10 b g Snurge—Egyptale (Crystal Glitters (USA))
1625[3] 2202[8] 2609[10] 3007[8] 3832[4] 4178[2] 4963[4] 5718[2] (6071) 6527[7] 7223[4]

Spice Gardens (IRE) *W Jarvis* a39 61
4 ch m Indian Ridge—Lime Gardens (Sadler's Wells (USA))
2337[6]

Spice Route *Roger L Attfield* a109 114
4 ch g King's Best(USA) —Zanzibar (IRE) (In The Wings)
1077[3] 1427[2] 1921[3] 2325[3] 6506a[2]

Spice Run *C G Cox* a63 29
5 b g Zafonic(USA) —Palatial (Green Desert (USA))
5278[12] 5995[8]

Spice Trade *J Noseda* a63 73
3 ch c Medicean—Nutmeg (IRE) (Lake Coniston (IRE))
253[4]

Spic 'n Span *R A Harris* a71 66
3 b g Piccolo—Sally Slade (Dowsing (USA))
170[U] 706[4] 965[6] 1255[2] 1529[6] 1897[6] 2099[5] 2240[3] 3346[7] 3608[13] 3782[4] 4028[6] 4324[8] 4725[3] 5141[2] 5749[6] 6707[3] 6907[6] 7444[2] (7527) 7644[7] 7672[5]

Spider Silk *W Jarvis* a58 80
3 b g Lomitas—Silken Brief (IRE) (Ali-Royal (IRE))
2199[10] 3654[5] (4249) 4906[4] 5464[7] 7091[4] 7515[12]

Spiders Star *Miss Kate Milligan* 47
5 br m Cayman Kai(IRE) —Kiss In The Dark (Starry Night (USA))
(4698) 5385[14] 6309[6] 6550[9]

Spin Again (IRE) *R M Beckett* a73 78
3 b g Intikhab(USA) —Queen Of The May (IRE) (Nicolotte)
1036[2] (1311) 2014[6] 2974[7] 4083[3] 4369[2] (4637) 5248[2]

Spin Around (AUS) *S Cooper* 114
8 ch g Spinning World(USA) —Be Yourself (USA) (Noalcoholic (FR))
2234a[7]

Spin Cycle (IRE) *B Smart* 106
2 b c Exceed And Excel(AUS) —Spinamix (Spinning World (USA))
1813[5] ◆ (2140) ◆ (2838) 3152[2] 4507[5] 5226[12] 6644[14]

Spinight (IRE) *M Botti* a65 60
2 b c Spinning World(USA) —Adjtiya (IRE) (Green Desert (USA))
5316[4] 5784[8] 5939[5] 6986[4] 7205[8]

Spinners End (IRE) *K R Burke* 67
2 b c Royal Applause—Needwood Epic (Midyan (USA))
4164[7] 5499[4] 6212[2] 6426[22]

Spinning *T D Barron* a87 87
5 ch g Pivotal—Starring (FR) (Ashkalani (IRE))
992[2] (1450) (3453) ◆ 3972[8] 4876[10] 5390[5] 6482[8] 6841[9] 7127[3] (7278) (7564) 7750[3]

Spinning Belle (IRE) *J W Hills* a63 55
2 ch f Spinning World(USA) —Hishmah (Nashwan (USA))
5048[6] 5535[9] 6080[12] 6697[6] 7205[13] 7652[9]

Spinning Game *Mrs R A Carr* a44 50
4 b m Mind Games—Spindara (IRE) (Spinning World (USA))
46[9] 106[7] 1675[6] 2036[8] 2748[11] 3952[6] 4383[7] 4967[9]

Spinning Joy *J R Boyle* a29
2 b f Josr Algarhoud(IRE) —Den's-Joy (Archway (IRE))
5996[11] 6602[13]

Spinning Lucy (IRE) *B W Hills* 100
3 ch f Spinning World(USA) —Dolara (IRE) (Dolphin Street (FR))
1401[5] 1830[14] 3927[7] 4590[10] 5829[5] 6271[15] 6782[10]

Spinning Ridge (IRE) *R A Harris* a68 61
3 ch c Spinning World(USA) —Summer Style (IRE) (Indian Ridge)
918[11] 1530[3] 1696[10] 7729[5]

Spinning Waters *Eve Johnson Houghton* 60
2 b g Vettori(IRE) —Secret Waters (Pharly (FR))
4776[3] 5468[15] 6198[9]

Spin Sister *J Gallagher* a36
2 b f Umistim—Gloaming (Celtic Swing)
7312[11] 7561[10]

Spira (IRE) *A P O'Brien* 61
2 b f Sadler's Wells(USA) —Spring Flight (USA) (Miswaki (USA))
5132a[9] 6318a[13]

Spiritina (IRE) *Noel Lawlor* a84 55
3 b f Invincible Spirit(IRE) —Clairification (IRE) (Shernazar)
(7586) ◆

Spirito Del Vento (FR) *J-M Beguigne* a97 119
5 b g Indian Lodge(IRE) —Heavenly Song (FR) (Machiavellian (USA))
1108a[3] 1761a[3] (2876a) 3100[7] 4212a[2] 5738a[2] (6498a) 7684a[4]

Spirit Of Adjisa (IRE) *Pat Eddery* a77 83
4 br g Invincible Spirit(IRE) —Adjisa (IRE) (Doyoun)
2369[3] 2764[5] 3802[6] 4662[2] 5370[3] 5773[4] 6203[3] 6551[8] (6898)

Spirit Of A Nation (IRE) *S Parr* 91
3 b c Invincible Spirit(IRE) —Fabulous Pet (Somethingfabulous (USA))
1068[5] 1295[5] (1750) (3442)

Spirit Of Coniston *P T Midgley* a73 73
5 b g Lake Coniston(IRE) —Kigema (IRE) (Case Law)
994[6] 1047[7] 1309[4] 1624[18] 1901[4] 2270[7] 3112[10] 3546[6] 4047[12] 4293[10] (6310) 6546[2] 6840[3] 7218[4] 7517[6]

Spirit Of Dubai (IRE) *D M Simcock* 59
2 b f Cape Cross(IRE) —Questina (FR) (Rainbow Quest (USA))
6392[7] ◆ 6884[7]

Spirit Of Duke (GER) *C Von Der Recke*
2 ch c Bachelor Duke(USA) —See Me Well (IRE) (Common Grounds)
5686a[6]

Spirit Of France (IRE) *D Carroll* 74
6 b g Anabaa(USA) —Les Planches (Tropular)
3928[12] 4460[8]

Spirit Of Sharjah (IRE) *Miss J Feilden* 107
3 b g Invincible Spirit(IRE) —Rathbawn Realm (Doulab (USA))
1400[8] 2404[11] 4617[8] 6239[14] 6971[17]

Spiritofthestorm (USA) *R A Teal* a70 43
3 b f Mizzen Mast(USA) —Southern Issue (USA) (Southern Halo (USA))
1270[5] 1412[6] 1721[7] 3065[13] 3562[9] 5145[7] 5684[4]

Spiritofthewest (IRE) *S Parr* 83
2 b c Invincible Spirit(IRE) —Rosie's Guest (IRE) (Be My Guest (USA))
4647[10] (6010) 6644[15] 6972[7] 7241[15]

Spirit One (FR) *P Demercastel* a116 122
4 b h Anabaa Blue—Lavayssiere (FR) (Sicyos (USA))
(912a) 1240a[2] 1665a[4] 3053a[2] (4889a)

Spiritonthemount (USA) *P W Hiatt* a70 77
3 bb g Pulpit(USA) —Stirling Bridge (USA) (Prized (USA))
1173[2] 2336[5] 3168[4] 3671[2] 6897[7] 7216[7] 7366[10]

Spirit's Awakening *M J Attwater* 22
9 b g Danzig Connection(USA) —Mo Stopher (Sharpo)
5267[13]

Spiritual Art *S A Callaghan* a74 60
2 b f Invincible Spirit(IRE) —Oatey (Master Willie)
5099[4] 5572[8] 6030[13] 6579[2] (7543) ◆ (7645)

Spiritual Bond *R A Harris* a48 20
2 b f Monsieur Bond(IRE) —Country Spirit (Sayf El Arab (USA))
3358[10] 4321[9] 6574[10] 6709[5] 7370[9]

Spiritual Treasure (USA) *M A Magnusson* a74
2 bb c Perfect Soul(IRE) —Storm Runner (USA) (Miswaki (USA))
6731[10] (7023)

Spit And Polish *J L Dunlop* a61 68
2 b g Polish Precedent(USA) —Brooklyn's Sky (Septieme Ciel (USA))
3519[6] 4769[3] 5184[5] 5959[5] 6414[10] 6732[5]

Spitfire *J R Jenkins* a72 101
3 b g Mujahid(USA) —Fresh Fruit Daily (Reprimand)
1328[2] 1834[9] 3047[5] 3850[2] 4842[5] 5102[7] 6005[6]

Spitfire Jane (IRE) *K R Burke* a59
3 br f Xaar—Hope Of Pekan (IRE) (Sri Pekan (USA))
597[2] 820[5]

Splashdown *L M Cumani* a75 96
2 ch f Falbrav(IRE) —Space Time (FR) (Bering)
(6167) 7144[3]

Splash Mountain (IRE) *A Trybuhl* 103
3 br f Peintre Celebre(USA) —Secret Dream (IRE) (Zafonic (USA))
3073a[2] 3705a[8]

Splash The Cash *K A Ryan* a66 70
3 b g Lomitas—Bandit Queen (Desert Prince (IRE))
17[3] 170[6] 629[4] 1306[3] 2366[3] 3298[4] 3564[3] 3825[2] (4118) 4397[7] 7040[2] 7428[11]

Splendidio *A Crook* a50 55
4 b m Zamindar(USA) —Diddymu (IRE) (Revoque (IRE))
2676[16] 3139[15]

Splendorinthegrass (IRE) *R Charlton* 91
2 ch c Selkirk(USA) —Portelet (Night Shift (USA))
6122[7] 6979[5] ◆

Splinter Cell (USA) *M Botti* 82
2 bb c Johannesburg(USA) —Rock Salt (Selkirk (USA))
4296[3] (4780) ◆

Splinter Group *S A Callaghan* a35 56
4 ch g Inchinor—Haiyfoona (Zafonic (USA))
1172[12] 1853[10] 2832[11]

Split The Wind (USA) *Miss Sheena West* a59 61
4 ch m Just A Cat(USA) —Maple Hill Jill (USA) (Executive Pride)
1243[8] 1692[13] 2003[4] 2510[8] 2861[3] 2930[2] 3343[5] 3572[5] 4182[2] 4409[3] 4635[2] (4774) 6019[6] 6728[6] 6768[6] 7217[5] 7792[10]

Spoilt Madame *P D Evans* a34 32
3 b f Bertolini(USA) —Madame Jones (IRE) (Lycius (USA))
5426[12]

Sponge *P R Chamings* a38 53
3 b g Zaha(CAN) —Glensara (Petoski)
3484[8] 4057[4] 5150[5]

Spoof Master (IRE) *C R Dore* a81 81
4 b g Invincible Spirit(IRE) —Talbiya (IRE) (Mujtahid (USA))
4[7] 459[2] 554[2] 726[2] 1033[4] 1242[2] 1386[2] 1901[3] 2710[6] 3374[7] 4025[8] 4958[10] (5401) 5775[2] 6046[7] 6840[11] 7182[11] 7346[6] 7471[6] 7679[5]

Spooky *W Storey* 39
3 br g Vettori(IRE) —Aneen Alkamanja (Last Tycoon)
4077[10] 4901[8] 6111[9]

Sporting Gesture *M W Easterby* 78
11 ch g Safawan—Polly Packer (Reform)
1482[3] 2107[4] 2585[6] 3010[2] 3440[5] 3864[3] 4457[2] 6243[10] 6551[10]

Spotty Muldoon (IRE) *R M Beckett* 77
3 b c Mull Of Kintyre(USA) —Fashion Guide (IRE) (Bluebird (USA))
997[4] 4195[2] (5652)

Spouk *L M Cumani* a76 64
3 b f Pivotal—Souk (IRE) (Ahonoora)
2413[7] ◆ 7344[2] (7474)

Spring Adventure *E A L Dunlop* 76
2 b f Dr Fong(USA) —Yavari (IRE) (Alzao (USA))
6565[3] ◆

Spring Breeze *M Dods* 62
7 ch g Dr Fong(USA) —Trading Aces (Be My Chief (USA))
3545[4] 3863[6] 4652[7]

Spring Buck (IRE) *M Johnston* a76
3 b c Acclamation—Torosay Spring (First Trump)
7074[3]

Spring Charm (IRE) *Irene J Monaghan* a28 65
6 ch m Inchinor—Arabis (Arazi (USA))
(4848)

Spring City (GER) *Saeed Bin Suroor* a88 95
4 ch h Monsun(GER) —Spirit Of Eagles (USA) (Beau's Eagle (USA))
2711[6]

Spring Dream (IRE) *A King* a77 90
5 gr m Kalanisi(IRE) —Zest (USA) (Zilzal (USA))
1697[2] (2241) 2682[2] 2952[2] 3685[2] (3884) 4426[2] 4771[2] 6646[15] (7108)

Springfield Lass *Mrs A Duffield* a7 39
3 b f Compton Place—Mouchez Le Nez (IRE) (Cyrano De Bergerac)
1222[10] 1490[9] 2929[5]

Springfort (IRE) *Tracey Collins* 75
3 ch f Captain Rio—Second Guess (Ela-Mana-Mou)
(5873a)

Spring Goddess (IRE) *A P Jarvis* a83 83
7 b m Daggers Drawn(USA) —Easter Girl (Efisio)
124[4] 969[5] ◆ 6537[3] 6738[8] (6950) 7210[2] 7419[6]

Spring Green *H Morrison*
2 b f Bahamian Bounty—Star Tulip (Night Shift (USA))
4251[16]

Spring House (USA) *Julio C Canani* a104 115
6 bb g Chester House(USA) —Spring Star (BRZ) (Itajara (BRZ))
1091a[10] 7000a[9]

Spring Of Fame (USA) *M A Magnusson* a81 76
2 b c Grand Slam(USA) —Bloomy (USA) (Polish Numbers (USA))
5469[5] ◆ (6000) ◆

Spring Quartet *Pat Eddery* a42 59
2 b g Captain Rio—Alice Blackthorn (Forzando)
2893[14] 3882[7] 4926[5] 5213[8] 6207[11] 7693[5]

Spring Season *H R A Cecil* 27
3 b f Dansili—Midsummer (Kingmambo (USA))
4447[6]

Spring Secret *B Palling* 61
2 b g Reset(AUS) —Miss Brooks (Bishop Of Cashel)
3164[6] 4151[10] 6745[6]

Spring Tale (USA) *M J Wallace* a59 86
2 b f Stravinsky(USA) —Sadler's Profile (USA) (Royal Academy (USA))
1413[4] ◆ 2534[2] (2845) 4190[10] 4434[8] 6102[8]

Spring Touch (USA) *F Head*
3 b f Elusive Quality(USA) —Spring Star (FR) (Danehill (USA))
4674a[9]

Spruzzo *C W Thornton* 25
2 b g Emperor Fountain—Ryewater Dream (Touching Wood (USA))
6858[14] 7172[8]

Spume (IRE) *S Parr* a60 80
4 b g Alhaarth(IRE) —Sea Spray (IRE) (Royal Academy (USA))
2185[9] 2510[9] 3399[3] 5154[4] 5478[11] 5712[5] 6019[5] 6812[10] 7189[12] 7270[6] 7658[7] 7731[7] (7787) 7827[3]

Spy Eye (USA) *Sir Michael Stoute* 74
2 ch f Tale Of The Cat(USA) —Surya (USA) (Unbridled (USA))
(4643)

Spy Gun (USA) *T Wall* a53 51
8 ch g Mt. Livermore(USA) —Takeover Target (USA) (Nodouble (USA))
103[5] 115[4] 284[5] 2988[13] 4683[11]

Squad *Pat Eddery* 61
2 ch g Choisir(AUS) —Widescreen (USA) (Distant View (USA))
4890[7] 5649[4] 6198[10]

Square Dealer *J R Norton* a46 60
7 b g Vettori(IRE) —Pussy Foot (Red Sunset)
283[5] 600[8]

Square Eddie (CAN) *Doug O'Neill* a115 83
2 ch c Smart Strike(CAN) —Forty Gran (USA) (El Gran Senor (USA))
2254[3] ◆ 3103[11] (4274) 5693[2] ◆ (6503a) 6997a[2]

Squiffy *P D Cundell* a62 58
5 br g Kylian(USA) —Cebwob (Rock City)
179[3] 461[2] 600[12]

Squire Boldwood (IRE) *D R C Elsworth* a49 53
3 b g Nayef(USA) —Lanelle (USA) (Trempolino (USA))
1748[11] 2199[16] 2668[11] 3873[11] 4278[6] 5161[11] 5574[9] 6436[12]

Squirtle (IRE) *W M Brisbourne* a70 69
5 ch m In The Wings—Manilia (FR) (Kris)
152[3] (3589) (4029) 4391[6] 4652[2] (4924) 5367[8] 5498[4] 5718[6] 5887[5] 6606[6] 6824[3] 7293[3] 7366[5] 7455[8] 7827[2]

Sr. Henry (USA) *Michael Stidham* 93
3 b g Straight Man(USA) —B T Delite (USA) (Cahill Road (USA))
4887a[9]

Sri Kandi *P F I Cole* a73 74
2 ch f Pivotal—Aunt Pearl (USA) (Seattle Slew (USA))
4643[10] 5570[2] (6013)

Sri Kuantan (IRE) *P F I Cole* a80 27
4 ch g Spinning World(USA) —Miss Asia Quest (Rainbow Quest (USA))
22[2] (134) (316) 406[2] ◆ 504[6] 1904[8] 2200[7]

Sri Putra *M A Jarvis* 105
2 b c Oasis Dream—Wendylina (IRE) (In The Wings)
(2972) ◆ (5507) 6474[8] 6973[8]

Staceys Girl *T P Tate* 38
2 b f Timeless Times(USA) —Lavernock Lady (Don't Forget Me)
4328[11] 5256[10] 5715[14]

Stafford Charlie *J G M O'Shea* a29 32
2 ch c Silver Patriarch(IRE) —Miss Roberto (IRE) (Don Roberto (USA))
6893[10] 7699[13]

Stafford Will (IRE) *J G M O'Shea* 53
4 b g Rossini(USA) —Firstrusseofsummer (USA) (Summer Squall (USA))
4023[7]

Stage Acclaim (IRE) *B R Millman* a69 76
3 b g Acclamation—Open Stage (IRE) (Sadler's Wells (USA))
2678[14] 3183[8] (3845) 4332[4] 4766[4] 5428[9] 5961[11] 6400[5]

Stagecoach Emerald *R W Price* a70 46
6 ch g Spectrum(IRE) —Musician (Shirley Heights)
5154[12] 5833[14]

Stagecoach Topaz (USA) *M Johnston* a59 70
3 b g Stravinsky(USA) —Indian Fashion (USA) (General Holme (USA))
178[7] 416[11]

Stage Gift (IRE) *Saeed Bin Suroor* a82 117
5 ch g Cadeaux Genereux—Stage Struck (IRE) (Sadler's Wells (USA))
3683[4]

Stagnite *D L Williams* a47 47
8 ch g Compton Place—Superspring (Superlative)
3021[14] 3608[16]

Staked A Claim (IRE) *T D Barron* 62
4 ch g Danehill Dancer(IRE) —Twany Angel (Double Form)
1827[4] ◆ (2491) 2936[9] 3454[10] 4018[8] 4540[10]

Stalking Shadow (USA) *Saeed Bin Suroor* a81 91
3 b c Storm Cat(USA) —Strategic Maneuver (USA) (Cryptoclearance (USA))
3796[3] (4378) (4976) 6467[8]

Stalking Tiger (IRE) *R Charlton* a67 72
4 b g King's Best(USA) —Obsessed (Storm Bird (CAN))
1383[11] 5476[5] 6400[12]

Stamford Blue *R A Harris* a46 92
7 b g Bluegrass Prince(IRE) —Fayre Holly (IRE) (Fayruz)
1145[12] 1278[7] 1683[10] 2339[2] 2644[2] 3024[3] 3093[7] 3418[4] 3905[8] 5121[6] 5400[9]

Stamford Street (IRE) *J R Gask* a58
5 ch g Distant Music(USA) —Exemplaire (FR) (Polish Precedent (USA))
1416[2]

Stand Guard *P Howling* a86 58
4 b g Danehill(USA) —Protectress (Hector Protector (USA))
441[5] 700[5] 879[13] 5837[4] 6374[3] (6768) (7189) (7354) 7493[4] 7753[3]

Stand In Flames *Pat Eddery* a45 84
3 b f Celtic Swing—Maid Of Arc (USA) (Patton (USA))
2563[2] 3023[2] 3563[4] 4180[3] (4863) (5088) 5580[8] 5841[6] 6200[10] (6864) 7018[2] 7436[6]

Standpoint *Sir Michael Stoute* a73 75
2 b g Oasis Dream—Waki Music (USA) (Miswaki (USA))
5696[4] 6253[4] 6701[2]

St Andrews (IRE) *M A Jarvis* a94 93
8 b g Celtic Swing—Viola Royale (IRE) (Royal Academy (USA))
1723[P] (Dead)

Stanley Goodspeed *J W Hills* a85 93
5 ch g Inchinor—Flying Carpet (Barathea (IRE))
6699[10] 7390[4]

Stanley Rigby *C F Wall*
2 b g Dr Fong(USA) —Crystal (IRE) (Danehill (USA))
5246[19]

Stan's Cool Cat (IRE) *P F I Cole* a62 79
2 b f One Cool Cat(USA) —Beautiful France (IRE) (Sadler's Wells (USA))
2253[2] ◆ 2627[4] 3085[2] (4367) 5016[3] 6319a[21]

Stanstill (IRE) *G A Swinbank* 54
2 b g Statue Of Liberty(USA) —Fervent Wish (Rainbow Quest (USA))
6480[10] 6723[4]

Star Acclaim *T Keddy* a47 67
3 b f Acclamation—Tropical Lass (IRE) (Ballad Rock)
931[10] 1423[7] 3916[5] 5317[11]

Star Berry *T Wall* a38 55
5 b m Mtoto—Star Entry (In The Wings)
778[8] 4026[9]

Starbougg *K G Reveley* 35
4 b m Tobougg(IRE) —Celestial Welcome (Most Welcome)
5637[15] 6725[5]

Starburst *A M Balding* a59 61
3 b f Fantastic Light(USA) —Rasmalai (Sadler's Wells (USA))
3530[4] 7583[9] 7822[3] ◆

Star Choice *J Pearce* a69 49
3 ch g Choisir(AUS) —Bay Queen (Damister (USA))
1073[4] 1298[10] 1535[12] (6492) ◆ 6685[3] 7010[2] 7526[12]

Starcross Maid *A G Juckes* a61 61
6 ch m Zaha(CAN) —Maculatus (USA) (Sharpen Up)
(77) 171[3] 368[4] 658[3] 851[2] 1184[7] 1704[3] 2290[7] 2867[4] 3687[4] 4123[6] 7608[8]

Star Crowned (USA) *R Bouresly* a108 115
5 b h Kingmambo(USA) —Fashion Star (USA) (Chief's Crown (USA))
(566a) 670a[4] 814a[2] 1089a[3] 2235a[5]

Stardom Bound (USA) *Christopher S Paasch* a118
2 rg f Tapit(USA) —My White Corvette (USA) (Tarr Road (USA))
(6967a)

Starfala *P F I Cole* a89 89
3 gr f Galileo(IRE) —Farfala (FR) (Linamix (FR))
3688[2] (4342) (5573) 6127[5] 6415[2] 7108[7]

Starfinch *J J Bridger* a42 39
3 br f Fraam—Mockingbird (Sharpo)
2126[6] 4083[10] 5086[11] 5269[14] 5607[8] 6018[12]

Stargazer Jim (FR) *W J Haggas* a89 83
6 br g Fly To The Stars—L'Americaine (USA) (Verbatim (USA))
3132[9] 3896[8] 4309[2] 4532[7] (Dead)

Stargazy *W G M Turner* a54 51
4 b g Observatory(USA) —Romantic Myth (Mind Games)
101[5] 254[2] (289) 392[5] 663[4] 1154[9] 1248[3] 5152[11] 5797[14] 6335[5] 6913[11]

Star Grazer *C F Wall* a61 65
3 ch f Observatory(USA) —Oatey (Master Willie)
665^3 ◆ 2052^8 2833^7 3655^4 (4259) 4992^2 5537^9 5868^8

Stark Contrast (USA) *M D I Usher* a70 73
4 ch g Gulch(USA) —A Stark Is Born (USA) (Graustark)
51^6 316^4 504^3 941^9 4936^2 5145^8 5478^{10} 6364^9 (7167) 7405^8 7559^6 7750^7

Starla Dancer (GER) *R A Fahey* 45
2 b f Danehill Dancer(IRE) —Starla (GER) (Lando (GER))
6383^3 6858^{13}

Starlarks (IRE) *W J Knight* a87 88
2 b f Mujahid(USA) —Violet (IRE) (Mukaddamah (USA))
2835^7 3032^2 (3632) 3967^4 4640^2 (5937) 6439^8

Starlight Gazer *J A Geake* a62 87
5 b g Observatory(USA) —Dancing Fire (USA) (Dayjur (USA))
1069^9 2565^6 3138^6 3904^4 4865^5 5267^{11} 5779^4 (6537) 7021^5

Starlight Girl *T D Easterby* 65
3 ch f Fantastic Light(USA) —Intervene (Zafonic (USA))
2269^{10} 3230^9 3960^{15}

Starlight Prince *R Hollinshead* 61
3 b g Forzando—Inchtina (Inchinor)
2779^4

Starlight Wish *E F Vaughan* a62 12
2 ch c Fantastic Light(USA) —Aliena (IRE) (Grand Lodge (USA))
3444^{10} 3848^8 4304^6 5606^8 (Dead)

Star Links (USA) *R Hannon* a82 76
2 b c Bernstein(USA) —Startarette (USA) (Dixieland Band (USA))
5754^4 6077^4 6398^2 (7098)

Starlish (IRE) *E Lellouche* 113
3 b c Rock Of Gibraltar(IRE) —Stylish (Anshan)
1887a^2 2654a^{14} 3356a^6 5302a^6 6664a^7

Starlit Sands *Sir Mark Prescott* a103 106
3 b f Oasis Dream—Shimmering Sea (Slip Anchor)
4059^3 ◆ 4550^4 5553a^3 6429^P

Star Of Gibraltar *J L Dunlop* 85
3 b f Rock Of Gibraltar(IRE) —Fallen Star (Brief Truce (USA))
1599^5 2920^6 3500^6 4152^6 (5024) 5900^3 6542^9

Star Of Pompey *A B Haynes* a55 58
4 b m Hernando(FR) —Discerning (Darshaan)
934^{13} 1643^{11} 2125^3

Star Of Rosanna *Doug Watson* a74 65
3 b f Bertolini(USA) —Etma Rose (IRE) (Fairy King (USA))
201a^{14} 496a^5 744a^7

Star Of Sophia (IRE) *Mrs A Duffield* a39 7
2 b f Hawk Wing(USA) —Sofia Aurora (USA) (Chief Honcho (USA))
5304^{10} 5590^{11} 6133^4 7269^7

Star Of The Desert (IRE) *Mrs K Walton* a56 56
5 bb g Desert Story(IRE) —Cindy's Star (IRE) (Dancing Dissident (USA))
2144 521^{11} (Dead)

Star Pattern (USA) *J H M Gosden* 63
3 ch c Seeking The Gold(USA) —Starlore (USA) (Spectacular Bid (USA))
1172^7 1367^6 1622^4 3183^7 3525^{13}

Starpix (FR) *H J Brown* a62 85
6 gr g Linamix(FR) —Star's Proud Penny (USA) (Proud Birdie (USA))
384a^{15}

Starr Flyer *A Bailey* a44 51
4 b g Star Of Persia(IRE) —Madame Butterfly (Reprimand)
451^5

Star Rocker *J H M Gosden* 80
3 ch c Galileo(IRE) —Rockerlong (Deploy)
4620^3 5463^2 5814^3 6413^7

Starry Sky *Sir Mark Prescott* a75 75
2 b f Oasis Dream—Succinct (Hector Protector (USA))
4080^4 ◆ 4289^2 (4720) 5511^4 7067^4 7229^4

Star Strider *Miss Gay Kelleway* a77 73
4 gr g Royal Applause—Onefortheditch (USA) (With Approval (CAN))
(19) 126^4 334^3 539^8 1040^5 1312^6 2350^5 3345^4 4162^9 4772^3 5101^2 5639^3 6178^9 6336^{10} (7591) 7670^2 ◆ 7821^8

Starstruck Peter (IRE) *S Curran* a61 58
4 b g Iron Mask(USA) —Daraliya (IRE) (Kahyasi)
129^4 (374) 544^7 1246^3 1726^4 2053^3

Startengo (IRE) *Miss Suzy Smith* a62 62
5 ch g Nashwan(USA) —Virgin Hawk (USA) (Silver Hawk (USA))
51^7 207^{10} 881^8

Stash *R Hollinshead* a78
2 b g Bold Edge—Gemtastic (Tagula (IRE))
(7501)

State Banquet (USA) *H Morrison* 78
2 br c Fusaichi Pegasus(USA) —Gracie Lady (IRE) (Generous (IRE))
(6397)

State Function (IRE) *G Prodromou* 60
3 b g Grand Slam(USA) —Well Designed (IRE) (Sadler's Wells (USA))
2981^5 5160^8

State General (IRE) *Miss J Feilden* a74 64
2 b c Statue Of Liberty(USA) —Nisibis (In The Wings)
3274^6 5068^8 6524^7 7069^2 7623^2 7718^6

Staten (USA) *T D Barron* 56
3 b g Century City(IRE) —Lever To Heaven (IRE) (Bluebird (USA))
1379^8

State Shinto (USA) *R Bouresly* a90 90
12 bb g Pleasant Colony(USA) —Sha Tha (USA) (Mr Prospector (USA))
204a^{16}

Stateside (CAN) *R A Fahey* a12 47
3 b f El Corredor(USA) —Double Trick (USA) (Phone Trick (USA))
5837^9 6337^{10}

State Treasure (USA) *Neil J Howard* a75
2 b f Mineshaft(USA) —Private Status (USA) (Alydar (USA))
6613a^{11}

Station Place *A B Haynes* a26 55
3 b f Bahamian Bounty—Twin Time (Syrtos)
500^8 3445^2 (4412) 7433^{12}

Statute Book (IRE) *S Kirk* a54
2 b c Statue Of Liberty(USA) —Velvet Slipper (Muhtafal (USA))
6253^9 6574^4 7164^2

Staying On (IRE) *W R Swinburn* a84 108
3 b g Invincible Spirit(IRE) —Lakatoi (Saddlers' Hall (IRE))
1443^4 (1875) ◆ (2403) 3156^2 6074^6 6440^8 6816^{11}

Steady Gaze *M A Allen* 28
3 b g Zamindar(USA) —Krisia (Kris)
3161^{14} 3894^{14} 4085^8

Stealth Project *A M Hales* a45 65
3 b g Elmaamul(USA) —Guardee (Hector Protector (USA))
1516^2 1962^{15} 6596^{10}

Steam Cuisine *M G Quinlan* a70 101
4 ch m Mark Of Esteem(IRE) —Sauce Tartar (Salse (USA))
1993^6 2666^5 2890^3 3415^9 3500^5 4841^7 5096^7 5896^6 6271^9 6981^7

Steel Blue *R M Whitaker* a54 81
8 b g Atraf—Something Blue (Petong)
1015^{13} 1261^6 1485^{11} 1952^9 2891^6 2968^2 3271^6 3454^4 3998^6 (4327) (4608) 5067^{12} 5260^4 5634^8 6724^9 7152^4

Steel City Boy (IRE) *D Shaw* a78 75
5 b g Bold Fact(USA) —Balgren (IRE) (Ballad Rock)
1476^3 1624^7 1677^4 2036^3 2293^3 2583^{11} 2891^{11} 3171^7 3374^5 3819^9 (3890) 4117^2 4218^6 4440^{10} 4700^7 4971^4 5222^{13} 5648^3 5867^4 5930^8 6164^6 6634^{12} 7152^2 7182^4 7562^5 7730^7

Steelcut *R A Fahey* 85
4 b g Iron Mask(USA) —Apple Sauce (Prince Sabo)
983^7 1451^{10} 1624^6 (2145) 2828^{12} 3336^9 3868^9 4246^2 4502^2 5250^6 5467^3

Steele Tango (USA) *R A Teal* a78 108
3 ch c Okawango(USA) —Waltzing Around (IRE) (Ela-Mana-Mou)
(163) 1598^2 (3038) 3877^2 4552^5 4867^2

Steel Grey *M Brittain* a55 24
7 gr g Grey Desire—Call Me Lucky (Magic Ring (IRE))
33^6 193^4 282^9 468^3 578^9 640^8 1032^{10} 3795^8

Steel Mask (IRE) *M Brittain* a31 47
3 b c Iron Mask(USA) —Thorn Tree (Zafonic (USA))
1454^3 1795^{15} 2187^{14} 7528^7

Steel Silk (IRE) *D H Brown* a48 60
4 b g Desert Style(IRE) —Dear Catch (IRE) (Bluebird (USA))
1902^5

Steel Stockholder *M Brittain* 64
2 b c Mark Of Esteem(IRE) —Pompey Blue (Abou Zouz (USA))
1967^4 2108^5 2581^4 2845^4

Steely Dan *Mrs L C Jewell* a74 70
9 b g Danzig Connection(USA) —No Comebacks (Last Tycoon)
(122) 1048^{10} 1164^4 1411^2 1564^6 2073^5

Steenberg (IRE) *M H Tompkins* 92
9 ch g Flying Spur(AUS) —Kip's Sister (Cawston's Clown)
1517^8 2818^{14} 3491^{12} 3812^{10} 4854^{16}

Steer *M Brittain* 41
2 b c Reset(AUS) —Honours Even (Highest Honor (FR))
4536^7 6212^9

Stefer (USA) *D Smaga* 103
2 ch f Johannesburg(USA) —Ardere (USA) (El Prado (IRE))
(7185a)

Steig (IRE) *Carl Llewellyn* a69 74
5 b g Xaar—Ring Of Kerry (IRE) (Kenmare (FR))
(144) 248^3 344^2 526^3 660^4 697^2 852^5 1048^6 (1345) 2995^{13} 3648^3 4386^2 (4807) 5170^9

Stella Di Quattro *U Ostmann* 104
4 b m Best Of The Bests(IRE) —Search For Love (FR) (Groom Dancer (USA))
6691a^2 7348a^{12}

Stellando (IRE) *T D Easterby*
3 b g Hernando(FR) —La Stellina (IRE) (Marju (IRE))
2488^{11}

Stellarina (IRE) *G A Swinbank* a69 52
2 b f Night Shift(USA) —Accelerating (USA) (Lear Fan (USA))
3456^{13} 6808^5 7095^3

Stellino (GER) *N J Henderson* 82
5 b g Monashee Mountain(USA) —Sweet Tern (GER) (Arctic Tern (USA))
1947^{13}

Stellite *J S Goldie* a71 76
8 ch g Pivotal—Donation (Generous (IRE))
(1775) (2251) 2841^2 3548^5 4605^6

Stepaside (IRE) *A D Brown* a55 62
4 gr g Fasliyev(USA) —Felicita (IRE) (Catrail (USA))
2^2 66^2 147^7 530^2

Step Dancing *Mrs Prunella Dobbs* a54 56
3 b f Distant Music(USA) —Light Step (USA) (Nureyev (USA))
4715a^7

Step Fast (USA) *M Johnston* a35 46
2 ch f Giant's Causeway(USA) —Nannerl (USA) (Valid Appeal (USA))
5672^{10} 6291^{11} 7117^9

Stephenson (FR) *W Baltromei* 106
7 br g Platini(GER) —Sternina (IRE) (Runnett)
2346a^8

Steph The Ref *R A Fahey* 57
3 bb f Rossini(USA) —Fairy Ring (IRE) (Fairy King (USA))
2928^{14} 3079^{15}

Step It Up (IRE) *J R Boyle* a73 61
4 ch g Daggers Drawn(USA) —Leitrim Lodge (IRE) (Classic Music (USA))
(7478) 7621^6 7743^8

Steppe Dancer (IRE) *D J Coakley* a114 106
5 b h Fasliyev(USA) —Exemina (USA) (Slip Anchor)
1944^6

Stepping Up (IRE) *E Charpy* a90 99
5 ch h Soviet Star(USA) —Rise And Fall (Mill Reef (USA))
563a^4 647a^3

Step Softly *J-C Rouget* a73 99
3 b f Golan(IRE) —Step Aloft (Shirley Heights)
1664a^5

Step This Way (USA) *M Johnston* a83 92
3 ch f Giant's Causeway(USA) —Lady In Waiting (USA) (Woodman (USA))
2109^7 2840^6 (3045) 3505^{13} 3930^5 4742^{15}

Sterling Sound (USA) *M P Tregoning* a67 71
2 b f Street Cry(IRE) —Lady In Silver (USA) (Silver Hawk (USA))
2835^2 ◆ 3349^4 4088^2 4521^3 5214^4

Stern Opinion (USA) *P Bary* 112
3 rg c Mizzen Mast(USA) —Helstra (USA) (Nureyev (USA))
2034a^4 (3243a) 3938a^2 5556a^4 5955a^3 7187a^5

Sterope (FR) *D Sepulchre* 71
3 b f Hernando(FR) —Sacred Song (USA) (Diesis)
2257^6 2800^6 3326^4 3843^2 4427^4 4762^5 7551a^5

Stetchworth Prince *E Charpy* a8 86
6 b g Cadeaux Genereux—Elfin Laughter (Alzao (USA))
290a^4

Steve's Champ (CHI) *Rune Haugen* 107
8 b h Foxhound(USA) —Emigracion (CHI) (Semenenko (USA))
3451^8 5957a^7

Stevie Gee (IRE) *G A Swinbank* a85 96
4 b g Invincible Spirit(IRE) —Margaree Mary (CAN) (Seeking The Gold (USA))
680^6 791^5 1069^7 (1327) 1517^3 1774^5 2538^2 3040^3 3491^6 4145^7 4437^5 5503^{14} 5831^7 6069^8

Stevie Junior *P W Chapple-Hyam* a88 74
2 b c Monsieur Bond(IRE) —Song Of Skye (Warning)
5066^5 (5870) ◆ (6376)

Stevies Song *D Flood*
2 b f Mark Of Esteem(IRE) —Turf Moor (IRE) (Mac's Imp (USA))
4536^9 6730^{11} 6837^{11}

Stevie Thunder *G A Swinbank* a64 94
3 ch g Storming Home—Social Storm (USA) (Future Storm (USA))
1161^2 ◆ (1306) 1750^2 1868^4 (3039) (3494) 3919^4 4783^4 5273^5

Stevil (USA) *Nicholas Zito* a109
3 gr c Maria's Mon(USA) —Company Storm (USA) (Storm Creek (USA))
2215a^5

Sticky Tape *J A Osborne* 51
4 b m Royal Applause—Golden Symbol (Wolfhound (USA))
2917^6 6335^{13}

Still Calm *N J Vaughan* a51 62
4 b g Zamindar(USA) —Shining Water (Kalaglow)
2446^4 2949^{10} 6185^9

Still Dreaming *R J Price* a61 61
4 ch m Singspiel(IRE) —Three Green Leaves (IRE) (Environment Friend)
127^3 (215) 485^2 664^2 771^4 1086^3 1408^{12} 2641^3 3059^3 3698^{10} 4105^8 7400^{12}

Still Life (IRE) *T F Lacy* 51
4 b g Orpen(USA) —Kristabelle (IRE) (Elbio)
2283^7

Stimulation (IRE) *H Morrison* 118
3 b c Choisir(AUS) —Damiana (IRE) (Thatching)
(1400) 1808^7 2409^2 3119^4 4506^2 5742a^3 (6814) ◆

Stir Crazy (IRE) *D W Barker* a64 65
4 b g Fath(USA) —La Captive (IRE) (Selkirk (USA))
596^7 806^{11} 1338^{10} 2040^{12} 2658^{13} 3139^{14}

Stirling Castle *M J Wallace* a81 79
2 b c Dubai Destination(USA) —Craigmill (Slip Anchor)
3568^4 4214^4 (4861) 5274^5 6058^7

St Jean Cap Ferrat *G Wragg* a76 92
3 bb c Domedriver(IRE) —Miss Cap Ferrat (Darshaan)
1014^2 1243^3 (1477) 2464^2 3745^4 4621^{12} 5502^2 6582^6 6704^5 6949^3

St Johns Wood *M W Easterby* a31 65
3 b g Singspiel(IRE) —Mamounia (IRE) (Green Desert (USA))
1490^8 1814^6 2008^{11} 2675^P 3174^3 3335^7

St Michael's Mount *M P Tregoning* a65 13
3 b g Mark Of Esteem(IRE) —Marithea (IRE) (Barathea (IRE))
1410^4 1701^7 2311^{12} 5268^6 6091^{10}

Stockman *H Morrison* a12
4 b g Kylian(USA) —Fabriana (Northern State (USA))
7721^8

Stock Market (USA) *E A L Dunlop* 78
3 ch c Rahy(USA) —Two Marks (USA) (Woodman (USA))
1367^4 1814^4 (2143) 2699^{10} 3038^8 3736^8 5472^{10}

Stoic (IRE) *J Noseda* 65
2 b c Green Desert(USA) —Silver Bracelet (Machiavellian (USA))
6438^5

Stoic Leader (IRE) *R F Fisher* a73 87
8 b g Danehill Dancer(IRE) —Starlust (Sallust)
990^{13} 1138^2 1774^4 2251^7 2400^3 (2445) 2913^5 2969^5 3548^4 3599^9 4219^8

Stolen Light (IRE) *A Crook* a78 40
7 ch g Grand Lodge(USA) —Spring To Light (USA) (Blushing Groom (FR))
1798^{10} 2525^3 3296^9 6054^{13} 7042^{14}

Stolt (IRE) *N Wilson* a83 93
4 b g Tagula(IRE) —Cabcharge Princess (IRE) (Rambo Dancer (CAN))
84^5 301^7 359^2 580^6 1195^2 (1451) 1802^8 2212^7 (2583) 3009^5 3472^2 3931^5

Stoneacre Baby (USA) *Peter Grayson* a29
3 ch f Stravinsky(USA) —Katiba (USA) (Gulch (USA))
298^7

Stoneacre Boy (IRE) *Peter Grayson* a76 36
5 ch g City On A Hill(USA) —Sans Ceriph (IRE) (Thatching)
29^{10} 414^6 620^5 1037^9

Stoneacre Chris (USA) *Peter Grayson* a55 49
3 ch f Belong To Me(USA) —Fonage (Zafonic (USA))
412^2 ◆ 734^2 928^6 1120^5 4308^4 4852^2 5393^3 5679^7 6308^6 6405^4 7369^{13} 7528^8

Stoneacre Donny (IRE) *Peter Grayson* a54
4 br h Lend A Hand—Election Special (Chief Singer)
(119) 174^6 372^8 522^7 7049^{12} 7288^{10} 7636^{11}

Stoneacre Gareth (IRE) *J Jay* a74 62
4 b g Grand Lodge(USA) —Tidal Reach (USA) (Kris S (USA))
318^5 ◆ 522^6 627^3 770^7 808^6 1643^{15}

Stoneacre Lad (IRE) *Peter Grayson* a106 104
5 b h Bluebird(USA) —Jay And-A (IRE) (Elbio)
907^3 1442^9 (2712) 4840^9 6468^{10} 6653^{16}

Stoneacre Ma *Peter Grayson* a44 16
3 b f Dubai Destination(USA) —Silent Tribute (IRE) (Lion Cavern (USA))
412^7 734^7 882^7 932^4 1081^2 1169^4 1487^4

Stoneacre Paddy (IRE) *Peter Grayson* a42
3 ch c Golan(IRE) —Nocturnal (FR) (Night Shift (USA))
734^8 5679^{10} 6433^{11}

Stoneacre Pat (IRE) *Peter Grayson* a63 51
3 b c Iron Mask(USA) —Sans Ceriph (IRE) (Thatching)
(412) 612^5 952^6 1066^5 1635^{12} 2074^{10} (3332) 3609^6 4852^5 5141^4 5201^4 5911^2 7679^8 7835^4

Stoneacre Sarah *Peter Grayson* a63 44
3 b f Cadeaux Genereux—Tropical (Green Desert (USA))
5431^0 (734) 882^3 2527^6 3609^5 4308^9 7416^{12} 7836^5

Stonehaugh (IRE) *J Howard Johnson* 85
5 b g King Charlemagne(USA) —Canary Bird (IRE) (Catrail (USA))
2389^2 2938^{11} 4500^8 4961^4

Stone Of Scone *E A L Dunlop* a88 68
3 b c Pivotal—Independence (Selkirk (USA))
1418^6 ◆ (1748) ◆

Stones Of Venice (IRE) *R M Whitaker* a47 47
3 b f Barathea(IRE) —Midnight Fever (IRE) (Sure Blade (USA))
2536^7 2926^9 4537^9

Stones River (USA) *J Larry Jones* a104
3 rg c Monarchos(USA) —Little Bold Belle (USA) (Silver Buck (USA))
6373a^6

Stoop To Conquer *A W Carroll* a77 80
8 b g Polar Falcon(USA) —Princess Genista (Ile De Bourbon (USA))
405^4 540^{11} 810^3 1267^8 1472^9 1798^6 4105^2 5385^2 5613^4

Stop Making Sense *A Fabre* a101 104
6 b g Lujain(USA) —Freeway (FR) (Exit To Nowhere (USA))
5555a^7

Stop On *M R Channon* a60 76
3 b g Fraam—Tourmalet (Night Shift (USA))
1342^4 (1741) 2840^{13}

Stop The Power (GER) *Ruaidhri Joseph Tierney* a24 40
3 ch g Platini(GER) —Stalima (GER) (Lemhi Gold (USA))
2868^8

Storey Hill (USA) *D Shaw* a81 53
3 bb g Richter Scale(USA) —Crafty Nan (USA) (Crafty Prospector (USA))
756^8 924^{10} (1284) 1707^7 2732^4

Stormbeam (USA) *G A Butler* a63 67
3 b c Tale Of The Cat(USA) —Broad Smile (USA) (Broad Brush (USA))
2981^{10} 3525^3 4377^6 4991^2

Stormburst (IRE) *A J Chamberlain* a64 57
4 b m Mujadil(USA) —Isca (Caerleon (USA))
54^5 213^3 539^{11} 620^6 933^{10} 1338^7 1489^2 2670^3 2802^7 3033^{12} 3608^6

Storming Sioux *W J Haggas* a66 65
2 b f Storming Home—Sueboog (IRE) (Darshaan)
6789^2 ◆ 7227^4

Stormin Heart (USA) *M Johnston* a50 56
3 br g Stormin Fever(USA) —Heart Beats True (USA) (Cherokee Run (USA))
1453^{14} 2008^{14} 4076^9 4533^2 4797^{12} 5544^7 7180^5 7368^6

Storm Mission (USA) *J Mackie* a49 65
4 bb g Storm Creek(USA) —Bemissed (USA) (Nijinsky (CAN))
40^5 127^7

Storm Mist (IRE) *P F I Cole* a26 56
2 ch c Giant's Causeway(USA) —Madeira Mist (IRE) (Grand Lodge (USA))
3682^{10} 4151^{12} 5404^{13}

Storm Mountain (IRE) *B Grizzetti* 110
5 b h Montjeu(IRE) —Lady Storm (IRE) (Mujadil (USA))
6325a^3 7263a^{12}

Storm Sir (USA) *B J Meehan* a90 84
3 ch c Johannesburg(USA) —Robust (USA) (Conquistador Cielo (USA))
2620^{12} 3694^2 ◆ 4128^7 4423^7 (5140) (5908) 6283^2

Storm Treasure (USA) *Steven Asmussen* a105 116
5 ch h Storm Boot(USA) —Boogie Beach Blues (USA) (Cure The Blues (USA))
6994a^3

Stormy Journey *Mrs K Walton* 67
3 b g Mujahid(USA) —Sabonis (USA) (The Minstrel (CAN))
1560[14] 2661[9] 3079[14] 3577[6]

Stormy Summer *R W Price* a35 30
3 b g Observatory(USA) —Khambani (IRE) (Royal Academy (USA))
6280[6] 6584[8]

Stormy View (USA) *J H M Gosden* a70 76
3 bb f Cozzene(USA) —Another Storm (USA) (Gone West (USA))
2328[8] 2956[2] 3611[3] 3841[7] 5155[7] 6126[4] 6437[9]

Stormy Weather (FR) *J-L Pelletan* 98
2 gr c Highest Honor(FR) —Stormy Moud (USA) (Storm Bird (CAN))
6642a[6] 7449a[2]

Storyland (USA) *W J Haggas* a94 93
3 b f Menifee(USA) —Auspice (USA) (Robellino (USA))
(1751) (2190) 2920[3] 3433[3] 5472[5] (6127) (6415) ◆ 7100[6]

Stotsfold *W R Swinburn* a95 119
5 b g Barathea(IRE) —Eliza Acton (Shirley Heights)
1422[5] 1921[5] 3121[6] 3741[6] 4585[7] (5289)

Stow *H Morrison* a67 85
3 ch g Selkirk(USA) —Spry (Suave Dancer (USA))
1516[3] (2244) 3004[3] 4621[9] 6078[5] 6446[2]

St Petersburg *J R Boyle* a75 85
8 ch g Polar Falcon(USA) —First Law (Primo Dominie)
3612[12] 3887[7] 4927[9] 5478[3] 5915[10] 6675[6] 7202[5] 7461[2] 7702[9]

Strabinios King *M Wigham* a74 73
4 b g King's Best(USA) —Strawberry Morn (CAN) (Travelling Victor (CAN))
(806) ◆ 2263[11] (2758) 2983[3] 3757[7] 7677[10] ◆ 7829[3] ◆

Straboe (USA) *S C Williams*
2 b g Green Desert(USA) —Staff Nurse (USA) (Arch (USA))
6553[13]

Straight (IRE) *M Brittain* a62 61
3 b c King Charlemagne(USA) —Fun Of The Fair (Mistertopogigo (IRE))
993[2] (1120) 1548[6] 3564[9] 3819[7] 3960[14] 4782[10]

Straight And Level (CAN) *Miss Jo Crowley* a76 63
3 gr c Buddha(USA) —Azusa (USA) (Flying Paster (USA))
799[4] 1443[7] 1745[7] 3004[11] 5999[10] 7302[4] 7603[6] 7771[4]

Straight Face (IRE) *Miss Gay Kelleway* a61 53
4 b g Princely Heir(IRE) —Dakota Sioux (IRE) (College Chapel)
147[8] 160[8] 693[2] (922) (1053) (1248) 1313[2] 1602[12] 3572[3] 3839[7] 4084[5] 4891[2] 5157[8] 7766[7]

Straight Sets (IRE) *M R Channon* 76
4 b m Pivotal—Flying Squaw (Be My Chief (USA))
4651[3] (5057) 5639[2] 6056[3] 6487[5]

Straitjacket *R Hannon* a57 72
2 b f Refuse To Bend(IRE) —Thara'A (IRE) (Desert Prince (IRE))
2306[2] 2835[5] 3378[6] 5432[7] 6023[5] 6231[8]

Strait Of Mewsina (IRE) *Larry Rivelli* 95
3 b c Spartacus(IRE) —Siraka (FR) (Grand Lodge (USA))
4887a[5]

Straits Of Hormuz (USA) *E J O'Neill* 23
2 rg f War Chant(USA) —Tjinouska (USA) (Cozzene (USA))
4897[7]

Strategic Mission (IRE) *P F I Cole* 99
3 b c Red Ransom(USA) —North East Bay (USA) (Prospect Bay (CAN))
(2194) ◆ 3157[16] 4160[6] 4404[9]

Strategic Mount *P F I Cole* a63 106
5 b g Montjeu(IRE) —Danlu (USA) (Danzig (USA))
3249[12] 4191[7] (4844) 5494[2] ◆ 5885[3] 6444[9]

Strategic Mover (USA) *P F I Cole* 92
3 ch g Grand Slam(USA) —Efficient Frontier (USA) (Mt. Livermore (USA))
1803[2] 2427[4] 2919[4]

Strathcal *H Morrison* a66 57
2 b g Beat Hollow—Shall We Run (Hotfoot)
5365[6] 6375[6] 6876[5] 7190[7]

Strathmore (IRE) *R A Fahey* a73 73
4 gr g Fath(USA) —In The Highlands (Petong)
4[3] (71) 286[2] ◆ 370[2] 466[6] 1129[2] 1485[13] 1561[4] 1775[9] 2703[4]

Strathtay *M G Rimell* a33
6 ch m Pivotal—Cressida (Polish Precedent (USA))
5308[10] 5676[7]

Stratn Jack *B G Powell* a47
4 b g Rambling Bear—Strat's Quest (Nicholas (USA))
99[10] 607[7] 776[11] 935[8]

Stravita *R Hollinshead* a70 63
4 b m Weet-A-Minute(IRE) —Stravsea (Handsome Sailor)
3738[6] 4031[4] 5593[7] 6189[2] 6395[7] (6719) 7039[3] 7401[5] 7512[5] 7688[10] (7776)

Stravonian *D A Nolan* 47
8 b g Luso—In The Evening (IRE) (Distinctly North (USA))
982[6] 2286[10] 2752[8] 3216[4] 3545[9] 3718[8] 4947[4] 5415[4] 6071[6] 6309[7]

Strawberry Moon (IRE) *B Smart* 74
3 b f Alhaarth(IRE) —Dancing Drop (Green Desert (USA))
1519[2] 1951[2] 2673[3] 3280[3] 4383[3] 4782[3] (5636) 6411[3] (6792)

Straw Boy *R Brotherton* 56
4 gr g Hunting Lion(IRE) —Sky Light Dreams (Dreams To Reality (USA))
2988[P]

Stream Cat (USA) *George R Arnold II* a108 117
5 bb h Black Minnaloushe(USA) —Water Course (USA) (Irish River (FR))
4889a[6]

Street Boss (USA) *Bruce Headley* a120
4 ch h Street Cry(IRE) —Blushing Ogygian (USA) (Ogygian (USA))
6999a[3]

Street Crime *A M Balding* a66 65
3 b g Tagula(IRE) —Brandon Princess (Waajib)
3894[10] 4581[3] 4941[3] 5477[2] 6400[7]

Street Devil (USA) *P A Blockley* 73
3 gr c Street Cry(IRE) —Math (USA) (Devil's Bag (USA))
1125[12] 2786[3] 3312[6] 4153[8] 4920[2] 6537[8]

Street Diva (USA) *P A Blockley* a64
3 ch f Street Cry(IRE) —Arctic Valley (USA) (Arctic Tern (USA))
4669[10] 5616[7] 5998[8] 6377[11] 6683[12]

Street Hero (USA) *Myung Kwon Cho* a115
2 b c Street Cry(IRE) —Squall Linda (USA) (Summer Squall (USA))
6997a[3]

Street Life (IRE) *W J Musson* a73 76
10 ch g Dolphin Street(FR) —Wolf Cleugh (IRE) (Last Tycoon)
28[7] 180[6] 811[7] (1159) 1281[2] 1521[4] 2682[4] 4930[8] 6050[P] (Dead)

Streetline (IRE) *Miss S Collins* 76
2 b f Choisir(AUS) —Sidecar (IRE) (Spectrum (IRE))
6320a[8]

Street Of Hope (USA) *George Baker* a61 58
2 bb f Street Cry(IRE) —Cycle Of Life (USA) (Spinning World (USA))
1762[4] 2309[5] 3331[4] 5581[6]

Street Power (USA) *J R Gask* a69 31
3 bb g Street Cry(IRE) —Javana (USA) (Sandpit (BRZ))
4431[8] 6047[9]

Streets Apart (USA) *W R Swinburn* a72 70
3 b f Street Cry(IRE) —Saintly Speaking (USA) (Dahar (USA))
5463[6] 6280[2] 6762[3]

Street Star (USA) *J R Fanshawe* a87 85
3 b f Street Cry(IRE) —Domludge (USA) (Lyphard (USA))
1999[11] 2993[8] 3838[2] 4345[7] 5648[10]

Strensall *R E Barr* a32 76
11 b g Beveled(USA) —Payvashooz (Ballacashtal (CAN))
1893[10] 2212[9] 2777[9] 3112[8] 3759[6] 4294[6] 6546[7]

Stretton (IRE) *J D Bethell* a66 86
10 br g Doyoun—Awayil (USA) (Woodman (USA))
1947[10] 3010[6] 3440[4]

Strevelyn *Mrs A Duffield* 48
2 br g Namid—Kali (Linamix (FR))
2569[11] 6481[9] 6811[6]

Strictly *Sir Michael Stoute* a68
2 b f Falbrav(IRE) —Dance On (Caerleon (USA))
5835[2]

Strictly Elsie (IRE) *J R Norton* 59
3 b f No Excuse Needed—Sophrana (IRE) (Polar Falcon (USA))
2208[11] 2911[16] 3081[11] 3416[9] 4112[9] 6585[13]

Strictly Royal *M R Channon* 15
2 ch g Imperial Dancer—Royal Logic (Royal Applause)
1276[4] 1377[6] 3706[7] 4063[9]

Striding Edge (IRE) *W R Muir* a69 68
2 bb g Rock Of Gibraltar(IRE) —For Criquette (IRE) (Barathea (IRE))
1523[8] 1955[5] (3158) 3967[3] 5432[2] 6087[4] 6700[2] 7190[3]

Strike Command (USA) *R Charlton* a68 49
2 b c Van Nistelrooy(USA) —Craftimae (USA) (Crafty Prospector (USA))
4480[13] 4926[8] 5431[3] 5997[12]

Strike Force *K F Clutterbuck* a70 65
4 b g Dansili—Miswaki Belle (USA) (Miswaki (USA))
148[11] 270[7] 1842[15] 2243[3] 2640[12] 4491[7] 5145[6] 5407[2] (5712) (6090) 6629[7] 7094[4] 7385[5] 7606[2] 7800[9]

Strikemaster (IRE) *J W Hills* a55 52
2 b c Xaar—Mas A Fuera (IRE) (Alzao (USA))
2150[11] 3821[7] 4827[6] 5909[4] 6394[8] 7079[3] 7353[4] 7666[8]

Striker Torres (IRE) *B Smart* 80
2 ch c Danehill Dancer(IRE) —Silver Skates (IRE) (Slip Anchor)
3997[4] 6230[3] 6481[2] 6944[2]

Strike The Deal (USA) *J Noseda* a106 112
3 ch c Van Nistelrooy(USA) —Countess Gold (USA) (Mt. Livermore (USA))
1088a[5] 1808[9] 3119[5] 4188[4] 5275[3] 5891[9] 6304[5]

Strike Up The Band *D Nicholls* a112 110
5 b g Cyrano De Bergerac—Green Supreme (Primo Dominie)
959[12] 1157[4] 1917[7] 2129[8] 2828[7] 3336[2] 3680[4] 3943[2] 4445[2] (4840) 5890[7] 6184[2] 6518a[4]

Striking Force (IRE) *V C Ward* a76 84
6 b g Danehill(USA) —Trusted Partner (USA) (Affirmed (USA))
(3286a)

Striking Spirit *B W Hills* 95
3 b g Oasis Dream—Aspiring Diva (USA) (Distant View (USA))
1404[6] 2162[3] 3047[16] 6239[6]

Stringsofmyheart *Miss Gay Kelleway* a81 82
4 b m Halling(USA) —Heart's Harmony (Blushing Groom (FR))
14[12] 1577[2] (2078) (2453) (2718) 2990[6] 3163[3] 3630[3] 3900[3] 4178[4] 4426[P] 6248[11]

Striving (IRE) *Sir Michael Stoute* 66
3 bb f Danehill Dancer(IRE) —Wannabe (Shirley Heights)
2199[9] 2603[6] 3095[3] 3552[2] 4282[9]

Striving Storm (USA) *P W Chapple-Hyam* 93
4 bb g Stormin Fever(USA) —Sugars For Nanny (USA) (Brocco (USA))
2133[5] 3413[8]

Strobe *Mrs L B Normile* a76 81
5 ch g Fantastic Light(USA) —Sadaka (USA) (Kingmambo (USA))
2135[13]

Strongarm *A Bailey* 49
2 b g Refuse To Bend(IRE) —Surf The Net (Cape Cross (IRE))
4826[15] 5316[7] 6580[8]

Strong Storm (USA) *J Noseda* 48
2 ch c Giant's Causeway(USA) —Sweeping Story (USA) (End Sweep (USA))
6425[14]

Strong Survivor (USA) *P R Webber* a73 69
5 b g Kingmambo(USA) —Summer Survivor (IRE) (Caerleon (USA))
1340[2] 1933[8] 3059[8]

Stroppi Poppi *Jean-Rene Auvray* a37 7
4 b m Mtoto—Capricious Lass (Corvaro (USA))
1266[11]

Strut The Stage (IRE) *B W Duke* a61 76
4 b g Lil's Boy(USA) —Eva Luna (IRE) (Double Schwartz)
276[3] 356[3] 663[2] 937[7] 1533[9] 2128[10]

St Savarin (FR) *B R Johnson* a93 101
7 ch g Highest Honor(FR) —Sacara (GER) (Monsagem (USA))
418[5] 968[4] 1080[5] 1544[5] 7717[6]

St Trinians *E F Vaughan* a95 77
3 b f Piccolo—Cherrycombe-Row (Classic Cliche (IRE))
3318[3] (3823) 5108[3] 5595[5] (6256) (6491) 6663[3]

Stubbs Art (IRE) *D R C Elsworth* 113
3 ch c Hawk Wing(USA) —Rich Dancer (Halling (USA))
1595[5] 1808[3] 2418a[3] 3102[6] 6237a[6] 6440[5] 6780[9]

Student Council (USA) *Steven Asmussen* a117 101
6 b h Kingmambo(USA) —Class Kris (USA) (Kris S (USA))
7001a[11]

Sturgis (IRE) *Paul W Flynn* a49 53
5 b g Factual(USA) —Vannuccis Daughter (IRE) (Perugino (USA))
7072[4]

Style Award *W J H Ratcliffe* a87 87
3 b f Acclamation—Elegant (IRE) (Marju (IRE))
(798) ◆ 1484[6] 1623[12] 1911[4] 2171[4] 2594[5] 3009[9] 3320[7] 4074[5] 4922[4] 5397[5] 7040[9]

Style Icon *D R C Elsworth* a62 62
3 ch g Mark Of Esteem(IRE) —Break Point (Reference Point)
1403[7] 1763[4] 2198[13] 3117[4]

Stylish Dream (USA) *J R Fanshawe* a65 68
2 bb f Elusive Quality(USA) —Stylelistick (USA) (Storm Cat (USA))
3456[6] ◆ 5673[3]

Stylistic (IRE) *W A Murphy* a32 21
7 b m Daggers Drawn(USA) —Treasure (IRE) (Treasure Kay)
5452[13]

Suakin Dancer (IRE) *H Morrison* a58 60
2 ch f Danehill Dancer(IRE) —Wedding Morn (IRE) (Sadler's Wells (USA))
4149[10] 5097[9] 5788[9] 6473[15]

Suba (USA) *Saeed Bin Suroor* a74 71
2 b f Seeking The Gold(USA) —Zomaradah (Deploy)
5097[3] 6076[8] 7097[2]

Subadar *M Botti* a64 60
4 b g Zamindar(USA) —Valencia (Kenmare (FR))
192[5] 361[3] 728[9] 879[7] 938[10]

Subitodopo *M Gasparini* 102
4 ch h Fraam—Comtesse Noire (CAN) (Woodman (USA))
1667a[4] 2027a[5] 6325a[7]

Subpoena *A Al Raihe* a61 102
6 b h Diktat—Trefoil (Kris)
666a[8] 741a[7] 814a[12]

Sub Prime (IRE) *J A Osborne* a64 55
2 b c Danetime(IRE) —Primo Supremo (IRE) (Primo Dominie)
1078[2] 1341[4] 2049[2] 2459[4] (2882) 4768[9] 5567[10]

Sub Rose (IRE) *A De Royer-Dupre* 110
3 b f Galileo(IRE) —Amazing Krisken (USA) (Kris S (USA))
(2650a)

Subsidise (IRE) *F P Murtagh* a39 48
5 br g Key Of Luck(USA) —Haysong (IRE) (Ballad Rock)
345[11]

Subtle Shimmer *Ms Joanna Morgan* 88
4 b m Danehill Dancer(IRE) —Clipper (Salse (USA))
3619a[12]

Suburban Cool *Thomas O'Neill* a30 45
4 b g Desert Style(IRE) —Flounce (Unfuwain (USA))
508[8]

Such Optimism *R M Beckett* 87
2 b f Sakhee(USA) —Optimistic (Reprimand)
(5021) 5641[2] 6982[10]

Sudan (IRE) *Robert Frankel* 120
5 ch h Peintre Celebre(USA) —Sarabande (USA) (Woodman (USA))
3995a[4]

Sudden Impact (IRE) *Paul Green* 96
3 bb f Modigliani(USA) —Suddenly (Puissance)
2605[8] 3999[2] 4074[2] 4408[2] 4842[7] 5259[5] 6160[6] 7181[9] 7243[11]

Sudden Impulse *A D Brown* a76 78
7 b m Silver Patriarch(IRE) —Sanshang (FR) (Astronef)
51[2] 132[4] 586[5] 1909[4] 2155[2] 2499[6] 3029[9] 3624[8] 4244[7] 4701[3] 5308[6] (5543) 6007[7] 7280[4] 7447[4] 7620[10] 7777[3]

Suede *Pat Eddery* a53 69
3 b f Zamindar(USA) —Blue Gentian (USA) (Known Fact (USA))
2800[3] 3801[2] 4461[3] 5019[9] 6331[4]

Sue's Hawk (IRE) *A P Jarvis* a12
3 ch f Hawk Wing(USA) —Desert Blues (IRE) (Desert Prince (IRE))
1499[8]

Sugarbaby Princess (IRE) *S W James* a24
2 gr f Verglas(IRE) —Alkifaf (USA) (Mtoto)
7098[11]

Sugar Free (IRE) *T Stack* 99
2 b f Oasis Dream—Much Faster (IRE) (Fasliyev (USA))
3123[5] ◆ 5549a[5] 6441[10]

Sugar Mint (IRE) *B W Hills* 101
3 b f High Chaparral(IRE) —Anna Karenina (USA) (Atticus (USA))
(1265) 1915[2] 2792[12] 3742[4] 4395[5] ◆ 4623[9]

Sugar Mom (USA) *Wayne Catalano* a100 100
2 b f Monarchos(USA) —Plenty Of Sugar (CAN) (Ascot Knight (CAN))
6966a[7]

Sugar Ray (IRE) *Sir Michael Stoute* 110
4 b g Danehill(USA) —Akuna Bay (USA) (Mr Prospector (USA))
(1531) 2168[3] (3249) 4444[8] 6303[2]

Suhayl Star (IRE) *P Burgoyne* a68 51
4 b g Trans Island—Miss Odlum (IRE) (Mtoto)
402[10] 536[6] 624[7] 713[2] 808[2] 877[5] 972[2] 1053[4] 1275[10]

Suitably Accoutred (IRE) *Mrs A Duffield* 49
2 b f Acclamation—Cliveden Gail (IRE) (Law Society (USA))
6291[10] 6722[8]

Suite Francaise *Sir Mark Prescott* a51 61
3 gr f Hernando(FR) —Entente Cordiale (USA) (Affirmed (USA))
4303[5] 4762[2] 5223[3] 6060[8] 6386[6]

Suits Me *T P Tate* a112 101
5 ch g Bertolini(USA) —Fancier Bit (Lion Cavern (USA))
962[4] 1072[8] 1569[6] 1970[5] 2970[2] 3627[3] 4856[11] 5382[3] 5858[9] 6249[2] 6763[2] (7127) (7291) (7496) (7579) 7741[2]

Sularno *H Morrison* a78 57
4 ch g Medicean—Star Precision (Shavian)
1554[5] 1933[7] (2870) (3162) 3691[11] 4529[4] 7184[4] 7650[7]

Sultan Of The Sand *C C Bealby* a39 34
3 b g High Estate—Desert Bloom (FR) (Last Tycoon)
837[11] 1453[12] 7616[6]

Sultans Way (IRE) *P F I Cole* 70
2 b g Indian Ridge—Roses From Ridey (IRE) (Petorius)
3926[6] (4697) 5274[6] 6344[7]

Sumani (FR) *S Dow* a57 54
2 b g Della Francesca(USA) —Sumatra (IRE) (Mukaddamah (USA))
4861[6] 5641[7]

Sumbe (USA) *M P Tregoning* 69
2 bb c Giant's Causeway(USA) —Sumoto (Mtoto)
5246[6] ◆

Summer Bounty *F Jordan* a59 52
12 b g Lugana Beach—Tender Moment (IRE) (Caerleon (USA))
934[11] 1206[4] 1459[10] 1692[8] 2512[3] 3084[5] 3606[10] 6594[9] 6753[5] 7322[6] 7473[5] 7608[4] 7688[9]

Summercove (IRE) *John Joseph Murphy* a72 66
3 b f Cape Cross(IRE) —Reasonably Devout (CAN) (St Jovite (USA))
7398[7]

Summer Dancer (IRE) *D R C Elsworth* a83 84
4 br g Fasliyev(USA) —Summer Style (IRE) (Indian Ridge)
2787[2] 3367[12] 4364[6] 4603[9] 5789[10] 6177[5] 6867[10]

Summer Fete (IRE) *B Smart* 100
2 gr f Pivotal—Tamarillo (Daylami (IRE))
(4685) ◆ 6102[4] (6982)

Summer Gift *J O'Reilly* a31 49
5 b m Cadeaux Genereux—Summer Exhibition (Royal Academy (USA))
1561[10] 2491[14] 2664[8]

Summer Gold (IRE) *E J Alston* 84
4 b m Barathea(IRE) —Eman's Joy (Lion Cavern (USA))
(2155) 3367[14] (3866) 4841[4] 6431[8]

Summer Lodge *A J McCabe* a74 62
5 b g Indian Lodge(IRE) —Summer Siren (FR) (Saint Cyrien (FR))
4936[3] 5593[3] 5971[5] (6493) 6662[3] 7376[11] 7455[5] 7686[3] 7797[7]

Summer Loving (IRE) *Mrs L C Jewell* a24 51
4 b m Barathea(IRE) —Tree House (USA) (Woodman (USA))
4730[11] 5150[4]

Summer Of Love (IRE) *Mrs S J Humphrey* a63 76
4 b m Fasliyev(USA) —Overboard (IRE) (Rainbow Quest (USA))
(2071) 2354[2] 2921[4] 3220[2]

Summerofsixtynine *J G M O'Shea* a59
5 b h Fruits Of Love(USA) —Scurrilous (Sharpo)
78[4] 272[5] 1165[8]

Summer Recluse (USA) *J M Bradley* a65 68
9 gr g Cozzene(USA) —Summer Retreat (USA) (Gone West (USA))
2933[11] 3363[5] 3608[3] 4186[7] 4903[7] 5121[9] 5871[4] 6255[5] 6335[3] 6693[P] (Dead)

Summer Rose *R M H Cowell* a56 19
3 gr f Kyllachy—Roses Of Spring (Shareef Dancer (USA))
2981[16] 3502[8] 3867[6] 4308[7] 5015[4] 7528[2] 7648[5] (7835)

Summer's Lease *M L W Bell* 86
3 b f Pivotal—Finlaggan (Be My Chief (USA))
(5076) 6605[3] 7242[8]

Summer Soul (IRE) *Miss Lucinda V Russell* 78
6 b g Danehill(USA) —Blend Of Pace (IRE) (Sadler's Wells (USA))
3198[3]

Summers Target (USA) *B J Meehan* a36 87
2 ch g Mr Greeley(USA) —She's Enough (USA) (Exploit (USA))
4360[2] 5469[2] ◆ 6083[5] 6575[11]

Summerstrand (IRE) *M A Jarvis* a86 86
3 b f Cape Cross(IRE) —Flamelet (USA) (Theatrical)
(4161) 4694[4] ◆ 5309[5] 6170[3] 6467[11]

Summer Winds *T G Mills* a82 81
3 ch g Where Or When(IRE) —Jetbeeah (IRE) (Lomond (USA))
(903) 1244[2] 1839[3] 2327[2] 6866[6] 7211[5] 7314[8] 7526[3] 7752[2]

Summit Surge (IRE) *G M Lyons* a109 110
4 b g Noverre(USA) —Lady Peculiar (CAN) (Sunshine Forever (USA))
2026a[4] (2961a) 3536a[7] 6814[8]

Summon Up Theblood (IRE) *M R Channon* a65 97
3 b g Red Ransom(USA) —Diddymu (IRE) (Revoque (IRE))
1208[6] (1685) (2209) (3251) ◆ 3919[12] 4553[16] 5360[9] 5907[10]

Sun Catcher (IRE) *P G Murphy* a81 81
5 b g Cape Cross(IRE) —Taalluf (USA) (Hansel (USA))
901[6] 1040[7] 1260[2] 1842[10] 2101[9] (2289) 2533[12] 3612[11] 4390[11] 5799[7] 6356[12] 6888[8] 7194[8]

Sun Classique (AUS) *M F De Kock* 122
5 ch m Fuji Kiseki(JPN) —Elfenjer (AUS) (Last Tycoon)
(475a) ◆ (672a) (1091a)

Sundae *C F Wall* a57 99
4 b g Bahamian Bounty—Merry Rous (Rousillon (USA))
2195[12] 3056[4] 3680[9] 3881[11] 5930[11]

Sunday's Brunch (IRE) *B Grizzetti* 108
5 ch g Indian Lodge(IRE) —Pinky Mouse (IRE) (Machiavellian (USA))
2656a[5]

Sundowner (IRE) *G A Butler* a82 89
3 b c Galileo(IRE) —Sunsetter (USA) (Diesis)
(909) 1524[7] 2194[6] 2840[2] (Dead)

Sun In Splendour (USA) *A P Jarvis* a43 36
3 ch c Hold That Tiger(USA) —Fit To Win (USA) (Fit To Fight (USA))
1504[10] 1855[10] 2486[8] 3791[5]

Sunisa (IRE) *J Mackie* a66 84
7 b m Daggers Drawn(USA) —Winged Victory (IRE) (Dancing Brave (USA))
1072[10]

Sunley Smiles *D R C Elsworth* a50
3 ch f Arkadian Hero(USA) —Sunley Scent (Wolfhound (USA))
590[5] 705[7] 885[5] 976[11]

Sunley Sovereign *Mrs R A Carr* a61 56
4 b g Josr Algarhoud(IRE) —Pharsical (Pharly (FR))
4919[13] 5770[8] 6039[8] (6159) 6382[6] 6546[13] 7197[13] 7218[11]

Sunniva Duke (IRE) *R Hannon* a76 74
2 b c Bachelor Duke(USA) —Amandian (IRE) (Indian Ridge)
5929[4] 6246[5] (7191) 7460[6] 7538[8] 7739[2]

Sunny Future (IRE) *M S Saunders* a75 78
3 b c Masterful(USA) —Be Magic (Persian Bold)
3568[3] ◆ 4360[3] 5021[2] 5461[7] 5827[14]

Sunny Peace *B G Powell* 75
3 b f Vision Of Night—Three Gifts (Cadeaux Genereux)
1621[10] 1876[8] 2328[2] 2772[2] ◆

Sunny Power (AUS) *K W Lui* 117
6 b g Honour And Glory(USA) —Zebra (AUS) (Palace Music (USA))
7683a[5]

Sunnyside Tom (IRE) *R A Fahey* 81
4 b g Danetime(IRE) —So Kind (Kind Of Hush)
2445[4] (2841) (3214) 3367[4] 3972[7] 4627[11] 6052[11] 6363[11] 6813[12]

Sunny Spells *S C Williams* a65 52
3 b g Zamindar(USA) —Bright Spells (Salse (USA))
936[5] 1125[7] 1960[11] 2695[12] 5105[10] 5168[4] 5837[2] ◆ (6044)

Sunny Sprite *J M P Eustace* a70 69
3 b g Lujain(USA) —Dragon Star (Rudimentary (USA))
1194[5] 2546[4] 3117[8] 5964[12]

Sun Of The Sea *N P Littmoden* a83 80
4 b g Best Of The Bests(IRE) —Gem (Most Welcome)
(139) 428[2] 888[2] 1256[5] 3474[6]

Sun Quest *I W McInnes* a45 44
4 b g Groom Dancer(USA) —Icaressa (Anabaa (USA))
988[5] 1121[3] 1262[9]

Sunrise Safari (IRE) *R A Fahey* a66 106
5 b g Mozart(IRE) —Lady Scarlett (Woodman (USA))
497a[7] 670a[8] 3248[15] 4145[11] 4437[13] 5542[3] 6069[10]

Sunset Boulevard (IRE) *Miss Tor Sturgis* a66 75
5 b g Montjeu(IRE) —Lucy In The Sky (IRE) (Lycius (USA))
1768[5] 7711[5]

Sunset Crest *Mrs A Duffield* 80
2 b f Reel Buddy(USA) —Day Star (Dayjur (USA))
2845[2] (3259) 4175[2] 5359[6] 5855[12]

Sunset Resort (IRE) *A Berry* 8
3 b g King's Best(USA) —Summer Dreams (IRE) (Sadler's Wells (USA))
6163[6] 6762[14]

Sunshine Ellie *D Shaw* a46 51
2 ch f Desert Sun—Lindoras Glory (USA) (Gone West (USA))
5344[8] 5643[9] 6197[8] 7833[7]

Sunshine Lady (IRE) *D Haydn Jones* a58 39
3 b f Captain Rio—Damezao (Alzao (USA))
262[4] ◆ 2052[10] 2639[14] 6492[11] 6660[9]

Sun Ship (IRE) *R Hannon* 90
2 b c Xaar—Silky Dawn (IRE) (Night Shift (USA))
1439[3] 1714[3] (2124) 3152[9] 3634[5] 5226[10] 5496[4] 5827[21]

Supa Seeker (USA) *A W Carroll*
2 bb c Petionville(USA) —Supamova (USA) (Seattle Slew (USA))
6425[17]

Supaseus *H Morrison* 112
5 b g Spinning World(USA) —Supamova (USA) (Seattle Slew (USA))
1828[4] 2103[3] (3195) 3974[15] 4436[3] 5289[7] 5528a[8]

Supaverdi (USA) *H Morrison* a69 48
3 br f Green Desert(USA) —Supamova (USA) (Seattle Slew (USA))
7084[5] 7344[3] (7609)

Supera (IRE) *M H Tompkins* a43 41
2 ch f Spartacus(IRE) —Lauretta Blue (IRE) (Bluebird (USA))
5835[12] 6885[11]

Super Al *M Wigham* a20 15
3 b g Largesse—Palmstead Belle (IRE) (Wolfhound (USA))
700[8] 1581[10] 5049[8] 5627[8] 6015[10] 6337[11] 6447[7]

Supercast (IRE) *N J Vaughan* a82 79
5 b g Alhaarth(IRE) —Al Euro (FR) (Mujtahid (USA))
214[2] ◆ 323[2] (560) 811[3] 1449[DSQ] 2262[4] 2749[4] (3257) (3579) 4219[7] 5418[3] 6346[3] 6758[6] (7502) 7758[3]

Superduper *R Hannon* 85
3 b f Erhaab(USA) —I'm Magic (First Trump)
2067[3] 2622[2] (2991) ◆ 3462[5] (4252) 5310[2] 5839[4] 6402[11]

Super Flight *P W Chapple-Hyam* 64
2 b c Exceed And Excel(AUS) —Strings (Unfuwain (USA))
5068[7] 5882[8] 6524[13]

Superfling *H J Manners* a24 42
7 ch g Superpower—Jobiska (Dunbeath (USA))
4104[16]

Super Fourteen *R Hannon* 63
2 b c Lucky Story(USA) —Beechnut (IRE) (Mujadil (USA))
2324[8] 2893[11] 3693[4] 4828[3] 5511[5] 5960[3] (6333)

Super Frank (IRE) *J Akehurst* a86 77
5 b g Cape Cross(IRE) —Lady Joshua (IRE) (Royal Academy (USA))
26[4] 313[2] 456[2] (717) 969[9] 1566[7] 1996[11] 2203[12] 2556[9] 6627[10] 7299[10] 7507[5] 7837[9]

Super Hornet (JPN) *Y Yahagi* 124
5 b h Rodrigo De Triano(USA) —You Sun Polish (JPN) (El Senor (USA))
7684a[5]

Superior Duchess *Jane Chapple-Hyam* a44 57
3 b f Superior Premium—Downclose Duchess (King's Signet (USA))
4929[5] 5652[3] 7321[5] 7590[9]

Superior Star *N Wilson* a63 74
5 b g Superior Premium—Lindfield Belle (IRE) (Fairy King (USA))
659[5] 996[4] 4048[13] 4172[5] 4650[12] 4850[7] (5454) 6162[7] 6385[7] 6482[21]

Superius (IRE) *T Stack* a84 99
3 b g High Chaparral(IRE) —Zing Ping (IRE) (Thatching)
3805a[5] 5729a[6] 6261a[11]

Super King *A D Brown* 26
7 b g Kingsinger(IRE) —Super Sisters (AUS) (Call Report (USA))
3557[9]

Superman (DEN) *Hanne Bechmann*
3 b c Palatal(USA) —Skee The Feen (Viking (USA))
4918a[5]

Supermassive Muse (IRE) *E S McMahon* a90 93
3 br g Captain Rio—Cautionary (IRE) (Warning)
1611[3] 1911[2] 2407[7] 3000[4] 3455[4] (4000) 4595[6] 4922[6] (5493) 5886[2] 6449[3] 6810[2]

Super Midge *B J Meehan* 52
2 b f Royal Applause—Sabina (Prince Sabo)
3625[6] 4149[12]

Supernoverre (IRE) *Mrs A J Perrett* a71 71
2 b c Noverre(USA) —Caviare (Cadeaux Genereux)
2972[15] 3164[4] 3519[5] 5460[5] 6199[4] 6674[11] 7069[4] (7353) 7505[2]

Super Sleuth (IRE) *B J Meehan* 99
3 ch f Selkirk(USA) —Enemy Action (USA) (Forty Niner (USA))
5241[7] 6076[2] ◆ 6439[5] 7144[2]

Supersonic Dave (USA) *B J Meehan* a94 109
4 bb h Swain(IRE) —Vickey's Echo (CAN) (Clever Trick (USA))
1944[2] 2625[8] 3975[8] 5288[4] 5694[8] 6286[7]

Super Starlet (IRE) *M Botti* a43 24
3 b f Statue Of Liberty(USA) —Wings To Soar (USA) (Woodman (USA))
20[P]

Superstitious Me (IRE) *B Palling* a49 52
2 b f Desert Prince(IRE) —Royal Rival (IRE) (Marju (IRE))
2663[7] 4534[3] 4931[4] 5606[14] 6135[8]

Support Fund (IRE) *Eve Johnson Houghton* a65 81
4 ch m Intikhab(USA) —Almost A Lady (IRE) (Entitled)
1345[3] 1641[2] (1867) 2128[3] 3507[9] 3892[3] 4174[10] 4433[5] 4723[10] 5069[6] 5600[7] (6671) 6899[3] 7307[10]

Supporting Role (IRE) *E S McMahon* a57 54
3 b g Marju(IRE) —Intercession (Bluebird (USA))
976[2] ◆ 1343[5] 1696[14] 2639[7] 3126[14] 3569[3]

Supremely Blessed *D W Thompson* 8
4 b m Supreme Sound—Far Howe (Respect)
3282[15] 6055[14] 6217[14] 7131[9]

Supreme Speedster *M Brittain* a62 59
4 br h Superior Premium—Effervescent (Efisio)
84[9] 370[4] 636[5] 766[8] 2583[9] 2596[11] 2950[10]

Surprende Espere *Jennie Candlish* a13
8 b g Espere D'Or—Celtic Dream (Celtic Cone)
3688[7]

Surprise Gift *J J Quinn* 35
2 b f Intikhab(USA) —Digamist Girl (IRE) (Digamist (USA))
6213[9] 6787[15]

Surdoue *J G M O'Shea* a58 45
8 b g Bishop Of Cashel—Chatter's Princess (Cadeaux Genereux)
2863[7] 3131[8]

Surdoue (USA) *Robert Collet* 75
2 b c Gone West(USA) —La Promenade (ARG) (Southern Halo (USA))
7163a[11]

Surething (FR) *M Rolland* a92 95
3 b c Zieten(USA) —Moldava (FR) (Saumarez)
1712a[6]

Surf Cat (USA) *Bruce Headley* a121 100
6 bb h Sir Cat(USA) —Trust Greta (USA) (Centrust (USA))
6995a[12]

Surprise Act *P R Chamings* a61 69
4 gr g Act One—Surprise Surprise (Robellino (USA))
1898[13] 2477[10] 5816[4] 6364[12]

Surprise Package (FR) *H J L Dunlop* a53 69
3 ch c Cadeaux Genereux—Red Yellow Blue (USA) (Sky Classic (CAN))
5023[2] 5366[3]

Surprise Party *C F Wall* 69
2 b f Red Ransom(USA) —Surprise Visitor (IRE) (Be My Guest (USA))
3959[4] 4328[3] 6552[5] 6924[13]

Surprise Pension (IRE) *J J Quinn* 66
4 b g Fruits Of Love(USA) —Sheryl Lynn (Miller's Mate)
4219[15] (6161) 6786[4] 7039[2]

Surrealism *J H M Gosden* 86
3 gr f Pivotal—Dali's Grey (Linamix (FR))
6055[5] ◆ 6275[3] ◆ (6896) 7242[6]

Surrounded *R W Price* a33 69
2 b f Distant Music(USA) —Vacance (Polish Precedent (USA))
6084[3] 6580[4] 7093[8]

Suruor (IRE) *M Johnston* 73
2 b c Intikhab(USA) —Kismah (Machiavellian (USA))
2507[5] 3107[2] (4014) 4589[7] 5511[10] ◆ 5883[3]

Survivor's Song *D K Ivory* a55 73
2 b c Falbrav(IRE) —Linda's Schoolgirl (IRE) (Grand Lodge (USA))
2146[9] 4982[6] 6084[4] 7011[5]

Surwaki (USA) *R M H Cowell* a67 79
6 b g Miswaki(USA) —Quinella (Generous (IRE))
1449[2] 1729[5] 2533[6] 3691[7] 5069[11] 7433[2] 7677[8] 7803[3]

Sushisan (AUS) *J M P Eustace* 119
6 ch g Fuji Kiseki(JPN) —Meine Tochter (AUS) (Bataan (AUS))
494a[2] 739a[3] 1091a[6] 6074[5]

Susiedil (IRE) *S T Mason* a18 46
7 b m Mujadil(USA) —Don't Take Me (IRE) (Don't Forget Me)
2[5] 2658[10] 3281[12] 4679[8] 7596[11]

Susie May *G L Moore* a69 98
4 ch m Hernando(FR) —Mohican Girl (Dancing Brave (USA))
(1148) (2354) ◆ 3220[3] 3562[2] 4549[4] 5264[6] 6241[4] 7100[10]

Sussex Dancer (IRE) *J A Osborne* a71 11
2 ch f Danehill Dancer(IRE) —Wadud (Nashwan (USA))
5570[3] 6982[12] 7422[3] 7726[3]

Susurrayshaan *Mrs G S Rees* 52
2 b g Dilshaan—Magic Mistral (Thowra (FR))
4593[13] 4960[10] 5590[13] 6292[9] 6534[6] 7229[5]

Sutania *P F I Cole* a39 45
2 b f Nayef(USA) —Suta (GER) (Lomitas)
4643[11] 5571[10] 6081[17]

Sutra (GER) *Mario Hofer* 89
3 ch f Big Shuffle(USA) —Simply Red (GER) (Dashing Blade)
2655a[7] 6692a[8]

Suzie Quw *K R Burke* 77
2 ch f Bahamian Bounty—Bonkers (Efisio)
3365[6] (4113) 4857[2] ◆ 6067[5]

Suzi's Decision *P W D'Arcy* 102
3 gr f Act One—Funny Girl (IRE) (Darshaan)
2118[2] (2376) 2840[8] (3351) (3729) 4435[3] (4667)

Suzi Spends (IRE) *H J Collingridge* a86 73
3 b f Royal Applause—Clever Clogs (Nashwan (USA))
2665[9] 2956[7] 4061[3] 4795[4] (5019) 5630[2] 5964[9] 6424[3] (6758) 6904[2] (7305)

Svindal (IRE) *K A Ryan* a63 60
2 ch g Tomba—Princess Sadie (Shavian)
1907[4] 5072[9] 5778[9] 5966[3] 6709[2] 7164[5] 7283[2] 7443[2] 7659[2]

Swallow Forest *T D Barron* a66 58
3 b f Averti(IRE) —Sangra (USA) (El Gran Senor (USA))
487[6] 917[5] 1120[2] (1257) 1475[9] 1754[2] 4383[6] 4609[7] 5457[2] 6159[7] 6890[10] 7444[9] (7615) 7698[6]

Swallow Senora (IRE) *M C Chapman* a22 37
6 b m Entrepreneur—Sangra (USA) (El Gran Senor (USA))
346[5] 479[6] 2491[9] 7616[7] 7727[8]

Swallow Star *R Bouresly* a68 75
3 b f Observatory(USA) —Swift Baba (USA) (Deerhound (USA))
201a[8] 496a[12] 812a[8]

Swanky Lady *R Hannon* a74 78
3 b f Cape Cross(IRE) —Lady Links (Bahamian Bounty)
1745[5] 2428[11]

Swan Queen *J L Dunlop* a46 99
5 b m In The Wings—Bronzewing (Beldale Flutter (USA))
1841[3] 2346a[9] 3209[7] 3942[7] 5853[11] 6817[21]

Sway Yed (KSA) *Saud Saad Alkahtani* a106
7 b h Nisnas(IRE) —Eidah (KSA) (Caerwent)
1092a[10]

Swayze (IRE) *M Quinn* a55 67
5 b g Marju(IRE) —Dance Of Love (IRE) (Pursuit Of Love)
57[6] 640[13]

Sweet Afton (IRE) *M S Saunders* 92
5 b m Mujadil(USA) —Victory Peak (Shirley Heights)
1698[3] ◆ 2326[3] 2773[5]

Sweet Andromeda *T J Fitzgerald* a39 49
3 ch f Observatory(USA) —Smooth Princess (IRE) (Roi Danzig (USA))
439[12] (Dead)

Sweet And Sour (IRE) *Robert Collet* a67 91
3 b f Kalanisi(IRE) —Graten (IRE) (Zieten (USA))
7431a[3] 7450a[12]

Sweet Applause (IRE) *A P Jarvis* a76 82
2 b f Acclamation—Nice Spice (IRE) (Common Grounds)
1967[9] 2759[5] 3123[8] 3792[2] 4403[16] 5204[7] 5466[8] 5680[4] 6603[11] 6696[4] 6769[4] ◆ 7113[2] 7575[7]

Sweet Demerara *P Butler* a19
4 ch m Sugarfoot—Scotland Bay (Then Again)
273[6] 909[12] 7553[12] 7801[12]

Sweet Destiny *M H Tompkins*
3 b f Namid—Cinnamon Lady (Emarati (USA))
3810[10] 4166[14]

Sweet Gale (IRE) *Mike Murphy* a82 81
4 b m Soviet Star(USA) —Lady Moranbon (USA) (Trempolino (USA))
4022[10] 5144[9] 5697[7] 6178[7] 6734[11]

Sweetheart *Jamie Poulton* a73 73
4 b m Sinndar(IRE) —Love And Adventure (USA) (Halling (USA))
1017[7]

Sweet Hearth (USA) *R Betti* 101
2 ch f Touch Gold(USA) —Sweet Gold (USA) (Gilded Time (USA))
5951a[4]

Sweet Hollow *C G Cox* 69
2 b f Beat Hollow—Three Piece (Jaazeiro (USA))
6945[4]

Sweet Hope (USA) *K A Ryan* a99 80
3 bb f Lemon Drop Kid(USA) —High Heeled Hope (USA) (Salt Lake (USA))
217[4]

Sweet Kiss (USA) *M J Attwater* a66 81
3 gr f Yes It's True(USA) —Always Freezing (USA) (Robyn Dancer (USA))
1925[10] 2276[7] 2981[4] 3268[3] 3727[6] 6380[6] 7027[5] 7194[9] 7490[11]

Sweet Lightning *W R Muir* a93 93
3 b g Fantastic Light(USA) —Sweetness Herself (Unfuwain (USA))
1243[2] (1563) 2109[9] 2665[4] (3471) ◆ 3633[3] 5111[3] 5573[4] 5938[4] 6355[6]

Sweet Lilly *M R Channon* a74 113
4 b m Tobougg(IRE) —Maristax (Reprimand)
475a[4] 672a[9] 1801[3] 2325[2] 3088[5] 3720[8] (4395) 4667[5] 4977[2] 5332a[7] 6106[5] 6781[8]

Sweet Mind *R A Fahey* a41 59
3 b f Mind Games—Cape Charlotte (Mon Tresor)
1132[3] 2282[10]

Sweet Mujahid *R A Harris* a21 2
2 b g Mujahid(USA) —Sweet Angeline (Deploy)
1555[5] 2049[5] 2450[8]

Sweet Pickle *J R Boyle* a87 84
7 b m Piccolo—Sweet Wilhelmina (Indian Ridge)
(72) 111[2] 173[2] 2504[4] 2831[4] 2993[10] 4016[7] 4483[7]

Sweet Possession (USA) *A P Jarvis* 73
2 b f Belong To Me(USA) —Bingo Meeting (USA) (General Meeting (USA))
3674[9] 4359[3] 4868[11] 6305[7]

Sweet Refrain *M J Attwater* a49
3 ch f Tobougg(IRE) —Steppin Out (First Trump)
772[9] 1050[6] 1270[10] 1959[11] 2756[14] 3342[P]

Sweet Request *Dr J R J Naylor* a68 71
4 ch m Best Of The Bests(IRE) —Sweet Revival (Claude Monet (USA))
2641[8] 2990[8] 3448[9] 4105[11]

Sweet Sara *C E Brittain* a75 77
3 b f Mark Of Esteem(IRE) —Mild Deception (IRE) (Glow (USA))
2973[4] (3644) 4170[9] 5449[6] 5999[7] 6703[10]

Sweet Seville (FR) *Mrs G S Rees* a24 46
4 b m Agnes World(USA) —Hispalis (IRE) (Barathea (IRE))
2571[7] 3089[9] 5593[9] 6248[9] 7174[4] 7400[9] 7661[6]

Sweet Sixteen (IRE) *A P O'Brien* 89
3 b f Sadler's Wells(USA) —User Friendly (Slip Anchor)
2113a[5] 3805a[11] 4100a[10] 4833a[8]

Sweet Smile (IRE) *K A Ryan* a57 70
2 b c Catcher In The Rye(IRE) —Quivala (USA) (Thunder Gulch (USA))
1987[4] (2730) 3576[6] 4816[2] 5632[19] 6730[5]

Sweet Virginia (USA) *K R Burke* a37 27
2 bb f Arch(USA) —Hey Hey Sunny (USA) (Known Fact (USA))
2775[8] 3125[6] 4740[9] 7298[7] 7467[6]

Sweet World *B J Llewellyn* a64 69
4 b g Agnes World(USA) —Douce Maison (IRE) (Fools Holme (USA))
122[4] 139[6] 512[6] 653[2] 1041[3] 1895[9] 2277[8] 2932[4] 3474[7] 3844[5] 4023[6] (4899) 5221[2] 5603[8]

Swift Acclaim (IRE) *K R Burke* a53 50
3 b f Acclamation—Swift Chorus (Music Boy)
2141[9] 2660[8] 3086[7] 3395[2] 4242[7] 4686[13] 5015[9]

Swift Chap *B R Millman* 81
2 b g Diktat—Regent's Folly (IRE) (Touching Wood (USA))
2769[6] (3645) 4589[5] (5511) 6082[8]

Swift Cut (IRE) *D Burchell* a65 70
4 ch g Daggers Drawn(USA) —Jugendliebe (IRE) (Persian Bold)
512[5] 622[3] 794[7] 914[5] 1044[7] 1898[6] 2664[5] 2988[2] 3329[5] 3822[11]

Swift Gift *B J Meehan* a89 92
3 b g Cadeaux Genereux—Got To Go (Shareef Dancer (USA))
1834[3] 2104[4] 2624[2] 3039[5] 6783[4] 7418[6] 7470[5]

Swift Princess (IRE) *K R Burke* 91
4 b m Namid—Swift Chorus (Music Boy)
1430[10] (1755) ◆ 2598[8] 3554[2] 3973[3] 4240[12] 5503[2] 5831[20] 6160[7] 7222[7]

Swift Sailing (USA) *Patrick Allen* a48 75
7 b g Storm Cat(USA) —Saytarra (USA) (Seeking The Gold (USA))
4003a[14]

Swimandyouwin (IRE) *Shaun Harley* a42
5 b g Xaar—Mouette (FR) (Fabulous Dancer (USA))
127[6] 144[11]

Swinbrook (USA) *R A Fahey* a83 85
7 ch g Stravinsky(USA) —Dance Diane (USA) (Affirmed (USA))
1015[2] (1134) ◆ 1327[4] 1617[2] 1796[3] 2210[6] 2698[4] 3281[4] 4476[2] 4586[13] 5708[4]

Swindler (IRE) *A M Balding* 79
2 b c Sinndar(IRE) —Imitation (Darshaan)
3853[2] ◆

Swindon Town Flyer (IRE) *A B Haynes* a49 68
3 b g Captain Rio—Baltic Breeze (USA) (Labeeb)
848[7] (1536) 2068[5] 2690[6] 3575[7] 4325[8] 5217[7] 5393[6] 6190[8] 7636[12]

Swing And Rock (IRE) *A Trybuhl* 65
3 b f Rock Of Gibraltar(IRE) —Saldenschwinge (GER) (In The Wings)
6742a[6]

Swingfire (USA) *R M H Cowell* a59 72
2 b c Doneraile Court(USA) —Incoming Missile (USA) (Touch Gold (USA))
1399[10] 1778[7] 3158[2] 3689[3] 4079[8] (4373) 5274[15] (5581) 6082[5] 6362[9] 6756[9]

Swinging Sixties (IRE) *M A Jarvis* 105
3 b c Singspiel(IRE) —Velvet Lady (Nashwan (USA))
(2119) ◆ 3048[4] (3527) 4519[7] 5830[5] (6445) ◆

Swing It Ruby (IRE) *Miss V Haigh* a48 42
2 br f Celtic Swing—Golconda (IRE) (Lahib (USA))
5857[12] 6089[6] 6789[15]

Swingkeel (IRE) *J L Dunlop* a84 86
3 ch g Singspiel(IRE) —Anniversary (Salse (USA))
1398[12] 1840[4] 2454[3] 2997[10] 3685[3] (4087) 4866[6] 5698[4] 6361[4]

Swing That Cat (USA) *F Reuterskiold*
3 b c Cat Thief(USA) —Incha (Nashwan (USA))
(4918a)

Swiss Art (IRE) *R A Harris* a61
2 b g One Cool Cat(USA) —Alpine Park (IRE) (Barathea (IRE))
6574[2] 6910[8] 7165[4] 7468[6] 7645[5]

Swiss Diva *D R C Elsworth* a82 84
2 br f Pivotal—Swiss Lake (USA) (Indian Ridge)
3219[7] 6776[3] 7020[2] 7104[2] (7388)

Swiss Franc *D R C Elsworth* a105 107
3 br c Mr Greeley(USA) —Swiss Lake (USA) (Indian Ridge)
2605[3] 3063[6] 7421[3] 7703[9]

Swiss Lake Sweetie (USA) *George Baker* a47 67
2 ch f Action This Day(USA) —Almost Blue (USA) (Mr Greeley (USA))
5394[5] ◆ 5838[6] 7734[4]

Swop (IRE) *L M Cumani* a91 104
5 b g Shinko Forest(IRE) —Changing Partners (Rainbow Quest (USA))
1936[2] (3054) 4509[2] 5508[3] 6476[3]

Swords *R E Peacock* a71 56
6 b g Vettori(IRE) —Pomorie (IRE) (Be My Guest (USA))
2051[8] 2755[4] 4029[7] (4391) (4477) 4935[2] (5154) (5476) 6472[9] 7364[8] 7515[5] 7647[2] 7722[4]

Sworn (USA) *J Noseda* 68
2 b f Yes It's True(USA) —Take The Lady Out (USA) (Take Me Out (USA))
5240[10] 6198[4]

Sworn Pro (GER) *Mario Hofer*
2 br f Protektor(GER) —Sweet Tern (GER) (Arctic Tern (USA))
(7006a)

Sydney (DEN) *Birgitte Nielsen* a62
3 b f Academy Award(IRE) —Kirobel (GER) (Robellino (USA))
4917a[6]

Sydney Cove (IRE) *M Johnston* a38 47
2 b c Cape Cross(IRE) —First Fleet (USA) (Woodman (USA))
6481[11] 6760[9] 7011[11]

Sydneyroughdiamond *M Mullineaux* a36 52
6 b g Whittingham(IRE) —November Song (Scorpio (FR))
3952[5] 4538[9] 4746[5] 5454[9] 7267[9]

Sydneysider *Eve Johnson Houghton* 67
3 b g Averti(IRE) —Cajole (IRE) (Barathea (IRE))
2919[8] 3916[3] 4431[4]

Sylvias Grove *B Smart* a46 72
3 b f Royal Applause—Branston Fizz (Efisio)
2014[2] ◆ 2366[5] 2670[5] 7018[10] 7513[6]

Symonette *M Johnston* a58
2 b c Cape Cross(IRE) —Gombay Girl (USA) (Woodman (USA))
7709[7]

Synergy (FR) *Y Durepaire* 98
3 b f Victory Note(USA) —Kuddam (IRE) (Doyoun)
7431a[2]

Synonymy *M Blanshard* a66 64
6 b g Sinndar(IRE) —Peony (Lion Cavern (USA))
212[5] 1062[8] 1267[3] (1408) 1856[8] (2012) 2393[6] 2643[5] 3137[9] 4775[4] 4935[6] 5651[7] 6060[11] 6252[6] 6824[5] 7455[9] 7827[8]

Syriana *A Bailey* 52
3 b f Dubai Destination(USA) —Syrian Dancer (IRE) (Groom Dancer (USA))
2573[7] 3058[8] 3624[12] 4498[6] 4722[14]

Syrinx (IRE) *J Noseda* a68 73
2 b f One Cool Cat(USA) —Latest Chapter (IRE) (Ahonoora)
2713[5] 5066[3] 5788[4]

Syrup (IRE) *P D Evans* 43
2 b f Pyrus(USA) —Sweet Chat (IRE) (Common Grounds)
1264[3] 1480[5] 1555[2] 2216[8] 2459[5] 3309[5] (Dead)

Sytygre *Miss J A Camacho* a30
2 gb g Paris House—Blue Wraith (Bluegrass Prince (IRE))
7227[10] 7425[10]

Syvilla *Rae Guest* 88
3 b f Nayef(USA) —Dance Steppe (Rambo Dancer (CAN))
1964[13] 2717[2] 3810[2] 4909[2] (5750) 6921a[6]

Szaba *J Akehurst* a51 28
3 ch f Tipsy Creek(USA) —Compton Alice (Compton Place)
271[6] 498[5] 1295[8] 1672[4] 1897[9] 7022[7] 7759[8]

Taameer *M P Tregoning* 105
2 b c Beat Hollow—Vayavaig (Damister (USA))
(6075) ◆ 6648[2]

Taarab *Saeed Bin Suroor* 82
2 ch c Refuse To Bend(IRE) —Tanzania (USA) (Darshaan)
7054[2]

Taaresh (IRE) *J L Dunlop* 80
3 b c Sakhee(USA) —Tanaghum (Darshaan)
4349[2] (5361) 5865[7]

Taazur *M Johnston* 79
2 b c Needwood Blade—Mouchez Le Nez (IRE) (Cyrano De Bergerac)
2281[2] 2696[5] 3400[3] 4143[3] 4626[2] 6002[3] 6480[4] 6885[2]

Tabadul (IRE) *M Al Muhairi* a106 101
7 b g Cadeaux Genereux—Amaniy (USA) (Dayjur (USA))
650a[16]

Tabaret *R M Whitaker* a99 101
5 ch g Bertolini(USA) —Luanshya (First Trump)
1393[8] 2129[6] 2538[11] 2626[4] 3009[14] (3228) 3680[2] 4445[12] 5509[13] 5906[10] 6184[6] 6285[4] 6902[11]

Tableau Vivant (IRE) *Sir Michael Stoute* a86 86
3 b f Pivotal—Sea Picture (IRE) (Royal Academy (USA))
1372[3] 1721[2] 2929[2] (3870) 4433[2] 5071[2] 5683[4]

Taboor (IRE) *R M H Cowell* a61 58
10 b g Mujadil(USA) —Christoph's Girl (Efisio)
86[3] 247[5] 641[4] 857[4] (1028) 1185[12] 1706[7] 2075[8] 4064[10] (4285) 4703[9] 5319[3] 5626[7] 6595[4] 7522[8] 7836[4]

Tabulate *P Howling* a66 33
5 b m Dansili—Let Alone (Warning)
76[4] 269[3] (400) 518[7] 686[7] 769[6] 1031[2] 1282[6] 1505[5] 2078[6] 2832[6] (4182) 5087[3] 5787[2] 6019[7] 7217[4] 7342[6] 7596[5] 7626[6]

Tactful (IRE) *R M Beckett* a89
3 b f Intikhab(USA) —Crozon (Peintre Celebre (USA))
(6047) (6684) ◆ 7635a[7]

Tactic *J L Dunlop* 76
2 b c Sadler's Wells(USA) —Tanaghum (Darshaan)
6117[4] ◆ 6604[3]

Tactical Move *Miss V Haigh* 61
3 b c Diktat—My Mariam (Salse (USA))
1298[2] 1573[6] 1781[10] (Dead)

Tadalavil *M R Channon* a76 85
3 gr g Clodovil(IRE) —Blandish (USA) (Wild Again (USA))
926[5] 1167[9] 2460[7] 2883[4] 3324[3] 3782[5] 4252[8] 4782[2] (5028) 5056[10] 5510[3] 5839[3] 5962[2] 6402[13] 6532[3]

Tadlil *J M Bradley* a56 52
6 b g Pivotal—Pretty Poppy (Song)
1522[14] 1872[14] 2798[13] 2968[12] 3608[10] 4125[13] 4903[8] 5152[4] 5797[11] 5916[5] 7369[2] 7509[4] 7615[9] 7637[2] 7746[6]

Tae Kwon Do (USA) *E A L Dunlop* a63 60
2 b g Thunder Gulch(USA) —Judy's Magic (USA) (Wavering Monarch (USA))
4062[9] 4304[4] 4636[4] 5432[5] 5914[7] 6394[12] 6632[8]

Tafaool (IRE) *M P Tregoning* a65
2 b f Green Desert(USA) —Sundus (USA) (Sadler's Wells (USA))
6620[7]

Tagalura (IRE) *J O'Reilly*
2 b g Tagula(IRE) —Allurah (IRE) (Goldmark (USA))
1987[11]

Tag Team (IRE) *John A Harris* a73 53
7 ch g Tagula(IRE) —Okay Baby (IRE) (Treasure Kay)
(4) 241[2] 554[6] 1040[10] 2081[5] 2293[8] 2950[6] 3169[7] 3819[8]

Tagula Blue (IRE) *Ian Williams* a52 72
8 b g Tagula(IRE) —Palace Blue (IRE) (Dara Monarch)
5058[8] (5367) 5934[6]

Tagula Breeze (IRE) *I W McInnes* 80
2 b c Tagula(IRE) —Pearl Egg (IRE) (Mukaddamah (USA))
2035[10] 2362[4] (2909) 3809[3] 4626[4] 5226[9] 5794[7]

Tagula King (IRE) *D Carroll* 36
3 b g Tagula(IRE) —Isla (IRE) (Turtle Island (IRE))
2669[P] 3166[10]

Tagula Minx (IRE) *J Pearce* a52 20
2 b f Tagula(IRE) —Persian Fantasia (Alzao (USA))
6887[12] 7259[6]

Tagula Night (IRE) *W R Swinburn* a70 36
2 ch c Tagula(IRE) —Carpet Lady (IRE) (Night Shift (USA))
4024[11] 7333[10] 7465[2]

Tagula Sands (IRE) *J C Fox* a42
4 b g Tagula(IRE) —Pomme Pomme (USA) (Dayjur (USA))
11[11] 120[9] 1836[10] 2528[14] 3675[6] 4181[6] 7801[10]

Tagula Sunrise (IRE) *R A Fahey* a69 94
6 ch m Tagula(IRE) —Lady From Limerick (IRE) (Rainbows For Life (CAN))
85[7] 280[7] 733[6]

Tagula Sunset (IRE) *P T Midgley* 50
2 b f Tagula(IRE) —My Mimi (USA) (Diesis)
1447[5] 1794[5] 2134[9] 5381[10] 6009[10]

Tahfeez (IRE) *Sir Michael Stoute* a60
2 b f Alhaarth(IRE) —Ghazal (USA) (Gone West (USA))
7311[7] 7458[6]

Tahkeem *M P Tregoning* a15
2 b f Green Desert(USA) —Katayeb (IRE) (Machiavellian (USA))
7311[11]

T'Ai Chi *John A Harris*
7 b m Pursuit Of Love—Trojan Desert (Troy)
172[P]

Taikoo *H Morrison* a92 81
3 b g Dr Fong(USA) —So True (So Blessed)
(172) 1678[2] 1962[8] 4021[11] (5900) 6355[5] 6974[5] 7314[4] (7664)

Tajaaweed (USA) *Sir Michael Stoute* 115
3 br c Dynaformer(USA) —Uforia (USA) (Zilzal (USA))
(1943) ◆ 2829[8] 4436[5]

Tajdeef (USA) *B W Hills* 111
3 gr c Aljabr(USA) —Tabheej (IRE) (Mujtahid (USA))
1718[2] 2148[2] 2605[2] 3041[6] 4617[3]

Tajneed (IRE) *D Nicholls* 103
5 b g Alhaarth(IRE) —Indian Express (Indian Ridge)
1300[3] (1430) 1809[11] (5109) 6104[2]

Tajweed (IRE) *M Johnston* 91
3 ch g Pivotal—Mannakea (USA) (Fairy King (USA))
991[2] (1307) ◆ (1753) 2825[12] 6445[6]

Takaamul *K A Morgan* a59 54
5 ch g Almutawakel—Mafaatin (IRE) (Royal Academy (USA))
(209) 267[8] 728[12] 7706[11]

Takaatuf (IRE) *M Johnston* 81
2 b c Dubai Destination(USA) —Karlaka (IRE) (Barathea (IRE))
2592[13] 5842[5] (6234)

Take A Mile (IRE) *C Gordon* a59 59
6 ch g Inchinor—Bu Hagab (IRE) (Royal Academy (USA))
330[10] (420) 541[9] 1643[3] 3084[12]

Takeanoteofthat (IRE) *D Burchell* a29
6 b g Victory Note(USA) —Classic Queen (IRE) (Classic Secret (USA))
130[8] 326[6] 715[4] 1259[5] 2259[11]

Take It Easee (IRE) *G A Swinbank* 65
3 b f Noverre(USA) —Fairy Lore (IRE) (Fairy King (USA))
1519[7] 1869[8] 2038[3] 2490[5] 2911[4] 5544[4]

Take It There *A J Lidderdale* a61 47
6 ch m Cadeaux Genereux—Feel Free (IRE) (Generous (IRE))
219[3] 356[9]

Take Me There *John Berry* a71
5 b g Cape Cross(IRE) —Mill Path (Mill Reef (USA))
(7721) ◆

Takemor (FR) *J-J Boutin* 18
2 ch c Take Risks(FR) —Makzane (FR) (Nikos)
385a[8]

Taken (IRE) *Miss Gay Kelleway* a76 79
3 b g Red Ransom(USA) —Heart's Harmony (Blushing Groom (FR))
(130) 458[5] 799[2] 3461[2] 3745[11] 6021[6] 6528[7] 6905[5] 7111[8] 7506[2] 7604[P]

Takeover Bid (USA) *M Johnston* a72 68
2 b c Empire Maker(USA) —Seba (Alzao (USA))
6714[3] ◆ 6926[6] (7170) 7475[8]

Takeover Target (AUS) *J Janiak* 122
9 b g Celtic Swing—Shady Stream (AUS) (Archregent (CAN))
(2235a) 3101[2] 3247[4]

Takestan (IRE) *Patrick O Brady* a28 49
5 b g Selkirk(USA) —Takariya (IRE) (Arazi (USA))
1105a[20]

Take That *S P Griffiths* 13
3 b g Kasakov—Baby Be (Bold Arrangement)
6114[11] 7528[13]

Take The Hint *J H M Gosden* 83
2 b f Montjeu(IRE) —Insinuate (USA) (Mr Prospector (USA))
6081[7] (6887)

Take The Micky *W J Knight* a74 66
2 b c Beat Hollow—Ailincala (IRE) (Pursuit Of Love)
5246[7] 6031[8] (6876)

Take To The Skies (IRE) *Miss Tracy Waggott* a63 53
4 b g Lujain(USA) —To The Skies (USA) (Sky Classic (CAN))
2487[9] 3037[9] 3551[13] 3839[11] 5380[5] 6163[4]

Takhir (IRE) *P Schiergen*
2 b c Lando(GER) —Tocopilla (FR) (Medaaly)
5686a[3]

Takitwo *P D Cundell* a67 71
5 b g Delta Dancer—Tiama (IRE) (Last Tycoon)
149[7] 576[10] 2917[3] 3383[11] 4807[5] 4979[3] 5639[6] 6208[2] 6560[9] 7382[3] 7653[9]

Takyro (FR) *J-P Pelat* 88
2 br c Take Risks(FR) —Ninazeyra (FR) (Sheyrann)
3774a[6]

Talamahana *A B Haynes* a63 55
3 b f Kyllachy—Bahawir Pour (USA) (Green Dancer (USA))
23[7] 92[4] (306) 425[3] (583) 709[3] 797[5] 876[8] 2260[11] 3678[14] 4278[12] 4725[7] 5832[12] 6751[8]

Talayeb *M P Tregoning* a44 81
3 bb g Nayef(USA) —Paper Chase (FR) (Machiavellian (USA))
1283[4] 1539[8] 2302[12] 3275[2] 4085[3]

Talcen Gwyn (IRE) *M F Harris* a50 65
6 b g Fayruz—Cheerful Knight (IRE) (Mac's Imp (USA))
4106[7] 4370[13] 4580[11] 6328[6] 7196[11] 7292[12]

Talenti (IRE) *Miss E C Lavelle* 96
5 b g Sadler's Wells(USA) —Sumoto (Mtoto)
1568[3] 6817[15]

Tale Of Ekati (USA) *Barclay Tagg* a116
3 b c Tale Of The Cat(USA) —Silence Beauty (JPN) (Sunday Silence (USA))
1820a[4] 2858a[6]

Tale Of Silver (IRE) *G A Swinbank* 84
2 b g Pyrus(USA) —Bajan Belle (IRE) (Efisio)
2035[9] 3669[3] 4415[2] ◆ (5539) (6038)

Tale Of Two Cities (IRE) *A P O'Brien* a71 96
3 b c Sadler's Wells(USA) —Kasora (IRE) (Darshaan)
1398[7]

Talking Hands *S Kirk* a90 100
2 b g Mujahid(USA) —With Distinction (Zafonic (USA))
2146[7] 3331[2] (3568) (3941) ◆ (4402) 5359[5] 5507[4] 5827[5] 6284[3] 6648[6]

Talk Of Saafend (IRE) *P Monteith* a78 83
3 b f Barathea(IRE) —Sopran Marida (IRE) (Darshaan)
2190[2] 2412[9] 2761[7] 3031[9] 4158[6] (4429) 4872[2] 5149[4] (5607) (6001) (6152) 6311[3]

Tallest Peak (USA) *M G Quinlan* a57
3 b g Giant's Causeway(USA) —Hum Along (USA) (Fappiano (USA))
1410[7] 1701[8] 1854[8] 2613[6] ◆ 2833[9] 3397[3] 5574[3] 7500[9]

Tallulah's Secret *J Gallagher* 20
2 b f Bertolini(USA) —Ascend (IRE) (Glint Of Gold)
4530[7] 5165[9] 6245[11]

Tallulah Sunrise *M D I Usher* a69 36
3 b f Auction House(USA) —Tallulah Belle (Crowning Honors (CAN))
12[3] 281[3]

Talon (IRE) *G A Swinbank* a48 59
3 ch g Indian Ridge—Brief Lullaby (IRE) (Brief Truce (USA))
1221[6] 1558[5] 2247[3] 4737[6] 4901[5] (5544) 6042[8] 7166[10] 7382[11]

Talsarnau (IRE) *W M Brisbourne* 36
2 b g Kheleyf(USA) —Ezilana (IRE) (Shardari)
2569[10] 3107[11] 4658[8]

Talulah Bells *A W Carroll* a18 44
2 br f Superior Premium—Hullo Mary Doll (Lidhame)
1264[6] 1384[5] 1574[4] 2450[4] 2548[6] 2720[4]

Tamagin (USA) *K A Ryan* a107 106
5 b g Stravinsky(USA) —Luia (USA) (Forty Niner (USA))
2530[2] 3248[5] 3946[10] 4437[10] 5109[3] 5890[9] 6104[9] 6269[8]

Tamarah *Miss D Mountain* 73
2 b f Beat Hollow—Valagalore (Generous (IRE))
2368[7] 3292[7] 6029[2] 6818[14]

Tamara Moon (IRE) *M R Channon* a64 77
3 b f Acclamation—Non Ultra (USA) (Peintre Celebre (USA))
1074[11] 2302[6] 2622[9] 3407[7]

Tamasou (IRE) *Garry Moss* a77 69
3 b g Tamarisk(IRE) —Soubresaut (IRE) (Danehill (USA))
484[4] 1396[4] 1819[6] 2429[5] 3206[4] (3790) 4180[2] 5224[4] 6042[4] 6287[8]

Tamayuz *F Head* 125
3 ch c Nayef(USA) —Al Ishq (FR) (Nureyev (USA))
(1361a) 2032a[9] (4010a) (5138a) 6270[4]

Tamborim (USA) *William Mott*
2 bb c Belong To Me(USA) —Miu Miu (USA) (Kris S (USA))
6502a[5]

Tamburello (ARG) *P Wahl* 98
5 br g Lode(USA) —Tatibitati (ARG) (Fitzcarraldo (ARG))
5957a[2]

Tamdiid (USA) *C E Brittain* a67 51
3 b f Horse Chestnut(SAF) —Ladue (USA) (Demons Begone (USA))
5445[4] 5803[7] 6018[7] 6227[10] 6735[10]

Tamerlano (USA) *M Johnston* 53
3 ch c Singspiel(IRE) —Innuendo (IRE) (Caerleon (USA))
2336[7]

Tamimi's History *P D Evans* 105
4 b g Kalanisi(IRE) —Polish Pink (IRE) (Polish Precedent (USA))
4845[7] 6120[12]

Taminas Desert *M Botti* a54
3 b f Green Desert(USA) —Tamise (USA) (Time For A Change (USA))
3133[6] ◆

Tamino (IRE) *P Howling* a66 80
5 b g Mozart(IRE) —Stop Out (Rudimentary (USA))
150[7] 404[6] 639[7] 1209[6] 1528[8] 2350[4] 2511[8] 2983[7] 6046[5] 7509[2] 7706[6] 7809[3]

Tampa Boy (IRE) *M F Harris* a66
6 b g Montjeu(IRE) —Tirolean Dance (IRE) (Tirol)
7583[5] 7721[6]

Tampopo (IRE) *D J S Ffrench Davis* a49 43
3 ch g Tamarisk(IRE) —Pumpona (USA) (Sharpen Up)
5023[6] 5426[6] 5748[5] 6332[5] 7018[9] 7373[8]

Tamrai Dancer *R M Beckett* 71
3 b f Tamure(IRE) —Rail Cat (Catrail (USA))
1128[3] 1530[10] 2603[5] 3393[14] 4859[11] 5148[6]

Tamreen (IRE) *R J Price* a84 34
7 b g Bahhare(USA) —Na-Ayim (IRE) (Shirley Heights)
6395[14]

Tamworth (IRE) *E J Creighton* a63 53
6 b g Perugino(USA) —Faiblesse (Welsh Saint)
120[8]

Tancredi (SWE) *N B King* a76 73
6 b g Rossini(USA) —Begine (IRE) (Germany (USA))
91[5] ◆ 207[3] 874[2] 879[5] 973[6] 1165[6]

Tanforan *B P J Baugh* a70 66
6 b g Mujahid(USA) —Florentynna Bay (Aragon)
49[2] 235[8] 395[5] 1708[3] 2373[11] 2925[8] 3329[6] 3431[6] 3757[4] 3951[3] 4683[7] (4813) 5045[5] 5198[2] 6408[6] 6585[3] 6867[4]

Tang *W G M Turner* a55 35
4 ch m Bahamian Bounty—Hymne (FR) (Saumarez)
254[9] 285[2] 353[2] 445[5] 535[4] 642[10] 1035[7]

Tangaspeed (FR) *R Laplanche* 109
3 b f Vertical Speed(FR) —Fitanga (FR) (Fijar Tango (FR))
2650a[9] 5039a[4] 5952a[6] 7037a[4] 7348a[4]

Tangerine Trees *B Smart* a65 72
3 b g Mind Games—Easy To Imagine (USA) (Cozzene (USA))
1452[7] 1971[2] 2466[6] 3231[3] 3455[12] 4615[9] 6218[6] 6486[3] (6707) 7276[5] 7428[3] 7671[4]

Tangible *Liam McAteer* a65 69
6 b m Hernando(FR) —Trinity Reef (Bustino)
4511a[13]

Tango Foxtrot (IRE) *W P Mullins* a90 90
6 bb g Foxhound(USA) —Tango Two Thousand (IRE) (Sri Pekan (USA))
3531a[10]

Tank Commander *W R Muir* a25 62
3 b g Polish Precedent(USA) —Herminoe (Rainbow Quest (USA))
2197[8] 2669[10] 3094[9] 3671[15] 4281[8] 5077[11] 5603[2] 5813[5] 6032[4] 6541[3] 6757[9] 6927[9]

Tanley *J F Coupland* a60 62
3 gr g Compton Admiral—Schatzi (Chilibang)
1452[8] 1674[2] 2380[4] 3030[10] 3298[10] 4703[6] 5307[11] 5457[3] 5911[4] 6308[2] (6595) 6766[7] 7197[3] 7295[3] 7529[7] 7618[8]

Tanning *M Appleby* a33 53
6 b m Atraf—Gerundive (USA) (Twilight Agenda (USA))
129[7] 322[8]

Tanoura (IRE) *John M Oxx* 89
2 b f Dalakhani(IRE) —Takarouna (USA) (Green Dancer (USA))
5924a[3]

Tante Dora (FR) *F-X de Chevigny*
2 b f Canyon Creek(IRE) —Tangshan (CAN) (Zilzal (USA))
7549a[0]

Tanto Faz (IRE) *W J Haggas* a88 90
3 b c Rock Of Gibraltar(IRE) —Sharakawa (IRE) (Darshaan)
3051[2] (3628) 4790[3] 5942[5] 6445[5]

Tantris (IRE) *J A Osborne* a68 63
3 b g High Chaparral(IRE) —Emerald Cut (Rainbow Quest (USA))
1410[5] ◆ 1737[7] 2340[10] 3781[2] 4086[7] 4646[6]

Tanweer (USA) *Sir Michael Stoute* 89
3 ch g Seeking The Gold(USA) —Fitted Crown (USA) (Chief's Crown (USA))
2104[6] 3046[12] 4197[8]

Tapaellya (IRE) *J E Long* a51 64
4 ch m Tobougg(IRE) —Confines (IRE) (Acatenango (GER))
3321[13] 5183[9] 6007[13] 6421[4] 7285[9] 7587[8] 7696[6]

Tapas Lad (IRE) *G J Smith* a62 57
3 b c Modigliani(USA) —Missish (Mummy's Pet)
156[3] (195) 288[5] 360[4] 464[6] 607[4] 704[4] 820[6] 976[7] 1193[2] 1533[5] 1870[3] (1938) 2613[8] 3397[8] 4533[12] 5378[13] 6173[12] 6752[5] 7373[6] 7581[7] 7599[2] 7663[6]

Tapis Wizard *M W Easterby* 76
2 b g Alhaarth(IRE) —Just Call Me (NZ) (Blues Traveller (IRE))
3411[5] 3976[3] 4415[6] 4733[4] 5447[9]

Taqdeyr *M A Jarvis* a88 77
3 ch g Dubai Destination(USA) —Pastorale (Nureyev (USA))
6393[5] ◆ 6791[2] (7321)

Taqseem (IRE) *M Al Muhairi* a101 104
5 b g Fantastic Light(USA) —Elshamms (Zafonic (USA))
291a[8]

Tara's Force (IRE) *J J Quinn* 53
3 b f Acclamation—Tara's Girl (IRE) (Fayruz)
3867[7]

Tara's Garden *M Blanshard* a17 61
3 b f Dr Fong(USA) —Tremiere (FR) (Anabaa (USA))
1869[2] 2451[4] 3095[11] 3845[4] 4344[10] 4708[6] 6956[8]

Tarawa Atoll *M R Channon* a52 48
2 b f Imperial Dancer—Musical Capers (Piccolo)
995[14] 1264[2] 1384[4] 4387[4] 5909[5] 6059[3] 7258[6] 7338[4] 7415[7]

Tariq *P W Chapple-Hyam* 119
4 ch h Kyllachy—Tatora (Selkirk (USA))
2193[3] 3100[9] 4518[5]

Tarkamara (IRE) *P F I Cole* a69 61
4 ch m Medicean—Tarakana (USA) (Shahrastani (USA))
5604[13] 6251[11] 7469[8] (7678) 7792[3]

Tarkheena Prince (USA) *G A Swinbank* a103 98
3 b g Aldebaran(USA) —Tarkheena (USA) (Alleged (USA))
(1573) ◆ 2819[9] (3493) ◆ 4021[7] 5391[3] (6107) 6527[3] (7150)

Tarraburn (USA) *G C H Chung* a37 72
4 ch g Eltish(USA) —Rahy's Wish (USA) (Rahy (USA))
4051[11] 4478[13] 5161[8] 6036[5] 6752[8]

Tarruji (IRE) *P W Chapple-Hyam* a26 60
2 gr c Verglas(IRE) —Polish Affair (IRE) (Polish Patriot (USA))
6117[15] 6600[4] 7465[10]

Tartan Bearer (IRE) *Sir Michael Stoute* 125
3 ch c Spectrum(IRE) —Highland Gift (IRE) (Generous (IRE))
(1621) (2131) ◆ 2829[2] 3535a[3]

Tartan Gigha (IRE) *M Johnston* a82 82
3 b g Green Desert(USA) —High Standard (Kris)
1073[11] 1429[8] 1748[3] 2269[2] (4454) 5397[6] 6052[8] 6598[4]

Tartan Gunna *M Johnston* a79 56
2 b g Anabaa(USA) —Embraced (Pursuit Of Love)
5387[7] 7726[2] ◆ 7812[2] ◆

Tartan Tie *M Johnston* a93 83
4 b g Grand Lodge(USA) —Trois Graces (USA) (Alysheba (USA))
105[3] ◆ 315[9] (1026) ◆ 1212[8] 1544[4] 1812[8] 2379[2]

Tartan Turban (IRE) *R Hannon* a48 65
2 b c Invincible Spirit(IRE) —Tappen Zee (Sandhurst Prince)
2592[15] (4024) 5228[10] 5647[7] 7212[5] 7361[8] 7600[8]

Tartatartufata *J G Given* a91 78
6 b m Tagula(IRE) —It's So Easy (Shaadi (USA))
(5) (84) 411[10] 593[5] 866[7] 907[8] 983[4] ◆ 1366[3] 1624[5] 1818[14] 2082[3] 6486[11] 7151[11] 7394[7] 7614[6]

Tarzan (IRE) *M Johnston* 68
2 ch g Spinning World(USA) —Run To Jane (IRE) (Doyoun)
3476[5] 5316[3] 6197[4]

Tasdeer (USA) *M A Jarvis* a103 103
3 b g Rahy(USA) —Mehthaaf (USA) (Nureyev (USA))
905[2] (1328) 2409[6] (3396) 3946[11] 5368[7]

Tasheba *P W Chapple-Hyam* a91 91
3 ch g Dubai Destination(USA) —Tatanka (IRE) (Lear Fan (USA))
1389[4] 1962[2] 2977[3] (3393) ◆ (3697) 4955[3]

Tashkandi (IRE) *Mrs S J Humphrey* a69 84
8 gr g Polish Precedent(USA) —Tashiriya (IRE) (Kenmare (FR))
2076[6]

Task Complete *Jean-Rene Auvray* a59 53
5 ch m Bahamian Bounty—Taskone (Be My Chief (USA))
327[5] 624[9]

Tasman Gold *A M Balding* a55
2 ch c Piccolo—Silken Dalliance (Rambo Dancer (CAN))
2502[6] 4274[13] 5430[10]

Tastahil (IRE) *B W Hills* a94 101
4 ch g Singspiel(IRE) —Luana (Shaadi (USA))
1719[2] ◆ 2103[2] 5349[3] 5894[2] 6646[8] 7244[3] ◆

Taste Of Honey (IRE) *D W P Arbuthnot* a39 36
2 b f Deportivo—Long Tall Sally (IRE) (Danehill Dancer (IRE))
6327[9] 6933[11]

Taste The Wine (IRE) *J R Best* 61
2 gr c Verglas(IRE) —Azia (IRE) (Desert Story (IRE))
2150[10] 4184[11] 6083[7] 6700[8] 7016[13]

Tatbeeq (IRE) *M A Jarvis* a78 77
3 b f Invincible Spirit(IRE) —Announcing Peace (Danehill (USA))
2221[2] 2954[2] (3629) 4082[2] ◆ 4872[4]

Tathkaar *C E Brittain* a79 89
3 ch f Dr Fong(USA) —Royal Patron (Royal Academy (USA))
905[6] (1144) ◆ 1470[7] 1993[7] 2655a[S] 3124[8] 3849[12] 4869[9]

Tatillius (IRE) *J M Bradley* 11
5 ch g King Charlemagne(USA) —Aunty Eileen (Ahonoora)
1529[13]

Tattercoats (FR) *D M Simcock* a43
2 b f Whywhywhy(USA) —Driscilla (USA) (Stately Don (USA))
7380[13] 7577[5] 7734[10]

Taurus Twins *W G M Turner* a18 55
2 b g Deportivo—Intellibet One (Compton Place)
1640[7] 1955[4] 2458[6] 3846[8]

Tavalu (USA) *G L Moore* a72 68
6 b g Kingmambo(USA) —Larrocha (IRE) (Sadler's Wells (USA))
(3160) 4366[9] 5913[7]

Taverny *S Wattel* a90 94
3 b c Rock Of Gibraltar(IRE) —Tigertail (FR) (Priolo (USA))
6664a[8] 7551a[3]

Tawaash (USA) *M A Jarvis* a78 101
3 bb c Storm Cat(USA) —Victory Ride (USA) (Seeking The Gold (USA))
(1957) ◆ (2624) 3119[10] 3850[3] 4553[11] 5102[4]

Tawzeea (IRE) *M Johnston* 86
3 ch c Cadeaux Genereux—Kismah (Machiavellian (USA))
997[2] 1623[3] (1951) 2481[7] 3141[3] (3601) 4145[15] 4900[7]

Tax Dodger (IRE) *J L Spearing* 56
2 b g Catcher In The Rye(IRE) —Stonor Lady (USA) (French Deputy (USA))
3882[6] 5021[8] 5365[5] 6534[10]

Tax Free (IRE) *D Nicholls* a89 121
6 b g Tagula(IRE) —Grandel (Owington)
959[5] 1495a[2] 1783a[2] 2404[4] (2685a) (3533a)

Taxman (IRE) *A G Newcombe* a57 77
6 ch g Singspiel(IRE) —Love Of Silver (USA) (Arctic Tern (USA))
344[8] 540[10] 1246[7] 5917[5] 7169[9] 7688[2]

Tayman (IRE) *Carl Llewellyn* a69 69
6 bb g Sinndar(IRE) —Sweet Emotion (IRE) (Bering)
600[5] 4365[4]

Tayseer *J E Hammond* 101
3 ch g Medicean—Rohita (IRE) (Waajib)
(6064a)

Tayyab (USA) *M F De Kock* a86
3 b c Belong To Me(USA) —Atyab (USA) (Mr Prospector (USA))
(6822)

Tazbar (IRE) *K G Reveley* 73
6 b g Tiraaz(USA) —Candy Bar (IRE) (Montelimar (USA))
6527[6] 7174[7]

Tazeez (USA) *J H M Gosden* 113
4 bb g Silver Hawk(USA) —Soiree Russe (USA) (Nureyev (USA))
(2509) ◆ 3413[7] 4422[3] (4867) 5508[4] 6120[10] (6476) ◆

T-Bird (SAF) *Doug Watson* a67 80
7 ch h Special Preview(SAF) —Lady Greystoke (SAF) (Lords (SAF))
290a[9] 472a[11] 666a[9]

Tcherina (IRE) *T D Easterby* 85
6 b m Danehill Dancer(IRE) —Forget Paris (IRE) (Broken Hearted)
2107[11] 2585[7] 2822[3] 3143[5] (3624) (4170) 4645[6]

Tchic Cove (FR) *A Junk* a24 60
3 b c Chichicastenango(FR) —Turtle Cove (IRE) (Catrail (USA))
385a[9] 549a[5]

Tea Cake (IRE) *H J L Dunlop* a60 58
3 b f Compton Place—Griddle Cake (IRE) (Be My Guest (USA))
1671[5] 2898[7] 3381[5] ◆ 3678[10] 4338[5] 5015[10] 6878[6]

Teachers Choice (IRE) *Adrian McGuinness* a56 83
5 b g Fruits Of Love(USA) —Son Chou (Cyrano De Bergerac)
4004a[8]

Teacht An Earraig (USA) *J S Bolger* 103
3 b f Galileo(IRE) —Autumn Banner (USA) (Summer Squall (USA))
1356a[6] 3070a[8] 6298a[13] 7157a[8]

Teadancer (IRE) *J G Portman* a53 39
3 b f Traditionally(USA) —Dance Up A Storm (USA) (Storm Bird (CAN))
1553[5] 2719[11] 3206[9] 6206[9]

Tears Of A Clown (IRE) *J A Osborne* a85 96
5 b g Galileo(IRE) —Mood Swings (IRE) (Shirley Heights)
1569[5] 2599[6] 3104[P] (Dead)

Teasing *J Pearce* a86 73
4 b m Lujain(USA) —Movieland (USA) (Nureyev (USA))
233[5] 357[6] 417[4] 807[2] (870) 1143[2] 1286[3] 3317[8] 4181[3] 5144[11] 5799[5] 6490[5] 6771[4] 7309[4] 7642[2] 7786[5]

Tebheagnaneilan (SWE) *L Reuterskiold Jr* a40
4 b m Nicolotte—Fernet-Branca (SWE) (Diligo (FR))
4917a[8]

Tecktal (FR) *P M Phelan* a47 48
5 ch m Pivotal—Wenge (USA) (Housebuster (USA))
7217[12]

Teddy West (IRE) *Mrs L Williamson* 55
2 b g Trans Island—Duckmore Bay (IRE) (Titus Livius (FR))
6655[13] 7080[9]

Tee Gee Cee *T D Easterby* 54
2 b c Tiger Hill(IRE) —Flamingo Queen (GER) (Surumu (GER))
2569[8] 3055[5] 5500[12]

Teeky *J H M Gosden* 65
2 b f Daylami(IRE) —Las Flores (IRE) (Sadler's Wells (USA))
4256[5] 6945[5] ◆

Teen Ager (FR) *P Burgoyne* a80 66
4 b g Invincible Spirit(IRE) —Tarwiya (IRE) (Dominion)
887[9] 1112[6] 1409[5] 1641[6] 1954[8] 2255[4] 2556[5] 2758[6] 3033[14]

Teen Spirit (IRE) *J W Hills* 60
3 b g Sinndar(IRE) —Whitefoot (Be My Chief (USA))
1684[7] 2197[12] 2468[6] 2997[5] 3697[5]

Telepathic (IRE) *A Berry* a44 49
8 b g Mind Games—Madrina (Waajib)
15[8] 153[6] 236[6] 289[8] 305[7] 2936[13] 4451[12]

Telephonist *J R Best* a51 51
3 b f Forzando—Telegram Girl (Magic Ring (IRE))
2560[10] 4412[3] 5086[10] 6338[12] 6912[4] 7088[5] 7379[9] 7522[10]

Tell *J L Dunlop* 114
5 b h Green Desert(USA) —Cephalonie (USA) (Kris S (USA))
1326[5] 1631[4] 2607[5] 3683[5]

Telling *Mrs A Duffield* a41 52
4 b g Josr Algarhoud(IRE) —Crystal Canyon (Efisio)
8[9] 33[11] 438[13]

Telling Stories (IRE) *M Johnston* a55 35
2 b f Lucky Story(USA) —Yes Virginia (USA) (Roanoke (USA))
6923[8] 7148[4] 7341[10] 7514[11] 7607[9] 7666[4]

Tell Me What (FR) *D J S Ffrench Davis* a52 44
3 b f Diktat—Galgarina (FR) (Double Bed (FR))
931[9] 1247[9] 1416[8] 2988[14]

Tempelstern (GER) *H R A Cecil* a94 115
4 gr h Sternkoenig(IRE) —Temple Esprit (Esprit Du Nord (USA))
1468[3] 1944[7] 4880a[2] 5094[2] 5736a[6] 6286[5]

Tempeltanzer (GER) *Frau Z Kubovicova* 102
6 b h Devil River Peek(USA) —Trueville (GER) (Top Ville)
4470a[7]

Temperence Hall (USA) *J R Best* a69 66
2 ch g Graeme Hall(USA) —Sue's Temper (USA) (Temperence Hill (USA))
2754[4] ◆ 3444[9] 4256[3] 4933[7] 5432[3] 5671[7]

Temple Lord (FR) *Y De Nicolay* 92
2 gr c Califet(FR) —Temple Queen (GER) (Local Suitor (USA))
5139a[3] 6147a[5]

Temple Of Thebes (IRE) *E A L Dunlop* a90 93
3 b f Bahri(USA) —Franglais (GER) (Lion Cavern (USA))
(1499) (2428) 3850[8] 4198[3] 5310[6] 6430[5] 7047[2] 7181[6] 7477[5] 7641[4]

Temple Place (IRE) *D McCain Jnr* 98
7 b g Sadler's Wells(USA) —Puzzled Look (USA) (Gulch (USA))
960[21] 1920[9] 3474[10]

Templet (USA) *W G Harrison* a52 44
8 b g Souvenir Copy(USA) —Two Step Trudy (USA) (Capote (USA))
2523[10] 2867[11] 3204[7] 5415[7]

Templetuohy Max (IRE) *J D Bethell* a66 53
3 b g Orpen(USA) —Eladawn (IRE) (Ela-Mana-Mou)
1073[10] 1429[10] 2221[7] 2926[7] 4077[3] 4457[8] 5379[3] 5868[2] 6956[4] 7274[2] (7654) 7786[6] ◆

Temtation (IRE) *J A Pickering* a56 51
4 b m Trans Island—Ish (IRE) (Danehill (USA))
33[3] 79[10] 254[3] 363[3] 642[4] 808[7] 972[5] 1550[7] 1906[7] 3422[10] 4125[14]

Tenacious Greg (IRE) *A Kinsella* a80 78
5 ch g Miswaki(USA) —Pattimech (USA) (Nureyev (USA))
4514a[8]

Tenancy (IRE) *R C Guest* a61 58
4 b g Rock Of Gibraltar(IRE) —Brush Strokes (Cadeaux Genereux)
65[4] 82[11] 191[10] 278[2] (371) 846[9] 951[4] 1338[12] 1378[9] 1675[2] 1906[2] 2075[2] 4479[9] 4683[9] 5088[10] 5797[13] 5916[10] 7049[U] (7218) 7286[8] (7369)

Tencendur (IRE) *D Nicholls* a79 81
4 ch g King Charlemagne(USA) —Jallaissine (IRE) (College Chapel)
992[8] (1138) 1327[11] 1552[2] 1891[3] 2733[7] 3006[12]

Ten Cents A Dance *T D Easterby* 42
2 b g Carnival Dancer—Whittle Woods Girl (Emarati (USA))
2362[8] 2909[14] 3334[6] 5632[20]

Tendalay (USA) *D Carroll* a78 53
4 b g Red Ransom(USA) —Mandalay Point (USA) (Gilded Time (USA))
2499[7] 3006[14] (Dead)

Tender Falcon *R J Hodges* a68 85
8 br g Polar Falcon(USA) —Tendresse (IRE) (Tender King)
6594[3] 7064[4] 7216[5] 7296[3]

Tender Moments *B Smart* 60
4 br m Tomba—Cherish Me (Polar Falcon (USA))
2841[7] 4597[8] 5108[5] 5308[2]

Tender Process (IRE) *R A Fahey* a71 68
5 b g Monashee Mountain(USA) —Appledorn (Doulab (USA))
994[9] 1129[5] 3819[12] 4958[3] 5260[6] 6766[10] 7043[4] (7228) 7316[5] 7466[5] 7675[5]

Tender The Great (IRE) *H J Collingridge* a92 84
5 br m Indian Lodge(IRE) —Tender Guest (IRE) (Be My Guest (USA))
336[5] 456[5] 3855[9] 4110[5] 4422[9] 4723[3] 5071[7] 5600[11] 5908[3] 6266[13] 6684[5]

Ten Down *M Quinn* a85 81
3 b g Royal Applause—Upstream (Prince Sabo)
(324) 798[2] (835) (1707) 1945[8] 2529[7] 3462[8] 4127[7] 4347[3] 4787[7] 5531[8] 7393[11] 7562[8] 7743[5]

Tendulkar's Diva (IRE) *A Berry* 40
3 b f Tendulkar(USA) —Daring Connection (Danzig Connection (USA))
3438[8] 3712[16] 4615[12]

Tenement (IRE) *Jamie Poulton* a56 53
4 b g Mull Of Kintyre(USA) —Afifah (Nashwan (USA))
3036[4] 3265[6] 4182[12] 4811[13] 5787[4] 6421[12] 7217[8] 7473[9] 7707[4] 7816[6]

Teneo Vestri *A B Haynes* 51
2 ch g Monsieur Bond(IRE) —Splicing (Sharpo)
2349[DSQ] 3412[6] 4720[7] 6059[11]

Ten For Tosca (IRE) *R A Harris* a23 54
4 b g Distant Music(USA) —Errazuriz (IRE) (Classic Music (USA))
19[7]

Ten Hour Lunch *S Lycett* a51
3 br g Averti(IRE) —Long Tall Sally (IRE) (Danehill Dancer (IRE))
221[9] 311[7] 867[11] 1163[10] 4247[17]

Tenjack King *J A Osborne* a80 77
3 b c Kyllachy—Rash (Pursuit Of Love)
396[3] 737[2] (900)

Ten Pole Tudor *R A Harris* a79 78
3 b g Royal Applause—Amaniy (USA) (Dayjur (USA))
723[7] 975[U] 1868[3] 2276[5] 2481[8] 3560[4] 3969[6] 4369[7] 6380[8] 6749[3] 7358[14] 7513[7]

Tenraninthemist (IRE) *B R Johnson* a38
3 gr f Tendulkar(USA) —Saranyu (IRE) (Rusticaro (FR))
1271[7] 1586[P]

Tense (IRE) *J A Osborne* a68 64
3 b f Invincible Spirit(IRE) —Roses From Ridey (IRE) (Petorius)
2946[4] 3731[4]

Tension Mounts (IRE) *J A Osborne* a74
3 b g Daggers Drawn(USA) —Dazzling Maid (IRE) (Tate Gallery (USA))
265[2] 705[4] 923[4]

Tension Point *D L Williams* a65 68
4 b g Hernando(FR) —Blessed (IRE) (Jurado (USA))
779[9]

Tenson (IRE) *R Brogi* 87
3 b c Intikhab(USA) —Strategic Tactics (IRE) (Bigstone (IRE))
1513a[12]

Ten Spot (IRE) *Stef Liddiard* a64 43
3 b f Intikhab(USA) —Allergy (Alzao (USA))
262[3] (556) 644[P] 1128[7] 5119[15] 6928[14] 7634[7] 7744[8]

Tenth Night (IRE) *P T Midgley* 49
3 b c Mujadil(USA) —Starlight Venture (IRE) (Hernando (FR))
998[7] 1169[6] 1626[6]

Ten To The Dozen *P W Hiatt* a55 66
5 b g Royal Applause—Almost Amber (USA) (Mt. Livermore (USA))
3383[14] (3648) 4121[8] 4597[7] 4807[4] 5170[2] 5533[2] 6208[13] 6335[2] 6749[6] 6928[7] 7180[3] 7373[7] 7441[9]

Teorban (POL) *Mrs N S Evans* a64 35
9 b g Don Corleone—Tabaka (POL) (Pyjama Hunt)
2643[11] 4935[7]

Tepmokea (IRE) *K R Burke* a71 70
2 ch c Noverre(USA) —Eroica (GER) (Highest Honor (FR))
3049[4] ◆ 3364[2] 4625[11] 5274[8] 5895[9] 6761[7] (6954)

Tequila Sheila (IRE) *M A Allen* a37 61
6 ch m Raise A Grand(IRE) —Hever Rosina (Efisio)
219[8] 392[12]

Terandeil *J G M O'Shea* 25
4 b m Auction House(USA) —Frisson (Slip Anchor)
3139[6] 4793[15]

Terenzium (IRE) *Micky Hammond* a52 55
7 br g Cape Cross(IRE) —Tatanka (ITY) (Luge)
4501[7]

Terminate (GER) *Ian Williams* a64 66
6 ch g Acatenango(GER) —Taghareed (USA) (Shadeed (USA))
559[3] (771) 1044[4] 1374[2] 1639[2] (2100) ◆ 2185[4] 2568[7] 2908[7] 4813[7] 5429[6] 6364[8] 7427[5] 7806[3]

Terracos Do Pinhal *M Johnston* a61 65
3 b g Selkirk(USA) —Sister Bluebird (Bluebird (USA))
157[3] 1060[6] 2037[8] 3715[3]

Terracotta Warrior *J Jay* a47 47
2 ch g Dubai Destination(USA) —Tamesis (IRE) (Fasliyev (USA))
3158[4] 3669[12] 4421[7] 7258[9] 7693[9]

Terrain (USA) *Albert Stall Jr* a113
2 ch g Sky Mesa(USA) —Minery (USA) (Forty Niner (USA))
6503a[2] 6997a[4]

Terra Incognita *Y De Nicolay* 100
4 b m Rock Of Gibraltar(IRE) —Terre A Terre (FR) (Kaldounevees (FR))
5114a[5] 6237a[4]

Terrasini (FR) *J Howard Johnson* 59
3 gr g Linamix(FR) —Trazando (Forzando)
2941[4] 4247[9] 5399[8]

Terrific Challenge (USA) *Doug Watson* a103 105
6 ch h Royal Academy(USA) —Clever Empress (Crafty Prospector (USA))
295a[8] 472a[8] 670a[7]

Terry's Tip (IRE) *Mrs L Stubbs* 84
3 b g Namid—Kadarassa (IRE) (Warning)
1795[3] 2824[2]

Tertio Bloom (SWE) *F Reuterskiold*
3 ch c Tertullian(USA) —Yankee Bloom (USA) (El Gran Senor (USA))
4918a[2]

Tertullus (FR) *Rune Haugen* 105
5 br g Monsun(GER) —Tryphosa (IRE) (Be My Guest (USA))
2708a[6] 5335a[2]

Teslin (IRE) *Saeed Bin Suroor* 109
4 b g In The Wings—Yukon Hope (USA) (Forty Niner (USA))
296a[2] 383a[9] 739a[4]

Testimonial *B G Powell* a49 66
3 b f Singspiel(IRE) —Endorsement (Warning)
1599[7] 2973[7] 3326[8] 4527[9] 5320[2] 7010[11]

Test Match (IRE) *M P Tregoning* a73
2 b c Exceed And Excel(AUS) —Reunion (IRE) (Be My Guest (USA))
6621[5] 6877[3] ◆

Tetragon (IRE) *A M Hales* a46 66
8 b g Octagonal(NZ) —Viva Verdi (IRE) (Green Desert (USA))
269[8] 930[5] 1246[10]

Tevez *Miss Amy Weaver* a78 71
3 b g Sakhee(USA) —Sosumi (Be My Chief (USA))
(158) 376[2] 6256[10] 6683[10] 7115[6] 7771[8]

Tewin Green *M D Squance* a58 6
3 ch f Zaha(CAN) —Green Run (USA) (Green Dancer (USA))
1669[12] 1937[5] 2528[5] 2984[15] 3841[10] 4182[14] 5407[7] 6044[10] 6228[11]

Tewitfield Lass *K W Hogg* a27 32
6 b m Bluegrass Prince(IRE) —Madam Marash (IRE) (Astronef)
3718[12]

Tewkesbury (IRE) *Mrs K Waldron* a40
4 b g King's Best(USA) —Zeferina (IRE) (Sadler's Wells (USA))
144[7] 238[5] 471[3] 661[11]

Texaline (FR) *D De Watrigant* 63
3 b f Alzao(USA) —Texalouna (FR) (Kaldoun (FR))
7635a[10]

Texan Dream (IRE) *J De Roualle* a84 69
3 b c Oasis Dream—Texalina (FR) (Kaldoun (FR))
6064a[0]

Thabaat *J M Bradley* a62 87
4 ch g Pivotal—Maraatib (IRE) (Green Desert (USA))
1174[11] 1800[9] 2013[11] 3443[10] 4103[3] 4535[8] 5121[8] 6209[6] 7012[4] 7383[6] 7497[2] 7651[3] 7766[5]

Thankful *Rae Guest* a56
3 b f Diesis—La Martina (Atraf)
52[5] 529[8] 931[6] ◆

Thankfully (IRE) *W M Brisbourne* 38
3 b f Green Desert(USA) —Your Welcome (Darshaan)
3058[12] 4461[5]

Thanks Again (IRE) *J De Roualle* 95
3 ch f Anabaa Blue—Exciting Times (FR) (Jeune Homme (USA))
5038a[8]

Thankuforthemusic (IRE) *C Tinkler* a58
3 b g Shinko Forest(IRE) —Auriga (Belmez (USA))
543[8] 704[3] 1054[5] 1343[4] 1478[16] 2613[12] 3264[11]

Thannaan (USA) *B W Hills* a57 82
3 gr c Elusive Quality(USA) —Lady Aloma (CAN) (Cozzene (USA))
(1535) 2333[10] 3612[9]

Thanxforthat (USA) *J J Quinn* a27 60
3 gr g Alphabet Soup(USA) —Paper Princess (USA) (Flying Paster (USA))
2208[8] 3557[5] 4560[5] 6843[6]

Tharawaat (IRE) *B W Hills* a65 77
3 b g Alhaarth(IRE) —Sevi's Choice (USA) (Sir Ivor (USA))
961[5] 1283[3]

That Boy Ronaldo *A Berry* a47 55
2 b f Pyrus(USA) —Red Millennium (IRE) (Tagula (IRE))
2331[6] 2903[6] 3470[6] 4594[6] 4857[7] 5384[5] 5746[7] 5988[6] 6245[9] 7179[9] 7318[7] 7370[6] 7530[2] 7687[5] 7694[7]

That'll Do Nicely (IRE) *N G Richards* a63
5 b g Bahhare(USA) —Return Again (IRE) (Top Ville)
6956[5] 7344[6] 7749[2]

That Look *D E Cantillon* a61 64
5 b g Compton Admiral—Mudflap (Slip Anchor)
(3863) 4490[2] 4935[3] ◆ (6060)

That's Hot (IRE) *G M Lyons* a94 110
5 b m Namid—Smoke Lady (IRE) (Barathea (IRE))
2738a[7]

Thatwasthepension (IRE) *B Storey*
2 b c Milan—Biondo (IRE) (College Chapel)
4847[9] 5387[11] 5716[11]

Thaumatology (USA) *M Botti* a59
2 ch f Distorted Humor(USA) —Crystal Ballet (USA) (Royal Academy (USA))
6375[9] 6876[6] 7332[6] 7514[9]

The Age Of Anxiety (USA) *Edward Lynam* a71
2 br c Bernstein(USA) —Conspiring (USA) (Grand Slam (USA))
7699[8]

Theatre Royal *Mouse Hamilton-Fairley* a58 65
5 b m Royal Applause—Rada's Daughter (Robellino (USA))
299[7] 2354[5] 2641[7] 3361[5] 3631[6] 4409[5]

Theatre Street (IRE) *J Noseda* a68
2 b f Invincible Spirit(IRE) —Markova (IRE) (Marju (IRE))
7769[2]

The Bear *R Johnson* a35 78
5 ch g Rambling Bear—Precious Girl (Precious Metal)
1261[7] 1485[16] (1826) 2444[4] 2751[2] 3454[3] 3868[10] 4418[3] 5719[8] 6066[3] 6164[10] 6486[14]

The Beat Is On *J M Bradley* 12
2 b f Beat All(USA) —Lady Ezzabella (Ezzoud (IRE))
1523[11] 3267[14] 3674[15]

Thebes *M Johnston* a93 97
3 ch c Cadeaux Genereux—See You Later (Emarati (USA))
505[2] (616) (918) ◆ (967) ◆ 3155[22] 3850[10] 4405[22] (5102) ◆ 5270[5] 5495[4] 5731a[3] 6069[27] 6478[7] 7181[7]

The Best Day Ever (USA) *Kenneth McPeek*
2 br f Brahms(USA) —Added Asset (USA) (Lord At War (ARG))
6613a[4]

The Betchworth Kid *M L W Bell* a83 106
3 b g Tobougg(IRE) —Runelia (Runnett)
1424[11] 2256[2] 2610[3] 2840[3] 3157[12] 4351[3] (4955) (5853) 6427[3] 7244[2]

The Bodhran Beat (IRE) *P J Rothwell* a23 26
4 b g Tendulkar(USA) —Bella Galiana (ITY) (Don Roberto (USA))
7559[8] 7587[12]

The Bogberry (USA) *A De Royer-Dupre* 118
3 ch c Hawk Wing(USA) —Lahinch (IRE) (Danehill Dancer (IRE))
1421[3] (5729a) 6499a[3] 7682a[4]

The Bonus King *J Jay* a65 58
8 b g Royal Applause—Selvi (Mummy's Pet)
724[9]

The Brat *Miss Tracy Waggott* 41
4 b m Perryston View—Kalarram (Muhtarram (USA))
7527[10]

The Bull Hayes (IRE) *Mrs John Harrington* 97
2 b c Sadler's Wells(USA) —No Review (USA) (Nodouble (USA))
6317a[5] 7158a[4]

The Bully Wee *J Jay* 45
2 b c Bishop Of Cashel—Red Barons Lady (IRE) (Electric)
7221[5]

The Canny Dove (USA) *T D Barron* 35
2 b g Monashee Mountain(USA) —Who's Sorry Now (USA) (Ogygian (USA))
2746[5] 3277[8] 3590[14] 4203[6]

The Carlton Cannes *G Wragg* a98 91
4 b h Grand Lodge(USA) —Miss Riviera Golf (Hernando (FR))
(970) 1547[2] 6079[3] 6698[2]

The Carpet Man *A W Carroll* a53 48
4 b g Iron Mask(USA) —Yarrow Bridge (Selkirk (USA))
151[10] 247[8] 318[6] 372[7] 445[7] 523[11] 558[3] 690[9] 713[4] 877[10]

The Cayterers *A W Carroll* a80 80
6 b g Cayman Kai(IRE) —Silky Smooth (IRE) (Thatching)
2992[7] 3313[12] 4051[9] (6046) 6706[11] 7435[2] (7677)

The Cheka (IRE) *Eve Johnson Houghton* 104
2 b c Xaar—Veiled Beauty (USA) (Royal Academy (USA))
(3939) ◆ 5507[2]

The Chip Chopman (IRE) *Seamus G O'Donnell* a27 73
6 b g Sri Pekan(USA) —Firstrusseofsummer (USA) (Summer Squall (USA))
4655a[11]

The City Kid (IRE) *Miss Gay Kelleway* a69 59
5 b m Danetime(IRE) —Unfortunate (Komaite (USA))
173[4] 2758[2] 3826[5] 4306[6] 4946[4] 7345[4] 7440[5] 7656[7] 7779[2]

The Composer *M Blanshard* a60 63
6 b g Royal Applause—Superspring (Superlative)
(4275) 4704[12] 5489[4] 6022[2] 6329[4] 6740[4]

The Cube *J Balding* a53 54
4 b g Mind Games—Nite-Owl Dancer (Robellino (USA))
1675[11] 2824[9] 3231[2] 3712[7] 4107[9] 4542[13] 7292[10] 7527[4] 7629[6] 7648[4]

The Cuckoo *M Quinn* a74
2 b c Invincible Spirit(IRE) —Aravonian (Night Shift (USA))
4474[3] 4634[7] 5904[4] (6350) 6469[11] 7825[5]

The Dagger *G L Moore* a61 61
4 ch g Daggers Drawn(USA) —Highland Blue (Never So Bold)
716[9] 1280[12] 1345[4] 1747[12] 2069[4] 2352[12]

The Desert Saint *A M Balding* a72 60
2 b g Dubai Destination(USA) —Maria Theresa (Primo Dominie)
1851[2] 2124[7]

The Dial House *J A Osborne* a77 77
2 b g Tagula(IRE) —Marliana (IRE) (Mtoto)
1413[2] 1722[2] (2859) 4079[6] 4373[4]

The Diamond Bond *G R Oldroyd* a48 51
4 bl g Josr Algarhoud(IRE) —Alsiba (Northfields (USA))
144[6] 277[3] 552[4]

The Dragon (IRE) *M Quinn* a45 10
3 b f Statue Of Liberty(USA) —Noble Rocket (Reprimand)
885[8] 1132[6]

The Fairy (GER) *J Hirschberger* 87
4 b m Night Shift(USA) —Tucana (GER) (Acatenango (GER))
2879a[9] 5334a[4]

The Fifth Member (IRE) *J R Boyle* a87 95
4 b g Bishop Of Cashel—Palace Soy (IRE) (Tagula (IRE))
2203[9] 2693[4] 3167[3] (3612) ◆ (3840) 4509[3] 4853[2] 5695[4] (6675)

Thefillyfromepsom *P M Phelan* a58
2 b f Royal Academy(USA) —For Love (USA) (Sultry Song (USA))
7554[5] 7622[8]

The Fisio *G D Blake* a72 47
8 b g Efisio—Misellina (FR) (Polish Precedent (USA))
1242[4] 1312[3] 1703[9] 1901[9]

The Fist Of God (IRE) *Noel Meade* a87 90
3 b g Sadler's Wells(USA) —Hula Angel (USA) (Woodman (USA))
2435a[8]

The Flying Cowboy (IRE) *Jane Chapple-Hyam* a62 74
4 b g Tagula(IRE) —Sesame Heights (IRE) (High Estate)
1349[4] 1725[7] 2483[9] 3089[12] 5087[10] 6217[7]

Theflyingscottie *D Shaw* a55 57
6 gr g Paris House—Miss Flossa (FR) (Big John (FR))
220[5]

The Fonz *Sir Michael Stoute* a75 65
2 b c Oasis Dream—Crystal Cavern (USA) (Be My Guest (USA))
4598[3] 6621[4]

The Gaikwar (IRE) *R A Harris* a45 73
9 b g Indian Ridge—Broadmara (IRE) (Thatching)
724[8] 1898[8] 2101[11] 2477[4] 2640[9] 2795[3] 3025[11] 3360[7] 3604[4] 4707[2] 5429[2] (5604) 6228[14] 6336[9] 6570[11] 6867[14]

The Galloping Shoe *J Noseda* 80
3 b g Observatory(USA) —My Way (IRE) (Marju (IRE))
(1344)

The Game *Tom Dascombe* a98 86
3 b g Compton Place—Emanant (Emarati (USA))
228[3] 470[2] 1707[3] 1925[12] 2794[10] 3394[6] (4375) 5102[8] 7477[2] (7592) (7716)

The Geester *S R Bowring* a65 51
4 b g Rambling Bear—Cledeschamps (Doc Marten)
109[2] 191[6] 521[4] (790) 858[3] 1024[2] 1189[5] 5260[9] 6353[11] 6955[6] (7444) 7615[4] 7746[8]

Thegirlsgonewild (USA) *H J L Dunlop* a52
2 bb f Gone West(USA) —Coconut Girl (USA) (Cryptoclearance (USA))
6696[9]

The Graig *J R Holt* a53 57
4 b g Josr Algarhoud(IRE) —Souadah (USA) (General Holme (USA))
1207[5] 1602[9] 2375[7] 2449[8] 3162[4] 3569[5] 4162[5] 4597[10] 6693[8]

The Grey One (IRE) *J M Bradley* a70 70
5 gr g Dansili—Marie Dora (FR) (Kendor (FR))
996[8] 1160[9] 1644[8] 1898[7] 2001[8] 3025[8] 3361[9] 3698[4] 4485[4] 4568[4] 4820[3] 5020[3] 5489[7] 5653[3] 5912[7] 6228[8] (6913) (7112) 7368[2] 7441[5] 7532[2]

The Hague *J H M Gosden* 58
2 b c Xaar—Cox Orange (USA) (Trempolino (USA))
6080[13] 6342[12]

The Happy Hammer (IRE) *T Keddy* 58
2 b c Acclamation—Emma's Star (ITY) (Darshaan)
6077[6] 6885[7]

The History Man (IRE) *M Mullineaux* a42 76
5 b g Titus Livius(FR) —Handsome Anna (IRE) (Bigstone (IRE))
1677[6] 1818[7] 2356[7] 3759[2] 4171[15] 4385[7] (4609) 4743[4] 4858[9] 4981[9] 5719[9] 6766[8] 7043[12]

The Honorable (IRE) *R A Fahey* 31
3 b c Sadler's Wells(USA) —Bonita Francita (CAN) (Devil's Bag (USA))
6762[11]

The Hoofer (IRE) *I A Wood* a62 59
3 b f Vision Of Night—Dance In The Sun (Halling (USA))
1279[6] 2922[6] 3293[7] 3764[7] (4298) (4569) 4772[10] 5377[6] 5607[10] 5799[9] 6173[6] 6419[3] 6681[10] (7022)

The Illies (IRE) *Saeed Bin Suroor* 107
4 b g Fasliyev(USA) —Velvet Appeal (IRE) (Petorius)
384a[7] 477a[4] 669a[4] 739a[7]

The Iron Giant (IRE) *Dr J R J Naylor* a56 54
6 b g Giant's Causeway(USA) —Shalimar (IRE) (Indian Ridge)
1902[4] 2072[4] 3360[4] 3780[4] 4414[8]

The Jailer *J G M O'Shea* a64 67
5 b m Mujahid(USA) —Once Removed (Distant Relative)
115[7] 408[2] 571[2] 1143[4] 1285[3] 1670[3] (2069) 2556[2] 2860[6] 3648[4] 3842[5] 4767[7] 6773[9] 7382[12]

The Jobber (IRE) *M Blanshard* a93 106
7 b g Foxhound(USA) —Clairification (IRE) (Shernazar)
2326[6] 3056[13] 3680[10] 3881[9] 4957[6] 5493[5] ◆ 5796[10] (6006) 6174[5] 6557[2] 6971[12] 7365[2]

The Jostler *B W Hills* a85 91
3 b f Dansili—The Jotter (Night Shift (USA))
1868[7] 2276[2] 2624[9] 3636[3] 4300[2] (5071) 5795[10] 6772[9] 7146[15] 7737[5]

The Kiddykid (IRE) *P D Evans* a94 105
8 b g Danetime(IRE) —Mezzanine (Sadler's Wells (USA))
1723[4] 1942[5] ◆ 2163[7] 2905[11] 3435[2] 3646[4] (4661) 5446[4] 6277[10] 6710[7] 7439[5] 7564[8]

The Kilkenny Kat (IRE) *T D Easterby* 62
2 b g Hold That Tiger(USA) —Strategy (Machiavellian (USA))
1794[7] 2584[4] 3107[5] 5632[18] 5966[10]

The King And I (IRE) *Miss E C Lavelle* a81 81
4 b g Monashee Mountain(USA) —Scrimshaw (Selkirk (USA))
510 [4] 701[5] (1704) 1904[5] 2621[3] 4526[6] 5092[2] 6838[7]

The Kyllachy Kid *T P Tate* 82
2 b g Kyllachy—All Business (Entrepreneur)
3078[5] 4497[5] 4960[3] 5497[3] 6112[2] (6407) 7173[3]

The Lady Granuaile (USA) *K A Ryan* 71
3 b f More Than Ready(USA) —Marlene (USA) (Theatrical)
2067[5] 2911[15]

The Lady Lapwing *G Wragg* a39 34
3 b f Mark Of Esteem(IRE) —Lonely Shore (Blakeney)
1965[10]

The Last Bottle (IRE) *W M Brisbourne* a66 65
3 ch g Hawk Wing(USA) —Mesmerist (USA) (Green Desert (USA))
1396[10] 2014[9] 2805[2] 3436[6] 3817[5] 4382[4] 4663[3] 5868[3] 6092[3] 6447[2]

The Last Drop (IRE) *B W Hills* 109
5 b h Galileo(IRE) —Epping (Charnwood Forest (IRE))
1070[P] 1944[11] 3721[10] 5853[6] (6479)

The Last Hurrah (IRE) *Mrs John Harrington* 82
8 b g In The Wings—Last Exit (Dominion)
4003a[2]

The Legal Blonde (IRE) *Tom Dascombe* 91
2 b f Elusive City(USA) —Virgin Stanza (USA) (Opening Verse (USA))
3959[6] 4402 [2] ◆ 4868[6]

The Little Fizzer (IRE) *P D Evans* a63 63
3 ch f Fayruz—Villaminta (IRE) (Grand Lodge (USA))
(9) 243[3] 397[4] 1155[3] 1475[4] 1769[6] 3000[7] 3577[4] 4028[3] 4370[8] 4725[2] 5421[6] 6218[3] 6405[5] 6658[5] 6823[6] 7508[8] 7522[3] 7615[6]

The Little Master (IRE) *D R C Elsworth* a59 54
4 bb g Tendulkar(USA) —Minatina (IRE) (Ela-Mana-Mou)
6126[5] 6400[11] 6725[4] 7310[3] 7626[9] 7701[2]

The Loan Express (IRE) *T Stack* 100
3 b f Choisir(AUS) —Mamma's Too (Skyliner)
1783a[3] 2685a[6] 3252[7]

The London Gang *W M Brisbourne* a64 43
5 b g Mind Games—Nom Francais (First Trump)
770[10] 1025[11] 1269[12] 1636[2] 4748[13] 4797[13]

The Lord *W G M Turner* a34 95
8 b g Averti(IRE) —Lady Longmead (Crimson Beau)
824[9] 2598[7] 2760[8] 4957[7]

The Magic Blanket (IRE) *Stef Liddiard* a67 63
3 b g Bahamian Bounty—Zietunzeen (IRE) (Zieten (USA))
(928) 2127[8] 2506[8] 2710[12] 3585[5] 4272[9] 4725[12]

The Magic Of Rio *Peter Grayson* a88 88
2 b f Captain Rio—Good Health (Magic Ring (IRE))
1627[5] 2048[3] 2462[3] 3114[2] (3734) 4190[18] (4768) (5204) 6281[6] 6540[2] 7464[4] (7628) 7788[3]

Themelie Island (IRE) *A Trybuhl* 98
3 b f Montjeu(IRE) —Thelema (IRE) (Caerleon (USA))
2065a[5] 2655a[6] 3623a[7] 4675a[15] 5737a[2] 6691a[4]

The Mighty Ogmore *R C Guest* a47 59
4 ch m Dr Fong(USA) —Welsh Dawn (Zafonic (USA))
375 [5] 238[8] 637[3]

The Miniver Rose (IRE) *R Hannon* 87
2 b f High Chaparral(IRE) —Bloemfontain (IRE) (Cape Cross (IRE))
4870[7] (5859) 6473[3]

The Mumbo *W Jarvis* a27
2 b f Bahamian Bounty—Mandolin (IRE) (Sabrehill (USA))
7674[7]

The Music Queen *C W J Farrell* a31 32
7 ch m Halling(USA) —Sadly Sober (IRE) (Roi Danzig (USA))
919[9]

Themwerethedays *S Kirk* a69 69
3 b g Olden Times—Zither (Zafonic (USA))
974[5] 1252[2] 1504[4] 1896[9] 2678[9] (3333) 3799[8] 5146[7] 5639[5] 6048[4] 6211[5] 6712[3] 6908[5] 6985[7]

The Name Is Frank *J W Mullins* 71
3 b g Lujain(USA) —Zaragossa (Paris House)
1839[13] 2974[11] 3313[13] 3678[12] 5748[6] 6024[4] 6706[13]

The Nawab (IRE) *Barry Potts* a17 83
6 ch g Almutawakel—Eschasse (USA) (Zilzal (USA))
810[4]

Thenford Flyer (IRE) *C Roberts* a48
8 b g Oscar(IRE) —Broadway Baby (Some Hand)
5913[11]

The Nifty Fox *T D Easterby* 87
4 b g Foxhound(USA) —Nifty Alice (First Trump)
1818[5] 2212[6] 2489[2] 2843[3] 3009[7] (3401) 3708[5] 4171[13] 4240[15] 5455[2] 5831[18] 6069[11]

The Oil Magnate *M Dods* 85
3 ch g Dr Fong(USA) —Bob's Princess (Bob's Return (IRE))
(1298) 2624[10] 3494[9] 3864[2] 4205[5] 5202[4] (6012)

Theola (IRE) *M H Tompkins* a52
2 b f Kalanisi(IRE) —Third Dimension (FR) (Suave Dancer (USA))
7069[7]

Theologist (IRE) *Mrs A J Perrett* 55
2 b c Galileo(IRE) —Medina (IRE) (Pennekamp (USA))
6083[9] 6443[9]

Theonebox (USA) *N J Vaughan* a86 78
3 ch g Johannesburg(USA) —Khalifa Of Kushog (USA) (Air Forbes Won (USA))
2360[7] 4606[2] 6949[10] 7202[13] (7610)

Theoretical *A J McCabe* a62 56
4 b m Marju(IRE) —Relativity (IRE) (Distant Relative)
49[7]

Theoricienne (FR) *Mme C Head-Maarek* 89
2 bl f Kendor(FR) —Theorie (FR) (Anabaa (USA))
7103a[6]

Theory *J H M Gosden* 71
3 b f Oasis Dream—Insinuate (USA) (Mr Prospector (USA))
1957[6] 2307[3] 2919[3] 3918[4] 4651[4] 5402[P] (Dead)

The Osteopath (IRE) *M Dods* 92
5 ch g Danehill Dancer(IRE) —Miss Margate (IRE) (Don't Forget Me)
(992) ◆ (1174) 1481[7] 1816[7] 3261[8] 3491[2] 4853[9] 5419[DSQ] 6070[4] 6482[2]

The Pirate (DEN) *Niels Petersen* a68 95
5 b h Primatico(USA) —Medinova (Mas Media)
383a[7] 568a[6] 745a[8] 2708a[5] 5335a[5]

The Plainsman *P W Hiatt* a36 45
6 b g Atraf—Mylania (Midyan (USA))
2394[6] 2667[8] 3604[7] 4503[14]

The Pott Reidy (USA) *T J O'Mara* 65
3 ch g Johannesburg(USA) —The Heebster (USA) (Bonus Money)
4494a[12]

The Power Of Phil *Miss Joanne Priest* a47
4 b g Komaite(USA) —Starboard Tack (FR) (Saddlers' Hall (IRE))
8[4] 145[10] 578[3] 770[9] 862[3] 930[7]

The Quantum Kid *T J Etherington* 61
4 b h Desert Prince(IRE) —Al Hasnaa (Zafonic (USA))
2286[6] 3059[12]

The Real Guru *Miss Tor Sturgis* a56 71
3 b g Ishiguru(USA) —Aloma's Reality (USA) (Proper Reality (USA))
1426[18] 3696[7] 4163[15] 4979[10] 5626[8] 6024[11]

The Riddler (IRE) *J A Osborne* a69 76
3 b c Daylami(IRE) —Wimple (USA) (Kingmambo (USA))
454[3]

Thermidor (USA) *Lady Herries* a67 56
5 ch g Giant's Causeway(USA) —Langoustine (AUS) (Danehill (USA))
608[6] 1058[6] 1345[8] 2597[9] 3265[9] 3482[6]

The Salwick Flyer (IRE) *I Semple* a64 64
5 b g Tagula(IRE) —Shimla (IRE) (Rudimentary (USA))
32[2] (214) 560[4] 2251[4] 2846[11] 4453[2] 4683[3] 5389[6] 6116[6] 7228[7] 7663[9]

The Saucy Snipe *P Winkworth* a66 59
2 b f Josr Algarhoud(IRE) —The Dark Eider (Superlative)
1680[6] 2709[6] 3019[4] 4185[9] 5567[8] 6432[5]

The Scorching Wind (IRE) *S C Williams* 57
2 b c Fasliyev(USA) —Rose Of Mooncoin (IRE) (Brief Truce (USA))
6885[13] 7240[8]

The Slider *Mrs L C Jewell* a49 15
4 b m Erhaab(USA) —Cottage Maid (Inchinor)
152[8] 269[5] 415[10] 691[9] 4250[10] 4772[11] 5787[11]

The Snatcher (IRE) *R Hannon* a96 96
5 b h Indian Danehill(IRE) —Saninka (IRE) (Doyoun)
(1532) 1719[5] 2565[2] 3319[2] 3899[5] 4509[16] 5096[2] 5896[4] 6103[2] 7019[10]

The Staffy (IRE) *N J Vaughan* a50
3 b g Redback—Lady Charlotte (Night Shift (USA))
7759[5]

The Tatling (IRE) *J M Bradley* a91 106
11 b g Perugino(USA) —Aunty Eileen (Ahonoora)
3336[13] 4445[19] 4962[4] 5151[5] 5648[9] 5757[6] 6006[8] 6650[3] (6925) 7222[6] 7456[5] 7584[4] (7697) 7826[5]

Theta Wave (USA) *J R Gask* a44
2 ch g Buckhar(USA) —Let's Dance (USA) (Thorn Dance (USA))
7501[9]

The Thrifty Bear *C W Fairhurst* 45
5 ch g Rambling Bear—Prudent Pet (Distant Relative)
2751[16] 3080[15] 4542[18] 6411[10]

The Tinker Man *M D I Usher* a48 54
4 b g Killer Instinct—Sporting Affair (IRE) (Ashkalani (IRE))
7441[12] 7469[6] 7692[13]

The Tooth Fairy (IRE) *Michael Mulvany* a58 74
2 b c Statue Of Liberty(USA) —Fairy Lore (IRE) (Fairy King (USA))
6320a[5]

The Trader (IRE) *M Blanshard* 104
10 ch g Selkirk(USA) —Snowing (Tate Gallery (USA))
1442[2] 2195[8] 2652a[10] 3063[9] 3943[5] 4840[8] 5509[14] 5781[3] 5990[6]

The Twelve Steps *G A Swinbank* a67 79
3 b c Diktat—Polygueza (FR) (Be My Guest (USA))
1426[3] 1995[6] 2705[7] 4741[9] 5258[7] (5714) 5962[5] 6724[16]

Thewaytosanjose (IRE) *S Kirk* a56 41
2 b f Fasliyev(USA) —Soltura (IRE) (Sadler's Wells (USA))
3674[13] 4339[8] 5066[9] (7659) 7789[7]

Thewayyouare (USA) *A Fabre* 117
3 b c Kingmambo(USA) —Maryinsky (IRE) (Sadler's Wells (USA))
2032a[6] 2654a[10]

The Which Doctor *J Noseda* a91 89
3 b g Medicean—Oomph (Shareef Dancer (USA))
1524[3] ◆ 2302[9] 2714[10] 4128[3] (4571) ◆ 5033[5] 6130[5] (6625)

Thewhirlingdervish (IRE) *T D Easterby* 84
10 ch g Definite Article—Nomadic Dancer (IRE) (Nabeel Dancer (USA))
1137[6] 1625[7] 2135[7] 2628[7] 2888[4] 3296[2] 3710[3] 4046[5] 4452[3] 5498[6] 6054[3] 6861[7]

The Willowy Wigeon *P Winkworth* a27 62
3 b f Josr Algarhoud(IRE) —The Dark Eider (Superlative)
2639[2] 3183[4] 3397[14] 5167[9] 6541[7] 6908[8]

The Wily Woodcock *G L Moore* a71 65
4 b g Mark Of Esteem(IRE) —Lonely Shore (Blakeney)
2261[2] 2533[4] 3914[9] 4343[11] 4946[11] 6091[3] 6585[12] 6821[6] 7654[3] 7749[4]

The Wolverine (NZ) *Leon Corstens* 106
5 ch g Stravinsky(USA) —Arena Pride (NZ) (Nassipour (USA))
6922a[6]

The Wonkey Donkey *K J Burke* a12 26
2 ch f Pursuit Of Love—Basheera (Bahhare (USA))
2049[6] 2508[5] 2720[5]

The World *A Fabre* 84
3 b f Dubai Destination(USA) —Bright Tiara (USA) (Chief's Crown (USA))
7431a[6] 7635a[0]

They All Laughed *P W Hiatt* a82 78
5 ch g Zafonic(USA) —Royal Future (IRE) (Royal Academy (USA))
540[3] (617) (854) 1026[6] 1299[9] 1744[3] 1998[5] 2621[10] 2952[3] 3523[2] ◆ 3884[10] 4432[9]

The Young Fella *S A Callaghan* a35 43
3 ch g Compton Place—Centre Court (Second Set (IRE))
3268[9] 3502[5] ◆ 3916[10] 4301[9] 5832[11] 6751[7]

Thief *L M Cumani* 64
2 b c Falbrav(IRE) —Eurolink Raindance (IRE) (Alzao (USA))
5068[9] 6892[8]

Thinking Robins (IRE) *I Bugattella* 88
5 b h Plumbird—Rose Jasmine (ITY) (Sikeston (USA))
7349a[15]

Thin Red Line (IRE) *E A L Dunlop* a78 78
2 b c Red Ransom(USA) —Albaiyda (IRE) (Brief Truce (USA))
6777[6] ◆ 7227[7] 7333[7] (7524)

Third Set (IRE) *Saeed Bin Suroor* a100 114
5 b g Royal Applause—Khamseh (Thatching)
203a[2] (495a) (745a) 5025[5] 5265[3] 6780[12]

Thirtyfourthstreet (IRE) *W R Muir* 36
3 gr f Beat Hollow—Peacock Alley (IRE) (Salse (USA))
2257[14] 2328[13] 3482[8]

This Ones For Eddy *S Parr* a77 66
3 b g Kyllachy—Skirt Around (Deploy)
1960[4] 2187[6] 2380[5] 2823[10] 4207[18] 4538[3] 4724[2] 4952[7] 6339[4] 6792[12] 7228[6] 7416[4] 7544[6] (7618) 7698[2] 7829[4]

This Ones For Pat (USA) *S Parr* a67 39
3 bb g Proud Citizen(USA) —Lace Curtain Irish (USA) (Cryptoclearance (USA))
6791[8] 7074[7] 7213[6] 7357[9] 7383[9] 7518[13] (7644) 7746[4] (7774) 7799[8]

Thoas (GR) *Jane Chapple-Hyam* a13
3 b c Filandros(GR) —Xirolia (GR) (Busted)
5047[8]

Thomas Lawrence (USA) *P A Blockley* a46 64
7 ch g Horse Chestnut(SAF) —Olatha (USA) (Miswaki (USA))
1534[7] 2243[13] 2478[13]

Thomas Malory (IRE) *Miss V Haigh* a65 63
3 b c Mujadil(USA) —Isca (Caerleon (USA))
767[4] (876) 1155[7] 1274[2] 1548[5] 1743[8] 2282[7] 2660[9] 3217[3] 3441[4] 4107[7]

Thompsons Walls (IRE) *P C Haslam* a59 79
3 b g Trans Island—Nordic Living (IRE) (Nordico (USA))
(1823) 3963[6]

Thornaby Green *T D Barron* a65 67
7 b g Whittingham(IRE) —Dona Filipa (Precocious)
3175[12] 3450[15] 3814[6] 4261[2] 4420[2] 4936[11] 6162[2] 6726[11] 6786[2] 7085[10] 7132[8] 7516[5] 7634[3] 7692[2]

Thorns Of Life (USA) *Robert Collet* 84
2 ch f Fusaichi Pegasus(USA) —After Taxes (USA) (Nureyev (USA))
3749a[4] 4441a[6]

Thorn Song (USA) *Dale Romans* 116
5 rg h Unbridled's Song(USA) —Festal (USA) (Storm Bird (CAN))
(6504a) 6996a[9]

Thorny Mandate *W M Brisbourne* a68 69
6 b g Diktat—Rosa Canina (Bustino)
1086[6] 1639[5] 2053[2] 2364[6] (2908) 3650[7] 4295[3] 4501[4] 4592[6] 5450[4] 6136[2] 6279[2] 6493[5]

Thought Is Free *P F I Cole* a69 94
3 b f Cadeaux Genereux—Dayville (USA) (Dayjur (USA))
2566[3] 4249[5] 4606[6]

Thoughtless Moment (IRE) *D K Weld* 101
4 ch m Pivotal—Celebrity Style (USA) (Seeking The Gold (USA))
5731a[6]

Thoughtsofstardom *P S McEntee* a81 71
5 b g Mind Games—Alustar (Emarati (USA))
29[5] 54[7] 263[6] 372[3] 437[3] 628[2] (690) 774[2] 875[4] 1646[4] 1842[7] 1996[8] 2205[3] 2551[3] (2881) 2934[2] 3159[2] 3271[8] 3405[6] 4159[5] 4313[9] 4809[5] 5250[5] 5401[2] 5474[5] 7286[10] 7471[10] (7589) 7621[2] (7672) (7743)

Thousand Miles (IRE) *P W Chapple-Hyam* 67
2 br c Danehill Dancer(IRE) —Mille Miglia (IRE) (Caerleon (USA))
6029[5] ◆ 6580[2]

Three Boars *S Gollings* a79 67
6 ch g Most Welcome—Precious Poppy (Polish Precedent (USA))
(78) 260[7] 443[6] (954) 1017[10] 6662[8] 6838[10] 7271[5] 7455[7]

Threecheersforanby (IRE) *S Parr* a1 31
3 br g Elnadim(USA) —Joud (Dancing Brave (USA))
1298[6] 1751[8] 1960[10] 2552[15] 2704[10]

Three Ducks *L M Cumani* a70 67
2 b f Diktat—Three Terns (USA) (Arctic Tern (USA))
7015[4] 7380[3] (7578)

Three Gold Leaves *J G Given* a52 38
3 ch g Zaha(CAN) —Tab's Gift (Bijou D'Inde)
2528[9] 2847[11]

Three Half Crowns (IRE) *M S Saunders* a47 39
4 b g Barathea(IRE) —My-Lorraine (IRE) (Mac's Imp (USA))
1031[12] 1148[10]

Three Moons (IRE) *H J L Dunlop* a74 85
2 b f Montjeu(IRE) —Three Owls (IRE) (Warning)
5048[2] 5643[2] ◆ 6081[2] ◆ 6720[2] 7144[8]

Three Rocks (IRE) *J S Bolger* a83 84
3 b c Rock Of Gibraltar(IRE) —Top Crystal (IRE) (Sadler's Wells (USA))
6315a[9] 6516a[6]

Threestepstoheaven *B W Hills* 74
2 b g Haafhd—Bella Bianca (IRE) (Barathea (IRE))
2592[11] 3164[2] 5857[7] 6480[2]

Threestoneburn (USA) *J R Boyle* a56 68
3 b f Johannesburg(USA) —White Bridle (IRE) (Singspiel (IRE))
184[7] 225[6] 2559[6] 2695[11] 3574[5] 3780[7] 6175[2] 6541[9] 6747[2] 6927[3] 7050[6] 7260[6] 7506[7]

Three Strings (USA) *P D Niven* a65 63
5 b g Stravinsky(USA) —Just Cause (Law Society (USA))
1521[3] 2001[13] 2927[6] 3814[8] 4785[3] (5456) 5971[4] 6812[5] 7039[4] (7376) 7630[7]

Three Thieves (UAE) *M S Saunders* a76 55
5 ch g Jade Robbery(USA) —Melisendra (FR) (Highest Honor (FR))
185[8] 224[8] 344[7] 485[7] 695[11] 2051[7] 2832[8]

Three Way Stretch (IRE) *J T Gorman* 89
2 b c Intikhab(USA) —Chapka (IRE) (Green Desert (USA))
5546a[7] 6317a[13]

Throne Of Power (USA) *M A Magnusson* a84 99
3 bb c Pulpit(USA) —Lakabi (USA) (Nureyev (USA))
(500) ◆ 1834[8] ◆ (2189) 3155[10] 3919[17] 5907[9] 6666[6] 6984[4]

Throw The Dice *A Berry* a29 63
6 b g Lujain(USA) —Euridice (IRE) (Woodman (USA))
3668[9] 4561[10] 5044[8] 5452[12]

Thumberlina *Mrs C A Dunnett* a23 40
2 b f Choisir(AUS) —Capstick (JPN) (Machiavellian (USA))
6885[12] 7452[9]

Thumbs Up *L M Cumani* a77 86
3 gr g Intikhab(USA) —Exclusive Approval (USA) (With Approval (CAN))
1763[7] 2546[3] 2981[8] (4061) ◆ 4741[2] (5935) 6202[7] 6582[7]

Thunderball *A J McCabe* a85 85
2 ch g Haafhd—Trustthunder (Selkirk (USA))
2592[8] 3476[3] 4213[2] 4733[3] (5404) 5895[2] 6284[5] 6946[14]

Thunder Bay *R A Fahey* a62 87
3 b g Hunting Lion(IRE) —Floral Spark (Forzando)
3336[10] 3909[4] 4418[7] 5510[11] 5886[6] 6823[2] 6990[8] 7225[7]

Thunder Gorge (USA) *Mouse Hamilton-Fairley* a74 76
3 b g Thunder Gulch(USA) —Renaissance Fair (USA) (Theatrical)
2481[5] 2976[9] 3563[6] 4128[2] 4310[2] 4724[3] 5168[5] (5588) 6242[3] 6675[8]

Thundering Star (SAF) *M F De Kock* 111
5 b g Fort Wood(USA) —Lightning Duel (SAF) (Foveros)
1663a[8] 2542[7] 3154[7]

Thunder Jodys (USA) *B Grizzetti*
2 b c Thunder Gulch(USA) —Jodys Deelite (USA) (Afternoon Deelites (USA))
2745a[12]

Thunderousapplause *A J McCabe* a68 85
4 b m Royal Applause—Trustthunder (Selkirk (USA))
1552[3] 1676[2] 1903[5] 2787[8] 7152[7]

Thunderous Mood (USA) *P F I Cole* 102
2 bb c Storm Cat(USA) —Warm Mood (USA) (Alydar (USA))
2424[3] ◆ (2581) 3103[18] 4507[7] 5383[2] 5850a[2]

Thunder Storm Cat (USA) *M Rulec* a85 94
4 b h Storm Cat(USA) —Tenga (USA) (Mr Prospector (USA))
5115a[0] 5743a[8]

Thunderstruck *K A Ryan* a75 81
3 b g Bertolini(USA) —Trustthunder (Selkirk (USA))
1395[5] 1576[5] 2378[8] 5202[7] 5888[5] 6188[6] 6250[4] 6629[3] 6950[9]

Thunderwing (IRE) *James Moffatt* a73 65
6 bb g Indian Danehill(IRE) —Scandisk (IRE) (Kenmare (FR))
1219[4] 1824[7] 4142[3] 4850[6]

Thurston (IRE) *D J S Ffrench Davis* a66
2 ch c Barathea(IRE) —Campiglia (IRE) (Fairy King (USA))
7020[12] 7389[8] 7649[2]

Tiago (USA) *John Shirreffs* a123
4 b h Pleasant Tap(USA) —Set Them Free (USA) (Stop The Music (USA))
7001a[3]

Tia Mia *M Botti* a93 90
3 ch f Dr Fong(USA) —Giusina Mia (USA) (Diesis)
926[3] 1075[4] 2000[5] 2993[3] 3460[4] 4198[8] 5206[3] 5906[9] 6699[5] 7477[10]

Tian Shan (IRE) *D K Weld* 108
4 b h Barathea(IRE) —Most Charming (FR) (Darshaan)
2026a[5] 6516a[5] 7157a[5]

Tiara Boom De Ay (IRE) *D J Wintle* a44 55
4 b m Fasliyev(USA) —Fez (Mujtahid (USA))
354[8] 590[9] 857[9] 1369[9] 1694[13]

Tibinta *P D Evans* a47 57
4 b m Averti(IRE) —Bint Albadou (IRE) (Green Desert (USA))
46[6] 100[7] 119[4]

Tibroso (ITY) *U Rispoli* 92
4 ch h Tibullo(USA) —Calabrosa (IRE) (Barathea (IRE))
7253a[10]

Ticking *T Keddy* a58 22
5 ch g Barathea(IRE) —Tuning (Rainbow Quest (USA))
81[3] 804[7] 1342[5] 1504[9] 1700[7] 3834[13] 7068[8]

Ticmosic (FR) *Eva Sundbye* a81 55
5 br g Musical Fappi(USA) —Ticket To Ride (Prince Sabo)
2232a[3]

Tidal Force (USA) *P F I Cole* 78
2 ch g High Yield(USA) —Shady Waters (CAN) (Rahy (USA))
4024[8] (4425) 5511[11]

Tidy (IRE) *Micky Hammond* a56 64
8 b g Mujadil(USA) —Neat Shilling (IRE) (Bob Back (USA))
69[10] 229[2] 559[7] 769[2] 822[2] 1391[4] 1521[10] 4075[4] 4701[7] 4966[10]

Tiegan An Josh *A Crook*
3 b f Lahib(USA) —Poungada (FR) (Tropular)
3835[7] 5505[10] 6530[13] 6843[9]

Tiegs (IRE) *P W Hiatt* a52 47
6 ch m Desert Prince(IRE) —Helianthus (Groom Dancer (USA))
(269) 206[11] 7272[9] 7626[10]

Tiepie *J Akehurst* a65 41
3 ch c Tomba—Contrary Mary (Mujadil (USA))
514[4] 714[6] 797[2] ◆ 1060[4] 1670[7] 2069[8] 2277[7]

Tifernati *W J Haggas* a86 94
4 b g Dansili—Pain Perdu (IRE) (Waajib)
1793[3] 2264[3] (2939) ◆ 3925[4] 6061[4] 6479[3]

Tiffany Diamond (IRE) *A P O'Brien* 100
3 gr f Sadler's Wells(USA) —Niyla (IRE) (Darshaan)
2113a[2] 2792[14] 3196[4]

Tiffany Lady *M D I Usher* a38
2 ch f Generous(IRE) —Art Deco Lady (Master Willie)
7699[11]

Tiffin Deano (IRE) *H J Manners* a25 29
6 b g Mujadil(USA) —Xania (Mujtahid (USA))
394[6]

Tiger Dream *K A Ryan* a51 88
3 b g Oasis Dream—Grey Way (USA) (Cozzene (USA))
(2008) 2403[7] 3039[6] 4407[9] 4867[4] 5257[9] 6170[11]

Tiger Eye (IRE) *M A Jarvis* 98
2 b f Danehill Dancer(IRE) —Pink Stone (FR) (Bigstone (IRE))
6030[4] ◆ (6473) ◆ (Dead)

Tiger Flash *W J Haggas* 63
2 b c Dansili—Miss Penton (Primo Dominie)
7051[5]

Tiger Goddess (IRE) *W J Haggas* a71 71
2 gr f Verglas(IRE) —Googoosh (IRE) (Danehill (USA))
2783[5] 4339[2] 4968[5] 6809[3] 6970[6]

Tiger King (GER) *P Monteith* 68
7 b g Tiger Hill(IRE) —Tennessee Girl (GER) (Big Shuffle (USA))
7177[7]

Tiger Reigns *M Dods* 65
2 b g Tiger Hill(IRE) —Showery (Rainbow Quest (USA))
6213[3] 6723[3]

Tiger Spice *W J Haggas* a65 64
3 b f Royal Applause—Up And About (Barathea (IRE))
30[3] 325[7]

Tiger's Rocket (IRE) *S Gollings* a71 66
3 b c Monashee Mountain(USA) —Brown Foam (Horage)
178[4] (360) 589[2] 712[3] (1124) 1395[4] 1750[5] 7752[5]

Tiger Trail (GER) *Mrs N Smith* a51 67
4 b g Tagula(IRE) —Tweed Mill (Selkirk (USA))
1265[10] 1835[3] 2128[8] 2692[4] 3847[6] 4313[10]

Tighnabruaich (IRE) *M A Jarvis* a58 89
3 b c Rainbow Quest(USA) —Miss Mistletoes (IRE) (The Minstrel (CAN))
(1446) 1919[4] 3719[8] 5423[11]

Tight Precision (USA) *Thomas F Proctor* 92
3 b f Pure Precision(USA) —Come Tight (USA) (Artistry I (SAF))
5744a[4]

Tightrope (IRE) *T D McCarthy* a48 30
2 b c Refuse To Bend(IRE) —Sisal (IRE) (Danehill (USA))
1736[9] 3001[12] 5929[11] 6282[10] 6876[12]

Tigim (IRE) *Noel Henley* a58 69
9 b g Fayruz—Rousalong (Rousillon (USA))
126[7]

Tignello (IRE) *D R C Elsworth* a68 50
3 b g Kendor(FR) —La Genereuse (Generous (IRE))
5463[9] 6018[6] 6571[6] 7012[2]

Tikka Masala (IRE) *Tom Dascombe* a55 51
2 b f One Cool Cat(USA) —Raysiza (IRE) (Alzao (USA))
6764[5] 7168[4]

Tilapia (IRE) *Miss Gay Kelleway* a92 77
4 ch g Daggers Drawn(USA) —Mrs Fisher (IRE) (Salmon Leap (USA))
43[3] 531[3] (626) 735[5] 908[6] 3896[10] 4269[6] 4894[8] 5209[12] 5675[8] 6210[9] 6607[15]

Tilerium's Dream (IRE) *G A Swinbank*
2 b g Tillerman—Thai Princess (IRE) (Hamas (IRE))
3976[9]

Tillagirl *G G Margarson* 31
2 b f Tillerman—Emaura (Dominion)
3114[8] 3652[5] 6986[11]

Tillers Satisfied (IRE) *R Hollinshead* a60 65
2 b f Tillerman—Lady Of Pleasure (IRE) (Marju (IRE))
2903[3] 3417[6] 4321[6] 5200[4] (6489) 7205[12] (7687) 7794[6]

Tilletudlem (FR) *J S Goldie* a30 38
2 gr g Kutub(IRE) —Queenhood (FR) (Linamix (FR))
7221[6] 7735[7]

Tilly Ann (IRE) *Peter Grayson* a41 9
3 b f Turtle Island(IRE) —Buckland Filleigh (IRE) (Buckskin (FR))
412[8] 486[2] 623[6] 780[8] 1169[5] 1251[7]

Tilly's Dream *G C Bravery* a81 83
5 ch m Arkadian Hero(USA) —Dunloe (IRE) (Shaadi (USA))
1021[2] 1386[4] 1698[7] 1901[5] 2504[3] 2993[2] 3271[7] 3883[4] 5884[7]

Tilos Gem (IRE) *M Johnston* 73
2 ch c Trans Island—Alpine Flair (IRE) (Tirol)
4360[8] 6057[3] 7080[6]

Tilsworth Charlie *J R Jenkins* a68 68
5 br m Dansili—Glossary (Reference Point)
13[4] 89[3] 211[2] 349[4] 584[2] 677[12] 933[2] 2055[5] 2355[4] (2798) 3026[5] 3608[17] (4383) 4779[5] 5073[5] 5801[7] 6564[12] (7102) 7254[10] 7433[8] 7591[9] 7764[9]

Tilt *B Ellison* a94 99
6 b g Daylami(IRE) —Tromond (Lomond (USA))
1568[2] 1916[3] 3490[11] 3942[9] 4508[14] 6817[6] 7404[2]

Timbaa (USA) *Rae Guest* a33 49
2 b g Anabaa(USA) —Timber Ice (USA) (Woodman (USA))
6375[12] 6714[14] 7105[13]

Timbalier (USA) *D M Simcock* a60 71
3 ch c Dixieland Band(USA) —Gabacha (USA) (Woodman (USA))
1403[6] 2996[6] ◆ 3737[2] 4112[3]

Timber Creek *H Candy* a64 68
3 b g Tobougg(IRE) —Proserpine (Robellino (USA))
1684^{6} ◆ 2046^{6} 2994^{5} 3563^{8} 3886^{12} 4524^{4} 4727^{3} ◆ 5069^{3} 5816^{5} 6417^{7}

Timber Treasure (USA) *Paul Green* a69 85
4 bb g Forest Wildcat(USA) —Lady Ilsley (USA) (Trempolino (USA))
860^{8} 1030^{4} 1708^{6} 2005^{2} 2356^{3} (2968) 3171^{5} 3626^{15} (4502) 7290^{9}

Time Control *L M Cumani* 77
3 b f Sadler's Wells(USA) —Time Away (IRE) (Darshaan)
3479^{3} 4166^{2} 4871^{3} (5445) 6241^{10}

Time Dancer (IRE) *H A McWilliams* a31
4 ch g Desert Sun—With Finesse (Be My Guest (USA))
821^{8} 1305^{13} 2395^{10}

Time For Old Time *I A Wood* a59 59
2 b f Olden Times—Pink Supreme (Night Shift (USA))
3091^{4} ◆ (3570) 4389^{2}

Timeless Dream *P W Chapple-Hyam* a55 69
2 b f Oasis Dream—Simply Times (USA) (Dodge (USA))
5240^{14} 6785^{2} 7546^{7}

Time Loup *S R Bowring* a45 58
2 b g Loup Sauvage(USA) —Bird Of Time (IRE) (Persian Bold)
2458^{5} 2754^{10} (4120) 4956^{7} 5204^{9} 5591^{10} 5715^{5} 6009^{8} 7372^{12}

Time Medicean *M R Channon* 66
2 rg c Medicean—Ribbons And Bows (IRE) (Dr Devious (IRE))
5649^{3}

Time Share (IRE) *M Wigham* a60 59
4 b m Danetime(IRE) —Clochette (IRE) (Namaqualand (USA))
50^{6} 82^{7} 106^{4} 297^{4} 338^{6} 696^{3} 725^{2} 871^{4} 883^{2} 1706^{3} 2088^{5} 2547^{5} 3405^{13} 3460^{7}

Times Up *J L Dunlop* 84
2 b g Olden Times—Princess Genista (Ile De Bourbon (USA))
6778^{2} ◆

Times Vital (IRE) *E J O'Neill* a65 93
3 b c Danetime(IRE) —Flying Freedom (IRE) (Archway (IRE))
1194^{3} 2912^{4} 3628^{4} (4179) 5865^{2} ◆ (6079) 6563^{7} (6974)

Timetable *H R A Cecil* a85 91
3 b c Observatory(USA) —Clepsydra (Sadler's Wells (USA))
2413^{2} (2912) 3919^{15} 4783^{10} 6035^{2} 6467^{4} (6949)

Timeteam (IRE) *S Kirk* a87 80
2 b c Danetime(IRE) —Ceannanas (IRE) (Magical Wonder (USA))
2759^{6} 3019^{2} ◆ 3315^{2} 3902^{3} (4579) 5466^{4} 6118^{5} 6426^{6} 6603^{2} (6931) (7024) 7334^{4}

Time To Beat (GER) *W Baltromei* 95
3 b f Areion(GER) —Torbay (IRE) (Surumu (GER))
5038a^{6} 7431a^{14}

Time To Play *T T Clement* a62 68
3 b g Best Of The Bests(IRE) —Primavera (Anshan)
5426^{4} 6280^{4} 6762^{6} 7300^{3} 7504^{5}

Time To Regret *I W McInnes* a69 63
8 b g Presidium—Scoffera (Scottish Reel)
916^{3} 1032^{3} 1391^{14} 1605^{9} 3201^{9} 3593^{4} 4386^{7} (4919) 5157^{2} 5604^{9} 6211^{12} 6821^{4} 7267^{3} 7340^{10} 7634^{12}

Timewatch *Miss J E Foster* a37 62
3 b g Fantastic Light(USA) —Maybe Forever (Zafonic (USA))
7184^{8} 7518^{12}

Timocracy *M Johnston* 84
3 br c Cape Cross(IRE) —Tithcar (Cadeaux Genereux)
4606^{5} 5366^{7} (5815) 6050^{2} 6195^{2} ◆ 6416^{3} 6657^{5}

Timpanist *P W Chapple-Hyam* a67 62
2 ch f Beat Hollow—Messila Rose (Darshaan)
5225^{12} 5812^{2} 6205^{3} 6700^{14}

Tina's Best (IRE) *R Hannon* a64 79
3 b f King's Best(USA) —Phantom Waters (Pharly (FR))
1738^{3} 2047^{2} 2429^{10} 2974^{6} (3266) 3345^{2} 3679^{4} 6124^{4} 6675^{11} 6864^{7}

Tina's Ridge (IRE) *R Hollinshead* a60 63
4 ch g Indian Ridge—Phantom Waters (Pharly (FR))
323^{8} 550^{4} 601^{8} 844^{6} 996^{5} 1160^{8} 1391^{6} 1776^{7}

Tinkerbelle (IRE) *J L Dunlop* 42
2 br f Marju(IRE) —Pershaan (IRE) (Darshaan)
3349^{14} 5534^{11} 6580^{11}

Tinnarinka *R Hannon* a77 61
4 ch m Observatory(USA) —Dancing Fire (USA) (Dayjur (USA))
736^{2} (1182) 1329^{7} 1932^{10} 2718^{5} 3132^{10} 3903^{11} 6396^{6} 6738^{10} 7009^{9}

Tinshu (IRE) *D Haydn Jones* a47
2 ch f Fantastic Light(USA) —Ring Of Esteem (Mark Of Esteem (IRE))
7424^{8} 7773^{5}

Tinted View (USA) *W S Kittow* a44 18
4 ch m Distant View(USA) —Gombeen (USA) (Private Account (USA))
5912^{11} 6175^{8}

Tin Town Boy (IRE) *H Rogers* a53 76
7 b g Danehill Dancer(IRE) —Sushari (IRE) (Shardari)
4799a^{4}

Tioga Gold (IRE) *L R James* a57 46
9 b g Goldmark(USA) —Coffee Bean (Doulab (USA))
67^{3} (345) 600^{11} 2051^{10}

Tipsy Prince *David Pinder* a75 73
4 b g Tipsy Creek(USA) —Princess Of Garda (Komaite (USA))
2081^{9} 2556^{6} 2988^{11}

Tip Toes (IRE) *M J Gingell* a52 52
6 b m Bianconi(USA) —Tip Tap Toe (USA) (Pleasant Tap (USA))
76^{9}

Tiramisu (TUR) *S Tasbek* 109
5 b m Marlin(USA) —Dan Dancing (FR) (Groom Dancer (USA))
5741a^{7}

Tirol Livit (IRE) *N Wilson* a44 50
5 ch g Titus Livius(FR) —Orange Royale (IRE) (Exit To Nowhere (USA))
657^{5} 804^{3} 821^{4}

Tishtar *R Hannon* a82 82
2 br c Kyllachy—Xtrasensory (Royal Applause)
1987^{3} (2338) ◆ 4626^{7} 5466^{6} 6118^{13} (6575)

Tis Mighty (IRE) *P J Prendergast* a96 97
5 bb m Fruits Of Love(USA) —Floating Agenda (USA) (Twilight Agenda (USA))
1105a^{13} 4007a^{10} (5550a) 6689a^{6} 7328a^{10} 7492^{3}

Titan Triumph *W J Knight* a91 83
4 b h Zamindar(USA) —Triple Green (Green Desert (USA))
1566^{5} 1809^{20} 2329^{4} 4944^{10} 5051^{3} 5675^{4} 6471^{12} 6675^{14} (7068) (7302) (7525) (7821)

Titfer (IRE) *A W Carroll* a57 65
3 ch g Fath(USA) —Fur Hat (Habitat)
1478^{6} 2475^{7} (3183) 3407^{5} 4049^{7} 4377^{8} 4710^{10} 6757^{10}

Titillate (IRE) *Saeed Bin Suroor* 25
3 b f Barathea(IRE) —Most Charming (FR) (Darshaan)
2800^{9}

Titinius (IRE) *Micky Hammond* 69
8 ch g Titus Livius(FR) —Maiyria (IRE) (Shernazar)
2155^{5} 2446^{2} 2848^{10} 3226^{10} 4172^{9}

Title Deed (USA) *A P Jarvis* a74 62
4 b g Belong To Me(USA) —Said Privately (USA) (Private Account (USA))
1411^{4} 1856^{6} 1972^{3} 2467^{13} 3137^{10} 3820^{9} 4490^{7} 4664^{6}

Title Role *P F I Cole* a78 77
3 b g Mark Of Esteem(IRE) —No Comebacks (Last Tycoon)
(1243) 1527^{4} 2151^{11} 2996^{3} 3327^{8} 4344^{6} 5428^{2} 5605^{2} 6256^{5} 6704^{8}

Tito (IRE) *T D Barron* 69
3 b g Diktat—T G's Girl (Selkirk (USA))
5636^{2} 6150^{6} 6543^{4} 6792^{9}

Tito Gobbi *Mrs Marjorie Fife* 52
2 ch g Lomitas—Nellie Melba (Hurricane Sky (AUS))
1727^{4} 2140^{6} 2910^{4} 4292^{7} 5715^{13}

Tittle *H Candy* a37 57
3 b f Tobougg(IRE) —Poppy's Song (Owington)
3177^{5} 3765^{4} 4107^{17} 4725^{11} 5679^{4} 6595^{10}

Titus Andronicus (IRE) *K A Ryan* 73
2 b g Danetime(IRE) —Scarlet Empress (Second Empire (IRE))
2275^{5} 2696^{3} 3949^{2} 4175^{3} 4434^{3} 5363^{4} 6274^{5} (6548)

Titus Gent *J Ryan* a59
3 ch g Tumbleweed Ridge—Genteel (IRE) (Titus Livius (FR))
6633^{2} 6822^{7} 7074^{8} 7536^{11}

Titus Shadow (IRE) *B Grizzetti* 102
4 ch h Titus Livius(FR) —Mujadil Shadow (IRE) (Mujadil (USA))
(2029a) 7253a^{7} 7349a^{3}

Tiza (SAF) *A De Royer-Dupre* a91 114
6 b g Goldkeeper(USA) —Mamushka (SAF) (Elliodor (FR))
2214a^{3} 2637a^{3} 3938a^{4} 4915a^{8} (5556a) 6518a^{7} 7187a^{2}

Tizdejavu (USA) *Gregory Fox* 111
3 b c Tiznow(USA) —Remember When (USA) (Dixie Brass (USA))
4887a^{3}

Tiz Elemental (USA) *Carla Gaines* a107
4 b m Cee's Tizzy(USA) —Blending Element (IRE) (Great Commotion (USA))
6965a^{13}

Tizzy May (FR) *B Ellison* a66 78
8 ch g Highest Honor(FR) —Forentia (Formidable (USA))
989^{3} 1521^{8} 1729^{7} 2250^{10} 2394^{2} 2617^{3} 2782^{5} 3450^{12} 4048^{2} 4503^{8} 5008^{9} 6189^{6}

Tizzy's Tune (USA) *Ronald McAnally* a103
5 bb m Tiznow(USA) —Flowing Melody (USA) (Eternal Prince (USA))
6965a^{5}

To Arms *K J Burke* a7 70
6 b g Mujahid(USA) —Toffee (Midyan (USA))
6672^{3}

Toasted Special (USA) *W McCreery* a52 80
3 ch f Johannesburg(USA) —Sajjaya (USA) (Blushing Groom (FR))
4467a^{12} (6366a)

Tobago Bay *Miss Sheena West* a49 63
3 b g Tobougg(IRE) —Perfect Dream (Emperor Jones (USA))
325^{8} 674^{4} 865^{3} 940^{8} 5269^{2} 6329^{3}

Tobago Reef *Mrs L Stubbs* a75 35
4 b g Tobougg(IRE) —Silly Mid-On (Midyan (USA))
127^{5}

Toballa *H J Collingridge* a40 51
3 b f Tobougg(IRE) —Ball Gown (Jalmood (USA))
2954^{10} 3161^{11} 4992^{4} 5379^{5} 6007^{8} 6762^{12} 7111^{11}

Tobanjaro (HUN) *Z Nagy*
5 ch h Bakharoff(USA) —Tubarozsa (HUN) (Gilmore (FR))
421a^{4} 603a^{6}

Tobar Suil Lady (IRE) *J L Spearing* a70 71
3 b f Statue Of Liberty(USA) —Stellarette (IRE) (Lycius (USA))
924^{6} 1819^{14} 4163^{14} 4702^{4} 5867^{12} (7358) ◆ 7548^{5}

To Be Or Not To Be *John Berry* a73
3 b f Tobougg(IRE) —Lady Mayor (Kris)
6935^{6} 7344^{4} (7490) (7748)

Toberogan (IRE) *W A Murphy* a47 63
7 b g Docksider(USA) —Beltisaal (FR) (Belmez (USA))
1103a^{6}

Tobizzy *J R Jenkins* a10 51
2 ch f Tobougg(IRE) —Isabella D'Este (IRE) (Irish River (FR))
2691^{8} 3869^{10} 4907^{10} 6333^{3} 6770^{10} 7542^{9} 7832^{11}

Toboggan Lady *Mrs A Duffield* a46 70
4 b m Tobougg(IRE) —Northbend (Shirley Heights)
1136^{2} 1518^{4} 2572^{6} 2849^{8} 6115^{8}

Tobond (IRE) *M Botti* a90
2 b g Tobougg(IRE) —Rajmata (IRE) (Prince Sabo)
5344^{7} (6375) 6756^{3} 7067^{2} (7426) ◆

Tobouggornotobougg *D Shaw* a47
3 ch g Tobougg(IRE) —Douce Maison (IRE) (Fools Holme (USA))
184^{10} 288^{6} 439^{4} 556^{7} 656^{6} 797^{11}

To Bubbles *A G Newcombe* a71 39
3 b f Tobougg(IRE) —Effervescent (Efisio)
483^{6} 662^{6} 2084^{2} (3818) 4782^{9} 5638^{9} 7534^{10}

Toby Tyler *P T Midgley* 71
2 b g Best Of The Bests(IRE) —Pain Perdu (IRE) (Waajib)
(1727) 2154^{3} 2392^{4} 4733^{10} 5381^{6} 5632^{13}

Today's The Day *M A Jarvis* a74 64
2 b f Alhaarth(IRE) —Dayville (USA) (Dayjur (USA))
2691^{9} 3373^{3} 3837^{2} 4525^{5} 5165^{2} 6240^{18} 7371^{3} 7638^{2} 7769^{3} 7830^{3}

Todber *M P Tregoning* a65 68
3 b f Cape Cross(IRE) —Dominica (Alhaarth (IRE))
3379^{7} 4090^{6} 4524^{8} 5574^{7} (5911) (6308)

Todwick Owl *J G Given* a53 1
4 b g Namid—Blinding Mission (IRE) (Marju (IRE))
88^{5} (369) 550^{5} 868^{5} 1391^{13}

Toggle *Ms V S Lucas* a51 66
4 b g Tobougg(IRE) —Niggle (Night Shift (USA))
5002a^{4}

Toho Alan (JPN) *H Fujiwara* 114
5 b h Dance In The Dark(JPN) —Hidden Dance (USA) (Nureyev (USA))
7511a^{10}

Toirneach (USA) *J S Bolger* a60 99
3 b f Thunder Gulch(USA) —Wandering Pine (USA) (Country Pine (USA))
2024a^{4} 2435a^{6}

Toldo (IRE) *G M Moore* 81
6 gr g Tagula(IRE) —Mystic Belle (IRE) (Thatching)
3007^{5} ◆ 3929^{8} 5718^{9} 6361^{P}

Toledo Gold (IRE) *E J Alston* 72
2 ch c Needwood Blade—Eman's Joy (Lion Cavern (USA))
3997^{8} (4536) 5451^{3} 6247^{8}

Toll Road *E A L Dunlop* a54
2 b f Dubai Destination(USA) —Endorsement (Warning)
7812^{5}

Tomatina *C F Wall* 35
3 ch f Kyllachy—Sunningdale (IRE) (Indian Ridge)
4987^{11} 5278^{15} 6003^{10}

Tombalina *C J Teague* a55 50
5 ch m Tomba—Ashkernazy (IRE) (Salt Dome (USA))
5961^{2}

Tombi (USA) *J Howard Johnson* 110
4 b g Johannesburg(USA) —Tune In To The Cat (USA) (Tunerup (USA))
(2172) 3248^{25} 4437^{2} 6484^{2} 6653^{6}

Tombov (FR) *A King* 73
2 bb c Laveron—Zamsara (FR) (Zino)
4780^{11} (5184)

Tomina *Miss E C Lavelle* a76 80
8 b g Deploy—Cavina (Ardross)
(2715) 3884^{2} 4516^{4}

Tomintoul Flyer *H R A Cecil* a100 86
3 br c Dr Fong(USA) —Miller's Melody (Chief Singer)
2610^{5} (3134) ◆ 3877^{13} 4621^{8} 5349^{2} 5682^{4} 6012^{2} 6202^{5} 6582^{10}

Tomintoul Star *H R A Cecil* 60
2 gr f Dansili—Lixian (Linamix (FR))
6358^{8} 6884^{5}

Tomorrow's World (IRE) *M S Saunders* a67 70
3 b f Machiavellian(USA) —Follow That Dream (Darshaan)
2109^{8} 6896^{6} 7387^{9} 7446^{7}

Toms Laughter *R A Harris* a78 102
4 ch g Mamalik(USA) —Time Clash (Timeless Times (USA))
30^{4} (681) (875) (964) 1261^{5} (2484) (2692) 3042^{6} 3418^{2} 3728^{2} 3898^{11} (4445) 4555^{4} 5890^{11} 6121^{3} 6290^{5}

Tom Tower (IRE) *A C Whillans* 53
4 b g Cape Cross(IRE) —La Belle Katherine (USA) (Lyphard (USA))
1818^{17} 3370^{12} 4018^{11} 4846^{10} 5420^{12}

Toni Alcala *N B King* a60 58
9 b g Ezzoud(IRE) —Etourdie (USA) (Arctic Tern (USA))
1518^{6}

Tonic Star (FR) *Christian Wroe* a61 99
5 b m Enrique—Tonic Stream (FR) (Bering)
200a^{4} 384a^{12} 493a^{13}

Tony Douglas (IRE) *A Di Dio* 58
4 h Elnadim(USA) —Zilwaki (USA) (Miswaki (USA))
2029a^{10}

Tony James (IRE) *K O Cunningham-Brown* a93 101
6 b h Xaar—Sunset Ridge (FR) (Green Tune (USA))
925^{8} 1800^{10} 2339^{4} 2995^{14}

Tony The Tap *W R Muir* a95 91
7 b g Most Welcome—Laleston (Junius (USA))
2195^{11} 3009^{18} 3680^{6} 4201^{3} 4555^{5} 4668^{4} 5206^{12} (6174) (6449) 6971^{18}

Too Grand *J J Bridger* a62 53
3 ch f Zaha(CAN) —Gold Linnet (Nashwan (USA))
23^{5} 266^{4} 419^{6} 709^{2} 876^{5} 1051^{2} 2563^{10} 3678^{9} 4083^{7} 4637^{5} 4777^{5} 5607^{2} 7310^{8} 7392^{8} 7535^{11} 7707^{7}

Too Hot To Handle (IRE) *J M P Eustace* a42 51
3 br f Elnadim(USA) —Tropical Zone (Machiavellian (USA))
3847^{7} 4301^{8} 5318^{10}

Toolittleyourlate (USA) *S Seemar* a68 91
3 bb c Harlan's Holiday(USA) —Spirit In The Sky (USA) (Gulch (USA))
292a^{11} 567a^{15} 813a^{7}

Too Much To Do *T D McCarthy* a23
3 b g Tobougg(IRE) —Dodona (Lahib (USA))
223^{9} 1054^{10} 1669^{11} 2528^{P} 3161^{15}

Too Much Trouble *M R Channon* 76
2 b c Barathea(IRE) —Tentpole (USA) (Rainbow Quest (USA))
(5029)

Toon Army *Miss D Mountain* a30 34
3 gr f Tobougg(IRE) —Align (Petong)
1423^{15} 1869^{14} 2611^{6} 3264^{10} 3687^{8}

Too Risky *P W Chapple-Hyam* a61
2 b f Fasliyev(USA) —Muwasim (USA) (Meadowlake (USA))
223^{3}

Too Rye Ay (IRE) *Mrs A M O'Shea* a54 54
3 b f Chevalier(IRE) —Toordillon (IRE) (Contract Law (USA))
4613a^{9}

Too Tall *L M Cumani* 68
2 b c Medicean—Embark (Soviet Star (USA))
4421^{2} 4982^{4} 6057^{4}

Toparudi *M H Tompkins* a49 87
7 b g Rudimentary(USA) —Topatori (IRE) (Topanoora)
7717^{P} (Dead)

Topazes *M L W Bell* a69 92
3 ch c Cadeaux Genereux—Topkamp (Pennekamp (USA))
1298^{9} (1592) (1740) (2047) 2761^{2} 3494^{2} (3627) (3969) 4783^{6} 5862^{5} 6526^{5}

Topazleo (IRE) *J Wade* 52
4 ch g Peintre Celebre(USA) —Mer Noire (IRE) (Marju (IRE))
3339^{11}

Top Bid *T D Easterby* a60 78
4 b g Auction House(USA) —Trump Street (First Trump)
3050^{19} 3626^{17} 6219^{12} 6486^{17} 7090^{4} (7197) 7517^{7}

Topclas (FR) *P Demercastel* 107
2 b c Kutub(IRE) —Noble Presence (FR) (Fasliyev (USA))
6147a^{4} 6642a^{3} 7294a^{7}

Topcroft *Mrs C A Dunnett* 16
2 b g Mujahid(USA) —Starminda (Zamindar (USA))
6031^{11}

Top Draw (USA) *M L W Bell* a74 69
3 b f Elusive Quality(USA) —Cala (FR) (Desert Prince (IRE))
(543) 1060^{4} 1216^{2} 2705^{4} 3487^{4} 4306^{11}

Topenhall (IRE) *Daniel O'Connell* a69 52
7 b g Topanoora—Jrred Up (IRE) (Jurado (USA))
7686^{4} 7829^{8}

Topflightcoolracer *Mrs G S Rees* a83 86
4 b m Lujain(USA) —Jamarj (Tyrnavos)
3998^{3} 4171^{12} 4854^{7} 5493^{4} 5884^{4} 6278^{12} 6532^{2} 6782^{14}

Topflightrebellion *Mrs G S Rees* a56 43
3 b f Mark Of Esteem(IRE) —Jamarj (Tyrnavos)
74^{3} 2333^{12} 2659^{7} 4179^{6} 4479^{6} 4964^{5}

Top Flight Splash *Mrs G S Rees* a49 45
2 b f Bertolini(USA) —Making Waves (IRE) (Danehill (USA))
5989^{13} 6488^{9} 7038^{8} (7281) 7531^{9} 7728^{4}

Tophorsnopedigree *E J Creighton* 16
3 b g Teofilio(IRE) —Happy And Blessed (IRE) (Prince Sabo)
6003^{12} 6543^{13}

Top Jaro (FR) *Mrs R A Carr* a7 77
5 b g Marathon(USA) —Shahmy (USA) (Lear Fan (USA))
978^{2} 1160^{5} 6152^{5} (6217) (6312) 6585^{8} 7374^{8} 7799^{12}

Topkapi Diamond (IRE) *E Kurdu* 77
3 b f Acclamation—Anthyllis (IRE) (Night Shift (USA))
5334a^{7} 6743a^{7}

Top Lock *A M Balding* a77 111
3 ch c Nayef(USA) —Ermine (IRE) (Cadeaux Genereux)
(1272) ◆ 1632^{4} 2303^{3} ◆ 3193^{3} 3773a^{3} 5263^{2} ◆ 5892^{11}

Top Man Dan (IRE) *D Carroll* 64
3 b g Danetime(IRE) —Aphra Benn (IRE) (In The Wings)
1380^{8} 2008^{8} 3717^{14} 4049^{2} 4455^{4} 4738^{7} 4902^{5} 5399^{3} 7039^{12}

Topolski (IRE) *M Johnston* 65
2 b g Peintre Celebre(USA) —Witching Hour (IRE) (Alzao (USA))
2845^{7} 3853^{11} 6014^{4}

Topor (TUR) *H Demirkiran* a73 92
4 b h Sri Pekan(USA) —Shiero (TUR) (Castle Rising I)
205a^{9} 474a^{12}

Top Seed (IRE) *Ian Williams* a68 72
7 b g Cadeaux Genereux—Midnight Heights (Persian Heights)
646^{6} 999^{9} (1528) ◆ 1692^{3} (2949) 3029^{2} 7786^{9}

Top Spec (IRE) *J Pearce* a79 67
7 b g Spectrum(IRE) —Pearl Marine (IRE) (Bluebird (USA))
344^{6} 778^{4} 963^{7} 1281^{8} 1554^{2}

Topsy Maite *P A Blockley* 29
4 b m Komaite(USA) —Noble Soul (Sayf El Arab (USA))
2015^{10} 5117^{10}

Top The Charts *A J Martin* a71 78
6 b g Singspiel(IRE) —On The Tide (Slip Anchor)
6817[16]

Top Ticket (IRE) *D M Simcock* a69 82
3 ch c Alhaarth(IRE) —Tathkara (USA) (Alydar (USA))
1342[2] (1695) 2327[3] 3471[6] 4984[7] 5773[2] 6542[7] 6898[8]

Top Tiger *M H Tompkins* a67 68
4 b g Mtoto—Topatori (IRE) (Topanoora)
6050[10] ◆ 6790[5] 7272[4] 7401[2] 7545[10] 7715[8]

Top Tinker *M H Tompkins* a49 35
2 b g Vettori(IRE) —Topatori (IRE) (Topanoora)
6789[16] 6944[14] 7434[10]

Top Toss (IRE) *Y De Nicolay* 112
3 gr f Linamix(FR) —Tossup (USA) (Gone West (USA))
1323a[2] 2877a[7] 3775a[2] (4657a) 7037a[9]

Top Town Girl *R M Beckett* 84
2 b f Efisio—Halland Park Girl (IRE) (Primo Dominie)
5097[14] (5838) ◆ 6102[12] 6603[3]

Top Tribute *T P Tate* 66
3 b g Acclamation—Mary Hinge (Dowsing (USA))
5361[2] 6114[14] 6393[11] 6792[2] 7131[6]

Top Vision *M R Channon* 71
3 ch f Medicean—Perfect Partner (Be My Chief (USA))
1899[4] 2272[6] 3057[3] 3672[4]

Topwell *R C Guest* a42 36
7 b g Most Welcome—Miss Top Ville (FR) (Top Ville)
481[6] 657[4] 843[8] 1518[8] 1726[9]

Toque De Queda *M Delzangles* 108
4 b m Dansili—Bazbina (FR) (Highest Honor (FR))
4212a[4] 4888a[3] 6505a[5]

Tora Bora (GER) *B G Powell* 16
6 bb g Winged Love(IRE) —Tower Bridge (GER) (Big Shuffle (USA))
6361[9]

Tora Petcha (IRE) *R Hollinshead* a44 76
5 b g Bahhare(USA) —Magdalene (FR) (College Chapel)
7695[10]

Torch Of Freedom (IRE) *Sir Mark Prescott* a76 72
3 b g Statue Of Liberty(USA) —Danse Royale (IRE) (Caerleon (USA))
3286a[3]

Tori's Secret (IRE) *G A Swinbank* 71
2 br g Tillerman—Grey Pursuit (IRE) (Pursuit Of Love)
3365[3] 3714[6]

Tornadodancer (IRE) *T G McCourt* a86 85
5 b g Princely Heir(IRE) —Purty Dancer (IRE) (Foxhound (USA))
6514a[4] 6963a[9] 7325a[5]

Torphichen *M A Jarvis* 93
3 ch g Alhaarth(IRE) —Genoa (Zafonic (USA))
2681[2] ◆ (5780) 6107[2] ◆ 6563[4]

Torquemada (IRE) *M J Attwater* a78 71
7 ch g Desert Sun—Gaelic's Fantasy (IRE) (Statoblest)
2615[6] 2837[7] 3165[6] 4268[P] 5170[3] 6178[16] 6749[11] 7102[4] 7382[8] 7437[9] 7766[2]

Torrens (IRE) *P D Evans* a82 84
6 b g Royal Anthem(USA) —Azure Lake (USA) (Lac Ouimet (USA))
3474[5] 4217[11] 4541[2] 4701[6] 6825[7] 7217[2] 7355[2] 7590[5] 7608[2] 7744[4] 7806[4]

Torrid Hell (FR) *Y De Nicolay* a94 101
3 b c Vettori(IRE) —Heleniade (FR) (Entrepreneur)
5529a[5] 7643a[14]

Torver *Dr J D Scargill* a49 13
4 br m Lake Coniston(IRE) —Billie Blue (Ballad Rock)
1687[13]

Tosen Captain (JPN) *Katsuhiko Sumii* 110
4 gr h Jungle Pocket(JPN) —Sunday Picnic (JPN) (Sunday Silence (USA))
7511a[15]

Toshi (USA) *P Monteith* a57 71
6 b g Kingmambo(USA) —Majestic Role (FR) (Theatrical)
4848[11]

Tosho Courage (JPN) *Kaneo Ikezoe* 112
6 b h Last Tycoon—Rose Tosho (JPN) (Sakura Bakushin O (JPN))
7683a[9]

Toss The Caber (IRE) *K G Reveley* 47
6 ch g Dr Devious(IRE) —Celtic Fling (Lion Cavern (USA))
1559[10] 1892[8] 2467[6] 3602[7]

Total Gallery (IRE) *J S Moore* 101
2 b c Namid—Diary (IRE) (Green Desert (USA))
2796[2] 3105[6] ◆ (3707) 4588[5] 6068[2] (6483)

Total Impact *R A Fahey* a82 95
5 ch g Pivotal—Rise 'n Shine (Night Shift (USA))
1023[4] (2596) ◆ 3009[2] 3228[2] 3931[3] 4445[3] (4555) 5503[16] 5831[14] 6289[13] 6810[15] 7047[5] ◆

Totally Focussed (IRE) *S Dow* a87 64
3 rg g Trans Island—Premier Place (USA) (Out Of Place (USA))
1208[2] 1546[2] ◆ 2161[9] 2756[2] (3376) 5350[3] 5695[5] 6242[16] 6467[6] 7211[3] 7821[4] ◆

Totally Free *M D I Usher* a63 58
4 ch g Woodborough(USA) —Barefooted Flyer (USA) (Fly So Free (USA))
109[9] 304[6] 460[9] 530[9] 663[11] 792[5] 844[14]

Totem Flower (IRE) *R Charlton* a70 78
3 ch f Indian Ridge—Tree Peony (Woodman (USA))
1721[4] 2261[5] 5098[2] 5964[2] 6530[4]

To The Max (IRE) *Mrs C A Dunnett* a57 12
4 b g Spectrum(IRE) —Pray (IRE) (Priolo (USA))
1458[6] 1725[8] 2533[15] 3034[17] 3162[8] 3612[13] 5157[13]

To The Point *E S McMahon* 82
2 b f Refuse To Bend(IRE) —Be Decisive (Diesis)
(1866) 2167[7] 3528[3] 6540[6] 6807[2]

Tot Hill *C N Kellett* 29
5 b m Syrtos—Galava (CAN) (Graustark)
3168[RR] 3688[12] 4523[8] 5203[7] 6275[10]

Totoman *G G Margarson* a67 78
3 b c Mtoto—Norcroft Lady (Mujtahid (USA))
1573[9] 1876[5] (2090) 3459[10] 5502[6] 6379[5] 6703[8]

Toto Skyllachy *T P Tate* 86
3 b g Kyllachy—Little Tramp (Trempolino (USA))
1576[2] 1923[6] 2953[5] 3493[8]

Tottie *Mrs A J Perrett* a53 94
2 b f Fantastic Light(USA) —Katy Nowaitee (Komaite (USA))
6166[8] 6391[4] (6745) ◆ 7144[5]

Touchdown *M Johnston* a76 85
3 b c Singspiel(IRE) —Salim Toto (Mtoto)
1272[2] ◆ 1539[5] (2207)

Touched By Madness (USA) *Lorne Richards* a101 101
6 b g Sword Dance(USA) —Marilyn's Madness (USA) (Shananie (USA))
2472a[10]

Touchet Marie (IRE) *M Marcialis*
2 b f Touch Of The Blues(FR) —Tofarella (IRE) (Fools Holme (USA))
2744a[3]

Touching (IRE) *R Hannon* a79 93
2 b f Kheleyf(USA) —Feminine Touch (IRE) (Sadler's Wells (USA))
3558[3] (3837) 4348[3] 6025[3] 6439[6]

Touch Of Mida *G Pucciatti* 101
3 ch c Atticus(USA) —Akka Brava (IRE) (Royal Academy (USA))
1513a[4] 7262a[7]

Touch Of Style (IRE) *J R Boyle* a81 70
4 b g Desert Style(IRE) —No Hard Feelings (IRE) (Alzao (USA))
47[3] 3132[11] 3561[7] 4155[2] 4645[4] 4953[5] 7261[11] 7376[7] 7573[8] 7807[7]

Tough Love *T D Easterby* 76
9 ch g Pursuit Of Love—Food Of Love (Music Boy)
1449[10] 2003[3] 3339[6]

Tour D'Amour (IRE) *R Craggs* a63 63
5 b m Fruits Of Love(USA) —Touraneena (Robellino (USA))
258[5] 478[5] 1024[5] 1679[5] 2364[7] 4537[3]

Tourism (IRE) *M Johnston* 77
3 b c Dubai Destination(USA) —Ribot's Guest (IRE) (Be My Guest (USA))
(982) 1618[5] 2310[5] 2675[8]

Tourist *B W Hills* 80
3 b g Oasis Dream—West Devon (USA) (Gone West (USA))
2571[4] (2954) 3494[11]

Tournedos (IRE) *D Nicholls* a64 105
6 b g Rossini(USA) —Don't Care (IRE) (Nordico (USA))
1917[12] (2129) 2828[10]

Tous Les Deux *G L Moore* a78 70
5 b g Efisio—Caerosa (Caerleon (USA))
2082[7] 3585[8] 3956[8] 4182[10] (5157) 6090[8] (6377) 6631[10] 6773[3] (7194) 7507[7] 7821[2]

Towerofcharlemagne (IRE) *Miss E C Lavelle* a64 47
5 ch g King Charlemagne(USA) —Nozet (Nishapour (FR))
4078[7] 5465[11] 5802[3] 6022[4]

Town And Gown *S C Williams* a73 50
3 br f Oasis Dream—Degree (Warning)
261[3] 3224[11] 3447[3] 4272[4] 4308[5] 4639[13] 5141[6] 5911[9]

Town House *B P J Baugh* a53 57
6 gr m Paris House—Avondale Girl (IRE) (Case Law)
318[4] 522[3] 641[2] 857[5] 971[6] (3405) 3724[8] 4285[6] 5074[6] 6546[6]

Townkab (IRE) *N P Littmoden* a51 66
3 b g Intikhab(USA) —Town Girl (IRE) (Lammtarra (USA))
1161[17] 2559[8] 2982[7] 3397[4] 4053[8] 6173[14]

Towy Boy (IRE) *I A Wood* a71 70
3 b g King Charlemagne(USA) —Solar Flare (IRE) (Danehill (USA))
1315[3] 1548[9] 3564[12] 4102[2] 4324[6] 4793[2] 5217[2] 6046[2] 6707[5] 6773[8]

Towy Girl (IRE) *A W Carroll* a71 55
4 b m Second Empire(IRE) —Solar Flare (IRE) (Danehill (USA))
2991[8] 3329[3] 3507[8] 3816[2] 4368[4] 4529[B]

Towy Valley *C G Cox* a73 40
3 b f Bertolini(USA) —Ulysses Daughter (IRE) (College Chapel)
6543[9] 7074[2]

Toy Top (USA) *M Dods* a14 71
5 rg m Tactical Cat(USA) —I'll Flutter By (USA) (Concorde's Tune (USA))
1378[11] 1893[11] 2159[3] 2676[5] 2777[7] (3112) 3546[12] 4385[8] 5398[12] 6218[9]

Tracer *M W Easterby* a49 61
4 br g Kyllachy—Western Sal (Salse (USA))
341[7]

Trachonitis (IRE) *J R Jenkins* a84 86
4 b g Dansili—Hasina (IRE) (King's Theatre (IRE))
96[9] 260[6] ◆ 443[2] ◆ (588) 810[2] (2414) 3523[3] 4314[5] 5017[8] 6079[12]

Trackattack *M Appleby* a47 44
6 ch g Atraf—Verbena (IRE) (Don't Forget Me)
145[7] 197[3] 394[4] 606[13] 661[6]

Track Record *A Fabre* 98
3 b c Montjeu(IRE) —Prove (Danehill (USA))
5685a[7]

Trading Nation (USA) *R Charlton* 24
2 b c Tiznow(USA) —Nidd (USA) (Known Fact (USA))
4430[5]

Traditionalist (IRE) *T T Clement* a58 56
4 ch g Traditionally(USA) —Rouberia (IRE) (Alhaarth (IRE))
2423[7]

Trafalgar Bay (IRE) *K R Burke* 88
5 b g Fruits Of Love(USA) —Chatsworth Bay (IRE) (Fairy King (USA))
6069[20] 7127[5]

Trafalgar Square *M J Attwater* a80 96
6 b g King's Best(USA) —Pat Or Else (Alzao (USA))
958[3] 1469[8] 1982[14] 2163[6] 3197[25] 4927[8] 5290[6] 5588[6] 6380[4] 6695[8] 7077[10] 7360[6] 7494[2] (7603) 7813[5]

Traffic Guard (USA) *Jane Chapple-Hyam* a106 121
4 b h More Than Ready(USA) —Street Scene (IRE) (Zafonic (USA))
294a[5] 494a[4] 671a[8] 818a[3] 1422[2] 2234a[10] 5289[2] ◆ 5732a[2] 6816[5]

Traitor's Gate *M Johnston* a58 40
3 b g Machiavellian(USA) —Wilayif (USA) (Danzig (USA))
74[6] 484[3] 619[7]

Trance (IRE) *T D Barron* a39 87
8 ch g Bahhare(USA) —Lady Of Dreams (IRE) (Prince Rupert (FR))
1305[6] 1482[13] 1773[3] 1998[11] 2628[10] 2844[4] 4735[3] 4848[6] 5637[11] 6727[5] 7045[5]

Tranquil Tiger *H R A Cecil* 117
4 ch h Selkirk(USA) —Serene View (USA) (Distant View (USA))
1468[14] 1829[4] (2192) 2625[2] (3295) 3497[2] 4585[5] (6201) 6780[5]

Transcend *J H M Gosden* a100 103
4 ch g Beat Hollow—Pleasuring (Good Times (ITY))
(1481) ◆ 1765[4] ◆ 2163[3]

Transcendent (IRE) *J D Bethell* a49 50
3 b c Trans Island—Shannon Dore (IRE) (Turtle Island (IRE))
23[3] 306[3] 534[4] 803[7]

Transcentral *W M Brisbourne* a54 69
2 ch f Kheleyf(USA) —Khafayif (USA) (Swain (IRE))
995[4] ◆ 1168[3] 1515[4] 2048[4] 3670[6] (3910) 4389[6] 6274[12] 6666[4] 7113[5]

Transfer *A M Balding* a89 76
3 br g Trans Island—Sankaty Light (USA) (Summer Squall (USA))
(2756) ◆ 3475[5] 4404[10] 4682[9] 6911[9]

Transfered (IRE) *Lucinda Featherstone* a44 44
2 b f Trans Island—Second Omen (Rainbow Quest (USA))
1778[9] 4256[7] 5778[3] 7468[5] 7659[8] 7718[7]

Transformation (IRE) *J R Weymes* 26
2 b f Trans Island—Gleam (Green Desert (USA))
1889[6] 2485[8] 2924[6] 3225[7] 3830[7] 4203[14]

Transformer (IRE) *W J Knight* a58
2 b c Trans Island—Lady At War (Warning)
7336[11] 7593[7]

Transmission (IRE) *B Smart* a66 77
3 b g Galileo(IRE) —Individual (USA) (Gulch (USA))
1572[5] 2665[13] 6114[5] 6408[2] 6726[5] 7461[6] 7613[3] 7799[4]

Transporter (IRE) *T D Easterby* 24
2 b g Trans Island—Ascoli (Skyliner)
6187[11] 6381[9] 6789[14]

Trans Siberian *P F I Cole* a93 89
4 b h Soviet Star(USA) —Dina Line (USA) (Diesis)
1365[2] 1630[2] (1874) ◆ 2540[4] 3003[2] 3398[2] 4642[6] 5207[5] 6238[6] 6582[6]

Trans Sonic *A J Lockwood* a78 70
5 ch g Trans Island—Sankaty Light (USA) (Summer Squall (USA))
1048[4] 1559[5] 2927[12] 3450[14] 4048[12] (4898) 5258[8] 5638[7] (6116) 6585[9] 7284[4] 7650[5]

Transvestite (IRE) *J W Hills* a93 84
6 b g Trans Island—Christoph's Girl (Efisio)
97[6] (2558) 3060[7] 3650[8] 4771[12] 5092[16]

Traphalgar (IRE) *P F I Cole* a93 88
3 br g Cape Cross(IRE) —Conquestadora (Hernando (FR))
1213[3] 1595[9] 3251[7] 3969[2] 7551a[0]

Traprain (IRE) *D Carroll* 82
6 b g Mark Of Esteem(IRE) —Nassma (IRE) (Sadler's Wells (USA))
1793[4] 1998[7] (Dead)

Travelling Light (USA) *R Charlton* a32 54
3 b f Gone West(USA) —Gaily Tiara (USA) (Caerleon (USA))
1445[7] 1854[10] 2954[11]

Trawlerman (IRE) *M H Tompkins* a38 73
3 b c High Chaparral(IRE) —Forest Lair (Habitat)
867[12] 3530[2] 4303[6] 4691[7] 5603[3]

Treasure (FR) *Mme C Head-Maarek* 101
2 b f Anabaa(USA) —Treasure Queen (USA) (Kingmambo (USA))
(5112a) 5850a[3] 6713a[4] 7186a[4]

Treasure Islands (IRE) *S W Hall* a56 52
3 b f Trans Island—Gold Prospector (IRE) (Spectrum (IRE))
223[4] 464[8] 1870[7] 2613[10]

Treasure Isle *R A Fahey* a54 46
4 ch m Bahamian Bounty—South Rock (Rock City)
(1606) ◆ 2078[5]

Treat *E A L Dunlop* 108
4 b m Barathea(IRE) —Cream Tease (Pursuit Of Love)
2890[9] 4395[7] 5120[10]

Treat Gently *A Fabre* 116
3 b f Cape Cross(IRE) —Kid Gloves (In The Wings)
2650a[2] (3543a) 5331a[2] 5952a[3] 6521a[4]

Treeko (IRE) *Francis Ennis* a28 72
3 b g Alhaarth(IRE) —Allegheny River (USA) (Lear Fan (USA))
6511a[13]

Trees Of Green (USA) *M Wigham* a50 78
4 bb g Elusive Quality(USA) —Grazia (Sharpo)
329[10] 777[8] 1541[9] 2081[7] 3506[13] 3825[10] 4605[11]

Treetops Hotel (IRE) *L R James* a70 60
9 ch g Grand Lodge(USA) —Rousinette (Rousillon (USA))
18[3] 198[6] 373[6] 1310[6] 2053[9] 3226[3] 3642[8] 6309[8]

Tremoto *F & L Camici* 100
3 b f Generous(IRE) —Therese Chenu (IRE) (Local Suitor (USA))
2439a[4] 3076a[17] 5331a[10]

Trenchant *J R Fanshawe* a78 72
3 b g Medicean—Tromond (Lomond (USA))
1380[5] 2199[8] 2695[6] 3873[2] 4156[4] 4992[5] 6934[2]

Trenchtown (IRE) *R Charlton* 91
3 b c King's Best(USA) —Barbuda (Rainbow Quest (USA))
1600[8] 2194[7] 2610[2] 3157[6] 3719[6] 4519[4] 5249[4]

Tres Borrachos (USA) *C Beau Greely* a117 84
3 b g Ecton Park(USA) —Pete's Fancy (CAN) (Peteski (CAN))
2215a[9]

Tres Chic (FR) *S Curran*
2 gr f Kaldounevees(FR) —Chic Emilie (FR) (Policeman (FR))
6760[13]

Tres Rapide (IRE) *H-A Pantall* 113
3 b f Anabaa Blue—Tres Ravi (GER) (Monsun (GER))
4675a[4] 5597a[2] 6495a[2] 7037a[3]

Trevelez (IRE) *F-X de Chevigny* a96 84
3 b c Alhaarth(IRE) —Agapimou (IRE) (Spectrum (IRE))
687a[2] 1712a[4] 6064a[9]

Trevian *Tim Vaughan* a60 60
7 ch g Atraf—Ascend (IRE) (Glint Of Gold)
2353[11] 3025[3] 3360[6] 3563[5] 4635[6]

Trew Style *M H Tompkins* a64 72
6 ch g Desert King(IRE) —Southern Psychic (USA) (Alwasmi (USA))
3523[4] 5934[4] 6361[10] 6957[9]

Trianon *R Charlton* 80
3 ch f Nayef(USA) —Trying For Gold (USA) (Northern Baby (CAN))
1839[4] 2327[4] 2675[7] 4619[5] 5464[2] 5887[8]

Tribe *P R Webber* a73 83
6 b g Danehill(USA) —Leo Girl (USA) (Seattle Slew (USA))
1583[5] 1984[9] 2888[7] 6054[4] 6329[6]

Tribiani (IRE) *P A Blockley* a44 49
4 b m Alzao(USA) —Suzette (Zilzal (USA))
144[8] 375[10] 578[7] 1025[5] 1643[6]

Tri Chara (IRE) *R Hollinshead* a68 64
4 ch g Grand Slam(USA) —Lamzena (IRE) (Fairy King (USA))
(48) 2007[17] 5198[8] 5712[12] 6116[10] 6951[3] 7287[7] 7503[4] (7663) 7745[2] 7829[9]

Tricien (FR) *L Urbano-Grajales* a92 95
4 b h Lomitas—Cherry Moons (FR) (Alysheba (USA))
7643a[11]

Trickle (USA) *Miss D Mountain* a67 60
4 ch m Rahy(USA) —Avitrix (USA) (Storm Bird (CAN))
164[6] 267[9]

Trick Or Two *S Kirk* a68
2 gr g Desert Style(IRE) —Vax Star (Petong)
7273[9] 7402[12] 7689[5] (7795)

Tricky Situation *J G Given* 72
2 b f Mark Of Esteem(IRE) —Trick Of Ace (USA) (Clever Trick (USA))
6392[2] ◆

Tricky Trev (USA) *S Curran* a64 49
2 ch c Toccet(USA) —Lady Houston (USA) (Houston (USA))
4616[6] 5430[5] 6531[8] 7205[10] 7454[5] 7832[6]

Triel *J R Holt*
5 b h Tout Ensemble—Winter Greeting (Hello Gorgeous (USA))
7690[5]

Trifti *Miss Jo Crowley* a78 51
7 b g Vettori(IRE) —Time For Tea (IRE) (Imperial Frontier (USA))
(1039) 1583[P] 4390[3] 5156[9] 5999[5] 7096[2] 7526[6]

Trigger Express (AUS) *S Burridge* 103
7 b g Citidancer—Rich Resource (AUS) (Chanteclair (AUS))
2234a[11]

Trigger McCann *J S Moore* a70 49
2 b c Royal Applause—Roses Of Spring (Shareef Dancer (USA))
2916[7] ◆ 6281[5] ◆ 6661[2] 7044[3] (7475) 7760[3]

Trigger's Friend *Jamie Poulton* a50 63
4 b m Double Trigger(IRE) —Four-Legged Friend (Aragon)
(2832) 3321[4] (3871) ◆ (4105) 4775[5] 5613[5] 5934[3] 6672[13]

Trimaran (IRE) *M Johnston* a69
3 b f Red Ransom(USA) —Moonlight Sail (USA) (Irish River (FR))
447[2] (748) ◆ 900[5]

Trimlestown (IRE) *P D Evans* a76 83
5 b g Orpen(USA) —Courtier (Saddlers' Hall (IRE))
910[8] 1771[9] 3443[7] 3928[3] 4393[11] 4858[5] 5389[2] (6736) 7041[11] 7378[5] 7557[9] (7671) 7748[6]

Tri Nations (UAE) *J W Hills* 88
3 ch g Halling(USA) —Six Nations (USA) (Danzig (USA))
(1417) 2121[7] 3676[7] (4565) 5279[11] 6078[6]

Trincot (FR) *P Demercastel* 113
3 b c Peintre Celebre(USA) —Royal Lights (FR) (Royal Academy (USA))
(2096a) 2654a[7] 4010a[6] 6148a[3] (6499a) 7685a[10]

Trinculo (IRE) *R A Harris* a67 71
11 b g Anita's Prince—Fandangerina (USA) (Grey Dawn II)
41[5] 256[2] (1634) 1842[9] (2010) 2330[8] 2478[3] 2950[7] 3313[4] 3608[4] 3966[10] 4639[4] 5091[7] 5398[3] 5601[2] 6864[10] 7225[9]

Trinity College (USA) *M F De Kock* 108
4 ch h Giant's Causeway(USA) —City College (USA) (Carson City (USA))
4177[3] 4644[3]

Trinkila (USA) *P F I Cole* a69 73
3 b f Cat Thief(USA) —Que Belle (CAN) (Seattle Dancer (USA))
1412[9] 2920[10] 3562[8] 4607[7] 5378[12] 5602[3] 5803[5] 6436[4] 6754[4] 7010[4] 7310[2] 7427[8]

Triple Aspect (IRE) *W J Haggas* 105
2 b c Danetime(IRE) —Wicken Wonder (IRE) (Distant Relative)
(4346) (5487) ◆ (5850a)

Triple Axel (IRE) *J Noseda* a64 54
4 b m Danehill Dancer(IRE) —Across The Ice (USA) (General Holme (USA))
(7798)

Triple Bluff *J D Frost* a43 36
5 b g Medicean—Trinity Reef (Bustino)
3606[13]

Triple Cee (IRE) *M R Channon* 71
2 b f Cape Cross(IRE) —Karri Valley (USA) (Storm Bird (CAN))
3349[3] ◆ 3913[10] 5241[9] 6231[6]

Triple Dream *J L Dunlop* a68 47
3 ch g Vision Of Night—Triple Joy (Most Welcome)
2198[16] 4412[7] *5995[4]* ◆ *6422[8]* *6905[9]*

Triple Shadow *M A Peill* a60 66
4 ch g Compton Place—Arctic High (Polar Falcon (USA))
2597[19] 3112[12] 3668[4] *3819[11]*

Tripod Molly (IRE) *P J McBride* a71 48
3 ch f King Charlemagne(USA) —Pericolo (IRE) (Kris)
343[3] *543[6]* *796[5]* *1959[9]* 2495[4] *(3483)* *3614[4]*

Trip The Light *R A Fahey* a36 72
3 b g Fantastic Light(USA) —Jumaireyah (Fairy King (USA))
976[8] 1186[5] *1710[4]* (2468) 3666[3] ◆ (4501) (4879) ◆ *5406[5]* 5967[5]

Trip To Glory (FR) *J-C Rouget* 109
3 gr f Where Or When(IRE) —Trip To Fame (FR) (Lordmare (FR))
1664a[6] 5038a[2]

Trireme (IRE) *K A Morgan* 53
4 b g Fantastic Light(USA) —Dreamboat (USA) (Mr Prospector (USA))
2571[6] 2954[9] 3312[5] 4991[7] 5262[7]

Triskaidekaphobia *Miss J R Tooth* a71 75
5 b g Bertolini(USA) —Seren Teg (Timeless Times (USA))
126[6] *(230)* *286[7]* *488[5]* *939[3]* *1037[4]* *6711[13]* *7295[12]* *7346[3]* 7589[5] 7836[3]

Tritonville Lodge (IRE) *Miss E C Lavelle* a78 79
6 b g Grand Lodge(USA) —Olean (Sadler's Wells (USA))
1744[5] 3104[10] 6606[5] 6948[9]

Triumphant Welcome *G F Bridgwater* a66 68
3 b g Piccolo—Shoof (USA) (Dayjur (USA))
4388[3] (5268) *5617[7]* 5861[10] 6357[14] 6706[14]

Trivia (IRE) *Ms J S Doyle* a81 81
4 br m Marju(IRE) —Lehua (IRE) (Linamix (FR))
124[9] *246[8]* *731[4]* *899[8]* *1038[7]* *1253[4]* *1565[8]* *2758[13]* 3064[10] *3371[3]* 3583[11] 3842[12] 4182[11]

Trois Rois (FR) *F Head* 111
3 b c Hernando(FR) —Trevise (FR) (Anabaa (USA))
2064a[3] 2654a[16] 6664a[4]

Trojan Flight *R A Fahey* 87
7 ch g Hector Protector(USA) —Fairywings (Kris)
2210[8] 2538[9] 3050[2] 3489[8] 4375[9]

Trojan Hero (IRE) *S W Hall* a34 44
3 b g Royal Applause—Anne Boleyn (Rainbow Quest (USA))
2673[10] 3549[5] 4381[4] *7676[10]*

Tropical Bachelor (IRE) *D W P Arbuthnot* a54
2 b g Bachelor Duke(USA) —Tropical Coral (IRE) (Pennekamp (USA))
7709[8]

Tropical Blue *Jennie Candlish* 73
2 b c Fath(USA) —Tropical Zone (Machiavellian (USA))
2608[6] 3164[3] 3597[2] 4214[6] 6808[2]

Tropical Duke (IRE) *D W P Arbuthnot* a39
2 ch c Bachelor Duke(USA) —Tropical Dance (USA) (Thorn Dance (USA))
7312[12]

Tropical Paradise (IRE) *P Winkworth* a89 85
2 gr f Verglas(IRE) —Ladylishandra (IRE) (Mujadil (USA))
2309[3] 2691[2] (5147) 5855[6] *(7075)*

Tropical Strait (IRE) *D W P Arbuthnot* a102 105
5 b g Intikhab(USA) —Tropical Dance (USA) (Thorn Dance (USA))
1841[2] *2711[7]* (5054) 5229[2] 5853[13] (7244) *7491[3]*

Tropical Tradition (IRE) *D W P Arbuthnot* a67
3 ch g Traditionally(USA) —Tropical Coral (IRE) (Pennekamp (USA))
5995[12] *6433[6]* *6757[6]* *(7310)* *7604[3]*

Troque (FR) *F Doumen* a98 102
4 b g Enrique—The Trollop (FR) (Double Bed (FR))
5115a[9]

Trotting Weasel (IRE) *M Halford* a63 62
5 b g Bold Fact(USA) —Eves Temptation (IRE) (Glenstal (USA))
6366a[25]

Troubadour (IRE) *W Jarvis* a103 97
7 b g Danehill(USA) —Taking Liberties (IRE) (Royal Academy (USA))
62[4] *227[5]* *418[4]* *502[5]* *678[9]* *834[3]* 958[14] *1724[2]* 3684[7] 4364[2] 5495[13]

Trouble Mountain (USA) *M W Easterby* a57 72
11 br g Mt. Livermore(USA) —Trouble Free (USA) (Nodouble (USA))
1159[4] 1383[6] 1963[7] (2848) 3450[11] 3965[7] 5391[9] 6050[3] 6726[10] 7085[6]

Troubletimestwo (FR) *H J L Dunlop* 54
2 gr c Linamix(FR) —Time Of Trouble (FR) (Warning)
6715 [6] 6978[14]

Troy G (USA) *Kenneth McPeek*
2 ch c Cape Canaveral(USA) —Caveat Apt (CAN) (Chief's Crown (USA))
6502a[2]

True And Fair (IRE) *Tom Dascombe*
3 b f Xaar—Quintellina (Robellino (USA))
1445[11] 2126[10]

True Bliss (USA) *John C Kimmel*
2 b f Yes It's True(USA) —Brief Bliss (USA) (Navarone (USA))
6613a[2]

Trueblue Wizard (IRE) *W R Muir* a71
2 ch c Bachelor Duke(USA) —Truly Bewitched (USA) (Affirmed (USA))
(7773)

True Britannia *S Kirk* a57 53
2 b f Lujain(USA) —Surf Bird (Shareef Dancer (USA))
1955[3] 3032[8] *3837[10]* *6697[7]* *6906[9]* *(7257)* *7467[7]* *7659[6]* *(7760)* *7824[3]*

True Cause (USA) *Saeed Bin Suroor* 115
5 ch h Storm Cat(USA) —Dearly (Rahy (USA))
3995a[5]

True Decision *S Kirk* a39
2 b g Reset(AUS) —True Precision (Presidium)
3848[10]

True To Tradition (USA) *Scott Lake* 111
6 b g Rahy(USA) —Successful Dancer (USA) (Fortunate Prospect (USA))
6994a[7]

Truism *Mrs A J Perrett* 79
2 b g Daylami(IRE) —Real Trust (USA) (Danzig (USA))
5225[6] (6412)

Trully Belle (IRE) *D Smaga* 81
3 b f Bahri(USA) —Truly A Gift (IRE) (Arazi (USA))
7450a[15]

Truly Divine *E A L Dunlop* a45 64
3 b g Invincible Spirit(IRE) —Shabarana (FR) (Nishapour (FR))
4195[7] 5160[5] 5561[3] 6063[4] *6773[10]*

Truly Fruitful (IRE) *Dr R D P Newland* a72 71
5 ch g Fruits Of Love(USA) —Truly Flattering (Hard Fought)
978[5] 1305[2] *1405[2]* 1895[11]

Truly Mine (IRE) *D K Weld* a97 101
4 ch m Rock Of Gibraltar(IRE) —Truly Yours (IRE) (Barathea (IRE))
1104a[9] *(1199a)*

Trumpet Lily *J G Portman* a67 86
3 b f Acclamation—Periwinkle (FR) (Perrault)
1685[4] 2118[9] 2974[2] 4022[2] (4872) 6027[7] 6605[9]

Trumpstoo (USA) *R A Fahey* 72
2 b c Perfect Soul(IRE) —Cozzy Love (USA) (Cozzene (USA))
6187[5] (6723)

Trusted Friend (USA) *M Johnston* 13
3 ch g Hennessy(USA) —Miss Bridget Jones (USA) (Peaks And Valleys (USA))
441[8] 5395[8] 6806[P]

Trusted Venture (USA) *J R Best* a58 14
2 b c Trust N Luck(USA) —Afleet Canadian (CAN) (Bucksplasher (USA))
6197[12] *6661[6]* *7356[10]* *(7789)* ◆

Truxton King (IRE) *W P Mullins* a88 81
3 gr g Clodovil(IRE) —Robinia (USA) (Roberto (USA))
3861a[2]

Try Me (UAE) *C E Brittain* a89 91
3 bb f Singspiel(IRE) —Cunas (USA) (Irish River (FR))
1042[3] *1542[2]* 1915[5] 3076a[12] 4196[10] 4618[8] 6266[9] 6605[14] *(6904)*

Tryst *Sir Michael Stoute* 82
3 gr c Highest Honor(FR) —Courting (Pursuit Of Love)
1417[2]

Trysting Grove (IRE) *E G Bevan* a60 63
7 b m Cape Cross(IRE) —Elton Grove (IRE) (Astronef)
(415) *579[2]* *695[3]* *802[2]* 999[2] *1148[4]* 1383[7] *1639[3]* *2707[6]* *2949[11]* 3698[5] (4055) 4365[8] 4704[4] 5058[5] 5232[2]

Tsar De Russie (IRE) *E Lellouche* 102
3 b c Montjeu(IRE) —Tamariyya (IRE) (Alzao (USA))
4959a[5] 5685a[4] 6494a[6]

Tsaroxy (IRE) *J Howard Johnson* 80
6 b g Xaar—Belsay (Belmez (USA))
992[3] 2447[8] 5563[5] 6487[8]

Tuanku (IRE) *A King* 76
3 b g Tagula(IRE) —Be My Lover (Pursuit Of Love)
(4978)

Tubby Isaacs *P J Makin* a82 71
4 b g Cyrano De Bergerac—Opuntia (Rousillon (USA))
4313[6] ◆ *(4824)* ◆ *(5610)* 6340[5] *7315[2]*

Tubular Bells (USA) *H-A Pantall* 90
3 gr f Kingmambo(USA) —Summer Symphony (IRE) (Caerleon (USA))
7431a[10]

Tudor Court (IRE) *H-A Pantall* 93
3 b f Cape Cross(IRE) —Rise And Fall (Mill Reef (USA))
7450a[7]

Tudor Key (IRE) *Mrs A J Perrett* 88
2 br g Key Of Luck(USA) —Anne Boleyn (Rainbow Quest (USA))
2146[4] ◆ 3245[4] 3968[5] (6085)

Tudor Prince (IRE) *A W Carroll* a69 85
4 bb g Cape Cross(IRE) —Savona (IRE) (Cyrano De Bergerac)
1300[8] 1617[6] 1928[14] 3626[8] 3904[3] 3998[9] 5247[9] 5648[8] 5751[5] 6200[13] *7288[2]*

Tufton *R A Fahey* a94 94
5 b g King's Best(USA) —Mythical Magic (Green Desert (USA))
309[3] (2335) (4217) 5005[5] *5910[6]*

Tugalu (IRE) *K A Ryan* a78 75
3 b g Tagula(IRE) —Merci (IRE) (Cadeaux Genereux)
1027[2] 1454[8] 3231[4] 4207[12] 4632[4] *5015[6]* 5395[5] *6251[8]*

Tulipa Di Job (BRZ) *A Selvaratnam* a60 64
6 b m Job Di Caroline(BRZ) —Fiore Di Capitaine (BRZ) (Oui Mon Capitaine (USA))
200a[5] 475a[10]

Tumbleweed Di *G R Oldroyd* a47 50
4 ro m Tumbleweed Ridge—Peggotty (Capricorn Line)
2038[9] 2283[6] 2928[8] 3231[6] 3340[4] 3665[9]

Tump Mac *N Bycroft* 61
4 ch g Compton Admiral—Petite Elite (Anfield)
2912[5] 3438[6] 3600[10] 4172[15] 6791[11] *7442[12]*

Tune Up The Band *R J Hodges* 60
4 b h Bandmaster(USA) —Name That Tune (Fayruz)
3021[2]

Tungsten Strike (USA) *Mrs A J Perrett* 116
7 ch g Smart Strike(CAN) —Bathilde (IRE) (Generous (IRE))
1980[4] 2625[9] 3743[3] 4551[2] (5264) 5956a[4] 6306[8]

Tuning Fork *M J Attwater* a53 4
8 b g Alzao(USA) —Tuning (Rainbow Quest (USA))
219[6] *392[2]* *624[3]* *795[9]* *898[6]* *937[6]* *1248[8]* 2355[14] *4529[6]* 4979[8] *7705[4]* 7818[9]

Tuppenny Piece *W R Swinburn* a48
2 ch f Sakhee(USA) —Tuppenny (Salse (USA))
7380[9] *7561[7]*

Tuppenny's Jeanie *Rae Guest* a55
2 b f Dubai Destination(USA) —Tahirah (Green Desert (USA))
7708[9]

Turban Heights (IRE) *E J O'Neill* a86 79
4 ch m Golan(IRE) —Turban (Glint Of Gold)
5017[5] ◆ 6293[3] 6607[10] *7046[3]* *(7183)* *(7459)* *7639[6]* *7770[7]*

Turbo Linn *G A Swinbank* 113
5 b m Turbo Speed—Linns Heir (Leading Counsel (USA))
2144[2] ◆ 2791[7] 3720[5]

Turfani (IRE) *W J Knight* a59 61
3 b f Danetime(IRE) —Tuhfah (Cadeaux Genereux)
2123[8] 2566[6] 3322[10] 4278[9] *5019[2]* *5575[6]*

Turfrose (GER) *A Fabre* 111
4 b m Big Shuffle(USA) —Turfquelle (IRE) (Shaadi (USA))
1761a[2] 2238a[4] 4914a[2] 5952a[10] 6521a[11]

Turfshuffle (GER) *Ian Williams* 78
5 b g Big Shuffle(USA) —Turfquelle (IRE) (Shaadi (USA))
4661[12] 4853[11] 5382[9] 5992[6] 6279[10]

Turfwolke (GER) *J W Hills* 60
3 b f Medicean—Turfaue (GER) (Big Shuffle (USA))
5057[6] 5471[2] 6275[4] 6671[16]

Turgenjew (IRE) *H J Groschel*
2 ch c Big Shuffle(USA) —Tamarita (GER) (Acatenango (GER))
7264a[5]

Turin Lady (IRE) *Tracey Collins* a69 98
2 ch f Alhaarth(IRE) —Miss Lorilaw (FR) (Homme De Loi (IRE))
7294a[11]

Turjuman (USA) *W J Musson* a10 80
3 ch g Swain(IRE) —Hachiyah (IRE) (Generous (IRE))
5505[4] 6055[11] 6703[15] *6991[11]*

Turk (IRE) *G M Lyons* a79 67
3 ch g Dr Fong(USA) —Input (Primo Dominie)
4715a[4]

Turkish Lokum *J M P Eustace* 67
2 b f Bertolini(USA) —Malabarista (FR) (Assert)
4251[10] 5959[4] 6426[27]

Turkish Sultan (IRE) *J M Bradley* a60 62
5 b g Anabaa(USA) —Odalisque (IRE) (Machiavellian (USA))
(1533) 1900[10] 2003[6] 2355[8] 2917[9] 5755[11] *6208[4]* 6335[10] *6570[2]* *6768[2]* *6912[6]* *6951[4]* *7322[9]* *7581[3]* 7691[3]

Turn And River (IRE) *M Brittain* a14 67
3 b f Viking Ruler(AUS) —Scatter Brain (Risk Me (FR))
849[8] 1306[10] 1754[3] (2660) 3030[14]

Turner's Touch *G L Moore* a76 73
6 ch g Compton Place—Chairmans Daughter (Unfuwain (USA))
540[8] *(794)* *921[3]* *1164[2]* *1564[2]* *3687[11]* 4371[3] 4691[9] *5913[8]* 6243[16] *7009[14]* 7473[3] 7512[6] 7831[8]

Turnham Green *S Curran*
2 b c Groom Dancer(USA) —Pie In The Sky (Bishop Of Cashel)
7699[14]

Turning For Home (FR) *H-A Pantall* 107
3 ch f Spinning World(USA) —Nanty (IRE) (Nashwan (USA))
5331a[4] 6322a[6] 7162a[14]

Turning Top (IRE) *S A Callaghan* a60
2 b f Pivotal—Pietra Dura (Cadeaux Genereux)
7097[8]

Turnkey *D Nicholls* 102
6 br g Pivotal—Persian Air (Persian Bold)
1300[6] (1517) 1796[4] 6104[22] 6289[9]

Turn Me On (IRE) *T D Walford* a70 80
5 b g Tagula(IRE) —Jacobina (Magic Ring (IRE))
(2400) 2925[3] 3599[6] 3834[2] 4172[2] 4605[3] (5400) 6314[4] 6813[3]

Turn Of Phrase (IRE) *N Wilson* a68 79
9 b g Cadeaux Genereux—Token Gesture (IRE) (Alzao (USA))
260[11] 963[16] 1482[9] 1559[4] 2006[8]

Turn On The Style *J Balding* a112 107
6 ch g Pivotal—Elegant Rose (Noalto)
5[5] (492a) 649a[4] 741a[8] 5793[5] 6971[20] *7192[7]* *(7614)* *(7805)*

Turn To Dreams *P D Evans* a52 53
2 b f Auction House(USA) —Seren Teg (Timeless Times (USA))
4251[11] 4480[11] 4705[4] 5287[3] 5488[2] *5834[5]* 6191[6] *6489[8]* *6572[4]* *7065[7]* *7212[3]* *7361[11]* *7600[4]* 7760[4] 7832[7]

Turtle Dove *M Botti* a60 62
3 b f Tobougg(IRE) —Inseparable (Insan (USA))
694[3] *931[2]* *1252[10]* 2090[5] 2208[4] 2982[10]

Tuscan Evening (IRE) *John Joseph Murphy* 109
3 b f Oasis Dream—The Faraway Tree (Suave Dancer (USA))
2433a[4] 3194[9]

Tuscan Treaty *R W Price* a22 52
8 b m Brief Truce(USA) —Fiorenz (USA) (Chromite (USA))
11[9] *289[9]* 1644[3] 2072[7] 2863[5] 4282[5] 4772[2] *7267[8]*

Tusculum (IRE) *A P Stringer* 32
5 b g Sadler's Wells(USA) —Turbaine (USA) (Trempolino (USA))
3209[8] 3630[9] 4200[7] 5651[13]

Tuxedo *P W Hiatt* a67 40
3 ch g Cadeaux Genereux—Serengeti Bride (USA) (Lion Cavern (USA))
3094[12] 3813[9] *4302[12]* *7088[7]* *(7541)* *(7763)*

Tvara *M J Wallace* a6
4 b m In The Wings—Timiram (IRE) (Runnett)
1053[12]

Twelfth Night (IRE) *J R Best* a68 22
4 ch m Namid—Charm The Stars (Roi Danzig (USA))
633[3] 2800[10]

Twenty Score *Miss J R Tooth* a69
2 ch f Lear Spear(USA) —Milladella (FR) (Nureyev (USA))
7546[2] *7593[5]*

Twice Over *H R A Cecil* 121
3 b c Observatory(USA) —Double Crossed (Caerleon (USA))
(1421) 2131[3] 3102[3] (4473a) 5302a[7] 6816[2]

Twiglet (IRE) *George Baker* a62 59
3 b f Choisir(AUS) —Regal Opinion (USA) (Gone West (USA))
1222[6] *1638[2]* 1867[13] *2261[12]* 4531[12]

Twilight Belle (IRE) *K R Burke* a57 58
3 b f Fasliyev(USA) —Pretty Sharp (Interrex (CAN))
59[4] *70[7]* *480[8]*

Twilight Dawn *L Lungo* 72
4 ch m Muhtarram(USA) —Indigo Dawn (Rainbow Quest (USA))
(1222) 1732[5] 2848[9] 3552[12]

Twilight Star (IRE) *R A Teal* a84 89
4 b g Green Desert(USA) —Heavenly Whisper (IRE) (Halling (USA))
910[5] ◆ 1365[11] *1936[4]* 2545[6] (2762) *3319[8]* 3529[6] *6471[11]* 7143[8] *7390[5]* *7525[4]* *7712[9]*

Twill (IRE) *G L Moore* a80 83
5 ch g Barathea(IRE) —Khafaya (Unfuwain (USA))
2567[12]

Twinkle De Star *J S Moore* a24
2 b f Imperial Dancer—Windy Breeze (IRE) (Mujadil (USA))
2720[3] 2980[8]

Twinned (IRE) *Mike Murphy* a59 45
5 ch g Soviet Star(USA) —Identical (IRE) (Machiavellian (USA))
318[2] *581[4]* *690[2]* *1028[3]* *1706[6]* *2802[9]* *7648[11]* *7774[4]*

Twin Prince (IRE) *J-M Lefebvre*
3 b g Desert Prince(IRE) —Twin Island (IRE) (Standaan (FR))
7551a[0]

Twist Bookie (IRE) *S Lycett* a64 63
8 br g Perugino(USA) —Twist Scarlett (GER) (Lagunas)
31[5] 3084[2] 5512[10]

Twisted *J H M Gosden* 64
2 ch c Selkirk(USA) —Winding (USA) (Irish River (FR))
6083[5] ◆

Two Imposters (USA) *J R Best* a36 55
3 bb g Gulch(USA) —Queen Of Women (USA) (Sharpen Up)
2495[10] *2833[13]* *3264[9]*

Two Left Feet *W R Swinburn* a72 68
3 b g Groom Dancer(USA) —Sardegna (Pharly (FR))
837[2] *974[3]* 6346[8] 6721[13]

Twos And Eights (IRE) *G D Blake* a53 20
2 bb g Kyllachy—Docklands Grace (USA) (Honour And Glory (USA))
1363[9] *1722[4]* 3603[13] *6017[10]*

Twosheetstothewind *C R Dore* a68 70
4 ch m Bahamian Bounty—Flag (Selkirk (USA))
29[4] *1129[7]* *1373[6]* 1476[2] 4693[8] 5319[5] *5401[12]* 6766[9] *6907[8]*

Two Step Salsa (USA) *Julio C Canani* a122
3 bb c Petionville(USA) —Two To Waltz (Seattle Slew (USA))
6995a[3]

Tycoon's Buddy *E J O'Neill* a29
3 ch g Reel Buddy(USA) —Tycoon's Last (Nalchik (USA))
1751[11] *3823[9]* 4076[11] *6224[11]*

Tyfos *W M Brisbourne* a74 77
3 b g Bertolini(USA) —Warminghamsharpish (Nalchik (USA))
2407[4] 2883[2] 3202[4] 3999[7] 5886[9] *7428[6]*

Tykie Two *S Wynne* a58 52
4 ch m Primo Valentino(IRE) —Tycoon's Last (Nalchik (USA))
1282[11] 1890[12] *(2290)* *2707[3]* *3820[8]* 6812[14] *7169[13]* *7322[8]* *7499[7]* *7613[4]* *7647[6]* 7776[9]

Tyler *W M Brisbourne* a32 40
2 b g Bertolini(USA) —Fly Like The Wind (Cyrano De Bergerac)
1392[8] 2011[12] 3091[5] *3815[6]* 3889[4] 4764[8]

Tyrana (GER) *J L Spearing* a57
5 ch m Acatenango(GER) —Tascalina (GER) (Big Shuffle (USA))
506[9] *730[9]* *879[12]* *7189[8]*

Tyrannosaurus Rex (IRE) *D Shaw* a66 66
4 b g Bold Fact(USA) —Dungeon Princess (IRE) (Danehill (USA))
990[6] *1209[10]* *1416[9]* 4207[2] *4478[9]* (5074) 5319[7] *5401[4]* *7323[8]* *7521[5]* *7778[8]*

Tyrrells Wood (IRE) *T G Mills* a73 77
3 b g Sinndar(IRE) —Diner De Lune (IRE) (Be My Guest (USA))
3004[7] (3781) 4573[7] 4985[5] *5406[2]*

Tyrur Ted *John A Quinn* a57 76
3 b g Val Royal(FR) —Spanish Serenade (Nashwan (USA))
826a[11]

Tyzack (IRE) *Stef Liddiard* a77 81
7 b g Fasliyev(USA) —Rabea (USA) (Devil's Bag (USA))
3457[9] 5170[5]

Uace Mac *N Bycroft* 70
4 b m Compton Place—Umbrian Gold (IRE) (Perugino (USA))
2270[11] 2597[13] 3977[3] 4207[6] (4877) 5634[7] 6219[16]

Ubenkor (IRE) *B Smart* a31 73
3 b c Diktat—Lucky Dancer (FR) (Groom Dancer (USA))
2786^{13} 3282^{2} 3955^{3} 4236^{2} (4702) 5258^{6} 6813^{4} 7131^{8}

Ubi Ace *T D Walford* 72
2 b g First Trump—Faithful Beauty (IRE) (Last Tycoon)
4780^{3} (6008) 6549^{12}

Ubiquitous *S Dow* 48
3 b f Erhaab(USA) —Lady Isabell (Rambo Dancer (CAN))
2046^{11} 2885^{8} 3484^{10} 4338^{11} 4774^{8} 5537^{11} 6337^{7} 6896^{10}

Ubiquitous Bounty *Miss Z C Davison* 20
3 b g Bahamian Bounty—In A Twinkling (IRE) (Brief Truce (USA))
7721^{1}

Ucantmissme *D W P Arbuthnot* a75
2 ch g Compton Place—Simply Sooty (Absalom)
5939^{7} ◆ 6620^{2} 7402^{8}

Ucetek (IRE) *Sir Michael Stoute* a53 74
3 b f Kalanisi(IRE) —Dragnet (IRE) (Rainbow Quest (USA))
2119^{3} 2862^{5}

Ugenius *Mrs C A Dunnett* a70 55
4 b g Killer Instinct—I'm Sophie (IRE) (Shalford (IRE))
(792) 844^{8} 864^{7} 1266^{13} 2703^{3} 2866^{2} 3822^{6} 4748^{3} 5045^{11} 6208^{10} 6913^{2} 7320^{2} 7437^{2} (7619) 7764^{3}

Ugly Betty *Bruce Hellier* 25
3 b f Where Or When(IRE) —Dancing Steps (Zafonic (USA))
3262^{7} 4849^{6} 6411^{9} 6836^{8}

Uhuru Peak *M W Easterby* a51 61
7 ch g Bal Harbour—Catherines Well (Junius (USA))
3732^{5} 4491^{2} 4679^{10} (5008) 5458^{2} 6396^{13} 7441^{10}

Uig *H S Howe* a68 73
7 ch m Bien Bien(USA) —Madam Zando (Forzando)
1406^{2} ◆ 1697^{6} (1959) 2125^{2} 2990^{2} 3132^{6} 3944^{8} 6090^{11} 6605^{12} 6667^{11} 7009^{10}

Ukrainian (BRZ) *A Cintra Pereira* a93
4 b h Urban Habitat(USA) —Masmorra (BRZ) (Choctaw Ridge (USA))
$292a^{15}$ $563a^{3}$ $648a^{6}$ (812a) $1088a^{7}$

Ultimate *H Morrison* a71 58
2 b c Anabaa(USA) —Nirvana (Marju (IRE))
6977^{13} 7424^{6} 7660^{3}

Ultimate Quest (IRE) *Sir Mark Prescott* a51 63
3 ch g Rainbow Quest(USA) —Crepe Ginger (IRE) (Sadler's Wells (USA))
74^{9} 175^{10} 265^{9} ◆ 3393^{4} 3873^{7} 4067^{2}

Ulysees (IRE) *Miss L A Perratt* a52 56
9 b g Turtle Island(IRE) —Tamasriya (IRE) (Doyoun)
1952^{12} 2524^{9} 2940^{9} 3201^{13} 3255^{10} 4630^{2} 5456^{6} 6040^{U} 7132^{3}

Ul Zincarlin (IRE) *S Santella* 98
5 b h Definite Article—Flying Petrel (USA) (Storm Bird (CAN))
$7263a^{6}$

Umirage (GER) *H Blume* 101
3 br f Monsun(GER) —Ungarin (GER) (Goofalik (USA))
$3705a^{3}$ $4675a^{9}$

Umpa Loompa (IRE) *B J McMath* a47 65
4 ch g Indian Lodge(IRE) —Bold Fashion (FR) (Nashwan (USA))
370^{9} 596^{6} 2289^{6} 2597^{20} 3033^{16} 4535^{13}

Umverti *N Bycroft* 59
3 b f Averti(IRE) —Umbrian Gold (IRE) (Perugino (USA))
2041^{12} (3081) 3717^{8} 4219^{12} 6116^{11}

Una Auroraborealis *S W James* a42 50
3 br f Fantastic Light(USA) —Aly McBe (USA) (Alydeed (CAN))
1124^{8} 1364^{11} 1586^{4} 1937^{6} 2089^{2} 2907^{6} 3458^{8} 6047^{12} 6583^{10} 7050^{7}

Unawatuna *Mrs K Walton* 55
3 b f Golden Snake(USA) —Laylee (Deploy)
3479^{9} 4166^{11} 4689^{7} 5637^{9} 6386^{2} 6861^{3}

Unbiased (IRE) *J L Dunlop* a68 69
3 b c Olden Times—Sharp Mode (USA) (Diesis)
1418^{5} 4484^{3} 4877^{4} 5652^{8} 6091^{2} 6571^{2} 6843^{2}

Unbreak My Heart (IRE) *R Charlton* 97
3 ch g Bahamian Bounty—Golden Heart (Salse (USA))
1595^{2} 2403^{13} 3919^{14} 4783^{2} 5257^{7} 5795^{12} 6526^{3}

Unbridled Belle (USA) *Todd Pletcher* a117
5 b m Broken Vow(USA) —Little Bold Belle (USA) (Silver Buck (USA))
$6523a^{9}$

Uncle Bulgaria (IRE) *G C Bravery* a49
6 b g Alhaarth(IRE) —Istibshar (USA) (Mr Prospector (USA))
2866^{3} 5712^{8}

Uncle Fred *P R Chamings* a74 43
3 b c Royal Applause—Karla June (Unfuwain (USA))
5023^{5} 5608^{3} 5995^{6}

Uncle Harry *J J Quinn* 43
3 b g Mind Games—Lapadar (IRE) (Woodborough (USA))
3600^{8} 4379^{6} 4964^{6} 5399^{9}

Unconsoled *K J Condon* a20 65
2 b f Ishiguru(USA) —Chantilly (FR) (Sanglamore (USA))
$5294a^{17}$

Undaunted Affair (IRE) *K A Ryan* 88
2 ch f Spartacus(IRE) —Party Bag (Cadeaux Genereux)
1961^{3} ◆ (2357) ◆ $2686a^{3}$

Under Fire (IRE) *A W Carroll* a70 66
5 b g Lear Spear(USA) —Kahyasi Moll (IRE) (Brief Truce (USA))
10^{2} 125^{2} 180^{4} 387^{2} (517) (537) 730^{3} 879^{6} 996^{8} 1565^{12} 2097^{4} 2642^{9} 3181^{4} 3360^{5} 4055^{3} 4365^{3} 5783^{3} 6364^{2} 6928^{2} 7076^{2} 7354^{13} 7591^{12}

Under The Rainbow *B W Hills* 107
5 gr m Fantastic Light(USA) —Farfala (FR) (Linamix (FR))
1829^{9} 2130^{2} 2402^{2} 3195^{10} 3415^{11} 5826^{6} 6241^{2} 6819^{4} 7145^{5}

Under The Table *Miss J E Foster*
2 ch f Bertolini(USA) —Over The Counter (IRE) (Persian Bold)
2924^{7} 4474^{13}

Underworld *M Johnston* a93 107
3 ch g Cadeaux Genereux—Mythic (Zafonic (USA))
(705) (975) ◆ 3251^{2} ◆ 4405^{21} (5096) 5495^{5} 6103^{11} 6269^{16}

Unepetitehistoire (FR) *Robert Collet* a68 78
2 b f Sagacity(FR) —Petite Ancre (FR) (Slip Anchor)
$1886a^{3}$

Unilateral (IRE) *B Smart* 103
3 ch f Rock Of Gibraltar(IRE) —Mira Adonde (USA) (Sharpen Up)
2605^{7}

Union Island (IRE) *K A Ryan* 80
2 b c Rock Of Gibraltar(IRE) —Daftiyna (IRE) (Darshaan)
4780^{2} ◆ 5859^{2} 6292^{3} 6760^{2}

Union Jack Jackson (IRE) *John A Harris* a56 63
6 b g Daggers Drawn(USA) —Beechwood Quest (IRE) (River Falls)
437^{8} 596^{11} 792^{13} 872^{11} 1675^{7} 1906^{3} 2751^{11} 2866^{6} 3691^{13} 3952^{9} 7369^{12}

Unique (IRE) *N P Littmoden* 36
3 b g Invincible Spirit(IRE) —Licorne (Sadler's Wells (USA))
2763^{10} 3530^{10} 5320^{7}

United Nations *N Wilson* a73 80
7 ch g Halling(USA) —Congress (IRE) (Dancing Brave (USA))
4813^{10} 6090^{4} 6450^{9} 7656^{8} (7799)

Universal Ruler (AUS) *Darren McAuliffe* 99
4 b h Scenic—Rulings (AUS) (Hurricane Sky (AUS))
$2235a^{8}$

Unleashed (IRE) *H R A Cecil* a94 99
3 br c Storming Home—Uriah (GER) (Acatenango (GER))
(2528) (2948) 3196^{10} 3875^{4}

Unlicensed *R Hannon* a68 39
3 ch g Hawk Wing(USA) —Multicolour (Rainbow Quest (USA))
58^{6} 3675^{7}

Unlimited *A W Carroll* a66 73
6 b g Bold Edge—Cabcharge Blue (Midyan (USA))
(149) 235^{2} 446^{3} 515^{4} 749^{8} 938^{5} (1900) 2101^{2} 2243^{4} 2860^{7} 3165^{4} 3797^{7} 5198^{4} 5315^{6}

Unnefer (FR) *H R A Cecil* 114
3 b c Danehill Dancer(IRE) —Mimalia (USA) (Silver Hawk (USA))
(1443) 1943^{2} (2408) 3156^{8} 5289^{3}

Uno Dos Tres *Jane Chapple-Hyam* a48
3 ch c Night Shift(USA) —Sartigila (Efisio)
483^{7}

Unshakable (IRE) *Bob Jones* a96 99
9 b g Eagle Eyed(USA) —Pepper And Salt (IRE) (Double Schwartz)
2789^{2} 3740^{7} (5279) 6120^{15} 6476^{17} 7146^{14}

Unsung Heroine (IRE) *T Stack* 116
3 b f High Chaparral(IRE) —Thermopylae (Tenby) (4833a) 5892^{2} 6819^{2} ◆

Until When (USA) *B Smart* a70 73
4 b g Grand Slam(USA) —Chez Cherie (Wolfhound (USA))
2749^{8} 4013^{2} 4385^{11} 5110^{4}

Unwritten Rule (IRE) *D K Weld* 99
3 gr c Dalakhani(IRE) —Triple Try (IRE) (Sadler's Wells (USA))
(1233a) $1509a^{3}$ $3805a^{9}$

Up And Coming (IRE) *J E Pease* a87 90
4 b g Compton Place—Uplifting (Magic Ring (IRE))
$5113a^{10}$

Up Dee Creek *W M Brisbourne* a39 40
6 ch m Tipsy Creek(USA) —Sandra Dee (IRE) (Be My Guest (USA))
236^{4} 401^{7} 578^{8} 769^{10} 822^{9}

Up In Arms (IRE) *P Winkworth* a73 72
4 b g Daggers Drawn(USA) —Queenliness (Exit To Nowhere (USA))
2952^{8}

Upper Class (IRE) *M Johnston* a93 72
3 b g Fantastic Light(USA) —Her Ladyship (Polish Precedent (USA))
489^{4} ◆ (723) ◆ 1074^{3}

Upper Village *John Halley* a70 78
4 ch g Bertolini(USA) —Magic Dawn (AUS) (Bletchley Park (IRE))
$4514a^{15}$

Upstairs *D R C Elsworth* a68 59
4 ch g Sugarfoot—Laena (Roman Warrior)
1581^{5} 2187^{8} 2510^{5} 3037^{4} 3162^{5} 7437^{7} 7591^{5} (7766) ◆

Upstanding *M Brittain* a66 65
3 b f Acclamation—Uplifting (Magic Ring (IRE))
112^{3} 397^{3} (721) (767) 7182^{14}

Upstart (IRE) *H R A Cecil* a32
3 b g Vettori(IRE) —Foxglove (Hernando (FR))
1669^{10} 3530^{9} 6909^{8}

Up The Chimney *A P Jarvis* a53 57
4 gr g Kyllachy—Simply Sooty (Absalom)
5837^{10} 6571^{9} 6733^{6} 7018^{15} 7180^{8}

Upton Grey (IRE) *J H M Gosden* a71 94
3 gr c Dalakhani(IRE) —Rosse (Kris)
1428^{5} 2953^{4} $3535a^{9}$ (4160) 4552^{7} 5279^{8} 5903^{5} 6276^{2} 6816^{8}

Upton Seas *R D E Woodhouse* a49 45
2 b f Josr Algarhoud(IRE) —Crystal Seas (Zamindar (USA))
5590^{6} 6187^{6} 6524^{8}

Uramazin (IRE) *G A Swinbank* 81
2 ch c Danehill Dancer(IRE) —Uriah (GER) (Acatenango (GER))
2444^{3} (2951) 3412^{3}

Urban Farmer *R A Fahey* 53
3 b c Fantastic Light(USA) —Petonica (IRE) (Petoski)
2269^{4}

Urban Space *B G Powell* 46
2 ch g Sulamani(IRE) —Rasmalai (Sadler's Wells (USA))
5579^{10} 6026^{11} 6234^{5}

Urban Warrior *Ian Williams* a74 75
4 b g Zilzal(USA) —Perfect Poppy (Shareef Dancer (USA))
660^{2} 1065^{3} 2483^{5} 3060^{6} 3650^{2} 4220^{2} 5027^{5} 5465^{6} 7366^{9}

Ursis (FR) *S Gollings* a62 80
7 b g Trempolino(USA) —Bold Virgin (USA) (Sadler's Wells (USA))
1580^{4} 1909^{5} 2822^{7} 3613^{7} 5993^{2}

Ursula (IRE) *K R Burke* 75
2 b f Namid—Fritta Mista (IRE) (Linamix (FR))
5416^{4} (5988)

Ursus *C R Wilson* 63
3 ch g Rambling Bear—Adar Jane (Ardar)
1139^{9} 1453^{10} 2367^{11} (3283) (3454) 3833^{4} 4684^{8} 5775^{4} 6218^{8} 6382^{4} 7197^{9}

Usetheforce (IRE) *M J Wallace* a53 35
3 ch g Black Minnaloushe(USA) —Polynesian Goddess (IRE) (Salmon Leap (USA))
175^{7} 590^{8} 6048^{12} 6716^{11} 6878^{7}

US Ranger (USA) *A P O'Brien* 122
4 b h Danzig(USA) —My Annette (USA) (Red Ransom (USA))
$1355a^{3}$ 2106^{4} ◆ 3247^{5} 3922^{2} $4915a^{5}$ 5891^{11} $6496a^{3}$ $6996a^{5}$

Usual Suspects *Peter Grayson* a38 46
2 b f Royal Applause—Soft Breeze (Zafonic (USA))
2903^{7} 3315^{7} 4279^{4} 4628^{6} 5567^{12}

Utmost Respect *R A Fahey* 116
4 b g Danetime(IRE) —Utmost (IRE) (Most Welcome)
(1483) ◆ 2106^{9} 2390^{4} (3488) ◆ $4915a^{4}$ 5891^{3} $6496a^{6}$ (7187a)

Uvinza *W J Knight* a71 95
2 ch f Bertolini(USA) —Baddi Heights (FR) (Shirley Heights)
5241^{2} 5828^{5} (6432)

Uvpaintedupyurlips (IRE) *Peter Henley* 44
2 b f Fasliyev(USA) —Marefonic (Zafonic (USA))
$3509a^{12}$

Vacare (USA) *Christophe Clement* 113
5 b m Lear Fan(USA) —Appealing Storm (USA) (Valid Appeal (USA))
$6968a^{5}$

Vacation (IRE) *S Curran* a94 91
5 b g King Charlemagne(USA) —Lady Peculiar (CAN) (Sunshine Forever (USA))
1026^{9}

Vaccaria (GER) *W Hickst* 71
3 ch f Pentire—Valentine Rose (GER) (Platini (GER))
$6742a^{4}$

Vadsalina (IRE) *A De Royer-Dupre* 101
3 b f Sagacity(FR) —Vadaza (FR) (Zafonic (USA))
$1323a^{6}$

Vaglefield *J H M Gosden* a57
2 b c Montjeu(IRE) —Photogenic (Midyan (USA))
7343^{8}

Vahhare (FR) *J-P Perruchot* 20
3 b c Bahhare(USA) —Verte Rive (FR) (Green Tune (USA))
$549a^{8}$

Vainglory (USA) *D M Simcock* a96 96
4 ch h Swain(IRE) —Infinite Spirit (USA) (Maria's Mon (USA))
6^{3} $380a^{4}$ $650a^{8}$ 1920^{3} 2531^{2} ◆ 2789^{3} 3972^{6} 4405^{23} 5405^{5} 5772^{7} 6130^{8} 6352^{4} ◆

Valart *M R Bosley* a42 57
5 ch m Bien Bien(USA) —Riverine (Risk Me (FR))
76^{5} 166^{11} 776^{9} 1109^{5} 6226^{10} 6899^{11}

Valassini *J W Mullins* 39
8 b m Dr Massini(IRE) —Running Valley (Buckskin (FR))
3343^{6}

Valatrix (IRE) *C F Wall* a84 83
3 b f Acclamation—Dramatic Entry (IRE) (Persian Bold)
(2546) 4090^{3} 5142^{2} 5510^{2} 6650^{8}

Valdan (IRE) *P D Evans* a71 86
4 b g Val Royal(FR) —Danedrop (IRE) (Danehill (USA))
990^{20} 1138^{7} 1371^{5} 2285^{10} 2446^{3} 2568^{2} 2782^{6} 3143^{4} 3257^{6} 3755^{3} 4215^{5} 4679^{6} (5837) 6134^{10} 6577^{5} 6599^{11} 7076^{9} 7261^{2} 7354^{4} 7620^{2} (7711) 7791^{6}

Val De Flores *E F Vaughan* a60 62
2 b f Oasis Dream—My Lass (Elmaamul (USA))
3207^{8} 3528^{5} 5004^{8} 5567^{2} 5834^{9} 6017^{7} 6666^{2} 6933^{8}

Valdemar *A D Brown* a59
2 ch g Tobougg(IRE) —Stealthy Times (Timeless Times (USA))
4474^{10} 5539^{10} 6010^{13} 6351^{4} 6879^{11} 7179^{6} 7372^{10}

Valdemar Victory *D Nicholls*
4 b g Inchinor—Park Crystal (IRE) (Danehill (USA))
1125^{11} 1701^{10}

Valdino (GER) *U Ostmann* 114
3 b g Black Sam Bellamy(IRE) —Valdina (GER) (Lomitas)
(4911a) (5625a) (6517a)

Valeesha *M S Saunders* a7 46
4 b m Erhaab(USA) —Miss Laetitia (IRE) (Entitled)
2350^{7} 2556^{7} 2753^{13}

Valentine Bay *M Mullineaux* a22 44
2 b f Reel Buddy(USA) —Bullion (Sabrehill (USA))
5004^{10} 5650^{6} 5989^{9} 6788^{8} 7170^{8} 7734^{9}

Valentine Blue *A B Haynes* a40 56
3 ch g Tobougg(IRE) —Blue Topaz (IRE) (Bluebird (USA))
4724^{7} 5379^{10} 5813^{4} 6185^{3} 6929^{8}

Valentine Hill (IRE) *Adrian Maguire* a86 89
3 b f Mujadil(USA) —First Nadia (Auction Ring (USA))
$1230a^{9}$ $2024a^{8}$

Valentino Rossi (BRZ) *J M P Eustace* 38
6 b h New Colony(USA) —Great Sola (BRZ) (Duke Of Marmalade (USA))
5264^{7}

Valentino Swing (IRE) *Miss T Spearing* a69 73
5 ch g Titus Livius(FR) —Farmers Swing (IRE) (River Falls)
1368^{13} 1900^{6} 2615^{2} 2837^{3} 3842^{8} 5458^{11} 5779^{9} 6132^{3} 6628^{6} 6889^{11} 7228^{8} 7359^{7} 7513^{2} 7619^{7}

Valento *Eve Johnson Houghton* a69 70
3 ch g Noverre(USA) —My Valentina (Royal Academy (USA))
1957^{5} 2991^{15} 4338^{3} 4637^{2} 4777^{2} 6001^{2} 6336^{4} 6544^{4} 6741^{4}

Valery Borzov (IRE) *D Nicholls* a93 108
4 b g Iron Mask(USA) —Fay's Song (IRE) (Fayruz)
1069^{8} 1415^{2} (1567) (2210) ◆ 2698^{2} 3489^{9} 4145^{5} 4586^{10} (4854) 5109^{2} 6104^{11}

Valferno (IRE) *Mrs P Sly* 71
3 b f Val Royal(FR) —Golden (FR) (Sanglamore (USA))
1279^{2} 2015^{4} 3796^{4} 4741^{5}

Valhillen *M D I Usher* a74 72
3 ch g Bertolini(USA) —Dancing Nelly (Shareef Dancer (USA))
38^{2} (199) ◆ 364^{5} 612^{3} 756^{2} 798^{4} 924^{2} 1066^{2} 1284^{3} 1584^{4} 1934^{4} 2099^{2} (2555) 2998^{9} 3330^{4} 3615^{7} 4083^{4} 4476^{6} 4904^{3} 5028^{4} 5592^{8} 6774^{9}

Valiance (USA) *M F De Kock* a90 69
4 ch g Horse Chestnut(SAF) —Victoria Cross (IRE) (Mark Of Esteem (IRE))
$295a^{7}$ $379a^{13}$ $473a^{16}$ $738a^{9}$

Valiant Romeo *R Bastiman* a15 56
8 b g Primo Dominie—Desert Lynx (IRE) (Green Desert (USA))
1772^{6} 2881^{6} 3340^{8} 3784^{3} 4013^{8} 5452^{9}

Valid Point (IRE) *Sir Mark Prescott* a36 48
2 b g Val Royal(FR) —Ricadonna (Kris)
6885^{9} 7038^{10} 7640^{8} 7769^{9}

Val Jaro (FR) *S Morineau* a72 105
5 b g Le Triton(USA) —Valana (USA) (Valanour (IRE))
$3243a^{6}$ $3938a^{9}$

Valkyrie (IRE) *N P Littmoden* a57 23
2 b f Danehill Dancer(IRE) —Ridotto (Salse (USA))
5271^{12} 6253^{6}

Vallemeldee (IRE) *P W D'Arcy* a77 68
4 b m Bering—Vassiana (FR) (Anabaa (USA))
96^{8} 510^{6}

Valletta *J H M Gosden* a60 68
2 b f Cape Cross(IRE) —Vituisa (Bering)
6291^{5} 7337^{8}

Valley Observer (FR) *W R Swinburn* a72 72
4 ch g Observatory(USA) —Valleyrose (IRE) (Royal Academy (USA))
128^{8}

Valley Of The Moon (IRE) *R A Fahey* a80 84
4 b m Monashee Mountain(USA) —Unaria (Prince Tenderfoot (USA))
(1373) 1755^{5} (2219) 2583^{14} 3056^{10} 3554^{7} 3973^{13}

Vallorcine (FR) *G Martin*
5 b m Loup Solitaire(USA) —Valluga (USA) (Roar (USA))
$422a^{10}$

Valrhona (IRE) *J Noseda* a80 86
4 bb m Spectrum(IRE) —Minerva (IRE) (Caerleon (USA))
1329^{4} ◆ 1981^{4} ◆ (2895)

Valtraud (FR) *M Simondi*
2 b f Lord Of Men—Val Ferret (FR) (Rusticaro (IRE))
$2744a^{5}$

Value Of Time (IRE) *R Donohoe* a56 71
3 b f Xaar—Astuti (IRE) (Waajib)
7656^{12} 7667^{10}

Valverde (IRE) *George Baker* a24 58
5 b g Sinndar(IRE) —Vert Val (USA) (Septieme Ciel (USA))
2513^{15} (4102) 4653^{9} 5871^{11} 6036^{12} (Dead)

Valvignеres (IRE) *E A L Dunlop* a67 67
3 gr g Dalakhani(IRE) —Albacora (IRE) (Fairy King (USA))
2681^{12} 3873^{4}

Vamos (IRE) *J R Gask* a60
2 b g Royal Applause—Feather Boa (IRE) (Sri Pekan (USA))
5628^{6}

Vampress (IRE) *Liam McAteer* 43
9 b m Marju(IRE) —Sharenara (USA) (Vaguely Noble)
$4655a^{16}$

Vanadium *G L Moore* a70 71
6 b g Dansili—Musianica (Music Boy)
1842^{3} (2128) 2337^{8} 3966^{11} 4428^{10} 5267^{5} ◆ 5755^{4} 6132^{4} 7226^{7} 7651^{2} 7803^{9}

Vanatina (IRE) *W M Brisbourne* a53 46
4 b m Tagula(IRE) —Final Trick (Primo Dominie)
1313^{6} 1602^{7} 1869^{4} 2781^{7} 3127^{7} 3624^{11} 3951^{7} 6843^{5} 7178^{4} 7369^{4} 7631^{4} 7706^{5} 7746^{9}

Van Bossed (CAN) *D Nicholls* a88 101
3 ch g Van Nistelrooy(USA) —Embossed (CAN) (Silver Deputy (CAN))
967^{8} 1284^{2} (1426) (1623) ◆ 1949^{3} 3047^{19} 5890^{18} 6239^{2}

Vanderlin *A M Balding* a108 108
9 ch g Halling(USA) —Massorah (FR) (Habitat)
1387^{3} 1767^{3} 2600^{8} 3946^{5} 5208^{4} 5495^{2} 6269^{12}

Vanishing Dancer (SWI) *Mrs D Thomas* a55 56
11 ch g Llandaff(USA) —Vanishing Prairie (USA) (Alysheba (USA))
198^{4} 287^{4} 374^{10} 695^{10} 1246^{8} 6708^{6} 7216^{12}

Van Lear Rose (CAN) *Catherine Day-Phillips* a105
2 bb f Stroll(USA) —Devaluation (USA) (Conquistador Cielo (USA))
$6967a^{6}$

Vanquisher (IRE) *Ian Williams* a52 79
4 br g Xaar—Naziriya (FR) (Darshaan)
2970[4] 3258[4] 3630[5] 3950[4] 4432[7] 4785[6] 7447[7] 7573[11] 7667[4] 7787[4]

Van Ruymbeke (IRE) *D J Murphy* a54 41
4 ch g Indian Ridge—Badrah (USA) (Private Account (USA))
42[6] 82[5] 256[8]

Vaqueras (FR) *Mrs John Harrington* 90
5 b g Pennekamp(USA) —Las Americas (FR) (Linamix (FR))
1105a[2]

Vaquero (USA) *Michael P Leahy* 102
2 bb c Orientate(USA) —Sambra (USA) (Storm Cat (USA))
6998a[6]

Varadouro (BRZ) *Tom Dascombe* a87 77
6 b g A Good Reason(BRZ) —Orquidea Vermelha (BRZ) (Lucence (USA))
1015[4] ◆ 1327[14] (1703) ◆ 1952[11] 2293[2] 4058[5] (4476) 7317[7]

Varevees *R Gibson* 112
5 b m Kahyasi—Danse Bretonne (FR) (Exit To Nowhere (USA))
2653a[6] 4041a[9] 5333a[8] 7188a[14]

Varinia (IRE) *M Brittain* a46 62
3 b f Spartacus(IRE) —Bucaramanga (IRE) (Distinctly North (USA))
2803[2] 3030[16] 4241[10] (5501) 7618[7]

Varsa (IRE) *K R Burke* 35
2 b f Refuse To Bend(IRE) —For Evva Silca (Piccolo)
3085[8] 5241[15] 6244[10]

Varsity *C F Swan* a98 99
5 b m Lomitas—Renowned (IRE) (Darshaan)
4576a[4] 5547a[4] 6298a[6] 7235a[2]

Vassinella (FR) *Mme C Head-Maarek* 72
3 b f Anabaa(USA) —Vassia (USA) (Machiavellian (USA))
6743a[6]

Vattene (IRE) *M Gasparini* 103
3 br f Kendor(FR) —Voglia Matta (IRE) (Second Set (IRE))
2231a[2] 3775a[8] 7253a[15]

Veddasca (IRE) *L Brogi* 57
3 b f Polish Precedent(USA) —Imco Imagination (IRE) (Darshaan)
2231a[14]

Veenwouden *E F Vaughan* a81 109
4 b m Desert Prince(IRE) —Delauncy (Machiavellian (USA))
1158[7] 2169[7] 5264[8] 6479[9]

Vegano (FR) *C Von Der Recke*
7 bb h Waky Nao—Vega Sicilia (Environment Friend)
422a[2] 605a[5]

Vehari *Ian Williams* a35 35
5 ch g Tomba—Nannie Annie (Persian Bold)
2642[13] 5059[7] 5489[12]

Veiled *Sir Mark Prescott* a58
2 b f Sadler's Wells(USA) —Evasive Quality (FR) (Highest Honor (FR))
6167[9] 6423[7] 6622[11] 6901[7]

Veiled Applause *J J Quinn* a85 92
5 b g Royal Applause—Scarlet Veil (Tyrnavos)
1072[2] 1910[6] (2220) 2582[5] 3046[7] 3294[5] 4688[7] 5382[2]

Vella *H J L Dunlop* a44
2 b f Mtoto—Villella (Sadler's Wells (USA))
7259[8]

Velma Kelly *W R Swinburn* a54 27
4 b m Vettori(IRE) —Possessive Artiste (Shareef Dancer (USA))
3088[7]

Veloso (FR) *A J McCabe* a72
6 gr g Kaldounevees(FR) —Miss Recif (IRE) (Exit To Nowhere (USA))
5999[9] (6594) 6985[2] (7089) 7280[2]

Velox Vixen (IRE) *M Blanshard*
2 b f Muhtarram(USA) —Pretiosa (IRE) (Royal Abjar (USA))
4339[10] 5650[11]

Velvet Heights (IRE) *J L Dunlop* a103 91
6 b h Barathea(IRE) —Height Of Fantasy (IRE) (Shirley Heights)
1501[4] 3044[6] 4866[7]

Velvet Revolver (IRE) *L Riccardi* a71 98
5 b m Mujahid(USA) —Noble Kara (FR) (Noblequest (FR))
1659a[12]

Veneer (IRE) *Mrs N S Evans* a50 56
6 b g Woodborough(USA) —Sweet Lass (Belmez (USA))
8[3] 145[11] 1031[10] 1702[4]

Venelina (IRE) *J S Bolger* a66 62
3 ch f King's Best(USA) —Kentmere (FR) (Galetto (FR))
6366a[26]

Venetian Lady *Mrs A Duffield* a58 19
2 b f Tobougg(IRE) —Perfect Partner (Be My Chief (USA))
4169[11] 5500[8] 5771[8] 6661[4] 6987[7]

Veni Bidi Vici *A M Balding* a54 36
3 ch f Horse Chestnut(SAF) —Wily Bid (USA) (Spectacular Bid (USA))
897[8] 3823[3] 4566[5] 5119[12] 5407[10] 6173[13]

Venir Rouge *M Salaman* a80 81
4 ch g Dancing Spree(USA) —Al Awaalah (Mukaddamah (USA))
2304[8] 2764[3] 2990[5] 5092[7] 6898[12] 7230[5] 7385[12]

Ventana (IRE) *D Gambarota* 92
3 ch f Fath(USA) —Beyond Doubt (Belmez (USA))
2231a[17]

Ventana (USA) *Bob Baffert* a95
2 b c Toccet(USA) —Full Figure (USA) (Polish Numbers (USA))
6501a[10] 7751a[11]

Ventura (USA) *Robert Frankel* a121 116
4 bb m Chester House(USA) —Estala (Be My Guest (USA))
(6965a)

Venture Capitalist *L M Cumani* a63 47
2 b c Diktat—Ventura Highway (Machiavellian (USA))
5227[14] 6197[10] 7170[3] ◆

Veracity *Saeed Bin Suroor* a73 115
4 ch h Lomitas—Vituisa (Bering)
5885[5] (6527) (6820) 7008a[3]

Vera Lilley (IRE) *M J Grassick* a22 69
2 gr f Verglas(IRE) —La Tintoretta (IRE) (Desert Prince (IRE))
6320a[17]

Veras Joy *Miss Z C Davison* a38 14
3 b f Piccolo—Fly South (Polar Falcon (USA))
2932[8] 3342[6] 7260[8] 7379[6] 7506[12]

Verba (FR) *R Gibson* 105
3 gr f Anabaa(USA) —Tambura (FR) (Kaldoun (FR))
1993[2] 7450a[2]

Verbatim *A M Balding* a62 66
4 b m Vettori(IRE) —Brand (Shareef Dancer (USA))
88[4]

Verdant (USA) *George R Arnold II*
2 b f Pleasantly Perfect(USA) —Rift Valley (USA) (Gulch (USA))
6613a[6]

Verinco *B Smart* a67 78
2 b g Bahamian Bounty—Dark Eyed Lady (IRE) (Exhibitioner)
2035[4] 2521[2] 2746[U] 3400[2] 3809[6] 4874[3] 6525[6] 7130[2] 7426[6]

Verlegen (IRE) *R Hannon* 70
2 b f Royal Applause—Petite Epaulette (Night Shift (USA))
2204[3] 2479[4] 2999[6] 4346[3] 4768[6]

Vermilion (JPN) *S Ishizaka* a120 104
6 br h El Condor Pasa(USA) —Scarlet Lady (JPN) (Sunday Silence (USA))
1092a[12]

Veronicas Boy *G M Moore* 71
2 br c Diktat—Thamud (IRE) (Lahib (USA))
1392[2] (1821) 2154[6] 2775[6] 3576[2] 4072[6] 5381[5] 5632[14] 6101[4]

Veronicas Way *G J Smith* 61
3 b f High Estate—Mimining (Tower Walk)
1396[6] 2282[8] 2781[11] 3281[9] 5501[6] 6562[6] 7267[13] 7815[10]

Veroon (IRE) *J G Given* 68
2 b g Noverre(USA) —Waroonga (IRE) (Brief Truce (USA))
4740[5] 5277[3] 6080[7] 7241[6]

Versaki (IRE) *R Hannon* 93
2 gr g Verglas(IRE) —Mythie (FR) (Octagonal (NZ))
(2601) ◆ 3103[17] 3879[4] 5228[3] 5641[5] 6082[12] 6717[7]

Vertigineux (FR) *Mme C Dufreche* 113
4 b h Nombre Premier—Very Gold (FR) (Goldneyev (USA))
(3357a) 4915a[15] (7162a)

Verumontanum (IRE) *Henry De Bromhead* 60
3 b g Bach(IRE) —Emma O (IRE) (Dr Devious (IRE))
4715a[8]

Very Distinguished *M G Quinlan* 67
2 b f Diktat—Dignify (IRE) (Rainbow Quest (USA))
2618[9] ◆ 4337[2] 5225[7] 5895[5] 6231[7] 6761[5] 7142[6]

Very Green (FR) *Mrs A L M King* 60
6 b g Barathea(IRE) —Green Bend (USA) (Riverman (USA))
4704[6] 5163[6] 5367[11] 5752[4] 7775[9]

Very Well Red *P W Hiatt* a69 74
5 b m First Trump—Little Scarlett (Mazilier (USA))
148[8] 537[6] 3557[8] 3903[10] (4567) 4895[11] 5119[3] 5492[7] 6056[10] 6255[7] 6336[14] 6671[5] 6899[8] 7320[6] 7601[4] 7663[2] 7766[4] 7772[10]

Very Wise *W J Haggas* a98 107
6 b g Pursuit Of Love—With Care (Warning)
960[14] 1133[8] 1633[9] 1816[10] 2200[8] 2545[5] 2604[3] 3840[7] 4509[20] 6215[18]

Vesuve (IRE) *E Lellouche* 86
2 b c Green Tune(USA) —Verveine (USA) (Lear Fan (USA))
6147a[6]

Vesuvio *C W Thornton* a45 63
4 br g Efisio—Polo (Warning)
1189[12] 1775[2] 2782[4] 3757[6] 4018[3] 4683[5] 4736[6]

Vettorenjoy *M Botti* a82 62
3 b g Vettori(IRE) —Veiled Beauty (USA) (Royal Academy (USA))
(223) ◆ 573[6] 966[7] 1746[8] 3458[3]

Vhujon (IRE) *P D Evans* a96 94
3 b g Mujadil(USA) —Livius Lady (IRE) (Titus Livius (FR))
(1075) 1404[14] 2162[5] 2390[5] 2594[2] 3047[17] 3905[10] 4201[13] 4893[7] 5424[9] (6169) 6471[5] 6902[9] 7365[7] 7576[7] 7697[7] 7826[8]

Viable *Mrs P Sly* a63 64
6 b g Vettori(IRE) —Danseuse Davis (FR) (Glow (USA))
3964[3] 4797[8]

Via Galilei (IRE) *J S Bolger* a87 101
3 b c Galileo(IRE) —Manger Square (IRE) (Danehill (USA))
5136a[7]

Vial De Kerdec (FR) *M Bradstock* a41
5 bb g Poliglote—Love For Ever (FR) (Kaldoun (FR))
7526[11]

Via Mantua *P J Rothwell* a76 83
4 b m Halling(USA) —Isabella Gonzaga (Rock Hopper)
1199a[6]

Via Mia *P F I Cole* a71 62
2 b f Namid—Coming Home (Vettori (IRE))
4763[3] (6089) 6809[8]

Vibrato (USA) *C J Teague* a61 49
6 b g Stravinsky(USA) —She's Fine (USA) (Private Account (USA))
1024[11]

Vica Pota (IRE) *H Rogers* 62
3 b f King Charlemagne(USA) —Acidanthera (Alzao (USA))
4715a[16]

Vice Admiral *M W Easterby* a39 64
5 ch g Vettori(IRE) —Queen Of Scotland (IRE) (Mujadil (USA))
1136[10] 1892[9] 3589[11] 4924[10]

Vice Consul *M Johnston* a72 64
3 b g In The Wings—Wajina (Rainbow Quest (USA))
903[4] ◆ 1059[5] 1330[4] 1962[11]

Vicious Warrior *R M Whitaker* a72 91
9 b g Elmaamul(USA) —Ling Lane (Slip Anchor)
1816[8] 2218[6] 2733[6] 3367[7] 3864[4] 4204[4] 5005[2] 5391[4] 5843[9] 6250[3] 6582[8] 7184[5]

Victoria Montoya *A M Balding* a78 84
3 br f High Chaparral(IRE) —Spurned (USA) (Robellino (USA))
1205[2] 1542[3] 2164[3] (2997) 3930[3] (4351) ◆ 5464[8] 5938[5] 6272[5]

Victorian Bounty *Stef Liddiard* a73 97
3 b g Bahamian Bounty—Baby Bunting (Wolfhound (USA))
1170[4] 1404[7] (1837) 2410[6] 3047[2] 3850[17] 5102[11] 5403[11]

Victorian Tycoon (IRE) *E J O'Neill* a64 56
2 b c Choisir(AUS) —New Tycoon (IRE) (Last Tycoon)
2502[7] 3334[5] 4780[8] ◆ 5914[2] 6101[5] 6632[2]

Victoria Reel *R Hannon* a90 89
3 ch f Danehill Dancer(IRE) —New Assembly (IRE) (Machiavellian (USA))
2307[2] ◆ 2566[2] 3312[2] 3971[2] (4433) 6242[9] 6576[2] 7215[12] 7419[3]

Victorias *A Crook* 20
3 gr f Tamayaz(CAN) —Paper Flight (Petong)
1429[11] 1628[10] 2207[11] 2468[13] 2941[8]

Victoria Sponge (IRE) *R Hannon* a72 70
2 b f Marju(IRE) —Trill (Highest Honor (FR))
4251[2] ◆ 4521[5] 4980[3] (6732)

Victor Trumper *Jim Best* a61 39
4 b g First Trump—Not So Generous (IRE) (Fayruz)
218[8] 1049[8] 1109[2] 1260[8] 1670[8] 2069[5]

Victory Mile (USA) *M F Harris* a56 54
4 b g Victory Gallop(CAN) —Viva Girl (USA) (Deputy Minister (CAN))
212[10] 455[5] 544[11]

Victory Quest (IRE) *Mrs S Lamyman* a76 67
8 b g Victory Note(USA) —Marade (USA) (Dahar (USA))
3[2] 159[3] 260[10] 638[5] 854[4] 3820[2] 4439[5] 6054[14] 6527[8] 6838[2] (7045) 7271[4] 7366[3] 7515[6] 7617[3] (7696)

Victory Shout (USA) *J R Best* a44 57
3 b g Victory Gallop(CAN) —Lu Lu's Lullaby (USA) (Palace Music (USA))
98[8] 184[11] 5379[7] 5833[15]

Victory Spirit *I Semple* a57 55
4 b g Invincible Spirit(IRE) —Tanouma (USA) (Miswaki (USA))
5045[14] 7114[2] 7765[4]

Victram (IRE) *Adrian McGuinness* a84 87
8 b g Victory Note(USA) —Lady Tristram (Miami Springs)
1105a[3]

Vie A Deux (FR) *W Storey*
5 b m Jeune Homme(USA) —Callithea (Fools Holme (USA))
1305[10] 1890[14]

Vien (IRE) *R Hannon* a54 52
2 br c Captain Rio—Fairy Free (Rousillon (USA))
2759[10] 3267[9] 5314[8] 7391[5] 7514[10]

Vienna Affair *J R Fanshawe* 67
3 b f Red Ransom(USA) —Wiener Wald (USA) (Woodman (USA))
2620[3] ◆ 5261[9] 6003[4] 7055[13]

Viewed (AUS) *Bart Cummings* 116
5 b h Scenic—Lovers Knot (NZ) (Khozaam (USA))
6835a[10] (7188a)

Viewforth *M Wigham* a11 63
10 b g Emarati(USA) —Miriam (Forzando)
1378[12] 1966[15] 3665[10] 7636[10] 7778[9]

Vigano (IRE) *S Kirk* a74 73
3 b g Noverre(USA) —Perugia (IRE) (Perugino (USA))
(397) 2945[8] (3571) 4252[9] 4369[6] 5056[6] 5346[4] 5713[11] 6137[3] 6420[4] 6867[3] 6880[2]

Vignelaure Rose (IRE) *Charles O'Brien* a45 63
3 b f Danehill Dancer(IRE) —Vignelaure (IRE) (Royal Academy (USA))
3861a[6]

Viking Awake (IRE) *J W Unett* a46 67
2 b c Almutawakel—Norwegian Queen (IRE) (Affirmed (USA))
4296[5] 4780[5] 5882[4] 6988[9]

Viking Rock (IRE) *M Salaman* a58 46
2 ch g Viking Ruler(AUS) —Polar Rock (Polar Falcon (USA))
6333[7] 6665[7] 7023[9] 7258[10] 7789[8]

Viking Spirit *W R Swinburn* a107 108
6 b g Mind Games—Dane Dancing (IRE) (Danehill (USA))
1809[18] (2598) 3248[18] 4059[4] 5109[12] 6468[11]

Vilasol (IRE) *Kevin Prendergast* a83 98
2 gr g Verglas(IRE) —Pitrizza (IRE) (Machiavellian (USA))
4353a[3] 5296a[10] 6637a[6] 7029a[8]

Vilna (USA) *S A Callaghan* a75 57
3 b g Hold That Tiger(USA) —Not To Be Outdone (USA) (Damascus (USA))
3836[2] 4344[5] (4527) 4732[2] 5017[7] 5605[4]

Vinando *C R Egerton* 95
7 ch g Hernando(FR) —Sirena (GER) (Tejano (USA))
3104[13] 4362[6]

Vincenzio (IRE) *C R Egerton* a53 73
4 b g Galileo(IRE) —Mystic Lure (Green Desert (USA))
1559[8] 3029[4] 3574[3] 3891[6] 4075[2] 6594[7]

Vinces *T D McCarthy* a69 71
4 b g Lomitas—Vadinaxa (FR) (Linamix (FR))
(1994) 2886[7] 3896[7] 4309[5] 5017[3] 5576[2] 5934[9] 7071[12] 7545[2] 7711[9]

Vin De Rose *S W Hall*
2 b g Tipsy Creek(USA) —Rosewings (In The Wings)
7054[15]

Vinea Federspiel (IRE) *C Bocksai* 101
4 b m Singspiel(IRE) —Far Fetched (IRE) (Distant Relative)
2438a[8] 3623a[6] 5596a[6]

Vine Street (IRE) *M A Jarvis* a82 69
3 ch f Singspiel(IRE) —Wood Vine (USA) (Woodman (USA))
5231[2] 5612[2] 6280[3] 7342[2] (7580) (7642) 7712[10]

Vineyard *W J Haggas* a83 77
3 b g Alhaarth(IRE) —Abime (USA) (Woodman (USA))
2261[6] (2678) (4335) 4984[5] 6758[2] ◆

Vineyard Haven (USA) *Robert Frankel* a116
2 gr c Lido Palace(CHI) —Princess Aloha (USA) (Aloha Prospector (USA))
(6501a)

Vintage (IRE) *J Akehurst* a87 66
4 b g Danetime(IRE) —Katherine Gorge (USA) (Hansel (USA))
(1541) 1928[7] 2615[10] 2947[5] 3587[2] 4307[2] 4944[2] (5433) 5936[5] 6624[2] ◆

Vintage Quest *D Burchell* a47 45
6 b m Diktat—Sadly Sober (IRE) (Roi Danzig (USA))
147[4] 249[2] 400[6] 579[6] 770[12] 7776[11]

Vintage Steps (IRE) *R A Fahey* 75
2 b f Bahamian Bounty—Red Melodica (USA) (Red Ransom (USA))
(1390) 3625[9]

Viola Rosa (IRE) *D Shaw* a42 35
3 b f Fraam—Bleu Cerise (Sadler's Wells (USA))
12[8]

Violent Velocity (IRE) *J J Quinn* a71 85
5 b g Namid—Lear's Crown (USA) (Lear Fan (USA))
990[10] 1450[3] 1900[2] 2087[2] 2400[2] 2778[4] 3108[4] 3443[3] (3591) 3972[2] 4440[4] 4661[4] 4876[4] 5717[4] 6052[4] 6482[14] 6813[10] 7175[8]

Violet's Pride *N Tinkler* a51 54
4 b m Kyllachy—Majalis (Mujadil (USA))
2088[8] 2159[7] 2491[5] 3231[8] 3953[2] 4285[11] 4703[8] 5074[7]

Violon Sacre (USA) *J-C Rouget* 100
3 b c Stravinsky(USA) —Histoire Sainte (FR) (Kendor (FR))
4719a[6]

Viper *R Hollinshead* 96
6 b g Polar Prince(IRE) —Maradata (IRE) (Shardari)
(6413) (7110)

Virana (IRE) *A De Royer-Dupre* 95
3 b f King's Best(USA) —Vereva (IRE) (Kahyasi)
6567a[7]

Virginias Best *M Botti* a48
3 b f King's Best(USA) —La Virginia (GER) (Surumu (GER))
3318[8]

Virginia's Choice *Jane Chapple-Hyam* 63
2 b f Big Shuffle(USA) —Never Enough (GER) (Monsun (GER))
4598[5] 5048[12] 5640[6] 6343[5]

Virtual *J H M Gosden* 117
3 b c Pivotal—Virtuous (Exit To Nowhere (USA))
(1403) 2544[3] 3155[17] (5896) (6664a) (7147)

Virtuality (USA) *B Smart* 60
3 bb f Elusive Quality(USA) —Hold To Ransom (USA) (Red Ransom (USA))
1817[6] 2008[10] 3438[2] 3960[5] 5561[8]

Viscaya (IRE) *Mrs A Duffield* 57
3 b f Xaar—Fearfully Grand (Grand Lodge (USA))
3640[2] 5380[7]

Visconte (GER) *J Pearce* a42
3 b g Law Society(USA) —Vicenca (USA) (Sky Classic (CAN))
674[6] 823[4]

Viscountess (IRE) *M Johnston* a67 76
3 b f Green Desert(USA) —Maria Isabella (USA) (Kris)
1050[2] 1302[5] 2282[3] (4989) 5267[7] 5504[8]

Viscount Monty *N Tinkler* 39
3 b g Sugarfoot—Desert Loch (IRE) (Desert King (IRE))
1397[8] 1626[11] 2221[15]

Viscount Rossini *S Gollings* a50 50
6 bb g Rossini(USA) —Spain (Polar Falcon (USA))
1062[7] 1643[5] 2100[8] 2770[4] 3182[6] 3820[3] 3965[6] 5593[6] 5869[8]

Visionaire (USA) *Michael Matz* a114
3 ch c Grand Slam(USA) —Scarlet Tango (USA) (French Deputy (USA))
1820a[12]

Vision D'Etat (FR) *E Libaud* 124
3 b c Chichicastenango(FR) —Uberaba (FR) (Garde Royale)
(2654a) (5953a) 6522a[5]

Visionist (IRE) *M Al Muhairi* a103 98
6 b g Orpen(USA) —Lady Taufan (IRE) (Taufan (USA))
294a[3]

Visions Of Johanna (USA) *J Noseda* a88 82
3 b c Johannesburg(USA) —Belle Turquoise (FR) (Tel Quel (FR))
1854[2] 2834[2] (4349) 5051[4] 7556[5] ◆

Visit *Sir Michael Stoute* 114
3 b f Oasis Dream—Arrive (Kahyasi)
3742[2] (4590) 6475[3] 6968a[4]

Visite Royale (USA) *Sir Michael Stoute* a66
2 b f Danehill Dancer(IRE) —Fantasy Royale (USA) (Pleasant Colony (USA))
7312[4]

Visit Wexford (IRE) *John E Kiely* 69
7 b g Entrepreneur—Elida (IRE) (Royal Academy (USA))
4003a[19] 4493a[14]

Visterre (IRE) *B Smart* 83
2 ch f Noverre(USA) —Twiggy's Sister (IRE) (Flying Spur (AUS))
2443^{4} 3364^{9} (3547) (4558) ◆ 5306^{3} (6656) 7219^{5}

Vital Link (IRE) *W J Haggas* 14
3 gr g Pivotal—Attachment (USA) (Trempolino (USA))
2199^{15}

Vital Statistics *D R C Elsworth* 102
4 br m Indian Ridge—Emerald Peace (IRE) (Green Desert (USA))
3927^{10} 4198^{5} 4590^{12} 4841^{5} 5644^{3} 6053^{2} 6271^{5} 6782^{5} 6981^{9} 7146^{12}

Vita Mia *P C Haslam* a35 38
2 b f Central Park(IRE) —Ma Vie (Salse (USA))
6480^{9} *7117^{8}*

Vitamina Plus (ITY) *R Giorgetti* 96
4 ch m Cameron(IRE) —Pammukale (IRE) (Tirol)
1659a^{5}

Vitoria (IRE) *M J Wallace* a79 91
2 b f Exceed And Excel(AUS) —Karayb (IRE) (Last Tycoon)
4080^{2} ◆ (4380) 6473^{2}

Vitruvian Man *John M Oxx* 104
2 b c Montjeu(IRE) —Portrait Of A Lady (IRE) (Peintre Celebre (USA))
7029a^{2}

Vitznau (IRE) *R Hannon* a108 105
4 b h Val Royal(FR) —Neat Dish (CAN) (Stalwart (USA))
960^{10} *(1334)* *1767^{5}* ◆ 2789^{4} 3248^{14} 3635^{4} 4587^{6} 4869^{5}

Vivaldi (IRE) *A P O'Brien* 99
3 b c Montjeu(IRE) —Parvenue (FR) (Ezzoud (IRE))
1922^{6}

Viva Macau (FR) *J Moore* 113
5 bb h Sendawar(IRE) —Diyawara (IRE) (Doyoun)
818a^{4} 1666a^{10} 7685a^{12}

Viva Pataca *J Moore* a84 126
6 b g Marju(IRE) —Comic (IRE) (Be My Chief (USA))
1091a^{2} 1666a^{3} 7685a^{4}

Viva Ronaldo (IRE) *R A Fahey* 99
2 b c Xaar—Papaha (FR) (Green Desert (USA))
1924^{2} 2581^{2} (3005) 3876^{4} (5496) ◆ 5827^{6} 6483^{7}

Viva Vettori *D R C Elsworth* a95 79
4 ch h Vettori(IRE) —Cruinn A Bhord (Inchinor)
(1857) 2200^{6} *2711^{9}*

Viva Volta *T D Easterby* a83 84
5 b g Superior Premium—La Volta (Komaite (USA))
1430^{9} 2535^{5} 3443^{6} 4245^{10} 4440^{9} 4875^{6}

Vive Les Rouges *C F Wall* 95
3 b f Acclamation—Bible Box (IRE) (Bin Ajwaad (IRE))
2606^{6} 3273^{9}

Vlasta Weiner *J M Bradley* a59 14
8 b g Magic Ring(IRE) —Armaiti (Sayf El Arab (USA))
211^{9} *327^{12}* *641^{8}* *696^{6}* *871^{7}* *1370^{7}* 3346^{10} 4324^{12}

Vlavianus (CZE) *M Weiss* 61
7 b g Rainbows For Life(CAN) —Vlnka (CZE) (Amyndas)
(604a)

Vodka (JPN) *Katsuhiko Sumii* 121
4 b m Tanino Gimlet(JPN) —Tanino Sister (JPN) (Rousillon (USA))
1090a^{4} 7511a^{3}

Vodka Shot (USA) *M L W Bell* a49
2 bb f Holy Bull(USA) —Absoluta (IRE) (Royal Academy (USA))
7318^{8} *7425^{5}* *7602^{9}* *7699^{7}*

Vogarth *B R Millman* a67 59
4 ch g Arkadian Hero(USA) —Skara Brae (Inchinor)
2491^{12} 3034^{12} 3733^{8} 4428^{4} 5090^{7} 5749^{3} *6208^{9}* *6836^{2}* *7178^{2}* *(7442)* *7698^{9}* *7799^{9}*

Voice Coach (IRE) *Sir Michael Stoute* 99
3 ch c Alhaarth(IRE) —Drama Class (IRE) (Caerleon (USA))
2681^{6} ◆ (3043) ◆ 4867^{7} 6536^{2} 6974^{2}

Voie De Printemps (FR) *D Smaga* 94
2 b f Della Francesca(USA) —Vallee De Joux (FR) (Welkin (CAN))
5300a^{7}

Voila Ici (IRE) *V Caruso* 114
3 gr c Daylami(IRE) —Far Hope (Barathea (IRE))
2028a^{5} 3075a^{2} (6325a)

Voitudon *D Prod'Homme* a82 76
3 b f Lujain(USA) —Muramixa (FR) (Linamix (FR))
687a^{4}

Volaticus (IRE) *A D Brown* a65 59
7 b g Desert Story(IRE) —Haysel (IRE) (Petorius)
3175^{6} 3795^{5} *4031^{3}* 4420^{9}

Vola Vola (IRE) *R Feligioni* 53
4 br m Danehill Dancer(IRE) —Mistress Thames (Sharpo)
1659a^{14}

Voliere *S C Williams* a96 90
5 b m Zafonic(USA) —Warbler (Warning)
678^{7}

Volo Cat (FR) *B Olsen* a70 84
4 ch h Volochine(IRE) —The Cat Eater (FR) (Tagel (USA))
2233a^{9} 5335a^{4} 5958a^{4}

Volochkova (USA) *J R Fanshawe* a68
2 b f War Chant(USA) —Ballerina Princess (USA) (Mr Prospector (USA))
7341^{5} *7561^{2}*

Volo Prince (FR) *J Parize* 55
3 ch g Volochine(IRE) —Princesse Rooney (FR) (Baby Turk)
549a^{6}

Volvoretas Rainbow *P C Haslam* 52
3 ch f Rainbow Quest(USA) —Volvoreta (Suave Dancer (USA))
2536^{6}

Vondova *D A Nolan* 63
6 b m Efisio—Well Proud (IRE) (Sadler's Wells (USA))
3952^{8} 4631^{8} 4967^{7}

Vortex *Miss Gay Kelleway* a111 113
9 b g Danehill(USA) —Roupala (USA) (Vaguely Noble)
62^{3} *204a^{9}* *382a^{6}* 474a^{9} *680^{4}* *904^{7}* 2595^{10} 3197^{17} 3498^{5} 3635^{8} *4089^{4}*

Voulez Vous *E J O'Neill* a58 71
2 b f Bahamian Bounty—Ligne D'Amour (Pursuit Of Love)
1474^{5} 1961^{4} 2534^{6} 3734^{7} *7298^{5}* *7524^{6}*

Vraiment Rouge (FR) *C Laffon-Parias* 95
3 b f Red Ransom(USA) —Red Stella (FR) (Rainbow Quest (USA))
5597a^{9}

Vraona *D Sepulchre* a83 82
3 ch f Fantastic Light(USA) —Laughing Girl (USA) (Woodman (USA))
3018a^{8}

Waahej *J L Dunlop* 63
2 b g Haafhd—Madam Ninette (Mark Of Esteem (IRE))
2972^{5} 4164^{6} 4974^{5}

Waarid *G L Moore* 66
3 b g Alhaarth(IRE) —Nibbs Point (IRE) (Sure Blade (USA))
1628^{8} 2669^{6} 3168^{5} 5169^{8}

Wabbraan (USA) *D M Simcock* a65 59
3 b g Aldebaran(USA) —Madame Modjeska (USA) (Danzig (USA))
2161^{12} *2805^{F}* 4427^{8} 4750^{3} *6757^{2}*

Wabi Sabi (IRE) *B W Hills* a63 61
2 b f Xaar—Taroudannt (IRE) (Danehill (USA))
4359^{4} ◆ *6000^{3}* 6360^{6} 6857^{7}

Wadnagin (IRE) *I A Wood* a67 62
4 b m Princely Heir(IRE) —Band Of Colour (IRE) (Spectrum (IRE))
609^{6} *1209^{8}* 2285^{9} *2806^{7}* *4030^{4}* *4306^{7}* *4862^{7}* *5157^{7}* *5797^{3}* ◆ *6751^{4}*

Waffle (IRE) *J Noseda* 107
2 ch c Kheleyf(USA) —Saphire (College Chapel) (1616) 4588^{7} 4857^{5} 5103^{2} 6644^{2}

Wahan (USA) *C E Brittain* a57 44
2 b c Theatrical—Abrade (USA) (Mr Prospector (USA))
6438^{10} *6731^{12}*

Waheeba *J L Dunlop* 64
2 b f Pivotal—Winsa (USA) (Riverman (USA))
6084^{13} 6559^{13} 6945^{6}

Wahoo Sam (USA) *P D Evans* a68 74
8 ch g Sandpit(BRZ) —Good Reputation (USA) (Gran Zar (MEX))
1520^{15} (2003) 2597^{10} 2642^{8} 2933^{3} (3360) 3431^{14} *4268^{3}* *4529^{3}* *4862^{4}* 4895^{10} *5478^{13}* *5708^{12}* *5799^{13}* *7790^{5}*

Waikato (NZ) *L Laxon* 116
5 b g Pins(AUS) —Skywalker Wilkes (USA) (Skywalker (USA))
2235a^{4} 7683a^{13}

Wait And See (FR) *Robert Collet* 105
3 b f Montjeu(IRE) —Dareen (IRE) (Rahy (USA))
1664a^{2} 2237a^{7} 2877a^{6} *7635a^{9}*

Wait A While (USA) *Todd Pletcher* a115 116
5 rg m Maria's Mon(USA) —Flirtatious (USA) (A.P. Indy (USA))
6968a^{3}

Wait For The Light *Mrs S Leech* a74 84
4 b g Fantastic Light(USA) —Lady In Waiting (Kylian (USA))
4963^{8} *5913^{3}* *6210^{2}* *6662^{9}*

Wait For The Will (USA) *G L Moore* a74 77
12 ch g Seeking The Gold(USA) —You'd Be Surprised (USA) (Blushing Groom (FR))
27^{2} *675^{5}* *886^{3}* *1151^{5}* *(1405)* 1929^{3} 2304^{9} *(2832)*

Wajaha (IRE) *J H M Gosden* a81 61
2 ch f Haafhd—Amanah (USA) (Mr Prospector (USA))
6443^{4} *(6901)*

Wake Me Now (IRE) *R M Beckett* a71 59
2 b f Almutawakel—Shiyra (Darshaan)
4763^{2} *6016^{3}* *6682^{2}*

Wake Up Maggie (IRE) *Julio C Canani* a106 112
5 b m Xaar—Kalagold (IRE) (Magical Strike (USA))
6523a^{5}

Wakita (IRE) *Aidan Anthony Howard* a62 48
5 b m Bold Fact(USA) —Pleasant Outlook (USA) (El Gran Senor (USA))
(7114) *7287^{4}* *7497^{3}*

Waky Love (GER) *Frau Jutta Mayer* 103
4 b m Royal Dragon(USA) —Waky Su (IRE) (Konigsstuhl (GER))
3623a^{4} 4916a^{3} 5596a^{5} 6323a^{3} 6692a^{6}

Waldorf (IRE) *W R Muir* a48
3 b c Sadler's Wells(USA) —Durrah Green (Green Desert (USA))
7757^{7}

Waldvogel (IRE) *A Wohler* 106
4 ch g Polish Precedent(USA) —Wurftaube (GER) (Acatenango (GER))
1237a^{6} 2346a^{2} 5625a^{4} 6517a^{7}

Walhalla (IRE) *M P Tregoning* a29 45
3 b c Sinndar(IRE) —Imitation (Darshaan)
4730^{10} 5182^{8} 5491^{11} (Dead)

Walking In Memphis (IRE) *C P Morlock*
4 b g Golan(IRE) —Delta Blues (IRE) (Digamist (USA))
2832^{13}

Walking Talking *H R A Cecil* a99 99
4 b g Rainbow Quest(USA) —Wooden Doll (USA) (Woodman (USA))
5894^{3} ◆ *6171^{3}*

Wallonia (IRE) *K A Ryan* a63 66
3 b f Barathea(IRE) —Flanders (IRE) (Common Grounds)
(4651) *5378^{6}* *6683^{5}* *7070^{4}* *7441^{11}*

Wall To Wall (IRE) *Patrick Carey* a41 50
5 b m Orpen(USA) —La Soeur D'Albert (Puissance)
640^{12}

Walragnek *J G M O'Shea* a59 53
4 gr g Mind Games—Eastern Lyric (Petong)
598^{5} *928^{5}* *1162^{2}* *1259^{2}* 2240^{4} 2991^{10} 3600^{5} *4388^{5}* 4812^{9} 5101^{15} *7231^{6}* *7774^{10}*

Walton House (USA) *A M Balding* a41
3 ch g Mutakddim(USA) —Dominant Dancer (Primo Dominie)
1351^{1} *447^{4}*

Waltzing Buddy *P T Midgley* 40
2 ch f Reel Buddy(USA) —Waltzing Star (IRE) (Danehill (USA))
3049^{9}

Walzertraum (USA) *J Hirschberger* 101
3 b c Rahy(USA) —Walzerkoenigin (USA) (Kingmambo (USA))
(2880a) 3773a^{15} 5624a^{4} 6461a^{3}

Wanderin Boy (USA) *Nicholas Zito* a121
7 ch h Seeking The Gold(USA) —Vid Kid (CAN) (Pleasant Colony (USA))
5558a^{3} *6373a^{2}*

Wandle *T G Mills* a89 85
4 b h Galileo(IRE) —Artistic Blue (USA) (Diesis)
6984^{8}

Wannabe Free *J Noseda* a74 70
3 b f Red Ransom(USA) —Wannabe Grand (IRE) (Danehill (USA))
225^{2} *632^{4}* *(823)*

Wannabe King *D R Lanigan* 80
2 b c King's Best(USA) —Wannabe Grand (IRE) (Danehill (USA))
3219^{5} (4062)

Wannarock (IRE) *M C Chapman* a17 72
3 bb g Rock Of Gibraltar(IRE) —Propensity (Habitat)
1527^{8} 7201^{5} *7321^{10}*

Wanted (GER) *B R Millman* a46 51
2 b f Ransom O'War(USA) —Wassiliki (IRE) (Night Shift (USA))
4251^{12} 5650^{4} *6167^{13}*

Waqaarr *Lady Herries* a67 60
4 b g Tobougg(IRE) —Seeking Utopia (Wolfhound (USA))
150^{4} *326^{2}* *537^{3}* *938^{6}* 1932^{16}

War And Peace (IRE) *Jane Chapple-Hyam* a77 77
4 b g Danehill(USA) —Pipalong (IRE) (Pips Pride)
5160^{2} 5634^{2} *6020^{8}* 6340^{11} *7811^{3}*

War Anthem *J R Boyle* a71 69
4 br g Vettori(IRE) —Lucy Boo (Singspiel (IRE))
4930^{11} 5603^{6} *(6909)* *7183^{11}* *7462^{7}* *7715^{P}*

War Artist (AUS) *J M P Eustace* a116 120
5 b g Orpen(USA) —Royal Solitaire (AUS) (Brocco (USA))
832^{2} ◆ 1420^{6} ◆ 2106^{2} 3247^{2} 3922^{3}

Warden Fizz *D R C Elsworth* a34 73
3 b g Efisio—Miss Rimex (IRE) (Ezzoud (IRE))
1581^{6} 3502^{6} 4194^{2} 4566^{6} 4989^{5} 6192^{12} *6433^{8}*

Wardy's Wonder (IRE) *P D Evans* a41 69
3 ch f Choisir(AUS) —Beucaire (IRE) (Entrepreneur)
7536^{12} *7582^{8}*

War Echo (USA) *Steven Asmussen* a99
2 ch f Tapit(USA) —Wild Vision (USA) (Wild Again (USA))
6500a^{4}

War Feather *G C Bravery* a55 19
6 b g Selkirk(USA) —Sit Alkul (USA) (Mr Prospector (USA))
8^{10} *269^{12}* *303^{9}* *415^{8}* 5148^{16}

Warming Up (IRE) *C E Brittain* a67 64
3 b c Kalanisi(IRE) —Sound Asleep (USA) (Woodman (USA))
(940) *1244^{5}* 2045^{7}

War Monger (USA) *William Mott* 113
4 b h War Chant(USA) —Carnival Delight (USA) (Half A Year (USA))
6504a^{3} 6996a^{7}

Warm Tribute (USA) *A G Foster* 56
4 ch g Royal Anthem(USA) —Gentle Mind (USA) (Seattle Slew (USA))
2246^{7} 3200^{5} 3638^{12} 5561^{7}

War Native (IRE) *J Noseda* a97 83
2 b c Cape Cross(IRE) —Walkamia (FR) (Linamix (FR))
(4598) *(5143)* 5889^{7}

Warners Bay (IRE) *R Bastiman* a38 60
3 b g Iron Mask(USA) —Romangoddess (IRE) (Rhoman Rule (USA))
3298^{8} 3834^{12}

War Officer (USA) *J-C Rouget* a107 111
3 bb c Grand Slam(USA) —Wonder Woman (USA) (Storm Cat (USA))
(1712a) 3119^{8}

War Of The Roses (IRE) *R Brotherton* a94 54
5 b g Singspiel(IRE) —Calvia Rose (Sharpo)
(27) *358^{2}* *630^{2}* *1151^{2}* *1744^{6}* 4331^{7} 5058^{9} *(5999)* *6626^{2}* *7025^{2}* *7595^{6}*

Warringah *Sir Michael Stoute* a62 100
3 b g Galileo(IRE) —Threefold (USA) (Gulch (USA))
1621^{2} 2207^{4} (2977) ◆ 3380^{2} ◆ 5892^{13}

Warrior Conquest *C A Horgan* a49
3 b g Alhaarth(IRE) —Eilean Shona (Suave Dancer (USA))
6378^{6}

Warrior Nation (FR) *G M Lyons* a66 75
2 br g Statue Of Liberty(USA) —Tadawul (USA) (Diesis)
5294a^{18}

Warrior One *J Howard Johnson* 84
2 gr g Act One—River Cara (USA) (Irish River (FR))
4415^{5} (4968) 5895^{4}

Warriors Key (IRE) *S Seemar* a95 97
4 b h Key Of Luck(USA) —Warrior Wings (Indian Ridge)
651a^{7} 818a^{12}

Warsaw (IRE) *M F De Kock* a109 100
3 ch c Danehill Dancer(IRE) —For Evva Silca (Piccolo)
(5347)

Warsaw Waltz *J G Given* 60
3 b f Polish Precedent(USA) —Generous Diana (Generous (IRE))
2468^{5} 2997^{13}

Wartime *J H M Gosden* a64
2 ch g Bertolini(USA) —Follow Flanders (Pursuit Of Love)
5939^{6}

Wasalat (USA) *D W Barker* a68 76
6 b m Bahri(USA) —Saabga (USA) (Woodman (USA))
(340) *526^{5}* *811^{8}*

Wasan *E A L Dunlop* a70 104
3 ch c Pivotal—Solaia (USA) (Miswaki (USA))
(1572) ◆ 1923^{3} (3261) 3877^{7} (5830)

Washington Irving (IRE) *A P O'Brien* 114
3 b c Montjeu(IRE) —Shouk (Shirley Heights)
1233a^{2} 2023a^{2} 2829^{5} 3535a^{11} 5136a^{2} 5892^{6}

Wasp (AUS) *W Jarvis* a92 86
6 bb g Octagonal(NZ) —Establishment (AUS) (Star Watch (AUS))
6478^{6} *(6710)* 7146^{18}

Wassiljew (IRE) *K Schafflutzel* 101
4 b h Zinaad—Wassiliki (IRE) (Night Shift (USA))
423a^{5} 5528a^{4}

Wassily Kandinsky *A P O'Brien* 90
3 b c Montjeu(IRE) —Lady Storm (IRE) (Mujadil (USA))
1922^{8} (Dead)

Watamu (IRE) *P J Makin* a109 111
7 b g Groom Dancer(USA) —Miss Golden Sands (Kris)
1076^{10} *(1212)* ◆ *(1766)* ◆ 2168^{5} 3195^{8} 4504^{3} 5508^{13} 6476^{11}

Watar (IRE) *F Head* a86 115
3 b c Marju(IRE) —Ombrie (Zafonic (USA))
1362a^{3} 3191a^{3} (4959a) 5685a^{3} (6494a) ◆ 7008a^{5}

Watchmaker *Miss Tor Sturgis* a73 62
5 b g Bering—Watchkeeper (IRE) (Rudimentary (USA))
(207) *586^{6}* *747^{3}* *860^{3}* *1039^{8}* 1963^{8} *5630^{11}*

Watch Out *G A Ham* a47 45
4 b g Observatory(USA) —Ballet Fame (USA) (Quest For Fame)
471^{2} *661^{3}*

Watch The Master *B I Case* a60
2 b g Passing Glance—Fine Arts (Cadeaux Genereux)
7402^{5} *7720^{7}*

Watch This Place *K R Burke* a25 27
3 b g Compton Place—Swissmatic (Petong)
1311^{10} 1894^{12} 2268^{10} 2463^{20}

Watch What Happens (FR) *S P C Woods* a81 107
5 bb h Stravinsky(USA) —Eaton Place (IRE) (Zafonic (USA))
815a^{10} *1087a^{11}*

Watercolours (IRE) *G L Moore* 59
3 b f High Chaparral(IRE) —Emerald Waters (Kings Lake (USA))
5463^{8} 5750^{5} 6705^{10} 6883^{7}

Watergate (IRE) *Sir Mark Prescott* a79 84
2 gr g Verglas(IRE) —Moy Water (IRE) (Tirol)
2569^{4} ◆ 2783^{4} (3597) ◆ 4666^{6} *7214^{4}*

Water Hen (IRE) *R Charlton* a65 65
2 b f Diktat—Waterfall One (Nashwan (USA))
5227^{6} 5640^{12} *6622^{8}*

Waterline Twenty (IRE) *P D Evans* a86 78
5 b m Indian Danehill(IRE) —Taisho (IRE) (Namaqualand (USA))
53^{2} *208^{4}* *(302)* *730^{6}* *941^{7}* 996^{2}

Waterloo Corner *R Craggs* a65 58
6 b g Cayman Kai(IRE) —Rasin Luck (Primitive Rising (USA))
128^{3} *368^{6}* 4537^{4} 6786^{13}

Waterloo Dock *M Quinn* a58 50
3 b g Hunting Lion(IRE) —Scenic Air (Hadeer)
23^{2} *98^{2}* 2041^{17} *3397^{10}* *7102^{12}* *7759^{3}*

Watermill (IRE) *Mrs R A Carr* a30 9
5 b g Daylami(IRE) —Brogan's Well (IRE) (Caerleon (USA))
843^{9} *863^{13}*

Water Pistol *M C Chapman* 34
6 b g Double Trigger(IRE) —Water Flower (Environment Friend)
2623^{11}

Waterside (IRE) *S Curran* a108 96
9 ch g Lake Coniston(IRE) —Classic Ring (IRE) (Auction Ring (USA))
(245) *(331)* 6791^{0} *870^{3}*

Waterstown (IRE) *R A Fahey* a37
2 ch g Noverre(USA) —Twany Angel (Double Form)
7168^{7} *7319^{5}*

Water Violet *J R Fanshawe* a58 45
3 b f Dubai Destination(USA) —Spring (Sadler's Wells (USA))
2191^{14} *4342^{7}* 5612^{6} *6436^{6}* (Dead)

Watson's Bay *Miss Tor Sturgis* a71 70
3 b c Royal Applause—Multaka (USA) (Gone West (USA))
7026^{6} *7360^{4}* *7494^{6}*

Wattys The Craic *G Prodromou* a51
4 ch g Erhaab(USA) —La Puce Volante (Grand Lodge (USA))
624^{8} *808^{8}*

Wave Aside *B J Meehan* 100
2 b g Reset(AUS) —Crinkle (IRE) (Distant Relative)
3323^{8} (6077) ◆ 6483^{3}

Wave Hill (IRE) *A Berry* a59 59
3 b g Mujadil(USA) —Bryna (IRE) (Ezzoud (IRE))
924^{9} *1315^{4}* 1740^{10} 2268^{6} *2803^{9}* 5110^{14} 5307^{13}

Wavertree One Off *J Ryan* a48 43
6 b g Diktat—Miss Clarinet (Pharly (FR))
166^{4} *322^{6}* *415^{4}*

Wavertree Princess (IRE) *N P Littmoden* a72 74
3 gr f Invincible Spirit(IRE) —Blushing Queen (IRE) (Desert King (IRE))
1284^{4} 2122^{6} *2506^{7}* *5142^{8}* 5531^{5} 6204^{15} 6765^{12}

Wavertree Warrior (IRE) *N P Littmoden* a92 91
6 br g Indian Lodge(IRE) —Karamana (Habitat)
124^{7} *314^{8}* 2995^{11} *3317^{4}* 3972^{14} *5144^{4}* 6867^{12} *7307^{7}* *7525^{3}*

Wayra (GER) *R Rohne*
2 b f Second Set(IRE) —Western Gold (GER) (Gold And Ivory (USA))
7549a[0]

Wazir (USA) *L Reuterskiold Jr* a86 90
6 bb g Pulpit(USA) —Top Order (USA) (Dayjur (USA))
2233a[11]

Weald *P Bary* 98
3 b c Bering—New Abbey (Sadler's Wells (USA))
3191a[7] 4959a[8]

Weald Park (USA) *R Hannon* 100
2 ch c Cozzene(USA) —Promptly (IRE) (Lead On Time (USA))
2411[2] (3495) 3920[2] 6474[10] 6647[2] 6973[7]

Weatherstaff (USA) *M Johnston* a107 86
2 ch c Elusive Quality(USA) —Secret Garden (IRE) (Danehill (USA))
(4237) ◆ 5693[3] ◆

Webbow (IRE) *T D Easterby* a69 98
6 b g Dr Devious(IRE) —Ower (IRE) (Lomond (USA))
3278[4] 4853[3] 5360[2] 6130[13]

Wedding List *W J Haggas* a82 42
2 ch f Pivotal—Confetti (Groom Dancer (USA))
6885[10] 7333[2] (7458)

Wednesdays Boy (IRE) *P D Niven* a9 61
5 b g Alhaarth(IRE) —Sheen Falls (IRE) (Prince Rupert (FR))
1159[6] 1394[5] 1776[5] 2290[12] 2870[12] 4015[5] (4851) (5420) 5454[5] 6408[4] 7132[4]

Wee Bizzom *A Berry* a44 44
2 b f Makbul—Lone Pine (Sesaro (USA))
3547[7] 4113[5] 4449[6] 4948[4] 5414[6] 5541[5] 6489[7] 7168[6] 7279[6] 7689[4]

Wee Buns *P Burgoyne* a69 59
3 b g Piccolo—Gigetta (IRE) (Brief Truce (USA))
257[5] (403) 582[3] (714) 732[2] 835[3] 924[7] 1060[3] 1216[7] 1670[10]

Wee Charlie Castle (IRE) *G C H Chung* a71 77
5 b g Sinndar(IRE) —Seasonal Blossom (IRE) (Fairy King (USA))
332[2] 541[2] 1148[2] 1639[8] (3113) 3347[2] 3965[2] (4309) 4771[8] 5512[2] 6033[6] 6472[5]

Wee Ellie Coburn *M Mullineaux* a55 51
4 ch m Bold Edge—Wathbat Mtoto (Mtoto)
1116[11] 1825[6] 2053[12] 2491[8] 2966[12] 3473[7] 3947[14]

Wee Giant (USA) *K A Ryan* a74 60
2 ch c Giant's Causeway(USA) —Christmas In Aiken (USA) (Affirmed (USA))
6759[7] (7165)

Weekend Hussler (AUS) *Ross McDonald* 125
4 b g Hussonet(USA) —Weekend Beauty (AUS) (Helissio (FR))
6835a[12]

Wee Sonny (IRE) *Tom Dascombe* a78
2 b c Refuse To Bend(IRE) —Coup De Coeur (IRE) (Kahyasi)
7336[6] 7552[3]

Weet A Surprise *R Hollinshead* a76 69
3 b f Bertolini(USA) —Ticcatoo (IRE) (Dolphin Street (FR))
470[5] 3028[6] 4000[2] 4347[6] 4767[8] 5594[11] 6011[4] ◆ 6232[9] 6840[10]

Weet By Far *R Hollinshead* a63 63
3 b f Bertolini(USA) —Shaiybara (IRE) (Kahyasi)
(141) 656[5]

Weet For Ever (USA) *W M Brisbourne* a56 17
5 bb g High Yield(USA) —Wild Classy Lady (USA) (Wild Again (USA))
39[5] 144[3] 231[3] 352[8] 481[4] 657[6] 4503[12] 4932[9]

Weetfromthechaff *R Hollinshead* a56 61
3 gr g Weet-A-Minute(IRE) —Weet Ees Girl (IRE) (Common Grounds)
81[4] 141[4] 237[4] 339[5] 397[2] 557[4] 634[9] 780[7]

Weet In Nerja *R Hollinshead* a58 26
2 b g Captain Rio—Persian Fortune (Forzando)
4027[6] 4474[4] 4931[3] 5591[11] 6579[13]

Weet Yer Tern (IRE) *W M Brisbourne* a58 36
6 b g Brave Act—Maxime (IRE) (Mac's Imp (USA))
1282[9] 1606[10] 4503[9] 4936[6]

We Have A Dream *W R Muir* a79 84
3 bb c Oasis Dream—Final Shot (Dalsaan)
1110[6] (1277) 1584[2] 1837[5] (2460) (2883) 3324[6] 3999[9] 4408[9] 4864[6] 5403[12] 5962[10] 6340[16]

Welcome Applause (IRE) *M G Quinlan* a57 60
2 b f Acclamation—Waseyla (IRE) (Sri Pekan (USA))
3411[9] 4296[6] 4792[6] 5432[6] 5774[8] 6207[10] 7257[10]

Welcome Approach *J R Weymes* a64 76
5 b g Most Welcome—Lucky Thing (Green Desert (USA))
1908[10] 2270[10] 2596[9] 2892[7] 3255[8] 3546[11] 4013[4] 4246[8] 4462[5] 4561[5] (5152) 6251[5] 6679[6] 6907[5] (7118) 7288[4] 7414[8]

Welcome Cat (USA) *A D Brown* a75 73
4 b g Tale Of The Cat(USA) —Mangano (USA) (Quiet American (USA))
229[6] 1518[9] 2364[9] 3335[10]

Welcome Releaf *P Leech* a63 64
5 ch g Most Welcome—Mint Leaf (IRE) (Sri Pekan (USA))
369[4] 550[7] 790[5] (1259) 1455[3] (1705) 1780[6] 2870[6] 4910[7] 6036[9] 6353[8] 7287[6] 7469[9] 7637[7]

Welcome Return (IRE) *T D Easterby* 73
3 b f Mull Of Kintyre(USA) —Aiaie (Zafonic (USA))
1395[6] 2209[7] 3081[2] 3481[3] 3672[2] 4741[6] 6528[3]

Well Armed (USA) *Eoin Harty* a124 97
5 b g Tiznow(USA) —Well Dressed (USA) (Notebook (USA))
1092a[3] 6995a[3]

We'll Come *M A Jarvis* 100
4 b g Elnadim(USA) —Off The Blocks (Salse (USA))
1982[4] ◆ 3122[14] 4177[2] 4522[3] 4853[6] 6269[3] 6783[13] 7245[4]

Wellesley *W R Swinburn* a65
2 b c Bertolini(USA) —Markova's Dance (Mark Of Esteem (IRE))
7498[6] 7709[5]

Well Informed *E J O'Neill* a59 50
3 b f Averti(IRE) —May Light (Midyan (USA))
1764[8] 2676[15] 3455[9] 5710[2] 6032[5] 6248[2] (6729) 6930[4] 7010[10] 7149[3] 7280[5]

Wellington Square *H Morrison* a86 80
4 b g Millkom—Tempestosa (Northern Tempest (USA))
4695[3] 5463[3] 6280[7] 6949[14] (7256) (7526) 7753[5]

Well Of Echoes *A J McCabe* 60
2 b f Diktat—Seeker (Rainbow Quest (USA))
1987[6] 2821[10] 4109[9] 6214[14]

Wells Lyrical (IRE) *B Smart* 94
3 b c Sadler's Wells(USA) —Lyrical (Shirley Heights)
1628[2] 1814[3] 2336[3] 2675[3] (4116) (6313) (6948) ◆

Well Styled *W J Knight* 4
3 b c Oasis Dream—Summer Fashion (Moorestyle)
1835[10]

Welsh Anthem *W R Muir* 67
2 b f Singspiel(IRE) —Khubza (Green Desert (USA))
6392[4]

Welsh Emperor (IRE) *T P Tate* a89 116
9 b g Emperor Jones(USA) —Simply Times (USA) (Dodge (USA))
1387[2] 1989[7] 2637a[4] 3946[4] (4177) 5095[6] 5586[2] 5893[4] 6496a[5] 6975[2] 7243[5]

Welsh Guard (USA) *G P Enright* 44
5 ch g Silver Hawk(USA) —Royal Devotion (USA) (His Majesty (USA))
166[9]

Welsh Opera *S C Williams* a68 57
3 b f Noverre(USA) —Welsh Diva (Selkirk (USA))
3507[13] 3906[5] 4524[6] 5019[2] 5378[10] 6955[8] 7362[2] 7508[3] 7536[8] 7705[2] 7809[2]

Welsh Passion *D Flood* 13
2 b f Marju(IRE) —Focosa (ITY) (In The Wings)
5812[8] 6135[11] 6273[11]

Welsh Whisper *S A Brookshaw* a47 44
9 b m Overbury(IRE) —Grugiar (Red Sunset)
145[9] 251[7] 579[8]

Wendy Craig *J Balding*
3 ch f Arkadian Hero(USA) —Millie's Lady (IRE) (Common Grounds)
3180[10] 3640[10] 4388[12]

We'Re Delighted *T D Walford* a55 77
3 b g Tobougg(IRE) —Samadilla (IRE) (Mujadil (USA))
(2366) 2674[8] 3263[9] 4174[6] 4650[8] 5964[5] 6186[2] 6385[8]

Wessex (USA) *P A Blockley* a97 88
8 ch g Gone West(USA) —Satin Velvet (USA) (El Gran Senor (USA))
233[7] 280[2] ◆ 442[9] 791[3] 833[7]

West Act *A & G Botti* 93
3 ro f Act One—West One (Gone West (USA))
2439a[5]

West End Lad *S R Bowring* a72 71
5 b g Tomba—Cliburnel News (IRE) (Horage)
39[7] 239[3] 369[2] (844) 1679[10] 2703[5] 3175[2] 3738[7] (3964) 4650[4] 4785[7] (5303) 5779[3] 6186[5] 6889[3] 7284[2] 7532[3]

Wester Lodge (IRE) *J M P Eustace* a59 77
6 ch g Fraam—Reamzafonic (Grand Lodge (USA))
7787[5]

Western Art (USA) *P W Chapple-Hyam* 99
3 bb g Hennessy(USA) —Madam West (USA) (Gone West (USA))
2409[8]

Western Roots *A M Balding* a74 73
7 ch g Dr Fong(USA) —Chrysalis (Soviet Star (USA))
44[4] 128[4] 234[7] 330[9] 611[5] 753[6] (1282) 1673[4] (2073) 2978[2] (3518) 4254[3] (4664) 5312[3] 5512[7] 6450[11]

Wester Ross (IRE) *J M P Eustace* 75
4 b g Fruits Of Love(USA) —Diabaig (Precocious)
1365[9] 1963[10] 2482[4] 3518[3] 4276[6] 5058[4] 5465[3] 5934[5] 6403[3]

West Leake (IRE) *B W Hills* a58 58
2 b g Acclamation—Kilshanny (Groom Dancer (USA))
3798[11] 4024[6] 4474[2] 4956[10] 6223[2] 7016[6] 7451[3]

West Lorne (USA) *E J O'Neill* a59 44
3 b f Gone West(USA) —Meniatarra (USA) (Zilzal (USA))
343[2] 483[3] 885[11] 1540[7] 2041[11] 5537[5] 5868[4] 6044[4] 6768[5]

Westphalia (IRE) *A P O'Brien* 112
2 b c Danehill Dancer(IRE) —Pharapache (USA) (Lyphard (USA))
(3509a) 4005a[2] (4804a) 5296a[7] (5889) 6998a[2]

Westport *K A Ryan* a83 85
5 b g Xaar—Connemara (IRE) (Mujadil (USA))
210[2] 574[4] 992[17] 1409[4] 1969[2] 3615[2] 4117[7] 4849[7] 5400[5] 6448[6]

West Side Bernie (USA) *Kelly Breen* a111
2 bb c Bernstein(USA) —Time Honored (USA) (Gilded Time (USA))
6997a[6]

West Virginia (USA) *S Seemar* a70 104
7 bb h Tomorrows Cat(USA) —Wild And Wonderful (USA) (Kennedy Road (USA))
476a[12] 667a[5]

West Wind *Saeed Bin Suroor* 116
4 ch m Machiavellian(USA) —Red Slippers (USA) (Nureyev (USA))
1091a[15]

West With The Wind *T P Tate* a83 88
3 b c Fasliyev(USA) —Midnight Angel (GER) (Acatenango (GER))
2119[2] ◆ 2840[5] 3633[6] 6126[3] 6948[16] 7174[2] (7446)

West With The Wind (USA) *P W Chapple-Hyam* a68 75
2 b f Gone West(USA) —Opera Aida (IRE) (Sadler's Wells (USA))
6030[7] 6559[3] 7095[11]

Westwood *D Haydn Jones* a74 89
3 ch g Captain Rio—Consignia (IRE) (Definite Article)
2410[13] 3041[9] 3324[9] 4983[8] 5962[7] 6554[3] 6952[11] 7448[12] 7534[2] 7615[2]

Westwood Dawn *D Shaw* a59
3 gr g Clodovil(IRE) —Ivory Dawn (Batshoof)
112[5] 1743[11] 3686[5] 4056[4] 4413[9] 5015[2] 5421[5] 5592[3] 7648[2] 7808[9]

Wetherby Place (IRE) *R M Beckett* 56
2 ch f King's Best(USA) —Summer Sunset (IRE) (Grand Lodge (USA))
4643[15] 5459[7]

Weybridge Light *Eoin Griffin* a76 57
3 b g Fantastic Light(USA) —Nuryana (Nureyev (USA))
(7296) (7545) 7639[2] 7715[4]

Whaston (IRE) *J D Bethell* a58 58
3 b g Hawk Wing(USA) —Sharafanya (IRE) (Zafonic (USA))
141[2] 321[2] 785[6] 1592[8] 2367[8] 3737[6] (4241) 4533[7] 5378[4] 6227[12]

What A Day *J J Quinn* 71
2 b g Daylami(IRE) —Sensation (Soviet Star (USA))
4780[7] 5364[10] 6014[2] 6381[5]

What A Fella *Mrs A Duffield* 67
2 b c Lujain(USA) —Fred's Dream (Cadeaux Genereux)
2657[2] 3365[5] 4014[3] 4113[4] 5306[6] 6350[13] 6807[7]

Whatalotofbuts *B De Haan* a45 40
3 ch g Kirkwall—Wontcostalotbut (Nicholas Bill)
727[9] 1549[8] 1938[7] 2719[12]

Whatami *E A L Dunlop* 56
2 bg f Daylami(IRE) —Wosaita (Generous (IRE))
6759[6]

What Budget *A Lund* a77 65
4 br m Halling(USA) —Baked Alaska (Green Desert (USA))
5336a[5]

What Do You Know *A M Hales* a82 87
5 b g Compton Place—How Do I Know (Petong)
94[4] 187[5] 676[8] 1047[3] (1646) (2166) 2583[8] 3945[8] 5250[9] 5861[13] 6881[6]

What Katie Did (IRE) *J M Bradley* a78 68
3 b g Invincible Spirit(IRE) —Chatterberry (Aragon)
(1110) 1934[6] 2998[11] 3136[8] 3733[5] 4028[11] 6448[3] 6878[5] 7254[6] 7416[3] 7522[4] 7745[4]

What's For Tea *P Butler* a67 53
3 b f Beat All(USA) —Come To Tea (IRE) (Be My Guest (USA))
257[2] (424) (589) 737[5] 1115[4] 1412[8] 1937[2] 2559[5] 4181[7] 4664[15] 5086[9] 7506[11]

Whatsthescript (IRE) *John W Sadler* a97 116
4 b h Royal Applause—Grizel (Lion Cavern (USA))
6996a[3]

What's Up Doc (IRE) *Mrs T J Hill* a82 79
7 b g Dr Massini(IRE) —Surprise Treat (IRE) (Shalford (IRE))
4576a[17] (5577) 6663[5]

What's Up Pussycat (IRE) *David Wachman* 96
2 b f Danehill Dancer(IRE) —Sangita (Royal Academy (USA))
3466a[3] 5294a[3] 6318a[4] 7029a[5]

Whatyouwoodwishfor (USA) *R A Fahey* a74 72
2 ch c Forestry(USA) —Wishful Splendor (USA) (Smart Strike (CAN))
2134[5] 2584[8] 3049[7] 6525[2] (7335) 7426[5]

Whaxaar (IRE) *R Ingram* a68 68
5 b g Xaar—Sheriyna (FR) (Darshaan)
91[6] (273) 881[10] 1181[5] 1459[3] (1726) 2567[3] 3137[14] 5367[9] 5676[6] 5917[4] 6421[3]

Whazzis *D Selvaratnam* a80 107
4 br m Desert Prince(IRE) —Wosaita (Generous (IRE))
475a[5] 672a[7]

Wheelavit (IRE) *B G Powell* a64 71
5 b g Elnadim(USA) —Storm River (USA) (Riverman (USA))
970[5] 1210[3] 1256[4]

When Doves Cry *B W Hills* a53 61
2 b f Grandera(IRE) —Deeply (IRE) (Darshaan)
3669[6] 4328[4] 7397[9]

Whenever *R T Phillips* 89
4 ch g Medicean—Alessandra (Generous (IRE))
3044[2] 3942[5] ◆ 4866[4] 6272[8] 6817[23]

Whenineedyou *I A Wood* a42 5
3 ch f Best Of The Bests(IRE) —Party Turn (Pivotal)
645[8] 903[12] 2704[11] 3359[11] 4052[14]

Whentodream *M Botti* a65
3 b c Where Or When(IRE) —Snow Shoes (Sri Pekan (USA))
6757[3]

When Yer Ready (IRE) *T D Easterby* 61
3 b g Val Royal(FR) —Rachel Green (IRE) (Case Law)
1750[3] 2041[8] 2785[12]

Where's Dids *M R Channon* 42
3 b f Piccolo—Who Goes There (Wolfhound (USA))
1835[6] 2341[11] 2620[14] 3030[9] 3406[4]

Where's Killoran *Peter Grayson* a45
3 b f Iron Mask(USA) —Calypso Lady (IRE) (Priolo (USA))
92[3] 306[8]

Where's Reiley (USA) *T D Barron* 69
2 bb g Doneraile Court(USA) —Plateau (USA) (Seeking The Gold (USA))
1821[2] ◆ 2186[8]

Where's Susie *D K Ivory* a60 66
3 ch f Where Or When(IRE) —Linda's Schoolgirl (IRE) (Grand Lodge (USA))
1525[4] 1876[4] 2678[12] 3845[9] 4524[7] 6868[8]

Where To Now *Mrs C A Dunnett* a25 29
3 b f Where Or When(IRE) —Starminda (Zamindar (USA))
3161[13] 5320[6]

Where With All (IRE) *E Charpy* 98
6 b g Montjeu(IRE) —Zelding (IRE) (Warning)
296a[6]

Where You Will *S W Hall* a42 55
2 ch f Where Or When(IRE) —Red Duchess (Halling (USA))
6923[4] 7602[8]

Wherry (USA) *M A Jarvis* a64
3 b f Cherokee Run(USA) —Whist (Mr Prospector (USA))
146[6] 311[3]

Whinhill House *D W Barker* a69 72
8 ch g Paris House—Darussalam (Tina's Pet)
1309[8] 1893[3] 2248[6] 2356[4] 3080[2] (3212) 3759[4] (4294) 5398[7]

Whipma Whopma Gate (IRE) *D Carroll* 49
3 b f Rossini(USA) —The Gibson Girl (IRE) (Norwich)
2221[5] 4166[9] 4461[7] 6015[11]

Whiskey Creek *C A Dwyer* a63 56
3 ch g Tipsy Creek(USA) —Judiam (Primo Dominie)
5911[7] 6334[5] 6679[3] 6890[6] 7022[2] (7705) 7746[5]

Whiskey Junction *A M Balding* a94 88
4 b g Bold Edge—Victoria Mill (Free State)
1529[5] (2240) (2773) (3374) (3587) 4240[13] 5206[8] 5990[5]

Whisky Galore *C G Cox* 72
2 ch c Kyllachy—Owdbetts (IRE) (High Estate)
6026[6] 6604[6] 6893[3]

Whisky Jack *W R Muir* a70 70
2 b g Bahamian Bounty—Dress Design (IRE) (Brief Truce (USA))
3798[2] ◆ 4176[10] 5277[8] 5960[7] 6341[3] 6535[3] 6879[2] 7191[4]

Whispering Angel *B J Meehan* 97
2 b c Hawk Wing(USA) —Savignano (Polish Precedent (USA))
3853[3] ◆ (4150) ◆ 5093[4] 6648[4]

Whispering Death *J Howard Johnson* a92 94
6 br g Pivotal—Lucky Arrow (Indian Ridge)
2939[5] 3490[16] 4439[7]

Whispering Desert *P T Midgley* a48 63
3 b f Distant Music(USA) —Nullarbor (Green Desert (USA))
2171[11] 2660[14] 4686[12]

Whispering Spirit (IRE) *Mrs A Duffield* a58 64
2 b f Catcher In The Rye(IRE) —Celtic Guest (IRE) (Be My Guest (USA))
3714[2] 5384[3] 6089[4] 6362[13]

Whistful Miss *P Howling* a44 31
3 b f First Trump—Mise En Scene (Lugana Beach)
425[5] 462[5]

Whistledownwind *J Noseda* a106 106
3 b c Danehill Dancer(IRE) —Mountain Ash (Dominion)
1632[2] 2303[4] 5892[12] 6444[10] 7146[8] 7594[3] ◆

Whistleupthewind *J M P Eustace* a26 60
5 b m Piccolo—The Frog Queen (Bin Ajwaad (IRE))
2550[11] 7316[9] 7497[12]

Whiston Pat *S R Bowring* a23
3 ch g Lomitas—Fille De Bucheron (USA) (Woodman (USA))
7631[8]

Whitbarrow (IRE) *B R Millman* a81 90
9 b g Royal Abjar(USA) —Danccini (IRE) (Dancing Dissident (USA))
1415[8] 2293[4] 2692[6] 4058[2] 4478[5] 6137[5] 6420[5] 7153[2] 7286[3] 7510[9]

Whitcombe Flyer (USA) *Miss M E Rowland* a54 47
3 bb g Fusaichi Pegasus(USA) —Bakewell Tart (IRE) (Tagula (IRE))
222[4] 298[3] 557[5] 583[3] 767[8] 845[2] 950[5] 1135[4] 1416[10] 1487[6]

Whitcombe Minister (USA) *Jamie Poulton* a96 98
3 b c Deputy Minister(CAN) —Pronghorn (USA) (Gulch (USA))
902[2] ◆ 1632[8] 2194[5] 2600[4] 3156[12] 3880[7] 5941[7] 6649[5] 6784[7]

Whitcombe Spirit *Jamie Poulton* a65 40
3 b c Diktat—L'Evangile (Danehill (USA))
464[3] 940[4]

Whiteball Wonder (IRE) *M Halford* a61 65
2 b g Tagula(IRE) —Notanother (Inchinor)
6320a[10]

White Bear (FR) *C R Dore* a72 72
6 ch g Gold Away(IRE) —Danaide (FR) (Polish Precedent (USA))
356[6] 508[2] 537[8] 686[8]

White Deer (USA) *D Nicholls* a83 101
4 b g Stravinsky(USA) —Brookshield Baby (IRE) (Sadler's Wells (USA))
958[11] 1218[8] 1481[6] 1816[9] 2969[7] 4627[2] 5221[5] 5717[5] 6314[5] 6490[3] 6841[6]

White Elephant *W Storey* 10
4 gr g Daylami(IRE) —Never A Doubt (Night Shift (USA))
1894[13] 2283[13] 2747[9]

White Ledger (IRE) *R E Peacock* a55 50
9 ch g Ali-Royal(IRE) —Boranwood (IRE) (Exhibitioner)
46[10] 363[2] 641[9] 857[2] 1028[7] 2010[5] 2869[10] 3405[10]

White Lightening (IRE) *J Wade* 72
5 ch g Indian Ridge—Mille Miglia (IRE) (Caerleon (USA))
3810[7]

White Lightning (GER) *U Stech* 100
6 gr h Sternkoenig(IRE) —Whispering Grass (GER) (Konigsstuhl (GER))
1237a[3] 6461a[4] 6992a[2]

White Moss (IRE) *M H Tompkins* a60 67
4 b m Peintre Celebre(USA) —Saint Ann (USA) (Geiger Counter (USA))
4902[2] (5262)

Whiteoak Lady (IRE) *J L Spearing* 76
3 ch f Medecis—French Toast (IRE) (Last Tycoon)
1277[6] 1781[5] 2452[3] 3893[3] (4782) 4988[4] 5714[3] 6124[7]

White Rose (ITY) *M Bucci* a95 93
4 ch m Handsome Ridge—Pursuit Of Rose (FR) (Pursuit Of Love)
1659a[7]

White Rose George *J O'Reilly*
3 b g Primo Valentino(IRE) —Amber's Bluff (Mind Games)
1519[14] 2269[11] *7178[11]*

White Ross (IRE) *Neill McCluskey* a38 47
3 ch f Rossini(USA) —White-Wash (Final Straw)
4972[8]

White Shift (IRE) *P D Evans* a87 88
2 b f Night Shift(USA) —Ivy Queen (IRE) (Green Desert (USA))
(1722) ◆ 1914[3] (2254) 2497[9] 3123[12] 3528[2] 3681[6] *5693[11]* 6483[14]

White Snow (IRE) *G Miliani* 100
4 b m Orpen(USA) —Trop Chere (IRE) (Distinctly North (USA))
(7253a)

White Spire (FR) *F Rohaut* a90 90
3 b f Septieme Ciel(USA) —White Love (FR) (Northern Crystal)
6743a[2]

White's Ruby *G D Blake* a52 47
4 gr m Iron Mask(USA) —Negligee (Night Shift (USA))
858[12] 1259[6]

Whittinghamvillage *Mrs H O Graham* 58
7 b m Whittingham(IRE) —Shaa Spin (Shaadi (USA))
3201[11] 3450[13] 4142[8] 4540[14]

Who Art Thou (USA) *P A Blockley* 52
2 bb g More Than Ready(USA) —Silk Sails (USA) (Ocean Crest (USA))
2972[14] 3997[6] 4430[4] 6058[10]

Whodouthinkur (IRE) *Mrs C A Dunnett* a24 49
3 b g Beckett(IRE) —Scarletta (USA) (Red Ransom (USA))
950[7] 1193[9] 3115[6] 3572[7] 4066[7]

Whodunit (UAE) *P W Hiatt* a56 47
4 b g Mark Of Esteem(IRE) —Mystery Play (IRE) (Sadler's Wells (USA))
6956[6] 7261[6] 7559[9] (7605) 7702[7]

Who Needs A Hand (IRE) *Patrick J Flynn* a37 49
3 b g Lend A Hand—Carols Choice (Emarati (USA))
4715a[10]

Whos Counting *R J Hodges* a43
4 ch m Woodborough(USA) —Hard To Follow (Dilum (USA))
401[8] 691[10]

Who's Shirl *C W Fairhurst* 41
2 b f Shinko Forest(IRE) —Shirl (Shirley Heights)
4897[9] 6212[6] 6524[14]

Who's This (IRE) *W R Swinburn* a78 83
4 b g Xaar—Tarafiya (USA) (Trempolino (USA))
(4085) ◆ 4894[6] *5908[6] 6170[10]*

Who's Winning (IRE) *B G Powell* a60 86
7 ch g Docksider(USA) —Quintellina (Robellino (USA))
2798[9] 3363[9] (3446) 3761[5] 4102[4] 4273[11] (4808) 5166[7] 5533[7] 5601[9] 6024[7] 6334[8] *6681[2] 7013[4] 7255[3] 7359[10]*

Whozart (IRE) *A Dickman* a54 63
5 b g Mozart(IRE) —Hertford Castle (Reference Point)
1827[12] *2706[2] 2869[3]* 3112[14] 3340[3] 3638[8] 4073[3] 4294[3] 4653[13] 5044[4] 5452[2] 5770[2] 6382[7] (6546) 7176[5]

Why Be (AUS) *L Laxon* 109
6 b g Success Express(USA) —Charybdis (AUS) (Royal Academy (USA))
2235a[11]

Why Nee Amy *Miss Gay Kelleway* a65 47
2 ch f Tipsy Creek(USA) —Ashleen (Chilibang)
2979[6] *7179[8] 7402[2] 7823[4]*

Wibbadune (IRE) *D Shaw* a82 80
4 ch m Daggers Drawn(USA) —Becada (GER) (Cadeaux Genereux)
86[9] 307[4] 479[5] (883) 1021[5] 1706[2] (2088) (2616) (2836) 3042[2] 3931[6] 4631[4] *5046[11]* 5796[19] 6388[12] 6658[2] (6881) 7066[6]

Wicked Daze (IRE) *Ian Williams* a95 96
5 ch g Generous(IRE) —Thrilling Day (Groom Dancer (USA))
(1) (96) ◆ *410[2] (630)* (4362) 5229[20] 6817[20] 7244[20]

Wickedish *M J Gingell* a49 55
4 b m Medicean—Sleave Silk (IRE) (Unfuwain (USA))
277[8] 851[5] 3113[12] 3460[6] 3764[9] 3952[12]

Wicked Lady (UAE) *B J McMath* a50 56
5 b m Jade Robbery(USA) —Kinsfolk (Distant Relative)
3874[2] 4774[5] 5321[2]

Wickedly Fast (USA) *George Baker* a49
2 b f Gulch(USA) —Need More Business (IRE) (Alzao (USA))
6709[3] 7164[9]

Wicked Uncle *S Gollings* a73 61
9 b g Distant Relative—The Kings Daughter (Indian King (USA))
49[5] 191[9] 230[3] 1061[3] 1338[3] 1634[7] 1706[5]

Wicked Wilma (IRE) *A Berry* a44 64
4 b m Tagula(IRE) —Wicked (Common Grounds)
1755[6] 2356[9] 2777[4] 2928[13] 3546[2] 3581[6] 4013[6] 4385[9] 4703[4] ◆ 5260[8] 5452[6] (5770) 6039[10] 6218[2] 6405[3] 7043[2] *7182[10]*

Wicklewood *Mrs C A Dunnett*
2 b g Mujahid(USA) —Pinini (Pivotal)
5905[P] 6389[11]

Wicksy Creek *G C H Chung* a25 50
3 b g Tipsy Creek(USA) —Bridal White (Robellino (USA))
1054[11] 1672[10] 2074[5] 3118[8] *3686[9]*

Wi Dud *K A Ryan* 113
4 b h Elnadim(USA) —Hopesay (Warning)
959[3] 1483[5] 2106[14] 3739[4] 4188[7] 5551a[3] 5891[10] 6121[2] 6518a[16]

Wiesenpfad (FR) *W Hickst* 116
5 ch h Waky Nao—Waldbeere (Mark Of Esteem (IRE))
(3306a) 4470a[8] 5528a[3] 6692a[2]

Wigan Pier *M D Squance* a43 58
2 b f Gulch(USA) —Kiralik (Efisio)
1610[6] 2357[7] 3027[4] ◆ 3788[5] 4175[5] 4558[6] *6573[12] 7168[8] 7303[4] 7600[9]*

Wiggy Smith *H Candy* a84 81
9 ch g Master Willie—Monsoon (Royal Palace)
6028[3] ◆ 6346[7] (6721)

Wightgold *H J L Dunlop* a25 46
2 ch f Golden Snake(USA) —Main Brand (Main Reef)
7015[8] *7259[12]*

Wigram's Turn (USA) *A M Balding* a87 87
3 ch g Hussonet(USA) —Stacey's Relic (USA) (Houston (USA))
967[2] 1336[2] ◆ 2104[5] 3850[6] 4983[5] *5697[5]*

Wigwam Willie (IRE) *K A Ryan* 92
6 b g Indian Rocket—Sweet Nature (IRE) (Classic Secret (USA))
1016[4] 1218[3] 1469[11] 1910[12] 2733[3] (3142) 3758[3] 4204[8] 4856[4] 6041[3]

Wikaala (USA) *M P Tregoning* a79 80
3 ch g Diesis—Roseate Tern (Blakeney)
2834[3] (3338) 4621[6] 5309[4] 6130[10] *6683[2] 6936[11]*

Wilbury Star (IRE) *R Hannon* a78 81
2 b c Trans Island—Gold Blended (IRE) (Goldmark (USA))
3444[3] 3760[2] (4296) 4828[7] 5447[6] 6665[2] *7067[5]*

Wilby (IRE) *Mrs C A Dunnett* 19
3 b g Chevalier(IRE) —Solo Symphony (IRE) (Fayruz)
5160[10]

Wild And Innocent (IRE) *J T Gorman* a39 59
2 b c Tagula(IRE) —Alvor Lass (IRE) (Namid)
3509a[18]

Wildbach (IRE) *Miss Sheena West* a27
6 b g Law Society(USA) —Wurfspiel (GER) (Lomitas)
7695[9]

Wild Bill Tracey *M J Wallace* a72 72
3 b g Bahamian Bounty—Travel Secret (Blakeney)
59[3] 279[2] 444[2]

Wild By Nature *P Leech*
3 b f Tipsy Creek(USA) —Kinraddie (Wuzo (USA))
6280[P]

Wildcat Island (IRE) *T D Easterby* a17
3 b f Statue Of Liberty(USA) —Green Green Grass (Green Desert (USA))
616[4] 1019[13] 1754[11]

Wildcat Wizard (USA) *P F I Cole* 98
2 b c Forest Wildcat(USA) —Tip the Scale (USA) (Valiant Nature (USA))
(3049) (3439) 4402[4] 5486a[3] 6401[5]

Wild Desert (FR) *Ian Williams* 89
3 br c Desert Prince(IRE) —Sallivera (IRE) (Sillery (USA))
5070[9] 6078[14]

Wildfahrte (GER) *P Rau*
2 ch f Mark Of Esteem(IRE) —Wurfspiel (GER) (Lomitas)
7006a[3]

Wild Fell Hall (IRE) *A D Brown* a87 81
5 ch g Grand Lodge(USA) —Genoa (Zafonic (USA))
692[9] 1137[9] *1585[8]* 2249[5] 2447[4] 3010[9] 3785[5] *4343[8]*

Wild Pitch *Stef Liddiard* a94 77
7 ch g Piccolo—Western Horizon (USA) (Gone West (USA))
2059[4] *2264[5]* 2667[5] *3160[4]*

Wild Rhubarb *C G Cox* 76
3 ch f Hernando(FR) —Diamant Noir (Sir Harry Lewis (USA))
3894[2] 4821[3] ◆

Wild Savannah *E Charpy* a85 105
6 b h Singspiel(IRE) —Apache Star (Arazi (USA))
739a[9]

Wilford Maverick (IRE) *Garry Moss* a33 28
6 b g Fasliyev(USA) —Lioness (Lion Cavern (USA))
365[12] 1338[8] *1636[6] 2753[12]*

Wilfred Pickles (IRE) *Mrs A J Perrett* 75
2 ch c Cadeaux Genereux—Living Daylights (IRE) (Night Shift (USA))
5314[13] 6122[3] 6359[2]

Wilki (FR) *A De Royer-Dupre* 101
3 b f Oasis Dream—Khumba Mela (IRE) (Hero's Honor (USA))
2034a[6] 2637a[5] 3938a[8]

Willaby Lad *D Shaw* 15
3 b g Celtic Swing—Deerskin (USA) (Diesis)
2786[14] 3338[6] 3813[11]

Will Be (IRE) *B Bo* a84 84
5 bb m In The Wings—Bintalshaati (Kris)
5336a[4]

Will He Wish *S Gollings* a89 87
12 b g Winning Gallery—More To Life (Northern Tempest (USA))
124[3] (218) 259[5] 417[2] 502[3] 6710[12] 7014[3] 7278[6] 7507[6] 7758[7]

Willhewiz *W M Brisbourne* a68 71
8 b g Wizard King—Leave It To Lib (Tender King)
149[9] 2242[11] 2710[9] 3021[8] 3363[12] *3565[6]* 3948[8] *5152[2]* ◆ *(6419) 6679[9]* 6895[11] *7226[8] 7292[3]* 7444[8] 7509[6] 7710[3] 7745[6]

William Blake *M Johnston* a93 93
3 b c Rainbow Quest(USA) —Land Of Dreams (Cadeaux Genereux)
(529) ◆ *(799)* ◆ (1395) 2194[11] 2610[10] 3896[3] 4363[2] 4519[5] 5005[6] *5677[8] 6698[4]* 6984[9]

William Hogarth *A P O'Brien* a74 85
3 b c High Chaparral(IRE) —Mountain Holly (Shirley Heights)
4042a[13]

William's Way *I A Wood* a85 89
6 b g Fraam—Silk Daisy (Barathea (IRE))
3613[11] 4191[10] 5092[6] 5900[8] 6203[8] *6626[11] 6839[7]* 6898[9] *7385[4]* ◆ *7563[3] 7711[10]*

Willie Ever *B Ellison* a76 56
4 b g Agnes World(USA) —Miss Meltemi (IRE) (Miswaki Tern (USA))
251[4] 1602[2] 2491[2] *(3569) (3826) (4390) 5156[10]*

Willin Dillon (IRE) *W Storey* 9
2 b g Dilshaan—Saratoga Splendour (USA) (Diesis)
2671[9] 3225[9] 6109[8]

Willingly (GER) *M Trybuhl* 106
9 b h Second Set(IRE) —Winara (GER) (Konigsstuhl (GER))
3515a[8] 4233a[4] 4916a[5]

Willkandoo (USA) *D M Simcock* a87 78
3 bb g Unbridled's Song(USA) —Shannkara (IRE) (Akarad (FR))
1817[11] 2221[6] 2915[3] (3126) (3407) ◆ 3525[5] 4818[6] (5397) *5910[3]* 6124[3] *(6511a) 6710[5] 7423[3] 7737[3]*

Willoughby Bay (IRE) *P J Prendergast* a73 74
3 b g Invincible Spirit(IRE) —Grand Morning (IRE) (King Of Clubs)
6366a[3]

Willow Dancer (IRE) *W R Swinburn* a84 95
4 ch g Danehill Dancer(IRE) —Willowbridge (IRE) (Entrepreneur)
1383[8] 1932[3] (2642) 3090[2] *3376[2]* (4310) 4694[2] *5695[8]* (6431)

Willridge *Tom Dascombe* a38 72
3 ch g Tumbleweed Ridge—Minnina (IRE) (In The Wings)
3823[7] 4431[3] (5023) 6899[12]

Willyn (IRE) *J S Goldie* a48 63
3 b f Lujain(USA) —Lamasat (USA) (Silver Hawk (USA))
1306[5] 2041[4] 3126[4] 3578[5] 3790[4] 4019[2] 4560[2] 4952[2] 5544 [6] 6042[7]

Willywell (FR) *J-P Gauvin* a99 109
6 br h Jimble(FR) —Basilissa (FR) (Gay Minstrel (FR))
4320a[6] *7643a[6]*

Wilmington *Mrs J C McGregor* a69 60
4 ch g Compton Place—Bahawir Pour (USA) (Green Dancer (USA))
1771[7] 2246[3] 2524[7] 3402[6]

Wiltshire (IRE) *P T Midgley* a65 61
6 br g Spectrum(IRE) —Mary Magdalene (Night Shift (USA))
32[6] 402[5] (625) 718[3] 1189[7] 1641[3] 2040[6] 3079[2] 3638[6] 4327[6] 4653[7]

Winchester (USA) *D K Weld* 118
3 b c Theatrical—Rum Charger (IRE) (Spectrum (IRE))
3193[8] 3535a[7] (4887a) 7000a[7]

Wind Flow *C A Dwyer* a75 58
4 b g Dr Fong(USA) —Spring (Sadler's Wells (USA))
(180) ◆ *248[2] 728[4] 1039[4] 1165[4] (1340) 1768[3] (1933)* 2414[5] *4726[7] 5017[9]* (5913) 6210[4] 6472[8] 6985[9] (7473) 7711[6] (7831)

Windjammer *T D Easterby* a64 76
4 b g Kyllachy—Absolve (USA) (Diesis)
1485[14] 1624[8] 2005[6] 2596[7] (2777) 3080[10] 3171[4] 3594[7] 3787[6] 4291[5] 5398[13] 5719[6] 5970[4] 6218[18] 6486[7] *6711[3]*

Windpfeil (IRE) *J H M Gosden* a58
2 b g Indian Ridge—Flying Kiss (IRE) (Sadler's Wells (USA))
7336[12] 7438[5] 7622[7]

Wind Shuffle (GER) *J S Goldie* 82
5 b g Big Shuffle(USA) —Wiesensturmerin (GER) (Lagunas)
1138[9] 1775[3] 2285[3] 2662[4] 3082[3] (3366) (3716) 3758[4] (4148) (4633) 5564[3] (6108) 6582[4] 7127[4] 7224[2]

Windsor Palace (IRE) *A P O'Brien* a83 98
3 b c Danehill Dancer(IRE) —Simaat (USA) (Mr Prospector (USA))
4518[6] *7235a[6]*

Wind Star *G A Swinbank* 94
5 ch g Piccolo—Starfleet (Inchinor)
2220[11] 2582[8] 3368[3] 3649[2] 4422[5] 4699[5] (5968)

Wine 'n Dine *G L Moore* a86 73
3 b g Rainbow Quest(USA) —Seasonal Splendour (IRE) (Prince Rupert (FR))
1840[8] *7387[2]* ◆ *7539[2] (7704)* ◆

Wingbeat (USA) *Saeed Bin Suroor* 100
3 b c Elusive Quality(USA) —Infinite Spirit (USA) (Maria's Mon (USA))
(2162) ◆ 2594[3]

Wing Collar *T D Easterby* 103
7 b g In The Wings—Riyoom (USA) (Vaguely Noble)
1629[3] 1916[6] 2609[9] 3975[4] 5229[15]

Wing Diva (IRE) *B Smart* a62 51
3 b f Hawk Wing(USA) —Sasimoto (USA) (Saratoga Six (USA))
7084[4] *7721[2]*

Winged D'Argent (IRE) *B J Llewellyn* 87
7 bb g In The Wings—Petite-D-Argent (Noalto)
1472[2] 2628[6] (3414) 3942[10] 5718[8]

Winged Farasi *Miss J E Foster* a58 66
4 b h Desert Style(IRE) —Clara Vale (IRE) (In The Wings)
143[2] 176[7] 521[2] 844[5] 1142[9] 1626[7] *7114[3] 7180[4] 7442[8]*

Winged Flight (USA) *M Johnston* a68 87
4 b g Fusaichi Pegasus(USA) —Tobaranama (IRE) (Sadler's Wells (USA))
274[8]

Winged Harriet (IRE) *W J Haggas* 80
2 bb f Hawk Wing(USA) —Hawala (IRE) (Warning)
6080[2] 6473[4]

Wing Express (IRE) *L M Cumani* 117
4 b h Montjeu(IRE) —Eurobird (Ela-Mana-Mou) (1841)

Wing Home (IRE) *Tom Dascombe* 69
2 ch c Hawk Wing(USA) —Talbiya (IRE) (Mujtahid (USA))
2011[3] ◆ 4907[6]

Wingman (IRE) *G L Moore* a87 85
6 b g In The Wings—Precedence (IRE) (Polish Precedent (USA))
2830[5]

Wing Play (IRE) *H Morrison* a76 76
3 b g Hawk Wing(USA) —Toy Show (IRE) (Danehill (USA))
2665[11] 3421[3] *4303[4]* 4984[9] *6134[11]* 6337[8] *(6936) 7115[2] 7277[2] 7466[6]*

Wingstar (IRE) *Robert Collet* 88
4 b m In The Wings—Thirtysomething (USA) (Thirty Six Red (USA))
7487a[5]

Wingwalker *H R A Cecil* 106
2 b c Dansili—Emplane (USA) (Irish River (FR))
(4826) ◆ (6025) ◆ 6428[5] (Dead)

Winker Watson *P W Chapple-Hyam* 116
3 ch c Piccolo—Bonica (Rousillon (USA))
4010a[7] 4518[4] 5275[8] 6270[5]

Winkle (IRE) *M Delzangles* 102
3 b f High Chaparral(IRE) —Bernique (USA) (Affirmed (USA))
5623a[3] (6921a)

Winners Chant (IRE) *Sir Michael Stoute* a75 60
3 b f Dalakhani(IRE) —Delilah (IRE) (Bluebird (USA))
2717[7] *3688[5] 4342[3]* 4985[10] 5750[7]

Winning Band (IRE) *B J Meehan* 52
2 ch g Dr Fong(USA) —Band (USA) (Northern Dancer (CAN))
6062[7] 6246[6] 6600[6] 6886[7]

Winning Brew (USA) *Francis J Vitale* a84
2 b f Milwaukee Brew(USA) —Winning Kiss (USA) (Grand Slam (USA))
6500a[7]

Winning Show *C Gordon* a69 70
4 b g Muhtarram(USA) —Rose Show (Belmez (USA))
1345[2] *1747[2]* 2243[5] *2533[8]* 4156[6] 4820[4] 6364[11]

Winsome Hearts *M W Easterby* a23 56
2 b g Erhaab(USA) —Boulevard Rouge (USA) (Red Ransom (USA))
3976[6] 4536[4] 4960[6] *5591[12]* 5774[5] 6787[17]

Winter Bloom (USA) *H R A Cecil* a82 87
3 b f Aptitude(USA) —Bionic (Zafonic (USA))
1746[3] 2256[5] 2920[9] 5100[9]

Winterbourne *M Blanshard* 45
2 ch f Cadeaux Genereux—Snowing (Tate Gallery (USA))
2614[8] 5860[6] 6244[7]

Winterbrook King *J R Best* a59 39
2 b g Gleaming(IRE) —Alice Holt (Free State)
5798[8] 6282[9] 6553[9] *7257[2] 7505[11]*

Winter Cruise (IRE) *Ian Williams* a59 20
4 b g Lil's Boy(USA) —Arundhati (IRE) (Royal Academy (USA))
125[10] 533[8] 722[6] 3089[14]

Winter Dream (IRE) *Robert Collet* 101
4 b h Act One—Settler (Darshaan)
1663a[5]

Winterfell *C F Wall* 43
2 b f Haafhd—It Girl (Robellino (USA))
3349[10]

Winter Lane *J R Norton* a2 36
4 b g Hernando(FR) —Winding (USA) (Irish River (FR))
7045[11]

Winter Miss (USA) *J Noseda* a68 14
3 bl f Theatrical—Snowy Range (USA) (Seattle Slew (USA))
5047[3] 5612[8] *7387[7]*

Winthorpe (IRE) *J J Quinn* a71 75
8 b g Tagula(IRE) —Zazu (Cure The Blues (USA))
4[2] 71[6] 347[6] (1015) 1188[6] 1431[8] (2005) 2188[6] 2444[9] 2891[13] 3050[13] 3708[2] 4174[12] 4246[9] 5260[2] 5400[4] 5775[3] 6011[10] (Dead)

Wisdom's Kiss *J D Bethell* a84 71
4 b g Ocean Of Wisdom(USA) —April Magic (Magic Ring (IRE))
537[2] (703) 872[2] 1085[5] 1578[8] *(2259) (2533)* 3591[9] *(4934)* 5156[8] 5965[4] *6663[2]* 7278[10]

Wise Dennis *A P Jarvis* a107 113
6 b g Polar Falcon(USA) —Bowden Rose (Dashing Blade)
474a[3] ◆ (671a) (743a) 4192[8] 5025[7] 6106[9]

Wise Hawk *C J Down* a63 76
3 b g Hawk Wing(USA) —Dombeya (IRE) (Danehill (USA))
1957[4] 3117[2] 3407[8] *4732[5]*

Wise Lee *W J Haggas* a64
3 b g Zilzal(USA) —Ayunli (Chief Singer)
1748[6]

Wiseman's Diamond (USA) *P T Midgley* a68 65
3 b f Wiseman's Ferry(USA) —Aswhatilldois (IRE) (Blues Traveller (IRE))
131[3] 849[4] 1823[2] 3081[3] *3819[5]* 4961[7] *6088[5]* 6585[10]

Wise Melody *W J Haggas* a90 89
3 b f Zamindar(USA) —Swellegant (Midyan (USA))
1999[9] 2428[4] 2896[2] ◆ (3141) 3850[20] 5102[3] ◆ *5403[2]*

Wise Owl *D E Pipe* a90 75
6 b g Danehill(USA) —Mistle Thrush (USA) (Storm Bird (CAN))
3523[6]

Wish You Luck *D R Lanigan* 30
2 b f Dubai Destination(USA) —Noble Lily (USA) (Vaguely Noble)
5643[13]

Witch Of The Wave (IRE) *Miss J S Davis* a46
2 ch f Dr Fong(USA) —Clipper (Salse (USA))
7402[9] 7699[10]

Witchry *A G Newcombe* a25 71
6 gr g Green Desert(USA) —Indian Skimmer (USA) (Storm Bird (CAN))
1872[10] (2478) 2923[4] 3626[4] 5101[5] (5751) 6039[4] 6556[8] *7286[9]*

With Interest *Saeed Bin Suroor* 113
5 b h Selkirk(USA) —With Fascination (USA) (Dayjur (USA))
294a[4] (565a) (739a) 5070[4] 5792[2] 6123[3] (6654) (7145)

Without A Prayer (IRE) *R M Beckett* a108 105
3 ch c Intikhab(USA) —Prayer (IRE) (Rainbow Quest (USA))
1471[8] (2121) 3156[5] 7147[7] *(7643a)*

Without Equal *A Dickman* 21
2 ch f Tobougg(IRE) —Sans Egale (FR) (Lashkari)
3277[10] 3792[8] 4290[8] 4873[12]

Without Excuse (USA) *M Botti* a78 79
4 ch g Woodman(USA) —Dixie Jewel (USA) (Dixieland Band (USA))
196[4] 331[5] 512[2] (750)

Without Precedent (FR) *Y De Nicolay* 91
3 b f Polish Precedent(USA) —Sue Generoos (IRE) (Spectrum (IRE))
3018a[4]

Without Prejudice (USA) *J Noseda* a85 79
3 ch g Johannesburg(USA) —Awesome Strike (USA) (Theatrical)
2427[3] 2966[2] (4638) 6125[12] (6695) 6952[10]

With Touch (USA) *Luis E Seglin*
2 gr f With Approval(CAN) —Miss U Mama (USA) (Minshaanshu Amad (USA))
6613a[12]

Wivny (USA) *P A Blockley* 42
3 b f Yonaguska(USA) —Mostly Sassy (USA) (Green Dancer (USA))
2198[17] 2955[8] 3326[9]

Wizard Looking *D E Cantillon* a69 61
7 b g Wizard King —High Stepping (IRE) (Taufan (USA))
(606) 934[12] 1459[8] (2053) 2290[2] (2884) 3131[5] 3820[4] 4477[5]

Wizard Of Us *M Mullineaux* a53 63
8 b g Wizard King—Sian's Girl (Mystiko (USA))
(377) 720[7] 779[5]

Wizby *Ms Deborah J Evans* a51 54
5 b m Wizard King—Diamond Vanessa (IRE) (Distinctly North (USA))
40[7] 66[6] 120[2] 267[7] 328[7] 400[3] 518[3] 535[2] 621[4] 691[2] 711[4] 3604[2] 4168[7] 5303[11]

Wodhill Be *D Morris* a54 50
8 b m Danzig Connection(USA) —Muarij (Star Appeal)
189[8]

Wodhill Gold *D Morris* a71 46
7 ch g Dancing Spree(USA) —Golden Filigree (Faustus (USA))
7[2] (80) 351[4] (639)

Wodhill Schnaps *D Morris* a69 66
7 b g Danzig Connection(USA) —Muarij (Star Appeal)
42[3] ◆ 193[3] 465[4] 640[2] (1116) (1258) 1590[4] 2087[3] 2510[6] 2837[9] 3653[3] 4428[7] 5161[10] 5478[7]

Wogan's Sister *D R C Elsworth* a65 75
3 b f Lahib(USA) —Dublivia (Midyan (USA))
(873) ◆ 2247[7] 3569[7] 4386[5] (4750) (4991) 5232[3] 5630[7]

Wohaida (IRE) *M R Channon* 74
2 b f Kheleyf(USA) —Cambara (Dancing Brave (USA))
2691[5] 3292[4] (3778) 4640[5] 5242[10]

Wolf Pack *D A Nolan* a23 23
6 b g Green Desert(USA) —Warning Shadows (IRE) (Cadeaux Genereux)
3200[8] 4632[9] 4969[7]

Wolverton (IRE) *N P Littmoden* 5
2 ch c Alhaarth(IRE) —Debbie's Next (USA) (Arctic Tern (USA))
6674[14]

Womaniser (IRE) *T Keddy* a42
4 br g Rock Of Gibraltar(IRE) —Top Table (Shirley Heights)
1311[9] 5020[11] 7310[6]

Won More Night *D J Wintle* 55
6 b m Kayf Tara—Wonderfall (FR) (The Wonder (FR))
5231[7] 5750[8] 6055[17]

Wood Chorus *M L W Bell* a76 97
3 b f Singspiel(IRE) —Woodbeck (Terimon)
1372[2] 1905[2] (2735) 3415[3] 3875[9] 4977[6] 6241[11]

Woodcote (IRE) *P R Chamings* a93 93
6 b g Monashee Mountain(USA) —Tootle (Main Reef)
1346[3] 1802[9] 1985[10] 2326[4] 2773[9] 3062[9] 3587[4] 4025[3] 4693[6] (5046) 5757[4] 5886[5] 6174[6] 6623[6] 7290[8] 7477[6] 7621[8] 7768[4]

Woodcote Place *P R Chamings* a89 93
5 b g Lujain(USA) —Giant Nipper (Nashwan (USA))
3040[10] 3646[2] 3898[5] 4501[13] 4723[12] 5290[3] 5697[2] ◆ 6471[2]

Woodcraft *D McCain Jnr* 84
4 ch g Observatory(USA) —Woodwardia (USA) (El Gran Senor (USA))
5450[11]

Woodcutter (IRE) *J H M Gosden* 90
3 gr c Daylami(IRE) —Cinnamon Rose (USA) (Trempolino (USA))
3094[3] 3854[2] ◆ (4372) 4784[6]

Wooden King (IRE) *P D Evans* a58 56
3 b g Danetime(IRE) —Olympic Rock (IRE) (Ballad Rock)
1548[11] 1558[13] 2922[10] 2991[7] 4163[12] 4207[14] 5045[12] 5162[5] 6173[5] 6562P 6771[6] 7194[13] 7382[10] 7535[3] (7817)

Woodland Mist *M Dods* a48
3 b f Tobougg(IRE) —Aker Wood (Bin Ajwaad (IRE))
698[6] 845[3]

Woodland Violet *I A Wood* a40
2 b f Reset(AUS) —Be My Tinker (Be My Chief (USA))
6709[8]

Woodlark Island (IRE) *M P Tregoning* a70 58
2 b g Tagula(IRE) —Be My Lover (Pursuit Of Love)
6978[12] 7204[4]

Woodnook *J A R Toller* a99 86
5 b m Cadeaux Genereux—Corndavon (USA) (Sheikh Albadou)
226[5] 677[5] 2008[6] 2530[5] 3554[5]

Woodsley House (IRE) *A G Foster* a61 76
6 b g Orpen(USA) —Flame And Shadow (IRE) (Turtle Island (IRE))
990[14] 1775[10] 2251[6] 2936[10] (4903) (5392) (5634) 5991[6] 6724[13]

Wood White (USA) *R Menichetti* 94
2 b c Aljabr(USA) —Off You Go (USA) (Seattle Slew (USA))
7449a[6]

Woodygo *J R Best* a64 45
4 ch g Tobougg(IRE) —Woodrising (Nomination)
3089[10]

Woody Valentine (USA) *Mrs Dianne Sayer* 44
7 ch g Woodman(USA) —Mudslinger (USA) (El Gran Senor (USA))
1891[12] 2568[11] 4679[13] 5776[7] 6727[11]

Woody Waller *J Howard Johnson* 75
3 ch g Lomitas—Reamzafonic (Grand Lodge (USA))
3402[2] (3835) 6113[4]

Woolfall Blue (IRE) *G G Margarson* a67 87
5 gr h Bluebird(USA) —Diamond Waltz (IRE) (Linamix (FR))
5115a[0] 6346[12] 7314[11]

Woolfall Treasure *G L Moore* 94
3 gr c Daylami(IRE) —Treasure Trove (USA) (The Minstrel (CAN))
1526[2] 1811[3] (2156) 2425[2] 3157[15] 4621[7] 5054[2]

Woolston Ferry (IRE) *M R Channon* a80 77
2 b g Fath(USA) —Cathy Garcia (IRE) (Be My Guest (USA))
2562[2] 2796[3] 3199[3] 3669[5] (5432) 6058[5] 6112[7] 6549[5] 7065[2] (7275) 7389[3]

Woqoodd *D Shaw* a70 72
4 b g Royal Applause—Intervene (Zafonic (USA))
1431[4] 1624[20] 2270[12] 4118[3] 4327[8] 4542[6] 7615[10] 7705[5] 7835[2]

Working Late *Mike Hammond* a44 47
6 b g Night Shift(USA) —All The Luck (USA) (Mr Prospector (USA))
1086[5] 1246[13]

World Delight (NZ) *S Burridge* 116
6 ch g Mellifont(USA) —Lady Anne (NZ) (Grosvenor (NZ))
2234a[4]

Worldly Wise *Patrick J Flynn* a94 97
5 b g Namid—Tina Heights (Shirley Heights)
3531a[12]

World Of Choice (USA) *M W Easterby* a45 69
3 b g Distorted Humor(USA) —Palace Weekend (USA) (Seattle Dancer (USA))
7317[13] 7532[8] 7665[5]

World Ruler *A Fabre* 105
3 b g Dansili—Revealing (Halling (USA))
3356a[4] 4719a[3]

World Time *J H M Gosden* a57 76
3 ch c Dalakhani(IRE) —Time Ahead (Spectrum (IRE))
1382[4] ◆ 1621[8] 2291[8] 2603[11] (2984) ◆ 3327[6] 6678[5]

World Tour *Miss L A Perratt* 60
3 b g Spinning World(USA) —Seven Wonders (USA) (Rahy (USA))
5388[7]

World View (IRE) *M P Tregoning* a46 54
3 br f Golan(IRE) —Athene (IRE) (Rousillon (USA))
2756[10] 3379[6]

Worth A King'S *Sir Michael Stoute* a72 50
2 b g Red Ransom(USA) —Top Romance (IRE) (Entrepreneur)
3495[11] 5404[3] 6057[9] 6756[U] (7067)

Wotashirtfull (IRE) *K A Ryan* a81 85
3 ch g Namid—Madrina (Waajib)
2240[2] (2850) (3171) 3794[3] 4591[11] 4922[3] 5417[4] 7811[2]

Wotatomboy *R M Whitaker* a62 68
2 ch f Captain Rio—Keen Melody (USA) (Sharpen Up)
3598[7] 4449[2] 4647[4] 5004[7] 6051[5] (7044)

Wotavadun (IRE) *I W McInnes* a33 22
5 ch g King Of Kings(IRE) —Blush With Love (USA) (Mt. Livermore (USA))
6421[1]

Wotchalike (IRE) *Jim Best* a65 60
6 ch g Spectrum(IRE) —Juno Madonna (IRE) (Sadler's Wells (USA))
1726[2] 3871[4] 4105[3] 4366[2]

Woteva *B Ellison* a67 74
2 b f Kyllachy—Happy Omen (Warning)
1390[2] ◆ 1627[6] 2534[8] 3597[5] 4434[11] 5006[6] 5632[7] (5774) 6101[3] 6857[6] 6954[5]

Wouldn'Titbenice *V Smith* 57
3 ch f Dr Fong(USA) —Krista (Kris)
2994[7] 3844[4] 4280[3]

Wovoka (IRE) *D W Barker* a81 89
5 b g Mujadil(USA) —Common Cause (Polish Patriot (USA))
9921[6] 1217[4] 1308[6] 1815[12] 2155[9] 3261[3] 3493[9] 3758[2] 4001[7] 4219[2] 4440[6] 4876[11] 5390[8] 6052[16] 6385[2] 6482[17]

Wraith *H R A Cecil* a81 76
4 b h Maria's Mon(USA) —Really Polish (USA) (Polish Numbers (USA))
1690[4] 1998[10] 2623[7]

Wrecker's Moon (IRE) *T J Etherington* a12
3 b f Shinko Forest(IRE) —Coast Is Clear (IRE) (Rainbow Quest (USA))
4378[9] 5426[9] 6909[9]

Wrecking Crew (IRE) *B R Millman* a58 66
4 b g Invincible Spirit(IRE) —Rushing (Deploy)
5491[3] 5915[11]

Wreningham *T Keddy* a69 62
3 br g Diktat—Slave To The Rythm (IRE) (Hamas (IRE))
3000[10] 3564[10] 4056[2] 4271[2] 5049[6] 5627[2] (6224) (7092) 7295[9] 7621[7]

Wrens Hope *N Bycroft* 44
2 ch f Shinko Forest(IRE) —Star Dancer (Groom Dancer (USA))
5633[9] 5989[10] 6183[4]

Wrighty Almighty (IRE) *P R Chamings* a76 76
6 b g Danehill Dancer(IRE) —Persian Empress (IRE) (Persian Bold)
148[2] (246) 452[2] 548[3] 730[8] 2722[11] 3360[2] 4081[13] 4428[3] 4946[6] 5915[4] ◆ 6336[2] 6671[11] 7309[6] 7580[7]

Writ (IRE) *Miss L A Perratt* a65 60
6 ch g Indian Lodge(IRE) —Carnelly (IRE) (Priolo (USA))
5968[11] 6491[10] 6826[10]

Writingonthewall (IRE) *M L W Bell* 75
3 b c Danetime(IRE) —Badee'A (IRE) (Marju (IRE))
1448[11] 2161[11] 3441[5] 4641[7] 5162[4]

Wujood *Mrs L J Young* 38
6 b g Alzao(USA) —Rahayeb (Arazi (USA))
5583[8]

Wulimaster (USA) *D W Barker* a59 63
5 br g Silver Hawk(USA) —Kamaina (USA) (Mr Prospector (USA))
1521[5] 1559[7] (1913) 2752[5] 3131[6] 3279[6] 3666[2] ◆ 4048[7] 4457[10] 4879[3] 5396[4] 5869[2] 6550[7] 6812[9]

Wunder Strike (USA) *M J Wallace* a40 34
2 b g Smart Strike(CAN) —Bishop's Mate (USA) (Lyphard (USA))
6010[11] 6545[7] 6755[5]

Wusuul *C E Brittain* 69
3 br f Kyllachy—Cartuccia (IRE) (Doyoun)
3379[3] 3854[7] 4300[11] 4724[5] 6363[9]

Wyatt Earp (IRE) *R A Fahey* a91 100
8 b g Piccolo—Tribal Lady (Absalom)
1393[6] 2172[11] 3056[11] 3477[6] 3812[7] (4218) 4460[6] 4854[8] 5247[4] 5831[8] 6125[3] (6278) ◆ 6624[11] 6845a[13] 7245[21]

Wychwood Wanderer (IRE) *M Halford* 83
5 b m Barathea(IRE) —Calamander (IRE) (Alzao (USA))
4467a[8]

Wyeth *G L Moore* a70 67
4 ch g Grand Lodge(USA) —Bordighera (USA) (Alysheba (USA))
1692[2] ◆ 2361[5] 2921[7] 3650[6] 4691[5] (5752) 6672[5] (7520)

Wynberg (IRE) *S A Callaghan* a73 66
3 b g Danetime(IRE) —Jayzdoll (IRE) (Stravinsky (USA))
23[8] 237[3] (298) (333) ◆ (425) 2068[4] 2690[2] 3000[5] 3136[4] 4272[3] 5046[6] 5374[6] 6190[11] 6907[7]

Wysiwyg Lucky (FR) *J-L Gay* a89 100
5 b m Ultimately Lucky(IRE) —Les Estelles (FR) (Dress Parade)
7643a[18]

Xaaroon (IRE) *Rae Guest* 30
2 br f Xaar—Swoon (Night Shift (USA))
3923[8] 4665[11] 6559[12]

Xandra (IRE) *C F Wall* a53 44
3 b f Xaar—Talah (Danehill (USA))
4987[13] 5205[3] 5402[6] 6003[7] 6935[7]

Xaravella (IRE) *J G M O'Shea* a40 61
3 b f Xaar—Walnut Lady (Forzando)
1870[15] 2922[7] 4326[6] 4810[11] 5215[7] 6541[12]

Xpres Boy (IRE) *S R Bowring* a23 11
5 b g Tagula(IRE) —Highly Motivated (Midyan (USA))
821[7]

Xpres Maite *S R Bowring* a96 84
5 b g Komaite(USA) —Antonias Melody (Rambo Dancer (CAN))
41[2] ◆ 190[5] (235) (342) 636[7] 1015[5] (1188) (1590) (1708) 2082[2] 2406[3] 2593[7] 5208[7] 5424[7] 5717[6] 6354[7] 6710[10] 6842[4] 7633[7]

Xtra Torrential (USA) *D M Simcock* a77 100
6 b g Torrential(USA) —Offering (USA) (Majestic Light (USA))
5051[11] 7560[9]

Xtravaganza (IRE) *J W Hills* a59 68
3 b f Xaar—Royal Jubilee (IRE) (King's Theatre (IRE))
1479[2] 2288[10] 3065[5] (3874) 4669[5] 5058[10] 6558[2]

Yab Adee *M P Tregoning* a67 58
4 b g Mark Of Esteem(IRE) —Kotdiji (Mtoto)
4078[6] 4568[7] 5321[7] 7217[7] ◆ (7379)

Yacht Woman (USA) *E Borromeo* 96
3 gr f Mizzen Mast(USA) —Yacht Club (USA) (Sea Hero (USA))
2231a[6] 7253a[11] 7349a[10]

Yaddree *M A Jarvis* a76 110
3 ch c Singspiel(IRE) —Jathaabeh (Nashwan (USA))
1686[2] (2412) ◆ 3155[3] 4404[2] ◆ (6123) 6476[5] 6780[10]

Yahrab (IRE) *C E Brittain* a116 104
3 gr c Dalakhani(IRE) —Loire Valley (IRE) (Sadler's Wells (USA))
292a[16] 743a[5] 1402[5] 1922[7] (5942) (7208) (7420)

Yahwudhee (FR) *P W Chapple-Hyam* 79
3 b g Zamindar(USA) —Lady Marshall (FR) (Octagonal (NZ))
2198[4] (2455) 3999[8]

Yakama (IRE) *Mrs C A Dunnett* a62 58
3 b g Indian Danehill(IRE) —Working Progress (IRE) (Marju (IRE))
998[3] 1193[4] 1478[3] 2552[7] 2988[4] 3359[4] 3817[8] 3963[3] 4280[2] 4750[8] 5020[15] 6001[3] 6716[3] 6888[6] 7256[4] 7591[2] 7759[4]

Yakhy (FR) *B De Montzey* 86
2 b f Ballingarry(IRE) —Faintly (FR) (Dominion)
6891a[5]

Yakimov (USA) *Ollie Pears* a93 74
9 ch g Affirmed(USA) —Ballet Troupe (USA) (Nureyev (USA))
(463) (653) (851) (1700) 1902[2] 2083[2] 2867[3] 7309[12] 7695[4] 7723[2]

Yaldas Girl (USA) *J R Best* 51
2 rg f Unbridled's Song(USA) —Marina De Chavon (USA) (Exploit (USA))
1419[10] 4164[11] 4926[7]

Yali (IRE) *Francis Ennis* 93
3 b f Orpen(USA) —Klang (IRE) (Night Shift (USA))
1230a[4] 1847a[5]

Yamal (IRE) *M Johnston* a75 101
3 b g Green Desert(USA) —Pioneer Bride (USA) (Gone West (USA))
(1036) ◆ 1546[5] 2209[5] (3108) 3416[2] (3907) (4104) 4404[3] (4509) 4853[8]

Yamanmickmccann *R Hannon* a72 48
3 b c Desert Style(IRE) —Cashel Kiss (Bishop Of Cashel)
25[5] 136[10] 266[5]

Yankee Bravo (USA) *Patrick Gallagher* a112 82
3 bb c Yankee Gentleman(USA) —Vickey Jane (USA) (Royal Academy (USA))
2215a[10]

Yankee Storm *P W D'Arcy* a81 62
3 b g Yankee Gentleman(USA) —Yes Virginia (USA) (Roanoke (USA))
(70) 170[5] 2141[6] (2506) 3224[12] 3394[2] 3587[3] 3838[5] 4440[13] 7398[5] 7462[8] 7603[8]

Yanza *J R Gask* 72
2 b f Bahamian Bounty—Locharia (Wolfhound (USA))
4763[4] 5214[2] 5746[3]

Yarastar *H-A Pantall* 100
3 b f Cape Cross(IRE) —Yara (IRE) (Sri Pekan (USA))
(2743a) 3705a[6] 5331a[8]

Yarqus *C E Brittain* a99 97
5 b g Diktat—Will You Dance (Shareef Dancer (USA))
678[5] 834[5] 1211[2] 1545[5] 2465[8] 3122[13] 4642[3] 5207[2] 5908[2] 6287[9]

Yasoodd *D Selvaratnam* a87 105
5 br g Inchinor—Needwood Epic (Midyan (USA))
203a[4] 383a[3] 565a[3] 818a[7]

Yathreb (USA) *J L Dunlop* 81
3 bb c Kingmambo(USA) —Thawakib (IRE) (Sadler's Wells (USA))
1614[5] 2151[12] (3221) 3607[2] 4310[4]

Yatir (FR) *E F Vaughan* a71 61
3 b f Red Ransom(USA) —Tycoon's Dolce (IRE) (Rainbows For Life (CAN))
2341[12] 3260[11]

Yattendon *S Kirk* a61 49
3 ch g Compton Place—Arian Da (Superlative)
1026 557[8] 582[5] 797[10] 835[5]

Yeaman's Hall *A M Balding* 103
4 b g Galileo(IRE) —Rimba (USA) (Dayjur (USA))
960[7]

Yeats (IRE) *A P O'Brien* 126
7 b h Sadler's Wells(USA) —Lyndonville (IRE) (Top Ville)
(1655a) (3154) (4551) 6497a[5] (7008a)

Yeldham Lady *A J Chamberlain* a34 18
6 b m Mujahid(USA) —Future Options (Lomond (USA))
2421[0]

Yellow Printer *Tom Dascombe* a76 59
2 b c Royal Applause—Robsart (IRE) (Robellino (USA))
6677[5] 7165[2] (7593)

Yellow River (USA) *S A Callaghan* a47
2 ch f Johannesburg(USA) —Ascension (IRE) (Night Shift (USA))
7546[8]

Yellowstone (IRE) *Jane Chapple-Hyam* 118
4 b h Rock Of Gibraltar(IRE) —Love And Affection (USA) (Exclusive Era (USA))
1091a[14] 1829[8] 3246[5] (3975) 5229[3] 5921a[8]

Yellow Thunder (IRE) *Luke Comer* a53 59
3 ch c On The Ridge(IRE) —Mother Nellie (USA) (Al Nasr (FR))
1398[15] 1748[9] 2191[9] 4613a[14]

Yem Kinn *S Seemar* a54 92
3 b c Dubai Destination(USA) —Nova Cyngi (USA) (Kris S (USA))
292a[12]

Yenaled *J M Bradley* a48 59
11 gr g Rambo Dancer(CAN) —Fancy Flight (FR) (Arctic Tern (USA))
101[6] 145[6] 691[8]

Yeoman Blaze *A M Balding* 56
2 b g Needwood Blade—Gymcrak Flyer (Aragon)
2893[6] 3358[6] 3895[8] 7016[16]

Yeoman Of England (IRE) *B Smart* a64 64
2 b c Pyrus(USA) —Regal Lustre (Averti (IRE))
4921[8] 5539[4] 6187[4] 6761[12] 6988[3]

Yerevan *M Mullineaux* a64 81
4 b m Iron Mask(USA) —Unfuwaanah (Unfuwain (USA))
2679[14] 3165[5] 4052[3] 4891[5] 5201[8] 5566[6]

Yes Eighteen (IRE) *J W Hills* a69 44
3 b c Diktat—Siskin (IRE) (Royal Academy (USA))
909[8] 1194[4] 2261[8] 4727[7] 5086[12] 5799[2] 6227[7] (6685) (6882)

Yes Mate (FR) *R Gibson* 84
2 b f Lord Of Men—Zigalixa (FR) (Linamix (FR))
5300a[9]

Yes Meg *P F I Cole* a45 57
3 b f Sagamix(FR) —Segsbury Belle (Petoski)
1147[13] 2475[12]

Yes Mr President (IRE) *M Johnston* a82 85
3 b g Montjeu(IRE) —Royals Special (IRE) (Caerleon (USA))
350[4] (702) ◆ 1919[8] 2840[4] 3459[7] 4448[3]

Yes One (IRE) *K A Ryan* a78 87
4 ch g Peintre Celebre(USA) —Copious (IRE) (Generous (IRE))
(752) ◆ 852[3] 1030[2] 1450[2] (1815) 2271[4]

Yes She Can Can *Peter Grayson* a32
2 ch f Monsieur Bond(IRE) —Antonia's Folly (Music Boy)
6434[7] 7501[10] 7689[9]

Yes Sir (IRE) *P Bowen* 57
9 b g Needle Gun(IRE) —Miss Pushover (Push On)
3310[6] 3813[7]

Yetholm (USA) *J R Fanshawe* 80
3 rg g Dynaformer(USA) —Gypsy (USA) (Marfa (USA))
5076[6] 5864[3] 6584[4] 6950[2]

Yirga *Saeed Bin Suroor* a71 69
2 b c Cape Cross(IRE) —Auratum (USA) (Carson City (USA))
7051[2] 7311[3]

Ykikamoocow *G A Harker* 66
2 b f Cape Town(IRE) —Pigeon (Casteddu)
(1555) 2775[4] 4119[7] 4648[5] 6362[3]

Ymir *M J Attwater* a65
2 b c Zaha(CAN) —Anastasia Venture (Lion Cavern (USA))
7011^{4} 7380^{6} 7602^{5}

Yokozuna *Mrs R A Carr* a52 65
2 b g Efisio—Celt Song (IRE) (Unfuwain (USA))
2086^{2} ◆ 2502^{5} 2979^{5} 3334^{4} 3645^{5} 4063^{2} 5447^{8} 5591^{5} 6214^{9} 6549^{9} 6886^{9}

Yonder *H Morrison* 61
4 br m And Beyond(IRE) —Dominance (Dominion)
2123^{9} 2363^{3}

Yorgunnabelucky (USA) *M Johnston* 76
2 b c Giant's Causeway(USA) —Helsinki (Machiavellian (USA))
3277^{2} ◆ 3926^{7}

York Cliff *W M Brisbourne* a63 67
10 b g Marju(IRE) —Azm (Unfuwain (USA))
1184^{4} 1459^{7} 2776^{4} 3328^{3} 3871^{5} (4026) 4592^{7} 4932^{2} 5040^{10} 5450^{3} 5583^{3} 6279^{4} 7265^{2} 7512^{10} 7608^{6}

Yorke's Folly (USA) *C W Fairhurst* a38 49
7 b m Stravinsky(USA) —Tommelise (USA) (Dayjur (USA))
2676^{6} 2928^{11} 3665^{13} 4462^{6} 6232^{10} 6791^{14}

York Key Bar *B Ellison* a46 70
2 b g Presidium—Onemoretime (Timeless Times (USA))
6010^{3} 6383^{2} 6807^{3} 7044^{4}

Yorkshire Blue *J S Goldie* a43 86
9 b g Atraf—Something Blue (Petong)
1430^{8} 1826^{5} 1952^{7} 2251^{9} 2535^{6} 2751^{3} ◆ 2938^{4} 3129^{5} 3443^{2} 3757^{12} 4239^{2} 4327^{11} 4875^{4} 5222^{6} 5392^{10} 5562^{3} 6043^{9} 6411^{4} 7131^{5}

Yorksters Girl (IRE) *M G Quinlan* 96
2 ch f Bachelor Duke(USA) —Isadora Duncan (IRE) (Sadler's Wells (USA))
4062^{2} 4868^{7} 5825^{3} (6381) 6982^{3}

Yorktown (FR) *J-C Rouget* a89 113
3 b c Red Ransom(USA) —Wedding Night (FR) (Valanour (IRE))
$2032a^{4}$ $2875a^{3}$ $4010a^{12}$

Yorokobi (BRZ) *H J Brown* a79 75
5 b g Burooj—Fancy Lady (BRZ) (Executioner (USA))
$379a^{10}$ $493a^{11}$

Yossi (IRE) *M H Tompkins* 83
4 b g Montjeu(IRE) —Raindancing (IRE) (Tirol)
2822^{10} 3630^{2} 3884^{8} 4955^{2}

You Avin A Laugh *C A Dwyer* 33
2 ch g Bertolini(USA) —High Stepping (IRE) (Taufan (USA))
1832^{7}

Youmeanddupree (IRE) *K J Burke*
6 b g Supreme Leader—Beau Belle (IRE) (Beau Sher)
715^{6} 787^{8}

Youmzain (IRE) *M R Channon* 128
5 b h Sinndar(IRE) —Sadima (IRE) (Sadler's Wells (USA))
$1091a^{5}$ 2791^{2} (3542a) 4406^{3} $6522a^{2}$

Young Bertie *H Morrison* a72 78
5 ch g Bertolini(USA) —Urania (Most Welcome)
1520^{4} 2308^{3} 6052^{13} 6336^{13} 6867^{11} 7360^{5} (7771)

Young Dottie *P M Phelan* a75 67
2 b f Desert Sun—Auntie Dot Com (Tagula (IRE))
2893^{3} 3522^{4} 4296^{2} 4925^{7} 6432^{2} (6877)

Young Gladiator (IRE) *Miss J A Camacho* a66 65
3 b g Spartacus(IRE) —Savona (IRE) (Cyrano De Bergerac)
505^{3} 700^{3} 848^{2} (1674) 3118^{3} 3416^{3} 3691^{10} 4044^{8} 5638^{5} 6353^{9}

Young Ivanhoe *C A Dwyer* a70 65
3 b g Oasis Dream—Cybinka (Selkirk (USA))
(706) 924^{11} 1110^{7} 1277^{10} 2429^{16} 3564^{8} 3779^{4} 4684^{12} 5015^{8} 5248^{4} 5684^{11} 6595^{6} 6680^{8}

Young Mick *G G Margarson* a99 112
6 br g King's Theatre(IRE) —Just Warning (Warning)
1980^{8} 2169^{8} 2797^{7} 3249^{4} 3721^{2} 4444^{2} 5229^{5} 5694^{9} 6302^{2} 6646^{10} (7017) 7491^{11}

Young Ollie *E A Wheeler* 14
3 ch f Piccolo—Miss Michelle (Jalmood (USA))
2257^{13} 2449^{13} 6345^{12}

Young Pretender (FR) *Saeed Bin Suroor* 112
3 b c Oasis Dream—Silent Heir (AUS) (Sunday Silence (USA))
2131^{5} 2788^{3}

Young Scotton *J D Bethell* a71 58
8 b g Cadeaux Genereux—Broken Wave (Bustino)
320^{3} 533^{9} 722^{2} 988^{6}

You'relikemefrank *J Balding* a26
2 ch c Bahamian Bounty—Proudfoot (IRE) (Shareef Dancer (USA))
7082^{8} 7279^{7} 7689^{7}

You'resothrilling (USA) *A P O'Brien* 113
3 bb f Storm Cat(USA) —Mariah's Storm (USA) (Rahy (USA))
$5730a^{4}$ $6521a^{8}$

Your Golf Travel *J S Wainwright* a39 40
3 b f Bertolini(USA) —Scottish Spice (Selkirk (USA))
1068^{7} 1302^{8} 1971^{8} 2946^{7} 3549^{4} 4043^{8} 4381^{12}

Your Old Pal *J Noseda* 98
2 ch c Rock Of Gibraltar(IRE) —Questabelle (Rainbow Quest (USA))
(6978) ◆

Your Pleasure (USA) *A M Balding* a57 73
3 ch f Forest Wildcat(USA) —Pleasure Center (USA) (Diesis)
1284^{6}

Your Round (USA) *M Hubley* a99 99
3 b c Distorted Humor(USA) —Another Round (USA) (Affirmed (USA))
$4887a^{6}$

You Say I Say (USA) *Sir Michael Stoute* 61
2 bb f Unbridled's Song(USA) —Insight (FR) (Sadler's Wells (USA))
7140^{8}

You've Been Mowed *D K Ivory* a68 69
2 ch f Ishiguru(USA) —Sandblaster (Most Welcome)
1680^{5} 2638^{7} 4126^{2} 4411^{3} 5466^{5} 5997^{3} 6350^{3} 6863^{9}

Ysing Yi *K A Ryan* a75 43
2 b c Singspiel(IRE) —Hsi Wang Mu (IRE) (Dr Fong (USA))
4960^{7} 5344^{2} 5590^{3} 6621^{3} 6837^{6}

Yughanni *C E Brittain* 46
2 b f Oasis Dream—Bedazzling (IRE) (Darshaan)
6885^{8}

Yungaburra (IRE) *S Parr* a92 95
4 b g Fath(USA) —Nordic Living (IRE) (Nordico (USA))
5^{6} 84^{7} 162^{2} 329^{9} 676^{9} 824^{5} 983^{12} 1071^{17} 2188^{7} 3401^{3} 3668^{6} 3868^{13} 5398^{8} 5796^{16} (6137) ◆ 6310^{9} 6357^{3} 6813^{14} 7206^{5} 7290^{3} 7384^{5} (7456) 7584^{3} 7614^{9} 7793^{6} 7828^{3}

Yurchenko *M Wellings* a42
4 b m Mamalik(USA) —Rajmata (IRE) (Prince Sabo)
50^{11} 363^{9} 386^{4} 690^{6} 1035^{9}

Yvonne Evelyn (USA) *J R Gask* a67
3 rg f Cozzene(USA) —One Great Lady (USA) (Fappiano (USA))
5995^{10} 7344^{7} 7474^{6} 7620^{3}

Yxes (IRE) *E J Creighton* a25
3 br f Lend A Hand—Woodenitbenice (USA) (Nasty And Bold (USA))
6878^{9}

Zaafira (SPA) *E J Creighton* a58
4 b m Limpid—Hot Doris (IRE) (Fayruz)
24^{6} 229^{7}

Zaahid (IRE) *B W Hills* 107
4 ch h Sakhee(USA) —Murjana (IRE) (Pleasant Colony (USA))
958^{4} 1469^{3} ◆ (1982) 3921^{11} 4405^{16} 6269^{11}

Zaaqya *J L Dunlop* 79
2 b f Nayef(USA) —Classical Dancer (Dr Fong (USA))
3349^{6} (4109) ◆ 5242^{6} (6231) 6946^{5}

Zaarmit (IRE) *D M Simcock* a65 67
3 b c Xaar—Tender Is Thenight (IRE) (Barathea (IRE))
1344^{4} 1876^{10} 2455^{4} (3342) 3763^{8} 4533^{10} 5162^{8} 6631^{5} 6936^{6}

Zabeel House *John A Harris* a69 50
5 b g Anabaa(USA) —Divine Quest (Kris)
7^{3} 148^{7} 601^{4} 809^{5} 2870^{11} 4254^{13} 7691^{10}

Zabeel Tower *R Allan* a55 80
5 b g Anabaa(USA) —Bint Kaldoun (IRE) (Kaldoun (FR))
(2009) (2285) 2523^{5} 2846^{2} (3211) (3431) 3957^{3} 4453^{4} (4951) 5419^{4} 6314^{3} 6724^{17} 7041^{6} 7175^{5}

Zabougg *D W Barker* 66
3 b g Tobougg(IRE) —Double Fault (IRE) (Zieten (USA))
991^{8} 1449^{9} 2002^{6} 2208^{5} 2911^{6} 3126^{10} 4049^{9} 4381^{6} 4741^{8} 4919^{9}

Zach's Harmoney (USA) *Miss M E Rowland* a63 69
4 ch g Diesis—Cool Ashlee (USA) (Mister Baileys)
758^{9} 874^{5} 1621^{6} 2001^{6} 2483^{2} 2863^{2} 3518^{9} 4309^{6} 4458^{4} 4710^{11} 7532^{14}

Zacinto *Sir Michael Stoute* 111
2 b c Dansili—Ithaca (USA) (Distant View (USA))
(3682) 5889^{2}

Zack Dream (FR) *M Delzangles* 104
3 b c Dream Well(FR) —Halawa (IRE) (Dancing Brave (USA))
$2654a^{9}$ $3191a^{2}$ $4880a^{7}$

Zadounevees (FR) *W Gulcher* 93
5 ch h Kaldounevees(FR) —Zurs (GER) (Lando (GER))
$4496a^{5}$

Zafayra (IRE) *John M Oxx* a80 99
3 b f Nayef(USA) —Zafayana (IRE) (Mark Of Esteem (IRE))
$1847a^{2}$ $4007a^{6}$

Zaffaan *E A L Dunlop* a88 84
2 ch g Efisio—Danceabout (Shareef Dancer (USA))
3219^{8} (3895) 4374^{4} 5016^{2} 5827^{18}

Zaffeu *A G Juckes* a69 65
7 ch g Zafonic(USA) —Leaping Flame (USA) (Trempolino (USA))
(76) 171^{4} (394) (787) (1121) 7617^{7}

Zafisio (IRE) *P A Blockley* 110
2 b c Efisio—Goldthroat (IRE) (Zafonic (USA))
5029^{3} (5387) (5898) $6855a^{4}$ (7163a) $7294a^{5}$

Zafonical Storm (USA) *B W Duke* a84 80
4 ch g Aljabr(USA) —Fonage (Zafonic (USA))
357^{4} 910^{11} 1365^{10} 6363^{13} 7307^{11}

Zaftig (USA) *James Jerkens* a117
3 rg f Gone West(USA) —Zoftig (USA) (Cozzene (USA))
$6965a^{3}$

Zaftil (IRE) *H S Howe* 12
2 b f Tillerman—Zafine (Zafonic (USA))
2638^{16} 3358^{11} 4321^{7} 4975^{11}

Zaham (USA) *M Johnston* a91 116
4 ch g Silver Hawk(USA) —Guerre Et Paix (USA) (Soviet Star (USA))
906^{14} 1468^{2} ◆

Zaif (IRE) *Simon Earle* 87
5 b g Almutawakel—Colourful (FR) (Gay Mecene (USA))
2107^{5} 2304^{3} 2764^{4} 3461^{5} 3896^{6} 4645^{8}

Zain (IRE) *J G Given* a49 66
4 b g Alhaarth(IRE) —Karenaragon (Aragon)
999^{13} 1394^{8} 3964^{6} 4172^{6}

Zakhaaref *M Johnston* 96
3 gr c Daylami(IRE) —Shahaamah (IRE) (Red Ransom (USA))
1598^{4} 2403^{9} 3475^{7} 4312^{2} 4893^{2} 5313^{7}

Zakocity (USA) *J Smith Jr* a109
7 b h Precocity(USA) —Zakcat (USA) (Vilzak (USA))
$1087a^{4}$

Zalkani (IRE) *J Pearce* a66 47
8 ch g Cadeaux Genereux—Zallaka (IRE) (Shardari)
4026^{5} 4267^{9} 5145^{4} 5631^{9} ◆ (5869) (6136) ◆ 6493^{10} 7499^{6} (7806)

Zalzaar (IRE) *R T Phillips* a40 54
6 b g Xaar—Zalamalec (USA) (Septieme Ciel (USA))
37^{8}

Zamalik (USA) *Mrs A Duffield* a47 73
5 bb g Machiavellian(USA) —Ashbilya (USA) (Nureyev (USA))
2968^{13} 4073^{6} 5965^{13} 6116^{5} 7043^{8} 7176^{3} 7320^{10}

Zambezi Sun *P Bary* 123
4 b h Dansili—Imbabala (Zafonic (USA))
$1665a^{6}$ $2653a^{2}$ $3542a^{4}$ (5954a) $6522a^{15}$

Zamboozle (IRE) *A King* a76 79
6 ch g Halling(USA) —Blue Sirocco (Bluebird (USA))
358^{4} 1668^{3}

Zania (FR) *M Delzangles* 89
3 b f Kahyasi—Zafarana (FR) (Shernazar)
$2902a^{6}$ $6744a^{6}$

Zantic *P R Chamings* a44 55
3 ch g Zaha(CAN) —Suta (GER) (Lomitas)
2772^{6} 3342^{4} 3823^{10} 6735^{11}

Zaplamation (IRE) *D W Barker* a40 48
3 b g Acclamation—Zapatista (Rainbow Quest (USA))
998^{5} 1343^{6} 1912^{3} 2750^{4} 3126^{6} 3555^{8} 4019^{3} 4420^{3} 4738^{3} 5399^{7}

Zappa (USA) *John W Sadler* a117
6 b g Afternoon Deelites(USA) —Julies Angel (USA) (Theatrical)
$6993a^{7}$

Zariyan (FR) *T Doumen* a92 105
5 b h Anabaa(USA) —Zarkana (IRE) (Doyoun)
$7643a^{12}$

Zarkava (IRE) *A De Royer-Dupre* 129
3 b f Zamindar(USA) —Zarkasha (IRE) (Kahyasi)
(1360a) (2033a) (2877a) (5952a) ◆ (6522a)

Zarkozy (IRE) *D Broad* 48
3 br c Odyle(USA) —Another Baileys (Deploy)
5967^{9}

Zarrado (GER) *U Ostmann* 89
2 b c Big Shuffle(USA) —Zanana (Zafonic (USA))
$5686a^{7}$

Zaruschka *R M Beckett* 35
2 b f Xaar—Zanella (IRE) (Nordico (USA))
3674^{17} 3968^{9} 5811^{8}

Zarzu *C R Dore* a86 83
9 b g Magic Ring(IRE) —Rivers Rhapsody (Dominion)
715^{5} 241^{6}

Zaskar *John Terranova II* a87 95
3 b f Anabaa(USA) —Bezzaaf (Machiavellian (USA))
(2505) ◆ $3018a^{2}$ $3807a^{10}$ $5164a^{7}$

Zaungast (IRE) *W Hickst* 106
4 b h Alkalde(GER) —Zauberwelt (Polar Falcon (USA))
(6156a) $6461a^{2}$ $6992a^{6}$

Zavite (NZ) *Anthony Cummings* 109
6 b h Zabeel(NZ) —Miss Vita (USA) (Alleged (USA))
$6922a^{7}$

Zaya (GER) *A Wohler* 88
3 b f Diktat—Zayala (Royal Applause)
$2065a^{7}$ $5334a^{2}$ $6323a^{9}$

Zayyir (IRE) *R A Harris* a38 43
4 b h Indian Ridge—Lurina (IRE) (Lure (USA))
1036^{5} 1265^{9} 1533^{12}

Za Za *H R A Cecil* 11
2 br f Barathea(IRE) —Madiyla (Darshaan)
6391^{14}

Zazous *J J Bridger* a64 63
7 b g Zafonic(USA) —Confidentiality (USA) (Lyphard (USA))
54^{4} 149^{10} 446^{9} 628^{5} 937^{3} 1038^{3} 1154^{8} 1641^{9} 2128^{15} 4824^{7} 5088^{7} 5267^{6} 5797^{8} 5916^{7} (6912) 7360^{13}

Zebra Crossing (SAF) *N L Bruss* 67
7 ch g Jallad(USA) —Teclafields (SAF) (Northfields (USA))
6307^{7}

Zebrano *Miss E C Lavelle* a75 78
2 br g Storming Home—Ambience Lady (Batshoof)
2324^{10} 2754^{3} ◆ 3444^{2} 4305^{3} 5753^{2} 6198^{2}

Zed Candy (FR) *J T Stimpson* a69 64
5 b g Medicean—Intrum Morshaan (IRE) (Darshaan)
533^{5} 789^{5} 4238^{6} (4817) 5559^{4}

Zeeran *C E Brittain* a39 31
3 b c Barathea(IRE) —Mrs Marsh (Marju (IRE))
1298^{8} 2199^{14} 3654^{8} 4338^{9} 5186^{10} 7396^{3} 7636^{7}

Zeeuw (IRE) *D J Coakley* a43 62
4 b g Xaar—Lucky Bet (IRE) (Lucky Guest)
777^{9} 1143^{8} 4580^{6} 4808^{7}

Zeffirelli *M Quinn* a59 59
3 ch g Tomba—Risky Valentine (Risk Me (FR))
864^{3} 1124^{2} 1587^{2} 2805^{4} 3333^{7} 3817^{3} 5248^{3} (6004) 7111^{4} 7270^{10}

Zegna (IRE) *B Smart* 79
2 gb g Clodovil(IRE) —Vade Retro (IRE) (Desert Sun)
6407^{5} 6858^{2} 7038^{3}

Zeitgeist (IRE) *Miss L A Perratt* a41 78
7 b g Singspiel(IRE) —Diamond Quest (Rainbow Quest (USA))
6154^{7} 6410^{5} 6985^{8}

Zellers *W J Haggas* a36 31
2 b f Efisio—Council Rock (General Assembly (USA))
5147^{14} 5609^{8}

Zelloof (IRE) *Saeed Bin Suroor* a74 74
2 b f Kheleyf(USA) —Belle Genius (USA) (Beau Genius (CAN))
4251^{5} ◆ 4636^{2} 5672^{4} 6525^{5} (6837)

Zelos (IRE) *D G Bridgwater* a70 77
4 b g Mujadil(USA) —First Degree (Sabrehill (USA))
4568^{9} 7385^{11} 7512^{12}

Zelos Diktator *J G Given* 49
2 br g Diktat—Chanterelle (IRE) (Indian Ridge)
4740^{7} 6760^{8}

Zelos Girl (IRE) *Rae Guest* a52 72
2 ch f Exceed And Excel(AUS) —Sedna (FR) (Bering)
4020^{3} (4681) 5204^{8}

Zeloso *M F Harris* a50 57
10 b g Alzao(USA) —Silk Petal (Petorius)
1408^{3} 1726^{7} 2245^{3} (3710) 5651^{9} 6672^{16}

Zemlinsky (IRE) *B Grizzetti*
2 b c Galileo(IRE) —River Missy (USA) (Riverman (USA))
$2745a^{10}$

Zendaro *C C Bealby* a63 58
6 b g Danzero(AUS) —Countess Maud (Mtoto)
258^{9}

Zen Factor *J G Portman* 69
3 b g Josr Algarhoud(IRE) —Zabelina (USA) (Diesis)
1128^{2} 1527^{6} 1696^{6} 2340^{8}

Zennerman (IRE) *G A Swinbank* a79 79
5 b g Observatory(USA) —Precocious Miss (USA) (Diesis)
807^{7} 914^{4} 1030^{5} 1371^{6} 1752^{2} 2285^{5} 2662^{9} 3339^{3} 4919^{4} (5198)

Zenone (IRE) *Laura Grizzetti* 104
4 b h Orpen(USA) —Luna D'Estate (Alzao (USA))
$7162a^{9}$ $7253a^{9}$

Zenyatta (USA) *John Shirreffs* a124
4 bb m Street Cry(IRE) —Vertigineux (USA) (Kris S (USA))
(6969a)

Zero Cool (USA) *G L Moore* a83 87
4 br g Forestry(USA) —Fabulous (USA) (Seeking The Gold (USA))
1212^{6} 1473^{7} 1799^{4} 2545^{3} 2762^{7} 3319^{3} 3836^{6} 4627^{9} 6738^{3} 7553^{2} 7707^{3}

Zero Money (IRE) *R Charlton* 68
2 ch c Bachelor Duke(USA) —Dawn Chorus (IRE) (Mukaddamah (USA))
4973^{3}

Zero Point Seven (USA) *J S Bolger* 74
2 b f Saarland(USA) —Eshaarat (Zafonic (USA))
$5546a^{8}$

Zero Tolerance (IRE) *T D Barron* a77 103
8 ch g Nashwan(USA) —Place De L'Opera (Sadler's Wells (USA))
1910^{2} ◆ 3413^{3} $3531a^{2}$ ◆ (4853) $5550a^{3}$ 6103^{5} 6649^{10} 7146^{13}

Zeyadah (IRE) *M A Jarvis* 43
2 b f Red Ransom(USA) —Beraysim (Lion Cavern (USA))
7240^{10}

Zezao *B J Meehan* a94 93
2 b c Fasliyev(USA) —Graffiti Girl (IRE) (Sadler's Wells (USA))
2042^{6} (2239) 4908^{4} 5359^{3} 5693^{7}

Z Fortune (USA) *Steven Asmussen* a116
3 gr c Siphon(BRZ) —Fortunate Faith (USA) (Fortunate Prospect (USA))
$1820a^{10}$

Zhebe *P J McBride* a70 60
3 br c Dr Fong(USA) —Krajina (FR) (Holst (USA))
1398^{14} 2261^{10} 2695^{10} 3116^{8}

Zhukhov (IRE) *T G McCourt* a50 81
5 ch g Allied Forces(USA) —Karameg (IRE) (Danehill (USA))
$4514a^{5}$ $6845a^{5}$

Z Humor (USA) *William Mott* a114
3 b c Distorted Humor(USA) —Offtheoldblock (USA) (A.P. Indy (USA))
$1820a^{14}$

Zia Sofi (FR) *Mme M Bollack-Badel* a83 79
3 b f Le Balafre(FR) —Zayine (IRE) (Polish Patriot (USA))
$6743a^{9}$

Zia Zabel (IRE) *M G Quinlan* 66
3 b f Rock Of Gibraltar(IRE) —Blu Meltemi (ITY) (Star Shareef)
2164^{9} 2668^{8} 3562^{7} 4410^{2} 6703^{P}

Zibeling (IRE) *Robert Collet* 71
2 b f Cape Cross(IRE) —Zelding (IRE) (Warning)
$7430a^{10}$

Zidane *J R Fanshawe* a94 113
6 b g Danzero(AUS) —Juliet Bravo (Glow (USA))
(1420) 1831^{5} 3247^{8} 3488^{2} 3922^{11} 6304^{12} 6645^{2} 7243^{12}

Ziggy Lee *S C Williams* 52
2 b g Lujain(USA) —Mary O'Grady (USA) (Swain (IRE))
3485^{3} 5213^{13}

Zim Ho *J Akehurst* a69
2 b c Zilzal(USA) —Robanna (Robellino (USA))
6876^{4} 7311^{6} (7767)

Zina Blue (FR) *J De Roualle* 96
3 ch f Anabaa Blue—Vezina (FR) (Bering)
$4657a^{10}$

Zion (USA) *Steven Asmussen* a92
2 ch c Thunder Gulch(USA) —Riverkeeper (USA) (Awesome Again (CAN))
$6503a^{7}$

Zippi Jazzman (USA) *R M Beckett* a77 81
3 ch g Dixieland Band(USA) —Redeem (USA) (Devil's Bag (USA))
1584^{5} 4252^{7} 4765^{5} 4943^{2} 5708^{10}

Zipping (AUS) *John D Sadler* 120
7 b g Danehill(USA) —Social Scene (IRE) (Grand Lodge (USA))
$7188a^{9}$

Zomerlust *J J Quinn* 103
6 b g Josr Algarhoud(IRE) —Passiflora (Night Shift (USA))
1071^{13} 1517^{11} 2172^{15} 3491^{8} ◆ (3973) 4145^{13} 4854^{15} 5503^{5} 6105^{5} 6277^{9} 6947^{8} 7239^{15}

Zonergem *Lady Herries* a95 94
10 ch g Zafonic(USA) —Anasazi (IRE) (Sadler's Wells (USA))
2059^{2} 3505^{10}

Zoom (GER) *C Von Der Recke* 92
5 ch m Lomitas—Zizi Top (Robellino (USA))
$421a^{3}$ $603a^{9}$

Zoriana (FR) *F Rohaut* 82
3 b f Danehill Dancer(IRE) —Amarige (FR) (Lesotho (USA))
4881a^{0}

Zorn *P Howling* a55 60
9 br g Dilum(USA) —Very Good (Noalto)
749^{12} *858*^{9} *898*^{4} *933*^{11} *1029*^{6} *1142*^{6} *1260*^{5} *1591*^{3} *1906*^{11} 2075^{9} 2703^{13} 3037^{2} 3162^{6} 3371^{6} 3842^{7} 4268^{2} 4635^{14}

Zowington *C F Wall* a29 91
6 gr g Zafonic(USA) —Carmela Owen (Owington)
1537^{6} (1956) 2760^{11} 3881^{4} 4601^{10} 5101^{11} 5757^{5} 6650^{6}

Zulu Chief (USA) *A P O'Brien* a95 106
3 b c Fusaichi Pegasus(USA) —La Lorgnette (CAN) (Val De L'Orne (FR))
1418^{3} ◆ (3861a) ◆ 5135a^{3} 5944a^{4} *6261a*^{8}

Zulu Moon *A M Balding* a68 56
2 b g Passing Glance—Mory Kante (USA) (Icecapade (USA))
6602^{6} *7023*^{4}

Zulu Princess (IRE) *J S Moore* a56 69
3 b f Hawk Wing(USA) —Try To Catch Me (USA) (Shareef Dancer (USA))
3487^{5} (3906) 4253^{4} 4613a^{3}

Zuwaar *Ian Williams* a73 76
3 b g Nayef(USA) —Raheefa (USA) (Riverman (USA))
2199^{12} *2612*^{6} (3573) 4419^{8} 6400^{4} 6703^{9} 6862^{15} *7089*^{2} *7293*^{2} *7400*^{8} *(7587)* *(7827)*

Zuzu (IRE) *M A Jarvis* 93
2 b f Acclamation—Green Life (Green Desert (USA))
3625^{3} (4164) (5107) ◆ 6483^{18}

INDEX TO MEETINGS FLAT 2008

† Abandoned
* All-Weather
(M) Mixed meeting

Leading Turf Flat Trainers 2008

(22 March – 8 November 2008)

NAME	WINS-RUNS	2nd	3rd	4th	WIN £	TOTAL £	£1 STAKE
A P O´Brien	20-107 (19%)	6	8	11	2,683,152	3,276,097	-32.74
R Hannon	183-1338 (14%)	172	132	162	1,845,503	2,917,124	-256.86
Sir Michael Stoute	88-460 (19%)	66	54	47	1,511,580	2,758,918	-93.52
J H M Gosden	94-486 (19%)	69	53	52	1,839,812	2,589,635	+27.80
M Johnston	152-1087 (14%)	140	135	107	1,298,018	2,008,270	-219.26
J S Bolger	7-20 (35%)	4	3	0	1,530,661	1,810,106	+21.93
M A Jarvis	99-462 (21%)	73	65	48	1,188,020	1,668,868	-5.13
B J Meehan	69-581 (12%)	57	43	54	561,436	1,294,031	-166.03
Saeed Bin Suroor	58-313 (19%)	60	47	31	758,692	1,268,210	-56.42
R A Fahey	112-947 (12%)	115	96	108	748,959	1,239,591	-269.27
M R Channon	93-966 (10%)	93	126	114	666,281	1,239,189	-271.88
H R A Cecil	52-281 (19%)	43	37	30	472,381	1,179,512	-39.67
J Noseda	57-272 (21%)	32	28	36	858,383	1,070,362	-11.13
W J Haggas	82-407 (20%)	52	48	32	778,683	1,038,026	+100.68
B W Hills	70-617 (11%)	71	67	55	441,423	931,611	-221.16
L M Cumani	54-327 (17%)	50	45	40	521,941	924,076	-64.46
K A Ryan	104-841 (12%)	106	128	90	543,658	922,984	-207.67
M L W Bell	70-468 (15%)	55	57	48	605,534	917,194	-33.56
D Nicholls	68-532 (13%)	62	58	44	563,945	862,024	+79.83
A M Balding	66-421 (16%)	59	50	49	502,990	855,142	+24.31
K R Burke	57-552 (10%)	76	48	65	344,668	654,719	-118.29
P Chapple-Hyam	33-262 (13%)	44	32	26	252,232	606,886	-143.10
R M Beckett	41-330 (12%)	40	36	35	377,439	548,812	-1.32
R Charlton	33-277 (12%)	30	31	34	362,048	547,358	-80.86
T D Easterby	50-586 (9%)	35	55	44	298,599	508,286	-111.74
P F I Cole	53-421 (13%)	36	42	38	360,179	501,709	-78.37
J R Fanshawe	32-293 (11%)	38	41	35	182,695	496,640	-106.44
J R Best	26-381 (7%)	23	37	35	339,506	494,851	+19.44
J L Dunlop	37-453 (8%)	38	48	40	287,471	488,470	-163.56
B Smart	55-423 (13%)	56	42	41	303,753	487,192	-71.75
M P Tregoning	34-244 (14%)	25	35	22	236,970	456,266	-34.85
H Morrison	39-335 (12%)	40	34	39	297,562	453,171	+6.80
J S Goldie	39-384 (10%)	48	44	48	202,407	430,388	-99.54
D R C Elsworth	28-325 (9%)	30	33	30	150,840	398,501	-79.26
W R Swinburn	34-316 (11%)	36	41	31	264,805	392,363	-93.35
J G Given	35-353 (10%)	35	34	21	274,091	384,388	-22.66
P D Evans	72-727 (10%)	67	80	90	240,337	376,771	-150.88
E A L Dunlop	42-402 (10%)	39	43	40	214,544	366,297	-156.77
G A Swinbank	45-391 (12%)	43	46	42	229,788	362,994	-121.10
Mrs A J Perrett	32-286 (11%)	30	29	46	225,012	360,680	-43.97
C E Brittain	34-338 (10%)	17	27	25	251,453	360,464	-53.08
W R Muir	40-346 (12%)	36	41	35	175,926	360,130	+12.53
S Kirk	44-375 (12%)	35	27	38	225,468	356,170	-73.00
M Botti	42-277 (15%)	28	36	33	251,410	354,120	+48.31
G L Moore	74-503 (15%)	50	41	42	243,483	353,492	-98.16
J J Quinn	31-333 (9%)	40	35	35	174,069	345,439	-73.54
M H Tompkins	29-355 (8%)	30	35	37	228,248	340,249	-117.28
H Candy	32-218 (15%)	21	25	32	232,541	332,352	+36.32
M Dods	47-406 (12%)	34	49	50	213,555	323,901	-42.50
C F Wall	34-211 (16%)	29	16	23	161,789	309,117	+39.13

Leading Turf Flat Jockeys 2008

(22 March – 8 November 2008)

NAME	WIN-RIDES	2nd	3rd	4th	WIN £	TOTAL £	£1 STAKE
Ryan Moore	186-992 (19%)	142	115	98	2,065,629	3,581,641	-92.60
Richard Hughes	117-775 (15%)	112	80	74	1,122,840	2,030,242	-68.70
Jamie Spencer	113-723 (16%)	96	83	58	847,636	1,674,955	-212.59
N Callan	109-790 (14%)	113	113	86	594,882	1,073,588	-170.01
Paul Hanagan	91-778 (12%)	81	90	94	505,671	900,124	-186.12
Seb Sanders	89-614 (14%)	72	58	56	921,787	1,264,939	-115.25
Jimmy Fortune	82-569 (14%)	83	58	60	1,359,697	2,190,614	-120.59
Dane O´Neill	79-715 (11%)	92	71	90	639,773	1,027,367	-89.67
Tom Eaves	78-759 (10%)	91	72	74	418,471	661,579	-237.86
Darryll Holland	76-523 (15%)	43	66	59	640,814	913,776	-44.55
Jim Crowley	76-735 (10%)	70	69	96	558,451	882,133	-56.93
Ted Durcan	75-665 (11%)	77	60	60	587,510	1,372,653	-179.65
Philip Robinson	74-393 (19%)	53	46	42	996,555	1,319,406	-21.14
Eddie Ahern	73-659 (11%)	60	69	76	511,207	968,919	-97.00
George Baker	70-446 (16%)	62	54	45	354,623	505,940	-28.90
Joe Fanning	69-636 (11%)	49	57	55	494,881	697,530	-140.13
Chris Catlin	68-891 (8%)	80	90	86	289,263	510,149	-348.38
L Dettori	67-403 (17%)	74	40	36	1,441,387	2,247,841	-120.37
R Hills	66-410 (16%)	68	51	38	677,400	1,158,127	-48.98
Alan Munro	65-613 (11%)	65	67	47	543,176	919,593	-126.31
Steve Drowne	64-716 (9%)	67	67	78	544,269	939,865	-96.18
T P Queally	62-639 (10%)	51	68	57	489,811	814,206	-138.13
David Allan	61-549 (11%)	51	54	47	324,803	574,173	+7.04
Martin Dwyer	58-591 (10%)	59	70	53	924,243	1,374,910	-87.07
Hayley Turner	58-619 (9%)	60	65	66	449,645	707,318	-154.27
Pat Cosgrave	57-485 (12%)	39	40	47	323,175	456,058	-8.15
Shane Kelly	57-522 (11%)	52	42	54	400,462	623,664	-145.80
Jimmy Quinn	57-674 (8%)	64	68	67	484,799	773,997	-239.42
Richard Mullen	56-466 (12%)	38	53	41	301,078	478,149	-119.71
Paul Mulrennan	56-700 (8%)	50	67	75	232,953	393,909	-250.97
Robert Winston	55-611 (9%)	73	64	59	315,222	573,315	-194.33
David Probert	50-443 (11%)	52	35	51	234,792	342,318	-68.83
William Buick	50-545 (9%)	51	51	46	324,861	564,912	-157.76
L P Keniry	49-592 (8%)	48	54	52	333,459	483,814	-193.68
Greg Fairley	48-411 (12%)	37	30	32	274,134	498,358	-29.05
Adam Kirby	48-512 (9%)	64	59	46	318,845	509,703	-174.47
Michael Hills	45-401 (11%)	38	38	36	258,833	546,615	-139.71
Tony Hamilton	43-467 (9%)	45	45	56	154,405	298,573	-183.32
Micky Fenton	43-508 (8%)	49	45	50	203,374	367,958	-97.67
J-P Guillambert	41-388 (11%)	50	31	42	169,993	288,866	-54.10
Liam Jones	41-496 (8%)	52	46	48	304,869	505,040	-50.88
Francis Norton	40-399 (10%)	34	42	43	332,311	479,837	-88.00
John Egan	40-410 (10%)	39	39	32	243,468	459,330	-5.88
Royston Ffrench	40-559 (7%)	66	64	36	320,019	567,586	-252.06
Fergus Sweeney	39-431 (9%)	42	43	49	162,661	332,517	-136.00
P J McDonald	38-381 (10%)	42	39	37	172,965	267,213	-3.29
T P O´Shea	38-419 (9%)	42	37	41	183,882	305,341	-26.99
Neil Brown	37-279 (13%)	30	29	30	186,143	245,943	+35.78
Kirsty Milczarek	37-335 (11%)	27	34	44	157,187	222,838	+52.63
Rich'd Kingscote	36-347 (10%)	35	29	30	242,128	346,205	-30.83

Leading Flat Owners 2008

(22 March – 8 November 2008)

NAME	WINS-RUNS	2nd	3rd	4th	WIN £	TOTAL £
H R H Princess Haya Of Jordan	38-215 (18%)	35	27	20	1,895,716	2,167,296
K Abdulla	69-318 (22%)	43	36	28	863,678	1,694,027
Hamdan Al Maktoum	105-699 (15%)	100	89	71	866,935	1,524,339
Godolphin	58-313 (19%)	60	47	31	758,692	1,268,210
Mrs John Magnier & M Tabor	3-6 (50%)	0	1	0	837,358	858,898
Ballymacoll Stud	15-65 (23%)	14	6	8	551,976	964,515
Cheveley Park Stud	37-199 (19%)	25	23	29	453,966	1,039,231
D Smith, Mrs J Magnier, M Tabor	10-47 (21%)	5	4	5	637,708	803,081
Sheikh Hamdan Bin Mohammed	83-414 (20%)	46	52	43	595,746	804,589
Sheikh Ahmed Al Maktoum	52-261 (20%)	37	38	24	528,566	755,810
Mrs John Magnier	3-9 (33%)	1	2	1	525,123	595,753
Mrs J S Bolger	5-10 (50%)	2	0	0	485,525	565,009
Saeed Suhail	9-68 (13%)	9	10	9	457,670	540,965
Highclere Thor'bred Racing (VC2)	2-5 (40%)	0	0	1	436,090	436,467
M Tabor, D Smith & Mrs J Magnier	5-18 (28%)	1	0	0	348,000	399,362
George Strawbridge	11-40 (28%)	3	2	3	297,753	319,307
A D Spence	18-173 (10%)	18	23	20	193,713	355,350
J H Richmond-Watson	4-28 (14%)	6	4	3	221,691	295,953
Stonerside Stable Llc	4-14 (29%)	5	1	2	162,617	332,026
Saleh Al Homaizi & Imad Al Sagar	8-73 (11%)	12	7	7	117,886	369,690
J Reddam Mrs C Burrell J Harvey	1-2 (50%)	1	0	0	122,623	344,223
John Mayne	2-15 (13%)	0	3	0	215,219	244,634
Mme J-L Giral	1-2 (50%)	0	0	0	227,080	232,143
Jaber Abdullah	19-168 (11%)	13	30	17	101,360	348,386
Mountgrange Stud	11-75 (15%)	13	6	6	174,034	275,042
Saeed Manana	22-208 (11%)	11	19	16	180,004	257,894
Stefan Friborg	1-1 (100%)	0	0	0	212,888	212,888
The Calvera Partnership No 2	5-12 (42%)	1	1	3	209,399	215,652
Noodles Racing	5-19 (26%)	0	1	2	199,821	203,953
Sheikh Rashid Bin Mohammed	16-83 (19%)	11	5	11	85,936	312,960
Mrs J Magnier & Mrs David Nagle	2-2 (100%)	0	0	0	198,695	198,695
Matthew Green	32-187 (17%)	33	17	19	125,249	262,785
Mrs Susan Roy	11-62 (18%)	5	3	5	155,261	204,568
Malcolm & Mrs Penny Brown	4-9 (44%)	2	1	0	161,413	192,314
J C Smith	14-138 (10%)	12	21	20	89,020	244,830
Dab Hand Racing	5-26 (19%)	4	2	3	149,737	174,738
Mrs J Magnier, M Tabor & D Smith	1-12 (8%)	1	0	1	113,540	197,477
Tagg/Mrs Magnier/Meduri/G Moffitt	1-1 (100%)	0	0	0	154,698	154,698
Niarchos Family	8-42 (19%)	5	5	4	115,995	190,001
The Queen	14-78 (18%)	18	6	9	119,096	174,041
J Acheson	1-5 (20%)	0	0	1	141,925	150,786
P J McGee	1-2 (50%)	1	0	0	123,300	153,156
The Matthewman Partnership	5-32 (16%)	3	8	4	123,175	149,078
Derek J Willis & Rae Guest	1-1 (100%)	0	0	0	134,971	134,971
Sir Evelyn De Rothschild	6-16 (38%)	3	1	1	130,370	134,608
H R H Sultan Ahmad Shah	12-95 (13%)	7	12	9	103,891	150,973
Coleman Bloodstock Limited	3-23 (13%)	4	0	2	120,178	134,282
R A Green	9-40 (23%)	4	2	4	122,572	131,219
Exors Of The Late Mrs P W Harris	12-109 (11%)	15	14	10	100,588	150,387

Leading All-Weather Flat Jockeys

(11 Nov 2007 – 30 March 2008)

NAME	WIN-RIDES	2nd	3rd	4th	WIN £	TOTAL £	£1 STAKE
Chris Catlin	72-563 (13%)	63	59	45	204,127	281,490	-141.90
Kirsty Milczarek	42-221 (19%)	32	36	27	118,759	158,882	+42.63
T P Queally	41-265 (15%)	34	29	34	109,652	163,888	-86.19
Jim Crowley	41-273 (15%)	37	37	23	108,677	157,331	-30.40
George Baker	39-190 (21%)	22	18	23	109,178	140,378	+20.14
Hayley Turner	39-317 (12%)	32	36	44	122,493	178,743	-49.13
N Callan	38-174 (22%)	34	20	22	129,389	182,997	+6.20
James Doyle	30-191 (16%)	24	22	16	78,347	115,618	+26.35
Phillip Makin	29-129 (22%)	22	14	15	85,453	104,917	+50.20
Step'n Donohoe	28-205 (14%)	12	30	23	76,191	97,385	+8.95
Greg Fairley	25-179 (14%)	28	23	22	65,355	100,349	-65.43
Micky Fenton	25-255 (10%)	29	27	23	80,139	120,927	-116.29
Liam Jones	25-273 (9%)	26	27	28	72,675	109,860	-72.48
Pat Cosgrave	24-147 (16%)	23	24	12	51,626	78,456	-63.49
Adam Kirby	24-187 (13%)	30	19	19	50,505	88,207	-27.75
Andrew Elliott	24-212 (11%)	33	27	19	66,967	103,794	-43.36
Fergus Sweeney	21-175 (12%)	21	24	19	51,825	94,147	-68.63
Jamie Spencer	20-71 (28%)	9	8	11	136,211	172,729	-9.28
Paul Mulrennan	20-194 (10%)	22	29	20	62,712	101,211	-67.40
Jimmy Quinn	20-202 (10%)	30	18	27	40,966	75,252	+28.13
Seb Sanders	19-90 (21%)	16	9	10	141,853	177,197	+8.93
John Egan	19-138 (14%)	28	15	14	50,102	94,997	-20.21
Tolley Dean	19-157 (12%)	11	15	12	57,855	76,203	-54.14
T G McLaughlin	19-205 (9%)	18	21	28	47,058	75,076	-58.88
Steve Drowne	19-208 (9%)	30	26	19	67,478	123,530	-83.90
L P Keniry	19-277 (7%)	27	31	25	50,795	90,428	-104.50
Richard Hughes	18-98 (18%)	14	13	13	85,772	121,705	+10.97
Jerry O´Dwyer	18-142 (13%)	10	22	16	34,842	49,389	-23.21
Dane O´Neill	18-171 (11%)	18	18	25	53,797	77,308	-88.33
Dean McKeown	18-225 (8%)	34	26	26	37,453	80,009	-117.14
Eddie Ahern	17-103 (17%)	16	10	13	70,276	98,124	+38.16
Rich'd Kingscote	16-87 (18%)	15	12	7	35,225	50,381	-26.89
J-P Guillambert	15-145 (10%)	21	21	20	35,231	72,361	-32.00
Robert Havlin	14-132 (11%)	14	17	20	39,354	56,098	-76.99
Rus. Kennemore	12-104 (12%)	8	13	11	37,026	45,625	-21.72
Paul Doe	11-105 (10%)	9	11	11	23,365	38,541	-26.23
Neil Chalmers	11-145 (8%)	13	16	25	23,215	38,416	-36.67
Joe Fanning	10-37 (27%)	4	2	7	43,671	57,581	+2.95
Jamie Jones	10-64 (16%)	6	8	4	22,959	29,979	+36.28
Nicky Mackay	10-65 (15%)	10	8	6	21,793	33,788	-27.78
Francis Norton	10-96 (10%)	13	14	16	24,664	42,550	-39.88
James O´Reilly	9-43 (21%)	6	6	4	26,402	32,764	+13.00
T Quinn	9-45 (20%)	6	4	4	37,127	47,443	+12.53
Mark Lawson	9-51 (18%)	2	9	7	17,350	21,100	+16.43
Daniel Tudhope	9-64 (14%)	3	8	6	31,417	37,174	-4.13
Patrick Donaghy	9-96 (9%)	7	6	15	30,489	38,355	-29.00
Ashley Hamblett	8-31 (26%)	2	6	1	15,675	18,776	-0.13

Leading All-Weather Trainers

(11 Nov 2007 – 30 March 2008)

NAME	WINS-RUNS	2nd	3rd	4th	WIN £	TOTAL £	£1 STAKE
M Johnston	29–164 18%	32	28	20	93,727	£149,165	-42.48
D Shaw	34–296 11%	36	39	24	97,413	£148,228	-58.90
R Hannon	17–102 17%	18	11	15	84,234	129,807	-26.49
K A Ryan	23–173 13%	30	30	22	71,654	127,930	-73.36
C E Brittain	8–32 25%	1	5	7	88,051	99,717	+27.35
A J McCabe	18–132 14%	14	24	18	66,989	96,641	-16.60
G L Moore	26–145 18%	23	12	14	64,194	96,291	-46.01
P D Evans	21–211 10%	22	30	31	56,315	91,712	-23.17
K R Burke	19–130 15%	19	20	16	47,396	87,546	-14.63
M Botti	12–85 14%	8	15	13	63,130	83,104	+11.51
Miss G Kelleway	16–94 17%	7	16	16	60,835	81,326	-20.78
N P Littmoden	16–74 22%	9	13	10	55,304	78,780	-11.30
M W Easterby	8–42 19%	7	4	10	60,461	73,868	-10.75
M Wigham	23–90 26%	14	12	13	55,801	73,082	-5.40
M A Jarvis	9–43 21%	11	5	5	43,238	72,204	-15.37
J R Boyle	22–112 20%	19	22	14	47,793	71,753	-3.68
R Hollinshead	20–116 17%	14	12	13	57,634	70,291	+10.74
J R Best	17–167 10%	13	19	19	49,030	68,918	-64.68
P A Blockley	17–93 18%	7	11	9	45,495	56,495	+4.87
J A Osborne	17–68 25%	8	12	9	41,385	53,052	+25.43
P W Hiatt	18–83 22%	11	10	6	43,058	53,038	+43.10
W M Brisbourne	17–110 15%	14	19	15	37,044	52,921	-19.30
E J O'Neill	11–35 31%	6	6	3	42,554	50,376	+8.91
W J Haggas	9–43 21%	4	9	4	35,752	50,298	-4.61
P F I Cole	10–48 21%	4	5	8	37,875	49,137	+16.08
A W Carroll	14–173 8%	26	19	26	26,922	48,161	-61.79
R A Fahey	9–102 9%	14	14	10	23,173	47,113	+0.11
T D Barron	11–59 19%	4	2	8	41,317	44,745	+4.00
D K Ivory	12–71 17%	7	9	5	32,278	43,716	+1.50
J S Moore	7–45 16%	9	5	10	25,257	43,670	-13.00
Sir M Prescott	11–43 26%	6	6	4	32,375	42,960	-7.71
R A Harris	12–141 9%	16	9	21	28,694	42,832	-61.75
I A Wood	8–74 11%	9	8	7	24,654	42,434	+17.00
Stef Liddiard	9–82 11%	9	11	9	26,765	41,835	-16.88
M R Channon	7–54 13%	5	7	10	26,809	40,587	-7.67
J Akehurst	8–71 11%	15	6	7	20,973	40,056	-6.42
M D I Usher	9–83 11%	13	15	5	20,583	39,002	-25.52
W Jarvis	9–39 23%	3	5	5	22,319	38,210	+10.21
S Kirk	11–63 17%	5	9	10	29,422	36,698	-5.00
S Gollings	8–38 21%	8	8	0	21,423	33,033	+33.38
J G Given	10–50 20%	7	5	3	22,654	32,961	-4.50
B P J Baugh	9–84 11%	9	5	9	25,580	32,810	-2.00
S C Williams	5–81 6%	12	12	7	12,955	32,360	-42.25
I W McInnes	10–67 15%	7	4	10	24,846	30,860	+2.88
Tom Dascombe	10–34 29%	11	3	2	18,530	29,642	-14.94
G Wragg	2–15 13%	3	2	0	18,432	29,085	-6.75
P Howling	8–118 7%	10	6	16	17,589	28,496	-60.75
M J Wallace	9–48 19%	7	8	8	19,653	28,331	-4.86

Racing Post Top Rated 2008

(Best performance figures recorded between 1 January and 31 December 2008)

New Approach (IRE)....131
Curlin (USA)....131
Raven's Pass (USA)....131
Duke Of Marmalade (IRE)....130
Zarkava (IRE)....129
Youmzain (IRE)....128
Midnight Lute (USA)....128
Henrythenavigator (USA)....128
Big Brown (USA)....128
Conduit (IRE)....127
Paco Boy (IRE)....127
Yeats (IRE)....126
Viva Pataca....126
Papal Bull....126
Commentator (USA)....126
Marchand D'Or (FR)....126
Soldier Of Fortune (IRE)....126
Phoenix Tower (USA)....126
Sacred Kingdom (AUS)....126
Colonel John (USA)....126
It's Gino (GER)....126
Montmartre (FR)....126
Good Ba Ba (USA)....125
Getaway (GER)....125
Tamayuz....125
Goldikova (IRE)....125
Weekend Hussler (AUS)....125
Tartan Bearer (IRE)....125
Mambo In Seattle (USA)....125
Absolute Champion (AUS)....124
Well Armed (USA)....124
Apache Cat (AUS)....124
Super Hornet (JPN)....124
Ask....124
Eagle Mountain....124
Zenyatta (USA)....124
Vision D'Etat (FR)....124
Cesare....123
Heatseeker (IRE)....123
Go Between (USA)....123
Grand Couturier....123
Saddex....123
Mount Nelson....123
Sirmione (AUS)....123
Bankable (IRE)....123
Frozen Fire (GER)....123
Tiago (USA)....123
Haradasun (AUS)....123
Ginger Punch (USA)....123
Adlerflug (GER)....123
Kingsgate Native (IRE)....123
Fleeting Spirit (IRE)....123
Sageburg (IRE)....123
Lady Marian (GER)....123
Bob Black Jack (USA)....123
Jay Peg (SAF)....123
Lucky Island (ARG)....123
Overdose....123
Linngari (IRE)....122
Takeover Target (AUS)....122
Racing To Win (AUS)....122
Meisho Samson (JPN)....122
Admire Monarch (JPN)....122
Archipenko (USA)....122
Macarthur....122
Spirit One (FR)....122
Kip Deville (USA)....122
Lucarno (USA)....122
Darjina (FR)....122
Matsurida Gogh (JPN)....122
Mr. Nightlinger (USA)....122
Famous Name....122
Falco (USA)....122
Maldivian (NZ)....122
Proud Spell (USA)....122
Eishin Deputy (JPN)....122
Sun Classique (AUS)....122
Two Step Salsa (USA)....122
Music Note (USA)....122
Borderlescott....121
Better Talk Now (USA)....121
Doctor Dino (FR)....121
Tax Free (IRE)....121
Company (JPN)....121
Wanderin Boy (USA)....121
Inti Raimi (JPN)....121
Surf Cat (USA)....121
Septimus (IRE)....121
Red Rocks (IRE)....121
Creachadoir (IRE)....121
Traffic Guard (USA)....121
Sakhee's Secret....121
Pompeii Ruler (AUS)....121
Ventura (USA)....121
Armada (NZ)....121
Monterey Jazz (USA)....121

Raceform Median Times 2008

ASCOT

5f 1m 0.5
6f 1m 14.4
7f 1m 28.0
1m Str 1m 40.6
1m Rnd 1m 40.8
1m 2f 2m 9.8
1m 4f 2m 35.5
2m 3m 32.6
2m 4f 4m 20.6

AYR

5f 1m 0.1
6f 1m 13.6
7f 50y 1m 33.4
1m 1m 43.8
1m 1f 20y 1m 58.4
1m 2f 2m 12.0
1m 5f 13y 2m 56.6
1m 7f 3m 20.4
2m 1f 105y 4m 5.7

BATH

5f 11y 1m 2.5
5f 161y 1m 11.2
1m 5y 1m 40.8
1m 2f 46y 2m 11.0
1m 3f 144y 2m 30.6
1m 5f 22y 2m 52.0
2m 1f 34y 3m 51.9

BEVERLEY

5f 1m 3.5
7f 100y 1m 33.8
1m 100y 1m 47.6
1m 1f 207y 2m 7.0
1m 4f 16y 2m 40.9
2m 35y 3m 39.8

BRIGHTON

5f 59y 1m 2.3
5f 213y 1m 10.2
6f 209y 1m 23.1
7f 214y 1m 36.0
1m 1f 209y 2m 3.6
1m 3f 196y 2m 32.7

CARLISLE

5f 1m 0.8
5f 193y 1m 13.7
6f 192y 1m 27.1
7f 200y 1m 40.0
1m 1f 61y 1m 57.6
1m 3f 107y 2m 23.1
1m 6f 32y 3m 7.5
2m 1f 52y 3m 53.0

CATTERICK

5f 59.8s
5f 212y 1m 13.6
7f 1m 27.0
1m 3f 214y 2m 38.9
1m 5f 175y 3m 3.6
1m 7f 177y 3m 32.0

CHEPSTOW

5f 16y 59.3s
6f 16y 1m 12.9
7f 16y 1m 23.2
1m 14y 1m 36.2
1m 2f 36y 2m 10.6
1m 4f 23y 2m 39.0
2m 49y 3m 38.9
2m 2f 4m 3.6

CHESTER

5f 16y 1m 1.0
6f 18y 1m 13.8
7f 2y 1m 26.5
7f 122y 1m 33.8
1m 2f 75y 2m 12.2
1m 3f 79y 2m 26.6
1m 4f 66y 2m 41.0
1m 5f 89y 2m 55.7
1m 7f 195y 3m 29.9
2m 2f 147y 4m 10.9

DONCASTER

5f 1m 0.5
5f 140y 1m 7.4
6f 1m 13.6
7f 1m 26.3
1m Str 1m 39.3
1m Rnd 1m 41.0
1m 2f 60y 2m 11.2
1m 4f 2m 35.1
1m 6f 132y 3m 6.7
2m 110y 3m 35.5
2m 2f 3m 58.2

EPSOM

5f 55.7s
6f 1m 9.4
7f 1m 23.3
1m 114y 1m 46.1
1m 2f 18y 2m 9.7
1m 4f 10y 2m 38.9

FOLKESTONE

5f 1m
6f 1m 12.7
7f 1m 27.3
1m 1f 149y 2m 4.9
1m 4f 2m 40.9
1m 7f 92y 3m 29.7
2m 93y 3m 37.2

GOODWOOD

5f 58.4s
6f 1m 12.2
7f 1m 27.4
1m 1m 39.9
1m 1f 1m 56.3
1m 1f 192y 2m 8.0
1m 3f 2m 28.3
1m 4f 2m 38.4
1m 6f 3m 3.6
2m 3m 33.2
2m 5f 4m 33.1

GREAT LEIGHS

5f 1m 0.2
6f 1m 13.7
1m 1m 39.9
1m 2f 2m 8.6
1m 5f 66y 2m 53.6
1m 6f 3m 3.2
2m 3m 30.0

HAMILTON

5f 4y 1m
6f 5y 1m 12.2
1m 65y 1m 48.4
1m 1f 36y 1m 59.7
1m 3f 16y 2m 25.6
1m 4f 17y 2m 38.6
1m 5f 9y 2m 53.9

HAYDOCK

5f 1m 0.5
6f 1m 14.0
7f 30y 1m 30.2
1m 30y 1m 43.8
1m 2f 120y 2m 16.7
1m 3f 200y 2m 33.2
1m 6f 3m 4.3
2m 45y 3m 37.0

KEMPTON (AW)

5f 1m 0.5
6f 1m 13.1
7f 1m 26.0
1m 1m 39.8
1m 2f 2m 8.0
1m 3f 2m 21.9
1m 4f 2m 34.5
2m 3m 30.1

LEICESTER

5f 2y 1m
5f 218y 1m 13.0
7f 9y 1m 26.2
1m 60y 1m 45.1
1m 1f 218y 2m 7.9
1m 3f 183y 2m 33.9

LINGFIELD (TURF)

5f 58.2s
6f 1m 11.2
7f 1m 23.3
7f 140y 1m 32.3
1m 1f 1m 56.6
1m 2f 2m 10.5
1m 3f 106y 2m 31.5
1m 6f 3m 10.0
2m 3m 34.8

LINGFIELD (AW)

5f 58.8s
6f 1m 11.9
7f 1m 24.8
1m 1m 38.2
1m 2f 2m 6.6
1m 4f 2m 33.0
1m 5f 2m 46.0
2m 3m 25.7

MUSSELBURGH

5f 1m 0.4
7f 30y 1m 30.3
1m 1m 41.2
1m 1f 1m 54.7
1m 4f 2m 39.7
1m 5f 2m 52.0
1m 6f 3m 5.3
2m 3m 36.1

NEWBURY

5f 34y 1m 1.4
6f 8y 1m 13.0
7f 1m 25.7
1m 1m 39.7
1m 1f 1m 55.5
1m 2f 6y 2m 8.8
1m 3f 5y 2m 21.2
1m 4f 5y 2m 35.5
1m 5f 61y 2m 52.0
2m 3m 36.9

NEWCASTLE

5f 1m 0.7
6f 1m 15.2
7f 1m 29.0
1m Rnd 1m 43.7
1m 3y Str 1m 43.7
1m 1f 9y 1m 58.1
1m 2f 32y 2m 13.5
1m 4f 93y 2m 45.6
1m 6f 97y 3m 11.3
2m 19y 3m 36.2

NEWMARKET (ROWLEY)

5f 59.1s
6f 1m 12.2
7f 1m 25.4
1m 1m 38.6
1m 1f 1m 50.6
1m 2f 2m 5.8
1m 4f 2m 33.5
1m 6f 2m 58.5
2m 3m 30.8
2m 2f 3m 54.8

NEWMARKET (JULY)

5f 59.1s
6f 1m 12.5
7f 1m 25.7
1m 1m 40.0
1m 2f 2m 5.5
1m 4f 2m 32.9
1m 6f 175y 3m 11.3
2m 24y 3m 27.0

NOTTINGHAM
5f 13y.........................1m 0.7
6f 15y.........................1m 15.1
1m 54y........................1m 45.6
1m 1f 213y..................2m 10.7
1m 6f 15y...................3m 7.3
2m 9y..........................3m 33.6

PONTEFRACT
5f 1m 3.3
6f 1m 16.9
1m 4y..........................1m 45.9
1m 2f 6y.....................2m 13.7
1m 4f 8y.....................2m 40.8
2m 1f 22y...................3m 51.6
2m 1f 216y.................4m 3.9
2m 5f 122y.................5m 8.8

REDCAR
5f 58.6s
6f 1m 11.8
7f 1m 24.5
1m 1m 38.0
1m 1f 1m 53.0
1m 2f 2m 7.1
1m 3f 2m 21.7
1m 6f 19y...................3m 4.7
2m 4y..........................3m 31.4

RIPON
5f 1m 0.7
6f 1m 13.0
1m 1m 41.4
1m 1f 170y.................2m 5.4
1m 4f 10y...................2m 36.7
2m 3m 31.8

SALISBURY
5f 1m 0.8
6f 1m 14.8
6f 212y.......................1m 29.0
1m 1m 43.5
1m 1f 198y.................2m 9.9
1m 4f 2m 38.0
1m 6f 21y...................3m 7.4

SANDOWN
5f 6y...........................1m 1.6
7f 16y.........................1m 29.5
1m 14y........................1m 43.3
1m 1f 1m 56.3
1m 2f 7y.....................2m 10.5
1m 6f 3m 6.6
2m 78y........................3m 39.5

SOUTHWELL (TURF)
6f 1m 15.8
7f 1m 29.4
1m 2f 2m 13.1
1m 3f 2m 27.8
1m 4f 2m 41.7
2m 3m 38.6

SOUTHWELL (AW)
5f 59.7s
6f 1m 16.5
7f 1m 30.3
1m 1m 43.7
1m 3f 2m 28.0
1m 4f 2m 41.0
1m 6f 3m 8.3
2m 3m 45.5

THIRSK
5f 59.6s
6f 1m 12.7
7f 1m 27.2
1m 1m 40.1
1m 4f 2m 36.2
2m 3m 33.4

WARWICK
5f 59.6s
5f 110y.......................1m 5.9
7f 26y.........................1m 24.6
1m 22y........................1m 41.0
1m 2f 188y.................2m 21.1
1m 4f 134y.................2m 44.6
1m 6f 213y.................3m 19.0
2m 39y........................3m 33.8

WINDSOR
5f 10y.........................1m 0.3
6f 1m 13.0
1m 67y........................1m 44.7
1m 2f 7y.....................2m 8.7
1m 3f 135y.................2m 29.5

WOLVERHAMPTON (AW)
5f 20y.........................1m 2.3
5f 216y.......................1m 15.0
7f 32y.........................1m 29.6
1m 141y......................1m 50.5
1m 1f 103y.................2m 1.7
1m 4f 50y...................2m 41.1
1m 5f 194y.................3m 6.0
2m 119y......................3m 41.8

YARMOUTH
5f 43y.........................1m 2.2
6f 3y...........................1m 14.4
7f 3y...........................1m 26.6
1m 3y..........................1m 40.6
1m 2f 21y...................2m 10.5
1m 3f 101y.................2m 28.7
1m 6f 17y...................3m 7.6
2m 3m 34.6

YORK
5f 59.3s
6f 1m 11.9
7f 1m 25.3
1m 1m 38.8
1m 208y......................1m 52.0
1m 2f 88y...................2m 12.5
1m 4f 2m 33.2
1m 6f 3m 0.2
2m 2f 3m 58.4

Raceform Flat Record Times

ASCOT

Distance	Time	Age	Weight	Going	Horse	Date
5f	59.77 sec	2	9-3	Gd To Firm	Drawnfromthepast(IRE)	Jun 19 2007
5f	57.44 sec	6	9-1	Gd To Firm	Miss Andretti (AUS)	Jun 19 2007
6f	1m 12.46	2	9-1	Gd To Firm	Henrythenavigator(USA)	Jun 19 2007
6f	1m 12.46	2	9-1	Gd To Firm	Henrythenavigator(USA)	Jun 19 2007
7f	1m 26.76	2	7-12	Gd To Firm	Relative Order	Aug 11 2007
7f	1m 25.89	4	8-9	Gd To Firm	Dabbers Ridge (IRE)	Jly 29 2006
1m (R)	1m 40.59	2	8-12	Good	Jukebox Jury (IRE)	Sep 27 2008
1m (R)	1m 38.70	3	9-0	Gd To Firm	Henrythenavigator(USA)	Jun 17 2008
1m (S)	1m 37.21	5	9-0	Gd To Firm	Ramonti (FR)	Jun 19 2007
1m 2f	2m 4.150	4	8-7	Gd To Firm	I'm So Lucky	Jun 23 2006
1m 4f	2m 27.24	3	8-9	Gd To Firm	Linas Selection	Jun 23 2006
2m	3m 25.52	6	9-0	Gd To Firm	Tungsten Strike (USA)	May 2 2007
2m 4f	4m 18.29	8	9-1	Gd To Firm	Full House (IRE)	Jun 19 2007
2m 5f 159y	4m 49.07	4	9-5	Gd To Firm	Honolulu (IRE)	Jun 21 2008

AYR

Distance	Time	Age	Weight	Going	Horse	Date
5f	56.9 secs	2	8-11	Good	Boogie Street	Sep 18 2003
5f	55.68 secs	3	8-11	Gd to Firm	Look Busy (IRE)	Jun 21 2008
6f	69.7 secs	2	7-10	Good	Sir Bert	Sep 17 1969
6f	68.37 secs	5	8-6	Gd to Firm	Maison Dieu	Jun 21 2008
7f	1m 25.7	2	9-0	Gd to Firm	Jazeel	Sep 16 1993
7f	1m 24.9	5	7-11	Firm	Sir Arthur Hobbs	Jun 19 1992
7f 50y	1m 28.9	2	9-0	Good	Tafaahum (USA)	Sep 19 2003
7f 50y	1m 28.2	4	9-2	Gd to Firm	Flur Na H Alba	Jun 21 2003
1m	1m 39.2	2	9-0	Gd to Firm	Kribensis	Sep 17 1986
1m	1m 36.0	4	7-13	Firm	Sufi	Sep 16 1959
1m 1f 20y	1m 50.3	4	9-3	Good	Retirement	Sep 19 2003
1m 2f	2m 4.0	4	9-9	Gd to Firm	Endless Hall	Jly 17 2000
1m 2f192y	2m 13.3	4	9-0	Gd to Firm	Azzaam	Sep 18 1991
1m 5f 13y	2m 45.8	4	9-7	Gd to Firm	Eden's Close	Sep 18 1993
1m 7f	3m 13.1	3	9-4	Good	Romany Rye	Sep 19 1991
2m 1f105y	3m 45.0	4	6-13	Good	Curry	Sep 16 1955

BATH

Distance	Time	Age	Weight	Going	Horse	Date
5f 11y	59.50 secs	2	9-2	Firm	Amour Propre	Jly 24 2008
5f 11y	58.75 secs	3	8-12	Firm	Enticing (IRE)	May 1 2007
5f 161y	68.70 secs	2	8-12	Firm	Qalahari (IRE)	Jly 24 2008
5f 161y	68.1 secs	6	9-0	Firm	Madraco	May 22 1989
1m 5y	1m 39.7	2	8-9	Firm	Casual Look	Sep 16 2002
1m 5y	1m 37.2	5	8-12	Gd to Firm	Adobe	Jun 17 2000
1m 5y	1m 37.2	3	8-7	Firm	Alasha (IRE)	Aug 18 2002
1m 2f 46y	2m 5.8	3	9-0	Gd to Firm	Connoisseur Bay(USA)	May 29 1998
1m 3f144y	2m 25.74	3	9-0	Hard	Top Of The Charts	Sep 8 2005
1m 5f 22y	2m 47.2	4	10-0	Firm	Flown	Aug 13 1991
2m 1f 34y	3m 43.4	6	7-9	Firm	Yaheska (IRE)	Jun 14 2003

BEVERLEY

Distance	Time	Age	Weight	Going	Horse	Date
5f	61.0 secs	2	8-2	Gd to Firm	Addo (IRE)	Jly 17 2001
5f	60.1 secs	4	9-5	Firm	Pic Up Sticks	Apr 16 2003
7f 100y	1m 31.1	2	9-7	Gd to Firm	Champagne Prince	Aug 10 1995
7f 100y	1m 31.1	2	9-0	Firm	Majal (IRE)	Jly 30 1991
7f 100y	1m 29.5	3	7-8	Firm	Who's Tef	Jly 30 1991
1m 100y	1m 43.3	2	9-0	Firm	Arden	Sep 24 1986
1m 100y	1m 42.2	3	8-4	Firm	Legal Case	Jun 14 1989
1m 1f 207y	2m 1.8	3	9-7	Firm	Rose Alto	Jly 5 1991
1m 3f 216y	2m 30.8	3	8-1	Hard	Coinage	Jun 18 1986
1m 4f 16y	2m 35.8	4	9-3	Gd to Firm	Red River Rebel	Aug 25 2002
2m 35y	3m 29.5	4	9-2	Gd to Firm	Rushen Raider	Aug 14 1996

BRIGHTON

Distance	Time	Age	Weight	Going	Horse	Date
5f 59y	60.1 secs	2	9-0	Firm	Bid for Blue	May 6 1993
5f 59y	59.3 secs	3	8-9	Firm	Play Hever Golf	May 26 1993
5f 213y	68.1 secs	2	8-9	Firm	Song Mist (IRE)	Jly 16 1996
5f 213y	67.3 secs	3	8-9	Firm	Third Party	Jun 3 1997
5f 213y	67.3 secs	5	9-1	Gd to Firm	Blundell Lane	May 4 2000
6f 209y	1m 19.9	2	8-11	Hard	Rain Burst	Sep 15 1988
6f 209y	1m 19.4	4	9-3	Gd to Firm	Sawaki	Sep 3 1991
7f 214y	1m 32.8	2	9-7	Firm	Asian Pete	Oct 3 1989
7f 214y	1m 30.5	5	8-11	Firm	Mystic Ridge	May 27 1999
1m 1f 209y	2m 4.7	2	9-0	Gd to Soft	Esteemed Master	Nov 2 2001
1m 1f 209y	1m 57.2	3	9-0	Firm	Get The Message	Apr 30 1984
1m 3f 196y	2m 25.8	4	8-2	Firm	New Zealand	Jly 4 1985

CARLISLE

Distance	Time	Age	Weight	Going	Horse	Date
5f	60.1 secs	2	8-5	Firm	La Tortuga	Aug 2 1999
5f	58.8 secs	3	9-8	Gd to Firm	Esatto	Aug 21 2002
5f 193y	1m 12.45	2	9-6	Gd to Firm	Musical Guest (IRE)	Sep 11 2005
5f 193y	1m 10.83	4	9-0	Gd to Firm	Bo McGinty (IRE)	Sep 11 2005
6f 192y	1m 24.3	3	8-9	Gd to Firm	Marjurita (IRE)	Aug 21 2002
6f 206y	1m 26.5	2	9-4	Hard	Sense of Priority	Sep 10 1991
6f 206y	1m 25.3	4	9-1	Firm	Move With Edes	Jly 6 1996
7f 200y	1m 37.34	5	9-7	Gd to Firm	Hula Ballew	Aug 17 2005
7f 214y	1m 44.6	2	8-8	Firm	Blue Garter	Sep 9 1980
7f 214y	1m 37.3	5	7-12	Hard	Thatched (IRE)	Aug 21 1995
1m 1f 61y	1m 53.8	3	9-0	Firm	Little Jimbob	Jun 14 2004
1m 3f 107y	2m 22.46	3	8-5	Gd to Firm	Regal Connection(USA)	Aug 2 2006
1m 4f	2m 28.8	3	8-5	Firm	Desert Frolic (IRE)	Jun 27 1996
1m 6f 32y	3m 2.2	6	8-10	Firm	Explosive Speed	May 26 1994
2m 1f 52y	3m 46.2	3	7-10	Gd to Firm	Warring Kingdom	Aug 25 1999

CATTERICK

Distance	Time	Age	Weight	Going	Horse	Date
5f	57.6 secs	2	9-0	Firm	H Harrison	Oct 8 2002
5f	57.1 secs	4	8-7	Fast	Kabcast	Jly 7 1989
5f 212y	1m 11.4	2	9-4	Firm	Captain Nick	Jly 11 1978
5f 212y	69.8 secs	9	8-13	Gd to Firm	Sharp Hat	May 30 2003
7f	1m 24.1	2	8-11	Firm	Lindas Fantasy	Sep 18 1982
7f	1m 22.5	6	8-7	Firm	Differential (USA)	May 31 2003
1m 3f 214y	2m 30.5	3	8-8	Gd to Firm	Rahaf	May 30 2003
1m 5f 175y	2m 54.8	3	8-5	Firm	Geryon	May 31 1984
1m 7f 177y	3m 20.8	4	7-11	Firm	Bean Boy	Jly 8 1982

CHEPSTOW

Distance	Time	Age	Weight	Going	Horse	Date
5f 16y	57.6 secs	2	8-11	Firm	Micro Love	Jly 8 1986
5f 16y	56.8 secs	3	8-4	Firm	Torbay Express	Sep 15 1979
6f 16y	69.4 secs	2	9-0	Fast	Royal Fifi	Sep 9 1989
6f 16y	68.1 secs	3	9-7	Firm	America Calling (USA)	Sep 18 2001
7f 16y	1m 20.8	2	9-0	Gd to Firm	Royal Amaretto (IRE)	Sep 12 1996
7f 16y	1m 19.3	3	9-0	Firm	Taranaki	Sep 18 2001
1m 14y	1m 33.1	2	8-11	Gd to Firm	Ski Academy (IRE)	Aug 28 1995
1m 14y	1m 31.6	3	8-13	Firm	Stoli (IRE)	Sep 18 2001
1m 2f 36y	2m 4.1	5	8-9	Hard	Leonidas	Jly 5 1983
1m 2f 36y	2m 4.1	5	7-8	Gd to Firm	It's Varadan	Sep 9 1989
1m 2f 36y	2m 4.1	3	8-5	Gd to Firm	Ela Athena	Jly 23 1999
1m 4f 23y	2m 31.0	3	8-9	Gd to Firm	Spritsail	Jly 13 1989
1m 4f 23y	2m 31.0	7	9-6	Hard	Maintop	Aug 27 1984
2m 49y	3m 27.7	4	9-0	Gd to Firm	Wizzard Artist	Jly 1 1989
2m 2f	3m 56.4	5	8-7	Gd to Firm	Laffah	Jly 8 2000

CHESTER

Distance	Time	Age	Weight	Going	Horse	Date
5f 16y	60.06 secs	2	8-9	Gd to Firm	Not For Me (IRE)	Jly 14 2006
5f 16y	59.2 secs	3	10-0	Firm	Althrey Don	Jly 10 1964
6f 18y	1m 12.8	2	8-10	Gd to Firm	Flying Express	Aug 31 2002
6f 18y	1m 12.7	3	8-3	Gd to Firm	Play Hever Golf	May 4 1993
6f 18y	1m 12.7	6	9-2	Good	Stack Rock	Jun 23 1993
7f 2y	1m 25.2	2	9-0	Gd to Firm	Due Respect (IRE)	Sep 25 2002
7f 2y	1m 23.75	5	8-13	Gd to Firm	Three Graces (GER)	Jly 9 2005
7f 122y	1m 32.2	2	9-0	Gd to Firm	Big Bad Bob (IRE)	Sep 25 2002
7f 122y	1m 30.91	3	8-12	Gd to Firm	Cupid's Glory	Aug 18 2005
1m 2f 75y	2m 7.15	3	8-8	Gd to Firm	Stotsfold	May 7 2002
1m 3f 79y	2m 22.5	3	8-9	Gd to Firm	Rockerlong	Sep 23 2006
1m 4f 66y	2m 33.7	3	8-10	Gd to Firm	Fight Your Corner	May 7 2002
1m 5f 89y	2m 45.4	5	8-11	Firm	Rakaposhi King	May 7 1987
1m 7f 195y	3m 20.3	4	9-0	Gd to Firm	Grand Fromage (IRE)	Jly 13 2002
2m 2f 147y	3m 58.89	7	9-2	Gd to Firm	Greenwich Meantime	May 9 2007

DONCASTER

Distance	Time	Age	Weight	Going	Horse	Date
5f	58.4 secs	2	9-5	Firm	Sing Sing	Sep 11 1959
5f	58.4 secs	2	9-0	Good	D'Urberville	Sep 13 1967
5f	57.2 secs	6	9-12	Gd to Firm	Celtic Mill	Sep 9 2004
5f 140y	67.2 secs	2	9-0	Gd to Firm	Cartography (IRE)	Jun 29 2003
5f 140y	65.6 secs	9	9-10	Good	Halmahera (IRE)	Sep 8 2004
6f	69.6 secs	2	8-11	Good	Caesar Beware (IRE)	Sep 8 2004
6f	69.6 secs	2	8-11	Good	Caesar Beware (IRE)	Sep 8 2004
6f 110y	1m 17.42	2	8-2	Gd to Firm	Royal Confidence	Sep 12 2007
7f	1m 22.6	2	9-1	Good	Librettist (USA)	Sep 8 2004
7f	1m 21.6	3	8-10	Gd to Firm	Pastoral Pursuits	Sep 9 2004
1m	1m 36.5	2	8-6	Gd to Firm	Singhalese	Sep 9 2004
1m (R)	1m 35.4	2	8-10	Good	Playful Act (IRE)	Sep 9 2004

1m	1m 35.3	3	9-0	Gd to Firm	Gneiss	May 2 1994
1m (R)	1m 36.6	7	9-9	Gd to Firm	Invader	Jun 29 2003
1m 2f 60y	2m 13.4	2	8-8	Good	Yard Bird	Nov 6 1981
1m 2f 60y	2m 4.81	4	8-13	Gd to Firm	Red Gala	Sep 12 2007
1m 4f	2m 27.7	3	8-12	Gd to Firm	Takwin (IRE)	Sep 9 2000
1m 6f 132y	3m 1.07	3	8-7	Gd to Firm	Hi Calypso (IRE)	Sep 13 2007
2m 2f	3m 48.41	4	9-4	Gd to Firm	Septimus (IRE)	Sep 14 2007

EPSOM

Distance	Time	Age	Weight	Going	Horse	Date
5f	55.0 secs	2	8-9	Gd to Firm	Prince Aslia	Jun 9 1995
5f	53.6 secs	4	9-5	Firm	Indigenous	Jun 2 1960
6f	67.8 secs	2	8-11	Gd to Firm	Showbrook	Jun 5 1991
6f	67.3 secs	5	8-12	Good	Loyal Tycoon (IRE)	Jun 7 2003
7f	1m 21.3	2	8-9	Gd to Firm	Red Peony	Jly 29 2004
7f	1m 20.1	4	8-7	Firm	Capistrano	Jun 7 1972
1m 114y	1m 42.8	2	8-5	Gd to Firm	Nightstalker	Aug 30 1988
1m 114y	1m 40.7	3	8-6	Gd to Firm	Sylva Honda	Jun 5 1991
1m 2f 18y	2m 3.5	5	7-13	Good	Crossbow	Jun 7 1967
1m 4f 10y	2m 32.3	3	9-0	Gd to Firm	Lammtarra	Jun 10 1995

FOLKESTONE

Distance	Time	Age	Weight	Going	Horse	Date
5f	58.4 secs	2	9-2	Gd to Firm	Pivotal	Nov 6 1995
5f	58.23 secs	3	9-4	Gd to Firm	Millisecond	Sep 2 2007
6f	1m 10.8	2	8-9	Good	Boomerang Blade	Jly 16 1998
6f	69.38 secs	4	9-8	Gd to Firm	Munaddam (USA)	Sep 18 2006
6f 189y	1m 23.7	2	8-11	Good	Hen Harrier	Jly 3 1996
6f 189y	1m 21.4	3	8-9	Firm	Cielamour (USA)	Aug 9 1988
7f	1m 25.01	2	9-0	Gd to Firm	Dona Alba (IRE)	Sep 2 2007
7f	1m 23.76	3	8-11	Gd to Firm	Welsh Cake	Sep 18 2006
1m 1f 149y	1m 59.7	3	8-6	Gd to Firm	Dizzy	Jly 23 1991
1m 4f	2m 33.2	4	8-8	Hard	Snow Blizzard	Jun 30 1992
1m 7f 92y	3m 23.1	3	9-11	Firm	Mata Askari	Sep 12 1991
2m 93y	3m 34.9	3	8-12	Gd to Firm	Candle Smoke (USA)	Aug 20 1996

GOODWOOD

Distance	Time	Age	Weight	Going	Horse	Date
5f	57.5 secs	2	8-12	Gd to Firm	Poets Cove	Aug 3 1990
5f	56.0 secs	5	9-0	Gd to Firm	Rudi's Pet	Jly 27 1999
6f	69.8 secs	2	8-11	Gd to Firm	Bachir (IRE)	Jly 28 1999
6f	69.18 secs	4	9-0	Good	Tax Free (IRE)	Sep 9 2006
7f	1m 24.9	2	8-11	Gd to Firm	Ekraar	Jly 29 1999
7f	1m 23.8	3	8-7	Firm	Brief Glimpse (IRE)	Jly 25 1995
1m	1m 37.21	2	9-0	Good	Caldra (IRE)	Sep 9 2006
1m	1m 35.6	3	8-13	Gd to Firm	Aljabr (USA)	Jly 28 1999
1m 1f	1m 52.8	3	9-6	Good	Vena (IRE)	Jly 27 1995
1m 1f 192y	2m 2.81	3	9-3	Gd to Firm	Road To Love (IRE)	Aug 3 2006
1m 3f	2m 23.0	3	8-8	Gd to Firm	Asian Heights	May 22 2001
1m 4f	2m 31.5	3	8-10	Firm	Presenting	Jly 25 1995
1m 6f	2m 58.5	4	9-2	Gd to Firm	Mowbray	Jly 27 1999
2m	3m 21.55	5	9-10	Gd to Firm	Yeats (IRE)	Aug 3 2006
2m 4f	4m 11.7	3	7-10	Firm	Lucky Moon	Aug 2 1990

GREAT LEIGHS (A.W)

Distance	Time	Age	Weight	Going	Horse	Date
5f	60.36	2	8-12	Standard	Rublevka Star (USA)	Oct 23 2008
5f	59.34	6	9-0	Standard	Almaty Express	May 28 2008
6f	1m 13.13	2	8-9	Standard	Calahonda	Nov 15 2008
6f	1m 11.52	6	9-1	Standard	Nota Bene	May 29 2008
1m	1m 39.24	2	9-0	Standard	Shampagne	Sep 27 2008
1m	1m 37.16	3	8-8	Standard	Roaring Forte (IRE)	Sep 27 2008
1m 2f	2m 5.02	4	8-12	Standard	Mutajarred	May 28 2008
1m 5f 66y	2m 48.87	5	9-7	Standard	Red Gala	Sep 27 2008
1m 6f	3m 0.73	3	9-7	Standard	Detonator	Sep 14 2008
2m	3m 28.69	4	9-1	Standard	Whaxaar (IRE)	Apr 30 2008

HAMILTON

Distance	Time	Age	Weight	Going	Horse	Date
5f 4y	58.0 secs	3	7-8	Firm	Fair Dandy	Sep 25 1972
5f 4y	58.0 secs	5	8-6	Firm	Golden Sleigh	Sep 6 1972
6f 5y	1m 10.0	2	8-12	Gd to Firm	Break The Code	Aug 24 1999
6f 5y	69.3 secs	4	8-7	Firm	Marcus Game	Jly 11 1974
1m 65y	1m 45.8	2	8-11	Firm	Hopeful Subject	Sep 24 1973
1m 65y	1m 42.7	6	7-7	Firm	Cranley	Sep 25 1972
1m 1f 36y	1m 53.6	5	9-6	Gd to Firm	Regent's Secret	Aug 10 2005
1m 3f 16y	2m 19.32	3	9-0	Gd to Firm	Captain Webb	May 16 2008
1m 4f 17y	2m 32.0	4	10-0	Firm	Hold Tight	Aug 22 1983
1m 4f 17y	2m 32.0	4	7-4	Firm	Fine Point	Aug 24 1981
1m 5f 9y	2m 45.1	6	9-6	Firm	Mentalasanythin	Jun 14 1995

HAYDOCK

Distance	Time	Age	Weight	Going	Horse	Date
5f	59.2 secs	2	9-4	Firm	Money For Nothing	Aug 21 1964
5f	57.15 secs	3	8-11	Gd to firm	Fleeting Spirit (IRE)	May 24 2008
6f	1m 10.9	4	9-9	Gd to Firm	Wolfhound (USA)	Sep 4 1993
6f	69.9 secs	4	9-0	Gd to Firm	Iktamal (USA)	Sep 7 1996
7f 30y	1m 29.4	2	9-0	Gd to Firm	Apprehension	Sep 7 1996
7f 30y	1m 26.8	3	8-7	Gd to Firm	Lady Zonda	Sep 28 2002
1m 30y	1m 40.6	2	8-12	Gd to Firm	Besiege	Sep 7 1996
1m 30y	1m 40.1	3	9-2	Firm	Untold Riches (USA)	Jly 11 1999
1m 2f 120y	2m 22.2	2	8-11	Soft	Persian Haze	Oct 9 1994
1m 2f 120y	2m 8.5	3	8-7	Gd to Firm	Fahal (USA)	Aug 5 1995
1m 3f 200y	2m 26.4	5	8-2	Firm	New Member	Jly 4 1970
1m 6f	2m 58.46	3	8-10	Gd to Firm	Meshtri (IRE)	Sep 27 2008
2m 45y	3m 27.0	4	8-13	Firm	Prince of Peace	May 26 1984
2m 1f 130y	3m 55.0	3	8-12	Good	Crystal Spirit	Sep 8 1990

KEMPTON (A.W)

Distance	Time	Age	Weight	Going	Horse	Date
5f	60.29 sec	2	9-1	Standard	Inflight (IRE)	Aug 23 2006
5f	59.77 sec	5	8-7	Standard	Harry Up	Dec 10 2006
6f	1m 11.91	2	9-0	Standard	Elnawin	Sep 6 2008
6f	1m 11.11	4	9-4	Standard	Edge Closer	May 29 2008
7f	1m 25.93	2	9-0	Standard	Boscobel	Nov 22 2006
7f	1m 23.91	3	8-4	Standard	BomberCommand(US)	Nov 24 2006
1m	1m 38.56	2	9-0	Standard	Rallying Cry (USA)	Sep 30 2006
1m	1m 37.47	3	9-1	Standard	Evident Pride (USA)	Nov 29 2006
1m 2f	2m 3.77	6	8-13	Standard	Kandidate	Mar 29 2008
1m 3f	2m 17.74	4	9-9	Standard	Ajhar (USA)	Sep 5 2008
1m 4f	2m 30.48	3	8-11	Standard	Dansant	Nov 3 2007
2m	3m 27.49	4	9-2	Standard	Velvet Heights (IRE)	Apr 26 2006

LEICESTER

Distance	Time	Age	Weight	Going	Horse	Date
5f 2y	58.4 secs	2	9-0	Firm	Cutting Blade	Jun 9 1986
5f 2y	59.85 secs	5	9-5	Gd to Firm	The Jobber (IRE)	Sep 18 2006
5f 218y	1m 10.1	2	9-0	Firm	Thordis (IRE)	Oct 24 1995
5f 218y	69.4 secs	3	8-12	Gd to Firm	Lakeland Beauty	May 29 1990
7f 9y	1m 22.8	2	8-6	Good	Miss Dragonfly (IRE)	Sep 22 1997
7f 9y	1m 20.8	3	8-7	Firm	Flower Bowl	Jun 9 1986
1m 60y	1m 44.05	2	8-11	Gd to Firm	Congressional (IRE)	Sep 6 2005
1m 60y	1m 42.49	3	9-2	Gd to Firm	Street Warrior (IRE)	Sep 18 2006
1m 1f 218y	2m 5.3	2	9-1	Gd to Firm	Windsor Castle	Oct 14 1996
1m 1f 218y	2m 2.4	3	8-11	Firm	Effigy	Nov 4 1985
1m 1f 218y	2m 2.4	4	9-6	Gd to Firm	Lady Angharad (IRE)	Jun 18 2000
1m 3f 183y	2m 27.1	5	8-12	Gd to Firm	Murghem (IRE)	Jun 18 2000

LINGFIELD (TURF)

Distance	Time	Age	Weight	Going	Horse	Date
5f	57.1 secs	2	8-9	Good	Emerald Peace	Aug 6 1999
5f	56.2 secs	3	9-1	Gd to Firm	Eveningperformance	Jly 25 1994
6f	68.6 secs	2	9-3	Firm	The Ritz	Jun 11 1965
6f	68.2 secs	6	9-10	Firm	Al Amead	Jly 2 1986
7f	1m 21.3	2	7-6	Firm	Mandav	Oct 3 1980
7f	1m 20.1	3	8-7	Gd to Firm	Zelah (IRE)	May 13 1998
7f 140y	1m 29.9	2	8-12	Firm	Rather Warm	Nov 7 1978
7f 140y	1m 26.7	3	8-6	Fast	Hiaam	Nov 7 1978
1m 1f	1m 52.4	4	9-2	Gd to Firm	Quandary (USA)	Jly 15 1995
1m 2f	2m 4.6	3	9-3	Firm	Usran	Jly 15 1989
1m 3f 106y	2m 23.9	3	8-5	Firm	Night-Shirt	Jly 14 1990
1m 6f	2m 59.1	5	9-5	Firm	Ibn Bey	Jly 1 1989
2m	3m 23.7	3	9-5	Gd to Firm	Lauries Crusader	Aug 13 1988

LINGFIELD (A.W)

Distance	Time	Age	Weight	Going	Horse	Date
5f	58.46 secs	2	8-2	Standard	Ruby Tallulah	Aug 12 2008
5f	57.26 secs	8	8-12	Standard	Magic Glade	Feb 24 2007
6f	1m 10.75	2	9-4	Standard	Global City (IRE)	Oct 15 2008
6f	69.61	6	9-0	Standard	Excusez Moi (USA)	Feb 23 2008
7f	1m 23.68	2	8-4	Standard	Young Dottie	Oct 21 2008
7f	1m 22.19	4	8-7	Standard	Red Spell	Nov 19 2005
1m	1m 36.5	2	9-5	Standard	San Pier Niceto	Nov 30 1989
1m	1m 34.77	4	9-3	Standard	Baharah (USA)	Oct 30 2008
1m 2f	2m 1.79	5	9-0	Standard	Cusoon	Feb 24 2007
1m 4f	2m 28.10	3	8-10	Standard	Falcativ	Oct 27 2008
1m 5f	2m 42.47	3	9-2	Standard	Raffaas	July 3 2007
2m	3m 20.0	3	9-0	Standard	Yenoora	Aug 8 1992

MUSSELBURGH

Distance	Time	Age	Weight	Going	Horse	Date
5f	57.7 secs	2	8-2	Firm	Arasong	May 16 1994
5f	57.3 secs	3	8-12	Firm	Corunna	Jun 3 2000

7f 30y	1m 28.4	2	8-8	Firm	Sand Bankes	Jun 26 2000
7f 30y	1m 26.3	3	9-5	Firm	Waltzing Wizard	Aug 22 2002
1m	1m 40.3	2	8-12	Gd to Firm	Succession	Sep 26 2004
1m	1m 38.8	6	9-4	Gd to Firm	Sea Storm (IRE)	May 29 2004
1m 1f	1m 50.8	3	9-2	Firm	Short Respite	Aug 22 2002
1m 4f	2m 33.7	3	9-11	Firm	Alexandrine	Jun 26 2000
1m 5f	2m 47.51	6	9-11	Gd to Firm	Dimashq	Jly 31 2008
1m 6f	2m 59.2	3	9-7	Firm	Forum Chris	Jly 3 2000
2m	3m 26.6	5	9-6	Gd to Firm	Jack Dawson (IRE)	Jun 1 2002

NEWBURY

Distance	Time	Age	Weight	Going	Horse	Date
5f 34y	59.1 secs	2	8-6	Gd to Firm	Superstar Leo	Jly 22 2000
5f 34y	59.2 secs	3	9-5	Gd to Firm	The Trader (IRE)	Aug 18 2001
6f 8y	1m 11.19	2	8-9	Gd to Firm	Mixed Blessing	Jly 23 2005
6f 8y	69.42 secs	3	8-11	Gd to Firm	Nota Bene	May 13 2005
7f	1m 23.0	2	8-11	Gd to Firm	Haafhd	Aug 15 2003
7f	1m 21.5	3	8-4	Gd to Firm	Three Points	Jly 21 2000
1m	1m 37.5	2	9-1	Gd to firm	Winged Cupid (IRE)	Sep 16 2005
1m	1m 33.59	6	9-0	Firm	Rakti	May 14 2005
1m 1f	1m 49.6	3	8-0	Gd to Firm	Holtye	May 21 1995
1m 2f 6y	2m 1.2	3	8-7	Gd to Firm	Wall Street (USA)	Jly 20 1996
1m 3f 5y	2m 16.5	3	8-9	Gd to Firm	Grandera (IRE)	Sep 22 2001
1m 4f 5y	2m 28.26	4	9-7	Gd to Firm	Azamour (IRE)	Jul 23 2005
1m 5f 61y	2m 44.9	5	10-0	Gd to Firm	Mystic Hill	Jly 20 1996
2m	3m 25.4	8	9-12	Gd to Firm	Moonlight Quest	Jly 19 1996

NEWCASTLE

Distance	Time	Age	Weight	Going	Horse	Date
5f	58.8 secs	2	9-0	Firm	Atlantic Viking (IRE)	Jun 4 1997
5f	58.0 secs	4	9-2	Firm	Princess Oberon	Jly 23 1994
6f	1m 12.18	2	9-0	Gd to Firm	Stepping Up (IRE)	Sep 5 2005
6f	1m 10.6	8	9-5	Firm	Tedburrow	Jly 1 2000
7f	1m 24.2	2	9-0	Gd to Firm	Iscan (IRE)	Aug 31 1998
7f	1m 23.3	4	9-2	Gd to Firm	Quiet Venture	Aug 31 1998
1m	1m 38.9	2	9-0	Gd to Firm	Stowaway	Oct 2 1996
1m	1m 38.9	3	8-12	Firm	Jacamar	Jly 22 1989
1m 3y	1m 37.1	2	8-3	Gd to Firm	Hoh Steamer (IRE)	Aug 31 1998
1m 3y	1m 37.3	3	8-8	Gd to Firm	Its Magic	May 27 1999
1m 1f 9y	2m 3.2	2	8-13	Soft	Response	Oct 30 1993
1m 1f 9y	1m 52.3	3	6-3	Good	Ferniehurst	Jun 23 1936
1m 2f 32y	2m 6.5	4	8-9	Fast	Missionary Ridge	Jly 29 1990
1m 4f 93y	2m 37.3	5	8-12	Firm	Retender	Jun 25 1994
1m 6f 97y	3m 6.4	3	9-6	Gd to Firm	One Off	Aug 6 2003
2m 19y	3m 24.3	4	8-10	Good	Far Cry (IRE)	Jun 26 1999

NEWMARKET (ROWLEY)

Distance	Time	Age	Weight	Going	Horse	Date
5f	58.7 secs	2	8-5	Gd to Firm	Valiant Romeo	Oct 3 2002
5f	56.8 secs	6	9-2	Gd to Firm	Lochsong	Apr 30 1994
6f	69.56 secs	2	8-12	Gd to Firm	Bushranger (IRE)	Oct 3 2008
6f	69.56 secs	2	8-12	Gd to Firm	Bushranger (IRE)	Oct 3 2008
7f	1m 22.39	2	8-12	Gd to Firm	Ashram (IRE)	Sep 21 2004
7f	1m 22.2	4	9-5	Gd to Firm	Perfolia	Oct 17 1991
1m	1m 35.7	2	9-0	Gd to Firm	Forward Move (IRE)	Sep 21 2004
1m	1m 34.07	4	9-0	Gd to Firm	Eagle Mountain	Oct 3 2008
1m 1f	1m 47.2	4	9-5	Firm	Beauchamp Pilot	Oct 5 2002
1m 2f	2m 4.6	2	9-4	Good	Highland Chieftain	Nov 2 1985
1m 2f	2m 0.13	3	8-12	Good	New Approach (IRE)	Oct 18 2008
1m 4f	2m 27.1	5	8-12	Gd to Firm	Eastern Breeze	Oct 3 2003
1m 6f	2m 51.59	3	8-7	Good	Art Eyes (USA)	Sep 29 2005
2m	3m 19.5	5	9-5	Gd to Firm	Grey Shot	Oct 4 1997
2m 2f	3m 47.5	3	7-12	Hard	Whiteway	Oct 15 1947

NEWMARKET (JULY)

Distance	Time	Age	Weight	Going	Horse	Date
5f	58.5 secs	2	8-10	Good	Seductress	Jly 10 1990
5f	57.3 secs	6	8-12	Gd to Firm	Rambling Bear	Jan 1 1999
6f	1m 10.35	2	8-11	Good	Elnawin	Aug 22 2008
6f	69.5 secs	3	8-13	Gd to Firm	Stravinsky (USA)	Jly 8 1999
7f	1m 24.01	2	9-0	Good	Golden Stream (IRE)	Aug 22 2008
7f	1m 22.5	3	9-7	Firm	Ho Leng (IRE)	Jly 9 1998
1m	1m 39.0	2	8-11	Good	Traceability	Aug 25 1995
1m	1m 35.5	3	8-6	Gd to Firm	Lovers Knot	Jly 8 1998
1m 110y	1m 44.1	3	8-11	Good	Golden Snake	Apr 15 1999
1m 2f	2m 0.9	4	9-3	Gd to Firm	Elhayq (IRE)	May 1 1999
1m 4f	2m 25.11	3	8-11	Good	Lush Lashes	Aug 22 2008
1m 6f 175y	3m 4.2	3	8-5	Good	Arrive	Jly 11 2001
2m 24y	3m 20.2	7	9-10	Good	Yorkshire	Jly 11 2001

NOTTINGHAM

Distance	Time	Age	Weight	Going	Horse	Date
5f 13y	57.9 secs	2	8-9	Firm	Hoh Magic	May 13 1994
5f 13y	57.6 secs	6	9-2	Gd to firm	Catch The Cat (IRE)	May 14 2005
6f 15y	1m 11.4	2	811	Firm	Jameelapi	Aug 8 1983
6f 15y	1m 10.0	4	9-2	Firm	Ajanac	Aug 8 1988
1m 54y	1m 40.8	2	9-0	Gd to Firm	King's Loch	Sep 2 1991
1m 54y	1m 39.6	4	8-2	Gd to Firm	Blake's Treasure	Sep 2 1991
1m 75y	1m 43.35	3	9-1	Gd To Firm	Scuffle	Jun 11 2008
1m 1f 213y	2m 5.6	2	9-0	Firm	Al Salite	Oct 28 1985
1m 1f 213y	2m 2.3	2	9-0	Firm	Ayaabi	Jly 21 1984
1m 2f 50y	2m 10.27	3	9-0	Gd To Firm	Hunting Country	Jly 5 2008
1m 6f 15y	2m 57.8	3	8-10	Firm	Buster Jo	Oct 1 1985
2m 9y	3m 24.0	5	7-7	Firm	Fet	Oct 5 2036
2m 2f 18y	3m 55.1	9	9-10	Gd to Firm	Pearl Run	May 1 1990

PONTEFRACT

Distance	Time	Age	Weight	Going	Horse	Date
5f	61.1 secs	2	9-0	Firm	Golden Bounty	Sep 20 2001
5f	60.8 secs	4	8-9	Firm	Blue Maeve	Sep 29 2004
6f	1m 14.0	2	9-3	Firm	Fawzi	Sep 6 1983
6f	1m 12.6	3	7-13	Firm	Merry One	Aug 29 1970
1m 4y	1m 42.8	2	9-13	Firm	Star Spray	Sep 6 1983
1m 4y	1m 42.8	2	9-0	Firm	Alasil (USA)	Sep 26 2002
1m 4y	1m 40.6	4	9-10	Gd to Firm	Island Light	Apr 13 2002
1m 2f 6y	2m 10.1	2	9-0	Firm	Shanty Star	Oct 7 2002
1m 2f 6y	2m 8.2	4	7-8	Hard	Happy Hector	Jly 9 1979
1m 2f 6y	2m 8.2	3	7-13	Hard	Tom Noddy	Aug 21 1972
1m 4f 8y	2m 33.72	3	8-7	Firm	Ajaan	Aug 8 2007
2m 1f 22y	3m 40.67	4	8-7	Gd to Firm	Paradise Flight	June 6 2005
2m 1f 216y	3m 51.1	3	8-8	Firm	Kudz	Sep 9 1986
2m 5f 122y	4m 47.8	4	8-4	Firm	Physical	May 14 1984

REDCAR

Distance	Time	Age	Weight	Going	Horse	Date
5f	56.9 secs	2	9-0	Firm	Mister Joel	Oct 24 1995
5f	56.01 secs	10	9-3	Firm	Henry Hall	Sep 20 2006
6f	68.8 secs	2	8-3	Gd to Firm	Obe Gold	Oct 2 2004
6f	68.6 secs	3	9-2	Gd to Firm	Sizzling Saga	Jun 21 1991
7f	1m 21.28	2	9-3	Firm	Karoo Blue	Sep 20 2006
7f	1m 21.0	3	9-1	Firm	Empty Quarter	Oct 3 1995
1m	1m 34.37	2	9-0	Firm	Mastership	Sep 20 2006
1m	1m 32.42	4	10-0	Firm	Nanton	Sep 20 2006
1m 1f	1m 52.4	2	9-0	Firm	Spear (IRE)	Sep 13 2004
1m 1f	1m 48.5	5	8-12	Firm	Mellottie	Jly 25 1990
1m 2f	2m 10.1	2	8-11	Good	Adding	Nov 10 1989
1m 2f	2m 1.4	5	9-2	Firm	Eradicate	May 28 1990
1m 3f	2m 17.2	3	8-9	Firm	Photo Call	Aug 7 1990
1m 5f 135y	2m 54.7	6	9-10	Firm	Brodessa	Jun 20 1992
1m 6f 19y	2m 59.81	4	9-1	Gd to Firm	Esprit De Corps	Sep 11 2006
2m 4y	3m 24.9	3	9-3	Gd to Firm	Subsonic	Oct 8 1991
2m 3f	4m 10.1	5	7-4	Gd to Firm	Seldom In	Aug 9 1991

RIPON

Distance	Time	Age	Weight	Going	Horse	Date
5f	57.8 secs	2	8-8	Firm	Super Rocky	Jly 5 1991
5f	57.6 secs	5	8-5	Good	Broadstairs Beauty	May 21 1995
6f	1m 10.4	2	9-2	Good	Cumbrian Venture	Aug 17 2002
6f	69.8 secs	4	9-8	Gd to Firm	Tadeo	Aug 16 1997
6f	69.8 secs	5	7-10	Firm	Quoit	Jly 23 1966
1m	1m 39.79	2	8-6	Good	Top Jaro (FR)	Sep 24 2005
1m	1m 36.62	4	8-11	Gd to Firm	Granston (IRE)	Aug 29 2005
1m 1f 170y	1m 59.12	5	8-9	Gd to Firm	Wahoo Sam (USA)	Aug 30 2005
1m 2f	2m 2.6	3	9-4	Firm	Swift Sword	Jly 20 1990
1m 4f 10y	2m 32.06	4	8-8	Good	Hearthstead Wings	Apr 29 2006
2m	3m 27.07	5	9-12	Gd to Firm	Greenwich Meantime	Aug 30 2005

SALISBURY

Distance	Time	Age	Weight	Going	Horse	Date
5f	59.3 secs	2	9-0	Gd to Firm	Ajigolo	May 12 2005
5f	59.3 secs	2	9-0	Gd to Firm	Ajigolo	May 12 2005
6f	1m 12.1	2	8-0	Gd to Firm	Parisian Lady (IRE)	Jun 10 1997
6f	1m 11.3	3	8-1	Firm	Bentong (IRE)	May 7 2006
6f 212y	1m 25.9	2	9-0	Firm	More Royal (USA)	Jun 29 1995
6f 212y	1m 24.9	3	9-7	Firm	High Summer (USA)	Sep 5 1996
1m	1m 40.4	2	8-13	Firm	Choir Master (USA)	Sep 17 2002
1m	1m 38.29	3	8-7	Gd to Firm	Layman (USA)	Aug 11 2005
1m 1f 198y	2m 4.9	3	8-6	Gd to Firm	Zante	Aug 12 1998
1m 4f	2m 31.6	3	9-5	Gd to Firm	Arrive	Jun 27 2001
1m 6f 15y	2m 59.4	3	8-6	Gd to Firm	Tabareeh	Sep 2 1999

SANDOWN

Distance	Time	Age	Weight	Going	Horse	Date
5f 6y	59.4 secs	2	9-3	Firm	Times Time	Jly 22 1982
5f 6y	58.8 secs	6	8-9	Gd to Firm	Palacegate Touch	Sep 17 1996
7f 16y	1m 26.56	2	9-0	Gd to Firm	Raven's Pass (USA)	Sep 1 2007
7f 16y	1m 26.3	3	9-0	Firm	Mawsuff	Jun 14 1983
1m 14y	1m 41.1	2	8-11	Fast	Reference Point	Sep 23 1986

Distance	Time	Age	Weight	Going	Horse	Date
1m 14y	1m 39.0	3	8-8	Firm	Linda's Fantasy	Aug 19 1983
1m 1f	1m 54.6	2	8-8	Gd to Firm	French Pretender	Sep 20 1988
1m 1f	1m 52.4	7	9-3	Gd to Firm	Bourgainville	Aug 11 2005
1m 2f 7y	2m 2.1	4	8-11	Firm	Kalaglow	May 31 1982
1m 3f 91y	2m 21.6	4	8-3	Fast	Aylesfield	Jly 7 1984
1m 6f	2m 56.9	4	8-7	Gd to Firm	Lady Rosanna	Jly 19 1989
2m 78y	3m 29.9	6	9-2	Firm	Sadeem	May 29 1989

SOUTHWELL (TURF)

Distance	Time	Age	Weight	Going	Horse	Date
6f	1m 15.03	2	9-3	Good	Trepa	Sep 6 2006
6f	1m 13.48	4	8-10	Good	Paris Bell	Sep 6 2006
7f	1m 27.56	2	9-7	Good	Hart Of Gold	Sep 6 2006
7f	1m 25.95	3	9-0	Good	Aeroplane	Sep 6 2006
1m 2f	2m 7.470	3	8-11	Good	Desert Authority(USA)	Sep 6 2006
1m 3f	2m 20.13	4	9-12	Good	Sanchi	Sep 6 2006
1m 4f	2m 34.4	5	9-3	Gd to Firm	Corn Lily	Aug 10 1991
2m	3m 34.1	5	9-1	Gd to Firm	Triplicate	Sep 20 1991

SOUTHWELL (A.W)

Distance	Time	Age	Weight	Going	Horse	Date
5f	58.89 secs	2	8-6	Standard	Egyptian Lord	Dec 15 2005
5f	57.14 secs	5	9-5	Standard	Godfrey Street	Jan 24 2008
6f	1m 14.00	2	8-5	Standard	Panalo	Nov 8 1989
6f	1m 13.50	4	10-02	Standard	Saladan Knight	Dec 30 1989
7f	1m 27.10	2	8-2	Standard	Mystic Crystal	Nov 20 1990
7f	1m 26.80	5	8-4	Standard	Amenable	Dec 13 1990
1m	1m 38.00	2	8-9	Standard	Alpha Rascal	Nov 13 1990
1m	1m 38.00	2	8-10	Standard	Andrew's First	Dec 30 1989
1m	1m 37.25	3	8-6	Standard	Valira	Nov 3 1990
1m 3f	2m 21.50	4	9-7	Standard	Tempering	Dec 5 1990
1m 4f	2m 33.90	4	9-12	Standard	Fast Chick	Nov 8 1989
1m 6f	3m 1.60	3	7-8	Standard	Erevnon	Dec 29 1990
2m	3m 37.60	9	8-12	Standard	Old Hubert	Dec 5 1990

THIRSK

Distance	Time	Age	Weight	Going	Horse	Date
5f	57.2 secs	2	9-7	Gd to Firm	Proud Boast	Aug 5 2000
5f	56.9 secs	5	9-6	Firm	Charlie Parkes	April 11 2003
6f	69.2 secs	2	9-6	Gd to Firm	Westcourt Magic	Aug 25 1995
6f	68.8 secs	6	9-4	Firm	Johayro	Jly 23 1999
7f	1m 23.7	2	8-9	Firm	Courting	Jly 23 1999
7f	1m 22.8	4	8-5	Firm	Silver Haze	May 21 1988
1m	1m 37.9	2	9-0	Firm	Sunday Symphony	Sep 4 2004
1m	1m 34.8	4	8-13	Firm	Yearsley	May 5 1990
1m 4f	2m 29.9	5	9-12	Firm	Gallery God	Jun 4 2001
2m	3m 22.3	3	8-11	Firm	Tomaschek	Jly 17 1981

WARWICK

Distance	Time	Age	Weight	Going	Horse	Date
5f	57.95 secs	2	8-9	Gd to Firm	Amour Propre	Jun 26 2008
5f	57.7 secs	4	9-6	Gd to Firm	Little Edward	Jly 7 2002
5f 110y	63.6 secs	5	8-6	Gd to Firm	Dizzy In The Head	Jun 27 2004
6f	1m 11.22	2	9-3	Gd to Firm	Hurricane Hymnbook	Sep 15 2007
6f	69.44	5	8-12	Gd to Firm	Peter Island	Jun 26 2008
7f 26y	1m 22.9	2	9-0	Firm	Country Rambler(USA)	Jun 20 2004
7f 26y	1m 20.7	4	8-8	Good	Etlaala	Apr 17 2006
1m 22y	1m 37.1	3	8-11	Firm	Orinocovsky (IRE)	Jun 26 2002
1m 2f 188y	2m 14.98	4	8-12	Gd to Firm	Ronaldsay	Jun 16 2008
1m 4f 134y	2m 39.5	3	8-13	Gd to Firm	Maimana (IRE)	Jun 22 2002
1m 6f 135y	3m 7.5	3	9-7	Gd to Firm	Burma Baby (USA)	Jly 2 1999
2m 39y	3m 27.9	3	8-1	Firm	Decoy	Jun 26 2002

WINDSOR

Distance	Time	Age	Weight	Going	Horse	Date
5f 10y	58.75 secs	2	8-12	Gd to Firm	Hoh Mike (IRE)	May 15 2006
5f 10y	58.3 secs	5	7-10	Gd to Firm	Beyond The Clouds	Jun 2 2001
6f	1m 10.5	2	9-5	Gd to Firm	Cubism (USA)	Aug 17 1998
6f	1m 10.26	5	9-1	Gd to Firm	Baltic King	May 23 2005
1m 67y	1m 42.78	2	8-11	Gd to Firm	Sequillo	Sep 29 2008
1m 67y	1m 40.27	4	9-3	Gd to Firm	Librettist (USA)	Jul 1 2006
1m 2f 7y	2m 3.0	2	9-1	Firm	Moomba Masquerade	May 19 1990
1m 3f 135y	2m 21.5	3	9-2	Firm	Double Florin	May 19 1980

WOLVERHAMPTON (A.W.)

Distance	Time	Age	Weight	Going	Horse	Date
5f 20y	61.13 sec	2	8-8	Std to Fast	Yungaburra (IRE)	Nov 8 2006
5f 20y	60.56 sec	3	8-10	Standard	King Orchisios (IRE)	Oct 29 2006
5f 216y	1m 12.61	2	9-0	Std to Fast	Prime Defender	Nov 8 2006
5f 216y	1m 13.32	5	8-12	Standard	Desert Opal	Sep 17 2005
7f 32y	1m 27.70	2	9-5	Standard	Billy Dane	Aug 14 2006
7f 32y	1m 26.86	6	9-3	Standard	Border Music	Mar 10 2007
1m 141y	1m 48.08	2	8-9	Std to Fast	Worldly	Aug 30 2006
1m 141y	1m 46.71	4	8-12	Standard	Cimyla	Nov 11 2005
1m 1f 103y	2m 0.76	2	9-0	Standard	Mr Excel (IRE)	Nov 14 2005
1m 1f 103y	1m 57.34	4	8-13	Standard	Bahar Shumaal (IRE)	Aug 31 2006
1m 4f 50y	2m 35.71	3	9-2	Std to Fast	Steppe Dancer (IRE)	Aug 30 2006
1m 5f 194y	2m 59.85	6	9-12	Std to Fast	Valance (IRE)	Aug 30 2006
2m 119y	3m 35.85	5	8-11	Std to Fast	Market Watcher (USA)	Nov 21 2006

YARMOUTH

Distance	Time	Age	Weight	Going	Horse	Date
5f 43y	60.4 secs	2	8-6	Gd to Firm	Ebba	Jly 26 1999
5f 43y	59.8 secs	4	8-13	Gd to Firm	Roxanne Mill	Aug 25 2002
6f 3y	1m 10.4	2	9-0	Fast	Lanchester	Aug 15 1988
6f 3y	69.9 secs	4	8-9	Firm	Malhub (USA)	Jun 13 2002
7f 3y	1m 22.2	2	9-0	Gd to Firm	Warrshan	Sep 14 1988
7f 3y	1m 22.12	4	9-4	Gd to Firm	Glenbuck (IRE)	Apr 26 2007
1m 3y	1m 36.3	2	8-2	Gd to Firm	Outrun	Sep 15 1988
1m 3y	1m 33.9	3	8-8	Firm	Bonne Etoile	Jun 27 1995
1m 1f	1m 54.85	3	9-1	Gd To Firm	Riqaab (IRE)	Jly 15 2008
1m 2f 21y	2m 2.83	3	8-8	Firm	Reunite (IRE)	Jul 18 2006
1m 3f 101y	2m 23.1	3	8-9	Firm	Rahil	Jly 1 1993
1m 6f 17y	2m 57.8	3	8-2	Gd to Firm	Barakat	Jly 24 1990
2m	3m 26.7	4	8-2	Gd to Firm	Alhesn (USA)	Jly 26 1999
2m 2f 51y	3m 56.8	4	9-10	Firm	Provence	Sep 19 1991

YORK

Distance	Time	Age	Weight	Going	Horse	Date
5f	57.3 secs	2	7-8	Gd to Firm	Lyric Fantasy	Aug 20 1992
5f	56.1 secs	3	9-3	Gd to Firm	Dayjur	Aug 23 1990
6f	69.5 secs	2	9-0	Gd to Firm	Indiscreet (CAN)	Aug 22 1996
6f	68.58 secs	7	9-4	Firm	Cape Of Good Hope	Jun 16 2005
7f	1m 23.29	2	8-10	Good	Vital Equine (IRE)	Sep 9 2006
7f	1m 21.98	5	9-6	Good	Iffraaj	Sep 9 2006
1m	1m 39.20	2	8-1	Gd to Firm	Missoula (IRE)	Aug 31 2005
1m	1m 36.35	3	9-1	Gd to Firm	Mostashaar (FR)	Jun 16 2005
1m 208y	1m 46.76	5	9-8	Gd to Firm	Echo Of Light	Sep 5 2007
1m 2f 88y	2m 6.09	4	8-11	Gd to Firm	Imperial Stride	Jun 17 2005
1m 4f	2m 26.28	6	8-9	Firm	Bandari (IRE)	Jun 18 2005
1m 5f 194y	2m 51.8	3	8-7	Gd to Firm	Tuning	Aug 19 1998
1m 7f 195y	3m 18.4	3	8-0	Gd to Firm	Dam Busters	Aug 16 1988

Raceform Flat Speed Figures 2008

(Best time performances achieved between1 January and 31 December 2008 (min rating 110, 2-y-o 105)

THREE YEAR-OLDS AND UPWARDS – TURF

Aahayson 114 (6f,Don,GS,Mar 22)
Abraham Lincoln 112 (6f,Cur,F,May 24)
Ace Of Hearts 110 (8f,San,GF,Jly 5)
Admire Aura 113 (9f,Nad,G,Mar 29)
African Rose 117 (6f,Don,S,Sep 13)
Against The Grain 110 (6f,Ayr,HY,Sep 19)
Age Of Chivalry 110 (6f,Cur,GF,Jly 27)
Ajaan 113 (12f,Nmk,G,May 3)
Ajigolo 110 (6f,Nmk,G,May 25)
Akua'Ba 110 (6f,Cur,GF,Jly 27)
Al Khaleej 110 (7f,Asc,GF,May 10)
Al Qasi 113 (7f,Cur,GY,Jly 12)
Alamanni 112 (10f,Lon,GS,Oct 5)
Alarazi 112 (10f,Cur,GY,May 5)
Albisola 113 (9f,Lon,HY,Apr 6)
Aleagueoftheirown 111 (6f,Cur,GF,Jly 27)
Alessandro Volta 115 (12f,Cur,GY,Jun 29)
Alexandros 111 (8½f,Eps,G,Jun 6)
All The Aces 115 (12f,Chs,GF,May 8)
All The Good 111 (13f,Nby,GS,Aug 22)
Allegretto 116 (15½f,Lon,GS,Oct 26)
Allied Powers 112 (12f,Chs,G,May 7)
Almass 111 (7f,Leo,S,Nov 2)
Almuraad 110 (7½f,Nad,G,Feb 7)
Alnadana 111 (7f,Lon,GS,Sep 7)
Always Bold 112 (13f,Ham,G,Jly 18)
Amber Queen 112 (7f,Yor,HY,Jly 12)
Americain 113 (15f,Lon,GS,Sep 5)
American Trilogy 110 (12f,Lon,HY,Apr 13)
Ancien Regime 115 (6f,Don,S,Sep 13)
Appalachian Trail 111 (7f,Hay,G,May 10)
Aqlaam 110 (7f,Asc,GF,Jun 18)
Arabian Gleam 112 (7f,Don,S,Sep 13)
Arc Bleu 110 (16f,Ncs,S,Jun 28)
Archipenko 116 (9f,Nad,G,Mar 29)
Ascalon 115 (16f,Asc,G,Sep 27)
Ask 112 (10f,Asc,GF,Jun 18)
Ask The Butler 112 (10f,San,G,Aug 30)
Assertive 116 (6f,Don,S,Sep 13)
Astrologie 113 (12½f,Lon,G,Oct 4)
Astronomer Royal 113 (6f,Cur,F,May 24)
Athanor 111 (8f,Cha,G,Jun 8)
Atlantic Sport 110 (8f,Goo,GF,Aug 2)
Avanti Polonia 112 (12½f,Dea,S,Aug 10)
Azabara 110 (8f,Lon,G,May 11)

Bahar Shumaal 111 (8f,Lei,GF,Jun 19)
Baharah 111 (8½f,Eps,G,Jun 7)
Balius 111 (10f,Lon,HY,Apr 6)
Balkan Knight 110 (16f,Asc,G,Sep 28)
Balladeuse 115 (12½f,Lon,G,Oct 4)
Balthazaar's Gift 111 (6f,Nmk,GF,Aug 23)
Bankable 112 (8f,Nmk,GF,Oct 3)
Bannaby 116 (15½f,Lon,GS,Oct 26)
Barshiba 112 (10f,Nmk,G,Oct 17)
Bashkirov 113 (12f,Cur,GY,Jun 29)
Beach Bound 111 (9f,Leo,GF,May 21)
Beach Bunny 110 (10f,Cur,SH,Sep 13)
Beckermet 111 (6f,Yor,GF,May 14)
Bel Cantor 112 (6f,Hay,HY,Aug 9)
Believe Me 113 (10½f,Lon,HY,Apr 3)
Bellifiore 113 (6½f,Dea,S,Aug 10)
Benbaun 114 (5f,Cur,GY,Jun 29)
Bermuda Rye 110 (8f,Sai,HY,Nov 2)
Big Timer 110 (6f,Asc,GF,Jun 21)
Birkside 110 (12f,Pon,G,Aug 6)
Blue Bresil 114 (11f,Lon,GS,May 5)
Blue Monday 112 (11f,Nby,G,Sep 19)
Blue Sky Basin 111 (7f,Goo,GF,Jly 31)
Blythe Knight 112 (8½f,Eps,G,Jun 6)
Borderlescott 115 (5f,Nmk,G,Aug 22)
Boris De Deauville 113 (10f,Dea,GS,Aug 16)
Brave Prospector 110 (6f,Yor,G,Jun 14)
Bronze Cannon 112 (10f,Nmk,G,Apr 17)
Bullish Luck 111 (9f,Nad,G,Mar 29)
Bustan 110 (8f,Yar,GF,May 12)

Campanologist 115 (10f,San,GF,Jly 5)
Camps Bay 112 (12f,Nmk,G,May 3)
Candy Gift 113 (12½f,Dea,G,Aug 31)
Cape Amber 116 (10f,Yar,G,Sep 17)
Cape Colony 110 (12f,Pon,G,Jun 30)
Capt Chaos 120 (8f,Cur,GY,Jun 29)
Captain Gerrard 114 (5f,Nmk,GF,May 4)
Captain Webb 112 (11f,Ham,GF,May 16)
Captain's Lover 113 (7f,Lon,GS,Sep 7)
Caracciola 110 (18f,Nmk,G,Oct 18)
Carribean Sunset 113 (7f,Leo,Y,Apr 6)
Carrie McCurry 112 (6f,Cur,HY,Apr 13)
Casual Conquest 115 (12f,Cur,GY,Jun 29)
Cat Junior 111 (8f,Cha,G,Jly 13)
Caudillo 112 (15f,Dea,GS,Aug 24)
Cesare 111 (8f,Asc,GF,Jun 17)
Charlie Farnsbarns 111 (10f,San,S,May 29)
Cheshire Prince 110 (12f,Chs,G,Aug 3)
Cheyenne Star 111 (7f,Leo,G,Jly 2)
Chinchon 111 (10f,Msn,G,Jly 27)
Chinese White 110 (12f,Cur,G,Jly 13)
Choose Your Moment 111 (8f,Pon,GF,Jly 27)
Cicerole 111 (8f,Lon,GS,May 5)
Cima De Triomphe 110 (12f,Lon,GS,Oct 5)
City Leader 111 (10f,Msn,G,Jly 27)
Claire Et Bleu 116 (10½f,Lon,HY,Apr 3)
Clifton Dancer 110 (7f,War,GF,Jun 26)
Coastal Path 119 (15½f,Lon,S,Apr 27)
Collection 110 (10f,Msn,G,Jly 27)
Colony 112 (12f,Asc,GF,Jun 19)
Concentric 110 (10½f,Lon,HY,Apr 3)
Conduit 119 (10f,Eps,G,Jun 7)
Conquest 111 (6f,Asc,GS,Oct 11)
Corrybrough 116 (5f,San,G,Jun 14)
Creachadoir 114 (9f,Nad,G,Mar 29)
Crime Scene 111 (12f,Nad,G,Mar 6)
Crooked Throw 111 (8f,Cur,HY,Mar 30)
Crossharbour 113 (10f,Lon,G,Jun 14)
Crystal Capella 113 (12f,Asc,G,Sep 26)
Curtain Call 113 (12f,Cur,GY,Jun 29)

Dandy Man 112 (5f,Asc,GF,Jun 17)
Danehill Music 113 (8f,Cur,GY,Jun 29)
Dar Re Mi 115 (12f,Nmk,G,Aug 22)
Darjina 119 (8f,Lon,GS,Sep 7)
Dark Missile 111 (6f,Nmk,G,Apr 17)
Democrate 115 (11f,Lon,GS,May 5)
Derison 110 (5f,Lon,G,May 11)
Desert Lord 110 (5f,Cur,GY,Jun 29)
Desert Sea 111 (14f,San,G,Jun 14)
Diabolical 113 (6f,Don,S,Sep 13)
Diamond Quest 110 (12f,Nad,G,Mar 6)
Dijeerr 112 (9f,Nad,G,Feb 22)
Distinction 113 (22f,Asc,GF,Jun 21)
Divine Jury 111 (7½f,Nad,G,Jan 24)
Doctor Dino 114 (12f,Sai,GS,Jun 29)
Doctor Fremantle 116 (12f,Chs,GF,May 8)
Don't Panic 110 (8f,Don,S,Apr 12)
Donegal 111 (12f,Chs,GF,May 8)
Downhiller 114 (16f,Asc,G,Sep 27)
Dream Desert 110 (12f,Asc,GF,Jun 19)
Dubai's Touch 110 (8f,San,GF,Jly 5)
Duke Of Marmalade 118 (12f,Asc,GF,Jly 26)
Dunaskin 110 (12f,Pon,GF,Jun 22)
Dunelight 111 (8f,Wdr,GF,Jun 28)

Eagle Mountain 113 (8f,Nmk,GF,Oct 3)
Ebadiyan 112 (14f,Leo,G,Jly 16)
Edge Closer 112 (6f,Nmk,GF,Aug 23)
Electrolyser 111 (12f,Lei,S,Oct 7)
Elletelle 112 (6f,Cur,GF,Jly 27)
Emily Blake 111 (7f,Cur,YS,May 5)
Emirates Skyline 110 (10f,Eps,G,Jun 6)
Enforce 111 (8½f,Eps,G,Jun 7)
Enticing 113 (5f,Goo,GF,Jly 31)
Equiano 114 (5f,Cha,S,Jun 1)
Eradicate 111 (10½f,Yor,HY,Jly 12)
Expresso Star 112 (9f,Ham,S,Sep 22)
Ezdiyaad 111 (10½f,Yor,HY,Jly 12)
Ezima 112 (10f,Cur,GY,May 5)

Fair Breeze 110 (10f,Cha,VS,Apr 29)
Falco 113 (8f,Lon,G,May 11)
Fat Boy 110 (6f,Hay,G,May 31)
Feared In Flight 112 (12f,Chs,GF,May 8)
Fifteen Love 111 (8f,Goo,GF,Aug 1)
Finsceal Beo 114 (9f,Nad,G,Mar 29)
Firestreak 110 (7f,Goo,GF,Jly 30)
First Avenue 113 (10f,Eps,G,Jun 7)
First Buddy 111 (9f,Mus,GS,May 2)
Fiulin 110 (14f,Nmk,GF,Oct 2)
Fleeting Spirit 115 (5f,Hay,GF,May 24)
Floral Pegasus 114 (9f,Nad,G,Mar 29)
Flying Clarets 113 (8f,Pon,G,Jun 9)
Fontcia 110 (10½f,Lon,HY,Apr 3)
Foxhaven 111 (12f,Chs,GS,Sep 13)
Fragrancy 111 (10f,Nmk,G,Oct 17)
Frozen Fire 117 (12f,Cur,GY,Jun 29)
Full Of Gold 111 (11f,Lon,GS,May 5)
Furmigadelagiusta 110 (12f,Don,S,Mar 29)
Furnace 111 (7f,Asc,G,Sep 27)
Fyodor 111 (6f,Yar,GF,Apr 28)

Gagnoa 111 (12f,Cur,G,Jly 13)
Galistic 114 (14f,Leo,G,Jly 16)
Garnica 113 (7f,Lon,S,May 31)
General Eliott 112 (8f,Nmk,GF,Oct 3)
Geojimali 111 (6f,Don,G,May 3)
Georgebernardshaw 112 (7f,Cur,GY,Jly 12)
Getaway 115 (12½f,Dea,G,Aug 31)
Glen Nevis 111 (10f,Nad,G,Feb 22)
Goldikova 120 (8f,Lon,GS,Sep 7)
Gower Song 114 (12f,Nad,G,Mar 6)
Grande Caiman 113 (16f,Asc,G,Sep 27)
Gravitas 113 (12f,Nad,G,Mar 6)
Grecian Dancer 116 (8f,Cur,F,May 24)
Green Tango 110 (15f,Dea,GS,Aug 24)
Gris De Gris 115 (8f,Sai,VS,May 1)
Gulf Express 113 (10f,Goo,G,Jly 29)
Gull Wing 110 (14f,Yor,HY,Jly 12)

Hala Bek 112 (10f,Not,GS,Jly 10)
Halfway To Heaven 114 (8f,Nmk,GF,Oct 4)
Halicarnassus 112 (10½f,Yor,GF,Jly 26)
Hamish McGonagall 110 (5f,Yor,GF,May 16)
Haradasun 113 (8f,Asc,GF,Jun 17)
Hasanka 112 (10f,Cur,GY,May 5)
Hearthstead Maison 111 (10½f,Yor,GF,Jly 26)
Heaven Sent 111 (8f,Nmk,GS,Jly 9)
Hendersyde 110 (14f,San,GS,Aug 13)
Henrythenavigator 117 (8f,Lon,GS,Sep 7)
Hi Calypso 113 (15f,Dea,GS,Aug 24)
High Maintenance 114 (15½f,Lon,S,Apr 27)
High Rock 113 (10f,Lon,HY,Apr 13)
Highland Legacy 110 (16f,Rip,G,Apr 26)
Hoh Mike 111 (5f,Asc,GF,Jun 17)
Hold Me Love Me 112 (14f,Leo,G,Jly 16)
Holocene 110 (8f,Sai,VS,May 1)
Honolulu 114 (22f,Asc,GF,Jun 21)
Howdigo 111 (12f,Goo,GF,Jly 30)
Hue 110 (16f,Asc,GF,May 10)

Ice Queen 112 (12f,Cur,G,Jly 13)
Icelandic 114 (6f,Don,S,Nov 8)
Ideal World 110 (10f,Msn,G,Jly 27)
Idle Power 110 (6f,Goo,GS,May 3)
Illustrious Blue 110 (12f,Nad,G,Mar 6)
Imperial Star 111 (12f,Nad,G,Mar 6)
Impossible Dream 112 (6f,Cur,HY,Apr 13)
Incanto Dream 116 (15½f,Lon,S,Apr 27)
Infallible 112 (8f,Nmk,GS,Jly 9)
Instant Recall 111 (7½f,Nad,G,Feb 7)
Intrepid Jack 113 (6f,Nby,G,Jly 19)
Inxile 113 (5f,San,G,Jun 14)
It's Gino 112 (12f,Lon,GS,Oct 5)

Jalmira 118 (8f,Cur,GY,Jun 29)
Jamboretta 110 (8f,San,G,Apr 26)
Jay Peg 117 (9f,Nad,G,Mar 29)
Jewelled Dagger 110 (8f,Rip,GF,May 18)
Jimmy Styles 110 (6f,Asc,GF,May 10)
Joseph Henry 110 (6f,Don,G,May 3)
Judge 'n Jury 110 (5f,Don,G,Oct 25)
Jumbajukiba 121 (8f,Cur,GY,Jun 29)

Kalahari Gold 110 (7f,Nmk,GF,Aug 2)
Kandahar Run 111 (8f,Cha,G,Jly 13)
Kasbah Bliss 113 (15½f,Lon,GS,Sep 14)
Kasumi 114 (8f,Pon,G,Jun 9)
Katiyra 115 (10f,Lon,GS,Oct 5)

King Of Rome 115 (10f,Leo,GF,Jly 24)
Kingsdale Orion 110 (8f,Ncs,GS,Jun 26)
Kingsgate Native 117 (6f,Asc,GF,Jun 21)
Kirklees 110 (10f,Nmk,GS,Nov 1)
Konig Turf 113 (8f,Sai,HY,Mar 30)
Krataios 112 (8f,Sai,VS,May 1)
Kylayne 112 (7f,Lin,GF,May 10)
Kyniska 112 (6f,Leo,HY,Aug 17)

La Boum 111 (12½f,Lon,G,Oct 4)
Laa Rayb 113 (8f,Dea,G,Aug 31)
Lady Deauville 111 (8f,Bat,GS,Aug 17)
Lady Gloria 114 (10f,Lon,GS,Oct 5)
Lady Marian 118 (10f,Lon,GS,Oct 5)
Lang Shining 111 (10f,San,G,Aug 30)
Latin Mood 114 (15½f,Lon,S,Apr 27)
Le Cadre Noir 110 (5f,Cur,GY,Jun 29)
Le Miracle 115 (15½f,Lon,S,Apr 27)
Leo's Starlet 112 (12½f,Lon,G,Oct 4)
Lesson In Humility 111 (6f,Goo,S,Sep 13)
Light Green 113 (10f,Lon,GS,Oct 5)
Linngari 113 (7½f,Nad,G,Jan 24)
Lion Sands 112 (12f,Nmk,F,Jun 28)
Lisvale 124 (8f,Cur,GY,Jun 29)
Literato 111 (9f,Nad,G,Mar 29)
Little White Lie 112 (8½f,Eps,G,Jun 6)
Look Busy 113 (5f,Cur,S,Aug 31)
Look Here 116 (12f,Eps,G,Jun 6)
Lord Admiral 114 (9f,Nad,G,Mar 6)
Lost Soldier Three 110 (12f,Cat,GS,Sep 20)
Loup Breton 116 (9f,Lon,GS,May 18)
Love Galore 114 (12f,Goo,GF,Jly 30)
Lovelace 112 (8f,San,GF,Jly 5)
Lucarno 112 (12f,Sai,GS,Jun 29)
Lucifer Sam 116 (8f,Cur,GY,Jun 29)
Lucky Dance 110 (8f,Nmk,GS,Nov 1)
Lush Lashes 116 (12f,Nmk,G,Aug 22)

Maal 113 (10f,Leo,G,Jun 18)
Macarthur 115 (12f,Asc,GF,Jun 21)
Mad About You 113 (10f,Cur,Y,Jun 28)
Mad Rush 114 (15f,Dea,GS,Aug 24)
Magadan 112 (12f,Lon,G,Jly 14)
Magadino 111 (12½f,Dea,G,Aug 31)
Magicalmysterytour 112 (12f,Don,S,Sep 13)
Magnum Force 115 (9f,Leo,GF,May 21)
Major Cadeaux 111 (8f,Dea,GS,Aug 17)
Many Volumes 111 (10f,San,GF,Jly 4)
Maraahel 113 (10f,San,S,May 29)
Marchand D'Or 117 (6½f,Dea,S,Aug 10)
Mariol 113 (6f,Dea,S,Jly 11)
Marjalina 110 (8f,Cur,HY,Mar 30)
Markab 110 (7f,Ncs,GS,Apr 5)
Masaalek 110 (8f,San,GF,Jly 5)
Masiyma 112 (12f,Leo,Y,Sep 7)
Masta Plasta 111 (5f,Cur,GY,Jly 13)
Mastership 110 (7f,Nmk,G,Jly 11)
Matsunosuke 110 (5f,Nmk,GF,May 4)
Mawatheeq 110 (8f,Nmk,GF,Aug 23)
Medicine Path 111 (8f,Don,S,Apr 12)
Metaphoric 111 (16f,Asc,G,Sep 28)
Mezzanisi 110 (12f,Lei,S,Oct 7)
Mia's Boy 110 (8f,Don,S,Mar 29)
Michita 112 (12f,Nmk,G,Aug 22)
Midships 110 (10f,Nmk,GF,Sep 20)
Minkowski 112 (16f,Asc,G,Sep 27)
Miss Gorica 110 (6f,Cur,GF,Jly 27)
Modern Look 110 (8f,Lon,G,May 11)
Montmartre 115 (12f,Lon,G,Jly 14)
Mood Music 111 (5f,Lon,G,May 11)
Moon Sister 112 (10f,Yar,G,Sep 17)
Moonquake 110 (12f,Asc,GF,Jun 19)
Moonstone 114 (15½f,Lon,GS,Oct 26)
Mooretown Lady 111 (8f,Cur,F,May 24)
Moorhouse Lad 114 (5f,Lon,GS,Oct 5)
Mores Wells 112 (10f,Cur,GY,May 5)
Morinqua 112 (5f,Bat,S,Apr 29)
Mount Nelson 117 (10f,San,GF,Jly 5)
Mourilyan 113 (12f,Nad,G,Mar 6)
Mujood 111 (6f,Goo,GS,May 3)
Multidimensional 114 (12f,Asc,GF,Jun 21)
Munsef 110 (12f,Asc,GF,May 10)
Mustameet 111 (10f,Leo,GF,Jly 24)
Mutamarres 112 (6f,Nad,G,Feb 28)

Nahoodh 114 (8f,Nmk,GS,Jly 9)
Nanton 111 (9f,Nmk,GF,Oct 4)
Natagora 115 (8f,Lon,GS,Sep 7)
National Colour 114 (5f,Nmk,G,Aug 22)
Navajo Moon 111 (9f,Leo,G,Jun 18)
New Approach 118 (10f,Nmk,G,Oct 18)
Niconero 112 (9f,Nad,G,Mar 29)
Night Hour 111 (12f,Pon,G,Aug 6)
Noble Prince 110 (12f,Lon,HY,Apr 13)
Not Just Swing 112 (12f,Sai,GS,Jun 29)

Once Upon A Grace 110 (7f,Lin,GF,May 10)
One Great Cat 111 (8f,Cur,GY,Jun 29)
Only Answer 113 (5f,Lon,G,May 11)
Oracle West 113 (12f,Nad,G,Mar 6)
Ordnance Row 112 (8f,Nmk,GF,Oct 3)
Orion Star 118 (15½f,Lon,S,Apr 27)
Orpenindeed 113 (6f,Yar,GF,Apr 28)

Paco Boy 118 (8f,Lon,GS,Sep 7)
Pampas Cat 112 (12f,Chs,GF,May 8)
Papal Bull 117 (12f,Asc,GF,Jly 26)
Passage Of Time 110 (12f,Nmk,G,Aug 22)
Patkai 111 (12f,Hay,GF,May 31)
Peace Offering 111 (5f,Not,S,Aug 12)
Peppertree Lane 114 (14f,Leo,G,Jly 16)
Perfect Flight 111 (6f,Goo,S,Sep 14)
Perfect Treasure 110 (7f,Bri,GF,Jun 8)
Perks 113 (10½f,Hay,HY,Aug 9)
Persian Storm 110 (8f,Sai,VS,May 1)
Petara Bay 110 (12f,Asc,GF,May 10)
Philario 110 (5f,San,G,Jun 14)
Phoenix Tower 116 (10f,San,GF,Jly 5)
Pinpoint 112 (10f,Goo,G,Jly 29)
Pipedreamer 116 (10f,San,GF,Jly 5)
Plan 119 (8f,Cur,GY,Jun 29)
Ponte Tresa 117 (15½f,Lon,S,Apr 27)
Poseidon Adventure 113 (12½f,Dea,G,Aug 31)
Power Of Future 112 (14f,Leo,G,Jly 16)
Pressing 112 (10f,Asc,GF,Jun 18)
Prima Luce 112 (7f,Cur,YS,May 5)
Prime Defender 115 (6f,Don,S,Sep 13)
Profound Beauty 117 (14f,Leo,G,Jly 16)
Promising Lead 116 (10½f,Yor,GF,May 15)
Prospect Wells 112 (12f,Lon,G,Jly 14)
Proviso 113 (10f,Lon,GS,Oct 5)

Quench The Flame 112 (6f,Cur,HY,Apr 13)
Quijano 112 (12f,Nad,G,Mar 6)

Racinger 113 (8f,Msn,G,Jly 19)
Ramona Chase 114 (10f,Eps,G,Jun 7)
Raven's Pass 117 (8f,Asc,G,Sep 27)
Red Gala 111 (13½f,Chs,GF,Aug 30)
Red Moloney 112 (10f,Cur,S,Apr 13)
Red Rock Canyon 111 (12f,Asc,GF,Jly 26)
Red Rocks 110 (12f,Eps,G,Jun 6)
Regal Parade 111 (6f,Ayr,HY,Sep 20)
Regime 113 (10f,Cur,GY,May 5)
Relative Order 110 (7f,Nmk,GF,Aug 23)
Reverence 112 (6f,Don,S,Sep 13)
Rio De La Plata 112 (8f,Cha,G,Jly 13)
River Proud 113 (8f,Goo,GF,Aug 2)
Rob Roy 115 (10f,San,GF,Jly 5)
Rock Harmonie 112 (5f,Lon,GS,Sep 14)
Rock Moss 111 (6f,Leo,HY,Aug 17)
Ronaldsay 111 (12f,Asc,G,Sep 26)
Rosbay 110 (12f,Pon,G,Aug 6)
Rosenreihe 110 (10f,Lon,GS,Oct 5)
Royal Oath 112 (9f,Nad,G,Mar 6)
Royal Rock 114 (6f,Yar,GF,Apr 28)
Russian Cross 112 (10f,Dea,G,Aug 23)
Ryan 110 (15½f,Lon,GS,Oct 26)

Sabana Perdida 115 (7f,Lin,GF,May 10)
Saddex 112 (10½f,Lon,S,Apr 27)
Sagara 112 (16f,Goo,GF,Jly 31)
Sageburg 119 (9f,Lon,GS,May 18)
Sakhee's Secret 113 (5f,Nmk,GF,May 4)
Salsa Steps 111 (7f,Lin,GF,May 10)
Samuel 111 (14f,Yor,G,May 31)
Saoirse Abu 111 (8f,Nmk,GF,May 4)
Savarain 113 (12f,Goo,GF,Jly 30)
Savile's Delight 110 (6f,Goo,GS,May 3)
Seachange 114 (9f,Nad,G,Mar 29)
Seal Bay 110 (9f,Lon,HY,Apr 6)
Selinka 111 (8½f,Eps,G,Jun 7)
Sentinelese 111 (8f,Nad,G,Jan 31)
Septimus 113 (14f,Cur,SH,Sep 13)
Shaimaa 112 (10f,Leo,G,Jun 18)
Shemima 112 (15f,Lon,GS,Sep 5)
Shipmaster 113 (16f,Asc,S,Apr 30)
Siberian Tiger 113 (10f,Eps,G,Jun 7)
Signor Peltro 110 (7f,Goo,S,Aug 24)
Silver Seeker 111 (16f,Mus,GF,May 19)
Silver Suitor 111 (12f,Nmk,G,May 3)
Sir Gerry 114 (6f,Asc,GF,Jun 21)
Smokey Oakey 114 (10f,San,S,May 29)
Snaefell 113 (6f,Leo,HY,Aug 17)
Soapy Danger 112 (12f,Don,S,Mar 29)
Soldier Of Fortune 116 (12f,Eps,G,Jun 6)
Sommertag 112 (12½f,Dea,G,Aug 31)
Sonny Red 113 (6f,Don,GS,Mar 22)
Southpaw Lad 110 (11f,Goo,GF,Aug 2)
Spacious 111 (8f,Nmk,GF,May 4)
Spanish Moon 111 (12f,Asc,GF,May 10)
Speed Gifted 110 (12f,Asc,GF,Jun 21)
Spinning 110 (8f,Ncs,S,Jun 27)
Spirit One 112 (10f,Lon,HY,Apr 6)
Spirito Del Vento 113 (8f,Cha,G,Jun 8)
Starlish 114 (11f,Lon,GS,May 5)
Steam Cuisine 110 (8f,Pon,G,Jun 9)
Step Softly 110 (9f,Lon,HY,Apr 6)
Stern Opinion 111 (5f,Cha,S,Jun 20)
Stimulation 112 (7f,Nmk,G,Oct 18)
Stop Making Sense 110 (8f,Lon,GS,May 5)
Stotsfold 114 (10f,San,GF,Jly 5)
Strategic Mount 110 (13½f,Chs,GF,Aug 30)
Strike The Deal 112 (6f,Don,S,Sep 13)
Strike Up The Band 112 (5f,Lon,GS,Oct 5)
Stubbs Art 110 (8f,Cur,F,May 24)
Suailce 111 (12f,Leo,Y,Sep 7)
Summit Surge 115 (8f,Cur,GY,Jun 29)
Sun Classique 113 (12f,Nad,G,Mar 29)
Supaseus 112 (10½f,Yor,GF,Jly 26)
Sushisan 110 (12f,Nad,G,Mar 29)
Susie May 110 (12f,Asc,G,Sep 26)
Sweet Lightning 110 (12f,Chs,G,Jun 28)
Swop 110 (9f,Nmk,GF,Oct 4)

Tajaaweed 111 (10½f,Yor,GF,Jly 26)
Takeover Target 113 (5f,Asc,GF,Jun 17)
Tamayuz 117 (8f,Dea,GS,Aug 17)
Tartan Bearer 115 (12f,Cur,GY,Jun 29)
Tastahil 110 (12f,Don,S,Sep 13)
Tax Free 116 (5f,Cur,GY,Jun 29)
Tazeez 112 (9f,Nmk,GF,Oct 4)
Third Set 111 (8f,Nad,G,Feb 28)
Thundering Star 114 (15½f,Lon,S,Apr 27)
Tian Shan 111 (8f,Leo,GY,Apr 20)
Tiza 112 (7f,Lon,S,May 31)
Tombi 111 (6f,Yor,GF,May 16)
Top Lock 110 (12f,Asc,F,Jun 20)
Top Toss 110 (10f,Dea,S,Aug 2)
Traffic Guard 113 (9f,Nad,G,Mar 6)
Tranquil Tiger 111 (12f,Pon,GF,Jun 22)
Treat Gently 115 (10f,Lon,GS,Oct 5)
Tres Rapide 114 (12½f,Lon,G,Oct 4)
Tropical Strait 110 (12f,Don,S,Nov 8)
Tungsten Strike 113 (16f,Goo,GF,Jly 31)
Turbo Linn 110 (12f,Eps,G,Jun 6)
Turfrose 115 (9f,Lon,GS,May 18)
Turn On The Style 111 (6f,Nad,G,Feb 8)
Twice Over 115 (8f,Nmk,G,Apr 17)
Tyrur Ted 113 (6f,Cur,HY,Apr 13)

US Ranger 112 (6f,Nmk,G,Jly 11)
Under The Rainbow 113 (10½f,Yor,GF,May 15)
Unshakable 111 (8½f,Eps,G,Jun 6)
Utmost Respect 115 (6f,Don,S,Sep 13)

Vainglory 111 (8½f,Eps,G,Jun 6)
Valery Borzov 113 (6f,Hay,HY,Aug 9)
Vaqueras 110 (8f,Cur,HY,Mar 30)
Varsity 111 (10f,Cur,G,Jly 13)
Veracity 116 (15½f,Lon,GS,Oct 26)
Verba 113 (7f,Lin,GF,May 10)
Vertigineux 113 (8f,Sai,HY,Nov 2)
Victoria Montoya 111 (16f,Asc,G,Sep 27)
Vision D'Etat 111 (12f,Lon,GS,Oct 5)
Visionist 111 (7½f,Nad,G,Jan 24)
Visit 112 (8f,Nmk,GF,Oct 4)
Viva Macau 112 (9f,Nad,G,Mar 6)
Viva Pataca 111 (12f,Nad,G,Mar 29)
Vivaldi 111 (12f,Chs,GF,May 8)
Vodka 115 (9f,Nad,G,Mar 29)

War Artist 115 (6f,Asc,GF,Jun 21)
Watamu 111 (10f,Goo,G,Jly 29)
Watar 115 (15½f,Lon,GS,Oct 26)
Welsh Emperor 111 (7f,Lon,S,May 31)
Wi Dud 111 (6f,Don,GS,Mar 22)
Winter Dream 116 (15½f,Lon,S,Apr 27)
Wise Dennis 113 (9f,Nad,G,Feb 22)
With Interest 112 (10f,Nad,G,Feb 14)
Woodcutter 111 (12f,Nmk,GF,Jly 25)

Yahrab 110 (12f,Chs,GF,May 8)
Yeats 117 (16f,Goo,GF,Jly 31)
Yellowstone 111 (14f,Yor,HY,Jly 12)
You'resothrilling 113 (10f,Lon,GS,Oct 5)
Youmzain 117 (12f,Sai,GS,Jun 29)
Young Pretender 110 (8½f,Eps,G,Jun 6)

Zaahid 111 (7f,Asc,GF,May 10)
Zack Dream 111 (12f,Lon,G,Jun 19)
Zambezi Sun 113 (12f,Sai,GS,Jun 29)
Zarkava 115 (8f,Lon,G,May 11)
Zidane 112 (6f,Nmk,G,Apr 17)

THREE YEAR-OLDS AND UPWARDS – SAND

A P Arrow 112 (10f,Nad,FT,Mar 29)
Ajhar 112 (11f,Kem,SD,Sep 5)
Ajigolo 110 (6f,Kem,SD,Mar 18)
Alfresco 117 (8f,Lin,SD,Feb 16)
Algarade 112 (10f,Grl,SD,Jun 19)
Alpes Maritimes 111 (10f,Lin,SD,Jan 26)
Another Genepi 114 (6f,Sth,SD,Mar 12)
Armure 110 (11f,Kem,SD,Sep 6)
Ascot Lime 111 (11f,Kem,SD,Sep 5)
Asiatic Boy 113 (6f,Nad,FT,Jan 24)
Atlantic Story 114 (8f,Lin,SD,Feb 16)

Baharah 112 (8f,Lin,SD,Oct 30)
Ballinteni 113 (10f,Lin,SD,Apr 4)
Barbecue Eddie 111 (6f,Nad,FT,Mar 29)
Barton Sands 110 (10f,Lin,SD,Jan 30)
Bavarica 110 (10f,Grl,SD,Jun 19)
Baylini 111 (10f,Lin,SD,Mar 15)
Bazroy 112 (7f,Lin,SD,Feb 6)
Beat The Bell 110 (6f,Grl,SD,Oct 2)
Benandonner 110 (8f,Sth,SD,Apr 1)
Benllech 111 (6f,Kem,SD,Mar 18)
Benny The Bull 118 (6f,Nad,FT,Mar 29)
Bentley Brook 110 (11f,Kem,SD,Feb 6)
Blackat Blackitten 113 (8f,Nad,FT,Mar 6)
Bomber Command 111 (8f,Lin,SD,Feb 16)
Bonnie Prince Blue 110 (6f,Sth,SD,Jan 8)
Bonus 111 (6f,Lin,SD,Feb 23)
Boss Hog 110 (8f,Sth,SD,Dec 13)
Boundless Prospect 112 (8f,Sth,SD,Dec 13)
Boz 110 (12f,Kem,SD,Oct 13)
Bussell Up 110 (6f,Lin,SD,Jan 30)

Capable Guest 110 (8f,Lin,SD,Feb 16)
Casual Affair 110 (12f,Wol,SD,Jan 28)
Celtic Spirit 115 (10f,Lin,SD,Apr 4)
Ceremonial Jade 112 (6f,Lin,SD,Feb 23)
Classic Legend 110 (8f,Kem,SD,Nov 29)
Cold Turkey 111 (12f,Lin,SD,Feb 4)
Come Out Fighting 110 (6f,Lin,SD,Jan 19)
Commander Cave 114 (8f,Kem,SD,Nov 29)
Cornus 110 (7f,Lin,SD,Feb 6)
Councellor 113 (8f,Lin,SD,Feb 16)
Count Ceprano 112 (7f,Wol,SD,Apr 16)
Curlin 119 (10f,Nad,FT,Mar 29)

Dance The Star 110 (12f,Lin,SD,Jly 23)
Dansant 113 (10f,Lin,SD,Dec 20)
Detonator 110 (14f,Grl,SD,Sep 14)
Diabolical 112 (6f,Nad,FT,Mar 6)

Diamond Stripes 113 (8f,Nad,FT,Mar 29)
Diriculous 110 (6f,Grl,SD,Oct 22)
Divertimenti 110 (7f,Wol,SD,Jan 19)
Don Renato 110 (8f,Nad,FT,Mar 29)
Dream Lodge 110 (10f,Lin,SD,Mar 15)
Dreams Jewel 110 (16f,Sth,SD,Mar 20)
Dubai Ace 113 (16f,Lin,SD,Feb 13)
Dubai's Touch 113 (10f,Lin,SD,Mar 15)
Duff 111 (6f,Lin,SD,Nov 22)
Dvinsky 110 (6f,Grl,SD,Dec 21)

Ebraam 111 (5f,Grl,SD,Dec 18)
Eddie Jock 112 (8f,Grl,SD,Sep 14)
Edge Closer 112 (6f,Kem,SD,Mar 29)
Ellmau 111 (11f,Sth,SD,Oct 19)
Elusive Warning 114 (8f,Nad,FT,Mar 6)
Evens And Odds 116 (6f,Sth,SD,Feb 12)
Excusez Moi 114 (6f,Lin,SD,Feb 23)

Falcativ 110 (12f,Lin,SD,Oct 27)
Familiar Territory 110 (10f,Nad,FT,Feb 14)
Fiesta Lady 110 (7f,Nad,FT,Jan 17)

Flame Creek 111 (16f,Lin,SD,Jan 23)
Flores Sea 110 (7f,Sth,SD,Jan 10)
Fregate Island 111 (11f,Kem,SD,Feb 6)
Fromsong 110 (5f,Kem,SD,Jan 25)
Frosty Secret 110 (6f,Nad,FT,Feb 22)
Fusili 110 (10f,Lin,SD,Jan 26)

Gala Evening 111 (16f,Kem,SD,Apr 12)
Gallantry 116 (8f,Lin,SD,Feb 16)
Gloria De Campeao 113 (10f,Nad,FT,Mar 6)
Grand Passion 113 (10f,Lin,SD,Mar 15)
Grande Caiman 111 (12f,Lin,SD,Mar 15)
Great Hawk 114 (10f,Lin,SD,Mar 15)
Great Hunter 111 (10f,Nad,FT,Mar 29)
Green Coast 111 (7½f,Nad,FT,Feb 21)

Happy Boy 113 (8f,Nad,FT,Jan 17)
Happy Runner 112 (7½f,Nad,FT,Jan 17)
Harry Up 112 (5f,Grl,SD,Dec 18)
Harvest Queen 111 (8f,Lin,SD,Oct 30)
Hattan 116 (10f,Lin,SD,Mar 15)
Holbeck Ghyll 110 (6f,Kem,SD,Apr 17)
Honour Devil 115 (9f,Nad,FT,Mar 29)
Hora 110 (16f,Sth,SD,Jan 24)

Idiot Proof 115 (6f,Nad,FT,Mar 29)
Il Grande Maurizio 110 (8f,Kem,SD,Nov 29)
Il Warrd 110 (8f,Kem,SD,Apr 12)
Illustrious Blue 114 (10f,Kem,SD,Mar 29)
Impeller 111 (10f,Kem,SD,Mar 29)
Imperial Echo 110 (8f,Lin,SD,Feb 16)
Internationaldebut 112 (6f,Lin,SD,Nov 28)
Inventor 110 (12f,Kem,SD,Sep 1)
Irish Mayhem 111 (8f,Grl,SD,Sep 13)
Irish Pearl 113 (6f,Sth,SD,Nov 4)
Ivory Silk 110 (5f,Wol,SD,Dec 30)

Jack Sullivan 113 (7f,Wol,SD,Mar 8)
Jalil 115 (10f,Nad,FT,Mar 6)
Jeer 113 (10f,Lin,SD,Apr 4)
John Terry 115 (12f,Lin,SD,Feb 2)

Kabeer 111 (7f,Sth,SD,Jan 22)
Kames Park 112 (12f,Lin,SD,Feb 2)
Kandidate 115 (10f,Kem,SD,Mar 29)
Keenes Day 110 (16½f,Wol,SD,Oct 24)
King Of Dixie 110 (7f,Lin,SD,Apr 5)
Kylayne 110 (8f,Lin,SD,Oct 30)

Lisathedaddy 110 (10f,Lin,SD,Jan 26)
Lone Wolfe 111 (6f,Grl,SD,Dec 6)
Lord Of Dreams 112 (10f,Lin,SD,Feb 13)
Lordswood 111 (10f,Lin,SD,Jan 30)
Luberon 116 (10f,Lin,SD,Apr 4)
Lucky Find 113 (10f,Nad,FT,Mar 6)

Mac Love 115 (8f,Kem,SD,Nov 29)
Majuro 110 (7f,Lin,SD,Nov 22)
Many Volumes 111 (10f,Grl,SD,May 28)
Markab 110 (7f,Lin,SD,Nov 22)
Maslak 111 (12f,Lin,SD,Feb 16)
Master Of Arts 111 (8f,Lin,SD,Jly 16)
Mataram 110 (10f,Lin,SD,Feb 2)
Matsunosuke 112 (5f,Grl,SD,Dec 18)
Medicine Path 110 (8f,Kem,SD,Feb 3)
Merchant Of Dubai 112 (12f,Sth,SD,Sep 30)
Mezzanisi 110 (12f,Sth,SD,Sep 30)
Millville 114 (12f,Lin,SD,Feb 2)
Mischief Making 110 (13f,Lin,SD,Oct 30)
Miswaatt 111 (8½f,Nad,FT,Feb 21)
Monkey Glas 116 (8f,Lin,SD,Feb 16)
Moon Quest 111 (10f,Grl,SD,Jun 26)
Mr Aviator 117 (10f,Lin,SD,Apr 4)
Mr Lambros 114 (7f,Wol,SD,Jan 19)
Muhannak 113 (11f,Kem,SD,Aug 25)
Murfreesboro 111 (12f,Lin,SD,Mar 15)
Mutajarred 112 (10f,Grl,SD,May 28)

Nanton 110 (9½f,Wol,SD,Nov 12)
Neardown Beauty 114 (8f,Lin,SD,Feb 16)
Nightjar 110 (7f,Sth,SD,Dec 10)
Nota Bene 111 (6f,Grl,SD,May 29)
Numaany 110 (9f,Nad,FT,Mar 6)

Orchard Supreme 112 (10f,Lin,SD,Mar 15)
Orpenindeed 111 (6f,Grl,SD,Nov 13)
Orpsie Boy 111 (6f,Kem,SD,Jan 28)

Persian Peril 110 (11f,Sth,SD,Oct 19)
Philatelist 112 (11f,Kem,SD,Mar 29)
Plum Pudding 114 (8f,Lin,SD,Feb 16)

Polish Power 110 (12f,Lin,SD,Feb 2)
Precision Break 110 (13f,Grl,SD,Oct 30)
Premio Loco 111 (8f,Kem,SD,Sep 6)
Press The Button 111 (12f,Wol,SD,Nov 21)
Prohibit 111 (6f,Grl,SD,Oct 22)
Proper 112 (11f,Kem,SD,Apr 9)
Pur Sucre 113 (10f,Kem,SD,Mar 29)

Rapidity 110 (8f,Lin,SD,Feb 15)
Rationale 113 (11f,Kem,SD,Feb 6)
Reclamation 110 (12f,Kem,SD,Sep 1)
Red Gala 110 (13f,Grl,SD,Sep 27)
Regional Counsel 110 (12f,Lin,SD,Mar 15)
Resplendent Nova 110 (7f,Kem,SD,Nov 28)
Rhapsilian 111 (6f,Kem,SD,Apr 22)
Rosberg 114 (8½f,Nad,FT,Feb 21)
Royal Jet 110 (11f,Kem,SD,Sep 5)
Royal Vintage 112 (9f,Nad,FT,Mar 6)

Safari Sundowner 114 (10f,Lin,SD,Feb 13)
Sailor King 111 (7f,Lin,SD,Jan 26)
Salaam Dubai 111 (6f,Nad,FT,Jan 24)
Salut Saint Cloud 112 (16f,Lin,SD,Feb 13)
Samuel Charles 110 (7f,Lin,SD,Jan 23)
Scamperdale 115 (10f,Lin,SD,Apr 4)
Sgt Schultz 114 (12f,Lin,SD,Feb 2)
Silver Hotspur 111 (7f,Sth,SD,Mar 12)
Silver Pivotal 114 (10f,Lin,SD,Mar 15)
Smarty Socks 111 (7f,Sth,SD,Nov 2)
Smokey The Bear 110 (10f,Kem,SD,Feb 10)
Sophia Gardens 112 (7f,Sth,SS,Jan 15)
Speedy Sam 110 (10f,Lin,SD,Jan 26)
Spice Route 114 (10f,Kem,SD,Mar 29)
Star Crowned 112 (6f,Nad,FT,Mar 29)
Starfala 112 (12f,Kem,SD,Sep 1)
Suits Me 111 (10f,Lin,SD,Dec 20)
Sun Catcher 110 (8f,Sth,SD,May 20)
Super Frank 111 (7f,Lin,SD,Feb 6)
Sweet Pickle 111 (7f,Sth,SS,Jan 15)

The Game 113 (5f,Grl,SD,Dec 18)
Three Boars 111 (16f,Sth,SD,Mar 20)
Tilapia 110 (12f,Lin,SD,Mar 15)
Tilt 111 (12f,Wol,SD,Nov 21)
Tis Mighty 111 (8f,Kem,SD,Nov 29)
Tomintoul Flyer 112 (11f,Kem,SD,Aug 25)
Trans Siberian 110 (10f,Grl,SD,Jun 26)

Vintage 112 (6f,Kem,SD,Apr 22)

Well Armed 112 (10f,Nad,FT,Mar 29)
Wicked Daze 114 (12f,Lin,SD,Feb 2)

Xpres Maite 110 (7f,Wol,SD,Apr 29)

Zakocity 110 (8f,Nad,FT,Mar 29)

TWO YEAR-OLDS – SAND

Elnawin 106 (6f,Kem,SD,Sep 6)

Rainbow Seeker 106 (5f,Wol,SD,Oct 31)
Rowayton 106 (6f,Kem,SD,Oct 29)

Square Eddie 105 (6f,Kem,SD,Sep 6)
Swiss Diva 105 (6f,Lin,SD,Nov 19)

Tropical Paradise 107 (6f,Kem,SD,Oct 29)

Weatherstaff 105 (6f,Kem,SD,Sep 6)

TWO YEAR-OLDS – TURF

Again 109 (7f,Leo,HY,Aug 17)
Amour Propre 106 (5f,Bat,F,Jly 24)
Anglezarke 106 (5f,Don,S,Sep 12)
Arazan 105 (7f,Cur,HY,Aug 23)
Art Connoisseur 110 (6f,Asc,GF,Jun 17)
Ashram 109 (7f,Nmk,GF,Oct 2)
Aspen Darlin 105 (6f,Nmk,GF,Oct 3)

Bushranger 108 (6f,Nmk,GF,Oct 3)

Call Me Alice 107 (5f,Cur,GF,Jly 27)
Calvados Blues 108 (8f,Sai,HY,Nov 2)
Chintz 112 (7f,Cur,Y,Sep 28)
Cityscape 108 (8f,Asc,G,Sep 27)
Copperbeech 105 (8f,Lon,GS,Oct 5)

Crowded House 105 (8f,Don,G,Oct 25)

Damien 105 (6f,Nby,G,Sep 20)
Danehill Destiny 105 (5f,Don,S,Sep 12)
Definightly 105 (6f,Nby,G,Sep 20)
Delegator 105 (7f,Nmk,G,Oct 18)
Donativum 105 (7f,Nmk,GF,Oct 4)

Elnawin 105 (6f,Nmk,G,Aug 22)
Elusive Wave 106 (8f,Lon,GS,Oct 5)
Enticement 106 (8f,Nmk,GS,Nov 1)
Evasive 105 (7f,Nby,S,Oct 25)

Finjaan 106 (7f,Nmk,G,Oct 18)
Fuisse 108 (8f,Sai,HY,Nov 2)

Gallagher 109 (6f,Goo,GF,Aug 1)

Hallie's Comet 107 (7f,Cur,Y,Sep 28)
Harry Patch 105 (5f,Not,GS,Oct 16)
Henderson Park 106 (8f,Don,G,Oct 24)
Himalya 106 (6f,Asc,GF,Jun 17)

Imperial Guest 105 (6f,Don,G,Oct 25)
Infamous Angel 105 (5f,Nby,G,Jly 19)
Intense Focus 107 (6f,Asc,GF,Jun 17)

Jargelle 106 (5f,Nby,G,Jly 19)
Jobe 106 (6f,Ayr,GS,Aug 9)
Jukebox Jury 109 (8f,Asc,G,Sep 27)

Kingship Spirit 106 (6f,Nmk,GF,Oct 2)

Lahaleeb 110 (7f,Cur,Y,Sep 28)
Le Havre 108 (8f,Sai,HY,Nov 2)
Lord Shanakill 109 (6f,Nby,G,Sep 20)
Lui Rei 106 (5½f,Msn,G,Jly 27)

Madame Trop Vite 107 (5f,Don,S,Sep 12)
Magic Cat 109 (5f,Ayr,HY,Sep 19)
Maid For Music 105 (7f,Sal,GF,Jly 4)
Marine Boy 108 (6f,Nby,G,Aug 3)
Mastercraftsman 106 (7f,Lon,GS,Oct 5)
Milanais 108 (7f,Lon,GS,Oct 5)
Moonlife 106 (7f,Nmk,GF,Oct 3)
Mythical Border 106 (5f,Don,S,Sep 12)

Naaqoos 109 (7f,Lon,GS,Oct 5)
Nashmiah 105 (7f,Nmk,GF,Oct 3)
Nasri 107 (6f,Nby,G,Sep 20)

On Our Way 107 (8f,Nmk,G,Oct 17)
Oui Say Oui 105 (6f,Cur,Y,Jly 12)

Pasar Silbano 109 (5f,Cur,GF,Jly 27)
Percolator 105 (5½f,Msn,G,Jly 27)
Plumania 105 (8f,Lon,GS,Oct 5)
Prince Siegfried 110 (8f,Sai,HY,Nov 2)
Prolific 110 (6f,Goo,GF,Aug 1)
Proportional 109 (8f,Lon,GS,Oct 5)
Pyrrha 105 (6f,Nmk,GF,Oct 2)

Rainbow View 109 (7f,Nmk,GS,Aug 9)
Rayeni 107 (7f,Leo,YS,Oct 27)
Reve De Soleil 109 (6f,Goo,GF,Aug 1)

Rievaulx World 105 (5f,Rip,GF,Jun 18)
Rileyskeepingfaith 106 (6f,Goo,GF,Aug 1)

Salsa Star 105 (5f,Ayr,HY,Sep 19)
Saxford 108 (6f,Goo,GF,Aug 1)
Sayif 108 (6f,Nby,G,Sep 20)
Senor Mirasol 105 (5f,Nby,G,Jly 19)
Serious Attitude 106 (6f,Nmk,GF,Oct 3)
Serva Jugum 105 (8f,Sai,HY,Nov 2)
Shaweel 106 (7f,Nmk,G,Oct 18)
Silver Frost 110 (8f,Sai,HY,Nov 2)
Silver Shoon 107 (5f,Cur,GF,Jly 27)
Skid Solo 105 (6f,Nby,G,Sep 20)
Smart Coco 106 (7f,Cur,Y,Sep 28)
Sohcahtoa 105 (7f,Goo,GF,Aug 1)
Soul City 105 (7f,Cur,Y,Sep 28)
Souter's Sister 107 (7f,Nmk,GF,Oct 3)
Spin Cycle 105 (5f,Ham,GF,May 16)
Splashdown 105 (8f,Nmk,GS,Nov 1)
Super Sleuth 105 (8f,Nmk,GS,Nov 1)

Tiger Eye 108 (7f,Nmk,GF,Oct 4)
Total Gallery 106 (6f,Goo,GF,Aug 1)

Vitruvian Man 105 (7f,Leo,YS,Oct 27)

Waffle 105 (5f,Asc,GS,Oct 11)
What's Up Pussycat 107 (7f,Cur,Y,Sep 28)

Your Old Pal 108 (8f,Nby,S,Oct 25)

Zafisio 111 (8f,Sai,HY,Nov 2)